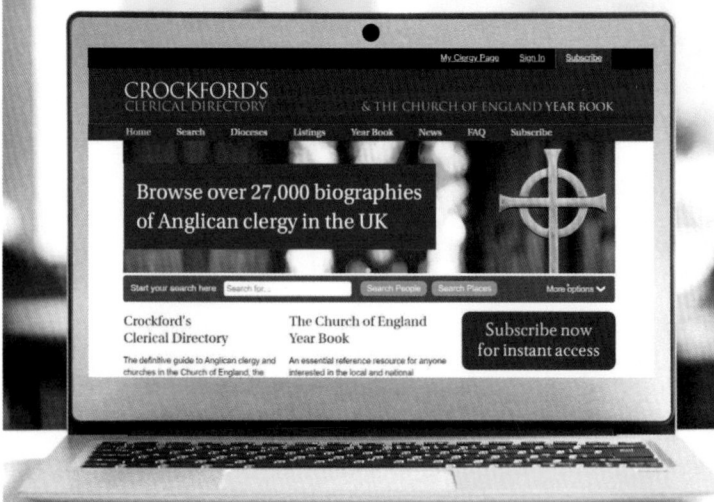

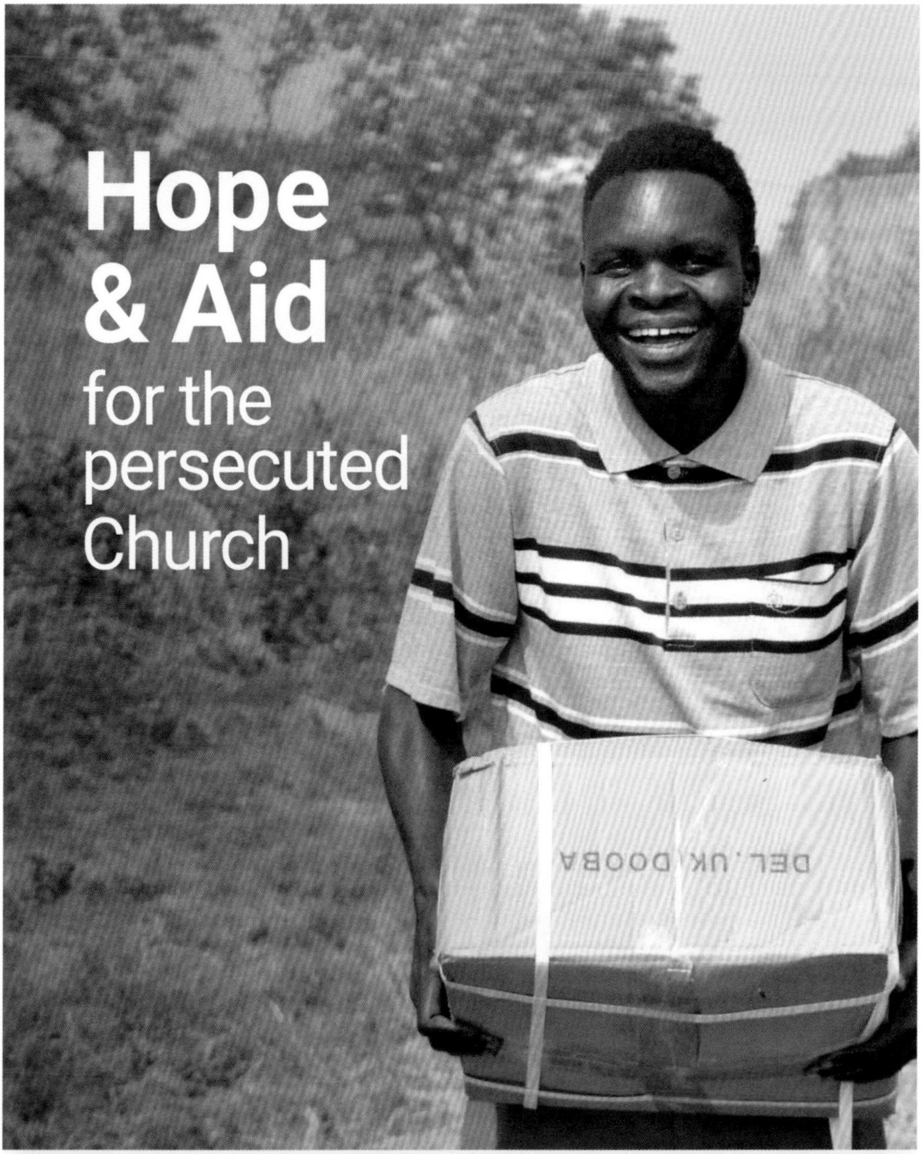

Hope & Aid
for the persecuted Church

English Clergy Association

Founded 1938

www.clergyassoc.co.uk

The Association seeks to be a Church of England mutual resource and support for clergy (with Freehold or on Common Tenure) patrons and churchwardens requiring information or insight.

It publishes a journal *Parson & Parish* that is free to memebers. Membership is equally open to men and women, clergy and laity.

The Association administers a charitable *Benefit Fund* to provide holiday grants for clergy (Registered Charity No. 258559). Donations, legacies, etc. to support the charitable work of the Association are very much appreciated.

Membership enquiries
to the Revd. Mark Binney
Reverend-mark-binney@hotmail.co.uk

For information concerning the holiday benefit fund
please contact the Revd. Richard Hall
revrichardhall45@gmail.com or at
45 Howard Park, Greystoke CA11 0TU

If you are considering a donation or legacy
please contact the
Revd. Canon Peter Johnson
petrd867@gmail.com or at
4 St John's Road, Windsor, SL4 3QN.

General enquiries to Dr. Peter Smith at P.M.Smith@exeter.ac.uk, or 36 High Street, Silverton, Exeter, EX5 4JD.

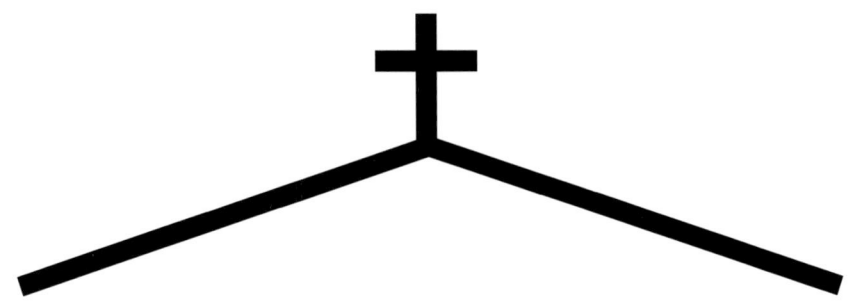

BUILDING CONSERVATION UK LTD

All Church maintenance

Roofing - Guttering - Decoration

0800 0521030

www.buildingconservationukltd.com

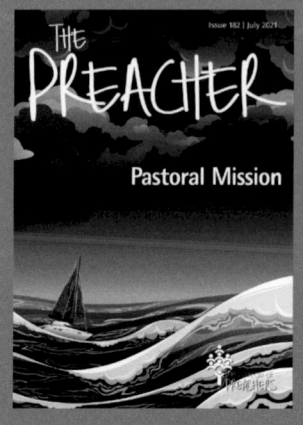

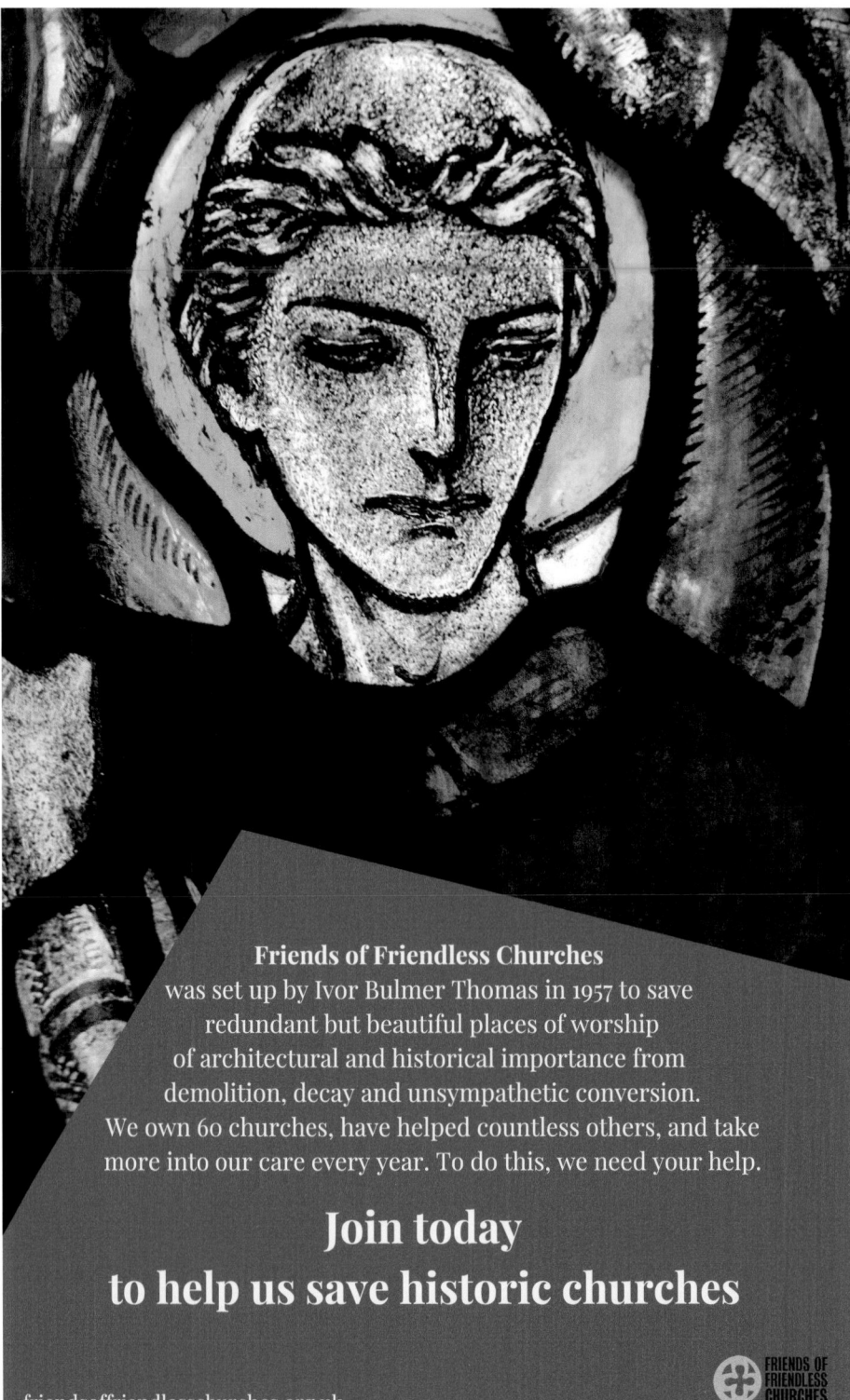

Friends of Friendless Churches
was set up by Ivor Bulmer Thomas in 1957 to save
redundant but beautiful places of worship
of architectural and historical importance from
demolition, decay and unsympathetic conversion.
We own 60 churches, have helped countless others, and take
more into our care every year. To do this, we need your help.

Join today
to help us save historic churches

FRIENDS OF
FRIENDLESS
CHURCHES

friendsoffriendlesschurches.org.uk

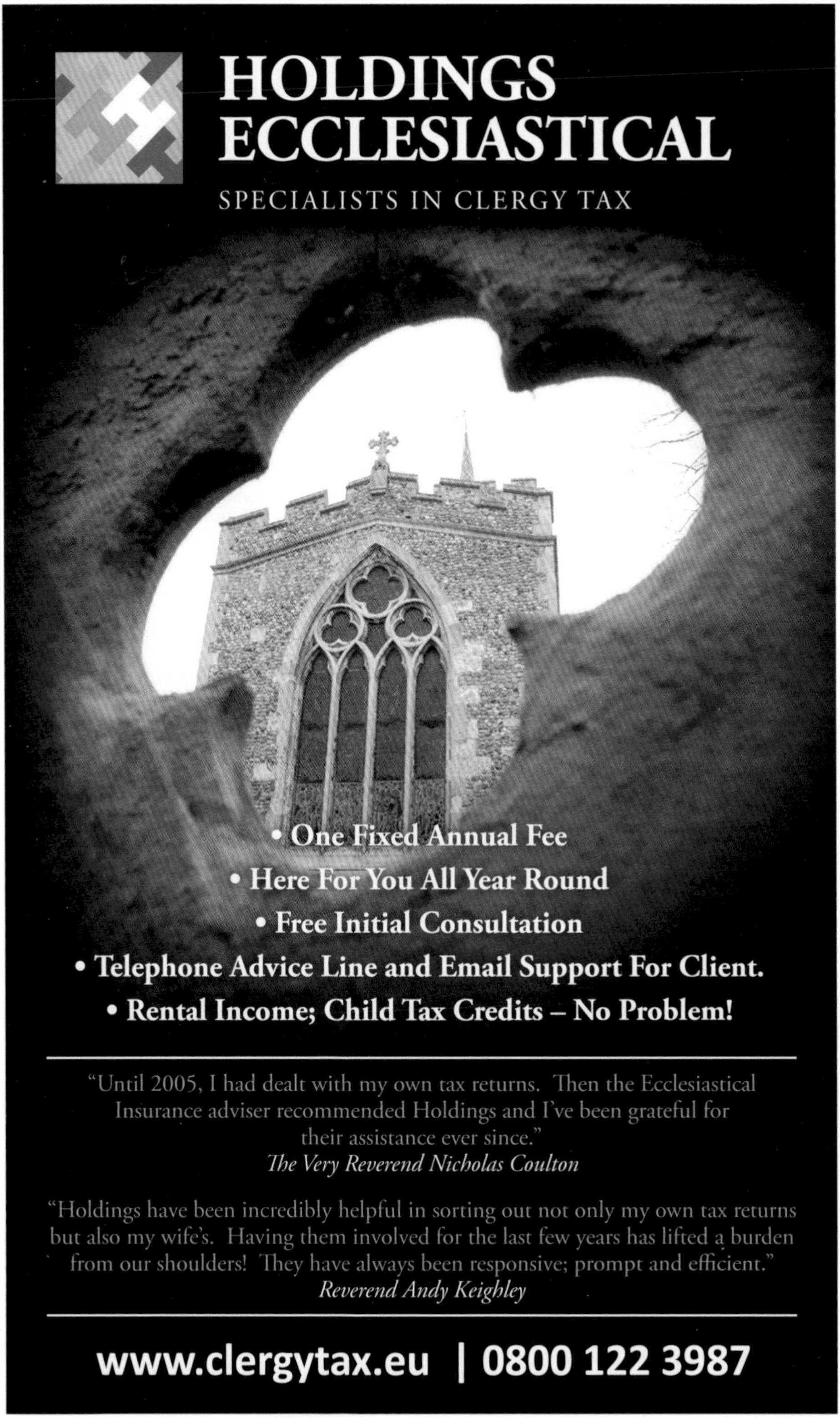

Common Worship Apps

Our user-friendly apps for iOS and Android phones and tablets help you use Common Worship wherever you are.

Reflections on the Psalms

Explore all 150 Psalms with thoughtful commentaries.

£8.99

Time to Pray

Provides Prayer During the Day and Night Prayer, with audio recordings in full and seasonal variations.

FREE TO USE

Daily Prayer

Presents Morning, Evening and Night Prayer in full, in both Contemporary and Traditional Language.

FREE TO USE ONLINE
OFFLINE ACCESS –
12 MONTHS FOR £2.99

Lectionary

Presents the Common Worship Lectionary readings in full, plus Collects and Post Communions.

ONLINE ACCESS -
12 MONTHS FOR £4.99
OFFLINE ACCESS -
12 MONTHS FOR £8.99

Reflections for Daily Prayer

Daily Bible reflections based on one of the day's readings for Common Worship Morning Prayer.

12 MONTHS
FOR £12.99

Sunday Worship

View the Bible readings, Collect and post Communion prayers for Sundays only.

ONLINE ACCESS -
12 MONTHS FOR 99P
OFFLINE ACCESS -
12 MONTHS FOR £1.99

 CHURCH HOUSE PUBLISHING   www.chpublishing.co.uk/apps

the ministry
experience scheme

If you are aged 18-30 why not spend a year serving God through the Ministry Experience Scheme.

You will have the opportunity to explore your calling and learn more about yourself, whilst gaining experience of Christian ministry and developing your leadership skills.

It is free to do, with accommodation and living expenses provided.

Local schemes are based in many locations across the Church of England.

**Where is God sending you?
Find out more at cofe.io/mes**

ministry
empower | equip | enable

 THE CHURCH
OF ENGLAND

CROCKFORD'S
CLERICAL DIRECTORY

2022–2023

CROCKFORD'S

CLERICAL DIRECTORY
107TH EDITION

2022–2023

A directory of the clergy
of the Church of England
the Church of Wales
the Scottish Episcopal Church
the Church of Ireland

SINCE 1858

CHURCH HOUSE PUBLISHING

Crockford's Clerical Directory published December 2021 for The Archbishops' Council by:

Church House Publishing
Church House
Great Smith Street
London SW1P 3AZ

107th edition (2022–2023) © The Archbishops' Council 2021.

Please send any corrections to the Compiler, Crockford (address as above), Tel (020) 7898 1012
E-mail crockford@churchofengland.org

ISBN   978 0 7151 1184 0

Typeset by   Printed by
RefineCatch Ltd,   William Clowes Ltd,
Bungay, Suffolk   Beccles, Suffolk

Contents

INTRODUCTION

This, the one hundred and seventh edition of *Crockford's Clerical Directory*, provides details as at 23 August 2021 of all Anglican clergy and deaconesses in the British Isles and overseas who have given their consent under the General Data Protection Regulation (GDPR), including those Michaelmas ordinands of whom we have received advance notice.

First published in 1858, the publication of *Crockford* now spans over one-and-a-half centuries. The Oxford University Press purchased the copyright for *Crockford* in 1921, publishing thirty-six editions before transferring ownership to the Church Commissioners and the Central Board of Finance, on economic grounds, sixty years later. This is the ninth edition under the sole ownership of the Archbishops' Council.

The publishing, design, advertising, selling and distribution of the directory are carried out by Church House Publishing in partnership with the *Crockford* Department, who are responsible for maintaining the data published here and *via* the *Crockford* on-line subscription service (www.crockford.org.uk), first launched in 2004. The information that generates the biographical entries is stored on a database, which is updated daily. The website is also updated after each working day. Much of the information is obtained indirectly from the Church Commissioners' central clergy pay-roll. However, about one-third of the clergy are not on the central pay-roll. These are principally non-stipendiary ministers, those engaged in some form of ministry outside the parochial system (such as hospital, university, prison or service chaplains) and those serving in Wales, Scotland and Ireland. In maintaining the records of these clergy, we continue to rely greatly on the assistance of bishops' secretaries and diocesan offices, and information contained in diocesan directories, year books and the Church Press. We are also grateful for the help provided by the central authorities of the Church in Wales, the Scottish Episcopal Church, the Church of Ireland, the Ministry of Defence, the Hospital Chaplaincies Council, and our various overseas contacts.

A tremendous amount of help has come from the clergy themselves. This is the second print edition of *Crockford* to appear since the introduction of GDPR in 2018, and we have received notification from well over 24,000 clergy of their data permissions and preferences. It is also the first print edition since we introduced the 'My Clergy Page' facility (www.crockford.co.uk/my-clergy-page) which allows clergy to review their own published data without a subscription and to update their GDPR permissions online. Full details of our privacy policy can be found via www.crockford.org.uk/privacy.

We are enormously grateful to all those who have provided us with information, and have helped to minimize omissions and errors. We are also grateful to Richard Christmas, Angela Florence, Abigail Clausen and Mark Walsh, who have been responsible for most of the work in compiling this directory.

We are always glad to be informed of amendments to entries, and we particularly appreciate any information about clergy whose addresses are not currently known to us (see list on p. 1170). Information relating to omissions or amendments should be sent to the *Crockford* Department; requests for archival information from earlier editions should be addressed in writing to Lambeth Palace Library; for other information, please consult the Church of England's website at www.churchofengland.org.

Crockford Department
Church House
27 Great Smith Street
London SW1P 3AZ

Telephone (020) 7898 1012
E-mail: crockford@churchofengland.org

The Librarian
Lambeth Palace Library
15 Lambeth Palace Road
London SE1 7JT

Telephone (020) 7898 1400
E-mail: archives@churchofengland.org

JOHN CROCKFORD

John Crockford was the eldest child of a Somerset schoolmaster and his wife, John and Hannah Crockford; and by 1841 he was working as an attorney's clerk in Taunton, Somerset. John Crockford Sr was described in 1869 as Gentleman, of Rowbarton near Taunton. By his early twenties he was in business as a printer and publisher at 29 Essex Street, Strand; and it was from that address that Crockford was first published in 1858. On 6 December of the same year, John Crockford moved to new business premises at 346 Strand and 19 Wellington Street North.

His private address at that time was 16 Oakley Square, Hampstead Road; though by 1865 he had moved to 10 Park Road, Haverstock Hill.

Crockford's business association of more than two decades with Edward William Cox (1809–1879) had begun in 1843, when the *Law Times* first appeared. Both men are claimed as publisher – Crockford by Boase in *Modern English Biography*; Cox by the *Athenaeum* and by *Notes and Queries*. There is similar lack of agreement over other publications, such as the ill-fated *Critic*. "[Crockford] tried to establish a literary paper, the *Critic*. To this he brought all his great ability, but after fifteen years he gave it up in despair" (*Notes and Queries*): whereas the *Dictionary of National Biography* has it that Cox became "proprietor of . . . two other papers called respectively 'The Critic' and 'The Royal Exchange'."

The truth appears to be that the two men, who shared the same business address in Essex Street, were joint founders of a number of projects. Cox – the elder, more established and richer man – was often the financier and named publisher, with Crockford as the manager of the undertaking. Each had his own specialities: Cox, called to the bar in 1843, and successively Recorder of Helston & Falmouth (1857–1868) and of Portsmouth (1868–1879), was no doubt the leader in the establishment of the *Law Times*, to which, in *DNB*'s words, he "thenceforth devoted . . . the larger portion of his time and attention." But the legend which has arisen that Cox, restrained by professional ethics from using his own name, chose, almost at random, the name of one of his clerks to bear the title of his new clerical directory in 1858 – thus, in the words of the first postwar editor (probably Newman) bestowing "a more than tomb-stone meed of remembrance" – cannot be substantiated. As the jubilee account of the *Field* notes, Crockford was an equal partner in the success of the joint enterprises: "It was John Crockford who purchased the paper for Mr Cox. He obtained it from Mr Benjamin Webster for a trifling sum . . . In a short time the net profits amounted to 20,000*l.* a year. The management was placed under Crockford's control. He was a splendid man of business" (*Notes and Queries*).

The first *Clerical Directory* (1858), "A Biographical and Statistical Book of Reference for facts relating to the clergy and the Church", seems to have been assembled in a very haphazard fashion, with names added "as fast as they could be obtained", out of alphabetical order and with an unreliable index. By 1860 the *Directory* had become a very much more useful work of reference; and by 1917, with the absorption of its only serious rival, the *Clergy List*, reigned supreme.

No more than glimpses survive of Crockford's personality, and those mostly from the account of him given by John C. Francis, in the *Field* jubilee article already referred to. "I had occasion to call upon him a short time before his death, when we joined in a hearty laugh over his former furious attacks upon the *Athenaeum*. 'Dilke's Drag' he used to call it, and would accuse it of 'vulgar insolence and coxcombry' and 'the coarsest vulgarity'. As we parted he said, 'You have the *Athenaeum* to be proud of, and we have the *Field*.'"

John Crockford died suddenly at his home on 13 January 1865, at the age of 41. He left a widow, Annie (née Ellam) whom he married on 24 December 1847 at St Pancras Old Church. A daughter, Florence Annie, was born in St Pancras in 1852. (Florence married Arthur Brownlow in 1875 and had a son called Frederick.) His very brief will, proved 6 February 1865 at the Principal Probate Registry, left everything to his widow. His personal effects were valued at less than £1,000, but the family must have lived in some style, since one of the witnesses to the will was the resident coachman. Crockford's widow moved to 4 Upper Eton Place, Tavistock Hill, and died there on 26 July 1868.

BRENDA HOUGH

A request from the *Dictionary of National Biography* for a notice of the life of John Crockford led to the preparation of this article, a shorter version of which appeared in *The Dictionary of National Biography: Missing Persons*, 1993. For the information from the 1841 Census, and the record of Crockford's daughter Florence, we are indebted to Mr Ken Rhoades, of Kent.

A USER'S GUIDE TO *CROCKFORD*

Who is included in Crockford?
Crockford includes details of clergy and deaconesses of the Church of England, the Church in Wales, the Scottish Episcopal Church and the Church of Ireland who have given their consent under GDPR. Clergy currently serving overseas qualify for inclusion if they have trained or have been licensed in this country (see **Overseas clergy**). Clergy who have died since the last edition are listed on p. 1173 Generally, clergy who have resigned their offices (but not their orders) are included unless they are known to have been received into another Church. A small number of clergy are excluded at their own request.

Readers and lay workers are not included: please consult diocesan directories. The *Who's Who* section of *The Church of England Year Book* (published on-line by Church House Publishing and covering most aspects of the life and institutions of the Church of England) lists members of General Synod and principal members of staff of the Church's central organizations.

Addresses and telephone numbers
Where more than one land line telephone number is given, the first will normally relate to the address shown.

Addressing the clergy
See p. *12*.

Appointment details in the *Biographies* section
These reflect the legal pastoral situation prevailing at 23 August 2021, the date of the compilation of this edition of *Crockford*. Conventional districts, proprietary chapels and local ecumenical projects are also recorded. Benefice names are only recorded once in a biographical entry when they apply to successive appointments.

Crockford does not record group ministries, informal local arrangements, areas of special responsibility, emeritus appointments (except as reflected in the style of address), licence or permission to officiate when held in conjunction with another appointment from the same diocese, commissary appointments, examining chaplaincies, or secular appointments (except for educational or charitable posts).

Appointments held before ordination are not included (apart from service as a deaconess) unless they straddle the date of ordination.

Archdeaconries
See *Archdeaconries, deaneries and rural/area deans* on p. 938.

Archdeacons
Look up the place name in *Biographies*: this is cross-referenced to a personal name.

Bishops (diocesan, area, suffragan, and provincial episcopal visitors)
Look up the place name in *Biographies*: this is cross-referenced to a personal name. See also p. 888, which lists the diocesan, area, suffragan and assistant bishops by diocese, as well as provincial episcopal visitors.

Bishops (assistant)
See *Bishops in England, Wales, Scotland and Ireland* on p. 888.

Bishops in the House of Lords
See p. 892.

Bishops overseas
See *Provincial offices of the Anglican Communion* on p. 1168. Further information about the Anglican Communion, including individual dioceses and their bishops, can be found in *The Church of England Year Book*.

Bishops and archbishops, former
A list of former archbishops and bishops (diocesan and suffragan) will be found on p. 893.

Boundaries, provincial and diocesan
Maps of England and Wales, Scotland and Ireland, showing provincial and diocesan boundaries and cathedral cities, will be found on pp. 1180–1183.

Cathedral clergy
See *Cathedrals* on p. 931 for full-time cathedral clergy. The list does not include honorary appointments.

Chapel Royal
See *Royal Peculiars* on p. 933.

Christian names
The name by which a person prefers to be known, if not the first Christian name, is underlined (for example, SMITH, David John prefers to be called John). Names 'in religion' or names not part of a person's legal name are shown in parentheses.

Church: how to find the names of clergy responsible for a particular church
Look up the place name in the appropriate *Benefices and churches* section, see p. 946: if the entry is in bold type, the names of all clergy are listed and can be cross-referenced in the *Biographies* section; if the place name is not in bold type, the name of the benefice is given where the names of all clergy will be found.

Church: how to find the names of clergy responsible for a particular church when there is a vacancy
If the benefice is vacant, the telephone number of the clergy house is usually given in the appropriate *Benefices and churches* section to enable contact to be made with a new incumbent or priest-in-charge. The deanery reference (e.g. *Guildf 2*) following the benefice name cross-refers to *Archdeaconries, deaneries and rural deans* on p. 938 by means of which the name of the rural dean responsible for the vacant benefice can be found.

College chaplains
See p. 1164 for chaplains at universities, colleges of further education, colleges of higher education, sixth-form colleges, and schools.

Corrections
Clergy can now register free to view their own published data and GDPR preferences in Crockford free of charge via www.crockford.co.uk/my-clergy-page. This can also be used to notify us of updates.

Alternatively, corrections can be sent to:
Crockford Compiler, Church House, 27 Great Smith Street, London SW1P 3AZ
T: (020) 7898 1012   E: crockford@churchofengland.org

Crockford
The full title is *Crockford's Clerical Directory*. *Crockford* (not *Crockford's*) is an accepted abbreviation. See also the biography of John Crockford on p. 7.

Deaconesses
See separate section on p. 887.

Deacons
See *Biographies* section.

Deaneries
See rural or area deans below.

Deans

Look up the place name in *Biographies*: this is cross-referenced to a personal name. See also *Cathedrals* on p. 931, and *Royal Peculiars* on p. 933.

Diocesan offices

Details of the diocesan offices in England, Wales, Scotland and Ireland can be found on p. 934

E-mail addresses

These are provided where known. See after the telephone and/or fax number.

Europe, chaplains in

See *Diocese in Europe* on p. 1150.

Fax numbers

The exchange number is only given if different from that of the preceding telephone number.

Hospital chaplains

Whole-time and part-time hospital chaplains are listed under their NHS trusts on p. 1157. Cross-references have been inserted for individual hospitals.

Lay workers

Lay workers are not included in *Crockford*: please consult diocesan directories.

London churches

See English benefices and churches on p. 946. City and Guild churches are listed under LONDON CITY CHURCHES and LONDON GUILD CHURCHES. In other cases, see under church name (e.g. LANGHAM PLACE (All Souls), WESTMINSTER (St Matthew)).

Married or single?

Crockford does not provide information on marital status. However, we have included the form of address Miss, Mrs or Ms where requested. Where there has been a change of surname, a cross-reference may be found from the previous name.

National Register

In 2021 the Church of England introduced a National Register of all Church of England Clergy who are authorized to carry out ministry within the Church of England. Unlike Crockford, this does not include contact or biographical information. The register can be found at: www.churchofengland.org/about/national-register-clergy.

Non-stipendiary clergy

Non-stipendiary clergy are listed in the main *Biographies* section.

Ordination courses

See *Theological colleges and courses* on p. 1167.

Overseas clergy

Clergy who are on the *Crockford* database and who are currently serving overseas qualify for inclusion. Service overseas has in the past been recorded simply by country, though higher office (e.g. as bishop or archdeacon) has also been noted. Other eligible appointments are now being added on request.

Overseas addresses and telephone numbers are given as required by a user in the UK, and include the international access and country codes, as well as the area code. If dialling from within the country concerned, the user will need to omit the international access and country codes, and dial zero immediately before the area code.

Patronage

The patron of each benefice is listed under the benefice name in *English benefices and churches* on p. 946.

Prison chaplains
See p. 1155.

Proprietary chapels
See *English benefices and churches* on p. 946.

Provincial episcopal visitors
Look up the place name in *Biographies*: this is cross-referenced to a personal name. See also p. 888, which lists the diocesan, area, suffragan and assistant bishops and provincial episcopal visitors.

Provosts
Look up the place name in *Biographies*: this is cross-referenced to a personal name. See also *Cathedrals* on p. 931.

Queen's Chaplains
See *Royal Peculiars* on p. 933.

Readers
Readers are not included in *Crockford*: please consult diocesan directories.

Religious orders
For members of religious orders where the Christian name alone is commonly used (e.g. Brother Aidan) a cross-reference is provided to the surname. Names 'in religion' not forming part of a person's legal name will be shown in parentheses. Details of religious communities are provided in *The Church of England Year Book*.

Retired clergy
The description 'rtd' does not imply that ministry has ceased, only that clergy so described are now in receipt of a pension. All eligible appointments are now recorded.

Rural or area deans
See *Archdeaconries, deaneries and rural/area deans* on p. 938. To find who is the rural dean of a particular church, look up the place or benefice name in the appropriate *Benefices* section: the deanery reference (e.g. *Guildf 2*) following the benefice name cross-refers to *Archdeaconries, deaneries and rural deans* on p. 938 where the name of the rural dean responsible can be found.

School chaplains
See p. 1165 for chaplains in schools.

Service chaplains
See p. 1153.

Sixth-form colleges
See p. 1165.

Theological colleges and courses
See p. 1167.

University chaplains
See p. 1164.

HOW TO ADDRESS THE CLERGY

In offering the advice below, we do not intend to imply that other practices are necessarily to be discouraged (for example, the use of Father as in 'Father Smith' or 'Father Alan'). A good deal depends on circumstances, and, where a personal preference is known, it is usually good practice to follow it.

The following notes show acceptable current usage

(a) on an envelope or formal listing
(b) in starting a social letter or in speech, and
(c) when referring to a member of the clergy

Category (a) is not open to much variation, owing to the formality of the context, but categories (b) and (c) will often vary according to circumstances. It is always acceptable to use the appropriate Christian name in place of initials (for example, the Revd Alice Smith). In the absence of any style or title conferred by a post, all deacons and priests are styled 'The Reverend', and all who have been consecrated bishop are styled 'The Right Reverend'.

For abbreviations, see paragraph 13 below.

1 **Deacons and Priests**
   (a) The Reverend A B Smith
   (b) Mr/Mrs/Miss/Ms Smith (unless it is known that some other style is preferred— the title Vicar or Rector is acceptable only if the person so addressed really is the incumbent of the parish where you live or worship)
   (c) The Reverend A B Smith at the first mention, and Mr/Mrs/Miss/Ms Smith thereafter

   Notes 1 The form 'Reverend Smith' or 'The Reverend Smith' should never be used this side of the Atlantic. If the Christian name or initials are not known, the correct forms are
      (a) The Reverend — Smith, or The Reverend Mr/Mrs/Miss/Ms Smith
      (b) Mr/Mrs/Miss/Ms Smith
      (c) The Reverend Mr/Mrs/Miss/Ms Smith at the first mention, and Mr/Mrs/Miss/Ms Smith thereafter

   2 There is no universally accepted way of addressing an envelope to a married couple of whom both are in holy orders. We recommend the style 'The Reverend A B and the Reverend C D Smith'.
   3 Where the husband is in holy orders and the wife is not, the customary style is 'The Reverend A B and Mrs Smith'.
   4 Where the wife is in holy orders and the husband is not, we recommend the style 'Mr A B Smith and the Reverend Mrs Smith'.

2 **Prebendaries**
   (a) The Reverend Prebendary A B Smith
   (b) Prebendary Smith
   (c) Prebendary Smith

3 **Canons (both Residentiary and Honorary)**
   (a) The Reverend Canon A B Smith
   (b) Canon Smith
   (c) Canon Smith

4 **Archdeacons**
   (a) The Venerable the Archdeacon of X
   (b) Archdeacon, or more formally Mr/Madam Archdeacon
   (c) The Archdeacon of X at the first mention, and the Archdeacon thereafter

   Notes 1 In the case of an archdeacon (or dean/provost, bishop, or archbishop) in office, the style above is to be preferred. The personal name should be used only for the purpose of identification.
   2 For an archdeacon emeritus, the correct forms are
      (a) The Venerable A B Smith
      (b) Archdeacon
      (c) Archdeacon Smith

5 Deans and Provosts
(a) The Very Reverend the Dean/Provost of X
(b) Dean/Provost, *or more formally* Mr/Madam Dean/Provost
(c) The Dean/Provost of X at the first mention, and the Dean thereafter (see also note 1 to paragraph 4 above)

6 Bishops, Diocesan and Suffragan
(a) The Right Reverend the Bishop of X, *or* The Right Reverend the Lord/Lady Bishop of X
(b) Bishop, *or more formally* My Lord/Lady
(c) The Bishop of X at the first mention, and the Bishop thereafter (see also note 1 to paragraph 4 above)

Notes   1 It is a matter of individual preference whether the title 'Lord/Lady' should be used.
        2 The Bishop of London is a Privy Councillor, and has the style 'The Right Reverend and Right Honourable the Lord Bishop of London'.
        3 The Bishop of Meath and Kildare is styled 'The Most Reverend'.

7 Assistant and Retired Bishops
(a) The Right Reverend A B Smith
(b) Bishop
(c) Bishop Smith

8 Archbishops
(a) The Most Reverend the Lord Archbishop of X
(b) Archbishop, *or more formally* Your Grace
(c) (His Grace) the Archbishop of X at the first mention, and the Archbishop thereafter (see also note 1 to paragraph 4 above)

Notes   1 The Archbishops of Canterbury and York, being Privy Councillors, also have 'Right Honourable' included in their style (for example, The Most Reverend and Right Honourable the Lord Archbishop of Canterbury).
        2 The presiding bishop of the Scottish Episcopal Church is the Primus, and the correct forms are
           (a) The Most Reverend the Primus
           (b) Primus
           (c) Primus
        3 A retired archbishop properly reverts to the status of bishop, but may be given as a courtesy the style of an archbishop.

9 Chaplains to the Armed Services
(a) The Reverend A B Smith RN (*or* CF *or* RAF)
(b) Padre, *or* Padre Smith
(c) The Padre, *or* Padre Smith

10 Titled Clerics
Where a member of the clergy also holds a temporal title, this is always preceded in writing by the ecclesiastical one.

Barons (other than retired archbishops)
(a) The Reverend the Lord Smith of X
(b) Lord Smith
(c) The Reverend the Lord Smith at the first mention, and Lord Smith thereafter

Baronets
(a) The Reverend Sir Alan Smith Bt
(b) Sir Alan Smith or Sir Alan
(c) The Reverend Sir Alan Smith at the first mention, and Sir Alan thereafter

Knights
An ordained priest may be appointed to an order of knighthood, but will not normally receive the accolade or title. The appropriate designation will follow the name or ecclesiastical title, e.g. The Right Reverend the Bishop of X, KCVO. If he was knighted *before* he was ordained, he will retain his title, and will be addressed in much the same manner as a baronet.

Dames
(a) The Reverend Dame Alice Smith
(b) Dame Alice Smith or Dame Alice
(c) The Reverend Dame Alice Smith at the first mention, and Dame Alice thereafter

Wives of Barons, Baronets and Knights
(a) The Reverend Lady Smith (of X)
(b) Lady Smith
(c) The Reverend Lady Smith at the first mention, and Lady Smith thereafter

Sons and daughters of peers
(a) The Reverend the Honourable Jocelyn Smith, *or* The Reverend Lord/Lady Jocelyn Smith (as appropriate)
(b) Mr/Mrs/Miss/Ms Smith, *or* Lord/Lady Jocelyn Smith
(c) The Reverend J K Smith at the first mention, and Mr/Mrs/Miss/Ms Smith thereafter; *or* the Reverend Lord/Lady Jocelyn Smith at the first mention, and Lord/Lady Jocelyn thereafter.

11 Ordained Members of Religious Orders
(a) The Reverend Alan/Alice Smith XYZ; The Reverend Brother Alan/Sister Alice XYZ
(b) Father, Father Smith, *or* Father Alan; Mother, Mother Smith, *or* Mother Alice; Brother Alan/Sister Alice
(c) The Reverend Alan/Alice Smith; Father Alan Smith; Mother Alice Smith; Father Smith; Brother Alan/Sister Alice

Notes 1 A name 'in religion', shown in parentheses in the biographical entry, should be used in preference to the baptismal name or initials. Sometimes the surname is not used. In this Directory, however, the entry will be found under the surname, whether it is normally used or not, and, if appropriate, a cross-reference is given under the Christian name.
2 Some orders use 'Brother' and 'Sister' for lay and ordained members without distinction, along with Christian names.
3 It is customary to specify the religious order by giving the appropriate letters after the name.

12 Academics
When a member of the clergy holds more than one title, the ecclesiastical one is normally used.

Professor   (a) The Reverend Canon A B Smith
also Canon   (b) Canon Smith, *or* Professor Smith, according to context
                 (c) Canon Smith, *or* Professor Smith, according to context
Canon   (a) The Reverend Canon A B Smith (degree)
also Doctor   (b) Canon Smith, *or* Dr Smith, according to context
                 (c) Canon Smith, *or* Dr Smith, according to context

13 Abbreviations
The following abbreviations are in common use

Reverend: Revd *or* Rev
Father: Fr
Right Reverend: Rt Revd *or* Rt Rev
Prebendary: Preb
Venerable: Ven

Reverend, Right Reverend, Very Reverend, Most Reverend and Venerable, whether abbreviated or not, should always be preceded by the definite article.

ABBREVIATIONS USED IN CROCKFORD'S CLERICAL DIRECTORY

A

AAAI .... Associate, Institute of Administrative Accountants
AB .... Bachelor of Arts (USA)
Ab .... (Diocese of) Aberdeen and Orkney
ABEng .... Associate Member of the Association of Building Engineers
Aber .... Aberdeen
ABIA .... Associate, Bankers' Institute of Australasia
ABIPP .... Associate, British Institute of Professional Photography
ABIST .... Associate, British Institute of Surgical Technology
ABM .... Advisory Board of Ministry (now Ministry Division)
Abp .... Archbishop
ABPsS .... Associate, British Psychological Society (now see AFBPsS)
ABSM .... Associate, Birmingham and Midland Institute School of Music
Abth .... Aberystwyth
ACA .... Associate, Institute of Chartered Accountants
ACABE .... Associate, Chartered Association of Building Engineers (formerly ABEng)
ACC .... Anglican Consultative Council
ACCA .... Associate, Chartered Association of Certified Accountants (formerly AACCA)
ACCM .... Advisory Council for the Church's Ministry (now Ministry Division)
ACCS .... Associate, Corporation of Secretaries
ACCTS .... Association for Christian Conferences, Teaching, and Service
ACE .... Associateship of the College of Education
.... Member, Association of Conference Executives
ACF .... Army Cadet Force
ACIArb .... Associate, Chartered Institute of Arbitrators
ACIB .... Associate, Chartered Institute of Bankers (formerly AIB)
ACIBS .... Associate, Chartered Institute of Bankers in Scotland
ACII .... Associate, Chartered Insurance Institute
ACIOB .... Associate, Chartered Institute of Building
ACIPA .... Associate, Chartered Institute of Patent Agents
ACIPD .... Associate, Chartered Institute of Personnel and Development
ACIS .... Associate, Institute of Chartered Secretaries and Administrators
ACIT .... Associate, Chartered Institute of Transport
ACMA .... Associate, Chartered Institute of Management Accountants (formerly ACWA)
ACMI .... Associate, Chartered Management Institute (formerly AIMgt)
ACORA .... Archbishops' Commission on Rural Areas
ACP .... Associate, College of Preceptors
ACS .... Additional Curates Society

ACSM .... Associate, Camborne School of Mines
ACT .... Australian Capital Territory
.... Australian College of Theology
ACUPA .... Archbishops' Commission on Urban Priority Areas
AD .... Area Dean
Ad .... Advanced
AdDipEd .... Advanced Diploma in Education
Admin .... Administration
.... Administrative
.... Administrator
Adn .... Archdeacon
Adnry .... Archdeaconry
Adv .... Adviser
.... Advisory
AEdRD .... Associateship in Educational Research and Development
AFAIM .... Associate Fellow, Australian Institute of Management
AFBPsS .... Associate Fellow, British Psychological Society (formerly ABPsS)
AFC .... Air Force Cross
AFHEA .... Associate Fellow, Higher Education Academy
AFIMA .... Associate Fellow, Institute of Mathematics and its Applications
AFOM .... Associate, Faculty of Occupational Medicine
Agric .... Agricultural
.... Agriculture
AGSM .... Associate, Guildhall School of Music and Drama
AHSM or AHA ... Associate, Institute of Health Service Management (formerly Administrators)
AIA .... Associate, Institute of Actuaries
AIAS .... Associate, Incorporated Association of Architects and Surveyors
AIAT .... Associate, Institute of Animal Technicians
Aid .... Aidan
.... Aidan's
AIDS .... Acquired Immunity Deficiency Syndrome
AIFST .... Associate, Institute of Food Science and Technology
AIGCM .... Associate, Incorporated Guild of Church Musicians
AIIM .... Associate, Institute of Investment Management
AIL .... Associate, Institute of Linguists
AIMgt .... Associate, Institute of Management (now see ACMI)
AIMLS .... Associate, Institute of Medical Laboratory Sciences
AIMSW .... Associate, Institute of Medical Social Work
AIPM .... Associate, Institute of Personnel Management (now see ACIPD)
AITI .... Associate, Institute of Taxation in Ireland
AKC .... Associate, King's College London
ALA .... Associate, Library Association
ALAM .... Associate, London Academy of Music
ALBC .... Associate, London Bible College
ALCD .... Associate, London College of Divinity
ALCM .... Associate, London College of Music
ALSM .... Associate, Lancashire School of Music
alt .... alternate

AM .... Albert Medal
.... Master of Arts (USA)
AMA .... Associate, Museums Association
AMASI .... Associate Member of the Architects and Surveyors Institute
AMCST .... Associate, Manchester College of Science and Technology
AMCT .... Associate, Manchester College of Technology
AMIBF .... Associate Member, Institute of British Foundrymen
AMIC .... Associate Member, Institute of Counselling
AMICME .... Associate Member, Institute of Cast Metal Engineers
AMIDHE .... Associate Member, Institute of Domestic Heating Engineers
AMIEHO .... Associate Member, Institution of Environmental Health Officers
AMIM .... Associate Member, Institute of Metals
AMIMMM .... Associate Member, Institute of Materials, Minerals and Mining
AMInstT .... Associate Member, Institute of Transport
AMInstTA .... Associate Member, Institute of Transport Administration
AMITD .... Associate Member, Institute of Training and Development (now see ACIPD)
AMIW .... Associate Member, Institute of Welfare (formerly AMIWO)
AMRSH .... Associate Member, Royal Society of Health
AMSIA .... Associate Member, Society of Investment Analysts
AMusLCM .... Associate in Music, London College of Music
AMusTCL .... Associate in Music, Trinity College of Music London
ANC .... African National Congress
Andr .... Andrew
.... Andrew's
.... Andrews
Angl .... Anglican
.... Anglicans
Ant .... Anthony
.... Anthony's
AO .... Officer, Order of Australia
APhS .... Associate, Philosophical Society of England
Appt .... Appointment
ARAM .... Associate, Royal Academy of Music
ARCA .... Associate, Royal College of Art
ARCIC .... Anglican-Roman Catholic International Commission
ARCM .... Associate, Royal College of Music
ARCO .... Associate, Royal College of Organists
ARCO(CHM) .... Associate, Royal College of Organists with Diploma in Choir Training
ARCS .... Associate, Royal College of Science
ARCST .... Associate, Royal College of Science and Technology (Glasgow)
ARCT .... Associate, Royal Conservatory of Music Toronto
ARCUK .... Architects' Registration Council of the United Kingdom

Arg...................... (Diocese of) Argyll and The Isles
ARHistS................. Associate, Royal Historical Society
ARIAM............... Associate, Royal Irish Academy of Music
ARICS.................. Professional Associate, Royal Institution of Chartered Surveyors (now see MRICS)
Arm...................... (Diocese of) Armagh
ARMCM.............. Associate, Royal Manchester College of Music
ARPS .... Associate, Royal Photographic Society
ARSCM .... Associate, Royal School of Church Music
ARSM.................. Associate, Royal School of Mines
AS........................ Associate in Science (USA)
ASCA................... Associate, Society of Company and Commercial Accountants
Assn .... Association
Assoc.................. Associate
ASSP .... Society of All Saints Sisters of the Poor
Asst..................... Assistant
ASVA .... Associate, Incorporated Society of Valuers and Auctioneers
ATC .... Air Training Corps
ATCL .... Associate, Trinity College of Music London
ATD..................... Art Teacher's Diploma
ATh(SA).............. Associate in Theology (South Africa)
ATI...................... Associate, Textile Institute
ATII...................... Associate Member, Institute of Taxation
ATL .... Association of Teachers and Lecturers
ATV .... Associated Television
Aug..................... Augustine
.... Augustine's
Aus...................... Australian
Aux .... Auxiliaries
.... Auxiliary
AVCM .... Associate, Victoria College of Music

B

b .... Born
B & W.................. (Diocese of) Bath and Wells
B or Bapt............. Baptist
.... Baptist's
BA........................ Bachelor of Arts
BA(Econ)............. Bachelor of Arts in Economics
BA(Ed)................. Bachelor of Arts in Education
BA(QTS)............. Bachelor of Arts (Qualified Teacher Status)
BA(Theol)........... Bachelor of Arts in Theology
BA(ThM)............. Bachelor of Arts in Theology in Ministry
BAdmin.............. Bachelor of Administration
BAgr.................... Bachelor of Agriculture
BAgrSc............... Bachelor of Agricultural Science
BAI...................... Bachelor of Engineering (also see BE and BEng)
Ball..................... Balliol
Ban .... (Diocese of) Bangor
BAO .... Bachelor of Obstetrics
BAppSc .... Bachelor of Applied Science
BAppSc(Agric).... Bachelor of Applied Science (Agriculture)
BAppSc(OT)........ Bachelor of Applied Science (Occupational Therapy)
BArch .... Bachelor of Architecture
Barn .... Barnabas
.... Barnabas's
Bart .... Bartholomew
.... Bartholomew's
BAS .... Bachelor of Architectural Studies
BASc .... Bachelor of Applied Science
BATM.................. Bachelor of Arts in Theology and Ministry
BBA..................... Bachelor of Business Administration
BBC..................... British Broadcasting Corporation
BBS .... Bachelor of Business Studies
BC........................ British Columbia (Canada)

BCA..................... Bachelor of Commerce and Administration
BCC .... British Council of Churches (now CTBI)
BCE .... Bachelor of Civil Engineering
BCh or BChir....... Bachelor of Surgery (also see BS and ChB)
BChD.................. Bachelor of Dental Surgery
BCL...................... Bachelor of Civil Law
BCMS................... Bible Churchmen's Missionary Society (now Crosslinks)
BCom or BComm Bachelor of Commerce
BCombStuds .... Bachelor of Combined Studies
BCommWelf .... Bachelor of Community Welfare
BD........................ Bachelor of Divinity
Bd .... Board
BDA .... Bachelor of Dramatic Art
BDes .... Bachelor of Design
BDiv .... Bachelor of Divinity
BDQ..................... Bachelor of Divinity Qualifying Examination
BDS...................... Bachelor of Dental Surgery
BDSc.................... Bachelor of Dental Science
BE........................ Bachelor of Engineering (also see BAI and BEng)
BEc....................... Bachelor of Economics (Australia)
BEcon .... Bachelor of Economics (USA)
BEd .... Bachelor of Education
Bedf .... Bedford
BEdSt .... Bachelor of Educational Studies
Belf...................... Belfast
BEM..................... British Empire Medal
BEng .... Bachelor of Engineering (also see BAI and BE)
BèsL .... Bachelier ès lettres
BFA...................... Bachelor of Fine Arts
BFBS.................... British and Foreign Bible Society
BHSc .... Bachelor of Health Sciences
Bibl .... Biblical
BIE....................... Bachelor of Industrial Engineering (USA)
Birm .... (Diocese of) Birmingham
BL........................ Bachelor of Law
Blackb.................. (Diocese of) Blackburn
BLib..................... Bachelor of Librarianship
BLitt .... Bachelor of Letters
BM....................... Bachelor of Medicine (also see MB)
BM, BCh .... Conjoint degree of Bachelor of Medicine, Bachelor of Surgery
BMedSci .... Bachelor of Medical Science
BMet................... Bachelor of Metallurgy
BMin.................... Bachelor of Ministry
BMMF................. Bible and Medical Missionary Fellowship (now Interserve)
BMO..................... Bishop's Mission Order
BMU .... Board for Mission and Unity
BMus .... Bachelor of Music (also see MusB and MusBac)
BMusEd .... Bachelor of Music Education
BN........................ Bachelor of Nursing
BNC..................... Brasenose College
Bp .... Bishop
BPaed.................. Bachelor of Paediatrics
BPh or BPhil........ Bachelor of Philosophy
BPharm............... Bachelor of Pharmacy
BPhil(Ed)............. Bachelor of Philosophy (Education)
BPl....................... Bachelor of Planning
BPR&TM............. Bachelor of Parks, Recreation and Tourism Management
BPrimEd.............. Bachelor of Primary Education
BProfStud .... Bachelor of Professional Studies
Br .... British
Bradf................... (Diocese of) Bradford
Bre...................... (Diocese of) Brechin
BRE...................... Bachelor of Religious Education (USA)
BRF...................... Bible Reading Fellowship
Brig .... Brigadier
Bris...................... (Diocese of) Bristol
BS........................ Bachelor of Science (also see BSc)

.... Bachelor of Surgery (also see BCh, BChir and ChB)
BSB...................... Brotherhood of St Barnabas
BSc...................... Bachelor of Science (also see BS)
BSc(Econ) .... Bachelor of Science in Economics
BSc(Soc) .... Bachelor of Science (Sociology)
BScAgr................ Bachelor of Science in Agriculture
BScEcon.............. Bachelor of Science in Economics
BScEng................ Bachelor of Science in Engineering (also see BSE)
BScFor................. Bachelor of Science in Forestry
BScTech .... Bachelor of Technical Science
BSE...................... Bachelor of Science in Engineering (also see BScEng)
BSEd.................... Bachelor of Science in Education (USA)
BSocAdmin......... Bachelor of Social Administration
BSocSc................ Bachelor of Social Science (also see BSSc)
BSP...................... Brotherhood of St Paul
BSS...................... Bachelor of Social Studies
BSSc.................... Bachelor of Social Science (also see BSocSc)
BST .... Bachelor of Sacred Theology
BSW..................... Bachelor of Social Work
BT........................ Bachelor of Teaching
Bt .... Baronet
BTech.................. Bachelor of Technology
BTh or BTheol...... Bachelor of Theology (also see STB)
BTS .... Bachelor of Theological Studies
BUniv .... Bachelor of the University
BVetMed.............. Bachelor of Veterinary Medicine (also see VetMB)
BVM&S .... Bachelor of Veterinary Medicine and Surgery
BVSc.................... Bachelor of Veterinary Science

C

C.......................... Curate
c........................... Consecrated
C & O.................. (Diocese of) Cashel and Ossory (united dioceses of Cashel, Waterford, Lismore, Ferns and Leighlin)
C of E.................. Church of England
C of S.................. Church of Scotland
C&G .... City and Guilds
C, C & R .... (Diocese of) Cork, Cloyne and Ross
C, F & O .... (Diocese of) Cashel, Ferns and Ossory (united dioceses of Cashel, Waterford, Lismore, Ossory, Ferns and Leighlin)
c/o .... Care of
CA........................ Church Army
.... Member, Institute of Chartered Accountants of Scotland
CA(Z)................... Member, Institute of Chartered Accountants of Zimbabwe
CACTM............... Central Advisory Council for the Ministry (now Ministry Division)
Cam..................... Cambridge
Can .... Canon
Cand.................... Candidate
.... Candidate's
.... Candidates'
CANDL .... Church and Neighbourhood Development in London
Cant..................... (Diocese of) Canterbury

Capt.................... Captain
CARA .... Care and Resources for
people affected by AIDS/HIV
CARE................. Christian Action Research
and Education
Carl.................... (Diocese of) Carlisle
CASA................. Anglican Church of the
Southern Cone of America
Cath................... Catharine/Catherine
.... Catharine's/Catherine's
Cathl.................. Cathedral
CB.................... Companion, Order of the
Bath
CBDTI .... Carlisle and Blackburn
Diocesan Training Institute
CBE.................. Commander, Order of the
British Empire
CBIM................. Companion, British
Institute of Management
CBiol................. Chartered Biologist
CCBI .... Council of Churches for
Britain and Ireland (now see
CTBI)
CCC.................. Corpus Christi College
.... Council for the Care of
Churches
CCCS .... Commonwealth and
Continental Church Society
CChem .... Chartered Chemist
CCWA................ Churches Community Work
Alliance
CD .... Canadian Forces Decoration
.... Conventional District (also
see ED)
CDir.................. Chartered Director
Cdre.................. Commodore
CECD................. Church of England Council
for the Deaf
CECS .... Church of England Children's
Society (now known as the
Children's Society)
CEMS .... Church of England Men's
Society
Cen .... Centre
.... Center
.... Central
CEng................. Chartered Engineer
CEnv .... Chartered Environmentalist
Cert................... Certificate(e)
CertEd............... Certificate of Education
CertFE .... Certificate of Further
Education
CertHE .... Certificate in Higher
Education
CETD .... Certificate in the Education
of the Deaf
CF .... Chaplain to the Forces
CGA.................. Community of the Glorious
Ascension
CGeol................ Chartered Geologist
CH .... Companion of Honour
Ch..................... Christ
.... Christ's
.... Church
Ch Ch .... Christ Church
Chan.................. Chancellor
Chapl................. Chaplain
.... Chaplaincies
.... Chaplaincy
.... Chaplains
Chas.................. Charles
.... Charles's
ChB................... Bachelor of Surgery (also see
BChir and BS)
Chelmsf............. (Diocese of) Chelmsford
Chelt................. Cheltenham
Ches.................. (Diocese of) Chester
Chich................. (Diocese of) Chichester
Chmn .... Chairman
.... Chairwoman
Chpl.................. Chapel
Chr.................... Christian
.... Christians
Chris .... Christopher
.... Christopher's
Chrys .... Chrysostom
.... Chrysostom's
Chu................... Churchill
CIMA .... Chartered Institute of
Management Accountants
C-in-c................ Curate-in-charge
CIO .... Church Information Office
CIPFA .... Chartered Institute of Public
Finance and Accountancy
CITC .... Church of Ireland
Theological College

CITP .... Chartered Information
Technology Professional
CJGS .... Community of the
Companions of Jesus the
Good Shepherd
Clem.................. Clement
.... Clement's
Cl-in-c............... Cleric-in-charge
Cllr.................... Councillor/Counsellor
Clogh................. (Diocese of) Clogher
CMath .... Chartered Mathematician
CMD .... Cambridge Mission to Delhi
(now see USPG)
.... Continuing Ministerial
Development
CME.................. Continuing Ministerial
Education
CMG.................. Companion, Order of St
Michael and St George
CMgr .... Chartered Manager
CMIIA .... Chartered Member, Institute
of Internal Auditors
CMJ................... Church's Ministry among
Jewish People
CMP.................. Company of Mission Priests
CMS.................. Church Mission Society
(formerly Church
Missionary Society)
CNZM .... Companion, New Zealand
Order of Merit
Co...................... Company
.... County
.... Counties
Col..................... Colonel
Coll .... College
Colleg .... Collegiate
Comdr .... Commander
Comdr OM (Italy) Commander, Order of Merit
of the Italian Republic
Commn .... Commission
Commr............... Commissioner
Comp .... Comprehensive
Conf................... Confederation
.... Conference
Conn.................. (Diocese of) Connor
Co-ord .... Co-ordinator
.... Co-ordinating
COPEC.............. Conference on Politics,
Economics and Community
CORAT .... Christian Organizations
Research and Advisory Trust
CORE .... City Outreach through
Renewal Evangelism
Corp .... Corporation
Coun.................. Council
Cov.................... (Diocese of) Coventry
CP .... Community Priest
CPA.................... Chartered Patent Agent
(formerly FCIPA)
CPAS .... Church Pastoral Aid Society
CPEng............... Chartered Professional
Engineer (of Institution of
Engineers of Australia)
CPFA................. Member Chartered Institute
of Public Finance and
Accountancy (formerly IPFA)
CPhys................ Chartered Physicist of the
Institute of Physics
CPM.................. Colonial Police Medal
CPsychol............ Chartered Member, British
Psychological Society
CQSW................ Certificate of Qualification
in Social Work
CR .... Community of the
Resurrection (Mirfield)
CSA .... Community of St Andrew
CSC................... Community of the Sisters of
the Church
CSci .... Chartered Scientist
CSD................... Community of St Denys
CSF .... Community of St Francis
CSG .... Company of the Servants of
God
CSMV................ Community of St Mary the
Virgin
CSocSc.............. Certificate in Social Science
CSP .... Community of St Peter
CSS .... Certificate in Social Service
CSSM................ Children's Special Service
Mission

CStat................. Chartered Statistician
CSWG................ Community of the Servants
of the Will of God
CTA.................... Chartered Tax Adviser
CTABRSM .... Certificate of Teaching,
Associated Board of the
Royal Schools of Music
CTBI.................. Churches Together in
Britain and Ireland
(formerly CCBI)
CTE .... Churches Together in
England
Cttee.................. Committee
CUF................... Church Urban Fund
Cust .... Custodian
.... Custody
Cuth.................. Cuthbert
.... Cuthbert's
CVO................... Commander, Royal
Victorian Order
CWME .... Commission on World
Mission and Evangelism
CY..................... Church and Youth
CYCW .... Certificate in Youth and
Community Work
CYFA .... Church Youth Fellowships
Association
Cypr.................. Cyprian
.... Cyprian's

D

d.......................... Ordained Deacon
D & D .... (Diocese of) Down and
Dromore
D & G .... (Diocese of) Dublin and
Glendalough
D & R................ (Diocese of) Derry and
Raphoe
D&C.................. Dean and Chapter
DA...................... Doctor of Arts
DACE .... Diploma in Adult and
Continuing Education
DAES................. Diploma in Advanced
Educational Studies
DAPC .... Diploma in Advanced
Psychological Counselling
DArch .... Doctor of Architecture
Darw................. Darwin
DASAE............... Diploma of Advanced Study
in Adult Education
DASE................. Diploma in the Advanced
Study of Education
DASHE .... Diploma in Advanced
Studies in Higher Education
DASS................. Diploma in Applied Social
Studies
DASSc .... Diploma in Applied Social
Science
Dav .... David
.... David's
DB..................... Bachelor of Divinity (USA)
DBA .... Doctor of Business
Administration
DBE................... Dame Commander, Order of
the British Empire
DBF................... Diocesan Board of Finance
DBP................... Diocesan Board of Patronage
DC .... District of Columbia (USA)
DCC................... Diploma in Crisis Counselling
of the Institute of Counselling
DCE................... Diploma of a College of
Education
DCL................... Doctor of Civil Law
DCnL .... Doctor of Canon Law
DCouns.............. Doctor of Counselling
DCR(R).............. Diploma of the College of
Radiographers
DCYW............... Diploma in Community
and Youth Work
DD .... Doctor of Divinity
DDes.................. Doctor of Design
DDS................... Doctor of Dental Surgery
DEd.................... Doctor of Education (also
see EdD)
DEHC................ Diploma in the Education
of Handicapped Children
DEng.................. Doctor of Engineering
Dep.................... Deputy
Dept................... Department
DèS.................... Docteur ès sciences
DèsL................. Docteur ès lettres
Det..................... Detention

DFC..................... Distinguished Flying Cross
DFM..................... Distinguished Flying Medal (Canada)
DHA..................... District Health Authority
DHC..................... Doctor Honoris Causa
DHL .... Doctor of Humane Letters
DHSc.................... Doctor of Health Science
DHumLit............... Doctor of Humane Letters
Dio...................... Diocese
Dioc .... Diocesan
Dip...................... Diploma
DipAdEd .... Diploma in Advanced Education
DipAE.................. Diploma in Adult Education
DipCOT .... Diploma of the College of Occupational Therapists
DipEd.................. Diploma in Education
DipHE .... Diploma in Higher Education
DipOT .... Diploma in Occupational Therapy
DipSW .... Diploma in Social Work
Dir....................... Director
Distr..................... District
Div....................... Divinity
Div Test............... Divinity Testimonium
DL .... Deputy Lieutenant
DLC...................... Diploma of Loughborough College
DLitt.................... Doctor of Letters (also see LittD)
DLitt et Phil .... Doctor of Letters and Philosophy
DLSc .... Doctor of Legal Science
DM .... Doctor of Medicine
DMin .... Doctor of Ministry
DMinTh .... Doctor of Ministry and Theology
DMus................... Doctor of Music
Dn........................ Deacon
Dn-in-c .... Deacon-in-charge
DOE .... Department of the Environment
Dom .... Domestic
Down.................... Downing
DPhil................... Doctor of Philosophy (also see PhD)
DProf .... Doctor in Professional Studies
.... Professional Doctorate in Practical Theology
DPsych................ Doctor of Psychotherapy
DPT..................... Doctor of Practical Theology
Dr......................... Doctor
Dr rer nat............ Doctor of Natural Science
Dr Théol .... Doctor of Theology (France)
DRCOG................ Diploma of the Royal College of Obstetricians and Gynaecologists
DrTheol .... Doctor of Theology (Germany)
DSc .... Doctor of Science (also see ScD)
DSC .... Distinguished Service Cross
DSc(Eng) .... Doctor of Science in Engineering
DSM..................... Distinguished Service Medal
DSO..................... Companion, Distinguished Service Order
DSocSc .... Doctor of Social Science
Dss...................... Deaconess
dss...................... Admitted Deaconess
DST...................... Doctor of Sacred Theology (also see STD)
DSW..................... Doctor of Social Work
DTech .... Doctor of Technology
DTh *or* DTheol..... Doctor of Theology (also see ThD)
DThM *or* DThMin ... Doctor of Theology and Ministry
DTI....................... Department of Trade and Industry
Dub...................... Dublin
DUniv .... Doctor of the University
DUP .... Docteur de l'Université de Paris
Dur .... (Diocese of) Durham

E

E........................... East
.... Eastern
EAMTC .... East Anglian Ministerial Training Course
EC .... Emergency Commission
Ecum.................... Ecumenical

.... Ecumenics
.... Ecumenism
Ed........................ Editor
.... Editorial
ED........................ Ecclesiastical District (also see CD)
.... Efficiency Decoration
EdD...................... Doctor of Education (also see DEd)
Edin..................... (Diocese of) Edinburgh
Edm .... Edmund
.... Edmund's
EdM...................... Master of Education (USA) (also see MEd)
Educn .... Education
.... Educational
Edw...................... Edward
.... Edward's
Eliz .... Elizabeth
.... Elizabeth's
Em .... Emanuel
.... Emmanuel
Emb .... Embassy
EMMTC .... East Midlands Ministry Training Course
EN(G)................... Enrolled Nurse (General)
EN(M)................... Enrolled Nurse (Mental)
EngD.................... Doctor of Engineering
EngTech............... Engineering Technician
Episc .... Episcopal
.... Episcopalian
ERD..................... Emergency Reserve Decoration
ERMC................... Eastern Region Ministry Course
ESC .... École Supérieure de Commerce
ESMI .... Elderly, Sick and Mentally Infirm
Eur .... (Diocese in) Europe (formerly Diocese of Gibraltar in Europe)
.... European
EurIng................. European Engineer
Ev........................ Evangelist
.... Evangelist's
.... Evangelists
Evang................... Evangelical
.... Evangelism
Ex........................ (Diocese of) Exeter
Exam.................... Examining
Exec..................... Executive
Exor .... Executor
Ext....................... Extension
EYTS.................... Early Years Teacher Status

F

F&HE .... Further and Higher Education
FAA .... Fellow, Institution of Administrative Accountants
FACOG .... Fellow, American College of Obstetricians and Gynaecologists
FAcSS.................. Fellow, Academy of Social Sciences
FADO................... Fellow, Association of Dispensing Opticians
FAEB.................... Fellow, Academy of Environmental Biology (India)
FAIM .... Fellow, Australian Institute of Management
FAIWCW.............. Fellow, Australian Institute of Welfare and Community Workers
FASI..................... Fellow, Architects' and Surveyors' Institute
FBA .... Fellow, British Academy
FBCartS............... Fellow, British Cartographic Society
FBCO .... Fellow, British College of Ophthalmic Opticians (Optometrists)
FBCS .... Fellow, British Computer Society
FBDO................... Fellow, Association of British Dispensing Opticians
FBEng.................. Fellow, Association of Building Engineers
FBIM .... Fellow, British Institute of Management (formerly MBIM)
FBIS..................... Fellow, British Interplanetary Society

FBIST................... Fellow, British Institute of Surgical Technologists
FBOA .... Fellow, British Optical Association
FBPICS .... Fellow, British Production and Inventory Control Society
FBPsS .... Fellow, British Psychological Society
FBS...................... Fellow, Burgon Society
FCA...................... Fellow, Institute of Chartered Accountants
FCCA .... Fellow, Chartered Association of Certified Accountants (formerly FACCA)
FCFI..................... Fellow, Clothing and Footwear Institute
FCIArb................. Fellow, Chartered Institute of Arbitrators
FCIB .... Fellow, Chartered Institute of Bankers
.... Fellow, Corporation of Insurance Brokers
FCIE .... Fellow, Association of Charity Independent Examiners
FCIH.................... Fellow, Chartered Institute of Housing
FCII .... Fellow, Chartered Insurance Institute
FCILA .... Fellow, Chartered Institute of Loss Adjusters
FCIM.................... Fellow, Chartered Institute of Marketing (formerly FInstM)
FCIOB.................. Fellow, Chartered Institute of Building
FCIPD .... Fellow, Chartered Institute of Personnel and Development
FCIS .... Fellow, Institute of Chartered Secretaries and Administrators
FCIT .... Fellow, Chartered Institute of Transport
FCMA .... Fellow, Chartered Institute of Management Accountants
FCMI.................... Fellow, Chartered Management Institute (formerly FIMgt)
FCO .... Foreign and Commonwealth Office
FCollP .... Fellow, College of Preceptors
FCollT.................. Fellow, College of Teachers
FCOptom .... Fellow, College of Optometrists
FCP...................... Fellow, College of Preceptors
FCT .... Fellow, Association of Corporate Treasurers
FDS .... Fellow in Dental Surgery
FDSRCPSGlas....... Fellow in Dental Surgery, Royal College of Physicians and Surgeons of Glasgow
FDSRCS............... Fellow in Dental Surgery, Royal College of Surgeons of England
FE........................ Further Education
FEI....................... Fellow, Energy Institute
Fell...................... Fellow
FEPA.................... Fellow, Evangelical Preachers' Association
FETC .... Further Education Teacher's Certificate
FFA...................... Fellow, Institute of Financial Accountants
FFAEM................. Fellow, Faculty of Accident and Emergency Medicine
FFARCS .... Fellow, Faculty of Anaesthetists, Royal College of Surgeons of England
FFChM................. Fellow, Faculty of Church Music
FFCI..................... Fellow, Faculty of Clinical Informatics
FFDRCSI............... Fellow, Faculty of Dentistry, Royal College of Surgeons in Ireland
FFHom................. Fellow, the Faculty of Homoeopathy
FFOM................... Fellow, Faculty of Occupational Medicine
FFPH .... Fellow, Faculty of Public Health (formerly FFPHM)
FFPHM................. Fellow, Faculty of Public Health Medicine (*now see* FFPH)

FFPM.................. Fellow, Faculty of Pharmaceutical Medicine
FGA..................... Fellow, Gemmological Association
FGMS................. Fellow, Guild of Musicians and Singers
FGS .... Fellow, Geological Society of London
FHA..................... Fellow, Institute of Hospital Administrators (now see FHSM)
.... Fellow, Historical Association
FHCIMA.............. Fellow, Hotel Catering and Institutional Management Association
FHEA .... Fellow, Higher Education Academy
FHSM................. Fellow, Institute of Health Services Management
FIA...................... Fellow, Institute of Actuaries
FIBMS .... Fellow, Institute of Biomedical Sciences
FICE .... Fellow, Institution of Civil Engineers
FIChemE .... Fellow, Institution of Chemical Engineers
FICM.................. Fellow, Institution of Commercial Managers
FICS .... Fellow, International College of Surgeons
FIDiagE .... Fellow, Institute of Diagnostic Engineers
FIED .... Fellow, Institution of Engineering Designers
FIEE .... Fellow, Institution of Electrical Engineers (formerly FIERE)
FIEEE .... Fellow, Institute of Electrical and Electronics Engineers (NY)
FIERE .... Fellow, Institution of Electronic and Radio Engineers (now see FIEE)
FIET.................... Fellow, Institution of Engineering and Technology
FIFireE .... Fellow, Institution of Fire Engineers
FIHEEM .... Fellow, Institute of Healthcare Engineering and Estate Management (formerly FIHospE)
FIHT................... Fellow of the Institution of Highways and Transportation
FIIM .... Fellow, Institution of Industrial Managers (formerly FIPlantE)
FIL .... Fellow, Institute of Linguists
FIMA.................. Fellow, Institute of Mathematics and its Applications
FIMarEST .... Fellow, Institute of Marine Engineering, Science and Technology
FIMechE.............. Fellow, Institution of Mechanical Engineers
FIMI .... Fellow, Institute of the Motor Industry
FIMLS................ Fellow, Institute of Medical Laboratory Sciences
FIMM................. Fellow, Institution of Mining and Metallurgy (now see FIMMM)
FIMMM .... Fellow, Institute of Materials, Minerals and Mining
FIMS .... Fellow, Institute of Management Specialists
FInstAM............. Fellow, Institute of Administrative Management
FInstD .... Fellow, Institute of Directors
FInstE................ Fellow, Institute of Energy
FInstLEx .... Fellow, Institute of Legal Executives
FInstLM.............. Fellow, Institute of Leadership and Management
FInstMC............. Fellow, Institute of Measurement and Control
FInstP................ Fellow, Institute of Physics
FInstSMM .... Fellow, Institute of Sales and Marketing Management
FInstTT.............. Fellow, Institute of Travel and Tourism
FINucE............... Fellow, Institution of Nuclear Engineers (now see FNucI)
FIOSH .... Fellow, Institute of Occupational Safety and Health

FIPD .... Fellow, Institute of Personnel Development
FIPEM .... Fellow, Institute of Physics and Engineering in Medicine
FIQA................... Fellow, Institute of Quality Assurance
FISM .... Fellow, Institute of Supervisory Management
FISSR................. Fellow, International Society for Science and Religion
FIST.................... Fellow, Institute of Science and Technology
FIStructE .... Fellow, Institution of Structural Engineers
Fitzw .... Fitzwilliam
FKC..................... Fellow, King's College London
FLA...................... Fellow, Library Association
FLAME................ Family Life and Marriage Education
FLCM.................. Fellow, London College of Music
FLIA.................... Fellow, Life Insurance Association
FLS .... Fellow, Linnean Society
FLSW.................. Fellow, Learned Society of Wales
FMA.................... Fellow, Museums Association
FMedSci.............. Fellow, Academy of Medical Sciences
FNI...................... Fellow, Nautical Institute
FNMSM .... Fellow, North and Midlands School of Music
FNucI .... Fellow, Nuclear Institute (formerly FINucE)
FPhS.................... Fellow, Philosophical Society of England
FPS .... Fellow, Pharmaceutical Society of Great Britain
FRACI................. Fellow, Royal Australian Chemical Institute
FRAeS................. Fellow, Royal Aeronautical Society
FRAgS .... Fellow, Royal Agricultural Societies
FRAI.................... Fellow, Royal Anthropological Institute
FRAM.................. Fellow, Royal Academy of Music
Fran..................... Francis
.... Francis's
FRAS.................... Fellow, Royal Asiatic Society
.... Fellow, Royal Astronomical Society
FRCA................... Fellow, Royal College of Anaesthetists
FRCGP................. Fellow, Royal College of General Practitioners
FRCM.................. Fellow, Royal College of Music
FRCO .... Fellow, Royal College of Organists
FRCOG................. Fellow, Royal College of Obstetricians and Gynaecologists
FRCOphth .... Fellow, Royal College of Ophthalmologists
FRCP .... Fellow, Royal College of Physicians
FRCP(C).............. Fellow, Royal College of Physicians of Canada
FRCPath.............. Fellow, Royal College of Pathologists
FRCPCH .... Fellow, Royal College of Paediatrics and Child Health
FRCPEd .... Fellow, Royal College of Physicians Edinburgh
FRCPGlas .... Fellow, Royal College of Physicians and Surgeons, Glasgow (also see FRCSGlas)
FRCPsych............ Fellow, Royal College of Psychiatrists
FRCR .... Fellow, Royal College of Radiologists
FRCS .... Fellow, Royal College of Physicians and Surgeons of England
FRCSE or FRCSEd. Fellow, Royal College of Surgeons of Edinburgh
FRCSGlas .... Fellow, Royal College of Physicians and Surgeons, Glasgow (also see FRCPGlas)
FRCSI .... Fellow, Royal College of Surgeons in Ireland
FRCVS .... Fellow, Royal College of Veterinary Surgeons

FREng.................. Fellow, Royal Academy of Engineering
FRGS .... Fellow, Royal Geographical Society
FRHistS................ Fellow, Royal Historical Society
FRHS .... Fellow, Royal Horticultural Society
FRIAS................... Fellow, Royal Incorporation of Architects of Scotland
FRIBA .... Fellow, Royal Institute of British Architects
FRICS .... Fellow, Royal Institution of Chartered Surveyors (formerly FLAS and FSI)
FRIN.................... Fellow, Royal Institute of Navigation
FRINA.................. Fellow, Royal Institution of Naval Architects
FRIPH .... Fellow, Royal Institute of Public Health
FRMetS .... Fellow, Royal Meteorological Society
FRPharmS .... Fellow, Royal Pharmaceutical Society
FRPS.................... Fellow, Royal Photographic Society
FRS...................... Fellow, Royal Society
FRSA.................... Fellow, Royal Society of Arts
FRSAI................... Fellow, Royal Society of Antiquaries of Ireland
FRSB.................... Fellow, Royal Society of Biology (formerly FIBiol)
FRSC .... Fellow, Royal Society of Canada
.... Fellow, Royal Society of Chemistry (formerly FRIC)
FRSCM................. Honorary Fellow, Royal School of Church Music
FRSE.................... Fellow, Royal Society of Edinburgh
FRSH .... Fellow, Royal Society for Public Health
FRSL.................... Fellow, Royal Society of Literature
FRSM .... Fellow, Associated Board of the Royal Schools of Music
FRSocMed .... Fellow, Royal Society of Medicine
FRTPI.................. Fellow, Royal Town Planning Institute
FSA .... Fellow, Society of Antiquaries
FSAScot............... Fellow, Royal Society of Antiquaries of Scotland
FSCA.................... Fellow, Royal Society of Company and Commercial Accountants
FSJ....................... Fellowship of St John the Evangelist
FSR...................... Fellowship Diploma of the Society of Radiographers
FSS .... Fellow, Royal Statistical Society
FTC .... Flying Training Command
FTCL .... Fellow, Trinity College of Music London
FTII..................... Fellow, Institute of Taxation
FVCM.................. Fellow, Victoria College of Music
FWeldI................. Fellow, Institute of Welding

G

G&C .... Gonville and Caius
Gabr.................... Gabriel
.... Gabriel's
GB........................ Great Britain
GBSM .... Graduate of the Birmingham School of Music
GCVO .... Knight Grand Cross, Royal Victorian Order
Gd........................ Good
Gen..................... General
Geo...................... George
.... George's
GFS .... Girls' Friendly Society
GGSM .... Graduate Diploma of the Guildhall School of Music and Drama
Gib....................... Gibraltar
GIBiol.................. Graduate of the Institute of Biology
GIFireE .... Graduate of the Institute of Fire Engineers
GIMechE.............. Graduate of the Institution of Mechanical Engineers

GInstP .... Graduate of the Institute of Physics
GIPE .... Graduate of the Institution of Production Engineers
Glam..................... Glamorgan
Glas...................... (Diocese of) Glasgow and Galloway
.... Glasgow
GLCM................... Graduate Diploma of the London College of Music
Glos .... Gloucestershire
Glouc................... (Diocese of) Gloucester
GM .... George Medal
GMus.................... Graduate Diploma in Music
GMusRNCM .... Graduate in Music of the Royal Northern College of Music
GNSM.................. Graduate of the Northern School of Music
Gov...................... Governor
Gp........................ Group
Gr......................... Grammar
GradCIPD .... Graduate of the Chartered Institute of Personnel and Development
GradICSA............. Graduate of the Institute of Chartered Secretaries and Administrators
GradIPM .... Graduate of the Institute of Personnel Management
Greg .... Gregory
.... Gregory's
GRIC .... Graduate Membership, Royal Institute of Chemistry
GRNCM .... Graduate of the Royal Northern College of Music
GRSC .... Graduate of the Royal School of Chemistry
GRSM .... Graduate of the Royal Schools of Music
GSM .... (Member of) Guildhall School of Music and Drama
Gt.......................... Great
GTCL .... Graduate Diploma of Trinity College of Music, London
Gtr .... Greater
Guildf.................... (Diocese of) Guildford

H

H.......................... Holy
H&FE .... Higher and Further Education
HA........................ Health Authority
Hatf...................... Hatfield
HCIMA................. Hotel and Catering International Management Association
Hd........................ Head
HDipEd .... Higher Diploma in Education
HE........................ Higher Education
Heref.................... (Diocese of) Hereford
Hertf .... Hertford
Hist .... Historic
.... Historical
.... History
HIV....................... Human Immunodeficiency Virus
HM....................... Her (or His) Majesty
HMI...................... Her (or His) Majesty's Inspector (or Inspectorate)
HMS.................... Her (or His) Majesty's Ship
Ho........................ House
Hon...................... Honorary
.... Honourable
Hon GCM .... Honorary Member, Guild of Church Musicians
HonDLaws........... Honorary Doctor of Laws
HonFChS .... Honorary Fellow, Society of Chiropodists
HonRCM.............. Honorary Member, Royal College of Music
HonRSCM............ Honorary Member, Royal School of Church Music
Hosp .... Hospital
HQ........................ Headquarters
HTV...................... Harlech Television
HVCert.................. Health Visitor's Certificate

I

I............................ Incumbent
IAAP .... International Association for Analytical Psychology

IBA .... Independent Broadcasting Authority
ICF .... Industry Churches Forum (formerly Industrial Christian Fellowship)
ICM....................... Irish Church Missions
ICS .... Intercontinental Church Society
IDC .... Inter-Diocesan Certificate
IDWAL.................. Inter-Diocesan West Africa Link
IEAB .... Igreja Episcopal Anglicana do Brasil
IEng .... Incorporated Engineer (formerly TEng(CEI))
IFES .... International Fellowship of Evangelical Students
ILEA..................... Inner London Education Authority
IME .... Initial Ministerial Education
IMMM .... Institute of Materials, Minerals and Mining
Imp....................... Imperial
Inc........................ Incorporated
Ind .... Industrial
.... Industry
Info .... Information
INSEAD .... Institut Européen d'Administration des Affaires
Insp...................... Inspector
Inst....................... Institut
.... Institute
.... Institution
Intercon .... Intercontinental
Internat................ International
Interpr.................. Interpretation
IPFA...................... Member, Chartered Institute of Public Finance and Accountancy
Is .... Island
.... Islands
.... Isle
.... Isles
ISO....................... Imperial Service Order
IT.......................... Information Technology
ITV........................ Independent Television
IVF........................ Inter-Varsity Fellowship of Evangelical Unions (now see UCCF)
IVS .... International Voluntary Service

J

Jas .... James
.... James's
JCD .... Doctor of Canon Law
JCL .... Licentiate in Canon Law
JD......................... Doctor of Jurisprudence
JEM .... Jerusalem and the East Mission (now see JMECA)
Jes .... Jesus
JMECA.................. Jerusalem and Middle East Church Association (formerly JEM)
Jo .... John
.... John's
Jos........................ Joseph
.... Joseph's
JP.......................... Justice of the Peace
Jt.......................... Joint
Jun .... Junior

K

K........................... King
.... King's
K, E & A .... (Diocese of) Kilmore, Elphin and Ardagh
KA .... Knight of St Andrew, Order of Barbados
Kath .... Katharine/Katherine
.... Katharine's/Katherine's
KBE .... Knight Commander, Order of the British Empire
KCB....................... Knight Commander, Order of the Bath
KCMG.................. Knight Commander, Order of St Michael and St George
KCVO.................... Knight Commander, Royal Victorian Order
KPM...................... King's Police Medal
Kt .... Knight

L

L & K .... (Diocese of) Limerick and Killaloe (united dioceses of Limerick, Ardfert, Aghadoe, Killaloe, Kilfenora, Clonfert, Kilmacduagh and Emly)
Lamp .... Lampeter
Lanc..................... Lancaster
LASI...................... Licentiate, Ambulance Service Institute
Laur...................... Laurence
.... Laurence's
Lawr...................... Lawrence
.... Lawrence's
LBIPP.................... Licentiate, British Institute of Professional Photography
LCC....................... London County Council
LCL .... Licentiate in Canon Law
LCP .... Licentiate, College of Preceptors
LCST .... Licentiate, College of Speech Therapists
LCTP .... Lancashire and Cumbria Theological Partnership
Ld......................... Lord
LDiv .... Licentiate in Divinity
Ldr .... Leader
LDS .... Licentiate in Dental Surgery
LEA....................... Local Education Authority
Lect...................... Lecturer
Leic .... (Diocese of) Leicester
Leon...................... Leonard
.... Leonard's
LEP .... Local Ecumenical Partnership
LèsL...................... Licencié ès lettres
LGCM .... Lesbian and Gay Christian Movement
LGSM.................... Licentiate, Guildhall School of Music and Drama
Lib........................ Librarian
.... Library
Lic........................ Licence
.... Licensed
.... Licentiate
LICeram .... Licentiate, Institute of Ceramics
Lich...................... (Diocese of) Lichfield
LicTh.................... Licence in Theology
LIMA.................... Licentiate, Institute of Mathematics and its Applications
Linc...................... (Diocese of) Lincoln
Lit........................ Literature
LittD..................... Doctor of Letters (also see DLitt)
Liturg .... Liturgical
Liv........................ (Diocese of) Liverpool
LLA....................... Lady Literate in Arts
LLAM .... Licentiate, London Academy of Music and Dramatic Art
Llan...................... (Diocese of) Llandaff
LLB....................... Bachelor of Laws
LLCM.................... Licentiate, London College of Music
LLCM(TD)............ Licentiate, London College of Music (Teachers' Diploma)
LLD .... Doctor of Laws
LLM...................... Master of Laws
LMH...................... Lady Margaret Hall
LMPA.................... Licentiate Master, Photographers' Association
LNSM.................... Local Non-stipendiary Minister (or Ministry)
Lon....................... (Diocese of) London
LOROS.................. Leicestershire Organization for the Relief of Suffering
Loughb.................. Loughborough
LRAM.................... Licentiate, Royal Academy of Music
LRCP..................... Licentiate, Royal College of Physicians
LRCPI .... Licentiate, Royal College of Physicians of Ireland
LRCSEng .... Licentiate of the Royal College of Surgeons in England
LRCSI .... Licentiate, Royal College of Surgeons in Ireland
LRPS .... Licentiate, Royal Photographic Society
LRSC .... Licentiate, Royal Society of Chemistry

LRSM .... Licentiate Diploma of the Royal Schools of Music
LSE .... London School of Economics and Political Science
LSHTM................. London School of Hygiene and Tropical Medicine
LSIAD.................. Licentiate, Society of Industrial Artists and Designers
LSocEth............... Licence en Sociologie-Ethnologie
Lt........................ Lieutenant
.... Little
LTCL.................... Licentiate, Trinity College of Music London
Ltd .... Limited
LTh...................... Licentiate in Theology (also see LST)
LtO...................... Licence to officiate
LVCM................... Licentiate, Victoria College of Music
LVO .... Lieutenant, Royal Victorian Order
LWCMD............... Licentiate, Welsh College of Music and Drama

M

M & K................. (Diocese of) Meath and Kildare
MA....................... Master of Arts
MA(Ed) .... Master of Arts in Education
MA(MM) .... Master of Arts in Mission and Ministry
MA(Theol) .... Master of Arts in Theology
MA(TS) .... Master of Arts in Theological Studies
MAAIS................. Member, Association of Archaeological Illustrators and Surveyors
MAAT................... Member, Association of Accounting Technicians
MACC.................. Member, Australian College of Chaplains
MACE................... Member, Australian College of Educators
MACT .... Member, Association of Corporate Treasurers
MAE .... Member, Academy of Experts
Magd................... Magdalen/Magdalene
.... Magdalen's/Magdalene's
MAgrSc................ Master of Agricultural Science
MAJA.................... Member, Association of Jungian Analysts
MAMIT .... Member, Associate of Meat Inspectors Trust
Man .... (Diocese of) Manchester
Man Dir .... Managing Director
Mansf................... Mansfield
MAPM .... Member, Association for Project Management
MAPsS................. Member, Australian Psychological Society
MArAd .... Master of Archive Administration
MArch.................. Master of Architecture
Marg.................... Margaret
.... Margaret's
MASI.................... Member, Architects and Surveyors Institute
MAT .... Master of Arts and Teaching (USA)
MATA................... Member, Animal Technicians' Association
MATCA .... Member, Air Traffic Control Association
MATM.................. Master of Arts in Theology and Ministry
Matt..................... Matthew
.... Matthew's
MB .... Bachelor of Medicine (also see BM)
MB,BS or MB,ChB Conjoint degree of Bachelor of Medicine, Bachelor of Surgery
MBA..................... Master of Business Administration
MBACP .... Member, British Association for Counselling and Psychotherapy
MBAOT................ Member, British Association of Occupational Therapists (formerly MAOT)

MBAP................... Member, British Association of Psychotherapists
MBASW .... Member, British Association of Social Workers
MBATOD .... Member, British Association of Teachers of the Deaf
MBC..................... Metropolitan (or Municipal) Borough Council
MBChA .... Member, British Chiropody Association
MBCS................... Member, British Computer Society
MBE .... Member, Order of the British Empire
MBEng................. Member, Association of Building Engineers
MBES .... Member, Biological Engineering Society
MBIM................... Member, British Institute of Management (later MIMgt)
MBiochem........... Master of Biochemstry
MBKSTS .... Member, British Kinematograph, Sound and Television Society
MBM .... Master of Business Management
MBPsS.................. Member, British Psychological Society
MC....................... Military Cross
MCA .... Member, Institute of Chartered Accountants
MCB..................... Master in Clinical Biochemistry
MCCDRCS .... Member in Clinical Community Dentistry, Royal College of Surgeons
MCD .... Master of Civic Design
MCE..................... Master of Civil Engineering
MCGI.................... Member, City and Guilds of London Institute
.... Member, City and Guilds of London Institute
MChap .... Masterof Chaplaincy
MChem .... Master of Chemistry
MChemA.............. Master in Chemical Analysis
MChOrth............. Master of Orthopaedic Surgery
MChS................... Member, Society of Chiropodists
MCIArb................ Member, Chartered Institute of Arbitrators
MCIBS.................. Member, Chartered Institute of Bankers in Scotland
MCIBSE................ Member, Chartered Institute of Building Service Engineers
MCIEEM .... Member, Chartered Institute of Ecology and Environmental Management (formerly MIEEM)
MCIEH .... Member, Chartered Institute of Environmental Health (formerly MIEH)
MCIH.................... Member, Chartered Institute of Housing (formerly MIH)
MCIJ..................... Member, Chartered Institute of Journalists
MCIL.................... Member, Chartered Institute of Linguists
MCIM................... Member, Chartered Institute of Marketing (formerly MInstM)
MCIOB................. Member, Chartered Institute of Building
MCIPD................. Member, Chartered Institute of Personnel and Development
MCIPR.................. Member, Chartered Institute of Public Relations (formerly MIPR)
MCIPS.................. Member, Chartered Institute of Procurement and Supply
MCIT..................... Member, Chartered Institute of Transport
MCIWEM............. Member, Chartered Institution of Water and Enviromental Management
MCL..................... Master of Canon Law
MCLIP.................. Member, Chartered Institute of Library and Information Professionals
MCMI................... Member, Chartered Management Institute (formerly MBIM and MIMgt)

MCollP................. Member, College of Preceptors
MCom .... Master of Commerce
MCommH .... Master of Community Health
MCS...................... Master of Christian Spirituality
.... Master of Christian Studies
MCSD .... Member, Chartered Society of Designers
MCSP.................... Member, Chartered Society of Physiotherapy
MCST.................... Member, College of Speech Therapists
MCT...................... Member, Association of Corporate Treasurers
MD .... Doctor of Medicine
MDA .... Master of Defence Administration
MDefStud............ Master of Defence Studies
MDiv.................... Master of Divinity
ME .... Master of Engineering (also see MEng)
MEd .... Master of Education
MEHS................... Member, Ecclesiastical History Society
MEng.................... Master of Engineering
Mert...................... Merton
MèsL.................... Lettres Modernes
Metrop .... Metropolitan
MFA .... Master of Fine Art
MFHom .... Member, Faculty of Homeopathy
MFOM.................. Member, Faculty of Occupational Medicine
MGDSRCS .... Membership in General Dental Surgery, Royal College of Surgeons of England
Mgt....................... Management
MHCIMA .... Member, Hotel Catering and Institutional Management Association
MHort (RHS)....... Master of Horticulture, Royal Horticultural Society
MHSc.................... Master of Health Science
MHSM .... Member, Institute of Health Services Management
MHums................. Master of Humanities
MIA...................... Malawi Institute of Architects
MIAAP.................. Member, International Association for Analytical Psychology
MIAAS................. Member, Incorporated Association of Architects and Surveyors
MIAM .... Member, Institute of Administrative Management
MIAP.................... Member, Institution of Analysts and Programmers
MIAT.................... Member, Institute of Asphalt Technology
MIBC.................... Member, Institute of Business Counsellors
MIBCO................. Member, Institution of Building Control Officers
MIBF .... Member, Institute of British Foundrymen
MIBiol................. Member, Institute of Biology
MICA.................... Member, International Cartographic Association
.... Member, International Compliance Association
MICAS .... Member, Institute of Chartered Accountants of Scotland
MICE.................... Member, Institution of Civil Engineers (formerly AMICE)
MICFM................. Member, Institute of Charity Fundraising Managers
MICFor................ Member, Institute of Chartered Foresters
Mich .... Michael
.... Michael's
.... Michael and All Angels
MIChemE .... Member, Institution of Chemical Engineers
MICM .... Member, Institute of Credit Management
MICorrST............ Member, Institution of Corrosion Science and Technology
MICS.................... Member, Institute of Chartered Shipbrokers
Midl .... Midlands

MIE .... Member, Institute of Engineers and Technicians
MIEAust .... Member, Institute of Engineers and Technicians Australia
MIED................... Member, Institute of Engineering Designers
MIEE .... Member, Institution of Electrical Engineers (formerly AMIEE & MIERE)
MIEEE................. Member, Institute of Electrical and Electronics Engineers (NY)
MIET .... Member, Institution of Engineering and Technology
MIEx .... Member, Institute of Export
MIHEEM .... Member, Institute of Healthcare Engineering and Estate Management
MIHM.................. Member, Institute of Healthcare Management
MIHT .... Member, Institution of Highways and Transportation
MIIA.................... Member, Institute of Internal Auditors
MIIExE................ Member, Institute of Incorporated Executive Engineers
MIIM.................... Member, Institute of Industrial Managers
MIInfSc .... Member, Institute of Information Scientists
MIL .... Member, Institute of Linguists
Mil .... Military
MILT .... Member, Institute of Logistics and Transport
MIM..................... Member, Institute of Metals (formerly Institution of Metallurgists)
MIMA .... Member, Institute of Management Accountants
.... Member, Institute of Mathematics and its Applications
MIMarEST........... Member, Institute of Marine Engineering, Science and Technology
MIMC .... Member, Institute of Management Consultants
MIMechE .... Member, Institution of Mechanical Engineers (formerly AMIMechE)
MIMI.................... Member, Institute of the Motor Industry
MIMunE............... Member, Institution of Municipal Engineers
Min .... Minister
.... Ministers
.... Ministries
.... Ministry
.... Minor
Min-in-c.............. Minister-in-charge
Minl .... Ministerial
MInstC(Glas) .... Member, Institute of Counselling (Glasgow)
MInstD................ Member, Institute of Directors
MInstE................ Member, Institute of Energy
MInstGA .... Member, Institute of Group Analysis
MInstP................ Member, Institute of Physics
MInstPI .... Member, Institute of Patentees and Inventors
MInstPkg .... Member, Institute of Packaging
MInstPS .... Corporate Member, Institute of Purchasing and Supply
MInstTA .... Member, Institute of Transport Administration
MINucE................ Member, Institute of Nuclear Engineers
MIOSH................ Member, Institution of Occupational Safety and Health
MIOT .... Member, Institute of Operating Theatre Technicians
MIPI .... Member, Institute of Private Investigators
MIProdE.............. Member, Institute of Production Engineers
MIQA................... Member, Institute of Quality Assurance
MIRSE .... Member, Institution of Railway Signal Engineers

MISE .... Member, Institute of Sales Engineers
MISM................... Member, Institute of Supervisory Management
Miss .... Mission
.... Missions
.... Missionary
Missr .... Missioner
MIStructE............ Member, Institute of Structural Engineers
MISW................... Member, Institute of Social Welfare
MITI .... Member, Institute of Translation and Interpreting
MITMA .... Member, Institute of Trade Mark Agents
MITPA .... Member, International Tax Planning Association
MIW..................... Member, Institute of Welfare (formerly MIWO)
ML .... Master of Leadership
MLI .... Member, Landscape Institute
MLib .... Master of Librarianship
MLitt.................... Master of Letters
MLL..................... Master of Laws
MLS .... Master of Library Studies
MM...................... Military Medal
MMath .... Master of Mathematics
MMCET .... Martyrs' Memorial and Church of England Trust
MMedSc .... Master of Medical Science
MMet................... Master of Metallurgy
MMin................... Master of Ministry
MMinTheol.......... Master in Ministry and Theology
MMS.................... Member, Institute of Management Services
MMus .... Master of Music (also see MusM)
MN .... Master of Nursing
MNI .... Member, Nautical Institute
MOD .... Ministry of Defence
Mon..................... (Diocese of) Monmouth
Mor...................... (Diocese of) Moray, Ross and Caithness
MPA .... Master of Public Administration
MPerf................... Master of Performance
MPH..................... Master of Public Health
MPhil .... Master of Philosophy
MPhilF .... Master of Philosophical Foundations
MPhys.................. Master of Physics
MProf................... Master of Professional Studies
.... Master in Professional Studies
MPS .... Master of Professional Studies
MPsychSc .... Master of Psychological Science
MRAC .... Member, Royal Agricultural College
MRAeS .... Member, Royal Aeronautical Society
MRCGP............... Member, Royal College of General Practitioners
MRCO.................. Member, Royal College of Organists
MRCOG............... Member, Royal College of Obstetricians and Gynaecologists
MRCP................... Member, Royal College of Physicians
MRCPath .... Member, Royal College of Pathologists
MRCPsych .... Member, Royal College of Psychiatrists
MRCS.................. Member, Royal College of Surgeons
MRCSE................ Member, Royal College of Surgeons of Edinburgh
MRCVS .... Member, Royal College of Veterinary Surgeons
MRelSc................ Master of Religious Science
MRes.................... Master of Research
MRIA................... Member, Royal Irish Academy
MRICS................. Member, Royal Institution of Chartered Surveyors (formerly ARICS)
MRIN .... Member, Royal Institute of Navigation
MRINA................ Member, Royal Institution of Naval Architects

MRIPHH .... Member, Royal Institute of Public Health and Hygiene
MRPharmS........... Member, Royal Pharmaceutical Society (formerly MPS)
MRSB .... Member, Royal Society of Biologists (formerly MSB)
MRSC................... Member, Royal Society of Chemistry (formerly MRIC)
MRSL .... Member, Order of the Republic of Sierra Leone
MRSPH................ Member, Royal Society for the Promotion of Health
MRST .... Member, Royal Society of Teachers
MRTPI .... Member, Royal Town Planning Institute
MRTvS .... Member, Royal Television Society
MS .... Master of Science (USA)
.... Master of Surgery
MSacMus............. Master of Sacred Music
MSAICE............... Member, South African Institution of Civil Engineers
MSc .... Master of Science
MSc(Econ)........... Master of Science in Economics
MSci..................... Master of Natural Sciences
MScRel................ Maitrise es Sciences Religieuses
MSE .... Master of Science in Engineering (USA)
.... Minister (or Ministers) in Secular Employment
MSERT .... Member, Society of Electronic and Radio Technicians
MSHAA .... Member, Society of Hearing Aid Audiologists
MSI .... Member, Securities Institute
MSIAD .... Member, Society of Industrial Artists and Designers
MSLIS.................. Master of Science in Library and Information Science
MSNTS .... Member, Society for New Testament Study
MSoc .... Maîtrise en Sociologie
MSocSc................ Master of Social Sciences (also see MSSc)
MSocWork........... Master of Social Work (USA)
MSOSc................. Member, Society of Ordained Scientists
MSOTS .... Member, Society for Old Testament Study
MSR .... Member, Society of Radiographers
MSSc.................... Master of Social Science (also see MSocSc)
MSSCh................. Member, School of Surgical Chiropody
MSSTh................. Member, Society for the Study of Theology
MSt .... Master of Studies
MSTSD................ Member, Society of Teachers of Speech and Drama
MSW.................... Master of Social Work
Mt........................ Mount
MTD .... Master of Transport Design
MTeach................ Master of Teaching
MTech.................. Master of Technology
MTh or MTheol ... Master of Theology (also see STM and ThM)
MThSt or MTS ..... Master of Theological Studies
MU....................... Mothers' Union
MusB or MusBac.. Bachelor of Music (also see BMus)
MusD or MusDoc. Doctor of Music
MusM .... Master of Music (also see MMus)
MVO .... Member, Royal Victorian Order

N

N.......................... North
.... Northern
NACRO............... National Association for the Care and Rehabilitation of Offenders
NASA .... National Aeronautics and Space Administration (USA)
Nat...................... National
Nath .... Nathanael/Nathaniel

.... Nathanael's/Nathaniel's
NCEC............... National Christian Education Council
NE...................... North East
NEITE................. North East Institute for Theological Education
NEOC .... North East Oecumenical Course (formerly North East Ordination Course)
Newc................. (Diocese of) Newcastle
NHS .... National Health Service
Nic..................... Nicholas/Nicolas
.... Nicholas's/Nicolas's
NIDA................. National Institute of Dramatic Art
NJ...................... New Jersey
NOC .... Northern Ordination Course
Nor .... (Diocese of) Norwich
Northn................ Northampton
Nottm................ Nottingham
NPQH .... National Professional Qualification for Headship
NS...................... Nova Scotia (Canada)
NSM .... Non-stipendiary Minister (or Ministry)
NSPCC............... National Society for the Prevention of Cruelty to Children
NSW .... New South Wales (Australia)
NT...................... New Testament
NTMTC.............. North Thames Ministerial Training Course
Nuff .... Nuffield
NUI.................... National University of Ireland
NUU................... New University of Ulster
NW .... North West/Northwestern
NWT .... North West Territories (Canada)
NY...................... New York (USA)
NZ .... New Zealand

O

OAM.................. Medal of the Order of Australia
OBE................... Officer, Order of the British Empire
OBI.................... Order of British India
OCF .... Officiating Chaplain to the Forces
OCM.................. Officiating Chaplain to the Military
Offg.................. Officiating
Offic.................. Officiate
OGS .... Oratory of the Good Shepherd
OH .... Ohio
OHP................... Order of the Holy Paraclete
OLM .... Ordained Local Minister (or Ministry)
OM .... Order of Merit
OM(Ger)............. Order of Merit of Germany
OMF .... Overseas Missionary Fellowship
ONZ .... Order of New Zealand
Ord .... Ordained
.... Ordinands
.... Ordination
Org .... Organization
.... Organizer
.... Organizing
OSB................... Order of St Benedict
OSP................... Order of St Paul
OT...................... Old Testament
Ox...................... (Diocese of) Oxford

P

P......................... Patron(s)
.... Priest
p .... Ordained Priest
P in O .... Priest in Ordinary
PACE .... Practical Assistance in Christian Education
Par .... Parish
.... Parishes
Paroch .... Parochial
Past.................... Pastoral
Patr .... Patrick
.... Patrick's
.... Patronage
PBS.................... Pengeran Bintang Sarawak (Companion of the Order of the Star, Sarawak)
PC .... Perpetual Curate

.... Privy Counsellor
PCC.................... Parochial Church Council
Pemb................. Pembroke
Penn .... Pennsylvania (USA)
Perm .... Permission
Pet .... (Diocese of) Peterborough
.... Peter
.... Peter's
Peterho .... Peterhouse
PEV.................... Provincial Episcopal Visitor
PGCE................. Postgraduate Certificate in Education
PGDE................. Professional Graduate Diploma in Education
PGTC................. Postgraduate Teaching Certificate
PhB .... Bachelor of Philosophy
PhC.................... Pharmaceutical Chemist
PhD.................... Doctor of Philosophy (also see DPhil)
PhD(Educ) .... Doctor of Philosophy in Education
Phil.................... Philip
.... Philip's
PhL.................... Licentiate of Philosophy
P-in-c .... Priest-in-charge
plc...................... public limited company
PM .... Priest Missioner
PO...................... Post Office
Poly.................... Polytechnic
Portsm .... (Diocese of) Portsmouth
PPRIBA.............. Past President, Royal Institute of British Architects
PQCSW.............. Post-Qualifying Certificate in Social Work
Preb .... Prebendary
Prec.................... Precentor
Prep .... Preparatory
Pres.................... President
Prin .... Principal
Pris .... Prison
.... Prisons
Prof .... Professor
.... Professorial
Progr.................. Program
.... Programme
.... Programmes
Prop .... Proprietary
Prov .... Province
.... Provincial
PsychD............... Professional Doctor of Counselling Psychology
Pt .... Point
PtO .... Permission to officiate
PV .... Priest Vicar

Q

QC...................... Queen's Counsel
QGM .... Queen's Gallantry Medal
QHC................... Honorary Chaplain to The Queen
Qld..................... Queensland
QN...................... Queen's Nurse
QPM .... Queen's Police Medal
QSM .... Queen's Service Medal
QSO.................... Queen's Service Order of New Zealand
Qu...................... Queen
.... Queen's
.... Queens'
QUB.................... The Queen's University of Belfast
QVRM................. Queen's Volunteer Reserve Medal

R

R......................... Rector
.... Royal
R and D .... Research and Development
R of O .... Reserve of Officers
R&SChTrust........ Rochester and Southwark Church Trust
RAAChD............. Royal Australian Army Chaplains' Department
RAAF .... Royal Australian Air Force
RAChD............... Royal Army Chaplains' Department
RAD or RADD..... Royal Association in Aid of Deaf People (formerly Deaf and Dumb)
RADA .... Royal Academy of Dramatic Art
RADICLE .... Residential and Drop-in Centre London Enterprises

RAEC.................. Royal Army Educational Corps
RAF .... Royal Air Force
RAFVR .... Royal Air Force Volunteer Reserve
RAM.................... (Member) Royal Academy of Music
RAN .... Royal Australian Navy
RANSR................ Royal Australian Naval Strategic Reserve
RAuxAF .... Royal Auxiliary Air Force
RC .... Roman Catholic
RCA..................... Royal College of Art
RCAF................... Royal Canadian Air Force
RCM..................... Royal College of Music
RCN .... Royal Canadian Navy
.... Royal College of Nursing
RCNT .... Registered Clinical Nurse Teacher
RCPS .... Royal College of Physicians and Surgeons
RCS .... Royal College of Surgeons of England
RCSE .... Royal College of Surgeons of Edinburgh
RD....................... Royal Navy Reserve Decoration
.... Rural Dean
RE....................... Religious Education
Reg .... Registered
Regt.................... Regiment
Rehab .... Rehabilitation
Relig................... Religion(s)
.... Religious
Relns .... Relations
Rem .... Remand
Rep .... Representative
Res .... Residence
.... Resident
.... Residential
.... Residentiary
Resp .... Responsibility
Resurr................. Resurrection
Revd.................... Reverend
RFN .... Registered Fever Nurse
RGN .... Registered General Nurse
RHV .... Registered Health Visitor
RIA .... Royal Irish Academy
RIBA .... (Member) Royal Institute of British Architects (formerly ARIBA)
Rich.................... Richard
.... Richard's
Ripon .... Ripon and Leeds
RLSMD............... Royal London School of Medicine and Dentistry
RM .... Registered Midwife
RMA or RMC....... Royal Military Academy (formerly College), Sandhurst
RMCM .... Royal Manchester College of Music
RMCS................. Royal Military College of Science, Shrivenham
RMHN................ Registered Mental Health Nurse
RMN .... Registered Mental Nurse
RN....................... Registered Nurse (Canada)
.... Royal Navy
RN(MH).............. Registered Nurse (Mental Health)
RNCM................. Royal Northern College of Music
RNIB................... Royal National Institute for the Blind
RNLI................... Royal National Lifeboat Institution
RNMH................. Registered Nurse Mental Health
RNR.................... Royal Naval Reserve
RNT.................... Registered Nurse Tutor
RNVR.................. Royal Naval Volunteer Reserve
RNZN .... Royal New Zealand Navy
Rob .... Robinson
Roch .... (Diocese of) Rochester
RS....................... Religious Studies
RSAMD .... Royal Scottish Academy of Music and Drama
RSCM.................. (Member) Royal School of Church Music
RSCN .... Registered Sick Children's Nurse
Rt .... Right
RTCert................. Certified Reality Therapist
Rtd or rtd .... Retired
RTE..................... Radio Telefís Éireann

RVC...... Royal Veterinary College
RVO ...... Royal Victorian Order

S

S...... South
.... Southern
S & B ...... (Diocese of) Swansea and Brecon
S & M ...... (Diocese of) Sodor and Man
SA ...... Salvation Army
Sacr...... Sacrist
.... Sacristan
SAMS...... South American Mission Society (now see CMS)
SAOMC...... St Albans and Oxford Ministry Course
SAP ...... (Member) Society of Analytical Psychologists
Sarum...... (Diocese of) Salisbury
Sav...... Saviour
.... Saviour's
ScD...... Doctor of Science (also see DSc)
Sch...... School
SCM...... State Certified Midwife
.... Student Christian Movement
SCRTP...... South Central Regional Training Partnership
SCTEI ...... South Central Theological Education Institution
SE...... South East
Sec...... Secretary
SEITE...... South East Institute for Theological Education
Selw...... Selwyn
Sem...... Seminary
Sen...... Senior
SEN...... State Enrolled Nurse
SFHEA ...... Senior Fellow, Higher Education Academy
.... Senior Fellow, Higher Education Academy
SHARE...... Shelter Housing and Renewal Experiment
Sheff ...... (Diocese of) Sheffield
Shep ...... Shepherd
SM ...... Master of Science (USA)
SMF ...... Society for the Maintenance of the Faith
SNTS...... Society for New Testament Studies
SNWTP ...... Southern North West Training Partnership
So...... Souls
.... Souls'
SOAS...... School of Oriental and African Studies
Soc...... Social
.... Society
SOMA...... Sharing of Ministries Abroad
SOSc...... Society of Ordained Scientists
Southn...... Southampton
SPCK...... Society for Promoting Christian Knowledge
SPG...... Society for the Propagation of the Gospel (now see USPG)
Sqn Ldr...... Squadron Leader
SRCh...... State Registered Chiropodist
SRD...... State Registered Dietician
SRN...... State Registered Nurse
SROT...... State Registered Occupational Therapist
SRP...... State Registered Physiotherapist
SS...... Saints
.... Saints'
.... Sidney Sussex
SSB...... Society of the Sisters of Bethany
SSC ...... Solicitor before the Supreme Court (Scotland)
SSEES ...... School of Slavonic and East European Studies
SSF ...... Society of St Francis
SSJ...... Society of St John of Jerusalem
SSJE...... Society of St John the Evangelist
SSM ...... Self-supporting Minister (or Ministry)
.... Society of the Sacred Mission
St ...... Saint

St Alb...... (Diocese of) St Albans
.... St Alban
.... St Alban's
St And...... (Diocese of) St Andrews, Dunkeld and Dunblane
St As...... (Diocese of) St Asaph
St D...... (Diocese of) St Davids
St E ...... (Diocese of) St Edmundsbury and Ipswich
STB ...... Bachelor of Theology (also see BTh)
STD...... Doctor of Sacred Theology (also see DST)
Ste...... Sainte
Steph ...... Stephen
.... Stephen's
STETS...... Southern Theological Education and Training Scheme
STh ...... Scholar in Theology (also see ThSchol)
.... Student in Theology
STL...... Reader (or Professor) of Sacred Theology
STM ...... Master of Theology (also see MTh or MTheol and ThM)
STV ...... Scottish Television
Sub ...... Substitute
Succ ...... Succentor
Suff ...... Suffragan
Supt ...... Superintendent
SW ...... South West
S'wark...... (Diocese of) Southwark
S'well...... (Diocese of) Southwell and Nottingham
.... Southwell
SWJ...... Servants with Jesus
SWMTC ...... South West Ministry Training Course
Syn...... Synod

T

T, K & A ...... (Diocese of) Tuam, Killala and Achonry
TA ...... Territorial Army
Tas...... Tasmania
TAVR ...... Territorial and Army Volunteer Reserve
TC...... Technician Certificate
TCD...... Trinity College, Dublin
TCert...... Teacher's Certificate
TD...... Team Deacon
.... Territorial Efficiency Decoration
TDip...... Teacher's Diploma
TEAR ...... The Evangelical Alliance Relief
Tech...... Technical
.... Technological
.... Technology
TEM ...... Territorial Efficiency Medal
temp...... temporarily
TEng ...... Senior Technician Engineer
Th ...... Theologian
.... Theological
.... Theology
ThA...... Associate of Theology
ThB ...... Bachelor of Theology (USA)
ThD...... Doctor of Theology (also see DTh)
ThL...... Theological Licentiate
ThM...... Master of Theology (also see MTh or MTheol and STM)
Thos...... Thomas
.... Thomas's
ThSchol...... Scholar in Theology (also see STh)
Tim ...... Timothy
.... Timothy's
TISEC ...... Theological Institute of the Scottish Episcopal Church
TM ...... Team Minister (or Ministry)
TP...... Team Priest
TR ...... Team Rector
Tr...... Trainer
.... Training
Treas ...... Treasurer
.... Treasurer's
Trin ...... Trinity
TS...... Training Ship
TSB ...... Trustee Savings Bank
TV ...... Team Vicar
.... Television
TVS ...... Television South

U

UAE...... United Arab Emirates
UCC...... University College, Cork
UCCF ...... Universities and Colleges Christian Fellowship of Evangelical Unions (formerly IVF)
UCD...... University College, Dublin
UEA...... University of East Anglia
UED ...... University Education Diploma
UK...... United Kingdom
UKRC ...... United Kingdom Register of Counsellors
UMCA...... Universities' Mission to Central Africa (now see USPG)
UMIST...... University of Manchester Institute of Science and Technology
UNISA ...... University of South Africa
Univ ...... University
UPA...... Urban Priority Area (or Areas)
URC ...... United Reformed Church
US or USA...... United States (of America)
USCL...... United Society for Christian Literature
USPG ...... United Society Partners in the Gospel (formerly SPG, UMCA, and CMD)
UWE...... University of the West of England
UWIC ...... University of Wales Institute, Cardiff
UWIST...... University of Wales Institute of Science and Technology

V

V ...... Vicar
.... Virgin
.... Virgin's
Ven...... Venerable
VetMB ...... Bachelor of Veterinary Medicine (also see BVetMed)
Vic...... Victoria (Australia)
Vin ...... Vincent
.... Vincent's
Voc...... Vocation(s)
.... Vocational
VR ...... Volunteer Reserve
VRD...... Royal Naval Volunteer Reserve Officers' Decoration

W

W ...... West
.... Western
w...... with
W/Cdr...... Wing Commander
Wadh ...... Wadham
Wakef...... (Diocese of) Wakefield
WCC ...... World Council of Churches
WEC...... Worldwide Evangelism Crusade
WEMTC ...... West of England Ministerial Training Course
Westf...... Westfield
Westmr ...... Westminster
Wilts...... Wiltshire
Win ...... (Diocese of) Winchester
Wm...... William
WMMTC...... West Midlands Ministerial Training Course
Wolfs...... Wolfson
Wolv ...... Wolverhampton
Worc ...... (Diocese of) Worcester
WRAF ...... Women's Royal Air Force

Y

YMCA ...... Young Men's Christian Association
YOI...... Young Offender Institution
YWAM...... Youth with a Mission

A

AAGAARD, Canon Angus Robert. b 64. CQSW 86. Ripon Coll Cuddesdon BTh 93. **d** 93 **p** 94. C Taunton St Andr *B & W* 93–97; TV Southampton (City Cen) *Win* 97–01; TR N Lambeth *S'wark* from 01; Hon Can Asante Mampong Ghana from 15; CF(V) from 15. *St Anselm's Vicarage, 286 Kennington Road, London SE11 5DU* T: (020) 7735 3415 F: 7735 3403 M: 07810-646644 E: angus.aagaard@gmail.com

ABAKUKS, Andris. b 49. Qu Coll Cam BA 70 MA 74 Sussex Univ DPhil 73 CStat 93. K Coll Lon BA 00 MA 03. **p** 02. In Latvian Evang Lutheran Ch from 02; PtO *Guildf* from 16. *4 Richmond Close, Epsom KT18 5EY* T: (01372) 811144 E: abakuks@ntlworld.com

ABAYOMI-COLE, Canon Bimbisara Alfred (Bimbi). b 58. CCC Ox BA 80 MA 85. Trin Coll Bris BA 94. **d** 94 **p** 95. C Deptford St Pet *S'wark* 94–98; V Crofton St Paul *Roch* from 98; Hon Can Roch Cathl from 15. *St Paul's Vicarage, 2 Oakwood Road, Orpington BR6 8JH* T: (01689) 852939 *or* 850697 E: bimbiabayomi_cole@hotmail.com

ABBOTT, Barry Joseph. b 59. Sunderland Univ BA 98 Sarum Coll MA 17 MCIEH. NEOC 89. **d** 92 **p** 93. NSM Bishopwearmouth Ch Ch *Dur* 92–98; NSM Silksworth 98–00; P-in-c Lumley 00–04; AD Chester-le-Street 02–04; P-in-c Whickham 04–08; R from 08; V Swalwell from 21. *The Rectory, Church Chare, Whickham, Newcastle upon Tyne NE16 4SH* T: 0191-488 7397 M: 07801-074909

ABBOTT, Christopher Ralph. b 38. Univ of Wales (Lamp) BA 59. Wells Th Coll 59. **d** 61 **p** 62. C Camberwell St Giles *S'wark* 61–67; C Portsea St Mary *Portsm* 67–70; V Portsea St Cuth 70–87; P-in-c Gt Milton *Ox* 87–88; P-in-c Lt Milton 87–88; R Gt w Lt Milton and Gt Haseley 88–93; R Chailey *Chich* 93–00; Chapl Chailey Heritage Hosp Lewes 95–00; rtd 00; PtO *Chich* 01–16; Hon C Purbrook *Portsm* 03–05; PtO 14–16; *Chich* from 17. *23 Ramsay Hall, 9-13 Byron Road, Worthing BN11 3HN* T: (01903) 214135

ABBOTT, Craig Andrew. b 75. St Martin's Coll Lanc BA 96. LCTP 10. **d** 12 **p** 13. C Lancaster St Thos *Blackb* 12–20; V Ellel from 16. *20 Highland Brow, Galgate, Lancaster LA2 0NB* M: 07813-903420

ABBOTT, Canon David John. b 52. CertEd. St Jo Coll Nottm. **d** 87 **p** 88. C Biddulph *Lich* 87–90; C Tunbridge Wells St Jas *Roch* 90–92; TV Tunbridge Wells St Jas w St Phil 92–98; V Sunnyside w Bourne End *St Alb* 98–16; RD Berkhamsted 04–09; Hon Can St Alb 15–16; rtd 16. *11 Stoberry Avenue, Wells BA5 2TF* T: (01749) 572356

ABBOTT, David Robert. b 49. Edin Univ BD 72. Qu Coll Birm 72. **d** 74 **p** 75. C Kirkby *Liv* 74–78; C Ditton St Mich 78–80; R Ashton-in-Makerfield H Trin 80–14; rtd 14; PtO *Liv* from 16. *65 Meadow Brook, Wigan WN5 8ED* T: (01942) 214006

ABBOTT (née Bush), Esther Rachma Hartley. b 66. LMH Ox BA 88 St Jo Coll Dur BA 04. Cranmer Hall Dur 04. **d** 04 **p** 05. C Bethnal Green St Matt w St Jas the Gt *Lon* 04–07; C Staines 07–10; P-in-c Westfield *B & W* 10–15; Chapl Norton Radstock Coll of FE 10–14; P-in-c Woodhill *Sarum* 15–19; C Lyneham w Bradenstoke 15–19; P-in-c 19; R Lyneham and Woodhill from 19. *The Vicarage, Clyffe Pypard, Swindon SN4 7PY* T: (01793) 731134 M: 07854-852806 E: reverendrachma@gmail.com

ABBOTT, Miss Geraldine Mary. b 33. SRN 55 SCM 58 Open Univ BA 77 Lon Univ MTh 85. Oak Hill Th Coll BA 82. **dss** 86 **d** 87 **p** 94. Tutor Oak Hill Th Coll 86–96; St Alb St Paul 86–94; Hon Par Dn 87–94; PtO from 94. *2 Wheatleys, St Albans AL4 9UE* T: (01727) 860869 E: mary@stpauls-stalbans.org

ABBOTT (née ROBERTS), Ms Judith. b 55. Collingwood Coll Dur BA 76 Goldsmiths' Coll Lon PGCE 77. SWMTC 00. **d** 03 **p** 04. C Burrington, Chawleigh, Cheldon, Chulmleigh etc *Ex* 03–06; C Axminster, Chardstock, All Saints etc 06–12; PtO *B & W* 13–14; NSM Chaffcombe, Cricket Malherbie etc from 14; Dioc Chapl MU from 16; RD Ilminster *B & W* from 19. *Braytons, Wreath Green, Tatworth, Chard TA20 2SN* T: (01460) 220689 E: judith754@btinternet.com

ABBOTT, Mrs Kathleen Frances. b 60. STETS 96. **d** 99 **p** 00. NSM St Helens and Sea View *Portsm* 99–02; P-in-c Wootton 02–14; AD W Wight 12–14; rtd 15; PtO *Portsm* 16–20; P-in-c Wroxall from 20; P-in-c Newchurch from 20;

P-in-c Arreton from 20. *The Vicarage, High Street, Newchurch, Sandown PO36 0NN* T: (01983) 867034 M: 07499-805359 E: abbott.kath@gmail.com

ABBOTT, Canon Nigel Douglas Blayney. b 37. Open Univ BA 87. Bps' Coll Cheshunt 58. **d** 61 **p** 62. C Northampton St Mich *Pet* 61–64; C Wanstead St Mary *Chelmsf* 64–66; Chapl St Jo Sch Tiffield 66–69; V Earls Barton *Pet* 69–73; V Cov H Trin 73–80; Provost St Jo Cathl Oban *Arg* 80–86; R Oban St Jo 80–86; TR Hemel Hempstead *St Alb* 86–96; RD 94–96; R Much Hadham 96–02; Hon Can St Alb 96–02; rtd 02; PtO *Ely* from 03. *1 Cambridge Road, Ely CB7 4HJ* T: (01353) 662256 E: ndba75@icloud.com

ABBOTT, Peter John. b 48. CQSW 86. St Mich Coll Llan 94. **d** 96 **p** 97. C Neath w Llantwit *Llan* 96–98; C Merthyr Tydfil Ch Ch 98–00; P-in-c Llangeinor w Nantymoel and Wyndham 00–02; V Cwm Ogwr 02–03; TV Ebbw Vale *Mon* 03–13; TV Upper Ebbw Valleys 13–14; rtd 14; PtO *Llan* from 15. *19 Pantglas, Llanbradach, Caerphilly CF83 3PD* T: (029) 2086 6434

ABBOTT, Rachma. *See* ABBOTT, Esther Rachma Hartley

ABBOTT, Stephen Anthony. b 43. K Coll Cam BA 65 MA 69 Edin Univ BD 68 Harvard Univ ThM 69. Edin Th Coll 66. **d** 69 **p** 70. C Deal St Leon *Cant* 69–72; Chapl K Coll Cam 72–75; C Cambridge St Matt *Ely* 75–76; Asst Chapl Bris Univ and Hon C Clifton St Paul 77–80; PtO *Bris* 81–04; P-in-c Mangotsfield 04–10; rtd 10; PtO *Bris* 10–17; *Glouc* from 11. *24 Melrose Close, Yate, Bristol BS37 7AY* T: (01454) 315073 E: abbott.steve@btinternet.com

ABBOTT, Stephen John. b 62. Qu Mary Coll Lon LLB 83. Linc Th Coll BTh 92. **d** 92 **p** 93. C E Dereham and Scarning *Nor* 92–95; TV Penistone and Thurlstone *Wakef* 95–97; R Brandon and Santon Downham w Elveden *St E* 97–00; P-in-c Gt Barton 00–04; PtO 04–08; R Bansfield 08–12; rtd 12; PtO *St E* from 18. *49 Bonsey Gardens, Wrentham, Beccles NR34 7LU* T: (01502) 675598 M: 07531-400347 E: fr.stephenabbott@gmail.com

ABBOTT, William John. b 68. Ex Univ BSc 89 Sheff Univ MSc 91 Cliff Coll MA 13. St Mellitus Coll 18. **d** 19 **p** 20. C Witham and Villages *Chelmsf* from 19. *The Vicarage, 18 Witham Lodge, Witham CM8 1HG* M: 07702-023144 E: will.vicarage@gmail.com

ABECASSIS, Canon Joanna Margaret. b 54. Girton Coll Cam BA 75 MA 79 PhD 81. WEMTC 99. **d** 02 **p** 03. C Tavistock and Gulworthy *Ex* 02–07; TV Totnes w Bridgetown, Berry Pomeroy etc 07–10; P-in-c Bradford-on-Avon H Trin *Sarum* 10–13; R Bradford on Avon H Trin, Westwood and Wingfield from 13; Can and Preb Sarum Cathl from 17. *Holy Trinity Vicarage, 18A Woolley Street, Bradford-on-Avon BA15 1AF* T: (01225) 864444 E: joanna.abecassis@cantab.net

ABELL, George Derek. b 31. Selw Coll Cam BA 54 MA 68. Qu Coll Birm 54. **d** 56 **p** 57. C Stoke upon Trent *Lich* 56–60; C Wolverhampton 60–64; R Bridgnorth St Mary *Heref* 64–70; P-in-c Oldbury 64–70; R Atherton N Australia 70–73; R Withington w Westhide and Weston Beggard *Heref* 73–81; R Withington w Westhide 81–83; P-in-c Sutton St Nicholas w Sutton St Michael 76–81; R 81–83; Preb Heref Cathl 82–83; V Basing *Win* 83–88; rtd 88; PtO *Heref* 88–04; *Ox* from 08. *25 Eastfield Court, Church Street, Faringdon SN7 8SL* T: (01367) 240731

ABERDEEN AND ORKNEY, Bishop of. *See* DYER, The Rt Revd Anne Catherine

ABERDEEN AND ORKNEY, Dean of. *See* BERK, The Very Revd Dennis Bryan Alban

ABERDEEN, Provost of. *See* POOBALAN, The Very Revd Isaac Munuswamy

ABERNETHY, The Rt Revd Alan Francis. b 57. QUB BA 78 BD 89. CITC. **d** 81 **p** 82 **c** 07. C Dundonald *D & D* 81–84; C Lecale Gp 84–86; I Helen's Bay 86–90; I Ballyholme 90–07; Preb Down Cathl 00–07; Cen Dir of Ords 04–07; Bp Conn 07–19; rtd 20. *The Walled Garden, 13 Worcester Lane, Bangor BT19 1GU* E: alanfabernethy@btopenworld.com

ABERNETHY, Cameron Peter. b 75. N Coll of Educn BEd 00 Ox Brookes Univ BA 14. Westcott Ho Cam 16. **d** 18 **p** 19. C Cockerton *Dur* from 18. *175 Brinkburn Road, Darlington DL3 9LD* M: 07725-314995 E: revdcam@gmail.com

ABLETT, Edwin John. b 37. Clifton Th Coll 64. **d** 67 **p** 68. C Sneinton St Chris w St Phil *S'well* 67–70; R High and Gd Easter w Margaret Roding *Chelmsf* 70–73; SAMS Chile 73–75; C Gt Baddow *Chelmsf* 75–78; V Newchapel *Lich* 78–82; V S Westoe *Dur* 82–86; V Tibshelf *Derby* 86–00; rtd 00; PtO *St D* 00–09; *Win* from 10. *Copihue, 18 Sherley Green, Bursledon, Southampton SO31 8FL* T: (023) 8040 6413 E: john.copihue4@gmail.com

ABLETT, Mrs Jennifer Vera. b 46. **d** 00 **p** 01. OLM Claydon and Barham *St E* 00–13; NSM 13–16; rtd 16. *10 Phillipps Road, Barham, Ipswich IP6 0AZ* T: (01473) 830205 E: jenny_and_mick@hotmail.com

ABRAHAM, Brian. b 42. **d** 00 **p** 01. OLM Burscough Bridge *Liv* 00–12; rtd 12; PtO *Liv* from 16. *4 Mere Court, Burscough, Ormskirk L40 0TQ* T: (01704) 892547

ABRAHAMS, Peter William. b 42. Southn Univ BA 77. Sarum Th Coll 77. **d** 78 **p** 79. C Bitterne Park *Win* 78–82; C Old Brumby *Linc* 82–84; V Mitcham Ascension *S'wark* 84–91; TV Riverside *Ox* 91–06; rtd 06; PtO *Ox* 06–12. *17 Snowberry Close, Wokingham RG41 4AQ* T: 0118-989 3072

ABRAM, Paul Robert Carrington. b 36. MVO 07. Keble Coll Ox BA 62 MA 65. Chich Th Coll 60. **d** 62 **p** 63. C Redcar *York* 62–65; CF 65–89; V Salcombe *Ex* 89–96; Miss to Seafarers from 89; rtd 96; Chapl to The Queen 96–06; Chapl St Pet-ad-Vincula at HM Tower of Lon 96–06; Dep P in O 96–06; PtO *Win* 09–19; *Sarum* 16–17. *Paddock End, Kimpton, Andover SP11 8PG* T: (01264) 772349 E: paul.jo@virgin.net *or* abran348@btinternet.com

ABRAM, Steven James. b 50. Lon Univ BD 76. Oak Hill Th Coll 71. **d** 76 **p** 77. C Biddulph *Lich* 76–79; C Heatherlands St Jo *Sarum* 79–83; Libya 83–84; C Stratford-on-Avon w Bishopton *Cov* 84; V Alderholt *Sarum* 84; V Daubhill *Man* 90–04; TV Mid Trent *Lich* 07–16; rtd 16; PtO *Eur* 17–20. *2 Rue André Malraux, 86400 Civray, France* E: sj@abram.org.uk

ABRAMS, Leonard John. b 54. **d** 14 **p** 15. NSM Purley St Mark *S'wark* 14–17; NSM Merstham, S Merstham and Gatton 17–20; P-in-c S Nutfield from 20. *136 Mid Street, South Nutfield, Redhill RH1 5RP* M: 07941-095086 E: revd.len@cc-nutfield.org.uk

ABREY, Mrs Barbara May. b 52. Trin Coll Bris 09. **d** 11 **p** 12. OLM Wroughton and Wichelstowe *Bris* from 11. *17 Edgar Row Close, Wroughton, Swindon SN4 9LR* T: (01793) 633024 E: barbaraabrey@hotmail.com

ABREY, Mark Evans John. b 66. Ripon Coll Cuddesdon BTh 93. **d** 93 **p** 94. C W Derby St Mary *Liv* 93–97; P-in-c Anfield St Marg 97–01; Chapl R Liverpool Children's NHS Trust 95–99; R Chase *Ox* from 01; P-in-c Chadlington and Spelsbury, Ascott under Wychwood 01–05; P-in-c Ascott under Wychwood 05–07. *The Vicarage, Church Road, Chadlington, Chipping Norton OX7 3LY* T: (01608) 676572 E: mark@abreys.com *or* rector@thechasebenefice.org.uk

ABREY, Canon Philip James. b 51. NOC 82. **d** 85 **p** 86. NSM Hindley All SS *Liv* 85–90; C Caversham St Pet and Mapledurham etc *Ox* 90–00; Min Caversham Park LEP 96–00; Co Ecum Officer (Berks) 96–00; PtO *Cov* 01–07; Chapl HM Pris The Mount 02–21; Hon Can St Alb 13–21; rtd 21. *Address withheld by request*

ACHESON, Andrew David. b 89. Sheff Univ BA 11 Middx Univ BA 21. Oak Hill Th Coll 18. **d** 21. C Stamford St Geo w St Paul *Linc* from 21. *17 Turnpole Close, Stamford PE9 1DT* E: andyacheson@hotmail.co.uk

ACHESON, Denise Mary. BTh. **d** 05 **p** 06. C Ballyholme *D & D* 05–08; I Dunmurry *Conn* 08–13; Treas Belf Cathl 13–16; Dean's V 13–16; C Lisburn Ch Ch Cathl *Conn* 16–17; P-in-c Belfast H Trin and St Silas 18–21; rtd 21. *45 West Park, Lisburn BT28 2BQ* T: (028) 9260 2400 E: revdacheson@gmail.com

ACHESON, James Malcolm. b 48. BNC Ox BA 70 MA 73. Sarum & Wells Th Coll 83. **d** 85 **p** 86. C Highgate St Mich *Lon* 85–88; TV Tisbury *Sarum* 88–94; R Storrington *Chich* 94–14; rtd 14; PtO *Chich* from 16. *Gilbert Lodge, 1A Gilbert Road, Eastbourne BN22 8JA* T: (01323) 733315

ACHONRY, Dean of. See GRIMASON, The Very Revd Alistair John

ACKERLEY, Daniel Thomas. b 91. Lindisfarne Regional Tr Partnership 16. **d** 19 **p** 20. NSM Croxdale and Tudhoe *Dur* 19–20; NSM Merrington 19–20; NSM Stockton St Pet from 20; NSM Elton from 20. *41 Kingsley Road, Stockton-on-Tees TS18 5AQ* M: 07720-613301 E: daniel.ackerley@hotmail.com

ACKERLEY, Glyn James. b 57. Kent Univ MA 04 K Coll Lon PhD 13. Cranmer Hall Dur 84. **d** 87 **p** 88. C Tonbridge SS Pet and Paul *Roch* 87–90; R Willingham *Ely* 90–94; R Rampton 90–94; V Chatham St Phil and St Jas *Roch* 94–09; P-in-c Shorne 09–12; V 12–16; Dioc Dir of Ords 09–16; V Bushmead *St Alb* 16–18; rtd 19; PtO *Pet* from

19. *3 Catlin Way, Rushden NN10 9FN* M: 07595-171748 E: g.ackerley@btconnect.com

ACKERMAN, David Michael. b 71. Westmr Coll Ox BTh 95 Brighton Univ PGCE 98 Cardiff Univ LLM 11. Pontificium Institutum Internationale Angelicum Rome STB 01 MA 02. **d** 01 **p** 02. In RC Ch 01–04; C Fairford and Kempsford w Whelford *Glouc* 05–08; P-in-c Sherborne, Windrush, the Barringtons etc 08–12; Dioc Ecum Officer 08–12; V Kensal Green St Jo *Lon* from 13. *St John's Vicarage, Kilburn Lane, London W10 4AA* T: (020) 8969 2615 M: 07882-824909 E: vicarstjohnskg@gmail.com

ACKFORD, Christopher Mark. b 60. Univ Coll Lon BDS 83 K Coll Lon MSc 89. Ripon Coll Cuddesdon 02. **d** 04 **p** 05. C Bracknell *Ox* 04–07; TV Aylesbury 07–14; V Bierton and Hulcott 15–18; P-in-c Stokenchurch and Ibstone 18–19; TR S Chilterns from 19. *The Vicarage, Wycombe Road, Stokenchurch, High Wycombe HP14 3RG* T: (01494) 266891 M: 07780-554032

ACKLAND, Canon John Robert Warwick. b 47. **d** 82 **p** 83. NSM Shooters Hill Ch Ch *S'wark* 82–88; NSM Mottingham St Andr w St Alban 82–94; NSM Woolwich St Thos 94–96; NSM Bellingham St Dunstan 96–03; Hon Chapl *S'wark* Cathl 98–03; P-in-c Perry Hill St Geo w Ch Ch and St Paul 03–04; V 04–12; TR Forest Hill w Lower Sydenham 12–15; Hon Can *S'wark* Cathl 05–15; rtd 15; PtO *S'wark* from 16. *39B Central Hill, London SE19 1BW* M: 07831-516662 E: johnackland100@btinternet.com

ACKROYD, David Andrew. b 66. Coll of Ripon & York St Jo BA 90 St Jo Coll Dur BA 97. Cranmer Hall Dur 94. **d** 97 **p** 98. C Lilleshall and Sheriffhales *Lich* 97–01; Asst Chapl R Wolv Hosps NHS Trust 01–02; C Ogley Hay *Lich* 02–03; PtO 10–11; TR Cheswardine, Childs Ercall, Hales, Hinstock etc 11–17; TR Wrockwardine Deanery from 17; RD Wrockwardine from 17. *The Rectory, Wrockwardine, Telford TF6 5DD* T: (01952) 252078 E: revandy320@btinternet.com

ACKROYD, Dennis. b 36. Cranmer Hall Dur 67. **d** 70 **p** 71. C Newcastle w Butterton *Lich* 70–73; C Horsell *Guildf* 73–77; P-in-c Moreton and Woodsford w Tincleton *Sarum* 77–82; R 82–86; RD Dorchester 79–85; R Ewhurst *Guildf* 86–94; V Cleckheaton St Luke and Whitechapel *Wakef* 94–02; rtd 02; PtO *Sarum* 03–15; *Nor* from 16. *35 Greengate, Swanton Morley, Dereham NR20 4AD* T: (01362) 638078 E: rev.dennis@me.com

ACKROYD, Canon Peter Michael. b 60. Jes Coll Cam BA 82 MA 86 Fontainebleau MBA 87 Edin Univ PhD 02. Wycliffe Hall Ox BA 93 MA 00. **d** 94 **p** 95. C Denton Holme *Carl* 94–97; Sec Proclamation Trust 97–00; V Wootton *St Alb* from 02; Hon Can St Alb from 15. *The Vicarage, Church Road, Wootton, Bedford MK43 9HF* T: (01234) 768391 E: peterackroyd@me.com

ACKROYD, Prof Ruth. b 49. St Aid Coll Dur BA 70 Man Univ MPhil 87 Sheff Univ DMinTh 03. **d** 04 **p** 05. NSM Hoole *Ches* 04–15; V Thornton-le-Moors w Ince and Elton 15–19; rtd 19; PtO *Ches* from 19. *3 Strathmore, Ashby Place, Hoole, Chester CH2 3AG*

ACLAND, Mrs Sophia Caroline Annabel. b 61. Somerville Coll Ox BA 11 MA 11. Ripon Coll Cuddesdon BA 12. **d** 11 **p** 12. NSM Cam w Stinchcombe *Glouc* from 11; NSM All Hallows by the Tower etc *Lon* from 14. *The Mount House, Alderley, Wotton-under-Edge GL12 7QT* T: (01453) 842233 *or* (020) 7481 2928 E: sophia@acland.force9.co.uk *or* sophia@ahbtt.org.uk

ACONLEY, Carole Ann. b 51. Hull Univ BTh 01. NEOC 99. **d** 02 **p** 03. NSM Langtoft w Foxholes, Butterwick, Cottam etc *York* 02–12; PtO from 13. *Hawthorn Farm, Langtoft, Driffield YO25 3BT* T: (01377) 267911 E: caroleaconley@me.com

ACREMAN, John. b 53. Oak Hill Th Coll 86. **d** 88 **p** 89. C Iver *Ox* 88–92; R Hook Norton w Gt Rollright, Swerford etc 92–18; rtd 18; PtO *Ox* from 21. *98 Grange Road, Banbury OX16 9AU* T: (01295) 267054 E: acreman@xalt.co.uk *or* john.acreman@btinternet.com

ACWORTH, The Ven Richard Foote. b 36. SS Coll Cam BA 62 MA 65. Cuddesdon Coll 61. **d** 63 **p** 64. C Fulham St Etheldreda *Lon* 63–64; C Langley All SS and Martyrs *Man* 64–66; C Bridgwater St Mary w Chilton Trinity *B & W* 66–69; V Yatton 69–81; V Yatton Moor 81; P-in-c Taunton St Jo 81–84; P-in-c Taunton St Mary 81–85; V 85–93; Preb Wells Cathl 87–93; Adn Wells, Can Res and Preb Wells Cathl 93–03; rtd 03; PtO *B & W* from 04. *Corvedale Cottage, Ganes Terrace, Croscombe, Wells BA5 3QJ* T: (01749) 342242 E: vendick@talktalk.net

ADAIR, Canon William Matthew. b 52. Open Univ BA. CITC 77. **d** 77 **p** 78. C Portadown St Mark *Arm* 77–78; Asst Chapl Miss to Seamen 78–80; C Lisburn Ch Ch Cathl *Conn* 80–84; I Kildress w Altedesert *Arm* 84–92; I Portadown St Columba from 92; Dioc Sec Min of Healing 95–99; Can

Arm Cathl from 08. *St Columba's Rectory, 81 Loughgall Road, Portadown, Craigavon BT62 4EG* T: (028) 3833 2746 E: billadair77@btinternet.com

ADAM, Andrew Keith Malcolm. b 57. Bowdoin Coll USA BA 79 Duke Univ (USA) PhD 91. Yale Div Sch MDiv 86 STM 87. **d** 86 **p** 86. Chapl St Thos Day Sch & C New Haven Ch Ch USA 86–87; Chapl Assoc Duke Univ 87–90; Asst Prof Eckerd Coll 90–94; P-in-c Tampa St Jas 91–92; Asst Prof Princeton Th Sem 94–99; Prof Seabury-Western Th Sem 99–08; P-in-c Evanston St Luke 01–02; Lect Glas Univ 09–13; NSM St Mary's Cathl 10–13; Tutor St Steph Ho Ox from 13. Lect Oriel Coll Ox from 13. *St Stephen's House, 16 Marston Street, Oxford OX4 1JX* T: (01865) 613500 M: 07514-800612 E: akm.adam@gmail.com

ADAM, Lawrence. b 38. NOC 82. **d** 82 **p** 83. C Thornton-le-Fylde *Blackb* 82–86; Dioc Video Production Co-ord 85–97; P-in-c Scorton 86–91; C W Burnley All SS 91–97; P-in-c Ashton St Jas *Man* 97–99; TV Ashton 00–03; rtd 03; PtO *Ches* from 03. *23 Dryden Avenue, Cheadle SK8 2AW*

ADAM, Lindsay Anne. *See* YATES, Lindsay Anne

ADAM, Canon Peter James Hedderwick. b 46. OAM 12. Lon Univ BD 73 MTh 76 Dur Univ PhD 81. Ridley Coll Melbourne ThL 69. **d** 70 **p** 71. C Ivanhoe St Jas Australia 70–72; C Rosanna 72; Hon C Holborn St Geo w H Trin and St Bart *Lon* 72–73; C Essendon St Thos Australia 73–74; Tutor Ridley Coll 73–74; Tutor St Jo Coll Dur 75–82; Hon C Dur St Cuth 75–82; P-in-c Carlton St Jude Australia 82–88; V 88–01; Adn Melbourne 88–91; Chapl Melbourne Univ 95–01; Prin Ridley Coll Melbourne 01–12; Can Melbourne 96–16; rtd 12. *PO Box 603, North Carlton VIC 3054, Australia* E: pjhadam@gmail.com

ADAM, William Jonathan. b 69. Man Univ BA 91 Univ of Wales (Cardiff) LLM 03 PhD 09 FRHistS 11. Westcott Ho Cam 92 Bossey Ecum Inst Geneva. **d** 94 **p** 95. C Beaconsfield *Ox* 94–97; C Witney 97–98; TV 98–02; P-in-c Girton *Ely* 02–07; R 07–10; Dioc Ecum Officer 02–10; V Winchmore Hill St Paul *Lon* 10–17; Abp Cant's Ecum Adv 17–21; Ecum Officer Coun for Chr Unity 17–19; Dir Unity, Faith and Order Angl Communion Office from 19; Dep Sec Gen from 21; PtO *Lon* from 17; *Chich* from 17. *Anglican Consultative Council, St Andrew's House, 16 Tavistock Crescent, London W11 1AP* T: (020) 7313 3930 E: william.adam@anglicancommunion.org

ADAMOLEKUN, Abimbola Abolade (Bola). b 72. St Jo Coll Nottm. **d** 14 **p** 15. NSM Shepherd's Bush St Steph w St Thos *Lon* 14–17; Chapl HM Pris Wandsworth 17–21; Chapl HM Pris Pentonville 18–21; Chapl HM Pris Brixton from 21. *HM Prison Brixton, Jebb Avenue, London SW2 5XF* T: (020) 8588 6052 E: abimbola.adamolekun@justice.gov.uk

ADAMS, Canon Alison Mary. b 51. Girton Coll Cam MA 73 Birm Univ BMus 76 CertEd 77 Sheff Univ MPhil 93. EMMTC 94. **d** 97 **p** 98. NSM Burbage w Aston Flamville *Leic* 97–05; Dir Bloxham Project 00–05; Chapl HM YOI Glen Parva 06–13; Dioc and Cathl Soc Resp Enabler *Leic* from 13; Hon Can Leic Cathl 15–16; Can Res Leic Cathl from 16; Past and Sub-Dean from 16. *29 Leicester Lane, Desford, Leicester LE9 9JJ* T: (01455) 823674 E: alison.adams@leccofe.org

ADAMS, Brian Hugh. b 32. Pemb Coll Ox BA 54 MA 57. Sarum & Wells Th Coll 77. **d** 79 **p** 80. Hon C Crediton *Ex* 79–81; Chapl St Brandon's Sch Clevedon 81–85; C Street w Walton *B & W* 86–88; V Baltonsborough w Butleigh and W Bradley 88–97; RD Glastonbury 86–97; rtd 97; PtO *B & W* from 97. *18 Hayes End Manor, South Petherton TA13 5BE* T: (01460) 242442 M: 07980-605284 E: adamsbj@btinternet.com

ADAMS, Canon Brian Peter. b 47. FInstD FRSA Avery Hill Coll CertEd 70. S'wark Ord Course 90. **d** 93 **p** 94. NSM Tonbridge SS Pet and Paul *Roch* 93–99; P-in-c Chatham St Mary w St Jo 99–14; Hon Can Roch Cathl 09–14; rtd 14; PtO *Roch* from 15. *3 St Davids Gate, Maidstone ME16 9EP* T: (01622) 728032 M: 07778-777824 E: bpadams@btinternet.com

ADAMS, Mrs Celia. b 39. R Holloway Coll Lon BSc 60 Cam Univ CertEd 61. Sarum & Wells Th Coll 86. **d** 88 **p** 94. NSM Canley *Cov* 88–91; NSM Cov N Deanery 91–92; C Coventry Caludon *Cov* 92–97; Asst to Dioc Dir of Educn 92–93; Asst Chapl Geo Eliot Hosp NHS Trust Nuneaton 97–01; rtd 01; PtO *Ban* from 01; *Cov* from 01. *Cefn-y-Mor, 102 Plas Edwards, Tywyn LL36 0AS* T: (01654) 711604 E: nigeladams864@btinternet.com

ADAMS, Christine Frances. *See* BULL, Christine Frances

ADAMS, Christopher John. b 40. **d** 98 **p** 99. C Luton St Fran *St Alb* 98–05; rtd 06; PtO *St Alb* from 06. *91 Byron Road, Luton LU4 0HX* T: (01582) 529373 E: chrisandsallyadams@ntlworld.com

ADAMS, David. *See* ADAMS, John David Andrew

ADAMS, David James. b 58. Trin Coll Bris 95. **d** 97 **p** 98. C Wirksworth *Derby* 97–00; P-in-c Seale and Lullington 00–02;

R Seale and Lullington w Coton in the Elms 02–05; CF from 05. *c/o MOD Chaplains (Army)* T: (01264) 383430 F: 381824

ADAMS, Donald John. b 46. St Jo Coll Nottm 86. **d** 88 **p** 89. C Byfleet *Guildf* 88–93; P-in-c E Molesey St Mary 93–03; PtO *S'wark* 96–03; rtd 03; PtO *Glouc* 15–20. *4 Boxbush Close, South Cerney, Cirencester GL7 5XS*

ADAMS, Douglas George. b 39. St Luke's Coll Ex CertEd 69 MEd 87 ALBC 65. SWMTC 86. **d** 89 **p** 90. NSM Bude Haven and Marhamchurch *Truro* 89–93; P-in-c St Mewan 93–04; P-in-c Mevagissey and St Ewe 00–04; Chapl Mt Edgcumbe Hospice 93–96; rtd 04; PtO *Truro* from 05; *Ex* from 10. *9 Arundel Terrace, Bude EX23 8LS* T: (01288) 353842 E: douglas-adams@talktalk.net

ADAMS, Gillian Linda. *See* WILTON, Gillian Linda

ADAMS, Godfrey Bernard. b 47. **d** 93 **p** 94. OLM Saddleworth *Man* 93–09; PtO from 09. *Shawfields House, Shaws, Uppermill, Oldham OL3 6JX* T: (01457) 875126 M: 07717-222042 E: godfreyadams1@btinternet.com

ADAMS, Hubert Theodore. b 28. FCA. **d** 98 **p** 99. OLM Blurton *Lich* 98–11; OLM Blurton and Dresden 11–13; PtO 14–20. *12 Wakefield Road, Stoke-on-Trent ST4 5PT* T: (01782) 415364 E: theoadams@live.co.uk

ADAMS, Ian Robert. b 57. R Holloway Coll Lon BA 79. Ridley Hall Cam 95. **d** 97 **p** 98. C Thame *Ox* 97–04; Ldr mayBe 04–09; Missional Community Developer CMS 09–15; Miss Spirituality Adv from 15; Tutor Ridley Hall Cam from 17; Chapl from 19; LtO *Ely* from 17. *Ridley Hall, Ridley Hall Road, Cambridge CB3 9HG* M: 07889-906983 E: ira21@cam.ac.uk *or* ianradams@icloud.com

ADAMS, Canon James Michael. b 49. Man Univ LLB 71 Lon Univ PGCE 79. St Jo Coll Nottm 80. **d** 82 **p** 83. C Luton St Mary *St Alb* 82–85; TV Cove St Jo *Guildf* 85–92; V Chislehurst Ch *Ch Roch* 92–14; Hon Can Roch Cathl 09–14; rtd 14; PtO *Carl* from 15; *Chich* from 18; *Roch* from 18. *20 Piltdown Way, Eastbourne BN23 8LB* T: (01323) 761141 M: 07511-268016 E: michaeladamsjma@gmail.com

ADAMS, Mrs Jayne Maxine. b 57. Westhill Coll Birm CertEd 78. WMMTC 94. **d** 97 **p** 98. NSM Cotteridge *Birm* 97–99; NSM Nechells 99–05; NSM Bournville 05–07; Asst Chapl Dudley Gp NHS Foundn Trust 07–13; NSM Selly Oak St Mary *Birm* from 14. *95 Mavis Road, Birmingham B31 2SB* T: 0121-574 0436 E: jaynevicar@aol.com

ADAMS, John David Andrew. b 37. TCD BA 60 MA 64 BD 69 Div Test 61 Reading Univ MEd 74. **d** 62 **p** 63. C Belfast St Steph *Conn* 62–65; Asst Master Lacunza Academy Spain 65–67; Asst Master Tower Ramparts Sch Ipswich 67–70; Asst Master Robert Haining Sch Surrey 70–74; Hd Master St Paul's Secondary Sch Addlestone 74–82; Hd Master Weydon Secondary Sch Farnham 82–98; NSM Bourne *Guildf* 80–99; NSM The Bourne and Tilford 99–07; Chapl to The Queen 94–07; Consultant to Secondary Schs 98–07; PtO *Guildf* 08–15. *Brookside Farm, Oast House Crescent, Farnham GU9 0NP* T: (01252) 726888

ADAMS, John Frederick. b 82. Univ Coll Ox BA 05. Wycliffe Hall Ox BA 12. **d** 13 **p** 14. C Wimbledon Em Ridgway Prop Chpl *S'wark* 13–20; V S Croydon Em from 20. *The Vicarage, 33 Hurst Way, South Croydon CR2 7AP* M: 07863-544228 E: johnfredadams@gmail.com *or* john.adams@emmanuelcroydon.org.uk

ADAMS, John Mark Arthur. *See* ADAMS, Mark

ADAMS, John Peter. b 42. Lon Univ BD 69. Oak Hill Th Coll 65. **d** 70 **p** 71. C Whitnash *Cov* 70–73; Hon Asst Chapl Basle *Eur* 73–74; Chapl Davos 74–75; Chapl Düsseldorf 75–76; C Gt Baddow *Chelmsf* 77–80; Miss Eur Chr Miss 80–91; PtO *Chelmsf* 80–91; Hon Asst Vienna w Prague *Eur* 90–91; Asst Chapl Zürich 91–95; P-in-c Harmondsworth *Lon* 95–99; TV Shebbear, Buckland Filleigh, Sheepwash etc *Ex* 99–02; rtd 02; PtO *Ex* 02–18; *Eur* 13–18; *Win* from 18. *21 Florence Court, Andover SP10 5HZ*

ADAMS, Jonathan Henry. b 48. St Andr Univ MA 73. Cranmer Hall Dur 73. **d** 76 **p** 77. C Upperby St Jo *Carl* 76–78; C Sunderland St Chad *Dur* 78–82; Soc Resp Officer 83–91; TV Willington *Newc* 91–96; Local Min Development Officer 91–96; P-in-c Byker St Silas *Newc* 96–01; PtO from 01; *Dur* from 01; rtd 13. *5A Tunstall Vale, Sunderland SR2 7HP* T: 0191-525 1881 M: 07903-911771 E: adams.j@icloud.com

ADAMS, Mark. b 67. Reading Univ BSc 89. St Jo Coll Nottm MA 98 MPhil 07. **d** 99 **p** 00. C Skegby *S'well* 99–02; C Bletchley *Ox* 02–07; P-in-c Mansfield St Jo *S'well* 07–10; P-in-c Ladybrook 09–10; V Mansfield St Jo w St Mary 10–16; AD Mansfield 10–15; V Norwell w Ossington, Cromwell etc 16–20; AD Newark and S'well 16–20; Hon Can S'well Minster 15–20. *Address temp unknown*

ADAMS, Martin Philip. b 57. Open Univ BA 99 K Coll Lon MA 13. Sarum & Wells Th Coll 88. **d** 90 **p** 91. C Sandringham w W Newton *Nor* 90–93; P-in-c Docking w The Birchams and Stanhoe w Barwick 93–95; V Docking, the Birchams, Stanhoe and Sedgeford 95–97; V Orrell *Liv* 97–03; R Aughton St Mich 03–08; Dir Dioc OLM Scheme 03–11; Dir Studies SNWTP 08–11; Dean of Studies All SS Cen for Miss and Min 11–14; Ed ROOTS for Churches Ltd from 15; Hon C Aughton St Mich and Bickerstaffe *Liv* 15–19. *73 Crossdale Street, Northrepps, Cromer NR27 9LB* T: (01263) 512986 M: 07939-396934 E: martin.adams@rootsontheweb.com or martin.p.adams@btopenworld.com

ADAMS, Michael. *See* ADAMS, James Michael

ADAMS, Canon Michael John. b 48. St Jo Coll Dur BA 77. Ripon Coll Cuddesdon 77. d 79 p 80. C Falmouth K Chas *Truro* 79–81; C St Buryan, St Levan and Sennen 81–83; P-in-c Lanlivery w Luxulyan 83–84; V 84–88; V St Agnes 88–99; V Newquay 99–14; RD Powder 90–96; rtd 14; Hon Can Truro Cathl from 03; PtO from 15. *5 Trevemper Road, Newquay TR7 2HR* T: (01637) 853930 E: m.j.adams20@gmail.com

ADAMS, Nicholas Stephen. b 68. K Coll Lon BA 04. Westcott Ho Cam 06. d 09 p 10. Partnership P E Bris 09–11; C Soundwell 11–13; NSM 13–15; NSM Cotham St Sav w St Mary and Clifton St Paul 15–18; TV Upper Islwyn *Mon* from 18. *The Vicarage, Central Avenue, Oakdale, Blackwood NP12 0JS* E: nickadams100@hotmail.com

ADAMS, Nigel Charles. b 60. St Jo Coll Dur BA 81 Greenwich Univ PGCE 92. Oak Hill Th Coll MA 14. d 14 p 15. C Barton Seagrave w Warkton *Pet* 14–17; P-in-c Braintree St Mich *Chelmsf* from 17. *St Michael's Vicarage, 10A Marshalls Road, Braintree CM7 2LL* T: (01376) 807662 E: revnigeladams@gmail.com

ADAMS, Nigel David. b 40. Sarum & Wells Th Coll 86. d 88 p 89. C Tile Hill *Cov* 88–91; C Coventry Caludon 91–92; TV 92–97; Asst Chapl HM YOI Onley 92–95; Sub Chapl HM Pris Birm 95–01; P-in-c Nuneaton St Mary *Cov* 97–01; rtd 01; PtO *Cov* from 01; *Ban* from 01; AD Ystumaner 05–09 and 13–15; AD Synod De Meirionnydd 15–18. *Cefn-y-Mor, 102 Plas Edwards, Tywyn LL36 0AS* T: (01654) 711604 E: nigeladams864@btinternet.com

ADAMS, Canon Olugboyega Adeoye. b 55. Univ of Illinois BSc 81 Univ of Kansas MSc 82 Lon Univ PhD 93 Nottm Univ MA 08 Birm Univ PhD 19. EMMTC 99. d 02 p 03. C Glenfield *Leic* 02–05; V Peckham St Mary Magd *S'wark* from 05; Hon Can S'wark Cathl from 20. *St Mary's Vicarage, 22 St Mary's Road, London SE15 2DW* T: (020) 7639 4596 E: oadams.smm@gmail.com

ADAMS, Canon Peter. b 37. K Coll Lon AKC 65 Trin Coll Cam MA 70. St Boniface Warminster 65. d 66 p 67. C Clapham H Trin *S'wark* 66–70; Chapl Trin Coll Cam 70–75; Warden Trin Coll Cen Camberwell 75–83; V Camberwell St Geo *S'wark* 75–83; RD Camberwell 80–83; P-in-c W Dulwich All SS and Em 83–85; V 85–92; V Addington 92–02; Hon Can S'wark Cathl 99–02; rtd 03; PtO *S'wark* 04–16. *26 Mansfield Road, South Croydon CR2 6HN* T: (020) 8680 3191 E: canon.adams@talk21.com

ADAMS, Canon Raymond William. b 58. Reading Univ BA 79. Oak Hill Th Coll BA 85. d 85 p 86. C Blackpool St Thos *Blackb* 85–88; C Padiham 88–90; TV Rodbourne Cheney *Bris* 90–02; RD Cricklade 97–99; V Haydon Wick from 02; AD Swindon 20–21; Hon Can Bris Cathl from 20. *The Vicarage, 54 Furlong Close, Swindon SN25 1QP* T: (01793) 634258 or 726000 E: r.adams4@ntlworld.com or r.adams3081@gmail.com

ADAMS, Richard John. b 48. Leeds Univ BA 70. SAOMC 94. d 97 p 98. C N Hinksey and Wytham *Ox* 97–01; V Fence-in-Pendle and Higham *Blackb* 01–11; rtd 11. *Tros y Mor, Llangoed, Beaumaris LL58 8SB* T: (01248) 490770 E: richard@gwyneth.net

ADAMS, Robin Thomas. b 54. QUB BSc 76. Oak Hill Th Coll BA 79. d 79 p 80. C Magheralin D & D 79–82; C Coleraine *Conn* 82–86; I Belfast St Aid 86–89; USA 89–18; V Gainesville Ch of the Word 98–18; Chapl Brittany *Eur* 18–21; rtd 21. *3516 Edland Drive, Orlando FL 32806-3418, USA*

ADAMS, Ruth. *See* OATES, Ruth

ADAMS, Ms Ruth Helen. b 73. St Jo Coll Dur BA 94 TCD BTh 97. CITC 94. d 97 p 98. C Drumragh w Mountfield D & R 97–99; Chapl Trin Coll Cam 00–06; P-in-c Bar Hill *Ely* 06–11; V Chesterton St Geo 12–21; Bp's Officer for Resilience in Conflict from 14. *Address temp unknown* E: rev.r.h.adams@gmail.com

ADAMS, Stephen Paul. b 56. Ex Univ BSc 78 Ches Univ DProf 20. Sarum & Wells Th Coll 85. d 87 p 88. C Swansea St Nic *S & B* 87–88; C Llwynderw 88–91; R Badby w Newham and Charwelton w Fawsley etc *Pet* 91–97; R Abington 97–06; RD Northn 01–06; Dean Min Development St Mich Coll Llan 06–15; TR Cowbridge *Llan* from 15. *The Rectory, 85 Broadway, Llanblethian, Cowbridge CF71 7EY* T: (01446) 771625 E: rector@cowbridgeparish.com

ADAMS (née DABIN), Susan. b 51. NTMTC 96. d 00 p 01. NSM Hullbridge *Chelmsf* 00–03 and 07–10; NSM Rawreth w Rettendon 07–10; NSM Ashingdon w S Fambridge 03–07; NSM Rettendon and Hullbridge 10–21; rtd 21; PtO *Chelmsf* from 21. *49 Crouch Avenue, Hullbridge, Hockley SS5 6BS* T: (01702) 231825 E: susansecretarybird@hotmail.co.uk

ADAMS, Theo. *See* ADAMS, Hubert Theodore

ADAMS, William Thomas. b 47. Ches Coll of HE CertEd 69 Open Univ BA 74 Leic Univ M1 FRSA 96. EAMTC 97. d 00 p 01. NSM Helmdon w Stuchbury and Radstone etc *Pet* 00–03; NSM Astwell Gp 03–05; R 05–12; rtd 12; PtO *Pet* from 12; *Worc* from 14. *Brookdale, Mill Road, Whitfield, Brackley NN13 5TQ* T: (01280) 850683 M: 07787-184510 E: will@adamsbrookdale.com

ADAMSON, Arthur John. b 38. Keble Coll Ox BA 61 MA 65. Tyndale Hall Bris 61. d 63 p 64. C Redhill H Trin *S'wark* 63–66; Chapl Trent Park Coll of Educn 66–69; C Enfield Ch Ch Trent Park Lon 66–70; Ind Chapl Battersea Power Station and V Battersea St Geo w St Andr *S'wark* 70–74; R Reedham *Nor* 74–80; Min Beighton and Moulton 75–80; P-in-c Cantley w Limpenhoe and Southwood 77–80; R Oulton St Mich 80–90; Chapl Lothingland Hosp 80–90; R Laceby *Linc* 90–98; R Laceby and Ravendale Gp 98–03; rtd 03; PtO *Pet* from 03. *24 Mill Lane, Cottesmore, Oakham LE15 7DL* T: (01572) 812816 E: ajohnadamson@aol.com

ADAMSON, Graham William. b 76. Robert Gordon Univ Aber BA 98. Trin Coll Bris 12. d 14 p 15. C Bushey St Alb 14–17; V Baswich *Lich* from 17; PtO Lon 16–17. *The Vicarage, 97 Baswich Lane, Stafford ST17 0BN* M: 07979-963707 E: frgraham@adamsonweb.com or frgrahamadamson@outlook.com

ADAMSON, Mrs Ruth Margaret. b 51. Anglia Poly Univ BSc 95 RGN 89 RHV 95. St Jo Coll Nottm 14 ERMC 15. d 16 p 17. NSM Aylmerton, Runton, Beeston Regis and Gresham *Nor* 16–19; P-in-c 19–20; PtO from 20. *5 Rookery Close, Mundesley, Norwich NR11 8QH* T: (01263) 722647 M: 07980-634826 E: ruth.adamson2@btinternet.com

ADAMSON-HILL, David William Dominic. b 91. Sheff Univ BA 17. Coll of Resurr Mirfield 14. d 17 p 18. C S'wark St Geo w St Alphege and St Jude 17–21; C Bermondsey St Hugh CD 17–21; C S'wark Cathl 17–21; C Croydon St Jo from 21. *Church House, Barrow Road, Croydon CR0 4EZ* M: 07792-409952 E: dave_adamson@me.com

ADAN, Howard Keith. b 62. d 01 p 02. C Amsterdam w Den Helder and Heiloo *Eur* 01–04; Asst Chapl 04–07; Angl Chapl Amsterdam Airport Schiphol 04–07; Chapl for Min Development Ostend and Bruges 08; Old Catholic Ch The Netherlands 08–09; Asst Chapl The Hague *Eur* 09–11; R Cedar St Phil Canada 11–13; Chapl Vancouver Internat Airport 13–16; Hd of Multi-Faith Chapl Heathrow Airport *Lon* 16–20; PtO *Eur* from 20. *Address temp unknown* M: (0031) 62-919 5495 E: howie.adan@gmail.com

ADÁN FERNÁNDEZ, Hugo Federico. b 75. San Dámaso Univ Madrid SThB 02 Comillas Pontifical Univ SThM 10 SThD 15. Westcott Ho Cam 13. d 03 p 04. In RC Ch 03–13; PtO *Ely* 14–17; C Catford St Laur *S'wark* 15–18; P-in-c S'wark H Trin w St Matt 18; R from 18. *The Rectory, Meadow Row, London SE1 6RG* T: (020) 7357 8532 M: 07593-310487 E: rector@stmatt.co.uk

ADDENBROOKE, Keith Paul. b 67. Warwick Univ BSc 90 MA 05 Lanc Univ MA 03 Ches Univ MTh 14. Qu Coll Birm BA 07. d 07 p 08. C Upton (Overchurch) *Ches* 07–10; V Tranmere St Paul w St Luke 10–15; V Hale and Ashley 15–18; V Birkenhead St Jas w St Bede from 18. *St James's Vicarage, 56 Tollemache Road, Prenton CH43 8SZ* T: 0151-652 1016 E: k.addenbrooke32@btinternet.com

ADDENBROOKE, Peter Homfray. b 38. Trin Coll Cam BA 59 MA 68 Ex Univ PGCE 60. Lich Th Coll 61. d 63 p 64. C Bakewell *Derby* 63–67; C Horsham *Chich* 67–73; P-in-c Colgate 73–98; Adv for Past Care and Counselling 73–93; rtd 98; PtO *Chich* from 99. *Ashworth, 10 Collingwood Road, Horsham RH12 2QW* T: (01403) 264818 M: 07970-888107 E: pha2000@wma2005.plus.com

ADDINGTON, David John. b 47. FInstLEx 72 FCIArb 96. St Jo Coll Nottm 98. d 01 p 03. Asst P Warwick St Mary Bermuda 03–08; Hon C St George St Pet from 08; Chapl Miss to Seafarers from 05; Hon C March St Jo *Ely* 08–11; Hon C Wisbech SS Pet and Paul 11–16; Hon C Downham Market and Stradsett from 16; Chapl RNM from 19. *Eben-Ezer Cottage, 79 New Park, March PE15 8RT* T/F: (01354) 650139 M: 07775-796543 E: fradders@btinternet.com

ADDIS, Rosemary Anne. b 70. Keele Univ BA 92 New Coll Edin BD 14. d 14 p 15. C Edin Gd Shep 14–17; C Edin St Jo from 17. *11A Cornwall Street, Edinburgh EH1 2EQ* M: 07795-225098 E: rosieaddis@yahoo.co.uk

ADDISON, David John Frederick. b 37. K Coll Dur BA 60 DipEd 62 Birm Univ MA 79 Bris Univ MLitt 93. Wells Th Coll 64. **d** 66 **p** 71. C Rastrick St Matt *Wakef* 66–67; PtO *Bradf* 67–71; Hon C Manningham St Luke 71–73; PtO *Glouc* 77–79; Hon C Bisley w Oakridge 79–81; V Newland and Redbrook w Clearwell 81–02; Chapl R Forest of Dean Coll 89–02; PtO *Glouc* 02–08; *Mon* 04–08; TV Langtree *Ox* 08–16; PtO *Lon* 17–19; *Glouc* from 19. *2 Lypiatt Road, Lypiatt Street, Cheltenham GL50 2UA* T: (01242) 238905 M: 07815-806313 E: davidaddison10@btinternet.com

ADDY, William Henry. b 54. SNWTP 09. **d** 12 **p** 13. NSM Fazakerley Em *Liv* 12–14; NSM Mossley Hill 14–17; NSM Liv Our Lady and St Nic from 17; AD Liv N from 20. *7 Broadacre Close, Liverpool L18 2JW* T: 0151-722 3417 M: 07836-225709 E: bill@addyfamily.com

ADEDIPE, Adewole Foluso. b 85. Obafemi Awolowo Univ BN 15 RN 05. **d** 12 **p** 13. C Ile-Ife St Matthias Nigeria 12–18; V Moro St Jos 18–20; PtO *Lich* from 20. *112 Flint House, Lomas Street, Wolverhampton WV1 1QU* M: 07545-566053 E: adewoleadedipe@yahoo.com *or* adewole.adedipe@nhs.net

ADEKUNLE, The Ven Elizabeth. Birm Univ BTh SOAS MA. Ridley Hall Cam. **d** 07 **p** 08. C Homerton St Luke *Lon* 07–11; Chapl St Mellitus Coll 07–11; Chapl Homerton Univ Hosp NHS Foundn Trust 07–11; Chapl St Jo Coll Cam 11–16; Adn Hackney *Lon* 16–21; P-in-c Shoreditch St Leon w St Mich 19–20; PtO from 21; Chapl to The Queen from 17. *Address temp unknown*

ADELAJA, Adebowale Oluwatunwase. b 56. Ibadan Univ Nigeria BSc 79 MSc 91 Strathclyde Univ MSc 82. **d** 12 **p** 13. Nigeria 12–20; NSM Fulham All SS *Lon* from 20. *5 Bensbury Close, London SW15 3TB* T: (020) 8780 1058 M: 07307-886608 E: revdbadelaja@gmail.com

ADELOYE, Emmanuel Olufemi Kehinde. b 60. Ilorin Univ Nigeria BA 85 Ibadan Univ Nigeria MA 95 Crowther Graduate Th Sem Abeokuta PhD 16. Immanuel Coll Ibadan 89. **d** 91 **p** 92. Chapl to Bp Egba Nigeria 91–92; C Egba Cathl 92–95; V Kemta All SS 95–99; Personal Asst to Bp Ibadan S 99–00; Adn Odo-Ona St Paul 00–06; PtO *S'wark* 07; C Lewisham St Mary 07–08; C Lagos Pentecost Nigeria 09–10; P-in-c 10; Adn Iju-Ishaga St Jo 10–12; V Jakande Estate Our Sav 12–13; Adn Ogunbiyi Memorial Ch 13–18; PtO *S'wark* 18–19; V Peckham St Jo w St Andr from 19. *10A Meeting House Lane, London SE15 2UN* T: (020) 3556 1095 M: 07428-460646 E: ven.eadeloye@yahoo.com

ADEMOLA, Canon Ade. b 62. Goldsmiths' Coll Lon BA 91 N Lon Univ MA 94. NTMTC 95. **d** 98 **p** 99. NSM Lt Ilford St Barn *Chelmsf* 98–02; V Leyton Em from 02; Can Ibadan from 03. *Emmanuel Vicarage, 149 Hitcham Road, London E17 8HL* T: (020) 8539 2200 M: 07941-029084 E: orison@ademola.eu

ADENEY, Mrs Susan Margaret Eliza. b 55. **d** 18 **p** 19. NSM Hanley Castle, Hanley Swan and Welland *Worc* from 18; NSM Upton-on-Severn, Ripple, Earls Croome etc from 18. *The Villa, Gilberts End, Hanley Castle, Worcester WR8 0AS*

ADENIRAN (née POWIS), Mrs Amy Victoria. b 87. Reading Univ BA 08. Trin Coll Bris BA 14. **d** 14 **p** 15. C Shirley *Win* 14–18; Min Whiteley CD *Portsm* 18–21; C Whiteley from 21. *47 Sorrel Drive, Whiteley, Fareham PO15 7JL*

ADESANYA, The Ven Stephen Adedotun. b 57. Ogun State Univ MEd 97 Ado-Ekiti State Univ PhD 03. Evang Th Faculty Osijek Croatia BTh 91. **d** 91 **p** 92. Nigeria 91–07; Adn Iwade and V Italupe Em 03–07; PtO *S'wark* 07–08; P-in-c Romaldkirk w Laithkirk *Ripon* 09–13; P-in-c Startforth and Bowes and Rokeby w Brignall 09–13; V Burnley St Cuth *Blackb* 13–20; V Brierfield 13–20; rtd 20; PtO *Liv* from 21. *11 Boswell Street, Bootle L20 4RP* M: 07411-899724 E: dsny57@gmail.com

ADETAYO, Mrs Abigail Olufunke. b 47. SRN 74 SCM 75 Greenwich Univ PGCE 01. SEITE 06. **d** 09 **p** 10. NSM Peckham St Mary Magd *S'wark* 09–17; PtO from 17. *158 Torridon Road, London SE6 1RD* T/F: (020) 8695 1713 M: 07746-033727 E: jadetayo@aol.com

ADEY HUISH, Helen Louise. b 59. Bris Univ BA 81 Qu Coll Cam PhD 87. SAOMC 01. **d** 04 **p** 05. NSM Banbury *Ox* 04–07; Chapl Ox Radcliffe Hosps NHS Trust 07–12; Chapl Ox Univ Hosps NHS Trust 12–13; Chapl Myton Hamlet Hospice 13–19; rtd 19; PtO *Ox* 09–17; NSM Banbury from 17. *Timberhurst, The Green, Shenington, Banbury OX15 6NE* T: (01295) 670285 E: louise.adeyhuish@btinternet.com

ADFIELD, Richard Ernest. b 31. Oak Hill Th Coll 62. **d** 64 **p** 65. C Bedworth *Cov* 64–67; V Whitehall Park St Andr Hornsey Lane *Lon* 67–77; V Kensington St Helen w H Trin 77–86; V Turnham Green Ch Ch 86–92; rtd 92; PtO *Chich* from 92; Chapl Brighton and Sussex Univ Hosps NHS Trust 02–03; Chapl Whittington Coll Felbridge 03–11. *363 Hangleton Road, Hove BN3 7LQ* T: (01273) 732538 E: ric_the_vic@hotmail.co.uk

ADIDE, Denis. b 86. Brunel Univ BA 11. Trin Coll Bris MA 16. **d** 16 **p** 17. C Turnham Green Ch Ch *Lon* 16–19; V Shepherd's Bush St Steph w St Thos from 19. *St Stephen's Vicarage, 1 Coverdale Road, London W12 8JJ* M: 07903-351319 E: denis.adide@ststephensw12.org

✠**ADIE, The Rt Revd Michael Edgar.** b 29. CBE 94. St Jo Coll Ox BA 52 MA 56 Surrey Univ DUniv 95. Westcott Ho Cam 52. **d** 54 **p** 55 **c** 83. C Pallion *Dur* 54–57; Abp's Dom Chapl *Cant* 57–60; V Sheff St Mark Broomhall 60–69; RD Hallam 66–69; R Louth w Welton-le-Wold *Linc* 69–75; P-in-c N w S Elkington 69–75; TR Louth 75–76; V Morton w Hacconby 76–83; Adn Linc 77–83; Can and Preb Linc Cathl 77–83; Bp Guildf 83–94; rtd 95; PtO *Portsm* from 95; Hon Asst Bp Portsm 95–14; Hon Asst Bp Chich from 96; LtO *Ab* from 14. *4 Lochnagar Way, Ballater AB35 5PB* T: (01339) 753709 M: 07787-571396 E: michael.adie@btinternet.com

ADKINS, Peter Vincent Alexander (Alex). b 44. Lanc Univ BA 71 Lon Inst of Educn CertEd 78. Kelham Th Coll 63. **d** 69 **p** 70. SSM 67–73; Tutor Kelham Th Coll 71–73; Perm to Offic Jerusalem 73–75; Hon C Cambridge St Giles w St Pet *Ely* 76–78; Hon C Northolt St Mary *Lon* 81–83; P-in-c Hanworth St Geo 83–86; R 86–88; Adult Educn Officer 83–86; Burford Priory 89–93; Warden Edw King Ho *Linc* 93–04; Gen Preacher 93–07; Hon Succ Linc Cathl 99–04; rtd 04. *4 Holly Cottages, Main Street, Horsington, Woodhall Spa LN10 5EX* T: (01526) 388448 E: alexad@tiscali.co.uk

ADLAM, David John. b 47. **d** 06 **p** 07. OLM Dickleburgh and The Pulhams *Nor* from 06. *The Cottage, Common Road, Dickleburgh, Diss IP21 4PJ* T: (01379) 741200 F: 741800 M: 07860-417158 E: john@adlams.net

ADLAM, Keith Richard. b 44. STETS 00. **d** 03 **p** 04. NSM Binstead and Havenstreet St Pet *Portsm* 03–07; NSM Northwood 07–11; NSM Gurnard 07–11; NSM Cowes St Faith 07–11; P-in-c Wroxall 11–18; rtd 18; PtO *Portsm* from 18. *71A Arctic Road, Cowes PO31 7PF* T: (01983) 296996 M: 07552-793366 E: revkeith@kjr-group.co.uk

ADLEY, Ernest George. b 38. Leeds Univ BA 61. Wells Th Coll 62. **d** 64 **p** 65. C Bideford *Ex* 64–67; C Yeovil St Mich *B & W* 67–70; V Taunton Lyngford 70–79; R Skegness and Winthorpe *Linc* 79–91; R Wantage Downs *Ox* 91–03; rtd 03; PtO *Ox* from 04. *13 Pixton Close, Didcot OX11 0BX* T: (01235) 210395

ADLEY, Nicholas James Douglas. b 67. Ripon Coll Cuddesdon 11. **d** 13 **p** 14. C Ross w Walford and Brampton Abbotts *Heref* 13–16; CF from 16. *c/o MOD Chaplains (Army)* T: (01264) 383430 M: 07877-886740

ADMAN, Fayaz. b 63. Pakistan Adventist Sem Sheikhupura BA 94. St Thos Th Coll Karachi 97. **d** 98 **p** 99. Dn St Jo Cathl Peshawar Pakistan 98–99; P 00–03; Presbyter Peshawar City All SS 99–00; Bp's Chapl 01–03; V Charsada, Shabqadar and Ghalana 00–04; C S Rochdale *Man* 04–07; P-in-c Bolton St Paul w Em 07–11; P-in-c Daubhill 07–11; TV W Bolton from 11. *Emmanuel Vicarage, Edward Street, Bolton BL3 5LQ* T: (01204) 393282 *or* 393282 E: fayaz.a@hotmail.co.uk

ADSHEAD, Adele Elizabeth. b 64. BEd. St Jo Coll Nottm. **d** 14 **p** 15. NSM Ashby-de-la-Zouch and Breedon on the Hill *Leic* 14–19; V Nanpantan St Mary in Charnwood from 19. *2 Spindle Road, Loughborough LE11 2DL* T: (01509) 232262 E: adele.adshead@gmail.com

AECHTNER, Rebecca Barbara. b 83. Calgary Univ BA 04 MA 06 Edin Univ PhD 11. St Mellitus Coll 14. **d** 16 **p** 17. C Lancaster St Mary w St John and St Anne *Blackb* 16–19; V Scotforth from 19. *St Paul's Vicarage, 24 Scotforth Road, Lancaster LA1 4ST* M: 07527-102772 E: raechtner@hotmail.com

ÆLRED, Brother. *See* ARNESEN, Raymond Halfdan

AFFLECK, Stuart John. b 47. AKC 69. St Aug Coll Cant. **d** 70 **p** 71. C Prittlewell St Mary *Chelmsf* 70–75; Asst Chapl Charterhouse Sch Godalming 75–78; Chapl 78–80; Warden Pilsdon Community 80–94; PtO *S'wark* 03–15; *St E* from 20. *Address temp unknown* E: stuartaffleck96@hotmail.com

AGAR, George. b 40. Edin Univ BSc 63 Ox Univ PGCE 64. NOC 92. **d** 94 **p** 95. Hd Biddulph High Sch Stoke-on-Trent 94–96; NSM Sandbach *Ches* 94–99; NSM Hartford from 99. *10 Maes y Ddawns, Llangadfan, Welshpool SY21 0GA* T: (01938) 820380 E: georgea@stjohnshartford.org

AGASSIZ, David John Lawrence. b 42. St Pet Hall Ox BA 64 MA 67 Imp Coll Lon PhD 94. Ripon Hall Ox 64. **d** 66 **p** 67. C Southampton St Mary w H Trin *Win* 66–71; V Enfield St Jas *Lon* 71–80; P-in-c Grays Thurrock *Chelmsf* 80–83; P-in-c Grays All SS 81–84; P-in-c Lt Thurrock St Mary 81–84; P-in-c W Thurrock 81–83; P-in-c Grays SS Pet and Paul, S Stifford and W Thurrock 83–84; TR Grays Thurrock 84–90; Hon Can Chelmsf Cathl 90–93; Dioc Development Rep 90–93; PtO 93–94; Kenya 98–00; PtO *S'wark* 02–07; *B & W* from 08. *The Garden House, Stafford Place, Weston-super-*

Mare BS23 2QZ T: (01934) 620486 M: 07813-566957
E: david.agassiz@gmail.com

AGBELUSI, Canon Dele Omotayo. b 51. Ahmadu Bello
Univ Zaria MSc 81 Oak Hill Th Coll BA 99 Spurgeon's Coll
MTh 09. Immanuel Coll Ibadan. **d** 86 **p** 87. Nigeria 86–96;
C Edmonton All SS w St Mich *Lon* 97–99; V Hornsey Ch
Ch 99–19; rtd 19; PtO *St Alb* from 19; Hon Can Akure
Nigeria from 08. *5 Cornflower Way, Hatfield AL10 9FY*
E: agbelusi@aol.com

AGER, Mrs Christabel Ruth. b 51. Bedf Coll Lon BA 73 Gipsy
Hill Coll of Educn PGCE 74 MCLIP 98. STETS BA 10. **d** 10
p 11. NSM Beercrocombe w Curry Mallet, Hatch Beauchamp
etc *B & W* 10–21; rtd 21. *14 Morgans Rise, Bishops Hull,
Taunton TA1 5HW* T: (01823) 335424 M: 07766-759131
E: crev1951@gmail.com

AGER, David George. b 52. Lon Univ BA 73 Ex Univ BTh 07
Solicitor 77. SWMTC 01. **d** 04 **p** 05. NSM Deane Vale
B & W 04–09; NSM Taunton St Jas 09–12; NSM Blackdown
12–16; Bp's Officer for Ord NSM (Taunton Adnry) 09–19;
PtO from 16; Bps' Adv for SSM Taunton Adnry 19–21;
Asst Dir of Ords 19–21. *14 Morgans Rise, Bishops Hull,
Taunton TA1 5HW* T: (01823) 335424 M: 07887-893918
E: drev1952@gmail.com

AGNEW, Kevin Raymond Christopher. b 59. Chich Th Coll.
d 94 **p** 95. C Eastbourne St Mary *Chich* 94–98; V Roughey
98–14; P-in-c Willingdon 14–19; V 19–21; rtd 21. *1 Grange
Lodge, Aldwick Street, Bognor Regis PO21 3AN*

AGNEW, Stephen Mark. b 54. Univ of Wales (Ban) BSc 76
Southn Univ BTh 81. Sarum & Wells Th Coll 76. **d** 79
p 80. C Wilmslow *Ches* 79–84; V Crewe St Jo 84–90;
Chapl Bromsgrove Sch 90–99; V Claines St Jo *Worc* 99–12;
P-in-c Old Swinford Stourbridge 12–18; rtd 18. *White
Cottage, 53B High Street, Martin, Lincoln LN4 3QY* M: 07762-
250749 E: revsmagnew@yahoo.com

A'HERNE-SMITH, Mrs Mary Catriona. b 65. Bris Univ BA 86
PGCE 88. Coll of Resurr Mirfield 13. **d** 14 **p** 15. C Sutton in
Ashfield St Mary *S'well* 14–16; TV Fosse Team *Leic* from 16.
20 Hoby Road, Thrussington, Leicester LE7 4TH M: 07948-
272669 E: mezcat@icloud.com

AIDLEY, Jessica-Jil Stapleton. b 42. Westf Coll Lon BSc 67
UEA PhD 73 PGCE 84. **d** 99 **p** 00. OLM High Oak, Hingham
and Scoulton w Wood Rising *Nor* 99–04; PtO *Mon* 04–05;
NSM Rockfield and Dingestow Gp 05–09; PtO *Chich* 09; NSM
Brighton St Nic 09–11; PtO 11–14; NSM New Shoreham and
Shoreham Beach from 14. *Myrtle, 2 Riverbank, Shoreham-by-
Sea BN43 5YH* T: (01273) 455445 E: j.aidley@gmail.com

AIKEN, Canon Nicholas John. b 58. Sheff Univ BA.
Wycliffe Hall Ox 80. **d** 82 **p** 83. C Ashtead *Guildf* 82–86;
Dioc Youth Officer 86–93; R Wisley w Pyrford from 93;
RD Woking 03–08; Hon Can Guildf Cathl from 10. *The
Rectory, Aviary Road, Woking GU22 8TH* T: (01932) 352914
E: rector@wisleywithpyrford.org

AIKEN, The Very Revd Simon Mark. b 62. St Andr Univ
MTheol 85 HonRSCM 15. Ripon Coll Cuddesdon 86. **d** 88
p 89. C Burnley St Matt w H Trin *Blackb* 88–91; C Heyhouses
on Sea 91–94; V Musbury 94–99; V Longridge 99–06; Sub
Dean Bloemfontein 06–10; Chapl Free State Univ S Africa
06–10; Adn Maluti 07–09; Dean Kimberley 10–14; Adn
Karoo 11–13; Dean Highveld from 13. *19 Mayor Avenue,
Benoni, Gauteng 1501, South Africa* T: (0027) (11) 420 3002
E: simonaiken@icloud.com

AIKENHEAD, Mary. See CANTACUZENE, Mary

AILWOOD, The Ven Frederick Charles. b 37. Univ of Qld
BA 81. St Fran Coll Brisbane. **d** 63 **p** 63. C Auchenflower
Australia 63–65; C Lutwyche 65–68; V Caboolture 68–74; R
Goondiwindi 74–80; R Pittsworth 80–84; R Gympie 84–92; R
Caloundra 92–00; R Toowoomba St Jas 00–06; Adn Wide Bay
and Burnett 89–93; Adn Wide Bay 93–00; Adn The Downs
00–06; PtO *Eur* 17–20. *Tongala, 13 Hickey Street, Toowoomba
QLD 4350, Australia* E: fandbailwood@bigpond.com

AINDOW, Philip Thomas. b 74. Trin Coll Bris 17.
d 19 **p** 20. C Liskeard and St Keyne *Truro* from 19.
E: longboat74@gmail.com

AINGE, Canon David Stanley. b 47. Ian Ramsey Coll
Brasted 68 Oak Hill Th Coll 70. **d** 73 **p** 74. C Bitterne *Win*
73–77; C Castle Church *Lich* 77–79; P-in-c Becontree St Alb
Chelmsf 79–89; P-in-c Becontree St Jo 85–89; TR Becontree S
89–91; RD Barking and Dagenham 86–91; V Leyton St Mary w
St Edw 91–96; P-in-c Leyton St Luke 91–96; V Leyton St Mary
w St Edw and St Luke 96–03; RD Waltham Forest 94–00; R
Gt Dunmow and Barnston 03–13; Hon Can Chelmsf Cathl
97–13; rtd 13; PtO *Chelmsf* from 15. *42 Abels Road, Church
End, Halstead CO9 1EW* T: (01787) 476486 E: davidainge@btinternet.com

AINSCOUGH, Malcolm Ralph. b 52. Liv Univ BEd 76. St Mich
Coll Llan 85. **d** 87 **p** 88. C Fleur-de-Lis *Mon* 87–90; C
Chepstow 90–91; TV Cwmbran 91–95; V Newport St Steph

and H Trin 95–03; R Hasland *Derby* 03–17; V Temple
Normanton 03–17; rtd 17. *79 Flowery Leys Lane, Alfreton
DE55 7HA* E: malcolmainscough@yahoo.com

AINSLIE, John Francis. b 58. Qu Coll Cam BA 79. Ox Min
Course 14. **d** 17 **p** 18. NSM The Cookhams *Ox* 17–21;
NSM Burchetts Green from 21. *6 Clifton Close, Maidenhead
SL6 1DG* T: (01628) 629827 E: revjohnainslie@gmail.com

AINSWORTH, Mrs Janina Helen Margaret. b 50. Homerton
Coll Cam CertEd 72 Newnham Coll Cam BEd 73 Lanc Univ
MA 74 FCollT 14. Ripon Coll Cuddesdon. **d** 05 **p** 06. Dioc
Dir of Educn *Man* 98–07; Chief Educn Officer Abps' Coun
07–14; NSM E Farnworth and Kearsley *Man* 05–07; PtO *Lon*
07–12; Hon C St Geo-in-the-East w St Paul 12–14; TV Turton
Moorland *Man* 14–20; rtd 20; PtO *Man* from 21. *4 Beech
Court, 4 Willow Bank, Manchester M14 6XN* T: 0161-217
9514 M: 07825-854945 E: janina.ainsworth@gmail.com

AINSWORTH, Canon Michael Ronald. b 50. K Coll Lon LLB 71
LLM 72 Trin Hall Cam BA 74 MA 79. Westcott Ho Cam 72.
d 75 **p** 76. C Scotforth *Blackb* 75–78; Chapl St Martin's Coll
of Educn 78–82; Chapl NOC 82–89; R Withington St Chris
Man 89–94; TR Worsley 94–07; AD Eccles 00–05; Hon Can
Man Cathl from 04; R St Geo-in-the-East w St Paul *Lon*
07–14; rtd 14; PtO *Man* from 15; *Blackb* 15–21. *4 Beech Court,
4 Willow Bank, Manchester M14 6XN* T: 0161-217 9514
E: rector.stgite@gmail.com

AIRD, Robert Malcolm. b 31. Lon Univ BSc 54. Westcott
Ho Cam 75. **d** 77 **p** 78. C Burnham *B & W* 77–79;
P-in-c Taunton Lyngford 79–84; V 84–87; R Dulverton and
Brushford 87–94; rtd 94. *Arran Cottage, East Street, Chulmleigh
EX18 7DD* T: (01769) 581042

AIREY, Mrs Dawn Janine. b 69. Reading Univ MA 02. Ridley Hall
Cam 15. **d** 17 **p** 18. C Wollaston w Strixton and Bozeat etc *Pet*
17–21; V Gleneagles from 21. *20 Ribble Close, Wellingborough
NN8 5XJ* E: vicar@gleneaglesanglicanchurch.co.uk

AIREY, Robert William. b 54. **d** 99 **p** 00. OLM Holcombe *Man*
99–08; OLM Holcombe and Hawkshaw from 09. *9 Smithy
Brow Court, Haslingden, Rossendale BB4 5DP* T: (01706)
224743

AIREY, Simon Christopher. b 60. Trin Coll Bris BA 87. **d** 87
p 88. C Wilton *B & W* 87–90; Chapl Scargill Ho 90–93; TV
Kingswood *Bris* 93–96; Asst P Nether Springs Northumbria
Community 96–98 and 02–03; C Bath Abbey w St Jas
B & W 98–02; C Nailsea Ch Ch w Tickenham 03–09; Chapl
Grey Coll Dur 09–11; P-in-c Criftins w Dudleston and
Welsh Frankton *Lich* 11–16; V 16–20; Chapl Robert Jones/
Agnes Hunt Orthopaedic and Distr Hosp NHS Trust from
20. *The Vicarage, Criftins, Ellesmere SY12 9LN* T: (01691)
690212 M: 07740-799191 E: getthevicar@yahoo.com

AISBITT, Joanne. See LISTER, Joanne

AISBITT, Michael. b 60. St Pet Coll Ox BA 81 MA 84. Westcott
Ho Cam 81. **d** 84 **p** 85. C Norton St Mary *Dur* 84–87; C
Kirkleatham *York* 87–90; V S Bank 90–96; R Whitby 96–97;
TR Whitby w Aislaby and Ruswarp 97–00; R Attleborough
w Besthorpe *Nor* 00–09; RD Thetford and Rockland
03–09. *16 The Acres, Stokesley, Middlesbrough TS9 5QA*
E: m_aisbitt@hotmail.com

AISBITT, Osmond John. b 35. St Chad's Coll Dur BA 57. **d** 61
p 62. C Ashington *Newc* 61–64; C Blyth St Mary 64–68; V
Cleckheaton St Jo *Wakef* 68–75; V Horbury 75–78; V Horbury
w Horbury Bridge 78–97; rtd 97; PtO *Carl* 97–00 and 02–11;
P-in-c Nerja and Almuñécar *Eur* 00–02. *8 Stonecross Gardens,
Ulverston LA12 7HA* T: (01229) 585622

AITCHISON, Charles Baillie. b 45. New Coll Dur BEd 85
Bede Coll Dur TCert 67 Newc Univ DAES 74 ACP 69.
LNSM course 85. **d** 93 **p** 98. NSM Peebles *Edin* from 93;
NSM Innerleithen from 93. *45 Whitehaugh Park, Peebles
EH45 9DB* T: (01721) 729750 *or* 724008 F: 724008
E: hall100@sky.com

AITKEN, Christopher William Mark. b 53. Dur Univ BA 75.
Westcott Ho Cam 76. **d** 79 **p** 80. C Finchley St Mary *Lon*
79–82; C Radlett *St Alb* 82–85; V Sprowston *Nor* 85–90; R
Beeston St Andr 85–90; R Sprowston w Beeston 90–93; Chapl
Sherborne Sch 93–04; Hd Master St Lawr Coll Ramsgate
04–12; Master R Foundn of St Kath in Ratcliffe 13–19; rtd 19.
24 Kilderkin Way, Norwich NR1 1RD E: cwmaitken@gmail.com

AITKEN, Deborah June. b 65. Qu Foundn (Course) 15. **d** 18
p 19. OLM Hanford *Lich* from 18. *13 Ampthill Place, Stoke-
on-Trent ST4 8NP* T: (01782) 644908 M: 07559-072882
E: debhanfordchurch@gmail.com

AITKEN, Janet. b 55. **d** 16 **p** 17. NSM Westleigh St Pet
Man 16–18; NSM Westleigh St Paul 16–18; NSM
Westleigh St Pet and St Paul from 18. *9 Browning Street,
Leigh WN7 5EF* T: (01942) 740740 M: 07977-661888
E: janetaitken55@hotmail.co.uk

AITKEN, Jonathan William Patrick. b 42. Ch Ch Ox MA 64
Wycliffe Hall Ox BTh 02. **d** 18 **p** 19. NSM Westmr St Matt *Lon*

from 18; Asst Chapl HM Pris Pentonville from 18. *83 Barkston Gardens, London SW5 0EU* T: (020) 7373 5800 M: 07590-827655 E: jonathanaitken@jwpaitken.co.uk

AITKEN, Valerie Anne. b 46. STETS 01. d 04 p 05. NSM Perivale *Lon* 04–17; P-in-c 14–17; rtd 17; PtO *Lon* from 17. *22 Woodfield Road, London W5 1SH* T: (020) 8997 6819 M: 07968-345992 E: valerie.aitken2@btinternet.com

AITON, Janice Hanan. Glas Univ MA 79 Jordanhill Coll Glas PGCE 80 Edin Univ MTh 04. TISEC 98. d 01 p 02. C St Andrews St Andr *St And* 01–04; Chapl NUI 04; R Dumfries *Glas* from 17. *St John's Rectory, 8 Newall Terrace, Dumfries DG1 1LW* T: (01387) 254126 E: janiceaiton1@gmail.com

AITON, Canon Robert Neilson. b 36. Univ of Wales BA 59 DipEd 60. Chich Th Coll 74. d 76 p 77. C E Grinstead St Swithun *Chich* 76–83; R Lavant 83–90; V Durrington 90–01; Chapl St Barn Hospice Worthing 90–95; rtd 01; Can and Preb Chich Cathl 99–11; LtO 01–11; PtO 11–20. *Fieldings, Joys Croft, Chichester PO19 4NJ* T: (01243) 781728 E: bob.aiton@btopenworld.com

AJAEFOBI, Joseph Obichukwu. b 63. Anambra State Univ of Tech Nigeria BEng 88 Loughb Univ PhD 04. Trin Coll Umuahia 90. d 92 p 93. Chapl Nkpor H Innocents Nigeria 92–00; PtO *Leic* 01–12; Asst Chapl Loughb Univ 05–16; LtO *S'wark* from 16; Chapl Nigerian Congregation *Lon* from 16. *79 Alderney Gardens, Northolt UB5 5BT* M: 07422-465558 E: joeajaefobi@yahoo.co.uk

AJAYI, Timothy Temitope. b 77. Lagos Univ BSc 01 Bedfordshire Univ MSc 08. Ridley Hall Cam 16. d 18 p 19. C Blackheath Park St Mich *S'wark* from 18. *123 Kidbrooke Park Road, London SE3 0DZ* M: 07517-570093 E: ajayitimothy@yahoo.com

AJIBADE, Ms Ijeoma. b 65. Univ of Nigeria LLB 87 S Bank Univ MA 96 Heythrop Coll Lon MA 09. SEITE BA 10. d 10 p 11. NSM Kensington St Mary Abbots w Ch Ch and St Phil *Lon* 10–14; Hon Min Can S'wark Cathl from 11; Regional Dir Miss to Seafarers from 16; PtO *S'wark* from 11; *Lon* from 14; *Eur* from 17. *25 Duffield Drive, London N15 4UH* T: (020) 8376 0598 M: 07757-913318 E: ijeomaajibade@gmail.com

AJUKA, Sampson Chikwere. b 72. Qu Coll Birm BA 08. d 08 p 09. C Venice w Trieste *Eur* 08–11; Dioc C and P-in-c Devenish w Boho *Clogh* from 12; Chapl to Bp Clogh from 12. *The Rectory, 10 Castletown Road, Monea, Enniskillen BT74 8GG* T: (028) 6634 1672 M: 07908-856207

AKERS, Miss Rachel Leanne. b 81. Ches Univ BA 13 MA 15. St Jo Coll Nottm 13. d 15 p 16. C Kidderminster E *Worc* 15–18; TV Dudley from 18; Area Sub-Dean Gtr Dudley from 21. *St Augustine's Vicarage, Hallchurch Road, Dudley DY2 0XH* M: 07578-340464 E: rachelakers1@aol.com

AKIBO-BETTS, Hannah Muriel. b 18 p 19. NSM Bletchley *Ox* from 18. *20 Silicon Court, Shenley Lodge, Milton Keynes MK5 7DL* E: hw2811@tiscali.co.uk

AKKER, Derek Alexander. b 46. Bradf Univ MA 83. NOC 85. d 88 p 89. C Mossley *Man* 88–90; C Bury St Pet 90–92; V Lever Bridge 92–97; TV Wolstanton *Lich* 97–99; V Hattersley *Ches* 99–09; rtd 09; PtO *Man* from 09; *Ches* from 10; *Eur* 11–16 and from 17. *54 Purbeck Drive, Bury BL8 1JQ* T: 0161-797 0105 M: 07970-646809 E: derekakker@icloud.com

AKRILL, Dean. b 71. York Univ BA 97. Ripon Coll Cuddesdon BTh 00. d 00 p 01. C Swinton *Sheff* 00–11; C Wath-upon-Dearne 01–04; V Mosborough 04–08; C Sprowston w Beeston Nor from 08. *The Newlands, 15 Blue Boar Lane, Norwich NR7 8RX* E: dean@sprowston.org.uk

AKWASI-YEBOAH, Kingsley Nana. b 76. Cam Univ BA 16. Ridley Hall Cam 14. d 16 p 18. C Rainham w Wennington *Chelmsf* 16–17; C Forest Gate Em w Upton Cross 17–19; Chapl RAF 19–20; P-in-c Eastwood *Chelmsf* from 20. *The Vicarage, Eastwoodbury Lane, Southend-on-Sea SS2 6UH* M: 07828-974417 E: revd.yeboah@gmail.com

ALAGOA, Ms Biobelemoye Susan (Belemo). b 56. E Lon Univ LLB 86 Warwick Univ LLM 88. SEITE 10. d 13 p 14. NSM N Lambeth *S'wark* 13–17; NSM Merton Priory from 17. *32 Lewis Road, Mitcham CR4 3DE* M: 07960-518381 E: belemo.alagoa@gmail.com

ALAN MICHAEL, Brother. See PATERSON, Alan Michael

ALASAUKKO-OJA, Tuomas. See MÄKIPÄÄ, Tuomas

ALBAN JONES, Canon Timothy Morris. b 64. MBE 03. Warwick Univ BA 85. Ripon Coll Cuddesdon 85. d 88 p 89. C Tupsley *Heref* 88–93; TV Ross 93–00; P-in-c Soham *Ely* 00–01; P-in-c Wicken 00–01; V Soham and Wicken 02–15; RD Fordham and Quy 10–15; Warden of Readers 12–15; Hon Can Ely Cathl 12–15; Bp's Chapl *Pet* from 15; Can Res Pet Cathl from 15; Vice Dean from 18; Dioc Ecum Officer from 17. *The Bishop's Office, The Palace, Minster Precincts, Peterborough PE1 1YA* T: (01733) 887014 E: tim.albanjones@peterborough-diocese.org.uk

ALBERS, Johannes Reynoud (Joop). b 47. Hogeschool Holland BTh 92 Amsterdam Univ MTh 98. EAMTC 99. d 00 p 01. C Voorschoten *Eur* 00–02; C Amsterdam w Den Helder and Heiloo 02–04; Asst Chapl 04–12; P-in-c Haarlem 12–15; PtO 15–20; Angl Chapl Amsterdam Airport Schiphol from 07. *Dorpsweg 134, 1697 KH Schellinkhout, The Netherlands* T: (0031) (22) 950 1611 *or* (61) 009 8239 E: joopalbers@quicknet.nl

ALBINSON, Thomas Roy. b 79. Ripon Coll Cuddesdon 09. d 12 p 13. C Littlemore *Ox* 12–16; C Ox St Giles and SS Phil and Jas w St Marg 16–18; C St Louis St Mich USA from 19. *6300 Wydown Boulevard, Clayton, St Louis MO 6315, USA* E: tomalbinson@gmail.com

ALBON, Lionel Frederick Shapland. b 31. CEng MIMechE 60. St Alb Minl Tr Scheme 80. d 83 p 84. NSM Bromham w Oakley *St Alb* 83–88; NSM Bromham w Oakley and Stagsden 88–89; Ind Chapl 89–96; rtd 96; LtO *St Alb* 96–09; PtO from 09. *38 Glebe Rise, Sharnbrook, Bedford MK44 1JB* T: (01234) 781560 E: lionelalbon@aol.co.uk

ALBONE, Mrs Joy Elizabeth. b 59. Roehampton Inst BA 80 Gwent Coll Newport PGCE 95. Sarum Th Coll 16. d 19 p 20. NSM Canalside Benefice *Sarum* from 19. *48 Primrose Drive, Melksham SN12 6GB* M: 07931-638524 E: canalsidecurate@gmail.com

ALBY, Harold Oriel. b 45. Witwatersrand Univ BA 68 MA 77. Sarum Th Coll 68. d 71 p 72. C Germiston St Boniface S Africa 71–74; C Johannesburg Cathl 74–75; R Ermelow w Pet Relief 75–78; R Potchefstroom 78–82; R Boksburg 82–89; P-in-c Forton *Portsm* 89–96; V Milton 96–10; rtd 11; Perm to Offic and Dioc Archivist George S Africa from 11. *7 Plover Road, Heatherlands, George, 6529 South Africa* T: (0027) (44) 873 0797 E: orielalby@hotmail.com

ALCOCK (née TOYNBEE), Claire Louise. b 65. Reading Univ BA 86 Ox Brookes Univ MA 15 Goldsmiths' Coll Lon PGTC 87. Ox Min Course 07. d 10 p 11. NSM Langtree *Ox* 10–19; V Reading St Jo from 19. *50 Talfourd Avenue, Reading RG6 7BP* M: 07519-861040 E: claire_alcock@hotmail.com

ALCOCK, Donald. b 52. McGill Univ Montreal BA 74 MA 76 Univ of S California PhD 85. Huron Coll Ontario MDiv 00. d 00 p 00. Canada 00–10; NSM Gt Amwell w St Margaret's and Stanstead Abbots *St Alb* 10–12; P-in-c Woore and Norton in Hales *Lich* 12–21; rtd 21. *6 Margetts Close, Kenilworth CV8 1EN* E: dga952@hotmail.com

ALCOCK, Edwin James. b 31. AKC 57. d 58 p 59. C Old St Pancras w Bedford New Town St Matt *Lon* 58–62; C Hillingdon St Andr 62–81; V N Acton St Gabr 81–01; rtd 01; PtO *Lon* from 01. *17 Westfields Road, London W3 0AX* T: (020) 8896 2748

ALDCROFT, Malcolm Charles. b 44. Leeds Univ MA 94. NOC 79. d 82 p 83. NSM Alverthorpe *Wakef* 82–85; NSM Horbury Junction 85–93; Sub Chapl HM Pris and YOI New Hall 94–97; Sub Chapl HM Pris Wakef 96–97; R Cupar and Ladybank *St And* 97–05; Chapl Stratheden Hosp Fife 97–05; Dioc Miss Officer and Min Development Co-ord *Mor* 05–07; Hon C Arpafeelie 05–07; Warden of Readers 06–07; Hon C St Andrews All SS *St And* from 08; TV Edin St Mich and All SS 08–11; LtO from 11. *14 Cherry Lane, Cupar KY15 5DA* T: (01334) 650264 E: mc33.aldcroft@gmail.com

ALDEN, Andrew Michael. b 65. Bris Univ BA 88 Lon Univ MA 94 Ex Univ PGCE 89. Wycliffe Hall Ox 01. d 03 p 04. C Weston-super-Mare St Paul *B & W* 03–07; V 07–20. *Somerset House, 20 Addiscombe Road, Weston-super-Mare BS23 4LT* E: revandrewalden@btinternet.com

ALDEN, Mrs Pamela Ann (Pat). b 42. St Gabr Coll Lon TCert 67. d 02 p 03. OLM Camberwell St Giles w St Matt *S'wark* 02–07; NSM Camberwell St Phil and St Mark 07–12; PtO 12–16; *Chich* from 15. *20 Kings Walk, Shoreham-by-Sea BN43 5LG* M: 07710-283710 E: pat@looksouth.net

ALDER, Mrs Alison Kirstine Ruth. b 62. d 19 p 20. NSM Blyth Valley *St E* from 19. *Address temp unknown* E: alisonalder@hotmail.com

ALDER, Mrs Anne-Louise (Louise). b 63. STETS 99. d 02 p 03. C Cowes H Trin and St Mary *Portsm* 02–05; C Cowes St Faith 05–06; C Newport St Thos 06–07; P-in-c Shipdham w Bradenham *Nor* 07–14; P-in-c Barnham Broom and Upper Yare 10–12; Dioc Fresh Expressions Asst 13–14; V Hellesdon from 14. *The Vicarage, Broom Avenue, Hellesdon, Norwich NR6 6LG* E: louise.alder@lineone.net *or* louise.alder63@gmail.com

ALDERMAN, Canon John David. b 49. Man Univ BA 71 Selw Coll Cam BA 79 MA 80 Lon Inst of Educn PGCE 72. Ridley Hall Cam 77. d 80 p 81. C Hartley Wintney, Elvetham, Winchfield etc *Win* 80–83; V Bursledon 83–92; R Dibden 92–05; AD Lyndhurst 04–05; Hon Can Win Cathl 01–05; Patr Sec CPAS 05–11; rtd 11; PtO *Cov* from

05. *32 Stuart Close, Warwick CV34 6AQ* T: (01926) 400743
E: jandgalderman@btinternet.com

ALDERSLEY, Ian. b 42. FIBMS 68. Wycliffe Hall Ox 89.
d 91 **p** 92. C Allestree *Derby* 91–94; R Brailsford w Shirley
and Osmaston w Edlaston 94–06; P-in-c Yeaveley 05–06;
P-in-c Ruishton w Thornfalcon *B & W* 06–10; P-in-c Creech
St Michael 08–10; rtd 10; Hon C Fenny Bentley, Thorpe,
Tissington, Parwich etc *Derby* 11–18; Retirement Chapl
12–15. *5 Clifford Close, Chesterfield S40 3PP* T: (01246)
568448 E: aldersley_ian@yahoo.co.uk

ALDERSON, Gary. b 65. ERMC. **d** 08 **p** 09. NSM
Wellingborough St Mark *Pet* 08–13; NSM Wellingborough
All SS 13–19; NSM Wellingborough All Hallows 13–19; NSM
Gt w Lt Harrowden and Orlingbury and Isham etc 19–21;
V Barnack w Ufford, Bainton, Helpston and Wittering
from 21. *The Rectory, Millstone Lane, Barnack, Stamford
PE9 3ET* M: 07503-975588

ALDERSON, Mrs Hannah Samantha Joy. b 86. Ex Univ
BA 08. Ripon Coll Cuddesdon MTh 13. **d** 13 **p** 14. C
Bridgwater H Trin and Durleigh *B & W* 13–16; Dioc Voc
Development Officer *Ex* 16–19; Chapl Ex Univ from
16. *3 Spicer Road, Exeter EX1 1SX* M: 07546-397981
E: hannahsjalderson@gmail.com *or* h.alderson@exeter.ac.uk

ALDERSON, Major Robin Edward Richard. b 44. **d** 04
p 05. OLM Alde River *St E* 04–07; NSM Brandeston w
Kettleburgh and Easton 07–13; rtd 13; PtO *St E* from
13. *Pipsfold House, Priory Road, Snape, Saxmundham
IP17 1SD* T: (01728)   688255   M: 07939-310242
E: robin.alderson@btinternet.com

ALDERSON, Roger James Ambrose. b 47. Lon Univ BD 70
AKC 71 Man Univ 76 Liv Inst of Educn PGCE 93. St Aug Coll
Cant. **d** 71 **p** 72. C Lawton Moor *Man* 71–75; C Barton w
Peel Green 75–76; R Heaton Norris St Thos 76–85; V Bedford
Leigh 85–92; V Cleadon Park *Dur* 99–07; rtd 07. *73 West
Drive, Sunderland SR6 7SL* T: 0191-536 1236 M: 07710-
722817

ALDERTON, Mary Louise. *See* PRICE, Mary Louise

ALDERTON-FORD, Canon Jonathan Laurence. b 57. St Jo
Coll Nottm BTh 85. **d** 85 **p** 86. C Gaywood, Bawsey and
Mintlyn *Nor* 85–87; C Herne Bay Ch Ch *Cant* 87–90; Min
Bury St Edmunds St Mary *St E* 90–91; Min Moreton Hall
Estate CD 91–94; V Bury St Edmunds Ch Ch from 94; Hon
Can St E Cathl from 08. *18 Heldhaw Road, Bury St Edmunds
IP32 7ER* T: (01284) 769956 *or* 725391 F: 725391
E: worship@ccmh.org.uk *or* revdjonathanford@gmail.com

ALDIS, John Arnold. b 43. Univ of Wales (Cardiff) BA 65 Lon
Univ BD 67. Clifton Th Coll 65. **d** 69 **p** 70. C Tonbridge
SS Pet and Paul *Roch* 69–72; C St Marylebone All So w SS
Pet and Jo *Lon* 72–77; Overseas Service Adv CMS 77–80;
C Welling *Roch* 77–80; V Leic H Trin w St Jo 80–89; Hon
Can Leic Cathl 88–89; V W Kowloon St Andr Hong Kong
89–99; Sen Chapl Protestant Ch Oman 00–01; V Watford
St Alb 02–08; rtd 08; PtO *Glouc* 14–19. *Address temp unknown*
E: john.aldis@btinternet.com

ALDIS, John Philip. b 83. Keble Coll Ox BA 05 Fitzw Coll
Cam BA 11 Peterho Cam MPhil 12 Called to the Bar
(Lincoln's Inn) 16. Ridley Hall Cam 09. **d** 12 **p** 13. C
Newbury St Nic and Speen *Ox* 12–15; PtO *Worc* 17–22. *10
Thetford Avenue, Worcester WR4 0RB* M: 07815-503485
E: johnaldis@gmail.com

ALDIS, Miss Rosemary Helen. b 40. Southn Univ BSc 62 Ox
Univ Inst of Educn DipEd 63 Keele Univ MSc 67 Open Univ
MA 99. All Nations Chr Coll 98. **d** 05 **p** 05. NSM Gabalfa *Llan*
05–10; PtO from 11; Hon Tutor St Mich Coll Llan 05–10;
Hon Chapl 11–16. *94 Glendower Court, Velindre Road, Cardiff
CF14 2TZ* T: (029) 2062 6337 E: aldisrosemary@gmail.com

ALDOUS, Alexander Charles Victor. b 56. Southn Univ BA 81
K Alfred's Coll Win PGCE 83. S Dios Minl Tr Scheme 91. **d** 94
p 95. Chapl Oundle Sch 94–97; Chapl Benenden Sch 98–01;
Chapl Oakham Sch 02–16; Chapl Shrewsbury Sch from 16;
Chapl Prestfelde Sch Shrewsbury from 18; PtO *Lich* from 18.
Shrewsbury School, Kingsland, Shrewsbury SY3 7BA T: (01743)
280500 E: chaplain@shrewsbury.org.uk

ALDOUS, Benjamin James. b 75. Liv Univ BA 98 Bris Univ
MA 02 Redcliffe Coll Glouc MA 12 Stellenbosch Univ
PhD 19. **d** 11 **p** 11. C Durban N S Africa 11–13; Min-
in-c Wynberg St Jo 13–18; Evang and Miss Officer CTE
from 19. *The Old Bookshop, 12-14 Temple Street, Sidmouth
EX10 9AY* M: 07547-395382 E: ben.aldous@cte.org.uk

ALDRIDGE, Mrs Anne Louise. b 59. Nottm Univ BEd 80.
EAMTC 96. **d** 99 **p** 00. NSM Milton *Ely* 99–03; Chapl Milton
Children's Hospice 99–03; Deputy Chapl Team Ldr Cam
Univ Hosps NHS Foundn Trust 03–11; Tutor Ridley Hall
Cam 10–18; rtd 18; PtO *Ely* from 18. *Address temp unknown*
E: anne@aldridge.biz

ALDRIDGE, Mrs Claire Maire. b 76. Liv Univ BSc 98.
St Mellitus Coll BA 21. **d** 21. C Roby *Liv* from 21. *111
Western Avenue, Huyton, Liverpool L36 4PP* M: 07783-329150
E: claire@stbartholomewsroby.org.uk

ALDRIDGE, Canon Harold John. b 42. Oak Hill Th Coll 65.
d 69 **p** 70. C Rawtenstall St Mary *Man* 69–72; CMJ
72–76; C Woodford Wells *Chelmsf* 76–79; TV Washfield,
Stoodleigh, Withleigh etc *Ex* 79–86; V Burton *Ches* 86–90;
P-in-c Shotwick 90; V Burton and Shotwick 91–07; Dioc
Clergy Widows and Retirement Officer 91–07; RD Wirral
S 96–06; Hon Can Ches Cathl 98–07; Chapl Clatterbridge
Hosp Wirral 86–91; Chapl Wirral Hosp NHS Trust 91–97;
Chapl Wirral and W Cheshire Community NHS Trust 97–03;
Chapl Cheshire and Wirral Partnerships NHS Trust 03–07;
rtd 07; PtO *Ches* from 08. *Tedda Junction, 9 Moorhouse Close,
Chester CH2 2HU* T: (01244) 371628

ALDRIDGE, Mark Richard. b 58. Oak Hill Th Coll BA 89.
d 89 **p** 90. C Combe Down w Monkton Combe and S
Stoke *B & W* 89–90; C Woodside Park St Barn *Lon* 90–94;
P-in-c Cricklewood St Gabr and St Mich 94–99; V 99–04;
Min Oak Tree Angl Fellowship 04–15; Dir New Wine
Internat Min from 15; Dir Ch Leadership Development
from 17; LtO from 15; PtO *Leic* from 18. *20 Swingbridge Street,
Foxton, Market Harborough LE16 7RH* M: 07957-204956
E: international@new-wine.org

ALDRIDGE-COLLINS, Murray Allan Leonard. b 73. UWE
BSc 09. St Steph Ho Ox 13. **d** 15 **p** 16. C Ilfracombe, Lee,
Woolacombe, Bittadon etc *Ex* 15–20; V Over Peover w
Lower Peover *Ches* from 20. *The Vicarage, Crown Lane,
Lower Peover, Knutsford WA16 9QB* M: 07872-889162
E: murrayaldridge-collins@hotmail.co.uk

ALDWINCKLE, Jonathan Frederick. b 62. ERMC 12. **d** 15
p 16. C Kettering Ch the King *Pet* 15–18; R Raunds,
Hargrave, Ringstead and Stanwick from 18. *The
Vicarage, High Street, Raunds, Wellingborough NN9 6HS*
E: revjonaldwinckle@btconnect.com

ALEXANDER, Alison. b 67. Bournemouth Univ BSc 07. Sarum
Coll 17. **d** 20 **p** 21. C Salisbury St Thos and St Edm *Sarum*
from 20. *4 St Joseph's Close, Bishopdown, Salisbury SP1 3FX*
E: revalialexander@gmail.com

ALEXANDER, Ann Maria. b 58. Surrey Univ BA 01.
Cuddesdon Coll 07. **d** 09 **p** 10. C Chiswick St Nic w St Mary
Lon 09–13; TV Ifield *Chich* 13–17; V Gossops Green and
Bewbush from 17. *St Alban's Vicarage, Gossops Drive, Crawley
RH11 8LD* M: 07961-853343 E: anejmi6@gmail.com

ALEXANDER, Christopher Aslan. b 73. Leic Univ BSc 97.
St Mellitus Coll 15 Wycliffe Hall Ox BA 17. **d** 17 **p** 18. C
Woodside Park St Barn *Lon* 17–20. *61 Lullington Garth,
London N12 7BB* M: 07462-101242

ALEXANDER, David Graham. b 61. Ridley Hall Cam 87.
d 89 **p** 90. C New Barnet St Jas *St Alb* 89–93; C Northwood
H Trin *Lon* 93–95; V Stopsley *St Alb* from 95. *The Vicarage,
702 Hitchin Road, Luton LU2 7UJ* T: (01582) 729194
E: stopsley@aol.com

ALEXANDER, James Crighton. b 43. Qu Coll Cam BA 65
MA 69. Cuddesdon Coll 66. **d** 68 **p** 69. C Much Wenlock w
Bourton *Heref* 68–72; V Oakington *Ely* from 72; P-in-c Dry
Drayton 85–95. *The Vicarage, 99 Water Lane, Oakington,
Cambridge CB24 3AL* T: (01223) 232396

ALEXANDER, Jane Louise. *See* MacLAREN, Jane Louise

ALEXANDER, Canon Loveday Constance Anne. b 47.
Somerville Coll Ox BA 69 MA 78 DPhil 78. NOC 98. **d** 99
p 00. NSM Alderley Edge *Ches* from 99; Can Th Ches Cathl
03–14; PtO *Sheff* from 00. *5 Nevill Road, Bramhall, Stockport
SK7 3ET* T: 0161-439 7946 E: l.c.alexander@sheffield.ac.uk

ALEXANDER, Canon Michael George. b 47. Open Univ
BA 90 DipEd 91. Sarum & Wells Th Coll 74. **d** 77 **p** 78. C
Wednesfield *Lich* 77–80; C Tettenhall Wood 80–83; Distr
Min 83–85; Dioc Adv in Adult and Youth Educn *Derby*
85–89; V Hazlewood 85–89; V Turnditch 85–89; Par Educn
Adv (Laity Development) 89–96; Dioc Laity Development
Adv 96–00; Dioc Dir Studies Bp's Centres of Learning 96–00;
P-in-c Ticknall, Smisby and Stanton-by-Bridge 00–01;
P-in-c Barrow-on-Trent w Twyford and Swarkestone 00–01;
V Ticknall, Smisby and Stanton by Bridge etc 01–07; RD
Melbourne 02–07; P-in-c Loscoe 07–12; C Morley w Smalley
and Horsley Woodhouse 07–12; RD Heanor 09–11; Hon
Can Derby Cathl 09–12; rtd 12. *79 Allerburn Lea, Alnwick
NE66 2NQ*

ALEXANDER, Nancy. b 58. **d** 16 **p** 17. OLM Droylsden St Mary
Man from 16; Chapl Pennine Acute Hosps NHS Trust from 17.
6 Longcroft Grove, Audenshaw, Manchester M34 5SD T: 0161-
317 9667 M: 07968-688585 E: nancya@milnerb.co.uk

ALEXANDER, Nancy Joan. *See* WALLACE, Nancy Joan

ALEXANDER, Nicholas Edward. b 68. Leic Poly BSc 90. Oak
Hill Th Coll BA 06. **d** 06 **p** 07. C Linc Minster Gp 06–12; C

Linc St Pet in Eastgate 12–15; C Bury St Edmunds St Mary *St E* 15–20; C Moulton *Pet* from 20. *1 High Street, Moulton, Northampton NN3 7SR* E: n.alexander@moultonchurch.co.uk

ALEXANDER, Peter John. b 36. CQSW 73. Oak Hill Th Coll 92. **d** 95 **p** 96. NSM Aspenden, Buntingford and Westmill *St Alb* 95–02; rtd 02; PtO *Nor* from 02. *Dell Gate, 4 The Dell, Bodham, Holt NR25 6NG* T: (01263) 588126 E: peter.brenda2@tiscali.co.uk

ALEXANDER, Mrs Rachel Clare. b 57. EAMTC 96. **d** 99 **p** 00. NSM Mattishall w Mattishall Burgh, Welborne etc *Nor* 99–02; PtO 02–03; NSM Rugby St Matt *Cov* 03–04; PtO *Nor* 11; NSM Thorpe Acre w Dishley *Leic* 11–15; PtO *Nor* 16–19; R Snettisham 19–20; C from 20. *The Rectory, 18 Park Lane, Snettisham, King's Lynn PE31 7NW* T: (01485) 542303 E: snettishamrector@gmail.com

ALEXANDER, Robert. b 37. Lon Univ LLB 60 St Cath Coll Ox BA 62. St Steph Ho Ox 60. **d** 63 **p** 64. C Kensington St Mary Abbots w St Geo *Lon* 63–68; C Notting Hill 71–74; TV 74–79; Australia from 79; rtd 02. *302/27 Neutral Street, North Sydney NSW 2060, Australia* T/F: (0061) (2) 9954 0543 E: robalexand@bigpond.com

ALEXANDER, Sarah Louise. b 72. Wycliffe Hall Ox 02. **d** 04 **p** 05. C Enfield Ch Ch Trent Park *Lon* 04–08; C Newbury *Ox* 08–14; C Redhill H Trin *S'wark* from 14. *3 Ringwood Avenue, Redhill RH1 2DY* E: sarah@htredhill.com

ALEXANDER, Wilfred Robert Donald. b 35. TCD BA 58 MA 80. **d** 63 **p** 63. C Raheny w Coolock *D & G* 63–67; Min Can St Patr Cathl Dublin 65–67; Hon C Herne Hill St Paul *S'wark* 68–70; Asst Master Gosforth Gr Sch 71–76; Hon C Long Benton St Mary *Newc* 74–76; Chapl St Mary and St Anne's Sch Abbots Bromley 76–80; V Cauldon *Lich* 80–83; V Waterfall 80–83; P-in-c Calton 80–83; P-in-c Grindon 80–83; V Blackb St Luke w St Phil 83–89; V Rainhill *Liv* 89–92; R Croft w Southworth 92–99; C Croft w Southworth and Newchurch 99–01; rtd 01. *16 Hawkshaw Close, Birchwood, Warrington WA3 7NF* T: (01925) 851472

ALEXANDER-WATTS, Tristan Nathaniel. b 66. SEITE 99. **d** 03 **p** 04. NSM Eltham H Trin *S'wark* 03–10; Chapl Qu Eliz Hosp NHS Trust 04–11; Chapl Bromley Hosps NHS Trust 05–09; Chapl Oxleas NHS Foundn Trust 05–09; Chapl S Lon Healthcare NHS Trust 09–11; Chapl Barts Health NHS Trust 11–19; Chapl Richard Ho Children's Hospice 11–19; Hd of Chapl Kent and Medway NHS and Soc Care Partnership Trust from 19. *Kent and Medway NHS and Social Care Partnership Trust, Greenacres, Bow Arrow Lane, Dartford DA2 6PB* M: 07970-016009 E: tristan.alexander-watts@nhs.net

ALEY, Simon John. b 61. Warwick Univ LLB 83 Leic Univ MBA 00. ERMC 17. **d** 20 **p** 21. C Oakham, Ashwell, Braunston, Brooke, Egleton etc *Pet* from 20. *Charnwood House, 34 Lyndon Road, Manton, Oakham LE15 8SR* T: (01572) 737482 M: 07860-414743 E: sialey@aol.com or simon@oakhamteam.org.uk

ALFORD, Kathryn. b 73. Man Univ BA 95. ERMC 17. **d** 20 **p** 21. C Bishop's Hatfield, Lemsford and N Mymms *St Alb* from 20. *1 Church Street, Hatfield AL9 5AR* M: 07971-057342 E: alfordkathryn@gmail.com

ALIDINA (née LINGARD), Jennifer Mary. b 59. Ox Min Course 05. **d** 07 **p** 08. C Chipping Norton *Ox* 07–10; Asst Chapl HM Pris Bullingdon 10–11; P-in-c Ellingham and Harbridge and Hyde w Ibsley *Win* 11–14; PtO *Sarum* 14–19; *Win* 14–16; C W Purbeck *Sarum* from 19. *Iris Hollow, New Road, Stoborough, Wareham BH20 5BB* T: (01929) 505007 E: revjennyalidina@gmail.com or jennyalidina@irishollow.co.uk

ALISON, Sister. See FRY, Alison Jacquelyn

ALKER, Canon Adrian. b 49. Wadh Coll Ox BA 70 Lanc Univ MA 71. Ripon Coll Cuddesdon 77. **d** 79 **p** 80. C W Derby St Mary *Liv* 79–83; Dioc Youth Officer *Carl* 83–88; V Sheff St Mark Broomhill 88–08; Dioc Dir of In-Service Tr 90–08; Hon Can Sheff Cathl 05–08; Dir Miss Resourcing *Ripon* 08–14; *Leeds* 14–15; rtd 15; PtO *Sheff* from 16. *23 Meadow Head, Sheffield S8 7UA* T: 0114-274 6246

ALKIRE, Sabina Marie. b 69. Univ of Illinois BA 89 Magd Coll Ox MPhil 94 MSc 95 DPhil 99. **d** 00 **p** 02. NSM Washington St Alb and St Phil USA 00–03; NSM Boston St Steph 03–07; Chapl Assoc Magd Coll Ox from 06; NSM Cowley St Jo *Ox* 08–19; PtO from 19. *3 Mansfield Road, Oxford OX1 3TB* T: (01865) 271529 F: 281801 M: 07792-505847 E: sabina.alkire@qeh.ox.ac.uk

ALLABY, Simon Arnold Kenworthy. b 65. St Chad's Coll Dur BA 88. Trin Coll Bris 88. **d** 90 **p** 91. C Preston on Tees *Dur* 90–93; C Chester le Street 93–99; R Ardingly *Chich* 99–05. *Fenners, Top Street, Bolney, Haywards Heath RH17 5PP* M: 07837-637113 E: simon@sixnineteen.co.uk

ALLAIN CHAPMAN, The Ven Justine Penelope Heathcote. b 67. K Coll Lon BA 88 AKC 88 PGCE 89 DThMin 11 Nottm Univ MDiv 93. Linc Th Coll 91. **d** 93 **p** 94. C Forest Hill *S'wark* 93–96; TV Clapham Team 96–01; V Clapham St Paul 02–04; Dir Miss and Past Studies SEITE 04–13; Vice Prin 07–13; Adn Boston *Linc* from 13. *Archdeacon's House, Castle Hill, Welbourn, Lincoln LN5 0NF* T: (01400) 273335 M: 07715-077993 E: justine.allainchapman@lincoln.anglican.org or archdeacon.boston@lincoln.anglican.org

ALLAN, Andrew John. b 47. Westcott Ho Cam 76. **d** 79 **p** 80. C Whitstable All SS w St Pet *Cant* 79–84; C Whitstable 84–86; P-in-c Littlebourne 86–87; P-in-c Ickham w Wickhambreaux and Stodmarsh 86–87; R Littlebourne and Ickham w Wickhambreaux etc 87–10; rtd 10. *The Moorings, Old Road, Liskeard PL14 6DL* T: (01579) 349074 E: johnallan014@aol.com

ALLAN, Donald James. b 35. Sarum & Wells Th Coll 63. **d** 65 **p** 66. C Royton St Paul *Man* 65–71; V Middleton Junction 71–78; P-in-c Finmere w Mixbury *Ox* 78–83; R Finmere w Mixbury, Cottisford, Hardwick etc 83; Chapl Westcliff Hosp 83–87; V Westcliff St Andr *Chelmsf* 83–87; R Goldhanger w Lt Totham 87–01; rtd 01; P-in-c St Goran w Caerhays *Truro* 01–06; PtO *Sarum* 06–15. *23 Stirrup Close, Wimborne BH21 2UQ* T: (01202) 880645 E: donald.allan2@btinternet.com

ALLAN, Janet Ross. b 57. Ex Univ BA 80 Open Univ MBA 06 MCLIP 88. St Mellitus Coll BA 13. **d** 13 **p** 14. C Thorpe Bay *Chelmsf* 13–17; V Swaffham and Sporle *Nor* from 17. *The Vicarage, White Cross Road, Swaffham PE37 7QY* T: (01760) 622241 M: 07958-534465 E: revdjanetallan@gmail.com

ALLAN, Jeanette Winifred. b 40. ALA 63. St And Dioc Tr Course 79. **dss** 81 **d** 86 **p** 94. NSM Hillfoot's TM St And 81–86; NSM Bridge of Allan *St And* 86–88; NSM Dunblane 88–98; R Glenrothes 98–06; rtd 06; LtO *St And* from 07. *Pernettya, Sinclairs Street, Dunblane FK15 0AH* T: (01786) 821151 M: 07990-947429 E: pernettya@gmail.com

ALLAN, John. See ALLAN, Andrew John

ALLAN, Preb John William. b 58. St Olaf Coll Minnesota BA 80 Birm Univ 86. Trin Lutheran Sem Ohio MDiv 84 Qu Coll Birm 90. **d** 91 **p** 92. In Lutheran Ch (USA) 84–86; C Newport w Longford and Chetwynd *Lich* 91–94; P-in-c Longdon 94–01; Local Min Adv (Wolverhampton) 94–01; V Alrewas from 01; V Wychnor from 01; RD Lich 04–14; Preb Lich Cathl from 11. *The Vicarage, Church Road, Alrewas, Burton-on-Trent DE13 7BT* T: (01283) 790486 E: revdjohnallan@revdjohnallan.plus.com

ALLAN, Kirsty Elizabeth. b 70. York St Jo Coll BEd 92 St Jo Coll Dur BA 18. Cranmer Hall Dur 16. **d** 18 **p** 19. C Wilmslow *Ches* 18–21; TV Hunstanton and Saxon Shore *Nor* from 21. *The Vicarage, Broad Lane, Brancaster, King's Lynn PE31 8AU* E: revkirsty@icloud.com

ALLAN, Peter Burnaby. b 52. Clare Coll Cam BA 74 MA 78 St Jo Coll Dur BA 82. Cranmer Hall Dur 80. **d** 83 **p** 84. C Chaddesden St Mary *Derby* 83–86; C Brampton St Thos 86–89; TV Halesworth w Linstead, Chediston, Holton etc *St E* 89–94; TR Trunch *Nor* 94–03; R Ansley and Arley *Cov* 03–16; RD Nuneaton 06–12; rtd 16; PtO *S'well* from 17. *26 Hazel Grove, Mapperley, Nottingham NG3 6DN* E: peterballan52@gmail.com

ALLAN, Peter George. b 50. Wadh Coll Ox BA 72 MA 76. Coll of Resurr Mirfield 72. **d** 75 **p** 76. C Stevenage St Geo *St Alb* 75–78; Chapl Wadh Coll and C Ox St Mary V w St Cross and St Pet 78–82; CR from 85; Prin Coll of Resurr Mirfield 11–19; C Bicton, Montford w Shrawardine and Fitz *Lich* from 19. *The Vicarage, Baschurch Road, Bomere Heath, Shrewsbury SY4 3PN* E: pallan@mirfield.org.uk

ALLARD, Roderick George. b 44. Lon Univ BA 77 Sheff Poly MSc 88 Loughb Coll of Educn CertEd 96. NOC 97. **d** 99 **p** 00. NSM Charlesworth and Dinting Vale *Derby* 99–13; NSM Glossop and Hadfield 11–13; PtO *Leic* from 14. *37 Sutton Lane, Sutton in the Elms, Broughton Astley, Leicester LE9 6QF* T: (01455) 289356 M: 07976-435160 E: r.allard@sky.com

ALLAWAY, Richard John. b 54. **d** 16 **p** 17. C Frome Valley *Heref* from 16. *Lower Court, Ullingswick, Hereford HR1 3JQ* M: 07969-699270 E: rja5204572fco@gmail.com

ALLBERRY, William Alan John. b 49. Ch Coll Cam BA 70 MA 71. Ripon Coll Cuddesdon 84. **d** 86 **p** 87. C Brixton St Matt *S'wark* 86–90; V Wandsworth St Paul 90–98; R Esher *Guildf* 98–12; RD Emly 01–06; rtd 12; Lect Tamilnadu Th Sem Madurai India from 12; PtO *Guildf* from 12; *S'wark* from 12; *St D* from 17. *48 Ditton Road, Surbiton KT6 6RB* T: (020) 8390 2019 E: williamallberry@hotmail.com

ALLCHIN, Miss Maureen Ann. b 50. Edge Hill Coll of HE CertEd 71 Sussex Univ MA 93. S Dios Minl Tr Scheme 88. **d** 91 **p** 94. Hd Past Faculty Steyning Gr Sch 79–92; NSM

Southwick St Mich *Chich* 91–93; C Storrington 93–95; TV Bridport *Sarum* 95–05; LtO 05–06; P-in-c Canalside Benefice 06–08; LtO 08–09 and 10–15; P-in-c Trowbridge H Trin 09–10; P-in-c Seend, Bulkington and Poulshot 15–17; rtd 17; PtO *Sarum* from 17. *4 Northfields, Bulkington, Devizes SN10 1SE* T: (01380) 828931 E: maureen@mallchin.co.uk

ALLCOCK, Jeremy Robert. b 63. Trin Coll Bris BA 92. **d** 92 **p** 93. C Walthamstow St Luke *Chelmsf* 92–96; V E Ham St Paul 96–05; V Paddington St Steph w St Luke *Lon* 05–18; V Bayswater 12–16; AD Westmr Paddington 11–16; R Birm St Martin w Bordesley St Andr from 18. *37 Barlows Road, Birmingham B15 2PN*

ALLCOCK, Philip. **p** 13. NSM Mayfair Ch Ch *Lon* 01–19; NSM Down Street Ch Ch from 19. *Christ Church Mayfair, Down Street, London W1J 7AN* E: phil@christchurchmayfair.org

ALLDRIDGE, Dimitri. b 81. Cov Univ BA 03. Gordon-Conwell Th Sem MDiv 13. **d** 13 **p** 14. C Gateshead H Trin S Africa 13–16; C Hartford *Ches* from 16. *The Propagator's House, Greenbank Lane, Hartford, Northwich CW8 1JJ* M: 07706-185297 E: dimitri.alldridge@gmail.com *or* dimitri@christchurchgreenbank.org

ALLDRITT, Nicolas Sebastian Fitz-Ansculf. b 41. St Edm Hall Ox BA 63 MA 69 DPhil 69. Cuddesdon Coll 72. **d** 72 **p** 73. C Limpsfield and Titsey *S'wark* 72–81; Tutor Linc Th Coll 81–96; Sub-Warden 88–96; R Witham *Gp Linc* 97–07; rtd 07; PtO *Pet* 07–12. *104 Orchard Hill, Little Billing, Northampton NN3 9AG* T: (01604) 407115

ALLDRITT, Richard James Lee. b 79. Somerville Coll Ox MEng 01. Oak Hill Th Coll 10. **d** 13 **p** 14. C Cambridge H Sepulchre *Ely* 13–18; V Oakwood St Thos *Lon* from 18. *2 Sheringham Avenue, London N14 4UE* M: 07788-952137 E: rich.alldritt@gmail.com

ALLEN, Andrew Michael. b 84. Ripon Coll Cuddesdon BA 09. **d** 10 **p** 11. C Aston Clinton w Buckland and Drayton Beauchamp *Ox* 10–13; Chapl and Fell Ex Coll Ox from 13; LtO Ox from 18. *Exeter College, Turl Street, Oxford OX1 3DP* T: (01865) 279600 E: andrew.allen@exeter.ox.ac.uk

ALLEN, Andrew Stephen. b 55. Nottm Univ BPharm 77 MPS. St Steph Ho Ox 78. **d** 81 **p** 82. C Gt Ilford St Mary *Chelmsf* 81–83; C Luton All SS w St Pet *St Alb* 83–86; TV Chambersbury 86–91; TV Brixham w Churston Ferrers and Kingswear *Ex* 91–01; TR 01–06; P-in-c Upton cum Chalvey *Ox* 06–08; TR 08–20; rtd 20; PtO *B & W* from 20. *44 Osborne Road, Weston-super-Mare BS23 3EJ*

ALLEN, Beverley Carole. See PINNELL, Beverley Carole

ALLEN, Brian. b 58. Oak Hill NSM Course 90. **d** 93 **p** 94. NSM W Norwood St Luke *S'wark* 93–02; NSM Gipsy Hill Ch Ch 02–08. *76 Bradley Road, London SE19 3NS* T: (020) 8771 4282 *or* 8686 8282 E: lonesomestone@hotmail.co.uk

ALLEN, Brian. *See* ALLEN, Frank Brian

ALLEN, Mrs Caroline Anne. b 59. ERMC 08. **d** 11 **p** 12. C Kesgrave *St E* 11–14; P-in-c Walton and Trimley 14–17; R 17–18; rtd 18. *Bethany Cottage, Dog Corner, Matlaske Road, Little Barningham, Norwich NR11 7DQ* T: (01263) 570283 M: 07970-737639 E: carolineallen121@gmail.com

ALLEN, Mrs Christine Anne. b 57. Avery Hill Coll CertEd 78 Cant Ch Ch Univ MA 12. St Aug Coll of Th 14. **d** 17 **p** 18. NSM S Gillingham *Roch* 17–20; NSM Rainham from 20. *74 Kingsway, Gillingham ME7 3AU* T: (01634) 853172 E: revchrisallen74@gmail.com

ALLEN, Christopher Dennis. b 50. Fitzw Coll Cam BA 73 MA 77. Cuddesdon Coll 74. **d** 76 **p** 77. C Kettering St Andr *Pet* 76–79; C Pet H Spirit Bretton 79–82; R Bardney *Linc* 82–87; V Knighton St Mary Magd *Leic* 87–11; V Cosby and Whetstone 11–20; P-in-c Shipley *Chich* from 20. *The Vicarage, Red Lane, Shipley, Horsham RH13 8PH* T: (01403) 432813 E: rev.c.allen@googlemail.com

ALLEN, Christopher Leslie. b 56. Leeds Univ BA 78. St Jo Coll Nottm 79. **d** 80 **p** 81. C Birm St Martin 80–85; Tr and Ed Pathfinders 85–89; Hd 89–92; Midl Youth Dept Co-ord CPAS 85–89; Hon C Selly Park St Steph and St Wulstan *Birm* 86–92; V Hamstead St Bernard 92–95; NSM Kidderminster St Mary and All SS w Trimpley etc *Worc* 03–11; NSM Ribbesford w Bewdley and Dowles and Wribbenhall 11–17. *The Brambles, Dowles Road, Bewdley DY12 2RD* T: (01299) 409057 M: 07956-303037 E: chris.allen@compass.uk.net

ALLEN, David Edward. b 70. Van Mildert Coll Dur BSc 91. Ripon Coll Cuddesdon BA 94 MA 11. **d** 95 **p** 96. C Grantham *Linc* 95–99; C W Hampstead St Jas *Lon* 99–01; C Kilburn St Mary w All So and W Hampstead St Jas 01–02; V Finsbury St Clem w St Barn and St Matt from 02; Chapl Moorfields Eye Hosp NHS Foundn Trust 04–17. *St Clement's Vicarage, King Square, London EC1V 8DA* T: (020) 7251 0706 E: davideallen@blueyonder.co.uk *or* frdavid@stclementfinsbury.org

ALLEN, Derek. b 57. MCIOB 89. **d** 99 **p** 00. OLM Bacup Ch Ch *Man* 99–04; OLM Bacup and Stacksteads 04–16; TV from 16. *180 New Line, Bacup OL13 9RU* T: (01706) 875960 E: allennewline@aol.com

ALLEN, Frank Brian. b 47. K Coll Lon BD AKC 71. **d** 71 **p** 72. C Leam Lane *Dur* 71–74; C Tynemouth Ch Ch *Newc* 74–78; Chapl Preston Hosp N Shields 74–78; Chapl Newc Poly 78–84; V Newc St Hilda 84–88; Chapl Nottm Mental Illness and Psychiatric Unit 88–89; Chapl for Mental Health Newc Mental Health Unit 89–94; Chapl Newc City Health NHS Trust 94–96; Chapl Team Leader 96–06; Chapl Team Leader Northumberland, Tyne and Wear NHS Foundn Trust 06–12; Visiting Fell Newc Univ 93–02; rtd 12; PtO *Newc* from 12. *43 Cherryburn Gardens, Newcastle upon Tyne NE4 9UQ* T: 0191-274 9335 E: brian_allen63@hotmail.com

ALLEN, Giles David. b 70. RCM BMus 91 Leeds Univ MA 05. Coll of Resurr Mirfield 92. **d** 95 **p** 96. C Palmers Green St Jo *Lon* 95–99; V Lund *Blackb* 99–12; CF from 12. *c/o MOD Chaplains (Army)* T: (01264) 383430 F: 381824 E: gilesallen@live.co.uk

ALLEN, Hugh Edward. b 47. Bp Otter Coll Chich CertEd 68. Sarum & Wells Th Coll 79. **d** 81 **p** 82. C Frome St Jo *B & W* 81–85; R Old Cleeve, Leighland and Treborough 85–97; RD Exmoor 92–97; P-in-c The Stanleys *Glouc* 97–99; PtO *B & W* 99–05; P-in-c Charlton Musgrove, Cucklington and Stoke Trister 05–10; RD Bruton and Cary 06–10; rtd 10; PtO *B & W* from 11; RD Tone 12–14. *Woodpeckers, Langley Marsh, Wiveliscombe, Taunton TA4 2UL* T: (01984) 624166 E: hallenarkwood@yahoo.co.uk

ALLEN, Jacqueline Lesley. *See* McKENNA, Jacqueline Lesley

ALLEN, Jamie. *See* ALLEN, Timothy James

ALLEN, Mrs Jane Rosemary. b 39. Cartrefle Coll of Educn BA 83 PGCE 84. St As & Ban Minl Tr Course 99. **d** 00 **p** 01. C Llandudno *Ban* 00–05; TV 05–09; rtd 09; PtO *St As* from 09. *39 Manor Park, Gloddaeth Avenue, Llandudno LL30 2SE* T: (01492) 860531

ALLEN, Joanna Elizabeth. b 86. Wycliffe Hall Ox BA 20. **d** 20 **p** 21. C Goring and Streatley w S Stoke *Ox* from 20. *7 The Bull Meadow, Streatley, Reading RG8 9QD* E: revjoallen@gmail.com

ALLEN, Johan. b 49. Lanc Univ CertEd 75 Roehampton Inst BEd 88. S'wark Ord Course 05. **d** 08 **p** 09. NSM W Streatham St Jas *S'wark* 08–12; NSM Furzedown 12–20; PtO from 20. *54 Leigham Vale, London SW16 2JQ* T: (020) 7564 8588 M: 07743-156786 E: hjohanallen@gmail.com

ALLEN, John Clement. b 32. K Coll Lon 54. **d** 58 **p** 59. C Middlesbrough St Martin *York* 58–60; C Northallerton w Kirby Sigston 60–64; V Larkfield *Roch* 64–70; R Ash 70–79; R Ridley 70–79; RD Cobham 76–79; R Chislehurst St Nic 79–97; rtd 97; PtO *Sarum* 97–19. *The Peppergarth, 9 Lane Fox Terrace, Penny Street, Sturminster Newton DT10 1DE* T: (01258) 473754 E: forestbear9@outlook.com

ALLEN, Jordan. b 94. Trin Coll Bris 16. **d** 19 **p** 20. C Rushden St Pet *Pet* from 19. *43 Melloway Road, Rushden NN10 6XX* M: 07446-219211 E: revjord@hotmail.com

ALLEN, Mrs Kathleen. b 46. Westmr Coll Ox MTh 02. NOC 88. **d** 91 **p** 94. NSM Colne H Trin *Blackb* 91–94; NSM Colne Ch Ch 94–98; NSM Colne and Villages 98–06; rtd 06; PtO *B & W* from 09. *80 Stoddens Road, Burnham-on-Sea TA8 2DB* T: (01278) 793627 E: krabos080@gmail.com

ALLEN, Malcolm. b 60. Open Th Coll BA 00. Trin Coll Bris 94. **d** 96 **p** 97. C Skirbeck H Trin *Linc* 96–00; TV Cheltenham St Mark *Glouc* 00–09; TR Bishop's Cleeve and Woolstone w Gotherington etc from 09; AD Tewkesbury and Winchcombe 16–19. *The Rectory, 4 Church Approach, Bishops Cleeve, Cheltenham GL52 8NG* T: (01242) 677851 E: malc.rector@gmail.com

ALLEN, Matthew Frederick James. b 82. Univ of Wales (Cardiff) BSc 03 St Jo Coll Dur BA 09 Dur Univ MA 11. Cranmer Hall Dur 07. **d** 10 **p** 11. C Kendal St Thos *Carl* 10–14; P-in-c Accrington Ch Ch *Blackb* 14–17; Dioc Dir of Studies 16–20; Dir IME2 18–20; Dir Tr from 20. *Diocesan Offices, Clayton House, Walker Industrial Estate, Walker Road, Guide, Blackburn BB1 2QE* T: (01254) 824940 M: 07739-465073 E: revmattallen@gmail.com *or* matt.allen@blackburn.anglican.org

ALLEN, Michael Stephen. b 37. Nottm Univ BA 60. Cranmer Hall Dur 60. **d** 62 **p** 63. C Sandal St Helen *Wakef* 62–66; Hon C Tile Cross *Birm* 66–70; V 72–84; Hon C Bletchley *Ox* 70–72; Vice-Prin Aston Tr Scheme 84–91; Hon C Boldmere *Birm* 85–91; P-in-c Easton w Colton and Marlingford *Nor* 91–93; Local Min Officer 91–93; Dioc Adv in Adult Educn *S'well* 93–02; rtd 02; PtO *S'well* from 02. *8 Grenville Rise, Arnold, Nottingham NG5 8EW* T: 0115-967 9515 E: msa1@sky.com

ALLEN, Patricia. *See* LEWER ALLEN, Patricia

ALLEN, Peter John. b 34. Leic Coll of Educn CertEd 74 Leic Univ BEd 75 MA 79. EAMTC 89. **d** 92 **p** 93. NSM Ketton w

Tinwell *Pet* 92–94; NSM Easton on the Hill, Collyweston w Duddington etc 94–96; Chapl St Pet Viña del Mar Chile 96–99; NSM Culworth w Sulgrave and Thorpe Mandeville etc *Pet* 00–04; rtd 04; PtO *Pet* from 04; *Eur* 16–20. *24 Holm Close, Weedon, Northampton NN7 4TJ* T: (01327) 349292 E: peterjallen@tinyworld.co.uk

ALLEN, Peter Richard. b 62. Qu Coll Birm BA 04. d 04 p 05. C Hackenthorpe *Sheff* 04–07; TV Gleadless 07–08; Chapl for Sport 07–13; TV Halstead Area *Chelmsf* 13–18; P-in-c Hackenthorpe *Sheff* from 19; P-in-c Gleadless from 19; P-in-c Woodhouse St Jas from 19. *S James's Vicarage, 65 Cardwell Avenue, Sheffield S13 7XB* T: 0114-269 0371 M: 07772-926278 E: prallen1962@gmail.com *or* woodhousestjames@gmail.com

ALLEN (née WADEY), Rachel Susan. b 71. Lanc Univ BA 94. St Steph Ho Ox BA 98. d 98 p 99. C Poulton-le-Fylde *Blackb* 98–01; C Blackpool H Cross 01–03; V Skerton St Chad 03–09; Chapl Prospect Park Hosp Reading 09–15; Chapl E and N Herts NHS Trust 15–18; Chapl Isabel Hospice 18–20; Chapl NE Lon Foundn Trust from 18; LtO *Chelmsf* from 20; PtO *St Alb* 15–21. *North-East London NHS Foundation Trust, Goodmayes Hospital, 157 Barley Lane, Ilford IG3 8XJ* T: 03005-551200 M: 07825-827100 E: rsw904@gmail.com *or* rachel.allen2@nelft.nhs.uk

ALLEN, Richard James. b 46. Wells Th Coll 69. d 71 p 72. C Upholland *Liv* 71–75; TV 76–79; TV Padgate 79–85; V Weston-super-Mare St Andr Bournville *B & W* 85–93; V Williton 93–10; P-in-c St Decumans 08–10; Chapl Somerset Primary Care Trust 93–10; rtd 10; PtO *B & W* from 10. *26 Causeway Terrace, Watchet TA23 0HP* T: (01984) 248119 M: 07789-242245 E: richzakers@uwclub.net

ALLEN, Richard John. b 62. Lon Univ BA 83 Ex Univ PGCE 84. SWMTC 05. d 91 p 93. In Free C of E 91–02; Chapl Millfield Sch Somerset 02–17; Chapl Ch Coll Brecon 17–21; NSM Ottery St Mary, Alfington, W Hill, Tipton etc *Ex* 06–19; NSM Dawlish w Holcombe, Cofton and Starcross 19–21; R Trelawny *Truro* from 21; PtO *B & W* 09–20; *Eur* from 16. *The Rectory, St Marnarchs Road, Lanreath, Looe PL13 2NR* M: 07383-621292 E: rev@trelawnybenefice.com

ALLEN, Richard Lee. b 41. Liv Inst of Educn TCert 67. NOC 80. d 83 p 84. NSM Colne Ch Ch *Blackb* 83–90; P-in-c Trawden 91–98; NSM Colne and Villages 98–06; Chapl Burnley Health Care NHS Trust 99–03; Chapl E Lancs Hosps NHS Trust 03–06; rtd 06; PtO *B & W* from 09. *30 Stoddens Road, Burnham-on-Sea TA8 2DB* T: (01278) 793627 E: krabos@talktalk.net

ALLEN, Roy Vernon. b 43. Open Univ BA 81 Birm Univ MA 84. Sarum Th Coll 67. d 70 p 71. C Hall Green Ascension *Birm* 70–74; V Temple Balsall 74–78; P-in-c Smethwick St Steph 78–81; V Smethwick St Mich 78–81; V Smethwick SS Steph and Mich 81–86; V Marston Green 86–13; rtd 13; PtO *Birm* from 13. *16 Orchard Close, Curdworth, Sutton Coldfield B76 9DX* T: (01675) 470629 E: roy_v_allen@hotmail.com

ALLEN, Rupert. b 63. Worc Coll of HE BA 87 Sussex Univ PGCE 88. Qu Foundn (Course) 15. d 17 p 18. OLM Chilvers Coton w Astley *Cov* from 17; *Leic* from 17. *24 Park Avenue, Nuneaton CV11 4PQ* T: (024) 7632 5372 E: rupert@allsaintscoton.org *or* rupert.allen@leicestercofe.org

ALLEN, Canon Steven. b 49. Nottm Univ BA 73 York St Jo Univ MA 08. St Jo Coll Nottm 73. d 75 p 76. C Gt Horton *Bradf* 75–80; V 89–02; V Upper Armley *Ripon* 80–89; RD Bowling and Horton *Bradf* 98–02; Dioc Tr Officer 02–14; *Leeds* 14; Hon Can Bradf Cathl 00–14; rtd 14; PtO *Leeds* from 17. *1 Hawkstone Avenue, Guiseley, Leeds LS20 8ET* T: (01943) 510653

ALLEN, Canon Susan Rosemary. b 47. Warwick Univ BSc 68 Trevelyan Coll Dur PGCE 69. Sarum Th Coll 93. d 96 p 97. C Goldsworth Park *Guildf* 96–01; TV Hemel Hempstead *St Alb* 01–09; TR 09–13; Hon Can St Alb 11–13; rtd 13; PtO *St Alb* 13–18; *Newc* from 13. *33 Swansfield Park Road, Alnwick NE66 1AT* E: revsue33@gmail.com

ALLEN, Mrs Suzanna Claire. b 75. St Jo Coll Nottm 09. d 11 p 12. C Wareham *Sarum* 11–15; C Horton, Chalbury, Hinton Martel and Holt St Jas 15; C Witchampton, Stanbridge and Long Crichel etc 15; C Wimborne Minster 15; C Wimborne Minster and Villages from 15. *The Rectory, Hinton Martel, Wimborne BH21 7HD* E: suzie-assocpriest@wimborneminster.org.uk

ALLEN, Thomas Henry. b 42. NOC 87. d 90 p 91. C Upholland *Liv* 90–93; TV Walton-on-the-Hill 93–07; rtd 07; PtO *Eur* 14–17; *Liv* from 16. *13 Crosgrove Road, Liverpool L4 8TE* T: 0151-476 9705

ALLEN, Timothy James. b 71. Warwick Univ BA 93. Ripon Coll Cuddesdon BTh 99. d 99 p 00. C Nuneaton St Mary *Cov* 99–02; V Seend, Bulkington and Poulshot *Sarum* 02–03; Hon C Winslow w Gt Horwood and Addington *Ox* 03–05; V Gt

Cornard *St E* 05–09; V New Plymouth St Mary NZ 09–10; Dean Taranaki 10–16. *3 Raleigh Street, Waitara 4320, New Zealand* E: jamie@taranakiretreat.org.nz

ALLEN, Zachary Edward. b 52. Warwick Univ BA 74. Ripon Coll Cuddesdon 78. d 81 p 82. C Bognor *Chich* 81–84; C Rusper and Roughey 84–86; TV Carl H Trin and St Barn 86–90; Chapl Strathclyde Ho Hosp Carl 86–90; V Findon w Clapham and Patching *Chich* 90–01; V Rustington 01–18; rtd 18. *Cherry Cottage, Westview Terrace, Nepcote Lane, Findon, Worthing BN14 0TY* E: zacharyallen753@gmail.com

ALLERTON, Patrick. b 78. NTMTC. d 10 p 11. C Onslow Square and S Kensington St Aug *Lon* 10–14; C Fulham St Dionis 14–17; V Notting Hill St Pet from 17. *St Peter's Church Office, 59A Portobello Road, London W11 3DB* T: (020) 7792 8227 E: pat@stpetersnottinghill.org.uk

ALLEYNE, Sir John Olpherts Campbell Bt. b 28. Jes Coll Cam BA 50 MA 55. d 55 p 56. C Southampton St Mary w H Trin *Win* 55–58; Chapl Cov Cathl 58–62; Chapl Clare Hall Cam 62–66; Chapl Bris Cathl 66–68; Area Sec (SW England) Toc H 68–71; V Speke All SS *Liv* 71–73; TR Speke St Aid 73–76; R Win St Matt 76–93; rtd 93; PtO *Guildf* from 93. *18 Ashbarn Crescent, Winchester SO22 4LW* T: (01962) 869472 E: jocalleyne@hotmail.com

ALLFORD, Canon Judith Mary. b 55. Sheff Univ BA Lon Univ BD. Trin Coll Bris 77. dss 86 d 87 p 94. Par Dn Deptford St Jo w H Trin *S'wark* 87–91; Asst Chapl Buckland Hosp 91–93; Asst Chapl King's Healthcare NHS Trust 93–95; Lead Chapl Ashford and St Pet Hosps NHS Foundn Trust 95–15; PtO *Guildf* 15–19; V Englefield Green from 19; Hon Can Guildf Cathl from 15. *The Vicarage, 21 Willow Walk, Englefield Green, Egham TW20 0DQ* T: (01784) 434133 M: 07928-362972 E: jallford@btinternet.com

ALLIES, Lorna Gillian. b 46. UEA BSc 93 Sheff Univ EdD 01. d 05 p 06. OLM Thurton w Ashby St Mary, Bergh Apton etc *Nor* 05–07; NSM Bunwell, Carleton Rode, Tibenham, Gt Moulton etc 07–09; P-in-c Rackheath and Salhouse 09–14; Dioc Rural Adv 06–09; rtd 14; PtO *Nor* 14–15; NSM Acle and Bure to Yare 15–19; PtO 19–20; NSM Nor St Pet Mancroft w St Jo Maddermarket from 20; Jt RD Nor E from 20. *426 Unthank Road, Norwich NR4 7QH* M: 07706-482284 E: lorna.allies@gmail.com

ALLINSON, Paul Timothy. b 63. CA Tr Coll 82 Edin Th Coll 89. d 91 p 92. C Peterlee *Dur* 91–94; C Shadforth and Sherburn w Pittington 94–97; P-in-c Byers Green 97–04; P-in-c Seaton Carew 04–17; P-in-c Greatham 09–17; Dioc Children's Adv 94–09; Chapl Greatham Hosp 09–17; V Ponteland *Newc* from 17. *The Vicarage, Thornhill Road, Ponteland, Newcastle upon Tyne NE20 9PZ* T: (01661) 612533 M: 07888-726535 E: vicar@pontelandstmary.co.uk

ALLISON, Alliandra Bingo. b 86. Keble Coll Ox BA 07 St Jo Coll Dur BA 16. Cranmer Hall Dur 13. d 16 p 20. C N Wingfield, Clay Cross and Pilsley *Derby* from 16. *Address temp unknown* M: 07818-841697

ALLISON, Benjamin John. See ALLISON, Alliandra Bingo

ALLISON, Elliott Desmond. b 36. UNISA BA 64 K Coll Lon MTh 74. S Africa Federal Th Coll. d 69 p 70. PtO *Leeds* 14–16. *Flat 1, 20 Southview Gardens, Worthing BN11 5JA*

ALLISON, Canon James Timothy. b 61. Man Univ BSc 83. Oak Hill Th Coll BA 89. d 89 p 90. C Walkden Moor *Man* 89–93; Chapl Huddersfield Univ *Wakef* 93–98; V Erringden 98–12; RD Calder Valley 06–12; P-in-c Coley 12–14; *Leeds* from 14; Bp's Rural Adv from 14; C Northowram 14–20; P-in-c from 20; Hon Can Wakef Cathl from 20. *The Vicarage, 1 Church Walk, Northowran, Halifax HX3 7HF* T: (01422) 202292 E: james.allison@leeds.anglican.org

ALLISON, Keith. b 34. Dur Univ BA 59. Ely Th Coll 59. d 61 p 62. C Sculcoates *York* 61–64; C Stainton-in-Cleveland 64–65; C Leeds St Pet *Ripon* 65–70; V Micklefield *York* 70–74; V Appleton-le-Street w Amotherby 74–78; P-in-c Barton le Street 77–78; P-in-c Salton 77–80; R Amotherby w Appleton and Barton-le-Street 78–82; Chapl Lister Hosp Stevenage 82–90; P-in-c St Ippolyts *St Alb* 82–85; V 85–90; Chapl Hitchin Hosp 86–90; Chapl Shotley Bridge Gen Hosp 90–94; Chapl NW Dur HA 90–94; Sen Chapl N Dur Acute Hosps NHS Trust 94–97; Sen Chapl N Dur Healthcare NHS Trust 98–00; rtd 00; PtO *Dur* from 00. *2 Middlewood Road, Lanchester, Durham DH7 0HL* T: (01207) 529046 M: 07413-298578

ALLISON, Rosemary Jean. See WHITLEY, Rosemary Jean

ALLISON, Susan Ann. b 61. EMMTC 06. d 06 p 07. C Gt and Lt Coates w Bradley *Linc* 06–09; P-in-c Fotherby 09–14; R 14–15; P-in-c Somercotes and Grainthorpe w Conisholme 09–14; R 14–15; RD Louthesk 11–15; R Bain Valley Gp from 15. *The Rectory, High Street, Coningsby, Lincoln LN4 4RA* T: (01526) 348505 M: 07920-133329 E: susan.333allison@btinternet.com

ALLISON, Mrs Susan Margaret. b 63. Ridley Hall Cam 18. d 19 p 20. C Newmarket All SS *St E* from 19. *4 Bunbury Terrace, All Saints Road, Newmarket CB8 8FL* M: 07904-491947 E: susanmallison54@gmail.com

✠**ALLISTER, The Rt Revd Donald Spargo.** b 52. Peterho Cam BA 74 MA 77 Ches Univ Hon DTh 11. Trin Coll Bris 74. d 76 p 77 c 10. C Hyde St Geo *Ches* 76–79; C Sevenoaks St Nic *Roch* 79–83; V Birkenhead Ch Ch *Ches* 83–89; R Cheadle 89–02; RD 99–02; Adn Ches 02–10; Bp Pet from 10. *Bishops Lodging, The Palace, Minster Precincts, Peterborough PE1 1YA* T: (01733) 562492 F: 890077 E: bishop@peterborough-diocese.org.uk

ALLISTER, John Charles. b 77. Ch Coll Cam BA 00 MA 03 MSci 00 St Anne's Coll Ox PGCE 01. Wycliffe Hall Ox BA 08. d 09 p 10. C Hurdsfield *Ches* 09–12; V Nottingham St Jude *S'well* from 12. *403 Woodborough Road, Nottingham NG3 5HE* T: 0115-960   4102   M: 07092-119317 E: john.allister@cantab.net *or* revjohnallister@gmail.com

ALLMAN, Mrs Susan. b 56. Bris Univ BA 77. WEMTC 93. d 96 p 97. NSM Henleaze *Bris* 96–99; C Southmead 99–02; V Two Mile Hill St Mich 02–08; Partnership P E Bris 08–10; P-in-c Titchfield *Portsm* 10–20; AD Fareham 13–17; rtd 20. *Address temp unknown* M: 07775-977298 E: susanrev@hotmail.co.uk

ALLMARK, Leslie. b 48. Open Univ BA 90. d 01 p 02. OLM Halliwell St Luke *Man* 01–08; rtd 08; PtO *Man* from 08. *75 Crosby Road, Bolton BL1 4EJ* T: (01204) 845795 *or* 528491 M: 07582-609735

ALLON-SMITH, Roderick David. b 51. Leic Univ BA PhD Cam Univ MA. Ridley Hall Cam 79. d 82 p 83. C Kinson *Sarum* 82–86; V Westwood *Cov* 86–96; RD Cov S 92–96; P-in-c Radford Semele 96–04; Dioc Dir Par Development and Evang 01–03; Dioc Missr *Dur* 04–10; AD Dur 08–10; R Lanercost, Walton, Gilsland and Nether Denton *Carl* 10–17; RD Brampton 12–15; rtd 17. *5 Glovers Crescent, Ripon HG4 2TB* T: (01765) 608220 E: allonsmith@btinternet.com

ALLRIGHT, Rebecca Jane. b 72. Aber Univ MA 96 Green Coll Ox MSc 01. St Hild Coll 16. d 18 p 19. C Carlton and Drax *York* from 18. *The Parsonage, 2 Church Dike Lane, Drax, Selby YO8 8NZ* T: (01904) 733829 M: 07984-742269 E: becky.allright@hotmail.co.uk

ALLS, Mrs Anna Kate. b 78. St Jo Coll Nottm BA 12. d 12 p 13. C Bestwood Em w St Mark *S'well* 12–14; C Brinsley w Underwood 14–16; C Eastwood 14–16; C Bilsthorpe 16–19; C Eakring 16–19; C Egmanton 16–19; C Kirton 16–19; C Kneesall w Laxton and Wellow 16–19; C Ollerton w Boughton 16–19; C Walesby 16–19; V Burton Joyce, Bulcote and Stoke Bardolph etc from 19. *The Vicarage, 9 Chestnut Grove, Burton Joyce, Nottingham NG14 5DP* M: 07535-017591 E: reverend.anna.alls@gmail.com

ALLSOP, Mrs Beryl Anne. b 45. EMMTC 94. d 97 p 98. NSM Clipstone *S'well* 97–00; NSM Blidworth w Rainworth 00–10; rtd 10; PtO *S'well* from 11; *Derby* 14–19. *The Old Post Office, Bottom Row, Pleasley Vale, Mansfield NG19 8RS* T: (01623) 811095 E: beryl@faithfulfish.co.uk

ALLSOP, David. b 50. d 10 p 11. NSM Musbury *Blackb* 10–20; NSM Haslingden w Grane and Stonefold 10–20; NSM Laneside 10–20; PtO from 20. *7 Elizabeth Drive, Haslingden, Rossendale BB4 4JB* T: (01706) 224663 M: 07986-004401 E: davidallsop@hotmail.com

ALLSOP, David George. b 48. Wycliffe Hall Ox. d 99 p 00. C Chenies and St Chalfont, Latimer and Flaunden *Ox* 99–02; P-in-c 02–08; R 08–17; rtd 17; PtO *Ox* from 17. *7 Elizabeth Drive, Haslingden, Rossendale BB4 4JB* T: (01706) 224663 M: 07818-441431 E: cheniesrectory@aol.com

ALLSOP, Peter William. b 33. Kelham Th Coll 58. d 58 p 59. C Woodford St Barn *Chelmsf* 58–61; C Upholland *Liv* 61–65; V Wigan St Geo 65–71; P-in-c Marham *Ely* 71–72; TV Fincham 72–76; V Trawden *Blackb* 76–90; C Marton 90–92; C S Shore H Trin 92–98; rtd 98; PtO *Blackb* from 98. *33 Grizedale Court, Forest Gate, Blackpool FY3 9AP* E: peter.w.allsop@talktalk.net

ALLSOPP, The Ven Christine. b 47. Aston Univ BSc 68. S Dios Minl Tr Scheme 86. d 89 p 94. C Caversham St Pet and Mapledurham etc *Ox* 89–94; C Bracknell 94; TV 94–98; P-in-c Bourne Valley *Sarum* 98–00; TR 00–05; RD Aldersbury 99–05; Can and Preb Sarum Cathl 02–05; Adn Northn *Pet* 05–13; Can Pet Cathl 05–13; rtd 13; PtO *Ox* from 13. *Mellor Cottage, 2 Walkers Lane, Lambourn, Hungerford RG17 8YE* T: (01488) 674108 M: 07801-096345 E: venchrisallsopp@gmail.com

ALLSOPP, Mark Dennis. b 66. Cuddesdon Coll 93. d 96 p 97. C Hedworth *Dur* 96–98; C Gt Aycliffe 98–00; TV Gt Aycliffe and Chilton 00–04; P-in-c Kirklevington and High and Low Worsall *York* 04–08; Chapl HM Pris Kirklevington Grange 04–08; Chapl RN from 08. *Royal Naval Chaplaincy Service Headquarters, Tanner Building, HMS Excellent, Whale Island, Portsmouth PO2 8ER* T: 0300-157 7544

ALLSOPP, Mrs Patricia Ann. b 48. St Mary's Coll Chelt CertEd 69. Qu Coll Birm. d 00 p 01. C Upton-on-Severn, Ripple, Earls Croome etc *Worc* 00–04; P-in-c Finstall 04–05; V 05–08; RD Bromsgrove 06–08; rtd 08; PtO *Leic* from 15. *18 Stuart Court, High Street, Kibworth Beauchamp, Leicester LE8 0LR* M: 07779-753908 E: pannbeth1@gmail.com

ALLSOPP, Stephen Robert. b 50. BSc 71 MSc 72 PhD 75. Mon Dioc Tr Scheme 81. d 84 p 85. NSM Trevethin *Mon* 84–88; Asst Chapl K Sch Roch 88–07; Chapl K Prep Sch Roch 99–07; rtd 07; Hon PV Roch Cathl 89–16. *579 Stonegate Road, Leeds LS17 6EJ* E: stephen@allsopps.net

ALLSWORTH, Peter Thomas. b 44. St Mich Coll Llan 93. d 93 p 94. C Prestatyn *St As* 93–96; V Esclusham 96–06; C Rhyl w St Ann 06–10; P-in-c Bodelwyddan 10; P-in-c Rhuddlan and Bodelwyddan 10–11; rtd 11; PtO *St As* from 11. *Subiaco, 10 Tirionfa, Rhuddlan, Rhyl LL18 6LT* T: (01745) 590683 E: peterallsworth@btinternet.com

ALLTON, Canon Paul Irving. b 38. Man Univ BA 60. d 63 p 64. C Kibworth Beauchamp *Leic* 63–66; C Reading St Mary V *Ox* 66–70; R Caston *Nor* 70–75; V Griston 70–75; P-in-c Sturston w Thompson and Tottington 70–75; P-in-c Merton 70–75; V Hunstanton St Mary w Lt Ringstead 75–80; V Holme-next-the-Sea 75–80; V Hunstanton St Mary w Ringstead Parva, Holme etc 80–85; RD Heacham and Rising 81–85; Hon Can Nor Cathl 85–93; TR Lowestoft and Kirkley 85–93; TR Keynsham *B & W* 93–96; TR Gaywood *Nor* 96–01; rtd 01; PtO *Nor* from 01; *Roch* from 16. *13 Bromley College, London Road, Bromley BR1 1PE* E: paulallton@btinternet.com

ALLUM, Jeremy Warner. b 32. Wycliffe Hall Ox 60. d 62 p 63. C Hornchurch St Andr *Chelmsf* 62–67; P-in-c W Derby St Luke *Liv* 67–69; V 69–75; P-in-c Boulton *Derby* 75–90; RD Melbourne 86–90; V Hathersage 90–98; rtd 98; PtO *Derby* from 98. *32 Sandown Avenue, Mickleover, Derby DE3 0QQ* T: (01332) 231253 E: jnmsandown@ntlworld.com

ALLWOOD, Linda Angela Fredrika. b 76. Newc Univ BA 00. Cranmer Hall Dur 01. d 03 p 04. C Northampton St Giles *Pet* 03–06; PtO *St E* 06–07. *Norrskensgatan 6, 37151 Karlskrona, Sweden* E: linda_allwood@hotmail.com

ALLWOOD, Martin Eardley. b 71. Natal Univ BSc 92. Ripon Coll Cuddesdon 08. d 10 p 11. C Hundred River *St E* 10–14; R The Street Par *York* 14–21; P-in-c Monifieth *Bre* from 21; P-in-c Carnoustie from 21. *123 Chapman Drive, Carnoustie DD7 6DY* M: 07565-298540 E: revmartinallwood@gmail.com

ALMOND, Kenneth Alfred. b 36. EMMTC 76 Linc Th Coll 78. d 79 p 80. C Boston *Linc* 79–82; V Surfleet 82–87; RD Elloe W 86–96; V Spalding St Jo w Deeping St Nicholas 87–98; rtd 98. *18 Century Court, 1 Wilford Lane, West Bridgford, Nottingham NG2 7TU* T: 0115-981 3788 E: ken.hilary@btopenworld.com

ALSBURY, Colin. b 54. Ch Ch Ox BA 77 MA 81. Ripon Coll Cuddesdon 77. d 80 p 81. C Oxton *Ches* 80–84; V Crewe All SS and St Paul 84–92; Ind Chapl 92–95; V Kettering St Andr *Pet* 95–02; V Frome St Jo *B & W* from 02; V Woodlands from 02; RD Frome 10–17. *St John's Vicarage, Vicarage Close, Frome BA11 1QL* T: (01373) 472853 E: colin.alsbury@btinternet.com

ALSOP, Barbara Lynn. b 48. d 11 p 12. NSM Epsom St Martin *Guildf* 11–15; PtO from 15. *15 Meadow Way, Bookham, Leatherhead KT23 3NY* T: (01372) 458492 E: revlynnalsop@talktalk.net

ALSTON, Stephen. b 67. R Holloway Coll Lon BSc 90 PhD 94 Goldsmiths' Coll Lon PGCE 97. Qu Foundn Birm 17. d 20 p 21. C Baschurch and Weston Lullingfield w Hordley *Lich* from 20. *5 South Hermitage, Shrewsbury SY3 7JR* T: (01743) 247728 E: stevealstonfish@gmail.com

ALTY, Jane Alida. b 55. St Hugh's Coll Ox BA 78 MA 17. St Aug Coll of Th BA 17. d 17 p 18. NSM Clapton St Jas *Lon* 17–20; Chapl St Joseph's Hospice Hackney from 18. *20 Meynell Crescent, London E9 7AS* T: (020) 8986 0601 M: 07710-095404 E: jane.alty3@gmail.com

AMAT-TORREGROSA, Gabriel José. b 42. R Superior Coll of Music Madrid MA 63. Bapt Th Sem Ruschlikon Zürich 64. d 71 p 72. Spain 71–98; Asst Chapl Zürich *Eur* 98–07; P-in-c Marseille w Aix-en-Provence 08–13; Chapl Agia Napa Cyprus from 15. *10 Tassou Markou, Apart 202, 5281 Paralimni, Cyprus* M: (00357) 9783 9349 E: gjamat@hotmail.com

AMBANI, Stephen Frederick. b 45. Univ of Wales (Lamp) BA 90. St Jo Coll Nottm 86 CA Tr Coll Nairobi 70. d 83 p 83. Kenya 83–93; C Glan Ely *Llan* 93–95; C Whitchurch 95–97; V Nantymoel w Wyndham 97–99; V Tonyrefail w Gilfach Goch and Llandyfodwg 99–03; V Tonyrefail w Gilfach Goch 04; rtd 05. *68 St Winifred's Road, Bridgend CF31 4PN* T: (01656) 653589

AMBROSE, James Field. b 51. Newc Univ BA 73. Cranmer Hall Dur. d 80 p 81. C Barrow St Geo w St Luke *Carl* 80–83; C

Workington St Jo 83–85; R Montford w Shrawardine and Fitz *Lich* 85–88; Ch Radio Officer BBC Radio Shropshire 85–88; Chapl RAF 88–92; Voc and Min Adv CPAS 92–99; TV Syston *Leic* 99–06; C Leic Martyrs 06–07; V Heald Green St Cath *Ches* 07–17; Chapl St Ann's Hospice Manchester 07–17; rtd 17; PtO *Ches* from 19. *51 Coppice Road, Poynton, Stockport SK12 1SL* E: jfambrose@btinternet.com

AMBROSE, John George. b 30. Lon Univ BD Ox Univ PGCE. **d** 74 **p** 75. C Rayleigh *Chelmsf* 74–79; V Hadleigh St Barn 79–95; rtd 95; PtO *Chelmsf* from 95. *9 Fairview Gardens, Leigh-on-Sea SS9 3PD*   T: (01702) 474632 E: johng.ambrose@btinternet.com

AMBROSE, Thomas. b 47. Sheff Univ BSc 69 PhD 73 Em Coll Cam BA 77 MA 84. Westcott Ho Cam 75. **d** 78 **p** 79. C Morpeth *Newc* 78–81; C N Gosforth 81–84; R March St Jo *Ely* 84–93; RD March 89–93; P-in-c Witchford w Wentworth 93–99; Dioc Dir of Communications 93–99; Chapl K Sch Ely 94–96; V Trumpington *Ely* 99–08; PtO 14–15; Hon C Cambridge Ascension from 15. *229 Arbury Road, Cambridge CB4 2JJ* M: 07711-263083

AMELIA, Alison. b 67. Hull Univ BA 03 St Jo Coll Dur BA 05. Cranmer Hall Dur 03. **d** 05 **p** 06. C Nunthorpe *York* 05–06; C Hessle 06–09; Chapl United Lincs Hosps NHS Trust from 09. *62 Glengarry Way, Greylees, Sleaford NG34 8XU* E: alison.amelia@ulh.nhs.uk

AMES, Jeremy Peter. b 49. K Coll Lon BD 71 AKC 71. **d** 72 **p** 73. C Kennington St Jo *S'wark* 72–75; Chapl RN 75–04; Chapl RN Engineering Coll 86–89; USA 91–93; Dir of Ords RN 00–04; QHC 02–04; Master St Nic Hosp Salisbury 04–11; PtO *Sarum* from 11. *Springfield, Stratford Road, Stratford sub Castle, Salisbury SP1 3LQ*   T: (01722) 322542 E: jeremyames9@gmail.com

AMES-LEWIS, Richard. b 45. Em Coll Cam BA 66 MA 70. Westcott Ho Cam 76. **d** 78 **p** 79. C Bromley St Mark *Roch* 78–81; C Edenbridge 81–84; V 84–91; P-in-c Crockham Hill H Trin 84–91; P-in-c Barnes St Mary *S'wark* 91–97; TR Barnes 97–00; RD Richmond and Barnes 94–00; TR E Dereham and Scarning *Nor* 00–06; P-in-c Swanton Morley w Beetley w E Bilney and Hoe 02–06; TR Dereham and Distr 06–09; RD Dereham in Mitford 03–08; Hon Can Nor Cathl 06–09; rtd 09; PtO *Ely* from 09. *21 Victoria Street, Cambridge CB1 1JP* T: (01223) 300615 E: ameslewis@btinternet.com

AMEY, Graham George. b 44. Lon Univ BD 70. Tyndale Hall Bris 67. **d** 71 **p** 72. C Hornsey Rise St Mary *Lon* 71–74; C St Helens St Helen *Liv* 74–79; V Liv All So Springwood 79–91; V Whiston 91–02; V Aigburth 02–12; rtd 12; PtO *Liv* from 16. *213 Rose Lane, Liverpool L18 5EA*   T: 0151-378 4687

AMEY, John Mark. b 59. Ripon Coll Cuddesdon 98. **d** 00 **p** 01. C Winchmore Hill St Paul *Lon* 00–04; V Sutton *Ely* 04–11; R Witcham w Mepal 04–11; V St Ives from 11; Chapl ATC 03–19; CF from 18. *The Vicarage, Westwood Road, St Ives PE27 6DH*   M: 07308-675777 E: vicar@stivesparishchurch.org.uk or vicar.stives@gmail.com or padre.amey@armymail.mod.uk

AMEY, Phillip Mark. b 73. Win Univ BA 11. STETS 03. **d** 06 **p** 07. C Southsea H Spirit *Portsm* 06–09; P-in-c Purbrook 09–12; P-in-c Southsea H Spirit 12–17; C Milton 12–17; Chapl RN from 17. *Royal Naval Chaplaincy Service Headquarters, Tanner Building, HMS Excellent, Whale Island, Portsmouth PO2 8ER*   T: 0300-157 7544 E: phillip.amey@sky.com

AMOROSO, Rebecca Mary Louise. b 75. St Martin's Coll Lanc BA 00 Newc Univ MA 12 Sheff Univ BA 14. Coll of Resurr Mirfield 12. **d** 14 **p** 15. C The Boldons *Dur* 14–18; Chapl HM Pris and YOI Stoke Heath 18; Chapl HM YOI Deerbolt 18–20; Chapl HM Pris Dur from 18. *HM Prison Durham, 19B Old Elvet, Durham DH1 3HU*   T: 0191-332 3400 E: rebecca.amoroso@justice.gov.uk

AMOS, Brother. *See* YONGE, James Mohun

AMOS, Colin James. b 62. Univ of Wales (Lamp) BA 83 CQSW 85. Ridley Hall Cam 93. **d** 93 **p** 94. C Aberdare *Llan* 93–96; V Port Talbot St Theodore 96–12; AD Margam 08–12; V Kilburn St Aug w St Jo *Lon* from 12. *St Augustine's Vicarage, Kilburn Park Road, London NW6 5XB*   T: (020) 7624 1637 E: fr.amos@sky.com

AMYES, Emma Charlotte. b 65. Redcliffe Coll BA 01. Ridley Hall Cam. **d** 04 **p** 05. C Hucclecote *Glouc* 04–10; TV Worle *B & W* 10–21. *21 Westmarch Way, Weston-super-Mare BS22 7JY* M: 07866-808635 E: emma.amyes@virgin.net

AMYS, Richard James Rutherford. b 58. Trin Coll Bris BA 90. **d** 90 **p** 91. C Whitnash *Cov* 90–93; P-in-c Gravesend H Family w Ifield *Roch* 93–95; R 95–99; R Eastington, Frocester, Haresfield etc *Glouc* 99–15; rtd 15; PtO *Glouc* from 15. *37 St Mary's Square, Gloucester GL1 2QT*   T: (01452) 503811 M: 07796-956050 E: richardjramys@aol.com

ANAN, Gabriel Jaja. b 48. Regents Th Coll BA 92 Univ of E Lon MA 96 PhD 08 Middx Univ BA 03 MCIT 92. NTMTC 00.

---

d 03 **p** 04. NSM Victoria Docks St Luke *Chelmsf* 03–07; NSM Forest Gate St Sav w W Ham St Matt 07–09; NSM N Woolwich w Silvertown 09–10; NSM E Ham St Geo 10–18; rtd 18. *67 Bedale Road, Romford RM3 9TU*   T: (01708) 349564 M: 07734-707887 E: gabriel58@hotmail.com

ANAND, Jessie Nesam Nallammal. b 54. Madurai Univ BSc 73 BEd 76 Annamalai Univ MA 84. Tamilnadu Th Sem BD 91 New Coll Edin MTh 94 EMMTC 02. **d** 03 **p** 04. NSM Birstall and Wanlip *Leic* 03–05; NSM Emmaus Par Team 05–07; PtO *S'wark* 07–11; C Bermondsey St Hugh CD 11–14; NSM Angell Town St Jo from 15. *All Saints' Vicarage, 100 Prince of Wales Drive, London SW11 4BD*   T: (020) 7622 3809 M: 07760-252655 E: jessieanand@yahoo.co.uk

ANAND, The Very Revd Sekar Anand Asir. b 53. Madurai Univ BSc 75 Serampore Univ BD 79 New Coll Edin MTh 93 Annamalai Univ MA 99. **d** 80 **p** 81. C Nayaith St Jo India 80–82; R Tuticorin St Paul 82–84; Sec Tirunelveli Children's Miss 84–91; C Edin St Pet 91–92; Hon C Burmantofts St Steph and St Agnes *Ripon* 92–93; C Edin St Mark 93–95; Provost Palayamcottai Cathl India 95–00; C Leic Resurr 00–07; C Battersea Fields *S'wark* from 07. *All Saints' Vicarage, 100 Prince of Wales Drive, London SW11 4BD*   T: (020) 7622 3809 M: 07711-492946 E: anandjessie@yahoo.co.uk

ANDERSON, Alice Calder. b 50. Moray Ho Coll of Educn DipEd 76. Local Minl Tr Course 90. **d** 93 **p** 95. NSM Edin St Barn from 93. *20 Pentland Road, Bonnyrigg EH19 2LG*   T: 0131-654 0506 E: alicelibby@gmail.com

ANDERSON, Canon Ann. b 57. Cranmer Hall Dur 01. **d** 03 **p** 04. C Chester le Street *Dur* 03–07; P-in-c Hetton-Lyons w Eppleton 07; R 07–18; TR Gt Aycliffe from 18; Hon Can Dur Cathl from 21. *St Clare's Rectory, St Cuthbert's Way, Newton Aycliffe DL5 5NT*   T: (01325) 315194 E: a.ann007@btinternet.com

ANDERSON, Preb Brian Arthur. b 42. Sarum Th Coll 75. **d** 78 **p** 79. C Plymouth St Jas Ham *Ex* 78–80; Org Sec CECS B & W, Ex and Truro 80–89; TV Saltash *Truro* 89–94; RD E Wivelshire 91–94; P-in-c St Breoke and Egloshayle 94–96; R 96–02; Dioc Officer for Evang 93–99; RD Trigg Minor and Bodmin 95–02; P-in-c Torpoint 02–09; P-in-c Antony w Sheviock 02–09; Preb St Endellion 99–09; rtd 09; PtO *Truro* from 14. *44 Essa Road, Saltash PL12 4EE*   T: (01752) 511271 M: 07710-231219 E: sheriock42@yahoo.co.uk

ANDERSON, David Richard. b 58. Lanc Univ BEd 79. EAMTC 96. **d** 99 **p** 00. C N Walsham w Antingham *Nor* 99–02; R Stalham, E Ruston, Brunstead, Sutton and Ingham 02–06; P-in-c Smallburgh w Dilham w Honing and Crostwight 05–06; TV Wrexham *St As* 06–11; Chapl St Jos High Sch Wrexham 06–11; V Romford St Edw *Chelmsf* 11–14; P-in-c Yeovil St Mich *B & W* 14–15; V from 15. *The Vicarage, 137 St Michael's Avenue, Yeovil BA21 4LW*   T: (01935) 474898 M: 07956-267265 E: fr.anderson.yeovil@gmail.com

ANDERSON, Digby Carter. b 44. Reading Univ BA Brunel Univ MPhil 73 PhD 77. **d** 85 **p** 86. NSM Luton St Sav *St Alb* 85–16; PtO from 16. *17 Hardwick Place, Woburn Sands, Milton Keynes MK17 8QQ*   T: (01908) 584526

ANDERSON, Donald Whimbey. b 31. Trin Coll Toronto BA 54 MA 58 LTh 57 STB 57 ThD 71. **d** 56 **p** 57. Canada 57–59 and 75–88; and from 96; Japan 59–74; Philippines 74–75; Dir Ecum Affairs ACC 88–96; rtd 96. *Conference on the Religious Life, PO Box 99, Little Britain ON K0M 2C0, Canada* T/F: (001) (705) 786 3330 E: dwa@nexicom.net

ANDERSON, Mrs Elizabeth Anne. b 68. Man Univ BA 90 Lanc Univ PGCE 92. SNWTP 14. **d** 17 **p** 18. C St Helens Town Cen *Liv* 17–20; V Blundellsands St Nic from 20. *All Saints' Vicarage, 17 Moor Coppice, Liverpool L23 2XJ* M: 07736-550818

ANDERSON, Mrs Gillian Ann. b 52. NTMTC 05. **d** 08 **p** 09. NSM Lambourne w Abridge and Stapleford Abbotts *Chelmsf* 08–09; NSM Loughton St Jo 09–11; P-in-c High Laver w Magdalen Laver and Lt Laver etc 11–17; rtd 17; PtO *St E* from 18. *Virginia Cottage, 25 Church Lane, Worlington, Bury St Edmunds IP28 8SG* M: 07954-429153 E: revgillanderson@gmail.com

ANDERSON, Gordon Stuart. b 49. St Jo Coll Nottm. **d** 82 **p** 83. C Hattersley *Ches* 82–86; C Dagenham *Chelmsf* 86–91; TV Mildenhall *St E* 91–01; V Southminster *Chelmsf* 01–11; P-in-c Steeple 08–11; V Southminster and Steeple 11–14; RD Maldon and Dengie 06–11; rtd 14; PtO *St E* from 14; *Ely* 14–19. *11 Yew Tree Close, Mildenhall, Bury St Edmunds IP28 7SJ*   T: (01638) 711260 M: 07549-539174 E: gandr42@btinternet.com

ANDERSON, Graeme Edgar. b 59. Poly of Wales BSc 82. St Jo Coll Nottm MA 02. **d** 02 **p** 03. C Brislington St Luke *Bris* 02–05; C Galleywood Common *Chelmsf* 05–09; P-in-c Radcliffe-on-Trent and Shelford *S'well* 09–11; V 11–17; AD E Bingham 15–16; V Cov H Trin 17–21; R Crick and Yelvertoft w Clay Coton and Lilbourne *Pet* from 21. *c/o The Bishop's Office, The Palace, Minster Precincts, Peterborough PE1 1YA* M: 07528-765027 E: church.graeme@gmail.com

ANDERSON, Hugh Richard Oswald. b 35. Roch Th Coll 68. **d** 70 **p** 71. C Minehead *B & W* 70–76; C Darley w S Darley *Derby* 76–80; R Hasland 80–94; V Temple Normanton 80–94; rtd 94; PtO *Derby* 94–18. *32 Barry Road, Brimington, Chesterfield S43 1PX* T: (01246) 551020

ANDERSON, Ivo Berisov. BA 03. **d** 15 **p** 16. OLM Stratford St Paul and St Jas *Chelmsf* 15–16; C 16–19; V from 19. *St Paul's Vicarage, Maryland Road, London E15 1JL* T: (020) 8923 4432 M: 07460-125933 E: rev.ivo.anderson@gmail.com

ANDERSON, James. b 36. Magd Coll Ox BA 59 MA 64 Leeds Univ MA 00. **d** 02 **p** 03. NSM Holme and Seaton Ross Gp *York* 02–08; P-in-c The Beacon 08–20; PtO 20–21. *61 Moor Lane, Carnaby, Bridlington YO16 4UT* T: (01262) 401688

ANDERSON, James Frederick Wale. b 34. G&C Coll Cam BA 58 MA 62. Cuddesdon Coll 60. **d** 62 **p** 63. C Leagrave *St Alb* 62–65; C Eastleigh *Win* 65–70; R Sherfield-on-Loddon 70–86; P-in-c Stratfield Saye w Hartley Wespall 75–86; R Sherfield-on-Loddon and Stratfield Saye etc 86–87; R Newton Valence, Selborne and E Tisted w Colemore 87–99; rtd 99; Chapl Surrey Hants Borders NHS Trust 01–04; Hon C Farnham *Guildf* 01–04; PtO 07–21; *Win* from 11. *1 Potter's Gate, Farnham GU9 7EJ* T: (01252) 710728

ANDERSON, Canon James Raffan. b 33. Edin Univ MA 54 FRSA 90. Edin Th Coll 56. **d** 58 **p** 59. Chapl St Andr Cathl *Ab* 58–59; Prec St Andr Cathl 59–62; CF (TA) 59–67; Chapl Aber Univ *Ab* 60–62; Chapl Glas Univ 62–69; Chapl Lucton Sch 69–71; Chapl Barnard Castle Sch 71–74; Asst Dir of Educn *Blackb* 74–78; P-in-c Whitechapel 74–78; Bp's Officer for Min *Cov* 78–87; Hon Can Cov Cathl 83–87; Miss Sec Gen Syn Bd for Miss and Unity 87–92; rtd 92; PtO *Blackb* 98–13. *Bramble Cottage, Lower Quinton, Stratford-upon-Avon CV37 8SG* T: (01789) 721779

ANDERSON, Jane Alison. b 71. **d** 14 **p** 15. NSM Woodhorn w Newbiggin *Newc* 14–17; Chapl Newcastle upon Tyne Hosps NHS Foundn Trust 17–20; rtd 20; PtO *Newc* from 20. *52 Castle Way, Pegswood, Morpeth NE61 6XH* E: jalison.anderson@outlook.com

ANDERSON (née FLAHERTY), Mrs Jane Venitia. b 68. Oak Hill Th Coll BA 92. **d** 93 **p** 94. C Timperley *Ches* 93–97; C Cheshunt *St Alb* 97–99; P-in-c N Springfield *Chelmsf* 99–18; P-in-c Pleshey 16–17; P-in-c Woldsburn *York* 19–20; R from 20. *The New Rectory, West End, Bainton, Driffield YO25 9NR* T: (01377) 219471 E: revjaney@talktalk.net

ANDERSON, Jeffrey. b 56. Cranmer Hall Dur. **d** 07 **p** 08. C Chester le Street *Dur* 07–11; PtO 14–19; TV Gt Aycliffe from 19. *St Clare's Rectory, St Cuthbert's Way, Newton Aycliffe DL5 5NT* T: (01325) 315194 E: jeff.and@btinternet.com

ANDERSON, Jeremy Dudgeon. b 41. Edin Univ BSc 63. Trin Coll Bris 75. **d** 77 **p** 78. C Bitterne *Win* 77–81; TV Wexcombe *Sarum* 81–91; Evang Enabler (Reading Deanery) *Ox* 91–96; V Epsom Common Ch Ch *Guildf* 96–00; C Kinson *Sarum* 00–06; rtd 06; PtO *Chich* 12–17. *The Croft, Church Road, Crowborough TN6 1ED* T: (01892) 655825

ANDERSON, Mrs Joanna Elisabeth. b 53. St Andr Univ MTheol 75. EMMTC 85. **d** 88 **p** 95. Par Dn Crosby *Linc* 88–92; Warden Iona Community *Arg* 92–95; R S Trin Broads *Nor* 95–02; Dir Body, Mind, Spirit Project 02–05; R Stiffkey and Bale *Nor* 05–09; C Hexham *Newc* 09–12; Is Cen Dir Iona Community *Arg* 12–15; TV Dudley *Worc* 15–18; rtd 18; PtO *York* from 20. *31 Middleton Road, Pickering YO18 8AN* T: (01751) 623304 M: 07774-446880 E: revjoannacam@gmail.com

ANDERSON, Julie. b 60. St Jo Coll Nottm 09. **d** 11 **p** 12. C Liv Ch Ch Norris Green 11–14; P-in-c Long Stanton w St Mich *Ely* 14–18; P-in-c Over 14–18; P-in-c Willingham 16–18; P-in-c Lolworth 17–18; P-in-c Swavesey 17–18; R Newsome and Armitage Bridge and S Crosland *Leeds* from 18; AD Almondbury and Kirkburton from 20. *The Vicarage, 42 Beaumont Park Road, Huddersfield HD4 5JS* E: julie_anderson51@yahoo.co.uk

ANDERSON, Canon Keith Bernard. b 36. Qu Coll Cam BA 60 MA 64. Tyndale Hall Bris 60. **d** 62 **p** 63. C Bootle St Leon *Liv* 62–65; Lect Can Warner Mem Coll Buye Burundi 66–73; Dir Th Educn by Ext Studies Dio Nakuru Kenya 74–77; Dir Th by Ext Studies Mt Kenya E 78–82; Hon Can Mt Kenya E from 82; P-in-c Newnham and Doddington w Wychling *Cant* 83–88; Chapl Cannes w Grasse *Eur* 88–94; Dir and Chapl Mulberry Ho High Ongar 94–95; TV Horley *S'wark* 96–01; rtd 01; PtO *S'wark* 01–05; *Chich* from 01. *93 Rusper Road, Horsham RH12 4BJ* T: (01403) 262185 E: kb.anderson@virgin.net

ANDERSON, Canon Keith Edward. b 42. Fitzw Coll Cam BA 77 MA 83 MRCS 83. Ridley Hall Cam 74. **d** 77 **p** 78. C Goodmayes All SS *Chelmsf* 77–80; Chapl Coll of SS

Mark and Jo Plymouth *Ex* 80–87; RD Plymouth Moorside 83–86; V Northampton H Sepulchre w St Andr and St Lawr *Pet* 87–98; RD Northn 92–98; Adv for Min Willesden *Lon* 98–03; Can Res Win Cathl and Adv for Ord Min Development *Win* 03–08; rtd 08; PtO *Win* from 08. *49 Chaundler Road, Winchester SO23 7HW* T: (01962) 853429 E: keith.anderson20@btinternet.com

ANDERSON, Mark Stuart. b 73. UEA BA 95 Lon Inst of Educn PGCE 05. St Mellitus Coll BA 17. **d** 17 **p** 18. C Oxted *S'wark* from 17. *St Mary's Church Office, Oxted Community Hall, 53 Church Lane, Oxted RH8 9NB* M: 07480-067756 E: oxtedcurate@gmail.com

ANDERSON, Martin Edward. b 73. Humberside Univ BA 95 St Jo Coll Dur BA 02. Cranmer Hall Dur 99. **d** 02 **p** 03. C Gt Aycliffe and Chilton *Dur* 02–05; TV Sunderland 05–07; Chapl Sunderland Minster 07–13; P-in-c Norton St Mary from 13; P-in-c Norton St Mich from 13. *2 Brambling Close, Norton, Stockton-on-Tees TS20 1TX* E: revmartin@outlook.com

ANDERSON, Canon Michael Garland. b 42. Clifton Th Coll 62. **d** 66 **p** 67. C Fareham St Jo *Portsm* 66–69; C Worting *Win* 69–74; V Hordle 74–07; RD Lyndhurst 82–00; Hon Can Win Cathl 92–07; rtd 07; PtO *Win* from 07. *20 Forestlake Avenue, Ringwood BH24 1QU* T: (01425) 471490

ANDERSON, Mrs Pearl Ann. b 46. St Andr Univ MA 68 MCIPD 74. Cant Sch of Min 90. **d** 93 **p** 00. Par Dn Epping St Jo *Chelmsf* 93–95; Adv to Coun for Soc Resp Roch and Cant 95–02; Asst Chief Exec Ch in Soc Roch and Cant 02–06; PtO *Roch* 95–02; Hon C Biddenden and Smarden Cant 00–06; rtd 06; PtO *Cant* from 06. *1 Gibbs Hill, Headcorn, Ashford TN27 9UD* T: (01622) 890043 M: 07811-209448 E: pearlaanderson@btinternet.com

ANDERSON, Peter John. b 44. Nottm Univ BA 65 BA 73 Ex Univ CertEd 66. St Jo Coll Nottm. **d** 74 **p** 75. C Otley *Bradf* 74–77; TV Marfleet *York* 77–84; V Greasbrough *Sheff* 84–95; I Clonmel Union *C, C & R* 95–02; I Rathcooney Union 95–02; Chapl Cannes *Eur* 02–09; rtd 09; PtO *Eur* 17–19. *23 Kentsford Road, Grange-over-Sands LA11 7AP* T: 07426-823940 E: pjhmander@yahoo.com

ANDERSON, Canon Philip Gregory. b 80. Keble Coll Ox BA 01. Ripon Coll Cuddesdon BA 04. **d** 05 **p** 06. C Prescot *Liv* 05–09; Chapl Liv Hope Univ 09–12; P-in-c Pemberton St Jo *Liv* 12–15; V 15–19; TV Wigan 20–21; AD 17–21; Can Res and Prec Liv Cathl from 21. *2 Cathedral Close, Liverpool L1 7BR* T: 0151-702 7203 E: philip.anderson@liverpoolcathedral.org.uk

ANDERSON, Canon Roderick Stephen. b 43. Cant Univ (NZ) BSc 63 PhD 67 New Coll Ox BA 72. Wycliffe Hall Ox 70. **d** 73 **p** 74. C Bradf Cathl 73–75; C Allerton 76–78; V Cottingley 78–94; V Heaton St Barn 94–09; C 09–11; RD Airedale 88–95; Chapl Bradf Univ and Bradf Coll 04–11; Hon Can Bradf Cathl 94–11; rtd 11; PtO *Bradf* 11–14; *Leeds* from 14. *40 Low Wood, Wilsden, Bradford BD15 0JS* M: 07900-675350

ANDERSON, Stephen George. b 54. Liv Univ BA 75 ACIB. NOC 05. **d** 08 **p** 09. NSM Gt Shelford *Ely* 08–12; PtO 12–14; NSM Cambridge St Clem 14–16; PtO 16–17; P-in-c Cambridge St Botolph 17–21; rtd 21; PtO *Eur* 12–17 and from 18. *Address temp unknown* M: 07889-003588 E: fr.stephen.anderson@gmail.com

ANDERSON, Timothy George. b 59. Ealing Coll of HE BA 82. Wycliffe Hall Ox 83. **d** 86 **p** 87. C Harold Wood *Chelmsf* 86–90; C Whitfield *Derby* 90–95; P-in-c Wolverhampton St Luke *Lich* 95–98; V 98–01; I Dundonald *D & D* from 01. *St Elizabeth's Rectory, 26 Ballyregan Road, Dundonald, Belfast BT16 1HY* T: (028) 9048 3153 *or* 9048 2644 E: t.j.anderson@btinternet.com

ANDERSON-MacKENZIE, Janet Melanie. b 70. Edin Univ BSc 93 PhD 97 Trin Coll Bris MA 07. WEMTC 01. **d** 04 **p** 05. C Woolavington w Cossington and Bawdrip *B & W* 04–05; C Wellington and Distr 05–08; P-in-c Box w Hazlebury and Ditteridge *Bris* from 08; C Colerne w N Wraxall from 11. *The Vicarage, Church Lane, Box, Corsham SN13 8NR* T/F: (01225) 744458 E: janet@anderson-mackenzie.co.uk

ANDERTON, Christopher David. b 86. Hertf Coll Ox MBiochem 09. Oak Hill Th Coll BA 17. **d** 17 **p** 18. C Blackb Redeemer 17–21; V from 21. *The Vicarage, 2 Kendall Close, Blackburn BB2 4FB* M: 07951-695257 E: christopher.anderton@gmail.com *or* chris.anderton@the-redeemer.org.uk

ANDERTON, David Edward. b 60. Leeds Poly BSc 92. St Jo Coll Nottm 02. **d** 04 **p** 05. C Daybrook *S'well* 04–06; C Hucknall Torkard 06–09; TV Newark w Coddington 09–16; V Collier Row St Jas and Havering-atte-Bower *Chelmsf* from 16; P-in-c Noak Hill from 21. *24 Lower Bedfords Road, Romford RM1 4DG* M: 07751-269412

ANDERTON, Elaine Irene. *See* de JONGE, Elaine Irene

ANDERTON, Peter. b 45. Sarum & Wells Th Coll 80. **d** 82 **p** 83. C Adel *Ripon* 82–86; P-in-c Dacre w Hartwith 86–90; P-in-c Thornthwaite w Thruscross and Darley 88–90; V Dacre w Hartwith and Darley w Thornthwaite 90–91; V Owton Manor *Dur* 91–02; V Torrisholme *Blackb* 02–03; P-in-c Hunslet St Mary *Ripon* 03; V Hunslet w Cross Green 03–07; rtd 07; PtO *Dur* from 09. *12 School Street, Darlington DL3 0UG* T: (01325) 465841 E: fatherpeteranderton@gmail.com

ANDREW, Christopher John. b 61. Cen Lancs Univ BA 87. St Mich Coll Llan 01. **d** 03 **p** 04. C Bingley H Trin *Bradf* 03–07; PtO 07–10; *Derby* 11–18; *Ches* 15–18; C Morton and Stonebroom w Shirland *Derby* 18–20; PtO from 20. *Garden Apartment, 3A Broad Walk, Buxton SK17 6JE* E: chris.mx@live.co.uk

ANDREW, David Geoffrey. b 64. St Mellitus Coll 20. **d** 21. C Stoneleigh *Guildf* from 21. *59 Stoneleigh Park Road, Epsom KT19 0QU* M: 07870-174888 E: geoffa2000@yahoo.co.uk

ANDREW, David Neil. b 62. Down Coll Cam BA 83 MA 87 PhD 88. Ridley Hall Cam 93. **d** 93 **p** 94. C Heatherlands St Jo *Sarum* 93–98; P-in-c White Waltham w Shottesbrooke *Ox* 98–18; P-in-c Waltham St Lawrence 07–11; NSM Maidenhead St Andr and St Mary 18–19; NSM Chesterton St Geo *Ely* from 19. *46 Kings Hedges Road, Cambridge CB4 2PA*

ANDREW, David Shore. b 39. Liv Univ BA 61 CertEd 62. OLM course 97. **d** 99 **p** 00. NSM Birkenshaw w Hunsworth *Wakef* 99–09; PtO *Leeds* 09–17; *Ches* from 18. *25 Summers Way, Knutsford WA16 9AP* T: (01565) 228921

ANDREW, Donald. b 35. Tyndale Hall Bris 63. **d** 66 **p** 67. C Croydon Ch Ch Broad Green *Cant* 66–69; C Ravenhead *Liv* 69–72; Scripture Union 72–77; V Rushen *S & M* 77–82; TR Heworth H Trin *York* 82–00; rtd 00; PtO *York* 05–15. *Address temp unknown*

ANDREW, Jeremy Charles Edward. b 68. St Jo Coll Dur BA 01. Cranmer Hall Dur 98. **d** 01 **p** 02. C Newquay *Truro* 01–04; P-in-c Perranzabuloe 04–10; P-in-c Crantock 05–06; C Crantock w Cubert 06–07; P-in-c 07–10; V Perranzabuloe and Crantock w Cubert 10–14; Dioc Dir of Ords 12–14; P-in-c Warmley, Syston and Bitton *Bris* 14–15; R from 15; AD Kingswood and S Glos from 19. *The Vicarage, Church Avenue, Warmley, Bristol BS30 5JJ* T: 0117-967 2724 E: j.andrew.102@btinternet.com

ANDREW, Jonathan William. b 50. Univ Coll Ox MA 78 FCA 80. Ripon Coll Cuddesdon 02. **d** 04 **p** 05. NSM Hersham *Guildf* 04–19; PtO from 19. *Orchard, 6 Westacres, Esher KT10 9JE* T: (01372) 479776 M: 07968-765188 E: jonathanandrew@stpetershersham.com

ANDREW, Paul Roland. b 70. Oak Hill Th Coll BA 06. **d** 06 **p** 07. C Plymouth Em, St Paul Efford and St Aug *Ex* 06–09; Chapl RN from 09. *Royal Naval Chaplaincy Service Headquarters, Tanner Building, HMS Excellent, Whale Island, Portsmouth PO2 8ER* T: 0300-157 7544

ANDREW, The Ven Philip John. b 62. Nottm Univ BSc 84. St Jo Coll Nottm MTh 02. **d** 02 **p** 03. C Reading Greyfriars *Ox* 02–06; V Reigate St Mary *S'wark* 06–17; Hon Can S'wark Cathl 16–17; Adn Cheltenham *Glouc* from 17. *8 Grace Gardens, Cheltenham GL51 6QE* M: 07498-052045 E: archdchelt@glosdioc.org.uk

ANDREW, Sydney William. b 55. Cranmer Hall Dur 82. **d** 85 **p** 86. C Horncastle w Low Toynton *Linc* 85–88; V Worlaby 88–93; V Bonby 88–93; V Elsham 88–93; rtd 93; LtO *Linc* 93–95; Hon C Brocklesby Park 95–04; Hon C Croxton 96–04; Hon C Caistor Gp 04–18; Hon C Caistor from 18. *10 Bentley Lane, Grasby, Barnetby DN38 6AW* T: (01652) 628586 E: sbec@revdoc.plus.com

ANDREWES, Nicholas John. b 64. Southn Univ BA 87 Man Univ MA 01 La Sainte Union Coll PGCE 88. Cranmer Hall Dur BTh 93. **d** 96 **p** 97. C Dovecot Liv 90–03; V Pendleton *Man* 00–03; P-in-c Lower Crumpsall w Cheetham St Mark 03–10; P-in-c Oldham St Paul 10–14; V Oldham St Paul and Werneth from 14; AD Oldham W 17–21. *St Paul's Vicarage, 55 Belgrave Road, Oldham OL8 1LU* T: 0161-624 1068 E: rev.nick@andrewes.org

ANDREWS, Benjamin. b 75. St Steph Ho Ox 97. **d** 00 **p** 01. C Whitchurch *Llan* 00–03; C Newton Nottage 03–05; C Cardiff St Mary and St Steph w St Dyfrig etc 05–12; R Cadoxton-juxta-Barry 12–16; TR Parish 16–20; TV Aberavon from 20. *St Theodore's Vicarage, Talbot Road, Port Talbot SA13 1LB* T: (01639) 883123 E: vicar@parishofaberavon.org

ANDREWS, Canon Brian Keith. b 39. Keble Coll Ox BA 62 MA 69. Coll of Resurr Mirfield 62. **d** 64 **p** 65. C Is of Dogs Ch Ch and St Jo w St Luke *Lon* 64–68; C Hemel Hempstead *St Alb* 68–71; TV 71–79; V Abbots Langley 79–88; RD Watford 88–94; Hon Can St Alb 94–05; rtd 05; PtO *Glouc* from 06. *High Pleck, Littleworth, Amberley, Stroud GL5 5AG* T: (01453) 873068

ANDREWS, Canon Christopher Paul. b 47. Fitzw Coll Cam BA 70 MA 73. Westcott Ho Cam 69. **d** 72 **p** 73. C Croydon St Jo *Cant* 72–75; C Gosforth All SS *Newc* 75–79; TV Newc Epiphany 80–87; RD Newc Cen 82–87; V Alnwick 87–96; Chapl Alnwick Infirmary 87–96; R Grantham St Wulfram *Linc* 96–13; P-in-c Grantham, Manthorpe 11–13; RD Grantham 09–11; Can and Preb Linc Cathl 04–13; Chapl United Lincs Hosps NHS Trust 99–01; rtd 13; Chapl to The Queen 09–17; PtO *St E* from 14. *74 Daisy Avenue, Bury St Edmunds IP32 7PH* T: (01284) 723785 E: candrews3007@gmail.com

ANDREWS, Clive Frederick. b 43. St Jo Coll Nottm 81. **d** 83 **p** 84. C Leic St Jas 83–86; Ind Chapl 86–90; Hon TV Melton Gt Framland 89–90; TV Clifton *S'well* 90–92; P-in-c Gamston w Eaton and W Drayton 92–98; R 94–08; P-in-c Elkesley w Bothamsall 92–08; Chapl Bramcote Sch Notts 92–08; rtd 08; PtO *S'well* 10–21. *15 Oakwood Grove, Edwinstowe, Mansfield NG21 9JT* E: cliveand@waitrose.com

ANDREWS, David Jonathan. b 85. Kent Univ BA 07 Northn Univ MA 16. St Mellitus Coll 19. **d** 21. C Church Stretton *Heref* from 21. *26 Churchill Road, Church Stretton SY6 6AE* T: (01694) 721355 E: david.andrews@strettonparish.org.uk *or* davidjandrews@pm.me

ANDREWS, Edward Robert. b 33. Brasted Th Coll 60 St Mich Coll Llan 62. **d** 64 **p** 65. C Kingswinford St Mary *Lich* 64–69; Chapl RAF 69–88; R St Just-in-Roseland w Philleigh *Truro* 88–99; rtd 99; PtO *Ex* 00–21. *2 Ingleside, Gunsdown Villas, Station Road, South Molton EX36 3EA* T: (01769) 572386

ANDREWS, Mrs Jean. b 48. Leic Univ BSc 70. NTMTC. **d** 10 **p** 11. NSM Downham w S Hanningfield *Chelmsf* 10–11; NSM Downham w S Hanningfield and Ramsden Bellhouse from 11. *3 Sewards End, Wickford SS12 9PB* T: (01268) 733817 E: jean@rjandrews.me.uk

ANDREWS, Preb John Colin. b 47. Open Univ BA 93. Sarum & Wells Th Coll 78. **d** 80 **p** 81. C Burnham *B & W* 80–84; V Williton 84–92; P-in-c Ashwick w Oakhill and Binegar 92–02; Dioc Communications Officer 92–12; TV Yatton Moor 02–12; Preb Wells Cathl 04–12; rtd 12; PtO *B & W* from 12. *Cherry Tree House, Kenn Street, Kenn, Clevedon BS21 6TN* T: (01275) 877806 M: 07971-484061 E: john.andrews150@btinternet.com

ANDREWS, John Elfric. b 35. Ex Coll Ox BA 59 MA 63. Wycliffe Hall Ox 59. **d** 61 **p** 62. C Pittville All SS *Glouc* 61–66; Cand Sec Lon City Miss 66–92; LtO *S'wark* 66–92; R Kingham w Churchill, Daylesford and Sarsden *Ox* 92–99; rtd 99; PtO *St E* 01–20. *4 St George's Road, Felixstowe IP11 9PL* T: (01394) 283557 E: jandsandrews@hotmail.co.uk

ANDREWS, John Francis. b 34. Jes Coll Cam BA 58 MA 62. S'wark Ord Course 78. **d** 81 **p** 82. NSM Upper Norwood All SS *S'wark* 81–87; NSM Dulwich St Barn 89–92; NSM S Dulwich St Steph 92–95; PtO 95–01; *Sarum* from 01. *1 Kennington Square, Wareham BH20 4JR* T: (01929) 555311 E: jeca.jfa@btinternet.com

ANDREWS, John George William. b 42. Qu Coll Birm 65. **d** 68 **p** 69. C Smethwick St Matt w St Chad *Birm* 68–71; CF 71–97; Asst Chapl Gen 95–97; QHC 95–97; P-in-c Lyme Regis *Sarum* 97–98; TV Golden Cap Team 98–03; rtd 03. *2 Sparnham Mews, West Street, Ashburton, Newton Abbot TQ13 7DU* T: (01364) 654101

ANDREWS, Judith Marie. b 47. Avery Hill Coll CertEd 68. **d** 00 **p** 01. OLM Wilford Peninsula *St E* 00–08; TV 08–15; rtd 15; PtO *St E* from 20. *Hillside, Tower Hill, Hollesley, Woodbridge IP12 3QX* T: (01394) 411642 E: judith.andrews@btopenworld.com

ANDREWS, Mrs Karen Margaret. b 59. Portsm Poly BSc 81 PGCE 82. All SS Cen for Miss & Min 17. **d** 19 **p** 20. NSM Kelsall *Ches* 19–21; C Marbury w Tushingham and Whitewell 21. *Castle View, Long Lane, Waverton, Chester CH3 7RA* T: (01244) 332028 E: karenmandrews5@gmail.com

ANDREWS, Margaret Jane. b 72. K Coll Cam MA 99. Westcott Ho Cam 18. **d** 21. C Putney St Mary *S'wark* from 21. *56A Burnbury Road, London SW12 0EL* M: 07811-430559 E: jane@janeandandy.plus.com

ANDREWS, Morey Alisdair Christopher. b 66. Leic Poly BSc 91 MRICS 91. St Jo Coll Nottm MA 99. **d** 99 **p** 00. C Yate New Town *Bris* 99–02; C Downend 02–06; V Eynsham and Cassington *Ox* 06–16; Miss Enabler Sedgemoor Deanery B & W from 16. *14 Tundra Walk, Bridgwater TA6 6FH* E: moreyandrews3@gmail.com

ANDREWS, Mrs Natalie Janis. b 78. Univ of Cen England in Birm BSc 00 Newman Univ MA 17. Ridley Hall Cam 10. **d** 12 **p** 13. C Loughborough All SS w H Trin *Leic* 12–13; C Loughborough Em and St Mary in Charnwood 13–14; C Loughborough Em 15; TV Ely 15–20; Project Officer Evang and Discipleship Abps' Coun from 20; PtO *Ely* from 21. *Church House, 27 Great Smith Street, London SW1P 3AZ* T: (020) 7898

1000 M: 07710-426744 E: revnatalieandrews@gmail.com *or* natalie.andrews@churchofengland.org

ANDREWS, Canon Paul Douglas. b 54. Univ of Wales (Abth) BLib 76 PhD 99. SAOMC. **d** 00 **p** 01. NSM Kempston and Biddenham *St Alb* 00–03; C Leighton Buzzard w Eggington, Hockliffe etc 03–05; TV Billington, Egginton, Hockliffe etc 06–08; P-in-c St Neots *Ely* 08–19; C Eynesbury 12–19; Min Ely St Pet Prop Chpl from 19; Asst Dir of Ords from 14; Hon Can Ely Cathl from 16. *15 Barton Road, Ely CB7 4DB* T: (01353) 656941 E: priest@elystpeterschurch.co.uk

ANDREWS, Peter Douglas. b 52. SEN 72 SRN 78. St Steph Ho Ox 86. **d** 88 **p** 89. C Perry Barr *Birm* 88–92; TV Swindon New Town *Bris* 92–98; V Streatham St Pet *S'wark* 98–19; rtd 19. *Meads, Musbury Road, Axminster EX13 5JR* T: (01297) 35605 E: frpeterandrews@aol.com

ANDREWS, Raymond Cyril. b 50. SEITE 00. **d** 03 **p** 04. C E Dulwich St Jo *S'wark* 03–07; P-in-c S'wark St Geo w St Alphege and St Jude 07–13; rtd 13; PtO *S'wark* 13–15; Chapl Greenwich and Bexley Cottage Hospice 13–15; TV Costa Blanca *Eur* 15–18; PtO from 18. *Carrer Sant Antoni 19, 03530 La Nucia, Alicante, Spain* E: revrayandrews@aol.com

ANDREWS, Canon Richard John. b 57. Bris Univ BA 78 CertEd 79. Ripon Coll Cuddesdon 82. **d** 84 **p** 85. C Kidderminster St Mary and All SS, Trimpley etc *Worc* 84–87; Chapl Derbyshire Coll of HE 87–89; Hon C Derby Cathl 87–89; V Chellaston 89–93; V Spondon 93–05; TR Dunstable *St Alb* 05–18; RD 09–14; Hon Can St Alb 17–18; Can for Liturgy Derby Cathl from 18. *Derby Cathedral Centre, 18-19 Iron Gate, Derby DE1 3GP* T: (01332) 341201 E: richard@derbycathedral.org

ANDREWS, Robert. *See* ANDREWS, Edward Robert

ANDREWS, Sharon Elaine. b 59. Qu Foundn Birm 16. **d** 18 **p** 19. NSM Glenfield and Newtown Linford *Leic* from 18. *13 Ainsdale Road, Leicester LE3 0UD* T: 0116-223 9265 E: sharon@stpetersglenfield.org.uk

ANDREWS, Stephen. b 69. **d** 11 **p** 12. OLM Gt Yarmouth *Nor* from 11; Chapl James Paget Univ Hosps NHS Foundn Trust from 17. *19 Forth Close, Caister-on-Sea, Great Yarmouth NR30 5UW* T: (01493) 377897 *or* 452408 M: 07973-468411 E: stephen.andrews@jpaget.nhs.uk *or* revdstephenandrews@gmail.com

ANDREYEV, Michael. b 62. Hatf Coll Dur BA 85. Wycliffe Hall Ox BA 93 MA 03. **d** 96 **p** 97. C Surbiton Hill Ch Ch *S'wark* 96–01; NSM Stapenhill w Cauldwell *Derby* 02–03; P-in-c 03–06; V from 06. *3 Stapenhill Road, Burton-on-Trent DE15 9AF* T: (01283) 530320 E: office@stpetersstapenhill.org.uk *or* andreyevs07@talktalk.net

ANETTS, Roy. b 55. Qu Coll Birm 06. **d** 09 **p** 10. NSM Acocks Green *Birm* 09–12; NSM Yardley St Cypr Hay Mill 12–13; P-in-c 13–17; P-in-c S Yardley St Mich 14–17; R Cupar *St And* from 17; R Ladybank from 17. *The Rectory of St James the Great, 13 Robertson Road, Cupar KY15 5YR* T: (01334) 653141 E: revroy@hotmail.com

ANGEL, Andrew Richard. b 67. St Pet Coll Ox BA 89 Surrey Univ MA 94 Cant Ch Ch Univ MA 06 Lon Inst of Educn PGCE 90. St Jo Coll Nottm PhD 04. **d** 02 **p** 03. C Dartford Ch Ch *Roch* 02–05; Tutor SEITE 05–10; Tutor St Jo Sch of Miss Nottm 10–16; V Burgess Hill St Andr *Chich* from 16; PtO *Eur* 11–16. *2 Cants Lane, Burgess Hill RH15 0LG* T: (01444) 232023 M: 07495-310768 E: vicar@standrewsbh.org.uk

ANGEL, Gervais Thomas David. b 36. Ch Ch Ox BA 59 MA 62 Bris Univ MEd 78 Lon Univ PGCE 72. Wycliffe Hall Ox 57. **d** 61 **p** 62. C Aberystwyth St Mich *St D* 61–65; Tutor Clifton Th Coll 65–71; Dean of Studies Trin Coll Bris 71–81; Dir of Studies 81–90; Area Sec (W and SW) SAMS 90–02; NSM Stoke Gifford *Bris* 92–02; rtd 02; PtO *Bris* from 02; *York* from 19. *Flat 1A, 9 Royal Crescent, Whitby YO21 3EJ* M: 07967-441426 E: gervais.angel@blueyonder.co.uk

ANGELICI, Ruben. b 80. S Nazarene Univ (USA) BSc 02 Man Univ BA 05 MA 06 Jes Coll Cam PhD 15 Edge Hill Univ PGCE 09. Westcott Ho Cam 11. **d** 15 **p** 16. C Sleaford *Linc* 15–17; C Linc St Jo 17–18; Chapl Denstone Coll Uttoxeter 18–19; V S Hinksey *Ox* 19–21. *Address temp unknown* M: 07741-453080 E: fr.ruben@outlook.com

ANGELL, Miss Elizabeth Patricia. b 54. Univ of Wales (Ban) BA 72. Trin Coll Bris BA 08. **d** 08 **p** 09. C Fosse Team *Leic* 08–11; TV Bridgnorth, Tasley, Astley Abbotts, etc *Heref* 11–16; R Whitwick, Thringstone and Swannington *Leic* 16–20; rtd 20; PtO *Glouc* from 20. *20 Sherwood Road, Tetbury GL8 8BU* T: (01666) 239361 E: angell304@btinternet.com

ANGIER, Patrick John Mark. b 61. Leic Univ BSc 83. Trin Coll Bris. **d** 03 **p** 04. C Stratford-upon-Avon, Luddington etc *Cov* 03–06; V Prestbury *Ches* from 06. *7 Northmead, Prestbury, Macclesfield SK10 4XD* T: (01625) 829288 M: 07971-923668

ANGLE, John Edwin George. b 42. Lon Bible Coll BD 65 Univ of Wales MEd 75 Liv Univ AdDipEd 73. WEMTC 92. **d** 94 **p** 95. NSM Clevedon St Andr and Ch Ch *B & W* 94–97; NSM Worle 97–98; P-in-c Camelot Par 98–01; R 01–06; Warden of Readers Wells Adnry 02–05; rtd 06; PtO *B & W* from 06. *2 Orchard Court, Claverham, Bristol BS49 4TB* T: (01934) 835521 M: 07970-968652 E: johnangle@btinternet.com

ANGUS, Canon Edward. b 39. Man Univ BA 60. Qu Coll Birm. **d** 62 **p** 63. C Chorley St Geo *Blackb* 62–65; C S Shore H Trin 65–68; R Bretherton 68–76; V Altham w Clayton le Moors 76–90; V Preesall 90–04; RD Garstang 96–01; Hon Can Blackb Cathl 98–04; rtd 04; PtO *Blackb* 04–17. *14 Lazenby Avenue, Fleetwood FY7 8QH* T: (01253) 686817 E: eandjandgus@hotmail.com

ANGUS, Mrs Sherine Victoria. b 74. Ox Brookes Univ BA 96 BA 12 UWE BSc 04. St Hild Coll 16. **d** 19 **p** 20. C Alford Gp *Linc* from 19. *55 South Street, Alford LN13 9AN* T: (01507) 824690 M: 07811-218086 E: sherineangus@yahoo.co.uk

ANI, Joel Osita. b 72. Qu Coll Birm BA 08. **d** 08 **p** 10. C Telford Park *S'wark* 08–09; C Clapham Park All SS 09–12; PtO *Lon* from 19. *27 Hornsey Park Road, London N8 0JU* M: 07903-234444 E: joel_ani123@yahoo.com

ANITA, Sister. *See* COOK, Anita Isabel

ANKER, Malcolm. b 39. Univ of Wales BA 61. Bps' Coll Cheshunt 61. **d** 63 **p** 64. C Marfleet *York* 63–66; C Cottingham 66–69; V Skirlaugh w Long Riston 69–74; V Elloughton and Brough w Brantingham 74–84; V Tadcaster 84–86; V Tadcaster w Newton Kyme 86–91; V Oatlands *Guildf* 91–05; rtd 05; PtO *Guildf* 05–13; *Sheff* from 15. *27 Ringstead Avenue, Sheffield S10 5SL* T: 0114-453 4858 E: malcolm.anker@gmail.com

ANKER-PETERSEN, Robert Brian. b 52. Aber Univ MTh 88. Wycliffe Hall Ox BA 79 MA 88. **d** 93 **p** 94. C Perth St Ninian *St And* 93–96; Bp's Researcher on Ch's Min of Healing 93–96; Dir Bield Retreat and Healing Cen from 93; Dioc Dir of Healing *St And* from 97. *Blackruthven House, Tibbermore, Perth PH1 1PY* T: (01738) 583238

ANKERS, Canon Charles William (Bill). b 42. FIMI. NEOC 89. **d** 93 **p** 95. NSM York St Luke 93–95; C Kexby w Wilberfoss 95–98; Asst Chapl HM Pris Full Sutton 95–98; V Norton juxta Malton *York* 98–11; Can and Preb York Minster 10–11; rtd 11; PtO *York* from 11. *10 Beechwood Road, Norton, Malton YO17 9EJ* T: (01653) 693930 E: canonbill-norton@hotmail.co.uk

ANKETELL, Jeyarajan. b 41. Lon Univ BSc 62 PhD 67 MInstP. Coll of Resurr Mirfield 69. **d** 73 **p** 74. Asst Chapl Newc Univ 73–75; Asst Chapl Lon Univ 75–77; Teacher 78–05; LtO *S'wark* 81–83; Chasetown High Sch 85–05; NSM Lich St Mary w St Mich 86–96; NSM Lich St Mich w St Mary and Wall 96–15; PtO 15–21. *7 Wissage Lane, Lichfield WS13 6DQ* T: (01543) 268897 E: jeyan.anketell@ntlworld.com

ANN-MARIE, Sister. *See* STUART, Ann-Marie Lindsay

✠ANNAS, The Rt Revd Geoffrey Peter. b 53. Sarum & Wells Th Coll. **d** 83 **p** 84 **c** 10. C S'wark H Trin w St Matt 83–87; TV Walworth 87–94; Warden Pemb Coll Miss Walworth 87–94; V Southampton Thornhill St Chris *Win* 94–10; Hon Can Win Cathl 07–10; Area Bp Stafford *Lich* 10–19; rtd 19; Hon Asst Bp Win from 20. *6 Hood Road, Southampton SO18 5PD*

ANNE, Sister. *See* PROUDLEY, Anne

ANNIS, Charles Richard Millar. b 86. Greyfriars Ox BA 08 Regent's Park Coll Ox BA 10 UEA MA 15 Leeds Univ MA 16. Coll of Resurr Mirfield 13. **d** 16 **p** 17. C Oldham St Mary w St Pet *Man* 16–19; PtO *Leeds* 21. *Community of the Resurrection, Stocks Bank Road, Mirfield WF14 0BN* M: 07546-773457 E: charlie.annis@gmail.com *or* cannis@mirfield.org.uk

ANNIS, Jennifer Mary. b 49. Middx Univ BA 95. Oak Hill Th Coll 92. **d** 95 **p** 97. NSM Digswell and Panshanger *St Alb* 95–97; NSM Codicote 97–98 and 99–00; Tanzania 98–99; Chapl ATC from 99; NSM Fishguard w Llanychar and Pontfaen w Morfil etc *St D* 10–18; NSM W Cemaes from 18. *Capel Newydd Dau, Dinas Cross, Newport SA42 0YB* T: (01348) 811121 E: jennie.annis@btinternet.com

ANNS, Pauline Mary. *See* HIGHAM, Pauline Mary

ANSAH, Canon Kwesi Gyebi Ababio (George). b 54. Oak Hill Th Coll BTh 97. Simon of Cyrene Th Inst 90. **d** 93 **p** 94. C Peckham St Mary Magd *S'wark* 93–96; V W Dulwich Em from 96; Hon Can Kumasi from 04. *Emmanuel Vicarage, 94 Clive Road, London SE21 8BU* T: (020) 8670 2793 M: 07771-783693 E: gkansa@aol.com

ANSCOMBE, John Thomas. b 51. Ex Univ BA 72. Cranmer Hall Dur. **d** 74 **p** 75. C Upper Armley *Ripon* 74–77; C Leeds St Geo 78–81; Exec Producer Scripture Union 81–96; Hon C Beckenham Ch Ch *Roch* 82–11; Dir Video Production Unit SA 01–16. *22 Hawthorndene Road, Bromley*

BR2 7DY   T/F: (020) 8462 4831   M: 07736-070160
E: john_anscombe@hotmail.com

ANSELL, John Christopher. b 49. Sarum & Wells Th Coll 79. **d** 81 **p** 82. C Dartford St Alb *Roch* 81–84; C Leybourne and Larkfield 84–88; TV Mortlake w E Sheen *S'wark* 88–98; V Mitcham SS Pet and Paul 98–14; rtd 14; PtO *Glouc* from 15. *Tankards Spring, High Street, Chalford, Stroud GL6 8DJ* M: 07974-432562 E: jsansell@hotmail.com

ANSELL, Mrs Mandy. b 47. **d** 04 **p** 05. OLM Rockland St Mary w Hellington, Bramerton etc *Nor* from 04. *44 The Street, Rockland St Mary, Norwich NR14 7AH* T: (01508) 538654 E: mandy.ansell44@gmail.com

ANSELL, Mark Stephen. b 68. Univ of Wales (Abth) BLib 89 Abth Univ PGCE 98. St Mich Coll Llan 12. **d** 14 **p** 15. C Henfynyw w Aberaeron and Llanddewi Aberarth etc *St D* 14–16; C Aberystwyth 16–17; TV 17–19; P-in-c from 19; AD from 19. *Fenton, Queen's Square, Aberystwyth SY23 2HL* T: (01970) 617849 E: revmarkansell@btinternet.com *or* mark@stmikes.net

ANSELL, Philip Harding. b 67. LMH Ox BA 89 Rob Coll Cam BA 92. Ridley Hall Cam. **d** 93 **p** 94. C Rainham w Wennington *Chelmsf* 93–97; C Rodbourne Cheney *Bris* 97–01; V Moseley St Agnes *Birm* from 01. *St Agnes' Vicarage, 5 Colmore Crescent, Birmingham B13 9SJ* T/F: 0121-449 0368 E: philip_ansell@live.co.uk

ANSLOW, Mrs Patricia Margaret. b 49. Yorks Min Course 08. **d** 11 **p** 12. NSM Bramham *York* from 11. *4 Pine Tree Avenue, Boston Spa, Wetherby LS23 6HA* T: (01937) 844789 M: 07903-262880 E: t.anslow@hotmail.co.uk

ANSON (née DRAX), Mrs Elizabeth Margaret. b 57. St Jo Coll Nottm 91. **d** 94 **p** 95. C Kimberworth *Sheff* 94–95; C Doncaster St Mary 95–97; rtd 97; PtO *Sheff* from 10. *62 School Green Lane, Sheffield S10 4GR* T: 0114-229 5478

ANSTEY, Nigel John. b 55. Cranmer Hall Dur 84. **d** 87 **p** 88. C Plumstead St Jo w St Jas and St Paul *S'wark* 87–91; TV Ipswich St Fran *St E* 91–97; TV Walthamstow *Chelmsf* 97–17; C Leyton St Mary w St Edw and St Luke 17–18; rtd 19; PtO *Chelmsf* from 19. *163 Larkshall Road, London E4 6PE* T: (020) 8529 9604 E: nigel.anstey@btinternet.com

ANSTICE, John Neville. b 39. Lon Univ BSc 63. Cuddesdon Coll 69. **d** 71 **p** 72. C Stonebridge St Mich *Lon* 71–74; Chapl Woodbridge Sch 74–76; TV Droitwich *Worc* 76–80; P-in-c Salwarpe 76–79; PtO *Chich* from 80; rtd 99. *5 Ash Grove, Wheathampstead, St Albans AL4 8DF* E: johnanstice@yahoo.com

ANTELL, Roger Howard. b 47. Lon Univ BD 71 Warwick Univ MSc 79 Ox Univ MTh 99. Ripon Coll Cuddesdon 97. **d** 99 **p** 00. C Ashchurch *Glouc* 99–03; R Stoke Prior, Wychbold and Upton Warren *Worc* 03–11; rtd 11. *Hafodwen, Dinas Cross, Newport SA42 0SG* T: (01348) 811391 E: roger.antell@btinternet.com

ANTHONY, Canon Ian Charles. b 47. NW Ord Course 76. **d** 79 **p** 80. NSM Lt Lever *Man* from 79; Dep Hd St Matt Primary Sch Lt Lever 79–97; Hd 97–07; Chapl St Ann's Hospice Manchester from 07; Hon Can Man Cathl 12–17; Dioc Officer for SSM 12–17. *36 Meadow Close, Little Lever, Bolton BL3 1LG* T: (01204) 791437 E: iancanthony@btinternet.com

ANTHONY, John Thomas. b 49. Trin Coll Carmarthen CertEd 71. **d** 15 **p** 16. NSM Cen Swansea *S & B* from 15. *11 Church Close, Neath SA10 7TF* T: (01639) 638434 E: johnanthony1@tiscali.co.uk

ANTHONY, Peter Benedict. b 79. Magd Coll Ox BA 02 MA 05 St Steph Ho Ox MSt 10 DPhil 15. St Steph Ho Ox 03 Ven English Coll Rome 05. **d** 06 **p** 07. C Hendon St Mary and Ch Ch *Lon* 06–09; Jun Dean St Steph Ho Ox 09–13; Jun Chapl Mert Coll Ox 10–13; P-in-c Kentish Town *Lon* 13–17; V 17–21; V St Marylebone All SS from 21. *All Saints' Vicarage, 7 Margaret Street, London W1W 8JG* T: (020) 7636 1788 M: 07949-005550 E: peterbanthony@hotmail.com

ANTHONY, Miss Sheila Margaret. b 79. Wycliffe Hall Ox BTh 04. **d** 04 **p** 05. C Bideford, Northam, Westward Ho!, Appledore etc *Ex* 04–08; P-in-c Bluntisham cum Earith w Colne and Woodhurst *Ely* 08–10; P-in-c Holywell w Needingworth 08–10; V Bluntisham cum Earith w Colne and Holywell etc from 10. *The Rectory, 6 Rectory Road, Bluntisham, Huntingdon PE28 3LN* T: (01487) 740456 E: sheila@saintintraining.net

ANTOINE, Emma Louise. b 72. Newc Univ BA 96. Westcott Ho Cam 02. **d** 05 **p** 06. C High Wycombe *Ox* 05–06; C Wokingham All SS 06–09; P-in-c Chorlton-cum-Hardy St Werburgh *Man* 12–14; PtO 14–18. *The Rectory, 6 Edge Lane, Manchester M21 9JF* T: 0161-881 3063 E: emma@mightyflood.org.uk

AOKO, Mrs Olushola Ibiwunmi. b 55. SEITE 03. **d** 06 **p** 07. C Bermondsey St Mary w St Olave, St Jo etc *S'wark* 06–11;

TV St Laur in Thanet *Cant* 10–17; TV Langley Marish *Ox* from 17. *Christ the Worker Vicarage, Parlaunt Road, Slough SL3 8BB* M: 07896-337578 E: shola_aoko@yahoo.co.uk

ap IORWERTH, Geraint. b 50. Univ of Wales (Cardiff) MPhil 90 Open Univ BA 78. Burgess Hall Lamp 69 Westmr Past Foundn 73 St Mich Coll Llan 73. **d** 74 **p** 75. C Holyhead w Rhoscolyn w Llanfair-yn-Neubwll *Ban* 74–78; R Pennal w Corris and Esgairgeiliog 78–12; rtd 12. *Oak Tree House, Dranllwyn Lane, Machen, Caerphilly CF83 8QS*

ap ROBERT, Rhun Gwynedd. **d** 14 **p** 15. C Aberavon *Llan* 14–17; TV 17–20; TV Neath from 20. *Y Ficerdy, 6 Trenewydd Rise, Cimla, Neath SA11 3TP* T: (01639) 417500 M: 07957-675918 E: vicar@parishofneath.org

ap SION, Tania. Ex Coll Ox BA 90 MA 96 Univ of Wales (Ban) MA 92 Warwick Univ PhD 10 Univ of Wales (Ban) PGCE 91. **d** 15 **p** 16. NSM Bro Tysilio *Ban* from 15. *Gelli Wen, Llanfairpwllgwyngyll LL61 6EQ* T: (01248) 715131 E: smc.taniaapsion@gmail.com

APARANGA, Herbert Okidi. b 59. Kingston Univ BA 97. Cranmer Hall Dur 10. **d** 12 **p** 13. C Blackheath St Jo *S'wark* 12–15; P-in-c Plumstead All SS 15–20; V from 20; Chapl Greenwich and Bexley Cottage Hospice from 15. *All Saints' Vicarage, 106 Herbert Road, London SE18 3PU* M: 07808-300795 E: h.o.okot@gmail.com *or* herbertaparanga@gbch.org.uk

APOKIS, Konstantinos Fotios. b 61. Monash Univ BA 82. Ridley Coll Melbourne BTh 87 ACT MTh 96. **d** 88 **p** 88. C Greythorn Australia 88–90; C Port Melbourne 90–91; P-in-c 91–10; Res Asst World Vision 93–95; Chapl Incolink Support Services Unit 96–99; Manager 96–99; Clergy Tr Officer *S'well* 10–12; Dir Educn and Tr CA 12; PtO *Sheff* 12–13; *Roch* 13–16; *Cant* 14–16. *1-17 College Crescent, Parkville VIC 3052, Australia* T: (0061) (3) 9349 0500 M: 07500-795477 E: capokis@sky.com

APOKIS, Sally-Ann. b 62. Dip Teaching. Ridley Coll Melbourne BMin 94. **d** 97. Chapl Camberwell Girls' Gr Sch Australia 97–00; Chapl Shelford Gr Sch 01–07; Chapl Melbourne Girls' Gr Morris Hall 08; Chapl Galilee Regional Catholic Sch 09; Asst Dn Port Melbourne H Trin 97–09; Chapl Sheff Univ 12–13; Hon C Crosspool 12–13; Chapl Medway Campus Kent, Greenwich and Cant Ch Ch Univ 13–16; Hon Can Roch Cathl 13–16; Chapl Qu Coll Melbourne Univ Australia from 16. *1-17 College Crescent, Parkville VIC 3052, Australia* T: (0061) (3) 9349 0500 M: (0061) 43-979 0480

APPADOO, Aneal Nathan. b 85. Oak Hill Th Coll BA 15. **d** 15 **p** 16. C Redhill H Trin *S'wark* 15–19; C Surbiton Hill Ch Ch from 19. *19 Dennan Road, Surbiton KT6 7RY* M: 07834-665887

APPELBE, Canon Frederick Charles. b 52. CITC 87. **d** 87 **p** 88. C Waterford w Killea, Drumcannon and Dunhill *C, F & O* 87–90; C Taney *D & G* 90–92; I Rathmichael 92–19; Can Ch Ch Cathl Dublin 02–19; rtd 19. *14 Bramble Glade, Ballinahinch, Ashford, Co Wicklow, A67 FD66, Republic of Ireland* T: (00353) (404) 40924 M: (00353) 87-248 2410 E: fcappelbe@gmail.com

APPIAH, Kuuku Andrew. b 77. Univ of Benin BSc 00 E Lon Univ MSc 14. Ridley Hall Cam 17. **d** 19 **p** 20. C Barkingside H Trin *Chelmsf* from 19. *32 Oakhurst Close, Ilford IG6 2LT* T: (01223) 678323 M: 07853-197937 E: rebuilding.in.christ@gmail.com

APPLEBY, Anthony Robert Nightingale. b 40. K Coll Lon AKC 62. St Boniface Warminster 62. **d** 63 **p** 64. C Cov St Mark 63–67; CF 67–95; R Dulverton and Brushford *B & W* 95–02; rtd 02; PtO *Ex* from 02. *19 Albatross Road, Exeter EX2 7SB* T: (01392) 874458 E: anthonyappleby@icloud.com

APPLEBY, David. b 60. St Jo Coll Dur BA 04. Cranmer Hall Dur 02. **d** 04 **p** 05. C W Acklam *York* 04–08; R Aylestone St Andr w St Jas *Leic* 08–14; TV Plymstock and Hooe *Ex* 14–21. *Address withheld by request*

APPLEBY, Janet Elizabeth. b 58. Bris Univ BSc 80 MSc 81 Newc Poly BA 90. Cranmer Hall Dur 01. **d** 03 **p** 04. C Newc H Cross 03–06; TV Willington 06–15; Dioc Ecum Officer 12–18; rtd 17; PtO *Newc* from 18. *38 Beech Grove, Whitley Bay NE26 3PL* E: jepd82@gmail.com

APPLEBY, Ms Jennie. b 58. Southlands Coll Lon CertEd 81. Cranmer Hall Dur 01. **d** 03 **p** 04. C Marton-in-Cleveland *York* 03–05; C Coatham and Dormanstown 05–08; R Emmaus Par Team *Leic* 08–14; TV Plymstock and Hooe *Ex* 14–17; TR from 17; RD Plymouth City from 20. *The Rectory, 5 Cobb Lane, Plymouth PL9 9BQ* T: (01752) 941844 E: applebyj5@gmail.com

APPLEBY, Mrs Melanie Jayne. b 65. RGN 86. Ripon Coll Cuddesdon 01. **d** 03 **p** 04. C Reddish *Man* 03–06; TV Wythenshawe 06–20; TR Egremont and Haile *Carl* from 20. *The Rectory, Grove Road, Egremont CA22 2LU* E: melanieappleby@hotmail.com

APPLEFORD, Kenneth Henry. b 30. Portsm Dioc Tr Course 91. d 92. NSM Portsea St Mary *Portsm* 92–00; rtd 00. *124 Stride Avenue, Portsmouth PO3 6HN* T: (023) 9281 4685

APPLEGATE, The Ven John. b 56. Bris Univ BSc 78. Trin Coll Bris PhD 85. d 84 p 85. C Collyhurst *Man* 84–87; Asst Chapl Monsall Hosp 84–87; C Broughton St Jas w St Clem and St Matthias *Man* 87–94; R Broughton St Jo 94–96; TR Broughton 96–02; AD Salford 97–02; Research Fell and Lect Man Univ from 00; Bp's Adv for Hosp Chapl 02–08; Adn Bolton 02–08; Prin SNWTP 08–12; Prin All SS Cen for Miss and Min from 12; PtO *Man* from 21. *University of Chester, Crab Lane, Warrington WA2 0DB* T: (01925) 534373 E: john.applegate@allsaintscentre.org

APPLEGATH, Canon Caroline Tracey. b 67. Lon Univ BMus 90 Edin Univ BD 94 MTh 07 MBACP. Edin Th Coll 91. d 94 p 95. C Edin St Martin 94–96; Hon C Edin St Pet 97–99; C 99–01; Chapl NHS Lothian 01–18; Prec St Ninian's Cathl *Edin* from 19; PtO *Edin* from 19; Hon Can St Mary's Cathl from 16. *Lauder House, 39 Jeffrey Street, Edinburgh EH1 1DH* T: 0131-556 3332 *or* 536 0144 M: 07889-981283 E: carrie.applegath@gmail.com *or* carrie.applegath@nhslothian.scot.nhs.uk

APPLETON, Mrs Bonita. b 55. Man Univ MA 08. St Jo Coll Nottm 91. d 93 p 94. C Camberley St Paul *Guildf* 93–96; Chapl Elmhurst Ballet Sch 95–96; TV Cove St Jo *Guildf* 96–03; Chapl Farnborough Sixth Form Coll 97–00; Dioc Par Resources Officer *Guildf* 03–10; NSM Knaphill w Brookwood 05–10; TR S Gillingham *Roch* 10–15; RD Gillingham 11–15; PtO 15–19; *Cant* 16–21; NSM Ashford Town from 21. *Elm Tree, Church Road, Kennington, Ashford TN24 9DQ* T: (01233) 646402 E: appletonbonnie@gmail.com

APPLETON, John Bearby. b 42. Linc Th Coll 74. d 76 p 77. C Selby Abbey *York* 76–79; C Epsom St Barn *Guildf* 79–82; V Linc All SS 82–94; rtd 02. *33 South End, Osmotherley, Northallerton DL6 3BN*

APPLETON, Ruth Elizabeth. *See* WALKER, Ruth Elizabeth

APPLIN, David Edward. b 39. Oak Hill Th Coll 63. d 65 p 66. C Ox St Clem 65–69; C Felixstowe SS Pet and Paul *St E* 69–71; LtO *Win* 71–91; Travelling Sec Ruanda Miss 71–74; Home Sec 74–77; Gen Sec 77–81; Dir Overseas Personnel Dept TEAR Fund 82–87; Overseas Dir 87–92; Hon C Kempshott *Win* 91–92; R Awbridge w Sherfield English 92–97; Exec Dir Samaritan's Purse Internat from 95. *27 Heath Lodge, Marsh Road, Pinner HA5 5PB* T: (020) 8429 2332

APPS, Bryan Gerald. b 37. Univ of Wales (Lamp) BA 59 St Cath Coll Ox BA 61 MA 65. Wycliffe Hall Ox 59. d 61 p 62. C Southampton St Alb *Win* 61–65; C Andover w Foxcott 65–69; P-in-c Freemantle 69–72; R 73–78; V Pokesdown All SS 78–03; rtd 03; PtO *Win* from 03. *14 Bartlett Drive, Bournemouth BH7 7JT* T: (01202) 418360 E: bryanapps@talk21.com

APPS, David Ronald. b 34. Univ of Wales (Lamp) BA 57. Sarum Th Coll 57. d 59 p 60. C Southbourne St Chris *Win* 59–62; C Weeke 62–67; V Alton All SS 67–80; V Charlestown *Truro* 80–97; Miss to Seamen 80–97; rtd 99; PtO *Ex* from 21. *12 Walnut Close, Exminster, Exeter EX6 8SZ* T: (01392) 824234

APPS-HUGGINS, Mrs Lorraine Georgina. b 63. Cant Ch Ch Univ BA 13. Local Minl Tr Course 07. d 10 p 11. OLM Deal St Geo *Cant* 10–14; NSM Downsfoot 14; V Shepherds Lees 14–17; Asst Chapl The Living Well 17–19; Chapl from 19; Bp's Adv for Healing and Wholeness *Cant* from 19. *Lenham Vicarage, Old Ashford Road, Lenham, Maidstone ME17 2PX* T: (01304) 842847 E: appshuggins@gmail.com

ARBER, Gerald Kenneth Walter. b 37. Open Univ BA 87. Oak Hill NSM Course 81. d 84 p 85. NSM Romford St Edw *Chelmsf* 84–95; NSM Cranham 95–14; PtO *Cant* from 13. *69 Parsonage Chase, Minster on Sea, Sheerness ME12 3JX* T: (01795) 872186 E: frgerryarber@btinternet.com

ARBUTHNOT, Paul Ian. b 81. TCD BA 03 MA 06 MLitt 07. CITC BTh 10. d 10 p 11. C Glenageary *D & G* 10–12; Chan V St Patr Cathl Dublin 11–12; PV Ch Ch Cathl Dublin *D & G* 11–12; Prec and Min Can St Alb Abbey 12–15; Min Can and Sacrist Westmr Abbey 15–17; I Cobh and Glanmire *C, C & R* from 18; Chapl Dioc Guild of Lay Min from 18; Min Can Cork Cathl from 19; Bp's Dom Chapl from 19. *The Rectory, Fota View, Ballycureen, Glounthaune, T45 Y898, Republic of Ireland* T: (00353) (21) 435 5208 M: 83-896 1465 E: paul.arbuthnot@gmail.com

ARCH, Ian Michael. b 75. Univ Coll Dur MSc 97 Peterho Cam BA 02. Westcott Ho Cam 00. d 03 p 04. C Bromborough *Ches* 03–05; Chapl Ches Univ 05–11; Dean of Chpl 10–11; V Marton, Siddington w Capesthorne, and Eaton etc 11–18; V Marton, Siddington w Capesthorne etc from 18. *The Vicarage, School Lane, Marton, Macclesfield SK11 9HD* T: (01260) 224447 E: revd.arch@gmail.com

ARCHER, David John. b 69. Reading Univ BSc 91 PhD 95 Cam Univ BTh 05. Ridley Hall Cam 02. d 05 p 06. C Abingdon *Ox* 05–09; R Purley from 09; AD Bradfield from 20. *The Rectory, 1 Westridge Avenue, Purley on Thames, Reading RG8 8DE* T: 0118-326 0839 E: david.archer@stmaryspurley.org.uk

ARCHER, Graham John. b 58. Lanc Univ BSc 79. St Jo Coll Nottm 82. d 85 p 86. C Ipswich St Matt *St E* 85–89; C Walton 89–95; P-in-c 95–99; Chapl Local Health Partnerships NHS Trust 96–99; P-in-c Portswood Ch Ch *Win* 99–05; V 05–12; P-in-c Portswood St Denys 00–02; Hon Can Win Cathl 11–12; Dir Min CPAS from 12; PtO *Cov* 13–15 and 18–21; LtO from 21; Acting Adn Malmesbury *Bris* 18–19. *CPAS, Unit 3, Sir William Lyons Road, University of Warwick Science Park, Coventry CV4 7EZ* T: 03001-230780 E: garcher@cpas.org.uk

ARCHER, Keith Malcolm. b 40. Man Univ BA 61 MA 81 PhD 91 Magd Coll Cam BA 67 MA 72. Ridley Hall Cam 66. d 68 p 69. C Newland St Jo *York* 68–72; Hon C Kersal Moor *Man* 72–79; Ind Chapl 72–93; V Weaste 93–09; TV Pendleton 08–09; TV Salford All SS 09–10; rtd 10; PtO *Man* from 11. *Flat 2, 86-88 Wellington Road, Eccles, Manchester M30 9GW* M: 07943-366502 E: keitharcher@hotmail.co.uk

ARCHER, Michael James. b 67. St Jo Coll Dur BA 90 St Edm Coll Cam PhD 95. Ridley Hall Cam 92. d 94 p 95. C Littleover *Derby* 94–97; C Edgware *Lon* 97–98; TV 98–01; P-in-c Bletchley *Ox* 01–08; R 08–13; P-in-c Portswood Ch Ch *Win* from 13; P-in-c Portswood St Denys from 16. *Highfield Vicarage, 36 Brookvale Road, Southampton SO17 1QR* T: (023) 8122 8151 E: mikearcher101@me.com

ARCHER, Neill John. b 61. UEA BA 82. NTMTC 96. d 99 p 00. C Ripley *Derby* 99–02; C Forster Tuncurry Australia 02–03; PtO *Lon* 03–04; P-in-c Malmesbury w Westport and Brokenborough *Bris* 04–16; C Gt Somerford, Lt Somerford, Seagry, Corston etc 09–16; V Malmesbury and Upper Avon 16–17; AD N Wilts 09–16; Chapl R United Hosps Bath NHS Foundn Trust 17–18; Chapl Univ Hosps Bris NHS Foundn Trust 18–20; Chapl Univ Hosps Bris and Weston NHS Foundn Trust from 20. *University Hospitals Bristol NHS Foundation Trust, Trust Headquarters, Marlborough Street, Bristol BS1 3NU* T: 0117-923 0000

ARCHER, Nicholas William. b 88. Univ Coll Lon BSc 11. St Steph Ho Ox BA 16. d 17 p 18. C Eastbourne St Sav and St Pet *Chich* 17–18; C Eastbourne St Mary 18; C St Leonards Ch Ch and St Mary etc from 18. *33 Park Lane Mansions, Eversfield Place, St Leonards-on-Sea TN37 6DD* E: nick@archer.gg

ARCHER, Norman Vivian. b 34. K Coll Lon AKC 57. d 60 p 61. C Baldock w Bygrave and Clothall *St Alb* 60–62; India 62–77; rtd 99. *29 Westcott Road, London SE17 3QY* T: (020) 7820 1725

ARCHER, Mrs Rachel Louise. b 72. Edin Univ BD 95 Moray Ho Edin PGCE 96. St Mellitus Coll MA 20. d 19 p 20. C Biggin Hill *Roch* from 19. *Address withheld by request* M: 07740-368225 E: rachel.vicarintraining@yahoo.com

ARCHER, Sarah Elizabeth. b 66. Charing Cross Hosp Medical Sch MB, BS 89 Heythrop Coll Lon MA 03 MRCGP 95. Ripon Coll Cuddesdon BA 99 MA 07. d 00 p 01. C Dulwich St Barn *S'wark* 00–03; C Shepherd's Bush St Steph w St Thos *Lon* 03–07; PV Westmr Abbey from 07; PtO *Lon* 07–08; *B & W* 08–11; NSM Bath Abbey w St Jas 11–15; V W Brompton St Mary w St Peter and St Jude *Lon* 15–16; Bp's Dom Chapl *Portsm* 16–17; PtO *Ex* 17–20; *Eur* from 18; *B & W* from 19; *Lon* 19–20; C N Harrow St Alb 20–21; V from 21. *Parish Office, St Alban's Church Hall, Norwood Drive, Harrow HA2 7PF* T: (020) 8429 1383

ARCHER, Sarah Jane. b 67. Dur Univ BA 89 Cam Univ PGCE 90. Win Sch of Miss 18. d 20 p 21. C N Stoneham and Bassett *Win* from 20. *36 Brookvale Road, Southampton SO17 1QR* T: (023) 8122 8151 M: 07846-230375 E: curate@nsab.org.uk

ARCHER, Simon Antony. b 65. Staffs Poly BA 90. Ripon Coll Cuddesdon 10. d 12 p 13. C Glouc St Paul and St Steph 12–16; TV Brierley Hill *Worc* 16–19; TV Kidderminster Ismere from 19. *22 Roden Avenue, Kidderminster DY10 2RF* M: 07815-164991 E: revsimonarcher@gmail.com

ARCHER, Simon Frank. b 75. d 16 p 17. C Erith Ch Ch *Roch* 16–19; P-in-c Belvedere All SS 19–20; V from 20. *All Saints' Vicarage, Nuxley Road, Belvedere DA17 5JE* T: (01322) 432169 M: 07506-464848 E: revsimonfarcher@gmail.com

ARCHIBALD, Peter Ben. b 83. Robert Gordon Univ Aber BSc 04. St Steph Ho Ox BTh 08. d 08 p 09. C Middlesbrough All SS *York* 08–11; Lead Chapl Middlesbrough Coll 09–11; P-in-c Kettering St Mary *Pet* 11–13; CF from 13. *c/o MOD Chaplains (Army)* T: (01264) 383430 F: 381824 E: frbenarchibald@gmail.com

ARDAGH-WALTER, Christopher Richard. b 35. Univ of Wales (Lamp) BA 58. Chich Th Coll 58. d 60 p 61. C Heavitree *Ex*

60–64; C Redcar *York* 64–67; C King's Worthy *Win* 67–69; C-in-c Four Marks 70–73; V 73–76; P-in-c Eling, Testwood and Marchwood 76–78; TR Totton 76–84; R The Sherbornes w Pamber 84–88; V Froyle and Holybourne 88–95; C Verwood *Sarum* 95–97; rtd 97; PtO *Win* 98–14; *Ox* 01–14; *Birm* 14–19. *1 Ashfield Gardens, Ashfield Road, Birmingham B14 7AS* T: 0121-449 9663 E: crawalter@btinternet.com

ARDILL, Robert William Brian. b 40. QUB BSc 63 PhD 67 SOSc. Ox NSM Course 80 St Jo Coll Nottm 84. **d** 83 **p** 85. NSM Sunninghill *Ox* 83–84; Hon Chapl R Holloway Coll *Lon* 83–84; C Lenton *S'well* 85–87; PtO *Leic* 92–95; C Harpenden St Nic *St Alb* 95–00; R N Tawton, Bondleigh, Sampford Courtenay etc *Ex* 00–10; rtd 10; PtO *Ex* 11–21. *8 Hanover Gardens, Cullompton EX15 1XA* T: (01884) 798386 E: brian.ardill@gmail.com

ARDING, Richard. b 52. ACIB 84. Oak Hill Th Coll 90. **d** 92 **p** 93. C Bromley Common St Aug *Roch* 92–96; V Wilmington 96–18; RD Dartford 07–13; rtd 18. *15 Mulberry Close, Tunbridge Wells TN4 9XR*

ARDIS, Canon Edward George. b 54. Dur Univ BA 76. CITC 76. **d** 78 **p** 79. C Dublin Drumcondra w N Strand and St Barn *D & G* 78–81; C Dublin St Bart w Leeson Park 81–84; I Ardamine w Kiltennel, Glascarrig etc *C, F & O* 84–89; Can Tuam Cathl *T, K & A* 89–03; Dean Killala 89–03; I Killala w Dunfeeny, Crossmolina etc 89–93; I Killala w Dunfeeny, Crossmolina, Kilmoremoy etc 94–03; Dir of Ords 95–03; I Dublin Irishtown w Donnybrook *D & G* 03–13; Dean's V Cork Cathl *C, C & R* from 13; Can Ch Ch Cathl Dublin *D & G* from 08; PtO *Eur* 16–17. *9 Dean Street, Cork, Republic of Ireland* T: (00353) (21) 241 6081 M: 87-637 6241 E: tedardis@yahoo.ie

ARDIS, John Kevin. **d** 06 **p** 07. C Dublin Ch Ch Cathl Gp *D & G* 06–08; Dean's V Cork St Fin Barre's Union *C, C & R* 08–11; Chapl Univ Coll Cork 11–13; I Abbeystrewry Union from 13; Bp's Dom Chapl from 14. *The Rectory, Coronea Drive, Skibbereen, Co Cork, Republic of Ireland* T: (00353) (28) 21234 M: 87-680 7289 E: abbeystrewryunion@gmail.com

ARDLEY, Annette Susan. *See* ROSE, Annette Susan

ARDOUIN, Timothy David Peter. Univ of Wales (Lamp) BA 94 Univ of Wales (Cardiff) MTh 08. St Mich Coll Llan. **d** 08 **p** 09. C Gorseinon *S & B* 08–11; P-in-c Llanrhidian w Llanyrnewydd 11–21; V N Gower from 21; Interfaith Officer *St D* from 16. *The Vicarage, Llanrhidian, Swansea SA3 1EH* T: (01792) 391353 M: 07871-420089 E: frtimardouin@btinternet.com

ARENS, Canon Johannes. b 69. Heythrop Coll Lon MTh 97. **d** 96 **p** 97. Old Catholic Ch Germany 96–04; TV Harrogate St Wilfrid *Ripon* 04–06; V Manston 06–11; Can Res Leic Cathl 11–20; Chapl De Montfort Univ from 19; C Leic H Spirit from 20; Hon Can Leic Cathl from 21; PtO *Eur* 16–21. *11 Dixon Drive, Leicester LE2 1RA* M: 07507-196629 E: fatherjohannes@gmail.com

ARGLES, Mrs Christine. b 57. Bris Univ BA 00. Trin Coll Bris 00. **d** 02 **p** 03. C Nailsea Ch Ch w Tickenham *B & W* 02–05; Chapl Weston Area Health NHS Trust 05–07; Chapl Cardiff and Vale NHS Trust 07–08; PtO *B & W* 08–17; Past Care Co-ord St Monica Trust Sandford Station 10–11; NSM Milton and Kewstoke *B & W* 17–18; rtd 18. *21 Hayward Avenue, West Wick, Weston-super-Mare BS24 7FR* T: (01934) 707291 M: 07763-476127 E: chrisargles@aol.com

ARGUILE, Canon Roger Henry William. b 43. Dur Univ LLB 64 Keble Coll Ox BA 70 MA 75. St Steph Ho Ox 69 Ripon Hall Ox 70. **d** 71 **p** 72. C Walsall *Lich* 71–76; TV Blakenall Heath 76–83; TV Stafford 83–95; P-in-c St Neots *Ely* 95–97; V 97–07; Hon Can Ely Cathl 01–07; RD St Neots 02–07; rtd 07; PtO *Nor* from 07. *10 Marsh Lane, Wells-next-the-Sea NR23 1EG* T: (01328) 711788 E: arguile@btinternet.com

ARGYLL AND THE ISLES, Bishop of. *See* RIGLIN, The Rt Revd Keith Graham

ARGYLL AND THE ISLES, Dean of. *See* CAMPBELL, The Very Revd Margaret Ruth

ARKELL, Kevin Paul. b 53. Leeds Univ MA 95 Preston Poly DipSW 81. Sarum & Wells Th Coll BTh 86. **d** 86 **p** 87. C S Petherton w The Seavingtons *B & W* 86–88; P-in-c Gt Harwood St Bart *Blackb* 88–90; V 90–95; TR Darwen St Pet w Hoddlesden 95–03; Acting RD Darwen 97–98; AD Blackb and Darwen 98–03; P-in-c Pokesdown All SS *Win* 03–11; P-in-c Bournemouth St Clem 08–11; V Newport St Thos *Portsm* 11–20; V Newport St Jo 11–17; Hon Can Portsm Cathl 18–20; rtd 20. *3 Rose in June Place, Mengham Avenue, Hayling Island PO11 9JB* M: 07971-800083 E: kevin@thearkells.co.uk

ARLIDGE, Canon Lucille Monica. b 56. WMMTC 04. **d** 07 **p** 08. NSM Birchfield *Birm* 07–11; PtO *Lich* 11–14 and 15–18; P-in-c Smethwick St Matt w St Chad *Birm* from 14; Hon Can

Birm Cathl from 16. *23 Willow Road, Great Barr, Birmingham B43 6LB* T: 0121-358 3321 E: lucyarlidge@yahoo.com

ARMAGH, Archbishop of. *See* MACDOWELL, The Most Revd Francis John

ARMAGH, Archdeacon of. *See* SCOTT, The Ven Terence

ARMAGH, Dean of. *See* DUNSTAN, The Very Revd Gregory John Orchard

ARMAN, Canon Brian Robert. b 54. St Jo Coll Dur BA 77. Cranmer Hall Dur 74. **d** 78 **p** 79. C Lawrence Weston *Bris* 78–82; C Bishopston 82–88; R Filton 88–15; P-in-c Horfield St Greg 03–05; Hon Can Bris Cathl 01–15; rtd 15. *59 Kenmore Crescent, Bristol BS7 0TP*

✠**ARMES, The Rt Revd John Andrew.** b 55. SS Coll Cam BA 77 MA 81 Man Univ PhD 96. Sarum & Wells Th Coll 77. **d** 79 **p** 80 **c** 12. C Walney Is *Carl* 79–82; Chapl to Agric 82–86; TV Greystoke, Matterdale and Mungrisdale 82–86; TV Watermillock 82–86; TV Man Whitworth 86–88; TR 88–94; Chapl Man Univ 86–94; P-in-c Goodshaw and Crawshawbooth 94–98; AD Rossendale 94–98; R Edin St Jo 98–12; Dean Edin 10–12; Bp Edin from 12. *Bishop's Office, 21A Grosvenor Crescent, Edinburgh EH12 5EL* T: 0131-538 7044 E: bishop@edinburgh.anglican.org

ARMITAGE, Richard Norris. b 51. Birm Univ PhD 10 AKC. St Aug Coll Cant 73. **d** 74 **p** 75. C Chapelthorpe *Wakef* 74–77; C W Bromwich All SS *Lich* 77–82; P-in-c Ketley 82–83; V Oakengates 82–83; V Ketley and Oakengates 83–89; V Evesham *Worc* 89–96; V Evesham w Norton and Lenchwick 96–05; RD Evesham 00–05; Chapl Wilts Constabulary *Bris* 05–16; rtd 16; PtO *Ox* from 17; *Bris* 17–19. *6 Witney Road, Long Hanborough, Witney OX29 8BJ*

ARMITSTEAD, Margaretha Catharina Maria. b 65. Free Univ of Amsterdam MA 89. SAOMC 00. **d** 03 **p** 04. C Littlemore *Ox* 03–06; P-in-c 06–20; V Littlemore w Sandford-on-Thames from 20. *The Vicarage, St Nicholas Road, Littlemore, Oxford OX4 4PP* T: (01865) 748003 *or* 779885 E: margreetarmitstead@btinternet.com

ARMITT, Andy John. b 68. Moorlands Bible Coll 88 Trin Coll Bris BA 00. **d** 00 **p** 01. C Millhouses H Trin *Sheff* 00–03; R Bisley and W End *Guildf* 03–20; Asst Chapl Doncaster and Bassetlaw Teaching Hosps NHS Foundn Trust from 20. *The Chaplaincy, Doncaster Royal Infirmary, Armthorpe Road, Doncaster DN2 5LT* T: (01302) 642237 M: 07725-516124 E: andyarmitt@gmail.com *or* andrew.armitt@nhs.net

ARMSTEAD, Canon Paul Richard. b 63. Ox Poly BA 85 ACA 89 FCA 99. St Steph Ho Ox BTh 11. **d** 08 **p** 09. C Northampton St Matt *Pet* 08–12; P-in-c Milton *Portsm* from 12; C Southsea H Spirit from 12; Can Ho Ghana from 18. *St James's Vicarage, 287 Milton Road, Southsea PO4 8PG* T: (023) 9273 2786 E: paularmstead@btinternet.com

ARMSTRONG, Adrian Christopher. b 48. LSE BSc 70 K Coll Lon PhD 80. EAMTC 84. **d** 87 **p** 88. NSM Linton *Ely* 87–95; P-in-c N and S Muskham *S'well* 95–00; P-in-c Averham w Kelham 95–00; PtO *B & W* 01–02; Hon C Wiveliscombe w Chipstable, Huish Champflower etc 02–06; Hon C Lydeard St Lawrence w Brompton Ralph etc 06–09; rtd 10; PtO *B & W* 15–18; *Dur* from 19. *11 The Paddock, Lanchester, Durham DH7 0HW* E: drmudpie@btinternet.com

ARMSTRONG, Alexander Milford. b 57. Local Minl Tr Course. **d** 95 **p** 95. NSM Livingston LEP *Edin* 95–97; C Cleator Moor w Cleator *Carl* 97–98; C Frizington and Arlecdon 97–98; C Crosslacon 98–99; V Westfield St Mary 99–10; P-in-c Aldingham, Dendron, Rampside and Urswick 10–17; rtd 17; PtO *Glas* 17–21; *Ab* from 21. *Innisfree, Bridge of Don, Aberdeen AB23 8BJ* M: 07762-215896 E: amvarmstrong@hotmail.com

ARMSTRONG, The Very Revd Christopher John. b 47. Nottm Univ BTh 75. Kelham Th Coll 72. **d** 75 **p** 76. C Maidstone All SS w St Phil and H Trin *Cant* 76–79; Chapl St Hild and St Bede Coll *Dur* 79–84; Abp's Dom Chapl and Dir of Ords *York* 85–91; V Scarborough St Martin 91–01; Dean Blackb 01–16; P-in-c Barrowden and Wakerley w S Luffenham etc *Pet* from 16. *The Rectory, 11 Church Lane, Barrowden, Oakham LE15 8ED* E: chris.armstrong@yahoo.com

ARMSTRONG, David Thomas. b 62. St Mellitus Coll BA 14. **d** 14 **p** 15. C Lexden *Chelmsf* 14–18; P-in-c St Botolph without Bishopsgate *Lon* 18–21; R from 21; PtO *S'wark* from 19. *42 Gilbert Road, London SE11 4NL* T: (020) 7588 3388 E: priest@botolph.org.uk

ARMSTRONG, Eileen. **d** 95 **p** 96. NSM Navan w Kentstown, Tara, Slane, Painestown etc *M & K* from 95. *Hennigan, Nobber, Co Meath, Republic of Ireland* T: (00353) (46) 905 2314 E: reveileen2@gmail.com

ARMSTRONG, John Edwin. b 51. Leic Univ CertEd 73 BEd 74. Ridley Hall Cam 91. **d** 93 **p** 94. C Fulbourn *Ely* 93–96; C Gt Wilbraham 93–96; C Lt Wilbraham 93–96; P-in-c Bassingbourn 96–02; V 02–04; P-in-c Whaddon 96–02;

V 02–04; P-in-c Southam *Cov* 04–16; P-in-c Ufton 04–16; RD Southam 08–11; C Kenilworth St Jo 16–17; rtd 17; Hon C Kenilworth St Jo *Cov* 17–19; PtO from 19; *Leic* from 20. *6 St Margaret's Drive, Leire, Lutterworth LE17 5HW* T: (01455) 202789 M: 07513-944468 E: revarmstrong@gmail.com

ARMSTRONG, John Gordon. b 64. Man Poly BSc 86 MSc 91 Man Univ MA 03. Wycliffe Hall Ox 95. **d** 97 **p** 98. C Pennington *Man* 97–01; P-in-c Holcombe and Hawkshaw Lane 01–07; TV Deane 07–18; P-in-c Bolton St Bede 16–18; R Wombwell *Sheff* from 18. *The Rectory, 1 Rectory Close, Wombwell, Barnsley S73 8EY* T: (01226) 891124 E: johngordonarmstrong1964@gmail.com

ARMSTRONG, Jonathan Oliver Lloyd. b 88. Middx Univ BA 21. Oak Hill Th Coll 18. **d** 21. C Hornsey Ch Ch *Lon* from 21. *Church Cottage B, Edison Road, London N8 8AE* M: 07584-072506 E: armstrongjol@gmail.com

ARMSTRONG (*formerly* READING), Mrs Lesley Jean. b 49. GNSM 70 Trent Park Coll of Educn CertEd 71. NOC 98. **d** 01 **p** 02. NSM Eccles *Man* 01–05; P-in-c Heywood St Jas 05–11; rtd 11; PtO *Man* 12–18; *Lich* from 19. *34 Stafford Road, Newport TF10 7LZ* T: (01952) 273210 M: 07760-202411 E: readinglesley@hotmail.com

ARMSTRONG, Mrs Margaret Betty. b 48. SRN 70 RSCN 71. Westcott Ho Cam 89. **d** 92 **p** 94. NSM Linton *Ely* 92–95; NSM Shudy Camps 92–95; NSM Castle Camps 92–95; NSM Bartlow 92–95; NSM N and S Muskham and Averham w Kelham *S'well* 95–00; P-in-c Lydeard St Lawrence w Brompton Ralph etc *B & W* 01–09; rtd 10; PtO *B & W* 15–18; *Dur* from 19. *11 The Paddock, Lanchester, Durham DH7 0HW*

ARMSTRONG, Canon Maurice Alexander. b 62. Ulster Poly BA 84. CITC 84. **d** 87 **p** 88. C Portadown St Mark *Arm* 87–90; I Sixmilecross w Termonmaguirke 90–95; I Richhill 95–01; I Tempo and Clabby *Clogh* from 01; Can Clogh Cathl from 12. *403 Tempo Road, Doon, Tempo, Enniskillen BT94 3GQ* T: (028) 8954 1232 M: 07704-518101

ARMSTRONG, Preb Nicholas Paul. b 58. Bris Univ BSc 79. Trin Coll Bris 91. **d** 93 **p** 94. C Filey *York* 93–97; P-in-c Alveley and Quatt *Heref* 97–98; R 98–15; RD Bridgnorth 13–15; V Tupsley w Hampton Bishop from 15; Preb Heref Cathl from 12. *The Vicarage, 107 Church Road, Hereford HR1 1RT* T: (01432) 353068 E: nicka@inbox.com

ARMSTRONG, Rosemary. *See* WYNN, Rosemary

ARMSTRONG, Susan Carol. b 64. Hull Univ BMus 85 Bretton Hall Coll PGCE 86 ALCM 82. St Hild Coll 19. **d** 21. NSM Rotherham *Sheff* from 21; NSM Masbrough from 21. *5 Farcroft Grove, Sheffield S4 8BP* T: 0114-249 7831 M: 07758-396904 E: suearmstrong2016@gmail.com

ARMSTRONG, Mrs Susan Elizabeth. b 45. **d** 05 **p** 06. OLM Tilstock, Edstaston and Whixall *Lich* 05–09; OLM Edstaston, Fauls, Prees, Tilstock and Whixall 09–15; OLM Whitchurch 13–15; rtd 15; PtO *Lich* 18–21. *Tarragon Cottage, Shrewsbury Street, Prees, Whitchurch SY13 2DH* T: (01948) 840039

ARMSTRONG, Mrs Valri. b 50. Man Univ BA 73. **d** 04 **p** 05. OLM Stoke by Nayland w Leavenheath and Polstead *St E* 04–13; NSM 13–18; rtd 18; PtO *St E* from 19. *Orchid House, 38 Bramble Way, Leavenheath, Colchester CO6 4UN* T: (01206) 262814

ARMSTRONG-MacDONNELL, Mrs Vivienne Christine. b 42. Open Univ BA 89 Ex Univ MEd 01 Lambeth MA 05. Ripon Coll Cuddesdon 88. **d** 90 **p** 94. C Crediton and Shobrooke *Ex* 90–93; Dioc Adv in Adult Tr 93–00; rtd 00; PtO *Ex* 00–07 and 09–19; Bp's Adv for Spirituality 07–09. *Strand House, Greenway, Woodbury, Exeter EX5 1LU* T/F: (01395) 232790

ARNALL-CULLIFORD, Jane Margaret. *See* CULLIFORD, Jane Margaret

ARNELL, Andrew. b 65. Hull Univ BA 88. **d** 19 **p** 20. NSM Hampstead Em W End *Lon* from 19. *65 Hale Grove Gardens, London NW7 3LT* E: andyarnell123@aol.com *or* andyarnell123@icloud.com

ARNESEN, Christopher **Paul**. b 48. Lon Univ BA 70 Sheff Univ MA 02. Sarum & Wells Th Coll 78. **d** 80 **p** 81. C Dalton-in-Furness *Carl* 80–83; C Ranmoor *Sheff* 83–86; R Distington *Carl* 86–93; TV Sheff Manor 93–97; Mental Health Chapl Sheff Care Trust 98–04; PtO *Sheff* 04–20; Bp's Adv in Past Care and Counselling 08–13; rtd 13. *39 Greystones Crescent, Sheffield S11 7JN* T: 0114-266 8836 E: paul.arnesen@me.com

ARNESEN, Raymond Halfdan (**Brother Ælred**). b 25. Qu Coll Cam BA 49 MA 54. Linc Th Coll 50. **d** 52 **p** 53. C Newc St Fran 52–55; SSF 55–66; Cistercian Monk from 66; Ewell Monastery 66–04; rtd 95. *2 Brentmead Close, London W7 3EW* T: (020) 8579 2074 E: aelred@arnesen.co.uk

ARNOLD, Briony Alice. *See* BOYDE, Briony Alice

ARNOLD, Christine Sabina. b 60. **d** 12 **p** 13. NSM St Peter-in-Thanet *Cant* 12–16; Asst Chapl The Living Well 16–17. *6 East Northdown Close, Margate CT9 3YA* T: (01843) 224449 E: chris.arnold06@btinternet.com

ARNOLD, David Alun. b 78. St Andr Univ MTheol 00 Leeds Univ MA 03. Coll of Resurr Mirfield 01. **d** 03 **p** 04. C Ribbleton *Blackb* 03–05; C Hawes Side and Marton Moss 05–07; Bp's Dom Chapl 07–12; V Adlington 12–21; P-in-c Chorley St Geo 17–18; AD Chorley 17–21; R Accrington St Andr, St Mary and St Pet and Church Kirk from 21; AD Accrington from 21; Asst Dir of Ords from 06. *St Peter's Vicarage, Willows Lane, Accrington BB5 0LR* M: 07786-168261 E: frdavidarnold@gmail.com

ARNOLD, Derek John. b 59. Wycliffe Hall Ox 01. **d** 03 **p** 04. C St Jo in Bedwardine *Worc* 03–06; TV Kidderminster St Jo and H Innocents 06–09; TR 09–14; P-in-c Ombersley w Doverdale 14–16; P-in-c Elmley Lovett w Hampton Lovett and Elmbridge etc 14–16; P-in-c Hartlebury 14–16; R Elmley Lovett w Hampton Lovett and Elmbridge w Rushock and Hartlebury and Ombersley w Doverdale 16–17; TR Appledore, Northam and Westward Ho! *Ex* from 17; RD Hartland from 19. *The Rectory, Fore Street, Northam, Bideford EX39 1AW* T: (01237) 721723 M: 07789-631346 E: darnold.rector@gmail.com

ARNOLD, Elisabeth Anne Truyens. b 44. TCert 66. **d** 91 **p** 94. OLM Ipswich St Thos *St E* 91–00; Chapl Dioc Min Course 00–01; OLM Tutor 01–06; rtd 06; PtO *St E* 06–19; *Bris* from 19. *6 Tallis Walk, Grange Park, Swindon SN5 6BQ*

ARNOLD, Frances Mary. b 64. R Holloway Coll Lon BA 86 Anglia Ruskin Univ MA 07 Dur Univ PGCE 90. Westcott Ho Cam 01. **d** 04 **p** 05. C Biggleswade *St Alb* 04–07; Exec Officer Abps' Coun 07–13; PtO *Lon* 08–13; V Sawbridgeworth *St Alb* 13–19; P-in-c Sutton *S'wark* from 19. *The Rectory, 34 Robin Hood Lane, Sutton SM1 2RG* T: (020) 8642 3499 E: rector.stnicholassutton@gmail.com

ARNOLD, Graham Thomas. b 62. Aston Tr Scheme 87 Ripon Coll Cuddesdon 89. **d** 92 **p** 93. C Margate St Jo *Cant* 92–95; TV Whitstable 95–00; PtO *S'wark* 07–09; NSM N Dulwich St Faith 09–12. *10B Franklin Road, London SE20 8HW* T: (020) 8289 0233 M: 07793-555017 E: grahamt62@btinternet.com

ARNOLD, Jane Elizabeth. b 50. **d** 11 **p** 12. NSM Kingswinford St Mary *Worc* 11–18; rtd 18. *9 Murdoch Drive, Kingswinford DY6 9HG* E: jane.arnold128@btinternet.com

ARNOLD, Sister Janet Rachel. b 64. **d** 14 **p** 15. CA from 88; C Woodchurch *Ches* 14–17; V Newchapel *Lich* from 17. *St James's Vicarage, 32 Pennyfields Road, Newchapel, Stoke-on-Trent ST7 4PN* T: (01782) 782837 E: vicar@stjamesnewchapel.co.uk

ARNOLD, The Very Revd John Robert. b 33. OBE 02. SS Coll Cam BA 57 MA 61 Lambeth DD 99. Westcott Ho Cam 58. **d** 60 **p** 61. C Millhouses H Trin *Sheff* 60–63; Chapl and Lect Southn Univ *Win* 63–72; Gen Sec Gen Syn Bd for Miss and Unity 72–78; Hon Can Win Cathl 74–78; Dean Roch 78–89; Dean Dur 89–02; rtd 03; PtO *Cant* from 02. *26 Hawks Lane, Canterbury CT1 2NU* T: (01227) 764703 E: arnold.jr@btinternet.com

ARNOLD, Jonathan Allen. b 69. St Pet Coll Ox BA 92 MA 99 K Coll Lon PhD 04 LTCL 89 LRAM 94. Ripon Coll Cuddesdon 03. **d** 05 **p** 06. NSM Chalgrove w Berrick Salome *Ox* 05–08; Chapl Worc Coll Ox 08–16; Dean Div and Fell Magd Coll Ox 16–19; Dir Communities and Partnerships Framework *Cant* from 19. *15 The Precincts, Canterbury CT1 2EL* T: (01227) 865228 M: 07939-093085 E: jarnold@diocant.org

ARNOLD, Mark James. b 75. Univ of Wales (Lamp) BA 97. St Mellitus Coll BA 17. **d** 17 **p** 18. NSM Sudbury St Andr *Lon* 17–20; NSM Pinner from 20. *108 Whittington Way, Pinner HA5 5JX* T: (020) 8966 9574 E: mjrarnold@hotmail.co.uk

ARNOLD, Mrs Norma. b 48. SNWTP 09. **d** 11 **p** 12. NSM Grassendale *Liv* 11–18; rtd 18. *28 Ambergate Road, Liverpool L19 9AU* T: 0151-427 2320

ARNOLD, Norman. *See* ARNOLD, Victor Norman

ARNOLD, Paul Andrew. b 79. Abth Univ LLB 01 Dur Univ MA 19 Barrister-at-Law (Gray's Inn). Ridley Hall Cam 15. **d** 18 **p** 19. C Preston-on-Tees and Longnewton *Dur* 18–21; P-in-c Stockton St Paul from 21. *The Vicarage, 65 Bishopton Road, Stockton-on-Tees TS18 4PE* M: 07784-780407 E: vicar@stpaulstockton.church

ARNOLD, Philip Robert. b 75. Qld Univ of Tech BN 96 Ches Univ MTh 10. St Jo Coll Nottm 07. **d** 09 **p** 10. C Pudsey St Lawr and St Paul *Bradf* 09–13; C Farsley 09–13; V Calverley Leeds 13–20; V Upper Armley from 20. *22 Hill End Crescent, Leeds LS12 3PW* T: 0113-808 0345 M: 07758-266922 E: revparnold@sky.com

ARNOLD, Canon Roy. b 36. St D Coll Lamp BA 62. **d** 63 **p** 64. C Brislington St Luke *Bris* 63–66; C Ches St Mary 67–70; V Brinnington w Portwood 71–75; V Sale St Paul 75–82; R Dodleston 82–84; V Sheff St Oswald 84–90; Dioc Communications Officer 84–97; Chapl w the Deaf 90–97; Hon Can Sheff Cathl 95–97; rtd 97; PtO *Ches* from 97. *49*

Crossfield Road, Bollington, Macclesfield SK10 5EA T: (01625) 575472

ARNOLD, Victor Norman. b 45. Oak Hill Th Coll 91. **d** 94 **p** 95. NSM Chigwell and Chigwell Row *Chelmsf* 94–98; C W Ham 98–04; C Hornchurch St Andr 04–10; rtd 10; PtO *Chelmsf* from 10. *Spring Cottage, 6 Spring Grove, Loughton IG10 4QA* T: (020) 8508 6572 E: standrews@me.com

ARNOLD-DAVIES, Mrs Elizabeth. Bp Grosseteste Coll TCert 58. St Mich Coll Llan 14. **d** 16. NSM Lampeter w Maestir and Silian and Llangybi and Betws Bledrws *St D* 16–19. *3 Queen Street, Aberaeron SA46 0BY* M: 07885-542524

ARNOTT, Preb David. b 44. Em Coll Cam BA 66. Qu Coll Birm 68. **d** 69 **p** 70. C Charlton St Luke w St Paul *S'wark* 69–73; C S Beddington St Mich 73–78; Chapl Liv Poly 78–82; V Bridgwater St Fran *B & W* 86–02; Preb Wells Cathl 00–02; V Yealmpton and Brixton *Ex* 02–09; P-in-c 09–11; RD Ivybridge 03–11; rtd 09. *14 Woodlands Avenue, Exmouth EX8 4QP* E: revdavid.arnott@btinternet.com

ARNOTT, Janine Beverley. b 69. Man Univ BSocSc 02 MRes 03 PhD 07 St Mellitus Coll MA 17. Cam Univ BTh 19. Ridley Hall Cam 17. **d** 19 **p** 20. C Stockport St Geo *Ches* from 19. *40 Beechfield Road, Stockport SK3 8SF* E: jba30@cam.ac.uk *or* rev.janinearnott@outlook.com

ARORA, Canon Arun. b 71. Birm Univ LLB 93 St Jo Coll Dur BA 06 Solicitor 96. Cranmer Hall Dur 04. **d** 07 **p** 08. C Harrogate St Mark *Ripon* 07–10; Abp's Dir of Communications *York* 06–09; Pioneer Min Wolv City Cen *Lich* 10–12; Dir Communications Abps' Coun 12–17; Public Preacher *St Alb* 13–17; V Dur St Nic from 17; Hon Can Dur Cathl from 21. *11 Beechways, Durham DH1 4LG* T: 0191-386 8346 M: 07984-334564 E: arunarora1@yahoo.co.uk

ARRAND, The Ven Geoffrey William. b 44. K Coll Lon BD 66 AKC 66. **d** 67 **p** 68. C Washington *Dur* 67–70; C S Ormsby w Ketsby, Calceby and Driby *Linc* 70–73; TV Gt Grimsby St Mary and St Jas 73–79; TR Halesworth w Linstead and Chediston *St E* 79–80; TR Halesworth w Linstead, Chediston, Holton etc 80–85; R Hadleigh w Layham and Shelley 85–94; Dean Bocking 85–94; RD Hadleigh 86–94; Adn Suffolk 94–09; Hon Can St E Cathl 91–09; rtd 09; PtO *St E* from 09; *Eur* from 10; *Linc* 17–20. *86 Broadway, Lincoln LN2 1SR* T: (01522) 826967 E: garrand@virginmedia.com

ARTHUR, Graeme Richard. b 52. Univ of NSW BCom 78 Heythrop Coll Lon MA 09. Linc Th Coll 93. **d** 93 **p** 94. C Witney *Ox* 93–97; R Westcote Barton w Steeple Barton, Duns Tew etc 97–18; rtd 18; PtO *Ox* from 19. *4 Margaret Road, Twyford, Banbury OX17 3JE* T: (01295) 812806 E: graemearthur0@gmail.com

ARTHUR, Canon Ian Willoughby. b 40. Lon Univ BA 63 BA 66 PGCE 64 Lambeth STh 94 Kent Univ MA 98. Ripon Coll Cuddesdon 78. **d** 80 **p** 81. C Kempston Transfiguration *St Alb* 80–83; R Potton w Sutton and Cockayne Hatley 83–96; P-in-c Sharnbrook and Knotting w Souldrop 96–98; R 98–04; RD Sharnbrook 97–04; Hon Can St Alb 99–04; rtd 04; PtO *St Alb* from 04; *Ox* 05–21; *Cov* from 09. *35 London Road, Chipping Norton OX7 5AX* T: (01608) 646839 E: iwarthur@btinternet.com

ARTHUR, Canon Kenneth Paul. b 64. Univ of Wales (Cardiff) BScEcon 86 Roehampton Inst PGCE 87 Cardiff Univ LLM 08. St Steph Ho Ox BTh 05. **d** 00 **p** 01. C Bodmin w Lanhydrock and Lanivet *Truro* 00–02; P-in-c Treverbyn and Boscoppa 02–06; P-in-c St Dennis from 06; RD St Austell 05–10; P-in-c Roche from 17; P-in-c Treverbyn from 17; Warden of Readers 05–10; Deputy Warden of Readers from 10; Dir Minl Formation and Development 06–16; Hon Can Truro Cathl from 13. *The Rectory, 16 Trelavour Road, St Dennis, St Austell PL26 8AH* T: (01726) 822317 E: clayparishes@gmail.com

ARTHY, Canon Nicola Mary. b 64. St Jo Coll Ox BA 85 MA 93. SEITE. **d** 00 **p** 01. C Guildf H Trin w St Mary 00–01; C Farncombe 01–04; P-in-c Toddington, Stanton, Didbrook w Hailes etc *Glouc* 04–05; TV Winchcombe 05–09; AD Tewkesbury and Winchcombe 07–09; P-in-c Glouc St Mary de Lode and St Mary de Crypt etc 09–10; P-in-c Hempsted 09–10; R Glouc City and Hempsted from 10; Can Res Glouc Cathl from 09. *The Rectory, Rectory Lane, Hempsted, Gloucester GL2 5LW* T: (01452) 523808 M: 07944-721835 E: nikkiarthy@btinternet.com

ARTISS, Rebecca Jane. b 72. **d** 18 **p** 19. NSM Four Rivers *St E* from 18. *Address temp unknown* M: 07484-630280

ARTLEY, Miss Pamela Jean. b 47. Hull Univ MEd 91 Worc Coll of Educn CertEd 68 ALCM 73. NEOC 99. **d** 02 **p** 03. NSM Bridlington Priory *York* 02–05; P-in-c Nafferton w Wansford 05–14; rtd 14; PtO *York* 14–19. *11 Bempton Drive, Bridlington YO16 7HG* E: revjeanartley@gmail.com

ARTUS, Stephen James. b 60. Man Poly BA 82 W Midl Coll of Educn PGCE 84. St Jo Coll Nottm MA 95. **d** 95 **p** 96. C Altrincham St Geo *Ches* 95–99; P-in-c Norton 99–05; V

05–07; C Wybunbury and Audlem w Doddington 10–12; PtO from 12. *Address withheld by request*

ARUNDEL, Canon Michael. b 36. Qu Coll Ox BA 60 MA 64. Linc Th Coll 60. **d** 62 **p** 63. C Hollinwood *Man* 62–65; C Leesfield 65–69; R Newton Heath All SS 69–80; RD N Man 75–80; P-in-c Eccles St Mary 80–81; TR Eccles 81–91; R Man St Ann 91–01; Hon Can Man Cathl 82–01; rtd 01; PtO *Man* from 01. *20 Kiln Brow, Bromley Cross, Bolton BL7 9NR* T: (01204) 591156 E: m.arundel555@btinternet.com

ARVIDSSON, Canon Carl Fredrik. b 66. Regents Th Coll 88 Chich Th Coll 92. **d** 92 **p** 93. C Southsea H Spirit *Portsm* 92–94; C Botley, Curdridge and Durley 94–96; P-in-c Ringwould w Kingsdown *Cant* 96–97; R 97–01; Sen Chapl K Sch Cant 01–17; Hon Min Can Cant Cathl from 01; Hon C Deal St Andr 13–15; Hon Can Antsiranana from 13; rtd 17; PtO *Cant* from 19. *Monks Hall, 177 Mongeham Road, Great Mongeham, Deal CT14 9LL* T: (01304) 694894 E: carlfredrikarvidsson@gmail.com

ASBRIDGE, Preb John Hawell. b 26. Dur Univ BA 47. Bps' Coll Cheshunt 47. **d** 49 **p** 50. C Barrow St Geo *Carl* 49–52; C Fort William *Arg* 52–54; C Lon Docks St Pet w Wapping St Jo 54–55; C Kilburn St Aug 55–59; V Northolt Park St Barn 59–66; V Shepherd's Bush St Steph w St Thos 66–96; Preb St Paul's Cathl 89–96; rtd 96; PtO *B & W* from 05. *Crystal Glen, The Old Mineral Line, Roadwater, Watchet TA23 0RL* T: (01984) 640211

ASBRIDGE, Nigel Henry. b 58. Bris Univ BA 80. Chich Th Coll 87. **d** 89 **p** 90. C Tottenham St Paul *Lon* 89; C W Hampstead St Jas 89–94; P-in-c Hornsey H Innocents 94–04; P-in-c Stroud Green H Trin 02–04; Nat Chapl-Missr Children's Soc 04–09; NSM Edmonton St Alphege and Ponders End St Matt *Lon* 06–10; P-in-c Edmonton St Mary w St Jo 10–13; V from 13; P-in-c Gt Cambridge Road St Jo and St Jas 13–17. *St John's Vicarage, Dysons Road, London N18 2DS* T: (020) 8807 2767 M: 07905-499323 E: nigelasbridge@hotmail.com

ASCOUGH, Mrs Susan Glynis. b 48. STETS 06. **d** 09 **p** 10. NSM Bishop's Cannings, All Cannings etc *Sarum* 09–12; NSM Cannings and Redhorn 12–18; Chapl HM Pris Erlestoke 09–18; rtd 18; PtO *Sarum* 18–21. *Address withheld by request* M: 07714-451992 E: davide.frenchman@btopenworld.com

ASH, Arthur Edwin. b 44. St Jo Coll Nottm 85. **d** 87 **p** 88. C Attleborough *Cov* 87–91; V Garretts Green *Birm* 91–02; rtd 02; PtO *Birm* 02–12; *Cov* 04–21. *1 Margetts Close, Kenilworth CV8 1EN* T: (01926) 853547 E: arthureash@yahoo.co.uk

ASH, Brian John. b 32. ALCD 62. **d** 62 **p** 63. C Plymouth St Andr *Ex* 62–66; Area Sec CMS Cant and Roch 66–73; V Bromley Common St Aug *Roch* 73–97; rtd 97; PtO *Chelmsf* 97–00. *The Vines, 95 Green Lane, Leigh-on-Sea SS9 5QU* T: (01702) 523644 E: brianash2@gmail.com

ASH, Christopher Brian Garton. b 53. Trin Hall Cam MA 76. Wycliffe Hall Ox BA 92. **d** 93 **p** 94. C Cambridge H Sepulchre *Ely* 93–97; P-in-c Lt Shelford 97–02; R 02–04; Dir Cornhill Tr Course 04–15; PtO *Lon* from 15; *Ely* from 17. *23 Fulbrooke Road, Cambridge CB3 9EE* T: (01223) 301165

ASH, David Nicholas. b 61. Southlands Coll Lon BA 82. Wycliffe Hall Ox BTh 03. **d** 03 **p** 04. C Walsall *Lich* 03–06; P-in-c Petton w Cockshutt, Welshampton and Lyneal etc 06–12; C Wellington All SS w Eyton 12–15; Local Par Development Adv Shrewsbury Area 10–15; V Prestatyn *St As* 15–17; P-in-c Bryn a Mor Miss Area from 18. *Address temp unknown*

ASH, John Christopher Garton. b 84. St Cuth Soc Dur BA 06. Wycliffe Hall Ox BA 13. **d** 14. C Ches Square St Mich w St Phil *Lon* 13–16; Chapl Dean Close Sch from 16. *Bayley House, Dean Close School, Shelburne Road, Cheltenham GL51 6HE* M: 07886-892995 E: john.ash06@gmail.com

ASH, Canon Nicholas John. b 59. Bath Univ BSc 81 Nottm Univ BTh 88. Linc Th Coll 85. **d** 88 **p** 89. C Hersham *Guildf* 88–93; P-in-c Flookburgh *Carl* 93–97; Dioc Officer for Stewardship 94–97; TV Cartmel Peninsula 97–98; Dir of Ords 97–03; P-in-c Dalston 98–00; P-in-c Wreay 98–00; P-in-c Raughton Head w Gatesgill 98–00; V Dalston w Cumdivock, Raughton Head and Wreay 01–03; Can Res Portsm Cathl 03–09; TR Cartmel Peninsula *Carl* 09–16. *28 Westmorland Rise, Appleby-in-Westmorland CA16 6SJ* E: nicholasash59@yahoo.co.uk

ASH, Nicholas Martin. b 62. Ch Ch Coll Cant BEd 86. SEITE 06. **d** 09 **p** 10. NSM Faversham *Cant* 09–13; Chapl Medway Secure Tr Cen 13–19; Chapl HM Pris Elmley from 20. *HM Prison Elmley, Church Road, Eastchurch, Sheerness ME12 4DZ* T: (01795) 802000 M: 07896-006282 E: nicholas.ash@justice.gov.uk

ASHBRIDGE, Clare Patricia Esther. *See* KAKURU, Clare Patricia Esther

ASHBURNER, David Barrington. b 26. Ch Coll Cam BA 51 MA 55. Wycliffe Hall Ox 51. **d** 53 **p** 54. C Coalville *Leic* 53–56; C Leic H Apostles 56–58; V Bucklebury w Marlston *Ox* 58–70; V Belton *Leic* 70–75; P-in-c Osgathorpe 73–75; R Belton and Osgathorpe 75–79; V Frisby-on-the-Wreake w Kirby Bellars 79–82; V Uffington w Woolstone and Baulking *Ox* 82–91; P-in-c Shellingford 83–91; RD Vale of White Horse 87–91; rtd 91; PtO *Glouc* 91–17; *Ox* 91–13. *7 Stonefern Court, Stow Road, Moreton-in-Marsh GL56 0DW* T: (01608) 650347

✠**ASHBY, The Rt Revd Godfrey William Ernest Candler.** b 30. Lon Univ AKC 54 BD 54 PhD 69. **d** 55 **p** 56 **c** 80. C St Helier *S'wark* 55–57; P-in-c St Mark's Miss Cape Town S Africa 58–60; Sub-Warden St Paul's Th Coll Grahamstown 60–66; R Alice 66–68; Sen Lect Rhodes Univ 68–75; Can Grahamstown Cathl 69–75; Dean and Adn Grahamstown 75–80; Bp St John's 80–85; Prof Div Witwatersrand Univ S Africa 85–88; Asst Bp Johannesburg 85–88; Asst Bp Leic 88–95; P-in-c Newtown Linford 92–95; Hon Can Leic Cathl 93–95; rtd 95; Asst Bp George S Africa 95–08; Hon Asst Bp Portsm 08–11; Hon Asst Bp Ex from 11. *The College of St Barnabas, Blackberry Lane, Lingfield RH7 6NJ* M: 07968-396195 E: godfreyashby@gmail.com

ASHBY, Canon Judith Anne Stuart. b 53. Man Univ BSc 74 MSc 76 Ox Brookes Univ PGCE 99. STETS 96. **d** 99 **p** 00. NSM Swindon Ch Ch *Bris* 99–05; P-in-c Cricklade w Latton 05–12; C Ashton Keynes, Leigh and Minety 07–12; rtd 12; Dean of Women's Min *Bris* 13–15; NSM Swindon Ch Ch 15–17; Adv for Women's Min and Asst Adv for Minl Support from 15; Hon Can Bris Cathl from 14; PtO from 20. *57 Greywethers Avenue, Swindon SN3 1QG* T: (01793) 978528 E: judith.ashby@tiscali.co.uk

ASHBY, Mrs Linda. b 48. Dartford Coll of Educn CertEd 70. **d** 03 **p** 04. OLM The Ch in the Woottons *Nor* from 03. *4 Melford Close, South Wootton, King's Lynn PE30 3XH* T: (01553) 672893 E: linda_ashby@tiscali.co.uk

ASHBY, Peter George. b 49. Univ of Wales (Cardiff) BSc(Econ) 70. Linc Th Coll 70. **d** 73 **p** 74. C Bengeo *St Alb* 73–75; Chapl Hatf Poly 76–79; C Apsley End 80; TV Chambersbury 80–82; Adn N Harare Zimbabwe 82–87; V Eskdale, Irton, Muncaster and Waberthwaite *Carl* 87–93; TR Sedgley All SS *Worc* 93–99; TV Tettenhall Regis *Lich* 99–04; V W Bromwich St Jas w St Paul 04–06; R Bradeley, Church Eaton, Derrington and Haughton 06–11; rtd 11; PtO *B & W* from 12. *24 Bryant Gardens, Clevedon BS21 5HE* T: (01275) 542677 M: 07756-897547 E: peter.g.ashby@gmail.com

ASHBY, Philip Charles. b 52. Birm Univ BSc 73 Lon Univ MSc 74 PhD 93. WEMTC 05. **d** 08 **p** 09. NSM Stratton St Margaret w S Marston etc *Bris* 08–11; NSM Garsdon, Lea and Cleverton and Charlton 11–12; NSM N Swindon St Andr from 14; NSM W Swindon and Lydiard Tregoze from 18. *57 Greywethers Avenue, Swindon SN3 1QG* T: (01793) 978528 E: phil.ashby@tiscali.co.uk

ASHCROFT, Ann Christine. b 46. Sheff Univ MA Sarum Coll MA Cov Coll of Educn TCert 68. NOC 82. **d** 87 **p** 94. Chapl Trin C of E High Sch Man 86–91; Burnage St Nic *Man* 86–95; Hon Par Dn 87–95; Dio Adv Man Coun for Educn 91–95; TV Wareham *Sarum* 95–02; Chapl Purbeck Sch Sarum 95–02; TR By Brook *Bris* 02–10; P-in-c Colerne w N Wraxall 06–10; Hon Can Bris Cathl 08–10; rtd 10. *Beckside, Baslow Road, Ashford-in-the-Water, Bakewell DE45 1QA*

✠**ASHCROFT, The Rt Revd Mark David.** b 54. Worc Coll Ox BA 77 MA 82 Fitzw Coll Cam BA 81. Ridley Hall Cam 79. **d** 82 **p** 83 **c** 16. C Burnage St Marg *Man* 82–85; Tutor St Paul's Sch of Div Kapsabet Kenya 86–89; Prin St Paul's Th Coll Kapsabet 90–96; R Harpurhey *Man* 96–09; R Harpurhey St Steph 96–06; AD N Man 00–06; Adn Man 09–16; Hon Can Man Cathl 04–09; Suff Bp Bolton from 16; Warden of Readers from 18. *Bishop's Lodge, Walkden Road, Worsley, Manchester M28 2WH* T: 0161-790 8289 M: 07810-272020

ASHDOWN, Andrew William Harvey. b 64. K Coll Lon BD 88 AKC 88 Heythrop Coll Lon MA 15 Win Univ PhD 19. Sarum & Wells Th Coll 88. **d** 90 **p** 91. C Cranleigh *Guildf* 90–94; V Ryhill *Wakef* 94–98; P-in-c Denmead *Portsm* 98–99; V 99–05; S Asia Regional Officer USPG 05–06; Hon C Tadley S and Silchester *Win* 05–06; P-in-c Knight's Enham and Smannell w Enham Alamein 06–09; TR 09–14; V Knight's Enham 14–15; PtO from 15. *The Vicarage, 33 Crescent Road, North Baddesley, Southampton SO52 9HU* T: (023) 8178 8031 E: andrewashdown@talktalk.net

ASHDOWN, Barry Frederick. b 42. St Pet Coll Ox BA 65 MA 69. Ridley Hall Cam 66. **d** 68 **p** 69. C Shipley St Pet *Bradf* 68–71; C Rushden w Newton Bromswold *Pet* 71–74; R Haworth *Bradf* 74–82; V Ore Ch Ch *Chich* 82–87; C Southwick St Mich 91–99; PtO from 17. *9 Bucknell Avenue, Pangbourne, Reading RG8 7JU* T: 0118-984 5129 M: 07888-996763 E: bazzaashdown@hotmail.co.uk

ASHDOWN, Ms Lucyann. b 64. LSE BSc 95 RGN 86 RM 88. NTMTC BA 08. **d** 08 **p** 09. C Stoke Newington St Mary and Brownswood Park *Lon* 08–11; P-in-c Blaenau Irfon *S & B* 11–14; P-in-c Irfon Valley 11–14; Chapl Farleigh Hospice 14–19; Chapl Weldmar Hospice 19–20; Chapl Ex Hospiscare from 21; PtO *St E* from 15; *Sarum* from 20. *Address temp unknown* E: lucyann.ashdown@gmail.com

ASHDOWN, Philip David. b 57. Imp Coll Lon BSc 79 NW Univ Chicago MS 80 Cranfield Inst of Tech PhD 85 ARCS 79. Ripon Coll Cuddesdon 91. **d** 93 **p** 94. C Houghton le Spring *Dur* 93–96; C Stockton and Chapl Stockton Campus Dur Univ 96–02; V Stockton St Pet *Dur* 02–15; P-in-c Elton 09–15; PtO *St D* from 16. *7 Denham Avenue, Llanelli SA15 4DB* T: (01554) 750628 E: pdashdown@aol.com

ASHE, The Ven Francis John. b 53. Sheff Univ BMet 74. Ridley Hall Cam 77. **d** 79 **p** 80. C Ashtead *Guildf* 79–82; S Africa 82–87; R Wisley w Pyrford *Guildf* 87–93; V Godalming 93–01; TR 01–09; RD 96–02; Hon Can Guildf Cathl 03–09; Adn Lynn *Nor* 09–18; Warden of Readers 15; rtd 18; PtO *Nor* from 18. *Kirkleigh Farmhouse, Virginstowe, Beaworthy EX21 5DZ*

ASHELBY, Mrs Sarah Elizabeth. b 84. Warwick Univ BA 06. St Mellitus Coll BA 20. **d** 20 **p** 21. C The Bridge, Cov from 20. *47 Glebe Close, Coventry CV4 8DJ* M: 07793-279709 E: sesarah@gmail.com

ASHFORD, Archdeacon of. See MILLER, The Ven Darren Noel

ASHFORD-OKAI, Fred. b 57. Nui BA 90 Lanc Univ MA 92 TCD HDipEd 93. St Pet Sem Ghana 79 NTMTC 06. **d** 84 **p** 85. NSM E Ham w Upton Park and Forest Gate *Chelmsf* 07–09; PtO 14–17; NSM E Ham H Trin 17–21; NSM Forest Gate All SS from 21. *5 Harold Mugford Terrace, Pearl Close, London E6 5AA* M: 07940-984883 E: fashfordokai@gmail.com

ASHFORTH, David Edward. b 37. Lon Univ BSc ARCS 59. Qu Coll Birm. **d** 61 **p** 62. C Scarborough St Columba *York* 61–65; C Northallerton w Kirby Sigston 65–67; V Keyingham 67–73; Chapl Imp Coll *Lon* 73–89; V Balderstone *Blackb* 89–01; Dir Post-Ord Tr 89–01; rtd 01; PtO *Ripon* 02–14; *Leeds* from 14. *Sunnyholme Cottage, Preston under Scar, Leyburn DL8 4AH* T: (01969) 622438 E: d.ashforth@btinternet.com

ASHLEY, Clive Ashley. b 54. Croydon Coll of Art and Design LSIAD 75 Lon Hosp SRN 80 E Ham Coll of Tech TCert 82. Aston Tr Scheme 81 Cranmer Hall Dur 84. **d** 86 **p** 87. C Withington St Paul *Man* 86–89; Chapl Freeman Hosp Newc 89–92; Chapl St Rich and Graylingwell Hosps Chich 92–98; Chapl Sussex Weald and Downs NHS Trust 95–98; Chapl and Bereavement Cllr R W Sussex Trust 98–01; R New Fishbourne *Chich* 01–10; P-in-c Appledram 01–10; P-in-c Lt Baddow *Chelmsf* 10–17; P-in-c Sandon 10–13; P-in-c Danbury 13–17; rtd 17. *3 Glencoyne Drive, Southport PR9 9TS* M: 07939-509628 E: cliveashley@btinternet.com

ASHLEY, Jane Isobel. See HULME, Jane Isobel

ASHLEY, Miss Victoria Lesley. St Mich Coll Llan. **d** 08 **p** 09. C Tredegar *Mon* 08–12; P-in-c Pontnewydd 12–16; P-in-c Cwmbran 16–17; TV Cowbridge *Llan* from 17. *The Vicarage, 2 Court Close, Aberthin, Cowbridge CF71 7EH* E: revvla@btinternet.com *or* vicar@cowbridgeparish.com

ASHLEY-ROBERTS, James. b 50. Lon Univ BD 77. Oak Hill Th Coll 75 Wycliffe Hall Ox 79. **d** 80 **p** 81. C Gt Warley Ch Ch *Chelmsf* 80–83; C E Ham St Paul 83–85; TV Holyhead w Rhoscolyn w Llanfair-yn-Neubwll *Ban* 85–88; TR 88–91; V Penrhyndeudraeth w Llanfrothen w Beddgelert 91–97; R Ffestiniog w Blaenau Ffestiniog 97–01; PtO 01–12; P-in-c Llangefni w Tregaean w Llanddyfnan 12–13. *26 Garrabost, Isle of Lewis HS2 0PW* M: 07881-770437 E: revjamesashleyroberts@sky.com

ASHMAN, Paul Andrew. b 70. Wycliffe Hall Ox 05. **d** 07 **p** 08. C Portswood Ch Ch *Win* 07–11; C Auckland St Paul NZ 11–14; V Panmure from 14. *5 Thompson Road, Panmure, Auckland 1072, New Zealand* M: (0064) 21-550104 E: ashmanpaul@gmail.com *or* vicar@stmatthias.org.nz

ASHMAN, Peter Michael. b 61. Ex Univ LLB 83 LLM 84 BTh(Min) 12 Called to the Bar (Inner Temple) 85. SWMTC 07. **d** 10 **p** 11. C Ex St Jas 10–13; P-in-c Ipplepen, Torbryan and Denbury 13–14; R Ipplepen w Torbryan, Denbury and Broadhempston w Woodland 14–17; R Weston super Mare St Jo *B & W* from 17. *St John's Rectory, 9D Cecil Road, Weston-super-Mare BS23 2NF* E: revpeterashman@gmail.com

ASHMAN, Mrs Vanessa Mary. b 53. Cant Ch Ch Univ BA 07. **d** 03 **p** 04. NSM Lyminge w Paddlesworth, Stanford w Postling etc *Cant* 03–13; C Bewsborough 13–16; rtd 17. *Address temp unknown* E: vanessa.ashman@btinternet.com

ASHTON, Anthony Joseph. b 37. Oak Hill Th Coll 62. **d** 65 **p** 66. C Crookes St Thos *Sheff* 65–68; C Heeley 68–73; V Bowling St Steph *Bradf* 73–78; R Chesterfield H Trin *Derby*

✠**ASHTON, The Rt Revd Cyril Guy.** b 42. Lanc Univ MA 86. Oak Hill Th Coll 64. **d** 67 **p** 68 **c** 00. C Blackpool St Thos *Blackb* 67–70; Voc Sec CPAS 70–74; V Lancaster St Thos *Blackb* 74–91; Lanc Almshouses 76–90; Dioc Dir of Tr *Blackb* 91–00; Hon Can Blackb Cathl 91–00; Suff Bp Doncaster *Sheff* 00–11; rtd 11; Hon Asst Bp Blackb and Liv from 11. *Charis, 17C Quernmore Road, Lancaster LA1 3EB* T: (01524) 848684 M: 07968-371596 E: bpcg.ashton@btinternet.com

ASHTON, David. b 52. Sarum Th Coll 93. **d** 96 **p** 97. NSM St Leonards Ch Ch and St Mary *Chich* 96–98; NSM Upper St Leonards St Jo 98–99; C Uckfield 99–02; V Langney 02–14; rtd 14; PtO *Chich* from 14. *3 Streatfield Road, Uckfield TN22 2BG* T: (01825) 768643 E: frdavidashton@aol.com

ASHTON, Eleanor Jane. *See* RANCE, Eleanor Jane

ASHTON, Grant. *See* ASHTON, William Grant

ASHTON, Hubert Samuel. b 86. Trin Coll Ox BA 08. Oak Hill Th Coll 12. **d** 15 **p** 16. C Chelsea St Jo w St Andr *Lon* 15–18. *The Old Farmhouse, Appledore Road, Tenterden TN30 7DF* M: 07789-870962 E: sam.ashton86@gmail.com

ASHTON, Janet Heather Hephzibah. b 52. Westcott Ho Cam. **d** 07 **p** 08. C Wenlock *Heref* 07–11; TV Kidderminster St Mary and All SS w Trimpley etc *Worc* 11–15; TV Kidderminster Ismere 15–16; rtd 16; PtO *Worc* 16; V Hightown *Liv* from 16. *St Stephen's Vicarage, St Stephen's Road, Hightown, Liverpool L38 0BL* T: 0151-929 3971 M: 07737-916499 E: janhhashton@gmail.com

ASHTON, Miss Joan Heather. b 54. Sheff Hallam Univ BA 10 Eaton Hall Coll of Educn CertEd 76. Cranmer Hall Dur 91. **d** 93 **p** 94. Par Dn Darnall-cum-Attercliffe *Sheff* 93–94; C Hillsborough and Wadsley Bridge 94–96; P-in-c Stainforth 96–98; P-in-c Arksey 98–03; Asst Chapl Doncaster R Infirmary and Montagu Hosp NHS Trust 98–01; Asst Chapl Doncaster and Bassetlaw Hosps NHS Foundn Trust 01–04; Co-ord Chapl Services Rotherham Gen Hosps NHS Trust 04–17; rtd 17; PtO *Sheff* from 17. *2 St Albans Court, Wickersley, Rotherham S66 1FG* T: (01709) 544626

ASHTON, Lesley June. b 49. York Univ BA 89. NEOC 00. **d** 04 **p** 05. C Roundhay St Edm *Ripon* 04–08; P-in-c Hawksworth Wood 08–11; TV Abbeylands 11–13; rtd 13; Hon C Fountains Gp *Ripon* 13–14; *Leeds* 14–16; Asst Dir of Ords 10–16; PtO from 17; *York* from 17. *53 The Green, Romanby, Northallerton DL7 8NL* M: 07910-002014 E: lesley493ashton@btinternet.com

ASHTON, Mrs Margaret Lucie. b 40. St Jo Coll Nottm 79. **dss** 83 **d** 87 **p** 94. Billericay and Lt Burstead *Chelmsf* 83–99; NSM 87–99; rtd 99; Hon C Fordingbridge and Breamore and Hale etc *Win* 01–05; PtO from 05. *3 Stephen Martin Gardens, Fordingbridge SP6 1RF* T: (01425) 656205

ASHTON, Mrs Mary Isabel. b 57. Robert Gordon Inst of Tech Aber BSc 78 Open Univ PGCE 96. St Steph Ho Ox 07. **d** 09 **p** 10. C Whitewater *Win* 09–13; V Guildf All SS 13–14; PtO *Blackb* 14–15; C Euxton 15–19; P-in-c Silverdale from 19. *The Vicarage, St John's Grove, Silverdale, Carnforth LA5 0RH* T: (01524) 701499 E: silverdalevicar@gmail.com

ASHTON, Nicholas Graham. b 87. Loughb Univ BA 09. Oak Hill Th Coll BA 19. **d** 19 **p** 20. C Down Street Ch Ch *Lon* from 19. *54 Hamilton Road, London NW10 1NE* M: 07745-622009 E: littleash51@hotmail.com

ASHTON, Canon Peter Donald. b 34. Lon Univ BD 62. ALCD 61. **d** 62 **p** 63. C Walthamstow St Mary *Chelmsf* 62–68; V Girlington *Bradf* 68–73; Dir Past Studies St Jo Coll Nottm 73–80; TR Billericay and Lt Burstead *Chelmsf* 80–99; Chapl Mayflower Hosp Billericay 80–99; Chapl St Andr Hosp Billericay 80–92; Chapl Thameside Community Healthcare NHS Trust 93–99; RD Basildon *Chelmsf* 89–99; Hon Can Chelmsf Cathl 92–99; rtd 99; Hon C Fordingbridge and Breamore and Hale etc *Win* 01–10; PtO 10–14 and from 17. *3 Stephen Martin Gardens, Fordingbridge SP6 1RF* T: (01425) 656205 E: peterd.ashton@btinternet.com

ASHTON, Samuel. *See* ASHTON, Hubert Samuel

ASHTON, Preb Samuel Rupert. b 42. Sarum & Wells Th Coll. **d** 83 **p** 84. C Ledbury w Eastnor *Heref* 83–86; R St Weonards w Orcop, Garway, Tretire etc 86–98; RD Ross and Archenfield 91–95 and 96–98; P-in-c Cradley w Mathon and Storridge 98–99; R 99–07; Preb Heref Cathl 97–07; rtd 07; PtO *Heref* from 08. *The Old Greyhound, Longtown, Hereford HR2 0LD* T: (01873) 860492

ASHTON (née JONES), Mrs Susan Catherine. b 48. Qu Coll Birm 09. **d** 11 **p** 12. NSM Knowle *Birm* 11–18; PtO from 18. *1467 Warwick Road, Knowle, Solihull B93 9LU* T: (01564) 776895 E: sue.ashton@yahoo.co.uk

ASHTON, Canon William Grant. b 57. St Chad's Coll Dur BA 79. Oak Hill Th Coll BA 85. **d** 85 **p** 86. C Lancaster St Thos *Blackb* 85–89; CF 89–14; Chapl R Memorial Chpl Sandhurst

06–07; QHC 11–14; V Euxton *Blackb* 14–19; Hon Can Blackb Cathl 18–19; rtd 19; PtO *Blackb* from 19. *The Vicarage, St John's Grove, Silverdale, Carnforth LA5 0RH* T: (01524) 701499 E: grant.ashton@blackburn.anglican.org

ASHURST, Mrs Judith Anne. b 57. St Aid Coll Dur BA 80 St Jo Coll Dur BA 08 Homerton Coll Cam PGCE 01 ACIB 83. Cranmer Hall Dur 06. **d** 08 **p** 09. C Belmont and Pittington *Dur* 08–11; C Chester le Street 11–16; P-in-c Upper Derwent *Carl* 17–19; rtd 20; PtO *Leeds* 20–21. *Address temp unknown* E: revjudi@icloud.com

ASHWELL, Anthony John. b 42. St Andr Univ BSc 65. Sarum & Wells Th Coll 86. **d** 88 **p** 89. C Plymstock *Ex* 88–91; C Axminster, Chardstock, Combe Pyne and Rousdon 91–92; TV 92–95; C Crediton and Shobrooke 95–97; TV Bride Valley *Sarum* 97–07; P-in-c Symondsbury 05–07; RD Lyme Bay 03–06; rtd 07; PtO *Sarum* 07–11; *Sheff* 16–21. *51 Kenbourne Road, Sheffield S7 1NJ* T: 0114-255 0568 E: antanna@btinternet.com

ASHWIN, Canon Vincent George. b 42. Worc Coll Ox BA 65 Nottm Univ BA 10 MA 12. Coll of Resurr Mirfield 65. **d** 67 **p** 68. C Shildon *Dur* 67–70; C Newc St Fran 70–72; R Mhlosheni Swaziland 72–75; R Manzini 75–79; V Shildon *Dur* 79–85; V Fenham St Jas and St Basil *Newc* 85–97; RD Newc W 89–97; V Haydon Bridge and Beltingham w Henshaw 97–04; RD Hexham 97–02; Hon Can Newc Cathl 00–04; rtd 04; PtO *S'well* from 04; *Leic* from 18. *83 Westgate, Southwell NG25 0LS* T: (01636) 813975 E: vincentashwin@tiscali.co.uk

ASHWIN-SIEJKOWSKI, Piotr Jan. b 64. Warsaw Univ PhD 97. Coll of Resurr Mirfield 98. **d** 91 **p** 92. Poland 92–98; C Tile Hill *Cov* 99–01; Chapl and Lect Univ Coll Chich 01–04; TV Richmond St Mary w St Matthias and St Jo *S'wark* 04–13; C Twickenham St Mary *Lon* 13–20; Chapl and Inter-Faith Adv Brunel Univ from 20. *21 Campbell Road, Twickenham TW2 5BY* T: (020) 8894 5102 E: piotrashwin@btinternet.com

ASHWORTH, Canon David. b 40. Nottm Univ BPharm 62. Linc Th Coll 63. **d** 65 **p** 66. C Halliwell St Thos *Man* 65–69; C Heywood St Jas 69–72; C-in-c Heywood St Marg CD 72–78; V Hale *Ches* 78–87; V Hale and Ashley 87–96; V Prestbury 96–05; RD Bowdon 87–95; RD Macclesfield 98–03; Hon Can Ches Cathl 94–05; rtd 05; PtO *Ches* 05–19. *12 Lime Close, Sandbach CW11 1BZ* T: (01270) 529187 E: david@davidashworth39.plus.com

ASHWORTH, Canon James Nigel. b 55. York Univ BA 77. Cranmer Hall Dur 93. **d** 93 **p** 94. C Rothwell *Ripon* 93–96; Chapl Campsfield Ho Oxon 96–99; Hon C Akeman *Ox* 96–99; V Kemsing w Woodlands *Roch* 99–08; R Man St Ann from 08; Hon Can Man Cathl from 17. *St Ann's Rectory, 44 George Leigh Street, Manchester M4 5DG* T: 0161-235 5206 or 834 0239 E: rector@stannsmanchester.com

ASHWORTH, John Russell. b 33. Lich Th Coll 57. **d** 60 **p** 61. C Castleford All SS *Wakef* 60–62; C Luton St Sav *St Alb* 63–67; V Clipstone *S'well* 67–70; V Bolton-upon-Dearne *Sheff* 70–82; V Thornhill Lees *Wakef* 82–98; rtd 98; PtO *Wakef* 99–14; *Leeds* from 14. *Walsingham, 2 Vicarage Road, Savile Town, Dewsbury WF12 9PD* T: (01924) 461269

ASHWORTH, Mark Stephen. b 71. Birm Univ BSocSc 91 Goldsmiths' Coll Lon PGCE 96. Oak Hill Th Coll BA 14. **d** 14 **p** 15. C Crowborough *Chich* from 14; P-in-c High Hurstwood from 17. *1 Mardens, Myrtle Road, Crowborough TN6 1EY* M: 07708-491289 E: mashworth71@gmail.com or mark@allsaintscrowborough.org

ASHWORTH, Canon Martin. b 41. AKC 63. **d** 64 **p** 65. C Wythenshawe Wm Temple Ch CD *Man* 64–71; R Haughton St Anne 71–83; V Prestwich St Marg 83–06; rtd 06; Can Res Bermuda 07–09; PtO *Man* 06–08 and from 15; *Leeds* from 17. *17 Plane Tree Nest Lane, Halifax HX2 7PL*

ASHWORTH, Nigel. *See* ASHWORTH, James Nigel

ASHWORTH, Timothy. b 52. Worc Coll of Educn CertEd 74. Oak Hill Th Coll BA 81. **d** 82 **p** 83. C Tonbridge St Steph *Roch* 82–85; C-in-c Whittle-le-Woods *Blackb* 85–90; Chapl Scargill Ho 90–96; V Ingleton w Chapel le Dale *Bradf* 96–03; TV Yate New Town *Bris* 03–08; NSM Lostock St Thos and St Jo and Bolton St Bede *Man* 09–13; Chapl HM Pris Forest Bank 12–15; Pilsdon at Malling Community 15–21. *40 Homefield, Yate, Bristol BS37 5US* E: timashworth52@gmail.com

ASHWORTH, Mrs Vivien. b 52. Worc Coll of Educn CertEd 73. Trin Coll Bris 79 Oak Hill Th Coll BA 82. **dss** 82 **d** 87 **p** 94. Tonbridge St Steph *Roch* 82–85; Whittle-le-Woods *Blackb* 85–90; Hon Par Dn 87–90; Chapl Scargill Ho 90–96; Hon C Ingleton w Chapel le Dale *Bradf* 96–03; Dioc Youth Adv 96–01; Hon C Yate New Town *Bris* 03–07; TV 07–08; Sub Chapl HM Pris Ashfield 04–09; P-in-c Lostock St Thos and St Jo *Man* 09–15; P-in-c Bolton St Bede 09–15; Guardian

Pilsdon at Malling Community 15–21; rtd 21. *40 Homefield, Yate, Bristol BS37 5US*

ASIEGBU, Mrs Eucharia Ifeoma. b 68. Univ of Nigeria BEd 92 Greenwich Univ PGCE 10 Chich Univ EYTS 14. St Aug Coll Cant 19. **d** 21. C Sidcup St Jo w Footscray *Roch* from 21. *St Andrew's Vicarage, St Andrew's Road, Sidcup DA14 4SA* M: 07908-069477 E: curatesjas@yahoo.com

ASINUGO, Mrs Christiana Chidinma. b 56. NTMTC. **d** 09 **p** 10. C Becontree St Mary *Chelmsf* 09–13; C W Ham St Matt 13–15; P-in-c 15–19; V from 19; C Stratford St Jo w Ch Ch from 15. *St Matthew's Vicarage, 38 Dyson Road, London E15 4JX* T: (020) 8221 0902 E: ccasinugo@yahoo.co.uk

ASIR, Jebamani Sekar Anand. *See* ANAND, Sekar Anand Asir

ASKEW, Miss Alison Jane. b 57. Dur Univ BA 78 PGCE 79 Win Univ MA 12. S Dios Minl Tr Scheme 93. **d** 95 **p** 96. NSM Kingsclere *Win* 95–96; Asst Chapl N Hants Hosps NHS Trust 95–99; Chapl 99–04; Sen Chapl Basingstoke and N Hants NHS Foundn Trust 04–10; P-in-c Kirby-on-the-Moor, Cundall w Norton-le-Clay etc *Ripon* 10–14; *Leeds* 14–15; V 15–20; rtd 20; PtO *Leeds* 20–21. *6 Mallorie Close, Ripon HG4 2QE*

ASKEW, Benjamin Paul. b 79. Sheff Univ BA 01 PGCE 03. St Mellitus Coll BA 13. **d** 13 **p** 14. Pioneer Min and Min Kairos BMO *Ripon* 13–14; *Leeds* from 14. *22 Harlow Oval, Harrogate HG2 0DS* T: (01423) 560558 E: askewben@gmail.com *or* ben@kairoschurch.net

ASKEW, Ms Catherine Clasen. b 75. Princeton Th Sem MDiv 01. Cranmer Hall Dur 08. **d** 10 **p** 11. NSM Amble *Newc* 10–12; NSM Bothal and Pegswood w Longhirst 12–15; NSM Chevington 15–17; Asst Dioc Dir of Ords from 17. *1 Lovaine Place, Alnwick NE66 1AQ* E: catherineaskew@gmail.com

ASKEW, Canon Peter Timothy. b 68. Ridley Hall Cam 00. **d** 02 **p** 03. C Bilton *Ripon* 02–06; C Harrogate St Mark and Chapl St Aid Sch Harrogate 06–09; PtO *Newc* 10–11; NSM Felton 11–17; Bp's Chapl from 17; Hon Can Newc Cathl from 18. *1 Lovaine Place, Alnwick NE66 1AQ* M: 07754-046029

ASKEY, John Stuart. b 39. Chich Th Coll 63. **d** 66 **p** 67. C Feltham *Lon* 66–69; C Epsom Common Ch Ch *Guildf* 69–72; C Chesterton Gd Shep *Ely* 72–74; R Stretham w Thetford 74–93; Dioc Spirituality Officer 75–98; Dioc Youth Officer 80–99; P-in-c Brinkley, Burrough Green and Carlton 93–97; P-in-c Westley Waterless 93–97; P-in-c Dullingham 93–97; P-in-c Stetchworth 93–97; R Raddesley Gp 97–99; Chapl Gothenburg w Halmstad, Jönköping etc *Eur* 99–04; rtd 04; PtO *Chich* 11–16; *York* from 17. *260 Boulevard, Hull HU3 3ED* T: (01482) 228685 E: johnaskey39@gmail.com

ASKEY, Matthew Robert. b 74. Loughb Coll BA 96 Bretton Hall Coll MA 99 Leeds Univ BA 09 Huddersfield Univ PGCE 06. Coll of Resurr Mirfield 07. **d** 09 **p** 10. C Elland *Wakef* 09–13; Chapl Minster Sch S'well 13–19; Chapl Worksop Coll Notts from 19. *Worksop College, Cuthbert's Avenue, Worksop S80 3AP* T: (01909) 537100 M: 07814-502034 E: frmaskey@btinternet.com

ASKEY, Mrs Susan Mary. b 44. Leeds Univ MA 00. NOC 99. **d** 99 **p** 00. C Golcar *Wakef* 99–02; P-in-c Drighlington 02–12; rtd 12; PtO *Leeds* from 17. *26 Handel Street, Golcar, Huddersfield HD7 4AB*

ASKWITH, Angela Catherine. b 58. St Mellitus Coll 16. **d** 18 **p** 19. NSM Frodsham *Ches* 18–20; R Delamere from 20. *The Rectory, Chester Road, Delamere, Northwich CW8 2HS* T: (01606) 882184 M: 07429-075283 E: revangelaaskwith@gmail.com

ASKWITH, Mrs Helen Mary. b 57. Thames Valley Univ BSc 00. ERMC 04. **d** 07 **p** 08. NSM Wembley St Jo *Lon* 07–10; NSM Northolt Park St Barn 10–12; V Wembley Park from 12. *St Augustine's Vicarage, 13 Forty Avenue, Wembley HA9 8JL* T: (020) 8908 5938 M: 07711-643220 E: revhelen.askwith@btinternet.com

ASKWITH, Joshua Christian. b 90. Stirling Univ BA 14. Cranmer Hall Dur 14. **d** 17 **p** 18. C Neston *Ches* 17–19; V Norbury from 19. *75 Chester Road, Hazel Grove, Stockport SK7 5PE* M: 07727-187987 E: jcaskwith@gmail.com

ASMELASH, Berhane Tesfamariam. b 56. Addis Ababa Univ MD 89 Lon Bible Coll MPhil 04. SEITE BA 08. **d** 08 **p** 09. C Upper Holloway *Lon* 08–12; NSM Dalston H Trin w St Phil and Haggerston All SS 12–13; C Plumstead Common S'wark from 13. *152 Kirkham Street, London SE18 2EN* M: 07838-167198 E: asmelash_b@ymail.com

ASPINALL, Christine Joyce. b 54. SNWTP 14. **d** 17 **p** 18. OLM Old Trafford St Jo *Man* from 17. *382 Kings Road, Stretford, Manchester M32 8GW*

ASPINALL, Philip Norman. b 51. Cam Univ MA ATI. WMMTC 86. **d** 89 **p** 90. NSM Cov E 89–98. *139 Wiltshire Court, Nod Rise, Mount Nod, Coventry CV5 7JP* T: (024) 7646 7509 E: philaspinall@gmail.com

ASQUITH, (née SHIPLEY), June Patricia. b 54. Liv Hope BA 00 PGCE 01. SNWTP 08. **d** 10 **p** 11. NSM Walton Breck

Liv 10–12; C Bootle 12–14; R Wavertree St Mary from 14. *St Mary's Rectory, 1 South Drive, Wavertree, Liverpool L15 8JJ* E: june150@btinternet.com

ASQUITH, Michael John. b 60. St D Coll Lamp BA 82 MPhil 91 Ch Ch Coll Cant PGCE 83. Cant Sch of Min 91. **d** 94 **p** 95. C S Ashford Ch Ch *Cant* 94–98; P-in-c Weldon w Deene *Pet* 98–00; P-in-c Corby Epiphany w St Jo 98–06; Dep Dioc Dir of Educn *Leic* 06–10; R Lowestoft St Marg *Nor* from 11; RD Lothingland from 18. *St Margaret's Rectory, 147 Hollingsworth Road, Lowestoft NR32 4BW* T: (01502) 573046 M: 07503-377360 E: mikeasq@aol.com *or* rector@stmargaretslowestoft.co.uk

ASQUITH, Simon Andrew. b 85. Cam Univ BTh 21. Westcott Ho Cam 19. **d** 21. C Merton Priory *S'wark* from 21. *The Vicarage, Beaford Grove, London SW20 9LB* E: simonpsalm34@gmail.com *or* curate@ht-sw.org.uk

ASSON, Geoffrey Ormrod. b 34. Univ of Wales (Ban) BA 54 St Cath Coll Ox BA 56 MA 61. St Steph Ho Ox 54. **d** 57 **p** 58. C Aberdare *Llan* 57–59; C Roath 59–61; R Hagworthingham w Asgarby and Lusby *Linc* 61–65; P-in-c Mavis Enderby w Raithby 62–65; V Friskney 65–69; R S Ormsby w Ketsby, Calceby and Driby 69–74; R Harrington w Brinkhill 69–74; R Oxcombe 69–74; R Ruckland w Farforth and Maidenwell 69–74; R Somersby w Bag Enderby 69–74; R Tetford and Salmonby 69–74; P-in-c Belchford 71–74; P-in-c W Ashby 71–74; V Riverhead w Dunton Green *Roch* 75–80; R Kington w Huntington *Heref* 80–82; RD Kington and Weobley 80–86; P-in-c Almeley 81–82; P-in-c Knill 81–82; P-in-c Old Radnor 81–82; R Kington w Huntington, Old Radnor, Kinnerton etc 82–86; V Mathry w St Edren's and Grandston etc St D 86–97; Bp's Rural Adv and Tourist Officer 91–95; rtd 96; PtO *St D* from 97. *Mimulus, Mutton Dingle, New Radnor, Presteigne LD8 2TL* T: (01544) 350358 E: goasson@btinternet.com

ASTBURY, Susan. b 61. St Hugh's Coll Ox BA 82 MA 85 DPhil 85. SWMTC 05. **d** 08 **p** 09. NSM Teignmouth, Ideford w Luton, Ashcombe etc *Ex* from 08. *3 The Strand, Shaldon, Teignmouth TQ14 0DL* T: (01626) 873807 E: sue.ast@btinternet.com

ASTIN, Howard Keith. b 51. Warwick Univ LLB. Trin Coll Bris 83. **d** 83 **p** 84. C Kirkheaton *Wakef* 83–88; V Bowling St Jo *Bradf* 88–14; *Leeds* 14–17; rtd 17. *4 Cocking Steps Mill, Cocking Steps Lane, Netherton, Huddersfield HD4 7EA* E: h.astin@virgin.net

ASTIN, The Ven Moira Anne Elizabeth. b 65. Clare Coll Cam BA 86 MA 90. Wycliffe Hall Ox BA 96. **d** 95 **p** 96. C Newbury *Ox* 95–99; C Thatcham 99–01; TV 01–05; TV Woodley 05–09; V Southlake 09–11; Angl Ecum Officer (Berks) 03–11; Dioc Ecum Officer 10–11; P-in-c Frodingham and New Brumby *Linc* 11–16; Can and Preb Linc Cathl 12–16; Adn Reigate *S'wark* from 16. *Croydon Episcopal Area Office, 6 St Peter's Road, Croydon CR0 1HD* T: (020) 8256 9630 E: moira.astin@southwark.anglican.org

ASTIN, Timothy Robin. b 58. St Edm Hall Ox BA 79 Darw Coll Cam PhD 82 FGS. Ox Min Course 90. **d** 93 **p** 94. NSM Reading St Jo *Ox* 93–95; NSM Newbury 95–99; NSM Beedon and Peasemore w W Ilsley and Farnborough 99–05; NSM Woodley 05–11; NSM Frodingham and New Brumby *Linc* 11–13; P-in-c Bottesford w Ashby 13–16; Public Preacher S'wark 16–17; V Tadworth from 17. *The Vicarage, 1 The Avenue, Tadworth KT20 5AS* E: tim.astin@virginmedia.com

ASTLEY, Prof Jeffrey. b 47. Down Coll Cam BA 68 MA 72 Dur Univ PhD 79. Qu Coll Birm 68. **d** 70 **p** 71. C Cannock *Lich* 70–73; Lect and Chapl St Hild Coll Dur 73–75; Sen Lect and Chapl SS Hild and Bede Coll Dur 75–77; Prin Lect and Hd RS Bp Grosseteste Coll Linc 77–81; Dir N of England Inst for Chr Educn 81–13; PtO *Dur* from 81; *Leeds* from 17. *8 Vicarage Court, Heighington Village, Newton Aycliffe DL5 6SD* E: jeff.astley@durham.ac.uk *or* jagdaa71@aol.com

ASTON, Heather Jane. b 54. Cen Lancs Univ MBA 02. SWMTC 10. **d** 13 **p** 14. C Meneage *Truro* 13–17; P-in-c Boscastle and Tintagel Gp 17–21; C Week St Mary Circle of Par 19–21; R Boscastle Gp from 21. *The Rectory, Forrabury, Boscastle PL35 0DJ* T: (01840) 250359 M: 07960-965787 E: heather_solo@msn.com

ASTON, John Bernard. b 34. Leeds Univ BA 55 PGCE 56. Qu Coll Birm 72. **d** 75 **p** 76. NSM Shenstone *Lich* 75–05; NSM Stonnall 00–05; Chapl HM YOI Swinfen Hall 90–99; PtO *Lich* 05–21. *4 Footherley Road, Shenstone, Lichfield WS14 0NJ* T: (01543) 480388 E: bradston@btinternet.com

ASTON, John Leslie. b 47. Open Univ BSc 99 Win Univ MA 06. Oak Hill Th Coll BA 80. **d** 80 **p** 81. C Trentham *Lich* 80–83; C Meir Heath 83–85; V Upper Tean 85–91; CF 91–02; C Andover w Foxcott *Win* 02–05; P-in-c Felixstowe SS Pet and Paul *St E* 05–11; V 11–17; rtd 17. *20 Princes Gardens, Felixstowe IP11 7RH* T: (01394) 246076 E: john@astfam.uk

ASTON, Michael James. b 48. Loughb Univ BSc 70 MBCS 85. NTMTC 98. **d** 01 **p** 02. NSM Writtle w Highwood *Chelmsf* 01–07; P-in-c W Hanningfield 07–11; rtd 11; PtO *Chelmsf* 11–19; P-in-c Pleshey from 19. *15 Weller Grove, Chelmsford CM1 4YJ* T: (01245) 442547 M: 07957-610235

ASTON, Roger. b 52. Ox Poly BEd 83. SAOMC 96. **d** 99 **p** 00. OLM Eynsham and Cassington *Ox* from 99. *9 Bell Close, Cassington, Witney OX29 4EP* T: (01865) 880757 E: rogera52@aol.com

ASTON, Ms Sheelagh Mary. Dur Univ BA 15. NEOC 02. **d** 05 **p** 06. C Windy Nook St Alb *Dur* 05–10; P-in-c Oxclose 10–16; Dioc Ecum Officer 10–16; P-in-c Blackb St Silas from 16; PtO *Eur* 17–20. *St Silas's Vicarage, Preston New Road, Blackburn BB2 6PS* T: (01254) 664722 E: revsmaston@gmail.com

ASTON, Simon Richard. b 57. SEITE 12. **d** 16 **p** 17. NSM Kidbrooke St Jas *S'wark* 16–19; NSM Linc St Pet in Eastgate from 20. *East Wing, Coleby Hall, Hall Drive, Coleby, Lincoln LN5 0FG* E: simonaston@chef.net

ASTON, Archdeacon of. *See* HEATHFIELD, The Ven Simon David

ASTON, Suffragan Bishop of. *See* HOLLINGHURST, The Rt Revd Anne Elizabeth

ATACK, Elaine. b 57. Man Univ BA 78. St Mich Coll Llan 09. **d** 12 **p** 13. C St As 12–14; Chapl St As Cathl 12–14; R Bala 14–17; C Edstaston, Fauls, Prees, Tilstock and Whixall *Lich* 17–20; C Whitchurch 17–20; V Frodsham *Ches* from 20. *The Vicarage, 6 Vicarage Lane, Frodsham WA6 7DU* T: (01928) 733378 M: 07579-821612 E: revelaine@nym.hush.com

ATACK, John Philip. b 49. Lanc Univ MA 91. Linc Th Coll 86. **d** 88 **p** 89. C Cleveleys *Blackb* 88–92; V Appley Bridge 92–96; P-in-c Mostyn w Ffynnongroyw *St As* 99–03; P-in-c Colwyn 03–08; R Colwyn and Llanelian 08–14; AD Rhos 09–12; AD Llanrwst and Rhos 12–14; Chapl Conwy and Denbighshire NHS Trust 05–10; Hon Chapl Miss to Seafarers 01–03; rtd 14; PtO St As 15–20; *Lich* 17–20; *Ches* from 20. *The Vicarage, 6 Vicarage Lane, Frodsham WA6 7DU* T: (01928) 733378 M: 07930-443602 E: revphil@nym.hush.com

ATALLAH, David Alexander. b 74. Ox Univ MPhys 97 Ex Univ MSc 99 PhD 03. Wycliffe Hall Ox 09. **d** 11 **p** 12. C Okehampton, Inwardleigh, Belstone, Sourton etc *Ex* 11–15; C Maidenhead St Andr and St Mary *Ox* 15–18; P-in-c White Waltham from 18; C Maidenhead St Andr and St Mary from 19. *The Vicarage, Waltham Road, White Waltham, Maidenhead SL6 3JD* T: (01628) 822000 E: vicar@atallahfamily.co.uk

ATFIELD, Gladys. b 39. Univ Coll Lon BSc 53. Gilmore Course. **dss** 79 **d** 87 **p** 94. Bexley St Mary *Roch* 79–01; Hon C 87–01; rtd 01; PtO *Roch* 01–16. *6 Clarendon Mews, High Street, Bexley DA5 1JS* T: (01322) 551741

ATFIELD, Graham Roy. b 60. Kent Univ BA 82. SEITE 08. **d** 11 **p** 12. NSM Rye *Chich* 11–15; Chapl E Sussex Healthcare NHS Trust from 15. *104 Elphinstone Road, Hastings TN34 2BS* T: (01424) 717382 M: 07810-554268 E: grahamatfield@hotmail.co.uk

ATFIELD, Tom David. b 80. Bris Univ BA 02 MPhil 10 Inst for Chr Studies Toronto MPhilF 06 Birm Univ ThD 11 PGCE 06. Qu Coll Birm 08. **d** 11 **p** 12. C Bromsgrove *Worc* 11–15; TV Dudley 15–19; V Shrewsbury H Cross *Lich* from 19. *1 Underdale Court, Underdale Road, Shrewsbury SY2 5DD* T: (01743) 245300 E: tomatfield@virginmedia.com *or* vicar@shrewsburyabbey.com

ATHA, Gareth William. b 83. Leeds Univ BSc 05 York St Jo Univ MA 10 Selw Coll Cam BTh 14. Westcott Ho Cam 11. **d** 14 **p** 15. C Beverley Minster *York* 14–17; V Elloe Stone *Linc* 17–20; V Pickering w Lockton and Levisham *York* from 20; AD N Ryedale from 21. *The Vicarage, Whitby Road, Pickering YO18 7HL* M: 07712-572073 E: gareth.atha@cantab.net

ATHERFOLD, Mrs Evelyne Sara. b 43. Leeds Inst of Educn CertEd 64. NOC 82. **dss** 85 **d** 92 **p** 94. Kirk Sandall and Edenthorpe *Sheff* 85–87; NSM Fishlake w Sykehouse and Kirk Bramwith etc 87–00; P-in-c 00–03; R 03–11; P-in-c 11–14; Hon C 14–15; Chapl HM YOI Hatfield 96–03; PtO *Sheff* from 15. *Runswick House, Hay Green, Fishlake, Doncaster DN7 5JY* T: (01302) 841396 M: 07980-282270 E: eve.atherfold@virgin.net

ATHERSTONE, Andrew Castell. b 74. Ch Coll Cam BA 95 MA 98 Wycliffe Hall Ox MSt 99 DPhil 01 FRHistS 08. **d** 01 **p** 02. C Abingdon *Ox* 01–05; NSM Eynsham and Cassington from 05; Research Fell Latimer Trust from 05; Tutor Wycliffe Hall Ox from 07. *44 Shakespeare Road, Eynsham, Witney OX29 4PY* T: (01865) 731239 E: andrew.atherstone@wycliffe.ox.ac.uk

ATHERSTONE, Canon Castell Hugh. b 45. Natal Univ BA 67. St Chad's Coll Dur MA 79. **d** 70 **p** 70. C Pietermaritzburg St Alphege S Africa 70–72; C Berea 72–75; C Kloof w Hillcrest 75–77; R Hillcrest 77–80; R Newcastle H Trin w Volksrust 80–82; Chapl Durban Univ 82–83; Dioc Stewardship Adv

Ely 83–87; P-in-c Doddington w Benwick 83–87; R Frant w Eridge *Chich* 87–95; P-in-c Rotherfield w Mark Cross 94–95; RD Rotherfield 90–94; V Seaford w Sutton 95–10; RD Lewes and Seaford 97–07; Can and Preb Chich Cathl 02–10; rtd 10; PtO *Ox* from 10. *9 The Tennis, Cassington, Witney OX29 4EL* T: (01865) 880475 E: hugh@atherstone.net

ATHERTON, Henry Anthony. b 44. Univ of Wales BSc 67 DipEd 68 Fitzw Coll Cam BA 72 MA 75 Heythrop Coll Lon MTh 00 FGS 68. Westcott Ho Cam 70. **d** 72 **p** 73. C Leamington Priors All SS *Cov* 72–75; C Orpington All SS *Roch* 75–78; V Gravesend St Mary 78–87; Chapl St Jas Hosp Gravesend 82–87; V Bromley St Andr *Roch* 87–10; rtd 10; PtO *Roch* from 10; *S'wark* from 12. *20 Laleham Road, London SE6 2HT* T: (020) 8695 0212 E: anthony6atherton@btinternet.com

ATHERTON, Lionel Thomas. b 45. Univ of Wales (Ban) BA 74 St Luke's Coll Ex. St Steph Ho Ox 74. **d** 76 **p** 77. C Chenies and Lt Chalfont *Ox* 76–79; C Fleet *Guildf* 79–84; V S Farnborough 84–89; TR Alston Team *Newc* 89–96; V Chorley St Pet *Blackb* 96–10; Bp's Adv on New Relig Movements 02–10; rtd 10; PtO *Derby* from 14. *36 Windsor Park Road, Buxton SK17 7NP* T: (01298) 74204 E: lionel.atherton@sky.com

ATHERTON, Paul Christopher. b 56. Chich Th Coll. **d** 82 **p** 83. C Orford St Marg *Liv* 82–86; CR 86–88; Chapl Univ of Wales (Cardiff) *Llan* 88–89; TV Walton St Mary *Liv* 89–92; C Westmr St Matt *Lon* 92–96; C Somers Town 96–97; V Bush Hill Park St Mark 97–19; P-in-c Bush Hill Park St Steph 13–19; Chapl N Middx Univ Hosp NHS Trust 97–19; rtd 19. *St Cedd, 41 Spring Road, Brightlingsea, Colchester CO7 0PJ* E: paulc.atherton@gmail.com

ATHERTON, Philip Gordon. b 47. NTMTC BA 07. **d** 07 **p** 08. NSM Hornsey H Innocents *Lon* 07–14; NSM Stroud Green H Trin 07–14; NSM Harringay St Paul 10–14; rtd 14; PtO *Cant* from 18. *12A Beach Court Park, Faversham Road, Seasalter, Whitstable CT5 4FE* M: 07901-555235

ATKINS, Austen Shaun. b 55. St Pet Coll Ox MA 82 Selw Coll Cam MA 85. Ridley Hall Cam 79. **d** 82 **p** 83. C S Mimms Ch Ch *Lon* 82–86; C Fulham St Matt 86–90; P-in-c Fulham St Dionis 91–03; V 03–04; C Ox St Andr 05–09; Chapl Bedford Sch 09–18; rtd 18; Hon C Wootton *St Alb* from 19. *6 The Crescent, Bedford MK40 2RU*

ATKINS, Canon David John. b 43. Kelham Th Coll 64. **d** 68 **p** 69. C Lewisham St Mary *S'wark* 68–72; Min Motspur Park 72–77; P-in-c Mitcham Ascension 77–82; V 82–83; P-in-c Downham w S Hanningfield *Chelmsf* 83–88; R 88–01; P-in-c W Hanningfield 90–93; RD Chelmsf S 93–01; V Maldon All SS w St Pet 01–09; Hon Can Chelmsf Cathl 00–09; rtd 09; PtO *Chelmsf* from 09; *St E* from 19. *19 The Green, Hadleigh, Ipswich IP7 6AE* T: (01473) 822535 E: atkins.d@hotmail.co.uk

ATKINS, Dean John. b 70. Univ of Wales (Cardiff) BD 93. St Steph Ho Ox 93. **d** 95 **p** 96. C Merthyr Dyfan *Llan* 95–99; V Aberaman and Abercwmboi w Cwmaman 99–01; Dioc Youth Officer 01–12; P-in-c Roath St Sav 08–12; V Cardiff St German w St Sav 12–16; P-in-c Cardiff St Mary from 16. *St Mary's Vicarage, 2 North Church Street, Cardiff CF10 5HB* T: (029) 2048 7777 E: deanjatkins@outlook.com

ATKINS, Forrest William (Bill). b 59. Ch Coll Cam MA 85 Lon Univ BD 84. Ridley Hall Cam 83. **d** 86 **p** 87. C Normanton *Derby* 86–90; C Stratford St Jo and Ch Ch w Forest Gate St Jas *Chelmsf* 90–97; Asst Chapl Dubai and Sharjah w N Emirates 97–03; I Mohill w Farnaught, Aughavas, Oughteragh etc *K, E & A* 03–13; Preb Elphin Cathl 08–13; I Killylea, Caledon, and Brantry *Arm* from 13. *154 Killylea Road, Armagh BT60 4LN* T: (028) 3756 8874 E: fwatkins@eircom.net *or* fwatkins123@btinternet.com

ATKINS, Jane Elizabeth. b 51. EMMTC 98. **d** 01 **p** 02. NSM Fenn Lanes Gp *Leic* 01–05; Sub Chapl HM Pris Leic 03–05; P-in-c Ashill w Saham Toney *Nor* 05–07; V Ashill, Carbrooke, Ovington and Saham Toney 07–21; rtd 21. *The Pightle, Comar Lane, Bradenham, Thetford IP25 7QD* E: revd.jane@btinternet.com

ATKINS, Joy Katherine. b 75. Lon Sch of Th BTh 97 Dur Univ PGCE 98. St Jo Coll Nottm MTh 09. **d** 09 **p** 10. C Uxbridge *Lon* 09–12; Chapl Twyford C of E High Sch Acton and Wm Perkin C of E High Sch 12–13; C Reading Greyfriars *Ox* 13–21; Chapl St Edm Sch Cant from 21. *St Edmund's School Canterbury, St Thomas Hill, Canterbury CT2 8HU* E: joyatkins@hotmail.com

ATKINS (*née* HARDING), Ms Lesley Anne. b 58. Westcott Ho Cam 98 SEITE 99. **d** 01 **p** 02. C Walmer *Cant* 01–03; C Broadstairs 03–04; PtO 05–07; NSM Barkston and Hough Gp *Linc* 07–10; P-in-c Hattersley *Ches* 10–18; V Marton *Blackb* from 18. *St Paul's Vicarage, 55 Vicarage Lane, Blackpool FY4 4EF* E: lesley@revlesleyanne.plus.com

ATKINS, Canon Nicholas Steven. b 60. Oak Hill Th Coll BA 88. **d** 88 **p** 89. C Shepton Mallet w Doulting *B & W* 88–91; C Combe Down w Monkton Combe and S Stoke 91–93; TV N Wingfield, Clay Cross and Pilsley *Derby* 93–98; V Essington *Lich* 98–05; P-in-c Ipswich St Matt *St E* 05–06; R Triangle, St Matt and All SS from 06; AD Ipswich from 17; Hon Can St E Cathl from 17. *St Matthew's Rectory, 3 Portman Road, Ipswich IP1 2ES* T: (01473) 251630 E: rector@smast.org.uk

ATKINS, Canon Paul Henry. b 38. St Mich Coll Llan 62. **d** 65 **p** 66. C Sheringham *Nor* 65–68; V Southtown 68–84; RD Flegg (Gt Yarmouth) 78–84; R Aylmerton w Runton 84–99; P-in-c Beeston Regis 98–99; P-in-c Gresham 98–99; R Aylmerton, Runton, Beeston Regis and Gresham 99–03; RD Repps 86–95; Hon Can Nor Cathl 88–03; rtd 03; PtO *Nor* from 03. *34 Regis Avenue, Beeston Regis, Sheringham NR26 8SW* T: (01263) 820147   E: paulatkins07@btinternet.com   *or* paulatkins07@hotmail.co.uk

ATKINS, Robert Brian. b 49. Open Univ BA 94 CIPFA 78. SAOMC 94. **d** 97 **p** 98. NSM Bicester w Bucknell, Caversfield and Launton *Ox* 97–18; PtO *Derby* from 19. *39 Gertrude Road, Chaddesden, Derby DE21 4JQ* T: (01332) 679985 M: 07905-814401 E: bob@frbob.co.uk

ATKINS, Roger Francis. b 30. AKC 54. **d** 55 **p** 56. C Bromley All Hallows *Lon* 55–58; C Eastleigh *Win* 58–62; Missr The Murray Australia 62–65; R Mossman 65–69; Adn Carpentaria 69–71; V Wolverley *Worc* 71–76; V S Hackney St Mich w Haggerston St Paul *Lon* 76–85; TV Gleadless *Sheff* 85–93; rtd 93; PtO *Sheff* 93–20. *19 Stuart Court, High Street, Kibworth Beauchamp, Leicester LE8 0LR*

ATKINS, Mrs Sarah Christine. b 83. Magd Coll Cam MA 09. Ridley Hall Cam 12. **d** 14 **p** 16. C Trumpington *Ely* 14–18; Chapl Magd Coll Cam from 18. *Magdalene College, Cambridge CB3 0AG* T: (01223) 332129 M: 07906-659655 E: sarah.atkins@cantab.net

ATKINS, Mrs Sarah Elizabeth. b 61. Univ Coll Lon LLB 82. St Aug Coll of Th 16. **d** 19 **p** 20. NSM Ham St Rich *S'wark* from 19. *138 Manor Road North, Thames Ditton KT7 0BH* T: (020) 8398 7730 M: 07597-959473 E: sarah.atkins@yahoo.co.uk

ATKINS, Shaun. *See* ATKINS, Austen Shaun

ATKINS, Stephen John. b 65. Nottm Univ BSc 88 MA 91 Glos Univ MA 18 Dur Univ MA 21. Sarum Coll 18. **d** 21. NSM Spetisbury w Charlton Marshall etc *Sarum* from 21. *139A Merley Ways, Wimborne BH21 1QR* T: (01202) 885988 M: 07825-566336 E: saeatkins@icloud.com

ATKINS, Timothy David. b 45. Ridley Hall Cam 71. **d** 74 **p** 75. C Stoughton *Guildf* 74–79; C Chilwell *S'well* 79–84; R Eastwood 84–91; V Finchley Ch Ch *Lon* 91–10; Chapl Barnet Healthcare NHS Trust 92–01; Chapl Enfield Primary Care Trust 01–10; rtd 10; PtO *Lon* 10–12; Hon C Uxbridge from 12. *75 Belmont Road, Uxbridge UB8 1QU* T: (01895) 231801 M: 07875-747760 E: timanneatkins@gmail.com

ATKINS, Timothy James. b 38. Worc Coll Ox BA 62. Cuddesdon Coll 62. **d** 64 **p** 65. C Stafford St Mary *Lich* 64–67; C Loughborough St Pet *Leic* 67–69; C Usworth *Dur* 69–71; LtO *Newc* 71–76; P-in-c Slaley 76–87; P-in-c Shotley 87–05; Dioc Child Protection Adv 98–06; PtO *Dur* 06–21. *5 Railway Terrace, Witton le Wear, Bishop Auckland DL14 0AL* T: (01388) 488626 E: kandtatk@gmail.com

ATKINS, William. *See* ATKINS, Forrest William

ATKINSON, The Ven Adam. b 67. Birm Univ BA 89. Wycliffe Hall Ox 05. **d** 07 **p** 08. C Shadwell St Paul w Ratcliffe St Jas *Lon* 07–10; P-in-c Bethnal Green St Pet w St Thos 10–11; V 11–19; Miss Dir Development Two Cities Area 19–20; Adn Charing Cross from 20. *St Peter's Vicarage, St Peter's Close, London E2 7AE* T: (020) 7229 0550 M: 07780-992112 E: adam.atkinson@london.anglican.org

ATKINSON, Ms Audrey. b 54. Univ of Wales (Lamp) BA 97 Trin Coll Carmarthen PGCE 98. Coll of Resurr Mirfield 06. **d** 08 **p** 09. C Beadnell and N Sunderland *Newc* 08–11; Dep Warden Launde Abbey *Leic* 11; TV Oakham, Ashwell, Braunston, Brooke, Egleton etc *Pet* 11–14; Chapl HM Pris Full Sutton 14–17; rtd 17; PtO *York* 18–19. *Address withheld by request* M: 07833-198968 E: audreyatkinson@hotmail.co.uk

ATKINSON, Brian Colin. b 49. Sarum & Wells Th Coll 85. **d** 87 **p** 88. C Up Hatherley *Glouc* 87–90; R Upper Stour *Sarum* 90–95; TR Trowbridge H Trin 95–04; P-in-c Fairford and Kempsford w Whelford *Glouc* 04–08; TV S Cotswolds 09–14; AD Fairford 04–11; rtd 14; Hon C Minchinhampton w Box and Amberley *Glouc* 14–16; PtO from 17. *54 Lypiatt View, Bussage, Stroud GL6 8DA* E: katki01225@aol.com

ATKINSON, Christopher John. b 57. Man Univ BA 80. Qu Coll Birm 82. **d** 85 **p** 86. C Stalybridge *Man* 85–88; P-in-c Westhall w Brampton and Stoven *St E* 88–89; P-in-c Sotterley, Willingham, Shadingfield, Ellough etc 88–89; P-in-c Hundred River Gp of Par 90–92; R Hundred

River 92–97; P-in-c Eye w Braiseworth and Yaxley 97–00; P-in-c Occold 97–00; P-in-c Bedingfield 97–00; R Eye 00–03; RD Hartismere 97–03; V Bourne *Linc* from 03; RD Beltisloe 13–20. *Bourne Vicarage, Church Walk, Bourne PE10 9UQ* T: (01778) 422412 E: chris_atk@yahoo.com

ATKINSON, Canon Christopher Lionel Varley. b 39. K Coll Lon 63. Chich Th Coll 65. **d** 67 **p** 68. C Sowerby Bridge w Norland *Wakef* 67–70; P-in-c Flushing *Truro* 70–73; Dioc Adv in RE 70–73; PtO *Worc* 74–78; TR Halesowen 78–88; RD Dudley 79–87; Hon Can Worc Cathl 83–88; V Cartmel *Carl* 88–97; TV Cartmel Peninsula 97–98; RD Windermere 94–98; Hon Can Carl Cathl 94–98; TR Bensham *Dur* 98–03; AD Gateshead 99–03; rtd 03; Bp's Adv Spiritual Development *Dur* 03–08; Hon Can Dur Cathl 01–03; PtO from 11. *64 Beacon Street, Gateshead NE9 5XN* T: 0191-447 1732 E: chris.atkinson@durham.anglican.org *or* canon.chris.atkinson@gmail.com

ATKINSON, Clive James. b 68. QUB BSc 90. CITC 90. **d** 93 **p** 94. C Belfast H Trin and Ardoyne *Conn* 93–95; C Belfast H Trin and St Silas 96–97; I Belfast Upper Falls 97–02; Chapl Vevey w Château d'Oex *Eur* 02–21; Hon Can 19–21; I Willowfield *D & D* from 21. *149A My Lady's Road, Belfast BT6 8FE*

ATKINSON, Prof David. b 44. Hull Univ BSc 66 Newc Univ PhD 69 CBiol FIBiol FRSA MIEEM FRCPEd. TISEC 03. **d** 05 **p** 06. C Aberdeen St Andr *Ab* 05–07; NSM Bieldside 07–09; NSM Auchindoir from 09; NSM Inverurie from 09; NSM Kemnay from 09. *33 Norman Gray Park, Blackburn, Aberdeen AB21 0ZR* T: (01224) 791163 E: atkinson390@btinternet.com

ATKINSON, Canon David James. b 41. K Coll Lon BD 63 AKC 63 Selw Coll Cam BA 65 MA 72. Linc Th Coll 65. **d** 66 **p** 67. C Linc St Giles 66–70; Asst Chapl Newc Univ 70–73; P-in-c Adbaston *Lich* 73–80; Adult Educn Officer 73–75; Dioc Dir of Educn 75–82; Preb Lich Cathl 79–82; Chapl Hull Univ York 82–87; Dioc Dir of Educn *Linc* 87–94; P-in-c Bishop Norton, Waddingham and Snitterby 94–01; PtO from 01; Can and Preb Linc Cathl 89–06; rtd 06. *4 The Orchards, Middle Rasen, Market Rasen LN8 3TL* T: (01673) 849979

✠**ATKINSON, The Rt Revd David John.** b 43. K Coll Lon BSc 65 AKC 65 PhD 69 Bris Univ MLitt 73 Ox Univ MA 85 MSOSc. Trin Coll Bris and Tyndale Hall Bris 69. **d** 72 **p** 73 **c** 01. C Halliwell St Pet *Man* 72–74; C Harborne Heath *Birm* 74–77; Lib Latimer Ho Ox 77–80; Chapl CCC Ox 80–93; Fell 84–93; Visiting Lect Wycliffe Hall Ox 84–93; Can Res and Chan S'wark Cathl 93–96; Adn Lewisham 96–01; Suff Bp Thetford *Nor* 01–09; rtd 09; Asst Bp S'wark from 09. *6 Bynes Road, South Croydon CR2 0PR* T: (020) 8406 0895 E: davidatkinson43@virginmedia.com

ATKINSON, David Steven. b 85. Nottm Univ BSc 06 Cam Univ BTh 20. Ridley Hall Cam 18. **d** 20 **p** 21. C Wallington Springfield Ch *S'wark* from 20. *5 Milton Road, Wallington SM6 9RP* M: 07871-705794 E: david@springfieldchurch.org.uk

ATKINSON, Donald. b 31. Magd Coll Cam BA 54 MA 57. Chich Th Coll. **d** 56 **p** 57. C Dorking w Ranmore *Guildf* 56–58; C Hillingdon St Andr *Lon* 59–60; Hd Master Friern Barnet Gr Sch 60–96; rtd 96. *9 Maxwell Close, Lichfield WS13 6TY*

ATKINSON, Mrs Heather Dawn. b 69. Leeds Univ BA 02. NOC 03. **d** 05 **p** 06. C Morley *Wakef* 05–08; P-in-c Moldgreen and Rawthorpe *Leeds* 08–16; V New Brighton St Jas w Em *Ches* from 16. *St James's Vicarage, 14 Albion Street, Wallasey CH45 9LF* T: 0151-639 5844 M: 07877-581092 E: revheatheratkinson@gmail.com

ATKINSON, Heather Mary Ann. b 66. Birm Univ BA 89 Nottm Univ PGCE 90. St Mellitus Coll BA 15. **d** 15 **p** 16. NSM S Hackney St Mich w Haggerston St Paul *Lon* 15–16; C 16–18; Chapl The Urswick Sch 14–16; C Bethnal Green St Pet w St Thos *Lon* 18–19; V from 19. *St Peter's Vicarage, St Peter's Close, London E2 7AE* T: (020) 7739 0550 M: 07970-197152 E: heather@stpetersbethnalgreen.org *or* atkinson.heather@gmail.com

ATKINSON, Ian. b 33. BNC Ox BA 58 MA 63. Coll of Resurr Mirfield 56. **d** 58 **p** 59. C Welling *S'wark* 58–62; C Camberwell St Giles 62–63; V Wandsworth Common St Mary 63–67; C Pretoria Cathl S Africa 67–68; C Oxted *S'wark* 68–69; Asst Chapl Ch Hosp Horsham 70–85; NSM Dalmahoy *Edin* 85–91; Asst Master Clifton Hall Sch 85–91; NSM Dunkeld *St And* 91–16; LtO from 16. *2 Pinel Lodge, Druids Park, Murthly, Perth PH1 4ES* T: (01738) 710561

ATKINSON, Jane Louise. b 66. **d** 13 **p** 14. NSM Kirkham *Blackb* 13–17; V Lt Thornton from 17. *St John's Vicarage, 35 Station Road, Thornton-Cleveleys FY5 5HY* T: (01253) 969492 E: revjaneatkinson@sky.com

ATKINSON, Canon Lewis Malcolm. b 34. Cranmer Hall Dur. d 82 **p** 83. C Chapeltown *Sheff* 82–85; V Sheff St Paul 85–93; Ind Chapl 85–99; RD Ecclesfield 90–93; V Oughtibridge 93–99; RD Tankersley 96–99; Hon Can Sheff Cathl 98–99; rtd 99; PtO *Sheff* from 99. *14 Rowan Close, Chapeltown, Sheffield S35 1QE*

ATKINSON, Marianne Rose. b 39. Girton Coll Cam BA 61 MA 64 Homerton Coll Cam CertEd 62. Linc Th Coll 86. d 88 **p** 94. C S w N Hayling *Portsm* 88–91; C Rainham *Roch* 91–92; Asst Chapl Salford R Hosps NHS Trust 92–97; Hon C Prestwich St Marg *Man* 94–97; Chapl R United Hosp Bath NHS Trust 97–00; rtd 00; PtO *B & W* 00–03; *St E* 03–21. *68 Barons Road, Bury St Edmunds IP33 2LW* T: (01284) 752075 E: torrensatkinson@aol.com

ATKINSON, Nigel Terence. b 60. Sheff Univ BA 82 St Jo Coll Dur MA 96. Westmr Th Sem (USA) MDiv 87 Cranmer Hall Dur 87. d 89 **p** 90. C Oakwood St Thos *Lon* 89–92; P-in-c Dolton *Ex* 92–95; P-in-c Iddesleigh w Dowland 92–95; P-in-c Monkokehampton 92–95; Warden Latimer Ho Ox 95–98; V Knutsford St Jo and Toft *Ches* from 98. *The Vicarage, 11 Gough's Lane, Knutsford WA16 8QL* T: (01565) 632834 F: 755160 E: nigel.atkinson@stjohnsknutsford.org.uk

ATKINSON, Canon Patricia Anne. b 47. EAMTC 86. d 89 **p** 01. NSM Nor St Steph 89–94; LtO 94–17; Chapl Norfolk Primary Care Trust from 00; Chapl Norfolk and Nor Univ Hosps NHS Foundn Trust 01–11; NSM Brundall w Braydeston and Postwick Nor 01–02; PtO from 17; Hon Can Nor Cathl from 06. *32 Berryfields, Brundall, Norwich NR13 5QE* T: (01603) 714720 E: patatkinson44@gmail.com

ATKINSON, Paul William. b 64. St Steph Ho Ox 07. d 09 **p** 10. C Castleford *Wakef* 09–13; C Smawthorpe 11–12; P-in-c Ravensthorpe and Thornhill Lees w Savile Town 13–14; *Leeds* 14–17; V Cookridge H Trin from 17. *Holy Trinity Vicarage, 53 Green Lane, Cookridge, Leeds LS16 7LW*

ATKINSON, Peter Duncan. b 41. Univ Coll Dur BA 62. Linc Th Coll 63. d 65 **p** 66. C Beckenham St Geo *Roch* 65–69; C Caversham *Ox* 69–75; P-in-c Millfield St Mark *Dur* 76–86; V Dedworth *Ox* 86–93; TV Aylesbury 93–95; rtd 05. *24 Grimbald Road, Knaresborough HG5 8HD* T: (01423) 866593

ATKINSON, The Very Revd Peter Gordon. b 52. St Jo Coll Ox BA 74 MA 78 Worc Univ Hon DLitt 14 FRSA 06. Westcott Ho Cam 77. d 79 **p** 80. C Clapham Old Town *S'wark* 79–83; P-in-c Tatsfield 83–90; R Bath H Trin *B & W* 90–91; Prin Chich Th Coll 91–94; Can and Preb Chich Cathl 91–97; R Lavant 94–97; Can Res and Chan Chich Cathl 97–07; Dean Worc from 07; PtO *Eur* from 01. *The Deanery, 10 College Green, Worcester WR1 2LH* T: (01905) 732939 *or* 732909 F: 732906 E: peteratkinson@worcestercathedral.org.uk

ATKINSON, Peter Michael. b 87. Trin Coll Bris BA 16. d 16 **p** 17. C Warrington W *Liv* 16–18; C St Helens Town Cen 18–20; Min Can Saram Cathl from 20. *Address withheld by request* M: 07950-878767 E: p.atkinson@salcath.co.uk

ATKINSON, Philip Stephen. b 58. K Coll Lon BD 80 AKC 80 Dur Univ MA 97. Ridley Hall Cam 81. d 83 **p** 84. C Barrow St Matt *Carl* 83–86; C Kirkby Lonsdale 86–89; R Redmarshall *Dur* 89–95; V Bishopton w Gt Stainton 89–95; C Kirkby Lonsdale *Carl* 95–97; Chapl Casterton Sch Lancs 95–09; NSM Kirkby Lonsdale *Carl* 97–09; Chapl Taunton Sch 09–11; R Odd Rode *Ches* from 11. *Odd Rode Rectory, Church Lane, Scholar Green, Stoke-on-Trent ST7 3QN* T: (01270) 882195 E: rector.oddrode@gmail.com

ATKINSON, Richard Timothy Kenneth. b 81. Leic Univ BA 03. Ridley Hall Cam 15. d 17 **p** 18. C Onslow Square and S Kensington St Aug *Lon* 17–18; V Aspley *S'well* from 18; P-in-c Bilborough and Strelley from 19; P-in-c Basford St Leodegarius and St Aid from 20. *319 Aspley Lane, Nottingham NG8 5GA* M: 07736-306980 E: rich@timetorebuild.co.uk

✠**ATKINSON, The Rt Revd Richard William Bryant.** b 58. OBE 02. Magd Coll Cam MA. Ripon Coll Cuddesdon. d 84 **p** 85 **c** 12. C Abingdon w Shippon *Ox* 84–87; TV Sheff Manor 87–91; TR 91–96; Hon Tutor Ripon Coll Cuddesdon 87–92; V Rotherham *Sheff* 96–02; Hon Can Sheff Cathl 98–02; Adn Leic 02–12; Suff Bp Bedford *St Alb* from 12. *Bishop's Lodge, Bedford Road, Cardington, Bedford MK44 3SS* T: (01234) 831432 F: 831484 E: bishopbedford@stalbans.anglican.org

ATKINSON, Mrs Ruth Alison. b 65. Ridley Hall Cam 13. d 16 **p** 17. C Thorley *St Alb* 16–20; P-in-c Penn Street *Ox* from 20. *The Vicarage, Penn Street, Amersham HP7 0PX* M: 07973-312892 E: r_atkinson1@hotmail.co.uk

ATKINSON, Miss Ruth Irene. b 58. Worc Coll of Educn BEd 80 Cant Ch Ch Univ MA 08. Qu Coll Birm 06. d 09 **p** 10. C Old Swinford Stourbridge *Worc* 09–14; V Bartley Green *Birm* from 14. *96 Romsley Road, Birmingham B32 3PS* T: 0121-476 5287 M: 07432-660538 E: revruthvicarbg@gmail.com

ATKINSON, Simon James. b 71. St Chad's Coll Dur BA 93 Ustinov Coll Dur PGCE 04. St Steph Ho Ox 93. d 95 **p** 96. C Norton St Mary *Dur* 95–96; C Hartlepool H Trin 96–99; TV Jarrow 99–01; V Chich St Wilfrid 01–03; PtO *Dur* 03–09; *Lon* 09–18; NSM Old St Pancras 10–17; NSM Colindale St Matthias from 17; Headteacher Hampstead Paroch C of E Primary Sch 10–15; Headteacher St Steph C of E Primary Sch 15–20; Hd of Primary Sch St Mary's and St Jo C of E Sch from 20; CMP 98–20. *22 Ascent House, 35 Boulevard Drive, London NW9 5QZ* M: 07453-299411 E: s.atkinson@smsj.london

ATKINSON, Mrs Valerie. b 50. d 12. NSM Teignmouth, Ideford w Luton, Ashcombe etc *Ex* 12–20; Asst Chapl HM Pris Ex from 20. *HM Prison Exeter, New North Road, Exeter EX4 4EX* T: (01392) 415650 E: valian09@btinternet.com

ATKINSON, Wendy Sybil. b 53. Man Univ BA 95. NOC 95. d 97 **p** 98. NSM Brinnington w Portwood *Ches* 97–99; C 99–01; NSM Werneth from 01. *8 Freshfield Close, Marple Bridge, Stockport SK6 5ES* T: 0161-427 5612 E: wendyatkinson33@yahoo.co.uk

ATKINSON-JONES, Mrs Susan Florence. b 64. Univ of Wales (Cardiff) BD 93. St Mich Coll Llan 96. d 98 **p** 99. C Bargoed and Deri w Brithdir *Llan* 98–05; TV Sanderstead *S'wark* 05–19; P-in-c Green Street Green and Pratts Bottom *Roch* 19–21; R Chelsfield w Green Street Green and Pratts Bottom from 21. *The Vicarage, 46 World's End Lane, Orpington BR6 6AG*

ATLING, Canon Edwood Brian. b 46. ACIB FCMI. Westcott Ho Cam 00. d 02 **p** 03. NSM Godmanchester *Ely* 02–04; P-in-c Abbots Ripton w Wood Walton 04–12; P-in-c Kings Ripton 04–12; P-in-c Houghton w Wyton 04–13; R Hartford and Houghton w Wyton 13–16; P-in-c Fen Drayton 17–18; P-in-c Fenstanton 17–18; P-in-c Fen Drayton w Fenstanton 18–19; RD Huntingdon 06–19; C Hemingford Abbots from 19; C Hemingford Grey from 19; Hon Can Ely Cathl from 10. *Ash Meadow, Meadow Lane, Hemingford Abbots, Huntingdon PE28 9AR* T: (01480) 493975 M: 07775-544679 E: atling@btopenworld.com

ATTLEY, Ronald. b 46. Open Univ BA 87. Brasted Th Coll 66 Chich Th Coll 68. d 70 **p** 71. C Heworth St Mary *Dur* 70–73; C Hulme Ascension *Man* 73–75; R Corozal and Orange Walk Belize 76–79; V Leadgate *Dur* 79–84; Chapl HM Rem Cen Ashford 84–87; Chapl HM Pris Ashwell 87–89; Chapl HM Pris Stocken 87–89; Chapl HM Pris Frankland 89–92; Chapl HM YOI Deerbolt 92–96; V Bath St Barn w Englishcombe *B & W* 96–00; Belize 00; V Brinnington w Portwood *Ches* 01–06; P Narrogin Australia 06–12; rtd 12. *103 Clayton Road, Narrogin WA 6312, Australia*

ATTWATER, Mrs Sallyanne. b 48. Westmr Coll Ox MTh 98. S Dios Minl Tr Scheme 86. d 94 **p** 95. Chapl Asst Eastbourne Distr Gen Hosp 94–95; Asst Chapl Princess Alice Hospice Esher 94–95; Asst Chapl All SS Eastbourne 94–95; C E Grinstead St Swithun *Chich* 95–98; P-in-c Bishop's Cannings, All Cannings etc *Sarum* 98–10; RD Devizes 07–10; rtd 10; PtO *Chich* from 16. *51 St Kitts Drive, Eastbourne BN23 5TL* T: (01323) 472266 E: sally.attwater@gmail.com

ATTWATER, Canon Stephen Philip. b 47. ALCM 67. Linc Th Coll 85. d 87 **p** 88. C Warrington St Elphin *Liv* 87–90; P-in-c Eccleston St Thos 90–94; V 94–99; V Padgate 99–13; AD Warrington 05–12; Hon Can Liv Cathl 01–13; rtd 13; PtO *Ches* from 13. *30 Rowcliffe Avenue, Chester CH4 7PW* M: 07523-492863 E: attwater292@btinternet.com

ATTWOOD, Preb Carl Norman Harry. b 53. Bris Univ BA 74. Cuddesdon Coll BA 76 MA 80. d 77 **p** 78. C Tupsley *Heref* 77–82; R Colwall w Upper Colwall and Coddington 82–08; Bp's Voc Officer 83–89; RD Ledbury 90–96; Chapl St Jas Sch Malvern 86–08; Preb Heref Cathl 97–08; rtd 08; PtO *Worc* 82–06; *Heref* from 08. *The Lodge, Old Colwall, Malvern WR13 6HF* T: (01604) 540788 E: carl@attwoods.org

ATTWOOD, David John Edwin. b 51. Dur Univ BA 76 Em Coll Cam BA 73 MA 77. Cranmer Hall Dur 74. d 77 **p** 78. C Rodbourne Cheney *Bris* 77–79; C Lydiard Millicent w Lydiard Tregoz 79–85; Dir and Lect Trin Coll Bris 85–97; V Prenton *Ches* 97–02; R Sundridge w Ide Hill and Toys Hill *Roch* 02–13; rtd 13; PtO *Chich* from 17. *65 The Ridge, Hastings TN34 2AB* T: (01424) 440635 E: david.attwood5@btinternet.com

ATTWOOD, Leslie Thomas. b 42. UWE MA 94 Cranfield Univ MBA MCIPD 76. St Steph Ho Ox. d 83 **p** 84. C Ascot Heath *Ox* 83–86; Dioc Tr Officer *Truro* 86–88; C Wallasey St Hilary *Ches* 98–00; C Devizes St Pet *Sarum* 00–02; TV Godrevy *Truro* 02–07; TR 07–09; rtd 09; PtO *Truro* from 15. *Chyrempter, Perranuthnoe, Penzance TR20 9NQ* T: (01736) 710449 E: leslie.attwood@gmail.com

ATTWOOD, Peter John. b 44. ACIB 68. SEITE 00. d 03 **p** 04. NSM Langton Green *Roch* 03–06; C S Molton w Nymet St George, High Bray etc *Ex* 06–12; RD S Molton 09–12; rtd

12; PtO *B & W* from 12. *Brome Cottage, 86 Castle Hill, Nether Stowey, Bridgwater TA5 1NB* T: (01278) 734588 M: 07714-026402 E: rev@podlea.co.uk

ATTY, Norman Hughes. b 40. Dur Univ BA 62. Cranmer Hall Dur 62. **d** 65 **p** 66. C Blackb St Gabr 65–67; Asst Master Billinge Sch Blackb 67–71; City of Leic Boys' Sch 71–73; P-in-c Elmley Lovett w Hampton Lovett *Worc* 73–78; P-in-c Elmbridge w Rushock 74–78; R Elmley Lovett w Hampton Lovett and Elmbridge etc 78–85; Hon Can Worc Cathl 81–85; rtd 05; PtO *Blackb* 05–20. *The Dog Inn, King Street, Whalley, Clitheroe BB7 9SP* T: (01254) 823009 E: attyaoahouse@gmail.com

✠**ATWELL, The Rt Revd Robert Ronald.** b 54. St Jo Coll Dur BA 75 Dur Univ MLitt 79. Westcott Ho Cam 76. **d** 78 **p** 79 **c** 08. C Mill Hill Jo Keble Ch Lon 78–81; Chapl Trin Coll Cam 81–87; OSB 87–98; LtO *Ox* 87–97; PtO *Ely* 97–98; V Primrose Hill St Mary w Avenue Road St Paul *Lon* 98–08; Suff Bp Stockport *Ches* 08–14; Bp Ex from 14. *The Palace, Exeter EX1 1HY* T: (01392) 272362 F: 430923 E: bishop.of.exeter@exeter.anglican.org

AUBREY-JONES, Adrian Frederick. b 51. ERMC 04. **d** 07 **p** 08. NSM Dersingham w Anmer and Shernborne *Nor* 07–10; TV Dereham and Distr 10–16; RD Dereham in Mitford 15–16; rtd 16; PtO *Nor* 17–20; Hon C Dersingham, Anmer, Ingoldisthorpe etc from 20. *23 Tudor Way, Dersingham, King's Lynn PE31 6LX* T: (01485) 542244 M: 07775-514567 E: a3351adrian@aol.com

AUCHMUTY, Canon John Robert. b 67. ACCA. CITC 89. **d** 92 **p** 93. C Dundela St Mark *D & D* 92–96; I Eglish w Killylea *Arm* 96–01; I Killaney w Carryduff *D & D* 01–07; I Knock from 07; Can Down Cathl from 16; Chan from 20. *St Columba's Rectory, 29 King's Road, Knock, Belfast BT5 6JG* T: (028) 9047 1514 E: rectorknock@down.anglican.org

AUCKEN, Mrs Hazel Margaret. b 61. New Hall Cam BA 83 MA 87 Lon Univ PhD 94. St Hild Coll 17. **d** 19 **p** 20. C Newbold de Verdun, Barlestone and Kirkby Mallory *Leic* 19–21; C Peckleton 19–21; C Newbold De Verdun, Barlestone, Kirkby Mallory and Peckleton from 21. *36 Main Street, Kirkby Mallory, Leicester LE9 7QB* M: 07976-808959 E: hazel.aucken@outlook.com

AUCKLAND, Mrs Susan Frances. **d** 12 **p** 13. OLM Scole, Brockdish, Billingford, Thorpe Abbots etc *Nor* 12–14; OLM Redenhall w Scole 14–21; PtO from 21. *Greenbanks, 8 Karen Close, Scole, Diss IP21 4DL* T: (01379) 740325 M: 07825-838403 E: susanauckland@btinternet.com *or* revsue@7churches.org.uk

AUCKLAND, Archdeacon of. *See* SIMPSON, The Ven Richard Lee

AUDIBERT, Canon Janice Elizabeth. b 56. **d** 99 **p** 00. OLM Oakdale *Sarum* 99–02; C N Poole Ecum Team 02–06; TV 06–16; P-in-c 16; V Creekmoor from 17; Can and Preb Sarum Cathl from 19. *24 Blackbird Close, Poole BH17 7YA* T: (01202) 389751 E: janiceaudibert@gmail.com *or* rev.janice@christchurchcreekmoor.org

AUDIBERT, Jean Robert Alain. b 58. Sarum Coll 15. **d** 17 **p** 18. NSM Creekmoor *Sarum* from 17. *24 Blackbird Close, Poole BH17 7YA* T: (01202) 389751 E: revjohn.aiw@gmail.com

AUDU, Ayodeji Ocholi Ibrahim Ada. b 77. Bucks New Univ LLB 07 Qu Mary Coll Lon LLM 08 Dur Univ BA 21. St Mellitus Coll 18. **d** 21. C Water Eaton *Ox* from 21. *3 Wraxall Way, Ashland, Milton Keynes MK6 4AF* E: a.o.a.audu@gmail.com

AULD, Jeremy Rodger. b 66. Edin Univ LLB 87 Solicitor 89 Barrister 97. TISEC BD 04. **d** 04 **p** 05. C Edin St Pet 04–06; Hon Chapl Edin Univ 04–06; R Dollar *St And* 06–10; Provost St Paul's Cathl Dundee *Bre* 10–20; Hon Chapl Dundee Univ 10–20; R Woodstock and Bladon *Ox* from 20; AD Woodstock from 20. *The Rectory, Rectory Lane, Woodstock OX20 1UQ* M: 07715-868960 E: jeremy.auld@btinternet.com

AULD, Mrs Sheila Edith. b 38. Newc Poly BA 87 Univ of Northumbria at Newc MA 99. NEOC 91. **d** 94 **p** 95. Project Worker Cedarwood Trust 88–02; NSM Newc St Gabr 94–02; rtd 02; PtO *Newc* from 02. *5 Gibson Fields, Hexham NE46 1AS* T: (01434) 602297 E: sheilaauld@ovidian.co.uk

AUSSANT, Mrs Jill Amaryllis. b 43. Ripon Coll Cuddesdon. **d** 07 **p** 08. NSM Crawley and Littleton and Sparsholt w Lainston *Win* 07–08; NSM The Downs 08–10; NSM Romsey 10–14; PtO from 14. *121 Hocombe Road, Chandler's Ford, Eastleigh SO53 5QD* T: (023) 8026 9799 E: jill@vaussant.plus.com

AUSTEN, Canon John. b 46. St Cath Coll Cam BA 69 MA 72. Qu Coll Birm. **d** 71 **p** 72. C Thornaby on Tees *York* 71–74; C Aston St Jas *Birm* 74–82; Chapl Aston Univ 82–88; C Handsworth St Andr 88–11; Hon Can Birm Cathl 06–11; rtd 11; PtO *Birm* from 11. *151 Church Lane, Handsworth, Birmingham B20 2RU* T: 0121-554 8882 E: johnausten151@hotmail.co.uk

AUSTEN, Matthew Robert George. b 85. St Steph Ho Ox 18. **d** 20 **p** 21. C Brentwood St Thos *Chelmsf* from 20. *Stokes House, 25-27 St Thomas Road, Brentwood CM14 4DF* M: 07756-378739 E: frmausten@gmail.com

AUSTEN, Simon Neil. b 67. Warwick Univ BSc 88. Wycliffe Hall Ox BA 93 MA 97. **d** 94 **p** 95. C Gt Chesham *Ox* 94–98; Chapl Stowe Sch 98–02; V Houghton *Carl* 02–13; R Ex St Leon w H Trin from 13. *St Leonard's Rectory, 27 St Leonard's Road, Exeter EX2 4LA* T: (01392) 286993 E: simon.austen@stleonards.church

AUSTERBERRY, Preb David Naylor. b 35. Birm Univ BA 58. Wells Th Coll 58. **d** 60 **p** 61. C Leek St Edw *Lich* 60–63; Iran 64–70; Chapl CMS Foxbury 70–73; V Walsall Pleck and Bescot *Lich* 73–82; R Brierley Hill 82–88; R Kinnerley w Melverley and Knockin w Maesbrook 88–99; RD Oswestry 92–95; Preb Lich Cathl 96–00; rtd 00; PtO *Lich* 00–21; *Heref* 01–08. *Chad Cottage, Dovaston, Kinnerley, Oswestry SY10 8DT* T: (01691) 682039

AUSTERBERRY, John Maurice. b 62. Birm Univ BA 83 Leeds Univ MA 01. Sarum & Wells Th Coll 84. **d** 86 **p** 87. C Clayton *Lich* 86–89; Asst Chapl Withington Hosp Man 89–95; Chapl Tameside and Glossop NHS Trust 95–99; Chapl Univ Hosp of N Staffs NHS Trust 99–17; Chapl Kath Ho Hospice Stafford 17–20; Bp's Adv on Healthcare Chapl *Lich* 11–19; V Alstonfield, Ilam and Wetton from 19. *The Vicarage, Alstonfield, Ashbourne DE6 2FX* M: 07766-042754 E: revjohn.aiw@gmail.com

AUSTIN (*née* JONES), Mrs Angela Mary. b 51. Man Univ BSc 00. WEMTC 10. **d** 13 **p** 14. NSM S Cerney w Cerney Wick, Siddington and Preston *Glouc* 13–17; NSM Kemble, Poole Keynes, Somerford Keynes etc from 19. *The Vicarage, Kemble, Cirencester GL7 6AG* T: (01285) 770654 M: 07776-101253 E: revangiemary@icloud.com

AUSTIN, David Samuel John. b 63. St Jo Coll Dur BATM 11 Sheff Univ MA 15. Cranmer Hall Dur 09. **d** 11 **p** 12. C Addingham *Leeds* 11–15; V New Catton St Luke w St Aug *Nor* 15–18; V Coldhurst and Oldham St Steph *Man* from 18. *Holy Trinity Vicarage, 46 Godson Street, Oldham OL1 2DB* M: 07740-922468 E: dsj.austin@hotmail.com

AUSTIN, Glyn. *See* AUSTIN, Ronald Glyn

AUSTIN, Miss Jane. b 43. SRN 64 SCM 66. **dss** 81 **d** 87 **p** 94. Tonbridge SS Pet and Paul *Roch* 81–98; C 87–98; Hon Can Roch Cathl 96–98; P-in-c Meltham *Wakef* 98–01; V 01–07; P-in-c Helme 00–01; RD Almondbury 01–06; rtd 07; PtO *Wakef* 08–14; *Leeds* from 14. *177 Bourne View Road, Netherton, Huddersfield HD4 7JS* T: (01484) 664212 E: revjaustin@aol.com

AUSTIN, Leslie Ernest. b 46. Trin Coll Bris 72. **d** 74 **p** 75. C Paddock Wood *Roch* 74–79; C Upper Armley *Ripon* 79–81; V Horton *Bradf* 81–85; V Long Preston w Tosside 85–97; TR Shirwell, Loxhore, Kentisbury, Arlington, etc *Ex* 97–12; RD Shirwell 10–12; rtd 12; PtO *Ches* 16–18. *7 Kennedy Close, Chester CH2 2PL* T: (01244) 314723 E: leslie.austin@btinternet.com

AUSTIN, Lucie. b 48. Th Ext Educn Coll. **d** 08 **p** 09. C Sunninghill St Steph S Africa 08–10; PtO *Ox* 11–12; NSM Icknield 12–18; PtO from 18. *20 Raven Road, Stokenchurch, High Wycombe HP14 3QP* T: (01494) 483729 M: 07906-684987 E: luciea48@gmail.com

AUSTIN, Ronald Glyn. b 52. Univ of Wales (Cardiff) BD 90 Univ of Wales MPhil 98. St Mich Coll Llan 88. **d** 90 **p** 91. C Llangynwyd w Maesteg *Llan* 90–91; C Barry All SS 91–93; V Nantymoel w Wyndham 93–97; V Pontyclun w Talygarn 97–02; Tutor St Mich Coll Llan 02–04; V Llansantffraid, Bettws and Aberkenfig *Llan* 04–06; PtO 07–15; Hon C Gtr Gower *S & B* from 15. *The Vicarage, Llangennith, Swansea SA3 1HU* T: (01792) 386782 E: glynaustin52@gmail.com

AUSTIN, Preb Rosemary Elizabeth. b 68. K Alfred's Coll Win BEd 91 Ex Univ BTh 14. SWMTC 08. **d** 11 **p** 12. C Fremington, Instow and Westleigh *Ex* 11–15; TR Shirwell, Loxhore, Kentisbury, Arlington, etc from 15; RD Shirwell from 18; Preb Ex Cathl from 20. *The Parsonage, 1 The Glebe, Bratton Fleming, Barnstaple EX31 4RE* T: (01598) 711962 E: rosieaustin@live.co.uk

AUSTIN, Mrs Susan Frances. b 47. Open Univ BA 81. Cant Sch of Min 87. **d** 92 **p** 94. Chapl Ch Ch High Sch Ashford 90–94; C Gt Chart *Cant* 92–94; C Ashford 92–94; C Estover *Ex* 94–96; V Stevenage All SS Pin Green *St Alb* 96–98; P-in-c Bredgar w Bicknor and Frinsted w Wormshill etc *Cant* 00–04; rtd 04; PtO *Cant* 04–13; *B & W* from 14. *Stepping Stones, Park Lane, Carhampton, Minehead TA24 6NL* T: (01643) 822550 M: 07443-948306 E: saraustin@btinternet.com

AVANN, Canon Penelope Joyce. b 46. **dss** 83 **d** 87 **p** 98. Southborough St Pet w Ch Ch and St Matt *Roch* 83–89; Par Dn 87–89; Warden Past Assts 89–10; Par Dn Beckenham St Jo *Roch* 89–94; C 94–02; C Green Street Green and Pratts

Bottom 02–16; Hon Can Roch Cathl 94–16; rtd 16; PtO *Chich* from 17. *53 Pilot Road, Hastings TN34 2AP* M: 07745-657557 E: pennyavann@btinternet.com

AVENT, Mrs Hilary. b 50. Sunderland Univ CertEd 03. **d** 20 **p** 21. NSM Hetton-Lyons w Eppleton *Dur* from 20. *19 Brookside, Houghton le Spring DH5 9NW* M: 07723-061078 E: hilary.avent@yahoo.co.uk

AVERAY, Philip Roger. b 75. **d** 14 **p** 15. C Drybrook, Lydbrook and Ruardean *Glouc* 14–17; V Chepstow *Mon* from 17. *The Vicarage, 25 Mount Way, Chepstow NP16 5NF* T: (01291) 620980 E: revphilipaveray@gmail.com

AVERY, Andrew James. b 58. Open Univ BA 81 Dudley Coll of Educn CertEd 79. St Jo Coll Nottm 06. **d** 08 **p** 09. C Brundall w Braydeston and Postwick *Nor* 08–11; TV Gt Yarmouth 11–13; P-in-c Greenhithe St Mary *Roch* 13–19; P-in-c Stanground and Farcet *Ely* from 19. *The Vicarage, Main Street, Farcet, Peterborough PE7 3AN* M: 07976-523554 E: revavery@hotmail.co.uk

AVERY, Carol Rosemary. b 58. BEM 19. Dur Univ BA 20. St Mellitus Coll 14. **d** 16 **p** 17. NSM Stone *Roch* 16–19; C Stanground and Farcet *Ely* from 19. *The Vicarage, Main Street, Farcet, Peterborough PE7 3AN* M: 07976-523555 E: carolavery131@gmail.com

AVERY, Derek Anthony. b 61. Lindisfarne Regional Tr Partnership 16. **d** 19 **p** 20. NSM Newc St Geo and St Hilda from 19. *15 Northumberland Gardens, Jesmond, Newcastle upon Tyne NE2 1HA* E: averyhrd@aol.com

AVERY, Mrs Lydia Dorothy Ann. b 57. Sheff Univ MA 03 Bath Spa Univ Coll PGCE 97. STETS BA 08. **d** 08 **p** 09. C Pilton w Croscombe, N Wootton and Dinder *B & W* 08–11; P-in-c Winscombe and Sandford 11–16; V 16–18; RD Locking 16–18; P-in-c Upper Tas Valley *Nor* from 18. *The Rectory, 16 The Fields, Tacolneston, Norwich NR16 1DG* E: ldavery@btinternet.com

AVERY, Richard Hugh. b 61. All SS Cen for Miss & Min 15. **d** 18 **p** 19. NSM Wallasey St Hilary *Ches* from 18. *90 Dingwall Drive, Wirral CH49 1SQ*

AVERY, Richard Julian. b 52. Keble Coll Ox BA 73. St Jo Coll Nottm 74. **d** 77 **p** 78. C Macclesfield St Mich *Ches* 77–80; Asst P Prince Albert St Dav Canada 82–83; C Becontree St Mary *Chelmsf* 84–87; R Hudson Bay Canada 87–90; R Duncan 90–97; TV Cheltenham St Mark *Glouc* 97–03; PtO 03–06; P-in-c Berkeley w Wick, Breadstone, Newport, Stone etc 06–11; V 11–18; rtd 18; PtO *Sarum* from 19. *Timberley, The Ridge, Redlynch, Salisbury SP5 2LN* T: (01725) 238327 E: averys@rjavery.co.uk

AVERY, Robert Edward. b 69. Magd Coll Cam BA 90. Ripon Coll Cuddesdon MPhil 93. **d** 93 **p** 94. C Cen Telford *Lich* 93–96; C Cambridge Gt St Mary w St Mich *Ely* 96–99; V Tamerton Foliot *Ex* 99–03; V Tunbridge Wells K Chas *Roch* 03–15; RD Tunbridge Wells 14–15; R Nor St Pet Mancroft w St Jo Maddermarket 15–17; Nat Discernment Adv Abps' Coun from 18. *23 Friezland Road, Tunbridge Wells TN4 8LJ* E: robertavery@me.com

AVESON, Ian Henry. b 55. Jes Coll Ox BA 77 MA 81 Univ Coll Dur PGCE 78 Birkbeck Coll Lon MSc 85. St Mich Coll Llan 88. **d** 97 **p** 98. C Penarth All SS *Llan* 97–99; TV Aberystwyth *St D* 99–07; V Llandingat w Myddfai 07–19; AD Llandeilo from 12; rtd 19. *18 Chestnut Drive, Abergavenny NP7 5JZ* E: ianaveson@hotmail.com

AVEYARD, Ian. b 46. Liv Univ BSc 68 Sheff Univ MEd 00. ALCD 72 St Jo Coll Nottm 71. **d** 71 **p** 72. C Bradley *Wakef* 71–74; C Knowle *Birm* 74–79; P-in-c Cofton Hackett 79; P-in-c Barnt Green 79; V Cofton Hackett w Barnt Green 80–94; Dioc Dir of Reader Tr 85–94; Warden of Readers 91–94; Course Leader St Jo Coll Nottm 96–99; P-in-c Thanington *Cant* 99–99; Dioc Dir of Ords 99–09; rtd 09; PtO *Glouc* from 10. *19 The Damsells, Tetbury GL8 8JA* T: (01666) 502278 E: ian.aveyard1@btinternet.com

AVIS, Elizabeth Mary. *See* BAXTER, Elizabeth Mary

AVIS, Paul David Loup. b 47. Lon Univ BD 70 PhD 76. Westcott Ho Cam 73. **d** 75 **p** 76. C S Molton, Nymet St George, High Bray etc *Ex* 75–80; V Stoke Canon, Poltimore w Huxham and Rewe etc 80–98; Preb Ex Cathl 93–08; Sub Dean Ex Cathl 97–08; Can Th Ex Cathl 08–13; Hon Prof Ex Univ 09–17; Hon Research Fell from 17; Hon Prof Dur Univ from 17; Gen Sec Coun for Chr Unity 98–11; Th Consultant Angl Communion Office 11–12; Chapl to The Queen 08–17; Ed *Ecclesiology* from 04. *Lea Hill, Membury, Axminster EX13 7AQ* T: (01404) 881881 E: reception@leahill.co.uk

AVRAMENKO, Andrew Richard. b 73. Derby Univ BSc 94 Leeds Univ MRes 97 Bath Spa Univ PGCE 08. Sarum Coll BA 20. **d** 20 **p** 21. C Charlcombe w Bath St Steph *B & W* from 20. *23 Lucklands Road, Bath BA1 4AX* T: (01225) 840064 M: 07908-485961 E: andrewavramenko@me.com

AWRE, Canon Richard William Esgar. b 56. Univ of Wales BA 78. Wycliffe Hall Ox 78. **d** 81 **p** 82. C Blackpool St Jo *Blackb* 81–84; Asst Dir of Ords and Voc Adv 84–89; C Altham w Clayton le Moors 84–89; V Longridge 89–99; V Kenilworth St Nic *Cov* 99–15; RD Kenilworth 01–09; Hon Can Cov Cathl 11–15; rtd 15; PtO *Blackb* 16–17. *9 Irwell Mews, Clitheroe BB7 2FR* T: (01200) 424061 E: richard.awre@gmail.com

AXE, Terence Arthur. b 46. **d** 14 **p** 15. NSM Constantine *Truro* 14–16; rtd 16; PtO *Truro* from 16. *Trebarvah Woon, Constantine, Falmouth TR11 5QJ* T: (01326) 340140 E: tvaxe123@gmail.com

AXELSON, Guy Anton. b 84. Cape Town Univ BCom 07. Wycliffe Hall Ox BTh 16. **d** 16 **p** 17. C Ches Square St Mich w St Phil *Lon* 16–21; V Kenilworth Ch Ch S Africa from 21. *Christ Church Kenilworth, 8 Richmond Road, Kenilworth, 7708 South Africa* T: (0027) (21) 797 6332 E: guyaxelson@gmail.com

AXFORD, Mrs Christine Ruth. b 53. Glam Coll of Educn BEd 75. STETS BTh 00. **d** 00 **p** 02. NSM Yeovil w Kingston Pitney *B & W* 00–01; NSM N Hartismere *St E* 02–08; NSM Tyndale *Glouc* 08–18; rtd 18; PtO *Glouc* from 19. *12 Cherry Road, Chipping Sodbury, Bristol BS37 6HJ* T: (01454) 321161 E: chris@robaxford.plus.com

AXFORD, Canon Robert Henry. b 50. Univ of Wales BEng 72 CEng 85. Sarum & Wells Th Coll 89. **d** 91 **p** 92. C Castle Cary w Ansford *B & W* 91–95; P-in-c Queen Camel w W Camel, Corton Denham etc 95–01; R 01–02; R N Hartismere *St E* 02–08; RD Hartismere 04–08; P-in-c Wotton-under-Edge w Ozleworth, N Nibley etc *Glouc* 08–11; V Tyndale 11–18; AD Wotton 09–13; Hon Can Glouc Cathl 13–18; rtd 18; PtO *Glouc* from 19. *12 Cherry Road, Chipping Sodbury, Bristol BS37 6HJ* T: (01454) 321161 E: rob@robaxford.plus.com

AXON, Andrew John. b 76. Univ of Wales (Lamp) BTh 97 Univ of Wales (Ban) MTh 09. Trin Coll Bris 99. **d** 01 **p** 02. C Sevenhampton w Charlton Abbots, Hawling etc *Glouc* 01–05; V Ruddington *S'well* 05–10; P-in-c Hucclecote *Glouc* 10–16; P-in-c Lamberhurst and Matfield *Roch* 16–18; V from 18; RD Paddock Wood from 19. *The Vicarage, 29 Hopgarden Close, Lamberhurst, Tunbridge Wells TN3 8DY* E: revandrew@mail.com

AXTELL, Stephen Geoffrey. b 57. Open Univ BSc 96. St Jo Coll Nottm 00. **d** 02 **p** 03. C Coseley Ch Ch *Worc* 02–06; Chapl Rotterdam *Eur* 06–12; Chapl Rotterdam w Schiedam Miss to Seafarers 06–12; V Westfield St Mary *Carl* from 12. *St Mary's Vicarage, Salisbury Street, Workington CA14 3TA*

AYERS, Canon John. b 40. FCollP Bris Univ BEd 75 Newton Park Coll Bath MEd 89 FRSA 94. **d** 77 **p** 78. NSM Corsham *Bris* 77–79; NSM Gtr Corsham 79–88; NSM Ditteridge 88–92; NSM Box w Hazlebury and Ditteridge 93–10; Hon Can Bris Cathl 94–10; rtd 10; PtO *Bris* 10–20. *Toad Hall, Middlehill, Box, Corsham SN13 8QP* T: (01225) 742123 E: middlehill@supanet.com

AYERS, Martin John. b 79. Trin Hall Cam MA 03 Solicitor 04. Oak Hill Th Coll 08. **d** 11 **p** 12. C Preston All SS *Blackb* 11–15; R Glas St Silas from 16. *St Silas' Church, 69 Park Road, Glasgow G4 9JE* T: 0141-337 2276 M: 07976-170916 E: martin.ayers@talk21.com *or* martin@stsilas.org.uk

AYERS, The Ven Paul Nicholas. b 61. St Pet Coll Ox BA 82 MA 86. Trin Coll Bris 83. **d** 85 **p** 86. C Clayton *Bradf* 85–88; C Keighley St Andr 88–91; V Wrose 91–97; V Pudsey St Lawr and St Paul 97–17; Adn Leeds from 17; Hon Can Bradf Cathl from 16. *2 Wike Ridge Avenue, Leeds LS17 9NL* T: 0113-269 0594 M: 07837-370678 E: paul.ayers@leeds.anglican.org

AYERST, Gabrielle Mary. b 52. St Luke's Coll Ex BEd 74. SEITE 97. **d** 00 **p** 01. NSM Surbiton St Andr and St Mark *S'wark* 00–08; PtO *Newc* from 08. *6 Bell Tower Park, Berwick-upon-Tweed TD15 1ND* T: (01289) 302680 E: gadrillea@paff.nsf.org.uk *or* gabrielleayerst@hotmail.com

AYLEN, Luke Jonathan. b 92. Dur Univ MA 20. Lon Sch of Th BA 14 Trin Coll Bris 18. **d** 21. NSM Heref St Pet w St Owen and St Jas from 21. *10 Holmer Manor Close, Hereford HR4 9QZ* E: luke.aylen@spsj.org.uk

AYLETT, Miss Barbara Celia. b 46. Open Univ BA 91 SRN 73 SCM 74 Surrey Univ PGCE 83. **d** 14 **p** 15. OLM Harlow Town Cen w Lt Parndon *Chelmsf* 14–18; NSM 18–20; PtO from 20. *105 Hare Street Springs, Harlow CM19 4AT* T: (01279) 413749 E: b.aylett@btinternet.com

AYLING, Mrs Ann Margaret. b 39. Edge Hill Coll of HE TCert 59. STETS 07. **d** 10 **p** 11. NSM Bridport *Sarum* 10–17; PtO 17–20. *4 Manor Farm Court, Walditch, Bridport DT6 4LQ* T: (01308) 424896 E: ann@bridport-team-ministry.org

AYLING, Miss Dallas Jane. b 53. Trin Coll Bris BA 94. **d** 98 **p** 99. C Ellesmere Port *Ches* 98–02; TV Birkenhead Priory 02–06; TR 06–07; R 07–16; RD Birkenhead 11–16; R Dawlish w Holcombe, Cofton and Starcross *Ex* from 16; RD Kenn from 19.

The Vicarage, 13 West Cliff Road, Dawlish EX7 9EB T: (01626) 867386 E: revddallasayling@yahoo.co.uk

AYO, Ms Margaret Florence Aceng. b 55. Buwalasi Teacher Tr Coll CertEd 75 Lon Metrop Univ MEd 03. St Mellitus Coll BA 15. **d** 15 **p** 16. NSM Notting Dale St Clem w St Mark and St Jas *Lon* 15–19; NSM Earl's Court Road St Phil from 19. *37 Mitchell House, White City Estate, London W12 7PF* T: (020) 8743 0896 M: 07904-045804 E: margaret.ayo@stclementsjames.org

AYODEJI, Olakunle. b 66. Obafemi Awolowo Univ BSc 86. Westcott Ho Cam 12. **d** 14 **p** 15. C Pinner *Lon* 14–17; V Highgate St Mich from 17. *St Michael's Church, South Grove, London N6 6BJ* T: (020) 8340 7279 M: 07790-504812 E: kunleayodeji@yahoo.co.uk *or* office@stmichaelshighgate.org

AYRES, Dean Matthew. b 68. Bris Univ BSc 89. Ridley Hall Cam 00. **d** 02 **p** 03. C Epsom Common Ch Ch *Guildf* 02–06; Chapl W Lon Univ 06–16; C Acton St Mary from 16. *11 Packington Road, London W3 8FB* T: (020) 8992 9384 E: dean.m.ayres@outlook.com

AZER, Ms Helen. b 77. Ch Ch Ox BA 00 MA 03. Wycliffe Hall Ox BTh 04. **d** 04 **p** 05. C Ox St Aldate 04–07; C Cumnor from 07. *St Michael's Church Office, 1 Abingdon Road, Cumnor, Oxford OX2 9QN* T: (01865) 861541 E: helen.azer@heartcry.co.uk

B

BABB, Canon Geoffrey. b 42. Man Univ BSc 64 MA(Theol) 74 Linacre Coll Ox BA 67. Ripon Hall Ox 65. **d** 68 **p** 69. C Heywood St Luke *Man* 68–71; C-in-c Loundsley Green Ascension CD *Derby* 71–76; TV Old Brampton and Loundsley Green 76–77; TV Stafford and Dioc Soc Resp Officer *Lich* 77–88; Preb Lich Cathl 87–88; P-in-c Salford Sacred Trin *Man* 88–99; Dir CME 88–99; TR Wythenshawe 99–06; TV 06–07; Hon Can Man Cathl 89–07; rtd 07; PtO *Man* 07–08 and 13–18; *Newc* 07–10; *Derby* 10–12; *Lich* 18–21. *The Vicarage, Clayton Lane, Newcastle ST5 3DW* M: 07751-472632 E: geoffrey-babb@outlook.com

BABB, Mrs Julia Bebbington. b 69. Man Univ BA 98 St Jo Coll Dur MA 00. Cranmer Hall Dur. **d** 00 **p** 01. C Langley and Parkfield *Man* 00–04; V Cowgate *Newc* 04–10; P-in-c Whittington *Derby* 10–11; R 12; Tr Officer CMD and IME 4-7 *Man* 12–18; V Clayton *Lich* from 18. *The Vicarage, Clayton Lane, Newcastle ST5 3DW* T: (01782) 614500 E: juliabbabb@icloud.com

BABBINGTON, David Paul Simon. b 66. Newman Univ MA 19. Qu Coll Birm BA 15. **d** 15 **p** 16. C Pelsall *Lich* 15–19; P-in-c Walsall Wood from 19. *The Vicarage, 2 St John's Close, Walsall Wood WS9 9NH* T: (01543) 360558 E: davidbabbington@me.com

BABER, Helen Charlotte. b 67. STETS 10. **d** 13 **p** 14. C Stratton St Margaret w S Marston etc *Bris* 13–17; R Lanteglos Pydar *Truro* from 17. *1 Tippett Meadow, St Columb TR9 6TY* M: 07767-310773 E: helenbaber@me.com

BABINGTON, Peter Gervase. b 69. Aston Univ BSc 91 Birm Univ MPhil 03 DPT 17. Cuddesdon Coll BTh 98. **d** 98 **p** 99. C Salter Street and Shirley *Birm* 98–02; V Bournville 02–20; AD Moseley 07–13; Hon Can Birm Cathl 15–20; P-in-c St Mary le Strand w St Clem Danes *Lon* from 20. *1 Amen Court, London EC4M 7BU* E: pgbabington@gmail.com

BACH, Mrs Frances Mary. b 48. Open Univ BA AIL. CITC BTh. **d** 94 **p** 95. NSM Ballynure and Ballyeaston *Conn* 94–96; C Larne and Inver 96–99; C Glynn w Raloo 96–99; I Armoy w Loughguile and Drumtullagh 99–12; rtd 13. *141A Ballinlea Road, Stranocum, Ballymoney BT53 8PX* T: (028) 2075 1081 E: frances.bach@btinternet.com

BACH, John Edward Goulden. b 40. JP. Dur Univ BA 66. Cranmer Hall Dur 66. **d** 69 **p** 70. C Bradf Cathl 69–72; Chapl and Lect NUU 73–84; Chapl and Lect Ulster Univ 84–15; rtd 15. *141A Ballinlea Road, Stranocum, Ballymoney BT53 8PX* T: (028) 2075 1081 E: revjegbach@hotmail.com

BACK, Esther Elaine. *See* McCAFFERTY, Esther Elaine

BACKHOUSE, Alan Eric. b 37. Keble Coll Ox BA 61 MA 67. Tyndale Hall Bris 61. **d** 64 **p** 65. C Burnage St Marg *Man* 64–67; C Cheadle Hulme St Andr *Ches* 67–70; V Buglawton 70–80; V New Ferry 80–87; V Tarvin 87–93; V Knypersley *Lich* 93–99; Patr Sec Ch Soc Trust 99–00; C Watford *St Alb* 99–02; rtd 02; PtO *St As* from 09. *Perelandra, Church Pitch, Llandyssil, Montgomery SY15 6LQ* T: (01686) 669963 E: alanbackhouse@yahoo.com

BACKHOUSE, Miss Carol Louisa. b 86. York Univ BSc 10. Westcott Ho Cam 13. **d** 16 **p** 17. C Northallerton w Kirby Sigston *York* 16–20; V Lancaster Ch Ch *Blackb* from 20. *Christ Church Vicarage, 1 East Road, Lancaster LA1 3EE* M: 07720-931415 E: revcarolbackhouse@gmail.com

BACKHOUSE, John. b 30. Univ Coll Southn BA 50. Wycliffe Hall Ox 51. **d** 53 **p** 54. C Eccleston St Luke *Liv* 53–55; C Maghull 55–58; V Lathom 58–64; Area Sec CMS Linc and Ely 64–71; PtO *Leic* 72–78; Cov 75–78; V Thorpe Acre w Dishley *Leic* 78–83; R Ab Kettleby Gp 83–89; P-in-c Bitteswell 89–94; RD Guthlaxton II 90–94; rtd 94; PtO *Leic* 94–15. *29 Peashill Close, Sileby, Loughborough LE12 7PT* T: (01509) 812016

BACKHOUSE, Jonathan Roland. b 60. Jes Coll Cam BA 82 MA 85. Trin Coll Bris 01. **d** 03 **p** 04. C Nailsea H Trin *B & W* 03–07; Chapl RN 07–15; Chapl Naples w Sorrento, Capri and Bari *Eur* 15–19; Chapl RNR from 20. *The Chaplaincy, HMS Sultan, Military Road, Gosport PO12 3BY* T: (023) 9254 3181 E: jonbackhouse53@gmail.com

BACON, David Gary. b 62. Leic Univ BA 83 Southn Univ BTh 88. Sarum & Wells Th Coll 85. **d** 88 **p** 89. C Bromley St Mark *Roch* 88–92; C Lynton, Brendon, Countisbury, Lynmouth etc *Ex* 92; TV 92–95; P-in-c Lapford, Nymet Rowland and Coldridge 95–99; P-in-c Dartford St Alb *Roch* 99–05; P-in-c Bramshaw and Landford w Plaitford *Sarum* 05–06; TV Forest and Avon from 06; RD Alderbury from 14. *The Rectory, Bramshaw, Lyndhurst SO43 7JF* T: (01794) 390256 E: davidbramrec@aol.com

BACON, Derek Robert Alexander. b 44. Birkbeck Coll Lon BA 92 MSc 94 Ulster Univ PhD 04. TCD Div Sch 69. **d** 71 **p** 72. C Templemore *D & R* 71–73; V Choral Derry Cathl 72–73; C Heeley *Sheff* 74–76; V Sheff St Pet Abbeydale 76–82; Chapl Gt Ormond Street Hosp for Children NHS Trust 82–95; Visiting Fell Ulster Univ 91–97; PtO *Conn* from 04; rtd 09. *19 Ballycairn Road, Coleraine BT51 3HX*

BACON, Janet Ann. b 57. Man Univ LLB 78. NTMTC 95. **d** 98 **p** 99. NSM Stifford *Chelmsf* 98–01; P-in-c Sandbach North w Wheelock *Ches* 01–03; V 03–12; V Cheadle Hulme All SS 12–19; rtd 20; PtO *Ches* from 20. *12 Darnhall School Lane, Winsford CW7 1JR* E: janetbacon23@sky.com

BACON, John Martindale. b 22. St Aid Birkenhead 54. **d** 57 **p** 58. C Bury St Paul *Man* 57–59; C-in-c Clifton Green St Thos CD 59–71; V Astley Bridge 71–87; rtd 87; PtO *Man* 87–00; *Blackb* 87–11. *21 Lichen Close, Charnock Richard, Chorley PR7 5TT* T: (01257) 792535 E: johnandcon.bacon@tiscali.co.uk

BACON, Mrs Julie Sara. b 65. Solicitor. Yorks Min Course. **d** 14 **p** 15. C Shipley St Pet *Leeds* 14–17; P-in-c Kildwick 17–19; P-in-c Cononley w Bradley 17–19; V Kildwick, Cononley and Bradley 19–21; Assoc Adn Sheff and Rotherham from 21. *Whiston Rectory, Doles Lane, Rotherham S60 4JA*

BADEN, Peter Michael. b 35. CCC Cam BA 59 MA 62. Cuddesdon Coll 58. **d** 60 **p** 61. C Hunslet St Mary and Stourton *Ripon* 60–63; Lic to Offic *Wakef* 63–64; C E Grinstead St Swithun *Chich* 65–68; V Brighton St Martin 68–74; TR Brighton Resurr 74–76; R Westbourne and V Stansted 76–84; V Copthorne 84–91; V Clifton and R Dean *Carl* 91–00; P-in-c Mosser 99–00; rtd 00; PtO *Pet* from 00; *Carl* 01–06. *62 Springfield Avenue, Thrapston, Kettering NN14 4TN* T: (01832) 733186 E: pmbaden@gmail.com

BADGER, Mark. b 65. Qu Coll Birm BTh 96. **d** 96 **p** 97. C Barbourne *Worc* 96–01; P-in-c Worc St Geo w St Mary Magd 01–05; Chapl R Gr Sch Worc 02–05; Chapl Thames Valley Police *Ox* 05–07; Man Dir Motov8 04–12; R Kempsey and Severn Stoke w Croome d'Abitot *Worc* from 12; AD Malvern and Upton from 21. *Appletree Cottage, 31 Napleton Lane, Kempsey, Worcester WR5 3PX* T: (01905) 820057 E: rector@severnsideparishes.co.uk

BADGER, Michael. b 64. Portsm Univ BSc 86. Trin Coll Bris 18. **d** 21. NSM Harnham *Sarum* from 21. *Hothfield, Coombe Road, Salisbury SP2 8BT* M: 07952-292192 E: michaelbadger505@gmail.com

BADGER-WATTS, Mrs Lorraine Gwyneth. b 76. De Montfort Univ BSc 99. St Mich Coll Llan BTh 13. **d** 13 **p** 14. C Petryal and Betws yn Rhos *St As* 13–16; V Gorsedd w Brynford, Ysgeifiog and Whitford 16; TV Estuary and Mountain Miss Area 17–19; R Colchester, New Town and The Hythe *Chelmsf* from 19. *The Rectory, 24 New Town Road, Colchester CO1 2EF* M: 07402-429991 E: revbadger.watts@hotmail.com

BADHAM, Prof Paul Brian Leslie. b 42. Jes Coll Ox BA 65 MA 69 Jes Coll Cam BA 68 MA 72 Birm Univ PhD 73. Westcott Ho Cam 66. **d** 68 **p** 69. C Edgbaston St Bart *Birm* 68–69; C Rubery 69–73; LtO *St D* from 73; Lect Th Univ of Wales (Lamp) 73–83; Sen Lect 83-88; Reader 88-91; Prof Th 91–07; rtd 07; Dir Alister Hardy Relig Experience Research Cen from 02. *11 Petherton Mews, Llantrisant Road, Llandaff, Cardiff CF5 2SJ* M: 07968-626902 E: pblbadham@hotmail.com

BAGE, Damon John. b 71. Teesside Univ BA 95. St Steph Ho Ox 01. **d** 03 **p** 04. C Stockton St Jo *Dur* 03–07; P-in-c Norton St Mich 07–13; Chapl John Snow Coll Dur 06–13; V Cockerton from 13. *St Mary's Vicarage, 17 Newton Lane, Darlington DL3 9EX* E: revddamon@icloud.com

BAGG, Marcus Christopher. b 75. Bath Univ BSc 96. Trin Coll Bris BA 07. **d** 07 **p** 08. C Stanmore *Win* 07–11; P-in-c Gatcombe *Portsm* 11–14; R 14–20; P-in-c Carisbrooke St Nic 11–14; V 14–20; P-in-c Carisbrooke St Mary 11–14; V 14–20; PtO *Dur* from 20. *3 Brass Thill, St Margaret's Garth, Durham DH1 4DS* T: 0191-383 9883 E: marcusbagg@yahoo.com

BAGGALEY, Mrs Patricia Anne. b 45. Open Univ BSc 96 RGN 68. ERMC 05. **d** 07 **p** 08. NSM Trunch *Nor* 07–11; C 11–15; C Trunch Group 15–16; rtd 16; PtO *Nor* from 16. *Anglesea, Rosebery Road, West Runton, Cromer NR27 9QW* T: (01263) 837490 E: patriciabaggaley@gmail.com

BAGGS, Steven. b 70. **d** 09 **p** 10. NSM White Horse *Sarum* 09–12; V Frome Valley *Heref* from 12. *The Vicarage, Bishop's Frome, Worcester WR6 5AP* T: (01885) 490582

BAGNALL, David Christopher Gordon. b 90. Cam Univ BA 13 MPhil 18 MA 20. Westcott Ho Cam 17. **d** 20 **p** 21. C Cambridge Gt St Mary w St Mich *Ely* from 20; Asst Chapl Em Coll Cam from 20. *59 Abbey Road, Cambridge CB5 8HH* M: 07892-714234 E: davidcgbagnall@gmail.com

BAGNALL, Katherine Janet. b 67. Sunderland Univ BEd 92. NEOC 02. **d** 05 **p** 06. NSM Monkwearmouth *Dur* 05–06; C Darlington St Mark w St Paul 06–10; P-in-c Sunderland St Mary and St Pet from 10. *The Clergy House, Springwell Road, Sunderland SR3 4DY* T: 0191-528 3754 E: katherine.bagnall@ntlworld.com

BAGOTT, Paul Andrew. b 61. Leeds Univ BA 85. Westcott Ho Cam 86. **d** 88 **p** 89. C Chingford SS Pet and Paul *Chelmsf* 88–91; C Pimlico St Sav *Lon* 91–95; P-in-c Clerkenwell H Redeemer and St Mark 95–01; V Clerkenwell H Redeemer 02–13; V Clerkenwell St Mark 02–13; P-in-c Earl's Court St Cuth w St Matthias from 13; PV Westmr Abbey from 08. *St Cuthbert's Clergy House, 50 Philbeach Gardens, London SW5 9EB* T: (020) 7370 3263

BAGSHAW, Paul Stanley. b 55. Selw Coll Cam BA 78 MA 81 CQSW 80. NOC 85. **d** 88 **p** 89. Ind Missr *Sheff* 86–90; C Handsworth Woodhouse 88–90; NSM 91–93; C Newark S'well 93–96; P-in-c Ordsall 96–98; C Byker St Ant *Newc* 12–14; V Billy Mill 14–19; V Marden w Preston Grange 14–19; rtd 20. *35 Victoria Terrace, Whitley Bay NE26 2QN*

BAGSHAWE, John Allen. b 45. St Jo Coll Dur BA 70. Cranmer Hall Dur 67. **d** 71 **p** 72. C Bridlington Priory *York* 71–75; C N Ferriby 75–79; V Kingston upon Hull St Matt w St Barn 79–10; AD W Hull 00–10; rtd 10; PtO *York* 10–15. *334 Southcoates Lane, Hull HU9 3TR* T: (01482) 702220 E: allen@bagshawe.karoo.co.uk

BAGULEY, Andrew James. b 72. Glas Univ BSc 94 Jordanhill Coll Glas PGCE 97. Ridley Hall Cam 13. **d** 15 **p** 16. C Belper *Derby* 15–19; P-in-c Ilkeston St Jo from 19; P-in-c Ilkeston St Mary from 19. *63B Manners Road, Ilkeston DE7 5HB* M: 07421-053654 E: revandrew@baguley.net

BAGULEY, David Mark. b 61. Man Univ BSc 83 MSc 86 Open Univ MBA 94 Wolfs Coll Cam PhD 05. ERMC 09. **d** 11 **p** 12. Visiting Prof Anglia Ruskin Univ *Chelmsf* from 10; NSM Milton *Ely* 11–17; NSM Waterbeach 11–17; NSM Landbeach 11–17; PtO *S'well* 17–18; NSM Sherwood from 18. *St Martin's Vicarage, 12 Trevose Gardens, Nottingham NG5 3FU* T: 0115-840 6454 E: david.baguley@nottingham.ac.uk

BAHADUR, Naeem. b 82. Punjab Univ BA 03 Gujranwala Th Sem MDiv 08. Qu Foundn Birm 15. **d** 17 **p** 18. C Hyson Green and Forest Fields *S'well* from 17. *8 Austen Avenue, Nottingham NG7 6PE* T: 0115-874 0727 M: 07538-129820 E: rev.bahadur@yahoo.com

BAILES, Kenneth. b 35. Dur Univ BA 69 DPhil. **d** 71 **p** 72. C Redcar *York* 71–73; TV Redcar w Kirkleatham 73–74; P-in-c Appleton Roebuck w Acaster Selby 74–80; P-in-c Sutton on the Forest 80–82; R Stamford Bridge Gp 82–90; V Healaugh w Wighill, Bilbrough and Askham Richard 90–95; rtd 95; PtO *York* 98–11. *Lawnwith House, Stuton Grove, Tadcaster LS24 9BD* T: (01937) 831245 M: 07764-614139 E: kb13@btinternet.com

BAILES, Mrs Rachel Jocelyn. b 60. Huddersfield Sch of Music BA 81 Kingston Poly PGCE 83 Leeds Univ MEd 96 BA 07. NOC 04. **d** 07 **p** 08. C Thornes and Lupset *Wakef* 07–11; Chapl Mid Yorks Hosps NHS Trust 11–16; Chapl York Teaching Hosp NHS Foundn Trust from 16. *York Hospitals NHS Foundation Trust, Wigginton Road, York YO31 8HE* T: (01904) 631313 E: rjbailes@tiscali.co.uk or rachel.bailes@york.nhs.uk

BAILEY, Preb Adrian Richard. b 57. Cranmer Hall Dur 89. **d** 91 **p** 92. C Oswestry St Oswald *Lich* 91–94; C Shobnall 94–99; C Burton 94–99; Town Cen Chapl 94–99; P-in-c Shobnall 99–01; P-in-c Hengoed w Gobowen 01–08; C Weston Rhyn and Selattyn 05–07; P-in-c Selattyn 07–08; P-in-c Selattyn and Hengoed w Gobowen 08–19; Chapl Robert Jones/Agnes Hunt Orthopaedic and Distr Hosp NHS Trust 01–19; RD Oswestry *Lich* 09–17; Preb Lich Cathl 13–19; rtd 19; PtO *Lich* 19–21. *16 Rowlands Close, Morda, Oswestry SY10 9RQ* E: arb2@totalise.co.uk or adrian.bailey@rjah.nhs.uk

BAILEY, Alan. See **BAILEY, Graham Alan**

BAILEY, Andrew Henley. b 57. AKC 78. Sarum & Wells Th Coll 79. **d** 80 **p** 81. C Romsey *Win* 80–83; V Bournemouth St Alb 83–93; R Milton from 93. *The Rectory, Church Lane, New Milton BH25 6QN* T/F: (01425) 615150 E: miltonrectory@gmail.com

BAILEY, Andrew John. b 37. Trin Coll Cam BA 61 MA. Ridley Hall Cam 60. **d** 63 **p** 64. C Drypool *York* 63–66; C Melton Mowbray w Thorpe Arnold *Leic* 66–69; C-in-c Skelmersdale Ecum Cen *Liv* 69–79; V Langley Mill *Derby* 79–90; V Gt Faringdon w Lt Coxwell *Ox* 90–02; AD Vale of White Horse 97–01; rtd 02; PtO *Ches* 02–17; from 18. *53 Vyner House, Front Street, Acomb, York YO24 3DW* T: (01904) 914516 E: 58abailey@gmail.com

BAILEY, Canon Angela. b 61. Kent Univ BA 82. Qu Coll Birm 83. **dss** 85 **d** 87 **p** 94. Reculver and Herne Bay St Bart *Cant* 85–88; Par Dn 87–88; Asst Chapl Hull Univ *York* 88–92; Sen Chapl 94–98; PtO 92–94; P-in-c Rowley w Skidby 98–09; R 10–14; V Walkington 10–14; P-in-c Bishop Burton 10–14; RD Beverley 07–12; Chapl E Riding Community Health Trust 98–04; Dioc Ecum Officer *York* 07–09; Dioc Adv for Lay Development 14–19; Tutor York Sch of Min from 19; Can and Preb York Minster from 03. *Diocesan House, Aviator Court, Clifton Moor, York YO30 4WJ* T: (01904) 699500 E: angela.bailey@yorkdiocese.org

BAILEY, Brendan John. b 61. Strathclyde Univ BSc 83 K Coll Lon MA 99. Ripon Coll Cuddesdon BTh 93. **d** 94 **p** 95. C Purley *Ox* 94–99; R Nettlebed w Bix, Highmoor, Pishill etc 99–17; P-in-c Nuffield 06–17; PtO 18–19; C Purley from 19. *St Mary's Church, St Mary's Avenue, Purley on Thames, Reading RG8 8BJ* E: brendan.bailey@stmaryspurley.org.uk

BAILEY, Canon Brian Constable. b 36. K Coll Lon AKC 62. **d** 63 **p** 64. C Mill Hill Jo Keble Ch *Lon* 63–66; C Gt Stanmore 66–69; C Gt Marlow *Ox* 69–72; R Burghfield 72–81; R Wokingham All SS 81–96; Hon Can Ch Ch 94–96; TV Pinhoe and Broadclyst *Ex* 96–00; rtd 00; V of the Close Sarum Cathl 00–01. *2 Rose Cottages, Maudlin Road, Totnes TQ9 5TG* T: (01803) 865992 E: brianbailey579@btinternet.com

BAILEY, Mrs Carolyn. b 64. Ox Min Course 07. **d** 10 **p** 11. NSM Gt Missenden w Ballinger and Lt Hampden *Ox* 10–17; V Ness Gp *Linc* from 17. *The Vicarage, 10 Church Street, Thurlby, Bourne PE10 0EH* M: 07841-583303 E: ness.rector@gmail.com

BAILEY, Mrs Christine Ann. b 55. All SS Cen for Miss & Min 11. **d** 14 **p** 15. OLM Urmston *Man* 14–15; OLM Davyhulme Ch Ch and Urmston from 15. *16 Westmorland Road, Urmston, Manchester M41 9HJ* T: 0161-747 5123 E: christine.bailey70@ntlworld.com

BAILEY, The Ven David Charles. b 52. Linc Coll Ox BA 75 MA 78 MSc 77. St Jo Coll Nottm BA 79. **d** 80 **p** 81. C Worksop St Jo *S'well* 80–83; C Edgware *Lon* 83–87; V S Cave and Ellerker w Broomfleet *York* 87–97; RD Howden 91–97; V Beverley Minster 97–08; P-in-c Routh 97–08; Can and Preb York Minster 98–08; Adn Bolton *Man* 08–18; rtd 18. *2 Field View, Clotherholme Road, Ripon HG4 2RH* T: (01765) 607045

BAILEY, David Ross. b 58. UNISA BTh 82. St Bede's Coll Umtata 80. **d** 82 **p** 82. C Somerset West S Africa 82–85; C Elgin 85–87; R Atlantis 87–95; R Salt River 95–08; P-in-c Honicknowle *Ex* 08–14; C Ernesettle 08–14; C Whitleigh 08–14; V Ernesettle, Whitleigh and Honicknowle from 14. *St Francis's Presbytery, 53 Little Dock Lane, Plymouth PL5 2LP* T/F: (01752) 773874 M: 07864-059302 E: fr.david@blueyonder.co.uk

BAILEY, Dennis. b 53. Man Univ BEd 74 BMus 74 TCD MA 06 PhD 11. St Jo Coll Nottm BTh 79. **d** 79 **p** 80. C Netherley Ch Ch CD *Liv* 79–83; PtO Natal S Africa from 83. *PO Box 625, Hilton, 3245 South Africa* T: (0027) 82-275 3641 E: dbaileysa@gmail.com

BAILEY, Derek William. b 39. Man Univ BA 96. Cranmer Hall Dur 64. **d** 67 **p** 68. C Sutton *Liv* 67–69; C Chapel-en-le-Frith *Derby* 69–73; V Hadfield 73–90; R Collyhurst *Man* 90–95; V Chaddesden St Mary *Derby* 95–02; rtd 02; PtO *York* from 03. *187 Bishopthorpe Road, York YO23 1PD* T: (01904) 628080 E: derekwbailey@btinternet.com

BAILEY, Edward Peter. b 35. Nottm Univ MA 93. Qu Coll Birm. **d** 62 **p** 63. C Ordsall *S'well* 62–66; C Clifton w Glapton 66–71; V Lady Bay 71–83; Relig Affairs Adv to Radio Trent 83–85; C Gedling 86–89; C Bilborough St Jo 89–00; rtd 00; PtO *York* 00–15. *Cragside Cottage, 18 Egton Road, Aislaby, Whitby YO21 1SU*

BAILEY, Elizabeth. b 47. **d** 03 **p** 04. OLM Bishop's Cannings, All Cannings etc *Sarum* 03–09; rtd 09; PtO *Sarum* from 09. *Lynden, The Street, Bishop's Cannings, Devizes SN10 2LD* T: (01380) 860400 E: liz@iftco.com

BAILEY, Mrs Elizabeth Carmen. b 45. EAMTC 89. **d** 93 **p** 94. NSM Roughton and Felbrigg, Metton, Sustead etc *Nor* 93–95 and 99–02; P-in-c 02–06; NSM Cromer and Gresham 95–99; C Buxton w Oxnead, Lammas and Brampton 06–07; C Bure Valley 07–10; rtd 10; PtO *Nor* from 12. *5 Warren Road, Southrepps, Norwich NR11 8UN* T: (01263) 833785

BAILEY, Faye. b 88. St Mellitus Coll BA 16. **d** 16 **p** 17. C Chelmsf Ascension w All SS 16–19; TR Becontree S from 19. *St Alban's Vicarage, Vincent Road, Dagenham RM9 6AL* T: (020) 8595 1042 M: 07718-881922 E: fayebailey09@gmail.com

BAILEY, Graham Alan. b 52. N Staffs Poly BSc 75. **d** 08 **p** 09. NSM Betley *Lich* from 08; NSM Madeley from 11. *10 Ladygates, Betley, Crewe CW3 9AN* T: (01270) 820043 E: alan.bailey@beulahscience.co.uk

BAILEY, Helen Louise. b 69. Hull Univ BA 92 PGCE 99 SS Coll Cam BA 09 MA 14. Westcott Ho Cam 07. **d** 10 **p** 11. C High Harrogate Ch Ch *Ripon* 10–14; R Minchinhampton w Box and Amberley *Glouc* 14–18; V Broadstone *Sarum* from 18. *St John's Vicarage, Macaulay Road, Broadstone BH18 8AR* E: revdhelenbailey@gmail.com

BAILEY, Canon Ivan John. b 33. Keble Coll Ox BA 57 MA 65. St Steph Ho Ox 57. **d** 59 **p** 60. C Ipswich All Hallows *St E* 59–62; Clerical Sec CEMS 62–66; V Cringleford *Nor* 66–81; RD Humbleyard 73–81; R Colney 80–81; Relig Adv Anglia TV 81–91; P-in-c Kirby Bedon w Bixley and Whitlingham *Nor* 81–92; Hon Can Nor Cathl 84–98; Chapl St Andr Hosp Norwich 92–94; Chapl Mental Health Unit Nor HA 92–94; Chapl Norfolk Mental Health Care NHS Trust 94–98; rtd 98; PtO *Nor* from 98. *21 Cranleigh Rise, Norwich NR4 6PQ* T: (01603) 453565 E: ivanbailey21@gmail.com

BAILEY, James Alexander. b 87. Ox Brookes Univ BSc 10. St Mellitus Coll BA 20. **d** 20 **p** 21. C Brighton St Pet *Chich* from 20. *27 Brentwood Crescent, Brighton BN1 7EU* M: 07516-707608 E: revjamesbailey@icloud.com *or* james.bailey@stpetersbrighton.org

BAILEY, Ms Jane Rome. b 50. Univ of Wales (Ban) BA 99 BTh 03. Ban Ord Course 00. **d** 03 **p** 04. C Llifon and Talybolion Deanery *Ban* 03–06; P-in-c Trefdraeth w Aberffraw, Llangadwaladr etc 06–10; TV Holyhead 10–13; C Bro Cybi from 13. *St Seiriol's House, 25 Gors Avenue, Holyhead LL65 1PB* T: (01407) 764780 E: jane.r.bailey@btinternet.com *or* jane.r.bailey3@gmail.com

BAILEY, Joyce Mary Josephine. *See* OUTEN, Joyce Mary Josephine

BAILEY, Judith Elizabeth Anne. *See* MILLER, Judith Elizabeth Anne

BAILEY, Justin Mark. b 55. Birm Univ BA 77 Southn Univ MTh 97 Wolv Poly PGCE 78. Ripon Coll Cuddesdon 90. **d** 92 **p** 93. C Oakdale *Sarum* 92–96; P-in-c Milton Abbas, Hilton w Cheselbourne etc 96–05; P-in-c Piddletrenthide w Plush, Alton Pancras etc 02–05; V Piddle Valley, Hilton, Cheselbourne etc 05–06; P-in-c Bruton and Distr *B & W* 06–17; R Bruton, Brewham, Pitcombe and Shepton Montague 17–19; rtd 19; PtO *Lich* from 21; *Heref* from 21. *The Crossing, Church Road, Jackfield, Telford TF8 7ND* E: frjustin@btinternet.com

BAILEY, Mrs Katharine Ann. b 55. SEITE 14. **d** 16 **p** 17. NSM Horsham *Chich* 16–19; P-in-c Lurgashall from 19; P-in-c N Chapel w Ebernoe from 19. *The Rectory, Northchapel, Petworth GU28 9HP* E: rev.kate@lnechurches.org.uk

BAILEY, Mark David. b 62. Ripon Coll Cuddesdon 87. **d** 90 **p** 91. C Leigh Park *Portsm* 90–93; C Fleet *Guildf* 93–95; TV Basingstoke *Win* 95–00; P-in-c Twyford and Owslebury and Morestead 00–08; R Lower Dever 08–21; P-in-c Ardeley,

Benington, Cottered w Throcking etc *St Alb* from 21. *Address temp unknown* E: mdbailey066@gmail.com

BAILEY, Martin Tristram. b 57. Oak Hill Th Coll 89. **d** 91 **p** 92. C Brundall w Braydeston and Postwick *Nor* 91–95; TV Plymouth St Andr and Stonehouse *Ex* 95–06; Chapl St Dunstan's Abbey Sch Plymouth 02–05; V Riseley w Bletsoe *St Alb* 06–18; C Harold Hill St Paul *Chelmsf* 18–21. *74 Colwell Drive, Witney OX28 5NQ*

BAILEY, Michael Joseph. b 78. Open Univ BSc 02 City Univ MSc 05 RN 96. St Steph Ho Ox BTh 11. **d** 10 **p** 11. C Holbrooks *Cov* 10–13; Pioneer P *Lon* 13–14; P-in-c Sidley *Chich* 14–18; V Sidley 18–20; P-in-c Lewisham St Steph and St Mark *S'wark* from 20. *St Stephen's Vicarage, Cressingham Road, London SE13 5AG* M: 07713-258429 E: frmichaelbailey@gmail.com

BAILEY, Nicholas Andrew. b 55. Open Univ BA 84 Nottm Univ CertEd 80. Ripon Coll Cuddesdon 88. **d** 90 **p** 91. C Guisborough *York* 90–92; Chapl Repton Prep Sch 92–15; rtd 15; PtO *Leeds* 16. *16 Willow Bridge Lane, Dalton, Thirsk YO7 3QQ* T: (01845) 595925 E: twonickleby@aol.com

BAILEY, Miss Patricia Laura. b 49. Wall Hall Coll Aldenham CertEd 72. NTMTC 95. **d** 98 **p** 99. NSM Hackney Marsh *Lon* 98–01; NSM S Hackney St Jo w Ch Ch 01–04; NSM Cosby and Whetstone *Leic* 04–11; P-in-c Ibstock w Heather 11–16; R 16–19; rtd 19; PtO *Leic* from 19. *Springbank, High Street, Stoke Golding, Nuneaton CV13 6HF*

BAILEY, Peter. *See* BAILEY, Edward Peter

BAILEY, Canon Peter Robin. b 43. St Jo Coll Dur BA 64. Trin Coll Bris 72. **d** 74 **p** 75. C Corby St Columba *Pet* 74–77; C Bishopsworth *Bris* 77–82; V Sea Mills 82–97; RD Westbury and Severnside 91–97; P-in-c Bishopston 97–98; P-in-c Bris St Andr w St Bart 97–98; TR Bishopston and St Andrews 98–09; Hon Can Bris Cathl 97–09; rtd 09; PtO *Bris* from 09; *B & W* from 10. *4 The Croft, Backwell, Bristol BS48 3LY* T: (01275) 790611 M: 07970-180460 E: peterandheather@blueyonder.co.uk

BAILEY, Robert David. b 71. Leeds Metrop Univ BA 95. Cranmer Hall Dur 15. **d** 17 **p** 18. C Elmete Trin *Leeds* 17–21; TR Allerton Bywater, Kippax and Swillington from 21. *The Rectory, Church Lane, Kippax, Leeds LS25 7HF* M: 07885-386932 E: rev.bob.bailey@gmail.com

BAILEY, Robert Henry. b 45. FCA 69. NOC 99. **d** 02 **p** 03. NSM Dewsbury *Wakef* 02–05; Sub Chapl HM Pris Leeds 02–05; NSM Felkirk *Wakef* 05–13; P-in-c 06–13; rtd 13; PtO *Leeds* from 17. *77 Bennett Lane, Dewsbury WF12 7DZ* E: robertbailey.minster@btinternet.com

BAILEY, Stella. b 76. Westhill Coll Birm BTheol 98. Ripon Coll Cuddesdon 07. **d** 09 **p** 10. C Walsgrave on Sowe *Cov* 09–13; V Cov St Mary 13–16; V Kenilworth St Nic from 16; AD Kenilworth from 18. *The Vicarage, 7 Elmbank Road, Kenilworth CV8 1AL* E: chacethedog@me.com

BAILEY, Stephen. b 39. Leic Univ BA 61. Clifton Th Coll 61. **d** 62 **p** 63. C Wellington w Eyton *Lich* 62–66; C Rainham *Chelmsf* 66–69; V Ercall Magna *Lich* 69–75; V Rowton 69–75; RD Wrockwardine 72–75; V W Bromwich Gd Shep w St Jo 75–83; P-in-c W Bromwich St Phil 80–81; V 81–83; R Chadwell *Chelmsf* 83–96; RD Thurrock 92–96; V Galleywood Common 96–04; rtd 04; PtO *Chelmsf* from 04. *64 Bridport Way, Braintree CM7 9FJ* T: (01376) 619347

BAILEY, Stephen Andrew. b 75. St Jo Coll Nottm 05. **d** 07 **p** 08. C Walton-on-Thames *Guildf* 07–11; TV Oadby *Leic* 11–17; P-in-c 17–19; TR from 19; Warden of Readers 13–18; AD Gartree from 19. *St Paul's House, Hamble Road, Oadby, Leicester LE2 4NX* T: 0116-271 0519 E: oadbyrector@gmail.com

BAILEY, Stephen John. b 57. Sarum & Wells Th Coll 88. **d** 90 **p** 91. C Redhill H Trin *S'wark* 90–95; Chapl E Surrey Coll 91–93; P-in-c Betchworth *S'wark* 95–00; V 00–06; P-in-c Buckland 95–00; R 00–06; R Hamilton H Trin Bermuda 06–13; R Guernsey Ste Marie du Castel *Win* 13–17; V Guernsey St Matt 13–17; rtd 17. *Brent Cottage, 38 Church Road, East Wittering, Chichester PO20 8PS*

BAILEY, Mrs Susan Mary. b 40. F L Calder Coll Liv CertEd 61. EAMTC 89. **d** 92 **p** 94. NSM Chelmsf Cathl 92–93; NSM Needham Market w Badley *St E* 93–95; NSM Belper *Derby* 96–00; NSM Allestree St Nic and Quarndon 00–05; Chapl Morley Retreat and Conf Ho Derby 00–05; rtd 05; PtO *Glouc* 14–20. *Beck House, Carlton, Leyburn DL8 4BD* T: (01969) 640679 E: susan.m.bailey@gmail.com

BAILEY, Yvonne Mary. *See* HOBSON, Yvonne Mary

BAILIE, Alison Margaret. b 62. Leeds Univ LLB 83. Trin Coll Bris BA 98. **d** 98 **p** 99. C Halliwell St Pet *Man* 98–05; P-in-c Droylsden St Mary 05–09; R 09–19; R Middleton and Thornham from 19; AD Heywood and Middleton 21. *St Mary's Rectory, Dunkirk Street, Droylsden, Manchester M43 7FB* T: 0161-370 1569

BAILLIE, Terence John. b 46. New Coll Ox BA 69 MA 78 Man Univ MSc 72 Cardiff Univ MTh 93. St Jo Coll Nottm 74. **d** 77 **p** 78. C Chadwell *Chelmsf* 77–80; C Bickenhill w Elmdon *Birm* 80–84; V Bedminster St Mich *Bris* 84–96; V Clevedon St Andr and Ch Ch *B & W* 96–12; rtd 12; PtO *B & W* from 13; *Bris* 17–19. *33 Belgrave Road, Weston-super-Mare BS22 8AJ* T: (01934) 643429 E: tandam.baillie@btinternet.com

BAILY, Linda Rosemary. d 06 **p** 07. NSM Llanaber w Caerdeon *Ban* 06–15; NSM Bro Ardudwy from 15. *Address temp unknown* E: lindarbaily@aol.com

BAILY, Mrs Sally. b 65. Kingston Univ MBA 97. Trin Coll Bris MA 14. **d** 13 **p** 14. C Gt Chesham *Ox* 13–16; TV Edgware *Lon* 16–21; V Hounslow H Trin from 21. *Holy Trinity Church, Trinity Parade, High Street, Hounslow TW3 1HG* T: (020) 8577 9048 M: 07836-251432 E: revsallybaily@gmail.com

BAIN, Alan. b 48. Thames Poly BSc 72. St Jo Coll Nottm. **d** 77 **p** 78. C Wakef St Andr and St Mary 77–81; V Bath Odd Down *B & W* 81–82; P-in-c Combe Hay 81–82; V Bath Odd Down w Combe Hay 82–18; rtd 18; PtO *B & W* from 19. *46 Stonehouse Lane, Bath BA2 5DW*

BAIN, Canon Andrew John. b 55. Newc Poly BA 77 Edin Univ MTh 89. Edin Th Coll 86. **d** 88 **p** 89. Chapl St Mary's Cathl Edin 88–91; C Edin St Mary 88–91; R Edin St Jas 91–98; P-in-c Edin St Marg 93–98; R Haddington 98–06; P-in-c Edin St Ninian 06–10; Dioc Dir of Ords 95–98 and 06–07; Chapl Emmaus Ho from 10; R Dunbar *Edin* 13–17; P-in-c Edin St Salvador from 18; P-in-c Edin St Dav from 19; Hon Can St Mary's Cathl from 21. *Emmaus House, 14 Gilmore Place, Edinburgh EH3 9NQ* T: 0131-228 1066 M: 07929-047896 E: andrewbain99@hotmail.com

BAIN, Canon John Stuart. b 55. Van Mildert Coll Dur BA 77. Westcott Ho Cam 78. **d** 80 **p** 81. C Washington *Dur* 80–84; C Dunston 84–86; V Shiney Row 86–92; V Herrington 86–92; P-in-c Whitworth w Spennymoor 92–97; P-in-c Merrington 94–97; AD Auckland 96–02; V Spennymoor, Whitworth and Merrington 97–02; Hon Can Dur Cathl 98–02; Adn Sunderland 02–18; P-in-c Hedworth 02–13; P-in-c E Boldon 09–13; P-in-c Boldon 10–13; C The Boldons 13–18; V Sunderland Minster 18–21; Can Dur Cathl 18–21; rtd 21. *20 Glentrool, Newton Stewart DG8 6SY* M: 07852-308175 E: stuart.bain@mac.com

BAIN, Lawrence John Weir. b 60. NTMTC BA 05. **d** 05 **p** 06. C Stoughton *Guildf* 05–09; P-in-c Camberley Heatherside from 09. *30 Yockley Close, Camberley GU15 1QH* T: (01276) 691127 M: 07913-076164 E: revlarrybain@aol.com

BAIN-DOODU, Canon Joseph Justice. b 56. Cape Coast Univ Ghana DipEd 01 MEd 09 Cardiff Univ LLM 11. St Nic Th Coll Ghana LTh 86. **d** 86 **p** 86. Ghana 86–97 and 99–08; Hon C Sheldon *Birm* 97–98; PtO *Portsm* 09–12. *Address temp unknown* M: 07532-104795 E: josephbaindoodu@gmail.com

BAINBRIDGE, Mrs Christine Susan. b 48. St Aid Coll Dur BA 70 K Coll Lon MA 99. SEITE 93. **d** 96 **p** 97. C S'wark H Trin w St Matt 96–99; Asst to Bp Woolwich (Greenwich Area) 99–03; C Lee Gd Shep w St Pet 99–03; P-in-c Deptford St Jo w H Trin 03–06; TR Deptford St Jo w H Trin and Ascension 06–13; rtd 13; PtO *S'wark* 13–14; *Ox* from 14. *16 The Mount, Reading RG1 5HL* T: 0118-931 1587 M: 07939-662980 E: bainbridgerev@gmail.com

BAINBRIDGE, David George. b 42. Wadh Coll Ox BA 63 MA 67 Lon Inst of Educn PGCE 67. Ridley Hall Cam 84. **d** 86 **p** 87. C Downend *Bris* 86–90; TV Yate New Town 90–01; Warden Lee Abbey Internat Students' Club Kensington 01–07; rtd 07; PtO *Glouc* from 08. *2 Kingsmead, Lechlade GL7 3BW* T: (01367) 250347 E: bainbridge1973@yahoo.co.uk

BAINBRIDGE, Mrs Phyllis Marion. Aber Univ BSc 81 Ches Univ BA 17. St Jo Coll Nottm 10. **d** 11 **p** 12. NSM Littleover *Derby* 11–12; NSM Mickleover All SS 12–14; NSM Mickleover St Jo 12–14; NSM Mickleover 14–15; NSM Heath from 15; C Hucknall Torkard *S'well* 18; PtO *Derby* 16–19; *S'well* 18–19; R Anslow, Rolleston and Tutbury *Lich* from 19. *Rolleston Rectory, Church Road, Rolleston-on-Dove, Burton-on-Trent DE13 9BE* T: (01283) 814802 E: revdphyllisbainbridge@gmail.com

BAINBRIDGE, Richard Densham. b 49. Ch Coll Cam BA 71 MA 75 Edge Hill Coll of HE PGCE 72. S'wark Ord Course 91. **d** 94 **p** 95. C Bermondsey St Jas w Ch Ch *S'wark* 94–99; V Lee Gd Shep w St Pet from 99–14; AD E Lewisham 06–13; rtd 14; PtO *Ox* from 14. *16 The Mount, Reading RG1 5HL* T: 0118-931 1587 E: revrdb@yahoo.com

BAINES, Alan William. b 50. S Bank Poly BSc 72. Trin Coll Bris 92. **d** 94 **p** 95. C Chenies and Lt Chalfont, Latimer and Flaunden *Ox* 94–98; V Eye *Pet* 98–05; Post Ord Tr Co-ord 00–05; TV Duston 05–15; rtd 15; PtO *Glouc*

BAINES, Derek Alfred. b 53. MCSP 75. CBDTI 99. **d** 02 **p** 03. NSM Lostock Hall *Blackb* 02–09; NSM Lostock Hall and Farington Moss 09–11; R Hoole 11–18; rtd 18; PtO *Blackb* 19–20; *York* from 19. *12 Airedale Drive, Bridlington YO16 6GL* T: (01262) 604240 M: 07774-200885

BAINES, John Charles. b 68. Ripon Coll Cuddesdon 00. **d** 02 **p** 03. C Morton and Stonebroom w Shirland *Derby* 02–06; P-in-c New Mills 06–12; V 12–18; RD Glossop 10–13; P-in-c Longnor, Quarnford, Sheen etc *Lich* 18; V from 18; RD Alstonfield from 20. *The Vicarage, Longnor, Buxton SK17 0PA* T: (01298) 83411

✠**BAINES, The Rt Revd Nicholas.** b 57. Bradf Univ BA 80. Trin Coll Bris BA 87. **d** 87 **p** 88 **c** 03. C Kendal St Thos *Carl* 87–91; C Leic H Trin w St Jo 91–92; V Rothley 92–00; RD Goscote 96–00; Adn Lambeth *S'wark* 00–03; Area Bp Croydon 03–11; Bp Bradf 11–14; Bp Leeds from 14; Hon Asst Bp York from 14. *Hollin House, Weetwood Avenue, Leeds LS16 5NG* T: 0113-284 4300 E: bishop.nick@leeds.anglican.org

BAINES, Mrs Sharon June. b 52. Sheff Hallam Univ MSc 05 MCSP 74. LCTP 06. **d** 09 **p** 10. NSM Penwortham St Leon *Blackb* 09–18; rtd 18; PtO *Blackb* 18–20; *York* from 19. *12 Airedale Drive, Bridlington YO16 6GL* T: (01262) 604240

BAIRD, Agnes Murry (Nancy). b 39. Man Univ CertEd 70. EAMTC 93. **d** 96 **p** 97. NSM Bramford *St E* 96–98; NSM Haughley w Wetherden and Stowupland 98–09; rtd 09; PtO *St E* 09–20. *1 Burls Yard, Crown Street, Needham Market, Ipswich IP6 8AJ* T: (01449) 720567 E: nancybaird39@gmail.com

BAIRD, Mrs Sally. b 53. St As Minl Tr Course 04. **d** 06. NSM Bistre *St As* 06–16; NSM Borderlands Miss Area from 17. *100 Park Avenue, Bryn-y-Baal, Mold CH7 6TP* T: (01352) 758831 E: sally.baird@btinternet.com

BAISLEY, George. b 45. Sarum & Wells Th Coll 78. **d** 80 **p** 81. C Glouc St Geo w Whaddon 80–83; R Welford w Weston and Clifford Chambers 83–87; Chapl Myton Hamlet Hospice 87–91; Chapl Warw Univ *Cov* 87–91; R Berkswell 91–03; RD Kenilworth 96–01; Chapl Bromley Coll 03–04; P-in-c Doddington, Newnham and Wychling *Cant* 04–07; P-in-c Teynham w Lynsted and Kingsdown 04–07; P-in-c Norton 04–07; rtd 07; PtO *Chelmsf* 07–08; P-in-c N Ockendon 08–12; PtO *Roch* from 13. *25 Bromley College, London Road, Bromley BR1 1PE* T: (020) 8290 0183 M: 07974-151056 E: george@baisley45.co.uk

BAKER, Albert George. b 30. Qu Coll Birm. **d** 61 **p** 62. C Merton St Mary *S'wark* 61–64; C Limpsfield and Titsey 64–65; C Chapel-en-le-Frith *Derby* 65–68; R Odd Rode *Ches* 68–76; V Holme Cultram St Mary *Carl* 76–78; R Blofield w Hemblington *Nor* 78–94; rtd 94. *240 Raedwald Drive, Bury St Edmunds IP32 7DN* T: (01284) 701802

BAKER, Alexander David Laing. b 74. **d** 11 **p** 12. C Edin Ch Ch 11–12; NSM Burnley St Matt w H Trin *Blackb* 12–14; PtO 14–16; NSM Gisburn 16–17; V 17; PtO 17–20; NSM Halsall, Lydiate and Downholland *Liv* from 18. *Victoria Cottage, Swan Lane, Aughton, Ormskirk L39 6SU* T: 0151-526 2292 E: alexbaker@priests.uk.net

BAKER, Alicia Mary. b 63. Cliff Coll MA 11. Trin Coll Bris BA 03. **d** 03 **p** 04. C E Ham St Paul *Chelmsf* 03–07; P-in-c Abercarn and Cwmcarn *Mon* 07–12; V Dudley Wood and Cradley Heath *Worc* 12–21; R Ironstone *Ox* from 21. *The Rectory, Church Street, Wroxton, Banbury OX15 6QE* T: (01295) 738593 E: rectorofironstone@gmail.com

BAKER, Andrew James. b 81. St Mellitus Coll 12. **d** 15 **p** 16. C Maghull and Melling *Liv* 15–16; C Haydock St Mark 16–18; C York St Mich-le-Belfrey from 18. *12 Muncastergate, York YO31 9LA* M: 07972-921587 E: andyjimbaker@gmail.com

BAKER, Angela Mary. b 42. **d** 91. Par Dn Battersea St Sav and St Geo w St Andr *S'wark* 91–94; C 94–96; C Battersea Fields 96–02; rtd 02; PtO *Roch* from 03. *Finches, Ide Hill, Sevenoaks TN14 6JW* T: (01732) 750470 E: angelabaker854@btinternet.com

BAKER, Mrs Ann Christine. b 49. Edin Univ BEd 71. CBDTI 98. **d** 01 **p** 02. NSM St Bees *Carl* 01–04; P-in-c Eskdale, Irton, Muncaster and Waberthwaite 04–09; V 09–12; rtd 12; PtO *Carl* from 13. *Heatherside, Abbey Road, St Bees CA27 0EG* T: (01946) 822498

BAKER, Anthony Peter. b 38. Hertf Coll Ox BA 59 MA 63. Clifton Th Coll 60. **d** 63 **p** 64. C Ox St Ebbe w St Pet 63–66; C Welling *Roch* 66–70; V Redland *Bris* 70–79; Lect Tyndale Hall Bris 70–71; Lect Trin Coll Bris 71–77; V Beckenham Ch Ch *Roch* 79–94; Chapl Beckenham Hosp 79–94; V Hove Bp Hannington Memorial Ch *Chich* 94–03; rtd 03; PtO *Chich* from 04. *12 Paradise Close, Eastbourne BN20 8BT* T: (01323) 438783

BAKER, Miss Barbara Ann. b 36. Linc Th Coll 85. **d** 87 **p** 94. Par Dn Hornchurch St Andr *Chelmsf* 87–94; C 94–97; rtd

97; PtO *Chelmsf* from 97. *120 Devonshire Road, Hornchurch RM12 4LN* T: (01708) 477759

BAKER, Benjamin Adam. b 89. Nottm Univ BA 12. Wycliffe Hall Ox MTh 18. d 18 p 19. C Headington St Mary *Ox* from 18. *4 Meadowsweet Way, Oxford OX3 9FW* M: 07981-769797 E: ben.baker68@gmail.com

BAKER, Canon Bernard George Coleman. b 36. Lon Univ BD 61. Oak Hill Th Coll 61. d 63 p 64. C Broadwater St Mary *Chich* 63–66; BCMS Miss P and Chapl Morogoro Em *Ch* Tanzania 66–79; V Moshi St Marg 79–84; Hon Can Morogoro from 77; Hon Can Mt Kilimanjaro from 82; C-in-c Ryde St Jas Prop Chpl *Portsm* 84–96; Crosslinks 96–01; Asst P Ruaha Cathl Tanzania 96–01; Teacher Amani Chr Tr Cen 96–01; rtd 01; PtO *Ex* 02–15; *Leic* 15–20. *70 Sedgefield Drive, Thurnby, Leicester LE7 9PS* T: 0116-241 9181 E: bernandjenbaker@yahoo.co.uk

BAKER, Prof Christopher James. b 54. St Cath Coll Cam BA 75 MA 78 PhD 78 CEng 83 FICE 96 FIHT 95. EMMTC 85. d 88 p 89. NSM Matlock Bath *Derby* 88–95; NSM Matlock Bath and Cromford 95; NSM Beeston *S'well* 95–98; PtO *Lich* 98–00; NSM Lich St Mich w St Mary and Wall 00–10; NSM Lich Ch Ch 10–13; PtO from 13. *15 Saddlers Close, Lichfield WS14 9ZW* T: (01543) 256320 *or* 262211 E: cjsmbaker@btinternet.com

BAKER, Christopher Peter. b 64. St Cuth Soc Dur BA 95 Greenwich Univ PGCE 96. SEITE 99. d 02 p 03. C Kennington St Mark *S'wark* 02–06; Chapl Greenwich Univ 07–13; PtO *Roch* 14–15; *Cant* 18–21. *Holy Trinity Vicarage, 241 High Street, Sheerness ME12 1UR*

BAKER, Christopher Richard. b 61. Man Univ BA 83 PhD 02 Southn Univ BTh 90 Heythrop Coll Lon MTh 92. Sarum & Wells Th Coll 86. d 89 p 93. C Dulwich St Barn *S'wark* 89–92; Tutor Sarum & Wells Th Coll 92–94; Dir Chr Tr Milton Keynes *Ox* 94–98; Dir Tr OLM 98–99; Development Officer Wm Temple Foundn 01–04; Research Dir from 04; Sen Lect Ches Univ 09–14; Wm Temple Prof 14–17; Wm Temple Prof Goldsmiths' Coll Lon *S'wark* from 17. *St Mary's Rectory, Stoke Newington Church Street, London N16 9ES* M: 07779-000021 E: cbhorizon61@gmail.com

BAKER, David Ayshford. b 66. St Aid Coll Dur BA 88. Wycliffe Hall Ox BTh 97. d 97 p 98. C Chadwell Heath *Chelmsf* 97–01; C Surbiton Hill Ch Ch *S'wark* 01–09; R E Dean w Friston and Jevington *Chich* from 09. *The Rectory, Gilberts Drive, East Dean, Eastbourne BN20 0DL* T: (01323) 423266 E: davidbaker1966@gmx.co.uk

BAKER, David Clive. b 47. Sarum & Wells Th Coll 76. d 78 p 79. C Shirley *Birm* 78–82; R Wainfleet All SS w St Thos *Linc* 82–83; P-in-c Wainfleet St Mary 82–83; P-in-c Croft 82–83; R The Wainfleets and Croft 83–86; V Stirchley *Birm* 86–96; PtO 97–98; V Handsworth St Mich 98–02; Chapl Aston Univ 99–02; C Codsall *Lich* 02–05; P-in-c Coven 04–05; V Bilbrook and Coven 05–12; rtd 12; PtO *Heref* 12–14; P-in-c Rickerscote *Lich* 14–18; V 18. *4 Camrose Close, Oakham LE15 6UW* M: 07958-468819 E: linda.david.baker@gmail.com

BAKER, David Daniel. b 77. St Jo Coll Dur BA 98 LSE MSc 01. St Mellitus Coll 18. d 20 p 21. C Woodford Wells *Chelmsf* from 20. *20 Highland Avenue, Loughton IG10 3AJ* M: 07790-037347 E: davidbkr77@gmail.com

BAKER, David John. b 27. LRAM 50 GRSM 51. Ely Th Coll 53. d 55 p 56. C Swanley St Mary *Roch* 55–58; C Guildf St Nic 58–63; Prec St Alb Abbey 63–67; P-in-c Colney St Pet 67–68; V Tattenham Corner and Burgh Heath *Guildf* 73–84; R Fetcham 84–96; rtd 96; PtO *Guildf* 96–18. *1 Terra Cotta Court, Quennels Hill, Wrecclesham, Farnham GU10 4SL* T: (01252) 734202

BAKER, David Peter. b 63. Plymouth Univ CertEd 03. SWMTC 99. d 02 p 03. NSM Parkham, Alwington, Buckland Brewer etc *Ex* 02–12; C S Molton w Nymet St George, High Bray etc 12–16; C Bishopsnympton, Rose Ash, Mariansleigh etc 12–16; TR Bishopsnympton, Charles, E Anstey, High Bray etc from 16. *The Vicarage, East Street, North Molton, South Molton EX36 3HX* T: (01598) 740325 E: davidbaker.sw@gmail.com

BAKER, Deborah Maureen. b 69. RMN 91. Lindisfarne Regional Tr Partnership 11. d 16. NSM Long Benton St Mary *Newc* 16–17; NSM Ulgham 17–20; NSM Widdrington 17–20; NSM Cresswell and Lynemouth from 20. *15 Bradbury Court, New Hartley, Whitley Bay NE25 0SW* M: 07910-087831 E: debbiebaker@gmail.com

BAKER, Dilly. *See* BAKER, Hilary Mary

BAKER, Canon Elizabeth May Janet Margaret. b 51. Bretton Hall Coll CertEd 73. Ox Min Course 04. d 07 p 08. NSM Watling Valley *Ox* 07–10; NSM Stantonbury and Willen 10–15; R Pitlochry *St And* from 15; R Strathtay from 15; R Kilmaveonaig from 15; R Kinloch Rannoch from 15; Hon

Can St Ninian's Cathl Perth from 20. *3 Knockard Place, Pitlochry PH16 5JF* T: (01796) 472005 M: 07896-263768 E: bethmaybaker@yahoo.co.uk

BAKER, Hilary Mary (Dilly). b 61. Man Univ BA 83 Keele Univ MA 09 CQSW 86. Sarum & Wells Th Coll 86. d 89 p 94. Par Dn E Dulwich St Jo *S'wark* 89–92; Tutor Sarum & Wells Th Coll 92–94; TV Stantonbury and Willen *Ox* 94–01; Warden Scargill Ho 01–08; P-in-c Kirkby-in-Malhamdale w Coniston Cold *Bradf* 08–09; P-in-c Kirkby-in-Malhamdale 09–13; Hon Can Bradf Cathl 12–13; R Stoke Newington St Mary *Lon* from 13. *St Mary's Rectory, Stoke Newington Church Street, London N16 9ES* T: (020) 7254 6072 M: 07773-192888 E: dillybaker@gmail.com

BAKER, Hugh Crispin. b 58. Open Univ BA 92. Linc Th Coll 95. d 95 p 96. C Birstall and Wanlip *Leic* 95–99; V Middlestown *Wakef* 99–09; P-in-c Mirfield 09–14; V 14; *Leeds* from 14; Dioc Rural Officer *Wakef* 04–14; Jt AD Dewsbury and Birstall *Leeds* 21. *The Vicarage, 3 Vicarage Meadow, Mirfield WF14 9JL* T: (01924) 505790 E: hughcbaker@gmail.com

BAKER, Hugh John. b 46. Birm Univ BSocSc 68. Cuddesdon Coll 69. d 71 p 72. C Binley *Cov* 71–74; C Pemberton St Mark Newtown *Liv* 74–78; TV Sutton 78–90; V Hints *Lich* 90–05; V Fazeley 90–13; V Canwell 05–13; R Drayton Bassett 05–13; rtd 13; PtO *Lich* from 13; Chapl S Staffs and Shropshire Healthcare NHS Foundn Trust 00–10; Chapl Burton Hosps NHS Foundn Trust from 10. *21 Reedmace, Tamworth B77 1BH* E: hughbaker@hughbaker.plus.com

BAKER, Iain. b 70. St D Coll Lamp BA 91. Oak Hill Th Coll BA 99. d 99 p 00. C Gt Clacton *Chelmsf* 99–03; V Kidsgrove *Lich* from 03. *St Thomas's Vicarage, 12 The Avenue, Kidsgrove, Stoke-on-Trent ST7 1AG* T: (01782) 772895 E: iain.baker@btinternet.com

BAKER, Canon James Henry. b 39. MBE 02. Kelham Th Coll 62. d 67 p 68. C Sheff Arbourthorne 67–70; C Pemberton St Jo *Liv* 70–71; Chapl and Prec St Mary's Cathl *Edin* 71–74; R Lochgelly *St And* 74–84; P-in-c Rosyth and Inverkeithing 76–84; Can St Ninian's Cathl Perth 83–84; TR Whitehaven *Carl* 84–04; RD Calder 96–01; rtd 04; Hon C Eskdale, Irton, Muncaster and Waberthwaite *Carl* 05–12; Hon Can Carl Cathl 96–12; PtO from 13. *Heatherside, Abbey Road, St Bees CA27 0EG* T: (01946) 822498

BAKER, Jenifer Marlene. b 44. Bris Univ BSc 65 Univ of Wales (Swansea) PhD 71 York St Jo Coll BA 05. d 05 p 06. OLM Ruyton XI Towns w Gt and Lt Ness *Lich* 05–16; rtd 16. *15 Gracey Court, Woodland Road, Broadclyst, Exeter EX5 3GA* T: (01392) 468170

BAKER, Jennifer Elizabeth. *See* ROBINSON, Jennifer Elizabeth

✠**BAKER, The Rt Revd Jonathan Mark Richard.** b 66. St Jo Coll Ox BA 88 MPhil 90. St Steph Ho Ox BA 92. d 93 p 94 c 11. C Ascot Heath *Ox* 93–96; C Reading St Mark 96; P-in-c 96–99; V 99–02; P-in-c Reading H Trin 96–99; V 99–02; Prin Pusey Ho 03–11; Hon C Ox St Thos 08–13; Suff Bp Ebbsfleet (PEV) *Cant* 11–13; Hon Asst Bp Ox 11–13; Asst Bp B & W 11–13; Suff Bp Fulham *Lon* from 13; P-in-c St Dunstan in the West 13–16. *5 St Andrew Street, London EC4A 3AF* T: (020) 7932 1130 E: bishop.fulham@london.anglican.org

BAKER, Canon Jonathan William. b 61. SS Coll Cam MA 85. Wycliffe Hall Ox BA 91. d 92 p 93. C Sanderstead All SS *S'wark* 92–96; P-in-c Scalby w Ravenscar and Staintondale *York* 96–97; V Scalby 97–04; P-in-c Hackness w Harwood Dale 96–97; V 97–04; P-in-c Scarborough St Luke 03–04; Can Res Pet Cathl 04–17; V Beverley Minster *York* 17–20; P-in-c Routh 17–20; R Beverley St Jo and St Martin w Routh All SS from 20. *The Minster Vicarage, Highgate, Beverley HU17 0DN* T: (01482) 881434 *or* 868540 E: vicar@beverleyminster.org.uk

BAKER, The Ven Julie Ann Louise. b 77. Univ of Wales (Lamp) BA 98. St Mich Coll Llan BTh 06. d 06 p 07. C Barry All SS *Llan* 06–09; PV Llan Cathl 09–13; P-in-c Pinjarra-Waroona Australia 13–16; Adn Bunbury from 16. *6 Wintersweet Place, Halls Head WA 6210, Australia* M: (0061) 45-947 1894 E: revjuliebaker@gmail.com

BAKER, Kate Justine. b 70. Ridley Hall Cam 16. d 18 p 19. C Huntingdon *Ely* 18–21. *Bramley House, High Street, Colne, Huntingdon PE28 3ND* M: 07793-554196 E: katejbaker@outlook.com

BAKER, Miss Laura Mary. b 89. St Jo Coll Dur BA 10. Westcott Ho Cam 11. d 14 p 15. C King's Lynn St Marg w St Nic *Nor* 14–18; P-in-c New Catton Ch Ch 18–20; PtO *Lon* from 20. *27 Marsh Road, Pinner HA5 5NL* E: laurabaker27@tiscali.co.uk

BAKER, Marc Crispin. b 75. Westmr Coll Ox BTh 96. Oak Hill Th Coll 00. d 02 p 03. C Upton (Overchurch) *Ches* 02–06; TV Cheltenham St Mary, St Matt, St Paul and H Trin *Glouc* 06–07; C Cheltenham St Mary w St Matt 07–12; C Cheltenham St Mary w St Matt and St Luke 12–13; P-in-c Kea *Truro* 13–16;

V from 16; RD Powder from 20. *St Kea House, Killiow, Truro TR3 6AE* T: (01872) 260134 E: vicar@stkea.org.uk

BAKER, Margaret. b 55. **d** 08 **p** 09. C Herringthorpe *Sheff* 08–10; C Rivers Team 10–12; TV 12–20; rtd 20. *3 Devenish Close, Weymouth DT4 8RU*

BAKER, Canon Miles Anthony. b 71. Brunel Univ BA 92. Ridley Hall Cam 99. **d** 02 **p** 03. C Paignton Ch Ch and Preston St Paul *Ex* 02–05; P-in-c Upton 05–08; Dioc Miss Enabler 08–14; Dir Miss *Pet* 14–17; Can Pet Cathl 15–17; R Allesley *Cov* 17–20; Dir of Min Kensington Area *Lon* from 20; Lic Preacher from 20. *Address temp unknown* E: revmilesbaker@outlook.com

BAKER, Canon Neville Duff. b 35. St Aid Birkenhead 60. **d** 63 **p** 64. C Stranton *Dur* 63–66; C Houghton le Spring 66–68; V Tudhoe Grange 68–07; P-in-c Merrington 84–87 and 91–94; RD Auckland 83–94; Hon Can Dur Cathl 90–07; rtd 07; PtO *Dur* from 09; *Newc* from 10. *2 The Bents, Sunderland SR6 7NX* T: 0191-529 4600

BAKER, Nicholas George. b 73. Kent Univ BA 94 York Univ MA 97 PhD 13 FRSA 13. St Hild Coll 17. **d** 20 **p** 21. C Wigston *Leic* from 20. *11 Portgate, Wigston LE18 3LQ* T: 0116-288 3395 M: 07754-068845 E: revnickbaker@gmail.com

BAKER, Noel Edward Lloyd. b 37. Sarum & Wells Th Coll 73. **d** 75 **p** 76. C Charlton Kings St Mary *Glouc* 75–79; V Clearwell 79–81; R Eastington and Frocester 81–97; RD Stonehouse 90–94; P-in-c Eastington and Frocester 97–98; P-in-c Standish w Haresfield and Moreton Valence etc 97–98; rtd 98; PtO *Glouc* 00–13. *Capel Court, The Burgage, Prestbury, Cheltenham GL52 3EL* T: (01242) 269484 E: noelbaker@greenbee.net

BAKER, Mrs Pamela Daphne. b 53. Ox Min Course. **d** 08. NSM Blackbird Leys *Ox* 08–14. *2 White Lodge, Oak Lane, Sevenoaks TN13 1UA* M: 07717-377516 E: pamelabaker53@gmail.com

BAKER, Paul Anthony. b 64. St Chad's Coll Dur BA 85. St Steph Ho Ox BA 88 MA 98. **d** 89 **p** 90. C Hartlepool St Aid *Dur* 89–93; TV Jarrow 93–98; V Sunderland Pennywell St Thos 98–04; V Darlington St Mark w St Paul from 04. *St Mark's Vicarage, 394 North Road, Darlington DL1 3BH* T: (01325) 382400

BAKER, Peter Colin. b 43. Sarum & Wells Th Coll. **d** 82 **p** 83. C Bridgemary *Portsm* 82–86; V Ash Vale *Guildf* 86–99; P-in-c Earlham St Anne *Nor* 99–08; P-in-c Earlham St Mary 99–08; rtd 08; PtO *Sarum* from 11. *15 Linden Close, Laverstock, Salisbury SP1 1PN* T: (01722) 501305 M: 07710-844243 E: peter.baker854@ntlworld.com

BAKER, Robert James. b 80. Oriel Coll Ox BA 04 MA 08. Wycliffe Hall Ox BA 07. **d** 08 **p** 09. C Chesham Bois *Ox* 08–12; R Stoke H Cross w Dunston, Arminghall etc *Nor* from 12. *Holy Cross Vicarage, Mill Road, Stoke Holy Cross, Norwich NR14 8PA* T: (01508) 492305 E: rob@venta-group.org

BAKER, Canon Robert John Kenneth. b 50. Southn Univ BSc 71 MICE 79. Oak Hill Th Coll 88. **d** 90 **p** 91. C Cromer *Nor* 90–94; R Pakefield 94–17; Hon Can Nor Cathl 07–17; rtd 17. *15 Basingbourne Road, Fleet GU52 6TE* E: bcbaker@sky.com

BAKER, Canon Robert Mark. b 50. Bris Univ BA 73. St Jo Coll Nottm 74. **d** 76 **p** 77. C Portswood Ch Ch *Win* 76–80; R Witton w Brundall and Braydeston *Nor* 80–89; P-in-c Buckenham w Hassingham and Strumpshaw 80–86; R Brundall w Braydeston and Postwick 89–05; RD Blofield 89–94; TR Thetford 05–16; Hon Can Nor Cathl 93–16; rtd 16; PtO *Nor* from 17. *32 Tantallon Drive, Attleborough NR17 2SN* T: (01953) 454215 E: bob-baker@hotmail.com

BAKER, Ronald Kenneth. b 43. Open Univ BA 80. St Jo Coll Nottm LTh 87. **d** 87 **p** 88. C Paddock Wood *Roch* 87–90; V Ramsgate St Mark *Cant* 90–95; P-in-c Ewhurst and Bodiam *Chich* 95–98; V 98–03; rtd 03; PtO *Chich* from 03. *49 Coneyburrow Gardens, St Leonards-on-Sea TN38 9RZ* T: (01424) 851870

BAKER, Roy David. b 36. St Aid Birkenhead 59. **d** 62 **p** 63. C Garston *Liv* 62–64; C N Meols 64–68; V Newton-le-Willows 68–73; V Crossens 73–82; V Blundellsands St Nic 82–01; rtd 01; PtO *Liv* from 03. *18 Ennerdale Road, Formby, Liverpool L37 2EA* T: (01704) 830622 E: rdbaker@talktalk.net

BAKER, Sarah Jane. b 59. Lon Univ MB, BS 82 Sheff Univ MPhil 00 Coll of Ripon & York St Jo MA 02. NOC 99. **d** 02 **p** 03. NSM Kinsley w Wragby *Wakef* 02–04; NSM Sandal St Cath 04–07; PtO 07–11; NSM Westbrook St Jas *Liv* 11–14; TR Warrington W 14–17; PtO *Portsm* from 19. *82 Whichers Gate Road, Rowland's Castle PO9 6BB* T: (023) 9241 3399 M: 07885-376182 E: sarah.baker17@btinternet.com *or* sarahbakercouk@gmail.com

BAKER, Canon Simon Nicholas Hartland. b 57. K Coll Lon BD 78. Qu Coll Birm 79. **d** 81 **p** 82. C Tupsley *Heref* 81–85; V Shinfield *Ox* 85–98; Prin Berks Chr Tr Scheme 93–98; Lay Min Adv and Warden of Readers *Win* 98–02; Dir of Min Development 02–07; Dir of Min and Past Planning

07–13; Hon Can Win Cathl 08–13; Adn Lich 13–19; R Lich St Mich w St Mary and Wall 13–21; Preb Lich Cathl 19–21; rtd 21. *1 School Lane, Seavington, Ilminster TA19 0QD* E: simonbaker57@outlook.com

BAKER, Canon William John. b 45. FCII 80. Cranmer Hall Dur 87. **d** 89 **p** 90. C Sale St Anne *Ches* 89–93; V Crewe St Andr w St Jo 93–15; P-in-c Crewe Ch Ch 07–13; RD Nantwich 06–13; Hon Can Ches Cathl 03–15; rtd 15; PtO *Ches* from 16. *16 Lyceum Way, Crewe CW1 3YF* T: (01270) 488063 M: 07768-843654 E: revbaker@sky.com

BAKEWELL, Jeremy Edgar. b 44. **d** 12 **p** 13. OLM Aldridge *Lich* from 12. *37 St Mary's Way, Walsall WS9 0AB* T: (01922) 459345 E: jeremyebakewell@gmail.com

BAKKER (née CAMPBELL), Mrs Jane Judith. b 68. Trin Coll Bris BA 01. **d** 01 **p** 02. NSM Lyddington and Wanborough and Bishopstone etc *Bris* 01–03; NSM Stratton St Margaret w S Marston etc 03–08; NSM Sholing *Win* 08–16; NSM Maybush and Southampton St Jude 16–19; P-in-c from 19; AD Southampton 13–19. *Maybush Vicarage, Sedbergh Road, Southampton SO16 9HJ* E: jjbakker@tiscali.co.uk

BALCH, Andrew Peter. b 85. Guildhall Sch of Music & Drama BMus 08 MMus 10 Middx Univ BA 18. Oak Hill Th Coll 18. **d** 21. C St Helen Bishopsgate w St Andr Undershaft etc *Lon* from 21. *19 Morgan Street, London E3 5AA* M: 07401-111007 E: drewbalch@me.com

BALCHIN, Michael John. b 38. Selw Coll Cam BA 60 MA 64. Wells Th Coll 60. **d** 62 **p** 63. C Bournemouth H Epiphany *Win* 62–65; C Bris St Mary Redcliffe w Temple etc 65–69; R Norton sub Hamdon *B & W* 69–70; P-in-c Chiselborough w W Chinnock 69–70; R Norton sub Hamdon w Chiselborough 70–77; P-in-c Chipstable w Huish Champflower and Clatworthy 77–82; R 82–88; PtO *Ban* from 88; rtd 03. *Crogbren, Llandyssil Hill Road, Kerry Road, Trefaldwyn SY15 6PD* T: (01686) 669738 E: balchin844@btinternet.com

BALDING, Christopher Matthew Noel. b 90. Sheff Univ BEng 11 Dur Univ BA 19. Ridley Hall Cam 16. **d** 19 **p** 20. C Roundhay St Edm *Leeds* 19–21; C Wortley and Farnley from 21. *14 Parkside Green, Leeds LS6 4NY* M: 07746-668140

BALDOCK, Reginald David. b 48. Oak Hill Th Coll 72. **d** 75 **p** 76. C Plymouth St Jude *Ex* 75–79; C Ardsley *Sheff* 79–85; V Rawthorpe *Wakef* 85–96; C Salterhebble All SS 96–98; P-in-c Bournemouth St Jo w St Mich *Win* 98–16; rtd 16; PtO *Sarum* 17–21. *95 Lulworth Avenue, Poole BH15 4DH* E: r.baldock1@ntlworld.com

BALDWIN, Colin Steven. b 61. Brighton Poly BA 85. St Jo Coll Nottm MTh 01. **d** 01 **p** 02. C Billericay and Lt Burstead *Chelmsf* 01–05; P-in-c Prittlewell St Steph from 05; P-in-c Prittlewell St Pet w Westcliff St Cedd from 16. *26 Eastbourne Grove, Westcliff-on-Sea SS0 0QF* T: (01702) 352448 M: 07789-511910 E: colin@lifestreams.org.uk

BALDWIN, Canon David Frederick Beresford. b 57. Ripon Coll Cuddesdon 93. **d** 95 **p** 96. C Uttoxeter w Bramshall *Lich* 95–97; C Uttoxeter Area 97–98; V Tilstock, Edstaston and Whixall 98–08; P-in-c Prees 03–08; P-in-c Fauls 03–08; Rural Chapl (Salop Adnry) 00–08; RD Wem and Whitchurch 06–08; P-in-c The Lulworths, Winfrith Newburgh and Chaldon *Sarum* 08–10; C Wool and E Stoke 09–10; TR Beaminster Area from 10; RD Lyme Bay from 16; Can and Preb Sarum Cathl from 16. *The Rectory, 3 Clay Lane, Beaminster DT8 3BU* T: (01308) 862150 E: revdavidbaldwin@gmail.com

BALDWIN, Mrs Frances Mary. b 49. SRN 71. SEITE 99. **d** 02 **p** 03. NSM Caterham *S'wark* 02–10; Asst Chapl E Sussex Healthcare NHS Trust 11–21; PtO *Chich* 16–18; NSM Westham 18–21; rtd 21. *46 Hawkhurst Way, Bexhill-on-Sea TN39 3SN* T: (01424) 842864 E: francesb3@btinternet.com

BALDWIN, John Charles. b 39. Bris Univ BSc 61 Sussex Univ DPhil 65 FBCS CEng. St Steph Ho Ox 82. **d** 83 **p** 84. C Llandaff w Capel Llanilltern *Llan* 83–90; V Ewenny w St Brides Major 90–92; LtO from 92; Hon Chapl Llan Cathl from 96; rtd 04. *60 Llantrisant Road, Llandaff, Cardiff CF5 2PX* T: (029) 2055 4457 F: 2038 7835 E: dovemaster@gmail.com

BALDWIN, Canon Jonathan Michael. b 58. Chich Th Coll 92. **d** 94 **p** 95. C Crawley *Chich* 94–96; C New Shoreham 96–02; C Old Shoreham 96–02; Chapl Gatwick Airport from 02; C Crawley 02–17; C W Green from 17; Can and Preb Chich Cathl from 12. *18 Aldingbourne Close, Ifield, Crawley RH11 0QJ* T: (01293) 406001 E: jonathan.baldwin@gatwickairport.com

BALDWIN, Julia Clare. b 81. St Chad's Coll Dur BA 02 Darw Coll Cam PGCE 05. Ripon Coll Cuddesdon BA 09 MA 17. **d** 10 **p** 11. C Bridge *Cant* 10–13; Chapl to Bp Dover 13–17; Abp's Chapl 13–17; Chapl and BNC Ox from 17. *Brasenose College, Radcliffe Square, Oxford OX1 4AJ* M: 07926-516476 E: revjuliabaldwin@gmail.com

BALDWIN, Mrs Maureen Teresa. b 64. Trin & All SS Coll Leeds BEd 82 Liv Univ MEd 95. All SS Cen for Miss & Min 17. **d** 19 **p** 20. C Chorley St Laur *Blackb* from 19. *St Aidan's Vicarage, Longworth Street, Bamber Bridge, Preston PR5 6GN* M: 07592-838726 E: mobaldwin@btinternet.com

BALDWIN, Peter Alan. b 48. Bede Coll Dur BA 70. Qu Coll Birm 72. **d** 73 **p** 74. C Hartlepool St Oswald *Dur* 73–75; C Darlington H Trin 75–78; OGS from 77; C-in-c Bishop Auckland Woodhouse Close CD *Dur* 78–82; V Ferryhill 82–88; V Pendleton St Thos *Man* 88–89; P-in-c Charlestown 88–89; TR Pendleton St Thos w Charlestown 89–90; TR Newton Aycliffe *Dur* 90–96; TR Gt Aycliffe 96–97; V The Trimdons 97–99; AD Sedgefield 96–99; P-in-c Bramley *Ripon* 99–00; TR 00–02; Hon C Harrogate St Wilfrid 02–03; Hon C Methley w Mickletown 03–04; Dom Chapl to Bp Horsham *Chich* 04–06; P-in-c Ashington, Washington and Wiston w Buncton 05–06; P-in-c Brightlingsea *Chelmsf* 06–11; rtd 11; Hon C Halifax *Wakef* 11–13; Hon C Todmorden w Cornholme and Walsden 13–14; *Leeds* 14–15; PtO *Dur* from 15. *61 Hutton Way, Durham DH1 5BW* T: 0191-375 0822 M: 07403-231333 E: peter.baldwin21@yahoo.co.uk

BALDWIN, Shaun. b 64. Man Univ BA 04. Ushaw Coll Dur 82. **d** 89 **p** 90. In RC Ch 89–00; NSM Hawes Side and Marton Moss *Blackb* 11–12; P-in-c Waterside Par 12–13; V 13–14; C Stalmine w Pilling 12–13; V 13–14; V Broughton 14–20; AD Preston 17–19; P-in-c Ingol 18–19; V Bamber Bridge St Aid and Walton-le-Dale St Leon from 20. *St Aidan's Vicarage, Longworth Street, Bamber Bridge, Preston PR5 6GN* T: (01772) 335310 E: vicar.saintaidlen@gmail.com

BALDWIN, Mrs Vivien Lindsay. b 50. SAOMC 97. **d** 98 **p** 99. NSM Westbury w Turweston, Shalstone and Biddlesden *Ox* 98–00; C W Buckingham 00–02; P-in-c Stoneleigh w Ashow *Cov* 02–07; Rural Life Officer 02–06; Chapl W Midl Police *Birm* 07–09; PtO *Pet* 07–12; Chapl Northants Police 12–19; PtO from 19; *Birm* from 19. *20 Castle Road, Woodford Halse, Daventry NN11 3RS* T: (01327) 264722 M: 07720-811477

BALDWIN, William. b 48. RMN 73 FRSH 83. NW Ord Course 75. **d** 78 **p** 79. C Royton St Anne *Man* 78–82; V Halliwell St Thos 82–87; TR Atherton 87–99; TR Atherton and Hindsford 99–02; TV Atherton and Hindsford w Howe Bridge 02–08; AD Leigh 01–08; TV Turton Moorland 08–13; rtd 13; PtO *Man* from 13. *51 Shorefield Mount, Egerton, Bolton BL7 9EW* T: (01204) 302924 M: 07552-931264

BALE, Kenneth John. b 34. Univ of Wales (Lamp) BA 58. Qu Coll Birm. **d** 60 **p** 61. C Mitcham St Olave *S'wark* 60–63; C Warlingham w Chelsham and Farleigh 63–67; V Battersea Rise St Mark 67–85; PtO 85–88; Hon C Balham St Mary and St Jo 88–90; V S Wimbledon All SS 90–01; Dioc Adv Min of Healing 91–01; rtd 01; PtO *Sheff* 01–18. *23 Selhurst Crescent, Bessacarr, Doncaster DN4 6EF* M: 07710-212263 E: grandfatherken@gmail.com

BALE, Mrs Louise Ann. b 63. Sarum Coll 17. **d** 20 **p** 21. Chapl Taunton and Somerset NHS Foundn Trust from 20; NSM Taunton St Mary and St Jo *B & W* from 20. *3 Windsor Road, Bridgwater TA6 4HA* M: 07679-234983 E: curatelouise@stmarymagdalenetaunton.org.uk

BALE, Mrs Sandra Jane. b 62. SEITE 12. **d** 15 **p** 16. NSM Forest Row *Chich* 15–19; NSM Crawley Down All SS from 19. *Borders, Herons Lea, Copthorne, Crawley RH10 3HE* T: (01342) 718303

BALE, Simon John. b 62. Univ of Wales (Cardiff) BSc 84 PhD 88. STETS 10. **d** 13 **p** 14. C Highbridge *B & W* 13–17; V Bridgwater St Fran 17–18; Dioc Inter Faith Adv 15–18; P-in-c Athelney from 21. *3 Windsor Road, Bridgwater TA6 4HA* M: 07970-936325 E: sj_bale@icloud.com

BALE, Canon Susannah. b 67. Univ of Wales (Cardiff) BA 90 BTh 06. St Mich Coll Llan 03. **d** 06 **p** 07. C Betws w Ammanford *St D* 06–08; C Bro Teifi Sarn Helen 08–10; P-in-c Llanybydder and Llanwenog w Llanllwni etc 10–18; P-in-c Betws w Ammanford 18–19; P-in-c Bro Aman from 19; AD from 19; Can St D Cathl from 18. *The Vicarage, Parc Henry Lane, Ammanford SA18 2EH* T: (01269) 592084 E: suzybale@hotmail.com

BALFOUR, David Ian Bailey. b 33. **d** 63 **p** 63. C Ashburton NZ 63–66; P-in-c Aranui-Wainoni 66–71; Asst P Christchurch 66–71; V Lyttelton 72–75; V Symonds Street 75–84; P-in-c Kaitaia 85; P-in-c Henderson 85–86; V Rangiora 90–93; V Timaru 93–98; Adn S Canterbury and V Marchwell 94–98; NSM Dumfries *Glas* 05–08; LtO from 08; LtO *Mor* from 08; NSM Keith 09–13. *1 Balleigh Wood, Edderton IV19 1LF* T: (01862) 821645 M: 07527-445156 E: david.loma@baileybalfour.com

BALFOUR, Hugh Rowlatt. b 54. SS Coll Cam BA 76. Ridley Hall Cam 78. **d** 81 **p** 82. C Bedford Ch Ch *St Alb* 81–86; P-in-c Camberwell Ch Ch *S'wark* 86–90; V from 90. *Christ*

Church Vicarage, 79 Asylum Road, London SE15 2RJ T: (020) 7639 5662 E: hrbalfours@btinternet.com

BALFOUR, Mark Andrew. b 66. York Univ BA 88 R Holloway Coll Lon PhD 98. Trin Coll Bris BA 01. **d** 02 **p** 03. C Churchdown *Glouc* 02–06; V Furze Platt *Ox* 06–16; CMS Guatemala from 16. *Church Mission Society, Watlington Road, Cowley, Oxford OX4 6BZ*

BALFOUR, Mrs Penelope Mary. b 47. St Andr Univ MA 69 St Jo Coll York DipEd 72. Coates Hall Edin 89 St Jo Coll Nottm 84. **d** 88 **p** 95. C Dundee St Marg *Bre* 88–94; Dioc AIDS Officer 90–94; NSM Invergowrie 94–96; C 00–07; Chapl Abertay Univ 94–97; C Dundee St Marg 96–00; PtO from 08. *10 Strathaird Place, Dundee DD2 4TN* T: (01382) 643114

BALFOUR, Rory John. b 93. Dur Univ BA 14 CCC Cam MPhil 17. Cranmer Hall Dur 17. **d** 19 **p** 20. C Hillside *Dur* from 19. *45 Shotley Gardens, Gateshead NE9 5DP* E: rory.j.balfour@durham.ac.uk

BALKWILL, Canon Michael Robert. b 67. Univ of Wales (Lamp) BD 89 Univ of Wales (Cardiff) MTh 92. St Mich Coll Llan 89 Bp Tucker Coll Mukono 91. **d** 91 **p** 92. C Llanrhos *St As* 91–97; Bp's Visitor from 94; R Llanfyllin and Bwlchycibau 97–11; AD Llanfyllin 05–11; Bp's Chapl and Press Officer from 11; Can Cursal and Can Res St As Cathl from 11. *The Vicarage, 1 Llys Trewithan, St Asaph LL17 0DJ* T: (01745) 583503 E: michaelbalkwill@churchinwales.org.uk

BALL, Alan. b 26. Qu Coll Birm 72. **d** 75 **p** 75. NSM Hamstead St Paul *Birm* 75–93; rtd 93; PtO *Portsm* from 93. *25 Tebourba Drive, Alverstoke, Gosport PO12 2NT* T: (023) 9260 1694 E: alanball72017@gmail.com

BALL, Andrew Thomas. b 54. K Coll Lon BD 75 AKC 75. Sarum & Wells Th Coll 76. **d** 77 **p** 78. C Ribbleton *Blackb* 77–80; C Sedgley All SS *Lich* 80–84; V Pheasey 84–90; Chapl Gd Hope Distr Gen Hosp Sutton Coldfield 90–94; Chapl Gd Hope Hosp NHS Trust Sutton Coldfield 94–06; Chapl Heart of England NHS Foundn Trust 07–18; rtd 18; PtO *Birm* from 18. *42 Falstone Road, Sutton Coldfield B73 6PJ* T: 0121-243 1948 E: andrew.ball7@virgin.net

BALL, Anthony Charles. b 46. Lon Univ BD 71. Chich Th Coll 72. **d** 73 **p** 74. C Heref St Martin 73–76; C Ealing St Pet Mt Park *Lon* 76–82; V Ruislip Manor St Paul 82–11; rtd 11; PtO *Chich* from 17. *44 Ashdown, Eaton Road, Hove BN3 3AQ*

BALL, Canon Anthony James. b 68. St Chad's Coll Dur BA 89 Heythrop Coll Lon MA 10. NTMTC 97. **d** 00 **p** 01. NSM Madrid *Eur* 00–03; Chapl Damascus 03–05; Apb Cant's Asst Sec for Internat, Ecum and Angl Communion Affairs 05–09; Abp's Sec for Internat and Inter-Relig Relns *Cant* 08–09; Abp's Chapl 09–11; Lic Preacher *Lon* 07–11; Public Preacher *S'wark* 10–11; R Worth, Pound Hill and Maidenbower *Chich* 11–16; Chapl Worth Sch 12–16; Can Westmr Abbey from 16; Can Steward 16–20; R Westmr St Marg from 20; Hon Can All SS Cathl Cairo from 07; Hon Can Madrid Cathl from 07; Lic Preacher *Lon* from 17. *5 Little Cloister, London SW1P 3PL* T: (020) 7654 4805 E: anthony.ball@westminster-abbey.org

BALL, Anthony Michael. b 46. Kelham Th Coll 66. **d** 70 **p** 71. C Kingswinford St Mary *Lich* 70–74; C W Bromwich All SS 74–76; P-in-c Priorslee 76–80; V 80–82; Asst Chapl HM Pris Liv 82–83; Chapl 88–95; Chapl HM Pris Lewes 83–88; Featherstone 95–00; The Verne 00–06; PtO *Sarum* from 06; rtd 11. *La Providence, 21 Portland Road, Weymouth DT4 9ES* T: (01305) 787027 E: tonyball2008@hotmail.co.uk

BALL, Frances Anne. See FINN, Frances Anne

BALL, Ian Raymond. b 45. CertEd Univ of Wales MPhil. Glouc Th Course 81. **d** 85 **p** 87. NSM Churchstoke w Hyssington and Sarn *Heref* 85–15; Lic to Bp Ludlow 87–15; LtO *St As* from 93; PtO *Heref* from 16. *Bachaethlon Cottage, Sarn, Newtown SY16 4HH* T: (01686) 670505 M: 07966-022404 E: ian@pathways-development.com *or* irball@btinternet.com

BALL, Mrs Imogen Kate. b 92. Bath Univ BSc 16. Trin Coll Bris MA 21. **d** 21. C Trull w Angersleigh *B & W* from 21. *5 Barton Green, Trull, Taunton TA3 7NA* M: 07511-690125 E: imogen.k.ball@gmail.com

BALL, Mrs Jane. b 68. Charlotte Mason Coll of Educn BEd 91. St Steph Ho Ox 01. **d** 03 **p** 04. C Bedale and Leeming *Ripon* 03–05; Hon C Devizes St Jo w St Mary *Sarum* 05–07; Chapl Godolphin Sch 07–14; V E Meon *Portsm* 14–21; V Langrish 14–21; C W Meon and Warnford 14–21; AD Petersfield 16–21. *Address temp unknown* M: 07771-804324 E: jandjball@btinternet.com

BALL, Mrs Jema Mary. b 83. Man Univ BSc 04. Trin Coll Bris BA 12. **d** 12 **p** 13. C Countesthorpe w Foston *Leic* 12–15; C Oundle w Ashton and Benefield w Glapthorn *Pet* 15–19; Dioc Young Voc Officer 16–19; V Stoke Bishop *Bris* from 19. *St Mary's Vicarage, Mariners Drive, Bristol BS9 1QJ* M: 07966-733836

BALL, John Kenneth. b 42. Lon Univ BSc 64 AKC 64. Linc Th Coll 69. **d** 71 **p** 72. C Garston *Liv* 71–74; C Eastham *Ches* 74–75; C Barnston 75–77; V Over St Jo 77–82; V Helsby and Dunham-on-the-Hill 82–94; RD Frodsham 88–94; P-in-c Alvanley 92–94; V Hoylake 94–98; rtd 98; P-in-c Downholme and Marske *Ripon* 00–05; C Richmond w Hudswell and Downholme and Marske 05–07; PtO *Blackb* from 06; *Eur* 09–13. *2 King Street, Longridge, Preston PR3 3RQ* T: (01772) 783172

BALL, John Roy. b 47. Fitzw Coll Cam MA 71. Wycliffe Hall Ox 83. **d** 85 **p** 86. C Stockport St Mary *Ches* 85–88; C Fazeley *Lich* 88–94; Res Min Drayton Bassett 89–94; Chapl Grenoble w Den Helder and Heiloo 05–12; rtd 12; PtO *Lich* 13–21; *Eur* from 18. *20 Robin Close, Uttoxeter ST14 8TP* T: (01889) 567459 E: royball77@gmail.com

BALL, Jonathan Philip. b 96. Bath Univ BSc 18. Trin Coll Bris MA 21. **d** 21. C Trull w Angersleigh *B & W* from 21. *5 Barton Green, Trull, Taunton TA3 7NA* M: 07419-741169 E: jonathanphilipball@yahoo.co.uk

BALL, Mrs Judith Anne. b 48. Nottm Univ BA 70 Liv Univ PGCE 71. NOC 98. **d** 01 **p** 02. C Upholland *Liv* 01–12; rtd 12; PtO *Liv* from 16. *31 Ryder Crescent, Aughton, Ormskirk L39 5EY* T: (01695) 421579

BALL, Kevin Harry. b 55. Linc Th Coll 92. **d** 94 **p** 95. C New Mills *Derby* 94–96; C Walthamstow St Sav *Chelmsf* 96–98; V Stocksbridge *Sheff* 98–00; C Barnsley St Mary *Wakef* 00–01; Chapl Barnsley Coll 00–01; P-in-c Sneinton St Cypr *S'well* 01–05; Chapl Notts Fire and Rescue Service 04–05; Sen Chapl Man Airport 05–11; R Calow and Sutton cum Duckmanton *Derby* 11–21; Jt Dioc Ecum Officer 12–21; rtd 21. *4 Blackberry Way, Brimington, Chesterfield S43 1DA* E: k.h.ball@outlook.com

BALL, Mrs Marion Elaine. b 68. Hertf Coll Ox BA 90 St Jo Coll Dur BA 99. Cranmer Hall Dur 97. **d** 02 **p** 03. C Kingston upon Hull H Trin *York* 02–11; PtO *Sheff* from 12; Chapl HM Pris Moorland from 19. *HM Prison Moorland, Bawtry Road, Hatfield Woodhouse, Doncaster DN7 6BW* T: (01302) 523000 E: marion.ball001@btinternet.com

BALL, Martin Francis. b 62. Wycliffe Hall Ox 06. **d** 08 **p** 09. C Woking Ch Ch *Guildf* 08–11; V Knutton *Lich* 11–13; V Newcastle St Geo from 11. *St George's Vicarage, 28 Hempstalls Lane, Newcastle ST5 0SS* M: 07816-398459 E: martball@gmail.com

✠**BALL, The Rt Revd Michael Thomas.** b 32. Qu Coll Cam BA 55 MA 59. **d** 71 **p** 71 **c** 80. CGA from 60; Prior Stroud Priory 64–76; C Whiteshill *Glouc* 71–76; LtO 76; P-in-c Stanmer w Falmer *Chich* 76–80; Chapl Sussex Univ 76–80; Suff Bp Jarrow *Dur* 80–90; Angl Adv Tyne Tees TV 84–90; Bp Truro 90–97; rtd 97; PtO *B & W* 01–10 and 15–17. *The Coach House, The Manor, Aller, Langport TA10 0RA*

BALL, Nicholas Edward. b 54. Man Univ BA 75 Ox Univ MA 85. Ripon Coll Cuddesdon 79. **d** 80 **p** 81. C Yardley Wood *Birm* 80–83; C Moseley St Mary 83–86; Chapl Cen 13 83–85; V Bartley Green *Birm* 86–95; P-in-c Hall Green St Pet 95–97; PtO 00–03; Chapl Birm Children's Hosp NHS Trust and Birm Heartlands and Solihull NHS Trust 03–09; rtd 09; Chapl Birm Children's Hosp NHS Foundn Trust 13–16; PtO *Birm* from 16. *12 Apsley Croft, Birmingham B38 0AF* T: 0121-243 1336 E: nicholaseball@hotmail.com

BALL, Norman. b 41. Liv Univ BA 63 Ch Coll Liv CertEd 72. Cuddesdon Coll 65. **d** 68 **p** 69. C Broseley w Benthall *Heref* 68–72; Hd RS Christleton High Sch 72–75; V Plemstall w Guilden Sutton *Ches* 75–79; Hd RS Neston Co High Sch 79–94; NSM Dodleston *Ches* 86–91; NSM Buckley *St As* 91–94; TV Hawarden 94–00; rtd 00; PtO *St As* from 00. *White Cottage, Lower Mountain Road, Penyffordd, Chester CH4 0EX* T: (01244) 661132

BALL, Peter Edwin. b 44. Lon Univ BD 65 DipEd. Wycliffe Hall Ox 75. **d** 77 **p** 78. C Prescot *Liv* 77–80; R Lawford *Chelmsf* 80–99; RD Harwich 91–96; P-in-c Broomfield 99–04; V 04–10; rtd 10; PtO *Chelmsf* from 10; *St E* from 11. *14 Merriam Close, Brantham, Manningtree CO11 1RY* T: (01206) 393316 E: pebblej@btinternet.com

BALL, Philip John. b 52. Bris Univ BEd 75 Ox Univ MTh 98. Ripon Coll Cuddesdon 79. **d** 82 **p** 83. C Norton St Mich *Dur* 82–84; C Greenford H Cross *Lon* 84–88; V Hayes St Edm 88–97; AD Hillingdon 94–97; TR Bicester w Bucknell, Caversfield and Launton *Ox* 97–07; AD Bicester and Islip 00–05; R Abington *Pet* 07–18; Asst Dir Ords 14–18; rtd 18. *Applegrove, 2 Manor Court, Brackley NN13 6EL* T: (01280) 840357 M: 07761-223506 E: phjobal07@gmail.com

BALL, Philip John. b 63. Coll of Ripon & York St Jo BA 91. Cranmer Hall Dur 97. **d** 99 **p** 00. C Linthorpe *York* 99–02; C Kingston upon Hull H Trin 02–07; N Humberside Ind Chapl 08–11; V Airmyn, Hook and Rawcliffe *Sheff* from 11. *The Vicarage, 12 Church Lane, Hook, Goole DN14 5PN* T: (01405) 767721 E: philip.ball@sheffield.anglican.org

BALL, Rita Enid. b 49. Sheff Univ LLB 69. SAOMC 94. **d** 97 **p** 98. NSM Newbury *Ox* 97–03; R Wantage Downs 03–09; TR Hermitage 09–17; AD Newbury 10–15; Hon Can Ch Ch 12–17; rtd 17; Hon C Newbury St Geo and St Jo *Ox* 17–19; PtO from 19. *240 Andover Road, Newbury RG14 6PT* T: (01635) 228072 E: ritaball65@gmail.com

BALL, Roy. *See* BALL, John Roy

BALL, Stephen Andrew. b 54. Wycliffe Hall Ox. **d** 05 **p** 06. C Hilperton w Whaddon and Staverton etc *Sarum* 05–07; C Canalside Benefice 07–08; P-in-c 08–12; R 12–15; P-in-c Sherfield-on-Loddon and Stratfield Saye etc *Win* 15–19; R 19–21; rtd 21. *Address temp unknown* M: 07943-014277 E: vicar.sb54rev@gmail.com

BALL, Susan. b 64. SNWTP 14. **d** 17 **p** 18. OLM Droylsden St Mary *Man* from 17. *72 Graver Lane, Manchester M40 1QW.* T: 0161-682 1439

BALL, Canon Timothy William. b 60. Trin Coll Bris 96. **d** 96 **p** 97. C Harlow St Mary and St Hugh w St Jo the Bapt *Chelmsf* 96–99; V Springfield H Trin 99–11; Ind Chapl 00–11; TR Loughrigg *Carl* 11–15; TV Gt Baddow *Chelmsf* 15–21; P-in-c from 21; AD Chelmsf S 17–20; AD Chelmsf N 19–20; AD Chelmsford from 21; Hon Can Chelmsf Cathl from 18. *62 Longmead Avenue, Chelmsford CM2 7EY* T: (01245) 901612 E: vicar@meadgatechurch.org.uk

BALLANTINE, Canon Peter Sinclair. b 46. Nottm Univ MTh 85. K Coll Lon BA 68 AKC 68 St Jo Coll Nottm 70 Lon Coll of Div ALCD 71 BD 73 LTh 74. **d** 73 **p** 74. C Rainham *Chelmsf* 73–77; C Wennington 73–77; TV Barton Mills, Beck Row w Kenny Hill etc *St E* 77–82; Chapl Liv Poly 83–86; Tr Officer Rugby Deanery *Cov* 86–97; P-in-c Churchover w Willey 86–97; P-in-c Clifton upon Dunsmore and Newton 86–97; Dir Buckingham Adnry Chr Tr Progr *Ox* 97–02; TV Stantonbury and Willen 02–15; Hon Can Ch Ch 12–15; rtd 15; PtO *Ox* from 15. *2 Carroll Close, Newport Pagnell MK16 8QQ* M: 07876-797507 E: pballarev@yahoo.com

BALLANTINE, Roderic Keith. b 44. Chich Th Coll 66. **d** 69 **p** 70. C Nunhead St Antony *S'wark* 69–72; C S Hackney St Jo w Ch Ch *Lon* 72–75; P-in-c Kensal Town St Thos w St Andr and St Phil 75–79; V Stoke Newington St Andr 79–05; rtd 05; PtO *Lon* from 06. *67 Savernake Road, London NW3 2LA* T: (020) 7267 2744

BALLANTYNE, Jane Elizabeth. *See* KENCHINGTON, Jane Elizabeth Ballantyne

BALLARD, The Ven Andrew Edgar. b 44. Dur Univ BA 66. Westcott Ho Cam 66. **d** 68 **p** 69. C St Marylebone St Mary *Lon* 68–72; C Portsea St Mary *Portsm* 72–76; V Haslingden w Haslingden Grane *Blackb* 76–82; V Walkden Moor *Man* 82–93; TR Walkden Moor w Lt Hulton 93–98; AD Farnworth 90–98; Chapl Salford Coll 82–92; P-in-c Rochdale *Man* 98–99; TR 00; Adn Rochdale 00–05; Adn Man 05–09; Hon Can Man Cathl 98–09; rtd 09; PtO *Linc* 16–21. *30 Swift Drive, Scawby Brook, Brigg DN20 9FL* T: (01652) 659560 E: ae.ballard@btinternet.com

BALLARD, Miss Anne Christina. b 54. LRAM 76 HonRCM 93 ARAM 94. Wycliffe Hall Ox 82. **dss** 85 **d** 87 **p** 94. Hove Bp Hannington Memorial Ch *Chich* 85–87; Chapl St Mich Sch Burton Park 87–89; Chapl RCM and Imp Coll *Lon* 89–93; Prec Ch Ch *Ox* 93–98; P-in-c Ivinghoe w Pitstone and Slapton 98–03; P-in-c Llanbadarn Fawr, Llandegley and Llanfihangel etc *S & B* 03–08; V Alstonfield, Butterton, Ilam etc *Lich* 08–16; V Middle Marches *Heref* 16–21; rtd 21. *9 Russell Street, Knighton LD7 1EU*

BALLARD, Duncan Charles John. b 65. Sheff Univ BSc 87. St Mich Coll Llan 00. **d** 02 **p** 03. C Worc St Barn w Ch Ch 02–06; TV Worc SE 06–11; P-in-c Hampton in Arden *Birm* 11–12; P-in-c Bickenhill 11–12; R Hampton-in-Arden w Bickenhill 12–17; Chapl Birm Airport 11–17; P-in-c Barston 15–17; AD Solihull 13–17; P-in-c Ashbourne St Oswald w Mapleton *Derby* from 17; P-in-c Ashbourne St Jo from 17; P-in-c Clifton from 17; P-in-c Norbury w Snelston from 17. *The Vicarage, 3 Spire Close, Ashbourne DE6 1DB* T: (01335) 343825 *or* (01332) 388670 E: duncan.ballard@me.com *or* duncan.ballard@derby.anglican.org

BALLARD, Canon Michael Arthur. b 44. Lon Univ BA 66. Westcott Ho Cam 68. **d** 70 **p** 71. C Harrow Weald All SS *Lon* 70–73; C Aylesbury *Ox* 73–78; V Eastwood *Chelmsf* 78–90; RD Hadleigh 83–90; R Southchurch H Trin 90–13; RD Southend 94–00; Hon Can Chelmsf Cathl 89–13; rtd 13; PtO *Chelmsf* 14–16; Hon C Southend 16–20; Hon C Southend St Jo from 21. *159 Kensington Road, Southend-on-Sea SS1 2SZ* T: (01702) 616950 E: michael.ballard473@btinternet.com

BALLARD, Nigel Humphrey. b 48. Linc Th Coll 92. **d** 94 **p** 95. C Old Brumby *Linc* 94; C Bottesford w Ashby 94–97;

P-in-c Helpringham w Hale 97–01; rtd 02; PtO *St E* from 14. *37A Alumhurst Road, Bournemouth BH4 8EN*

BALLARD, Peter James. b 55. SS Hild & Bede Coll Dur BEd 78. Sarum & Wells Th Coll 85. **d** 87 **p** 88. C Grantham *Linc* 87–90 and 91; R Port Pirie Australia 90; V Lancaster Ch Ch *Blackb* 91–98; RD Lancaster 94–98; Can Res Blackb Cathl 98–06; Adn Lancaster 06–10; Dioc Dir of Educn 98–10; PtO 16–17; P-in-c Shireshead from 17.

BALLARD, Steven Peter. b 52. Man Univ BA 73 MA 74 Philipps Univ Marburg DrTheol 98. St Steph Ho Ox 76. **d** 78 **p** 79. C Lancaster St Mary *Blackb* 78–81; C Blackpool St Mich 81–84; V Brierfield 84–94; PtO *Carl* 95–07; Hon C Dumfries *Glas* from 09. *Avalon, Bankend, Dumfries DG1 4RN* T: (01387) 770438 M: 07563-564695 E: revsteven@stjohnsdumfries.org

BALLARD-TREMEER, Mrs Margaret Eileen. b 39. K Alfred's Coll Win TDip 62. Th Ext Educn Coll 86. **d** 90 **p** 94. C St Mary's Cathl Johannesburg S Africa 90–03; C Bramley 03–05; PtO *Roch* from 05. *313 Pickhurst Lane, West Wickham BR4 0HW* T: (020) 8777 5694 E: margaret@ecoharmony.org

BALLENTINE, Ian Clarke. b 46. Aston Univ BSc 71 CEng. BTh. **d** 91 **p** 92. C Lurgan St Jo *D & D* 91–95; I Mallusk *Conn* 95–07; Nat Dir (Ireland) SOMA UK 07–17; rtd 17. *12 Gordonville, Coleraine BT52 1EF* T: (028) 7035 8328 M: 07479-544396 E: iancballentine@gmail.com

BALLINGER, Francis James. b 43. AKC 70. **d** 71 **p** 85. C Weston-super-Mare St Sav *B & W* 71–72; Dir Bd Soc Resp *Leic* 85–88; Hon C Bringhurst w Gt Easton 85–88; TV Melksham *Sarum* 88–93; P-in-c Coughton and Spernall, Morton Bagot and Oldberrow *Cov* 93–98; Dioc Rural Adv 93–98; R Kingstone w Clehonger, Eaton Bishop etc *Heref* 98–03; rtd 04; PtO *Sarum* 05–15. *4 Broxburn Road, Warminster BA12 8EX* T: (01985) 300316

BALLISTON THICKE, James. See THICKE, James Balliston

BALMER, Richard Ian. b 88. QUB BSc 11. Oak Hill Th Coll BA 16 MA 18. **d** 18 **p** 19. C Enderby w Lubbesthorpe and Thurlaston *Leic* from 18. *2 Jacques Close, Enderby, Leicester LE19 4RW* M: 07743-574882 E: richbalmer10@gmail.com

BAMBER, David Beverley. b 51. Univ of Wales (Lamp) BA 75. St Steph Ho Ox 75. **d** 77 **p** 78. C Altrincham St Geo *Ches* 77–80; C Oxton 80–81; PtO *Derby* 85–87; C Staveley and Barrow Hill 87–88; C W Retford *S'well* 89–90; C E Retford 89–90 and 91–92; rtd 12. *10 Marine Park, Wirral CH48 5HW* M: 07984-807663 E: davidbamber2@hotmail.com

BAMBER, Jeremy John. b 56. St Jo Coll Cam MA 82. STETS 06. **d** 09 **p** 10. NSM Southover *Chich* 09–17; NSM Trin in Lewes from 18. *29 Montacute Road, Lewes BN7 1EN* T: (01273) 474923 E: jjbj@bambers.net

BAMBER, Canon Sheila Jane. b 54. Univ of Wales (Lamp) BA 75 Sheff Univ MA 77 Open Univ MBA 94. Ripon Coll Cuddesdon 96. **d** 98 **p** 99. C Dur St Cuth 98–01; C Sacriston and Kimblesworth 01–02; TV Dur N 02–09; Hon C Lanchester 09–10; Dioc Dir of Educn 04–10; Adv for Women's Min 09–10; Hon Can Dur Cathl 06–10; Can Res Newc Cathl 10–12; Can Provost Sunderland Minster *Dur* 12–16; AD Wearmouth 15–16; LtO from 17; Hon Can Dur Cathl from 17. *23 Strothers Terrace, High Spen, Rowlands Gill NE39 2HL* T: (01207) 544547 M: 07989-542565 E: sheilab1554@gmail.com

BAMBERG, Robert William. b 43. Chu Coll Cam BA 65 PGCE 68. SWMTC 98. **d** 02 **p** 03. NSM Kingsteignton and Teigngrace *Ex* 01–08; PtO 08–10. *Tynyfford, Ystrad Meurig SY25 6AX* T: (01974) 831725 E: sallybamberg@gmail.com

BAMFORD, Geoffrey Belk. b 35. Lon Univ BA 57 Leic Coll of Educn PGCE 58. OLM Upper Holme Valley *Wakef* 99–09; PtO 09–15; *Leeds* from 15. *11 Flushouse, Holmbridge, Holmfirth HD9 2QY* T: (01484) 682532 E: jmgbbamford@gmail.com

BAMFORTH, Canon Marvin John. b 48. NOC 78. **d** 81 **p** 82. C Barnoldswick w Bracewell *Bradf* 81–84; V Cullingworth 84–88; V Mornington NZ 88–89; V Thornton in Lonsdale w Burton in Lonsdale *Bradf* 89–98; P-in-c Bentham St Jo 93–98; Dioc Chapl MU 91–94; Chapl Paphos Cyprus 98–05; rtd 06; Chapl Miss to Seafarers Limassol Cyprus 06–14; Hon C Ross w Walford and Brampton Abbotts *Heref* 17–18; Hon C NW Hants *Win* from 18; Hon Can Kinkizi from 08. *The Vicarage, 2 Flexford Close, Highclere, Newbury RG20 9PE*

BAMPING, Mrs Susan Janet. b 49. LCTP 08. **d** 11 **p** 12. NSM Cross Fell Gp *Carl* 11–15; PtO *Derby* from 15; *Man* from 18. *13 Hill End Road, Delph, Oldham OL3 5JA* T: (01768) 879085 E: alan.sue.bamping@btinternet.com

BAMPTON, Edward Thomas William. b 74. Pemb Coll Ox MBiochem 97 Wolfs Coll Ox MSc 98 DPhil 02. Qu Coll Birm 12. **d** 14 **p** 15. C Shepshed and Oaks in Charnwood *Leic* 14–17; R Groby and Ratby from 17.

23 Ferndale Drive, Ratby, Leicester LE6 0LH T: 0116-239 6520 E: rector@grobychurch.org.uk *or* revdredbampton@outlook.com

BANBURY, Canon David Paul. b 62. Coll of Ripon & York St Jo BA 84. Ridley Hall Cam 85. **d** 88 **p** 89. C Blackb St Jas 88–90; C Preston St Cuth 90–95; P-in-c Bradf St Clem 95–00; V 00; CPAS Evang 01–08; Dir Miss and Faith Stratford-upon-Avon, Luddington etc *Cov* 08–11; Ldr Par Miss Support *Blackb* 11–18; V Burscough Bridge *Liv* from 18; Hon Can Blackb Cathl from 17. *St John's Vicarage, 253 Liverpool Road South, Burscough, Ormskirk L40 7RE* T: (01704) 621022 M: 07803-184872 E: davidbanbury@icloud.com *or* david.banbury@blackburn.anglican.org

BANBURY, Ruth. See GIBBONS, Ruth Banbury

BANCROFT, Barbara Frances. b 57. **d** 16. NSM Bridlington Em and Barmston w Fraisthorpe *York* from 16. *28 Kingsgate, Bridlington YO15 3PU* T: (01262) 603599 E: bfbancroft@btinternet.com

BANCROFT, Mrs Patricia Ann. b 64. Win Univ MA 16. STETS. **d** 10 **p** 11. C Kingsclere and Ashford Hill w Headley *Win* 10–14; R Lynch w Iping Marsh and Milland *Chich* 14–17; P-in-c Stedham w Iping 16–17; R Linch w Iping Marsh, Milland and Rake etc from 17. *St Luke's Rectory, Fernhurst Road, Milland, Liphook GU30 7LU* E: trishbancroft@aol.com

BANDAWE, Mrs Christine. b 57. Liv Univ BTh 06. NOC 01. **d** 04 **p** 05. C Middleton St Mary *Ripon* 04–08; TV Seacroft 08–18; rtd 18. *30 Fearnville Road, Leeds LS8 3EA* E: christinebandawe@yahoo.co.uk

BANDS, Canon Leonard Michael. b 40. Rhodes Univ BA 64. St Paul's Coll Grahamstown. **d** 69 **p** 70. C Uitenhage S Africa 69–72; R Alexandria 72–75; Chapl Rhodes Univ 75–80; Chapl Dioc Sch for Girls Grahamstown 80–86; Chapl Dioc Coll Cape Town 87–94; Dean Bloemfontein 94–02; C Lockerbie *Glas* 03–11; C Moffat 03–11; rtd 11. *Montagu Cottage, 20 Princes Street, Lochmaben, Lockerbie DG11 1PQ* T: (01387) 811149 M: 07766-341094 E: michael.bands@btinternet.com *or* michael.bands41@gmail.com

BANFIELD, Andrew Henry. b 48. AKC 71. St Aug Coll Cant 72. **d** 73 **p** 74. C Crayford *Roch* 73–76; Youth Chapl *Glouc* 77–89; Soc Services Development Officer Glos Co Coun from 89; PtO *Glouc* from 15. *49 Cleevelands Drive, Cheltenham GL50 4QD*

BANGAY (formerly REAST), Mrs Eileen Joan. b 40. Open Univ BA 93. EMMTC 81. **dss** 84 **d** 87 **p** 94. Linc St Mary-le-Wigford w St Benedict etc 80–90; C 87–90; C Stamford All SS w St Jo 90–93; NSM Walesby 93–95; P-in-c Sutton Bridge 95–00; V 00; RD Elloe E 99–00; rtd 01; PtO *Linc* from 01. *15 Heath Court, Grampian Way, Sinfin, Derby DE24 9NG* T: (01332) 989779 E: enj.bangay@btinternet.com

BANGOR, Archdeacon of. See STALLARD, The Ven Mary Kathleen Rose

BANGOR, Bishop of. See JOHN, The Rt Revd Andrew Thomas Griffith

BANGOR, Dean of. See JONES, The Very Revd Kathy Louise

BANHAM, Richard Mark. b 69. Sheff City Poly BSc 92. Trin Coll Bris 04. **d** 06 **p** 07. C Wroughton *Bris* 06–10; P-in-c Wheathampstead *St Alb* 10–12; R from 12; RD 15–20 and from 21. *The Rectory, Old Rectory Gardens, Wheathampstead, St Albans AL4 8AD* T: (01582) 833144 E: richard@banham.org.uk

BANISTER, Desmond Peter. b 52. K Coll Lon BA 75 AKC 75. SAOMC 02. **d** 05 **p** 06. Hd Master Quainton Hall Sch Harrow 98–09; NSM Hatch End St Anselm *Lon* 05–08; NSM Hillingdon All SS 09; V from 09; AD Hillingdon 13–18; PtO *Ox* from 05. *All Saints' Vicarage, Ryefield Avenue, North Hillingdon, Uxbridge UB10 9BT* T: (01895) 239457 E: ppasnh@gmail.com

BANISTER, Jane Catherine. b 67. Man Univ BA 90 Em Coll Cam BA 96. Westcott Ho Cam 94. **d** 97 **p** 98. C Addington *S'wark* 97–00; C Wisley w Pyrford *Guildf* 00–02; PtO *St Alb* 03–08; NSM Tring 08–15; TV from 15. *The Rectory, 2 The Limes, Station Road, Tring HP23 5NW* T: (01442) 822170 E: jane@tringteamparish.org.uk

BANISTER, Canon Martin John. b 39. Worc Coll Ox BA 62 MA 68. Chich Th Coll 62. **d** 64 **p** 65. C Wellingborough All Hallows *Pet* 64–67; C Heene *Chich* 67–70; V Denford w Ringstead *Pet* 70–78; P-in-c Wilshamstead *St Alb* 78–80; P-in-c Houghton Conquest 78–80; V Wilshamstead and Houghton Conquest 80–89; RD Elstow 86–89; V Waltham Cross 89–04; RD Cheshunt 00–04; Hon Can St Alb 03–04; rtd 04; PtO *St Alb* from 04. *35 Cottonmill Lane, St Albans AL1 2BT* T: (01727) 847082

BANKS, Canon Allen James. b 48. CBDTI 98. **d** 01 **p** 02. OLM Kells *Carl* 01–05; NSM 05–20; RD Calder 14–20; rtd 20;

BANKS, Matthew Clayton. b 79. **d** 13 **p** 14. C St Helen Bishopsgate w St Andr Undershaft etc *Lon* 13–16; C Cape Town St Steph S Africa from 16. *c/o David Banks, 37 Riversmead, Hoddesdon EN11 8DP* E: matthewclaytonbanks@gmail.com

BANKS, Canon Michael Thomas Harvey. b 35. Ushaw Coll Dur 58 Open Univ BA 75. **d** 63 **p** 64. C Winlaton Dur 69–71; P-in-c Bishopwearmouth Gd Shep 71–75; TV Melton Mowbray w Thorpe Arnold *Leic* 75–80; TR Loughborough Em 80–88; Dir of Ords 83–97; Hon Can Leic Cathl 83–87; Can Res and Chan Leic Cathl 87–03; Assoc P Christianity S 93–95; Hon C Leic H Spirit 01–03; rtd 03; PtO *Glouc* 04–17. *Harvard House, 7 Harvard Close, Moreton-in-Marsh GL56 0JT* T: (01608) 650706

✠**BANKS, The Rt Revd Norman.** b 54. Oriel Coll Ox BA 76 MA 80. St Steph Ho Ox 79. **d** 82 **p** 83 **c** 11. C Newc Ch Ch w St Ann 82–87; P-in-c 87–90; V Tynemouth Cullercoats St Paul 90–00; V Walsingham, Houghton and Barsham *Nor* 00–11; P-in-c 11–12; RD Burnham and Walsingham 08–11; Chapl to The Queen 09–11; Suff Bp Richborough (PEV) *Cant* from 11; Hon Asst Bp Guildf from 12; Hon Asst Bp Nor from 12; Hon Asst Bp St E from 12; Hon Asst Bp Ely from 12; Hon Asst Bp St Alb from 13; Hon Asst Bp Linc from 15; PtO *Nor* from 17. *Parkside House, Abbey Mill Lane, St Albans AL3 4HE* T: (01727) 836358 E: bishop@richborough.org.uk

BANKS, Canon Philip Charles. b 61. NE Lon Poly BSc 85 Nottm Univ BTh 93 MRICS 87. Linc Th Coll 90. **d** 93 **p** 94. C Chelmsf Ascension 93–94; C Brentwood St Thos 94–98; P-in-c Elmstead 98–03; V Coggeshall w Markshall 03–12; Bp's Press Officer 97–05; Bp's Dom Chapl 01–04; RD Dedham and Tey 08–11; Can Res St E Cathl from 12. *1 Abbey Precinct, The Great Churchyard, Bury St Edmunds IP33 1RS* T: (01284) 748720 *or* 761982 M: 07798-681886 E: precentor@stedscathedral.org

BANKS, Stephen John. b 65. Newc Univ BSc 87. St Jo Coll Nottm MA 96. **d** 97 **p** 98. C Sheldon *Birm* 97–00; P-in-c Austrey and Warton 00–07; P-in-c Newton Regis w Seckington and Shuttington 06–07; R All So N Warks 07–19; AD Polesworth 02–07; Bp's Rural Adv 12–19; TR Binsey *Carl* from 19. *The Vicarage, Torpenhow, Wigton CA7 1HT* T: (016973) 71541 E: teamrector@binsey.org.uk

BANKS, Susan Angela. *See* GRIFFITHS, Susan Angela

BANKS, Mrs Susan June. b 60. NOC 03. **d** 06 **p** 07. C Medlock Head *Man* 06–09; TV Heywood 09–10; P-in-c Heywood St Marg and Heap Bridge 10–18; V 18–19; C Kelsall *Ches* 19–21; P-in-c from 21. *The Vicarage, Chester Road, Kelsall, Tarporley CW6 0SA* T: (01829) 752639 E: sbanks4@sky.com

BANKS, Vivienne Philippa. *See* BRIDGES, Vivienne Philippa

BANNER, John William. b 36. Open Univ BA 78. Tyndale Hall Bris 61. **d** 64 **p** 65. C Bootle St Leon *Liv* 64–66; C Wigan St Jas 66–69; C Stapleton *Bris* 69–70; Gen Sec Scripture Union Australia 70–72; V Liv Ch Ch Norris Green 72–82; V Tunbridge Wells H Trin w Ch Ch *Roch* 82–05; rtd 05. *Dormers, Southvew Road, Crowborough TN6 1HG* E: celiabanner@gmail.com

BANNER, Michael Charles. b 61. Ball Coll Ox BA 83 MA 86 DPhil 87. **d** 86 **p** 87. Fell St Pet Coll Ox 85–88; Dean Peterho Cam 88–94; Prof Moral and Soc Th K Coll Lon 94–04; NSM Balsham, Weston Colville, W Wickham etc *Ely* 01–04; Prof Edin Univ 04–06; Dean Trin Coll Cam from 06. *Trinity College, Cambridge CB2 1TQ* T: (01223) 338563 F: 338564 E: chapel@trin.cam.ac.uk

BANNISTER, Preb Anthony Peter. b 40. Ex Univ BA 62. Clifton Th Coll 63. **d** 65 **p** 66. C Uphill *B & W* 65–69; C Hove Bp Hannington Memorial Ch *Chich* 69–74; V Wembdon *B & W* 74–91; Youth Chapl 80–83; RD Bridgwater 80–89; V Taunton St Jas 91–05; Preb Wells Cathl 97–05; rtd 05; PtO *B & W* from 05. *6 Inwood Road, Wembdon, Bridgwater TA6 7PW* T: (01278) 287495 M: 07576-697889 E: apbannister@talktalk.net

BANNISTER, Clifford John. b 53. Hatf Coll Dur BA 76. Ripon Coll Cuddesdon 84. **d** 86 **p** 87. C Weymouth H Trin *Sarum* 86–89; TV Basingstoke *Win* 89–94; V Hedge End St Jo 94–09; AD Eastleigh 07–09; P-in-c Win St Bart 09–10; R Win St Bart and St Lawr w St Swithun 10–19; rtd 19. *Address withheld by request* E: cliffbannister@hotmail.co.uk

BANNISTER, Gregory Simon. b 80. LMH Ox BA 01 Homerton Coll Cam PGCE 03. Wycliffe Hall Ox BA 09 Ridley Hall Cam 11. **d** 14 **p** 15. C Enfield Ch Ch Trent Park *Lon* 14–17; C St Marg Lothbury and St Steph Coleman Street etc 18–20; C St Sepulchre w Ch Ch Greyfriars etc 18–20; P-in-c Spalding St Jo *Linc* from 21; C Stamford St Geo w St Paul from 21; PtO *Chelmsf* from 18. *5 Truro Way, Spalding PE11 1YB* M: 07522-322920 E: gsbannister@gmail.com

BANNISTER, John Leslie. b 55. Lanc Univ MA 99. CBDTI 95. **d** 98 **p** 99. C Flimby and Netherton *Carl* 98–00; C Whitehaven 00–02; TV 02–04; TR 04–13; PtO 13–14; *Blackb* 13–14; V Lund 14–20; PtO *St Alb* from 21. *Flat 11, 45 Avian Avenue, Curo Park, Frogmore, St Albans AL2 2FF* M: 07788-562488 E: johnlbannister@gmail.com

BANNISTER, Peter. *See* BANNISTER, Anthony Peter

BANNISTER, Peter Edward. b 38. Leeds Univ BSc 60. Linc Th Coll 72. **d** 74 **p** 75. C Norbury St Steph *Cant* 74–77; C Allington and Maidstone St Pet 77–80; R Temple Ewell w Lydden 80–86; TV Bracknell *Ox* 86–93; P-in-c Swallowfield 93–03; rtd 03; PtO *Bradf* 04–14; *Leeds* 14–20. *27 Oakdene, Lansdown Road, Cheltenham GL51 6PX* T: (01242) 300813

BANNISTER, Mrs Sophie Claire. b 81. Ch Coll Cam BA 04. Ridley Hall Cam 12 Oak Hill Th Coll 14. **d** 16 **p** 18. C St Sepulchre w Ch Ch Greyfriars etc *Lon* 16–20; PtO *Chelmsf* from 19. *5 Truro Way, Spalding PE11 1YB* M: 07813-080075 E: sophiecbannister@gmail.com

BANNISTER-PARKER, Mrs Charlotte Bridget Melander. b 63. Trevelyan Coll Dur BA 84 Dur Univ MA 92 Middx Univ BA 05. Westmr Past Foundn 00. **d** 05 **p** 06. NSM Ox St Mary V w St Cross and St Pet 05–13; NSM Summertown 13–16; NSM Ox St Mary V w St Cross and St Pet 16–21; Chapl Ch 21; NSM Ox St Mary V w St Cross and St Pet from 21. *8 Belbroughton Road, Oxford OX2 6UZ* T: (01865) 512252 M: 07745-347395 E: charlottebannisterparker@gmail.com

BANNON, Lyndon Russell. b 73. Ches Coll of HE BA 95 Univ Coll Ches PGCE 96 Leeds Univ MA 06 NPQH 20. NOC 04. **d** 06 **p** 07. NSM Leasowe *Ches* 06–10; NSM Willaston from 10; Bp's Officer for SSM from 18. *7 Nelson's Croft, Wirral CH63 3DU* T: 0151-334 9931 E: lyndonbannon123@btinternet.com *or* lyndon.bannon@chester.anglican.org

BANTING, Canon David Percy. b 51. Magd Coll Cam MA 74. Wycliffe Hall Ox MA 79. **d** 80 **p** 81. C Ox St Ebbe w H Trin and St Pet 80–83; Min St Jos Merry Hill CD *Lich* 83–90; V Chadderton Ch Ch *Man* 90–98; V Harold Wood *Chelmsf* 98–18; Hon Can Chelmsf Cathl 09–18; rtd 18; PtO *Chelmsf* from 18; *Derby* from 18; *Man* from 20; *Sheff* from 21. *29 Hallamshire Close, Sheffield S10 4FJ*

BANTING, Dawn Ann. b 70. STETS. **d** 13 **p** 14. NSM Portsm Cathl 13–20; Chapl Portsm Hosps NHS Trust 16–19; Lead Chapl Portsm Hosps Univ NHS Trust from 20; OCM from 13. *Trust Headquarters, Queen Alexandra Hospital, Southwick Hill Road, Cosham, Portsmouth PO6 3LY* T: (023) 9228 6000 M: 07980-489658 E: dawn.banting@porthosp.nhs.uk

BANTING, The Ven Kenneth Mervyn Lancelot Hadfield. b 37. Pemb Coll Cam BA 61 MA 65. Cuddesdon Coll 64. **d** 65 **p** 66. Asst Chapl Win Coll 65–70; C Leigh Park *Portsm* 70–72; TV Hemel Hempstead *St Alb* 73–79; V Goldington 79–88; P-in-c Renhold 80–82; RD Bedford 84–87; V Portsea St Cuth *Portsm* 88–96; RD Portsm 94–96; Adn Is of Wight 96–03; Hon Can Portsm Cathl 95–96; rtd 03; PtO *Portsm* 03–17; *Chich* from 04; RD Westbourne 09–11. *Furzend, 38A Bosham Hoe, Bosham PO18 8ET* T: (01243) 572340 E: furzend@merlinbanting.plus.com

BANTON, Gareth Richard. b 89. Liv Univ BA 12 Dur Univ BA 18. Ridley Hall Cam 15. **d** 18 **p** 19. C Newton *Liv* 18–21; TV Eccleston from 21. *St John's Vicarage, Crossley Road, St Helens WA10 3ND* M: 07444-811428 E: bantongareth@gmail.com

BANTRY WHITE, Robin. *See* WHITE, Robin Edward Bantry

BANYARD, Michael George. b 47. Ch Ch Coll *Cant* CertEd 69 Birm Univ BPhil 79 Open Univ MA 92. Westcott Ho Cam 01. **d** 03 **p** 04. NSM Chippenham *Ely* 03–08; NSM Fordham St Pet 07–08; NSM Isleham 07–08; NSM Kennett 07–08; NSM Snailwell 07–08; R Three Rivers Gp 08–17; Dioc Spirituality Officer 10–14; RD Fordham and Quy 15–17; rtd 17; PtO *Ely* from 17. *12A Cambridge Road, Ely CB7 4HL* E: banyardmg1@yahoo.co.uk

BARBER, Ms Annabel Ruth. b 58. Leeds Univ BSc 80 Anglia Ruskin Univ MA 10. NEOC 01. **d** 04 **p** 05. C Scawby, Redbourne and Hibaldstow *Linc* 04–07; Sen Chapl N Lincs and Goole Hosps NHS Trust 07–12; Lic Preacher *Linc* 12–14; R Waddington 14–20; Discipleship Development Adv 14–17; RD Graffoe 17–20. *Shepards Hill, Thorpe Lane, Tealby, Market Rasen LN8 3XJ* E: revannabelbarber@gmail.com

BARBER, Anne Louise. *See* STEWART, Anne Louise

BARBER, Canon Christopher Albert. b 33. Ch Coll Cam BA 53 MA 57. Coll of Resurr Mirfield 56. **d** 58 **p** 59. C Cov St Pet 58–61; C Stokenchurch and Cadmore End 61–64; V Royton St Paul *Man* 64–70; V Stapleford *Ely* 70–80; RD Shelford 76–80; V Cherry Hinton St Andr 80–88; Hon Can Ely Cathl 88–98; R Cottenham 88–92; RD N Stowe 90–92; V Terrington St John 92–98; V Tilney All Saints 92–98; rtd 98; PtO *Ely* from 98; Asst Rtd Clergy and Clergy Widow(er)s' Officer 00–07; Rtd Clergy Officer from 07; PV Ely Cathl from

03. *20 King Edgar Close, Ely CB6 1DP*   T: (01353) 612338
E: chrisbarber2@ntlworld.com

BARBER, Garth Antony. b 48. Southn Univ BSc 69 Lon Univ MSc 79 FRAS MSOSc. St Jo Coll Nottm. **d** 76 **p** 77. C Hounslow H Trin *Lon* 76–79; Chapl City of Lon Poly 79–86; P-in-c Twickenham All Hallows 86–97; Chapl Richmond Coll 87–97; Chapl UEA *Nor* 97–02; P-in-c Kingswood *S'wark* 02–11; V 11–13; AD Reigate 06–12; rtd 13; PtO *Cant* from 14. *11 Jasmine Close, Chartham, Canterbury CT4 7TF*   T: (01737) 507293 E: garth.barber@sky.com

BARBER, Canon Hilary John. b 65. Aston Tr Scheme 92 Sarum Th Coll 94. **d** 96 **p** 97. C Moston St Jo *Man* 96–00; R Chorlton-cum-Hardy St Clem 00–07; P-in-c Chorlton-cum-Hardy St Werburgh 05–07; Dioc Music Adv 03–07; V Halifax *Wakef* 07–14; *Leeds* 14–17; P-in-c Siddal *Wakef* 13–14; *Leeds* 14–17; V Halifax w Siddal from 17; Hon Can Wakef Cathl from 11. *The Vicarage, Kensington Road, Halifax HX3 0HN*   T: (01422) 365477 E: h.barber@halifaxminster.org.uk

BARBER, John Eric <u>Michael</u>. b 30. Wycliffe Hall Ox 63. **d** 65 **p** 66. C Lupset *Wakef* 65–68; C Halifax St Jo Bapt 68–70; V Dewsbury St Matt and St Jo 70–80; V Perry Common *Birm* 80–95; rtd 95; PtO *Sarum* 95–19. *21A Westhill Road, Weymouth DT4 9NB*   T: (01305) 786553

BARBER, Miss Marion. b 50. Birkbeck Coll Lon BSc 97 K Coll Lon MSc 03. **d** 07 **p** 08. NSM Lee St Mildred *S'wark* from 07. *12B Beechfield Road, London SE6 4NE*   T: (020) 8690 6035 E: marionbarber12@outlook.com

BARBER, Michael. *See* BARBER, John Eric Michael

BARBER, Neil Andrew Austin. b 63. Ealing Coll of Educn BA 85. NTMTC 94. **d** 98 **p** 98. St Mary's Chr Workers' Trust 95–01; NSM Eastrop *Win* 98–01; V Normanton *Derby* from 01. *St Giles's Vicarage, 16 Browning Street, Derby DE23 8DN*   T: (01332) 767483 E: neil.barber@stgiles-derby.org.uk

BARBER, Philip Kenneth. b 43. St Jo Coll Dur BA 65 Sheff Univ DipEd 66. NW Ord Course 74. **d** 76 **p** 77. NSM Burscough Bridge *Liv* 76–84; Asst Master Ormskirk Gr Sch 76–84; P-in-c Brigham *Carl* 84–85; V 85–89; P-in-c Mosser 84–85; V 85–89; P-in-c Borrowdale 89–94; Chapl Keswick Sch 89–94; P-in-c Beetham and Educn Adv *Carl* 94–99; P-in-c Brampton and Farlam and Castle Carrock w Cumrew 99–02; P-in-c Irthington, Crosby-on-Eden and Scaleby 99–02; P-in-c Hayton w Cumwhitton 99–02; TR Eden, Gelt and Irthing 02–04; rtd 04; PtO *Carl* 04–16; *Blackb* 05–21. *18 Holbeck Avenue, Morecambe LA4 6NP*   T: (01524) 401695 E: philipbarber326@gmail.com

BARBER, Ralph Warwick. b 72. Lon Guildhall Univ BA 94. Ripon Coll Cuddesdon 03. **d** 05 **p** 06. C Newquay *Truro* 05–08; Chapl RN from 08. *Royal Naval Chaplaincy Service Headquarters, Tanner Building, HMS Excellent, Whale Island, Portsmouth PO2 8ER*   T: 0300-157 7544 E: ralphwbarber@aol.com

BARBER, Royston Henry. b 38. Univ of Wales (Aberth) BD 86. United Th Coll Abth 83. **d** 86 **p** 87. NSM Tywyn w Aberdyfi *Ban* 86–92; NSM Cannington, Otterhampton, Combwich and Stockland *B & W* 93–98; PtO 98–14; *Ex* 00–13. *30 Carlton Court, Blenheim Road, Minehead TA24 5PL*   T: (01643) 708783

BARBOUR, Mrs Jennifer Louise. b 32. JP 67. St Hugh's Coll Ox BA 54 MA 57 Barrister-at-Law 55. Gilmore Course 80. **dss** 81 **d** 87 **p** 94. Bray and Braywood *Ox* 81–84; Hermitage and Hampstead Norreys, Cold Ash etc 84–87; Chapl Leeds Poly *Ripon* 87–92; Chapl Leeds Metrop Univ 92–95; rtd 95; NSM Shipton Moyne w Westonbirt and Lasborough *Glouc* 95–99; PtO *Bris* 95–04; *Glouc* from 99; *Cov* 00–05; *Worc* 00–12. *1 Newlands Court, Stow on the Wold, Cheltenham GL54 1HN*   T: (01451) 798165

BARBOUR, Walter Iain. b 28. Pemb Coll Cam BA 48 MA 53 FICE 65. Ox NSM Course 78. **d** 81 **p** 82. NSM Bray and Braywood *Ox* 81–84; NSM Thatcham 84–87; TV Moor Allerton *Ripon* 87–95; rtd 95; NSM Shipton Moyne w Westonbirt and Lasborough *Glouc* 95–98; PtO *Bris* 95–04; *Glouc* 98–01; *Cov* 00–06; *Worc* 00–12; *Glouc* from 16. *1 Newlands Court, Stow on the Wold, Cheltenham GL54 1HN*   T: (01451) 798165

BARBY, Canon Sheana Braidwood. b 38. Bedf Coll Lon BA 59. EMMTC 81. **dss** 84 **d** 87 **p** 94. NSM Derby St Paul 84–87; NSM Derby Cathl 87–03; Dioc Dir of Ords 90–97; Par Educn Adv 93–01; RD Derby N 00–05; Hon Can Derby Cathl 96–05; rtd 05; PtO *Derby* from 05. *2 Margaret Street, Derby DE1 3FE*   T: (01332) 383301 E: sheana@talktalk.net

BARCLAY, Adam John. b 61. **d** 18 **p** 19. NSM Stanton *St E* from 18. *Address temp unknown* E: adambarclay86@gmail.com

BARCLAY, Mrs Christine Ann. b 54. TISEC. **d** 07 **p** 08. C St Andrews All SS *St And* 07–10; R Tayport 10–12; R Bathgate *Edin* from 12; R Linlithgow from 12; Dioc Chapl MU 16–19.

The Rectory, 85 Acredales, Linlithgow EH49 6JA   T: (01506) 846069 E: christine.barclay28@gmail.com

BARCLAY, Ian Newton. b 33. Clifton Th Coll 58. **d** 61 **p** 62. C Cullompton *Ex* 61–63; C Ashill w Broadway *B & W* 63–66; V Chatham St Phil and St Jas *Roch* 66–69; C St Helen Bishopsgate w St Martin Outwich *Lon* 70–73; V Prestonville St Luke *Chich* 73–81; LtO 82–93; rtd 93; P-in-c Cannes *Eur* 98–02; PtO *Chich* from 13. *35 Marine Avenue, Hove BN3 4LH*

BARCROFT, Canon Ian David. b 60. UMIST BSc 83 Edin Univ BD 88 Glas Univ MTh 01. Edin Th Coll 85. **d** 88 **p** 89. Prec St Ninian's Cathl Perth *St And* 88–92; Min Perth St Ninian 88–92; P-in-c Aberdeen St Clem *Ab* 92–97; R Hamilton *Glas* 97–19; Dean Glas 10–19; Prov Dir of Ords from 19; Hon Can St Mary's Cathl *Glas* from 20. *Scottish Episcopal Church, General Synod Office, 21 Grosvenor Crescent, Edinburgh EH12 5EE*   T: 0131-225 6357 E: pdo@scotland.anglican.org

BARDELL, Alan George. b 39. City Univ BSc. **d** 92 **p** 93. OLM Addlestone *Guildf* 92–06; rtd 06; PtO *Guildf* from 07. *14 Dickens Drive, Addlestone KT15 1AW*   T: (01932) 847574 E: alanbardell@aol.com

BARDELL, Terence Richard. b 51. EMMTC 04. **d** 01 **p** 02. OLM Coningsby w Tattershall *Linc* 01–05; C Gt Grimsby St Mary and St Jas 05–06; TV 06–09; P-in-c Chapel St Leonards w Hogsthorpe 09–18; V Chapel St Leonards and Hogsthorpe etc 18–19; rtd 19; PtO *Glouc* from 20. *25 De Borg Close, Tetbury GL8 8TW*

BARDER, Joel Alexander Christopher Remilly. b 88. Abth Univ BA 09. Trin Coll Bris 13. **d** 16 **p** 17. C Tenby *St D* 16–19; P-in-c Carew and Cosheston and Nash and Redberth 19–20; P-in-c S W Pembrokeshire from 20. *9 Sageston Fields, Sageston, Tenby SA70 8TQ*   T: (01646) 650114 E: rev.jbarder@zoho.com

BARDWELL, Mrs Elaine Barbara. b 60. K Coll Lon BA 81 AKC 81. St Steph Ho Ox BA 85 MA 90. **dss** 86 **d** 87 **p** 95. Heref H Trin 86–89; C 87–89; Dir Past Studies St Steph Ho Ox 89–96; V New Marston *Ox* from 96; AD Cowley 02–07. *The Vicarage, 8 Jack Straws Lane, Headington, Oxford OX3 0DL*   T: (01865) 434340   M: 07779-086231 E: elaine.bardwell@ntlworld.com

BARDWELL, John Edward. b 53. Jes Coll Cam BA 75 MA 79 Ox Univ BA 85 MA 90. St Steph Ho Ox 83. **d** 86 **p** 87. C Heref H Trin 86–89; PtO *Ox* 90–96. *The Vicarage, 8 Jack Straws Lane, Headington, Oxford OX3 0DL*   T: (01865) 434340 E: je.bardwell@tiscali.co.uk

BAREHAM, Rowland. b 60. **d** 21. NSM Gt Cornard *St E* from 21. *28 Danes Court, Great Cornard, Sudbury CO10 0JW* E: revrowland@rbareham.co.uk

BAREHAM, Miss Sylvia Alice. b 36. Hockerill Coll Cam CertEd 59 Open Univ BA 83 Ox Univ DipEd 84. Ox Min Course 86. **d** 89 **p** 94. NSM N Leigh *Ox* 89–93; NSM Bampton w Clanfield 93–95; NSM Kedington *St E* 95–97; NSM Hundon w Barnardiston 95–97; NSM Haverhill w Withersfield, the Wrattings etc 95–97; NSM Stourhead 97–05; NSM Lark Valley 05–07; rtd 07; PtO *Chelmsf* 05–09; *St E* 07–21. *Davaar, Old Hall Lane, Fornham St Martin, Bury St Edmunds IP31 1SS*   T: (01284) 724899

BARFORD, Patricia Ann. b 47. Univ of Wales (Cardiff) BSc 68 PhD 73. WMMTC 95. **d** 98 **p** 99. NSM Stoke Prior, Wychbold and Upton Warren *Worc* 98–05; C Redditch H Trin 05–08; TV 08–09; rtd 09; PtO *Worc* from 09. *Greenfields, Church Road, Dodford, Bromsgrove B61 9BY*   T: (01527) 871614 E: thebarfords@hotmail.com

BARGE, Preb Ann Marina. b 42. S'wark Ord Course 89. **d** 96 **p** 97. C Ludlow *Heref* 96–12; Preb Heref Cathl 11–12; rtd 12; PtO *Heref* from 12. *8 Old Street, Ludlow SY8 1NP*   T: (01584) 877307 E: annbarge123@gmail.com

BARGE, David Robert. b 45. S Dios Minl Tr Scheme 92. **d** 95 **p** 96. NSM Westfield *B & W* 95–00; C Frome St Jo and St Mary 00; V Frome St Mary 01–10; RD Frome 08–10; rtd 10; PtO *B & W* from 10. *26 Charolais Drive, Bridgwater TA6 6EX*   T: (01278) 431655   M: 07772-559721 E: dbarge@btinternet.com

BARHAM, Ian Harold. b 40. Clifton Th Coll 64. **d** 66 **p** 67. C Broadwater St Mary *Chich* 66–69 and 72–76; Burundi 71–72; R Beyton and Hessett *St E* 76–79; PtO 79–81; Hon C Bury St Edmunds St Mary 81–84; Chapl St Aubyn's Sch Tiverton 84–96; Chapl Lee Abbey 96–99; rtd 00; PtO *Ex* from 00. *53 Sylvan Road, Exeter EX4 6EY*   T: (01392) 251643 E: ian.jacqui@barhams.co.uk

✠**BARHAM, The Rt Revd Kenneth Lawrence.** b 36. OBE 01. Clifton Th Coll BD 63. **d** 63 **c** 93. C Worthing St Geo *Chich* 63–65; C Sevenoaks St Nic *Roch* 65–67; C Cheltenham St Mark *Glouc* 67–70; V Maidstone St Luke *Cant* 70–79; S Area Sec Rwanda Miss 79–84; P-in-c Ashburnham w Penhurst *Chich* 84–01; Asst Bp Cyangugu (Rwanda) 93–96; Bp 96–01; rtd 01; Hon Asst Bp Chich from 05. *Rosewood,*

Canadia Road, Battle TN33 0LR   T/F: (01424) 773073 E: bishopken@btinternet.com

BARHAM, Peter. b 62. Selw Coll Cam MA 83. Linc Th Coll BTh 94. **d** 94 **p** 95. C Fornham All SS and Fornham St Martin w Timworth *St E* 94–97; P-in-c Cockfield w Bradfield St Clare, Felsham etc 97–01; Min Can St E Cathl 98–03; Chapl 01–03; Can Res St E Cathl 03–08; V Ponteland *Newc* 08–16; V Allestree St Edm and Darley Abbey *Derby* from 16; Dioc Ecum Officer from 17. *The Vicarage, King's Croft, Allestree, Derby DE22 2FN* E: revpeterbarham@btinternet.com

BARKER, Adele. b 69. Reading Univ BSc 90 ACA 94. St Mellitus Coll 12 Ridley Hall Cam 14. **d** 16 **p** 17. C Chatham St Phil and St Jas *Roch* 16–20; P-in-c Fawkham and Hartley from 20; P-in-c Longfield from 20. *The Rectory, 3 St John's Lane, Hartley, Longfield DA3 8ET* M: 07961-121648 E: adele.barker@cantab.net

BARKER, Anne Margaret. b 57. Leeds Univ BSc 78. EAMTC 96. **d** 99 **p** 00. C Greenstead w Colchester St Anne *Chelmsf* 99–04; TV 04–08; P-in-c Kingsley and Foxt-w-Whiston *Lich* 08–10; R Kingsley and Foxt-w-Whiston and Oakamoor etc 10–11; P-in-c Clifton and Southill *St Alb* 11–15; R 15–16; V Warmington, Tansor and Cotterstock etc *Pet* 16–19; rtd 19; PtO *St Alb* from 19; Chapl HM Pris Bedf from 20. *HM Prison Bedford, St Loyes Street, Bedford MK40 1HG* M: 07799-960259 E: annembarker2010@gmail.com

BARKER, Cameron Timothy. b 62. Rhodes Univ BA 83 Nottm Univ MA(TS) 96. St Jo Coll Nottm 94. **d** 96 **p** 97. C W Streatham St Jas *S'wark* 96–00; V Herne Hill 00–17; Chapl R Brompton and Harefield NHS Foundn Trust from 17. *Harefield Hospital, Hill End Road, Harefield, Uxbridge UB9 6JH* T: (01895) 823737 ext 6533 E: c.barker@rbht.nhs.uk

BARKER, Prof Charles Philip Geoffrey. b 50. Lon Univ MB, BS 75 MS 91 FRCS 79 FICS 92. S Dios Minl Tr Scheme 95. **d** 98 **p** 99. NSM Alverstoke *Portsm* 98–02; NSM The Lickey *Birm* 02–06; NSM Empangeni H Cross S Africa 06–10; NSM Maple Ridge St Jo Canada from 10. *36198 Cascade Ridge Drive, Mission BC V2V 7G9, Canada* T/F: (001) (604) 814 2072 E: barkerphilip30@gmail.com

BARKER, David Robert. b 45. Worc Coll Ox BA 67 MA 70. Virginia Th Sem BD 72. **d** 72 **p** 73. C Roehampton H Trin *S'wark* 72–75; Chapl Goldsmiths' Coll Lon 75–79; Min Tr Officer *Cov* 79–85; Selection Sec and Sec for Continuing Minl Educn ACCM 85–90; V Sutton Valence w E Sutton and Chart Sutton *Cant* 90–08; rtd 08. *1 Colletts Close, Corfe Castle, Wareham BH20 5HG* T: (01929) 481477 E: david_pennybarker@hotmail.com

BARKER, Gordon Frank. b 43. Heriot-Watt Univ MSc 75 Sheff Univ MA 98. S & M Dioc Tr Inst 91. **d** 94 **p** 95. NSM Malew *S & M* 94–00; V Grain w Stoke *Roch* 00–04; Through Faith Miss Ev 00–04; P-in-c Andreas and Jurby *S & M* 04–08; P-in-c Lezayre 04–05; rtd 08; PtO *S & M* from 10; Eur 17–21. *The Harp Inn, Cross Four Ways, Ballasalla, Isle of Man IM9 3DH* T: (01624) 824116

BARKER, Canon John Howard. b 36. Southn Univ BA 58. Ripon Coll Cuddesdon 80. **d** 82 **p** 83. C W Leigh *Portsm* 82–84; V Cosham 84–88; Bp's Dom Chapl 88–96; Hon Can Portsm Cathl 93–02; V St Helens and Sea View 96–02; rtd 02; PtO *Portsm* from 02. *Coniston Lodge, 2 Coniston Drive, Ryde PO33 3AE* T: (01983) 618674 M: 07802-281797

BARKER, John William. b 53. Newc Univ BSc 75 PhD 80 Qu Coll Ox MA 16. Ridley Hall Cam 13. **d** 13 **p** 14. Asst Chapl Vienna *Eur* 13–16; R Buxted and Hadlow Down *Chich* 16–19; V Harrow Weald All SS *Lon* from 19. *All Saints' Vicarage, 175 Uxbridge Road, Harrow HA3 6TP* T: (020) 3669 0022 or 8954 8865 M: 07391-028956 E: revjohnwbarker@gmail.com

BARKER, Jonathan. b 55. Hull Univ BA 79. Westcott Ho Cam 79. **d** 83 **p** 84. C Sketty *S & B* 83–86; Chapl Sport and Leisure 83–86; C Swansea St Mary w H Trin *S & B* 85–86; Bermuda 86–90; TV Liv Our Lady and St Nic w St Anne 90–93; P-in-c S Shore St Pet *Blackb* 93–98; Chapl Blackpool Victoria Hosp NHS Trust 93–98; V Cleckheaton St Jo *Wakef* 98–08; Chapl St Pancras Internat and K Cross Stations *Lon* 08–14; P-in-c Romaldkirk w Laithkirk *Leeds* 14–15; P-in-c Startforth and Bowes and Rokeby w Brignall 14–17; R Lower Teesdale from 17; P-in-c Eggleston *Dur* from 14; P-in-c Middleton-in-Teesdale w Forest and Frith from 14. *Ashbourne, Cotherstone, Barnard Castle DL12 9PR* T: (01833) 650761 M: 07896-934881 E: jonathanbarker19.jb@gmail.com

BARKER, Ms Joyce. b 46. Nottm Univ BPharm 68. Yorks Min Course 09. **d** 11 **p** 12. NSM Barnby Dun *Sheff* 11–13; NSM Hatfield 13–16; rtd 16; PtO *Sheff* from 16. *52A Harpenden Drive, Dunscroft, Doncaster DN7 4HN* T: (01302) 844970 E: joycebarkertwin@gmail.com

BARKER, Julian Roland Palgrave. b 37. Magd Coll Cam BA 61 MA 65. Westcott Ho Cam 61. **d** 63 **p** 64. C Stafford St Mary

Lich 63–66; Chapl Clare Hall Cam 66–69; Chapl Clare Coll Cam 66–70; Tutor St Aug Coll Cant 70–71; TV Raveningham *Nor* 71–78; TR 78–82; V Foremark *Derby* 82–02; V Repton 82–02; C Bretby w Newton Solney 01–02; V Foremark and Repton w Newton Solney 02–03; RD Repton 91–95; rtd 03; PtO *St E* from 06. *78 St Barnabas Road, Cambridge CB1 2DE* T: (01223) 501611 E: jrpbarker@gmail.com

BARKER, Canon Mark. b 62. ACIB 90. St Jo Coll Nottm BTh 95. **d** 95 **p** 96. C Barking St Marg w St Patr *Chelmsf* 95–98; C Cranham Park 98–04; V Tonbridge St Steph *Roch* from 04; Hon Can Roch Cathl from 18. *St Stephen's Vicarage, 6 Brook Street, Tonbridge TN9 2PJ* T: (01732) 353079 E: mark.barker@ststephens.org.uk

BARKER, Mrs May Winifred. b 65. Sarum Coll. **d** 16 **p** 17. C Pokesdown All SS *Win* 16–19; P-in-c Hatch Warren and Beggarwood 19–21; R N Mundham w Hunston and Merston *Chich* from 21. *The Rectory, Church Lane, Hunston, Chichester PO20 1AJ* M: 07922-516761 E: maybarker@virginmedia.com *or* revmaybarker@gmail.com

BARKER, Miriam Sarah Anne. b 62. Lon Univ MB, BS 86. SEITE 08. **d** 11 **p** 12. C Southborough St Pet w Ch Ch and St Matt etc *Roch* 11–15; Community Chapl Tonbridge Adnry and C Tonbridge St Steph from 15; AD Tonbridge from 18. *St Stephen's Vicarage, 6 Brook Street, Tonbridge TN9 2PJ* T: (01732) 353079 M: 07783-228275 E: miriambarker@live.co.uk

BARKER, Neil Anthony. b 52. St Andr Univ BSc 73. Ridley Hall Cam 74. **d** 77 **p** 78. C Leic H Apostles 77–81; C Camberley St Paul *Guildf* 81–86; R Bradfield *Ox* 86–88; R Bradfield and Stanford Dingley 88–92; R Woodmansterne *S'wark* 92–05; AD Reigate 05; Chapl MU 96–02; TR Modbury, Bigbury, Ringmore, Kingston etc *Ex* 05–15; R Modbury, Bigbury, Ringmore etc 15–17; RD Woodleigh 07–12; rtd 17. *Stonecot, Fore Street, Aveton Gifford, Kingsbridge TQ7 4LB* E: revbarker@btinternet.com

BARKER, The Ven Nicholas John Willoughby. b 49. Oriel Coll Ox BA 73 BA 75 MA 77. Trin Coll Bris 75. **d** 77 **p** 78. C Watford *St Alb* 77–80; TV Didsbury St Jas and Em *Man* 80–86; TR Kidderminster St Geo *Worc* 86–07; RD Kidderminster 01–07; Hon Can Worc Cathl 03–07; Adn Auckland and Can Dur Cathl 07–17; P-in-c Darlington H Trin 07–17; rtd 17; PtO *Dur* from 18. *4 Watson Park, Spennymoor DL16 6NB* T: (01388) 819487 E: nick.barker99@btinternet.com

BARKER, Paul. b 73. Ripon Coll Cuddesdon 14. **d** 16 **p** 18. C Sunderland St Chad *Dur* 16–20; P-in-c The Boldons from 20. *The Rectory, 13 Rectory Green, West Boldon, East Boldon NE36 0QD* E: revpaulbarker@gmail.com

BARKER, Philip. *See* BARKER, Charles Philip Geoffrey

BARKER, Capt Robert Gardiner. b 59. **d** 14 **p** 15. NSM Ellesmere Port *Ches* 14–17; P-in-c Kirby Misperton w Normanby and Salton *York* 17–21; V Ryce 21; P-in-c Middleton, Newton and Sinnington 17–21; R from 21. *St Andrew's House, 15 Middleton Carr Lane, Middleton, Pickering YO18 8PU* T: (01751) 476686 E: captainrgb@btinternet.com

BARKER, The Very Revd Timothy Reed. b 56. Qu Coll Cam BA 79 MA 82. Westcott Ho Cam 78. **d** 80 **p** 81. C Nantwich *Ches* 80–83; V Norton 83–88; V Runcorn All SS 88–94; Urban Officer 88–90; Dioc Communications Officer 91–98; Bp's Chapl 94–98; Hon P Asst Ches Cathl 94–98; V Spalding St Mary and St Nic *Linc* 98–09; P-in-c Spalding St Paul 07–09; RD Elloe W 00–09; RD Elloe E 08–09; Adn Linc 09–15; Can and Preb Linc Cathl 03–15; R Guernsey St Andr *Win* from 15; P-in-c Sark from 15; Dean Guernsey from 15; Hon Can Win Cathl from 16. *St Andrew's Rectory, Route de St Andre, St Andrew, Guernsey GY6 8XN* T: (01481) 238568 M: 07781-166095 E: dean@deanery.gg

BARKING, Archdeacon of. *See* BURKE, The Ven Christopher Mark

BARKING, Area Bishop of. *Vacant*

BARKS, Jeffrey Stephen. b 45. Cranmer Hall Dur 66. **d** 71 **p** 72. C Wootton *St Alb* 71–74; C Boscombe St Jo *Win* 74–76; C Ringwood 76–80; P-in-c Spaxton w Charlynch *B & W* 80; P-in-c Enmore w Goathurst 80; P-in-c Spaxton w Goathurst, Enmore and Charlynch 80–81; R 81–92; RD Bridgwater 89–94; V Wembdon 92–07; rtd 07. *77 Alfoxton Road, Bridgwater TA6 7NW* T: (01278) 423647 E: stephen.barks@alivecm.org.uk

BARLEY, Ann Christine. b 47. **d** 93 **p** 94. OLM Walton *St E* 93–00; OLM Walton and Trimley 00–08; rtd 08; PtO *St E* from 08. *3 Wolsey Court, Stanley Road, Felixstowe IP11 7DJ* E: carmel.ann@btinternet.com

BARLEY, Canon Christopher James. b 56. St Steph Ho Ox 91. **d** 93 **p** 94. C Upton cum Chalvey *Ox* 93–96; TV High Wycombe 96–01; V Swinton *Sheff* from 01; Dioc Chapl MU from 08; Hon Can Sheff Cathl from 10. *The Vicarage, 50 Golden*

Smithies Lane, Swinton, Mexborough S64 8DL   T: (01709) 582259 E: chris.barley@sheffield.anglican.org

BARLEY, Gordon Malcolm. b 59. Aston Tr Scheme 94 Oak Hill Th Coll 96. **d** 98 **p** 99. C Walthamstow St Jo *Chelmsf* 98–02; TV Barking St Marg w St Patr 02–12; V Ovenden *Wakef* 12–14; Leeds 14–19; rtd 19; PtO *York* from 21. *Flat 4, 27 West Street, Scarborough YO11 2QR* E: gordon_barley@ntlworld.com

BARLEY, Ivan William. b 48. Loughb Univ MA 01. **d** 93 **p** 94. OLM Walton *St E* 93–00; OLM Walton and Trimley 00–13; NSM 13–14; Dioc NSM/OLM Officer 02–10; rtd 14; PtO *St E* from 14. *3 Wolsey Court, Stanley Road, Felixstowe IP11 7DJ* E: iwbarley@outlook.com

BARLEY, Lynda Mary. b 53. York Univ BA 74 PGCE 75 Lon Univ MSc 76 Anglia Ruskin Univ DProf 14 FSS 77. S'wark Ord Course 93. **d** 96 **p** 97. NSM Lower Nutfield *S'wark* 96–97; NSM Littleham w Exmouth *Ex* 97–98; NSM Tedburn St Mary, Whitestone, Oldridge etc 98–00; Hd Research and Statistics Abps' Coun 00–11; NSM Cullompton, Willand, Uffculme, Kentisbeare etc *Ex* 03–11; Preb Ex Cathl 09–11; Can Res and Pastor Truro Cathl 11–20; C Truro St Mary 12–20; P-in-c Tresillian and Lamorran w Merther 12–20; P-in-c St Michael Penkevil 12–20; RD Powder 18–20; rtd 20; PtO *Truro* from 20; *Eur* from 10. *Skinners House, Bradfield, Willand, Cullompton EX15 2RB* T: (01884) 839354

BARLEY, Victor Laurence. b 41. St Jo Coll Cam MA 66 Ch Ch Ox DPhil 72 FRCSEd 75 FRCR 76. **d** 02 **p** 03. NSM Flax Bourton and Barrow Gurney *B & W* 02–06; NSM Clevedon St Jo 06–09; NSM Chew Stoke w Nempnett Thrubwell 09–16; rtd 16; PtO *Bris* from 13; *B & W* 16–17 and from 20. *Church Farm, Church Lane, Chew Stoke, Bristol BS40 8TU* T: (01275) 331086 M: 07443-923648 E: victor.barley@tiscali.co.uk

BARLING, Michael Keith. b 38. Oak Hill Th Coll 63. **d** 66 **p** 67. C Portman Square St Paul *Lon* 66–70; C Enfield Ch Ch Trent Park 70–74; V Sidcup St Andr *Roch* 74–78; Dir Fountain Trust 78–81; Chapl Bethany Fellowship and Roffey Place 81–88; Hon C Kennington St Mark *S'wark* 88–89; rtd 03. *Address temp unknown* M: 07855-231755

BARLOW, Clive Christopher. b 42. Linc Th Coll 67. **d** 70 **p** 71. C Surbiton St Mark *S'wark* 70–74; C Spring Park *Cant* 74–77; V Ash w Westmarsh 77–92; R Chartham 92–08; RD E Bridge 86–92; RD W Bridge 95–01; rtd 08; PtO *Cant* from 08. *5 Barton Road, Canterbury CT1 1YG* T: (01227) 784779 E: c.barlow@btinternet.com

BARLOW, Canon Darren. b 65. Ridley Hall Cam 96. **d** 98 **p** 99. C Rayleigh *Chelmsf* 98–01; TV Billericay and Lt Burstead 01–06; TR Grays Thurrock from 06; RD Thurrock from 11; Hon Can Chelmsf Cathl from 15. *The Rectory, 10 High View Avenue, Grays RM17 6RU* T: (01375) 377379 *or* 373215 E: revbarlow@talktalk.net *or* rev.darren@gttm.org

BARLOW, David. b 50. Leeds Univ BA 71 MA 99. Wycliffe Hall Ox 71. **d** 73 **p** 74. C Horninglow *Lich* 73–75; C Wednesfield St Thos 75–77; C Bloxwich 77–78; Chapl RN 78–08; Prin Armed Forces Chapl Cen Amport Ho 05–08; QHC 04–08; P-in-c Baughurst, Ramsdell, Wolverton w Ewhurst etc *Win* 08–14; R 14–19; rtd 19. *138 Ferry Road, Southsea PO4 9UD* E: barlow857@btinternet.com

BARLOW, Edward Rhys. b 83. Glas Univ MA 05 Heythrop Coll Lon MA 11 St Jo Coll Dur MA 17 York St Jo Univ PGCE 07. Cranmer Hall Dur 14. **d** 16 **p** 17. C Bedford Park *Lon* 16–19; TV Bexley *Roch* from 19. *St John's Vicarage, 29 Parkhill Road, Bexley DA5 1HX* M: 07939-834704 E: fr.edwardbarlow@gmail.com

BARLOW, James Derek. b 64. Ex Univ BA 87. Ripon Coll Cuddesdon 09. **d** 11 **p** 12. C Burnham *Ox* 11–15; C Bracknell 15–18; P-in-c 18–20; TR Totnes w Bridgetown, Berry Pomeroy etc *Ex* from 20. *The Rectory, Northgate, Totnes TQ9 5NX* E: fr.jim@totnesrectory.co.uk

BARLOW, Patricia Mary. b 60. Linc Sch of Th and Min 15. **d** 17 **p** 18. NSM Gt Grimsby St Mary and St Jas *Linc* from 17. *Address temp unknown* E: patbarlow60@hotmail.com

BARLOW, Paul Andrew. b 59. Imp Coll Lon BSc 80 UMIST PhD 84 Dub City Univ MA 14 PhD 19 Bolton Inst of HE PGCE 85. Aston Tr Scheme 89 Chich Th Coll 91. **d** 93 **p** 94. C Hale *Guildf* 93–97; C Christchurch *Win* 97–01; P-in-c Alton All SS 01–09; C Alton 10–11; Chapl Dublin Sandymount *D & G* from 11. *Gealán, Durham Road, Sandymount, Dublin 4, Republic of Ireland* T: (00353) (1) 516 3457 M: (00353) 85-284 9564 E: paul.barlow@upcmail.ie paul.barlow@outlook.ie

BARLOW, Paul Benson. b 31. Fitzw Coll Cam BA 73 MA 77 FRSA 94. **d** 64 **p** 65. C Bath Abbey w St Jas *B & W* 64–74; Dep Hd Master Leys High Sch Redditch 74–81; Hd Master Jo Kyrle High Sch Ross-on-Wye 82–96; PtO *Heref* 82–85; LtO 85–92; NSM Walford and St John w Bishopswood, Goodrich etc 92–97; PtO 97–19. *The Coach House, Hentland, Ross-on-Wye HR9 6LP*

BARLOW, Philip Alan. b 72. S Bank Univ BA 95. St Mellitus Coll 18. **d** 20 **p** 21. C New Haw *Guildf* from 20. *9 Parklands, Addlestone KT15 1LS* M: 07715-496305 E: philbarlow72@gmail.com

BARLOW, Robert Mark. b 53. St Jo Coll Nottm 84. **d** 86 **p** 87. C Colwich w Gt Haywood *Lich* 86–91; R Crick and Yelvertoft w Clay Coton and Lilbourne *Pet* 91–04; Bp's Rural Officer 98–04; Chapl to Agric and Rural Life *Worc* 04–10; C Worcs W Rural 05–10; P-in-c Teme Valley S 10–17; TR Dudley 17–19; rtd 19; PtO *Worc* from 19; *Heref* from 20. *Oak House, Rhyse Lane, Tenbury Wells WR15 8NH* M: 07947-600627

BARNARD, Canon Anthony Nevin. b 36. St Jo Coll Cam BA 60 MA 64. Wells Th Coll 61. **d** 63 **p** 64. C Cheshunt *St Alb* 63–65; Tutor Wells Th Coll 65–66; Chapl 66–69; Vice-Prin 69–71; Dep Prin Sarum & Wells Th Coll 71–77; Dir S Dios Minl Tr Scheme 74–77; Can Res and Chan Lich Cathl 77–06; Warden of Readers 77–91; Dir of Tr 86–91; rtd 06; PtO *Lich* 06–21. *Junction House, 264 Efflinch Lane, Barton under Needwood, Burton-on-Trent DE13 8DF* T: (01283) 711505 E: aandabarnard@tiscali.co.uk

BARNARD, Kevin James. b 52. Keble Coll Ox BA 77 MA 79 Sheff Univ PhD 14. Cranmer Hall Dur 77. **d** 79 **p** 80. C Swinton *Sheff* 79–83; TV Sheff Manor 83–90; V Bolsterstone 90–13; Bp's Adv on Issues Relating to Ageing 94–13; V King Cross Leeds 13–20; C Southowram 18–20; rtd 20; PtO *Leeds* 20–21. *4 The Wickets, Bradford BD2 3JW*

BARNARD, Timothy John William. b 53. Magd Coll Cam BA 75 MA 78. **d** 13 **p** 14. OLM Amersham *Ox* from 13. *2A Stanley Hill Avenue, Amersham HP7 9BD* T: (01494) 728478 M: 07971-871667 E: timbar_uk@yahoo.co.uk

BARNDEN, Saskia Gail. b 50. Waterloo Univ (Canada) BA 70 Victoria Univ (BC) MA 71 Indiana Univ PhD 88 Westmr Coll Ox CertEd 75. SAOMC 97. **d** 00 **p** 01. Asst Chapl Wycombe Abbey Sch 00–01; Chapl Haberdashers' Monmouth Sch for Girls 01–12; Chapl St Mary's Hospice 13–17; rtd 17; PtO *Birm* from 17. *47 Elvetham Road, Birmingham B15 2LY* T: 0121-440 5677 *or* 472 1191 M: 07813-616574

BARNE, Hugh Nicholas. b 84. Wycliffe Hall Ox 14. **d** 17 **p** 18. C Wargrave w Knowl Hill *Ox* from 17. *46 Fidlers Walk, Wargrave, Reading RG10 8BA*

BARNES, Brian. b 49. St Mich Coll Llan 93. **d** 93 **p** 94. C Betws w Ammanford *St D* 93–96; V Llanwnda, Goodwick w Manorowen and Llanstinan 96–15; rtd 15; PtO *St D* from 15. *Glan y Don, Penbanc, Fishguard SA65 9BJ* E: revb@hotmail.com

BARNES, Christopher. b 57. **d** 06 **p** 07. NSM Bowling St Jo *Bradf* 06–14; Leeds 14–20; PtO 20–21. *257 Bolling Hall Road, Bradford BD4 7TJ* T: (01274) 306230 E: chrisbarnes257@hotmail.co.uk

BARNES, David Keith. b 53. Linc Th Coll. **d** 89 **p** 90. C E Crompton *Man* 89–93; V Belfield 93–99; V Honley *Wakef* 99–12; P-in-c Bude Haven and Marhamchurch *Truro* 12–16; P-in-c Stratton and Launcells 12–16; R N Kernow 16–19; C 19–21; P-in-c Kilkhampton w Morwenstow 16–19; C Week St Mary Circle of Par 19–21; R Bude Coast and Country from 21; RD Stratton from 18. *The Rectory, The Glebe, Week St Mary, Holsworthy EX22 6UY* E: d.barnes645@btinternet.com

BARNES, Elizabeth. b 60. St Mellitus Coll BA 13. **d** 13 **p** 14. C Tolleshunt Knights w Tiptree and Gt Braxted *Chelmsf* 13; C Thurstable and Winstree 13–16; P-in-c Gt Oakley w Wix and Wrabness 16–17; C Tendring and Lt Bentley w Beaumont cum Moze 16–17; V Gt Oakley, Wix, Wrabness etc 17–21; AD Harwich 20–21; rtd 21. *47 Grove Road, Tiptree, Colchester CO5 0JL* T: (01621) 334561 E: liz_barnes@sky.com

BARNES, Mrs Helen Clark. b 61. Worc Coll of Educn BA 82. Ox Min Course 07. **d** 10 **p** 11. NSM Haddenham w Cuddington, Kingsey etc *Ox* 10–14; TV Cottesloe 14–19; TR Cherwell Valley from 19. *The Rectory, 104 Camp Road, Upper Heyford, Bicester OX25 5AG* T: (01869) 233687 E: helen.barnes1503@gmail.com

BARNES, Jennifer. b 45. Leeds Univ MA 96. NOC 94. **d** 96 **p** 97. C Thorne *Sheff* 96–99; C Clifton St Jas 99–01; Chapl HM Pris Featherstone 01–04; Chapl HM YOI Swinfen Hall 04–05; P-in-c Barnsley St Edw *Wakef* 05–07; Chapl HM Pris and YOI New Hall 07–08; rtd 08; PtO *Wakef* 07–09; NSM Lundwood 09–11; PtO *Sheff* from 14; Leeds from 17. *Carlton House, 71 Woodhead Road, Honley, Holmfirth HD9 6PP* T: (01484) 660876 E: jbjcb@tiscali.co.uk

BARNES, Jeremy Paul Blissard. b 70. Southn Univ BSc 92. Wycliffe Hall Ox BTh 99. **d** 99 **p** 00. C Brompton H Trin w Onslow Square St Paul *Lon* 99–05; C Shadwell St Paul w Ratcliffe St Jas 05–09; V E Twickenham St Steph from 09. *17 Claremont Road, Twickenham TW1 2QX* T: (020) 8892 5258 E: jezbarnes@st-stephens.org.uk

BARNES, John Christopher. b 43. MA ATI. Linc Th Coll 78. **d** 80 **p** 81. C Guiseley *Bradf* 80–83; TV Guiseley w Esholt

83–86; V Rawdon 86–92; R Armthorpe *Sheff* 92–98; TR Maltby 98–01; RD Doncaster 96–98; Hon Can Sheff Cathl 00–01; TR Blakenall Heath *Lich* 01–05; P-in-c Gomersal *Wakef* 05–09; P-in-c Cleckheaton St Jo 08–09; rtd 09; P-in-c Lundwood *Wakef* 09–11; PtO *Leeds* from 17. *Carlton House, 71 Woodhead Road, Honley, Holmfirth HD9 6PP* T: (01485) 660876 E: jbjcb@tiscali.co.uk

BARNES, Josephine Ella. b 39. **d** 12 **p** 13. OLM Hope, Castleton and Bradwell *Derby* from 12. *2 Cavedale Cottage, Market Place, Castleton, Hope Valley S33 8WQ* T: (01433) 621443 E: josephine.barnes1@btinternet.com

BARNES, Jules Ann. b 60. St Mary's Coll Dur BA 83 Dur Univ MBA 84 RGN 95. Ripon Coll Cuddesdon BTh 11. **d** 10 **p** 11. C Wilton w Netherhampton and Fugglestone *Sarum* 10–14; Bp's Chapl *Bris* 14–16; Min Can Bris Cathl 15–16; P-in-c Warnham *Chich* 16–21; Chapl Hamburg *Eur* from 21. *Englische Planke 1A, 20459 Hamburg, Germany* T: (0049) (40) 439 2334 M: 07415-000290 E: chaplain@anglican-church-hamburg.de

BARNES, Canon Katrina Crawford. b 52. K Coll Lon BA 98 AKC 98. Oak Hill Th Coll 90. **d** 93 **p** 94. NSM Bromley H Trin *Roch* 93–98; C Meopham w Nurstead 98–00; Assoc Staff Tutor SEITE 99–03; R Longfield *Roch* 01–06; V Bromley Common St Aug 06–17; P-in-c Bromley Common St Luke 17; V Bromley Common St Aug w St Luke 17–18; Bp's Adv for Ord Women's Min 05–11; AD Bromley 11–15; Hon Can Roch Cathl 05–18; rtd 18. *39 The Fairway, Bromley BR1 2JZ*

BARNES, Lee. b 74. Trin Coll Bris BA 03 MA 09. **d** 09 **p** 10. C Malmesbury w Westport and Brokenborough *Bris* 09–12; C Gt Somerford, Lt Somerford, Seagry, Corston etc 09–12; PtO 12–13; LtO 13–14; P-in-c Bris St Steph w St Jas and St Jo w St Mich etc 14–21; P-in-c Clifton H Trin, St Andr and St Pet 14–21. *Address temp unknown*

BARNES, Margaret Anne. b 56. **d** 13 **p** 14. OLM Oulton Broad *Nor* from 13. *53 Dell Road East, Lowestoft NR33 9LA* T: (01502) 538122 E: mooskieanddave09@hotmail.co.uk

BARNES, Mrs Mary Jane. b 48. St Jo Coll Nottm 97. **d** 99 **p** 00. C Harefield *Lon* 99–02; TV New Windsor *Ox* 02–10; C 10–15; P-in-c Old Windsor 14–15; rtd 15; PtO *Eur* 17–20. *24 rue des Philips, 46220 Prayssac, France* M: 07930-337407 E: rev.mbarnes@gmail.com

BARNES, Canon Matthew John. b 68. Leeds Univ MA 99. St Jo Coll Nottm BA 93. **d** 96 **p** 97. C Stanley *Wakef* 96–99; TV N Wingfield, Clay Cross and Pilsley *Derby* 99–08; R Brampton St Thos 08–20; RD Chesterfield 11–15; Dir of Discipleship, Miss and Min from 20; Hon Can Derby Cathl from 13. *Church House, Full Street, Derby DE1 3DR* M: 07711-964451 E: matt.barnes@derby.anglican.org

BARNES, Canon Neal Duncan. b 63. Leeds Univ BSc 84 Cranfield Inst of Tech PhD 92. Oak Hill Th Coll 93. **d** 95 **p** 96. C Biggleswade *St Alb* 95–99; V Anlaby St Pet *York* 99–10; V Kingston upon Hull H Trin 10–11; V 11–19; Hon Chapl Ambulance Service Hull 99–19; Can and Preb York Minster 13–19; Can Res Liv Cathl from 19. *4 Cathedral Close, Liverpool L1 7BR* M: 07581-280785 E: neal@anvic.karoo.co.uk

BARNES, Canon Neil. b 42. Kelham Th Coll 61 Bps' Coll Cheshunt 65. **d** 68 **p** 69. C Poulton-le-Fylde *Blackb* 68–72; C Ribbleton 72–75; V Knuzden 75–81; Chapl Prestwich Hosp Man 81–88; Chapl Salford Mental Health Services NHS Trust 88–04; Manager Chapl Services 94–04; Hon Can Man Cathl 96–04; rtd 04; PtO *Blackb* from 04; *Man* 04–19. *7 Bouldsworth Road, Burnley BB10 3JT* E: neilbarnes.leads@gmail.com

BARNES, Paul. *See* BYLLAM-BARNES, Paul William Marshall

BARNES, Peter Frank. b 52. St Jo Coll Nottm LTh 81. **d** 81 **p** 82. C Colne St Bart *Blackb* 81–83; C Melton Mowbray w Thorpe Arnold *Leic* 83–86; P-in-c Barlestone 86–89; V Broughton and Duddon *Carl* 89–98; V Shrewsbury St Geo w Greenfields *Lich* 98–00; P-in-c Bicton, Montford w Shrawardine and Fitz 98–00; P-in-c Myddle 08–11; P-in-c Broughton 08–11; P-in-c Loppington w Newtown 08–11; R St John's-in-the-Vale, Threlkeld and Wythburn *Carl* 11–17; rtd 17. *10 Stanley Road, Brampton CA8 1DT* E: peterbarnes52@tiscali.co.uk

BARNES, Philip Richard. b 73. Westmr Coll Ox BTh 94 Heythrop Coll Lon MA 99. St Steph Ho Ox 98. **d** 00 **p** 01. C Ruislip St Martin *Lon* 00–03; Shrine P Shrine of Our Lady of Walsingham 03–08; V Northwood Hills St Edm *Lon* 08–16; AD Harrow 13–15; P Admin Shrine of Our Lady of Walsingham 16–17; P-in-c S Kensington St Steph *Lon* from 17. *5 Thomas Place, London W8 5UG* M: 07833-132500 E: frphilipbarnes@btinternet.com

BARNES, Roland Peter. b 59. Ban Ord Course 01. **d** 03 **p** 04. NSM Bro Ddyfi Uchaf *Ban* 03–05; P-in-c 05–14; P-in-c Bro Cyfeiliog and Mawddwy 14–18; AD Cyfeiliog and Mawddwy

12–15; V Bro Moelwyn from 18. *Y Rheithordy, The Square, Blaenau Ffestiniog LL41 3UW* T: (01766) 831871

BARNES, Simon. b 63. Warwick Univ BA 86 Lon Univ MA 88. **d** 03 **p** 04. USA 03–13; Exec Vice-Pres American Bible Soc 07–13; PtO *B & W* from 13; Chief Exec Officer Send a Cow 13–16; R Louisville St Fran USA 18–20; PtO *Ex* from 21. E: sbarnes305@gmail.com

BARNES, Stephen. b 46. Hull Univ BA 69. Clifton Th Coll 69. **d** 72 **p** 73. C Girlington *Bradf* 72–74; TV Glyncorrwg w Afan Vale and Cymmer Afan *Llan* 74–79; R 79–86; V Aberavon 86–01; V Dulais Valley 01–13; rtd 13. *43 Heol Maes y Dre, Ystradgynlais, Swansea SA9 1HA* T: (01639) 841882 E: stephen.barnes41@btinternet.com

BARNES, Stephen John. b 59. Univ of Wales (Cardiff) BSc 80. Chich Th Coll 83. **d** 86 **p** 87. C Neath w Llantwit *Llan* 86–89; C Coity w Nolton 89–95; V Troedyrhiw w Merthyr Vale from 95. *The Vicarage, Nixonville, Merthyr Vale, Merthyr Tydfil CF48 4RF* T: (01443) 690249 E: light2house@btinternet.com

BARNES, Stephen William. b 53. Man Univ BSc. St Jo Coll Nottm. **d** 83 **p** 84. C Chadwell Heath *Chelmsf* 83–87; C Becontree St Alb 88–89; Deanery Youth Chapl 88–91; C Becontree S 89–91; TV Worth *Chich* 91–98; Chapl Willen Hospice Milton Keynes 99–18; rtd 18; PtO *Ox* from 18. *90 Bradwell Road, Bradville, Milton Keynes MK13 7AD*

BARNES, Thomas. *See* BARNES, William Thomas

BARNES, Timothy. b 56. Birm Univ BSc 78. Westcott Ho Cam 96. **d** 98 **p** 99. C Shrub End *Chelmsf* 98–02; V Leigh-on-Sea St Aid 02–11; P-in-c Bocking St Pet from 11. *The Vicarage, St Peter's in the Fields, Braintree CM7 9AR* T: (01376) 349267 E: timbarnes1@btinternet.com

BARNES, Canon William Thomas. b 39. Dur Univ BA 60. Wycliffe Hall Ox 60. **d** 62 **p** 63. C Scotforth *Blackb* 62–66; C Cleveleys 66–67; V Colne Ch Ch 67–74; V Bamber Bridge St Sav 74–04; Hon Can Blackb Cathl 00–04; rtd 04; PtO *Blackb* from 04. *12 Little Close, Farington Moss, Leyland PR26 6QU* T: (01772) 457646 E: tom.beryl.barnes@hotmail.co.uk

BARNES-CLAY, Peter John Granger. b 43. Cam Univ CertEd 69 MCollP. Chich Th Coll 72. **d** 75 **p** 82. C Earlham St Anne *Nor* 75–76; Asst Master Hewett Sch Nor 76–83; Chapl Nor Cathl from 80; Hon C Eaton 81–83; C 83–87; R Winterton w E and W Somerton and Horsey 87–92; R Weybourne Gp 92–03; RD Holt 95–02; rtd 03; PtO *Nor* 03–05; C Smallburgh w Dilham w Honing and Crostwight 05–06; P-in-c 06–08; PtO from 08; *St E* 14–18. *Hunters End, 1 Danby Close, Eaton Rise, Norwich NR4 6RH* T: (01603) 501199 E: becketsthree1@aol.com

BARNES-DAVIES, Daniel Simon. b 88. Southn Univ BA 09 Dur Univ BA 17. Westcott Ho Cam 14. **d** 17 **p** 18. C Romford St Edw *Chelmsf* 17–21; TV Barry *Llan* from 21. *21 Rectory Road, Barry CF63 3QB* M: 07375-392285 E: frdan@barnesdavies.co.uk

BARNET, Carole Ann. b 58. All SS Cen for Miss & Min 17. **d** 18 **p** 19. OLM Prestwich St Mary *Man* from 18. *7 Old Hall Road, Whitefield, Manchester M45 7QW*

BARNETT, Diana. b 56. Qu Foundn (Course) 16. **d** 19 **p** 20. NSM Petton w Cockshutt, Welshampton and Lyneal etc *Lich* from 19. *Sandstones, Baschurch Road, Bomere Heath, Shrewsbury SY4 3PN* T: (01939) 291052 M: 07736-420779 E: dianabarnett1704@gmail.com

BARNETT, Dudley Graham. b 36. Ch Ch Ox BA 62 MA 65. St Steph Ho Ox 62. **d** 64 **p** 65. C Abbey Hey *Man* 64–68; V Swinton H Rood 68–90; R Old Trafford St Hilda 90–01; R Firswood and Gorse Hill 01–02; rtd 02; PtO *Man* from 02. *6A Gilda Crescent Road, Eccles, Manchester M30 9AG* T: 0161-707 9767 E: dudleygbarnett@yahoo.co.uk

BARNETT, Mrs Elizabeth Anne. b 68. Trin Coll Bris 17. **d** 19 **p** 20. C Dulwich St Barn *S'wark* from 19. *41 Woodware Road, London SE22 8UN* M: 07765-074102 E: lizbarnett68@gmail.com

BARNETT, Mrs Gillian. b 62. Edge Hill Coll of HE BA 06. All SS Cen for Miss & Min 12. **d** 15 **p** 16. C Walmersley Road, Bury *Man* 15–18; P-in-c Belfield 18–21; V from 21; P-in-c Hamer and Wardley from 18; Borough Dean Rochdale from 20. *8 Lowerfold Drive, Rochdale OL12 7JA* T: (01706) 458506 *or* 642846 E: barnettgill@hotmail.co.uk

BARNETT, Canon John Raymond. b 51. Lon Univ LLB 74 BD 86 Birm Univ MA 98 De Montfort Univ MA 11 Birm Univ DPT 19. Westcott Ho Cam 74. **d** 77 **p** 78. C Northfield *Birm* 77–81; V Hamstead St Bernard 81–91; R The Quinton 91–03; AD Edgbaston 98–03; P-in-c Oldbury 03–07; P-in-c Langley St Jo 03–07; P-in-c Langley St Mich 03–07; P-in-c Londonderry 04–07; V Oldbury, Langley and Londonderry 07–09; Hon Can Birm Cathl 01–09; P-in-c Darlaston All SS *Lich* 09–13; C Moxley 09–13; C Darlaston St Lawr 09–13; P-in-c Pheasey 13–17; Interfaith Officer Wolverhampton Area 09–16;

rtd 17; PtO *Birm* from 17; *Worc* from 18. *1 Front Cottages, Withybed Green, Alvechurch, Birmingham B48 7RJ* M: 07967-166931 E: johnbarnett255@gmail.com

BARNETT (*née* **JACKSON**), **Canon Lisa Helen.** b 79. Reading Univ BA(Ed) 01 Cam Univ BA 06. Ridley Hall Cam 04. **d** 07 **p** 08. C Patcham *Chich* 07–11; P-in-c Scaynes Hill 11–15; V 15–20; TR Horsham from 20; Dep Dir of Ords 19; Can and Preb Chich Cathl from 18. *The Vicarage, Causeway, Horsham RH12 1HE* M: 07989-761575 E: revlisa@btinternet.com

BARNETT, Michael. *See* BARNETT, Raymond Michael

BARNETT, Peter Geoffrey. b 46. AKC 71. St Aug Coll Cant 71. **d** 72 **p** 73. C Wolverhampton *Lich* 72–77; P-in-c Caldmore 77–83; TR Bris St Agnes and St Simon w St Werburgh 83–87; P-in-c Bris St Paul w St Barn 83–87; TR Bris St Paul's 87–94; Warden Pilsdon Community 94–04; PtO *Roch* 04–13; *S & B* from 13. *Catchpool Cottage, Llanmadoc, Swansea SA3 1DE* T: (01792) 386767 E: thebarnettfamily@talktalk.net

BARNETT, Preb Raymond Michael. b 31. Man Univ BA 54. Wells Th Coll 54. **d** 56 **p** 57. C Fallowfield *Man* 56–59; Madagascar 59–60; V Blackrod *Man* 60–67; V Woolavington *B & W* 67–76; RD Bridgwater 72–76; V St Decumans 76–96; RD Quantock 78–86 and 93–95; Preb Wells Cathl 89–96; rtd 96; PtO *B & W* 96–08. *22 Fosbrooke House, Clifton Drive, Lytham St Annes FY8 5RQ*

BARNFATHER, Thomas Fenwick. b 52. Cant Ch Ch Univ BSc 09. Linc Th Coll 86. **d** 88 **p** 89. C Sedgefield *Dur* 88–91; TV E Darlington 91–92; CF 92–96; V Heybridge w Langford *Chelmsf* 96–98; Chapl HM YOI Dover 98–00; Chapl HM Pris Swaleside 00–01; P-in-c Aylesham w Adisham *Cant* 01–04; Asst Dir of Ords 02–05; PtO 04–09; P-in-c Westgate St Sav 09–12; P-in-c Lanzarote *Eur* 12–14; PtO *Leic* 15–16; Hon C Ilkeston H Trin *Derby* 16–20; Hon C Long Eaton St Laur 16–20; rtd 20; PtO *Leic* from 21. *61 Sharpley Avenue, Coalville LE67 4DU* M: 07513-060519 E: tombarnfather@gmail.com

BARNSLEY, David Edward. b 75. Ox Brookes Univ BSc 97. Oak Hill Th Coll BA 03. **d** 03 **p** 04. C Kilnhurst *Sheff* 03–06; C Duffield and Lt Eaton *Derby* 06–20; C Buxton w Burbage and King Sterndale from 20. *Address temp unknown*

BARNSLEY, Canon Melvyn. b 46. Dur Univ BA 67 Lon Univ CertEd. St Chad's Coll Dur 64. **d** 71 **p** 72. C Cov St Thos 71–74; C Cov St Jo 71–75; V New Bilton 75–82; R Stevenage St Andr and St Geo St Alb 82–14; RD Stevenage 89–99; Hon Can St Alb 00–14; rtd 14; PtO *St Alb* from 14; *Ely* from 14. *48 Hogsden Leys, St Neots PE19 6AD* T: (01480) 474498 E: melvynbarnsley@gmail.com

BARNSTAPLE, Archdeacon of. *Vacant*

BARON, Thomas Michael. b 63. St Steph Ho Ox 85. **d** 88 **p** 89. C Hartlepool St Paul *Dur* 88–92; Chapl Asst Hartlepool Gen Hosp 89–92; Asst Chapl Whittington Hosp NHS Trust 92–95; Chapl Enfield Community Care NHS Trust from 01; Chapl Chase Farm Hosps NHS Trust 95–99; Chapl Barnet and Chase Farm Hosps NHS Trust 99–14; Chapl Barnet, Enfield and Haringey Mental Health NHS Trust from 01; Chapl Enfield Primary Care Trust from 01. *The Chaplaincy, Chase Farm Hospital, The Ridgeway, Enfield EN2 8JL* T: (020) 8375 1078 *or* 8882 1195 E: frtom.baron@btinternet.com *or* tom.baron@nhs.net

BARON, Mrs Vanessa Lillian. b 57. City Univ BSc 79 Fitzw Coll Cam BA 84 MA 85 Birkbeck Coll Lon MA 06 SRN 79. Ridley Hall Cam 83. **dss** 86 **d** 87 **p** 94. Roxbourne St Andr *Lon* 86–89; Par Dn 87–89; NSM Roxeth 92–95; Lic Preacher 95–17; Asst Chapl Harrow Sch 95–04; Chapl St Paul's Girls' Sch Hammersmith 04–17; C Lyminster and Wick *Chich* from 17. *Lyminster Vicarage, 3 The Paddock, Lyminster, Littlehampton BN17 7QH*

BARR, Alan. b 59. TCD BTh 07. **d** 07 **p** 08. C Bray *D & G* 07–09; I Sixmilecross w Termonmaguirke *Arm* from 09. *St Michael's Rectory, 104 Cooley Road, Sixmilecross, Omagh BT79 9DH* T: (028) 8075 7097 M: 87-948 4408 E: alnbarr@gmail.com *or* sixmilecross@armagh.anglican.org

BARR, Jacqueline Anne. b 66. **d** 17 **p** 18. C Chinnor, Sydenham, Aston Rowant and Crowell *Ox* 17–20; R from 20. *Chinnor Rectory, High Street, Chinnor OX39 4DH* E: revd.jackybarr@gmail.com

BARR, Joanna Margaret Alice. *See* HEALEY, Joanna Margaret Alice

BARR, John. *See* BARR, Michael John Alexander

BARR (*née* **HAYTER**), **Mary Elizabeth.** b 58. Jes Coll Ox BA 80 CertEd 81 MA 84 Qu Coll Ox DPhil 85. Ridley Hall Cam 84. **dss** 86 **d** 87 **p** 94. Chapl Cam Univ Pastorate 86–91; Cambridge H Trin w St Andr Gt *Ely* 86–87; Par Dn 87–91; PtO 91–92; *Ex* 92–94; NSM Torquay St Luke 94–97; NSM Gt Malvern St Mary *Worc* 97–17; Chapl Worcs Community Healthcare NHS Trust 99–01; TV Melton Mowbray *Leic* from

17. *23 Melton Road, Waltham on the Wolds, Melton Mowbray LE14 4AJ* T: (01664) 464293 E: maryebarr17@gmail.com

BARR, Canon Michael John Alexander. b 60. Qu Coll Ox BA 82 MA 86 Pemb Coll Cam BA 86 MA 90. Ridley Hall Cam 84. **d** 87 **p** 88. C Earley St Pet *Ox* 87–89; C Cambridge Gt St Mary w St Mich *Ely* 89–92; Chapl Girton Coll Cam 90–92; P-in-c Torquay St Luke *Ex* 92–97; Dioc Communications Officer 92–97; P-in-c Gt Malvern St Mary *Worc* 97–99; V 99–17; RD Malvern 01–07; Hon Can Worc Cathl 15–17; R Ironstone Villages *Leic* from 17; AD Framland from 21. *23 Melton Road, Waltham on the Wolds, Melton Mowbray LE14 4AJ* T: (01664) 464265 E: johnbarr2817@gmail.com

BARR, Mrs Ruth. b 63. St Mellitus Coll BA 18. **d** 16 **p** 17. C Stopsley *St Alb* 16–19; TV Bishop's Hatfield, Lemsford and N Mymms from 19. *The Vicarage, North Mymms Park, North Mymms, Hatfield AL9 7TN* M: 07447-458526 E: ruthbarr77@gmail.com

BARRACLOUGH, Canon Barbara Amanda Juliet. b 61. Stirling Univ BA 83 Ches Coll of HE MA 00. NOC 97. **d** 00 **p** 01. C Lupset *Wakef* 00–04; V Ardsley 04–14; Leeds 14–15; R Sprotbrough *Sheff* from 15; AD Adwick 15–18; Dean of Women's Min from 18; Hon Can Sheff Cathl from 21. *The Rectory, 42A Spring Lane, Sprotbrough, Doncaster DN5 7QG* T: (01302) 854836 M: 07890-614579 E: amanda.barraclough1@btinternet.com *or* amanda.barraclough@sheffield.anglican.org

BARRACLOUGH, Mrs Naomi Hannah Shrine. b 88. Lanc Univ BSc 10. Cranmer Hall Dur 12. **d** 15 **p** 16. C Wirksworth *Derby* 15–17; C Carsington 18–19; C Stalmine w Pilling *Blackb* 19; C Waterside Par 19; C Over Wyre from 20. *7 Bluebell Avenue, Hambleton, Poulton-le-Fylde FY6 9FE* M: 07872-056471 E: nhsbarraclough@gmail.com

BARRACLOUGH, Canon Owen Conrad. b 32. Pemb Coll Cam BA 55 MA 59. Westcott Ho Cam 56. **d** 57 **p** 58. C Chippenham St Andr w Tytherton Lucas *Bris* 57–62; V Harringay St Paul *Lon* 62–70; Bp's Chapl for Community Relns *Cov* 70–77; P-in-c Baginton 72–77; V Swindon Ch Ch *Bris* 77–97; Chapl Princess Marg Hosp Swindon 77–89; Hon Can Bris Cathl 87–97; rtd 98; PtO *Bris* 98–02; *Glouc* 98–01; Jt P-in-c Staverton w Boddington and Tredington etc 01–04; Hon C Twigworth, Down Hatherley, Norton, The Leigh etc 04–06; Hon C Leckhampton SS Phil and Jas w Cheltenham St Jas 06–09; Hon C S Cheltenham 10–11; PtO from 17. *Robin Hollow, 10A Church Road, St Marks, Cheltenham GL51 7AN* T: (01242) 230855 E: obarraclough@btinternet.com

BARRATT, Mrs Elizabeth June. b 32. ACP 65. Trin Coll Bris 75. **dss** 78 **d** 87 **p** 94. W Kilburn St Luke w St Simon and St Jude *Lon* 78–87; Par Dn 87–94; C 94–98; rtd 98; Hon C Kensal Rise St Mark and St Martin *Lon* 99–11; Hon C Kensal Rise St Martin from 11. *68A Bathhurst Gardens, London NW10 5HY* T: (020) 8968 5951 M: 07763-474602 E: ejbarratt@hotmail.co.uk

BARRATT, Terrick. b 45. **d** 71 **p** 71. Paraguay 71–73; Argentina 73–80; Chile from 80; rtd 10; PtO *Ex* from 20. *57 Scalwell Park, Seaton EX12 2DB* T: (01297) 598203 E: terrick.barratt@gmail.com

BARRELL (*formerly* **WALLACE**), **Mrs Julie Michele.** b 58. Ox Univ MTh 93 Univ Coll Lon MSc 02. CA Tr Coll 77. **d** 88 **p** 94. Chapl Middx Poly *Lon* 86–90; Voc Adv CA 90–92; Member CA Counselling Service 92–96; Hon C Bellingham St Dunstan *S'wark* 91–96; TV Kidbrooke St Jas 96–99; PtO 99–01; Hon C Croydon Woodside 01–03; PtO *Llan* 09–11; C Treharris, Trelewis and Bedlinog w Llanfabon 11–12. *1 Ridgeway, Wyesham, Monmouth NP25 3JX* T: (01600) 773283 M: 07960-915047 E: julie.barrell@btinternet.com

BARRETT, Alan. b 48. Southn Univ BA 69. Wycliffe Hall Ox 74. **d** 77 **p** 78. C Conisbrough *Sheff* 77–80; C Lower Homerton St Paul *Lon* 80–81; C-in-c Houslow Gd Shep Beavers Lane CD 81–87; R Langdon Hills *Chelmsf* 87–97; P-in-c Tamworth *Lich* 97–03; V 03–13; RD 99–04; rtd 13; Corps Chapl ATC 10–15; PtO *Carl* from 14. *Neale House, Neale's Row, Great Urswick, Ulverston LA12 0SX* T: (01229) 582179 E: barrett.alan@btinternet.com

BARRETT, Alastair David. b 75. Trin Coll Cam BA 97 MA 01 Birm Univ BD 00 Vrije Univ Amsterdam PhD 17. Qu Coll Birm MA 01. **d** 01 **p** 02. C Sutton Coldfield St Chad *Birm* 01–04; C Oldbury, Langley and Londonderry 04–10; P-in-c Hodge Hill 10–13; TR from 13; Jt AD Coleshill 18–19; Jt AD Coleshill and Polesworth 19–20. *8 Dreghorn Road, Hodge Hill, Birmingham B36 8LJ* T: 0121-747 6982 E: hodgehillvicar@hotmail.co.uk

BARRETT, Alexandra Mary. b 75. Clare Coll Cam BA 96 MA 99. Westcott Ho Cam 00. **d** 03 **p** 04. C Godmanchester *Ely* 03–07; R Buckden w the Offords 07–14; USA 14–15; Tutor Westcott Ho Cam 15–19; Fell and Chapl St Cath

Coll Cam from 19. *St Catharine's College, Cambridge CB2 1RL* T: (01223) 338346 E: chaplain@caths.cam.ac.uk

BARRETT, Arthur. *See* BARRETT, Kenneth Arthur Lambart

BARRETT, Mrs Brigid. b 44. RN 90. STETS MA 11. **d** 11 **p** 12. NSM Parkstone St Pet and St Osmund w Branksea *Sarum* 11–15; NSM Wareham from 15; rtd 17; PtO *Sarum* 17–21. *1 Wyatts Lane, Wareham BH20 4NH* T: (01929) 553460

BARRETT, Christopher Paul. b 49. AKC 71 St Aug Coll Cant 71. **d** 72 **p** 73. C Tupsley *Heref* 72–75; C Ex St Thos 75–79; R Atherington and High Bickington 79–83; V Burrington 79–83; Asst Dir of Educn 79–87; P-in-c Sticklepath 83–84; TV Barnstaple 85–90; V Whipton 90–99; TV Ex St Thos and Em 99–05; Chapl Burton Hosps NHS Foundn Trust 05–14; PtO *Derby* 05–16; rtd 14; PtO *Bris* from 17. *51 Barter Close, Kingswood, Bristol BS15 8JN* M: 07557-091747 E: revcpbarrett@aol.com

BARRETT, Clive. b 55. Ox Univ BA 76 MA 80 CertEd 77 Leeds Univ PhD 98. St Steph Ho Ox 80. **d** 83 **p** 84. C Wakef Cathl 83–87; Asst Chapl Leeds Univ *Ripon* 87–97; Dioc Development Rep 89–92; P-in-c Middleton St Cross 98–07; Co Ecum Development Officer W Yorks *Leeds* 07–16; Hon C Headingley 08–18; PtO from 18; *Ox* 18–20. *81 Becketts Park Drive, Leeds LS6 3PJ* T: 0113-275 5497 M: 07966-540699 E: clivebarrett@hotmail.com

BARRETT, Ellen Marie (Sister Helena). b 46. Albertus Magnus Coll New Haven USA BA 70 NY Univ MA 72 MPhil 84 PhD 86. Gen Th Sem NY MDiv 75. **d** 75 **p** 77. C NY St Ignatius USA 92–96; C Bergen Episc Area Min 96–98; R 98–00; R S Orange 00–03; P-in-c Bronx Ch of the Mediator 02–04; P-in-c Union City St Jo 04–05; P-in-c Easton Trin Ch 12–14; 75–14; OSB from 13; PtO *Ox* 15–17; *Glas* from 17; Co-founder Companions of Our Lady and St Mungo from 18. *0/1 40 Merryland Street, Glasgow G51 2QD* M: 07943-937638 E: srhelenaosb@hotmail.com

BARRETT, John Joseph James. b 38. Lon Univ BD 65. Sarum & Wells Th Coll. **d** 78 **p** 78. C Danbury *Chelmsf* 78–80; Ind Chapl 80–89; C Dovercourt 80–83; TV Dovercourt and Parkeston 83–89; V Rubery *Birm* 89–04; rtd 04; PtO *Sheff* from 04. *4 Arran Hill, Thrybergh, Rotherham S65 4BH* T: (01709) 850288 E: rev.barrett@btinternet.com

BARRETT, Jonathan Murray. b 68. Oak Hill Th Coll BA 98. **d** 98 **p** 99. C Pennycross *Ex* 98–02; TV Plymouth Em, St Paul Efford and St Aug 02–08; V Thurnby w Stoughton *Leic* 08–13; P-in-c Houghton-on-the-Hill, Keyham and Hungarton 11–13; TR Cornerstone Team 13–17; AD Gartree I 16–17; AD Gartree II 16–17; Miss and Communications Enabler from 17. *15 Ruskington Drive, Wigston LE18 1LB* M: 07415-828278 E: jon.barrett@leccofe.org

BARRETT, Canon Kenneth. b 42. Univ of Wales (Lamp) BA 64. St Steph Ho Ox 65. **d** 67 **p** 68. C Poulton-le-Fylde *Blackb* 67–69; C S Shore H Trin 69–72; V Brierfield 72–83; V Chorley St Geo 83–07; Hon Can Blackb Cathl 03–07; rtd 07; PtO *Blackb* from 07. *24 Astley Road, Chorley PR7 1RR* T: (01257) 233421

BARRETT, Kenneth Arthur Lambart. b 60. CITC BTh 94. **d** 97 **p** 98. C Seagoe *D & G* 97–00; I Dublin Booterstown *D & G* 00–04; I Dublin Mt Merrion 00–04; I Boyle and Elphin w Aghanagh, Kilbryan etc *K, E & A* 04–08; I Taunagh w Kilmactranny, Ballysumaghan etc 04–08; I Rossorry *Clogh* 08–14; Dir of Ords 11–14; Can Clogh Cathl 12–14; Dean Raphoe *D & R* 14–21; I Raphoe w Raymochy and Clonleigh 14–21; I Arklow w Inch and Kilbride *D & G* from 21. *The Rectory, Emoclew Road, Arklow, Co Wicklow, Republic of Ireland* E: aikrector@gmail.com

BARRETT, Canon Marion Lily. b 54. Ex Univ BA 01 SRN 75. SWMTC 91. **d** 94 **p** 95. C St Mawgan w St Ervan and St Eval *Truro* 94–97; C St Breoke and Egloshayle 97–98; Asst Chapl R Cornwall Hosps Trust 98–99; Chapl 00–05; R St Mewan w Mevagissey and St Ewe *Truro* from 05; RD St Austell 10–19; Convenor Bp's Gp for Min of Healing from 11; Hon Can Truro Cathl from 13. *The Rectory, St Mewan Lane, St Mewan, St Austell PL26 7DP* T: (01726) 72679 E: marionstmewan@btinternet.com

BARRETT, Matthew Edward John. b 73. Ripon Coll Cuddesdon BTh 18. **d** 13 **p** 14. C Guernsey St Michel du Valle *Win* 13–16; R Guernsey St Peter Port from 16; V Guernsey St Jo from 16. *St John's Vicarage, Les Amballes, St Peter Port, Guernsey GY1 1WY* T: (01481) 720879 E: revmatthewbarrett@gmail.com

BARRETT, Paul. *See* BARRETT, Christopher Paul

BARRETT, Mrs Rachel Jeanne Alexandra. b 56. Ex Univ BA 78 MA 96 PGCE 79. SWMTC 92. **d** 95 **p** 96. NSM Ex St Mark, St Sidwell and St Matt 95–99; Chapl St Margaret's Sch Ex 99–05; Chapl Derby High Sch 05–16; rtd 16; PtO *Bris* from 17. *51 Barter Close, Kingswood, Bristol BS15 8JN* E: raebarrett@aol.com

BARRETT, Robert David. b 48. Linc Sch of Th and Min 08. **d** 11 **p** 12. OLM Alford w Rigsby *Linc* 11–18; OLM Well 11–18; OLM Saleby w Beesby and Maltby 11–18; OLM Bilsby w Farlesthorpe 11–18; OLM Hannah cum Hagnaby w Markby 11–18; OLM Willoughby 13–18. *14 East Street, Alford LN13 9EQ* T: (01507) 462135 E: revd.bob@btinternet.com

BARRETT, Ronald Reginald. b 30. Roch Th Coll 61. **d** 64 **p** 65. C Spring Park *Cant* 64–66; C Thornton Heath St Jude 66–68; V Greengates *Bradf* 68–73; V Shelf 73–79; V Embsay w Eastby 79–87; V Farndon and Coddington *Ches* 87–92; rtd 92; PtO *Bradf* 92–10; *Man* 10–13; *Sheff* from 13. *27A Kenwood Park Road, Sheffield S7 1NE* E: revrb30@gmail.com

BARRETT, Mrs Susan Lesley. b 56. E Sussex Coll of HE CertEd 77 BEd 78. WMMTC 03. **d** 06. NSM Bowbrook N *Worc* 06–07; NSM Droitwich Spa 07–10; NSM Ombersley w Doverdale 10–14; NSM Hartlebury 10–14; NSM Elmley Lovett w Hampton Lovett and Elmbridge etc 10–14; PtO 14–16; NSM Bowbrook N 16–17; NSM Bowbrook S 16–17; NSM Stoke Prior, Wychbold and Upton Warren 16–17; NSM Cleobury Mortimer w Hopton Wafers etc *Heref* from 17. *Little Detton, Cleobury Mortimer, Kidderminster DY14 8LW* T: (01299) 513211 M: 07825-030607

BARRETT, Victoria Louise. b 64. Ripon Coll Cuddesdon 15. **d** 17 **p** 18. C Bunbury and Tilstone Fearnall *Ches* 17–19; V Thornton Hough from 19. *54 Neston Road, Thornton Hough, Wirral CH63 1JF* T: 0151-336 2766 E: revvickybarrett@gmail.com *or* vicar@allsaintsth.org.uk

BARRETT FORD, Mrs Carol Mary. b 67. NUI BA 88 HDipEd 89 Lon Inst of Educn MA 07 St Jo Coll Dur BA 13. Cranmer Hall Dur 11. **d** 13 **p** 14. C Cowgate *Newc* 13–16; Chapl St Jo Coll Cam 16–19; V Kentish Town St Martin w St Andr *Lon* from 19. *St Martin's Vicarage, 26 Vicars Road, London NW5 4NL* E: vicar@stmartinsnw5.org

BARRIBAL, Richard James Pitt. b 45. Trin Coll Bris. **d** 80 **p** 81. C Northampton St Giles *Pet* 80–82; V Long Buckby w Watford 82–86; PtO 86–00; *Leic* 00–08; P-in-c Welham, Glooston and Cranoe and Stonton Wyville 08–10; PtO from 14. *The Thatched House, 6 Church Bank, Great Easton, Market Harborough LE16 8SN* T: (01536) 772127 E: richard.barribal@btinternet.com

BARRIE, John Arthur. b 38. K Coll Lon 58 Bps' Coll Cheshunt 59. **d** 63 **p** 64. C Southgate St Mich *Lon* 63–66; CF 66–88; Sen CF 88–93; Chapl Guards Chpl Lon 88–92; QHC 91–93; P-in-c Heref H Trin 93–96; P-in-c Breinton 95–96; V St Marylebone St Mark Hamilton Terrace *Lon* 96–10; Ecum Adv Two Cities Area 99–10; rtd 10; PtO *Lon* from 10. *The Vicarage, 4 Beaudesert Mews, West Drayton UB7 7PE* T: (01895) 442194 E: rosybarrie1@btinternet.com *or* john.barrie@london.anglican.org

BARRIE (née HEITZMANN), Mrs Pamela. b 58. Open Univ BA 90 Kingston Univ MA 05. STETS 09. **d** 12 **p** 13. NSM Shepperton and Littleton *Lon* 12–20; rtd 20. *131A Laleham Road, Staines TW18 2EG* M: 07806-762745 E: pamelabarrie3284@hotmail.co.uk

BARRIE, Mrs Rosemary Joan. b 62. Bris Univ BA 83 PGCE 84. Qu Coll Birm 87 Perkins Sch of Th (USA) 89. **d** 07 **p** 08. NSM W Kilburn St Luke and Kilburn St Mary w All So and W Hampstead St Jas *Lon* 07–08; NSM St Marylebone St Mark Hamilton Terrace 08–10; C Twickenham St Mary 10–13; Chapl St Mary's Sch Twickenham 10–13; V W Drayton *Lon* from 13. *The Vicarage, 4 Beaudesert Mews, West Drayton UB7 7PE* T: (01895) 442194 E: rosybarrie1@btinternet.com

BARRINGTON, The Very Revd Dominic Matthew Jesse. b 62. Hatf Coll Dur BA 84 MSc 85 LTCL. Ripon Coll Cuddesdon BA 94 MA 98 Ch Div Sch of Pacific MTS 95. **d** 95 **p** 96. C Mortlake w E Sheen *S'wark* 95–98; Chapl St Chad's Coll Dur 98–03; P-in-c Kettering SS Pet and Paul 03–10; R 10–15; Dean Chicago USA from 15. *St James Cathedral, 65 East Huron Street, Chicago IL 60611-2728, USA* T: (001) (312) 622 6808 M: 07720-704953 E: dean@saintjamescathedral.org

BARROCCU, Phillip Nicholas. b 52. **d** 20 **p** 21. NSM Bro Aman *St D* from 20. *Meadowbank, 8 Waungron Road, Ammanford SA18 2HU* T: (01269) 596316 E: nick.barroccu@btinternet.com

BARRON, Arthur Henry. b 45. Solicitor 72. SEITE 99. **d** 02 **p** 03. NSM Addiscombe St Mary Magd w St Martin *S'wark* 02–06; Chapl Asst St Mary's NHS Trust Paddington 05–09; Chapl Guy's and St Thos' NHS Foundn Trust 09–12; rtd 12; PtO *S'wark* 06–07 and from 15; NSM Woodmansterne 07–15; Hon Min Can S'wark Cathl from 13; PtO *Lon* 17–18; *Chich* from 19. *53 Seal Road, Selsey, Chichester PO20 0HU* M: 07710-275977 E: thebarrons23lwl@hotmail.com

BARRON, John William. b 66. Imp Coll Lon BSc 88. Cranmer Hall Dur 06. **d** 08 **p** 09. C Whickham *Dur* 08–11; V High Spen and Rowlands Gill 11–19; P-in-c Houghton le

Spring from 19. *The Rectory, 5 Lingfield, Houghton le Spring DH5 8QA* T: 0191-584 7657 E: jwbarron@btinternet.com

BARRON, Kurt Karl. b 60. Chich Th Coll BTh 92. **d** 92 **p** 93. C Bulwell St Mary *S'well* 92–97; TV Southend *Chelmsf* 97–01; P-in-c Mansfield St Lawr *S'well* 01–08; PtO from 19. *Address temp unknown* E: kurt.barron1@gmail.com

BARRON, Leslie Gill. b 44. ACII 69. Lich Th Coll 67. **d** 70 **p** 71. C Bishopwearmouth Ch Ch *Dur* 70–72; C Bishopwearmouth St Mary V w St Pet Coll CD 72–75; C Harton 75–77; V Lumley 77–88; P-in-c Hendon and Sunderland 88–90; R Hendon 90–94; P-in-c Ushaw Moor 94–95; V Bearpark and Ushaw Moor 95–04; PtO from 04; rtd 08. *34 Brecongill Close, Hartlepool TS24 8PH* T: (01429) 291197 E: l.barron7@ntlworld.com

BARRON, Richard Davidson. b 51. Lon Univ BSc 74. Trin Coll Bris 75. **d** 78 **p** 79. C Bradley *Wakef* 78–81; C Heworth H Trin *York* 81–82; TV 82–89; Chapl York Distr Hosp 82–86; R Greenhithe St Mary *Roch* 89–12; R Fairlight and Pett *Chich* 12–20; rtd 20. *Cobb House, 56 Manor Road, Worthing BN11 4SQ* E: rbarron100@yahoo.co.uk

BARRON, Mrs Sonia Patricia. b 55. Lon Univ BEd 80 Nottm Univ MA 00. St Mellitus Coll 08. **d** 11 **p** 12. C Chilwell *S'well* 11–14; R Claypole *Linc* 14–19; RD Loveden 14–19; Dioc Dir of Ords from 19; PtO *S'well* from 20. *55 Lucknow Drive, Nottingham NG3 5EJ* E: sonia.barron@lincoln.anglican.org

BARRON, Ms Sylvia. b 50. Maria Grey Coll Lon CertEd 72. All SS Cen for Miss & Min 11. **d** 14 **p** 15. NSM Spotland and Oakenrod *Man* from 14. *35 Holstein Avenue, Rochdale OL12 6DL* T: (01706) 658766 E: barronsylvia@yahoo.co.uk

BARROW, Christine. *See* BARROW, Margaret Christine

BARROW, Mrs Evelyne. b 68. Yorks Min Course 12. **d** 15 **p** 16. NSM Upper Holme Valley *Leeds* 15–20; NSM High Hoyland, Scissett and Clayton W from 20; NSM Skelmanthorpe from 20. *17 Windmill Hill Lane, Emley Moor, Huddersfield HD8 9TP* T: (01924) 848070 E: esb44@icloud.com

BARROW, Gillian Stephanie. *See* BARROW-JONES, Gillian Stephanie

BARROW, Jack Alexander. b 81. St Andr Univ BSc 03 MLitt 07 Heythrop Coll Lon MA 18. Ripon Coll Cuddesdon BA 12 MA 17. **d** 13 **p** 14. C Frodingham and New Brumby *Linc* 13–14; C Gt and Lt Coates w Bradley 14–17; TV Mortlake w E Sheen *S'wark* from 17; Dioc Voc Adv from 18; AD Richmond and Barnes from 20. *All Saints' Vicarage, 86 East Sheen Avenue, London SW14 8AU* T: (020) 8876 5801 M: 07971-669587 E: alexbarrow1@gmail.com

BARROW (*née* DONSON), Mrs Margaret Christine. b 44. Homerton Coll Cam CertEd 65. Westcott Ho Cam 08. **d** 09 **p** 10. NSM Girton *Ely* 09–14; NSM Madingley 12–14; PtO from 14. *2 Cockerton Road, Girton, Cambridge CB3 0QW* T: (01223) 575089 E: mcbarrow@mac.com

BARROW, Paul Beynon. b 48. Liv Univ LLB 69 Man Univ MA 01. St Steph Ho Ox 02. **d** 04 **p** 05. NSM Ches H Trin 04–05; P-in-c Hargrave 05–11; V 11–13; rtd 13; PtO *St As* 15–19; *Ches* from 16; *Lich* from 19. *Keepers Cottage, Eyton, Wrexham LL13 0SN* T: (01978) 781534 M: 07792-154388

BARROW-JONES, Mrs Gillian Stephanie. Regent's Park Coll Ox BA 98. Westcott Ho Cam 08. **d** 10 **p** 11. C Gainsborough and Morton *Linc* 10–13; R Wolverton *Ox* from 13. *Holy Trinity House, 28 Harvester Close, Greenleys, Milton Keynes MK12 6LE*

BARRY, Colin Lionel. b 49. Open Univ BSc 94. Bp Attwell Tr Inst 85. **d** 96 **p** 97. NSM Arbory *S & M* 96–13; NSM Arbory and Castletown from 13. *80 Ballabrooie Crescent, Ballabeg, Castletown, Isle of Man IM9 4ER* T: (01624) 823080

BARRY, Ms Jacqueline Françoise. Univ of Bordeaux II LSocEth 86 MSoc 87 York Univ PGCE 91. Ridley Hall Cam. **d** 99 **p** 00. C Sydenham H Trin *S'wark* 99–03; C W Kilburn St Luke w St Simon and St Jude *Lon* 03–13; C Paddington Em Harrow Road 03–13; C W Kilburn St Luke and Harrow Road Em from 13. *Emmanuel Vicarage, 44C Fermoy Road, London W9 3NH* T: (020) 8969 0438 E: jackiefbarry@yahoo.co.uk

BARRY, Jonathan Peter Oulton. b 47. TCD BA 70 MA 73 Hull Univ BA 73 QUB PhD 84. Ripon Hall Ox 73. **d** 74 **p** 75. C Dundela St Mark *D & D* 74–79; I Ballyphilip w Ardquin 79–85; Dioc Info Officer 80–90; I Comber 85–01; Preb St Audoen St Patr Cathl Dublin 01–18; rtd 18. *32 Magheraknock Park, Ballynahinch BT24 8FG* M: 07754-508587 E: jpobarry@icloud.com

BARRY, Nicholas Brian Paul. b 61. Leic Univ BA 83. St Steph Ho Ox 84. **d** 87 **p** 88. C St John's Wood *Lon* 87–90; Chapl RAF 90–15; Dep Chapl-in-Chief 09–15; QHC 09–15; V Jersey St Luke w St Jas *Win* from 15. *Longueville Farm, Longueville Road, St Saviour, Jersey JE2 7WG* T: (01534) 851445 E: frnickbarry@gmail.com

BARRY, Ruth Mary. b 79. Bris Univ BSc 01 Darwin Coll Cam PhD 07. Ridley Hall Cam 17. **d** 19 **p** 20. C Cherry

Hinton St Andr *Ely* from 19. *39 Eland Way, Cambridge CB1 9XQ* M: 07808-165121 E: ruth.barry@yahoo.co.uk

BARSLEY, Canon Margaret Ann. b 39. Totley Hall Coll CertEd 60. EMMTC 79. **dss** 83 **d** 87 **p** 94. Kirton in Holland *Linc* 83–89; NSM 87–89; NSM Skirbeck Quarter 89–96; P-in-c Swineshead 96–99; V 99–04; RD Holland W 97–04; Can and Preb Linc Cathl from 00; rtd 04. *44 Sentance Crescent, Kirton, Boston PE20 1XF* T: (01205) 723824

BARTER, Christopher Stuart. b 49. Chich Th Coll. **d** 84 **p** 85. C Margate St Jo *Cant* 84–88; V Whitwood and Chapl Castleford, Normanton and Distr Hosp 88–95; P-in-c Ravensthorpe *Wakef* 95–98; AIDS Cllr W Yorks HA 95–98; TV Gt Yarmouth *Nor* 98–02; R Somersham w Pidley and Oldhurst *Ely* 02–10; V Somersham w Pidley and Oldhurst and Woodhurst 10–13; P-in-c Holywell w Needingworth 07–08; RD St Ives 06–10; rtd 13; PtO *Ely* from 14. *Address temp unknown* E: eandm477@btinternet.com

BARTER, The Very Revd Donald. b 34. St Fran Coll Brisbane ThL 69 ACT ThSchol 74. **d** 69 **p** 70. C Townsville Australia 69–72; R Mareeba 72–76; R Ingham 76–81; Adn of the W and R Mt Isa 81–86; Dean Townsville 86–90; Chapl Miss to Seamen 86–90; Appeals Dir SPCK 90–93; LtO *Leic* 90–93; Australia from 93; Asst to Dean St Jas Cathl 94–00. *49 Macrossan Street, South Townsville Qld 4810, Australia* T/F: (0061) (7) 4772 7036 M: 414-989593 E: dba18613@bigpond.net.au

BARTER, Geoffrey Roger. b 41. Bris Univ BSc 63. Clifton Th Coll 65. **d** 67 **p** 68. C Normanton *Derby* 67–70; C Rainham *Chelmsf* 70–75; V Plumstead St Jo w St Jas and St Paul *S'wark* 75–82; V Frogmore *St Alb* 82–01; rtd 01; PtO *Chich* from 02. *45 West Front Road, Pagham, Bognor Regis PO21 4SZ* T: (01243) 262522 E: geoff.barter@gmail.com

BARTER, Susan Kathleen. Open Univ MBA 97 Anglia Ruskin Univ MA 09. Ridley Hall Cam 01. **d** 03 **p** 04. C Happisburgh, Walcott, Hempstead w Eccles etc *Nor* 03–06; C Bacton w Edingthorpe w Witton and Ridlington 04–06; C Ward End w Bordesley Green *Birm* 06–21; Chapl Whiteley Village Walton-on-Thames from 21. *Whiteley Homes Trust, Eliza Palmer Hub, Octagon Road, Whiteley Village, Hersham, Walton-on-Thames KT12 4ES* T: (01932) 842360 M: 07778-063644

BARTHOLOMEW, David Grant. b 50. Univ of Wales (Lamp) BA 77. Chich Th Coll 91. **d** 93 **p** 94. C Petersfield *Portsm* 93–96; R Etton w Helpston and Maxey *Pet* 96–98; R Burghclere w Newtown and Ecchinswell w Sydmonton *Win* 98–19; rtd 20; PtO *Win* from 20. *6A Rokeby Close, Newbury RG14 7UE* E: davidrectory@twang.co.uk

BARTLEM, Gregory John. b 68. Ox Brookes Univ BA 05. Qu Coll Birm 07. **d** 09 **p** 10. NSM Cheylesmore *Cov* 09–11; C Cov Cathl 11–18; R Walton d'Eiville from 18; V Wellesbourne from 18. *St Peter's Vicarage, Church Street, Wellesbourne, Warwick CV35 9LS* M: 07414-675159 E: gregjbartlem@gmail.com

BARTLETT, Aidan Dominic. b 84. Van Mildert Coll Dur BA 07. St Steph Ho Ox BA 18. **d** 18 **p** 20. C Clerkenwell H Redeemer *Lon* from 18; C Clerkenwell St Mark from 18. *24 Exmouth Market, London EC1R 4QE* T: (020) 7837 1861 E: fr.aidan.bartlett@gmail.com

BARTLETT, Canon Alan Bennett. b 58. G&C Coll Cam BA 81 MA 85 Birm Univ PhD 87 St Jo Coll Dur BA 90. Cranmer Hall Dur 88. **d** 91 **p** 92. C Newc H Cross 91–94; C Newburn 94–96; Tutor Cranmer Hall Dur 96–08; V Dur St Giles 08–17; P-in-c Shadforth and Sherburn 08–17; Min Development Adv from 17; Hon Can Dur Cathl from 11. *Diocese of Durham, Cuthbert House, Stonebridge, Durham DH1 3RY* T: 0191-374 6012 M: 07384-214576 E: alan.bartlett@durham.anglican.org

BARTLETT, Anthony Martin. b 43. Cranmer Hall Dur 74. **d** 77 **p** 78. C Heworth St Mary *Dur* 77–80; V Cleadon 80–84; CF (TA) 81–90; Prec Dur Cathl 85–87; V Harton 87–95; P-in-c Hendon 95–96; R 96–97; V Greenlands *Blackb* 01–12; rtd 12; PtO *Blackb* 12–19. *3 Keats Close, Thornton-Cleveleys FY5 2SA* T: (01253) 273471 E: bcressell@aol.com

BARTLETT, David John. b 36. Pemb Coll Ox BA 61. Linc Th Coll 63. **d** 65 **p** 66. C Wollaton *S'well* 65–70; V Woodthorpe 70–83; V Farnsfield 83–01; P-in-c Kirklington w Hockerton 83–01; RD S'well 83–93; Chapl Rodney Sch Kirklington 83–01; rtd 01; PtO *S'well* from 01. *6 De Havilland Way, Farndon Road, Newark NG24 4RF* T: (01636) 651582

BARTLETT, David William. b 59. Trin Coll Bris 89. **d** 91 **p** 92. C Frinton *Chelmsf* 91–95; TV Eston w Normanby *York* 95–96; Assoc P Worksop St Jo *S'well* 96–01; TV Trunch *Nor* 01–14; P-in-c Overstrand, Northrepps, Sidestrand etc 12–14; R Bardney *Linc* 14–21; P-in-c Wiske Benefice *Leeds* from 21. *New Rectory, Great Smeaton, Northallerton DL6 2EP* E: revdb@btinternet.com

BARTLETT, Ms Jane Louise. b 63. Warwick Univ BA 84 Win Univ MA 10. St Mellitus Coll BA 17. **d** 17 **p** 18. C New

Shoreham and Shoreham Beach *Chich* from 17. *The Vicarage, West Beach, Shoreham-by-Sea BN43 5GL* M: 07935-538085 E: bartlett.jane@ntlworld.com

BARTLETT, Prof John Raymond. b 37. BNC Ox BA 59 MA 62 BLitt 62 TCD MA 70 LittD 94. Linc Th Coll 61. d 63 p 64. C W Bridgford *S'well* 63–64; Lect Div TCD 66–86; Assoc Prof Bibl Studies 86–92; Fell 75–92; Prof Past Th 90–01; Prin CITC 89–01; Treas Ch Ch Cathl Dublin *D & G* 86–88; Prec 88–01; rtd 01. *102 Sorrento Road, Dalkey, Co Dublin, Republic of Ireland* T: (00353) (1) 284 7786 E: jrbartlett@eircom.net

BARTLETT, Kenneth Vincent John. b 36. OBE 93. Oriel Coll Ox BA 61 BTh 63. Ripon Hall Ox 61. d 63 p 64. C Paddington St Jas *Lon* 63–67; LtO from 67; rtd 01. *25 Tudor Road, Kingston-upon-Thames KT2 6AS* T: (020) 8974 5453 E: ken.bartlett3@btinternet.com

BARTLETT, Michael Fredrick. b 52. Ex Univ BA 74 Liv Univ BPhil 75. Ven English Coll Rome 78 Ripon Coll Cuddesdon BA 79 MA. d 79 p 80. C Kirkby *Liv* 79–82; C Wordsley *Lich* 82–83; TV 83–88; Chapl Wordsley Hosp 82–88; TV Redditch, The Ridge *Worc* 88–05; TR Redditch Ch the K 05–20; rtd 20. *47 Myton Drive, Shirley, Solihull B90 1HD* T: 0121-574 1476

BARTLETT, Canon Richard Charles. b 68. St Kath Coll Liv BA 90 Surrey Univ MA 01. Westcott Ho Cam 91. d 94 p 95. C Wareham *Sarum* 94–98; Assoc V Ealing All SS *Lon* 98–02; Chapl Twyford C of E High Sch Acton 98–02; USPG Brazil 02–05; Hon Can Brasilia Cathl from 05; V Northwood H Trin *Lon* 05–16; AD Harrow 07–13; PtO from 16; *St Alb* from 16; Dir Miss Engagement USPG from 16; Public Preacher *S'wark* from 16. *USPG, Rise House, 5 Trinity Street, London SE1 1DB* T: (020) 7921 2236 M: 07711-701910 E: richardb@uspg.org.uk

BARTON, Andrew Edward. b 53. St Jo Coll Ox MA 77 DPhil 80 Idaho Univ MTh 06 MRSC. Ridley Hall Cam 87. d 90 p 91. C Ringwood *Win* 90–94; R Baughurst, Ramsdell, Wolverton w Ewhurst etc 95–07; Lect K Alfred's Coll Win 95–98; R Auchterarder and Muthill *St And* 07–14; Chapl N Police Convalescent Homes 07–14; P-in-c Headley All SS *Guildf* 14–18; R 18–21; rtd 21; LtO Adelaide Australia from 09. *Address withheld by request* E: james.kessog@gmail.com

BARTON, Canon Arthur Michael. b 33. CCC Cam BA 57 MA 61. Wycliffe Hall Ox 57. d 59 p 60. Min Can Bradf Cathl 59–61; C Maltby *Sheff* 61–63; V Silsden *Bradf* 63–70; V Moor Allerton *Ripon* 70–81; TR 81–82; V Wetherby 82–98; Chapl HM YOI Wetherby 82–89; RD Harrogate *Ripon* 88–95; Hon Can Ripon Cathl 89–98; rtd 98; PtO *Ripon* 98–14; *Leeds* from 14. *42 Church Square Mansions, Church Square, Harrogate HG1 4SS* T: (01423) 520105 E: teambarton@btinternet.com

BARTON, The Ven Charles John Greenwood. b 36. ALCD 63. d 63 p 64. C Cant St Mary Bredin 63–66; V Whitfield w W Langdon 66–75; V S Kensington St Luke *Lon* 75–83; AD Chelsea 80–83; Chief Broadcasting Officer for C of E 83–90; Adn Aston *Birm* 90–03; Can Res Birm Cathl 90–02; P-in-c Bickenhill 02–03; rtd 03; PtO *Cant* from 03; Abp's Communications Adv *York* 05–06; Acting Prin Adv to Abp *York* 07; Abp's Chapl and Researcher 08. *7 The Spires, Canterbury CT2 8SD* M: 07743-118544 E: venjohnbarton@gmail.com

BARTON, Dale. b 49. Selw Coll Cam BA 71 MA 76. Linc Th Coll 71. d 73 p 74. C Gosforth All SS *Newc* 73–77; Lesotho 77–81; Dep Warden CA Hostel Cam 82–83; C Shepton Mallet w Doulting *B & W* 83–88; TV Preston St Steph *Blackb* 88–96; V 96–99; Bp's Adv on Inter-Faith Relns 99–07; P-in-c Bradf St Clem 07–14; *Leeds* 14–16; P-in-c Bradf St Aug Undercliffe 07–14; *Leeds* 14–16; rtd 16; PtO *Leeds* from 17. *84 Park Road, Bingley BD16 4EJ* T: (01274) 297419 M: 07871-992324 E: dale.barton720@gmail.com

BARTON, David Gerald Story. b 38. Selw Coll Cam BA 62 MA 66. Cuddesdon Coll 63. d 65 p 66. C Cowley St Jas *Ox* 65–67; C Hambleden 67–70; Hon C Hammersmith St Jo *Lon* 72–77; Hon C Paddington St Jas 77–81; Hd Master Soho Par Sch 81–88; Hon C Westmr St Jas *Lon* 81–92; RE Project Officer Lon Dioc Bd for Schs 88–92; Dioc Schs Adv *Ox* 93–99; rtd 00; Warden Sisters of the Love of God Ox 01–09; Hon C Iffley *Ox* 93–06; PtO 06–09 and from 18. *254 Iffley Road, Oxford OX4 1SE* T: (01865) 240059 E: daviebarton@aol.com or davidbarton254@gmail.com

BARTON, Canon Geoffrey. b 27. Oriel Coll Ox BA 48 MA 52. Chich Th Coll 49. d 51 p 52. C Arnold *S'well* 51–53; C E Retford 53–54; V Hatfield Eastthorpe St Paul *Wakef* 54–60; V Boroughbridge w Roecliffe *Ripon* 60–73; V Aldborough w Boroughbridge and Roecliffe 73; P-in-c Farnham w Scotton and Staveley and Copgrove 73–74; R 74–77; Chapl Roundway Hosp Devizes 77–92; Can and Preb Sarum Cathl 86–92; rtd 92; PtO *Sarum* 01–10. *4B Willow House, Downlands Road, Devizes SN10 5EA* T: (01380) 725311

BARTON (née CRABB), Helen Maria. b 56. Lon Bible Coll BA 83 St Jo Coll Dur MA 04 St Mary's Coll Strawberry Hill PGCE 98. Cranmer Hall Dur 01. d 03 p 04. C Wisley w Pyrford *Guildf* 03–04; C Lanchester *Dur* 04–06; C Hexham *Newc* 06–08; V Widdrington 08–15; P-in-c Barlaston *Lich* 15–16; Master St Jo Hosp Lich 16–21. *1 Seckham Road, Lichfield WS13 7AN* E: helen@the-bartons.com

BARTON, Prof John. b 48. Keble Coll Ox BA 69 MA 73 Mert Coll Ox DPhil 74 St Cross Coll Ox DLitt 88. d 73 p 73. Jun Research Fell Mert Coll Ox 73–74; Lect St Cross Coll Ox 74–89; Fell 74–91; Chapl 79–91; Lect Th Ox Univ 74–89; Reader 89–91; Oriel and Laing Prof of Interpr of H Scripture from 91; Fell Oriel Coll Ox from 91; Can Th Win Cathl 91–03; PtO *Ox* from 18. *11 Withington Court, Abingdon OX14 3QA* T: (01235) 525925 E: john.barton@oriel.ox.ac.uk

BARTON, John. *See* BARTON, Charles John Greenwood

BARTON, John Michael. b 40. TCD BA 62 Div Test. d 63 p 64. C Coleraine *Conn* 63–68; C Portadown St Mark *Arm* 68–71; I Carnteel and Crilly 71–83; I Derryloran 83–97; Bp's C Acton and Drumbanagher 97–09; Can Arm Cathl 94–09; Treas 98–01; Chan Arm Cathl 01–09; rtd 09. *23 Strand Cottages, Sheskburn Avenue, Ballycastle BT54 6HR* T: (028) 2076 9673 E: jm7mabarton@talktalk.net

BARTON, Mrs Margaret Ann Edith. b 48. Newc Univ BA 71. EMMTC 95. d 98 p 99. NSM Castle Bytham w Creeton *Linc* 98–04; P-in-c Corby Glen 04–12; rtd 12; PtO *Linc* from 13. *Blanchland House, 15 Swinstead Road, Corby Glen, Grantham NG33 4NU* T: (01476) 550763

BARTON, Michael. *See* BARTON, Arthur Michael

BARTON, Michael James. b 78. Sheff Univ MEng 01 Man Univ BSc 06. Wycliffe Hall Ox 11. d 13 p 14. C Claygate *Guildf* 13–17; V Longridge *Blackb* from 17. *The Vicarage, Church Street, Longridge, Preston PR3 3WA* M: 07866-508697 E: revmikebarton@gmail.com

BARTON, Paul Michael Benson. b 60. d 14 p 15. NSM Torquay St Matthias, St Mark and H Trin *Ex* from 14. *Rowdale, Ridge Road, Maidencombe, Torquay TQ1 4TD* T: (01803) 327504 E: revpaulbarton@gmail.com

BARTON (née McVEIGH), Canon Sandra. b 58. Reading Univ BA 80. Cranmer Hall Dur 93. d 95 p 96. C Stranton *Dur* 95–98; P-in-c Blackhall, Castle Eden and Monkhesleden 98–99; R 99–02; PtO *Blackb* 02–06; *Ely* 06–10; *St E* 08–11; C Mildenhall 11–20; Dioc Environment Officer 17–20; Hon Can St E Cathl 15–20; rtd 20; PtO *St E* from 21. *The Old Village Stores, 6 The Street, Freckenham, Bury St Edmunds IP28 8HZ* T: (01638) 720048 E: revsandiebarton@gmail.com

BARTON, Stephen Christian. b 52. Macquarie Univ (NSW) BA 75 DipEd 75 Lanc Univ MA 78 K Coll Lon PhD 92. Cranmer Hall Dur 91. d 93 p 94. NSM Neville's Cross St Jo CD *Dur* 93–00; NSM Dur St Marg and Neville's Cross St Jo 00–06; PtO *Newc* 06–15; *Lich* from 15. *1 Seckham Road, Lichfield WS13 7AN* E: stephen@the-bartons.com

BARTON, Trevor James. b 50. St Alb Minl Tr Scheme 79. d 87 p 88. NSM Hemel Hempstead *St Alb* from 87. *Address temp unknown* E: trevorbarton@hotmail.com

BARWELL, Brian Bernard Beale. b 30. Preston Poly CertEd 79. AKC 59 St Boniface Warminster 59. d 60 p 61. C Heywood St Jas *Man* 60–63; V Smallbridge 63–69; V Farington *Blackb* 69–72; C-in-c Blackb St Luke w St Phil 72–75; V Standish 75–76; LtO 76–92; rtd 92; PtO *Blackb* 92–11. *70 Claytongate, Coppull, Chorley PR7 4PS* T: (01257) 794251

BARWICK, Lester Mark. b 56. Washington Coll (USA) BA 78. Wesley Th Sem Washington MDiv 89. d 09 p 10. Belgium 09–17; Chapl Strasbourg *Eur* from 17. *15 rue d'Austerlitz, 67000 Strasbourg, France* T: (033) 3 69 57 40 03 E: anglican.chaplaincy.strasbourg@gmail.com or mark.barwick@gmail.com

BARWOOD, Jonathan Paul. b 71. All SS Cen for Miss & Min 17. d 20. NSM Arbory and Castletown *S & M* from 20. *11 Glen Maye Park, Glen Maye, Isle of Man IM5 3AX* M: 07624-233966 E: jon.barwood@sodorandman.im

BASH, Anthony. b 52. Bris Univ LLB 73 LLM 76 Glas Univ BD 88 Clare Hall Cam PhD 96. Westcott Ho Cam 94. d 96 p 97. C Kingston upon Hull H Trin *York* 96–99; V N Ferriby 99–04; Chapl to Legal Profession 97–04; Hon Fell Hull Univ 97–04; Chapl and Fell Univ Coll Dur 05–06; TR Dur N 06–08; Chapl and Tutor Hatf Coll Dur 08–12; Chapl and Vice-Master 12–20; Hon Research Fell Dur Univ 08–15; Hon Prof from 15; PtO from 20. *Address temp unknown* E: anthony.bash@gmail.com

BASHAM, Lawrence David. b 72. Cliff Coll BA 15. St Hild Coll 18. d 20 p 21. C Keswick St Jo w Borrowdale *Carl* from 20. *The Vicarage, Bassenthwaite, Keswick CA12 4QH* M: 07981-001592 E: lawrencebasham@gmail.com

BASHFORD, Robert Thomas. b 49. Ch Coll Cam BA 70 MA 74 Lon Univ BD 84 Wadh Coll Ox PGCE 72. Oak Hill Th Coll

MPhil 89. **d** 88 **p** 89. C Frinton *Chelmsf* 88–91; C Galleywood Common 91–96; V Clapham *St Alb* 96–02; P-in-c Westgate St Jas *Cant* 02–06; V 06–12; rtd 12; PtO *Pet* from 13; *Leic* from 16. *66 Grosvenor Way, Barton Seagrave, Kettering NN15 6TZ* T: (01536) 723056 E: bashford66@outlook.com

BASHFORTH, Canon Alan George. b 64. Ex Univ MA. Ripon Coll Cuddesdon BTh 96. **d** 96 **p** 97. C Calstock *Truro* 96–98; C St Ives 98–01; V St Agnes and Mount Hawke w Mithian 01–14; P-in-c St Clement 12–14; RD Powder 04–12; Hon Can Truro Cathl 13–14; Can Res and Chan Truro Cathl from 14; Hon C Truro St Mary from 15. *The Cathedral Office, 14 St Mary's Street, Truro TR1 2AF* T: (01872) 245012 E: alanbashforth@trurocathedral.org.uk

BASINGSTOKE, Suffragan Bishop of. *See* WILLIAMS, The Rt Revd David Grant

BASKERVILLE, Philip Duncan. b 58. St Chad's Coll Dur BSc 79 Oriel Coll Ox PGCE 80. Trin Coll Bris BA 87. **d** 88 **p** 89. C Roby *Liv* 88–93; Tutor St Paul's Th Coll Kapsabet Kenya 93–98; C Barnston *Ches* 98–05; Chapl St Andr Sch Turi Kenya 05–08; P-in-c Guernsey St Sampson *Win* 08–13; In Bapt Min 13–17; PACE Co-ord Guernsey 17–20; PtO *Cant* from 18. *Sables d'Olonne, Route Isabelle, St Peter Port, Guernsey GY1 1QR* M: 07496-027601 E: philbaskie@live.co.uk

BASON, Carol. b 44. De Montfort Univ BSc 96. **d** 09 **p** 10. OLM S Lawres Gp *Linc* from 09. *Walnut Tree Cottage, 15 Church Lane, Reepham, Lincoln LN3 4DQ* T: (01522) 753282 M: 07403-875952 E: cbason@tiscali.co.uk

BASS, Colin Graham. b 41. Liv Univ BSc 62 Fitzw Ho Cam BA 64 MA 68. Ox NSM Course 84. **d** 87 **p** 88. Dir of Studies Leighton Park Sch Reading 87–97; NSM Earley St Pet *Ox* 87–92; NSM Reading Deanery 92–11; PtO 11–21. *9 Bramley Close, Reading RG6 7PL* T: 0118-966 3732 E: colin.bass@cantab.net

BASS, George Michael. b 39. Ely Th Coll 62. **d** 65 **p** 66. C Romaldkirk *Ripon* 65–68; C Kenton Ascension *Newc* 68–71; CF 71–94; Chapl Northumbria Healthcare NHS Trust 95–02; rtd 02; PtO *Newc* from 02. *35 Kelso Drive, North Shields NE29 9NS* T: 0191-258 2514

BASS, Mrs Rosemary Jane. b 38. Linc Th Coll 76. dss 79 **d** 87 **p** 94. Bedford All SS *St Alb* 79–84; Leavesden 84–94; Par Dn 87–94; C 94–95; V Luton St Andr 95–01; rtd 01; PtO *St Alb* from 01. *3 Highfield Road, Oakley, Bedford MK43 7TA* T: (01234) 822126 E: roanj@btinternet.com

BASSETT, Mrs Rosemary Louise. b 42. STETS. **d** 00 **p** 01. NSM The Winterbournes and Compton Valence *Sarum* 00–08; P-in-c 03–08; NSM Dorchester 08–14; rtd 14; PtO *Sarum* from 14. *12 Lime Close, Dorchester DT1 2HQ* T: (01305) 262615 E: rosemary.bassett42@gmail.com

BASTABLE, Richard Michael. b 83. Ex Univ BA 04 St Edm Coll Cam MPhil 08. Westcott Ho Cam 06. **d** 08 **p** 09. C Ruislip St Martin *Lon* 08–10; C St Andr Holborn 10–13; V Hammersmith St Luke from 13. *St Luke's Vicarage, 450 Uxbridge Road, London W12 0NS* T: (020) 8749 7523 M: 07816-074597 E: rbastable@gmail.com

BASTEN, Richard Henry. b 40. Codrington Coll Barbados 60. **d** 63 **p** 64. Br Honduras 63–67; Barbados 68–72; C Hartlepool H Trin *Dur* 72–73; Chapl Bedstone Coll 73–88; C Clun w Chapel Lawn *Heref* 73–77; P-in-c Clungunford 77–78; R Clungunford w Clunbury and Clunton, Bedstone etc 78–88; R Rowde and Poulshot *Sarum* 88–95; rtd 95; PtO *Glouc* 95–12. *41 Bewley Way, Churchdown, Gloucester GL3 2DU* T: (01452) 859738

BASTON, The Ven Caroline Jane. b 56. Birm Univ BSc 78 CertEd 79. Ripon Coll Cuddesdon 87. **d** 89 **p** 94. Par Dn Southampton Thornhill St Chris *Win* 89–94; C 94–95; R Win All SS w Chilcomb and Chesil 95–06; Dioc Communications Officer 95–98; Dioc Dir of Ords 99–06; Hon Can Win Cathl 00–06; Adn Is of Wight *Portsm* 06–11; P-in-c N Swindon St Andr *Bris* 11–16; Warden CSMV from 13; PtO *Ox* 13–21; Warden Community of Hopeweavers from 15; PtO *Win* 16–19; P-in-c Fawley 19–21; Master St Nic Hosp Salisbury from 21. *The Master's House, St Nicholas Hospital, 5 St Nicholas Road, Salisbury SP1 2SW* T: (01722) 340369 M: 07780-877895 E: cjbaston17@gmail.com

BATCHELOR, Andrew George. b 59. St Jo Coll Nottm 07. **d** 09 **p** 10. C Ulverston St Mary w H Trin *Carl* 09–13; V Walney Is 13–20; P-in-c Barrow St Jo 18–20; P-in-c Harbury and Ladbroke *Cov* from 20; P-in-c Ufton from 20. *The Rectory, 2 Vicarage Lane, Harbury, Leamington Spa CV33 9HA* T: (01926) 612377 M: 07934-483439 E: rev.andyb@gmail.com

BATCHELOR, John Millar. CITC 76. **d** 78 **p** 79. C Belfast All SS *Conn* 78–80; I Eglish w Killylea *Arm* 80–96; I Ballyhalbert w Ardkeen *D & D* 96–01; rtd 01. *Rhone Brae, 102 Eglish Road, Dungannon BT70 1LB* T: (028) 8775 0177 E: jm_batchelor@outlook.com

BATCHELOR, Canon Martin John. b 67. Plymouth Poly BSc 91. St Jo Coll Nottm MA 95. **d** 95 **p** 96. C Brecon St Mary and Battle w Llanddew *S & B* 95–97; Min Can Brecon Cathl 95–97; C Sketty 97–00; TV Hawarden *St As* 00–05; V Bistre 05–16; I Borderlands Miss Area from 17; AD Hawarden from 10; Can Cursal St As Cathl from 19. *Bistre Vicarage, Mold Road, Buckley CH7 2NH* T: (01244) 550947 E: martinbtchlr@gmail.com

BATCHELOR, Michael Patrick. b 55. Qu Coll Birm 11. **d** 13 **p** 14. OLM Willenhall St Steph *Lich* from 13. *24 Rockland Gardens, Willenhall WV13 3HP* T: (01902) 606615 E: m.batchelor922@btinternet.com

BATCHELOR, Veronica. b 69. **d** 10 **p** 11. NSM Forest and Avon *Sarum* from 10. *Arwood, Hale Purlieu, Fordingbridge SP6 2NN* T: (01725) 513878 E: batchelor446@btinternet.com

BATCHFORD, Canon Philip John. b 71. Sheff Univ BA 99. Ridley Hall Cam 00. **d** 02 **p** 03. C Sheff St Mary Bramall Lane 02–05; V Netherthorpe St Steph 05–13; P-in-c Sheff St Bart 11–13; V Sheffield Vine 13–17; C Rotherham 13–17; C Rotherham 17–19; V from 19; C Masbrough 17–19; P-in-c from 19; AD Rotherham from 20; Hon Can Sheff Cathl from 21. *St Paul's Vicarage, 256 Kimberworth Road, Rotherham S61 1HG* T: (01709) 325781 E: phil.batchford@sheffield.anglican.org

BATCOCK, Neil Gair. b 53. UEA BA 74. Westcott Ho Cam 94. **d** 96 **p** 97. C Barton upon Humber *Linc* 96–99; TV Totnes w Bridgetown, Berry Pomeroy etc *Ex* 99–06; P-in-c Blakeney w Cley, Wiveton, Glandford etc *Nor* 06–10; R 10–13; P-in-c Walpole St Peter w Walpole St Andrew *Ely* 13–15; P-in-c W Walton 13–15; rtd 15; PtO *Nor* from 15. *104 London Road, King's Lynn PE30 5ES* T: (01553) 768547 M: 07584-070123 E: gair2@aol.com

BATE, Dylan Griffin. b 48. Mon Dioc Tr Scheme 91. **d** 94 **p** 95. NSM Fleur-de-Lis *Mon* 94–96; NSM Bedwellty 96–97; C Pontypool 97–99; C Tenby *St D* 99–02; R Begelly w Ludchurch and Crunwere 02–05; C Risca *Mon* 05–13; rtd 13; PtO from 18. *23 Larch Lane, Tredegar NP22 4FA* T: (01495) 718677

BATE, Preb Lawrence Mark. b 40. Univ Coll Ox BA 63. Coll of Resurr Mirfield 65. **d** 67 **p** 68. C Benwell St Jas *Newc* 67–69; C Monkseaton St Pet 69–72; TV Withycombe Raleigh *Ex* 72–84; RD Aylesbeare 81–84; R Alphington 84–00; RD Christianity 95–99; TV Heavitree w Ex St Paul 00–02; TV Heavitree and St Mary Steps 02–05; Preb Ex Cathl 02–10; rtd 05; PtO *Ex* from 15. *Chapple Court, Kenn, Exeter EX6 7UR* T: (01392) 833485 E: francisurch70@gmail.com

BATE, Michael Keith. b 42. Lich Th Coll 67. **d** 69 **p** 70. C W Bromwich St Jas *Lich* 69–73; C Thornhill *Wakef* 73–76; V Wrenthorpe 76–82; V Upper Gornal *Lich* 82–93; V Upper Gornal *Worc* 93–05; TV Gornal and Sedgley 05–08; Chapl Burton Road Hosp Dudley 82–94; Chapl Dudley Gp of Hosps NHS Trust 94–00; rtd 08; PtO *Lich* 09–21. *44 Wentworth Road, Wolverhampton WV10 8EF*

BATE, Stephen Donald. b 58. Sheff Univ BSc 79 Cov Univ PhD 92 CEng 97 MIET 97. **d** 05 **p** 06. OLM Whitnash *Cov* 05–12; C Stratford-upon-Avon, Luddington etc 12–16; R Albury, Lt Hadham and Much Hadham *St Alb* from 16. *The Rectory, Hightrees, Station Road, Much Hadham SG10 6AX* M: 07773-583356 E: sbate@aol.com

BATEMAN, Adrian. b 61. **d** 14 **p** 15. C Goole *Sheff* 14–15; C Armthorpe 15–17; V Worsbrough Common w Worsbrough St Thos from 17. *St Thomas's Vicarage, 80 Kingwell Road, Worsbrough, Barnsley S70 4HG* M: 07738-536046 E: adrian.bateman@sheffield.anglican.org

BATEMAN, James Edward. b 44. Univ Coll Lon BSc 65. Trin Coll Bris BA 74. **d** 75. C Woodlands *Sheff* 74–77; C Rushden w Newton Bromswold *Pet* 77–84; R Vange *Chelmsf* 84–94; V Southminster 94–01; P-in-c Nazeing and Roydon 01–03; Warden Stacklands Retreat Ho W Kingsdown 03–05; C Rainham *Roch* 05–09; rtd 09; PtO *Pet* 11–14. *11 Ryeburn Way, Wellingborough NN8 3AH* T: (01933) 440106 E: lizandjim.bateman@gmail.com

BATEMAN, Nest Wynne. Univ of Wales (Cardiff) BA 71 CQSW 73. Westcott Ho Cam 08. **d** 09 **p** 10. NSM Lich Cathl 09–17; rtd 17; PtO *Lich* 17–21. *21 Christchurch Lane, Lichfield WS13 8BA* T: (01543) 257681 M: 07729-256364

BATEMAN, Patrick John. b 64. Ches Univ BA 14. St Jo Coll Nottm 99. **d** 01 **p** 02. C Wallington *S'wark* 01–05; P-in-c Chipstead 05–11; R 11–12; V Ilkley All SS *Bradf* 12–14; Leeds 14–18; V Claygate *Guildf* from 18. *The Vicarage, Church Road, Claygate, Esher KT10 0JP* M: 07764-171400

BATEMAN, Richard George. b 46. Cranmer Hall Dur. **d** 82 **p** 83. C Wolviston *Dur* 82–85; C Greenside 85–87; V Newburn *Newc* 87–00; TV Cramlington 00–08; rtd 08; PtO

Dur 08–18; *Worc* from 19. *9 Ripley Road, Stockton-on-Tees TS20 1NX* T: (01642) 356493 E: rgb158@gmail.com

BATEMAN, Rocky. d 17 **p** 18. C Estuary and Mountain Miss Area *St As* from 17. *4 Yr Aber, Holywell CH8 7RN* T: (01352) 386604

BATEMAN, Timothy William. b 91. Regent's Park Coll Ox BA 13. St Mellitus Coll 14. **d** 16 **p** 17. C Ox St Aldate 16–20; C Birm St Luke from 20. *29 Bradshaw Close, Birmingham B15 2DD* M: 07702-088118 E: timothy.bateman1@gmail.com

BATES, Alice Bella Jane. b 54. LMH Ox MA 76. St Aug Coll of Th BA 20. **d** 20 **p** 21. NSM St Peter-in-Thanet *Cant* from 20. *92 Manor Road, Deal CT14 9DB* T: (01304) 268424 M: 07790-903316 E: alicebates2@hotmail.com

BATES, Carol. *See* BATES, Trini Mari Carolina

BATES, David Frederick. b 61. Univ Coll Lon BSc 86 K Coll Lon PGCE 87. St Mellitus Coll BA 15. **d** 15 **p** 16. NSM Mardyke *Chelmsf* 15–19; Chapl Basildon and Thurrock Univ Hosps NHS Foundn Trust from 17; PtO *Chelmsf* from 19. *Basildon University Hospital, Nethermayne, Basildon SS16 5NL* T: (01268) 524900 E: david.bates@btuh.nhs.uk

BATES, Canon Elaine Austwick. b 57. Newc Univ BSc 79 MSc 80 Cumbria Univ BA 12 Lanc Univ PGCE 00. LCTP 06. **d** 10 **p** 11. NSM Barrow St Paul *Carl* from 10; Hon Can Carl Cathl from 18. *17 Harrel Lane, Barrow-in-Furness LA13 9LN* T: (01229) 822149 E: elaine.bates@carlislediocese.org.uk

✠**BATES, The Rt Revd Gordon. b** 34. Kelham Th Coll 54. **d** 58 **p** 59 **c** 83. C New Eltham All SS *S'wark* 58–62; Asst Youth Chapl *Glouc* 62–64; Youth Chapl *Liv* 65–69; Chapl Liv Cathl 65–69; V Huyton St Mich 69–73; Can Res and Prec Liv Cathl 73–83; Dir of Ords 73–83; Suff Bp Whitby *York* 83–99; rtd 99; Hon Asst Bp Carl and Blackb 99–09; NSM Kirkby Lonsdale *Carl* 03–09; Hon Asst Bp York from 12. *116 Turker Lane, Northallerton DL6 1QD* E: gordonbates606@btinternet.com

BATES, James. b 46. Linc Th Coll 73. **d** 75 **p** 76. C Ewell *Guildf* 75–77; C Farncombe 77–80; V Pet St Mary Boongate 80–92; V Kingston All SS w St Jo *S'wark* 92–05; P-in-c Win St Faith w St Cross 05–07; Master St Cross Hosp 05–07; V Offerton *Ches* 07–12; rtd 12. *166 Donaghadee Road, Bangor BT20 4PB* T: (028) 9147 3068 E: bates289@btinternet.com

BATES, James Paul. b 64. QUB BSc PGCE Cranfield Univ MSc MPhil. **d** 06. NSM Bangor Abbey *D & D* 06–07. *16 Craigowen Road, Holywood BT18 0DL* T: (028) 9042 2077 E: paul_tssf@hotmail.com *or* paul-bates@live.co.uk

BATES, Mrs Nichola Jane. b 63. Trin Coll Bris 09. **d** 11 **p** 12. C Freiston, Butterwick w Bennington, and Leverton *Linc* 11–14; C Old Leake w Wrangle 11–14; C Friskney 11–14; C Stamford Ch Ch 14–15; C Stamford St Geo w St Paul 14–15; V Stamford Ch Ch 15–18; V Bestwood Em and St Mark w Rise Park *S'well* from 18. *10 Church View Close, Arnold, Nottingham NG5 9QP* T: 0115-920 8879 E: revnikkibates@gmail.com

BATES, Robert John. b 50. FRICS 81. EAMTC 99. **d** 02 **p** 03. NSM Pet St Mary Boongate 02–05; C Ketton, Collyweston, Easton-on-the-Hill etc 05–09; Chapl Algarve *Eur* 09–14; Chapl Oporto 14–15; rtd 15; PtO *Eur* from 15; *Heref* from 16. *24 Woodfield Gardens, Belmont, Hereford HR2 9RN* T: (01432) 487485 M: 07751-015391 E: frbobbates@gmail.com

BATES, Stuart Geoffrey. b 61. Univ of Wales (Lamp) BA 82 City Univ MSc 11. St Steph Ho Ox 83. **d** 85 **p** 86. C Bromley St Mark *Roch* 85–88; C Westmr St Matt *Lon* 88–89; C Gt Ilford St Mary *Chelmsf* 89–95; V Crofton Park St Hilda w St Cypr *S'wark* from 95. *St Hilda's Vicarage, 35 Buckthorne Road, London SE4 2DG* T: (020) 8699 1277 E: father.bates@sainthildas.org

BATES, Mrs Susan Rita. b 65. City Univ BSc 89. ERMC 12. **d** 15 **p** 16. C Yoxmere *St E* 15–17; R Debenham and Helmingham from 17. *The Rectory, 6 Raedwald Way, Debenham, Stowmarket IP14 6SN* T: (01728) 860222 M: 07944-159606 E: revsusanbates@icloud.com

BATES, Thomas Henry Robert St John. *See* BATES-BOURNE, Thomas Henry Robert St John

BATES, Trini Mari Carolina (Carol). b 68. Liv Poly BSc 92 Dur Univ MA 20 Liv Univ PGCE 93. St Aug Coll of Th 17. **d** 19 **p** 20. C E Wickham *S'wark* from 19. *44 Northdown Road, Welling DA16 1NA* M: 07772-394855 E: trinibates@icloud.com

BATES, William Frederic. b 49. St Jo Coll Dur BSc 72 BA 74 MA 97. Cranmer Hall Dur. **d** 75 **p** 76. C Knutsford St Jo and Toft *Ches* 75–78; C Ripley *Derby* 78–80; R Nether and Over Seale 81–93; V Lullington 81–93; V Allestree St Nic 93–16; Bp's Adv on New Relig Movements 99–16; P-in-c Quarndon 00–16; RD Duffield 09–10; rtd 16. *20*

Main Avenue, Allestree, Derby DE22 2EG* T: (01332) 603605 E: williamfbates@gmail.com

BATES-BOURNE, Thomas Henry Robert St John. b 83. Univ of Wales BMus 07 Cardiff Univ BTh 15. St Mich Coll Llan 11. **d** 14 **p** 15. C Merthyr Tydfil St Dav and Abercanaid *Llan* 14–16; C Eglwysilan and Caerphilly 16–17; C Abergavenny H Trin *Mon* 17–20; C Abergavenny St Mary w Llanwenarth Citra 17–20; C Grimethorpe w Brierley *Leeds* from 20; C Ryhill from 20; C S Kirkby from 20. *St Luke's Vicarage, 7 St Luke's Road, Grimethorpe, Barnsley S72 7FN* M: 07540-250720 E: frtombates@gmail.com

BATESON, Jack William. b 75. Kent Univ BA 97. St Aug Coll of Th BA 17. **d** 17 **p** 18. C Calehill w Westwell *Cant* 17–20; Chapl Benenden Sch from 20; PtO *Roch* from 19; *Cant* from 20. *Benenden School, Cranbrook Road, Benenden, Cranbrook TN17 4AA* M: 07523-819190 E: revjackbateson@gmail.com

BATESON, Canon James Howard. b 36. Qu Mary Coll Lon BSc 57 MSOSc 88. EMMTC 85. **d** 87 **p** 88. NSM W Bridgford *S'well* 87–88; NSM Wilford Hill 88–95; Dioc Officer for NSMs 94–04; P-in-c Kilvington 96–04; P-in-c Staunton w Flawborough 96–04; Hon Can S'well Minster 99–04; rtd 04; PtO *S'well* from 04. *Adelfa, 48E Alford Road, West Bridgford, Nottingham NG2 6HP* T: 0115-923 5256 E: hbateson@talktalk.net

BATESON, Keith Nigel. b 43. **d** 00 **p** 01. OLM Wonersh w Blackheath *Guildf* 00–13; PtO from 13. *Advent Cottage, Blackheath Lane, Wonersh, Guildford GU5 0PN* T: (01483) 892753 E: keith@batesonfamily.net

BATEY, Caroline Elizabeth. b 52. **d** 08 **p** 09. OLM Warrington H Trin *Liv* 08–14; OLM Warrington H Trin and St Ann from 14. *22 Fairclough Avenue, Warrington WA1 2JS* E: cabethbatey@hotmail.com

BATH, David James William. b 43. Oak Hill NSM Course 87. **d** 89 **p** 90. NSM Henley *Ox* 89–90; Gen Manager Humberside Gd News Trust 90–96; NSM Anlaby St Pet *York* 96–04; P-in-c Anlaby Common St Mark 04–10; rtd 10; PtO *York* from 11. *24 Lawnswood, Hessle HU13 0PT* E: davidjwbath@hotmail.com

BATH AND WELLS, Bishop of. *Vacant*

BATH, Archdeacon of. *See* YOUINGS, The Ven Adrian

BATLEY-GLADDEN, Dane Christopher. b 68. St Steph Ho Ox 96. **d** 99 **p** 00. C Hendon St Alphage *Lon* 99–01; C-in-c Grahame Park St Aug CD 01–14; V Swanley St Mary *Roch* from 14. *St Mary's Vicarage, London Road, Swanley BR8 7AQ* T: (01322) 662201 E: vicar@swanleyparish.org.uk

BATSON, Canon Lee Paul. b 77. R Holloway Coll Lon BA 99 MA 00 Selw Coll Cam BA 03 MA 06. Westcott Ho Cam 01. **d** 04 **p** 05. C Saffron Walden w Wendens Ambo, Littlebury etc *Chelmsf* 04–08; P-in-c Boreham 08–17; Co Ecum Officer 08–14; C N Springfield 14–17; P-in-c E Hanningfield 15–17; TR Epping Distr from 17; P-in-c N Weald Bassett from 20; RD Epping Forest and Ongar from 18; Hon Can Chelmsf Cathl from 19. *The Vicarage, Hartland Road, Epping CM16 4PD* T: (01992) 561517 M: 07526-915645 E: lbatson@chelmsford.anglican.org

BATSON, Paul Leonard. b 47. Southn Univ BTh 79. Sarum & Wells Th Coll 73. **d** 75 **p** 76. C Chesham St Mary *Ox* 75–79; Dioc Youth Adv *Newc* 79–85; V Earley St Pet *Ox* 85–93; PtO *Sarum* 01–08; Hon C N Bradford on Avon and Villages 10–15; PtO from 15. *Maple Cottage, 78 Murhill, Limpley Stoke, Bath BA2 7FB* T: (01225) 722721 E: plbatson@gmail.com

BATSTONE, Bruce. b 70. Bris Univ BA 92. St Steph Ho Ox 98. **d** 00 **p** 01. C Leigh-on-Sea St Marg *Chelmsf* 00–03; C Old St Pancras *Lon* 03–07; TV 07–11; Chapl Camden and Islington NHS Foundn Trust 03–11; R Hornsey St Mary w St Geo *Lon* from 11; PtO *Nor* from 21. *Hornsey Rectory, 140 Cranley Gardens, London N10 3AH* T: (020) 8883 6486 E: fr.bruce@hornseyparishchurch.org

BATT, Canon Joseph William. b 39. Keele Univ BA 62. Ripon Hall Ox 63. **d** 64 **p** 65. C Bushbury *Lich* 64–68; C Walsall 68–71; Tr Officer and Youth Chapl Dio Ibadan Nigeria 71–75; Hon Can Oke-Osun from 94; Area Sec CMS Guildf and Chich 75–84; V Ottershaw *Guildf* 84–04; rtd 04; PtO *Bradf* 07–14; *Leeds* from 14. *8 Parkwood Road, Shipley BD18 4SS* T: (01274) 589775 E: joe@jbatt.force9.co.uk

BATT, Canon Kenneth Victor. b 41. Wycliffe Hall Ox 68. **d** 71 **p** 72. C Yateley *Win* 71–76; R The Candover Valley 76–82; R Durrington *Sarum* 82–89; V Kempshott *Win* 89–00; P-in-c Bournemouth H Epiphany 00–05; V 05–08; rtd 08; Hon Can Win Cathl 07–15; Hon C Tadley w Pamber Heath and Silchester 08–15; PtO from 16. *4 Thumwood, Chineham, Basingstoke RG24 8TE* T: (01256) 351592 E: kenneth.batt@btinternet.com

BATT, Mrs Linda. d 14 **p** 15. NSM Magor *Mon* 14–17; NSM Newport Maindee and Lliswerry from 17. *44 Goossens Close, Newport NP19 9JN* T: (01633) 783344

BATTE, Mrs Kathleen. b 47. Homerton Coll Cam TCert 68. NEOC 91. **d** 94 **p** 95. NSM Newc St Gabr 94–96; NSM Wilford Hill *S'well* 96–99; P-in-c Cinderhill 99–05; Bp's Adv for Self-Supporting Min 05–07; Chapl Crowhurst Chr Healing Cen 07–10; Sen Chapl 10–12; rtd 12; PtO *S'well* from 17. *10 Bracey Rise, West Bridgford, Nottingham NG2 7AX* T: 0115-923 4503 E: kath.batte@outlook.com

BATTEN, Ms Sibylle. b 62. Sheff Univ BA 88 MA 90 CQSW 90. St Hild Coll 17. **d** 19 **p** 20. NSM Sheff Manor from 19; Chapl Methodist Homes for the Aged from 21. *The Vicarage, 4 St Mark's Crescent, Sheffield S10 2SG* M: 07966-293303 E: sibylle.batten@manorparish.co.uk

BATTEN, Stuart William. b 73. Univ of Wales (Abth) BD 94 MTh 96. Trin Coll Bris 96. **d** 98 **p** 99. C Northolt St Jos *Lon* 98–01; TV Hucknall Torkard *S'well* 01–06; P-in-c Wickham Bishops w Lt Braxted *Chelmsf* 06–14; P-in-c Barkingside H Trin 14–20; V 20–21; P-in-c Barkingside St Fran 15–21; Asst Dir of Ords 06–21; Dioc Dir of Ords from 21. *Address temp unknown* E: stuart.batten@btinternet.com

BATTERSBY, David George Sellers. b 32. AKC 57. St Boniface Warminster 57 Lambeth STh 81. **d** 58 **p** 59. C Glas St Marg 58–60; C Burnley St Pet *Blackb* 60–62; V Warton St Paul 62–71; Chapl K Wm's Coll Is of Man 71–91; C Ashchurch *Glouc* 91–97; rtd 97; PtO *Worc* 97–02; *Ox* 03–18; St E 19–21. *Denehouse, Whatfield Road, Elmsett, Ipswich IP7 6LT* T: (01473) 657467

BATTERSBY, Richard David. b 69. Sheff Univ BA 13 FCCA. Yorks Min Course 10. **d** 13 **p** 14. NSM Brayton *York* 13–16; C Rural Ainsty from 16. *The Old Vicarage, Main Street, Healaugh, Tadcaster LS24 8DB* T: (01937) 918259 M: 07795-302119 E: revdrichardb@gmail.com

BATTERSBY, Simon Charles. *See* CROMPTON-BATTERSBY, Simon Jackson

BATTERSHELL, Mrs Anne Marie. b 33. Ox Poly BEd 83. SAOMC 95. **d** 98 **p** 99. NSM Goring w S Stoke *Ox* 98–01; NSM Brafferton w Pilmoor, Myton-on-Swale etc *York* 01–03; rtd 03; PtO *Wakef* 04–14; *Leeds* from 14; *Man* 07–18. *26 Winterbutlee Grove, Todmorden OL14 7QU* T: (01706) 839848 E: rev.anne@hotmail.co.uk

BATTERSHELL, Rachel Damaris. b 65. RN 88. SNWTP 08. **d** 11 **p** 12. C Coldhurst and Oldham St Steph *Man* 11–14; TV Ashton 14–17; V Dearnley, Wardle and Smallbridge from 17. *Dearnley Vicarage, Arm Road, Littleborough OL15 8NJ* T: (01706) 378466 M: 07563-630594 E: rev.rachel@hotmail.co.uk

BATTEY, Alexander Robert Fenwick. b 77. St Andr Univ MA 99. Ripon Coll Cuddesdon BA 04 MA 08. **d** 05 **p** 06. C Whitby w Aislaby and Ruswarp *York* 05–08; CF 08–12 and from 18; V Old Basing and Lychpit *Win* 12–18. *c/o MOD Chaplains (Army)* M: 07823-323315 E: alec.battey@gmail.com

BATTISON, David John. b 62. ACIB 93. St Jo Coll Nottm 07. **d** 09 **p** 10. C Matlock Bath and Cromford *Derby* 09–11; C Matlock Bank and Tansley 11–21; Pioneer Min 13–20; TV Daventry *Pet* from 21. *The Vicarage, Church Street, Staverton, Daventry NN11 6JJ* M: 07971-506088 E: davidbattison@btinternet.com

BATTLE, Dean of. *See* DUCKETT, The Very Revd Lee Christopher James

BATTS-NEALE, Sara Louise. b 72. Nottm Univ BSc 95 City Univ MSc 06 Loughb Univ PhD 13 Nottm Univ MA 20. Westcott Ho Cam 14. **d** 16 **p** 17. C Chingford St Edm *Chelmsf* 16–18; C Coggeshall w Markshall 18–20; C Cressing w Stisted and Bradwell etc 18–20; Chapl Essex Univ from 20; C Colchester, New Town and The Hythe from 20; C Greenstead w Colchester St Anne from 20; C Wivenhoe from 20. *Mariners, Rectory Hill, Wivenhoe, Colchester CO7 9LB* E: rev.dr.batts@gmail.com

BATTY, John Ivan. b 35. Clifton Th Coll 59. **d** 62 **p** 63. C Clayton *Bradf* 62–67; V Toxteth Park St Clem *Liv* 67–73; R Darfield *Sheff* 73–90; Chapl Düsseldorf *Eur* 90–95; V The Marshland *Sheff* 95–00; rtd 00; PtO *Sheff* 00–15; *Linc* 00; *Eur* from 01. *4 St Lawrence Way, Tallington, Stamford PE9 4RH* T/F: (01780) 740151

BATTY, Leslie. b 48. Univ of Wales (Ban) BSc 70 Hull Univ PGCE 71 MSc 93 Univ of Wales MPhil 92. Linc Sch of Th and Min 10. **d** 14 **p** 15. OLM Ringstone in Aveland Gp *Linc* 14–16; OLM Grantham, Harrowby w Londonthorpe from 16. *12 Scotney Drive, Grantham NG31 9UA* T: (01476) 578829 M: 07890-010735 E: batty527@btinternet.com

BATTYE, Mrs Alison Jill. b 65. Rob Coll Cam BA 86 Sheff Univ BA 16 PGCE 87. Yorks Min Course 13. **d** 16 **p** 17. C Whitkirk *Leeds* 16–19; R Adel from 19. *Adel Rectory, 25 Church Lane, Adel, Leeds LS16 8DQ* M: 07717-564542 E: alison.battye65@btinternet.com *or* alison.battye@leeds.anglican.org

BATTYE, Canon Lisa Katherine. b 55. Man Univ BN 78 MA(Theol) 96 Liv Univ MTh 00 Ches Univ MProf 14 RM 79. NOC 96. **d** 99 **p** 00. C Clifton *Man* 99–02; R Kersal Moor 02–17; AD Salford 13–17; TV Didsbury St Jas and Em from 17; Chapl St Mellitus NW from 19; Hon Can Man Cathl from 16. *453 Parrs Wood Road, Didsbury, Manchester M20 5NE* T: 0161-434 9886 M: 07539-775483 E: lisabattye@stjamesandemmanuel.org

BAUDON, Raymond Jean Grigor. b 78. Glas Univ LLB 03. Ripon Coll Cuddesdon 16. **d** 18 **p** 19. C E Dulwich St Jo *S'wark* 18–21; Dioc Voc Adv 19–21; Bp's Adv (Shared Discernment Process) from 21. *Trinity House, 4 Chapel Court, London SE1 1HW* T: (020) 7939 9400 E: raymond.baudon@southwark.anglican.org

BAUER, Jonathan Nathaniel. b 72. Bp Grosseteste Coll BA 96 Drew Univ New Jersey DMin 12. Ripon Coll Cuddesdon 97. **d** 00 **p** 01. C Spalding St Mary and St Nic *Linc* 00–02; C Sanderstead St Mary *S'wark* 02–03; P-in-c 03–05; TV Sanderstead 05–06; V E Crompton *Man* 06–09; R Broughty Ferry *Bre* 09–11; Chapl St Mich Hospice Harrogate 11–13; Bereavement Support Worker 13–16; Manager St Leon Hospice York 16–20; PtO *Ripon* 13–14; NSM Ripon Cathl Benefice *Leeds* 14–16; PtO *York* 14–15; *Leeds* 17–21; *Man* 17–21; R Chislehurst St Nic *Roch* from 21. *The Rectory, 2 Cardinal Close, Chislehurst BR7 6SA* T: (020) 8467 4405 E: revjbauer@gmail.com

BAUGHEN, Andrew Jonathan. b 64. City of Lon Poly BA 87 City Univ Lon MBA 13. Wycliffe Hall Ox BTh 94. **d** 94 **p** 95. C Battersea Rise St Mark *S'wark* 94–97; P-in-c Clerkenwell St Jas and St Jo w St Pet *Lon* 97–00; V 00–18; LtO 18–20; C St Edm and St Mary Woolnoth etc from 20. *St Edmund the King Church, Lombard Street, London EC3V 9EA* E: a.j.baughen@city.ac.uk

BAUGHEN, Elizabeth Jane. b 62. Lon Sch of Th BA 08. St Mellitus Coll. **d** 16 **p** 17. C Enfield St Andr *Lon* 16–18; C Whetstone St Jo 18–19; PtO from 19. *21 Hyde Close, Barnet EN5 5TJ* T: (020) 8449 6134 M: 07803-008090 E: lizziebaughen@btinternet.com

✠**BAUGHEN, The Rt Revd Michael Alfred.** b 30. Lon Univ BD 55. Oak Hill Th Coll 51. **d** 56 **p** 57 **c** 82. C Hyson Green *S'well* 56–59; C Reigate St Mary *S'wark* 59–61; Ord Cand Sec CPAS 61–64; R Rusholme H Trin *Man* 64–70; TV St Marylebone All So w SS Pet and Jo *Lon* 70–75; R 75–82; AD Westmr St Marylebone 78–82; Preb St Paul's Cathl 79–82; Bp Ches 82–96; rtd 96; Hon Asst Bp Lon 96–06; Hon Asst Bp Guildf from 06; PtO *S'wark* 97–02. *23 The Atrium, Woolsack Way, Godalming GU7 1EN* T: (01483) 808151 M: 07990-275563 E: michaelbaughen23@gmail.com

BAULCOMB, Canon Geoffrey Gordon. b 46. K Coll Lon BD 86. AKC 68. **d** 69 **p** 70. C Crofton Park St Hilda w St Cypr *S'wark* 69–74; TV Padgate *Liv* 74–79; R Whitton and Thurleston w Akenham *St E* 79–03; Hon Can St E Cathl 03; rtd 03; PtO *St E* from 03; *Chich* from 04. *Greenlands, 39 Filching Road, Eastbourne BN20 8SE* T: (01323) 641746 M: 07880-731232 E: geoffreybaulcomb@hotmail.com

BAUN, Jane Ralls. b 60. Yale Univ BA 83 Catholic Univ of America MA 89 Princeton Univ PhD 97. Ripon Coll Cuddesdon 08. **d** 10 **p** 11. NSM Abingdon *Ox* 10–18; PtO 18; Lect Ripon Coll Cuddesdon 13–18; Chapl Wadh Coll Ox from 18. *Wadham College, Parks Road, Oxford OX1 3PN* T: (01865) 244559 E: jane.baun@theology.ox.ac.uk

✠**BAVIN, The Rt Revd Timothy John.** b 35. Worc Coll Ox BA 59 MA 61 FRSCM 91. Cuddesdon Coll 59. **d** 61 **p** 62 **c** 74. C Pretoria Cathl S Africa 61–64; Chapl 65–69; C Uckfield *Chich* 69–71; V Brighton Gd Shep Preston 71–73; Dean and Adn Johannesburg 73–74; Bp Johannesburg 74–85; Bp Portsm 85–95; OGS 87–97; OSB from 96; PtO *Win* 96–14; Hon Asst Bp Portsm from 12; Hon Asst Bp Win from 13; PtO *Portsm* from 16. *Abbey of Our Lady and St John, Abbey Road, Beech, Alton GU34 4AP* T: (01420) 562145 *or* 563575 F: 561691 E: tjbavin@gmail.com

BAVINGTON, Canon John Eduard. b 68. Loughb Univ BEng 91. Trin Coll Bris BA 99. **d** 99 **p** 00. C W Ealing St Jo w St Jas *Lon* 99–02; V Bradf St Clem 02–06; Chapl Giggleswick Sch 06–13; V Gt Horton *Bradf* 13–14; *Leeds* 14–19; C Bradf St Wilfrid w St Columba 17–19; V Gt Horton and Lidget Green from 20; AD Inner Bradf from 19; Hon Can Bradf Cathl from 17. *St Wilfrid's Vicarage, St Wilfrid's Road, Bradford BD7 2LU* M: 07704-854978 E: john.bavington@leeds.anglican.org *or* revjohnbav@stjohnsgreathorton.com

BAWDEN, Sheila Irene. b 55. **d** 11 **p** 12. NSM Bodmin w Lanhydrock and Lanivet *Truro* 11–16; Public Preacher 16–17; NSM Lostwithiel Parishes from 17. *Chimes, 8 Church Lane, Lostwithiel PL22 0EQ* M: 07879-551046 E: sheila.stevens55@btinternet.com

BAWTREE, Andrew James. b 66. Univ of Wales BD 91 Ch Ch Coll Cant PGCE 92. St Jo Coll Nottm MA 95. d 96 p 97. C Hoddesdon *St Alb* 96–99; R S Boston Trin Ch USA 00–07; P-in-c River *Cant* from 07; Asst Dir of Ords from 17; AD Dover from 17. *The Vicarage, 23 Lewisham Road, Dover CT17 0QG* T: (01304) 822037 E: rockabillyrev@hotmail.com

BAXANDALL, Canon Peter. b 45. Tyndale Hall Bris 67. d 70 p 72. C Kidsgrove *Lich* 70–71; C St Helens St Mark *Liv* 71–75; C Ardsley *Sheff* 75–77; Rep Leprosy Miss E Anglia 77–86; P-in-c March St Wendreda *Ely* 86–87; R 87–11; P-in-c March St Jo 09–11; RD March 93–09; Hon Can Ely Cathl 07–11; rtd 12; PtO *Nor* from 11. *22 Westland Road, Lowestoft NR33 9AB* T: (01502) 583228 E: peterbaxandall@sky.com

BAXENDALE, Rodney Douglas. b 45. Ex Univ BA 66 Cardiff Univ MTh 10 Leeds Univ PGCE 68. Linc Th Coll 78. d 80 p 81. C Maidstone All SS and St Phil w Tovil *Cant* 80–83; Chapl RN 83–03; Chapl Plymouth Hosps NHS Trust 06–08; Sen Chapl 08–13; rtd 13; Chapl St Luke's Hospice Plymouth 14–15; PtO *Ex* from 13. *17 Valletort Road, Plymouth PL1 5PH* T: (01752) 500573 E: thebaxendales@blueyonder.co.uk

BAXFIELD, Christopher Richard Collie. b 78. Victoria Univ (BC) BA 02 Univ of Alberta MA 04 Leeds Univ PhD 11. Wycliffe Hall Ox 15. d 17 p 18. C Moor Allerton and Shadwell *Leeds* 17–21; C Greengates and Thorpe Edge from 21; C Idle from 21; C Wrose from 21. *St Cuthbert's Vicarage, 71 Wrose Road, Bradford BD2 1LN* M: 07752-331228 E: revchrisbaxfield@gmail.com

BAXTER, Alexander. b 74. Westcott Ho Cam 10. d 13 p 14. C Eastbourne St Andr *Chich* 13–17; R Clayton w Keymer from 17. *The Rectory, 1 The Crescent, Hassocks BN6 8RB* M: 07957-848378 E: alexbaxter66@yahoo.co.uk

BAXTER, Mrs Alison Gilmour. b 70. Nene Coll Northn BSc 93 Cov Univ MSc 02. Ox Min Course 16. d 19 p 20. C Kenilworth St Nic *Cov* from 19. *19 Leyes Lane, Kenilworth CV8 2DD* M: 07910-404475 E: baxter.alison@gmail.com

BAXTER, Anthony. b 54. SEITE 99. d 02 p 08. NSM Romford Ascension Collier Row *Chelmsf* 02–07; NSM Hutton from 07. *44 Prower Close, Billericay CM11 2BU* T: (01277) 655514 M: 07909-984675

BAXTER, Carlton Edwin. d 07 p 08. NSM Lurgan Ch the Redeemer *D & D* 07–10; NSM Maghaberry 10–17; C Magheralin w Dollingstown 17–21; I Kilmore St Aid w St Sav *Arm* from 21. *The Rectory, 38 Vicarage Road, Portadown, Craigavon BT62 4HF* E: carltoneb@icloud.com

BAXTER (née AVIS), Elizabeth Mary. b 69. Leeds Metrop Univ MA 93 Win Univ MPhil 13 CYCW 77. NOC 81. dss 84 d 87 p 94. Leeds St Marg and All Hallows *Ripon* 84–93; Par Dn 87–93; Chapl Abbey Grange High Sch 85–93; Par Dn Topcliffe *York* 93–94; C 94–96; C Thirsk 96–07; Jt Dir H Rood Ho Cen for Health and Past Care 93–07; Exec Dir from 07; PtO *Ripon* 93–14; *Dur* 94–15; *Newc* from 94; *Sheff* 95–12; *Bradf* 95–04; *Wakef* 97–14; *Leeds* 14–16; *York* 08–17. *5 Glendale Road, Wooler NE71 6DN* T: (01668) 283125 *or* (01845) 522580 E: elizabethbaxter@gmail.co.uk

BAXTER, Canon Jane Elizabeth. b 51. EAMTC 98. d 01 p 02. C Clare w Poslingford, Cavendish etc *St E* 01–04; P-in-c Lyddington w Stoke Dry and Seaton etc *Pet* 04–10; C Bulwick, Blatherwycke w Harringworth and Laxton 04–10; V Lyddington, Bisbrooke, Caldecott, Glaston etc from 10; RD Rutland from 18; Can Pet Cathl 18–21. *The Rectory, 4 Windmill Way, Lyddington, Oakham LE15 9LY* T: (01572) 822717 E: revjanebaxter@gmail.com

BAXTER, John Richard. b 44. ACII 66. STETS 96. d 99 p 00. NSM Banstead *Guildf* 99–03; TV Surrey Weald 03–11; rtd 11; PtO *Guildf* from 12. *11 Arundel Avenue, Epsom KT17 2RF* T: (020) 8393 6767 M: 07974-692334 E: revdjohn@virginmedia.com

BAXTER, Stephen Richard. b 63. d 14 p 15. NSM St Olave Hart Street w All Hallows Staining etc *Lon* 14–18; P-in-c St Steph Walbrook and St Swithun etc from 18; PtO *Chelmsf* 16–21. *5 Elm Court, Elmdon, Saffron Walden CB11 4NP* T: (01763) 838278 M: 07739-658327 E: priest@ststephenwalbrook.net

BAXTER, Stuart. b 43. Liv Univ BA 65 Nottm Univ PGCE 66. Cuddesdon Coll 66. d 70 p 71. C Kirkby *Liv* 70–73; C Ainsdale 73–76; CMS 76–77 and 83–84; Sierra Leone 77–83; V Nelson in Lt Marsden *Blackb* 84–92; V Lostock Hall 92–99; P-in-c Hatton *Derby* 99–04; Asst Chapl HM Pris Sudbury 99–03; Asst Chapl HM Pris Foston Hall 03–06; rtd 06; PtO *Derby* from 06. *11 Pingle Crescent, Belper DE56 1DY* T: (01773) 827309

BAXTER, Terence Hugh. b 48. Leeds Poly BSc 74. NOC 89. d 92 p 93. NSM Guiseley w Esholt *Bradf* 92–04; NSM Weston w Denton 04–08; NSM Leathley w Farnley, Fewston and Blubberhouses 04–08; NSM Washburn and Mid-Wharfe 08–09; PtO *Eur* 11–20. *Avenida Juan Carlos 1, Puerta 86, La Marina Oasis, 03177 San Fulgencio (Alicante), Spain* M: (0034) 634 300 679 E: telbaxter@googlemail.com

BAXTER FIELDING, Mrs Joanna Nicola. b 67. St Hugh's Coll Ox BA 89 MA 15. d 12 p 13. C Roslyn St Jo NZ 13; P-in-c Otago Peninsula 13–19; PtO *Ox* 18–20; NSM Marsden and Slaithwaite w E Scammonden *Leeds* from 20. *Outbarn, Laund Road, Slaithwaite, Huddersfield HD7 5UU* T: (01484) 847545 M: 07561-823135

BAYCOCK, Philip Louis. b 33. Wells Th Coll 64. d 66 p 67. C Kettering SS Pet and Paul 66–68; C St Peter-in-Thanet *Cant* 68–72; V Bobbing w Iwade 72–73; PtO 73–76; V Thanington w Milton 77–84; R Chagford w Gidleigh and Throwleigh *Ex* 84–01; rtd 01; PtO *Ex* from 01. *7 Grove Meadow, Sticklepath, Okehampton EX20 2NE* T: (01837) 840617

BAYES, Frederick Alan. b 60. Imp Coll Lon BSc 81 St Jo Coll Dur BA 92. Cranmer Hall Dur 92. d 93 p 94. C Talbot Village *Sarum* 93–97; Chapl St Hild and St Bede Coll *Dur* 97–03; Bp's Adv in Interfaith Matters 02–03; V Penllergaer *S & B* 03–16; Chapl Whitgift Sch and Ho Croydon from 16; C Croydon St Jo S'*wark* from 16. *Whitgift School, Haling Park, South Croydon CR2 6YT* T: (020) 8688 9222

✠**BAYES, The Rt Revd Paul.** b 53. Birm Univ BA 75. Qu Coll Birm 76. d 79 p 80 c 10. C Tynemouth Cullercoats St Paul *Newc* 79–82; Chapl Qu Eliz Coll *Lon* 82–87; Chapl Chelsea Coll 85–87; TV High Wycombe *Ox* 87–90; TR 90–94; TR Totton *Win* 95–04; AD Lyndhurst 00–04; Nat Miss and Evang Adv Abps' Coun 04–10; Hon Can Worc Cathl 07–10; Suff Bp Hertford *St Alb* 10–14; Bp Liv from 14. *Bishop's Lodge, Woolton Park, Liverpool L25 6DT* T: 0151-421 0831 F: 428 3055 E: bishopslodge@liverpool.anglican.org

BAYLEY, Anne Christine. b 34. OBE 86. Girton Coll Cam BA 55 MB, ChB 58 FRCS 66 FRCSEd 86. St Steph Ho Ox 90. d 91 p 94. NSM Wembley Park St Aug *Lon* 91–97; PtO *York* 97–05; *Heref* 05–19. *Address temp unknown*

BAYLEY, Michael John. b 36. CCC Cam BA 60 MA 64 Sheff Univ PhD 73. Linc Th Coll 60. d 62 p 63. C Leeds Gipton Epiphany *Ripon* 62–66; NSM Sheff St Mark Broomhill 67–93; C Sheff St Mary w Highfield Trin 93–95; C Sheff St Mary Bramall Lane 95–00; rtd 00; PtO *Sheff* from 03. *27 Meadowbank Avenue, Sheffield S7 1PB* T: 0114-258 5248 E: mjbayley@btinternet.com

BAYLEY, Oliver James Drummond. b 49. Mansf Coll Ox MA PGCE. St Jo Coll Nottm 81. d 83 p 84. C Bath Weston St Jo w Kelston *B & W* 83–88; P-in-c Bathampton 88–93; P-in-c Claverton 92–93; R Bathampton w Claverton 93–96; Chapl Dauntsey's Sch Devizes 96–02; rtd 02; PtO *Win* from 01. *19 Treeside Road, Southampton SO15 5FY* T: (023) 8178 1962 E: ojdb80@hotmail.com

BAYLEY, Canon Raymond. b 46. Keble Coll Ox BA 68 MA 72 Ex Univ PhD 86. St Chad's Coll Dur 68. d 69 p 70. C Mold *St As* 69–74; Lay Tr Officer 71–74; C Llandaff w Capel Llanilltern *Llan* 74; PV Llan Cathl and Lay Tr Officer 74–77; V Cwmbach 77–80; Dir Past Studies St Mich Coll Llan 80–84; Lect Univ of Wales (Cardiff) *Llan* 80–84; V Ynysddu *Mon* 84–86; V Griffithstown 86–92; Tutor Dioc Minl Tr Course 84–92; V Rhosymedre *St As* 92–96; Warden and R Ruthin w Llanrhydd 96–09; Tutor Dioc Minl Tr Course 92–06; Dir CME 94–01; Warden of Readers 02–09; Hon Can St As Cathl 04–09; rtd 09; PtO *St As* from 09; S'*wark* from 15. *11 Maes Glanrafon, Brook Street, Mold CH7 1RJ* T: (01352) 752345 M: 07944-274154 E: raymond.bayley537@btinternet.com

BAYLIS (née LOFTS), Mrs Sally Anne. b 55. Kent Univ BA 78 K Coll Lon MA 80 Nottm Univ PGCE 93. St Jo Coll Nottm 01. d 03 p 04. C Gedling S'*well* 03–07; P-in-c Daybrook 07–11; V 11–21; rtd 21; PtO S'*well* from 21. *Address temp unknown* E: sally504@btinternet.com

BAYLISS, Geoffrey Brian Tudor. b 60. R Holloway Coll Lon BSc 83 Univ of Wales (Swansea) PGCE 85 Univ of Wales (Ban) MA 11 Glyndŵr Univ DMin 16. EAMTC 96. d 99 p 00. NSM Panfield and Rayne *Chelmsf* 99–04; TV Halstead Area 04–10; RD Hinckford 08–10; P-in-c Tolleshunt D'Arcy and Tolleshunt Major 10–11; P-in-c Tollesbury w Salcot Virley 10–11; V N Blackwater 11–15; RD Witham 11–15; Hon Can Chelmsf Cathl 15; TR Cowley St Jas *Ox* from 15; AD Cowley from 18. *Cowley Rectory, 11 Beauchamp Lane, Oxford OX4 3LF* M: 07759-393023 E: g.bayliss41@btinternet.com

BAYLISS, Canon Grant David. b 75. Ex Univ BA 96 Wolfs Coll Ox DPhil 05 Ox Univ MA 05. Ripon Coll Cuddesdon BA 99. d 03 p 04. C Prestbury and All SS *Glouc* 03–07; Chapl St Jo Coll Cam 07–11; Lect Ripon Coll Cuddesdon 11–17; Can Res and Prec Ch Ch *Ox* 17–20; Dir of IME (2) from 20; *Church House Oxford, Langford Locks, Kidlington OX5 1GF* T: (01865) 208200 grant.bayliss@oxford.anglican.org

BAYLOR, Canon Nigel Peter. b 58. NUI BA 80 TCD MPhil 88. d 84 p 86. C Carrickfergus *Conn* 84–87; C Dundela St Mark

D & D 87–89; I Galloon w Drummully *Clogh* 89–94; Adult Educn Adv 91–94; I Carnmoney *Conn* 94–03; I Jordanstown from 03; Can Belf Cathl from 12. *The Rectory, 120A Circular Road, Jordanstown, Newtownabbey BT37 0RH* T: (028) 9086 2119 E: nigel_stpatricks@outlook.com

BAYLY, Mrs Janet. b 43. d 08. OLM Schorne *Ox* 08–15; PtO from 15. *2B Granborough Road, North Marston, Buckingham MK18 3PN* T: (01296) 670245 E: janet.bayly@gmail.com

BAYMAN, Canon Brynn Alton. b 66. Witwatersrand Univ BA 87 PGCE 88. Ripon Coll Cuddesdon 09. d 11 p 12. OLM Finchampstead and California *Ox* 11–15; Chapl Framlingham Coll from 16; Hon Can St E Cathl from 20. *Framlingham College, College Road, Framlingham, Woodbridge IP13 9EY* E: bbayman@framcollege.co.uk

BAYNE, Canon David William. b 52. St Andr Univ MA 75. Edin Th Coll 88. d 90 p 91. C Dumfries *Glas* 90–92; P-in-c 92–93; R 93–99; Chapl Dumfries and Galloway Primary Care NHS Trust 92–99; Chapl Crichton R Hosp Dumfries 92–99; Chapl HM Pris Dumfries 96–99; R Castle Douglas *Glas* 99–17; P-in-c Dalbeattie 14–17; Can St Mary's Cathl 99–17; rtd 17; Hon Can St Mary's Cathl *Glas* from 17. *Adrigole, 2 Waterside Close, Askamore, Co Wexford, Republic of Ireland* T: (00353) (53) 941 4543 E: dwbayne@aol.com

BAYNE, Mrs Felicity Meriel. b 47. WEMTC 91. d 94 p 95. NSM Cheltenham Ch Ch *Glouc* 94–98; NSM Leckhampton St Pet 98–09; Chapl Glenfall Ho 09–13; rtd 13; PtO *Glouc* from 16. *Hamfield House, Ham Road, Charlton Kings, Cheltenham GL52 6NG* T: (01242) 237074 E: felicity.bayne@btinternet.com

BAYNE-JARDINE, Anthea Mary. See GRIGGS, Anthea Mary

BAYNES, Mrs Clare. b 57. Reading Univ BA 79. SAOMC 01. d 04 p 05. NSM Chambersbury *St Alb* 04–08; NSM St Alb St Steph 08–16; PtO from 16; *Leeds* from 17. *4 Pilgrim Close, Park Street, St Albans AL2 2JD* T: (01727) 875524 E: clarebaynes@gmail.com

BAYNES, Simon Hamilton. b 33. New Coll Ox BA 57 MA 62. Wycliffe Hall Ox 57. d 59 p 60. C Rodbourne Cheney *Bris* 59–62; Japan 63–80; C Keynsham *B & W* 80–84; P-in-c Winkfield *Ox* 84–85; V Winkfield and Cranbourne 85–99; rtd 99; LtO *Ox* 99–02; Hon C Thame 02–21. *23 Moorend Lane, Thame OX9 3BQ* T: (01844) 213673 E: baynes@psa-online.com *or* baynes@clearmail.net

BAYNES, William Hendrie. b 39. Adelaide Univ BA 60. S'wark Ord Course 77. d 79 p 80. C Notting Hill All SS w St Columb *Lon* 79–85; PtO 86–87 and 99–00; Hon C Paddington St Sav 88–94; Asst Chapl St Mary's NHS Trust Paddington 94–99; Hon C Paddington St Jas *Lon* 00–10; PtO 10–18. *39E Westbourne Gardens, London W2 5NR* T: (020) 7727 9530 E: will.baynes@london.anglican.org

BAYNHAM, Matthew Fred. b 57. BNC Ox BA 78 Birm Univ MPhil 00. Wycliffe Hall Ox 80. d 83 p 84. C Yardley St Edburgha *Birm* 83–87; TV Bath Twerton-on-Avon *B & W* 87–93; V Reddal Hill St Luke *Worc* 93–00; RD Dudley 98–00; Chapl Bp Grosseteste Coll Linc 00–05; Assoc Chapl Liv Univ 05–07; Sen Res Tutor from 07; P-in-c Llanllwchaearn and Llanina *St D* 11–19; P-in-c Glyn Aeron (Coastal) from 19. *Y Ficerdy, Penrhiwgaled Lane, Cross Inn, Llandysul SA44 6NS* T: (01545) 561878 E: mbaynham@cardigan-bay-churches.org

BAYS, Mrs Helen Margaret. b 48. Kent Univ BA 69 RGN 71 RHV 73. STETS 97. d 00 p 01. NSM Calne and Blackland *Sarum* 00–02; NSM Dawlish *Ex* 02–12; rtd 12; PtO *Ex* from 12. *14 Stockton Hill, Dawlish EX7 9LP* T: (01626) 862860 E: hbays@talktalk.net

BAZELY, Stephen William. b 80. Ox Brookes Univ BSc 05. Oak Hill Th Coll BA 11. d 11 p 12. C Deane *Man* 11–14; PtO 14–15; P-in-c Willaston *Ches* 15–21. *Address temp unknown*

BAZELY, William Francis. b 53. Sheff Univ BEng 75. St Jo Coll Nottm 78. d 81 p 82. C Huyton St Geo *Liv* 81–84; TV Netherthorpe *Sheff* 84–92; Chapl Lambeth Healthcare NHS Trust 92–98; Chapl Guy's and St Thos' Hosps NHS Trust Lon 98–01; C Rotherham *Sheff* 01–03; Chapl Rotherham Gen Hosps NHS Trust 01–03; Chapl Doncaster and S Humber Healthcare NHS Trust 01–03; Sen Chapl Norfolk & Waveney Mental Health NHS Foundn Trust 03–11; Sen Chapl Norfolk and Suffolk NHS Foundn Trust 12–14; rtd 14; Hon C Brampton St Thos *Derby* 15–19. *18 Bulling Lane, Crich, Matlock DE4 5DX* M: 07702-974680 E: wbazely@gmail.com

✠**BAZLEY, The Rt Revd Colin Frederick.** b 35. St Pet Coll Ox BA 57 MA 61. Tyndale Hall Bris 57. d 59 p 60 c 69. C Bootle St Leon *Liv* 59–62; SAMS Miss Chile 62–00; Adn Cautin and Malleco 67–69; Asst Bp Cautin and Malleco 69–75; Asst Bp Santiago 75–77; Bp Chile 77–00; Primate CASA Chile 77–83; Primate Inglesia Anglicana del Cono Sur 89–95; rtd 00; Hon Asst Bp Ches from 00; Warden of Readers 00–05; RD Wallasey 09–11. *121 Brackenwood Road, Higher Bebington,*

Wirral CH63 2LU T: 0151-608 1193 M: 07866-391333 E: cfbazley@gmail.com

BAZLINTON, Stephen Cecil. b 46. Lon Univ BDS RCS LDS. Ridley Hall Cam 78. d 85 p 86. NSM Stebbing w Lindsell *Chelmsf* 85–04; NSM Stebbing and Lindsell w Gt and Lt Saling 04–08; PtO from 08. *St Helens, High Street, Stebbing, Dunmow CM6 3SE* T: (01371) 856495 E: revbaz@phonecoop.coop

BEACH, Jonathan Mark. b 67. Essex Univ BSc 89. Trin Coll Bris BA 94. d 94 p 95. C Oulton Broad *Nor* 94–97; Chapl RAF 97–13; Chapl St Mary's Sch Calne from 13. *St Mary's School, 63 Curzon Street, Calne SN11 0DF* T: (01249) 857200 E: jbeach@stmaryscalne.org

BEACH, Mark Howard Francis. b 62. Kent Univ BA 83 Nottm Univ MA 95 K Coll Lon DMin 11. St Steph Ho Ox 85. d 87 p 88. C Beeston *S'well* 87–90; C Hucknall Torkard 90–93; R Gedling 93–01; R Netherfield 96–01; Bp's Chapl *Wakef* 01–03; TR Rugby *Cov* 03–12; Dean Roch 12–15; Dir Blackfriars Settlement 15–17; Dir of Care The Haven + London from 18. *17 Hickmire, Wollaston, Wellingborough NN29 7SL* M: 07957-584856 E: mark.beach62@gmail.com

BEACH, Stephen John. b 58. Man Univ BA 81 BD 88 Didsbury Coll of Educn PGCE 82. NOC 92. d 93 p 94. C Harwood *Man* 93–97; TV Westhoughton and Wingates 97–01; P-in-c Devonport St Budeaux *Ex* 01–02; V from 02. *St Budeaux Vicarage, Agaton Road, Plymouth PL5 2EW* T: (01752) 361019 E: stephenbeach@btinternet.com

BEACHAM, Peter Martyn. b 44. OBE 08. Ex Coll Ox BA 65 MA 70 Lon Univ MPhil 67 FSA 92 MRTPI 69. Sarum Th Coll 70. d 73 p 74. NSM Ex St Martin, St Steph, St Laur etc 73–74; NSM Cen Ex 74–90; PtO from 99. *Bellever, Barrack Road, Exeter EX2 6AB* T: (01392) 435074 E: peter-beacham1@live.co.uk

BEACON, Canon Ralph Anthony. b 44. St Mich Coll Llan 70. d 71 p 72. C Neath w Llantwit *Llan* 71–74; TV Holyhead w Rhoscolyn w Llanfair-yn-Neubwll *Ban* 74–78; R Llanenddwyn w Llanddwywe, Llanbedr w Llandanwg 78–99; V Harlech and Llanfair-juxta-Harlech etc 99–11; RD Ardudwy 89–02; AD 02–12; Hon Can Ban Cathl 91–97; Can Cursal Ban Cathl 97–11; Can and Preb Ban Cathl 03–11; rtd 11. *Hen Tyrpeg, Harlech LL46 2UU* T: (01766) 780031 M: 07713-421858 E: sbeacon@hotmail.co.uk

BEACON, Canon Stephanie Kathleen Nora. b 49. Univ of Wales (Ban) BA 70 PGCE 71. NW Ord Course 94. d 96 p 97. NSM Llanenddwyn w Llanddwywe, Llanbedr w Llandanwg *Ban* 96–98; C Ardudwy 98–99; P-in-c Llanenddwyn w Llanddwywe, Llanbedr w Llandanwg 99–01; R 01–11; R Bro Ardudwy Uchaf 11–13; Can Cursal Ban Cathl 11–13; rtd 13. *Hen Tyrpeg, Harlech LL46 2UU* T: (01766) 780031 M: 07713-421858 E: sbeacon@hotmail.co.uk

BEADLE, Canon Janet Mary. b 52. Philippa Fawcett Coll CertEd 74. EAMTC 91. d 94 p 95. C Kingston upon Hull H Trin *York* 94–98; V Ness Gp *Linc* 98–16; Bp's Adv in Women's Min 00–08; Can and Preb Linc Cathl from 03; PtO *York* from 17. *28 Manor Park Road, York YO30 5UD* T: (01904) 903126 E: reverendcanonjanetbeadle@gmail.com

BEADLE, Liam Paul. b 84. St Pet Coll Ox BA 07 MA 11 St Jo Coll Dur MA 10. Cranmer Hall Dur 07. d 09 p 10. C Enfield St Andr *Lon* 09–13; V Honley *Leeds* 13–17; PtO 17–19; P-in-c Toller Lane St Chad from 19; PtO *York* from 19. *25 Hirst Wood Crescent, Shipley BD18 4BY* E: liam.beadle@gmail.com

BEADLE, Mrs Lorna. b 40. NEOC 92. d 95 p 96. NSM Ashington *Newc* 95–10; PtO from 10; Chapl MU from 02. *9 Arundel Square, Ashington NE63 8AW* T: (01670) 816467

BEADLE, Capt Richard Alan. b 68. Wilson Carlile Coll 95 St Jo Coll Nottm 15. d 16 p 17. Kildallon and Swanlinbar *K, E & A* 16–17; C Cloonclare w Killasnett, Lurganboy and Drumlease from 17. *309 Lattone Road, Lattone, Belcoo, Enniskillen BT93 5ER* T: (028) 6638 1943 M: 07392-844721 *or* (00353) 86-842 1190 E: rbeadleca@gmail.com

BEAHAN, Alan. b 64. Birm Univ BA 87 St Jo Coll Dur BA 07 York Univ PGCE 89. Cranmer Hall Dur 05. d 07 p 08. C Warrington St Elphin *Liv* 07–10; P-in-c Hindley All SS 10–16; P-in-c Hindley St Pet 13–15; P-in-c Ormskirk 16–17; C Kirkby 17–18; R Calton, Cauldon, Grindon, Waterfall etc *Lich* from 18. *The Vicarage, Waterfall Lane, Waterhouses, Stoke-on-Trent ST10 3HT* T: (01538) 308506 M: 07908-709405 E: alanbeahan@yahoo.co.uk

BEAKE, The Ven Stuart Alexander. b 49. Em Coll Cam BA 72 MA 76. Cuddesdon Coll 72. d 74 p 75. C Hitchin St Mary *St Alb* 74–76; C Hitchin 77–79; TV Hemel Hempstead 79–85; Bp's Dom Chapl *S'well* 85–87; V Shottery St Andr *Cov* 87–00; RD Fosse 93–99; Dioc Dir of Ords 96–00; Hon Can Cov Cathl 98–00; Can Res and Sub-Dean Cov Cathl 00–05; Adn Surrey *Guildf* 05–17; Warden CSP 08–17; rtd 17; Hon Can Guildf Cathl 05–10; Can Res Guildf Cathl from 10; Sub-Dean from

16. *Hollyhocks Barn, Hollyhocks Cottage, High Street, Bramley, Guildford GU5 0HB* E: sabeake@msn.com

BEAKEN, Robert William Frederick. b 62. SS Paul & Mary Coll Cheltenham BA 83 Lambeth STh 90 MA 01 K Coll Lon PhD 09 FSAScot 01 FRHistS 12. Ripon Coll Cuddesdon 85 Ven English Coll & Pontifical Gregorian Univ Rome 87. **d** 88 **p** 89. C Forton *Portsm* 88–92; C Shepshed *Leic* 92–94; V Colchester St Barn *Chelmsf* 94–02; P-in-c Gt and Lt Bardfield from 02. *The Vicarage, Braintree Road, Great Bardfield, Braintree CM7 4RN* T: (01371) 810267 E: robert@webform.co.uk

BEAL, David Michael. b 61. St Jo Coll Nottm BTh 89. **d** 89 **p** 90. C Marton *Blackb* 89–92; C Darwen St Pet w Hoddlesden 92–93; TV 93–97; R Itchingfield w Slinfold *Chich* 97–09; R W Chiltington 09–16; RD Storrington 11–16; V Billingshurst from 16; RD Horsham from 18. *The Vicarage, East Street, Billingshurst RH14 9PY* T: (01403) 785743 E: vicar@stmarysbillingshurst.org

BEALE, Miss Fiona Jane. b 71. Moorlands Coll BA 16. Wycliffe Hall Ox 17. **d** 19 **p** 20. C Beaminster Area *Sarum* from 19. *Orchard Cottage, Mosterton, Beaminster DT8 3HH* M: 07581-233772 E: revfionabeale@gmail.com

BEALES, Canon Christopher Leader Day. b 51. St Jo Coll Dur BA 72. Cranmer Hall Dur 72. **d** 76 **p** 77. C Upper Armley and Ind Chapl *Ripon* 76–79; Ind Chapl *Dur* 79–84; Sen Chapl 82–84; Sec Ind Cttee of Gen Syn Bd for Soc Resp 85–91; Sec Inner Cities Relig Coun (DOE) 92–94; Dir Churches' Regional Commn in the NE Newc and *Dur* 94–98; Consultant Dir 98; Chief Exec Employment Focus 99–07; C Thamesmead *S'wark* 99–01; PtO 01–10; Chief Exec Afghan Action 05–16; P-in-c Woburn Sands *St Alb* 08–12; V 12–17; Hon Can St Alb 14–17; rtd 17; PtO *Eur* from 98; *Dur* from 17; Visiting Fell St Jo Coll Dur from 17; Wm Leech Research Fell Dur Univ 17–19. *68 Arncliffe Gardens, Hartlepool TS26 9JF* T: (01429) 861518 M: 07597-135593 E: cbeales@outlook.com

BEALES, John David. b 55. SS Hild & Bede Coll Dur BA 77 Univ of W Aus DipEd 79. St Jo Coll Nottm 81. **d** 83 **p** 84. C Scarborough Australia 83–86; Dioc Youth Chapl Perth 86–89; Dir Educn and Tr Philo Trust 89–90; NSM Nottingham St Nic *S'well* 89–95; Dir Creative Communications Trust 90–95; Dir Evang Melbourne Australia 95–00; PtO *Chelmsf* 99–01; Public Preacher 01–14 and from 18; Pioneer Min 14–18. *52 Wellesley Road, Colchester CO3 3HF* T: (01206) 530934 M: 07791-684699 E: davidbeales@icloud.com

BEAMENT, Canon Owen John. b 41. MBE 01. Bps' Coll Cheshunt 61. **d** 64 **p** 65. C Deptford St Paul *S'wark* 64–68; C Peckham St Jo 69–73; C Vauxhall St Pet 73–74; V Hatcham Park All SS 74–18; Hon Can S'wark Cathl 97–18; rtd 19; PtO *S'wark* from 19. *85 Kynaston Road, Orpington BR5 4JY* E: owenbeament@aol.com

BEAN, David Andrew. b 65. Linc Sch of Th and Min 15. **d** 18. NSM Retford Area *S'well* 18–19; NSM Ordsall and Retford St Mich from 19. *197 Albert Road, Retford DN22 7AW* M: 07973-864027 E: d.a.bean@btinternet.com

BEANE, The Ven Andrew Mark. b 72. St Jo Coll Nottm BA 02. **d** 02 **p** 03. C Thorpe St Matt *Nor* 02–05; P-in-c Horsham St Faith, Spixworth and Crostwick 05–06; R 06–12; P-in-c Aylsham 12–17; P-in-c Cawston w Booton and Brandiston etc 12–17; C Lt Barningham, Blickling, Edgefield etc 15–17; P-in-c Bure Valley 16–17; TR Aylsham and Distr 17–19; RD Ingworth 13–18; RD Sparham 17–18; RD Ingworth and Sparham 18–19; Hon Can Nor Cathl 15–19; Adn Ex from 19. *Emmanuel House, Station Road, Ide, Exeter EX2 9RS* T: (01392) 425577 M: 07898-932654 E: andrew.beane@btinternet.com or archdeacon.of.exeter@exeter.anglican.org

BEANEY, Canon John. b 47. Trin Coll Bris 77. **d** 79 **p** 80. C Bromley Ch Ch *Roch* 79–84; V Broadheath *Ches* 84–08; Chapl Altrincham Gen Hosp 91–94; Chapl Trafford Healthcare NHS Trust 94–98; P-in-c Norton *Ches* 08–14; Ecum Officer (Gtr Man) 02–14; Hon Can Ches Cathl 10–14; rtd 14; PtO *Ches* from 14. *5 Wivern Place, Runcorn WA7 1RZ* T: (01928) 411801 E: jjbea68@gmail.com

BEARCROFT, Bramwell Arthur. b 52. Homerton Coll Cam BEd 82. EAMTC 87. **d** 90 **p** 91. Chapl and Hd RS Kimbolton Sch Cambs 88–94; NSM Tilbrook *Ely* 90–94; NSM Covington 90–94; NSM Catworth Magna 90–94; NSM Keyston and Bythorn 90–94; NSM Cary Deanery *B & W* 94–02; Hd Master Hazlegrove Sch 94–02; Asst Chapl Aquitaine *Eur* 10–16; PtO 16–20. *1 Lotissement de la Caussade, 33270 Floirac, France* T: (0033) 5 56 40 05 12 E: jenniferbearcroft@hotmail.com

BEARD, Christopher Robert. b 47. Chich Th Coll 81. **d** 83 **p** 84. C Chich St Paul and St Pet 83–86; V Haywards Heath St Rich 91–99; P-in-c Donnington 99–12; Chapl St Wilfrid's Hospice Eastbourne 99–12; rtd 12; PtO *Chich*

12–17. *70 Victoria Road, Chichester PO19 7JA* T: (01243) 696034 M: 07845-482779

BEARD, Laurence Philip. b 45. Lon Univ BA 68. Trin Coll Bris 88. **d** 90 **p** 91. C Trentham *Lich* 90–94; V Wolverhampton St Matt 94–01; P-in-c Hartshill *Cov* 01–08; rtd 08; PtO *St Alb* 09–18. *14 Beechcroft Avenue, Croxley Green, Rickmansworth WD3 3EQ* T: (01923) 222312 E: lpbeard@talk21.com

BEARDSLEY, Christina. b 51. Sussex Univ BA 73 St Jo Coll Cam PhD 99 Leeds Univ MA 07. Westcott Ho Cam 76. **d** 78 **p** 79. C Portsea N End St Mark *Portsm* 78–85; V Catherington and Clanfield 85–00; Chapl Worthing and Southlands Hosps NHS Trust 00–01; Asst Chapl Chelsea and Westmr Hosp NHS Foundn Trust 01–04; Chapl 04–08; Hd Multi-Faith Chapl 08–16; rtd 16; Visiting Lect St Mary's Univ Twickenham *Lon* from 10; PtO from 16. *Flat 7, 81 Belgrave Road, London SW1V 2BG* M: 07904-162312 E: belgravetina@gmail.com

BEARN, Hugh William. b 62. Man Univ BA 84 MA 98. Cranmer Hall Dur 86. **d** 89 **p** 90. C Heaton Ch Ch *Man* 89–92; Chapl RAF 92–96; V Tottington *Man* from 96; CF (TA) 96–02; Chapl Bury Hospice from 99; CF (ACF) from 06; Chapl to The Queen from 06; Chapl Man Univ from 19; Chapl Man Univ NHS Foundn Trust from 20. *St Anne's Vicarage, Chapel Street, Tottington, Bury BL8 4AP* T: (01204) 883713 E: hughbearn@aol.com

BEARPARK, Canon John Michael. b 36. Ex Coll Ox BA 59 MA 63. Linc Th Coll 59. **d** 61 **p** 62. C Bingley H Trin *Bradf* 61–64; C Baildon 64–67; V Fairweather Green 67–77; Chapl Airedale NHS Trust 77–94; V Steeton *Bradf* 77–94; Hon Can Bradf Cathl 89–01; V Bentham St Marg 94–01; P-in-c Bentham St Jo 99–01; RD Ewecross 94–00; rtd 01; PtO *Bradf* 01–14; *Leeds* from 14. *31 Northfields Crescent, Settle BD24 9JP* T: (01729) 822712 E: johnbearpark@gmail.com

BEASLEY, Canon Elizabeth Parish. b 58. Wake Forest Univ USA BA 79 Univ of the S STM 04. Harvard Div Sch MDiv 89. **d** 98 **p** 99. V Honolulu St Geo USA 98–01; P-in-c Kapaa All SS 02–05; V Kaneohe St Jo 05–07; Can for Min Development Dio Hawaii 07–11; Can to the Ordinary 11–14; I Adare and Kilmallock w Kilpeacon, Croom etc *L & K* from 14; Chan Can Limerick, Killaloe and Clonfert Cathls from 18. *The Rectory, Adare, Co Limerick, Republic of Ireland* T: (00353) (61) 396227 E: revlizadare@gmail.com

✠**BEASLEY, The Rt Revd Noel Michael Roy.** b 68. Imp Coll Lon BSc 91 Oriel Coll Ox DPhil 95 St Jo Coll Dur BA 98. Cranmer Hall Dur 96. **d** 99 **p** 00 **c** 15. C Newport w Longford, Chetwynd and Forton *Lich* 99–03; Chapl Westcott Ho Cam 03–07; Vice Prin 07–10; Dioc Dir of Miss *Ox* 10–15; Hon Can Ch Ch 14–15; Suff Bp Hertford *St Alb* from 15. *Bishopswood, 3 Stobarts Close, Knebworth SG3 6ND* T: (01438) 817260 E: bishophertford@stalbans.anglican.org

BEATON, Canon Mark Timothy. b 61. Univ of Wales (Ban) BA 83. Trin Coll Bris 03. **d** 05 **p** 06. C Swindon St Jo and St Andr *Bris* 05–08; P-in-c New Radnor and Llanfihangel Nantmelan etc *S & B* 08–11; R from 11; AD Maelienydd 14–15; AD Radnor and Builth from 16; Hon Can Brecon Cathl from 16. *The Rectory, School Lane, New Radnor, Presteigne LD8 2SS* T: (01544) 350342 E: revmarkbeaton@gmail.com

BEATTIE, Angus James. b 65. Northumbria Univ BA 92 PGCE 96. St Mellitus Coll BA 19. **d** 19 **p** 20. NSM Ruislip St Mary *Lon* from 19. *69 The Fairway, Ruislip HA4 0SP* T: (020) 8422 7126 M: 07508-482909 E: ajbeattie@hotmail.co.uk

BEATTIE, David George. b 42. MIMechE 76. CITC 01. **d** 04 **p** 05. NSM Belfast H Trin and St Silas *Conn* 04–09; NSM Whitehouse 09–10; Chapl Belfast Health and Soc Care Trust 10–16; NSM Ematris w Rockcorry, Aghabog and Aughnamullan *Clogh* 11–16; rtd 16; LtO *Conn* from 16. *12 Donegall Crescent, Whitehead, Carrickfergus BT38 9LS* T: (028) 9303 9664 E: beattie5@talktalk.net

BEATTIE, Margaret. *See* BREWSTER, Margaret

BEATTIE, Canon Noel Christopher. b 41. TCD BTh 65 Cranfield Inst of Tech MSc 86. **d** 68 **p** 69. C Belfast H Trin *Conn* 68–70; C Belfast St Bart 70–73; C Doncaster St Mary *Sheff* 73–77; TV Northampton Em *Pet* 77–88; Ind Chapl 85–88; Ind Chapl *Linc* 88–92; Ind Chapl *Roch* 92–04; Hon Can Roch Cathl 00–04; rtd 04; PtO *Heref* from 05. *6 Oaks Road, Church Stretton SY6 7AX* T: (01694) 725530

BEATTIE, Pamela. b 61. **d** 12. OLM Linc St Jo 12–14; C Linc St Giles 15–19; Chapl United Lincs Hosps NHS Trust from 15. *Chaplaincy Services, Lincoln County Hospital, Greetwell Road, Lincoln LN2 5QY* T: (01522) 573080 E: pamela.beattie@ulh.nhs.uk

BEATTIE, Sheila Rachel. b 57. All SS Cen for Miss & Min 17. **d** 18 **p** 19. OLM Bury St Mary *Man* from 18; OLM Bury St Paul from 18. *12 Brandon Close, Bury BL8 1XL*

BEATTY, Jeremy Sean. b 67. Univ of Cen England in Birm BA 95. All SS Cen for Miss & Min 16. **d** 19 **p** 20. C Marple All SS *Ches* from 19. *42 Edgeley Road,*

Stockport SK3 9NQ T: 0161-718 3493 M: 07914-448760 E: jeremyseanbeatty@gmail.com

BEAUCHAMP, Anthony Hazlerigg Proctor. b 40. Trin Coll Cam BA 62 MA 66 MICE 68. St Jo Coll Nottm 73. **d** 75 **p** 76. C New Humberstone *Leic* 75–77; C-in-c Polegate *Chich* 77–80; Chapl Bethany Sch Goudhurst 80–86; Chapl Luckley-Oakfield Sch Wokingham 86–88; Chapl Clayesmore Sch Blandford 89–93; R Kirby-le-Soken w Gt Holland *Chelmsf* 93–00; Asst P Wetheral w Warwick *Carl* 00–01; rtd 01; PtO *Carl* 00–01; *Chich* from 01. *58 Charger Road, Trumpington, Cambridge CB2 9EA* T: (01223) 840017 E: tony.beauchamp@askomil.com

BEAUCHAMP, Gerald Charles. b 55. Hull Univ BA 78 K Coll Lon MA 96. Coll of Resurr Mirfield 78. **d** 80 **p** 81. C Hatcham St Cath *S'wark* 80–83; S Africa 83–86; C Ealing St Steph Castle Hill *Lon* 86–88; P-in-c Brondesbury St Anne w Kilburn H Trin 88–89; V 89–93; Chapl Kilburn Coll 88–93; C Chelsea St Luke and Ch Ch *Lon* 93–96; V W Brompton St Mary w St Pet 96–04; AD Chelsea 02–04; SSJE 04–07; C St Marylebone All SS *Lon* 07–10; P-in-c St Marylebone St Cypr 10–20; P-in-c St Marylebone Annunciation Bryanston Street 10–16; V 16–20; rtd 20; PtO *Lon* from 20. *Uus 17-9, 10111 Tallinn, Estonia* E: geraldcharles.beauchamp@gmail.com

BEAUCHAMP, Preb John Nicholas. b 57. Wycliffe Hall Ox 92. **d** 94 **p** 95. C Ipswich St Jo *St E* 94–97; TV Beccles St Mich 97–05; P-in-c Beccles St Mich and St Luke 05–08; R 08–15; V Canonbury St Steph *Lon* 15–21; Dioc Disability Min Enabler from 21; Preb St Paul's Cathl from 21. *2 Anatola Road, London N19 5HN* E: revjohnbeauchamp@gmail.com

BEAUCHAMP, Julian Thomas Proctor. b 68. Ex Univ BA 91. Oak Hill Th Coll BA 05. **d** 05 **p** 06. C Cheadle *Ches* 05–08; R Waverton w Aldford and Bruera from 08. *The Rectory, Village Road, Waverton, Chester CH3 7QN* T: (01244) 336668 M: 07974-397022 E: jules@stpeterswaverton.org.uk

BEAUMONT, Adam John. b 75. Bris Univ BSc 97 PGCE 01. Trin Coll Bris MA 12. **d** 12 **p** 13. C Westbury-on-Trym H Trin *Bris* 12–15; TV Gtr Corsham and Lacock 15–20; R Gauzebrook from 20. *The Vicarage, Green Lane, Sherston, Malmesbury SN16 0NP* M: 07903-672067 E: adamjbeaumont@gmail.com

BEAUMONT, Catherine Grace La Touche. See BOND, Catherine Grace La Touche

BEAUMONT, Mrs Jane. b 56. Ches Coll of HE BTh. NOC 01. **d** 04 **p** 05. NSM Chadkirk *Ches* 04–08; C Ashton-upon-Mersey St Mary Magd 08–21; rtd 21. *Highgate, Higher Chisworth, Chisworth, Glossop SK13 5SA*

BEAUMONT, Ms Jennifer Mary. b 76. Man Metrop Univ BA 98 Ches Univ MA 18. All SS Cen for Miss & Min 15. **d** 18 **p** 19. C Davyhulme St Mary *Man* from 18. *76 Whitelake Avenue, Urmston, Manchester M41 5QW* M: 07396-376134 E: jennicarrbeau@gmail.com

BEAUMONT, Stephen Martin. b 51. K Coll Lon BD 73 AKC 74. St Aug Coll Cant 73. **d** 74 **p** 75. C Benwell St Jas *Newc* 74–77; Asst Chapl Marlborough Coll 77–81; R Ideford, Luton and Ashcombe *Ex* 81–84; Bp's Dom Chapl 81–84; Chapl Taunton Sch 85–91; Chapl Haileybury Coll 92–00; Second Chapl and Hd Div Tonbridge Sch 00–04; Sen Chapl Taunton Sch 04–11; P-in-c Chiddingstone w Chiddingstone Causeway *Roch* 11–12; R 12–17; rtd 17; PtO *B & W* 18–19; Hon C Wellington and Distr from 19. *Hilltop, Butts Way, Milverton, Taunton TA4 1JR* T: (01823) 400127

BEAUMONT, Canon Terence Mayes. b 41. Lon Univ BA 63. Linc Th Coll 68. **d** 71 **p** 72. C Hitchin St Mary *St Alb* 71–74; C Harpenden St Nic 75–79; V Stevenage St Pet Broadwater 79–87; V St Alb St Mich 87–06; Hon Can St Alb 05–06; rtd 06; PtO *St Alb* from 06. *65 Weatherby, Dunstable LU6 1TP* T: (01582) 661333 E: terrybeaumont@ymail.com

BEAUMONT, Mrs Veronica Jean. b 38. Ox Min Course 90. **d** 93 **p** 94. NSM High Wycombe Ox 93–03; NSM W Wycombe w Bledlow Ridge, Bradenham and Radnage from 03; Fundraising Manager (Oxon) Children's Soc 95–00. *Edgehill, Upper Stanley Road, High Wycombe HP12 4DB* T: (01494) 523697 M: 07958-701913 E: veronica.beaumont@virgin.net

BEAVAN, Canon Edward Hugh. b 43. Ex Coll Ox BA 70 MA 74 Solicitor 66. Cuddesdon Coll 69. **d** 71 **p** 72. C Ashford St Hilda *Lon* 71–74; C Newington St Mary *S'wark* 74–76; R Sandon *Chelmsf* 76–86; V Thorpe Bay 86–98; P-in-c Bradwell on Sea 98–05; P-in-c St Lawrence 98–05; V Burnham 05–09; Ind Chapl 98–05; RD Maldon and Dengie 00–05; Hon Can Chelmsf Cathl 02–09; rtd 09; PtO *Chelmsf* from 09. *19 Wordsworth Road, Colchester CO3 4HR* T: (01206) 564577 E: hugh@beavan.go-plus.net

BEAVER, William Carpenter. b 45. Colorado Coll BA Wolfs Coll Ox DPhil 76. Ox NSM Course 79. **d** 82 **p** 83. NSM Kennington St Jo w St Jas *S'wark* 82–95; NSM Avonmouth

St Andr *Bris* 96–97; NSM Bris St Mary Redcliffe w Temple etc 95–08; NSM St Andr Holborn *Lon* 01–04; Dir Communications for C of E 97–02; Dir Communications for Br Red Cross 02–04; Speech Writer to the Ld Mayor of Lon 04–10; NSM Iffley *Ox* 10–19; Offg Chapl Household Cavalry Mounted Regt 09–15; Chapl Light Cavalry Hon Artillery Co 15–19; PtO *Lon* from 16; *Ox* from 19. *Townsend Close, 50 Church Way, Iffley, Oxford OX4 4EF* T: (01865) 778061 E: williambeaver01@gmail.com

BEAVIS, Adrian Neill. b 74. Worc Coll Ox BA 97. Wycliffe Hall Ox MTh 00. **d** 00 **p** 01. C E Twickenham St Steph *Lon* 00–08; V S Kensington St Luke 08–20; V Woking Ch Ch *Guildf* from 20. *Christ Church Vicarage, 10 Russetts Close, Woking GU21 4BH* E: adrian.beavis@gmail.com

BEAVIS, Sandra Kathleen. b 51. Univ Coll Chich BA 01. **d** 98 **p** 07. C Southbourne w W Thorney *Chich* 98–05; C Bedhampton *Portsm* 05–09; PtO 09–10; P-in-c Soberton w Newtown 10–16; OCM 02–16; rtd 16. *1 Princess Gardens, Waterlooville PO8 9PT* E: sandrabeavis@btinternet.com

BEAZLEY, Prof John Milner. b 32. Man Univ MB, ChB 57 MRCOG 62 FRCOG 73 FACOG 89 MD 64. St Deiniol's Hawarden 83. **d** 86 **p** 87. NSM W Kirby St Bridget *Ches* 86–89; NSM Newton 89–92; NSM Hayton w Cumwhitton *Carl* 92–98; rtd 99; PtO *Carl* 99–19; *Ox* from 15. *The Stables, High Street, Great Linford, Milton Keynes MK14 5AX* T: (01908) 665005

BEAZLEY-LONG, Clive. b 77. Greenwich Univ BSc 99. Trin Coll Bris 08. **d** 10 **p** 11. C Chertsey, Lyne and Longcross *Guildf* 10–14; V Erith St Paul *Roch* from 14. *The Vicarage, 44A Colyers Lane, Erith DA8 3NP* E: revclive@hotmail.co.uk

BEBB, Erica Charlotte. b 61. STETS. **d** 09 **p** 10. NSM Sea Mills *Bris* 09–13; NSM Clifton Ch Ch w Em from 13. *21 Bramble Drive, Bristol BS9 1RE* T: 0117-968 2153 E: erica.bebb@ccweb.org.uk

BEBBINGTON, Julia. See BABB, Julia Bebbington

BECK, Amanda Ruth. b 68. Liv Univ BA 91 Birm Univ BD 93. Qu Coll Birm 91. **d** 94 **p** 95. C W Derby Gd Shep *Liv* 94–99; Asst Chapl Voorschoten *Eur* 99–02; P-in-c Kingston Vale St Jo *S'wark* 03–12; TV Kingston from 12; Chapl SW Lon and St George's Mental Health NHS Trust from 13. *St John's Vicarage, Robin Hood Lane, London SW15 3PY* T: (020) 8546 4079 E: mandy.beck@alty.org

BECK, Mrs Gillian Margaret. b 50. Sheff Univ CertEd 71 Nottm Univ BTh 78. Linc Th Coll 74. **dss** 78 **d** 87. Gt Grimsby St Mary and St Jas *Linc* 78–83; St Paul's Cathl *Lon* 84–87; Hon Par Dn St Botolph Aldgate w H Trin Minories 87–88; Par Dn Monkwearmouth St Andr *Dur* 88–94; C 94–96; NSM Eppleton and Hetton le Hole 97–04; NSM E Rainton 04–11; NSM W Rainton 04–11; PtO from 13. *3 Ten Fields, Hetton-le-Hole, Houghton le Spring DH5 9NB* T: 0191-526 3886 E: mgtbex@gmail.com

BECK, Ms Karen Maureen. b 53. R Holloway Coll Lon BA 74. St Alb Minl Tr Scheme 88. **d** 92 **p** 94. Par Dn Royston *St Alb* 92–94; C 94–96; TV Chipping Barnet w Arkley 96–02; P-in-c Heddon-on-the-Wall *Newc* 02–07; Chapl Northumbria Police 02–07; P-in-c Didcot All SS *Ox* 07–18; rtd 18. *35 Oulton Lane, Liverpool L36 4QX* E: karen.beck140@gmail.com

BECK, Michael Leonard. b 50. K Coll Lon BD 77 AKC 77 Seabury-Western Th Sem DMin 04. Linc Th Coll 77. **d** 78 **p** 79. C Gt Grimsby St Mary and St Jas *Linc* 78–83; Min Can and Succ St Paul's Cathl *Lon* 83–88; V Monkwearmouth St Andr *Dur* 88–96; TR Monkwearmouth 97; R Eppleton and Hetton le Hole 97–04; AD Houghton 97–04; P-in-c Lyons 00–04; P-in-c W Rainton 04–15; P-in-c E Rainton 04–15; Dir Reader Min 04–09; Tutor Lindisfarne Regional Tr Partnership 09–16; rtd 16; PtO *Dur* from 16. *3 Ten Fields, Hetton-le-Hole, Houghton le Spring DH5 9NB* T: 0191-526 3886 M: 07793-462896 E: mlbparish@gmail.com

BECK, Rachel Gillian. b 80. Bp Grosseteste Coll BA 05 Selw Coll Cam BTh 16. Westcott Ho Cam 14 Yale Div Sch 16. **d** 17 **p** 18. C Linc St Giles 17–21; V Glouc St Geo w Whaddon from 21. *St George's Vicarage, Grange Road, Tuffley, Gloucester GL4 0PE* M: 07753-389865 E: rgbeck@btinternet.com

BECK, Roger William. b 48. Chich Th Coll 79. **d** 81 **p** 82. C St Marychurch *Ex* 81–85; TV Torre 85–88; V Torquay St Jo and Ellacombe 88–94; C Plympton St Mary 94–16; TV Plympton 16–17; rtd 18. *81 Fore Street, Plympton, Plymouth PL7 1NB* T: (01752) 336393

BECK, Mrs Sandra Veronica. b 52. St Jo Coll Nottm 97. **d** 00 **p** 01. NSM Digswell and Panshanger *St Alb* 00–04; NSM Codicote 04–08; PtO 08–09; Chapl E and N Herts NHS Trust 09–13; PtO *St Alb* 13–16; NSM Welwyn from 16. *4 Grange Rise, Codicote, Hitchin SG4 8YR* T: (01438) 820191 E: sckbeck@btinternet.com

BECKERLEG, Ms April Cornelia. b 62. Worc Coll of HE BEd 83. Ripon Coll Cuddesdon 15. **d** 17 **p** 18. C Bicester w

Bucknell, Caversfield and Launton *Ox* 17–20; V Earley St Nic from 20. *The Vicarage, 53 Sutcliffe Avenue, Earley, Reading RG6 7JN* M: 07951-119271 E: april@stnicolas.org.uk

BECKETT, Bonnie. *See* BECKETT, Yvonne Janine

BECKETT (formerly **MARTIN), Mrs Caroline Evelyn.** b 76. York Univ BA 98 Homerton Coll Cam PGCE 99. St Mellitus Coll BA 15. **d** 15 **p** 16. C Berechurch St Marg w St Mich *Chelmsf* 15–18; V Brightlingsea from 18. *The Vicarage, Richard Avenue, Brightlingsea, Colchester CO7 0LP* T: (01206) 308726 E: revcarolinebeckett@gmail.com

BECKETT, Glynis Joy. b 49. **d** 10 **p** 11. OLM Radley and Sunningwell *Ox* 10–15; OLM Radley, Sunningwell and Kennington from 15. *18 Sadlers Court, Abingdon OX14 2PA* T: (01235) 529505

BECKETT, Graham. b 49. St As Minl Tr Course 95. **d** 99 **p** 00. NSM Hawarden *St As* 99–01; C 01–07; V Gorsedd w Brynford, Ysgeifiog and Whitford 07–14; P-in-c Mostyn 13–14; AD Holywell 11–14; rtd 14; PtO *St As* from 16. *Hillview, Church Lane, Aston Hill, Ewloe, Deeside CH5 3BF* T: (01244) 535269 E: g147beckett@btinternet.com

BECKETT, John Adrian. b 61. Bris Univ BVSc 85. Trin Coll Bris. **d** 00 **p** 01. C Harrogate St Mark *Ripon* 00–04; P-in-c Sevenhampton w Charlton Abbots, Hawling etc *Glouc* 04–14; P-in-c Torquay St Matthias, St Mark and H Trin *Ex* 14–15; R from 15. *The Rectory, Wellswood Avenue, Torquay TQ1 2QE* T: (01803) 293119 M: 07513-346521 E: jandrbeckett@btinternet.com

BECKETT, Michael Shaun. b 55. ACA 79. Oak Hill Th Coll BA 88. **d** 88 **p** 89. C Cambridge St Barn *Ely* 88–93; P-in-c Cambridge St Paul 93–94; V 94–21; rtd 21. *Address temp unknown*

BECKETT, Mrs Patricia Ann. b 44. **d** 00 **p** 01. NSM Cheddleton *Lich* 00–06; NSM Upper Tean 06–12; PtO 13–21. *10 Wallis Way, Stoke-on-Trent ST2 7JQ* T: (01782) 769718 E: revpatbeckett@btinternet.com

BECKETT, Mrs Yvonne Janine (Bonnie). b 50. Qu Coll Birm 13. **d** 15 **p** 16. OLM Walsall Pleck and Bescot *Lich* 15–21; PtO from 21. *1 Newhall Crescent, Cannock WS11 7ZD* T: (01543) 270011 M: 07730-599633 E: bonniebeckett@talktalk.net

BECKINSALE, Mrs Pamela Rachel. b 46. Man Univ BSc 69. Cant Sch of Min 88. **d** 91 **p** 94. NSM Sittingbourne St Mich *Cant* 91–96; Hon Chapl Thames Gateway NHS Trust 96–98; Chapl 98–16; Chapl Kent and Medway NHS and Soc Care Partnership Trust from 16; PtO *Cant* from 16. *8 Glovers Crescent, Bell Road, Sittingbourne ME10 4DU* T: (01795) 471632 E: revpambeckinsale@tiscali.co.uk

BECKLES, Miss Natasha Selina. Univ of N Lon BA 99 Roehampton Inst PGCE 01. St Mellitus Coll BA 20. **d** 20 **p** 21. C Oseney Crescent St Luke *Lon* from 20. *Address withheld by request* E: revdnatashabeckles@gmail.com

BECKLEY, Peter William (Pedr). b 52. Lon Univ BSc 73 CertEd. Trin Coll Bris 76. **d** 79 **p** 80. C Plymouth St Jude *Ex* 79–83; C Ecclesall *Sheff* 83–88; V Greystones 88–18; P-in-c Endcliffe 11–15; rtd 18; PtO *Bris* from 19. *69 Hill View, Henleaze, Bristol BS9 4QF* E: pedrwb@gmail.com

BECKLEY, Simon Richard. b 38. Lon Univ BA 61. Oak Hill Th Coll 58. **d** 63 **p** 64. C Watford St Luke *St Alb* 63–67; C New Ferry *Ches* 67–70; C Chadderton Ch Ch *Man* 70–73; V Friarmere 73–80; V Tranmere St Cath *Ches* 80–03; Chapl Wirral Community Healthcare NHS Trust 80–97; Chapl Wirral and W Cheshire Community NHS Trust 97–03; rtd 03; PtO *Ches* 04–19. *14 Gracey Court, Woodland Road, Broadclyst, Exeter EX5 3GA* T: (01392) 461237

BECKWITH, John James. b 53. UMIST BSc 74 Newc Univ PGCE 88. **d** 02 **p** 03. OLM Bothal and Pegswood w Longhirst *Newc* 02–04; C Morpeth 04–07; V Belford and Lucker 07–18; rtd 18; PtO *Newc* from 18. *9 Kenmore Crescent, Greenside, Ryton NE40 4QY* M: 07989-102458 E: john_ang@hotmail.co.uk

BECKWITH, Roger Thomas. b 29. St Edm Hall Ox BA 52 MA 56 BD 85 Lambeth DD 92. Ripon Hall Ox 51 Tyndale Hall Bris 52 Cuddesdon Coll 54. **d** 54 **p** 55. C Harold Wood *Chelmsf* 54–57; C Bedminster St Luke w St Silas *Bris* 57–59; Tutor Tyndale Hall Bris 59–63; Lib Latimer Ho Ox 63–73 and from 94; Warden 73–94; Lect Wycliffe Hall Ox 71–94; Hon C Wytham *Ox* 88–89; Hon C N Hinksey and Wytham 90–96; rtd 94; Hon C Ox St Mich w St Martin and All SS 97–03; PtO 03–18. *310 Woodstock Road, Oxford OX2 7NR* T: (01865) 557340

BEDBOROUGH, Sarah. b 54. **d** 15 **p** 15. Chapl Weldmar Hospice 07–18; C Parkstone St Pet and St Osmund w Branksea *Sarum* from 15. *375 Wimborne Road, Poole BH15 3ED* T: (01202) 245463 E: sarah.bedborough@sky.com

BEDFORD, Christopher John. b 40. CEng 68 MIStructE 68. **d** 05 **p** 06. OLM Chobham w Valley End *Guildf* 05–10; PtO from 10. *23 Swallow Rise, Knaphill, Woking GU21 2LG* T: (01483) 480127 E: ahbedford@hotmail.com

BEDFORD, Michael Anthony. b 38. Reading Univ BSc 59 Heythrop Coll Lon MA 00. **d** 01 **p** 02. NSM Ruislip St Martin *Lon* 01–11; NSM Ruislip St Mary 11–18; PtO from 18. *7 Chandos Road, Eastcote, Pinner HA5 1PR* T: (020) 8866 4332 E: mabedford7cr@waitrose.com

BEDFORD, Rachel Jayne. b 85. Regent's Park Coll Ox BA 06 Cant Ch Ch Univ Coll QTS 07. St Mellitus Coll 13. **d** 16 **p** 17. C Kensal Rise St Mark *Lon* 16–19; C E Twickenham St Steph from 20; PtO 19–20. *92 St Margarets Grove, Twickenham TW1 1JG* M: 07799-624534 E: rachel.bedford@hotmail.co.uk

BEDFORD, Miss Susan Frances. b 55. Furzedown Coll of Educn CertEd 77. Yorks Min Course 15. **d** 17 **p** 18. NSM Doncaster St Geo *Sheff* 17–20; PtO from 21. *16 Granby Crescent, Doncaster DN2 6AN* M: 07503-186929 E: susan.bedford@doncasterminster.org.uk

BEDFORD, Archdeacon of. *See* MIDDLEBROOK, The Ven David John

BEDFORD, Suffragan Bishop of. *See* ATKINSON, The Rt Revd Richard William Bryant

BEE, Canon Judith Mary. b 52. STETS 03. **d** 06 **p** 07. NSM Hambledon *Portsm* 06–10; NSM Buriton from 10; NSM Petersfield from 11; Hon Can Portsm Cathl from 20. *St Mary's House, 41 North Lane, Buriton, Petersfield GU31 4RS* T: (01730) 269390 E: judith.bee@clara.co.uk

BEE, Mark Hilton. b 64. **d** 20 **p** 21. NSM Beccles St Mich and St Luke *St E* 20–21; NSM Beccles w Worlingham, N Cove and Barnby from 21. *69 London Road, Beccles NR34 9YT* E: mark.bee@btinternet.com

BEEBEE, Meyrick Richard Legge. b 43. SAOMC 99. **d** 02 **p** 03. NSM Gerrards Cross and Fulmer *Ox* from 02. *Lychgate House, 34 Austenway, Chalfont St Peter, Gerrards Cross SL9 8NW* T: (01753) 424375 M: 07956-435025 E: meyrick.beebee@saintjames.org.uk

BEEBY, Matthew David. b 77. Nottm Univ BA 99. Oak Hill Th Coll BA 11. **d** 11 **p** 12. NSM Mayfair Ch Ch *Lon* 11–19; R Gerrards Cross and Fulmer *Ox* from 19. *St James's Church, Oxford Road, Gerrards Cross SL9 7DJ* T: (01753) 883311 M: 07967-107228 E: matt.beeby@saintjames.org.uk

BEECH, Miss Ailsa. b 44. N Co Coll Newc TDip 65. Trin Coll Bris 78. **dss** 80 **d** 87 **p** 94. Pudsey St Lawr and St Paul *Bradf* 80–88; Par Dn 87–88; C Attleborough *Cov* 88–89; Par Dn Cumnor *Ox* 89–92; Asst Chapl Walsgrave Hosp Cov 92–94; Asst Chapl Walsgrave Hosps NHS Trust 94–96; Chapl 96–00; Chapl Univ Hosps Cov and Warks NHS Trust 00–04; rtd 04; PtO *York* 04–21. *Oxenby, Whitby Road, Pickering YO18 7HL* T: (01751) 472689 E: beecha71@gmail.com

BEECH, Preb Charmian Patricia. b 45. RGN 66 RHV 70 TCert 74. St As Minl Tr Course 99. **d** 02 **p** 03. C Connah's Quay *St As* 02–04; P-in-c Hodnet *Lich* 04–14; Dioc Child Protection Officer 04–14; RD Hodnet 11–14; Preb Lich Cathl 13–14; rtd 14; PtO *Heref* from 15; *Lich* 15–19. *3 Church Meadow, Ditton Priors, Bridgnorth WV16 6TH* E: salop@charmianbeech14.plus.com *or* charmianbeech@icloud.com

BEECH, John. b 41. St Jo Coll Nottm. **d** 83 **p** 83. C York St Paul 83–84; P-in-c Bubwith w Ellerton and Aughton 84–85; P-in-c Thorganby w Skipwith and N Duffield 84–85; V Bubwith w Skipwith 85–87; V Acomb H Redeemer 87–00; P-in-c Westleigh St Pet *Man* 00–01; rtd 01; PtO *York* 04–18. *6 Water Ark Cottages, Goathland, Whitby YO22 5JZ* E: jobe69@btinternet.com

BEECH, John Thomas. b 38. St Aid Birkenhead 64. **d** 67 **p** 68. C Burton St Paul *Lich* 67–70; Chapl RN 70–85; V Ellingham and Harbridge and Ibsley *Win* 85–94; Chapl Whiteley Village *Guildf* 94–03; rtd 03. *10 Friars Walk, Barton-on-Sea, New Milton BH25 7DA*

BEECH, Peter John. b 34. York St Jo Univ Hon BEd 19. Bps' Coll Cheshunt 58. **d** 61 **p** 62. C Fulham All SS *Lon* 61–64; Prec Kimberley Cathl S Africa 64–68; Dom Chapl to Bp Kimberley and Kuruman 64–68; V S Hackney St Mich *Lon* 68–71; P-in-c Haggerston St Paul 68–71; V S Hackney St Mich w Haggerston St Paul 71–75; V Wanstead H Trin Hermon Hill *Chelmsf* 75–89; P-in-c St Mary-at-Latton 89–90; V 90–99; rtd 99; PtO *Ely* 99–19. *10 Stuart Court, High Street, Kibworth Beauchamp, Leicester LE8 0LR*

BEECH-GRÜNEBERG, Keith Nigel. b 72. CCC Ox BA 93 MA 96 St Jo Coll Dur BA 97 PhD 02. Cranmer Hall Dur 95. **d** 01 **p** 02. C Pangbourne w Tidmarsh and Sulham *Ox* 01–04; Dir Studies Dioc Bd Stewardship 04–11; Dir Local Min Tr 11–16; IME Pathways Adv Min Division from 16. *Ministry Division, Church House, 27 Great Smith Street, London SW1P 3AZ* T: (020) 7898 1000 M: 07731-894344 E: keith.beech-gruneberg@churchofengland.org

BEECHAM, Mrs Sally-Anne. b 72. Open Univ MA 02. St Hild Coll 16. **d** 19 **p** 20. C Chesterfield SS Aug *Derby* from 19; C

Bakewell, Ashford w Sheldon and Rowsley 19–20; C Walton St Jo from 20. *161 Old Road, Chesterfield S40 3QL* M: 07849-110495 E: revsalbeecham@gmail.com

BEECROFT, Benjamin Harold. b 77. Trin Coll Bris BA 98. **d** 00 **p** 01. C Stapleford *S'well* 00–04; C Warfield *Ox* 04–07; V Addlestone *Guildf* from 07; AD Runnymede from 20. *The Vicarage, 140 Church Road, Addlestone KT15 1SJ* T: (01932) 842879 E: ben.beecroft@btinternet.com

BEECROFT, Mrs Christine Mary. b 62. RGN 85. Trin Coll Bris BA 97 MA 99. **d** 98 **p** 99. C Roxeth *Lon* 98–00; PtO *S'well* 00–02; C Stapleford 02–04; NSM Warfield *Ox* 04–07; C Addlestone *Guildf* from 09. *The Vicarage, 140 Church Road, Addlestone KT15 1SJ* T: (01932) 842879 E: chrisbeecroft@btinternet.com

BEECROFT, Mrs Miriam Joanna. Univ of Wales (Abth) BSc(Soc) 07. St Mich Coll Llan 11. **d** 15 **p** 16. C Bro Ardudwy *Ban* 15–18; V Bro Cyfeiliog and Mawddwy from 18. *16 Pencaemawr, Penegoes, Machynlleth SY20 8PF* T: (01654) 638096 E: miriam@esgobaethbangor.net

BEEDELL, Trevor Francis. b 31. ALCD 65. **d** 65 **p** 66. C Walton *St E* 65–68; R Hartshorne *Derby* 68–79; RD Repton 74–79; V Doveridge 79–86; Chapl HM Det Cen Foston Hall 79–80; Dioc Dir of Chr Stewardship *Derby* 79–97; rtd 97; PtO *Derby* 97–18. *185 High Lane West, West Hallam, Ilkeston DE7 6HP* T: 0115-932 5589

BEEDON, David Kirk. b 56. Birm Univ BA 89 MPhil 93 DPT 20. Qu Coll Birm 86. **d** 89 **p** 90. C Cannock *Lich* 89–92; V Wednesbury St Bart 92–99; R Lich St Mich w St Mary and Wall 99–12; P-in-c Lich Ch Ch 07–09; Chapl HM Pris Ranby 12–18; rtd 18; PtO *S'well* 18–19; *Lich* from 19. *Address withheld by request* E: david.beedon59@btinternet.com

BEER, Anthony Mark. St Mich Coll Llan. **d** 09 **p** 10. NSM Caerau w Ely *Llan* 09–11; C Llantwit Major 11–13; TV 13–16; P-in-c Laleston and Merthyr Mawr w Penyfai from 16. *The Vicarage, Rogers Lane, Laleston, Bridgend CF32 0LB* T: (01656) 859487 E: blammp2013@gmail.com

BEER, Ms Deborah Marion. SEITE 12. **d** 15 **p** 16. NSM Hurstpierpoint *Chich* from 15; Dioc Environment Officer from 19. *Address withheld by request* M: 07530-039299 E: revdebbiebeer@gmail.com

BEER, Mrs Janet Margaret. b 43. Goldsmiths' Coll Lon CertEd 64. Oak Hill Th Coll 83. dss 86 **d** 87 **p** 94. London Colney *St Alb* 86–97; Hon C 87–97; Chapl St Alb High Sch for Girls 87–89; Chapl Middx Univ *Lon* 94–97; NSM Northaw and Cuffley *St Alb* 97–09; rtd 09; PtO *Portsm* from 09. *L'Auberge, 15 Seymour Road, Lee-on-the-Solent PO13 9EG* T: (023) 9255 0264 E: j.m.beer@btinternet.com

BEER, The Ven John Stuart. b 44. Pemb Coll Ox BA 65 MA 70 Fitzw Coll Cam MA 78. Westcott Ho Cam 69. **d** 71 **p** 72. C Knaresborough St Jo *Ripon* 71–74; Chapl Fitzw Coll and New Hall Cam 74–80; Fell Fitzw Coll 77–80; Bye-Fell from 01; P-in-c Toft w Caldecote and Childerley *Ely* 80–83; R 83–87; P-in-c Hardwick 80–83; R 83–87; V Grantchester 87–97; Dir of Ords, Post-Ord Tr and Student Readers from 88; Hon Can Ely Cathl from 89; Adn Huntingdon 97–04; Acting Adn Wisbech 02–04; Adn Cam 04–14; rtd 14. *Fitzwilliam College, Storey's Way, Cambridge CB3 0DG* E: johnbeer1@btinternet.com

BEER, Kevin Lionel Charles. b 74. SWMTC 09. **d** 12 **p** 13. C Parkham, Alwington, Buckland Brewer etc *Ex* 12–14; NSM 14–20; NSM Bideford, Landcross, Littleham etc from 20. *3 Bevil Close, Bideford EX39 5XN* T: (01237) 421823 E: mrkevinlcbeer@btinternet.com

BEER, Kevin Vincent. b 65. Ox Min Course 09. **d** 12 **p** 13. C Beaconsfield *Ox* 12–16; TV Wallingford from 16. *The Vicarage, 34 Thames Mead, Crowmarsh Gifford, Wallingford OX10 8EY* M: 07740-869501 E: kvbeer@gmail.com

BEER, Matthew James. b 89. Ridley Hall Cam 13. **d** 16 **p** 17. C Bletchley *Ox* 16–19; Pioneer Min Telford *Lich* from 19. *95 Ernest Dawes Avenue, Priorslee, Telford TF2 9XA* M: 07891-567518 E: beermatt89@gmail.com

BEER, Michael Trevor. b 44. Chich Th Coll 66. **d** 69 **p** 70. C Leagrave *St Alb* 69–73; C St Geo Cathl Kingstown St Vincent 73–74; C Thorley w Bishop's Stortford H Trin *St Alb* 74–80; V London Colney 80–97; V Northaw and Cuffley 97–09; rtd 09; PtO *Portsm* from 09. *L'Auberge, 15 Seymour Road, Lee-on-the-Solent PO13 9EG* T: (023) 9255 0264 E: michael@mbwoodcarving.co.uk

BEER, Nigel David. b 62. Portsm Poly BSc 84. St Jo Coll Nottm MA 93. **d** 93 **p** 94. C Rastrick St Matt *Wakef* 93–96; C Bilton *Ripon* 96–98; TV Moor Allerton 98–09; TV Moor Allerton and Shadwell 09–13; Asst Dir of Ords 05–13; V Stanwix *Carl* from 13; RD Carl from 16. *The Vicarage, Dykes Terrace, Carlisle CA3 9AS* T: (01228) 514600 E: revbeer@hotmail.co.uk

BEER, William Barclay. b 43. ACT ThA 68 St Steph Ho Ox. **d** 71 **p** 72. C St Marychurch *Ex* 71–76; V Pattishall w Cold Higham

Pet 76–82; V Northampton St Benedict 82–85; V Chislehurst Annunciation *Roch* 85–12; rtd 12; PtO *Lon* from 14. *St Mary's Vicarage, Lansdowne Road, London N17 9XE* T: (020) 8808 6644 E: williambarclaybeer@gmail.com

BEERE, Adrian Mark. b 69. St Mellitus Coll BA 17. **d** 19 **p** 20. C Charlton Kings St Mary *Glouc* from 19. *2 Royal Crescent, Cheltenham GL50 3DA* M: 07788-725331 E: adrian.beere@icloud.com

BEESLEY, Aran Paul. b 71. Linc Sch of Th and Min 11 Westcott Ho Cam 14. **d** 15 **p** 16. C Stamford All SS w St Jo *Linc* 15–18; R Uffington Gp from 18. *67 Main Road, Uffington, Stamford PE9 4SN* M: 07590-055905 E: aran.beesley@gmail.com

BEESLEY, Daniel Edward. b 76. Man Univ BA 01. Wycliffe Hall Ox 13. **d** 15 **p** 16. C Risborough *Ox* 15–19; P-in-c Bierton and Hulcott from 19. *The Vicarage, 5 St James Way, Bierton, Aylesbury HP22 5ED* M: 07590-123603 E: revdbeesley@gmail.com

BEESLEY, Mrs Gemma Louise. b 79. Ox Min Course 15. **d** 18 **p** 19. C Cowley St Jas *Ox* 18–21; R Bernwode from 21. *The Vicarage, 7 High Street, Brill, Aylesbury HP18 9ST* M: 07894-637020 E: rector@bernwodebenefice.com

BEESLEY, John Stanley. b 70. St Martin's Coll Lanc BSc 92. WEMTC 06. **d** 09 **p** 10. C Ludlow *Heref* 09–12; R Corvedale Benefice from 12. *St Michael's Rectory, Park Lane, Munslow, Craven Arms SY7 9EU* T: (01584) 841488 E: revjbeesley@gmail.com

BEESLEY, Michael Frederick. b 37. K Coll Cam BA 59. Westcott Ho Cam 60. **d** 61 **p** 64. C Eastleigh *Win* 61–69; rtd 02; PtO *Sarum* 09–22. *11 Coy Pond Road, Poole BH12 1JT* T: (01202) 776915 E: michaelbeesley97@gmail.com

BEESON, Christopher George. b 48. Man Univ BSc 70. Qu Coll Birm 72. **d** 75 **p** 76. C Flixton St Mich *Man* 75–78; C Newton Heath All SS 78–80; R Gorton St Jas 80–90; Dioc Communications Officer *Blackb* 91–92; C Ribbleton 92–93; rtd 93; PtO *Blackb* from 93. *24 Arnold Close, Ribbleton, Preston PR2 6DX* T: (01772) 702675 E: cbeeson@cix.co.uk

BEESON, The Very Revd Trevor Randall. b 26. OBE 97. K Coll Lon MA 76 FKC 87 Southn Univ Hon DLitt 99. **d** 51 **p** 52. C Leadgate *Dur* 51–54; C Norton St Mary 54–56; C-in-c Stockton St Chad CD 56–60; V Stockton St Chad 60–65; C St Martin-in-the-Fields *Lon* 65–71; V Ware St Mary *St Alb* 71–76; Can Westmr Abbey 76–87; Treas Westmr Abbey 78–82; I Westmr St Marg 82–87; Chapl to Speaker of Ho of Commons 82–87; Dean *Win* 87–96; rtd 96; PtO *Win* 96–21. *69 Greatbridge Road, Romsey SO51 8FE* T: (01794) 514627 E: alison.beeson@gmail.com

BEESTON, Andrew Bernard. b 41. RMN 64 RGN 67. NEOC 99. **d** 01 **p** 02. NSM Cullercoats St Geo *Newc* 01–06; NSM Long Benton 06–09; NSM Earsdon and Backworth 09–11; PtO from 11. *21 Deepdale Road, Cullercoats, North Shields NE30 3AN* T: 0191-259 0431 E: werdnabeeston@btinternet.com

BEET, Duncan Clive. b 65. LLB. Ridley Hall Cam 98. **d** 01 **p** 02. C Northampton Em *Pet* 01–04; P-in-c Mears Ashby and Hardwick and Sywell etc 04–17; R Sileby, Cossington and Seagrave *Leic* from 17. *St Mary's Rectory, 11 Mountsorrel Lane, Sileby, Loughborough LE12 7NF* T: (01509) 815640 E: scsparishes@gmail.com

BEEVER, Miss Alison Rosemary. b 59. Man Univ BA 80. Linc Th Coll 88. **d** 90 **p** 94. Par Dn Watford Ch Ch *St Alb* 90–94; C 94–96; V Tilehurst St Cath *Ox* 96–01; P-in-c Cen Ex and Dioc Dir of Ords *Ex* 01–04; rtd 04. *7 Langridge Road, Paignton TQ3 3PT* T: (01803) 553645 E: abeever59@icloud.com

BEEVERS, Preb Colin Lionel. b 40. K Coll Lon BSc 62 PhD 66 CEng 70 MIET 70 MBIM 73. Sarum & Wells Th Coll 87. **d** 89 **p** 90. C Ledbury w Eastnor *Heref* 89–93; C Lt Marcle 89–93; Asst Dir of Tr 92–96; P-in-c Kimbolton w Hamnish and Middleton-on-the-Hill 93–96; P-in-c Bockleton w Leysters 93–96; P-in-c Ledbury w Eastnor 96–98; P-in-c Much Marcle 96–98; TR Ledbury 98–05; RD 96–02; Preb Heref Cathl 02–05; Chapl Herefordshire Primary Care Trust 96–05; rtd 05; PtO *Worc* from 06; *Heref* 16–19. *3 St Wulfstan Avenue, Bristol BS10 6TN* T: 0117-959 0122 E: colinandann.beevers@btinternet.com

BEGBIE, Prof Jeremy Sutherland. b 57. Edin Univ BA 77 Aber Univ BD 80 PhD 87 LRAM 80 ARCM 77 MSSTh. Ridley Hall Cam 80. **d** 82 **p** 83. C Egham *Guildf* 82–85; Chapl Ridley Hall Cam 85–87; Dir Studies 87–92; Vice-Prin 93–00; Assoc Prin 00–09; Hon Reader St Andr Univ 00–09; Research Prof Th Duke Div Sch USA from 09; PtO *Ely* from 15. *Duke University Divinity School, Box 90968, Durham NC 27708, USA* T: (001) (919) 660 3591 E: jeremy.begbie@duke.edu

BEGLEY, Mrs Helen. b 59. Kingston Poly BA 81. NOC 87. **d** 89 **p** 94. Par Dn Leeds H Trin *Ripon* 89–90; Chapl to the Deaf 89–96; Par Dn Leeds City 91–94; C 94–96; Chapl to the Deaf (Wilts) *Sarum* 96–06; NSM Upper Wylye Valley 03–11; NSM

Melksham from 11. *Beckerley View, 196 The Common, Holt, Trowbridge BA14 6QN* T: (01225) 783543 M: 07540-314852 E: begleyhelen4@gmail.com

BEGLEY, Canon Peter Ernest Charles. b 55. St Mellitus Coll BA 10. **d** 10 **p** 11. C New Thundersley *Chelmsf* 10–15; P-in-c Southminster and Steeple 15–19; V from 19; RD Maldon and Dengie from 19; Hon Can Chelmsf Cathl from 20. *The Vicarage, Burnham Road, Southminster CM0 7ES* T: (01621) 772300 E: pf.begley@btinternet.com *or* vicar@stleonardsouthminster.org.uk

BEGLEY, Sally Anne Jane. b 55. St Mellitus Coll 16. **d** 17 **p** 18. NSM Waltham H Cross *Chelmsf* from 17. *33 Byron Avenue, London E18 2HH* T: (020) 7421 3854 M: 07572-111387 E: jane.begley@irwinmitchell.com

BEHENNA, Canon Gillian Eve. b 57. CertEd 78 Bris Univ MSc 15. S Dios Minl Tr Scheme 82. **dss** 85 **d** 87 **p** 94. Chapl to the Deaf *Sarum* 85–90; Chapl w Deaf People *Ex* 90–04; Preb Ex Cathl 02–04; Chapl w Deaf Community *Bris* from 05; Nat Deaf Min Adv Abps' Coun from 13; Hon Can Bris Cathl from 11; PtO *B & W* from 16. *1 Saxon Way, Bradley Stoke, Bristol BS32 9AR* T: (01454) 202483 M: 07715-707135 E: gillbehenna@me.com

BEHREND, Michael Christopher. b 60. St Jo Coll Cam BA 82 MA 86 PGCE 83. Oak Hill Th Coll 93. **d** 97 **p** 98. C Hensingham *Carl* 97–02; TV Horwich and Rivington *Man* from 02; C Blackrod 11–16. *St Catherine's House, Richmond Street, Horwich, Bolton BL6 5QT* T: (01204) 697162

BELCADE, Joshua Good. BNC Ox BA. S'wark Ord Course 10. **d** 13 **p** 14. NSM S Wimbledon All SS *S'wark* from 13; Hon Chapl Epsom Racecourse from 13. *5A Edge Hill, London SW19 4LR* T: (020) 7898 1610 M: 07766-341663 E: jbelcade@gmail.com

BELCHER, Mrs Catherine Jane Allington. b 53. Charlotte Mason Coll of Educn CertEd 75. EAMTC 02. **d** 05 **p** 06. NSM Nor St Mary Magd w St Jas 05–11; PtO 11–13; NSM Nor Lakenham St Jo and All SS and Tuckswood 13–18; PtO from 18. *70 Mill Hill Road, Norwich NR2 3DS* M: 07708-650897 E: revkatebelcher@yahoo.co.uk

BELCHER, David John. b 44. Ch Ch Ox BA 65 MA 69. Cuddesdon Coll 68. **d** 70 **p** 71. C Gateshead St Mary *Dur* 70–72; C Stockton St Pet 73–76; LtO *Lich* 76–81; P-in-c W Bromwich Ch Ch 81–85; P-in-c W Bromwich Gd Shep w St Jo 85–89; V 89–95; RD W Bromwich 90–94; R Bratton, Edington and Imber, Erlestoke etc *Sarum* 95–03; rtd 03; Hon C Smestow Vale *Lich* 03–07; PtO 09–14. *81 The Lindens, Newbridge Crescent, Wolverhampton WV6 0LS* T: (01902) 750903

BELCHER, Canon Derek George. b 50. Univ of Wales (Cardiff) MEd 86 LLM 04 Newman Univ BA 15 Open Univ BSc 18 Lon Univ PGCE 82 MRSPH 73 MBIM 82 FRSPH 00. Chich Th Coll 74. **d** 77 **p** 78. C Newton Nottage *Llan* 77–81; PV Llan Cathl 81–87; V Margam 87–01; RD 99–01; TR Cowbridge 01–15; AD Vale of Glam 08–11; rtd 15; P-in-c Penmark w Llancarfan w Llantrithyd *Llan* 15–20; Can Llan Cathl from 97. *Ty Seren, 23 St Mary's View, Coychurch, Bridgend CF35 5HL* T: (01656) 860784 M: 07796-170671 E: dgbelc@gmail.com

BELDER, Jacob John. b 83. Redeemer Univ Coll Hamilton BA 06 Reformed Th Sem (USA) MDiv 10 St Jo Coll Dur DThM 18. Cranmer Hall Dur 14. **d** 18 **p** 18. C Selby Abbey *York* 18–20; P-in-c Pocklington Wold 20–21; R from 21. *The Vicarage, 29 The Balk, Pocklington, York YO42 2QQ* E: jake.belder@gmail.com

BELDING, Cheryl Pauline. b 54. ERMC 16. **d** 18. NSM Newmarket St Mary w Exning St Agnes *St E* from 18. *28 Heasman Close, Newmarket CB8 0GR* M: 07801-499179 E: cherylbelding@gmail.com

BELFAST, Archdeacon of. *See* FORDE, The Ven Barry George
BELFAST, Dean of. *See* FORDE, The Very Revd Stephen Bernard

BELHAM, John Edward. b 42. K Coll Lon BSc 65 AKC 65 PhD 70. Oak Hill Th Coll 69. **d** 72 **p** 73. C Cheadle Hulme St Andr *Ches* 72–75; C Cheadle 75–83; R Gressenhall w Longham w Wendling etc *Nor* 83–08; P-in-c Mileham 07–08; rtd 08; PtO from 08. *6 Brentwood, Norwich NR4 6PW* T: (01603) 456925 E: johnbelham@lords-prayer.co.uk

BELHAM, Michael. b 23. Lon Univ BScEng 50. **d** 67 **p** 68. C Northwood Hills St Edm *Lon* 67–69; C Hendon St Mary 69–73; V Tottenham H Trin 73–78; V Hillingdon St Jo 78–85; P-in-c Broughton *Ox* 85; R Broughton w N Newington and Shutford 85–90; Chapl Horton Gen Hosp 85–90; rtd 90; PtO *Pet* 90–01; *Ox* 90–01; Sec DBP 95–01; PtO *B & W* 01–13. *24 Carlton Court, Wells BA5 1SF* T: (01749) 675236

BELL, Adrian Christopher. b 48. AKC 70. St Aug Coll Cant 70. **d** 71 **p** 72. C Sheff St Aid w St Luke 71–74; C Willesborough w Hinxhill *Cant* 74–78; P-in-c Bredgar w Bicknor and Frinsted w Wormshill etc 78; P-in-c Hollingbourne w Hucking 78–82;

P-in-c Leeds w Broomfield 79–82; V Hollingbourne and Hucking w Leeds and Broomfield 82–84; V Herne Bay Ch Ch 84–91; R Washingborough w Heighington and Canwick *Linc* 91–01; R Fakenham w Alethorpe *Nor* 01–14; rtd 14; PtO *Nor* 14–17 and from 21; P-in-c Caston, Griston, Merton, Thompson etc 17–21. *Orchard House, 19 Whitsands Road, Swaffham PE37 7BJ* T: (01760) 627039 M: 07706-480489 E: adrian.bell4@uwclub.net

BELL, Canon Alan John. b 47. Liv Univ BA 68. Ridley Hall Cam 69. **d** 72 **p** 73. C Speke St Aid *Liv* 72–77; Min Halewood St Mary CD 77–81; R Wavertree St Mary 81–88; Chapl Mabel Fletcher Tech Coll and Olive Mt Hosp 81–88; R Fakenham w Alethorpe *Nor* 88–00; RD Burnham and Walsingham 92–00; TR Stockport SW *Ches* 00–07; V Stockport St Geo 07–12; RD Stockport 05–12; Hon Can Ches Cathl 08–12; rtd 12; PtO *Ely* from 13; *Nor* from 14. *24 Hall Road, Clenchwarton, King's Lynn PE34 4AT* T: (01553) 278106 E: vicaralanbell@aol.com

BELL, Arthur James. b 33. Ch Coll Cam BA 57 MA 60. Coll of Resurr Mirfield 57. **d** 59 **p** 60. C New Cleethorpes *Linc* 59–63; C Upperby St Jo *Carl* 63–66; P-in-c Wabasca Canada 67–72; 77–83; PtO *Ely* 73–75; LtO *Carl* 75–76; Warden Retreat of the Visitation Rhandirmwyn 83–99; PtO *Dur* 00–21. *Burnside, 22 Rose Terrace, Stanhope, Bishop Auckland DL13 2PE* T: (01388) 526514 E: abell178@btinternet.com

BELL, Barnaby. *See* BELL, Simon Barnaby

BELL, Bede. *See* BELL, William Wealands

BELL, Benjamin Lawrence. b 74. K Coll Lon MA 13. Westcott Ho Cam 15. **d** 17 **p** 18. C Poplar *Lon* 17–19; V Hoxton St Anne w St Columba from 19. *St Ann's Vicarage, 37 Hemsworth Street, London N1 5LF* M: 07739-487721 E: revbenbell@gmail.com

BELL, Brian Thomas Benedict. b 64. Newc Poly BA 87 Newc Univ PGCE 88 Univ of Northumbria at Newc MA 93 Leeds Univ BA 97. Coll of Resurr Mirfield. **d** 97 **p** 98. C Tynemouth Cullercoats St Paul *Newc* 97–01; V Horton 01–08; V Horbury w Horbury Bridge *Wakef* 08–14; *Leeds* 14–16; V Monk Bretton from 16. *The Vicarage, Burton Road, Barnsley S71 2HQ* E: fatherbrian@virginmedia.com

BELL, Charles John McKinnon. b 89. Cam Univ BA 11 MA 15 PhD 16 MB, BChir 17. St Mellitus Coll 18 St Aug Coll Cant 19. **d** 21. NSM Kennington St Jo w St Jas *S'wark* from 21. *3 Parish Mews, 126 Parish Lane, London SE20 7JH* M: 07962-021067 E: cb561@cam.ac.uk

BELL, Charles William. b 43. TCD Div Test 66 BA 66 MA 69. CITC 64. **d** 67 **p** 68. C Newtownards *D & D* 67–70; C Larne and Inver *Conn* 70–74; C Ballymena w Ballyclug 74–80; Bp's C Belfast Ardoyne 80–87; Bp's C Belfast Ardoyne w H Redeemer 88; I Eglantine 89–11; S Conn Dioc Info Officer 89–11; Preb Conn Cathl 04–11; rtd 11. *2 Beechwood Crescent, Moira, Craigavon BT67 0LA* T: (028) 9261 9834 E: norma.bell@virgin.net

BELL, Colin Douglas. b 65. QUB BTh 94 TCD MPhil 96 Cardiff Univ MTh 15. CITC 94. **d** 96 **p** 97. C Dundonald *D & D* 96–98; C Knock 98–00; I Lack *Clogh* 00–02; I Rathcoole *Conn* 02–05; CF 05–07 and from 08; I Aghadrumsee w Clogh and Drumsnatt 07–08. *c/o MOD Chaplains (Army)* T: (01264) 383430 F: 381824

BELL, Darren Morgan. b 69. Northumbria Univ LLB 01 Newc Univ MPhil 07. Ox Min Course 15. **d** 17 **p** 18. C Seghill *Newc* from 17. *15 Backworth Court, Backworth, Newcastle upon Tyne NE27 0RP* M: 07401-797179 E: revdarrenbell@gmail.com

BELL, David. b 52. **d** 12 **p** 13. NSM Hampton Hill *Lon* 12–15; NSM Kingston *S'wark* from 15; PtO *Lon* from 15; *Truro* from 14. *20 Vicarage Road, Hampton Wick, Kingston upon Thames KT1 4ED* T: (020) 8977 2482 M: 07986-245313 E: davidbell@bell5.co.uk

BELL, David Bain. b 57. Bp Otter Coll BEd 82. Ox Min Course 04. **d** 07 **p** 08. NSM Stantonbury and Willen *Ox* 07–10; TV Watling Valley 10–15; PtO 15–20; V Silsoe, Pulloxhill and Flitton *St Alb* 15–19; rtd 19; PtO *Ox* from 21. *The Studio House, 141 High Street, Brackley NN13 7BN*

BELL, Canon David Owain. b 49. Dur Univ BA 69 Fitzw Coll Cam BA 72 MA 80. Westcott Ho Cam 70. **d** 72 **p** 73. C Houghton le Spring *Dur* 72–76; C Norton St Mary 76–78; P-in-c Worc St Clem 78–84; R 84–85; R Old Swinford Stourbridge 85–97; TR Kidderminster St Mary and All SS w Trimpley etc 97–13; RD Stourbridge 90–96; Hon Can Worc Cathl 96–13; PtO from 13; rtd 14. *60A Main Road, Kempsey WR5 3JF* T: (01905) 820209 E: dowainbell@yahoo.co.uk

BELL, Canon Donald Jon. b 50. DL 12. Sarum & Wells Th Coll 73. **d** 76 **p** 77. C Jarrow *Dur* 76–80; C Darlington St Cuth w St Hilda 80–83; V Wingate Grange 83–89; V Sherburn w Pittington 89–95; R Shadforth 94–95; P-in-c Dur St Cuth 95–97; V 97–02; R Witton Gilbert 97–02; TR Dur N 02–05; AD Dur 93–05; Chapl Dur and Darlington Fire and Rescue Brigade 95–05; Bp's Sen Chapl and Exec Officer 05–12;

P-in-c Kelloe and Coxhoe 12–16; P-in-c Chilton 12–16; Hon Can Dur Cathl 01–16; rtd 16; PtO *Dur* from 16. *20 St Phillips Close, Auckland Park, Bishop Auckland DL14 8BD* M: 07973-829491 E: jonb22@btinternet.com

BELL, Dorothy Jane. b 53. Teesside Univ BSc 93. Cranmer Hall Dur 01. d 03 p 04. C Washington *Dur* 03–07; P-in-c Stockton St Jo 07–15; P-in-c Stockton St Jas 07–15; P-in-c Stockton Christchurch 15–17; P-in-c Scarborough St Columba *York* 17–20; P-in-c Scarborough St Jas w H Trin 17–20; V Scarborough St Columba and St Jas w H Trin from 20. *34 Box Hill, Scarborough YO12 5NG*

BELL, Duncan John. b 83. Sheff Univ MEng 06 PhD 11. Oak Hill Th Coll BA 14. d 14 p 15. C Woodseats St Chad *Sheff* 14–17; C Leyland St Andr *Blackb* from 17. *11 Stokes Hall Avenue, Leyland PR25 3FA* T: (01772) 622964 M: 07833-448014 E: duncan.j.bell@gmail.com

BELL, Evelyn Ruth. b 52. Univ of Wales (Cardiff) BSc(Econ). SAOMC 97. d 00 p 01. C Waltham Cross *St Alb* 00–03; Chapl HM Pris Edmunds Hill 03–11; Chapl HM Pris Highpoint 11–15; rtd 15; PtO *St E* 17–20; R Bansfield from 20. *Address withheld by request* M: 07815-441304 E: evie.bell@icloud.com

BELL, Georgiana Mary. b 48. K Coll Lon BD 81 AKC 81 MTh 93. Westcott Ho Cam 81. dss 83 d 87 p 94. Cobbold Road St Sav w St Mary *Lon* 83–85; St Botolph Aldgate w H Trin Minories 85–87; Par Dn 87; PtO *S'wark* 88–93; Par Dn Kidbrooke St Jas 93–95; Tutor S'wark Ord Course 93–94; Tutor SEITE 94–98; Teacher Eltham Coll 98–02; Asst Chapl Qu Eliz Hosp NHS Trust 03–11; Asst Chapl S Lon Healthcare NHS Trust 11–13; Tutor St Aug Coll of Th 13–17; Hon Chapl S'wark Cathl 95–17; rtd 17; Hon Min Can S'wark Cathl from 17; Public Preacher 12–18; PtO from 18; *Ex* from 21. *4 Roupell Street, London SE1 8SP* T: (020) 7642 1161 M: 07776-122350 E: georgianambell@gmail.com

BELL, Mrs Glynis Mary. b 44. Leeds Univ BA 66. SAOMC 99. d 02 p 03. OLM Newport Pagnell w Lathbury and Moulsoe *Ox* 02–14; PtO from 14. *6 Kipling Drive, Newport Pagnell MK16 8EB* T: (01908) 612971 E: gmbell@screaming.net

BELL, Godfrey Bryan. b 44. TD 00. Oak Hill Th Coll 72. d 75 p 76. C Penn Fields *Lich* 75–79; R Dolton *Ex* 79–89; R Iddesleigh w Dowland 79–89; R Monkokehampton 79–89; R Tollard Royal w Farnham, Gussage St Michael etc *Sarum* 89–96; TV Washfield, Stoodleigh, Withleigh etc *Ex* 96–06; TR 06–09; CF (ACF) 83–87; CF (TA) 87–99; rtd 09; PtO *Ex* from 10. *Bethany, 3 Alstone Road, Tiverton EX16 4JL* T: (01884) 252874 E: m.bell.bethany@gmail.com

BELL, Graham Dennis Robert. b 42. K Coll Lon BSc 63 AKC 63 Nottm Univ MTh 73 ALCM 76 Lambeth STh 01. Tyndale Hall Bris 65. d 68 p 69. C Stapleford *S'wark* 68–71; C Barton Seagrave *Pet* 71–73; C Barton Seagrave w Warkton 73–76; PtO *Nor* 76–82; V Wickham Market *St E* 82–86; V Wickham Market w Pettistree and Easton 86–98; R Thrapston *Pet* 98–07; rtd 07; PtO *Pet* from 11. *22 Cottesmore Avenue, Barton Seagrave, Kettering NN15 6QX* T: (01536) 725924 E: bellgood@talktalk.net

✠BELL, The Rt Revd James Harold. b 50. St Jo Coll Dur BA 72 St Pet Hall Ox BA 74 MA 78. Wycliffe Hall Ox 72. d 75 p 76 c 04. Hon C Ox St Mich w St Martin and All SS 75–76; Chapl and Lect BNC Ox 76–82; R Northolt St Mary *Lon* 82–93; AD Ealing 91–93; Adv for Min Willesden 93–97; Dioc Dir of Min and Tr *Ripon* 97–99; Dioc Dir of Miss 99–04; Can Res Ripon Cathl 97–99; Hon Can from 99; Suff Bp Knaresborough *Ripon* 04–15; Suff Bp Ripon *Leeds* 15–17; rtd 17. *Stone Croft, Bolton, Appleby-in-Westmorland CA16 6AL*

BELL, James Samuel. b 40. MBE 71. RMA 59 St Chad's Coll Dur BA 69. Coll of Resurr Mirfield 71. d 72 p 73. C Lambeth St Phil *S'wark* 72–73; C N Lambeth 74; P-in-c Invergordon St Ninian *Mor* 74–77; P-in-c Dornoch 74–77; P-in-c Brora 74–77; V Pet H Spirit Bretton 77–83; P-in-c Marholm 82–83; Sen Chapl Tonbridge Sch 83–00. *Clocktower House, Edderton, Tain IV19 1LJ* T: (01862) 821305

BELL, Jane. *See* BELL, Dorothy Jane

BELL, Canon Jeffrey William. b 37. Buckingham Univ MA 93. Sarum Th Coll 60. d 63 p 64. C Northampton St Matt *Pet* 63–66; C Portishead *B & W* 66–68; C Digswell *St Alb* 68–72; V Pet St Jude 72–79; V Buckingham *Ox* 79–93; RD 84–88 and 89–90; V Portsea N End St Mark *Portsm* 93–03; Hon Can Portsm Cathl 00–03; rtd 03; Hon C The Bourne and Tilford *Guildf* 03–13; PtO *Portsm* from 13. *164 Northern Parade, Portsmouth PO2 9LT* T: (023) 9265 0033 E: jeffnlinda@btinternet.com

BELL, Jennifer Kathryn. *See* McWHIRTER, Jennifer Kathryn

BELL, John. *See* BELL, Donald Jon

BELL, John George. b 74. Surrey Univ BEng 99. ERMC 16. d 19 p 20. C Bedford Ch Ch *St Alb* from 19. *161*

Dudley Street, Bedford MK40 3SY T: (01234) 401509 E: curate@ccbedford.org

BELL, John Holmes. b 50. Sheff City Coll of Educn CertEd 71. Oak Hill Th Coll BA 80. d 80 p 81. C Leic St Phil 80–83; C Portswood Ch Ch *Win* 83–86; TV S Molton w Nymet St George, High Bray etc *Ex* 86–01; V Stoke Fleming, Blackawton and Strete 01–15; rtd 15; PtO *Ex* 15–20. *40 Balmoral Crescent, Okehampton EX20 1GN* T: (01837) 53084 E: johnbell40@icloud.com

BELL, Jonathan Robert. b 84. Nottm Univ BA 06. Oak Hill Th Coll BA 14. d 14 p 15. C Stanton-by-Dale w Dale Abbey and Risley *Derby* 14–19; Min-in-c Grace Ch Highlands from 19. *2 Firs Lane, London N21 2HU* T: (020) 8374 6534

BELL, Joshua Russell Edmund. b 91. Cliff Coll BA 13. Westcott Ho Cam 15. d 18 p 19. C S and W Lynn *Nor* from 18; PtO *Ely* from 19; Chapl RN from 21. *Royal Naval Chaplaincy Service Headquarters, Tanner Building, HMS Excellent, Whale Island, Portsmouth, PO2 8ER* T: 03001-577544 M: 07476-848994 E: frjoshuabell@outlook.com

BELL, Julia Claire. b 68. Down Coll Cam BA 90. ERMC 18. d 21. C Stockton Par Ch *Dur* from 21. *36 Hills Drive, Stockton-on-Tees TS20 2GE* E: julia@twanbell.co.uk

BELL, Kenneth Murray. b 30. Sarum & Wells Th Coll 75. d 74 p 76. PtO *Guildf* 74–76; C Hartley Wintney and Elvetham *Win* 76–77; C Hartley Wintney, Elvetham, Winchfield etc 77–80; V Fair Oak 80–95; rtd 96; PtO *Win* from 96. *12 Hill Meadow, Overton, Basingstoke RG25 3JD* T: (01256) 770890 E: k_m_bell@btinternet.com

BELL, Kevin David. b 58. Newc Univ MA 93 Univ of Wales (Lamp) MA 06 FRSA 11. Aston Tr Scheme 78 Sarum & Wells Th Coll 80. d 83 p 84. C Weoley Castle *Birm* 83–87; C Acocks Green 87–89; CF 89–07; Asst Chapl Gen 07–15; Chapl Guards Chpl Lon 12–14; Dir of Ords 07–11; V Twickenham All Hallows *Lon* from 15. *All Hallows' Vicarage, 138 Chertsey Road, Twickenham TW1 1EW* T: (020) 8892 1322 M: 07764-541364 E: kevin.bell@allhallowstwick.org.uk

BELL, Mrs Leanne Alix. b 78. Northumbria Univ LLB 02. Ripon Coll Cuddesdon 15. d 17 p 18. C Monkseaton St Pet *Newc* 17–18. *15 Backworth Court, Backworth, Newcastle upon Tyne NE27 0RP* M: 07411-665195 E: revleannebell@gmail.com

BELL, Canon Nicholas Philip Johnson. b 46. St Jo Coll Dur BSc 69. St Jo Coll Nottm 70. d 73 p 74. C Chadderton Ch Ch *Man* 73–77; C Frogmore St Alb 77–81; V Bricket Wood 81–91; RD Aldenham 87–91; V Luton St Mary 91–12; Hon Can St Alb 01–12; rtd 12; PtO *St Alb* from 12; Nor from 14. *8C Sheringham House, Cremers Drift, Sheringham NR26 8HZ* T: (01263) 821443 M: 07968-049366 E: revnickbell@gmail.com

BELL, Owain. *See* BELL, David Owain

BELL, Mrs Rebecca Mary. b 79. UWE BSc 00. Trin Coll Bris 10. d 13 p 14. C Charlton Kings H Apostles *Glouc* 13–16; P-in-c St Neot and Warleggan w Cardynham *Truro* 16–17; V St Neot and Warleggan 17–19; P-in-c St Cleer from 16; C St Ive and Pensilva w Quethiock 16–19; P-in-c from 19; P-in-c Menheniot from 19. *Angrouse House, Miners Way, Liskeard PL14 3ET* E: revbeccabell@gmail.com

BELL, Prof Richard Herbert. b 54. Univ Coll Lon BSc 75 PhD 79 Tubingen Univ DrTheol 91. Wycliffe Hall Ox BA 82 MA 87. d 83 p 84. C Edgware *Lon* 83–86; W Germany 86–90; Lect Th Nottm Univ 90–97; Sen Lect 97-05; Reader 05-08; Prof from 08. *Department of Theology and Religious Studies, University Park, Nottingham NG7 2RD* T: 0115-951 5858 F: 951 5887 E: richard.bell@nottingham.ac.uk

BELL, Robert Mason. b 35. Lon Coll of Div 66. d 68 p 69. C Burgess Hill St Andr *Chich* 68–78; R Lewes St Jo sub Castro 78–00; rtd 00. *10 Rufus Close, Lewes BN7 1BG* T: (01273) 470561

BELL, Mrs Shena Margaret. b 49. EAMTC. d 00 p 01. C Earls Barton *Pet* 00–04; P-in-c Raunds 04–07; P-in-c Ringstead and Stanwick w Hargrave 04–07; R Raunds, Hargrave, Ringstead and Stanwick 07–17; rtd 17; PtO *Pet* from 18. *28 High Street, Upton, Northampton NN5 4EH* T: (01604) 586107 E: shena.m.bell@gmail.com

BELL, Simon Barnaby. b 48. Bris Univ CertEd 70. Sarum & Wells Th Coll 87. d 89 p 90. C Ewyas Harold w Dulas, Kenderchurch etc *Heref* 89–93; P-in-c Clungunford w Clunbury and Clunton, Bedstone etc 93–01; R 01–11; P-in-c Hopesay 02–11; rtd 11; PtO *Heref* from 12. *49 Warden Close, Presteigne LD8 2DH*

BELL, Canon Stuart Rodney. b 46. Ex Univ BA 67. Tyndale Hall Bris 69. d 71 p 72. C Henfynyw w Aberaeron and Llanddewi Aberarth *St D* 71–74; V 81–88; V Llangeler 74–80; TR Aberystwyth 88–13; Chapl Aberystwyth Univ from 94; Ev St Teilo Trust from 95; AD Llanbadarn Fawr 12–14; Can St D Cathl 01–13; rtd 13; PtO *St D* from 13; *Eur* from 14. *Gwel Enlli, Borth SY24 5NS* E: stuart@prudence45.plus.com

BELL, Mrs Susan. b 62. Lindisfarne Regional Tr Partnership 13. d 15 p 16. NSM Darlington St Hilda and

St Columba *Dur* 15–18; Chapl HM Pris Holme Ho from 18. *HM Prison Holme House, Holme House Road, Stockton-on-Tees TS18 2QU* T: (01642) 744000 M: 07850-675877 E: suebell158@hotmail.co.uk

BELL (née STEWART), Mrs Susan Catherine. b 57. St Martin's Coll Lanc BEd 80. LCTP 08. **d** 10 **p** 11. C Longridge *Blackb* 10–14; I Ballywalter w Inishargie *D & D* from 14. *15 Westland Drive, Ballywalter, Newtownards BT22 2TH* T: (028) 4275 7579 M: 07738-305129 E: bellsue9@gmail.com *or* vicarofballywalter@gmail.com

BELL, Terrance James. b 63. Toronto Univ BA 92. Trin Coll Toronto MDiv 97. **d** 97 **p** 98. C Wedmore w Theale and Blackford *B & W* 97–01; C Hampstead St Jo *Lon* 01–06; Chapl Eden Hall Marie Curie Hospice 01–06; P-in-c King's Walden and Offley w Lilley *St Alb* 06–11; V from 11. *Millstone Corner, Salusbury Lane, Offley, Hitchin SG5 3EG* T: (01462) 768123 E: kwol@btinternet.com

BELL, Timothy John Keeton. b 59. Trin Coll Bris BA 02. **d** 02 **p** 03. C Saltford w Corston and Newton St Loe *B & W* 02–06; Chapl Bath Spa Univ 04–06; P-in-c Wick w Doynton and Dyrham *Bris* from 06. *The Vicarage, 57 High Street, Wick, Bristol BS30 5QQ* T: 0117-937 3581 E: tim.vicar@gmail.com

BELL, Timothy Liam. b 73. Trin Coll Bris 15. **d** 17 **p** 18. C Hastings H Trin *Chich* 17–20; P-in-c Ore St Helen and St Barn from 20; P-in-c Ore Ch Ch from 20. *St Helen's Rectory, 23 Ore Place, Hastings TN34 2LR* E: timbell68@gmail.com

BELL, William. *See* BELL, Charles William

BELL, William Wealands. b 63. York Univ BA 86 Dur Univ PGCE 87 Leeds Univ BA 99. Coll of Resurr Mirfield 97. **d** 99 **p** 00. C Jarrow *Dur* 99–02; Novice CR 02–04; Chapl Aldenham Sch Herts 04–07; Can Res Lich Cathl 07–14; P-in-c Croydon St Andr *S'wark* 14–15; V 15–17; Chapl St Andr C of E High Sch Croydon 14–17; Chapl Magd Coll Sch Ox from 17. *Magdalen College School, Cowley Place, Oxford OX4 1DZ* T: (01865) 242191 E: wealandsbell@gmail.com

BELL-WINFROW, James Leo. b 89. Cliff Coll BA 10. Ripon Coll Cuddesdon 16. **d** 18 **p** 19. C Aller, High w Low Ham and Huish Episcopi cum Langport *B & W* 18–21; Chapl RN from 21. *Royal Naval Chaplaincy Service Heaquarters, Tanner Building, HMS Excellent, Whale Island, Portsmouth PO2 8ER* T: 0300-157 7544 M: 07531-386352 E: jamesbellwinfrow@gmail.com

BELLAMY, Canon David Quentin. b 62. Univ of Wales (Cardiff) BMus 84 Univ of Wales (Ban) MA 93. Ripon Coll Cuddesdon 87 Ch Div Sch of the Pacific (USA). **d** 90 **p** 91. C Rhyl w St Ann *St As* 90–94; V Llay 94–04; V Prestatyn 04–15; AD St As 10–15; R Colwyn and Llanelian 15–16; TV Aled Miss Area 17–20; Can Cursal St As Cathl 14–20; rtd 21. *Iscoed, 21 Woodland Road West, Colwyn Bay LL29 7DH* T: (01492) 209311 M: 07590-573547 E: dqbellamy@yahoo.co.uk

BELLAMY, Mrs Janet Mary. b 45. Westf Coll Lon BA 66 Birm Univ BLitt 98 MEd 93 Cam Univ PGCE 67. **d** 09 **p** 10. NSM Hope Bowdler w Eaton-under-Heywood *Heref* 09–13; NSM Apedale Gp 13–15; PtO from 16. *7 The Park, Hereford HR1 1TF* T: (01432) 359308 E: revjanetbellamy@gmail.com

BELLAMY, John Stephen. b 55. Jes Coll Ox BA 77 MA 81 Liv Univ PhD 06. St Jo Coll Nottm. **d** 84 **p** 85. C Allerton *Liv* 84–87; C Southport Ch Ch 87–89; Bp's Dom Chapl 89–91; V Birkdale St Jas 91–08; V Dur St Nic 08–16; V Gt Faringdon w Lt Coxwell *Ox* from 16. *The Vicarage, Coach Lane, Faringdon SN7 8AB* T: (01367) 240106 E: revsbellamy@gmail.com

BELLAMY, Mrs Norma Edna. b 44. Birm Univ CertEd 75 Open Univ BA 83. **d** 10 **p** 11. OLM Shareshill *Lich* 10–16; PtO 16–21. *10 Meadowlark Close, Hednesford, Cannock WS12 1UE* T: (01543) 876809 M: 07866-431211 E: revnorma.bellamy4@gmail.com

BELLAMY, Peter Charles William. b 38. Birm Univ MA 70 PhD 79 AKC 61. **d** 62 **p** 63. C Allestree *Derby* 62–65; Chapl All SS Hosp Birm 65–73; Chapl St Pet Coll of Educn Saltley 73–78; Chapl and Lect Qu Eliz Hosp Birm 78–90; Lect Past Psychology Birm Univ 79–92; Manager HIV Services Birm Cen HA 90–92; Commr for Public Health Cen and S Birm HA 92–96; Research Fell Birm Univ 97–02; Local Min Development Adv *Heref* 01–06; Dioc Co-ord for Min of Deliverance 06–19; PtO from 11. *7 The Park, Hereford HR1 1TF* T: (01432) 359308 E: petercbellamy@googlemail.com

BELLAMY, Quentin. *See* BELLAMY, David Quentin

BELLAMY, Richard William. b 62. SEITE 07. **d** 10 **p** 11. NSM Cheriton St Martin *Cant* 10–11; NSM Cheriton w Newington 11–12; NSM Folkestone Trin 12–17; TV Ashford Town from 17; Chapl Ashford Sch from 17. *Ashford Town Centre Vicarage, Church Yard, Ashford TN23 1QG* M: 07548-021371 E: r.w.bellamy@btinternet.com

BELLAMY, Stephen. *See* BELLAMY, John Stephen

BELLAMY-KNIGHTS, Peter George. b 41. Leic Univ BSc 63 Man Univ MSc 67 PhD 70 Lon Univ BD 03 CMath 91 FIMA 91 CEng 94 FRAeS 98. Man OLM Scheme 03. **d** 04 **p** 05. NSM Man Cathl 04–11; rtd 11; PtO *Man* from 11. *113 Old Hall Lane, Manchester M14 6HL* T: 0161-224 2702 *or* 833 2220 E: peter.bellamyknights@manchestercathedral.org

BELLENES, Peter Charles. b 49. Thurrock Coll Essex CQSW 72. Linc Th Coll 79. **d** 81 **p** 90. C Penistone *Wakef* 81–82; Hon C Liskeard, St Keyne, St Pinnock, Morval etc *Truro* 89–91; Hon C Menheniot 91–99; P-in-c Marldon *Ex* 99–03; TV Totnes w Bridgetown, Berry Pomeroy etc 03–09; rtd 09; C Duloe, Herodsfoot, Morval and St Pinnock *Truro* 15–17; R Duloe and Herodsfoot 17–18. *Little Grove, Harrow Barrow, Callington PL17 8JN* T: (01822) 833508 E: pbellenes@aol.com

BELLINGER, Richard George. b 47. Univ of Wales (Abth) BSc(Econ) 69. S Dios Minl Tr Scheme 91. **d** 94 **p** 95. NSM Guernsey St Steph *Win* 94–96; NSM Guernsey St Martin 96–09; PtO 09–14 and from 16. *La Maison des Vinaires, Rue des Vinaires, St Pierre du Bois, Guernsey GY7 9EZ* T: (01481) 63203 F: 66989 E: praisethelord@cwgsy.net

BELLIS, Andrew David. b 89. Oak Hill Th Coll BA 20. **d** 20 **p** 21. C Harold Wood *Chelmsf* from 20. *48 Harold Court Road, Romford RM3 0YX* E: andrew.bellis@stpetersharoldwood.org

BELLIS, Huw. b 72. Univ of Wales (Lamp) BA 94. Westcott Ho Cam 96. **d** 98 **p** 99. C Merrow *Guildf* 98–02; TV Tring *St Alb* 02–08; TR from 08. *The Rectory, 2 The Limes, Station Road, Tring HP23 5NW* T: (01442) 822170 E: huw@tringteamparish.org.uk

BELOE, Mrs Jane. b 46. STETS. **d** 04 **p** 05. NSM Shedfield *Portsm* 04–06; NSM Bishop's Waltham from 06; NSM Upham from 06. *Roughay Cottage, Popes Lane, Upham, Southampton SO32 1JB* T: (01489) 860452

BELSHAW, Patricia Anne. b 47. **d** 05 **p** 06. OLM Leyland St Jas *Blackb* 05–07; NSM 07–10; NSM Darwen St Pet 10–13; rtd 13; PtO *Blackb* from 13. *9 The Laund, Leyland PR26 7XX* T: (01772) 453624 E: patriciabelshaw@yahoo.co.uk

BEMENT, Peter James. b 43. Univ of Wales (Cardiff) BA 64 PhD 69. Wycliffe Hall Ox 92. **d** 94 **p** 95. C Hubberston *St D* 94–97; V Llandeilo Fawr and Taliaris 97–08; rtd 08; PtO *St D* from 08; *Eur* 15–19. *21 Chandler's Yard, Burry Port SA16 0FE* T: (01554) 833905

BENBOW, Susan Catherine. *See* TURNER, Susan Catherine

BENCE, Helen Mary. b 44. Leic Univ BA 65 PGCE 66. EMMTC 93. **d** 97 **p** 98. NSM Humberstone *Leic* 97–02; NSM Thurnby Lodge 01–02; TV Oadby 03–08; NSM Thurnby w Stoughton 08–13; NSM Cornerstone Team from 13. *The Grange, 126 Shanklin Drive, Leicester LE2 3QB* T: 0116-270 7820 E: helenbence@outlook.com

BENDALL, Robin Andrew. b 64. Qu Mary Coll Lon BA 86. SEITE 08. **d** 11 **p** 13. NSM Sandwich and Worth *Cant* from 11. *24 Delfside, Sandwich CT13 9RL* T: (01304) 617458 E: robinbendall@hotmail.com

BENDELL, David James. b 38. ACIB 74. S'wark Min Course 84. **d** 87 **p** 88. NSM Surbiton Hill Ch Ch *S'wark* 87–03; PtO 10–14; *Guildf* 12–15; *Ely* from 17. *58 North Lodge Park, Milton, Cambridge CB24 6UB* E: bendell@talktalk.net *or* dbendell58@gmail.com

BENDOR-SAMUEL, David Carey. b 57. Ox Min Course 13. **d** 15 **p** 16. C Beckley, Forest Hill, Horton-cum-Studley and Stanton St John *Ox* 15–17; C Albury w Tiddington etc from 17. *25 Littleworth Road, Wheatley, Oxford OX33 1NW* T: (01865) 872102. M: 07806-724335

BENDREY (née BRIGNALL), Elizabeth Jane. b 69. St Mary's Coll Twickenham BA 91 Heythrop Coll Lon MA 02 Cam Univ BTh 06. Westcott Ho Cam 04. **d** 06 **p** 07. C Witham *Chelmsf* 06–09; P-in-c Black Notley 09–12; R 12–16; C Panfield and Rayne 15–16; V Black Notley, Gt Notley and Rayne 16–20; RD Braintree 13–18; Hon Can Chelmsf Cathl 15–20; Chapl Gtr Lisbon *Eur* from 20. *Rua João de Deus no 5, Alcoitão, 2645-128 Alcabideche, Portugal* T: (00351) 932 101 805 M: 07940-516741 E: bethbendrey@hotmail.co.uk

BENDREY, Iain Robert. b 73. Bp Grosseteste Coll BA 96 Birm Univ MEd 03. ERMC 06. **d** 08 **p** 09. NSM Wickham Bishops w Lt Braxted *Chelmsf* 08–12; NSM Bocking St Pet 12–16; NSM Black Notley, Gt Notley and Rayne 16–20; PtO *Eur* 20–21; Asst Chapl Gtr Lisbon from 21. *Rua João de Deus no 5, Alcoitão, 2645-128 Alcabideche, Portugal* T: (00351) 911 979 007 E: bezzerbendrey@gmail.com

BENEDICT, Brother. *See* WINSPER, Arthur William

BENFIELD, Paul John. b 56. Newc Univ LLB 77 Southn Univ BTh 89 Barrister-at-Law (Lincoln's Inn) 78. Chich Th Coll 86. **d** 89 **p** 90. C Shiremoor *Newc* 89–92; C Hexham 92–93; TV Lewes All SS, St Anne, St Mich and St Thos *Chich* 93–97; R Pulborough 97–00; V Fleetwood St Nic *Blackb* 00–18; C Burnley St Andr w St Marg and St Jas from 18; C Burnley St Mark from 18; Dioc Registrar 18–20. *234A*

Todmorden Road, Burnley BB11 3EZ T: (01282) 424725
E: benfield@btinternet.com

✠BENFORD, The Rt Revd Steven Charles. b 61. Leic
Univ MB, ChB 86. NEOC 97. d 00 p 01 c 17. NSM
Northallerton w Kirby Sigston *York* 00–04; P-in-c York
St Luke 04–14; V Northolt St Jos *Lon* 14–17; Bp Dunedin
NZ from 17. *1A Howden Street, Green Island, Dunedin 9052,
New Zealand* T: (0064) (3) 425 8389 M: 22-074 9923
E: bishop.steven@calledsouth.org.nz

BENHAM, Canon Sandra Rhys. Westcott Ho Cam 04.
d 06 p 07. C Gainsborough and Morton *Linc* 06–09;
P-in-c Quarrington w Old Sleaford 09–15; P-in-c Silk
Willoughby 09–15; P-in-c Cranwell 09–11; V Baildon
Leeds from 15; AD Airedale 16; AD Aire and Worth from
17; Hon Can Wakef Cathl from 19. *The Vicarage, Church
Hill, Baildon, Shipley BD17 6NE* T: (01274) 589005
E: sandrabenham@btinternet.com

BENISON, Canon Brian. b 41. K Coll Lon 61. Bps' Coll
Cheshunt 63. d 66 p 67. C Tynemouth Ch Ch *Newc* 66–70;
C Gosforth All SS 70–72; TV Cullercoats St Geo 73–81; V
Denton 81–93; V Blyth St Mary 93–04; RD Bedlington
98–03; Chapl Cheviot and Wansbeck NHS Trust 93–98;
Chapl Northumbria Healthcare NHS Trust 98–04; Hon
Can Newc Cathl 01–04; rtd 04; PtO *Newc* from 04. *64
Monks Wood, North Shields NE30 2UA* T: 0191-257 1631
E: brian.benison@btinternet.com

BENJAMIN, Adrian Victor. b 42. Wadh Coll Ox BA 66 MA 68.
Cuddesdon Coll 66. d 68 p 69. C Gosforth All SS *Newc*
68–71; C Stepney St Dunstan and All SS *Lon* 71–75; V Friern
Barnet All SS 75–12; Relig Ed ITV Oracle 83–92; rtd 12; PtO
Linc 14–20. *Carlton Cottage, 75 Church Lane, Sutton-on-Sea,
Mablethorpe LN12 2JA*

✠BENN, The Rt Revd Wallace Parke. b 47. UCD BA 69.
Trin Coll Bris 69. d 72 p 73 c 97. C New Ferry *Ches* 72–76;
C Cheadle 76–82; V Audley *Lich* 82–87; V Harold Wood
Chelmsf 87–97; Chapl Harold Wood Hosp Chelmsf 87–96;
Area Bp Lewes *Chich* 97–12; Can and Preb Chich Cathl
97–12; rtd 12; PtO *Pet* 13–20. *10 Glade Close, Burton Latimer,
Kettering NN15 5YG* E: twobenns@gmail.com

BENNER, Joanna Susan. *See* HOVER, Joanna Susan

BENNET, Hadley Jane. b 66. d 09 p 10. NSM Grayshott *Guildf*
09–13; Chapl Alton Coll 13–16; PtO *Guildf* from 18. *Landfall,
Three Gates Lane, Haslemere GU27 2ET* T: (01428) 658166
E: hadleybennet@yahoo.co.uk

BENNET, Canon Mark David. b 62. SS Coll Cam BA 84 MA 92
Anglia Poly Univ MA 04 ACA 89. Westcott Ho Cam 98.
d 01 p 02. C Chapel Allerton *Ripon* 01–05; TV Gt Parndon
Chelmsf 05–07; P-in-c 07–09; TR 09–11; TR Thatcham *Ox*
from 11; AD Newbury 15–20; Hon Can Ch Ch from 21. *The
Rectory, 2 Rectory Gardens, Thatcham RG19 3PR* T: (01635)
867342 E: markbennet@btinternet.com

BENNETT, Alan Robert. b 31. Roch Th Coll 62. d 64 p 65.
C Asterby w Goulceby *Linc* 64–67; C St Alb St Pet 67–70;
R Banham *Nor* 70–72; CF 72–77; P-in-c Colchester St Mary
Magd *Chelmsf* 77; TV Colchester St Leon, St Mary Magd and
St Steph 77–81; R Colne Engaine 81–88; P-in-c Stoke Ferry w
Wretton *Ely* 88–89; V 89–96; V Whittington 88–96; rtd 96;
Hon C Wimbotsham w Stow Bardolph and Stow Bridge etc
Ely 96–00; PtO from 00. *34 West Way, Wimbotsham, King's
Lynn PE34 3PZ* T: (01366) 385958

BENNETT, Canon Alan William. b 42. Sarum Th Coll 65.
d 68 p 69. C Fareham H Trin *Portsm* 68–71; C Brighton
St Matthias *Chich* 71–73; C Stanmer w Falmer and
Moulsecoomb 73–75; C Moulsecoomb 76; V Lower
Sandown St Jo *Portsm* 76–80; V Soberton w Newtown 80–87;
R Aston Clinton w Buckland and Drayton Beauchamp *Ox*
87–07; RD Wendover 94–04; Hon Can Ch Ch 03–07; rtd 07;
Asst Chapl Costa Almeria and Costa Calida *Eur* from 10. *2
Chapman Close, Aylesbury HP21 8FY* T: (0034) 678 022 986
E: canonbennett@hotmail.co.uk

BENNETT, Alexander Steven Frederick. b 69. Hull Univ BA 91
Birm Univ MA 03 Cardiff Univ MTh 17. Westcott Ho Cam 93.
d 95 p 96. C Whitton and Thurleston w Akenham *St E* 95–99;
OGS from 99; C Oswestry *Lich* 99–01; V Oswestry H Trin
01–04; CF from 04. *c/o MOD Chaplains (Army)* T: (01264)
383430 F: 381824 E: armypadre@hotmail.com

BENNETT, Mrs Alison. b 63. Open Univ BSc 03 DipSW 99.
STETS 05. d 08 p 09. C Bramshott and Liphook *Portsm*
08–12; TV Basingstoke *Win* 12–21; P-in-c Fawley from 21.
Address temp unknown

BENNETT, Ms Anne Yvonne. b 62. Open Univ MSc 95 Imp
Coll Lon MBA 00 Dur Univ MA 08. Cranmer Hall Dur 06.
d 08 p 09. C Harton *Dur* 08–12; C Cleadon Park 09–12; V
Borstal *Roch* 12–17; Chapl HM Pris Cookham Wood 12–17;
TV Deptford St Jo w H Trin and Ascension *S'wark* from 17.
40 Dartmouth Row, London SE10 8AW E: btavicar@gmail.com

BENNETT, Anthony Richard. b 68. Sheff Univ BSc 91
Cranfield Inst of Tech MSc 92 Open Univ MBA 04.
St Mellitus Coll 17. d 19 p 20. C Haworth and Cross
Roads cum Lees *Leeds* from 19. *Swallow Barn, Sawood,
Oxenhope, Keighley BD22 9SP* T: (01535) 279624
E: anthony.bennett@leeds.anglican.org

BENNETT, Arnold Ernest. b 29. K Coll Lon BD 59 AKC 53.
d 54 p 55. C S w N Hayling *Portsm* 54–59; C Stevenage *St Alb*
59–64; R N w S Wootton *Nor* 64–74; V Hykeham *Linc* 74–85;
V Heckfield w Mattingley and Rotherwick *Win* 85–99; rtd
99; PtO *Win* 99–20. *24 Cricket Green, Hartley Wintney, Hook
RG27 8PP* T: (01252) 843147

BENNETT, Avril Elizabeth Jean. b 63. UCD BEd. d 00 p 01.
NSM Dublin Crumlin w Chapelizod *D & G* 00–03; NSM
Tallaght from 03. *17 Ardeevin Court, Lucan, Co Dublin, Republic
of Ireland* T: (00353) (1) 628 2353 E: avrilfred@eircom.net

BENNETT, Mrs Christina Mary. b 45. d 07 p 08. NSM Henfield
w Shermanbury and Woodmancote *Chich* 07–18; PtO from
18. *17 Gresham Place, Henfield BN5 9QJ* T: (01273) 492222
E: revd.christina@henfield.org

BENNETT, Christopher Ian. b 75. TCD BA 98 BTh 00.
CITC 97. d 00 p 01. C Larne and Inver *Conn* 00–03; C
Holywood *D & D* 03–09; Bp's C Belfast Titanic Quarter 09–19;
P-in-c Belfast St Clem 12–15; C Belvoir from 19. *29 Loughview
Terrace, Greenisland, Carrickfergus BT38 8RE* T: (028) 9085
2895 M: 07980-885991 E: cands2000@hotmail.com

BENNETT, David Edward. b 35. Fitzw Ho Cam BA 56 MA 60
Lon Univ PGCE. Wells Th Coll 58. d 60 p 61. C Lightcliffe
Wakef 60–62; NE Area Sec Chr Educn Movement 62–68; Gen
Insp RE Nottm Co Coun 68–00; Hon C Holme Pierrepont w
Adbolton *S'well* 71–85; NSM Radcliffe-on-Trent and Shelford
etc 85–00; rtd 00; PtO *S'well* 04–14. *The Old Farmhouse, 65
Main Street, Gunthorpe, Nottingham NG14 7EY* T: 0115-966
3451

BENNETT, Elizabeth Mary. b 44. d 10 p 11. NSM Broughton
Gifford, Gt Chalfield and Holt *Sarum* 10–14; NSM Hordle *Win*
14–19; rtd 19; C Batheaston w St Cath *B & W* from 19; PtO
Sarum from 20. *Gaston House, 388 Gaston, Holt, Trowbridge
BA14 6QA* T: (01225) 783119 E: revelizabeth1@gmail.com

BENNETT, Garry Raymond. b 46. K Coll Lon 66 St Aug Coll
Cant 69. d 70 p 71. C Mitcham St Mark *S'wark* 70–73; C
Mortlake w E Sheen 73–75; TV 76–78; V Herne Hill St Paul
78–88; P-in-c Ruskin Park St Sav and St Matt 82–88; V
Herne Hill 89; Sen Dioc Stewardship Adv *Chelmsf* 89–94;
TR Southend 94–98; Dir and Chapl Herne Hill Sch *S'wark*
98–10; PtO *St D* from 00; *Sarum* from 16. *Netherton, Higher
Street, Iwerne Minster, Blandford Forum DT11 8LY* T: (01747)
812151 E: phyll.bennett@btinternet.com

BENNETT, Canon Geoffrey Kenneth. b 56. Ex Univ
MA 01. Oak Hill Th Coll. d 89 p 90. C Ipswich St Matt
St E 89–92; R St Ruan w St Grade and Landewednack
Truro 92–98; V Budock from 98; P-in-c Mawnan 03–13;
RD Carnmarth S from 12; Hon Can Truro Cathl from 14.
*The Vicarage, Merry Mit Meadow, Budock Water, Falmouth
TR11 5DW* T: (01326) 376422 E: g.k.bennett@amserve.net
or rev.bennett@talk21.com

BENNETT, Canon George Edward. b 51. Univ of Wales
(Abth) BA 72. St Steph Ho Ox 73. d 76 p 77. C Clifton All SS
w Tyndalls Park *Bris* 76–78; C Clifton All SS w St Jo 78–82;
Chapl Newbury and Sandleford Hosps 82–93; TV Newbury
Ox 82–93; V Llwynderw *S & B* 93–06; V Newton St Pet 06–16;
AD Clyne 98–12; Hon Can Brecon Cathl 00–02; Can Res
Brecon Cathl 02–16; rtd 16; PtO *S & B* from 16. *20 Dol y Coed,
Dunvant, Swansea SA2 7UG* E: bennettgandr@gmail.com

BENNETT, Graham Eric Thomas. b 53. Sarum & Wells
Th Coll 88. d 90 p 91. C Baswich *Lich* 90–94; C Codsall
94–00; P-in-c Willenhall St Steph 00–05; V 05–18; AD
Wolverhampton 05–11; rtd 18; PtO *Lich* 18–21.

BENNETT, Handel Henry Cecil. b 33. Cant Sch of Min 79.
d 82 p 83. NSM St Margarets-at-Cliffe w Westcliffe etc
Cant 82–85; Dir Holy Land Chr Tours 85–94; Holy Land
Consultant F T Tours 95–96; Sen Travel Consultant Raymond
Cook Chr Tours from 96; PtO *St Alb* 85–99; *Ex* 99–18. *Camps
Bay, 2 Victoria Road, Sidmouth EX10 8TZ* T: (01395) 514211

BENNETT, Helen Anne. *See* EDWARDS, Helen Anne

BENNETT, Herbert Montagu. b 63. Dur Univ BA 17.
SEITE 13. d 16 p 17. NSM Kemp Town St Mary *Chich*
from 16; PtO *Lon* from 19. *6 Southover Manor House,
Southover High Street, Lewes BN7 1HT* T: (01273) 470341
E: revherbert.bennett@gmail.com

BENNETT, Ivan. b 64. Qu Coll Birm 17. d 19 p 20.
NSM Emmaus Par Team *Leic* from 19. *102 Dumbleton
Avenue, Leicester LE3 2EH* T: 0116-223 9730
E: ivanbennettsaysgodlovesyou@gmail.com

BENNETT, James Duncan. b 58. St Aug Coll of Th BA 17. d 17
p 18. NSM Slade Green *Roch* 17–19; C 19; P-in-c 19–20; V

from 20. *59 Hillingdon Road, Bexleyheath DA7 6LN* T: (01322) 553421 M: 07787-292094 E: jdbbarnehurst@aol.com

BENNETT, John David. b 58. Ox Univ BA 79 MA 83. Westcott Ho Cam 81. **d** 83 **p** 84. C Taunton St Andr *B & W* 83–86; Chapl Trowbridge Coll *Sarum* 86–90; Asst P Studley 86–90; V Yeovil H Trin *B & W* 90–95; R Yeovil H Trin w Barwick 95–02; R Sprowston w Beeston *Nor* 02–10; RD Nor N 05–10; V Spalding St Mary and St Nic *Linc* from 10; P-in-c Spalding St Paul 10–12. *The Parsonage, 1 Halmer Gate, Spalding PE11 2DR* T: (01775) 719668 E: jdbennett@gmail.com

BENNETT, John Dudley. b 44. Open Univ BA 87 Lanc Univ MA 92 Huddersfield Univ PGCE 04. Coll of Resurr Mirfield 08. **d** 09 **p** 09. NSM Bolton Abbey *Bradf* 09–14; rtd 14; PtO *Leeds* from 15; *Eur* from 15. *Honeysuckle Cottage, The Green, Linton, Skipton BD23 5HJ* T: (01756) 753763 E: brj.linton@virgin.net

BENNETT, Canon John Seccombe. b 59. Wye Coll Lon BSc 81 Leic Poly CertEd 84. Trin Coll Bris. **d** 00 **p** 01. C Llanrhian w Llanhywel and Carnhedryn etc *St D* 00–01; C Dewisland 01–02; TV 02–11; V Cardigan w Mwnt and Y Ferwig w Llangoedmor 11–18; P-in-c Bro Teifi from 18; Min Can St D Cathl from 00; AD Cemais and Sub-Aeron 14–18; AD Bro Teifi from 18; Can St D Cathl from 20. *The Vicarage, Maesydderwen, Cardigan SA43 1PE* T: (01239) 615466 E: jsbkbennett@btinternet.com

BENNETT, Mark Ian. b 61. K Coll Cam BA 83 MA 86. Trin Coll Bris BA 94. **d** 94 **p** 95. C Selly Park St Steph and St Wulstan *Birm* 94–97; C Harrow Trin St Mich *Lon* 97–99; Hon C Redland *Bris* 99–00; TV Drypool *York* 00–06; V Gee Cross *Ches* 06–16; V Shenley Green *Birm* 16–21; Dioc Coaching Lead from 21. *49 Shenley Green, Birmingham B29 4HH* M: 07435-927821 E: markbennett@cofebirmingham.com

BENNETT, Mark Stephen. b 66. Cant Univ (NZ) MusB 89 Cant Ch Ch Univ BA 14. SEITE 07. **d** 10 **p** 11. NSM Staplehurst Cant 10–12; Chapl Dulwich Prep Sch Cranbrook 10–12; Chapl St Edm Sch Cant 13–20; Hon Min Can Cant Cathl 11–12 and 18–20; Min Can 13–18; rtd 21. *Address temp unknown* M: 07709-376668

BENNETT, Michael John. b 43. AKC 66. St Boniface Warminster 66. **d** 67 **p** 68. C Chester le Street *Dur* 67–71; C Portland All SS w St Pet *Sarum* 71–74; V Portland St Jo 74–85; Chapl Portland Hosp Weymouth 74–85; R Alveley and Quatt *Heref* 85–92; Dep Chapl HM YOI Glen Parva 93–95; TV Wrexham 'St A 95–99; V Llansantffraid-ym-Mechain and Llanfechain 99–05; C Rhyl w St Ann 05–09; rtd 09; Hon C Redmarley D'Abitot, Bromesberrow, Pauntley etc *Glouc* 09–12; PtO from 13. *65 Robert Raikes Avenue, Tuffley, Gloucester GL4 0HL* T: (01452) 301337 E: sheilabennett123@btinternet.com

BENNETT, Milen George Penev. Bulgarian Evang Th Inst BA 03. **d** 15 **p** 16. OLM Stratford St Paul and St Jas *Chelmsf* 15–16; C 17–19; C Forest Gate All SS from 19. *79 Claremont Road, London E7 0QA* M: 07951-321563 E: milebennett7@gmail.com

BENNETT, Nigel John. b 47. Oak Hill Th Coll 66. **d** 71 **p** 72. C Tonbridge St Steph *Roch* 71–75; C Heatherlands St Jo *Sarum* 75–79; P-in-c Kingham w Churchill, Daylesford and Sarsden *Ox* 79; R 80–85; Chapl Blue Coat Sch Reading 85–08; rtd 08; PtO *Ox* 08–09; Hon C Southsea St Jude *Portsm* 09–14; PtO from 14. *19 Ashburton Road, Southsea PO5 3JS* T: (023) 9242 1463 E: nigelbennett@virginmedia.com

BENNETT, Paul. b 55. Southn Univ BTh 94. St Steph Ho Ox 95. **d** 97 **p** 98. C Willingdon *Chich* 97–00; C Hangleton 00–04; R Letchworth *St Alb* 04–18; rtd 18; PtO *Ely* from 19. *162 Cavalry Park, March PE15 9DL* E: revpaulbennett@ntlworld.com

BENNETT, Paul William. b 61. Linc Th Coll 95. **d** 95 **p** 96. C Thornton-le-Fylde *Blackb* 95–00; V Wesham 00–03; P-in-c Treales 00–03; V Wesham and Treales 03–08; Chapl Dunkirk Miss to Seafarers *Eur* 08–14; P-in-c Meir *Lich* 14–17; P-in-c Longton 14–17; R Longton and Meir from 17. *The Rectory, Rutland Road, Stoke-on-Trent ST3 1EH* T: (01782) 595098 E: mowbreck@aol.com

BENNETT, Miss Rachel Elizabeth. b 56. W Sussex Inst of HE CertEd 79. **d** 04. NSM Littlehampton and Wick *Chich* 04–05; C Durrington 05–07; Chapl Worthing and Southlands Hosps NHS Trust 08–09; Chapl W Sussex Hosps NHS Foundn Trust from 09. *Worthing Hospital, Lyndhurst Road, Worthing BN11 2DH* T: (01903) 205111 M: 07810-350098 E: rachel.bennett@wsht.nhs.uk

BENNETT, Robert Geoffrey. b 43. FCA. **d** 05 **p** 06. OLM Woking St Jo *Guildf* 05–13; PtO from 13. *10 Barricane, Woking GU21 7RB* T: (01483) 722832 E: rgb1215@btinternet.com

BENNETT, Sarah Grace. b 91. Ches Univ BTh 13. Qu Foundn Birm MA 19. **d** 19 **p** 20. C Glascote and Stonydelph *Lich* from 19. *9 Friars Walk, Tamworth B77 2FH*

BENNETT, Stephen. *See* BENNETT, Mark Stephen

BENNETT, Ms Toni Elizabeth. b 56. Worc Coll of Educn BA 81 Sheff Poly 87. St Jo Coll Nottm MA 94. **d** 96 **p** 97. C Heanor *Derby* 96–00; TV Bedworth *Cov* 00–08; R Montgomery and Forden and Llandyssil *St As* 08–17; P-in-c Pool Miss Area 18; AD Pool 10–15; rtd 18. *3A Runnings Park, Croft Bank, Malvern WR14 4DU* E: tonibrev@gmail.com

BENNETT, William Leslie. b 52. TCD Div Sch. **d** 90 **p** 91. C Carrickfergus *Conn* 90–93; I Lisnaskea *Clogh* 93–00; I Newcastle w Newtownmountkennedy and Calary *D & G* 00–20; rtd 20. *Kilmurray North, Kilmacanogue, Bray, Co Wicklow, A98 PH99, Republic of Ireland* M: (00353) 87-948 0317 E: bennettwilliam1@gmail.com

BENNETT-SHAW, Miss Anne Elizabeth. b 38. **d** 02 **p** 03. OLM Upper Wylye Valley *Sarum* 02–08; rtd 08; PtO *Sarum* 08–19. *5 Hospital of St John, Heytesbury, Warminster BA12 0HW* T: (01985) 840339 E: revannebennettshaw@btinternet.com

BENNETTS, Ms Rachel Mary. b 69. Homerton Coll Cam BEd 91. Trin Coll Bris BA 01. **d** 02 **p** 03. C Wroughton *Bris* 02–06; TV N Farnborough *Guildf* 06–17; Chapl Farnborough Sixth Form Coll 07–17; Prior Community of the Tree of Life from 17. *The Community of the Tree of Life, St Martin's House, 7 Peacock Lane, Leicester LE1 5PZ* M: 07749-045449 E: rachelmbennetts@gmail.com *or* info@leicestertreeoflife.org

BENNIE, Stanley James Gordon. b 43. Edin Univ MA 65. Coll of Resurr Mirfield 66. **d** 68 **p** 69. C Ashington *Newc* 68–70; Prec St Andr Cathl Inverness *Mor* 70–74; Itinerant Priest 74–81; R Portsoy *Ab* 81–84; R Buckie 81–84; R Stornoway *Arg* 84–10; R Eoropaidh 84–95; rtd 10. *St Lennan, 13A Scotland Street, Stornoway HS1 2JN* T: (01851) 703259 M: 07768-660612 E: gm4ptq@btinternet.com

BENNISON, Andrew Mark Kinsey. b 92. Trin Coll Ox BA 13 MA 17. Lon Inst of Educn PGCE 14. Ripon Coll Cuddesdon BA 18. **d** 19 **p** 20. C Burnage St Nic *Man* 19–20; C Stretford All SS from 20. *31 Bowness Street, Stretford, Manchester M32 0EA* M: 07904-132517 E: revandrewbennison@outlook.com

BENNISON, Philip Owen. b 42. Dur Univ BA 64. Coll of Resurr Mirfield 64. **d** 66 **p** 67. C Guisborough *York* 66–67; C S Bank 67–71; C Thornaby on Tees St Paul 71–72; TV Thornaby on Tees 72–74; R Skelton in Cleveland 74–78; R Upleatham 75–78; Chapl Freeman Hosp Newc 78–84; V Ashington *Newc* 84–93; Chapl N Tees Health NHS Trust Stockton-on-Tees 93–98; Chapl N Tees and Hartlepool NHS Trust 99–02; P-in-c Newton Flowery Field *Ches* 02–10; P-in-c Hyde St Thos 02–10; rtd 10; PtO *York* from 10; *Dur* from 12. *62 Glaisdale Road, Yarm TS15 9RP* T: (01642) 646624 M: 07740-852832 E: philip_bennison@hotmail.com

BENOY, Canon Stephen Michael. b 66. Clare Coll Cam BA 87 MA 90. Trin Coll Bris BA 93. **d** 96 **p** 97. C New Malden and Coombe *S'wark* 96–02; Kingston Borough Youth Project 00–02; V Kettering Ch the King *Pet* 02–11; Dir of Ords and Voc from 11; Dir Voc and Formation from 17; Can Pet Cathl from 13. *Diocese of Peterborough, Bouverie Court, 6 The Lakes, Bedford Road, Northampton NN4 7YD* T: (01604) 887047 E: steve.benoy@peterborough-diocese.org.uk

BENSKIN, David Peter. b 53. Qu Coll Birm 11. **d** 13 **p** 14. C Heart of England *Cov* 13–17; P-in-c Aston Cantlow and Wilmcote w Billesley from 17; Asst Chapl Rainsbrook Secure Tr Cen 13–15; Chapl 15–18. *The Vicarage, Church Road, Wilmcote, Stratford-upon-Avon CV37 9XD* M: 07375-566185 E: thebenskins@gmail.com

BENSON, Ashley Dawn. *See* ROSS, Ashley Dawn

BENSON, Christopher Hugh. b 53. Bath Academy of Art BA 75 Keble Coll Ox BA 78 MA 87. Chich Th Coll 78. **d** 80 **p** 81. C Heavitree w Ex St Paul 80–83; P-in-c Broadclyst 83–85; TV Pinhoe and Broadclyst 85–90; V Kingsteignton and Teigngrace 90–08; Chapl Plymouth Univ 92–95; RD Newton Abbot and Ipplepen 01–07; C Baslow w Curbar and Stoney Middleton *Derby* 08–11; C Ashford w Sheldon and Longstone 08–11; V Longstone, Curbar and Stony Middleton 11–14; rtd 14. *1 Leighon Cottages, Manaton, Newton Abbot TQ13 9UP* T: (01629) 640257 E: chbfiftythree@gmail.com

BENSON, Gareth Neil. b 47. Jordan Hill Coll Glas TCert 80. St And NSM Tr Scheme 77. **d** 81 **p** 82. NSM Glenrothes *St And* 81–88; NSM Kirkcaldy 88–04; P-in-c 04–12; NSM Kinghorn 88–04; P-in-c 04–12; rtd 12; PtO *St And* from 12. *129 Waverley Drive, Glenrothes KY6 2LZ* T: (01592) 769869 E: fathergareth@btinternet.com

BENSON, The Ven George Patrick (Paddy). b 49. Ch Ch Ox BA 70 Lon Univ BD 77 Open Univ MPhil 94. St Jo Coll Nottm 89. **d** 91 **p** 92. C Upton (Overchurch) *Ches* 91–95; V Barnston 95–11; RD Wirral N 98–08; Hon Can Ches Cathl 09–11; Adn Heref 11–18; rtd 18. *26 West Park Drive, Leeds LS16 5BL* T: 0113-450 7856 E: muhunjia@aol.com

BENSON, Mrs Hilary Christine. b 51. Man Univ BA 72 Hughes Hall Cam PGCE 73. Trin Coll Bris 81. **dss** 84 **d** 87 **p** 94. Starbeck *Ripon* 84–86; Birm St Martin w Bordesley St Andr 86–91; NSM 87–91; NSM Brandwood 91–97; Chapl Birm Univ 92–97; Chapl St Edw Sch Ox 97–00; Chapl Qu Anne's Sch Caversham 00–13; rtd 14; PtO *Derby* from 14. *50 Cardigan Road, Southport PR8 4SF* T: (01704) 553960 E: hilarybenson@icloud.com

BENSON, John Patrick. b 51. Univ of Wales (Ban) BSc 72. Trin Coll Bris 83. **d** 85 **p** 86. C Stoke Damerel *Ex* 85–88; P-in-c Petrockstowe, Petersmarland, Merton and Huish 88; TV Shebbear, Buckland Filleigh, Sheepwash etc 89–94; RD Torrington 93–94; P-in-c Newport, Bishops Tawton and Tawstock 94–97; TV Barnstaple 97–07; R Knockholt w Halstead *Roch* 07–16; rtd 16; PtO *Heref* from 17. *The Mill House, Monkland, Leominster HR6 9DB* T: (01568) 720035 M: 07982-627206 E: john.benson3@btinternet.com

BENSON, Canon John Patrick. b 52. Ch Coll Cam BA 73 MA 76 PhD 76. Trin Coll Bris 78. **d** 81 **p** 82. C Walmley *Birm* 81–84; C Chadkirk *Ches* 84–86; V St Geo Singapore 87–95; Dir of Tr 95–01; V Chpl of Resurr 01–07; Hon Can Singapore 96–07; Dean Cambodia 93–05; Dean Laos 98–00; rtd 07; PtO *Ches* from 09. *Cherry Trees, Queens Park Road, Chester CH4 7AD* T: (01244) 671170 E: johnpbenson@gmail.com

BENSON, Nicholas Henry. b 53. Man Univ BSc 75 Leeds Univ MSc 77. Trin Coll Bris 81. **d** 84 **p** 85. C Starbeck *Ripon* 84–86; C Birm St Martin w Bordesley St Andr 86–91; Chapl to the Markets 86–91; V Brandwood 91–97; PtO *Ox* 99–01; NSM Reading St Jo 01–14; PtO *Derby* from 14. *50 Cardigan Road, Southport PR8 4SF* T: (01704) 553960

BENSON, Nigel Anthony Stewart. b 58. St Hild Coll 18. **d** 19 **p** 20. NSM Haxby and Wigginton *York* from 19. *28 Oaken Grove, Haxby, York YO32 3QZ* E: revnas@btinternet.com

BENSON, Patrick. *See* BENSON, George Patrick

BENSON, Philip Richard. b 85. QUB BTh 06 MTh 09 TCD MTh 15. **d** 14 **p** 15. Finaghy *Conn* 14–15; C Larne and Inver 15–18; P-in-c Kilwaughter and Cairncastle w Craigy Hill from 18. *9 Oakdene, Larne BT40 2FD* M: 07850-345156

BENSON, Philip Steven. b 59. Ulster Univ BSc 81 LLCM 80. S Dios Minl Tr Scheme 88. **d** 92 **p** 93. Producer Relig Broadcasting Dept BBC 91–94; NSM W Ealing St Jo w St Jas *Lon* 92–94; Relig Progr Producer BBC Man from 94. *6 Sudlow Barns, Sudlow Lane, Tabley, Knutsford WA16 0TN* T: (01565) 652513 F: 641695 E: steven@benson5.co.uk

BENSON, Mrs Rachel Candia. b 43. JP 76. TCD MA 66 Lon Univ PGCE 67. S'wark Ord Course 84. **d** 87 **p** 94. NSM Putney St Marg *S'wark* 87–97; NSM Sand Hutton and Whitwell w Crambe, Flaxton and Foston *York* 97–07; PtO from 07. *Grange Farm, Westow, York YO60 7NJ* T: (01653) 658296 F: 658456 E: rachelbenson43@gmail.com

BENSON, Richard John. b 55. Birm Coll of Educn CertEd 78. Ripon Coll Cuddesdon 92. **d** 94 **p** 95. C Alford w Rigsby *Linc* 94–97; R Partney Gp 97–12; V Taddington, Chelmorton and Monyash etc *Derby* 12–19; rtd 19. *Address temp unknown* E: parson_benson@yahoo.co.uk

BENSON, Steven. *See* BENSON, Philip Steven

BENT, David Michael. b 55. Leeds Univ BSc 77. Trin Coll Bris BA 94. **d** 96 **p** 97. C Gorleston St Andr *Nor* 96–00; TR Brinsworth w Catcliffe and Treeton *Sheff* 00–03; TR Rivers Team 03–19; P-in-c Walgrave w Hannington and Wold and Scaldwell *Pet* 19–21; R from 21. *The Rectory, Lower Green, Walgrave, Northampton NN6 9QF* T: (01604) 781667 E: davidbent99@btinternet.com

BENT, Helen Margaret. b 56. Sheff Univ BMus 77 Trent Poly PGCE 78 Suffolk Poly BA 00. EAMTC 97. **d** 98 **p** 99. C Gorleston St Mary *Nor* 98–00; C Brightside w Wincobank *Sheff* 00–04; Bp's Adv in Music and Worship 05–15; Hd Minl Tr RSCM from 15; C Rivers Team *Sheff* 15–19; Hon Can Sheff Cathl 15–19; C Walgrave w Hannington and Wold and Scaldwell *Pet* from 19. *The Rectory, Lower Green, Walgrave, Northampton NN6 9QF* T: (01604) 780334 E: helen@thebents.co.uk

BENT, The Very Revd Michael Charles. b 31. Kelham Th Coll 51. **d** 55 **p** 56. C Wellingborough St Mary *Pet* 55–60; NZ 60–85; Adn Taranaki 76–85; Dean H Trin Cathl Suva Fiji 85–89; Can St Pet Cathl Hamilton NZ 90–94; Papua New Guinea 94–96; NZ from 96. *34 Brooklands Road, New Plymouth 4310, New Zealand* T: (0064) (6) 753 5507 E: miro@clear.net.nz

BENTALL, Canon Jill Margaret. b 44. MCSP 66. S Dios Minl Tr Scheme 91. **d** 94 **p** 95. NSM Knights Enham *Win* 94–02; C Andover w Foxcott 02–09; P-in-c Pastrow 09–14; RD Andover 06–10; Hon Can Win Cathl 11–14; rtd 14; PtO *Win* from 14; *Sarum* 15–19. *Old Farm Cottage, 102 Enham Lane, Charlton, Andover SP10 4AN* T: (01264) 351998

BENTHAM, Philip John (Ben). b 55. Hull Univ BA 83 PGCE 85. Trin Coll Bris MA 96. **d** 96 **p** 97. C Wrockwardine Deanery *Lich* 96–00; P-in-c Chipinge and Chimanimani Zimbabwe 00–03; Chapl Viña del Mar St Pet Chile 03–07; Chapl Bethany Sch Goudhurst 08–13; Chapl Dur Sch 13–14; C Stockton Country Par *Dur* 15–16; V Wye Brooks Benefice *Heref* from 17. *The Vicarage, Llangrove, Ross-on-Wye HR9 6EZ* T: (01989) 770454 M: 07437-447054 E: benbentham@yahoo.co.uk

BENTLEY, Frances Rymer. *See* COCKER, Frances Rymer

BENTLEY, The Ven Frank William Henry. b 34. AKC 57. **d** 58 **p** 59. C Shepton Mallet *B & W* 58–62; R Kingsdon w Podymore-Milton 62–66; P-in-c Yeovilton 62–66; P-in-c Babcary 64–66; V Wiveliscombe 66–76; RD Tone 73–76; V St Jo in Bedwardine *Worc* 76–84; P-in-c Worc St Mich 82–84; RD Martley and Worc W 80–84; Hon Can Worc Cathl 81–84; Adn Worc and Can Res Worc Cathl 84–99; rtd 99; PtO *Worc* from 04; Chapl to The Queen 94–04. *Willow Cottage, Station Road, Fladbury, Pershore WR10 2QW* T: (01386) 861847 E: f.bentley123@btinternet.com

BENTLEY, The Ven Ian Robert. b 55. Sheff Univ BA 76 Sheff City Poly PGCE 78. Cranmer Hall Dur 93. **d** 95 **p** 96. C Mattishall w Mattishall Burgh, Welborne etc *Nor* 95–98; R Ditchingham, Hedenham, Broome, Earsham etc 98–06; V Oulton Broad 06–17; RD Lothingland 10–14; P-in-c Nor St Pet Mancroft w St Jo Maddermarket 17–18; Adn Lynn from 18; Hon Can Nor Cathl 10–16; Chapter Can from 16. *Holly Tree House, Whitwell Road, Sparham, Norwich NR9 5PN* T: (01362) 688032 E: archdeacon.lynn@dioceseofnorwich.org

BENTLEY, Ian Ronald. b 51. BA 79. Oak Hill Th Coll 76. **d** 79 **p** 80. C Northwood Em *Lon* 79–85; C St Marylebone All So w SS Pet and Jo 85–88; C Langham Place All So 88–91; V Eynsham and Cassington *Ox* 91–05; V Chineham *Win* 05–17; rtd 17; PtO *Glouc* from 18. *22 Fosseway Avenue, Moreton-in-Marsh GL56 0EA* E: ibentley4@googlemail.com

BENTLEY, Lesley. b 55. Univ of Wales (Lamp) BA 76 RMN 80. St Jo Coll Nottm MTh 82. **dss** 82 **d** 87 **p** 94. Mickleover St Jo *Derby* 82–84; Thornton *Liv* 84–89; Par Dn 87–89; Dir Diaconal Mins 89–92; Par Dn Farnworth 92–94; C 94–95; V Westbrook St Phil 95–01; Hon Can Liv Cathl 99–01; V Bilton *Ripon* 01–03; TR 03–09; Initial Minl Educn Officer 03–09; Dir Min Development *Lich* 09–10; Dir Min 10–19; P-in-c Mid Trent 19–20; rtd 20; PtO *Lich* from 20. *Address temp unknown* E: lesley_bentley@btinternet.com

BENTLEY, Canon Paul. b 48. Sarum & Wells Th Coll. **d** 93 **p** 94. C Ex St Dav 93–96; P-in-c Marlpool *Derby* 96–01; V 01–02; Chapl Derbyshire Community Health Services 96–00; Chapl Amber Valley Primary Care Trust 00–02; Chapl Mansfield Distr Primary Care Trust 02–13; P-in-c Mansfield St Lawr *S'well* 13–17; Hon Can S'well Minster 11–17; rtd 17; PtO *S'well* from 18. *27 Sandringham Road, Mansfield Woodhouse, Mansfield NG19 9HN* E: revpaulb@aol.com

BENTLEY, Paul Nicholas. b 80. Man Univ BA 03. St Jo Coll Nottm MTh 14. **d** 14 **p** 15. C Frankby w Greasby *Ches* 14–17; R Birkenhead Priory from 17. *10 Cavendish Road, Birkenhead CH41 8AX* M: 07967-672778 E: paulnbentley@gmail.com

BENTON-EVANS, Martin James William. b 69. K Coll Lon BA 90 Anglia Poly Univ PGCE 97. Ripon Coll Cuddesdon BTh 03. **d** 03 **p** 04. C Ivybridge w Harford *Ex* 03–06; P-in-c St Teath *Truro* 06–12; P-in-c Lanteglos by Camelford w Advent 06–12; Chapl Sir Jas Smith's Community Sch Camelford 10–12; R Peebles *Edin* 12–18; R Innerleithen 12–18; P-in-c Glas E End from 18; Dioc Youth Chapl from 18; Chapl Swinton Primary Sch from 19. *38 Old Gartloch Road, Gartcosh, Glasgow G69 8ET* M: 07702-842727 E: jimbentonevans@gmail.com

BENWELL, Michael Patrick. b 55. Jes Coll Cam BA 77 Glas Univ PhD 80. Sarum & Wells Th Coll BTh 92. **d** 92 **p** 93. C Eastleigh *Win* 92–95; Chapl Leeds Metrop Univ *Ripon* 95–99; TV Seacroft 99–06; TR 06–14; Leeds 14–20; AD Whitkirk *Ripon* 09–14; *Leeds* 14–16; rtd 20. *Dunnock Croft, Carroch, Kirriemuir DD8 4RN* E: mike.p.benwell@gmail.com

BENYON, Oliver William Yates. b 80. Ox Brookes Univ BA 02. Wycliffe Hall Ox 13. **d** 15 **p** 16. C Cambridge H Trin *Ely* from 15. *42 Pretoria Road, Cambridge CB4 1HE* M: 07739-710947 E: olibenyon@me.com

BENYON, Thomas Yates. b 74. Edin Univ MA 98 Lon Inst of Educn PGCE 99. Trin Coll Bris. **d** 15 **p** 16. C Peasedown St John w Wellow and Foxcote etc *B & W* 15–19; C Stoke Gifford *Bris* from 19. *21 Hermitage Wood Road, Bristol BS16 1BF* M: 07725-037435 E: tybenyon@mac.com

BENZIES, Neil Graham. b 43. Bede Coll Dur. Cranmer Hall Dur 93. **d** 95 **p** 96. NSM Stockton St Pet *Dur* 95–08; PtO from 15. *62 Fairwell Road, Stockton-on-Tees TS19 7HX* T: (01642) 582322

BERDINNER, Clifford. b 24. SS Mark & Jo Univ Coll Plymouth BA 88 Ex Univ MPhil 95. **d** 64 **p** 65. C Leic St Pet 64–67; R Heather 67–72; NSM Totnes and Berry Pomeroy *Ex* 86–91; NSM Totnes, Bridgetown and Berry Pomeroy etc 91–94; rtd 89; PtO *Ex* 89–09. *Little Croft, 30 Droridge, Dartington, Totnes TQ9 6JQ* T: (01803) 732518

BERESFORD, Anthea Christine. b 63. **d** 16 **p** 17. NSM Cinderford w Littledean *Glouc* 16–20; V Beckley, Forest Hill, Horton-cum-Studley and Stanton St John *Ox* from 20. *The New Vicarage, Cox Lane, Stanton St John, Oxford OX33 1HW* T: (01865) 351839 E: anthea@fourparishes.org.uk

BERESFORD, Charles Edward. b 45. St Jo Coll Nottm. **d** 86 **p** 87. C Bushbury *Lich* 86–90; TV Glascote and Stonydelph 90–98; TR N Wingfield, Clay Cross and Pilsley *Derby* 98–11; rtd 11. *8 Spring Close, Belper DE56 2TY* T: (01773) 826519 E: charles.belper@uwclub.net

BERESFORD, David Charles. b 56. Leeds Univ BA 09 ACIB 93. Coll of Resurr Mirfield 07. **d** 09 **p** 10. C Lancing w Coombes *Chich* 09–11; C Bury w Houghton and Coldwaltham and Hardham 11–13; P-in-c Marsh Farm *St Alb* 13–16; R Springfield Redeemer USA 16–19; R Wilmington St Barn 19–20. *507 East Back Road, Wilmington DE 19807, USA* E: davidberesford@gmail.com

BERESFORD, Patrick Larner. b 53. Lon Bible Coll BA 77. **d** 10 **p** 11. NSM Weston super Mare St Jo *B & W* 10–12; TV Horsham *Chich* 12–18; rtd 18; PtO *Guildf* 18–21. *128 Cranleigh Mead, Cranleigh GU7 6JX* E: paddyjfj04@btinternet.com

BERESFORD, Peter Marcus de la Poer. b 49. Cranmer Hall Dur 74. **d** 77 **p** 78. C Walney Is *Carl* 77–80; C Netherton 80–83; TV Wednesfield *Lich* 83–88; TV Rugby *Cov* 88–97; Chapl Rugby Hosps 88–97; R Barby w Kilsby *Pet* 97–14; rtd 14; PtO *Cov* from 15. *The Barn, 41C School Street, Long Lawford, Rugby CV23 9AT* T: (01788) 570229 E: petermberesford@hotmail.co.uk

BERESFORD-PEIRSE, Mark de la Poer. b 45. Qu Coll Birm 73. **d** 76 **p** 77. C Garforth *Ripon* 76–79; C Beeston 79–83; V Barton and Manfield w Cleasby 83–90; V Pannal w Beckwithshaw 90–01; Dioc Chapl MU 91–98; R W Tanfield and Well w Snape and N Stainley 01–09; rtd 09; PtO *Leeds* from 17. *15 Eastfield Avenue, Richmond DL10 4NH* T: (01748) 826649 E: b_peirse@hotmail.com

BERESFORD-WEBB, Miss Petra May Elizabeth Broomé. b 66. Cardiff Univ BTh 14 NE Wales Inst of HE CertEd 01. St Mich Coll Llan 09. **d** 12 **p** 13. C E Radnor *S & B* 12–14; C Blaenau Irfon 14–15; P-in-c from 16; C Irfon Valley 14–15; P-in-c from 16; P-in-c Upper Wye from 16; Bp's Officer for Min to Children and Families from 14. *9 Cae Nant, Newbridge-on-Wye, Llandrindod Wells LD1 6LQ* T: (01597) 860842 M: 07966-799546 E: petra.beresfordwebb@yahoo.com

BERG, John Russell. b 36. MBE 78. Sarum Th Coll 57. **d** 60 **p** 61. C Ipswich St Aug *St E* 60–64; C Whitton and Thurleston w Akenham 64–65; Miss to Seafarers 65–04; Hong Kong 65–68; Japan 68–04; rtd 01; PtO *St E* 04–19. *23 Old Maltings Court, Old Maltings Approach, Melton, Woodbridge IP12 1AE* T: (01394) 383748 E: johnberg270@gmail.com

BERGQUIST, Anders Karim. b 58. Peterho Cam BA 79 MA 83 PhD 90. St Steph Ho Ox BA 85 MA 90. **d** 86 **p** 87. C Abbots Langley *St Alb* 86–89; Hon C Cambridge St Mary Less *Ely* 89–97; Tutor Westcott Ho Cam 89–95; Vice-Prin 95–97; Can Res St Alb 97–02; Minl Development Officer 97–02; V St John's Wood *Lon* from 02. *St John's House, St John's Wood High Street, London NW8 7NE* T: (020) 7722 4378 *or* 7586 3864 E: vicar.stjohnswood@london.anglican.org

BERK, The Very Revd Dennis Bryan Alban. b 65. Wheaton Coll Illinois BA 86 Toronto Univ MDiv 90. Lanc Th Sem Penn DMin 98. **d** 90 **p** 91. C Brockville St Pet Canada 90–92; C Tamworth 92–94; NSM Reading St Mary USA 94–96; R 96–01; Lect St Jo Sem Kitwe Zambia 03–06; USA 06–09; CR 09–18; R Ellon *Ab* from 18; R Cruden Bay from 18; Dean Ab from 20. *The Rectory, 1 South Road, Ellon AB41 9NP* T: (01358) 720366 M: 07717-804481 E: rector@stmarystjames.org

BERKSHIRE, Archdeacon of. See PULLIN, The Ven Stephen James

BERMUDA, Archdeacon of. See DOUGHTY, The Ven Andrew William

BERMUDA, Bishop of. See DILL, The Rt Revd Nicholas Bayard Botolf

BERNARDI, Frederick John. b 33. JP 75. Chich Th Coll 55. **d** 58 **p** 59. C Blackb St Luke 58–60; C Ribbleton 60–63; V Brinsley w Underwood *S'well* 63–66; V St Leon Barbados 67–71; V Sparkbrook St Agatha *Birm* 71–77; P-in-c Sparkbrook Ch Ch 73–75; V Haywards Heath St Wilfrid *Chich* 77–80; TR 80–87; Chapl Madrid *Eur* 87–90; NSM Tooting All SS *S'work* 90–91; V Hanger Hill Ascension and W Twyford St Mary *Lon* 91–95; rtd 95; PtO *Chich* from 95. *42 Woodlands*

Way, Southwater, Horsham RH13 9HZ T: (01403) 733335 E: stella@knights-templar.org.uk

BERNERS-WILSON, Preb Angela Veronica Isabel. b 54. St Andr Univ MTheol 76. Cranmer Hall Dur 77. **dss** 79 **d** 87 **p** 94. Southgate Ch Ch *Lon* 79–82; St Marylebone Ch Ch 82–84; Ind Chapl 82–84; Chapl Thames Poly *S'wark* 84–91; Chapl Bris Univ 91–95; C Bris St Mich and St Paul 94–95; P-in-c Colerne w N Wraxall 95–01; R 01–04; Chapl Bath Univ *B & W* 04–16; R Quantock Towers from 16; Preb Wells Cathl from 09. *The Rectory, 11 Trendle Lane, Bicknoller, Taunton TA4 4EG* T: (01984) 656067 E: a.bernerswilson@btinternet.com

BERNHARD, Peter James. b 55. Magd Coll Ox BA 76 MA 80. SAOMC 03. **d** 06 **p** 07. NSM Homerton St Luke *Lon* 06–08; Hon Chapl Homerton Univ Hosp NHS Foundn Trust Lon 07–08; PtO *Ox* 08–10; *Lon* 09–15; NSM Clerkenwell H Redeemer 15–17; Dir of Ords 15–19; rtd 19; PtO *Lon* from 19. *16 Doves Yard, London N1 0HQ* M: 07970-855354 E: souldernspring@tiscali.co.uk

BERRETT, Michael Vincent. b 56. St Chad's Coll Dur BA 78. Ox Min Course 06. **d** 09 **p** 10. NSM Wantage *Ox* 09–17; NSM Stokenham, Slapton, Charleton w Buckland etc *Ex* from 17. *The Vicarage, Stokenham, Kingsbridge TQ7 2ST* T: (01548) 580908 E: mvberrett@gmail.com

BERRIDGE, Grahame Richard. b 38. S'wark Ord Course 71. **d** 72 **p** 73. NSM S Beddington St Mich *S'wark* 72–75; NSM Merton St Jas 75–81; PtO from 81. *11 Cedar Walk, Kingswood, Tadworth KT20 6HW* T: (01737) 358882

BERRIMAN, Brinley John. b 50. Univ Coll Lon BSc 71. SWMTC 95. **d** 98 **p** 99. NSM Ives and Halsetown *Truro* 98–00; P-in-c Lanteglos by Camelford w Advent 00–05; P-in-c St Buryan, St Levan and Sennen 05–12; rtd 12; PtO *Truro* from 15. *Bosorne House, Bosorne, St Just, Penzance TR19 7NR* T: (01736) 787322 E: brin@dreckly.net

BERRIMAN, Gavin Anthony. b 60. S'wark Ord Course 87. **d** 90 **p** 91. C Greenwich St Alfege w St Pet and St Paul *S'wark* 90–94; V Lee St Aug from 94. *St Augustine's Vicarage, 336 Baring Road, London SE12 0DU* T: (020) 8857 4941 E: gavin.staug@hotmail.co.uk

BERRY, Canon Adrian Charles. b 50. Mert Coll Ox BA 71 MA 78. Cuddesdon Coll 72. **d** 75 **p** 76. C Prestbury *Glouc* 75–79; C Cirencester 79–83; V Cam w Stinchcombe 83–88; Dioc Ecum Officer 83–95; P-in-c Twyning 88–95; R Leckhampton St Pet 95–02; Dioc Min Development Officer *Llan* 02–14; P-in-c Wenvoe and St Lythans 02–09; R Barry All SS 09–14; Can Llan Cathl 02–14; rtd 14. *70 Meek Road, Newent GL18 1DX* T: (01531) 820981

BERRY, Anthony Nigel. b 53. Lon Bible Coll BA 80. Sarum & Wells Th Coll 84. **d** 87 **p** 88. NSM Howell Hill *Guildf* 87–90; C 90; C Farnham 90–93; R Abinger cum Coldharbour 93–14; R Abinger and Coldharbour and Wotton and Holmbury St Mary from 15; Tr Officer for Past Assts from 94. *The Rectory, Abinger Lane, Abinger Common, Dorking RH5 6HZ* T: (01306) 730746 E: revanberry@aol.com

BERRY, David Llewellyn Edward. b 39. St Jo Coll Cam BA 61 MA 65. Wells Th Coll 64. **d** 66 **p** 67. C Poplar All SS w St Frideswide *Lon* 66–69; C Ellesmere Port *Ches* 69–73; V Brafferton w Pilmoor and Myton-on-Swale *York* 73–79; P-in-c Thormanby 78–79; R Skelton w Upleatham 79–87; Chapl Barrow St Aid *Carl* 87–97; Rotterdam *Eur* 97–99; rtd 99; PtO *Carl* from 04. *22 Pele Court, Friargate, Penrith CA11 7XT* T: (01768) 867150 E: dandjberry3944@btinternet.com

BERRY, David Nicholas. b 77. York Univ BA 00 St Jo Coll Dur BA 10. Cranmer Hall Dur 08. **d** 10 **p** 11. C Mansfield St Jo w St Mary *S'well* 10–14; V Bentley *Sheff* from 14; AD Adwick from 21. *Bentley Vicarage, 3A High Street, Bentley, Doncaster DN5 0AA* T: (01302) 876272 M: 07733-127698 E: dave.b@stpetersbentley.org

BERRY, Mrs Diane Jayne. b 62. York Sch of Min 14. **d** 19. NSM S Holderness Coast *York* from 19. *Berry House, 96A Queen Street, Withernsea HU19 2HB* T: (01964) 613212 M: 07709-000556 E: dianejayneberry@hotmail.com

BERRY, Prof Frank John. b 47. Lon Univ BSc 72 PhD 75 DSc 88 FRSC 84. Qu Coll Birm 96. **d** 99 **p** 00. Prof Inorganic Chemistry Open Univ from 91; Hon Prof Chemistry Birm Univ from 07; NSM Rednal 99–04; NSM Birm St Martin w Bordesley St Andr 04–07; NSM Moseley St Mary and St Anne 07–17; PtO from 17. *44 Middle Park Road, Selly Oak, Birmingham B29 4BJ* T: 0121-475 2718 E: frank_berry44@hotmail.com

BERRY, Miss Heather Evelyn. b 45. Lon Univ BA 67 Ex Univ PGCE 68. **d** 00 **p** 01. OLM Gaywood *Nor* 00–14; C Gt w Lt Massingham, Harpley, Rougham etc 14–15; R Rougham, Weasenham and Wellingham 15–16; rtd 16; PtO *Nor* from

16. *12 Kent Road, King's Lynn PE30 4AF*   T: (01553) 764098
E: heberry@talktalk.net
BERRY, Canon Ian Thomas Henry. b 73. QUB BSc 94.
CITC BTh 98. **d** 98 **p** 99. C Bangor Abbey *D & D* 98–02;
I Monaghan w Tydavnet and Kilmore *Clogh* from 02; Preb
Clogh Cathl from 11; Chan from 19. *The Rectory, Clones
Road, Monaghan, Republic of Ireland*   T: (00353) (47) 81136
E: monaghan@clogher.anglican.org
BERRY, John. b 41. Dur Univ BA 62. Oak Hill Th Coll 63. **d** 65
p 66. C Burnage St Marg *Man* 65–68; C Middleton 68–70;
Travelling Sec IVF 70–73; V Derby St Pet 73–76; P-in-c Derby
St Pet and Ch Ch w H Trin 73–76; V 76–81; Bp's Officer
for Evang *Carl* 81–86; P-in-c Bampton w Mardale 81–86;
Evang Sec N Wingfield, Pilsley and Tupton *Derby* 86–89;
Evang Alliance 89–92; V Guernsey H Trin *Win* 92–98;
TR Broadwater *Chich* 98–07; rtd 07; PtO *Ox* from 08. *27
Blythe Close, Newport Pagnell MK16 9DN*   T: (01908) 217631
E: reverendjohn@sky.com
BERRY, Paul Edward. b 56. NOC 91. **d** 94 **p** 95. C Halliwell
St Luke *Man* 94–98; TV Horwich and Rivington 98–08;
TV Edgware *Lon* 08–16; TR 16–18; AD W Barnet 16–18;
Chapl Trin Hospice in the Fylde from 18. *Trinity Hospice,
Low Moor Road, Blackpool FY2 0BG*   T: (01253) 358881
E: paul.berry@trinityhospice.co.uk
BERRY, Mrs Philippa Raines. b 51. Man Univ BA 72 Univ
of Wales (Cardiff) CertEd 73. St Jo Coll Nottm 82. **d** 95
p 96. NSM Leic H Apostles 95–04; P-in-c 04–17; rtd
17; PtO *Leic* from 17. *37 The Glade, Leicester LE3 2WB*
E: pipberry@hotmail.com
BERRY, Simon David. b 86. G&C Coll Cam BA 09 MPhil 10.
Wycliffe Hall Ox 13. **d** 17 **p** 18. C Pet St Mark 17–21;
P-in-c Becontree St Geo *Chelmsf* from 21. *St George's Church,
86 Rogers Road, Dagenham RM10 8JX*
BERRY, Sister Susan Patricia (Sister Sue). b 49. Bris Univ
BA 70 Hughes Hall Cam PGCE 72. Qu Coll Birm 77. **dss** 86
d 87 **p** 94. Chapl Barn Fellowship Whatcombe Ho 86–89;
Chapl Lee Abbey 89–91; NSM Thatcham *Ox* 93–95; CSF from
95; PtO *B & W* 96–97 and 98–10; Chapl Guy's and St Thos'
Hosps NHS Trust Lon 97–98; PtO *S'wark* 97–98 and from
10; Hon Min Can S'wark Cathl from 12. *St Alphege Clergy
House, Pocock Street, London SE1 0BJ*   T: (020) 7928 8910
E: suecsf@franciscans.org.uk
BERRY-DAVIES, Charles William Keith. b 48. MIOT 71.
Linc Th Coll. **d** 83 **p** 84. C Hythe *Cant* 83–86; Chapl
RAF 86–09; rtd 09; PtO *B & W* from 09. *11 Stafford
Place, Weston-super-Mare BS23 2QZ*   T: (01934) 621344
E: keith.vicarage@btinternet.com
BERSWEDEN, Judith Anne. b 63. St Jo Coll Dur BA 84.
Ripon Coll Cuddesdon BA 91. **d** 92 **p** 94. Par Dn
Mirfield *Wakef* 92–94; NSM Robert Town 94–97; NSM
Roberttown w Hartshead 97–00; NSM Alderbury
Deanery *Sarum* 00–18; Chapl Bp Wordsworth's Sch
Salisbury 01–18; NSM Merton St Mary *S'wark* from 18.
3 Arthur Road, London SW19 7DL   T: (020) 3665 8746
E: judithbersweden@stmarysmerton.org.uk
BERSWEDEN, Nils Herry Stephen. b 57. Newc Univ BSc 78.
Ripon Coll Cuddesdon 88. **d** 90 **p** 91. C Mirfield *Wakef*
90–93; P-in-c Purlwell 93–94; P-in-c Robert Town 94–97; V
Roberttown w Hartshead 97–00; P-in-c Winterslow *Sarum*
00–01; TV Clarendon 01–08; TR 08–18; Hon C Wimbledon
S'wark from 18. *3 Arthur Road, London SW19 7DL*   T: (020)
3665 8746
BERWICK, Suffragan Bishop of. *See* WROE, The Rt Revd Mark
BESSANT, Christopher Dixon. b 69. Nottm Univ MA 14.
Ridley Hall Cam 07. **d** 09 **p** 10. C Gt Bookham *Guildf*
09–13; V Chobham w Valley End 13–19; R Haslemere and
Grayswood from 19; Tutor Local Min Progr from 14. *24
Pine View Close, Haslemere GU27 1DU*   M: 07800-719405
E: rector@haslemereparish.org
BESSANT, Canon Idwal Brian. b 39. Cardiff Coll of Art
ATD 62. St Mich Coll Llan 65. **d** 68 **p** 69. C Llantwit Major
and St Donat's *Llan* 68–73; R Llangammarch w Garth,
Llanlleonfel etc *S & B* 73–77; V Crickhowell 77–78; CMS
Miss 78–83; Cyprus 80–83; V Crickhowell w Cwmdu and
Tretower *S & B* 83–91; RD Crickhowell 86–91; V Llanwrtyd
w Llanddulas in Tir Abad etc 91–04; Can Res Brecon Cathl
98–04; RD Builth 02–04; rtd 04. *10 Bronant, Bronllys Road,
Talgarth, Brecon LD3 0HF*   T: (01874) 712380
BESSANT, Canon Simon David. b 56. Sheff Univ BMus 77
MA 00. St Jo Coll Nottm. **d** 81 **p** 82. C Litherland St Jo and
St Jas *Liv* 81–84; C Holloway Em w Hornsey Road St Barn *Lon*
84–86; C Holloway St Mark w Em 86–91; V Blackb Redeemer
91–98; Acting RD Blackb 97–98; Dir Miss and Evang 98–07;
Dir CME 02–07; Hon Can Blackb Cathl 06–07; V Ecclesall
Sheff 07–12; V Mortomley St Sav High Green 12–19;
P-in-c Grenoside 14–19; Miss Development Officer *Man* 19;

Hd of Discipleship and Evang from 20; PtO *Ches* from 19.
68 Kennedy Avenue, Macclesfield SK10 3DE   M: 07959-211319
E: simon.bessant@gmail.com
BESSANT, Stephen Michael. b 53. St Seiriol Cen 13. **d** 14
p 15. NSM Llanstadwel *St D* 14–16; NSM Burton and
Rosemarket 14–16; NSM Llanstadwel and Burton and
Rosemarket 16–19; NSM Roose from 19. *28 Greenhall
Park, Johnston, Haverfordwest SA62 3PT*   T: (01437) 890701
E: smbessant@btinternet.com
BESSENT, Preb Stephen Lyn. b 53. Bris Univ BA 75. Wycliffe
Hall Ox 75. **d** 77 **p** 78. C Patchway *Bris* 77–80; TV Swindon
St Jo and St Andr 80–83; TV Eston w Normanby *York* 83–90;
V Cogges *Ox* 90–94; P-in-c S Leigh 90–94; V Cogges and S
Leigh 94–01; P-in-c Alphington, Shillingford St George and
Ide *Ex* 01–12; R H Christianity 06–12; Preb Ex Cathl
09–17; rtd 17; PtO *Ox* from 17. *25 Lancaster Place, Carterton
OX18 3ET* E: stephenbessent@btinternet.com
BEST, Gary John. b 62. SEITE 13. **d** 16 **p** 17. C Bexley
Roch 16–19; V Shortlands from 19. *St Mary's Church,
Kingswood Road, Bromley BR2 0HG*   M: 07493-072695
E: revgarybest@gmail.com
BEST, Canon Raymond. b 42. Sarum & Wells Th Coll 71.
d 74 **p** 75. C Whorlton *Newc* 74–78; C Seaton Hirst 78–83;
C Benwell St Jas 83–85; TV Benwell 85–89; V Walker
89–00; P-in-c Byker St Martin 96–99; V Haltwhistle and
Greenhead 00–10; Hon Can Newc Cathl 97–10; AD Hexham
02–06; rtd 10; PtO *Newc* from 10. *The Annexe, 3 Admiral
Close, Swarland, Morpeth NE65 9GZ*   T: (01670) 783434
E: canonbest@aol.com
BESTELINK, Canon William Meindert Croft. b 48. Hull
Univ BA 70 FRSA 78. Cuddesdon Coll 71. **d** 73 **p** 74. C Holt
Nor 73–74; C E Dereham w Hoe 74–76; C Thorpe St Andr
76–80; R Colby w Banningham and Tuttington 80–90;
R Felmingham 80–90; R Suffield 80–90; P-in-c Roydon
St Remigius 90–04; P-in-c Scole, Brockdish, Billingford,
Thorpe Abbots etc 02–04; P-in-c Gillingham w Geldeston,
Stockton, Ellingham etc 04–09; RD Redenhall 00–03; Dioc
Rural Officer 99–09; Hon Can Nor Cathl 02–09; rtd 09; PtO
Nor from 09. *4 Francis Close, Cromer NR27 0HR*   T: (01263)
514045 M: 07909-690073
BESTER, Michael Adam Milton. b 70. Cape Town Univ
BAS 91 BArch 94 Nottm Univ MA 19. **d** 13 **p** 18. Athlone
St Geo S Africa 13–15; C St Geo Cathl Cape Town 15–16;
C Observatory St Mich 17; C Devils Peak Ascension 18–20;
PtO *Ox* from 20. *St Stephen's House, 16 Marston Street, Oxford
OX4 1JX*   M: 07768-410590 E: michael.bester@ssho.ox.ac.uk
BESTLEY, Peter Mark. b 60. Qu Coll Cam MA Univ of Wales
(Cardiff) MPhil 92. St Mich Coll Llan 89. **d** 92 **p** 93. C
Hampton All SS *Lon* 92–95; Chapl W Middx Univ Hosp NHS
Trust 95–99; Hon C Bracknell *Ox* 04–06; C Easthampstead
06–17; rtd 17; PtO *Ox* from 17. *40 Parkway, Crowthorne
RG45 6EW*   M: 07792-928624 E: peter.bestley@gmail.com
BESWETHERICK, Andrew Michael. b 55. Ex Univ BEd 80.
S'wark Ord Course 87. **d** 90 **p** 91. Dep Hd Maze Hill Sch
Greenwich 88–98; NSM Blackheath St Jo *S'wark* from
90; Hd Sixth Form Rosemary Sch Islington from 98.
112 Charlton Road, London SE7 7EY   T: (020) 8853 0853
E: andrewbmh@gmail.com
BESWICK, Canon Gary Lancelot. b 38. ALCD 63. **d** 63 **p** 64.
C Walthamstow St Mary *Chelmsf* 63–67; C Laisterdyke *Bradf*
67–70; V Idle 70–78; Area Sec (NW England) SAMS 78–92;
Area Sec (N Thames) 92–97; Hon Can N Argentina from 87;
R Gt Smeaton w Appleton Wiske and Birkby etc *Ripon* 97–03;
rtd 03. *14 Bolton Way, Boston Spa, Wetherby LS23 6PT*
BESWICK, Jane. *See* VOST, Jane
BESWICK, Jonathan Warwick. b 67. Jes Coll Cam BA 95.
Westcott Ho Cam 91. **d** 95 **p** 96. C Dudley St Fran *Worc*
95–96; C Brookfield St Mary and Brookfield St Anne,
Highgate Rise *Lon* 96–99; C St John's Wood 99–02; R
Catsfield and Crowhurst *Chich* 02–08; P-in-c Ox St Barn and
St Paul 08–15; P-in-c Ox St Thos 11–15; V Ox St Barn and
St Paul w St Thos 15–18; R Lon Docks St Pet w Wapping
St Jo from 18. *St Peter's Clergy House, Wapping Lane, London
E1W 2RW*   T: (020) 7481 2985
BESWICK PALLISTER, John Jorge. b 81. Coimbra Univ
(Portugal) BA 05. Ridley Hall Cam 16. **d** 18 **p** 19. C Betley
Lich from 18; C Madeley from 18. *St John's Vicarage, High
Street, Alsagers Bank, Stoke-on-Trent ST7 8BQ*   M: 07923-
135787 E: longobedience@gmail.com
BETSON, Christopher James. b 81. Writtle Agric Coll
BSc 03 St Jo Coll Dur BA 09. Cranmer Hall Dur 06. **d** 09
p 10. C Anston *Sheff* 09–12; V Tickhill w Stainton 12–17;
NSM Kidderminster St Jo and H Innocents *Worc* from 20.
The Vicarage, 9 Sutton Park Road, Kidderminster DY11 6LB
E: chrisbetson@outlook.com

BETSON (née BIDDINGTON), Mrs Laura Claire. b 84. Trin Coll Cam BA 05 St Jo Coll Dur MA 08. Cranmer Hall Dur 06. **d** 08 **p** 09. C Aston cum Aughton w Swallownest and Ulley *Sheff* 08–12; PtO 12–17; TV Kidderminster St Jo and H Innocents *Worc* from 17. *The Vicarage, 9 Sutton Park Road, Kidderminster DY11 6LB* T: (01562) 228712 M: 07984-960749 E: laura.betson@yahoo.co.uk

BETSON, Mark John. b 77. Univ Coll Lon BSc 99 Birkbeck Coll Lon PhD Cam Univ BA 06. Westcott Ho Cam 04. **d** 07 **p** 08. C Southwick *Chich* 07–10; P-in-c Lower Beeding 10–15; V 15–19; Nat Rural Officer Miss and Public Affairs from 19; PtO *Pet* from 19. *Church House, 27 Great Smith Street, London SW1P 3AZ* T: (020) 7898 1000 M: 07801-273074 E: m.betson@hotmail.co.uk

BETSON, Stephen. b 53. Sarum & Wells Th Coll 89. **d** 91 **p** 92. C Sittingbourne St Mich *Cant* 91–95; V Fairweather Green *Bradf* 95–01; R Hockwold w Wilton *Ely* 01–06; R Weeting 01–06; P-in-c Stanground 06–12; P-in-c St Mary Cray and St Paul's Cray *Roch* 12–14; rtd 14; PtO *Chich* from 15. *1 Purbeck Close, Eastbourne BN23 8EX* E: stephenbetson@hotmail.co.uk

BETTELEY, John Richard. b 46. Sarum & Wells Th Coll 81. **d** 83 **p** 84. C Auchterarder *St And* 83–85; C Dunblane 83–85; Chapl RAF 85–89; R Callander *St And* 89–94; P-in-c Aberfoyle 89–94; P-in-c Doune 89–94; R Ballachulish *Arg* 94–04; R Glencoe 94–04; R Onich 94–04; Dioc Youth Officer 94–01; Syn Clerk 99–04; Can St Jo Cathl Oban 99–04; Can Cumbrae 99–04; R Aboyne *Ab* 04–06; R Ballater 04–06; R Braemar 04–06; PtO *Mor* from 12. *Camusfearna, 3 School Street, Fearn, Tain IV20 1SX* T: (01862) 832774 M: 07713-914602 E: camus3jrb@gmail.com

BETTERIDGE, The Ven Kelly Anne. b 69. Roehampton Inst BA 92. Qu Coll Birm MA 10. **d** 10 **p** 11. C Nuneaton St Nic *Cov* 10–14; V 14–21; P-in-c Weddington and Caldecote 14–21; Adn Bodmin *Truro* from 21. *4 Park Drive, Bodmin PL31 2QF* E: revkells@gmail.com *or* kelly.betteridge@truro.anglican.org

BETTERIDGE, Simon Frank. b 66. St Jo Coll Nottm. **d** 00 **p** 01. C Studley *Cov* 00–02; C Leamington Priors St Paul 02–04; Chapl Univ Hosps Cov and Warks NHS Trust from 04. *61 Ambleside Way, Nuneaton CV11 6AU* M: 07743-870601 E: simon.betty@yahoo.com *or* simon.betteridge@uhcw.nhs.uk

BETTINSON, Philip Keith. b 79. Univ of Wales (Abth) BEng 01. St Mich Coll Llan BTh 11. **d** 11 **p** 12. C Cilcain, Gwernaffield, Llanferres etc *St As* 11–14; C Wrexham 14–17; TV Offa Miss Area from 17. *The Vicarage, Wrexham Road, Johnstown, Wrexham LL14 1PE* T: (01978) 846204 E: rev@jara23.co.uk

BETTIS, Canon Margaret Jean. b 42. Gilmore Ho 72. **dss** 77 **d** 87 **p** 94. Kenya 77–79; Tutor Crowther Hall CMS Tr Coll Selly Oak 79–82; Hodge Hill *Birm* 82–87; Par Dn 87; Par Dn Flitwick *St Alb* 87–93; P-in-c Westoning w Tingrith 93–94; V 94–04; Hon Can St Alb 97–04; rtd 04; PtO *St Alb* 04–05; *Glouc* 05–06; Hon C Cirencester from 06. *58 Aldsworth Close, Fairford GL7 4LB* T: (01285) 238992 E: canmjb42@talktalk.net

BETTRIDGE, Canon Graham Winston. b 39. Kelham Th Coll 60. **d** 65 **p** 66. C Burley in Wharfedale *Bradf* 65–67; C Baildon 67–70; V Harden and Wilsden 70–81; TR Kirkby Lonsdale *Carl* 81–06; Hon Can Carl Cathl 89–06; rtd 06; Chapl Cumbria Constabulary *Carl* 96–09; PtO *Bradf* 06–14; *Leeds* from 14; *Carl* 09–20; *Blackb* 14–20. *Moorgate Cottage, Maypole Green, Long Preston, Skipton BD23 4PJ* T: (01729) 841113 E: canongraham@mintegrity.co.uk

BETTS, Alan John. b 55. Portsm Poly BSc 77 St Martin's Coll Lanc PGCE 81. St Jo Coll Nottm 93. **d** 93 **p** 94. C Cannock *Lich* 93–01; P-in-c Endon w Stanley 01–04; V Bagnall w Endon 04–20; P-in-c Brown Edge from 15; rtd 20. *Address temp unknown*

BETTS, David John. b 38. Lon Univ BSc 61. Oak Hill Th Coll 63. **d** 65 **p** 66. C Slough *Ox* 65–70; C Welling *Roch* 70–75; V Swanley St Paul 75–93; R Nottingham St Nic *S'well* 93–98; TV Canford Magna *Sarum* 98–04; rtd 04; PtO *Sarum* 05–19. *290 Rempstone Road, Wimborne BH21 1SZ* T: (01202) 840537

BETTS, Edmund John. b 51. St Chad's Coll Dur BA 72 Lanc Univ MA 81 Ches Univ DProf 15. Qu Coll Birm 73. **d** 76 **p** 77. C Leagrave *St Alb* 76–79; Asst Chapl R Albert Hosp Lanc 79–81; Chapl Lea Castle Hosp Kidderminster 81–86; Chapl Kidderminster Gen Hosp 81–86; Prov Officer Educn for Min Ch in Wales 86–88; Exec Sec for Min 88–90; TR Haverhill w Withersfield, the Wrattings etc *St E* 90–97; V Haverhill w Withersfield 97–06; RD Clare 91–06; Hon Can St E Cathl 02–06; CUF Link Officer 02–06; V Altrincham St Geo *Ches* 06–16; P-in-c Altrincham St Jo 07–16; V Altrincham 17–21; rtd 21. *8 Woodyatt Way, Lymm WA13 9DF* T: (01925) 982886 E: edmund.betts1@btinternet.com

BETTS, Ivan Ringland. b 38. TCD BA 61 MA 67. **d** 62 **p** 63. C Ballyholme *D & D* 62–65; C Dundela St Mark 65–69; Miss to Seamen 69–73; Sudan 69–71; Trinidad and Tobago 71–73; C Drumglass *Arm* 73–81; I Augher w Newtownsaville and Eskrahoole *Clogh* 81–86; Bp's C Ballymacarrett St Martin *D & D* 86–02; rtd 02. *56 Norwood Drive, Belfast BT4 2EB* T: (028) 9065 0723 E: ivanbetts@btinternet.com

BETTS, Jordon Alexander Mark. b 91. Sheff Univ BA 14 Ox Univ BA 20. Wycliffe Hall Ox 18. **d** 21. C Wadsley *Sheff* from 21. *15 Northwood, Sheffield S6 1RX* E: jordanbetts34@gmail.com

BETTS, Mrs Patricia Joyce. b 43. St Kath Coll Lon CertEd 64 FRSA 96. S Dios Minl Tr Scheme 90. **d** 96 **p** 97. NSM Bath Widcombe *B & W* 96–00; P-in-c 00–05; PtO from 05. *Hunter's Lodge, North Road, Bath BA2 6HP* T: (01225) 464918 M: 07545-350565 E: candpbetts@talktalk.net

BETTS, The Ven Steven James. b 64. York Univ BSc 86. Ripon Coll Cuddesdon 87. **d** 90 **p** 91. C Bearsted w Thurnham *Cant* 90–94; Bp's Chapl *Nor* 94–97; V Old Catton 97–05; RD Nor N 01–05; Bp's Officer for Ord and Initial Tr 05–12; Adn Norfolk from 12; Hon Can Nor Cathl from 08. *8 Boulton Road, Thorpe St Andrew, Norwich NR7 0DF* T: (01603) 559199 E: archdeacon.norfolk@dioceseofnorwich.org

BETTS, Stewart David. b 75. St Jo Coll Nottm BA 14. Ripon Coll Cuddesdon 16. **d** 18 **p** 19. C Ashby-de-la-Zouch and Breedon on the Hill *Leic* 18–21; C Cosby and Whetstone from 21. *5 Ulleswater Crescent, Ashby-de-la-Zouch LE65 1FH* M: 07919-890094 E: stewb_1@hotmail.com

BEURKLIAN-CARTER, Mrs Santou. b 70. McMaster Univ Ontario BA 92 Toronto Univ MDiv 02. St Mellitus Coll 10. **d** 12 **p** 13. C Gt Ilford St Jo *Chelmsf* 12–14; C Woodford St Mary w St Phil and St Jas 14–17; Chapl Guy's and St Thos' NHS Foundn Trust from 18; Chapl Forest Healthcare NHS Trust Lon from 18. *116 Blythswood Road, Ilford IG3 8SG* T: (020) 8599 0399 M: 07939-876045 E: sbcarter@btinternet.com

BEVAN, Andrew Paul. b 68. ERMC 16. **d** 19 **p** 20. OLM Stalham, E Ruston, Brunstead, Sutton and Ingham *Nor* from 19; OLM Smallburgh w Dilham w Honing and Crostwight from 19. *The Saplings, New Road, Catfield, Great Yarmouth NR29 5BQ* T: (01692) 582358 E: apbevan@btinternet.com

BEVAN, Christopher Jeremy. Lon Inst BA 89 Lon Guildhall Univ MA 97 Cardiff Univ BA 11. **d** 11 **p** 12. C Llanelli *S & B* 11–15; P-in-c from 16. *Llanelly Rectory, Abergavenny Road, Gilwern, Abergavenny NP7 0AD* T: (01873) 830280 E: christopher.bevan@btinternet.com

BEVAN, David Graham. b 34. Univ of Wales (Lamp) BA 54 LTh 56. Gen Th Sem (NY) MDiv 57. **d** 57 **p** 58. C Llanelli *St D* 57–60; CF 60–76; rtd 99. *148 Bromley Heath Road, Bristol BS16 6JJ* T: 0117-956 0946

BEVAN, Esther Rose. b 73. Dur Univ BA 21. St Mellitus Coll 18. **d** 21. NSM Dartford St Edm *Roch* from 21; NSM Dartford St Alb from 21. *126 Shepherd Street, Northfleet, Gravesend DA11 9PR* M: 07748-168191 E: estherrose3@gmail.com

BEVAN, Janet Mary. See MOORE, Janet Mary

BEVAN, Judith Anne. See EGAR, Judith Anne

BEVAN, Paul John. b 49. Bris Sch of Min 84. **d** 87. NSM Bishopsworth *Bris* 87–96. *10 Brookdale Road, Headley Park, Bristol BS13 7PZ* T: 0117-964 6330

BEVAN, Peter John. b 54. K Coll Lon BA 76 AKC 76. St Steph Ho Ox BA 79 MA 86. **d** 80 **p** 81. C Brighouse *Wakef* 80–83; C Chapelthorpe 83–86; V Scholes 86–95; V Potters Bar *St Alb* 95–15; V Gt and Lt Torrington and Frithelstock *Ex* 15–21; rtd 21. *3 Nibble-n-Clinck, Hidcote Road, Ebrington, Chipping Campden GL55 6LH* E: peter.bevan900@gmail.com

BEVAN, Philip Frank. b 41. Brasted Th Coll 63 Chich Th Coll 65. **d** 67 **p** 68. C Walton St Mary *Liv* 67–71; P-in-c Long Is SS Pet and Paul Bahamas 71–73; R Nassau St Matt 73–78; PtO *S'wark* 00–17; Ox 16–20; *Lon* 17–21. *32 Collingwood House, 103 New Cavendish Street, London W1W 6XH* T: (020) 7436 8010 M: 07970-961539 E: fr.philip@btinternet.com

BEVAN, Mrs Rebecca Anne. b 64. Reading Univ BA 86. Ox Min Course 04. **d** 07 **p** 08. NSM Thatcham *Ox* 07–10; R Aldermaston and Woolhampton 10–17; V Newbury St Geo and St Jo from 17. *The Vicarage, 206 Andover Road, Newbury RG14 6NU* E: bbevan.awb@gmail.com

BEVAN, Rodney. b 57. Leeds Univ BA 80 Keele Univ PGCE 81 Open Univ MA 99. Cranmer Hall Dur 97. **d** 99 **p** 00. C Ogley Hay *Lich* 99–03; TV Rossendale Middle Valley *Man* 03–04; TR 04–17; V Edgeside from 17; AD Rossendale 18–21. *St Anne's Vicarage, Ashworth Road, Rossendale BB4 9JE* T: (01706) 221889 M: 07837-608637 E: revrodbev@hotmail.com

BEVER, Canon Michael Charles Stephen. b 44. Selw Coll Cam BA 66 MA 70. Cuddesdon Coll 67. **d** 69 **p** 70. C Steeton *Bradf* 69–72; C Northampton St Mary *Pet* 72–74; Niger 75–79; P-in-c Elmstead *Chelmsf* 80–83; V 83–85; V

Bocking St Pet 85–96; P-in-c Odiham *Win* 96–07; rtd 07; Hon Can Awka from 93; PtO *Portsm* from 08; *Win* 07–14. *68A Drift Road, Waterlooville PO8 0NX* T/F: (023) 9259 6895 E: mcsb@ozala.plus.com

BEVERIDGE, Mrs Freda Joy. b 38. Qu Mary Coll Lon BA 59 Lon Inst of Educn PGCE 60. Ripon Coll Cuddesdon 83. **dss** 85 **d** 87 **p** 94. Ox St Giles and SS Phil and Jas w St Marg 85–88; Par Dn 87–88; Par Dn Woughton 88–94; C 94–95; TR 95–97; C Woodham *Guildf* 97–00; rtd 00; PtO *Sarum* from 01. *Moonraker Cottage, 27 New Road, Chiseldon, Swindon SN4 0LX* T: (01793) 741064 E: freda.27@btinternet.com

BEVERLEY, Anne Ruth. b 76. Cen Lancs Univ BA 97 Cumbria Univ BA 14. LCTP 11. **d** 14 **p** 15. NSM S Shore H Trin *Blackb* 14–18; NSM S Shore St Pet 14–18; V Wesham from 18. *Christ Church Parish Office, Garstang Road North, Wesham, Preston PR4 3DE* M: 07841-742022 E: anne.beverley@btinternet.com

BEVERLEY, David John. b 46. Univ of Wales (Lamp) BA 68. Linc Th Coll 71. **d** 73 **p** 74. C Cov E 73–76; C Immingham *Linc* 76–84; V Bracebridge Heath 84–86; Ind Chapl 86–97; P-in-c Scunthorpe Resurr 97–01; V 01–02; R Trentside E 02–11; rtd 11; PtO *Linc* 17–20. *73 Peveril Avenue, Scunthorpe DN17 1BG* T: (01724) 279914

BEVERLEY, Sister. See DAVIES, Beverley

BEVERLEY, Suffragan Bishop of (Provincial Episcopal Visitor). See WEBSTER, The Rt Revd Glyn Hamilton

BEVERLY, George Charles. b 89. SS Hild & Bede Coll Dur BA 11 Dur Univ BA 21. St Mellitus Coll 18. **d** 21. Chapl K Sch Bruton from 17; NSM Yeovil w Kingston Pitney *B & W* from 21. *4 Brue Close, Bruton BA10 0HY* M: 07731-392153 E: georgecbeverly@gmail.com

BEVERLY, Sue. b 53. Cardiff Univ BTh 08. St Mich Coll Llan 05. **d** 07 **p** 08. NSM Coity, Nolton and Brackla *Llan* 07–12; Asst Dir of Min 10; AD Bridgend 11–12; R Broseley w Benthall, Jackfield, Linley etc *Heref* 12–16; NSM Malvern Link w Cowleigh *Worc* 16–19; V Otumoetai NZ from 19. *St John's Anglican Church, 94 Bureta Road, Otumoetai, Tauranga 3110, New Zealand* T: (0064) (7) 576 9923 E: sue.beverly@waiapu.com

BEVINGTON, David John. b 51. Ch Coll Cam BA 72 MA 76. Trin Coll Bris 73. **d** 76 **p** 77. C Tulse Hill H Trin *S'wark* 76–79; C Galleywood Common *Chelmsf* 79–82; TV Hanley H Ev *Lich* 82–90; TV Hemel Hempstead *St Alb* 90–99; V Calbourne w Newtown *Portsm* 99–16; V Shalfleet 99–16; rtd 16; PtO *Ox* from 17. *35 Gainsborough Green, Abingdon OX14 5JH* T: (01235) 521133 E: dbevington@lineone.net

BEWES, Anthony Charles Neill. b 71. Birm Univ BA 93. Wycliffe Hall Ox 96. **d** 99 **p** 00. C Sevenoaks St Nic *Roch* 99–05; Team Ldr Titus Trust from 05. *45 Lonsdale Road, Oxford OX2 7ES* T: (01865) 553625 E: anthony@bewes.com

BEWES, Helen Catherine. See SCAMMAN, Helen Catherine

BEWICK, Lisa Marie. b 83. Ex Univ BA 05 Surrey Univ PGCE 06. Sarum Coll MA 18. **d** 18 **p** 19. NSM Waterloo St Jo w St Andr *S'wark* from 18. *21 Windmill House, Windmill Walk, London SE1 8LX* E: lisa@stjohnswaterloo.org

BEWLEY, Canon Robin John. b 63. St Jo Coll Ox BA 86 MA 95 Fitzw Coll Cam BA 99 MA 05 PhD 05. Ridley Hall Cam. **d** 00 **p** 01. NSM Histon and Impington *Ely* 00–04; C Harborne Heath *Birm* 04–11; V Kettering Ch the King *Pet* from 11; Can Pet Cathl from 21. *The Vicarage, Deeble Road, Kettering NN15 7AA* T: (01536) 512828 M: 07307-897891 E: rob@thebewleys.co.uk or vicar@ctk.org.uk

BEXON, Valerie Joan. See THORNE, Valerie Joan

BEYNON, Lois Claire. b 92. Dur Univ BA 21. Cranmer Hall Dur 18. **d** 21. C Broseley w Benthall, Jackfield, Linley etc *Heref* from 21. *3 Blakeaway Close, Broseley TF12 5SS* T: (01852) 882728 E: revd.loisbeynon@gmail.com

BEYNON, Malcolm. b 36. Univ of Wales (Lamp) BA 56 Univ of Wales (Cardiff) PGCE 71. St Mich Coll Llan 56. **d** 59 **p** 60. C Aberavon *Llan* 59–62; C Whitchurch 63–68; V Llanwynno 68–73; Chapl Old Hall Sch Wellington Shropshire 74–75; Chapl Nevill Holt Sch Market Harborough 77–82; Chapl Denstone Coll Prep Sch Uttoxeter 82–93; V Dale and St Brides w Marloes *St D* 93–01; rtd 01. *22 Ostrey Bank, St Clears, Carmarthen SA33 4AH* T: (01994) 231872

BEYNON, Melissa Jane. b 67. Brunel Univ BSc 85. Qu Foundn Birm 19. **d** 21. C Halas *Worc* from 21. *89 Stourbridge Road, Halesowen B63 3UA* M: 07891-779871 E: melissa04@live.co.uk

BEYNON, Paul John. b 66. SWMTC 09. **d** 12 **p** 13. C Boscastle w Davidstow *Truro* 12–15; C Boscastle and Tintagel Gp 15–16; P-in-c Lostwithiel Parishes from 16. *The Rectory, 3 Springfield Close, Lostwithiel PL22 0RW* T: (01208) 623577 M: 07730-037113 E: p-beynon@sky.com

BEYNON, Canon Vincent Wyn. b 54. Anglia Poly Univ MA 04 Hockerill Coll Cam CertEd 76 Lambeth STh 97. St Mich Coll

Llan 78. **d** 81 **p** 82. C Llantrisant *Llan* 81–83; C Caerphilly 84–85; R Gelligaer 85–88; TV Gtr Corsham *Bris* 88–97; R Potton w Sutton and Cockayne Hatley *St Alb* 97–08; RD Biggleswade 01–06; P-in-c Stoke Prior, Wychbold and Upton Warren *Worc* 12–20; C Bowbrook N 14–20; C Bowbrook S 14–20; V Wychebrook 20–21; RD Droitwich 18–21; Hon Can Worc Cathl 19–21; rtd 21; P-in-c Churchill-in-Halfshire w Blakedown and Broome *Worc* from 21; Hon C Belbroughton w Fairfield and Clent from 21. *89 Stourbridge Road, Halesowen B63 3UA* M: 07595-313035 E: wynbeynon@gmail.com

BEZERRA SPEEKS, Mark William. b 62. Ex Univ BA 82 Ex Coll Ox MSt 83 Yale Univ MDiv 02 Worc Coll Ox MPhil 20. **d** 02 **p** 02. C Los Angeles St Alban USA 02–03; NSM Kilburn St Mary w All So and W Hampstead St Jas *Lon* 04–08; NSM St Botolph Aldgate w H Trin Minories 08–10; CF from 10; NSM Belsize Park *Lon* 10–16; NSM S Hampstead St Sav 10–16; Hon Chapl Ch Ch *Ox* from 17. *c/o MOD Chaplains (Army)* T: (01264) 383430 F: 381824 M: 07800-742786 E: mspeeks@hotmail.com

BHATTI, Javed. b 51. **d** 71 **p** 08. Pakistan 71–00; PtO *Leic* 16–21. *59 Ravenhouse Road, Dewsbury WF13 3QW* T: (01924) 467466 M: 07966-885643 E: javedbhatti_4540@yahoo.co.uk

BHUTTA, Mrs Patricia Frances Mary. b 52. Kent Univ BA 74. Ox Min Course 08. **d** 10 **p** 11. NSM Cumnor *Ox* 10–13; NSM Aldermaston and Woolhampton 13–19; rtd 19; PtO *Ox* from 19. *2 The Garth, Oxford OX2 9AL* M: 07968-089566 E: pat@patbhutta.co.uk or pbhutta.awb@gmail.com

BIANCHI, Matthew Robert. b 87. Dur Univ BA 19. Wycliffe Hall Ox 16. **d** 19 **p** 20. C Hartley Wintney, Elvetham, Winchfield etc *Win* from 19. *40 Pool Road, Hartley Wintney, Hook RG27 8RD* T: (01252) 492129 E: thebianchis@ymail.com

BIANCHI, Robert Frederick. b 56. St Jo Coll Dur BA 77. Cranmer Hall Dur 78. **d** 80 **p** 81. C Chester le Street *Dur* 80–83; C W Pelton 83–86; P-in-c 86–95; PtO from 95. *8 Lindisfarne, Washington NE38 7JR* T: 0191-417 0852 E: robbianchi56@gmail.com

BICK, David Jim. b 33. ALCD 59 LTh 74. **d** 59 **p** 60. C Glouc St Cath 59–61; C Coleford w Staunton 61–63; R Blaisdon w Flaxley 63–72; V Coaley 72–83; P-in-c Arlingham 80–83; P-in-c Frampton on Severn 80–83; Hon C Saul w Fretherne and Framilode 83–84; rtd 98. *St Joseph's, Prinknash Park, Cranham, Gloucester GL4 8EU* T: (01452) 812973

BICK (née GRIFFITHS), Mrs Sarah. b 75. Ex Univ BA 96 Homerton Coll Cam PGCE 99. Qu Coll Birm 07. **d** 09 **p** 10. C Coleford, Staunton, Newland, Redbrook etc *Glouc* 09–13; V from 13. *40 Boxbush Road, Coleford GL16 8DN* T: (01594) 835476 M: 07773-651893 E: sarah@thebickerage.org.uk

BICKERSTAFF, Denise Mary. See ACHESON, Denise Mary

BICKERSTETH, David Craufurd. b 50. Wycliffe Hall Ox 71. **d** 75 **p** 76. C Beverley Minster *York* 75–79; C Farnborough *Guildf* 79–81; P-in-c Dearham *Carl* 81–85; V 85–86; R Gosforth w Nether Wasdale and Wasdale Head 86–93; P-in-c Harraby 93–97; V Maryport 98–04; TR Maryport, Netherton and Flimby 04–06; Dioc Chapl MU 94–97; R Draycott-le-Moors w Forsbrook *Lich* 06–15; P-in-c Upper Tean 08–14; rtd 15. *Sunnybrae, Greenodd, Ulverston LA12 7RG* T: (01229) 861184 E: david.bickersteth@btinternet.com

BICKERSTETH, Edward Piers. b 56. MRICS 80. Wycliffe Hall Ox 89. **d** 91 **p** 92. NSM Bebington *Ches* 91–92; C 92–94; Proclamation Trust 94–98; P-in-c Arborfield w Barkham *Ox* 98–02; R from 02. *The Rectory, Church Lane, Arborfield, Reading RG2 9HZ* T: 0118-976 0285

BICKERSTETH, Simon Craufurd. b 77. St Jo Coll Dur BA 98. Wycliffe Hall Ox 99. **d** 01 **p** 02. C Windermere St Martin *Carl* 01–05; TV Walsall St Matt *Lich* 05–11; V Walsall St Martin 11–16; P-in-c Denton Holme *Carl* 16–20; V from 20. *St James's Vicarage, Goschen Road, Carlisle CA2 5PF* M: 07752-853148 E: simon.bickersteth@talktalk.net

BICKLEY, Mrs Alice Elizabeth Ann. b 60. Qu Coll Birm 06. **d** 09 **p** 10. C Leagrave *St Alb* 09–13; P-in-c Hexagon *Leic* 13–16; R from 16. *The Rectory, Honeypot Lane, Husbands Bosworth, Lutterworth LE17 6LY* T: (01858) 880351 M: 07977-601437 E: lizbickley@btinternet.com

BICKLEY, Mrs Pamela. b 59. Birm Univ BPhil 99. WEMTC 06. **d** 09 **p** 10. NSM Minsterley *Heref* 09–13; NSM Habberley 09–13; NSM Minsterley, Habberley and Hope w Shelve 13–19; Dioc Voc Adv 12–14; rtd 19; PtO *Heref* from 19. *High Ridge, Gorsty Bank, Snailbeach, Shrewsbury SY5 0LX* T: (01743) 792824

BICKLEY-PERCIVAL, Helena Jane. b 92. St Hilda's Coll Ox BA 13 R Holloway Coll Lon MMus 15. St Steph Ho Ox BA 19. **d** 20 **p** 21. C Westmr St Steph w St Jo *Lon* from 20. *Flat C, 16 Hide Place, London SW1P 4NJ* M: 07825-659348 E: curate@sswsj.org or revdhelena@gmail.com

BICKNELL (née RIDING), Mrs Pauline Alison. b 61. SEN 82. Oak Hill Th Coll BA 90. d 90 p 96. Par Dn Moor Allerton *Ripon* 90–93; Par Dn Leeds St Aid 93–94; C 94–96; C Rothwell 96–99; TV Drypool *York* 99–05; P-in-c Slyne w Hest *Blackb* 05–06; R Slyne w Hest and Halton w Aughton 06–17; P-in-c Ormskirk *Liv* from 17. *18 Chestnut Grange, Ormskirk L39 4YG* E: pauline.bicknell@outlook.com

BIDDINGTON, Laura Claire. *See* BETSON, Laura Claire

BIDDINGTON, Terence Eric. b 56. Hull Univ BA 77 Trin & All SS Coll Leeds PGCE 78 Leeds Univ PhD 86 Nottm Univ BTh 88 Man Univ MA(Theol) 96 MCollP 83 FRSA 15. Linc Th Coll 85. d 88 p 89. C Harpenden St Jo *St Alb* 88–90; Chapl Keele Univ *Lich* 90–93; Freelance Th Educator and Asst Lect Keele Univ 94–99; Assoc Min Betley and Keele *Lich* 90–93; Asst Dir Cornerstone St Aug Man 95–96; Mental Health Advocate Stockport 96–98; Dir and Sen Advocate Stockport MIND 99–16; PtO *Man* 99–01; P-in-c Heaton Norris Ch w All SS 01–02; C Heatons 02–03; Asst Chapl Manchester Mental Health and Soc Care Trust 01–03; Chapl Man Univ 03–16; Chapl Man Metrop Univ 03–16; Chapl RNCM 03–16; Dean of Spiritual Life Win Univ from 17. *Theology Department, The University of Winchester, Sparkford Road, Winchester SO22 4NR* T: (01962) 827063 E: terry.biddington@winchester.ac.uk

BIDDINGTON, Mrs Wendy Elizabeth. b 51. Cov Univ BSc 93 SRN 73 SCM 74. Qu Coll Birm 07. d 09 p 10. OLM Wellesbourne *Cov* 09–12; NSM from 12; PtO *Ox* from 17. *72 Mountford Close, Wellesbourne, Warwick CV35 9QQ* T: (01789) 840953 E: w.nbiddington701@btinternet.com

BIDDISCOMBE, Neil. b 69. Univ of Wales BSc 92 Nottm Univ LLM 14. Sarum Coll 18. d 21. NSM Three Saints *B & W* from 21. *6 Marlborough Court, Burnham-on-Sea TA8 2PZ* E: neil.biddiscombe@outlook.com

BIDDLE, Joanna Elizabeth. *See* JEPSON, Joanna Elizabeth

BIDDLE, Nicholas Lawrence. *See* JEPSON-BIDDLE, Nicholas Lawrence

BIDDLECOMBE, Francis William. b 30. St Mich Coll Llan 57. d 59 p 60. C Llangynwyd w Maesteg *Llan* 59–62; C Roath 62–65; V Llanddewi Rhondda w Bryn Eirw 65–71; V Berse and Southsea *St As* 71–79; P-in-c Teme Valley S *Worc* 79–85; rtd 92; PtO *Heref* 92–13; *Worc* 92–09. *Four Winds, New Road, Highley, Bridgnorth WV16 6NN* T: (01746) 861746 E: fwbiddlecombe@hotmail.com

BIDDLESTONE, Simon Christopher. b 77. York Univ BA 99 Coll of Ripon & York St Jo PGCE 00. Cranmer Hall Dur 15. d 17 p 18. C Tadcaster *York* 17–20; P-in-c Nether w Upper Poppleton from 20; P-in-c Acomb H Redeemer from 20. *St Mary's House, Church Street, Church Fenton, Tadcaster LS24 9RD* M: 07738-975927 E: revsimonbiddlestone@hotmail.com

BIDDULPH, John Whitmore. b 66. Lon Univ BPharm 87 MSc 91. St Mellitus Coll 16. d 19 p 20. OLM Doddinghurst *Chelmsf* from 19; OLM Bentley Common, Kelvedon Hatch and Navestock from 19. *100 Longfields, Ongar CM5 9DE* T: (01277) 364927 E: johnwbiddulph@btinternet.com

BIDE, Preb Mary Elizabeth. b 53. St Anne's Coll Ox BA 74 MA 78. S Dios Minl Tr Scheme 91. d 94 p 95. C Gt Bookham *Guildf* 94–98; P-in-c Frimley Green 98–01; V Frimley Green and Mytchett 02–03; Year Tutor Dioc Min Course 96–03; Prec Ch Ch *Ox* 03–07; TR Wimbledon *S'wark* 07–16; rtd 16; PtO *B & W* from 16; Sub-Dean and Preb Wells Cathl from 20; Chapl to The Queen from 13. *73 Portway, Wells BA5 2BJ* T: (01749) 679197 E: mary.bide@gmail.com

BIDEN, Neville Douglas. b 31. S'wark Ord Course 76. d 79 p 80. C Ash *Guildf* 79–82; NSM Surbiton St Andr and St Mark *S'wark* 87–91; Chapl Asst Long Grove Hosp Epsom 90–91; PtO *Guildf* 90–91 and 97–06; C Coulsdon St Jo *S'wark* 91–96; rtd 96; PtO *Heref* 95–97; *Win* from 01. *5 Taylor Drive, Bramley, Tadley RG26 5XB* T: (01256) 880459 E: rev.biden@gmail.com

BIDGOOD, Julian Paul. b 71. Sussex Univ BA 92. Oak Hill Th Coll BA 03. d 03 p 04. C Ox St Ebbe w H Trin and St Pet 03–08; C Arborfield w Barkham from 08. *5 Somerville Close, Wokingham RG41 4SW* M: 07779-296511 E: julian@abch.org.uk

BIELBY, Canon Elaine Elizabeth. b 57. Surrey Univ MSc 83. Ripon Coll Cuddesdon 96. d 98 p 99. C Marton-in-Cleveland *York* 98–01; P-in-c Welton w Melton 01–12; V from 12; Tr Officer E Riding from 01; Dean of Women's Min from 08; Can and Preb York Minster from 10. *St Helen's Vicarage, Cowgate, Welton, Brough HU15 1ND* T: (01482) 666677 E: ebielby@ebielby.karoo.co.uk

BIENFAIT, Alexander. b 61. Hatf Poly BSc 86. Sarum & Wells Th Coll BTh 94. d 94 p 95. C Battersea St Luke *S'wark* 94–96; C Clapham Team 96–99; TV Whitstable *Cant* 99–07;

P-in-c Biddenden and Smarden 07–21; AD Romney and Tenterden 19–21; PtO from 21. *Tilia, 9 Singleton Road, Great Chart, Ashford TN23 3BA* M: 07817-892005

BIERBAUM, Ms Ruth Anne. b 67. RN 89. Trin Coll Bris BA 98. d 99 p 00. C Filey *York* 99–02; C Coxheath, E Farleigh, Hunton, Linton etc *Roch* 02–08; Lead Mental Health Chapl Kent and Medway NHS and Soc Care Partnership Trust from 08; PtO *Roch* from 08; *Cant* from 08. *Room 314, Priory House, Hermitage Lane, Maidstone ME16 9PH* T: (01622) 722180 E: ruth.bierbaum@kmpt.nhs.uk

BIGG, Andrew John. *See* KRAUSS, Andrew John

BIGG, Howard Clive. b 40. Fitzw Coll Cam BA 68 MA 72. Ridley Hall Cam 73. d 74 p 75. C Worksop St Jo *S'well* 74–76; Min Can St Alb 76–77; PtO *Ches* 78–82; *Ely* 82–99; Vice-Prin Romsey Ho Cam 86–89; NSM Cambridge St Benedict *Ely* 99–01; rtd 05; PtO *Ely* 08–13 and from 15. *4 Pershore Road, Hardwick, Cambridge CB23 7XQ* T: (01954) 211673 E: hcbigg40@gmail.com

BIGG, Michael David. b 81. Dur Univ BA 07 Wolfs Coll Cam MPhil 08 PGCE 09 Dur Univ MA 17. Ridley Hall Cam 15. d 17 p 18. C E Leightonstone *Ely* 17–20; R Girton from 20; V Madingley from 20. *The Rectory, 42 Church Lane, Girton, Cambridge CB3 0JP* T: (01223) 202145 M: 07380-809377 E: rector@girton.church *or* vicar@madingleychurch.org

BIGGAR, Prof Nigel John. b 55. CBE 21. Worc Coll Ox BA 76 MA 88 Chicago Univ AM 80 PhD 86 Regent Coll Vancouver MCS 81. d 90 p 91. Lib Latimer Ho Ox 85–91; Asst Lect Chr Ethics Wycliffe Hall Ox 87–94; Chapl Oriel Coll Ox 90–99; Prof Th Leeds Univ *Ripon* 99–04; Prof Th TCD 04–07; Can Ch Ch Cathl Dublin *D & G* 05–07; Regius Prof Moral and Past Th Ox Univ from 07; Can Res Ch Ch *Ox* from 07. *Christ Church, Oxford OX1 1DP* T: (01865) 276219 E: nigel.biggar@chch.ox.ac.uk

BIGGS, David James. b 55. St Jo Coll Auckland LTh 82. d 81 p 82. NZ 81–86; C Stevenage St Andr and St Geo *St Alb* 86–89; TV Moulsecoomb *Chich* 89–99; C Brighton St Pet w Chpl Royal 99–02; P-in-c 02–09; V Brighton Chpl Royal from 09; Chapl St Mary's Hall Brighton 03–09. *The Chapel Royal, 164 North Street, Brighton BN1 1EA* T: (01273) 774492 *or* 328767 E: frbiggs@gmail.com

BIGGS, David James. b 93. Teesside Univ BSc 15. Ridley Hall Cam 15. d 18 p 19. C Thirsk *York* 18–21; P-in-c Sessay from 21; P-in-c Sowerby from 21; P-in-c Thirkleby w Kilburn and Bagby from 21. *The Vicarage, The Close, Sowerby, Thirsk YO7 1JA* M: 07857-143881 E: david.biggs@hotmail.com

BIGGS, Philip John. b 51. Ripon Hall Ox 74. d 77 p 78. C Maidstone All SS w St Phil and H Trin *Cant* 77–80; Dioc Youth Officer Truro 80–84; Chapl St Hilda's Angl Sch Australia 84–87; R Bicton 87–91; R Mosman Park 92–10; Hon Chapl Miss to Seafarers 84–10; Can Res and Chan Blackb Cathl 10–11; Poland 11–12; P-in-c Lytham St Cuth *Blackb* 12–15; Hon C St Neot and Warleggan *Truro* from 15; Hon C St Cleer 15–19. *The Vicarage, St Neot, Liskeard PL14 6NG* T: (01579) 320472 M: 07521-282876

BIGNELL, Alan Guy. b 39. Lon Univ BA 64. Ox NSM Course 78. d 81 p 82. NSM Upton cum Chalvey *Ox* 81–90; NSM Burnham and Slough Deanery 90–10; PtO from 10. *Little Gidding, 2 Turners Road, Slough SL3 7AN* T: (01753) 523005 E: abignell@waitrose.com

BILES, David George. b 35. AKC 58 Open Univ BA 75 Lambeth STh 91 Leeds Univ MA 96. d 59 p 60. C Cockerton *Dur* 59–62; C Winlaton 62–67; P-in-c Dipton 67–74; R Wolviston 74–89; P-in-c Thirkleby w Kilburn and Bagby *York* 89–90; V 90–00; RD Thirsk 90–91; RD Mowbray 91–00; rtd 00; PtO *York* 00–20; *Sheff* 11–13. *10 King Rudding Close, Riccall, York YO19 6RY* T: (01757) 248829 E: biles.cofferwood10@gmail.com

BILES, Canon Kathleen Anne. b 52. Bradf Univ BA 74. St Jo Coll Nottm 98. d 04 p 06. C Ch Ch Cathl Stanley Falkland Is from 04; Can Ch Ch Cathl from 19. *PO Box 166, 14 Kent Road, Stanley FIQQ 1ZZ, Falkland Islands* T/F: (00500) 21897 E: kbiles@horizon.co.fk

BILES, Canon Timothy Mark Frowde. b 35. MBE 20. St Mich Coll Llan 60. d 64 p 66. C Middleton St Cross *Ripon* 64–66; Chapl St Fran Sch Hooke 66–72; P-in-c Toller Porcorum w Hooke *Sarum* 72–79; P-in-c Melplash w Mapperton 74–79; P-in-c Beaminster 77–79; TR Beaminster Area 79–00; Can and Preb Sarum Cathl 83–00; RD Beaminster 84–89; rtd 00; PtO *Sarum* from 01. *36 Hound Street, Sherborne DT9 3AA* T: (01935) 816247 E: timbiles35@gmail.com

BILINDA, Mrs Lesley Anne. b 59. Aber Univ MA 81 All Nations Chr Coll BA 98. Ripon Coll Cuddesdon MA 13. d 13 p 14. C Fulham St Andr *Lon* 13–16; V from 16; Dean of Women's Min Kensington Area from 17. *St Andrew's Vicarage, 10 St Andrew's Road, London W14 9SX* T: (020) 7385 5023 M: 07956-587176 E: vicar@standrewsfulham.com

BILL, Alan. b 29. K Coll Lon BD 66 AKC 66. **d** 67 **p** 68. C Gt Burstead *Chelmsf* 67–70; TV Thornaby on Tees *York* 71–76; R E Gilling 76–81; V Ormesby 81–91; rtd 91; PtO *Newc* from 91. *13 Wilmington Close, Tudor Grange, Newcastle upon Tyne NE3 2SF* T: 0191-242 4467 E: alanbill_uk@yahoo.co.uk

BILL, Canon Thomas Andrew Graham. b 47. Dur Univ BA 76. Cranmer Hall Dur. **d** 77 **p** 78. C Penwortham St Mary *Blackb* 77–80; C Torrisholme 80–82; P-in-c Accrington St Pet 82–89; P-in-c Haslingden St Jo Stonefold 82–89; V Skerton St Chad 89–03; R Burnley St Pet 03–11; P-in-c Burnley St Steph 08–11; R Burnley St Pet and St Steph 11–13; Hon Can Blackb Cathl 03–13; rtd 13; PtO *Blackb* from 13. *26 Thornton Road, Morecambe LA4 5PE* T: (01524) 417117

BILLETT, Canon Anthony Charles. b 56. Bris Univ BEd. Wycliffe Hall Ox 82. **d** 85 **p** 86. C Waltham Abbey *Chelmsf* 85–88; C Nor St Pet Mancroft w St Jo Maddermarket 88–91; V Stalham and E Ruston w Brunstead 91–00; R Stalham, E Ruston, Brunstead, Sutton and Ingham 00–01; R Diss 01–14; TR from 14; RD Redenhall 06–15; P-in-c Winfarthing w Shelfanger w Burston w Gissing etc 21; Hon Can Nor Cathl from 10. *The Rectory, 26 Mount Street, Diss IP22 4QG* T: (01379) 642072 E: disschurch2@btconnect.com

BILLETT (née RANDALL), Mrs Elizabeth Nicola. b 55. RGN 75 SCM 81. EAMTC 94. **d** 97 **p** 98. C Loddon, Sisland w Hales and Heckingham *Nor* 97–98; C Loddon, Sisland, Chedgrave, Hardley and Langley 98–01; TV Hempnall from 02. *The Flat, George's House, The Street, Woodton, Bungay NR35 1LZ* T: (01508) 482366

BILLETT, Mrs Justine Elizabeth Stearman. b 82. Reading Univ BSc 08. Ripon Coll Cuddesdon 34–15. **d** 15 **p** 17. C Banwell *B & W* 15–17; C Congresbury w Puxton and Hewish St Ann 15–17; C Backwell w Chelvey and Brockley 17–19. *15 Marsh Farm Road, Twickenham TW2 6SH* M: 07778-049265 E: rev.j.billett@gmail.com

BILLIN, David Robert. b 55. S Bank Poly BSc 77 CEng 82 MIET 82 MIRSE 86 EurIng 89. **d** 06 **p** 07. NSM Carshalton S'wark 06–19; NSM Sutton from 19. *33 Beeches Avenue, Carshalton SM5 3LJ* T: (020) 8647 5046 M: 07946-609387 E: davidbillin@outlook.com

BILLIN, Mrs Susan Lynn. b 59. S Bank Univ BSc 99 Greenwich Univ CertEd 96 RGN 82. SEITE 02. **d** 05 **p** 06. NSM S Beddington and Roundshaw S'wark 05–16; P-in-c Hackbridge and Beddington Corner 16–19; V from 19. *33 Beeches Avenue, Carshalton SM5 3LJ* M: 07816-140385 E: lynnbillin234@hotmail.co.uk

BILLINGHURST, Richard George. b 48. St Jo Coll Cam BA 70 MA 74 FIA 76. Ridley Hall Cam 76. **d** 79 **p** 80. C Caverswall *Lich* 79–81; C Cullompton *Ex* 81–84; R Redgrave cum Botesdale w Rickinghall *St E* 84–92; R Skellingthorpe w Doddington *Linc* 92–17; RD Graffoe 94–02 and 14–17; rtd 17; PtO *Linc* from 18. *12 Chiltern Road, Lincoln LN5 8SD* M: 07971-590378 E: acorns@clara.co.uk

BILLINGS, Canon Alan Roy. b 42. Em Coll Cam BA 65 MA 69 Bris Univ PGCE 66 Leic Univ MEd 75 NY Th Sem DMin 87. Linc Th Coll 66. **d** 68 **p** 69. C Knighton St Mary Magd *Leic* 68–72; P-in-c Sheff Gillcar St Silas 72–76; V Beighton 76–77; Hd RE Broadway Sch Barnsley 77–81; PtO *Sheff* 77–81; V Walkley 81–86; Dir Ox Inst for Ch and Soc 86–92; PtO *Ox* 86–92; Vice-Prin Ripon Coll Cuddesdon 88–92; Prin WMMTC 92–94; V Kendal St Geo *Carl* 94–07; C Grayrigg 06–07; Warden of Readers 96–03; Dir Cen for Ethics and Relig Lanc Univ 00–07; Hon Can Carl Cathl 05–07; rtd 07; PtO *Sheff* from 07. *43 Northfield Court, Sheffield S10 1QR* T: 0114-267 6549 E: alanbillingsuk@yahoo.co.uk

BILLINGS, Roger Key. b 41. ACIB. Oak Hill Th Coll BA 80. **d** 80 **p** 81. C Tunbridge Wells St Jas *Roch* 80–84; V Chatham St Paul w All SS 84–95; V Carterton *Ox* 95–03; TR Brize Norton and Carterton 03–07; AD Witney 03–07; rtd 07; PtO *Nor* from 07. *Maudville, Norwich Road, Cromer NR27 9JU* T: (01263) 519055 E: rogerbillings@btinternet.com

BILLINGS, Mrs Valerie Ann. b 52. Nottm Trent Univ CertEd 02. EMMTC 07. **d** 09 **p** 10. NSM Ockbrook *Derby* 09–14; PtO from 15. *14 Conway Avenue, Borrowash, Derby DE72 3GT* T: (01332) 726285 E: valbillings1@gmail.com

BILLINGTON, George. b 45. St Jo Coll Nottm 92. **d** 94 **p** 95. C Accrington St Jo w Huncoat *Blackb* 94–98; C Whittle-le-Woods 98–00; V Stalmine w Pilling 00–10; rtd 10; PtO *Ex* from 11. *Brookvale, Sterridge Valley, Berrynarbor, Ilfracombe EX34 9TB* T: (01271) 883546

BILLSON, Jennifer Ann Margaret. b 46. **d** 16 **p** 17. NSM Crowland *Linc* from 16. *2 Ambury Gardens, Crowland, Peterborough PE6 0ET* E: annie@maildaemon.co.uk

BILLSON, Kevin Michael. b 58. Lon Univ BD 81. Qu Coll Birm 10. **d** 11 **p** 12. C Brereton and Rugeley *Lich* 11–15; R Blofield *Nor* from 15; C Broadside from 21; PtO *Eur* 16–21. *The*

Rectory, 10 Oak Wood, Blofield, Norwich NR13 4JQ T: (01603) 712299 M: 07941-341911 E: kevin.billson@eraith.net

BILTON, Canon Paul Michael. b 52. AKC 74. St Aug Coll Cant 74. **d** 75 **p** 76. C Skipton Ch Ch *Bradf* 75–79; Ind Chapl *Worc* 79–81; V Greetland and W Vale *Wakef* 81–88; R Mablethorpe w Trusthorpe *Linc* 88–91; V Bradf St Wilfrid Lidget Green 91–04; P-in-c Bradf St Columba w St Andr 00–04; V Bradf St Wilfrid w St Columba 04–14; *Leeds* 14–17; RD Bowling and Horton *Bradf* 02–14; AD *Leeds* 14; Hon Can Bradf Cathl 04–17; rtd 17. *7 Middle Burn End, Stonehaugh, Hexham NE48 3DY* E: paulmichaelbiltonbb@gmail.com

BIMSON, Sara Margaret. b 56. St Jo Coll Nottm BA. **d** 03 **p** 04. C Maidstone St Martin *Cant* 03–08; rtd 08; Voc Officer *Cant* 08–10; PtO from 08; Hon Min Can Cant Cathl from 12. *166 Westwood Drive, Canterbury CT2 7US* T: (01227) 760655 E: sara.bimson@canterbury-cathedral.org

BINDING, Ms Frances Mary. b 59. York Univ BA 81 Newc Poly PGCE 82. WEMTC 98. **d** 02 **p** 03. C Bromyard *Heref* 02–07; TV Worc SE 07–13; P-in-c Wraxall *B & W* 13–15; R 15–20; Hon C Yatton Moor from 20. *Kingfisher Cottage, Back Lane, Kingston Seymour, Clevedon BS21 6XB* E: franmbinding@gmail.com

BINDOFF, Ms Anna. b 70. Leeds Univ BA 94. Ripon Coll Cuddesdon BA 97. **d** 98 **p** 99. Asst Chapl New Coll Ox 98–01; Hon C Blackbird Leys *Ox* 98–01; C 01–04. *23 Brook Street, Watlington OX49 5JH* T: (01491) 613327 E: abindoff@btinternet.com

BING, Canon Alan Charles. b 56. St Edm Hall Ox BA 78 MA 91 Ex Univ MA 96. Oak Hill Th Coll 89. **d** 91 **p** 92. C Fremington *Ex* 91–94; C-in-c Roundswell CD 94–97; TV Barnstaple 97–99; Chapl N Devon Coll Barnstaple 96–99; P-in-c Ulverston St Mary w H Trin *Carl* 99–04; R from 04; RD Furness 10–19; Hon Can Carl Cathl from 09. *The Rectory, 15 Ford Park Crescent, Ulverston LA12 7JR* T/F: (01229) 584331 E: alanbing@live.co.uk *or* rector@ulverstonparishchurch.org

BINKS, Robert Peter. b 73. Trin Coll Bris 08. **d** 10 **p** 11. C Basildon St Andr w H Cross *Chelmsf* 10–14; P-in-c Warley Ch Ch and Gt Warley St Mary 14–18. *Address temp unknown* E: rob.binks@me.com

BINKS, Susan Jane. b 59. Edin Univ MA 81. Yorks Min Course 13. **d** 15 **p** 16. NSM Kirkdale w Harome, Nunnington and Pockley *York* 15–18; V from 18. *Helleborus Cottage, Main Street, Harome, York YO62 5JF* T: (01439) 770523 M: 07908-747796 E: binksharome@btinternet.com

BINLEY, Miss Teresa Mary. b 37. Dalton Ho Bris 61. **d** 87 **p** 94. Par Dn Ashton-upon-Mersey St Mary Magd *Ches* 87–92; Bp's Officer for Women in Min 87–92; C Chaddesden St Mary *Derby* 92–98; rtd 98; PtO *Derby* 98–19. *27 Hindscarth Crescent, Mickleover, Derby DE3 9NN* T: (01332) 511146

BINNEY, Mark James Gurney. b 58. K Coll Lon BD 80. Qu Coll Birm 84. **d** 86 **p** 87. C Hornchurch St Andr *Chelmsf* 86–89; C Hutton 89–91; V Pheasey *Lich* 91–96; TV Wombourne w Trysull and Bobbington 96–99; V Wilnecote 99–08; P-in-c Hampton w Sedgeberrow and Hinton-on-the-Green *Worc* 08–18; P-in-c Bengeworth 12–18; R Bengeworth and Hampton etc from 18. *St Andrew's Vicarage, 54 Pershore Road, Evesham WR11 2PQ* T: (01386) 446381 E: reverend-mark-binney@hotmail.co.uk

BINNS, Miss Elizabeth Ann. b 55. MBE 06. Man Metrop Univ BA 87 RGN 77. **d** 05 **p** 06. OLM Bury St Jo w St Mark *Man* 05–10; OLM Walmersley Road, Bury 10–14; NSM Radcliffe 14–20; TV 17–20; rtd 20. *36 Raymond Avenue, Bury BL9 6NN* T: 0161-764 5071 M: 07976-818157 E: elizabethannbinns@gmail.com

BINNS, Canon Janet Victoria. b 57. ACIB 96. Ox Min Course 04. **d** 07 **p** 08. C Slough *Ox* 07–10; C Eton w Eton Wick, Boveney and Dorney 10–11; Olympics Co-ord 11–12; PtO 13; R Hedsor and Bourne End from 13; Hon Can Ch Ch from 21. *34 Fieldhead Gardens, Bourne End SL8 5RN* T: (01628) 523046 E: revjanetbinns@btinternet.com

BINNS, Canon John Richard Elliott. b 51. St Jo Coll Cam MA 76 K Coll Lon PhD 89. Coll of Resurr Mirfield 74. **d** 76 **p** 77. C Clapham Old Town *S'wark* 76–80; TV Mortlake w E Sheen 80–87; V Upper Tooting H Trin 87–94; V Cambridge Gt St Mary w St Mich *Ely* 94–17; RD Cambridge N 07–11; Hon Can Ely Cathl 07–17; rtd 17; PtO *Lich* from 17. *Laburnum Cottage, 197 Chase Road, Burntwood WS7 0EB* T: (01543) 670217 E: johnrbinns@gmail.com

BINNS, Peter Rodney. b 44. St Andr Univ MA 66. Ox NSM Course 72. **d** 75 **p** 76. NSM Amersham on the Hill *Ox* 75–90; NSM Wingrave w Rowsham, Aston Abbotts and Cublington 90–97; NSM Hawridge w Cholesbury and St Leonard 90–97; NSM Amersham on the Hill from 97. *16 Turnfurlong Row, Turnfurlong Lane, Aylesbury HP21 7FF* T: (01296) 330836 F: 337965 E: peter.binns166@btinternet.com

BINNY, Canon John Wallace. b 46. Univ of Wales (Lamp) BA 70. St Mich Coll Llan 69. **d** 71 **p** 72. C Llantrisant *Llan*

71–77; V Troedyrhiw w Merthyr Vale 77–82; R Eglwysbrewis w St Athan, Flemingston, Gileston 82–95; R Eglwysbrewis w St Athan w Gileston 95–03; V Pentyrch w Capel Llanilltern 03–11; rtd 11; PtO *Llan* from 11; Hon Can St Helena from 18. *Oakdene, 27 Porthamal Road, Cardiff CF14 6AQ* T: (029) 2062 0360 E: johnbinny@live.co.uk

BIRBECK, Anthony Leng. b 33. MBE 90. Linc Coll Ox BA 59 MA 61. Linc Th Coll 58. **d** 60 **p** 61. C Redcar *York* 60–73; C Redcar w Kirkleatham 73–74; Chapl Teesside Ind Miss 62–74; Can Res and Treas Wells Cathl *B & W* 74–78; NSM Wells St Thos w Horrington 89–98; rtd 98; PtO *B & W* from 98; RD Shepton Mallet 07–11. *Beeches, Cannards Grave Road, Shepton Mallet BA4 4LX* T: (01749) 330382 M: 07802-725024 E: tony-birbeck@msn.com

BIRBECK, John Trevor. b 49. ACIB 77. St Jo Coll Nottm 86. **d** 88 **p** 89. C Eccleshill *Bradf* 88–92; V Hurst Green and Mitton 92–03; R Rawmarsh w Parkgate *Sheff* 03–16; C Greasbrough 10–16; C Kimberworth and Kimberworth Park 10–16; rtd 16; PtO *Guildf* 17–20; *Blackb* from 18. *3 Winston Avenue, Lytham St Annes FY8 3NS* T: (01253) 985986 E: susan4john@gmail.com

BIRCH, Barry. b 46. Sheff Univ CertEd 69 Lon Univ BA 74 MIL 84 MCollP 85. **d** 06 **p** 07. NSM Cantley *Sheff* 06–08; P-in-c Eastchurch w Leysdown and Harty *Cant* 08–12; Hon C W Sheppey 12; rtd 12; PtO *Eur* 13–18. *Richard Holstraat 133, 2551 HR Gravenhage, The Netherlands* T: (0031) (70) 213 4042 E: barrybirch@hotmail.com

BIRCH, Graham James. b 62. NOC BTh 94. **d** 97 **p** 98. C Southport St Phil and St Paul *Liv* 97–01; P-in-c Wigan St Cath 01–07; V Ainsdale 07–19; V Gt Harwood *Blackb* from 19. *The Vicarage, Church Lane, Great Harwood, Blackburn BB6 7PU*

BIRCH, Mark Russell. b 70. Bris Univ BVSc 93 Em Coll Cam BA 99. Westcott Ho Cam 97. **d** 00 **p** 01. C Cirencester *Glouc* 00–03; Chapl and Fell Ex Coll Ox 03–06; Chapl Helen and Douglas Ho Ox 06–10; Chapl Treloar Coll of FE 10–12; P-in-c Win St Faith w St Cross 12–14; Chapl St Cross Hosp 12–14; Min Can and Chapl Westmr Abbey from 14; Prec from 20. *The Chapter Office, 20 Dean's Yard, London SW1P 3PA* T: (020) 7654 4968 E: mark.birch@me.com or mark.birch@westminster-abbey.org

BIRCH, Richard Arthur. b 51. Brighton Poly BSc 73 Chelsea Coll Lon MSc 76. SEITE 98. **d** 01 **p** 02. NSM Folkestone St Jo *Cant* 01–04; NSM Hawkinge w Acrise and Swingfield 04–07; NSM Hythe 07–08; NSM Doddington, Newnham and Wychling 08–14; NSM Kingsdown and Creekside 14–19; rtd 19; PtO *Cant* from 19. *42 Robins Close, Lenham, Maidstone ME17 2LD* T: (01622) 858050 E: richarda.birch@gmail.com

BIRCH, Thomas David Keith. b 81. Glas Univ MA 03 Edin Univ MSc 06. Ripon Coll Cuddesdon BA 14. **d** 14 **p** 15. C Gosforth St Nic *Newc* 14–17; P-in-c Wylam 17–18; P-in-c Ovingham 17–18; V Ovingham and Wylam from 18; C Heddon-on-the-Wall from 21. *The Vicarage, Church Road, Wylam NE41 8AT* T: (01661) 853254 M: 07976-047707 E: revdtombirch@gmail.com

BIRCHALL, John Dearman. b 70. St Andr Univ MA 93. Wycliffe Hall Ox BTh 99. **d** 99 **p** 00. C Purley Ch Ch *S'wark* 99–02; C Fisherton Anger *Sarum* 02–08; V Surbiton Hill Ch Ch *S'wark* 08–20. *Address temp unknown*

BIRCHALL, Robert Gary. b 59. Sheff Univ BA 81. St Jo Coll Nottm 85. **d** 88 **p** 89. C Manston *Ripon* 88–91; C Leic Martyrs 91–94; C New Humberstone 94–95; V Burnopfield *Dur* 95–14; V Burnopfield and Dipton 14; AD Lanchester 06–14; V Boldmere *Birm* from 14. *209 Station Road, Sutton Coldfield B73 5LE* T: 0121-354 4501 E: garybirchall1@gmail.com

BIRCHARD, Canon Thaddeus Jude. b 45. Louisiana State Univ BA 66. Kelham Th Coll 66. **d** 70 **p** 71. C Devonport St Mark Ford *Ex* 70–73; C Southend St Jo w St Mark, All SS w St Fran etc *Chelmsf* 73–76; TV Poplar *Lon* 76–80; V Paddington St Jo w St Mich 80–01; Hon Can Louisiana from 90; rtd 01; PtO *Lon* 02–13 and from 18. *142 Dibdin House, Maida Vale, London W9 1QG* T: (020) 7328 2380 E: thaddeus@birchard.co.uk

BIRD, Andrew. b 95. St Mellitus Coll 16 Trin Coll Bris 19. **d** 21. C Chorlton-cum-Hardy St Werburgh *Man* from 21. *Address temp unknown* M: 07767-304123 E: andrew.bird578@gmail.com

BIRD, The Very Revd David John. b 46. St D Coll Lamp BA 70 Duquesne Univ PhD 87. Gen Th Sem (NY) STM 74. **d** 70 **p** 71. C Kidderminster St Geo *Worc* 70–72; Chapl Trin Sch New York USA 72–78; V Rochdale Ch Ch 78–79; R New Kensington St Andr 79–89; R Washington Grace Ch 89–03; Dean Trin Cathl San Jose from 03. *Trinity Cathedral, 81 North 2nd Street, San Jose, CA 95113-1205, USA* T: (001) (408) 293 7953 F: 293 4993 E: david3933@aol.com

BIRD, Canon David Ronald. b 55. York Univ BA 76. St Jo Coll Nottm 83. **d** 86 **p** 87. C Kinson *Sarum* 86–90; R

Thrapston *Pet* 90–97; P-in-c Islip 94–95; RD Higham 94–97; V Northampton St Giles 97–12; Can Pet Cathl 01–12; P-in-c Tollington *Lon* 12–14; TR 14–19; rtd 19. *5C Kidbrooke Park Road, London SE3 0LR* E: drbirdis@gmail.com

BIRD, Douglas Norman. b 38. **d** 92 **p** 93. OLM New Bury *Man* 92–06; PtO *Blackb* 06–14; *Man* from 06. *10 Hawthorne Avenue, Horwich, Bolton BL6 6JD* T: (01204) 695916 M: 07737-136306 E: aviary1712@outlook.com

BIRD, Canon Frederick Hinton. b 38. St Edm Hall Ox BA 62 MA 66 Univ of Wales MEd 81 PhD 86. St D Coll Lamp BD 65. **d** 65 **p** 66. C Mynyddislwyn *Mon* 65–67; Min Can St Woolos Cathl 67–70; Chapl Anglo-American Coll Farringdon 70–71; PtO *Ox* 70–78; *Cant* 72–78; *Mon* 76–82; V Rushen *S & M* 82–03; Can St German's Cathl 93–03; rtd 03; PtO *S & M* from 04. *Conrhenny, 56 Selborne Drive, Douglas, Isle of Man IM2 3NL* T: (01624) 621624 E: hinton.bird@gmail.com

BIRD, Geoffrey. b 44. Dioc OLM tr scheme 97. **d** 99 **p** 00. Asst Chapl HM YOI and Remand Cen Brinsford 99; Sen Chapl 99–04; Chapl HM Pris Shepton Mallet 04–09; rtd 09. *2 Hosey Road, Sturminster Newton DT10 1QP* T: (01258) 472904 E: revgeoffbird@gmail.com

BIRD, Henry John Joseph. b 37. ARCO 58 Qu Coll Cam BA 59 MA 63. Linc Th Coll 62. **d** 64 **p** 65. C Harbledown *Cant* 64–68; C Skipton H Trin *Bradf* 68–70; V Oakworth 70–81; Chapl Abingdon Sch 81–82; P-in-c Doncaster St Geo *Sheff* 82–85; V 85–02; rtd 02; PtO *Sheff* from 05; *Wakef* 14; *Leeds* from 14. *332 Thorne Road, Doncaster DN2 5AL* T: (01302) 365589 E: hbird588@btinternet.com

BIRD, Hinton. *See* BIRD, Frederick Hinton

BIRD, Ian Nicholas. b 62. Qu Eliz Coll Lon BSc 83 Newc Univ PhD 87 Heythrop Coll Lon MA 10. SAOMC 03. **d** 06 **p** 07. C Chandler's Ford *Win* 06–10; V from 10. *The Vicarage, 30 Hursley Road, Chandler's Ford, Eastleigh SO53 2FT* T: (023) 8025 4739 M: 07733-213535 E: ianbird@parishcf.church

BIRD, Jeremy Paul. b 56. Ex Univ BSc 77 Hull Univ MA 88. Sarum Th Coll 78. **d** 80 **p** 81. C Tavistock and Gulworthy *Ex* 80–83; Chapl Teesside Poly *York* 83–88; R Chipstable w Huish Champflower and Clatworthy *B & W* 88–93; Rural Affairs Officer 88–93; V Uffculme *Ex* 93–01; P-in-c Dawlish 01–09; P-in-c Exwick 09–20; V from 20. *The Vicarage, Exwick Hill, Exeter EX4 2AQ* T: (01392) 255500 M: 07960-491668

BIRD, Joel Timothy. b 88. St Mellitus Coll BA 18. **d** 18 **p** 19. C Dronfield w Holmesfield *Derby* from 18. *43 Firthwood Road, Coal Aston, Dronfield S18 3BW* M: 07888-657529 E: joeltbird88@gmail.com or joel.bird@dwhparish.org.uk

BIRD, John. *See* BIRD, Henry John Joseph

BIRD, John Anthony. b 45. EMMTC 00. **d** 03 **p** 04. NSM Thringstone St Andr *Leic* 03–09; NSM Whitwick and Swannington 07–09; NSM Whitwick, Thringstone and Swannington 09–11; NSM Shepshed and Oaks in Charnwood from 11. *8 Buckingham Drive, Loughborough LE11 4TE* T: (01509) 234962

BIRD, Mrs Margaret Kathleen. b 48. SAOMC 04. **d** 06 **p** 07. NSM Cox Green *Ox* 06–10; NSM New Windsor 10–18; AD Maidenhead and Windsor 14–17; rtd 18; PtO *Win* from 18. *47 Boundary Road, Bournemouth BH10 4HH* T: (01202) 251896 M: 07881-712611 E: margretkbird@gmail.com

BIRD, Canon Nicholas William Randle. b 70. Univ of Cen England in Birm BSc 99 RGN 92. NEOC 02. **d** 05 **p** 06. C Thirsk *York* 05–09; P-in-c Dunnington 09–12; P-in-c Stockton-on-the-Forest w Holtby and Warthill 09–12; R Rural E York from 12; RD Derwent from 16; Can and Preb York Minster from 21. *The Rectory, 30 Church Street, Dunnington, York YO19 5PW* T: (01904) 489349 E: revnickbird@gmail.com

BIRD, Patricia Moira. b 53. RGN 75. **d** 19 **p** 20. NSM Charlbury w Shorthampton *Ox* from 19. *4 Elm Crescent, Charlbury, Chipping Norton OX7 3PZ* E: tish@stmaryscharlbury.co.uk

BIRD, Canon Peter Andrew. b 40. Wadh Coll Ox BA 62 MA 68. Ridley Hall Cam 63. **d** 65 **p** 66. C Keynsham w Queen Charlton *B & W* 65–68; C Strood St Nic *Roch* 68–72; TV Strood 72–79; V S Gillingham 79–89; V Westerham 89–02; Hon Can Roch Cathl 01–02; PtO 02–05; *Derby* 05–18. *Iona, Prospect Terrace, Stanedge Road, Bakewell DE45 1DG* T: (01629) 813087 E: pabird@gmail.com

BIRDSALL, Sandra. **d** 15 **p** 16. C Penarth All SS *Llan* 15–19; V Llansawel, Briton Ferry from 19. *14 The Avenue, Neath SA11 2FD* T: (01639) 644241 E: sandra.birdsall@btinternet.com

BIRDSEYE, Miss Jacqueline Ann. b 55. Sussex Univ BEd 78 Southn Univ BTh 88 K Coll Lon MTh 93. Sarum & Wells Th Coll 85. **d** 88 **p** 94. C Egham Hythe *Guildf* 88–91; C Fleet 91–92; C Shottermill 92–95; C Leavesden *St Alb* 95–98; R Ashwell w Hinxworth and Newnham 98–05; R Moreton, Woodsford and Crossways w Tincleton *Sarum* 05–19; rtd 19. *Address withheld by request*

BIRKENHEAD, Suffragan Bishop of. *See* CONALTY, The Rt Revd Julie Anne

BIRKETT, Christine Joy. b 53. Univ of Wales (Cardiff) BTheol 99 PGCE 01. Trin Coll Bris 07. d 08 p 09. NSM Berkeley w Wick, Breadstone, Newport, Stone etc *Glouc* 08–10; NSM Cainscross w Selsley 10–12; NSM Rodborough and The Stanleys w Selsley 12–13; P-in-c Upton St Leonards 13–16; rtd 16; PtO *Glouc* from 16. *7 Ann Edwards Mews, Abbeydale, Gloucester GL4 4FG* E: cjoyb1953@yahoo.co.uk

BIRKETT, Mrs Joyce. b 38. WMMTC 84. d 87 p 94. Par Dn Hill *Birm* 87–91; Asst Chapl Highcroft Hosp Birm 87–91; Par Dn Rowley Regis *Birm* 91–94; C 94–96; V Londonderry 96–01; rtd 01; PtO *Birm* from 01. *83 Callowbrook Lane, Rubery, Rednal, Birmingham B45 9HP* T: 0121-457 9759

BIRKETT, Mrs Julie Anne. b 56. SWMTC. d 10 p 11. NSM Hutton and Locking *B & W* 10–13; NSM Weston super Mare St Jo 13–19; NSM Weston super Mare Ch Ch and Em from 19. *19 Stanhope Road, Weston-super-Mare BS23 4LP* T: (01934) 625587 M: 07763-335481 E: rebelrevd@gmail.com

BIRKETT, Neil Warren. b 45. Lanc Univ BEd 74 Southn Univ MA 84. Kelham Th Coll 65. d 77 p 77. NSM Win St Matt 77–15; PtO from 15. *Corrymeela, 132 Teg Down Meads, Winchester SO22 5NS* T: (01962) 864910

BIRKIN, Mrs Angela Elizabeth. b 58. New Hall Cam BA 79 MB, BChir 82 MRCGP 86. Yorks Min Course 15. d 17 p 18. NSM Headingley *Leeds* 17–21; TV Headingley and All Hallows from 21. *2 Lakeside View, Rawdon, Leeds LS19 6RN* T: 0113-414 6835 M: 07506-056185 E: ange.birkin1@sky.com

BIRKIN, Mrs Elspeth Joyce (Joy). b 36. CertEd 58. WMMTC 95. d 96 p 97. NSM Hanley Castle, Hanley Swan and Welland *Worc* 96–01; NSM Berrow w Pendock, Eldersfield, Hollybush etc 01–04; PtO 04–13; *Llan* from 13. *11 Spitzkop, Llantwit Major CF61 1RD* E: revjoy@uwclub.net

BIRKIN, Ms Julie. b 65. Qu Foundn (Course) 16. d 19 p 20. NSM Stoke-upon-Trent and Fenton *Lich* 19–21; NSM Hanley H Ev from 21. *87 Constance Avenue, Stoke-on-Trent ST4 8TE* T: (01782) 924728 M: 07748-856180 E: juliebirkin519@sky.com

BIRKINSHAW, Ian George. b 58. Pemb Coll Ox BA 81 Leeds Univ MA 97 Sheff Univ PGCE 82. NOC 93. d 96 p 97. NSM Chapeltown *Sheff* 96–97; C Normanton *Wakef* 98–01; C York St Mich-le-Belfrey 01–08; TR Huntington 08–10; R from 10. *The Rectory, Chestnut Court, Huntington, York YO32 9RD* T: (01904) 766550 or 768006 E: ian.birkinshaw@huntingtonparish.org.uk

BIRKS, Andrew Graham James. b 75. Dur Univ BA 17. SEITE 11. d 16 p 17. NSM Portslade St Nic and St Andr and Mile Oak *Chich* 16–19; C Bexhill St Barn 19–20; C Sidley 19–20; P-in-c Chidham from 20; P-in-c Funtington and W Stoke w Sennicotts from 20. *The Vicarage, Cot Lane, Chidham, Chichester PO18 8TA* M: 07795-117270 E: agb.75@hotmail.com

BIRMINGHAM, Archdeacon of. *See* TOMLINSON, The Ven Jennifer Clare

BIRMINGHAM, Bishop of. *See* URQUHART, The Rt Revd David Andrew

BIRMINGHAM, Dean of. *See* THOMPSON, The Very Revd Matthew

BIRNIE, Ms Ruth Burdett. b 41. Glas Univ MA 64 Jordanhill Coll Glas PGCE 65 Leeds Univ MA 73. NEOC 02. d 04 p 05. NSM Gosforth All SS *Newc* 04–11; PtO from 11. *20 Delaval Terrace, Newcastle upon Tyne NE3 4RT* T: 0191-284 1393 E: ruthbirnie27@gmail.com

BIRON-SCOTT, Laura Rebecca. b 83. Qu Coll Cam BA 06 St Jo Coll Cam MPhil 08 PhD 10. SEITE 16. d 16 p 17. C Kidlington w Hampton Poyle *Ox* 16–19; V Headington Quarry from 19. *The Vicarage, 46 Quarry Road, Headington, Oxford OX3 8NU* E: laura.biron@gmail.com

BIRT, Herbert Michael. b 56. ERMC 14. d 17 p 18. NSM Woolpit w Drinkstone *St E* 17–20; P-in-c Monks Eleigh w Chelsworth and Brent Eleigh etc from 20. *The Rectory, The Street, Monks Eleigh, Ipswich IP7 7AU* E: mikebirt856@btinternet.com

BIRT, Richard Arthur. b 43. Ch Ch Ox BA 66 MA 69. Cuddesdon Coll 67. d 69 p 70. C Sutton St Mich *York* 69–71; C Wollaton *S'well* 71–75; R Kirkby in Ashfield 75–80; P-in-c Duxford *Ely* 80–87; R 87–88; P-in-c Hinxton 80–87; V 87–88; P-in-c Ickleton 80–87; V 87–88; V Weobley w Sarnesfield and Norton Canon *Heref* 88–00; P-in-c Letton w Staunton, Byford, Mansel Gamage etc 88–00; PtO *Heref* 00–19. *8 Queens Hill Gardens, Hereford HR4 0EZ*

BIRTWISTLE, Lesley Sutherland. b 44. LLB. EMMTC 00. d 00 p 01. NSM Appleby Gp *Leic* 00–07; NSM Measham 07–08; NSM Packington w Normanton-le-Heath 07–08; NSM Donisthorpe and Moira w Stretton-en-le-Field 07–08;

NSM Woodfield 08–16; PtO 16–21. *14 Nethercroft Drive, Packington, Ashby-de-la-Zouch LE65 1WT* T: (01530) 413309

BISCOE, Mrs Erika Jayne. b 66. Ox Min Course 12. d 15 p 16. C Bicester w Bucknell, Caversfield and Launton *Ox* from 15. *8 Pippin Close, Bicester OX27 8AX* T: (01869) 369473 M: 07867-515900 E: erika.biscoe@gmail.com

BISCOE, Ian Rowland. b 68. Ox Min Course 06. d 07 p 08. C Cherwell Valley *Ox* 07–12; TV Bicester w Bucknell, Caversfield and Launton from 12. *8 Pippin Close, Bicester OX27 8AX* M: 07971-519234 E: ian.biscoe@googlemail.com

BISH, Jonathan James Peter. b 88. Ball Coll Ox BA 09 Peterho Cam BA 12. Westcott Ho Cam 10. d 13 p 14. C Halifax *Leeds* 13–17; C Outwood 17; C Outwood, Stanley and Wrenthorpe 17–20; C N Wakefield from 20. *The Vicarage, 121 Wrenthorpe Road, Wrenthorpe, Wakefield WF2 0JS* T: (01924) 373758 M: 07772-601259 E: frjonathanbish@gmail.com

BISHOP, Canon Andrew Scott. b 70. Leeds Univ BA 93 Heythrop Coll Lon MTh 02 K Coll Lon DThMin 14. St Steph Ho Ox BTh 93. d 96 p 97. C Westmr St Steph w St Jo *Lon* 96–99; C Kensington St Mary Abbots w St Geo 99–03; V Old Basing and Lychpit *Win* 03–11; AD Basingstoke 08–11; Can Res Guildf Cathl 11–18; Chapl Surrey Univ 11–18; P-in-c Croydon St Jo *S'wark* from 18; P-in-c Croydon St Andr 18–20; Hon Can S'wark Cathl from 20. *84 Higher Drive, Purley CR8 2HJ* T: (020) 8688 8104

BISHOP, Canon Anthony John. b 43. G&C Coll Cam BA 66 MA 69 Lon Univ MTh 69. ALCD 67. d 69 p 70. C Eccleston St Luke *Liv* 69–73; C Gt Baddow *Chelmsf* 73–77; CMS Nigeria 77–84; Lect Lon Bible Coll 84–85; TV Chigwell *Chelmsf* 85–93; P-in-c Walthamstow St Jo 93–98; V 98–09; rtd 09; Hon Can Kano from 00; PtO *Chelmsf* from 12. *7 High Meadows, Chigwell IG7 5JY* T: (020) 8501 4998 E: tony_bishop@talktalk.net

BISHOP, Canon Christopher. b 48. St Aug Coll Cant 71. d 72 p 73. C Gt Ilford St Mary *Chelmsf* 72–75; C Upminster 75–78; Adn's Youth Chapl 77–80; Dioc Youth Officer 80–86; Chapl Stansted Airport 86–13; P-in-c Manuden w Berden 86–03; P-in-c Manuden w Berden and Quendon w Rickling 03–13; RD Newport and Stansted 89–05; Hon Can Chelmsf Cathl 99–13; rtd 13; PtO *Chelmsf* from 14. *2 St Mary's View, Saffron Walden CB10 2GF* T: (01799) 523722 E: chrismitre@hotmail.com

BISHOP, Craig. *See* BISHOP, Stephen Craig

BISHOP, David. b 65. St Jo Coll Nottm 01. d 03 p 04. C Boulton *Derby* 03–07; V Ogley Hay *Lich* 07–19; TV Stroudwater *Glouc* from 19. *The Vicarage, Elm Road, Stonehouse GL10 2NP* T: (01453) 822332

BISHOP, Mrs Evelyn Joy. b 43. d 01 p 02. NSM Penkridge *Lich* 01–04; NSM Baswich 04–18; PtO 18–21. *21 Farmdown Road, Stafford ST17 0AP* T: (01785) 603074

BISHOP, Huw Daniel. b 49. Univ of Wales (Lamp) BA 71. Bp Burgess Hall Lamp 71. d 73 p 74. C Carmarthen St Pet *St D* 73–77; Prov Youth Chapl Wales 77–79; V Llanybydder and Llanwnog w Llanwnnen *St D* 79–80; Youth and Community Officer 80–81; Hd RS Carre's Gr Sch Sleaford 81–85; Hd RS K Sch Pet 85–91; Assoc Hd Teacher St Pet Colleg Sch Wolv 91–98; Hd Teacher St Teilo's High Sch Cardiff 98–01; Prin St Pet Colleg Sch Wolv 01–10; Asst Dioc Dir of Educn *Lich* 10–13; PtO 11–19; *St D* 13–14; CF (VR) from 85. *Ger y Bryn, 217 Waterloo Road, Penygroes, Llanelli SA14 7RB*

BISHOP, The Ven Ian Gregory. b 62. Portsm Poly BSc 84 MRICS 87. Oak Hill Th Coll BA 91. d 91 p 92. C Purley Ch Ch *S'wark* 91–95; P-in-c Saxlingham Nethergate and Shotesham *Nor* 95–97; TR Newton Flotman, Swainsthorpe, Tasburgh, etc 98–01; V Middlewich w Byley *Ches* 01–11; RD Middlewich 05–10; Adn Macclesfield from 11. *57A Sandbach Road, Congleton CW12 4LH* T: (01260) 272875 M: 07715-102519 E: ian.bishop@chester.anglican.org

BISHOP, Jeremy Simon. b 54. Nottm Univ BSc 75 Yonsei Univ S Korea 84. All Nations Chr Coll 82 Wycliffe Hall Ox 89. d 91 p 92. C Macclesfield Team *Ches* 91–98; R Carlton Colville w Mutford and Rushmere *Nor* 98–99; V Carlton Colville and Mutford 99–19; RD Lothingland 14–18; rtd 19; PtO *Nor* from 20. *Corner Cottage, 14 Church Street, Trimingham, Norwich NR11 8AL* E: jeremybishop532@gmail.com

BISHOP, John Charles Simeon. b 46. Chich Th Coll 77. d 79 p 79. SSF 66–86; P-in-c Edin St Dav 82–86; Chapl to the Deaf *Birm* 86–99; C Portsea N End St Mark *Portsm* 99–01; Chapl to the Deaf *Linc* 01–11; rtd 11; PtO *Dur* from 11; *Newc* 14–19. *66 York Crescent, Durham DH1 5PU* T: 0191-384 8838 E: jcsbishop@btinternet.com

BISHOP, Joy. *See* BISHOP, Evelyn Joy

BISHOP, Kathleen Rachel. b 51. Open Univ BA 88 Saffron Walden Coll CertEd 76. ERMC 05. d 08 p 09. NSM Raddesley Gp *Ely* 08–12; NSM Balsham, Weston Colville, W Wickham etc 12–18; NSM Gt w Lt Abington 12–18;

NSM Hildersham 12–18; NSM Granta Vale Gp from 18. *14 Granta Vale, Linton, Cambridge CB21 4LB* T: (01223) 892288 E: revkathy@hotmail.co.uk *or* michael.bishop@virgin.net

BISHOP, Mrs Louise Suzanne. b 64. St Aug Coll of Th 16. **d** 19 **p** 20. C Weybridge *Guildf* from 19. *87 Greenlands Road, Weybridge KT13 8PS* M: 07974-018160 E: louisebshp@aol.com

BISHOP, Mandy Louise. b 61. Univ of E Lon BA 00. NTMTC BA 09. **d** 09 **p** 10. C Moulsham St Luke *Chelmsf* 09–13; V Ormesby St Marg w Scratby, Ormesby St Mich etc *Nor* 13–19; R Kessingland, Gisleham and Rushmere from 19; Jt RD Lothingland 20–21. *The Rectory, 1 Wash Lane, Kessingland, Lowestoft NR33 7QZ* T: (01502) 743154 M: 07854-790234 E: revdmandy@btinternet.com

BISHOP, His Honour Judge Mark Andrew. b 58. Down Coll Cam BA 80 MA 83 Barrister 81. EAMTC 99. **d** 02 **p** 03. Dep Chan *Roch* from 01; NSM Cambridge St Mary Less *Ely* from 02; Chan *Linc* from 07. *Inner London Crown Court, Sessions House, Newington Causeway, London SE1 6AZ* T: (01223) 264527 *or* (020) 7234 3100

BISHOP, Mark Christopher. b 81. Sheff Hallam Univ BA 03. **d** 08 **p** 09. C Oak Tree Angl Fellowship *Lon* 08–11; LtO 11–14; Pioneer Min from 14. *19 Larch Avenue, London W3 7LH* M: 07779-585105 E: revmarkbishop@gmail.com

BISHOP, Philip Michael. b 47. Lon Univ BD 69 AKC 69. St Aug Coll Cant 70. **d** 71 **p** 72. C Mansfield Woodhouse *S'well* 71–76; C Liscard St Mary w St Columba *Ches* 76–78; V Thornton-le-Moors w Ince and Elton 78–90; V Sutton w Carlton and Normanton upon Trent etc *S'well* 90–96; P-in-c Ch Broughton w Barton Blount, Boylestone etc *Derby* 96–98; P-in-c Longford, Long Lane, Dalbury and Radbourne 96–98; R Boylestone, Church Broughton, Dalbury, etc 98–17; rtd 17; PtO *S'well* from 18. *17 Beech Avenue, Keyworth, Nottingham NG12 5DE* T: 0115-937 5637 E: rev@michael.bishop.name

BISHOP, Philip William. b 67. Loughb Univ BSc 90. St Mellitus Coll 18. **d** 20 **p** 21. C Weaverham *Ches* from 20. *272 Chester Road, Hartford, Northwich CW8 1QW* M: 07716-887442 E: pwbishop@hotmail.com

BISHOP, Phillip Leslie. b 44. K Coll Lon BD 66 AKC 66. **d** 67 **p** 68. C Albrighton *Lich* 67–70; C St Geo-in-the-East St Mary *Lon* 70–71; C Middlesbrough Ascension *York* 71–73; P-in-c Withernwick 73–77; Ind Chapl 73–82; V Gt Ayton w Easby and Newton-in-Cleveland 82–89; RD Stokesley 85–89; R Guisborough 89–08; Chapl S Tees Community and Mental Health NHS Trust 90–99; Chapl Tees and NE Yorks NHS Trust 99–08; Chapl Langbaurgh Primary Care Trust 02–08; rtd 08; PtO *York* 08–18; *Dur* from 13. *2 Sunny Side Grove, Stockton-on-Tees TS18 5DH* T: (01642) 582281 E: 317bishop@gmail.com

BISHOP, Roger John. b 49. SEITE 06. **d** 09 **p** 10. NSM Lamberhurst and Matfield *Roch* 09–19; rtd 19. *Brambletye, Maidstone Road, Five Oak Green, Tonbridge TN12 6QR* T: (01892) 833232 E: rogerjbishop@hotmail.com

BISHOP, Simeon. *See* BISHOP, John Charles Simeon

BISHOP, Stephen Craig. b 68. Wye Coll Lon BSc 90 Man Univ MA 92 Ex Univ MPhil 97 Glos Univ PGCE 98. Wycliffe Hall Ox 03. **d** 05 **p** 06. C Thornbury and Oldbury-on-Severn w Shepperdine *Glouc* 05–09; TV S Cotswolds 09–14; TR Vale and Cotswold Edge from 14. *The Vicarage, Church Street, Chipping Campden GL55 6JG* T: (01386) 840677 E: scriagbishop@hotmail.com

BISHOP, Stephen John. b 62. Hull Univ BA 84 PGCE 86. Ripon Coll Cuddesdon 90 Ch Div Sch of the Pacific (USA) 90. **d** 92 **p** 93. C Spixton *Leic* 92–95; C Market Harborough 95–97; TV Market Harborough and The Transfiguration etc 97–00; R Six Saints circa Holt from 00; Rural Officer (Leic Adnry) from 01. *The Rectory, Rectory Lane, Medbourne, Market Harborough LE16 8DZ* T: (01858) 565933 M: 07590-829902 E: rector@sixsaintscircaholt.org

BISHOP, Stephen Patrick. b 60. Dioc OLM tr scheme 99. **d** 02 **p** 03. OLM Purley Ch Ch *S'wark* from 02. *Elmwood, 117 Mitchley Avenue, South Croydon CR2 9HP* T: (020) 8651 2840 E: bishopelmwood@aol.com

BISHOP, Mrs Susan Linda. b 66. Trin Coll Bris 12. **d** 15 **p** 16. NSM Filton *Bris* 15–17; NSM Warmley, Syston and Bitton 17–20; PtO *Heref* from 21. *Appletree House, Hereford Street, Presteigne LD8 2AT* E: revsusiebishop.uk@gmail.com

BISSET, Michael Davidson. b 55. NTMTC 96. **d** 99 **p** 00. C Ickenham *Lon* 99–03; P-in-c Penn *Ox* 03–04; P-in-c Tyler's Green 03–04; V Penn and Tylers Green from 04. *The Vicarage, Church Road, Penn, High Wycombe HP10 8NU* T: (01494) 816700 E: vicar@holytrinityandstmargarets.co.uk

BISSETT, William Campbell. b 68. Westmr Coll Lon BA 89 PGCE 90 Cliff Coll MA 98 GradICSA 04. STETS 10. **d** 12 **p** 13. NSM Virginia Water *Guildf* 12–19; NSM Egham from

19. Cedar Cottage, Mount Lee, Egham TW20 9PD T: (01784) 434873 M: 07900-227748 E: w.bissett@ntlworld.com

BISSEX, Mrs Janet Christine Margaret. b 50. Westhill Coll Birm CertEd 72. Trin Coll Bris 76. **dss** 86 **d** 87 **p** 94. Toxteth Park St Bede *Liv* 86–93; Par Dn 87–93; Dn-in-c Kirkdale St Mary and St Athanasius 93–94; P-in-c 94–03; C Litherland St Andr 03; TV Bootle 04–12; rtd 12; PtO *Liv* from 16. *4 Garth Court, Haigh Road, Liverpool L22 3XL* T: 0151-538 4767 E: revjanetb@yahoo.co.uk

BISSON, Joyce Elaine. b 52. Liv Univ BTh 98 Nottm Coll of Educn TCert 73. NOC 06. **d** 08 **p** 09. NSM Gt Meols *Ches* 08–11; NSM Bromborough 11–16; PtO from 17. *14 Howbeck Drive, Prenton CH43 6UY* T: 0151-652 7888 E: elainebisson@yahoo.co.uk

BISTRAN, Petrica. b 85. Pentecostal Inst Bucharest BA 08 St Jo Coll Dur BA 15 MATM 16. Cranmer Hall Dur 13. **d** 16 **p** 17. C Silksworth *Dur* 16–18; C Sunderland St Matt and St Wilfrid 18–19. *2 Windmill Road, London N18 1PA* M: 07772-028520 E: petricabistran@yahoo.com

BJARNASON, Bjarni Thor. b 62. Univ of Iceland MSc 10. **p** 91. Iceland 91–97 and from 01; C Brumby *Linc* 99–01; PtO *Eur* 07–13; P-in-c Angl Congregation Iceland from 13. *Fannafold 87, 112 Reykjavík, Iceland* T: (00354) 565 8290 M: (00354) 899 6979 E: srbjarni@seltjarnarneskirkja.is

BLACK, Canon Alexander Stevenson. b 28. Glas Univ MA 53. Edin Th Coll 53. **d** 55 **p** 56. C Dumfries *Glas* 55–58; Chapl Glas Univ 58–61; C Glas St Mary 58–61; P-in-c E Kilbride 61–69; R Edin St Columba 69–79; TV Edin St Jo 79–83; R Haddington 83–93; R Dunbar 83–93; rtd 93; Can St Mary's Cathl *Edin* 88–00; Hon Can St Mary's Cathl from 00. *3 Bass Rock View, Canty Bay, North Berwick EH39 5PJ* T: (01620) 894771 E: alexander3black@btinternet.com

BLACK, David Roger. b 46. **d** 12 **p** 13. NSM Tattenhall w Burwardsley and Handley *Ches* 12–14; NSM Tilston and Shocklach 14–16; rtd 16; PtO *Ches* from 16. *Woodcroft, Church Road, Tilston, Malpas SY14 7HB* T: (01829) 250615 E: revdavidblack@mail.com

BLACK, Canon Dominic Paul. b 70. S Bank Univ BSc 95 St Jo Coll Dur BA 98 MA 11. Cranmer Hall Dur 95. **d** 98 **p** 99. C N Hull St Mich *York* 98–04; V N Ormesby 04–20; RD Middlesbrough 11–20; P-in-c Kingston upon Hull H Trin 20–21; V from 21; Can and Preb York Minster from 21. *22 Corinthian Way, Hull HU9 1UF* M: 07445-395806 E: dominic.black@hullminster.org

BLACK, The Very Revd Ian Christopher. b 62. Kent Univ BA 85 Nottm Univ MDiv 93. Linc Th Coll 91. **d** 93 **p** 94. C Maidstone All SS and St Phil w Tovil *Cant* 93–96; P-in-c The Brents and Davington w Oare and Luddenham 96–02; Hon Min Can Cant Cathl 97–02; Asst Dir Post-Ord Tr 98–02; V Whitkirk *Ripon* 02–12; Capitular Can Ripon Cathl 08–12; Can Res Pet Cathl 12–21; V Pet St Jo 12–21; RD Pet 15–20; Dean Newport *Mon* from 21. *The Deanery, 105 Stow Hill, Newport NP20 4ED* T: (01633) 259990 E: ianblack@churchinwales.org.uk

BLACK, Miss Imogen Nadine Laura. b 79. Trin Coll Ox BA 02 MA 05 MSt 03. St Steph Ho Ox 08–11 **p** 12. C Belper Ch Ch w Turnditch *Derby* 11–15; P-in-c Somercotes from 15; C Alfreton from 15; AD Hardwick from 21. *St Thomas's Vicarage, 114 Nottingham Road, Somercotes, Alfreton DE55 4LY* T: (01773) 603793 E: imogen.black@trinity-oxford.com

BLACK (formerly NAPIER), Jennifer Beryl. b 39. S Dios Minl Tr Scheme 89. **d** 93 **p** 96. NSM Itchen Valley *Win* 93–01; PtO from 02; Hon C Cupar *St And* from 05. *Forresters Cottage, Edenwood, Cupar KY15 5NX* T: (01334) 653159 *or* (01962) 771702 E: jenniblackedenwood@yahoo.co.uk

BLACK, Canon Neville. b 36. MBE 97. Oak Hill Th Coll 61. **d** 64 **p** 65. C Everton St Ambrose w St Tim *Liv* 64–69; P-in-c Everton St Geo 69–71; V 71–81; P-in-c Everton St Benedict 70–72; P-in-c Everton St Chad w Ch Ch 70–72; Nat Project Officer Evang Urban Tr Project 74–81; TR St Luke in the City *Liv* 81–04; Chapl Liv Women's Hosp NHS Trust 82–04; Tutor NOC 82–89; Dir Gp for Urban Min and Leadership *Liv* 84–95; P-in-c Edgehill St Dunstan 98–04; Hon Can Liv Cathl 87–04; rtd 05; PtO *Liv* from 05. *19 Montfort Drive, Liverpool L19 3RJ* T: 0151-427 9803 M: 07970-235817 E: nevilleblack55a@me.com

BLACK, Samuel James. b 38. CITC 84. **d** 68 **p** 69. C Cloughfern *Conn* 68–72; C Lisburn St Paul 72–78; I Rasharkin w Finvoy 78–82; I Belfast Upper Malone (Epiphany) 82–95; I Ballymore *Arm* 95–05; rtd 05. *Toberhewny Hall, 22 Toberhewny Lane, Lurgan, Craigavon BT66 8JZ* T: (028) 3834 3267 E: sblack381@btinternet.com

BLACK, William Henry. St Deiniol's Hawarden. **d** 88 **p** 89. NSM Malahide w Balgriffin *D & G* 88–89; NSM Dublin St Ann and St Steph 89–94; C 94–00; Hon Asst Chapl Miss to Seamen 89–00; I Dublin Drumcondra w N Strand *D & G*

00–07; rtd 07. *27 Greendale Avenue, Dublin 5, Republic of Ireland* T: (00353) (1) 832 3141 M: 86-150 3747

BLACKALL, Mrs Ivy Margaret. b 38. St Kath Coll Lon CertEd 58. EAMTC 82. **dss** 86 **d** 87 **p** 94. NSM Wickham Market w Pettistree and Easton *St E* 86–88; Par Dn Leiston 88–92; Par Dn Gt and Lt Glemham, Blaxhall etc 92–94; P-in-c 94–96; R 96–02; P-in-c Sternfield w Benhall and Snape 98–02; rtd 03; PtO *St E* 03–21. *6 Orchard Place, Wickham Market, Woodbridge IP13 0RU* T: (01728) 747326 M: 07850-632900 E: mgtblack@globalnet.co.uk *or* margaret@mgtblack.plus.com

BLACKBURN, Anne Dorothy. *See* WOOD, Anne Dorothy

BLACKBURN, David James. b 45. Hull Univ BA 67. Trin Coll Bris 85. **d** 87 **p** 88. C Bromsgrove St Jo *Worc* 87–90; V Cradley 90–01; R Kinver and Enville *Lich* 01–12; rtd 12; PtO *Worc* from 12. *39 Milestone Drive, Hagley, Stourbridge DY9 0LW* T: (01562) 720389 E: davidblackburn43@gmail.com

BLACKBURN, Helen Claire. b 55. Leeds Univ BA 76 MA 99 PGCE 78 ARCM 75. NOC 96. **d** 99 **p** 00. C Sheff Cathl 99–01; Asst Chapl Cen Sheff Univ Hosps NHS Trust 01–04; Chapl Sheff Teaching Hosps NHS Trust 04–06; C Ranmoor *Sheff* 06–07; P-in-c Abbeydale St Jo 07–09; Lead Chapl Willowbrook Hospice 10–13; TR E Widnes *Liv* 13–17; rtd 17; PtO *Sheff* 18–19 and from 21; Chapl Sheff Teaching Hosps NHS Foundn Trust 19–20. *9 Ventnor Place, Sheffield S7 1LA* M: 07714-329638 E: helen_blackburn@hotmail.co.uk

BLACKBURN, Jane Elizabeth. *See* PROUDFOOT, Jane Elizabeth

BLACKBURN, Jay Johnson. b 54. Univ of Wales BA 06 N Staffs Poly BA 76. Lindisfarne Regional Tr Partnership 19. **d** 19. NSM Haughton le Skerne *Dur* from 19; NSM Sadberge from 19. *34 Troon Avenue, Darlington DL1 3HY* T: (01325) 460151 M: 07900-984302 E: paddlerjay@aol.com

BLACKBURN, The Ven John. b 47. CB 04. Open Univ BA 88. St Mich Coll Llan 66. **d** 71 **p** 72. C Risca *Mon* 71–76; CF (TA) 73–76; CF 76–99; Dep Chapl-Gen 99–00; Chapl-Gen 00–04; Adn for the Army 99–04; QHC from 96; Hon Can Ripon Cathl 01–04; V Risca *Mon* 04–13; V Lower Islwyn 13; rtd 13; PtO *Mon* from 14. *St Hilary, 11 Gelli Avenue, Risca, Newport NP11 6QF* E: venblackburn@aol.com

BLACKBURN, Sister Judith Elizabeth. b 58. SEITE 99. **d** 02 **p** 03. NSM Old Ford St Paul and St Mark *Lon* 02–05; P-in-c Bethnal Green St Pet w St Thos 05–11; NSM Bethnal Green St Matt w St Jas the Gt from 11. *St Saviour's Priory, 18 Queensbridge Road, London E2 8NX* T: (020) 7739 9976 M: 07855-510393 E: judithblackburn@aol.com

BLACKBURN, Keith Christopher. b 39. K Coll Lon BD 63 AKC 63. St Boniface Warminster 63. **d** 64 **p** 65. C Surbiton St Andr *S'wark* 64–66; C Battersea St Mary 67–70; Teacher Sir Walter St John Sch Battersea 67–70; Hon C Eltham H Trin *S'wark* 70–76; Hd of Ho Crown Woods Sch Eltham 70–76; Dep Hd Master Altwood C of E Sch Maidenhead 76–82; LtO *Ox* 76–82; Hd Master and Chapl St Geo Sch Gravesend 83–93; Hon C Fawkham and Hartley *Roch* 83–93; V Seal SS Pet and Paul 93–05; rtd 05; PtO *Heref* 05–16. *The College of St Barnabas, Blackberry Lane, Lingfield RH7 6NJ* T: (01342) 872848 E: revkcb@btinternet.com

✠**BLACKBURN, The Rt Revd Richard Finn.** b 52. St Jo Coll Dur BA 74 Hull Univ MA 97. Westcott Ho Cam 81. **d** 83 **p** 84 **c** 09. C Stepney St Dunstan and All SS *Lon* 83–87; P-in-c Isleworth St Jo 87–92; V Mosborough *Sheff* 92–99; RD Attercliffe 96–99; Hon Can Sheff Cathl 98–99; Adn Sheff and Rotherham 99–09; Can Res Sheff Cathl 99–05; Suff Bp Warrington *Liv* 09–18; rtd 18; PtO *Sheff* from 18; Hon Asst Bp Sheff from 19. *9 Ventnor Place, Sheffield S7 1LA* E: bishoprichard.blackburn@hotmail.com

BLACKBURN, Archdeacon of. *See* IRELAND, The Ven Mark Campbell

BLACKBURN, Bishop of. *See* HENDERSON, The Rt Revd Julian Tudor

BLACKBURN, Dean of. *See* HOWELL JONES, The Very Revd Peter

BLACKBURNE, John. b 62. Lanc Univ LLB 84 Leic Univ MBA 09. St Aug Coll of Th 17. **d** 20 **p** 21. NSM Notting Hill All SS w St Columb *Lon* from 20; NSM Notting Hill St Mich and Ch Ch from 20. *18 Monroe House, Lorne Close, London NW8 7JN* M: 07939-076594 E: blackburnejohn@hotmail.com

BLACKDEN, Mrs Diane Janice. b 40. **d** 06. NSM Buxted and Hadlow Down *Chich* 06–18; rtd 18; PtO *Chich* from 18. *Oak Hill, Five Ashes, Mayfield TN20 6HL* T: (01435) 872082

BLACKER, Herbert John. b 36. Bris Univ BSc 59. Cranmer Hall Dur. **d** 61 **p** 62. C Wednesbury St Bart *Lich* 61–63; C Chasetown 63–65; C Chigwell *Chelmsf* 65–69; TV Barnham Broom w Kimberley, Bixton etc *Nor* 69–76; P-in-c Garveston w Thuxton 69–76; R Burgh Parva w Briston 76–92; C Melton

Constable w Swanton Novers 86–92; R Briston w Burgh Parva and Melton Constable 92–01; rtd 01; PtO *Nor* from 01; *St E* 04–10. *Webdor, Olney Road, Dereham NR19 2BZ*

BLACKETT, James Gilbert. b 27. Tyndale Hall Bris 52. **d** 55 **p** 56. C Heworth H Trin *York* 55–57; C Newburn *Newc* 57–58; C Newc St Barn and St Jude 58–61; V Broomfleet *York* 61–67; V Ledsham 67–74; V Burton All SS *Lich* 74–82; V Burton All SS w Ch Ch 82–92; rtd 92; PtO *Ox* 92–11; *Pet* from 92. *103 Milford Avenue, Stony Stratford, Milton Keynes MK11 1EZ* T: (01908) 265149 E: jjgblackett@gmail.com

BLACKETT, Robert Peter. b 63. Dur Univ BSc 85 Open Univ BSc 07. Ripon Coll Cuddesdon BTh 95. **d** 95 **p** 96. C Wigton *Carl* 95–00; R Bowness-on-Solway, Kirkbride and Newton Arlosh 00–19; PtO *York* from 19. *Lyngreen, Moor Lane, Cloughton, Scarborough YO13 0AH*

BLACKFORD, Barry Douglas. b 52. Southn Inst BSc 96 MCMI 00 MBCS 04. STETS 05. **d** 08 **p** 09. C N Poole Ecum Team *Sarum* 08–12; TV Melksham 12–14; TR 14–19; rtd 19. *Meadowcroft, 103 Church Road, Laverstock, Salisbury SP1 1RB* M: 07866-430428 E: revbor@hotmail.co.uk

BLACKLEDGE, David John. b 51. Oak Hill Th Coll 89. **d** 92 **p** 93. NSM Woodford Wells *Chelmsf* from 92. *Hornbeam, 143 Monkhams Lane, Woodford Green IG8 0NW* T: (020) 8262 7690 E: davidjblackledge@aol.com

BLACKLEY, Miles. b 69. Wycliffe Hall Ox. **d** 05 **p** 06. C Ches Square St Mich w St Phil *Lon* 05–08; C St Olave Hart Street w All Hallows Staining etc 08–10; C St Kath Cree 08–10; PtO *S'wark* from 11. *22 Assembly Apartments, 24 York Grove, London SE15 2NZ* E: milesblackley@gmail.com

BLACKMAN, Clive John. b 51. Hull Univ BSc 73 MSc 74. Qu Coll Birm 75. **d** 78 **p** 79. C Folkestone St Sav *Cant* 78–81; Chapl Birm Univ 81–86; V Thorpe St Matt *Nor* 86–94; R Cringleford w Colney and Bawburgh 94–98; Asst Dir Lay and Reader Tr 98–03; Dir Reader Tr 03–11; Chapl Nor City Coll of F&HE 03–15; rtd 15. *13 Norvic Drive, Norwich NR4 7NN* T: (01603) 505776

BLACKMAN, Michael Orville. b 46. Univ of W Ontario BMin 80. Codrington Coll Barbados 67. **d** 71 **p** 71. C St Jo Cathl Antigua 71–73; R H Innocents w St Sav Barbados 73–78; Hon C Westminster St Jas Canada 78–80; P-in-c St Patr Barbados 80–86; TV E Ham w Upton Park and Forest Gate *Chelmsf* 86–91; R St Pet Barbados 91–97; V Dalton *Sheff* 97–03; P-in-c Raynes Park St Sav *S'wark* 03–10; P-in-c S Wimbledon All SS 03–10; V Raynes Park St Sav and S Wimbledon All SS 10–16; rtd 16; PtO *S'wark* from 16. *80 Phyllis Avenue, New Malden KT3 6JZ* T: (020) 3737 0196 E: michaelblackman1@sky.com

BLACKMORE, Miss Eunice Sheila. b 57. Bris Univ BSc 79. All SS Cen for Miss & Min 12. **d** 16 **p** 17. NSM Higher Bebington *Ches* from 16. *4 Elms Park, Thingwall, Wirral CH61 9PJ* T: 0151-648 5343 M: 07763-890840 E: euniceblackmore@talktalk.net

BLACKMORE, Frank Ellis. b 43. Univ of Wales (Lamp) BA 66 Univ of Wales (Trin St Dav) MTh 12. Wells Th Coll 65. **d** 67 **p** 68. C S'wark St Geo 67–70; Hon C Camberwell St Giles 70–79; Pet 77–79; LtO 79–13; PtO *Ex* from 13; *Lon* from 13. *Address temp unknown*

BLACKMORE, Robert Ivor. b 37. Univ of Wales (Lamp) 59 Open Univ BA 78 Univ of Wales MTh 94. **d** 62 **p** 63. C Llangynwyd w Maesteg *Llan* 62–65; C Dowlais 65–67; C Neath w Llantwit 67–71; V Fochriw w Deri 71–73; V Troedrhiwgarth 73–80; V Seven Sisters 80–00; rtd 02. *28 Hen Parc Lane, Upper Killay, Swansea SA2 7EY*

BLACKSHAW, Brian Martin. b 43. Lanc Univ MA 74 Ch Ch Ox BA 95 MA 96. Ox NSM Course 87. **d** 90 **p** 91. NSM Amersham *Ox* 90–93; C Hatch End St Anselm *Lon* 93–95; V Cheshunt *St Alb* 96–07; rtd 07; PtO *St Alb* from 13; *Lon* from 13. *Holly Bush, Flaunden Lane, Flaunden, Hemel Hempstead HP3 0PQ* T: (01442) 832254 E: brianblackshaw@f2s.com

BLACKWALL, David d'Arcy Russell. b 35. Southn Univ BSc 60. Wycliffe Hall Ox 63. **d** 65 **p** 66. C Southampton Thornhill St Chris *Win* 65–68; V Long Sutton 69–72; Chapl Lord Wandsworth Coll Hook 69–74; Hon C Odiham w S Warnborough *Win* 72–75; Chapl St Lawr Coll Ramsgate 75–95; Hd Jun Sch 95–97; rtd 97; PtO *Sarum* from 98; *Eur* 09–18. *3 Constable Way, Salisbury SP2 8LN* T: (01722) 335695 E: dandmblackwall@btopenworld.com

BLACKWELL-SMYTH, Charles Peter Bernard. b 42. TCD BA 64 MA 71 MB 73. Gen Th Sem (NY) MDiv 65. **d** 65 **p** 66. C Bangor Abbey *D & D* 65–67; C Dublin Ch Ch Leeson Park *D & G* 67–69; P-in-c Carbury *M & K* 73–75; Hon C St Stephen in Brannel *Truro* 87–94; PtO from 94. *Parcgwyn, Rectory Road, St Stephen, St Austell PL26 7RL* T: (01726) 822465 E: blackwellsmyth@gmail.com

BLACOE, Brian Thomas. b 36. Open Univ BA. Oak Hill Th Coll 63. **d** 66 **p** 67. C Dundonald *D & D* 66–69; C Drumcree

Arm 69–74; I Ardtrea w Desertcreat 74–78; I Annalong *D & D* 78–95; I Knocknamuckley 95–08; Can Dromore Cathl 93–08; Prec 02–08; rtd 08. *91 Richmond Drive, Tandragee, Craigavon BT62 2GW* T: (028) 3884 2029 M: 07745-564056 E: briantblacoe@icloud.com

BLADE, Mrs Susan Joan. b 58. SEITE 97. **d** 00 **p** 01. NSM Wateringbury and Teston *Roch* 00–02; Asst Chapl Maidstone and Tunbridge Wells NHS Trust 00–02; Sen Chapl 02–06; Chapl Cant Ch Chr Univ 07–10; P-in-c Sampford Peverell, Uplowman, Holcombe Rogus etc *Ex* 10–11; TR 11–17. *The Molehole, South Pool, Kingsbridge TQ7 2RW* M: 07960-104173 E: sue.blade@gmail.com

BLADEN, Mrs Catherine Robin. b 64. ERMC 12. **d** 15 **p** 16. C Sancroft *St E* 15–18; R Hepworth, Hinderclay, Wattisfield and Thelnetham 18; R Stanton, Hopton, Market Weston, Barningham etc 18; R Stanton from 18. *The Rectory, 1 Old Rectory Gardens, Stanton, Bury St Edmunds IP31 2JH* T: (01359) 250239 E: revcathybladen@gmail.com

BLAGDEN, Ms Susan. b 64. Ox Min Course 89 Ripon Coll Cuddesdon 97. **d** 99 **p** 00. C Grantham St Wulfram *Linc* 99–03; Asst Chapl Stoke Mandeville Hosp NHS Trust 03–10; R Bangor Monachorum, Worthenbury and Marchwiel *St As* 10–12; R Bro Enlli *Ban* 12–14; Tr and Voc Officer 14–15; C Dwylan 14–15; Tutor St Padarn's Inst from 15. *Address withheld by request* E: blagdensm@gmail.com

BLAINE, Alastair John Park. b 79. Westmr Coll of Educn BEd 03. Ripon Coll Cuddesdon 11. **d** 13 **p** 14. C Witney *Ox* 13–17; Chapl RN from 17; PtO *Ex* from 20. *Royal Naval Chaplaincy Service Headquarters, Tanner Building, HMS Excellent, Whale Island, Portsmouth PO2 8ER* T: 0300-157 7544 E: rev.alastair.blaine@gmail.com

BLAINE (*née* King), **Helen Sarah Elizabeth.** b 81. Middx Univ BSc 04. Ripon Coll Cuddesdon BA 15. **d** 15 **p** 16. C Aldenham, Radlett and Shenley *St Alb* 15–18; P-in-c Ashreigney *Ex* from 18; P-in-c Broadwoodkelly from 18; P-in-c Brushford from 18; P-in-c Winkleigh from 18. *The Vicarage, Torrington Road, Winkleigh EX19 8HR* T: (01837) 83710 E: revhelenblaine@outlook.com

BLAIR, Catherine Jill. b 62. Nottm Univ BA 84 BArch 87 RIBA 88. St Jo Coll Nottm MA 02. **d** 02 **p** 03. C Goldsworth Park *Guildf* 02–06; C Woking St Paul 06–16; RD Woking 10–16; Jt V Walton-on-Thames from 16. *The Vicarage, 27 Bowes Road, Walton-on-Thames KT12 3HT* T: (01932) 917736 E: cathy@waltonparish.org.uk

BLAIR, Henry. *See* BLAIR, William Henry

BLAIR, John Wallace. b 48. Lon Univ BSc 70. Qu Coll Birm 79. **d** 81 **p** 82. C Chorlton-cum-Hardy St Werburgh *Man* 81–83; CF 83–97; I Faughanvale *D & R* 97–13; Can Derry Cathl 09–13; rtd 13; Chapl Madeira *Eur* 14–17; PtO *Ox* 18–20; TV Langtree from 20. *The Vicarage, Crabtree Corner, Ipsden, Wallingford OX10 6BN* E: revjwblair@gmail.com

BLAIR, Jonathan Lewis. Nottm Univ BA 84 ACA 88. St Jo Coll Nottm. **d** 02 **p** 03. C Goldsworth Park *Guildf* 02–06; P-in-c Woking St Paul 06–16; Jt V Walton-on-Thames from 16. *The Vicarage, 27 Bowes Road, Walton-on-Thames KT12 3HT* T: (01932) 917736 E: jonny@waltonparish.org.uk

BLAIR, William Henry. b 66. QUB BAgr 89 TCD BTh 04. CITC 01. **d** 04 **p** 05. C Monaghan w Tydavnet and Kilmore *Clogh* 04–06; C Magheraculmoney 06–11; I 11–19; Can Clogh Cathl 15–19; I Tullaniskin w Clonoe *Arm* from 19. *The Rectory, 215 Brackaville Road, Dungannon BT71 4EJ* T: (028) 8774 1297 M: 07842-070152 E: henry1blair@gmail.com

BLAIR-CHAPPELL, Mrs Elcineide. b 47. Sao Paulo Univ Brazil 74 Birm Poly PGCE 88. WMMTC 00. **d** 03 **p** 04. NSM Erdington Birm 03–08; NSM Birm St Martin w Bordesley St Andr from 08; Hon Chapl Birm Children's Hosp NHS Foundn Trust from 07. *18 Kempson Avenue, Sutton Coldfield B72 1HJ* T: 0121-682 5340

BLAKE, Ian Martyn. b 57. Oak Hill Th Coll BA 79. **d** 80 **p** 81. C Widford *Chelmsf* 80–84; C Barton Seagrave w Warkton *Pet* 84–90; V Sneinton St Chris w St Phil *S'well* 90–01; C Howell Hill w Burgh Heath *Guildf* 01–06; PtO 06–12; *S'wark* 08–12; P-in-c Thornton Heath St Paul 12–15; V Skirbeck H Trin *Linc* 15–18. *42 Bartlemere, Barnard Castle DL12 8LR* M: 07904-340783

BLAKE, Mrs Margaret. b 48. Open Univ BA 87. S'wark Ord Course 92. **d** 95 **p** 96. C Farnham *Guildf* 95–01; P-in-c Farncombe 01–05; R 05–09; rtd 09. *Tan-y-Llan, Llanfihangel-Nant-Bran, Brecon LD3 9NA* T: (01874) 636390 E: tanyllan2@gmail.com

BLAKE, Peter Stanley. **d** 18 **p** 19. Belfast Whiterock *Conn* 18–19; C Antrim All SS from 19. *16 Monaville Drive, Lisburn BT28 2DR* T: (028) 9264 0142 M: 07751-338331 E: rev.peterblake@gmail.com

BLAKE, Stephen. b 59. Ch Coll Cam MA 85 Wadh Coll Ox BM, BCh 84 MRCGP 88. Ox Min Course 07. **d** 10

p 11. NSM Burford w Fulbrook, Taynton, Asthall etc *Ox* 10–13; NSM Chipping Norton 13–15; NSM Broadwell, Evenlode, Oddington, Adlestrop etc *Glouc* from 15; Chapl HM Pris Long Lartin from 15. *HM Prison Long Lartin, South Littleton, Evesham WR11 8TZ* T: (01386) 295100 E: sb@evenlodevalechurches.org

BLAKELEY, John Michael. b 77. Lanc Univ BA 99 PGCE 00. St Mellitus Coll 17. **d** 19 **p** 20. C Nottingham St Nic *S'well* 19–21; P-in-c Sneinton St Steph w St Matthias from 21. *The Vicarage, 19 Marston Road, Nottingham NG3 7AN* M: 07722-713450 E: jmblakeley1998@gmail.com

BLAKELEY, Lynda Jean. b 76. St Martin's Coll Lanc BA 99 Middx Univ MA 21. St Mellitus Coll 19. **d** 21. C Sneinton St Steph w St Matthias *S'well* from 21; C Nottingham St Nic from 21. *The Vicarage, 19 Marston Road, Nottingham NG3 7AN* E: chattolynda@gmail.com

BLAKELY, Denise Irene. *See* CADDOO, Denise Irene

BLAKELY, Mark Francis James. b 75. Wolv Univ LLB 98 Lon Metrop Univ MA 09 Solicitor 01. St Mellitus Coll BA 15. **d** 15 **p** 16. C Becontree S *Chelmsf* 15–18; Bp's Chapl 18–19; V Lamorbey H Trin *Roch* from 19. *Holy Trinity Vicarage, 1 Hurst Road, Sidcup DA15 9AE* T: (020) 8300 8231 M: 07979-863409 E: mfjblakely@gmail.com

BLAKEMAN, Mrs Janet Mary. b 36. Man Univ BA 57 CertEd 58. Carl Dioc Tr Course 87. **d** 90 **p** 97. NSM Wetheral w Warwick *Carl* 90–97; NSM Thornthwaite cum Braithwaite, Newlands etc 97–01; rtd 01; PtO *Carl* 01–14; *Leeds* 17. *1 The Coach House, Romaldkirk, Barnard Castle DL12 9ED* T: (01833) 650143

BLAKESLEY, John. b 50. Keble Coll Ox BA 72 MA 76. St Steph Ho Ox 72. **d** 74 **p** 75. C Egremont *Carl* 74–77; C Doncaster Ch Ch *Sheff* 77–79; V Auckland St Helen *Dur* 79–94; Chapl Tindale Crescent Hosp Dur 90–94; Tutor St Chad's Coll Dur 95–00; C Ch the King *Newc* 00–03; V Cambois and Sleekburn 03–12; rtd 12; PtO *York* from 12; Lect Th Dur Univ from 91. *11 Clarence Road, Nunthorpe, Middlesbrough TS7 0DA* T: (01642) 318995 E: jblakesley@btinternet.com

BLAKEY, Cedric Lambert. b 54. Fitzw Coll Cam BA 76 MA 80. St Jo Coll Nottm 77. **d** 79 **p** 80. C Cotmanhay *Derby* 79–83; C-in-c Blagreaves St Andr CD 83–89; P-in-c Sinfin Moor 84–89; V Heanor 89–97; RD 94–97; Bp's Dom Chapl 97–05; NSM Derby Cathl 05–10; Hon Can Derby Cathl 02–10; Vice Provost St Mary's Cathl *Glas* 10–18; Dioc Interfaith Adv 14–18; Can St Mary's Cathl *Glas* 17–18; rtd 18; PtO *Edin* from 19. *11 Glenbenna, Walkerburn EH43 6DD* E: revcanclb@gmail.com

BLAKEY, William George. b 51. Southn Univ BSc 72 PGCE 73. Oak Hill Th Coll BA 82. **d** 82 **p** 83. C Cheltenham St Mark *Glouc* 82–85; P-in-c Parkham, Alwington, Buckland Brewer etc *Ex* 85–86; R 86–94; TR 94–01; P-in-c Lundy Is 92–01; RD Hartland 89–96; TR Wareham *Sarum* 01–07; TR Brize Norton and Carterton *Ox* 07–18; AD Witney 08–13; rtd 18; PtO *Glouc* from 19. *7 Chiltern Avenue, Bishops Cleeve, Cheltenham GL52 8XP* T: (01242) 678305 M: 07905-757920 E: bill@theblakeys.co.uk

BLAKEY WILLIAMS, Mrs Diane Patricia. b 53. MBE 08. Univ CertEd 74 Lanc Univ MA 84. Cranmer Hall Dur 84. dss 86 **d** 87 **p** 94. Clubmoor *Liv* 86–90; Par Dn 87–90; Dioc Lay Tr Officer 90–96; Par Dn Everton St Geo 90–94; Assoc P 94–96; Chapl Lanc Univ *Blackb* 96–00; Chapl Edin Univ 00–10; Ldr Still Paths 11–16; PtO *Leeds* from 17. *Meadowcroft, Kettlewell, Skipton BD23 5RL* T: (01756) 761864 E: diwilliams.labyrinth@gmail.com

BLAMEY, Mark Kendall. b 62. Bris Poly BSc 84 MRICS 86. Ripon Coll Cuddesdon 99. **d** 01 **p** 02. C Cowley St Jo *Ox* 01–04; P-in-c Goring w S Stoke 04–07; V Goring and Streatley w S Stoke 07–13; PtO *Win* 14–18; Manager Jersey Alzheimer's Assn from 14; PtO *Cant* 19–22. *6 Gros Puits, Fountain Lane, St Saviour, Jersey JE2 7RL* T: (01534) 631875 E: mkblamey@gmail.com

BLAMIRE, Jean. *See* PROSSER, Jean

BLAMIRE, Philip Gray. b 50. St Pet Coll Birm CertEd 71 Wall Hall Coll Aldenham BEd 76 UEA MA 91. EAMTC 00. **d** 03 **p** 04. C Swaffham *Nor* 03–07; P-in-c Weybourne Gp 07–10; R 10–19; RD Holt 17–19; rtd 20; PtO *Nor* from 20. *13 Rushmer Way, Sheringham NR26 8YA*

BLANCH, Michael Dennis. b 46. TD and Bar 88. Birm Univ BSocSc 69 PhD 75 DipEd 70. Yorks Min Course 07. **d** 09 **p** 10. NSM Askrigg w Stallingbusk *Ripon* 09–12; NSM Hawes and Hardraw 09–12; NSM Eastbourne St Mich *Chich* 12–13; P-in-c Hampden Park and The Hydneye 13–17; PtO 17–18; Hon C Isfield 18–19. *4 Ashburnham Road, Eastbourne BN21 2HU* M: 07792-240684

BLANCH, Paul Frederick. b 56. St Cuth Soc Dur BA 97. Chich Th Coll 83. **d** 86 **p** 87. C Chaddesden St Phil *Derby* 86–88; C Auckland St Andr and St Anne *Dur* 88–91; P-in-c Hunwick

91–94; Chapl HM Pris Edin 98–02; P-in-c Edin St Salvador 98–00; R 00–02; P-in-c Wester Hailes St Luke 00–02; P-in-c Melton *St E* 02–03; P-in-c Ufford w Bredfield and Hasketon 02–03; R Melton and Ufford 03–05; V Meir Heath and Normacot *Lich* 05–09; R Schenectady St Geo USA 09–14; R Redding All SS 14–17; V Kirton in Holland w Algarkirk and Fosdyke *Linc* 17–19; R Ramsgate H Trin *Cant* from 19; R Deal St Andr from 21. *Holy Trinity Rectory, 18 Winterstoke Way, Ramsgate CT11 8AG* T: (01843) 654102 E: ppstfrancis@gmail.com

BLANCHARD, Canon Christopher John. b 46. Univ of Wales (Lamp) BA 70. St Mich Coll Llan 86. **d** 79 **p** 80. NSM Chepstow *Mon* 79–81; NSM Itton and St Arvans w Penterry and Kilgwrrwg etc 81–86; TV Ebbw Vale 87–89; R Llangenni and Llanbedr Ystrad Yw w Patricio *S & B* 89–98; V Chepstow *Mon* 98–17; Hon Can St Woolos Cathl 14–17; rtd 17; Hon C Ross w Walford and Brampton Abbotts *Heref* from 17. *The Vicarage, Walford, Ross-on-Wye HR9 5QP* T: (01989) 762368 M: 07711-961237 E: frchris2@icloud.com

BLANCHARD, Frank Hugh. b 30. St Jo Coll Dur BA 54 MA 62. **d** 55 **p** 56. C Bottesford *Linc* 55–58; CMS 58–65; C Kirby Grindalythe *York* 65–67; V 67–71; C N Grimston w Wharram Percy and Wharram-le-Street 65–67; V 67–71; P-in-c Thorpe Bassett 67–71; P-in-c Settrington 67–68; V Scarborough St Jas 71–79; P-in-c Scarborough H Trin 78–79; V Scarborough St Jas and H Trin 79–86; R Stockton-on-the-Forest w Holtby and Warthill 87–94; rtd 94; P-in-c Rothesay *Arg* 94–96; PtO *York* 00–16. *23 Front Street, Sowerby, Thirsk YO7 1JG* T: (01845) 574446

BLANCHARD, Canon Lawrence Gordon. b 36. Edin Univ MA 60. Linc Th Coll 63. **d** 65 **p** 66. C Woodhouse *Wakef* 65–67; C Cannock *Lich* 67–70; Chapl Waterford Sch Mbabane Swaziland 70–72; R Mbabane All SS 72–75; Lic to Offic 75–76; TV Raveningham *Nor* 76–80; V Ancaster *Linc* 80–87; Dir LNSM 80–87; Can and Preb Linc Cathl 85–88; Dir of Tr CA 88–93; V Roxton w Gt Barford *St Alb* 93–98; rtd 98; PtO *St E* 99–09; *Ely* 09–19. *7A Barton Road, Ely CB7 4HZ* T: (01353) 654133

BLANCHARDE, Hilary Mary. b 61. STETS. **d** 09 **p** 10. NSM Horfield H Trin *Bris* 09–18; PtO 18–20. *149 Abbey Road, Bristol BS9 3QH* E: hilaryblancharde@talktalk.net

BLAND, Caroline Anne. b 61. Glos Univ BEd 04. WEMTC 10. **d** 15 **p** 16. C Wotton St Mary *Glouc* 15–19; V Nailsworth w Shortwood, Horsley etc from 19. *The Vicarage, 3 Vicarage Gardens, Nailsworth, Stroud GL6 0QS* T: (01453) 836536 E: rev.carolinebland@gmail.com

BLAND, Mrs Elizabeth Anne. b 63. Collingwood Coll Dur BA 85. SAOMC 01. **d** 04 **p** 05. C N Shields *Newc* 04–08; V Ashington 08–15; TV Gt Aycliffe *Dur* 15–19; TV Upper Skerne from 19. *St Alban's Vicarage, Trimdon Grange, Trimdon Station TS29 6EX* T: 07497-434304 E: elizabeth.a.bland@gmail.com

BLAND, Jean Elspeth. b 42. K Coll Lon BA 63. Glouc Sch of Min 87. **d** 90 **p** 94. Par Dn Cen Telford *Lich* 90–94; Asst Chapl HM Pris Shrewsbury 92–94; Chapl HM Pris and YOI Doncaster 94–98; C Goole *Sheff* 99; P-in-c Purleigh, Cold Norton and Stow Maries *Chelmsf* 99–08; rtd 08; PtO *Chelmsf* from 11. *33 Seagers, Great Totham, Maldon CM9 8PB* T: (01621) 829646 E: ebland@prowselyon.plus.com

BLAND, Mrs Lesley Nicole. b 57. Ch Ch Coll Cant BEd 78. ERMC 10. **d** 13 **p** 14. NSM Kym Valley *Ely* 13–16; NSM S Leightonstone 17; Chapl Kimbolton Sch 13–17; V The Staughtons w Hail Weston *Ely* from 17; RD St Neots from 21. *The Vicarage, Causeway, Great Staughton, St Neots PE19 5BF* M: 07805-078992 E: revlesnicki@gmail.com

BLANDFORD-BAKER, Canon Neil James. b 64. Dundee Univ BSc 86. St Jo Coll Nottm BTh 92. **d** 93 **p** 94. C The Quinton *Birm* 93–96; V E Acton St Dunstan w St Thos *Lon* 96–06; Dir of Ords Willesden Area 02–06; V Histon *Ely* from 06; P-in-c Impington 06–17; V from 17; RD N Stowe from 07; RD Bourn 16–17; Hon Can Ely Cathl from 16. *The Vicarage, 9A Church Street, Histon, Cambridge CB24 9EP* T: (01223) 320425 or 320420 E: jamesbb@me.com

BLANEY, Laurence. b 41. Open Univ BA 85 Essex Univ MA 88 PhD 95. Oak Hill Th Coll 66. **d** 69 **p** 70. C Leyton St Mary w St Edw *Chelmsf* 69–73; P-in-c Wimbish w Thunderley 73–77; P-in-c Mayland 77–82; P-in-c Steeple 77–82; R Pitsea 82–95; R Pitsea w Nevendon 95–96; P-in-c Mayland 96–06; P-in-c Steeple 96–06; rtd 06; PtO *Chelmsf* 06–12; P-in-c Purleigh 12–15. *14 Piercys, Basildon SS13 3HN* T: (01268) 552254 E: laurie@blaney.info

BLATCHLEY, Ms Elizabeth. b 62. Wycliffe Hall Ox 01. **d** 03 **p** 04. C Northolt St Jos *Lon* 03–06; C Telford Park S'wark 06–11; V Homerton St Luke *Lon* 11–18; C Battersea Fields *S'wark* from 18. *11 Cupar Road, London SW11 4JW* E: betsy.blatchley@southwark.anglican.org

BLATCHLY, Owen Ronald Maxwell. b 30. Bps' Coll Cheshunt 62. **d** 64 **p** 65. C Boxmoor St Jo *St Alb* 64–67; C Boreham Wood All SS 67–69; C Frimley *Guildf* 69–77; V Manaccan w St Anthony-in-Meneage *Truro* 77–82; R Binfield *Ox* 82–97; rtd 97; PtO *Truro* 97–21. *1 Rose Cottages, East Road, Stithians, Truro TR3 7BD* T: (01209) 860845

BLAY, Canon Ian. b 65. Man Univ BA 88. Westcott Ho Cam 89. **d** 91 **p** 92. C Withington St Paul *Man* 91–94; C Elton All SS 94–96; R Droylsden St Andr 96–05; Dioc Ecum Officer 98–05; R Mobberley *Ches* from 05; RD Knutsford from 16; Hon Can Asante Mampong Ghana from 15. *The Rectory, Church Lane, Mobberley, Knutsford WA16 7RA* T: (01565) 873218 M: 07776-195176 E: ianblay@btinternet.com

BLAY, Linda Jean. Warwick Univ DipEd 89 Essex Coll of Educn CertEd. Trin Coll Bris 98. **d** 00 **p** 01. C Foleshill St Paul *Cov* 00–04; C Bilton 04–08; R Fenn Lanes Gp *Leic* 08–21; rtd 21. *Address temp unknown* E: lindablay@hotmail.com

BLEAKLEY, Melvyn Thomas. b 43. K Coll Lon BD 66 AKC 66 Reading Univ TCert 78. **d** 67 **p** 68. C Cross Heath *Lich* 67–70; TV High Wycombe *Ox* 70–77; PtO 77–00; NSM Chalfont St Giles 00–15; NSM Chalfont St Giles, Seer Green and Jordans from 15. *294 Hughenden Road, High Wycombe HP13 5PE* T: (01494) 529315 E: melvynbleakley@gmail.com

BLEASE, Mariama Oluseun. See IFODE-BLEASE, Mariama Oluseun

BLEASE, Oliver Robert. b 86. Leic Univ LLB 10 Ox Univ BA 18 Dur Univ MA 21. Ripon Coll Cuddesdon 15. **d** 18 **p** 19. C R Wootton Bassett *Sarum* 18–21; TV Aldenham, Radlett and Shenley *St Alb* from 21. *The Vicarage, Church Field, Watling Street, Radlett WD7 8EE* T: (01923) 289720

BLEAZARD, John George. b 57. Univ of Wales (Abth) BA 79 Qu Coll Birm MA 06. Ripon Coll Cuddesdon 06. **d** 08 **p** 10. C Gt Cornard *St E* 08–11; R W Kirby St Bridget *Ches* 11–20; rtd 20. *Cefn Bryniau Uchaf, Bryniau Terrace, Mynydd Llandygai, Bangor LL57 4BJ* E: johnbleazard@hotmail.com

BLEWETT, Martin Arthur. b 60. Keele Univ BA 82 Glos Univ MA 04. Trin Coll Bris 07. **d** 09 **p** 10. C Seaford w Sutton *Chich* 09–13; P-in-c Timsbury w Priston, Camerton and Dunkerton *B & W* 13–20; R from 20; Asst Dir of Ords 19–20. *The Rectory, South Road, Timsbury, Bath BA2 0EJ* T: (01761) 472448 M: 07854-273489 E: martinblewett@gmail.com

BLEWETT, Timothy John. b 67. Surrey Univ BA 88 Cam Univ BA 92 MA 92 Coll of Ripon & York St Jo MA 96 Buckingham Univ MA 11. Westcott Ho Cam 89. **d** 92 **p** 93. C Knaresborough *Ripon* 92–95; V Hanmer, Bronington, Bettisfield, Tallarn Green *St As* 95–98; Can Res and Can Cursal St As Cathl 98–03; Asst Dioc Dir of Ords 98–00; 00–03; Dioc Officer for Min and Adv for CME 98–03; CF 03–04; P-in-c Loddington *Leic* 04–12; Warden Launde Abbey 04–12; Dir and Chapl Ark Trust 12–15. *Sycamore House, New Road, Burton Lazars, Melton Mowbray LE14 2UU* M: 07971-528915

BLICK, John Harold Leslie. b 36. Univ of Wales (Lamp) BA 61. Bps' Coll Cheshunt 61. **d** 63 **p** 64. C Radlett *St Alb* 63–66; Min St Cem Miss Labrador Canada 66–71; Min Marsh Farm CD *St Alb* 71–76; R Shaw cum Donnington *Ox* 76–89; rtd 96; PtO *Mon* from 99. *Springwood, Cleddon, Trelleck NP25 4PN* T: (01600) 860094 F: 869045

BLID-MACKENZIE, Ylva Helena Birgitha. b 66. Stockholm Univ MArch 92. St Aug Coll of Th 17. **d** 20 **p** 21. NSM Benenden and Sandhurst *Cant* from 20. *Madrona Nursery, Pluckley Road, Bethersden, Ashford TN26 3EG* T: (01233) 820100 M: 07766-711957 E: rev.ylva@gmail.com

BLIGH, Philip Hamilton. b 36. Lon Univ BSc 57 PhD 61 MEd 79 St Cath Coll Ox BA 63 MInstP 75. S'wark Ord Course 86. **d** 88 **p** 89. C Abington *Pet* 88–90; V Bozeat w Easton Maudit 90–99; R Hackett Australia 99–01; rtd 01; PtO Nor from 02. *49 Norwich Road, Cromer NR27 0EX* T: (01263) 511385 E: philipbligh752@btinternet.com

BLIGHT, Francis Charles. b 71. Newc Univ BA 94. Oak Hill Th Coll 84. **d** 08 **p** 09. C Virginia Water *Guildf* 08–12; Asst Chapl Amsterdam w Den Helder and Heiloo *Eur* 12–19; C Fordham *Chelmsf* 19–20; R from 20. *The Rectory, Wood Lane, Fordham Heath, Colchester CO3 9TR* T: (01206) 621576 or 243266 E: francis.blight@fordhamchurch.org.uk

BLISS, Canon David Charles. b 52. Aston Univ BSc 75 Cranfield Inst of Tech MSc 82. St Jo Coll Nottm 87. **d** 89 **p** 90. C Burntwood *Lich* 89–93; Chapl St Matt Hosp Burntwood 89–93; TV Aston cum Aughton w Swallownest, Todwick etc *Sheff* 93–02; R Todwick 02–08; AD Laughton 03–08; Chapl among Deaf People 97–08; V Rotherham 08–17; AD 08–11; Hon Can Sheff Cathl 06–17; rtd 17; PtO *Sheff* from 18. *5 Hanging Bank Court, North Anston, Sheffield S25 4DG* T: (01909) 566551 E: bliss.david@me.com

BLISS, John Derek Clegg. b 40. Sarum Th Coll. **d** 68 **p** 69. C Wymondham *Nor* 68–73; V Easton 73–80; R Colton 73–80;

R Madera H Trin USA 80–89; Human Outreach Agency Hayward 92–96; rtd 01; C Coconut Grove St Steph USA from 01. *4 Edgewater Hillside, Westport CT 06880-6101, USA* T: (001) (203) 222 1879 E: jb106600@aol.com

BLISS, Mrs Lyn Elizabeth. b 54. SS Mark & Jo Univ Coll Plymouth CertEd 76. Ox Min Course 06. **d** 09 **p** 10. NSM Bradfield and Stanford Dingley *Ox* from 09; NSM Bucklebury w Marlston from 09. *Holly Hedges, 2 Broad Lane, Upper Bucklebury, Reading RG7 6QJ* T: (01635) 862281 M: 07824-741225 E: toccata1428@gmail.com

BLISSARD-BARNES, Christopher John. b 36. ARCO 55 Linc Coll Ox BA 61 MA 64. Ridley Hall Cam 61. **d** 63 **p** 64. C Woking St Paul *Guildf* 63–67; C Orpington Ch Ch *Roch* 67–71; P-in-c Heref St Jas 71–78; Chapl Heref Gen Hosp 71–78; R Hampreston *Sarum* 78–88; TR 88–89; RD Wimborne 80–85; P-in-c Hambledon *Guildf* 89–94; R Newdigate 94–01; Warden of Readers 93–99; rtd 01; PtO *Win* from 02. *148 Olivers Battery Road South, Winchester SO22 4LF* T: (01962) 862082 E: chrisandfreda@virginmedia.com

BLOCKLEY, Christopher John Hamilton. b 72. UWE LLB 96 Rob Coll Cam BTh 04 Barrister-at-Law (Gray's Inn) 98. Ridley Hall Cam 01. **d** 04 **p** 05. C Kingswood *Bris* 04–07; Chapl Bps' Coll Glouc 07–15; PtO *Glouc* 15–20. *29 Wellesley Street, Gloucester GL1 4QP* T: (01452) 539956 M: 07984-072630 E: chrisjhblockley@outlook.com

BLODWELL, Ms Christine Maria. b 46. Open Univ BA Jo Dalton Coll Man CertEd 71. NOC 04. **d** 05 **p** 06. NSM Marple All SS *Ches* 05–15; rtd 16; PtO *Leic* 17–21. *5 White Hart Close, Billesdon, Leicester LE7 9AU* T: 0116-259 9606 M: 07931-714130 E: revchrisb@hotmail.com

BLOGG, Kevin Derek. b 55. Ch Ch Coll Cant BSc 82 PGCE 87. Franciscan Ho of Studies. **d** 84 **p** 85. NSM Eythorne and Elvington w Waldershare etc *Cant* 89–92; Orchard Sch Cant 89–90; Harbour Sch Dover 92–93; NSM Colkirk w Oxwick w Pattesley, Whissonsett etc *Nor* 95–02; NSM Gressenhall w Longham w Wendling etc 02–18; NSM Launditch and the Upper Nar from 18; Sidestrand Hall Sch Nor from 94. *Mill House, The Street, Mileham, King's Lynn PE32 2RB* T: (01328) 701124 E: bloggbarn@aol.com

BLOKLAND, Janneke Hendrika. b 82. Radboud Univ Nijmegen MSc 06 PhD 10 Utrecht Univ BA 10 Nottm Univ MA 14. Westcott Ho Cam 12. **d** 14 **p** 15. C Marlborough *Sarum* 14–17; Asst Chapl Marlborough Coll 17–20; Chapl Hurstpierpoint Coll from 20. *Woodard House, Chalkers Lane, Hurstpierpoint, Hassocks BN6 9LR* M: 07554-486575 E: jblokland@gmail.com

BLOOD, David John. b 36. G&C Coll Cam BA 60 MA 64. Westcott Ho Cam 60. **d** 62 **p** 63. C Rushmere *St E* 62–66; C Harringay St Paul *Lon* 66–70; LtO 71–81; rtd 01. *42 Churston Gardens, London N11 2NL*

BLOOD, Canon Michael William. b 44. AKC 67. **d** 69 **p** 70. C Moseley St Agnes *Birm* 69–75; V Cotteridge 75–09; Relig Progr Producer BBC Radio W Midl 76–06; Hon Can Birm Cathl 97–09; rtd 09; PtO *Birm* 09–18. *19 Nursery Drive, Birmingham B30 1DR* T: 0121-458 2815 E: michaelblood@blueyonder.co.uk

BLOOM, Mrs Lara Susan. b 67. Ripon Coll Cuddesdon 13. **d** 15 **p** 16. C Redmarley D'Abitot, Bromesberrow, Pauntley etc *Glouc* 15–17; C Abenhall w Mitcheldean 17–18; P-in-c Huntley and Longhope, Churcham and Bulley from 18. *56 Byfords Road, Huntley, Gloucester GL19 3EL* M: 07901-003575 E: rev.larabloom@gmail.com

BLOOMER, Ms Sherry Lesley. b 50. TD 91. Liv Jo Moores Univ BA 91 Wolv Poly CertEd 83 RN 73 RM 74 RHV 78. Westcott Ho Cam 95. **d** 97 **p** 98. C Llangollen w Trevor and Llantysilio *St As* 97–00; R Cilcain and Nannerch and Rhydymwyn 00–04; V Worc St Clem and Lower Broadheath 04–12; Chapl Worc Univ 04–12; rtd 12; PtO *St As* from 14. *13 Furrocks Lane, Neston CH64 4EH* T: 0151-336 1686 E: sherrybloomer@btinternet.com

BLOOMFIELD, Mrs Brenda Elizabeth. b 41. Gipsy Hill Coll of Educn TCert 63. **d** 07 **p** 08. NSM Upper Weardale *Dur* 07–11; rtd 11; PtO *Dur* 11–20. *1 Broadwood View, Frosterley, Bishop Auckland DL13 2RT* T: (01388) 527980

BLOOMFIELD, John Stephen. b 56. Chich Th Coll 83. **d** 86 **p** 87. C Chich St Paul and St Pet 86–89; TV Littlehampton and Wick 89–98; V Hunstanton St Edm w Ringstead *Nor* 98–19; P-in-c Flegg Coastal Benefice from 19. *The Rectory, Somerton Road, Winterton-on-Sea, Great Yarmouth NR29 4AW* T: (01493) 393628 E: jonstefanfield@btinternet.com

BLOOR, The Ven Amanda Elaine. b 62. Leic Univ BA 83 York Univ MA 02 K Coll Lon PhD 12 Open Univ PGCE 96. Ripon Coll Cuddesdon 02. **d** 04 **p** 05. C Hambleden Valley *Ox* 04–07; Bp's Dom Chapl 07–13; Dioc Adv for Women's Min and Dir of Ords (Berks) 13–15; P-in-c Bembridge

Portsm 15–20; Assoc Dir of Ords 15–20; Adn Cleveland *York* from 20. *46 Langbaurgh Road, Hutton Rudby, Yarm TS15 0HL* T: (01642) 706095 E: amandaebloor@gmail.com *or* adcl@yorkdiocese.org

BLOOR, Preb Terence Bernard. b 62. Liv Univ BTh 02. NOC 99. **d** 02 **p** 03. C Hadley *Lich* 02–06; Chapl N Staffs Combined Healthcare NHS Trust 06–13; P-in-c Basford *Lich* 06–19; V 19–20; P-in-c Wolstanton 16–20; RD Newcastle 11–20; Interim Min Stafford Area from 20; Preb Lich Cathl from 15. *16 Crediton Avenue, Stoke-on-Trent ST6 7NE* M: 07890-980749 E: terry.bloor@btinternet.com

BLORE, Canon John Francis. b 49. Jes Coll Ox BA 72 MA 76. Wycliffe Hall Ox 73. **d** 75 **p** 76. C Waltham Abbey *Chelmsf* 75–78; C E Ham St Geo 78–81; R Colchester St Mich Myland 81–00; Chapl Oxley Parker Sch Colchester 81–00; P-in-c Halstead St Andr w H Trin and Greenstead Green *Chelmsf* 00–04; TR Halstead Area 04–15; RD Hinckford 03–08; Hon Can Chelmsf Cathl 09–15; rtd 15; PtO *Nor* from 15. *Alden Cottage, Lexham Road, Litcham, King's Lynn PE32 2QQ* T: (01328) 701242 E: jf.blore@btinternet.com

BLOUNT, Robin George. b 38. Lon Coll of Div 61 Wycliffe Hall Ox 67. **d** 68 **p** 69. C Bletchley *Ox* 68–71; C Washington *Dur* 71–74; TV Chelmsley Wood *Birm* 74–76; Ind Chapl *Worc* 76–89; Asst P Dudley St Jo 76–88; Asst P Dudley St Thos and St Luke 88–89; Ind Chapl (Eurotunnel Development) *Cant* 89–03; rtd 03; PtO *Cant* 03–20. *1 Meadowlands, Clitheroe BB7 2ND* T: (01200) 538476 E: robin.blount38@gmail.com

BLOWEY, Mrs Judith Ann. b 55. SWMTC 14. **d** 17 **p** 18. C Tavistock, Gulworthy and Brent Tor *Ex* from 17. *Higher Woodley Farm, Sydenham Damerel, Tavistock PL19 8QU* T: (01822) 832374 E: jablowey@gmail.com

BLUNDELL, Linzi Marie Clare. b 72. Cen Lancs Univ BA. Cranmer Hall Dur 19. **d** 21. C Swaledale *Leeds* from 21. *Mill House, Swale Hall Lane, Grinton, Richmond DL11 6HL* T: (01748) 884491 E: linzi.blundell@leeds.anglican.org

BLUNDELL, Peter Grahame. b 61. Ealing Coll of Educn BA 83. Oak Hill NSM Course 91. **d** 94 **p** 95. NSM Kensington St Barn *Lon* 94–97; Zimbabwe 97–99; Assoc Min Romford Gd Shep *Chelmsf* 99–04; I Richmond Hill St Jo Canada from 04. *19 Waldron Crescent, Richmond Hill ON L4E 4A3, Canada* T: (001) (289) 809 1450 E: peter@ecclesiact.com

BLUNDEN, Jacqueline Ann. *See* MILLER, Jacqueline Ann

BLUNDEN, Canon Jeremy Augustine. b 61. BSc CEng 88 MIStructE 88. SEITE 99. **d** 99 **p** 00. NSM Sydenham St Bart *S'wark* 99–01; C 01–03; V Clapham H Spirit 03–12; TR Warlingham w Chelsham and Farleigh 12–16; R Beckenham St Geo *Roch* 16–18; R Beckenham St Geo and St Barn from 18; AD Beckenham from 19; Bp's Adv for Black, Asian and Minority Ethnic Affairs from 18; Hon Can Roch Cathl from 18. *The Rectory, 14 The Knoll, Beckenham BR3 5JW* T: (020) 8650 0983 E: jeremy.blunden@btinternet.com

BLUNSUM, Charles Michael. b 28. ACIB 51 MBIM 86. **d** 74 **p** 75. C Stoke Bishop *Bris* 74–79; Chapl Brunel Manor Chr Cen Torquay 79–94; rtd 94; PtO *Ex* from 94. *16A Hollywater Close, Torquay TQ1 3TN* T: (01803) 214371

BLUNT, Christopher John Scawen. b 73. Rob Coll Cam MA 97 MEng 97. St Jo Coll Nottm MTh 13. **d** 13 **p** 14. C Ches St Paul w St Luke 13–17; V from 17. *St Luke's Vicarage, 14 Celandine Close, Huntington, Chester CH3 6DT* T: (01244) 460058 M: 07503-706906 E: chrisblunt.jas@gmail.com

BLUNT, Jeremy William. b 49. Birm Univ MEd 85 GRNCM 73. **d** 07 **p** 08. OLM Streetly *Lich* 07–15; PtO from 16. *63 Lindrosa Road, Sutton Coldfield B74 3LB* T: 0121-353 9712 M: 07849-689180

BLUNT, Joshua Henry John. b 89. Birm City Univ BA 11. Wycliffe Hall Ox BA 20. **d** 20 **p** 21. C Goole *Sheff* from 20. *40 Olive Road, Goole DN14 5AD* M: 07907-388219 E: joshua@stjohnsgoole.org.uk

BLYDE, Ian Hay. b 52. Liv Univ BSc 74 Edin Univ BD 80. Edin Th Coll 77. **d** 80 **p** 81. C Ainsdale *Liv* 80–83; Chapl Birkenhead Sch 83–90; V Over St Chad *Ches* 90–93; Chapl Ex Sch and St Marg Sch 93–98; NSM Littleham w Exmouth *Ex* 03–06; TV Brixham w Churston Ferrers and Kingswear 06–13; TR 13–19; rtd 19. *2 Hulham Road, Exmouth EX8 3HR*

BLYTH, Florence Anne. b 56. ERMC 16. **d** 19 **p** 20. NSM Nor Colegate and Tombland from 19. *2 Willow Lane, Norwich NR2 1EU* M: 07904-188948 E: rev.annie.blyth@gmail.com

BLYTH, Graham. *See* BLYTH, Michael Graham

BLYTH, Kenneth Henry. b 35. Oak Hill Th Coll 58. **d** 61 **p** 62. C St Alb St Paul 61–65; P-in-c Aspenden and Layston w Buntingford 65–66; R 66–72; R Washfield, Stoodleigh, Withleigh etc *Ex* 72–82; P-in-c Cruwys Morchard 72–74; RD Tiverton 76–82; C Eastbourne H Trin *Chich* 82–00; rtd 00; PtO *Ex* from 00. *Hamslade House, Bampton, Tiverton EX16 9JA* T: (01398) 351461

BLYTH, Canon Michael Graham. b 53. Jes Coll Ox BA 75 MA 78 Dur Univ PhD 79. Qu Coll Birm 82. **d** 84 **p** 85. C Nantwich *Ches* 84–86; C Coppenhall 86–88; TV Southend *Chelmsf* 88–95; P-in-c Danbury 95–11; R 11–12; RD Chelmsf S 01–07; Hon Can Chelmsf Cathl 07–12; rtd 12; PtO *Chelmsf* from 14. *Selkirk House, 8 Rennie Walk, Heybridge, Maldon CM9 4QH* T: (01621) 854068 E: michaelg@canongate.org.uk

BOAG, David. b 46. Edin Th Coll 69. **d** 72 **p** 73. C Edin Old St Paul 72–75; P-in-c Edin St Andr and St Aid 75–88; LtO from 88. *13 Fleming Place, Fountainhall, Galashiels TD1 2TA* T: (01578) 760606 E: daviebfree@gmail.com

BOAG, Michael John. b 61. Leeds Univ BA 00. Coll of Resurr Mirfield 98. **d** 00 **p** 01. C Howden *York* 00–03; Min Can and Succ Windsor 03–11; Chapl St Geo Sch Windsor 03–06; Dean's V 06–11; R Upper Coquetdale *Newc* 11–17; R Worth, Pound Hill and Maidenbower *Chich* from 17. *Worth Rectory, Church Road, Worth, Crawley RH10 7RT* T: (01293) 882229 E: rector@worthparish.org

BOAKES, Canon Norman. b 50. Univ of Wales (Swansea) BA 71 Univ of Wales (Lamp) LTh 73 Ox Univ MTh 96. Bp Burgess Hall Lamp 71. **d** 73 **p** 74. C Swansea St Mary w H Trin *S & B* 73–78; Chapl Univ of Wales (Swansea) 76–78; Chapl K Alfred Coll *Win* 78–82; V Colbury 82–91; Chapl Ashurst Hosp 82–91; Chapl Mental Handicap Services Unit 82–91; V Southampton Maybush St Pet *Win* 91–06; P-in-c Southampton St Jude 04–06; V Maybush and Southampton St Jude 06–07; Bp's Adv for Hosp Chapl 87–00; AD Southampton 02–07; CMD Officer 08–14; Hon Can Win Cathl 11–14; PtO 14–19; Archdeacons' Nat Exec Officer 14–19; Hon C N Stoneham and Bassett *Win* from 19; Chapl Gen SSB from 19; PtO *Portsm* from 19. *21 Redcourt, Chetwynd Road, Southampton SO16 3TX* T: (023) 8076 7735 E: norman.boakes@btinternet.com

BOARDMAN, Jonathan Thomas. b 63. Magd Coll Cam BA 89 Magd Coll Ox MA 90. Westcott Ho Cam 87. **d** 90 **p** 91. C W Derby St Mary *Liv* 90–93; Prec St Alb Abbey 93–96; TR Catford (Southend) and Downham *S'wark* 96–99; RD E Lewisham 99; Chapl Rome *Eur* 99–18; Sen Tutor Angl Cen Rome 01–14; Can Gib Cathl *Eur* 07–18; Adn Italy and Malta 09–16; P-in-c Padova 13–18; V Clapham St Paul *S'wark* from 18; P-in-c Clapham St Pet from 20; PtO *Eur* from 18. *St Paul's Vicarage, 6A Rectory Grove, London SW4 0DZ* T: (020) 7207 9546 M: 07946-085977 E: vicar@stpaulsclapham.org

BOARDMAN, Miss Kathryn Louise. b 72. Hull Univ BA 94 MA 95 Cam Univ BTh 12 FHEA 07. Westcott Ho Cam 10. **d** 12 **p** 13. C Heworth St Mary *Dur* 12–16; P-in-c Harton from 16; P-in-c Cleadon Park from 16. *3 Page Avenue, South Shields NE34 0SY* T: 0191-455 4682 E: kate.boardman@durham.anglican.org

BOARDMAN, Philippa Jane. b 63. MBE 11. Jes Coll Cam BA 85 MA 89. Ridley Hall Cam 87. **d** 90 **p** 94. Par Dn Walthamstow St Mary w St Steph *Chelmsf* 90–93; C Hackney Wick St Mary of Eton w St Aug *Lon* 93–96; P-in-c Old Ford St Paul and St Mark 96–03; V 03–13; Dean of Women's Min Stepney Area 94–02; Preb St Paul's Cathl 02–13; Can Res and Treas St Paul's Cathl 13–17; P-in-c Wandsworth Common St Mary *S'wark* 17–19; V from 19. *The Vicarage, 291 Burntwood Lane, London SW17 0AP* E: info@smmwandsworth.org.uk

BOCKING (Essex), Dean of. Vacant

BOCKING (Suffolk), Dean of. *See* DELFGOU, The Very Revd Jonathan Hawke

BODDAM-WHETHAM, Paul Nathaniel. b 52. Em Coll Cam BA 73. ERMC 09. **d** 12 **p** 13. NSM St Alb Ch Ch 12–16; R Ducklington *Ox* 16–21; rtd 21. *Address temp unknown* M: 07713-069876 E: paulbw32@icloud.com

BODDAM-WHETHAM, Tudor Alexander. b 76. St Aid Coll Dur BA 97. Wycliffe Hall Ox 06. **d** 08 **p** 09. C Houghton Carl 08–11; P-in-c Barony of Burgh from 11. *The Rectory, Burgh-by-Sands, Carlisle CA5 6AW* T: (01228) 576324 E: vicartudor@gmail.com

BODDINGTON, Canon Alan Charles Peter. b 37. Oak Hill Th Coll 63. **d** 66 **p** 67. C Bedworth *Cov* 66–69; Bp's Officer for Min 69–75; Bp's Chapl for Miss 69–73; P-in-c Wroxall and Honiley 72–75; V Westwood 75–85; Asst Chapl Warw Univ 78–85; TR N Farnborough *Guildf* 85–02; RD Aldershot 88–93; Hon Can Guildf Cathl 92–02; rtd 02; PtO *Cov* from 02. *Tremar, Hathaway Lane, Stratford-upon-Avon CV37 9BJ* T: (01789) 263643 M: 07866-909092 E: bodds4@btinternet.com

BODDY, Alan Richard. b 47. Ripon Coll Cuddesdon. **d** 84 **p** 85. C Eastcote St Lawr *Lon* 84–87; C Kensington St Mary Abbots w St Geo 87–90; Chapl HM Pris Brixton 90–91; Chapl HM Pris Send 91–92; Chapl HM Pris Downview 91–92; Chapl HM Pris High Down 92–98; Chapl HM Pris Wormwood Scrubs 98–02; rtd 02; PtO *Lon* from 02; *Ox* 02–04; *S'wark* 02–13; PV Westmr Abbey from 02. *105 Valiant House, Vicarage Crescent, London SW11 3LX* E: arboddy@btinternet.com

BODDY, David. b 57. Linc Th Coll 92. **d** 92 **p** 93. C Peterlee *Dur* 92–95; C Penshaw 95–97; P-in-c Shiney Row 95–98; P-in-c Herrington 95–98; TV S Shields All SS 98–04; V Haswell, Shotton and Thornley 04–13; P-in-c Somerleyton, Ashby, Fritton, Herringfleet etc *Nor* 13–16; rtd 16. *455 Felixstowe Road, Ipswich IP3 9DQ* T: (01473) 720196 M: 07971-304622 E: davidboddy1@gmail.com

BODEKER, Brian Mark. b 60. Cant Univ (NZ) BCom 82. Ox Min Course 09. **d** 12 **p** 13. NSM Didcot All SS *Ox* 12–14; C from 14. *1 Holly Lane, Harwell, Didcot OX11 6DA* T: (01235) 816501 M: 07970-111110

BODLE, Richard Talbot. b 70. Southn Univ LLB 91. Wycliffe Hall Ox BTh 98. **d** 98 **p** 99. C S Mimms Ch Ch *Lon* 98–02; TV Edgware 02–08; V Churt and Hindhead *Guildf* from 08. *St Alban's Vicarage, Wood Road, Hindhead GU26 6PX* T: (01428) 605305 E: vicar@stalbanshindhead.org.uk

BODMIN, Archdeacon of. *See* BETTERIDGE, The Ven Kelly Anne

BODY, Andrew. b 46. Pemb Coll Cam BA 68 MA 71. Ridley Hall Cam 68. **d** 70 **p** 71. C New Bury *Man* 70–73; TV Droylsden St Mary 73–78; V Low Harrogate St Mary *Ripon* 78–92; TR Redhorn *Sarum* 92–97; V Chobham w Valley End *Guildf* 97–12; RD Surrey Heath 06–11; rtd 12; PtO *Heref* from 12. *Holyrood, 17 Temeside Estate, Ludlow SY8 1LD* T: (01584) 877465 E: corpora12@btinternet.com

BODY, Mrs Shuna Jane. b 67. MBE 14. SEITE 98. **d** 01 **p** 02. NSM Brookland, Fairfield, Brenzett w Snargate etc *Cant* 01–19; NSM Romney Marsh from 20. *Hope Farm, Snargate, Romney Marsh TN29 9UQ* T: (01797) 343977 M: 07747-142115 E: shunabody@hotmail.com

BODYCOMBE, Stephen John. b 58. Lanchester Poly Cov BA. St Mich Coll Llan. **d** 83 **p** 84. C Cardiff St Jo *Llan* 83–86; V Dinas and Penygraig w Williamstown 86–00; V Dyffryn from 00. *The Vicarage, Dyffryn, Neath SA10 7AZ* T: (01792) 814237

BOGGUST, Mrs Patricia Anne. b 42. Portsm Dioc Tr Course. **d** 90 **p** 98. NSM Hook w Warsash *Portsm* 90–94; NSM Locks Heath 94–09; Chapl Univ Hosp Southn NHS Foundn Trust from 01. *21 Beverley Close, Park Gate, Southampton SO31 6QU* T: (01489) 573586 E: anniebb.boggust@btinternet.com

BOGLE, Ms Elizabeth. b 47. York Univ BA 68 Leeds Univ PGCE 69. S'wark Ord Course 93. **d** 96 **p** 97. NSM E Greenwich *S'wark* 96–00; NSM Hatcham St Jas 00–06; NSM Newington St Paul 06–14; PtO from 14. *96 Grierson Road, London SE23 1NX* T: (020) 8699 9996 E: elizabethbogle@hotmail.com

BOGLE, James Main Lindam Linton. b 33. Peterho Cam BA 56 MA 60. Wells Th Coll 59. **d** 61 **p** 62. C Bermondsey St Anne *S'wark* 61–65; Chapl York Univ 65–72; V Brayton 72–76; V Forest Hill St Aug *S'wark* 76–83; C Hatcham St Cath 83–85; Hon C 91–03; C Herne Hill St Paul 86–87; rtd 87; PtO *S'wark* 04–17. *96 Grierson Road, London SE23 1NX* T: (020) 8699 9996 E: jamesmllbogle@hotmail.com

BOGLE, The Very Revd Paul David. b 57. CITC BTh 10. **d** 10 **p** 11. C Dunboyne and Rathmolyon *M & K* 10–13; I Trim and Athboy Gp from 13; Dean Clonmacnoise from 14. *St Patrick's Deanery, St Loman's Street, Trim, Co Meath, Republic of Ireland* T: (00353) (46) 943 6698 E: pdbogle@gmail.com

BOHAN, Kimberly. b 72. St Andr Univ MA 93 Smith Coll (USA) MAT 94 St Andr Univ BD 99 Edin Univ MTh 03. **d** 03 **p** 04. C Glas St Ninian 03–06; R Dunoon *Arg* 06–09; P-in-c Rothesay 06–09; P-in-c Tighnabruaich 06–09; R Dunblane *St And* 09–12; P-in-c Waltham *Linc* 13–14; P-in-c Barnoldby le Beck 13–14; P-in-c New Waltham 13–14; C Laceby and Ravendale Gp 13–14; R Waltham Gp from 14; RD Haverstoe from 20. *The Rectory, 95 High Street, Waltham, Grimsby DN37 0PN* E: kimberly@walthamgroupchurches.co.uk

BOL, Ann Kathleen Ruth. b 60. **d** 16 **p** 17. NSM Shingay Gp *Ely* from 16. *36 Hillfield, Foxton, Cambridge CB22 6RZ* T: (01223) 871058 M: 07733-468436 E: ann.bol@btinternet.com

BOLAND, Christopher Paul. b 75. Hertf Coll Ox MPhys 97. Ridley Hall Cam BTh 01. **d** 01 **p** 02. C Skirbeck H Trin *Linc* 01–05; P-in-c Grantham, Harrowby w Londonthorpe 05–18; RD Grantham 12–18; P-in-c Fulwood Ch Ch *Blackb* from 18. *Christ Church Vicarage, 19 Vicarage Close, Fulwood, Preston PR2 8EG* M: 07791-702537 E: cpboland@outlook.com

BOLAND, Geoffrey. b 56. Open Univ BA 03. Oak Hill Th Coll 87. **d** 89 **p** 90. C Ormskirk *Liv* 89–94; C Woodside Park St Barn *Lon* 94–99; TV Canford Magna *Sarum* 99–21; rtd 21; PtO *Eur* from 17. *Address temp unknown* E: brevgeoff@ntlworld.com

BOLD, Peter Edward. b 64. Sheff Univ BEng 86 PhD 90. Cranmer Hall Dur BA 94. **d** 95 **p** 96. C Grenoside *Sheff* 95–97; C Rotherham and Dioc Communications Officer 97–01; P-in-c Brampton Bierlow 01–05; V 05–11; TR Dronfield w

Holmesfield *Derby* from 11. *The Rectory, 24 Church Street, Dronfield S18 1QB* T: (01246) 411531 E: pebold@talk21.com

BOLDING, Alan Frederick. b 40. NTMTC. **d** 07 **p** 07. NSM Woodford Bridge *Chelmsf* 07–13; PtO from 13. *21 Portman Drive, Woodford Green IG8 8QN* T: (020) 8550 2070 M: 07932-797983 E: apbolding@onetel.com

BOLE, Malcolm Dennis. b 30. Oak Hill Th Coll 65. **d** 67 **p** 68. C Bridlington Priory *York* 67–70; Lect Stanley Smith Th Coll Gahini Rwanda 71; Prin 71-72; Lect École de Théologie Butare 72–73; P-in-c Combe Hay *B & W* 74–81; V Bath Odd Down 74–81; P-in-c Taunton St Jas 81–84; V 84–90; R Bicknoller w Crowcombe and Sampford Brett 90–98; rtd 98; PtO *B & W* from 01. *7 Putsham Mead, Kilve, Bridgwater TA5 1DZ* T: (01278) 741297 E: mjbole@btinternet.com

BOLEN, Mrs Susan Melanie. INSEAD MBA 91 K Coll Lon MA 11. ERMC 12. **d** 15 **p** 16. C Frimley *Guildf* 15–19; P-in-c Wandsworth St Paul *S'wark* 19–20; V from 20. *St Paul's Vicarage, 116 Augustus Road, London SW19 6EW* M: 07540-383081 E: revsusan@stpaulsparkside.org.uk

BOLGER, Ann Elise. b 88. Coll of Resurr Mirfield 18. **d** 20 **p** 21. Asst Chapl Brussels *Eur* from 20. *rue Capitaine Crespel 29, 1050 Bruxelles, Belgium* M: (0032) 48-587 5088 E: annie.bolger@holytrinity.be

BOLLARD, Canon Richard George. b 39. Fitzw Ho Cam BA 61 MA 65 K Coll Lon BD 63 AKC 63. **d** 64 **p** 65. C Southampton Maybush St Pet *Win* 64–68; Chapl Aston Univ *Birm* 68–74; TR Chelmsley Wood 74–82; V Coleshill and Maxstoke 82–04; RD Coleshill 82–92; Hon Can Birm Cathl 85–04; Dioc Ecum Officer 97–02; rtd 04; PtO *Heref* 05–19. *15 Riverdale Gardens, Otley LS21 2SX* T: (01432) 267414

BOLLEY, Michael Francis. b 55. St Cath Coll Ox BA 76 MSc 77 MA 92. Ripon Coll Cuddesdon 90. **d** 92 **p** 93. C Pinner *Lon* 92–95; C Eastcote St Lawr 95–99; P-in-c Southall H Trin 99–06; V from 06. *Holy Trinity Vicarage, Park View Road, Southall UB1 3HJ* T: (020) 8571 7329 E: vicar.htsouthall@gmail.com

BOLSTER, Christopher David. b 77. St Mary's Coll Twickenham BA 99. STETS MA 11. **d** 11 **p** 12. C Stanwix *Carl* 11–15; V Clifton *Man* 15–19; V Barking St Patr *Chelmsf* from 19; P-in-c Becontree St Elisabeth from 21. *St Patrick's Vicarage, 79 Sparsholt Road, Barking IG11 7YG* T: (020) 8281 6059 M: 07970-943244 E: chrisdbolster@virginmedia.com

BOLSTER, David Richard. b 50. BA. St Jo Coll Nottm. **d** 84 **p** 85. C Luton Lewsey St Hugh *St Alb* 84–87; V Woodside w E Hyde 87–01; V Edmonton St Aldhelm *Lon* 01–10; PtO *Blackb* from 15. *3 Arnside Crescent, Morecambe LA4 5PP* T: (01524) 923861 E: davidbolster50@gmail.com

BOLSTER, (née NICHOLSON), Mrs Lucy Clare. b 74. Sheff Univ BMedSci 97. St Jo Coll Nottm 12. **d** 15 **p** 16. NSM Sheffield Vine *Sheff* 15–19; LtO *Sarum* from 19. *38 Links Road, Poole BH14 9QS* M: 07948-403155

BOLT, George Henry. b 34. Lon Univ BSc 60 Bath Univ MSc 75 CPhys 75 MInstP 75. S Dios Minl Tr Scheme 85. **d** 88 **p** 89. NSM Oldbury *Sarum* 88–89; Chapl Chippenham Tech Coll 89–90; C Kington St Michael *Bris* 90–92; P-in-c Aldenham *St Alb* 92–98; rtd 98; PtO *Ban* 98–17. *Ty Capel Ffrwd, Llanfachreth, Dolgellau LL40 2NR* T: (01341) 422006 E: georgebolt34@gmail.com

BOLT, Mrs Mary Veronica. b 36. S Dios Minl Tr Scheme 90. **d** 93 **p** 94. NSM Aldenham *St Alb* 93–98; Sub-Chapl HM Pris The Mount 93–98; rtd 98; PtO *Ban* 98–99; P-in-c Maentwrog w Trawsfynydd 99–03. *Ty Capel Ffrwd, Llanfachreth, Dolgellau LL40 2NR* T: (01341) 422006 E: maryboltminstrel@gmail.com

BOLTON, Canon Jane Elizabeth. b 53. Leic Univ BA 75. Ripon Coll Cuddesdon 95. **d** 97 **p** 98. C Sheff St Mark Broomhill 97–02; P-in-c Dinnington 02–04; P-in-c Laughton w Throapham 03–04; P-in-c Dinnington w Laughton and Throapham 04–05; R 05–11; AD Laughton 08–11; P-in-c Ravenfield, Hooton Roberts and Braithwell 11–16; SSM Officer 11–16; Hon Can Sheff Cathl 10–16; rtd 16; PtO *Sheff* 16–18; *York* from 16. *3 Stakesby Manor, Manor Close, Whitby YO21 1HG* E: mail@janebolton.co.uk

BOLTON, John. b 43. SS Paul & Mary Coll Cheltenham DipEd 64. Trin Coll Bris 83. **d** 85 **p** 86. C Minehead *B & W* 85–89; R Winford w Felton Common Hill 89–98; C-in-c Locking Castle CD 98–06; rtd 06; PtO *B & W* 06–20. *The Poppies, 13 Cornlands, Sampford Peverell, Tiverton EX16 7UA* T: (01884) 821445 E: johnbolton455@btinternet.com

BOLTON, Mrs Judith Ann. b 48. ERMC 12. **d** 13 **p** 14. NSM Hemingford Abbots *Ely* 13–18; NSM Hemingford Grey 13–18; rtd 18; PtO *Ely* from 18. *10 Westmeare, Hemingford Grey, Huntingdon PE28 9BZ* T: (01480) 370036 E: judithbolton10@gmail.com

BOLTON, Kelvin. b 53. Wilson Carlile Coll 88 Trin Coll Bris BA 98. **d** 98 **p** 99. C Walton Breck Ch Ch *Liv* 98–01; V Goose Green 01–08; P-in-c Walton Breck 08–17; rtd 17. *4 Woodland*

Drive, Ashton-in-Makerfield, Wigan WN4 8LX* T: (01942) 583273

BOLTON, Paul Edward. b 71. St Jo Coll Ox BA 94 MA 98 Peterho Cam BA 97. Ridley Hall Cam 95. **d** 98 **p** 99. C Lowestoft Ch Ch *Nor* 98–01; Titus Trust 01–21; LtO *Ox* 05–20; C Ox St Ebbe w H Trin and St Pet from 20. *33 Wharton Road, Headington, Oxford OX3 8AL* T: (01865) 756334 E: paulbolton1971@gmail.com

BOLTON, Richard David Edward. b 52. MA. St Steph Ho Ox 79. **d** 81 **p** 82. C Rawmarsh w Parkgate *Sheff* 81–84; Chapl Wellingborough Sch 85–92; Chapl Merchant Taylors' Sch Northwood 91–11; P-in-c Winchmore Hill H Trin *Lon* from 12; P in O from 96. *Holy Trinity Vicarage, 6 King's Avenue, London N21 3NA* T: (020) 8364 1583 E: rdeb2010@btinternet.com

BOLTON, Archdeacon of. See BURGESS, The Ven Jean Ann

BOLTON-DEBBAGE, Grant William Vivian. b 86. St Aid Coll Dur BA 08. Ripon Coll Cuddesdon 12. **d** 14 **p** 15. C Gt Yarmouth *Nor* 14–18; C Upper Chelsea H Trin and St Sav *Lon* 18–20; V Hatcham Park All SS *S'wark* from 20. *22 Erlanger Road, London SE14 5TG* E: gboltondebbage@gmail.com

BOLTON, Suffragan Bishop of. See ASHCROFT, The Rt Revd Mark David

BOMFORD, Canon Rodney William George. b 43. BNC Ox BA 64 MA 68. Coll of Resurr Mirfield 67 Union Th Sem (NY) STM 69. **d** 69 **p** 70. C Deptford St Paul *S'wark* 69–77; V Camberwell St Giles w St Matt 77–01; RD Camberwell 87–97; Hon Can S'wark Cathl 93–01; rtd 01. *The Manor House, Modbury, Ivybridge PL21 0RA* T: (01548) 831277 E: rodney@bomford.eclipse.co.uk

BOMYER, Julian Richard Nicholas Jeffrey. b 55. AKC 78 Sarum & Wells Th Coll 78. **d** 79 **p** 80. C Rugby *Cov* 79–84; TV 85–88; P-in-c Clifton upon Dunsmore w Brownsover 84–85; Prec Ch Ch *Ox* 88–93; V Hampton *Worc* 93–01; P-in-c Sedgeberrow w Hinton-on-the-Green 00–01; R Hampton w Sedgeberrow and Hinton-on-the-Green 01–06; rtd 06; PtO *Worc* from 15. *52 Elmside, Evesham WR11 3DZ* T: (01386) 421559 M: 07900-824264 E: julian@bomyer.co.uk

BOND, Andrew James Douglas. b 81. Ridley Hall Cam 11. **d** 14 **p** 15. C Penge Lane H Trin *Roch* 14–17; C Derby St Alkmund and St Werburgh from 17; C Mackworth St Fran from 20. *St Paul's Vicarage, 6 Old Chester Road, Derby DE1 3SA* M: 07939-051990 E: andy.bond@stwderby.org

BOND, Andrew Thomas. b 50. Leeds Univ BA 74 Solicitor 79. Ox Min Course 09. **d** 12 **p** 13. NSM Pangbourne w Tidmarsh and Sulham *Ox* 12–16; NSM Reading St Mary the Virgin from 16. *Heron Lodge, 32 The Moors, Pangbourne, Reading RG8 7LP* T: 0118-984 5297 M: 07917-623444 E: at.bond@btinternet.com

BOND, Anne. See BOND, Sybilla Anne

BOND, Catherine Grace La Touche. b 60. SS Coll Cam MA 83 Darw Coll Cam PGCE 83 Solicitor 87. **d** 09 **p** 10. OLM Clopton w Otley, Swilland and Ashbocking *St E* 09–13; OLM Carlford 13–17. *230 Ferry Road, Felixstowe IP11 9RU* M: 07801-342336 E: beachhut1412@gmail.com

BOND, David. b 36. Oak Hill Th Coll 72. **d** 74 **p** 75. C Leyton St Mary w St Edw *Chelmsf* 74–78; C Slough *Ox* 78–80; V Selby St Jas *York* 80–93; P-in-c Wistow 80–82; V 82–93; RD Selby 89–93; P-in-c Northiam *Chich* 93–94; R 94–99; rtd 99; PtO *Chich* from 00. *24 The Sackville, De La Warr Parade, Bexhill-on-Sea TN40 1LS*

BOND, David Hugh Tremayne. b 64. Ripon Coll Cuddesdon 13. **d** 15 **p** 16. C Kingsbridge, Dodbrooke, and W Alvington *Ex* 15–19; R Queen Thorne *Sarum* from 19. *The Rectory, Trent, Sherborne DT9 4SL* T: (01935) 850201 M: 07875-781709 E: trentrectory@gmail.com

BOND, David Matthew. b 38. Leic Univ BA 59 Leeds Univ PGCE 67 Nottm Univ MA 85. Sarum Th Coll 59. **d** 61 **p** 62. C Leic St Anne 61–64; E England Sec SCM 64–66; Hon C Nor St Pet Mancroft 64–67; Lect and Hd of Section Pet Regional Coll 67–96; Lect Pet Coll of Adult Educn from 96; Hon C Stamford All SS w St Pet *Linc* 74–81; Hon C Stamford All SS w St Jo from 81; PtO *Pet* 85–07 and 12–17. *2 The Courtyard, Cotterstock, Peterborough PE8 5HD* T: (01832) 226255 E: david@dbond.me.uk

BOND, David Warner. b 32. MA BSc(Econ). Cant Sch of Min 79. **d** 82 **p** 83. NSM Otham w Langley *Cant* 82–10; PtO from 11. *6 Denton Close, Maidstone ME15 8ER* T: (01622) 202239 E: dwbond@blueyonder.co.uk or dwbond@bigfoot.com

BOND, David William. b 46. New Coll Edin BD 99. **d** 18 **p** 18. NSM S Hetton *Dur* 18–21; PtO from 21. *23 Pinedale Drive, South Hetton, Durham DH6 2XG* T: 0191-526 9604 E: david.columba53@outlook.com

BOND, Mrs Gita Deborah. b 57. N Lon Poly BSc 80 Chelsea Coll Lon PGCE 81. Ridley Hall Cam 06. **d** 08 **p** 09. C

The Ramseys and Upwood *Ely* 08–16; NSM W Green Ch Ch w St Pet *Lon* from 16. *Christ Church Vicarage, Waldeck Road, London N15 3EP* M: 07977-555895 E: gitabond@hotmail.com

BOND, Gordon. b 44. Chich Th Coll 68. **d** 71 **p** 72. C Wisbech St Aug *Ely* 71–74; C Wembley Park St Aug *Lon* 74–77; C York Town St Mich *Guildf* 77–80; TV Haywards Heath St Wilfrid *Chich* 80–82; V Lower Beeding 82–86; V E Grinstead St Mary 86–96; RD E Grinstead 98–04; rtd 06; PtO *Chich* 12–17; *Eur* 16–21. *6 St Andrew's Close, Reigate RH2 7JF* T: (01737) 340193 E: frgordon@hotmail.co.uk

BOND, Mrs Hilary Rowenna. b 65. W Lon Inst of HE BA 86 Sussex Univ PGCE 87. Sarum Coll BA 17. **d** 17 **p** 18. NSM The Lytchetts and Upton *Sarum* 17–20; NSM Wareham from 20. *Holme Priory, East Holme, Wareham BH20 6AG* T: (01929) 551219 M: 07766-228189 E: hilary.bond@mac.com

BOND, Mrs Jill Margaret. b 45. Newton Park Coll Bath TCert 67. WEMTC 04. **d** 06 **p** 07. OLM Redmarley D'Abitot, Bromesberrow, Pauntley etc *Glouc* 06–11; NSM from 11. *Southfield, Hawcross, Redmarley, Gloucester GL19 3JQ* T: (01452) 840202 E: rev.jbond@googlemail.com

BOND, The Very Revd John Frederick Augustus. b 45. Open Univ BA 75. CITC 64. **d** 67 **p** 69. C Lisburn St Paul *Conn* 67–70; C Finaghy 70–77; I Ballynure and Ballyeaston 77–99; I Skerry w Rathcavan and Newtowncrommelin 99–16; Can Conn Cathl 96–98; Prec 98–01; Dean Conn 01–16; rtd 16; Dioc C *Conn* from 19. *3 Rectory Green, Broughshane, Ballymena BT42 4LH* T: (028) 2586 1415 M: 07711-285728 E: jfa.bond@btinternet.com

BOND, Canon Lawrence. b 53. ACIB 77. Sarum & Wells Th Coll 92. **d** 92 **p** 93. C Saffron Walden w Wendens Ambo and Littlebury *Chelmsf* 92–95; TV 96–00; P-in-c Takeley w Lt Canfield 00–04; R 04–09; RD Dunmow and Stansted 02–09; P-in-c Sible Hedingham w Castle Hedingham 09–15; RD Hinckford 10–15; rtd 15; PtO *Chelmsf* 15–19; Hon C Frinton from 19; AD St Osyth from 19; Hon Can Chelmsf Cathl from 20. *34 Cedar Close, Walton on the Naze CO14 8NJ* T: (01255) 484741 E: revlbond@hotmail.com

BOND, Linda. b 52. Nottm Univ BEd 80 Lon Inst of Educn MA 89. EAMTC 96. **d** 99 **p** 00. C Brackley St Pet w St Jas *Pet* 99–03; C Skegness Gp *Linc* 03–09; P-in-c Bromham w Oakley and Stagsden *St Alb* 09–17; rtd 17; PtO *Pet* from 18. *Address withheld by request* E: revdlinda@talktalk.net

BOND, Mrs Marian Nancy Hamlyn. b 49. Univ of Wales (Cardiff) BSc(Econ) 71 Westmr Coll Ox PGCE 72 Ex Univ MEd 77. SEITE BA 06. **d** 06 **p** 07. NSM Marden *Cant* 06–09; NSM Len Valley 09–11; NSM Tunstall and Bredgar 11–16; Asst Dir of Ords 09–16; rtd 16; PtO *Nor* from 16; *Truro* from 16; *Cant* from 20. *The Granary, 1 Monks Walk, Charing, Ashford TN27 0HT* M: 07966-442181 E: mnhbond@gmail.com

BOND, Mark Francis Wilson. b 53. Sarum & Wells Th Coll 89. **d** 91 **p** 92. C Taunton Lyngford *B & W* 91–95; V Highbridge 95–02; R Jersey St Brelade *Win* from 02. *The Rectory, La Marquanderie Hill, St Brelade, Jersey JE3 8EP* T: (01534) 742302 F: 490878 E: rector@stbreladeschurch.com

BOND, Paul Maxwell. b 36. TD 73. Glos Univ BA 00 ACIB 56. Oak Hill Th Coll 76. **d** 79 **p** 80. NSM Wisley w Pyrford *Guildf* 79–91; Org Children's Soc SW Lon 88–91; C Egham *Guildf* 91–93; C Horsell 93–94; V Rockfield and St Maughen's w Llangattock etc *Mon* 94–99; rtd 99; PtO S w Charlton on Otmoor, Oddington, Noke etc *Ox* 99–01; Hon C Ray Valley 01–04; Nat Liaison Officer Ch Tourism Assn 99–04; PtO *Glouc* from 05; *Guildf* 08–13. *Fosters, Pyrford Heath, Pyrford, Woking GU22 8SS* T: (01932) 351137 E: revdpaul007@gmail.com

BOND, Mrs Susan Fraser. b 55. SS Hild & Bede Coll Dur BEd 78 Leeds Univ MA 00. NOC 96. **d** 99 **p** 00. C Tickhill w Stainton *Sheff* 99–02; R Warmsworth 02–10; AD W Doncaster 06–07; V Ampleforth w Oswaldkirk, Gilling E etc *York* 10–16; rtd 16; PtO *York* from 17. *Swan View, Wrelton, Pickering YO18 8PF* T: (01751) 475885 E: sfbond007@gmail.com

BOND, Mrs Sybilla Anne. b 44. **d** 12 **p** 13. NSM Corfe Castle, Church Knowle, Kimmeridge etc *Sarum* 12–17; NSM Swanage and Studland 12–17; rtd 17; PtO *Sarum* from 17. *51 West Street, Corfe Castle, Wareham BH20 5HA* T: (01929) 480249

BONE, David Hugh. b 39. Worc Coll Ox BA 63 MA 67. **d** 06 **p** 07. OLM Almondsbury and Olveston *Bris* 06–19; PtO 19–20; NSM N Severnside from 20; NSM S Severnside from 20. *3 Hardy Lane, Tockington, Bristol BS32 4LJ* T: (01454) 614601 M: 07958-414729 E: david.bone10@btinternet.com

BONE, Mrs Evelyn Mary. b 48. WEMTC 05. **d** 08 **p** 09. NSM Draycot *Bris* 08–18; rtd 18; PtO *Bris* 19–20; *Lich* from 21. *4 Swan Court, Church Eaton, Stafford ST20 0AP* T: (01785) 822623 E: revelyn@hotmail.co.uk

BONE, Janet Mary. York Univ BA 71 Univ of Wales BTh 06. St Mich Coll Llan. **d** 05 **p** 06. NSM Trellech and Penallt

Mon 05–09; NSM Monmouth w Overmonnow etc 09–14; P-in-c Llanishen w Trellech Grange and Llanfihangel etc 14–20; rtd 20; PtO *Mon* from 20. *St Denis Vicarage, Llanishen, Chepstow NP16 6QE* M: 07748-344161 E: revjanetbone@gmail.com

BONE, Peter Joseph George. b 60. St Aug Coll of Th 15. **d** 18 **p** 19. C St Laur in Thanet *Cant* 18–21; P-in-c Clifton w Newton and Brownsover *Cov* from 21. *Address temp unknown* E: peterbone617@gmail.com

BONE, Canon Simon Adrian. b 78. Ripon Coll Cuddesdon BA 09. **d** 09 **p** 10. C Newquay *Truro* 09–11; C Chacewater w St Day and Carharrack 11–14; P-in-c 14–19; C Devoran 11–14; P-in-c 14–19; C Feock 11–14; P-in-c 14–19; C St Stythians w Perranarworthal and Gwennap 11–14; P-in-c 14–19; Asst Rural Link Officer 13–19; Hon Can Truro Cathl 18–19. *Address temp unknown* M: 07971-270615 E: fathersimon@btinternet.com

BONHAM, Mrs Valerie. b 47. ALA 94. SAOMC 94. **d** 97 **p** 98. NSM Newbury *Ox* 97–98; C Cookham 98–02; P-in-c Coleford w Holcombe *B & W* 02–14; rtd 14; PtO *B & W* from 15. *89 Balch Road, Wells BA5 2BX* T: (01749) 676326 E: valerie.bonham@zen.co.uk

BONIFACE, Timothy Roger. b 82. Ex Univ BA 05 Nottm Univ MA 12 St Chad's Coll Dur PhD 17. Westcott Ho Cam 12. **d** 16 **p** 17. C Chislehurst St Nic *Roch* 16–20; Chapl Girton Coll Cam from 20. *Girton College, Cambridge CB3 0JG* T: (01223) 338999 E: tim.r.boniface@gmail.com

BONNEY, The Very Revd Mark Philip John. b 57. St Cath Coll Cam BA 78 MA 82. St Steph Ho Ox BA 84 MA 89. **d** 85 **p** 86. C Stockton St Pet *Dur* 85–88; Chapl St Alb Abbey 88–90; Prec 90–92; V Eaton Bray w Edlesborough 92–96; R Gt Berkhamsted 96–04; RD Berkhamsted 02–04; Can Res and Treas Sarum Cathl 04–12; Dean Ely from 12. *The Deanery, The College, Ely CB7 4DN* T: (01353) 660316 E: m.bonney@elycathedral.org

BONNEYWELL, Miss Christine Mary. b 57. Univ of Wales (Lamp) BA 78 LTh 80. Sarum & Wells Th Coll 80. **d** 81 **p** 94. C Swansea St Pet *S & B* 81–84; C Llangyfelach 84–86; Chapl Univ of Wales (Lamp) *St D* 86–90; Educn Officer Wells Cathl *B & W* 90–95; C Yeovil H Trin w Barwick 95–97; Chapl Yeovil Distr Hosp 95–97; Chapl Pilgrim Health NHS Trust Boston 97–01; Chapl United Lincs Hosps NHS Trust 01–19; rtd 19. *4 Hospital Lane, Boston PE21 9BY* T: (01205) 355151

BONSEY, Hugh Richmond Lowry. b 49. Win Univ MA 12. Sarum & Wells Th Coll 74. **d** 76 **p** 77. C Bris St Mary Redcliffe w Temple etc 76–80; TV Sutton *Liv* 80–88; P-in-c Yatton Keynell *Bris* 88–89; P-in-c Biddestone w Slaughterford 88–89; P-in-c Castle Combe 88–89; P-in-c W Kington 88–89; P-in-c Nettleton w Littleton Drew 88–89; C Westbury-on-Trym H Trin 89–90; V Peasedown St John w Wellow *B & W* 90–04; rtd 18; C Sherborne w Castleton, Lillington and Longburton *Sarum* 18–21; PtO from 21. *67 Acreman Street, Sherborne DT9 3PH* E: hughbonsey@gmail.com

BOOKER, Canon Alison Susan Wray. b 74. Worc Coll of Educn BA 95 York St Jo Coll MA 04. Westcott Ho Cam 06. **d** 08 **p** 09. C Countesthorpe w Foston *Leic* 08–11; C Church Langton cum Tur Langton etc 11–13; C Houghton-on-the-Hill, Keyham and Hungarton 11–13; V Coplow from 13; Warden Past Assts 14–17; AD Launde from 17; AD Gartree II 17–19; Hon Can Leic Cathl from 18. *The Vicarage, Gaulby Road, Billesdon, Leicester LE7 9AG* T: 0116-259 6321 E: alisonbooker@btinternet.com

BOOKER, Michael Charles. b 36. LLCM 57 ARCO 58. Lon Coll of Div LTh 63. **d** 63 **p** 64. C Royston *St Alb* 63–66; C Mildenhall *St E* 66–68; Min Can St E Cathl 68–83; Prec 70–83; Chapl Framlingham Coll 84–99; rtd 99; PtO *St E* 99–16. *29 The Mowbrays, Framlingham, Woodbridge IP13 9DL* T: (01728) 723122 E: mail@michaelbooker.plus.com

BOOKER, Canon Michael Paul Montague. b 57. Jes Coll Ox BA 79 Bris Univ PGCE 80. Trin Coll Bris BA 87. **d** 87 **p** 88. C Cant St Mary Bredin 87–91; V Leamington Priors St Mary *Cov* 91–96; Dir Miss and Past Studies Ridley Hall Cam 96–05; P-in-c Comberton *Ely* 05–10; P-in-c Toft w Caldecote and Childerley 05–10; TR Lordsbridge 10–16; RD Bourn 13–16; Bp's Change Officer w Resp for Market Towns 16–21; rtd 21; Hon C Huntingdon *Ely* from 21; Hon Can Ely Cathl from 15. *The Rectory, 6 Common Lane, Hemingford Abbots, Huntingdon PE28 9AN* T: (01480) 467046 E: mike.booker@elydiocese.org

BOOKLESS, Andrew Pitcairn. b 63. Sheff Univ BA 85. St Jo Coll Nottm 90. **d** 92 **p** 93. C Llantrisant *Llan* 92–95; C Llangynwyd w Maesteg 95–97; V Bargoed and Deri w Brithdir 97–12; R Hubberston *St D* 12–14; I Hubberston and Herbrandston 15–19; V Roose from 19. *The Rectory, 35 Westaway Drive, Hakin, Milford Haven SA73 3EQ* T: (01646) 696914 E: ahbookless@googlemail.com

BOOKLESS, Mrs Anne Karen. b 68. St Mellitus Coll 16. d 19 p 20. C Norwood St Mary *Lon* from 19. *The Rectory, 26A Tentelow Lane, Southall UB2 4LE* E: revdannebookless@gmail.com

BOOKLESS, David John Charles. b 62. Jes Coll Cam MA 83 Cam Univ PhD 19 PGCE. Trin Coll Bris MA 91. d 91 p 92. C Southall Green St Jo *Lon* 91–99; P-in-c Southall St Geo 99–01; Nat Dir A Rocha UK 01–11; Dir Th A Rocha Internat from 11; Hon C Southall Green St Jo *Lon* 03–18; P-in-c Norwood St Mary from 18. *The Rectory, 26A Tentelow Lane, Southall UB2 4LE* M: 07974-212713 E: dave.bookless@gmail.com

BOOKLESS, Mrs Rosemary. b 26. Westf Coll Lon BA 47 DipEd 49 Serampore Univ BD 72. St Mich Ho Ox 56. dss 80 d 91 p 94. Willoughby-on-the-Wolds w Wysall and Widmerpool *S'well* 80–85; rtd 85; PtO *Leic* 85–89; Loughborough Em 89–91; NSM 91–95; NSM Loughborough Em and St Mary in Charnwood 95–97; PtO 97–03; *Glouc* 16–17. *19 Capel Court, The Burgage, Prestbury, Cheltenham GL52 3EL* T: (01242) 236937 E: rosemary.bookless926@btinternet.com

BOON, Mrs Linda Margaret Claire. b 57. Buckingham Univ BA 79 Birm Univ PGCE 80 MEd 91 Sheff Univ MA 12. Yorks Min Course 09. d 12 p 13. NSM Ripon Cathl 12–14; *Leeds* 14–17; NSM Bishop Thornton, Burnt Yates, Markington etc from 17; Tutor St Hild Coll from 17. *Cowgate Manor Barn, Shaw Mills, Harrogate HG3 3HP* T: (01423) 779179 M: 07961-893163 E: revd.linda.boon@gmail.com

BOON, Marion. *See* SIMMONS, Marion

BOON, Stephen David. b 81. Em Coll Cam MA 04. Wycliffe Hall Ox BA 10. d 12 p 13. NSM Tunbridge Wells St Jo *Roch* 12–16; Tutor Cornhill Tr Course from 16. *10 Dunstan Grove, Tunbridge Wells TN4 9ND* T: (01892) 528451 E: stephen.boon@cantab.net

BOON, William John. b 54. Glouc Sch of Min 84. d 88 p 89. NSM Matson *Glouc* 88–91; C Gt Witcombe 91–95; C Brockworth 91–96; P-in-c Sharpness w Purton and Brookend 96–99; P-in-c Slimbridge 97–99; R Sharpness, Purton, Brookend and Slimbridge from 00; AD Dursley 02–07. *The Vicarage, Sanigar Lane, Newtown, Berkeley GL13 9NF* T: (01453) 811360 E: bill.boon@btinternet.com

BOOT, Felicity Olivia. b 43. TCert 64. STETS 94. d 97 p 98. NSM Lyndhurst and Emery Down and Minstead *Win* 97–04; Chapl Southn Univ Hosps NHS Trust 04–09; rtd 09; PtO *Win* from 09. *The Firs, Pikes Hill, Lyndhurst SO43 7AY* T: (023) 8028 2616 E: felicityboot@hotmail.com *or* felicityboot@yahoo.com

BOOTH, Charles. *See* BOOTH, Ewart Charles

BOOTH, David. b 44. Coll of Resurr Mirfield 72. d 74 p 75. C Osmondthorpe St Phil *Ripon* 74–77; C Armley w New Wortley 77–79; V Leeds St Wilfrid 79–95; V Royton St Paul *Man* 95–09; rtd 09. *13 Lyon Street, Shaw, Oldham OL2 7RU* T: (01706) 661172 E: davidbooth6@live.co.uk

BOOTH, Derek. b 36. LTCL ALCM AKC 61. d 62 p 63. C Woodchurch *Ches* 62–65; C Penrith St Andr *Carl* 65–67; C Tranmere St Paul *Ches* 67–70; C Wilmslow 70–72; V Micklehurst 73–97; C Staveley and Barrow Hill *Derby* 97–01; rtd 01; PtO *Derby* from 01. *9 Ilam Close, Inkersall, Chesterfield S43 3EW* T: (01246) 475421 E: delbooth@talktalk.net

BOOTH, Eric James. b 43. Open Univ BA 84. NOC 86. d 89 p 90. NSM Nelson St Phil *Blackb* 89–93; NSM Fence and Newchurch-in-Pendle 93–97; NSM Hapton w Padiham and Padiham Green 97–03; rtd 03; PtO *Blackb* 04–17. *5 Round Hill Place, Cliviger, Burnley BB10 4UA* T: (01282) 450708 E: ericjbooth1@yahoo.co.uk

BOOTH, Ewart Charles. b 67. LTCL 85 K Coll Lon LLB 88. Sarum & Wells Th Coll BTh 93. d 93 p 95. NSM Tadley St Pet *Win* 93–95; C Highclere w Hinton Admiral 95–00; R W Parley *Sarum* from 00. *The Rectory, 250 New Road, West Parley, Ferndown BH22 8EW* T: (01202) 873561

BOOTH, Graham Richard. b 55. Birm Univ BSocSc 75. St Jo Coll Nottm 89. d 91 p 92. C Woodthorpe *S'well* 91–96; P-in-c Trowell 96–02; P-in-c Awsworth w Cossall 00–02; R Trowell, Awsworth and Cossall 02–05; Warden Open Gate Retreat Ho 05–15; Guardian Community of Aid and Hilda from 12; NSM Burravoe *Ab* from 19; NSM Lerwick from 19. *The Glebe, Fetlar, Shetland ZE2 9DJ* T: (01957) 733380

BOOTH, Ian George. b 64. Chich Th Coll 85 Linc Th Coll 87. d 88 p 89. C Pet St Mary Boongate 88–90; C Hawley H Trin *Guildf* 90–94; V Willesden St Mary *Lon* 94–03; P-in-c Gosport H Trin *Portsm* 03–05; V 05–06; V Gosport Ch Ch 05–06; RD Gosport 03–06; V Leigh-on-Sea St Marg *Chelmsf* 09–17; TR Wood Green St Mich w Bounds Green St Gabr etc *Lon* from 17; P-in-c Alexandra Park from 21; AD E Haringey 17–20; AD Haringey from 20. *The Rectory, 1A Selborne Road, London N22 7TL* E: frianbooth@gmail.com

BOOTH, Martin Allison. b 54. K Coll Lon MA 06. SEITE. d 09 p 10. C Wimbledon *S'wark* 09–12; V Riverhead w Dunton Green *Roch* 12–19; RD Sevenoaks 16–19; rtd 19; PtO *Guildf* from 19. *2 Russet Grove, Cranleigh GU6 7FT*

BOOTH, Paul Harris. b 49. St Jo Coll Nottm. d 79 p 80. C Thorpe Edge *Bradf* 79–82; P-in-c Frizinghall 82–83; TV Shipley St Paul and Frizinghall 83–97; rtd 97; PtO *Bradf* 97–14; *Leeds* from 14; Hon Chapl Bradf Cathl from 14. *11 Derwent Avenue, Wilsden, Bradford BD15 0LY* T: (01535) 958939

BOOTHBY, Mrs Julia. b 64. St Andr Univ MTheol 87. SAOMC 02. d 04 p 05. C Welwyn *St Alb* 04–08; TV Ouzel Valley 08–11; TV Bishop's Hatfield, Lemsford and N Mymms 11–18; P-in-c Dingwall *Mor* from 18; P-in-c Strathpeffer from 18; P-in-c Invergordon St Ninian from 18. *4 Castle Street, Dingwall IV15 9HU* M: 07952-514228 E: juliabby@sky.com *or* julia.boothby@btinternet.com

BOOTHROYD, Callum. b 69. All SS Cen for Miss & Min 17. d 19 p 20. C Hyde St Geo w St Thos *Ches* from 19. *72 Market Street, Mottram, Hyde SK14 6JG* M: 07881-026594 E: revcallum@outlook.com

BOOYS, Canon Susan Elizabeth. b 56. Bris Univ BA 78 LMH Ox PGCE 79. SAOMC 92. d 95 p 96. C Kidlington w Hampton Poyle *Ox* 95–99; TV Dorchester 99–05; TR from 05; TV Warborough 99–05; TR from 05; AD Aston and Cuddesdon 07–12; Hon Can Ch Ch from 08. *The Rectory, Manor Farm Road, Dorchester-on-Thames, Wallingford OX10 7HZ* T/F: (01865) 340007 E: rector@dorchester-abbey.org.uk

BOREHAM, Harold Leslie. b 37. S'wark Ord Course. d 72 p 73. C Whitton and Thurleston w Akenham *St E* 72–77; R Saxmundham 77–85; V Felixstowe SS Pet and Paul 85–96; Chapl Felixstowe Hosp 85–96; Chapl Bartlet Hosp Felixstowe 95–96; P-in-c Ramsgate St Mark *Cant* 96–01; V 01–03; Chapl E Kent NHS and Soc Care Partnership Trust 98–03; rtd 03; PtO *St E* from 03; *Chelmsf* from 05. *313 St John's Road, Colchester CO4 0JR* T: (01206) 853769 E: harrylboreham@googlemail.com

BORLEY, Mark Letchford. b 61. Lon Univ BSc 83 PhD 87. St Jo Coll Nottm MTh 03. d 04 p 05. C W Swindon and the Lydiards *Bris* 04–05; C Swindon St Aug and Swindon All SS w St Barn 05–07; C Cricklade w Latton 07–09; P-in-c Allington and Maidstone St Pet *Cant* 09–12; PtO 12–14; C W Sheppey 14–15; V Ewell St Fran *Guildf* 15–18; P-in-c Stoneleigh 18–19; P-in-c Hoo St Werburgh *Roch* from 20. *The Vicarage, Vicarage Lane, Hoo, Rochester ME3 9BB* T: (01634) 250291 E: revborley@gmail.com *or* vicar@hoochurch.org.uk

BORMAN, Alexander John. b 88. Linc Sch of Th and Min 17. d 19 p 20. NSM Branston w Nocton and Potterhanworth *Linc* 19–20; NSM Boultham from 20. *2 Bottesford Close, Lincoln LN6 3YR* T: (01522) 688496 E: aborman3.142@gmail.com

BORROWDALE, Geoffrey Nigel. b 61. Southn Univ BSc 83 W Sussex Inst of HE PGCE 94. Chich Th Coll 87. d 90 p 99. C Tilehurst St Mich *Ox* 90–91; PtO *Chich* 93–97; NSM Sunninghill *Ox* 98–99; C Bracknell 99–01; P-in-c Theale and Englefield 01–11; C The Churn 11–13; V Hayes St Anselm *Lon* 13–19; R Hasland *Derby* from 19; V Temple Normanton from 19. *The Rectory, 49 Church Side, Hasland, Chesterfield S41 0JX* T: (01246) 232486 E: frgeoffrey@stpaulshasland.com

BORTHWICK, Anne Christine. *See* ROWLEY, Anne Christine

BORTHWICK, Kirsty Louise. b 91. Regent's Park Coll Ox BA 13 St Andr Univ MLitt 15. Westcott Ho Cam 17. d 21. C Ouzel Valley *St Alb* from 21. *138 Brooklands Drive, Leighton Buzzard LU7 3PG* E: revdkirstyborthwick@gmail.com

BOSHER, Philip Ross. b 61. Greenwich Univ CertEd 03 Univ of Wales MTh 07. Sarum & Wells Th Coll 84. d 87 p 88. C Warminster St Denys *Sarum* 87–88; C Warminster St Denys, Upton Scudamore etc 88–90; P-in-c Farley w Pitton and W Dean w E Grimstead 90–91; TV Alderbury Team 91–96; CF 96–16; P-in-c Winshill *Derby* 16–19; C Hartshorne and Bretby 16–19; V Winshill and Bretby from 20; AD Mercia 20–21. *The Vicarage, 54 Mill Hill Lane, Burton-on-Trent DE15 0BB* M: 07906-956883 E: prbosher@gmail.com

BOSLEY, Mrs Susan. b 65. Birm Univ BA 87 Open Univ PGCE 96. St Mellitus Coll BA 20. d 20 p 21. C Horley *S'wark* from 20. *84 Balcombe Road, Horley RH6 9AY* M: 07909-525873 E: suebosley1@gmail.com

BOSS, Mrs Ann. b 42. Cen Lancs Univ BA 93. CBDTI 99. d 02 p 03. NSM Scorton and Barnacre and Calder Vale *Blackb* 02–05; P-in-c Hanmer Springs NZ 05–10; PtO *Blackb* from 10. *School House Barn, Inglewhite Road, Inglewhite, Preston PR3 2LD* T: (01995) 643146 E: ann.boss227@btinternet.com

BOSSWARD, Eric Paul. b 63. CQSW 90. Trin Coll Bris BA 99. d 99 p 00. C Ecclesall *Sheff* 99–01; C Netherthorpe St Steph 01–04; Co-ord Chapl HM YOI Castington 04–12; V Preston St Cuth *Blackb* 12–16; V Headington St Mary *Ox* from 16.

St Mary's Vicarage, Bayswater Road, Headington, Oxford OX3 9EY M: 07982-264424 E: eric.bossward@talktalk.net
BOSTON, Archdeacon of. *See* ALLAIN CHAPMAN, The Ven Justine Penelope Heathcote
BOSWELL, Canon Colin John Luke. b 47. Sarum & Wells Th Coll 72. **d** 74 **p** 75. C Upper Tooting H Trin *S'wark* 74–78; C Sydenham St Phil 78–79; C St Helier 80–83; P-in-c Caterham 83–95; P-in-c Chaldon 85–95; RD Caterham 85–95; V Croydon St Jo 95–16; RD Croydon Cen 00–06; rtd 16; Chapl St Dunstan's Coll Catford from 16; Hon C Sydenham H Trin and St Aug *S'wark* 16–19; P-in-c Honor Oak Park St Aug from 19; Hon Can S'wark Cathl from 99. *129A Honor Oak Park, London SE23 3LD* T: (020) 8699 4469 M: 07854-265277 E: colinlukeboswell@outlook.com
BOSWELL, Stephen James. b 84. Oak Hill Th Coll 15. **d** 18 **p** 19. C Normanton *Derby* from 18. *23 Nevinson Drive, Sunnyhill, Derby DE23 1GX* E: steve.boswell@stgiles-derby.org.uk
BOTHAM, Arthur. b 53. St Jo Coll Nottm. **d** 00 **p** 01. C Hartley Wintney, Elvetham, Winchfield etc *Win* 00–04; TV Basingstoke 04–14; V Popley w Limes Park and Rooksdown from 14; AD Basingstoke 11–15. *The Vicarage, 25 Tewkesbury Close, Popley, Basingstoke RG24 9DU* T: (01256) 324734 E: arthur.botham@btinternet.com
BOTT, Graham Paul. b 49. Staffs Univ MBA 95. NOC 00. **d** 03 **p** 04. NSM Rickerscote *Lich* 03–13; P-in-c Hoar Cross w Newchurch from 13; Chapl Abbots Bromley Sch 14–19. *Church Cottage, Maker Lane, Hoar Cross, Burton-on-Trent   DE13 8QR*   T: (01283)   576058 E: graham.pbott@btopenworld.com
BOTTERILL, David Darrell. b 45. Open Univ BA. Sarum & Wells Th Coll. **d** 83 **p** 84. C Blandford Forum and Langton Long etc *Sarum* 83–86; TV Shaston 86–00; Chapl HM YOI Guys Marsh 89–91; P-in-c Portland St Jo *Sarum* 00–09; Asst Chapl N Dorset Primary Care Trust 01–09; rtd 09; Hon Chapl Miss to Seafarers from 02; PtO *Sarum* from 10. *41 Hawthorn Avenue, Gillingham SP8 4ST*   T: (01747) 821601   M: 07970-371757 E: david.botterill45@btinternet.com   *or* ddbotterill@gmail.com
BOTTING, Paul Lloyd. b 43. Brasted Th Coll 67 St Mich Coll Llan 69. **d** 71 **p** 72. C Hucknall Torkard *S'well* 71–74; C Cen Torquay *Ex* 74–76; P-in-c Sutton in Ashfield St Mich *S'well* 76; V 77–88; Chapl King's Mill Hosp Sutton-in-Ashfield 85–88; NSM Vale of Belvoir *Leic* 95–97; C High Framland Par 97–01; C Waltham on the Wolds, Stonesby, Saxby etc 97–01; C Wymondham w Edmondthorpe, Buckminster etc 97–01; P-in-c High Framland Par 01–10; rtd 10; PtO *Leic* 10–21; *S'well* from 11. *9 Orchard Close, Radcliffe-on-Trent, Nottingham NG12 2BN* T: 0115-933 2591 M: 07770-853762 E: plbpixie@gmail.com
BOTTLEY, Canon Kate. b 75. Trin & All SS Coll Leeds BA 97 Open Univ MTh 08. St Jo Coll Nottm LTh 08. **d** 08 **p** 09. C Skegby w Teversal *S'well* 08–11; P-in-c Blyth and Scrooby w Ranskill 11–13; V 13–16; Chapl N Notts Coll of FE 11–16; NSM Retford Area 17–19; NSM Retford St Sav from 19; Hon Can S'well Minster from 21. *Address withheld by request*
BOTTOMER, Sally Ann. b 68. **d** 14 **p** 15. C Aston Clinton w Buckland and Drayton Beauchamp *Ox* 14–18; R from 18. *The Rectory, 23 New Road, Aston Clinton,   Aylesbury   HP22 5BB*   M: 07967-208181 E: revsally.bottomer@btinternet.com
BOTWRIGHT, Canon Adrian Paul. b 55. St Jo Coll Ox MA PGCE. Westcott Ho Cam 80. **d** 82 **p** 83. C Chapel Allerton *Ripon* 82–85; Chapl Chapel Allerton Hosp 82–85; C Bourne *Guildf* 85–88; V Weston 88–94; R Skipton H Trin *Bradf* 94–13; P-in-c Embsay w Eastby 05–13; Hon Can Bradf Cathl 02–13; PtO from 14; *Leeds* from 17. *24 Ripon Way, Carlton Miniott, Thirsk YO7 4LR* T: (01845) 523491 E: adrianbotwright@gmail.com
BOUCHER, Geoffrey John. b 61. Warwick Univ BA 82 K Coll Lon 94 ACA 87. Ridley Hall Cam 94. **d** 96 **p** 97. C Tavistock and Gulworthy *Ex* 96–01; P-in-c W Monkton *B & W* 01–11; R W Monkton w Kingston St Mary, Broomfield etc 11–15; RD Taunton 10–15; R Hartford and Houghton w Wyton *Ely* from 16. *The Rectory, 3 Rectory Lane, Wyton, Huntingdon PE28 2AQ* T: (01480) 461846 E: geoffboucher@btinternet.com
BOUDIER, Rosemary. *See* TALLOWIN, Rosemary
BOUGHTON, Mrs Elisabeth Mary Victoria. b 66. St Anne's Coll Ox BA 87 MA 93. Ridley Hall Cam 89. **d** 91 **p** 94. C Guildf Ch Ch 91–95; Chapl St Cath Sch Bramley 92–97; NSM Fetcham *Guildf* 97–14; Chapl Guildf YMCA 04–14; Tutor CME *Guildf* 08–14; PtO *Ox* from 14. *91 Marlborough Road, Oxford OX1 4LX*
BOUGHTON, Canon Michael John. b 37. Kelham Th Coll 57. **d** 62 **p** 63. C Grantham St Wulfram *Linc* 62–66; C Kingsthorpe *Pet* 66–68; C Linc St Nic w St Jo Newport 68–72;

V Scunthorpe All SS 72–79; V Crowle 79–89; TR Bottesford w Ashby 89–02; Can and Preb Linc Cathl from 00; rtd 02; PtO *Linc* from 02. *45 Albion Crescent, Lincoln LN1 1EB* T: (01552) 569653 E: mboughton@aol.com
BOUGHTON, Miss Ruth Frances. b 52. Ox Brookes Univ BA 10. Birm Bible Inst 71. **d** 07 **p** 08. OLM Chenies and Lt Chalfont, Latimer and Flaunden *Ox* 07–10; NSM from 10. *17 Bell Lane, Amersham HP7 9PF* T: (01494) 764221 E: revboughton@live.co.uk
BOULLIER, Canon Kenneth John. b 51. Trin Coll Bris 82. **d** 84 **p** 85. C Heref St Pet w St Owen and St Jas 84–87; V Nutley *Chich* 88–93; R Maresfield 88–93; NZ 93–97; R Nailsea H Trin *B & W* 97–08; P-in-c St Just-in-Roseland and St Mawes *Truro* 08–18; RD Powder 13–17; Hon Can Truro Cathl 15–18; rtd 18. *7 Carnjewey Way, St Austell PL25 4FU* E: revkjb@hotmail.co.uk
BOULT, David Ronald. b 51. Bris Univ BSc 73. St Mich Coll Llan 04. **d** 07 **p** 08. NSM Llantwit Major *Llan* 07–10; NSM Cowbridge 11–16; PtO from 16. *52 The Verlands, Cowbridge CF71 7BY*   T/F: (01446)   772166   M: 07767-818257 E: daveboult@hotmail.co.uk
BOULT, Geoffrey Michael. b 56. Southn Univ BTh 88 Bris Univ MA 92 Birm Univ MSc 96 PGCE 98. Sarum & Wells Th Coll 77. **d** 80 **p** 81. C Newark w Hawton, Cotham and Shelton *S'well* 80–83; TV Melksham *Sarum* 83–90; P-in-c Charminster and Stinsford 90–95; PtO *Birm* 95–96; *Sarum* 95–98; Hon C Bradford Peverell, Stratton, Frampton etc 09–14; P-in-c Arlesey w Astwick *St Alb* 14–17; V from 17. *The Rectory, 77 Church Lane, Arlesey SG15 6UX* T: (01462) 731227 M: 07970-371757 E: vicar@arlesey.org.uk
BOULTER, Adam Charles. b 71. Bath Coll of HE BA 93 Kingston Univ MA 04 Fitzw Coll Cam BA 07 MA 11. Westcott Ho Cam 05. **d** 08 **p** 09. C Battersea St Mary *S'wark* 08–12; Port Chapl Aqaba Jordan 12–16; PtO *S'wark* 16–17; P-in-c Poitou-Charentes *Eur* 16–19; Dean and Prin St Patr Bible Coll Toliara Madagascar from 19. *Diosesin'ny Toliara, BP 408, 601 Toliara, Madagascar* E: adamboulter@cantab.net
BOULTER, Michael Geoffrey. b 32. Lon Univ BD 56. Tyndale Hall Bris 53. **d** 57 **p** 58. C Tranmere St Cath *Ches* 57–60; R Cheetham Hill *Man* 60–65; R Tollard Royal w Farnham *Sarum* 65–66; Chapl Alderney Hosp Poole 66–96; V Branksome St Clem *Sarum* 66–96; rtd 96. *7 Temple Trees, 13 Portarlington Road, Bournemouth BH4 8BU* T: (01202) 768718
BOULTER, Paul Roger. b 81. St Jo Coll Dur BA 03. Ridley Hall Cam 12. **d** 15 **p** 16. C Bedford Ch Ch *St Alb* 15–18; V Caton w Littledale *Blackb* from 18; V Over Kellet 18–21. *The Vicarage, 153 Brookhouse Road, Brookhouse, Lancaster LA2 9NX* T: (01524) 770300 E: revpaulboulter@gmail.com
BOULTON, Mrs Alison Peta. b 55. St Mich Coll Sarum CertEd 76. All SS Cen for Miss & Min 16. **d** 18 **p** 19. NSM Middlewich w Byley *Ches* from 18. *21 Main Road, Moulton, Northwich CW9 8NU* T: (01606) 591559 M: 07879-681827 E: alisonb_b@yahoo.co.uk
BOULTON, Christopher David. b 50. Keble Coll Ox BA 71 MA 80. Cuddesdon Coll 71. **d** 74 **p** 75. C St Mary-at-Latton *Chelmsf* 74–77; C Shrub End 77–80; P-in-c Gt Bentley 80–83; V 83–89; V Cherry Hinton St Andr *Ely* 89–04; P-in-c Teversham 90–04; P-in-c Much Hadham *St Alb* 04–05; TR Albury, Braughing, Furneux Pelham, Lt Hadham etc 06–12; RD Bishop's Stortford 07–12; Chapl Bromley Coll 12–19; rtd 19. *7 Stamford Drive, Coalville LE67 4TA* T: (01530) 451001 M: 07580-137977 E: boultonc50@gmail.com
BOULTON, Kingsley Garth. b 50. Sheff Univ BA 72 MA 74 MCLIP 74. **d** 18. NSM York All SS Pavement w St Crux and St Mich from 18; NSM York St Denys from 18; NSM York St Helen w St Martin from 18; NSM York St Olave w St Giles from 18. *15 Blakeney Place, York YO10 3HZ* T: (01904) 411535 E: kingsley.boulton@gmail.com
BOULTON, Ms Louise Jane. b 74. Goldsmiths' Coll Lon BA 93 Heythrop Coll Lon MA 98. SEITE 02. **d** 05 **p** 06. NSM Wandsworth St Anne *S'wark* 05–08; NSM Wandsworth St Anne w St Faith 08–10; PtO from 12. *17 Somers Road, London SW2 2AE* T: (020) 7096 1646 M: 07989-333016 E: louise@trespassersw.net
BOULTON-LEA, Peter John. b 46. St Jo Coll Dur BA 68. Westcott Ho Cam 69. **d** 71 **p** 72. C Farlington *Portsm* 72–75; C Darlington St Jo *Dur* 75–77; R E and W Horndon w Lt Warley *Chelmsf* 77–82; V Herefnsade *Guildf* 82–91; R Kirk Sandall and Edenthorpe *Sheff* 91–96; RD Doncaster 95–96; V Campsall 96–97; R Burghwallis and Campsall 97–98; V Tattenham Corner and Burgh Heath *Guildf* 98–03; V Thorne *Sheff* 03–08; rtd 08; PtO *Ox* from 08. *25 Larkfields, Headington, Oxford OX3 8PF* T: (01865) 744302
BOULTON-REYNOLDS, Mrs Jean. b 49. Univ of Wales (Lamp) MA 04. Sarum Th Coll 93. **d** 96 **p** 97. C Harnham *Sarum* 96–99; C Salisbury St Mark 99–01; TV Westborough *Guildf*

01–05; TV Barnes *S'wark* 05–11; rtd 11; PtO *Sarum* from 12; *Bris* 15–19; Dioc Adv in Spiritual Direction *Sarum* from 16. *21 Andover Road, Orpington BR6 8BW* M: 07921-924499 E: jeanboultonreynolds@gmail.com

BOUMENJEL, Nejib. b 73. St Jo Coll Nottm. **d** 14 **p** 15. C Birm St Geo 14–18; V Hall Green Ascension from 18. *The Vicarage, 592 Fox Hollies Road, Hall Green, Birmingham B28 9DX* M: 07769-624598 E: b_nejib2002@yahoo.co.uk

BOUNDY, Canon Gerald <u>Neville</u>. b 36. BA. Linc Th Coll. **d** 65 **p** 66. C Bris St Mary Redcliffe w Temple etc 65–70; P-in-c Southmead 70–72; V 72–81; V Cotham St Sav w St Mary 81–99; Hon Can Bris Cathl 96–99; rtd 99; PtO *Bris* from 99. *10 Morley Road, Southville, Bristol BS3 1DT* M: 07502-225506 E: neville.boundy@icloud.com

✠**BOURKE, The Rt Revd Michael Gay.** b 41. CCC Cam BA 63 MA 67. Cuddesdon Coll 65. **d** 67 **p** 68 **c** 93. C Gt Grimsby St Jas *Linc* 67–71; C Digswell *St Alb* 71–73; C-in-c Panshanger CD 73–78; Course Dir St Alb Minl Tr Scheme 75–87; V Southill *St Alb* 78–86; Adn Bedford 86–93; Area Bp Wolverhampton *Lich* 93–06; rtd 07; PtO *Heref* from 07; Hon Asst Bp Heref from 08. *The Maltings, Little Stretton, Church Stretton SY6 6AP* T: (01694) 722910

BOURKE, Canon Ronald Samuel James. b 50. MA HDipEd. **d** 79 **p** 80. C Portadown St Mark *Arm* 79–83; I Carnteel and Crilly 83–90; I Mountmellick w Coolbanagher, Rosenallis etc *M & K* 90–97; I Kingscourt w Syddan 97–09; Chan Kildare Cathl 00–09; Can Meath 00–09; I Boyle and Elphin w Aghanagh, Kilbryan etc *K, E & A* 09–16; Preb Tipper St Patr Cathl Dublin 00–16; Can Elphin Cathl *K, E & A* 12–16; rtd 16. *Mullaghnabreena, Collooney, Co Sligo, Republic of Ireland* T: (00353) (71) 916 7596 M: 89-458 1920 E: rsjbourke@hotmail.com

BOURKE, Stanley Gordon. b 48. CITC 78. **d** 78 **p** 79. C Dundonald *D & D* 78–80; C Lurgan Ch the Redeemer 81–82; I Dungiven w Bovevagh *D & R* 82–89; I Lurgan St Jo *D & D* 89–03; I Inishmacsaint *Clogh* 03–14; Preb Clogh Cathl 06–14; Chan Clogh Cathl 11–14; rtd 14. *63 Church Avenue, Bangor BT20 3EG* M: 07975-993213 E: sgbourke@hotmail.co.uk

BOURNE, Anne Clare. b 63. Univ of Wales (Cardiff) BEd 85. SEITE 08. **d** 11 **p** 12. NSM Sevenoaks St Luke *Roch* 11–18; C 18–19; C W Sevenoaks 19–21; TV from 21. *St Luke's Vicarage, 30 Eardley Road, Sevenoaks TN13 1XT* M: 07512-734224 E: rev.annebourne@gmail.com

BOURNE, Mrs Carole Sylvia. b 47. York Univ BA 68 LSE MSc 79 PhD 85. SEITE 99. **d** 02 **p** 03. C Epsom St Martin *Guildf* 02–05; NSM E Molesey 05–12; RD Emly 10–12; PtO 13–16 and from 18; *S'wark* from 14. *Flat 21, 9 St Mary's Road, Surbiton KT6 4JG* M: 07957-295864 E: cbeezles@me.com

BOURNE, Colin Douglas. b 56. Culham Coll of Educn CertEd 77. Oak Hill Th Coll BA 04. **d** 04 **p** 05. C Wellington All SS w Eyton *Lich* 04–08; P-in-c Toton *S'well* 08–11; V 11–21; AD Nottm S from 19; Public Preacher from 21. *95 Stapleford Lane, Beeston, Nottingham NG9 6FZ* T: 0115-973 1138 M: 07821-967879 E: revcolinbourne@gmail.com

BOURNE, David James. b 54. Reading Univ BA 76. Trin Coll Bris 77. **d** 79 **p** 80. C W Bromwich Gd Shep w St Jo *Lich* 79–84; V Riseley w Bletsoe *St Alb* 84–05; V Hailsham *Chich* from 05. *St Mary's Vicarage, Vicarage Road, Hailsham BN27 1BL* T: (01323) 842381 E: davidjbourne@googlemail.com

BOURNE, Canon Dennis <u>John</u>. b 32. Ridley Hall Cam 58. **d** 60 **p** 61. C Gorleston St Andr *Nor* 60–64; Min Gorleston St Mary CD 64–79; V Costessey 79–86; R Hingham w Wood Rising w Scoulton 86–97; RD Hingham and Mitford 90–95; Hon Can Nor Cathl 93–97; rtd 97; PtO *Nor* 97–06. *Amron, Star Lane, Long Stratton, Norwich NR15 2XH* T: (01508) 530863 E: johnbourne@onetel.com

BOURNE, Mrs Diana Mary. b 46. St Jo Coll York BEd 68. S Dios Minl Tr Scheme 92. **d** 95 **p** 96. C Pinner *Lon* 95–00; V Lamberhurst and Matfield *Roch* 00–06; rtd 07; PtO *Roch* 07–17; *Cant* from 07. *The Pump House, Angley Road, Cranbrook TN17 2PN* T: (01580) 712005 E: revdbourne@hotmail.com

BOURNE, Hugh Edward. b 86. Sussex Univ BSc 08. Oak Hill Th Coll BA 15. **d** 15 **p** 16. C Lindfield *Chich* from 15. *2 Church Close, Francis Road, Lindfield, Haywards Heath RH16 2JB* T: (01444) 483945 M: 07879-620322 E: revhughbo@gmail.com

BOURNE, The Ven Ian Grant. b 32. Univ of NZ BA 55 Otago Univ BD 75. **d** 56 **p** 57. NZ 56–65 and from 67; Adn Wellington 78–86 and 90–95; C Epsom St Martin *Guildf* 65–67. *19 Nisson Street, Riccarton, Christchurch 8011, New Zealand* T: (0064) (4) 233 0466 E: ian.marg@bourne.co.nz

BOURNE, John. *See* BOURNE, Dennis John

BOURNE, Nigel Irvine. b 60. St Jo Coll Ox BA 82 MA 86 Open Univ MBA 09. Trin Coll Bris BA 92. **d** 92 **p** 93. C Bedhampton *Portsm* 92–94; C Newport St Jo 94–98; V Chalk *Roch* from

98; RD Gravesend from 18. *The Vicarage, 2A Vicarage Lane, Gravesend DA12 4TF* T: (01474) 567906 F: 745147 E: vicarofchalk@hotmail.com

BOURNE, Canon Philip John. b 61. Sussex Univ BEd 83 Aber Univ MLitt 86 Ex Univ MEd 96 Liv Univ DMin 00 FRSA 97. Cranmer Hall Dur 85. **d** 87 **p** 88. C Gildersome *Wakef* 87–89; Chapl Ex Univ 89–93; Assoc Chapl The Hague and Voorschoten *Eur* 94–95; Chapl Voorschoten 96–06; Can Brussels Cathl 04–06; Dir of Ords *Chich* 07–14; TR Sidmouth, Woolbrook, Salcombe Regis, Sidbury etc *Ex* 14–18; Chapl Oporto *Eur* 18–21; rtd 21. *The Old School, Whittingham, Alnwick NE66 4UP* T: (01665) 574008 M: 07415-673231 E: philipjohnbourne@gmail.com

BOURNE, Mrs Sarah Madeleine. b 66. New Hall Cam BA 88 PGCE 89 MA 92. Wycliffe Hall Ox 12. **d** 15 **p** 16. Asst Chapl Tudor Hall Sch from 12; C Shipston-on-Stour w Honington and Idlicote *Cov* 15–18; PtO *Ox* 15–19; C Cov Cathl 17–18; NSM Banbury *Ox* from 19; Chapl for the Arts Banbury from 21; PtO *Cov* from 18. *2 Home Farm, Willington, Shipston-on-Stour CV36 5AS* T: (01608) 661249 E: revsarahbourne@gmail.com

BOURNEMOUTH, Archdeacon of. *Vacant*

BOURNER, Paul. b 48. CA Tr Coll. **d** 90 **p** 91. CA from 79; C Ipswich St Mary at Stoke w St Pet *St E* 90–93; R Ufford w Bredfield and Hasketon 93–01; V Ipswich St Thos 01–14; rtd 14; PtO *St E* from 15. *62 Dereham Avenue, Ipswich IP3 0QF* E: paul.bourner@ntlworld.com

BOUSFIELD, Andrew Michael. b 70. Middx Univ BA 92. Oak Hill Th Coll BA 00. **d** 00 **p** 01. C Beckenham Ch Ch *Roch* 00–03; C Surbiton Hill Ch Ch *S'wark* 03–07; C Patcham *Chich* 07–18; V Salisbury St Mark and Laverstock *Sarum* from 18. *St Mark's Vicarage, 62 Barrington Road, Salisbury SP1 3JD* M: 07866-434117 E: vicar@stmarkstandrew.org

BOUSKILL, David Walter. b 72. Westcott Ho Cam 95. **d** 98 **p** 99. C Henley w Remenham *Ox* 98–02; TV Bicester w Bucknell, Caversfield and Launton 02–08; TV Horsham *Chich* from 08. *Holy Trinity House, Blunts Way, Horsham RH12 2BL* T: (01403) 265401 E: fr.david@bouskill.co.uk

BOUTLE, David Francis. b 44. Leeds Univ BSc 67. Cuddesdon Coll 69. **d** 72 **p** 73. C Boston *Linc* 72–77; C Waltham 77–80; P-in-c Morton 80–81; V 81–94; Chapl W Lindsey NHS Trust 80–94; Local Mental Health Chapl 88–94; P-in-c Heckington Gp *Linc* 94–10; rtd 10; PtO *Linc* 17–20. *3 Hengist Close, Quarrington, Sleaford NG34 8WU* T: (01529) 415384 E: boutle.heck@btinternet.com

BOUTLE, Toby Jefferson. b 79. Magd Coll Ox BA 00 MA 11 Barrister 04. St Steph Ho Ox BA 15. **d** 16 **p** 17. C Whyke w Rumboldswhyke and Portfield *Chich* 16–20; P-in-c Swindon New Town *Bris* from 20. *18 Park Lane, Swindon SN1 5EL* M: 07773-377503 E: toby_boutle@yahoo.co.uk

BOVEY, Denis Philip. b 29. Ely Th Coll 50. **d** 53 **p** 54. C Southwick St Columba *Dur* 53–57; PtO *Ov* 57–59; LtO *Chich* 62–64; C W Hartlepool St Aid *Dur* 64–66; R Aberdeen St Jas *Ab* 66–74; R Old Deer 74–89; R Longside 74–89; R Strichen 74–89; Can St Andr Cathl 75–88; Syn Clerk 78–83; Dean *Ab* 83–88; R Alford 89–94; R Auchindoir 89–94; R Inverurie 89–94; P-in-c Dufftown 89–94; P-in-c Kemnay 89–94; rtd 94. *15 Loskin Drive, Glasgow G22 7QW* T: 0141-574 3603

BOVILL, Francis William. b 34. St Aid Birkenhead 55. **d** 58 **p** 59. C Bispham *Blackb* 58–61; C Crosthwaite Keswick *Carl* 61–64; V Radcliffe St Andr *Man* 64–68; P-in-c Woodside St Steph *Glouc* 68; V 69–73; V Scotby *Carl* 73–96; P-in-c Cotehill and Cumwhinton 94–96; rtd 96; PtO *Carl* from 96. *Crosthwaite, West Road, Wigton CA7 9RG* T: (016973) 43410

BOWDEN, Andrew. *See* BOWDEN, Robert Andrew

BOWDEN, Andrew David. b 59. Newc Univ BA 80 BArch 83. Cranmer Hall Dur 95. **d** 97 **p** 98. C Monkseaton St Pet *Newc* 97–01; V Whorlton 01–09; PtO *York* 10–11; P-in-c Weaverthorpe w Helperthorpe, Luttons Ambo etc 11–19; V from 19; C Malton and Old Malton 11–19. *Chapel House, Back Lane, West Lutton, Malton YO17 8TF* M: 07544-705064 E: andy@woldsvalley.plus.com

BOWDEN, Andrew John. b 77. Nottm Trent Univ BSc 99. Wycliffe Hall Ox 09. **d** 11 **p** 12. C Laleham *Lon* 11–15; Chapl All SS Academy Plymouth 15–19; V Buckland Monachorum *Ex* from 19. *The Vicarage, Buckland Monachorum, Yelverton PL20 7LQ*

BOWDEN, John-Henry David. b 47. Magd Coll Cam BA 69 MA 73 MIL 78. S Dios Minl Tr Scheme 81. **d** 84 **p** 85. NSM Redlynch and Morgan's Vale *Sarum* 84–88; NSM Cuckfield *Chich* 88–92; NSM St Mary le Bow w St Pancras Soper Lane etc *Lon* 92–98; NSM Chailey *Chich* 98–04; P-in-c Venice w Trieste *Eur* 04–09; rtd 09; P-in-c Málaga *Eur* 11–13; PtO from 13; *Chich* from 15; *Portsm* from 15. *Heathlyn, West Broyle Drive, West Broyle, Chichester PO19 3PP* T: (01243) 783204

BOWDEN, Lynne. b 53. Bris Univ BA 77 PGCE 78 Ban Univ BTh 09 Heythrop Coll Lon MA 12. **d** 06 **p** 07. OLM Oatlands *Guildf* from 06; NSM 06–15; CMD Tutor for Past Assts 08–14; PtO *Ches* 16–17 and from 18; NSM High Lane 17–18; Tutor for Past Worker Tr from 16; PtO *Derby* from 18. *Sitch House Farm, Taxal, Whaley Bridge, High Peak SK23 7EA* T: (01663) 732097 E: a.curate@btinternet.com

BOWDEN, Mrs Mary Eiluned. **d** 07 **p** 08. NSM Gipsy Hill Ch Ch *S'wark* 07–09; C W Dulwich All SS 09–11; P-in-c Haslemere and Grayswood *Guildf* 11–16; R 16–19; rtd 19; PtO *Glouc* from 19. *1 Wood Stanway Drive, Bishop's Cleeve, Cheltenham GL52 8TL* M: 07921-315894 E: revmarybowden@btconnect.com

BOWDEN, Canon Robert Andrew. b 38. Worc Coll Ox BA 62 MA 67 BDQ 68. Cuddesdon Coll 63. **d** 65 **p** 66. C Wolverhampton St Geo *Lich* 65–69; C Duston *Pet* 69–72; R Byfield 72–79; Chapl R Agric Coll Cirencester 79–93; R Coates, Rodmarton and Sapperton etc *Glouc* 79–04; Bp's Adv on Rural Soc 81–93; Local Min Officer 93–04; rtd 04; Hon C Kemble, Poole Keynes, Somerford Keynes etc *Glouc* 04–08; Chapl to The Queen 97–08; Hon Can Glouc Cathl 90–08; PtO from 08. *Washbrook Cottage, Caudle Green, Cheltenham GL53 9PW* T: (01285) 821067 E: bowdencoates@btinternet.com

BOWDEN-PICKSTOCK, Mrs Susan Mary. b 63. Bp Otter Coll BA 85 RGN 88. Ridley Hall Cam 09. **d** 11 **p** 12. C Bluntisham cum Earith w Colne and Holywell etc *Ely* 11–14; P-in-c Hunstanton St Mary w Ringstead Parva etc *Nor* 14–19; C Harston w Hauxton and Newton *Ely* from 19. *The Vicarage, Church Street, Harston, Cambridge CB22 7NP* M: 07912-293905 E: revroses@gmail.com

BOWEN, Daniel Joseph George. b 51. St Mich Coll Llan 96. **d** 98 **p** 99. C Gorseinon *S & B* 98–00; C Cen Swansea 00–01; TV 01–02; V Birchfield *Birm* 02–07; rtd 07. *Dryslwyn, 41 Station Road, Ystradgynlais, Swansea SA9 1NX* T: (01639) 843020 E: dejagebe@gmail.com

BOWEN, David Gregory. b 47. Lanchester Poly Cov BSc 69. Cuddesdon Coll 69. **d** 74 **p** 75. C Rugby St Andr *Cov* 74–77; C Charlton St Luke w H Trin *S'wark* 78–80; TV Stantonbury *Ox* 80–82; PtO *B & W* 82–07; Ab 08–19; *B & W* from 19. *7 Corner Croft, Clevedon BS21 5DB* T: (01275) 876201 M: 07762-569920 E: dbowenuk@btinternet.com

BOWEN, Ms Delyth. b 54. St D Coll Lamp BA 90. St Mich Coll Llan. **d** 91 **p** 97. C Llandybie *St D* 91–95; Dn-in-c Llanllwni 95–97; V Llanybydder and Llanwenog w Llanllwni 97–02; V Betws w Ammanford 02–11; V Cynwyl Gaeo w Llansawel and Talley etc 11–12; rtd 12. *6 Roderick Close, Townhill, Swansea SA1 6AJ* T: (01792) 920081

BOWEN, Gareth James. b 60. Lon Guildhall Univ BA 99 FRPS 00 FRSA 19. NTMTC 99. **d** 02 **p** 04. C Leyton St Cath and St Paul *Chelmsf* 02–05; C Upminster 05–07; V Barnehurst *Roch* from 07. *St Martin's Vicarage, 93 Pelham Road, Bexleyheath DA7 4LY* T: (01322) 523344 M: 07775-674504 E: gareth@bowen.to *or* fathergareth@me.com

BOWEN, Canon Jennifer Ethel. b 46. Liv Univ BSc 68 CertEd 69. NOC 80. **dss** 83 **d** 87 **p** 94. Blundellsands St Nic *Liv* 83–86; W Derby St Mary 86–94; Par Dn 87–94; C 94–08; AD W Derby 01–08; Hon Can Liv Cathl 03–08; rtd 08; PtO *Liv* from 16. *6 Springhill Court, Liverpool L15 9EJ* T: 0151-291 0845

BOWEN, John Roger. b 34. St Jo Coll Ox BA 59 MA 62. Tyndale Hall Bris 59. **d** 61 **p** 62. C Cambridge St Paul *Ely* 61–65; Tanzania 65–76; Kenya 76–80; Dir Past Studies St Jo Coll Nottm 80–85; Tutor 85–95; Gen Sec Crosslinks 96–00; rtd 99; PtO *Ely* from 01; Asst Rtd Clergy Officer from 09. *26 Lingholme Close, Cambridge CB4 3HW* T: (01223) 352592 E: bowenrw26@gmail.com

BOWEN, Julie Elizabeth. b 64. S Glam Inst HE BEd 86. SEITE 09. **d** 12 **p** 13. C Bexley *Roch* 12–16; V Bromley St Andr from 16; Chapl St Olave's Gr Sch Orpington from 15. *St Martin's Vicarage, 93 Pelham Road, Bexleyheath DA7 4LY* T: (01322) 523344 M: 07775-674503 E: julie@bowen.to

BOWEN, Mark Franklin. b 61. Coll of H Cross (USA) BA 79 Univ of S Florida MA 89. **d** 93. Asst Chapl Univ of S Florida USA 93–96; C Tampa St Andr 96–97; PtO *S'wark* 07–09; Co-ord Inclusive Ch *Eur* from 09; Teacher Internat Sch of Basel from 09. *309 Guterstrasse, Basel 4053, Switzerland* T: (0041) (61) 331 0961 E: markfbowen@hotmail.com

BOWEN, Roger. *See* BOWEN, John Roger

BOWEN, Canon Stephen Allan. b 51. Leic Univ BA 72. Glouc Sch of Min 88. **d** 91 **p** 92. NSM Bream *Glouc* 91–92; NSM Tidenham w Beachley and Lancaut 91–94; C Glouc St Jas and All SS 94–97; P-in-c Woodchester and Brimscombe 97–00; R 00–11; AD Stonehouse 07–08; AD Stroud 08–11; TR Cheltenham St Mark 11–16; Hon Can Glouc Cathl 09–16;

Community Can Glouc Cathl 16–17; rtd 17. *1 Clifford Villas, Scotts Lane, Wellington TA21 8PH* E: sabowen75@gmail.com

BOWER, Allen Cleeve. b 71. Trin Coll Bris 10. **d** 12 **p** 13. C Kensal Rise St Mark *Lon* 12–15; V Tipton St Matt *Lich* 15–18; V Tipton St Matt w St Martin and St Paul 19–20; V Upper Sunbury St Sav *Lon* from 20. *St Saviour's Vicarage, 205 Vicarage Road, Sunbury-on-Thames TW16 7TP* E: revallenb@gmail.com

BOWERMAN, Canon Andrew Mark. b 67. Southn Univ BSc 88 Brunel Univ MSW 91 Glos Univ MA 15. Wycliffe Hall Ox 00. **d** 02 **p** 03. C Bradf St Aug Undercliffe 02–05; Miss P Bradf Adnry 05–09; P-in-c Wareham *Sarum* 09–12; TR 12–14; Exec Dir Angl Alliance 14–18; Hon C Hardington Vale *B & W* 15–18; Regional Dir Miss to Seafarers from 18; PtO *B & W* from 19; Hon Can Peshawar Pakistan from 14. *6 Victoria Street, Shaftesbury SP7 8AG* M: 07720-398659 E: andy.bowerman@missiontoseafarers.org

BOWERMAN, Mrs Lynn Joan. b 56. STETS 12. **d** 15 **p** 16. C Branksome St Clem *Sarum* from 15. *6 Tree Hamlets, Poole BH16 5SA*

✠**BOWERS, The Rt Revd Dale Arthur.** b 69. MBE 12. St Steph Ho Ox BTh 04. **d** 04 **p** 07 **c** 18. C St Paul's St Helena 04–10; V 10–11; V Jamestown St Jas 10–18; Adn St Helena 11–18; Bp St Helena from 18. *Bishopsholme, PO Box 62, St Helena* T: (00290) 24471 E: dale.penny@helanta.co.sh

BOWERS, Canon David. b 56. Man Univ BA 79. Wycliffe Hall Ox 82. **d** 84 **p** 85. C Lawton Moor *Man* 84–87; C Walmsley 87–93; V Milnrow 93–98; P-in-c Deerhurst and Apperley w Forthampton etc *Glouc* 98–04; V 04–08; Assoc Dir of Ords 98–08; V S Cerney w Cerney Wick, Siddington and Preston *Glouc* 08–16; R Sodbury Vale from 16; Hon Can Glouc Cathl from 12. *The Vicarage, Horseshoe Lane, Chipping Sodbury, Bristol BS37 6ET* T: (01454) 313519 *or* 325160 E: dbowers@btinternet.com *or* office@svbcofe.org.uk

BOWERS, Denise Frances. *See* BROWN, Denise Frances

BOWERS, Canon Francis Malcolm. b 44. Chan Sch Truro 79. **d** 82 **p** 83. NSM Penzance St Mary w St Paul *Truro* 82–83; C 86–88; NSM Madron 83–86; TV Redruth w Lanner and Treleigh 88–91; V St Blazey 91–15; P-in-c Lanlivery w Luxulyan 01–08; P-in-c Luxulyan 08–15; P-in-c Tywardreath w Tregaminion 02–15; RD St Austell 96–05; Hon Can Truro Cathl 01–15; rtd 15; PtO *Truro* from 15. *10 The Green, St Austell PL25 4TB* T: (01276) 624901 M: 07974-818631 E: canonmalcolm@gmail.com

BOWERS, Canon John Edward William. b 32. St Aid Birkenhead 60. **d** 63 **p** 64. C Bromborough *Ches* 63–68; Ind Chapl 68–74; P-in-c Crewe St Pet 69–71; V Crewe St Mich 71–74; TR Ellesmere Port 74–79; V Hattersley 79–91; Hon Can Ches Cathl 80–02; RD Mottram 88–91; V Bunbury and Tilstone Fearnall 91–98; P-in-c Leasowe 98–02; rtd 02; PtO *Ches* from 02. *2 Shalford Grove, Wirral CH48 9XY* T: 0151-625 4831

BOWERS, Canon Julian Michael. b 48. Middx Univ BA 97 Goldsmiths' Coll Lon MA 00. Edin Th Coll 69. **d** 72 **p** 73. C Chippenham St Andr w Tytherton Lucas *Bris* 72–74; C Henbury 74–77; Chapl Kandy H Trin Sri Lanka 77–82; P-in-c Evercreech w Chesterblade and Milton Clevedon *B & W* 82–83; V 83–89; V Enfield St Jas *Lon* 89–04; Chapl St Andr Hosp Northn 04–12; Can Pet Cathl 10–12; rtd 12; Past Care and Counselling Adv Pet 13–18; Hon C Brigstock w Stanion and Lowick and Sudborough 13–17; PtO from 17; *Lich* 20–21. *13 The Leasowe, Lichfield WS13 7HD* T: (01543) 300075 E: revjbowers@gmail.com

BOWERS, Preb Peter. b 47. Linc Th Coll 72. **d** 76 **p** 77. C Mackworth St Fran *Derby* 76–78; C Maidstone St Martin *Cant* 78–83; V Elmton *Derby* 83–89; R Swimbridge w W Buckland and Landkey *Ex* 89–10; RD Shirwell 01–10; Preb Ex Cathl 07–10; rtd 10; PtO *York* from 11. *Endellion, 30 Kingsgate, Bridlington YO15 3PU* T: (01262) 676096 E: pbowers62@btinternet.com *or* pebo@live.co.uk *or* endellion47@icloud.com

BOWERS, Mrs Rosemary Christine. b 49. Ripon Coll Cuddesdon 99. **d** 01 **p** 02. C Rossendale Middle Valley *Man* 01–04; P-in-c Micklehurst *Ches* 04–09; P-in-c Kinnerley w Melverley and Knockin w Maesbrook *Lich* 09–12; P-in-c Maesbury 11–12; rtd 12; Hon C Ripponden *Wakef* 12–14; Hon C Barkisland w W Scammonden 12–14; TV Rossendale Middle Valley *Man* 14–15; PtO from 15. *7 Bowler Way, Greenfield, Oldham OL3 7FQ* T: (01457) 514172 E: revrosie86@sky.com

BOWES, Mrs Beryl Sylvia. b 48. Hull Univ BTh 89 Leeds Univ MA 06 SRN 70 RSCN 71. NEOC 89. **d** 91 **p** 94. NSM Kirk Ella *York* 91–99; Chapl R Hull Hosps NHS Trust 93–99; P-in-c Kexby w Wilberfoss *York* 99–04; S the Street Par 04–12; rtd 12; PtO *York* from 12; *B & W* from 19. *Apartment 1, 33 Great Pulteney Street, Bath BA2 4BX* T: (01225) 462490 M: 07410-627223 E: bsbowes@gmail.com

BOWES, Canon John Anthony Hugh. b 39. Ch Ch Ox BA 62 MA 65. Westcott Ho Cam 63. **d** 65 **p** 66. C Langley All SS and Martyrs *Man* 65–68; Asst Chapl Bris Univ 68–73; TV Cramlington *Newc* 73–76; P-in-c Oldland *Bris* 76–80; TR 80–84; V Westbury-on-Trym St Alb 84–05; Hon Can Bris Cathl 02–05; rtd 05; PtO *Bris* 05–19. *4 Royal Albert Road, Bristol BS6 7NY* T: 0117-973 5844

BOWES, Peter Hugh. b 48. Hull Univ LLB 69 Dur Univ MA 05 DThM 12 Solicitor 72. Cranmer Hall Dur 02. **d** 03 **p** 04. NSM Pocklington and Owsthorpe and Kilnwick Percy etc *York* 03–04; NSM The Street Par 04–07; NSM New Malton 06–07; P-in-c 07–13; C Old Malton 10–13; C Weaverthorpe w Helperthorpe, Luttons Ambo etc 11–13; Assoc Dir of Ords 05–10; RD S Ryedale 11–13; rtd 13; PtO *York* from 13; *B & W* from 19. *Apartment 1, 33 Great Pulteney Street, Bath BA2 4BX* T: (01225) 462490 M: 07775-757723 E: peter.bowes@123mail.org

BOWES-SMITH, Edward Michael Crispin. b 67. K Coll Lon LLB 89 AKC 89 Selw Coll Cam BA 96 Solicitor 90. Ridley Hall Cam 94. **d** 97 **p** 98. C Combe Down w Monkton Combe and S Stoke *B & W* 97–00; C Enfield Ch Ch Trent Park *Lon* 00–03; P-in-c Linc Minster Gp 03–12; V Linc St Pet in Eastgate 12–20; V Linc St Pet in Carlton 17–20; Can and Preb Linc Cathl 18–20; TR Gt Chesham *Ox* from 20. *The Rectory, Church Street, Chesham HP5 1HY* T: (01494) 794258 E: bowessmith@btinternet.com

BOWETT, Canon Richard Julnes. b 45. EAMTC 86. **d** 89 **p** 90. C Hunstanton St Mary w Ringstead Parva, Holme etc *Nor* 89–93; C King's Lynn St Marg w St Nic 93–95; V Watton w Carbrooke and Ovington 95–02; RD Breckland 99–02; P-in-c Ashill w Saham Toney 00–01; Dioc Sec 02–09; rtd 09; Hon Can Nor Cathl 05–13; PtO from 13. *The Red House, 9 Acorn Drive, Gayton, King's Lynn PE32 1XG* T: (01553) 636020 E: richard.bowett@sky.com

BOWIE, Michael Nicholas Roderick. b 59. Sydney Univ BA 78 CCC Ox DPhil 90. St Steph Ho Ox MA 90. **d** 91 **p** 92. C Swanley St Mary *Roch* 91–93; C Penarth w Lavernock *Llan* 93–96; Australia 96–00; R Norton *Sheff* 00–05; TR Gt Berkhamsted, Gt and Lt Gaddesden etc *St Alb* 05–14; RD Berkhamsted 09–14; C St Marylebone All SS *Lon* from 14. *6 Margaret Street, London W1W 8RQ* T: (020) 7636 1788 M: 07581-180963 E: mnrbowie@gmail.com

BOWIE, Sara. b 53. Open Univ BA 83 Surrey Univ BA 02. STETS 99. **d** 02 **p** 03. NSM Camberley St Mich Yorktown *Guildf* 02–07; C Coity, Nolton and Brackla *Llan* 07–10; P-in-c Essington *Lich* 10–18; P-in-c Shareshill 10–18; rtd 18; PtO *Cov* from 19. *2 Parkfield Road, Rugby CV21 1EN*

BOWKER, Prof John Westerdale. b 35. Worc Coll Ox BA 58. Ripon Hall Ox. **d** 61 **p** 62. C Endcliffe *Sheff* 61–62; Fell Lect and Dir of Studies CCC Cam 62–74; Lect Div Cam Univ 70–74; Prof RS Lanc Univ 74–86; Hon Prov Can Cant Cathl 85–03; Dean of Chpl Trin Coll Cam 86–91; rtd 91; LtO *Cant* 91–94; PtO *Ely* 94–00. *14 Bowers Croft, Cambridge CB1 8RP*

BOWKETT, Graham Philip. b 67. Open Univ BSc 99 Win Univ MA 19. NEOC 06. **d** 09 **p** 10. C Thirsk *York* 09–12; P-in-c Upper Itchen *Win* 12–15; R 15–18; RD Alresford 16–18; V Charlton Kings St Mary *Glouc* from 18. *St Mary's Vicarage, 63 Church Street, Charlton Kings, Cheltenham GL53 8AT* T: (01242) 253402 E: po@stmarysck.org.uk *or* vicar@stmarysck.org.uk

BOWLER, Christopher Peter. **d** 12 **p** 13. C Upper Ithon Valley *S & B* 12–14; C Vale of Gwrynne 14–15; P-in-c from 16; Bp's Officer for Min to Children and Families from 14. *The Rectory, Llangenny, Crickhowell NP8 1HD* T: (01873) 810591 E: revchrisbowler@gmail.com

BOWLER, Christopher William. *See* JAGE-BOWLER, Christopher William

BOWLER, David Edward. b 53. Northumbria Univ BA 04 RMN 80. NEOC 05. **d** 08 **p** 09. NSM Cramlington *Newc* 08–13; Chapl Northgate and Prudhoe NHS Trust 10–13; Chapl Northumberland, Tyne and Wear NHS Foundn Trust 10–13; V Delaval *Newc* 13–21; rtd 21. *Address temp unknown* E: djbowler@sky.com

BOWLER, David Henderson. b 54. Kent Univ BA 75. St Jo Coll Nottm 75. **d** 78 **p** 79. C Bramcote *S'well* 78–82; TV Kirby Muxloe *Leic* 82–88; V Quorndon 88–21; rtd 21. *22A Costock Road, East Leake, Loughborough LE12 6LY* E: dhb300154@aol.com

BOWLER, Preb Kenneth Neville. b 37. K Coll Lon 57. **d** 61 **p** 62. C Buxton *Derby* 61–67; R Sandiacre 67–75; V E Bedfont *Lon* 75–87; AD Hounslow 82–87; V Fulham All SS 87–02; Preb St Paul's Cathl 85–02; rtd 02; PtO *St Alb* 04; *Sheff* from 06. *The Coach House, 22 Brincliffe Crescent, Sheffield S11 9AW* T: 0114-250 0043 E: kenneth@kandsbowler.plus.com

BOWLER, Neil. b 70. Nottm Trent Univ LLB 92 Leeds Univ BA 05 Solicitor 93. Coll of Resurr Mirfield 03. **d** 05 **p** 06. C Doncaster St Jude *Sheff* 05–08; R Whiston 09–13; AD Rotherham 11–13; V Ranmoor 13–17; Hon C Bramley 17–20; Hon C Ravenfield, Hooton Roberts and Braithwell 17–20; Hon C Thrybergh 17–20; Hon C Wickersley 17–20; Hon Can Sheff Cathl 15–20; Bp's Adv in Spirituality 16–17; R Wykeham *Ox* from 21. *2 Sycamore Close, Sibford Gower, Banbury OX15 5SB* T: (01295) 788005 E: nbowler34@yahoo.co.uk *or* revneil@wykehambenefice.org.uk

BOWLES, David Gordon Desmond. **d** 13 **p** 15. Taney *D & G* 13–15; C Douglas Union w Frankfield *C, C & R* 15–19; P-in-c Moviddy Union from 19. *Moviddy Rectory, Rathard, Aherla, Cork, P31 TR04, Republic of Ireland* M: (00353) 89-236 4969 E: dgd_bowles@yahoo.co.uk

BOWLES, Peter John. b 39. Lon Univ BA 60. Linc Th Coll 71. **d** 73 **p** 74. C Clay Cross *Derby* 73–76; C Boulton 76–79; R Brailsford w Shirley 79–85; P-in-c Osmaston w Edlaston 81–85; R Brailsford w Shirley and Osmaston w Edlaston 85–89; TR Old Brampton and Loundsley Green 89–98; V Hope, Castleton and Bradwell 98–04; rtd 04; PtO *Nor* from 04. *3 Blackhorse Yard, Wells-next-the-Sea NR23 1BN* T: (01328) 711119 E: peterbowles23@gmail.com

BOWMAN, Canon Alison Valentine. b 57. St Andr Univ MA 79. St Steph Ho Ox 86. **d** 89 **p** 94. Par Dn Peacehaven *Chich* 89–94; C 94–95; Chapl to Bp Lewes 93–95; TV Rye 95–03; P-in-c Preston St Jo w Brighton St Aug and St Sav 03–09; V from 09; Can and Preb Chich Cathl from 15. *St John's Vicarage, 33 Preston Drove, Brighton BN1 6LA* T: (01273) 555033 E: avbow@aol.com

BOWMAN, Clifford William. b 57. St Jo Coll Dur BA 78 Nottm Univ MA 96. Ridley Hall Cam 80. **d** 82 **p** 83. C Sawley *Derby* 82–85; C Hucknall Torkard *S'well* 85–89; R Warsop 89–00; Dioc Chapl amongst Deaf People 00–06; TV Uxbridge *Lon* 06–17; rtd 17; PtO *Leeds* from 17. *10 Mallorie Park Drive, Ripon HG4 2QD* E: cliff.bowman@btinternet.com

BOWMAN, Canon Ivelaw Alexander. b 46. **d** 97 **p** 98. OLM Stockwell Green St Andr *S'wark* 97–03; OLM Stockwell St Andr and St Mich 03–16; Chapl S Lon and Maudsley NHS Foundn Trust 03–07; Hon Can S'wark Cathl 05–16; PtO from 16. *16 Horsford Road, London SW2 5BN* T: (020) 7733 2309 E: ivelawbowman@hotmail.com

BOWMAN-EADIE, Preb Russell Ian. b 45. K Coll Lon BD 71 AKC 71 ACP 68 FCP. St Aug Coll Cant 71. **d** 72 **p** 73. C Hammersmith St Pet *Lon* 72–74; V Leic St Nic 74–81; Chapl Leic Univ 74–81; Adult Educn Adv *Dur* 81–84; Dir of Tr *B & W* 84–09; Preb Wells Cathl 90–09; Can Res and Treas Wells Cathl 02–09; rtd 10. *8 Shaftesbury Place, Rustington, Littlehampton BN16 2GA* T: (01903) 774580

BOWN, Nicola Jenny. b 62. N Lon Poly BA 90 Sussex Univ MA 91 DPhil 96. ERMC 13. **d** 16 **p** 17. C Linton *Ely* 16–19; C Gt Shelford 19–20; R Cottingham *York* from 20. *The RectorY, Hallgate, Cottingham HU16 4DD* T: (01482) 847668 M: 07414-595160 E: nicolabown@icloud.com

BOWNASS (née FRYER), Alison Jane. b 56. Univ Coll of Swansea BSc 78 Birm Poly PGCE 90. Qu Coll Birm 05. **d** 07 **p** 08. C The Quinton *Birm* 07–10; PtO 10–11; C Hill 11–14; PtO from 14. *41 Silvermead Road, Sutton Coldfield B73 5SR* T: 0121-321 1600 M: 07958-911378 E: alison@bownass.co.uk

BOWNESS, William Gary. b 48. Warwick Univ BSc 69 Chicago State Univ DMin 98. Ripon Coll Cuddesdon 80. **d** 82 **p** 83. C Lancaster St Mary *Blackb* 82–86; V Lostock Hall 86–91; V Whittington w Arkholme and Gressingham 91–02; RD Tunstall 93–99; Dir Post-Ord Tr 00–02; R Alderley w Birtles *Ches* 02–07; P-in-c Henbury 07–13; rtd 13; PtO *Ches* from 13; P-in-c Skerton St Luke *Blackb* 17–19; PtO from 19. *7 Fife Street, Lancaster LA1 5TT* T: (01524) 849453 E: garybowness@btinternet.com

BOWRING, Stephen John. b 55. R Holloway Coll Lon BMus 77 St Mary's Coll Twickenham PGCE 78. EMMTC 89. **d** 92 **p** 93. C Thurmaston *Leic* 92–95; V Shepshed 95–02; R River *Cant* 02–06; P-in-c Charlton-in-Dover 05–06; AD Dover 03–06; Hon Min Can Cant Cathl 04–06; V Chesterton St Geo *Ely* 06–11; R Kym Valley 11–16; C E Leightonstone 14–16; V S Leightonstone 17–18; rtd 18; PtO *Ely* from 21. *4 The Bank, Somersham, Huntingdon PE28 3DJ* M: 07879-465205

BOWRON, Hugh Mark. b 52. Cant Univ (NZ) BA 74 MA 76 Otago Univ MTh 16. Coll of Resurr Mirfield 76. **d** 79 **p** 80. C Northampton St Mary *Pet* 79–82; V Ellesmere NZ 82–86; V Addington St Mary 86–95; V Wellington St Pet 95–05; V Avonside H Trin 05–12; V Caversham St Pet from 12. *57 Baker Street, Caversham, Dunedin 9012, New Zealand* T: (0064) (3) 455 3961 *or* 27-755 5831 E: hugh.bowron@xtra.co.nz

BOWRY, Nicholas John. b 60. FCIPD. TISEC. **d** 16 **p** 17. C Aberdeen St Clem *Ab* 16–19; C Aberdeen St Ninian

18–19; R Penicuik *Edin* from 19; R W Linton from 19. *The Rectory, 23 Broomhill Road, Penicuik EH26 9EE*   T: (01968) 678254   M: 07950-607574   E: nick.bowry@yahoo.co.uk *or* rector.pandwl@gmail.com

BOWSER, Alan. b 35. Univ of Wales (Lamp) BA 60. **d** 63 **p** 64. C Gateshead St Chad Bensham *Dur* 63–67; C Owton Manor CD 67–72; V Horden 72–02; rtd 02. *Kengarth House, Coast Road, Blackhall Colliery, Hartlepool TS27 4HF*   T: 0191-586 1753

BOWSHER, Andrew Peter. b 59. Reading Univ BA 81. St Jo Coll Nottm 83. **d** 86 **p** 87. C Grenoside *Sheff* 86–89; C Darfield 89–91; P-in-c Haley Hill *Wakef* 91–96; V Bradf St Aug Undercliffe 96–99; Chapl Bradf Univ and Bradf Coll 99–04; PtO *Dur* 04–19; Tutor St Jo Coll Nottm 07–11; Chapl Northumbria Univ *Newc* from 11. *52 Fern Avenue, Jesmond, Newcastle upon Tyne NE2 2QX*   T: 0191-209 9705   M: 07876-401339 E: andii.bowsher@northumbria.ac.uk

BOWSKILL, Mrs Amanda. b 49. STETS 96. **d** 99 **p** 00. NSM Winklebury *Win* 99–03; NSM Tadley S and Silchester 03–04; NSM Kempshott 05–10; PtO from 10. *10 Portway Place, Basingstoke RG23 8DT*   T: (01256) 327301 E: mandy.bowskill@ntlworld.com

BOWSKILL, Robert Preston. b 48. S Dios Minl Tr Scheme 88. **d** 91 **p** 92. NSM Eastrop *Win* 91–94; NSM Winklebury 94–05; NSM Kempshott 05–10; PtO from 10. *10 Portway Place, Basingstoke RG23 8DT*   T: (01256) 327301

BOWTELL, Paul William. b 47. Lon Univ BSc 68. St Jo Coll Nottm 80. **d** 82 **p** 83. C Gorleston St Andr *Nor* 82–85; TV Forest Gate St Sav w W Ham St Matt *Chelmsf* 85–91; R Spitalfields Ch Ch w All SS *Lon* 91–02; Co-ord Transform Newham 02–06; Chapl to Bp Barking *Chelmsf* 06–14; C Leyton St Cath and St Paul 07–14; rtd 14; PtO *Chelmsf* from 15. *14 Chapel Street, Rowhedge, Colchester CO5 7JS*   T: (01206) 729073 E: paul.bowtell@gmail.com

BOWYER, Andrew Derek. b 83. R Melbourne Inst of Tech BBA 04 Chas Sturt Univ NSW BTh 09 Sydney Univ MA 13 Edin Univ PhD 16. **d** 08 **p** 09. C Sapphire Coast Australia 08–10; C Sydney St Jas 10–12; Hon C Edin Old St Paul 12–15; Chapl Trin Coll Cam 15–19; Tutor Westcott Ho Cam 17–19; Dean of Div and Chapl Magd Coll Ox from 19; LtO *Ox* from 19. *Magdalen College, High Street, Oxford OX1 4AU*   M: 07833-762626 E: andrew.bowyer@gmail.com *or* andrew.bowyer@magd.ox.ac.uk

BOWYER, Arthur Gustavus Frederick. b 36. **d** 00 **p** 01. NSM Kingswood *S'wark* 00–09; PtO from 09; Guildf from 17. *41 Tattenham Grove, Epsom KT18 5QT*   T: (01737)   357913   M: 07939-533506 E: arthurbowyer578@btinternet.com

BOWYER, Geoffrey Charles. b 54. ACA 79 ATII 82 Lanc Univ BA 76. St Jo Coll Nottm 85. **d** 87 **p** 88. C Walton *St E* 87–89; C Macclesfield Team *Ches* 89–91; V Cinderford St Steph w Littledean *Glouc* 91–95; V Brockenhurst *Win* 95–98; Hon C Trull w Angersleigh *B & W* 00–15; PtO from 15. *36 Bakers Close, Bishops Hull, Taunton TA1 5HD*   T: (01823) 335289   M: 07709-268431

BOWYER, Canon Gerry. b 60. Cliff Th Coll MA 10. **d** 10 **p** 10. C Aberdeen St Ninian *Ab* 10; Bp's Ev for Fresh Expressions and Ch Planting from 11; R Bieldside from 18; Can St Andr Cathl from 18. *St Devenick's Rectory, 2 Baillieswells Road, Bieldside, Aberdeen AB15 9AP*   T: (01224) 861552   M: 07956-098566 E: gerry.caf4e@outlook.com *or* gerry.bowyer@live.com

BOX, Mrs Patricia Jane. b 54. ERMC 12. **d** 15 **p** 16. NSM Bures w Assington and Lt Cornard *St E* 15–20; PtO from 21. *Water House, 4 Croftside, Bures CO8 5LL*   T: (01787) 227528 E: triciajbox@gmail.com

BOXALL, Canon Martin Alleyne. b 37. Wells Th Coll 65. **d** 67 **p** 68. C Crowthorne *Ox* 67–70; C Tilehurst St Mich 70–76; V Tilehurst St Cath 76–78; V Padstow *Truro* 78–00; Miss to Seafarers from 78; RD Pydar *Truro* 93; Hon Can Truro Cathl from 93; rtd 01; Dioc Officer for Unity *Truro* 01; PtO from 16. *Jandy, Tregye Road, Carnon Downs, Truro TR3 6JH*   T: (01872) 863241 E: martinboxall@aol.com

BOXALL, Simon Roger. b 55. St Jo Coll Cam BA 76 MA 80. Ridley Hall Cam 77. **d** 79 **p** 80. C Eaton *Nor* 79–82; SAMS Brazil 82–04; P-in-c Belo Horizonte St Pet 84–88; P-in-c Santiago St Tim 88–91; P-in-c Horizontina H Spirit 88–91; C Bagé Crucifixion 93–94; R Jaguarao Ch Ch 94–98; English Chapl Rio de Janeiro 99–04; TV Thamesmead *S'wark* 05–14; V Chesterton *Lich* 14–21; rtd 21. *65 Wenlock Rise, Bridgnorth WV16 5EA*

BOXER, Caroline Victoria. *See* SKELTON, Caroline Victoria

BOXLEY, Christopher. b 45. K Coll Lon BD 68 AKC 68 Southn Univ CertEd 73 Reading Univ MA 84. **d** 69 **p** 70. C Bitterne Park *Win* 69–73; Hd RS Midhurst Gr Sch from 73; Dir Midhurst and Petworth RS Cen from 78; PtO *Chich* 73–78; P-in-c Heyshott 78–15; PtO from 16. *1 Pinewood*

Court, Church Road, West Lavington, Midhurst GU29 0EH E: boxley@talktalk.net

BOYCE, Christopher Allan. b 44. ARIBA 69. S Dios Minl Tr Scheme 84. **d** 87 **p** 88. NSM Eastbourne All SS *Chich* 87–93; C Upton (Overchurch) *Ches* 93–96; V New Brighton St Jas w Em 96–02; P-in-c New Brighton All SS 98–02; TV Bicester w Bucknell, Caversfield and Launton *Ox* 02–11; rtd 11. *4 Freshwaters, 92/94 Sturgeon Street, Ormiston QLD 4160, Australia* E: christopher.boyce468@gmail.com

BOYCE, Joy. b 46. **d** 05 **p** 06. NSM Streatham Ch Ch w St Marg *S'wark* 05–09; NSM Southfields St Barn 09–21; PtO from 21. *60 Westover Road, London SW18 2RH*   T: (020)   8874   1905   M: 07867-830273 E: joy@redzonecommunications.com

BOYCE, Ms Susan. b 59. Ch Ch Coll Cant MA 00 Birm Univ BPhil 06 Univ of Cen England in Birm DipSW 96. Ripon Coll Cuddesdon 05. **d** 06 **p** 07. NSM Rushall *Lich* 06–11; PtO 11–16; *Win* from 16; PtO 18–19; P-in-c Willenhall St Anne from 19; P-in-c Willenhall St Giles from 19; C Willenhall St Steph from 19. *The Vicarage, Walsall Street, Willenhall WV13 2ER*   T: (01902) 473273   M: 07941-927245 E: sueboyceca@hotmail.com *or* sue.boyce@lichfield.anglican.org

BOYCE-TILLMAN, Prof June Barbara. b 43. MBE . St Hugh's Coll Ox BA 65 Lon Inst of Educn PGCE 66 PhD 87 LRAM 74. Dioc OLM tr scheme. **d** 06 **p** 07. NSM Streatham St Paul *S'wark* 06–10; PtO from 10; *Win* from 10. *108 Nimrod Road, London SW16 6TQ*   F: (020) 8677 8752   M: 07850-208721 E: junebt@globalnet.co.uk

BOYD, Alan McLean. b 50. St Jo Coll Nottm BTh 79. **d** 79 **p** 80. C Bishop's Waltham *Portsm* 79–83; Chapl Reading Univ *Ox* 83–88; Chapl E Birm Hosp 88–94; Chapl Birm Heartlands and Solihull NHS Trust 94–14; rtd 14. *38 Rodborough Road, Dorridge, Solihull B93 8EF*   T: (01564) 730115

BOYD, Canon Alexander Jamieson. b 46. St Chad's Coll Dur BSc 68 Nottm Univ PGCE 69 MRSB FSAScot. Coll of Resurr Mirfield 69. **d** 79 **p** 80. NSM Musselburgh *Edin* 79–83; CF 83–00; P-in-c Loddington *Leic* 00–03; Warden Launde Abbey 00–03; P-in-c Mareham-le-Fen and Revesby *Linc* 03–06; P-in-c Hameringham w Scrafield and Winceby 03–06; P-in-c Mareham on the Hill 03–06; R Fen and Hill Gp 06–14; P-in-c Bain Valley Gp 12–14; RD Horncastle 06–11; Can and Preb Linc Cathl 09–14; rtd 14; PtO *Arg* from 16. *Springfield, 14B Bute Terrace, Millport, Isle of Cumbrae KA28 0BA*   T: (01475) 530151 E: canonalec@btinternet.com

BOYD, Allan Gray. b 41. St Jo Coll Nottm 84. **d** 87 **p** 88. Hon Chapl Miss to Seafarers from 87; NSM Glas St Gabr 87–93; NSM Greenock 93–96; NSM Paisley St Barn 96–00; NSM Paisley H Trin 96–00; NSM Alexandria 00–01; NSM Clydebank 02–08; rtd 09; LtO *Glas* from 09. *47 Holms Crescent, Erskine PA8 6DJ*   T: 0141-812 2754

BOYD, Canon David Anthony. b 42. Sarum & Wells Th Coll 72. **d** 75 **p** 76. C Ches H Trin 75–79; R 85–93; V Congleton St Jas 79–85; V Farndon and Coddington 93–97; RD Malpas 97–04; Hon Can Ches Cathl 02–07; rtd 07; PtO *Ches* from 08. *68 St James Avenue, Upton, Chester CH2 1NL*   T: (01244) 348800 E: tony.boyd42@googlemail.com

BOYD, David George. b 37. Cant Univ (NZ) BSc 62 LTh 64. St Aug Coll Cant. **d** 63 **p** 64. NZ 63–66; St Aug Coll Cant 66–67; Chapl RAF 67–71; NZ from 71; Adn Mid-Canterbury 92–96. *Flat 4, 100 Park Terrace, Christchurch Central, Christchurch 8013, New Zealand*   T: (0064) (3) 974 0826 E: daboyd@slingshot.co.nz

BOYD, Mrs Hannah Ruth. b 81. St Martin's Coll Lanc BA 05. St Mellitus Coll BA 15 MA 16. **d** 16 **p** 17. C Layton and Staining *Blackb* 16–19; V Higher Walton from 19; V Hoghton from 19. *All Saints' Vicarage, Blackburn Road, Higher Walton, Preston PR5 4EA*   T: (01772)   335138 E: revhannahboyd@gmail.com

BOYD, James. *See* BOYD, William James

BOYD, Canon Julie Marie. b 67. Ox Poly BSc 89. ERMC 09. **d** 12 **p** 13. C Dersingham w Anmer and Shernborne *Nor* 12–15; C Dersingham, Anmer, Ingoldisthorpe etc 15–16; TR Gaywood 16–21; TR Aylsham and Distr from 21; Bp's Adv for Women's Min from 21; Hon Can Nor Cathl from 20. *The Vicarage, Cawston Road, Aylsham, Norwich NR11 6NB*   M: 07923-473103

BOYD, Canon Samuel Robert Thomas. b 62. **d** 90 **p** 91. NSM Derryloran *Arm* 90–95; C 95–97; I Woodschapel w Gracefield 97–05; I Killyman 05–17; Can Arm Cathl 13–17; I Glendermott *D & R* from 17; Can Derry Cathl from 20. *Glendermott Rectory, 11 Church Brae, Altnagelvin, Londonderry BT47 2LS*   T: (028) 7134 3001 E: robert449@btinternet.com

BOYD, William James. b 45. **d** 07 **p** 08. C Magheralin w Dollingstown *D & D* 07–11; I Dromore *Clogh* 11–15; V Willowfield *D & D* 15–18; I Derryvolgie *Conn* from 18.

35 Kirkwoods Park, Lisburn BT28 3RR T: (028) 9267 1662
E: revjamesboyd@gmail.com

BOYD-WILLIAMS, Anthony Robert. b 46. St Mich Coll Llan 86. **d** 88 **p** 89. C Tonyrefail w Gilfach Goch *Llan* 88–91; V Treharris w Bedlinog 91–96; V Ocker Hill *Lich* 96–05; RD Wednesbury 05; rtd 05; PtO *Cov* 05–15; *Cant* 17–20. *1 Sir John Killick Road, Ashford TN23 3SL* M: 07393-902646 E: stratters@btinternet.com

BOYDE (née Arnold), Briony Alice (Bee). b 79. Univ of E Lon BA 01. BA 14. **d** 14 **p** 15. C Cov St Fran N Radford 14–17; R Cov St Pet 17–20; V Sandbach *Ches* from 20. *The Vicarage, 15 Offley Road, Sandbach CW11 1GY* M: 07872-326008 E: revbeeboyde@gmail.com

BOYDEN, Peter Frederick. b 41. Lon Univ BSc 62 AKC 62 Em Coll Cam BA 64 MA 68 MLitt 69. Ridley Hall Cam 63. **d** 66 **p** 67. C Chesterton St Andr *Ely* 66–68; C Wimbledon *S'wark* 68–72; Chapl K Sch Cant 72–89; Asst Chapl Radley Coll 89–02; rtd 02; PtO *Derby* 02–17; *Birm* from 17. *1 Longdon Croft, Warwick Road, Knowle, Solihull B93 9LJ* E: pandjboyden@aol.com

BOYES, Matthew John. b 70. Roehampton Inst BA 91. Wycliffe Hall Ox BTh 99. **d** 99 **p** 00. C Bury St Edmunds Ch Ch *St E* 99–02; P-in-c Penn Street *Ox* 02–06; V Turnham Green Ch Ch Lon 06–11; Chapl HM YOI Feltham from 11; PtO *Lon* from 20. *HM Young Offender Institution, Bedfont Road, Feltham TW13 4ND* T: (020) 8844 5000 F: 8844 5001 E: matt.boyes@justice.gov.uk *or* mattboyesw4@gmail.com

BOYLAND, David Henry. b 58. TCD BA 79 BAI 79. TCD Div Sch BTh 91. **d** 91 **p** 92. C Seapatrick *D & D* 91–94; I Celbridge w Straffan and Newcastle-Lyons *D & G* 94–98; I Kilmakee *Conn* from 98. *Kilmakee Rectory, 60 Killeaton Park, Dunmurry, Belfast BT17 9HE* T: (028) 9061 0505 *or* 9061 1024

BOYLAND, Peter James. b 68. TCD BA 92 MA 07. St Steph Ho Ox 07. **d** 09 **p** 10. C Towcester w Caldecote and Easton Neston etc *Pet* 09–11; R Claremont Australia from 11. *The Rectory, 2 Queenslea Drive, Claremont WA 6010, Australia* T: (0061) (8) 9384 9244 M: 40-680 3152 E: frboyland@gmail.com

BOYLE, Charles Robert. b 69. Edin Univ MA 92. Ridley Hall Cam 08. **d** 10 **p** 11. C Kea *Truro* 10–13; V Branksome Park All SS *Sarum* from 13. *The Vicarage, 28 Western Road, Poole BH13 7BP* T: (01202) 041147 M: 07979-857200 E: vicarallsaints@gmail.com

✠**BOYLE, The Rt Revd Christopher John.** b 51. AKC 75. St Aug Coll Cant 75. **d** 76 **p** 77 **c** 01. C Wylde Green *Birm* 76–80; Bp's Dom Chapl 80–83; R Castle Bromwich SS Mary and Marg 83–01; AD Coleshill 92–99; P-in-c Shard End 96–97; Hon Can Birm Cathl 96–01; Bp N Malawi 01–09; Asst Bp Leic 09–17; rtd 17; Hon Asst Bp Leic from 17. *5 The Pastures, Anstey, Leicester LE7 7QR* T: 0116-234 1473 E: bishopboyle@gmail.com

BOYLE, Mrs Lynn. b 58. Leeds Univ BEd 79 BA 07. NOC 04. **d** 07 **p** 08. NSM Stockport St Sav *Ches* 07–11; V Werneth from 11. *St Paul's Vicarage, Compstall Brow, Compstall, Stockport SK6 5HU* T: 0161-427 1259 M: 07971-390019 E: lynnboyle1@aol.com

BOYLE, Robert Leslie. b 52. EMMTC 97. **d** 00 **p** 01. NSM Derby St Anne and St Jo 00–08; C Paignton St Jo, St Andr and St Boniface *Ex* 08–13; P-in-c Douglas St Matt *S & M* 13–14; V 14–17; Assoc P Dartmouth and Dittisham *Ex* 17–20; rtd 21; PtO *Derby* from 21. *61 Rowditch Avenue, Derby DE22 3LE* T: (01332) 989245 E: frbobboyle@gmail.com

BOYLE, Sharon. b 73. Southn Univ BSc 00. Sarum Coll 17. **d** 20 **p** 21. NSM Wimborne Minster and Villages *Sarum* from 20. *98 Cutlers Place, Wimborne BH21 2HZ* M: 07875-677971 E: shalor0824@gmail.com

BOYLES, Peter John. b 59. Univ of Wales (Lamp) BA 84. Sarum & Wells Th Coll 86. **d** 88 **p** 89. C Ches St Mary 88–91; C Neston 91–95; R Lavendon w Cold Brayfield, Clifton Reynes etc *Ox* 95–99; V Dent w Cowgill *Bradf* 99–12; V Dent w Cowgill *Carl* 12–17; C Heart of Eden from 17. *The Vicarage, Appleby-in-Westmorland CA16 6QW* T: (01768) 354161

BOYLING, The Very Revd Mark Christopher. b 52. Keble Coll Ox BA 74 MA 78. Cuddesdon Coll BA 76. **d** 77 **p** 78. C Kirkby *Liv* 77–79; P-in-c 79–80; TV 80–85; Bp's Dom Chapl 85–89; V Formby St Pet 89–94; Can Res and Prec Liv Cathl 94–04; Dean Carl from 04. *The Deanery, The Abbey, Carlisle CA3 8TZ* T: (01228) 523335 F: 548151 E: dean@carlislecathedral.org.uk

BOYNS, Martin Laurence Harley. b 26. St Jo Coll Cam BA 49 MA 51. Ridley Hall Cam 50. **d** 52 **p** 53. C Woodmansterne *S'wark* 52–55; C Folkestone H Trin w Ch Ch Cant 55–58; V Duffield *Derby* 58–71; V Rawdon *Bradf* 71–76; Chapl Woodlands Hosp Rawdon 71–76; R Melton *St E* 76–85; R Gerrans w St Anthony in Roseland *Truro* 85–92; Miss to Seamen 85–92; rtd 92; PtO *Truro* from 92. *Bojunda, Boscaswell Village, Pendeen, Penzance TR19 7EP* T: (01736) 788390

BOYNS, Timothy Martin Harley. b 58. Warwick Univ BA 80 Nottm Univ BCombStuds 84. Linc Th Coll 81. **d** 84 **p** 85. C Oxhey St Matt *St Alb* 84–87; TV Solihull *Birm* 87–94; V Lillington *Cov* 94–06; RD Warwick and Leamington 99–06; V Hessle *York* 06–18; AD W Hull 10–17; RD Hull 11–18; PtO *Lich* from 19. *11 Alamein Way, Lichfield WS14 0GG* T: (01543) 257329 E: timboyns@timboyns.karoo.co.uk

BRABIN-SMITH, Ms Lorna Daphne. b 54. Leeds Univ BSc 75. Westcott Ho Cam 03. **d** 05 **p** 06. C Emmaus Par Team *Leic* 05–08; TV Fosse Team 08–16; R Branston w Nocton and Potterhanworth *Linc* from 16. *The Rectory, Abel Smith Gardens, Branston, Lincoln LN4 1NN*

BRABY (née QUINTON), Rosemary Ruth. b 53. Univ Coll Lon BA 75 Lon Inst of Educn PGCE 79. **d** 06 **p** 07. OLM Old Catton *Nor* 06–09; PtO 09–10; NSM Trowse 10–19; P-in-c from 19. *49 Woodland Drive, Norwich NR6 7AZ* T: (01603) 427165 E: rosemary.braby@ntlworld.com

BRACE, Alistair Andrew. b 53. Newc Univ MB, BS 76. WMMTC 90. **d** 94. NSM Broseley w Benthall, Jackfield, Linley etc *Heref* 94–98. *58 Spout Lane, Benthall, Broseley TF12 1QY* T: (01952) 884031 E: braceali@aol.com

BRACEGIRDLE, Canon Christopher Andrew. b 56. Dur Univ BEd 79 St Edm Ho Cam BA 84 MA 89 Cov Univ PhD 05. Ridley Hall Cam 82. **d** 85 **p** 86. C Livesey *Blackb* 85–88; TV E Farnworth and Kearsley *Man* 88–92; V Astley and Chapl Wigan and Leigh Health Services NHS Trust 92–98; P-in-c Walkden Moor w Lt Hulton *Man* 98–99; TR Walkden and Lt Hulton 99–03; V Heaton Ch Ch 03–10; Tutor Dioc OLM and Reader Course 97–06; AD Bolton 05–10; Bp's Sen Chapl 10–14; TR Daisy Hill, Westhoughton and Wingates 14–16; TR Blackrod, Daisy Hill, Westhoughton and Wingates 16–18; Warden of Readers 08–18; V Bolton St Pet w St Phil from 18; Borough Dean Bolton from 18; Hon Can Man Cathl from 07. *130 Green Lane, Bolton BL3 2HX* T: (01204) 396298 E: vicar@boltonparishchurch.co.uk

BRACEGIRDLE, Canon Cynthia Wendy Mary. b 52. LMH Ox BA 73 MA 77 Liv Univ DipAE 82. NOC. **d** 87 **p** 94. Chapl Asst Man R Infirmary 85–88; Dir Dioc OLM Scheme *Man* 89–02; Hon Can Man Cathl 98–02; rtd 03; PtO *Carl* from 03. *Drigg Hall, Drigg, Holmrook CA19 1XG* T: (019467) 24366 E: cwmb@sky.com

BRACEGIRDLE, Robert Kevin Stewart. b 47. Univ Coll Ox BA 69 MA 73. St Steph Ho Ox 70. **d** 73 **p** 74. C Dorchester *Sarum* 73–75; C Woodchurch *Ches* 75–78; V Bidston 78–82; P-in-c Salford St Ignatius *Man* 82–86; R Salford St Ignatius and Stowell Memorial 86–02; P-in-c Salford Ordsall St Clem 99–02; P-in-c Millom *Carl* 02–06; V 06–13; rtd 13; PtO *Carl* from 13. *Drigg Hall, Drigg, Holmrook CA19 1XG* T: (019467) 24366 E: cwmb@sky.com

BRACEWELL, Canon David John. b 44. Leeds Univ BA 66 Man Univ MA 82. Tyndale Hall Bris 67. **d** 69 **p** 70. C Tonbridge St Steph *Roch* 69–72; C Shipley St Pet *Bradf* 72–75; V Halliwell St Paul *Man* 75–84; R Guildf St Sav 84–10; Hon Can Guildf Cathl 05–10; rtd 10; PtO *Guildf* 12–18. *350 Kedleston Road, Derby DE22 2TE*

BRACEWELL, Howard Waring. b 35. FRGS 73. Tyndale Hall Bris. **d** 63 **p** 63. Canada 63–72; Travel Missr World Radio Miss Fellowship 72–77; P-in-c Ashill *Nor* 72–74; Hon C Bris St Phil and St Jacob w Em 77–84; PtO *St Alb* 84–86; R Odell 86–88; V Pavenham 86–88; LtO *Man* 88–93; Assoc Min St Andrew's Street Bapt Ch Cambridge 94–99; Assoc Min Halliwell St Luke *Man* 99–01; rtd 01; PtO *Man* 01–14. *16 Avon Road, Melksham SN12 8AY* T: (01225) 353692

BRACEWELL, Mrs Norma Lesley. b 47. SEITE 08. **d** 10 **p** 11. OLM Cant All SS 10–12; NSM 12–13; PtO *Derby* 13–15; C Derby St Andr w St Osmund 15–16; C Allenton and Shelton Lock 15–16; PtO from 16. *33 Sinfin Avenue, Derby DE24 9JA* T: (01332) 704195 E: norma@bracewell.org

BRACEY, David Harold. b 36. AKC 63. **d** 64 **p** 65. C Westleigh St Pet *Man* 64–67; C Dunstable *St Alb* 67–70; V Benchill *Man* 70–76; V Elton St Steph 76–87; V Howe Bridge 87–00; rtd 00; PtO *Ban* from 06. *Rhiw Awel, Sarn, Pwllheli LL53 8EY* T: (01758) 730381

BRACEY, Dexter Lee. b 70. Lanc Univ BA 92. St Steph Ho Ox BTh 11. **d** 09 **p** 10. C St Marychurch *Ex* 09–13; P-in-c Swindon New Town *Bris* 13–17; R Cov St Jo from 17. *St John's Rectory, 9 Davenport Road, Coventry CV5 6QA* E: dexter_bracey@yahoo.co.uk

BRACHER, Paul Martin. b 59. Solicitor 84 Ex Univ LLB 80. Trin Coll Bris BA 90. **d** 90 **p** 91. C Sparkhill w Greet and Sparkbrook *Birm* 90–93; Chapl Birm Women's Hosp 92–93; P-in-c Lea Hall *Birm* 93–98; V 98–18; V Garretts Green and Lea Hall from 18. *St Richard's Vicarage, Hallmoor Road, Birmingham B33 9QY* T: 0121-783 2319 E: richard1552@aol.com

BRACKENBURY, The Ven Michael Palmer. b 30. Linc Th Coll 64. **d** 66 **p** 67. C S Ormsby w Ketsby, Calceby and Driby *Linc* 66–69; V Scothern w Sudbrooke 69–77; RD Lawres 73–78; Bp's Personal Asst 77–88; Dioc Dir of Ords 77–87; Can and Preb Linc Cathl 79–95; Dioc Lay Min Adv 86–87; Adn Linc 88–95; rtd 95. *18 Lea View, Ryhall, Stamford PE9 4HZ* T: (01780) 752415

✠**BRACKLEY, The Rt Revd Ian James.** b 47. Keble Coll Ox BA 69 MA 73. Cuddesdon Coll 69. **d** 71 **p** 72 **c** 96. C Bris Lockleaze St Mary Magd w St Fran 71–74; Asst Chapl Bryanston Sch 74–77; Chapl 77–80; V E Preston w Kingston *Chich* 80–88; RD Arundel and Bognor 82–87; TR Haywards Heath St Wilfrid 88–96; RD Cuckfield 89–95; Suff Bp Dorking *Guildf* 96–15; Hon Can Guildf Cathl 96–15; rtd 15; Hon Asst Bp Portsm from 16; PtO *Chich* from 16; Portsm from 16. *1 Bepton Down, Petersfield GU31 4PR* T: (01730) 266465 E: ijbrackley@gmail.com

BRADBERRY, Canon John Stephen. b 47. Hull Univ BSc 70 Leeds Univ CertEd 71 MEd 86 Bradf Univ PhD 91. NW Ord Course 76. **d** 79 **p** 80. NSM Warley *Wakef* 79–14; *Leeds* 14–16; Chapl H Trin Sch Holmfield 91–06; Chapl Rishworth Sch Ripponden from 06; Bp's Officer for NSMs *Wakef* 95–04; RD Halifax 07–14; AD *Leeds* 14–17; NSM Warley and Halifax St Hilda 16–17; Hon Can Wakef Cathl 13–17; PtO *York* from 19. *7 Chestnut Avenue, Hemingbrough, Selby YO8 6UG* T: (01757) 335221 E: sbradberry@tiscali.co.uk

BRADBROOK, Mrs Averyl. b 46. Girton Coll Cam BA 67 MA 88 Man Univ PGCE 69 MA(Theol) 96. NOC 90. **d** 93 **p** 94. C Heaton Ch Ch *Man* 93–96; P-in-c Elton St Steph 96–02; Bp's Adv on Women in Min 01–02; V Moseley St Mary *Birm* 02–05; P-in-c Moseley St Anne 04–05; TR Eden, Gelt and Irthing *Carl* 05–10; rtd 10; PtO *Carl* from 11. *Turnmire House, Plains Road, Wetheral, Carlisle CA4 8JY* T: (01228) 562011 M: 07808-290817 E: abradbrook@btinternet.com

BRADBROOK, Peter David. b 33. Kelham Th Coll 54. **d** 60 **p** 61. C Ches St Oswald St Thos 60–63; C Fulham St Etheldreda *Lon* 64–65; V Congleton St Jas *Ches* 65–79; V Wheelock 79–92; V Crewe All SS and St Paul 92–98; rtd 98; PtO *Ches* from 00. *Address temp unknown*

BRADBURY, Jane. b 58. Liv Univ BA 80 Wolfs Coll Cam BTh 13. Westcott Ho Cam 11. **d** 13 **p** 14. C Helston and Wendron *Truro* 13–16; P-in-c S Weald *Chelmsf* 16–21; V from 21; P-in-c Brentwood St Geo from 21. *The Vicarage, Wigley Bush Lane, South Weald, Brentwood CM14 5QP* T: (01277) 212054 E: revdjane2902@gmail.com

BRADBURY, Julian Nicholas Anstey. b 49. BNC Ox BA 71 MA 75 Birm Univ MA 84 Cardiff Univ PhD 07. Cuddesdon Coll 71. **d** 73 **p** 74. C S'wark H Trin 73–74; C S'wark H Trin w St Matt 74–76; USA 76–79; V Tottenham H Trin *Lon* 79–85; Dir Past Th Sarum & Wells Th Coll 85–90; P-in-c Yatton Keynell *Bris* 90–97; P-in-c Biddestone w Slaughterford 90–97; P-in-c Castle Combe 90–97; P-in-c W Kington 90–97; P-in-c Nettleton w Littleton Drew 90–97; R Horfield H Trin 97–02; Fell K Fund 02–07; Sen Fell 07–12; Dir Nursing and Cross-Sector Leadership Development NHS Leadership Academy 13–17; PtO *Ox* 02–09 and from 16; Hon C Ox St Giles and SS Phil and Jas w St Marg 09–16; Dir Humanum from 17. *8 Osberton Road, Oxford OX2 7NU* T: (01865) 580823 M: 07900-607099 E: nicholas@nicholasbradbury.co.uk or nicholas@humanum.co.uk

BRADBURY, Justin Robert Grant. b 66. St Andr Univ MA 92. Wycliffe Hall Ox 06. **d** 08 **p** 09. C Southbroom *Sarum* 08–12; CF from 12. *c/o MOD Chaplains (Army)* T: (01264) 383430 F: 381824

BRADBURY, Canon Matthew Laurence. b 58. Kent Univ BA 79 Solicitor 83. EAMTC 00. **d** 03 **p** 04. NSM Sutton and Witcham w Mepal *Ely* 03–06; NSM Haddenham and Wilburton 06–08; V Wisbech St Mary and Guyhirn w Ring's End etc 08–16; P-in-c Wisbech SS Pet and Paul 16–20; V from 20; V Wisbech St Aug from 20; RD Wisbech Lynn Marshland 11–19; Hon Can Ely Cathl from 12. *The Vicarage, Love Lane, Wisbech PE13 1HP* T: (01945) 739680 M: 07704-139898

BRADBURY, Nicholas. See BRADBURY, Julian Nicholas Anstey

BRADBURY, Paul. b 72. St Cath Coll Cam BA 93 N Lon Univ MA 99. Trin Coll Bris BA 04. **d** 04 **p** 05. C Bitterne Park *Win* 04–08; Pioneer Min Poole Old Town *Sarum* from 08. *43 Green Road, Poole BH15 1QH* E: bradsare@btinternet.com

BRADBURY, Robert Douglas. b 50. Ripon Coll Cuddesdon 75. **d** 76 **p** 77. C Harlescott *Lich* 76–81; V Ruyton 81–88; P-in-c Gt w Lt Ness 84–88; V Ruyton XI Towns w Gt and Lt Ness 88–99. *Fairview, Holyhead Road, Froncysyllte, Llangollen LL20 7PU* T: (01691) 777898

BRADDOCK, Canon Andrew Jonathan. b 71. SS Coll Cam BA 92 MA 96 PhD 13. Ridley Hall Cam 95. **d** 98 **p** 99. C Ranworth w Panxworth, Woodbastwick etc *Nor* 98–01; R

Cringleford and Colney 01–08; RD Humbleyard 04–08; Miss and Evang Officer *Glouc* 08–13; Hon Can Glouc Cathl 11–13; Dir Miss and Min from 13; Can Res Glouc Cathl from 13. *Church House, College Green, Gloucester GL1 2LY* T: (01452) 835549 E: abraddock@glosdioc.org.uk

BRADDY, Andrew Richard. b 67. Birm Univ BA 88 City Univ MA 89 Goldsmiths' Coll Lon PhD 99 ABSM 88. SEITE BA 10. **d** 10 **p** 11. C Whitstable *Cant* 10–14; V Wantsum Gp from 14; Jt AD Thanet from 18. *The Vicarage, St Mildred's Road, Minster, Ramsgate CT12 4DE* T: (01843) 821250 M: 07813-384972 E: arichard.braddy@gmail.com

BRADFORD, John. b 34. Lon Univ BA 60 Birm Univ MEd 81 FRSA FRGS. Oak Hill Th Coll 55. **d** 60 **p** 61. C Walcot *B & W* 60–64; Asst Master Wendover C of E Primary Sch 64–65; Hd RE Dr Challoner's High Sch Lt Chalfont 65–69; PtO *Ox* 66–70; Lect St Pet Coll of Educn Saltley 70–77; PtO *Birm* 70–71 and from 05; Lic F11–03; PtO *Cov* from 77; Nat Chapl-Missr Children's Soc 77–99; PtO Ch in Wales from 89; rtd 99. *27 Marsh Lane, Solihull B91 2PG* T: 0121-704 9895 E: revjohnbradford@btinternet.com

BRADFORD, Mark James. b 78. York Univ BA 00. St Jo Coll Nottm 10. **d** 13 **p** 14. C Ripon H Trin 13–14; *Leeds* 14–16; V Preston St Cuth *Blackb* from 16. *66 Kings Drive, Fulwood, Preston PR2 3HQ* M: 07967-740536 E: markjamesbradford@googlemail.com or mark.bradford@stcuthbertschurch.net

BRADFORD, Nicola Diane. b 65. Matlock Coll of Educn BEd 87. Sarum Coll 18. **d** 21. C Aisholt, Enmore, Goathurst, Nether Stowey etc *B & W* from 21. *16 Bagborough Drive, Bridgwater TA6 6UW* T: (01823) 337690 M: 07588-672198 E: nicki.bradford@gmail.com

BRADFORD, Phillip James. b 81. York Univ BA 02 MA 04 PhD 08. Westcott Ho Cam 07. **d** 10 **p** 11. C Worc SE 10–13; C St Jo in Bedwardine 13–15; P-in-c Worc Dines Green St Mich and Crown E, Rushwick 15–21; P-in-c St Jo in Bedwardine 18–21; TR Worc City W from 21. *The Rectory, 124 Laugherne Road, Worcester WR2 5LT*

BRADFORD, Simon. b 77. **d** 12 **p** 13. NSM Milton *Ely* from 12; NSM Waterbeach from 12; NSM Landbeach from 12. *22 Heron Walk, Waterbeach, Cambridge CB25 9BZ* E: sd_bradford@hotmail.com

BRADFORD, Steven John. b 59. Open Univ MBA 01. St Jo Coll Nottm 06. **d** 08 **p** 09. C Bearsted w Thurnham *Cant* 08–11; V Gorleston St Andr *Nor* 11–15; P-in-c Folkestone St Jo *Cant* 15–19; V 19–20; rtd 20. *75 Poulders Gardens, Sandwich CT13 0AJ* E: stevejbradford@btinternet.com

BRADFORD, Archdeacon of. See JOLLEY, The Ven Andrew John

BRADFORD, Dean of. *Vacant*

BRADFORD, Suffragan Bishop of. See HOWARTH, The Rt Revd Toby Matthew

BRADING, Christopher. b 58. St Steph Ho Ox 12. **d** 14 **p** 15. C Swinton *Sheff* 14–17; V Haywards Heath St Rich *Chich* from 17. *St Richard's Vicarage, Queens Road, Haywards Heath RH16 1EB* T: (01444) 413621

BRADING, Jeremy Clive. b 74. Birm Univ BA 95 MPhil 98. Westcott Ho Cam 00. **d** 02 **p** 03. C Man Clayton St Cross w St Paul 02–05; TV Pendleton 05–07; P-in-c Daisy Hill 07–12; C Westhoughton and Wingates 11–12; R Chickerell w Fleet *Sarum* 12–21; P-in-c Abbotsbury, Portesham and Langton Herring 12–21; R Kings Bromley, The Ridwares and Yoxall *Lich* from 21. *The Rectory, Savey Lane, Yoxall, Burton-on-Trent DE13 8PD* M: 07985-416140 E: jeremybrading@gmail.com

BRADISH, Christopher James. b 85. Birm Univ LLB 07 Solicitor 10. Ripon Coll Cuddesdon BA 15. **d** 16 **p** 17. C Alton *Win* 16–18; C Onslow Square and S Kensington St Aug *Lon* 18–19; P-in-c Andover *Win* 19; V from 19. *The Vicarage, 1 Church Close, Andover SP10 1DP* T: (01264) 366373 E: chris.bradish@stmarysandover.org

BRADISH, Paul Edward. b 61. Reading Univ LLB 83. Ripon Coll Cuddesdon MA 07. **d** 07 **p** 08. C Wokingham St Sebastian *Ox* 07–08; C Upper Kennet *Sarum* 08–10; R Shiplake w Dunsden and Harpsden *Ox* 10–15; P-in-c Headbourne Worthy *Win* 15–19; R Martyr Worthy 15–19; R from 19; P-in-c King's Worthy 15–19; R from 19; P-in-c Upper Dever 16–19. *The Rectory, 4 Campion Way, Kings Worthy, Winchester SO23 7QP* T: (01962) 882166 M: 07469-392397 E: worthysrev@gmail.com

BRADLEY, Andrew Robert. b 65. Clare Coll Cam BA 88. St Jo Coll Nottm MA 94. **d** 94 **p** 95. C Burnage St Marg *Man* 94–98; TV Didsbury St Jas and Em 98–04; Nat Co-ord Acorn Chr Foundn 04–11; Chapl Christie NHS Foundn Trust Man from 11; P-in-c Northenden *Man* from 16. *Northenden Rectory, Ford Lane, Northenden, Manchester M22 4NQ* T: 0161-998 2615 M: 07342-230797 E: stwilfridspc@gmail.com

BRADLEY, Anthony Edward. b 39. Perth Bible Coll 93. **d** 89 **p** 96. Dn-in-c Ravensthorpe Australia 95-96; P-in-c 96–99;

C Wotton St Mary *Glouc* 00–04; rtd 04. *PO Box 1083, Bridgetown WA 6255, Australia* T: (0061) (8) 9761 2917 E: tonychris@westnet.com.au

BRADLEY, Colin John. b 46. Edin Univ MA 69. Sarum & Wells Th Coll 72. **d** 75 **p** 76. C Easthampstead *Ox* 75–79; V Shawbury *Lich* 79–90; R Moreton Corbet 80–90; P-in-c Stanton on Hine Heath 81–90; Can Res Portsm Cathl and Dir of Ords *Portsm* 90–98; C Chich 98–00; C Chich St Paul and Westhampnett 00–01; P-in-c Cocking, Bepton and W Lavington 01–14; rtd 14. *26 Kenwyn Street, Truro TR1 3BU* E: zen101842@zen.co.uk

BRADLEY (née DRAPER), Mrs Elizabeth Ann. b 38. Nottm Univ BTh 75. Linc Th Coll 71. **dss** 84 **d** 87 **p** 94. Ind Chapl *Linc* 84–91; Bracebridge 84–91; Hon C 87–91; GFS Ind Chapl *Lon* 91–96; Hon Chapl GFS 96–98; Riverside Chapl *S'wark* 96; C Leighton Buzzard w Eggington, Hockliffe etc *St Alb* 98–01; PtO 01–02; Chapl Luton and Dunstable Univ Hosp NHS Foundn Trust from 02; PtO *St Alb* from 10. *14 Wren Terrace, Wixams, Bedford MK42 6BP* E: elizabeth.bradley@ldh-tr.anglox.nhs.uk

BRADLEY, Gary Scott. b 53. Lon Univ LLB 75. Ripon Coll Cuddesdon 75. **d** 78 **p** 79. C St John's Wood *Lon* 78–83; V Paddington St Sav 83–11; P-in-c Paddington St Mary 95–11; P-in-c Paddington St Mary Magd 98–03; V Lt Venice from 11. *24 Formosa Street, London W9 2QA* T: (020) 7723 1968 *or* 7262 3787 F: 7724 5332 M: 07957-140371 E: vicar@parishoflittlevenice.com

BRADLEY, Mrs Jennifer Vivienne. b 73. St Hild Coll 18. **d** 21. C Kairos BMO *Leeds* from 21. *5 Greengate Drive, Knaresborough HF5 9EN* M: 07534-688975 E: jennifer.bradley@leeds.anglican.org

BRADLEY, Joy Elizabeth. *See* COUSANS, Joy Elizabeth

BRADLEY, Mrs Julie Caroline. b 59. Ex Univ BSc 80. WEMTC 00. **d** 03 **p** 04. NSM Stoke Gifford *Bris* from 03. *113 North Road, Stoke Gifford, Bristol BS34 8PE* T: 0117-979 3418 E: cjcbradley@icloud.com

BRADLEY, Mrs Mary. **d** 12 **p** 13. NSM Meanwood *Ripon* 12–14; *Leeds* from 14. *3 Dale Park Close, Leeds LS16 7PR*

BRADLEY, Canon Michael Frederick John. b 44. Qu Coll Birm 76. **d** 77 **p** 78. C Sheff St Cuth 77–78; C Alford w Rigsby *Linc* 78–83; V Bracebridge 83–90; V Flitwick *St Alb* 90–14; RD Ampthill and Shefford 08–13; Hon Can St Alb 10–14; rtd 14; PtO *St Alb* from 14. *14 Wren Terrace, Wixams, Bedford MK42 6BP* E: revmichael@virginmedia.com

BRADLEY, Michael Louis. b 54. Dartington Coll of Arts BA 77 K Coll Lon MMus 84. ERMC. **d** 11 **p** 12. NSM Loughton St Jo *Chelmsf* 11–15; C Barkingside St Fran from 15. *144 Fencepiece Road, Ilford IG6 2LA* T: (020) 8500 2970 E: mikebradley03@yahoo.co.uk *or* frmichael@stfrancisbarkingside.org

BRADLEY, The Ven Peter David Douglas. b 49. Nottm Univ BTh 79. Ian Ramsey Coll Brasted 74 Linc Th Coll 75. **d** 79 **p** 80. C Upholland *Liv* 79–83; TR 94–01; V Dovecot 83–94; Dir CME 89–02; Hon Can Liv Cathl 00–15; Adn St Helens and Warrington 01–15; TR Upholland 01–11; rtd 15; PtO *Liv* from 17. *30 Sandbrook Road, Orrell, Wigan WN5 8UD* T: (01695) 624131 E: peterddbradley@gmail.com

BRADLEY, Peter Edward. b 64. Trin Hall Cam BA 86 MA 90 FRSA 02. Ripon Coll Cuddesdon 86. **d** 88 **p** 89. C Northampton St Mich w St Edm *Pet* 88–91; Chapl G&C Coll Cam 91–95; TV Abingdon *Ox* 95–98; TV High Wycombe 98–03; TR 03; Dean Sheff 03–20; PtO from 21; *Lon* from 21. *Address temp unknown*

BRADLEY, Mrs Susan Kathleen. b 47. Hull Coll of Educn TCert 68 Open Univ BA 84 MA 96. **d** 05 **p** 06. OLM S Lawres Gp *Linc* 05–19; PtO from 19. *17 Holly Close, Cherry Willingham, Lincoln LN3 4BH* T: (01522) 750292 E: rev.s.bradley@gmail.com

BRADLEY, Miss Wendy Jayne. b 66. All SS Cen for Miss & Min 12. **d** 15 **p** 16. NSM Aspley *S'well* 15–18; C 18–19; V Bilton St Pet *York* from 19; V Sutton St Mich from 19. *751 Marfleet Lane, Hull HU9 4TJ* M: 07971-770836 E: wendyjayne.bradley@gmail.com

BRADLEY-STOW, Mrs Alexandra Elizabeth. b 89. Dur Univ MA 21. Ridley Hall Cam 18. **d** 21. C Cherwell Valley *Ox* from 21. *13 Miller Close, Upper Heyford, Bicester OX25 5AQ* M: 07920-144904 E: lex.bradley@hotmail.co.uk

BRADNUM, Canon Ella Margaret. b 41. CertEd 64 St Hugh's Coll Ox MA 65. **dss** 69 **d** 87 **p** 94. Illingworth *Wakef* 69–72; Batley All SS 72–73; Lay Tr Officer 77–82; Min Tr Officer 82–88; Sec Dioc Bd of Min *Wakef* 88–06; Warden of Readers 88–02; Co-ord Lay Tr 88–02; Hon Can Wakef Cathl 94–06; Prin Wakef Min Scheme 97–06; rtd 06. *4 Southlands Drive, Huddersfield HD2 2LT* T: (01484) 420721

BRADNUM, Richard James. b 39. Pemb Coll Ox BA 62 MA 67. Ridley Hall Cam 62. **d** 64 **p** 65. C Birm St Martin

64–68; C Sutton St Jas *York* 68–69; PtO *Wakef* 71–72; C Batley All SS 72–74; V Gawthorpe and Chickenley Heath 74–86; V Mixenden 86–97; rtd 97; PtO *Wakef* 97–99; Hon Retirement Officer 99–12. *4 Southlands Drive, Huddersfield HD2 2LT* T: (01484) 420721

BRADSHAW, Benjamin James. b 86. Sheff Univ BA 12. Coll of Resurr Mirfield 09. **d** 13 **p** 19. C Braunton *Ex* 13–15; Bp's Chapl *S & M* 17–20; PtO *Man* 17–18; Shrine P Shrine of Our Lady of Walsingham from 20. *The Shrine of Our Lady of Walsingham, The College, 1 Knight Street, Walsingham NR22 6EF* T: (01328) 824204 E: shrine.pr@olw-shrine.org.uk

BRADSHAW, Charles Anthony. b 44. Qu Coll Birm MA 76. **d** 75 **p** 76. C Whickham *Dur* 75–78; C Bilton *Cov* 78–81; TV Coventry Caludon 81–89; R Birstall and Wanlip *Leic* 89–99; TR Vale of Belvoir 00–04; TV Caterham *S'wark* 04–12; rtd 12; PtO *S'wark* from 13. *39 Mill Lane, Hurst Green, Oxted RH8 9DF* T: (01883) 724742 E: charles@bradshaw39.plus.com

BRADSHAW, Denis Matthew. b 52. Chich Th Coll 77. **d** 80 **p** 81. C Ruislip St Martin *Lon* 80–84; C Northolt Park St Barn 84–86; V Northolt St Jos 86–01; P-in-c Hayes St Nic CD 94–00; V Kennington St Jo w St Jas *S'wark* 01–09; V Burgess Hill St Edw *Chich* 09–19; rtd 19; PtO *Chich* from 19. *4 Lily Gardens, Worthing BN13 2FB* E: denis.bradshaw1@btinternet.com

BRADSHAW, Graham. b 58. Edin Univ BD 86. Edin Th Coll 83. **d** 86 **p** 87. C Thornton-le-Fylde *Blackb* 86–89; C Kirkby Lonsdale *Carl* 89–91; V Langford *St Alb* 91–97; Papua New Guinea 97–99; R Aspley Guise w Husborne Crawley and Ridgmont *St Alb* 00–21. *Address temp unknown* E: gbradshaw@tinyworld.co.uk

BRADSHAW (née DAY), Mrs Jennifer Ann. b 67. Aber Univ BSc 89. Wycliffe Hall Ox BTh 95. **d** 95 **p** 96. C Whitburn *Dur* 95–98; C Monkwearmouth 98–99; TV 99–01; NSM Silksworth 02–12; TV N Wearside from 12. *The Rectory, 2A Park Avenue, Sunderland SR6 9PU* M: 07443-228077 E: jenniferabradshaw@btinternet.com

BRADSHAW, Julia Dawn. b 60. ERMC 16. **d** 19. NSM Gtr Athens *Eur* from 19. *PO Box 32, Kalyves, 73003 Chania, Crete, Greece* T: (0030) (2825) 022733 E: juliaworld21@yahoo.co.uk

BRADSHAW, Canon Paul Frederick. b 45. Clare Coll Cam BA 66 MA 70 K Coll Lon PhD 71 Ox Univ DD 94 FRHistS 91. Westcott Ho Cam 67. **d** 69 **p** 70. C W Wickham St Jo *Cant* 69–71; C Cant St Martin and St Paul 71–73; Tutor Chich Th Coll 73–78; V Flamstead *St Alb* 78–82; Dir of Minl Tr Scheme 78–82; Vice-Prin Ripon Coll Cuddesdon 83–85; USA 85–95; Prof Th Notre Dame Univ 85–13; Hon Can N Indiana from 90; PV Westmr Abbey 95–13; PtO *Guildf* 96–13; Dioc Liturg Officer *Eur* 07–13; rtd 13. *367 Pine Valley Drive, Fairview TX 75069, USA* T: (001) (214) 856 0799 E: bradshaw.1@nd.edu

BRADSHAW, Philip Hugh. b 39. Qu Coll Ox BA 64 MA 67. S'wark Ord Course 88. **d** 91 **p** 92. NSM Bletchingley *S'wark* 91–98; Ldr Community of Celebration 91–98; NSM Redhill St Jo *S'wark* 98–10; PtO from 10. *35 Cavendish Road, Redhill RH1 4AL* T: (01737) 778760 E: bradshaws@ccct.co.uk

BRADSHAW, Richard Gordon Edward. b 66. Southn Univ LLB 90. Wycliffe Hall Ox BTh 94. **d** 97 **p** 98. C Bishopwearmouth St Gabr *Dur* 97–00; C Silksworth 00–01; P-in-c 01–03; V 03–12; TR Monkwearmouth from 12; AD Wearmouth 08–15. *The Rectory, 2A Park Avenue, Sunderland SR6 9PU* T: 0191-548 6607

BRADSHAW, Roy John. b 49. Sarum & Wells Th Coll 85. **d** 87 **p** 88. C Gainsborough All SS *Linc* 87–90; V New Waltham 90–94; R Killamarsh *Derby* 94–06; C Barlborough and Renishaw 05–06; rtd 06; PtO *Derby* from 07. *22 St Peter's Close, Duckmanton, Chesterfield S44 5JJ* T: (01246) 822280 E: rbradshaw@hotmail.com

BRADSHAW, Timothy. b 50. Keble Coll Ox BA 72 MA 78 PhD. St Jo Coll Nottm BA 75. **d** 76 **p** 77. C Clapton Park All So *Lon* 76–79; Lect Trin Coll Bris 80–91; Hon C Sea Mills *Bris* 83–91; Tutor Regent's Park Coll Ox from 91; NSM Ox St Aldate w St Matt 91–94; NSM Ox St Matt 95–18; rtd 18. *Address temp unknown* E: timothy.bradshaw@regents.ox.ac.uk

BRADSHAW, Veronica. *See* CAROLAN, Veronica

BRADWELL, Area Bishop of. *See* PERUMBALATH, The Rt Revd John

BRADY, Benjamin Eric. b 88. Leeds Univ BA 10 St Jo Coll Dur BA 16. Cranmer Hall Dur 14. **d** 17 **p** 18. C Ashton Ch Ch *Man* 17–21; C Linc St Swithin from 21; C Linc St Faith and St Martin w St Pet from 21. *165C Carholme Road, Lincoln LN1 1RU* M: 07792-052783 E: benjamin.e.brady@gmail.com

BRADY, Ian. b 59. Ridley Hall Cam. **d** 01 **p** 02. C Cromer *Nor* 01–04; V Belmont *Lon* 04–09; P-in-c Douglas St Thos *S & M* 09–14; V 14–16; Can St German's Cathl 14–16; R Doddington w Benwick and Wimblington *Ely* 16–19;

P-in-c Christchurch and Manea and Welney 16–19; R Six Fen Churches from 20. *The Rectory, 8 Church Street, Wimblington, March PE15 0QS* T: (01354) 740627 E: revianbrady@btinternet.com

BRADY, Jennifer Adrienne. b 70. Ches Univ BA 07. All SS Cen for Miss & Min 19. d 21. NSM Liv Our Lady and St Nic from 21. *Address withheld by request*

BRADY, Karen. b 62. Newc Univ BSc 85 Open Univ MBA 97 MA 08. All SS Cen for Miss & Min 10. d 17 p 18. C Macclesfield Team *Ches* 17–20; V Runcorn St Mich from 20. *145 Greenway Road, Runcorn WA7 4NR* E: revkarenbrady@gmail.com

BRADY, Lynda. b 60. SRN 83. SA Internat Tr Coll 87 Oak Hill Th Coll 07. d 07 p 08. NSM Belmont *Lon* 07–09; NSM Douglas St Thos *S & M* 09–16; Chapl Hospice Is of Man 09–16; C Christchurch and Manea and Welney *Ely* 16–19; C Six Fen Churches from 20. *The Rectory, 8 Church Street, Wimblington, March PE15 0QS* T: (01354) 740627 M: 07974-995561 E: revbrady@btinternet.com

BRADY, Mrs Natasha Dawn. b 71. St Mellitus Coll BA 15. d 15 p 16. C Rushden St Mary w Newton Bromswold *Pet* 15–18; V Stoke Bruerne Gp *Ox* from 18. *The Rectory, Victoria Road, Farnham Common, Slough SL2 3NJ* M: 07539-424821 E: natasha_brady@btinternet.com

BRAGG, Annette Frances. *See* STICKLEY, Annette Frances

BRAGG, The Hon Marie-Elsa Beatrice Roche. UEA MA 16. Ripon Coll Cuddesdon 06. d 07 p 09. NSM St Marylebone St Paul *Lon* 07–08; NSM Kilburn St Mary w All So and W Hampstead St Jas 08–14; PtO 14–18. *Address withheld by request* E: marieelsabragg@gmail.com

BRAGG, Mrs Rosemary Eileen. b 41. MRPharmS 64. St Steph Ho Ox 99. d 00 p 01. NSM Boyne Hill *Ox* 00–06; NSM Golden Cap Team *Sarum* 06–11; rtd 11; PtO *Sarum* 11–22. *Dove Inn Cottage, 48 Silver Street, Lyme Regis DT7 3HR* T: (01297) 442403 E: rosie@bragg.eu

BRAID, Simon. b 54. SS Coll Cam MA 76 FCA 79. SEITE 06. d 09 p 10. NSM Hildenborough *Roch* 09–19; Lic Preacher 19–20; P-in-c Hever, Four Elms and Mark Beech from 20. *Petresfield, Fordcombe Road, Penshurst, Tonbridge TN11 8DL* T: (01892) 871453 M: 07802-809849 E: simonbraid@uwclub.net

BRAILSFORD, Matthew Charles. b 64. Newc Univ BSc 86 St Jo Coll Dur BA 95. Cranmer Hall Dur 92. d 95 p 96. C Hull St Jo Newland *York* 95–06; P-in-c N Ferriby 06–14; V from 14; Adv in Evang and Fresh Expressions from 10; AD W Hull from 17. *The Vicarage, 20 Aston Hall Drive, North Ferriby HU14 3EB* T: (01482) 631306 E: matthewcbrailsford@icloud.com

BRAITHWAITE, Catherine Anne. *See* HALE-HEIGHWAY, Catherine Anne

BRAITHWAITE, Canon Michael Royce. b 34. Linc Th Coll 71. d 73 p 74. C Barrow St Geo w St Luke *Carl* 73–77; V Kells 77–88; RD Calder 84–88; V Lorton and Loweswater w Buttermere 88–96; Ldr Rural Life and Agric Team 93–96; Member Rural Life and Agric Team 96–99; RD Derwent 94–98; Hon Can Carl Cathl 94–99; rtd 99; PtO *Carl* from 00. *High Green Farm, Bothel, Carlisle CA7 2JA* T: (016973) 23429

BRAITHWAITE, Canon Roy. b 34. Dur Univ BA 56. Ridley Hall Cam 58. d 60 p 61. C Blackb St Gabr 60–63; C Burnley St Pet 63–66; V Accrington St Andr 66–74; V Blackb St Jas 74–95; RD Blackb 86–91; Hon Can Blackb Cathl 93–98; V Garstang St Helen Churchtown 95–98; Dioc Ecum Officer 95–98; rtd 98; PtO *Blackb* from 98. *9 Barker Lane, Mellor, Blackburn BB2 7ED* T: (01254) 240724

BRALESFORD, Nicholas Robert. b 53. St Jo Coll Nottm LTh 79 BTh 79. d 79 p 80. C Leic St Chris 79–82; C Heeley *Sheff* 82–85; TV Kings Norton *Birm* 85–90; V Chapel-en-le-Frith *Derby* 90–13; rtd 13; PtO *Blackb* from 13. *Flat 4, Anselm Court, Pembroke Avenue, Blackpool FY2 9QD* T: (01253) 500474 M: 07505-338853 E: nrb24601@hotmail.co.uk

BRALEY, Robert James. *See* RILEY-BRALEY, Robert James

BRAMHALL, Eric. b 39. St Cath Coll Cam BA 61 MA 65. Tyndale Hall Bris 61. d 63 p 64. C Eccleston St Luke *Liv* 63–66; C Bolton Em *Man* 66–69; PtO *Ches* 70–74; V Aughton Ch Ch *Liv* 75–92; Chapl Ormskirk Children's Hosp 75–92; V Childwall All SS *Liv* 92–04; rtd 04; PtO *St As* from 09. *Henfaes, Prior Street, Ruthin LL15 1LT* T: (01824) 702757

BRAMHALL, John. b 52. d 08. NSM Greenham *Ox* from 08. *56 Greyberry Copse Road, Thatcham RG19 8XB* T: (01635) 42348 E: johnbramuk@yahoo.co.uk

BRAMLEY, Mrs Elizabeth. b 46. Bedf Coll Lon BA 68 Lon Inst of Educn PGCE 70. St Mich Coll Llan 11. d 15 p 16. OLM The Beacons *S & B* from 15; OLM Llyn Safaddan from 15. *Weatheroak, Llanhamlach, Brecon LD3 7YB* T: (01874) 665267 E: liz.bramley@icloud.com

BRAMLEY, Thomas Antony. b 44. BSc PhD. TISEC 95. d 96 p 97. NSM Penicuik *Edin* 96–12; NSM W Linton 96–12;

LtO 12–15; PtO from 15. *70 The Links, Hyde SK14 4GR* E: tbramley44@sky.com

BRAMMER, David John. b 62. d 99 p 00. C Acton St Mary *Lon* 99–02; C Ealing All SS and Chapl Twyford C of E High Sch Acton 02–09; R Acton St Mary *Lon* 09–14; Chapl Twyford C of E High Sch Acton from 17; Chapl Wm Perkin C of E High Sch from 17. *Twyford C of E Academies Trust Ealing, Twyford C of E High School, Twyford Crescent, London W3 9PP* T: (020) 8752 0141 E: rev.d.brammer@btinternet.com or dbrammer@twyfordacademies.org.uk

BRAMPTON, Canon Fiona Elizabeth Gordon. b 56. St Jo Coll Dur BA 78 BA 83. Cranmer Hall Dur 81. dss 84 d 87 p 94. Bris St Andr Hartcliffe 84–90; Par Dn 87–90; C Orton Waterville *Ely* 90–96; C-in-c Orton Goldhay CD 90–96; TV The Ortons, Alwalton and Chesterton 96–00; V Haddenham 00–19; V Wilburton 00–19; P-in-c Witchford w Wentworth 08–19; RD Ely 03–09; C N Leightonstone from 19; Chapl Lt Gidding from 19; Hon Can Ely Cathl from 05. *The Rectory, 29 Church Road, Great Stukeley, Huntingdon PE28 4AL*

BRAMPTON, Timothy John Gordon. b 59. Coll of SS Mark and Jo Plymouth BA 01 Sheff Univ BA 12. Coll of Resurr Mirfield 10. d 12 p 13. C Standish *Blackb* 12–15; P-in-c Marks Gate *Chelmsf* 15–18; V 18–19; P-in-c Basildon St Martin from 19. *The Rectory, St Martin's Square, Basildon SS14 1DX* M: 07450-962688 E: timbrampton@btinternet.com

BRANCHE, Caren Teresa. *See* TOPLEY, Caren Teresa

BRAND, Peter John. b 32. Lon Univ BSc 54. Edin Dioc NSM Course 75. d 83 p 84. NSM Edin St Jo from 83. *24 Drum Brae Park, Edinburgh EH12 8TF* T: 0131-339 4406

BRAND, The Ven Richard Harold Guthrie. b 65. Univ Coll Dur BA 87 St Jo Coll Dur MA 16. Ripon Coll Cuddesdon 87. d 89 p 90. C N Lynn w St Marg and St Nic *Nor* 89–92; C King's Lynn St Marg w St Nic 92–93; C Croydon St Jo *S'wark* 93–96; TV Fendalton NZ 96–98; P-in-c Hambledon *Portsm* 98–06; Dir of Ords 98–06; P-in-c Market Harborough and The Transfiguration etc *Leic* 06–08; TR 08–16; AD Gartree I 13–16; AD Gartree II 13–16; Hon Can Leic Cathl 16; Adn Win from 16. *22 St John's Street, Winchester SO23 0HF* T: (01962) 710960 E: richard.brand@winchester.anglican.org

BRANDES, Simon Frank. b 62. Univ of Wales (Ban) BA 83. Edin Th Coll 83. d 85 p 86. C Barton w Peel Green *Man* 85–88; C Longsight St Jo w St Cypr 88–90; R 90–94; Asst Dioc Youth Officer 88–94; V Lt Lever 94–02; P-in-c Lydgate w Friezland 02–03; TR Saddleworth 03–07; V Chiswick St Nic w St Mary *Lon* from 07. *Chiswick Vicarage, Chiswick Mall, London W4 2PJ* T: (020) 8995 4717 M: 07775-526285

BRANDON, Helen Beatrice. b 55. Heythrop Coll Lon MA 02 Lambeth DD 12. SAOMC 03. d 06 p 07. NSM Burton Latimer *Pet* 06–07; NSM Earls Barton 07–09; Abps' Adv for Healing Min from 07; PtO *Lon* 07–13; *Pet* 09–19; *Carl* from 13; *Linc* from 13; Abp's Adv and Adv to Bps for Deliverance and Healing Ch in Wales from 16; NSM Aldwincle, Clopton, Pilton, Stoke Doyle etc *Pet* from 19. *Clopton Manor, Clopton, Kettering NN14 3DZ* T: (01832) 720346 E: beatrice@healingministry.com

BRANDSMA, Michael John. b 55. Trin Coll Bris 12. d 14 p 15. C Hartshill and Galley Common *Cov* 14–17; P-in-c Atherstone 17–18; V from 18. *40 Holte Road, Atherstone CV9 1HN* T: (01827) 437292 M: 07979-680213 E: visionhope@live.co.uk

BRANFORD, Jack Oliver. b 89. Sheff Univ BA 11 Trin Coll Cam BA 15. Westcott Ho Cam 13. d 16 p 17. C Aylsham *Nor* 16–17; C Aylsham and Distr 17–20; Chapl Gresham's Sch Holt from 20. *82 Grove Lane, Holt NR25 6ED* T: (01263) 713817 M: 07855-759024 E: jackbranford1@hotmail.com

BRANSCOMBE, Michael Peter. b 65. St Jo Coll Cur BA 95 Trin Episc Sch for Min DMin 08. Cranmer Hall Dur 92. d 95 p 96. C Ogley Hay *Lich* 95–01; Dioc Voc Officer 98–01; Asst R Palm Harbor USA 01–03; Assoc R Clearwater Ascension 03–15; C Birm St Martin 15–18; P-in-c Cobham and Stoke D'Abernon *Guildf* 18–19; V Cobham from 19. *The Vicarage, St Andrew's Walk, Cobham KT11 3EQ* M: 07481-726762 E: mike@branscombe.us

BRANSON, Robert David. b 46. Linc Th Coll 74. d 77 p 78. C Kempston Transfiguration *St Alb* 77–80; C Goldington 80–82; V Marsh Farm 82–91; V Aylsham *Nor* 91–11; RD Ingworth 00–10; Chapl Norfolk Primary Care Trust 99–11; rtd 11; PtO *Nor* from 11. *28 Alford Grove, Norwich NR7 8XB* T: (01603) 418177 E: rdlbransons@gmail.com

BRANSTON, Ms Anna Louise. b 63. WEMTC 12. d 15 p 16. C Heref S Wye 15–18; R Pembridge w Moor Court, Shobdon, Staunton etc from 18. *The Rectory, Manley Crescent, Pembridge, Leominster HR6 9EB* T: 07777-692458 E: abranston2002@gmail.com

BRANT, Jonathan David. b 70. K Coll Lon MA 02 Trin Coll Ox MPhil 06 DPhil 09. St Mellitus Coll 09. **d** 11 **p** 12. Chapl Ox Pastorate from 11; NSM Ox St Clem 11–15; PtO 15. *33 Jack Straw's Lane, Headington, Oxford OX3 0DL* T: (01865) 426778 M: 07854-771041 E: jonathan.brant@oxfordpastorate.org

BRASCHI, Lawrence. b 77. Bris Univ BSc 98 SOAS Lon MA 04 Ox Univ MTh 18. Wycliffe Hall Ox 12. **d** 14 **p** 15. C Plymouth St Andr and Stonehouse *Ex* 14–18; V Pennycross from 19; Bp's Adv on Urban Miss from 19. *St Pancras' Vicarage, 66 Glentor Road, Plymouth PL3 5TR* M: 07773-429467 E: lawrence.braschi@stps.org.uk

BRASIER, Ralph Henry (Jim). b 30. Cant Sch of Min 82. **d** 85 **p** 86. C S Ashford Ch Ch *Cant* 85–89; V Pembury *Roch* 89–95; rtd 95; PtO *Win* 95–14; *Portsm* from 95. *52 The Grove, Herne Bay CT6 7QD*

BRASIER (née Rudge), Mrs Susannah Mary. b 84. Trin Coll Ox MA 10 Jes Coll Cam MPhil 10. Westcott Ho Cam 08. **d** 10 **p** 11. C Bournville *Birm* 10–15; R Upminster *Chelmsf* from 15. *The Rectory, 4 Gridiron Place, Upminster RM14 2BE* T: (01708) 220174 E: susannah.brasier@gmail.com

BRASSIL, Seán Adrian. b 56. Westf Coll Lon BSc 79. STETS 97. **d** 00 **p** 01. NSM Westborough *Guildf* 00–04; NSM Woking St Jo 04–05; C Addlestone 05–10; P-in-c Whitchurch *Ex* from 10. *The Vicarage, 204 Whitchurch Road, Tavistock PL19 9DQ* T: (01822) 612936 E: priest.incharge@standrewandjames.org

BRASSIL, Thomas James. b 83. Ex Univ BSc 05. Wycliffe Hall Ox 11. **d** 14 **p** 15. C Elburton *Ex* from 14. *3 Vinery Lane, Plymouth PL9 8DD* T: (01752) 547492 M: 07725-972584 E: tom@sherfordchurch.net

BRATTON, Mark Quinn. b 62. Lon Univ BA 84 K Coll Lon MA 98 Warwick Univ PhD 12 Barrister-at-Law (Middle Temple) 87. Pontifical Gregorian Univ 93 Wycliffe Hall Ox BA 94. **d** 94 **p** 95. C W Ealing St Jo w St Jas *Lon* 94–98; Chapl Warw Univ *Cov* 98–09; AD Cov S 02–09; P-in-c Berkswell 09–14; R from 14; AD Kenilworth 13–18. *The Rectory, Meriden Road, Berkswell, Coventry CV7 7BE* T: (01676) 533766 or 533605 M: 07540-604225 E: markbratton@berkswellchurch.org.uk

BRAUN, Sasha Louise. See REEVES, Sasha Louise

BRAVERY, Christine Louise. See WILSON, Christine Louise

BRAVINER, William Edward. b 66. Leic Poly BSc 88 St Jo Coll Dur BA 94 MA 10 ACA 91 FCA 11. Cranmer Hall Dur 92. **d** 95 **p** 96. C Royton St Anne *Man* 95–99; R Lansallos *Truro* 99–03; V Talland 99–03; P-in-c Duloe, Herodsfoot, Morval and St Pinnock 01–03; TR Jarrow *Dur* 03–14; P-in-c S Shields St Simon 09–13; AD Jarrow 05–14; TV Billingham 14–17; P-in-c Stockton St Pet 17–21; V from 21; P-in-c Elton 17–21; V from 21. *11 Lorne Court, Stockton-on-Tees TS18 3UB* M: 07825-385982 E: bill@braviner.com or bill.braviner@durham.anglican.org

BRAY, Christopher Laurence. b 53. Leeds Univ BSc 74 Qu Univ Kingston Ontario MSc 76. St Jo Coll Nottm 78. **d** 81 **p** 82. C Aughton Ch Ch *Liv* 81–84; Hon C Scarborough St Mary w Ch Ch and H Apostles *York* 84–88; Chapl Scarborough Coll 84–88; V St Helens St Matt Thatto Heath *Liv* 88–98; V Southport All SS and All So 98–02; rtd 02; PtO *Liv* from 03; *Ches* from 12. *6 Ford Close, Wirral CH49 9AR* E: clb53@mac.com

BRAY, Gerald Lewis. b 48. McGill Univ Montreal BA 69 Sorbonne Univ Paris LittD 73. Ridley Hall Cam 76. **d** 78 **p** 79. C Canning Town St Cedd *Chelmsf* 78–80; Tutor Oak Hill Th Coll 80–92; Ed *Churchman* 83–18; Angl Prof Div Beeson Div Sch Samford Univ Alabama 93–06; Research Prof Div from 06. *16 Manor Court, Cambridge CB3 9BE* T: (01223) 311804 or (001) (205) 726 2585 F: (01223) 566608 or (001) (205) 726 2234 E: glbray@samford.edu

BRAY, Jason Stephen. b 69. SS Hild & Bede Coll Dur BA 90 MA 91 Fitzw Coll Cam PhD 96 MSOTS 97. Westcott Ho Cam 95. **d** 97 **p** 98. C Abergavenny St Mary w Llanwenarth Citra *Mon* 97–99; Min Can St Woolos Cathl 99–02; V Blaenavon w Capel Newydd 02–15; P-in-c Abersychan and Garndiffaith 09–11; TV Wrexham *St As* from 15. *The Rectory, 7 Westminster Drive, Wrexham LL12 7AT* T: (01978) 350971 E: jasonbray@aol.com

BRAY, Jeremy Grainger. b 40. Man Univ BA 62. Wells Th Coll 62. **d** 64 **p** 65. C Bris St Andr w St Bart 64–67; C Bris H Cross Inns Court 67–71; C-in-c Stockwood CD 71–73; V Bris Ch the Servant Stockwood 73–83; RD Brislington 79–83; P-in-c Chippenham St Pet 83–88; V 88–93; V Fishponds St Jo 93–04; rtd 04; PtO *Bris* from 04. *46 Charter Road, Chippenham SN15 2HA* T: (01249) 655661 E: jg.bray@btinternet.com

BRAY, Mrs Madeline Mary Elizabeth. b 54. SWMTC 10. **d** 13 **p** 14. NSM Bideford, Northam, Westward Ho!, Appledore etc *Ex* 13–17; NSM Bideford, Landcross, Littleham etc 17–18; TV Parkham, Alwington, Buckland Brewer etc from 18. *The Vicarage, 5 Manor Court, Parkham, Bideford EX39 5PG* T: (01237) 451445 M: 07812-957971 E: revmadelinebray@gmail.com

BRAY, Rachel Elizabeth. b 63. York Univ BA 86. All SS Cen for Miss & Min 18. **d** 21. NSM Southport St Phil and St Paul *Liv* from 21. *45 Arbour Street, Southport PR8 6SQ* T: (01704) 535586 M: 07504-806760 E: rachbray@blueyonder.co.uk

BRAY, Richard Antony. b 77. CCC Ox MA 05. Oak Hill Th Coll BA 09. **d** 09 **p** 10. C St Botolph without Aldersgate *Lon* 09–14; R Limehouse from 14. *Limehouse Rectory, 5 Newell Street, London E14 7HP* T: (020) 7987 1502 M: 07798-940554 E: brayra2001@yahoo.co.uk

BRAY, Simon Lee. b 77. Birm Univ BMus 00 St Jo Coll Dur BA 15. Cranmer Hall Dur 13. **d** 15 **p** 16. C Beverley St Nic *York* 15–18; Abp's Dom Chapl 18–21; P-in-c Bishopthorpe from 21; P-in-c York St Chad from 21; C York St Clem w St Mary Bishophill from 21. *St Chad's Vicarage, 36 Campleshon Road, York YO23 1EY* M: 07816-448030

BRAY, Mrs Wendy Elizabeth. b 60. UEA BEd 83 Bris Univ MA 14. Trin Coll Bris 12. **d** 14 **p** 15. C Pennycross *Ex* 14–17; C Clifton All SS w St Jo *Bris* from 18. *1 Ardern Close, Bristol BS9 2QT* M: 07887-987159 E: wendyebray@hotmail.co.uk

BRAYBROOKE, Marcus Christopher Rossi. b 38. Magd Coll Cam BA 62 MA 65 Lon Univ MPhil 68 Lambeth DD 04. Wells Th Coll 63. **d** 64 **p** 65. C Highgate St Mich *Lon* 64–67; C Frindsbury w Upnor *Roch* 67–72; TV 72–73; P-in-c Swainswick w Langridge and Woolley *B & W* 73–76; R 76–79; Dir of Tr 79–84; Hon C Bath Ch Ch Prop Chpl 84–91; Exec Dir Coun of Chrs and Jews 84–87; rtd 88; PtO *Bris* 88–93; Preb Wells Cathl *B & W* 90–93; Chapl Bath St Mary Magd Holloway 92–93; Hon C Dorchester *Ox* 93–05; PtO from 07; *Ex* from 16. *17 Courtiers Green, Clifton Hampden, Abingdon OX14 3EN* T: (01865) 407566

BRAZELL, Denis Illtyd Anthony. b 42. Trin Coll Cam BA 64 MA 68. Wycliffe Hall Ox 78. **d** 80 **p** 81. C Cheltenham Ch Ch *Glouc* 80–84; V Reading St Agnes w St Paul *Ox* 84–96; PtO *Guildf* 96–97; Warden and Chapl Acorn Chr Healing Trust 97–99; rtd 99; Co-Dir Word for Life Trust from 99; PtO *Glouc* 02–09; Lead Chapl St Andr Healthcare 09–15; rtd 16; PtO *Birm* from 16. *129 Balden Road, Harborne, Birmingham B32 2EL* T: 0121-427 2934 M: 07980-813159 E: denisbrazell@mac.com

BRAZIER, Annette Michaela. See HAWKINS, Annette Michaela

BRAZIER, Catharine Honor. b 67. ERMC 09. **d** 12 **p** 13. NSM Thrapston, Denford and Islip *Pet* 12–13; NSM Aldwincle, Clopton, Pilton, Stoke Doyle etc 13–16; R Barnwell, Hemington, Luddington in the Brook etc from 16. *Beechcroft, Barnwell, Peterborough PE8 5PU* E: cathy.h.brazier@btopenworld.com

BRAZIER, Eric James Arthur. b 37. Qu Coll Birm 84. **d** 86 **p** 87. C Lighthorne *Cov* 86–89; P-in-c 89–92; P-in-c Chesterton 89–92; P-in-c Newbold Pacey w Moreton Morrell 89–92; R Astbury and Smallwood *Ches* 92–99; rtd 99; PtO *Ches* 99–14; *Lich* 00–11; *Heref* from 00; *St As* 12–18. *Wolf's Head Cottage, Chirbury, Montgomery SY15 6BP* T: (01938) 561450

BRAZIER, Canon Raymond Venner. b 40. Wells Th Coll 68. **d** 71 **p** 72. C Horfield St Greg *Bris* 71–75; P-in-c Bris St Matt and St Nath 75–79; V 79–05; RD Horfield 85–91; P-in-c Bishopston 93–97; Hon Can Bris Cathl 94–05; rtd 05; PtO *Bris* from 05; Chapl to The Queen 98–10. *51 Chalks Road, Bristol BS5 9EP* T: 0117-329 4611 E: rayvb@tiscali.co.uk

BRAZIER, Thomas Ian. b 72. Natal Univ BSc 95 MSc 97. Cranmer Hall Dur 10. **d** 12 **p** 13. C Washington *Dur* 12–16; V Greenside from 16; AD Gateshead W from 18. *St John's Vicarage, Greenside, Ryton NE40 4AA* M: 07799-217775 E: greensidevicar@firstsolo.net

BRAZIER-GIBBS, Samantha Elizabeth. b 78. Ridley Hall Cam 03. **d** 06 **p** 08. C Grays Thurrock *Chelmsf* 06–09; NSM Harlow St Mary and St Hugh w St Jo the Bapt 10–12; NSM Church Langley 10–12; C Fyfield, Moreton w Bobbingworth etc 12–15; C Chipping Ongar w Shelley 12–15; V Blackmore and Stondon Massey from 15. *The Vicarage, Church Street, Blackmore, Ingatestone CM4 0RN* T: (01277) 821464 M: 07894-948867 E: revsbg@mac.com

BRAZIL, Ms Esther DaPonte. b 86. Qu Coll Ox MA 08 R Academy of Music MA 11. Ripon Coll Cuddesdon 19. **d** 21. C Ox St Mary Magd from 21. *64 London Road, Headington, Oxford OX3 7PD* M: 07896-460905 E: marymagscurate@gmail.com

BREADEN, Robert William. b 37. Edin Th Coll 58. **d** 61 **p** 62. C Broughty Ferry *Bre* 61–65; R 72–07; R Carnoustie 65–72; Can St Paul's Cathl Dundee 77–07; Dean Bre 84–07; rtd 07; P-in-c Portree *Arg* 07–12; PtO *Mor* from 13. *6 Chapel Road, Evanton, Dingwall IV16 9XT*

BREADMORE, The Ven Martin Christopher. b 67. Lon Univ LLB 89. Wycliffe Hall Ox BTh 93. d 93 p 94. C Herne Bay Ch Ch *Cant* 93–97; C Camberley St Paul *Guildf* 97–01; Chapl Elmhurst Ballet Sch 97–98; C Wallington S'wark 01–10; Dir Lic Min Kensington Area *Lon* 10–19; Adn Dorking *Guildf* from 19. *Old Cricketers, Portsmouth Road, Ripley, Woking GU23 6ER* M: 07850-649255 E: archdeacon.dorking@cofeguildford.org.uk

BREADON, John Desmond. b 73. St Andr Univ BD 96 Birm Univ PhD 02. Westcott Ho Cam 99. d 01 p 02. C W Bromwich All SS *Lich* 01–05; Chapl St Geo Post 16 Cen *Birm* 05–08; Nat Adv for FE/Chapl Abps' Coun 08–10; PtO *Birm* 11–12; Asst Chapl and Dir Eton Dorney Project Eton Coll 11–16. *94 Ermine Road, Chester CH2 3PW* E: johnbreadon@hotmail.co.uk

BREALEY, Mrs Frances Elizabeth. b 56. Univ of Wales (Lamp) BA 77 Univ of Wales (Trin St Dav) MA 14 Dur Univ PGCE 79. Sarum Coll 17. d 18 p 19. NSM Lawrence Weston and Avonmouth *Bris* from 18. *123 Sylvan Way, Bristol BS9 2LX* T: 0117-968 5479 M: 07948-676581 E: fran.brealey@btinternet.com

BREAREY, Mrs Heather Gay. b 66. Sarum Coll 16. d 18 p 19. C Amesbury *Sarum* 18–19; C Avon River from 19. *26 Harvard Way, Amesbury, Salisbury SP4 7XE* M: 07760-386677 E: heatherbrearey@gmail.com

BREBNER, Martin James. b 47. OBE 02. Imp Coll Lon BSc 68 ARCS 68. St Alb Minl Tr Scheme 87. d 90 p 91. Hon C Letchworth St Paul w Willian *St Alb* 90–94; Hon C St Ippolyts 95–01; PtO 01–02; *Linc* from 02. *Willowcroft, Greatford, Stamford PE9 4QA* T: (01778) 561145 F: 561157 E: martinbrebner@yahoo.com

BRECHIN, Bishop of. See SWIFT, The Rt Revd Andrew Christopher

BRECHIN, Dean of. See BRIDGER, The Very Revd Francis William

BRECKLES, Robert Wynford. b 48. St Edm Hall Ox BA 72 MA 74 CertEd. Cranmer Hall Dur. d 79 p 80. C Bulwell St Mary *S'well* 79–84; V Lady Bay 84–05; V Lady Bay w Holme Pierrepont and Adbolton 06–12; rtd 12; PtO *S'well* from 13. *25 Goodwood Road, Nottingham NG8 2FT* T: 0115-854 3795

BRECKNELL, David Jackson. b 32. Keble Coll Ox BA 53 MA 57. St Steph Ho Ox 56. d 58 p 59. C Streatham St Pet *S'wark* 58–62; C Sneinton St Steph w St Alb *S'well* 62–64; C Solihull *Birm* 64–68; V Streatham St Paul *S'wark* 68–75; R Rumboldswyke *Chich* 75–81; P-in-c Portfield 79–81; R Whyke w Rumboldswhyke and Portfield 81–95; rtd 95; PtO *Chich* from 95; P-in-c Boxgrove 98–99. *8 Priory Close, Boxgrove, Chichester PO18 0EA* T: (01243) 784841 E: davidjbrecknell@gmail.com

BRECON, Archdeacon of. See JEVONS, The Ven Alan Neil

BRECON, Dean of. See SHACKERLEY, The Very Revd Albert Paul

BREED, Canon Verena. b 69. d 02 p 02. NSM Prestbury *Ches* 02–04; V Bosley and N Rode w Wincle and Wildboarclough 04–14; RD Macclesfield 12–14; TR Bicester w Bucknell, Caversfield and Launton *Ox* from 14; Hon Can Ch Ch from 19. *The Rectory, 6 Thames Lane, Bicester OX26 6ES* T: (01869) 240744 E: verenabreed@talktalk.net

BREEDS, Christopher Roger. b 51. Lon Univ CertEd 73 LGSM 83. Chich Th Coll 84. d 87 p 88. C E Grinstead St Swithun *Chich* 87–90; TV Aldrington 90–92; P-in-c Hove St Andr Old Ch 92–93; TV Hove 93–99; V Wivelsfield 99–16; RD Cuckfield 06–11; rtd 16; PtO from 16; *Eur* from 17. *67 South Undercliff, Rye TN31 7HN* T: (01797) 224765 E: christopher.breeds@icloud.com

BREEN, Alan Terence. d 14 p 15. Greystones *D & G* 14–15; C 15–17; I Kill from 17. *The Rectory, Kill Lane, Deansgrange, Blackrock, Co Dublin, Republic of Ireland* M: (00353) 86-805 4818 E: alanwfc@me.com

BREENE, Timothy Patrick Brownell. b 59. Kent Univ BA 81 CCC Cam BA 89 MA 90. Ridley Hall Cam 87. d 90 p 93. C Hadleigh w Layham and Shelley *St E* 90–95; C Martlesham w Brightwell 95–03; rtd 03. *85 Cliff Road, Felixstowe IP11 9SQ* T: (01394) 283718

BREFFITT, Geoffrey Michael. b 46. CChem MRIC 72 Trent Poly CertEd 77. Qu Coll Birm 87. d 89 p 90. C Prenton *Ches* 89–92; V Frankby w Greasby 92–01; Dioc Ecum Officer 00–01; V German St Jo *S & M* 01–08; V Foxdale 01–08; V Patrick 01–08; RD Castletown and Peel 04–08; P-in-c Westow *Ches* 08–13; rtd 13. *181 Marion Road, Prestatyn LL19 7DG* E: geoff.breffitt@sky.com

BRENCHER, Lucy Jane. b 71. Ex Univ BA 94. St Hild Coll 15. d 18 p 19. NSM Rural Ainsty *York* 18–19; C from 19; C Tadcaster from 20. *3 Fairfax Close, Bolton Percy,*

York YO23 7AY T: (01904) 744281 M: 07940-514492 E: ruralainstycurate@gmail.com

BRENNAN, John Lester. b 20. MRCP 51 FRCPath 77 Barrister-at-Law (Middle Temple) 71 Lon Univ MB, BS 44 MD 52 LLM 86. St Aug Coll Cant 54. d 55 p 56. India 55–65; Hon C Woodside Park St Barn *Lon* 65–69; LtO *Lich* 69–88; P-in-c Chrishall *Chelmsf* 88–89; Hon C 89–91; Hon C Heydon, Gt and Lt Chishill, Chrishall etc 91–93; PtO *St Alb* from 93. *16 Butterfield Road, Wheathampstead AL4 8PU* T: (01582) 832230

BRENNAND (née PUNSHON), Ms Carol Mary. b 59. Liv Inst of Educn BEd 83. Ridley Hall Cam 92. d 94 p 95. C Bushey *St Alb* 94–97; C Watford Ch Ch 97–00; P-in-c Ash Vale *Guildf* 00–06; V 06–07; P-in-c Claybrooke cum Wibtoft and Frolesworth *Leic* 07–08; P-in-c Leire w Ashby Parva and Dunton Bassett 07–08; C Upper Soar 08–09; R 09–18; P-in-c W Leightonstone *Ely* 18–20; R from 20. *Brington Rectory, Church Lane, Brington, Huntingdon PE28 5AE* E: carolbrennand@btinternet.com

BRENNAND, Ian Peter. b 55. Univ of Wales (Trin St Dav) BA 12. STETS 01. d 04 p 05. C Frimley *Guildf* 04–07; Chapl Univ Hosps Leic NHS Trust 08–18; rtd 18; PtO *Leic* 18; *Ely* from 18; RD Huntingdon from 19. *Brington Rectory, Church Lane, Brington, Huntingdon PE28 5AE* E: ianbrennan@btinternet.com

BRENTFORD, Philip Bernard. d 15 p 16. C St Botolph without Aldersgate *Lon* 15–19; C Leyton Ch Ch *Chelmsf* from 19. *Christ Church, 73 Francis Road, London E10 6PL* T: (020) 8539 0193

BRERETON, Catherine Louise. See WILLIAMS, Catherine Louise

BRETHERTON, Canon Anthony Atkinson. b 51. Cant Univ (NZ) BA 74 Waikato Univ (NZ) MMS 97. St Jo Th Coll (NZ) LTh 74 STh 76. d 75 p 76. Asst C Ashburton NZ 75–78; Asst P St Geo-in-the-East w St Paul *Lon* 79–80; V Te Kauwhata NZ 80–85; V Cam 85–91; Can St Pet Cathl Waikato 88–90; Offg Min Waikato 91–01; LtO *L & K* 02–07; PtO *B & W* 07–10. *Address temp unknown* M: 07738-993809 E: tonybretherton@hotmail.com

BRETT, Dennis Roy Anthony. b 46. Sarum & Wells Th Coll 86. d 88 p 89. C Bradford-on-Avon H Trin *Sarum* 88–92; P-in-c Bishopstrow and Boreham 92–01; R 01–15; Chapl Warminster Hosp 92–14; rtd 16; PtO *Sarum* from 16. *50 Gipsy Lane, Warminster BA12 9LR* T: (01985) 301366 M: 07742-059704 E: revdb@yahoo.co.uk

BRETT, Canon Paul Gadsby. b 41. St Edm Hall Ox BA 62 MA 66. Wycliffe Hall Ox 64. d 65 p 66. C Bury St Pet *Man* 65–68; Asst Ind Chapl 68–72; Ind Chapl *Worc* 72–76; Sec Ind Cttee of Gen Syn Bd for Soc Resp 76–84; Dir Soc Resp *Chelmsf* 85–94; Can Res Chelmsf Cathl 85–94; R Shenfield 94–08; rtd 08. *23 Stothert Avenue, Bath BA2 3FF* T: (01225) 312678 E: paul.brett@btinternet.com

BRETT, Canon Peter Graham Cecil. b 35. Em Coll Cam BA 59 MA 63. Cuddesdon Coll 59. d 61 p 62. C Tewkesbury w Walton Cardiff *Glouc* 61–64; C Bournemouth St Pet *Win* 64–66; Chapl Dur Univ 66–72; R Houghton le Spring 72–83; RD Houghton 80–83; Can Res Cant Cathl 83–01; rtd 01; PtO *Cant* from 01. *3 Appledore Road, Tenterden TN30 7AY* T: (01580) 761794 E: pandgbrett@btinternet.com

BRETT, Steven Anthony. Univ of Wales (Lamp) BA 98 Cardiff Univ BTh 16. St Mich Coll Llan. d 16 p 17. C Llantrisant *Llan* 16–20; P-in-c Narberth and Tenby LMA *St D* from 20. *Address temp unknown* E: revstevebrett@gmail.com

BREUSS, Mrs Kristin Lynn. b 68. Univ of N Carolina BA 90 Columbia Univ MBA 98. St Mellitus Coll BA 14. d 14 p 15. C W Hampstead Trin *Lon* from 14. *29 Netherhall Gardens, London NW3 5RL* T: (020) 7435 0083 M: 07932-770239 E: kristinbreuss@gmail.com *or* kristin@lighthouselondon.org

BREW, Canon William Kevin Maddock. b 49. d 78 p 79. C Raheny w Coolock *D & G* 78–80; Bp's C Dublin Finglas 80–83; I Mountmellick w Coolbanagher, Rosenallis etc *M & K* 83–89; I Ahoghill w Portglenone *Conn* 89–05; I Howth *D & G* from 05; Can Ch Ch Cathl Dublin from 17. *The Rectory, 94 Howth Road, Howth, Co Dublin, Republic of Ireland* T: (00353) (1) 832 3019 E: howth@dublin.anglican.org

BREW, William Philip. b 43. Derby Coll of Educn CertEd 64 FCollP 84. NOC 84. d 87 p 88. In Independent Methodist Ch 70–83; Hd Master Birtenshaw Sch 78–90; NSM Holcombe *Man* 87–90; TV Horwich 91–93; TV Horwich and Rivington 93–97; V Lostock St Thos and St Jo 97–08; P-in-c Bolton St Bede 04–08; AD Deane 98–08; PtO *Wakef* 08–14; *Leeds* from 14; *Eur* 12–18. *22 Deganwy Drive, Kirkheaton, Huddersfield HD5 0NG* T: (01484) 301295 E: brewsp@gmail.com

BREWER, Barry James. b 44. Oak Hill Th Coll 72. d 75 p 76. C Hove Bp Hannington Memorial Ch *Chich* 75–78; C

Church Stretton *Heref* 78–81; TV Bishopsnympton, Rose Ash, Mariansleigh etc *Ex* 81–87; R Swynnerton and Tittensor *Lich* 87–07; RD Stone 01–07; rtd 07; PtO *Lich* 14–15; *Ex* from 15. *2 Hazel Close, Seaton EX12 2UG* T: (01297) 24880 E: barrybrewer29@gmail.com

BREWER, Canon Susan Comport. b 55. LMH Ox MA 76 Cant Ch Ch Univ MA 10. SEITE 99. d 02 p 03. C Dartford St Edm *Roch* 02–07; V Milton next Gravesend Ch Ch 07–18; RD Gravesend 13–18; P-in-c Borstal 13–21; Can Res Roch Cathl from 18. *46 The Fort, Rochester ME1 2FE* T: (01634) 923836 M: 07930-492323 E: suec@brewer86.plus.com *or* sue.brewer@rochestercathedral.org

BREWER-LENNON, Oliver Thomas. b 75. Kentucky Univ BMus 97 Roch Univ NY MMus 00. Scottish Episc Inst 13. d 16. C Edin St Pet 16–18; C Edin St Ninian 18–19; Vice Provost St Mary's Cathl *Glas* from 19. *St Mary's Cathedral, 300 Great Western Road, Glasgow G4 9JB* T: 0141-339 6691 M: 07954-314374

BREWERTON, Andrew Robert. b 70. Oak Hill Th Coll BA 05. d 05 p 06. C Gt Clacton *Chelmsf* 05–09; V Kilnhurst *Sheff* from 09; AD Wath from 12. *The Vicarage, Highthorn Road, Kilnhurst, Mexborough S64 5TX* T: (01709) 589674 E: andy@brewerton.org

BREWIN, David Frederick. b 39. Leic Poly BSc PhD. Lich Th Coll. d 66 p 67. C Shrewsbury H Cross *Lich* 66–69; C Birstall *Leic* 69–73; V Eyres Monsell 73–79; V E Goscote 79–82; V E Goscote w Ratcliffe and Rearsby 82–90; R Thurcaston 90–91; R Thurcaston w Cropston 92–05; rtd 05; PtO *Leic* 05–16; *Pet* 06–17. *28 Welland Way, Oakham LE15 6SL* T: (01572) 720073

BREWIN, Canon Donald Stewart. b 41. Ch Coll Cam BA 62 MA 66. Ridley Hall Cam 68. d 71 p 72. C Ecclesall *Sheff* 71–75; V Anston 75–81; V Walton H Trin *Ox* 81–89; TR 89–94; RD Aylesbury 90–94; Nat Dir SOMA UK 94–07; PtO *St Alb* from 94; rtd 07; Hon Can Boga from 17. *Wickham Cottage, Gaddesden Turn, Great Billington, Leighton Buzzard LU7 9BW* T: (01525) 373644 M: 07816-362797 E: donsbrewin@gmail.com

BREWIN, Karan Rosemary. b 42. CA Tr Coll 77 Glas NSM Course 80. dss 84 d 85 p 15. Clarkston *Glas* 84–89; Hon C 86–89 and 91–97; OHP 89 and 98–02 and from 11; PtO *York* 01–02 and from 13; PtO Johannesburg S Africa 03–05; PtO Swaziland 06–11. *St Agnes' Vicarage, 1 Broughton Avenue, Middlesbrough TS4 3PX* E: karanohp@gmail.com

BREWIN, Wilfred Michael. b 45. Nottm Univ BA 69. Cuddesdon Coll 69. d 70 p 71. C Walker *Newc* 70–73; C Alnwick St Paul 73–74; C Alnwick w Edlingham and Bolton Chpl 74–77; Fell Sheff Univ 77–79; C Greenhill *Sheff* 79; P-in-c Eggleston *Dur* 79–81; V Norton St Mich 81–87; V Headington *Ox* 87–10; rtd 10; PtO *Newc* from 14; *Eur* from 18. *Rose Cottage, New Road, Chatton, Alnwick NE66 5PU* T: (01668) 215319 E: michael.brewin@hotmail.co.uk

BREWIS, Mrs Kalantha Katherine. b 67. Em Coll Cam BA 89 MA 94 Dur Univ BA 20. WEMTC 13. d 16 p 17. C Worc St Barn w Ch Ch 16–20; P-in-c Hallow and Grimley w Holt 20–21; R Hallow and Grimley w Holt etc from 21; C Worc St Clem and Lower Broadheath 20–21. *Court Close, Main Road, Hallow, Worcester WR2 6PW* M: 07808-295457 E: rev.kalantha@gmail.com

BREWIS, Robert David. b 81. Lanc Univ BSc 03. Oak Hill Th Coll MTh 11. d 11 p 12. C Washfield, Stoodleigh, Withleigh etc *Ex* 11–14; NSM Chadderton Ch Ch *Man* 14–21; NSM Haughton St Mary from 21. *58 Oakbank Avenue, Chadderton, Oldham OL9 0PP* E: rbrewis@hotmail.com

BREWSTER, Christine Elaine. b 45. Newc Univ BA 67 CertEd 68 Lon Univ MA 84 DipEd 82 Univ of Wales (Ban) PhD 07 ALCM 76 LTCL 78. SAOMC 95. d 98 p 99. NSM Aylesbury *Ox* 98–00; NSM Dacre w Hartwith and Darley w Thornthwaite *Ripon* 00–01; C Wetherby 01–04; PtO 04–08; P-in-c Llanwnnog and Caersws w Carno *Ban* 08–12; rtd 12; PtO *Ban* 12–16; *Heref* from 13; Visiting Research Fell Glyndŵr Univ from 11. *Michaelmas Cottage, Lingen, Bucknell SY7 0DY* T: (01544) 267338 E: cbmichaelmas@gmail.com

BREWSTER, David Thomas. b 68. GLCM 90 ALCM 89. Cranmer Hall Dur BA 99. d 99 p 00. C Bidston *Ches* 99–03; TV Stockport SW 03–07; V Edgeley and Cheadle Heath from 07; RD Stockport from 17. *St Mark's Vicarage, 66 Berlin Road, Stockport SK3 9QF* T: 0161-480 5896 E: dtbrewster@talktalk.net

BREWSTER, Canon Jonathan David. b 67. Bucks Coll of Educn BA 89 Bris Univ BA 94 K Coll Lon MA 01. Trin Coll Bris 91. d 94 p 95. C Gt Horton *Bradf* 94–98; Chapl Univ of Westmr 98–03; V Highbury Ch Ch w St Jo and St Sav 03–17; AD Islington 14–17; Can Res and Treas St Paul's Cathl from 17. *St Paul's Cathedral, The Chapter House,*

St Paul's Churchyard, London EC4M 8AD M: 07977-127244 E: treasurer@stpaulscathedral.org.uk

BREWSTER, Mrs Lucinda Anne Morrine. b 68. GLCM 90. St Mellitus Coll 17. d 19 p 20. C Partington and Carrington *Ches* from 19. *66 Berlin Road, Stockport SK3 9QF* T: 0161-480 5896 M: 07436-017841 E: lucybrewster@talktalk.net

BREWSTER (*née* **BEATTIE), Margaret.** b 43. S'wark Ord Course 90. d 93 p 94. NSM S'wark H Trin w St Matt 93–97; NSM Newington St Paul 97–04; NSM Dunstable *St Alb* 04–07; rtd 07; PtO *Linc* from 07. *39 Glen Drive, Boston PE21 7QB* T: (01205) 351298 E: m.brewster789@btinternet.com

BREWSTER, Samuel Paul William. b 86. Selw Coll Cam MA 11. Wycliffe Hall Ox MTh 13. d 13 p 14. C Maidenhead St Andr and St Mary *Ox* 13–18; C Henley H Trin from 18. *29 Gainsborough Hill, Henley-on-Thames RG9 1ST* M: 07899-843461 E: sam@thebrewsters.org.uk

BRIAN, Stephen Frederick. b 54. Sussex Univ BEd 77 Open Univ MA 90 Lanc Univ MPhil 97 Surrey Univ PhD 03. Qu Coll Birm 82. d 85 p 86. C Scotforth *Blackb* 85–88; V Freckleton 88–97; V Bagshot *Guildf* 97–06; Chapl Heathfield St Mary's Sch Wantage 06–07; P-in-c Mid Loes *St E* 07–08; R 08–20; RD Loes 13–14; rtd 20; PtO *Lon* from 20. *27 Percy Avenue, Ashford TW15 2PB* M: 07502-291759 E: sfb4510@aol.com

BRICE, Christopher John. b 48. St Edm Ho Cam MA 80. Wycliffe Hall Ox 82. d 82 p 83. C N Hinksey *Ox* 82–86; Chapl Nuff Coll Ox 84–86; V S Hackney St Mich w Haggerston St Paul *Lon* 86–93; Dir Dioc Bd for Soc Resp 93–00; Adv for Soc Justice 01–08; Hon C De Beauvoir Town St Pet 93–08; P-in-c Kentish Town St Martin w St Andr 08–13; V 13–18; rtd 18; PtO *Lon* from 18. *9 Beresford Road, London N5 2HS* T: (020) 7226 3834 M: 07913-733669

BRICE, Derek William Fred. b 39. Poly Cen Lon MA 87 MCIM 89 FCMI 82. d 02 p 03. OLM Cheam *S'wark* 02–09; PtO from 09. *Mallow, Parkside, Cheam, Sutton SM3 8BS* T: (020) 8642 0241 *or* 8693 4324 E: derekbrice@blueyonder.co.uk

BRICE, Jonathan Andrew William. b 61. d 92 p 93. C Buckhurst Hill *Chelmsf* 92–96; C Victoria Docks Ascension 96; P-in-c 96–98; V 98–06; Chapl Felsted Sch 06–11; R Aspen Ch Ch USA 11–19. *Address temp unknown*

BRICE, Canon Neil Alan. b 59. Man Univ BA 81 Hughes Hall Cam CertEd 87. Westcott Ho Cam 82. d 84 p 85. C Longton *Lich* 84–86; Hd of Relig Studies Coleridge Community Coll Cam 87–89; NSM Cherry Hinton St Andr *Ely* 88–89; C Fulbourn 89–92; C Gt Wilbraham 89–92; C Lt Wilbraham 89–92; V Arrington 92–00; R Orwell 92–00; R Wimpole 92–00; R Croydon w Clopton 92–00; P-in-c Barrington 98–00; R Orwell Gp 00–09; R Lerwick *Ab* from 10; P-in-c Burravoe from 10; Can St Andr Cathl from 19. *St Magnus' Rectory, 14 Greenfield Place, Lerwick, Shetland ZE1 0AQ* T: (01595) 693862 M: 07713-259262 E: revnab@btinternet.com

BRICE, Paul Earl Philip. b 54. Bath Univ BSc 77. Wycliffe Hall Ox 83. d 86 p 87. C Gt Baddow *Chelmsf* 86–89; Chapl Imp Coll Lon and St Mary's Hosp Med Sch 89–95; Chapl R Coll of Art 90–95; Sec HE/Chapl C of E Bd of Educn 95–02; Hon C S Kensington St Jude *Lon* 95–02; R Hartfield w Coleman's Hatch *Chich* 02–12; Chapl Zürich *Eur* from 15. *St Andrew, Promenadengasse 9, 8001 Zürich, Switzerland* T: (0041) (44) 261 2241 *or* (44) 252 6024 E: pbrice@anglican.ch

BRICKMAN, Mark. b 60. Jes Coll Cam MA 81. Trin Coll Bris 10. d 12 p 13. C Ox St Aldate 12–16; NSM from 16. *25 Norreys Avenue, Oxford OX1 4ST* T: (01865) 254800 E: mark.brickman@staldates.org

BRIDEWELL, Mrs Alison Clare. b 66. Win Univ BA 11. STETS 11. d 14 p 15. C Bemerton *Sarum* 14–17; P-in-c Potterne w Worton and Marston 17–18; R Wellsprings from 18. *The Rectory, 9 Coxhill Lane, Potterne, Devizes SN10 5PH* M: 07847-952868

BRIDGE, Mrs Sheila Margaret. b 62. St Jo Coll Nottm. d 11 p 12. C Rugby W *Cov* 11–13; Min Rugby St Pet and St Jo CD 13–19; V Rugby St Pet and St Jo from 19; C Heart of England from 21. *St Peter's Vicarage, 63A Lower Hillmorton Road, Rugby CV21 3TQ* E: sheila@peterjohnchurch.org.uk

BRIDGE, Siobhan Claire. b 80. K Alfred's Coll Win BA 02. Qu Foundn Birm 14. d 16 p 17. C Erdington St Barn *Birm* 16–19; V Hamstead St Paul from 19. *St Paul's Vicarage, 840 Walsall Road, Great Barr, Birmingham B42 1ES* M: 07403-843585 E: revdsiobhanbridge@gmail.com

BRIDGE, Susan. BA LLB MBA BTh Regent's Park Coll Ox MPhil. d 09 p 10. C Canberra Australia 10–15; PtO *Ox* 16–18; Asst Chapl New Coll Ox from 17. *New College, Holywell Street, Oxford OX1 3BN* M: 07402-123473 E: susan.bridge@theology.ox.ac.uk

BRIDGEN, John William. b 40. K Coll Cam BA 62 MA 66. Ripon Hall Ox 66. d 70 p 72. C Headstone St Geo *Lon* 70–71;

C Hanwell St Mary 71–75; C Tolladine *Worc* 75; TV *Worc* St Barn w Ch Ch 76; R Barrow *St E* 76–83; V Denham St Mary 76–83; PtO *Ely* 84–88 and 91–16; rtd 88; PtO *Glas* 89–91. *57 St Philip's Road, Cambridge CB1 3DA* T: (01223) 571748 E: j.bridgen@ntlworld.com

BRIDGEN, Mark Stephen. b 63. K Coll Lon BD 85. Cranmer Hall Dur 86. **d** 88 **p** 89. C Kidderminster St Jo and H Innocents *Worc* 88–92; C Nor St Pet Mancroft w St Jo Maddermarket 92–94; V Longbridge *Birm* 94–00; V Wednesbury St Bart *Lich* 00–07; P-in-c Gnosall and Moreton 08–10; R Adbaston, High Offley, Knightley, Norbury etc 10–15; R Paston *Pet* 15–20; TR W Sevenoaks *Roch* from 20. *St Mary's Vicarage, 59 Kippington Road, Sevenoaks TN13 2LL* T: (01732) 452112 E: revmarkbridgen@gmail.com

BRIDGER, The Very Revd Francis William. b 51. Pemb Coll Ox BA 73 MA 78 Bris Univ PhD 81. Trin Coll Bris 74. **d** 78 **p** 79. C Islington St Jude Mildmay Park *Lon* 78–82; Lect St Jo Coll Nottm 82–90; V Woodthorpe *S'well* 90–99; Prin Trin Coll Bris 99–05; Prof Fuller Th Sem USA 05–08; PtO *Nor* 11–12; R Broughty Ferry *Bre* from 12; Dean Bre from 13; P-in-c Dundee St Jo 16–17; P-in-c Dundee St Martin from 16. *3 Wyvis Place, Broughty Ferry, Dundee DD5 3SX* T: (01382) 739035 M: 07507-885476 E: fbridger@yahoo.ie

BRIDGER, Canon Gordon Frederick. b 32. Selw Coll Cam BA 53 MA 58. Ridley Hall Cam 54. **d** 56 **p** 57. C Islington St Mary *Lon* 56–60; C Cambridge St Sepulchre *Ely* 60–62; V Fulham St Mary S End *Lon* 62–69; C Edin St Thos 69–76; R Heigham H Trin *Nor* 76–87; RD Nor S 79–86; Hon Can Nor Cathl 84–87; Prin Oak Hill Th Coll 87–96; rtd 96; PtO *Nor* from 96. *The Elms, 4 Common Lane, Sheringham NR26 8PL* T: (01263) 823522 E: gordonbridger123@btinternet.com

BRIDGER, Mrs Helen Ruth. b 68. Bradf Univ BA 91. Trin Coll Bris BA 06. **d** 05 **p** 06. C Altadena USA 05–06; C Arcadia Transfiguration 06–08; C Nuthall and Kimberley *S'well* 08–10; Chapl Qu Eliz Hosp King's Lynn NHS Foundn Trust 10–12; C Broughty Ferry *Bre* from 12; C Dundee St Jo from 16; C Dundee St Martin from 16. *3 Wyvis Place, Broughty Ferry, Dundee DD5 3SX* T: (01382) 739035 E: helenbridger@yahoo.com

BRIDGES, John Malham. b 57. TD. Goldsmiths' Coll Lon BSc 80. Ridley Hall Cam 03. **d** 05 **p** 06. C Cranleigh *Guildf* 05–08; Chapl RN 08–18; rtd 18; Chapl RNR from 18; PtO *Lon* 18–19; NSM Northwood H Trin from 19. *50 Moor Lane, Rickmansworth WD3 1LG* T: (01923) 775306 E: revdjohnbridges@gmail.com

BRIDGES, Simon Patrick (Sid). b 73. Ox Brookes Univ BA 04. Ridley Hall Cam 13. **d** 14 **p** 15. C Orton Longueville w Bottlebridge *Ely* 14; C The Ortons 14–18; PtO 19; *Pet* 19. *The Rectory, 67 Church Drive, Orton Waterville, Peterborough PE2 5HE* T: (01733) 233402 M: 07851-609020 E: sidbridges@live.co.uk

BRIDGES (née BANKS), Mrs Vivienne Philippa. b 46. Somerville Coll Ox BA 69. SAOMC 02. **d** 05 **p** 06. NSM Wolvercote *Ox* 05–10; NSM Wolvercote and Wytham 10–16; PtO from 16. *6 Haslemere Gardens, Oxford OX2 8EL* T: (01865) 558705

BRIDGEWATER, Guy Stevenson. b 60. Ch Ch Ox BA 83. Trin Coll Bris BA 87. **d** 87 **p** 88. C Radipole and Melcombe Regis *Sarum* 87–90; Chapl Lee Abbey 90–93; V Cranbrook *Cant* 93–98; Dioc Officer for Par Resources (Miss and Lay Tr) *Glouc* 98–07; Dioc Can Res Glouc Cathl 02–07; TR Horsham *Chich* 07–18; RD 09–18; R Bath Abbey w St Jas *B & W* from 18. *12 Cleveland Walk, Bath BA2 6JX* T: (01225) 422462 E: rector@bathabbey.org

BRIDGEWATER, Robert. b 69. Sheff Hallam Univ BEd 92 MSc 97. Oak Hill Th Coll BA 15. **d** 15 **p** 16. C Chapeltown *Sheff* 15–18; LtO from 18. *7 Haugh Lane, Sheffield S11 9SA* M: 07595-938138 E: rob@bridgewaterfamily.me.uk *or* robert.bridgewater@sheffield.anglican.org

BRIDGEWOOD, Bruce William. b 41. K Coll Lon BA 02 Heythrop Coll Lon MA 06. St Paul's Coll Grahamstown LTh 67. **d** 67 **p** 68. C Plumstead S Africa 67–69; C Somerset W 70–71; Hon C Stanmer w Falmer *Chich* 81–86; Hon C Westmr St Matt *Lon* 90–93; Hon C Alexandra Park 93–04; P-in-c Friern Barnet St Pet le Poer 04–13; rtd 13; PtO *Ox* 13–16; *Cant* 16–19. *Flat 2, 54 Bouverie West, Folkestone CT20 2RL* T: (01303) 680432 E: brucebridgewood@gmail.com

BRIDGMAN, James William. b 85. Man Univ BA 06. Trin Coll Bris BA 09 MA 10. **d** 10 **p** 11. C Heswall *Ches* 10–13; V Timperley 13–21; R Tarporley from 21. *The Rectory, High Street, Tarporley CW6 0AG* E: revjimb1017@gmail.com

BRIDGMAN (née JOYCE), Mrs Jennifer Claire. b 84. Man Univ BA 06. Trin Coll Bris BA 08 MPhil 10. **d** 10 **p** 11. C Heswall *Ches* 10–13; Young Voc Adv 11–13; C Broadheath 13–14; C Timperley 14–21; Asst Dioc Dir of Ords 16–20; Dir Studies for Past Workers from 20; IME2 Officer from 21. *The*

Rectory, High Street, Tarporley CW6 0AG M: 07546-304644 E: revjb99@gmail.com

BRIDGWATER, Philip Dudley. b 31. St Alb Minl Tr Scheme 88. **d** 91 **p** 92. NSM Buxton w Burbage and King Sterndale *Derby* 91–94 and 98–01; NSM Fairfield 94–98; PtO 01–18. *Millstone, 9 College Road, Buxton SK17 9DZ* T: (01298) 72876

BRIDLE, Canon Geoffrey Peter. b 52. CITC 87. **d** 87 **p** 88. C Lurgan Ch the Redeemer *D & D* 87–91; I Carnteel and Crilly *Arm* 91–99; I Cleenish w Mullaghdun *Clogh* from 99; Can Clogh Cathl from 15. *Cleenish Rectory, Bellanaleck, Enniskillen BT92 2BA* T: (028) 6634 8259 F: 6634 8620 E: geoffreypbridle@email.com *or* geoffreypeterbridle@me.com

BRIDSON, Canon Raymond Stephen. b 58. Southn Univ BTh 82. Chich Th Coll. **d** 82 **p** 83. C St Luke in the City *Liv* 82–86; TV Ditton St Mich 86–98; V Anfield St Columba 98–19; Asst Dioc Dir of Ords 90–02; AD Walton 02–13; Hon Can Liv Cathl 03–19; rtd 19; PtO *Ches* from 19; *Liv* from 19. *Inglenook, 119 Newton Cross Lane, Wirral CH48 9XG* T: 0151-625 0017 E: frray@blueyonder.co.uk

BRIDSTRUP, Juergen Walter. b 44. St Alb Minl Tr Scheme 84. **d** 87 **p** 88. C Leagrave *St Alb* 87–90; V Goff's Oak St Jas 90–98; TV Cheshunt 08–09; rtd 09; PtO *Heref* from 09. *4 The Vineyard, Lower Broad Street, Ludlow SY8 1PH* T: (01584) 876992 E: juergen.bridstrup@btinternet.com

BRIEN, John Richard. b 57. Kingston Poly BSc 80. EAMTC 98. **d** 01 **p** 02. NSM Mistley w Manningtree and Bradfield *Chelmsf* from 01. *2 Elmdale Drive, Manningtree CO11 2HP* T: (01206) 397549 E: brienfamily@btinternet.com

BRIERLEY, Michael William. b 73. CCC Cam BA 94 MA 98 Birm Univ PhD 07. Ripon Coll Cuddesdon BA 98. **d** 98 **p** 99. C Marnhull *Sarum* 98–01; C Okeford 98–01; Bp's Dom Chapl *Ox* 01–07; P-in-c Tavistock and Gulworthy *Ex* 07–14; Can Res and Prec Worc Cathl 14–21; Dir Formation Ripon Coll Cuddesdon from 21. *Ripon College, Cuddesdon, Oxford OX44 9EX*

BRIERLEY, Philip. b 49. Salford Univ BSc 74. **d** 92 **p** 93. OLM Stalybridge *Man* 92–13; P-in-c 13–16; V 16–19; rtd 19; PtO *Man* from 19. *30 Cranworth Street, Stalybridge SK15 2NW* T: 0161-338 2368 E: philip.brierley@yahoo.co.uk

BRIGGS, Christopher Ronald. b 58. K Coll Lon BD 79 AKC 79 PGCE 80. Sarum & Wells Th Coll 87. **d** 89 **p** 90. C Horsell *Guildf* 89–93; Hong Kong 93–97; V Norton St Alb 97–00; Sen Chapl Haileybury Coll 00–19; Chapl Shiplake Coll Henley from 19. *Shiplake College, Shiplake Court, Shiplake, Henley-on-Thames RG9 4BW* T: 0118-940 5258 E: cbriggs@shiplake.org.uk

BRIGGS, Enid. b 50. CBDTI 03. **d** 06 **p** 07. NSM Walton-le-Dale St Leon w Samlesbury St Leon *Blackb* 06–13; NSM Walton-le-Dale St Leon 12–14; NSM Bamber Bridge St Aid 11–14; LtO 14–20; PtO from 20. *Ground Floor Flat, 169 Manchester Road, Burnley BB11 4HR* E: enid_briggs@hotmail.com

BRIGGS, George William. b 76. Wadh Coll Ox BA 98 Fitzw Coll Cam BA 02. Ridley Hall Cam 00. **d** 03 **p** 04. C Old Trafford St Bride *Man* 03–06; P-in-c Clapham Park All SS *S'wark* 06–11; V 11–14; P-in-c Kendal St Thos *Carl* from 14; P-in-c Crook from 14. *St Thomas's Vicarage, South View Lane, Kendal LA9 4QN* T: (015395) 83058 E: georgebriggs.work@gmail.com

BRIGGS, Gordon John. b 39. CIPFA. SAOMC 95. **d** 98 **p** 99. OLM Farnham Royal w Hedgerley *Ox* 98–11; PtO from 11. *52 Freemans Close, Stoke Poges, Slough SL2 4ER* T: (01753) 662536 E: revgordon@hotmail.co.uk

BRIGGS, Canon John. b 39. Edin Univ MA 61. Ridley Hall Cam 61. **d** 63 **p** 64. C Jesmond Clayton Memorial *Newc* 63–66; Schs Sec Scripture Union 66–79; Tutor St Jo Coll Dur 67–74; LtO *Dur* 67–74; LtO *Edin* 74–79; V Chadkirk *Ches* 79–88; RD 85–88; TR Macclesfield Team 88–04; Hon Can Ches Cathl 96–04; Chapl W Park Hosp Macclesfield 90–99; rtd 04; PtO *Ches* from 04. *16 Lostock Hall Road, Poynton, Stockport SK12 1DP* T: (01625) 267228 E: briggsjohn63@gmail.com

BRIGGS, Richard Stephen. b 66. Hertf Coll Ox BA 88 MA 95 Lon Bible Coll MA 95 Nottm Univ PhD 00. Yorks Min Course 14. **d** 15 **p** 16. NSM Dur St Giles 15–20; NSM Shadforth and Sherburn 15–20; NSM Dur St Nic from 20; Prior Community of St Cuth from 20. *St Nicholas' Church, Market Place, Durham DH1 3NJ* E: prior@stnics.org.uk

BRIGGS, William James. b 75. Univ of Tasmania BE 97. Ridley Coll Melbourne BMin 03. **d** 02 **p** 03. C Burnie Australia 02–08; Project P Somerset Project 04–11; P-in-c Wynyard 05–07; P-in-c Burnie 10–11; C Hobart Cathl 11–15; C Newbury St Nic and Speen *Ox* 15–18; V Sheffield Vine *Sheff* from 18. *The Vicarage, 115 Upperthorpe Road, Sheffield S6 3EA* T: 0114-275 1480 M: 07548-050745 E: will.briggs@gmail.com

BRIGHT, George Frank. b 50. Peterho Cam BA 71 MA 75 LSE MSc 83 SAP 99. Coll of Resurr Mirfield 71. **d** 74 **p** 75. C Notting Hill *Lon* 74–77; PtO 77–84; P-in-c Kentish Town St Benet and All SS 84–89; P-in-c Kensington St Jo 89–93; V 93–06. *The Vicarage, 176 Holland Road, London W14 8AH* T: (020) 7602 4655 E: gfb@dircon.co.uk

BRIGHTON, Terrence William. b 43. SWMTC 85. **d** 88 **p** 89. C Dawlish *Ex* 88–92; P-in-c Newton Poppleford w Harpford 92–94; V Newton Poppleford, Harpford and Colaton Raleigh 94–98; RD Ottery 96–98; P-in-c W Lavington and the Cheverells *Sarum* 98–02; Rural Officer (Ramsbury Area) 98–02; P-in-c Charleton w Buckland Tout Saints etc *Ex* 02–05; R 05–08; RD Woodleigh 03–07; rtd 08. *30 Millway, Chudleigh, Newton Abbot TQ13 0JN* M: 07974-294044 E: twb@madasafish.com

BRIGHTWELL, Miss Elaine. b 57. STETS 09. **d** 12 **p** 13. NSM Pilton w Croscombe, N Wootton and Dinder *B & W* 12–17; TV Nadder Valley *Sarum* from 17. *The Vicarage, 11A Tyndales Meadow, Dinton, Salisbury SP3 5HU* M: 07986-639230 E: elainebri57@gmail.com

BRIGHTWELL, Johanna Clare. *See* CLARE, Johanna Howard

BRIGNALL, Elizabeth Jane. *See* BENDREY, Elizabeth Jane

BRIGNALL, Simon Francis Lyon. b 54. St Jo Coll Dur BA 78. Wycliffe Hall Ox 80. **d** 83 **p** 84. C Colne St Bart *Blackb* 83–86; SAMS Peru 86–96; P-in-c Tetsworth, Adwell w S Weston, Lewknor etc *Ox* 96–98; TV Thame 98–09; P-in-c Wriggle Valley *Sarum* 09–13; TV Three Valleys 13–15; Chapl St Pet Viña del Mar Chile 15–20; NSM S Cotswolds *Glouc* from 20. *The Vicarage, Church Lane, Coln St Aldwyns, Cirencester GL7 5AG* T: (01285) 750332 M: 07718-627674 E: sflbrignall@gmail.com

BRIMACOMBE, Keith John. b 59. Open Univ BA 92 Westmr Coll Ox MTh 00. SWMTC 99. **d** 01 **p** 03. NSM Ottery St Mary, Alfington, W Hill, Tipton etc *Ex* 01–07; Trinidad and Tobago 07–09; Perm to Offic Cyprus and the Gulf 09–10; Chapl Ahmadi St Paul Kuwait 11–13; C Fremington, Instow and Westleigh *Ex* 13–20. *Banklea, Exeter Road, Newton Poppleford, Sidmouth EX10 0BJ* T: (01395) 568404 E: brimacombe.keith@gmail.com

BRIMICOMBE, Mark. b 44. Nottm Univ BA 66 CertEd. SWMTC 83. **d** 85 **p** 86. NSM Plympton St Mary *Ex* 85–14; rtd 14; PtO *Ex* 14–20. *4 David Close, Stoggy Lane, Plympton, Plymouth PL7 3BQ* T: (01752) 338454 E: mark@thebrambles.eclipse.co.uk

BRIMSON, Dawn Diana. b 44. Ex Univ BTh 08. SWMTC 02. **d** 05 **p** 06. NSM Quantoxhead *B & W* 05–07; NSM Quantock Coast 07–14; PtO from 14. *5 Ridges, Holford, Bridgwater TA5 1DU* T: (01278) 741413 E: ddbrimson70@btinternet.com

BRINDLE, Keith Joseph. b 69. Middx Univ BSc 93 Wolv Univ MSc 95 Cranfield Univ PhD 98. Trin Coll Bris 10. **d** 12 **p** 13. C Deane Vale *B & W* 12–16; V Southbroom *Sarum* from 16. *The Vicarage, 31 Fruitfields Close, Devizes SN10 5JY* T: (01380) 721441 E: vicar@stjamesdevizes.org

BRINDLE, Peter John. b 47. MIStructE 72 FLS 05. NOC 78. **d** 81 **p** 82. NSM Bingley All SS *Bradf* 81–84; NSM Bingley H Trin 84–86; V Keighley All SS 86–91; V Kirkstall *Ripon* 91–96; V Beeston 96–02; TR 02–04; TR Leic Presentation 04–09; P-in-c Leic St Chad 04–07; P-in-c N Evington 07–09; rtd 09; PtO *York* 14–18. *5 Showfield Close, Sherburn in Elmet, Leeds LS25 6LW* T: (01977) 680026 M: 07860-157363 E: peter.brindle23@gmail.com

BRINDLEY, Angela Mary. *See* SPEEDY, Angela Mary

BRINDLEY, The Very Revd David Charles. b 53. K Coll Lon BD 75 AKC 75 MTh 76 MPhil 81 Open Univ MA 16. St Aug Coll Cant 75. **d** 76 **p** 77. C Epping St Jo *Chelmsf* 76–79; Lect Coll of SS Paul and Mary Cheltenham 79–82; Dioc Dir of Tr *Leic* 82–86; V Quorndon 82–86; Prin WEMTC *Glouc* 87–92 and 92–94; Dir of Minl Tr 87–94; Dioc Officer for NSM 88–94; Hon Can Glouc Cathl 92–94; TR Warwick *Cov* 94–02; Dean Portsm 02–18; rtd 18. *8 Rookwood Gardens, Fordingbridge SP6 1TA* T: (01425) 650090 E: davidbrindley3@gmail.com

BRINICOMBE, Matthew Jon. b 93. Man Univ BA 18 Dur Univ MA 21. Nazarene Th Coll Man 15 Trin Coll Bris 19. **d** 21. C Salford St Phil w St Steph *Man* from 21. *The Vicarage, 1 Parsonage Close, Salford M5 3GS* M: 07905-205984 E: matthew.brinicombe@gmail.com

BRINKLEY, Mrs Penelope Heather. b 57. ERMC 13. **d** 16 **p** 17. NSM Felixstowe St Jo *St E* from 16; Chapl to the Deaf from 20. *70 Leopold Road, Felixstowe IP11 7NR* M: 07901-950768 E: rev.pennybrinkley@yahoo.com

BRINKWORTH, Canon Christopher Michael Gibbs. b 41. Lanc Univ BA 70. Kelham Th Coll 62. **d** 67 **p** 68. C Lancaster St Mary *Blackb* 67–70; C Milton *Portsm* 70–74; V Ault Hucknall *Derby* 74–84; V Derby St Anne and St Jo 84–96; Hon Can Derby Cathl 00–06; rtd 06; PtO *Derby*

from 06. *3 Westfield Grove, Derby DE22 3SG* T: (01332) 208478 E: michaelbrinkworth@btinternet.com *or* michaelbrinkworth@icloud.com

BRION, Martin Philip. b 33. Ex Univ BA 55. Ridley Hall Cam 57. **d** 59 **p** 60. C Balderstone *Man* 59–62; C Morden S'wark 62–66; V Low Elswick *Newc* 66–73; P-in-c Giggleswick *Bradf* 73–77; V 77–80; V Camerton H Trin W Seaton *Carl* 80–86; V Dearham 86–95; rtd 95; PtO *Carl* 95–19. *7 Falcon Place, Moresby Parks, Whitehaven CA28 8YF* T: (01946) 691912

BRISCOE, Allen. b 42. Liv Univ BSc 64 CertEd 65. Coll of Resurr Mirfield 90. **d** 92 **p** 93. C Shiremoor *Newc* 92–95; V Barnsley St Pet and St Jo *Wakef* 95–10; Asst Dioc Ecum Officer 01–03; Bp's Adv for Ecum Affairs 03–06; RD Barnsley 04–09; rtd 10; Hon C Goldthorpe w Hickleton *Sheff* from 11; PtO *Leeds* from 17. *37 Holly Grove, Goldthorpe, Rotherham S63 9LA* T: (01709) 896739 E: abriscoe@talk21.com

BRISCOE, Canon Frances Amelia. b 35. Univ of Wales CertEd 55 Man Univ BA 71 MA 74. Gilmore Course 74. **dss** 77 **d** 87 **p** 94. Gt Crosby St Luke *Liv* 77–81; Dioc Lay Min Adv 81–87; Chapl Liv Cathl 81–89; Dir Diaconal Mins 87–89; Lect St Deiniol's Minl Tr Scheme 88–00; Hon Can Liv Cathl 88–00; AD Sefton 89–00; Dir of Reader Studies 89–00; Dn-in-c Hightown *Liv* 92–94; P-in-c 94–00; rtd 00; PtO *Liv* from 01. *5 Derwent Avenue, Formby, Liverpool L37 2JT* T: (01704) 830075

BRISCOE, Mark. b 71. Coll of Ripon & York St Jo BA 95. Ripon Coll Cuddesdon 05. **d** 07 **p** 08. C Saxilby Gp *Linc* 07–10; P-in-c Corringham and Blyton Gp 10–14; P-in-c Glentworth Gp 10–14; V Trentcliffe Gp from 14. *The Vicarage, Church Lane, Blyton, Gainsborough DN21 3JZ* T: (01427) 629105 E: markbriscoe71@gmail.com

BRISON, The Ven William Stanley. b 29. Alfred Univ NY BSc 51 Connecticut Univ MDiv 57 STM 71. Berkeley Div Sch. **d** 57 **p** 57. USA 57–72; V Davyhulme Ch Ch *Man* 72–81; R Newton Heath All SS 81–85; AD N Man 81–85; Hon Can Man Cathl 82–85; Adn Bolton 85–92; TV E Farnworth and Kearsley 85–89; C Bolton St Thos 89–92; CMS 92–94; Nigeria 92–94; P-in-c Pendleton St Thos w Charlestown *Man* 94–95; TR Pendleton 95–98; rtd 98; PtO *Man* 99–17. *2 Scott Avenue, Bury BL9 9RS* T: 0161-764 3998

BRISTOL, Archdeacon of. *See* WARWICK, The Ven Neil Michael

BRISTOL, Bishop of. *See* FAULL, The Rt Revd Vivienne Frances

BRISTOL, Dean of. *See* FORD, The Very Revd Amanda Kirstine

BRISTOW, Keith Raymond Martin. b 56. Ex Univ BA 78. Chich Th Coll 87. **d** 89 **p** 90. C Kirkby *Liv* 89–93; C Portsea St Mary *Portsm* 93–03; R Ash *Guildf* from 03. *The Rectory, Ash Church Road, Ash, Aldershot GU12 6LU* T: (01252) 321517

BRISTOW, Malcolm William. b 49. JP 94. SNWTP 11. **d** 12 **p** 13. OLM Bolton St Bede *Man* 12–19; rtd 19; PtO *Man* from 19. *8 Winton Grove, Bolton BL3 4UX* T: (01204) 659816 M: 07702-519007 E: malcolm.bristow@ntlworld.com

BRISTOW, Canon Peter Edmund. b 49. Pontificium Institutum Internationale Angelicum Rome JCL 77 St Jos Coll Upholland 67. **d** 72 **p** 73. In RC Ch 72–87; C Poplar *Lon* 89–92; Lay Tr Officer 89–90; TV Droitwich Spa *Worc* 92–94; TR 94–00; V Boston Spa *York* 00–11; P-in-c Bramham 09–11; P-in-c Thorp Arch w Walton 00–11; V Bramham 11–17; RD New Ainsty 06–11; Can Asante Mampong Ghana from 14; rtd 17; PtO *York* from 18. *Craiglea, 8 Church Lane, Ormesby, Middlesbrough TS7 9AH* E: pebristow49@gmail.com

BRISTOW, Roger. b 60. Aston Tr Scheme 81 Ridley Hall Cam 83. **d** 86 **p** 87. C Leyton St Mary w St Edw *Chelmsf* 86–90; TV Kings Norton *Birm* 90–98; V Bromley H Trin *Roch* from 98. *Holy Trinity Vicarage, Church Lane, Bromley BR2 8LB* T: (020) 8462 1280 M: 07778-397224 E: vicar@htc-bc.org.uk

BRITCLIFFE, Christine Elizabeth. b 61. Lindisfarne Coll of Th 18. **d** 21. NSM E Rainton *Dur* from 21; NSM W Rainton from 21; NSM Lumley from 21; NSM Chilton Moor from 21. *Gilpin Flat, Kepier Hall, Church Street, Houghton le Spring DH4 4DN* M: 07517-450672 E: kotzebue82@yahoo.co.uk *or* christine.britcliffe@nhs.net

BRITCLIFFE, James Andrew. b 65. All SS Cen for Miss & Min 18. **d** 21. C Alsager St Mary *Ches* from 21. *80 Kestrel Drive, Crewe CW1 3YX* T: (01270) 588659 M: 07536-184155 E: jim.britcliffe@btinternet.com

BRITT, Eric Stanley. b 47. St Jo Coll Nottm BTh 75. **d** 74 **p** 75. C Chorleywood Ch Ch *St Alb* 74–78; C Frimley *Guildf* 78–80; P-in-c Alresford *Chelmsf* 80–88; R Takeley w Lt Canfield 88–93; Asst Chapl R Free Hosp Lon 93–96; Chapl Mid-Essex Hosp Services NHS Trust 96–00; Chapl Algarve *Eur* 01–06; rtd 06; PtO *Ely* from 16. *5 De Lisle Close, Papworth Everard, Cambridge CB23 3UT* E: e.britt@btinternet.com

BRITT, Thomas Allen. b 90. Leeds Univ BA 12. Ripon Coll Cuddesdon BA 18. d 18 p 19. C Wanstead St Mary w Ch Ch *Chelmsf* from 18. *17 St David's Court, Grosvenor Road, London E11 2HH* E: tomallenbritt@gmail.com

BRITT, William Thomas. b 60. Westmr Coll Fulton (USA) BA 82. St Mellitus Coll BA 11. d 11 p 12. C Kempston Transfiguration *St Alb* 11–15; V Stotfold and Radwell from 15; RD Hitchin from 20. *The Vicarage, 61 Church Road, Stotfold, Hitchin SG5 4NE* E: revd.bill.britt@gmail.com

BRITTON, Christine Mary. *See* BEECROFT, Christine Mary

BRITTON, Canon David Robert. b 80. Leeds Univ BA 03 Fitzw Coll Cam BA 09. Ridley Hall Cam 07. d 10 p 11. C W Streatham St Jas *S'wark* 10–12; C Furzedown 12–14; V Leytonstone St Jo *Chelmsf* from 14; AD Waltham Forest from 19; Hon Can Chelmsf Cathl from 20. *St John's Vicarage, 44 Hartley Road, London E11 3BL* T: (020) 8279 7738 M: 07732-135178 E: rev.britton@gmail.com

BRITTON, John Timothy Hugh. b 50. Dundee Univ BSc 73. Trin Coll Bris 73. d 76 p 77. C Cromer *Nor* 76–79; P-in-c Freethorpe w Wickhampton 79–82; P-in-c Beighton and Moulton 79–82; P-in-c Halvergate w Tunstall 79–82; CMS 82–89; Uganda 83–89; R Allesley *Cov* 89–02; P-in-c Offchurch 02–15; P-in-c Long Itchington and Marton 02–15; P-in-c Wappenbury w Weston under Wetherley 02–15; P-in-c Hunningham 02–15; rtd 15; PtO *Nor* from 16; *Chelmsf* 16–21. *49 Clifton Park, Cromer NR27 9BG* T: (01263) 512776 E: tim@brittonfamily.org.uk

BRITTON, Neil Bryan. b 35. Em Coll Cam BA 59 MA 63. Clifton Th Coll 61. d 63 p 64. C Eastbourne All SS *Chich* 63–67; C Ashtead *Guildf* 67–70; Chapl Scargill Ho 70–74; Chapl Aiglon Coll and Asst Chapl Villars Eur 74–78; In Reformed Ch of Switzerland 78–98; rtd 00; USA 01–05; PtO *Win* from 10. *Rose Cottage, 7 Newbury Road, Kingsclere, Newbury RG20 5SP* T: (01635) 297687 M: 07903-120368 E: britton.neil@gmail.com

BRITTON, Canon Paul Anthony. b 29. SS Coll Cam BA 52 MA 57. Linc Th Coll 52. d 54 p 55. C Upper Norwood St Jo *Cant* 54–57; C Wantage *Ox* 57–61; V Stanmore *Win* 61–70; V Bitterne Park 70–80; Can Res Win Cathl 80–94; Lib Win Cathl *Worc* 81–85; Can Res and Treas Win Cathl 85–94; rtd 94; PtO *Sarum* 94–19. *Pemberton, High Street, Hindon, Salisbury SP3 6DR* T: (01747) 820406 E: paul.britton02@virgin.net

BRITTON, Robert. b 37. Oak Hill Th Coll 78. d 79 p 80. C St Helens St Helen *Liv* 79–83; V Lowton St Mary 83–02; AD Winwick 89–01; rtd 02; PtO *Man* 03–14; *Liv* from 03. *15 Balmoral Avenue, Lowton, Warrington WA3 2ER* T: (01942) 711135

BRITTON, Ronald George Adrian Michael (Robert). b 24. Univ of State of NY BSc 78 Lambeth STh 82. St D Coll Lamp 63. d 82 p 82. Arabia 82–85; Chapl Alassio *Eur* 85–90; 92–93; Chapl San Remo 86; Hon C Southbourne St Kath *Win* 90–92; rtd 96; PtO *Bris* from 97. *2 Cherry Tree Road, Bristol BS16 4EY* T: 0117-965 5734 E: nonalienum@talktalk.net

BRITTON, Stephen Paul. b 55. Trin Coll Bris. d 12 p 13. OLM Longwell Green *Bris* from 12. *15 Central Avenue, Bristol BS15 3PG* T: 0117-961 4796 E: revds.britton@gmx.com

BRITTON, Timothy. *See* BRITTON, John Timothy Hugh

BRIXTON, Miss Corinne Jayne. b 63. Ex Univ BSc 84. Wycliffe Hall Ox BTh 95. d 95. C Leytonstone St Jo *Chelmsf* 95–00; C Buckhurst Hill 00–15; PtO *Win* 16–19; C Hampstead St Jo Downshire Hill Prop Chpl *Lon* from 19. *88 Upper Park Road, London NW3 2UJ* E: corinne@sjdh.org

BRIXWORTH, Suffragan Bishop of. *See* HOLBROOK, The Rt Revd John Edward

BROAD, Canon Christine Jane. b 63. Leeds Univ BSc 86 BA 06. NOC 03. d 06 p 07. C Newchapel *Lich* 06–09; TV Hanley H Ev 09–13; TR 13–16; C Oxton *Ches* 16–19; R Woodchurch from 19; Dean of Women in Min from 19; Hon Can Ches Cathl from 21. *Woodchurch Rectory, 1 Church Lane, Upton, Wirral CH49 7LS* E: christinejanebroad@virginmedia.com

BROAD, Canon Hugh Duncan. b 37. Lich Th Coll 64. d 67 p 68. C Heref H Trin 67–72; Asst Master Bp's Sch Heref 72–73; C Fareham SS Pet and Paul *Portsm* 74–76; V Heref All SS 76–90; R Matson *Glouc* 90–97; V Glouc St Geo w Whaddon 97–03; Hon Can Glouc Cathl 02–03; rtd 03; P-in-c Costa Almeria and Costa Calida *Eur* 03–13; Hon Can Gib Cathl 13. *44 Vensfield Road, Quedgeley, Gloucester GL2 4FX* E: hugh.broad@yahoo.co.uk

BROAD, Canon William Ernest Lionel. b 40. Ridley Hall Cam 64. d 66 p 67. C Ecclesfield *Sheff* 66–69; Chapl HM Pris Wormwood Scrubs 69; Chapl HM Pris Albany 70–74; Chapl HM Rem Cen Risley 74–76; V Ditton St Mich *Liv* 76–81; TR 82–83; P-in-c Mayland and Steeple *Chelmsf* 83–91; V Blackhall *Dur* 91–97; TR Gt Aycliffe 97–03; P-in-c Chilton 03; TV Gt Aycliffe and Chilton 03–04; Hon Can Dur Cathl 02–04; rtd 04; PtO *Dur* from 04. *Moorcote, Thornley,*

Tow Law, Bishop Auckland DL13 4NU T: (01388) 731350 E: broad054@gmail.com

BROADBENT, Mrs Doreen. b 36. d 94 p 95. OLM Stalybridge *Man* 94–02; PtO 02–14. *37 Ladysmith Road, Ashton-under-Lyne OL6 9DJ* T: 0161-330 9085

BROADBENT, Gerald. b 44. LRAM 64. Westcott Ho Cam 66. d 68 p 69. C Tilbury Docks *Chelmsf* 68–71; C Woodford St Mary w St Phil and St Jas 71–74; rtd 09. *7 West Terrace, Richmond DL10 4EQ* T: (01748) 824047 E: gerrybroad@aol.com

BROADBENT, Neil Seton. b 53. Qu Coll Birm. d 81 p 82. C Knaresborough *Ripon* 81–84; C Leeds Gipton Epiphany 84–87; Lic to Offic 87–89; Chapl Minstead Community *Derby* 89; PtO from 89; Dir Sozein from 93. *The Old Vicarage, Church Lane, Horsley Woodhouse, Ilkeston DE7 6BB* T: (01332) 780598 E: neil.broadbent@sozein.org.uk

BROADBENT, Paul John. b 41. Oak Hill Th Coll 83. d 85 p 86. C Duston *Pet* 85–88; TV Ross w Brampton Abbotts, Bridstow and Peterstow *Heref* 88–91; R Pattishall w Cold Higham and Gayton w Tiffield *Pet* 91–10; rtd 10; P-in-c Fairwarp *Chich* 10–16; PtO from 16; S'wark from 17; *Guildf* from 18. *1 Glebe Cottages, Village Street, Newdigate, Dorking RH5 5AA* T: (01306) 631687 M: 07786-865015 E: pj.broadbent1@btinternet.com

✠BROADBENT, The Rt Revd Peter Alan. b 52. Jes Coll Cam BA 74 MA 78. St Jo Coll Nottm 74. d 77 p 78 c 01. C Dur St Nic 77–80; C Holloway Em w Hornsey Road St Barn *Lon* 80–83; Chapl N Lon Poly 83–89; Hon C Islington St Mary 83–89; V Harrow Trin St Mich 89–94; AD Harrow 94; Adn Northolt 95–01; P-in-c Southall H Trin 98–99; Area Bp Willesden 01–21; rtd 21. *63 Tring Avenue, London W5 3QD* M: 07950-299685

BROADBENT, Ralph Andrew. b 55. K Coll Lon BD 76 AKC 76 Birm Univ PhD 04. Chich Th Coll 77. d 78 p 79. C Prestwich St Mary *Man* 78–82; R Man Miles Platting 82–84; CF 84–87; TV Wordsley *Lich* 88–93; Chapl Wordsley Hosp 88–93; Chapl Ridge Hill Hosp 88–93; V Wollescote *Worc* 93–15; rtd 15. *273 route des Corbières, 16100 Boutiers-Saint-Trojan, France* E: ralphbroadbent1@icloud.com

BROADBENT, Thomas William. b 45. Chu Coll Cam BA 66 MA 70 PhD 70. Ridley Hall Cam 75. d 78 p 79. C Allington and Maidstone St Pet *Cant* 78–82; Chapl Mid Kent Coll of H&FE 80–82; C Kings Heath *Birm* 82–84; Hon C Pendleton St Thos *Man* 84–89; TV Pendleton St Thos w Charlestown 89–92; Chapl Salford Univ 84–92; P-in-c Claydon and Barham *St E* 92–08; P-in-c Coddenham w Gosbeck and Hemingstone w Henley 99–08; P-in-c Gt and Lt Blakenham w Baylham and Nettlestead 02–08; Chapl Suffolk Coll 92–00; P-in-c Witham Gp *Linc* 08–14; rtd 14; PtO *Linc* 15–18. *8 Abbey Road, Bardney, Lincoln LN3 5XA* T: (01526) 397101 E: broadbentevans@btinternet.com

BROADBENT, Timothy Robert Harry. b 79. K Coll Lon MA 11. St Aug Coll of Th MA 20. d 20 p 21. C Becontree St Mary *Chelmsf* from 20. *St Elisabeth's Vicarage, Hewett Road, Dagenham RM8 2XT* M: 07890-770002 E: timbroadbent@mac.com

BROADHEAD, Mrs Lynn. b 59. Yorks Min Course 08. d 11 p 12. NSM Thorpe Hesley *Sheff* 11–13; NSM Greasbrough 13–15; V Thorpe Hesley from 15; P-in-c Kimberworth and Kimberworth Park from 21. *The Vicarage, 30 Barnsley Road, Thorpe Hesley, Rotherham S61 2RR* T: 0114-246 3487 M: 07811-336183 E: revd.lynn.broadhead@sky.com

BROADHURST, Dorothy Bronwyn. b 48. Lon Univ LLB 70 MPhil 76. d 19. NSM Pocklington Wold *York* from 19; NSM Londesborough Wold 19–21. *21 Pinewood Road, Pocklington, York YO42 2UZ* T: (01759) 307479 M: 07950-049891 E: bronnie.broadhurst@hotmail.com

BROADHURST, Jonathan Robin. b 58. Univ Coll Ox BA 81 MA 86. Wycliffe Hall Ox 85. d 88 p 89. C Hull St Jo Newland *York* 88–91; P-in-c Burton Fleming w Fordon, Grindale etc 91–92; V 92–98; C Kingston upon Hull H Trin 98–01; P-in-c Rastrick St Jo *Wakef* 01–06; rtd 06; PtO *Leeds* from 17. *1 Moravian Terrace, Halifax HX3 8AL* T: (01422) 209549 M: 07790-899195

BROADIE, Stephen Kim. b 76. Leeds Univ BA 99 Bris Univ PGCE 03. Ridley Hall Cam 10. d 12 p 13. C Welling *Roch* 12–16; C Farnborough from 16. *Church House, Leamington Avenue, Orpington BR6 9QB* M: 07722-428553 E: sjwcurate@gmail.com

BROADLEY, Michael John. b 66. Roehampton Inst BA 87. Trin Coll Bris 93. d 96 p 97. C Egham *Guildf* 96–01; TV Horsham *Chich* 01–10; P-in-c Loughborough Em and St Mary in Charnwood *Leic* 10–14; P-in-c Loughborough Em from 15. *Emmanuel Rectory, 47 Forest Road, Loughborough LE11 3NW* T: (01509) 263264 E: broadley@bigfoot.com

BROADWAY, Mark Philip. b 87. Glam Univ LLB 09 Cardiff Univ MTh 14. St Mich Coll Llan 14. **d** 17 **p** 18. C Coity, Nolton and Brackla w Coychurch *Llan* 17–20; C Newton Nottage from 20. *5B West End Avenue, Porthcawl CF36 3NE* E: frmark@parishofporthcawl.org

BROCK, Michael John. b 52. Birm Univ BSc 74. St Jo Coll Nottm BA 77. **d** 78 **p** 79. C Stapleford *S'well* 78–82; C Bestwood St Matt 82–86; TV Bestwood 86–90; R Epperstone 90–05; R Gonalston 90–05; V Oxton 90–05; P-in-c Woodborough 02–05; RD S'well 93–96; Dioc Adv in Rural Affairs 97–02; R Dersingham w Anmer and Shernborne *Nor* 05–15; RD Heacham and Rising 07–11; C Snettisham w Ingoldisthorpe and Fring 14–15; rtd 15; P-in-c Sutton Bonington w Normanton-on-Soar *S'well* 15–19; PtO from 19. *133 Ashby Road, Loughborough LE11 3AB*

BROCKBANK, Arthur Ross. b 51. NOC 87. **d** 90 **p** 91. C Haughton St Mary *Man* 90–93; V Bircle 93–12; P-in-c Walmersley 04; Chapl Bury Healthcare NHS Trust 93–02; Chapl Co-ord Pennine Acute Hosps NHS Trust 02–03; rtd 12; Chapl Jospice from 14; Chapl Alder Hey Children's NHS Foundn Trust from 14; PtO *Liv* from 14. *12 Dickinson Road, Liverpool L37 4BX* T: (01704) 461346

BROCKBANK, Donald Philip. b 56. Univ of Wales (Ban) BD 78. Sarum & Wells Th Coll 79. **d** 81 **p** 82. C Prenton *Ches* 81–85; TV Birkenhead Priory 85–91; V Altrincham St Jo 91–96; Urban Officer 91–96; Dioc Ecum Officer *Lich* 96–98; C Lich St Mich w St Mary and Wall 96–98; V Acton and Worleston, Church Minshull etc *Ches* 98–06; rtd 07; Dioc Adv in Spirituality *Ches* 07–12; PtO from 12. *1 Plover Avenue, Winsford CW7 1LA* T: (01606) 593651 E: brockbankrev@gmail.com

BROCKBANK, John Keith. b 44. Dur Univ BA 65. Wells Th Coll 66. **d** 68 **p** 69. C Preston St Matt *Blackb* 68–71; C Lancaster St Mary 71–73; V Habergham All SS 73–83; P-in-c Gannow 81–83; V W Burnley All SS 83–86; Dioc Stewardship Adv 86–92; P-in-c Shireshead 86–92; V Kirkham 92–09; rtd 09; PtO *Blackb* from 09. *44 Esthwaite Gardens, Lancaster LA1 3AW* T: (01524) 847520 E: revjkb@talktalk.net

BROCKBANK, John Stanley. b 41. CBDTI 97. **d** 00 **p** 01. OLM Arnside *Carl* 00–11; rtd 11; PtO *Carl* from 11. *Hough Close, 5 Ash Meadow Road, Arnside, Carnforth LA5 0AE* T: (01524) 761634

BROCKHOUSE, Canon Grant Lindley. b 47. Adelaide Univ BA 71 Ex Univ MA 81. St Barn Coll Adelaide 70. **d** 73 **p** 74. C Edwardstown w Ascot Park Australia 73–74; Tutor St Barn Coll Belair 74–78; C Ex St Jas 78–80; Asst Chapl Ex Univ 80–83; V Marldon 83–98; Dep PV Ex Cathl 81–98; RD Torbay 95–98; V Higham Ferrers w Chelveston *Pet* 98–13; RD Higham 03–11; Can Pet Cathl 07–13; rtd 13; PtO *Pet* from 14. *71 Bishops Road, Peterborough PE1 5AS* T: (01733) 753339 E: grantbrockhouse@gmail.com

BROCKIE, Canon William James Thomson. b 36. Pemb Coll Ox BA 58 MA 62. Linc Th Coll 58. **d** 60 **p** 61. C Lin St Jo Bapt CD *Linc* 60–63; V Gt Staughton *Ely* 63–68; Chapl HM Borstal Gaynes Hall 63–68; TV Edin St Jo 68–76; Chapl Edin Univ 71–76; USA 76–79; R Edin St Martin 76–01; P-in-c Wester Hailes St Luke 79–90; Hon Can St Mary's Cathl from 98; rtd 00; Hon C Edin St Hilda and Edin St Fillan 02–03. *31 Hollybank Terrace, Edinburgh EH11 1SP* T: 0131-337 6482 E: billjennybrockie@hotmail.com

BROCKLEHURST, Ian Christopher. b 62. Nottm Univ BMedSci 83 BM, BS 85 FRCA 93. All SS Cen for Miss & Min 12. **d** 15 **p** 16. NSM Coldhurst and Oldham St Steph *Man* 15–18; NSM Mossley from 18; NSM Roughtown from 18. *4 Higher Lydgate Park, Grasscroft, Oldham OL4 4EF* M: 07742-558236 E: iancb53@btinternet.com

BROCKLEHURST, Simon. b 63. Cranmer Hall Dur 86. **d** 89 **p** 90. C Clifton *S'well* 89–93; TV 93–96; P-in-c Mabe *Truro* 96–99; Miss to Seamen 96–99; V Ham St Andr *S'wark* 99–16; P-in-c Southwick w Boarhunt *Portsm* from 16; Inland Hon Chapl Miss to Seafarers from 00. *White House, 13 High Street, Southwick, Fareham PO17 6EB* T: (023) 9238 0802 E: revsimonb@btinternet.com

BRODIE, Miss Ann. b 55. Ex Univ BA 76 PGCE 77. St Jo Coll Nottm 03. **d** 05 **p** 06. C Putney St Marg *S'wark* 05–09; P-in-c 09–12; V 12–17; PtO from 18. *1 Alfriston Road, London SW11 6NS*

BRODIE, Frederick. b 40. Leic Teacher Tr Coll TCert 61. St Jo Coll Nottm 90. **d** 92 **p** 93. C Lutterworth w Cotesbach *Leic* 92–95; P-in-c Mountsorrel Ch Ch and St Pet 95–97; V 97–03; rtd 03; PtO *Leic* 03–21. *7 Stuart Court, High Street, Kibworth Beauchamp, Leicester LE8 0LR* M: 07710-461865 E: fesbrodie@btinternet.com

BROGGIO, Bernice Muriel Croager. b 35. Bedf Coll Lon BA 57 K Coll Lon BD 66 Glas Univ DASS 72. **dss** 84 **d** 87 **p** 94. Bris St Paul w St Barn 84–87; Hon Par Dn Bris St Paul's

87–88; C Charlton St Luke w H Trin *S'wark* 88–95; V Upper Tooting H Trin 95–03; Hon Can S'wark Cathl 95–03; RD Tooting 96–02; TV Bensham *Dur* 03–05; rtd 06; PtO *Dur* from 06; *Eur* from 10. *86 Woodburn, Gateshead NE10 8LY* T: 0191-495 0959 M: 07900-327316 E: b.broggio@btinternet.com

BROKENSHIRE, Phillip Laurence. b 87. Ex Univ BSc 10. Wycliffe Hall Ox BTh 16. **d** 16. C Ex H Trin from 16. *48 Mulligan Drive, Exeter EX2 7SJ* M: 07401-867876 E: phillipbrokenshire@yahoo.co.uk

BROMFIELD, Michael. b 32. Kelham Th Coll 54 Lich Th Coll 59. **d** 62 **p** 63. C Sedgley All SS *Lich* 62–64; C Tunstall Ch Ch 64–67; P-in-c Grindon 67–70; R 70–80; P-in-c Butterton 67–70; V 70–80; R Hope Bowdler w Eaton-under-Heywood *Heref* 80–97; V Cardington 80–97; V Rushbury 80–97; rtd 98; PtO *Lich* 98–20. *11 Walklate Avenue, Newcastle ST5 0PR* T: (01782) 630716 E: pbromfield@btinternet.com

BROMFIELD, Nicholas Robert. b 60. St Jo Coll Cam MA 82. WEMTC 98. **d** 02 **p** 03. C Tidenham w Beachley and Lancaut *Glouc* 02–07; C St Briavels w Hewelsfield 05–07; R Drybrook, Lydbrook and Ruardean 07–16; TR N Cheltenham from 16. *The Rectory, Tatchley Lane, Prestbury, Cheltenham GL52 3DQ* E: bromfields@email.msn.com *or* revbromfield@btinternet.com

BROMFIELD, Richard Allan. b 47. Sussex Univ MA 96 LVCM 85. Chich Th Coll 86. **d** 88 **p** 89. C Durrington *Chich* 88–95; V Woodingdean 95–12; Chapl Nuffield Hosp Brighton 96–12; rtd 12; PtO *Chich* 12–17. *34 Rowan Way, Angmering, Littlehampton BN16 4FW* E: r.a.bromfield@btinternet.com

BROMILEY, Philip Arthur. b 73. Westmr Coll Ox BTh 94 St Jo Coll Dur MA 98. Cranmer Hall Dur 95. **d** 98 **p** 99. C Marton *Blackb* 98–01; Assoc P Calne and Blackland *Sarum* 01–06; P-in-c Oldbury 06–08; R 08–17; TR Avon River from 17. *The Rectory, Church Street, Durrington, Salisbury SP4 8AL* T: (01980) 258549 E: philbromiley@gmail.com

BROMLEY, Deborah Joan. See SCOTT-BROMLEY, Deborah Joan

BROMLEY, Mrs Janet Catherine Gay. b 45. Surrey Univ BSc 68 Bradf Univ MSc 72 Brunel Tech Coll Bris FE TCert 86. S Dios Minl Tr Scheme 91. **d** 94 **p** 96. C Westbury-on-Trym H Trin *Bris* 94–96; C Wroughton 96–00; Dean of Women's Min 98–00; R Dursley *Glouc* 00–13; AD 07–09; rtd 13. *40 Kings Fee, Monmouth NP25 5BW* T: (01600) 713847 E: revdjanet@googlemail.com

BROMLEY, Richard William. b 60. Birm Chr Coll MA 02. Qu Foundn Birm 08. **d** 08 **p** 09. NSM Binley *Cov* 08–11 and from 21; PtO 11–20; Miss Dir ICS from 13; PtO *Eur* from 16. *Intercontinental Church Society, Unit 11, Ensign Business Centre, Westwood Way, Westwood Business Park, Coventry CV4 8JA* T: (024) 7646 3940 M: 07772-496029 E: rbromley@ics-uk.org

BROMLEY, Mrs Tracy Le Couteur. STETS 06. **d** 09 **p** 10. NSM Jersey St Clem *Win* from 09; Chapl Jersey Gp of Hosps from 10. *11 Oakland Vineries, Rue du Presbytere, St Clement, Jersey JE2 6RB* T: (01534) 857693 E: tracylecouteur@hotmail.com

BROMLEY AND BEXLEY, Archdeacon of. See WRIGHT, The Ven Paul

BRONNERT, Preb David Llewellyn Edward. b 36. Ch Coll Cam BA 57 MA 61 PhD 61 Lon Univ BD 62. Tyndale Hall Bris 60. **d** 63 **p** 64. C Cheadle Hulme St Andr *Ches* 63–67; C Islington St Mary *Lon* 67–69; Chapl N Lon Poly 69–75; V Southall Green St Jo 75–01; Preb St Paul's Cathl 89–01; P-in-c Southall St Geo 92–99; AD Ealing W 84–90; rtd 01; PtO Ox from 04. *101 Walton Way, Aylesbury HP21 7JP* T: (01296) 484048 E: david.bronnert@talk21.com

BRONNERT, John. b 33. Man Univ MA(Theol) 84 Univ of Wales (Lamp) PhD 98 ACA 57 FCA 68. Tyndale Hall Bris 65. **d** 68 **p** 69. C Hoole *Ches* 68–71; P-in-c Parr *Liv* 71–73; TV 73–85; V Runcorn St Jo Weston *Ches* 85–98; rtd 98; PtO *Liv* 85–04; *Man* 98–14. *Tyndale, 15 Craig Avenue, Flixton, Urmston, Manchester M41 5RS* T: 0161-748 7061

BROOK, David Thomas. b 46. **d** 11 **p** 12. OLM Lt Aston *Lich* 11–15; OLM Burntwood, Chase Terrace etc 15–16; rtd 16; PtO *Lich* 16–21. *16 Brentnall Drive, Sutton Coldfield B75 5BB* T: 0121-353 6106 E: dtbrook@gmail.com

BROOK, John Brendan Paul. b 79. CCC Ox MEng 01. Oak Hill Th Coll BA 06. **d** 06 **p** 07. C Hailsham *Chich* 06–10; Min The Haven CD 10–20; C Eastbourne H Trin 15–20; V Worthing St Geo from 20. *St George's Vicarage, 14 Pendine Avenue, Worthing BN11 2NB* T: (01903) 348843 E: revjbrook@bfol.org

BROOK, Neville. See BROOK, William Neville

BROOK, Peter Geoffrey (Brother Simon). b 47. NOC 91. **d** 94 **p** 95. CGA from 71; NSM Heywood and Middleton Deanery 94–96; PtO *Ex* from 96. *1 Curlew Way, Dawlish EX7 0FT*

BROOK, Priestly. b 42. CBDTI 04. **d** 07 **p** 08. NSM Colne and Villages *Blackb* 07–12; rtd 12; PtO *Blackb* from 12;

Bradf 13–14; *Leeds* from 14. *The Coach House, Foulds Road, Trawden, Colne BB8 8NT* T: (01282) 869876 E: priestlybrook1@btinternet.com

BROOK, Stephen Edward. b 44. Univ of Wales (Abth) BSc 65 DipEd 66. Wycliffe Hall Ox 71 All Nations Chr Coll 85. **d** 74 **p** 75. C Heworth H Trin *York* 74–77; C Linthorpe 77–80; TV Deane *Man* 80–85; Crosslinks 86–96; Portugal 88–96; P-in-c Bacup St Sav *Man* 96–03; P-in-c Tunstead 99–03; V Blackpool St Mark *Blackb* 03–12; P-in-c Blackpool St Mich 10–12; V Layton and Staining 12; rtd 12; PtO *Leic* 13–21. *35 Oakham Grove, Ashby-de-la-Zouche LE65 2QP* E: revstephenbrook@gmail.com

BROOK, William Neville. b 31. S'wark Ord Course 66. **d** 69 **p** 70. C Maidstone St Martin *Cant* 69–75; V Hartlip w Stockbury 75–80; R Willesborough w Hinxhill 80–87; R Willesborough 87–89; V Gt Staughton and Hail Weston *Ely* 89–96; rtd 96; PtO *Chich* from 96. *73 Drummond Grove, Willesborough, Ashford TN24 0US* T: (01233) 632765

BROOKE, Ailsa Rosanne. b 47. Yorks Min Course 10. **d** 12 **p** 13. NSM Upper Holme Valley *Wakef* 12–14; *Leeds* from 14. *20 Fulstone Hall Lane, New Mill, Holmfirth HD9 7DW* T: (01484) 681155 E: ailsabrooke@tinyworld.co.uk

BROOKE, Miss Bridget Cecilia. b 31. Coll of Resurr Mirfield 88. **d** 89 **p** 94. Hon Par Dn Ranmoor *Sheff* 89–94; Hon C 94–04; Bp's Adv for NSMs 94–01; PtO 04–20. *3 Magnolia Court, 10 Storth Lane, Sheffield S10 3HN* T: 0114-230 2147 E: revbridgetbrooke@gmail.com

BROOKE, David Fewsdale. b 43. St Paul's Coll Grahamstown 80. **d** 90 **p** 90. Asst Chapl Dioc Coll Cape Town S Africa 90–92; NSM Crawford St Jo 93–97; NSM Sea Point St Jas 98–99; PtO *Newc* 00; C Norham and Duddo 01–04; C Cornhill w Carham 01–04; C Branxton 01–04; R Dunkeld *St And* 04–13; R Strathtay 04–13. *43 Innewan Gardens, Bankfoot, Perth PH1 4AZ* M: 07840-183707

BROOKE, David Martin. b 58. Selw Coll Cam BA 80 MA 83 Lon Inst of Educn PGCE 81. SAOMC 96. **d** 99 **p** 00. C Luton Lewsey St Hugh *St Alb* 99–00; NSM Sunnyside w Bourne End 00–02; C 02–04; V Bishopton w Gt Stainton *Dur* 04–13; R Redmarshall 04–13; R Grindon and Stillington 04–13; R Stockton Country Par 14–16; P-in-c Billingham St Mary 10–13; AD Stockton 07–16; NSM Stockton St Thos 16–18; Lead Miss Support Partner 16–18; Hon Can Dur Cathl 16–18; TR Chapelfields *Liv* 18–19; TV Wigan from 20. *10 St Nathaniel's Close, Platt Bridge, Wigan WN2 3FT* M: 07967-326085 E: hubleader.east@churchwigan.org

BROOKE, Canon Katherine Margaret. b 58. GRSM 79 LRAM 80 ARCM 80. SAOMC 01. **d** 04 **p** 05. C Auckland St Andr and St Anne *Dur* 04–07; C Stranton 07–11; Chapl HM Pris Holme Ho 11–18; Managing Chapl from 18; Hon Can Dur Cathl from 21. *HM Prison Holme House, Holme House Road, Stockton-on-Tees TS18 2QU* T: (01642) 744000 M: 07973-539729 E: katherine.brooke@justice.gov.uk

BROOKE, Canon Robert. b 44. Qu Coll Birm 70. **d** 73 **p** 74. C Man Resurr 73–76; C Bournville *Birm* 76–77; Chapl Qu Eliz Coll *Lon* 77–82; C Bramley *Ripon* 82–85; TV 85–86; V Hunslet Moor St Pet and St Cuth 86–93; Chapl People w Learning Disabilities 86–10; TV Seacroft 93–03; TV Beeston 03–10; Chapl Leeds Mental Health Teaching NHS Trust 94–03; Hon Can Ripon Cathl 01–10; rtd 10. *103 Crossgates Road, Leeds LS15 7PA* E: bob.brooke@hotmail.co.uk

BROOKE, Canon Rosemary Jane. b 53. Newnham Coll Cam BEd 75 Open Univ BA 84. NOC 86. **d** 89 **p** 94. NSM Poynton *Ches* 89–05; Bp's Adv for Women in Min 96–05; P-in-c Werneth 05–10; Can Res Ches Cathl from 10. *3 Bridge Place, Chester CH1 1SA* T: (01244) 351432 E: scrolls2@btinternet.com

BROOKE, Timothy Cyril. b 38. Jes Coll Cam BA 60 MA 70 Middx Poly CQSW 76. Ripon Coll Cuddesdon 84. **d** 86 **p** 87. C Hillmorton *Cov* 86–90; V Earlsdon 90–98; V Cov St Fran N Radford 98–05; rtd 05; PtO *Cov* from 05; *Eur* from 05; *Leic* 15–20. *80 Broadway, Coventry CV5 6NU* T: (024) 7667 9126 E: brooke@care4free.net

BROOKE, Vernon. b 41. St Aid Birkenhead 62. **d** 65 **p** 66. C Crofton Park St Hilda w St Cypr *S'wark* 65–68; C Eccleshill *Bradf* 68–70; Ind Chapl *Linc* 70–84; Ind Chapl *Derby* 84–97; Ind Chapl *Chich* 97–06; rtd 06; PtO *Pet* 06–21. *5 Blakesley Close, Northampton NN2 8PA* T: (01604) 845585 E: vernonbrooke@yahoo.co.uk

BROOKE-TAYLOR, John Drury Arthur. b 48. Cam Univ BA 69 MA 73 Solicitor 72. Trin Coll Bris 11. **d** 13 **p** 14. OLM Clifton H Trin, St Andr and St Pet *Bris* 13–20; NSM 20; OLM Bris St Steph w St Jas and St Jo w St Mich etc 14–20; NSM 20; PtO from 20. *2 Oldfield Road, Bristol BS8 4QQ* T: 0117-926 5517 E: drbrooketaylor@outlook.com

BROOKER, Canon Anna Lesley. b 56. York Univ BA 78 MA 79 York St Jo Univ MA 13 Homerton Coll Cam PGCE 80.

Ridley Hall Cam 01. **d** 03 **p** 04. C Brentford *Lon* 03–06; P-in-c Isleworth All SS 06–11; V 11–15; Dean of Women's Min Kensington Area 12–15; P-in-c Haswell and Shotton *Dur* 15–19; P-in-c S Hetton 18–19; P-in-c Brancepeth from 19; Chapl St Jo Coll Dur from 19; Hon Can Dur Cathl from 21. *The Rectory, Brancepeth, Durham DH7 8EL* E: albrooker@email.com *or* anna.brooker@durham.ac.uk

BROOKES, Colin Stuart. b 70. Lon Bible Coll BA 93. Ridley Hall Cam 00. **d** 02 **p** 03. C Cambridge St Barn *Ely* 02–06; C Woodside Park St Barn *Lon* 06–19; C Oseney Crescent St Luke from 19. *St Barnabas' Vicarage, 68 Westbury Road, London N12 7PD* T: (020) 8343 6144 M: 07973-840340

BROOKES, David Charles. b 45. St Mich Coll Llan 84. **d** 86 **p** 87. C Llanishen and Lisvane *Llan* 86–88; TV Brighouse St Martin *Wakef* 89–92; TV Brighouse and Clifton 92–94; V Hollingbourne and Hucking w Leeds and Broomfield *Cant* 94–03; rtd 03. *19 Orchards Rise, Richards Castle, Ludlow SY8 4EZ* T: (01584) 831276

BROOKES, Edwin William. b 39. St Mark & St Jo Coll Lon TCert 63 Birm Univ BPhil(Ed) 85 Open Univ BA 73 BA 93. OLM course 95. **d** 98 **p** 99. OLM Cen Wolverhampton *Lich* 98–19; PtO 19–21. *104 Napier Road, Wolverhampton WV2 3DX* T: (01902) 654979 F: 562616 E: ed.brookes@blueyonder.co.uk

BROOKES, Laurence. b 33. **d** 02 **p** 03. OLM Flockton cum Denby Grange *Wakef* 02–06; OLM Emley 02–06; PtO 06–14; *Leeds* from 14. *Treetops, 6 Chessington Drive, Flockton, Wakefield WF4 4TJ* T: (01924) 848238 E: lauriemarybrookes@supanet.com

BROOKES, Steven David. b 60. Lanc Univ BA 81. Ripon Coll Cuddesdon 82. **d** 85 **p** 86. C Stanley *Liv* 85–88; C W Derby St Mary 88–90; Chapl RN 90–94; R Weybridge *Guildf* 94–03; P-in-c Liv Our Lady and St Nic w St Anne 03–07; R Liv Our Lady and St Nic 07–13; Chapl R Hosp Chelsea from 13; Dep P in O from 19. *15 College Court, Royal Hospital Chelsea, Royal Hospital Road, London SW3 4SR* T: (020) 7881 5238 *or* 7881 5234 M: 07930-855146 E: chaplain@chelsea-pensioners.org.uk

BROOKFIELD, Patricia Anne. *See* HARDACRE, Patricia Anne

BROOKS, Mrs Christine Anne. b 62. STETS. **d** 09 **p** 10. C N Poole Ecum Team *Sarum* 09–13; C Kinson and W Howe 13–14; TV from 14. *41 Moore Avenue, Bournemouth BH11 8AT* T: (01202) 581135 *or* 911962 E: christine.brooks3@uwclub.net

BROOKS, Mrs Christine Ellen. b 43. Sheff Univ BA 65 Lon Univ BD 81 Lambeth STh 81. EAMTC 86. **d** 88 **p** 94. NSM Palgrave w Wortham and Burgate *St E* 88–89; Par Dn Thorndon w Rishangles, Stoke Ash, Thwaite etc 89–94; P-in-c Aldringham w Thorpe, Knodishall w Buxlow etc 94–04; R Whinlands 04–13; Asst P Sternfield w Benhall and Snape 98–03; P-in-c Alde River 03–06; rtd 13; PtO *St E* from 13. *Far End Cottage, Low Road, Friston, Saxmundham IP17 1PW* T: (01728) 688972 M: 07752-652833 E: cebwhinlands@btinternet.com

BROOKS, David Edward. b 73. **d** 09 **p** 10. OLM Middleton and Thornham *Man* from 09. *32 Sedgley Avenue, Rochdale OL16 4TY* M: 07904-520906 E: revdavidbrooks@middletonparishchurch.com *or* revrave73@gmail.com

BROOKS, Dorothy Anne. *See* MOORE BROOKS, Dorothy Anne

BROOKS, Glen. b 62. Ripon Coll Cuddesdon 12. **d** 14 **p** 15. C Northampton H Trin and St Paul *Pet* 14–17; P-in-c Somerleyton, Ashby, Fritton, Herringfleet etc *Nor* 17–18; R from 18; CF (ACF) from 16. *The Rectory, The Street, Somerleyton, Lowestoft NR32 5PT* T: (01502) 732420 E: frglen@outlook.com

BROOKS, Hannah Victoria. *See* HIGGINSON, Hannah Victoria

BROOKS, Jeremy Paul. b 67. Leic Univ LLB 88 Clare Coll Cam BA 96 MA 01 K Coll Lon MA 00 DMin 12. Ridley Hall Cam 94. **d** 97 **p** 98. C Highgate St Mich *Lon* 97–01; P-in-c Hoddesdon *St Alb* 01–07; V 07–10; TR Beaconsfield *Ox* from 10. *The Rectory, Wycombe End, Beaconsfield HP9 1NB* T: (01494) 730876 E: rector@stmarysbeaconsfield.org.uk

BROOKS, Judith Anne. b 71. City Univ MSc 10. St Aug Coll of Th 17. **d** 20 **p** 21. C Redhill St Matt *S'wark* from 20. *6 Lismore Road, South Croydon CR2 7QA* M: 07870-904035 E: judith.brooks@ymcaeastsurrey.org.uk

BROOKS, Malcolm David. b 45. **d** 71 **p** 72. C Pontlottyn w Fochriw *Llan* 71–72; C Caerphilly 72–78; V Ferndale w Maerdy 78–81; C Port Talbot St Theodore 82–84; V Ystrad Mynach 84–85; V Ystrad Mynach w Llanbradach 85–06. *33 Heol y Gors, Whitchurch, Cardiff CF14 1HF*

BROOKS (née LEWIS), Mrs Marjorie Ann. b 47. Liv Univ BA 68 Man Univ CertEd 69. WEMTC 07. **d** 13 **p** 14. OLM

Bridgnorth, Tasley, Astley Abbotts, etc *Heref* 13–16; NSM Bridgnorth and Morville Par 16–21; rtd 21; PtO *Heref* from 21. *2 The Hawthorns, Bridgnorth WV16 5JG* T: (01746) 761942 M: 07751-553736 E: marjorie.brooks47@gmail.com

BROOKS, Michael. b 57. K Coll Lon BSc 78 MB, BS 81 AKC 81 Cant Ch Ch Univ MA 13. SEITE 05. **d** 08 **p** 09. NSM Sydenham H Trin and St Aug *S'wark* 08–19; NSM Honor Oak Park St Aug from 19; AD W Lewisham from 17. *28 Frankfurt Road, London SE24 9NY* M: 07730-885187 E: michael@mybroadbandmail.com

BROOKS, Patrick John. b 27. Man Univ BA 49 DipEd. Oak Hill Th Coll 78. **d** 77 **p** 79. Burundi 77–80; PtO *Ex* 80–83; P-in-c Phillack w Gwithian and Gwinear *Truro* 83–88; R 88–93; rtd 93; PtO *Chich* from 93. *Abbots, Claigmar Road, Rustington, Littlehampton BN16 2NL* T: (01903) 784660 E: pbrooks08@googlemail.com

BROOKS, Paul John. b 59. Loughb Univ BSc 81. St Jo Coll Nottm 87. **d** 90 **p** 91. C Long Eaton St Jo *Derby* 90–94; Min Jersey St Paul Prop Chpl *Win* from 94. *5 Claremont Avenue, St Saviour, Jersey JE2 7SF* T: (01534) 880393

BROOKS, Penelope Ann. b 69. St Mellitus Coll 17. **d** 20 **p** 21. NSM Cranham *Chelmsf* from 20. *159 Usk Road, Aveley, South Ockendon RM15 4NT* T: (01708) 531337 E: penbenstrikesagain@yahoo.co.uk

BROOKS, Canon Peter. b 55. St Mich Coll Llan 97. **d** 99 **p** 00. C Morriston *S & B* 99–01; P-in-c Rhayader and Nantmel 01–02; P-in-c Cwmdauddwr w St Harmon and Llanwrthwl 02–05; P-in-c Llanwrthwl w St Harmon, Rhayader, Nantmel etc 05–08; V Gwastedyn 08–11; V Three Cliffs from 11; AD Gower 14–15; AD Gtr Gower from 16; Can Res Brecon Cathl from 15. *The Vicarage, 88 Pennard Road, Pennard, Swansea SA3 2AD* T: (01792) 232928 E: peter.brooks256@btinternet.com

BROOKS, Philip. b 82. Reading Univ BA 03 MA 04 K Coll Lon MA 10. Ridley Hall Cam 10. **d** 13 **p** 14. C Oxted *S'wark* 13–16; TV Sutton from 16. *Christchurch Vicarage, 14C Christchurch Park, Sutton SM2 5TN* M: 07969-066906 E: phil_brooks1982@hotmail.com

BROOKS, Philip David. b 52. MA Cam Univ MTh. St Jo Coll Nottm 80. **d** 83 **p** 84. C Ipsley *Worc* 83–87; V Fulford w Hilderstone *Lich* 87–95; Chapl Stallington Hosp 87–95; P-in-c Crich *Derby* 95–01; V Crich and S Wingfield 01–17; Dioc Adv Past Care and Counselling 03–09; RD Alfreton 09–16; rtd 17; PtO *Dur* from 18. *10 Bedale Close, Durham DH1 2BB* E: philipdbro@aol.com

BROOKS, Mrs Rachael. b 68. Nottm Univ BA 89 Nottm Poly PGCE 90. St Hild Coll 17. **d** 20 **p** 21. C Littleover *Derby* from 20; C Blagreaves from 20. *48 Jackson Avenue, Mickleover, Derby DE3 9AT* T: (01332) 605081 M: 07305-140573 E: rachael@stpeterlittleover.org.uk *or* rachael.brooks@ntlworld.com

BROOKS, Mrs Susan Vera. b 51. NOC 87. **d** 90 **p** 94. Par Dn Carleton and E Hardwick *Wakef* 90–94; TV Almondbury w Farnley Tyas 94–98; Chapl Huddersfield NHS Trust 98–01; Chapl Calderdale and Huddersfield NHS Trust 01–03; Lead Chapl 03–12; NSM Crosland Moor and Linthwaite *Wakef* 12–14; *Leeds* 14–16; rtd 16. *5 Miry Lane, Thongsbridge, Holmfirth HD9 7SA* T: (01484) 768178

BROOKS, Mrs Vivien June. b 47. Univ of Wales (Ban) BA 68 Southn Univ MA 70. Ridley Hall Cam 87. **d** 89 **p** 95. C Exning St Martin w Landwade *St E* 89–92; Par Dn Hermitage and Hampstead Norreys, Cold Ash etc *Ox* 92–94; C 94–95; P-in-c Cox Green 95–03; Co Ecum Officer (Berks) 00–03; P-in-c Earls Colne w White Colne and Colne Engaine *Chelmsf* 03–04; TV Halstead Area 04–12; rtd 12; PtO *St E* 13–18; *Chelmsf* 14–18; *Sarum* from 18. *104 Castleview Road, Chiseldon, Swindon SN4 0NT* T: (01793) 741286 E: vivienbrooks@gmail.com

BROOKS, Vivienne Christine. *See* ARMSTRONG-MacDONNELL, Vivienne Christine

BROOKSBANK, Alan Watson. b 43. Univ of Wales (Lamp) BA 64 Edin Univ MEd 76. Edin Th Coll 64. **d** 66 **p** 67. C Cleator Moor w Cleator *Carl* 66–70; V Dalston 70–80; P-in-c Greystoke, Matterdale and Mungrisdale 80–81; R 81–83; R Watermillock 81–83; R Hagley *Worc* 83–95; Bp's Officer for NSM 88–95; V Claines St Jo 95–98; rtd 98. *169 Northfields Lane, Brixham TQ5 8RD* E: awbrooksbank@gmail.com

BROOKSHAW, Miss Janice Chitty. b 48. Anglia Ruskin Univ MA 12 MCIPD 90. Ripon Coll Cuddesdon 96. **d** 98 **p** 99. C Beaconsfield *Ox* 98–02; P-in-c The Stodden Churches *St Alb* 02–03; R 03–14; rtd 14; PtO *Win* 14–15; C Upper Itchen from 16. *3 The Old Dairy, Easton, Winchester SO21 1EU* T: (01962) 779988 E: revjanb@gmail.com

BROOM, The Ven Andrew Clifford. b 65. Keele Univ BSocSc 86. Trin Coll Bris BA 92. **d** 92 **p** 93. C Wellington All SS w Eyton *Lich* 92–96; C Brampton St Thos *Derby* 96–00; V

Walton St Jo 00–09; Dir of Miss and Min 09–14; Hon Can Derby Cathl 11–14; Adn E Riding *York* from 14. *Brimley Lodge, 27 Molescroft Road, Beverley HU17 7DX* T: (01482) 881659 E: ader@yorkdiocese.org

BROOME, Mildred Dorothy. b 43. **d** 00 **p** 01. NSM Malden St Jo *S'wark* 00–13; PtO from 13. *124 The Manor Drive, Worcester Park KT4 7LW* T: (020) 8337 1572 E: m.broome@hotmail.co.uk

BROOMFIELD, Iain Jonathan. b 57. Univ Coll Ox MA 87. Wycliffe Hall Ox 80. **d** 83 **p** 84. C Beckenham Ch Ch *Roch* 83–87; Sen Schs Worker Titus Trust 87–00; V Bromley Ch Ch *Roch* from 00. *Christ Church Vicarage, 18 Highland Road, Bromley BR1 4AD* T: (020) 8313 9882 *or* 8464 1898 F: 8464 5846 E: iain.broomfield@christchurchbromley.org

BROOMHEAD, Mark Roger. b 71. Nottm Univ BSc 00. St Jo Coll Nottm 06. **d** 08 **p** 09. C N Wingfield, Clay Cross and Pilsley *Derby* 08–10; C Brampton St Thos from 10; C Chesterfield St Mary and All SS from 11; C Chesterfield H Trin and Ch Ch from 11; C Chesterfield SS Aug 11–15; P-in-c 15–16; Pioneer Development Officer from 21. *35 Whitecotes Park, Chesterfield S40 3RT* T: (01246) 555988 E: mark@theorderoftheblacksheep.com

BROSNAN, Mark. b 61. St Martin's Coll Lanc BA 83 RMN 88 Otley Agric Coll. EAMTC 92. **d** 95 **p** 96. C Rushmere *St E* 95–98; PtO *Chelmsf* 01–05; Hon C W w E Mersea 05–08; Hon C Peldon w Gt and Lt Wigborough 05–08; P-in-c Hadleigh St Barn 08–12; P-in-c Kirkbymoorside w Gillamoor, Farndale etc *York* 12; V from 12; C Kirby Misperton w Normanby and Salton from 12. *The Vicarage, Church Street, Kirkbymoorside, York YO62 6AZ* T: (01751) 431452 E: gohiking@hotmail.co.uk

BROSTER, Godfrey David. b 52. Ealing Tech Coll BA 75. Ripon Coll Cuddesdon 78. **d** 81 **p** 82. C Crayford *Roch* 81–82; C Brighton Resurr *Chich* 82–86; C-in-c The Hydneye CD 86–91; R Plumpton w E Chiltington 91–93; R Plumpton w E Chiltington cum Novington 93–20; rtd 20. *Address temp unknown*

BROTHERSTON, Miss Isabel Mary. b 42. Cranmer Hall Dur 81. **dss** 83 **d** 87 **p** 94. Coleshill *Birm* 83–87; Par Dn Duddeston w Nechells 87–92; Par Dn Harlescott *Lich* 92–94; C 94–04; R Llanddulas and Llysfaen *St As* 04–08; rtd 08; PtO *St As* from 08. *3 Marlow Terrace, Mold CH7 1HH* T: (01352) 756011 E: mbrother@live.co.uk

BROTHERTON, The Ven John Michael. b 35. St Jo Coll Cam BA 59 MA 63. Cuddesdon Coll 59. **d** 61 **p** 62. C Chiswick St Nic w St Mary *Lon* 61–65; Chapl Trin Coll Port of Spain Trinidad and Tobago 65–69; R Diego Martin 69–75; V Cowley St Jo *Ox* 76–81; Chapl St Hilda's Coll Ox 76–81; RD Cowley *Ox* 78–81; V Portsea St Mary *Portsm* 81–91; Hon Can Kobe Japan from 86; Adn Chich 91–02; rtd 02; PtO *Lon* 03–20; *Chich* from 03. *Flat 2, 23 Gledhow Gardens, London SW5 0AZ* T: (020) 7373 5147 E: jmbrotherton@yahoo.co.uk

BROTHERTON, Michael. b 56. MBE 93. Univ of Wales (Abth) BD 80. Wycliffe Hall Ox 80. **d** 81 **p** 82. Hon Chapl Miss to Seamen 81–84; C Pembroke Dock *St D* 81–84; Chapl RN 84–11; rtd 11; PtO *St D* from 13. *North Studdock Farm House, Angle, Pembroke SA71 5AZ* T: (01646) 641438 M: 07887-534666 E: entopan007@gmail.com

BROTHWELL, Ruth. b 60. **d** 10 **p** 12. NSM Merrow *Guildf* 10–13; NSM Worplesdon 13–15 and 17–20; PtO 15–17 and from 20. *Foxgrove, Burnt Common Lane, Ripley, Woking GU23 6HD* T: (01483) 223571 E: ruth@worplesdonparish.com

BROTHWOOD, Ian Sidney. b 56. K Coll Lon BD 84. Linc Th Coll 87. **d** 89 **p** 90. C Selsdon St Jo w St Fran *S'wark* 89–93; P-in-c S Norwood St Alb 93–97; V 97–99; V Reigate St Mark 99–04; P-in-c Selsdon St Jo w St Fran from 04; R 06–12; V Croydon St Mich w St Jas 12–15; rtd 16; PtO *Eur* 17–21. *The Barns, 5 Devon Lane, Bottesford, Nottingham NG13 0BZ*

BROUARD, Ms Susanna. New Hall Cam MA 94 Heythrop Coll Lon MA 94 Anglia Ruskin Univ DProf 15. Ripon Coll Cuddesdon 18. **d** 20 **p** 21. C Kidlington w Hampton Poyle *Ox* from 20. *Address temp unknown* M: 07951-917814

BROUGH (née CROWLE), Mrs Sarah Ann. b 65. Ripon Coll Cuddesdon BTh 99. **d** 99 **p** 00. C Godalming *Guildf* 99–03; Chapl Godalming Coll 01–03; R Chiddingfold *Guildf* 03–18; PtO 18–21. *Robinlea, Friday Street, Ockley, Dorking RH5 5TE* M: 07747-031524 E: sarahbrough@btinternet.com

BROUGHTON, James Roger. b 48. Leeds Univ BA 71 Liv Univ MEd 00 Nottm Univ CertEd 72. Wycliffe Hall Ox 87. **d** 89 **p** 90. C Stoneycroft All SS *Liv* 89–92; P-in-c Carr Mill 92–94; V 94–96; Chapl Duke of York's R Mil Sch Dover 96–08; rtd 08; PtO *Cant* from 08. *Woodstock, St Vincent Road, St Margarets-at-Cliffe, Dover CT15 6ET* T: (01304) 853840 M: 07934-560557 E: james@broughtonfamily.co.uk

BROUGHTON, Lynne Mary. b 46. Melbourne Univ BA 67 PhD 79. EAMTC 99. **d** 00 **p** 01. NSM Wood Ditton w Saxon Street *Ely* 00–07; NSM Kirtling 00–07; NSM Cheveley 00–07; NSM Ashley w Silverley 00–07; PtO from 07. *85 Richmond Road, Cambridge CB4 3PS* T: (01223) 322014 E: lmb27@hermes.cam.ac.uk *or* lmb27@cam.ac.uk

BROUGHTON, Matthew David. b 88. Sheff Univ BA 10 Trin Hall Cam BTh 17. Ridley Hall Cam 15. **d** 18 **p** 19. C Ireland Wood *Leeds* from 18. *11 Bedford View, Leeds LS16 6DL* M: 07982-197632 E: mbroughton1088@gmail.com

BROUGHTON, Canon Stuart Roger. b 36. Wilson Carlile Coll 59 St Mich Coll Llan 61. **d** 64 **p** 65. C Bromley Ch Ch *Roch* 64–67; SAMS 67–79 and 86–95; Miss Paraguayan Chaco Paraguay 67–70; R Salvador Gd Shep Brazil 70–79; V Stoke sub Hamdon *B & W* 79–83; Hon CF 82–86; V Blackb Ch Ch w St Matt 83–86; R Alcacer do Sal Portugal 86–91; Chapl Rio de Janeiro Brazil 91–95; rtd 96; Chapl Agia Napa Cyprus 96; Chapl Ch Ch Cathl Falkland Is 97–98; P-in-c Corfu *Eur* 98–01; Hon C Jersey St Paul Prop Chpl *Win* 01–03; Chapl to Abp Congo 03–06; Hon Can Bukavu from 04; LtO Sydney Australia 06–11; PtO *St Alb* 11–14; *Liv* 14–19; *Ches* from 18; *Blackb* from 19. *27 Burey Court, Barnacre Road, Longridge, Preston PR3 2PF* T: (01772) 785760 E: stuartrbroughtonsouthport@gmail.com

BROWELL (*née* SHILLINGTON), Mrs Maureen Lesley. b 57. MIH 89. NEOC 02. **d** 05 **p** 06. Soc Resp Officer *Ripon* 99–08; NSM Hoylandswaine and Silkstone w Stainborough *Wakef* 05–08; TV Almondbury w Farnley Tyas 08–12; Dioc Co-ord for Soc Resp 08–10; V Hoylandswaine and Silkstone w Stainborough 12–14; *Leeds* 14–16; V W Barnsley from 16; Dean of Women's Min Wakef Area from 17. *The Vicarage, 12 High Street, Silkstone, Barnsley S75 4JN* T: (01226) 492294 M: 07930-194421 E: maureenbrowell@sky.com

BROWN, Mrs Ailsa Elizabeth. b 64. Hull Univ BA 94 Nottm Univ MA 10. EMMTC 07. **d** 10 **p** 11. NSM Barton upon Humber *Linc* 14–18; C Barrow and Goxhill 18–21; P-in-c from 21; Asst Dioc Dir of Ords from 13. *21 Ferriby Road, Barton-upon-Humber DN18 5LE* T: (01652) 634855 M: 07805-694614 E: brown5le@btinternet.com

BROWN, Canon Alan. b 37. Tyndale Hall Bris 59. **d** 63 **p** 64. C Braintree *Chelmsf* 63–66; C Tooting Graveney St Nic *S'wark* 66–68; C Chesham St Mary *Ox* 68–70; V Hornsey Rise St Mary *Lon* 70–75; V Sidcup Ch Ch *Roch* 75–88; V Newport St Jo *Portsm* 88–01; P-in-c Newport St Thos 96–99; V 99–01; RD W Wight 91–96; Hon Can Portsm Cathl 95–01; rtd 01. *65 Sherbourne Avenue, Ryde PO33 3PW* T: (01983) 566956

BROWN, Alan George. b 51. Bradf Univ BSc 84 Leeds Univ CertEd 81 MBA 92 SRN 72 RMN 75 RNT 81. NOC 92. **d** 95 **p** 96. NSM Ilkley St Marg *Bradf* 95–10; Hd of Division Applied Health Studies Leeds Univ 98–07; Bp's Adv for Hosp Chapl *Bradf* 03–14; LtO 10–14; Bp's Inspector for Minl Tr *Wakef* 10–14; *Leeds* from 14; PtO *York* from 14. *Argyll Lodge, High Street, Scalby, Scarborough YO13 0PT* T: (01723) 503122 E: brown.alan.george@gmail.com

BROWN, Alec George. b 53. Univ of Wales (Cardiff) MSc(Econ) 87 Univ of Zimbabwe DipSW 80. St Deiniol's Hawarden 88 NOC 90. **d** 93 **p** 94. C Stockton Heath *Ches* 93–96; C Thelwall 96–97; V 97–01; V Gt Budworth from 01; P-in-c Antrobus from 13; RD Gt Budworth 10–20. *The Vicarage, High Street, Great Budworth, Northwich CW9 6HF* T: (01606) 891324 E: alecgbrown@gmail.com

BROWN, Allan James. b 47. K Coll Lon BD 69 AKC 69 MTh 70. St Aug Coll Cant 69. **d** 73 **p** 74. Chapl St Geo Sch Jerusalem 73–74; Chapl St Marg Sch Nazareth 74–75; C Clifton *S'well* 75–77; CF 77–99; Asst Chapl Gen 99–00; V Ilkeston St Mary *Derby* 00–10; P-in-c Ilkeston St Jo 05–10; rtd 10; PtO *S'well* 10–20. *63 Highfield Road, Nottingham NG2 6DR*

BROWN, The Ven Andrew. b 55. St Pet Coll Ox BA 80 MA 82. Ridley Hall Cam 79. **d** 80 **p** 81. C Burnley St Pet *Blackb* 80–82; C Elton All SS *Man* 82–86; P-in-c Ashton St Pet 86–93; V 94–96; V Halliwell St Luke 96–03; Can Th Derby Cathl and Dioc CME Adv *Derby* 03–11; Adn of Man *S & M* 11–21; V Douglas St Geo 11–14; V Douglas St Geo and All SS 15–21; rtd 21. *62 Holloway, Repton, Derby DE65 6RH* E: andiebfc@me.com

BROWN, Andrew (**Bod**). b 66. Man Univ BSc 87. Oak Hill Th Coll BA 02. **d** 03 **p** 04. C Hyde St Geo *Ches* 03–06; V Weaverham 06–18; V Shevington *Blackb* from 18. *St Ann's Vicarage, Gathurst Lane, Shevington, Wigan WN6 8HW* T: (01257) 252136

BROWN, Andrew James. b 60. Univ of Wales (Ban) BA 81. Ripon Coll Cuddesdon 07. **d** 09 **p** 10. C Castle Bromwich SS Mary and Marg *Birm* 09–13; P-in-c Charnock Richard 13–19; P-in-c Charnock Richard 13–19; R Eccleston and Charnock Richard from 19. *The Rectory, 30 Lawrence Lane, Eccleston, Chorley PR7 5SJ* T: (01257) 452777 E: rector@ecclestonstmaryschurch.org

BROWN, Andrew Paul. See GREAVES-BROWN, Andrew Paul

BROWN, Andrew Robert James. b 90. Cant Ch Ch Univ BA 13. Ripon Coll Cuddesdon 16. **d** 18 **p** 19. C Ashford Town *Cant* from 18. *The Vicarage, 66 Church Road, Willesborough, Ashford TN24 0JG* E: rev.arjbrown@gmail.com

BROWN, Mrs Angela. b 58. SWMTC 11. **d** 14 **p** 15. C Redruth w Lanner and Treleigh *Truro* 14–18; Public Preacher from 18. *22 Trescobeas Road, Falmouth TR11 2JE* M: 07729-118696 E: angelabythesea@icloud.com

BROWN, Canon Anne Elizabeth. b 61. SWMTC 06. **d** 09 **p** 10. C Probus, Ladock and Grampound w Creed and St Erme *Truro* 09–12; P-in-c Three Rivers 12–16; P-in-c St Agnes and Mount Hawke w Mithian from 16; P-in-c Perranzabuloe and Crantock w Cubert from 16; Hon Can Truro Cathl from 15. *The Vicarage, Cox Hill, Cocks, Perranporth TR6 0AT* T: (01872) 572654

BROWN, Anthony Frank Palmer. b 31. Fitzw Ho Cam BA 56 Fitzw Coll Cam MA 84. Cuddesdon Coll 56. **d** 58 **p** 59. C Aldershot St Mich *Guildf* 58–61; C Chiswick St Nic w St Mary *Lon* 61–66; Asst Chapl Lon Univ 65–70; LtO 70–72; C-in-c Hammersmith SS Mich and Geo White City Estate CD 72–74; P-in-c Upper Sunbury St Sav *Lon* V 80–01; rtd 01; PtO *Chich* 02–18. *Room 6, Terrys Cross House, Brighton Road, Woodmancote, Henfield BN5 9SX* T: (01273) 491226

BROWN, Preb Anthony Paul. b 55. Reading Univ BSc 75 MRICS 87. Qu Coll Birm 77. **d** 80 **p** 81. C Pelsall *Lich* 80–83; C Leighton Buzzard w Eggington, Hockliffe etc *St Alb* 83–87; TV Langley Marish *Ox* 87–93; V Pet St Mary Boongate 93–98; TR Wombourne w Trysull and Bobbington *Lich* 98–02; TR Smestow Vale from 02; Preb Lich Cathl from 09. *The Vicarage, School Road, Wombourne, Wolverhampton WV5 9ED* T: (01902) 892234 *or* 897700 E: prebpbrown@gmail.com

BROWN, Barry Ronald. b 48. Ridley Coll Melbourne ThL 72. **d** 73 **p** 74. Australia 73–77 and 82–95; C Richmond St Mary w St Matthias *S'wark* 78–79; C Richmond St Mary w St Matthias and St Jo 79; C Edin Old St Paul 79–80; Chapl Belgrade w Zagreb *Eur* 81–82; Canada from 95. *52 Queen Street, Belleville ON K8N 1T7, Canada* T: (001) (613) 968 9873 E: bbrownhome@hotmail.com

BROWN, Benjamin Brumas Martin. b 71. Goldsmiths' Coll Lon BA 99 Jes Coll Cam BA 11. Westcott Ho Cam 09. **d** 12 **p** 13. C Cheam *S'wark* 12–15; TV Merstham, S Merstham and Gatton 15–21; R Lewes St Anne and St Mich and St Thos etc *Chich* from 21. *Address temp unknown* M: 07890-858121 E: brownoctopus@yahoo.com

BROWN, Bill Charles Balfour. b 44. Linc Th Coll 87. **d** 89 **p** 90. C Moulsham St Luke *Chelmsf* 89–91; C Prittlewell St Mary 91–94; V Worksop St Paul *S'well* 95–12; rtd 12. *46 Holding, Worksop S81 0TD* E: fatherbill@btopenworld.com

BROWN, Bod. See BROWN, Andrew

BROWN (*née* BRYCE), Mrs Brenda Dorothy. b 48. **d** 11 **p** 13. NSM Trowell, Awsworth and Cossall *S'well* 11–18; rtd 18; PtO *S'well* from 18. *41 Park Hill, Awsworth, Nottingham NG16 2RD* T: 0115-932 9328 E: brenda.brown1408@outlook.com

BROWN, Caroline Ann. b 59. FCCA 08. ERMC 19. **d** 21. C The Hedinghams and Upper Colne *Chelmsf* from 21. *1 Hedingham Place, Spring Way, Sible Hedingham, Halstead CO9 3SW* T: (01787) 469161 E: seychelles85@hotmail.com

BROWN, Caroline Joy. b 81. Bris Univ BA 14. St Hild Coll 18. **d** 20 **p** 21. C Yeadon *Leeds* from 20. *37 Millbank, Yeadon, Leeds LS19 7AY* M: 07990-521682 E: caroline.brown@leeds.anglican.org

BROWN, Caryll Diane. b 50. **d** 13 **p** 14. NSM E w W Harling, Bridgham w Roudham, Larling etc *Nor* 13–20; rtd 20; PtO *Nor* from 20. *Carrick House, 7 West Harling Road, East Harling, Norwich NR16 2SL* T: (01953) 717451 E: c@trickhouse.com

BROWN, Charles Henry. b 48. Tulane Univ (USA) BA 70 Ch Coll Cam BA 75 MA 81. Westcott Ho Cam. **d** 00 **p** 01. C Boston *Linc* 00–03; Lect 03–05; Lic Preacher 05–06; P-in-c Crowland from 06. *The Abbey Rectory, East Street, Crowland, Peterborough PE6 0EN* T: (01733) 211763

BROWN, Mrs Christine Ann. b 42. Keele Univ CertEd 72. LCTP 10. **d** 11 **p** 12. NSM Dent w Cowgill *Bradf* 11–12; NSM Dent w Cowgill *Carl* 12–19; rtd 19; PtO *Carl* from 19. *Dale View, Laning, Dent, Sedbergh LA10 5QJ* T: (015396) 25418 E: christinelucy2014@gmail.com

BROWN, Canon Christine Lilian. b 54. Ex Univ BA 75 Newc Univ MA 93. NEOC 01. **d** 04 **p** 05. NSM Ponteland *Newc* from 04; Chapl St Oswald's Hospice Newc 08–14; AD Newc W from 17; Hon Can Newc Cathl from 17. *4 Woodlands, Ponteland, Newcastle upon Tyne NE20 9EU* T: (01661) 824196

BROWN, Christopher. b 43. Linc Th Coll 79. **d** 81 **p** 82. C Stafford St Jo *Lich* 81–85; V Alton w Bradley-le-Moors and Oakamoor w Cotton 85–94; Chapl Asst Nottm City Hosp NHS Trust 94–05; Sen Chapl 05–06; rtd 06. *3 Kingsbury Drive, Nottingham NG8 3EP* T: 0115-929 4821 E: christopher.brown20@sky.com

BROWN, Christopher. *See* BROWN, Paul David Christopher

BROWN, Christopher Charles. b 58. Univ of Wales (Cardiff) LLB 79 Solicitor 82. Westcott Ho Cam 87. **d** 90 **p** 91. C Taunton St Mary *B & W* 90–94; R Timsbury and Priston 94–00; P-in-c Urmston *Man* 00–10; AD Stretford 05–10; TR Radcliffe 10–14; V Fishguard w Llanychar and Pontfaen w Morfil etc *St D* 14–18; P-in-c W Cemaes from 18; AD Dewisland and Fishguard 15–18; AD W Cemaes from 18. *The Vicarage, High Street, Fishguard SA65 9AU* T: (01348) 875536 E: revchrisbrown4@gmail.com

BROWN, Christopher David. b 49. Birm Univ BEd 72. St Mich Coll Llan 92. **d** 94 **p** 95. C Swansea St Thos and Kilvey *S & B* 94–96; C Swansea St Jas 96–98; St Helena 99–01; Chapl and Hd RS Epsom Coll 01–03; Chapl Ellesmere Coll 03–05. *Flat 1, 13 Worcester Road, Malvern WR14 4QY* E: kristophdavid@hotmail.com

BROWN, Christopher Edgar Newall. b 31. Oak Hill Th Coll 51. **d** 55 **p** 56. C Surbiton Hill Ch Ch *S'wark* 55–57; C Gipsy Hill Ch Ch 57–61; V Plumstead All SS 61–70; V Sissinghurst *Cant* 70–73; P-in-c Frittenden 72–73; R Sissinghurst w Frittenden 73–76; PtO *S & M* 84–91 and 96–10; Bp's Dom Chapl 91–95; rtd 96. *21 College Green, Castletown, Isle of Man IM9 1BE* T: (01624) 822364

BROWN, Christopher Howard. b 49. **d** 03 **p** 04. OLM Uttoxeter Area *Lich* from 03. *21 Carter Street, Uttoxeter ST14 8EY* T: (01889) 567492 E: revchrishbrown@aol.co.uk

BROWN, Christopher Stephen. b 70. Trin Coll Bris BA 20. **d** 20 **p** 21. C Clifton Ch Ch w Em *Bris* from 20. *60 Clifton Park Road, Bristol BS8 3HN* M: 07419-847038 E: chris@vine-cottage.org.uk

BROWN, Daniel James. b 83. Sheff Univ BA 06 MA 13. Yorks Min Course 10. **d** 13 **p** 14. C Philadelphia St Thos *Sheff* 13–15; C Wadsley 15–17; P-in-c from 17. *The Vicarage, 91 Airedale Road, Sheffield S6 4AW* E: dan.brown@sheffield.anglican.org *or* danbrown@wadsleychurch.com

BROWN, David Andrew. b 72. York Univ MA 93. Wycliffe Hall Ox BTh 04. **d** 04 **p** 05. C Rugby St Matt *Cov* 04–07; C Rugby W 08; P-in-c Budbrooke 08–14; V from 14. *23 Robins Grove, Warwick CV34 6RF* T: (01926) 497298

BROWN, David Charles Girdlestone. b 42. Solicitor 67. S'wark Ord Course 87. **d** 90 **p** 91. NSM Milford *Guildf* 90–92; NSM Haslemere 92–01; PtO *Chich* 02–04 and from 14; LtO 04–08; P-in-c Barlavington, Burton w Coates, Sutton and Bignor 08–14; rtd 14. *Sunnyside, South Harting, Petersfield GU31 5LD* T: (01730) 825413 E: dbrown501@btinternet.com

BROWN, David George. b 55. Lon Univ BD 75 Sussex Univ MSc 06 MInstLM 03. Lon Bible Coll 72. **d** 15 **p** 15. OLM Woodside Park St Barn *Lon* 15–17; PtO 17–18; *Portsm* 17–18; C Warfield *Ox* from 19. *2 Dorset Vale, Warfield, Bracknell RG42 3JL* M: 07490-089255 E: davidgbrown@outlook.com

BROWN, David Lloyd. b 44. TCD BTh 90. **d** 86 **p** 87. C Cregagh *D & D* 86–91; Bp's C Knocknagoney 91–12; I 12–19; Can Down Cathl 07–19; rtd 19. *19 Old Holywood Road, Belfast BT4 2HJ* E: davidlloydbrown@googlemail.com

BROWN, David Mark. b 67. Bp Grosseteste Coll BSc 93. Oak Hill Th Coll 05. **d** 07 **p** 08. C Sidmouth, Woolbrook, Salcombe Regis, Sidbury etc *Ex* 07–11; P-in-c Stevenage St Nic and Graveley *St Alb* 11–15; V from 15. *St Nicholas' House, 2A North Road, Stevenage SG1 4AT* T: (01438) 354355 M: 07814-911937 E: rector@saintnicholaschurch.org.uk

BROWN, David Victor Arthur. b 44. Em Coll Cam BA 66 MA 70 CertEd. Linc Th Coll 72. **d** 74 **p** 75. C Bourne *Linc* 74–77; Chapl St Steph Coll Broadstairs 77–79; Chapl Asst N Gen Hosp Sheff 81–84; C Sheff St Cuth 81–84; Chapl Ridge Lea Hosp Lanc 84–92; Chapl Lanc Moor Hosp 84–92; Chapl Lanc R Infirmary 87–92; Chapl Lanc Priority Services NHS Trust and Lanc Acute Hosps NHS Trust 92–98; Chapl Morecambe Bay Hosps NHS Trust and Morecambe Bay Primary Care Trust 98–09; Hon C Scorton and Barnacre and Calder Vale *Blackb* 06–09; P-in-c 09–12; V 12–14; P-in-c Warsaw *Eur* from 14. *ul Dorotowska 7/5, Warsaw 02-347, Poland* M: (0048) 880-580628 E: dlgbrown@aol.com *or* chaplain@anglicanchurch-poland.org

BROWN, Prof David William. b 48. Edin Univ MA 70 Oriel Coll Ox BA 72 Clare Coll Cam PhD 76 FBA 02. Westcott Ho Cam 75. **d** 76 **p** 77. Chapl, Fell and Tutor Oriel Coll Ox 76–90; Van Mildert Prof Div Dur Univ 90–07; Can Res Dur Cathl 90–07; Wardlaw Prof St Andr Univ *St And*

07–15; LtO from 09. *Mansfield, 1A Grey Street, Tayport DD6 9JF* T: (01382) 550063

BROWN (née BOWERS), Lady (Denise Frances). b 50. City Univ BSc 72. SAOMC 99. **d** 02 **p** 03. NSM Beedon and Peasemore w W Ilsley and Farnborough *Ox* 02–10; NSM Brightwalton w Catmore, Leckhampstead etc 05–10; NSM E Downland 10–17; rtd 17; PtO *Ox* from 17. *Bridleway Cottage, Stanmore, Beedon, Newbury RG20 8SR* T/F: (01635) 281825 M: 07884-493923 E: denisefbrown@gmail.com

BROWN, Derek. b 42. Lindisfarne Regional Tr Partnership 10. **d** 10 **p** 11. NSM Gateshead St Helen *Dur* 10–15; PtO from 15. *29 Heathfield Road, Gateshead NE9 5HH* T: 0191-487 5922 M: 07985-512766 E: derekderekb@aol.com

BROWN, Derek Henry Pridgeon. b 46. Cam Coll of Art and Tech BA 67 Leeds Univ PGCE 71. St Steph Ho Ox 90. **d** 92 **p** 93. C Finchley St Mary *Lon* 92–95; C W Hampstead St Jas 95–99; V Eyres Monsell *Leic* 99–08; TV Leic Presentation 08–09; Min Leic St Barn CD 09–13; rtd 13; PtO *Leic* 13–21. *38 Gainsborough Road, Leicester LE2 3DE* T: 0116-270 9750 M: 07526-124023 E: dbrown@leicester.anglican.org

BROWN, Canon Donald Fryer. b 31. St Jo Coll Dur BA 56. Cranmer Hall Dur 60. **d** 61 **p** 62. Min Can Bradf Cathl 61–64; C Bingley All SS 64–66; V Low Moor H Trin 66–97; Hon Can Bradf Cathl 85–97; RD Bowling and Horton 87–95; rtd 97; PtO *Bradf* 97–14; *Leeds* from 14. *3 Northfield Gardens, Wibsey, Bradford BD6 1LQ* T: (01274) 671869 E: donaldandiris@hotmail.co.uk

BROWN, Douglas Adrian Spencer. b 29. Univ of W Aus BA 50 MA 71 K Coll Lon MTh 90. St Mich Th Coll Crafers 50. **d** 53 **p** 54. SSM 54–00; Chapl St Mich Th Coll Crafers Australia 54–60; Chapl Kelham Th Coll 60–66; Chapl Univ of W Aus Australia 66–71; P-in-c Canberra St Alb 71–75; Warden St Mich Th Coll Crafers 75–82; P-in-c Adelaide St Jo 78–82; Academic Dean Adelaide Coll of Div 79–81; Visiting Scholar Union Th Sem NY 82; President Adelaide Coll of Div 88; PtO *Lon* 88–90; Chapl Bucharest w Sofia *Eur* 90–91; Dir Angl Cen Rome 91–95; Chapl Palermo w Taormina *Eur* 95–96; Lect Newton Th Coll Papua New Guinea 97; PtO *Dur* 97–00; *S'wark* 99–00; Dir Nor Cathl Inst 00–02; Hon PV Nor Cathl 00–02; PtO 01–02. *6 Gilmour Road, Roleystone WA 6111, Australia* E: brown.douglas75@gmail.com

BROWN, Mrs Elizabeth Alexandra Mary Gordon. b 67. Westcott Ho Cam 06. **d** 08 **p** 09. C Merrow *Guildf* 08–11; NSM Bedlington *Newc* 12–18; PtO 18–19; NSM Morpeth from 19; Chapl Northumbria Healthcare NHS Foundn Trust from 17. *68 Shields Road, Morpeth NE61 2RZ* T: (01670) 515556 M: 07768-075803 E: lizzieegg@hotmail.co.uk

BROWN, Ms Elizabeth Ann. b 48. **d** 00 **p** 01. OLM W Bromwich All SS *Lich* 01–08; OLM Wednesbury St Paul Wood Green 08–10; rtd 10; PtO *Lich* from 11. *307 Beaconview Road, West Bromwich B71 3PS* T: 0121-588 7530 E: elizabethbrown630@gmail.com

BROWN, Elizabeth Grant. b 86. Cant Ch Ch Univ BA 09. Westcott Ho Cam 14. **d** 17 **p** 18. C Southgate Ch Ch *Lon* 17–18; C Southgate St Andr 17–21; C Becontree S *Chelmsf* from 21. *Address withheld by request* M: 07753-660680 E: motherlizn14@gmail.com

BROWN, Mrs Elizabeth Mary Godwin. b 48. St Matthias Coll Bris CertEd 69. WEMTC 07. **d** 10 **p** 11. NSM Leominster *Heref* 10–18; PtO 18–20. *Fairleigh House, Hereford Terrace, Leominster HR6 8JP* T: (01568) 613636 M: 07971-917141 E: elizabethmgbrown@hotmail.com

BROWN, Eric. b 28. Leeds Univ BA 98. NW Ord Course 73. **d** 76 **p** 77. NSM S Kirkby *Wakef* 76–83; NSM Knottingley 83–94; NSM Kellington w Whitley 89–94; Sub Chapl HM Pris Lindholme 90–94; PtO *Wakef* 94–14; *Leeds* from 14. *8 Ashfield House, Southmoor Road, Hemsworth, Pontefract WF9 4SQ* T: (01977) 618987 E: josephinehunter42@gmail.com

BROWN, Geoffrey Alan. b 34. **d** 99 **p** 00. OLM Bury St Edmunds St Mary *St E* 99–07; rtd 07; PtO *St E* 07–21. *Rodenkirchen, 12A Sharp Road, Bury St Edmunds IP33 2NB* T: (01284) 769725

BROWN, Geoffrey Gilbert. b 38. Dur Univ BA 62 DipEd 63 Fitzw Coll Cam BA 69 MA 73 FBIS. Westcott Ho Cam 67. **d** 70 **p** 71. C Gosforth All SS *Newc* 70–73; Chapl Dauntsey's Sch Devizes 73–76; Chapl St Paul's Colleg Sch Hamilton NZ 76–78; V Barrow St Aid *Carl* 79–86; Chapl Ch Coll Canterbury NZ 86–90; C Digswell and Panshanger *St Alb* 91–93; Chapl E Herts Hospice Care 94–07; rtd 07. *32 Uplands, Welwyn Garden City AL8 7EW* T: (01707) 327565

BROWN, Mrs Harriet Nina. b 37. Open Univ BA 77 Lon Univ CertEd 57. Gilmore Course 80 Oak Hill Th Coll 83. **dss** 83 **d** 87 **p** 94. Greenstead *Chelmsf* 83–90; Par Dn 87–90; Asst Chapl R Hosp Sch Holbrook 90–93; PtO *Chelmsf* from 93; *St E* 93–96; P-in-c Gt and Lt Blakenham w Baylham and

Nettlestead 96–01; rtd 01. *Spindles, Larksfield Road, Stutton, Ipswich IP9 2RZ* E: adhnbrown@tiscali.co.uk

BROWN, Ian Barry. *See* KING-BROWN, Ian Barry

BROWN, Ian David. b 53. UEA BA 76. Wycliffe Hall Ox BA 80. d 81 p 82. C Southsea St Jude *Portsm* 81–84; Chapl Coll of SS Paul and Mary Cheltenham 84–89; V Lt Heath *St Alb* 89–05; V Frindsbury w Upnor and Chattenden *Roch* 05–14; P-in-c Chalfont St Giles *Ox* 14–15; P-in-c Seer Green and Jordans 14–15; R Chalfont St Giles, Seer Green and Jordans 15–21; rtd 21. *32 East Street, Thame OX9 3 JT* E: ianandjuliebrown@gmail.com

BROWN, Canon Jack Robin. b 44. Linc Th Coll 67. d 69 p 70. C Canning Town St Cedd *Chelmsf* 69–72; C Dunstable *St Alb* 72–78; V Luton St Andr 78–85; V Kempston Transfiguration 85–00; RD Bedford 92–98; Hon Can St Alb 97–09; Dioc Officer for Local Min 00–09; rtd 10; P-in-c Mill End and Heronsgate w W Hyde *St Alb* 10–11; Asst Dir of Ords from 11. *9 Westmead, Princes Risborough HP27 9HP* T: (01844) 347178 E: randvbrown44@btinternet.com

BROWN, Mrs Jacqueline Kay. b 43. Saffron Walden Coll CertEd 65. d 08 p 09. OLM Newton Longville, Mursley, Swanbourne etc *Ox* from 08. *5 Berry Way, Newton Longville, Milton Keynes MK17 0AS* T: (01908) 270159 E: jackie.br@tiscali.co.uk

BROWN, James Christie. b 86. Van Mildert Coll Dur BSc 07 Peterho Cam BA 14. Ridley Hall Cam 12. d 17 p 18. C Harpenden St Jo *St Alb* 17–20; C Harpenden St Nic from 20. *10 Cross Way, Harpenden AL5 4RA* M: 07813-464643

BROWN, James Douglas. b 52. S'wark Ord Course 93. d 96 p 97. NSM Shooters Hill Ch Ch *S'wark* 96–01; P-in-c E Malling *Roch* 02–07; P-in-c Wateringbury and Teston 02–07; V E Malling, Wateringbury and Teston 07–15; RD Malling 07–14; rtd 15; PtO *Roch* from 16. *Summer Cottage, Teston Road, Offham, West Malling ME19 5NS* M: 07957-906297 E: jamesbrown.brown21@gmail.com

BROWN, Mrs Jane Catherine Deborah. b 65. York Univ BA 89. Cranmer Hall Dur 13. d 15 p 16. C Bramham *York* 15–18; R Garforth *Leeds* from 18. *The Rectory, Croft Foulds Court, Garforth, Leeds LS25 1NQ* T: 0113-286 3737 M: 07535-067056 E: janebrown160@live.com *or* jane.brown@leeds.anglican.org

BROWN, Jane Madeline. *See* SHARP, Jane Madeline

BROWN, Mrs Janice Elizabeth. b 65. Univ of Wales (Ban) BTh 04. d 04 p 05. C Botwnnog w Bryncroes w Llangwnnadl w Penllech *Ban* 04–05; C Llyn and Eifionydd 05–07; P-in-c Denio w Abererch 07–09; V 09–12; V Dwylan 12–20; P-in-c Aled Miss Area from 20. *The Rectory, 2 Rhodfa Wen, Llysfaen, Colwyn Bay LL29 8LE* T: (01492) 339781 M: 07969-655497

BROWN, Mrs Jean Louise. b 49. WEMTC 05. d 08 p 09. NSM Lechlade *Glouc* 08; NSM S Cotswolds 09–17; TV 11–17; Chapl Gt Western Hosps NHS Foundn Trust 16–17; rtd 17; PtO *Glouc* from 18. *5 Manor Gardens, Lechlade GL7 3EQ* T: (01367) 250361

BROWN, Mrs Jennifer Elizabeth. b 70. Geo Mason Univ Virginia BSc 91 Heythrop Coll Lon MA 09. SAOMC 02. d 05 p 06. C Ox St Clem 05–08; Chapl Jes Coll Ox 09; LtO *Ox* 09–16; NSM Kidlington w Hampton Poyle 12–14; NSM The Churn 14–19; NSM Abingdon from 19; Tutor Ripon Coll Cuddesdon from 10; Dir Tr Coll of Preachers from 19. *St John's Cottage, 45 Little Wittenham Road, Long Wittenham, Abingdon OX14 4QT* T: (01865) 407167 *or* 877455 E: jen.brown@rcc.ac.uk *or* training@collegeofpreachers.co.uk

BROWN, Ms Jodie Natasha. b 94. LSE BSc 15. Qu Foundn Birm MA 20. d 20 p 21. C Hall Green St Pet *Birm* from 20; C Hall Green St Mich from 20. *4 Etwall Road, Birmingham B28 0LE* E: jodie@stpetershg.onmicrosoft.com

BROWN, Canon John Bruce. b 42. Nottm Univ BA 64 MA 68. Cuddesdon Coll 64. d 66 p 67. C Warwick St Nic *Cov* 66–71; C Bp's Hatfield *St Alb* 71–78; V Watford St Mich 78–08; RD Watford 94–99; Hon Can St Alb 02–08; rtd 08; PtO *St Alb* 08–18; *Ox* from 09. *Broomfield Cottage, Poffley End, Hailey, Witney OX29 9US* T: (01993) 703029 E: patandjohnb@yahoo.co.uk

BROWN, Canon John Duncan. b 43. St Pet Coll Ox BA 64 BA 66 MA 68 Lon Univ BSc. Wycliffe Hall Ox 65. d 67 p 68. C Kingston upon Hull H Trin *York* 67–69; C St Leonards St Leon *Chich* 69–72; Hon C Norbiton *S'wark* 72–75; C Kirkcaldy *St And* 75–78; Prec and Chapl Chelmsf Cathl 78–86; P-in-c Kelvedon Hatch 86–92; P-in-c Navestock 86–92; P-in-c Fryerning w Margaretting 92–99; P-in-c Mountnessing 92–99; Bp's ACORA Officer 92–99; Hon Can Chelmsf Cathl 93–03; rtd 99; PtO *Chelmsf* from 09. *556 Galleywood Road, Chelmsford CM2 8BX* T: (01245) 358185 E: canonjbrown@mac.com

BROWN, Jonathan. b 60. Univ Coll Dur BA 83 MA 85 Ex Univ CertEd 86. Ripon Coll Cuddesdon 86 Ch Div Sch of the Pacific (USA) 88. d 89 p 90. C Esher *Guildf* 89–97; TV Crawley *Chich* 97–04; Chapl St Cath Hospice Crawley 97–04; V Earlsfield St Andr *S'wark* from 04. *22 St Andrew's Court, Waynflete Street, London SW18 3QF* T: (020) 8946 4214

BROWN, Jonathan. QUB BA 01 MTh 09 TCD MTh 19. d 18. Dromore Cathl *D & D* 18–19; C Hillsborough from 19. *54 Bishopshill, Dromore BT25 1FL* M: 07307-859336 E: revdjonathanbrown@gmail.com

BROWN, Prof Judith Margaret. b 44. Girton Coll Cam MA 69 PhD 68 Natal Univ Hon DSocSc 01. Ripon Coll Cuddesdon 09. d 09 p 10. NSM Osney *Ox* 09–10; Past Assoc to Chapl Ball Coll Ox from 09; Chapl BNC Ox 17; PtO *Ox* from 14. *97 Victoria Road, Oxford OX2 7QG* T: (01865) 514486 E: judith.brown@history.ox.ac.uk

BROWN, Mrs Kathleen Margaret. b 40. MBE 07. QUB BD BTh. d 88 p 90. C Carrickfergus *Conn* 88–92; 1 Belfast St Paul w St Barn 92–07; Can Belf Cathl 00–07; rtd 07. *3 The Avenue, Carrickfergus BT38 8LT* T: (028) 9336 6787 E: kbrown117@btinternet.com

BROWN, Mrs Kathleen Mary. b 49. Goldsmiths' Coll Lon BA 70 PGTC 71. York Sch of Min 16 St Hild Coll 20. d 21. NSM Cowesby *York* from 21; NSM Felixkirk w Boltby from 21; NSM Kirkby Knowle from 21; NSM Leake w Over and Nether Silton and Kepwick from 21; NSM Osmotherley w Harlsey and Ingleby Arncliffe from 21. *19 The Green, Kirklevington, Yarm TS15 9NW* T: (01642) 784918 M: 07554-288251 E: katebrown6@sky.com

BROWN, Keith Michael. b 42. d 07 p 08. OLM Earlham *Nor* 07–12; rtd 12; PtO *Nor* from 12. *115 Colman Road, Norwich NR4 7HF* T: (01603) 464707 E: keith.brown93@ntlworld.com

BROWN, Kenneth Roger. b 48. St Chad's Coll Dur BA 69. Liturg Inst Trier 72. d 73 p 74. C Patchway *Bris* 73–77; C Fishponds St Jo 77–79; Chapl RAF 79–95; Chapl HM Pris Pentonville 95–96; Chapl HM Pris Wellingborough 96–98; PtO *B & W* 99–00; P-in-c Crook Peak 00–11; R 11–14; rtd 14; PtO *B & W* from 16. *21 Crossmoor Road, Axbridge BS26 2DY* E: ken958@outlook.com

BROWN, Kim. b 68. Lanc Univ BA 89 Bradf Univ MSc 90. Ripon Coll Cuddesdon MA 15. d 15 p 16. C Tetbury, Beverston, Long Newnton etc *Glouc* 15–18; Pioneer Min 18–19; Public Preacher 19–20; Co-ord Min Experience Scheme 19–20; TV S Cotswolds *Glouc* from 20. *The Parsonage, High Street, Kempsford, Fairford GL7 4ET* T: (01285) 810954 E: revkimbrown10a@gmail.com

BROWN, Lloyd John. b 95. Trevelyan Coll Dur BA 17. Cranmer Hall Dur 19. d 21. C Darlington St Hilda and St Columba *Dur* from 21; C Darlington St Jo from 21. *30 Smithfield Road, Darlington DL1 4DD* M: 07840-811737 E: fr.lloydbrown@gmail.com

BROWN, Canon Malcolm Arthur. b 54. Oriel Coll Ox BA 76 MA 82 Man Univ PhD 00. Westcott Ho Cam 77. d 79 p 80. C Riverhead w Dunton Green *Roch* 79–83; TV Southampton (City Cen) *Win* 83–91; Assoc Dir Wm Temple Foundn 91–93; Exec Sec 93–00; Hon C Heaton Moor *Man* 95–00; Prin EAMTC *Ely* 00–05; Prin ERMC 05–07; Dir Miss and Public Affairs Abps' Coun from 07; Hon Can Ely Cathl from 14; Hon Can Man Cathl from 15. *Church House, 27 Great Smith Street, London SW1P 3AZ* T: (020) 7898 1000 E: malcolm.brown@churchofengland.org

BROWN, Canon Mandy Kathleen. b 57. SEITE. d 10 p 11. C Bishop's Hatfield, Lemsford and N Mymms *St Alb* 10–13; V Bishop's Stortford 13–21; RD 17–21; Hon Can St Alb 19–21; rtd 21. *14 Chancery Court, Downs Avenue, Dartford DA1 1SX* M: 07772-121277

BROWN (née PATTERSON), Preb Marjorie Jean. b 54. Wooster Coll USA BA 76 K Coll Lon MA 04. S Dios Minl Tr Scheme 92. d 95 p 96. C Poplar *Lon* 95–99; P-in-c Stamford Hill St Thos 99–02; V 02–09; P-in-c Upper Clapton St Matt 06–08; Dean of Women's Min Stepney Area 02–07; V Primrose Hill St Mary w Avenue Road St Paul from 09; Asst Dir of Ords Edmonton Area 14–16; Dir Ords 16–21; Preb St Paul's Cathl from 17. *St Mary's Vicarage, 44 King Henry's Road, London NW3 3RP* T: (020) 7722 3062 E: vicar@smvph.org.uk

BROWN, Canon Mark Edward. b 61. Southn Univ BSc 83 Cam Univ PGCE 84 Brunel Univ MTh 98. Trin Coll Bris BA 88. d 88 p 89. C Egham *Guildf* 88–92; C Northwood Em *Lon* 92–96; Assoc V 96–02; Bp's Officer for Evang 96–02; Can Missr *S'well* 02–07; Hon Can S'well Minster 02–07; P-in-c Tonbridge SS Pet and Paul *Roch* 07–10; V 10–21; AD Tonbridge 10–18; Hon Can Roch Cathl 16–21; P-in-c Ecclesall *Sheff* from 21; AD from 21. *All Saints' Vicarage, Ringinglow Road, Sheffield S11 7PQ* T: 0114-236 0084 E: mark.brown@allsaintsecclesall.org.uk

BROWN, Michael Brian. b 56. Trin Coll Bris BA 97 Coll of Resurr Mirfield 98. **d** 99 **p** 00. C Trowbridge St Jas *Sarum* 99–02; C Bruton and Distr *B & W* 02–09; C Bickleigh and Shaugh Prior *Ex* 09–12; Chapl Plymouth Hosps NHS Trust 09–12; P-in-c St John w Millbrook *Truro* 12–18; P-in-c Maker w Rame 12–18; R Rame Peninsula 18–19; R Maker w Rame, Millbrook, St John and Torpoint from 19; C Torpoint 12–15. *The Vicarage, Newport Street, Millbrook, Torpoint PL10 1BW* T: (01752) 822264 E: fr.michaelbrown1662@gmail.com

BROWN, Murray. *See* BROWN, Phillip Murray

BROWN, Nerys Ann. b 62. Univ of Wales (Abth) BA 83 PhD 87. TISEC 06. **d** 15 **p** 16. C Perth St Jo *St And* 15–18; R Dunblane from 18. *St Mary's Rectory, Smithy Loan, Dunblane FK15 0HQ* T: (01786) 824225 E: rector@stmarysdunblane.org

BROWN, Canon Nicholas James Watson. b 76. R Holloway Coll Lon BMus 98 Dur Univ MA 17 FTCL 08 Lon Inst of Educn PGCE 99. Ripon Coll Cuddesdon BTh 11. **d** 09 **p** 10. C Warminster St Denys and Upton Scudamore *Sarum* 09–13; P-in-c Louth *Linc* 13; TR 13–20; RD Louthesk 17–20; Can Res and Prec Linc Cathl from 20. *2 Pottergate, Lincoln LN2 1PH* M: 07901-852198

BROWN, Nina. *See* BROWN, Harriet Nina

BROWN, Canon Norman Charles Harry. b 27. Univ of Wales BSc 46. St Mich Coll Llan 48. **d** 50 **p** 51. C Canton St Jo Llan 50–57; C Llanishen and Lisvane 58–63; V Miskin 63–97; RD Aberdare 82–97; Can Llan Cathl 86–97; rtd 97; PtO *Llan* from 04. *33 Bron y Deri, Mountain Ash CF45 4LL* T: (01443) 476631 E: normanbrown234@btinternet.com

BROWN, Canon Norman John. b 34. Thames Poly MA 90. Ripon Hall Ox 72. **d** 74 **p** 75. C High Wycombe *Ox* 74–78; V Tilehurst St Cath 78–82; V Boyne Hill 82–04; Chapl Windsor and Maidenhead Coll 87–89; Hon Can Ch Ch *Ox* 03–04; rtd 04; PtO *Ox* 04–18. *Bosbury, 1 St James Close, Pangbourne, Reading RG8 7AP* T: 0118-984 5823 E: revbrown@waitrose.com

BROWN, Patricia Valerie. b 37. CertEd 58. STETS BTh 95. **d** 98 **p** 99. NSM Tadley St Pet *Win* 98–02; NSM Tadley S and Silchester 02–07; rtd 07; PtO *Win* 10–16 and from 17. *58 Bowmonts Road, Tadley, Basingstoke RG26 3SB* T: 0118-981 4860 E: pvbrown@tinyonline.co.uk

BROWN, Paul. *See* BROWN, Anthony Paul

BROWN, Paul David Christopher. b 50. Lon Univ LLB 71. EMMTC 81. **d** 84 **p** 85. NSM Wollaton *S'well* 84–13; PtO *Chelmsf* 13–14; NSM Thaxted 14–17; P-in-c 14–15; NSM Thaxted, The Sampfords, Radwinter and Hempstead *Chelmsf* 17–20; rtd 20; PtO *Chelmsf* from 20. *6 Bellrope Meadow, Sampford Road, Thaxted, Dunmow CM6 2FE* T: (01371) 831515 M: 07734-605921 E: pdchrisbrown@yahoo.co.uk

BROWN, Canon Penelope Jane. b 57. St Steph Ho Ox 94. **d** 96 **p** 97. C Croydon St Jo *S'wark* 96–99; V Croydon St Matt 99–09; AD Croydon Cen 07–09; P-in-c Limpsfield and Titsey 09–10; TR Limpsfield and Tatsfield 10–12; Hon Can S'wark Cathl 08–12; PtO 12–15; *St E* 12–13; Hon C Woodbridge St Mary 13–14; PtO 14–16; Hon C Melton and Ufford 16–20; PtO 20–21. *Vale House, 71 Ipswich Road, Woodbridge IP12 4BT* T: (01394) 388472 M: 07710-883787 E: canpennyb@btinternet.com

BROWN, Canon Peter. b 47. RMN 69. Kelham Th Coll 69. **d** 74 **p** 75. CMP from 75; C Hendon *Dur* 74–80; C Byker St Ant *Newc* 80–90; C Brandon and Ushaw Moor *Dur* 90–05; V 05–12; Hon Can Dur Cathl 01–12; rtd 12; PtO *Dur* from 12. *29 Willow Green, Sunderland SR2 7NL* T: 0191-903 1863 M: 07719-545522 E: 47peterbrown@gmail.com

BROWN, Peter. b 38. Leeds Univ BSc 62 ThD 65. Nashotah Ho 85. **d** 87 **p** 88. R Minneapolis St Andr USA 87–89; C Sprowston w Beeston *Nor* 89–92; P-in-c W Winch w Setchey and N Runcton 92–98; P-in-c Middleton w E Winch 96–98; P-in-c Nor St Andr and Nor St Geo Colegate 98–99; Chapl Norfolk and Nor Health Care NHS Trust 98–99; rtd 00; PtO *Leic* 00–12. *41 Main Street, Cosby, Leicester LE9 1UW* T: 0116-286 6184 E: peter@pbrownrev.plus.com

BROWN, Peter Russell. b 43. Oak Hill Th Coll. **d** 71 **p** 72. C Gt Faringdon w Lt Coxwell *Ox* 71–73; C Reading Greyfriars 73–74; V Forty Hill Jes Ch *Lon* 74–81; V Laleham 81–09; rtd 09; PtO *Cant* from 10. *42A Tothill Street, Minster, Ramsgate CT12 4AJ* T: (01843) 822294 E: revprb43@gmail.com

BROWN, Philip Anthony. b 54. Oak Hill Th Coll BA 91. **d** 91 **p** 92. C Rock Ferry *Ches* 91–95; V Hattersley 95–98; V Harold Hill St Geo *Chelmsf* 98–09; V Chartham *Cant* 09–14; P-in-c Stone Street Gp 11–14; V Chartham and Upper Hardres w Stelling 14–20; Asst Dir of Ords 09–20; rtd 20; PtO *Cant* from 20. *Address temp unknown* E: filbrown@ymail.com

BROWN, Phillip John. b 75. Univ of Wales (Lamp) BTh 10 Nottm Univ MA 14 PhD 20. WEMTC 05. **d** 08 **p** 09. C Heref

S Wye 08–13; TV 13–18; P-in-c Burghill 18–20; P-in-c Pipe-cum-Lyde and Moreton-on-Lugg 18–20; P-in-c Stretton Sugwas 18–20; R Burghill Gp from 20. *The Vicarage, Burghill, Hereford HR4 7SG* E: burghillchurch@gmail.com *or* revpjbrown.777@gmail.com

BROWN, Phillip Murray. b 59. Keele Univ BSc 80. Trin Coll Bris. **d** 87 **p** 88. C Greasbrough *Sheff* 87–91; Ind Chapl 87–93; V Thorne 91–99; V Norton Lees St Paul from 99; C Norton from 17; C Greenhill from 17; C Woodseats St Chad from 17. *St Paul's Vicarage, 6 Angerford Avenue, Sheffield S8 9BG* T: 0114-255 1945 E: murray.stpauls@btinternet.com

BROWN, Raymond John. b 49. Ox Univ BEd 71. Wycliffe Hall Ox 72. **d** 75 **p** 76. C Barking St Marg w St Patr *Chelmsf* 75–78; C Walton H Trin *Ox* 78–82; V Enfield St Mich *Lon* 82–91; Chapl St Mich Hosp Enfield 82–91; R Springfield All SS *Chelmsf* 91–14; rtd 14; PtO *York* 15–20; *Cov* from 19. *18 Sidney Road, Rugby CV22 5LB* E: raymondjohnbrown@talktalk.net

BROWN, Richard Alexander Hamilton. b 74. **d** 13 **p** 14. NSM N Thornaby *York* 13–14; NSM Middlesbrough Ascension 14–17; NSM Grangetown 17–18; P-in-c Marsh Farm *St Alb* from 18. *Holy Cross Vicarage, Buckle Close, Luton LU3 3RT* T: (01582) 257647 M: 07867-494688 E: fr.richard.brown@gmail.com

BROWN, Robert. b 47. Man Univ BSc 72 Open Univ BA 86 Dur Univ MA 87. NEOC 95. **d** 98 **p** 99. C Yarm *York* 98–01; V Ormesby 01–12; rtd 12. *The Old School House, 7 High Street, Bishopton, Stockton-on-Tees TS21 1EZ* E: robert.cuthbert@gmail.com

BROWN, Robert Peter Cameron. b 63. K Coll Lon BSc 84 Imp Coll Lon MSc 87 Lon Bible Coll BA 97 Dur Univ PhD 13. Cranmer Hall Dur 01. **d** 03 **p** 04. C Upper Weardale *Dur* 03–08; PtO *Carl* 09–13; NSM Bewcastle, Stapleton and Kirklinton etc 13–18; P-in-c from 18. *Greenholme, Bewcastle, Carlisle CA6 6PW* T: (016977) 48438 E: rob@bewcastlehouseofprayer.org.uk

BROWN, Robin. b 38. Leeds Univ BA 60 MPhil 69. Qu Coll Birm 89. **d** 91 **p** 92. C Far Headingley St Chad *Ripon* 91–94; V Hawksworth Wood 94–00; rtd 00; PtO *Ripon* 00–14; *Leeds* from 14. *Dale Edge, 2A Harbour View, Bedale DL8 2DQ* T/F: (01677) 425483 M: 07960-277495 E: robin.stel1@btinternet.com

BROWN, Robin. *See* BROWN, Jack Robin

BROWN, Capt Roger George. b 37. CQSW. CA Tr Coll SEITE 92. **d** 95 **p** 96. C Maidstone St Martin *Cant* 95–97; C Oakham, Hambleton, Egleton, Braunston and Brooke Pet 97–04; rtd 04; Asst Chapl Kettering Gen Hosp NHS Foundn Trust 04–12; Chapl 12–20; PtO Pet from 21. *5 Valley Walk, Kettering NN16 0LY* T: (01536) 524954

BROWN, Canon Roger Lee. b 42. Univ of Wales (Lamp) BA 63 Univ Coll Lon MA 73 Univ of Wales (Ban) DLitt 08 FSA 01. Wycliffe Hall Ox 66. **d** 68 **p** 69. C Dinas and Penygraig w Williamstown *Llan* 68–70; C Bargoed and Deri w Brithdir 70–72; TV Glyncorrwg w Afan Vale and Cymmer Afan 72–74; R 74–79; V Tongwynlais 79–93; R Welshpool w Castle Caereinion *St As* 93–07; AD Pool 01–07; Can Cursal St As Cathl 02–07; rtd 07. *St As* from 09. *14 Berriew Road, Welshpool SY21 7SS* T: (01938) 552161

BROWN, Canon Rosalind. b 53. Lon Univ BA 74. Yale Div Sch MDiv 97. **d** 97 **p** 97. V Canonsburg St Thos USA 97–99; Vice-Prin OLM Scheme *Sarum* 99–05; Tutor STETS 99–05; Can Res Dur Cathl 05–18; rtd 18; PtO *Dur* from 19. *Birdsong, Hillcrest, Durham DH1 1RB* T: 0191-384 9200 E: rosalindbrown.durham@googlemail.com

BROWN, Preb Rosémia. b 53. Ripon Coll Cuddesdon 97. **d** 99 **p** 00. C Shoreditch St Leon and Hoxton St Jo *Lon* 99–00; C Shoreditch St Leon w St Mich 00–02; TV Hackney 02–03; V Clapton St Jas from 03; AD Hackney 15–20; Preb St Paul's Cathl from 13. *St James's Vicarage, 105 Mayola Road, London E5 0RG* T: (020) 7686 3861 *or* 8985 1750 M: 07896-964693 E: office@stjamesclapton.co.uk *or* rosemia.brown@sky.com

BROWN, Sandra Ann. b 51. **d** 04 **p** 05. NSM Linc St Geo Swallowbeck 04–14; PtO from 16. *10 Station Road, North Hykeham, Lincoln LN6 9AQ* T: (01522) 870065 E: sandra.brown77@ntlworld.com

BROWN, The Very Revd Sarah Romilly Denner. b 65. Nottm Univ BA 86. ERMC 05. **d** 08 **p** 09. NSM Welford w Sibbertoft and Marston Trussell *Pet* 08–11; TV Daventry, Ashby St Ledgers, Braunston etc 11–16; TV Daventry 16–18; RD 13–18; Can Pet Cathl 15–18; Can Res Pet Cathl 18–21; Adv in Women's Min 18–21; Dean Heref from 21. *The Deanery, Cathedral Close, Hereford HR1 2NG* T: (01432) 374203 E: dean@herefordcathedral.org

BROWN, Sharon Lesley. b 63. Leeds Univ BA 86 Sheff Univ BA 14 MA 17 Bretton Hall Coll PGCE 88. Yorks Min Course 11. **d** 14 **p** 15. C Abbeylands *Leeds* 14–18;

P-in-c Brotherton from 18; P-in-c Ferrybridge from 18. *St Andrew's Vicarage, 5 Pontefract Road, Ferrybridge, Knottingley WF11 8PN* M: 07951-708937 E: sharondrums@sky.com *or* sharon.brown@leeds.anglican.org

BROWN, Canon Simon Nicolas Danton. b 37. Clare Coll Cam BA 61 MA 65. S'wark Ord Course 61 Linc Th Coll 63. d 64 p 65. C Lambeth St Mary the Less *S'wark* 64–66; Chapl and Warden LMH Settlement 66–72; P-in-c Southampton St Mary w H Trin *Win* 72–73; TV Southampton (City Cen) 73–79; R Gt Brickhill w Bow Brickhill and Lt Brickhill *Ox* 79–84; TR Burnham w Dropmore, Hitcham and Taplow 84–04; RD Burnham and Slough 87–02; Hon Can Ch Ch 94–04; Dioc Consultant for Deanery Development 97–04; Sen Exec Asst to Bp Buckingham 02–04; rtd 04; PtO *St E* 04–21. *Seagulls, Pin Mill Road, Chelmondiston, Ipswich IP9 1JN* T: (01473) 780051 E: sandrseagulls@btinternet.com

BROWN, Sonya Helen Joan. *See* WRATTEN, Sonya Helen Joan

BROWN, Stephen Charles. b 60. Leeds Univ BA 83 BA 89 Reading Univ PGCE 89. Coll of Resurr Mirfield 87. d 90 p 91. C Whitkirk *Ripon* 90–93; Asst Youth Chapl 92–95; C Chapel Allerton 93–95; R Stanningley St Thos 95–01; Chapl MU 98–01; V Laneside *Blackb* from 01; AD Accrington 20–21; Hon Chapl ATC 03–07. *St Peter's Vicarage, Helmshore Road, Haslingden, Rossendale BB4 4BG* T: (01706) 213838 E: stephenlaneside@gmail.com

BROWN, Stephen George. b 54. STETS 13. d 15 p 16. NSM Kilburn St Aug w St Jo *Lon* 15–17; NSM Hayes St Mary 17–19; P-in-c Edmonton St Alphege from 19; P-in-c Ponders End St Matt 19–21; PtO *Man* 15–19. *St Alphage Vicarage, Rossdale Drive, London N9 7LG* T: 07966-427213 *or* (020) 8374 8205 E: frstephenb@outlook.com

BROWN, Stephen James. b 44. Bradf Univ BSc 69. Westcott Ho Cam 71. d 72 p 73. C Seaton Hirst *Newc* 72–75; C Marton-in-Cleveland *York* 75–77; Dioc Youth Adv *Dur* 77–82; V Thorner *Ripon* 82–92; Dioc Officer for Local Min 90–01; P-in-c Ripley w Burnt Yates 92–09; Chapl Yorkshire TV 89–09; rtd 09; PtO *York* from 10. *88 Prince Rupert Drive, Tockwith, York YO26 7QS* T: (01423) 359142 M: 07521-705350 E: stephenbrown83@hotmail.co.uk

BROWN, Susan Gertrude. b 48. Univ of Wales (Swansea) BA 71 Roehampton Inst PGCE 72. St Mich Coll Llan 98. d 02 p 03. NSM Gelligaer *Llan* 02–04; NSM Eglwysilan 04–07; LtO 07–08; NSM Caerphilly 08–13; Dioc Adv for NSM 10–13; rtd 14; PtO *Llan* from 14. *2 Caerleon Court, Caerphilly CF83 2UF* T: (029) 2140 3773 E: suebrown27_uk@yahoo.com

BROWN, Terence George Albert. b 49. SS Mark & Jo Univ Coll Plymouth BEd 75. ERMC 04. d 06 p 09. NSM Langdon Hills *Chelmsf* 06–09; NSM Gt Wakering w Foulness 09–13; NSM Barling w Lt Wakering 09–13; P-in-c Sandon 13–17; R from 17; P-in-c E Hanningfield from 17. *The Vicarage, St Augustine's Way, Chelmsford CM1 6GX* T: (01245) 698988 M: 07944-444675 E: tgabrown@hotmail.com

BROWN, Terry Frederick. b 51. d 16 p 17. OLM Canvey Is *Chelmsf* from 16. *59 Lionel Road, Canvey Island SS8 9DJ* E: terry.f.brown@blueyonder.co.uk

BROWN, Thomas Andrew. b 86. Essex Univ BA 08. Oak Hill Th Coll BA 18. d 18 p 19. C Kilnhurst *Sheff* 18–21; P-in-c Barnby Dun, Kirk Sandall and Edenthorpe from 21. *The Rectory, 31 Doncaster Road, Kirk Sandall, Doncaster DN3 1HP* M: 07825-913286 E: tom.brown371@gmail.com

BROWN, Thomas Edward. b 86. Clare Coll Cam MSci 09. Oak Hill Th Coll 15. d 18 p 19. C Lutterworth w Cotesbach and Bitteswell *Leic* from 18. *The Vicarage, Lutterworth Road, Bitteswell, Lutterworth LE17 4RX* M: 07818-404287 E: tebrown39@gmail.com

✠BROWN, The Rt Revd Thomas John. b 43. San Francisco Th Sem DMin 84. St Jo Coll Auckland. d 72 p 73 c 91. C Christchurch St Alb NZ 72–74; C Leic St Jas 74–76; V Upper Clutha NZ 76–79; V Roslyn 79–85; V Lower Hutt St Jas 85–91; Adn Belmont 87–91; Asst Bp Wellington 91–97; Bp Wellington 97–12; rtd 12. *38 Saddleback Grove, Karori, Wellington 6012, New Zealand* T: (0064) 21-444875 E: tommitre10@gmail.com

BROWN, Mrs Verity Joy. b 68. Qu Mary Coll Lon BA 89. Ripon Coll Cuddesdon BTh 93. d 93 p 94. C Barnard Castle w Whorlton *Dur* 93–95; C Bensham 95–97; PtO 97–10; NSM Hartlepool St Hilda 10–16; P-in-c from 16. *The Rectory, Church Close, Hartlepool TS24 0PW* T: (01429) 423186 M: 07846-064456 E: veritybrwn@gmail.com

BROWN, Mrs Veronica Mary. b 60. Rowan Univ (USA) BA 83 St Jos Univ (USA) MBA 94 Win Univ MA 14. STETS 09. d 12 p 13. C Newport St Thos *Portsm* 12–14; C Newport St Jo 12–14; C Whippingham w E Cowes 14–15; P-in-c Binstead 15–16; R 16–20; P-in-c Havenstreet St Pet 15–16; V 16–20; P-in-c Wootton 15–16; R 16–20; V Highcliffe *Win* from 20.

33 Nea Road, Christchurch BH23 4NB M: 07921-514906 E: vbrown.brownassociates@gmail.com

BROWN, Victor Charles. b 31. S'wark Ord Course 67. d 71 p 72. C Pinhoe *Ex* 71–73; C Egg Buckland 73–74; C Oakdale St Geo *Sarum* 74–77; R Old Trafford St Hilda *Man* 77–83; R Chigwell Row *Chelmsf* 83–92; R Fenny Bentley, Kniveton, Thorpe and Tissington *Derby* 92–96; rtd 96; PtO *Sarum* 96–08. *5 Gracey Court, Woodland Road, Broadclyst, Exeter EX5 3GA* T: (01392) 462799

BROWN, Wallace. b 44. Oak Hill Th Coll 77. d 79 p 80. C Oadby *Leic* 79–85; V Quinton Road W St Boniface *Birm* 85–03; Hon Can Birm Cathl 01–03; TR Ipsley *Worc* 03–09; rtd 09; PtO *Heref* from 09. *2 Coppice Close, Withington, Hereford HR1 3PP*

BROWN, Wendy Anne. *See* WALE, Wendy Anne

BROWNE, Arnold Samuel. b 52. St Jo Coll Ox BA 73 MA 77 SS Coll Cam PhD 87 Surrey Univ MSc 89 MBPsS 92. Westcott Ho Cam 76. d 78 p 79. C Esher *Guildf* 78–81; C Worplesdon 81–86; Chapl R Holloway and Bedf New Coll 86–92; Fell and Dean of Chpl Trin Coll Cam 92–06; PtO *Nor* from 06. *18 Riverside Road, Norwich NR1 1SN* T: (01603) 629362 E: arnoldbrowne@btinternet.com

BROWNE, Ian Cameron. b 51. St Cath Coll Ox BA 74 MA 78 Fitzw Coll Cam BA 76 MA 80. Ridley Hall Cam 74. d 77 p 78. C Cheltenham Ch Ch *Glouc* 77–80; Hon C Shrewsbury St Chad *Lich* 80–83; Asst Chapl Shrewsbury Sch 80–83; Chapl Bedford Sch 83–96; Sen Chapl Oundle Sch 97–11; rtd 11; PtO *Pet* from 12; *Ely* from 19. *46C North Street, Oundle, Peterborough PE8 4AL* T: (01832) 273541 E: the.revb@virgin.net

BROWNE, Leonard Joseph. b 58. St Cath Coll Cam BA 81 MA 84. Trin Coll Bris 87. d 89 p 90. C Reading Greyfriars *Ox* 89–92; V Cambridge St Barn *Ely* 92–00; Sen Chapl Dean Close Sch 00–04; Hd Master Dean Close Prep Sch 04–14; Asst Chapl Dean Close Sch 14–16; V Harborne Heath *Birm* from 16. *99 Wentworth Road, Birmingham B17 9ST* T: 0121-427 4601 M: 07584-680910 E: leonardbrowne@stjohns-church.co.uk

BROWNE, Peter Clifford. b 59. Bris Univ BA 80 SRN 82. Ripon Coll Cuddesdon 88. d 90 p 91. C Southgate Ch Ch *Lon* 90–92; NSM Kemp Town St Mary *Chich* 93–95; Chapl United Bris Healthcare NHS Trust 96–98; NSM Southmead *Bris* 98–02; Chapl HM Pris Preston 02–10; Chapl HM Pris Shepton Mallet 10–13; Chapl HM Pris and YOI Guys Marsh from 13. *HM Prison Guys Marsh, Shaftesbury SP7 0AH* T: (01747) 856400 E: peter.browne@justice.gov.uk

BROWNE, Miss Tracy Bindi. b 67. St Mellitus Coll 15 Qu Coll Birm 17. d 20 p 21. C Is of Dogs Ch Ch and St Jo w St Luke *Lon* from 20. *St Mildred's House, Roserton Street, London E14 3PG* M: 07956-827293 E: tracybrowne3@yahoo.co.uk

BROWNHILL, Mrs Diane. b 56. Dioc OLM tr scheme 03. d 06 p 07. C Man Apostles w Miles Platting 06–09; TV Heatons from 09. *St Thomas' Rectory, 6 Heaton Moor Road, Stockport SK4 4NS* T: 0161-432 1912 M: 07505-781530 E: gldbrownhill@aol.com

BROWNING, Derek. *See* BROWNING, Robert Derek

BROWNING, Edward Barrington Lee (Barry). b 42. St Pet Coll Saltley TCert 65. Ripon Coll Cuddesdon 90. d 92 p 93. C Falmouth K Chas *Truro* 92–96; R Roche and Withiel 96–01; P-in-c Manaccan w St Anthony-in-Meneage and St Martin 01–06; P-in-c Cury and Gunwalloe w Mawgan 01–06; rtd 06; PtO *Truro* 06–10; P-in-c St Goran w Caerhays 10–13; PtO from 14. *73 Park Way, St Austell PL25 4HR* T: (01726) 65194 E: barry.browning@btinternet.com

✠BROWNING, The Rt Revd George Victor. b 42. Chas Sturt Univ NSW DLitt 07. St Jo Coll Morpeth ThL 66. d 66 p 67 c 85. C Inverell Australia 66–68; C Armidale 68–69; V Warialda 69–73; Vice Prin St Jo Coll Morpeth 73–76; R Singleton and Adn Upper Hunter 76–84; R Woy Woy and Adn Cen Coast 84–85; Asst Bp Brisbane 85–93; Prin St Fran Th Coll 88–91; Bp Canberra and Goulburn 93–08; Dir Aus Cen Christianity and Culture 96–08; P-in-c Wriggle Valley *Sarum* 08–09; rtd 09. *24 Henry Place, Long Beach NSW 2536, Australia* T: (0061) (2) 4472 7470 E: gandmbrowning@bigpond.com

BROWNING, Canon Jacqueline Ann. b 44. Sarum Th Coll 93. d 96 p 97. NSM New Alresford w Ovington and Itchen Stoke *Win* 96–02; Past Asst Win Cathl 02–12; Min Can Win Cathl 06–09; Hon Can Win Cathl 09–12; rtd 13; PtO *Win* 16–21. *1 Paddock Way, Alresford SO24 9PN* T: (01962) 734372 *or* 857237 E: alresfordjackie@gmail.com

BROWNING, Julian. b 51. St Jo Coll Cam BA 72 MA 76. Ripon Coll Cuddesdon 77. d 80 p 81. C Notting Hill *Lon* 80–81; C W Brompton St Mary w St Pet 81–84; PtO 84–91; NSM Paddington St Sav 99–06; NSM St Marylebone St Cypr 06–14; NSM St Marylebone All SS from 14. *82 Ashworth*

Mansions, Grantully Road, London W9 1LN T: (020) 7286 6034 E: julian.browning@yahoo.co.uk

BROWNING, Kevin John. b 56. Ridley Hall Cam 96. **d** 98 **p** 99. C Northampton Em *Pet* 98–01; P-in-c Hardwick *Ely* 01–09; C Cranham Park *Chelmsf* 10–18; V S Hornchurch St Jo and St Matt from 18. *St John's Vicarage, South End Road, Rainham RM13 7XT* T: (01708) 555260 E: rev.kevinbrowning@stjohnsparishchurch.org

BROWNING, Miss Rachel. b 69. Oak Hill Th Coll BA 08. **d** 09. NSM Hastings Em and St Mary in the Castle *Chich* from 09; PtO *Ely* from 15. *11A Emmanuel Road, Hastings TN34 3LB* T: (01424) 430980 M: 07939-126955 E: rach.browning@gmail.com *or* rach@emmanuelhastings.org.uk

BROWNING, Robert Derek. b 42. Guildf Dioc Min Course 98. **d** 01 **p** 02. OLM Lightwater *Guildf* 01–12; PtO from 12. *16 Guildford Road, Lightwater GU18 5SN* T: (01276) 474345 E: derekandcarol.b@tiscali.co.uk

BROWNING, Mrs Rosheen Elizabeth. b 76. Middx Univ BA 98 Cant Ch Ch Univ Coll PGCE 03. Ridley Hall Cam 13. **d** 15 **p** 16. C Paddock Wood *Roch* 15–19; P-in-c Camborne, Tuckingmill and Penponds *Truro* from 19; P-in-c Crowan and Treslothan from 19. *The Vicarage, 37 Trethannas Gardens, Praze, Camborne TR14 0LL* T: (01209) 831175 M: 07701-085736 E: rev.rosh@icloud.com *or* rev.rosh@cambornecluster.org.uk

BROWNLIE, Miss Caroline Heddon. b 47. CQSW 75. Qu Coll Birm IDC 81. **d** 87 **p** 94. Asst Chapl Fairfield Hosp Hitchin 87–91; NSM Ashwell w Hinxworth and Newnham *St Alb* 92–98; Chapl HM Rem Cen Low Newton 99–01; PtO *St Alb* 04–05; P-in-c Gilling and Kirkby Ravensworth *Ripon* 05–07; rtd 07; PtO *Ely* from 07. *13 Vicarage Close, Melbourn, Royston SG8 6DY* T: (01763) 263375 E: carolineatno9@john-lewis.com

BROWNSELL, Preb John Kenneth. b 48. Hertf Coll Ox BA 69 BA 72 MA 89. Cuddesdon Coll 70. **d** 73 **p** 74. C Notting Hill All SS w St Columb *Lon* 73–74; C Notting Hill 74–76; TV 76–82; V Notting Hill All SS w St Columb 82–18; AD Kensington 84–92; Dir of Ords 95–12; Preb St Paul's Cathl 92–18; rtd 18. *2 Morley College, Market Street, Winchester SO23 9LF* T: (01962) 867315 E: jkb194805@gmail.com

BROWNSMITH, Colin David. b 47. Cranfield Univ MBA 86 ACMA 78 FCMA 83. St Jo Coll Nottm 14. **d** 19 **p** 20. Enniskillen *Clogh* 19–20; OLM Lisbellaw from 20. *327 Lough Shore Road, Cosbystown, Enniskillen BT93 7ER* T: (028) 6864 1997 M: 07425-150828 E: colin.brownsmith@btinternet.com

BROXHAM, Ms Ann. b 47. York St Jo Coll BA 03. Westcott Ho Cam 10. **d** 10. NSM Littleport *Ely* 10–13; NSM Crosland Moor and Linthwaite *Leeds* 13–18; rtd 18. *45 Edale Avenue, Newsome, Huddersfield HD4 6LN* T: (01484) 420365 E: annbroxham@yahoo.co.uk

BRUCE, Adam. *See* BRUCE, Henry Adam Francis

BRUCE, Canon Amanda Jane. b 67. Liv Univ BSc 87 Southn Univ PGCE 89 Chelt & Glouc Coll of HE AdDipEd 01 Liv Hope Univ MA 19. Wycliffe Hall Ox 06. **d** 08 **p** 09. C Haydock St Mark *Liv* 08–12; TR Sutton 12–16; V Gt Crosby St Luke from 16; Dean of Women's Min from 18; Hon Can Liv Cathl from 19. *St Luke's Vicarage, 71 Liverpool Road, Crosby, Liverpool L23 5SE* T: 0151-932 9253 E: revamandabruce@gmail.com

BRUCE, David Crosby. b 72. SS Coll Cam MA 94 PGCE 95 Bris Univ MEd 05. Trin Coll Bris 10. **d** 12 **p** 13. C Meole Brace *Lich* 12–16; TR Malvern Chase *Worc* from 16. *48 Longridge Road, Malvern WR14 3JB* E: davecbruce@gmail.com *or* dave.bruce@chaseteam.org

BRUCE, The Hon Henry Adam Francis. b 62. Trin Coll Ox MA 89. **d** 17 **p** 18. NSM Llan-llwch w Llangain and Llangynog and Llansteffan etc *St D* 17–18; NSM Bro Sancler from 18. *St Davids Court, Llanboidy Road, Meidrim, Carmarthen SA33 5QF* T: (01994) 231470 M: 07976-829111 E: hafbruce@hotmail.com

BRUCE, James Hamilton. b 57. Dur Univ BSc 78 Newc Univ MSc 79 St Andr Univ PhD 99. Trin Coll Bris 81. **d** 84 **p** 85. C Walmley Birm 84–86; PtO *Carl* 87–95; W Cumbria Sch Worker N Schs Chr Union 87–93; Nat Development Officer Wales Scripture Union 93–94; Chapl Turi St Andr Kenya 95–96; NSM St Andrews St Andr *St And* 96–99; R Penicuik and W Linton *Edin* 99–03; PtO *Win* 03–06; V Lyndhurst and Emery Down and Minstead 06–17; P-in-c Cartmel Peninsula *Carl* 18–21. *Applebeck, Glebe Road, Bowness-on-Windermere, Windermere LA23 3HB* E: bruces@talktalk.net

BRUCE, John Cyril. b 41. EMMTC 95. **d** 98 **p** 99. NSM Spalding St Mary and St Nic *Linc* 98–05; P-in-c Grantham, Manthorpe 05–08; rtd 09; PtO *Linc* from 16. *5 Welwyn Close, Grantham NG31 7JU* T: (01476) 561546 M: 07947-156933 E: jcb.churchmail@gmail.com

BRUCE, Kathrine Sarah. b 68. Leeds Univ BA 89 St Jo Coll Dur BA 01 MATM 07 Dur Univ PhD 14 Trin & All SS Coll Leeds PGCE 91. Cranmer Hall Dur 98. **d** 01 **p** 02. C Ripon H Trin 01–04; Chapl Trevelyan Coll *Dur* 04–08; Chapl Van Mildert Coll 04–08; NSM Dur St Oswald 04–06; NSM Dur St Oswald and Shincliffe 06–08; Chapl St Jo Coll Dur 08–13; Dep Warden and Tutor 13–18; Chapl RAF from 18. *Chaplaincy Services (RAF), HQ Air Command, RAF High Wycombe HP14 4UE* T: (01494) 496800 E: katebruce971@gmail.com

BRUCE, Mrs Susan Elizabeth. b 52. **d** 08 **p** 09. OLM Haughton le Skerne *Dur* 08–14; NSM Middleton St George 14–16; rtd 16; PtO *Dur* from 16. *14 Haughton Green, Darlington DL1 2DF* T: (01325) 281567 M: 07810-720490 E: sue.bruce.014@gmail.com

BRUECK, Canon Jutta. b 61. LSE MSc 89 Heythrop Coll Lon MA 92 Fitzw Coll Cam BA 96 MA 00. Westcott Ho Cam 94. **d** 97 **p** 98. C Is of Dogs Ch Ch and St Jo w St Luke *Lon* 97–01; Chapl Guildhall Sch of Music and Drama 01–06; Chapl Fitzw Coll Cam 06–08; P-in-c Cambridge St Jas *Ely* 08–15; P-in-c Ipswich St Thos *St E* 15–21; Dean WITH Community from 21; PtO *St E* from 21; Hon Can St E Cathl from 20. *Lavinia House, Belsey Bridge Road, Ditchingham, Bungay NR35 2DZ* T: (01986) 892749 M: 07958-360564 E: jutta.brueck@cofesuffolk.org

BRUMFITT, Catherine. b 70. Qu Foundn (Course) 14. **d** 17 **p** 18. C Watershed *Lich* 17–20; R Bradeley, Church Eaton, Derrington and Haughton from 20. *The Rectory, Rectory Lane, Haughton, Stafford ST18 9HU* T: (01785) 780125 E: revcathbrumfitt@gmail.com

BRUMWELL, Suzanne. **d** 16 **p** 17. C Cowbridge *Llan* 16–19; V Llansantffraid, Bettws and Aberkenfig from 19. *13 Highland Court, Bryncethin, Bridgend CF32 9US* T: (01656) 728523 E: vicar.lbaparish@gmail.com

BRUNNER-ELLIS (formerly WHIFFIN), Vanessa Janet. b 68. Birm Univ BMus 89 ABSM 87. STETS 10. **d** 14 **p** 15. C Marshfield w Cold Ashton and Tormarton etc *Bris* 14–17; TV Witney *Ox* from 17. *Address withheld by request* E: ness@witneyparish.org.uk

BRUNNING, Canon David George. b 32. St D Coll Lamp BA 53. St Mich Coll Llan 53. **d** 55 **p** 56. C Llantwit Major and St Donat's *Llan* 55–59; C Usk and Monkswood w Glascoed Chpl and Gwehelog *Mon* 59–62; V Abercarn 62–71; V Pontnewydd 71–89; RD Pontypool 89–97; R Panteg 90–98; Can St Woolos Cathl from 94; rtd 98; LtO *Mon* from 98; PtO *Llan* from 98. *6 Spitzkop, Llantwit Major CF61 1RD* T: (01446) 792124

BRUNO, Canon Allan David. b 34. AKC 59. St Boniface Warminster 59. **d** 60 **p** 61. C Darlington H Trin *Dur* 60–64; C Kimberley Cathl and Chapl Bp's Hostel S Africa 64–65; Asst Chapl Peterhouse Dioc Boys' Sch Rhodesia 65–70; Overseas Chapl Scottish Episc Ch 70–75; C Edin Old St Paul 75–76; Dir of Miss Prov of S Africa 76–80; Namibia 80–86; Dean Windhoek 81–86; R Falkirk *Edin* 86–95; Hon Can Kinkizi from 95; Bp's Dom Chapl *Bradf* 96–99; Bp's Past Asst 99–01; rtd 01; PtO *Bradf* 01–14; *Leeds* from 14; *Blackb* 02–14; Bp's Officer for Rtd Clergy and Widows Craven Adnry *Bradf* 10–14; *Leeds* from 14. *Pond House, 5 Twine Walk, Burton in Lonsdale, Carnforth LA6 3LR* T: (015242) 61616 E: davidmaggiebruno@gmail.com

BRUNSKILL, Neil Peter. b 95. Liv Hope Univ BA 17 Sheff Univ BA 20. Coll of Resurr Mirfield 18. **d** 21. C Southport H Trin *Liv* from 21; C Southport St Luke from 21. *97 Station Road, Banks, Southport PR9 8AY* M: 07792-454868 E: nbrunskill@outlook.com

BRUNSWICK, Canon Robert John. b 38. TD 86. St Aid Birkenhead 60. **d** 63 **p** 64. C Neston *Ches* 63–66; CF (TA - R of O) 65–96; C Warrington St Paul *Liv* 66–68; V Liv St Paul Stoneycroft 68–78; V Southport St Luke 78–87; R Croston *Blackb* 87–01; R Croston and Bretherton 01–05; Chapl Bp Rawstorne Sch Preston 88–05; Hon Can Koforidua from 94; rtd 05. *60 St Clements Avenue, Farington, Leyland PR25 4QU* T: (01772) 426094

BRUNT, Alison. b 60. Nottm Univ BSc 82 K Coll Lon MA 01 ,SS Coll Cam BTh 12. Westcott Ho Cam 10. **d** 12 **p** 13. C S. Croydon St Pet and St Aug *S'wark* 12–15; V Norbury St Oswald from 15. *The Vicarage, 2B St Oswald's Road, London SW16 3SB* T: (020) 8764 2853 E: rev.alison@outlook.com

BRUNT, Prof Peter William. b 36. OBE 94 CVO 01. Liv Univ MB 59 MD 67 Lon Univ FRCP 74 FRCPEd. Ab Dioc Tr Course. **d** 96 **p** 97. NSM Bieldside *Ab* 96–07; PtO *Carl* from 08; *Ab* from 11. *81 Wansdyke, Morpeth NE61 3QY*

BRUNT, Canon Philippa Ann. b 53. Leeds Univ BA 74 Leeds and Carnegie Coll PGCE 75. WEMTC 95. **d** 98 **p** 99. C Cinderford St Steph w Littledean *Glouc* 98–01; V Parkend and Viney Hill 01–17; AD Forest S 09–15; Hon Can Glouc Cathl 10–17; rtd 17; PtO *Glouc* from 18. *4 Hill*

Crest, Highnam, Gloucester GL2 8LS T: (01452) 501966
E: pabrunt@btinternet.com
BRUSH, Canon Sally. b 47. Lon Univ BD 75 Univ of Wales
MPhil 96. Trin Coll Bris 73. **dss** 76 **d** 80 **p** 97. Flint *St As*
76–83; C 80–83; C Cefn 83–87; C St As and Tremeirchion
83–87; Chapl St As Cathl 83–87; Dn-in-c Cerrigydrudion w
Llanfihangel Glyn Myfyr etc 87–97; V 97–07; RD Edeirnion
98–04; Hon Can St As Cathl 01–07; rtd 07; PtO *St As* 09–19;
Ban 10–17. *Persondy, 1 Tyddyn Terrace, Cerrigydrudion, Corwen
LL21 9TN* T: (01490) 420048
BRUSH (née HAMILTON), Sarah Louise. b 74. Reading
Univ BA 97 MA 98 PhD 01. Qu Coll Birm MA 14. **d** 14
p 15. C Halas *Worc* 14–18; Lect Ripon Coll Cuddesdon
from 18. *3 Church Close, Cuddesdon, Oxford OX44 9HD*
E: sarahbrush@hotmail.co.uk or sarah.brush@rcc.ac.uk
BRYAN, Angela Edwina. b 82. York Univ BA 03 York St Jo Coll
PGCE 04. St Jo Coll Nottm 07. **d** 10 **p** 11. C Tipton St Matt
Lich 10–14; P-in-c Kirkholt *Man* 14–18; C Saddleworth 18–20;
V Blurton and Dresden *Lich* from 20. *The Vicarage, School
Lane, Stoke-on-Trent ST3 3DU* T: (01782) 942454 M: 07522-
316952 E: vicar@blurtonparish.com
BRYAN, Christopher. See BRYAN, Michael John Christopher
BRYAN, The Ven Christopher Paul. b 75. Univ Coll Ox BA 96
St Jo Coll Dur BA 99. Cranmer Hall Dur 97. **d** 00 **p** 01. C
Old Swinford Stourbridge *Worc* 00–04; P-in-c Lechlade *Glouc*
04–08; TV Fairford Deanery 09–10; Chapl Sherston Magna,
Easton Grey, Luckington etc *Bris* 10–16; P-in-c Hullavington,
Norton and Stanton St Quintin 10–16; R Gauzebrook 16–19;
AD N Wilts 17–19; Adn Malmesbury from 19. *Diocese of Bristol,
First floor, Unit 1500, Bristol Parkway North, Newbrick Road,
Stoke Gifford, Bristol BS34 8YU* T: 0117-906 0100 M: 07581-
447927 E: christopher.bryan@bristoldiocese.org
BRYAN, David John. b 56. Liv Univ BSc 77 Hull Univ BTh 85
Qu Coll Ox DPhil 89. Ox Min Course 89. **d** 90 **p** 91. C
Abingdon *Ox* 90–93; Tutor Qu Coll Birm 93–01; Dean
of Studies 95–01; R Haughton le Skerne *Dur* 01–11; Dir
Studies Lindisfarne Reg Tr Partnership 11–17; Dean 17–18;
Prin Lindisfarne Coll of Th from 18. *2 Kingfisher Close, Esh
Winning, Durham DH7 9AN* T: 0191-373 9698 *or* 270 4150
E: davidbryan@lindisfarnect.org
BRYAN, Mrs Helen Ann. b 68. ACIB 92. NTMTC BA 07. **d** 07
p 08. NSM Laindon w Dunton *Chelmsf* 07–13; P-in-c E and
W Horndon w Lt Warley and Childerditch 13–18; V 18–19;
TV Cheshunt *St Alb* from 19. *4 Haddestoke Gate, Cheshunt,
Waltham Cross EN8 0XJ* T: (01992) 479882 M: 07838-
377357 E: vicaratstclements@gmail.com
BRYAN, Judith Claire. See STEPHENSON, Judith Claire
BRYAN, Michael John Christopher. b 35. Wadh Coll Ox
BA 58 BTh 59 MA 63 Ex Univ PhD 83 Univ of the S Hon
DD 08. Ripon Hall Ox 59. **d** 60 **p** 61. C Reigate St Mark
S'wark 60–64; Tutor Sarum & Wells Th Coll 64–69; Vice-
Prin 69–71; Lect Virginia Th Sem USA 71–74; Sen Officer
Educn and Community Dept *Lon* 74–79; Chapl Ex Univ
79–83; Prof NT Univ of the S USA 83–08; rtd 08; Ed Sewanee
Theological Review 90–20; PtO *Ex* from 19. *Address withheld
by request* M: 07484-786074 E: cbryan@sewanee.edu
BRYAN, Patrick Joseph. b 41. St Jo Coll Cam BA 63 MA 67.
St Steph Ho Ox 73. **d** 75 **p** 76. C Rushall *Lich* 75–78; C Brierley
Hill 78–80; P-in-c Walsall St Mary and All SS Palfrey 80–87; PtO
13–21. *12 Derwent Road, Wolverhampton WV6 9ES* T: (01902)
689550 E: pjjmbryan@blueyonder.co.uk
BRYAN, Canon Sherry Lee. b 49. Open Univ BA 12.
WMMTC 88. **d** 91 **p** 94. Par Dn St Columb Minor and
St Colan *Truro* 91–94; C 94–95; P-in-c St Teath 95–05;
P-in-c Blisland w St Breward 05–15; P-in-c Helland 05–15;
R Blisland w Temple, St Breward and Helland 15–17;
P-in-c St Tudy w St Mabyn and Michaelstow 16–17; Adv for
Women's Min 92–99; Chapl Cornwall Fire Brigade 93–95;
Chapl Cornwall Healthcare NHS Trust 99–02; RD Trigg
Minor and Bodmin *Truro* 02–13; Hon Can Truro Cathl
03–17; rtd 17. *Address withheld by request*
BRYAN, Canon Timothy Andrew. b 56. St Edm Hall Ox
MA 80. S'wark Ord Course 93. **d** 96 **p** 97. NSM Morden
S'wark 96–99; NSM Carshalton Beeches 99–05; NSM Sutton
05–08; Resettlement Chapl HM Pris Wandsworth 07–08;
Co-ord Chapl 08–17; Chapl Adv HM Pris and Probation
Service (Midl, Yorks and NE) 17–20; rtd 20; Bp's Adv for
Pris Chapl *S'wark* from 20; Hon Can S'wark Cathl from 15;
PtO *Heref* from 17. *Sycamores, Carding Mill Valley, Church
Stretton SY6 6JF* T: (01694) 723192 M: 07974-366810
E: timbryan57@gmail.com
BRYAN, Canon Andrew Watts. b 57. St Jo Coll Dur BA 78
Birm Univ MA 81. Qu Coll Birm 80. **d** 83 **p** 84. C Pelsall *Lich*
83–87; NSM 91–94; PtO 87–92; NSM Streetly 94–96; NSM
Beckbury, Badger, Kemberton, Ryton, Stockton etc 96–99;
R Worplesdon *Guildf* 99–09; Chapl Merrist Wood Coll of

Agric and Horticulture 01–09; TR Portishead *B & W* 09–15;
Can Res Nor Cathl from 15; P-in-c Nor St Mary in the Marsh
15–16. *52 The Close, Norwich NR1 4EG* T: (01603) 218331
E: canon.missionandpastoral@cathedral.org.uk
BRYANT, Benjamin Mark. b 82. RCM BMus 05. St Mellitus
Coll BA 16. **d** 16 **p** 17. C Portsea St Alb *Portsm* 16–18; C
Onslow Square and S Kensington St Aug *Lon* from 18.
23 Pooles Lane, London SW10 0RH M: 07887-868445
E: ben.bryant@htb.org
BRYANT, Canon Christopher. b 32. K Coll Lon AKC 60. **d** 61
p 62. C Fareham H Trin *Portsm* 61–65; C Yatton Keynell
Bris 65–71; C Biddestone w Slaughterford 65–71; C Castle
Combe 65–71; V Chirton, Marden and Patney *Sarum* 71–76;
V Chirton, Marden, Patney, Charlton and Wilsford 76–78;
P-in-c Devizes St Jo w St Mary 78–79; R 79–97; RD Devizes
83–93; Can and Preb Sarum Cathl 87–04; rtd 97; Master
St Nic Hosp Salisbury 97–04; PtO *Sarum* from 06. *34 Mill
Road, Salisbury SP2 7RZ* T: (01722) 502336
BRYANT, Canon Edward Francis Paterson. b 43. S'wark Ord
Course 75. **d** 78 **p** 79. NSM Hadlow *Roch* 78–84; C Dartford
St Alb 84–87; R Hollington St Leon *Chich* 87–93; V Bexhill
St Aug 93–99; TR Bexhill St Pet 99–12; P-in-c Sedlescombe
w Whatlington 02–05; rtd 12; RD Battle and Bexhill *Chich*
98–04 and 10–13; Can and Preb Chich Cathl from 00. *14
Highwater View, St Leonards-on-Sea TN38 8EL* T: (01424)
853687 F: 07970-991268 M: 07824-859044
BRYANT, Graham Trevor. b 41. Keble Coll Ox BA 63 MA 67.
Chich Th Coll 64. **d** 66 **p** 67. C Leeds St Wilfrid *Ripon* 66–69;
C Haywards Heath St Wilfrid *Chich* 69–74; V Crawley Down
All SS 74–79; V Bexhill St Aug 79–85; V Charlton Kings
St Mary *Glouc* 85–02; rtd 02; PtO *Glouc* from 03. *6 The Close,
Cheltenham GL53 0PQ* T: (01242) 520313
⊞**BRYANT, The Rt Revd Mark Watts.** b 49. St Jo Coll Dur
BA 72. Cuddesdon Coll 72. **d** 75 **p** 76 **c** 07. C Addlestone
Guildf 75–79; C Studley *Sarum* 79–83; V 83–88; Chapl
Trowbridge Coll 79–83; Voc Development Adv and Dioc
Dir of Ords *Cov* 88–96; Hon Can Cov Cathl 93–01; TR
Coventry Caludon 96–01; AD Cov E 99–01; Adn Cov
01–07; Can Res Cov Cathl 06–07; Suff Bp Jarrow *Dur* 07–18;
rtd 18; PtO *Newc* from 18; Hon Asst Bp Newc from 19. *59
Eastfield Avenue, Whitley Bay NE25 8NQ* T: 0191-252 2429
E: markbryant@dunelm.org.uk
BRYANT, Patricia Ann. b 36. Qu Mary Coll Lon BA 58. St Mich
Coll Llan 94. **d** 91 **p** 97. NSM Llanbadoc *Mon* 91–93; NSM
Llangybi and Coedypaen w Llanbadoc *Mon*; C 94–98;
Asst Chapl Gwent Tertiary Coll 94–98; V Merthyr Cynog
and Dyffryn Honddu etc 98–02; rtd 03. *5 Trebarried
Court, Llandefalle, Brecon LD3 0NB* T: (01874) 754087
E: email@peterpatbryant.plus.com
BRYANT, Canon Richard Kirk. b 47. Ch Coll Cam BA 68
MA 72. Cuddesdon Coll 70. **d** 72 **p** 73. C Newc St Gabr
72–75; C Morpeth 75–78; C Benwell St Jas 78–82; V Earsdon
and Backworth 82–93; V Wylam 93–97; Prin Local Min
Scheme 97–11; Prin Reader Tr 97–11; Hon Can Newc Cathl
97–11; rtd 11; PtO *Newc* from 11. *60 Old Campus Close,
Newcastle upon Tyne NE7 7QB* E: rkbryant28@gmail.com
BRYANT, Richard Maurice. b 46. MAAIS 80. WMMTC 90.
d 93 **p** 94. NSM The Stanleys *Glouc* 93–98; NSM Glouc
St Geo w Whaddon 98–04; NSM Twigworth, Down
Hatherley, Norton, The Leigh etc 04–08; NSM Bisley,
Chalford, France Lynch, and Oakridge 08–11; rtd 11; PtO
Glouc from 11. *6 Church Street, Kings Stanley, Stonehouse
GL10 3HW* T: (01453) 823172
BRYANT, Sarah Elizabeth. See WOOD-ROE, Sarah Elizabeth
BRYANT-SCOTT, Canon David Bruce. b 62. Trin Coll Toronto
BA 84 MDiv 88 Harvard Div Sch ThM 03. **d** 88 **p** 89. C
Welland St Dav Canada 88–90; C St Catharine St Geo 90–95;
R Gulf Is Pender and Saturna 95–04; Dioc Adn BC 04–12;
R Victoria St Matthias 14–17; P-in-c Cobble Hill St Jo 17;
P-in-c Victoria St Dunstan 17–18; Asst Chapl Gtr Athens
Eur from 18. *Box 421, Gavalohori, Chania 73008, Crete,
Greece* T: (0030) (2825) 023270 M: (0030) 6947-600686
E: bbryantscott@gmail.com
BRYARS, Peter John. b 54. St Jo Coll Nottm. **d** 84 **p** 85. C Hull St Martin w Transfiguration *York* 84–87; TV
Drypool 87–90; TV Glendale Gp *Newc* 90–94; P-in-c Heddon-
on-the-Wall 94–01; Adult Educn Adv 94–01; V Delaval
01–11; AD Bedlington 03–09; Dioc Chapl MU 02–07; rtd 12;
PtO *Newc* from 12; Bp's Adv for Healing Min from 06. *36
Newlands Road, Blyth NE24 2QJ* E: pjbryars@btinternet.com
BRYCE, Brenda Dorothy. See BROWN, Brenda Dorothy
BRYCE, Michael Adrian Gilpin. b 47. TCD BA 71 MA 95.
CITC 74. **d** 78 **p** 79. C Clondalkin w Tallaght *D & G* 77–79;
C Ch Ch Cathl and Chapl Univ Coll Dub 79–82; I Ardamine
w Kiltennel, Glascarrig etc *C, F & O* 82–84; CF 84–00;
I Lisbellaw *Clogh* 00–05; R Bolam w Whalton and Hartburn

w Meldon *Newc* 05–16; V Nether Witton 05–16; Chapl Kirkley Hall Coll 05–16; rtd 16; PtO *Newc* from 19. *5 Church View, Longhorsley, Morpeth NE65 8UH*

BRYDON, Michael Andrew. b 73. St Chad's Coll Dur BA 95 MA 96 PhD 00. St Steph Ho Ox BA 01. **d** 02 **p** 03. C Bexhill St Pet *Chich* 02–06; C Brighton St Paul 06–08; Dioc Adv for Educn and Tr of Adults 06–08; R Catsfield and Crowhurst 08–21; Bp's Chapl *S & M* from 21. *62 Ballabrooie Way, Douglas, Isle of Man IM1 4HB* T: (01624) 622108 E: chaplain@sodorandman.im

BRYER, Anthony Colin. b 51. Qu Eliz Coll Lon BSc 72. Trin Coll Bris 72. **d** 75 **p** 76. C Preston St Cuth *Blackb* 75–78; C Becontree St Mary *Chelmsf* 78–81; TV Loughton St Mary and St Mich 81–88; C Clifton St Paul *Bris* 88–91; P-in-c 91–94; R Bris St Mich and St Paul 94–96; In C of S and LtO *Edin* 96–04; P-in-c Towcester w Caldecote and Easton Neston *Pet* 04–07; C Greens Norton w Bradden and Lichborough 06–07; V Towcester w Caldecote and Easton Neston etc 07–11; Hon Chapl *Edin* 11–16; rtd 16; LtO *Edin* from 16. *4 Yewlands Gardens, Edinburgh EH16 6TA* T: 0131-672 2232 M: 07814-832004 E: tony.bryer51@gmail.com

BRYER, The Ven Paul Donald. b 58. Sussex Univ BEd 80 Nottm Univ MA 96. St Jo Coll Nottm. **d** 90 **p** 91. C Tonbridge St Steph *Roch* 90–94; TV Camberley St Paul *Guildf* 94–99; V Camberley St Mary 99–01; V Dorking St Paul 01–14; RD Dorking 09–14; Adn Dorking 14–19; Hon Can Guildf Cathl 14–19; Adn Cornwall *Truro* from 19. *The Vicarage, 2 Devoran Lane, Devoran, Truro TR3 6PA* E: paul.bryer@truro.anglican.org

BRYSON, James Ferguson. b 55. NE Lon Poly BSc 79 Glas Univ DipArch 89 RIBA 93. SEITE 04. **d** 07 **p** 08. C Old Ford St Paul and St Mark *Lon* 07–10; P-in-c Eltham St Jo *S'wark* 11–19; R Alyth St And 19–20; R Blairgowrie 19–20; R Coupar Angus 19–20; rtd 21. *9/2 Leven Terrace, Edinburgh EH3 9LW* M: 07805-795331 E: fergusonbryson@btinternet.com

BRYSON, Neil Dominic. b 50. Open Univ BA 76 Lon Inst of Educn MA 84 St Matthias Coll Bris CertEd 71. Ox Min Course 10. **d** 12 **p** 13. NSM Boyne Hill *Ox* 12–16; PtO 16–17; V Maidstone St Mich *Cant* from 17. *The Vicarage, 416 Tonbridge Road, Maidstone ME16 9LW* T: (01622) 721123 M: 07553-091225 E: frneil@ymail.com

BRYSON, Philip Neil William. b 82. Man Metrop Univ BA 05. St Jo Coll Nottm 12. **d** 15 **p** 16. C Bedford St Paul *St Alb* 15–18; Lay Min Officer from 18. *St John's Rectory, 36 St John's Street, Bedford MK42 0DH* E: fr.phil.bryson@outlook.com

BRYSON (née O'NEILL), Victoria Elaine. b 82. Lanc Univ BA 05. St Jo Coll Nottm 12. **d** 15 **p** 16. C Kempston Transfiguration *St Alb* 15–18; R Bedford St Jo and St Leon from 18. *St John's Rectory, 36 St John's Street, Bedford MK42 0DH* E: rev.vicki.bryson@outlook.com

BRYZAK, Nicholas. b 46. **d** 16. OLM Stratford St Jo w Ch Ch *Chelmsf* 16–19; PtO from 21. *4 Caledonian Wharf, London E14 3EW* T: (020) 7987 5106 E: nicholas.citred.90@gmail.com

BUBB, David Michael. b 68. Nottm Univ BEng 90 Cant Ch Ch Univ MA 17 Nottm Univ PGCE 91. St Aug Coll of Th 18. **d** 20. C Bidborough St Lawr and Southborough St Pet *Roch* from 20; C Southborough Ch Ch from 20. *54 Holden Park Road, Tunbridge Wells TN4 0EP* M: 07967-200825 E: dave.bubb68@gmail.com *or* dave@christchurchsouthborough.com

BUBBERS, Richard David. b 55. Keble Coll Ox BA 78 MA 93 Solicitor 81. St Jo Coll Nottm 10. **d** 12 **p** 13. C Ipsley *Worc* 12–15; P-in-c Alvechurch 15–19; R 19–21; Ind Chapl 15–21; rtd 21. *Address withheld by request* E: rdbubbers@gmail.com

BUCHAN, Ms Janet Elizabeth Forbes. b 56. Ex Univ BA 79 K Coll Lon MSc 90 Surrey Univ PGCE 93. SEITE 08. **d** 11 **p** 12. C W Hackney *Lon* 11–14; P-in-c Goodmayes St Paul *Chelmsf* 14–19; V from 19. *St Paul's Vicarage, 20 Eastwood Road, Ilford IG3 8XA* T: (020) 8590 6596 M: 07749-104870 E: janetbuchan@gmail.com

BUCHAN, Matthew Alexander John. b 69. St Andr Univ MA 92. Wycliffe Hall Ox BTh 95. **d** 98 **p** 99. C Horninglow *Lich* 98–01; TV Moulsecoomb *Chich* 01–04; Bp's Chapl *Glouc* 04–06; P-in-c Leybourne *Roch* 06–14; R 14–20; RD Malling 14–19; Hon Can Roch Cathl 18–20; Chapl RAuxAF 11–20; Chapl RAF from 20. *Chaplaincy Services (RAF), HQ Air Command, RAF High Wycombe HP14 4UE* T: (01494) 496800 E: frstag@hotmail.co.uk

BUCHANAN, Andrew Derek. b 64. Stirling Univ BA 90. Wycliffe Hall Ox 98. **d** 01 **p** 02. C Plas Newton *Ches* 01–03; C Ches Ch Ch 03–06; C Plas Newton w Ches Ch Ch 07–11; Asst Chapl Ches Univ 03–11; V Ruddington *S'well* from 11. *The Vicarage, Wilford Road, Ruddington, Nottingham NG11 6EL* T: 0115-921 4522 E: rev_buchan@hotmail.com

✠**BUCHANAN, The Rt Revd Colin Ogilvie.** b 34. Linc Coll Ox BA MA Lambeth DD 93. Tyndale Hall Bris 59. **d** 61 **p** 62 **c** 85. C Cheadle *Ches* 61–64; Tutor St Jo Coll Nottm 64–85; Lib 64–69; Registrar 69–74; Dir of Studies 74–75; Vice-Prin 75–78; Prin 79–85; Hon Can S'well Minster 81–85; Suff Bp Aston *Birm* 85–89; Asst Bp Roch 89–96; Asst Bp S'wark 90–91; V Gillingham St Mark *Roch* 91–96; Area Bp Woolwich *S'wark* 96–04; rtd 04; Hon Asst Bp Bradf 04–14; Ripon 05–14; Leeds from 14. *21 The Drive, Alwoodley, Leeds LS17 7QB* T: 0113-267 7721 E: cobdleeds@btinternet.com

BUCHANAN, Eoin George. b 59. Glyndŵr Univ MA 11. Qu Coll Birm 98. **d** 00 **p** 01. C Dovercourt and Parkeston w Harwich *Chelmsf* 00–04; C Ramsey w Lt Oakley 02–04; TR N Hinckford 04–12; R Flegg Coastal Benefice *Nor* 12–13; P-in-c Kirkley St Pet and St Jo 16; R 16–19; rtd 19; PtO *Dur* from 19. *Low Allers Cottage, 5 Low Allers, Cowshill, Bishop Auckland DL13 1DF* M: 07740-051812 E: okyan12@icloud.com

BUCHANAN, Stephanie Joan. b 65. Linc Coll Ox BA 88 MA 02 Selw Coll Cam BA 01 Goldsmiths' Coll Lon PGCE 93. Ridley Hall Cam 99. **d** 02 **p** 03. C Mirfield *Wakef* 02–06; TV Em TM 06–12; V Wakef St Jo 12–14; Leeds from 14. *St John's Vicarage, 65 Bradford Road, Wakefield WF1 2AA* T: (01924) 371029 E: stephanie.buchanan@leeds.anglican.org

BUCHANAN, Canon Thomas Oliver. b 67. **d** 13 **p** 14. NSM St Marg Lothbury and St Steph Coleman Street etc *Lon* 13–17; PtO *Ely* 14–17; NSM Cambridge St Phil 17–20; Chapter Can Ely Cathl from 19; PtO from 20. *60 Panton Street, Cambridge CB2 1HS* T: (01223) 357416 M: 07974-982366 E: revtbuchanan@gmail.com

BUCK, Mrs Jacqueline Rosemary. b 66. ERMC 06. **d** 09 **p** 10. NSM Cople, Moggerhanger and Willington *St Alb* 09–12; NSM Goldington 12–16; R Gt Doddington and Wilby and Ecton *Pet* from 16. *The Rectory, 72 High Street, Great Doddington, Wellingborough NN29 7TH* T: (01933) 631232 E: jackiebuck@hotmail.co.uk

BUCK (née JONES), Kathryn Mary. b 59. Birm Univ BA 81 MEd 91 Sheff Univ PGCE 82. Ripon Coll Cuddesdon. **d** 99 **p** 00. C Uttoxeter Area *Lich* 99–00; C Scotforth *Blackb* 00–03; TV Cannock *Lich* 03–09; TV Cannock and Huntington 09–10; C Hednesford 05–10; V Lightcliffe and Hove Edge *Wakef* 11–14; Leeds from 14. *The Vicarage, Wakefield Road, Lightcliffe, Halifax HX3 8TH* T: (01422) 202424

BUCK, Canon Nicholas John. b 57. Leic Univ BScEng 79. Ridley Hall Cam 81. **d** 84 **p** 85. C Oakwood St Thos *Lon* 84–87; C Darnall and Attercliffe *Sheff* 87–90; V Kimberworth 90–96; Chapl Scargill Ho 96–01; P-in-c Bassingham Gp *Linc* 01–06; R 06–15; P-in-c Branston w Nocton and Potterhanworth 12–15; P-in-c Metheringham w Blankney and Dunston 12–15; RD Graffoe 09–14; V Linc St Giles from 15; Can and Preb Linc Cathl from 10; Chapl to The Queen from 18. *The Vicarage, 25 Shelley Drive, Lincoln LN2 4BY* E: stgileslincoln@gmail.com

BUCK, Samuel Reuben. b 87. Lon Sch of Th BA 11 K Coll Lon MA 16. St Mellitus Coll MA 20. **d** 20 **p** 21. C Crawley *Chich* from 20. *1 Crossways, Crawley RH10 1QF* M: 07743-411619 E: sam.buck@ymail.com

BUCKINGHAM, The Ven Hugh Fletcher. b 32. Hertf Coll Ox BA 57 MA 60. Westcott Ho Cam 55. **d** 57 **p** 58. C Halliwell St Thos *Man* 57–60; C Sheff Gillcar St Silas 60–65; V Hindolveston *Nor* 65–70; V Guestwick 65–70; R Fakenham w Alethorpe 70–88; Chmn Dioc Bd Soc Resp 81–88; RD Burnham and Walsingham *Nor* 81–87; Hon Can Nor Cathl 85–88; Adn E Riding *York* 88–98; Can and Preb York Minster 88–01; rtd 98; PtO *York* from 01. *Orchard Cottage, Rectory Corner, Brandsby, York YO61 4RJ* T: (01347) 888202

BUCKINGHAM, Richard Arthur John. b 49. Univ of Wales (Cardiff) BA 71 PGCE 72. Chich Th Coll 73. **d** 76 **p** 77. C Llantwit Major *Llan* 76–80; C Leigh-on-Sea St Marg *Chelmsf* 80–84; C Westmr St Matt *Lon* 84–87; R Stock Harvard *Chelmsf* 87–02; PtO *Lon* from 02. *3 Priory Close, London N3 1BB* T: (020) 8371 0178 E: rbuckingham@waitrose.com

BUCKINGHAM, Terence John. b 52. Aston Univ BSc 73 MSc 75 PhD 78 FCOptom 74. Coll of Resurr Mirfield 01. **d** 03 **p** 04. NSM Harrogate St Wilfrid *Ripon* 03–09; P-in-c Nidd 09–10; NSM Leeds St Wilfrid 10–19; NSM Harrogate St Wilfrid from 19. *Woodstock, Thorpe Lane, Guiseley, Leeds LS20 8LE* T: (01943) 876066 M: 07815-994017 E: terry.j.buckingham@btopenworld.com

BUCKINGHAM, Archdeacon of. See ELSMORE, The Ven Guy Charles

BUCKINGHAM, Area Bishop of. See WILSON, The Rt Revd Alan Thomas Lawrence

BUCKLE, Graham Charles. b 59. ERMC 08. **d** 11 **p** 12. NSM Silverstone and Abthorpe w Slapton etc *Pet* 11–16; P-in-c Castle Bytham w Creeton *Linc* 16–18; C

Witham Gp 16–18; P-in-c Riversmeet *St Alb* from 18; RD Biggleswade from 21. *The Rectory, Park Lane, Blunham, Bedford MK44 3NJ* T: (01767) 640412 M: 07901-660593 E: dovecote10@btinternet.com

BUCKLE, Graham Martin. b 62. Southn Univ BTh 89 Sheff Univ MMinTheol 04. Sarum & Wells Th Coll 85. **d** 89 **p** 90. C Paddington St Jas *Lon* 89–94; P-in-c Paddington St Pet 94–00; R St Marylebone St Paul 00–14; Dir of Ords Two Cities Area 99–08; V Westmr St Steph w St Jo from 14. *21 Vincent Square, London SW1P 2NA* T: (020) 7834 1300 E: vicar@sswsj.org

BUCKLER, Andrew Jonathan Heslington. b 68. Trin Coll Ox BA 89 MA 96 Protestant Inst Th France MTh 02. Wycliffe Hall Ox BTh 93. **d** 96 **p** 97. C Ox St Aldate 96–00; Crosslinks France 00–17; V Kensington St Barn *Lon* from 17. *23 Addison Road, London W14 8LH* T: (020) 7471 7000 E: andy@stbk.org.uk

BUCKLER, Canon Guy Ernest Warr. b 46. ACA 69 FCA 79. Linc Th Coll 71. **d** 74 **p** 75. C Dunstable *St Alb* 74–77; C Houghton Regis 77–86; TV Willington *Newc* 86–88; TR 88–95; Chapl N Tyneside Coll of FE 88–95; R Bedford St Pet w St Cuth *St Alb* 95–05; R Bushey 05–11; RD Aldenham 08–11; Hon Can St Alb 10–11; rtd 11; PtO *St Alb* from 11. *18 Deans Close, Abbots Langley WD5 0HL* M: 07791-955657 E: gbuckler@hotmail.com

BUCKLER, Miss Jennifer Anne. b 82. Reading Univ BA 06. Trin Coll Bris 15. **d** 17 **p** 18. C Bath Widcombe *B & W* 17–21; PtO from 21. *Pear Ash Farm, Pear Ash Lane, Pen Selwood, Wincanton BA9 8LX* T: (01747) 840377 M: 07753-785930 E: revjennybuckler@gmail.com

BUCKLER, Kenneth Arthur. b 50. S Bank Univ MSc 94. NTMTC 95. **d** 98 **p** 99. C Welwyn w Ayot St Peter *St Alb* 98–01; P-in-c Kimpton w Ayot St Lawrence 01–05; Asst Chapl E Herts NHS Trust 99–00; Asst Chapl E and N Herts NHS Trust 00–04; Chapl Team Ldr 04–05; V Hounslow W Gd Shep *Lon* 05–12; rtd 12; PtO *Lon* from 12. *104 Royal Lane, Uxbridge UB8 3QY* M: 07909-970545 E: kenbuckler@ymail.com

BUCKLER, The Very Revd Philip John Warr. b 49. St Pet Coll Ox BA 70 MA 74 Bp Grosseteste Univ Hon DUniv 15. Cuddesdon Coll 70. **d** 72 **p** 73. C Bushey Heath *St Alb* 72–75; Chapl Trin Coll Cam 75–81; Min Can and Sacr St Paul's Cathl *Lon* 81–87; V Hampstead St Jo 87–99; AD N Camden 93–98; Can Res St Paul's Cathl 99–07; Treas 00–07; Dean Linc 07–16; rtd 16; PtO *St E* from 17. *Green Acre, Whelp Street, Preston St Mary, Sudbury CO10 9NL* T: (01787) 249760 E: pjwb@hotmail.co.uk

BUCKLES, Ms Jayne Elizabeth. b 53. **d** 07 **p** 08. NSM Penrhyndeudraeth and Llanfrothen w Maentwrog etc *Ban* 07–10; R St Edm Way *St E* 10–16; rtd 16; PtO *Sarum* from 17. *The Old Coach House, 3 Church Lane, Codford, Warminster BA12 0PJ* E: jaynebuckles@btinternet.com

BUCKLEY, Alexander Christopher Nolan. b 67. Univ of Wales (Abth) BD 89 Man Univ MA 06. St Mich Coll Llan. **d** 91 **p** 94. C Llandudno *Ban* 91–92; C Ynyscynhaearn w Penmorfa and Porthmadog 92–93 and 94–96; Jesuit Volunteer Community Manchester 93–94; C Caerau w Ely *Llan* 96–01; V Trowbridge Mawr *Mon* 01–03; Chapl ATC 96–03; PtO *Mon* 03–09; *Man* 04–09; R Llanllyfni *Ban* 09–12; P-in-c Leeds Belle Is St Jo and St Barn *Ripon* 12–14 and 14–18; C Hunslet w Cross Green *Ripon* 12–14; *Leeds* 14–18; V Belle Isle and Hunslet from 18; CMP from 02. *The Vicarage, 30 Low Grange View, Leeds LS10 3DT* E: father-chris@ssjbchurchleeds.org.uk *or* chris.buckley@leeds.anglican.org

BUCKLEY, Anthony Graham. b 63. Keble Coll Ox BA 84 MA 90 Cant Ch Ch Univ Coll MA 03 Keble Coll Ox PGCE 85. Wycliffe Hall Ox 96. **d** 98 **p** 99. C Folkestone St Jo *Cant* 98–00; V 00–08; AD Elham 05–08; Hon Can Cant Cathl 08; Chapl Alleyn's Sch Dulwich 08–19; Hon C Dulwich St Barn *S'wark* 08–19; Dir of IME Woolwich Area 09–19; V Ox St Mich w St Martin and All SS from 19; AD Ox from 19. *37 Lonsdale Road, Oxford OX2 7ES* T: (01865) 240940 M: 07841-800609 E: vicar@smng.org.uk

BUCKLEY, Mrs Catherine Anne. **d** 17 **p** 18. OLM Hartshorne and Bretby *Derby* 17–19; OLM Swadlincote 17–19; OLM Swadlincote and Hartshorne from 20; OLM Seale and Lullington w Coton in the Elms from 17; OLM Stapenhill Immanuel from 17; OLM Walton-on-Trent w Croxall, Rosliston etc from 17. *22 Ordish Street, Burton-on-Trent DE14 3SA* T: (01283) 531257 M: 07753-751882 E: katebuckley9@gmail.com

BUCKLEY, Christine Judith. **d** 15 **p** 16. NSM Poynton *Ches* from 15. *74 Vernon Road, Poynton, Stockport SK12 1YR* M: 07709-032435 E: bcklyc@aol.com

BUCKLEY, Christopher Ivor. b 48. Chich Th Coll 84. **d** 86 **p** 87. C Felpham w Middleton *Chich* 86–89; C Jersey St Brelade *Win* 89–93; V Jersey St Mark 93–06; Chapl Jersey Airport 00–06; V E Radnor *S & B* 06–10; rtd 11; PtO *Win* from 10. *A*

Cappella, 15 Byron Road, St Helier, Jersey JE2 4LQ T: (01534) 738265 M: 0797-714595 E: revcbuckley@gmail.com

BUCKLEY, David Rex. b 47. Ripon Coll Cuddesdon 75. **d** 77 **p** 78. C Witton *Ches* 77–81; V Backford 81–85; Youth Chapl 81–85; V Barnton 85–93; P-in-c Bickerton w Bickley 93–97; P-in-c Harthill and Burwardsley 93–97; V Bickerton, Bickley, Harthill and Burwardsley 97–01; P-in-c Sandbach 01–03; V 03–07; rtd 08; Chapl Cheshire Constabulary *Ches* 08–12; PtO 15–19; *Ely* from 18. *39 The Croft, Fulbourn, Cambridge CB21 5DR* T: (01223) 882338 M: 07810-791417 E: padrerex@btinternet.com

BUCKLEY, Canon Debra. b 59. Birm Poly BA 81. Qu Coll Birm 08. **d** 10 **p** 11. C Balsall Heath and Edgbaston SS Mary and Ambrose *Birm* 10–14; V Smethwick from 14; AD Warley 17–20; Co-AD Warley and Edgbaston 20–21; Hon Can Birm Cathl from 19. *The Vicarage, 93A Church Road, Smethwick B67 6EE* T: 0121-558 1763 E: debbuckley@phonecoop.coop

BUCKLEY, Ernest Fairbank. b 25. Jes Coll Cam BA 49 MA 50 Jes Coll Ox BLitt 53. Westcott Ho Cam 55. **d** 55 **p** 56. C Rochdale *Man* 55–58; V Hey 58–64; V Baguley 64–79; V Clun w Chapel Lawn, Bettws-y-Crwyn and Newcastle *Heref* 79–87; RD Clun Forest 82–87; rtd 88. *The Old Barn, Brassington, Matlock DE4 4HL* T: (01629) 540821 E: buckley@w3z.co.uk

BUCKLEY, Rex. *See* BUCKLEY, David Rex

BUCKLEY, Richard Francis. b 44. FRSA. Ripon Hall Ox 69. **d** 72 **p** 73. C Portsea St Cuth *Portsm* 72–75; C Portsea All SS w St Jo Rudmore 75–79; Chapl RN 79–00; PtO *B & W* 00–15; *Glouc* from 13. *2 Nourse Close, Cheltenham GL53 0NQ* T: (01242) 220805 M: 07990-836802 E: r.f.buckley@me.com

BUCKLEY, Richard Simon Fildes. b 63. WMMTC 97. **d** 00 **p** 01. NSM Moseley St Mary *Birm* 00–04; NSM Soho St Anne w St Thos and St Pet *Lon* 05–09 and 12–13; P-in-c from 13; PtO 09–12. *St Anne's Rectory, 55 Dean Street, London W1D 6AF* T: (020) 7437 1012 M: 07976-290351 E: simon@simonbuckley.co.uk

BUCKLEY, Canon Stephen Richard. b 45. Cranmer Hall Dur 82. **d** 84 **p** 85. C Iffley *Ox* 84–88; TV Halesowen *Worc* 88–00; TR Sedgley All SS 00–05; TR Gornal and Sedgley 05–15; P-in-c Sedgley St Mary 10–15; Hon Can Worc Cathl 12–15; rtd 15; PtO *Worc* from 15; PV Westmr Abbey from 17. *70 Blenheim Road, Worcester WR2 5NG* T: (01905) 428802 M: 07746-206905

BUCKLEY, Timothy Denys. b 57. BA. St Jo Coll Nottm. **d** 83 **p** 84. C S Westoe *Dur* 83–85; C Paddington Em Harrow Road *Lon* 85–88; C Binley *Cov* 88–98; Min Binley Woods LEP 88–98; V Belton Gp *Linc* 98–13; P-in-c Crowle Gp 09–12; PtO *Chich* from 14. *34 Outerwyke Road, Bognor Regis PO22 8HX* T: (01243) 278731 E: revtimbuckley@gmail.com

BUCKLEY, Timothy John. b 67. Jes Coll Cam BA 90 MA 94 Lambeth MA 11. Wycliffe Hall Ox BTh 99. **d** 99 **p** 00. C Langdon Hills *Chelmsf* 99–02; P-in-c Devonport St Mich and St Barn *Ex* 02–15; V 15–19; V Devonport St Mich and St Barn w St Aubyn from 19. *St Barnabas' Vicarage, 10 De la Hay Avenue, Plymouth PL3 4HU* T: (01752) 666544 E: rev.tim@virgin.net

BUCKLEY, Timothy Simon. b 72. St Mellitus Coll. **d** 11 **p** 12. C Combe Down w Monkton Combe and S Stoke *B & W* 11–14; C Bath Widcombe 11–14; P-in-c 14–16; V from 16. *The Orchard, Forefield Rise, Bath BA2 4PL* E: tim@timbuck2.co.uk

BUCKMAN, Stephen Leslie. b 55. Open Univ BA 99 Chich Univ MA 19 Sussex Univ PGCE 01. SEITE 09. **d** 12 **p** 13. NSM Roughey *Chich* 12–15; P-in-c Corby Glen *Linc* 15–20; V Corby Glen Par from 20; RD Beltisloe from 20. *The Rectory, 14 Mussons Close, Corby Glen, Grantham NG33 4NY* T: (01476) 550884 M: 07768-116563 E: revstephen@btinternet.com

BUCKNALL, Allan. b 35. St Matthias Coll Bris CertEd 73. ALCD 62. **d** 62 **p** 63. C Harlow New Town w Lt Parndon *Chelmsf* 62–69; Chapl W Somerset Miss to Deaf 69–71; PtO *Bris* 71–77; P-in-c Wisborough Green *Chich* 77–79; R Tillington 78–86; R Duncton 82–86; R Upwaltham 82–86; C Henfield w Shermanbury and Woodmancote 86–89; Asst Chapl Princess Marg Hosp Swindon 89–96; Angl Chapl Swindon and Marlborough NHS Trust 96–00; rtd 00; PtO *Bris* 00–19. *5 The Willows, Highworth, Swindon SN6 7PG* T: (01793) 762721

BUCKNALL, Miss Ann Gordon. b 32. K Coll Lon BSc 53 Hughes Hall Cam DipEd 54. Qu Coll Birm 80. **dss** 81 **d** 87 **p** 94. Birm St Aid Small Heath 81–85; Balsall Heath St Paul 85–92; Par Dn 87–92; C Handsworth St Jas 92–95; rtd 95; PtO *Lich* 95–19. *29 The Oaks, St John's Hospital, St John Street, Lichfield WS13 6PB* T: (01543) 257382 E: bucknall20ann@talktalk.net

BUDD, Canon John Christopher. b 51. QUB BA 73. CITC. **d** 82 **p** 83. C Ballymena w Ballyclug *Conn* 82–85; C Jordanstown w Monkstown 85–88; I Craigs w Dunaghy and Killagan 88–97; Dioc Info Officer 89–97; Bp's Dom Chapl

94–02; I Derriaghy w Colin 97–18; Can Conn Cathl 11–18; Treas 16–18; Prec 16–18; rtd 18; PtO *Conn* from 18. *26 Causeway End Road, Lisburn BT28 1UB* T: (028) 9258 3691

BUDD, Philip John. b 40. St Jo Coll Dur BA 63 MLitt 71 Bris Univ PhD 78. Cranmer Hall Dur. **d** 66 **p** 67. C Attenborough w Chilwell *S'well* 66–69; Lect Clifton Th Coll 69–71; Lect Trin Coll Bris 72–80; Tutor Ripon Coll Cuddesdon 80–88; Asst Chapl and Tutor Westmr Coll Ox 88–00; Lect 88–00; Asst Chapl and Tutor Ox Brookes Univ 00–03; Lect 00–03; Hon C N Hinksey and Wytham 03–06; PtO 06–21. *4 Clover Close, Oxford OX2 9JH* T: (01865) 863682 E: budds@talk21.com

BUDD, Robert John. b 77. Nottm Univ BA 99 Warwick Univ PGCE 05. Trin Coll Bris 11. **d** 13 **p** 14. C Cov H Trin 13–16; C Warwick 16–17; C Whitnash 17–18; V Heathcote from 18. *72 Banquo Approach, Heathcote, Warwick CV34 6GB* T: (01926) 335367 M: 07811-945647 E: revrobbudd@gmail.com

BUDDEN, Alexander Mark. b 60. UEA BA 84. SEITE 01. **d** 04 **p** 05. NSM Mitcham St Barn *S'wark* 04–08; PtO 09–11; NSM Wimbledon 11–17; NSM Merton St Jas from 17. *29 Dane Road, London SW19 2NB* T: (020) 8542 0622 M: 07738-290534 E: markbudden@sky.com

BUDDEN, Carl James. b 57. SWMTC 12. **d** 15 **p** 16. C Egg Buckland *Ex* 15–17; C Eggbuckland w Estover 17–19; TV Plymstock and Hooe from 19. *Merrivale, Woodside, Plymouth PL4 8QE* M: 07525-210645 E: carljamesbudden@gmail.com

BUDGELL, Mrs Anne Margaret. b 44. RGN 66. STETS 07. **d** 10 **p** 11. NSM Vale of White Hart *Sarum* 10–13; NSM Three Valleys 13–18; PtO from 18. *7 Fox's Close, Holwell, Sherborne DT9 5LH* T: (01963) 23428 E: budgells@hotmail.co.uk

BUDGELL, Peter Charles. b 50. Lon Univ BD 74. **d** 83 **p** 84. C Goodmayes All SS *Chelmsf* 83–86; C Chipping Barnet w Arkley *St Alb* 86–88; R Luton St Anne 88–06; V Luton St Anne w St Chris 06–16; rtd 17; PtO *Ex* from 17. *5 Vicarage Road, Sidmouth EX10 8TS* T: (01395) 513770 E: pcbudgell@aol.com

BUIKE, Desmond Mainwaring. b 32. Ex Coll Ox BA 55 MA 69 Leeds Univ CertEd 72. **d** 57 **p** 58. C Man St Aid 57–60; C Ox SS Phil and Jas 60–63; V Queensbury *Bradf* 63–71; PtO 71–85; V Glaisdale *York* 85–93; rtd 93; PtO *York* from 93. *2 Pentland Grove, Wakefield WF2 8JX*

BULL, Andrew David. b 70. Hull Univ BSc 91 Sheff Univ PGCE 92. Regents Th Coll BA 99. **d** 07 **p** 08. C Macclesfield Team *Ches* 07–10; P-in-c Bredbury St Mark 10–21; V from 21. *St Mark's Vicarage, 61 George Lane, Bredbury, Stockport SK6 1AT* T: 0161-406 6552 E: ukbulls@aol.com

BULL, Mrs Christine. b 45. Bedf Coll Lon BA 67. NOC 91. **d** 94 **p** 95. NSM High Lane *Ches* 91–94; NSM Stockport SW 98–99; PtO *Derby* 98–04; *Ches* 99–04; *Man* 00–06; C Hale and Ashley *Ches* 04–07; NSM Wormhill, Peak Forest w Peak Dale and Dove Holes *Derby* 07–08; P Pastor Ches Cathl 08–13; rtd 13; PtO *Ches* from 07; *Derby* 09–18. *2 River Sett Cottages, Hyde Bank Road, New Mills, High Peak SK22 4BF* T: (01663) 740847 E: revchristinebull@yahoo.co.uk

BULL (née ADAMS), Canon Christine Frances. b 53. Cam Inst of Educn CertEd 74. NEOC 97. **d** 00 **p** 01. NSM St Oswald in Lee w Bingfield *Newc* 00–21; P-in-c 07–19; NSM Chollerton w Birtley and Thockrington *Newc* 19–21; Hon Can Newc Cathl 14–21; rtd 21. *East Side Lodge, Bingfield, Newcastle upon Tyne NE19 2LG* T: (01434) 672303 E: bull.christine4@gmail.com

BULL, Christopher Bertram. b 45. Lon Bible Coll BA 87. Wycliffe Hall Ox 88. **d** 90 **p** 91. C Leominster *Heref* 90–95; P-in-c Westbury 95–02; R 02–10; P-in-c Yockleton 95–02; R 02–10; P-in-c Gt Wollaston 95–02; V 02–07; P-in-c Worthen 07–10; rtd 10; PtO *Lich* 12–14 and from 18. *12 Aldersley Way, Ruyton XI Towns, Shrewsbury SY4 1NE* T: (01939) 260059 E: cbbull@live.co.uk

BULL, Canon Christopher David. b 59. Univ of Wales MA 08. St Jo Coll Nottm 89. **d** 91 **p** 92. C Bowbrook S *Worc* 91–95; P-in-c Flackwell Heath *Ox* 95–00; V 00–20; RD Wycombe 97–05; Asst Adn Buckingham 17–20; Assoc Adn from 20; Hon Can Ch Ch from 19. *The Vicarage, 245 Micklefield Road, High Wycombe HP13 7HU* M: 07481-343440 E: christopher.bull@oxford.anglican.org

BULL, Canon David Thomas. b 72. Worc Coll Ox BA 94. Wycliffe Hall Ox BA 07. **d** 08 **p** 09. C Reigate St Mary *S'wark* 08–12; TR Gt Marlow w Marlow Bottom, Lt Marlow and Bisham *Ox* from 12; AD Wycombe from 16; Hon Can Ch Ch from 21. *The Rectory, The Causeway, Marlow SL7 2AA* T: (01628) 471650 E: dave.bull@4u-team.org

BULL, John. *See* BULL, Michael John

BULL, Malcolm George. b 35. Portsm Dioc Tr Course 87. **d** 87 **p** 98. NSM Farlington *Portsm* 87–90; NSM Widley w Wymering 92–93; NSM S Hayling 93–97; NSM Hayling Is St Andr 97–00; Bp's Adv for Cults and New Relig Movements 99–00; rtd 00; PtO *Portsm* 00–01 and from 04; P-in-c Greatworth and Marston St Lawrence etc *Pet* 01–04.

20 Charleston Close, Hayling Island PO11 0JY T: (023) 9246 2025 E: bullmg@hotmail.co.uk

BULL, Malcolm Harold. b 44. BDS. St Alb Minl Tr Scheme. **d** 83 **p** 84. NSM Bedford St Paul *St Alb* 83–93. *27 Cardington Road, Bedford MK42 0BN* T: (01234) 368163

BULL, Martin Wells. b 37. Worc Coll Ox BA 61 MA 68. Ripon Hall Ox 61. **d** 63 **p** 64. C Blackley St Andr *Man* 63–67; C Horton *Bradf* 67–68; V Ingrow w Hainworth 68–78; RD S Craven 74–77; V Bingley All SS 78–80; TR 80–92; P-in-c Gargrave 92–02; rtd 02; PtO *Ripon* 03–14; *Leeds* from 14. *21 Magdalen's Close, Ripon HG4 1HH* T: (01765) 601422 M: 07870-138386

BULL, Michael John. b 35. Roch Th Coll 65. **d** 67 **p** 68. C N Wingfield *Derby* 67–69; C Skegness *Linc* 69–72; R Ingoldmells w Addlethorpe 72–79; Area Sec USPG S'wark 79–85; Area Org RNLI (Lon) 86–88; C Croydon St Jo *S'wark* 89–93; P-in-c Mitcham Ch Ch 93–97; V Colliers Wood Ch Ch 97–00; rtd 00; PtO *Nor* 00–04; Hon C Guiltcross 04–08; P-in-c 08–13. *21 Buckshorn Lane, Eye IP23 7AZ* T: (01379) 871509 E: mjbull@waitrose.com

BULL, Canon Robert David. b 51. Westmr Coll Ox MTh 03 Ches Univ DProf 16. Ripon Coll Cuddesdon 74. **d** 77 **p** 78. C Worsley *Man* 77–80; C Peel 80–81; TV 81–86; P-in-c Wisbech St Aug *Ely* 86–88; V 88–02; RD Wisbech 92–02; R Lich St Chad 02–11; P-in-c Longdon 08–10; Can Res Bris Cathl 11–17; rtd 18; PtO *Lich* from 18. *1 Myford Cottages, Myford, Horsehay, Telford TF4 3BU* T: (01952) 507414 E: robertdb8083@gmail.com

BULL, Mrs Ruth Lois Clare. b 54. Univ of Wales (Lamp) BA 76 W Midl Coll of Educn PGCE 77. Qu Coll Birm 08. **d** 11 **p** 12. NSM Burntwood *Lich* 11–12; NSM Lich St Mich w St Mary and Wall from 12. *36 Broadlands Rise, Lichfield WS14 9SF* T: (01543) 319296 E: dkbrlcb@hotmail.com

BULL, Stephen Andrew. b 58. St Jo Coll Nottm 91. **d** 93 **p** 94. C Wroughton *Bris* 93–96; P-in-c Eyemouth *Edin* 96–98; LtO from 98. *12 Craigs Court, Torphichen, Bathgate EH48 4NU* T: (01506) 650070 E: stvbull@btinternet.com

BULL, Miss Susan Helen. b 58. Qu Mary Coll Lon BSc 79 All Hallows Coll Dublin MA 11 ACIS 84. STETS BTh 98. **d** 98 **p** 99. NSM Epsom St Barn *Guildf* 98–04; Chapl Surrey and Borders Partnership NHS Foundn Trust 04–18; Chapl Epsom and St Helier Univ Hosps NHS Trust 18; PtO *S'wark* from 06; *Guildf* 18–21. *41 Stamford Green Road, Epsom KT18 7SR* T: (01372) 742703 E: shbull@btinternet.com

BULL, Canon Timothy Martin. b 65. Worc Coll Ox BA 87 MA 93 Dur Univ PhD 94 Fitzw Coll Cam BA 98 MA 07 K Coll Lon PhD 11 FRSA 96 CEng 94 MBCS 96. Ridley Hall Cam 96. **d** 99 **p** 00. C Bath Walcot *B & W* 99–03; P-in-c Langham w Boxted *Chelmsf* 03–13; Colchester Area CME Adv 03–13; Dir Min and Min Development Officer *St Alb* from 13; Can Res St Alb from 13. *43 Holywell Hill, St Albans AL1 1HD* T: (01727) 818151 E: canondrtim@gmail.com *or* tbull@stalbans.anglican.org

BULL, Mrs Wendy Jane. b 63. Birm Chr Coll MA 08. Ripon Coll Cuddesdon 11. **d** 13 **p** 14. C Gt Marlow w Marlow Bottom, Lt Marlow and Bisham *Ox* 13–16; C High Wycombe 16; TV from 16. *9 Chapel Road, Flackwell Heath, High Wycombe HP10 9AA* M: 07450-737438 E: revwbull@gmail.com

BULLAMORE, John Richard. b 41. Linc Coll Ox BA 69 MA 69. Wycliffe Hall Ox 74. **d** 95 **p** 95. NSM Eoropaidh *Arg* 95–98; NSM Bath St Sav w Swainswick and Woolley *B & W* 98–08; NSM Knaresborough *Ripon* 08–12; rtd 12; PtO *Ripon* 12–14; *Leeds* 14–17. *21 Hornbeam Way, Leeds LS14 2HP* T: 0113-318 9756 E: john.bullamore@hotmail.co.uk

BULLEN, Mrs Jacqueline. b 61. Westcott Ho Cam 11. **d** 13 **p** 14. C Fosse Team *Leic* 13–17; V Longthorpe *Pet* from 17. *Longthorpe Vicarage, 315 Thorpe Road, Peterborough PE3 6LU* T: (01733) 263016 M: 07729-706157 E: jacqbullen@aol.com

BULLEN, Marilyn Patricia. *See* MARTIN, Marilyn Patricia

BULLEN, Neil Geoffrey Osbourne. b 64. Qu Coll Birm 13. **d** 15 **p** 16. C Knighton *Leic* 15–18; R Ringstone in Aveland Gp *Linc* from 18. *The Vicarage, 46A High Street, Morton, Bourne PE10 0NR* M: 07729-004642 E: revdneil@yahoo.com

BULLIMORE, Canon Christine Elizabeth. b 46. Nottm Univ BA 67. St Jo Coll Nottm 96. **d** 96 **p** 97. Bp's Adv Past Care and Counselling *Wakef* 92–99 and 01–14; *Leeds* from 14; NSM S Ossett *Wakef* 96–99; P-in-c Emley and Flockton cum Denby Grange 99–11; RD Kirkburton 05–11; Hon Can Wakef Cathl 08–11; rtd 11. *5 Snowgate Head, New Mill, Holmfirth, Huddersfield HD9 7DH* T: (01484) 521025 M: 07921-588276 E: chrisbullimore@sky.com

BULLIMORE, Matthew James. b 77. Em Coll Cam BA 99 MA 03 PhD 02 Man Univ MPhil 02. Harvard Div Sch 99 Westcott Ho Cam 01. **d** 05 **p** 06. C Roberttown w Hartshead *Wakef* 05–07; Bp's Dom Chapl 07–11; V Royston 11–14; *Leeds*

14–16; P-in-c Felkirk *Wakef* 13–14; *Leeds* 14–16; V Royston and Felkirk 16–17; Widening Participation Officer Chu Coll Cam from 18; Chapl CCC Cam from 20; PtO *Ely* from 20. *Corpus Christi College, Cambridge CB2 1RH* T: (01223) 338002 E: mjb56@cantab.net

BULLOCK, Andrew Belfrage. b 50. Univ of Wales (Ban) BSc 73 MEd 81 Westmr Coll Ox PGCE 79. Wycliffe Hall Ox 94. d 97 p 98. C Sandhurst *Ox* 97–02; P-in-c Ashford, Lulsley, Suckley, Leigh and Bransford *Worc* 02–08; TV Worcs W Rural 09–14; rtd 15; PtO *Heref* from 18. *Gladstone House, Whitbourne, Worcester WR6 5SP* M: 07958-654331 E: ochse6@waitrose.com

BULLOCK, Andrew Timothy. b 56. Southn Univ BTh 91. Sarum & Wells Th Coll 89. d 91 p 92. C Erdington St Barn *Birm* 91–94; TV Solihull 94–03; P-in-c Acocks Green 03–08; V from 08; AD Yardley and Bordesley 12–19; AD Yardley and Solihull 20–21. *The Vicarage, 34 Dudley Park Road, Acocks Green, Birmingham B27 6QR* T/F: 0121-706 9764 E: andrewbullock2@blueyonder.co.uk

BULLOCK, Gary Kenneth. b 64. Staffs Univ BA 87 Wycliffe Hall Ox 06. d 16 p 17. NSM Heapey and Withnell *Blackb* from 16. *2 Richmond Close, Brinscall, Chorley PR6 8PY* T: (01254) 830575 E: gary@bowdenash.net

BULLOCK, Ian. b 74. York St Jo Univ BA 11. Cranmer Hall Dur. d 08 p 09. C Pontefract St Giles *Wakef* 08–11; P-in-c Heckmondwike 11–12; P-in-c Liversedge w Hightown 11–12; V Heckmondwike (w Norristhorpe) and Liversedge 12–15; V Littleborough *Man* from 15. *The Vicarage, 4 Stansfield Hall, Littleborough OL15 9RH* T: (01706) 375322 E: rev.ian@btinternet.com

BULLOCK, Jude Ross. b 58. Heythrop Coll Lon BD 89. Allen Hall 84. d 89 p 90. In RC Ch 89–97; C Lt Ilford St Mich *Chelmsf* 01–05; V Chingford St Anne from 05. *St Anne's Vicarage, 200A Larkshall Road, London E4 6NP* T: (020) 8529 4740 M: 07976-395732 E: juderbullock1@yahoo.co.uk

BULLOCK, Canon Michael. b 49. Hatf Coll Dur BA 71. Coll of Resurr Mirfield 72. d 75 p 76. C Pet St Jo 75–79; Zambia 79–86; V Longthorpe *Pet* 86–91; Chapl Naples w Sorrento, Capri and Bari *Eur* 91–99; OGS from 93; P-in-c Liguria *Eur* 99–00; Chapl Gtr Lisbon 00–12; Can Malta Cathl 98–12; PtO 12–17; Chapl Bonn w Cologne 17–20; PtO *Linc* from 13. *22 Georgian Court, Spalding PE11 2QT* T: (01775) 714454 E: bullock583@btinternet.com

BULLOCK, Philip Mark. b 59. Qu Coll Birm 05. d 08 p 09. C Cov E 08–10; TV 10–13; P-in-c S Shields St Aid and St Steph *Dur* 13–19; P-in-c Rekendyke 13–19; P-in-c Greatham from 19; P-in-c Seaton Carew from 19. *12 Dauntless Close, Hartlepool TS25 1EX* M: 07831-147822 E: rev.philip@virginmedia.com

BULLOCK, Miss Rosemary Joy. b 59. Portsm Poly BA 81 Southn Univ BTh 94. Sarum & Wells Th Coll 89. d 91 p 94. Par Dn Warblington w Emsworth *Portsm* 91–94; C 94–95; C Gt Parndon *Chelmsf* 95–98; TV Beaminster Area *Sarum* 98–03; P-in-c Ridgeway 03–04. *82 Green Lane, Shanklin PO37 7HD* T: (01983) 863345

✠**BULLOCK (née WHEALE), The Rt Revd Sarah Ruth.** b 64. Surrey Univ BA 86 St Jo Coll Dur BA 93. Cranmer Hall Dur 90. d 93 p 94 c 15. C Kersal Moor *Man* 93–98; P-in-c Whalley Range St Edm 98–04; P-in-c Moss Side St Jas w St Clem 99–04; R Whalley Range St Edm and Moss Side etc 04–13; Dioc Voc Adv 98–05; Chapl MU 00–06; Bp's Adv for Women's Min *Man* 09–13; Borough Dean *Man* 10–12; AD Hulme 12–13; Hon Can Man Cathl 07–13; Adn York 13–19; Area Bp Shrewsbury *Lich* from 19. *Athlone House, 68 London Road, Shrewsbury SY2 6PG* T: (01743) 235867 E: bishop.shrewsbury@lichfield.anglican.org

BULLOCK, Stephanie Clair. b 64. St Mary's Hosp Medical Sch Lon MB, BS 70. Ripon Coll Cuddesdon 90. d 92 p 94. Par Dn Cuddesdon *Ox* 92–94; Tutor Ripon Coll Cuddesdon 92–94; Asst Chapl Ox Radcliffe Hosp NHS Trust 94–97; Chapl Ox Radcliffe Hosps NHS Trust 97–03; Hon C Headington St Mary *Ox* 03–09; PtO from 09. *Church Farm, Church Lane, Old Marston, Oxford OX3 0PT* T: (01865) 722926 E: stephaniebullock9@gmail.com

BULLOCK, Canon Victor James Allen. b 67. Southn Univ BTh 90 St Mary's Coll Twickenham PGCE 91. St Steph Ho Ox 92. d 94 p 95. C Cowley St Jas *Ox* 94–95; C Reading St Giles 95–99; V Fenny Stratford from 99; Canon Ruvuma Tanzania from 13. *The Vicarage, Manor Road, Milton Keynes MK2 2HW* T: (01908) 372825 E: saintmartinschurch@hotmail.com *or* victorbullock@talktalk.net

BULLWORTHY, Rita Irene. b 48. Glos Univ BA 09. SWMTC 05. d 11. NSM N Tawton, Bondleigh, Sampford Courtenay etc *Ex* 11–13; NSM Chagford, Gidleigh, Throwleigh etc 13–20; PtO from 20. *Rivendell House, Sampford Courtenay, Okehampton EX20 2TF* T: (01837) 89168 E: ritabullworthy@yahoo.co.uk

BUNCE, Christopher Edward. b 82. Westcott Ho Cam. d 12 p 13. C Hammersmith St Pet *Lon* 12–15; R Stevenage St Andr and St Geo *St Alb* 15–19; RD Stevenage 16–19; TR Hitchin and St Paul's Walden from 19. *21 West Hill, Hitchin SG5 2HZ* M: 07539-101957 E: cebunce@gmail.com

BUNCE (née HOW), Gillian Carol. b 53. K Coll Lon MB, BS 77 MRCGP 82 MFHom 96. STETS 04. d 07 p 08. NSM Worle *B & W* from 07; Dioc Healing Adv from 20. *85 Clevedon Road, Tickenham, Clevedon BS21 6RD* T: (01275) 810610 E: gill.how@blueyonder.co.uk

BUNCH, Canon Andrew William Havard. b 53. Selw Coll Cam BA 74 MA 78 PhD 79. Ox NSM Course 84. d 87 p 88. NSM Wantage *Ox* 87–91; C New Windsor 91–93; TV 93–97; V Ox St Giles and SS Phil and Jas w St Marg 97–21; Hon Can Ch Ch 09–20; rtd 21; PtO *Ox* from 21. *113 Church Road, Long Hanborough, Witney OX29 8JF* T: (01993) 880449 E: awhbunch@gmail.com

BUNDAY, Mrs Janet Lesley. b 56. Nottm Univ BA 78 Univ of Wales (Lamp) MA 08 Lon Inst of Educn PGCE 79 Anglia Ruskin Univ MA 12. Ridley Hall Cam 08. d 10 p 11. NSM Potton w Sutton and Cockayne Hatley *St Alb* 10–12; C Blyth Valley *St E* 12–13; TV 13–19. *Address withheld by request* E: jan@bunday.co.uk

BUNDAY, Richard William. b 76. Lanc Univ BA 98 MA 04 PhD 19. Cranmer Hall Dur 98. d 00 p 01. C Redcar *York* 00–01; C Marton *Blackb* 01–04; P-in-c Ashton-on-Ribble St Mich w Preston St Mark 04–06; TR W Preston 06–10; P-in-c Kirkham 10–11; V 11–20; AD 15–17; Chapl HM Pris Garth from 20. *HM Prison Garth, Ulnes Walton Lane, Leyland PR26 8LW* T: (01772) 443300

BUNDOCK, Canon Anthony Francis. b 49. Qu Coll Birm 81. d 83 p 84. C Stansted Mountfitchet *Chelmsf* 83–86; TV Borehamwood *St Alb* 86–94; TR Seacroft *Ripon* 94–05; AD Whitkirk 00–05; TR Leeds City 05–14; Hon Can Ripon Cathl 05–14; rtd 14; TV Risborough *Ox* from 14. *The Vicarage, 1 Church Lane, Lacey Green, Princes Risborough HP27 0QX* E: tony.pat.bundock@virgin.net

BUNDOCK, Edward Leigh. b 52. Keble Coll Ox BA 73 Open Univ PhD 94 MAAT. St Steph Ho Ox 74. d 76 p 77. C Malvern Link w Cowleigh *Worc* 76–80; C-in-c Portslade Gd Shep CD *Chich* 80–88; V Wisborough Green 88–94; PtO *Guildf* 96–97; P-in-c E and W Rudham, Houghton-next-Harpley etc *Nor* 97–99; R E w W Rudham, Helhoughton etc from 99. *The Rectory, South Raynham Road, West Raynham, Fakenham NR21 7HH* T: (01328) 838385

BUNDOCK, Canon John Nicholas Edward. b 45. Wells Th Coll 66. d 70 p 71. C Chingford SS Pet and Paul *Chelmsf* 70–74; P-in-c Gt Grimsby St Matt Fairfield CD *Linc* 74–81; V Hindhead *Guildf* 81–99; RD Farnham 91–96; V Bramley and Grafham 99–15; RD Cranleigh 04–12; Chapl Gosden Ho Sch 99–15; Hon Can Guildf Cathl 09–15; rtd 15; PtO *Guildf* from 15; *Chich* from 15. *18 Hall Hurst Close, Loxwood, Billingshurst RH14 0BE* M: 07789-487695 E: jnebundock@gmail.com

BUNDOCK, Nicholas John. b 73. Sheff Univ BSc 94 PhD 98 Fitzw Coll Cam BA 01. Ridley Hall Cam 99. d 02 p 03. C Mortomley St Sav High Green *Sheff* 02–05; TV Didsbury St Jas and Em *Man* 05–10; TR from 10. *St James's Rectory, 9 Didsbury Park, Manchester M20 5LH* T: 0161-434 6518 *or* 446 4150 E: nickbundock@stjamesandemmanuel.org

BUNDOCK, Ronald Michael. b 44. Leeds Univ BSc 65. Ox NSM Course 87. d 90 p 91. NSM Buckingham *Ox* 90–98; NSM Stowe 98–14; P-in-c 03–14; PtO from 14; AD Buckingham 11–17. *1 Holton Road, Buckingham MK18 1PQ* T: (01280) 813887

BUNGARD, Mrs Rosemary Felicity. GTCL 72. TISEC 12. d 15 p 16. C Portree *Arg* 15–19; P-in-c 19–21; Hon C from 21. *Ceòl na Mara, West Suisnish, Isle of Raasay, Kyle IV40 8NX* T: (01478) 660248 M: 07719-585732 E: ceolmara@waitrose.com

BUNKER (née HARDING), Mrs Elizabeth. b 45. Chelsea Coll Lon BSc 67 MSc 69. SAOMC 04. d 06 p 07. NSM Baldock w Bygrave and Weston *St Alb* 06–10; NSM St Paul's Walden 10–16; NSM Hitchin and St Paul's Walden 16–18; rtd 18; PtO *St Alb* from 18. *Arana, 6 Hitchin Road, Letchworth Garden City SG6 3LL* T: (01462) 686808 F: 679276 M: 07850-413724 E: elizabethbunker@hotmail.com

BUNN, Mrs Rosemary Joan. b 60. EAMTC 94. d 97 p 98. NSM Sprowston w Beeston *Nor* 97–01; R Stoke H Cross w Dunston, Arminghall etc 01–11; R Belton and Burgh Castle from 11. *The Rectory, Beccles Road, Belton, Great Yarmouth NR31 9JQ* T: (01493) 780210 E: rosie@rosiebunn.co.uk

BUNNELL, Adrian. b 49. Univ of Wales (Abth) BSc 72. St Mich Coll Llan 74. d 75 p 76. C Wrexham *St As* 75–78; C Rhyl w St Ann 78–79; CF 79–95; R Aberfoyle and Callander *St And* 95–03; R Newport-on-Tay 03–06; rtd 06. *4 Williamsburgh Cottages, Forneth, Blairgowrie PH10 6SP* T: (01350) 724317

BUNTER, Andrew Stuart. b 84. Univ of Wales (Abth) LLB 05. St Mellitus Coll BA 19. **d** 19 **p** 20. C Sprowston w Beeston *Nor* 19–21; C Oulton Broad from 21. *St Michael's Rectory, Christmas Lane, Lowestoft NR32 3JX* M: 07425-154454

BUNTING, Canon Ian David. b 33. Ex Coll Ox BA 58 MA 61. Tyndale Hall Bris 57 Princeton Th Sem ThM 59. **d** 60 **p** 61. C Bootle St Leon *Liv* 60–63; V Waterloo St Jo 64–71; Dir Past Studies St Jo Coll Dur 71–78; R Chester le Street *Dur* 78–87; RD Chester-le-Street 79–84; Kingham Hill Fellow 87–89; Dioc Dir of Ords *S'well* 90–99; C Lenton 90–97; Hon Can S'well Minster 93–99; Bp's Research Officer 97–00; rtd 00; PtO *S'well* 00–19 and from 21. *8 Crafts Way, Southwell NG25 0BL* T: (01636) 813868 E: ibunting@waitrose.com

BUNTING (née SIMPSON), Mrs Rachel Victoria. b 89. Ban Univ BD 11 Cardiff Univ MTh 14. St Mich Coll Llan 11. **d** 13 **p** 14. C Llantwit Major *Llan* 13–16; Bp's Officer for Family Min *S & B* from 16; PtO from 16. *The Vicarage, Lewis Street, St Thomas, Swansea SA1 8BP* T: (01792) 652891 E: revrachelbunting@hotmail.co.uk

BUNYAN, David Richard. b 48. Edin Th Coll 93. **d** 96 **p** 97. NSM Musselburgh *Edin* 96–98; NSM Prestonpans 96–98; C Edin St Dav 98–00; R Grangemouth 00–13; P-in-c Bo'ness 00–13; rtd 13; LtO *Edin* from 14. *14 Clerwood Bank, Edinburgh EH12 8PZ* T: 0131-476 6586 E: bunyandr@gmail.com

BUQUÉ, Mrs Helena Margareta. b 55. Chich Inst of HE BEd 95. SEITE 09. **d** 12 **p** 13. NSM Findon w Clapham and Patching *Chich* 12–15; P-in-c 15–20; V from 20; RD Worthing from 17. *The Rectory, School Hill, Findon, Worthing BN14 0TR* T: (01903) 873601 M: 07504-333853 E: findoncprectory@gmail.com

BURBERRY, The Very Revd Frances Sheila. b 60. ACII 83. TISEC 03. **d** 06 **p** 07. C Edin St Pet 06–11; R Edin St Ninian from 11; Chapl Edin Univ from 06; Syn Clerk 16–17; Can St Mary's Cathl from 16; Dean Edin from 17. *163 Craigleith Road, Edinburgh EH4 2EB* T: 0131-315 0404 E: frances.burberry@ed.ac.uk *or* dean@dioceseofedinburgh.org

BURBIDGE, Barry Desmond. b 52. STETS 94. **d** 97 **p** 98. NSM Fleet *Guildf* 97–03; NSM Crondall and Ewshot 03–11; Chapl Frimley Park Hosp NHS Foundn Trust 06–14; Chapl Frimley Health NHS Foundn Trust from 14; PtO *Guildf* from 19. *Frimley Park Hospital, Portsmouth Road, Frimley, Camberley GU16 7UJ* T: (01276) 604604 E: padrebarry@hotmail.com

BURBIDGE, Richard John. b 52. Lon Guildhall Univ BSc 00. Oak Hill Th Coll BTh 11. **d** 11 **p** 12. C Lowestoft Ch Ch *Nor* 11–14; C Moulton *Pet* 14–16; R Billing from 16. *25 Church Walk, Great Billing, Northampton NN3 9ED* M: 07973-801254 E: richburbidge@googlemail.com

BURBRIDGE, The Very Revd John Paul. b 32. K Coll Cam BA 54 MA 58 New Coll Ox BA 54 MA 58 FSA 89. Wells Th Coll 58. **d** 59 **p** 60. C Eastbourne St Mary *Chich* 59–62; V Choral York Minster 62–66; Can Res and Prec York Minster 66–76; Adn Richmond *Ripon* 76–83; Can Res Ripon Cathl 76–83; Dean Nor 83–95; rtd 95; PtO *Ripon* 95–06; LtO *Glas* from 08. *The Clachan Bothy, Newtonairds, Dumfries DG2 0JL* T: (01387) 820403 E: fremington124@yahoo.co.uk *or* revpaul@stjohnsdumfries.org

BURBRIDGE, Richard James. b 47. Univ of Wales (Ban) BSc 68. Oak Hill Th Coll 68. **d** 72 **p** 73. C Rodbourne Cheney *Bris* 72–75; C Downend 75–78; P-in-c Bris H Cross Inns Court 78–83; P-in-c Fishponds All SS 83–86; V 86–97; RD Stapleton 89–95; C Bishopston 97–98; C Bris St Andr w St Bart 97–98; TV Bishopston and St Andrews 98–12; rtd 12; PtO *Bris* from 12. *10 Scandrett Close, Bristol BS10 7SS* T: 0117-950 4945 E: burbridge466@btinternet.com

BURBURY, Canon Janet. b 56. Sunderland Univ CertEd 02. Cranmer Hall Dur 05. **d** 07 **p** 08. C Hart w Elwick Hall *Dur* 07–11; P-in-c from 11; AD Hartlepool from 13; Hon Can Dur Cathl from 16. *The Vicarage, Hart, Hartlepool TS27 3AP* T: (01429) 262340 M: 07958-131271 E: janetb_231@hotmail.co.uk

BURCH, Caroline Mary Louise. b 71. Newnham Coll Cam BA 93. St Mellitus Coll BA 21. **d** 21. C Fleet *Guildf* from 21. *40 Poltimore Road, Guildford GU2 7PN* T: (01483) 546266 M: 07880-594740 E: caroline_burch@hotmail.com

BURCH, Charles Edward. b 57. Trin Coll Cam MA 80 Lon Business Sch MBA 87. ERMC 05. **d** 07 **p** 08. NSM Harpenden St Jo *St Alb* 07–11; V Bovingdon from 11; Dioc Voc Officer from 11. *10 Church Street, Bovingdon, Hemel Hempstead HP3 0LU* E: charlesburch57@hotmail.com

BURCH, Canon Peter John. b 36. ACA 60 FCA 71. Ripon Hall Ox 62. **d** 64 **p** 65. C Brixton St Matt *S'wark* 64–67; Chapl Freetown St Aug Sierra Leone 68–72; P-in-c Chich St Pet 72–76; V Broadwater Down 76–85; V Steyning 85–94; R Ashurst 85–94; Hon Can Bauchi from 93; V Broadway *Worc* 94–96; V Broadway w Wickhamford 96–02; rtd 02; PtO *Glouc*

03–20; *Worc* from 04. *6 Jordan's Close, Willersey, Broadway WR12 7QD* T: (01386) 853837 E: pj_pjburch@hotmail.com

BURCH, Stephen Roy. b 59. St Jo Coll Nottm 82. **d** 85 **p** 86. C Ipswich St Aug *St E* 85–89; Youth Chapl *Cov* 89–94; P-in-c Kinwarton w Gt Alne and Haselor 89–99; R 99–04; P-in-c Coughton 02–04; RD Alcester 99–04; V Fletchamstead from 04; AD Cov S 10–18; AD Kenilworth 10–13. *St James's Vicarage, 395 Tile Hill Lane, Coventry CV4 9DP* T: (024) 7646 6262 E: vicar@stjamesfletch.org.uk

BURCHELL, Mrs Elizabeth Susan. b 53. Sheff Univ BSc 74 De Montfort Univ MA 13. SAOMC 04. **d** 07 **p** 08. NSM Banbury St Leon *Ox* 07–10; P-in-c 10–13; V from 13. *St Leonard's Vicarage, 46A Middleton Road, Banbury OX16 4RG* T: (01295) 271008 M: 07709-754914 E: revsueb@btinternet.com

BURDEN, Miss Anne Margaret. b 47. Ex Univ BSc 69 CQSW 72. Linc Th Coll 89. **d** 91 **p** 94. Par Dn Mill Hill Jo Keble Ch *Lon* 91–94; C 94; TV Basingstoke *Win* 94–02; Dioc Adv for Women's Min 00–02; TV Brixham w Churston Ferrers and Kingswear *Ex* 02–10; rtd 10; PtO *Ex* from 11. *Ainsdale, Dornafield Road, Ipplepen, Newton Abbot TQ12 5SJ* T: (01803) 813520 E: anne.burden276@btinternet.com

BURDEN, Derek Ronald. b 37. Sarum Th Coll 59. **d** 62 **p** 63. C Cuddington *Guildf* 62–64; C Leamington Priors All SS *Cov* 64–66; C Stamford All SS w St Pet *Linc* 66–74; C-in-c Stamford Ch Ch CD 71–74; P-in-c Ashbury w Compton Beauchamp *Ox* 74–77; V 77–81; V Ashbury, Compton Beauchamp and Longcot w Fernham 81–84; V Wokingham St Sebastian 84–97; P-in-c Wooburn 97–02; rtd 02; PtO *Sarum* 03–05; *Win* from 06. *5 Cranford Park Drive, Yateley GU46 6JR* T: (01252) 890657

BURDEN, Ms Joanna Margaret. b 93. York Univ BSc 15 St Jo Coll Dur BA 20. Cranmer Hall Dur 17. **d** 20 **p** 21. C W Heref from 20. *79 Bridle Road, Hereford HR4 0PW* M: 07587-172563 E: joanna@burden.name

BURDEN, Lucy Angela Margaret. Cumbria Univ BA. CITI. **d** 16 **p** 17. Mt Merrion *D & D* 16–17; C Portadown St Mark *Arm* from 17. *9 Willow Drive, Portadown, Craigavon BT62 3SD* M: 07541-953148 E: curate@stmarksportadown.org

BURDEN, Paul. b 62. Rob Coll Cam BA 84 MA 88 Univ of Wales MTh 05 AMIMechE 87 AFHEA 17. Wycliffe Hall Ox BA 91. **d** 92 **p** 93. C Clevedon St Andr and Ch Ch *B & W* 92–96; R Bathampton w Claverton 96–14; Warden of Readers Bath Adnry 06–14; Tutor STETS 14–15; Dir Contextual Learning Sarum Coll from 15; LtO *Sarum* from 14; PtO *B & W* from 15. *Sarum College, 19 The Close, Salisbury SP1 2EE* T: (01722) 424816 E: pburden@sarum.ac.uk

BURDEN, Thomas. b 71. Ox Univ BA 95 MA 12. Wycliffe Hall Ox 20. **d** 21. C Fordingbridge and Hyde and Breamore etc *Win* from 21. *19 Falconmoor Close, Fordingbridge SP6 1TB* T: (01425) 652340 E: curate@avonvalleychurches.org.uk

BURDETT, Rachel Clare. b 66. Coll of Resurr Mirfield 19. **d** 21. C Belper Ch Ch w Turnditch *Derby* from 21. *26 Leighton Way, Belper DE56 1SX* M: 07340-990483 E: belpercurate@gmail.com

BURDETT, Canon Stephen Martin. b 49. AKC 72. St Aug Coll Cant 73. **d** 74 **p** 75. C Walworth St Pet *S'wark* 74–75; C Walworth 75–77; C Benhilton 77–80; P-in-c Earlsfield St Jo 80–83; V 83–89; V N Dulwich St Faith 89–99; Ldr Post Ord Tr Woolwich Area 96–99; TR Southend *Chelmsf* 99–15; Hon Can Chelmsf Cathl 09–15; RD Southend 10–15; rtd 15; PtO *Chelmsf* from 15. *51 Admirals Walk, Shoeburyness, Southend-on-Sea SS3 9HR* T: (01702) 294454 E: revstephenburdett@gmail.com

BURDITT, Jeffrey Edward. b 46. Ex Univ BA 67 CertEd 68 Lon Univ MPhil 79. Westcott Ho Cam 86. **d** 88 **p** 89. C Saffron Walden w Wendens Ambo and Littlebury *Chelmsf* 88–92; V Hatfield Peverel w Ulting 92–95; PtO from 21. *34 Maldon Road, Burnham-on-Crouch CM0 8NS* T: (01621) 786154 E: j.burditt@intamail.com

BURDON, Anthony James. b 46. Ex Univ LLB 67 Lon Univ BD 73. Oak Hill Th Coll 71. **d** 73 **p** 74. C Ox St Ebbe w St Pet 73–76; C Church Stretton *Heref* 76–78; Voc Sec CPAS and Hon C Bromley Ch Ch *Roch* 78–81; V Filkins w Broadwell, Broughton, Kelmscot etc *Ox* 81–84; R Broughton Poggs w Filkins, Broadwell etc 84–85; V Reading St Jo 85–96; C California and Adv for Spirituality (Berks) 96–98; Warden and P-in-c Cumbrae (or Millport) *Arg* 98–04; V Burstwick w Thorngumbald *York* 04–11; P-in-c Roos and Garton w Tunstall, Grimston and Hilston 08–11; RD S Holderness 06–09; rtd 11; PtO from 11. *22 Wheatlands Close, Pocklington, York YO42 2UT* T: (01759) 304290 E: pamandtonyburdon@btinternet.com

BURDON, Canon Christopher John. b 48. Jes Coll Cam BA 70 MA 74 Glas Univ PhD 95. Coll of Resurr Mirfield 71.

d 74 **p** 75. C Chelmsf All SS 74–78; TV High Wycombe *Ox* 78–84; P-in-c Olney w Emberton 84–90; R 90–92; Lto *Glas* 92–94; Lay Tr Officer *Chelmsf* 94–99; Prin NOC 00–07; Can Th and CME Adv *St E* 07–13; rtd 13; PtO *Chelmsf* 14–16; *Sarum* from 17. *24 Newman Road, Devizes SN10 5LE* E: cjburdon@btinternet.com

BURDON, Mrs Pamela Muriel. b 46. Ex Univ BA 68 Reading Univ DipEd 69. Wycliffe Hall Ox 88. **d** 90 **p** 94. Par Dn Reading St Jo *Ox* 90–94; C 94–96; P-in-c California 96–98; NSM Cumbrae (or Millport) *Arg* 98–04; NSM Burstwick w Thorngumbald *York* 04–11; C Preston and Sproatley in Holderness 05–06; P-in-c 06–11; C Roos and Garton w Tunstall, Grimston and Hilston 08–11; rtd 11; PtO *York* from 12. *22 Wheatlands Close, Pocklington, York YO42 2UT* T: (01759) 304290

BURFORD, Anthony Francis. b 55. Oak Hill Th Coll BA 98. **d** 98 **p** 99. C Cov H Trin 98–02; P-in-c Rye Park St Cuth *St Alb* 02–07; V 07–11; V S Hornchurch St Jo and St Matt *Chelmsf* 11–16; rtd 16; PtO *Chelmsf* 17–18; Hon C Grays Thurrock 18–21; PtO from 21. *14 Chelmer Drive, South Ockendon RM15 6EE* M: 07500-007479 E: revdtonyburford@gmail.com

BURGE, Edward Charles Richard. b 70. Liv Univ BA 92. Ridley Hall Cam 93. **d** 96 **p** 97. C Cayton w Eastfield *York* 96–99; P-in-c Lythe w Ugthorpe 99–03; Children's Officer (Cleveland Adnry) 99–03; Hon Chapl Miss to Seafarers 02–03; Dioc Youth and Children's Work Co-ord *Wakef* 04–10; P-in-c Roberttown w Hartshead 10–12; P-in-c Scholes 10–12; V Hartshead, Hightown, Roberttown and Scholes 12–14; *Leeds* 14–19; TR Harden and Wilsden, Cullingworth and Denholme from 19. *The Vicarage, Wilsden Old Road, Harden, Bingley BD16 1JD* T: (01535) 273758 E: richard.burge@leeds.anglican.org

BURGE, Stephen Russell. b 81. St Andr Univ MA 03 Edin Univ MSc 04 PhD 09 FRAS 10 FHEA 16. ERMC 16. **d** 18 **p** 19. NSM Eaton Bray w Edlesborough *St Alb* from 18. *67 Grasmere Road, Leighton Buzzard LU7 2QL* T: (020) 7756 2766 E: sburge@iis.ac.uk

BURGE-THOMAS, Mrs Ruth Anne. b 66. **d** 04 **p** 05. C Clapham H Spirit *S'wark* 04–14; V from 14; Chapl St Mark's C of E Academy Mitcham from 10. *The Vicarage, 15 Elms Road, London SW4 9ER* E: ruth@burgethomas.com *or* office@holyspirit-clapham.org.uk

BURGESS, Alan James. b 51. Ridley Hall Cam 87. **d** 89 **p** 90. C Glenfield *Leic* 89–92; V Donisthorpe and Moira w Stretton-en-le-Field 92–06; RD Akeley W 00–06; RD Akeley S 05–06; C Ravenstone and Swannington 06–09; P-in-c Thringstone St Andr 06–09; P-in-c Whitwick St Jo the Bapt 07–09; R Whitwick, Thringstone and Swannington 09–15; rtd 15. *242 Hearthcote Road, Swadlincote DE11 9DU* T: (01283) 213251 E: sylvanus06@gmail.com

BURGESS, Andrew Graham. b 84. Middx Univ BA 08. Wycliffe Hall Ox BA 19. **d** 19 **p** 20. C Bushey *St Alb* from 19. *2 University Close, Bushey WD23 3AL* M: 07539-409959 E: a_burgess@mac.com

BURGESS, Charles Anthony Robert. b 58. STETS. **d** 11 **p** 12. NSM Bath Weston All SS w N Stoke and Langridge *B & W* 11–15; NSM Bathford 15–16; PtO 16–18; Hon C Corfe Mullen *Sarum* from 17. *The Rectory, 32 Wareham Road, Corfe Mullen, Wimborne BH21 3LE* T: (01202) 699319 M: 07895-860399 E: burgesscj5@gmail.com

BURGESS, David James. b 58. Southn Univ BSc 80. St Jo Coll Nottm. **d** 89 **p** 90. C S Mimms Ch Ch *Lon* 89–93; C Hanwell St Mary w St Chris 93–97; P-in-c Hawridge w Cholesbury and St Leonard *Ox* 97–08; R 08–19; P-in-c The Lee 97–08; V 08–19; rtd 19. *3A Avondale, 8 Chesterfield Road, Eastbourne BN20 7NU* E: d.burgess@clara.net

BURGESS, Preb David John. b 39. Trin Hall Cam BA 62 MA 66 Univ Coll Ox MA 66 FRSA 91. Cuddesdon Coll 62. **d** 65 **p** 66. C Maidstone All SS w St Phil *Cant* 65; Asst Chapl Univ Coll Ox 66–70; Chapl 70–78; Can and Treas Windsor 78–87; V St Lawr Jewry *Lon* 87–08; Preb St Paul's Cathl 02–08; Chapl to The Queen 87–09; rtd 08. *62 Orbel Street, London SW11 3NZ* T: (020) 7585 1572

BURGESS, Mrs Denise. b 49. **d** 00 **p** 01. OLM Glascote and Stonydelph *Lich* 00–06; NSM 06–07; NSM Elford 07–15; NSM Mease Valley 15; rtd 16; PtO *Cov* from 16. *37 Greendale Road, Nuneaton CV11 6RH* M: 07818-890184 E: burgess.denise@virgin.net

BURGESS, Canon Edwin Michael. b 47. Ch Coll Cam BA 69 MA 73. Coll of Resurr Mirfield 70. **d** 72 **p** 73. C Beamish *Dur* 72–77; C Par *Truro* 77–80; P-in-c Duloe w Herodsfoot 80–83; R 83–86; Jt Dir SWMTC 80–86; Subwarden St Deiniol's Lib Hawarden 86–91; V Oughtrington *Ches* 91–05; P-in-c Warburton 93–05; R Oughtrington and Warburton from 05; CME Officer 99–03; Hon Can Ches Cathl from 10.

The Rectory, Stage Lane, Lymm WA13 9JB T: (01925) 752388 E: m.burgess154@btinternet.com

BURGESS, Mrs Geraldine Mary. b 54. Ox Univ BA 75 Southn Univ PGCE 76. SEITE 12. **d** 15 **p** 16. NSM Ifield *Chich* 15–17; NSM Gossops Green and Bewbush 17–18; P-in-c Amberley w N Stoke and Parham, Wiggonholt etc from 18. *Amberley New Vicarage, School Road, Amberley, Arundel BN18 9NA* E: revgerryburgess@gmail.com

BURGESS, Hugh Nigel. b 55. Edin Univ BSc 76 Aber Univ MA 79. Ox Minl Tr Course. **d** 06 **p** 07. NSM Halkyn w Caerfallwch w Rhesycae *St As* 06–16; P-in-c 07–16; TV Estuary and Mountain Miss Area from 17. *The Chimneys, 7 Leete Park, Rhydymwyn, Mold CH7 5JJ* T: (01352) 741646

BURGESS, Jane Ellen. b 63. Chelsea Coll Lon BSc 85. STETS BA 10. **d** 07 **p** 08. C Frome H Trin *B & W* 07–10; P-in-c Bathford 10–16; Asst RD Bath 15–17; R Corfe Mullen *Sarum* from 17. *The Rectory, 32 Wareham Road, Corfe Mullen, Wimborne BH21 3LE* ~~T: (01202) 699319~~ E: revjaneb@gmail.com

BURGESS, The Ven Jean Ann. b 62. Nottm Univ MA 03. EMMTC 00. **d** 03 **p** 04. C Gresley *Derby* 03–09; C Derby St Alkmund and St Werburgh 09–13; P-in-c 13–18; V 18; Dean of Women's Min 13–18; Asst Adn Derby 17; Hon Can Derby Cathl 16–18; Adn Bolton *Man* from 18; Adn Salford from 20. *The Vicarage, 14 Springside Road, Bury BL9 5JE* T: 0161-761 6117 E: archbolton@manchester.anglican.org

BURGESS, John David. b 51. Ex Univ BSc 73 Sussex Univ PGCE 94. Trin Coll Bris 07. **d** 08 **p** 09. NSM Westfield and Guestling *Chich* 08–15; NSM Brede w Udimore and Beckley and Peasmarsh 15–17; rtd 17. *25 Fairlight Gardens, Fairlight, Hastings TN35 4AY* E: revd.john.burgess@gmail.com

BURGESS, John Michael. b 36. ALCD 61. **d** 61 **p** 62. C Eccleston St Luke *Liv* 61–64; C Avondale St Mary Magd Rhodesia 64–68; R Marlborough 68–74; V Nottingham St Andr *S'well* 74–79; Bp's Adv on Community Relns 77–79; V Earlestown *Liv* 79–87; RD Warrington 82–87; TR Halewood 87–94; V Southport St Phil and St Paul 94–01; AD N Meols 95–00; rtd 01; PtO *Liv* from 03. *38 Brunlees Court, 19-23 Cambridge Road, Southport PR9 9DH*

BURGESS, Kate Lamorna. b 64. Man Poly BA 86 Leeds Univ MA 97. NEOC 99. **d** 02 **p** 03. OHP 92–03; C Hessle *York* 02–06; TV Howden 06–10; P-in-c Stretford St Matt *Man* 10–18; R from 18. *St Matthew's Rectory, 39 Sandy Lane, Stretford, Manchester M32 9DB* T: 0161-865 2535 E: kburgess1@tiscali.co.uk

BURGESS, Laura Jane. *See* JØRGENSEN, Laura Jane

BURGESS, Michael. *See* BURGESS, Edwin Michael

BURGESS, Canon Michael James. b 42. Coll of Resurr Mirfield 74. **d** 76 **p** 77. C Leigh-on-Sea St Marg *Chelmsf* 76–79; C St Peter-in-Thanet *Cant* 79–82; Chapl Royal St Geo Coll Toronto Canada 82–89; R Toronto Epiphany and St Mark 89–04; R Toronto Transfiguration from 04; Can Toronto from 01. *318W-118 Montgomery Avenue, Toronto ON M4R 1E3, Canada* T: (001) (416) 482 2462 *or* (416) 489 7798 F: 489 3272 E: michaelburgess@sympatico.ca

BURGESS, Canon Neil. b 53. Univ of Wales (Lamp) BA 75 Nottm Univ MTh 87 PhD 93. St Mich Coll Llan 75. **d** 77 **p** 78. C Cheadle *Lich* 77–79; C Longton 79–82; TV Hanley H Ev 82–86; C Uttoxeter w Bramshall 86–87; Lect Linc Th Coll 87–95; Hon C Linc Minster Gp 88–95; Dioc Dir of Clergy Tr *S'well* 95–00; C Newark 97–00; PtO *Linc* 00–06; Hon C Linc St Pet-at-Gowts and St Andr 06–21; Hon C Linc St Botolph 06–21; Hon C Linc St Pet-at-Gowts w St Andr and St Botolph from 21; Hon C Linc St Swithin from 06; Hon C Linc St Faith and St Martin w St Pet 06–15; Hon C Linc St Mary-le-Wigford w St Benedict etc from 06; Min Team Ldr from 13; Can and Preb Linc Cathl 18–21; Can Res Linc Cathl from 21; Vice-Chan from 21. *Edward King House, The Old Palace, Lincoln LN2 1PU* T: (01522) 539408 E: neil.burgess@lincoln.anglican.org

BURGESS, Prof Paul Christopher James. b 41. Qu Coll Cam BA 63 MA 67. Lon Coll of Div 66. **d** 68 **p** 69. C Islington St Mary *Lon* 68–72; C Church Stretton *Heref* 73–74; Lect Gujranwala Th Sem Pakistan 74–83; Warden Carberry Tower (Ch of Scotland) 84–86; Progr Co-ord 86–88; TV Livingston LEP *Edin* 88–92; Prof and Lib Gujranwala Th Sem 94–08; rtd 08. *Springvale, Halket Road, Lugton, Kilmarnock KA3 4EE* T: (01505) 850254 E: paulandcathie@gmail.com

BURGESS, Peter Alan. b 40. St Edm Ho Cam BA 86 MA 89 MPhil 86 St Jo Coll York MA 99. Cranmer Hall Dur 02. **d** 03 **p** 04. NSM Wheldrake w Thorganby *York* 03–08; NSM Derwent Ings 08–14; PtO from 14. *2 Derwent Drive, Wheldrake, York YO19 6AL* T: (01904) 448309 E: burgesspr@btinternet.com

BURGESS, Roy. b 32. S Dios Minl Tr Scheme 80. **d** 83 **p** 84. NSM Bentworth and Shalden and Lasham *Win* 83–89; R

Ingoldsby *Linc* 89–97; RD Beltisloe 93–97; rtd 97; PtO *Nor* from 98. *8 Windmill Court, St Mary's Close, Alton GU34 1EQ*

BURGESS, Roy Graham. b 47. Birm Univ CertCYW 72. Ox Min Course 91. **d** 94 **p** 95. C Easthampstead *Ox* 94–99; C Wokingham St Paul 99–04; P-in-c Owlsmoor 04–09; V 09–14; rtd 15; PtO *Ox* from 15. *Strathpeffer, 4 Appletree Place, Bracknell RG42 1YN* T: (01344) 304993 E: revroy@btinternet.com

BURGESS, Mrs Tina. b 61. St Hild Coll 14. **d** 17 **p** 18. NSM Ormesby *York* 17–18; C Redcar 18–21; V Middlesbrough St Martin w St Cuth from 21. *9 Emerson Avenue, Middlesbrough TS5 7QW* E: revtinaburgess@gmail.com

BURGON, Canon George Irvine. b 41. Open Univ BA 92. Edin Th Coll 62 Univ of the S (USA) 63. **d** 65 **p** 66. C Dundee St Mary Magd *Bre* 65–68; C Wellingborough All Hallows *Pet* 68–71; P-in-c Norton 71–73; TV Daventry w Norton 73–75; V Northampton St Mary 75–98; R Rothwell w Orton, Rushton w Glendon and Pipewell 98–08; Can Pet Cathl 95–08; rtd 08; PtO *Pet* 09–13. *47 Woodlands Avenue, Barton Seagrave, Kettering NN15 6QS* T: (01536) 722193 E: georgeburgon@yahoo.co.uk

BURGON, Mrs Lynne. b 58. RGN 80 RM 83. SWMTC 03. **d** 06 **p** 07. NSM Fremington *Ex* 06–07; C Okehampton w Inwardleigh, Bratton Clovelly etc 07–11; V Bampton, Morebath, Clayhanger, Petton etc 11–14; PtO 14–21. *2 Barton Cottages, Monkleigh, Bideford EX39 5JX* E: lynneburgon@live.co.uk

BURHOLT, Adrian Peter. b 65. Kent Univ BSc 87. Sarum Coll 17. **d** 20 **p** 21. C Wellsprings *Sarum* from 20. *83 Netherstreet, Bromham, Chippenham SN15 2DW* M: 07537-185095 E: adrian.burholt@btinternet.com

BURKE, Calum Joseph. b 87. Ridley Hall Cam 18. **d** 21. C Dudley *Worc* from 21. *27 Somery Road, Dudley DY1 4BD* E: calum@topchurch.co.uk

BURKE, The Ven Christopher Mark. b 65. Cov Poly LLB 87 Heythrop Coll Lon MA 06. Ripon Coll Cuddesdon 89. **d** 92 **p** 93. C Nunthorpe *York* 92–96; V S Bank 96–02; R Stepney St Dunstan and All SS *Lon* 02–10; Can Res Sheff Cathl 10–13; Can Res and Prec Sheff Cathl 13–19; Vice Dean 14–19; Adn Barking *Chelmsf* from 19. *11 Bridgefields Close, Hornchurch RM11 1GQ* T: (01708) 474951 M: 07950-434333 E: a.barking@chelmsford.anglican.org

BURKE, Colin Douglas. b 41. Bp Otter Coll CertEd 64. **d** 92 **p** 93. OLM Fressingfield, Mendham, Metfield, Weybread etc *St E* 92–99; P-in-c Oare w Culbone *B & W* 99–19; rtd 19; PtO *B & W* 19–20. *Victoria Church Cottage, Parson's Street, Porlock, Minehead TA24 8QJ* M: 07810-563529 E: colin.barbara.burke@googlemail.com

BURKE, Elisabeth Ann. b 44. St Matthias Coll Bris CertEd 66. **d** 05 **p** 06. OLM E Horsley and Ockham w Hatchford and Downside *Guildf* 05–14; PtO from 14. *39 Copse Road, Cobham KT11 2TW* T: (01932) 863886 E: elisabethb@ntlworld.com

BURKE, Mrs Elizabeth Mary Ann. b 72. Liv Univ BA 95 Surrey Univ MBA 06 Anglia Ruskin Univ MA 12. Westcott Ho Cam 12. **d** 13 **p** 14. C Bickleigh and Shaugh Prior *Ex* 13–14; C Plymouth Crownhill Ascension 14–17; P-in-c Holsworthy, Hollacombe, Pyworthy etc 17–20; R from 20. *The Rectory, Bodmin Street, Holsworthy EX22 6BH* T: (01409) 255490 M: 07990-978485 E: elizabethmaburke@icloud.com

BURKE, Jonathan. b 53. Lon Univ BEd. Westcott Ho Cam 79. **d** 82 **p** 83. C Weymouth H Trin *Sarum* 82–85; R Bere Regis and Affpuddle w Turnerspuddle 85–92; NSM Talbot Village 04–08; TR White Horse 08–15; RD Heytesbury 13–15; rtd 15; PtO *Sarum* from 15. *10 Graycot Close, Bournemouth BH10 7BU* E: jonathan_burke2003@yahoo.co.uk

BURKE, Kelvin Stephen. b 56. Man Univ BA 77 FCA 81. Cranmer Hall Dur. **d** 99 **p** 00. C Stanley *Wakef* 99–02; P-in-c Wakef St Andr and St Mary 02–06; Asst Chapl Leeds Teaching Hosps NHS Trust 06–10; PtO *Portsm* 11–14; Chapl Isle of Wight NHS Trust from 12. *7 Steephill Court Road, Ventnor PO38 1UH* T: (01983) 854261 M: 07793-979907

BURKE, Michael Robert. b 61. Leeds Univ BA 83. Trin Coll Bris BA 89. **d** 89 **p** 90. C Anston *Sheff* 89–92; V Crosspool 92–00; V Hucclecote *Glouc* 00–09; PtO 09–15; TV Keynsham *B & W* from 15. *9 Chelmer Grove, Keynsham, Bristol BS31 1QA* T: 0117-909 9425 M: 07432-530153 E: mikburke1@outlook.com *or* mikeburke@keynshamparish.org.uk

BURKE, Canon William Spencer Dwerryhouse. b 46. Ripon Coll Cuddesdon 90. **d** 92 **p** 93. C Watford St Mich *St Alb* 92–95; R Castor w Sutton and Upton w Marholm *Pet* 95–15; Can Pet Cathl 07–15; rtd 15; PtO *Ely* 12–16; *Pet* from 15; *Sarum* 15–17; RD Fincham and Feltwell *Ely* 17–21; V Gt w Lt Tew and Heythrop *Ox* from 21. *The Vicarage, New Road, Great Tew, Chipping Norton OX7 4AG* E: wsdburke@outlook.com

BURKETT, Canon Christopher Paul. b 52. Warwick Univ BA 75 Westmr Coll Ox MTh 93 Liv Univ PhD 10. Qu Coll Birm 75. **d** 78 **p** 79. C Streetly *Lich* 78–81; C Harlescott

81–83; TV Leek and Meerbrook 83–89; Chapl Leek Morlands Hosp 83–89; Area Sec USPG Ches 89–92; V Whitegate w Lt Budworth *Ches* 92–00; Asst CME Officer 93–00; Can Res Ches Cathl 00–10; Hon Can Ches Cathl from 11; Bp's Chapl 00–10; Dioc Dir of Min 10–21; C Ches H Trin from 10. *1 Newton Hall Drive, Chester CH2 1PQ* M: 07494-787689 E: cpb@theosoc.com

BURKILL, Mark Edward. b 56. MA PhD. Trin Coll Bris. **d** 84 **p** 85. C Cheadle *Ches* 84–88; C Harold Wood *Chelmsf* 88–91; V Leyton Ch Ch 91–21; rtd 21. *Address temp unknown* E: m.burkill@ntlworld.com

BURKITT, Paul Adrian. b 49. RMN 75 SRN 77. St Steph Ho Ox 84. **d** 86 **p** 87. C Whitby *York* 86–90; V Egton w Grosmont 90–93; V Newington w Dairycoates 93–96; P-in-c Kingston upon Hull St Mary 96–07; P-in-c Sculcoates 04–07; rtd 07; PtO *York* 07–14; P-in-c Kingston upon Hull St Mary 14–16; PtO from 16. *2 Plane Tree Way, Filey YO14 9PA* E: paul2planetrees@gmail.com

BURKITT-GRAY, Mrs Joan Katherine. b 47. Portsm Poly BSc 68 Southn Univ MPhil 74. SEITE 00. **d** 04 **p** 05. NSM Lee St Marg *S'wark* 04–17; Hon Asst Chapl St Chris Hospice Lon 08–09; PtO *S'wark* from 17. *7 Foxes Dale, London SE3 9BD* T: (020) 8463 0365 *or* 8768 4500

BURLAND, Clive Beresford. b 37. Sarum & Wells Th Coll 81. **d** 85 **p** 86. C Warblington w Emsworth *Portsm* 85–87; C Cowes St Mary 87–92; V Gurnard 92–98; R Northwood 93–98; rtd 98; PtO *Portsm* from 98. *5A Orchard Close, Freshwater PO40 9BQ* T: (01983) 753949 E: clive.burland@talktalk.net

BURLEIGH, Walter Coleridge. b 41. WMMTC 89. **d** 89 **p** 90. NSM N Evington *Leic* 90–96; PtO from 96. *20 Border Drive, Leicester LE4 2JH* T: 0116-235 9230

BURLES, Robert John. b 54. Bris Univ BSc 75. St Jo Coll Nottm LTh 86. **d** 88 **p** 89. C Mansfield SS Pet and Paul *S'well* 88–91; C The Lydiards *Bris* 91–92; TV W Swindon and the Lydiards 92–97; TR Swindon St Jo and St Andr 97–11; AD Swindon 06–11; Hon Can Bris Cathl 04–11; P-in-c Takeley w Lt Canfield *Chelmsf* 11–21; Lead Chapl Stansted Airport 16–21; rtd 21. *Denmar, Frome Park Road, Stroud GL5 3LF* M: 07432-104702 E: rob@burles.org.uk

BURLEY, John Roland James. b 46. St Jo Coll Cam BA 67 MA 70. Trin Episc Sch for Min Ambridge Penn MDiv 88. **d** 81 **p** 82. SAMS Chile 81–90; TV Southgate *Chich* 90–99; R Alfold and Loxwood *Guildf* 99–07; P-in-c 08–11; rtd 11; PtO *Heref* from 11. *72 Dahn Drive, Ludlow SY8 1XZ* T: (01584) 873155 E: john@burleys.co.uk

BURLEY, Michael. b 58. Ridley Hall Cam 86. **d** 89 **p** 90. C Scarborough St Mary w Ch Ch and H Apostles *York* 89–92; C Drypool 93; TV 93–97; V Sutton St Mich 97–03; V Burley in Wharfedale *Bradf* 03–13; Assoc Dioc Dir of Ords 07–13; P-in-c Staines *Lon* 13–18; V Staines St Mary and St Pet 18–19; V Staines Ch Ch from 19. *The Vicarage, 44 Kenilworth Gardens, Staines-upon-Thames TW18 1DR* M: 07415-054353 E: michael.burley@btinternet.com

BURLTON, Aelred Harry. b 49. Sarum & Wells Th Coll 75. **d** 78 **p** 79. C Feltham *Lon* 78–82; Chapl Heathrow Airport 83–94; P-in-c Harmondsworth 92–94; R St Buryan, St Levan and Sennen *Truro* 94–05; rtd 05; PtO *Truro* from 14. *Farway Barn, Hellangove Farm, Gulval, Penzance TR20 8XD* T: (01736) 330426 E: zoeb.sing@hotmail.co.uk

BURMAN, Philip Harvey. b 47. Kelham Th Coll 66. **d** 70 **p** 71. C Huyton St Mich *Liv* 70–75; C Farnworth 75–77; TV Kirkby 77–83; V Hindley All SS 83–93; V Middlesbrough St Martin *York* 93–97; V Middlesbrough St Martin w St Cuth 97–99; P-in-c Eccleston St Thos *Liv* 99–08; V Liv St Chris Norris Green 08–16; rtd 16; PtO *York* from 17; Hon C Heaton Ch Ch w Halliwell St Marg *Man* from 17. *1 Somerset Road, Bolton BL1 4NE* E: philip.h.burman@googlemail.com

BURMESTER, Stephen John. b 66. Leeds Univ BSc 87. Wycliffe Hall Ox 96. **d** 98 **p** 99. C Lenton *S'well* 98–02; C Bebington *Ches* 02–08; V Handforth from 08. *The Vicarage, 36 Sagars Road, Handforth, Wilmslow SK9 3EE* T: (01625) 250559 *or* 532145

BURN, Geoffrey Livingston. b 60. Sydney Univ BSc 83 Imp Coll Lon PhD 87 St Jo Coll Dur BA 95. Cranmer Hall Dur 93. **d** 96 **p** 97. C St Austell *Truro* 96–03; PtO *Cant* 03–06; P Forest S Deanery *Glouc* 06–11; Hon C Cinderford St Jo 06–11; Hon C Cinderford w Littledean 10–11; Chapl Glos Primary Care Trust 06–11; Chapl HM YOI Roch 11–17; Chapl HM Pris Maidstone from 17. *HM Prison, 36 County Road, Maidstone ME14 1UZ* T: (01622) 775300 E: geoffrey.burn@justice.gov.uk

BURN, Canon Helen Mary. b 64. Down Coll Cam BA 86 New Coll Ox PGCE 88 Ex Univ MA 02 PhD 11. SWMTC 00. **d** 03 **p** 04. C Eythorne and Elvington w Waldershare etc *Cant* 03–06; Dir of Studies Local Min Tr Scheme 03–06; Dir Reader Tr *Glouc* 06–11; Tutor WEMTC 06–12; Dir of Studies

Ripon Coll Cuddesdon 11–12; Sen Lect Glos Univ *Glouc* 09–12; V Roch St Justus from 12; AD Roch from 17; Hon Can Roch Cathl from 21. *St Justus's Vicarage, 1 Binnacle Road, Rochester ME1 2XR*   T: (01634) 841183   M: 07818-492553   E: helenmburn@gmail.com

BURN, Leonard Louis. b 44. K Coll Lon BD 67 AKC 67. **d** 68 **p** 69. C Kingswinford St Mary *Lich* 68–70; C S Ascot *Ox* 70–72; C Caversham 72–76; Chapl Selly Oak Hosp Birm 76–81; Chapl Bris City Hosp 81–82; P-in-c Bris St Mich 81–83; R Peopleton and White Ladies Aston w Churchill etc *Worc* 83–88; V Bengeworth 88–97; Chapl St Richard's Hospice Worc 88–97; Chapl Evesham Coll 90–97; rtd 97; PtO *Glouc* 97–20; *Worc* 97–98; Chapl Worcs Community and Mental Health Trust 98–11. *Beckford Rise, Beckford, Tewkesbury GL20 7AN*   T/F: (01386) 881160   M: 07734-505663 E: leonard.burn@btinternet.com

BURN, Michael Campbell. b 46. JP 01. City of Leeds Coll of Educn CertEd 68 Open Univ MA 88 Univ of Wales (Trin St Dav) LTh 12. Yorks Min Course 12. **d** 12 **p** 13. NSM Rotherham *Sheff* 12–14; NSM Wath-upon-Dearne 14–16; rtd 16; PtO *Sheff* from 16; *Leeds* from 17. *6 Greenway, Honley, Holmfirth HD9 6NQ*   M: 07712-620303   E: michaelcburn@btinternet.com

BURN, Richard James Southerden. b 34. Pemb Coll Cam BA 56. Wells Th Coll 56. **d** 58 **p** 59. C Cheshunt *St Alb* 58–62; C Leighton Buzzard 65–66; C Glastonbury St Jo *B & W* 66–68; P-in-c Prestonpans *Edin* 68–71; P-in-c Stokesay *Heref* 71–75; P-in-c Dorrington 75–81; P-in-c Stapleton 75–81; P-in-c Leebotwood w Longnor 75–81; P-in-c Smethcott w Woolstaston 81; TR Melbury *Sarum* 81–87; P-in-c Quendon w Rickling and Wicken Bonhunt *Chelmsf* 87–92; R Quendon w Rickling and Wicken Bonhunt etc 92–95; rtd 95; V Isleworth St Fran *Lon* 95–00; Hon C S Warks Seven Gp *Cov* 06–09; PtO *Heref* 12–20. *The Old School House, 29 Lydbury North, Craven Arms SY7 8AU*   T: (01588) 680465   E: richard.burn58@yahoo.co.uk

BURN, Robert Pemberton. b 34. Peterho Cam BA 56 MA 60 Lon Univ PhD 68. CMS Tr Coll Chislehurst 60. **d** 63 **p** 81. India 63–71; PtO *Ely* 71–81; P-in-c Foxton 81–88; PtO *Ex* from 89. *Sunnyside, Barrack Road, Exeter EX2 6AB*   T: (01392) 430028

BURNAGE, Arthur Gavin. b 63. Ulster Univ BA 85 Cam Univ MA 05. Wycliffe Hall Ox 05. **d** 07 **p** 08. C Aldridge *Lich* 07–12; C Walsall St Pet 12–13; P-in-c 13–18; V from 18. *2 Brewer Street, Walsall WS2 8BH*   T: (01922) 640955   E: gav.burnage@gmail.com

BURNE, Sambrooke Roger. b 47. Lon Univ MB, BS 70 MRCGP 74. SAOMC 03. **d** 06 **p** 07. NSM Chalfont Leys *Ox* 06–14; PtO *Pet* from 14. *43 Glebe Rise, Kings Sutton, Banbury OX17 3PH*   T: (01295) 811936   M: 07901-882957   E: rogerburne@gmail.com

BURNETT (formerly DRURY), Mrs Caroline Norah. b 60. SAOMC 00. **d** 03 **p** 04. C Leavesden *St Alb* 03–09; C Bushey 09–13; P-in-c Compton w Shackleford and Peper Harow *Guildf* 13–19; PtO *Leic* from 20; NSM Guilsborough and Hollowell and Cold Ashby etc *Pet* from 21. *The Vicarage, 15 Church Mount, Guilsborough, Northampton NN6 8QA*   M: 07722-921973 E: caroline_burnett@btinternet.com

BURNETT, Paul Christian. b 73. St Hild Coll 18. **d** 21. C Whitby w Ruswarp *York* from 21. *2 Heather Drive, Whitby YO22 4DZ*   M: 07917-880232 E: paul.burnett59@yahoo.com

BURNETT, Susan Mary. b 50. Lon Univ BEd 73. Cranmer Hall Dur 76. **dss** 78 **d** 87 **p** 94. Welling *S'wark* 78–83; E Greenwich Ch Ch w St Andr and St Mich 83–91; Par Dn 87–91; Par Dn Sydenham All SS 91–94; C 94–95; C Lower Sydenham St Mich 91–95; V 95–09; rtd 09; PtO *Chich* from 19. *9 Grove Park, Chichester PO19 3HY*   T: (01243) 532748

BURNETT-HALL, Mrs Karen. b 46. Bp Grosseteste Coll CertEd 68 Lon Univ BD 82. Oak Hill Th Coll 86. **d** 89 **p** 94. Par Dn Norbury *Ches* 89–92; NSM York St Paul 93–95; NSM York St Barn 95–99; P-in-c 00–09; P-in-c Wimbotsham w Stow Bardolph and Stow Bridge etc *Ely* 11–17; PtO from 16. *8 The Vineyards, Ely CB7 4QG*   T: (01353) 665249   E: karen.bh@btinternet.com

BURNHAM, Adam Henry. b 83. Moody Bible Inst Chicago BSc 09 Sheff Univ BA 16. Westcott Ho Cam 13 Coll of Resurr Mirfield 14. **d** 16 **p** 17. C Taunton H Trin *B & W* 16–20; C Hanslope w Castlethorpe *Ox* from 20. *2 Western Drive, Hanslope, Milton Keynes MK19 7LD*   T: (01908) 510336   E: fatherburnham@gmail.com

BURNHAM, Stephen Patrick James. b 75. Ch Ch Ox BA 97. Westcott Ho Cam 00. **d** 02 **p** 03. C Vale of Belvoir *Leic* 02–05; TV Leic Resurr 05–12; V Leic St Anne, St Paul w St Aug 12–18; Chapl LOROS Hospice from 19. *76 Fielding Road, Birstall, Leicester LE4 3AL*

BURNIE, Judith. *See* SWEETMAN, Judith

BURNINGHAM, Richard Anthony. b 47. Keele Univ BA 70 Aber Univ CQSW 77 Roehampton Inst PGCE 85. All Nations Chr Coll 82 Oak Hill Th Coll 94. **d** 96 **p** 97. C Reigate St Mary *S'wark* 96–00; V Weston *Win* 00–12; rtd 12; PtO *Win* 12–19; Hon C Somborne w Ashley from 19. *The New Vicarage, Romsey Road, King's Somborne, Stockbridge SO20 6PR* E: vicarstpeterandstpaulks@outlook.com

BURNISTON, Aubrey John. b 53. St Jo Coll Dur BA 82 Leeds Univ MA 03. Cranmer Hall Dur 79. **d** 83 **p** 84. C Owton Manor *Dur* 83–86; TV Rugby *Cov* 86–93; V Heaton St Martin *Bradf* 93–09; Bp's Adv in Liturgy 00–09; V Islington St Jas w St Pet *Lon* from 09. *St James's Vicarage, 1A Arlington Square, London N1 7DS*   T: (020) 7226 4108   E: vicar@stjamesislington.org

BURNLEY, Suffragan Bishop of. *See* NORTH, The Rt Revd Philip John

BURNS, Arthur. *See* BURNS, Williams Arthur

BURNS, Canon Edward Joseph. b 38. Liv Univ BSc 58 St Cath Soc Ox BA 61 MA 64. Wycliffe Hall Ox 58. **d** 61 **p** 62. C Leyland St Andr *Blackb* 61–64; C Burnley St Pet 64–67; V Chorley St Jas 67–75; V Fulwood Ch Ch 75–03; RD Preston 79–86; Chapl Sharoe Green Hosp Preston 81–94; Hon Can Blackb Cathl 86–03; Bp's Adv on Hosp Chapls 89–94; rtd 03; PtO *Blackb* from 03. *2 Brook Croft, Ingol, Preston PR2 3TW*   T: (01772) 725528 E: ejburns3tw@btinternet.com

BURNS, Canon James Denis. b 43. Lich Th Coll 69. **d** 72 **p** 73. C Gt Wyrley *Lich* 72–75; C Atherton *Man* 75–76; Asst Chapl Sheff Ind Miss 76–79; C-in-c Masborough St Paul w St Jo 76–78; C-in-c Northfield St Mich 76–78; V Rotherham St Paul, St Mich and St Jo Ferham Park 78–79; V Lancaster Ch Ch *Blackb* 79–81; V Lancaster Ch Ch w St Jo and St Anne 81–86; V Chorley St Pet 86–96; R Rufford 96–07; Warden Past Assts 96–06; C Croston and Bretherton 06–07; rtd 07; Hon C Hesketh w Becconsall *Blackb* 07–09; Hon Can Blackb Cathl 99–09; PtO from 09; *Man* from 09. *81 Church Road, Uppermill, Oldham OL3 6DY*   M: 07940-850982 E: jimdburns@sky.com

BURNS, Mrs Jane Elizabeth. b 64. ERMC 15. **d** 18 **p** 19. NSM Finedon *Pet* 18–21; NSM Kettering SS Pet and Paul from 21; NSM Kettering All SS from 21. *51 Broadway, Kettering NN15 6DE*   T: (01536) 524936 E: janeburns2211@gmail.com

BURNS, Mark John. b 64. York St Jo Coll MA 00. Yorks Min Course 15. **d** 17 **p** 18. NSM Barnsley St Mary *Leeds* 17–18; NSM Cen Barnsley 18–20; NSM Grimethorpe w Brierley *Wakef* from 21; Ryhill *Leeds* from 21; NSM S Kirkby from 21; Asst Chapl Doncaster and Bassetlaw Teaching Hosps NHS Foundn Trust 17–18; Chapl HM Pris Wakef from 18. *HM Prison Wakefield, 5 Love Lane, Wakefield WF2 9AG*   T: (01924) 612000   E: mark.burns@leeds.anglican.org   or markjohn.burns@justice.gov.uk

BURNS, Matthew. b 79. Leeds Univ BA. Coll of Resurr Mirfield. **d** 05 **p** 06. C Wrexham *St As* 05–08; V Towyn 08–10; P-in-c 10–11; TV Wrexham 11–15; TV Leominster *Heref* from 15. *118 Buckfield Road, Leominster HR6 8SQ* E: matthew@jmburns.co.uk

BURNS, Michael John. b 53. AKC 76. Chich Th Coll 76. **d** 77 **p** 78. C Broseley w Benthall *Heref* 77–81; C Stevenage All SS Pin Green *St Alb* 81–84; V Tattenham Corner and Burgh Heath *Guildf* 84–92; C and Chapl Younger People Milton Keynes *Ox* 92–00; P-in-c Potters Bar K Chas *St Alb* 00–12; V 12–17; AD Barnet 11–16; Hon Can St Alb 13–17; P-in-c W Wimbledon Ch Ch *S'wark* 17–18; V from 18. *46 Pepys Road, London SW20 8PF*   T: (020) 8946 5954   E: ccww.vicar@gmail.com

BURNS, Canon Stuart Keith. b 66. Bp Grosseteste Coll BEd 88 Lon Univ BD 94 Leeds Univ MA 95 PhD 99. St Jo Coll Nottm. **d** 03 **p** 04. C Gt Bowden w Welham, Glooston and Cranoe etc *Leic* 03–06; Hd Sch for Min 06–16; Dir Miss and Min Dept from 16; Hon Can Leic Cathl from 17. *The Rectory, 3 Stonton Road, Church Langton, Market Harborough LE16 7SZ*   T: (01858) 540202 E: stuart.burns@leccofe.org

BURNS, The Rt Revd Stuart Maitland. b 46. Leeds Univ BA 67. Coll of Resurr Mirfield 67. **d** 69 **p** 70. C Wyther *Ripon* 69–73; Asst Chapl Leeds Univ and Leeds Poly 73–77; P-in-c Thornthwaite w Thruscross and Darley 77–84; V Leeds Gipton Epiphany 84–89; OSB from 89; Prior Burford Priory 96–01; Abbot 01–17; LtO *Ox* 89–08; PtO *Worc* from 10. *Mucknell Abbey, Mucknell Farm Lane, Stoulton, Worcester WR7 4RB*   T: (01905) 345900   E: stuart@mucknellabbey.org.uk

BURNS, Stuart Sandeman. b 62. Natal Univ BA 85 Ball Coll Ox BA 89 MA 94. St Paul's Coll Grahamstown. **d** 89 **p** 90. C Stanger S Africa 90–91; Dir Scripture Union Ind Schs 92–94; R Drakensberg 95–97; Chapl W Prov Prep Sch 98–99; I Kinneigh Union *C, C & R* 99–02; TV Bourne Valley *Sarum* 02–08; I Down H Trin w

Hollymount *D & D* 08–16; Min Can Down Cathl 10–16; R Cheddar, Draycott and Rodney Stoke *B & W* from 16. *The Vicarage, Station Road, Cheddar BS27 3AH* T: (01934) 743649 M: 07796-493174 E: stuart.burns01@gmail.com *or* cheddardraycottandrodneystoke@gmail.com

BURNS, William Arthur. b 51. CITC 08. **d** 11 **p** 12. NSM Glendermott *D & R* from 11. *33 Sevenoaks, Londonderry BT47 6AL* T: (028) 7134 4354 M: 07917-358317 E: arthurburns33@hotmail.co.uk

BURNSIDE, Mrs Melanie. b 73. St Hild Coll BA 21. **d** 21. C Kirkdale w Harome, Nunnington and Pockley *York* from 21. *The Rectory, Normanby, Sinnington, York YO62 6RH* T: (01751) 269667 E: revmelburnside@gmail.com

BURR, Mrs Ann Pamela. b 39. S Dios Minl Tr Scheme 83. **dss** 86 **d** 87 **p** 94. Fareham H Trin *Portsm* 86–06; Hon C 87–06; Hon Asst Chapl Knowle Hosp Fareham 86–90; Asst Chapl Qu Alexandra Hosp Portsm 90–92; Chapl Portsm Hosps NHS Trust 92–00; rtd 06; PtO *Portsm* from 06. *3 Bruce Close, Fareham PO16 7QJ* T: (01329) 281375 E: ann.burr@hotmail.co.uk

BURR, Mrs Anna Victoria. b 58. Southn Univ BA 80 Leeds Univ MA 07. NOC 04. **d** 07 **p** 08. NSM Fulford *York* 07–11; P-in-c Haddlesey w Hambleton and Birkin from 11; P-in-c Carlton and Drax from 18. *The Rectory, Millfield Road, Chapel Haddlesey, Selby YO8 8QF* T: (01757) 270325 E: burrannav@gmail.com

BURR, Christopher Edward. b 68. Univ of Wales (Cardiff) BTh 01. St Mich Coll Llan 98. **d** 01 **p** 02. C Llantrisant *Llan* 01–04; P-in-c Pwllgwaun and Llanddewi Rhondda 04–10; V Lisvane 10–19; Tutor St Padarn's Inst from 19. *St Padarn's Institute, 54 Cardiff Road, Llandaff, Cardiff CF5 2YJ* T: (029) 2056 3379 E: christopher.burr@stpadarns.ac.uk

BURR, Paul David. b 62. Birm Univ LLB 83. St Jo Coll Nottm MA 99. **d** 99 **p** 00. C Newark *S'well* 99–02; C Eaton *Nor* 02–05; P-in-c Swardeston w E Carleton, Intwood, Keswick etc 05–09; R from 09; RD Humbleyard 15–18. *The Vicarage, The Common, Swardeston, Norwich NR14 8EB* T: (01508) 570550 E: pburr100@gmail.com

BURR, Raymond Leslie. b 43. NEOC 82 Edin Th Coll 84. **d** 85 **p** 86. C Hartlepool St Paul *Dur* 85–87; C Sherburn w Pittington 87–89; R Lyons 89–95; RD Houghton 94–96; V S Shields St Hilda w St Thos 95–08; rtd 08. *57 Pierremont Road, Darlington DL3 6DN* T: (01325) 463666 E: ray@burr.org.uk

BURRELL, David Philip. b 56. Southn Univ BTh 90. Sarum & Wells Th Coll 85. **d** 88 **p** 89. C Ixworth and Bardwell *St E* 88–91; P-in-c Haughley w Wetherden 91–96; P-in-c Culford, W Stow and Wordwell w Flempton etc 96–98; R Lark Valley 98–14; R Four Rivers from 14. *The Vicarage, 15 Noyes Avenue, Laxfield, Woodbridge IP13 8EB* T: (01986) 798136 E: theparsnips@gmail.com

BURRELL, Martin John. b 51. Cant Ch Ch Univ Coll MA 00 ARCM 71. Trin Coll Bris BA 95. **d** 95 **p** 96. C Cant St Mary Bredin 95–99; V Cranbrook 99–09; Asst Dir of Ords 06–09; P-in-c Bushmead *St Alb* 09–14; V 14–15; Chapl to Gypsies, Travellers and Roma 15–18; rtd 18; PtO *Cant* from 20; Bp's Adv to Gypsy, Traveller and Roma Communities from 20. *6 Bastien Mews, Canterbury CT1 3BY* M: 07791-536713 E: mburrell51@gmail.com

BURRELL, Timothy Graham. b 43. JP 83. St Steph Ho Ox 69. **d** 72 **p** 07. C Haltwhistle *Newc* 72–73; NSM Harrogate St Wilfrid *Ripon* 06–13; rtd 13; PtO *Ripon* 13–14; *Leeds* from 14; Chapl to Bp Beverley *York* from 19. *8 St Hilda's Road, Harrogate HG2 8JY* T: (01423) 883832 M: 07885-681379 E: tim.burrell@virgin.net

BURRIDGE, Matthew Guy. b 73. Univ Coll Lon BSc 94 MB, BS 97. NTMTC BA 08. **d** 08 **p** 09. NSM Kentish Town St Silas and H Trin w St Barn *Lon* 08–14; NSM Tottenham St Benet Fink from 14; NSM Tottenham St Phil from 14. *Health E1 Homeless Medical Centre, 9-11 Brick Lane, London E1 6PU* T: (020) 7247 0090 E: fr.matthewburridge@googlemail.com

BURRIDGE, Prof Richard Alan. b 55. Univ Coll Ox BA 77 MA 81 Nottm Univ CertEd 78 PhD 89. St Jo Coll Nottm 82. **d** 85 **p** 86. C Bromley SS Pet and Paul *Roch* 85–87; Chapl Ex Univ 87–94; Dean K Coll Lon 94–19; Visiting Prof Bibl Interpr from 19; Lic Preacher *Lon* from 94; PtO *S'wark* from 98; *Chelmsf* from 05; Can Th Sarum Cathl from 13; NSM St Mary le Strand w St Clem Danes *Lon* 17–19; PtO from 21. *26 Lockside, Marple, Stockport SK6 6BN* E: richard.burridge@kcl.ac.uk

BURRIDGE-BUTLER, Paul David. *See* BUTLER, Paul David

BURROW, Miss Alison Sarah. b 59. Homerton Coll Cam BEd 82. Westcott Ho Cam 84. **d** 87 **p** 03. Par Dn Hebden Bridge *Wakef* 87–88; Par Dn Prestwood and Gt Hampden *Ox* 88–90; Par Dn Olney w Emberton 90–92; rtd 92; Hon C Bedford St Pet w St Cuth *St Alb* 02–07; P-in-c Renhold 07–16; PtO *Ox* 16–20; *St Alb* from 17; Chapl Anjulita Court Care

BURROW, Canon Margaret Anne. b 46. Open Univ BA 82 Leeds Univ MSc 85 Lon Univ TCert 68. Coll of Resurr Mirfield 06. **d** 07 **p** 08. NSM Douglas St Ninian *S & M* 07–08; NSM St German's Cathl 08–13; Bp's Chapl 14–17; Can St German's Cathl 14–16; rtd 17; PtO *S & M* from 18. *Balley Beg, 24A Derby Road, Peel, Isle of Man IM5 1HW* T: (01624) 662173 M: 07624-235711 E: burrow.margaret@gmail.com

BURROW, Ronald. b 31. Univ Coll Dur BA 55. St Steph Ho Ox 83. **d** 85 **p** 86. C Dawlish *Ex* 85–87; TV Ottery St Mary, Alfington, W Hill, Tipton etc 87–91; P-in-c Pyworthy, Pancrasweek and Bridgerule 91–95; rtd 95; PtO *Ex* 95–21. *Abbeyfield Society, Apartment 1, Marjorie Baker House, Vicarage Street, Colyton EX24 6LJ* T/F: (01297) 553882

BURROW, Stephen Paul. b 62. Univ Coll Dur BA 84. Trin Coll Bris 09. **d** 11 **p** 12. C Chilcompton w Downside and Stratton on the Fosse *B & W* 11–15; R Heyford w Stowe Nine Churches and Flore etc *Pet* from 15; RD Daventry from 20. *The Rectory, Church Lane, Nether Heyford, Northampton NN7 3LQ* T: (01327) 344436 M: 07511-544375 E: s_p_burrow@yahoo.co.uk

BURROWS, Clive Robert. b 60. Bath Coll of HE BEd 82 Ches Coll of HE BA 04. NOC 01. **d** 04 **p** 05. C N Wingfield, Clay Cross and Pilsley *Derby* 04–09; P-in-c Hyson Green and Forest Fields *S'well* 09–11; V from 11. *St Stephen's Vicarage, 18 Russell Road, Nottingham NG7 6HB* T: 0115-978 4480 E: clive@revburrows.plus.com

BURROWS, Canon David. b 62. Leeds Univ BA 85 MA 03. Linc Th Coll 86. **d** 88 **p** 89. C Kippax w Allerton Bywater *Ripon* 88–91; C Manston 91–95; Chapl Killingbeck Hosp 94; V Halifax St Anne Southowram *Wakef* 95–00; P-in-c Charlestown 95–00; V Southowram and Claremount 00–02; Chapl Overgate Hospice 02–14; TV Elland *Wakef* 02–05; TR 05–12; R 12–14; *Leeds* from 14; C Greetland and W Vale *Wakef* 08–14; C Stainland w Outlane 06–14; RD Brighouse and Elland 08–15; Hon Can Wakef Cathl from 10. *All Saints' Vicarage, Charles Street, Elland HX5 0JF* T: (01422) 373184 M: 07928-895668 E: david.burrows@leeds.anglican.org

BURROWS, David MacPherson. b 43. NOC. **d** 82 **p** 83. NSM Newburgh *Liv* 82–93; NSM Newburgh w Westhead 93–12; Dioc Adv NSM 03–11; rtd 12; PtO *Liv* from 12. *34 Woodrow Drive, Newburgh, Wigan WN8 7LB* T: (01257) 462948

BURROWS, Diane. b 48. **d** 05 **p** 06. NSM Saltash *Truro* 05–18. *20 Andrews Way, Hatt, Saltash PL12 6PE* T: (01752) 842540 E: revdburrows@gmail.com

BURROWS, Graham Charles. b 47. Leeds Univ CertEd 69 Open Univ BA 81. NOC 87. **d** 90 **p** 91. C Chorlton-cum-Hardy St Clem *Man* 90–93; TV Horwich 93; TV Horwich and Rivington 93–94. *20 Glazebury Drive, Westhoughton, Bolton BL5 3JZ* T: (01942) 550404

BURROWS, Graham John. b 63. Jes Coll Cam BA 84 MA 88 Goldsmiths' Coll Lon PGCE 94. Oak Hill Th Coll 07. **d** 09 **p** 10. C Polegate *Chich* 09–13; P-in-c Burton and Holme *Carl* 13–19; V from 19. *St James's Vicarage, Glebe Close, Burton, Carnforth LA6 1PL* T: (01524) 781210 M: 07740-622962 E: vicarburtonholme@gmail.com

BURROWS, Jean. b 54. CertEd 75. Trin Coll Bris 89. **d** 91 **p** 94. C Allesley *Cov* 91–95; C Thorley *St Alb* 95–99; P-in-c Harrold and Carlton w Chellington 99–06; R 06–07; P-in-c Boughton under Blean w Dunkirk and Hernhill *Cant* 07–16; P-in-c Goodnestone w Graveney 15–16; V Boughton-under-Blean w Dunkirk etc 16–21; rtd 21. *Address temp unknown* E: jeanburrows@jeanius.me.uk

BURROWS, Canon John Edward. b 36. Leeds Univ BA 60 PGCE 63. Coll of Resurr Mirfield. **d** 63 **p** 65. C Much Hadham *St Alb* 63–65; Hon C Haggerston St Mary w St Chad *Lon* 65–73; P-in-c Finsbury St Clem w St Barn and St Matt 73–76; Chapl Woodbridge Sch 76–83; V Ipswich St Bart *St E* 83–03; Hon Can St E Cathl 01–03; rtd 03; PtO *St E* from 03; *Chelmsf* 14–16. *Flat 518, 1 Coprolite Street, Ipswich IP3 0BN* T: (01473) 216629

✠**BURROWS, The Rt Revd Michael Andrew James.** b 61. TCD BA 82 MA 85 MLitt 86. **d** 87 **p** 88 **c** 06. C Douglas Union w Frankfield *C, C & R* 87–91; Dean of Res TCD 91–94; Min Can St Patr Cathl Dublin 91–94; I Bandon Union *C, C & R* 94–02; Can Cork and Cloyne Cathls 96–02; Dean Cork and I Cork St Fin Barre's Union 02–06; Bp *C, F & O* from 06. *Bishop's House, Troysgate, Kilkenny, Republic of Ireland* T: (00353) (56) 778 6633 E: cfobishop@gmail.com

BURROWS, Canon Paul Anthony. b 55. Nottm Univ BA 77 Gen Th Sem NY STM 88. St Steph Ho Ox 77. **d** 79 **p** 80. C Camberwell St Giles *S'wark* 79–81; C St Helier 81–83; C Fareham SS Pet and Paul *Portsm* 83–85; V Union St Luke and All SS New Jersey USA 85–90; R Temple Hills St Barn

Maryland 90–95; P-in-c Des Moines St Mark Iowa 95–01; Can Des Moines Cathl 98–01; R San Francisco Advent of Ch the K 01–15; rtd 15. *51 Learmonth Grove, Edinburgh EH4 1BX* M: 07746-827791 E: paulburrows1@mac.com

BURROWS, Philip Geoffrey. b 59. Birm Univ BSc 80. Oak Hill Th Coll 90. **d** 92 **p** 93. C Poynton *Ches* 92–96; Min Cheadle Hulme Em CD 96–03; V Mottram in Longdendale 03–11; CF from 11. *c/o MOD Chaplains (Army)*   T: (01264)   383430   M: 07817-314979 E: philipburrows@man4god.co.uk

BURROWS, Samuel Reginald. b 30. AKC 57. **d** 58 **p** 59. C Shildon *Dur* 58–62; C Heworth St Mary 62–67; C-in-c Leam Lane CD 67–72; C-in-c Bishopwearmouth St Mary V w St Pet CD 72–77; R Bewcastle and Stapleton *Carl* 77–82; R Harrington 82–90; P-in-c Millom 90; V 90–95; rtd 95. *40 Lindisfarne Road, Durham DH1 5YQ*

BURROWS, Victoria Elizabeth. b 61. STETS 01. **d** 04 **p** 05. C The Bourne and Tilford *Guildf* 04–07; R Long Ditton 07–14; P-in-c R Wootton Bassett *Sarum* 14–15; V 15–16; RD Calne 14–16; V Bramley and Grafham *Guildf* 16–18; C Pendoylan w Welsh St Donats *Llan* 18–19; C Peterston-super-Ely w St Brides-super-Ely 18–19; P-in-c Radyr from 19; R St Fagans and Michaelston-super-Ely from 20. *The Rectory, Rectory Close, Radyr, Cardiff CF15 8EW* M: 07515-965781 E: vicki.burrows@me.com

BURSELL, Michael Hingston McLaughlin. b 70. K Coll Cam MA 96 Open Univ MBA 02. ERMC 05. **d** 08 **p** 09. NSM Halstead Area *Chelmsf* 08–16; NSM Upper Colne 16–17; NSM Sible Hedingham w Castle Hedingham 16–17; NSM The Hedinghams and Upper Colne from 17. *Bowyer's, North Road, Great Yeldham, Halstead CO9 4QD* T: (01787) 237486   F: 08700-517360   M: 07971-926937 E: mike.bursell@anglicanpriest.org

BURSELL, His Honour the Revd Canon Rupert David Hingston. b 42. QC 86. Ex Univ LLB 63 St Edm Hall Ox BA 67 MA 72 DPhil 72. St Steph Ho Ox 67. **d** 68 **p** 69. NSM St Marylebone w H Trin *Lon* 68–69; NSM Almondsbury *Bris* 69–71; NSM Bedminster St Fran 71–75; NSM Bedminster 75–82; NSM Bris Ch Ch w St Ewen and All SS 83–88; NSM City of Bris 83–88; LtO 88–95; LtO *B & W* 72–92; Chan *Dur* 89–17; Chan *B & W* 92; Chan St Alb 92–02; Hon Can St Alb 96–02; NSM Cheddar *B & W* 93–11; Dep Chan *York* 94–02; Hon CF 96–01; Chan *Ox* 02–13; Hon Can Ch Ch from 11; LtO from 11; rtd 17. *Pear Tree Cottage, Hatchet Leys Lane, Thornborough, Buckingham MK18 2BU*

BURSON-THOMAS, Canon Michael Edwin. b 52. Sarum & Wells Th Coll 84. **d** 86 **p** 87. C Bitterne Park *Win* 86–89; V Lockerley and E Dean w E and W Tytherley 89–95; P-in-c Fotherby *Linc* 95–99; Asst Local Min Officer 95–99; V Horncastle w Low Toynton 99–06; R Greetham w Ashby Puerorum 99–06; V High Toynton 99–06; R Horncastle Gp 06–07; RD Horncastle 01–06; Spirituality Adv Adnry Stow and Lindsey 07–14; P-in-c Scotter w E Ferry *Linc* 07–14; P-in-c Scotton w Northorpe 07–14; RD Is of Axholme 11; RD Manlake 11; rtd 14; Gen Preacher *Linc* 14–20; Can and Preb Linc Cathl 12–20; PtO *Win* from 21. *5 Shrubbs Hill Gardens, Lyndhurst SO43 7DL* T: (023) 8028 2311 M: 07777-641357 E: mbursonthomas@btinternet.com

BURSTON, Canon Robert Benjamin Stuart. b 45. St Chad's Coll Dur BA 68. **d** 70 **p** 71. C Whorlton *Newc* 70–77; V Alwinton w Holystone and Alnham 77–83; TR Glendale Gp 83–15; Hon Can Newc Cathl 95–15; rtd 15; PtO *Newc* from 16. *Woodbine Cottage, Holystone, Morpeth NE65 7AJ*

BURT, David Alan. b 44. Southn Univ BTh 98. STETS 95. **d** 98 **p** 99. C Goring-by-Sea *Chich* 98–06; P-in-c Lyminster 06–10; rtd 10; PtO *Chich* from 15. *15 Fernhurst Drive, Goring-by-Sea, Worthing BN12 5AH*

BURT, Canon Paul Andrew. b 52. Leeds Univ BA 74 K Coll Lon MA 02 Univ of Wales (Ban) PhD 09. Ridley Hall Cam 82. **d** 84 **p** 85. C Edin St Thos 84–88; CMS Bahrain 88–90; R Melrose *Edin* 91–00; Chapl Borders Gen Hosp NHS Trust 93–98; Ho Master Win Coll 00–04; Hd RS Pilgrims' Sch 00–04; Chapl and Hd RE K Coll Sch Cam 04–06; Sen Chapl Win Coll 06–12; Sen Chapl Miss to Seafarers Dubai 12–18; Regional Dir Gulf and S Asia Miss to Seafarers 14–18; Hon Can St Paul's Cathl Nicosia from 18. *The Angel Appeal, The Mission to Seafarers, Dubai, United Arab Emirates* M: (00971) 50-552 6044 E: paul.burt.mts@gmail.com

BURT, Roger Malcolm. b 45. MBE 91. St Jo Coll Auckland. **d** 73 **p** 74. V Tinui NZ 73–80; P-in-c Colton *Nor* 80; P-in-c Easton 80; V Easton w Colton and Marlingford 80–88; CF 88–01; P-in-c E Coker w Sutton Bingham and Closworth *B & W* 01–10; rtd 10; PtO *B & W* 15–16; Chapl Yeovil Distr Hosp NHS Foundn Trust from 16; PtO *Sarum* 16–18; *B & W* from 20. *Hugh Sexey's Hospital, Bruton BA10 0AS* E: rogermburt@gmail.com

BURTON, Andrew John. b 63. St Kath Coll Liv BA 84. Cranmer Hall Dur 86. **d** 88 **p** 89. C Harlescott *Lich* 88–91; C Ches H Trin 91–94; P-in-c Congleton St Jas 94–01; R Calton, Cauldon, Grindon, Waterfall etc *Lich* 01–08; RD Alstonfield 03–08; V Bushey Heath *St Alb* from 08. *St Peter's Vicarage, 19 High Road, Bushey Heath, Bushey WD23 1EA* T: (020) 8950 1424 E: fr.burton@btinternet.com

BURTON, Miss Barbara Louise. b 57. Leic Univ LLB 81 Solicitor 84. ERMC 03. **d** 06 **p** 07. NSM March St Jo *Ely* 06–10; P-in-c Barton Bendish w Beachamwell and Shingham 10–16; P-in-c Wereham 10–16; P-in-c Fincham 10–16; P-in-c Shouldham 10–16; P-in-c Shouldham Thorpe 10–16; P-in-c Boughton 10–16; P-in-c Marham 10–16; P-in-c Watlington 14–16; P-in-c Holme Runcton w S Runcton and Wallington 14–16; P-in-c Tottenhill w Wormegay 14–16; RD Fincham and Feltwell 12–16; P-in-c W Walton 16–18; R from 18; P-in-c Walpole St Peter w Walpole St Andrew 16–18; R from 18; R Clenchwarton from 20. *The Rectory, Church Road, Walpole St Peter, Wisbech PE14 7NS* E: barbaraburton@btinternet.com

BURTON, Charles Edmund. b 71. Newc Univ BSc 95. St Hild Coll 16. **d** 19 **p** 20. C Wath-upon-Dearne *Sheff* from 19. *The Vicarage, Church Drive, Wentworth, Rotherham S62 7TW*   T: (01226)   102729   M: 07803-219746 E: charlesburton@uk2.net

BURTON, Daniel John. b 96. St Jo Coll Cam BA 17 MA 21 MPhil 21. Westcott Ho Cam 19. **d** 21. C Carshalton *S'wark* from 21. *37 St Barnabas Road, Sutton SM1 4NS* M: 07582-565032   E: curateofcarshalton@gmail.com   or danieljohnburton@gmail.com

BURTON, Canon Daniel John Ashworth. b 63. Regent's Park Coll Ox BA 88 MA 93 Heythrop Coll Lon MTh 93. St Mich Coll Llan 93. **d** 94 **p** 95. C Mountain Ash *Llan* 94–97; R St Brides Minor w Bettws 97–02; R St Brides Minor w Bettws w Aberkenfig 02–03; P-in-c Cheetham *Man* 03–12; AD N Man 10–12; TR Salford All SS from 12; AD Salford 17–21; Hon Can Man Cathl from 13. *The Rectory, 92 Fitzwarren Street, Salford M6 5RS* T: 0161-745 7608 E: ashworthburton@hotmail.com

BURTON, David Alan. b 53. St Jo Coll Dur BA 75. Westcott Ho Cam 81. **d** 84 **p** 85. C Bedford St Andr *St Alb* 84–87; C Leighton Buzzard w Eggington, Hockliffe etc 87–91; V Kingsbury Episcopi w E Lambrook *B & W* 91–94; V Kingsbury Episcopi w E Lambrook, Hambridge etc 94–95; R Bishops Lydeard w Bagborough and Cothelstone 95–03; rtd 04; C Dawlish and Kenton, Mamhead, Powderham, Cofton and Starcross *Ex* 06–11; P-in-c Hemyock w Culm Davy, Clayhidon and Culmstock 11–18; PtO *B & W* from 19. *5 Clay Court, Uffculme, Cullompton EX15 3FE* T: (01884) 841379 E: dave.burton@mac.com

BURTON, Desmond Jack. b 49. Sarum & Wells Th Coll 70. **d** 73 **p** 74. C Lakenham St Jo *Nor* 73–77; C Gt Yarmouth 77–80; R Tidworth *Sarum* 80–83; Chapl HM Pris Pentonville 83–84; Chapl HM Pris Standford Hill 84–88; Chapl HM Pris Swaleside 88–93; Chapl HM Pris Roch 93–99; Chapl HM Pris Whitemoor 99–05; Chapl HM Pris Whatton 05–09; P-in-c Balcombe *Chich* 09–17; rtd 17. *6 Goldring Avenue, Hellingly, Hailsham BN27 4BX*

BURTON, Graham John. b 45. Bris Univ BA 69. Tyndale Hall Bris 69. **d** 71 **p** 72. C Leic St Chris 71–75; C Southall Green St Jo *Lon* 75–79; CMS Pakistan 80–92; P-in-c Basford w Hyson Green *S'well* 92–98; P-in-c Hyson Green and Forest Fields 98–01; Assoc P 01–07; Dir Rainbow Project 01–07; rtd 07; PtO *S'well* from 07. *6 Meadow Brown Road, Nottingham NG7 5PH* E: burtongraham2@gmail.com

BURTON, Hugh Anthony. b 56. Edin Univ BD 79. Cranmer Hall Dur 81. **d** 83 **p** 84. C Coalville and Bardon Hill *Leic* 83–87; P-in-c Packington w Normanton-le-Heath 87–92; V 92–96; V Dudley St Jo *Worc* 96–08; TV Kidderminster St Geo 96–08; P-in-c 08–12; TR Kidderminster E 12–19; RD Kidderminster 13–19; TR Dudley from 19. *50 Laurel Road, Dudley DY1 3ER*

BURTON, Karen. b 68. Graduate Soc Dur MA 92 PhD 98. ERMC 13. **d** 16 **p** 17. NSM Bury St Edmunds All SS w St Jo and St Geo *St E* 16–19; NSM Lark Valley 16–19; TR Blackbourne from 19. *The Vicarage, Commister Lane, Ixworth, Bury St Edmunds IP31 2HE* E: revkarenburton@outlook.com

BURTON, Michael John. b 55. Leeds Univ BSc 76 Leeds Poly BSc 80. St Jo Coll Nottm 86. **d** 88 **p** 89. C Charles w Plymouth St Matthias *Ex* 88–92; V Paignton St Paul Preston 92–99; TV Almondbury w Farnley Tyas *Wakef* 99–02; V Roade and Ashton w Hartwell *Pet* 02–11; C Collingtree w Courteenhall and Milton Malsor 09–11; V Salcey 11–20; RD Towcester 03–09; rtd 20. *Address temp unknown* E: michaelburton5@aol.com

BURTON, Nicholas Guy. b 69. Bris Univ BSc 91 ACCA 00. Ridley Hall Cam 03. **d** 05 **p** 06. C Ore St Helen and

St Barn *Chich* 05–09; C Bexhill St Steph 09–11. *6 Hilbert Close, Tunbridge Wells TN2 3SN* M: 07851-742049 E: ngb.cofe@tiscali.co.uk

BURTON, Nicholas John. b 52. St Steph Ho Ox 77. **d** 80 **p** 81. C Leic St Matt and St Geo 80–82; C Leic Resurr 82–83; TV 83–88; C Narborough and Huncote 88–90; R 90–10; rtd 10. *Address withheld by request* E: mrnjb@talktalk.net

BURTON, Richard Peter. b 56. Nottm Univ BA 80. Cranmer Hall Dur 80. **d** 82 **p** 83. C Linthorpe *York* 82–85; R Bishop Burton w Walkington 85–91; V Tadcaster w Newton Kyme 91–96; RD New Ainsty 01–06; Par Miss Development Officer *Ches* 06–11; C Ches St Mary 06–11; PtO *Lich* 11–16; C Whittington and W Felton w Haughton 16–19; Miss Area Ldr Tanat-Vyrnwy *St As* from 20. *The Vicarage, 8 Parc Bronhyddon, Llansantffraid SY22 6DZ* T: (01691) 829116 M: 07443-910608 E: everthankful9@gmail.com

BURTON, Mrs Sarah Elizabeth. b 59. Nottm Univ BMedSci 80 Dur Univ PGCE 82. NOC 05. **d** 08 **p** 09. C Eastham *Ches* 08–11; R Whittington and W Felton w Haughton *Lich* 11–19; P-in-c Vyrnwy Miss Area *St As* 19–20; P-in-c Tanat-Vyrnwy from 20. *8 Parc Bronhyddon, Llansantffraid SY22 6DZ*

BURTON, Mrs Virginia Ann. b 55. St As Minl Tr Course 00. **d** 03 **p** 04. C Llanrhos *St As* 03–08; C Colwyn Bay w Brynymaen 08–12; P-in-c Towyn 12–15; C Llanddulas and Llysfaen 12–15; C Abergele and St George 12–15; rtd 15; Hon C Llanrwst, Llanddoged w Capel Garmon etc *St As* 15–16; Hon C Aberconwy Miss Area 17 and from 18; PtO 17–18. *Siabod, Ffordd Trwyn Swch, Llanddoged, Llanrwst LL26 0DZ* T: (01492) 642778 E: ginnyburton@hotmail.co.uk

BURTON EVANS, David. *See* EVANS, David Burton

✠**BURTON-JONES, The Rt Revd Simon David.** b 62. Em Coll Cam BA 84 MA 88. St Jo Coll Nottm BTh 92 MA 93. **d** 93 **p** 94 **c** 18. C Darwen St Pet w Hoddlesden *Blackb* 93–96; C Biggin Hill *Roch* 96–98; P-in-c Plaistow St Mary 98–00; V 00–05; R Chislehurst St Nic 05–10; AD Bromley 01–06; Adn Roch 10–18; Can Res Roch Cathl 10–18; Suff Bp Tonbridge from 18. *Bishop's Lodge, 25 Shoesmith Lane, Kings Hill, West Malling ME19 4FF* E: bishop.tonbridge@rochester.anglican.org

BURTT, Andrew Keith. b 50. Massey Univ (NZ) BA 72 MA 74 DipEd 76. St Jo Coll (NZ) LTh 82. **d** 81 **p** 82. NZ 81–83; CF 84–92; Sen Chapl Brighton Coll 93–03; Chapl Portsm Gr Sch 03–16; Par P Paphos Cyprus and the Gulf from 16. *PO Box 61083, Kato Paphos, 8130 Paphos, Cyprus* T: (00357) (26) 953373 E: chaplain.acp@cytanet.com.cy

BURTWELL, Stanley Peter. b 32. Leeds Univ BA 55. Coll of Resurr Mirfield 55. **d** 57 **p** 58. C Leeds St Hilda *Ripon* 57–61; S Africa 61–72; P-in-c Gt Hanwood *Heref* 72–78; R 78–83; RD Pontesbury 80–83; V Upper Norwood St Jo *Cant* 83–84; V Upper Norwood St Jo *S'wark* 85–90; RD Croydon N 85–90; TR Bourne Valley *Sarum* 90–97; rtd 97; PtO *Sarum* 97–20. *Splinters, 116 High Street, Swanage BN19 2NY* T: (01929) 421785 E: pburtwell@yahoo.co.uk

BURY, Dennis Richard. b 43. Man Univ BA 66. Andover Newton Th Coll MA 71 Sarum Th Coll 66. **d** 69 **p** 71. C Southport H Trin *Liv* 69–71; C Gt Crosby St Faith 71–72; PtO *Lon* 92–98 and from 03; Hon C Belsize Park 02–03; rtd 08. *47 Mayfield Road, London N8 9LL* T: (020) 8348 9181 E: d.bury@rhul.ac.uk *or* dennisscience@hotmail.com

BURY, Miss Dorothy Jane. b 53. Lanc Univ BA 96 MA 98 St Hild Coll Dur CertEd 75. Ripon Coll Cuddesdon 00. **d** 02 **p** 03. C Thornton-le-Fylde *Blackb* 02–06; P-in-c Wigan St Anne *Liv* 06–12; Chapl Deanery C of E High Sch Wigan 06–12; V Fence-in-Pendle and Higham *Blackb* 12–18; rtd 18; PtO *Blackb* from 18. *1 Feilden's Farm Lane, Mellor Brook, Blackburn BB2 7PD* T: (01254) 659526 M: 07715-560031 E: tillybury@btinternet.com

BURY, The Very Revd Nicholas Ayles Stillingfleet. b 43. Qu Coll Cam BA 65 MA 69 Ch Ch Ox MA 71. Cuddesdon Coll. **d** 68 **p** 69. C Liv Our Lady and St Nic 68–71; Chapl Ch Ch *Ox* 71–75; V Stevenage St Mary Shephall *St Alb* 75–84; V St Peter-in-Thanet *Cant* 84–97; RD Thanet 93–97; Hon Can Cant Cathl 94–97; Dean Glouc 97–10; rtd 10; PtO *Heref* from 11. *122 The Homend, Ledbury HR8 1BZ* T: (01531) 636075 E: n.bury95@btinternet.com

BUSBY, John. b 38. St Cath Coll Cam MA 60 CEng. **d** 93 **p** 94. OLM Worplesdon *Guildf* 93–02; OLM Pirbright 02–04; PtO from 06. *Iona, Fox Corner, Worplesdon, Guildford GU3 3PP* T: (01483) 234562 E: john.busby@ionafoxcorner.plus.com

BUSBY, Nicola Jane. b 68. Qu Foundn (Course) 15. **d** 18 **p** 19. OLM Mease Valley *Lich* from 18. *Bramble Cottage, Church Lane, Chilcote, Swadlincote DE12 8DL* T: (01827) 373390 M: 07740-822095 E: busbynicola@gmail.com

BUSFIELD, Miss Lynn Maria. b 60. Trin Coll Bris BA 99. **d** 99 **p** 00. C Scartho *Linc* 99–03; TV Marlborough *Sarum* 03–05; Chapl Mt Edgcumbe Hospice 05–08; P-in-c Fladbury, Hill

and Moor, Wyre Piddle etc *Worc* 09–11; P-in-c Peopleton and White Ladies Aston w Churchill etc 11–13; C Fladbury, Hill and Moor etc and Abberton, The Flyfords, Naunton Beauchamp etc 11–13; Chapl Heart of England NHS Foundn Trust from 13. *60 Horrell Road, Birmingham B26 2PD* T: 0121-742 2895 E: lynnbusfield@btinternet.com

BUSH, Caspar James Barnard. b 68. Newc Univ BSc 90. SWMTC 09. **d** 12 **p** 13. C Perranzabuloe and Crantock w Cubert *Truro* 12–15; TR Redruth w Lanner and Treleigh from 15; RD Carnmarth N from 17. *1 Wheal Uny, Trewirgie Road, Redruth TR15 2TD* T: (01209) 216958 E: casparbush@gmail.com

BUSH, George Raymond. b 57. St Jo Coll Cam BA 81 MA 84 Univ of Wales LLM 95. Ripon Coll Cuddesdon BA 84 MA 88. **d** 85 **p** 86. C Leeds St Aid *Ripon* 85–89; Chapl St Jo Coll Cam 89–94; V Hoxton St Anne w St Columba *Lon* 94–02; R St Mary le Bow w St Pancras Soper Lane etc from 02. *The Rector's Lodgings, Cheapside, London EC2V 6AU* T: (020) 7248 5139 F: 7248 0509 E: grbush@london.anglican.org

BUSH, Kieran John Christopher. b 80. Ch Coll Cam BA 01 MA 05. Oak Hill Th Coll MTh 11. **d** 11 **p** 12. C Dagenham *Chelmsf* 11–15; V Walthamstow St Jo from 15. *The Vicarage, 18 Brookscroft Road, London E17 4LH* M: 07709-119325 E: kieranbush@hotmail.com

BUSH, Rachma. *See* ABBOTT, Esther Rachma Hartley

BUSH, The Very Revd Roger Charles. b 56. K Coll Lon BA 78 Leeds Univ BA 85. Coll of Resurr Mirfield 83. **d** 86 **p** 87. C Newbold w Dunston *Derby* 86–90; TV Leic Resurr 90–94; TR Redruth w Lanner and Treleigh *Truro* 94–04; RD Carnmarth N 96–03; Hon Can Truro Cathl 03–04; Can Res Truro Cathl 04–12; Adn Cornwall 06–12; Dean Truro from 12. *Westwood House, Tremorvah Crescent, Truro TR1 1NL* T: (01872) 225630 E: dean@trurocathedral.org.uk

BUSH, Lt Col Walter Patrick Anthony. b 39. **d** 07 **p** 08. OLM Watercombe *Sarum* 07–11; NSM 11–17; PtO from 17. *Holworth Farmhouse, Holworth, Dorchester DT2 8NH* T: (01305) 852242 E: bushinarcadia@yahoo.co.uk

BUSHAU, Reginald Francis. b 49. Shimer Coll Illinois AB 71. St Steph Ho Ox BA 73 MA 98. **d** 74 **p** 75. C Deptford St Paul *S'wark* 74–77; C Willesden St Andr and Gladstone Park St Fran *Lon* 77–82; P-in-c Brondesbury St Anne w Kilburn H Trin 83–88; V Paddington St Mary Magd 88–97; AD Westmr Paddington 92–97; P-in-c S Kensington St Steph 96–98; V 98–16; rtd 16; PtO *Lon* from 16; *Chelmsf* 17–21. *236 Prospect Road, Woodford Green IG8 7NQ* E: bushrf@aol.com

BUSHBY, Michael Reginald. b 42. LSE BSc 70 Leeds Univ MA 97. **d** 02 **p** 03. NSM S Cave and Ellerker w Broomfleet *York* 02–05; P-in-c Newbald from 05. *The Vicarage, 7 Dot Hill Close, North Newbald, York YO43 4TS* T: (01430) 801068 M: 07976-493359 E: michaelbushby@btinternet.com

BUSHELL, Anthony Colin. b 59. Pemb Coll Ox MA 82 Barrister 83. S'wark Ord Course 93. **d** 96 **p** 97. NSM Felsted and Lt Dunmow *Chelmsf* 96–98; NSM Stanway 98–06; NSM Greenstead w Colchester St Anne 06–14; P-in-c Stanway from 14. *Pump Hall, Middle Green, Wakes Colne, Colchester CO6 2BJ* F: (01787) 222361 M: 07484-265258 E: vicar@stalbrights.org

BUSHELL, Mrs Linda Mary. b 52. Bradf and Ilkley Coll BEd 91. STETS 06. **d** 09 **p** 10. NSM Bembridge *Portsm* 09–16; NSM Brighstone and Brooke w Mottistone 16–19; NSM Shorwell w Kingston 16–19; NSM W Wight 19–20; rtd 20; PtO *Portsm* from 20. *Old School, Fine Lane, Shorwell, Newport PO30 3JY* E: linda.bushell1@btinternet.com

✠**BUSHYAGER (née TWITCHEN), The Rt Revd Ruth Kathleen Frances.** b 77. Bris Univ MSci 99. Wycliffe Hall Ox BA 04. **d** 05 **p** 06 **c** 20. C Wilford *S'well* 05–07; NSM Abingdon *Ox* 08; Asst Chapl St Edw Sch Ox 08–10; Area Missr Kensington Area *Lon* 10–14; V Dorking St Paul *Guildf* 14–20; AD Dorking 19–20; Area Bp Horsham *Chich* from 20. *Bishop's House, 21 Guildford Road, Horsham RH12 1LU* E: bishop.horsham@chichester.anglican.org

BUSK, David Westly. b 60. Magd Coll Cam BA 83 St Jo Coll Dur BA 88. Cranmer Hall Dur 86. **d** 89 **p** 90. C Old Swinford Stourbridge *Worc* 89–93; USPG Japan 94–95; C Fukuoka Cathl 95–96; P-in-c Nagasaki H Trin 96–06; P-in-c Godmanchester *Ely* 06–13; P-in-c Hilton 11–13; V Godmanchester and Hilton from 13. *The Vicarage, 59 Post Street, Godmanchester, Huntingdon PE29 2AQ* T: (01480) 436400 *or* 453354 F: 453354 M: 07765-851757 E: dwbusk@hotmail.com

BUSK, Horace. b 34. Clifton Th Coll 56. **d** 60 **p** 61. C Burton All SS *Lich* 60–63; Paraguay 63–66; C Silverhill St Matt *Chich* 66–67; LtO *Sarum* 67–69; C W Kilburn St Luke w St Simon and St Jude *Lon* 69–74; TV Ashwellthorpe w Wreningham *Nor* 74–81; P-in-c Meysey Hampton w Marston Meysey and

Castle Eaton *Glouc* 81–82; R 82–04; rtd 04; PtO *Glouc* from 04. *23 Eastcote Road, Cirencester GL7 2DB* T: (01285) 650884

BUSSELL, Canon Ian Paul. b 62. Reading Univ BA 84 Kingston Poly PGCE 85. Qu Coll Birm MA 98. **d** 98 **p** 99. C Twickenham St Mary *Lon* 98–01; TV Godalming *Guildf* 01–07; P-in-c Leckhampton SS Phil and Jas w Cheltenham St Jas *Glouc* 07–09; TV S Cheltenham 10–11; Dioc Dir of Ords 11–19; Hd Minl Development from 19; Hon Can Glouc Cathl from 18. *4 College Green, Gloucester GL1 2LR* T: (01452) 835545 E: ianbussell@gmail.com *or* ibussell@glosdioc.org.uk

BUSSELL, Ronald William. b 34. CA Tr Coll 57 St Deiniol's Hawarden 81. **d** 83 **p** 84. C Claughton cum Grange *Ches* 83–85; P-in-c Preston St Oswald *Blackb* 85–87; V Fleetwood St Nic 87–93; Dioc Chapl MU 91–95; R Tarleton 93–95; rtd 95; PtO *Blackb* 95–19. *4 Willoughby Avenue, Thornton-Cleveleys FY5 2BW* T: (01253) 820067 E: ron.bussell@talk21.com

BUSSEY, Diane Jean. b 57. **d** 07 **p** 08. OLM Clifton w Newton and Brownsover *Cov* 07–16; NSM Newbold on Avon from 16; Chapl Rainsbrook Secure Tr Cen from 09. *2 Teasel Close, Rugby CV23 0TJ* T: (01788) 339278 E: diane.bussey1@ntlworld.com

BUSTIN, Canon Peter Ernest. b 32. Qu Coll Cam BA 56 MA 60. Tyndale Hall Bris 56. **d** 57 **p** 58. C Welling *Roch* 57–60; C Farnborough *Guildf* 60–62; V Hornsey Rise St Mary *Lon* 62–70; R Barnwell *Pet* 70–78; RD Oundle 76–84; P-in-c Luddington w Hemington and Thurning 77–78; R Barnwell w Thurning and Luddington 78–84; V Southwold *St E* 84–97; RD Halesworth 90–95; Hon Can St E Cathl 91–97; rtd 97; PtO *St E* 97–19. *55 College Street, Bury St Edmunds IP33 1NH* T: (01284) 767708 E: bustin@saintedmunds.vispa.com

BUTCHER, Andrew John. b 43. Trin Coll Cam BA 66 MA 69. Cuddesdon Coll 66. **d** 68 **p** 69. C Sheff St Mark Broomhall 68–70; P-in-c Louth H Trin *Linc* 70–72; Chapl RAF 72–87; LtO *Ox* 85–87; TR Cove St Jo *Guildf* 87–91; V Egham Hythe 91–98; V Docking, the Birchams, Stanhoe and Sedgeford *Nor* 98–08; rtd 08; PtO *Nor* from 08. *67 The Street, Hindringham, Fakenham NR21 0PR* T: (01328) 878526 M: 07887-506876 E: andrewj.butcher2@btinternet.com

BUTCHER, Mrs Caroline. b 56. **d** 19 **p** 20. NSM Mildenhall *St E* 19–20; NSM Forest Heath from 20. *9 Courier Close, Mildenhall, Bury St Edmunds IP28 7SB* T: (01638) 515665 M: 07879-857015 E: caroline@butchermail.com

BUTCHER, David Alan. b 56. **d** 18 **p** 19. NSM Mildenhall *St E* 18–19; C 19–20; TV Forest Heath from 21. *9 Courier Close, Mildenhall, Bury St Edmunds IP28 7SB* T: (01638) 515665 M: 07747-816038 E: revdavidbutcher@gmail.com

BUTCHER, Dawn Marie. b 74. Portsm Univ BA 95 Ches Univ MA 18. St Mellitus Coll 18 Westmr Th Cen 15. **d** 21. C Broomfield *Chelmsf* from 21. *65 School Lane, Broomfield, Chelmsford CM1 7DR* M: 07899-023359   E: revdawnbutcher@gmail.com   or dawnbutcher59@gmail.com

BUTCHER (formerly POTTS), Canon Heather Dawn. b 52. **d** 98 **p** 99. C Attleborough w Besthorpe *Nor* 98–01; R Bunwell, Carleton Rode, Tibenham, Gt Moulton etc 01–09; RD Depwade 03–09; R Cringleford and Colney 09–16; P-in-c Litcham w Kempston, E and W Lexham, Mileham etc 16–18; P-in-c Gressenhall w Longham w Wendling etc 16–18; P-in-c Wellingham 17–18; TR Launditch and the Upper Nar *Nor* 18–20; Bp's Adv for Women's Min 11–20; Hon Can Nor Cathl 13–20; rtd 21; P-in-c Scarrowbeck *Nor* from 21. *25 Muskett Way, Aylsham, Norwich NR11 6GF* E: canonhdb@gmail.com

BUTCHER (née Martin), Michelle Karen. b 81. Ripon Coll Cuddesdon 11. **d** 14 **p** 15. C Bris St Aid w St Geo 14–17; C Fishponds St Jo 14–17; C Two Mile Hill St Mich 14–17; PtO *B & W* 17–20. *3 Home Farm, Tatworth, Chard TA20 2SH* E: revmiche22@gmail.com

BUTCHER, Philip Ian Christopher. b 77. Seale-Hayne Agric Coll BSc 01. Ripon Coll Cuddesdon 11. **d** 13 **p** 14. C Honiton, Gittisham, Combe Raleigh, Monkton etc *Ex* 13–17; V Chaffcombe, Cricket Malherbie etc *B & W* from 17. *3 Home Farm, Tatworth, Chard TA20 2SH* M: 07775-762376 E: twoshiresrector@gmail.com

BUTCHER, Philip Warren. b 46. Trin Coll Cam BA 68 MA 70. Cuddesdon Coll 68. **d** 70 **p** 71. C Bris St Mary Redcliffe w Temple etc 70–73; Hon C W Wickham St Fran *Cant* 73–78; Chapl Abingdon Sch 78–85; Chapl Nor Sch 85–98; V Horsford and Horsham w Newton St Faith *Nor* 98–04; rtd 04; P-in-c Barningham w Matlaske w Baconsthorpe etc *Nor* 05–09; PtO from 09. *25 Muskett Way, Aylsham, Norwich NR11 6GF* E: pw.butcher@btinternet.com

BUTCHER, Roger John. b 71. St Steph Ho Ox 10. **d** 12 **p** 13. C Wyke Regis *Sarum* 12–16; V Piddle Valley, Hilton and Ansty, Cheselbourne etc from 16. *The Vicarage, Church Lane, Piddletrenthide, Dorchester DT2 7QY* T: (01300) 348211 M: 07502-118210 E: roger_butcher@hotmail.com

BUTCHER, Mrs Sallie Eleanor. b 58. Open Univ MBA 99. WEMTC 14. **d** 16 **p** 17. NSM Teme Valley N *Worc* 16–17; NSM Shrawley, Witley, Astley and Abberley 16–17; NSM Mamble w Bayton, Rock w Heightington etc 17–18; C 18–19; P-in-c from 19. *Summerhill, The Village, Abberley, Worcester WR6 6BN* T: (01299) 896837 M: 07850-062911 E: vicar@wyreforestwest.org.uk

BUTCHER-TUSET, Richard James. b 69. Westcott Ho Cam 15. **d** 17 **p** 18. C Sidley *Chich* 17–19; C Bexhill St Barn 17–19; C Brighton St Mich and St Paul 19–20; R Ovingdean from 20. *21 Ainsworth Avenue, Ovingdean, Brighton BN2 7BG*

BUTCHERS, Preb Mark Andrew. b 59. Trin Coll Cam BA 81 K Coll Lon MTh 90 PhD 06. Chich Th Coll BTh 87. **d** 87 **p** 88. C Chelsea St Luke and Ch Ch *Lon* 87–90; C Mitcham SS Pet and Paul *S'wark* 90–93; R N Tawton, Bondleigh, Sampford Courtenay etc *Ex* 93–99; Chapl and Fell Keble Coll Ox 99–05; C Wolvercote w Summertown *Ox* 05–07; P-in-c Wolvercote 07–10; V Wolvercote and Wytham 10–15; AD Ox 12–15; Adn Barnstaple *Ex* 15–20; Prin SWMTC from 20; Public Preacher *Truro* from 21. *SWMTC, Riverside Church and Conference Centre, 13-14 Okehampton Street, Exeter EX4 1DU* T: (01392) 272544 E: admin@swmtc.org.uk

BUTLAND, Canon Cameron James. b 58. UEA BA 79 Open Univ MA 12. Ripon Coll Cuddesdon BA 84. **d** 84 **p** 85. C Tettenhall Regis *Lich* 84–88; V Bodicote *Ox* 88–95; TR Witney 95–04; RD 97–02; R Grasmere *Carl* 04–15; V Rydal 04–15; Chapl Rydal Hall 04–15; Dioc Ecum Officer 11–14; Bp's Dom Chapl from 15; Hon Can Carl Cathl from 14. *The Rectory, Clifton, Penrith CA10 2EA* T: (01768) 201027 E: cdsa03@gmail.com

BUTLAND, Canon Godfrey John. b 51. Grey Coll Dur BA 72. Wycliffe Hall Ox 73. **d** 75 **p** 76. C Much Woolton *Liv* 75–78; Bp's Dom Chapl 78–81; V Everton St Geo 81–94; AD Liv N 89–94; V Allerton 94–05; P-in-c Mossley Hill St Barn 04–05; TV Mossley Hill 05–06; TR 06–15; AD Liv South-Childwall 00–06; Hon Can Liv Cathl 03–06; TR Cockermouth Area *Carl* from 15; rtd 20; Hon Can Carl Cathl from 18. *9 Broughton Lodge, Broughton Road, Dalton-in-Furness LA15 8RB* T: (01229) 463236 M: 07906-552631 E: gof15@btinternet.com

BUTLAND, Hazel Judith. b 56. Sheff Univ MB, ChB 79 MRCGP 85. SWMTC 18. **d** 20. NSM Tavistock, Gulworthy and Brent Tor *Ex* from 20. *Wheal Friendship, Bal Lane, Mary Tavy, Tavistock PL19 9PE* T: (01822) 811045 M: 07904-327258 E: hbutland@doctors.org.uk

BUTLER, Canon Alan. b 53. Carl Dioc Tr Inst 89. **d** 89 **p** 90. NSM Flookburgh *Carl* 89–93; C Maryport 93–96; C Flimby 93–96; P-in-c 96–98; TV Saltash *Truro* 98–09; TR 09–15; P-in-c Landrake w St Erney and Botus Fleming 12–15; C St Germans 12–15; Hon Can Truro Cathl 10–15; rtd 15; PtO *Sarum* 16–21. *Ashways, 3 Ashurst Road, West Moors, Ferndown BH22 0LR* T: (01202) 874641 M: 07890-717136

BUTLER, Angela Madeline. b 47. Oak Hill NSM Course 87. **d** 90 **p** 94. Hon Par Dn Chipperfield St Paul *St Alb* 90–93; Dn-in-c 93–94; P-in-c 94–01; Staff Oak Hill Th Coll 93–97; Springboard Missr 97–01; C Hempsted and Dioc Springboard Missr *Glouc* 01–07; rtd 07; PtO *Truro* from 14. *22 Esplanade Road, Newquay TR7 1QB* T: (01637) 859238 E: angelambutler@btinternet.com

BUTLER, Catherine Elizabeth. b 46. Nottm Univ MA 06. **d** 06 **p** 07. NSM Waltham Gp *Linc* 06–16; rtd 20; PtO *Linc* from 16. *8 Danesfield Avenue, Waltham, Grimsby DN37 0QE* T: (01472) 587692 E: elsiebutlerdane@msn.com

BUTLER, Cecil Anthony. b 37. Sarum Th Coll 65. **d** 68 **p** 69. C Gillingham *Sarum* 68–70; CF 70–74; R Whittington St Jo *Lich* 74–83; rtd 02; PtO *S & M* from 10. *The Mines House, The Mines Yard, Laxey, Isle of Man IM4 7NJ* T: (01624) 860085 M: 07967-497721 E: dorsetoak@gmail.com

BUTLER, Charles Hugh. b 87. Fitzw Coll Cam BA 08 MA 13. Oak Hill Th Coll BA 18 MA 19. **d** 19 **p** 20. C Edgbaston St Bart *Birm* from 19. *31 Vicarage Road, Harborne, Birmingham B17 0SN* M: 07388-685561 E: charlie.butler@edgbastonoldchurch.org.uk

BUTLER, Christine Jane. b 66. Cranmer Hall Dur. **d** 10 **p** 11. C Cheddar, Draycott and Rodney Stoke *B & W* 10–14; P-in-c Pilton w Croscombe, N Wootton and Dinder 14–18; R from 18. *The Rectory, Pilton, Shepton Mallet BA4 4DX* M: 07910-479145 E: butlerchristine19@gmail.com

BUTLER, Christopher. b 67. St Jo Coll Nottm 99. **d** 01 **p** 02. C Retford *S'well* 01–05; P-in-c Holbeck *Ripon* 05–12; P-in-c Beeston Hill and Hunslet Moor 11–12; V Ripon H Trin *Leeds* from 12. *Holy Trinity Vicarage, 3 College Road, Ripon HG4 2AE* T: (01765) 605865 E: chris.butler@holytrinityripon.org.uk

BUTLER, Colin Sydney. b 59. MBE 10. Bradf Univ BSc 81 Cardiff Univ MTh 09 PhD 17. Wycliffe Hall Ox 81. **d** 84 **p** 85. C Farsley *Bradf* 84–87; C Bradf St Aug Undercliffe 87–89; P-in-c Darlaston All SS *Lich* 89–95; Ind Missr 89–95; TR Chell 95–99; CF 99–15; PtO *Birm* from 14; P-in-c Ankara *Eur* 16–17; V Worc St Martin w St Swithun and St Paul from 18. *33 Cotton Lane, Birmingham B13 9SB* M: 07808-476982 E: revcsb@btopenworld.com

BUTLER, Derek John. b 53. Aston Univ BSc 74 St Jo Coll York PGCE 75. Cranmer Hall Dur 79. **d** 82 **p** 83. C Bramcote *S'well* 82–86; Lon and SE Co-ord CPAS 86–88; NSM Bromley Ch Ch *Roch* 88–91; NSM Chesham Bois *Ox* 92–10; PtO from 10. *121 Woodside Road, Amersham HP6 6AL* T: (01494) 724577 M: 07801-662110 E: derek@derekbutler.tv

BUTLER, Edward Daniel. b 42. Rhodes Univ BA 65 MA 70. Qu Coll Birm. **d** 68 **p** 69. C Edgbaston St Bart *Birm* 68–72; PtO 72–73; *Chich* 74–99. *Address temp unknown*

BUTLER, Elizabeth. *See* BUTLER, Catherine Elizabeth

BUTLER, George James. b 53. AKC 74 Kent Univ MA 95. St Aug Coll Cant 75. **d** 76 **p** 77. C Ellesmere Port *Ches* 76–79; C Eastham 79–81; Chapl RAF 81–83; C W Kirby St Bridget *Ches* 83–84; V Newton 84–86; CF 86–91; V Folkestone St Sav *Cant* 91–99; P-in-c Wool and E Stoke *Sarum* 99–04; P-in-c Mansfield St Mark *S'well* 04–10; AD Mansfield 05–10; V Goring-by-Sea *Chich* 10–18; rtd 18. *1 Redcotts, St Botolphs Road, Worthing BN11 4JW* E: revgjb@icloud.com

BUTLER, George William. b 52. CITC. **d** 90 **p** 91. C Drung w Castleterra, Larah and Lavey etc *K, E & A* 90–93; I 93–95; I Castlemacadam w Ballinaclash, Aughrim etc *D & G* 95–18; Can Ch Ch Cathl Dublin 03–18; rtd 18. *Dunamon, Fiddler's Lane, Ballinabarney, Redcross, Co Wicklow, A67 YC99, Republic of Ireland* M: (00353) 87-679 5625 E: gwbut2@gmail.com

BUTLER, Mrs Helen Carole. b 66. Bath Coll of HE BEd 87. Dioc OLM tr scheme 02. **d** 04 **p** 05. NSM Mirfield *Wakef* 04–14; *Leeds* from 14. *19 Woodbottom, Mirfield WF14 8HG* M: 07495-181509 E: revhelenb@gmail.com

BUTLER, Huw. b 63. Univ of Wales (Ban) BSc 84. St Mich Coll Llan BTh 95. **d** 95 **p** 96. C Llantwit Fardre *Llan* 95–00; R Llangynhafal w Llanbedr DC and Llanychan *St As* 00–02; R Llanbedr DC w Llangynhafal, Llanychan etc 02–10; P-in-c Llanynys 10; AD Dyffryn Clwyd 10; TR Llantwit Major *Llan* 10–16; V Llay, Rossett and Isycoed *St As* 16; TV Alyn Miss Area from 17. *The New Vicarage, First Avenue, Llay, Wrexham LL12 0TN* T: (01446) 794670 E: huwbutler63@gmail.com

BUTLER, Jane. *See* BUTLER, Linda Jane

BUTLER, John Frederick. b 53. Yorks Min Course. **d** 14 **p** 15. NSM Heaton St Barn *Leeds* from 14; NSM Heaton St Martin from 14; NSM Manningham 16–18; NSM Shipley St Paul from 18. *34 Queens Rise, Bradford BD2 4BS* T: (01274) 967532 M: 07305-651464 E: revdjohnbutler@icloud.com

BUTLER, John Philip. b 47. Leeds Univ BA 70. Coll of Resurr Mirfield 70. **d** 72 **p** 73. C Elton All SS *Man* 72–75; C Bolton St Pet 75–78; Chapl Bolton Colls of H&FE 75–78; Asst Chapl Bris Univ 78–81; Hon C Clifton St Paul 78–81; V Llansawel w Briton Ferry *Llan* 81–84; Warden Bp Mascall Cen *Heref* 84–88; Vice-Prin Glouc Sch for Min 85–88; Chapl Univ of Wales (Ban) 88–07; rtd 07; PtO *Ban* 11–17. *Cefn Engan, Llangybi, Pwllheli LL53 6LZ* T: (01766) 810046 E: johnbutler@phonecoop.coop

BUTLER, Mrs Lesley Ann. b 52. Cov Univ BSc 75 Nottm Univ MA 05. EMMTC 08. **d** 10 **p** 12. NSM Loughborough Em and St Mary in Charnwood *Leic* 10–11; NSM Kegworth, Hathern, Long Whatton, Diseworth etc 11–17; rtd 17; PtO *Man* from 18; *Leic* from 18. *1 Cheriborough Road, Castle Donington, Derby DE74 2RY* T: (01332) 391780 M: 07505-384527

BUTLER, Mrs Linda. b 51. Liv Univ CertEd 72. Cranmer Hall Dur 01. **d** 03 **p** 04. C Middlewich w Byley *Ches* 03–06; R Ditchingham, Hedenham, Broome, Earsham etc *Nor* 06–12; P-in-c Hartlepool St Luke *Dur* 12–17; rtd 17; PtO *Newc* from 18. *6 Gresham Close, Cramlington NE23 6EJ* T: (01670) 735371 E: revlbutler@gmail.com

BUTLER, Canon Linda Jane. b 56. SRN 77. St Jo Coll Nottm 85. **d** 88 **p** 94. C Burbage w Aston Flamville *Leic* 88–91; Asst Chapl Leic R Infirmary 91–93; Asst Chapl Towers Hosp Humberstone 93–95; Chapl 95–97; Chapl Leics and Rutland Healthcare NHS Trust 97–03; Chapl amongst Deaf People *Pet* 03–10; P-in-c Kingsthorpe 10–14; TR from 14; Can Pet Cathl from 14. *The Rectory, 16 Green End, Kingsthorpe, Northampton NN2 6RD* T: (01604) 717133 M: 07773-018260 E: revjane94@me.com

BUTLER, Mrs Louise Gail Nesta. b 53. **d** 04 **p** 05. OLM Blewbury, Hagbourne and Upton *Ox* 04–06; OLM S w N Moreton, Aston Tirrold and Aston Upthorpe 05–06; OLM The Churn from 06. *Penridge, Church Road, Blewbury, Didcot OX11 9PY* T: (01235) 851011 E: revlouiseb@aol.com

BUTLER, Malcolm. b 40. Linc Th Coll 76. **d** 78 **p** 79. C Whickham *Dur* 78–82; V Leam Lane 82–87; R Penshaw 87–90; rtd 90; PtO *Dur* from 90. *Lincoln Lodge, Front Street, Castleside, Consett DH8 9AR* T: (01207) 507672

BUTLER, Canon Michael. b 41. St Mich Coll Llan 62 St Deiniol's Hawarden 63. **d** 64 **p** 65. C Welshpool *St As* 64; C Welshpool w Castle Caereinion 65–73; TV Aberystwyth *St D* 73–80; Chapl Univ of Wales (Abth) 73–80; V St Issell's and Amroth 80–09; V St Issell's and Amroth w Crunwere 09–12; V St Issell's and Amroth w Crunwere and Marros 12–13; AD Narberth 94–09; AD Pembroke 10–13; Can St D Cathl 01–13; rtd 13; PtO *St D* from 13. *Roxborough, 45 Whitlow, Saundersfoot SA69 9AE* T: (01834) 810475

BUTLER, Canon Michael Weeden. b 38. Clare Coll Cam BA 60 MA 65. Westcott Ho Cam 63. **d** 65 **p** 66. C Bermondsey St Mary w St Olave, St Jo etc *S'wark* 65–68; Ind Chapl 68–72; Sierra Leone 73–77; Ind Chapl and R Gt Chart *Cant* 77–86; RD E Charing 81–86; V Glouc St Jas and All SS 86–04; RD Glouc City 94–99; Hon Can Glouc Cathl 96–04; rtd 04; Dioc Clergy Retirement Officer *Glouc* 05–17. *121 London Road, Gloucester GL2 0RR* T: (01452) 421563 M: 07761-586588 E: butlermichael121@gmail.com

BUTLER, Ms Pamela. b 53. Nottm Univ BTh 86 CertEd 74. Linc Th Coll 83. **dss** 86 **d** 87 **p** 94. Rotherhithe H Trin *S'wark* 86–87; Par Dn 87–88; Par Dn Old Trafford St Jo *Man* 88–89; Par Dn Claremont H Angels 90–94; C 94–95; C Pendleton 95–97; Chapl Asst S Man Univ Hosps NHS Trust 96–00; rtd 00. *St Mary's Vicarage, 18 Rushcroft Road, Shaw, Oldham OL2 7PP* T: (01706) 847455

BUTLER, Patrick. b 61. All Nations Chr Coll 89. **d** 07 **p** 07. V Asunción St Andr Paraguay 07–09; C Stoughton *Guildf* 09–13; Min Elvetham Heath LEP from 13. *1 Dunley Drive, Fleet GU51 1BH* T: (01252) 695067 M: 07847-121092 E: patrickbutler61@hotmail.com

BUTLER, Paul David. b 67. Sheff Univ BA 88. Linc Th Coll 92. **d** 92 **p** 93. C Handsworth Woodhouse *Sheff* 92–96; V Bellingham St Dunstan *S'wark* 96–06; AD E Lewisham 99–06; R Deptford St Paul from 06; AD Deptford 13–16. *St Paul's Rectory, Mary Ann Gardens, London SE8 3DP* T: (020) 8692 7449 E: paulredbutler@btinternet.com

BUTLER, Paul Harnett. b 58. Perkins Sch of Th (USA) MTS 96 Girton Coll Cam MPhil 99. Ridley Hall Cam 05. **d** 07 **p** 08. C Histon and Impington *Ely* 07–11; C Landbeach from 12; C Waterbeach from 12. *The Vicarage, 8 Chapel Street, Waterbeach, Cambridge CB25 9HR* T: (01223) 860353 M: 07903-904599 E: revpbutler@gmail.com

✠**BUTLER, The Rt Revd Paul Roger.** b 55. Nottm Univ BA 77. Wycliffe Hall Ox BA 82. **d** 83 **p** 84 **c** 04. C Wandsworth All SS *S'wark* 83–87; Inner Lon Ev Scripture Union 87–92; Dep Hd of Miss 92–94; NSM E Ham St Paul *Chelmsf* 87–94; P-in-c Walthamstow St Mary w St Steph 94–97; P-in-c Walthamstow St Luke 94–97; TR Walthamstow 97–04; AD Waltham Forest 00–04; Suff Bp Southampton *Win* 04–09; Bp S'well and Nottm 09–14; Bp Dur from 14; Hon Can Byumba from 01. *Auckland Castle, Bishop Auckland DL14 7NR* T: (01388) 602576 F: 605264 E: bishop.of.durham@durham.anglican.org

BUTLER, Perry Andrew. b 49. York Univ BA 70 Lon Univ PGCE 75 Jes Coll Ox DPhil 78 FRHistS. Linc Th Coll 78 Ven English Coll & Pontifical Gregorian Univ Rome 79. **d** 80 **p** 81. C Chiswick St Nic w St Mary *Lon* 80–83; C S Kensington St Steph 83–87; V Bedford Park 87–95; Angl Adv Lon Weekend TV 87–99; P-in-c Bloomsbury St Geo w Woburn Square Ch Ch *Lon* 95–02; R 02–09; Dioc Dir of Ords 96–09; rtd 09; PtO *Cant* from 10; Hon Fell Kent Univ from 13. *6 Mikyle Court, 39 South Canterbury Road, Canterbury CT1 3LH* T: (01227) 767692 E: holmado@aol.com

BUTLER, Canon Robert Edwin. b 37. Ely Th Coll 60. **d** 62 **p** 63. C Lewisham St Jo Southend *S'wark* 62–65; C Eastbourne St Elisabeth *Chich* 65–69; V Langney 69–86; TR 86–96; Can and Preb Chich Cathl 94–97; rtd 96; PtO *Chich* from 97. *10 Langdale Close, Langney, Eastbourne BN23 8HS* T: (01323) 461135

BUTLER, Sandra. *See* BARTON, Sandra

BUTLER, Canon Simon. b 64. UEA BSc 86 RN Coll Dartmouth 86. St Jo Coll Nottm MA 92. **d** 92 **p** 93. C Chandler's Ford *Win* 92–94; C Northolt St Jos *Lon* 94–97; V Streatham Immanuel and St Andr *S'wark* 97–04; RD Streatham 01–04; Lambeth Adnry Ecum Officer 99–02; P-in-c Sanderstead All SS 04–05; TR Sanderstead 05–11; V Battersea St Mary from 11; Hon Can S'wark Cathl from 06. *St Mary's Vicarage, 32 Vicarage Crescent, London SW11 3LD* T: (020) 7228 8141 M: 07941-552407 E: simon.butler7@gmail.com

BUTLER, Simon Richard. b 80. Oak Hill Th Coll BA 03 Ripon Coll Cuddesdon MTh 06. **d** 06 **p** 07. C W Bridgford *S'well*

06–10; C Ashtead *Guildf* 10–16; R N Hants Downs *Win* from 16. *The Vicarage, Church Street, Upton Grey, Basingstoke RG25 2RB* M: 07803-909284 E: nhdbrector@gmail.com *or* simon@fairtradeclergyshirts.co.uk

BUTLER, Mrs Susan Jane. b 60. Anglia Ruskin Univ BA 99. Ridley Hall Cam 08. **d** 11 **p** 12. C Cambridge St Phil *Ely* 11–14; Pioneer Min 11–19; PtO from 19. *The Vicarage, 8 Chapel Street, Waterbeach, Cambridge CB25 9HR* T: (01223) 635316 M: 07985-406371 E: susybu@gmail.com

✠**BUTLER, The Rt Revd Thomas Frederick.** b 40. Leeds Univ BSc 61 MSc 62 PhD 72. Coll of Resurr Mirfield 62. **d** 64 **p** 65 **c** 85. C Wisbech St Aug *Ely* 64–66; C Folkestone St Sav *Cant* 66–67; Lect Univ of Zambia 68–73; Chapl Kent Univ *Cant* 73–80; Six Preacher Cant Cathl 79–84; Adn Northolt *Lon* 80–85; Area Bp Willesden 85–91; Bp Leic 91–98; Bp S'wark 98–10; rtd 10; Hon Asst Bp Wakef 10–14; Asst Bp Leeds from 14. *Overtown Grange Cottage, The Balk, Walton, Wakefield WF2 6JX* E: tom.butler5340@gmail.com

BUTLER, Valerie Joyce. *See* WHITE, Valerie Joyce

BUTLER GALLIE, Fergus Bruce. b 91. St Jo Coll Ox BA 14 MA 18 Em Coll Cam BA 17. Westcott Ho Cam 15. **d** 18 **p** 19. C Liv Our Lady and St Nic 18–20; NSM Upper Chelsea H Trin and St Sav *Lon* from 21. *11 Fernleigh Court, 30 Duke of York Square, London SW3 4LZ* M: 07557-683727 E: butlergalliefb@gmail.com

BUTLIN, David Francis Grenville. b 55. Bris Univ BA 77 Ox Univ CertEd 78. Sarum & Wells Th Coll 85. **d** 87 **p** 88. C Bedford St Andr *St Alb* 87–90; C Milton *Portsm* 90–92; V Hurst Green *S'wark* 92; RD Godstone 04–08; Chapl Heart of Kent Hospice 12–17; PtO *S'wark* from 13. *10 Florence Road, South Croydon CR2 0PP* M: 07910-261757 E: david@butlin3.plus.com

BUTLIN, Timothy Greer. b 53. St Jo Coll Dur BA 75 Spurgeon's Coll MTh 05 Ox Univ CertEd 76. Wycliffe Hall Ox 85. **d** 87 **p** 88. C Eynsham and Cassington *Ox* 87–91; V Loudwater 91–18; rtd 18. *149 South Road, Taunton TA1 3ED* T: (01823) 353874

BUTT, Adrian. b 37. **d** 71 **p** 72. C Umtata Cathl S Africa 71–76; C Ilkeston St Mary *Derby* 76–79; R N and S Wheatley w W Burton *S'well* 79–84; P-in-c Bole w Saundby 79–84; P-in-c Sturton w Littleborough 79–84; R N Wheatley, W Burton, Bole, Saundby, Sturton etc 84–85; R Kirkby in Ashfield 85–05; rtd 05; PtO *Derby* 14–18; *S'well* from 19. *25 Searby Road, Sutton-in-Ashfield NG17 5JQ* T: (01623) 555650

BUTT, Mrs Catherine. b 76. St Hilda's Coll Ox BA 99 MA 02 St Jo Coll Dur BA 02. Cranmer Hall Dur 00. **d** 03 **p** 04. C Bletchley *Ox* 03–17; P-in-c Water Eaton from 17. *38 Mill Road, Bletchley, Milton Keynes MK2 2LD* T: (01908) 630599 M: 07878-411584 E: revcatherinebutt@yahoo.co.uk *or* mkcatherinebutt@gmail.com

BUTT, Canon Christopher Martin. b 52. St Pet Coll Ox BA 74 Fitzw Coll Cam BA 77. Ridley Hall Cam 75. **d** 79 **p** 80. C Cambridge St Barn *Ely* 79–82; Chapl St Jo Cathl and P-in-c Em Ch Hong Kong 82–89; P-in-c Windermere St Martin *Carl* 89–98; TR S Gillingham *Roch* 98–09; Dean St Chris Cathl Bahrain 09–19; rtd 19; Hon Can Bahrain from 19; PtO *Birm* from 19. *46 Regent Road, Harborne, Birmingham B17 9JU* E: revbutt@ymail.com

BUTT, Martin James. b 52. Sheff Univ LLB 75. Trin Coll Bris 75. **d** 78 **p** 79. C Aldridge *Lich* 78–84; C Walsall 84–87; TV 87–94; P-in-c Farewell 94–12; P-in-c Gentleshaw 94–12; C Hammerwich 96–03; P-in-c 03–12; rtd 12; PtO *Cov* from 15. *36 Buttermere Avenue, Nuneaton CV11 6ET* T: (024) 7767 6068

BUTT, Nicola Mary. b 60. Sarum Coll 15. **d** 17 **p** 18. NSM Exmoor *B & W* from 17. *Little Hawkwell, Wheddon Cross, Minehead TA24 7EF* E: rev.nicola@icloud.com

BUTT, William Arthur. b 44. Kelham Th Coll 70 Linc Th Coll 71. **d** 71 **p** 72. C Mackworth St Fran *Derby* 71–75; C Aston cum Aughton *Sheff* 76–79; V Dalton 79–88; TR Staveley and Barrow Hill *Derby* 88–11; rtd 12. *17 Ramsey Avenue, Chesterfield S40 3EF* T: (01246) 239131

BUTTANSHAW, Graham Charles. b 59. TCD BA(Econ) 80 BA 85. St Jo Coll Nottm 88. **d** 91 **p** 92. C Toxteth St Cypr w Ch Ch *Liv* 91–94; CMS 94–99; Uganda 95–99; V Otley *Bradf* 99–14; *Leeds* from 14. *The Vicarage, Vicarage Gardens, Otley LS21 3PD* T: (01943) 462240 E: graham.buttanshaw@leeds.anglican.org

BUTTER, Jan Hendrik. b 75. St Mellitus Coll 18. **d** 21. NSM W Blatchington *Chich* from 21. *Springfield, Shoreham Road, Small Dole, Henfield BN5 9YG* M: 07889-400889 E: jhb9002@gmail.com

BUTTERFIELD, Amanda Helen. *See* DIGMAN, Amanda Helen

BUTTERFIELD, David John. b 52. Lon Univ BMus 73. St Jo Coll Nottm. **d** 77 **p** 78. C Southport Ch Ch *Liv* 77–81; Min Aldridge St Thos CD *Lich* 81–91; V Lilleshall, Muxton and

Sheriffhales 91–07; RD Edgmond 97–00; RD Shifnal 99–00; RD Edgmond and Shifnal 01–06; Adn E Riding *York* 07–14; Can and Preb York Minster 07–14; Adn for Generous Giving and Can Res York Minster 14–17; rtd 17. *18 Kirkby Drive, Ripon HG4 2DP* T: (01765) 609394 E: david@justanote.co.uk

BUTTERFIELD, Mrs Katharine Mary. Aston Univ BSc 78 Cumbria Univ BA 18 FCOptom 79. LCTP 13. **d** 15 **p** 16. NSM Morland, Thrimby, Gt Strickland and Cliburn *Carl* 15–17; NSM N Westmorland 17–18; R Kirkoswald, Renwick w Croglin, Gt Salkeld etc from 18; C Cross Fell Gp from 18. *The Vicarage, Kirkoswald, Penrith CA10 1DQ* M: 07867-533131 E: kmbutterfield@btinternet.com

BUTTERFIELD, Peter Graham. b 60. Lanc Univ BSc 82 Trent Poly PGCE 83 CPhys 87 MInstP 90. SWMTC 11. **d** 13 **p** 14. NSM Gulval and Madron *Truro* from 13. *Stable Cottage, St Buryan, Penzance TR19 6DJ* T: (01736) 810528 M: 07812-959460 E: peter.butterfield@physics.org

BUTTERWORTH, Canon Antony James. b 51. Hull Univ BSc 73. Trin Coll Bris 73. **d** 76 **p** 77. C Halliwell St Pet *Man* 76–81; V Werneth 81–90; V Tonge Fold 90–06; V Pennington 06–16; Hon Can Man Cathl 11–16; rtd 16; PtO *Man* from 16. *28 Marlborough Road, Atherton, Manchester M46 9LT* T: (01942) 790612 M: 07960-794291

BUTTERWORTH, David Frederick. b 48. Oak Hill Th Coll BA 88. **d** 88 **p** 89. R Telegraph Creek Canada 88–92; R Barrhead and Westlock 92–94; R Yellowknife 94–98; V Hanmer, Bronington, Bettisfield, Tallarn Green *St As* 98–04; PtO from 09; *Ches* from 20. *Bettisfield Hall, Bettisfield, Whitchurch SY13 2LB* T: (01948) 710525 E: butterworthdavef@aol.com

BUTTERWORTH, George John. b 58. Liv Univ BA 85. Chich Th Coll 92. **d** 92 **p** 93. C Mayfield *Chich* 92–93; C Hastings St Clem and All SS 93–96; TV Brighton Resurr 96–02; P-in-c Saltdean 02–09; V 09–14; rtd 15; PtO *Chich* from 16. *2 Harlech Close, Worthing BN13 3QS* E: george.butterworth1@ntlworld.com

BUTTERWORTH, Canon George Michael. b 41. Man Univ BSc 63 Lon Univ BD 67 PhD 89 Nottm Univ MPhil 71. Tyndale Hall Bris. **d** 67 **p** 68. C S Normanton *Derby* 67–71; India 72–79; Lect United Th Coll Bangalore 72–77; Lect Oak Hill Th Coll 80–96; Prin SAOMC *Ox* 97–05; Prin Ox Min Course 05–06; Prin ERMC 05–06; Hon Can St Alb 02–06; PtO from 80; *Ox* from 11; Hon C Walton H Trin 06–09; Hon C Broughton 09–11. *3 Horseshoe Close, Cheddington, Leighton Buzzard LU7 0SB* T: (01296) 661903 M: 07870-242250 E: mikebutterworth@waitrose.com

BUTTERWORTH, Ian Eric. b 44. Aber Univ MA 67 MTh 79. Edin Th Coll 67. **d** 69 **p** 70. C Langley All SS and Martyrs *Man* 69–71; Prec St Andr Cathl *Ab* 71–75; V Bolton St Matt w St Barn *Man* 75–85; C-in-c Lostock CD 85–92; Laity Development Officer (Bolton Adnry) 85–92; Teacher Fairfield High Sch Droylsden 92–99; PtO *Man* 96–99; Hon C Sudden St Aidan 00–05; P-in-c Castleton Moor 00–05; V 05–10; AD Heywood and Middleton 07–10; rtd 10; PtO *Man* from 10. *7 Bruce Street, Rochdale OL11 3NH* T: (01706) 522264 E: ianbutterworth70@gmail.com

BUTTERWORTH, James Kent. b 49. Southn Univ BTh 79 PGCE 12. Chich Th Coll 75. **d** 79 **p** 80. C Heckmondwike *Wakef* 79–83; V Wrenthorpe 83–95; V Staincross 95–14; *Leeds* from 14; CF (TA) 82–86; rtd 14; PtO *Leeds* 14–19. *Address withheld by request* E: jim@radiouk.com

BUTTERWORTH, Mrs Janet Mary. b 49. Bris Univ CertEd 70. SNWTP 09. **d** 12 **p** 13. OLM Heatons *Man* 12–19; rtd 19; PtO *Man* from 19. *71 Berwick Avenue, Stockport SK4 3AA* T: 0161-431 3851 E: janetmbutterworth@gmail.com

BUTTERWORTH, Canon Julia Kay. b 42. Edin Univ MA 64 Bris Univ CertEd 66. Linc Th Coll 73. **dss** 77 **d** 87 **p** 94. Cov E 77–79; Cant Cathl 79–84; Dioc Adv in Women's Min 82–92; Faversham 84–92; Par Dn 87–92; Team Dn Whitstable 92–94; TV 94–97; P-in-c Tenterden St Mich 97–07; Dioc Adv in Spirituality 97–07; Hon Can Cant Cathl 96–07; rtd 07; PtO *Cant* from 07. *14 Cobham Close, Canterbury CT1 1YL* T: (01227) 472806 E: jkbutterworth@btinternet.com

BUTTERWORTH, Michael. *See* BUTTERWORTH, George Michael

BUTTERWORTH, Mrs Nicola Jane. b 70. All SS Cen for Miss & Min 16. **d** 19 **p** 20. C Horwich and Rivington *Man* from 19. *St Elizabeth's Vicarage, Cedar Avenue, Horwich, Bolton BL6 6HT* M: 07706-979393 E: n.butterworth@outlook.com

BUTTERY, Bernard. b 36. Culham Coll Ox CertEd 58 LCP 75. OLM course 96. **d** 99 **p** 00. OLM Stafford *Lich* 99–11; rtd 11; PtO *Lich* 12–21. *7 Dearnsdale Close, Tillington, Stafford ST16 1SD* T: (01785) 244771 E: bb.ngb@talktalk.net

BUTTERY, Canon Graeme. b 62. York Univ BA 84. St Steph Ho Ox 85. **d** 88 **p** 89. C Peterlee *Dur* 88–91; C Sunderland 91–92;

TV 92–94; V Horsley Hill St Lawr 94–05; AD Jarrow 01–05; V Hartlepool St Oswald from 05; Hon Can Dur Cathl from 10. *St Oswald's Clergy House, Brougham Terrace, Hartlepool TS24 8EY* T: (01429) 273201 E: g_buttery@sky.com

BUTTERY, Nathan James. b 72. Em Coll Cam BA 94 MA 97. Wycliffe Hall Ox BA 98. **d** 00 **p** 01. C Hull St Jo Newland *York* 00–08; C Cambridge H Sepulchre *Ely* 09–17; V Preston All SS *Blackb* from 17. *All Saints' Vicarage, 94 Watling Street Road, Fulwood, Preston PR2 8BP* E: nathan.buttery@gmail.com

BUTTIMER, Mrs Cynthia Margaret. b 45. STETS 07. **d** 08 **p** 09. OLM Clarendon *Sarum* 08–12; NSM 12–15; rtd 15; PtO *Sarum* from 15. *Willow Cottage, Gunville Road, Winterslow, Salisbury SP5 1PP* T: (01980) 862017 E: cynthiabuttimer@hotmail.com

BUTTON, Daniel Christopher. b 65. Bethel Univ BA 89 Univ of Minnesota BA 89 Columbia Internat Univ MDiv 98. **d** 04 **p** 06. Uganda 04–11; PtO *Glouc* 12–17 and from 18; NSM Churchdown St Jo and Innsworth 17–18. *113 Denmark Road, Gloucester GL1 3JW* T: (01452) 549271 M: 07580-571274 E: danielbutton2011@gmail.com

BUTTRESS, Andrew Kevin. b 63. Lon Sch of Th MA 16. Cranmer Hall Dur 17. **d** 18 **p** 19. C Triangle, St Matt and All SS *St E* 18–21; C Ipswich Deanery from 21. *19 Dales View Road, Ipswich IP1 4HJ* E: andy.buttress@bridgechurchipswich.org.uk

BUXTON, Francis Edmund. b 42. Trin Coll Cam MA 68 Sheff Univ MA 93. Linc Th Coll 65. **d** 67 **p** 68. C Wanstead St Mary *Chelmsf* 67–70; C Cambridge Gt St Mary w St Mich *Ely* 70–73; C Barking St Marg w St Patr *Chelmsf* 74–75; Chapl Vellore Hosp S India 75–79; Chapl Bath Univ *B & W* 79–89; TR Willenhall H Trin *Lich* 89–96; Chapl Team Leader Univ Hosp Birm NHS Foundn Trust 96–07; rtd 07; Hon C St Briavels w Hewelsfield *Glouc* 08–12. *Bridge Cottage, Mill Lane, Govilon, Abergavenny NP7 9SA* T: (01873) 831424 M: 07899-673096 E: fjbuxton@yahoo.co.uk

BUXTON, James Andrew Denis. b 64. Newc Univ BA 86 CCC Cam MA 11. Westcott Ho Cam 95. **d** 97 **p** 98. C Portsea St Mary *Portsm* 97–01; Succ S'wark Cathl 01–07; Chapl Guy's Campus K Coll Lon 01–07; Fell CCC Cam 07–17; Chapl 07–11; Dean of Chpl 11–17; Tutor Westcott Ho Cam 08–15; Chapl Izmir (Smyrna) w Bornova *Eur* from 17. *1458 Sokak 32 Daire 6, Alsancak, 38210 Izmir, Turkey* M: (0090) 537-772 1964 E: james.buxton@mtsmail.org

BUXTON, Nicholas Alexander Vavasseur. b 66. Wolfs Coll Cam BA 02 Trin Hall Cam MPhil 03 PhD 07. St Steph Ho Ox MTh 08. **d** 08 **p** 09. C and Hon Min Can Ripon Cathl 08–12; P-in-c Newc St Jo 12–18; Dioc Ch and Soc Adv 12–18; Dir St Ant Priory Dur from 18; PtO *Newc* from 18; LtO *Dur* from 19. *St Antony's Priory, 74 Claypath, Durham DH1 1QT* T: 0191-384 3747 E: buxton.nicholas@gmail.com

BUXTON, Richard Fowler. b 40. Lon Univ BScEng 62 Linacre Coll Ox BA 67 MA 71 Ex Univ PhD 73 Surrey Univ Hon BUniv 11. St Steph Ho Ox 65. **d** 68 **p** 69. C Whitley Ch Ch Ox 68–70; C Pinhoe Ex 70–71; Asst Chapl Ex Univ 71–73; Tutor Sarum & Wells Th Coll 73–77; Vice-Prin 77; PtO *Ches* 77–97; Lect Liturgy Man Univ 80–94; PtO *Man* 81–94; Subwarden St Deiniol's Lib Hawarden 94–97; PtO *Ban* from 96; *St As* 97–10; *Ely* 13–18. *Golygfa'r Orsaf, 6 Garth Terrace, Porthmadog LL49 9BE* T: (01766) 514782 E: cynhaearn@gmail.com

BUXTON, Canon Trevor George. b 57. Ex Univ BEd 78. Chich Th Coll 81. **d** 83 **p** 84. C Hove All SS *Chich* 83–87; C Burgess Hill St Jo 87–91; V Brighton St Aug and St Sav 91–03; P-in-c Sidley 92–04; V 04–11; V Brighton St Martin w St Wilfrid and St Alban from 11; Can and Preb Chich Cathl from 01. *St Martin's Vicarage, Upper Wellington Road, Brighton BN2 3AN* T: (01273) 604687 M: 07885-942901 E: hojoe@waitrose.com

BUYERS, Stanley. b 39. Leeds Univ CertEd 71 Sunderland Poly BEd 78 Newc Univ MEd 90. NEOC 97. **d** 00 **p** 01. NSM E Boldon *Dur* 00–03; P-in-c Boldon 03–09; rtd 09; PtO *Dur* from 09. *37 Tarragon Way, South Shields NE34 8TB* T: 0191-536 5452 M: 07979-693153 E: stanbuyers@btinternet.com

BYARD, Nigel Gordon. b 65. Leic Poly BEng 88 CEng MIMechE. Ox Min Course 06. **d** 09 **p** 10. NSM Sunningdale *Ox* 09–11; TV Penrith w Newton Reigny and Plumpton Wall *Carl* 11–14; P-in-c Droitwich Spa *Worc* 14–19; P-in-c Salwarpe and Hindlip w Martin Hussingtree 14–19; TR Droitwich, and Salwarpe and Hindlip w Martin Hussingtree from 19. *The Rectory, Salwarpe, Droitwich WR9 0AH* T: (01905) 778265 E: nigelbyard@btinternet.com

BYATT, John William. b 55. St Jo Coll Nottm 99. **d** 01 **p** 02. C Heanor *Derby* 01–05; C Ilkeston St Jo 05–07; P-in-c Whipton *Ex* 07–21; rtd 21. *1 Case Gardens, Seaton EX12 2AP* M: 07773-906919 E: john.byatt1@btinternet.com

BYE, Paul Andrew. b 82. Nottm Univ BSc 04. Wycliffe Hall Ox BTh 12. **d** 12 **p** 13. C Blackb Ch Ch w St Matt 12–16;

V Fairhaven from 16. *The Vicarage, 83 Clifton Drive, Lytham St Annes FY8 1BZ* M: 07923-552339 E: p_bye@hotmail.com

BYE, Canon Peter John. b 39. Lon Univ BD 65. Clifton Th Coll 62. **d** 67 **p** 68. C Hyson Green *S'well* 67–70; C Dur St Nic 70–73; V Lowestoft Ch Ch *Nor* 73–80; V Carl St Jo 80–04; Hon Can Carl Cathl 98–04; RD Carl 00–04; Chapl Carl Hosps NHS Trust 80–94 and 94–98; rtd 04; PtO *Carl* 08–18. *21 McIlmoyle Way, Carlisle CA2 5GY* T: (01228) 596256 E: peterbye@mcilmoyleway.plus.com

BYFORD, The Ven Edwin Charles. b 47. Aus Nat Univ BSc 70 Melbourne Coll of Div BD 73 Univ of Chicago MA 76 Man Univ PhD 85. Trin Coll Melbourne 70. **d** 73 **p** 73. C Qeanbeyan Ch Ch Australia 73–75; Chapl Univ of Chicago USA 75–76; Hon C Chorlton-cum-Hardy St Werburgh *Man* 76–79; Australia from 79; Chapl Woden Valley Hosp 80–83; Asst P Wagga Wagga 83–84; Asst P Ainslie All SS 84–87; Chapl Aus Nat Univ 87–91; R Binda 91–95; R Broken Hill St Pet and Adn The Darling 95–05; R Coolamon w Ganmain 05–10; R Deniliquin 10–14; Adn Riverina 05–14; Dioc Admin 12–14; R Mulwala and Berrigan 14–17; rtd 17; PtO Riverina and Wangaratta from 17. *9 Bon Accord Track, Harrietville VIC 3741, Australia* M: (0061) 40-946 7981 E: e-byford-4@alumni.uchicago.edu

BYLLAM-BARNES, Preb Paul William Marshall. b 38. Birm Univ BCom Lon Univ MSc. Sarum & Wells Th Coll. **d** 84 **p** 85. C Gt Bookham *Guildf* 84–87; R Cusop w Blakemere, Bredwardine w Brobury etc *Heref* 87–03; Preb Heref Cathl 99–03; rtd 03. *90 Granger Avenue, Maldon CM9 6AN* T: (01621) 858978

BYNON, William. b 43. St Aid Birkenhead 63. **d** 66 **p** 67. C Huyton St Mich *Liv* 66–69; C Maghull 69–72; TV 72–75; V Highfield 75–82; V Southport All SS 82–88; P-in-c Southport All So 86–88; V Newton in Makerfield St Pet 88–94; V Caerhun w Llangelynin w Llanbedr-y-Cennin *Ban* 94–06; rtd 06. *Swn-y-Don, Maes Hyfryd, Moelfre LL72 8LR* T: (01248) 410749 E: williambynon@btinternet.com

BYRNE, David Patrick. b 48. PGCE 96. St Jo Coll Nottm 74. **d** 77 **p** 78. C Bordesley Green *Birm* 77–79; C Weoley Castle 79–82; TV Kings Norton 82–92; TV Hodge Hill 92–94; PtO 94–97; Chapl Asst Birm Heartlands and Solihull NHS Trust 96–98; Chapl NW Lon Hosp NHS Trust 98–13; Chapl Harrow and Hillingdon Healthcare NHS Trust 98–13; rtd 13; Hon C Greenhill St Jo *Lon* from 11. *214 Currie Court, Harrow HA1 3GX* E: dave.byrne7@gmail.com

BYRNE, David Rodney. b 47. St Jo Coll Cam BA 70 MA 73. Cranmer Hall Dur 71. **d** 73 **p** 74. C Maidstone St Luke *Cant* 73–77; C Patcham *Chich* 77–83; TV Stantonbury *Ox* 83–87; TV Stantonbury and Willen 87–92; TV Woodley 92–02; V Patchway *Bris* 02–10; rtd 11; PtO *Ex* from 11. *4 Pound Lane, Topsham, Exeter EX3 0NA* T: (01392) 758557 E: dbyrne47@outlook.com

BYRNE, Georgina Ann. b 72. Trin Coll Ox BA 92 MA 96 CCC Cam MPhil 98. Westcott Ho Cam. **d** 97 **p** 98. NSM W Bromwich All SS *Lich* 97–98; C 98–01; Hon Asst Chapl CCC Cam 97–98; Chapl to Bp Kensington *Lon* 01–04; Hon C Twickenham St Mary 01–04; TV Halas *Worc* 04–09; Can Res Worc Cathl 09–21; Dir of Ords 09–15; Convenor for Women's Min 05–16; Tutor Qu Foundn Birm from 21; Chapl to The Queen from 17. *15B College Green, Worcester WR1 2LH* T: (01905) 732938 M: 07740-706448 E: georginabyrne@worcestercathedral.org.uk

BYRNE, Ian Barclay. b 53. Ripon Coll Cuddesdon 01. **d** 03 **p** 04. C Blyth Valley *St E* 03–06; P-in-c Bungay H Trin w St Mary 06–13; C Wainford 06–13; V Bungay 13–20; C The Saints 14–20; rtd 20. *20 Holly Blue Road, Wymondham NR18 0XJ* E: rev.ib@btinternet.com

BYRNE, Canon John Victor. b 47. FCA. St Jo Coll Nottm LTh 73. **d** 73 **p** 74. C Gillingham St Mark *Roch* 73–76; C Cranham Park *Chelmsf* 76–80; V Balderstone *Man* 80–87; V Southsea St Jude *Portsm* 87–06; Hon Can Portsm Cathl 97–06; RD Portsm 01–06; V Branksome Park All SS *Sarum* 06–12; Chapl to The Queen 03–17; PtO *Portsm* from 13. *4 St Georges Terrace, Southwick Road, Denmead, Waterlooville PO7 6FR* T: (023) 9225 3621 E: byrne.jv@gmail.com

BYRNE, Canon Roy Harold. b 71. Westmr Coll Ox BTh 97 Irish Sch of Ecum MPhil 00. CITC 97. **d** 99 **p** 00. C Dublin Ch Ch Cathl Gp *D & G* 99–03; I Killeshin w Cloydagh and Killabban *C, F & O* 03–08; I Dublin Drumcondra w N Strand *D & G* 08–16; I Monkstown from 16; Can Ch Ch Cathl Dublin from 12; Prec from 17. *Winton Lodge, 62 Monkstown Road, Monkstown, Co Dublin, Republic of Ireland* T: (00353) (1) 280 6596 M: 86-346 7920 E: royhbyrne71@gmail.com

BYROM, Alan. b 51. Magd Coll Ox BA 72 Bris Univ MA 85 Man Univ MPhil 99 Leeds Univ PGCE 73. NOC 97. **d** 99 **p** 00. C Leyland St Andr *Blackb* 99–03; TV Solway Plain *Carl*

03–10; P-in-c Blackpool Ch Ch w All SS *Blackb* 10–13; V 13–19; rtd 19; PtO *Blackb* from 19. *5 Beech Avenue, Warton, Preston PR4 1BY* T: (01772) 633559

BYROM, Catherine Mary. b 66. Nottm Univ BA 88 MA 04. St Jo Coll Nottm 11. **d** 13 **p** 14. C Skegby w Teversal *S'well* 13–18; V Ravenshead from 18. *St Peter's Vicarage, 55 Sheepwalk Lane, Ravenshead, Nottingham NG15 9FD* M: 07527-548644 E: katebyrom@hotmail.co.uk

BYROM, Canon Malcolm Senior. b 37. Edin Th Coll 65. **d** 67 **p** 68. C Allerton *Bradf* 67–69; C Padstow *Truro* 69–72; V Hessenford 72–77; P-in-c St Martin by Looe 72–77; V Kenwyn 77–91; R Kenwyn w St Allen 91–99; Hon Can Truro Cathl 92–00; RD Powder 88–90; Sub-Warden Community of the Epiphany Truro 85–01; Warden 01; rtd 99; PtO *Truro* 00–16. *1 Barton Meadow, Truro TR1 3NJ* T: (01872) 242282 E: malcolm.byrom@btinternet.com

BYRON, Terence Sherwood. b 26. Keble Coll Ox BA 50 MA 54. Linc Th Coll 50. **d** 52 **p** 53. C Melton Mowbray w Burton Lazars, Freeby etc *Leic* 52–55; C Whitwick St Jo the Bapt 55–60; India 60–76; C-in-c Beaumont Leys (Extra-paroch Distr) *Leic* 76–85; V Beaumont Leys 85–86; RD Christianity N 86–92; P-in-c Leic St Phil 86–88; V 88–92; rtd 93; PtO *Leic* 93–15. *84 Flax Road, Leicester LE4 6QD* T: 0116-266 1922

BYSOUTH, Paul Graham. b 55. Oak Hill Th Coll. **d** 84 **p** 85. C Gorleston St Andr *Nor* 84–87; C Ripley *Derby* 87–91; TV N Wingfield, Clay Cross and Pilsley 91–00; V Blagreaves 00–17; TV Newton Tracey, Horwood, Alverdiscott etc *Ex* 17–20; rtd 20. *Address temp unknown* E: paemlu@gmail.com

BYTHEWAY, Phillip James. b 35. MIIExE 89 BA 93. **d** 97. OLM Church Stretton *Heref* 97–00; rtd 00; PtO *Heref* from 00. *Buxton Cottage, All Stretton, Church Stretton SY6 6JU* T: (01694) 723907 M: 07835-565052

BYWORTH, Mrs Ruth Angela. b 49. Cranmer Hall Dur BA 82. **dss** 83 **d** 92 **p** 94. Kirkby *Liv* 83–89; Aintree St Pet 89–97; Dn-in-c 92–94; P-in-c 94–97; P-in-c St Helens St Mark 97–98; C Sutton 98–03; TV 03–04; rtd 04; PtO *Liv* from 16. *11 Oakleigh, Skelmersdale WN8 9QU* T: (01744) 886481

C

CABLE, Kevin John. b 74. Ripon Coll Cuddesdon BA 08. **d** 08 **p** 09. C Bromley Common St Aug *Roch* 08–11; NSM Brenchley 12–14; C Perry Street 14–16; TV Northfleet and Rosherville 14–16; P-in-c Southbourne St Kath *Win* 16–19; V 19–21; CMS from 21; P-in-c Jaffa St Pet Israel from 21. *The Cathedral Church of St George the Martyr, Nablus Road 65, Jerusalem 91191, Israel* M: (00972) 50-359 0128 E: fr.kevin@btopenworld.com

CABLE, Patrick John. b 50. AKC 72. **d** 74 **p** 75. C Herne *Cant* 74–78; CF 78–05; Rtd Officer Chapl RAChD from 05. *c/o MOD Chaplains (Army)* T: (01799) 550466 E: paddycable@gmail.com

CACKETT, Janice Susan. b 39. Goldsmiths' Coll Lon BA 76 Surrey Univ MSc 83. SWMTC 99. **d** 99 **p** 00. NSM Clyst St Mary, Clyst St George etc *Ex* 99–03; P-in-c E Budleigh w Bicton and Otterton 03–10; rtd 10; PtO *Ex* from 10. *27 Elm Grove Road, Topsham, Exeter EX3 0EJ* T: (01392) 877468

CACOURIS, Alexander Xenophon. b 71. St Mellitus Coll. **d** 13 **p** 14. C E Twickenham St Steph *Lon* 13–16; Chapl Rio de Janeiro Ch Ch Brazil 16–19; C Dorking St Paul *Guildf* 19–21; V from 21. *The Vicarage, 7 South Terrace, Dorking RH4 2AB* T: (01306) 743378 E: acacouris@hotmail.co.uk *or* alex@stpaulsdorking.org.uk

CADDELL, Richard Allen. b 54. Auburn Univ Alabama BIE 77. Trin Coll Bris BA 88. **d** 88 **p** 89. C Uphill *B & W* 88–94; PtO 94–96; TV Beaconsfield *Ox* 96–07; P-in-c Lamp 07–09; R 09–20; AD Newport 13–15; rtd 20; PtO *B & W* from 21. *13 Matfurlong Close, Martock TA12 6LD* E: caddells@holtspur.plus.com

CADDEN, Brian Stuart. b 58. BSc BTh TCD. **d** 89 **p** 90. C Lecale Gp *D & D* 89–92; C Killowen *D & R* 92–95; I Muckamore *Conn* 95–06; I Castlewellan w Kilcoo *D & D* 06–21; rtd 21. *5 Cedar Heights, Bryansford, Newcastle BT33 0PJ* T: (028) 4372 3198 E: castlewellan@dromore.anglican.org

CADDEN, Canon Terence John. b 60. TCD BTh 89. CITC 86. **d** 89 **p** 90. C Coleraine *Conn* 89–92; C Lurgan Ch the Redeemer *D & D* 92–93; Past Dir 93–01; I Gilford 01–06; I Seagoe from 06; Bp's C Ardmore w Craigavon from 16; Can Dromore Cathl from 18. *Seagoe Rectory, 8 Upper Church Lane, Portadown, Craigavon BT63 5JE* T: (028) 3833 2538 *or* 3835 0583 F: 3833 0773 M: 07894-987702 E: cadden@talktalk.net *or* seagoechurch@btinternet.com

CADDICK, Jeremy Lloyd. b 60. St Jo Coll Cam BA 82 MA 86 K Coll Lon MA 93. Ripon Coll Cuddesdon BA 86 MA 91. **d** 87 **p** 88. C Kennington St Jo w St Jas *S'wark* 87–90; Chapl Lon Univ 90–94; Chapl R Free Medical Sch 90–94; Chapl R Veterinary Coll Lon 90–94; PV Westmr Abbey 92–94; Dean Em Coll Cam from 94. *Emmanuel College, Cambridge CB2 3AP* T: (01223) 334264 *or* 330195 F: 334426 E: jlc24@cam.ac.uk

CADDOO (née BLAKELY), Mrs Denise Irene. b 69. QUB BD 91 PGCE 92. CITC 93. **d** 95 **p** 96. C Holywood *D & D* 95–99; C Portadown St Columba *Arm* 99–00; I Carrowdore w Millisle *D & D* 00–04; C Holywood 04–06; I Gilford from 06. *The Vicarage, 18 Scarva Road, Gilford, Craigavon BT63 6BG* T: (028) 3883 1130

CADDY, Canon Michael George Bruce Courtenay. b 45. K Coll Lon. **d** 71 **p** 72. C Walton St Mary *Liv* 71–76; C Solihull *Birm* 76–79; TV 79–81; V Shard End 81–87; TR Shirley 87–00; P-in-c Tanworth St Patr Salter Street 97–00; TR Salter Street and Shirley 00–13; AD Shirley 97–02; Hon Can Birm Cathl 99–13; Dioc Chapl MU 07–11; rtd 13; Bps' Chapl *B & W* 13–15; PtO from 15. *12 Dial Hill Road, Clevedon BS21 7HJ* T: (01275) 219059 E: anncaddy60@gmail.com

CADDY, Ms Susan. b 50. Westcott Ho Cam 99. **d** 01 **p** 02. C Sutton in Ashfield St Mary *S'well* 01–05; P-in-c Shelton and Oxon *Lich* 05–10; TV Retford Area *S'well* 10–19; R Ordsall and Retford St Mich 19–20; rtd 20; PtO *S'well* from 21. *3 Sanderling Way, Forest Town, Mansfield NG19 0GL* E: suecee123@btinternet.com

CADE, Canon Simon Peter Vincent. b 69. Univ of Wales BA 90. Westcott Ho Cam 92. **d** 94 **p** 95. C Calne and Blackland *Sarum* 94–98; Chapl St Mary's Sch Calne 94–97; TV Basingstoke *Win* 98–05; TR Redruth w Lanner and Treleigh *Truro* 05–14; P-in-c 14; Dioc Dir of Educn and Discipleship 14–20; Dioc Sec from 20; Public Preacher from 14; Hon Can Truro Cathl from 19. *Church House, Woodlands Court, Truro Business Park, Threemilestone, Truro TR4 9NH* T: (01872) 247214 E: simon.cade@truro.anglican.org

CADMORE, Albert Thomas. b 42. Open Univ BA 81 UEA MA 94 Lon Inst of Educn CertEd 68. EAMTC 85. **d** 88 **p** 89. NSM Gorleston St Andr *Nor* 88–96; NSM Winterton w E and W Somerton and Horsey 94–96; NSM Flegg Coastal Benefice 96–12; rtd 12; PtO *Nor* from 12. *10 Upper Cliff Road, Gorleston, Great Yarmouth NR31 6AL* T: (01493) 668762 E: acadmore@ntlworld.com

CADOGAN, Paul Anthony Cleveland. b 47. AKC 74. **d** 75 **p** 76. C Fishponds St Jo *Bris* 75–79; C Swindon New Town 79–81; P-in-c Swindon All SS 81–82; V 82–90; R Lower Windrush *Ox* 90–94. *2 Malthouse Close, Ashbury, Swindon SN6 8PB* T: (01793) 710488 E: paul-anthony@hotmail.com

CADOGAN, Percil Lavine. b 41. WMMTC. **d** 01 **p** 02. NSM Bournville *Birm* 01–05; NSM Bordesley St Benedict 05–14; P-in-c 12–14; rtd 14; PtO *Birm* from 14. *76 Highbury Road, Birmingham B14 7QW* T: 0121-680 9595 E: percil.cadogan@gmail.com

CADWALLADER, Michael Godfrey. b 56. Bris Univ BEd 79 St Jo Coll Dur BA 06. Cranmer Hall Dur 05. **d** 07 **p** 08. C Kingston upon Hull St Aid Southcoates *York* 07–11; P-in-c Burton Dassett *Cov* 11–16; P-in-c Avon Dassett w Farnborough and Fenny Compton 11–16; P-in-c Gaydon w Chadshunt 11–16; TV Mid Trent *Lich* from 16. *2 Vicarage Way, Hixon, Stafford ST18 0FT* T: (01889) 270418 E: cadwalladermg@gmail.com

CADY, Mrs Susan Janet. b 68. Wycliffe Hall Ox 15. **d** 17 **p** 18. C Reading St Agnes w St Paul and St Barn *Ox* from 17. *60 Frances Street, Chesham HP5 3ES* M: 07977-219305 E: sjcady@sky.com *or* rev.sue.cady@gmail.com

CAFFYN (formerly MCNEIL), Mrs Ann. b 41. **d** 89 **p** 94. NSM Henfield w Shermanbury and Woodmancote *Chich* 89–99; PtO from 00. *6 Holbrook Close, Eastbourne BN20 7JT* T: (01323) 736018 E: ann@annmcneil.com

CAFFYN, Douglas John Morris. b 36. Peterho Cam MA 60 Nairobi Univ MSc 69 Westmr Coll Ox DipEd 61 ACIS 77. S Dios Minl Tr Scheme 87. **d** 90 **p** 91. NSM Hampden Park *Chich* 90–94; Chapl among Deaf People 94–97; Jt Sec Cttee for Min among Deaf People 95–97; PtO *Chich* from 97; rtd 01. *34 St Lawrence Forstal, Canterbury CT1 3PA*

CAGE, Doreen Anne. b 51. **d** 13 **p** 14. Asst Chapl Málaga *Eur* from 13. *Buzón 40, La Parrilla, 21930 Villanueva de Algaidas, (Málaga), Spain* T: (0034) 952 745 028 E: jmnct123@gmail.com

CAHILL-NICHOLLS, Benjamin. b 87. Selw Coll Cam BA 08 Cam Univ MA 12. St Aug Coll Cant 18. **d** 21. NSM Guildf H Trin w St Mary from 21; Chief Exec Clergy Support Trust from 20. *The Old Granary, 14 Mill Lane, Godalming GU7 1EY* T: (01483) 239965 M: 07718-613217 E: bencahillnicholls@gmail.com

CAHUSAC, Henry William James. b 73. Wycliffe Hall Ox BTh 06. **d** 06 **p** 07. C Tollington *Lon* 06–10; C Onslow Square and S Kensington St Aug 10–15; PtO from 15; *Guildf* from 15. *12 Rowly Edge, Cranleigh GU6 8PU* T: (01483) 613068 E: bill.cahusac@emmausrd.com

CAIN, Andrew David. *See* FORESHEW-CAIN, Andrew David

CAIN, Andrew Paul. b 76. St Jo Coll Nottm. **d** 08 **p** 09. C Hinckley H Trin *Leic* 08–11; C Bosworth and Sheepy Gp 11–12; V Cuddington *Guildf* 12–16; PtO *Leic* 17–21. *Address withheld by request*

CAIN, Frank Robert. b 56. Liv Univ MA 97. Oak Hill Th Coll BA 88. **d** 88 **p** 89. C Aughton Ch Ch *Liv* 88–91; P-in-c Toxteth Park St Clem 91–99; V Toxteth St Bede w St Clem 99–04; AD Toxteth and Wavertree 01–04; Hon Can Liv Cathl 03–04; Chapl N Mersey Community NHS Trust 96–04; V New Brighton St Jas w Em *Ches* 04–15; RD Wallasey 07–09; TR Halewood and Hunts Cross *Liv* 15–17; V Walton St Luke from 17. *65 Fazakerley Road, Liverpool L9 2AJ* E: vicarfrank@btinternet.com *or* frankcain100@btinternet.com

CAIN, Jonathan Michael Field. b 69. Nottm Univ BEng 90 Bradf Univ MBA 03. Yorks Min Course 13. **d** 15 **p** 16. C Bolton Abbey *Leeds* 15–18; V Woodside from 18. *55 Bridgland Avenue, Menston, Ilkley LS29 6PD* T: (01943) 871149 M: 07957-713387 E: jonathan.cain@leeds.anglican.org

CAIN, Michael Christopher. b 68. St Jo Coll Dur BA 90 K Coll Lon MA 92 Selw Coll Cam BA 94. Ridley Hall Cam 92. **d** 95 **p** 96. C Wimbledon Em Ridgway Prop Chpl *S'wark* 95–99; Asst Chapl Leipzig *Eur* 99–02; C Clifton Ch Ch w Em *Bris* 02–10; Pioneer Min Clifton Em from 11. *35 Walsingham Road, Bristol BS6 5BU* T: 0117-942 7385 E: mike@emmanuelbristol.org.uk

CAINE, Diane Audrey. b 56. Ex Univ BTh 12. SWMTC 09. **d** 12 **p** 13. NSM Dawlish *Ex* 12–15; NSM Dawlish, Cofton and Starcross 15–17; C Yelverton, Meavy, Sheepstor, Walkhampton, Sampford Spiney and Horrabridge 17–21; rtd 21. *2 Charlemont Road, Teignmouth TQ14 8RP* M: 07415-897502 E: rev.dicaine@outlook.com

CAINE, Mrs Helen. b 71. Open Univ BA 98. WEMTC 14. **d** 16 **p** 17. NSM S Cotswolds *Glouc* from 16. *17 Links View, Cirencester GL7 2NF* M: 07958-686621 E: hel.caine@btinternet.com

CAINES, Julia Clare. *See* CHARD, Julia Clare

CAIRNS, The Ven Dorothy Elizabeth. b 66. Wilson Carlile Coll 87 CITC 07. **d** 09 **p** 10. CA from 90; C Portadown St Columba *Arm* 09–11; I 11–13; I Mullavilly from 13; Adn Ardboe from 20. *The Rectory, 89 Mullavilly Road, Tandragee, Craigavon BT62 2LX* T: (028) 3884 0221 M: 07719-857187 E: revecairns@gmail.com

CAIRNS, Philip. b 91. Oak Hill Th Coll MTheol 20. **d** 20. C Plymouth St Andr and Stonehouse *Ex* from 20. *18 Glenhurst Rad, Plymouth PL3 5LT* E: pcairns123@gmail.com

CAISSIE, Mrs Elizabeth Anne. b 40. CBDTI 07. **d** 08 **p** 09. NSM Keighley St Andr *Bradf* 08–13; PtO 13–14; *Leeds* 14–16; *York* from 14. *2A Turner Avenue, Bridlington YO15 2HJ* T: (01262) 229763

CAITHNESS, Mrs Joyce Marigold. b 45. **d** 06 **p** 07. OLM Bris St Matt and St Nath 06–13; OLM Southmead 13–18; rtd 18. *383 Southmead Road, Westbury-on-Trym, Bristol BS10 5LT* T: 0117-983 3755 E: jm.caithness@blueyonder.co.uk

CAKE, Nichola Carla. *See* CHATER, Nichola Carla

CAKE, Simon Charles Eagle. b 61. Wilson Carlile Coll 91 Cranmer Hall Dur 08. **d** 10 **p** 11. C Hebburn St Jo *Dur* 10–14; TV Egremont and Haile *Carl* 14–19; Chapl N Cumbria Univ Hosps NHS Trust 14–19; C Galashiels *Edin* from 19; C Hawick from 19; C Selkirk from 19. *1 Parsonage Road, Galashiels TD1 3HS* M: 07710-523856 E: cakekands@btinternet.com

CALDER, David Ainsley. b 60. NE Lon Poly BSc 86 St Jo Coll Dur BA 95. Cranmer Hall Dur 93. **d** 96 **p** 97. C Ireland Wood *Ripon* 96–00; V Woodhouse and Wrangthorn 00–10;

Chapl Leeds Metrop Univ 02–10. *Address withheld by request* E: darlodave17@gmail.com

CALDER, Canon Ian Fraser. b 47. York Univ BA 68 Southn Univ CertEd 69. Glouc Sch of Min 84. **d** 87 **p** 88. NSM Lydney w Aylburton Glouc 87–91; C Cirencester 91–95; V Coney Hill 95–01; RD Glouc City 99–01; R Bishop's Cleeve 01–08; AD Tewkesbury and Winchcombe 02–07; Hon Can Glouc Cathl 03–08; rtd 08; PtO *Glouc* from 15. *11 Riversley Road, Elmbridge, Gloucester GL2 0QU* T: (01452) 537845 E: canonian@virginmedia.com

CALDERBANK, Martin Nicholas. St Aug Coll of Th 16. **d** 19 **p** 20. NSM Barnes *S'wark* from 19. *St Michael and All Angels Church, Elm Bank Gardens, London SW13 0NX* E: curate@stmichaelbarnes.org

CALDERWOOD, Emma Louise. *See* WILLIAMS, Emma Louise

CALDWELL, Jacob Wilson (Jim). b 84. St Andr Univ MA 07 AVCM 04. TCD Div Sch MTh 09. **d** 11 **p** 12. Intern Dn Magherafelt *Arm* 11–12; C Larne and Inver *Conn* 12–15; CF from 15. *c/o MOD Chaplains (Army)* T: 03001-539116 M: 07785-649577 E: jacob.caldwell101@mod.gov.uk

CALDWELL, Miss Janet Elizabeth. b 56. Hull Univ BA 78 PGCE 79. **d** 19. NSM Ormesby *York* from 19. *11 Normanby Road, Ormesby, Middlesbrough TS7 9NU* T: (01642) 454790 M: 07809-041169 E: janet926@btinternet.com

CALDWELL, Mrs Jill. b 47. Lon Univ BPharm 69 MRPharmS 70. S Dios Minl Tr Scheme 89. **d** 92 **p** 94. NSM Yiewsley *Lon* 92–97; NSM St Marylebone w H Trin 97–02; Chapl St Marylebone Girls' Sch Lon 97–98; Chapl R Academy of Music 97–98; Chapl Lon Sch of Pharmacy 97–98; Chapl Liv Cathl 03–04; PtO *Derby* 04–05; NSM Darley Abbey 05–10; NSM Allestree St Edm and Darley Abbey 10–13; PtO *Ox* 14–17. *1 Pheasants Ridge, Marlow SL7 3QT* E: jill-caldwell@talk21.com

CALDWELL, Sarah Louise. *See* HARE, Sarah Louise

CALE, Canon Clifford Roy Fenton. b 38. St Mich Coll Llan 65. **d** 67 **p** 68. C Griffithstown *Mon* 67–72; V Cwm 72–73; V Abersychan 73–79; V Abersychan and Garndiffaith 79–82; R Goetre w Llanover and Llanfair Kilgeddin 82–84; R Goetre w Llanover 85–01; RD Raglan-Usk 90–01; Can St Woolos Cathl 98–01; rtd 01; PtO *Mon* from 17. *3 Trelawny Close, Usk NP15 1SP* T: (01291) 672252 E: canonroycale@btinternet.com

CALE, Mrs Heather. b 68. Ches Coll of HE BEd 90. St Mich Coll Llan 12. **d** 14 **p** 15. NSM Haverfordwest St D 14–18; NSM Daugleddau LMA from 19. *Greenway Cottage, 79 Hill Mountain, Houghton, Milford Haven SA73 1NB* E: heather.cale@btinternet.com

CALEY, Clare Yvonne. **d** 17 **p** 18. C Inverness St Jo *Mor* 17–20; C Inverness St Mich 17–20; P-in-c Lochinver from 20; P-in-c Ullapool from 20. *25 Market Street, Ullapool IV26 2XE*

CALLADINE, Matthew Robert Michael. b 65. St Jo Coll Dur BSc 87 BA 95 Reading Univ MSc 89. Cranmer Hall Dur 93. **d** 96 **p** 97. C Blurton *Lich* 96–01; P-in-c Moston St Mary *Man* 01–16; R Burnage St Marg from 16. *St Margaret's Rectory, 250 Burnage Lane, Manchester M19 1FL* T: 0161-432 1844 E: matt.calladine@ntlworld.com

CALLAGHAN, Martin Peter. b 57. Edin Th Coll 91. **d** 93 **p** 94. C Ayr *Glas* 93–96; C Girvan 93–96; C Maybole 93–96; P-in-c Gretna from 96; P-in-c Eastriggs from 96; P-in-c Annan from 97; P-in-c Lockerbie from 97; P-in-c Moffat from 97; Clergy Ldr Annandale Gp from 03. *South Annandale Rectory, 28 Northfield Park, Annan DG12 5EZ* T: (01461) 202924 E: martinpcallaghan@btinternet.com

CALLAGHAN, Michael James. b 63. Clare Coll Cam BA 85. SEITE 94. **d** 97 **p** 98. NSM Blackheath Park St Mich *S'wark* 97–08; PtO *Guildf* 12–14; NSM Egham from 14; PtO *Lon* from 15. *3 College Avenue, Egham TW20 8NR* T: (01784) 435678

CALLAGHAN, Robert Paul. b 59. K Coll Lon BD 81 Kent Univ MA 04. Linc Th Coll 81. **d** 83 **p** 85. C Winchmore Hill St Paul *Lon* 83–85; C Paddington St Jo w St Mich 85–91; V Dartford St Edm *Roch* 91–11; Nat Co-ordinator Inclusive Ch 11–17; PtO *Glouc* from 14. *4 Ferney, Dursley GL11 5AB* T: (01453) 549955 M: 07989-178558 E: bcall@hotmail.co.uk

CALLAGHAN, Yvonne Susan. b 58. St Jo Coll Nottm 06. **d** 08 **p** 09. C Middleham w Coverdale and E Witton etc *Ripon* 08–13; V Easby w Skeeby and Brompton on Swale etc *Leeds* from 13; AD Richmond 17–19. *The Vicarage, St Paul's Drive, Brompton on Swale, Richmond DL10 7HQ* T: (01748) 810613 M: 07980-276226 E: revyvonnecallaghan@esbb.co.uk

CALLARD, Canon David Kingsley. b 37. St Pet Coll Ox BA 61 MA 65. Westcott Ho Cam 61. **d** 63 **p** 64. C Leamington Priors H Trin *Cov* 63–68; C Wyken 66–68; C Bp's Hatfield *St Alb* 68–73; R Bilton *Cov* 73–83; TR Swanage and Studland *Sarum* 83–93; TR Oakdale 93–02; Can and Preb Sarum Cathl 95–02; rtd 02; PtO *Sarum* from 04; B & W 05–15. *Woodlands,*

29 Folkestone Road, Salisbury SP2 8JP T: (01722) 501200
E: katcallard@ntlworld.com

CALLEN, Nicola Geraldine. b 48. Open Univ BA 85. Trin Coll Bris 09. **d** 11 **p** 12. OLM Fishponds St Jo Bris 11–20; OLM Bris St Aid w St Geo 15–20; OLM Two Mile Hill St Mich 15–20; OLM Bris St Aid w St Geo, Fishponds St Jo, and Two Mile Hill from 20. 164 Ridgeway Road, Bristol BS16 3EG

CALLIS, Gillian Ruth. See TURNER-CALLIS, Gillian Ruth

CALLON, Andrew McMillan. b 56. Chich Th Coll 77. **d** 80 **p** 81. C Wigan All SS Liv 80–85; V Abram 85–90; V Bickershaw 89–90; Chapl RN 90–12; rtd 12; PtO B & W from 13. Kings Living, Prigg Lane, South Petherton TA13 5BX T: (01460) 242537 M: 07777-670319 E: a.mcallon@btinternet.com

CALLWAY, Peter Stanley. b 55. SEITE 06. **d** 09 **p** 10. C Paddock Wood Roch 09–13; R Coxheath, E Farleigh, Hunton, Linton etc 13–21; rtd 21. 7 Heath Road, Langley, Maidstone ME17 3LH E: peter@callways.co.uk

CALOW, Jacqueline. b 60. SNWTP. **d** 11 **p** 12. C Langley Man 11–14; NSM Saddleworth 14–16; P-in-c Tonge w Alkrington 16–18; C Rhodes 16–18; V Tonge, Rhodes and Alkrington 18–21; PtO from 21. The New Vicarage, Boardman Lane, Middleton, Manchester M24 4TU T: 0161-655 1816 E: jackie.2026309@gmail.com

CALOW, Timothy. b 58. **d** 10 **p** 11. NSM Sutton w Cowling and Lothersdale Bradf 10–14; Leeds 14–16; NSM Embsay w Eastby from 16. 3 Laurel Close, Embsay, Skipton BD23 6RS T: (01756) 799517 E: tim@calows.me.uk

CALVELEY, Mrs Susan. b 47. **d** 02 **p** 03. OLM Birkdale St Pet Liv 02–06; NSM 06–11; rtd 11; PtO Liv from 16. 22 Warren Court, Southport PR8 2DE E: revd.sue@gmail.com

CALVER, Canon Gillian Margaret. b 47. Qu Eliz Coll Lon BSc 68. Cant Sch of Min 89. **d** 92 **p** 94. NSM Folkestone H Trin w Ch Ch Cant 92–95; P-in-c Alkham w Capel le Ferne and Hougham 95–01; V 01–02; Chapl Dover Coll 95–99; R Staplehurst Cant 02–11; AD Weald 06–10; Hon Can Cant Cathl 08–11; rtd 11; PtO Cant from 12; Chapl to The Queen 08–17. 6 Grand Court, Grand Parade, Littlestone, New Romney TN28 8NT T: (01797) 366082 E: gill.calver@btinternet.com

CALVER, Nicholas James. b 58. Nottm Univ BTh 83 Dur Univ MA 90. Cranmer Hall Dur 86. **d** 88 **p** 89. C Forest Hill Ch Ch S'wark 88–91; C Forest Hill 91–92; P-in-c Mottingham St Edw 92–95; V 95–97; Voc Adv Lewisham Adnry 94–97; V Redhill St Jo S'wark 97–14; P-in-c Burstow w Horne 14–15; C S Nutfield w Outwood 14–15; R The Windmill from 15. The Rectory, 5 The Acorns, Redehall Road, Smallfield, Horley RH6 9QJ T: (01342) 842224 E: nicholas.calver@btinternet.com

CALVERLEY, Mrs Denise Marie. b 66. Trin Coll Bris 10. **d** 12 **p** 13. C Saltford w Corston and Newton St Loe B & W 12–14; C Keynsham 14–16; P-in-c Publow w Pensford, Compton Dando and Chelwood from 16. The Rectory, Old Road, Pensford, Bristol BS39 4BB M: 07849-821588 E: dmcalverley@icloud.com

CALVERT, Geoffrey Richard. b 58. Edin Univ BSc 79 PhD 84 Leeds Univ BA 86. Coll of Resurr Mirfield 84. **d** 87 **p** 88. C Curdworth w Castle Vale Birm 87–90; C Barnsley St Mary Wakef 90–92; TV Halifax 92–94; V Halifax H Trin 95–99; V Luton St Aug Limbury St Alb 99–09; P-in-c Watford St Mich 09–12; V from 12. St Michael's Vicarage, 4 Mildred Avenue, Watford WD18 7DY T: (01923) 232460 E: geoffreycalvert@virginmedia.com

CALVERT, Canon Jean. b 34. Lightfoot Ho Dur IDC 63. dss 78 **d** 87 **p** 94. S Bank York 78–84; Chapl Asst Rampton Hosp Retford 84–88; Dn-in-c Dunham w Darlton, Ragnall, Fledborough etc S'well 88–94; P-in-c 94–04; Hon Can S'well Minster 93–04; rtd 04; PtO S'well 06–16. The Rafters, Lincoln Road, Darlton, Newark NG22 0TF T: (01777) 228758

CALVERT, John Raymond. b 44. Lon Coll of Div 64. **d** 67 **p** 68. C Kennington St Mark S'wark 67–70; C Southborough St Pet w Ch Ch and St Matt Roch 70–72; C Barton Seagrave Pet 72–73; C Barton Seagrave w Warkton 73–75; Asst Master Shaftesbury High Sch 78–79; Dioc Children's Officer Glouc 79–87; P-in-c S Cerney w Cerney Wick and Down Ampney 87–89; V 89–07; P-in-c Siddington w Preston 02–07; rtd 07. 46 Penn Lane, Brixham TQ5 9NR E: jrcalvertuk@googlemail.com

CALVERT, Mrs Judith. b 50. NOC 04. **d** 07 **p** 08. NSM Woodchurch Ches 07–12; NSM Neston from 12. 33 Centurion Drive, Wirral CH47 7AL T: 0151-632 4729 E: rev.judithcalvert@btinternet.com

CALVERT, Canon Peter Noel. b 41. Ch Coll Cam BA 63 MA 67. Cuddesdon Coll 64. **d** 66 **p** 67. C Brighouse Wakef 66–71; V Heptonstall 71–82; V Todmorden 82–07; P-in-c Cross Stone 83–93; RD Calder Valley 84–06; Hon Can Wakef Cathl 92–07; rtd 07; PtO Leven Valley Carl 07–11; TV Cartmel Peninsula 12–15; Chapl to The Queen 98–11; PtO Blackb from 16. 26

Stonemere Avenue, Todmorden OL14 5RW T: (01706) 817166
E: pncalvert@btinternet.com

CALVERT, Philip. b 62. St Steph Ho Ox 00. **d** 02 **p** 03. C Holbrooks Cov 02–06; P-in-c Kingstanding St Mark Birm 06–10; V from 10; AD Handsworth 14–19; Jt AD Handsworth and Central 19–20. St Mark's Clergy House, Bandywood Crescent, Birmingham B44 9JX T: 0121-360 7288 M: 07488-286290 E: frphilipcalvert@outlook.com

CALVIN, Canon Alison Noeleen. Ulster Univ BA QUB BTh PGCE. CITC. **d** 09 **p** 10. Bp's C Killeshandra w Killegar and Derrylane K, E & A 09–12; I 12–20; I Kilkeel D & D from 20; Can Kilmore Cathl K, E & A from 17. The Rectory, 44 Manse Road, Kilkeel, Newry BT34 4BN T: (028) 4176 5994 E: alisoncalvin@gmail.com

CALVIN-THOMAS, Canon David Nigel. b 43. Univ of Wales (Cardiff) BSc 64 Lon Univ BD 77. St Mich Coll Llan 77. **d** 78 **p** 79. C Pontypridd St Cath Llan 78–80; Malawi 81–84; V Rastrick St Matt Wakef 84–88; V Birchencliffe 88–93; Chapl Huddersfield R Infirmary 88–93; R Aberdeen St Pet Ab 93–01; P-in-c Cove Bay 93–01; TV Glenrothes St And 01–07; R 07–09; R Leven and Lochgelly 07–09; rtd 09. 2 Ruthin Way, Tonteg, Pontypridd CF38 1TF T: (01443) 203633 E: davidcalvinthomas@btinternet.com

CAM, Julian Howard. b 48. York Univ BA 69 Man Univ MA 99. Qu Coll Birm 73. **d** 75 **p** 76. C St Ives Truro 75–80; C Lelant 78–80; V Flookburgh Carl 80–82; V St Stephen by Saltash Truro 82–83; V Low Marple Ches 83–08; rtd 08; PtO Ches from 08; Derby from 08; Man 15–20. 14 High Lea Road, New Mills, High Peak SK22 3DP T: (01663) 744065 E: julian.angela.cam08@btinternet.com

CAMAIONI, Orazio. b 83. Chieti Univ BA 08 MA 11 Reading Univ PhD 15. St Steph Ho Ox 14. **d** 16 **p** 17. C Wantage Ox 16–19; R Wantage Downs from 19. The Rectory, Church Street, East Hendred, Wantage OX12 8LA M: 07449-968816 E: ocamaioni@gmail.com

CAMBER, Mrs Victoria Clare. b 69. Man Univ BA 91 Leeds Univ BA 10. Yorks Min Course 07. **d** 10 **p** 11. C Wales Sheff 10–12; C Todwick 12–13; P-in-c from 13; AD Laughton from 20. The Rectory, 15 Rectory Gardens, Todwick, Sheffield S26 1JU T: (01909) 771101 E: vicky_camber@yahoo.co.uk or vicky.camber@sheffield.anglican.org

CAMBRIDGE, Benedict Howard. b 73. Westmr Coll Ox BTh 95. Cranmer Hall Dur 99. **d** 01 **p** 02. C Chilwell S'well 01–05; Sen Chapl Staffs Univ Lich 05–12; TV Littleham w Exmouth Ex 12–13; C Lympstone and Woodbury w Exton 12–13; TV Littleham-cum-Exmouth w Lympstone from 13. The Vicarage, 96 Littleham Road, Exmouth EX8 2RD M: 07535-480077 E: rev.benedict@btinternet.com

CAMBRIDGE, Archdeacon of. See HUGHES, The Ven Alexander James

✠**CAMERON, The Rt Revd Andrew Bruce.** b 41. Edin Th Coll 61. **d** 64 **p** 65. C 92. C Helensburgh Glas 64–67; C Edin H Cross 67–71; Prov and Dioc Youth Chapl 69–75; Chapl St Mary's Cathl Edin 71–75; R Dalmahoy 75–82; Chapl Heriot-Watt Univ 75–82; TV Livingston LEP 82–88; R Perth St Jo St And 88–92; Convener Prov Miss Bd 88–92; Bp Ab 92–06; Primus 00–06; rtd 06; LtO St And from 07; PtO Ab from 19. 21/1 Barossa Place, Perth PH1 5HH M: 07715-323119 E: bruce2541@gmail.com

CAMERON, Andrew John. b 60. Lon Univ MB, BS 85 St Jo Coll Cam MA 85. St Mellitus Coll 17. St Aug Coll of Th 18. **d** 20. NSM Lamberhurst and Matfield Roch from 20. 10 Shandon Close, Tunbridge Wells TN2 3RE T: (01892) 528638 M: 07841-386034   E: sixcamerons@blueyonder.co.uk   or sixcamerons@gmail.com

CAMERON, David Alan. b 59. Glas Univ MA 81 DipEd 82 PGCE 82. Ripon Coll Cuddesdon 88. **d** 91 **p** 92. C Farncombe Guildf 91–95; C Guildf H Trin w St Mary 93–96; V Fenton Lich 96–15; R Forfar St And 15–17; R Lunan Head 15–17. Flat 1/1, 14 Darnley Road, Glasgow G41 4NB M: 07931-644143

CAMERON, David Alexander. b 42. Reading Univ BA 63 MRTPI. St And Dioc Tr Course 80. **d** 90 **p** 93. NSM Blairgowrie St And from 90; NSM Coupar Angus from 90; NSM Alyth from 90. Firgrove, Golf Course Road, Blairgowrie PH10 6LF T: (01250) 873272 or 874583 E: dacameron@talk21.com

✠**CAMERON, The Rt Revd Douglas MacLean.** b 35. Edin Th Coll 59. **d** 62 **p** 63 **c** 93. C Falkirk Edin 62–65; Miss P Eiwo Papua New Guinea 66–67; Miss P Movi 67–72; R Goroka and Adn New Guinea Mainland 72–74; P-in-c Edin St Fillan 74–78; R 78–88; R Edin St Hilda 77–88; R Dalkeith 88–92; R Lasswade 88–92; Can St Mary's Cathl 90–91; Syn Clerk 90–91; Dean Edin 91–92; Bp Arg 93–03; rtd 03; LtO Edin from 04. 23 Craigs Way, Rumford, Falkirk FK2 0EU T: (01324) 714137 E: dcamera@tiscali.co.uk

✠**CAMERON, The Rt Revd Gregory Kenneth.** b 59. Linc Coll Ox BA 80 MA 84 Down Coll Cam BA 82 MA 85 Univ of Wales (Cardiff) MPhil 92 LLM 95. St Mich Coll Llan 82. **d** 83 **p** 84 **c** 09. C Newport St Paul *Mon* 83–86; Tutor St Mich Coll Llan 86–89; C Llanmartin *Mon* 86–87; TV 87–88; Chapl Wycliffe Coll Glos 88–94; Dir Bloxham Project 94–00; Research Fell Cardiff Univ Cen for Law and Relig 98–00; Chapl to Abp Wales 00–03; Dir Ecum Relns ACC 03–04; Dep Sec 04–09; Hon Can St Woolos Cathl *Mon* 03–09; Bp St As from 09. *Esgobty, St Asaph LL17 0TW* T: (01745) 583503 E: bishop.stasaph@churchinwales.org.uk *or* bishop.stasaph@cinw.org.uk

CAMERON, Mrs Janice Irene. b 43. Reading Univ BA. TISEC 93. **d** 96 **p** 96. C Blairgowrie *St And* 96–98; C Coupar Angus 96–98; C Alyth 96–98; R Dunblane 99–08; Can St Ninian's Cathl Perth 05–08; rtd 08; LtO *St And* from 08. *Firgrove, Golf Course Road, Blairgowrie PH10 6LF* T: (01250) 873272 E: janicecameron@freeola.net

CAMERON, Mrs Laura Bluebell. b 55. SRN 77. STETS 10. **d** 13 **p** 14. NSM Shedfield and Wickham *Portsm* 13–16; NSM Fareham H Trin 16; NSM Portsdown from 19; NSM Purbrook from 19. *Wentworth, Heath Road, Wickham, Fareham PO17 6LA* T: (01329) 830145 M: 07562-217104 E: revdlauracameron@gmail.com

CAMERON, Lindy Jane. b 61. Sarum Coll 19 Cliff Th Coll MA 15. **d** 21. NSM Hilfield Friary from 21. *Society of St Francis, The Friary, Hilfield, Dorchester DT2 7BE* T: (01300) 341345 M: 07901-601547 E: lindyjane100@yahoo.co.uk

CAMERON, Preb Margaret Mary. b 48. Qu Mary Coll Lon BA 69 Ex Univ MA 95. SWMTC 87. **d** 90 **p** 94. NSM Budleigh Salterton *Ex* 90–95; C Whipton 95–97; R Hemyock w Culm Davy, Clayhidon and Culmstock 97–03; RD Cullompton 99–03; V Plympton St Mary 03–13; Preb Ex Cathl 05–13; rtd 13. *Belair, 9 Cyprus Road, Exmouth EX8 2DZ* T: (01395) 223395 E: margaretcameron271@btinternet.com

CAMERON, Michael John. b 41. Linc Th Coll 91. **d** 92 **p** 93. C Dinnington *Sheff* 92–96; V Beighton 96–06; AD Attercliffe 99–02; rtd 07; PtO *Sheff* 09–18. *17 Western Street, Barnsley S70 2BP* T: (01226) 249573 E: michaelcameron851@btinternet.com

CAMERON, Monica Eunice. b 58. Newc Univ BA 82 Solicitor 01. Westcott Ho Cam 12. **d** 15 **p** 16. C Gt Shelford *Ely* 15–18; V Erith Ch Ch *Roch* 18–21; P-in-c Deal St Leon w St Rich and Sholden etc *Cant* from 21. *St Leonard's Rectory, Addelam Road, Deal CT14 9BZ* M: 07985-304860 E: revmonicacameron@gmail.com

CAMERON, Ms Sheila. b 34. TCert 54. Gilmore Ho 65. **d** 98 **p** 99. NSM Catford St Laur *S'wark* 98–02; PtO from 02. *49 Keedonwood Road, Bromley BR1 4QJ* T: (020) 8695 5521 E: sheilacameron@rocketmail.com

CAMERON, Sheila Helen MacLeod. b 46. St Andr Univ MA 68 MLitt 15 Anglia Ruskin Univ MA 06. ERMC 04. **d** 06 **p** 07. NSM Cherry Hinton St Andr *Ely* 06–07; NSM Chesterton St Geo 07–09; P-in-c Dunbar *Edin* 09–12; NSM Lasswade and Dalkeith 12–13; NSM N Tyne and Redesdale *Newc* 13–16; rtd 16; PtO *Newc* from 16; *Edin* from 18. *1 Elderberry Cottages, Otterburn, Newcastle upon Tyne NE19 1LJ* T: (01830) 520071 M: 07432-504308 E: shmcameron@btinternet.com

CAMERON, Thomas Edward. b 46. **d** 06 **p** 10. NSM St Paul's Cathl *Lon* 06–11; NSM Clayton w Keymer *Chich* 11–20; PtO *Chelmsf* from 20. *Dresden House, 64 King Street, Aspatria, Wigton CA7 3AH* E: tom.cameron2@aol.com

CAMMIDGE, Jacqueline Ann. b 57. **d** 15 **p** 16. NSM Hampton Hill *Lon* from 15. *32 Uxbridge Road, Hampton TW12 3AD* E: cammidgeclan@blueyonder.co.uk *or* curate@stjames-hamptonhill.org.uk

CAMP, Lin. b 47. Loughb Univ MA 07. SNWTP 07. **d** 10 **p** 11. OLM Ormskirk *Liv* 10–17; rtd 17; PtO *Liv* from 17. *9 Whiterails Drive, Ormskirk L39 3BE* T: (01695) 574152

CAMP, Michael Maurice. b 52. Southn Univ BTh 83 K Coll Lon MA 99 Brentwood Coll of Educn CertEd 73. Sarum & Wells Th Coll 78. **d** 81 **p** 82. C Loughton St Jo *Chelmsf* 81–84; C Chingford SS Pet and Paul 84–87; V Northfleet *Roch* 87–94; V Hadlow 94–01; RD Paddock Wood 99–01; V Bromley SS Pet and Paul 01–12; AD Bromley 06–11; Hon Can Roch Cathl 11–13; Abp's Chapl *Cant* 12–13; Hon C Stockwell St Andr and St Mich *S'wark* 12–13; R Parkstone St Pet and St Osmund w Branksea *Sarum* 13–19; rtd 19. *24 Berkshire Road, Salisbury SP2 8NY* M: 07734-424996

CAMPBELL, Andrew Philip. b 82. QUB BA MTh PhD. **d** 12 **p** 13. C Belfast St Anne *Conn* 12–13; C Bangor Abbey *D & D* 13–16; I Skerry w Rathcavan and Newtowncrommelin *Conn* from 16. *The Rectory, 49 Rectory Gardens, Broughshane, Ballymena BT42 4LF* T: (028) 2586 1215 E: skerry@connor.anglican.org *or* revdrapcampbell@gmail.com

CAMPBELL, Mrs Brenda. b 47. St Jo Coll Nottm 92. **d** 94 **p** 95. C Rothley *Leic* 94–97; C Market Bosworth, Cadeby w Sutton Cheney etc 97–00; TV Bosworth and Sheepy Gp 00–07; rtd 07; PtO *Derby* 09–18; *Leic* 13–21. *28 Ashfield Drive, Moira, Swadlincote DE12 6HQ* T: (01530) 413534 E: brendajones101@sky.com

CAMPBELL, Christine Emily. b 78. Imp Coll Lon BSc 00. Westcott Ho Cam 16. **d** 18 **p** 19. C Cherry Hinton St Jo *Ely* from 18. *22 Levitt Lane, Waterbeach, Cambridge CB25 9AZ* T: (01223) 440014 M: 07383-512636 E: chris@revcc.uk

CAMPBELL, David. b 70. St Andr Univ MTheol 92 New Coll Edin MTh 94. Edin Th Coll 92. **d** 94 **p** 95. C Perth St Jo *St And* 94–96; P-in-c Tayport and Newport-on-Tay 96–99; R Dunfermline 99–07; Dioc Youth Officer 96–07; Can St Ninian's Cathl Perth 06–07; Chapl Fettes Coll Edin 07–12; Sen Chapl Marlborough Coll 12–17; Sen Chapl Sherborne Sch from 17. *Sherborne School, Abbey Road, Sherborne DT9 3AP* T: (01935) 810498 M: 07402-633600 E: david.campbell@sherborne.org

CAMPBELL, Miss Elizabeth Hume. b 53. Glas Univ MA 74 Hamilton Coll of Educn TCert 75. St Jo Coll Nottm 01. **d** 02 **p** 03. NSM Alstonfield, Butterton, Ilam etc *Lich* 02–08; NSM Stonehaven and Catterline *Bre* 08–10; P-in-c Dundee St Luke 10–12; Chapl Grampian Univ Hosp NHS Trust 12–13; NSM Muchalls, Stonehaven and Catterline *Bre* 12–15; P-in-c S Shields St Simon *Dur* 15–18; C Jarrow 15–17; rtd 18; PtO *Dur* 19. *Address temp unknown* M: 07809-830556 E: lizziecampbell18@gmail.com

CAMPBELL, George St Clair. b 32. Lon Univ BSc 53. Clifton Th Coll 58. **d** 60 **p** 61. C Tunbridge Wells St Pet *Roch* 60–64; C Clitheroe St Jas *Blackb* 64–70; V Tibshelf *Derby* 70–86; V W Bromwich H Trin *Lich* 86–97; Chapl Heath Lane Hosp 87–97; rtd 97; PtO *Guildf* 98–15. *1 Green Drive, Fulwood, Preston PR2 9SA*

CAMPBELL, Mrs Hilary Anne. b 58. UMIST BSc 80. SAOMC. **d** 01 **p** 02. C Goring w S Stoke *Ox* 01–05; TV Kidlington w Hampton Poyle 05–13; V Shires' Edge from 13. *The Vicarage, High Street, Cropredy, Banbury OX17 1NG* T: (01295) 750385

CAMPBELL, Ian George. b 47. FRICS 74 FBEng 93. SEITE 96. **d** 99 **p** 00. NSM Chilham w Challock and Molash *Cant* 99–01; P-in-c Crundale w Godmersham 01–12; NSM King's Wood 12–14; C A20 Benefice 14–17; rtd 17; PtO *Cant* from 18. *19 Quarry House, Calleywell Lane, Aldington, Ashford TN25 7FZ* T: (01233) 721445 E: campbellkent@gmail.com

CAMPBELL, James Duncan. b 55. Qu Eliz Coll Lon BSc 77 Oak Hill Th Coll MA 00. Cranmer Hall Dur 85. **d** 87 **p** 88. C Hendon St Paul Mill Hill *Lon* 87–92; V Stevenage St Hugh and St Jo *St Alb* 92–13; RD Stevenage 11–13; V Watford Ch Ch from 13. *Christ Church Vicarage, Leggatts Way, Watford WD24 5NQ* T: (01923) 674142 E: vicarccwatford@gmail.com

CAMPBELL, James Larry. b 46. Indiana Univ BSc 69 E Kentucky Univ MA 73 Hull Univ MA 91. Linc Th Coll 86. **d** 88 **p** 89. C N Hull St Mich *York* 88–92; C Hessle 92–95; V Burton Pidsea and Humbleton w Elsternwick 95–12; rtd 12; PtO *Linc* 15–18. *The Mullburys, Bardney Road, Wragby, Market Rasen LN8 5QZ* T: (01673) 857646 E: campbell822@aol.com

CAMPBELL, Canon James Malcolm. b 55. MRICS 81. Wycliffe Hall Ox 89. **d** 91 **p** 92. C Scole, Brockdish, Billingford, Thorpe Abbots etc *Nor* 91–95; R Bentley and Binsted *Win* 95–08; RD Alton 02–08; Hon Can Win Cathl 08; R The Lavingtons, Cheverells, and Easterton *Sarum* 08–16; R Withyham St Mich *Chich* from 16. *The Rectory, Withyham, Hartfield TN7 4BA* T: (01892) 770069 E: withyhamrector@gmail.com

CAMPBELL, James Norman Thompson. b 49. BTh MA. **d** 86 **p** 87. C Arm St Mark w Aghavilly 86–89; I Belfast H Trin and Ardoyne *Conn* 89–95; I Dundela St Mark *D & D* 95–01; I Portadown St Mark *Arm* 01–15; Can Arm Cathl 09–15; rtd 15. *41 Cavanacaw Manor, Armagh BT60 2FH* T: (028) 3731 0696 M: 07784-556026 E: jim.campbell149@sky.com

CAMPBELL, Jane Judith. See BAKKER, Jane Judith

CAMPBELL, Kenneth Scott. b 47. BA 82. Oak Hill Th Coll. **d** 82 **p** 83. C Aughton St Mich *Liv* 82–85; V Brough w Stainmore *Carl* 85–90; R Brough w Stainmore, Musgrave and Warcop 90–92. *4 Quarry Close, Kirkby Stephen CA17 4SS* T: (01768) 372390

CAMPBELL, Lerys William. b 85. Win Univ BA 06. Trin Coll Bris MA 14. **d** 14 **p** 15. C Ringwood *Win* 14–17; P-in-c Darby Green and Eversley from 17. *St Barnabas House, Green Lane, Frogmore, Camberley GU17 0NU* M: 07952-303970 E: revlerys@gmail.com *or* vicar@stmaryseversley.com

CAMPBELL, The Very Revd Margaret Ruth. b 62. Trin Coll Bris BA 02. **d** 02 **p** 03. C Yeovil w Kingston Pitney *B & W* 02–06; TV Wellington and Distr 06–11; R Backwell w Chelvey and

Brockley 11–18; RD Portishead 17–18; Provost St Jo Cathl Oban *Arg* from 18; R Ardbrecknish from 18; Can Cumbrae from 18; Dean Arg from 19. *The Rectory, Ardconnel Terrace, Oban PA34 5DJ* T: (01631) 562323 E: jmbt2001@hotmail.com *or* provostoban@argyll.angican.org

CAMPBELL, Roger Stewart. b 40. Birm Univ BSc 61 PhD 65 St Jo Coll Dur BA 71. Cranmer Hall Dur 68. **d** 71 **p** 72. C Jesmond Clayton Memorial *Newc* 71–77; V St Jo and St Marg Singapore 78–85; C Nottingham St Nic *S'well* 86–90; V Holloway St Mark w Em *Lon* 90–92; TR Tollington 92–97; Chapl Leeds Teaching Hosps NHS Trust 97–04; rtd 04; PtO *Carl* from 05. *Redesdale Cottage, Lazonby, Penrith CA10 1AJ* T: (01768) 870695 E: rogercampbell456@btinternet.com

CAMPBELL, Ms Roxanne Elizabeth. b 86. St Andr Univ MA 08. Scottish Episc Inst 17. **d** 19 **p** 20. C Dundee St Ninian *Bre* 19–20; C Dundee St Mary Magd from 20. *5 Oban Terrace, Dundee DD3 0GZ* M: 07764-212092 E: rev.roxanne.campbell@gmail.com

CAMPBELL, Stephen James. b 60. TCD BTh 91. CITC 88. **d** 91 **p** 92. C Lisburn Ch Ch *Conn* 91–95; I Kilcronaghan w Draperstown and Sixtowns *D & R* 95–00; I Dunluce *Conn* 00–03; PtO *Eur* 04–17. *23A Kirk Road, Ballymoney BT53 6PP* T: (028) 2766 3403 E: sjmimc@yahoo.com

CAMPBELL, Stephen Lloyd. b 46. St Andr Univ LLB 67 Solicitor 72. SEITE 95. **d** 98 **p** 99. NSM Quantoxhead *B & W* 98–07; NSM Quantock Coast 07–16; RD Quantock 06–12; PtO from 16. *Hoddescombe Lodge, Holford, Bridgwater TA5 1SA* T/F: (01278) 741329 M: 07523-350145 E: campbell1sa@btinternet.com

CAMPBELL-SMYTH, Jonathan David. QUB BSc. St Jo Coll Nottm MTh 11. **d** 11 **p** 12. C Coleraine *Conn* 11–13; C Jordanstown 13–17; I Ballynure and Ballyeaston from 17. *Ballynure Rectory, 11 Church Road, Ballynure, Ballyclare BT39 9UF* M: 07808-479649 E: jonathan@campbellsmyth.co.uk

CAMPBELL-TAYLOR, William Goodacre. b 65. Ox Univ BA 87 Cam Univ BA 93 MA 95 Princeton Th Sem DMin 11. Westcott Ho Cam 90. **d** 94 **p** 95. C Chingford SS Pet and Paul *Chelmsf* 94–97; Chapl Lon Guildhall Univ 97–02; Chapl Lon Metrop Univ 02–04; Research Fell St Ethelburga's Cen for Reconciliation and Peace 05–08; Hon C Hoxton St Anne w St Columba *Lon* 05–09; V Stamford Hill St Thos from 09; P-in-c Upper Clapton St Matt from 14; Hon C Stoke Newington Common St Mich from 16. *The Vicarage, 1 Clapton Terrace, London E5 9BW* T: (020) 8806 1463 E: fatherwilliamtaylor@hotmail.com

CAMPBELL-WILSON, Allan. b 43. Dur Univ BEd 74. NEOC 79. **d** 82 **p** 83. NSM Boosbeck w Moorsholm *York* 82–85; R Easington w Skeffling, Kilnsea and Holmpton 85–87; P-in-c Middlesbrough St Jo the Ev 89–95; V 95–99; V Cayton w Eastfield 99–12; rtd 12; PtO *York* from 12. *51 Oak Road, Scarborough YO12 4AP* T: (01723) 362426 E: campbellwilson165@btinternet.com

CAMPEN, William Geoffrey. b 50. Southn Univ BTh 81 Lon Univ MA 08 Liv Univ CertEd 71. Sarum & Wells Th Coll 76. **d** 79 **p** 80. C Peckham St Jo w St Andr *S'wark* 79–83; P-in-c Mottingham St Edw 83–92; R Charlwood 92–15; R Sidlow Bridge 92–15; rtd 15; PtO *Cant* 18–21. *41 Old Park Avenue, Canterbury CT1 1DN* T: (01227) 764340 E: campenwg@googlemail.com

CAMPION (formerly **HOUSEMAN), Mrs Patricia Adele.** b 58. St Mich Coll Llan. **d** 93 **p** 97. C St Issell's and Amroth *St D* 93–95; C Llanegryn w Aberdyfi w Tywyn *Ban* 95–97; rtd 97; PtO *St D* from 99. *3 Mariners Reach, The Strand, Saundersfoot SA69 9EX* T: (01834) 811047

CAMPION, Canon Peter Robert. b 64. Bp's Univ Canada BA 87 TCD BTh 90 MA 93 MPhil 97 Homerton Coll Cam PGCE 94. **d** 90 **p** 91. C Belfast H Trin and Ardoyne *Conn* 90–93; C Taney *D & G* 94–00; Dean's V St Patr Cathl Dublin 96–00; Chapl Netherwood Sch Rothesday Canada 00–05; Chapl K Hosp Sch Dub from 05; Treas St Patr Cathl Dublin 05–11; Prec Ch Ch Cathl Dublin *D & G* from 08; Prec St Patr Cathl Dublin from 15. *The King's Hospital, Palmerstown, Dublin 20, Republic of Ireland* T: (00353) (1) 626 5933 F: 626 0349 E: chaplain@thekingshospital.ie

CAMPION-SPALL, Ms Kathryn May. b 79. York Univ BA 02 Fitzw Coll Cam BA 09. Westcott Ho Cam 07. **d** 10 **p** 11. C Merton St Mary *S'wark* 10–14; C Bris St Mary Redcliffe w Temple etc from 14; Dean of Women's Min from 20. *2 Colston Parade, Bristol BS1 6RA* T: 0117-929 1519 *or* 929 1605 M: 07960-588015 E: kat.campion-spall@stmaryredcliffe.co.uk

CAMPLING, Camilla Anne. *See* CAMPLING-DENTON, Camilla Anne

CAMPLING, Michael. b 27. Trin Coll Cam BA 50 MA 61. Wells Th Coll 51. **d** 53 **p** 54. C Calne *Sarum* 53–57; C

Roehampton H Trin *S'wark* 57–61; V Crowthorne *Ox* 61–75; P-in-c Foleshill St Laur *Cov* 75–81; V Foleshill St Laur 81–83; R Old Alresford and Bighton *Win* 83–92; rtd 92; Chapl St Marg Convent E Grinstead 92–99; Hon C Bexhill St Pet *Chich* 99–05; PtO *Ox* from 05. *9 Orchard Grove, Bloxham, Banbury OX15 4NZ* T: (01295) 721599

CAMPLING-DENTON, Camilla Anne. b 76. St Andr Univ MA 98 Jes Coll Cam MPhil 04. Westcott Ho Cam 02. **d** 05 **p** 06. C Fountains Gp *Ripon* 05–07; C Caerleon w Llanhennock *Mon* 07–09; C Caerleon and Llanfrechfa 09–10; Hon C Washburn and Mid-Wharfe *Bradf* 10–14; R Walkingham Hill *Leeds* 14–17; P-in-c Forcett and Aldbrough and Melsonby 17–18; R from 18. *The Rectory, 1 Appleby Close, Aldbrough St John, Richmond DL11 7TT* T: (01325) 374634 M: 07817-386070 E: camilla.cd@cantab.net

CAMPOS DE SANTANA, Levy Henrique. b 85. **d** 13 **p** 14. C High Wycombe *Ox* 13–17; CMS from 17. *Rua El Greco, Qd 31, Lt 06, Casa 03, Setor Gentil Meireles, Goiania, GO 74575-140, Brazil* M: 07950-212347 E: levysantana@me.com

CANDLIN, David James. b 68. St Cath Coll Cam BA 89 Imp Coll Lon MBA 00. Ripon Coll Cuddesdon 16. **d** 18 **p** 19. C Epsom St Martin *Guildf* from 18. *12 Worple Road, Epsom KT18 5EE* E: revcandlin@gmail.com

CANDY, Julia Elaine. b 80. K Coll Cam BA 01 QUB PhD 06 Jes Coll Cam BA 09. Westcott Ho Cam 07. **d** 10 **p** 11. C Dur St Giles 10–13; C Shadforth and Sherburn 10–13; P-in-c Aberdeen St Jas *Ab* 13; P-in-c Aberdeen St Clem 13; Asst Chapl Univ Coll Lon Hosps NHS Foundn Trust 14–17; V W Hendon St Jo and Cricklewood St Pet *Lon* 17–20; PtO *Dur* from 21. *21 Bower Court, Coxhoe, Durham DH6 4JT* E: revd.dr.juliacandy@gmail.com

CANE, The Very Revd Anthony William Nicholas Strephon. b 61. Cape Town Univ BA 81 Birm Univ MPhil 93 PhD 03. Westcott Ho Cam 87. **d** 90 **p** 91. C Kings Heath *Birm* 90–93; Chapl Brighton Univ *Chich* 93–99; P-in-c Torquay St Luke *Ex* 99–01; Dioc Adv in Adult Tr 99–01; C Ringmer and Dioc Adv for Educn and Tr of Adults *Chich* 01–07; Can Res and Chan Chich Cathl 07–19; Dean Portsm from 19. *The Deanery, 13 Pembroke Road, Portsmouth PO1 2NS* T: (023) 9282 4400 E: anthony.cane@portsmouthcathedral.org.uk

CANESSA, Jonathan Graham. b 70. Ox Brookes Univ BA 02. Westcott Ho Cam 11. **d** 13 **p** 14. C Cambridge St Paul *Ely* 13–21; Bp's Officer for Homelessness 16–21; Min Can Newc Cathl from 21. *Cathedral House, 42 Mosley Street, Newcastle upon Tyne NE1 1DF* E: joncanessa@gmail.com *or* jon.canessa@newcastlecathedral.org.uk

CANEY, Canon Robert Swinbank. b 37. St Jo Coll Cam 57. Lich Th Coll 58. **d** 61 **p** 62. C Kingswinford H Trin *Lich* 61–64; C Castle Church 64–67; V Bradwell *Derby* 67–73; V Fairfield 73–84; RD Buxton 78–84; P-in-c Peak Forest and Wormhill 79–83; R Wirksworth w Alderwasley, Carsington etc 84–92; TR Wirksworth 92–02; Hon Can Derby Cathl 93–02; rtd 02; PtO *Derby* 02–18. *2 Erica Drive, South Normanton, Alfreton DE55 2ET* T: (01773) 581106 E: randjcaney@gmail.com

CANHAM, Frances Elizabeth. b 55. Cardiff Univ MTh 13 MCIPD 93. St Mich Coll Llan 05. **d** 07 **p** 08. NSM Thanington *Cant* 07–10; C Washington St Dav USA 07–10; Asst Chapl Salisbury NHS Foundn Trust 10–13; Chapl from 13. *Chaplain's Office, Salisbury District Hospital, Salisbury SP2 8BJ* T: (01722) 429271

CANNAM, Martin Stafford John. b 68. Jes Coll Ox BA 90 MA 95. Wycliffe Hall Ox 93. **d** 96 **p** 97. C Childwall All SS *Liv* 96–00; V Biddulph *Lich* 00–15; RD Leek 13–15; R Heswall *Ches* from 15. *The Rectory, Village Road, Heswall, Wirral CH60 0DZ* T: 0151-342 3471 M: 07999-594373

CANNELL, Anthea Marjorie. b 45. UEA MA 85. EAMTC 01. **d** 02 **p** 03. NSM Theydon Bois *Chelmsf* 02–10; P-in-c Roydon 10–15; rtd 15; PtO *Chelmsf* from 15. *118 High Street, Roydon, Harlow CM19 5EF* T: (01279) 792543 E: amcannell@btinternet.com

CANNING, Canon Arthur James. b 45. St Jo Coll Dur BA 66 Linacre Coll Ox BA 70 MA 74 Lambeth STh 90. Ripon Hall Ox 67. **d** 71 **p** 72. C Coleshill *Birm* 71–74; C Frome St Jo *B & W* 75–76; V Frizington and Arlecdon *Carl* 76–80; P-in-c Foleshill St Paul *Cov* 80–81; V 81–12; Hon Can Cov Cathl 00–12; rtd 12; PtO *Cov* 12–21; *Birm* from 21. *13 Broadlands Close, Coventry CV5 7AJ* T: (024) 7671 3220 E: jcxwx@aol.com

CANNING, Peter Christopher. b 52. Birm Poly CQSW. St Jo Coll Nottm 87. **d** 89 **p** 90. C Cov St Mary 89–93; V Hartshill 93–96; rtd 96. *Address withheld by request*

CANNINGS, Karen Rachel. *See* SKIDMORE, Karen Rachel

CANNON, Elizabeth Mary. b 50. EAMTC 94. **d** 97 **p** 98. NSM New Catton Ch Ch *Nor* 97–00; P-in-c Cross Roads cum Lees *Bradf* 00–06; TV Blyth Valley *St E* 06–15; rtd 15; PtO *Nor* from 16; *St E* from 17. *Address temp unknown*

CANNON, Mark Harrison. b 60. Keble Coll Ox BA 82. Cranmer Hall Dur 83. **d** 85 **p** 86. C Skipton Ch Ch *Bradf* 85–88; Dioc Youth Officer 88–92; C Baildon 88–92; P-in-c Church Coniston *Carl* 92–00; P-in-c Torver 92–00; P-in-c Brindle *Blackb* 00–10; Dioc Voc Adv 00–05; NSM E Lonsdale 10–11; P-in-c 11–16; V 16–20; R Addingham *Leeds* from 20. *The Rectory, Low Mill Lane, Addingham, Ilkley LS29 0QP* E: markhcannon1@gmail.com

CANNON, Ms Rebekah Lindsey. b 77. Man Metrop Univ BA 99 Middx Univ MA 06 PGCE 06 SS Coll Cam BTh 09. Westcott Ho Cam 07. **d** 10 **p** 11. C Whyke w Rumboldswhyke and Portfield *Chich* 10–14; Chapl RAF from 14. *Chaplaincy Services (RAF), HQ Air Command, RAF High Wycombe HP14 4UE* T: (01494) 496800 E: rebecca.cannon103@mod.gov.uk

CANNON, Tony Arthur. b 57. Oak Hill Th Coll 94. **d** 96 **p** 97. C Church Stretton *Heref* 96–00; P-in-c Kingham w Churchill, Daylesford and Sarsden *Ox* 00–01; TV Chipping Norton 01–10; V Woking St Jo *Guildf* 11–17; rtd 17. *42 Coach Barn Lane, Hailsham BN27 3YR* T: (01323) 398539

CANSDALE, Mrs Elspeth. b 72. Bradf Univ BA 95. St Hild Coll 16. **d** 20 **p** 21. C Oxenhope *Leeds* from 20. *St Mark's Vicarage, 64 Green Head Road, Keighley BD20 6ED* M: 07890-342991 E: elspeth.cansdale@gmail.com

CANSDALE, Canon Michael Cranmer. b 70. Bradf Univ BA 93 St Jo Coll Dur BA 06. Cranmer Hall Dur 04. **d** 06 **p** 07. C Silsden *Bradf* 06–09; P-in-c Morton St Luke 09–15; P-in-c Riddlesden 09–15; V Morton and Riddlesden *Leeds* 15–16; TR Keighley from 16; Hon Can Bradf Cathl from 19. *St Mark's Vicarage, 64 Green Head Road, Keighley BD20 6ED* T: (01535) 607003 M: 07545-566898

CANSDALE, Philip John. b 73. Keble Coll Ox BA 95 MA 99. Trin Coll Bris BA 98 MA 99. **d** 99 **p** 00. C East St Mary Bredin 99–03; C Penn Fields *Lich* 03–09; V Meole Brace from 09; RD Shrewsbury from 18. *The Vicarage, Vicarage Road, Shrewsbury SY3 9EZ* T: (01743) 231744

CANSDALE, Simon James Lee. b 68. Keble Coll Ox BA 90. Wycliffe Hall Ox 93. **d** 95 **p** 96. C Bletchley *Ox* 95–98; C Cambridge H Trin *Ely* 98–01; R W Bridgford *S'well* 01–08; TR Gt Chesham *Ox* 08–19; V Win Ch Ch from 19. *Christchurch Vicarage, Sleepers Hill, Winchester SO22 4ND* T: (01962) 857988 E: simon.cansdale@ccwinch.org.uk

CANT, Anthony David. b 59. Middx Univ BA 04. NTMTC 01. **d** 04 **p** 05. C Walthamstow *Chelmsf* 04–07; TV 07–10; Chapl Anglia Ruskin Univ 10–19; rtd 19; P-in-c Writtle w Highwood *Chelmsf* from 19; P-in-c Roxwell from 19. *The Vicarage, 19 Lodge Road, Writtle, Chelmsford CM1 3HY* E: revtonyc@gmail.com

CANT, Christopher Somerset Travers. b 51. Keble Coll Ox BA 72 MA 76 Ex Univ PGCE 77. All Nations Chr Coll 80 Wycliffe Hall Ox 93. **d** 87 **p** 90. C Tando Muhammad Khan Pakistan 87–90; P-in-c Badin 90–92; LtO *Cov* 92–93; Warden St Clem Family Cen *Cov* 93–95; C Gt Ilford St Andr *Chelmsf* 95–98; V Hainault 98–10; C Aylesbeare, Clyst St George, Clyst St Mary etc *Ex* 11–16. *15 Stoneborough Lane, Budleigh Salterton EX9 6HL* T: (01395) 488178 E: chriscant@tiscali.co.uk

CANT, Joseph Clifford. b 72. UEA BA 94 MA 98 DipSW 98 Cam Univ BTh 08. Westcott Ho Cam 06. **d** 08 **p** 09. C Hilton w Marston-on-Dove *Derby* 08–11; TV Uttoxeter Area *Lich* from 11. *The Parish Office, St Mary's Church, Bridge Street, Uttoxeter ST14 8AW* M: 07952-798649 E: joecant214@gmail.com

CANT, Miss Sheila Phyllis. b 59. All SS Cen for Miss & Min 13. **d** 15 **p** 16. OLM Denton St Lawr *Man* 15–21; PtO from 21. *3 Ashlands Drive, Audenshaw, Manchester M34 5EL* T: 0161-336 1566 E: sheila.cant@btinternet.com

CANTACUZENE, Mrs Mary. b 52. **d** 05 **p** 06. OLM Bures w Assington and Lt Cornard *St E* 05–13; NSM from 13. *Peartree Barn, Peartree Hill, Mount Bures, Bures CO8 5BA* T: (01787) 227616 F: 227220 M: 07932-033019 E: mary.cantacuzene@gmail.com

CANTERBURY, Archbishop of. See WELBY, The Most Revd and Rt Hon Justin Portal

CANTERBURY, Archdeacon of. *Vacant*

CANTERBURY, Dean of. See WILLIS, The Very Revd Robert Andrew

CANTLOW, Tony Loram. b 61. St Hild Coll 17. **d** 18. NSM Skipton Ch Ch w Carleton *Leeds* 18–20. *3 Spences Court, Main Street, Carleton, Skipton BD23 3BY*

CANTRILL, Mark James. b 67. Lanc Univ BEd 89. St Jo Coll Nottm 00. **d** 02 **p** 03. C Warsop *S'well* 02–07; TV Retford Area 07–19; R The Clays from 19. *Clarborough Vicarage, Church Lane, Clarborough, Retford DN22 9NA* T: (01777) 711530 M: 07985-160694 E: revmark.cantrill@btinternet.com

CANTY, Canon Katherine Anne. b 52. York Univ BA 74 Coll of Ripon & York St Jo PGCE 75. NOC 05. **d** 07 **p** 08. Asst Chapl HM Pris Altcourse 04–07; Chapl 07–16; NSM Gateacre *Liv* from 07; Dean Sector Min from 18; Hon Can Liv Cathl from 19. *c/o Crockford, Church House, 27 Great Smith Street, London SW1P 3AZ* E: katy.canty@liverpool.anglican.org

CAPEL, Luke Thomas. See IRVINE-CAPEL, Luke Thomas

CAPEL-EDWARDS, Maureen. b 36. Southn Univ BSc 60 Reading Univ PhD 69. St Alb Minl Tr Scheme 84. **d** 87 **p** 94. NSM Ware St Mary *St Alb* 87–90; Chapl Hertf Regional Coll of FE 87–00; NSM Hertford All SS *St Alb* 90–94; NSM Aspenden and Layston w Buntingford 94–95; NSM Aspenden, Buntingford and Westmill 95–00; P-in-c Ardeley 00–05; P-in-c Cottered w Broadfield and Throcking 00–05; rtd 05; PtO *Portsm* from 05. *Capeland, High Street, Soberton, Southampton SO32 3PN* T: (01489) 878192 E: capeland@waitrose.com

CAPERON, John Philip. b 44. Bris Univ BA 66 Open Univ MPhil 80 Ox Univ MSc 83 Kent Univ MA 99 Anglia Ruskin Univ DProf 13. Ox Min Course 80. **d** 83 **p** 84. NSM Hook Norton w Gt Rollright, Swerford etc *Ox* 83–86; NSM Knaresborough *Ripon* 86–92; Dep Hd St Aid Sch Harrogate 86–92; Hd and Chapl Bennett Memorial Dioc Sch Tunbridge Wells 92–04; rtd 04; PtO *Chich* 98–03 and 11–17; Hon C Mayfield 03–11; P-in-c Fairwarp from 17; Dir Bloxham Project 06–11; PtO *Roch* from 15; *Cant* 17–19. *Sarum, 5 Twyfords, Beacon Road, Crowborough TN6 1YE* T: (01892) 667207 E: johncaperon@btinternet.com

CAPES, Dennis Robert. b 34. Handsworth Coll Birm 55 Linc Th Coll 65. **d** 64 **p** 65. In Methodist Ch (Sarawak) 59–63; C Lt Coates *Linc* 64–66; R Miri Malaysia 66–69; V Gosberton Clough *Linc* 69–71; V Kirton in Holland 71–80; Area Sec USPG Cov, Heref and Worc 80–87; Chapl Copenhagen w Aarhus *Eur* 87–93; TV Liv Our Lady and St Nic w St Anne 93–99; rtd 99. *35 Hardwick Avenue, Newark NG24 4AW* T: (01636) 672874 E: dennis@capes.plus.com

CAPIE, Fergus Bernard. b 47. Auckland Univ BA 68 MA 71. Wycliffe Hall Ox BA 77. **d** 77 **p** 78. C Ox St Mich w St Martin and All SS 77–80; Chapl Summer Fields Sch Ox 80–91; Hon C Wolvercote w Summertown *Ox* 87–91; PtO *St E* 91; TV E Ham w Upton Park and Forest Gate *Chelmsf* 91–95; P-in-c Brondesbury St Anne w Kilburn H Trin *Lon* 95–01; V 01–12; Chapl NW Lon Coll 95–12; rtd 12; P-in-c Bure Valley *Nor* 13–16. *27 Olympus Way, Richmond 7020, Nelson, New Zealand* E: ferguscapie@yahoo.co.uk

CAPITANCHIK, Sophie Rebecca. See JELLEY, Sophie Rebecca

CAPLE, Stephen Malcolm. b 55. Chich Th Coll 86. **d** 88 **p** 89. C Newington St Mary *S'wark* 88–92; V Eltham St Sav 92–97; V Salfords 97–07; P-in-c S Kensington St Aug *Lon* 07–10; V Whitton St Aug 10–19; Dir Evang Kensington Area 07–19; rtd 19. *Address temp unknown*

CAPON, The Very Revd Gerwyn Huw. b 65. Liv Jo Moores Univ BSc 92. St Steph Ho Ox 01. **d** 03 **p** 04. C W Derby St Mary *Liv* 03–07; Dir of Ords *Llan* 07–09; Chapl to Abp Wales 07–09 and 12–14; P-in-c Bolton-le-Sands *Blackb* 09–12; Dean Llan from 14; V Llandaff from 14. *The Deanery, The Cathedral Green, Cardiff CF5 2YF* T: (029) 2056 1545 E: thedean@llandaffcathedral.org.uk

CAPORN, David Richard. b 78. St Jo Coll Cam BA 00 MA 04 ACA 03. Trin Coll Bris MA 13. **d** 13 **p** 14. C Highworth w Sevenhampton and Inglesham etc *Bris* 13–17; C Broad Blunsdon 13–17; TV Sidmouth, Woolbrook, Salcombe Regis, Sidbury etc *Ex* 17–19; TR from 19. *All Saints' Vicarage, All Saints Road, Sidmouth EX10 8ES* T: (01395) 515963 M: 07900-055390 E: david.caporn@sidvalley.org.uk

CAPPER, Alan. See CAPPER, William Alan

CAPPER, Mrs Katherine Frances. b 64. Warwick Univ BA 86. SEITE 07. **d** 10 **p** 11. NSM Horley *S'wark* 10–14; NSM Betchworth and Buckland 14–15; C Reigate St Mary from 15. *12 Beaufort Close, Reigate RH2 9DG* T: (01737) 217191 M: 07710-813177 E: revkate@thecappers.co.uk *or* kate.capper@stmaryreigate.org

CAPPER, Lorraine Alberta. Ulster Univ BTh. **d** 10 **p** 11. C Drumragh w Mountfield *D & R* 10–15; C Donagh w Tyholland and Errigal Truagh *Clogh* from 18. *The Rectory, 3 Castlebalfour Road, Lisnaskea, Enniskillen BT92 0LT* T: (028) 6772 2413 E: lorraine.capper@gmail.com

CAPPER, Canon Richard. b 49. Leeds Univ BSc 70 Fitzw Coll Cam BA 72 MA 79. Westcott Ho Cam 70. **d** 73 **p** 74. C Wavertree H Trin *Liv* 73–76; P-in-c Ince St Mary 76–79; V 79–83; V Gt Crosby St Faith 83–97; AD Bootle 89–97; Can Res Wakef Cathl 97–05; Can Res Nor Cathl 05–14; P-in-c Nor St Mary in the Marsh 05–14; rtd 15; PtO *Nor* from 15; *S'wark* from 16; *Eur* 17–20. *3 Kingfisher Walk, Loddon, Norwich NR14 6FB* T: (01508) 520046 E: richardcapper49@gmail.com

CAPPER, Canon Robert Melville. b 52. Chu Coll Cam BA 74 MA 80. Wycliffe Hall Ox 74. **d** 77 **p** 78. C Maindee Newport *Mon* 77–80; TV Aberystwyth *St D* 80–87; Chapl Univ of Wales (Abth) 80–87; V Malpas *Mon* 87–00; V Gabalfa *Llan* 00–17; P-in-c Tremorfa St Phil CD 05–17; AD Cardiff 13–17; Hon Can Llan Cathl 14–17; rtd 17. *Cleddau View, Haven View, Neyland, Milford Haven SA73 1LS* T: (01646) 562804

CAPPER, William Alan. QUB BTh. **d** 88 **p** 89. C Dundonald *D & D* 88–91; C Lisburn Ch Ch *Conn* 91–94; I Tamlaght O'Crilly Upper w Lower *D & R* 94–96; I Lack *Clogh* 03–09; I Lisnaskea from 09. *The Rectory, 3 Castlebalfour Road, Lisnaskea, Enniskillen BT92 0LT* T: (028) 6772 2413 *or* 6772 3977 E: lisnaskea@clogher.anglican.org

CAPPLEMAN, Graham Robert (Sam). b 56. Chelsea Coll Lon BSc 79 Sheff Univ PhD 83. SAOMC 94. **d** 97 **p** 98. NSM Bedf St Mark *St Alb* from 97; Bp's Dom Chapl from 19; AD Bedford from 20. *107 Dover Crescent, Bedford MK41 8QR* T: (01234) 266952 M: 07836-784051 E: sam_cappleman@hotmail.com

CAPPLEMAN, Mrs Jennifer Margaret. b 53. C F Mott Coll of Educn CertEd 74. SAOMC 97. **d** 00 **p** 01. NSM Bedford St Pet w St Cuth *St Alb* 00–03; C Goldington 03–07; TV Ouzel Valley 07–13; rtd 13; PtO *St Alb* 13–14; NSM Keysoe w Bolnhurst and Lt Staughton 14–15; NSM Bolnhurst w Keysoe 15–17; PtO from 17. *107 Dover Crescent, Bedford MK41 8QR* T: (01234) 266952 M: 07714-701008 E: jennie.cappleman@yahoo.co.uk

CAPRON, Canon David Cooper. b 45. Open Univ BA 80. Sarum & Wells Th Coll 71. **d** 75 **p** 76. C Cov St Mary 75–79; V Shottery St Andr 79–86; TV Stratford-on-Avon w Bishopton 79–86; V Shottery St Andr 86; V Newton Aycliffe *Dur* 86–89; TR 89–90; P-in-c Alcester and Arrow w Oversley and Weethley *Cov* 90–95; R 95–12; P-in-c Kinwarton w Gt Alne and Haselor 06–12; P-in-c Coughton 06–12; Hon Can Cov Cathl 07–12; Chapl Warks Fire and Rescue Service 93–09; rtd 13; PtO *Cov* from 13; *Worc* from 13. *19 Holbrook Road, Stratford-upon-Avon CV37 9DZ* T: (01789) 762904 M: 07780-707521 E: canon@caprons.co.uk

CAPRON, Mark Andrew. b 80. Staffs Univ BA 02. Ridley Hall Cam 09. **d** 12 **p** 13. C Pakefield *Nor* 12–16; C Carlton Colville and Mutford 12–16; R Dersingham, Anmer, Ingoldisthorpe etc from 16. *The Vicarage, Shernborne Road, Dersingham, King's Lynn PE31 6JA* E: revmarkcapron@gmail.com

CAPSTICK, Mrs Jean Rose. b 44. **d** 09 **p** 10. NSM Sodbury Vale *Glouc* 09–11; NSM Winterbourne *Bris* 12–13; NSM Frenchay and Winterbourne Down 12–13; NSM Frampton Cotterell and Iron Acton 12–13; NSM Coalpit Heath 12–13; PtO from 13; *Glouc* from 14. *Lerryn, Wotton Road, Rangeworthy, Bristol BS37 7LZ* T: (01454) 228236 E: jean.capstick@homecall.co.uk *or* jean@lescapstick.plus.com

CARBERRY, Leon Carter. b 54. Penn State Univ BSc 76. St Steph Ho Ox 81. **d** 84 **p** 85. C Peterlee *Dur* 84–87; C Newton Aycliffe 87–89; V Choral York Minster 89–94; Chapl St Pet Sch York 94–95; V Fylingdales and Hawsker cum Stainsacre York 95–01; Chapl Burrswood Chr Cen *Roch* 01–03; V Beckenham St Jas 03–16; P-in-c Beckenham St Mich w St Aug 15–16; V Beckenham St Jas w St Mich and St Aug from 16; AD Beckenham 12–15. *The Vicarage, 15 St James' Avenue, Beckenham BR3 4HF* T/F: (020) 8650 0420 E: leoncarberry@gmail.com

CARBY, Stuart Graeme. b 51. Man Univ BSc 73 Open Univ MA 96 Leeds Univ PGCE 74 CBiol 77 MRSB 77 LRSC 78. St Jo Coll Nottm 92. **d** 92 **p** 93. C Magor w Redwick and Undy *Mon* 92–96; TV Cyncoed 96–18; rtd 18. *10 Rectory Drive, Huddersfield HD5 0JT*

CARD-REYNOLDS, Charles Leonard. b 67. Lon Univ BD 92 Hughes Hall Cam BA 94 MA 98 FRSA 13. St Steph Ho Ox 96. **d** 98 **p** 99. C Reading H Trin *Ox* 98–06; C Reading St Mark 98–06; V Stamford Hill St Bart *Lon* from 06. *The Vicarage, 31 Craven Park Road, London N15 6AA* T: (020) 8800 1554 E: c.cardreynolds@me.com

CARDALE, Edward Charles. b 50. CCC Ox BA 72 MA 73. Cuddesdon Coll 72 Union Th Sem (NY) STM 74. **d** 74 **p** 75. C E Dulwich St Jo *S'wark* 74–77; Asst P Bainbridge Is USA 77–80; V Ponders End St Matt *Lon* 80–84; V Lytchett Minster *Sarum* 84–98; Dir Past Studies Coll of the Resurr Mirfield 98–02; P-in-c Lemsford *St Alb* 02–05; TV Bishop's Hatfield, Lemsford and N Mymms 05–14; Tutor SAOMC 02–05; Dir Past Studies ERMC 05–14; rtd 14; PtO *St Alb* from 14. *28 Warren Way, Welwyn AL6 0DH* E: edward.cardale@btopenworld.com

CARDELL-OLIVER, John Anthony. b 43. Em Coll Cam BA 67 MA 72 Univ of W Aus BEd 75 MEd 85 Murdoch Univ Aus PhD 15. Westcott Ho Cam 86. **d** 86 **p** 88. C Subiaco w Leederville Australia 86–88; PtO *Ely* 88–89; C Stansted Mountfitchet *Chelmsf* 89–92; R Langham

w Boxted 92–02; rtd 02. *40 Halesworth Road, Jolimont, Perth WA 6014, Australia* T: (0061) (0) 432 298 111 E: john.cardell-oliver@cantab.net

CARDIGAN, Archdeacon of. *See* DAVIES, The Ven Rachel Hannah Eileen

CARDINAL, Preb Ian Ralph. b 57. Qu Coll Birm 81. **d** 84 **p** 85. C Whitkirk *Ripon* 84–87; C Knaresborough 87–89; R Ancaster Wilsford Gp *Linc* 89–94; P-in-c Wigginton *Lich* 94–07; Warden of Readers 96–03; P-in-c Stone St Mich and St Wulfad w Aston St Sav 07–08; R from 08; RD Stone from 16; RD Eccleshall 17–18; Preb Lich Cathl from 18. *11 Farrier Close, Stone ST15 8XP* T: (01785) 812747 M: 07778-055993 E: rector@stmichaelschurchstone.co.uk

CARDWELL, Edward Anthony Colin. b 42. Trin Coll Cam BA 63 MA 68. St Jo Coll Nottm 73. **d** 75 **p** 76. C Stapenhill w Cauldwell *Derby* 75–78; C Bramcote *S'well* 78–81; V S'well H Trin 81–92; R Eastwood 92–07; rtd 07; PtO *S'well* from 08. *49 Bramcote Road, Beeston, Nottingham NG9 1DW* T: 0115-925 5866

CARDWELL, Joseph Robin. b 47. Qu Coll Cam BA 68 MA 77. Trin Coll Bris 73. **d** 76 **p** 77. C Bromley Ch Ch *Roch* 76–79; C Shirley *Win* 79–82; V Somborne w Ashley 82–90; V Derry Hill *Sarum* 90–94; V Derry Hill w Bremhill and Foxham 94–00; Community Affairs Chapl 90–94; V Lyddington and Wanborough and Bishopstone etc *Bris* 00–12; rtd 12; PtO *Ox* from 13. *Winter's Tale, 18 Stainswick Lane, Shrivenham, Swindon SN6 8DX* T: (01793) 783822

CARE, Benjamin Lewis. b 78. Warwick Univ BA 99 Lon Sch of Th MA 09. Wycliffe Hall Ox MTh 17. **d** 17 **p** 18. C Burton St Chad *Lich* from 17; C Stretton w Claymills from 17. *St Mary's Vicarage, Church Road, Stretton, Burton-on-Trent DE13 0HD* T: (01283) 565795 M: 07504-579953 E: curate@stchadstmary.org.uk

CAREW, Canon Richard Clayton. b 72. York Univ BA 94 PGCE 96 St Jo Coll Dur BA 04. Cranmer Hall Dur 02. **d** 05 **p** 06. C Beverley Minster *York* 05–10; Abp's Dom Chapl 10–18; V Dringhouses from 18; Can and Preb York Minster from 21. *St Edward's Vicarage, Tadcaster Road, Dringhouses, York YO24 1QG* T: (01904) 709111 M: 07725-239072 E: dringhousesvicar@hotmail.com

CAREY, Alan Lawrence. b 29. K Coll Lon AKC 53. **d** 54 **p** 55. C Radford *Cov* 54–57; C Burnham *Ox* 57–65; C-in-c Cippenham CD 65–77; rtd 94. *12 Ormsby Street, Reading RG1 7YR* T: 0118-961 2309

CAREY, Christopher Lawrence John. b 38. St Andr Univ BSc 61 Lon Univ BD 64. Clifton Th Coll 61. **d** 64 **p** 65. C Battersea Park St Sav *S'wark* 64–67; P-in-c Ukia Kenya 68–71; Warden Trin Coll Nairobi 72–76; CMS Rep Kenya 76–79; Overseas Regional Sec for E and Cen Africa CMS 79–98; NSM Chislehurst Ch Ch *Roch* 79–98; R Stickney Gp *Linc* 99–04; RD Bolingbroke 02–03; rtd 04; PtO *Mon* from 04. *83 Wentwood View, Caldicot NP26 4QH* T: (01291) 425010 E: crcandkili@tiscali.co.uk

CAREY, Donald Leslie. b 50. ACII 78. CBDTI 01. **d** 04 **p** 05. OLM Ashton-on-Ribble St Mich w Preston St Mark *Blackb* 04–06; OLM W Preston 06–07; NSM 07–08; P-in-c Fairhaven 08–11; V 11–15; rtd 15; PtO *Blackb* from 15. *31 Roman Way, Kirkham, Preston PR4 2YG* E: frdonaldcarey@gmail.com

CAREY, Mark Jonathan. b 65. St Jo Coll Nottm BTh 94. **d** 94 **p** 95. C S Ossett *Wakef* 94–97; C Chapeltown *Sheff* 97–99; V Grenoside 99–07; P-in-c Low Harrogate St Mary *Ripon* 07–13; Pioneer Min 13–14; *Leeds* 14–17; P-in-c Bessingby York 17–18; P-in-c Bridlington Quay Ch Ch 17–18; V Bridlington Ch Ch w Bessingby and Ulrome from 18. *Christ Church Vicarage, 21 Kingston Road, Bridlington YO15 3NF* E: mcarey@christchurchbrid.co.uk

CAREY, Philip John. b 46. NSM Rhosllanerchrugog and Penycae *St As* 15–16; NSM Offa Miss Area 17–18; NSM Valle Crucis Miss Area 18–21; P-in-c from 21. *The Rectory, Ffordd Ty Cerrig, Corwen LL21 9RP* T: (01978) 312604 E: carey711@btinternet.com

CAREY, Mrs Wendy Marion. b 45. Bris Univ BA 66 Lon Inst of Educn CertEd 67. WMMTC 90. **d** 93 **p** 94. NSM Milton Keynes *Ox* 93–96; Sub Chapl HM Pris Woodhill 93–96; Chapl HM Pris Bullingdon 96–00; Ecum Tr Officer HM Pris Service Chapl 00–06; rtd 06; PtO *Ox* from 00. *46 Parklands, Great Linford, Milton Keynes MK14 5DZ* T: (01908) 605997

✠**CAREY OF CLIFTON, The Rt Revd and Rt Hon Lord (George Leonard).** b 35. Th-ico. Lon Univ BD 62 MTh 65 PhD 71 Dur Univ Hon DD 93 Open Univ Hon DD 95 FRSA 91 FKC 93. ALCD 61. **d** 62 **p** 63 **c** 87. C Islington St Mary *Lon* 62–66; Lect Oak Hill Th Coll 66–70; Lect St Jo Coll Nottm 70–75; V Dur St Nic 75–82; Chapl HM Rem Cen Low Newton 77–81; Prin Trin Coll Bris 82–87; Hon Can Bris Cathl 84–87; Bp B & W 87–91; Abp Cant 91–02; rtd 02;

PtO *Ox* from 21. *16 Badsworth Gardens, Newbury RG14 6PH*
E: carey.george01@gmail.com

CAREY-SLATER, Paul John. b 73. St Jo Coll Nottm 10. **d** 12
p 13. C Skirbeck H Trin *Linc* 12–17; Min Grange Park LEP *Pet*
17–21; P-in-c Sutton Bridge and Tydd St Mary *Linc* from 21.
*St Matthew's Vicarage, 79 Bridge Road, Sutton Bridge, Spalding
PE12 9SD* M: 07863-164134 E: paul.slaterclan@sky.com

CARGILL, Christine Elizabeth. b 68. Chas Sturt Univ NSW
BA(Ed) 91 New England Univ NSW MLitt 99 Sydney Univ
MA 03. NTMTC 07. **d** 10 **p** 11. C Kilburn St Mary w All
So and W Hampstead St Jas *Lon* 10–13; V Brondesbury
St Anne w Kilburn H Trin from 13; P-in-c Brondesbury
Ch Ch and St Laur 20. *The Vicarage, 125A Salusbury Road,
London NW6 6RG* T: (020) 7624 5306 M: 07906-067569
E: motherchristinenw6@gmail.com

CARGILL THOMPSON, Edmund Alwyn James. b 72. St Jo
Coll Ox BA 94. Cranmer Hall Dur 98. **d** 00 **p** 01. C St Jo on
Bethnal Green *Lon* 00–03; V Barkingside H Trin *Chelmsf*
03–13; V Pimlico St Pet w Westmr Ch Ch *Lon* 13–14; V
Northolt Park St Barn from 14. *The Vicarage, Raglan Way,
Northolt UB5 4SX* T: (020) 8422 3775 M: 07908-949166

CARHART, John Richards. b 29. Bris Univ BA 50 Salford Univ
MSc 71 Liv Univ MTh 99 FRSA. St Deiniol's Hawarden 63.
d 65 **p** 66. C Ches St Oswald w Lt St Jo 65–72; Lect Ches
Coll of HE 63–72; Prin Lect from 72; Dean Academic
Studies 88–94; C Ches 72; LtO 73–85; Hon C Ches St Mary
85–00; rtd 00; PtO *Ches* from 00. *29 Abbot's Grange, Chester
CH2 1AJ* T: (01244) 380923 E: jcarhart@nepc.co.uk

CARLILL, Adam Jonathan. b 66. Keble Coll Ox BA 88. Linc
Th Coll 88. **d** 90 **p** 91. C Romford St Edw *Chelmsf* 90–94;
C Uckfield *Chich* 94–98; V Tilehurst St Geo *Ox* 98–12;
P-in-c Tilehurst St Mary 02–12; V Tilehurst St Geo and
St Mary from 12. *St George's Vicarage, 98 Grovelands Road,
Reading RG3 2PD* T: 0118-958 8354 E: adamcarlill@me.com

CARLILL, Richard Edward. b 38. Westcott Ho Cam 77. **d** 79
p 80. C Prittlewell St Mary *Chelmsf* 79–83; TV Saffron
Walden w Wendens Ambo and Littlebury 83–89; V Langtoft
w Foxholes, Butterwick, Cottam etc *York* 89–94; V Gt and
Lt Driffield 94–03; RD Harthill 99–02; rtd 03; PtO *Newc*
from 03. *31 Riverdene, Tweedmouth, Berwick-upon-Tweed
TD15 2JD* T: (01289) 303701

CARLIN, William Patrick Bruce. b 53. St Steph Ho Ox 75. **d** 78
p 79. C Penistone *Wakef* 78–81; C Barnsley St Mary 81–83; V
Stockton St Chad *Dur* 83–93; V Hedworth 93–01; TR Kippax
w Allerton Bywater *Ripon* 01–11; V Bury, Roch Valley *Man*
11–13; rtd 13; PtO *Leeds* from 17. *44 Frank Lane, Dewsbury
WF1 0JJ* T: (01924) 511066 E: brucecarlin@cooptel.net

CARLISLE, Matthew David. b 74. Man Univ BA 96. Westcott
Ho Cam 99. **d** 02 **p** 03. C E Crompton *Man* 02–06; TV
Heywood 06–11; V Heywood St Jo and St Luke 11–15; V
Gatley *Ches* from 15. *St James's Vicarage, 14 Elm Road, Gatley
SK8 4LY* M: 07870-760746 E: matthewcarlisle@aol.com

CARLISLE, Archdeacon of. *See* TOWNEND, The Ven Lee
Stuart

CARLISLE, Bishop of. *See* NEWCOME, The Rt Revd James
William Scobie

CARLISLE, Dean of. *See* BOYLING, The Very Revd Mark
Christopher

CARLSON, Blair Truett. b 52. Wheaton Coll Illinois BA 74.
Cranmer Hall Dur 00. **d** 02 **p** 03. C Hailsham *Chich* 02–05;
USA from 05; P-in-c Kiev *Eur* 14–15; Tunisia 20–21. *4619
Arden Avenue, Edina MN 55424, USA* T: (001) (952) 924 9062
E: btcarlson@gmail.com

CARLSON, Joshua Alan. b 79. St Jo Coll Cur BA 18.
Cranmer Hall Dur 16. **d** 18 **p** 19. C Heswall *Ches* from 18.
5 St Peter's Close, Wirral CH60 0DU M: 07736-370806
E: josh.carlson@mac.com *or* josh@heswallparish.co.uk

CARLSSON, Canon Susanne Fredrika. b 71. BA 96 MA 96.
d 97 **p** 98. Sweden 98–99; C Whitstable *Cant* 99–01;
PtO *Roch* from 08; Hon Can Roch Cathl from 15. *65
Maidstone Road, Chatham ME4 6DP* M: 07795-167603
E: susanne.carlsson@rochester.anglican.org

CARLTON, Preb Roger John. b 51. **d** 80 **p** 81. NSM Downend
Bris 80–83; NSM Heavitree w Ex St Paul 83–87; Chapl Ex
Sch and St Marg Sch 83–87; TV Bickleigh (Plymouth) *Ex*
87–91; TR 91–93; TR Bickleigh and Shaugh Prior 94–10;
RD Ivybridge 93–98; P-in-c Honicknowle 07; V Paignton
St Jo, St Andr and St Boniface 10–21; RD Torbay 16–21;
Preb Ex Cathl 06–21; rtd 21; P-in-c St Marychurch *Ex*
from 21. *Holwell Cottage, Middlemoor, Tavistock PL19 9DY*
E: roger.carlton@btinternet.com

CARLYON, Miss Catherine Rachel. b 67. RN 89. Ripon Coll
Cuddesdon BTh 06. **d** 02 **p** 03. C Launceston *Truro* 02–06;
C Crediton, Shobrooke and Sandford etc *Ex* 06–14; Chapl
w Deaf People 06–14; Chapl among Deaf and Deafblind
People *Lon* 14–20; P-in-c Bridgwater St Fran *B & W* from

20; PtO *Chelmsf* 16–21; *S'wark* from 16. *The Vicarage,
Saxon Green, Bridgwater TA6 4JA* M: 07855-098953
E: catherine@ccarlyon.uk

CARMAN, Philip Gordon. b 80. York St Jo Coll BA 01
St Jo Coll Dur BA 07. Cranmer Hall Dur 04. **d** 07 **p** 08.
C Acomb St Steph and St Aid *York* 07–10; C Huntington
10–16; V Starbeck *Leeds* from 16. *51 Bogs Lane, Harrogate
HG1 4AB* M: 07954-895731 E: philcarman3@gmail.com

CARMARTHEN, Archdeacon of. *See* DAVIES, The Ven Dorrien
Paul

CARMICHAEL (*née* Edwards), Mrs Anthea Mirenda. b 78. N
Lon Univ BSc 01. St Mellitus Coll 16. **d** 19 **p** 20. C Kensal
Rise St Mark *Lon* from 19. *82 Herbert Gardens, London
NW10 3BU* T: (020) 8960 3929 E: anthea@stmkr.org

CARMICHAEL, Elizabeth Dorothea Harriet. b 46. MBE 95.
LMH Ox MA 73 BM 73 BCh 73 Worc Coll Ox BA 83 Ox Univ
DPhil 91. **d** 00 **p** 92. S Africa 91–96; Chapl and Tutor St Jo
Coll Ox 96–11; rtd 11; Research Fell from 11; LtO Ox 15–18;
PtO from 20. *St John's College, Oxford OX1 3JP* T: (01865)
277351 F: 277435 E: liz.carmichael@sjc.ox.ac.uk

CARMICHAEL-DAVIS, Ms Caitlin Louise. b 88. Ball Coll Ox
BA 11 Sheff Hallam Univ PGCE 12. Ripon Coll Cuddesdon
BA 16 MSt 17. **d** 17 **p** 18. C Ripon Cathl *Leeds* 17–20; V
Skerton St Chad *Blackb* from 20; V Skerton St Luke from
20. *St Chad's Vicarage, 1 St Chad's Drive, Lancaster LA1 2SE*
E: revdcaitlin@gmail.com

CARMODY, Canon Dermot Patrick Roy. b 41. CITC 77. **d** 77
p 78. C Dublin Zion Ch *D & G* 77–79; I Dunganstown w
Redcross 79–84; TV Dublin Ch Ch Cathl Gp 84–93; Can
Ch Ch Cathl Dublin 84–92; Preb Ch Ch Cathl Dublin
92–93; I Mullingar, Portnashangan, Moyliscar, Kilbixy
etc *M & K* 93–08; Dir of Ords (Meath) 97–08; Can Meath
98–08; Can Kildare Cathl 98–08; Treas Kildare Cathl 00–08;
P-in-c Rathmolyon w Castlerickard, Rathcore and Agher
00–07; rtd 08. *32 The Mageough, Cowper Road, Rathmines,
Dublin 6, DO6 W6V4, Republic of Ireland* M: (00353) 86-829
0183 E: patkcarmody@gmail.com

CARMYLLIE, Mrs Kathryn Ruth. b 61. Cov Poly BA 84
CQSW 84 Univ Coll Ches BTh 04. NOC 01. **d** 04 **p** 05.
C Leigh St Mary *Man* 04–07; TV Worsley 07–12; TR
Atherton and Hindsford w Howe Bridge 12–14; PtO from
15; *Blackb* from 15; Chapl Pennine Acute Hosps NHS Trust
from 17. *The Vicarage, 40 The Sands, Whalley, Clitheroe
BB7 9TL* T: (01254) 824679 E: k.carmyllie@btinternet.com

CARMYLLIE, Robert Jonathan. b 63. Cov Poly BSc 85.
Cranmer Hall Dur 85. **d** 88 **p** 89. C Horwich *Man* 88–92;
P-in-c Edgeside 92–99; P-in-c astley 99–06; TR Astley,
Tyldesley and Mosley Common 06–15; AD Leigh 12–15;
V W Pendleside *Blackb* from 15; AD Whalley from 18. *The
Vicarage, 40 The Sands, Whalley, Clitheroe BB7 9TL* T: (01254)
824679 E: j.carmyllie@btinternet.com

CARNALL, Mrs Nicola Jane. b 66. St Jo Coll Nottm 99. **d** 01
p 02. C Edwinstowe *S'well* 01–05; P-in-c Sowerby *York*
05–12; V 12–19; P-in-c Sessay 05–12; R 12–19; V Thirkleby
w Kilburn and Bagby 12–19; V Mansfield Woodhouse *S'well*
19–21. *Address temp unknown* E: revnjcarnall@gmail.com

CARNEGIE, Canon Rachel Clare. b 62. New Hall Cam BA 84
Sussex Univ MA 94. SEITE 01. **d** 04 **p** 05. NSM Richmond
St Mary w St Matthias and St Jo *S'wark* 04–09; Abp's
Sec for Internat Development *Cant* 09–13; Co-Dir Angl
Alliance from 13; PtO *Ox* 17–20; NSM Dorchester from
20; Hon Can Ch Ch from 20. *Anglican Communion Office,
16 Tavistock Crescent, London W11 1AP* T: (020) 7313 3922
E: rachel.carnegie@aco.org

CARNELLEY, Ms Elizabeth Amy. b 64. St Aid Coll Dur
BA 85 Selw Coll Cam MPhil 87. Ripon Coll Cuddesdon 88.
d 90 **p** 94. Par Dn Sharrow St Andr *Sheff* 90–93; Par Dn Is
of Dogs Ch Ch and St Jo w St Luke *Lon* 93–94; C 94–95;
P-in-c Woolfold *Man* 95–99; TV Man Whitworth 99–02;
Chapl Man Univ and Man Metrop Univ 99–02; Policy
Officer Chs' Regional Commn for Yorks and the Humber
02–06; Chief Exec 06–11; Near Neighbours Progr Dir CUF
from 11; PtO *S'well* from 17. T: (01777) 248869 M: 07812-
984818 E: elizabeth.carnelley@cuf.org.uk

CARNEY, David Anthony. b 42. Salford Univ BSc 77. Linc Th
Coll 77. **d** 79 **p** 80. C Wythenshawe St Martin *Man* 79–81;
CF 81–84; Chapl Canadian Armed Forces Canada 84–87; R
Burford H Trin Ontario 87–91; P-in-c Whaplode *Linc* 91–97; V
97–02; P-in-c Holbeach Fen 91–97; V 97–02; R Colsterworth
Gp 02–05; P-in-c Kirton in Holland 05–09; rtd 09; PtO *Linc*
17–20. *6 South Road, Bourne PE10 9JD* T: (01778) 426061

CARNEY, Mrs Mary Patricia. b 42. Univ of Wales (Ban)
BSc 62. Wycliffe Hall Ox. **d** 90 **p** 94. Par Dn Carterton *Ox*
90–93; Par Dn Harwell w Chilton 93–94; C 94–01; P-in-c Ray
Valley 01–07; rtd 07; PtO *Ox* from 07. *104 Pensclose, Witney
OX28 2EQ* T: (01993) 358139

CAROLAN (*née* **STUART-BLACK**), **Mrs Veronica.** b 52. St Jo Coll Dur BA 75. Cranmer Hall Dur. **dss** 82 **d** 87 **p** 08. Borehamwood *St Alb* 82–84; Watford Ch Ch 84–85; Stevenage St Mary Shephall 85–86; Stevenage St Mary Shephall w Aston 86–87; Par Dn 87–88; Hon C 08–14; PtO 98–08; V Lower Esk *York* 14–19; PtO from 19. *2 Marlborough Avenue, Whitby YO21 3JE* T: (01947) 229304

CAROLIN CLARE, Sister. *See* CLAPPERTON, Carolin Beryl

CARPENTER, Canon Bruce Leonard Henry. b 32. Lon Univ BA 54. St Chad's Coll Dur. **d** 59 **p** 60. C Portsea N End St Mark *Portsm* 59–63; C Fareham SS Pet and Paul 63–67; V Locks Heath 67–74; TR Fareham H Trin 74–84; RD Alverstoke 71–76; Hon Can Portsm Cathl 79–84; V Richmond St Mary w St Matthias and St Jo *S'wark* 84–91; Chapl Ch Ch High Sch Ashford 91–93; P-in-c S Ashford Ch Ch *Cant* 94–97; rtd 97; Chapl Huggens Coll Northfleet 97–02; PtO *Portsm* from 02; Hon Chapl MU from 03. *48 Summerson Lodge, 94 Alverstone Road, Southsea PO4 8GS* T: (023) 9307 6722 E: angelbru@btinternet.com

CARPENTER, David James. b 52. Trin Coll Carmarthen CertEd 74. St Steph Ho Ox 74. **d** 76 **p** 77. C Newport St Julian *Mon* 76–77; C Pontypool 77–79; C Ebbw Vale 79–81; TV 81–85; V Pontnewynydd 85–88; V Bedwellty 88–00; Chapl Aberbargoed Hosp 88–99; V Staincliffe and Carlinghow *Wakef* 00–05; Chapl Yorks Ambulance Service 05–11; PtO *Wakef* 10–11; P-in-c Birkby and Woodhouse 11–14; *Leeds* 14–15; V 15–19; rtd 19; Hon C Halifax w Siddal *Leeds* from 19. *48A Stratton Road, Brighouse HD6 3TA* E: carpenterdj@aol.com

CARPENTER, Canon Derek George Edwin. b 40. K Coll Lon BD 62 AKC 62. **d** 63 **p** 64. C Friern Barnet All SS *Lon* 63–66; C Chingford SS Pet and Paul *Chelmsf* 66–70; V Dartford St Alb *Roch* 70–79; R Crayford 79–90; RD Erith 82–90; R Beckenham St Geo 90–02; Hon Can Roch Cathl 97–02; rtd 02; PtO *Roch* from 04. *39 Chatfield Way, East Malling, West Malling ME19 6QD* T: (01732) 874420

CARPENTER, Donald Arthur. b 35. Roch Th Coll 65. **d** 67 **p** 68. C Thornton Heath St Jude *Cant* 67–73; V Earby *Bradf* 73–78; V Skipton Ch Ch 78–88; V Baildon 88–91; P-in-c Perivale *Lon* 91–96; rtd 96; PtO *Lon* 96–05. *1 Bootham Green, Newborough Street, York YO30 7EJ* T: (01904) 623280 M: 07516-304390 E: donarth610@gmail.com

CARPENTER, Giles Michael Gerard. b 67. Trin Coll Bris BA 10. **d** 10 **p** 11. C Shottermill *Guildf* 10–14; V Eastbourne St Jo *Chich* from 14; P-in-c Eastbourne St Mich from 20. *9 Buxton Road, Eastbourne BN20 7LL* T: (01323) 721105 *or* 738671 M: 07710-498906 E: giles.rev@gmail.com *or* vicar@stjm.org.uk

CARPENTER, Canon Judith Margaret. b 47. Bris Univ BA 68 CertEd 69. Trin Coll Bris BA 95. **d** 95 **p** 96. C Warmley, Syston and Bitton *Bris* 95–99; V Withywood 99–12; Hon Can Bris Cathl 06–12; rtd 12; PtO *Glouc* from 16. *Dawes Orchard, Latchen, Longhope GL17 0QB*

CARPENTER, Leonard Richard. b 32. EMMTC 82. **d** 85 **p** 86. NSM Leic H Apostles 85–90; P-in-c Barlestone 90–98; rtd 98; PtO *Leic* 98–20; Derby 98–20. *10 Main Street, Albert Village, Swadlincote DE11 8EW* T: (01283) 229335

CARPENTER, Nicholas Andrew. b 61. St Aug Coll Cant 19. **d** 21. NSM The Six *Cant* from 21. *22 Wadham Place, Sittingbourne ME10 4LZ* T: (01795) 420845 M: 07979-748225 E: na.carpenter@outlook.com

CARPENTER, Thomas David Leonard. b 88. Mansf Coll Ox BA 09 MA 15 Keble Coll Ox MSt 10 DPhil 16. Coll of Resurr Mirfield 14. **d** 16 **p** 17. C Goldthorpe w Hickleton *Sheff* 16–18; C Sheff St Cath Richmond Road 18–19; V Southport H Trin *Liv* from 19; P-in-c Southport All SS from 19; P-in-c Southport St Luke from 21. *Holy Trinity Vicarage, 24 Roe Lane, Southport PR9 9DX* M: 07740-395154 E: thomasdcarpenter@gmail.com

CARR, Alan Cobban. b 49. Nottm Univ BTh 88. Linc Th Coll 85. **d** 88 **p** 89. C Rustington *Chich* 88–92; V Highbrook and W Hoathly 92–10; C St Giles-in-the-Fields *Lon* 10–15; R 15–19; rtd 19. *Address temp unknown* E: alancarr17@gmail.com

CARR, Canon Amanda Helen. b 70. Univ of Wales (Cardiff) BA 91 Kent Univ MA 97. SEITE 01. **d** 04 **p** 05. C Meopham w Nurstead *Roch* 04–07; P-in-c Lamberhurst and Matfield 07–09; V 09–15; RD Paddock Wood 12–13; V Sevenoaks Weald from 15; Bp's Adv for Ord Women's Min from 18; Hon Can Roch Cathl from 18. *St George's Vicarage, Church Road, Weald, Sevenoaks TN14 6LT* T: (01732) 463291 M: 07866-675015 E: mandy@carrfamilyonline.co.uk

CARR, David Scott. b 72. Derby Univ BA 97 MCIM 05. NEOC 06. **d** 09 **p** 10. NSM Horden *Dur* 09–14. *Glen View, 26 Station Avenue, Brandon, Durham DH7 8QQ* T: 0191-378 0126 M: 07990-775054 E: david.s.carr@btinternet.com

CARR, Derrick Charles. b 43. MCIPD. SAOMC 99. **d** 02 **p** 03. NSM Amersham *Ox* 02–13; AD 09–12; PtO from 13. *52 Warren Wood Drive, High Wycombe HP11 1EA* T/F: (01494) 452389 M: 07768-507391 E: carrd@btopenworld.com

CARR, Edward William Christopher. b 92. Coll of Resurr Mirfield 14. **d** 16 **p** 17. C Adlington *Blackb* 16–19; C Holborn St Alb w Saffron Hill St Pet *Lon* 19–21; V Rishton *Blackb* from 21. *The Vicarage, 4 Somerset Road, Rishton, Blackburn BB1 4BP* E: fatherecarr@gmail.com

CARR, Mrs Elaine Susan. b 46. LTCL 82. SAOMC 99. **d** 02 **p** 03. NSM High Wycombe *Ox* from 02; Bp's NSM Officer (Bucks) 09–15. *52 Warren Wood Drive, High Wycombe HP11 1EA* T/F: (01494) 452389 M: 07500-140935 E: revcarr@btinternet.com

CARR, Miss Eveline. b 45. Cranmer Hall Dur 91. **d** 93 **p** 95. NSM Eighton Banks *Dur* 93–98; NSM Gateshead 98–12; rtd 12; PtO *Dur* 12–21. *10 Lanchester Avenue, Gateshead NE9 7AJ* T: 0191-482 1157 E: eveline.c@blueyonder.co.uk

CARR, Jeremy Barnardo Quintin. b 75. Wycliffe Hall Ox 13. **d** 15 **p** 16. C St Margaret's-on-Thames *Lon* 15–18. *The Spinney, The Green, Cuddington, Aylesbury HP18 0AN*

CARR, Canon John Bernard. b 53. Lindisfarne Regional Tr Partnership 11. **d** 13 **p** 14. NSM Jesmond H Trin *Newc* 13–17; NSM Cornhill w Carham 17–20; NSM Branxton 17–20; Hon Can Newc Cathl 18–20; rtd 20; PtO *Leeds* 21. *14 Cavendish Street, Harrogate HG1 4NT* E: jbcarr@btinternet.com

CARR, Canon John Henry Percy. b 52. NTMTC 95. **d** 98 **p** 99. C Hackney Wick St Mary of Eton w St Aug *Lon* 98–01; R Walesby *Linc* 01–17; Can and Preb Linc Cathl 15–17; rtd 17; PtO *Nor* from 17. *19 Wades Way, Trunch, North Walsham NR28 0PW* E: carr.ide@btinternet.com

CARR, John Robert. b 40. ACII 62. Oak Hill Th Coll 63. **d** 66 **p** 67. C Tonbridge St Steph *Roch* 66–70; C Cheadle Hulme St Andr *Ches* 70–79; R Widford *Chelmsf* 79–87; TV Becontree W 87–93; V Basildon St Andr w H Cross 93–05; rtd 05; PtO *Chelmsf* from 06. *3 Windsor Way, Rayleigh SS6 8PE* T: (01268) 741065 E: johnandwendycarr3@hotmail.com

CARR, Mandy. *See* CARR, Amanda Helen

CARR, Paul Anthony. b 62. Univ of Wales MA 13. Aston Tr Scheme 93 Oak Hill Th Coll 95. **d** 97 **p** 98. C Handforth *Ches* 97–01; V Chadwell Heath *Chelmsf* 01–08; TR Billericay and Lt Burstead from 08. *The Rectory, 40 Laindon Road, Billericay CM12 9LD* T: (01277) 658055 E: revpaulcarr@btinternet.com

CARR, Mrs Wendy Dawn. b 70. Ridley Hall Cam 15. **d** 17 **p** 18. C Tonbridge SS Pet and Paul *Roch* from 17. *St Saviour's House, 13 Dry Hill Park Crescent, Tonbridge TN10 3BJ* M: 07971-048416 E: wdcarr6@gmail.com

CARRILLO, Fernando. b 92. Westmr Univ BA 16 Global Univ Missouri BA 18. St Mellitus Coll MA 20. **d** 20 **p** 21. C Onslow Square and S Kensington St Aug *Lon* from 20. *9 Mudie House, Forster Road, London SW2 4UX* M: 07426-749311 E: fernando.carrillo@htb.org

CARRINGTON, David John. b 63. Cam Univ MA 85 Reading Univ MSc 88. Trin Coll Bris BA 09. **d** 09 **p** 10. C Bovey Tracey SS Pet, Paul and Thos w Hennock *Ex* 09–12; C Brampford Speke, Cadbury, Newton St Cyres etc 12–15; TV Bideford, Northam, Westward Ho!, Appledore etc 15–17; TV Appledore, Northam and Westward Ho! 17–18; TV Ottery St Mary, Alfington, W Hill, Tipton etc from 18; Dir Lay Tr SWMTC from 18. *The Rectory, Station Road, Feniton, Honiton EX14 3DF* E: revdavidcarrington@gmail.com

CARRINGTON, Mrs Elizabeth Ashby. b 46. Open Univ BA 02. EMMTC 86. **d** 90 **p** 94. NSM Nottingham St Ann w Em *S'well* 90–91; C Basford w Hyson Green 92–97; Lect Nottingham St Mary and St Cath 97–00; LtO W Bingham Deanery 00; PtO 00–01; Chapl Woodford Ho Sch NZ 01–10; NSM Napier Cathl 03–06; rtd 11. T: 0115-891 2703 M: 07900-417275 E: ea.carrington@yahoo.co.nz

CARRINGTON, Margaret Elizabeth. b 44. **d** 09. NSM York St Luke 09–19; PtO from 19. *202 Boroughbridge Road, York YO26 6BD* T: (01904) 798916 E: carringtone@btinternet.com

CARRINGTON, Philip John. b 48. MBE 03. **d** 85 **p** 86. C W Acklam *York* 85–88; V Middlesbrough St Agnes 88–92; Chapl S Cleveland Hosp 88–92; Trust Chapl S Tees Hosps NHS Foundn Trust 92–06; V Guernsey St Steph *Win* 06–13; Hd Chapl Services States of Guernsey Health and Soc Care 07–13; rtd 13; PtO *Ripon* 13–14; *Leeds* from 14. *Stonecroft, Hackforth Road, Little Crakehall, Bedale DL8 1HY* T: (01677) 425077 E: philipjcarrington@gmail.com

CARRIVICK, Derek Roy. b 45. Birm Univ BSc 66. Ripon Hall Ox 71. **d** 74 **p** 75. C Enfield St Jas *Lon* 74–78; C-in-c Woodgate Valley CD *Birm* 78–83; TV Chelmsley Wood 83–92; Dioc Ecum Officer 86–96; R Baxterley w Hurley and Wood End and Merevale etc 92–99; AD Polesworth 96–99; P-in-c Helland

Truro 99–04; P-in-c Blisland w St Breward 99–04; Bp's Dom Chapl 04–09; rtd 09; P-in-c Devoran *Truro* 04–11; Hon C 11–12; Hon C Chacewater w St Day and Carharrack 11–12; Hon C Feock 11–12; Hon C St Stythians w Perranarworthal and Gwennap 11–12; PtO from 15. *30 Par Green, Par PL24 2AF* T: (01726) 813566 E: derek.carrivick@gmail.com

CARROLL, Anthony Joseph. b 65. **d** 99 **p** 99. NSM Folkestone St Mary, St Eanswythe and St Sav *Cant* 16–19; Dean Past Studies Coll of Resurr Mirfield 19–20; Dean Systematic Th from 20. *The College of the Resurrection, Stocks Bank Road, Mirfield WF14 0BW* T: (01924) 490441 E: tcarroll@mirfield.org.uk

CARROLL, John Hugh. b 31. Bris Univ BA 57. Tyndale Hall Bris 54. **d** 58 **p** 59. C Slough *Ox* 58–61; V S Lambeth St Steph *S'wark* 61–72; V Norwood St Luke 72–81; P-in-c Purley Ch Ch 81–85; V 85–93; rtd 93; PtO *S'wark* 93–13; *Guildf* 12–17. *11 Manormead, Tilford Road, Hindhead GU26 6RA* E: jonthelc@gmail.com

CARROLL, Ruth Ellen. b 68. **d** 14 **p** 15. C Boston *Linc* 14–15; C Alford w Rigsby 15–18; C Bilsby w Farlesthorpe 15–18; C Hannah cum Hagnaby w Markby 15–18; C Saleby w Beesby and Maltby 15–18; C Well 15–18; C Willoughby 15–18; V Stevenage H Trin *St Alb* from 18. *Holy Trinity Vicarage, 18 Letchmore Road, Stevenage SG1 3JD* T: (01438) 353229 E: vicar@holytrinity-stevenage.org.uk

CARROLL WALLIS, Ms Joy Ann. b 59. SS Mark & Jo Univ Coll Plymouth BEd 82. Cranmer Hall Dur 85. **d** 88 **p** 94. Par Dn Hatcham St Jas *S'wark* 88–93; Par Dn Streatham Immanuel and St Andr 93–94; C 94–97; USA from 97. *1305 Fairmont Street NW, Washington DC 20009, USA* T: (001) (202) 483 0119 E: joycwallis@aol.com

CARRUTHERS, John Alexander. b 69. Natal Univ BA 91 Bond Univ Aus MBA 06. Ripon Coll Cuddesdon 15. **d** 17 **p** 18. C Newington St Paul *S'wark* 17–20; P-in-c 20–21; V from 21. *St Paul's Vicarage, Lorrimore Square, London SE17 3QU* M: 07814-948325 E: john.carruthers1@gmail.com

CARSON, Alison Jane. b 61. Liv Hope BEd 97. All SS Cen for Miss & Min 19. **d** 21. NSM Haydock St Mark *Liv* from 21. *253 Liverpool Road, Haydock, St Helens WA11 9RT* T: (01744) 380201 M: 07741-453466 E: alisonjcarson@gmail.com *or* alison.carson@stmarkshaydock.org

CARSON, Claire. b 76. St Martin's Coll Lanc BA 98 Birm Univ MA 99. Qu Coll Birm 00. **d** 03 **p** 04. C Streetly *Lich* 03–04; C Stafford 04–05; C Lich St Mich w St Mary and Wall 05–07; Chapl R Free Hampstead NHS Trust 07–10; Chapl Imp Coll Healthcare NHS Trust 10–11; Chapl St Geo Healthcare NHS Trust Lon 11–18; Hd Spiritual Care 15–18; Hd Spiritual Care R Free London NHS Foundn Trust from 18; Bp's Adv for Healthcare Chapl *Lon* from 21. *Royal Free London NHS Foundation Trust, Royal Free Hospital, Pond Street, London NW3 2QG* T: (020) 7830 2742 E: clairecarson@nhs.net

CARSON, Canon James Irvine. b 59. TCD BA MTh. **d** 84 **p** 85. C Willowfield *D & D* 84–87; C Lecale Gp 87–89; I Devenish w Boho *Clogh* 89–95; Dioc Youth Adv 91–95; Dioc Communications Officer 93–95; I Belfast Upper Malone (Epiphany) *Conn* 95–99; I Lisburn St Paul 99–16; P-in-c Belfast St Steph w St Luke from 16; Preb Conn Cathl from 11. *12 Lansdowne Road, Belfast BT15 4AB* T: (028) 9077 3964 E: jamescarson203@btinternet.com

CARSON, Tom Patrick. b 83. Regent's Park Coll Ox MA 09 Heythrop Coll Lon MA 10 K Coll Lon PGCE 06. Ripon Coll Cuddesdon MTh 12. **d** 12 **p** 13. C Mortlake w E Sheen *S'wark* 12–15; Chapl Ex Sch 15–21; PtO *Truro* 15–21. *Address temp unknown* M: 07974-080946 E: tompcarson@gmail.com

CARSON-FEATHAM, Canon Lawrence William. b 53. AKC. **d** 78 **p** 79. SSM from 77; C Walton St Mary *Liv* 78–82; Chapl Bolton Colls of H&FE 82–87; C Bolton St Pet *Man* 82–87; TV Oldham 87–92; V Ashton St Jas 92–95; PtO *Liv* 95–97; C Leeds Belle Is St Jo and St Barn *Ripon* 97–01; TV Accrington Ch the King *Blackb* 01–13; V Accrington St Andr, St Mary and St Pet 13–16; R Accrington St Andr, St Mary and St Pet and Church Kirk 16–19; Hon Can Blackb Cathl 18–19; rtd 19; PtO *Blackb* from 20. *7 Woburn Road, Blackpool FY1 2PH* T: (01253) 318440 E: carsonfeatham@btinternet.com

CARTER, Ashley Stuart Bourn. b 79. Lanc Univ BA 00. Oak Hill Th Coll MTheol 14. **d** 14 **p** 15. C Mayfair Ch Ch *Lon* 14–18; R Kirk Ella and Willerby *York* from 18. *The Rectory, 2 School Lane, Kirk Ella, Hull HU10 7NR* T: (01482) 653040 M: 07908-779325 E: revdashcarter@gmail.com

CARTER, Barry Graham. b 54. K Coll Lon BD 76 AKC 76. St Steph Ho Ox 76. **d** 77 **p** 78. C Evesham *Worc* 77–81; C Amblecote 81–84; TV Ovingdean w Rottingdean and Woodingdean *Chich* 84–85; V Woodingdean 85–95; V Lancing St Mich 95–16; rtd 16; PtO *Chich* from 16. *Flat 2, 15 Parkhurst Road, Bexhill-on-Sea TN40 1DE* T: (01424) 211395 E: fatherbarrycarter@gmail.com

CARTER, Canon Benjamin Huw. b 77. Ex Univ BA 99 St Cath Coll Cam MPhil 00 Middx Univ PhD 04. Cranmer Hall Dur 08. **d** 10 **p** 11. C Monkseaton St Mary *Newc* 10–14; V Haydon Bridge and Beltingham w Henshaw 14–21; Can Res Carl Cathl from 21. *3 The Abbey, Carlisle CA3 8TZ* M: 07985-412542 E: benj_carter@yahoo.co.uk

CARTER, Carl. b 56. LCTP 11. **d** 14 **p** 15. NSM Millom *Carl* 14–20; C from 20. *13 Pepper Hall Walk, Haverigg, Millom LA18 4HT* T: (01229) 774427 M: 07738-618350

CARTER, Celia. b 38. JP 74 MBE 12. Glouc Sch of Min 86. **d** 89 **p** 94. NSM Avening w Cherington *Glouc* 89–13; P-in-c 95–13; Asst Chapl Severn NHS Trust 89–05; Asst Chapl Glos Primary Care Trust 05–13; rtd 13; PtO *Glouc* 16–20. *Avening Park, West End, Avening, Tetbury GL8 8NE* T: (01453) 836390 E: rev.celiacarter@gmail.com

CARTER (née SMITH), Mrs Christine Lydia. b 43. SRN 64 SCM 67. Trin Coll Bris 89. **d** 91 **p** 94. Par Dn Penkridge *Lich* 91–94; C 94–96; PtO *Blackb* 96–97; NSM Blackb Sav 97–01; Chapl Asst St Helens and Knowsley Hosps NHS Trust 97–01; NSM Elmdon St Nic *Birm* 01–11; rtd 11; PtO *Lich* 12–19. *Elmdon, 4 Goods Station Lane, Penkridge, Stafford ST19 5AU* T: (01785) 710809 E: chris@tworevs.co.uk

CARTER, Christopher Paul. b 43. CCC Cam BA 64. SAOMC 02. **d** 05 **p** 06. NSM W Buckingham *Ox* 05–13; rtd 13; PtO *Ox* 13–18. *The Mount, Upper Street, Tingewick, Buckingham MK18 4QN* T/F: (01280) 848291 E: rev.c.carter@btinternet.com *or* r.c.carter@btinternet.com

CARTER, Colin John. b 56. Fitzw Coll Cam BA 77 MB, BChir 80 MA 81 FRCS 86 FRCOphth 89. Trin Coll Bris BA 93. **d** 93 **p** 94. C Ripley *Derby* 93–97; TV Horsham *Chich* 97–00. *48 Swindon Road, Horsham RH12 2HD* T: (01403) 252146

CARTER, Duncan Robert Bruton. b 58. Univ of Wales (Cardiff) BA 79 Cam Univ BA 83 MA 89. Ridley Hall Cam 81. **d** 84 **p** 85. C Harold Wood *Chelmsf* 84–88; C S Kensington St Luke *Lon* 88–90; V Henley H Trin *Ox* from 90; AD Henley 02–06. *Holy Trinity Vicarage, Church Street, Henley-on-Thames RG9 1SE* T: (01491) 574822 E: drbcarter@hotmail.com

CARTER, Canon Edward John. b 67. Ex Univ BA 88. Ripon Coll Cuddesdon BA 96 MA 01. **d** 97 **p** 98. C Thorpe St Matt *Nor* 97–00; Min Can and Dean's V Windsor 00–04; P-in-c Didcot St Pet *Ox* 04–12; AD Wallingford 07–12; Can Th Chelmsf Cathl 12–18; R Nor St Pet Mancroft w St Jo Maddermarket from 18; Jt RD Nor E from 20. *37 Unthank Road, Norwich NR2 2PB* T: (01603) 610443 E: revedwardcarter@gmail.com *or* vicar@stpetermancroft.org.uk

CARTER, Grayson Leigh. b 53. Univ of S California BSc 76 Ch Ch Ox DPhil 90. Fuller Th Sem California MA 84 Wycliffe Hall Ox 89. **d** 90 **p** 91. C Bungay H Trin w St Mary *St E* 90–92; Chapl BNC Ox 92–96; Hon C Ox St Mary V w St Cross and St Pet 93–96; USA from 96; Assoc Prof Methodist Coll Fayetteville 96–02; Asst R Fayetteville H Trin 96–02; Assoc Prof Fuller Th Sem from 02. *1602 Palmcroft Drive SW, Phoenix AZ 85007-1738, USA* T: (001) (602) 252 5582 *or* (602) 220 0400 E: gcarter@fuller.edu

CARTER, Hazel June. b 48. Doncaster Coll of Educn CertEd 72. Carl Dioc Tr Inst 89. **d** 92 **p** 94. C Wreay *Carl* 92–98; C Dalston and Raughton Head w Gatesgill 92–98; TV Carl H Trin and St Barn 98–02; TR 02–07; PtO *Carl* from 08. *4 Wandales Lane, Natland, Kendal LA9 7QY* T: (015395) 60429

CARTER, Heather Ruth. b 62. Trin Coll Bris 85. **d** 02 **p** 04. Dn Montevideo Cathl Uruguay 02–04; Chapl among Deaf People 02–04; NSM Dalston w Cumdivock, Raughton Head and Wreay *Carl* 04–10; Chapl to the Deaf and Hard of Hearing 05–10; Chapl N Cumbria Acute Hosps NHS Trust 05–10; V Blackbird Leys *Ox* from 12. *Church House, 5 Cuddesdon Way, Oxford OX4 6JH* T: (01865) 778728 E: revhev2@gmail.com

CARTER, Ian Sutherland. b 51. Trin Coll Ox BA 73 MA 77 DPhil 77 Leeds Univ BA 80 Man Univ MA 05. Coll of Resurr Mirfield 78. **d** 81 **p** 82. C Shildon *Dur* 81–84; C Darlington H Trin 84–87; Chapl Liv Univ 87–93; V Hindley St Pet 93–98; Chapl Oldham NHS Trust 98–02; Chapl Pennine Acute Hosps NHS Trust 02–03; Chapl Salford R NHS Foundn Trust 03–14; P-in-c Hamer *Man* 14–15; P-in-c Healey 14–15; V Hamer and Healey 15–17; rtd 17. *Awel y Mor, 29 Lon Ceredigion, Pwllheli LL53 5PP* T: (01758) 701535 E: ianscarter@aol.com

CARTER, Mrs Jacqueline Ann. b 50. St Mich Coll Llan 01. **d** 03 **p** 04. C Ebbw Vale *Mon* 03–06; TV 06–11; V Rhosllannerchrugog *St As* 11; V Rhosllanerchrugog and Penycae 11–16; rtd 16; PtO *Llan* from 16. *50 Fox Hollows, Brackla, Bridgend CF31 2NG* T: (01656) 668303 E: jackiecarter16@hotmail.com

CARTER, Canon John Howard Gregory. b 55. York Univ BA 76 Leeds Univ CertEd 77 Nottm Univ MA 96. St Jo Coll Nottm LTh 87. **d** 87 **p** 88. C Nailsea H Trin *B & W* 87–91; TV

Camberley St Paul *Guildf* 91–97; Chapl Elmhurst Ballet Sch 91–97; Bp's Press Officer *Ripon* 00–14; Dioc Communications Officer 97–14; *Leeds* 14–18; Hon Can Ripon Cathl 10–18; rtd 18; PtO *Leeds* 20–21. *Seed Cottage, Manor Road, Harrogate HG2 0HP* T: (01423) 509859 M: 07798-652707 E: jhgcarter@aol.com

CARTER, Jonathan James. b 88. Nottm Univ BA 11. St Mellitus Coll BA 19. d 19 p 20. Pioneer Min *Lon* from 19. *479A Liverpool Road, London N7 8PG* T: (020) 3432 5396 E: jon.carter@kxc.org.uk

CARTER, Jonathan Mark. b 77. Imp Coll Lon MSci 99 PhD 04 Cam Univ MPhil 12 Edin Univ PhD 17. d 17 p 18. C Lowestoft Ch Ch *Nor* 17–20; P-in-c from 20. *10 Station Road, Lowestoft NR32 4QF* M: 07771-614836 E: jon@christ-church.info

CARTER, Katherine Elizabeth. b 71. Ripon Coll Cuddesdon 16. d 19 p 20. C Hoddesdon *St Alb* from 19. *134 Plomer Avenue, Hoddesdon EN11 9FS*

CARTER, Lewis. *See* CARTER, Stephen Lewis

CARTER, Mrs Linda Susan. b 61. STETS 11. d 14 p 15. C Broadstone *Sarum* 14–17; TV Marden Vale from 17. *The Vicarage, Church Road, Derry Hill, Calne SN11 9NN* E: lscarter@btinternet.com

CARTER, Marian. b 40. Whitelands Coll Lon TCert 61 Lon Univ BD 67 Nottm Univ MPhil 79 Man Univ MA 84 Ex Univ PhD 05. N Bapt Coll 81. d 92 p 96. Par Dn Kempshott *Win* 92–93; Tutor SWMTC 92–96; Tutor Coll of SS Mark and Jo Plymouth 93–00; NSM Plymstock and Hooe *Ex* 94–98; NSM Widecombe-in-the-Moor, Leusdon, Princetown etc 98–00; Chapl St Eliz Hospice Ipswich 00–05; rtd 05; PtO *St E* from 06. *Shalom, 80 Woodlands, Chelmondiston, Ipswich IP9 1DU* T: (01473) 780259 E: marian.carter@btinternet.com

CARTER, Melissa Jane. b 80. d 16 p 17. C N Downs *Cant* 16–19; TV Dover Town from 19. *339 Folkestone Road, Dover CT17 9JG* M: 07825-910116 E: melissa.j.carter@btinternet.com

CARTER, Canon Michael John. b 32. St Alb Minl Tr Scheme 81. d 84 p 85. NSM Radlett *St Alb* 84–88; Chapl SW Herts HA 88–94; Chapl Watford Gen Hosp 88–94; LtO *St Alb* 88–99; Chapl Mt Vernon and Watford Hosps NHS Trust 94–99; Bp's Adv for Hosp Chapl *St Alb* 95–99; Hon Can St Alb 96–99; rtd 99; PtO *St Alb* from 99; Hon Chapl Peace Hospice Watford from 99. *4 Field View Rise, Bricket Wood, St Albans AL2 3RT* T: (01923) 279870 E: mail@mjcarter.com

CARTER, Nicholas Adrian. b 47. Ripon Hall Ox 71. d 74 p 75. C Sowerby *Wakef* 74–79; V Hanging Heaton 79–83; CF 83–86; V Elton All SS *Man* 86–90; C Milton *Win* 90–94; P-in-c Boscombe St Andr 94–00; V 00–09; rtd 09; TV Winchcombe *Glouc* 09–17. *The Warren, Velindre, Brecon LD3 0TE* T: (01497) 842736 E: cdevildodger@aol.com

CARTER, Noel William. b 53. Birm Univ BSc 75 Bris Univ CertEd 76 Nottm Univ BSc 83. Linc Th Coll. d 83 p 84. C Penrith w Newton Reigny and Plumpton Wall *Carl* 83–86; C Barrow St Matt 86–87; V Netherton 87–91; TR Penrith w Newton Reigny and Plumpton Wall 91–97; P-in-c Jersey St Brelade *Win* 97–98; R 98–01; Vice-Dean Jersey 00–01; P-in-c Brymbo and Southsea *St As* 05–07; P-in-c Brymbo, Southsea and Tanyfron 07–14; AD Minera 08–12; TR Rhos-Cystennin 14–16; I Aberconwy Miss Area 17–20; AD Llanrwst and Rhos 15–20; PtO *Ban* from 15; rtd 20. *8 Llys Helyg, Deganwy, Conwy LL31 9BN* T: (01492) 339521

CARTER, Paul Joseph. b 67. St Chad's Coll Dur BA 88. St Steph Ho Ox 89. d 91 p 92. C Ipswich All Hallows *St E* 91; C Newmarket St Mary w Exning St Agnes 91–94; V Thorpe-le-Soken *Chelmsf* 94–04; V Ipswich St Bart *St E* from 04; PtO *Chelmsf* from 19. *St Bartholomew's Vicarage, Newton Road, Ipswich IP3 8HQ* T: (01473) 727441 E: frpaulcarter@hotmail.com

CARTER, Paul Rowley. b 45. Lon Univ BD 69 Lon Bible Coll ALBC 69 Southn Univ PGCE 70. Trin Coll Bris. d 91 p 92. C Penkridge *Lich* 91–96; V Blackb Sav 96–01; R Elmdon St Nic *Birm* 01–11; rtd 11; PtO *Birm* 11; *Lich* 12–18. *Elmdon, 4 Goods Station Lane, Penkridge, Stafford ST19 5AU* T: (01785) 710809 E: paul@tworevs.co.uk

CARTER, Richard Anthony. b 59. Univ of Wales (Abth) BA 80 Melbourne Coll of Div BD 94 Leeds Univ MA 02 Lon Inst of Educn PGCE 87. Bp Patteson Th Coll (Solomon Is) 90. d 91 p 92. Lect Bp Patteson Th Coll 91–00; Miss and Tr Co-ord Melanesian Brotherhood 00–05; Chapl 94–00 and 02–05; PtO *Lon* 00–06; C St Martin-in-the-Fields from 06. *Flat 1, 6 St Martin's Place, London WC2N 4JJ* T: (020) 7766 1100 F: 7839 5163 E: richard.carter@smitf.org

CARTER, Richard William. b 75. Newc Univ BSc 96. Westcott Ho Cam 04. d 07 p 08. C Llanbedr DC w Llangynhafal, Llanychan etc *St As* 07–10; P-in-c 10; P-in-c Clocaenog and

Gyffylliog 10–16; P-in-c Llanfair DC, Derwen, Llanelidan and Efenechtyd 10–16; TV Dyffryn Clwyd Miss Area from 17. *The Vicarage, Bron y Clwyd, Llanfair Dyffryn Clwyd, Ruthin LL15 2SB* T: (01824) 703867 M: 07769-727985 E: reverendcarter@gmail.com

CARTER, Robert Desmond. b 35. Cranmer Hall Dur 62. d 65 p 66. C Otley *Bradf* 65–69; C Keighley 69–73; V Cowling 73–00; rtd 00; PtO *Bradf* 00–14; *Leeds* 14–16. *1 Quincy Close, Eccleshill, Bradford BD2 2EP* T: (01274) 638385

CARTER, Robert Edward. b 44. Univ of Wales (Ban) BSc 66. St Jo Coll Nottm 79. d 81 p 82. C Caverswall *Lich* 81–86; V Biddulph 86–94; V Wolverhampton St Jude 94–10; rtd 11; PtO *Lich* 11–21; NSM Penn Fields 12–18. *17 The Spinney, Wolverhampton WV3 9HE* E: gear.carter@gmail.com

CARTER, Robin. b 46. Cam Univ MSt 02. Chich Th Coll 71. d 74 p 75. C Wortley-de-Leeds *Ripon* 74–76; C Hutton *Chelmsf* 76–78; V Wickford 78–81; TV Wickford and Runwell 81–83; Chapl HM Pris Leeds 83–85; Chapl HM Pris Reading 85–89; Chapl HM YOI Huntercombe and Finnamore 85–89; Chapl HM YOI Finnamore Wood Camp 86–89; Gov 5, Hd of Operations, HM Pris Channings Wood 89–94; Gov 4, Hd of Operations/Régime and Throughcare, HM Pris Woodhill 94–99; Gov HM Pris E Sutton Park 99–05; Sen Operational Pris Service Manager 05–08; Chapl Costa Blanca *Eur* 08–12; rtd 12; PtO *Ox* from 13. *1 Symington Court, Shenley Lodge, Milton Keynes MK5 7AN* E: robincarter@yahoo.com

CARTER, Russell James Wigney. b 29. Chich Th Coll 80. d 82 p 83. C Aldwick *Chich* 82–86; R Buxted and Hadlow Down 86–90; rtd 90; PtO *Chich* from 90. *1 Bishopsgate Walk, Chichester PO19 6FG* T: (01243) 931900

CARTER, Samuel Nicholas Cato. b 83. Mert Coll Ox BA 05 Trin Coll Cam BA 16 MPhil 17. Ridley Hall Cam 14. d 17 p 18. C Eastbourne All So *Chich* 17–21; R Barcombe from 21. *The Rectory, 1 The Grange, Barcombe, Lewes BN8 5AT* T: (01273) 400260 M: 07810-744528 E: snccarter@yahoo.co.uk

CARTER, Sarah Helen Buchanan. *See* GORTON, Sarah Helen Buchanan

CARTER, Stanley Reginald. b 24. St Jo Coll Dur BA 49. d 50 p 51. C Stoughton *Guildf* 50–53; C Bucknall and Bagnall *Lich* 53–56; R Salford St Matthias w St Simon *Man* 56–62; V Highbury New Park St Aug *Lon* 62–69; V Sneinton St Chris w St Phil *S'well* 69–89; rtd 89; PtO *S'well* 89–18. *31 Pateley Road, Nottingham NG3 5QF* T: 0115-953 2122 E: stan.carter@dunelm.org.uk

CARTER, Canon Stephen. b 56. Univ of Wales (Lamp) BA 77 Southn Univ BTh 81. Sarum & Wells Th Coll 78. d 81 p 82. C Halstead St Andr w H Trin and Greenstead Green *Chelmsf* 81–84; C Loughton St Jo 84–89; V N Shoebury 89–95; R Lexden 95–09; RD Colchester 01–06; V Maldon All SS w St Pet 09–20; P-in-c Woodham Mortimer w Hazeleigh 16–19; P-in-c Woodham Walter 16–19; Hon Can Chelmsf Cathl 07–20; rtd 20; PtO *Chelmsf* from 20. *28 Taylor Drive, Lawford, Manningtree CO11 2HU* E: revscarter@gmail.com

CARTER, Stephen Howard. b 47. City Univ BSc 72. St Jo Coll Nottm 83. d 85 p 86. C Helledson *Nor* 85–88; Chapl Birm Children's Hosp 88–91; Chapl Birm Maternity Hosp 88–91; TV Tettenhall Wood *Lich* 91–98; Chapl Compton Hospice 91–98; P-in-c Coalbrookdale, Iron-Bridge and Lt Wenlock *Heref* 98–00; R 00–07; Asst Dioc Co-ord for Evang 00–01; P-in-c Darby End *Worc* 07–08; V 08–12; P-in-c Netherton St Andr 07–08; V 08–12; V Darby End and Netherton 12–14; RD Dudley 10–13; rtd 14; PtO *Cov* from 15. *33 Manse Close, Exhall, Coventry CV7 9NT* T: (024) 7631 2831 M: 07811-222020 E: stevecarter@fastmail.net

CARTER, Stephen Lewis. b 86. Lon Sch of Th BA 09 Homerton Coll Cam MEd 12 PGCE 10. Trin Coll Bris 14. d 16 p 17. C Cant St Mary Bredin from 16. *14 Oxford Road, Canterbury CT1 3QF* M: 07950-969633 E: stephenlewiscarter@gmail.com or scarter@smb.org.uk

CARTER, Stephen Paul. b 55. Cartrefle Coll of Educn CertEd 76. Trin Coll Bris BA 88. d 98 p 99. Dn-in-c Montevideo H Spirit Uruguay 98–99; P-in-c 00–04; V Dalston w Cumdivock, Raughton Head and Wreay *Carl* 04–19; rtd 19; PtO *Carl* from 19. *60 Eden Street, Carlisle CA3 9LH*

CARTER, Stuart Conway. b 58. Lon Bible Coll 81 St Jo Coll Nottm 90. d 92 p 93. C Birm St Luke 92–96; C The Quinton 96–10; V Castle Bromwich St Clem 10–21; AD Coleshill 13–18; rtd 21. *Wain House, Habberley, Pontesbury, Shrewsbury SY5 0TP*

CARTER, Mrs Wendy Elise Grace. b 46. Battersea Coll of Educn TCert 67. Qu Coll Birm 01. d 04 p 05. C Kingshurst *Birm* 04–07; P-in-c High Wych and Gilston w Eastwick *St Alb* 07–10; rtd 10; PtO *St Alb* 11–14; Hon C Salter Street and Shirley 14–16; PtO from 16; P-in-c High Wych and Gilston w Eastwick *St Alb* 18–20; PtO 20–21. *134 Shakespeare Drive, Shirley, Solihull B90 2AR* E: revwendy@sky.com

CARTLEDGE, Margery. See TÖLLER, Elizabeth Margery

CARTLEDGE, Mark John. b 62. Lon Bible Coll BA 85 Trin Coll Carmarthen PhD 00. Oak Hill Th Coll MPhil 89. **d** 88 **p** 89. C Formby H Trin *Liv* 88–91; CMS Nigeria 91–93; Chapl Liv Univ 93–98; Chapl and Tutor St Jo Coll Dur 98–03; Lect Univ of Wales (Lamp) 03–06; PtO *St D* 03–06; *Birm* from 06; Sen Lect Th Birm Univ 08–15; Prof Practical Th Regent Univ USA 15–19; Prin Lon Sch of Th from 20; PtO *Lon* from 20. *London School of Theology, Green Lane, Northwood HA6 2UW* T: (01923) 456000 E: mark.cartledge@lst.ac.uk

CARTMELL, Canon Richard Peter Watkinson. b 43. Cranmer Hall Dur 77. **d** 79 **p** 80. C Whittle-le-Woods *Blackb* 79–85; V Lower Darwen St Jas 85–03; RD Darwen 91–96; P-in-c S Shore H Trin 03–08; Hon Can Blackb Cathl 98–08; rtd 08; PtO *Blackb* from 08. *4 Salwick Avenue, Blackpool FY2 9BT* T: (01253) 590083

CARTMILL, Canon Ralph Arthur. b 40. St Jo Coll Dur BA 62 Em Coll Cam MA 64. Ridley Hall Cam 63. **d** 65 **p** 66. C Dukinfield St Jo *Ches* 65–68; C Wilmslow 68–69; Warden Walton Youth Cen Liv 69–70; Asst Master Aylesbury Gr Sch 70–74; PtO *Ox* 72–74; V Terriers 74–85; P-in-c Chinnor w Emmington and Sydenham 85–86; R Chinnor w Emmington and Sydenham etc 86–98; Hon Can Ch Ch 97–98; rtd 98; PtO *Nor* from 00. *1 Stuart Court, High Street, Kibworth Beauchamp, Leicester LE8 0LR* T: 0116-279 3614 E: r.cartmill58@btinternet.com

CARTWRIGHT, Mrs Amanda Jane. b 58. St Jo Coll Nottm 00. **d** 02 **p** 03. C Beeston *S'well* 02–07; P-in-c Bilborough St Jo 07–13; V 13–15; P-in-c Bilborough w Strelley 07–13; R 13–15; R Bilborough and Strelley 15–16; V E Trent from 16. *The Rectory, 1 Vicarage Close, Collingham, Newark NG23 7PQ* E: revdmand@hotmail.com

CARTWRIGHT, Hannah Rosina. b 88. Ripon Coll Cuddesdon 14. **d** 18 **p** 19. C Littlemore *Ox* 18–20; C Littlemore w Sandford-on-Thames from 20. *20 Vicarage Close, Oxford OX4 4PL* E: hannahrosinacartwright@gmail.com

CARTWRIGHT, Julia Ann. b 58. Nottm Univ BA 80. Linc Th Coll 84. **dss** 86 **d** 87 **p** 94. Asst Chapl HM Pris Morton Hall 85–90; Linc St Jo 86–88; Hon C 87–88; Hon C Bardney 88–97; Chapl Linc Co Hosp 90–93; Chapl St Geo Hosp Linc 90–93; Chapl Linc Distr Health Services and Hosps NHS Trust 93–97; Chapl S Bucks NHS Trust 97–04; LtO *Ox* 97–04; Chapl S Warks Combined Care NHS Trust 04–12; Chapl N Devon Healthcare NHS Trust from 12. *North Devon District Hospital, Raleigh Park, Barnstaple EX31 4JB* T: (01271) 322362 E: juliecartwright1@nhs.net

CARTWRIGHT, Lydia. b 78. Nottm Univ BA 99. St Jo Coll Nottm 13. **d** 16 **p** 17. C Stapleford *S'well* 16–20; TR Clifton from 20. *The Rectory, 569 Farnborough Road, Nottingham NG11 9DG* M: 07305-820553 E: rev.lydiacartwright@gmail.com

CARTWRIGHT, Michael. See CARTWRIGHT, William Michael

CARTWRIGHT, Michael John. b 42. Qu Coll Birm 67. **d** 70 **p** 71. C Astwood Bank w Crabbs Cross *Worc* 70–75; P-in-c Worc St Mich 75–77; V Stockton St Paul *Dur* 77–87; V Market Rasen *Linc* 87–12; R Linwood 87–12; V Legsby 87–12; R Wickenby Gp 95–00; V Lissington 00–12; RD W Wold 89–01; rtd 12; PtO *Linc* 16–19. *The Coach House, Main Road, Welbourn, Lincoln LN5 0PA* T: (01400) 279062 E: pontiac57@hotmail.com or rostigcs7@outlook.com

CARTWRIGHT, Canon Paul. b 71. Leeds Metrop Univ BA 99 Leeds Univ BA 08 MA 13 Huddersfield Univ PGCE 06. Coll of Resurr Mirfield 06. **d** 08 **p** 09. C Athersley *Wakef* 08–11; C Carlton 10–11; P-in-c Barnsley St Pet and St Jo 11–14; *Leeds* 14–16; V 16–19; P-in-c Grimethorpe w Brierley from 19; P-in-c Ryhill from 19; P-in-c S Kirkby from 19; Hon Can Wakef Cathl from 17. *The Vicarage, 20 School Lane, Ryhill, Wakefield WF4 2DW* M: 07852-174303 E: fr.paul.cartwright@gmail.com

CARTWRIGHT, Ms Ruth. b 59. St Mellitus Coll BA 14. **d** 14 **p** 15. C Grays Thurrock *Chelmsf* 14–17; P-in-c Hadleigh St Barn from 17; P-in-c Hadleigh St Jas from 17. *The Rectory, 50 Rectory Road, Benfleet SS7 2ND* M: 07432-599404 E: ruth@cartmann.eclipse.co.uk

CARTWRIGHT, Simon John. b 71. R Holloway Coll Lon BA 93 Sheff Univ MA 95 Nottm Univ PhD 12. St Jo Coll Nottm MTh 05. **d** 06 **p** 07. C Ward End w Bordesley Green *Birm* 06–11; TV Walbrook Epiphany *Derby* from 11; AD Derby City from 20. *The Vicarage, 81 Palmerston Street, Derby DE23 6PF* T: (01332) 367690 M: 07720-769631 E: revscartwright@gmail.com

CARTWRIGHT, William Michael. b 44. Birm Univ CertEd 67. Coll of Resurr Mirfield 83. **d** 83 **p** 84. Hd Master Chacombe Sch 83–85; Hon C Middleton Cheney w Chacombe *Pet* 83–85; C Kettering SS Pet and Paul 85–86; PtO 86–88; Chapl Northaw Prep Sch Win 89–92; P-in-c Altarnon

w Bolventor, Laneast and St Clether *Truro* 92–97; V Treverbyn 97–01; V Bempton w Flamborough, Reighton w Speeton *York* 01–03; V Ampleforth w Oswaldkirk, Gilling E etc 03–09; rtd 09; P-in-c Barningham w Matlaske w Baconsthorpe etc *Nor* 09–14; PtO 14–16; Chapl Beeston Hall Sch 16–17; P-in-c Matlaske *Nor* 17–18; TV Heart of Norfolk from 18. *The Rectory, 1 Guist Road, Foulsham, Dereham NR20 5RZ*

CARUANA, Mrs Rosemary Anne. b 38. St Alb Minl Tr Scheme 81. **dss** 84 **d** 87 **p** 94. Hertford St Andr *St Alb* 84–87; Par Dn Hertingfordbury 87–94; C 94–98; P-in-c 98–05; rtd 05; PtO *St Alb* from 05. *36 Holly Croft, Hertford SG14 2DR* T: (01992) 306427 M: 07769-658756 E: rosemarycaruana2@sky.com

CARVETH, Mrs Marlene. b 51. Ex Univ BA 07. SWMTC 04. **d** 07 **p** 08. NSM Camborne *Truro* 07–13; NSM St Illogan from 14 and 15–21; rtd 21. *Trelowarren, 5 Rosevale Crescent, Camborne TR14 7LU* T: (01209) 713175 E: roseyvale@tiscali.co.uk

CARVOSSO, John Charles. b 45. ACA 71 FCA 79. Oak Hill Th Coll 75. **d** 78 **p** 79. C Chelsea St Jo w St Andr *Lon* 78–81; Chapl RAF 81–84; P-in-c Tawstock *Ex* 84–85; TV Newport, Bishops Tawton and Tawstock 85–96; TV Newton Tracey, Horwood, Alverdiscott etc 96–11; RD Torrington 97–02; rtd 11. *45 Trafalgar Drive, Torrington EX38 7AD* M: 07507-369127 E: revjcc@gmail.com

CASE, Preb Catherine Margaret. b 44. Ripon Coll Cuddesdon 86. **d** 88 **p** 94. C Blurton *Lich* 88–92; TD Hanley H Ev and Min to Hanley Care Agencies 92–94; P-in-c Wrockwardine Wood *Lich* 95–98; R 98–00; V Gnosall 00–06; V Gnosall and Moreton 06–07; Preb Lich Cathl 02–07; rtd 07; PtO *Lich* 07–14 and 17–21; C Barlaston 14–16. *2 Fulmar Place, Stoke-on-Trent ST3 7QF* T: (01782) 399291 E: preb.case@gmail.com

CASE, Clive Anthony. b 70. St Andr Univ MTheol 93 Surrey Univ BA 05 St Jo Coll Dur PGCE 94. STETS 02. **d** 05 **p** 06. NSM Epsom St Martin *Guildf* 05–11; Asst Chapl Epsom Coll 05–07; Chapl St Jo Sch Leatherhead 08–11; Sen Chapl Charterhouse Sch Godalming from 11. *Charterhouse School, Brook Hall, Charterhouse, Godalming GU7 2DX* T: (01483) 291741 M: 07801-288943 E: cac@charterhouse.org.uk

CASEBOW, Ronald Philip. b 31. Roch Th Coll 59. **d** 61 **p** 62. C Southgate Ch Ch *Lon* 61–64; C Oseney Crescent St Luke w Camden Square St Paul 64–70; Warden St Paul's Ho Student Hostel 64–70; V Colchester St Steph *Chelmsf* 70–74; V Burnham 74–89; rtd 89; PtO *Nor* from 95. *The Priory, Priory Road, Palgrave, Diss IP22 1AJ* T: (01379) 651804

CASEY, Christopher Noel. b 61. Open Univ BA 95. St Jo Coll Nottm BA 01. **d** 01 **p** 02. C Penrith w Newton Reigny and Plumpton Wall *Carl* 01–06; P-in-c Mirehouse 06–16; P-in-c Constable Lee *Man* 16–17; P-in-c Rawtenstall St Mary 16–17; V Rawtenstall and Constable Lee 17–20; Borough Dean Rossendale 16–20; V Holme-in-Cliviger w Worsthorne *Blackb* from 20; AD Burnley from 21. *St John's Vicarage, Gorple Road, Worsthorne, Burnley BB10 3NN* E: kcvicar@gmail.com

CASH, Simon Andrew. b 62. St Jo Coll Nottm 99. **d** 01 **p** 02. C Todwick *Sheff* 01–04; P-in-c Worksop St Anne *S'well* 04–16; P-in-c Norton Cuckney 05–16; AD Bassetlaw and Bawtry 14–16; TR Dewsbury *Leeds* from 16; AD 16–19; AD Birstall 18–19; AD Dewsbury and Birstall 20–21. *The Rectory, Oxford Road, Dewsbury WF13 4JT* T: (01909) 472069 E: simon_cash@sky.com

CASHEL, Dean of. See FIELD, The Very Revd Gerald Gordon

CASHEL, WATERFORD AND LISMORE, Archdeacon of. See GRAY, The Ven Robert James

CASHEL, WATERFORD, LISMORE, OSSORY, FERNS AND LEIGHLIN, Bishop of. See BURROWS, The Rt Revd Michael Andrew James

CASHMORE, Matthew James. b 80. Dur Univ BA 17. Ripon Coll Cuddesdon 14. **d** 17 **p** 18. C W Heref 17–19; C Kenton *Lon* 19–20; P-in-c Hayes St Anselm from 20. *St Anselm's Vicarage, 101 Nield Road, Hayes UB3 1SQ* T: (020) 3882 0553 E: father@matthewcashmore.com

CASSAM, Victor Reginald. b 33. Chich Univ BA 05. Chich Th Coll 59. **d** 62 **p** 63. C Portsea St Jo Rudmore *Portsm* 62–64; C W Leigh CD 64–66; C Torquay St Martin Barton *Ex* 66–69; C Stanmer w Falmer and Moulsecoomb *Chich* 69–73; P-in-c Catsfield 73–76; R Catsfield and Crowhurst 76–81; R Selsey 81–01; RD Chich 96–01; rtd 01; PtO *Chich* from 01; *Portsm* 01–15. *195 Oving Road, Chichester PO19 7ER* T/F: (01243) 783998 M: 07976-757451 E: frvictor@gmail.com

CASSELTON, John Charles. b 43. Univ of Wales (Swansea) MA 95. Oak Hill Th Coll 64. **d** 68 **p** 69. C Upton *Ex* 68–73; C Braintree *Chelmsf* 73–80; V Ipswich St Jo *St E* 80–92; RD Ipswich 86–92; Chapl St Clem Hosp Ipswich 92–98; Chapl St Eliz Hospice Ipswich 92–00; Dir Inspire

Chr Counselling 00–05; rtd 05; PtO *St E* 00–21. *54C Westerfield Road, Ipswich IP4 2UT*   M: 07421-143167 E: johnandmidge@hotmail.co.uk

✠**CASSIDY, The Rt Revd George Henry.** b 42. QUB BSc 65 Lon Univ MPhil 67. Oak Hill Th Coll 70. **d** 72 **p** 73 **c** 99. C Clifton Ch Ch w Em *Bris* 72–75; V Sea Mills 75–82; V Portman Square St Paul *Lon* 82–87; Adn Lon and Can Res St Paul's Cathl 87–99; P-in-c St Ethelburga Bishopgate 89–91; Bp S'well and Nottm 99–09; rtd 09; Hon Asst Bp B & W from 10; Hon Asst Bp Bris from 10. *Darch House, 17 St Andrew's Road, Stogursey, Bridgwater TA5 1TE*   T: (01278) 732625 E: georgecassidy123@btinternet.com

CASSON, David Christopher. b 41. Qu Coll Cam BA 64 MA 68. Ridley Hall Cam 65. **d** 67 **p** 68. C Birm St Martin 67–72; C Luton St Mary *St Alb* 72–77; P-in-c Luton St Fran 77; V 77–84; V Richmond H Trin and Ch Ch *S'wark* 84–97; R Acle w Fishley, N Burlingham, Beighton w Moulton *Nor* 97–04; rtd 04; PtO *Nor* from 04. *4 Mattock Way, Abingdon OX14 2PB*   T: (01235) 524226

CASSWELL, Canon David Oriel. b 52. Loughb Coll of Educn DipEd 74 CQSW 79. Oak Hill Th Coll 85. **d** 87 **p** 88. C Acomb St Steph and St Aid *York* 87–91; Dep Chapl HM Pris Leeds 91–92; Chapl HM Pris Everthorpe 92; Chapl HM Pris Wolds 92–98; V Clifton *York* 98–17; Can and Preb York Minster 13–17; rtd 17; PtO *York* from 18. *68 Seebohm Mews, York YO31 0SJ*

CASTER, John Forristall. b 71. Texas A&M Univ BA 93. St Steph Ho Ox BTh 05. **d** 05 **p** 06. C Hendon St Alphage *Lon* 05–09; TV Old St Pancras 09–12; P-in-c Tunbridge Wells St Barn *Roch* 12–17; V from 17. *The Clergy House, 114 Upper Grosvenor Road, Tunbridge Wells TN1 2EX*   T: (01892) 525656 E: john.caster@ssho.oxon.org

CASTILLO-BURLEY, Jassica Geraldine. b 67. Greenwich Univ BSc 96. Ridley Hall Cam 15. **d** 17 **p** 18. C Whittington and W Felton w Haughton *Lich* 17–21; C Cen Telford from 21. *32 Viscount Avenue, Telford TF4 3SW*   T: (01952)   957348   M: 07850-543446 E: princessjassica1@googlemail.com

✠**CASTLE, The Rt Revd Brian Colin.** b 49. Lon Univ BA 72 Ox Univ BA 77 MA 80 Birm Univ PhD 89. Cuddesdon Coll 74. **d** 77 **p** 78 **c** 02. C Limpsfield and Titsey *S'wark* 77–81; USPG Zambia 81–84; Lect Ecum Inst WCC Geneva 84–85; V N Petherton w Northmoor Green *B & W* 85–92; Dir Past Studies and Vice-Prin Cuddesdon Coll 92–01; Suff Bp Tonbridge *Roch* 02–15; Hon Can Roch Cathl 02–15; rtd 15; Hon Asst Bp B & W from 16. *Pound Cottage, Wootton Courtenay, Minehead TA24 8RH*   T: (01643) 841062 E: brian@briancastle.org

CASTLE, Canon Brian Stanley. b 47. Oak Hill Th Coll 70. **d** 73 **p** 74. C Barnsbury St Andr w St Thos and St Matthias *Lon* 73–76; C Lower Homerton St Paul 76–79; P-in-c Bethnal Green St Jas Less 79–82; V 82–98; V Tile Cross *Birm* 98–08; P-in-c Garretts Green 03–08; V Garretts Green and Tile Cross 08–17; P-in-c Sheldon 12–16; and Coleshill 06–13; Hon Can Birm Cathl 16–17; rtd 17; PtO *Ban* from 16; *Birm* 17. *Hafan, Penisarwaun, Caernarfon LL55 3BS*   T: (01286) 871705   M: 07710-251790 E: revbcastle@me.com

CASTLE, John Arthur. b 61. G&C Coll Cam BA 83 St Jo Coll Dur BA 95. Aston Tr Scheme 90 Cranmer Hall Dur 92. **d** 95 **p** 96. C Southborough St Pet w Ch Ch and St Matt *Roch* 95–99; Miss Partner CMS 99–04; P-in-c Sandhurst *Ox* 04–10; R from 10. *The Rectory, 155 High Street, Sandhurst GU47 8HR*   T: (01252) 872168 E: rector@stmichaels-sandhurst.org.uk

CASTLE, Louise Sarah. b 66. Birm Univ MB, ChB 90 MRCGP 94. St Hild Coll 16. **d** 18 **p** 19. NSM Mosborough *Sheff* from 18. *5 Southgate Court, Eckington, Sheffield S21 4LA*

CASTLE, Martin Roger. b 69. Leic Univ BA 92 Liv Univ MCD 95 St Edm Coll Cam BTh 09. Ridley Hall Cam. **d** 09 **p** 10. C Leic Martyrs 09–12; P-in-c Earl Shilton w Elmesthorpe from 12. *The Vicarage, Maughan Street, Earl Shilton, Leicester LE9 7BA*   T: (01455) 843961

CASTLE, Michael David. b 38. Wells Th Coll 69. **d** 71 **p** 72. C Acocks Green *Birm* 71–75; C Weoley Castle 76–78; V 78–08; rtd 08. *339 Bournville Gardens, 49 Bristol Road South, Birmingham B31 2FS*

CASTLE, Phillip Stanley. b 43. **d** 97 **p** 98. OLM E Farnworth and Kearsley *Man* 97–09; OLM Farnworth, Kearsley and Stoneclough 10–13; rtd 13; PtO *Man* 13–20. *73 Bradford Street, Farnworth, Bolton BL4 9JY*   T: (01204) 571439 E: phillip.castle43@gmail.com

CASTLE, Roger James. b 39. St Jo Coll Cam BA 62 MA 66. Clifton Th Coll 63. **d** 65 **p** 66. C Rushden w Newton Bromswold *Pet* 65–68; C Stapenhill w Cauldwell *Derby* 68–72; V Hayfield 72–89; R Coxheath, E Farleigh, Hunton, Linton etc *Roch* 89–04; Chapl Invicta Community Care NHS Trust 91–04; rtd 04; PtO *Bris* from 04. *10 College Park Drive, Bristol BS10 7AN*   T: 0117-950 7028

CASTLETON, Mark Peter. b 82. Bath Spa Univ BA 04 Cam Univ BTh 09. Ridley Hall Cam 06. **d** 09 **p** 10. C Salisbury St Mark *Sarum* 09–13; C Aldridge *Lich* 13–19; C Woodford Wells *Chelmsf* from 19. *3 Inmans Row, Woodford Green IG8 0NH* E: markcastleton@ymail.com

CASWELL, Roger John. b 47. St Chad's Coll Dur BA 70. St Steph Ho Ox 75. **d** 77 **p** 78. C Brighton Resurr *Chich* 77–83; TV Crawley 83–90; TR Littlehampton 90–18; Chapl Worthing Priority Care NHS Trust 90–18; rtd 18. *5 Magnolia Close, Worthing BN13 3PT*

CASWELL (formerly HARVEY), Mrs Tracey Louise. b 74. St Mellitus Coll 13. **d** 16 **p** 17. C Coggeshall w Markshall *Chelmsf* 16–20; C Cressing w Stisted and Bradwell etc 16–20; P-in-c N Blackwater from 20; P-in-c Gt Totham and Lt Totham w Goldhanger from 20. *The Vicarage, 37 Church Street, Tolleshunt d'Arcy, Maldon CM9 8TS*   M: 07742-999633 E: revtlharvey@gmail.com

CATALLO, Leon Peter. b 84. Down Coll Cam MSci 06. Wycliffe Hall Ox BA 14. **d** 15 **p** 16. C Plymouth St Andr *Ex* 15–18; C Ox St Ebbe w H Trin and St Pet 18–21; P-in-c Highfield from 21. *All Saints' Church, Lime Walk, Headington, Oxford OX3 7AB* E: leoncatallo@gmail.com

CATER, Lois May. b 37. S Dios Minl Tr Scheme 81. **dss** 84 **d** 87 **p** 94. Calne and Blackland *Sarum* 84–89; Hon Par Dn 87–89; Hon Par Dn Devizes St Jo w St Mary 89–94; Hon C 94–96; Hon TV Alderbury Team 96–01; Hon TV Clarendon 01–07; PtO from 06. *18 St Margaret's Close, Calne SN11 0UQ*   T: (01249) 819432

CATERER, James Albert Leslie Blower. b 44. New Coll Ox BA 67 MA 81. Sarum & Wells Th Coll 79. **d** 81 **p** 82. C Cheltenham St Luke and St Jo *Glouc* 81–85; V Standish w Haresfield and Moreton Valence etc 85–96; P-in-c Glouc St Steph 96–09; rtd 09. *Copelands, 180 Stroud Road, Gloucester GL1 5JX*   T/F: (01452)   524694 E: jimscicaterer@googlemail.com

CATHERALL, Mark Leslie. b 64. Chich Th Coll BTh 93. **d** 93 **p** 94. C Lancing w Coombes *Chich* 93–95; C Selsey 95–98; Chapl RN 98–04; V S Thornaby *York* 04–19; V Up Hatherley *Glouc* from 19. *The Vicarage, 336 Hatherley Road, Cheltenham GL51 6HX*   T: (01242)   210673 E: frmark.catherall@ntlworld.com

CATHIE, Sean Bewley. b 43. Dur Univ BA 67 Birkbeck Coll Lon MSc 03 K Coll Lon DThMin 15. Cuddesdon Coll 67. **d** 69 **p** 70. C Kensal Rise St Martin *Lon* 69–73; C Paddington H Trin w St Paul 73–75; P-in-c Bridstow w Peterstow *Heref* 76–79; Hon C Westmr St Jas *Lon* 85–97; Hon C St Marylebone w H Trin 99–06; Hon C St Marylebone St Cypr 99–06; rtd 06; PtO *Heref* from 09. *Address temp unknown* E: scathie@waitrose.com

CATLEY, Marc. b 59. Liv Univ BA 82 Lon Bible Coll BA 85 Man Poly PGCE 90. St Jo Coll Nottm MTh 06. **d** 07 **p** 08. C E Green *Cov* 07–11; V Packwood w Hockley Heath *Birm* from 11. *The Vicarage, Nuthurst Lane, Hockley Heath, Solihull B94 5RP*   T: (01564) 783121   M: 07952-456846 E: marc.catley@yahoo.co.uk

CATLING, Michael David. b 56. Goldsmiths' Coll Lon CertEd 77 DipEd 84 Newc Univ MLitt 06. Cranmer Hall Dur 88. **d** 90 **p** 91. C Cullercoats St Geo *Newc* 90–94; TV Glendale Gp 94–01; V Whittingham and Edlingham w Bolton Chapel 01–09; R Wigmore Abbey *Heref* from 09. *The Rectory, Watling Street, Leintwardine, Craven Arms SY7 0LL* T: (01547) 540235 E: mikecat7@btinternet.com

CATON, Philip Cooper. b 47. Oak Hill Th Coll 79. **d** 81 **p** 82. C Much Woolton *Liv* 81–85; TV Parr 85–98; V Birkdale St Jo 98–11; rtd 11; PtO *Liv* from 16. *Cooper's Cottage, 23 Alma Road, Southport PR8 4AN*   T: (01704) 565785 E: p.caton@sky.com

CATTELL, Angela Kathleen. b 48. Trin Coll Bris. **d** 12 **p** 13. OLM Stoke Bishop *Bris* 12–20; NSM from 20. *9 Eastmead Lane, Bristol BS9 1HW*   T: 0117-968 3069 E: angela.cattell@blueyonder.co.uk

CATTELL, Mrs Rosemary Ann. b 51. Open Univ BA 87 Univ Coll Chich BA 04 Chich Univ MA 09. SEITE 10. **d** 12 **p** 13. NSM Warnham *Chich* 12–16; NSM Itchingfield w Slinfold from 16. *Whitegates, Salisbury Road, Horsham RH13 0AL* T: (01403) 264396 E: r.a.cattell@btinternet.com *or* assocpriest@stnicolasitchingfield.org.uk

CATTERALL, David Arnold. b 53. Lon Univ BSc 74 ARCS 74. Cranmer Hall Dur. **d** 78 **p** 79. C Swinton St Pet *Man* 78–81; C Wythenshawe St Martin 81–83; R Heaton Norris Ch w All SS 83–88; I Fanlobbus Union *C, C & R* 88–95; Can Cork and Ross Cathls 93–95; Warden Ch's Min of Healing in Ireland 95–02; I Templemichael w Clongish, Clooncumber etc *K, E & A* 02–19; rtd 19. *28 St Albans, Battery Road, Longford, Co Longford, N39 R2T6, Republic of Ireland* T: (00353) (43) 334 9285 E: djcatt@eircom.net

CATTERALL, Canon Janet Margaret. b 53. Univ of Wales (Ban) BA 74. Cranmer Hall Dur 77. **dss** 81 **d** 87 **p** 90. Wythenshawe St Martin *Man* 81–83; Heaton Norris Ch w All SS 83–88; Par Dn 87–88; C Bandon Union *C, C & R* 88–89; Dioc Youth Adviser (Cork) 89–94; Dioc Youth Chapl 94–95; I Drung w Castleterra, Larah and Lavey etc *K, E & A* 95–02; P-in-c Mostrim w Granard, Clonbroney, Killoe etc 02–16; Preb Mulhuddart St Patr Cathl Dublin 05–16; rtd 16. *28 St Albans, Battery Road, Longford, Co Longford, N39 R2T6, Republic of Ireland* T: (00353) (43) 334 9285 E: djcatt@eircom.net *or* janetcatt@eircom.net

CATTERICK, Matthew John. b 68. W Sussex Inst of HE BA 90 Heythrop Coll Lon MA 11. St Steph Ho Ox BTh 95. **d** 95 **p** 96. C Colchester St Jas and St Paul w All SS etc *Chelmsf* 95–98; C Leic Resurr 98–99; TV 99–04; TR Wembley Park *Lon* 04–11; V Pimlico St Sav from 11. *59 Aylesford Street, London SW1V 3RY* T: (020) 7592 9733 E: vicar@stsp.org.uk

CATTERMOLE, Mrs Elke Brunhilde Emma. b 52. Anglia Ruskin Univ MSc 11 RN 74 RM 76. Westcott Ho Cam 16. **d** 17 **p** 18. NSM Lavenham w Preston *St E* 17–19; R Bildeston w Wattisham and Lindsey etc from 20. *The Rectory, 10 Crowcroft Road, Nedging Tye, Ipswich IP7 7HR* T: (01449) 403698 E: revdelkecattermole@gmail.com

CATTLE, David James. b 75. ACCA 00 FCCA 05. Trin Coll Bris BA 06 MA 07. **d** 07 **p** 08. C Firswood and Gorse Hill *Man* 07–10; TV Digswell and Panshanger *St Alb* 11–16; PtO *Nor* 16–18; V Galleywood Common *Chelmsf* from 18; C Widford from 18; C Moulsham St Luke from 18; C Moulsham St Jo from 18. *The Vicarage, 450 Beehive Lane, Chelmsford CM2 8RN* T: (01245) 265250 M: 07891-148884 E: revdcattle@gmail.com

CATTLE, Canon Richard John. b 40. WMMTC 88. **d** 90 **p** 91. NSM Brixworth Deanery *Pet* 90–91; NSM Welford w Sibbertoft and Marston Trussell 91–92; V 92–97; Bp's Dioc Chapl 97–00; Dioc Sec 98–00; Can Pet Cathl 98–02; rtd 01; PtO *Pet* 02–17; Dean's Asst 05–16. *Cedar Hay Farm, 3 School Lane, Yelvertoft, Northampton NN6 6LH* E: richardcattle1874@gmail.com

CATTLEY, Richard Melville. b 49. Trin Coll Bris. **d** 73 **p** 74. C Kendal St Thos *Carl* 73–77; Nat Sec Pathfinders CPAS 77–82; Exec Sec 82–85; V Dalton-in-Furness *Carl* 85–90; V Dulwich St Barn *S'wark* 90–99; Chapl Alleyn's Foundn Dulwich 90–99; V Milton Keynes *Ox* 99–05; AD 01–05; V Dorking w Ranmore *Guildf* 05–10; rtd 11; PtO *Ox* 13–20. *9 St Margaret's Road, Maidenhead SL6 5DZ*

CATTON, Canon Cedric Trevor. b 36. JP. Lambeth STh 94. Wells Th Coll 70. **d** 72 **p** 73. C Solihull *Birm* 72–74; R Hawstead and Nowton w Whepstead and Brockley *St E* 74–75; R Hawstead and Nowton w Stanningfield etc 74–79; Dioc Stewardship Adv 77–83; R Cockfield 79–83; V Exning St Martin w Landwade 83–99; Chapl Mid Anglia Community Health NHS Trust 85–99; Dioc Par Resources and Stewardship Officer *St E* 99–02; Hon Can St E Cathl 02; Hon Can St E Cathl 90–02; rtd 02; PtO *St E* 02–21; Dioc Clergy Retirement Officer 02–10; Acting Can Past St E Cathl 03–05; Asst Curate Past St E Cathl. *24 Manson Gardens, Northgate Street, Bury St Edmunds IP33 1HR*

CATTON, Stanley Charles. b 44. **d** 99 **p** 00. NSM Bermondsey St Jas w Ch Ch and St Crispin *S'wark* 99–13; NSM Bermondsey St Jas and St Anne 13–14; PtO from 14. *44 Old Farm Avenue, Sidcup DA15 8AF* E: scatton4@btinternet.com

CAUDELL, Juliet Lesley. *See* STRAW, Juliet Lesley

CAUDWELL, Lynn Fraser. b 62. Lon Univ BSc 83 Redcliffe Coll Glouc MA 13. Cranmer Hall Dur 18. **d** 19 **p** 20. C Corbridge w Halton and Newton Hall *Newc* from 19. *6 St Cuthbert's Terrace, Hexham NE46 2EL* M: 07824-558350 E: lynn.caudwell9@gmail.com

CAUNT, Mrs Margaret. b 55. Coll of Ripon & York St Jo MA 97. NOC 93. **d** 97 **p** 98. NSM Brightside w Wincobank *Sheff* 97–00; C Ecclesfield 00–02; TV Gleadless 02–07; V Anston 07–16; AD Laughton 15–16; V Arnold *S'well* from 16. *St Mary's Vicarage, 6 Church Lane, Arnold, Nottingham NG5 8HJ* M: 07543-563099 E: caunt@sky.com

CAVAGHAN, Dennis Edgar. b 45. Ex Univ MA 99. St Jo Coll Nottm BTh 74. **d** 74 **p** 75. C Hartford *Ches* 74–77; C Plymouth St Andr w St Paul and St Geo *Ex* 77–80; V Cofton w Starcross 80–88; P-in-c W Exe 88–93; PtO *B & W* 94–02; Hon C Taunton St Mary 02–14; Hon C Taunton St Mary and St Jo 14–16; PtO from 16. *Combe House, Corfe, Taunton TA3 7BU* T: (01823) 421013 M: 07810-796025 E: revdencav@gmail.com

CAVALCANTI, Canon Joabe Gomes. b 69. Federal Univ of Pernambuco BA 97 Trin Coll Bris MA 00. Nordeste Th Sem BA 91. **d** 98 **p** 98. PtO *Bris* 99; S'wark 01–05; Chapl St Sav and St Olave's Sch Newington 05–08; C Bermondsey St Hugh CD 05–08; V Mitcham St Barn from 08; Hon Can

Rio de Janeiro from 15. *St Barnabas' Vicarage, 46 Thirsk Road, Mitcham CR4 2BD* T: (020) 8648 2571 M: 07940-444241 E: joabec@gmail.com

CAVALIER, Mrs Sandra Jane. b 48. Guildf Dioc Min Course 98. **d** 00 **p** 01. OLM Guildf Ch Ch w St Martha-on-the-Hill 00–04; NSM Westborough 04–08; NSM Wrecclesham 08–18; PtO from 18. *17 Marston Road, Farnham GU9 7BN* T: (01252) 591068 M: 07828-072912 E: revcavalier@gmail.com

CAVAN, Lawrence Noel. b 38. Trin Coll Bris 72. **d** 75 **p** 76. C Lurgan Ch the Redeemer *D & D* 75–78; C Chorleywood Ch Ch *St Alb* 78–82; I Kilmocomogue w Snave, Durrus and Rooska *C, C & R* 82–85; I Portarlington w Cloneyhurke and Lea *M & K* 85–90; TV Eston w Normanby *York* 90–03; rtd 03; PtO *Derby* 05–13; *Sheff* 11–15. *22 Wentworth Road, Dronfield Woodhouse, Dronfield S18 8ZU* T: (01246) 418814 E: thecavans@hotmail.com

CAVANAGH, Anthony James. b 49. Ushaw Coll Dur 72. **d** 79 **p** 80. In RC Ch 79–95; C Goole *Sheff* 99–01; TV Cullercoats St Geo *Newc* 01–06; V Billy Mill 06–09; V Marden w Preston Grange 06–09; P-in-c Shilbottle 09–11; P-in-c Gosforth St Hugh 11–14; rtd 14; PtO *Newc* 14–20; *Dur* from 15. *7 Westfield Drive, Crook DL15 9NX* T: (01388) 762064 E: a.cavanagh258@btinternet.com

CAVANAGH, Lorraine Marie. b 46. Lucy Cavendish Coll Cam BA 97 MA 01 PhD 03. Ridley Hall Cam 00. **d** 01 **p** 02. PtO *Ely* 01–03; Chapl Fitzw Coll Cam 03; Chapl Cardiff Univ *Llan* 04–09; rtd 09. *Cae Hedd, Talycoed Lane, Llantilio Crossenny, Abergavenny NP7 8TL* T: (01600) 780244 E: lorraine@lorrainecavanagh.net

CAVANAGH, Canon Peter Bernard. b 49. Sarum & Wells Th Coll 71. **d** 73 **p** 74. C Gt Crosby St Faith *Liv* 73–76; C Stanley 76–79; V Anfield St Columba 79–97; V Lancaster St Mary w St John and St Anne *Blackb* 97–09; P-in-c Scorton and Barnacre and Calder Vale 06–09; Hon Can Blackb Cathl 00–09; rtd 09; PtO *Blackb* from 09; *Eur* from 16. *6 Lunesdale Court, Derwent Road, Lancaster LA1 3ET* T: (01524) 62786 E: manderley552@btinternet.com

CAVE, Bill. *See* CAVE-BROWNE-CAVE, Bernard James William

CAVE, Mrs Margaret. b 62. Van Mildert Coll Dur BSc 84 Cant Ch Ch Univ MA 15. SEITE 07. **d** 10 **p** 11. C Kidbrooke St Jas *S'wark* 10–13; TR E Greenwich from 13. *3 Hardy Road, London SE3 7NS* T: (020) 8853 3235 M: 07740-859958 E: vicar@christchurcheastgreenwich.org.uk

CAVE BERGQUIST, Julie Anastasia. b 59. St Jo Coll Dur BA 80 Franciscan Univ Rome STL 87. St Steph Ho Ox 85. **d** 87 **p** 98. Par Dn Kennington *Cant* 87–89; Chapl Trin Coll Cam 89–94; Chapl Westcott Ho Cam 94–97; C St Alb St Steph 98–02; P-in-c S Kensington H Trin w All SS *Lon* 02–06; Dir of Ords Two Cities Area 02–06; Nat Voc Adv and Selection Sec Min Division 06–10; PtO *Lon* 06–13; Dioc Dir of Ords *Ox* 10–15; PtO *Lon* from 19; *Eur* 19–20; Chapl Naples w Sorrento, Capri and Bari from 20; Asst Dir of Ords from 20. *via San Pasquale a Chiaia 15B, 80121 Naples, Italy* T: (0039) (081) 411842 M: (0047) 92-351561 E: vicar@christchurchnaples.org

CAVE-BROWNE-CAVE, Canon Bernard James William (Bill). b 54. Trin Hall Cam BA 76 MA 80 Bradf Univ MA 90 Open Univ LLB 14 LLM 18. Westcott Ho Cam 77. **d** 79 **p** 80. C Chesterton Gd Shep *Ely* 79–83; Chapl Lanc Univ *Blackb* 83–95; Chapl HM Pris Service 95–14; Chapl Wilts Police from 17; Dioc Inter-Faith Adv *Sarum* from 18; Can and Preb Sarum Cathl from 15. *Address withheld by request*

CAW (née FINLAY), Alison Mary. b 40. Natal Univ BA 62 Ox Univ PGCE 64. Ox Min Course 90. **d** 93 **p** 94. NSM Beaconsfield *Ox* 93–04; NSM Penn and Tylers Green 04–08; PtO 08–16; *Chelmsf* 16–21. *13 King Harold Lodge, Broomstick Hall Road, Waltham Abbey EN9 1LN* T: (01992) 700232 E: matopos@waitrose.com

CAW, Hannah Mary. *See* JEFFERY, Hannah Mary

CAWDELL, Dominic Austin. b 95. CCC Cam BA 16 MA 20. St Padarn's Inst 16. **d** 18 **p** 19. C Alyn Miss Area *St As* 18–20; P-in-c Estuary and Mountain Miss Area from 20; OGS from 19. *The Vicarage, 1 Llys Bychan, Holywell CH8 7SX* T: (01352) 712872 E: dominiccawdell@churchinwales.org.uk

CAWDELL, Mrs Sarah Helen Louise. b 65. St Hugh's Coll Ox BA 88 MA 91 Trin Coll Cam BA 94 MA 99 K Coll Lon MA 99. Ridley Hall Cam 92. **d** 95 **p** 96. C Belmont *S'wark* 95–98; PtO *Heref* 98–00; Hon C Claverley w Tuckhill 00–06; CME Officer 06–09; Public Preacher 06–17; TV Bridgnorth and Morville Par from 17; TR *Worc* 15–17; *Lich* from 15; *S'well* 16–17. *The Rectory, 16 East Castle Street, Bridgnorth WV16 4AL* T: (01746) 761573 E: sarah.h.l.cawdell@btinternet.com

CAWDELL, Preb Simon Howard. b 65. Univ Coll Dur BA 86 K Coll Lon MA 99. Ridley Hall Cam 91. **d** 94 **p** 95. C Cheam Common St Phil *S'wark* 94–98; V Claverley w Tuckhill *Heref* 98–10; TR Bridgnorth, Tasley, Astley Abbotts, etc 10–16; V

Morville w Aston Eyre 10–16; TR Bridgnorth and Morville Par from 16; RD Bridgnorth 09–13; Asst Adn Ludlow 20–21; Preb Heref Cathl from 15; PtO *Worc* from 17. *The Rectory, 16 East Castle Street, Bridgnorth WV16 4AL* T: (01746) 761573 E: s.h.cawdell@btinternet.com

CAWLEY, David Lewis. b 44. AKC 71 FSA 81. St Aug Coll Cant 71. **d** 72 **p** 73. C Sprowston *Nor* 72–75; Chapl HM Pris Nor 74–75; C Wymondham *Nor* 75–77; C Buckland in Dover w Buckland Valley *Cant* 77–83; V Eastville St Anne w St Mark and St Thos *Bris* 83–95; V Leic St Mary 95–09; TV Leic H Spirit 97–02; Chapl Trin Hosp Leic 96–09; rtd 09; C Margate All SS *Cant* 09–16; PtO from 17. *2B St John's Hospital, Northgate, Canterbury CT1 1BG* T: (01227) 479871 E: davidl.cawley@btinternet.com

CAWRSE, Christopher William. b 60. Birkbeck Coll Lon BA 97 Qu Mary and Westf Coll Lon MA 00. Westcott Ho Cam 82. **d** 84 **p** 85. C Stoke Newington St Mary *Lon* 84–86; Chapl St Mark's Hosp Lon 86–90; C Islington St Jas w St Pet *Lon* 86–90; Chapl Asst Charing Cross Hosp Lon 90–93; PtO *Lon* 93–06; P-in-c St Pancras H Cross w St Jude and St Pet 06–21; V from 21; Chapl Goodenough Coll from 21. *Holy Cross Vicarage, 47 Argyle Square, London WC1H 8AL* T: (020) 7278 6263 E: chriscawrse@blueyonder.co.uk

CAWTE, Martin Charles. b 51. Jes Coll Ox BA 73 MA 77 IPFA 76. SEITE 97. **d** 00 **p** 01. NSM Sanderstead All SS *S'wark* 00–03; NSM Greenham *Ox* 03–06; NSM Hermitage 06–12; P-in-c Lambourn 12–13; P-in-c Eastbury and E Garston 12–13; V Lambourn Valley 13–18; rtd 18; PtO *Ox* from 19. *9 Night Owls, Greenham, Thatcham RG19 8SB* T: (01635) 36736 E: martin_cawte@hotmail.com

CAWTHORNE, Paul Howarth. b 66. St Hild Coll Dur BA 88. Cuddesdon Coll 98. **d** 98 **p** 99. C Cen Telford *Lich* 98–01; TV Wrockwardine Deanery 01–13; TV Dorchester *Ox* 13–18; P-in-c Astley, Clive, Grinshill and Hadnall *Lich* from 18. *The Vicarage, Shrewsbury Road, Hadnall, Shrewsbury SY4 4AG* M: 07981-345820 E: paulcawthorne1966@gmail.com

CECIL, John Richard. b 75. Univ of Wales (Lamp) BA 97 Univ of Wales (Abth) PGCE 98. St Mich Coll Llan 11. **d** 13 **p** 14. NSM Hubberston *St D* 13–14; NSM Hubberston and Herbrandston 15; NSM Steynton 15–18; P-in-c 18–19; P-in-c Roose from 19; Dioc Dir of Educn from 18. *The Vicarage, Steynton, Milford Haven SA73 1AW* T: (01646) 692974 E: revjohncecil@btinternet.com

CECILE, Sister. *See* HARRISON, Cécile

CERMAKOVA, Ms Helena Maria Alija. b 43. **d** 88 **p** 95. NSM Roath *Llan* 88–91; Asst Chapl Univ Hosp of Wales NHS Trust 92–95; Chapl United Bris Healthcare NHS Trust 95–99; Lead Chapl Jersey Gp of Hosps 99–06; Tutor St Mich Coll Llan 06–12. *2 Royal Court, Den Crescent, Teignmouth TQ14 8BR* E: revhelena@icloud.com

CERRATTI, Christa Elisabeth. *See* PUMFREY, Christa Elisabeth

CERVAL-PENA, Anna Mary. b 81. Dur Univ BA 04. St Mellitus Coll 19. **d** 21. C Sutton, Wincle, Wildboarclough and Bosley *Ches* from 21. *4 Massey House, Hatton Street, Macclesfield SK11 6RZ* M: 07307-210080 E: curateanna@peakparishes.org.uk

CHABALA, Patches. b 78. St Jo Coll Nottm BA 11. **d** 11 **p** 12. C Plas Newton *Ches* 11–15; TV Hampreston *Sarum* from 15. *The Vicarage, 44 Albert Road, Ferndown BH22 9HE* T: (01202) 895099 M: 07791-2S0300

CHADD, Jeremy Denis. b 55. Jes Coll Cam BA 77 MA 81. Coll of Resurr Mirfield 78. **d** 81 **p** 82. C Seaton Hirst *Newc* 81–84; C N Gosforth 84–88; V Sunderland St Chad *Dur* 88–21; rtd 21. *8 Jubilee Estate, Ashington NE63 8SZ* T: (01670) 816719 E: jeremy.chadd@zoho.eu

CHADDER, Philip Thomas James. b 66. Ex Univ BA 88. Oak Hill Th Coll 01. **d** 03 **p** 04. C Gt Chesham *Ox* 03–07; Chapl HM Pris Brixton 07–15; Chapl Tr and Development Officer HM Pris Service from 15; PtO *St Alb* 16–21; *Ex* from 21. *Chaplaincy HQ, Post Point 8.34, 8th Floor Blue Zone, Ministry of Justice, 102 Petty France, London SW1H 9AJ* M: 07885-239812 E: phil.chadder@noms.gsi.gov.uk

CHADWICK, Canon Alan Michael. b 61. St Cath Coll Cam BA 83 MA 87. Wycliffe Hall Ox 96. **d** 98 **p** 99. C Hubberston *St D* 98–01; R 01–11; P-in-c Llanstadwell 11–16; P-in-c Llanstadwell and Burton and Rosemarket 16–19; P-in-c Roose from 19; AD from 10; Hon Can St D Cathl from 15. *The Vicarage, 68 Church Road, Llanstadwell, Milford Haven SA73 1EB* T: (01646) 600227 E: alanandmarychadwick@btinternet.com

CHADWICK, Carolyn Ann. b 52. Westhill Coll Birm CertEd 73 Birm Univ BMus 93 ABSM 78. WMMTC 04. **d** 07 **p** 08. NSM Pontesbury I and II Heref 07–08; NSM Minsterley 08–13; NSM Minsterley, Habberley and Hope w Shelve 13–17; PtO from 17; Lich from 20. *The Hermitage, Asterley, Minsterley,*

Shrewsbury SY5 0AW T/F: (01743) 792421 M: 07766-832547 E: carolyn.chadwick@gmail.com

CHADWICK, Canon Charles John Peter. b 59. Birm Univ BA 81 Southn Univ BTh 90. Sarum & Wells Th Coll 85. **d** 88 **p** 89. C Chalfont St Peter *Ox* 88–91; C Gt Marlow 91–93; TV Gt Marlow w Marlow Bottom, Lt Marlow and Bisham 93–95; P-in-c Stokenchurch and Ibstone 95–01; Asst Dir Chiltern Ch Tr Course 95–01; V Bridgwater St Mary and Chilton Trinity *B & W* 01–14; Preb Wells Cathl 11–14; Par Development Adv *Ox* from 14; Hon Can Ch Ch from 21. *Church House Oxford, Langford Locks, Kidlington OX5 1GF* T: (01865) 208200 E: charles.chadwick@oxford.anglican.org

CHADWICK, David Emmerson. b 73. Lincs & Humberside Univ BA 96. Ridley Hall Cam BTh 00. **d** 00 **p** 01. C Whickham *Dur* 00–06; V Ryhope from 06. *St Paul's Vicarage, Ryhope Street North, Sunderland SR2 0HH* T: 0191-523 7884

CHADWICK, David Guy Evelyn St Just. b 36. Bps' Coll Cheshunt 61. **d** 68 **p** 69. C Edmonton All SS *Lon* 68–71; C Edmonton St Mary w St Jo 71–72; C Greenhill St Jo 72–74; Bp's Dom Chapl Truro 74–79; Chapl Community of the Epiphany Truro 77–78; P-in-c Crantock *Truro* 79–83; R Clydebank *Glas* 83–87; R Renfrew 87–94; rtd 94. *Alverna, 1 Nithsdale Crescent, Bearsden, Glasgow G61 4DF*

CHADWICK, Helen Jane. *See* MARSHALL, Helen Jane

CHADWICK, Mark William Armstrong. b 67. Coll of Resurr Mirfield. **d** 05 **p** 06. C Colwyn Bay w Brynymaen *St As* 05–08; V Kerry, Llanmerewig, Dolfor and Mochdre 08–13; V Shrewsbury St Chad, St Mary and St Alkmund *Lich* 13–18; CF(V) 15–18; CF from 18. *c/o MOD Chaplains (Army)* T: (01264) 383430

CHAFFEY, Jane Frances. b 59. Somerville Coll Ox BA 80 MA 84 St Jo Coll Dur BA 86. Cranmer Hall Dur 84. **d** 88 **p** 94. Par Dn Roby *Liv* 88–90; NSM Finningley w Auckley *S'well* 95–96; PtO *Pet* 96–99; *Linc* 98–01; Chapl Wycombe Abbey Sch 08–18; PtO *Ox* from 18. *Stone Cottage, 133 Main Road, Naphill, High Wycombe HP14 4SA*

CHAFFEY, The Ven Jonathan Paul Michael. b 62. CB 18. St Chad's Coll Dur BA 83. Cranmer Hall Dur 84. **d** 87 **p** 88. C Gateacre *Liv* 87–90; Chapl RAF 90–14; Chapl-in-Chief RAF 14–18; Adn RAF 14–18; Can and Preb Linc Cathl 14–18; PtO *Ox* 18–20; Adn Ox and Can Res Ch Ch from 20. *Archdeacon's Lodgings, Christ Church, St Aldates, Oxford OX1 1DP* E: archdeacon.oxford.anglican.org

CHAFFEY, Michael Prosser. b 30. Lon Univ BA 51. St Steph Ho Ox 53. **d** 55 **p** 56. C Victoria Docks Ascension *Chelmsf* 55–59; C Leytonstone H Trin and St Aug Harrow Green 59–62; V Walthamstow St Mich 62–69; R Cov St Jo 69–85; P-in-c Cov St Thos 69–74; Hon C Bideford *Ex* 85; P-in-c Charlestown *Man* 85–88; V Sutton St Mich *York* 88–96; rtd 96; PtO *York* from 96. *17 Highcliffe Court, St Annes Road, Bridlington YO15 2JZ* T: (01262) 602758

CHALCRAFT, Mrs Sharon Anita. b 62. Ex Univ BTh 09. SWMTC 05. **d** 08 **p** 09. NSM Carbis Bay w Lelant, Towednack and Zennor Truro 08–09; NSM Breage w Godolphin and Germoe 09–14; Public Preacher from 14; NSM Godrevy from 15; C Maadi Egypt from 19. *Summerhill Cottage, Nancledra, Penzance TR20 8AY* T: (01736) 350779 M: 07889-406326 E: mrschalc@gmail.com

CHALLEN (née O'DONNELL), Paula Ella. b 72. ERMC 11. **d** 14 **p** 16. C Towcester w Caldecote and Easton Neston etc *Pet* 14–19; V from 19. *The Vicarage, Chantry Lane, Towcester NN12 6YY* E: revpaula@btinternet.com

CHALLEN, Canon Peter Bernard. b 31. Clare Coll Cam BA 56 MA 60 FRSA 94. Westcott Ho Cam 56. **d** 58 **p** 59. C Goole *Sheff* 58–61; V Dalton 61–67; Sen Ind Chapl *S'wark* 67–96; R *S'wark* Ch Ch 67–96; Hon Can *S'wark* Cathl 74–96; rtd 96; PtO *S'wark* 96–16. *Flat 12, Manormead, Tilford Road, Hindhead GU26 6RA* T: (01428) 601512 E: peterchallen@gmail.com

CHALLENDER, John Clifford. b 32. CITC 67. **d** 67 **p** 68. C Belfast St Luke *Conn* 67–70; Bp's V and Lib Kilkenny Cathl and C Kilkenny w Aghour and Odagh *C, F & O* 70–71; I Fenagh w Myshall and Kiltennel 71–76; I Fenagh w Myshall, Aghade and Ardoyne 76–79; I Crosspatrick Gp 79–95; Preb Ferns Cathl 85–88; Dioc Glebes Sec (Ferns) 86–91; Treas Ferns Cathl 88–91; Chan Ferns Cathl 91–95; I Killeshin w Cloydagh and Killabban 95–02; Can Ossory and Leighlin Cathls 00–02; rtd 02. *3 Adare Close, Killincarrig, Greystones, Co Wicklow, Republic of Ireland* T: (00353) (1) 201 7268 *or* 287 6359 M: 86-243 3678 E: challen1@eircom.net

CHALLENGER, Peter Nelson. b 33. St Jo Coll Cam BA 57 MA 61. Ripon Hall Ox 57. **d** 59 **p** 60. C Bushbury *Lich* 59–62; V Horsley Woodhouse *Derby* 62–67; V Derby St Barn 67–75; Brazil 75–80; TV New Windsor *Ox* 80–89; V Wootton (Boars Hill) 89–98; rtd 99; PtO *Ox* from 06. *39 Moorland Road, Witney OX28 6LS* T: (01993) 774630 E: peterleni@tiscali.co.uk

CHALLIS, Terence Peter. b 40. St Aid Birkenhead 65. **d** 68 **p** 69. C Billericay St Mary *Chelmsf* 68–71; Admin Sec Dio Maseno S Kenya 72–75; Bp's Chapl 72–74; P-in-c Sparkbrook Ch Ch *Birm* 76–80; V Enfield St Jas *Lon* 80–89; V Astley Bridge *Man* 89–98; P-in-c Leigh St Mary 98–02; P-in-c Leigh St Jo 98–02; rtd 02; PtO *Blackb* from 03. *48 Wilson Square, Thornton-Cleveleys FY5 1RF* T: (01253) 864534

CHALLIS, Canon William George. b 52. Keble Coll Ox BA 73 K Coll Lon MTh 75. Oak Hill Th Coll 73. **d** 75 **p** 76. C Islington St Mary *Lon* 75–79; Lect Trin Coll Bris 79–81; C Stoke Bishop *Bris* 79–81; Lect Oak Hill Th Coll 82; Burundi 82–85; P-in-c Bishopston *Bris* 86–89; TR 89–92; Vice-Prin Wycliffe Hall Ox 93–98; V Bitterne *Win* 98–03; Dir of Ords *Guildf* 03–19; Hon Can Guildf Cathl 13–19; rtd 19; PtO *B & W* from 20. *8 Kellaway Lane, Combe Down, Bath BA2 5EA* E: wg.challis@gmail.com

CHALMERS, Canon Brian. b 42. Oriel Coll Ox BA 64 MA 68 DPhil 70 BA 71 Lon Univ MA 06. Wycliffe Hall Ox 71. **d** 72 **p** 73. C Luton St Mary *St Alb* 72–76; Chapl Cranfield Inst of Tech 76–81; Chapl Kent Univ *Cant* 81–89; Six Preacher Cant Cathl 85–96; V Charing w Charing Heath and Lt Chart 89–05; AD Ashford 98–03; Hon Can Cant Cathl 97–05; rtd 05; PtO *Cant* from 05. *The Chantry, Pilgrims Lane, Chilham, Canterbury CT4 8AB* T: (01227) 730669

CHALMERS, Malcolm McMahon. b 65. Witwatersrand Univ BPrimEd 88 BEd 97 MA 08 ARSCM 13 FGMS 20. **d** 10 **p** 11. C Germiston S Africa 10–19; C Bracknell *Ox* from 19. *2 Buckhurst Hill, The Warren, Bracknell RG12 9YP* T: (01344) 249259 E: chantry.music@gmail.com

CHAMBERLAIN, Elizabeth Ann. b 58. St Jo Coll Nottm 08. **d** 10 **p** 11. C Walsall St Matt *Lich* 10–14; V Shenstone and Stonnall from 14. *The Vicarage, St John's Hill, Shenstone, Lichfield WS14 0JB* T: (01543) 480286 E: lizchamberlainuk@yahoo.co.uk

CHAMBERLAIN, Helen. b 66. **d** 09 **p** 10. NSM Farnham Royal w Hedgerley *Ox* 09–14; C The Cookhams from 14. *St John's House, Spring Lane, Cookham, Maidenhead SL6 9PN* T: (01628) 486744 E: revhec@zoho.com

CHAMBERLAIN, Preb Jane Louise. b 62. Bedf Coll Lon BSc 84. WEMTC 04. **d** 07 **p** 08. NSM Blagdon w Compton Martin and Ubley *B & W* 07–11; R 11–17; RD Chew Magna 14–17; Hd Min for Miss 19–21; Preb Wells Cathl 20–21; PtO from 21. *Thalassa, Upper Hermosa Road, Teignmouth TQ14 9JW* M: 07949-037548 E: revjanechamberlain@gmail.com

CHAMBERLAIN, The Ven Malcolm Leslie. b 69. York Univ BA 92 Liv Hope Univ MPhil 11. Wycliffe Hall Ox BTh 96. **d** 96 **p** 97. C Walsall Pleck and Bescot *Lich* 96–99; C Mossley Hill St Matt and St Jas *Liv* 99–02; Asst Chapl Liv Univ 99–02; Chapl Liv Univ and Dioc 18-30s Officer 02–08; P-in-c Wavertree St Mary 08–11; R 11–14; AD Toxteth and Wavertree 12–14; Adn Sheff and Rotherham from 14. *34 Wilson Road, Sheffield S11 8RN* T: 0114-418 3917 *or* (01709) 309110 E: malcolm.chamberlain@sheffield.anglican.org

✠**CHAMBERLAIN, The Rt Revd Nicholas Alan.** b 63. St Chad's Coll Dur BA 85 PhD 91 New Coll Edin BD 91. Edin Th Coll 88. **d** 91 **p** 92 **c** 15. C Cockerton *Dur* 91–94; C Newton Aycliffe 94–95; TV 95–96; TV Gt Aycliffe 96–98; P-in-c Burnmoor 98–06; Bp's Adv for CME 98–06; V Newc St Geo and St Hilda 06–15; Can and Preb Linc Cathl from 15; Suff Bp Grantham from 15. *The Bishops' Office, The Old Palace, Lincoln LN2 1PU* E: bishop.grantham@lincoln.anglican.org

CHAMBERLAIN, Paul Martin. b 74. Southn Univ MChem 97 Bris Univ PhD 02. Ripon Coll Cuddesdon 08. **d** 10 **p** 11. C Thame *Ox* 10–14; P-in-c Lee-on-the-Solent *Portsm* 14–18; V from 18; AD Gosport from 20. *8 Victoria Square, Lee-on-the-Solent PO13 9NF* T: (023) 9200 6184 E: revdr.paulchamberlain@gmail.com

CHAMBERLAIN, Roger Edward. b 53. Culham Coll of Educn BEd 75. Trin Coll Bris BA 87. **d** 87 **p** 88. C Plymouth Em w Efford *Ex* 87–90; C Selly Park St Steph and St Wulstan *Birm* 90–94; V Yardley St Cypr Hay Mill 94–96; PtO 96–10; P-in-c Baddesley Ensor w Grendon 10–14; V 14–19; rtd 19; PtO *Birm* from 19. *22 Hanbury Croft, Birmingham B27 6RX* M: 07749-266863 E: revrog@hotmail.co.uk

CHAMBERLAIN, Roy Herbert. b 44. Oak Hill Th Coll 91 NOC 95. **d** 96 **p** 97. C Gee Cross *Ches* 96–98; PtO *Blackb* 01–06. *125 Lancaster Road, Morecambe LA4 5QJ* T: (01524) 409070 E: rhchamberlain@btinternet.com

CHAMBERLAIN, Russell Charles. b 51. Univ of Wales (Cardiff) LLM 00. Oak Hill Th Coll 76. **d** 78 **p** 79. C Harold Hill St Geo *Chelmsf* 78–80; C Uckfield *Chich* 80–83; R Balcombe 83–90; V Okehampton w Inwardleigh *Ex* 90–94; TR Okehampton w Inwardleigh, Bratton Clovelly etc 94–01; RD Okehampton 93–98; R Wolborough and Ogwell 01–15; rtd 15; St Jo Hosp Heytesbury from 15. *6 Lea Mount Close,*

Dawlish EX7 9EP T: (01626) 864670 M: 07770-270019 E: russell.chamberlain70@gmail.com

CHAMBERLAIN, Ruth Margaret. b 66. Portsm Poly BSc 87 Open Univ BA 02 MA 10. ERMC 17. **d** 20 **p** 21. C Histon *Ely* from 20; C Impington from 20. *60 Impington Lane, Impington, Cambridge CB24 9NJ* M: 07759-816648 E: ruthm.chamberlain@gmail.com

CHAMBERLAIN, David John. b 56. MCMI 20. St Jo Coll Nottm. **d** 94 **p** 95. C Chatham St Phil and St Jas *Roch* 94–97; R Swardeston w E Carleton, Intwood, Keswick etc *Nor* 97–04; RD Humbleyard 03–04; R Milton *Ely* from 04; P-in-c Landbeach from 12; P-in-c Waterbeach from 12. *The Rectory, 24 Church Lane, Milton, Cambridge CB24 6AB* T: (01223) 861511 M: 07805-083300 E: rector@allsaintsmilton.org.uk *or* dc@revdc.net

CHAMBERLIN, John Malcolm. b 38. MRSC. Carl Dioc Tr Course 84. **d** 87 **p** 88. NSM Cockermouth w Embleton and Wythop *Carl* 87–97; Master St Mary Magd and H Jes Trust 97–05; Hon C Newc St Jo 98–05; rtd 05; PtO *Newc* from 05. *45 Wansbeck Avenue, North Shields NE30 3DU* T: 0191-253 0022 E: johnchamberlin@btinternet.com

CHAMBERLIN, Mrs Julia Joanne. b 61. UEA BA 02 PGCE 03. St Mellitus Coll BA 15. **d** 15 **p** 16. C Bluntisham cum Earith w Colne and Holywell etc *Ely* 15–16; C Ely 16–17; Chapl NW Anglia NHS Foundn Trust 17–21; Chapl Norfolk and Nor Univ Hosps NHS Foundn Trust from 21. *24 Church Lane, Milton, Cambridge CB24 6AB* T: (01223) 861511 *or* (01603) 286286 E: julia.chamberlin@nhs.net *or* julia@chamberlin.org.uk

CHAMBERLIN, Peter John. b 86. St Cath Coll Cam BA 09 MSci 09 MA 12. Oak Hill Th Coll BA 17. **d** 17 **p** 18. C New Ferry *Ches* 17–20; C Rock Ferry 17–20; C Woking St Jo *Guildf* from 20. *149 Hermitage Woods Crescent, Woking GU21 8UH* M: 07914-524278 E: peter.chamberlin@gmail.com

CHAMBERS, Canon Anthony Frederick John. b 40. ACII 69. Sarum Th Coll 69. **d** 71 **p** 72. C Hall Green St Pet *Birm* 71–74; C Holdenhurst *Win* 74–77; P-in-c Ropley w W Tisted 77–79; R Bishop's Sutton and Ropley and W Tisted 79–83; V Pokesdown St Jas 83–99; RD Bournemouth 95–99; P-in-c Heckfield w Mattingley and Rotherwick 99–02; V 02–04; Chapl N Foreland Lodge Sch Basingstoke 99–04; Hon Can Win Cathl 03–04; rtd 05; PtO *Ex* from 05. *4 J H Taylor Drive, Northam, Bideford EX39 1TU* T: (01237) 421306 E: anthonychambers701@gmail.com

CHAMBERS, Miss Barbara Ada. b 51. **d** 98 **p** 99. OLM Gt Crosby St Luke *Liv* 98–15; rtd 15; PtO *Liv* from 17. *12 Vale Road, Crosby, Liverpool L23 5RZ* T: 0151-924 5851

CHAMBERS, Mrs Barbara Mary Sinnott. b 43. SRN 65 RM 67 HVCert 75 Keele Univ TCert 77. WMMTC 87. **d** 93 **p** 94. Par Dn Blurton *Lich* 93–94; C 94–96; Chapl Asst Qu Medical Cen Nottm Univ Hosp NHS Trust 96–03; Chapl 03–07; Chapl United Lincs Hosps NHS Trust from 07; PtO *Linc* 17–19. *51 Mill Lane, Woodhall Spa LN10 6QZ* T: (01526) 354872 E: barbarachambers51@gmail.com

CHAMBERS, Carl Michael. b 68. Pemb Coll Cam BA 90 Oak Hill Th Coll BA 00 MA 02. **d** 01 **p** 02. C Hove Bp Hannington Memorial Ch *Chich* 01–05; Pioneer Min 05–16; V Wilmington *Roch* from 19. *The Vicarage, 1 Curate's Walk, Dartford DA2 7BJ* E: vicar.wilmington@gmail.com

CHAMBERS, Canon John Richard. b 50. EMMTC 01. **d** 04 **p** 05. C Farnsfield *S'well* 04–07; C Kirklington w Hockerton 04–07; C Bilsthorpe 04–07; C Eakring 04–07; C Maplebeck 04–07; C Winkburn 04–07; P-in-c Flintham 08–10; P-in-c Car Colston w Screveton 08–10; R Richmond w Hudswell and Downholme and Marske *Leeds* 10–17; AD Richmond 15–16; Hon Can Ripon Cathl 16–17; rtd 17; PtO *S'well* from 18; AD Newark and S'well from 21. *27 Fairway, Newark NG24 4RN* M: 07875-348245 E: john.chambers@southwell.anglican.org

CHAMBERS, Marion Patricia. *See* HINKS, Marion Patricia

CHAMBERS, Canon Peter Lewis. b 43. Imp Coll Lon BScEng 64. St Steph Ho Ox 64. **d** 66 **p** 67. C Llandaff w Capel Llanilltern *Llan* 66–70; Chapl Ch in Wales Youth Coun 70–73; Youth Chapl *Bris* 73–78; V Bedminster St Mich 78–84; RD Bedminster 81–84; Adv Ho of Bps Marriage Educn Panel Gen Syn 84–88; Dir Dioc Coun for Soc Resp *Guildf* 88–94; Hon Can Guildf Cathl 89–94; Dir Tr *Sheff* 95–00; P-in-c Harthill and Thorpe Salvin 00–07; Dioc Min Teams Officer 00–04; Hon Can Sheff Cathl 96–07; rtd 07; PtO *Bris* from 08. *5 Henley Grove, Bristol BS9 4EQ* T: 0117-307 9427

CHAMBERS, Rachel Jill. *See* GANNEY, Rachel Jill

CHAMBERS, Robert Anthony. b 46. **d** 05 **p** 06. OLM Kirkburton *Wakef* 05–12; rtd 12; PtO *Glas* from 12. *1/2 Kersland, South Street, Houston, Johnstone PA6 7ET*

CHAMBERS, Simon Paul. b 65. Liv Univ BEng 87 PhD 91. Ripon Coll Cuddesdon 00. **d** 02 **p** 03. C Parkstone St Pet and St Osmund w Branksea *Sarum* 02–05; P-in-c Ashwell w Hinxworth and Newnham *St Alb* 05–10; TV Shaftesbury *Sarum* 10–19; RD Blackmore Vale 17–19; TR Clarendon from 19. *The Rectory, West Winterslow, Salisbury SP5 1RE* T: (01980) 862231 E: simon@clarendoncofe.org

CHAMBERS, Timothy John Essex. b 69. St Jo Coll Cam MA 95. St Mellitus Coll BA 16. **d** 16 **p** 17. C W Bridgford *S'well* 16–20; V Whatton w Aslockton, Hawksworth, Scarrington etc from 20. *The Vicarage, Main Street, Aslockton, Nottingham NG13 9AL* M: 07946-526569

CHAMP, Darren David. b 60. Kent Univ BA 93. Linc Th Coll MA 95. **d** 95 **p** 96. C Ashford *Cant* 95–97; PtO 02–03. *154 Beaver Road, Ashford TN23 7SS* T: (01233) 663090 E: daz@dazchamp.co.uk

CHAMPION, Arthur. b 51. Loughb Univ BSc 76 Aston Univ MSc 77 CEng 88 MIMechE 88 FIOSH 88. WEMTC 03. **d** 08 **p** 09. NSM Badgeworth, Shurdington and Witcombe w Bentham *Glouc* 08–13; NSM Bourton-on-the-Water w Clapton etc 13–14; Environmental Adviser 14–21; Public Preacher 14–21; NSM Churn Valley 15–21; rtd 21. *18 George Rodgers Close, Hulland Ward, Ashbourne DE6 3GY* M: 07955-475303 E: championarthur@gmail.com

CHAMPNEYS, Michael Harold. b 46. LRAM 66 GRSM 67 ARCO 67. Linc Th Coll 69. **d** 72 **p** 73. C Poplar *Lon* 72–73; C Bow w Bromley St Leon 73–75; P-in-c Bethnal Green St Barn 75–76; C Tewkesbury w Walton Cardiff *Glouc* 76–78; V Bedford Park *Lon* 78–83; V Shepshed *Leic* 84–87; Community Educn Tutor Bolsover 88–93; PtO *Derby* 90–92; NSM Bolsover 92–93; V Potterspury, Furtho, Yardley Gobion and Cosgrove *Pet* 93–98; RD Towcester 94–98; V Shap w Swindale and Bampton w Mardale *Carl* 98–01; R Calow and Sutton cum Duckmanton *Derby* 01–10; rtd 10; P-in-c Wentworth *Sheff* 15–18. *1 New Road, Holymoorside, Chesterfield S42 7EW* T: (01246) 566172 E: michaelchampneys@yahoo.co.uk

CHANCE, David Newton. b 44. Univ of Wales (Lamp) BA 68. St Steph Ho Ox 68. **d** 70 **p** 71. C Selsdon St Jo w St Fran *Cant* 70–73; C Plymstock *Ex* 73–77; P-in-c Northam 77–79; TR Northam w Westward Ho! and Appledore 79–93; V Banstead *Guildf* 93–10; rtd 10; PtO *Cant* 11–21; *Ex* from 21. *4 Kingfisher Drive, Barnstaple EX32 8QW* T: (01271) 344803 E: andrea3david@yahoo.co.uk

CHAND, Richard. b 62. SAOMC 02. **d** 05 **p** 06. NSM Headington St Mary *Ox* 05–09; NSM Cowley St Jas 09–16; P-in-c Braintree St Paul *Chelmsf* from 20. *St Paul's Parsonage, 1A Hay Lane South, Braintree CM7 3DY* T: (01376) 619515 M: 07590-431903 E: richardwchand@outlook.com

CHANDLER, Anthony. b 43. Lon Inst of Educn CertEd 65. EAMTC 94. **d** 97 **p** 98. Dioc Youth Officer *Ely* 96–00; NSM March St Mary 97–00; R 00–12; P-in-c 12–15; NSM March St Pet 97–00; R 00–12; P-in-c 12–15; rtd 12; PtO *Ely* from 15. *17 St Peter's Road, March PE15 9NA* T/F: (01354) 652894 E: anthonychandler@btinternet.com

CHANDLER, Barbara Janet. b 58. Newc Univ BMedSci 79 MB, BS 82 MD 93 FRCP 00. NEOC 04. **d** 07 **p** 08. NSM Ponteland *Newc* 07–11; PtO *Mor* from 11. *Highfield House, Lentran, Inverness IV3 8RN* T: (01463) 704393 E: chandlernorth@gmail.com

CHANDLER, Derek Edward. b 67. Southn Univ BTh 91 Nottm Univ MDiv 93. Linc Th Coll 91. **d** 93 **p** 94. C Bitterne Park *Win* 93–97; C Sholing 97–00; R Emmer Green w Caversham Park *Ox* 00–21; Chapl Coll of St Barn Lingfield from 21. *The College of St Barnabas, Blackberry Lane, Lingfield RH7 6NJ* E: rev.derek.chandler@virgin.net

CHANDLER, Ian Nigel. b 65. K Coll Lon BD 89 AKC 89. Chich Th Coll 92. **d** 92 **p** 93. C Hove *Chich* 92–96; Bp's Dom Chapl 96–00; V Haywards Heath St Rich 00–10; RD Cuckfield 04–06; Adn Plymouth *Ex* 10–18; PtO *Lon* 19–20; V E Finchley All SS from 20. *All Saints' Vicarage, 1 Twyford Avenue, London N2 9NH* T: (020) 8893 9315 E: ianchandler@hotmail.com

CHANDLER, John. b 49. ACIB 73. NTMTC 05. **d** 07 **p** 08. NSM Colchester St Mich Myland *Chelmsf* 07–19; P-in-c Wormingford, Mt Bures and Lt Horkesley 14–19; NSM Colchester St Luke 18–19; NSM Langham w Boxted 18–19; NSM W Bergholt and Gt Horkesley 18–19; rtd 19; PtO *Chelmsf* from 19. *4 Longdryve, Wavell Avenue, Colchester CO2 7HH* T: (01206) 366930 M: 07951-160558 E: john@mylandchurch.org.uk

CHANDLER, John Charles. b 46. Solicitor. Oak Hill Th Coll 91. **d** 94 **p** 95. C Tonbridge St Steph *Roch* 94–98; V Felsted and Lt Dunmow *Chelmsf* 98–05; V Hildenborough *Roch* 05–13; rtd 13; PtO *Nor* from 13. *1 Beach Close, Overstrand, Cromer NR27 0PJ* T: (01263) 576970 E: chandlerjandm@gmail.com

CHANDLER, The Very Revd Michael John. b 45. Lambeth STh 80 K Coll Lon PhD 87. Linc Th Coll 70. **d** 72 **p** 73. C Cant St Dunstan w H Cross 72–75; C Margate St Jo 75–78; V Newington w Bobbing and Iwade 78–83; P-in-c Hartlip w Stockbury 80–83; V Newington w Hartlip and Stockbury 83–88; RD Sittingbourne 84–88; R Hackington 88–95; RD Cant 94–95; Can Res Cant Cathl 95–03; Dean Ely 03–11; rtd 11; PtO *Cant* from 12; Prior St Jo Hosp Cant from 16. *218 Tankerton Road, Whitstable CT5 2AT* T: (01227) 262937 E: deanemeritus@gmail.com

CHANDLER, Quentin David. b 62. Anglia Ruskin Univ MA 08 DProf 15. Aston Tr Scheme 87 Trin Coll Bris BA 92. **d** 92 **p** 93. C Goldington *St Alb* 92–96; TV Rushden w Newton Bromswold *Pet* 96–00; V Rushden St Pet 00–03; Dir Tr for Past Assts 03–08; Dir Studies Dioc Lay Min Course 08–11; R Burton Latimer 03–11; CME Officer and Lic Lay Min Officer 11–16; C Gt w Lt Harrowden and Orlingbury and Isham etc 12–16; Dir of Ords *St Alb* 16–20; P-in-c Marston Morteyne w Lidlington 16–18; R 18–20; Hon Can St Alb 18–20; Dioc Dir of Ords *Ox* from 20. *1 Cavalry Path, Aylesbury HP19 9RP* M: 07909-542060 E: quentin.chandler@oxford.anglican.org

CHANDLER, Samantha Jane. b 65. SCTEI 17. **d** 20 **p** 21. C Hartley Wintney, Elvetham, Winchfield etc *Win* from 20. *Hinon Lodge, Brackley Avenue, Hartley Wintney, Hook RG27 8QX* M: 07387-477005 E: sam.chandler@stjonhshw.org.uk

CHANDLER, Stephen Michael. b 54. NTMTC. **d** 09 **p** 10. NSM Victoria Docks St Luke *Chelmsf* 09–12; NSM W Ham 12–18; PtO from 19. *3 Charnock Close, Kirby Cross, Frinton-on-Sea CO13 0RT* E: rev.stephen@hotmail.co.uk

CHANDLER, Susan May. b 54. Newman Univ BA 15. WMMTC 06. **d** 09 **p** 10. NSM Olton *Birm* 09–20; NSM Solihull from 20. *14 Hollyberry Avenue, Solihull B91 3UA* T: 0121-709 1512 M: 07970-791288 E: j14chand@sky.com

CHANDRA, Kevin Douglas Naresh. b 65. Lon Bible Coll BA 91. Qu Coll Birm 94. **d** 96 **p** 97. C Walmley *Birm* 96–00; P-in-c Erdington St Chad 00–02; TV Erdington 02–05; Chapl St Pet Sch Ex 06–15; V Bampton, Morebath, Clayhanger, Petton etc *Ex* from 15. *The New Vicarage, Station Road, Bampton, Tiverton EX16 9NG* T: (01398) 332885 E: hukeleymissioncommunity@gmail.com

✠**CHANG HIM, The Most Revd French Kitchener.** b 38. OBE 14. Trin Coll Toronto LTh 75 Hon DD 91 Univ of Wales MPhil 10. Lich Th Coll. **d** 62 **p** 63 **c** 79. C Goole *Sheff* 62–63; R Praslin Seychelles 63–67; C Sheff St Leon Norwood 67–68; C Mahé Cathl Mauritius 68–70; Missr Praslin Seychelles 70–73; R S Mahé 73–74; R Anse Royale St Sav 73–79; Adn Seychelles 73–79; R Praslin and S Mahé Seychelles 75–79; P-in-c St Paul's Cathl 77–79; Bp Seychelles 79–04; Dean Prov of Indian Ocean 83–84; Abp Indian Ocean 84–95; Bp in charge Glacis St Jo Seychelles 05–20. *PO Box 44, Victoria, Seychelles* T: (00248) 248151 E: bishop@seychelles.net

CHANNER, Christopher Kendall. b 42. K Coll Lon BD 64 AKC 64. St Boniface Warminster 64. **d** 65 **p** 66. C Norbury St Steph *Cant* 65–68; C S Elmsall *Wakef* 68–70; V Dartford St Edm *Roch* 70–75; Chapl Joyce Green Hosp Dartford 73–75; V Bromley St Andr *Roch* 75–81; V Langton Green 81–94; Chapl Holmewood Ho Sch Tunbridge Wells 94–98; P-in-c Lewes All SS, St Anne, St Mich and St Thos *Chich* 98–00; R Lewes St Mich and St Thos at Cliffe w All SS 00–08; rtd 08; PtO *Chich* from 16. *Abbots Croft, Lower Lake, Battle TN33 0BE* T: (01424) 777396

CHANT, Harry. b 40. Oak Hill Th Coll. **d** 78 **p** 79. C Heatherlands St Jo *Sarum* 78–81; P-in-c Bramshaw 81–83; P-in-c Landford w Plaitford 81–83; R Bramshaw and Landford w Plaitford 83–87; V Fareham St Jo *Portsm* 87–00; rtd 00; PtO *Truro* from 00. *141 Pendeen Park, Helston TR13 0SL* T/F: (01326) 561916 E: tellharrychant@aol.com

CHANTREY, Preb David Frank. b 48. K Coll Cam BA 70 PhD 73 MA 74. Westcott Ho Cam 83. **d** 86 **p** 87. C Wordsley *Lich* 86–89; C Beckbury 89–90; P-in-c 90–93; C Badger 89–90; P-in-c 90–93; C Kemberton, Sutton Maddock and Stockton 89–90; P-in-c 90–93; C Ryton 89–90; P-in-c 90–93; R Beckbury, Badger, Kemberton, Ryton, Stockton etc 93–08; TR Wrockwardine Deanery 08–16; RD Wrockwardine 03–16; Preb Lich Cathl 99–16; rtd 16; PtO *Lich* from 18; *Heref* from 18. *85 Victoria Road, Bridgnorth WV16 4LD* T: (01746) 218892 M: 07785-524495 E: david01wdtm@talktalk.net

CHANTRY, Ms Helen Fiona. b 59. Bradf Univ BSc 82 Leeds Univ CertEd 83. Trin Coll Bris BA 89. **d** 89 **p** 94. NSM Hyde St Geo *Ches* 89–92; Dioc Youth Officer 92–00; NSM Barrow 94–99; C Acton and Worleston, Church Minshull etc 00–04; P-in-c Audlem 04–11; Bp's Adv for Women in Min 05–09; V Wybunbury and Audlem w Doddington 11–20; RD Nantwich 13–20; Hon Can Ches Cathl 10–20;

R Hucknall *S'well* from 20. *The Rectory, 60 Annesley Road, Hucknall, Nottingham NG15 7DE* T: 0115-874 7369 E: helenchantry@btopenworld.com

CHANTRY, Peter Thomas. b 62. Bradf Univ BSc 83. Trin Coll Bris BA 89. **d** 89 **p** 90. C Hyde St Geo *Ches* 89–92; Dioc Youth Officer 91–99; P-in-c Barrow 94–99; R Nantwich 99–12; PtO from 12; Hon C Edstaston, Fauls, Prees, Tilstock and Whixall *Lich* 13; V Betley 13–20; V Madeley 13–20; R Skegby w Teversal *S'well* from 20. *The Rectory, 60 Annesley Road, Hucknall, Nottingham NG15 7DE* T: (01623) 558800 E: peterchantry@hotmail.com

CHAPLIN, Colin. b 33. Edin Dioc NSM Course 74. **d** 76 **p** 77. NSM Penicuik *Edin* 76–91; P-in-c Peebles 89–90; NSM Bathgate 91–95; rtd 95; Asst P Edin St Mark 97–00; Asst P Innerleithen from 00; Asst P Peebles from 00; P-in-c Galashiels 02–03. *26 Broomhill Road, Penicuik, Edinburgh EH26 9EE* T: (01968) 672050

CHAPLIN, Canon Douglas Archibald. b 59. Em Coll Cam BA 81 MA 91 Birm Univ MPhil 98. St Jo Coll Nottm. **d** 86 **p** 87. C Glouc St Geo w Whaddon 86–89; C Lydney w Aylburton 89–93; R Worc St Clem 93–01; TV Droitwich Spa 01–13; Dioc Miss Development Officer 13–19; Dir Reader Tr 04–19; Discipleship and Lay Tr Officer *Worc* from 19; Hon Can Worc Cathl from 19. *16 Lowesmoor Wharf, Lowesmoor, Worcester WR1 2RS* T: (01905) 20537 M: 07858-501120 E: doug.chaplin@cofe-worcester.org.uk

CHAPLIN, Paul. b 57. Hull Univ BA 80 PGCE 81 K Coll Lon MA 89. St Steph Ho Ox 85. **d** 87 **p** 88. C Ex St Jas 87–90; C Wokingham St Paul *Ox* 90–98; V Stratfield Mortimer and Mortimer W End etc from 98. *The Vicarage, 10 The Avenue, Mortimer, Reading RG7 3QY* T: 0118-933 1718 *or* 933 3704 E: admin@mortimerbenefice.co.uk

CHAPMAN, Andrew John. b 81. Leeds Univ BA 03 St Jo Coll Dur BA 09. Cranmer Hall Dur 06. **d** 09 **p** 10. C Hykeham *Linc* 09–12; Chapl RAF from 12. *Chaplaincy Services (RAF), HQ Air Command, RAF High Wycombe HP14 4UE* T: (01494) 496800 E: a.j.chapman@live.co.uk

CHAPMAN, Barry Frank. b 48. Trin Coll Bris 83. **d** 82 **p** 83. NSM Bradford-on-Avon Ch Ch *Sarum* 82–11; NSM N Bradford on Avon and Villages 11–18; Assoc Chapl Bath Univ *B&W* 83–18; rtd 18. *16 Church Acre, Bradford-on-Avon BA15 1RL* T: (01225) 866861 E: ann.barry.chapman@btinternet.com

CHAPMAN, Canon Christopher Robin. b 37. Ripon Hall Ox 72. **d** 73 **p** 74. C Kidbrooke St Jas *S'wark* 73–77; V Corton *Nor* 77–80; V Hopton 77–80; V Hopton w Corton 80–92; RD Lothingland 80–86; P-in-c Loddon w Sisland 92–93; P-in-c Loddon, Sisland w Hales and Heckingham 93–98; P-in-c Chedgrave w Hardley and Langley 97–98; V Loddon, Sisland, Chedgrave, Hardley and Langley 98–03; RD Loddon 95–98; Hon Can Nor Cathl 96–03; Chapl Langley Sch Nor 00–03; rtd 04; PtO *Chelmsf* 04–06; *St E* 06–21. *Preveli, 16 Riley Close, Ipswich IP1 5QD* T: (01473) 462109 E: canons.chapman@btinternet.com

CHAPMAN, Colin Gilbert. b 38. St Andr Univ MA 60 Lon Univ BD 62 Birm Univ MPhil 94. Ridley Hall Cam 62. **d** 64 **p** 65. C Edin St Jas 64–67; Asst Chapl Cairo Cathl Egypt 68–73; Tutor Crowther Hall CMS Tr Coll Selly Oak 73–75; Prin 90–97; Lebanon 75–82; Chapl Limassol St Barn 82–83; Lect Trin Coll Bris 83–90; Dir Faith to Faith Consultancy 97–99; Lect Near E Sch of Th Lebanon 99–03; rtd 04; PtO *Ely* from 07. *12 Daniels Park, Milton, Cambridge CB24 6UD* T: (01223) 860317 E: beirutchapman@hotmail.com

CHAPMAN, Mrs Elizabeth Ann. b 57. SEITE 05. **d** 09 **p** 10. NSM Gillingham St Mary *Roch* 09–11; Chapl Pilgrims Hospice Cant 11–13; NSM Cant St Pet w St Alphege and St Marg etc 11–13; PtO 13–15; Chapl Ellenor Hospice Gravesend 15–17; PtO *Roch* from 17. *93 Hempstead Road, Hempstead, Gillingham ME7 3RH* T: (01634) 233477 M: 07961-337083 E: l.chapman431@btinternet.com

CHAPMAN, Preb Gorran. b 55. Dur Univ BA. Westcott Ho Cam 78. **d** 80 **p** 81. C Par *Truro* 80–82; C Kenwyn 82–84; P-in-c Penwerris 84–89; V 89–92; V Torquay St Martin Barton *Ex* 92–21; Preb Ex Cathl 07–21; rtd 21; PtO *Truro* from 21; *Ex* from 21. *Santosa, 11 Trencrom Lane, Carbis Bay, St Ives TR26 2TP*

CHAPMAN, Guy Godfrey. b 33. Southn Univ BSc 57. Clifton Th Coll 60. **d** 62 **p** 63. C Chadderton Ch Ch *Man* 62–67; V Edgeside 67–70; P-in-c Shipton Bellinger *Win* 70–72; V 72–83; RD Andover 75–85; Hon Can Win Cathl 79–91; R Over Wallop w Nether Wallop 83–91; V Ambrosden w Merton and Piddington *Ox* 91–00; RD Bicester and Islip 95–00; rtd 00; PtO *Sarum* 01–16; *Win* 01–15. *65 St Ann Place, Salisbury SP1 2SU* T: (01722) 335339

CHAPMAN, Henry Davison. b 31. Bris Univ BA 55. Tyndale Hall Bris 52. **d** 56 **p** 57. C St Helens St Mark *Liv* 56–60; R

Clitheroe St Jas *Blackb* 60–67; V Tipton St Martin *Lich* 67–68; SW Area Sec CPAS 68–72; V Eccleston St Luke *Liv* 72–78; P-in-c Ringshall w Battisford, Barking w Darmsden etc *St E* 78–80; R 80–93; RD Bosmere 87–91; rtd 93; PtO *Sarum* 93–10. *Daracombe, 4 The Clays, Market Lavington, Devizes SN10 4AY* T: (01380) 813774

CHAPMAN (née CRAVEN), Canon Janet Elizabeth. b 58. St Jo Coll Dur BSc 80 MA 92. Cranmer Hall Dur 84. **d** 87 **p** 95. Par Dn Darlington St Cuth *Dur* 87–92; NSM Edin Gd Shep 93–95; NSM Long Marston and Rufforth w Moor Monkton and Hessay *York* 95–98; Chapl Qu Ethelburga's Coll York 97–99; Chapl Harrogate Ladies' Coll 00; P-in-c Banbury *Ox* 01–08; Can Res Birm Cathl 08–16; R Northfield from 16; Hon Can Birm Cathl from 16. *The Rectory, Rectory Road, Birmingham B31 2NA* T: 0121-475 1518 E: stlaurence@btconnect.com

CHAPMAN, John Brown. b 54. Strathclyde Univ BSc 76 Lon Bible Coll BA 80. NTMTC 00. **d** 02 **p** 03. C W Ealing St Jo w St Jas *Lon* 02–05; C Northolt St Mary 05–08; Chapl for Internat Chs 08–13; Chapl Sharjah and Asst Chapl Dubai UAE 13–14; Chapl Barcelona *Eur* from 14. *St George, Horacio 38, 08022 Barcelona, Spain* T: (0034) 934 178 867 F: 932 128 433 E: info@st-georges-church.com

CHAPMAN (née WHITFIELD), Mrs Joy Verity. b 46. SRN 67 SCM 71. Trin Coll Bris BA 88. **d** 88 **p** 94. C Littleover *Derby* 88–92; Par Dn Bucknall and Bagnall *Lich* 92–94; TV 94–97; Chapl LOROS Hospice 97–03; rtd 03; PtO *Leic* from 03. *15 Templar Way, Rothley, Leicester LE7 7RB* T: 0116-230 1994

CHAPMAN, Mrs Lesley. b 61. NEOC 02. **d** 05 **p** 06. C Fenham St Jas and St Basil *Newc* 05–09; P-in-c Kenton Ascension 09–16; P-in-c Riding Mill 16–19; Bp's Adv for Spirituality and Spiritual Direction from 16; AD Corbridge 17–19. *Address temp unknown* E: lesley.chapman414@btopenworld.com

CHAPMAN, Mrs Linda. b 46. Lon Univ BSc 67 Lon Inst of Educn PGCE 68. Guildf Dioc Min Course 98. **d** 00 **p** 01. NSM Ewell St Fran *Guildf* 00–04; NSM Cheswardine, Childs Ercall, Hales, Hinstock etc *Lich* 04–14; TV 11–14; rtd 14; PtO *Newc* from 15. *Dalrigh, 12 Lords Mount, Berwick upon Tweed TD15 1LY* T: (01289) 307466 M: 07956-429116 E: rev.linda@btinternet.com

CHAPMAN, Linda Rosa. *See* HILLIER, Linda Rosa

CHAPMAN, Miss Lynn Marie. b 71. Coll of Ripon & York St Jo BEd 93 Cant Ch Ch Univ MA 98. ERMC 08. **d** 11 **p** 12. C Sheringham *Nor* 11–14; P-in-c Brooke, Kirstead, Mundham w Seething and Thwaite from 14; Asst Dioc Dir of Ords from 18; PtO *St E* from 19. *The Vicarage, 105 The Street, Brooke, Norwich NR15 1JU* T: (01508) 558479 E: chapman.lynn@btinternet.com

CHAPMAN, Margaret. *See* FLINTOFT-CHAPMAN, Margaret

CHAPMAN, Prof Mark David. b 60. Trin Coll Ox MA 83 DPhil 89. Ox Min Course 93. **d** 94 **p** 95. Lect Ripon Coll Cuddesdon from 92; Vice-Prin from 02; Prof Hist of Modern Th Ox Univ from 15; NSM Dorchester *Ox* 94–99; NSM Wheatley 99–14; NSM Garsington, Cuddesdon and Horspath from 14; Can Th Truro Cathl from 16. *Ripon College, Cuddesdon, Oxford OX44 9EX* T: (01865) 877405 E: mark.chapman@rcc.ac.uk

CHAPMAN, Nigel Leonard. b 58. York St Jo Coll MA 02. Cranmer Hall Dur 04. **d** 05 **p** 06. Dioc Youth Officer *York* 00–16; NSM Coxwold and Husthwaite 05–16; V Filey from 16. *5 Belle Vue Crescent, Filey YO14 9AD* T: (01723) 512645 M: 07877-793179 E: fileyvicar@gmail.com

CHAPMAN, Peter Harold White. b 40. AKC 64. **d** 65 **p** 66. C Havant *Portsm* 65–69; C Stanmer w Falmer and Moulsecoomb *Chich* 69–73; Chapl RN 73–86; Chapl Chigwell Sch Essex 86–90; P-in-c Stapleford Tawney w Theydon Mt *Chelmsf* 87–01. *Unit F, 33/F, Block 6, Tung Chung Crescent, 2 Mei Tung Street, Lantau, Hong Kong, China* E: phwchapman@aol.com

CHAPMAN, Peter John. b 50. ERMC 05. **d** 08 **p** 09. NSM Lt Barningham, Blickling, Edgefield etc *Nor* 08–11; NSM Trunch 11–12; NSM Roughton and Felbrigg, Metton, Sustead etc 12–17; NSM Aylsham and Distr 17–19; Chapl Qu Eliz Hosp King's Lynn NHS Foundn Trust 12–14; PtO *Nor* from 19. *Pump Cottage, The Street, Bessingham, Norwich NR11 7JR* T: (01263) 577782

CHAPMAN, Peter John. b 33. Dur Univ BA 56. Cranmer Hall Dur. **d** 59 **p** 60. C Boulton *Derby* 59–62; Uganda 63–70; P-in-c Southampton St Matt *Win* 71–73; TV Southampton (City Cen) 73–78; V Bilston St Leon *Lich* 78–79; P-in-c Bilston St Mary 78–79; TR Bilston 80–98; RD Wolverhampton 89–98; rtd 99; PtO *Glouc* 99–16; *Worc* 99–16. *Flat 10, Manormead Supported Housing, Tilford Road, Hindhead GU26 6RA*

CHAPMAN, Raymond. b 41. Linc Th Coll 68. **d** 71 **p** 72. C Dronfield *Derby* 71–74; C Delaval *Newc* 75–76; TV Whorlton 76–79; V Newc St Hilda 79–83; V Blyth St Cuth 83–89; Hon C Fareham SS Pet and Paul *Portsm* 95–98; PtO 98–00 and from 05; C Purbrook 00–05. *Address withheld by request*

CHAPMAN, Canon Rex Anthony. b 38. Univ Coll Lon BA 62 St Edm Hall Ox BA 64 MA 68. Wells Th Coll 64. **d** 65 **p** 66. C Stourbridge St Thos *Worc* 65–68; Chapl Aber Univ *Ab* 68–78; Can St Andr Cathl 76–78; Bp's Adv for Educn *Carl* 78–85; Dir of Educn 85–04; Can Res Carl Cathl 78–04; rtd 04; LtO *Ab* from 06; Chapl to The Queen 97–08. *Myreside Cottage, Finzean, Banchory AB31 6NB* T: (01330) 850485 E: rex.chapman@btinternet.com

CHAPMAN, Robert Bertram. b 68. St Jo Coll Nottm BA 00 Lambeth PhD 15. **d** 00 **p** 01. C Daybrook *S'well* 00–03; P-in-c Colwick and Netherfield 03–11; V Hanwell St Thos *Lon* from 11. *St Thomas's Vicarage, 182 Boston Road, London W7 2AD* T: (020) 3302 1040 E: fatherrobert@thomashanwell.org.uk *or* robertbchapman68@gmail.com

CHAPMAN, Rodney Andrew. b 53. AKC 75. St Aug Coll Cant 75. **d** 76 **p** 77. C Hartlepool St Aid *Dur* 76–81; LtO 81–83; C Owton Manor 83–87; P-in-c Kelloe 87–92; V Sharlston *Wakef* 92–01; V Stainland w Outlane 01–14; Stainland and Outlane *Leeds* from 14; C Elland *Wakef* 06–14; *Leeds* from 14. *The Vicarage, 345 Stainland Road, Stainland, Halifax HX4 9HF* T: (01422) 311848 E: stainlandvicarage@btinternet.com

CHAPMAN, Roger. b 60. Leic Univ BSc 82 Anglia Ruskin Univ BA 09. Westcott Ho Cam 04 Seabury-Western Th Sem 05. **d** 06 **p** 07. C Norton *St Alb* 06–09; P-in-c Eaton Bray w Edlesborough 09–10; rtd 10; PtO *St Alb* 11–18 and 19–21; Hon C Cheshunt 18–19; Hon C Bishop's Hatfield, Lemsford and N Mymms from 21. *13 The Pastures, Hatfield AL10 8PB* T: (01707) 882509 M: 07905-391890 E: revrogerchapman@gmail.com *or* rchapman27@virginmedia.com

CHAPMAN, Roger John. b 34. AKC 58. **d** 59 **p** 60. C Guildf Ch 59–61; Kenya 61–67; R S Milford *York* 68–77; RD Selby 72–77; V Beverley St Mary 77–88; RD Beverley 85–88; V Desborough *Pet* 88–95; R Brampton Ash w Dingley and Braybrooke 88–95; rtd 95; PtO *York* 95–15. *14 Scrubwood Lane, Beverley HU17 7BE* T: (01482) 881267

CHAPMAN, Ruth Elizabeth. b 84. St Jo Coll Dur BA 13. Cranmer Hall Dur 10. **d** 13 **p** 14. C Queen Thorne *Sarum* 13–17; PtO 17–18; C Preston Plucknett *B & W* from 19. *1 Old School Close, Yeovil BA21 3UB* M: 07739-161120 E: revruth@mail.com

CHAPMAN, Canon Sarah Jean. b 55. Lon Univ DipCOT 77. Sarum & Wells Th Coll 86. **d** 89 **p** 94. NSM Rogate w Terwick and Trotton w Chithurst *Chich* 89–94; NSM Easebourne 94–96; PtO *Portsm* 96–97; V Sheet 97–02; V Bitterne Park *Win* 02–12; Chapl The Living Well and Dioc Adv for Healing and Wholeness *Cant* 12–19; Hon Can Cant Cathl 16–19; rtd 19; PtO *Portsm* from 20. *2 Wyndham Mews, Portsmouth PO1 2NY* T: (023) 9204 4542 E: revsarah@sargil.co.uk

CHAPMAN, Stephen Gerard. b 61. Man Univ BSc 83 Sheff Univ BA 15. Yorks Min Course 13. **d** 15 **p** 16. C Sheff Manor 15–18; V Worsbrough w Elsecar from 18. *The Vicarage, Wath Road, Elsecar, Barnsley S74 8HJ* T: (01226) 744953 M: 07579-028798 E: vicar.stmaryswithholytrinity@gmail.com

CHAPMAN, Thomas Graham. b 33. Trin Coll Bris 73. **d** 75 **p** 76. C Branksome St Clem *Sarum* 75–81; V Quarry Bank *Lich* 81–93; V Quarry Bank *Worc* 93–99; rtd 99; PtO *Worc* from 99. *8 Somerset Drive, Wollaston, Stourbridge DY8 4RH* T: (01384) 373921 E: thomas.chapman1@btinternet.com

CHAPMAN, Tristan David. b 79. K Alfred's Coll Win BA 01. Ripon Coll Cuddesdon BTh 07. **d** 07 **p** 08. C Bocking St Mary *Chelmsf* 07–10; TV Chipping Barnet *St Alb* 10–21; TR from 21. *St Mark's Vicarage, 56 Potters Road, Barnet EN5 5HY* T: (020) 8440 7490 E: fr.tristan@googlemail.com

CHAPMAN, Miss Yvonne Hazel. b 35. Serampore Th Coll BRE 63 Brighton Coll of Educn CertEd 55. EAMTC 95. **d** 96 **p** 97. NSM Duston *Pet* 96–02; NSM Officer 99–02; rtd 02; PtO *Pet* from 02. *St Christopher's Home, Abington Park Crescent, Northampton NN3 3AD* E: rev.yhc@btinternet.com

CHARD, Mrs Julia Clare. b 54. Trin Coll Bris 09. **d** 11 **p** 12. OLM Soundwell *Bris* 11–16; OLM Fromeside from 17. *8 Glenside Close, Bristol BS16 2QY* T: 0117-902 1774 E: chardjulia7@gmail.com

CHARD, Reginald Jeffrey. b 40. Univ of Wales (Lamp) BA 62 CQSW 75. Coll of Resurr Mirfield 62. **d** 64 **p** 65. C Ystrad Mynach *Llan* 64–67; C Aberdare St Fagan 67–71; V Hirwaun 71–74; Hon C Stechford *Birm* 74–78; TV Banbury *Ox* 78–86; Ind Chapl 86–09; P-in-c Claydon w Mollington 86–96; R Ironstone 96–09; rtd 09. *15 The Glen, Yarmouth PO41 0PZ* T: (01983) 760554 E: jeffreychard@btinternet.com

CHARING CROSS, Archdeacon of. *See* ATKINSON, The Ven Adam

CHARKHAM, Miss Emily. b 90. Edin Univ MA 13. Trin Coll Bris MA 20. **d** 20 **p** 21. C Gamston and Bridgford *S'well* from 20. *9 Fountains Close, West Bridgford, Nottingham NG2 6LL* E: emily.charkham@gmail.com

CHARKHAM, Rupert Anthony. b 59. Ex Univ BA 81. Wycliffe Hall Ox 83. **d** 89 **p** 89. C Ox St Aldate w St Matt 89–92; P-in-c Fisherton Anger *Sarum* 92–99; R 99–03; V Cambridge H Trin *Ely* 03–20; V Ches Square St Mich w St Phil *Lon* from 20; Chapl to The Queen from 16. *St Michael's Church, Chester Square, London SW1W 9EF* T: (020) 7730 8889 E: rupert@smccs.org.uk

CHARLES, Ms Beverley Maria. b 65. FCCA 92. Trin Coll Bris 13. **d** 15 **p** 16. C Yate *Bris* 15–18; P-in-c Kingswood from 18; P-in-c Hanham from 18. *Holy Trinity Vicarage, 18 High Street, Kingswood, Bristol BS15 4AB* M: 07801-056553 E: charlesbeverley12@gmail.com

CHARLES, David Gordon. b 79. Ex Coll Ox BA 01 MA 04 CCC Cam BA 05 MA 09. Westcott Ho Cam 03. **d** 06 **p** 07. C Willingdon *Chich* 06–10; P-in-c Waldron 10–12; V Eastbourne Ch Ch and St Phil from 12; Chapl to Bp Lewes from 10. *Christ Church Vicarage, 18 Addingham Road, Eastbourne BN22 7DY* T: (01323) 728522 E: davidgcharles@hotmail.com *or* vicar@ccwithsp.org

CHARLES, James Richard. b 67. St Edm Hall Ox BA 90 CertEd 91. Oak Hill Th Coll BA 03. **d** 03 **p** 04. C Throop *Win* 03–07; P-in-c Bexleyheath St Pet *Roch* 07–11; V from 11. *St Peter's Vicarage, 50 Bristow Road, Bexleyheath DA7 4QA* T: (020) 8303 8713 E: jimrcharles@mac.com

CHARLES, Canon Jonathan. b 42. St Luke's Coll Ex CertEd 64. Ripon Hall Ox 72 Ripon Coll Cuddesdon 78. **d** 79 **p** 80. C Leagrave *St Alb* 79–82; Chapl Denstone Coll Uttoxeter 82–86; Chapl Malvern Girls' Coll 86–89; Chapl K Sch Worc 89–95; Min Can Worc Cathl 89–95; R Burnham Gp of Par *Nor* 95–09; RD Burnham and Walsingham 00–08; Hon Can Nor Cathl 05–09; rtd 09; PtO *Nor* from 09. *Michaelmas Cottage, 99 Burnham Road, North Creake, Fakenham NR21 9LB* T: (01328) 738249 E: revj.charles@virgin.net

CHARLES, Kevin. b 58. EMMTC 08. **d** 11 **p** 12. NSM Annesley w Newstead *S'well* 11–15; Chapl E Midl Ambulance Service from 15; NSM Sutton Bonington w Normanton-on-Soar *S'well* from 15. *6 Boughton Close, Sutton-in-Ashfield NG17 4NJ* T: (01623) 514294 E: kevin.charles1@btinternet.com

CHARLES, Meedperdas Edward. b 28. Fitzw Ho Cam BA 60 MA 64. Bangalore Th Coll BD 54. **d** 54 **p** 55. C Malacca Malaya 54–55; P-in-c St Paul and St Pet Singapore 55–58; PtO *Ely* 12–96; V Sheff St Bart Langsett Road 60–64; Chapl Univ of Singapore and Gen Sec Coun of Chs for Malaysia and Singapore 64–65; V Gravelly Hill *Birm* 66–78; V Endcliffe *Sheff* 79–90; rtd 91; PtO *Sheff* 91–20. *60 Ringinglow Road, Sheffield S11 7PQ* T: 0114-266 4980

CHARLES, Nathan John. b 80. Wycliffe Hall Ox. **d** 13 **p** 14. C Broadwell, Evenlode, Oddington, Adlestrop etc *Glouc* 13–16; Min Dalston St Barn BMO *Lon* from 16. *182B Amhurst Road, London E8 2AZ* M: 07968-975236 E: njcharles@gmail.com

CHARLES, Robert Sidney James. b 40. Lon Univ CertEd 72 Open Univ BA 79 Univ of Wales LLM 97. St Mich Coll Llan. **d** 65 **p** 66. C Merthyr Tydfil *Llan* 65–68; C Shotton *St As* 68–70; R Stock and Lydlinch *Sarum* 70–74; R Hubberston *St D* 74–76; PtO *Chelmsf* 81–83; C Crossens *Liv* 83–97; V Budleigh Salterton *Ex* 97–10; rtd 10; PtO *Ex* from 11. *8 Old Bystock Drive, Exmouth EX8 5RB* T: (01395) 223419 E: revrsjc@gmail.com

CHARLES, Mrs Susan Jane. b 67. Cant Ch Ch Univ BA 12. SEITE 05. **d** 08 **p** 09. NSM Eltham H Trin *S'wark* 08–13; NSM Mottingham St Edw 13–16; PtO from 16. *Address withheld by request* M: 07909-037690 E: susanjcharles@aol.com

CHARLESWORTH, Eric Charlesworth. b 29. Kelham Th Coll 49. **d** 54 **p** 56. C Woodbridge St Mary *St E* 54–57; Asst Chapl Oslo St Edm *Eur* 57–59; Canada 60–66; R Huntingfield w Cookley *St E* 66–70; R Slimbridge *Glouc* 70–96; rtd 96; PtO *Glouc* 96–16; Ox 04–12. *37 Pavilion Walk, South Street, Letcombe Regis, Wantage OX12 9SQ*

CHARLESWORTH, Philip. b 55. Sheff City Poly BSc 85 Anglia Poly MSc 92. **d** 07 **p** 08. OLM Sprowston w Beeston *Nor* 07–13; NSM Taverham 13–16; NSM Taverham w Ringland from 16. *63 Wroxham Road, Norwich NR7 8TN* T: (01603) 411316 M: 07545-968435 E: revdphilcharlesworth@gmail.com

CHARLTON, Mrs Elizabeth Anne. b 55. STETS BA 08. **d** 08 **p** 09. C W Moors *Sarum* 08–11; C Budleigh Salterton *Ex* 11–12; P-in-c 12–13; C E Budleigh w Bicton and Otterton 11–12; P-in-c 12–13; V Budleigh Salterton, E Budleigh w Bicton etc 13–17; P-in-c St Goran w Caerhays *Truro* 17–18; PtO *B & W* from 21. *43 Thomson Drive, Crewkerne TA18 8AQ* M: 07807-827781 E: eacharlton@btinternet.com

CHARLTON, Fraser Graham. b 67. Newc Univ BMedSci 88 MB, BS 91 PhD 97. Lindisfarne Regional Tr Partnership 12. **d** 15 p 17. NSM Wallsend St Jo *Newc* 15–16; NSM Newc St Gabr 16–19; NSM Long Benton from 19. *17 Northumberland Avenue, Forest Hall, Newcastle upon Tyne NE12 9NR* T: 0191-292 1033 M: 07783-402007 E: fraser.charlton@ncl.ac.uk

CHARLTON, Canon Hazel. b 66. Qu Coll Birm. d 12 p 13. C Worc SE 12–15; TV Halas from 15; Dean of Women's Min from 18; Hon Can Worc Cathl from 19. *10 Highland Ridge, Halesowen B62 8PH* T: 0121-550 1158 E: revhazel@halasteam.org.uk

CHARLTON, Helen Julie. b 56. d 09 p 10. NSM Wokingham All SS *Ox* 09–16; Asst Dioc Dir of Ords from 16; LtO from 16. *36 Rances Lane, Wokingham RG40 2LH* T: 0118-978 9153 M: 07706-931071 E: helenjcharlton@btinternet.com

CHARLTON, Thomas David. b 53. York St Jo Univ BA 12 IEng MIET 80. Cranmer Hall Dur 12. d 13 p 14. NSM Whorlton w Carlton and Faceby *York* 13–15; NSM Eston w Normanby 15–16; NSM Ingleby Barwick 16–20; rtd 20. *28 Brougham Close, Ingleby Barwick, Stockton-on-Tees TS17 5GH* T: (01642) 767176 M: 07805-388165 E: td.charlton@btinternet.com

CHARMAN, Canon Jane Ellen Elizabeth. b 60. St Jo Coll Dur BA 81 Selw Coll Cam BA 84 MA 88. Westcott Ho Cam 82. d 87 p 94. C Glouc St Geo w Whaddon 87–90; Chapl and Fell Clare Coll Cam 90–95; R Duxford *Ely* 95–04; V Hinxton 95–04; V Ickleton 95–04; RD Shelford 03–04; Dir of Min *Sarum* 04–07; Dir of Learning for Discipleship and Min 07–20; Can and Preb Sarum Cathl 07–20; TR Cockermouth Area *Carl* from 20. *Parish Office, Christ Church Rooms, South Street, Cockermouth CA13 9RU* T: (01900) 829926 E: office@grasmoormc.church

CHARMAN, Mrs Karen. b 71. Birm Univ BA 97 Newc Univ PGCE 98. Ripon Coll Cuddesdon 14. d 16 p 17. C Delaval *Newc* 16–20; V Garsington, Cuddesdon and Horspath *Ox* from 20. *The Rectory, 17 Southend, Garsington, Oxford OX44 9DH* T: (01865) 361146 E: rev.karen.charman@gmail.com

CHARMLEY, Mrs Tracy-Belinda. b 72. Ex Univ BA 93 St Luke's Coll Ex PGCE 95 Birm Univ MEd. Ripon Coll Cuddesdon 07. d 10 p 11. NSM Guernsey St Martin *Win* 10–14; NSM Guernsey W Par 14–16; NSM Guernsey St Philippe de Torteval from 16; NSM Guernsey St Sav from 16. *The Rectory, Le Neuf Chemin Road, St Saviour, Guernsey GY7 9FQ* T: (01481) 263045 E: charmley@cwgsy.net

CHARNLEY, Anthony Keith. b 49. Dur Univ BSc 71 PhD 76 FHEA 07. STETS. d 12 p 13. NSM N Bradford on Avon and Villages *Sarum* 12–20; PtO from 20; Visiting Prof Chongqing Univ China from 08. *41 Leigh Park Road, Bradford-on-Avon BA15 1TF* T: (01225) 866515 E: akeithcharnley@gmail.com

CHARNOCK, Deryck Ian. b 47. Oak Hill Th Coll 78. d 80 p 81. C Rowner *Portsm* 80–84; TV Southgate *Chich* 84–90; V Penge St Paul *Roch* 90–98; V Whitwick St Jo the Bapt *Leic* 98–06; R Hollington St Leon *Chich* 06–15; rtd 15; PtO *Roch* from 16. *10 Faraday Ride, Tonbridge TN10 4RL* T: (01732) 365617 E: deryckc@btinternet.com

CHARNOCK, Ms Tracy. b 75. Leeds Univ BA 97 BA 08. Coll of Resurr Mirfield 06. d 08 p 09. C Man Victoria Park 08–11; P-in-c S Shore H Trin *Blackb* 11–13; V from 13; P-in-c S Shore St Pet 11–13; V from 13. *92 Watson Road, Blackpool FY4 2DE* T: (01253) 344773 M: 07778-163920 E: tracy.charnock@hotmail.co.uk

CHARTERS, Alan Charles. b 35. Trin Hall Cam BA 60 MA 63 FCollP 88. Linc Th Coll 60. d 62 p 63. C Gt Grimsby St Mary and St Jas *Linc* 62–65; Chapl and Hd RE Eliz Coll Guernsey 65–70; P-in-c Guernsey St Jas the Less 65–70; Dep Hd Master Park Sen High Sch Swindon 70–73; Chapl St Jo Sch Leatherhead 73–83; Dep Hd Master 76; Visiting Lect and Tutor Lon Univ Inst of Ed 76–80; Headmaster The K Sch Glouc 83–92; V Aberedw w Llandeilo Graban and Llanbadarn etc *S & B* 92–00; Bp's Visitor to Schs 92–00; rtd 00; PtO *Eur* 00–03; P-in-c Dinard 03–06. *Crescent House, Church Street, Talgarth, Brecon LD3 0BL* T: (01874) 711135 E: ac.charters@btinternet.com

✠**CHARTRES, The Rt Revd and Rt Hon Lord (Richard John Carew).** b 47. PC 96 GCVO 19. Trin Coll Cam BA 68 MA 73 Lambeth BD 83 Hon DLitt 98 Hon DD 99 FSA 99 Hon FGCM 97. Cuddesdon Coll 69 Linc Th Coll 72. d 73 p 74 c 92. C Bedford St Andr *St Alb* 73–75; Bp's Dom Chapl 75–80; Abp's Chapl *Cant* 80–84; P-in-c Westmr St Steph w St Jo *Lon* 84–85; V 86–92; Dir of Ords 85–92; Prof Div Gresham Coll 86–92; Six Preacher Cant Cathl 91–97; Area Bp Stepney *Lon* 92–95; Bp Lon 95–17; rtd 17; Dean of HM Chpls Royal 95–19; Hon Asst Bp Eur from 17; Hon Asst Bp Sarum from 19; Hon Fell Trin Coll Cam from 17; PtO *Sarum* from 19; Lon from 19. *House of Lords, Houses of Parliament, London SW1A 0PW*

CHASE, Mrs Elisabeth. b 49. Wycliffe Hall Ox. d 09 p 10. NSM Headbourne Worthy *Win* 09–19; NSM King's Worthy 09–19;

rtd 19; PtO *Win* from 19. *The Vicarage, Sloe Lane, Micheldever, Winchester SO21 3DA* E: lis.chase@gmail.com

CHATER, John Augustus. b 43. SEITE 99. d 04 p 05. NSM St Peter-in-Thanet *Cant* 04–07; Ramsgate Town Cen Missr 07–13; rtd 13; PtO *Cant* from 13. *125 High Street, Ramsgate CT11 9UA* T: (01843) 596175 E: john.chater@gmail.com

CHATER, John Leathley. b 29. Qu Coll Cam BA 54 MA 58. Ridley Hall Cam 54. d 56 p 57. C Bath Abbey w St Jas *B & W* 56–60; V Bermondsey St Anne *S'wark* 60–64; Ind Chapl 60–64; V Heslington *York* 64–69; Chapl York Univ 64–69; V Lawrence Weston *Bris* 69–73; PtO 74–80; P-in-c Wraxall *B & W* 80–82; R 82–84; V Battle *Chich* 84–90; Dean Battle 84–90; RD Battle and Bexhill 86–90; R St Marylebone w H Trin *Lon* 90–96; rtd 96; PtO *Chich* 96–11. *Oak Lodge, 2 Saxonwood Road, Battle TN33 0EY* T: (01424) 772743 E: jlchater@icloud.com

CHATER (née CAKE), Nichola Carla. b 58. Liv Univ BSc 79 MB, ChB 85 MRCGP FRCP 08. Cranmer Hall Dur 05. d 07 p 08. NSM Dur St Marg, Neville's Cross St Jo and Bearpark from 07. *37 Hill Meadows, High Shincliffe, Durham DH1 2PE* T: 0191-383 1869 E: nicky_chater@yahoo.co.uk

CHATFIELD, Adrian Francis. b 49. Leeds Univ BA 71 MA 72 MPhil 89 PhD 97. Coll of Resurr Mirfield 71. d 72 p 73. Trinidad and Tobago 72–83; TV Barnstaple, Goodleigh and Landkey *Ex* 83–84; TV Barnstaple 85; TR 85–88; Lect St Jo Coll Nottm 88–95; S Africa 99–05; Tutor Wycliffe Hall Ox 05–07; Hon C Wallingford *Ox* 05–07; Co-ord Mixed Mode Tr Ridley Hall Cam 07–15; Tutor 15–16; Dir Simeon Cen 07–16; rtd 16; PtO *S'well* from 17. *63 Wesley Street, Ilkeston DE7 8QW* T: 0115-930 1065 E: adrian.chatfield@btinternet.com

CHATFIELD, Mrs Gillian. b 50. Leeds Univ BA 71 PGCE 72. St Jo Coll Nottm MA 94. d 94 p 95. C Greasley *S'well* 94–98; Miss Partner Th Coll by Ext S Africa 99–05; TV Wallingford *Ox* 05–07; Past Tutor Ridley Hall Cam 07–13; Hon C Lordsbridge *Ely* 13–15; PtO 15–16; *S'well* from 17. *63 Wesley Street, Ilkeston DE7 8QW* T: 0115-930 1065 M: 07758-591430 E: jill.chatfield@btinternet.com

CHATFIELD, Michael Francis. b 75. York Univ BSc 96 Fitzw Coll Cam BA 99 MA 03 Portsm Univ MSc 18. Ridley Hall Cam. d 00 p 01. C Attenborough *S'well* 00–03; P-in-c Chaguanas St Thos Trinidad and Tobago 04–09; Chapl RAF 09–19; Chapl RN from 19. *Royal Naval Chaplaincy Service Headquarters, Tanner Building, HMS Excellent, Whale Island, Portsmouth PO2 8ER* T: 0300-157 7544 M: 07540-848758 E: thechatalots@hotmail.com

CHATFIELD, Canon Norman. b 37. Fitzw Ho Cam BA 59 MA 68. Ripon Hall Ox 60. d 62 p 63. C Burgess Hill St Jo *Chich* 62–65; C Uckfield 65–69; V Lower Sandown St Jo *Portsm* 69–76; V Locks Heath 76–83; R Alverstoke 83–91; Hon Can Portsm Cathl 85–91; Can Res Glouc Cathl 91–02; rtd 02; PtO *Portsm* from 03. *Ellwood, Garfield Road, Bishop's Waltham SO32 1AT* T: (01489) 891995 E: chat.field@btinternet.com

CHATTELL, David Malcolm. b 63. St Luke's Coll Ex BEd 93. Wycliffe Hall Ox 03. d 05 p 06. C Bucklebury w Marlston *Ox* 05–11; R Farleigh, Candover and Wield *Win* from 11; RD Alresford from 19. *The Rectory, Alresford Road, Preston Candover, Basingstoke RG25 2EE* T: (01256) 389474 E: davidchattell172@btinternet.com

CHATTEN, Mrs Sophie. b 79. d 15 p 16. C Stoughton *Guildf* 15–20; C Falmouth All SS *Truro* from 20. *72 Dracaena Avenue, Falmouth TR11 2EN* M: 07969-604514 E: sophiebish@gmail.com

CHATTERLEY, Canon Marion Frances. b 55. Edin Th Coll 95. d 98 p 99. C Edin Gd Shep 98–00; C Edin Ch Ch 00–05; Hon C Edin St Mich and All SS 07–11; Chapl Edin Napier Univ 99–12; Dioc Dir of Ords 06–19; Hon Can St Mary's Cathl 16–20; Chapl Marie Curie Hospice Edinburgh from 18; Vice Provost St Mary's Cathl *Edin* from 20. *102 Relugas Road, Edinburgh EH9 2LZ* T: 0131-667 6847 M: 07771-982163 E: marion.chatterley@blueyonder.co.uk

CHATTERTON, Mrs Nicola Mary. b 63. Qu Coll Birm BA 15. d 14 p 15. NSM Stratford-upon-Avon, Luddington etc *Cov* 14–17; C Avon Dassett w Farnborough and Fenny Compton 17–18; P-in-c from 18; C Burton Dassett 17–18; P-in-c from 18; C Gaydon w Chadshunt 17–18; P-in-c from 18. *Burton Dassett Vicarage, Bottom Street, Northend, Southam CV47 2TH* M: 07769-871237 E: chat2rev.nicki@gmail.com

CHATTERTON, Thomas William. b 50. SEITE. d 99 p 00. Hon C Blackheath All SS *S'wark* 99–11 and from 15; Hon C Thamesmead 11–12; P-in-c 13–14; Chapl Greenwich Foundn 14–15. *44 Harland Road, London SE12 0JA* T: (020) 8851 6813 E: williamchatterton@hotmail.com

CHATWIN, Ronald Ernest. b 34. St Aid Birkenhead 58. d 60 p 61. C Selsdon *Cant* 60–64; C Crawley *Chich* 64–68; V Coldwaltham 68–74; TV Ovingdean w Rottingdean and

Woodingdean 74–83; V Saltdean 83–91; V Hellingly and Upper Dicker 91–02; rtd 02; PtO *Chich* from 03. *Cold Waltham, 29A New Road, Hellingly, Hailsham BN27 4EW* T: (01323) 843346 E: ronaldchatwin@hotmail.com

CHAUDHARY, Canon Jaisher Masih. b 56. Qu Coll Birm. d 08 p 09. NSM Handsworth St Mich *Birm* from 08; NSM Handsworth Good News Asian Ch from 12; Hon Can Birm Cathl from 19. *29 George Street, Handsworth, Birmingham B21 0EG* T: 0121-551 6279 E: jaisher@hotmail.com

CHAVE, Preb Brian Philip. b 51. Open Univ BA. Trin Coll Bris. d 84 p 85. C Cullompton *Ex* 84–87; TV Bishopsnympton, Rose Ash, Mariansleigh etc 87–93; Chapl for Agric *Heref* 93–96; Communications Adv and Bp's Staff Officer 97–01; Bp's Dom Chapl 97–01; TV W Heref 01–15; Bp's Dom Chapl from 15; RD Heref City 04–07; Preb Heref Cathl from 97; Can Heref Cathl 97–01. *The Bishop's Office, The Palace, Hereford HR4 9BN* T: (01432) 271355 E: b.chave@hereford.anglican.org

CHAVE-COX, Guy. b 56. St Andr Univ BSc 79. Wycliffe Hall Ox 83. d 86 p 87. C Wigmore Abbey *Heref* 86–88; C Bideford *Ex* 88–91; TV Barnstaple 91–97 and 08–17; C-in-c Roundswell CD 97–08; V Sticklepath w Roundswell from 17. *St Paul's Vicarage, Old Sticklepath Hill, Barnstaple EX31 2BG* T: (01271) 344400 E: vicar@barnstaple-st-paul.org.uk

CHAVNER, Robert. b 59. ALCM 82 AGSM 85 FGMS 00 FRSA 05. Linc Th Coll 90. d 92 p 93. C Beckenham St Geo *Roch* 92–96; V Sevenoaks St Luke 96–06; P-in-c Brighton St Nic *Chich* 06–11; V 11–16; rtd 16; PtO *Ex* from 17; *Eur* from 18. *The Old School, Whittingham, Alnwick NE66 4UP* M: 07714-653264 E: robertchavner@outlook.com

CHEATLE, Adèle Patricia. b 46. York Univ BA 73. Trin Coll Bris 76. d 87 p 98. Par Dn Harborne Heath *Birm* 87; NSM 92–93; PtO *Heref* 96–97; NSM Burghill and Stretton Sugwas 97–99; NSM Heref St Pet w St Owen and St Jas 99–04; NSM Ches Square St Mich w St Phil *Lon* 04–07; PtO *Birm* from 11. *26 Oakham Road, Harborne, Birmingham B17 9DG* T: 0121-427 5362 E: thecheatles@googlemail.com

CHEDZEY, The Ven Derek Christopher. b 67. Univ of Wales MA 12. Trin Coll Bris BA 93. d 93 p 94. C Bedgrove *Ox* 93–95; C Haddenham w Cuddington, Kingsey etc 95–98; TV High Wycombe 98–01; Deanery Tr Officer and C Washfield, Stoodleigh, Withleigh etc *Ex* 01–04; P-in-c Frenchay and Winterbourne Down *Bris* 04–06; Dioc Dir Lay Min 04–08; Adv for Initial Minl Educn 08–15; Warden of Readers 04–15; Hon C Yate 09–15; Asst Adn 13–15; Hon Can Bris Cathl 11–15; Hd of Min Development 15–18; Can Res Bris Cathl 15–18; Dioc Dir of Ords 15–18; Adn Heref from 18; Acting Adn Ludlow 20–21. *The Diocesan Office, The Palace, Hereford HR4 9BL* T: (01432) 373316 M: 07811-878774 E: archdeacon@hereford.anglican.org

CHEESEMAN (née DUNHAM), Mrs Angela Mary. b 40. New Hall Cam MB, BChir 66 MRCOG 74 FRCSEd 75 FRCOG 96. d 05 p 06. OLM Eastling w Ospringe and Stalisfield w Otterden *Cant* 05–10; PtO 11–17. *New House Farm, Otterden Road, Eastling, Faversham ME13 0BN* T: (01795) 890629

CHEESEMAN, Colin Henry. b 47. Reading Univ BA 69 Kent Univ PhD 00. Sarum & Wells Th Coll 82. d 84 p 85. C Cranleigh *Guildf* 84–87; C Godalming 87–89; V Cuddington 89–96; Chapl HM Pris Wealstun 96–97; P-in-c Tockwith and Bilton w Bickerton *York* 97–01; RD New Ainsty 99–01; P-in-c Roundhay St Jo *Ripon* 01–14; Dioc Ecum Adv 09–14; rtd 14; PtO *York* from 16. *Scatwell House, Church Fenton Lane, Ulleskelf, Tadcaster LS24 9DW* E: colin.cheeseman3@gmail.com

CHEESEMAN, Janet. *See* GOODAIR, Jan

CHEESEMAN, Trevor Percival. b 38. Auckland Univ PhD 64 Lon Univ BD 67. K Coll Lon and St Boniface Warminster AKC 67. d 68 p 69. C Warmsworth *Sheff* 68–71; C Manurewa NZ 71–73; P-in-c Birkdale-Beach Haven 73–77; V Meadowbank 77–85; Chapl K Coll Auckland 86–99; P-in-c Whitford 00–03; rtd 03; PtO *NZ* from 03. *Apartment 803, Betty Pyatt Building, 101 Shaftesbury Avenue, Selwyn Village, Point Chevalier, Auckland 1022, New Zealand* T: (0064) (9) 849 9303 M: (0064) 27-610 3768 E: trevor@middleearth.net.nz

CHEESMAN, Peter. b 43. ACS 63 FCA 76 MCMI. Ridley Hall Cam 66. d 69 p 70. C Herne Bay Ch Ch *Cant* 69–74; TV Lowestoft St Marg *Nor* 75–78; TV Lowestoft and Kirkley 79–81; Ind Chapl *Glouc* 81–84; P-in-c Saul w Fretherne and Framilode 84–85; V Frampton on Severn, Arlingham, Saul etc 85–08; rtd 08; PtO *Glouc* from 15. *Frampton Court, The Green, Frampton on Severn, Gloucester GL2 7EX* T: (01452) 740533 E: peter@the-cheesman.net

CHEESMAN, Samuel Graham. b 85. St Mellitus Coll 14. d 17 p 18. C Anchorsholme *Blackb* 17–19; NSM Salesbury from 19; Bp's Dom Chapl from 19. *Ayton, Whitehalgh Lane, Langho, Blackburn BB6 8ET* T: (01254) 248234

CHEETHAM, David Andrew. b 69. d 12 p 13. NSM Kenilworth St Jo *Cov* 12–13; NSM Olton *Birm* 13–16; NSM Birm Cathl from 16. *75 Solihull Road, Shirley, Solihull B90 3HJ* T: 0121-744 4407 E: d.cheetham@bham.ac.uk

CHEETHAM (née MUMFORD), Mrs Lesley Anne. b 51. Man Univ BA 73. NOC 01. d 04 p 05. C Halifax *Wakef* 04–08; V Easby w Skeeby and Brompton on Swale etc *Ripon* 08–12; Chapl Overgate Hospice 12–19; P-in-c Greetland and W Vale *Leeds* 15–19; rtd 19. *Mokes Barn, Wainstalls Lane, Halifax HX2 7TR* M: 07963-620391 E: lesley_cheetham@btinternet.com

✠**CHEETHAM, The Rt Revd Richard Ian.** b 55. CCC Ox BA 77 CertEd 78 MA 82 Lon Univ PhD 99. Ripon Coll Cuddesdon 85. d 87 p 88 c 02. C Newc H Cross 87–90; V Luton St Aug Limbury *St Alb* 90–99; RD Luton 95–98; Adn St Alb 99–02; Area Bp Kingston S'wark from 02. *Kingston Episcopal Area Office, 620 Kingston Road, London SW20 8DN* T: (020) 8545 2440 or 8789 3218 F: 8545 2441 E: bishop.richard@southwark.anglican.org

CHEGWIDDEN, James Peter. b 77. Sydney Univ LLB 04 Magd Coll Ox BCL 06 Ox Univ BA 20 Called to the Bar 08. St Steph Ho Ox 18 Ripon Coll Cuddesdon 20. d 21. C Earl's Court St Cuth w St Matthias *Lon* from 21. *51 Philbeach Gardens, London SW5 9EB* E: curate@saintcuthbert.org

CHEGWIN HALL, Elaine. *See* HALL, Elaine Chegwin

CHELASHAW, Godfrey Kiprotich (Kip). b 76. Oak Hill Th Coll BA 08 MA 10. d 10 p 11. C Audley *Lich* 10–15; C Talke 14–15; C Alsagers Bank 14–15; C Alsagers Bank, Audley and Talke 15; C E Dean w Friston and Jevington *Chich* 15–17; Kenya from 17. *PO Box 42383-00100, GPO Nairobi, Kenya* E: kchelashaw@yahoo.com

CHELMSFORD, Bishop of. *See* FRANCIS DEHQANI, The Rt Revd Gulnar Eleanor

CHELMSFORD, Dean of. *See* HENSHALL, The Very Revd Nicholas James

CHELTENHAM, Archdeacon of. *See* ANDREW, The Ven Philip John

CHERRY, David. b 30. Roch Th Coll 59. d 61 p 62. C Seacroft *Ripon* 61–67; R Bamford *Derby* 67–75; Chapl Málaga w Almuñécar *Eur* 83–91; rtd 91; NSM Waltham St Lawrence *Ox* 97–01; PtO *Leic* 01–21. *2 Church Lane, Rearsby, Leicester LE7 4YE* T: (01664) 424099

CHERRY, David Warwick. b 61. Cape Town Univ BMus 86 Leeds Univ BA 91. Coll of Resurr Mirfield 92. d 92 p 93. C Hammersmith SS Mich and Geo White City Estate CD *Lon* 92–01; C Hammersmith St Luke 94–01; Chapl Greenwich Univ S'wark 01–03; Chapl Univ of Westmr *Lon* 03–10; Hon C St Marylebone St Cypr 06–08; V Pimlico St Mary Bourne Street 10–15; V Pimlico St Barn 10–15; PtO 15–16; NSM Kilburn St Aug w St Jo 16–18; PtO 18. *The Curate's Flat, St Paul's Vicarage, 60 Park Lane, London N17 0JR* T: (020) 7624 1637 M: 07939-553547

CHERRY, Stephen Arthur. b 58. St Chad's Coll Dur BSc 79 Fitzw Coll Cam BA 85 MA 90 K Coll Lon PhD 95. Westcott Ho Cam 83. d 86 p 87. C Baguley and Asst Chapl Wythenshawe Hosp Man 86–89; Chapl K Coll Cam 89–94; R Loughborough All SS w H Trin *Leic* 94–06; RD Akeley E 96–99; Hon Can Leic Cathl 04–06; Dir Min and Tr *Dur* 06–14; Can Res Dur Cathl 06–14; Dean K Coll Cam from 14. *King's College, Cambridge CB2 1ST* T: (01223) 331419 E: sacherry@btinternet.com *or* dean@kings.cam.ac.uk

CHESHER, Michael. b 52. Open Univ BA 84. EAMTC 97. d 00 p 01. C Littleport *Ely* 00–03; V Chelmsf All SS 03–04; P-in-c W Walton *Ely* 04–11; P-in-c Walpole St Peter w Walpole St Andrew 04–11; PtO 11–16; C Spalding St Mary and St Nic *Linc* 12–16; C Spalding St Paul 12–16; C Cowbit 14–16; PtO from 20; P-in-c Culworth w Sulgrave and Thorpe Mandeville etc *Pet* from 21. *The Rectory, Queens Street, Culworth, Banbury OX17 2AT* T: (01295) 768626 M: 07751-801305 E: m.chesher559@btinternet.com

CHESHIRE, Mrs Charlotte Amy. b 77. St Jo Coll Nottm 11. d 14 p 15. C Shifnal and Sheriffhales *Lich* 14–16; C Tong 14–16; C Shifnal, Sheriffhales and Tong 16–17; C Wellington All SS w Eyton 17–18; P-in-c Moldgreen and Rawthorpe *Leeds* from 18; Chapl Huddersfield Univ from 18. *The Vicarage, 35 Church Lane, Moldgreen, Huddersfield HD5 9DL* T: (01484) 982373 E: rev.charlottecheshire@gmail.com

CHESHIRE, James Wilson. b 73. Univ of Florida BA 05. Gordon-Conwell Th Sem MDiv 00 CITC 13. d 14 p 15. C Bangor Abbey *D & D* 14–18; I Ballybeen from 18. *1 Grahams Bridge Road, Dundonald, Belfast BT16 2DB* T: (028) 9058 6939 M: 07751-576954 E: jim@stmarysballybeen.com

CHESHIRE, Lauren Marie. b 84. St Mellitus Coll 19. d 21. C Bournemouth St Jo w St Mich *Win* from 21. *72 West Cliff Road, Bournemouth BH4 8BE* M: 07429-105995 E: lauren_cheshire@live.com *or* lauren.cheshire@sjsm.org.uk

CHESNEY, Canon David Vince. b 69. UMIST BSc 99. NTMTC BA 08. **d** 08 **p** 09. C Springfield H Trin *Chelmsf* 08–12; V Victoria Docks Ascension from 12; AD Newham from 19; Hon Can Chelmsf Cathl from 20. *75 Baxter Road, London E16 3HJ* T: (020) 7511 1886 E: dave.chesney@btinternet.com

✠**CHESSUN, The Rt Revd Christopher Thomas James.** b 56. Univ Coll Ox BA 78 MA 82 Trin Hall Cam BA 82. Westcott Ho Cam. **d** 83 **p** 84 **c** 05. C Sandhurst *Ox* 83–87; C Portsea St Mary *Portsm* 87–89; Min Can and Chapl St Paul's Cathl *Lon* 89–93; Voc Adv 90–05; R Stepney St Dunstan and All SS 93–01; AD Tower Hamlets 97–01; Adn Northolt 01–05; Area Bp Woolwich *S'wark* 05–11; Bp S'wark from 11. *Bishop's House, 38 Tooting Bec Gardens, London SW16 1QZ* T: (020) 8769 3256 *or* 7939 9420 E: bishop.christopher@southwark.anglican.org

CHESTER, David Kenneth. b 50. Dur Univ BA 73 Aber Univ PhD 78 CGeol 92 FGS 88. NOC 93. **d** 96 **p** 97. NSM Hoylake *Ches* 96–04; NSM W Kirby St Bridget from 04; PtO *Liv* from 16. *Yenda, Grange Old Road, West Kirby, Wirral CH48 4ET* T: 0151-625 8004 E: jg54@liv.ac.uk

CHESTER, Irene Mary. See GREENMAN, Irene Mary

CHESTER, Letitia Irene. b 46. Yorks Min Course 08. **d** 10 **p** 11. NSM Clifton *York* 10–13; NSM Dringhouses 13–17; rtd 17; PtO *York* from 17. *6 Woodland Chase, York YO30 6RE* T: (01904) 692652 E: letitiachester@btinternet.com

CHESTER, Mark. b 55. Lanc Univ BA 79. Wycliffe Hall Ox 86. **d** 88 **p** 89. C Plymouth St Andr w St Paul and St Geo *Ex* 88–94; V Burney Lane *Birm* 94–99; V Camberley St Paul *Guildf* 99–15; Sen Chapl Waterways from 15; PtO *Guildf* from 15; Public Preacher *St Alb* from 15; PtO *Lon* from 20; CF (VR) 89–21. *Berisay, Guildford Road, Frimley Green GU16 6NS* E: markwith29@gmail.com

CHESTER, Maureen Olga. b 47. Univ of Wales (Swansea) BA 70. NEOC 94. **d** 97 **p** 98. NSM Morpeth *Newc* 97–11; rtd 11; PtO *Newc* from 11. *10 Leland Place, Morpeth NE61 2AN* T: (01670) 514569 E: mochester2001@yahoo.co.uk

CHESTER, Preb Philip Anthony Edwin. b 55. Birm Univ LLB 76. Cranmer Hall Dur 77. **d** 80 **p** 81. C Shrewsbury St Chad *Lich* 80–85; C St Martin-in-the-Fields *Lon* 85–88; Chapl K Coll Lon 88–95; P-in-c Westmr St Matt *Lon* 95–03; V from 03; P-in-c St Mary le Strand w St Clem Danes 14–20; AD Westmr St Marg from 05; PV Westmr Abbey from 90; Preb St Paul's Cathl *Lon* from 21. *St Matthew's House, 20 Great Peter Street, London SW1P 2BU* T: (020) 7222 3704 F: 7233 0255 E: paec@stmw.org

CHESTER, Archdeacon of. See GILBERTSON, The Ven Michael Robert

CHESTER, Bishop of. See TANNER, The Rt Revd Mark Simon Austin

CHESTER, Dean of. See STRATFORD, The Very Revd Timothy Richard

CHESTERFIELD, Archdeacon of. See COSLETT, The Ven Carol Ann

CHESTERFIELD-TERRY, John Darcy Francis Malcolm. b 82. Kingston Univ BEng 05. Ripon Coll Cuddesdon 12. **d** 15 **p** 16. C Portsea St Mary *Portsm* 15–19; V Colnbrook and Datchet *Ox* from 19. *St Mary's Vicarage, London Road, Datchet, Slough SL3 9JW* M: 07442-197723 E: vicar@colnbrookanddatchet.co.uk

CHESTERMAN, Canon George Anthony (Tony). b 38. Man Univ BSc 62 DipAdEd Nottm Univ PhD 89. Coll of Resurr Mirfield 62. **d** 64 **p** 65. C Newbold w Dunston *Derby* 64–68; C Derby St Thos 68–70; Adult Educn Officer 70–79; R Mugginton and Kedleston 70–89; Vice-Prin EMMTC 79–86; Can Res Derby Cathl and Dioc Clergy In-Service Tr Adv *Derby* 89–03; rtd 03; Chapl to The Queen 98–08; PtO *Newc* from 04. *7 Hillside, Lesbury, Alnwick NE66 3NR* T: (01665) 833124

✠**CHESTERS, The Rt Revd Alan David.** b 37. CBE 07. St Chad's Coll Dur BA 59 St Cath Soc Ox BA 61 MA 65 Ches Univ Hon DTheol 10. St Steph Ho Ox 59. **d** 62 **p** 63 **c** 89. C Wandsworth St Anne *S'wark* 62–66; Hon C 66–68; Chapl Tiffin Sch Kingston 66–72; Hon C Ham St Rich *S'wark* 68–72; Dioc Dir of Educn *Dur* 72–85; R Brancepeth 72–85; Hon Can Dur Cathl 75–85; Adn Halifax *Wakef* 85–89; Bp Blackb 89–03; rtd 03; Hon Asst Bp Ches 03–10; Eur 05–09; St As 09–10; S'wark 11–14; Chich from 11. *14 Pegasus Court, Deanery Close, Chichester PO19 1EA* T: (01243) 788053 M: 07768-955534 E: achesters1937@gmail.com

CHESTERS, David Nigel. b 45. OBE . BA FRSA FSAScot. **d** 04 **p** 05. NSM Wallasey St Hilary *Ches* 04–06; V Ches St Jo from 06. *St John's Rectory, 48 Elizabeth Crescent, Chester CH4 7AZ* T: (01244) 676567 E: office@parishofchester.com *or* rectorofchester@btinternet.com

CHESTERS, Simon. b 66. Rob Coll Cam BA 87 MA 91. Wycliffe Hall Ox BA 94. **d** 95 **p** 96. C Bidston *Ches* 95–99; P-in-c Runcorn St Jo Weston 99–03; Dioc Min Development Officer 03–09; Hon C Lache cum Saltney from 03; Dir Reader Tr 99–09; Regional Leadership Development Adv (NW) CPAS 10–11; Dir Studies Dioc Lifelong Learning *Liv* from 11; Lic Preacher *Man* from 10. *25 Marlston Avenue, Chester CH4 8HE* T: (01244) 679311 E: chesters.simon@gmail.com *or* simon.chesters@liverpool.anglican.org

CHESWORTH (née NAYLOR), Mrs Alison Louise. b 68. St Andr Univ MTheol 97 New Coll Edin MTh 99. TISEC 98. **d** 00 **p** 01. C Ayr, Girvan and Maybole *Glas* 00–03; R Glas All SS and P-in-c Glas H Cross 03–10; TV Ipswich St Mary at Stoke w St Pet and St Fran *St E* 10–17; P-in-c Penhill *Bris* 17–21; P-in-c Upper Stratton 17–21. *Address temp unknown* E: revd.alichesworth@gmail.com

CHESWORTH, John Martin. b 44. Leeds Univ BSc 67 PhD 71 FRSC 80. S Dios Minl Tr Scheme 90. **d** 92 **p** 93. Oman 92–95; PtO *Ab* 96–98; *Ches* 98–03; C Egremont St Jo 03–04; V Tranmere St Paul w St Luke 04–09; rtd 09; PtO *Lich* 10–21. *21 Oerley Way, Oswestry SY11 1TD* T: (01691) 653922 E: chez.ches@talktalk.net

CHEUNG SALISBURY, Matthew Robert. See SALISBURY, Matthew Robert Cheung

CHEVERTON, Miss Jill. b 48. Cranmer Hall Dur 93. **d** 93 **p** 94. Par Dn Bilton *Ripon* 93–94; C 94–96; V Burmantofts St Steph and St Agnes 96–03; Min Binley Woods LEP *Cov* 03–13; rtd 13; PtO *York* from 14. *51 Fairway, Selby YO8 9AF* T: (01757) 428876 E: jillcheverton@gmail.com

CHEVILL, Elizabeth Jane. See PITKETHLY, Elizabeth Jane

CHEW, Philip Vivian Frederick. b 62. St Martin's Coll Lanc BA 96. Qu Coll Birm 96. **d** 98 **p** 99. C Chorley St Laur *Blackb* 98–02; V Burnley St Steph 02–08; P-in-c Blackb St Fran and St Aid 08–10; R Llanbedr DC, Llangynhafal, Llanychan etc. *St As* 10–16; R Dyffryn Clwyd Miss Area 17–19; AD Dyffryn Clwyd 10–19; V Ribby cum Wrea and Weeton *Blackb* from 19. *The Vicarage, 1 Vicarage Close, Wrea Green, Preston PR4 2PQ* T: (01772) 687644 E: revpchew@gmail.com

CHICHESTER, Caroline Margaret. b 57. STETS. **d** 09 **p** 10. NSM Winterborne Valley and Milton Abbas *Sarum* 09–16; NSM Red Post from 16. *Kingston Farmhouse, West Street, Winterborne Kingston, Blandford Forum DT11 9AX* E: cmchichester@tiscali.co.uk

CHICHESTER, Archdeacon of. See IRVINE CAPEL, The Ven Luke Thomas

CHICHESTER, Bishop of. See WARNER, The Rt Revd Martin Clive

CHICHESTER, Dean of. See WAINE, The Very Revd Stephen John

CHIDLAW, Richard Paul. b 49. St Cath Coll Cam BA 71 MA. Ripon Hall Ox 72. **d** 74 **p** 81. C Ribbesford w Bewdley and Dowles *Worc* 74–76; NSM Coaley *Glouc* 81–83; NSM Frampton on Severn 81–83; NSM Arlingham 81–83; NSM Saul w Fretherne and Framilode 83–84; NSM Cam w Stinchcombe 85–90; PtO 90–91; NSM Berkeley w Wick, Breadstone, Newport, Stone etc 91–19; rtd 19. *38 May Lane, Dursley GL11 4HU* T: (01453) 547838

CHIDLOW, Ian Luke. b 90. Sheff Univ BA 11. Oak Hill Th Coll BA 19. **d** 19 **p** 20. C Cheadle *Ches* from 19. *39 Oakfield Avenue, Cheadle SK8 1EF* M: 07475-004360 E: ilchidlow@gmail.com

CHIDWICK, Alan Robert. b 49. MA MIL. Oak Hill NSM Course. **d** 84 **p** 85. NSM Pimlico St Pet w Westmr Ch Ch *Lon* 84–06; rtd 06; PtO *Nor* from 06; *Lon* from 14. *85 Claremont House, 14 Aerodrome Road, London NW9 5NW* T: (020) 8032 5402 E: deslannw9@gmail.com

CHIGUMIRA, Godfrey. St Mich Coll Llan. **d** 99 **p** 00. In RC Ch 99–08; C Hawarden *St As* 08–12; TV Rhos-Cystennin 12–16; C Aberconwy Miss Area 17–21; PtO *Ban* 15–17; TV Forton and Gosport *Portsm* from 21. *The Vicarage, 10 Spring Garden Lane, Gosport PO12 1HY* E: gchigumira@hotmail.co.uk

CHIKE, Canon Chigor. b 66. Glos Univ BA 93 Ox Univ MTh 07 Birm Univ PhD 11 Univ of Wales (Trin St Dav) MA 16. St Jo Coll Nottm 05. **d** 06 **p** 07. C Victoria Docks St Luke *Chelmsf* 06–10; V Forest Gate Em w Upton Cross from 10; P-in-c Forest Gate All SS 13–16; Hon Can Chelmsf Cathl from 20. *Emmanuel Vicarage, 2B Margery Park Road, London E7 9JY* T: (020) 8534 6796 M: 07905-155494 E: chigor.chike@sky.com

CHIKE, Mrs Obaka Echenim. b 70. Westmr Univ BSc 98 City Univ BSc 10. St Mellitus Coll 15. **d** 18 **p** 19. C E Ham St Paul *Chelmsf* from 18. *Emmanuel Vicarage, 2B Margery Park Road, London E7 9JY* T: (020) 8534 6796 M: 07981-435711 E: chikeobaka@yahoo.co.uk

CHILCOTT, Mark David. b 62. Ch Coll Cam BA 83 MA 87 PhD 88. Ripon Coll Cuddesdon BA 92. **d** 93 **p** 94. C Warrington St Elphin *Liv* 93–99; P-in-c Westbrook St Jas

99–01; V 01–02. *Estates Branch, Sedgley Park Centre, Sedgley Park Road, Prestwich, Manchester M25 0JT* T: 0161-856 0505 F: 856 0506

CHILD, Corin James. b 73. Man Univ BA 95. Trin Coll Bris BA 02 MA 03. **d** 03 **p** 04. C Sanderstead *S'wark* 03–07; V King's Lynn St Jo the Ev *Nor* 07–14; Chapl Coll of W Anglia 07–14; Chapl Nor Sch from 14; Hon PV Nor Cathl from 14. *The Chaplain's Office, Norwich School, 70 The Close, Norwich NR1 4DD* T: (01603) 728450 E: corin.child@sky.com *or* cchild@norwich-school.org.uk

CHILD, Canon David Francis. b 44. Birm Univ MB, ChB 67 FRCP 88. St As Minl Tr Course 02. **d** 04 **p** 05. NSM Gresford *St As* 04–07; NSM Bangor Isycoed Deanery 08–12; P-in-c Overton and Erbistock *St As* 12–16; TV Maelor Miss Area 17–18; AD Dee Valley 12–14; Hon Can St As Cathl 13–18; rtd 18. *11 Maelor Court, Overton, Wrexham LL13 0HE* E: d_f_child@yahoo.co.uk

CHILD, James John. b 79. St Jo Coll Ox BA 00. Oak Hill Th Coll BTh 10. **d** 10 **p** 11. C St Helen Bishopsgate w St Andr Undershaft etc *Lon* from 10; PtO *Chelmsf* 16–21. *4 Merrick Square, London SE1 4JB* E: jamiejchild@hotmail.com

CHILD, Margaret Mary. *See* MASLEN, Margaret Mary

CHILDS, Adam Raymond. b 90. Ridley Hall Cam 14. **d** 17 **p** 18. C Walthamstow *Chelmsf* from 17. *76 Brooke Road, London E17 9HH* M: 07807-908034 E: mr.a.childs@gmail.com *or* adam@walthamstowchurch.org.uk

CHILDS, Christopher. b 59. **d** 05 **p** 06. NSM Gt Finborough w Onehouse, Harleston, Buxhall etc *St E* 05–11; P-in-c 11–18; P-in-c Combs and Lt Finborough 13–18; R Combs and Finborough 18–21; TV Forest Heath from 21; RD Mildenhall from 21. *All Saints' Vicarage, The Street, Gazeley, Newmarket CB8 8RB* E: revcchilds@aol.com

CHILDS, David Robert. b 64. Univ Coll Lon BSc 86 Regent's Park Coll Ox MA 95 FRGS 21. Ripon Coll Cuddesdon 99. **d** 99 **p** 00. C Bloxham w Milcombe and S Newington *Ox* 99–02; TV Witney 02–06; TR 06–08; P-in-c Hadleigh St Jas *Chelmsf* 08–16; P-in-c Hadleigh St Barn 12–16; Chapl Southend Univ Hosp NHS Foundn Trust from 16. *Southend University Hospital NHS Foundation Trust, Prittlewell Chase, Westcliff-on-Sea SS0 0RY* T: (01702) 435555 E: dekm@sky.com *or* david.childs@southend.nhs.uk

CHILDS, Emma Jane. *See* WESTERMANN-CHILDS, Emma Jane

CHILDS, Ernest Edmund. b 23. Lich Th Coll 63. **d** 65 **p** 66. C Billesley Common *Birm* 65–68; C Elland *Wakef* 68–69; Clerical Org Sec CECS Pet, Leic and Ely 69–72; V Staverton w Helidon and Catesby *Pet* 72–76; rtd 77; PtO *Nor* 77–91; Hon C W Lynn *Ely* 92–94; P-in-c 94–95; PtO 95–00; *Nor* from 96. *4 Fieldview Court, Fakenham NR21 8PB* T: (01328) 856595

CHILDS, Mrs Frances Mary. b 54. MIOSH 98 GIFireE 09. Wycliffe Hall Ox 02 Ripon Coll Cuddesdon 15. **d** 16 **p** 17. OLM Didcot St Pet *Ox* from 16. *3 South Park Avenue, Didcot OX11 8NB* T: (01235) 816166 M: 07798-643962 E: fran.childs@btinternet.com

CHILDS, Michael Thomas. b 79. Hull Univ BA 01. St Steph Ho Ox BTh 10. **d** 10 **p** 11. C Swinton *Sheff* 10–13; C Edmonton St Alphege *Lon* 13–17; P-in-c 17–18; C Ponders End St Matt 13–17; P-in-c 17–18; V Morecambe St Barn *Blackb* from 18. *St Barnabas' Vicarage, 101 Regent Road, Morecambe LA3 1AG* T: (01524) 951521 E: westendpriest@gmail.com

✠**CHILLINGWORTH, The Rt Revd David Robert.** b 51. TCD BA 73 Oriel Coll Ox BA 75 MA 81. Ripon Coll Cuddesdon 75. **d** 76 **p** 77 **c** 05. C Belfast H Trin *Conn* 76–79; Ch of Ireland Youth Officer 79–83; C Bangor Abbey *D & D* 83–86; I Seagoe 86–05; Dean Dromore 95–02; adn Dromore 02–05; Bp St And 05–17; Primus 09–17; rtd 17; PtO *Edin* from 18. *9 Almondhill Steading, Kirkliston EH29 9LA* T: 0131-333 2038 E: david@chillingworth.org.uk

CHILTON, Janice Marguerite. b 43. **d** 08. NSM Wallingford *Ox* 08–13; rtd 13; PtO *Ox* from 13. *2 Fairthorne Memorial, West End, Brightwell-cum-Sotwell, Wallingford OX10 0RY* T: (01491) 836661 E: jchilton894@btinternet.com

CHINDABATA, Miss Unesu Audrey. b 74. Birkbeck Coll Lon BSc 06 K Coll Lon BA 13 AKC 13 Anglia Ruskin Univ MA 15. Westcott Ho Cam 13. **d** 15 **p** 16. C Is of Dogs Ch Ch and St Jo w St Luke *Lon* 15–18; V Thames View *Chelmsf* from 18; P-in-c Becontree St Cedd from 21. *Christ Church Vicarage, Bastable Avenue, Barking IG11 0NG* T: (020) 8594 1976 M: 07534-582578 E: rev@christchurch-thamesview.org.uk

CHIPLIN, Christopher Gerald. b 53. Lon Univ BSc 75. St Steph Ho Ox BA 77 MA 81. **d** 78 **p** 79. C Chesterfield St Mary and All SS *Derby* 78–80; C Thorpe St Andr *Nor* 80–84; V Highbridge *B & W* 84–94; V Midsomer Norton w Clandown 94–19; rtd 19. *74 St Ann Street, Salisbury SP1 2DX* E: cchi759070@aol.com

CHIPLIN, Howard Alan. b 43. Sarum & Wells Th Coll 84. **d** 86 **p** 87. C Caerleon *Mon* 86–89; V Ferndale w Maerdy *Llan* 89–91; V Ysbyty Cynfyn w Llantrisant and Eglwys Newydd *St D* 91–95; R Narberth w Mounton w Robeston Wathen and Crinow 95–02; V Grwp Bro Ystwyth a Mynach 02–08; rtd 08; PtO *St D* from 08; *Ban* 08–14; AD Arwystli 11–15; PtO from 15. *Minffordd, 15 Hafren Terrace, Llanidloes SY18 6AT* T: (01686) 413619

CHIPLIN, Malcolm Leonard. b 42. St Mich Coll Llan 86. **d** 88 **p** 89. C Newton Nottage *Llan* 88–91; V Pwllgwaun w Llanddewi Rhondda 91–03; V Mountain Ash and Miskin 03–08; rtd 08; PtO *Llan* from 08. *3 Maes y Ffynon Grove, Aberaman, Aberdare CF44 6PJ* T: (01685) 874720 E: malcolmchiplin@aol.com

CHIPPENDALE, Peter David. b 34. Dur Univ BA 55. Linc Th Coll 57. **d** 59 **p** 60. C St Claines *Worc* 59–63; V Defford w Besford 63–73; P-in-c Eckington 66–69; V 69–73; V Kidderminster St Geo 73–76; V The Lickey *Birm* 76–96; rtd 96. *1 Fairways, Pershore WR10 1HA* T: (01386) 553478

CHIPPER, Stanley Mark Edwin (Joe). b 63. Ripon Coll Cuddesdon 18. **d** 21. C Tupsley w Hampton Bishop *Heref* from 21. *25 Loder Drive, Hereford HR1 1DS* T: (01432) 649158 M: 07727-163074 E: streetpastor@live.co.uk *or* joe.chipper@rcc.ac.uk

CHISHOLM, Canon Ian Keith. b 36. AKC 62. **d** 63 **p** 64. C Lich St Chad 63–66; C Sedgley All SS 66–69; V Rough Hills 69–77; V Harrow Weald All SS *Lon* 77–88; V W Moors *Sarum* 88–01; Can and Preb Sarum Cathl 00–01; rtd 01; PtO *Sarum* from 02. *33 Meadway, Shrewton, Salisbury SP3 4HE* T: (01980) 620579 E: ian.chisholm250@btinternet.com

CHISHOLM, Ian Stuart. b 37. ALCD 63. **d** 63 **p** 64. C Worksop St Jo *S'well* 63–66; Succ Sheff Cathl 66–68; Bp's Chapl for Soc Resp 68–72; C Ox St Andr 72–76; Tutor Wycliffe Hall Ox 72–76; V Conisbrough *Sheff* 76–94; Chapl Conisbrough Hosp 76–94; RD W Doncaster *Sheff* 82–87 and 93–94; V Chilwell *S'well* 94–99; rtd 99; PtO *Sheff* 94–10; Linc from 00; *S'well* 03–08. *72 Broadbank, Louth LN11 0EW* T: (01605) 605970 E: ianchisholm700@btinternet.com

CHISLETT, David Edward. b 52. **d** 79 **p** 80. C Sydney St Laur Australia 79–80; C Warnambool 80–82; R Skipton 82–85; R Horsham 85–93; P-in-c S Ballarat 93–95; R Brisbane All SS 95–05; PtO The Murray 07–15; PtO *S'wark* 15–18; V Benhilton from 18. *All Saints' Vicarage, All Saints' Road, Sutton SM1 3DA* E: david@fministry.com

CHISLETT, David Norman Hilton. b 61. Kingston Poly BSc 83 UEA PGCE 84. Ridley Hall Cam 00. **d** 02 **p** 03. C Highley w Billingsley, Glazeley etc *Heref* 02–05; TV Eston w Normanby *York* 05–09; C Bridlington Quay Ch Ch 09–14; C Bessingby 09–14; rtd 14; PtO *York* from 19. E: dave.chislett@me.com

CHISLETT, David William. b 61. St Mellitus Coll MA 18. Ripon Coll Cuddesdon 19. **d** 21. NSM Warfield *Ox* from 21. *25 Queensbury Gardens, Ascot SL5 9GG* T: (020) 3282 7118 M: 07379-839720 E: E-mail addressdavid.chislett@warfield.org.uk

CHITHAM, Ernest John. b 57. LSE BSc 79 Leeds Univ PGCE 80 Dur Univ MA 84. NEOC 88. **d** 91 **p** 92. C Swanborough *Sarum* 91–94; CMS 94–99; R Beirut All SS Lebanon 95–98; TV Worthing Ch the King *Chich* 99–05; P-in-c 05–08; V Worthing St Matt 08–16; Bp's Dom Chapl *Blackb* 16–19; R Standon and The Mundens w Sacombe *St Alb* from 19. *The Vicarage, Kents Lane, Standon, Ware SG11 1PJ* M: 07940-498549 E: chitham.john@gmail.com *or* rector@ubsms.org

CHITHAM-MOSLEY, Conan Martin Maximillian. b 68. **d** 16 **p** 17. NSM Moseley St Mary and St Anne *Birm* 16–19; NSM Birm St Paul from 19; Chapl Birm Repertory Theatre from 16. *Burritt's House, 11 Victoria Road, Harborne, Birmingham B17 0AG* M: 07775-833884 E: revconan@burritt.co.uk *or* conan.chitham@stpaulsjg.church

CHITTY, Lynne. b 64. **d** 06. NSM Glouc Cathl 06–08. *Rocknell Manor Farm, Westleigh, Tiverton EX16 7ES* T: (01884) 829000 E: lynnechittyso@gmail.com

CHIUMBU, Esther Tamisa. *See* PRIOR, Esther Tamisa

CHIVERS, Canon Christopher Mark. b 67. Magd Coll Ox BA 88 MA 92 Selw Coll Cam BA 96 MA 00. Westcott Ho Cam 94. **d** 97 **p** 98. C Friern Barnet St Jas *Lon* 97–99; Can Prec St Geo Cathl Cape Town S Africa 99–01; Min Can and Prec Westmr Abbey 01–05; Can Res and Chan Blackb Cathl 05–10; V Mill Hill Jo Keble Ch *Lon* 10–15; C Mill Hill St Mich 11–15; AD W Barnet 14–15; PV Westmr Abbey from 12; Hon Can Salisbania Bay S Africa from 14; Prin Westcott Ho Cam 15–19. *Address temp unknown*

CHIVERS, Royston George. b 34. Glouc Th Course. **d** 83 **p** 84. NSM Gorsley w Cliffords Mesne *Glouc* 83–85; NSM Newent and Gorsley w Cliffords Mesne from 85. *Mayfield, Gorsley, Ross-on-Wye HR9 7SJ* T: (01989) 720492

CHMIELEWSKI, Dominik Abraham. b 79. Evang Sch of Th Wrocław BA 14. Ripon Coll Cuddesdon MA 19. **d** 19 **p** 20. C Arundel w Tortington and S Stoke *Chich* from 19. *Torton Springs, 44B Torton Hill Road, Arundel BN18 9HL* T: (01903) 882811 M: 07925-689788 E: dominikchmielewski@gmail.com

CHO, Paul Hang-Sik. b 61. Kent Univ MA 96 PhD 04. Chr Th Sem & Div Sch of Korea BTh 93. **d** 00 **p** 01. C Munster Square Ch Ch and St Mary Magd *Lon* 00–07; Chapl Angl Korean Community 00–07; Consultant for Institutional Advancement Ox Cen for Miss Studies 08–11; Prof St Andr Th Sem Philippines 10–15; PtO *Birm* 15–19; P-in-c W Heath from 19. *54A Lilley Lane, Birmingham B31 3JT* T: 0121-251 0123 M: 07445-985165 E: frpaulcho@gmail.com

CHOI, Soon-Han. b 64. Bapt Sem Seoul BA 94 Surrey Univ MA 99. **d** 10. NSM St Marylebone Annunciation Bryanston Street *Lon* 10–14; PtO from 14; Chapl Qu Mary Univ of Lon 16–17; Chapl W Lon Univ 17; PtO *Eur* from 18. *Flat 8, 33 Lexham Gardens, London W8 5JR* T: (020) 7373 5025 M: 07808-081179 E: soonpray@gmail.com

CHOLDCROFT, Graham Charles. b 49. Ripon Coll Cuddesdon 07. **d** 10 **p** 11. NSM Thame *Ox* from 10; Chapl Thames Valley Police from 10. *100 Aylesbury Road, Thame OX9 3AY* T: (01844) 216979 M: 07851-191842 E: graham-choldcroft@supanet.com

CHORLTON, Christopher James Woodard. b 73. Westmr Coll Ox BTh 94 Leeds Univ PGCE 98. **d** 10 **p** 12. C Cairo Cathl Egypt 10–16; C Maadi 14–16; C Manningham *Leeds* 16–18; C Heaton St Barn 16–18; C Girlington, Heaton and Manningham 18–19; R from 19. *The Vicarage, 130 Haworth Road, Bradford BD9 6LL* E: chris.chorlton@leeds.anglican.org

CHORLTON, John Samuel Woodard. b 45. Newc Univ BSc 67. Wycliffe Hall Ox 89. **d** 89 **p** 91. Jerusalem 79–92; C Ox St Aldate 92–04; AD Ox 99–04; TV W Slough 04–08; V Britwell 08–14; Voc Adv 98–14; rtd 14; PtO *Ox* from 14. *6 Martin Close, Botley, Oxford OX2 9GU* M: 07517-454433 E: jsw@chorlton.org

CHOW, Ms Katherine King Yee. b 82. Brunel Univ LLB 03. St Mellitus Coll 19. **d** 20 **p** 21. C Onslow Square and S Kensington St Aug *Lon* from 20. *Flat 2, The Vicarage, 117 Queen's Gate, London SW7 5LP* T: (020) 7052 0291 M: 07742-436889 E: katherine.chow@htb.org

CHOW, Ting Suie Roy. b 46. Brasted Th Coll 68 Sarum & Wells Th Coll 70. **d** 72 **p** 73. C Weaste *Man* 72–74; C Swinton St Pet 74–78; R Blackley St Paul 78–85; Sec SPCK (Dio Man) from 80; R Burnage St Nic *Man* 85–95; P-in-c Man Gd Shep 95–97; P-in-c Openshaw 95–97; R Manchester Gd Shep and St Barn 97–13; rtd 13; PtO *Man* from 13. *5 Towton Street, Manchester M9 4JA* T: 0161-205 3432 M: 07855-182990

CHRICH, Andrew James. b 70. Girton Coll Cam BA 92 MA 96. Cranmer Hall Dur BA 96. **d** 96 **p** 97. C Gerrards Cross and Fulmer *Ox* 96–99; Chapl Trin Coll Cam 99–04; R Linton in Craven *Bradf* 04–09; P-in-c Burnsall w Rylstone 04–09; V Trumpington *Ely* 09–18; V Highbury Ch Ch w St Jo and St Sav *Lon* from 18. *Christ Church Vicarage, 155 Highbury Grove, London N5 1SA* T: (020) 7226 2201 or 7354 0741 E: andychrich@virginmedia.com or vicar@christchurchhighbury.com

CHRISTENSEN, Mrs Carole Glenda. b 45. Qu Coll Birm 07. **d** 09 **p** 10. NSM Blackheath *Birm* 09–15; rtd 15; PtO *Man* from 15; *Birm* 15–20. *73 John Street, Rowley Regis B65 0EN* T: 0121-561 5561 E: christensen_250@hotmail.com or carolechristensen250@gmail.com

CHRISTENSEN, Nikolaj. b 86. Aarhus Univ BTh 11 MTh 13 Birm Univ PhD 17. Ripon Coll Cuddesdon 18. **d** 19 **p** 20. C Iffley *Ox* from 19. *Church House, The Oval, Oxford OX4 4SE* M: 07741-087877 E: nikolajchr@gmail.com

CHRISTENSEN, Canon Norman Peter. b 37. St D Coll Lamp BA 63. Ridley Hall Cam 63. **d** 65 **p** 66. C Barnston *Ches* 65–70; V Over St Jo 70–77; R Bromborough 77–92; RD Wirral S 86–92; Hon Can Ches Cathl 90–02; Chapl Arrowe Park Hosp Wirral 92–96; V Higher Bebington *Ches* 96–02; rtd 02; PtO *Ches* 02–19. *13 Howbeck Close, Prenton CH43 6TH* T: 0151-652 9869 E: canonpc@uwclub.net

CHRISTIAN, Daniel Chung. b 85. St Jo Coll Dur BA 07. Wycliffe Hall Ox MSt 10 DPhil 15. **d** 12 **p** 13. C Chester le Street *Dur* 12–16; C Ecclesall *Sheff* from 16. *162 Knowle Lane, Sheffield*

S11 9SJ M: 07841-835711 E: dan.christian@dunelm.org.uk *or* dan.christian@allsaintsecclesall.org.uk

CHRISTIAN, Helen. *See* HORNBY, Helen

CHRISTIAN, Mark Robert. b 58. Linc Th Coll 95. **d** 95 **p** 96. C Stockport SW *Ches* 95–98; CF 98–08; Sen CF 08–11; Dep Asst Chapl Gen 11–15; Hon C Whitchurch w Tufton and Litchfield *Win* from 15; Asst Chapl Naomi Ho Hospice 17–19. *Red House, Litchfield, Whitchurch RG28 7PR* T: (01256) 8969888 M: 07702-516518

CHRISTIAN, Paul. b 49. Cant Sch of Min 84. **d** 87 **p** 88. C Folkestone St Sav *Cant* 87–91; R Temple Ewell w Lydden 91–17; rtd 17. *The Sanctuary, 29 The Boulevard, Pevensey Bay, Pevensey BN24 6RP*

CHRISTIAN, Richard. b 37. Nottm Univ DipEd 74 Ox Univ MA 81. AKC 62. **d** 63 **p** 65. C Camberwell St Mich w All So w Em *S'wark* 63–66; C Woolwich St Mary w H Trin 66–70; Chapl and Lect Bp Lonsdale Coll Derby 70–74; P-in-c Hurley *Ox* 76–79; Chapl Lancing Coll 79–81; Chapl Harrow Sch 82–89; Chapl R W Sussex Hosp Chich 89–91; P-in-c Cowley *Lon* 91–95; Chapl Hillingdon Hosp NHS Trust 91–11; PtO *Leic* 12–16; *Pet* 12–17; *Lon* from 17. *3 Crown Street, Harrow HA2 0HT* T: (020) 8423 7970 E: r.christian10@gmail.com

CHRISTIAN-EDWARDS, Canon Michael Thomas. b 36. Down Coll Cam BA 60 MA 64. Clifton Th Coll 60. **d** 62 **p** 63. C Ex St Leon w H Trin 62–67; V Trowbridge St Thos *Sarum* 67–75; R Wingfield w Rowley 67–75; P-in-c Fisherton Anger 75–81; R 81–92; Ind Chapl 85–92; RD Salisbury 85–90; Can and Preb Sarum Cathl 87–92; V Crofton *Portsm* 92–00; rtd 00; PtO *Win* from 02. *Rivendell, Westbeams Road, Sway, Lymington SO41 6AE* T: (01590) 682353 E: mmce@ukpiglet.com *or* michaelchristianedwards@gmail.com

CHRISTIAN-IWUAGWU, Canon Amatu Onundu. b 73. Port Harcourt Univ Nigeria BEng 93. **d** 00 **p** 01. NSM Stonebridge St Mich *Lon* 00–03; St Alb 02–19; NSM Welwyn 04–05; Can Ideato from 03; NSM Stonebridge St Mich *Lon* 05–07; V Harmondsworth 07–21; P-in-c Bush Hill Park St Mark from 21; Missr for Racial Inclusion Edmonton Area from 21; Preb St Paul's Cathl from 20. *The Vicarage, 43A Village Road, Enfield EN1 2ET* M: 07429-863280 E: iwuagwuoa@yahoo.co.uk *or* amatu.christian-iwuagwu@london.anglican.org

CHRISTIANSON, Canon Rodney John (Bill). b 47. St Paul's Coll Grahamstown. **d** 72 **p** 73. C St Sav Cathl Pietermaritzburg S Africa 72–76; Miss to Seafarers 76–09; Min Sec Miss to Seamen 93–00; Sec Gen Miss to Seafarers 00–09; R Richard's Bay S Africa 82–91; Chapl Hull Miss to Seamen 91–93; LtO *Lon* 94–97; V St Mich Paternoster Royal 00–09; rtd 09; PtO *Lon* from 09; *S'wark* from 20; Hon Can Bloemfontein Cathl from 93. *45 Wimbledon Park Court, Wimbledon Park Road, London SW19 6NN* T: (020) 7251 1554 E: bill.christianson@btinternet.com

CHRISTIE, Alexander Robert. b 58. Qu Coll Cam BA 79 LLM 80. Oak Hill Th Coll 92. **d** 94 **p** 95. C W Norwood St Luke *S'wark* 94–98; C Wandsworth All SS 98–03; V Blackheath Park St Mich from 03. *St Michael's Vicarage, 2 Pond Road, London SE3 9JL* T: (020) 8852 5287 E: ar.christie@outlook.com

CHRISTIE (née MOUK), Mae Elizabeth. b 83. **d** 14 **p** 15. C Walworth St Chris *S'wark* 14–17; P-in-c Tooting All SS 17–19; V from 19. *84 Franciscan Road, London SW17 8DQ* T: (020) 8767 7705 M: 07500-309540 E: mae.mouk@icloud.com

CHRISTODOULOU, Kostakis. b 53. Southn Univ CertEd 76 BEd 76. St Mellitus Coll BA 10. **d** 10 **p** 11. NSM Edgware *Lon* from 10. *142 Summers Lane, London N12 0QD* M: 07972-058583 E: kostakis_christodoulou2002@yahoo.co.uk

CHRISTOPHER, Miss Barbara. b 58. Univ of Wales (Swansea) BA 80. **d** 09 **p** 10. OLM Saddleworth *Man* from 09. *2 St Mary's Crest, Greenfield, Oldham OL3 7DS* T: (01457) 876802 E: barbara.christopher@hotmail.com

CHRISTOU, Sotirios. b 51. St Jo Coll Nottm 84. **d** 88 **p** 92. C Berechurch St Marg w St Mich *Chelmsf* 88–89; C Goodmayes All SS 89–90; NSM Harston w Hauxton *Ely* 92–94; LtO 94–95; C Burgess Hill St Andr *Chich* 95–98; PtO *Ely* from 98. *18 Bullen Close, Cambridge CB1 8YU* T: (01223) 977764 E: christousotirios@hotmail.co.uk

CHRYSOSTOMOU, Stefan. b 87. R Holloway Coll Lon BA 08 SS Coll Cam BA 11. Westcott Ho Cam 09. **d** 12 **p** 13. C Finchley St Mary *Lon* 12–16; V Potters Bar *St Alb* from 16. *The Vicarage, 15 The Walk, Potters Bar EN6 1QN* E: revstef@me.com

CHUKUKA, Ifeanyi Emmanuel Chukwunonso. b 76. **d** 09 **p** 10. PtO *Chelmsf* 12–15; NSM Victoria Docks St Luke 15–17; Chapl Barts Health NHS Trust from 16; TV Forest Hill w Lower Sydenham *S'wark* from 17. *St Michael's Vicarage, Champion Crescent, London SE26 4HH* T: (020) 3601 7026 M: 07930-614660 E: ifeanchuks@yahoo.com

CHUMBLEY, Lore Elinor Jane. b 59. **d** 12 **p** 13. NSM Stockton Heath *Ches* 12–16; P-in-c Bath Ch Ch Prop Chpl *B & W* from 16. *8 St James's Street, Bath BA1 2TW* E: lore.chumbley@talktalk.net

CHUMU MUTUKU, Norbert. b 68. Urbanian Univ Rome BA 89 St Jo Fisher Coll USA MSc 00. St Mathias Mulumba Sem Kenya 89. **d** 93 **p** 94. In RC Ch 93–02; C Milton *Portsm* 03–06; C Pitsea w Nevendon *Chelmsf* 06–11; TV Wickford and Runwell 11–18; NSM Risborough Ox from 18. *The Rectory, Church End, Bledlow, Princes Risborough HP27 9PD* T: (01844) 344762 E: nchumu@yahoo.com

CHURCH, Mrs Annette Marie. b 56. **d** 09 **p** 10. C Caldicot *Mon* 09–14; P-in-c Shaldon, Stokeinteignhead, Combeinteignhead etc *Ex* 14–15; R 15–21; rtd 21. *14 Somerset Road, Brentford TW8 8BX* M: 07789-778312 E: anniechurch@hotmail.com *or* revannie@hotmail.co.uk

CHURCH, Janet May. b 60. Bris Univ BA 04. Sarum Coll 18. **d** 20 **p** 21. NSM Cannington, Otterhampton, Combwich and Stockland *B & W* from 20. *18 Ship Lane, Combwich, Bridgwater TA5 2QT* M: 07733-433526 E: mercifulezra@hotmail.com

CHURCH, Canon Linda Ann. b 51. MCSP 73. EMMTC 88. **d** 91 **p** 94. NSM Kirkby in Ashfield St Thos *S'well* 91–95; NSM Skegby and Teversal 95–98; P-in-c Annesley w Newstead 98–03; TR Hucknall Torkard 03–09; Hon Can S'well Minster 07–09; R Fowlmere, Foxton, Shepreth and Thriplow *Ely* 09–13; RD Shingay 13; Dir Min 14–20; Hon Can Ely Cathl 14–20; PtO 14–18; rtd 20; PtO *Nor* from 21. *10 Penrice Road, Little Plumstead, Norwich NR13 5FP* T: (01603) 570065 E: canonlinda.church@btinternet.com

CHURCH, Robert Hugh. b 89. K Coll Lon BA 11. Ripon Coll Cuddesdon BA 16. **d** 17 **p** 18. C Tetbury, Beverston, Long Newnton etc *Glouc* 17–20; Chapl RN from 20. *Royal Naval Chaplaincy Service Headquarters, Tanner Building, HMS Excellent, Whale Island, Portsmouth PO2 8ER* T: 0300-157 7544 M: 07854-656547 E: robert-church@hotmail.co.uk

CHURCH, William John. b 41. Qu Coll Cam MA 62 Solicitor. SAOMC 96. **d** 99 **p** 00. NSM Bengeo *St Alb* 99–01; NSM Gt Amwell w St Margaret's and Stanstead Abbots 01–05; NSM Hertford 05–18; PtO from 18. *115 Queen's Road, Hertford SG13 8BJ* T: (01992) 410469 F: 583079 E: bill.church@hertscc.gov.uk *or* churchwj@hotmail.com

CHURCHER, Ms Mandy. b 54. Brunel Univ MEd 92 Surrey Univ PGCE 87 RN 75 RM 77. NTMTC 96. **d** 99 **p** 00. C Wolverhampton St Matt *Lich* 99–02; Assoc Chapl Plymouth Hosps NHS Trust 02–06; Chapl S Devon Healthcare NHS Foundn Trust 06–11; NSM Malmesbury w Westport and Brokenborough *Bris* 11–16; NSM Malmesbury and Upper Avon 16–20. *The Old Squash Court, Holloway, Malmesbury SN16 9BA* T: (01666) 826666 E: mandy@malmesburyabbey.com

CHYNCHEN, John Howard. b 38. FRICS 72. Sarum & Wells Th Coll 88. **d** 89 **p** 90. Bp's Dom Chapl *Sarum* from 89; Hon Chapl Hong Kong Cathl 90–07; Chapl 07–14; Hon Chapl 14–18; Abp's Chapl for Internat Min Hong Kong from 19; PtO *Eur* from 10. *Bishop's House, 1 Lower Albert Road, Hong Kong* T: (00852) 3487 6155 F: 3487 6404 M: (00852) 9019 0495 E: john.chynchen@hkskh.org

CICILY ANTONY, Dioynisious. b 66. Urban Univ Rome BPh 88 BTh 94 Indira Gandhi Nat Open Univ MA 07 MBA 09 AKC 16. **d** 93. NSM Uxbridge *Lon* 17–19; NSM Hillingdon All SS from 19; PtO *Chelmsf* from 18. *10 Queens Road, Uxbridge UB8 2NN* T: (01895) 473942 M: 07775-503510 E: dinysca@yahoo.com

CIECHANOWICZ, Edward Leigh Bundock. *See* BUNDOCK, Edward Leigh

CINNAMOND, Andrew Victor. b 71. St Andr Univ MA 94 Lon Sch of Th PhD 12. Wycliffe Hall Ox BA 00. **d** 01 **p** 02. C Clapham H Trin and St Pet *S'wark* 01–05; C Wandsworth All SS 05–11; TV S Cotswolds *Glouc* from 11. *The Vicarage, Sherborne Street, Lechlade GL7 3AH* T: (01367) 253651 E: andrew_cinnamond@hotmail.com

CLACEY, Derek Phillip. St Jo Coll Nottm 76. **d** 79 **p** 80. C Gt Parndon *Chelmsf* 79–82; C Walton H Trin Ox 82–88; R Bramshaw and Landford w Plaitford *Sarum* 88–04; P-in-c Redlynch and Morgan's Vale 03–04; TV E Greenwich *S'wark* 04–13; rtd 13; PtO *Bris* from 15. *111 Forest Road, Fishponds, Bristol BS16 3ST* E: derekclacey@aol.com

CLACK (née JERWOOD), Mrs Eleanor Alice Jerwood. b 80. Bath Univ BSc 03. St Jo Coll Nottm MTh 09. **d** 08 **p** 09. C New Milverton *Cov* 08–11; PtO 11–18; LtO from 18; Dioc Communications Officer 13–15; Dioc Voc Adv from 15; Dioc Dir of Ords from 18. *Coventry Cathedral and Diocese, 1 Hill Top, Coventry CV1 5AB* T: (024) 7652 1374 M: 07802-657768 E: ellie.clack@covcofe.org

CLACK, Robert John Edmund. b 63. Lanc Univ BA 85 Ches Univ MA 14. Coll of Resurr Mirfield 89. **d** 92 **p** 93. C Bury St Pet *Man* 92–95; Chapl Bury Colls of FE 93–95; TV New Bury *Man* 95–97; R Ashton-upon-Mersey St Martin *Ches* 97–11; V Ches St Oswald and St Thos 11–16; Chapl Ches Univ 14–19; PtO *Liv* 17–19; R Wavertree H Trin from 19. *The Rectory, Hunters Lane, Liverpool L15 8HL* T: 0151-733 2172

CLAMMER, Canon Thomas Edward. b 80. Sussex Univ BA 01 CCC Cam BA 04 MA 09 Win Univ PhD 17 ARSCM 20. Westcott Ho Cam 02. **d** 05 **p** 06. C Wotton St Mary *Glouc* 05–08; P-in-c Deerhurst and Apperley w Forthampton etc 08–12; Dioc Worship Officer 08–12; C Tewkesbury w Walton Cardiff and Twyning 10–12; Can Res Sarum Cathl 12–19; PtO 19–21; *Glouc* from 19; *Lon* from 19. *6 Lime Kiln Way, Salisbury SP2 8RN* M: 07811-639741 E: tomclammer@gmail.com

CLAMPIN, Amanda Jane. b 68. St Aug Coll of Th 19. **d** 21. C Kingsdown *Roch* from 21. *Coach House, Vigo Road, Fairseat, Sevenoaks TN15 7LU* T: (01732) 823948 M: 07851-732489

CLAPHAM, Christopher Charles. b 69. Man Univ BA 91 St Jo Coll Dur BA 96 Man Univ PhD 04. Cranmer Hall Dur 94 Union Th Sem (NY) STM 98. **d** 99 **p** 00. NSM Withington St Chris *Man* 99–01; C Didsbury Ch Ch 01–03; P-in-c Swinton H Rood 03–08; Chapl Keele Univ *Lich* 08–12; TV Wolstanton 12–14; V 14–15; V Hammersmith St Pet *Lon* from 15. *17 Ravenscourt Road, London W6 0UH* M: 07979-093418 E: charles.clapham@sky.com

CLAPHAM, George Henry James. b 52. Trin Coll Bris. **d** 08 **p** 09. C Wellington and Distr *B & W* 08–12; V Wilton 12–19; rtd 19; PtO *B & W* from 20. *15 Shuteleigh, Wellington TA21 8PG* T: (01823) 664880 E: dispo_box@hotmail.com

CLAPHAM, John. b 47. Open Univ BA 76. Sarum & Wells Th Coll 77. **d** 80 **p** 81. Dep PV Ex Cathl 80–09; C Lympstone 85–87; P-in-c 87–99; P-in-c Woodbury 97–99; RD Aylesbeare 96–01; R Lympstone and Woodbury w Exton 99–09; rtd 09. *375 Topsham Road, Exeter EX2 6HB* T: (01392) 873345 E: johnclaphamuk@btinternet.com

CLAPHAM, Kenneth. b 47. Trin Coll Bris 76. **d** 78 **p** 79. C Pemberton St Mark Newtown *Liv* 78–81; C Darfield *Sheff* 81–83; P-in-c Over Kellet *Blackb* 83–88; V 88–16; rtd 16; PtO *Blackb* 16–17. *38 Fairhope Avenue, Morecambe LA4 6JZ* T: (01524) 415069 E: ukvicar@gmail.com

CLAPHAM, Stephen James. b 61. Portsm Poly BSc 84 Ches Coll of HE BTh 04. NOC 01. **d** 04 **p** 05. C Nantwich *Ches* 04–06; V Crewe All SS and St Paul w St Pet 07–15; P-in-c Church Lawton 15–20; R from 20; Dioc Ecum Officer from 15; RD Congleton from 18. *Alphabet House, Liverpool Road West, Church Lawton, Stoke-on-Trent ST7 3DZ* T: (01270) 876604 E: stevclapham@outlook.com

CLAPPERTON, Carolin Beryl (Sister Carolin Clare). b 43. Westcott Ho Cam 04. **d** 05 **p** 06. NSM Faversham *Cant* 05–08; NSM The Brents and Davington w Oare and Luddenham 08–11; rtd 11; PtO *Cant* 12–13; *Ox* 13–15 and from 19; OSC from 16. *St Mary's Convent, Wroslyn Road, Freeland, Witney OX29 8AJ* T: (01993) 881227 E: carolin@oscfreeland.co.uk

CLAPSON, Clive Henry. b 55. Leeds Univ BA 76. Trin Coll Toronto MDiv 79. **d** 79 **p** 80. C Belleville St Thos Canada 79–80; R Loughborough 80–83; V Alpine Ch the K USA 83–88; C Hawley H Trin *Guildf* 88–90; R Invergordon St Ninian *Mor* 90–00; Prin Moray Ord and Lay Tr Course 90–94; Can St Andr Cathl Inverness 97–00; R Aberdeen St Mary *Ab* 00–05; R Dundee St Salvador *Bre* 05–20; rtd 20. *5 George House, 14 Brown Street, Haddington EH41 3JH* E: cliveclapson@gmail.com

CLAPTON, Timothy. b 59. Westmr Coll Ox MTh 92. Westcott Ho Cam 96. **d** 98 **p** 99. C Wimborne Minster *Sarum* 98–02; Ecum Chapl Milton Keynes Gen NHS Trust 02–05; Milton Keynes Miss Partnership Development Chapl *Ox* 05–10; PtO *S'wark* 11–15; *Lon* 14–15; Hon C St Geo-in-the-East w St Paul from 15; PtO *S'wark* from 16; Chapl HM Pris Wandsworth from 17. *HM Prison Wandsworth, PO Box 757, London SW18 3HS* T: (020) 8588 4249 E: timothy.clapton@justice.gov.uk

CLARE, Christopher. b 52. Sheff Univ BSc 73 Nottm Univ PGCE 74. Ox Min Course 89. **d** 92 **p** 93. NSM Chesham Bois *Ox* from 92. *5 Lime Tree Walk, Amersham HP7 9HY* T: (01494) 766513 E: cc@challoners.com

CLARE, Ms Johanna Howard. b 64. Bris Univ BSc 86 Heythrop Coll Lon MA 98. Ridley Hall Cam 97. **d** 99 **p** 00. C Coulsdon St Jo *S'wark* 99–02; TV Morden 02–09; Dioc Continuing Professional Development Officer 09–14; PtO 14; *Truro* 14–18; P-in-c Mawnan from 18. *Trelowen, 16 Forth An Cos, Ponsanooth, Truro TR3 7RJ* T: (01872) 864129 M: 07919-186307 E: rev.johanna.clare@gmail.com

CLARE, Mrs Sarah Catherine Jane. b 57. Reading Univ BA 79. St Mellitus Coll BA 11. **d** 11 **p** 12. C St Helier's Bay NZ 11–17; PtO *Chelmsf* 17–20; C Gt Totham and Lt Totham w Goldhanger from 20; C N Blackwater from 20. *Mellwick,*

5 Monks Walk, Tollesbury, Maldon CM9 8XP T: (01621) 868819 M: 07762-840905 E: sarahclare8@gmail.com

CLARE, Sister. *See* LOCKHART, Clare Patricia Anne

CLARIDGE, Antony Arthur John. b 37. Hull Univ MA LRAM. Bris & Glouc Tr Course. **d** 84 **p** 85. NSM Keynsham *B & W* 84–97; Bp's Officer for NSMs 90–10; Min Bath Ch Ch Prop Chpl 97–10; rtd 10; PtO *B & W* from 11. *62 Cranwells Park, Bath BA1 2YE* T: (01225) 427462 M: 07988-745721 E: antony.claridge@btinternet.com

CLARIDGE, Michael John. b 61. MCIEH. Qu Coll Birm 89 Bossey Ecum Inst Geneva 91. **d** 92 **p** 93. C Harlescott *Lich* 92–95; P-in-c Wellington Ch Ch 95–97; V 97–03; V W Bromwich St Andr w Ch Ch 03–17; RD W Bromwich 15–17; P-in-c Cotteridge *Birm* from 17; Bp's Ecum Adv from 18. *118 Northfield Road, Kings Norton, Birmingham B30 1DX* T: 0121-433 5176 E: mjclaridge@me.com *or* mike.claridge@thecotteridgechurch.org.uk

CLARINGBULL (née DAVID), Canon Faith Caroline. b 55. St Aid Coll Dur BA 77. Ripon Coll Cuddesdon 87. **d** 89 **p** 94. Par Dn Is of Dogs Ch Ch and St Jo w St Luke *Lon* 89–93; Asst Chapl R Lon Hosps NHS Trust 93–98; NSM Wheatley *Ox* 98–00; Asst Dioc Dir of Ords *Worc* 00–04; Dioc CME Officer 02–04; Dioc Dir of Ords *Birm* 04–17; Dean of Women's Min 04–17; Hon Can Birm Cathl 05–17; PtO *Lich* 18–21. *3 King George Street, Stoke-on-Trent ST1 2DZ* M: 07539-217072 E: faithclaringbull@hotmail.co.uk

CLARINGBULL, Keith. b 49. Ripon Coll Cuddesdon 98. **d** 00 **p** 01. SSF 69–89; C Droitwich Spa *Worc* 00–04; P-in-c Hampton in Arden *Birm* 04–10; P-in-c Bickenhill 04–10; Chapl Univ Hosp Birm NHS Foundn Trust 13–14; PtO *Birm* 14–17. *3 King George Street, Stoke-on-Trent ST1 2DZ* T: (01782) 857380 M: 07946-150919 E: keithclaringbull@hotmail.com

CLARK, Andrew. b 76. Anglia Poly Univ BA 97. Oak Hill Th Coll BA 08. **d** 08 **p** 09. C Heref St Pet w St Owen and St Jas 08–11; C Barton Seagrave w Warkton *Pet* from 11. *Rectory Cottage, St Botolph's Road, Barton Seagrave, Kettering NN15 6SR* T: (01536) 660363 E: lurpak@aol.com *or* andy@stbots.church

CLARK, Antony. b 61. York Univ BA 83 St Andr Univ PhD. Wycliffe Hall Ox 84. **d** 88 **p** 89. C Ashton-upon-Mersey St Mary Magd *Ches* 88–92; Chapl Lee Abbey 92–95; LtO *Ex* 92–95; Chapl Univ of Westmr *Lon* 95–98; C Bletchley *Ox* 98–00; Chapl Fettes Coll Edin from 12. *Fettes College, Carrington Road, Edinburgh EH4 1QX* T: 0131-332 2281 E: a.clark@fettes.com

CLARK, Bernard Charles. b 34. Open Univ BA 81. S'wark Ord Course 65. **d** 68 **p** 69. C Pemberton St Jo *Liv* 68–71; C Winwick 71–73; P-in-c Warrington St Barn 74–76; V 76–78; V Hindley All SS 78–83; PtO 86–94; R Glazebury w Hollinfare 94–99; rtd 99; PtO *Man* 00–08 and 11–18. *31 Linkfield Drive, Worsley, Manchester M28 1JU* T: 0161-799 7998

CLARK, Canon Caroline Robbins (Robbin). b 45. Mt Holyoke Coll USA BA 67 Columbia Univ BS 70 Univ of California MS 74. Ch Div Sch of Pacific MDiv 81 Ripon Coll Cuddesdon 79. **d** 81 **p** 82. C Upland St Mark USA 81–84; R Santa Fé St Bede 85–90; R Berkeley St Mark 93–10; Dean of Women Clergy *Glouc* 11–16; Hon Can Glouc Cathl 12–16; rtd 16. *1907 Camino Lumbre, Santa Fe NM 87505, USA* T: (001) (510) 410 9998

CLARK, Cecil. b 44. Sarum Th Coll. **d** 98 **p** 99. OLM Canford Magna *Sarum* 98–15; PtO from 15. *Fermain Cottage, 133 Magna Road, Bearwood, Bournemouth BH11 9NE* T: (01202) 577898 *or* 663275 E: fermain133@btinternet.com

CLARK, Mrs Christine Margaret. b 44. SAOMC 01. **d** 01 **p** 02. NSM Croxley Green St Oswald *St Alb* 01–06; P-in-c Odell 06–14; rtd 14; PtO *St Alb* from 14. *99 High Street, Clapham, Bedford MK41 6AQ* T: (01234) 918985 M: 07812-524992

CLARK, Daniel Alastair. b 74. St Jo Coll Dur BA 96. Wycliffe Hall Ox BA 99. **d** 00 **p** 01. C Rusholme H Trin *Man* 00–06; NSM 04–06; C Clifton Ch Ch w Em *Bris* 06–12; P-in-c Shirley Win from 12. *The Vicarage, 2B Wordsworth Road, Southampton SO15 5LX*

CLARK, David. b 60. Coll of SS Mark and Jo Plymouth BEd 82. Qu Foundn (Course) 17. **d** 19 **p** 20. NSM Baswich *Lich* from 19. *140 Rickerscote Road, Stafford ST17 4HE* T: (01785) 253111 M: 07999-596590 E: david.clark@berkswich.org.uk

CLARK, David Humphrey. b 39. G&C Coll Cam BA 60. Wells Th Coll. **d** 64 **p** 65. C Leigh St Mary *Man* 64–68; Min Can and Prec Man Cathl 68–70; Ind Chapl *Nor* 70–85; P-in-c Nor St Clem and St Geo 70–76; P-in-c Nor St Sav w St Paul 70–76; V Norwich-over-the-Water Colegate St Geo 76–79; Hon Asst P Nor St Pet Mancroft 79–85; TR Oadby *Leic* 85–98; C Leic St Jas 98–04; rtd 04; PtO *Leic* 04–21. *46 St James Road, Leicester LE2 1HQ* T: 0116-255 8988 E: dhclark2@btinternet.com

CLARK, David John. b 61. Bretton Hall Coll BA 82 MA 06 PGCE 83 Sheff Univ BA 13. Yorks Min Course 10. **d** 13 **p** 14.

C Gildersome *Wakef* 13–14; *Leeds* 14–16; C Drighlington *Wakef* 13–14; *Leeds* 14–16; V Upper Wensleydale from 16. *The Vicarage, Burtersett Road, Hawes DL8 3NP* T: (01969) 667553 M: 07891-329614 E: davejclark61@gmail.com

CLARK, David John. b 40. Surrey Univ MPhil 75 CEng MIStructE. Ridley Hall Cam 81. **d** 83 **p** 84. C Combe Down w Monkton Combe and S Stoke *B & W* 83–89; Voc Adv Bath Adnry 89–96; R Freshford, Limpley Stoke and Hinton Charterhouse *B & W* 89–05; rtd 05; PtO *B & W* from 05. *14 Barn Close, Frome BA11 4ER* T: (01373) 461073 M: 07710-507327 E: david@astrorev.co.uk

CLARK, Diane Catherine. *See* FITZGERALD CLARK, Diane Catherine

CLARK, Edward Robert. b 39. Ex Coll Ox BA 61 MA 65. St Steph Ho *Ox* 61. **d** 63 **p** 64. C Solihull *Birm* 63–67; PtO *Bris* 67–69; *Leic* 69–71; *Ox* 71–80; *St Alb* 80–84; *Cant* from 84. *3 Hunters Bank, Old Road, Elham, Canterbury CT4 6SS* T: (01303) 840134 E: edward.clark.elham@gmail.com

CLARK, Ellen Jane. *See* CLARK-KING, Ellen Jane

CLARK, Ms Erin Marie. b 87. Houghton Coll USA BA 09 Lon Sch of Th MA 13. Westcott Ho Cam 13. **d** 16 **p** 17. C Bethnal Green St Matt w St Jas the Gt *Lon* 16–19; R from 19. *The Rectory, Hereford Street, London E2 6EX* M: 07974-010157 E: erin.clark@london.anglican.org

CLARK, Graham John. b 62. Westf Coll Lon BA 85 Brighton Poly PGCE 86. ERMC 16. **d** 19 **p** 20. NSM Stotfold and Radwell *St Alb* from 19. *17 Heathermere, Letchworth Garden City SG6 4QH* T: (01462) 625270 M: 07842-215560 E: graham.clark20@ntlworld.com

CLARK, Ian Duncan Lindsay. b 35. K Coll Cam BA 59 MA 63 PhD 64. Ripon Hall Ox 62. **d** 64 **p** 65. C Willington *Newc* 64–66; India 66–76; Lect Bp's Coll Calcutta 66; Vice-Prin 69–74; Chapl St Cath Coll Cam 76; Fell 77–85; Tutor 78–85; Dean of Chpl and Lect 80–85; Select Preacher Cam Univ 82; Hon Asst P Kelso *Edin* 85–06; Hon C from 16. *4 Yewtree Lane, Yetholm, Kelso TD5 8RZ* T: (01573) 420323 E: revbirdbath@gmail.com

CLARK, Jacqueline Mary. b 58. **d** 08 **p** 09. OLM Canalside Benefice *Sarum* 08–12; NSM Devizes St Jo w St Mary 12–19; Chapl HM Pris Erlestoke from 19. *HM Prison Erlestoke, Erlestoke, Devizes SN10 5TU* T: (01380) 814250 M: 07948-089865 E: jacqueline.clark3@justice.gov.uk

CLARK, Miss Janet Elizabeth. b 44. Derby Coll of Educn CertEd 65 Open Univ BA 75. Oak Hill Th Coll BA 92. **d** 92 **p** 94. Par Dn Edmonton All SS w St Mich *Lon* 92–94; C 94–96; V Ealing St Steph Castle Hill 96–08; rtd 08; PtO *Ox* from 09. *55 Cranwells Lane, Farnham Common, Slough SL2 3GW* T: (01753) 646546

CLARK, Mrs Jean Robinson. b 32. K Coll Lon AKC BD 79. dss 85 **d** 87 **p** 94. Cov E 85–88; C 87–88; NSM Upper Mole Valley Gp *S'wark* 89–90; Hon Par Dn Charlwood 89–90; LtO *Cov* 90–92; rtd 92; PtO *Cov* from 92. *12 Marlborough Road, Coventry CV2 4EP* T: (024) 7644 2400 E: david@revdgnc.plus.com

CLARK, John David Stanley. b 36. Dur Univ BA 64. Ridley Hall Cam 64. **d** 66 **p** 67. C Benchill *Man* 66–69; C Beverley Minster *York* 69–74; PtO *S'well* 74–76; LtO 76–77; Miss to Seamen 77–80; PtO *York* 80–83; V Egton w Grosmont 83–89; R Thornton Dale w Ellerburne and Wilton 89–01; R Thornton Dale w Allerston, Ebberston etc 01–05; rtd 05; PtO *York* from 05. *22 Swainsea Lane, Pickering YO18 8AP* T: (01751) 476118 E: jdsclark@btinternet.com

CLARK, John Edward Goodband. b 49. Leeds Univ MA 01. Chich Th Coll 70. **d** 73 **p** 74. C Thorpe St Andr *Nor* 73–76; C Earlham St Anne 76–78; Chapl RN 78–82; P-in-c Tittleshall w Godwick, Wellingham and Weasenham *Nor* 82–85; P-in-c Helhoughton w Raynham 82–85; R S Raynham, E w W Raynham, Helhoughton, etc 85–90; R Taverham w Ringland 90–96; V Eggleston and R Middleton-in-Teesdale w Forest and Frith *Dur* 96–03; AD Barnard Castle 00–03; R Caston, Griston, Merton, Thompson etc *Nor* 03–05; PtO from 07. *Old Orchards, Gateley Road, Brisley, Dereham NR20 5LR* T: (01362) 667879

CLARK, John Patrick Hedley. b 37. St Cath Coll Cam BA 61 MA 65 Worc Coll Ox BA 63 MA 72 BD 74 Lambeth Hon DD 89. St Steph Ho Ox 61. **d** 64 **p** 65. C Highters Heath *Birm* 64–67; C Eglingham *Newc* 67–72; P-in-c Newc St Anne 72–77; V Longframlington w Brinkburn 77–95; V Chevington 95–02; rtd 02; PtO *Dur* 02–21. *6 The Cottage, West Row, Greatham, Hartlepool TS25 2HW* T: (01429) 870203

CLARK, Canon John Ronald Lyons. b 47. TCD BA 69 MA 72. Div Hostel Dub 67. **d** 70 **p** 71. C Dundela St Mark *D & D* 70–72; CF 72–75; C Belfast St Aid *Conn* 75–76; I Stranorlar w Meenglas and Kilteevogue *D & R* 76–81; Chapl Wythenshawe Hosp Man 81–95; I Kilgariffe Union *C, C & R*

95–96; Chapl Blackb, Hyndburn and Ribble Valley NHS Trust 96–03; Chapl Co-ord E Lancs Hosps NHS Trust 03–09; Chapl E Lancs Hospice 96–05; Hon Can Blackb Cathl 06–09; rtd 09; PtO *Eur* 09–15. *25 Castle Meadow Drive, Cloughey, Newtownards BT22 1RT* T: (028) 4277 2431 M: 07823-380179 E: rcronnieclark@gmail.com

✠**CLARK, The Rt Revd Jonathan Dunnett.** b 61. Ex Univ BA 83 Bris Univ MLitt 90 Southn Univ MA 96. Trin Coll Bris 84. **d** 88 **p** 89 **c** 12. C Stanwix *Carl* 88–92; Chapl Bris Univ 92–93; Dir of Studies STETS 94–97; Chapl Lon Metrop Univ 97–03; AD Islington 99–03; R Stoke Newington St Mary 03–12; P-in-c Brownswood Park 04–11; Area Bp Croydon *S'wark* from 12. *Croydon Episcopal Area Office, 6 St Peter's Road, Croydon CR0 1HD* T: (020) 8256 9630 F: 8256 9631 M: 07968-845698 E: bishop.jonathan@southwark.anglican.org

CLARK, Jonathan Giles. b 72. **d** 14 **p** 16. C Stroud Team *Glouc* 14–15; C S Cotswolds 15–18; V Chineham *Win* from 18. *1 Hartswood, Chineham, Basingstoke RG24 8SJ* T: (01256) 474280 E: jonathan@christchurchchineham.org.uk

CLARK, Judith Alison. b 88. Man Univ BA 13 MA 14. Ripon Coll Cuddesdon 16. **d** 19 **p** 20. C Leeds City from 19. *Flat 5, 41 The Calls, Leeds LS2 7EY* M: 07968-730544 E: judith.clark@leedsminster.org

CLARK, Julia Ann. b 62. Linc Sch of Th and Min 10. **d** 13 **p** 14. NSM Brumby *Linc* from 13. *13 Rivelin Crescent, Scunthorpe DN16 2AL* T: (01724) 862273 E: julia.clark23@virginmedia.com

CLARK, Kenneth William. b 69. R Holloway Coll Lon BA 92 Trin Coll Cam BA 99 MA 04. Westcott Ho Cam 97. **d** 00 **p** 01. C Bromley St Mark *Roch* 00–04; R Stone from 04; RD Dartford 13–19. *The Rectory, Church Road, Greenhithe DA9 9BE* T: (01322) 382076 E: kenofkent@outlook.com

CLARK, Lance Edgar Dennis. b 52. MBE 93. Linc Th Coll 74. **d** 77 **p** 78. C Arnold *S'well* 77–82; V Brinsley w Underwood 82–87; Chapl RAF 87–02; Chapl Cardiff and Vale NHS Trust 02–10; rtd 10. *Hafod, Gileston, Vale of Glamorgan CF62 4HX* T: (01446) 751077 E: lanceedclark@aol.co.uk

CLARK, Lee Robert. b 82. St Steph Ho Ox BTh 15. **d** 15 **p** 16. C Pimlico St Gabr Lon 15–17; C Kentish Town 17–18; P-in-c Tottenham St Phil from 18. *226 Philip Lane, London N15 4HH* M: 07908-675619 E: lee.clark82@gmail.com

CLARK, Lynn. See PURVIS-LEE, Lynn

CLARK, Canon Martin Hudson. b 46. K Coll Lon BD 68 AKC 68 MTh 91 Birm Univ PGCE 89. **d** 71 **p** 72. C S'wark H Trin 71–74; C Parkstone St Pet w Branksea and St Osmund *Sarum* 74–77; V E Wickham *S'wark* 77–86; V Wandsworth St Anne 86–98; RD Wandsworth 90–95; V Angell Town St Jo 98–07; RD Brixton 01–05; Hon Can S'wark Cathl 05–07; rtd 07; PtO *Cant* 07–08 and from 11; Hon C Deal St Leon w St Rich and Sholden etc 08–10. *27 Century Walk, Deal CT14 6AL* T: (01304) 366586 E: eveandmartin@hotmail.com

CLARK, Melanie Louise. See HARRINGTON, Melanie Louise

CLARK, Michael Arthur. b 46. S Dios Minl Tr Scheme. **d** 83 **p** 84. NSM Monkton Farleigh, S Wraxall and Winsley *Sarum* 83–05; PtO *Chich* from 05. *5 Park West, Southdowns Park, Haywards Heath RH16 4SG* T: (01444) 440831 E: mike_clark55@hotmail.com

CLARK, Michael David. b 45. Ox Univ MA 68. Trin Coll Bris. **d** 72 **p** 73. C Cheadle *Ches* 72–76; Brazil 77–86; Bolivia 86–88; C Wilton *B & W* 89–90; TV 90–99; C Tollington *Lon* 99–01; TR Edgware 01–15; rtd 15; Hon C Bisley, Chalford, France Lynch, and Oakridge etc *Glouc* 15–18. *4 Coates Road, Exeter EX2 5RH* T: (01392) 795406

CLARK, Michael James. b 71. Univ of Wales (Cardiff) BSc 92. Trin Coll Bris BA 02. **d** 02 **p** 03. C Tiverton St Geo and St Paul *Ex* 02–07; TV Newton Tracey, Horwood, Alverdiscott etc 07–16; TR 16–19; Miss Community Development Adv from 19. *Address temp unknown* M: 07889-570159 E: mike.clark@exeter.anglican.org

CLARK, Miss Patricia Mary. b 36. Liv Univ BSc. **d** 88 **p** 94. Par Dn Leaswe *Ches* 88–92; Bp's Officer for Women in Min 89–97; Par Dn Davenham 92–94; C 94–97; rtd 97; PtO *Ches* 97–12; *Blackb* 12–19. *7 Fosbrooke House, 8 Clifton Drive, Lytham St Annes FY8 5RQ* T: (01253) 667052

CLARK, Peter. b 45. Sarum & Wells Th Coll 87. **d** 89 **p** 90. C Portsea St Cuth *Portsm* 89–92; TV Rye *Chich* 92–96 and 04–08; P-in-c Chiddingly w E Hoathly 96–98; R 98–04; rtd 08; PtO *Chich* from 14. *44 Ingrams Way, Hailsham BN27 3NP* T: (01323) 841809 E: clucksville@tiscali.co.uk

CLARK, Canon Peter. b 39. Ch Coll Cam BA 61 MA 65. Chich Th Coll 61. **d** 63 **p** 64. C Huddersfield SS Pet and Paul *Wakef* 63–67; C Notting Hill St Jo *Lon* 67–74; Grenada 75–79; C Hove All SS *Chich* 79; P-in-c Hove St Patr 79–82; V Hove St Patr w Ch Ch and St Andr 82–83; V Battersea Ch Ch and St Steph *S'wark* 83–08; RD Battersea 90–01; Hon Can

S'wark Cathl 96–08; rtd 08; PtO *S'wark* from 08. *46 Havil Street, London SE5 7RS* T: 020-7708 8915 M: 07506-095173 E: peterclark263@btinternet.com

CLARK, Peter. b 47. DipCOT 92. ERMC 04. **d** 07 **p** 08. NSM Vange *Chelmsf* 07–11; Public Preacher 11–13; NSM Thundersley 13–15; PtO from 15. *283 Church Road, Basildon SS14 2NE* T: (01268) 527570 M: 07828-642518 E: frpeterclark@hotmail.co.uk

CLARK, Peter Rodney. b 58. Oriel Coll Ox BA 81 Liv Univ MTh 03 Ches Univ MProf 18 MCIH 93. NOC 97. **d** 00 **p** 01. C Stone St Mich and St Wulfad w Aston St Sav *Lich* 00–03; TV Hanley H Ev 03–12; RD Stoke N 08–12; R Lich St Chad from 12; Bp's Adv for Deliverance Min from 19. *St Chad's Rectory, The Windings, Lichfield WS13 7EX* E: revrod.stchad@gmail.com

CLARK, Mrs Prudence Anne. b 44. Man Coll of Educn CertEd 78. NOC 89. **d** 92 **p** 94. NSM Royton St Anne *Man* 92–94; Hon C 94–95; NSM Haughton St Anne 95–09; PtO from 09. *1 Hereford Way, Stalybridge SK15 2TD* T: 0161-338 5275 E: prueclark1@btinternet.com

CLARK, Miss Rebekah Amy. b 91. UEA BA 12. Ridley Hall Cam 12. **d** 15 **p** 16. C Weston super Mare Ch Ch and Em *B & W* 15–20; C Woking St Mary *Guildf* from 20. *46 Hawthorn Road, Woking GU22 0BA* M: 07749-162996 E: rebekah.clark36@gmail.com

CLARK, Richard Martin. b 60. Ch Coll Cam MA 81 Nottm Univ MA 99. Trin Coll Bris BA 86. **d** 86 **p** 87. C Orpington Ch Ch *Roch* 86–89; C Marple All SS *Ches* 89–92; V Nottingham St Andr *S'well* 92–13; AD Nottingham Cen 08–11; TR Redditch H Trin *Worc* from 13; V Tardebigge from 15. *The Vicarage, Church Road, Webheath, Redditch B97 5PD* M: 07970-823462 E: trhtredditch@gmail.com

CLARK, Rodney. See CLARK, Peter Rodney

CLARK, Ronald. See CLARK, John Ronald Lyons

✠**CLARK, The Rt Revd Sarah Elizabeth.** b 65. Loughb Univ BA 86 Keele Univ MBA 94. St Jo Coll Nottm MA 97. **d** 98 **p** 99 **c** 19. C Porchester *S'well* 98–02; R Carlton-in-Lindrick and Langold w Oldcotes 02–09; AD Worksop 06–09; TR Clifton 09–14; Dean of Women's Min 10–14; Hon Can S'well Minster 10–14; Adn Nottingham 14–19; Suff Bp Jarrow *Dur* from 19. *Bishop's House, 25 Ivy Lane, Gateshead NE9 6QD* T: 0191-491 0917 E: bishop.of.jarrow@durham.anglican.org

CLARK, Simon Peter John. b 68. Westcott Ho Cam 95. **d** 98 **p** 99. C Bocking St Mary *Chelmsf* 98–02; C Edmonton St Alphege *Lon* 02–07; C Ponders End St Matt 02–07; P-in-c Noel Park St Mark 07–17; V from 17; Chapl Coll of Haringey, Enfield and NE Lon 07–12. *St Mark's Vicarage, Ashley Crescent, London N22 6LJ* T: (020) 8888 3442 E: fr.simon@btinternet.com

CLARK, Canon Stephen Kenneth. b 52. Bris Univ BEd 74. Wycliffe Hall Ox 80. **d** 83 **p** 84. C Pitsea *Chelmsf* 83–86; Chapl Scargill Ho 86–89; R Elmley Castle w Bricklehampton and Combertons *Worc* 89–96; Chapl Burrswood Chr Cen *Roch* 96–01; Chapl Team Ldr 01–07; I Annagh w Drumaloor, Cloverhill and Drumlane *K, E & A* 07–12; Can Kilmore Cathl 10–12; Dep Chapl Crowhurst Chr Healing Cen 12–17; rtd 17; PtO *Ely* from 18. *4 Tennyson Place, Ely CB6 3WE* E: skclar@googlemail.com

CLARK, Terence Paul. b 62. Leeds Univ BSc 85 PGCE 94 St Jo Coll Ox DPhil 91. Wycliffe Hall Ox 98. **d** 00 **p** 01. C Whitfield *Derby* 00–10; TR Deane *Man* from 10; P-in-c Lostock St Thos and St Jo 16–20; V from 20; AD Deane 12–19. *Deane Rectory, 234 Wigan Road, Bolton BL3 5QE* T: (01204) 61819 E: deanechurchoffice@btinternet.com *or* rectordeane@btinternet.com

CLARK-KING (née CLARK), Ellen Jane. b 62. Newnham Coll Cam BA 85 MA 89 Lon Univ MA 99 Lanc Univ PhD 03. Ripon Coll Cuddesdon 89. **d** 92 **p** 94. C Colwall w Upper Colwall and Coddington *Heref* 92–95; Chapl SS Coll Cam 95–00; NSM N Shields *Newc* 00–05; Asst Dioc Dir of Ords 01–05; Assoc P Ch Ch Cathl Vancouver Canada 05–12; Cathl V 12-14 and 15–16; Adn Burrard 07–14; Angl Dir Formation Vancouver Sch of Th 14–15; Exec Pastor Grace Cathl San Francisco USA 16–20; Dean K Coll Lon from 20. *King's College London, Strand, London WC2R 2LS* T: (020) 7848 2333 E: dean@kcl.ac.uk

CLARK-KING (formerly KING), Jeremy Norman. b 66. K Coll Lon BD 88 AKC 88 Lon Univ MA 99. Ripon Coll Cuddesdon 88. **d** 90 **p** 91. C Ashby-de-la-Zouch St Helen w Coleorton *Leic* 90–93; C Ledbury w Eastnor *Heref* 93–96; C Cambridge Gt St Mary w St Mich *Ely* 96–00; Chapl Girton Coll Cam 96–99; Chapl Cam Univ 96–99; V Byker St Ant *Newc* 00–05; St V Vancouver St Martin Canada 05–11; R Kerrisdale 12–16; P-in-c San Fransisco St Jo USA 16–20; Dioc IME2 Lead *S'wark* from 20; PtO *Lon* from 20. *Trinity House, 4*

Chapel Court, Borough High Street, London SE1 1HW T: (020) 7939 9400

CLARK MAXWELL, James Michael Gilchrist. b 75. Edin Univ BSc 98 MSc 99 Imp Coll Lon MB, BS 04. TISEC 06 St Jo Coll Nottm 06. **d** 11 **p** 18. NSM Dumfries *Glas* from 11. *Speddoch, Dumfries DG2 9UB* T: (01556) 610355 M: 07720-455253 E: james@speddoch.com

CLARKE, Adrian Melvin. b 68. Middx Univ MA 02. St Mellitus Coll 16. **d** 19 **p** 20. C Woodside Park St Barn *Lon* from 19. *11 Woodward Avenue, London NW4 4NU* M: 07976-373381

CLARKE, Alan John. b 55. St Jo Coll Dur BA 77 MA 85 PGCE. Westcott Ho Cam 78. **d** 80 **p** 81. C Heworth St Mary *Dur* 80–83; C Darlington St Jo 83–87; Asst Chapl Bryanston Sch 87–91; Chapl St Pet High Sch Ex 93–99; Chapl and Hd RS Reed's Sch Cobham 99–15; rtd 15; PtO *Dur* from 16. *Bear's Den, 22 Blackcliffe Way, Bearpark, Durham DH7 7TJ* T: 0191-659 9114 E: alanbearsden@gmail.com

CLARKE, Alexandra Naomi Mary. b 75. Trin Coll Cam BA 96 MA 99 MPhil 97 SS Hild & Bede Coll Dur PhD 02 Anglia Poly Univ BA 04. Westcott Ho Cam 02. **d** 05 **p** 06. C Papworth *Ely* 05–09; R Upper Itchen *Win* 09–11; TV Papworth *Ely* 11–16; Chapl St Bede's Sch Cam from 15. *St Bede's Inter-Church School, Birdwood Road, Cambridge CB1 3TD* T: (01223) 568816 E: aclarke@stbedes.cambs.sch.uk

CLARKE, Miss Alison Clare. b 33. MCST 54 Open Univ BA 85. EAMTC 90. **d** 93 **p** 94. NSM Lt Ilford St Mich *Chelmsf* 93–98; Asst Chapl Newham Healthcare NHS Trust Lon 93–98; PtO *Lon* 94–98; NSM Woodford St Mary w St Phil and St Jas *Chelmsf* 98–03; rtd 03; PtO *Chelmsf* 03–04 and from 07. *20 Manor Court Lodge, 175 High Road, London E18 2PD* T: (020) 8504 5106

CLARKE, Andrew John. b 58. New Coll Edin BD 82 Graduate Soc Dur PGCE 89. Linc Th Coll 84. **d** 86 **p** 87. C High Harrogate Ch Ch *Ripon* 86–88; RE Teacher Royds Hall High Sch Huddersfield 89–91; C Thornbury *Bradf* 91–93; P-in-c Bingley H Trin 93–99; V 99–14; *Leeds* from 14; RD Airedale *Bradf* 00–05. *6 Woodvale Crescent, Bingley BD16 4AL* T: (01274) 562278 E: andrew.clarke@leeds.anglican.org

CLARKE, Ann. See CLARKE, Geraldine Ann

CLARKE (née HARWOOD), Mrs Ann Jane. b 73. SEITE. **d** 08. C Winslow w Gt Horwood and Addington *Ox* 08–11; C Lee Gd Shep w St Pet *S'wark* 11–15; PtO from 15; Chapl Goldsmiths' Coll Lon from 19. *63 Bellingham Road, London SE6 2PW* M: 07903-652927 E: ann@leonandann.org

CLARKE, Anne. b 51. **d** 04 **p** 05. OLM E Dulwich St Jo *S'wark* from 04. *62 Oakhurst Grove, London SE22 9AQ* T: (020) 8693 8752 M: 07788-766783 E: anne@oakhurstgrove.com

CLARKE, Canon Barbara. Bradf Univ BA 87 Leeds Univ PGCE 89 MA 07. NOC 04. **d** 07 **p** 08. *3 Radley Court, Mirfield WF14 9FD* T: (01924) 489292 E: bclarke3@bclarke3.plus.com

CLARKE, Bernard Ronald. b 53. MBE 12. Nottm Univ MA 97 FRGS. Ridley Hall Cam 74. **d** 77 **p** 78. C Leigh Park *Portsm* 77–78; C Petersfield w Sheet 78–81; Chapl RN 81–13; Dir of Ords RN 93–03; Chapl RNR from 13; QHC from 08. *Royal Naval Chaplaincy Service Headquarters, Tanner Building, HMS Excellent, Whale Island, Portsmouth PO2 8ER* T: 0300-157 7544

CLARKE, Mrs Caroline Anne. b 49. Girton Coll Cam BA 75 MA 79 K Coll Lon PGCE 76. SEITE 97. **d** 00 **p** 01. NSM Clapham H Trin *S'wark* 00–19; Chapl Trin Hospice Lon 03–11; AD Lambeth N *S'wark* from 17; PtO from 19. *42 The Chase, London SW4 0NH* T: (020) 7622 0765 M: 07808-858674 E: clarkecaroline@hotmail.com *or* caroline.clarke@holytrinityclapham.org

CLARKE, Claire Margaret Alice. b 74. **d** 14 **p** 15. C Upper Sunbury St Sav *Lon* 14–17; V Hounslow St Paul and Gd Shep from 17. *183 Bath Road, Hounslow TW3 3BU* M: 07810-543197 E: claire@hwparish.org.uk

CLARKE, Canon David James. b 55. Univ of Wales (Abth) BSc(Econ) 77 Keele Univ MA 78 PhD 83. Trin Coll Bris. **d** 84 **p** 85. C Cardigan w Mwnt and Y Ferwig *St D* 84–87; P-in-c Llansantffraed and Llanbadarn Trefeglwys etc 87–88; V 88–91; Chapl Coll of SS Mark and Jo Plymouth 91–96; V Lindfield *Chich* 96–20; Can and Preb Chich Cathl 06–20; rtd 20. *1 Crossfield Cottage, Potmans Lane, Bexhill-on-Sea TN39 5JL* T: (01424) 552855 E: tavyd@aol.com

CLARKE, Dominic James. b 71. Surrey Univ BA 07. STETS 04. **d** 07 **p** 08. C Petersfield *Portsm* 07–11; P-in-c Blackmoor and Whitehill 11–16; V from 16; V Greatham 16–18; PtO *Guildf* 18–21. *The New Vicarage, Blackmoor, Liss GU33 6BN* T: (01420) 489418

CLARKE, Duncan James Edward. b 54. Wycliffe Hall Ox 75. **d** 78 **p** 79. C Newport St Andr *Mon* 78–80; C Griffithstown 80–82; Trinidad and Tobago 82–84 and 95–99; NSM Fleckney and Kilby *Leic* 92–95; USPG 99–15; C Wednesfield

Lich 99; TV 99–01; Asst Chapl HM Pris Wormwood Scrubs 01–02; Chapl HM Pris Haverigg 02–07; Chapl HM Pris Garth 07–09; P-in-c Leyland St Ambrose *Blackb* 09–11; V 11–20; rtd 20. *Address temp unknown* M: 07946-668786

CLARKE, Mrs Elizabeth Hazel. b 55. Ridley Hall Cam 02. **d** 04 **p** 05. C Frankby w Greasby *Ches* 04–09; P-in-c Dodleston 09–11; R from 11. *St Mary's Rectory, Pulford Lane, Dodleston, Chester CH4 9NN* T: (01244) 660257 E: hazelclarke@jcscomputers.co.uk

CLARKE, Fanta. See CLARKE, Kenneth Herbert

CLARKE (née GILMARTIN), Mrs Frances. b 53. Reading Univ BSc 75 PGCE 92. **d** 11 **p** 12. OLM Skellingthorpe w Doddington *Linc* from 11. *12 Shaftesbury Avenue, Lincoln LN6 0QN* T: (01522) 685487 E: frances_clarke@hotmail.co.uk

CLARKE, Francis Alfred. b 46. MCLIP 67 MCMI 82. **d** 08 **p** 09. OLM Weybourne Gp *Nor* 08–16; rtd 16; PtO *Nor* 16–20; P-in-c Weybourne Gp 20; PtO from 20. *7 Alexandra Road, Sheringham NR26 8HU* T: (01263) 825677 E: f.clarke46@btinternet.com

CLARKE, Geraldine Ann. b 46. Hockerill Coll of Educn CertEd 68 ACP 81. NTMTC 93. **d** 96 **p** 97. NSM Aldersbrook *Chelmsf* 96–01; TR Becontree S 01–09; P-in-c N Bersted *Chich* 09–17; Can and Preb Chich Cathl 14–17; Hon C Wanstead St Mary w Ch Ch *Chelmsf* 17–20; Preacher Charterhouse and Dep Master from 20. *The Preacher, The Charterhouse, Charterhouse Square, London EC1M 6AN* T: (020) 3817 4178 E: annclarke@talktalk.net

CLARKE, Hazel. See CLARKE, Elizabeth Hazel

CLARKE, Hilary James. b 41. JP. Univ of Wales (Lamp) BA 64 Ox Univ DipEd 65. St Steph Ho Ox 64. **d** 66 **p** 67. C Kibworth Beauchamp *Leic* 66–68; Chapl to the Deaf 68–71; Prin Officer Ch Miss for Deaf Walsall 71–73; Prin Officer & Sec Leic and Co Miss for the Deaf 73–89; Hon C Leic St Anne 73–98; TV Leic H Spirit 82–89; Hon Can Leic Cathl 88–98; Bp's Press Relns and Dio Communications Officer 95–96; Sec Gen Syn Coun for the Deaf 88–02; rtd 02; PtO *Carl* from 05. *The Gate House, Brough, Kirkby Stephen CA17 4DS* M: 07730-002570 E: hjclarke@compuserve.com

CLARKE, James. See CLARKE, David James

CLARKE, Jennifer Anna. b 78. Edge Hill Coll of HE BA 99. Ripon Coll Cuddesdon 16. **d** 18 **p** 19. C Bradshaw and Holmfield *Leeds* from 18. *3 Burnholme, Denhholme, Bradford BD13 4NJ* E: rev.jen@outlook.com

CLARKE, John Charles. b 31. St Jo Coll Nottm 91. **d** 92 **p** 93. NSM Winshill *Derby* 92–95; P-in-c Stanley 95–98; rtd 98; PtO *Win* 98–19. *4 Campion Drive, Romsey SO51 7RD* T: (01794) 523945

CLARKE, The Very Revd John Martin. b 52. Edin Univ BD 76 Hertf Coll Ox BA 89 MA 89. Edin Th Coll 73. **d** 76 **p** 77. C Kenton Ascension *Newc* 76–79; Prec St Ninian's Cathl Perth *St And* 79–82; Info Officer to Gen Syn of Scottish Episc Ch 82–87; Greece 87–88; V Battersea St Mary *S'wark* 89–96; Prin Ripon Coll Cuddesdon 97–04; Can and Preb Linc Cathl 00–04; Dean Wells *B & W* 04–15; rtd 16; PtO *Bris* from 16. *1 Blackbridge Road, Chippenham SN15 3LS* T: (01249) 709246

CLARKE, John Patrick Hatherley. b 46. Pemb Coll Ox BA 68 Man Univ MBA 73. St Jo Coll Nottm. **d** 83 **p** 84. C Leic H Trin w St Jo 83–87; C Selly Park St Steph and St Wulstan *Birm* 87–92; Hon C Woking St Mary *Guildf* 92–94; V Greenham *Ox* 94–14; rtd 14; Hon C The Churn *Ox* 14–20; PtO from 20. *27 Blewbury Road, East Hagbourne, Didcot OX11 9LE* E: jphclarke@gmail.com

CLARKE, Mrs Joy Irene. b 44. **d** 98 **p** 02. OLM Ditton St Mich w St Thos *Liv* 98–10; rtd 10; PtO *Ches* from 12. *55 Spinney Avenue, Widnes WA8 8LB* T: 0151-424 8747 E: jiclarke1144@gmail.com

CLARKE, Judith Irene. b 46. SRN 67 SCM 69. EAMTC 97. **d** 00 **p** 01. NSM Shingay Gp *Ely* 00–02; P-in-c Gt Staughton 02–05; P-in-c Hail Weston and Southoe 04–05; R Gt Staughton w Hail Weston w Southoe 05–15; V The Staughtons w Hail Weston 15–16; rtd 16; PtO *Ely* 16–21; *St Alb* from 14. *8 Munkman Close, Potton, Sandy SG19 2BY* E: judi195@btinternet.com

CLARKE (née PULLIN), Kathleen Jean Rebecca. b 58. Qu Coll Birm BA 07. **d** 07 **p** 08. C Kings Norton *Birm* 07–11; V Highters Heath 11–17; TR N Meols *Liv* from 17. *20 Moss Lane, Churchtown, Southport PR9 7QR* T: (01704) 233738 E: revdrebecca@hotmail.co.uk

✠**CLARKE, The Rt Revd Kenneth Herbert (Fanta).** b 49. TCD BA 71. **d** 72 **p** 73 **c** 01. C Magheralin *D & D* 72–75; C Dundonald 75–78; Chile 78–81; I Crinken *D & G* 82–86; I Coleraine *Conn* 86–01; Chmn SAMS (Ireland) 94–18; Can Conn Cathl 96–01; Adn Dalriada 98–01; Bp K, E & A 01–12; Miss Dir SAMS (Ireland) 13–18. *62 Taughrane Lodge, Dollingstown, Craigavon BT66 7UH* M: 07872-568161

CLARKE, Miss Kirsty Ann. b 81. Chich Univ BA 03. Qu Foundn Birm BA 15. d 15 p 16. C Leominster *Heref* 15–19; TV Shaftesbury *Sarum* 19–20. *Address temp unknown* M: 07720-323916 E: kclarke1981@yahoo.co.uk

CLARKE, Mrs Lynnette Jean. b 46. Qu Coll Birm 05. d 08 p 09. OLM Allesley Park and Whoberley *Cov* 08–13; OLM Cov E 13–16; PtO 16–21. *14 High Park Close, Coventry CV5 7BE* T: (024) 7646 7097 M: 07890-048210 E: lynnette@mountnod.co.uk

CLARKE, Martin Howard. b 47. AKC 70. St Aug Coll Cant 70. d 71 p 72. C Saffron Walden w Wendens Ambo *Chelmsf* 71–74; C Ely 74–78; V Messing w Inworth *Chelmsf* 78–90; V Layer de la Haye 90–96; R Layer de la Haye and Layer Breton w Birch etc 96–12; rtd 12; PtO *Chelmsf* from 14. *Saddlers, 2 Stable Close, West Mersea, Colchester CO5 8HP* T: (01206) 383952 E: martinandangela2@btinternet.com

CLARKE, Ms Mary Margaret. b 65. K Coll Lon BD 86 AKC 86. Linc Th Coll 89. d 89 p 94. Par Dn Northampton St Jas *Pet* 89–93; Chapl Nene Coll of HE Northn 92–93; Team Dn Coventry Caludon *Cov* 93–94; TV 94–01; PtO *Lon* 01–08 and from 20; C Notting Dale St Clem w St Mark and St Jas 12–19. *1 Porchester Gardens, London W2 3LA* T: (020) 7229 6359 E: revdmaryclarke@gmail.com

CLARKE, Maurice Harold. b 30. K Alfred's Coll Win CertEd 56 Sussex Univ MA 79 LCP 69. Cuddesdon Coll 65. d 67 p 68. Hd Master Co Sec Sch Cowplain (Lower Sch) 67–72; Dep Hd Master Thamesview High Sch 72–80; Hd Master Eltham Green Comp Sch 80–83; Hon C Waterlooville *Portsm* 67–70; Hon C Fareham SS Pet and Paul 70–72; Hon C Higham and Merston *Roch* 72–83; V Hamble le Rice *Win* 83–90; rtd 91; PtO *Win* 91–14; Chich from 92. *7 Henty Gardens, Chichester PO19 3DL* T: (01243) 775646

CLARKE, Canon Neil Malcolm. b 53. OBE 05. Solicitor 79. WMMTC 90. d 92 p 93. NSM Desborough, Brampton Ash, Dingley and Braybrooke *Pet* from 92; Can Pet Cathl from 04. *53 Breakleys Road, Desborough, Kettering NN14 2PT* T: (01536) 760667 E: revnclarke@aol.com

CLARKE, Nicholas John. b 57. Sarum Coll 15. d 17 p 18. NSM Merriott w Hinton, Dinnington and Lopen *B & W* 17–20; P-in-c Ham Hill Villages from 20. *The Vicarage, 1 Castle Street, Stoke-sub-Hamdon TA18 8RE* T: (01935) 824167 M: 07842-192402 E: revnickclarke@gmail.com

CLARKE, Nicholas John. b 57. Lon Univ BA 78 St Andr Univ MLitt 09 Lon Inst of Educn PGCE 80. Ridley Hall Cam 95. d 97 p 98. C Attleborough *Cov* 97–00; V Fillongley and Corley 00–07; Chapl Chantilly *Eur* 07–16; TR Radipole and Melcombe Regis *Sarum* from 16; RD Weymouth and Portland from 17. *39 Icen Road, Weymouth DT3 5JL* T: (01305) 520163 M: 07724-139601 E: nickclarke@radipole.church

CLARKE, Norman. b 28. Keble Coll Ox BA 52 MA 58. St Steph Ho Ox 52. d 54 p 55. C Ellesmere Port *Ches* 54–57; C Kettering St Mary *Pet* 57–60; Chapl and Tutor St Monica Mampong Ghana 60–62; C Friern Barnet All SS *Lon* 62–63; LtO *Leic* 63–74; C Knighton St Mary Magd 74–81; Dioc Communications Officer *St E* 81–88; P-in-c Sproughton w Burstall 81–88; P-in-c Dunsford and Doddiscombsleigh *Ex* 88–95; P-in-c Cheriton Bishop 88–95; rtd 95; PtO *Ex* 95–08; RD Ottery 02–03; Perm to Offic St Helena from 96. *78 Malden Road, Sidmouth EX10 9NA* T: (01395) 515849

CLARKE, Paul Ian. b 72. W Suffolk Coll BA 09. Trin Coll Bris BA 11. d 11 p 12. C Haughley w Wetherden and Stowupland *St E* 11–14; P-in-c Coxley w Godney, Henton and Wookey *B & W* 14–18; V 18–20; R Walton and Trimley *St E* from 20. *The Rectory, 15 Walton Hall Drive, Felixstowe IP11 9FA* M: 07456-936475 E: revpaulclarke@me.com

CLARKE, Rachel Frances. *See* HARTLAND, Rachel Frances

✠CLARKE, The Rt Revd Richard Lionel. b 49. TCD BA 71 MA 79 PhD 90 K Coll Lon BD 75 AKC 75. d 75 p 76 c 96. C Holywood *D & D* 75–77; C Dublin St Bart w Leeson Park *D & G* 77–79; Dean of Residence TCD 79–84; I Bandon Union C, C & R 84–93; Dir of Ords 85–93; Cen Dir of Ords 82–97; Can Cork and Ross Cathls C, C & R 91–93; Dean Cork 93–96; I Cork St Fin Barre's Union 93–96; Chapl Univ Coll Cork 93–96; Bp M & K 96–12; Abp Arm 12–20; Hon Can St Ninian's Cathl Perth *St And* 04–20; rtd 20. *Address temp unknown*

CLARKE, Robert Graham. b 28. S Dios Minl Tr Scheme 78. d 81 p 82. NSM Woolston *Win* 81–89; NSM Portswood St Denys 89–93; Chapl Torrevieja *Eur* 93–95; PtO *Win* 95–17; *Eur* from 95. *10 River Green, Hamble, Southampton SO31 4JA* T: (023) 8045 4230

CLARKE, Robert Michael. b 45. Oak Hill Th Coll BD 71 Sarum & Wells Th Coll 78. d 78 p 79. Hon C Glastonbury St Jo w Godney *B & W* 78–81; Asst Hd Master Edington Sch 78–81; Chapl Felsted Sch 81–84; Asst Chapl and Ho Master 85–92; Hd Master Brocksford Hall 92–94; Hd Master The Park Sch

Bath 94–96; Chapl Seaford Coll Petworth 96–99; Hd Master Bredon Sch 99–00; PtO *Lich* 01–19; Hon Chapl ATC 07–19. *4 West Road, Old Colwyn, Colwyn Bay LL29 9DU* T: (01492) 330921 E: revbclarke@hotmail.co.uk

CLARKE, Canon Robert William. b 56. CITC. d 83 p 84. C Cloughfern *Conn* 83–85; C Drumragh w Mountfield *D & R* 85–87; I Edenderry w Clanabogan from 87; Can Derry Cathl from 05. *Edenderry Rectory, 91 Crevenagh Road, Omagh BT79 0EZ* T: (028) 8224 5525 E: rev.clarke@btinternet.com

CLARKE, Roger Anthony. b 69. d 16 p 17. OLM Romford St Edw *Chelmsf* 16–20. *65 Birch Close, Romford RM7 8ES*

CLARKE, Canon Roger David. b 58. Man Univ BA Ox Univ MA. Ripon Coll Cuddesdon 80. d 83 p 84. C Frodsham *Ches* 83–86; C Wilmslow 86–88; V High Lane 88–93; V Heald Green St Cath 93–99; R W Kirby St Bridget 99–10; V Hale Barns w Ringway 10–15; R Eccleston and Pulford 15–21; Bp's Chapl 15–21; Hon Can Ches Cathl 15–21; rtd 21; PtO *Ches* from 21. *Lyndale, Ellesmere Lane, Penley, Wrexham LL13 0LP* E: yficerdy@btopenworld.com

CLARKE, Sandra Lea. b 62. N Illinois Univ BSc 84. St Mellitus Coll BA 19. d 19 p 20. C The Bourne and Tilford *Guildf* from 19. *4 Priory Court, 1 Frensham Road, Farnham GU9 8HA* M: 07806-624560 E: sandy.clarke@hotmail.com

CLARKE, Sheelagh Alison. b 56. Bulmershe Coll of HE BEd 79 Open Univ MA(Ed) 90. Gen Th Sem NY MDiv 05. d 05 p 06. C Gladstone St Luke USA 05–07; C Westfield St Paul 07–09; C Monmouth Junction St Barn 09–11; V Millburn St Steph 11–17; Co-ord Young Adult and Youth Min Newark 17–19; PtO *St Alb* from 19. *20 Browns Way, Aspley Guise, Milton Keynes MK17 8JA* M: 07835-514363 E: sheelaghclarke@hotmail.com

CLARKE, Stephen Robert. b 77. Southn Univ BA 99. Trin Coll Bris BA 10. d 10 p 11. C Pioneer Min Glouc City 10–14; V Whitehall Park *Lon* from 14. *St Andrew's Vicarage, 43 Dresden Road, London N19 3BG* T: (020) 3712 6501 E: steve@standrewsn19.org *or* stevecclarkey@gmail.com

CLARKE, Steven David. b 54. All SS Cen for Miss & Min 17. d 19 p 20. NSM Chapelfields *Liv* 19; NSM Wigan from 20. *120 Camberwell Crescent, Wigan WN2 1AT* T: (01942) 498861 M: 07958-077549 E: steven.clarke1@tiscali.co.uk

CLARKE (*formerly* GARDNER), Mrs Susan Carol. b 54. SRN 75. St Jo Coll Nottm 02. d 04 p 05. C Abington *Pet* 04–07; P-in-c Woodhouse *Wakef* 07–08; V Birkby and Woodhouse 08–10; P-in-c Thornhill and Whitley Lower 10–14; R *Leeds* 14–17; rtd 17; PtO *Leeds* 17–21; Hon C Cumberworth, Denby, Denby Dale etc from 21; Hon C Kirkburton and Shelley from 21; PtO *York* from 19. *Heselwood House, 199 Woodhead Road, Holmbridge, Holmfirth HD9 2NW* M: 07896-464417 E: sue.clarke@btinternet.com

CLARKE (*née* DAVIS), Susan Elizabeth Mary. b 50. St Thos Hosp Lon MB, BS 74 Univ Coll Lon MSc 81 FRCP 84 FRCR 03. SEITE 03. d 06 p 07. NSM W Streatham St Jas *S'wark* 06–12; NSM Streatham St Paul 10–12; Hon TV Furzedown 12–20; AD Tooting 16–20; Hon Can S'wark Cathl 15–20; rtd 20; PtO *S'wark* from 20. *26 Abbotsleigh Road, London SW16 1SP* T: (020) 8769 5117 M: 07710-744006 E: sue.clarke@kcl.ac.uk *or* semclarke@btinternet.com

CLARKE, Timothy John. b 69. Jes Coll Cam BA 91 MA 95 Barrister 92. WMMTC 00. d 03 p 04. NSM Birm Cathl 03–16; NSM Worc St Martin w St Swithun and St Paul from 16; PtO 10–16; *Birm* from 16; Dep Chan Derby 15–20; Chan from 20. *15B College Green, Worcester WR1 2LH* T: (01905) 732938 E: timclarke@waitrose.com

CLARKE, Mrs Yvonne Veronica. b 58. CA Tr Coll. dss 86 d 87 p 94. Nunhead St Silas *S'wark* 86–90; Par Dn 87–90; Par Dn Nunhead St Antony w St Silas 90–91; Par Dn Mottingham St Andr w St Alban 91–94; C 94–98; V Spring Park All SS from 98. *All Saints' Vicarage, 1 Farm Drive, Croydon CR0 8HX* T: (020) 8777 2775 F: 8777 5228

CLARKE-MOISLEY, Lisselle Roseanne Sarah. b 88. Trin Coll Bris 17. d 19 p 20. C Harwich Peninsula *Chelmsf* 19–21; C Colchester St Luke from 21. *99 Weetmans Drive, Colchester CO4 9EA* E: lissellecm@gmail.com

CLARKE-MOISLEY, Sarah Anne. b 60. St Mellitus Coll 15. d 17 p 18. NSM Hainault *Chelmsf* from 17. *6 Hannards Way, Ilford IG6 3TB* E: sclarkemoisley@gmail.com

CLARKSON, The Ven Alan Geoffrey. b 34. Ch Coll Cam BA 57 MA 61. Wycliffe Hall Ox 57. d 59 p 60. C Penn *Lich* 59–60; C Oswestry St Oswald 60–63; C Wrington *B & W* 63–65; V Chewton Mendip w Emborough 65–74; Dioc Ecum Officer 65–75; V Glastonbury St Jo w Godney 74–84; P-in-c W Pennard 80–84; P-in-c Meare 81–84; P-in-c Glastonbury St Benedict 82–84; V Glastonbury w Meare, W Pennard and Godney 84; Hon Can Win Cathl 84–99; Adn Win 84–99; V Burley Ville 84–99; rtd 99; PtO *Chelmsf* from 99; Ely from 99; *St E* 99–18. *Cantilena, 4 Harefield Rise, Linton, Cambridge*

CB21 4LS T: (01223) 892988 E: agclarkson@hotmail.co.uk *or* a.clarkson@talktalk.net

CLARKSON, Geoffrey. b 35. AKC 61. d 62 p 63. C Shildon *Dur* 62–65; Asst Chapl HM Pris Liv 65–66; Chapl HM Borstal Feltham 66–71; Development Officer Br Assn of Settlements 71–74; Dir Community Projects Foundn 74–87; Chapl HM Rem Cen Ashford 88–90; Chapl HM Pris Coldingley 90–99; Chapl HM Pris Send 92–94; rtd 00; Hon C Hampton St Mary *Lon* 71–05; PtO from 05. *109 Cambridge Road, Teddington TW11 8DF* T: (020) 8977 1434 E: geoffreyclarkson@virginmedia.com

CLARKSON, Mrs Julie Marie. b 60. York St Jo Univ BA 13 Sheff Univ MA 16. Yorks Min Course 13. d 16 p 17. C Barnoldswick w Bracewell *Leeds* 16–19; P-in-c Settle from 19; P-in-c Giggleswick and Rathmell w Wigglesworth from 19. *The Vicarage, 2 Town Head Way, Settle BD24 9RG* M: 07764-976431 E: julie.clarkson@btinternet.com

CLARKSON, Michael. *See* CLARKSON, Richard Michael

CLARKSON, Michael Livingston. b 48. California Univ BA 70 Loyola Univ JD 73. Wycliffe Hall Ox 87. d 89 p 90. C Kensington St Barn *Lon* 89–93; Min Oak Tree Angl Fellowship 93–04; Oman 04–06; C Bluffton Ch of the Cross USA 07–08; R Johns Island Our Saviour 08–16. *37 Maldon Road, London W3 6SZ* E: mikec@gulf-net.org

CLARKSON, Canon Richard. b 33. Man Univ BSc 54 Ball Coll Ox DPhil 57. Oak Hill Th Coll 89. d 91 p 92. NSM Sunnyside w Bourne End *St Alb* 91–03; RD Berkhamsted 97–02; Hon Can St Alb 02–03; rtd 03; PtO *St Alb* from 09. *Kingsmead, Gravel Path, Berkhamsted HP4 2PH* T: (01442) 873014 E: r.clarkson@btopenworld.com

CLARKSON, Richard Anthony. b 85. Nottm Univ BSc 06. Trin Coll Bris BA 14. d 14 p 15. C Whitchurch *Lich* 14–17; C Edstaston, Fauls, Prees, Tilstock and Whixall 14–17; R Adderley, Ash, Calverhall, lghtfield etc 17–20; R Kinver and Enville from 20. *The Rectory, Vicarage Drive, Kinver, Stourbridge DY7 6HJ* T: (01384) 872556 M: 07529-223962 E: revrichclarkson@gmail.com

CLARKSON, Richard Michael. b 38. St Jo Coll Dur BA 60 Lanc Univ PGCE 68. Cranmer Hall Dur 60. d 62 p 63. C Heyhouses on Sea *Blackb* 62–66; C Lancaster St Mary 66–68; Asst Master Kirkham Gr Sch 68–90; Asst Master Hurstpierpoint Coll 90–91; Asst Master St Mary's Hall Brighton 92–98; Chapl 96–98; rtd 93; PtO *Chich* from 93. *121 College Lane, Hurstpierpoint, Hassocks BN6 9AF* T: (01273) 834117

CLARKSON, Robert Christopher. b 32. Dur Univ BA 53 DipEd 54. S Dios Minl Tr Scheme 85. d 87 p 88. NSM Lower Dever Valley *Win* 87–03; PtO from 03. *22 Wrights Way, South Wonston, Winchester SO21 3HE* T: (01962) 881692

CLARRIDGE, Mrs Ann. b 44. Bournemouth Univ BSc 89 S Bank Univ MSc 94. SEITE 01. d 04 p 05. NSM Shepherd's Bush St Steph w St Thos *Lon* 04–07; NSM Whitton St Aug 07–11; NSM Northwood H Trin 11–18; NSM Cowley 18–20; NSM Ruislip Manor St Paul from 20. *18 Elgar Close, Ickenham, Uxbridge UB10 8HN* T: (01895) 349005 E: annclarridge@hotmail.co.uk

CLARRIDGE, Donald Michael. b 41. DipOT 86. Oak Hill Th Coll 63. d 66 p 67. C Newc St Barn and St Jude 66–70; C Pennycross *Ex* 70–76; R Clayhanger 76–83; R Petton 76–83; R Huntsham 76–83; V Bampton 76–83. *Winkley, Broad Road, Hambrook, Chichester PO18 8RF* T: (01243) 576535

CLASBY, Michael Francis Theodore. b 37. Univ Coll Lon BA 59. Chich Th Coll 59. d 61 p 62. C Leigh-on-Sea St Marg *Chelmsf* 61–64; C Forest Gate St Edm 64–69; V Walthamstow St Mich 69–70; Chapl Community of Sisters of the Love of God 87–89; PtO *St Alb* 87–89; NSM Hemel Hempstead 90–93; PtO 93–98; rtd 02. *2 Heritage Close, High Street, St Albans AL3 4EB* T: (01727) 869818 M: 07506-785442 E: michael.clasby@gmail.com

CLATWORTHY, Jonathan Richard. b 48. Univ of Wales BA 70 Man Univ MPhil 88. Sarum & Wells Th Coll 71. d 76 p 77. C Man Resurr 76–78; C Bolton St Pet 78–81; V Ashton St Pet 81–85; Chapl Sheff Univ 85–91; V Denstone w Ellastone and Stanton *Lich* 91–98; Chapl Liv Univ 98–02; rtd 02; PtO *Liv* from 04; *Leeds* 21. *9 Westward View, Aigburth, Liverpool L17 7EE* T: 0151-727 6291 E: jonathan@clatworthy.org

CLAVIER, Canon Mark Forbes Moreton. b 70. Coll of Wm & Mary (USA) AB 93 Duke Univ (USA) MTS 95 St Chad's Coll Dur PhD 11. d 09 p 09. C Langley Park, Hamsteels, Esh and Waterhouses *Dur* 09–10; P-in-c Steeple Aston w N Aston and Tackley *Ox* 11–13; Dean of Res St Mich Coll Llan 13–16; Vice-Prin St Steph Ho Ox 16–17; Can Res Brecon Cathl *S & B* from 17. *The Cathedral Office, Cathedral Close, Brecon LD3 9DP* M: 07531-856943 E: mark.clavier@gmail.com *or* rescanon@breconcathedral.org.uk

CLAXTON, Mrs Claire Marie. b 58. R Academy of Music BMus 79 LRAM 78 K Alfred's Coll Win PGCE 80. STETS 12.

d 14 p 15. C Guernsey St Martin *Win* 14–17; C Guernsey St Marguerite de la Foret 17–18; R from 18. *Carillon, Rue des Bailleuls, St Andrew, Guernsey GY6 8XB* T: (01481) 238815 M: 07781-433225 E: carillon@cwgsy.net

CLAY, Geoffrey. b 51. CertEd. Ridley Hall Cam. d 86 p 87. C Birstall *Wakef* 86–90; V Lupset 90–03; P-in-c Marsden 03–10; P-in-c Kirkburton 10–14; *Leeds* 14–15; P-in-c Cumberworth, Denby and Denby Dale *Wakef* 10–14; *Leeds* 14–15; Min Development Officer *Wakef* 03–14; *Leeds* 14–15; rtd 15. *3 The Chase, Coldwell End, Youlgrave, Bakewell DE45 1UY* E: geoffclay@me.com

CLAYDEN, David Edward. b 42. Oak Hill Th Coll 74. d 76 p 77. C Worksop St Jo *S'well* 76–79; V Clarborough w Hayton 79–84; C Bloxwich *Lich* 87–90; TV 90–93; TV Tollington *Lon* 93–99; P-in-c Thorndon w Rishangles, Stoke Ash, Thwaite etc *St E* 99–00; P-in-c Thornhams Magna and Parva, Gislingham and Mellis 99–00; R S Hartismere 00–06; rtd 06; PtO *S'well* 06–21. *151 Southview Road, Carlton, Nottingham NG4 3QT* T: 0115-987 2690

CLAYDON, Preb Graham Leonard. b 43. K Coll Lon BA 65. Clifton Th Coll 66. d 68 p 69. C Walthamstow St Mary w St Steph *Chelmsf* 68–71; C St Marylebone All So w SS Pet and Jo *Lon* 71–73; Hon C 73–81; Warden All So Clubhouse 71–81; V Islington St Mary *Lon* 81–99; Dioc Ev (Stepney) and C Highbury Ch Ch w St Jo and St Sav 99–03; Preb St Paul's Cathl 92–06; rtd 07; PtO *Chich* 12–17. *Acre End, Tangmere Road, Tangmere, Chichester PO20 2HW* T: (01243) 536789

CLAYDON, Mrs Marilyn Pamela. b 53. Middx Univ MA 04 RGN 74 HVCert 76. St Mellitus Coll 17. d 19 p 20. OLM Chingford SS Pet and Paul *Chelmsf* from 19. *25 Whitehall Gardens, London E4 6EH* T: (020) 8524 9173 M: 07931-967167 E: marilyn.claydon@ntlworld.com

CLAYTON, Adam Jonathan Barnett. b 56. d 06 p 07. OLM Icknield *Ox* 06–12; P-in-c Myddle *Lich* 12–18; R 18–20; P-in-c Broughton 12–18; V 18–20; P-in-c Loppington w Newtown 12–20; R Myddle and Broughton, Loppington and Newtown from 20; RD Wem and Whitchurch from 15. *The Rectory, Myddle, Shrewsbury SY4 3RX* T: (01939) 291801 E: revajbelayton@gmail.com

CLAYTON, Benjamin Theo. b 90. Nottm Univ BA 11. Wycliffe Hall Ox 13. d 15 p 16. C Nottingham St Jude *S'well* 15–18; C Retford Area 18–19; R Retford St Sav from 19. *St Saviour's Vicarage, 31 Richmond Road, Retford DN22 6SJ*

CLAYTON, Christopher Charles. b 81. Ripon Coll Cuddesdon BA 18. d 18 p 19. C High Harrogate St Pet *Leeds* from 18. *23 Azerley Grove, Harrogate HG3 2SY* M: 07407-258733 E: christopher.charles.clayton@gmail.com

CLAYTON, Geoffrey Buckroyd. b 26. Newc Univ BA 67. Roch Th Coll 62. d 64 p 65. C Newc St Geo 64–67; C Byker St Ant 67–68; Chapl Salonika *Eur* 68–69; C Cheddleton *Lich* 69–72; V Arbory *S & M* 72–97; RD Castletown 82–97; V Santan 88–97; rtd 97; PtO *St D* from 97. *The Cottage, Hendre Mynach Caravan Park, Llanaber Road, Barmouth LL42 1YR* T: (01341) 280409 E: revgbclayton@hotmail.co.uk

CLAYTON, Matthew Anthony. b 89. St Mellitus Coll BA 16. d 16 p 17. C Bournemouth Town Cen *Win* 16–19; C Ex St Matt w St Sidwell from 19. *2 Velwell Road, Exeter EX4 4LE* M: 07763-115512

CLAYTON, Paul. b 47. St Jo Coll Dur BA 08. Cranmer Hall Dur 03. d 04 p 05. NSM Elton and Preston-on-Tees and Longnewton *Dur* 04–06; NSM Bishopton w Gt Stainton 06–13; NSM Redmarshall 06–13; NSM Grindon, Stillington and Wolviston 06–13; NSM Billingham St Mary 09–13; rtd 13; PtO *Dur* from 13. *144 Darlington Lane, Stockton-on-Tees TS19 0NG* T: (01642) 607233 E: gandpclayton@btinternet.com

CLAYTON, Ross. b 47. EMMTC 82. d 85 p 86. C Cotmanhay *Derby* 85–89; TV Eckington w Handley and Ridgeway 89–90; PtO from 08; Spiritual Dir Derby Angl Cursillo from 18. *69 Beresford Road, Long Eaton, Nottingham NG10 3EF* T: 0115-946 0084 E: mosesclayton@sky.com

CLAYTON, William Terence. b 42. Lon Univ BSc 71 MSc 73. AKC 66. d 67 p 68. C Rotherhithe St Mary w All SS *S'wark* 67–71; Hon C Camberwell St Mich w All So w Em 71–76; Hon C Newington St Paul 71–76; Hon C Winterslow *Sarum* 76–77; rtd 07. *Dungarth, Middleton Road, Winterslow, Salisbury SP5 1QL* T: (01980) 862286 E: wtclayton@btinternet.com

CLEALL, Mary Jane Anne. *See* LINDSAY, Mary Jane Anne

CLEALL-HILL, Malcolm John. b 51. Salford Univ Man Metrop Univ. d 01 p 02. OLM Chorlton-cum-Hardy St Werburgh *Man* 01–11; rtd 11; PtO *Man* from 11. *62 Buckingham Road, Chorlton cum Hardy, Manchester M21 0RP* T: 0161-881 7024 *or* 247 2288 E: malcandmon@tiscali.co.uk

CLEATON, Mrs Nancy Thomas. b 45. Lon Bible Coll BD 67. WEMTC 05. d 07 p 08. NSM Church Stretton *Heref* 07–12; P-in-c Hope Bowdler w Eaton-under-Heywood 12–13;

P-in-c Rushbury 12–13; P-in-c Cardington 12–13; R Apedale Gp 13–19; rtd 19; PtO *Heref* from 20. *3 Brockhurst, Church Stretton SY6 6QY* E: nancy.cleaton@tiscali.co.uk

CLEATON, Sheena Faith. b 74. Colchester Inst BA 97 R Holloway Coll Lon MMus 02 PhD 07. Ripon Coll Cuddesdon BTh 14. **d** 11 **p** 12. C Bourne *Linc* 11–16; R Scartho from 16. *St Matthew's House, 8 Thirlmere Avenue, Grimsby DN33 3EA* E: sheena_cleaton@hotmail.com

CLEAVER, John Martin. b 42. K Coll Lon BD 64 AKC 64. St Boniface Warminster 61. **d** 65 **p** 66. C Bexley St Mary *Roch* 65–69; C Ealing St Steph Castle Hill *Lon* 69–71; P-in-c Bostall Heath *Roch* 71–76; V Green Street Green 76–85; Primary Adv Lon Dioc Bd for Schs 85–92; V Teddington St Mary w St Alb 92–08; rtd 08; PtO *Chich* from 13; *Lon* from 14. *5 Oaklands, Westham, Pevensey BN24 5AW* T: (01323) 769964 E: cleaverjohn@hotmail.com

CLEAVER, Stuart Douglas. b 46. ACIS. Oak Hill Th Coll. **d** 83 **p** 84. C Portsdown *Portsm* 83–86; C Blendworth w Chalton w Idsworth etc 86–88; P-in-c Whippingham w E Cowes 88–98; R 98–01; rtd 01. *The Crest, Soake Road, Waterlooville PO7 6HY* T: (023) 9226 2277 E: eandscleaver@gmail.com

CLEE, Mrs Norma. b 53. Lindisfarne Regional Tr Partnership 13. **d** 15 **p** 16. NSM Eighton Banks *Dur* from 15; P-in-c from 21. *19 Cromarty, Outston, Chester le Street DH2 1LA* T: 0191-492 0293 M: 07964-029986 E: normaclee@icloud.com

CLEEVE, Martin. b 43. Bp Otter Coll TCert 65 ACP 67 Open Univ BA 80. Oak Hill Th Coll 69. **d** 72 **p** 73. C Margate H Trin *Cant* 72–76; V Southminster *Chelmsf* 76–86; Teacher Castle View Sch Canvey Is 86–91; Hd RE Bromfords Sch Wickford 91–94; Hd RE Deanes Sch Thundersley 94–98; P-in-c Gt Mongeham w Ripple and Sutton by Dover *Cant* 99–04; rtd 04; PtO *Cant* from 04; Chapl Kent and Medway NHS and Soc Care Partnership Trust from 08. *Cottage Pie, Waldershare Road, Ashley, Dover CT15 5JA* T: (01304) 821705

CLEEVES, Canon David John. b 56. Univ of Wales (Lamp) BA Fitzw Coll Cam MA 85. Westcott Ho Cam. **d** 82 **p** 83. C Cuddington *Guildf* 82–85; C Dorking w Ranmore 85–87; V Ewell St Fran 87–94; P-in-c Rotherfield w Mark Cross *Chich* 94–01; V Masham and Healey *Ripon* 01–14; *Leeds* 14–21; P-in-c W Tanfield and Well w Snape and N Stainley 09–21; Jt AD Ripon 04–05; AD 05–09; Hon Can Ripon Cathl *Leeds* 19–21; rtd 21. *92 Dale Grove, Leyburn DL8 5GA* T: (01969) 625069 E: revdavidcleeves@gmail.com

CLEGG, Canon John Anthony Holroyd. b 44. Kelham Th Coll 65. **d** 70 **p** 71. C Heyhouses on Sea *Blackb* 70–74; C Lancaster St Mary 74–76; V Lower Darwen St Jas 76–80; TV Shaston *Sarum* 80–86; R Poulton-le-Sands w Morecambe St Laur *Blackb* 86–97; RD Lancaster 89–94; TR Cartmel Peninsula *Carl* 97–04; RD Windermere 01–04; P-in-c Appleby 04–08; P-in-c Ormside 04–08; TR Heart of Eden 08–09; RD Appleby 04–09; Hon Can Carl Cathl 01–09; rtd 09; PtO *Carl* 09–19; *Blackb* 10–19; *Sarum* 16–21. *10 Townsend Road, Swanage BH19 2PT* T: (01929) 425301 M: 07855-740928 E: anthonyhclegg@gmail.com

CLEGG, John Lovell. b 48. Qu Coll Ox BA 70 MA 74. Trin Coll Bris. **d** 75 **p** 76. C Barrow St Mark *Carl* 75–79; R S Levenshulme *Man* 79–98; P-in-c Blackley St Paul 98–10; rtd 10; PtO *Man* from 11. *5 Mough Lane, Chadderton, Oldham OL9 9NT* T: 0161-684 1226

CLEGG, Patricia Ann. b 45. STETS 96. **d** 99 **p** 00. NSM Harnham *Sarum* 99–03; PtO 03–05; NSM Bemerton 05–07; NSM Arle Valley *Win* 07–11; rtd 11; PtO *Sarum* from 11. *23 Richards Way, Salisbury SP2 8NT* T: (01722) 333573 E: pat.clegg@btinternet.com

CLEGG, Roger Alan. b 46. St Jo Coll Dur BA 68 Nottm Univ CertEd 69. St Jo Coll Nottm 75. **d** 78 **p** 79. C Harwood *Man* 78–81; TV Sutton St Jas and Wawne *York* 81–87; V Kirk Fenton w Kirkby Wharfe and Ulleskelfe 87–09; Chapl HM Pris Askham Grange 95–12; PtO *York* from 09. *8 Wolsey Grange, Cawood, Selby YO8 3SB* T: (01757) 268060 M: 07957-474030 E: rogclegg@dunelm.org.uk

CLEGHORN, Catherine Grace. b 79. Grey Coll Dur BA 02 Dur Univ MA 08. St Mellitus Coll 15. **d** 18 **p** 19. C Crewe St Andr w St Jo *Ches* 18–21; C Crewe All SS and St Paul w St Pet 18–21; V Leighton-cum-Minshull Vernon and Warmingham from 21. *The Vicarage, Middlewich Road, Minshull Vernon, Crewe CW1 4RD* M: 07813-117385 E: catherine.cleghorn@hotmail.com

CLELAND, Miss Lucy Eleanor. b 74. Aston Univ BSc 97 Cam Univ BTh 05. Ridley Hall Cam 02. **d** 05 **p** 06. C Yaxley and Holme w Conington *Ely* 05–08; P-in-c Landbeach and Waterbeach 08–11; Bp's Dom Chapl *S'well* 11–17; Chapl Scargill Ho 17–20; C Long Stanton w St Mich *Ely* 20–21; C Swavesey 20–21; C Over 20–21; C Willingham

20–21; TV 5folds from 21. *The New Rectory, High Street, Longstanton, Cambridge CB24 3BP* T: (01954) 277758 E: lucy@5folds.org.uk

CLELAND, Trevor. b 66. QUB BTh 94 TCD MPhil 97. CITC 94. **d** 96 **p** 97. C Lisburn Ch Ch *Conn* 96–99; C Carrickfergus 99–03; I Belfast Upper Falls 03–12; I Ballinderry from 12. *Ballinderry Rectory, 124 Ballinderry Road, Ballinderry Upper, Lisburn BT28 2NL* T: (028) 9265 0134 M: 07875-361682 E: tcleland@btinternet.com

CLEMAS, Preb Nigel Antony. b 53. Wycliffe Hall Ox. **d** 83 **p** 84. C Bootle St Mary w St Paul *Liv* 83–87; V Kirkdale St Mary and St Athanasius 87–91; TV Netherthorpe *Sheff* 91–93; V Netherthorpe St Steph 93–98; R Chapel Chorlton, Maer and Whitmore *Lich* from 98; RD Eccleshall 00–16; Preb Lich Cathl from 13. *The Rectory, Snape Hall Road, Whitmore, Newcastle ST5 5HS* T: (01782) 680258 E: nclemas@hotmail.com

CLEMENCE, Paul Robert Fraser. b 50. St Edm Hall Ox MA 90 MRTPI 82. Wycliffe Hall Ox 88. **d** 90 **p** 91. C Lancaster St Mary *Blackb* 90–94; Chapl HM Pris Lanc Castle 90–94; V Lt Thornton *Blackb* 94–16; AD Poulton 00–09; rtd 16; PtO *Blackb* from 16. *94 Victoria Road East, Thornton-Cleveleys FY5 5HH* E: p.clemence@tiscali.co.uk *or* p.clemence61@gmail.com

CLEMENT, Geoffrey Paul. b 64. **d** 94 **p** 96. Jardines del Hipódromo St Aug Uruguay 94–96; Colón St Jas Miss 95–97; Barrio Fátima Salto St Luke w H Spirit 97–01; TV Wilford Peninsula *St E* 01–07; R Holbrook, Stutton, Freston, Woolverstone etc 07–18; V Wychwood *Ox* from 18. *The Vicarage, Church Street, Shipton-under-Wychwood, Chipping Norton OX7 6BP* T: (01993) 832467 M: 07955-721332 E: revgclement@btinternet.com

CLEMENT, Paskal. b 63. Punjab Univ BA 92 Univ of Wales MA 08. Nat Catholic Inst of Th Karachi 82. **d** 88 **p** 88. Pakistan 88–01; NSM Hounslow H Trin w St Paul and St Mary *Lon* 04–08; C Oadby *Leic* 08–13; P-in-c Leic Resurr from 13. *St Alban's House, Weymouth Street, Leicester LE4 6FN* M: 07727-286905 E: paskalm@yahoo.com

CLEMENT, Canon Peter James. b 64. UMIST BSc 88 Man Univ MA 98. Qu Coll Birm 89. **d** 92 **p** 93. C Grange St Andr *Ches* 92–95; C Man Apostles w Miles Platting 95–97; TV Uggeshall w Sotherton, Wangford and Henham *St E* 97–99; TV Sole Bay 99–00; Dioc Youth Officer 01–02; V Fairweather Green *Bradf* 02–07; Assoc Dioc Dir of Ords 04–07; Dioc Dir of Ords *Ripon* 07–14; Dir of Ords *Leeds* 14–15; Voc Development Officer and Dir of Ords *Carl* from 15; Can Res Carl Cathl from 17. *Church House, 19-24 Friargate, Penrith CA11 7XR* T: (01768) 807777 E: peter.clement@carlislediocese.org.uk

CLEMENT, Richard Percy. b 63. Bris Univ BA 85. ERMC 04. **d** 06 **p** 08. C Framlingham w Saxtead *St E* 06–09; Chapl RAF from 09. *Chaplaincy Services (RAF), HQ Air Command, RAF High Wycombe HP14 4UE* T: (01494) 496800 E: richardclement98@yahoo.co.uk

CLEMENT, Thomas Gwyn. b 51. Lon Univ BMus 73 Goldsmiths' Coll Lon PGCE 74 LRAM 73 LTCL 74. St Steph Ho Ox. **d** 93 **p** 94. C Friern Barnet St Jas *Lon* 93–96; V Edmonton St Alphege 96–04; P-in-c Ponders End St Matt 02–04; AD Enfield 01–04; V Hendon St Mary and Ch Ch 04–18; Warden of Readers Edmonton Area 08–17; AD W Barnet 09–14; rtd 18; PtO *Lon* from 18. *46 Princes Avenue, London N3 2DB* T: (020) 8346 1119 E: ht.gwyn@btinternet.com

CLEMENT, Canon Timothy Gordon. b 54. Trin Coll Bris 92. **d** 94 **p** 95. C Chepstow *Mon* 94–97; R Bettws Newydd w Trostrey etc 97–14; R Raglan Gp from 14; Rural Min Adv from 02; AD Raglan-Usk from 05; Can St Woolos Cathl from 08. *The Rectory, Bettws Newydd, Usk NP15 1JN* T: (01873) 880258 E: timtherec@icloud.com

CLEMENTS, Alan Austin. b 39. Newc Univ MA 93 ACIB 66 FCIE 05. Linc Th Coll 74. **d** 76 **p** 77. C Woodley St Jo the Ev *Ox* 76–79; C Wokingham All SS 79–83; V Felton *Newc* 83–95; P-in-c Wallsend St Pet 95–01; rtd 01; PtO *Newc* from 01; *Blackb* from 07; *Man* from 09. *15 Carleton Road, Chorley PR6 8TQ* T/F: (01257) 271782 E: fralanclements@gmail.com

CLEMENTS, Andrew. b 48. K Coll Lon BD 72 AKC 72 Leeds Univ MA 02. St Aug Coll Cant 72. **d** 73 **p** 74. C Langley All SS and Martyrs *Man* 73–76; C Westhoughton 76–81; R Thornton Dale w Ellerburne and Wilton *York* 81–89; Prec Leic Cathl 89–91; V Market Weighton *York* 91–97; R Goodmanham 91–97; V Osbaldwick w Murton 97–19; RD Derwent 11–16; rtd 19. *89 Wetherby Road, York YO26 5BU* E: andrewrev73@gmail.com

CLEMENTS, Miss Christine Hilda. b 49. Ex Univ BTh 04. SWMTC 99. **d** 02 **p** 03. C Halsetown *Truro* 02–05; Zambia 05–07; PtO *Nor* 07; TR Thamesmead *S'wark* 07–13; rtd 13; PtO *Truro* from 16. *3 Torwood House, Old*

Torwood Road, Torquay TQ1 1PN T: (01803) 295469
E: revdchrisclements@gmail.com

CLEMENTS, Canon Doris Thomasina Sara. b 46. TCD BA 68
MA 90. CITC 92. **d** 95 **p** 96. NSM Killala w Dunfeeny,
Crossmolina, Kilmoremoy etc *T, K & A* 95–14; Dioc C from
14; Can Achonry Cathl 05–11 and from 13; Can Tuam
Cathl from 11. *Doobeg House, Bunninadden, Ballymote, Co
Sligo, Republic of Ireland* T: (00353) (71) 918 5425 F: 918
5255 M: 86-249 7806 E: doristsclements@gmail.com

CLEMENTS, Miss Mary Holmes. b 43. Bedf Coll Lon BA 64 Lon
Inst of Educn PGCE 69. Ox Min Course 92. **d** 94 **p** 95. NSM
High Wycombe *Ox* 94–01; C N Petherton w Northmoor Green
and N Newton w St Michaelchurch, Thurloxton etc *B & W*
01–03; C Alfred Jewel 03–10; rtd 10; PtO *B & W* from 12.
18 Meadway, Woolavington, Bridgwater TA7 8HA T: (01278)
683099 E: kharaclements@btinternet.com

CLEMENTS, Philip John Charles. b 42. Nottm Univ CertEd 64
Loughb Univ Hon BA 09. Ridley Hall Cam. **d** 85 **p** 86. C
Aylestone St Andr w St Jas *Leic* 85–87; P-in-c Swinford w
Catthorpe, Shawell and Stanford 87–91; V 91–99; Dioc Rural
Officer 91–96; RD Guthlaxton II 94–99; P-in-c N w S Kilworth
and Misterton 96–99; P-in-c Barrowden and Wakerley w
S Luffenham *Pet* 99–02; R Barrowden and Wakerley w S
Luffenham etc 03–06; RD Barnack 00–06; rtd 06; PtO *Pet*
from 06; *Leic* 07–20. *Clementine Cottage, 51 Laughton Road,
Lubenham, Market Harborough LE16 9TE* T/F: (01858)
432548 E: clements.philip@sky.com

CLEMENTS, Canon Roy Adrian. b 44. St Chad's Coll Dur
BA 68 MA 74. **d** 69 **p** 70. C Royston Wakef 69–73; V Clifton
73–77; V Rastrick St Matt 77–84; Dioc Communications
Officer 84–98; V Horbury Junction 84–92; Bp's Chapl
92–00; V Battyeford 00–08; Hon Can Wakef Cathl
94–08; rtd 08; PtO *Wakef* 08–14; *Leeds* from 14. *12 Castle
Crescent, Sandal, Wakefield WF2 7HX* T: (01924) 251834
E: royclements@live.co.uk

CLEMENTS, Mrs Virginia. b 47. Weymouth Coll of Educn
CertEd 68. **d** 13 **p** 14. OLM Apedale Gp *Heref* 13–20; rtd 20.
Address temp unknown E: virginia_clements@me.com

CLEMETT, Peter Thomas. b 33. Univ of Wales (Lamp) BA 60.
Sarum Th Coll 59. **d** 61 **p** 62. C Tredegar St Geo *Mon* 61–63;
Chapl St Woolos Cathl 63–66; CF 66–99; Chapl R Memorial
Chpl Sandhurst 84–88; rtd 88; OCM from 99; PtO *Win*
from 01. *Silver Birches, Gardeners Lane, East Wellow, Romsey
SO51 6AD* T: (023) 8081 4261

CLEMINSON, Lee James. b 84. Sheff Univ BA 16. Coll of
Resurr Mirfield 13. **d** 16 **p** 17. C Bothal and Pegswood w
Longhirst *Newc* 16–18; C Balkwell 19–20; P-in-c from 20; C
Tynemouth St Jo 19–20; P-in-c from 20. *St John's Vicarage, 35
St John's Terrace, North Shields NE29 6HS* M: 07976-296733
E: revleecleminson@gmail.com

CLEMOW (*née* WINDER)**, Cynthia Frances.** b 48. SWMTC 02.
d 05 **p** 06. NSM Bodmin w Lanhydrock and Lanivet *Truro*
05–17; TV Bodmin from 17. *Denton, 2 Boxwell Park, Bodmin
PL31 2BB* T: (01208) 73306

CLEPHANE, Alexander Honeyman. b 48. **d** 97 **p** 98. OLM
Flixton St Mich *Man* 97–11; NSM Stretford from
15; Dioc Officer for SSM 17–21; rtd 21; PtO *Man* from 21.
306 Church Road, Urmston, Manchester M41 6JJ T: 0161-747
8816 M: 07443-902511 E: alexclephane@gmail.com

CLEUGH, David Robert. b 80. New Coll Ox MA 07. Ripon
Coll Cuddesdon BTh 09. **d** 09 **p** 10. C Dorchester *Ox*
09–13; P-in-c Leadgate *Dur* 13–17; P-in-c Ebchester
14–17; P-in-c Medomsley 14–17; R Three Rivers Gp *Ely*
from 17; RD Fordham and Quy from 20. *The Vicarage, 24
Mildenhall Road, Fordham, Ely CB7 5NR* M: 07722-012314
E: davidrcleugh@gmail.com

CLEUGH, Hannah Felicity. b 81. Worc Coll Ox MA 08 MSt 04
DPhil 07. Ripon Coll Cuddesdon 07. **d** 09 **p** 10. C Dorchester
Ox 09–12; Chapl Univ Coll Dur 13–17; Bp's Sen Chapl *Ely*
from 17; Min Can Ely Cathl from 19. *The Bishop's House,
The College, Ely CB7 4DW* T: (01353) 662749 F: 669477
E: hannah.cleugh@elydiocese.org

CLEVELAND, Michael Robin. b 52. Warwick Univ BA 73.
St Jo Coll Nottm 86 Serampore Th Coll BD 88. **d** 88 **p** 89. C
Bushbury *Lich* 88–92; V Foleshill St Laur *Cov* 92–17; rtd 17.
88 Victoria Street, Exeter EX4 6JG

CLEVELAND, Archdeacon of. *See* BLOOR, The Ven Amanda
Elaine

CLEVERLEY, Michael Frank. b 36. Man Univ BScTech 57.
Wells Th Coll 61. **d** 63 **p** 64. C Halifax St Aug *Wakef*
63; C Huddersfield St Jo 63–66; C Brighouse 66–69; V
Gomersal 69–83; P-in-c Clayton W w High Hoyland 83–89;
P-in-c Scissett St Aug 83–89; R High Hoyland, Scissett
and Clayton W 89–96; rtd 96; Hon C Leathley w Farnley,
Fewston and Blubberhouses *Bradf* 96–04; PtO 04–14; *Leeds*
from 14. *86 Riverside Park, Otley LS21 2RW*

CLEVERLY, Canon Charles St George. b 51. St Jo Coll Ox
MA 75 Goldsmiths' Coll Lon PGCE 76. Trin Coll Bris 79.
d 82 **p** 83. C Cranham Park *Chelmsf* 82–89; V 89–92;
Crosslinks Paris Pastor Eglise Réformée de Belleville 92–02;
R Ox St Aldate 02–20; Hon Can Ch Ch 15–20; rtd 20;
PtO *Ox* from 21. *10 Harrison's Lane, Woodstock OX20 1SS*
E: charlie.cleverly@gmail.com

CLEWS, Nicholas. b 57. SS Coll Cam BA 80 MA 84 Leeds Univ
BA 87 CIPFA 85. Coll of Resurr Mirfield 85. **d** 88 **p** 89. C S
Elmsall *Wakef* 88–91; V Featherstone 91–07; P-in-c Purston
cum S Featherstone 04–07; P-in-c Thornbury *Bradf* 07–14;
Leeds 14–17; P-in-c Woodhall 07–17; V Thornbury,
Woodhall and Waterloo from 17; Prayer and Spirituality Co-
ord Bradf Area from 17. *St James's Vicarage, Galloway Lane,
Pudsey LS28 8JR* T: (01274) 662735 M: 07985-091748
E: nicholas.clews@leeds.anglican.org

CLIFF, Frank William. b 51. ERMC. **d** 14 **p** 15. NSM Gt
Yarmouth *Nor* from 14. *2 Barrack Road, Great Yarmouth
NR30 3DR* T: (01493) 851097 E: fwc1234@gmail.com

CLIFF, Mrs Sarah Jane. b 66. St Jo Coll Dur BA 18. Cranmer
Hall Dur 17. **d** 19 **p** 20. C Barnard Castle w Whorlton
Dur from 19. *17 Mayfield, Barnard Castle DL12 8EA*
E: revsarahcliff@gmail.com

CLIFFE, Canon Christopher George. b 47. CITC 94. **d** 97 **p** 98.
C Fiddown w Clonegam, Guilcagh and Kilmeaden *C, F & O*
97–00; I 00–13; Bp's Dom Chapl 97–13; Can Ossory Cathl
07–13; rtd 13. *Hawthorn, 51 Fan Glas, Kilmeaden, Waterford,
X91 E8N3, Republic of Ireland* T: (00353) (51) 399699 M: 87-
236 8682 E: cgc2@eircom.net *or* georgecliffe47@gmail.com

CLIFFORD, Bruce Douglas. b 52. Birm Univ BA 73 Southn
Univ MSocSc 76. Trin Coll Bris 09. **d** 11 **p** 12. NSM Glouc
St Cath 11–15; NSM Glouc St Geo w Whaddon 15; V 15–20;
rtd 20; PtO *Glouc* from 21. *20 Estcourt Close, Gloucester
GL1 3LT* M: 07855-228943 E: clifftopps@btinternet.com

CLIFFORD, Paula Margaret. b 45. **d** 11 **p** 12. NSM Ox
St Giles and SS Phil and Jas w St Marg 11–13; NSM
Akeman 13–14; P-in-c Minster Lovell 14–17; Deanery Miss
Enabler 14–16; rtd 17; PtO *Ox* from 17; Chapl Puerto de
la Cruz Tenerife *Eur* 18–19; Chapl Fontainebleau 20–21.
18 Boulevard André Maginot, 77300 Fontainebleau, France
E: paulaclifford4@gmail.com

CLIFFORD HILL, Timothy James. b 88. Cant Ch Ch Univ
BMus 10 Dur Univ BA 21. Sarum Coll 17. **d** 20 **p** 21. C
Cranleigh *Guildf* from 20. *The Curatage, 22 Orchard Gardens,
Cranleigh GU6 7LG* E: timcliffordhill@me.com

CLIFTON, Daphne Sheila. b 59. St Aug Coll of Th 14.
d 17 **p** 18. NSM Lee St Mildred *S'wark* from 17. *54
Shearman Road, London SE3 9HX* T: (020) 8318 3857
E: daphne@cliftonconsulting.com

CLIFTON, Canon Robert Walter. b 39. Solicitor. Westcott Ho
Cam 82. **d** 84 **p** 85. C Bury St Edmunds St Geo *St E* 84–87;
P-in-c Culford, W Stow and Wordwell 87–88; R Culford, W
Stow and Wordwell w Flempton etc 88–95; P-in-c Fornham
All SS and Fornham St Martin w Timworth 93–95; RD
Thingoe 93–95; P-in-c Orford w Sudbourne, Chillesford,
Butley and Iken 95–00; P-in-c Eyke w Bromeswell,
Rendlesham, Tunstall etc 98–99; TR Wilford Peninsula
00–05; RD Woodbridge 96–04; Hon Can St E Cathl 00–05;
rtd 05; PtO *Nor* from 05; *St E* 05–16. *12 Stan Petersen Close,
Norwich NR1 4QJ* T: (01603) 631758 M: 07713-237754
E: cliftonrobert@sky.com

CLIFTON, Canon Roger Gerald. b 45. ACA 70 FCA. Sarum
& Wells Th Coll 70. **d** 73 **p** 74. C Winterbourne *Bris* 73–76;
P-in-c Brislington St Cuth 76–83; P-in-c Colerne w N
Wraxall 83–95; RD Chippenham 88–94; Hon Can Bris Cathl
94–09; TR Gtr Corsham 95–01; TR Gtr Corsham and Lacock
01–09; rtd 09; PtO *Bris* 10–19; *B & W* from 11. *20 Southcot
Place, Bath BA2 4PE* T: (01225) 330211 M: 07762-324596
E: rogerclifton@btinternet.com

CLIFTON, Sharon. b 66. **d** 07 **p** 08. C St Illogan *Truro* 07–11;
TV Godrevy 11–13; TR from 13. *The Rectory, 22 Forth An
Tewennow, Phillack, Hayle TR27 4QE* T: (01736) 756377

CLIFTON-SMITH, Canon Gregory James. b 52. Goldsmiths'
Coll Lon BMus 82 GGSM 73 Lon Univ TCert 74 Leeds Univ
MA 02 Ches Univ DProf 13. Sarum & Wells Th Coll 87. **d** 89
p 90. C Welling *S'wark* 89–93; V Tattenham Corner and
Burgh Heath *Guildf* 93–97; Asst Chapl R Berks and Battle
Hosps NHS Trust 97–99; Chapl Isle of Wight NHS Primary
Care Trust 99–12; Close V Win Cathl 12–17; Min Can
Win Cathl 12–16; Hon Can Win Cathl 16–17; rtd 17; PtO
Portsm from 12; *Win* from 17. *46 Gills Cliff Road, Ventnor
PO38 1LH* M: 07790-089981 E: kontrabass@tiscali.co.uk

CLINCH, Christopher James. b 60. Nottm Univ BEd 82
BTh 89. Linc Th Coll 86. **d** 89 **p** 90. C Newc St Geo 89–92; C
Seaton Hirst 92–94; TV Ch the King 94–00; V Newc St Fran
00–09; Chapl K Sch Tynemouth 09–15; PtO *Newc* 15–16;

Chapl Northumbria Healthcare NHS Foundn Trust from 16. *Chaplains' Office, North Tyneside General Hospital, Rake Lane, North Shields NE29 8NH* T: 03448-118111

CLINES, Emma Christine. *See* LOUIS, Emma Christine

CLINES, Jeremy Mark Sebastian. b 68. Birm Univ PhD 11. Cranmer Hall Dur. **d** 97 **p** 98. C Birm St Martin w Bordesley St Andr 97–99; Chapl York St Jo Univ 99–10; Chapl Sheff Univ from 10. *Flat 1, 5 Ranmoor Park Road, Sheffield S10 3GX* E: jeremyclines@gmail.com *or* j.clines@sheffield.ac.uk

CLITHEROW, Canon Andrew. b 50. St Chad's Coll Dur BA 72 Ex Univ MPhil 87. Sarum & Wells Th Coll 78. **d** 79 **p** 80. Hon C Bedford Ch Ch *St Alb* 79–84; Asst Chapl Bedford Sch 79–84; Chapl Caldicott Sch Farnham Royal 84–85; C Penkridge w Stretton *Lich* 85–88; Min Acton Trussell w Bednall 85–88; Chapl Rossall Sch Fleetwood 89–94; V Scotforth *Blackb* 94–00; Dioc Dir of Tr and Can Res Blackb Cathl 00–07; Hon Can Blackb Cathl 07–20; P-in-c Lytham St Cuth 07–12; P-in-c Lytham St Jo 08–12; Chapl Cen Lancs Univ 12–20; Chapl to The Queen 08–20; rtd 20. *Address temp unknown*

CLOAKE, David Michael. b 72. Ox Brookes Univ BA 15. Ripon Coll Cuddesdon 07. **d** 08 **p** 09. C Aylesbury *Ox* 08–11; V Whitton SS Phil and Jas *Lon* from 11; P-in-c Hounslow St Steph from 20; CF (ACF) from 10. *The Vicarage, 205 Kneller Road, Twickenham TW2 7DY* T: (020) 8894 1932 M: 07758-289702 E: vicar@whittonchurch.com

CLOCKSIN (née HOYLE), Mrs Pamela Margaret. b 61. Nottm Univ BA 82. St Jo Coll Nottm 84. **d** 87 **p** 94. Par Dn Bulwell St Jo *S'well* 87–91; Cam Pastorate Chapl 91–95; C Cambridge H Trin *Ely* 91–95; PtO 95–01. *26 York Avenue, Oxford OX3 8NS* T: (01865) 766263 E: ella@clocksin.com

CLOCKSIN, Prof William Frederick. b 55. BA 76 St Cross Coll Ox MA 81 Trin Hall Cam MA 87 PhD 93. EAMTC 91. **d** 94 **p** 95. Asst Chapl Trin Hall Cam 94–01; Acting Dean 00–01; PtO *St Alb* 17–21. *Address temp unknown* E: wfc@me.com

CLOETE, Richard James. b 47. AKC 71. St Aug Coll Cant 72. **d** 72 **p** 73. C Redhill St Matt *S'wark* 72–76; V Streatham St Paul 76–84; P-in-c W Coker w Hardington Mandeville, E Chinnock etc *B & W* 84–88; R 88; R Wincanton and Pen Selwood 88–97; Sec and Treas Dioc Hosp Chapl Fellowship 91–97; PtO *Lon* 97–98; *Ex* 99–02; C Sampford Peverell, Uplowman, Holcombe Rogus etc 02–11; rtd 11; PtO *B & W* from 12. *19 Mount Nebo, Taunton TA1 4HG* T: (01823) 338428 M: 07855-493868 E: r.j.cloete@btinternet.com

CLOGHER, Archdeacon of. *See* HARPER, The Ven Brian John

CLOGHER, Bishop of. *See* ELLIS, The Rt Revd Ian William

CLOGHER, Dean of. *See* HALL, The Very Revd Kenneth Robert James

CLONMACNOISE, Dean of. *See* BOGLE, The Very Revd Paul David

CLOSE, Brian Eric. b 49. St Chad's Coll Dur BA 74 MA 76. Ridley Hall Cam 74. **d** 76 **p** 77. C Far Headingley St Chad *Ripon* 76–79; C Harrogate St Wilfrid 79–80; C Harrogate St Wilfrid and St Luke 80–82; P-in-c Alconbury cum Weston *Ely* 82–83; V 83–86; P-in-c Buckworth 82–83; R 83–86; P-in-c Upton and Copmanford 82–83; Chapl Reed's Sch Cobham 86–96; Chapl Malvern Coll 96–01; Chapl Uppingham Sch 01–04; R Easington, Easington Colliery and S Hetton *Dur* 04–09; rtd 09; PtO *Dur* from 19. *12 Mitford Close, High Shincliffe, Durham DH1 2QE* T: 0191-384 4931 E: brianclose777@btinternet.com

CLOSE (née HITCHEN), Mrs Carol Ann. b 47. St Mary's Coll Ban CertEd 69 St Martin's Coll Lanc DipEd 91 Ches Coll of HE BTh 02. NOC 99. **d** 02 **p** 03. NSM Hindley St Pet *Liv* 02–07; PtO *Man* 08–18; NSM Hindley Green *Liv* 11–14; NSM Newton from 15. *271 Warrington Road, Abram, Wigan WN2 5RQ* T: (01942) 861670 E: revclose@blueyonder.co.uk *or* revcarolclose@gmail.com

CLOSE, Mrs Jane. b 48. WMMTC 00. **d** 03 **p** 04. NSM Fillongley and Corley *Cov* 03–06; P-in-c Leam Valley 06–17; PtO *Leic* from 18. *129 Ashby Road, Hinckley LE10 1SH* T: (01455) 619843 M: 07958-685423 E: closejane35@gmail.com

CLOVER, Brendan David. b 58. G&C Coll Cam BA 79 MA 83 LTCL 74. Ripon Coll Cuddesdon 79. **d** 82 **p** 83. C Friern Barnet St Jas *Lon* 82–85; C W Hampstead St Jas 85–87; Chapl Em Coll Cam 87–92; Dean 92–94; P-in-c St Pancras w St Jas and Ch Ch *Lon* 94–99; P-in-c St Pancras H Cross w St Jude and St Pet 96–99; Can Res Bris Cathl 99–06; Sen Provost Woodard Corp 06–21; P-in-c Clevedon St Jo *B & W* from 21; PtO *Lich* from 06; *B & W* 16–21; *Llan* 17–18; *Lon* from 20. *St John's Vicarage, 11 St John's Road, Clevedon BS21 7TG*

CLOW, Laurie Stephen. b 65. Man Univ BA 86 MA 88. Wycliffe Hall Ox 96. **d** 98 **p** 99. C Trentham *Lich* 98–01; TV Hampreston *Sarum* 01–15; R Chesham Bois *Ox* from 15. *The Rectory, 1 Glebe Way, Amersham HP6 5ND* T: (01494) 728318 M: 07825-135616 E: rector@stleonardscb.org.uk

CLOWES, John. b 45. AKC 67. **d** 68 **p** 69. C Corby St Columba *Pet* 68–71; R Itchenstoke w Ovington and Abbotstone *Win* 71–73; R New Alresford w Ovington and Itchen Stoke 73–74; V Acton w Gt and Lt Waldingfield *St E* 74–80; Asst Dioc Chr Stewardship Adv 75–80; TV Southend St Jo w St Mark, All SS w St Fran etc *Chelmsf* 80–82; TV Southend 82–85; Ind Chapl 80–85; R Ashwick w Oakhill and Binegar *B & W* 85–91; P-in-c Brompton Regis w Upton and Skilgate 91–97; rtd 98. *The Tythings, Tythings Court, Minehead TA24 5NT* M: 07964-022682

CLOWES, Mrs Lindsay Joan. b 48. **d** 13 **p** 14. OLM Biddulph *Lich* 13–16; NSM 16–18; PtO from 18. *10 York Close, Biddulph, Stoke-on-Trent ST8 6SE* T: (01782) 514413 E: lindsay48@hotmail.co.uk

CLOYNE, Dean of. *See* GREEN, The Very Revd Susan Denise

CLUCAS, Anthony John. b 56. Portsm Poly BA 77. WMMTC 96. **d** 99 **p** 00. NSM Erdington *Birm* 99–04; NSM Nechells 04–05; P-in-c Shard End 05–12; V from 12. *Apartment 1, 11 York Crescent, Birmingham B34 7NS* T: 0121-747 3299 E: clucas@btinternet.com

CLUES, David Charles. b 66. K Coll Lon BD 87 Lon Univ PGCE 95. St Steph Ho Ox 88. **d** 90 **p** 91. C Notting Hill All SS w St Columb *Lon* 90–94; NSM 94–96; NSM Notting Hill St Mich and Ch Ch 96–98; Asst Chapl HM Pris Wormwood Scrubs 97–98; C Paddington St Mary Magd *Lon* 98–03; C Paddington St Mary 98–03; C Paddington St Sav 98–03; V Willesden St Mary 03–11; P-in-c Brighton St Bart *Chich* 11–16; Chapl Heathfield Sch Ascot from 16; PtO *Ox* from 16. *Heathfield School, London Road, Ascot SL5 8BQ* T: (01344) 898343 E: dcclues@btinternet.com

CLUETT, Preb Michael Charles. b 53. Kingston Poly BSc 78. St Steph Ho Ox 84. **d** 86 **p** 87. C Pontesbury I and II *Heref* 86–90; TV Wenlock 90–99; P-in-c Canon Pyon w Kings Pyon and Birley 99–04; V Canon Pyon w King's Pyon, Birley and Wellington 04–17; RD Leominster 08–14; Preb Heref Cathl 10–17; rtd 17; PtO *Heref* from 18. *1 Scholars Walk, Hereford HR4 0GH* E: m.charles802@btinternet.com

CLUNE, David Julian. b 60. Open Univ BSc 03. Wilson Carlile Coll 99 St Jo Coll Nottm LTh 07. **d** 07 **p** 08. C Spalding St Mary and St Nic *Linc* 07–11; TV Sutton St Jas and Wawne *York* 11–12; V Sutton St Jas 12–15; NSM Digby Gp *Linc* 16–17. *3 High Street, Howden le Wear, Crook DL15 8EZ* M: 07891-912450 E: me@davidclune.com

CLUTTERBUCK, Ms Elizabeth Lesieli. b 81. LSE BA 02 K Coll Lon MA 04. St Mellitus Coll BA 14 MA 15. **d** 15 **p** 16. C Highbury Ch Ch w St Jo and St Sav *Lon* 15–18; C Tollington 18–19; V Hornsey Road from 19. *Emmanuel Vicarage, 145 Hornsey Road, London N7 6DU* M: 07763-852258 E: liz.clutterbuck@gmail.com

CLUTTERBUCK, Marion Isobel. b 56. Oak Hill Th Coll BA 91. **d** 92 **p** 94. C Lindfield *Chich* 92–96; TV Alderbury Team *Sarum* 96–01; TV Clarendon 01–05; PtO *Win* 13–16 and from 17; P-in-c Six Pilgrims *B & W* 19–21; PtO from 21. *Jessamine Cottage, South Barrow, Yeovil BA22 7LN* T: (01963) 441604 E: mcdeanridge@icloud.com

CLUTTON, Canon Barbara Carol. b 47. WMMTC 00. **d** 04 **p** 05. NSM Draycote Gp *Cov* 04–14; P-in-c 14; Rural Life Officer 07–14; Hon Can Cov Cathl 11–14; rtd 14; Hon C Leam Valley *Cov* from 21. *Church Cottage, Main Street, Grandborough, Rugby CV23 8DQ* T: (01788) 810372 M: 07808-137550 E: barbaraclutton@gilberthouse.co.uk

COAD, Dominic John. b 82. Ex Univ BA 02 MA 06 PhD 10. Westcott Ho Cam 10. **d** 12 **p** 13. C Oakham, Ashwell, Braunston, Brooke, Egleton etc *Pet* 12–16; TV Benwell and Scotswood *Newc* from 16. *5 Lynnwood Avenue, Newcastle upon Tyne NE4 6XB* T: 0191-256 7020 M: 07713-165193

COAKLEY (née FURBER), Prof Sarah Anne. b 51. New Hall Cam BA 73 PhD 82. Harvard Div Sch ThM 75. **d** 00 **p** 01. Edw Mallinckrodt Jr Prof Div Harvard Div Sch 95–07; Visiting Prof 07–08; Hon C Waban The Gd Shep 00–08; Hon C Littlemore *Ox* 00–07; Norris-Hulse Prof Div Cam Univ from 07; LtO *Ely* 08–18; PtO from 18; Hon Can Ely Cathl 11–18. *Faculty of Divinity, West Road, Cambridge CB3 9BS* T: (01223) 763002 E: sc545@cam.ac.uk

COATES, Andrew Peter Richard. b 86. Warwick Univ BA 07 Down Coll Cam BTh 17. Westcott Ho Cam 15. **d** 18 **p** 19. C Wood Green St Mich w Bounds Green St Gabr etc *Lon* 18–21; C Alexandra Park from 21. *1B Selbourne Road, London N22 7TL* M: 07802-884707 E: revdandrewcoates@gmail.com

COATES, Archie. *See* COATES, Richard Michael

COATES, Canon Christopher Ian. b 59. Qu Coll Birm 81. **d** 84 **p** 85. C Cottingham *York* 84–87; TV Howden 87–91; V Sherburn in Elmet 91–94; V Sherburn in Elmet w Saxton 94–02; V Bishopthorpe 02–20; V Acaster Malbis 02–20; P-in-c Appleton Roebuck w Acaster Selby 07–12; V

12–20; RD New Ainsty 11–16; rtd 21; Hon Can Ho from 10; PtO *York* from 21. *65 Lady Edith's Avenue, Scarborough YO12 5RA* T: (01723) 378811 E: chris.coates@hotmail.co.uk

COATES, Mrs Clare Louise Gye. b 72. Trin Call Cam BA 94 Trin Coll Cam MA 98. Ridley Hall Cam 17. **d** 19 **p** 20. C Stapleford *Ely* from 19. *13 Hawthorn Avenue, Sawston, Cambridge CB22 3TE* M: 07917-845968 E: clareguecoates@btinternet.com

COATES, David Martin. b 57. Sheff Univ BSc 78 Reading Univ MSc 80 Birm Univ PhD 83. STETS 04. **d** 07 **p** 08. NSM Salisbury St Mark *Sarum* 07–10; NSM Bourne Valley 10–19; PtO from 19. *2 St Matthew's Close, Bishopdown, Salisbury SP1 3FJ* T: (01722) 325944 E: dmcoates@hotmail.co.uk

COATES, Jean. b 55. Linc Univ BA 10. **d** 13 **p** 14. OLM Bolingbroke Deanery *Linc* from 13. *The Vicarage, Church Street, Spilsby PE23 5EF* T: (01790) 752526 E: coatesjean@yahoo.co.uk

COATES, Canon Jean Margaret. b 47. Sussex Univ BSc 68 Reading Univ PhD 77 CBiol MRSB. SAOMC 93. **d** 96 **p** 97. C Wallingford *Ox* 96–99; P-in-c Watercombe *Sarum* 99–02; R 02–13; Rural Officer (Dorset) 99–13; Can and Preb Sarum Cathl 05–13; rtd 13; PtO *Sarum* 15–19. *Three Gables, Colesbrook, Gillingham SP8 4HH* T: (01747) 229168 E: jeanmcoates@gmail.com

COATES, Maxwell Gordon. b 49. Lon Univ CertEd 70 Open Univ BA 83 UEA MA 86. Trin Coll Bris. **d** 77 **p** 78. C Blackheath Park St Mich *S'wark* 77–79; Chapl Greenwich Distr Hosp Lon 77–79; Asst Teacher Saintbridge Sch Glouc 79–81; Teacher Gaywood Park High Sch King's Lynn 81–85; NSM Lynn St Jo *Nor* 81–85; Dep Hd Teacher Winton Comp Sch Bournemouth 85–90; Hd Teacher St Mark's Comp Sch Bath 90–97; NSM Canford Magna *Sarum* 85–90 and 99–05; NSM Stoke Gifford *Bris* 93–96; PtO *B & W* 91–96; rtd 96. *3 Oakley Road, Wimborne BH21 1QJ* T: (01202) 883162 E: maxgcoates@gmail.com

COATES, Michael David. b 60. Ches Coll of HE BTh 01. NOC 98. **d** 01 **p** 02. C Orrell Hey St Jo and St Jas *Liv* 01–07; P-in-c Edge Hill St Cypr w St Mary 07–10; C Liv All SS 11–14; V from 14. *The Vicarage, 48 John Lennon Drive, Liverpool L6 9HT* T: 0151-260 6351 E: mike@allsaintsliverpool.org

COATES, Canon Nigel John. b 51. Reading Univ BSc MA. Trin Coll Bris. **d** 83 **p** 84. C Epsom St Martin *Guildf* 83–86; C Portswood Ch Ch *Win* 86–88; Chapl Southn Univ 89–97; Chapl Southn Inst of HE 89–95; P-in-c Freemantle 97–00; R 00–05; Can Res S'well Minster 05–19; rtd 19; PtO *Win* from 20. *9 Bowerwood Road, Fordingbridge SP6 1BJ* T: (01425) 838503 E: nigeljcoates@icloud.com

COATES, Canon Peter Frederick. b 50. K Coll Lon BD 79 AKC 79. St Steph Ho Ox 79. **d** 80 **p** 81. C Woodford St Barn *Chelmsf* 80–83; C E and W Keal *Linc* 83–86; R The Wainfleets and Croft 86–94; R The Wainfleet Gp 94–03; RD Calcewaithe and Candleshoe 92–03; P-in-c Spilsby Gp 03–13; TR Bolingbroke Deanery from 14; RD Bolingbroke from 03; Can and Preb Linc Cathl from 12. *The Vicarage, Church Street, Spilsby PE23 5EF* T: (01790) 752526 E: peter.coates50@yahoo.com

COATES, Canon Richard Michael (Archie). b 70. Birm Univ BA 92. Wycliffe Hall Ox BA 99. **d** 00 **p** 01. C Ashtead *Guildf* 00–03; C Brompton H Trin w Onslow Square St Paul *Lon* 03–09; V Brighton St Pet *Chich* from 09; P-in-c Whitehawk from 13; Can and Preb Chich Cathl from 15. *10 West Drive, Brighton BN2 0GD* T: (01273) 695064 M: 07887-522402 E: archie@stpetersbrighton.org

COATES, Robert. b 63. St Steph Ho Ox 89. **d** 92 **p** 93. C Heavitree w Ex St Paul 92–95; Chapl RN 95–00; V Bexhill St Aug *Chich* from 00. *St Augustine's Vicarage, St Augustine's Close, Bexhill-on-Sea TN39 3AZ* T/F: (01424) 210785 E: robert.coates74@gmail.com

COATES, Robert Charles. b 44. Open Univ BA 76. Cant Sch of Min 83. **d** 86 **p** 87. C Deal St Leon and St Rich and Sholden *Cant* 86–89; V Loose 89–00; V Barnwood *Glouc* 00–06; rtd 06; PtO *B & W* from 06. *4 The Poplars, Weston-super-Mare BS22 6RB* T: (01934) 249387 M: 07874-202318 E: robert.coates@hotmail.co.uk

COATES, Stuart Murray. b 49. Lon Univ BA 70 Edin Univ MTh 91. Wycliffe Hall Ox 72. **d** 75 **p** 76. C Rainford *Liv* 75–78; C Orrell 78–79; V 79–86; Chapl Strathcarron Hospice Denny from 86; Hon C Stirling *Edin* 86–90; NSM Aberfoyle *St And* 89–94; NSM Doune 89–12; R 12–14; rtd 14. *Westwood Smithy, Chalmerston Road, Stirling FK9 4AG* T: (01786) 860531 *or* (01324) 826222 E: revsmc1@gmail.com

COATSWORTH, Mrs Deborah Margaret. b 58. **d** 13 **p** 14. NSM Baschurch and Weston Lullingfield w Hordley *Lich* from 13. *Oakmere House, 69 Hill Park, Dudleston Heath, Ellesmere SY12 9LB* T: (01691) 690261 E: deborahcoatsworth@btinternet.com

COATSWORTH, Nigel George. b 39. Trin Hall Cam BA 61 MA. Cuddesdon Coll 61. **d** 63 **p** 64. C Hellesdon *Nor* 63–66; Ewell Monastery 66–80; TV Folkestone H Trin and St Geo w Ch Ch *Cant* 83–85; C Milton next Sittingbourne 85–86; P-in-c Selattyn *Lich* 86–91; P-in-c Weston Rhyn 88–91; R Weston Rhyn and Selattyn 91–05; rtd 05; PtO *Lich* 05–09 and 16–19 and 20–21. *Oakmere House, 69 Hill Park, Dudleston Heath, Ellesmere SY12 9LB* T: (01691) 690261 E: rev.coatsworth@btinternet.com

COBB, George Reginald. b 50. Oak Hill Th Coll BA 81. **d** 81 **p** 82. C Ware Ch Ch *St Alb* 81–84; C Uphill *B & W* 84–89; R Alresford *Chelmsf* 89–99; Chapl Mt Vernon and Watford Hosps NHS Trust 99–00; Chapl E and N Herts NHS Trust 00–15; rtd 15; PtO *St Alb* from 15. *25 Church Meadows, St Neots PE19 1PR* M: 07890-091973 E: george.cobb@cobbweb.co.uk

COBB, Canon John Philip Andrew. b 43. Man Univ BSc 65 New Coll Ox BA 67 MA 71. Wycliffe Hall Ox 66. **d** 68 **p** 69. C Reading St Jo *Ox* 68–71; C Romford Gd Shep *Chelmsf* 71–73; SAMS Chile 74–08; Can from 99; Dioc Ecum Officer 00–06; rtd 08; Lic to Offic Chile from 08. *Casilla 330, Correo Paine, Paine, Región Metropolitana, Chile* T: (0056) (2) 259 4099 E: jn.cobb@yahoo.co.uk

COBB, Mark Robert. b 64. Lanc Univ BSc 86 Keele Univ MA 99 Liv Univ PhD 13. Ripon Coll Cuddesdon 88. **d** 91 **p** 92. C Hampstead St Jo *Lon* 91–94; Asst Chapl Derbyshire R Infirmary NHS Trust 94–96; Palliative & Health Care Chapl Derbyshire R Infirmary NHS Trust 96–98; Chapl Manager Cen Sheff Univ Hosps NHS Trust 98–02; Sen Chapl 98–04; Sen Chapl Sheff Teaching Hosps NHS Foundn Trust from 04. *Chaplaincy Services, Royal Hallamshire Hospital, Glossop Road, Sheffield S10 2JF* T: 0114-271 3327 E: mark.cobb@sth.nhs.uk

COBB, Peter Graham. b 27. St Jo Coll Cam BA 48 MA 52. Ridley Hall Cam 66. **d** 68 **p** 69. C Porthkerry *Llan* 68–71; P-in-c Penmark 71–72; V Penmark w Porthkerry 72–81; V Magor w Redwick and Undy *Mon* 82–95; rtd 95. *2 Talycoed Court, Talycoed, Monmouth NP25 5HR* T: (01600) 780309 E: petercobb@waitrose.com

COBBOLD, Richard Nevill. b 55. Bris Univ BScEng 76. Local Minl Tr Course. **d** 11 **p** 12. NSM N Farnborough *Guildf* 11–17; NSM Farnborough St Pet from 17. *4 Penns Wood, Farnborough GU14 6RB* T: (01252) 515547 M: 07776-352240 E: richard@cobbold.plus.com

COBLEY, Mrs Irene Patricia Mary. b 51. Ox Min Course 16. **d** 18 **p** 19. NSM Cogenhoe and Gt and Lt Houghton w Brafield *Pet* from 18. *1 Donovan Court, Northampton NN3 3DD* T: (01604) 402543 E: irene.cobley@sky.com *or* irene.cobley@theunitedbenefice.org.uk

COBURN, Dennis Anthony. b 70. **d** 18 **p** 19. NSM Brandon *St E* from 18. *Address temp unknown* E: dennis.coburn@me.com

COBURN, Canon Sharron Dawn. b 73. Trin Coll Bris BA 12 MA 13. **d** 13 **p** 14. C Stanton, Hopton, Market Weston, Barningham etc *St E* 13–16; C Brandon and Santon Downham w Elveden etc 16–17; V Brandon from 17; Asst Dioc Dir of Ords from 17; Hon Can St E Cathl from 20. *215 London Road, Brandon IP27 0LR* T: (01359) 221946 M: 07739-250135 E: sha.coburn@me.com

COCHRANE, Mrs Anthea Mary. b 38. **d** 02 **p** 03. OLM Clarendon *Sarum* 02–07; PtO 07–08 and from 14. *1 Home Farm Dairy, Shute End, Alderbury, Salisbury SP5 3DJ* T: (01722) 710503 E: a.cochrane03@btinternet.com

COCHRANE, Philip Andrew. b 70. Reading Univ BA 92 FRSA 17. Trin Coll Bris BA 07. **d** 07 **p** 08. C Fareham H Trin *Portsm* 07–09; TV 09–12; V Win St Barn 12–15; P-in-c Caerleon and Llanfrechfa *Mon* 15–16; R Banbury *Ox* 16–19; AD Deddington 17–19; R Vancouver St Paul Canada from 19. *1205-2020 Hard Street, Vancouver BC VG6 1J3, Canada* M: (001) (604) 685 6832

COCKAYNE, Canon Mark Gary. b 61. UEA LLB 82. St Jo Coll Nottm BTh 92 MA 93. **d** 93 **p** 94. C Armthorpe *Sheff* 93–96; V Malin Bridge 96–05; AD Hallam 02–05; C Haydock St Mark *Liv* 05–08; V 08–14; AD St Helens 06–14; Hon Can Liv Cathl 06–14; Dir Par Support Team *Sheff* from 14; Hon Can Sheff Cathl from 15. *16 Ormsby Close, Thurgoland, Sheffield S35 7BN* E: mark.cockayne@sheffield.anglican.org

COCKBILL, Douglas John. b 53. Chicago Univ BA 75. Gen Th Sem (NY) MDiv 78. **d** 78 **p** 79. Virgin Is 79–80; Bahamas 80–83; USA 84–90; P-in-c Roxbourne St Andr *Lon* 90–92; V 92–04; USA 05–06; Chapl Larnaca St Helena Cyprus 06–09; USA from 09. *428 King Street, Wenatchee WA 98801-2846, USA* E: dcockbill22@yahoo.com

COCKBURN, Kathleen. b 50. NEOC 04. **d** 07 **p** 08. NSM Walker *Newc* 07–10; NSM N Shields 10–15; rtd 16; PtO *Newc* from 16. *92 Paignton Avenue, Whitley Bay NE25 8SZ* T: 0191-252 0710 E: kath.cock@blueyonder.co.uk

COCKBURN, Sheron June. b 61. Leeds Univ BA 90. St Hild Coll 17. **d** 20 **p** 21. C Drighlington and

Gildersome *Leeds* 20–21; C Upper Armley from 21. *The Vicarage, Back Lane, Drighlington, Bradford BD11 1LS* E: june.cockburn@leeds.anglican.org

COCKCROFT, Mrs Carol Ann. b 62. Univ Coll Ox BA 85 Essex Univ MSc 06. St Mellitus Coll 17. d 20 p 21. NSM Grays Thurrock *Chelmsf* from 20. *5 Sadlers Close, Billericay CM11 1SB* T: (01277) 632181 M: 07952-826823 E: carol.cockcroft2@btinternet.com

COCKELL, Ms Helen Frances. b 69. Trin Hall Cam BA 90 MA 94. Qu Coll Birm BD 94. d 95. C Bracknell *Ox* 95–98; PtO *Cov* from 00; Chapl S Warks Gen Hosps NHS Trust from 09. *The New Rectory, Pool Close, Rugby CV22 7RN* T: (01788) 812613 E: nfchub-nellwork@yahoo.co.uk

COCKELL, Timothy David. b 66. Qu Coll Birm BTheol 95. d 95 p 96. C Bracknell *Ox* 95–98; C Rugby *Cov* 98–99; TV 99–04; P-in-c Bilton 04–08; R from 08; AD Rugby from 17. *The New Rectory, Pool Close, Rugby CV22 7RN* T: (01788) 812613 E: tim.cockell@btopenworld.com or rectorbilton@icloud.com

COCKER (née BENTLEY), Mrs Frances Rymer (Sister Frances Anne). b 22. Man Univ BSc 48 TDip 49 PGCE 49. d 95 p 95. Mother Superior CSD 87–00; PtO *Sarum* 95–15. *Braemar Lodge, 18-20 Stratford Road, Salisbury SP1 3JH* M: 07702-659609

COCKERELL, David John. b 47. Univ of Wales (Cardiff) BA 71 Univ of Wales (Swansea) MA 74 Qu Coll Cam BA 75. Westcott Ho Cam 73. d 76 p 77. C Chapel Allerton *Ripon* 76–79; C Farnley 79–81; TV Hitchin *St Alb* 81–89; TV Dorchester *Ox* 89–92; Adult Educn and Tr Officer *Ely* 92–00; R Raddesley Gp 00–06; rtd 06. *44 Humberley Close, Eynesbury, St Neots PE19 2SE* T: (01480) 218225 E: david@cockerell.co.uk

COCKETT, The Ven Elwin Wesley. b 59. Aston Tr Scheme 86 Oak Hill Th Coll BA 91. d 91 p 92. C Chadwell Heath *Chelmsf* 91–94; Chapl W Ham United Football Club 92–12; C Harold Hill St Paul *Chelmsf* 94–95; P-in-c 95–97; V 97–00; TR Billericay and Lt Burstead 00–07; RD Basildon 04–07; Adn W Ham from 07; PtO *B & W* from 19; Can Koforidua Ghana from 20. *86 Aldersbrook Road, London E12 5DH* T: (020) 8989 8557 E: a.westham@chelmsf.anglican.org

COCKFIELD, Mrs Marisa. b 54. d 14 p 15. NSM Staverton w Landscove, Littlehempston, Buckfastleigh and Dean Prior *Ex* 14–18; TV Bideford, Landcross, Littleham etc from 18. *The Rectory, Weare Giffard, Bideford EX39 4QP* E: mmacneish@hotmail.co.uk

COCKFIELD, Mrs Myrtle Jacqueline. b 51. S Bank Univ BSc 96. SEITE 05. d 08 p 09. NSM Mitcham SS Pet and Paul *S'wark* from 08. *28 Garden Avenue, Mitcham CR4 2EA* T: (020) 8646 2333 M: 07722-568604 E: jackiecockfield@yahoo.co.uk

COCKING, Ann Louisa. b 44. d 03 p 04. OLM The Lavingtons, Cheverells, and Easterton *Sarum* 03–12; rtd 12; PtO *Sarum* from 12. *High Acre, Eastcott, Devizes SN10 4PH* T: (01380) 812763 E: alc.highacre@btinternet.com

COCKING, Keith. b 59. Ripon Coll Cuddesdon 08. d 09 p 10. C Newbold w Dunston *Derby* 09–13; TV Buxton w Burbage and King Sterndale 13–21; R Elmton w Creswell and Whitwell w Steetley from 21. *The New Rectory, 31 High Street, Whitwell, Worksop S80 4RE* M: 07903-736791 E: keithcocking@live.co.uk

COCKING, Martyn Royston. b 53. Trin Coll Bris 83. d 85 p 86. C Weston-super-Mare Cen Par *B & W* 85–88; C Kingswood *Bris* 88–89; TV 89–93; V Pill w Easton in Gordano and Portbury *B & W* 93–96; PtO *Man* 12–13. *39 Down Green Road, Bolton BL2 3QD*

COCKS, Canon Howard Alan Stewart. b 46. St Barn Coll Adelaide 78. d 80 p 81. C Portland Australia 80–82; C Prestbury *Glouc* 82–87; P-in-c Stratton w Baunton 87–94; P-in-c N Cerney w Bagendon 91–93; R Stratton, N Cerney, Baunton and Bagendon 95–98; V Leic St Aid 98–04; RD Christianity S 01–04; R Winchelsea and Icklesham *Chich* 04–12; rtd 12; PtO *Lon* 13–19; *S'wark* 15–19; Can The Murray from 06; PtO Sydney from 19. *50 Cook Terrace, Mona Vale, Sydney NSW 2103, Australia* T: (0061) (2) 9997 1604 E: hascocks@gmail.com

COCKS, Michael Dearden Somers. b 28. Univ of NZ MA 50 St Cath Coll Ox BA 53 MA 57. Ripon Hall Ox. d 53 p 54. C Merivale NZ 53–56; V Geraldine 56–58; V Ross and S Westland 58–60; V Hinds 60–63; V St Martins 63–70; V Barrington Street w Speydon St Nic 70–79; V Hororata 79–93; Chapl Gothenburg w Halmstad, Jönköping etc *Eur* 93–98; rtd 98. *23 Fairfield Avenue, Addington, Christchurch 8024, New Zealand* T: (0064) (3) 981 7057 E: michaelandgertrud@gmail.com

COCKS, Simon Richard. b 63. Birm Poly BSc 88. Qu Foundn Birm 17. d 20 p 21. NSM Boldmere *Birm* from 20. *51 Melrose Avenue, Sutton Coldfield B73 6NS* T: 0121-681 2533 M: 07773-329875 E: simon@wildgoose.me.uk

COCKSEDGE, Simon Hugh. b 56. Univ Coll Lon BSc 78 New Coll Ox BM, BCh 81 Man Univ MD 03 FRCGP 96. NOC 05. d 07 p 08. NSM Hayfield and Chinley w Buxworth *Derby* 07–11; P-in-c Edale from 11; Chapl Blythe Ho Hospice from 13. *Glen Thorne, Barber Booth, Edale, Hope Valley S33 7ZL* E: cocksedge@doctors.org.uk

COCKSEDGE, Stuart John. b 78. Ex Univ BA 99 Univ Coll Lon MSc 07. St Jo Coll Nottm 11. d 13 p 14. C Hinckley St Jo *Leic* 13–17; TV Wareham *Sarum* from 17. *9 Keysworth Drive, Wareham BH20 7BD* M: 07779-345852 E: stuart.cocksedge@gmail.com

✠**COCKSWORTH, The Rt Revd Christopher John.** b 59. Man Univ BA 80 PhD 89 PGCE 81. St Jo Coll Nottm 84. d 88 p 89 c 08. C Mortlake w E Sheen *S'wark* 88–92; Chapl R Holloway and Bedf New Coll 92–97; Dir STETS 97–01; Hon Can Guildf Cathl 99–01; Prin Ridley Hall Cam 01–08; Bp Cov from 08. *The Bishop's House, 23 Davenport Road, Coventry CV5 6PW* T: (024) 7667 2244 F: 7671 3271 E: bishop@bishop-coventry.org

CODRINGTON-MARSHALL, Louise. b 64. Westcott Ho Cam 06. d 08 p 09. C Mortlake w E Sheen *S'wark* 08–11; P-in-c Deptford St Nic and St Luke 11–14; V from 14. *11 Evelyn Street, London SE8 5RQ* T: (020) 8876 7162 or 8692 2749 E: stnicholaschurchdeptford@gmail.com

CODY (née TAYLOR), Julia Mary. b 73. Reading Univ LLB 94. Ridley Hall Cam 06. d 08 p 09. C Penkridge *Lich* 08–12; TV Tettenhall Wood and Perton from 12; RD Trysull from 19. *Church House, 23 Portrush Road, Perton, Wolverhampton WV6 7YZ* T: (01902) 750232 M: 07990-976859 E: jules.m.taylor@googlemail.com

CODY, Paul James Luke. b 73. Westcott Ho Cam. d 08 p 09. C Cen Wolverhampton *Lich* 08–12; Chapl St Pet Colleg Sch Wolv 12–17; Chapl Kemp Hospice Kidderminster from 17; PtO *Lich* 18–21. *Church House, 23 Portrush Road, Perton, Wolverhampton WV6 7YZ* T: (01902) 750232 M: 07834-345269 E: paulcody@hotmail.co.uk

COE, Andrew Derek John. b 58. Nottm Univ BTh 86. St Jo Coll Nottm 83. d 86 p 87. C Pype Hayes *Birm* 86–88; C Erdington St Barn 88–91; C Birm St Martin w Bordesley St Andr 91–96; P-in-c Hamstead St Bernard 96; V 96–02; P-in-c Newdigate *Guildf* 02–03; TR Surrey Weald from 03; RD Dorking 04–09. *St Peter's Rectory, Church Lane, Newdigate, Dorking RH5 5DL* T: (01306) 631469 E: revdandrewdj.coe@btinternet.com

COE, David. b 45. d 69 p 70. C Belfast St Matt *Conn* 69–72; C Belfast St Donard *D & D* 72–75; I Tullylish 75–81; I Lurgan St Jo 81–89; I Ballymacarrett St Patr 89–02; I Richhill *Arm* 02–11; rtd 11. *49 Toberhewny Lodge, Lurgan, Craigavon BT66 7FL* T: (028) 3834 2579 M: 07794-356030 E: davidcoe144@aol.com

COE, Michael Stephen. b 63. Bath Univ BSc 85. Wycliffe Hall Ox. d 00 p 01. C Moulton *Pet* 00–03; P-in-c Silverhill St Matt *Chich* 03–05; R 05–18; P-in-c St Leonards St Ethelburga and St Leon 17–18; RD Hastings 13–18; V Ilkley All SS *Leeds* from 18; AD S Craven and Wharfedale 21. *58 Curly Hill, Ilkley LS29 0BA* T: (01943) 816035 E: vlear@ilkleyallsaints.org.uk

COE, Noelle Elizabeth. b 60. Anglia Ruskin Univ BA 10. d 08 p 09. NSM N Holmwood *Guildf* 08–10; NSM Westcott 10–12; NSM Surrey Weald from 12. *St Peter's Rectory, Church Lane, Newdigate, Dorking RH5 5DL* T: (01306) 631469 E: noellecoe@btinternet.com

COE, Stephen David. b 49. Ch Coll Cam MA 72 Oak Hill Th Coll MA 99. Ox Min Course 90. d 93 p 94. NSM Abingdon *Ox* 93–97; Assoc Min Ox St Andr 97–05; V Wallington H Trin *S'wark* 05–17; rtd 17; PtO *Ox* from 17. *Stile House, 53A Wootton Village, Boars Hill, Oxford OX1 5HP* E: sdcoe@btinternet.com

COEKIN, Philip James. b 64. Wye Coll Lon BScAgr 87. Oak Hill Th Coll BA 93. d 96 p 97. C Eastbourne All SS *Chich* 96–00; V Hastings Em and St Mary in the Castle 00–11; V Eastbourne H Trin from 11. *Holy Trinity Vicarage, 4 Hartington Place, Eastbourne BN21 3BE* T: (01323) 325421 E: pcoekin@gmail.com

COEKIN, Richard John. b 61. Solicitor 86 Jes Coll Cam BA 83 MA 87. Wycliffe Hall Ox 89. d 91 p 92. C Cheadle *Ches* 91–95; NSM Wimbledon Em Ridgway Prop Chpl *S'wark* 95–15; PtO *Lon* from 02; *S'wark* from 15. *264 Worple Road, London SW20 8RG* T: (020) 8545 2734 E: richard.coekin@dundonald.org

COFFEY, Helen Theresa. b 63. Salford Univ BA 08 Sheff Univ BA 12. Coll of Resurr Mirfield 10. d 12 p 13. C Ashton-in-Makerfield St Thos *Liv* 12–16; P-in-c Ashton-in-Makerfield H Trin 16–18; TR Eccleston from 18. *St James's Vicarage, 159A St Helen's Road, Eccleston Park, Prescot L34 2QB* M: 07742-590672 E: helentcoffey@gmail.com

COFFEY (formerly COOMBS), Patrick Michael Joseph. b 65. Sheff Univ MA 00 Brighton Univ MBA 04 Plymouth Univ

MA 11. St Steph Ho Ox BTh 94. **d** 94 **p** 95. C Torquay St Martin Barton *Ex* 94–95; C Goodrington 95–98; V Sheff St Cuth 98–99. *Thornbury Manor, Thornbury, Holsworthy EX22 7DD*   M: 07393-207977   E: coffey@coffey.cc   *or* admin@pmjcoffey.com

COFFIN, Pamela. *See* PENNELL, Pamela

COGGINS, Glenn. b 60. Warwick Univ BA 81. Cranmer Hall Dur 93. **d** 95 **p** 96. C Cley Hill Warminster *Sarum* 95–99; R Doddington w Benwick and Wimblington *Ely* 99–06; V E Ardsley *Wakef* 06–14; *Leeds* 14–19; V Outwood, Stanley and Wrenthorpe 19–20; P-in-c Alverthorpe 19–20; V N Wakefield from 20; Bp's Adv for Ecum Affairs *Wakef* 07–14; *Leeds* from 14. *St Paul's Vicarage, St Paul's Drive, Wakefield WF2 0BT*   M: 07951-651952 E: cogginsglenn@gmail.com

COGHLAN, Jennifer Mary. *See* WILTSHIRE, Jennifer Mary

COGLE, Ann Marie. b 62. Reading Univ BA 84 PGCE 85. St Mellitus Coll 19. **d** 21. NSM Reading St Mary the Virgin *Ox* from 21. *10A Victoria Road, Tilehurst, Reading RG31 5AD*   T: 0118-942   0322   M: 07906-606402 E: cogle@talktalk.net

COHEN, Grant Geoffrey. b 71. Regents Th Coll BA 08. Ridley Hall Cam 09. **d** 11 **p** 12. C Sale St Anne *Ches* 11–14; TV Sanderstead *S'wark* 14–18; V Sanderstead St Mary from 18; P-in-c Riddlesdown from 16. *St Mary's Vicarage, 85 Purley Oaks Road, South Croydon CR2 0NY*   M: 07717-170386 E: grant_cohen@hotmail.co.uk

COHEN, Canon Ian Geoffrey Holland. b 51. Nottm Univ BA 74. Ripon Coll Cuddesdon 77. **d** 79 **p** 80. C Sprowston *Nor* 79–83; TV Wallingford w Crowmarsh Gifford etc *Ox* 83–88; V Chalgrove w Berrick Salome 88–18; Hon Can Ch Ch 11–18; rtd 18. *19 Nun Street, St Davids, Haverfordwest SA62 6NS*   T: (01437) 729585 E: ianghcohen@hotmail.com

COHEN, Janet Elizabeth. *See* GASPER, Janet Elizabeth

COHEN, Malcolm Arthur. b 38. Canberra Coll of Min. **d** 78 **p** 79. C Moruya, Bega and Cootamundra Australia 79–80; R Braidwood 82–83; R Stifford *Chelmsf* 84–92; Chapl Asst Thurrock Community Hosp Grays 84–86; Hon Chapl ATC from 86; P-in-c Mayland and Steeple *Chelmsf* 92–95; C Prittlewell St Mary 95–99; C Greenstead 99–00; TV Greenstead w Colchester St Anne 00–03; rtd 03; PtO *Chelmsf* from 08. *177 Straight Road, Colchester CO3 5DG*   T: (01206) 573231 E: lynnpcohen@googlemail.com

COKER, Canon Barry Charles Ellis. b 46. K Coll Lon BD 69 AKC 69. **d** 70 **p** 71. C Newton Aycliffe *Dur* 70–74; R Marabella H Cross Trinidad and Tobago 74–78; R Matson *Glouc* 78–90; V Stroud and Uplands w Slad 90–11; P-in-c The Edge, Pitchcombe, Harescombe and Brookthorpe 00–01; RD Bisley 94–06; Hon Can Glouc Cathl 98–11; rtd 11; PtO *Glouc* from 14. *St Petroc, 30 Highfield Road, Lydney GL15 5NA*   T: (01594) 840890 E: fatherbarry@btinternet.com

COLAM (*née* TAVERNER)**, Mrs Lorraine Dawn.** b 61. SRN 82 RSCN 86. **d** 07 **p** 08. OLM Tilehurst St Cath and Calcot *Ox* 07–18; Chapl R Berks NHS Foundn Trust 14–18; NSM Burghfield *Ox* from 18. *120 Chapel Hill, Tilehurst, Reading RG31 5DH*   T: 0118-943 2001   M: 07790-076450 E: lorraine.colam@virginmedia.com

COLBROOK, Mrs Andrea Dorothy. b 70. Reading Univ BA 96 RGN 92. Ripon Coll Cuddesdon 17. **d** 19 **p** 20. C Ridgeway *Ox* from 19. *Fawler Paddock, Fawler, Wantage OX12 9QJ*   T: (01367)   820553   M: 07749-865052 E: revd.acolbrook@gmail.com

COLBY, Mrs Ruth Mary. b 61. ERMC 13. **d** 16 **p** 17. C Rothwell w Orton, Rushton w Glendon and Pipewell *Pet* 16–18; C Broughton w Loddington and Cransley etc 16–18; C Rothwell w Orton and Rushton w Glendon etc 18–19; P-in-c Car Colston w Screveton *S'well* from 19; P-in-c E Bridgford and Kneeton from 19; P-in-c Flintham from 19. *The Vicarage, Woods Lane, Flintham, Newark NG23 5LR*   T: (01636) 924383 E: revruthcolby@gmail.com

COLCHESTER, Archdeacon of. *See* PATTEN, The Ven Ruth Janet

COLCHESTER, Area Bishop of. *See* MORRIS, The Rt Revd Roger Anthony Brett

COLCLOUGH, The Rt Revd Michael John. b 44. Leeds Univ BA 69. Cuddesdon Coll 69. **d** 71 **p** 72 **c** 96. C Burslem St Werburgh *Lich* 71–75; C Ruislip St Mary *Lon* 75–79; P-in-c Hayes St Anselm 79–85; V 85–86; AD Hillingdon 85–92; P-in-c Uxbridge St Marg 86–88; P-in-c Uxbridge St Andr w St Jo 86–88; TR Uxbridge 86–92; Adn Northolt 92–94; P-in-c St Vedast w St Mich-le-Querne etc 94–96; P-in-c St Magnus the Martyr w St Marg New Fish Street 95–96; Bp's Sen Chapl 94–96; Dean of Univ Chapls 94–96; Dep P in O 95–96; Area Bp Kensington *Lon* 96–08; Can Res St Paul's Cathl 08–13; rtd 13; Hon Asst Bp Lon from 13; Hon Asst Bp Eur from 13; PtO from 18. *12 Grosvenor Court,*

99 Sloane Street, London SW1X 9PF   T: (020) 3612 3135 E: michaeljcolclough@gmail.com

COLDICOTT, Richard Spencer. b 69. Leeds Univ BSc 90 PhD 93 PGCE 94. Trin Coll Bris 06. **d** 08 **p** 09. C Aspley *S'well* 08–11; TV Horsham *Chich* 11–16; V Holbrook from 16. *St Mark's House, North Heath Lane, Horsham RH12 4PJ*   T: (01403) 260435   M: 07742-014444 E: vicar@stmarksholbrook.org.uk

COLDWELL, Canon John Philip. b 62. Trin Coll Bris 04. **d** 06 **p** 07. C Inglewood Gp *Carl* 06–09; P-in-c Douglas St Ninian *S & M* 09–13; V from 13; Dioc Communications Officer from 10; Hon Can St German's Cathl 15–16; Can St German's Cathl from 16. *St Ninian's Vicarage, 58 Ballanard Road, Douglas, Isle of Man IM2 5HE*   T: (01624) 621694   M: 07624-203395 E: media@sodorandman.im

COLDWELL, Rosemary Anne. b 52. Open Univ BA 82 Bretton Hall Coll CertEd 75 LTCL 74 LLCM 74. STETS 04. **d** 07 **p** 08. NSM Blandford Forum and Langton Long *Sarum* 07–12; PtO *Bradf* 12–13; *Sarum* 16–21. *Address temp unknown*   M: 07395-808035 E: rosemarycoldwell@btinternet.com

COLE, Canon Alan John. b 35. Bps' Coll Cheshunt 63. **d** 66 **p** 67. C Boreham Wood All SS *St Alb* 66–69; C St Alb St Mich 69–72; V Redbourn 72–80; R Thorley w Bishop's Stortford H Trin 80–87; Chapl St Edw K and Martyr Cam *Ely* 87–94; Chapl Arthur Rank Hospice Cam 87–94; P-in-c Gamlingay w Hatley St George and E Hatley *Ely* 94–99; Hon Can Ely Cathl 96–00; P-in-c Everton w Tetworth 98–99; R Gamlingay and Everton 99–00; rtd 01; PtO *St E* 01–15; *Ely* from 01. *73 Finchams Close, Linton, Cambridge CB21 4ND* E: alan703cole@btinternet.com

COLE, Alan Michael. b 40. Melbourne Univ DipEd 74 BA 74. ACT. **d** 66 **p** 67. Australia 66–75 and 90–97; Chapl Bp Otter Coll Chich 76–77; Chapl Ardingly Coll 77–82; Chapl Bonn w Cologne *Eur* 82–86; Chapl Helsinki w Moscow 86–90; P-in-c Ilkeston H Trin *Derby* 97–01; V 02–10; rtd 10; PtO *Pet* from 10; *Leic* from 10; *Eur* from 10. *30 St Mary's Paddock, Wellingborough NN8 1HJ*   T: (01933) 274650

COLE, Mrs Alice Alexandra Judith. b 87. St Andr Univ MMath 09 Lanc Univ MSc 10 PhD 15. St Mellitus Coll BA 17. **d** 17 **p** 18. C Lower Darwen St Jas *Blackb* from 17; C Over Darwen St Jas and Hoddlesden from 17. *81 Delphinium Way, Lower Darwen, Darwen BB3 0SX*   T: (01254) 671229   M: 07793-712757

COLE, Mrs Christine Anne. b 58. Homerton Coll Cam BEd 80. ERMC 19. **d** 20 **p** 21. NSM Cambridge St Martin *Ely* from 20. *135 Coleridge Road, Cambridge CB1 3PN*   T: (01223) 410824   M: 07552-232626 E: cacole2607@gmail.com

COLE, Guy Spenser. b 63. Univ of Wales (Ban) BA 84 Jes Coll Cam BA 88 MA 91. Westcott Ho Cam 85. **d** 88 **p** 89. C Eastville St Anne w St Mark and St Thos *Bris* 88–92; P-in-c Penhill 92–95; V 95–01; R Easthampstead *Ox* from 01; AD Bracknell from 19. *The Rectory, Crowthorne Road, Easthampstead, Bracknell RG12 7ER*   T: (01344) 423253 *or* 425205 E: guy.s.cole@btinternet.com

COLE, Jennifer Ann. b 52. Open Univ MBA 04. STETS 07. **d** 09 **p** 10. NSM Kilmersdon w Babington and Radstock w Writhlington *B & W* 09–13; PtO 13–14; NSM Wells St Cuth w Wookey Hole 14–19; PtO 19–20. *Address temp unknown* M: 07749-079276

COLE, John Gordon. b 43. Magd Coll Cam BA 65 MA 69. Cuddesdon Coll 66. **d** 68 **p** 69. C Leeds St Pet *Ripon* 68–71; C Moor Allerton 71–75; P-in-c Pendleton *Blackb* 75–86; Dioc Communications Officer 75–86; Dioc Missr *Linc* 86–98; Ecum Development Officer 98–02; Nat Adv for Unity in Miss 03–08; rtd 08. *5 Markham Way, Wrawby, Brigg DN20 8TE* E: jg.cole@tiscali.co.uk

COLE, John Spensley. b 39. Clare Coll Cam BA 62 MA 66 FCA 65. Linc Th Coll 78. **d** 80 **p** 81. C Cowes St Mary *Portsm* 80–83; C Portchester 83–87; V Modbury *Ex* 87–95; R Aveton Gifford 87–95; TR Modbury, Bigbury, Ringmore w Kingston etc 95–98; P-in-c Alne and Brafferton w Pilmoor, Myton-on-Swale etc *York* 98–05; rtd 05; PtO *S'well* from 14. *11 Long Meadow, Farnsfield, Newark NG22 8DR*   T: (01623) 883595 E: johncole@phonecoop.coop

COLE, Canon Michael John. b 34. St Pet Hall Ox BA 56 MA 60. Ridley Hall Cam 56. **d** 58 **p** 59. C Finchley Ch Ch *Lon* 58; C Leeds St Geo *Ripon* 58–61; Travelling Sec IVF 61–64; V Crookes St Thos *Sheff* 64–71; R Rusholme H Trin *Man* 71–75; V Woodford Wells *Chelmsf* 75–00; Chapl Leytonstone Ho Hosp 85–00; Hon Can Chelmsf Cathl 89–00; RD Redbridge 95–00; rtd 00; PtO *Chelmsf* 00–06; *Chich* from 13. *1 Paradise Drive, Eastbourne BN20 7SX*   T: (01323) 723425 E: canoncole@yahoo.com

COLE, Canon Norma Joan. b 46. EAMTC 93. **d** 96 **p** 97. C Ipswich St Mary at Stoke w St Pet *St E* 96–97; C Ipswich St Mary at Stoke w St Pet and St Fran 97–99; V Gt Cornard 99–04; V Rushen *S & M* 04–10; Hon Can St German's Cathl

09–10; rtd 10; PtO *Ches* 13–18; Hon C Pet St Mark from 19. *4 Lincoln Gate, Lincoln Road, Peterborough PE1 2RD* E: canon.norma678@gmail.com

COLE, Canon Peter George Lamont. b 27. Pemb Coll Cam BA 49 MA 52. Cuddesdon Coll 50. **d** 52 **p** 53. C Aldershot St Mich *Guildf* 52–55; C St Jo Cathl Bulawayo S Rhodesia 55–59; P-in-c Riverside All SS 55–59; R 59–62; Chapl St Steph Coll Balla Balla 63–65; V Bromley St Andr *Roch* 65–72; V Folkestone St Mary and St Eanswythe *Cant* 72–87; Hon Can Cant Cathl 80–87; V E and W Worldham, Hartley Mauditt w Kingsley etc *Win* 87–92; RD Alton 89–92; rtd 92; RD Petworth *Chich* 94–95; PtO from 95. *29 Swan View, Pulborough RH20 2BF* T: (01798) 873238 E: petergcole@outlook.com

COLE, Mrs Vanessa Anne. b 73. K Alfred's Coll Win BA 94. Trin Coll Bris BA 03. **d** 04 **p** 05. C Congresbury w Puxton and Hewish St Ann *B & W* 04–09; TV Portway and Danebury *Win* 09–21; PtO from 21. *The Rectory, Over Wallop, Stockbridge SO20 8HT* E: vanessa@cole.org.uk

COLE, William. b 45. Oak Hill Th Coll BA 96. **d** 96 **p** 97. NSM St Keverne *Truro* 96–99; P-in-c St Ruan w St Grade and Landewednack 99–10; rtd 10; PtO *Carl* 11–16; C Combe Martin, Berrynarbor, Lynton, Brendon etc *Ex* 16–18; C Ilfracombe SS Phil and Jas, Combe Martin and Berrynarbor 18–19. *16 Copperas Close, Lowca, Whitehaven CA28 6QU* M: 07792-932559 E: billcole124@btinternet.com

COLE-BAKER, Peter Massey. b 58. New Univ of Ulster BSc 80 TCD BTh 98. CITC 95. **d** 98 **p** 99. C Ballywillan *Conn* 98–01; I Templemore w Thurles and Kilfithmone *C, F & O* 01–14; Can Ossory Cathl 12–14; rtd 14. *The Bungalow, Springfield, Clonard Road, Wexford, Y35 X2R1, Republic of Ireland* E: pcolebaker@eircom.net

COLEBROOK, Canon Christopher John. b 36. Qu Mary Coll Lon BA 60 BD 69. St D Coll Lamp 60. **d** 62 **p** 63. C Llandeilo Tal-y-bont *S & B* 62–66; C Llansamlet 66–71; V Nantmel w St Harmon's and Llanwrthwl 71–76; V Glantawe 76–85; V Gowerton 85–01; RD Llwchwr 93–00; Hon Can Brecon Cathl 97–01; Prec 00–01; rtd 01. *79 Vivian Road, Sketty, Swansea SA2 0UN* T: (01792) 521966

COLEBROOKE, Andrew. b 50. Imp Coll Lon BSc 71 MSc 72 PhD 75. Ridley Hall Cam 92. **d** 94 **p** 95. C Shrub End *Chelmsf* 94–98; R Mistley w Manningtree and Bradfield 98–09; RD Harwich 04–09; R Icknield Way Villages 09–16; rtd 16; PtO *Chelmsf* 17–19. *42 Crabtrees, Saffron Walden CB11 3BH* T: (01799) 732970 E: andy.colebrooke@gmail.com

COLEBY, Andrew Mark. b 59. Linc Coll Ox MA 85 DPhil 85 Dur Univ BA 90 FRHistS 88. Cranmer Hall Dur 88. **d** 91 **p** 92. C Heeley *Sheff* 91–93; TV Gleadless 94–97; Chapl Ox Brookes Univ 97–01; P-in-c Didcot All SS 01–06; Dioc FE Officer and Chapl Abingdon and Witney Coll 06–09; Soc Resp Adv *St Alb* 09–13; R Shipston-on-Stour w Honington and Idlicote *Cov* 13–17; PtO *Ox* from 11; Min Tr Officer *Pet* from 17. *Silver Birches, Picklers Hill, Abingdon OX14 2BA* T: (01235) 528374 E: am.coleby@btopenworld.com

COLEMAN, Andrew David. b 78. Monash Univ BA 00. Melbourne Coll of Div MDiv 08. **d** 07 **p** 08. C Kilmore Australia 07–09; C Port Elliot w Goolwa 09–11; V Longford *Cov* 13–19; P-in-c Radford from 19; P-in-c Ansty and Shilton from 13. *The Vicarage, 65 Hurst Road, Longford, Coventry CV6 6EL* T: (024) 7636 6635 M: 07517-373587 E: andrewdavidcoleman@hotmail.com

COLEMAN, Mrs Ann Valerie. b 51. K Coll Lon BD 72 Heythrop Coll Lon MA 03. St Aug Coll Cant. **dss** 80 **d** 87 **p** 94. Hampstead Garden Suburb *Lon* 80–84; Golders Green 85–87; Selection Sec and Voc Adv ACCM 87–91; Teacher Bp Ramsey Sch 92–93; Chapl 93–99; Dir of Ords Willesden Area *Lon* 96–99; Course Leader NTMTC 99–04; Hon C Eastcote St Lawr *Lon* 93–04; Dir Wydale Hall *York* 04–08; Dioc Moderator Reader Tr 05–08; Tutor St Mellitus Coll *Lon* 08–12; Asst Dean St Mellitus Coll and Dir NTMTC 12–15; Hon C Doddinghurst *Chelmsf* 14–19; NSM Bentley Common, Kelvedon Hatch and Navestock from 14; Hon C 15–19. *The Rectory, Church Lane, Doddinghurst, Brentwood CM15 0NJ* T: (01277) 821366 E: annvcol@gmail.com

COLEMAN, Brian James. b 36. K Coll Cam BA 58 MA 61. Ripon Hall Ox 58. **d** 60 **p** 61. C Allestree *Derby* 60–65; V Allestree St Nic 65–69; Chapl and Lect St Mich Coll Salisbury 69–77; P-in-c Matlock Bank *Derby* 77–86; R Frimley *Guildf* 86–92; V Guildf All SS 92–02; rtd 02; PtO *Sarum* 03–15. *6 Kingfisher Close, Salisbury SP2 8JE* T: (01722) 410034

COLEMAN, David. b 61. **d** 14 **p** 15. C Horley S'wark 14–16; C S Nutfield 16–18; R W Chiltington *Chich* 18–19; V Steeton *Leeds* from 19. *The Vicarage, 2 Halsteads Way, Steeton, Keighley BD20 6SN* M: 07734-948469 E: vicarsteeton@gmail.com

COLEMAN, Preb David. b 49. K Coll Lon BD 72 AKC 72. St Aug Coll Cant 72. **d** 73 **p** 74. C Is of Dogs Ch Ch and

St Jo w St Luke *Lon* 73–77; C Greenford H Cross 77–80; V Cricklewood St Pet 80–85; V Golders Green 85–90; V Eastcote St Lawr 90–04; P-in-c Upper Ryedale and CME Officer Cleveland Adnry *York* 04–08; V Heston *Lon* 08–15; Preb St Paul's Cathl 13–15; rtd 15; PtO *Chelmsf* from 15. *The Rectory, Church Lane, Doddinghurst, Brentwood CM15 0NJ* T: (01227) 821366 E: frdavid.coleman@tiscali.co.uk

COLEMAN, David Kenneth. b 60. Ex Univ BTh 10. SWMTC 06. **d** 09 **p** 10. NSM Bickleigh and Shaugh Prior *Ex* 09–14; NSM Whitchurch 14–16; NSM Peter Tavy and Mary Tavy 14–16; TV S Molton w Nymet St George, Chittlehamholt etc from 16. *The Vicarage, Chittlehampton, Umberleigh EX37 9QL* E: revd.davecoleman@gmail.com

COLEMAN, Frank. b 58. Hull Univ BA 79. St Steph Ho Ox BA 83 MA 87. **d** 83 **p** 84. C Brandon *Dur* 83–85; C Newton Aycliffe 85–88; V Denford w Ringstead *Pet* 88–00; P-in-c Islip 95–00; V Caldecote, Northill and Old Warden *St Alb* from 00. *The Vicarage, 2A Biggleswade Road, Upper Caldecote, Biggleswade SG18 9BL* T: (01767) 315578 F: 317988 M: 07738-357458 E: frankcoleman@ntlworld.com

COLEMAN, Jonathan Mark. b 59. Kent Univ BA 81. Qu Coll Birm MA 99. **d** 99 **p** 00. C Warrington St Elphin *Liv* 99–02; P-in-c Liv St Chris Norris Green 02–07; Area Dean W Derby and Hon Can Liv Cathl 06–07; P-in-c W Derby St Mary 07–09; P-in-c W Derby St Jas 07–09; V W Derby St Mary and St Jas 09–14; R Rochdale *Man* 14–20; AD 15–17; Borough Dean Rochdale 16–20; rtd 20; PtO *Man* from 20. *40 Buxton Crescent, Rochdale OL16 4TU* M: 07795-202955 E: hellomarkcoleman@gmail.com

COLEMAN, Julie Victoria. b 62. Cant Ch Ch Univ PGCE 08. St Jo Coll Nottm 09. **d** 11 **p** 12. C Aylesham w Adisham and Nonington *Cant* 11–14; P-in-c Romney Marsh 14–18; V Palmers Green St Jo from 18. *The Vicarage, 1 Bourne Hill, London N13 4DA* T: (020) 8886 0847 M: 07583-774857 E: rev.jcoleman@hotmail.com

COLEMAN, Neil Geoffrey. b 77. Trin Coll Bris BA 11. **d** 11 **p** 12. C N Mundham w Hunston and Merston *Chich* 11–15; V St Paul's Cray St Barn *Roch* from 15. *The Vicarage, Rushet Road, Orpington BR5 2PU* M: 07826-850273 E: n-coleman@hotmail.co.uk

COLEMAN, Ms Nicola Jane. b 63. Goldsmiths' Coll Lon BA 86. Ripon Coll Cuddesdon 99. **d** 01 **p** 02. C Croydon St Jo *S'wark* 01–05; P-in-c S Norwood H Innocents 05–12; P-in-c The Lulworths, Winfrith Newburgh and Chaldon *Sarum* 12–16; P-in-c Barton Hill St Luke w Ch Ch and Moorfields *Bris* from 17; P-in-c E Bris St Ambrose and St Leon from 17. *St Luke's Vicarage, 60 Barton Hill Road, Bristol BS5 0AW* T: 0117-955 6678 M: 07985-659667 E: revncoleman@gmail.com

COLEMAN, Patrick Francis. b 58. Pontifical Univ Rome PhB 79 STB 82 STL 84. Ven English Coll Rome 77. **d** 82 **p** 83. In RC Ch 82–92; NSM Abergavenny St Mary w Llanwenarth Citra *Mon* 96–99; Asst Chapl Milan w Genoa and Varese *Eur* 99–01; R Goetre w Llanover *Mon* 01–06; Dir CME 01–06; P-in-c Abertillery w Cwmtillery 06–10; V Abertillery w Cwmtillery w Llanhilleth etc 10–14; V Chesterfield St Mary and All SS *Derby* from 14. *The Vicarage, 28 Cromwell Road, Chesterfield S40 4TH* T: (01246) 462866 E: abervicar@me.com

COLEMAN, Canon Peter Nicholas. b 42. St Mich Coll Llan 83. **d** 85 **p** 86. C Skewen *Llan* 85–88; R Ystradyfodwg 88–07; P-in-c Treorchy and Treherbert 04–07; RD Rhondda 96–04; Can Llan Cathl 04–07; rtd 07; PtO *Llan* from 07. *15 Pant Hendre, Pencoed, Bridgend CF35 6LN*

COLEMAN, Richard Ian. b 70. Open Univ BSc 00. Wycliffe Hall Ox 05. **d** 07 **p** 08. C Peterlee *Dur* 07–11; P-in-c Barton in Fabis *S'well* 11–19; P-in-c Gotham 11–19; P-in-c Kingston and Ratcliffe-on-Soar 11–19; P-in-c Thrumpton 11–19; R A453 churches of S Notts from 19. *The New Rectory, 39 Leake Road, Gotham, Nottingham NG11 0HW* T: 0115-983 0608 E: coleman@orpheusmail.co.uk

COLEMAN, Stephen Paul Losack. b 80. St Benet's Hall Ox BA 02 MSt 03 Cardiff Univ LLM 17. Westcott Ho Cam 12. **d** 14 **p** 15. C Winchmore Hill St Paul *Lon* 14–17; V Grange Park St Pet from 17. *The Vicarage, Langham Gardens, London N21 1DN* T: (020) 8360 2294 E: stephenplcoleman@hotmail.com

COLEMAN, Timothy. b 57. Southn Univ BSc 79 MBACP. Ridley Hall Cam 87. **d** 89 **p** 90. C Bisley and W End *Guildf* 89–93; C Hollington St Jo *Chich* 93–97; V Aldborough Hatch *Chelmsf* 97–02; Chapl Princess Alexandra Hosp NHS Trust 02–04; Chapl Barking, Havering and Redbridge Hosps NHS Trust 04–21; rtd 21; PtO *Chelmsf* from 21. *Address temp unknown*

COLERIDGE, William Paul Hugh. b 76. Newc Univ LLB 98 Solicitor 01. Wycliffe Hall Ox 07. **d** 09 **p** 10. C Ches Square St Mich w St Phil *Lon* 09–12; C Paddington St Steph w

St Luke 12–16; C Bayswater 12–16; V from 16. *The Vicarage, 27 St Petersburgh Place, London W2 4LA* T: (020) 7229 2192 E: will@stmatthewsbayswater.org.uk

COLES, Canon Alasdair Charles. b 67. St Andr Univ BSc 90 Ox Univ BTh 96 Homerton Coll Cam PGCE 91 Heythrop Coll Lon PhD 03. Ripon Coll Cuddesdon 96. d 96 p 97. C Wymondham *Nor* 96–99; Min Can and Sacr St Paul's Cathl *Lon* 99–04; P-in-c Pimlico St Mary Bourne Street 04–07; V 07–09; P-in-c Pimlico St Barn 04–07; V 07–09; Asst Vice Prin and Chapl All SS Academy Dunstable 09–15; PV Westmr Abbey 04–15; R St Andrews All SS *St And* from 15; Can St Ninian's Cathl Perth from 20; Hon Can Mampong Ghana from 14. *All Saints' Rectory, 39 North Street, St Andrews KY16 9AQ* T: (01334) 473153 M: 07729-962723 E: rector@allsaints-standrews.org.uk

COLES, Alasdair John. b 66. Pemb Coll Ox BA 87 Green Coll Ox BM, BCh 90 CCC Cam PhD 98 MRCP 94. ERMC 05. d 08 p 09. NSM Chesterton St Andr *Ely* from 08. *Department of Neurology, Box 165, Addenbrooke's Hospital, Cambridge CB2 2QQ* T: (01223) 216751 F: 336941 E: ajc1020@medschl.cam.ac.uk

COLES, Preb Alison Elizabeth. b 60. St Mary's Coll Dur BA 81. Ripon Coll Cuddesdon 95. d 97 p 98. C Leckhampton SS Phil and Jas w Cheltenham St Jas *Glouc* 97–00; Asst Chapl Dudley Gp of Hosps NHS Trust 00–04; Chapl Walsall Healthcare NHS Trust 04–20; Bp's Adv on Healthcare Chapl *Lich* from 19; Preb Lich Cathl from 15. *Address temp unknown*

COLES, Charlotte Lois. b 62. SEITE 11 St Aug Coll of Th 18. d 20 p 21. NSM Len Valley *Cant* from 20. *Park View, 27 Jemmett Road, Ashford TN23 4QD* T: (01233) 335829 M: 07805-092823 E: charlottecoles62@hotmail.com *or* curate@lvb.org

✠**COLES, The Rt Revd David John.** b 43. Auckland Univ MA 67 Otago Univ BD 69 MTh 71 Man Univ PhD 74. St Jo Coll Auckland 66. d 68 p 69 c 90. C Remuera NZ 68–70; Chapl Selwyn Coll Dunedin 70–71; Hon C Fallowfield *Man* 72–74; Chapl Hulme Gr Sch Oldham 73–74; V Glenfield NZ 74–76; V Takapuna 76–80; Dean Napier 80–84; Dean Christchurch 84–90; Bp Christchurch 90–08; V Wakatipu NZ 08–14; Chapl Denmark *Eur* 14–15; V Heathcote Mt Pleasant NZ from 15. *88 Canon Street, St Albans, Christchurch 8014, New Zealand* T: (0064) (3) 366 0359 M: (0064) 27-306 9961 E: vicar@heathcote-mtpleasant.org.nz *or* dandjcoles@gmail.com

COLES, Preb Francis Herbert. b 35. Selw Coll Cam BA 59 MA 63. Coll of Resurr Mirfield 59. d 61 p 62. C Wolvercote *Ox* 61–65; C Farnham Royal 65–69; V Lynton and Brendon *Ex* 69–73; V Countisbury 70; V Lynton, Brendon, Countisbury and Lynmouth 70–73; TR Lynton, Brendon, Countisbury, Lynmouth etc 73–76; P-in-c Iffley *Ox* 76–88; V Ivybridge w Harford *Ex* 88–00; Preb Ex Cathl from 98; rtd 00; PtO *Ex* 00–20 and from 21. *17 Gracey Court, Woodland Road, Exeter EX5 3GA* T: (01392) 461117

COLES, Graham Robert. b 60. Qu Coll Birm 07. d 09 p 10. C Lillington and Old Milverton *Cov* 09–12; P-in-c Cubbington 12–14; V from 14. *St Mary's Vicarage, 15 Pinehurst, Cubbington, Leamington Spa CV32 7XA* T: (01926) 330596

COLES, Preb John Spencer Halstaff. b 50. Hertf Coll Ox BA 72 MA 76. Wycliffe Hall Ox 72. d 75 p 76. C Reading Greyfriars *Ox* 75–79; C Clifton Ch Ch w Em *Bris* 79–82; V Woodside Park St Barn *Lon* 82–06; C 06–11; Dir New Wine Internat Min 11–15; LtO from 13; Preb St Paul's Cathl from 11. *33 Arnos Road, London N11 1AP* T: (020) 3441 5264 M: 07779-016930

COLES, Matthew Simon Robert. b 79. UEA BA 02 Cardiff Univ MTh 17. Ridley Hall Cam 06. d 09 p 10. C Gt Chesham *Ox* 09–12; CF from 12. *c/o MOD Chaplains (Army)* M: 07736-464537 E: mattsr7@yahoo.com

COLES, Mrs Olivia Mary Kana. b 64. Cen Sch Speech & Drama BEd 87. ERMC 12. d 15 p 16. NSM Histon *Ely* 15–18; NSM Impington 15–18; NSM Whittlesford from 18; Baptism Co-ord 17–19. *The Vicarage, 22A North Road, Whittlesford, Cambridge CB22 4NZ* T: (01223) 833128 M: 07720-985889 E: revoliviacoles@gmail.com

COLES, Mrs Pamela. b 39. Nottm Univ CertEd 59. NOC 04. d 05 p 06. NSM Clayton *Bradf* 05–09; PtO 09–14; *Leeds* from 14. *4 Ferndale Avenue, Clayton, Bradford BD14 6PG* T: (01274) 427956 E: pamcolesclayton@yahoo.com

COLES, Richard Keith Robert. b 62. K Coll Lon BA 94 AKC 94 Leeds Univ MA 05 Northn Univ Hon PhD 12 FRSA 12. Coll of Resurr Mirfield 03. d 05 p 06. C Boston *Linc* 05–07; C Wilton Place St Paul *Lon* 07–11; Chapl R Academy of Music 07–08; P-in-c Finedon *Pet* 11–15; V from 15; PtO *Lon* from 20. *St Mary's Vicarage, Church Hill, Finedon, Wellingborough NN9 5NR* T: (01933) 681786 E: revdrichardcoles@yahoo.co.uk

COLES, Canon Robert Reginald. b 47. Surrey Univ BSc 69. Cant Sch of Min 82. d 85 p 86. NSM Sittingbourne St Mich *Cant* 85–87; C St Laur in Thanet 87–93; P-in-c St Nicholas at Wade w Sarre and Chislet w Hoath 93–13; P-in-c Minster w Monkton 96–13; Hon Can Cant Cathl 09–13; rtd 13; PtO *Cant* from 14. *4 Millfield, St Margaret-at-Cliffe, Dover CT15 6JL* T: (01304) 852091

COLES, Preb Stephen Richard. b 49. Univ Coll Ox BA 70 MA 74 Leeds Univ BA 80. Coll of Resurr Mirfield 78. d 81 p 82. C Stoke Newington St Mary *Lon* 81–84; Chapl K Coll Cam 84–89; V Finsbury Park St Thos *Lon* 89–20; Preb St Paul's Cathl 13–20; rtd 20; PtO *Lon* from 20. *Address temp unknown* E: cardinal.jeoffry@btconnect.com

COLES, Mrs Sylvia Margaret. b 48. ERMC 04. d 07 p 08. NSM Northampton St Benedict *Pet* 07–10; NSM Duston 10–14; NSM Dallington 14–17; NSM Northampton St Jas 14–17; NSM Dallington and St James 17–18; rtd 18; PtO *Pet* from 21; Hon C Northampton St Mary from 21. *37 Delapre Crescent Road, Northampton NN4 8NG* T: (01604) 767305

COLEY (*née* JOHNSON), Mrs Emma Louise. b 76. Ex Univ BA 97 PGCE 98. Wycliffe Hall Ox BTh 04. d 04 p 05. C Wendover and Halton *Ox* 04–09; C Kennington 09–12; C Radley and Sunningwell 09–12; P-in-c Sandridge *St Alb* 12–14; V 14–19; Asst Dir of Ords 12–19; Young Voc Officer Nat Min Team Abps' Coun from 19. *National Ministry Team, Church House, 27 Great Smith Street, London SW1P 3AZ* T: (020) 7898 1554 E: emcoley@me.com *or* em.coley@churchofengland.org

COLEY, Peter Leonard. b 45. Bath Univ BSc 67 City Univ MSc 84 CEng MIMechE. Oak Hill Th Coll 85. d 87 p 88. C Mile Cross *Nor* 87–92; R Stratton St Mary w Stratton St Michael etc 92–01; R Kirby-le-Soken w Gt Holland *Chelmsf* 01–10; rtd 10; PtO *Portsm* from 11. *6 Forest Rise, Liss GU33 7AU* T: (01730) 300659 M: 07706-037108 E: rev.petercoley@googlemail.com

COLLEDGE, Ms Anthea June. b 78. St Jo Coll Ox BA 00 Imp Coll Lon MSc 06 MPhil 09 St Jo Coll Dur BA 10. Cranmer Hall Dur 08. d 10 p 11. C Wortley-de-Leeds *Ripon* 10–13; C Wortley and Farnley 13–14; Chapl Sheff Univ 14–17; PtO *Leeds* from 17; Chapl Leeds Univ from 19. *University of Leeds, Woodhouse Lane, Leeds LS2 9JT* M: 07518-319475 E: a.j.colledge@gmail.com

COLLEDGE, Christopher Richard. b 58. Chich Th Coll. d 82 p 83. C Deal St Leon and St Rich and Sholden *Cant* 82–85; Bermuda 85–88; TV Wickford and Runwell *Chelmsf* 88–90; Chapl Runwell Hosp Wickford 88–90; Chapl RAD 90–03; PtO *Wor* from 12; *Sarum* 12–22. *27 Grand Marine Court, Durley Gardens, Bournemouth BH2 5HS* M: 07901-686237 E: revdchriscolledge@gmail.com

COLLETT, Reginald Martin Vizor. b 50. Thames Poly CertEd 87. Sarum Coll 17. d 19 p 20. NSM Dulverton w Brushford, Brompton Regis etc *B & W* from 19. *5 Musgraves, Dulverton TA22 9EB* T: (01398) 324211 E: colletts36@btinternet.com

COLLETT-WHITE, Thomas Charles. b 36. Trin Coll Cam BA 61 MA 86. Ridley Hall Cam 60. d 62 p 63. C Gillingham St Mark *Roch* 62–66; V 79–90; C Normanton *Wakef* 66–69; V Highbury New Park St Aug *Lon* 69–76; R Huntingdon w Ormstown Canada 76–79; Chapl Medway Hosp Gillingham 79–85; P-in-c Clerkenwell St Jas and St Jo w St Pet *Lon* 90–96; rtd 01; PtO *Cant* 06–21. *4 Little Meadow, Upper Harbledown, Canterbury CT2 9BD* E: tcollettwhite@yahoo.co.uk

COLLEY, Elizabeth Jane. b 51. Open Univ BA 89 DipSW 96. d 13 p 14. NSM Crewe All SS and St Paul w St Pet *Ches* 13–16; P-in-c 16–19; rtd 19. *8 Tatton Drive, Sandbach CW11 1DR* T: (01270) 748669 M: 07404-778831 E: ejmmcc@aol.com

COLLEY, Graham Albert. b 46. Auckland Teachers' Coll TCert 68. St Jo Th Coll (NZ) LTh 71. d 70 p 71. C Papakura NZ 70–73; P-in-c Papakura 73; V Waimate N 73–83; P-in-c Ynysddu *Mon* 78; V Thames St Geo NZ 81–16; Adn Hunua 89–00; PtO 16–17; C Birchington w Acol and Minnis Bay *Cant* 17–18; rtd 18; P-in-c Buckland's Beach Cooperating NZ 18–20; PtO Auckland from 20. *Bay Tree House, 103 Victoria Street, Thames 3500, New Zealand* E: gandj.colley@gmail.com

COLLEY, Mrs Karen. b 68. Sheff Hallam Univ BA 96 Leeds Metrop Univ MSc 01. Yorks Min Course 11. d 13 p 14. NSM Sheff Manor from 13. *4 Bramley Hall Road, Handsworth, Sheffield S13 8TX* E: revdkaren@btinternet.com *or* karen.colley@manorparish.co.uk

COLLEY, Leonard Noel. b 51. Qu Coll Birm 12. d 15 p 16. NSM Nanpantan St Mary in Charnwood *Leic* 15–19; NSM Groby and Ratby from 19. *The Vicarage, 58 Pymm Ley Lane, Groby, Leicester LE6 0GZ*

COLLEY, Williamina Taylor. b 59. Nottm Univ BMedSci 80 BM, BS 83. Qu Foundn (Course) 16. d 19 p 20. NSM

Woodfield *Leic* from 19. *58 Pymm Ley Lane, Groby, Leicester LE6 0GZ* M: 07766-306227 E: revwilmacolley@gmail.com

COLLICUTT McGRATH, Canon Joanna Ruth. b 54. LMH Ox BA 76 MA 85 Lon Univ MPhil 78 Ox Brookes Univ PhD 98 K Coll Lon MA 17. Wycliffe Hall Ox 00 Ripon Coll Cuddesdon 05. **d** 06 **p** 07. NSM Witney *Ox* from 06; Tutor Ripon Coll Cuddesdon from 07; Lect from 10; Dioc Adv for Spiritual Care for Older People *Ox* from 10; Hon Can Ch Ch from 16. *Ripon College, Cuddesdon, Oxford OX44 9EX* T: (01865) 877404 E: jcollicutt@aol.com *or* joanna.collicutt@hmc.ox.ac.uk

COLLIER, Anthony Charles. b 45. Peterho Cam BA 68 MA 72 Whitelands Coll Lon PGCE 76. Cuddesdon Coll 68. **d** 71 **p** 72. C N Holmwood *Guildf* 71–75; PtO *S'wark* 75–79; Chapl Colfe's Sch Lon 80–10; rtd 10; Hon C Shirley St Jo *Cant* 80–84; Hon C Shirley St Jo *S'wark* 85–13; PtO from 13. *56 Bennetts Way, Croydon CR0 8AB* T: (020) 8777 6456 E: accollier@hotmail.com

COLLIER, Capt David Leslie. b 60. Wilson Carlile Coll 02 Qu Coll Birm 12. **d** 14 **p** 15. C Birkdale St Pet *Liv* 14–18; V Branston and Burton All SS w Ch Ch *Lich* from 18. *The Vicarage, Church Road, Branston, Burton-on-Trent DE14 3ER* E: davecollier3@gmail.com

COLLIER, Janice Margaret. b 57. MCSP 79. Cam Th Federation 99. **d** 01 **p** 02. C Formby H Trin *Liv* 01–05; P-in-c Hale 05–10; TR S Widnes 10–18; AD Widnes 13–18; Hon Can Liv Cathl 13–18; V Bampton w Clanfield *Ox* from 18. *The Vicarage, 5 Deanery Court, Broad Street, Brampton OX18 2LY*

COLLIER, John Alfred. **d** 13 **p** 13. NSM Mamhilad w Monkswood and Glascoed Chapel *Mon* 13–14; R from 14; R Goetre w Llanover from 14. *The Rectory, Nantyderry, Abergavenny NP7 9DW* T: (01873) 880378 E: collierjohn1@aol.com

COLLIER, Richard John Millard. b 45. FRSA 92. EAMTC 78. **d** 81 **p** 82. NSM Nor St Pet Mancroft w St Jo Maddermarket 81–97; NSM Thurton w Ashby St Mary, Bergh Apton etc 99–09; NSM Rockland St Mary w Hellington, Bramerton etc 09–12; PtO 12–14; NSM Docking, the Birchams, Stanhoe and Sedgeford 14–15; NSM Docking, The Birchams, Fring etc from 15. *The Old Buck, Church Lane, Sedgeford, Hunstanton PE36 5NA* T: (01485) 579091 E: rjsjc@yahoo.com

COLLIER, Stephen John. b 46. St Pet Coll Ox MA 68 Univ of Wales (Cardiff) DipSW 74. Qu Coll Birm 92. **d** 94 **p** 95. C Thorpe St Andr *Nor* 94–98; C Nor St Pet Mancroft w St Jo Maddermarket 98–01; R Kessingland, Gisleham and Rushmere 01–05; rtd 05; Hon C N Greenford All Hallows *Lon* 06–16; PtO from 16. *9 Drew Gardens, Greenford UB6 7QF* T: (020) 8903 9697

COLLIER, Steven Philip. Roehampton Univ BA 07. Wycliffe Hall Ox BTh 12. **d** 12 **p** 13. C Upper Sunbury St Sav *Lon* 12–13; C Isleworth All SS 13–15; TV Broadwater *Chich* 15–18; C 18–19; C Westcliff St Mich *Chelmsf* 19–21; C Southend St Jo from 21. *62 Leigh Road, Leigh-on-Sea SS9 1LF* T: (01702) 480736 E: steve@stjohnssouthend.org

COLLIER, Susan Margaret. b 47. Cam Univ MB, BChir 73. NOC 95. **d** 98 **p** 99. NSM Dringhouses *York* 98–12; PtO from 12. *12 St Helen's Road, York YO24 1HP* T: (01904) 706064 F: 708052 E: susan.collier@me.com

COLLIN, Mrs Fiona Maria. b 62. RGN 83. Cranmer Hall Dur 11. **d** 13 **p** 14. C Sunderland Minster *Dur* 13–16; TV Dur N 16–19; Chapl Newcastle upon Tyne Hosps NHS Foundn Trust from 19. *The Newcastle upon Tyne Hospitals NHS Foundation Trust, Freeman Hospital, Freeman Road, High Heaton, Newcastle upon Tyne NE7 7DN* T: 0191-233 6161 M: 07743-589429 E: fionamariacollin@gmail.com

COLLIN, Terry. b 39. St Aid Birkenhead 65. **d** 67 **p** 68. C Bolton St Jas w St Chrys *Bradf* 67–71; C Keighley 71–74; V Greengates 74–04; rtd 04; PtO *Bradf* 05–11. *275 Leeds Road, Eccleshill, Bradford BD2 3LD* T: (01274) 200855

COLLING, Terence John. b 47. Linc Th Coll 84. **d** 86 **p** 87. C Wood End *Cov* 86–90; V Willenhall 90–02; V Wolvey w Burton Hastings, Copston Magna etc 02–14; rtd 14; PtO *Cov* 14–21; *Leic* from 14. *2 Roman Close, Claybrooke Magna, Lutterworth LE17 5DU* T: (01455) 209712 E: terencecolling@btinternet.com

COLLINGBOURNE, David Edward. b 42. St D Coll Lamp. **d** 01. Treas Dioc Coun of Educn *Mon* from 94; NSM Bishton 01–06; NSM Newport Ch Ch 06–08; NSM Bedwas w Machen w Rudry 08–12; P-in-c Marshfield w St Bride's Wentloog from 12. *The Gables, Llanwern, Newport NP18 2DS* T: (01633) 411883 E: davidcollingbourne42@tiscali.co.uk

COLLINGBOURNE, Mrs Susan Lynne. b 48. Caerleon Coll of Educn TCert 75 Univ of Wales (Cardiff) BEd 82 MEd 94. **d** 09 **p** 10. NSM Maesglas and Duffryn *Mon* 09–12; P-in-c Marshfield w St Bride's Wentloog from

12; Dioc Child Protection Officer from 98. *The Gables, Llanwern, Newport NP18 2DS* T: (01633) 411883 E: susan.collingbourne@tinyworld.co.uk

COLLINGE, Mrs Christine Elizabeth. b 47. Doncaster Coll of Educn CertEd 68. SAOMC 95. **d** 98 **p** 99. NSM W Slough *Ox* 98–04; TV Stantonbury and Willen 04–12; rtd 12; PtO *Ox* from 13. *26 Bell Close, Slough SL2 5UQ* T: (01753) 575332 E: chriscollinge@hotmail.com

COLLINGRIDGE, Graham Ian. b 58. Pemb Coll Ox BA 80 MA 84 Bedf Coll Lon MSc 84 Anglia Ruskin Univ MA 10. Ridley Hall Cam 07. **d** 09 **p** 10. C Bitterne Park *Win* 09–13; V Long Buckby w Watford and W Haddon w Winwick *Pet* from 13. *The Vicarage, 10 Hall Drive, Long Buckby, Northampton NN6 7QU* T: (01327) 842204 E: vicar.longbuckby@btinternet.com

COLLINGRIDGE, Susan Rachel. b 61. St Mary's Coll Dur BA 83 Ches Univ DProf 20. Cranmer Hall Dur 85. **d** 88 **p** 94. Par Dn Luton St Mary *St Alb* 88–93; PtO *Ex* 93–94; NSM Parkham, Alwington, Buckland Brewer etc 94–98; TV Cove St Jo *Guildf* 98–03; V Guildf Ch Ch w St Martha-on-the-Hill 03–11; PtO *Ches* 11–14; NSM Antrobus 14–16; PtO Portsm 17–18; NSM Steep and Froxfield w Privett from 18. *18 Silent Garden Road, Liphook GU30 7GU* M: 07734-879224 E: susie.collingridge@gmail.com

COLLINGS, Ms Helen Mary. b 67. Warwick Univ BA 88 St Jo Coll Dur BA 06 Jes Coll Ox PGCE 90. Cranmer Hall Dur 04. **d** 06 **p** 07. C Ossett and Gawthorpe *Wakef* 06–09; P-in-c Sandal St Cath 09–14; *Leeds* 14–15; V Sutton w Cowling and Lothersdale from 15. *The Vicarage, Main Street, Sutton-in-Craven, Keighley BD20 7JS* T: (01535) 636679 M: 07708-066063 E: revd.helen.collings@gmail.com

COLLINGTON, Cameron James. b 68. Wycliffe Hall Ox BTh 01. **d** 01 **p** 02. C Ealing St Paul *Lon* 01–05; V Hammersmith St Simon from 05; AD Hammersmith and Fulham from 20. *153 Blythe Road, London W14 0HL* M: 07739-489118 E: cameron@stsimons.co.uk

COLLINGWOOD, Canon Christopher Paul. b 54. Birm Univ BMus 76 PGCE 77 Ox Univ BA 82 MA 87 K Coll Lon MA 01 PhD 07 LRSM 04. Ripon Coll Cuddesdon 80. **d** 83 **p** 84. C Tupsley *Heref* 83–86; Prec St Alb Abbey 86–90; V Bedford St Paul 90–97; Can Res and Prec Guildf Cathl 97–99; Hon C Loughton St Jo *Chelmsf* 99–09; Chapl Chigwell Sch Essex 99–09; Sen Tutor 01–09; R Minchinhampton w Box and Amberley *Glouc* 09–13; AD Stroud 11–13; Can Res and Chan York Minster 13–20; rtd 20; PtO *York* from 21. *Hill Brow, 11 Lead Lane, Brompton, Northallerton DL6 2TZ* M: 07309-624924 E: christopherpcollingwood@gmail.com

COLLINGWOOD, Deryck Laurence. b 50. St Jo Coll Cam BA 72. Edin Th Coll BD 85. **d** 85 **p** 85. Chapl Napier Poly *Edin* 85–88; C Edin Ch Ch 85–88; TV 88–89; Tutor Edin Th Coll 89–94; Asst P Edin St Hilda and Edin St Fillan 94–03; Chapl Edin Napier Univ 95–03; P-in-c Dalmahoy 03–06; R 06–16; rtd 16; LtO *Edin* from 18. *40 Hunter Avenue, Loanhead EH20 9SN* T: 0131-448 0240 E: dcollingwood131@btinternet.com

COLLINGWOOD, Graham Lewis. b 63. Open Univ BA 92 Ex Univ MA 98. St Steph Ho Ox 92. **d** 95 **p** 96. C Heavitree w Ex St Paul 95–97; CF 97–99; C St Marychurch *Ex* 99–00; C Cottingham *York* 00–02; Chapl RAF 02–11; V New Rossington *Sheff* 11–13; CF from 13. *c/o MOD Chaplains (Army)* T: (01264) 383430 F: 381824 E: rafglc@hotmail.co.uk

COLLINS, Mrs Ann Maureen. b 62. St Pet Coll Ox BA 83 Cam Univ PGCE 84. St Jo Coll Nottm MA 13. **d** 13 **p** 14. C Wilford *S'well* 13–17; V Nottingham St Ann w Em from 18. *The Vicarage, 17 Robin Hood Chase, Nottingham NG3 4EY* M: 07988-079224 E: revmaureen@live.com

COLLINS, Anthony James. b 63. NEOC 04. **d** 07 **p** 08. NSM Fountains Gp *Ripon* 07–08; NSM Dacre w Hartwith and Darley w Thornthwaite 08–14; *Leeds* from 14; NSM Washburn and Mid-Wharfe 17–19; AD Ripon 19–21. *Harvest Cottage, Sawley, Ripon HG4 3EQ* T: (01765) 620393 M: 07549-950924 E: tony.collins@leeds.anglican.org

COLLINS, Barry Douglas. b 47. Kelham Th Coll 66. **d** 70 **p** 71. C Peel Green *Man* 70–73; C Salford St Phil w St Steph 73–75; R Blackley H Trin 75–79; PtO *Ripon* 80–82; *Pet* 83–93; Cov 85–93; *Ox* 93–97; P-in-c Bengeworth *Worc* 98–99; V 99–11; rtd 11; PtO *Cov* 12–21. *9 Holbrook Avenue, Rugby CV21 2QG* T: (01788) 878993 E: barry2047@btinternet.com

COLLINS, Canon Cheryl Anne. b 62. Rob Coll Cam BA 85 MA 89 MCA 90. Ripon Coll Cuddesdon 91. **d** 93 **p** 94. C Sharrow St Andr *Sheff* 93–95; Chapl Sheff Univ 95–01; Hon C Endcliffe 96–01; P-in-c Barton *Ely* 01–10; P-in-c Coton 01–10; P-in-c Dry Drayton 01–10; RD Bourn 03–10; Miss P Red Lodge *St E* 10–12; P-in-c Chevington w Hargrave, Chedburgh w Depden etc 12–15; R 15–16;

Acting RD Clare 14–16; P-in-c Sudbury and Chilton 16–20; R from 20; P-in-c Sudbury w Ballingdon and Brundon from 19; Hon Can St E Cathl from 15. *The Rectory, Christopher Lane, Sudbury CO10 2AS* T: (01787) 375027 E: cheryl62collins@btinternet.com

COLLINS, Christopher. b 46. K Coll Lon BSc 67 AKC 67 Pemb Coll Ox BA 70. St Steph Ho Ox 68. **d** 71 **p** 72. C Pennywell St Thos and Grindon St Oswald CD *Dur* 71–74; C Pallion, Millfield St Mary and Bishopwearmouth Gd Shep 74–76; C Harton Colliery 76–78; TV Winlaton 78–85; V Grangetown 85–11; rtd 12; PtO *Dur* from 15. *15 Linthorpe Avenue, Seaham SR7 7JW* T: 0191-581 7186 E: christopher_collins@lineone.net

COLLINS, Canon Christopher David. b 43. Sheff Univ BA(Econ) 64. Tyndale Hall Bris 65. **d** 68 **p** 69. C Rusholme H Trin *Man* 68–71; C Bushbury *Lich* 71–74; V Fairfield *Liv* 74–81; V Tunbridge Wells St Jo *Roch* 81–92; R Luton Ch Ch and Chapl Thames Gateway NHS Trust 92–05; Chapl Medway NHS Trust 92–99; RD Roch 94–00; P-in-c Cobham w Luddesdowne and Dode 05–08; Hon Can Roch Cathl 98–08; rtd 08. *2 Courtenay Gardens, Alphington, Exeter EX2 8UH* T: (01392) 203975 E: canonchris@blueyonder.co.uk

COLLINS, Darren Victor. b 69. NTMTC. **d** 05 **p** 06. C Chingford SS Pet and Paul *Chelmsf* 05–07; Min Can St Alb Abbey 07–11; P-in-c Norton 11–13; V 13–16; TR Bishop's Hatfield, Lemsford and N Mymms from 16. *The Rectory, 1 Fore Street, Hatfield AL9 5AN* T: (01707) 256638 M: 07453-624061 E: frdarren@yahoo.co.uk

COLLINS, Donard Michael. b 55. Oak Hill Th Coll BA 83. **d** 83 **p** 84. C Lurgan Ch the Redeemer *D & D* 83–87; I Ardmore w Craigavon 87–98; I Killowen *D & R* from 98. *St John's Rectory, 4 Laurel Hill, Coleraine BT51 3AT* T: (028) 7034 2629 E: revdonard@yahoo.co.uk

COLLINS, Earl Martin. b 60. QUB BA 82 PhD 90. **d** 94 **p** 95. Chapl Westcott Ho Cam 17–18; C Chesterton St Andr *Ely* 18–19; P-in-c Hove St Jo *Chich* 19–21; V from 21; CMD Officer from 19. *The Rectory, 119 Holland Road, Hove BN3 1JS* T: (01273) 725811 M: 07810-576853 E: earlcollins@hotmail.com

COLLINS, Elaine Judith. b 56. **d** 12 **p** 13. NSM The Bourne and Tilford *Guildf* 12–20; NSM Haslemere and Grayswood from 20. *49 Carlton Road, Headley Down, Bordon GU35 8JT* T: (01428) 714385 E: elainecollins25@btinternet.com

COLLINS, Gary Steven. b 69. Ripon Coll Cuddesdon 14. **d** 16 **p** 17. C Reading St Jo *Ox* 16–19; C Newbury St Geo and St Jo from 19. *69B Chapel Street, Thatcham RG18 4JS* T: (01635) 827526 M: 07986-901879

✠**COLLINS, The Rt Revd Gavin Andrew.** b 66. Trin Hall Cam BA 89 MA 93. Trin Coll Bris BA 96 MA 97. **d** 97 **p** 98 **c** 21. C Cambridge St Barn *Ely* 97–02; V Chorleywood Ch Ch St Alb 02–11; RD Rickmansworth 06–11; Hon Can St Alb 09–11; Adn The Meon *Portsm* 11–21; Warden of Readers 14–21; Area Bp Dorchester *Ox* from 21. *Church House Oxford, Langford Locks, Kidlington OX5 1GF* T: (01865) 208218 E: bishopdorchester@oxford.anglican.org

COLLINS, Helen Marie. b 83. Magd Coll Ox BA 04 K Coll Lon MA 08 Bris Univ PhD 17. Trin Coll Bris 10. **d** 12 **p** 13. C Bris Ch the Servant Stockwood 12–15; Dioc Dir of Ords 15–17; Warden of Readers 15–17; NSM Hengrove 16–17; Tutor Trin Coll Bris from 17. *Trinity College, Stoke Hill, Bristol BS9 1JP* T: 0117-968 2803 E: h.collins@trinitycollegebristol.ac.uk

COLLINS, Canon Ian Geoffrey. b 37. Hull Univ BA 60 CertEd. Sarum Th Coll 60. **d** 62 **p** 63. C Gainsborough All SS *Linc* 62–65; Min Can Windsor 65–81; Succ Windsor 67–81; R Kirkby in Ashfield *S'well* 81–85; Can Res S'well Minster 85–02; P-in-c Edingley w Halam 91–00; rtd 02. *2 Marston Moor Road, Newark NG24 2GN* T: (01636) 702866 E: iancollins1908@outlook.com

COLLINS, Preb John Theodore Cameron Bucke. b 25. Clare Coll Cam BA 49 MA 52. Ridley Hall Cam 49. **d** 51 **p** 52. C St Marylebone All So w SS Pet and Jo *Lon* 51–57; V Gillingham St Mark *Roch* 57–71; Chapl Medway Hosp Gillingham 70–71; V Canford Magna *Sarum* 71–80; RD Wimborne 79–80; V Brompton H Trin w Onslow Square St Paul *Lon* 80–85; C 85–89; AD Chelsea 84–88; Preb St Paul's Cathl 85–89; rtd 89; PtO *Lon* 89–90; *Win* 89–97. *3 Laundry Cottages, Adlestrop Park, Adlestrop, Moreton-in-Marsh GL56 0YN* T: (01608) 658605 E: jtcollins@gmail.com

COLLINS, John William Michael. b 54. Bp Otter Coll 95. **d** 98 **p** 07. NSM S Patcham *Chich* 98–06; NSM Moulsecoomb w Bevendean and Coldean from 06. *2 Buxted Rise, Brighton BN1 8FG* T: (01273) 509388

COLLINS, Mrs Joy Christina. b 53. K Coll Lon MA. STETS. **d** 14 **p** 15. NSM Westfield and Guestling *Chich* from 14;

P-in-c from 20. *23 Croft Road, Hastings TN34 3HP* T: (01424) 447643

COLLINS, Ms Linda Kathleen. b 56. Girton Coll Cam BA 77 MA 80 Bris Univ PGCE 78. WMMTC 99. **d** 02 **p** 03. C Harborne St Pet *Birm* 02–05; C Cen Wolverhampton *Lich* 05–09; TV 09–10; Chapl K Sch Wolv and St Pet Colleg Sch Wolv 05–10; C Lich St Mich w St Mary and Wall 10–19; rtd 19; PtO *Lich* from 20. *17 Leyfields, Lichfield WS13 7NJ* M: 07985-033476 E: lindacollins@hotmail.co.uk

COLLINS, Mrs Lindsay Rosemary Faith. b 70. K Coll Lon BD 91 AKC 91 PGCE 92. Ripon Coll Cuddesdon MTh 95. **d** 97 **p** 98. C Witney *Ox* 97–99; NSM 00–01; Chapl Cokethorpe Sch Witney 00–01; Chapl and Hd RE St Paul's Girls' Sch Hammersmith 01–04; Chapl K Coll Sch Wimbledon 04–10; Hon C Barnes *S'wark* 04–10; Chapl Sherborne Sch 10–17; PtO *B & W* 13–18; Chapl K Sch Cant from 17. *The King's School, 25 The Precincts, Canterbury CT1 2ES* T: (01227) 595501 E: lrfcollins@gmail.com

COLLINS, Martin. See COLLINS, William Francis Martin

COLLINS, Maureen. See COLLINS, Ann Maureen

COLLINS, Canon Norman Hilary. b 33. Mert Coll Ox BA 55 MA 58. Wells Th Coll 58. **d** 60 **p** 61. C Ystrad Mynach *Llan* 60–62; C Gelligaer 62–67; V Maerdy 67–77; R Penarth w Lavernock 77–98; RD Penarth and Barry 87–98; Can Llan Cathl 92–98; rtd 98; PtO *Llan* from 04. *4 Llys Steffan, Llantwit Major CF61 2UF* T: (01446) 794976

COLLINS, Paul Michael. b 71. St Jo Coll Nottm 06. **d** 08 **p** 09. C Chenies and Lt Chalfont, Latimer and Flaunden *Ox* 08–10; Chapl RAF 10–14; C Warfield *Ox* 14–17; Min Chich Immanuel BMO from 17. *12 Palmers Field Avenue, Chichester PO19 6UW* M: 07973-838003 E: pmcollins2@yahoo.co.uk *or* paul@immanuelchichester.com

COLLINS, Peter Graham. b 60. Anglia Ruskin Univ MA 07. EMMTC 99 Westcott Ho Cam 05. **d** 07 **p** 08. C S Lawres Gp *Linc* 07–11; P-in-c Upper Wreake *Leic* 11–14; R Hykeham Linc from 14. *The Rectory, Mill Lane, North Hykeham, Lincoln LN6 9PA* M: 07740-039048 E: revdpeter@msn.com

COLLINS, Canon Philip Howard Norton. b 50. AKC 73. St Aug Coll Cant 73. **d** 74 **p** 75. C Stamford Hill St Thos *Lon* 74–78; C Upwood w Gt and Lt Raveley *Ely* 78–81; C Ramsey 78–81; R Leverington 81–92; P-in-c Wisbech St Mary 89–92; RD Wisbech 90–92; TR Whittlesey and Pondersbridge 92–95; TR Whittlesey, Pondersbridge and Coates 95–02; R New Alresford w Ovington and Itchen Stoke *Win* 02–07; R Arle Valley 07–16; RD Alresford 09–16; Hon Can Win Cathl 14–16; rtd 16; PtO *Win* from 17. *9 River Close, Four Marks, Alton GU34 5XB* T: (01420) 563489 E: philcollinsrector@yahoo.co.uk

COLLINS, Roger Richardson. b 48. Birm Univ BPhil 88. WMMTC 78. **d** 81 **p** 82. NSM Cotteridge *Birm* from 81. *6 Chesterfield Court, Middleton Hall Road, Birmingham B30 1AF* T: 0121-459 4009

COLLINS, Prof Ross Nicoll Ferguson. b 64. Edin Univ MA 87 Ven English Coll Rome 91 Pontifical Gregorian Univ 91. Ripon Coll Cuddesdon BA 91 MA 13. **d** 92 **p** 93. C Goring w S Stoke *Ox* 92–96; P-in-c N Leigh 96–01; TR Barnes *S'wark* 01–10; NSM Sherborne w Castleton, Lillington and Longburton *Sarum* 10–17; Prof Nat Univ Asunción Paraguay from 18. *Le Paraguayen 4D, Profesor Manuel Riquelme, Asunción, Paraguay* M: (00595) 9-8133 2732 E: rossnfcollins@btinternet.com

COLLINS, Thomas Daniel. b 82. Ox Univ MEng 05 Surrey Univ MSc 07. Trin Coll Bris 16. **d** 18 **p** 19. C Balham Hill Ascension *S'wark* from 18. *124 Alderbrook Road, London SW12 8AA* M: 07947-270785 E: who2tom@hotmail.com

COLLINS, Timothy Paul. b 58. Open Univ BA 92. SWMTC 15. **d** 18 **p** 19. C Dawlish w Holcombe, Cofton and Starcross *Ex* from 18. *14 Shillingate Close, Dawlish EX7 9SQ* T: (01626) 862383 E: revtimpaul@btinternet.com

COLLINS, Canon William Francis Martin. b 43. St Cath Coll Cam BA 66 MA 70. Cuddesdon Coll 68. **d** 70 **p** 71. C Man Victoria Park 70–73; P-in-c Ancoats 73–78; Chapl Abraham Moss Cen 78–91; Hon C Cheetham Hill 81–84; Chs' FE Officer for Gtr Man 84–91; V Norbury *Ches* 91–08; Hon Can Ches Cathl 05–08; rtd 08. *9 Milldale Avenue, Buxton SK17 9BE* T: (01298) 74906 M: 07866-505589

COLLINS, Winfield St Clair. b 41. Univ of W Indies BA 83 Man Univ BA 88 MEd 91. Codrington Coll Barbados. **d** 76 **p** 76. Asst Chapl HM Pris Wakef 76; C St Jo Barbados 76; P-in-c St Mark and St Cath 77–84; Asst Chapl HM Pris Wandsworth 85; Chapl HM YOI Thorn Cross 85–91; Chapl HM Pris Pentonville 91–01; Can Res Barbados 01–02; rtd 02; PtO *Lon* 09–18. *92 Barclay Road, London N18 1EQ* T: (020) 8245 4145

COLLINSON, Mrs Amanda. b 74. Luton Univ BA 96. Ripon Coll Cuddesdon 07. **d** 09 **p** 10. C Catherington and

Clanfield *Portsm* 09–13; P-in-c Gurnard 13–14; P-in-c Cowes St Faith 13–14; V Gurnard w Cowes St Faith from 14; P-in-c Northwood 13–14; R from 14; AD Is of Wight 19–21. *The Rectory, Chawton Lane, Cowes PO31 8PR* T: (01983) 294913 E: amandacollinson01@gmail.com

COLLINSON, Canon Mark Peter Charles. b 68. City Univ BSc 90 Fitzw Coll Cam BA 97 MA 01 Vrije Univ Amsterdam MA 10 PhD 21. Ridley Hall Cam 95. **d** 98 **p** 99. C Ashton-upon-Mersey St Mary Magd *Ches* 98–01; Chapl Amsterdam w Den Helder and Heiloo *Eur* 01–15; Hon Can 12–15; Can Res Win Cathl 15–20; Prin Win Sch of Miss 15–20; Dir Min from 21; PtO *Eur* from 18. *5 Roman Road, Twyford, Winchester SO21 1QW* T: (01962)   710985   M: 07469-859517 E: mark.collinson@winchester.anglican.com

COLLINSON, Roger Alfred. b 36. St Jo Coll Dur BA 58. Cranmer Hall Dur 60. **d** 63 **p** 97. C Liv St Mich 63–64; NSM Ormside *Carl* 97–06; NSM Appleby 97–06; PtO from 06. *1 Caesar's View, Appleby-in-Westmorland CA16 6SH* T: (017683) 52886

COLLIS, Janet Mary. b 57. Plymouth Poly BA 78 PhD 83 SS Mark & Jo Univ Coll Plymouth MA 03. SWMTC 08. **d** 10 **p** 11. NSM Plympton St Mary *Ex* 10–12; Chapl Plymouth Community Healthcare Trust from 12; Chapl Plymouth Hosps NHS Trust from 13. *Department of Pastoral and Spiritual Care, Level 7, Derriford Hospital, Derriford Road, Derriford, Plymouth PL6 8DH* T: (01752) 439044 E: j.collis@nhs.net

COLLIS, Jonathan. b 69. Selw Coll Cam BA 91 MA 94. Aston Tr Scheme 96 Westcott Ho Cam 97. **d** 99 **p** 00. C St Neots *Ely* 99–02; Chapl Jes Coll Cam 02–09; V Thorpe Bay *Chelmsf* 09–21; P-in-c N Shoebury 16–17; RD Southend 15–21; Hon Can Chelmsf Cathl 15–21; PtO *Ely* from 21. *279 Campkin Road, Cambridge CB4 2LE* E: jonathan.collis@cantab.net

COLLISHAW, Ashley Stuart. b 66. Wycliffe Hall Ox 03. **d** 05 **p** 06. C Worc City 05–09; Hon C Cheltenham H Trin and St Paul *Glouc* 09–15; LtO 15–19; V Charlton Kings H Apostles from 19; P-in-c Cheltenham St Mich from 19. *7 Cirencester Road, Charlton Kings, Cheltenham GL53 8EP* T: (01242) 237882 M: 07932-045598 E: ashley@holyapostles.org.uk

COLLISON, Christopher John. b 48. Oak Hill Th Coll 68. **d** 72 **p** 73. C Cromer *Nor* 72–75; C Costessey 76–78; V 87–95; C Heckmondwike *Wakef* 78–79; P-in-c Shepley and Dioc Communications Officer 79–83; Chapl Flushing Miss to Seamen *Eur* 83–85; Asst Min Sec Miss to Seamen 85–87; C St Mich Paternoster Royal *Lon* 85–87; P-in-c Swainsthorpe w Newton Flotman *Nor* 95–97; TV Newton Flotman, Swainsthorpe, Tasburgh, etc 98–02; R Henfield w Shermanbury and Woodmancote *Chich* 02–09; Dioc Evang Officer *Nor* 95–01; RD Hurst *Chich* 04–09; P-in-c Hartlepool St Hilda *Dur* 09–15; AD Hartlepool 10–13; Chapl Miss to Seafarers 09–15; rtd 15; PtO *Chich* from 15; *Dur* 17–18. *17 Blatchington Road, Seaford BN25 2AB* M: 07931-646745 E: cjc72@btinternet.com

COLLISON, Ms Elizabeth. b 38. Man Univ CertEd 58. NOC 85. **d** 88 **p** 94. C Huyton St Mich *Liv* 88–94; C Rainhill 94–05; rtd 05; PtO *Liv* from 16. *25 Lowther Drive, Rainhill, Prescot L35 0NG* T: 0151-426 3853 E: liz_collison@yahoo.co.uk

COLLYER, Leon John. b 72. SS Hild & Bede Coll Dur BSc 95 Leeds Univ BA 00. Coll of Resurr Mirfield 98. **d** 01 **p** 02. C Airedale w Fryston *Wakef* 01–04; P-in-c Crofton and Warmfield 04–10; C Reading St Agnes w St Paul and St Barn *Ox* 10–19; P-in-c The Saints *St E* from 19. *Parsonage House, Low Street, Ilketshall St Margaret, Bungay NR35 1QZ* M: 07714-986462 E: leoncollyer@gmail.com

COLMAN, Susan Elizabeth. b 59. **d** 12 **p** 13. NSM Onslow Square and S Kensington St Aug *Lon* 12–19; PtO *Win* 14–19; NSM Oakley w Wootton St Lawrence from 19; PtO *Lon* from 21. *Malshanger House, Malshanger, Basingstoke RG23 7EY* E: sue.colman@stmellitus.ac.uk

COLMER, Andrew John. b 68. De Montfort Univ Leic BSc 90. St Jo Coll Nottm MA 96 LTh 97. **d** 97 **p** 98. C Roby *Liv* 97–01; C Litherland St Andr 01–02; P-in-c Liv All So Springwood 02–10; Chapl Enterprise S Liv Academy 10–19; V Childwall All SS *Liv* from 19. *42 Buttermere Road, Liverpool L16 2NN* M: 07305-842257   E: andrewcolmer@hotmail.co.uk   *or* vicar.allsaintschildwall@gmail.com

COLMER, The Ven Malcolm John. b 45. Sussex Univ MSc 67. St Jo Coll Nottm BA 73. **d** 73 **p** 74. C Egham *Guildf* 73–76; C Chadwell *Chelmsf* 76–79; V S Malling *Chich* 79–85; V Hornsey Rise St Mary w St Steph *Lon* 85–87; TR Hornsey Rise Whitehall Park Team 87–96; AD Islington 90–94; Adn Middx 96–05; Adn Heref 05–10; Can Res Heref Cathl 05–10; rtd 10; PtO *Lon* from 12–15. *59 Station Road, Pershore WR10 1PE* T: (01386) 556583

COLPUS (*née* EDWARDS), Mrs Anita Carolyn. b 71. Trin Coll Bris 01. **d** 03 **p** 04. C Notting Hill St Pet *Lon* 03–06; NSM Sittingbourne St Mary and St Mich *Cant* 07–10; P-in-c Reigate St Luke S'wark 10–17; V from 17; AD Reigate from 19; Jt Dir

of IME Croydon Area 13–19. *St Luke's Church, 5 Church Road, Reigate RH2 8HY* T: (01737) 243846 M: 07786-2686123 E: anitacolpus@gmail.com

COLSON, Ian Richard. b 65. Wolv Poly BSc 86 Nottm Univ BTh 89 Warwick Univ MA 03. Linc Th Coll 86. **d** 89 **p** 90. C Nunthorpe *York* 89–92; C Thornaby on Tees 92–93; Chapl RAF 93–00; V Sunbury *Lon* 00–02; Chapl Ardingly Coll 02–09; Sen Chapl Ch Hosp Horsham 09–10; CF(V) 08; CF from 10. *c/o MOD Chaplains (Army)* T: (01264) 383430 F: 381824 E: ianrcolson@aol.com

COLSTON, Canon John Edward. b 43. Open Univ BA 91 Leeds Univ MA 94. Lich Th Coll 65. **d** 68 **p** 69. C Bromsgrove All SS *Worc* 68–71; C Tettenhall Wood *Lich* 71–74; V Alrewas 74–88; V Wychnor 74–88; R Ainderby Steeple w Yafforth and Kirby Wiske etc *Ripon* 88–95; V High Harrogate Ch Ch 95–07; Warden of Readers 90–96; AD Harrogate 01–05; Hon Can Ripon Cathl 06–07; rtd 08; PtO *Leeds* from 14. *15 Sycamore Road, Ripon HG4 2LR* T: (01765) 600747 M: 07769-938735 E: john.colston@yahoo.co.uk

COLTON, Mrs Christine Ann. b 56. Univ of Wales (Cardiff) BA 00. St Mich Coll Llan 01. **d** 06 **p** 07. NSM Cen Cardiff *Llan* 06–07; NSM Radyr 07–13; PtO S'wark 14; P-in-c Kingswood from 14. *St Mark's Vicarage, 8 Alma Road, Reigate RH2 0DA* T: (01737) 241161 M: 07941-011337 E: chriscolton@ntlworld.com

COLTON, Christopher Francis. b 52. **d** 12 **p** 14. NSM Holme-in-Cliviger w Worsthorne *Blackb* 12–13; NSM Oswaldtwistle 13–16; PtO 16–17. *357 Newbrook Road, Atherton, Manchester M46 9HN* E: fr.chriscolton@gmail.com

COLTON, Martin Philip. b 67. Sheff Univ BMus 89 MMus 92 FRCO 92 Open Univ PGCE 97. St Mich Coll Llan BA 03. **d** 03 **p** 04. C Whitchurch *Llan* 03–06; TV Canton Cardiff 06–14; V Reigate St Mark *S'wark* from 14. *St Mark's Vicarage, 8 Alma Road, Reigate RH2 0DA* T: (01737) 241161 E: martin.colton@ntlworld.com

✠**COLTON, The Rt Revd William Paul.** b 60. NUI BCL 81 TCD MPhil 87 Univ of Wales (Cardiff) LLM 06 Cardiff Univ PhD 13. **d** 84 **p** 85 **c** 99. C Lisburn St Paul *Conn* 84–87; Bp's Dom Chapl 85–90; V Choral Belf Cathl 87–90; Min Can Belf Cathl 89–90; PV, Registrar and Chapter Clerk Ch Ch Cathl Dub *D & G* 90–95; I Castleknock and Mulhuddart w Clonsilla 90–99; Co-ord Protestant Relig Progr RTE 93–99; Hon Chapl Actors' Ch Union 94–96; Area Chapl (Ireland) Actors' Ch Union 96–97; Can Ch Ch Cathl Dublin *D & G* 97–99; Bp C, C & R from 99. *St Nicholas' House, 14 Cove Street, Cork, Republic of Ireland* T: (00353) (21) 500 5080 F: 432 0960 E: bishop@corkchurchofireland.com

COLVER, Mrs Sarah Marianne. b 63. RGN 85. Westcott Ho Cam. **d** 13 **p** 14. C Aston cum Aughton w Swallownest and Ulley *Sheff* 13–16; C Sheff St Mark Broomhill 16–20; R Old Brampton and Gt Barlow *Derby* from 20; P-in-c Loundsley Green   from   20. *25   Oldridge   Close,   Chesterfield S40 4UF* M: 07975-689403 E: smcolver@hotmail.com

COLWELL, Ms Katherine Elizabeth. b 57. Man Univ BA 78 Nottm Univ MA 08 Man Poly PGCE 79. EMMTC 05. **d** 08 **p** 09. C Barton upon Humber *Linc* 08–11; P-in-c Kirton in Lindsey w Manton 11–13; R from 13; P-in-c Grayingham 11–13; R from 13; P-in-c Bishop Norton, Waddingham and Snitterby 11–13; R from 13; Dioc Ecum Officer from 17. *The Vicarage, 28 South Cliff Road, Kirton Lindsey, Gainsborough DN21 4NR* T: (01652) 640595 E: katherinecolwell57@outlook.com

COLWILL, Canon James Patrick (Jay). b 68. Man Poly BA 91. St Jo Coll Nottm BTh 93 MA 94. **d** 94 **p** 95. C Reading St Agnes w St Paul *Ox* 94–97; C Easthampstead 97–03; V Orpington Ch Ch *Roch* 03–18; AD Orpington 10–14; Dir Miss and Can Res S'wark Cathl from 18. *483A Southwark Park Road, London SE16 2JP* M: 07952-988312 E: jay.colwill@southwark.anglican.org

COLYER, Kevin Peter. b 70. CMS 16. **d** 18 **p** 19. C Furze Platt *Ox* 18–20; C Bray and Braywood from 20. *46 Belmont Park   Avenue,   Maidenhead   SL6 6JS* M: 07967-105273 E: kevin@thecolyers.com

COMBE, Edward Charles. b 40. Man Univ MSc PhD QUB DSc. NOC. **d** 89 **p** 90. NSM Broadheath *Ches* 89–94; USA from 94. *1760 Southwind Lane, Maplewood MN 55109, USA* T: (001) (651) 773 3066 E: combe001@gold.tc.umn.edu

COMBE, The Very Revd John Charles. b 33. TCD BA 53 MA 56 BD 57 MLitt 65 PhD 70. **d** 56 **p** 57. C Cork St Luke w St Ann *C, C & R* 56–58; C Ballynafeigh St Jude *D & D* 58–61; I Crinken *D & G* 61–66; Hon Clerical V Ch Ch Cathl Dublin 63–66; C Belfast St Bart *Conn* 66–70; I Belfast St Barn 70–74; I Portadown St Mark *Arm* 74–84; I Arm St Mark w Aghavilly 84–90; Can Arm Cathl 85–90; Dean Kilmore *K, E & A* 90–96; I Kilmore w Ballintemple, Kildallan etc 90–96; rtd 96. *c/o Ms*

M Macleod, 104 Beechfield Avenue, Bangor BT19 7ZX T: (028) 9185 4537

COMBER, The Ven Anthony James. b 27. Leeds Univ BSc 49 MSc 52. St Chad's Coll Dur 53. **d** 56 **p** 57. C Manston *Ripon* 56–60; V Oulton 60–69; V Hunslet St Mary 69–77; RD Armley 72–75 and 79–81; R Farnley 77–82; Hon Can Ripon Cathl 80–92; Adn Leeds 82–92; rtd 92; PtO *Bradf* 93–99; *Ripon* 92–14; *Leeds* from 14. *28 Blayds Garth, Woodlesford, Leeds LS26 8WN* T: 0113-288 0489 M: 07840-763818 E: tonycomber20@gmail.com

COMBES, The Ven Roger Matthew. b 47. K Coll Lon LLB 69. Ridley Hall Cam 72. **d** 74 **p** 75. C Onslow Square St Paul *Lon* 74–77; C Brompton H Trin 76–77; C Cambridge H Sepulchre w All SS *Ely* 77–86; R Silverhill St Matt *Chich* 86–03; RD Hastings 98–02; Adn Horsham 03–14; rtd 14; PtO *Chich* from 14. *3 Aldingbourne Close, Ifield, Crawley RH11 0QJ* T: (01293) 538161 E: rogercombes@gmail.com

COMER-STONE, Mrs Caroline. b 53. St Hild Coll 19. **d** 21. NSM Sherburn in Elmet w Saxton *York* from 21; NSM Aberford w Micklefield from 21. *2 Victoria Close, Sherburn in Elmet, Leeds LS25 6NR* T: (01977) 680894 M: 07775-868189 E: caroline.cs@btinternet.com

COMERFORD, Canon Patrick. b 52. Pontifical Univ Maynooth BD 87 FRSAI 87. CITC 99. **d** 00 **p** 01. NSM Dublin Whitechurch *D & G* 00–17; Dir Spiritual Formation CITC 06–11; Lect 11–17; Can Ch Ch Cathl Dublin *D & G* 07–17; Dir CME and P-in-c Rathkeale w Askeaton, Kilcornan and Kilnaughtin *L & K* from 17; Can Limerick Cathl from 17. *The Rectory, Church Street, Askeaton, Co Limerick, Republic of Ireland* M: (00353) 87-663 5116 E: revpatrickcomerford@gmail.com *or* rathkeale@limerick.anglican.org

COMFORT, Alan. b 64. Ridley Hall Cam 91. **d** 94 **p** 95. C Chadwell Heath *Chelmsf* 94–97; C Buckhurst Hill 97–98; TV 98–03; V Loughton St Mary 03–09; TR Gt Baddow 09–10; V Walthamstow St Jo 10–14; R Standon and The Mundens w Sacombe *St Alb* 14–18; V Upper Holloway *Lon* from 18. *St John's Vicarage, 51 Tytherton Road, London N19 4PZ* E: alancomfort11@gmail.com

COMLEY, Thomas Hedges. b 36. Leeds Univ BA 62. Coll of Resurr Mirfield 62. **d** 64 **p** 65. C Leadgate *Dur* 64–67; C Shirley *Birm* 67–71; V Smethwick St Alb 71–76; PtO 76–82; V N Wembley St Cuth *Lon* 82–92; V Taddington, Chelmorton and Flagg, and Monyash *Derby* 92–01; rtd 01; PtO *Derby* from 01. *19 Wentworth Avenue, Walton, Chesterfield S40 3JB* T: (01246) 270911

COMMANDER, David James. b 58. Cranfield Inst of Tech MSc 84. SEITE 07. **d** 10 **p** 11. C Tunbridge Wells St Jas *Roch* 10–13; V Benenden and Sandhurst *Cant* from 13. *The Rectory, The Green, Benenden, Cranbrook TN17 4DL* T: (01580) 240658 M: 07710-416978 E: revdavidcommander@gmail.com

COMMIN, Robert William. b 47. Cape Town Univ BA 79. St Paul's Coll Grahamstown. **d** 70 **p** 71. S Africa 70–80 and from 89; Chapl Loretto Sch Musselburgh 80–84; TV Thetford *Nor* 84–89. *42 Earl Street, Woodstock, 7925 South Africa* M: (0027) 82-202 5303 E: bcommin@netactive.co.za

COMPTON, Barry Charles Chittenden. b 33. Linc Th Coll 60. **d** 62 **p** 63. C Beddington *S'wark* 62–65; C Limpsfield and Titsey 66–68; Hon C 71–94; rtd 94; R Rotherwick 69–70; R Ash 69–70; PtO *S'wark* 70–16; *Roch* from 11. *14 Hallsland Way, Oxted RH8 9AL* T: (01883) 714896 F: 722842 E: bcccompton@aol.com

✠CONALTY, The Rt Revd Julie Anne. b 63. SEITE. **d** 99 **p** 00 **c** 21. NSM E Wickham *S'wark* 99–04; NSM Charlton 04–10; C Plumstead Common 10–12; V Erith Ch Ch *Roch* 12–17; AD Erith 14–17; Bp's Adv for Ord Women's Min 13–17; Hon Can Roch Cathl 16–17; Adn Tonbridge 17–21; Suff Bp Birkenhead *Ches* from 21. *Pinewood, Vyner Road North, Prenton CH43 7PZ* E: bpbirkenhead@chester.anglican.org

CONANT, Alan Richard. b 67. Kent Univ BSc 89 PhD 92. St Jo Coll Nottm 09. **d** 11 **p** 12. C Maghull and Melling *Liv* 11–14; V Rainhill from 14. *The Vicarage, 1 View Road, Rainhill, Prescot L35 0LE* T: 0151-426 4666 E: revd_al@btinternet.com

CONANT, Fane Charles. b 44. Oak Hill Th Coll 83. **d** 85 **p** 86. C Hoole *Ches* 85–89; V Kelsall 89–01; P-in-c Seer Green and Jordans *Ox* 01–06; rtd 06; PtO *Heref* from 06; Partner Evang Luis Palau Evang Assn from 06. *1 Spring Bank, Shrewsbury Road, Church Stretton SY6 6HA* T: (01694) 722610 E: fanesue@aol.com

CONANT (née PARR), Mrs Vanessa Caroline. b 78. Lanc Univ BA 00. Trin Coll Bris BA 07. **d** 08 **p** 09. C Hoddesdon *St Alb* 08–11; C Edin St Paul and St Geo 11–15; TR Walthamstow *Chelmsf* from 15. *The Rectory, 117 Church Hill, London E17 3BD* T: (020) 3722 2041 M: 07811-444435 E: vcconant@gmail.com

CONAWAY, Barry Raymond. b 41. CertEd 69 Nottm Univ BEd 70. Sarum & Wells Th Coll 86. **d** 88 **p** 89. C Ross w Brampton Abbotts, Bridstow and Peterstow *Heref* 88–91; R Bishop's Frome w Castle Frome and Fromes Hill 91–96; P-in-c Acton Beauchamp and Evesbatch w Stanford Bishop 91–96; P-in-c Charminster and Stinsford *Sarum* 96–01; rtd 01; PtO *Glouc* 01–02; *Sarum* 03–11. *9 Constable Way, West Harnham, Salisbury SP2 8LN* T: (01722) 334870

CONDER, Paul Collingwood Nelson. b 33. St Jo Coll Cam BA 56 MA 60. Ridley Hall Cam 56. **d** 58 **p** 59. C Grassendale *Liv* 58–61; Tutor St Jo Coll Dur 61–67; R Sutton *Liv* 67–74; TR 74–75; V Thames Ditton *Guildf* 75–86; RD Emly 82–86; V Blundellsands St Mich *Liv* 86–99; rtd 99; PtO *York* 00–15; *Ches* 14–19. *21 Bowling Green Court, Brook Street, Chester CH1 3DP* T: (01244) 460151 E: pconder787@gmail.com

✠CONDRY, The Rt Revd Edward Francis. b 53. UEA BA 74 Ex Coll Ox BLitt 77 DPhil 80 Open Univ MBA 02. Linc Th Coll 80. **d** 82 **p** 83 **c** 12. C Weston Favell *Pet* 82–85; V Bloxham w Milcombe and S Newington *Ox* 85–93; TV Rugby *Cov* 93–02; Can Res Cant Cathl 02–12; Dir Post-Ord Tr 02–06; Treas and Dir of Educn 06–12; Area Bp Ramsbury *Sarum* 12–18; Can and Preb Sarum Cathl 12–18; rtd 18; Hon Asst Bp *Pet* from 18. *The Meadow, 16 Westhorpe Lane, Byfield, Daventry NN11 6XB* T: (01327) 438729

CONEY, Joanna Margery. b 39. Culham Coll of Educn CertEd 75 Open Univ BA 83. Ox Min Course 90. **d** 93 **p** 94. C Wolvercote w Summertown *Ox* 93–97; Hon C New Marston 97–06; Hon C Wolvercote w Summertown 06–07; Hon C Wolvercote 07–10; OLM Tr Officer (Ox Adnry) 97–00; Dioc Portfolio Officer 00–04; rtd 04; Dioc Adv to Lic Lay Min *Ox* 02–09; NSM Voc Adv from 09; Min Prov (Eur) Third Order SSF 09–12; Hon C Wolvercote and Wytham *Ox* 10–17; PtO from 17. *4 Rowland Close, Wolvercote, Oxford OX2 8PW* T/F: (01865) 556456 E: joanna.coney@gmail.com

CONEYS, Canon Stephen John. b 61. Sheff Univ LLB 82. St Jo Coll Nottm 87. **d** 90 **p** 91. C Plymouth Em w Efford *Ex* 90–92; C Plymouth Em, Efford and Laira 93–94; TV Whitstable *Cant* 94–02; TR 02–17; Jt AD Reculver 12–17; Dioc Miss and Growth Adv from 17; Hon Can Cant Cathl from 08. *Diocesan House, Lady Wootton's Green, Canterbury CT1 1NQ* T: (01227) 459401 E: steveconeys@btinternet.com

CONEYS, Mrs Victoria Susan. b 60. St Mary's Coll Dur BA 83. St Aug Coll of Th 14. **d** 17 **p** 18. C Wantsum Gp *Cant* 17–21. *1 Warwick Drive, Ramsgate CT11 0JP* M: 07583-684338 E: vickysconeys@hotmail.com

CONLIN, Tiffany Jane Kate. b 71. K Coll Lon BA 93 MA 94 PhD 00 AKC 93. Westcott Ho Cam 03. **d** 05 **p** 06. C Wisbech St Aug and Wisbech SS Pet and Paul *Ely* 05–08; Chapl Fitzw Coll Cam 08–11; Dir Past Studies Westcott Ho Cam 11–14; Chapl HM Pris Wakef 15–18; Chapl HM Pris Northd from 18. *HM Prison Northumberland, Acklington, Morpeth NE65 9XG* T: (01670) 762300

CONLON, Shaun. b 69. Birm Univ BA 90. Ripon Coll Cuddesdon 91. **d** 93 **p** 94. C Castle Bromwich SS Mary and Marg *Birm* 93–97; C Hockerill *St Alb* 97–00; V St Mary-at-Latton *Chelmsf* 00–07; V Prittlewell St Mary 07–14; P-in-c Ashton-upon-Mersey St Martin *Ches* 14–20; P-in-c Prestwich St Mary *Man* from 20. *67 Scholes Lane, Prestwich, Manchester M25 0AW* T: 0161-773 2912

CONN, Christopher Kenneth. b 83. Dur Univ BSc 05. Oak Hill Th Coll BA 15. **d** 15 **p** 16. C Laleham *Lon* 15–18; C Fulwood *Sheff* 18–20. *38 Stone Delf, Sheffield S10 3QX* M: 07917-191303 E: c.conn@hotmail.co.uk

CONNELL, Anthony. **d** 12. NSM Dolton *Ex* 12–15; NSM Iddesleigh w Dowland 12–15; NSM Monkokehampton 12–15; NSM Dolton, Dowland, Iddesleigh etc 15–19; PtO 19–21. *12 Martins Paddock, West Cranmore, Shepton Mallet BA4 4QY* T: (01749) 880972 E: tonyandjeanconnell@gmail.com

CONNELL, Clare. *See* CONNELL, Penelope Clare

CONNELL, John Richard. b 63. K Coll Lon BD 84. St Mich Coll Llan 92. **d** 94 **p** 96. C Caldicot *Mon* 94–97; C Risca 97–00; V Llantilio Pertholey w Bettws Chpl etc 00–05; P-in-c Wokingham St Paul *Ox* 05–11; Chapl R Berks NHS Foundn Trust 11–12; R Chingford SS Pet and Paul *Chelmsf* 12–15; P-in-c Rumney *Mon* 15–21; AD Bassaleg 17–21; V Abergavenny St Mary w Llanwenarth Citra from 21; V Abergavenny H Trin from 21; P-in-c Govilon w Llanfoist w Llanellen from 21. *St Mary's Vicarage, Monk Street, Abergavenny NP7 5ND* T: (01873) 853168 E: frjohn@stmarys-priory.org

CONNELL, Mrs Penelope Clare. b 44. EMMTC. **d** 03 **p** 04. NSM Whatton w Aslockton, Hawksworth, Scarrington etc *S'well* 03–06; NSM Nottingham St Ann *S'well* 06–07; NSM Ironstone Villages *Leic* 07–12; rtd 12; PtO *Leic* from 12; *S'well* from 14. *Colston Bassett House, Church Gate, Colston Bassett,*

Nottingham NG12 3FE T: (01949) 81424 M: 07866-495720 E: clare2connell@icloud.com

CONNELL, Sister Sharon Margaret. b 65. Cardiff Univ MTh 11. Wilson Carlile Coll 86 St Jo Coll Nottm BA 03. d 03 p 04. C S Hackney St Jo w Ch Ch *Lon* 03–06; C Stepney St Dunstan and All SS 06–08; Ecum Chapl Chelsea and Westmr Hosp NHS Foundn Trust 08–13; Dep Hd Multi-Faith Chapl 13–15; Chapl St Nic Hospice Care Bury St Edmunds from 15; PtO *St E* from 09; Bp's Adv for Healthcare Chapl from 16; Hon Can St E Cathl from 20. *St Nicholas Hospice Care, Macmillan Way, Hardwick Lane, Bury St Edmunds IP33 2QY* T: (01284) 715551 E: sharon.connell@stnh.org.uk

CONNER, Mrs Cathryn. b 42. Birm Univ BSc 64. NEOC 91. d 94 p 95. NSM Bainton w N Dalton, Middleton-on-the-Wolds etc *York* 94–98; NSM Woldsburn 98–04; rtd 04; PtO *York* from 04. *Deepdale, Main Street, North Dalton, Driffield YO25 9XA* T: (01377) 217430 E: cathrynconner@hotmail.co.uk

✠**CONNER, The Rt Revd David John.** b 47. KCVO 10. Ex Coll Ox BA 69 MA 77. St Steph Ho Ox 69. d 71 p 72 c 94. Asst Chapl St Edw Sch Ox 71–73; Chapl 73–80; Hon C Summertown *Ox* 71–76; TV Wolvercote w Summertown 76–80; Chapl Win Coll 80–87; V Cambridge Gt St Mary w St Mich *Ely* 87–94; RD Cambridge 89–94; Suff Bp Lynn *Nor* 94–98; Dean Windsor and Dom Chapl to The Queen from 98; Bp HM Forces 01–09. *The Deanery, Windsor Castle, Windsor SL4 1NJ* T: (01753) 865561 F: 819002 E: david.conner@stgeorges-windsor.org

CONNING, Dowell Paul. b 64. Univ of Wales (Cardiff) MTh 12. Ripon Coll Cuddesdon BTh 00. d 00 p 01. C Leckhampton St Pet *Glouc* 00–03; CF 03–21; Hon Min Can Ripon Cathl 05–14; Chapl Guards Chpl Lon 14–16; R Dulverton w Brushford, Brompton Regis etc *B & W* from 21. *The Vicarage, High Street, Dulverton TA22 9DW* E: dconning@gmail.com

CONNOLL, Miss Helen Dorothy. b 45. Oak Hill Th Coll BA 86. dss 86 d 87 p 94. Leytonstone St Jo *Chelmsf* 86–90; Par Dn 87–90; Asst Chapl Grimsby Distr Gen Hosp 90–93; Chapl Kent and Cant Hosp 93–94; Chapl Kent and Cant Hosps NHS Trust 94–99; Chapl E Kent Hosps NHS Trust 99–01; Hon C Aylesham w Adisham *Cant* 01–09; Hon C Nonington w Wymynswold and Goodnestone etc 01–09; rtd 09; PtO *Cant* from 09; Chapl St Jo Hosp Cant from 16. *1 St Nicholas Hospital, Church Hill, Harbledown, Canterbury CT2 9AD* T: (01227) 379806 E: helen.therev@virgin.net

CONNOLLY, Catherine Hannah Victoria. b 90. Anglia Ruskin Univ BA 13. Ripon Coll Cuddesdon BA 17. d 18 p 19. C Ipswich St Thos *St E* from 18. *176 Fircroft Road, Ipswich IP1 6PS* T: (01473) 422528 E: revcatconnolly@gmail.com

CONNOLLY, Daniel. b 51. BEng. St Jo Coll Nottm 82. d 84 p 85. C Bedgrove *Ox* 84–87; C-in-c Crookhorn Ch Cen CD *Portsm* 87–88; V Crookhorn 88–97; R Sutton Coldfield H Trin *Birm* 97–98; V Reigate St Mary *S'wark* 98–05; RD Reigate 03–05; P-in-c Kenilworth St Jo *Cov* 05–08; Adnry Miss Enabler 08–09; P-in-c Blackpool St Jo *Blackb* 09–13; V 13–16; rtd 16; PtO *Man* from 16. *26 Ashley Drive, Leigh WN7 5HP* E: dan@famcon.co.uk

CONNOLLY, Canon Lynne. b 53. Aston Tr Scheme 88 Linc Th Coll 92. d 92 p 94. Par Dn Hurst *Man* 92–94; C 94–96; R Burnage St Nic 96–02; V Spotland 02–10; P-in-c E Crompton 10–14; V 14–15; Hon Can Man Cathl 15; rtd 15; PtO *Man* from 15; *Leeds* from 17. *5 Cross Bank, Skipton BD23 6AH* T: (01756) 796657 E: tyc@clara.co.uk

CONNOLLY, Canon Sydney Herbert. b 40. Leeds Univ BA 66. Coll of Resurr Mirfield 66. d 68 p 69. C W Derby St Mary *Liv* 68–71; C Prescot 71–74; V Burtonwood 74–80; V Walker *Newc* 89–96; TR Whorlton 89–96; V Chapel House 96–99; TR N Shields 99–04; Hon Can Newc Cathl 04–06; rtd 06; PtO *Newc* from 06. *222 Brunton Walk, Newcastle upon Tyne NE3 2TL* T: 0191-271 1473 E: sydandpat@kingstonpark.plus.com

CONNOP PRICE, Martin Randall. *See* PRICE, Martin Randall Connop

CONNOR, Canon Geoffrey. b 46. K Coll Lon BD 73 AKC 73. St Aug Coll Cant. d 74 p 75. C Cockerton *Dur* 74–79; Dioc Recruitment Officer 79–87; Chapl St Chad's Coll 84–87; R Edin St Mary and Vice Provost St Mary's Cathl *Edin* 87–90; Dioc Dir of Ords Edin and Arg 87–90; V Whitechapel w Admarsh-in-Bleasdale *Blackb* 90–00; Dir of Ords 90–00; TR Epping Distr *Chelmsf* 00–16; RD Epping Forest 04–16; Hon Can Chelmsf Cathl 12–16; rtd 16; PtO *Chelmsf* 16–19. *18 Milestone Road, Newhall, Harlow CM17 9NW* M: 07787-568529 E: geoffrey_connor@priest.com

CONNOR, Archdeacon of. *See* MACBRIDE, The Ven Stephen Richard

CONNOR, Bishop of. *See* DAVISON, The Rt Revd George Thomas William

CONNOR, Dean of. *See* WRIGHT, The Very Revd William Samuel

CONRAD, Canon Paul Derick. b 54. Worc Coll Ox BA 76 MA 82. St Steph Ho Ox 78. d 80 p 81. C Wanstead St Mary *Chelmsf* 80–83; C Somers Town *Lon* 83–85; P-in-c Kentish Town St Martin w St Andr 85–91; V 91–95; P-in-c Hampstead Ch Ch 95–97; V from 97; Chapl R Free London NHS Foundn Trust from 95; Can Wiawso Ghana from 09. *Christ Church Vicarage, 10 Cannon Place, London NW3 1EJ* T/F: (020) 7435 6784 E: paulconrad@btinternet.com

CONROY, Kevin Paul. d 14 p 16. Stillorgan w Blackrock *D & G* 14–16; NSM Dalkey St Patr from 16. *St Patrick's, Harbour Road, Dalkey, Co Dublin, Republic of Ireland* T: (00353) (1) 284 5941 M: 86-040 6256 E: revkvn@gmail.com

CONSTABLE, Douglas Brian. b 40. Linc Univ BA 62 Southn Univ MPhil 05. Linc Th Coll 63. d 65 p 66. C Stockwood CD *Bris* 65–70; Asst Chapl Bris Univ 70–72; Hon C Clifton St Paul 70–72; Chapl Lee Abbey 72–77; V Derby St Thos 77–85; TV Southampton (City Cen) *Win* 85–92; rtd 92; PtO *Win* 92–05; *St D* from 05. *Y Bwthyn, 9 Church Street, Llandeilo SA19 6BH* T: (01558) 823518 E: douglasconstable@btinternet.com

CONSTABLE, Mrs Sharon Joanne. b 57. STETS 95. d 98 p 99. NSM Hutton *B & W* 98–01; Bp's Officer for NSMs 01–04; C E Clevedon w Clapton in Gordano etc 01–04; Chapl St Jo Cathl Hong Kong 04–10; TV Melton Mowbray *Leic* 10–15; Bp's Adv for Women's Min 10–14; P-in-c Broughton Astley and Croft w Stoney Stanton 15–18; R from 18; P-in-c Avon-Swift 20–21; RD Guthlaxton 18–21. *The Rectory, St Mary's Close, Broughton Astley, Leicester LE9 6ES* T: (01455) 644779 E: sharonconstable@msn.com

CONVERY, Canon Arthur Malcolm. b 42. Sheff Univ BSc 63 DipEd 64. NOC 79. d 82 p 83. NSM Parr *Liv* 82–87; V Marown *S & M* 87–04; V Onchan 04–10; Can St German's Cathl 99–10; rtd 10; P-in-c German St Jo *S & M* 10–12; C Michael 10–12. *50 Faaie ny Cabbal, Kirk Michael, Isle of Man IM6 2HU* T: (01624) 878855

CONWAY, Canon Glyn Haydn. b 38. St Mich Coll Llan. d 65 p 66. C Wrexham *St As* 65–71; TV 71–77; V Holywell 77–83; V Upton Ascension *Ches* 83–05; rtd 05; Hon Can Accra from 03; PtO *Ches* from 05; *St As* from 07; *St D* from 10. *18 Salmon Leap, Chester CH4 7JJ* T: (01244) 678298

CONWAY, The Very Revd John Arthur. b 67. Leeds Univ BEng 90 Edin Univ BD 97. Linc Th Coll 94 TISEC 95. d 97 p 98. C Edin St Mary 97–01; R Edin St Martin 01–17; Dioc IME Co-ord 04–07 and from 09; Chapl Edin Sick Children's NHS Trust 98–99; Chapl Lothian Univ Hosps NHS Trust 99–01; Provost St Mary's Cathl *Edin* from 17; R Edin St Mary from 17. *8 Lansdowne Crescent, Edinburgh EH12 5EQ* T: 0131-225 2978 *or* 225 6293 M: 07791-508103 E: provost@cathedral.net

CONWAY, Philip James. b 66. Liv Inst of Educn BA 91. St Steph Ho Ox 92. d 95 p 96. C High Harrogate Ch Ch *Ripon* 95–99; P-in-c Menheniot *Truro* 99–08; C St Ive and Pensilva w Quethiock 02–08; P-in-c Lostwithiel, St Winnow w St Nectan's Chpl etc 08–15; P-in-c Lanlivery 08–15; C Lanreath, Pelynt and Bradoc 08–15; Public Preacher 15–18; Chapl Abbots Bromley Sch 16–19; PtO *Lich* from 19; *Truro* from 19; *Ex* 19–20; P-in-c Lifton, Broadwoodwidger, Stowford etc from 20. *The Rectory, Lifton PL16 0BJ* M: 07717-717786 E: liftonpriest@yahoo.com

CONWAY, Robert. b 51. Bris Poly MBA 90. Trin Coll Bris 09. d 12 p 13. OLM Filton *Bris* 12–17; OLM Fromeside from 17; Chapl N Bris NHS Trust from 17. *71 Juniper Way, Bradley Stoke, Bristol BS32 0BR* T: (01454) 612661 M: 07733-228878 E: bob.conway1@btinternet.com

CONWAY, Mrs Sandra Coralie. b 45. Bris Univ BA 66. S'wark Ord Course 89. d 92 p 00. NSM Kenley *S'wark* 92–05; PtO 06–07; *Guildf* 07–09; NSM E Horsley and Ockham w Hatchford and Downside 09–15; rtd 15; PtO *Guildf* from 15. *Rowan Tree Cottage, Norrels Drive, East Horsley, Leatherhead KT24 5DR* T: (01483) 281497 E: sandyconwayrtc@btinternet.com

✠**CONWAY, The Rt Revd Stephen David.** b 57. Keble Coll Ox BA 80 MA 84 CertEd 81 Selw Coll Cam BA 85. Westcott Ho Cam 83. d 86 p 87 c 06. C Heworth St Mary *Dur* 86–89; C Bishopwearmouth St Mich w St Hilda 89–90; Dir of Ords and Hon C Dur St Marg 90–94; P-in-c Cockerton 94–96; V 96–98; Bp's Sen Chapl and Communications Officer 98–02; Adn Dur and Can Res Dur Cathl 02–06; Area Bp Ramsbury *Sarum* 06–10; Bp Ely from 10. *The Bishop's House, The College, Ely CB7 4DW* T: (01353) 662749 F: 669477 E: bishop@elydiocese.org

COOGAN, The Ven Robert Arthur William. b 29. Univ of Tasmania BA 51. St Jo Coll Dur 51. d 53 p 54. C Plaistow St Andr *Chelmsf* 53–56; R Bothwell Australia 56–62; V N

Woolwich *Chelmsf* 62–73; P-in-c W Silvertown St Barn 62–73; V Hampstead St Steph *Lon* 73–77; P-in-c N St Pancras All Hallows 74–77; RD S Camden 75–81; P-in-c Old St Pancras w Bedford New Town St Matt 76–80; V Hampstead St Steph w All Hallows 77–85; P-in-c Kentish Town St Martin w St Andr 78–81; AD N Camden 78–83; Preb St Paul's Cathl 82–85; Adn Hampstead 85–94; rtd 94; PtO *Chich* 94–00. *46 The Gilberts, Sea Road, Rustington, Littlehampton BN16 2LY*

COOK, Alan. b 27. St Deiniol's Hawarden 79. **d** 80 **p** 81. Hon C Gatley *Ches* 80–83; Chapl Man R Eye Hosp 83–86; Chapl Asst Man R Infirmary 80–83 and 86–88; V Congleton St Jas *Ches* 89–93; rtd 93; PtO *Ches* 93–09. *15 Buttermere Road, Gatley, Cheadle SK8 4RQ* T: 0161-428 4350

COOK, Alan James. b 61. Univ Coll Ox BA 83. Wycliffe Hall Ox 86. **d** 00 **p** 01. C Fonthill Canada 00–02; R St Catharine's 02–06; Chapl St Monica Trust Westbury Fields from 16. *Gate Lodge, Cote Lane, Bristol BS9 3UN* T: 0117-962 8372 M: 07397-150680 E: alancook61@hotmail.com

COOK, Mrs Alison Mary. b 63. Leeds Univ BEd 85. St Hild Coll 17. **d** 19 **p** 20. NSM Stannington *Sheff* from 19. *20 Hanmoor Road, Stannington, Sheffield S6 6BL* T: 0114-234 3463 M: 07951-470911 E: alison42cook@hotmail.co.uk

COOK, Anesia. *See* NASCIMENTO DE JESUS COOK, Anesia

COOK, Sister Anita Isabel. b 44. Whitelands Coll Lon CertEd 66 Toronto Univ BA 93. **d** 06 **p** 07. CSC from 67; PtO *S'wark* 10–15; Hon C E Clevedon w Clapton in Gordano etc *B & W* 10–19; rtd 19; PtO *B & W* from 19. *St Gabriel's, 27A Dial Hill Road, Clevedon BS21 7HL* T: (01275) 544471 M: 07588-684380 E: anita@sistersofthechurch.org.uk

COOK, Benjamin William. b 85. St Mellitus Coll 14. **d** 17 **p** 18. C Walmley *Birm* from 17. *2 Geoffrey Close, Sutton Coldfield B76 1GB* M: 07545-309018 E: bencookw@gmail.com *or* benc@stjw.org.uk

COOK, Brian Robert. b 43. Chich Th Coll 83. **d** 85 **p** 86. C Whyke w Rumboldswhyke and Portfield *Chich* 85–87; C Worth 87–90; TV 90–94; P-in-c Chidham 94–99; V 99–04; RD Westbourne 99–04; P-in-c E Blatchington 04–08; R E Blatchington and Bishopstone 08–11; rtd 11; Hon C Wymering *Portsm* 11–15; Hon C Cosham 11–15; PtO *B & W* from 16. *49 Parkhouse Road, Minehead TA24 8AD* T: (01643) 703518 M: 07795-055204 E: fbparkhead49@btinternet.com

COOK, Celia Jane. b 66. Anglia Ruskin Univ BA 88 BA 13 DipCOT 94. ERMC 07. **d** 10 **p** 11. C Aldeburgh w Hazlewood *St E* 10–14; TV Thurstable and Winstree *Chelmsf* 14–15; P-in-c Gt and Lt Bealings w Playford and Culpho *St E* 15–18; Chapl E Suffolk and N Essex NHS Foundn Trust from 18; PtO *Chelmsf* from 19. *26 St Edmunds Road, Ipswich IP1 3RD* T: (01473) 878104 M: 07857-823617 E: thecooksonline@hotmail.co.uk

COOK, Christopher. *See* COOK, James Christopher Donald

COOK, Christopher Charles Holland. b 56. K Coll Lon BSc 77 MB, BS 81 MD 95 MRCPsych 87. SEITE 97. **d** 00 **p** 01. Prof Psychiatry Alcohol Misuse Kent Inst of Medicine and Health Science 97–03; NSM Otham w Langley *Cant* 00–03; Chapl and Prof Fell St Chad's Coll Dur 03–05; Prof Research Fell Dur Univ from 05; Tutor and Lect Cranmer Hall Dur 08–13; Hon Min Can Dur Cathl 13–19; PtO from 20. *Department of Theology and Religion, Abbey House, Palace Green, Durham DH1 3RS* T: 0191-334 3885 E: c.c.h.cook@durham.ac.uk

COOK, David. b 46. Hertf Coll Ox BA MA 72. Wycliffe Hall Ox 69. **d** 73 **p** 74. C Stranton *Dur* 74–75; Lect Qu Coll Birm 75–81; Chapl Cranbrook Sch Kent 81–11; rtd 11; PtO *Cant* from 11. *33 Oatfield Drive, Cranbrook TN17 3LA* T: (01580) 713310 E: senor_aardvark@hotmail.com

COOK, Canon David Charles Murray. b 41. MA. Wycliffe Hall Ox 65. **d** 67 **p** 68. C Chatham St Phil and St Jas *Roch* 67–71; S Africa 71–89; TR Newbury *Ox* 89–02; RD 98–02; Hon Can Ch 02; P-in-c Chipping Campden w Ebrington *Glouc* 02–13; rtd 13; PtO *Glouc* from 17. *Laverton Cottage, Lansdowne, Bourton-on-the-Water, Cheltenham GL54 2AR*

COOK, David Smith. b 47. Hull Univ BTh 88 MA 93. Lich Th Coll 68. **d** 71 **p** 72. C Tudhoe Grange *Dur* 71–75; C Bishopwearmouth St Mary V w St Pet Cd 75–77; V Copley *Wakef* 77–80; V Birstall 80–83; V Holme upon Spalding Moor *York* 83–98; R Holme and Seaton Ross Gp 98–01; RD S Wold 96–01; V Copmanthorpe 01–07; P-in-c Askham Bryan 01–07; Chapl Askham Bryan Coll 01–04; P-in-c Eskdaleside w Ugglebarnby and Sneaton *York* 07–09; V Lower Esk 09–13; RD Whitby 08–13; rtd 13; PtO from 13. *15 Farndale Drive, Guisborough TS14 8JD* T: (01287) 619296 E: farndalecook@gmail.com

COOK, Elspeth Jean. b 34. Edin Univ BSc 56 PhD 66. S Dios Minl Tr Scheme 85. **d** 88 **p** 94. C Yateley *Win* 88–91; Assoc Chapl Ld Mayor Treloar Hosp Alton 91–93; NSM Dunfermline *St And* 93–99; P-in-c Aberdour 96–01; rtd 01.

12 River View, Dalgety Bay, Dunfermline KY11 9YE T: (01383) 825222 E: andrewandjean.cook@btinternet.com

COOK, Helen Jane. b 63. SEITE 13. **d** 16 **p** 17. NSM Redhill St Matt *S'wark* 16–20; TR Limpsfield and Tatsfield from 20. *The Rectory, High Street, Limpsfield, Oxted RH8 0DG* M: 07530-609511 E: hjwcook@yahoo.co.uk

COOK, Ian. b 63. Trin Coll Bris. **d** 09 **p** 10. C Plymouth St Jude *Ex* 09–13; P-in-c Karori NZ from 13. *5 Birdwood Street, Karori, Wellington, New Zealand* E: ianruthcook@aol.com *or* ian@karoriananglican.org.nz

COOK, Preb Ian Brian. b 38. Aston Univ MSc 72 Birm Univ MA 76 MBIM 73. Kelham Th Coll 58. **d** 63 **p** 64. C Langley Marish *Ox* 63–66; C Stokenchurch and Cadmore End 66–68; V Lane End 68–72; P-in-c Ibstone w Fingest 68–72; Tutor W Bromwich Coll of Comm and Tech 72–74; Sen Tutor 74–80; NSM W Bromwich St Pet *Lich* 77–80; R Wednesbury St Jas and St Jo 80–03; Dir St Jas Tr Inst 81–03; RD Wednesbury *Lich* 88–03; Preb Lich Cathl 94–03; rtd 03; PtO *Lich* 03–21; RD Penkridge 06–11; P-in-c Tipton St Martin and St Paul 17–18; PtO *Leeds* 19–21. *10 Horsforde View, Leeds LS13 1FE* M: 07783-011242 E: prebyxkel@btinternet.com

COOK, Canon James Christopher Donald. b 49. Ch Ch Ox BA 70 MA 74. St Steph Ho Ox 79. **d** 80 **p** 81. C Witney *Ox* 80–83; CF 83–04; P-in-c Toxteth Park St Agnes and St Pancras *Liv* 04–06; V 06–16; rtd 16; Can Wiawso Ghana from 09; PtO *Liv* from 17. *8 Princes Park Mansions, Croxteth Road, Liverpool L8 3SA* T: 0151-727 5723 E: leoclericus@aol.com

COOK, James Daniel. b 87. Ox Univ BA 10 MPhil 12 DPhil 16. Ridley Hall Cam 17. **d** 20 **p** 21. C Eaton St Andr *Nor* from 20. *12 Fulton Close, Norwich NR4 6HX*

COOK, James Robert. b 45. ACCA 68 FCCA 73. Ox Min Course 05. **d** 08 **p** 09. NSM Newbury *Ox* 08–10; NSM W Woodhay w Enborne, Hampstead Marshall etc 10–11; NSM Kintbury w Avington 10–11; NSM Walbury Beacon 11–13; P-in-c Totland Bay *Portsm* 13–18; rtd 18; PtO from 19. *St Blasius Rectory, Rectory Road, Shanklin PO37 6NX* T: (01983) 867887 M: 07919-125647 E: jamesrobertcook@aol.com

COOK, Jean. *See* COOK, Elspeth Jean

COOK, Mrs Joan Lindsay. b 46. SRN 70. Cranmer Hall Dur 86. **d** 88 **p** 94. Par Dn Hartlepool St Hilda *Dur* 88–93; Dn-in-c 93–94; P-in-c 94–96; rtd 96. *10 Peakston Close, Hartlepool TS26 0PN* T: (01429) 231778 E: joancook14@gmail.com

COOK, John. b 32. Linc Th Coll 87. **d** 89 **p** 90. C Bourne *Linc* 89–92; R Colsterworth Gp 92–02; rtd 02; PtO *Linc* 17–20. *24 Portrush Drive, Grantham NG31 9GD* T: (01476) 569063

COOK, John Edward. b 35. AKC 61. **d** 62 **p** 63. C York Town St Mich *Guildf* 62–67; Singapore 67–71; P-in-c Beoley *Worc* 78–83; V 83–89; V Bromsgrove All SS 89–01; rtd 01; PtO *Cov* 02–18. *86 Winton Road, Reading RG2 8HJ* T: 0118-901 2262 E: jcook120@btinternet.com

COOK, John Richard Millward. b 61. St Jo Coll Dur BA. Wycliffe Hall Ox 83. **d** 85 **p** 86. C Brampton St Thos *Derby* 85–89; C Farnborough *Guildf* 89–92; C Langham Place All So *Lon* 92–98; V Chelsea St Jo w St Andr 98–08; V Wargrave w Knowl Hill *Ox* from 08; PtO *Lon* from 19. *The Vicarage, Station Road, Wargrave, Reading RG10 8EU* T: 0118-940 2202 E: johnrmcook@btconnect.com

COOK, Kenneth Hugh. b 30. ALAM. AKC 55. **d** 56 **p** 57. C Netherfield *S'well* 56–59; C Newark w Coddington 59–61; V Basford St Aid 61–67; V Gargrave *Bradf* 67–77; Dir of Ords 77–89; Can Res Bradf Cathl 77–95; rtd 95; PtO *Ripon* 95–14; *Leeds* 14–19. *25 Hollins Close, Hampsthwaite, Harrogate HG3 2EH* T: (01423) 772521

COOK (née McCLEAN), Mrs Lydia Margaret Sheelagh. b 72. Ball Coll Ox BA 94 MA 98. Cuddesdon Coll 94. **d** 96 **p** 97. C Brackley St Pet w St Jas *Pet* 96–99; Chapl Cranford Ho Sch Ox 99–02; NSM Wallingford *Ox* 99–01; NSM Wallingford Deanery 01–04; NSM Sandford-on-Thames 04–06; NSM Sturminster Newton, Hinton St Mary and Lydlinch *Sarum* 06–15; R Okeford 15–21; RD Blackmore Vale 19–21; TR Ottery St Mary, Alfington, W Hill, Tipton etc *Ex* from 21. *The Vicar's House, The College, Ottery St Mary EX11 1DQ* M: 07725-046700 E: lydia@revrock.net

COOK, Marcus John Wyeth. b 41. Chich Th Coll 67. **d** 70 **p** 71. C Friern Barnet St Jas *Lon* 70–73; Hon C St Geo-in-the-East w St Paul 73–00. *3 Hugh Platt House, Patriot Square, London E2 9NS* M: 07890-207726

COOK, Matthew Brian. b 78. Oak Hill Th Coll. **d** 06 **p** 07. C Bispham *Blackb* 06–10; P-in-c Preston St Steph 10–11; V 11–16; C Leyland St Andr from 17. *8 St Andrew's Close, Leyland PR25 3BJ* T: (01772) 622964 E: matt.cook@standrewsleyland.org.uk

COOK, Mrs Myrtle Bridget Weigela. b 47. BA I.LM. EMMTC. **d** 04 **p** 05. NSM Kibworth and Smeeton Westerby and Saddington *Leic* 04–08; NSM Church Langton cum Tur Langton etc 08–13; P-in-c 11–13; P-in-c Thundridge *St Alb*

13–17; P-in-c High Cross 13–17; rtd 17; PtO *Leic* from 18. *1 Highcroft, Husbands Bosworth, Lutterworth LE17 6LF* E: mchighcroft@aol.com

COOK, Nicholas Leonard. b 59. Nottm Univ BCombStuds 84 Greenwich Univ PGCE 01 MCGI 12. Linc Th Coll 81. **d** 84 **p** 85. C Leic St Pet 84–85; C Knighton St Mich 85–86; Chapl Asst Towers Hosp Humberstone 86–89; Sen Chapl Leics Mental Health Services Unit 89–91; Chapl Quainton Hall Sch Harrow 91–94; CF(V) 88–94; CF 94–14; Chapl Duke of York's R Mil Sch Dover 14–16; Chapl Woodbridge Sch 16–18; Chapl RAuxAF from 14. *Chaplaincy Services (RAF), HQ Air Command, RAF High Wycombe HP14 4UE* T: (01494) 496800 F: 496343 E: carlton.hayes@btinternet.com

COOK, Paul Raymond. See McLAREN-COOK, Paul Raymond

COOK, Peter John. b 57. Ridley Hall Cam 93. **d** 95 **p** 96. C Romford Gd Shep *Chelmsf* 95–98; C Colchester St Jo 98–06; V Bangkok Ch Ch Thailand 06–15; Miss P Singapore from 15. *11 St Andrew's Road, Singapore, S178959* T: (0065) (9) 335 5520 E: peterjcook@gmail.com

COOK, Peter Ralph. b 69. Portsm Univ BA 92 Kent Univ BA 06. SEITE 03. **d** 06 **p** 07. C Hadlow *Roch* 06–09; V Docking, the Birchams, Stanhoe and Sedgeford *Nor* 09–15; P-in-c Fring 14–15; R Docking, The Birchams, Fring etc from 15; P-in-c Snettisham from 20; RD Heacham and Rising from 19. *The Vicarage, Sedgeford Road, Docking, King's Lynn PE31 8PN* T: (01485) 517157 E: t2andnor@supanet.com

COOK, Mrs Rachel Elizabeth. b 48. **d** 11 **p** 12. NSM Haydon Wick *Bris* 11–13; NSM N Swindon St Andr 13–15; Chapl RAF 15–21; V Tyndale *Glouc* from 21. *Charnwood, Coombe, Wootton-under-Edge GL12 7ND* M: 07495-491953 E: revdrachel@gmail.com

COOK, Canon Richard John Noel. b 49. Univ Coll Ox BA 70 MA 74 PGCE 72 Brunel Univ MTh 06. Wycliffe Hall Ox MA 77. **d** 78 **p** 79. C Fulwood *Sheff* 78–80; C Bolton St Paul w Em *Man* 81–86; TV 86–93; V Goldsworth Park *Guildf* 93–14; RD Woking 99–03; Bp's Adv in Interfaith Relns 07–14; Hon Can Guildf Cathl 10–14; rtd 14; PtO *Ox* from 15. *7 Rye Close, Banbury OX16 1XG* T: (01295) 367944 E: cookingwok@gmail.com

COOK, Mrs Ruth Anna Margaret. b 52. Bedf Coll of Educn CertEd 74. **d** 08 **p** 09. OLM Smestow Vale *Lich* 08–12. *Le Havre, 315 rue Johé Gormand, Toury, 71250 Cortambert, France* T: (0033) 3 85 36 11 70 E: ruthfromstourbridge@gmail.com

COOK, Simon David James. b 74. St Cath Coll Ox BA 97 St Jo Coll Dur BA 08. Cranmer Hall Dur 06. **d** 08 **p** 09. C Broughton *Man* 08–11; V Kirklees Valley 11–21; Borough Dean Bury 12–17; AD Bury 16–21; C Bolton St Pet w St Phil from 21. *195B Harrowby Street, Farnworth, Bolton BL4 9QU* M: 07745-232662 E: simondjcook@aol.com

COOK, Stephen. b 62. JP 05. Brunel Univ BSc(Econ) 84 Open Univ LLB 12. S'wark Ord Course 89. **d** 92 **p** 93. Hon C Forest Hill St Aug *S'wark* 92–98; P-in-c Eltham St Barn 98–10; V from 11; CF (TA) 00–03; Lead Chapl Greenwich Univ *S'wark* from 14. *St Barnabas' Vicarage, 449 Rochester Way, London SE9 6PH* T: (020) 8856 8294 E: cooksca@aol.com

COOK, Stephen William. b 57. Bris Univ BA 80 Lambeth STh 86. Trin Coll Bris 82. **d** 85 **p** 86. C Heref St Pet w St Owen and St Jas 85–89; TV Keynsham *B & W* 89–95; V Hanham *Bris* 95–02; RD Bitton 98–99; AD Kingswood and S Glos 99–02; TR Okehampton w Inwardleigh, Bratton Clovelly etc *Ex* 02–11; TR Okehampton, Inwardleigh, Belstone, Sourton etc from 12; RD Okehampton 05–12; Chapl R Devon and Ex NHS Foundn Trust from 09. *The Rectory, 1 Church Path, Okehampton EX20 1LW* T: (01837) 659297 E: scook9673@aol.com

COOK, Tom Adrian. b 86. Glos Univ BA 12. Trin Coll Bris MA 19. **d** 19 **p** 20. C W Cheltenham *Glouc* 19–20; C N Cheltenham from 20. *50 Robert Burns Avenue, Cheltenham GL51 6NT* M: 07538-048647 E: revtomcook@gmail.com

COOK, Trevor Vivian. b 43. Sarum Th Coll 67. **d** 69 **p** 70. C Lambeth St Phil *S'wark* 69–73; C St Buryan, St Levan and Sennen *Truro* 73–75; V The Ilketshalls *St E* 75–79; P-in-c Rumburgh w S Elmham 75–79; R Rumburgh w S Elmham w the Ilketshalls 79–84; TR Langport Area *B & W* 84–96; P-in-c Rode Major 96–02; C Hardington Vale 02–04; rtd 04; PtO *B & W* from 04. *Hedge End, 5 Queen Street, Keinton Mandeville, Somerton TA11 6EH* T: (01458) 224448   E: sandracook838@btinternet.com   *or* sandracook838@outlook.com

COOKE, Alan. b 50. Nottm Univ BTh 74 Lanc Univ PGCE 75. Kelham Th Coll 69. **d** 75 **p** 76. C Tyldesley w Shakerley *Man* 75–78; C Langley All SS and Martyrs 80–82; TV Langley and Parkfield 82–83; P-in-c Chadderton St Mark 83–85; V 85–14; rtd 14; PtO *Man* 14–17. *6 Hallet Court, Hughes Hallet*

Street, Sliema SLM 3142, Malta GC T: (00356) 2783 6339 E: theplookes@gmail.com

COOKE, Angela Elizabeth. b 42. SRN 65 SCM 67. St Jo Coll Nottm 85. **d** 87 **p** 94. Par Dn Walton H Trin *Ox* 87–92; Par Dn Bexleyheath Ch Ch *Roch* 92–94; C 94–97; V St Mary Cray and St Paul's Cray 97–05; rtd 05; PtO *Chich* from 15. *7 Maytree Gardens, Bexhill-on-Sea TN40 2PE* T: (01424) 213268

COOKE (née LEA), Canon Carolyn Jane. b 65. Nottm Univ BA 88 PGCE 90. St Jo Coll Nottm MTh 02. **d** 02 **p** 03. C Hyson Green and Forest Fields *S'well* 02–06; TV Clifton 06–10; P-in-c La Côte *Eur* from 10; Hon Can from 19. *Chemin des Saules 1, 1260 Nyon, Switzerland* T: (0041) (22) 364 0030 E: carolyn.cooke@lacotechurch.ch

COOKE, Christopher Stephen. b 54. Lon Univ BA 76 MA 77 Ox Univ BA 81 MA 88. Ripon Coll Cuddesdon 79. **d** 82 **p** 83. C Cen Telford *Lich* 82–86; R Uffington, Upton Magna and Withington 86–95; RD Wrockwardine 92–01; TR Wrockwardine Deanery 95–01; P-in-c Wem and Lee Brockhurst 01–13; P-in-c Loppington w Newtown 01–02; rtd 13; PtO *Heref* from 14. *Broomfield, Station Road, Pontesbury, Shrewsbury SY5 0QY* E: christophercooke@mscsolutions.co.uk

COOKE, Claire. b 80. St Mellitus Coll 14. **d** 17 **p** 18. C Lancaster St Thos *Blackb* from 17. *97 Barton Road, Lancaster LA1 4EN*

COOKE, Daniel Benedict. b 84. Hull Univ BA 06 Leeds Univ MA 12. St Jo Coll Nottm 06. **d** 08 **p** 09. C W Acklam *York* 08–11; R Brimington *Derby* from 11. *The Rectory, Church Street, Brimington, Chesterfield S43 1JG* T: (01246) 273103 E: danielbcooke@hotmail.com

COOKE, David John. b 31. Linc Th Coll 60. **d** 62 **p** 63. C Brighton Gd Shep Preston *Chich* 62–65; C Clayton w Keymer 65–70; R Stone w Hartwell w Bishopstone *Ox* 70–77; R Stone w Dinton and Hartwell 77–07; rtd 07; PtO *Ox* from 08. *5 Astronomy Way, Aylesbury HP19 7WD* T: (01296) 392296 E: david.j.cooke@btinternet.com

COOKE, David Michael Randle. b 68. Newc Univ BA 90. Wycliffe Hall Ox 05. **d** 07 **p** 08. C Richmond H Trin and Ch Ch *S'wark* 07–12; TV Barnes from 12. *162 Castelnau, London SW13 9ET* T: (020) 8741 7330 M: 07766-900267 E: davidcooke2003@hotmail.com *or* david@htbarnes.com

COOKE, Ms Gillian Freda. b 39. Lon Univ BD 73 Leeds Univ MA 87. Linc Th Coll 74. **dss** 78 **d** 87 **p** 94. Cricklewood St Pet CD *Lon* 78–80; Chapl Middx Poly 78–80; Chapl Leeds Poly *Ripon* 80–87; N Humberside Ind Chapl *York* 87–90; Asst Chapl HM Pris Hull 90–94; Chapl Keele Univ *Lich* 94–97; Assoc Min Betley and Keele 94–97; Chapl Rampton Hosp Retford 97–99; rtd 99; PtO *York* 00–12; Chapl HM Pris Wolds 05–12. *7 Northfield, Swanland, North Ferriby HU14 3RG* T: (01482) 633971

COOKE, Heather Ann. QUB BEd. **d** 17 **p** 20. Belfast St Steph w St Luke *Conn* 17–20; C Carrickfergus from 20. *23 Westmount Avenue, Carrickfergus BT38 3DQ* T: (028) 9336 0370   M: 07745-688605   E: hcooke84@hotmail.com   *or* cookehe@tcd.ie

COOKE (née MORRALL), Mrs Heather Lynne. b 55. LMH Ox BA 76 MA 80 MCIPR 88. Dioc OLM tr scheme 96. **d** 99 **p** 00. OLM Martlesham w Brightwell *St E* 99–12; PtO from 12. *9 Swan Close, Martlesham Heath, Ipswich IP5 3SD* T: (01473) 623770 M: 07703-568051 E: hcookema@aol.com

COOKE, James Martin. b 46. Trin Coll Ox BA 67 Ox Univ DipEd 68. **d** 07 **p** 08. OLM Wonersh w Blackheath *Guildf* 07–16; PtO from 16. *7 Durnsford Way, Cranleigh GU6 7LN* T: (01483) 276049 E: james.cooke2015@gmail.com

COOKE, John Stephen. b 35. K Coll Lon BD 58 AKC 58. **d** 59 **p** 60. C W Bromwich St Fran *Lich* 59–62; C Chalfont St Peter *Ox* 62–66; V Cross Heath *Lich* 66–72; R Haughton 72–86; P-in-c Ellenhall w Ranton 72–80; V Eccleshall 86–00; Sub Chapl HM Pris Drake Hall 89–95; rtd 00; PtO *Lich* 00–21. *34 Stone Road, Eccleshall, Stafford ST21 6DL* T: (01785) 850189 E: jstephencooke@btinternet.com

COOKE, Mrs Katherine Mary. b 69. Univ of Wales (Lamp) BA 92. Ox Min Course 08. **d** 12 **p** 13. C Eynsham and Cassington *Ox* 12–16; C N Abingdon from 16. *102 Gibson Close, Abingdon OX14 1XT* M: 07540-568055 E: revkathcooke@gmail.com

COOKE, Lesley Elizabeth. b 49. **d** 12 **p** 13. NSM Hawarden *St As* 12–15; PtO *Ches* from 14; *St As* from 15. *University of Chester, Parkgate Road, Chester CH1 4BJ* T: (01244) 511136 E: l.cooke@chester.ac.uk

COOKE, Lorraine Mary. b 48. **d** 12 **p** 13. OLM Droylsden St Martin *Man* 12–14; NSM Audenshaw St Steph 14–16; NSM Denton Ch Ch 14–16; NSM Denton St Lawr 14–16; NSM Haughton St Anne 14–16; PtO from 16. *Address withheld by request* E: revlmcooke@gmail.com

COOKE, Michael David. b 46. New Coll Ox BA 68 MA 71 DPhil 71. Ox NSM Course 75. **d** 78 **p** 79. NSM Newport

Pagnell *Ox* 78–79; NSM Newport Pagnell w Lathbury 79–85; NSM Newport Pagnell w Lathbury and Moulsoe 85–88; NSM Beckenham Ch Ch *Roch* 90–96; P-in-c Seal St Lawr 96–10; P-in-c Underriver 96–10; rtd 10; PtO *Cant* from 11. *92 Dumpton Park Drive, Broadstairs CT10 1RL* T: (01843) 863293 E: mcooke.92@btinternet.com

COOKE, Michael John. b 39. Ab Dioc Tr Course 78. **d** 80 **p** 81. NSM St Andr Cathl *Ab* 80–81; Chapl Miss to Seamen 81–88; Miss to Seamen Tilbury 88–91; Hon C Immingham *Linc* 81–88; Ind Chapl Teesside *Dur* 91–97; V Kelloe and Coxhoe 97–06; rtd 06. *36 Nuneaton Drive, Hemlington, Middlesbrough TS8 9PR* E: mikecooke8@yahoo.co.uk

COOKE, Patrick Arthur. b 45. **d** 12. NSM Winterton Gp *Linc* from 12. *10 West Street, Winterton, Scunthorpe DN15 9QQ* T: (01724) 734885

COOKE, Philip George. b 66. Plymouth Univ BSc 88 Univ of Wales (Lamp) PhD 96. Lon Bible Coll 99 Ox Min Course 10. **d** 12 **p** 13. NSM Hanborough and Freeland *Ox* 12–16; PtO 16–17; NSM N Abingdon from 17; Dir Local Min Tr from 16. *102 Gibson Close, Abingdon OX14 1XT* T: (01235) 536024 M: 07857-822053 E: revphilcooke@gmail.com *or* phil.cooke@oxford.anglican.org

COOKE, Raymond. b 34. Liv Univ BSc 56. Wells Th Coll 58. **d** 60 **p** 61. C Newton Heath All SS *Man* 60–64; C-in-c Failsworth H Family CD 64–75; R Failsworth H Family 75–83; P-in-c Man Gd Shep 83–88; V Westleigh St Pet 88–99; rtd 99; PtO *Man* from 00. *136 Victoria Avenue East, Manchester M9 6HF* T: 0161-740 0664

COOKE, Canon Richard James. b 60. Pemb Coll Ox BA 82 MA 88 Bris Univ PhD 96. Trin Coll Bris 85. **d** 88 **p** 89. C Rugby St Matt *Cov* 88–92; V Fletchamstead 92–04; Dir Initial Tr for Readers 97–02; CME Adv *Cov* 04–06; CME Lay Development and Local Min Adv 07–08; Dir of Discipleship Development 09–10; Prin Dioc Tr Partnership from 10; C Warmington w Shotteswell and Radway w Ratley 07–14; C Kineton 07–14; C Combroke w Compton Verney 07–14; C Edgehill Churches from 14; Gen LtO from 18; Hon Can Cov Cathl from 10. *Diocesan Office, 1 Hill Top, Coventry CV1 5AB* T: (024) 7652 1200 *or* 7652 1316 E: richard.cooke@covcofe.org

COOKE, Roger. b 68. Heriot-Watt Univ BA 90 BArch 91 Edin Univ MTh 02. TISEC 98. **d** 99 **p** 00. C Prestonpans *Edin* 99–02; R 02–09; C Musselburgh 99–02; R 02–09; I Coleraine *Conn* from 09. *St Patrick's Rectory, 28 Mountsandel Road, Coleraine BT52 1JE* T: (028) 7034 3429 E: carrington20@aol.com

COOKE, Stephen. *See* COOKE, John Stephen

COOKE, Miss Susan Marilyn. b 76. K Coll Lon BA 97 MA 02 AKC 97 PGCE 98. Ridley Hall Cam 10. **d** 12 **p** 13. C Sunningdale *Ox* 12–16; V Ewell *Guildf* 16–21; P-in-c Tolland Park *S'wark* from 21; V from 22. *2 Thornton Road, London SW12 0JU* M: 07780-606124 E: revsuecooke@gmail.com

COOKE, Mrs Susan Patricia. b 63. Ox Brookes Univ MA 99. WEMTC 10. **d** 13 **p** 14. C Barnwood *Glouc* 13–17; R Badgeworth, Shurdington and Witcombe w Bentham from 17. *The Vicarage, School Lane, Shurdington, Cheltenham GL51 4TF* T: (01242) 321806 E: revsusancooke@gmail.com

COOKE, Mrs Suzanne. b 65. Westmr Coll Ox BTh 96 Anglia Ruskin Univ MA 13. Westcott Ho Cam 08. **d** 10 **p** 11. C Watton *Nor* 10–13; P-in-c Upper Tas Valley 13–16; V 16–17; V Doddington, Ilderton, Kirknewton and Wooler *Newc* from 17. *2 Queens Road, Wooler NE71 6DR* E: suzanne@cookehouse.co.uk

COOKSEY, Miss Diane Marie. b 75. Univ of Cen England in Birm BA 97. St Jo Coll Nottm 09. **d** 11 **p** 12. C Churchill-in-Halfshire w Blakedown and Broome *Worc* 11–14; C Warndon St Nic from 14; RD Worc E 18–21; AD Worc from 21. *4 Daty Croft, Home Meadow, Worcester WR4 0JB* M: 07974-556514 E: diane_cooksey@hotmail.com

COOKSEY, Mrs Emma. b 80. Qu Foundn (Course) 15. **d** 18 **p** 19. C Lichfield and Longdon *Lich* 18–21; TV Newport and Carisbrooke *Portsm* from 21; C Gatcombe from 21. *Shalfleet Vicarage, 4 Manor Green, Shalfleet, Newport PO30 4QT* E: emma.cooksey@sky.com

COOKSON, Canon Diane Veronica. b 51. NOC 81. **dss** 84 **d** 87 **p** 94. Gt Sutton *Ches* 84–86; Neston 86–87; Par Dn 87–94; C 94–96; V Stockport St Sav from 96; Ecum Adv (Gtr Man) 00–02; RD Stockport 12–17; Hon Can Ches Cathl from 04. *St Saviour's Vicarage, 22 St Saviour's Road, Great Moor, Stockport SK2 7QE* T: 0161-483 2633 E: st.saviours@virgin.net

COOKSON, Canon Graham Leslie. b 37. Bernard Gilpin Soc *Dur* 63 Sarum Th Coll 64. **d** 67 **p** 68. C Upton Ascension *Ches* 67–69; C Timperley 69–75; V Godley cum Newton Green 75–83; R Tarporley 83–07; Hon Can Ches Cathl 04–07; rtd 07; PtO *Ches* from 08. *15 Dolphin Court, Chester CH4 8JX* T: (01244) 671044 E: g.cookson532@btinternet.com

COOKSON, Canon William. b 61. **d** 98 **p** 99. C Haydock St Mark *Liv* 98–02; Min Wallington Springfield Ch *S'wark* 02–17; Public Preacher from 17; Dioc Dean for Fresh Expressions from 15; Hon Can S'wark Cathl from 15. *Christ Church Vicarage, 52 Earlswood Street, London SE10 9ES* T: (020) 7939 9414 E: willcookson@blueyonder.co.uk

COOLING (née YOUNG), Mrs Margaret Dorothy. b 37. K Coll Lon BA 59 AKC Lon Univ BD 69 PGCE 70 MSc 10 Univ of Wales (Cardiff) MEd 81. Mon Dioc Tr Scheme 89. **d** 90 **p** 95. NSM Bettws *Mon* 90–95; NSM Purleigh, Cold Norton and Stow Maries *Chelmsf* 95–98; rtd 98; PtO *Mon* from 98; *Glouc* from 01. *St Thomas Cottage, The Fence, St Briavels, Lydney GL15 6QG* T: (01594) 530926 E: maggieandderrick@outlook.com

COOMBER, Ian Gladstone. b 47. Southn Univ BTh 79 Ch Ch Coll Cant CertEd 68. Sarum & Wells Th Coll 73. **d** 76 **p** 77. C Weeke *Win* 76–79; TV Saffron Walden w Wendens Ambo and Littlebury *Chelmsf* 79–82; V Weston *Win* 82–90; R Bedhampton *Portsm* 90–96; R Botley and Durley 96–05; V Curdridge 96–05; RD Bishop's Waltham 98–03; TR Cartmel Peninsula *Carl* 05–09; rtd 09; PtO *B & W* 09–19. *28 Hebron Court, 35 Hill Lane, Southampton SO15 5WE* T: (023) 8071 5128 E: iancoomber747@outlook.com

COOMBS, Christopher. b 48. UWIC MSc 05. Trin Coll Bris 10. **d** 12 **p** 13. OLM Rodbourne Cheney *Bris* 12–19; PtO *Ex* from 21. *Farthings, Bay View Road, Woolacombe EX34 7DQ* M: 07789-514310 E: chris.coombs8@gmail.com

COOMBS, John Allen. b 46. Portsm Poly BSc 70. Oak Hill Th Coll 86 Sarum & Wells Th Coll 89. **d** 89 **p** 90. C Leverington and Wisbech St Mary *Ely* 89–93; P-in-c Emneth 93–96; V Emneth and Marshland St James 96–99; P-in-c Papworth Everard 99–00; TV Papworth 00–02; Chapl Papworth Hosp NHS Foundn Trust 99–06; P-in-c Roche *Truro* 06–12; rtd 12; PtO *Ex* 13–14; *Portsm* from 14. *The Little Haven, Castle Road, Ventnor PO38 1LG* T: (01983) 854290 E: john.coombs.7@gmail.com

COOMBS, John Kendall. b 47. Culham Coll Ox BEd 73. Sarum & Wells Th Coll 75. **d** 77 **p** 78. C Fareham H Trin *Portsm* 77–80; C Petersfield w Sheet 80–83; TV Beaminster Area *Sarum* 83–87; TR Preston w Sutton Poyntz, Littlemoor etc 87–97; TR Hermitage *Ox* 97–05; P-in-c Hurst 05–11; rtd 11; PtO *Ox* from 11. *65 Rosedale Gardens, Thatcham RG19 3LF*

COOMBS, Martin. *See* COOMBS, Walter James Martin

COOMBS, Matthew Robert. b 90. Heythrop Coll Lon BA 11. St Mellitus Coll 15. **d** 18 **p** 19. C Bryanston Square St Mary w St Marylebone St Mark *Lon* from 18. *St Mary's Church Office, 255 Old Marylebone Road, London NW1 5QT* T: (020) 7258 5040 M: 07889-793536 E: matt@stmaryslondon.com

COOMBS, Patrick Michael Joseph. *See* COFFEY, Patrick Michael Joseph

COOMBS, Richard Murray. b 63. St Chad's Coll Dur BSc 85 Rob Coll Cam BA 89 MA 90. Ridley Hall Cam 87. **d** 90 **p** 91. C Enfield Ch Ch Trent Park *Lon* 90–94; C St Helen Bishopsgate w St Andr Undershaft etc 94–98; P-in-c St Pet Cornhill 95–98; V Burford w Fulbrook, Taynton, Asthall etc *Ox* 98–18; R Cheltenham St Mary w St Matt and St Luke *Glouc* from 18. *38 Sydenham Villas Road, Cheltenham GL52 6DZ* T: (01242) 703154 E: rmcoombs@btinternet.com

COOMBS, Canon Walter James Martin. b 33. Keble Coll Ox BA 57 MA 61. Cuddesdon Coll 59. **d** 61 **p** 62. C Kennington St Jo *S'wark* 61–64; Chapl Em Coll Cam 64–68; Bp's Dom Chapl *S'wark* 68–70; V E Dulwich St Jo 70–77; V Pershore w Pinvin, Wick and Birlingham *Worc* 77–92; Hon Can Worc Cathl 84–92; RD Pershore 85–91; TV Dorchester *Ox* 92–98; rtd 98; PtO *Ox* from 01. *54 Divinity Road, Oxford OX4 1LJ* T: (01865) 243865

COONEY, Canon Michael Patrick. b 55. City of Lon Poly BA 77. Ripon Coll Cuddesdon 77. **d** 80 **p** 81. C Cov E 80–83; C Old Brumby *Linc* 83–85; V Linc St Jo 85–90; V Frodingham 90–05; RD Manlake 99–10; RD Is of Axholme 05–10; Ind Chapl 05–19; P-in-c Gainsborough and Morton 12–19; Can and Preb Linc Cathl 04–19; rtd 19; PtO *York* from 20. *Address withheld by request* E: mccooney593@gmail.com

COONEY, William Barry. b 47. K Coll Lon 69. **d** 70 **p** 71. C W Bromwich All SS *Lich* 70–73; C Wolverhampton St Pet 73–75; C Rugeley 75–78; V Sneyd Green 78–87; R Sandiacre *Derby* 87–11; rtd 11; PtO *S'well* from 11. *15 Newthorpe Common, Newthorpe, Nottingham NG16 2BX* T: (01773) 711549 E: rosemary.c@talk21.com

COOPER, Alexander James Goodenough. b 47. Bath Univ BSc 69. WEMTC 04. **d** 06 **p** 07. NSM Soundwell *Bris* from 06. *1 Deerhurst, Bristol BS15 1XH* T: 0117-973 9441 E: linsand@blueyonder.co.uk

COOPER, Andrew John. b 62. W Sussex Inst of HE BA 87 Greenwich Univ PGCE 03 FRSA 14. St Steph Ho Ox 88. **d** 91 **p** 92. C Rawmarsh w Parkgate *Sheff* 91–93; C Mosborough

93–95; P-in-c Donnington Wood *Lich* 95–96; CF 96–14; PtO *Bris* from 10; *Sarum* from 18. *Address withheld by request* E: revajcooper@btinternet.com

COOPER, Andrew John Gearing. b 48. Sir John Cass Coll Lon BSc 70. Ripon Coll Cuddesdon 73. **d** 76 **p** 77. C Potternewton *Ripon* 76–79; Antigua 79–81; Anguilla 81–87; V W Bromwich St Andr w Ch Ch *Lich* 88–92. *Address withheld by request*

COOPER, Andrew Richard James. b 81. Lon Metrop Univ BSc 04. Ridley Hall Cam 07. **d** 10 **p** 11. C S Harrow St Paul *Lon* 10–13; Chapl HM YOI Feltham 13–17; PtO *Lon* 17–18 and from 19; Chapl R Brompton and Harefield NHS Foundn Trust 18–19. *106 Acton Lane, London NW10 8TX* M: 07947-722277 E: arjcooper@aim.com

COOPER, Angela. d 18 **p** 19. NSM Pendoylan w Welsh St Donats *Llan* 18–19; NSM Peterston-super-Ely w St Brides-super-Ely 18–19; NSM St Nicholas w Bonvilston and St George-super-Ely 18–19; NSM E Vale from 19. *The Old Vicarage, Church Road, Llanblethian, Cowbridge CF71 7JF* M: 07811-018685 E: angelacooper03@gmail.com

COOPER, Miss Angela Jean. b 56. SWMTC 09. **d** 12 **p** 13. C St Just-in-Roseland and St Mawes *Truro* 12–16; P-in-c Lanteglos by Camelford w Advent 16–19; P-in-c St Teath 16–19; R Camel-Allen from 19. *Fairway View, Helstone, Camelford PL32 9RL* T: (01840) 212468 M: 07753-517304 E: angelajeancooper@hotmail.com

COOPER, Anne. *See* COOPER, Margaret Anne

COOPER, The Ven Annette Joy. b 53. Open Univ BA 80 Dur Univ MA 13 CQSW 84. S'wark Ord Course 85. **d** 88 **p** 94. NSM Pembury *Roch* 88; Chapl Asst Kent and Sussex Hosp Tunbridge Wells 88–91; Chapl Asst Leybourne Grange Hosp W Malling 88–91; Chapl Bassetlaw Hosp and Community Services NHS Trust 91–96; P-in-c Edwinstowe *S'well* 96–04; Chapl Center Parcs Holiday Village 96–01; AD Worksop 99–04; Hon Can S'well Minster 02–04; Adn Colchester *Chelmsf* 04–19; rtd 19; PtO *St E* from 19; *Chelmsf* 19–21; RD Woodbridge *St E* from 20. *1 Fox Hill, Hollesley, Woodbridge IP12 3RD*

COOPER, Arthur. b 47. **d** 15 **p** 15. C Stoneycroft All SS *Liv* 15–16; P-in-c 16–18; rtd 18; Hon C Glazebury w Hollinfare *Liv* from 18. *The Vicarage, 468 Manchester Road, Rixton, Warrington WA3 6HY* T: 0161-775 8368 E: akc@f2s.com or sthelenhollinfare@gmail.com

COOPER, Barrie Keith. b 56. Oak Hill Th Coll. **d** 85 **p** 86. C Partington and Carrington *Ches* 85–89; V Stockport St Mark 89–93; Chapl HM YOI Stoke Heath 93–01; Chapl HM Pris Acklington 01–08; Chapl HM Pris Dur 08–11; Chapl Dur Sch 11–15; PtO *Newc* 17–18; NSM Lesbury w Alnmouth from 18; NSM Longhoughton w Howick from 20; NSM Embleton w Rennington and Rock from 20. *4 Island View, Amble, Morpeth NE65 0SE* M: 07969-514982

COOPER, Canon Bede Robert. b 42. Ex Univ BA 69. Coll of Resurr Mirfield 69. **d** 71 **p** 72. C Weymouth H Trin *Sarum* 71–74; P-in-c Broad Town 74–79; V Wootton Bassett 74–86; R Wilton w Netherhampton and Fugglestone 86–07; Can and Preb Sarum Cathl 88–07; rtd 07; PtO *B & W* 09–19; *Win* 11–14; *Sarum* 13–18. *205 High Street, Milborne Port, Sherborne DT9 5AG* T: (01963) 250503 E: b.cooper789@btinternet.com

COOPER, Benedict Christopher. b 68. K Coll Cam BA 90 Wolfs Coll Ox MPhil 94 DPhil 97 W Sydney Univ PhD 10. Oak Hill Th Coll BA 03. **d** 03 **p** 04. C St Helen Bishopsgate w St Andr Undershaft etc *Lon* 03–07; Australia 07–10; C Fulwood *Sheff* 10–20; Tutor Cornhill Tr Course from 20. *The Cornhill Training Course, 140-148 Borough High Street, London SE1 1LB* M: 07402-065857

COOPER, Clive Anthony Charles. b 38. Lon Univ BEd 74. ALCD 62. **d** 62 **p** 63. C Morden *S'wark* 62–65; SAMS Argentina 65–71; Asst Master St Nic Sch Cranleigh 74–92; Hon C Cranleigh *Guildf* 78–79; Hon C Ewhurst 80–82; Hon Chapl Duke of Kent Sch Ewhurst 83–92; Chapl Felixstowe Coll 92–93; PtO *Ex* 94–95; Chapl Puerto Pollensa *Eur* 95–02; P-in-c Instow and Westleigh *Ex* 09–18; PtO *Eur* 08–12; *Ex* 09–12. *64 Benfer Road, Victoria Point QLD 4165, Australia* E: clivecooper141@yahoo.com.au

COOPER, Colin. b 55. Open Univ BA. St Jo Coll Nottm 83. **d** 86 **p** 87. C Cheadle Hulme St Andr *Ches* 86–89; C Tunbridge Wells St Jo *Roch* 89–93; V Whitfield *Derby* 93–11; TR N Wingfield, Clay Cross and Pilsley 11–21; rtd 21. *19 Moores Close, Debenham, Stowmarket IP14 6RU* E: revccooper@gmail.com

COOPER, Colin Charles. b 40. Middx Univ BA 94. Oak Hill Th Coll 62. **d** 66 **p** 67. C Islington St Andr w St Thos and St Matthias *Lon* 66–69; Bermuda 69–76; V Gorleston St Andr *Nor* 76–79; R Emporia Ch Ch w Purdy Grace USA 94–12; rtd 12. *2608 South Anchor Lane, Nags Head NC 27959, USA* T: (001) (434) 430 0107 E: colincooper9540@gmail.com

COOPER, Mrs Corynne Elizabeth. b 54. Kent Univ BA 76 PGCE 77 Nottm Univ MA 98. EMMTC 95. **d** 98 **p** 99. NSM Kneesall w Laxton and Wellow *S'well* 98–01; C Widecombe-in-the-Moor, Leusdon, Princetown etc *Ex* 01–05; TV Ashburton, Bickington, Buckland in the Moor etc 05–15. *15 Amberley Close, Ashburton, Newton Abbot TQ13 7JE* T: (01364) 653812

COOPER, David. b 44. AKC 69. **d** 69 **p** 70. C Wortley-de-Leeds *Ripon* 73–83; LtO *Ox* 84–04; Chapl Eton Coll 85–04; rtd 09; PtO *Ox* from 11. *Old Shute, Dulverton TA22 9RJ* T: (01398) 323624 E: godshot@btinternet.com

COOPER, David Philip. b 65. York Univ BA 86. Qu Coll Birm BTheol 94. **d** 94 **p** 95. C Burslem *Lich* 94–98; TV Cen Wolverhampton and Dioc Inter-Faith Officer 98–05; P-in-c Arnside *Carl* 05–19; Dioc Ecum Officer 14–19; TR Walkden and Lt Hulton *Man* from 19. *St John's Vicarage, Algernon Road, Worsley, Manchester M28 3RD* E: revdavidcooper@btinternet.com

COOPER, Derek Edward. b 30. Bps' Coll Cheshunt 61. **d** 62 **p** 63. C Bishop's Stortford St Mich *St Alb* 62–66; V Westcliff St Cedd *Chelmsf* 66–89; R Camerton w Dunkerton, Foxcote and Shoscombe *B & W* 89–95; rtd 95; PtO *Win* 95–14. *6 Caerleon Drive, Andover SP10 4DE* T: (01264) 362807

COOPER, Frances. b 57. Lindisfarne Regional Tr Partnership 15. **d** 17 **p** 18. NSM Gainford *Dur* 17–18; NSM Winston 17–18; NSM Bishop Auckland 18–20; NSM Shildon from 20. *4 Riverside, South Church, Bishop Auckland DL14 6XT* E: frances.cooper@durham.anglican.org

COOPER, Gavin Ashley. b 85. Chich Univ BA 06. St Steph Ho Ox BA 10 MA 15. **d** 11 **p** 12. C Old St Pancras *Lon* 11–14; C Stamford St Mary and St Martin *Linc* 14–16; R 16–20. *Address temp unknown* E: frgavincooper@gmail.com

COOPER, Gordon William. b 54. Aston Tr Scheme 93 Ripon Coll Cuddesdon 95. **d** 97 **p** 98. C Kippax w Allerton Bywater *Ripon* 97–01; V Wyther 01–08; P-in-c Garforth 08–12; R 12–14; Leeds 14–17; rtd 17; PtO *Leeds* from 17. *18 Neville Grove, Swillington, Leeds LS26 8QN* M: 07896-329055 E: gordon.cooper1954@gmail.com

COOPER, Graham Denbigh. b 48. Nottm Univ BTh 75. St Jo Coll Nottm LTh 75. **d** 75 **p** 76. C Collyhurst *Man* 75–78; C Stambermill *Worc* 78–80; V The Lye and Stambermill 80–90; P-in-c Frome H Trin *B & W* 90; V 91–95; Appeals Organiser Children's Soc 95–97; Area Manager Save the Children Fund from 97. *9 Maxwell Road, Shepton Mallet BA4 5RF* T: (01749) 938156

COOPER, Mrs Gwenda. d 11 **p** 12. NSM Colwyn and Llanelian St As 11–16; NSM Aled Miss Area 17–18; P-in-c from 18. *Bron Digain, Llangernyw, Abergele LL22 8PP* T: (01745) 860349 E: brondigain@googlemail.com

COOPER, Heather Dawn. *See* BUTCHER, Heather Dawn

COOPER, Ian. b 57. St Jo Coll Nottm 00. **d** 02 **p** 03. C Mildenhall *St E* 02–05; TV 05–06; V Blacklands Hastings Ch Ch and St Andr *Chich* 06–10; P-in-c Peacehaven and Telscombe Cliffs 10–13; P-in-c Piddinghoe 10–13; P-in-c Telscombe Village 10–13; V Peacehaven and Telscombe Cliffs w Piddinghoe etc 13–14; Chapl HM Pris Wayland 15–16; Chapl HM Pris Bure from 16. *HM Prison Bure, Jaguar Drive, Badersfield, Norwich NR10 5GB* T: (01603) 326180 E: ian@rpmo.co.uk *or* ian.cooper5@justice.gov.uk

COOPER, Ian Clive. b 48. Ex Univ BA 76 K Coll Lon MTh 94 FCA. Linc Th Coll 76. **d** 78 **p** 79. C Sunbury *Lon* 78–81; P-in-c Astwood Bank *Worc* 81–85; P-in-c Feckenham w Bradley 82–85; TV Hemel Hempstead *St Alb* 85–95; R Bushey 95–04; TR Witney *Ox* 04–06; TV Marlborough *Sarum* 06–13; rtd 13; Learning for Discipleship Support Officer *Sarum* 13–15; PtO *Glouc* from 17. *73 Bowridge Lane, Stroud GL5 2JL* T: (01453) 298364 E: iancoopermth@talktalk.net

COOPER, James Peter. b 61. Westf Coll Lon BSc 82 Portsm Univ BA 04 Heythrop Coll Lon MA 12. Sarum & Wells Th Coll 82. **d** 85 **p** 86. C Durrington *Chich* 85–88; C Clayton w Keymer 88–95; TV Chich and Chapl Chich Coll of Tech 95–01; Chapl R W Sussex NHS Trust 01–11; R Cessnock Australia 11–15; P-in-c Donnington *Chich* 15–17; V from 17; Chapl St Wilfrid's Hospice Chich from 15. *The Vicarage, 34 Graydon Avenue, Chichester PO19 8RF* T: (01243) 788321 E: lizandjimcooper@gmail.com

COOPER, Mrs Jennifer Ann Lisbeth. b 45. MCSP 67. **d** 04 **p** 05. OLM Ashwellthorpe, Forncett, Fundenhall, Hapton etc *Nor* 04–13; rtd 13; PtO *Nor* 13–16; *Derby* from 17. *Address temp unknown*

COOPER, Jennifer Elaine. b 62. Toronto Univ BA 83 Ottawa Univ MA 90 Keble Coll Ox DPhil 05. Ripon Coll Cuddesdon 05. **d** 06 **p** 07. C Cotham St Sav w St Mary and Clifton St Paul *Bris* 06–09; Lect and Tutor Coll of Resurr Mirfield 09–18; Visiting Lect Leeds Univ 09–18; Dir IME

166

Newc from 19. *Church House, St John's Terrace, North Shields NE29 6HS* T: 0191-270 4100

COOPER, Jeremy Llewellyn John. b 51. Lanc Univ BA 73 Sussex Univ PGCE 74 York Univ MSc 87. **d** 07 **p** 08. OLM Morpeth *Newc* from 07; Chapl Northumbria Healthcare NHS Foundn Trust 11–17. *Southdown, 13 Curlew Hill, Morpeth NE61 3SH* E: jeremylcooper@aol.com

COOPER, Jill Mary. b 49. Qu Foundn (Course) 14. **d** 17 **p** 18. OLM Milton *Lich* 17–19; OLM Milton and Norton 19–21; PtO from 21. *16 Kirkwall Grove, Stoke-on-Trent ST2 7PH* E: jillcooper777@hotmail.com

COOPER, John. b 47. Sarum & Wells Th Coll 71. **d** 74 **p** 75. C Spring Grove St Mary *Lon* 74–77; C Shepherd's Bush St Steph w St Thos 77–82; V Paddington St Pet 82–89; V Darwen St Cuth w Tockholes St Steph *Blackb* 89–96; V Northampton St Mich w St Edm *Pet* 96–99; PtO *St Alb* from 99; *Lon* 02–15. *The Charterhouse, Charterhouse Square, London EC1M 6AN* T: (020) 3560 1336 M: 07749-502929 E: buster6913@yahoo.co.uk

COOPER, Canon John Leslie. b 33. Lon Univ BD 65 MPhil 78. Chich Th Coll 59. **d** 62 **p** 63. C Kings Heath *Birm* 62–65; Asst Chapl HM Pris Wandsworth 65–66; Chapl HM Borstal Portland 66–68; Chapl HM Pris Bris 68–72; P-in-c Balsall Heath St Paul *Birm* 73–81; V 81–82; Adn Aston and Can Res Birm Cathl 82–90; Adn Coleshill 90–93; C Sutton Coldfield H Trin 93–97; Hon Can Birm Cathl 93–97; rtd 97; PtO *Derby* from 98; *Chich* from 17. *9 Ramsay Hall, 9-13 Byron Road, Worthing BN11 3HN* T: (01903) 207939 E: jl612cooper@gmail.com

COOPER, John Northcott. b 44. Ox Min Course 89. **d** 92 **p** 93. NSM Burghfield *Ox* 92–99; P-in-c Wootton (Boars Hill) 99–00; V Wootton and Dry Sandford 00–10; AD Abingdon 02–07; rtd 10; PtO *Sarum* 14–20. *Dinosaur Footprints, 21 Townsend Road, Swanage BH19 2PU* T: (01929) 423591 E: dinofoot@hotmail.com

COOPER, Jonathan Charles. b 91. Fitzw Coll Cam BA 13 MEng 13 MA 17. Coll of Resurr Mirfield BA 16. **d** 17 **p** 18. C Newc St Fran 17–20; PtO from 20. *45 Cherryburn Gardens, Newcastle upon Tyne NE4 9UQ* E: revjoncooper@gmail.com

COOPER, Jonathan Mark Eric. b 62. Man Univ BSc 83 Edin Univ BD 88. Edin Th Coll 85. **d** 88 **p** 89. C Stainton-in-Cleveland *York* 88–91; C W Bromwich All SS *Lich* 91–93; P-in-c Ingleby Barwick CD *York* 93–98; P-in-c Hinderwell w Roxby 98–03; R Kirby Misperton w Normanby, Edston and Salton 03–10; V Brompton w Deighton from 10; R Rounton w Welbury from 10. *The Vicarage, Northallerton Road, Brompton, Northallerton DL6 2QA* T: (01609) 772436 E: j.m.e.c@btinternet.com

COOPER, Joseph Edward. b 87. St Hild Coll 15. **d** 18 **p** 19. C Stannington *Sheff* 18–20; C Handsworth 20–21; C Worksop Priory S'well from 21; C Worksop St Paul from 21. *St Paul's Vicarage, Cavendish Road, Worksop S80 2ST* M: 07340-280460 E: revjoecooper@gmail.com

COOPER, Judith Mary. b 52. Leeds Univ BA 09. NOC 06. **d** 09 **p** 10. C Prestwich St Mary *Man* 09–12; P-in-c Westleigh St Pet 12–15; V 15–18; P-in-c Westleigh St Paul 12–18; V Westleigh St Pet and St Paul 18–20; rtd 20; PtO *Man* from 21. *92 Gilda Road, Worsley, Manchester M28 1BP* M: 07752-676007 E: judith.cooper5@virginmedia.com

COOPER, Ms Louise Helena. b 68. Leeds Univ BA 90. Qu Coll Birm. **d** 93 **p** 94. Par Dn Dovecot *Liv* 93–94; C 94–96; Dep Chapl HM YOI Glen Parva 96–01; Chapl HM Pris Styal 01–02; Chapl HM Pris Man 02–09; Chapl HM Pris Nottm 09–11; Chapl HM Pris Dartmoor from 11. *The Chaplaincy, HM Prison Dartmoor, Princetown, Yelverton PL20 6RR* T: (01822) 322000

COOPER, Marc Ashley Rex. b 62. Leeds Univ BA 85 MA 95. Linc Th Coll 92. **d** 92 **p** 93. C Bolton St Jas w St Chrys *Bradf* 92–96; P-in-c Fishtoft *Linc* 96–97; R from 97; RD Holland E 03–09. *The Rectory, Rectory Close, Fishtoft, Boston PE21 0RZ* T/F: (01205) 363216 E: rector@fishtoftchurch.org.uk

COOPER, Mrs Margaret Anne. b 54. SRN 76. STETS 11. **d** 14 **p** 15. NSM Guildf St Nic 14–18; PtO 18–19; *Ox* from 21. *Four Acres, Green End Road, Radnage, High Wycombe HP14 4BZ* E: anne.cooper9@btinternet.com

COOPER, Mark Gareth Ashley. b 89. St Jo Coll Dur BA 10. St Mellitus Coll BA 19. **d** 19 **p** 20. C Hinckley H Trin *Leic* from 19. *5 King Richard Road, Hinckley LE10 0HJ* M: 07896-706329 E: mark.cooper40@gmail.com

COOPER, Canon Michael Leonard. b 30. St Jo Coll Cam BA 53 MA 58. Cuddesdon Coll 53. **d** 55 **p** 56. C Croydon St Jo *Cant* 55–61; V Spring Park 61–71; V Boxley 71–82; RD Sutton 74–80; V Cranbrook 82–92; Hon Chapl to Bp Dover 93–97; Asst Chapl Kent and Cant Hosps NHS Trust 94–97; Hon Can Cant Cathl 76–97; PtO *Roch* 97–06; rtd 00. *West View, Wark, Hexham NE48 3LG*

COOPER, Canon Michael Sydney. b 41. Univ of Wales (Lamp) BA 63. Westcott Ho Cam 63. **d** 65 **p** 66. C Farlington *Portsm* 65–69; Pakistan 70–71; Mauritius 71–73; C-in-c Hayling St Pet CD *Portsm* 74–81; V Carisbrooke St Mary 81–92; V Carisbrooke St Nic 81–92; V Hartplain 92–98; V Portchester 98–06; RD Fareham 99–04; Hon Can Portsm Cathl 02–06; rtd 06; PtO *Portsm* from 06. *122 Paxton Road, Fareham PO14 1AE* T: (01329) 822152

COOPER, Nicholas John. Wycliffe Hall Ox. **d** 06 **p** 07. C Tenterden St Mildred w Smallhythe *Cant* 06–09; C Tenterden St Mich 07–09; P-in-c Saltwood 09–13; R Aldington w Bonnington and Bilsington etc 10–13; R Lympne and Saltwood 13–15; V Frindsbury w Upnor and Chattenden *Roch* from 15. *Frindsbury Vicarage, 4 Parsonage Lane, Rochester ME2 4UR* T: (01634) 717580 E: vicar@allsaintsfrindsbury.org.uk

COOPER, Canon Nigel Scott. b 53. Qu Coll Cam BA 75 MA 79 PGCE 76 CEnv FRSB FLS. Ripon Coll Cuddesdon BA 83 MA 88. **d** 83 **p** 84. C Moulsham St Jo *Chelmsf* 83–88; R Rivenhall 88–05; Chapl Anglia Ruskin Univ *Ely* from 05; Hon Can Ely Cathl from 13. *The Chaplaincy Office, Anglia Ruskin University, East Road, Cambridge CB1 1PT* T: (01223) 698398 E: nigel.cooper@anglia.ac.uk

COOPER, Canon Peter David. b 48. Sarum & Wells Th Coll 70. **d** 73 **p** 74. C Yateley *Win* 73–78; C Christchurch 78–81; P-in-c Southampton St Mark 81–83; V 83–98; P-in-c Tadley St Pet 98–02; R Tadley S and Silchester 02–13; rtd 13; PtO *Win* from 13; Hon Can Ife Nigeria from 00. *42 Tuckton Road, Bournemouth BH6 3HS* T: (01202) 986894 E: peter.clairecooper@gmail.com

COOPER, Canon Richard Thomas. b 46. Leeds Univ BA 69. Coll of Resurr Mirfield 69. **d** 71 **p** 72. C Rothwell *Ripon* 71–75; C Adel 75–78; C Knaresborough 78–81; P-in-c Croft 81–90; P-in-c Eryholme 81–90; P-in-c Middleton Tyas and Melsonby 81–90; RD Richmond 86–90; V Aldborough w Boroughbridge and Roecliffe 90–98; RD Ripon 93–96; R Richmond w Hudswell 98–05; R Richmond w Hudswell and Downholme and Marske 05–09; Hon Can Ripon Cathl 97–09; rtd 09; Chapl to The Queen 03–16; PtO *Leeds* from 17. *13 Ash Bank Road, Ripon HG4 2EQ* E: richard@hargill.plus.com

COOPER, The Ven Robert Gerard. b 68. Univ of Wales (Abth) BD 91. Linc Th Coll 93. **d** 93 **p** 94. C Whitkirk *Ripon* 93–96; C Leeds Richmond Hill 96–97; Chapl Agnes Stewart C of E High Sch Leeds 96–97; Chapl Chigwell Sch Essex 97–98; V Lightcliffe *Wakef* 98–05; V Pontefract St Giles 05–14; *Leeds* 14–18; RD Pontefract *Wakef* 06–14; AD *Leeds* 14–18; Hon Can Wakef Cathl 08–18; Adn Sunderland *Dur* from 18; Can Mara Tanzania from 17. *St Nicholas' Vicarage, Hedworth Lane, Boldon Colliery NE35 9JA* T: 0191-536 2300 M: 07384-510731 E: robert_cooper@msn.com *or* archdeacon.of.sunderland@durham.anglican.org

COOPER, Robert James. b 52. Bris Univ BA 75. Ridley Hall Cam 76. **d** 78 **p** 79. C Street w Walton *B & W* 78–82; C Batheaston w St Cath 82–86; P-in-c Sadberge *Dur* 86–03; Asst Chapl Arts and Recreation 86–05; Chapl 05–08; Lic to AD Stockton 08–18; Chapl N Tees and Hartlepool NHS Foundn Trust 14–18; rtd 18; PtO *Dur* from 20. *12 Hutton Close, Fishburn, Stockton-on-Tees TS21 4HE* T: (01740) 622788 E: cooperphoto@btinternet.com

COOPER, Canon Roger Charles. b 48. GRSM ARMCM 69 PGCE 70. Coll of Resurr Mirfield 79. **d** 81 **p** 82. C Monkseaton St Mary *Newc* 81–83; C Morpeth 83–87; Min Can and Prec Man Cathl 87–90; V Blackrod 90–15; AD Deane 05–12; C Horwich and Rivington 11–15; Hon Can Man Cathl 11–15; rtd 15; PtO *Man* from 15. *62 Belmont Road, Adlington, Chorley PR6 9PU* T: (01257) 434373 E: revrog17@gmail.com

COOPER, Sarah Fiona Louise. b 69. Coll of SS Mark and Jo Plymouth BEd 92. Qu Foundn Birm 15. **d** 17 **p** 18. C Perry Barr *Birm* 17–20. *Address temp unknown*

COOPER, Canon Seth William. b 62. Westcott Ho Cam 94. **d** 96 **p** 97. C Golders Green *Lon* 96–00; TV Uxbridge 00–05; V Walmer *Cant* 05–18; R Walmer and Cornilo from 18; AD Sandwich 10–19; Hon Can Cant Cathl from 17. *Elizabeth House, 32 St Mary's Road, Walmer, Deal CT14 7QA* T: (01304) 366605 E: sethandjen@tinyworld.co.uk *or* vicar@walmerparishchurches.org

COOPER, Stephen. b 54. Bernard Gilpin Soc Dur 73 Chich Th Coll 74. **d** 77 **p** 78. C Horbury *Wakef* 77–78; C Horbury w Horbury Bridge 78–81; C Barnsley St Mary 81–84; TV Elland 84–91; Hon C Huddersfield St Thos 93–94; P-in-c Middlesbrough St Columba w St Paul *York* 94–08; V from 09; P-in-c Middlesbrough St Jo the Ev 05–08; V from 09; Chapl S Tees Hosps NHS Foundn Trust 94–05. *St Columba's Vicarage, 115 Cambridge Road, Middlesbrough TS5 5HF* T: (01642) 824779 E: fr_s_cooper@hotmail.com

COOPER, Stephen Paul Crossley. b 58. Trin Coll Bris 91. d 93 p 94. C Blackb Redeemer 93–95; C Altham w Clayton le Moors 95–98; V Langho Billington 98–03; Chapl Rossall Sch Fleetwood 03–09; TV Fellside Team *Blackb* 09–15; TR from 15. *The Vicarage, Goosnargh Lane, Goosnargh, Preston PR3 2BN* T: (01722) 865274 E: office.fellside@gmil.com

COOPER, Mrs Susan Elizabeth Courtenay. b 50. Open Univ BA 94 LLAM 70. d 10 p 12. NZ 01–13; NSM Rotherfield Peppard and Kidmore End etc *Ox* 14–16; P-in-c Purleigh *Chelmsf* 16–18; rtd 18; Hon C W Rotorua NZ from 18. *43/15 Hodgkins Street, Pukehangi, Rotorua 3015, New Zealand* E: revdsusancooper@gmail.com

COOPER, Mrs Susan Mary. b 45. Westcott Ho Cam 01. d 03 p 04. C Syston *Leic* 03–06; R Chipping Ongar w Shelley *Chelmsf* 06–14; rtd 14; PtO *Leic* 14–16; NSM Market Harborough and The Transfiguration etc from 16. *89 Scotland Road, Market Harborough LE16 8AY* E: scoople@btinternet.com

COOPER, Susan Mira. *See* RAMSARAN, Susan Mira

COOPER, Mrs Suzanne Tracey. b 62. Ripon Coll Cuddesdon 13. d 15 p 16. C Blisworth, Alderton, Grafton Regis etc *Pet* 15–19; R Aynho and Croughton w Evenley etc from 19. *The Rectory, Croughton Road, Aynho, Banbury OX17 3BD* T: (01869) 810903 E: revsue.cooper@gmail.com

COOPER, Thomas Joseph Gerard Strickland. b 46. Lanc Univ PhD 85. Ven English Coll & Pontifical Gregorian Univ Rome PhB 66 PhL 67 STB 69 STL 71. d 70 p 70. In RC Ch 70–92; Chapl St Woolos Cathl *Mon* 93–95; V Llandaff N *Llan* 95–08; rtd 08; PtO *St D* from 08. *Arwel, Cwmdegwel, St Dogmaels, Cardigan SA43 3JH* T: (01239) 614156 E: woolos@gmail.com

COOPER, Ms Wendy. b 58. d 12 p 14. NSM Salisbury St Thos and St Edm *Sarum* 12–15; PtO from 16. *Parish Office, St Thomas's House, St Thomas's Square, Salisbury SP1 1BA* E: mukinge.minstead@yahoo.co.uk

COOPER, William Douglas. b 42. Open Univ BA 83 BSc 11 St Andr Univ MA 09. St Jo Coll Nottm 88 Qu Coll Birm 93. d 94 p 95. NSM Melbourne *Derby* 94–97; C Penwortham St Mary *Blackb* 97–00; P-in-c Smeeth w Monks Horton and Stowting and Brabourne *Cant* 00–04; rtd 04. *18A Market Street, St Andrews KY16 9NS* T: (01334) 460678

COORE, Jonathan. b 71. LTCL 93 GTCL 94 Lon Inst of Educn PGCE 97. Trin Coll Bris 05. d 07 p 08. C Heref St Pet w St Owen and St Jas 07–12; Bp's Dom Chapl 08–12; Min Can and Succ St Paul's Cathl *Lon* 12–14; R S'wark Ch Ch 14–19; PV Westmr Abbey 16–19; Hon Min Can S'wark Cathl 14–19; Min Can and Succ Windsor from 19; Chapl St Geo Sch Windsor from 19. *16 Horseshoe Cloisters, Windsor Castle, Windsor SL4 1NJ* T: (01753) 865553 M: 07786-431451 E: jonathancoore@gmail.com

COOTE, Bernard Albert Ernest. b 28. Lon Univ BD 53. Chich Th Coll 54. d 55 p 56. C Addiscombe St Mary *Cant* 55–57; C Hawkhurst 57–59; C Sanderstead All SS *S'wark* 59–63; Chapl HM Borstal E Sutton Park 63–74; V Sutton Valence w E Sutton *Cant* 63–76; P-in-c Chart next Sutton Valence 71–76; P-in-c Sutton Valence w E Sutton and Chart Sutton 76; Chapl and Dir R Sch for the Blind Leatherhead 76–91; rtd 91; PtO *Chich* from 91; *Guildf* 91–05. *25 Raphael Road, Hove BN3 5QP* T: (01273) 640732

COPE, Elizabeth Ruth. b 80. Ch Coll Cam BA 04 MSci 04 MA 07 PhD 10. Ridley Hall Cam 14. d 16 p 17. C Lordsbridge *Ely* 16–18; C Long Stanton w St Mich 18–19; C Swavesey 18–19; C Willingham 18–19; C Over 18–19; Pioneer Min from 19. *6 Woodpecker Close, Northstowe, Cambridge CB24 1AW* T: (01954) 261181 E: beth.cope@northstowe.church

COPE, James Brian Andrew. b 58. Chich Th Coll 80. d 83 p 84. C Poulton-le-Fylde *Blackb* 83–86; C Fleetwood St Pet 86–87; V Fleetwood St Dav 87–94; P-in-c Somercotes *Derby* 94–99; V Watford St Jo *St Alb* 99–07; V Castle Vale w Minworth *Birm* from 07. *St Cuthbert's Vicarage, St Cuthbert's Place, Birmingham B35 7PL* T: 0121-747 4041 E: fr.jamescopessc@outlook.com

COPE, Judith Diane. b 50. St Hilda's Coll Ox BA 72 Lon Univ MB, BS 75 MRCGP 80. SAOMC 00. d 03 p 04. NSM Lt Berkhamsted and Bayford, Essendon etc *St Alb* 03–13; rtd 13; PtO *St Alb* 13–18. *23 Gresley Court, Hawkshead Road, Potters Bar EN6 1LF* T: (01707) 644391 E: m_cope@btinternet.com

COPE, Canon Melia Lambrianos. b 53. Cape Town Univ BSocSc 73. St Jo Coll Nottm 80 WMMTC 83. dss 86 d 93 p 94. W Bromwich All SS *Lich* 86–93; NSM 93–94; NSM W Bromwich St Mary Magd CD 93–94; TV Cen Telford 94–02; Chapl HM Pris Shrewsbury 95–98; P-in-c Stokesay *Heref* 02–12; P-in-c Halford w Sibdon Carwood 02–12; P-in-c Acton Scott 02–12; P-in-c Wistanstow 06–12; V E Radnor *S & B* 12–18; V Beacon Hill 16–18; Can Res Brecon

Cathl 17–18; rtd 18; PtO *Heref* from 20. *37 Beech Close, Ludlow SY8 2PD* T: (01584) 873467 E: revdmeliacope@gmail.com

COPE, Miss Olive Rosemary. b 29. MBE 17. Gilmore Ho 63. dss 69 d 87 p 94. Kentish Town St Martin w St Andr *Lon* 69–72; Enfield St Andr 73–99; Par Dn 87–89; Hon Par Dn 89–94; Hon C W 94–99; PtO 99–18. *7 Calder Close, Enfield EN1 3TS* T: (020) 8363 8221 E: oliveclose2003@yahoo.co.uk

COPE, Mrs Patricia Millicent. b 51. Man Univ BEd 73 MEd 88. SNWTP 10. d 12 p 13. NSM Knutsford St Cross *Ches* 12–15; NSM Rostherne w Bollington from 15; NSM High Legh from 15; NSM Over Tabley from 15; rtd 22. *23 North Drive, High Legh, Knutsford WA16 6LX* T: (01925) 754787 M: 07703-470101 E: trishcope2012@btinternet.com

COPE, Peter John. b 42. Mert Coll Ox BA 64 MA 67 Lon Univ MSc 74 Man Univ PhD 91. Cuddesdon Coll 64. d 66 p 67. C Chapel Allerton *Ripon* 66–69; Ind Chapl *Lon* 69–76; Ind Chapl *Worc* 76–85; Min Can Worc Cathl 76–85; P-in-c Worc St Mark 76–81; Ind Chapl W Bromwich and Min W Bromwich St Mary Magd CD *Lich* 85–94; Telford Town Cen Chapl 94–07; W Midl FE Field Officer 94–97; Churches Ind Officer 97–07; rtd 07; PtO *Heref* 96–05, from 12; *S & B* from 12. *37 Beech Close, Ludlow SY8 2PD* T: (01584) 873467 E: peter.cope123@btinternet.com

COPE, Canon Stephen Victor. b 60. St Jo Coll Ox BA 81 MA 87. Chich Th Coll 86. d 89 p 90. C Newmarket St Mary w Exning St Agnes *St E* 89–92; C Northampton St Matt *Pet* 92–94; V Rudston w Boynton and Kilham *York* 94–98; V Rudston w Boynton, Carnaby and Kilham 98–06; P-in-c Burton Fleming w Fordon, Grindale etc 00–06; RD Bridlington 98–03; P-in-c Owthorne and Rimswell w Withernsea 06–07; P-in-c Easington w Skeffling, Kilnsea and Holmpton 06–07; R Withernsea w Owthorne and Easington etc 07–14; P-in-c Roos and Garton w Tunstall, Grimston and Hilston 12–14; V Withernsea w Owthorne, Garton-in-Holderness etc 14; RD S Holderness 09–14; R Holme and Seaton Ross Gp from 14; Can and Preb York Minster from 10. *The Vicarage, Market Weighton Road, Holme-on-Spalding-Moor, York YO43 4AG* T: (01964) 611462 E: stephenvcope@tiscali.co.uk

COPELAND, Annabel Susan Mary. b 64. Roehampton Inst BEd 87. Wycliffe Hall Ox 03. d 05 p 06. C Billericay and Lt Burstead *Chelmsf* 05–08; TV St Baddow 08–14; P-in-c Tidworth *Sarum* 14–17; Chapl Wellington Academy 14–17; Chapl Bluecoat Sch Nottm 17–18; Pioneer Min *Lon* 18–20; C Oundle w Ashton and Benefield w Glapthorn *Pet* from 20. *41 Hillfield Road, Oundle, Peterborough PE8 4QR* T: (01832) 358079 E: copeland321@btinternet.com

COPELAND, Christopher Paul. b 38. AKC 64. d 65 p 66. C Luton St Andr *St Alb* 65–67; C Droitwich St Nic w St Pet *Worc* 67–71; C Kings Norton *Birm* 71–72; TV 73–78; V Tyseley 78–88; P-in-c Grimley w Holt *Worc* 88–96; Dioc Stewardship Missr 88–96; P-in-c Forest of Dean Ch Ch w English Bicknor *Glouc* 96–03; rtd 03; PtO *Worc* from 03. *6 Capel Court, The Burgage, Prestbury, Cheltenham GL52 3EL* T: (01242) 471088 E: chriscopeland@mypostoffice.com

COPESTAKE, Mrs Sharon Louise. b 70. Cov Univ BA 94 Cant Ch Ch Univ BA 12. SEITE 09. d 12 p 13. C Chatham St Phil and St Jas *Roch* 12–15; V Strood St Fran from 15; RD Strood from 17. *The Vicarage, Galahad Avenue, Rochester ME2 2YS* T: (01634) 717162 E: vicar.stfrancisstrood@gmail.com

COPLEY, Paul. b 58. NEOC 97. d 99 p 00. C Hessle *York* 99–02; TV Sutton St Jas and Wawne 02–07; P-in-c Kingston upon Hull St Nic 07–14; V from 14; P-in-c Newington w Dairycoates 07–10. *St Nicholas' Vicarage, 898 Hessle High Road, Hull HU4 6SA* T: (01482) 504088 E: copleypaul@hotmail.com

COPLEY, Ross Stephen. b 88. Derby Univ BA 09. St Steph Ho Ox BA 20. d 20 p 21. C Linc All SS from 20. *3 Middleton Fields, Lincoln LN2 1QP* M: 07517-494434 E: curate@allsaints-monkskool.com

COPPEN, Colin William. b 53. BCombStuds 85. Linc Th Coll. d 85 p 86. C Tokyngton St Mich *Lon* 85–88; C Somers Town 88–90; P-in-c Edmonton St Alpheage 90–92; V 92–95; P-in-c W Hampstead St Jas 95–97; P-in-c Kilburn St Mary w All So 95–97; TR Wood Green St Mich w Bounds Green St Gabr etc 97–16; C Munster Square Ch Ch and St Mary Magd 16–18; rtd 18; PtO *Birm* from 19. *20 Wood Street, Tipton DY4 9BQ*

COPPEN, George. *See* COPPEN, Robert George

COPPEN, Canon Martin Alan. b 48. Ex Univ BA 69. St Jo Coll Nottm 83. d 85 p 86. C Bitterne *Win* 85–88; V St Mary Bourne and Woodcott 88–99; V Hurstbourne Priors, Longparish etc 00–13; RD Whitchurch 98–03; Hon Can Win Cathl 04–13; rtd 13; PtO *Win* from 14. *5 Acre Path, Andover SP10 1HJ*

COPPEN, Robert George. b 39. Cape Town Univ BA 66. Cranmer Hall Dur 79. **d** 81 **p** 82. C Douglas St Geo and St Barn *S & M* 81–84; TV Kidlington w Hampton Poyle *Ox* 84–05; Chapl HM Detention Cen Campsfield Ho 84–91; Chapl Campsfield Ho Immigration and Detention Cen 94; rtd 05; LtO *Mor* from 05. *Taobh Mol, Kildary, Invergordon IV18 0NJ* T: (01862) 842381 E: coppen@dunelm.org.uk

COPPING, Canon Adrian Walter Alexander. b 52. Ridley Hall Cam. **d** 00 **p** 01. C Royston *St Alb* 00–04; R Bangor Monachorum, Worthenbury and Marchwiel *St As* 04–09; AD Bangor Isycoed 05–09; R Cilcain, Gwernaffield, Llanferres etc 09–16; AD Mold 11–16; Can St As Cathl 14–16; rtd 16; PtO *St E* from 17. *57 Briar Hill, Woolpit, Bury St Edmunds IP30 9SD* E: adriancopping@hotmail.com

COPPING, Mary Catriona. b 50. STETS. **d** 12 **p** 13. NSM Win St Matt 12–20; PtO from 20. *2 Churchill Close, King's Worthy, Winchester SO23 7PD* T: (01962) 881342   E: marycopping@btinternet.com *or* youth@stmatthewstpaul.org

COPSEY, Canon Christine. b 51. Nottm Univ CertEd 73. ERMC 04. **d** 07 **p** 08. NSM Fakenham w Alethorpe *Nor* 07–08; NSM King's Lynn St Marg w St Nic 08–11; Chapl Ind Miss 11–20; Chapl Support Co-ord from 13; Dioc Co-ord Soc, Environmental and Community Concerns from 16; Hon Can Nor Cathl from 17; PtO from 21. *5 Back Lane, Castle Acre, King's Lynn PE32 2AR* T: (01760) 755558 E: chriscopsey@btinternet.com

COPSEY, Nigel John. b 52. K Coll Lon BD 75 AKC 75 Surrey Univ MSc 88 Middx Univ DProf 01. St Aug Coll Cant 72. **d** 76 **p** 77. C Barkingside St Fran *Chelmsf* 76–78; C Canning Town St Cedd 78–80; P-in-c Victoria Docks Ascension 80–87; Chapl E Surrey Mental Health Unit 87–90; Hd Past and Spiritual Care E Surrey Priority Care NHS Trust from 90; Co-ord Past Care Surrey Oaklands NHS Trust 99–05; Hd Past and Spiritual Care Surrey and Borders Partnership NHS Foundn Trust from 08; Co-ord Relig Care Newham Community Health Services NHS Trust 99–01; Co-ord Relig Care Newham Primary Care Trust from 01; Team Ldr Spiritual, Relig & Cultural Care E Lon NHS Foundation Trust from 08. *Newham Centre for Mental Health, Glen Road, London E13 8SP* T: (020) 7540 4380 F: 7540 2970 E: nigel.copsey@eastlondon.nhs.uk

COPUS, Brian George. b 36. AKC 59. **d** 60 **p** 61. C Croydon St Mich *Cant* 60–63; C Swindon New Town *Bris* 63–69; V Colebrooke *Ex* 69–73; P-in-c Hittisleigh 69–73; R Perivale *Lon* 73–82; V Ruislip St Mary 82–01; rtd 01; PtO *Win* 02–11. *Le Bec, 84 Carbery Avenue, Bournemouth BH6 3LQ* T: (01202) 428943

COPUS, John Cecil. b 38. TCert 64 Maria Grey Coll Lon DipEd 71 Open Univ BA 78. Cant Sch of Min. **d** 83 **p** 84. Hon C Folkestone H Trin and St Geo w Ch Ch *Cant* 83–85; C Midsomer Norton w Clandown *B & W* 85–91; Dioc Adv for Children's Work *Ex* 91–98; Hon C Aylesbeare, Rockbeare, Farringdon etc 95–98; P-in-c 98–01; rtd 01; PtO *Ex* 01–17; Clergy Widow(er)s Officer 02–13; C N Creedy 08–10. *6 Gracey Court, Woodland Road, Broadclyst, Exeter EX5 3GA* T: (01392) 460238

COPUS, Jonathan Hugh Lambert. b 44. BNC Ox BA 66 MA 71 LGSM 66 MInstPI 94. S'wark Ord Course 68. **d** 71 **p** 72. C Horsell *Guildf* 71–73; Producer Relig Progr BBC Radio Solent 73–87; V Maenclochog and New Moat etc *St D* 06–07; V Martletwy w Lawrenny and Minwear etc 07; PtO 07–11; rtd 10; P-in-c Crymych Gp *St D* 11–19. *Llys Myrddin, Efailwen, Clynderwen SA66 7XG* T: (01994) 438414 M: 07828-510283 E: revjc@dentron.co.uk

CORBETT, The Very Revd Ian Deighton. b 42. St Cath Coll Cam BA 64 MA 67 Salford Univ MSc 83 Cam Univ PGCE 65. Westcott Ho Cam 67. **d** 69 **p** 70. C New Bury *Man* 69–72; C Bolton St Pet 72–75; Chapl Bolton Colls of H&FE 72–75; R Man Victoria Park 75–80; Chapl Salford Univ 80–83; Dioc FE Officer 74–83; R Salford Sacred Trin 83–87; Dir CME and Hon Can Man Cathl 83–87; Warden Lelapa la Jesu Sem Lesotho 88–91; Can Missr Harare Zimbabwe 92–93; Can Missr Botswana 93–95; R Kuruman St Mary S Africa 95–97; Dean Tuam *T, K & A* 97–99; I Tuam w Cong and Aasleagh 97–99; R Whitesands Canada 99–01; V Utah Region USA 01–08; Hon C E Clevedon w Clapton in Gordano etc *B & W* 09–13; PtO *Worc* from 13. *6 The Quadrangle, Newland, Malvern WR13 5AX* T: (01684) 574091 E: iancorbett123@btinternet.com

CORBETT, Jocelyn Rory. **d** 05 **p** 06. Aux Min Aghalee *D & D* 05–06; NSM Donaghcloney w Waringstown 06–13; NSM Seapatrick from 13. *Badger Hill, 23 Magherabeg Road, Dromore BT25 1RS* T: (028) 9269 2067 *or* 4062 2744 E: rory.corbett23@gmail.com *or* office@seapatrickparish.com

CORBETT, Philip Peter. b 81. St Andr Univ MTheol 03 Yale Univ STM 04 Keble Coll Ox MPhil 06. Coll of Resurr Mirfield 06. **d** 08 **p** 09. C Worksop Priory *S'well* 08–11; P Lib and Chapl Pusey Ho 11–13; P-in-c Lewisham St Steph and St Mark *S'wark* 13–16; V 16–19; P-in-c Notting Hill All SS w St Columb *Lon* 19–21; V from 21; P-in-c Notting Hill St Mich and Ch Ch from 19. *All Saints' Vicarage, Clydesdale Road, London W11 1JE* M: 07929-750054 E: philippetercorbett@gmail.com

CORBETT, Rory. *See* CORBETT, Jocelyn Rory

CORBYN, Canon John. b 58. Man Univ BA 79 Ven English Coll & Pontifical Gregorian Univ Rome 83. Wycliffe Hall Ox BA 83 MA 87. **d** 84 **p** 85. C Deane *Man* 84–87; C Lancaster St Mary *Blackb* 87–90; Sub-Chapl HM Pris Lanc 89–90; V Blackb St Gabr 90–01; V Bearsted w Thurnham *Cant* 01–16; TR N Downs from 16; AD from 18; Hon Can Cant Cathl from 16. *The Vicarage, Church Lane, Bearsted, Maidstone ME14 4EF* T: (01622) 737135 E: vicar@holycrosschurch.co.uk

CORCORAN, Daniel Chad. b 71. Man Metrop Univ BA 93. St Jo Coll Nottm 04. **d** 06 **p** 07. C Stapleford *S'well* 06–10; C Bilborough and Strelley 10–17; C Broxtowe 14–17; PtO *Cant* 17–19; C Faversham from 19. *22 Priory Road, Faversham ME13 7EJ* M: 07963-332221 E: danchad@gmail.com

CORCORAN, Jennifer Miriam. b 78. Lanc Univ BA 01. St Jo Coll Nottm MA(MM) 07. **d** 07 **p** 08. C Chilwell *S'well* 07–10; NSM Chilwell and Lenton Abbey 10–13; Tutor St Jo Coll Nottm 13–17; Chapl to Bp Dover *Cant* from 17; Abp's Chapl from 17. *The Bishop of Dover's Office, The Old Palace, The Precincts, Canterbury CT1 2EE* T: (01227) 459382 E: jenny.corcoran@bishcant.org

CORCORAN, Michael Patrick. b 65. Man Univ BSocSc 86. St Jo Coll Nottm MTh 17. **d** 14 **p** 15. C Brunswick *Man* 14–17; Chapl Man Univ NHS Foundn Trust 17–21; C Withington St Paul *Man* 19–21; Chapl Kettering Gen Hosp NHS Foundn Trust from 21. *Chaplains' Office, Kettering General Hospital NHS Trust, Rothwell Road, Kettering NN16 8UZ* T: (01536) 492000 M: 07825-153455 E: corkie@sky.com

CORCORAN, Mrs Valerie A'Court. b 46. UEA BA 68 Lon Inst of Educn PGCE 69. STETS 99. **d** 02 **p** 03. NSM Boyatt Wood *Win* 02–10; rtd 10; PtO *Win* from 13. *Ashley, Finches Lane, Twyford, Winchester SO21 1QB* T: (01962) 712951 F: 715770 M: 07736-459500 E: v.corcoran@btinternet.com

CORDELL, Derek Harold. b 34. Chich Th Coll 57. **d** 60 **p** 61. C Whitstable All SS *Cant* 60–63; C Moulsecoomb *Chich* 63–69; Chapl Bucharest *Eur* 69–71; V Brighton St Wilfrid *Chich* 71–74; Chapl HM Borstal Roch 74–80; Asst Chapl HM Pris Man 80–81; Chapl HM Pris The Verne 81–89; Chapl HM Pris Channings Wood 89–90; Chapl Milan w Genoa and Varese *Eur* 90–91; Chapl Mojácar 91–94; PtO 95–14; rtd 97; PtO *B & W* 15–20. *27 Scalwell Mead, Seaton EX12 2DW* T: (01297) 624182

CORFE, David Robert. b 35. Pemb Coll Cam BA 58 MA 60 Lambeth STh 70. Cuddesdon Coll 58. **d** 60 **p** 61. C Wigan All SS *Liv* 60–63; SPG Miss India 63–68; V Lucknow Ch Ch w All SS and St Pet 70–75; C Northwood Em *Lon* 75; V Westwell and Eastwell w Boughton Aluph *Cant* 75–80; V Hildenborough *Roch* 80–91; Lic Preacher Stretford St Bride *Man* 91–98; Interserve 98–00; rtd 00; PtO *Win* 03–21; *Birm* 18–20. *1 Hartley Court, 12 Winn Road, Southampton SO17 1EN* T: (023) 8058 5557 E: davidrobertcorfe@gmail.com

CORIO, Alec Stephen. b 82. Qu Coll Cam BA 05 MA 09 MPhil 07 Open Univ PhD 14. Westcott Ho Cam 13. **d** 16 **p** 17. C Stockport St Geo *Ches* 16–19; R E Barnet *St Alb* from 19. *1 Spring Close, Barnet EN5 2UR* T: (020) 8440 3231 E: rector.stmaryeastbarnet@gmail.com

CORK, CLOYNE AND ROSS, Archdeacon of. *See* WILKINSON, The Ven Adrian Mark

CORK, CLOYNE AND ROSS, Bishop of. *See* COLTON, The Rt Revd William Paul

CORK, Dean of. *See* DUNNE, The Very Revd Nigel Kenneth

CORKE, Andrew John. b 55. Bris Univ LLB 77. **d** 98 **p** 99. NSM Canford Magna *Sarum* 98–10; TV Swanage and Studland 10–20; rtd 20; PtO *Sarum* from 21. *2 Silverwood Close, Wimborne BH21 1QZ* T: (01202) 840815 M: 07711-898723 E: andrewjcorke@gmail.com

CORKE, Colin John. b 59. St Pet Coll Ox BA 81. Cranmer Hall Dur 83. **d** 85 **p** 86. C Chapel Allerton *Ripon* 85–88; C Burmantofts St Steph and St Agnes 88–91; P-in-c Tatsfield *S'wark* 91–01; Reigate Adnry Ecum Officer 92–01; V Longbridge *Birm* from 01; Dioc Ecum Officer 02–05; AD Kings Norton 06–12; Ind Chapl from 08. *St John's Vicarage, 220 Longbridge Lane, Birmingham B31 4JT* T: 0121-475 3484 E: colincorke@gmail.com

CORKE, Canon Louise Dorothy. b 59. Southn Univ BSc 80 PGCE 81. Trin Coll Bris BA 94. **d** 97 **p** 98. C Ipsley *Worc* 97–01; TV Bradgate Team *Leic* 01–15; C Groby and Ratby 15–17; TV Kegworth, Hathern, Long Whatton, Diseworth etc from 17; Bp's NSM Officer from 13; Hon Can Leic Cathl from 18. *The Vicarage, Presents Lane, Belton, Loughborough LE12 9UN* T: (01530) 588868

CORKE, Roderick Geoffrey. b 58. UEA BEd 79 Open Univ MA 96. St Jo Coll Nottm 90. **d** 92 **p** 93. C Trimley *St E* 92–95; C Walton 95–00; TR Walton and Trimley 00–05; P-in-c Taunton St Mary *B & W* 05–08; V 08–14; V Taunton St Mary and St Jo 14–18; V Gt Malvern St Mary *Worc* from 18. *Priory Vicarage, 7 Clarence Road, Malvern WR14 3EN* E: vicar@greatmalvernpriory.org.uk

CORKER, Mrs Elizabeth Jane. b 42. **d** 99 **p** 00. OLM Martlesham w Brightwell *St E* 99–10; OLM Felixstowe St Jo 10–12; rtd 12. *12 Fairfield Avenue, Felixstowe IP11 9JN* T: (01394) 210793 E: e.corker@ntlworld.com

CORKER, John Anthony. b 37. TD 93. AKC 63 ACIB 75. K Coll Lon 1960 St Boniface Warminster 63. **d** 64 **p** 65. C Lindley *Wakef* 64–68; V Brotherton 68–72; PtO 72–82; CF (TA) 80–93; Hon C Askham Bryan *York* 82–91; TV York All SS Pavement w St Crux and St Martin etc 91–96; Chapl York Health Services NHS Trust 91–96; Chapl Dudley Gp of Hosps NHS Trust 96–99; Asst P Amblecote *Worc* 96–01; Asst P Dudley St Barn 01–02; rtd 02; PtO *Worc* from 02. *15 Holly Grove, Stourbridge DY8 1UF* T: (01384) 897378 E: the.corkers@talktalk.net

CORLETT, Daniel James. b 77. Birm Univ MEng 00. Wycliffe Hall Ox 17. **d** 19 **p** 20. C Arden Marches *Cov* from 19. *6 Lansdowne Road, Studley B80 7RB* M: 07543-370637 E: curate@ardenmarches.co.uk

CORLEY, Claire Marie. b 76. St Mary's Coll Dur BA 98. St Hild Coll 14. **d** 17 **p** 18. C Roundhay St Edm *Leeds* 17–20; P-in-c Wortley and Farnley from 20. *2A Ryder Gardens, Leeds LS8 1JS* T: 0113-268 0260 M: 07811-151027

✠**CORLEY, The Rt Revd Samuel Jon Clint.** b 76. St Aid Coll Dur BA 97 MA 98 Hughes Hall Cam PGCE 99. St Jo Coll Nottm MA 04. **d** 04 **p** 05 **c** 21. C Lancaster St Thos *Blackb* 04–08; Asst Dioc Missr 08–11; P-in-c Ellel w Shireshead 08–11; Can Res Bradf Cathl *Leeds* 11–15; Chapl Bradf Univ 11–15; P-in-c Leeds City 15–17; R 17–21; Hon Can Ripon Cathl 15–21; Suff Bp Stockport *Ches* from 21. *Bishop's Lodge, Back Lane, Dunham Town, Altrincham WA14 4SG* M: 07878-371897 E: bpstockport@chester.anglican.org

CORMACK, Donald Stuart. b 45. Brock Univ Ontario TCert 67 McMaster Univ Ontario BA 71. Regent Coll Vancouver MTh 85. **d** 92 **p** 93. C St Geo Singapore 92–93; P-in-c Phnom Penh Cambodia 93–96; PtO *Glouc* 06–15; *Chich* from 15. *Address withheld by request* E: doncormack@aol.com

CORNE, Ronald Andrew. b 51. Sarum & Wells Th Coll 87. **d** 89 **p** 90. C Bitterne Park *Win* 89–93; R Headbourne Worthy and King's Worthy 93–01; P-in-c Broughton, Bossington, Houghton and Mottisfont 01–03; R 03–17; RD Romsey 06–13; rtd 17; PtO *Win* from 17; Clergy Retirement Officer 18–20; PtO *Eur* 17–20; Chapl Puerto de la Cruz Tenerife from 20. *Sociedad de la Iglesia Anglicana, Calle Parque Taora, 38400 Puerto de la Cruz, Santa Cruz de Tenerife, Canary Islands, Spain* T: (0034) 922 384 038 E: cronandrew@aol.com

CORNELL, Nicholas Simon. b 78. Trin Hall Cam BA 00 MA 03. Oak Hill Th Coll MTh 08. **d** 08 **p** 09. C Eastbourne All SS *Chich* 08–12; R Maresfield 12–18; V Nutley 12–18; C Southborough St Pet w Ch Ch and St Matt etc *Roch* 18–19; R Southborough Ch Ch from 19. *The Rectory, 86 Prospect Road, Southborough, Tunbridge Wells TN4 0EG* T: (01825) 769004 M: 07946-220638 E: nscornell@gmail.com *or* revnickcornell@gmail.com

CORNES, Alan Stuart. b 70. Open Univ BA 98. St Jo Coll Nottm MA 00. **d** 01 **p** 02. C Meole Brace *Lich* 01–04; P-in-c Halliwell St Luke *Man* 04–11; P-in-c Halliwell 06–11; TR W Bolton 11–15; Salford Miss Support P 15–18; V Disley *Ches* from 18. *Disley Vicarage, 1A Red Lane, Disley, Stockport SK12 2NP* T: (01663) 635273 E: ascornes@yahoo.co.uk

CORNES, Canon Andrew Charles Julian. b 49. CCC Ox BA 70 MA 74. Wycliffe Hall Ox 70 Cranmer Hall Dur 72. **d** 73 **p** 74. C York St Mich-le-Belfrey 73–76; C St Marylebone All So w SS Pet and Jo *Lon* 76–85; R Pittsburgh Ascension USA 85–88; V Crowborough *Chich* 89–15; RD Rotherfield 97–03; Can and Preb Chich Cathl 00–15; Chapl Eastbourne and Co Healthcare NHS Trust 89–02; Chapl Sussex Downs and Weald Primary Care Trust 02–15; rtd 15; PtO *Chich* 15–17. *20 Gorringe Road, Eastbourne BN22 8XL* T: (01323) 732561

CORNESS, Andrew Stuart. b 69. Bp Otter Coll Chich BA 91 Westmr Coll Ox PGCE 93. Wycliffe Hall Ox BA 00 MA 05. **d** 01 **p** 02. C Ewood *Blackb* 01–04; Chapl RN from 04. *Royal Naval Chaplaincy Service Headquarters, Tanner Building, HMS Excellent, Whale Island, Portsmouth PO2 8ER* T: 0300-157 7544 E: andrewcorness@hotmail.com

CORNFIELD, Richard James. b 67. St Jo Coll Nottm BA 96. **d** 96 **p** 97. C Cheltenham Ch Ch *Glouc* 96–00; C Aldridge *Lich* 00–03; R 03–11; C Edin St Paul and St Geo 11–17; Dioc Dir of Ords 12–19; Pioneer P Mustard Seed Edinburgh from 17; P-in-c Edin St Marg from 21. *24 North Fort Street, Edinburgh EH6 4HD* M: 07966-165043 E: rich.cornfield@gmail.com

CORNISH, Gillian Lesley. b 45. ACIB 77. **d** 96 **p** 97. OLM Moston St Mary *Man* 96–08; OLM Blackley St Pet 08–10; rtd 10; PtO *Man* from 10. *11 Rishworth Drive, New Moston, Manchester M40 3PS* T: 0161-681 2839 E: revd.gillian@talktalk.net

CORNISH, Graham Peter. b 42. Dur Univ BA 67 FLA. NEOC 82. **d** 84 **p** 85. NSM Harrogate St Wilfrid and St Luke *Ripon* 84–96; PtO *York* 84–96; NSM Bilton *Ripon* 96–09; rtd 09; PtO *Leeds* from 17. *5 Hill Top Drive, Harrogate HG1 3BU* T: (01423) 431186

CORNISH, Ivor. b 40. Reading Univ BSc 61 DipEd 62. Ox Min Course 86. **d** 89 **p** 90. NSM Aston Clinton w Buckland and Drayton Beauchamp *Ox* 89–97; NSM The Lee and Hawridge w Cholesbury and St Leonard 97–10; PtO from 10; *St Alb* from 11. *79 Weston Road, Aston Clinton, Aylesbury HP22 5EP* T: (01296) 630345 E: rev.ivor@btinternet.com

CORNISH, Peter Andrew. b 55. Ch Ch Ox BA 77 MA 80 Ex Univ CertEd 78. St Jo Coll Nottm 84. **d** 87 **p** 88. C Sanderstead All SS *S'wark* 87–92; TV Cen Telford *Lich* 92–98; R Sturry w Fordwich and Westbere w Hersden *Cant* 98–21; Jt AD Cant 11–14; rtd 21. *42 Folks Wood Way, Lympne, Hythe CT21 4EW* E: peter.a.cornish@gmail.com

CORNISH, Mrs Rachel. b 54. **d** 14 **p** 15. NSM Felixstowe St Jo *St E* 14–15; NSM Combs and Lt Finborough 15–17; NSM Gt Finborough w Onehouse, Harleston, Buxhall etc 15–17; P-in-c Alde River 17–18; R from 18. *The Rectory, Great Glemham Road, Stratford St Andrew, Saxmundham IP17 1LJ* T: (01728) 768136 E: rev.rachelcornish@gmail.com

CORNWALL, Valerie Cecilia. *See* SAUNDERS, Valerie Cecilia

CORNWALL, Archdeacon of. *See* BRYER, The Ven Paul Donald

CORNWELL, Christopher Richard. b 43. Dur Univ BA 67. Cuddesdon Coll 67. **d** 69 **p** 70. C Cannock *Lich* 69–75; P-in-c Hadley 75–80; V 80–81; Bp's Dom Chapl 81–86; Subchanter Lich Cathl 81–86; V Ellesmere 86–89; V Welsh Frankton 86–89; V Ellesmere and Welsh Frankton 89–92; TV Leeds City *Ripon* 92–00; AD Allerton 94–97; V Ireland Wood 00–08; AD Headingley 01–07; Hon C Bishop Monkton and Burton Leonard 08–13; Hon Min Can Ripon Cathl *Leeds* from 08; PtO from 14. *41 Skelldale Close, Ripon HG4 1UH* T: (01765) 602837 E: cr.cornwell43@btinternet.com

CORNWELL, Lisa Michele. b 70. Lon Bible Coll BA 94 Westmr Coll Ox PGCE 95 K Coll Lon MA 99 PhD 18. Ridley Hall Cam 00. **d** 02 **p** 03. C Newport Pagnell w Lathbury and Moulsoe *Ox* 02–06; V Crowthorne from 06. *The Vicarage, 56 Duke's Ride, Crowthorne RG45 6NY* T: (01344) 772413 E: revlisacornwell@aol.com

CORP, Ronald Geoffrey. b 51. OBE 12. Ch Ch Ox MA 77. STETS. **d** 98 **p** 99. NSM Kilburn St Mary w All So and W Hampstead St Jas *Lon* 98–02; NSM Hendon St Mary and Ch Ch 02–07; NSM Holborn St Alb w Saffron Hill St Pet from 07. *The Clergy House, 18 Brooke Street, London EC1N 7RD* M: 07956-847792 E: ronald.corp@btconnect.com

CORRIE, John. b 48. Imp Coll Lon BScEng 69 MSc 70 PhD 73 Nottm Univ MTh 86. Trin Coll Bris 74. **d** 77 **p** 78. C Kendal St Thos *Carl* 77–80; C Attenborough *S'well* 80–86; ICS Peru 86–91; Tutor and Lect All Nations Chr Coll Ware 91–02; Lect/Development Officer Cen for Angl Communion Studies Selly Oak 02–05; Abp's Internat Project Officer *Cant* 05–06; Tutor Trin Coll Bris 07–17; PtO *Birm* 03–17; rtd 17. *Brambles, Higher Batson, Salcombe TQ8 8NF* E: revjohncorrie@gmail.com

CORRIE, Paul Allen. b 43. St Jo Coll Nottm 77. **d** 79 **p** 80. C Beverley Minster *York* 79–82; V Derby St Werburgh 82–84; V Derby St Alkmund and St Werburgh 84–95; Singapore 95–99; R Hawkwell *Chelmsf* 00–05; rtd 06; PtO *Bradf* 06–14; *Leeds* from 14. *5 Airedale Ings, Cononley, Keighley BD20 8LF*

CORRIE, Richard Tom. b 73. Cumbria Chr Learning 19. **d** 21. NSM Caldbeck, Castle Sowerby and Sebergham *Carl* from 21; NSM Westward, Rosley-w-Woodside and Welton from 21. *Tonrie, Grinsdale, Carlisle CA5 6DS* T: (01228) 934994 E: reverendrichardcorrie@outlook.com

CORSIE, Andrew Russell. b 57. Middx Univ BA 97 Birkbeck Coll Lon MSc 11. Trin Coll Bris 91. **d** 93 **p** 94. C Northolt Park St Barn *Lon* 93–97; C Perivale 97–01; P-in-c 01–06; R 06–14; AD Ealing 03–10; Dir Tr and Development Willesden Area from 14. *37 Ridding Lane, Greenford UB6 0JX* T: (020) 8991 9571 M: 07940-722144 E: andrew.corsie@london.anglican.org

CORY, Valerie Ann. *See* DAWSON, Valerie Ann

COSGRAVE-HANLEY, Máirt Joseph. *See* HANLEY, Máirt Joseph

COSH, Roderick John. b 56. Lon Univ BSc 78 Heythrop Coll Lon MA 03. St Steph Ho Ox 78. **d** 81 **p** 82. C Swindon New Town *Bris* 81–86; Chapl Asst R Marsden Hosp 86–91; V Whitton St Aug *Lon* 91–00; P-in-c Staines St Mary and St Pet 00–05; P-in-c Staines Ch Ch 04–05; V Staines 06–13; AD Spelthorne 04–10; AD Burnham and Slough *Ox* 13–20; C Colnbrook and Datchet 13–20; Hon Can Ch Ch 16–20; Lead Chapl St Monica Trust *Bris* from 20. *St Monica Trust, Cote Lane, Bristol BS9 3UN* T: 0117-949 4000 M: 07771-527141 E: rod@tommiez.com

COSLETT, Anthony Allan. b 49. Cuddesdon Coll. **d** 84 **p** 85. C Notting Hill St Clem and St Mark *Lon* 84–85; C Brentford 85–87; C-in-c Hounslow Gd Shep Beavers Lane CD 87–90; V Hounslow W Gd Shep 90–92; CF 92–08; TR Leic Resurr 08–12; C Broughton Astley and Croft w Stoney Stanton 12–17; rtd 17. *Ty am Byth, 62 Strathmore Road, Hinckley LE10 0LR* T: (01455) 611896

COSLETT (*née* SLATER), **The Ven Carol Ann.** b 63. Univ of Wales (Ban) BD 85 Jes Coll Cam PGCE 86 Lon Inst of Educn MA 92. Ripon Coll Cuddesdon 01. **d** 03 **p** 04. C Horsell *Guildf* 03–07; R Betchworth and Buckland *S'wark* 07–18; P-in-c Merstham, S Merstham and Gatton 13–15; Hon Can S'wark Cathl 16–18; Adn Chesterfield *Derby* from 18. *4 Woodnook Close, Ashgate, Chesterfield S42 7JB* T: (01246) 569764 *or* (01332) 388658 M: 07736-196315 E: ccoslett@btinternet.com *or* archchesterfield@derby.anglican.org

COSS, Oliver James. b 82. Hull Univ BSc 04 Leeds Univ BA 06 MA 09 FRSA 18. Coll of Resurr Mirfield 04. **d** 07 **p** 08. C Cottingham *York* 07–11; V Small Heath *Birm* 11–16; R Northampton All SS w St Kath and St Pet *Pet* from 16. *7 Towpath Avenue, Northampton NN4 9DW* T: (01604) 632845 E: oliver.coss@gmail.com

COSSAR, David Vyvyan. b 34. Lon Univ BA 63. Chich Th Coll 63. **d** 65 **p** 66. C Upper Clapton St Matt *Lon* 65–68; C Withycombe Raleigh *Ex* 68–72; V Honicknowle 72–78; V Brixham w Churston Ferrers 78–86; P-in-c Kingswear 85–86; TR Brixham w Churston Ferrers and Kingswear 86–90; V Lamorbey H Trin *Roch* 90–03; rtd 03; PtO *Roch* from 03. *11 Wells Court, Morden College, 19 St Germans Place, London SE3 0PW* M: 07741-406407 E: davidanddianec4@talktalk.net

COSSEY, David James. b 86. Redcliffe Coll Glouc BA 08. Ridley Hall Cam 17. **d** 19 **p** 20. C Dersingham, Anmer, Ingoldisthorpe etc *Nor* from 19. *6 Paiges Close, Dersingham, King's Lynn PE31 6UF* T: (01485) 297102 E: revdavecossey@gmail.com

COSSINS, John Charles. b 43. Hull Univ BSc 65. Oak Hill Th Coll 65. **d** 67 **p** 68. C Kenilworth St Jo *Cov* 67–70; C Huyton St Geo *Liv* 70–73; TV Maghull 73–79; Chapl Oakwood Hosp Maidstone 79–85; Maidstone Hosp 85–88; Chapl Park Lane Hosp Maghull 88–03; Chapl Moss Side Hosp Liv 88–03; Chapl Ashworth Hosp Maghull 88–03; rtd 03; PtO *Liv* 03–16; *Guildf* from 17. *68 Brookwood Farm Drive, Knaphill, Woking GU21 2FW* T: (01483) 480570 E: jcossins@gmail.com

COSSINS, Roger Stanton. b 40. K Coll Lon BD 67 AKC 67. **d** 68 **p** 69. C Bramley *Ripon* 68–71; C W End *Win* 71–76; V Bramley 76–91; C-in-c Bournemouth H Epiphany 91–94; V 94–00; rtd 00. *5 Allen Court, Trumpington, Cambridge CB2 9LU* T: (01223) 841726

COSTER, Canon Catherine Anne. b 47. Bris Poly BEd 85. WEMTC 97. **d** 00 **p** 01. NSM Yate New Town *Bris* 00–04; NSM Warmley, Syston and Bitton 04–17; Hon Min Can Bris Cathl 04–13; Hon Can 13–17; rtd 17; PtO *Bris* from 17; *Glouc* from 17. *31 Vayre Close, Chipping Sodbury, Bristol BS37 6NT* T: (01454) 329377 M: 07762-349691 E: catherinecoster3@gmail.com

COSTERTON, Alan Stewart. b 40. Bris Univ BA 67. Clifton Th Coll 67. **d** 69 **p** 70. C Peckham St Mary Magd *S'wark* 69–73; C Forest Gate St Sav w W Ham St Matt *Chelmsf* 73–76; TV 76–79; V Thornton cum Bagworth *Leic* 79–85; V Thornton, Bagworth and Stanton 85–95; TR Sileby, Cossington and Seagrave 95–04; R 04–05; rtd 05; PtO *Leic* from 14. *71 Fowke Street, Leicester LE7 7PJ* T: 0116-234 1026 E: alan.costerton@gmail.com

COSTIGAN, Esther Rose. *See* FOSS, Esther Rose

COSTIN, Pamela Lindsay. *See* REEVES, Pamela Lindsay

COSTIN, Richard George Charles. b 38. Liv Univ CertEd 59 Anglia Poly BEd 85 ACP 67 FCollP 82. Coll of Resurr Mirfield 04. **d** 05 **p** 06. NSM Scarborough St Martin *York* 05–16; PtO from 16; *Chelmsf* from 18. *64 Dame Mary Walk, Halstead CO9 2FF* T: (01787) 829118 M: 07768-856175 E: rcos38@hotmail.com

COTMAN, John Sell Granville (Jan). b 44. St Jo Coll Dur BA 69. Wells Th Coll 70. **d** 73 **p** 74. C Leigh St Mary *Man*

73–76; P-in-c Coldhurst 76–78; TV Oldham 78–82; TV E Ham w Upton Park and Forest Gate *Chelmsf* 82–85; C Hove All SS *Chich* 88–93; TV Hove 93–00; TV W Slough *Ox* 01–08; V Manor Park and Whitby Road 08–13; rtd 13. *6 Riley Close, Aylesbury HP20 2TH*

COTTEE, Christopher Paul. b 54. Newc Univ BSc 75. Wycliffe Hall Ox 77. **d** 80 **p** 81. C Much Woolton *Liv* 80–84; C Prescot 84–88; NSM Parr 89–91; V Watford St Pet *St Alb* 91–19; rtd 19. *98 Linaker Street, Southport PR8 5DG* E: chris.cottee1@ntlworld.com

COTTEE, Mary Jane. b 43. Open Univ BA 81 CertEd 64. Oak Hill Th Coll 87. **d** 90 **p** 94. NSM Gt Baddow *Chelmsf* 90–95; P-in-c Woodham Ferrers and Bicknacre 95–11; rtd 11; PtO *Chelmsf* from 11. *12 Mitchell Avenue, Halstead CO9 1DS* M: 07735-975423 E: marycottee@gmail.com

COTTELL, Avril Jane. *See* GAUNT, Avril Jane

COTTER, Preb Graham Michael. b 50. Univ of Wales (Ban) BA 72. Ridley Hall Cam 75. **d** 78 **p** 79. C Headley All SS *Guildf* 78–81; C Plymouth St Andr w St Paul and St Geo *Ex* 81–84; V Buckland Monachorum 84–18; RD Tavistock 93–98; Preb Ex Cathl 16–18; rtd 18. *9 Lakes Down, Upton Pyne, Exeter EX5 5BD* E: cotters@onetel.com

COTTER, Robert Edmund. **d** 05 **p** 06. NSM Mossley *Conn* 05–09; NSM Skerry w Rathcavan and Newtowncrommelin 09–13; Aux Min Belfast St Mary Magd from 13. *33 Deerfin Road, Ballymena BT42 4HP* T: (028) 2563 1303 E: bobcotter56@icloud.com

COTTERELL, Michael Clifford. b 54. Oak Hill Th Coll 81. **d** 84 **p** 85. C Lutterworth w Cotesbach *Leic* 84–87; C Belper *Derby* 87–91; V Locking *B & W* 91–98; V Slough *Ox* 98–19; rtd 19; PtO *Lich* 19–21. *5 Sycamore Drive, Whitchurch Road, Wem, Shrewsbury SY4 5AQ* E: mikeccotterell@gmail.com

COTTERILL, John Glyn. b 58. **d** 10 **p** 11. NSM Baswich *Lich* 10–13; NSM Stone St Mich and St Wulfad w Aston St Sav from 14. *11 Bracken View, Brocton, Stafford ST17 0TF* T: (01785) 664072 E: john-cotterill@hotmail.com

COTTERILL, Joseph Charles. b 17. AMCT 38 Lon Univ BD California Coll Peking MA 46. Ox Min Course 92. **d** 93 **p** 94. NSM Marcham w Garford *Ox* 93–98; PtO 98–20. *8 Draycott Road, Southmoor, Abingdon OX13 5BY* T: (01865) 820436

COTTERILL, Steven Derek. b 64. **d** 16 **p** 17. NSM Annesley w Newstead and Kirkby Woodhouse *S'well* from 16. *1 Bracken Close, Kirkby-in-Ashfield, Nottingham NG17 8NU* E: stevencotterill@hotmail.co.uk

COTTON, Charles Anthony. b 50. Linc Coll Ox BA 72 MA 77 PGCE 73. Ridley Hall Cam 89. **d** 91 **p** 92. C Hendon St Paul Mill Hill *Lon* 91–96; C Wandsworth All SS *S'wark* 96–97; V Clapham St Jas 97–08; rtd 08; PtO *S'wark* from 08. *9 Woodcote Avenue, Wallington SM6 0QR* T: (020) 8669 1143 E: revdcharlie@btinternet.com

COTTON, David John. b 65. Linc Sch of Th and Min 12. **d** 14 **p** 16. OLM Lea Gp *Linc* from 14. *42 Meadow Rise, Saxilby, Lincoln LN1 2HW* T: (01522) 702634 M: 07944-669166 E: david.cotton500@ntlworld.com

COTTON, John William. b 53. Oak Hill Th Coll 86. **d** 86 **p** 87. C New Clee *Linc* 86–89; Chapl St Andr Hospice Grimsby 88–89; R Middle Rasen Gp *Linc* 89–95; P-in-c Broughton 95–97; R 97–10; Chapl Humberside Airport 99–00; rtd 11; PtO *Linc* 11–18; Chapl United Lincs Hosps NHS Trust 11–12. *Address withheld by request* E: coulingwill@yahoo.com

COTTON, Mrs Margaret Elizabeth. b 30. JP 79. Newnham Coll Cam BA 53 MA 66. St Alb Minl Tr Scheme 78. **dss** 82 **d** 87 **p** 94. Lt Berkhamsted and Bayford, Essendon etc *St Alb* 82–87; Hon Par Dn 87–94; Hon C 94–96; rtd 96; PtO *St Alb* from 96. *49 Sherrardspark Road, Welwyn Garden City AL8 7LD* T: (01707) 321815

COTTON, Miss Michelle Susan. b 77. Ox Brookes Univ BA 13. Ripon Coll Cuddesdon 09. **d** 11 **p** 12. C Weston Favell *Pet* 11–15; P-in-c Wellingborough St Andr 15–16; V 16–18; V Wellingborough St Andr and St Barn from 18. *St Andrew's Vicarage, Berrymoor Road, Wellingborough NN8 2HU* T: (01933) 222634 M: 07817-905423 E: michelle.cotton123@btinternet.com

COTTON, Miss Patricia Constance. b 32. Gilmore Ho 54. **dss** 60 **d** 87 **p** 94. Forest Gate St Edm *Chelmsf* 60–64; Reading St Giles *Ox* 64–65; Basildon St Martin w H Cross and Laindon *Chelmsf* 65–79; Gt Burstead 79–87; Par Dn Maldon All SS w St Pet 87–91; rtd 92; NSM Holland-on-Sea *Chelmsf* 94–96; PtO from 96. *29 Alexander Mews, Sandon, Chelmsford CM2 7TT* T: (01245) 473983

COTTON, Patrick Arthur William. b 46. Essex Univ BA 67 Down Coll Cam MA 73 Homerton Coll Cam PGCE 96. Linc Th Coll 68. **d** 71 **p** 72. C Earlham St Anne *Nor* 71–73; Chapl Down Coll Cam 73–78; V Eaton Socon *St Alb* 78–84; TR Newc Epiphany 84–90; V Tunstall w Melling and Leck *Blackb* 90–95; Chapl Pet High Sch 01–05; P-in-c Debenham and Helmingham *St E* 06–16; rtd 16; PtO *Ely* 16–21. *4 Brook Lane, Coton, Cambridge CB23 7PY* T: (01954) 210285

COTTON, Peter John. b 45. BNC Ox BA 66 CQSW 76. Cuddesdon Coll 67. **d** 69 **p** 70. C Salford St Phil w St Steph *Man* 69–73; Asst Educn Officer *St Alb* 73–75; C Bris St Geo 75; C-in-c Portsea St Geo CD *Portsm* 76–80; Soc Resp Adv 78–88; Can Res Portsm Cathl 84–88; V St Laur in Thanet *Cant* 88–93; TR 93–97; Hon Min Can Cant Cathl 93–97; TR Hemel Hempstead *St Alb* 97–09; RD 03–08; Hon Can St Alb 08–09; rtd 09; PtO *Portsm* from 09. *7 Armory Lane, Portsmouth PO1 2PE* T: (023) 9281 6075 E: petercotton172@btinternet.com

COTTON, Canon Robert Lloyd. b 58. Mert Coll Ox MA 79. Westcott Ho Cam 81. **d** 83 **p** 84. C Plaistow St Mary *Roch* 83–86; C Bisley and W End *Guildf* 87–89; P-in-c E Molesey St Paul 89–96; Dir of Reader Tr from 90; R Guildf H Trin w St Mary from 96; Hon Can Highveld S Africa from 06; Hon Can Guildf Cathl from 10. *Holy Trinity Rectory, 9 Eastgate Gardens, Guildford GU1 4AZ* T: (01483) 575489 E: rector@holytrinityguildford.org.uk

COTTON-BETTERIDGE, Mrs Fiona Jane Marson. b 56. Nottm Univ MA 05. EMMTC 02. **d** 05 **p** 06. NSM Burton Joyce w Bulcote and Stoke Bardolph *S'well* 05–08; P-in-c Old Leake w Wrangle *Linc* 08–20; P-in-c Friskney 08–20; NSM Barrow upon Soar w Walton le Wolds *Leic* from 20; NSM Wymeswold and Prestwold w Hoton from 20. *Address temp unknown* E: fionacb@aol.com

COTTRELL, Matthew Brian. b 80. Ban Univ BTh 09. Ripon Coll Cuddesdon 11. **d** 14 **p** 16. C Thornbury and Oldbury-on-Severn w Shepperdine *Glouc* 14–17; C Glouc St Paul and St Steph 17–19. *11 Hackett Close, Swindon SN2 7UB* M: 07491-951538 E: revmattcottrell@gmail.com

✠**COTTRELL, The Most Revd Stephen Geoffrey.** b 58. Poly Cen Lon BA 79 St Mellitus Coll MA 19. St Steph Ho Ox 81. **d** 84 **p** 85 **c** 04. C Forest Hill Ch Ch *S'wark* 84–88; P-in-c Parklands St Wilfrid CD *Chich* 88–93; Asst Dir Past Studies Chich Th Coll 88–93; Dioc Missr *Wakef* 93–98; Bp's Chapl for Evang 93–98; Springboard Missr and Consultant in Evang 98–01; Can Res Pet Cathl 01–04; Area Bp Reading *Ox* 04–10; Bp Chelmsf 10–20; Abp York from 20. *Bishopthorpe Palace, Bishopthorpe, York YO23 2GE* T: (01904) 707021 E: office@archbishopofyork.org

COTTRILL, Derek John. b 43. MA. Qu Coll Birm. **d** 82 **p** 83. C Southampton Maybush St Pet *Win* 82–85; V Barton Stacey and Bullington etc 85–92; R Bishopstoke 92–06; Asst Chapl Win and Eastleigh Healthcare NHS Trust 92–06; rtd 06; PtO *Sarum* 14–21. *St John's Almshouse, Half Moon Street, Sherborne DT9 3LJ* E: revdc@live.co.uk

COTTRILL, Mrs Sarah. b 64. **d** 14 **p** 15. C St Jo in Bedwardine *Worc* 14–18; C Worc St Clem and Lower Broadheath 18–21; TV Worc City W from 21. *7 Manor Road, Worcester WR2 4PD* E: salocot@gmail.com

COUCH, Ms Felicity Anne. b 59. CQSW 85. SEITE 00. **d** 03 **p** 04. NSM Stockwell St Andr and St Mich *S'wark* 03–08; P-in-c Ulceby Gp, Croxton and Brocklesby Park *Linc* 08–11; R Orwell Gp *Ely* from 11; RD Shingay from 15. *The Rectory, Fishers Lane, Orwell, Royston SG8 5QX* T: (01223) 207212 M: 07745-905417 E: fcouch@btinternet.com

COUCH, John. b 46. Trin Coll Carmarthen BEd 85. **d** 14 **p** 15. NSM Llansadwrn w Llanwrda and Manordeilo *St D* 14–18; PtO from 18. *35 Llandybie Road, Ammanford SA18 2DP* T: (01269) 592096 M: 077443-610033 E: john@wales123.plus.com

COUCHMAN, Anthony Denis. b 37. Sarum Th Coll 66. **d** 69 **p** 70. C Barkingside St Fran *Chelmsf* 69–71; C Chingford SS Pet and Paul 71–76; P-in-c Walthamstow St Barn and St Jas Gt 76–80; V 80–07; rtd 07; PtO *Nor* from 08. *Friarscot, Church Street, King's Lynn PE30 5EB* T: (01553) 766643 E: anthony.couchman@btinternet.com

COUCHMAN, Kathryn. b 60. Open Univ BA 92 Coll of Ripon & York St Jo MA 00 MBPsS. NOC 02. **d** 06 **p** 07. C Wetherby *Ripon* 06–08; C Collingham w Harewood 08–10; C Spofforth w Kirk Deighton 08–10; Chapl HM YOI Wetherby 08–11; NSM Bishop Thornton, Burnt Yates, Markington etc *Ripon* 11–12; R Middleham w Coverdale and E Witton etc 12–15; Chapl St Mich Hospice Harrogate 15–20; NSM Fountains Gp *Leeds* from 21. *Garth Heads, Grassgill, West Witton, Leyburn DL8 4LY* M: 07435-882112 E: kathy.couchman@leeds.anglican.org

COUGHTREY, Miss Sheila Frances. b 48. RSCN 73 SRN 73 S Bank Poly BSc 79. Qu Coll Birm 79. dss 81 **d** 87 **p** 94. Sydenham St Bart *S'wark* 81–85; Roehampton H Trin 85–91; Par Dn 87–91; Par Dn Brixton Hill St Sav 91–94; P-in-c 94–01; Min King's Acre LEP 91–01; RD Brixton *S'wark* 99–01; P-in-c Pleshey *Chelmsf* 01–15; Warden Dioc Retreat

Ho 01–15; rtd 15; PtO *Chelmsf* from 19. *7 Hereward Way, Wethersfield, Braintree CM7 4EG* T: (01371) 580378

COULDRIDGE, Janice Evelyn. *See* FOX, Janice Evelyn

COULSON, Kenneth. b 51. **d** 15 **p** 16. NSM Windy Nook St Alb *Dur* from 15; NSM Gateshead Fell from 18. *13 Beaconsfield Avenue, Low Fell, Gateshead NE9 5XT* T: 0191-487 1544

COULSON, Renée Yvonne. b 45. **d** 03 **p** 04. OLM Potterne w Worton and Marston *Sarum* 03–09; P-in-c Seend, Bulkington and Poulshot 09–15; rtd 15; PtO *Sarum* from 15. *40 Highlands, Potterne, Devizes SN10 5N* T: (01380) 725208 E: renee.coulson.2@googlemail.com *or* revren.d@btinternet.com *or* rycoulson40@gmail.com

COULSON, Canon Stephen Hugh. b 60. St Edm Hall Ox BA 82 MA 88 Lon Univ CertEd 83. Wycliffe Hall Ox 85. **d** 88 **p** 89. C Summerfield *Birm* 88–91; PtO 91–92; CMS Uganda 92–01; Asst V Namirembe 92–96; Can from 96; Prin Uganda Martyrs Sem Namugongo 96–01; V Mitcham St Mark *S'wark* 01–12; AD Merton 09–12; V Kennington St Mark from 12. *St Mark's Vicarage, 56 Kennington Oval, London SE11 5SW* T: (020) 7735 1801 E: vicar@stmarkskennington.org

COULSON, Tony Erik Frank. b 32. St Edm Hall Ox BA 55 MA 59. Wycliffe Hall Ox 55. **d** 57 **p** 58. C Walthamstow St Mary *Chelmsf* 57–60; C Reading St Jo *Ox* 60–63; V Iver 63–86; R White Waltham w Shottesbrooke 86–97; rtd 97; PtO *Ox* from 98. *30 Ravensbourne Drive, Reading RG5 4LH* T: 0118-969 3556 E: tefcoulson@gmail.com

COULTER, Edmond James. b 60. CQSW 86. **d** 87 **p** 88. C Ballymena w Ballyclug *Conn* 87–90; C Knockbreda *D & D* 90–92; I Belfast Upper Falls *Conn* 92–97; I Milltown *Arm* 97–03; Supt Dublin Irish Ch Miss *D & G* 03–16; I Lambeg *Conn* from 16. *Lambeg Rectory, 58 Belfast Road, Lisburn BT27 4AT* T: (028) 9266 3872

COULTER, Canon Ian Herbert Young. b 54. TCD BA 77 HDipEd 78. **d** 99 **p** 00. LtO Cashel, Waterford and Lismore *C, F & O* 99–10; NSM Castlecomer w Colliery Ch, Mothel and Bilboa 10–13; NSM Templemore w Thurles and Kilfithmone 13–16; NSM Clonenagh w Offerlane, Borris-in-Ossory etc 16–20; P-in-c Templemore w Thurles and Kilfithmone from 20; Can Ossory Cathl from 20. *22 Rose Hill Court, Kilkenny, Co Kilkenny, Republic of Ireland* T/F: (00353) (56) 776 2675 M: 86-813 0290 E: ianhycoulter@gmail.com

COULTER (née REEVES), Mrs Maria Elizabeth Ann. b 72. Leeds Univ BA 95 Heythrop Coll Lon MTh 03 Buckingham Univ PGCE 18. St Steph Ho Ox 96. **d** 98 **p** 99. C Newington St Mary *S'wark* 98–02; V Dulwich St Clem w St Pet 02–17; Asst Chapl Oundle Sch from 17. *2 Cricketers Way, Oundle, Peterborough PE8 4JU* E: meareeves@hotmail.com

COULTER, Miss Marilyn Judith. b 48. City of Birm Coll BEd 70 Qu Coll Birm BA 05. WMMTC 02. **d** 05 **p** 06. NSM Brewood *Lich* 05–19; NSM Bishopswood 05–19; Chapl Mid Staffs NHS Foundn Trust 08–14; PtO *Lich* 19–21. *14 St Chad's Close, Brewood, Stafford ST19 9DA* T: (01902) 851168 E: coulter14@aol.com

COULTHARD, Miss Nina Marion. b 50. CertEd 71 Bp Lonsdale Coll BEd 72. Trin Coll Bris 89. **d** 91 **p** 94. Par Dn Cant St Mary Bredin 91–94; C 94–95; C Bath Abbey w St Jas *B & W* 95–99; Chapl R Nat Hosp for Rheumatic Diseases NHS Trust 95–99; C Northwood Em *Lon* 99–06; V Loughton St Mich *Chelmsf* 06–18; rtd 18; PtO *Cant* from 19. *22 Grays Way, Canterbury CT1 3XY* M: 07956-513615 E: revninac@gmail.com

COULTHURST, Jeffrey Evans. b 38. Man Univ BA 61 Leeds Univ PGCE 62. **d** 84 **p** 85. OLM Ancaster *Linc* 84–89; OLM Ancaster Wilsford Gp 89–05. *152 Cirencester Road, Charlton Kings, Cheltenham GL53 8DY* E: jeff.coulthurst38@gmail.com

COULTON, David John. b 45. St Jo Coll Cam BA 67 MA 71 Glos Univ MA 04 CertEd 69. WEMTC 07. **d** 09 **p** 10. NSM Tewkesbury w Walton Cardiff and Twyning *Glouc* 09–18; Succ and Chapl Tewkesbury Abbey 16–18; NSM Deerhurst and Apperley w Forthampton etc *Glouc* 12–16; rtd 18; PtO *Glouc* from 21. *4 Conigree Lane, Abbots Road, Tewkesbury GL20 5TF* T: (01684) 293523 E: davidcoulton@btinternet.com

COULTON, David Stephen. b 41. Bernard Gilpin Soc Dur 63 Sarum Th Coll 64. **d** 67 **p** 68. C Guildf H Trin w St Mary 67–70; Asst Chapl St Luke's Hosp Guildf 67–70; Asst Chapl Radley Coll 70–83; Sen Chapl 83–01; Chapl Eton Coll 01–04; rtd 04; PtO *Sarum* from 06. *Address withheld by request*

COULTON, The Very Revd Nicholas Guy. b 40. Lon Univ BD 72 Ox Univ MA 07. Cuddesdon Coll 65. **d** 67 **p** 68. C Pershore w Wick *Worc* 67–70; Bp's Dom Chapl *St Alb* 71–75; P-in-c Bedford St Paul 75–79; V 79–90; Hon Can St Alb 89–90; Provost Newc 90–01; Dean Newc 01–03; Can

Res and Sub-Dean Ch Ch *Ox* 03–08; rtd 08. *123 Merewood Avenue, Headington, Oxford OX3 8EQ* T: (01865) 763790 E: ngc@proscenia.co.uk

COULTON, Philip Ernest. b 31. St Cath Coll Cam BA 54 MA 58 TCD BD 68 Open Univ BA 84. Ely Th Coll 55. **d** 57 **p** 58. Asst Master Perse Sch Cam 54–55; Asst Master Bradf Gr Sch 57; C Newark w Coddington *S'well* 57–61; Min Can and Sacr Cant Cathl 61–63; Min Can Ripon Cathl 63–68; Hd of RE Ashton-under-Lyne Gr Sch 69–84; V Ulceby Gp *Linc* 85–89; P-in-c Ingatestone w Buttsbury *Chelmsf* 89–99; P-in-c Fryerning w Margaretting 89–92; rtd 99; PtO *Sarum* from 01; *B & W* 02–06. *90 Boreham Road, Warminster BA12 9JW* T: (01985) 219353 E: pecoulton@talktalk.net

COUPAR, Thomas. b 50. BA 71 ACE 80 Edin Univ MTh 15. Edin Dioc NSM Course 77. **d** 80 **p** 81. NSM Dunbar *Edin* 80–86; NSM Haddington 80–86; Hd Master Pencaitland Primary Sch E Lothian 80–81; Hd Master K Meadow Sch E Lothian 81–87; Asst Dioc Supernumerary *Edin* 87–89; Primary Educn Adv Fife Coun 88–06; Dioc Supernumerary *Edin* 90–96 and 13–15; rtd 19; LtO *Edin* from 19. *21/9 Rennie's Isle, Edinburgh EH6 6QB* M: 07765-431321 E: tcoupar@hotmail.com

COUPE, Christopher John. b 57. Cumbria Univ BA 15. LCTP 10. **d** 12 **p** 13. NSM Lower Darwen St Jas *Blackb* 12–16; V Chell *Lich* from 16. *The Rectory, 203 St Michael's Road, Stoke-on-Trent ST6 6JT* E: vicar@chellparish.org.uk

COUPER (née WOOD), Mrs Audrey Elizabeth. b 54. Edin Univ BSc 75 Westmr Coll of Educn PGCE 76. ERMC 05. **d** 08 **p** 09. NSM Digswell and Panshanger *St Alb* 08–13; NSM Luton St Fran 13–14; PtO *Edin* from 15. *2 St Ninian's Way, Linlithgow EH49 7BU* E: audreycouper@gmail.com

COUPER, Jonathan George. b 51. St Jo Coll Dur BA 73. Wycliffe Hall Ox 73. **d** 75 **p** 76. C Clifton *York* 75–78; C Darfield *Sheff* 78–81; V Bridlington Quay Ch Ch *York* 81–16; P-in-c Bessingby 99–12; V 12–16; rtd 16; PtO *York* from 18. *3 Tudor Close, Bridlington YO15 3TA* E: jc1066@outlook.com

COUPLAND, Robert Lee. b 92. Dur Univ BA 16. Westcott Ho Cam 13. **d** 16 **p** 17. C Brighton St Mich and St Paul *Chich* 16–19; Min Can and Sacr St Paul's Cathl *Lon* from 19. *St Paul's Cathedral, The Chapter House, St Paul's Churchyard, London EC4M 8AD* E: robertleecoupland@yahoo.com

COUPLAND, Simon Charles. b 59. St Jo Coll Cam BA 82 MA 85 PhD 87 Dur Univ PGCE 83. Ridley Hall Cam 88. **d** 91 **p** 92. C Bath St Luke *B & W* 91–95; TV Broadwater *Chich* 95–04; V Kingston Hill St Paul *S'wark* 04–18; AD Kingston 12–16; P-in-c Ham St Rich 18–20; V from 20. *28 Dysart Avenue, Kingston upon Thames KT2 5RB* T: (020) 8546 1438 E: strichardsvicar@btinternet.com

COURT, Carol Ann. b 61. St Padarn's Inst. **d** 19 **p** 20. NSM Bro Sancler *St D* from 19. *62 Lon Hafren, St Clears, Carmarthen SA33 4BU* T: (01994) 230233 M: 07961-273409 E: carolcourt21@gmail.com

✠**COURT, The Rt Revd David Eric.** b 58. Southn Univ BSc 80 PhD 83 PGCE 84. Oak Hill Th Coll BA 91. **d** 91 **p** 92 **c** 14. C Barton Seagrave w Warkton *Pet* 91–94; C Kinson *Sarum* 94–97; P-in-c Mile Cross *Nor* 97–99; V 99–03; V Cromer 03–14; RD Repps 10–14; Hon Can Nor Cathl 10–14; Suff Bp Grimsby *Linc* from 14. *The Bishops' Office, The Old Palace, Lincoln LN2 1PU* E: revdavidcourt@btinternet.com *or* bishop.grimsby@lincoln.anglican.org

COURT, Canon Kenneth Reginald. b 36. AKC 60. **d** 61 **p** 62. C Garforth *Ripon* 61–63; C Harrogate St Wilfrid 63–65; V Thornbury *Bradf* 65–73; Prec Leic Cathl 73–76; V Douglas St Matt *S & M* 76–84; V Syston *Leic* 84–93; TR 93–98; RD Goscote 90–95; Hon Can Leic Cathl 92–98; rtd 98; PtO *Leic* 99–12; *Linc* 01–03; *Pet* 03–08. *12 Lord Burghley's Hospital, Station Road, Stamford PE9 2LD* T: (01780) 754372 E: kenneth.court554@gmail.com

COURT, Martin Jeremy. b 61. GRNCM 84 Nottm Univ BTh 89. Linc Th Coll 86. **d** 89 **p** 90. C Thurmaston *Leic* 89–92; C Leic St Jas 92–93; TV Leic Resurr 93–98; V Scraptoft from 98; P-in-c Leic St Chad from 08; Dioc Interim Tech Co-ord from 96. *All Saints' Vicarage, 331 Scraptoft Lane, Scraptoft, Leicester LE5 2HU* T: 0116-241 3205 M: 07798-876837 E: mcourt@leicester.anglican.org

COURT, Canon Nicholas James Keble. b 56. Chich Th Coll 86. **d** 88 **p** 89. C Golders Green *Lon* 88–91; C Westbury-on-Trym H Trin *Bris* 91–94; PV Llan Cathl 94–96; V Graig 96–02; P-in-c Cilfynydd 96–01; Miss P Mor

09–11; Can St Andr Cathl Inverness 13–20; rtd 20. *Cair Paravel, Ardmair, Ullapool IV26 2TN* T: (01854) 612506 E: nicholas.court@btinternet.com

COURT, Richard Leonard. b 54. Univ of Wales (Ban) BTh 04. EAMTC 94. **d** 97 **p** 98. NSM Framlingham w Saxtead *St E* 97–05; V Badsey w Aldington and Offenham and Bretforton *Worc* 05–15; RD Evesham 10–15; rtd 15; PtO *St E* from 14. *Brookside, Green Lane, Redlingfield, Eye IP23 7QT* T: (01379) 678772 M: 07751-775917 E: rev.richard.court@icloud.com

COURTIE, John Malcolm. b 42. BNC Ox BA 65 DPhil 72 St Jo Coll Dur BA 76. Cranmer Hall Dur 74. **d** 77 **p** 78. C Mossley Hill St Matt and St Jas *Liv* 77–80; V Litherland St Paul Hatton Hill 80–84; Wellingborough Sch 84–89; Hon C Wollaston and Strixton *Pet* 84–89; V Woodford Halse w Eydon 89–99; R Blisworth and Stoke Bruerne w Grafton Regis etc 99–02; rtd 02; Hon C NW Hants *Win* 09–10; PtO *Ex* from 11. *12 Case Gardens, Seaton EX12 2AP* E: thecourties@hotmail.com

COURTNEY, Canon Brian Joseph. b 44. BD 92 MA 97. CITC 70. **d** 73 **p** 74. C Willowfield *D & D* 73–75; P-in-c Knocknagoney 75–78; I Aghavea *Clogh* 78–83; I Carrickfergus *Conn* 83–95; I Enniskillen *Clogh* 95–09; Prec Clogh Cathl 95–09; rtd 09. *10 Berkeley Road, Carrickfergus BT38 9DS* T: (028) 9335 5139 E: briancourtney09@googlemail.com

COURTNEY, Miss Louise Anita Hodd. b 48. Ex Univ BTh 04. SWMTC 99. **d** 02 **p** 03. C St Keverne *Truro* 02–05; P-in-c Lanteglos by Fowey 05–15; P-in-c Lansallos 05–15; P-in-c Talland 10–15; C Lanreath, Pelynt and Bradoc 13–15; rtd 15. *131 Le Pinet, 24500 Razac-d'Eymet, France* E: louiseanitacourtney@gmail.com

COURTNEY, Martin Horace. b 34. SAOMC 95. **d** 98 **p** 99. OLM Flackwell Heath *Ox* from 98. *1 Green Crescent, Flackwell Heath, High Wycombe HP10 9JQ* T: (01628) 526354 E: martin@ccfh.org.uk

COUSANS (née BRADLEY), Mrs Joy Elizabeth. b 63. Sheff Univ BA 85 Fitzw Coll Cam BA 91 MA 95. Ridley Hall Cam 89. **d** 92 **p** 94. Par Dn Wadsley *Sheff* 92–94; C 94–96; C Mosborough 96–97; V Hillsborough and Wadsley Bridge 97–06; P-in-c High Hoyland, Scissett and Clayton W *Wakef* 06–14; Leeds 14–17; Asst Dir of Ords 08–17; V Eaton Bray w Edlesborough *St Alb* from 17. *The Vicarage, 11 High Street, Eaton Bray, Dunstable LU6 2DN* T: (01525) 220261 E: vicar@stmaryseatonbray.org.uk

COUSINS, Mrs Deborah Ann. b 52. LCST 74. ERMC 06. **d** 09 **p** 10. C Earlham *Nor* 09–13; C Bure Valley 13–17; TV Aylsham and Distr 17–19; rtd 19; PtO *Nor* from 19. *c/o Mrs Forkes, Greenways, Sandpit Lane, Thorpe Market, Norwich NR11 8TJ* M: 07814-282307 E: debstherev@gmail.com

COUSINS, Canon Graham John. b 55. Oak Hill Th Coll BA 91. **d** 91 **p** 92. C Birkenhead St Jas w St Bede *Ches* 91–95; C Bebington 95–01; R Moreton from 01; RD Wallasey 11–18; Hon Can Ches Cathl from 12. *The Rectory, Dawpool Drive, Moreton, Wirral CH46 0PH* T: 0151-641 0303 *or* 604 0049 E: rector@christchurchmoreton.org.uk

COUSINS, Canon Philip John. b 35. K Coll Cam BA 58 MA 62. Cuddesdon Coll 59. **d** 61 **p** 62. C Marton *Blackb* 61–63; PV Truro Cathl 63–67; USPG Ethiopia 67–75; V Henleaze *Bris* 75–84; RD Clifton 79–84; Provost All SS Cathl Cairo 84–89; Chan Malta Cathl *Eur* 89–95; Chapl Valletta w Gozo 89–95; R Llandudno *Ban* 95–04; rtd 04; PtO *York* from 04; *Eur* from 05. *17 Chalfonts, York YO24 1EX* T: (01904) 700316 E: janet.philip1@gmail.com

COUSINS, Stephen Michael. b 53. SAOMC 98. **d** 01 **p** 02. OLM Caversham St Jo *Ox* 01–03; PtO 03–04; NSM Shiplake w Dunsden and Harpsden 04–11; Chapl Shiplake Coll Henley 09–19; NSM Benson w Ewelme *Ox* from 19. *The Parsonage, Ewelme, Wallingford OX10 6HP* M: 07753-166687 E: stephen.cousins@btinternet.com

COUSINS, Suzanne Jane. **d** 15 **p** 16. Newtownards *D & D* 15–16; C Moville w Greencastle, Donagh, Cloncha etc *D & R* 16–19; I Clonfeacle, Derrygortreavy and Eglish *Arm* from 19. *The Rectory, 4 Clonfeacle Road, Dungannon BT71 7LQ* E: sjcousinshome@gmail.com *or* benburbgroup@armagh.anglican.org

COUTTS, Diana Angela. *See* COUTTS-PAULING, Diana Angela

COUTTS, James Allan. b 58. Fitzw Coll Cam MA. St Jo Coll Nottm MTh 84. **d** 84 **p** 85. C Thorpe Acre w Dishley *Leic* 84–88; TV Kirby Muxloe 88–99; P-in-c Trowbridge St Thos and W Ashton *Sarum* 99–07; V from 07; Chapl Wilts and Swindon Healthcare NHS Trust 99–08; Chapl Gt Western Hosps NHS Foundn Trust from 08. *St Thomas's Vicarage, York Buildings, Trowbridge BA14 8PT* T: (01225) 754826 E: allan@stthomastrowbridge.org

COUTTS, Canon Mandy Rosalind. b 65. Ox Poly BSc 87 St Jo Coll Dur BA 06 Leeds Univ MA 11 Bath Univ PGCE 88. Cranmer Hall Dur 04. **d** 06 **p** 07. C Chapel Allerton *Ripon*

06–10; TV Bramley 10–14; Can Res Bradf Cathl *Leeds* from 15. *2 Cathedral Close, Bradford BD1 4EG* T: (01274) 777728 E: mandy.coutts@virgin.net

COUTTS, Canon Robin Iain Philip. b 52. Portsm Univ MA 00. Sarum & Wells Th Coll 80. **d** 83 **p** 84. C Alverstoke *Portsm* 83–86; Min Leigh Park St Clare CD 86–88; V Warren Park 89–91; V Purbrook 91–04; RD Havant 00–04; P-in-c Blendworth w Chalton w Idsworth 04–06; P-in-c Hambledon 06–17; Dioc Dir NSM 04–17; Dioc Dir of Ords 06–16; Hon Can Portsm Cathl 06–17; rtd 17; PtO *Portsm* from 18; *Sarum* from 18. *3 Oakwood Grove, Alderbury, Salisbury SP5 3BN* E: robin.rocket@btinternet.com

COUTTS-PAULING, Diana Angela. Cant Ch Ch Univ BA 11. **d** 07 **p** 08. Chapl Qu Mary's Sidcup NHS Trust 07–08; Chapl S Lon Healthcare NHS Trust 09–13; rtd 13; PtO *Roch* from 14. *16 Darwin Close, Orpington BR6 7EP* T: (01689) 853122 E: revdacp@gmail.com

COUTURE (*née* MAWBEY), Mrs Diane. b 55. Birm Univ MMedSc 97. Cranmer Hall Dur. **d** 89 **p** 94. Par Dn Menston w Woodhead *Bradf* 89–92; C Barnoldswick w Bracewell 92–93; Chapl Asst Birm Children's Hosp 93–96; Chapl Asst Birm Maternity Hosp 93–96; Chapl Birm Women's Healthcare NHS Trust 96–98; R The Whitacres, Lea Marston, and Shustoke *Birm* 98–15; rtd 15; PtO *Birm* from 15. *14 Atherstone Road, Hurley, Atherstone CV9 2HU* T: (01827) 873223 M: 07710-281648 E: diane.couture@btinternet.com

COUVELA, Ms Stephanie Joy. b 68. Sheff City Poly BA 89. Ridley Hall Cam 95. **d** 98 **p** 99. C Upper Holloway *Lon* 98–01; TV 01–04; C Busbridge and Hambledon *Guildf* 04–10; Chapl Scargill Ho 10–15; Chapl Keele Univ *Lich* from 15. *51 Quarry Bank Road, Keele, Newcastle ST5 5AG* T: (01782) 734919 E: s.couvela@keele.ac.uk

COUZENS (*formerly* WATERS), Brenda Mary. b 51. Bp Otter Coll. **d** 99. NSM Whyke w Rumboldswhyke and Portfield *Chich* 99–04; NSM Chich Cathl 05–14; PtO 14–18; Chapl St Wilfrid's Hospice Chich 01–18; NSM Chich St Paul and Westhampnett from 18. *12 Peacock Close, Chichester PO19 6YD* E: brendacouzens51@gmail.com

COUZENS, Mrs Carolyn Mary. b 67. St Mellitus Coll 13. **d** 15 **p** 16. C Lilliput *Sarum* 15–19; P-in-c Bridge Par 19–21; P-in-c Spetisbury w Charlton Marshall etc from 19. *The Old Post Office, High Street, Spetisbury, Blandford Forum DT11 9DW* M: 07590-552311 E: revcarolyncouzens@gmail.com

COVENTRY, Archdeacon of. See FIELD, The Ven Susan Elizabeth

COVENTRY, Bishop of. See COCKSWORTH, The Rt Revd Christopher John

COVENTRY, Dean of. See WITCOMBE, The Very Revd John Julian

COVERLEY, Mrs Cheryl Joy. b 62. SS Hild & Bede Coll Dur BA 83 PGCE 84. St Jo Coll Nottm MA 07. **d** 05 **p** 06. C Birkenhead St Jas w St Bede *Ches* 05–07; V Newton from 07; Asst Warden of Readers from 08. *St Michael's Vicarage, 56 Queensbury, Wirral CH48 6EP* T: 0151-625 8517 E: vicar.stmaa@gmail.com *or* cheryl.coverley@tiscali.co.uk

COVINGTON, Canon Michael William Rock. b 38. Open Univ BA 78. Sarum Th Coll 60. **d** 63 **p** 64. C Daventry *Pet* 63–66; C Woolwich St Mary w H Trin *S'wark* 66–68; C Northampton All SS w St Kath *Pet* 68–71; V Longthorpe 71–86; Hon Min Can Pet Cathl 75–86; V Warmington, Tansor, Cotterstock and Fotheringhay 86–95; Warden of Readers 87–95; RD Oundle 89–95; V Oakham, Hambleton, Egleton, Braunston and Brooke 95–03; P-in-c Langham 97–03; RD Rutland 02–03; Can Pet Cathl 86–03; rtd 03; PtO *Leic* 05–06 and 10–13 and from 16; C Burrough Hill Pars 07–10; P-in-c S Framland 13–16. *Hall Farm House, Burrough Road, Little Dalby, Melton Mowbray LE14 2UG* T: (01664) 454015

COWAN, David John. b 47. Selw Coll Cam BA 69 MA 73. SEITE 06. **d** 09 **p** 10. NSM Dorking w Ranmore *Guildf* 09–17; PtO from 17. *25 Falkland Road, Dorking RH4 3AB* T: (01306) 885341 E: mave@uwclub.net

COWAN, Helen Jane. b 42. **d** 00 **p** 01. OLM Redhill H Trin *S'wark* 00–12; PtO from 12. *15 Westway Gardens, Redhill RH1 2JA* T: (01737) 762543

COWAN, John Conway. b 71. Liv Univ BA 93 Liv Inst of HE PGCE 94. Trin Coll Bris BA 03. **d** 03 **p** 04. C Redcar *York* 03–07; V Hull St Cuth from 07; Chapl Hull Univ from 10; AD Cen and N Hull from 17; AD Hull from 18. *The Vicarage, 112 Marlborough Avenue, Hull HU5 3JX* T: (01482) 342848 E: cowanjohnc@yahoo.com

COWAN, Mrs Lynda Barbette. b 55. ALAM 77. Ban Ord Course 02. **d** 05 **p** 06. C Arwystli Deanery Ban 05–08; P-in-c Llandinam w Trefeglwys w Penstrowed Ban 08–10; V 10–14; V Bro Arwystli 14–21; rtd 21. *The Coach House,*

Old Hall Road, Llanidloes SY18 6PQ T: (01686) 413099 E: lyndacowan@pc-q.net

COWAN, Malcolm. b 60. Ches Coll of HE BTh 04. NOC 01. **d** 04 **p** 05. C W Kirby St Bridget *Ches* 04–07; V Witton 07–11; R Christleton 11–18; Chapl Wirral Univ Teaching Hosp NHS Foundn Trust from 18. *44 Westbourne Road, West Kirby, Wirral CH48 4DH* E: jandmcowan@gmail.com *or* malcolm.cowan@nhs.net

COWAN, Malcolm. b 45. CBDTI. **d** 00 **p** 01. NSM Keswick St Jo *Carl* 00–05; TV Whitehaven 05–07; P-in-c Kirkby Ireleth 07–15; C Dalton-in-Furness and Ireleth-with-Askam 07–15; rtd 15; PtO *Carl* from 16. *The Spinney, Bridekirk, Cockermouth CA13 0PF*

COWAN, Paul Hudson. b 69. Ripon Coll Cuddesdon BTh 05. **d** 02 **p** 03. C Wokingham All SS *Ox* 02–05; C Kimberley Cathl S Africa 05–06; TV Newbury *Ox* 06–15; V Newbury St Geo and St Jo 15–17; Bp's Dom Chapl from 17. *Church House Oxford, Langford Locks, Kidlington OX5 1GF* T: (01865) 208221 E: paul.cowan@oxford.anglican.org

COWAN, Shirley. b 64. **d** 12 **p** 13. C Gateacre *Liv* 12–16; V Warrington H Trin and St Ann from 16. *St Ann's Vicarage, 1A Fitzherbert Street, Warrington WA2 7QG* T: (01925) 631781

COWAN, Sophie Valentine. b 87. Wycliffe Hall Ox BA 18. **d** 19 **p** 20. C Desborough, Brampton Ash, Dingley and Braybrooke *Pet* from 19. *134 Pioneer Avenue, Desborough, Kettering NN14 2PB* M: 07800-909768 E: cowansophie@icloud.com

COWARD, Colin Charles Malcolm. b 45. MBE 14. Kingston Poly DArch 72. Westcott Ho Cam 75. **d** 78 **p** 79. C Camberwell St Geo *S'wark* 78–82; P-in-c Wandsworth St Faith 82–90; V 90–96; Chapl Richmond, Twickenham and Roehampton NHS Trust 96–97; Co-ord Changing Attitude 97–03; Dir 03–15; PtO *Sarum* 07–10; rtd 15. *6 Norney Bridge, Mill Road, Worton, Devizes SN10 5SF* T: (01380) 724908 E: ccmcoward@aol.com

COWELL, Anthony. See COWELL, Neil Anthony

COWELL, Irene Christine. b 58. RGN 80. Ridley Hall Cam 92. **d** 94 **p** 95. C Litherland St Phil *Liv* 94–98; R Sefton and Thornton 98–11; P-in-c Southport Em 11–17; Dioc Adv on HIV/AIDS and Sexual Health 97–06; Dioc Dir CME 02–17; Dir Leadership and Management Tr 05–17; V Arbory and Castletown *S & M* from 17; Dioc Dir CME from 17. *The Vicarage, Arbory Road, Castletown, Isle of Man IM9 1ND* T: (01624) 823509 E: irene.cowell@sodorandman.im *or* cmd@sodorandman.im

COWELL, Neil Anthony. b 61. **d** 98 **p** 99. OLM New Bury *Man* 98–06; OLM New Bury w Gt Lever 06–20; PtO from 20. *16 Castle Mews, Farnworth, Bolton BL4 9JX* T: (01204) 706957 E: revtonycowell@yahoo.co.uk

COWEN, Canon Brian. b 45. Nottm Univ BTh 77. Linc Th Coll 73. **d** 77 **p** 78. C Hexham *Newc* 77–80; C Ledbury w Eastnor *Heref* 80–81; TV Glendale Gp *Newc* 81–90; V Lesbury w Alnmouth 90–98; V Longhoughton w Howick 98–08; AD Alnwick 93–05; Hon Can Newc Cathl 01–08; rtd 08; PtO *Newc* from 08; *Edin* from 14. *13 Fenton Grange, Wooler NE71 6AW* T: (01668) 281991 E: rev.cowen@btopenworld.com

COWGILL, Canon Michael. b 48. Linc Th Coll 84. **d** 86 **p** 87. C Bolton St Jas w St Chrys *Bradf* 86–89; V Buttershaw St Paul 89–93; P-in-c Cullingworth 93–97; Dir Dioc Foundn Course 93–97; V Sutton 97–07; V Sutton w Cowling and Lotherskale 07–14; *Leeds* 14; rtd 14; PtO *Leeds* from 17. *2 Garforth Avenue, Steeton, Keighley BD20 6SP* T: (01535) 652363 E: michael@cowgill.force9.co.uk

COWIE, Andrew Cameron. b 66. Wycliffe Hall Ox. **d** 11 **p** 12. C Woking St Paul *Guildf* 11–15; V Thames Ditton from 15; AD Emly from 18. *The Vicarage, Summer Road, Thames Ditton KT7 0QQ* T: (020) 8398 9641 E: stnicparishoffice@btinternet.com

COWIE, Mrs Catherine Anne. b 87. Ripon Coll Cuddesdon BA 19. **d** 20 **p** 21. C The Guitings, Cutsdean, Farmcote etc *Glouc* from 20. *1 Greenbank Gardens, Piccadilly, Guiting Power, Cheltenham GL54 5UU* E: revcatherinecowie@gmail.com

COWIE, David James. b 87. Ches Univ BEd 09. Ripon Coll Cuddesdon BTh 14. **d** 14 **p** 15. C Ches H Trin 14–16; C Ches St Mary 16–17; P-in-c High Framland Par *Leic* from 17; P-in-c S Framland from 17. *The Rectory, 7 Sycamore Lane, Wymondham, Melton Mowbray LE14 2AZ* M: 07377-873837 E: revd.david.cowie@gmail.com

COWIE, Derek Edward. b 33. S'wark Ord Course 70. **d** 73 **p** 74. C Maldon All SS w St Pet *Chelmsf* 73–76; R Bowers Gifford w N Benfleet 76–79; V Chelmsf Ascension 79–84; V Shrub End 84–95; P-in-c Gosfield 95–03; RD Hinckford 01–03; rtd 03; PtO *Nor* from 03. *Bruar Cottage, 68 Wash Lane, Kessingland, Lowestoft NR33 7QY* T: (01502) 740989 M: 07788-662211 E: revcowie73@outlook.com

COWIE, Margaret Harriet. See KING, Margaret Harriet

COWLES, Richard Martin. b 53. Birm Univ BSc 74. Ripon Coll Cuddesdon 91. d 93 p 94. C Iffley Ox 93–96; TV Wheatley 96–08; V Bray and Braywood 08–17; rtd 17; PtO Llan from 17. The Dower House, Gwern-y-Domen Farm Lane, Caerphilly CF83 3RN

COWLEY, Anne. See COWLEY, Judith Anne

COWLEY, Mrs Elizabeth Mary. b 47. Bris Univ PQCSW 84. WMMTC 89. d 92 p 94. NSM Wolston and Church Lawford Cov 92–97; Soc Resp Officer 97–02; P-in-c Churchover w Willey 97–02; TV Daventry, Ashby St Ledgers, Braunston etc Pet 02–13; Adv for Healing Min (Northn Adnry) 06–13; rtd 13; PtO Pet from 14; Cov 15–21. 57 Daventry Road, Barby, Rugby CV23 8TP T: (01788) 891411 E: liz.cowley@btinternet.com

COWLEY, Ian Michael. b 51. Natal Univ BCom 72 BA 75 Sheff Univ MA 83. Wycliffe Hall Ox 75. d 78 p 79. C Scottsville S Africa 78–81; C Norton Woodseats St Chad Sheff 81–83; R Hilton S Africa 83–94; R Milton Ely 94–03; RD Quy 00–02; V Yaxley and Holme w Conington 03–08; Co-ord of Voc and Spirituality Sarum 08–16; Hon C Clarendon 15–16; rtd 16; PtO Ely from 17. 12 Stockwell Avenue, Stamford PE9 2WH T: (01780) 755612 E: iancowley3@outlook.com

COWLEY, Jean Louie Cameron. See HERRICK, Jean Louie Cameron

COWLEY, Mrs Judith Anne. b 59. Nottm Univ BSc 80. Ox Min Course. d 08 p 09. NSM Shepherd's Bush St Steph w St Thos Lon 08–18; NSM Fulham St Andr from 18. 10 Barlby Road, London W10 6AR T: (020) 8960 9587 M: 07824-511029 E: anne.cowley@btinternet.com or anne@standrewsfulham.com

COWLEY, Paul William. b 55. MBE 15. Middx Univ BA 02. NTMTC 99. d 02 p 03. C Brompton H Trin w Onslow Square St Paul Lon 02–11; C Onslow Square and S Kensington St Aug from 11; Pioneer Min from 18; Bps' Adv for Pris and Penal Affairs from 18. 72 Archel Road, London W14 9QP T: (020) 7386 5140 or 08456-447544 M: 07860-146552 E: paul.cowley@htb.org

COWLEY, Peter. b 53. NOC 06. d 08 p 09. NSM Prescot Liv 08–12; NSM Knowsley 12–14; NSM Stockbridge Village 12–14; NSM Huyton St Geo 12–14; NSM W Derby St Luke 12–14; NSM 4Saints Team 14–15; NSM Prescot 15–20; rtd 20. 17 Kingsway, Prescot L35 5BG T: 0151-426 5441 E: petercowley@blueyonder.co.uk

COWLEY, Samuel Henry. b 44. St Jo Coll Nottm 85. d 87 p 88. C Hadleigh w Layham and Shelley St E 87–91; P-in-c Ipswich St Mich 91–99; P-in-c Westerfield and Tuddenham w Witnesham 99–10; rtd 10; PtO St E from 10. 44 Hunters End, Trimley St Mary, Felixstowe IP11 0XH T: (01394) 200462

COWLIN, Clare Margaret. b 54. d 13 p 14. NSM Wells St Thos w Horrington B & W 13–17; NSM Chewton Mendip w Ston Easton, Litton etc 15–17; PtO 17–18 and from 21; NSM Wells St Cuth w Wookey Hole 18–21. Garden Cottage, The Liberty, Wells BA5 2SU T: (01749) 678022 E: clare.cowlin@outlook.com

COWLING, Mark Alasdair. b 71. Loughb Univ BA 92 Man Metrop Univ MA 94. Trin Coll Bris BA 10. d 10 p 11. C Halliwell St Pet Man 10–13; Young Adults Missr 13–17; TR New Bury w Gt Lever Man from 17. 130A Highfield Road, Farnworth, Bolton BL4 0AJ T: (01204) 572334 M: 07701-089420 E: mark@sevensaints.org

COWLING, The Very Revd Simon Charles. b 59. G&C Coll Cam BA 80 MA 88 K Coll Lon PGCE 82. Linc Th Coll BTh 91. d 91 p 92. C Potternewton Ripon 91–94; C Far Headingley St Chad 94–96; V Roundhay St Edm 96–07; AD Allerton 04–07; Can Res and Prec Sheff Cathl 07–13; R Bolton Abbey Bradf 13–14; Leeds 14–18; Hon Can Ripon Cathl 15–18; Dean Wakef from 18; V Wakef Cathl Benefice from 18. The Deanery, 1 Cathedral Close, Wakefield WF1 2DP T: (01924) 373923 E: dean@wakefield-cathedral.org.uk

COWLING-GREEN, Felicity Gabrielle. b 87. SOAS Lon BA 10 Chu Coll Cam BTh 16 Dur Univ MA 18. Ridley Hall Cam 14. d 17 p 18. C Ashton-in-Makerfield St Thos Liv 17–19; USA 19–20; PtO Man from 20; TR Almondbury w Farnley Tyas Leeds from 21. Parish Office, All Hallows Church, Westgate, Almondbury, Huddersfield HD5 8XF T: (01484) 541837 M: 07568-342606 E: felicitycowlinggreen@gmail.com

COWLING-GREEN, Samuel John McKibbin. b 90. d 16 p 17. C Ashton-in-Makerfield St Thos Liv 16–19; USA 19–20; PtO Man from 20; Chapl Leeds and York Partnership NHS Foundn Trust from 21. The Rectory, 2 Westgate, Almondbury, Huddersfield HD5 8XE M: 07553-936123 E: samhcsp@gmail.com

COWPER, Christopher Herbert. b 44. Open Univ BA 76. AKC 67. d 68 p 69. C Pitsmoor Sheff 68–71; C Ulverston St Mary w H Trin Carl 71–74; R Kirklinton w Hethersgill and Scaleby 74–83; V Bridekirk and Chapl Dovenby Hall Hosp Cockermouth 83–94; P-in-c Wetheral w Warwick Carl 94–98; R Barningham w Hutton Magna and Wycliffe Ripon 98–09; rtd 09; PtO Leeds from 17. 6 Darnborough Gate, Ripon HG4 2TF T: (01765) 692221 E: chrisjchrish@gmail.com

COWPER, Peter James. See SELLICK, Peter James

COX, Alan John. b 34. Lon Coll of Div ALCD 65 LTh. d 65 p 66. C Kirkheaton Wakef 65–67; C Keynsham w Queen Charlton B & W 67–71; R Chipstable w Huish Champflower and Clatworthy 71–76; TV Strood Roch 76–80; V Strood St Fran 80–83; R Keston 83–95; rtd 95; PtO Roch from 00. 12 Beech Court, 46 Copers Cope Road, Beckenham BR3 1LD T: (020) 8639 0082

COX, Alison Hilda. b 57. Coll of Ripon & York St Jo BEd 79 Nottm Univ MA 02. EMMTC 99. d 02 p 03. NSM Bakewell Derby 02–04; NSM Walton St Jo 04–05; TV Buxton w Burbage and King Sterndale 05–07; Lay Tr Officer S'well 07–17; PtO Derby from 16. The Cruck Barn, 191 Old Road, Chesterfield S40 3QH T: (01246) 211179

COX, Canon Anthony James Stuart. b 46. BNC Ox BA 68 MA 74. Qu Coll Birm 69. d 71 p 72. C Smethwick St Matt w St Chad Birm 71–74; Chapl Liv Univ 74; Chapl Malosa Secondary Sch Malawi 75–79; Hd Master 80–87; Hon Can S Malawi from 80; Chapl Loughborough Gr Sch 87–09; rtd 09; PtO Leic from 87; S'well from 97. Orchard House, 169 Main Street, Willoughby on the Wolds, Loughborough LE12 6SY T: (01509) 880861 E: tonycox149@gmail.com

COX, Brian Leslie. b 49. S Dios Minl Tr Scheme 91. d 94 p 95. C Southampton Maybush St Pet Win 94–98; P-in-c Knights Enham 98–05; R Knight's Enham and Smannell w Enham Alamein 05–06; P-in-c Freemantle Win 06–09; R 09–14; rtd 14; PtO Win 14–19; Portsm from 14. 2 Arden Close, Gosport PO12 3RS M: 07796-070850 E: brianandlys@icloud.com

COX, Colin John. b 57. Open Univ BSc 97 Dur Univ BA 18. St Aug Coll of Th 14. d 17 p 18. NSM Findon w Clapham and Patching Chich from 17. 40 Hide Gardens, Rustington, Littlehampton BN16 3NP T: (01903) 771981 M: 07716-117905 E: colin@cjcox.name

COX, David John. b 51. Lon Univ BD 97 Man Univ MA 04. Qu Coll Birm 76. d 79 p 80. C Brampton Bierlow Sheff 79–82; Miss Partner CMS 82–88; V N Perak W Malaysia 83–88; V Friarmere Man 88–96; P-in-c Denton Ch 96–06; rtd 06; PtO Carl 07–20. 5 Main Street, St Bees CA27 0DE T: (01946) 821601 E: davidj.cox@hotmail.co.uk

COX (née FRANKLIN), Mrs Dianne Mary. b 48. UEA BA 69 Univ Coll of Swansea PGCE 70. NEOC 03. d 06 p 07. NSM Osbaldwick w Murton York 06–09; Chapl Aiglon Coll Switzerland 09–10; NSM Berne Eur 11–13; rtd 13; Chapl York Teaching Hosp NHS Foundn Trust from 14; PtO York from 14; Eur from 14. 101 Old Orchard, Haxby, York YO32 3DS T: (01904) 421556 E: diannecoxuk@yahoo.co.uk

COX, Elizabeth Anne. b 55. SEITE 01. d 04 p 05. NSM Newington w Hartlip and Stockbury Cant 04–09; Chapl HM Pris Standford Hill 11–13; Chapl HM Pris Swaleside 13–19; P-in-c Gillingham St Barn Roch from 19; P-in-c Gillingham St Mary from 19. The Vicarage, 27 Gillingham Green, Gillingham ME7 1SS T: (01634) 850529 E: revlizcox@outlook.com

COX, Canon Eric William. b 30. Dur Univ BA 54. Wells Th Coll 54. d 56 p 57. C Sutton in Ashfield St Mary S'well 56–59; Asst Chapl Brussels Eur 59–62; V Winnington Ches 62–71; V Middlewich 71–76; Chapl Mid Cheshire Hosps Trust 73–95; P-in-c Biley Ches 73–76; V Middlewich w Byley 76–95; RD Middlewich 80–94; Hon Can Ches Cathl 84–95; rtd 95; PtO Ches 95–09; Lich 96–14. Lovel Hollow, Church Road, Baschurch, Shrewsbury SY4 2EE T: (01939) 261258 E: ewcox@hotmail.co.uk

COX, Geoffrey Sidney Randel. b 33. Mert Coll Ox BA 56 MA 60. Tyndale Hall Bris. d 58 p 59. C St Paul's Cray St Barn CD Roch 58–61; C Bromley Ch Ch 61–64; V Gorsley w Cliffords Mesne Glouc 64–79; V Hucclecote 79–89; V Wollaston and Strixton Pet 89–96; rtd 96; PtO Glouc 96–19. 32 Murvagh Close, Cheltenham GL53 7QY T: (01242) 251604 E: g.cox25@btinternet.com

COX, Hugh Teversham. b 42. Keble Coll Ox BA 76 MA 82 Trin Evang Div Sch (USA) DMin 99. Moore Th Coll Sydney. d 69 p 70. C Manuka St Paul Australia 70–71; P-in-c Kameruka 71–74; PtO Ox 75–76; P-in-c Canberra Ch Ch Australia 76–82; Tutor and Lect St Mark's Nat Th Cen 77–87; R Lane Cove 82–87; R Castle Hill St Paul 87–01; Tervuren Eur 01–06; R E Sydney Australia 06–10; Asst to Bp S Sydney 10–16; rtd 16; PtO Eur 13–19. Weemalah, 201 Mt Lindsay Road, Barraba NSW 2347, Australia T: (0061) (2) 6783 1406 M: (0061) 42-389 5810 E: htevershamcox@hotmail.com

COX, James David Robert. b 65. Lanc Univ BA 88. Qu Coll Birm BD 92. d 93 p 94. C Harborne St Pet Birm 93–96; C Chelmsley Wood 96–97; TV 97–00; V Smethwick Resurr 00–07; V Taunton St Andr B & W 07–09; V Selly Oak St Mary

Birm 09–18; C S Quantock *B & W* from 18; RD Taunton from 20. *55 Batt Drive, Cheddon Fitzpaine, Taunton TA2 8FY* E: jimcox11@gmail.com

COX, Janet. b 48. CBDTI 04. **d** 05 **p** 06. NSM Long Marton w Dufton and w Milburn *Carl* 05–08; NSM Heart of Eden 08–13; rtd 13; PtO *Carl* 13–19; *Leeds* from 19. *86 Ainsty Road, Wetherby LS22 7FY* E: peter_janet_cox@hotmail.com

COX, John Anthony. b 45. Hull Univ BA 67. Qu Coll Birm 71. **d** 73 **p** 74. C Buckingham *Ox* 73–76; C Whitley Ch Ch 76–81; V Reading St Agnes w St Paul 81–83; V Chaddesley Corbett and Stone *Worc* 83–10; rtd 10; PtO *Worc* from 11. *7 Burlington Close, Kidderminster DY10 3DQ* T: (01562) 637966 E: jacm.cox@ukgateway.net

COX, The Ven John Stuart. b 40. Fitzw Ho Cam BA 62 MA 66 Linacre Coll Ox BA 67. Wycliffe Hall Ox 64. **d** 68 **p** 69. C Prescot *Liv* 68–71; C Birm St Geo 71–73; R 73–78; Selection Sec ACCM 78–83; Hon C Orpington All SS *Roch* 78–83; Dioc Dir of Ords *S'wark* 83–91; Can Res and Treas S'wark Cathl 83–91; V Roehampton H Trin 91–95; Adn Sudbury *St E* 95–06; rtd 06; PtO *St E* 06–21; Dioc Dir of Educn 07–10. *2 Bullen Close, Bury St Edmunds IP33 3JP* T/F: (01284) 766796

COX, Julie Margaret. b 55. SAOMC. **d** 00 **p** 01. NSM Luton St Chris Round Green *St Alb* 00–06; NSM Luton St Anne w St Chris 06–08; PtO 08–21; *Leeds* 21. *Belisama, 4 Riverside View, Settle BD24 9FP* E: revjuliecox@hotmail.com

COX, Mrs Linda Jayne. b 66. RGN 88. Qu Coll Birm 10. **d** 12 **p** 13. C Woodfield *Leic* 12–16; R Baschurch and Weston Lullingfield w Hordley *Lich* from 16; RD Ellesmere from 17. *The Rectory, Nobold, Baschurch, Shrewsbury SY4 2EB* T: (01939) 260305 E: lindac40@btinternet.com

COX, Martin Brian. b 64. Keele Univ BA 91 CQSW 91. St Jo Coll Nottm 01. **d** 03 **p** 04. C Sale St Anne *Ches* 03–05; V Sandiway 05–10; P-in-c Chorley St Laur *Blackb* 10–11; R 11–16; TR Astley, Tyldesley and Mosley Common *Man* from 16; AD Leigh 19–21; C Bedford Leigh from 21. *The Rectory, 7 Holbeck, Astley, Tyldesley, Manchester M29 7DU* T: (01942) 883313

COX, Martin Lloyd. b 57. Wilson Carlile Coll and Sarum & Wells Th Coll. **d** 88 **p** 89. C Risca *Mon* 88–91; TV Pontypool 91–96; V Monkton *St D* 96–04; TR 04–10; V Gorseinon *S & B* 10–16; AD Llwchwr 13–15; P-in-c Narberth w Mounton w Robeston Wathen etc *St D* 16–20; P-in-c Narberth and Tenby LMA from 20; AD Narberth and Tenby from 19. *New Rectory, Adams Drive, Narberth SA67 7AE* T: (01834) 861192 E: martinlloydcox@btinternet.com

COX, Noel Stanley Bertie. b 65. Auckland Univ LLB 88 LLM 95 PhD 01 MTheol 08 Lambeth MA 05 Univ of Wales (Lamp) LTh 07 Otago Univ MChap 19 FRHistS 04. St Mich Coll Llan 10. **d** 12 **p** 13. Prof Law Aberystwyth Univ *St D* 10–14; NSM Llanbadarn Fawr and Elerch and Penrhyncoch etc 12–15; NZ from 15. *4/170 St Heliers Bay Road, St Heliers, Auckland 1071, New Zealand* E: noel.cox34@gmail.com

COX, Ms Patricia Jean. b 44. WEMTC. **d** 00 **p** 01. NSM Coleford, Staunton, Newland, Redbrook etc *Glouc* 00–07; NSM Lydney 07–13; rtd 14; PtO *Glouc* from 14. *67 Primrose Hill, Lydney GL15 5SW* T: (01594) 843852

COX, Canon Peter Allard. b 55. Univ of Wales (Lamp) BA 76. Wycliffe Hall Ox 77. **d** 79 **p** 80. C Penarth All SS *Llan* 79–82; V Aberpergwm and Blaengwrach 82–86; V Bargoed and Deri w Brithdir 86–97; V Penarth All SS 97–21; AD Penarth and Barry 11–16; Can Llan Cathl 21; PtO *Llan* from 21. *4 Durell Street, Llantwit Major CF61 1AD* E: peterallard.cox@ntlworld.com

COX, Miss Rosemary Jennifer. b 54. St Aid Coll Dur BA 75 Lon Bible Coll BTh 97 Trin Coll Bris MA 99. Cranmer Hall Dur 01. **d** 03 **p** 04. C Leeds All SS w Osmondthorpe *Ripon* 03–05; C Ireland Wood 05–07; PtO *Dur* from 05. *7 The Paddock, Waterhouses, Durham DH7 9AW* T: 0191-373 1539 E: rosemaryjcox@aol.com

COX, Sheila Margaret. b 54. Nottm Univ BA 76 Reading Univ PGCE 77 Win Univ MA 15. SEITE 00. **d** 03 **p** 04. NSM Cranbrook *Cant* 03–08; NSM Mersham w Hinxhill and Sellindge 08–12; NSM Smeeth w Monks Horton and Stowting and Brabourne 08–12; R G7 Benefice 12–19; Asst Dir of Ords 08–19; Bp's Adv for Women's Min 13–19; Hon Can Cant Cathl 14–19; rtd 19; PtO *Heref* from 20. *Stoneycroft, Hope Bowdler, Church Stretton SY6 7DD* T: (01694) 724960 M: 07985-003095 E: sheila.m.cox@btopenworld.com

COX, Mrs Sheila Stuart. b 41. Aber Coll of Educn CertEd 63. Edin Dioc NSM Course 85. **d** 88 **p** 94. NSM Livingston LEP *Edin* 88–93; Asst Chapl St Jo and Bangour Hosps W Lothian 89–93; Chapl 96–98; Hon C Edin St Mark 93–96; Missr Edin St Andr and St Aid 95–96; NSM Eyemouth 98–05; rtd 05; LtO *Edin* 06–17. *5 Northfield Farm Cottages, St Abbs, Eyemouth TD14 5QF* T: (01890) 771764

COX, Canon Simon John. b 53. Qu Mary Coll Lon BSc 74 Liv Univ PhD 81 Selw Coll Cam BA 81 MA 85 Lanc Univ MA 87 CBiol 79 MRSB 79. Ridley Hall Cam 79. **d** 82 **p** 83. C Livesey *Blackb* 82–85; C Cheadle Hulme St Andr *Ches* 85–89; V Disley 89–94; R Bispham *Blackb* 94–20; P-in-c S Shore St Pet 05–07; AD Blackpool 04–19; P-in-c Copp w Inskip 19–20; Hon Can Blackb Cathl from 07; rtd 20; PtO *Blackb* from 20. *16 Wolverton Avenue, Bispham, Blackpool FY2 9NT* T: (01253) 464795 M: 07703-475586 E: drsjcox@yahoo.co.uk

COX, Stephen John Wormleighton. b 54. New Coll Ox MA 79 Fitzw Coll Cam BA 79. Ridley Hall Cam 77. **d** 80 **p** 81. C Clapton Park All So *Lon* 80–85; V Holloway St Mary w St Jas 87–88; P-in-c Barnsbury St Dav w St Clem 87–88; V Holloway St Mary Magd 88–97; AD Islington 95–99; TR Upper Holloway 97–10; Preb St Paul's Cathl 07–10; Local Miss Adv *Guildf* 10–18; rtd 18; PtO *Guildf* from 19. *17 Glenmount Road, Mytchett, Camberley GU16 6AY* T: (01483) 790330 E: stephenj.cox@virgin.net

COXALL, Mrs Jayne. b 66. Open Univ BSc 09. All SS Cen for Miss & Min 14. **d** 17 **p** 18. C Bredbury St Mark *Ches* 17–19; C Aber-Morfa Miss Area *St As* from 19. *18 Tirionfa, Rhuddlan, Rhyl LL18 6LT* T: (01745) 590883 M: 07896-652261 E: jaynecoxall@aol.com

COYNE, Deborah Margaret. b 88. Cranmer Hall Dur 12. **d** 15 **p** 16. C Rural E York 15–18; C Tadcaster 18–19; P-in-c Alne from 19; P-in-c Brafferton w Pilmoor, Myton-on-Swale etc from 19; C Coxwold and Husthwaite from 19; C Crayke w Brandsby and Yearsley from 19; C Easingwold w Raskelf from 19; C Forest of Galtres from 19; C Skelton w Shipton and Newton on Ouse from 19; C Strensall from 19. *1 Hollygarth, Brafferton, York YO61 2NZ* M: 07704-855759 E: rev.deborah.coyne@gmail.com

COYNE, John Edward. b 55. Sheff Univ MA 98. Oak Hill Th Coll BA 79. **d** 79 **p** 80. C Cheadle Hulme St Andr *Ches* 79–81; C Macclesfield St Mich 81–83; V Stalybridge H Trin and Ch Ch 83–88; Chapl RAF 88–03; Command Chapl RAF 03–05; RAF Adv in Evangelism 93–98; Hon C Hemingford Grey *Ely* 96–98; Dean of Coll St Jo Coll Nottm 05–09; Dir Local and Regional Delivery CPAS 09–12; R Aldridge *Lich* 12–17; Patr Leadership Specialist CPAS 17–20; PtO *Cov* from 21; *Ox* from 21. *Windrush House, London Road, Moreton-in-Marsh GL56 0HB* T: (01608) 652159 E: j2scoyne@hotmail.com

COZENS (née FULLER), Mrs Alison Jane. b 61. St Andr Univ MTheol 84. Edin Th Coll 85. **d** 87 **p** 94. C Selkirk *Edin* 87–89; C Melrose 87–89; C Galashiels 87–89; C Edin H Cross 89–92; Dn-in-c Edin St Columba 92–94; R 94–10; Chapl Edin Univ 96–00; P-in-c Leic Presentation 10–15; R Dunfermline *St And* 15–18; P-in-c Birm St Geo 18–20; P-in-c Lozells St Paul and St Silas 18–20; P-in-c Lozells and Newtown from 20. *St James's Vicarage, 21 Austin Road, Birmingham B21 8NU* T: 0121-551 3470 E: revalisonjanecozens18@gmail.com

COZENS, Daniel Harry. b 44. Oak Hill Th Coll. **d** 71 **p** 72. C St Paul's Cray St Barn *Roch* 71–74; C Deptford St Nic w Ch Ch *S'wark* 74–76; C Deptford St Nic and St Luke 76–78; Rees Missr *Ely* 78–09; rtd 09; PtO *Ely* 09–19; Six Preacher Cant Cathl 94–04. *Walnut Top, High Street, Bury, Ramsey, Huntingdon PE26 2NR* T: (01487) 814533

COZENS, Canon Michael Graeme. b 59. Chich Th Coll 91. **d** 93 **p** 94. C Emscote *Cov* 93–96; C Prestbury *Glouc* 96–03; TV Prestbury and All SS 03–06; P-in-c 06–08; TR N Cheltenham 08–14; P-in-c Dursley 14–18; R Dursley, Uley, Owlpen etc from 18; Hon Can Glouc Cathl from 10. *The Rectory, Broadwell, Dursley GL11 4JE* T: (01453) 542035

COZIER, Christopher Eugene. b 83. Wycliffe Hall Ox. **d** 16 **p** 17. C Harold Hill St Geo *Chelmsf* 16–18; C Cranham Park 18–21. *21 Small Heath Avenue, Romford RM3 7FB* M: 07881-900487 E: magpie83@live.co.uk

CRABB, Helen Maria. *See* BARTON, Helen Maria

CRABB, Paul Anthony. b 58. St Chad's Coll Dur BSc 79 Leeds Univ PGCE 80. Qu Coll Birm 90. **d** 91 **p** 92. C Gomersal *Wakef* 91–95; V Drighlington 95–01; TV Dewsbury 01–09; P-in-c Hanging Heaton 09–12; P-in-c Batley St Thos 09–12; P-in-c Bramley *Ripon* 14; *Leeds* 14–17; R from 17. *The Vicarage, 8 Hough Lane, Leeds LS13 3NE* T: 0113-257 8590 *or* 225 8562 M: 07946-530415 E: paulthepriest.pc@gmail.com

CRABTREE, Hazel. b 40. SRN 82 Yorks & Humberside Assn for F&HE TCert 89. **d** 07 **p** 08. OLM Went Valley *Wakef* 07–10; PtO 10–14; *Leeds* 14–16. *11 Hillcroft Close, Darrington, Pontefract WF8 3BD* T: (01977) 793268 E: hazel@darringtonchurch.com *or* rev.hcrabtree@gmail.com

CRABTREE, Martine Charmaine. b 74. Glas Bible Coll BA 96 St Jo Coll Nottm MTh 02. **d** 02 **p** 03. C Kippax w Allerton Bywater *Ripon* 02–06; P-in-c Sowerby *Wakef* 06–12; P-in-c Norland 09–12; P-in-c Lupset 12–14; *Leeds* from 14; P-in-c Thornes *Wakef* 12–14; *Leeds* from 14; Adv on Urban

Issues from 12. *Lupset Vicarage, 23C Broadway, Wakefield WF2 8AA* T: (01422) 832830 E: martinecrabtree@aol.com
CRACKNELL, Heather Louise. b 76. UEA BSc 97. ERMC 08. d 11 p 12. C Cringleford and Colney *Nor* 11–17; V Nor Heartsease St Fran 17–19; Hd of Development Fresh Expressions Abps' Coun from 19; PtO *Nor* from 20. *Church House, 27 Great Smith Street, London SW1P 3AZ* T: (020) 7898 1000 E: heather.cracknell@gmail.com *or* heather.cracknell@churchofengland.org
CRADDOCK, Lesley-Ann. b 58. Ridley Hall Cam 10. d 12 p 13. C Hatfield Hyde *St Alb* 12–15; P-in-c Glas St Oswald 15–18; P-in-c Dunkeld *St And* from 20; PtO *Mor* 19–20. *Address temp unknown* M: 07903-020509 E: lesley.craddock@btinternet.com
CRADDUCK, Stuart William. b 74. Bp Otter Coll Chich BA 97. Ripon Coll Cuddesdon BTh 00. d 00 p 01. C W Leigh *Portsm* 00–03; Min Can St Alb Abbey 03–07; R Whyke w Rumboldswhyke and Portfield *Chich* 07–14; R Grantham St Wulfram *Linc* from 14; P-in-c Grantham, Manthorpe from 14; RD Grantham from 19. *The Rectory, Church Street, Grantham NG31 6RR* T: (01476) 569582 E: rector@stwulframs.com
CRAFER, Mrs Jeanette Angela. b 48. Keswick Hall Coll CertEd 78. EAMTC 99. d 01 p 02. C Ashmanhaugh, Barton Turf etc *Nor* 01–05; P-in-c Martham and Repps w Bastwick, Thurne etc 05–07; V 07–13; rtd 13; PtO *Nor* from 14. *Whispers, Chapel Road, Sea Palling, Norwich NR12 0UQ* T: (01692) 598590 E: rev.jeanette@btinternet.com
CRAFT, William Newham. b 46. Lon Univ BSc 68 MCIPD 70. Oak Hill Th Coll 87. d 89 p 90. C Werrington *Pet* 90–93; C-in-c Norfolk Park St Leonard CD *Sheff* 93–02; P-in-c Sheff St Jo 99–02; V 02–03; V Stapleford *S'well* 03–09; AD Beeston 07–09; rtd 09; PtO *Sheff* from 09. *435 Redmires Road, Sheffield S10 4LF* T: 0114-230 2718 E: billncraft@gmail.com
CRAGG, Edward William Adrian. b 55. St Cath Coll Cam BA 77 MA 81. Cranmer Hall Dur 97. d 99 p 00. C Clifton *York* 99–02; R Skelton w Shipton and Newton on Ouse 02–09; Chapl York Hosps NHS Foundn Trust 02–09; R Bridlington Priory *York* 09–12; V Wyke *Bradf* 12–14; rtd 18. *6 Ward Street, Skipton BD23 2EY*
CRAGG, Mrs Sandra Anne. b 45. St Hugh's Coll Ox BA 67. SEITE 94. d 97 p 98. NSM Kingston All SS w St Jo *S'wark* 97–12; NSM Kingston 12–15; PtO from 15. *10 Lingfield Avenue, Kingston upon Thames KT1 2TN* T: (020) 8546 1997 F: 8541 5281 E: sandycragg26@gmail.com
CRAGGS, Michael Alfred. b 43. Open Univ BA 79. St Mich Coll Llan 66. d 69 p 70. C Clee *Linc* 69–72; C Old Brumby 72–76; TV Kingsthorpe w Northampton St Dav *Pet* 76–83; P-in-c Gt w Lt Addington 83–89; RD Higham 88–89; TR Corby SS Pet and Andr w Gt and Lt Oakley 89–02; V Corby SS Pet and Andr 02–08; RD Corby 90–95; rtd 08. *1 Johnson Drive, Scotter, Gainsborough DN21 3HA* T: (01724) 764200 E: mikeccorb@aol.com
CRAGO, Geoffrey Norman. b 44. Linc Th Coll 67. d 70 p 71. C Matson *Glouc* 70–75; V Dean Forest H Trin 75–80; Relig Progr Producer Radio Severn Sound 80–85; P-in-c Huntley *Glouc* 80–82; PtO 82–90; Dioc Communications Officer 84; Gen Syn Broadcasting Dept 85–88; Hon C Highnam, Lassington, Rudford, Tibberton etc *Glouc* 90–08; Relig Progr Producer BBC Radio Gloucestershire 94–03; Bp's Press Officer and Dioc Communications Officer *Glouc* 97–01; rtd 09; PtO *Glouc* from 16. *Milestones, 2 Two Mile Lane, Highnam, Gloucester GL2 8DW* T: (01452) 750575 F: 08700-940404 E: g.crago@btinternet.com
CRAIG, Canon Alan Stuart. b 38. Leeds Univ BA 59. Cranmer Hall Dur. d 61 p 62. C Newcastle w Butterton *Lich* 61–65; C Scarborough St Mary w Ch Ch, St Paul and St Thos *York* 65–67; V Werrington *Lich* 67–72; Asst Chapl HM Pris Man 72–73; Chapl HM Borstal Hindley 73–78; Chapl HM Pris Acklington 78–84; V Longhirst *Newc* 84–90; R Morpeth 90–99; RD 84–95; Dir of Ords and Bp's Chapl 99–02; Hon Can Newc Cathl 90–02; Chapl Northd Mental Health NHS Trust 90–99; Chapl to The Queen 95–08; rtd 02; PtO *Newc* from 02. *5 Springfield Meadows, Alnwick NE66 2NY* T: (01665) 602806 M: 07779-519040
CRAIG, Andrew John. b 54. Selw Coll Cam BA 76 MA 80 PhD 80 Dur Univ MBA 92. NEOC 00. d 03 p 04. NSM Stranton *Dur* 03–19; rtd 19; PtO *Dur* from 20. *25 Egerton Road, Hartlepool TS26 0BW* T: (01429) 422461 E: revdrandrewcraig@gmail.com
CRAIG, Gillean Weston. b 49. York Univ BA 72 Qu Coll Cam BA 76 MA 80. Westcott Ho Cam 76. d 77 p 78. C St Marylebone Ch Ch *Lon* 77–82; C Ealing St Barn 82–88; P-in-c St Geo-in-the-East w St Paul 88–89; R 89–02; V Kensington St Mary Abbots w St Geo 02–06; V Kensington St Mary Abbots 06–18; Preb St Paul's Cathl 16–18; rtd

18; PtO *Cant* 19–20; P-in-c Littlebourne and Ickham w Wickhambreaux etc 20; C Canonry 20. *61 Cromwell Road, Whitstable CT5 1NN*
CRAIG, James Owen Maxwell. b 72. Open Univ BA 98. Cranmer Hall Dur 99. d 02 p 03. C Ch the K *Dur* 02–05; Gateshead and Bensham Community Chapl to Arts 05–16; TV Gateshead 11–16; Chapl Guy's Campus K Coll Lon from 16; C S'wark St Geo w St Alphege and St Jude 16–17; NSM St Mary le Strand w St Clem Danes *Lon* from 17. *11 Wilkinson Street, London SW8 1DD* T: (020) 7091 0292 M: 07918-659088 E: rev.jim@btopenworld.com *or* jim.craig@kcl.ac.uk
CRAIG, Canon John Newcome. b 39. Selw Coll Cam BA 63 MA 67. Linc Th Coll 63. d 65 p 66. C Cannock *Lich* 65–71; V Gt Wyrley 71–79; TR Wednesfield 79–91; Prec Leic Cathl 91–03; Hon Can Leic Cathl 93–03; Can Res Leic Cathl 03–04; rtd 04; PtO *Birm* from 04; *Lich* 19–21. *231 Beacon Park Village, Lower Sandford Street, Lichfield WS13 6JZ* E: john.olivia.craig@lineone.net
CRAIG, Judy Howard. See CRAIG PECK, Judy Howard
CRAIG, Julie Elizabeth. See EATON, Julie Elizabeth
CRAIG, Richard Harvey. b 31. Em Coll Cam BA 58. Linc Th Coll. d 60 p 61. C Bottesford *Linc* 60–65; Bp's Ind Chapl 65–69; Dioc Adv on Laity Tr *Bris* 69–74; V Whitchurch 74–86; TV N Lambeth *S'wark* 86–96; Bp's Ecum Adv 88–96; Ecum Officer 90–96; rtd 96; PtO *St Alb* 96–99; *S'wark* 01. *18 Holst Court, Westminster Bridge Road, London SE1 7JQ* T: (020) 7928 0495
CRAIG, Robin Joseph. b 43. TCD BA 65 Div Test 66 Birm Univ CertEd 70. d 66 p 67. C Carrickfergus *Conn* 66–69; Chapl Lord Wandsworth Coll Hook 75–85; Vice Prin and Chapl K Sch Macclesfield 85–01; LtO *Ches* 85–01; rtd 01. *5 Winston Court, Lavant Road, Chichester PO19 5RG* T: (01243) 778636
CRAIG PECK, Judy Howard. b 57. Lon Univ MB, BS 81 MRCGP 86. WMMTC 97. d 00 p 01. NSM Billing *Pet* 00–07; NSM Yardley Hastings, Denton and Grendon etc 07–15; NSM Officer 03–10; C Guilsborough and Hollowell and Cold Ashby etc from 15. *14 Pine Court, Little Brington, Northampton NN7 4EZ* M: 07714-401695 E: judy@revpeck.co.uk
CRAIGHEAD, Mrs Patricia Anne. b 60. Northumbria Univ BSc 02 St Jo Coll Dur MATM 12. NEOC 05. d 08 p 09. C Monkseaton St Pet *Newc* 08–12; V Long Benton St Mary 12–21; rtd 21. *23 Airedale, Wallsend NE28 8TL* M: 07967-316615 E: patcraighead@hotmail.co.uk
CRAMERI, Mrs Mary Barbara. b 44. K Coll Lon BD 65 AKC 91 Lon Inst of Educn PGCE 66. S Dios Minl Tr Scheme 86. d 88 p 94. C Whitton SS Phil and Jas *Lon* 88–91; Tutor STETS 91–97; Vice-Prin 93–96; Acting Prin 96–97; Dep Dir and Minl Formation Officer 97–98; Par Dn Bemerton *Sarum* 91–92; TV Pewsey and Swanborough 98–00; TR Whitton 00–01; rtd 01; PtO *Sarum* 02–05; *Ox* 10–12; *Cov* from 10; Hon C Chase *Ox* 05–10. *6 Browning Close, Stratford-upon-Avon CV37 7PF* T: (01789) 296650 E: mary.crameri@btinternet.com
CRAMPTON, John Leslie. b 41. CITC 64. d 67 p 68. C Lurgan Ch the Redeemer *D & D* 67–71; C Dundela St Mark 71–73; C Umtali Rhodesia 73–76; R Fort Victoria 73–76; I Killanne w Killegney, Rossdroit and Templeshanbo *C, F & O* 82–88; Preb Ferns Cathl 85–88; Chapl Wilson's Hosp Sch Multyfarnham *M & K* 88–91; C Mullingar, Portnashangan, Moyliscar, Kilbixy etc 89–91; I Athy w Kilberry, Fontstown and Kilkea *D & G* 91–01; Can Ch Ch Cathl Dublin 95–01; I Geashill w Killeigh and Ballycommon *M & K* 01–06; rtd 06. *41 Beech Avenue, The Paddock, Enniscorthy, Co Wexford, Y21 Y6H9, Republic of Ireland* T: (00353) (53) 923 2589 M: 87-907 7981 E: cramptonj41@gmail.com
CRANE, Mrs Judith. b 53. Matlock Coll of Educn BCombStuds 81. Cranmer Hall Dur 94. d 96 p 97. C Tadcaster w Newton Kyme *York* 96–99; TV Brayton 99–02; V Blackwell w Tibshelf *Derby* 02–08; Asst Dir of Ords 06–09; LtO 09–18; rtd 18; PtO *Derby* from 19. *12 Laund Close, Belper DE56 1ET* E: judithcrane@yahoo.co.uk
CRANFIELD, Charlotte Clare. b 60. d 16 p 21. NSM Easingwold w Raskelf *York* from 16; NSM Skelton w Shipton and Newton on Ouse from 17; NSM Alne from 17; NSM Brafferton w Pilmoor, Myton-on-Swale etc from 17; NSM Coxwold and Husthwaite from 17; NSM Crayke w Brandsby and Yearsley from 17; NSM Strensall from 17; NSM Forest of Galtres from 17. *12 Penny Lane, Easingwold, York YO61 3RR* T: (01347) 824399
CRANFIELD, Canon Nicholas William Stewart. b 56. Mert Coll Ox BA 77 MA 81 DPhil 88 Leeds Univ BA 81 Selw Coll Cam PhD 95 FSA 07. Coll of Resurr Mirfield 79 Union Th Sem (NY) STM 84. d 86 p 87. C Ascot Heath *Ox* 86–89; Prin Berks Chr Tr Scheme 89–92; Hon C Reading St Mary the Virgin 89–92; Chapl and Fell Selw Coll Cam 92–99; Dean of Chpl 94–99; Chapl Newnham Coll Cam 92–99; V

Blackheath All SS S'wark from 99; Chapl St Dunstan's Coll Catford 00–05; Hon Can S'wark Cathl from 17. *All Saints' Vicarage, 10 Duke Humphrey Road, London SE3 0TY* T: (020) 8852 4280

CRANKSHAW, Ronald. b 41. Coll of Resurr Mirfield 74. **d** 76 **p** 77. C Orford St Andr *Liv* 76; C N Meols 76–79; V Abram 79–85; V Wigan St Anne 85–99; AD Wigan W 94–99; V Heston *Lon* 99–07; rtd 07; PtO *Carl* 09–16; *Liv* from 16. *Address temp unknown* E: roncrankshaw@sky.com

CRANMER, Ms Elaine. b 56. Hockerill Coll Cam CertEd 77. SEITE 97. **d** 00 **p** 01. C Charlton S'wark 00–03; P-in-c Eltham Park St Luke 03–10; V 11–14; AD Eltham and Mottingham 06–13; TR S Chatham H Trin *Roch* from 14. *The Rectory, 18 Marion Close, Chatham ME5 9QA* T: (01634) 685556 E: elaine.cranmer@gmail.com

CRANSHAW, Trevor Raymond. b 58. Trin Coll Bris 00. **d** 03 **p** 04. C Westbury-on-Trym H Trin *Bris* 03–07; P-in-c Wheathill Priory Gp *B & W* 07–14; P-in-c Clevedon St Andr and Ch Ch 14–18; V Clevedon St Andr and St Pet from 18; Warden of Readers Bath Adnry from 17. *The Vicarage, 10B Coleridge Road, Clevedon BS21 7TB* T: (01275) 871458 *or* 872982 M: 07872-496300 E: trevcranshaw@hotmail.com *or* vicar@standrews-clevedon.org.uk

CRANSTON, Andrew David. b 79. Ex Univ MEng 02 PGCE 04 Cam Univ BTh 11. Ridley Hall Cam 08. **d** 11 **p** 12. C Stone Ch Ch and Oulton *Lich* 11–14; Chapl Oswestry Sch 14–20; PtO *Lich* 20–21; C Criftins w Dudleston and Welsh Frankton from 21. *Offa's View, Trefonen, Oswestry SY10 9DQ*

CRANSTON, Miss Margaret Elizabeth. b 56. Newnham Coll Cam BEd 78 Ex Univ BTh 10. SWMTC 04. **d** 07 **p** 08. NSM Heanton Punchardon w Marwood *Ex* 07–13; NSM Isle Valley *B & W* 13–16; rtd 16; PtO *Ex* from 17. *17 South Park, Braunton EX33 2HT* T: (01271) 813295 E: mecranston@btinternet.com

CRANWELL, Brian Robert. b 32. Sheff Poly MSc Sheff Hallam Univ MPhil 06. Cranmer Hall Dur. **d** 84 **p** 85. C Ecclesfield *Sheff* 84–86; V Handsworth Woodhouse 86–99; rtd 99; PtO *Sheff* 99–20; *Derby* 00–05. *9 Westview Close, Totley, Sheffield S17 3LT* T: 0114-262 1499 E: brian_cranwell@lineone.net

CRASKE, Leslie Gordon Hamilton. b 29. AKC 54 Lambeth STh 80. St Boniface Warminster 54. **d** 55 **p** 56. C Malden St Jo S'wark 55–58; C Streatham St Leon 58–60; SPG S Rhodesia 60–65; SPG Rhodesia 65–66; V Upper Norwood St Jo *Cant* 67–83; R Guernsey St Sav *Win* 83–97; rtd 97; PtO *Win* from 97. *La Gruterie, 3 Mount Row, St Peter Port, Guernsey GY1 1NS* T: (01481) 716027

CRASTON (née FULLALOVE), Mrs Brenda Hurst. b 33. Open Univ BA 75 Man Univ MPhil 86. St Mich Ho Ox 58. **dss** 80 **d** 87 **p** 94. Bolton St Paul w Em *Man* 80–93; Par Dn 87–93; rtd 93; PtO *Man* from 94. *12 Lever Park Avenue, Horwich, Bolton BL6 7LE* T: (01204) 699972 E: colbrencraston@gmail.com

CRAVEN, Colin Peter. b 48. Dartmouth RN Coll. St Steph Ho Ox 83. **d** 85 **p** 86. C Holbeach *Linc* 85–88; Chapl Fleet Hosp 86–97; TV Grantham *Linc* 88–97; P-in-c Fairfield *Derby* 97–03; OCM 88–03; CF 03–06; Rtd Officer Chapl RAChD 06–14; rtd 14. *29A Cranford Avenue, Exmouth EX8 2QA* E: revcp@hotmail.com

CRAVEN, David Alex. b 80. Univ of Wales (Ban) BA 01. Wycliffe Hall Ox BTh 06. **d** 06 **p** 07. C Holme Eden and Wetheral w Warwick *Carl* 06–09; R 09–17; C Croglin 06–09; P-in-c 09–12; R Rufford and Tarleton *Blackb* 17–19; C Preston St Jo and St Geo from 19. *97 Garstang Road, Preston PR1 1LD* E: dacraven@hotmail.com

CRAVEN, Janet Elizabeth. *See* CHAPMAN, Janet Elizabeth

CRAVEN, Mrs Janet Mary. b 43. Bp Otter Coll TCert 64. **d** 06 **p** 07. OLM Shelley and Shepley *Wakef* 06–14; Leeds 14–16; OLM Kirkburton and Shelley from 16. *70 Jenkyn Lane, Shepley, Huddersfield HD8 8AW* T: (01484) 604107

CRAVEN, Rebecca Clare. b 58. Bris Univ BDS 80 Glas Univ MPH 90 Man Univ PhD 97 RCPS FDS 97. **d** 01 **p** 02. OLM Reddish *Man* 01–06; NSM 06–07; NSM Salford Sacred Trin and St Phil 07–16; NSM Salford Sacred Trin from 16. *201 Thornton Road, Fallowfield, Manchester M14 7NS* T: 0161-225 7336 E: rebecca.c.craven@manchester.ac.uk

CRAW, Jane Mary. b 53. Stockwell Coll of Educn CertEd 76 Lon Inst of Educn BEd 77. STETS BA 13. **d** 10 **p** 11. NSM Sherborne w Castleton, Lillington and Longburton *Sarum* 10–16; TV from 16. *Jubilee Cottage, Lower Kingsbury, Milborne Port, Sherborne DT9 5ED* T: (01963) 251527 E: jane@jubileecottage.plus.com

CRAWFORD, Alexander Ian George. b 88. Univ Coll Dur BA 11 Sheff Univ MA 18. Coll of Resurr Mirfield 16. **d** 18 **p** 19. C Bensham and Teams *Dur* from 18; C Gateshead St Helen from 18. *St Columba House, Peterborough Close, Gateshead NE8 1NL* M: 07450-507956 E: revd.crawford@outlook.com *or* aigc88@hotmail.com

CRAWFORD, Mrs Anne Elizabeth. b 59. SAOMC 01. **d** 04 **p** 05. C Billington, Egginton, Hockliffe etc *St Alb* 04–08; R Toddington and Chalgrave 08–16; TV Richmond St Mary w St Matthias and St Jo *S'wark* from 16. *St Matthias' House, 22 Cambrian Road, Richmond TW10 6JQ* T: (020) 8948 7217 E: annie.anselm@btinternet.com

CRAWFORD, Canon Ivy Elizabeth. b 50. Trin Coll Bris 83. **dss** 85 **d** 87 **p** 94. Collier Row St Jas *Chelmsf* 85; Collier Row St Jas and Havering-atte-Bower 86–89; Par Dn 87–89; Par Dn Harlow New Town w Lt Parndon 89–94; C Harlow Town Cen w Lt Parndon 94–95; V Blackmore and Stondon Massey 95–09; RD Ongar 06–09; P-in-c Broxted w Chickney and Tilty etc 09–16; CME Adv 09–16; Hon Can Chelmsf Cathl 98–16; rtd 16; PtO *Lon* from 19. *118B Holden Road, London N12 7EA* T: (020) 3560 1299 E: ivycrawford@btinternet.com

CRAWFORD, James Robert Harry. b 55. Cumbria Univ BA 08. CBDTI 00. **d** 03 **p** 04. NSM Lower Darwen St Jas *Blackb* 03–10; C Colne and Villages 10–14; C Pendle Deanery 14–16; C Bispham *Blackb* from 16. *89 Ashfield Road, Blackpool FY2 0EN* T: (01253) 592166 E: jayjay644@btinternet.com *or* jrcrawford645@gmail.com

CRAWFORD, Kenneth Ian. b 48. Melbourne Univ BMus 77 Columbia Univ MA 79 MEd 80 MACE 84. Trin Coll Melbourne BD 86. **d** 87 **p** 87. C Ringwood St Paul Australia 87–89; C Cheltenham St Matt 89–90; P-in-c Vermont S H Name 90–93; Can Prec Melbourne Cathl 93–97; P-in-c Warndon St Nic *Worc* 97–03; V Pershore w Pinvin, Wick and Birlingham 03–14; P-in-c Darlington St Jas *Dur* 14–20; P-in-c Newc St Jo from 20. *The Vicarage, 3 Crossway, Jesmond, Newcastle upon Tyne NE2 3QH* E: kenneth.priest@stjohnthebaptistnewcastle.co.uk

CRAWFORD, Louise Dorothy Anita. *See* CRAWFORD-McCAFFERTY, Louise Dorothy Anita

CRAWFORD, Michael Davis. b 45. Oak Hill Th Coll BA 97 K Coll Lon PGCE 98. **d** 00 **p** 01. NSM New Barnet St Jas *St Alb* 00–04; C Limassol St Barn Cyprus 04–08; Chapl SE Cyprus 08–11; PtO *Eur* from 11; Cyprus and the Gulf from 11; PtO *Nor* from 18. *3 Brewers Green Lane, Diss IP22 4QP* M: 07572-615268 E: rev.michaelcrawford@gmail.com

CRAWFORD JONES, Neil. *See* JONES, Neil Crawford

CRAWFORD-McCAFFERTY, Louise Dorothy Anita. b 60. Oak Hill Th Coll BA 91 Princeton Th Sem MDiv 00. Irish Sch of Ecum MPhil 02. **d** 02 **p** 03. C Drumragh w Mountfield *D & R* 02–05; I Aghadowey w Kilrea 05–17; I Aghadowey from 17. *40 Brone Road, Garvagh, Coleraine BT51 4EQ* T: (028) 7086 9277 M: 07725-908117 E: louisecrawfordmccafferty@yahoo.com

CRAWLEY, Alan John. b 58. Trin Coll Cam MA 83. SAOMC 04. **d** 07 **p** 08. NSM Gt Marlow w Marlow Bottom, Lt Marlow and Bisham *Ox* 07–08; C Amersham on the Hill 08–11; P-in-c Badshot Lea and Hale *Guildf* 11–15; NSM from 15. *The Rectory, 25 Upper Hale Road, Farnham GU9 0NX* T: (01252) 820537 E: reverend.alan@gmail.com

CRAWLEY, Canon David. b 47. TD . St Steph Ho Ox 75. **d** 78 **p** 79. C Solihull *Birm* 78–81; TV Newbury *Ox* 81–84; LtO 84–95; Chapl Stoke Mandeville Hosp Aylesbury 84–95; Distr Chapl 88–95; Hd Chapl Services W Suffolk Hosps NHS Trust 95–11; Bp's Adv on Hosp Chapl *St E* 00–11; Hon Can St E Cathl 05–17; Chapl 11–17; PtO from 18. *22 Westbury Avenue, Bury St Edmunds IP33 3QE* T: (01284) 750526 E: davidandrew@davidandrew.plus.com

CRAWLEY (née FELLOWS), Lesley June. b 70. Salford Univ BEng 91 New Coll Ox DPhil 01. Ox Min Course 04. **d** 07 **p** 08. C Bernwode *Ox* 07–11; NSM Badshot Lea and Hale *Guildf* 12–15; R from 15. *The Rectory, 25 Upper Hale Road, Farnham GU9 0NX* T: (01252) 820537 E: revdlesley@gmail.com

CRAWLEY, Nicholas Simon. b 58. Southn Univ BSc 79 ACIB 82. AIIM 85. Wycliffe Hall Ox 85. **d** 88 **p** 89. C E Twickenham St Steph *Lon* 88–93; R Avondale Zimbabwe 93–99; P-in-c Netherthorpe St Steph *Sheff* 99–04; Network Miss P (Bris Adnry) *Bris* from 04; P-in-c Clifton H Trin, St Andr and St Pet 10–12; NSM Redland from 17. *27 Carnarvon Road, Bristol BS6 7DU* T: 0117-944 1980 E: nick.crawley@blueyonder.co.uk

✠**CRAY, The Rt Revd Graham Alan.** b 47. Leeds Univ BA 68. St Jo Coll Nottm 69. **d** 71 **p** 72 **c** 01. C Gillingham St Mark *Roch* 71–75; N Area Co-ord CPAS Youth Dept 75–78; C York St Mich-le-Belfrey 78–82; V 82–92; Prin Ridley Hall Cam 92–01; Six Preacher Cant Cathl 97–01; Suff Bp Maidstone 01–09; Abps' Missr and Team Ldr Fresh Expressions 09–14; rtd 14; Hon Asst Bp Cant 09–14; Hon Asst Bp York from 09; Hon Asst Bp Roch 11–14. *The Dovecote, Main Street, Kirby Misperton, Malton YO17 6XL* T: (01653) 669365 E: grahamcray@me.com

CRAY, Mrs Jacqueline. b 49. Glos Coll of Educn CertEd 70. SEITE 01. **d** 04 **p** 05. NSM Gt Chart *Cant* 04–08;

P-in-c Maidstone St Faith 08–14; Asst Dir of Ords 09–14; rtd 14; PtO *York* from 14. *The Dovecote, Main Street, Kirby Misperton, Malton YO17 6XL* T: (01653) 669365 M: 07889-742973 E: jackiecray@hotmail.co.uk

CREAN, Patrick John Eugene. b 38. TCD BA 81 MA 84. Edin Th Coll 82. **d** 84 **p** 85. C Perth St Jo *St And* 84–86; P-in-c Liv St Phil w St Dav 86–87; V 87–90; R Cupar and Ladybank *St And* 90–92; P-in-c Sefton *Liv* 92–97; Dioc Children's Officer 92–03; V Aintree St Giles 97–98; V Aintree St Giles w St Pet 98–03; rtd 03; PtO *Liv* from 03. *36 Lingfield Close, Netherton, Bootle L30 1BB* T: 0151-525 8838 E: paddycrean@hotmail.co.uk

CREASER, Canon David Edward. b 35. St Cath Coll Cam BA 58 MA 62. Clifton Th Coll 59. **d** 61 **p** 62. C Cheadle *Ches* 61–67; V Weston *Bradf* 67–69; P-in-c Denton 67–69; V Weston w Denton 69–74 and 82–02; Dir Educn 73–96; V Frizinghall 74–82; Hon Can Bradf Cathl 80–02; P-in-c Leathley w Farnley, Fewston and Blubberhouses 96–02; rtd 02; PtO *Bradf* 03–14; *Leeds* from 14. *Rose Cottage, Pant Lane, Austwick, Lancaster LA2 8BH* T: (01542) 51536 E: david@creaser.com

CREASEY, Mrs Alison Frances. b 72. Yorks Min Course 12. **d** 15 **p** 16. NSM Dore *Sheff* 15–19; NSM Totley from 18. *142 Meadowhead, Sheffield S8 7UF* M: 07496-451687 E: alison.creasey@sheffield.anglican.org

CREASEY, Graham. See GOLDSTONE-CREASEY, Graham

CREBER, Preb Arthur Frederick. b 45. NOC 84. **d** 87 **p** 88. C Rickerscote *Lich* 87–91; V Gt Wyrley 91–99; RD Rugeley 94–98; P-in-c Newcastle w Butterton 99–07; R 07–08; Preb Lich Cathl 04–08; rtd 08; PtO *St As* from 09. *22 Malvern Rise, Rhos-on-Sea, Colwyn Bay LL28 4RX* T: (01492) 547761 E: arthur.creber@btinternet.com

CREBER-DAVIES, Matthew James. b 84. UEA BA 07 Cam Univ BTh 19. Ridley Hall Cam 17. **d** 20 **p** 21. C Cornerstone Team *Leic* from 20. *59 Somerby Road, Thurnby, Leicester LE7 9PR* M: 07739-171984

CREDITON, Suffragan Bishop of. See SEARLE, The Rt Revd Jacqueline Ann

CREE, John Richard. b 44. Open Univ BA 74 Lanc Univ MA 92. Coll of Resurr Mirfield. **d** 83 **p** 84. C Blackb St Jas 83–86; V Feniscowles 86–01; Chapl Blackb Coll 86–01; R Chorley St Laur *Blackb* 01–09; rtd 09; PtO *Bre* from 86; *Blackb* from 09. *5 Bromley Green, Chorley PR6 8TX* T: (01257) 263398 E: john.cree@tiscali.co.uk

CREEDON, Anna Clare. b 90. Cardiff Univ BA 12 K Coll Lon MA 15 Aber Univ PhD 19 Southn Univ PGCE 13. Trin Coll Bris 16. **d** 19 **p** 20. C Camelot Par *B & W* from 19. *Fourposts, Long Street, Galhampton, Yeovil BA22 7AZ* E: annaclarecreedon@gmail.com

CREER, Irene. See SHAW, Irene

CREES, David Paul. b 68. Southn Univ BSc 89. Trin Coll Bris BA 99 MA 00. **d** 00 **p** 01. C Patcham *Chich* 00–04; CF 04–17; Sen CF from 17; Chapl R Memorial Chpl Sandhurst from 17. *c/o MOD Chaplains (Army)* T: (01276) 686540 E: rmcrmas@gmail.com

CREES, Geoffrey William. b 35. Open Univ BA 85. Cranmer Hall Dur 65. **d** 67 **p** 68. C Hoddesdon *St Alb* 67–70; C Harwell and Chilton All SS *Ox* 70–73; V Greenham 73–82; TR Marfleet and AD E Hull *York* 82–88; TR Rodbourne Cheney Bris 88–99; rtd 99; PtO *Glouc* from 99. *The Thatch, New Road, Popes Hill, Newnham GL14 1JT* T: (01452) 760843 M: 07551-201617 E: creesjean@gmail.com

CREGAN, Mark. b 59. Lon Bible Coll BA 91. Wycliffe Hall Ox 95. **d** 97 **p** 98. C Chippenham St Pet *Bris* 97–01; P-in-c Stapleton 01–05; Asst Chapl Colston's Sch Bris 01–03; Chapl 03–05; Chapl Stanley Bay All SS Egypt 05–07; P-in-c Casablanca *Eur* 07–12; PtO *B & W* 13; R Clutton w Cameley, Bishop Sutton and Stowey from 13. *Cameley Rectory, Main Road, Temple Cloud, Bristol BS39 5DA* T: (01761) 451315 M: 07770-295461 E: r.cregan59@gmail.com

CREGEEN, Canon Gary Marshall. b 62. Oak Hill Th Coll BA 00. **d** 00 **p** 01. C Carl St Jo 00–03; P-in-c Scotby and Cotehill w Cumwhinton 03–05; V 06–12; N Area Chapl Cumbria Constabulary 04–12; RD Brampton 09–12; TR S Barrow 12–19; RD Barrow 12–19; TV Penrith w Newton Reigny and Plumpton Wall from 19; Hon Can Carl Cathl from 14. *7 Park Close, Penrith CA11 8ND* E: gary@gandjcregeen.co.uk

CREIGHTON, Frederick David. b 50. TCD BTh 88 QUB MSSc 00 ACII 74. **d** 88 **p** 89. C Lisburn Ch Ch *Conn* 88–91; I Drumclamph w Lower and Upper Langfield *D & R* 91–00; I Glendermott 00–16; Can Derry Cathl 08–16; rtd 16. *22 Greenmount Drive, Coleraine BT51 3QE* T: (028) 7035 7275

CREIGHTON, Mrs Judith. b 36. Reading Univ BSc 57. Trin Coll Bris 80 Edin Th Coll 81. **dss** 83 **d** 87 **p** 94. Greenock *Glas* 83–85; Lawrence Weston *Bris* 85–87; Par Dn Kingswood 87–90; Chapl Stoke Park and Purdown Hosps Stapleton 90–91; Chapl Phoenix NHS Trust 92–93; Hon C Marshfield w

Cold Ashton and Tormarton etc *Bris* 93–97; rtd 96; PtO *Bris* 97–15. *Rose Cottage, West Littleton, Marshfield, Chippenham SN14 8JE* T: (01225) 891021

CREIGHTON, Ms Rachel Margaret Maxwell. b 64. Br Is Nazarene Coll BTh 86 BD 87 Lon Bible Coll MA 89 Man Univ MA. Cranmer Hall Dur 92. **d** 94 **p** 95. C Basford w Hyson Green *S'well* 94–96; C Nottingham All SS 96–98; P-in-c Broxtowe 98–02; Chapl HM Pris Bedf 02–04; Chapl HM Pris Wellingborough 04–09; I Belfast H Trin and St Silas *Conn* 09–18; R Hollington St Leon *Chich* from 18; RD Hastings 18–20. *Hollington Rectory, Tilebarn Road, St Leonards-on-Sea TN38 9PA* T: (01424) 854535 M: 07748-063770 E: rachelcreighton16@yahoo.com

CRELLIN, Gary Paul. b 67. Kingston Poly BSc 88 Aston Business Sch MBA 06. WEMTC 11. **d** 14 **p** 15. NSM Stoke Prior, Wychbold and Upton Warren *Worc* 14–16; C 16–18; R Powick and Guarlford and Madresfield w Newland from 18. *The Vicarage, 31 The Greenway, Powick, Worcester WR2 4RZ* M: 07708-488705 E: revgarycrellin@gmail.com

CREMIN (née LAKE), Mrs Eileen Veronica. b 58. Aston Tr Scheme 83 Sarum & Wells Th Coll 85. **d** 88 **p** 94. Par Dn Islington St Mary *Lon* 88–92; Asst Chapl Homerton Hosp Lon 92–94; Asst Chapl Hackney Hosp Gp Lon 92–94; P-in-c Brondesbury Ch Ch and St Laur *Lon* 94–01; C Douglas Union w Frankfield *C, C & R* 01–06; I Fermoy Union 06–18; rtd 18. *2 Bearna Deara, Limerick Road, Kildorrery, Co Cork, P67 YR91, Republic of Ireland* T: (00353) (22) 40919 M: 86-333 0206 E: evcremin@eircom.net *or* ecremin@hotmail.com *or* ecremin23@gmail.com

CRESSEY, Canon Roger Wilson. b 35. Chich Th Coll 72. **d** 74 **p** 75. C Pontefract St Giles *Wakef* 74–77; Hon C Dewsbury All SS 77–80; Chapl Pinderfields Gen Hosp Wakef 80–94; Chapl Carr Gate Hosp Wakef 80–94; Chapl Fieldhead Hosp Wakef 80–94; Chapl Pinderfields and Pontefract Hosps NHS Trust 94–00; Hon Can Wakef Cathl 98–00; rtd 00. *1 Wellhead Mews, Chapelthorpe, Wakefield WF4 3JG* T: (01924) 258972 E: roger-cressey@supanet.com *or* rwcressey@gmail.com

CRESSWELL, Howard Rex. b 31. Ely Th Coll 56. **d** 59 **p** 60. C Dovercourt *Chelmsf* 59–61; C Victoria Docks Ascension 61–64; V 64–71; R E w W Harling *Nor* 71–72; TV Quidenham w Eccles and Snetterton 72–75; V Arminghall 75–82; R Caistor w Markshall 75–82; V Trowse 75–82; V Heigham St Barn w St Bart 82–91; rtd 91; PtO *Nor* from 91. *61 Field Acre Way, Long Stratton, Norwich NR15 2WE* E: enesp11@gmail.com

CRESSWELL, Jane Stella. b 62. Bris Univ BA 84. SEITE 04. **d** 07 **p** 08. C Sutton *S'wark* 07–11; P-in-c Nork *Guildf* 11–17; V Taplow and Dropmore *Ox* from 17. *The Rectory, Rectory Road, Taplow, Maidenhead SL6 0ET* T: (01628) 661182 E: janecresswell523@gmail.com

CRESSWELL, Canon Jeremy Peter. b 49. St Jo Coll Ox BA 72 MA 78 K Coll Lon MA 83. Ridley Hall Cam 73. **d** 75 **p** 76. C Wisley w Pyrford *Guildf* 75–78; C Weybridge 78–82; P-in-c E Clandon 82–83; P-in-c W Clandon 82–83; R E and W Clandon 83–90; V Oxshott 90–15; RD Leatherhead 03–08; Hon Can Owerri from 01; Hon Can Guildf Cathl 10–15; rtd 15; PtO *Sarum* 16–21; *Bris* from 17; *B & W* from 18. *Grant's House, 13A Castle Street, Calne SN11 0DX* T: (01249) 814350 E: jeremy.cresswell@outlook.com

CRESSWELL, Mark Charles Stewart. b 63. **d** 18 **p** 19. NSM Carlford *St E* from 18; P-in-c 20–21. *15 Gurdon Road, Grundisburgh, Woodbridge IP13 6XA* T: (01473) 738313 E: mark@carlfordchurches.com

CRESSWELL, Richard James. b 78. Liv Univ BDS 01 Ches Univ MTh 17. St Jo Coll Nottm 13. **d** 15 **p** 16. C Lilleshall and Muxton *Lich* 15–18; P-in-c Moreton Corbet 18–19; R from 19; P-in-c Shawbury 18–19; V from 19; P-in-c Stanton on Hine Heath 18–19; V from 19. *36 Millbrook Drive, Shawbury, Shrewsbury SY4 4PQ* M: 07974-157862 E: revrichcresswell@gmail.com

CRETNEY, Mrs Antonia Lois. b 48. York Univ BA 69 Bris Univ BA 87 PGCE 89. S Dios Minl Tr Scheme 92. **d** 94 **p** 95. NSM Bedminster *Bris* 94–96; C 96–97; P-in-c Beedon and Peasemore w W Ilsley and Farnborough *Ox* 97–99; R 99–04; Deanery P Wantage from 04; Bp's Adv for Women in Ord Min *Ox* from 05; PtO from 14. *8 Elm Farm Close, Grove, Wantage OX12 9FD* T: (01235) 763192 E: antcret@aol.com

CREW, Ruan John. b 70. Bris Univ BSc 92 PGCE 93 All Nations Chr Coll BA 99 Anglia Ruskin Univ MA 10. ERMC 07. **d** 10 **p** 11. C Almondsbury and Olveston *Bris* 10–13; C Pilning w Compton Greenfield 10–13; Chapl Voorschoten *Eur* from 13. *Chopinlaan 17, 2253 BS Voorschoten, Netherlands* T: (0031) (71) 561 3020 E: ruancrew@gmail.com

CREWES, Jennifer Ruth. b 86. Glas Univ MA 08 MTh 09. Qu Foundn Birm MA 17. **d** 17 **p** 18. C Hodge Hill *Birm* 17–20; V Warley Woods from 20. *St Hilda's Vicarage,*

269 Abbey Road, Smethwick B67 5NQ M: 07377-363915
E: revjennicrewes@gmail.com
CRIBB, Mrs Karen Elisabeth. b 63. Liv Univ BA 85 Leeds
Univ BA 10. Yorks Min Course 97. **d** 10 **p** 11. NSM Sheff
St Mary Bramall Lane from 10; Bp's Adv for SSM from
14. *40 Whirlow Lane, Sheffield S11 9QF* T: 0114-262 1876
E: revkaren@stmarys-church.co.uk
CRICK, Peter. b 39. Lon Univ BD 68 NY Univ DMin 84.
Wells Th Coll 66. **d** 67 **p** 68. C Horsham *Chich* 67–71;
Asst Dioc Youth Officer *Ox* 71–73; Dioc Youth Officer
73–75; R Denham 75–88; Bp's Adv for CME *Dur* 88–97;
P-in-c Coniscliffe 88–97; Hon Can Dur Cathl 93–97; R City
of Bris 97–04; Ind Chapl 97–04; rtd 04; PtO *Win* from 06;
Portsm from 16. *7 Westfield Common, Hamble, Southampton
SO31 4LB* T: (023) 8045 7025
CRIDDLE, Richard Benjamin. b 86. Imp Coll Lon MEng 09.
Oak Hill Th Coll BA 18. **d** 19 **p** 20. C Rusholme H Trin *Man*
from 19. *1 Aldwych Avenue, Manchester M14 5NL* M: 07963-
428932 E: richard@plattchurch.org
CRIDLAND, Clarissa Rosemary Dorothea. b 55. STETS 03.
d 06 **p** 07. NSM Coleford w Holcombe *B & W* 06–20;
P-in-c from 20. *The Vicarage, Church Street, Coleford,
Radstock BA3 5NG* T: (01373) 812705 M: 07800-578967
E: clarissacridland@hotmail.co.uk
CRINKS, Kevin David. b 63. Aston Tr Scheme 86 Sarum &
Wells Th Coll BTh 91. **d** 93 **p** 94. C Aylesford *Roch* 93–96;
C Hessle *York* 96–97; TV Upholland *Liv* 97–00; V Platt
Bridge 00–09; P-in-c Leigh St Mary *Man* 09–12; V from
12; Borough Dean Wigan 10–13. *St Mary's Vicarage, 34
Vicarage Square, Leigh WN7 1YD* T: (01942) 603603
E: kcrinks@btinternet.com
CRIPPS, Martyn Cyril Rowland. b 46. Birm Univ LLB 68
Solicitor 71. Wycliffe Hall Ox 80. **d** 82 **p** 83. C Canford
Magna *Sarum* 82–86; V Preston St Cuth *Blackb* 87–94;
Warden Les Cotils *Win* 94–96; V Gipsy Hill Ch Ch *S'wark*
96–00; R Ashmanhaugh, Barton Turf etc *Nor* 00–04;
P-in-c Davenham *Ches* 04–06; R 06–14; rtd 14; PtO *Blackb*
from 14. *11 Lancaster Road, Pilling, Preston PR3 6AU*
E: mandmc2@btopenworld.com
CRISPIN, Mrs Mavis Avril. b 46. Open Univ BA 75 Stranmillis
Coll TCert 69. Lon Sch of Th BA 03. **d** 06 **p** 09. Peru 06–09;
NSM Finchley St Paul and St Luke *Lon* 09–21; PtO from 21.
47 Etchingham Park Road, London N3 2EB T: (020) 8346 8698
E: mavecrispin@yahoo.co.uk
CRITCHELL, Denise Eileen. b 49. SAOMC 96. **d** 99
p 00. C Flackwell Heath *Ox* 99–03; TV Risborough
03–13; rtd 13; PtO *Cant* 14–18 and from 20. *3 Somerset
Close, Whitstable CT5 4RA* T: (01227) 771885
E: denisecritchell@btconnect.com
CRITCHLEY, Colin. b 41. Dur Univ BA 63 Liv Univ MA 69
AFBPsS 94. NW Ord Course 75. **d** 78 **p** 79. NSM Halewood
Liv 78–06; Dioc Child Protection Adv 96–06; rtd 06;
PtO *Liv* from 16. *53 Elwyn Drive, Halewood, Liverpool
L26 0UX* T: 0151-487 5710 F: 280 4937
CRITCHLEY, Mrs Patsy Eva. b 49. Reading Univ CertEd 70.
ERMC 04. **d** 07 **p** 08. NSM Meppershall and Shefford
St Alb 07–10; NSM Henlow and Langford 10–15; rtd 15;
PtO *St Alb* from 15. *39 Rooktree Way, Haynes, Bedford
MK45 3PT* T: (01234) 381510 E: patsy@critchley04.plus.com
CRITCHLOW, Anne-Louise. b 51. Westf Coll Lon BA 73 Qu
Mary Coll Lon MA 75 Leeds Univ MA 05 Grenoble Univ
MèsL 74 Man Univ PhD 15 Cam Univ PGCE 76. NOC 03.
d 05 **p** 06. C Eccles *Man* 05–08; TV 08–17; SW Chapl
Abbeyfield from 17; PtO *Bris* from 18. *25 Meg Thatcher's
Green, Bristol BS5 8ND* E: malcritch@gmail.com
CRITCHLOW, Melville Mark. b 54. SS Coll Cam BA 77 MA 81
Sheff Univ PhD 15 PGCE 82. Trin Coll Bris 17. **d** 18. NSM
Bris St Aid w St Geo 18–20; NSM Fishponds St Jo 18–20;
NSM Two Mile Hill St Mich 18–20; NSM Bris St Aid w
St Geo, Fishponds St Jo, and Two Mile Hill from 20. *25
Meg Thatchers Green, Bristol BS5 8ND* M: 07745-033144
E: mmcritchlow@btinternet.com
CRITCHLOW (*née* **KHARITONOVA**), **Mrs Natalia** (**Tasha**).
b 74. St Petersburg State Univ MA 98 Dallas Th Sem MTh 04.
Westcott Ho Cam 07. **d** 09 **p** 10. C Brondesbury Ch Ch
and St Laur *Lon* 09–12; PtO from 12; Chapl Barts Health
NHS Trust 15–21; Chapl Cam Univ Hosps NHS Foundn
Trust from 21. *St Dunstan's Rectory, Rectory Square, London
E1 3NQ* M: 07540-588860 E: tasha.critchlow@gmail.com
CRITCHLOW, Trevor Francis. b 61. Lanc Univ BA 83 K Coll
Lon MA 96. Westcott Ho Cam 88. **d** 90 **p** 91. C Croydon St Jo
S'wark 90–92; C Lewisham St Mary *S'wark* Dioc *Ely* 94–05;
Development Dir Westmr St Matt Lon 95–99; TV Wembley
Park *Lon* 05–11; CME Officer Willesden Area 06–10; R
Stepney St Dunstan and All SS from 11. *St Dunstan's Rectory,*

Rectory Square, London E1 3NQ T: (020) 3290 1920 F: 07850-
578193 M: 07850-578193 E: rector@stdunstanstepney.com
CRITTALL, Richard Simon. b 47. Sussex Univ BA 69 Linacre
Coll Ox BA 71. St Steph Ho Ox 69. **d** 72 **p** 73. C Oswestry
H Trin *Lich* 72–75; C E Grinstead St Mary *Chich* 75–78;
TV Brighton Resurr 78–83; R E Blatchington 83–95; V
Heathfield St Rich 95–07; Dioc Ecum Officer *Ex* 07–12;
P-in-c Broadhembury, Payhembury and Plymtree 07–12; rtd
12; PtO *Sarum* 12–16; *Ex* 13–18; *Derby* from 16; *S'well* from
18. *7 Laurel Grove, Broadmeadows, South Normanton, Alfreton
DE55 3LT*
CROAD, Arthur Robert. b 35. Down Coll Cam BA 58 MA 61.
Clifton Th Coll 58. **d** 61 **p** 62. C Sneinton St Chris w St Phil
S'well 61–64; C Kinson *Sarum* 64–72; R Sherfield English *Win*
72–74; R Awbridge w Sherfield English 74–92; P-in-c Hinton
Ampner w Bramdean and Kilmeston 92–01; rtd 01; PtO *Win*
from 10. *2 Nursery House, 26 Hursley Road, Chandler's Ford,
Eastleigh SO53 2RQ* T: (023) 8184 8646
CROAD, David Richard. b 31. Reading Univ BSc 55. Clifton
Th Coll. **d** 57 **p** 58. C Iver *Ox* 57–60; C Rushden *Pet* 60–63; V
Loudwater *Ox* 63–72; SW Area Sec CPAS 72–78; V Bovingdon
St Alb 78–91; Min Hampstead St Jo Downshire Hill Prop Chpl
Lon 91–94; rtd 94; PtO *Guildf* 97–07; *Win* 97–20. *8 Compass
Court, 42 Winn Road, Southampton SO17 1EZ* T: (023) 8058
2022
CROCKER, Mrs Fiona Jane. b 64. Southn Univ BN 87 Univ of
Wales (Lamp) BA 14 RGN 87. St Jo Coll Nottm. **d** 14 **p** 15.
C Brailsford w Shirley, Osmaston w Edlaston etc *Derby*
14–17; V Cam w Stinchcombe *Glouc* from 17. *The Vicarage,
Church Road, Cam, Dursley GL11 5PQ* M: 07817-021196
E: fionacrocker@aol.com
CROCKER, The Very Revd Jeremy Robert. b 67. S Bank
Univ MA 94 Heythrop Coll Lon MA 98 MCIM 92. Westcott
Ho Cam 94 CITC 96. **d** 97 **p** 98. C Stevenage H Trin *St Alb*
97–00; TV Bp's Hatfield 00–04; TR Elstow 04–15; PtO 15–19;
Dean St Paul's Cathl and Chapl Nicosia from 15. *St Paul's
Cathedral, PO Box 22014, 1516 Nicosia, Cyprus* T: (00357)
(22) 677897 E: jeremy.crocker@live.co.uk
CROCKER, Richard Campbell. b 54. Nottm Univ BSc 76.
Wycliffe Hall Ox BA 81 MA 85. **d** 82 **p** 83. C Summerfield
Birm 82–84; Chapl K Edw Sch Birm 84–91; R Council Bluffs
USA 91–99; C Truro Ch Falmure *Truro* 99–08; R Newport Beach St Jas
08–17; Gen Sec Evang Fellowship in the Angl Communion
18–19. *10229 Shiloh Street, Fairfax VA 22030, USA* T: (001)
(949) 873 3101 E: revcrocker@icloud.com
CROCKFORD, Ian David. b 63. Local Minl Tr Course 19.
d 21. OLM Hall Green St Mich *Birm* from 21. *62
Lakey Lane, Birmingham B28 9DS* T: 0121-777 2890
E: ian.crockford@hotmail.co.uk
CROCKFORD, James Robert William. b 86. Nottm Univ BA 07
Trin Hall Cam BA 13 MA 18 MPhil 15 FRSM. Ridley Hall
Cam 11. **d** 14 **p** 15. C Crayford *Roch* 14–17; C Ox St Mary
V w St Cross and St Pet 17–19; Chapl Magd Coll Ox 18–19;
Dean of Chapl Jes Coll Cam from 19. *Jesus College, Cambridge
CB5 8BL* T: (01223) 339433 E: j.crockford@jesus.cam.ac.uk
CROFT, James Stuart. b 57. K Coll Lon BD 80 Leeds Univ
MA 95. Ripon Coll Cuddesdon 83. **d** 85 **p** 86. C Friern
Barnet St Jas *Lon* 85–88; R Lea *Linc* 88–93; V Knaith 88–93; V
Upton 88–93; R Gate Burton 88–93; R Lea Gp 93–97; Chapl
N Lincs Coll 90–93; V Froyle and Holybourne *Win* 97–10;
P-in-c Chesterfield SS Aug *Derby* 10–15; P-in-c Brampton
St Mark 10–15; V Longstone, Curbar and Stony Middleton
from 15. *The Vicarage, Church Lane, Great Longstone, Bakewell
DE45 1TB* T: (01629) 640257 E: jamescroft80@gmail.com
CROFT, Jennifer Sara. b 69. Leeds Univ BSc 94. Ripon Coll
Cuddesdon 99. **d** 01 **p** 02. C Lillington *Cov* 01–05; Chapl
Cov Univ 05–11; Chapl amongst Deaf People 03–08; V Over
Tabley *Ches* 11–14; V High Legh 11–14; Sen Research Fell
Warw Univ *Cov* 11–14; Chapl Countess of Chester Hosp NHS
Foundn Trust 13–14; V Ormesby *York* 14–20; V Blackwell All
SS and Salutation *Dur* from 20; V Coniscliffe from 20. *104
Blackwell Lane, Darlington DL3 8QQ*
CROFT, Michael Peter. b 60. GradIPM MCIPD 95 FCIPD 08.
Trin Coll Bris BA 88. **d** 88 **p** 89. C Drypool *York* 88–91;
P-in-c Sandal St Cath *Wakef* 91–95; V 95–07; PtO 07–14;
Leeds from 14. *5 College Terrace, Ackworth, Pontefract
WF7 7LB* T: (01977) 611251 M: 078139-59066
E: michael@innovationpeople.co.uk
CROFT, Richard Gary. b 64. **d** 15 **p** 16. NSM Clifton H Trin,
St Andr and St Pet *Bris* from 15; NSM Bris St Steph w St Jas
and St Jo w St Mich etc from 15. *7 Henleaze Avenue, Bristol
BS9 4EU* T: 0117-962 9262 E: revdrichardcroft@gmail.com
CROFT, Robert Frank. St Jo Coll Dur BSc 75 Liv Univ MSc 01.
All SS Cen for Miss & Min 14 Qu Foundn Birm 19. **d** 20
p 21. NSM Christleton *Ches* from 20. *2 Fairford Road,*

Chester CH4 8EQ T: (01244) 683926 M: 07745-624323 E: robcroft@hotmail.co.uk

CROFT, Ronald. b 30. St Aid Birkenhead 61. **d** 63 **p** 64. C Lawton Moor *Man* 63–65; C Withington St Crispin 65–66; R 74–86; C Prestwich St Marg 66–67; V Oldham St Ambrose 67–71; P-in-c Oldham St Jas 67–68; V 68–71; V Prestwich St Hilda 71–74; P-in-c 96–00; R Heaton Norris St Thos 86–96; rtd 00; PtO *Man* from 00. *St Hilda's Vicarage, 55 Whittaker Lane, Prestwich, Manchester M25 1ET* T: 0161-773 1642

CROFT, Mrs Sally Ann. b 66. **d** 20 **p** 21. C Ingatestone w Fryerning *Chelmsf* from 20. *The Vicarage, Penny's Lane, Margaretting, Ingatestone CM4 0HA* M: 07850-361101 E: revsally.croft@gmail.com

CROFT, Simon Edward Owen. b 51. Ch Ch Coll Cant CertEd 73. St Steph Ho Ox 75. **d** 78 **p** 79. C Heavitree w Ex St Paul 78–83; V Seaton 83–93; P-in-c Ex St Mark 93–96; P-in-c Ex St Sidwell and St Matt 96; R Ex St Mark, St Sidwell and St Matt 96–09; C Dawlish 09–10; P-in-c 10–15; R Dawlish, Cofton and Starcross 15; rtd 15; Hon C Ashburton, Bickington, Buckland in the Moor etc *Ex* 17; PtO from 18. *16 Madison Avenue, Exeter EX1 3AH* T: (01392) 667877 E: simoncdevon@yahoo.co.uk

✠**CROFT, The Rt Revd Steven John Lindsey.** b 57. Worc Coll Ox BA 80 MA 83 St Jo Coll Dur PhD 84. Cranmer Hall Dur 80. **d** 83 **p** 84 **c** 09. C Enfield St Andr *Lon* 83–87; V Ovenden *Wakef* 87–96; Dioc Miss Consultant 94–96; Warden Cranmer Hall Dur 96–04; Abps' Missr and Team Ldr Fresh Expressions 04–09; Bp Sheff 09–16; Bp Ox from 16. *Bishop's Office, Church House Oxford, Langford Locks, Kidlington OX5 1GF* T: (01865) 208222 E: bishop.oxford@oxford.anglican.org

CROFT, Canon William Stuart. b 53. Trin Hall Cam BA 76 MA 79 K Coll Lon MTh 88. Ripon Coll Cuddesdon BA 80. **d** 80 **p** 81. C Friern Barnet St Jas *Lon* 80–83; Tutor Chich Th Coll 83–92; Vice-Prin 88–92; V Fernhurst *Chich* 92–98; Dir of Ords *Pet* 98–03; Prec and Min Can Pet Cathl 98–01; Can Res and Prec 01–04; Liturg Officer 03–04; Non-res Can 04–20; P-in-c Longthorpe *Pet* 04–16; P-in-c Pet H Spirit Bretton 11–20; rtd 20; PtO *Pet* from 20. *5 Woodfield Road, Peterborough PE3 6HD* E: williamsbill_croft@hotmail.com

CROFTON, Edwin Alan. b 46. Univ Coll Ox BA 68 MA 72. Cranmer Hall Dur. **d** 73 **p** 74. C Hull St Jo Newland *York* 73–77; C Worksop St Jo *S'well* 77–81; Chapl Kilton Hosp Worksop 80–81; V Scarborough St Mary w Ch Ch and H Apostles *York* 81–91; Miss to Seamen 81–91; Chapl St Mary's Hosp Scarborough 82–91; V Cheltenham Ch Ch *Glouc* 91–02; RD Cheltenham 95–00; Hon Can Glouc Cathl 01–02; TR Eccles *Man* 02–11; P-in-c Hope St Jas 07–09; AD Eccles 05–11; rtd 11; PtO *Worc* from 12. *177 Leigh Sinton Road, Malvern WR14 1LB* T: (01886) 833376 E: ea_crofton@msn.com

CROFTON, Robert Edwin. b 75. UEA BSc 98. Ridley Hall Cam 03. **d** 06 **p** 07. C Churchdown *Glouc* 06–09; TV Cheltenham St Mark 09–18; V Barnwood from 18. *The Vicarage, 27A Barnwood Avenue, Gloucester GL4 3AB* T: (01452) 668761 M: 07810-338542 E: rob.crofton@tiscali.co.uk

CROFTS, David Thomas. b 47. Cheshire Coll of Educn CertEd 68 Open Univ BA 76. **d** 99 **p** 00. OLM Bury St Edmunds St Mary *St E* 99–13; NSM 13–17; PtO from 19. *8 Linton Gardens, Bury St Edmunds IP33 2DZ* T: (01284) 761801 M: 07545-120915 E: dtc01@icloud.com

CROFTS, Ian Hamilton. b 55. BSc. St Jo Coll Nottm 79. **d** 82 **p** 83. C Leamington Priors St Paul *Cov* 82–86; C Oadby *Leic* 86; TV 86–91; V Maidstone St Faith *Cant* 91–07; V Forty Hill Jes Ch *Lon* from 07. *The Vicarage, Forty Hill, Enfield EN2 9EU* T: (020) 8363 1935 E: ian.crofts@gmail.com

CROFTS, Mrs Sharon Lucy. b 65. Qu Foundn (Course) 15. **d** 18 **p** 19. C Hartshill and Galley Common *Cov* 18–21; NSM from 21. *4 Burton Close, Allesley, Coventry CV5 9EG* M: 07855-551004

CROFTS, Stephen Andrew. b 76. Ch Ch Coll Cant BA 98 Ox Brookes Univ MA 09. Ripon Coll Cuddesdon 07. **d** 09 **p** 10. C Birstall and Wanlip *Leic* 09–14; PtO 14–16; C St Andr Cathl Shibakoen Japan 14–15; C Wakabayashi 14–17; C Asagaya 17–18; P-in-c Asagaya 18–21; P-in-c Cheriton w Newington *Cant* from 21. *St Martin's Rectory, Horn Street, Folkestone CT20 3JJ* E: crofts.stephen@icloud.com

CROISDALE-APPLEBY, Mrs Carolynn Elizabeth. b 46. Ch Ch Coll Cant CertEd 68. SAOMC 01. **d** 04 **p** 05. NSM Amersham and Gt Coxwell w Buscot, Coleshill etc *Ox* 04–07; NSM Beaconsfield 07–16; PtO from 16. *Abbotsholme, Hervines Road, Amersham HP6 5HS* T: (01494) 725194 F: 725474 E: revcarolynn@aol.com

CROMARTY, Andrew Robert McKean. b 63. Newc Univ MB, BS 86 Homerton Coll Cam PGCE 89 St Jo Coll Dur BA 04. Cranmer Hall Dur 02. **d** 06 **p** 07. NSM Crook *Dur* 06–10; C Upper Weardale 10–14; V Hipswell *Leeds* from

14. The Vicarage, 7 Forest Drive, Colburn, Catterick Garrison DL9 4PN E: andrew.cromarty63@btinternet.com

CROMBIE, Calum Dugald Ferguson. b 81. Nazarene Th Coll Man BA 05 Keele Univ MA 13. LCTP 12. **d** 13 **p** 14. NSM Leyland St Ambrose *Blackb* from 13; Chapl HM Pris Preston 13–15; Chapl HM Pris Wymott from 15. *Chaplaincy Office, HM Prison Wymott, Ulnes Walton Lane, Leyland PR26 8LW* T: (01772) 442000 E: calum.crombie@justice.gov.uk

CROMPTON (*née* KILGOUR), **Mrs Christine Mary.** b 39. Newnham Coll Cam BA 61 MA York Univ MA 86 Lon Inst of Educn PGCE 62. **d** 06 **p** 07. OLM Newc St Geo and St Hilda 06–18; PtO from 18. *11 South Bend, Newcastle upon Tyne NE3 5TR* T: 0191-236 3679

CROMPTON, Gillian Kay. *See* STANNING, Gillian Kay

CROMPTON, Canon Roger Martyn Francis. b 47. Sheff Univ BA 69 PGCE 73 St Jo Coll Dur BA 84. Cranmer Hall Dur 82. **d** 85 **p** 86. C Woodford Wells *Chelmsf* 85–89; V Golcar *Wakef* 89–12; P-in-c Longwood 10–12; RD Huddersfield 99–09; Hon Can Wakef Cathl 06–12; rtd 12. *16 Colders Green, Meltham, Holmfirth HD9 5JH* T: (01484) 859320

CROMPTON-BATTERSBY, Holly Jo. b 74. Bath Coll of HE BA 95. Wycliffe Hall Ox BTh 01. **d** 01 **p** 02. C Luton Lewsey St Hugh *St Alb* 01–04; Chapl Bennett Memorial Dioc Sch Tunbridge Wells 04–07; Chapl Bedgebury Sch Kent 05–06; Chapl St Bede's Sch Cam 09–15; Chapl Ipswich Sch from 15. *Ipswich School, 25 Henley Road, Ipswich IP1 3SG* T: (01473) 408300 ext 338 M: 07447-913109 E: hollycrompton@hotmail.com *or* hcb@ipswich.suffolk.sch.uk

CROMPTON-BATTERSBY, Simon Jackson. b 64. Wycliffe Hall Ox BTh 01. **d** 01 **p** 02. C Askern *Sheff* 01–03; Chapl Bethany Sch Goudhurst 03–07; Chapl Culford Sch Bury St Edmunds 08–18; P-in-c Elmsett w Aldham, Hintlesham, Chattisham etc *St E* from 18. *The Rectory, Hadleigh Road, Elmsett, Ipswich IP7 6ND* M: 07894-488315 E: rev@kind.church

CRONIN, Alan. b 57. NSM Borderlands Miss Area *St As* from 18. *8 Little Meadows, Bradley, Wrexham LL11 4AR* T: (01978) 750440 E: 794alan@gmail.com

CRONIN, Mrs Janie. b 62. **d** 16 **p** 17. C Guildf St Sav 16–19; C Onslow Square and S Kensington St Aug *Lon* 19–20; C Rochdale *Man* 20–21. *Address temp unknown* M: 07799-824707 E: janiecronin@gmail.com

CRONIN, Mrs Linda Nancy. b 61. NTMTC BA 08. **d** 08 **p** 09. C Barrow St Mark *Carl* 08–10; C S Barrow 10–11; TV 11–13; Chapl All SS Academy Cheltenham 13–14; NSM Cheltenham St Mark *Glouc* 13–14; P-in-c Madeley *Heref* 14–20; I Glenavy w Tunny and Crumlin *Conn* from 20. *30 Crumlin Road, Glenavy, Crumlin BT29 4LG* M: 07817-678775 E: linda@thecronins.org.uk *or* linda.cronin@tf7.org.uk

CROOK, Colin. b 44. JP 78. Lon Univ BSc(Econ) 74 ALA 67 FLA 93. S'wark Ord Course 87. **d** 90 **p** 91. NSM Dartford Ch Ch *Roch* 90–97; P-in-c Crockenhill All So 97–05; Dioc Ecum Officer 96–04; rtd 05; Chapl Crowhurst Chr Healing Cen from 05; PtO *Chich* from 06. *57 Martello Court, 3-15 Jevington Gardens, Eastbourne BN21 4SD*

CROOK, David Robert. b 64. Liv Univ BA 85 PGCE 86 Univ of Wales (Swansea) PhD 01. Westcott Ho Cam 13. **d** 15 **p** 16. C Easebourne, Lodsworth and Selham *Chich* 15–19; P-in-c Stopham and Fittleworth from 19; P-in-c Tillington from 21; P-in-c Duncton from 21; P-in-c Upwaltham from 21. *The Rectory, Church Lane, Fittleworth, Pulborough RH20 1HL* T: (01798) 865473 M: 07902-485877 E: david.crook15@btinternet.com

CROOK, Dennis Eric. b 40. AKC 65. **d** 66 **p** 67. C Penwortham St Mary *Blackb* 66–69; C Kirkham 69–71; V Accrington St Jo 72–89; RD Accrington 82–90; P-in-c Huncoat 86–89; Hon Can Blackb Cathl 89–96; V Accrington St Jo w Huncoat 89–96; rtd 00; PtO *Blackb* from 13. *224 Pleckgate Road, Blackburn BB1 8QW* T: (01254) 248720

CROOK, Mrs Diana Elizabeth. b 47. Hull Univ BA 73 Open Univ BSc 93 City Univ MSc 97 Middx Univ BA 03 RGN 70 CPsychol. NTMTC 00. **d** 03 **p** 04. NSM Waltham H Cross *Chelmsf* 03–07; P-in-c Uley w Owlpen and Nympsfield *Glouc* 07–17; rtd 17. *Upper Redlap, Redlap, Dartmouth TQ6 0JR* E: revdiana@dianacrook.org

CROOK, Graham Leslie. b 49. Chich Th Coll 74. **d** 76 **p** 77. C Withington St Crispin *Man* 76–79; C Prestwich St Marg 79–82; V Nelson St Bede *Blackb* 82–92; Chapl Southend Health Care NHS Trust 92–15; Bp's Adv for Hosp Chapl (Bradwell Area) *Chelmsf* 98–04; LtO 92–09; PtO from 09; *Lon* from 20. *Ebenezer, 249 Woodgrange Drive, Southend-on-Sea SS1 2SQ* T: (01702) 613429

✠**CROOK, The Rt Revd John Michael.** b 40. Univ of Wales (Lamp) BA 62. Coll of Resurr Mirfield 62. **d** 64 **p** 65 **c** 99. C Horninglow *Lich* 64–66; C Bloxwich 66–70; R Inverness St Mich *Mor* 70–78; R Inverness St Jo 74–78; Dioc Youth

Chapl *St And* 78–86; R Aberfoyle 78–87; R Doune 78–87; R Callander 78–87; Can St Ninian's Cathl Perth 85–99; R Bridge of Allan 87–99; Syn Clerk 97–99; Bp Mor 99–06; rtd 06; LtO *St And* from 07. *163 Lothian Crescent, Stirling FK9 5SG* E: johnmcook99@gmail.com

CROOK, Malcolm Geoffrey. b 53. St Steph Ho Ox 88. **d** 90 **p** 91. C Pet St Jude 90–93; C Barrow St Matt *Carl* 93–96; TV Langley and Parkfield *Man* 96–97; R Man Apostles w Miles Platting 97–03; P-in-c Sneinton St Steph w St Alb *S'well* 03–04; P-in-c Sneinton St Matthias 03–04; V Sneinton St Steph w St Matthias 04–11; P-in-c Sculcoates *York* 11–16; P-in-c Hull St Mary Sculcoates 15–16; R Glas E End 16–17; LtO from 17. *228 Myreside Street, Glasgow G32 6DX* T: 0141-554 5398 E: malccrook@hotmail.com

CROOK, Rowland William. b 39. Tyndale Hall Bris 61. **d** 64 **p** 65. C Penn Fields *Lich* 64–68; C Lower Broughton St Clem w St Matthias *Man* 68–70; C Bucknall and Bagnall *Lich* 70–76; V New Shildon *Dur* 76–86; V Northwich St Luke and H Trin *Ches* 86–99; P-in-c Helsby and Dunham-on-the-Hill 99–04; rtd 04; PtO *Ches* from 04. *14 Bollington Avenue, Northwich CW9 8SB* T: (01606) 45177 E: rowland.crook@talktalk.net

CROOK, Simon Charles. b 72. Imp Coll Lon BSc 95 Ox Brookes Univ PGCE 97 Sheff Univ BA 14. Coll of Resurr Mirfield 12. **d** 14 **p** 15. C Huddersfield St Pet *Leeds* 14–18; V Golcar and Longwood from 18. *The Vicarage, Church Street, Golcar, Huddersfield HD7 4PX* M: 07742-177610 E: vicar@stjohnschurchgolcar.org

CROOK, Timothy Mark. b 68. Oak Hill Th Coll BA 00. **d** 00 **p** 01. C Charles w Plymouth St Matthias *Ex* 00–03; C Harold Wood *Chelmsf* 03–09; V S w N Bersted *Chich* from 09. *121 Victoria Drive, Bognor Regis PO21 2EH* T: (01243) 862018 E: timothycrook@hotmail.com

CROOKS, Christopher John (Kip). b 53. St Bede's Coll Dur CertEd 75. Trin Coll Bris BA 90. **d** 90 **p** 91. C The Quinton *Birm* 90–93; V Ince Ch Ch *Liv* 93–03; R Much Woolton from 03; AD Liv South-Childwall 06–14; Hon Can Liv Cathl 06–14. *The Rectory, 67 Church Road, Woolton, Liverpool L25 6DA* T: 0151-428 1853 E: rector@stpeters-woolton.org.uk

CROOKS, Canon David William Talbot. b 52. TCD BA 75 MA 78 BD 83. **d** 77 **p** 78. C Glendermott *D & R* 77–81; C Edin Old St Paul 81–84; I Taughboyne, Craigadooish, Newtowncunningham etc *D & R* from 84; Bp's Dom Chapl 88–07; Can Raphoe Cathl from 91; Can St Patr Cathl Dublin from 17. *Taughboyne Rectory, Churchtown, Carrigans, Lifford, Co Donegal, Republic of Ireland* T: (00353) (74) 914 0135 M: 86-212 5670 E: dcrooks@eircom.net

CROOKS, Mrs Jayne Barbara. b 52. Birm Univ BSc 73 Avery Hill Coll PGCE 74. WMMTC 01. **d** 04 **p** 05. NSM Kings Norton *Birm* 04–08; C 08–11; TV 11–15; rtd 15; PtO *Birm* from 15. *15 Chalgrove Avenue, Birmingham B38 8YP* T: 0121-459 3733 E: jayne.crooks@blueyonder.co.uk

CROOKS, Kenneth Robert. b 36. CEng FIEE FCMI FCIM. S'wark Ord Course 80. **d** 83 **p** 84. NSM Wisley w Pyrford *Guildf* 83–92; PtO *Ex* 98–21. *1 Glenside, Manor Road, Sidmouth EX10 8FG* T: (01395) 489254 E: revken.sidmouth@talktalk.net

CROOKS, Kip. *See* CROOKS, Christopher John

CROOKS, Peter James. b 50. MBE 09. St Jo Coll Cam BA 72. Cranmer Hall Dur. **d** 76 **p** 77. C Onslow Square St Paul *Lon* 76–77; C Brompton H Trin w Onslow Square St Paul 77–79; C Wembley St Jo 79–82; CMS 82–92; Lebanon 83–89; Syria 85–89; Dean Jerusalem 89–92; P-in-c Hunningham and Wappenbury w Weston under Wetherley *Cov* 92–01; P-in-c Offchurch 96–01; V Long Itchington and Marton 96–01; CMS Iran 01–02; TV Dolgellau w Llanfachreth and Brithdir etc *Ban* 02–04; Chapl Aden Ch Ch Yemen 04–09; Dir Ras Morbat Clinics 04–09; rtd 09; P-in-c Arthog w Fairbourne w Llangelynnin w Rhoslefain *Ban* 09–10; PtO 10–16; *Ox* from 14. *25 Radstock Road, Reading RG1 3PS* T: 0118-375 3103 M: 07866-276562 E: petercrooks781@btinternet.com *or* crookspeter300@gmail.com

CROOS, Sebastian John Princely. b 59. Madurai Univ BA 82. Oak Hill Th Coll BA 04. **d** 04 **p** 05. C Becontree St Mary *Chelmsf* 04–07; C E Ham St Paul 07–08; Chapl Lon City Miss 08–11; NSM Forest Gate St Mark *Chelmsf* 11–13; P-in-c N Woolwich w Silvertown 13–19; rtd 19; PtO *Chelmsf* from 20; *Lon* from 20. *St John's Vicarage, Manwood Street, London E16 2JY* M: 07449-043579 E: sprincecroos@hotmail.com

CROSBIE, Andrew. b 62. St Steph Ho Ox 96. **d** 98 **p** 99. C St Paul's Cathl St Helena 98–00; CF 00–03; PtO *Blackb* 03–11; Chantry P Shrine of Our Lady of Haddington from 08. *The Parish Office, 92 Whitesands, Dumfries DG1 2RX* M: 07791-540535 E: dumfriesanglican@gmail.com

CROSBIE, Timothy John. b 44. Univ of Wales (Ban) BTheol 04 Univ of Wales (Lamp) MA 11 ACMA 72. **d** 00 **p** 01. OLM

Shotley *St E* 00–08; OLM Shoreline 08–13; NSM 13–14; rtd 14; PtO *St E* from 15. *5 Mill Rise, Holbrook, Ipswich IP9 2QH* T: (01473) 328297 E: txb44@btinternet.com

CROSBY, Mrs Anne Denise. b 58. Dur Univ BA 14 De Montfort Univ CertEd 02. Linc Sch of Th and Min 11. **d** 14 **p** 15. NSM Birstall and Wanlip *Leic* 14–17; V Luton St Anne w St Chris *St Alb* from 17. *St Christopher's Vicarage, 33 Felix Avenue, Luton LU2 7LE* T: (01582) 850125 M: 07946-178087 E: revdanneluton@gmail.com

CROSBY, Bernard Edward. b 47. Oak Hill Th Coll 86. **d** 88 **p** 89. C Springfield H Trin *Chelmsf* 88–91; C Penn Fields *Lich* 91–94; V St Leonards St Ethelburga *Chich* 94–02; R Fairlight, Guestling and Pett 02–10; rtd 10; PtO *Chich* from 15. *4 Willowbed Walk, Hastings TN34 2QL* T: (01424) 435800 E: bernardcrosby@supanet.com

CROSBY, David Edward. b 48. SAOMC 96. **d** 99 **p** 00. NSM Newbury *Ox* 99–01; C The Bourne and Tilford *Guildf* 01–04; P-in-c Hurst Green and Mitton *Bradf* 04. *7 Murfitt Way, Gamlingay, Sandy SG19 3EW* T: (01767) 651787 M: 07936-703541 E: davidec@live.co.uk

CROSLAND, Sarah Rosita. *See* WILLIAMS, Sarah Rosita

CROSS, Preb Elizabeth Mary. b 46. Leeds Univ BA 69 CertEd 70. Sarum Th Coll 80. **dss** 83 **d** 87 **p** 94. Wootton Bassett *Sarum* 83–86; Westbury 86–87; Par Dn 87–89; C Glastonbury w Meare, W Pennard and Godney *B & W* 89–95; Asst Dir of Ords 89–95; Preb Wells Cathl 93–07; V Wedmore w Theale and Blackford 95–07; rtd 07; PtO *Sarum* 08–20. *10 Manor Farm Court, Martinstown, Dorchester DT2 9JN* T: (01305) 889194 E: lizmcross@btinternet.com

CROSS, Canon Greville Shelly. b 49. Sarum & Wells Th Coll 73. **d** 76 **p** 77. C Kidderminster St Mary *Worc* 76–80; P-in-c Worc St Mark 80–81; TV Worc St Martin w St Pet, St Mark etc 81–85; R Inkberrow w Cookhill and Kington w Dormston 85–98; RD Evesham 93–97; R Old Swinford Stourbridge 98–11; RD Stourbridge 01–04; rtd 11; NSM Upton-on-Severn, Ripple, Earls Croome etc *Worc* 11–14; NSM Hanley Castle, Hanley Swan and Welland 11–14; Hon Can Worc Cathl from 05. *4 Oakland Close, Upton-upon-Severn, Worcester WR8 0ES* T: (01905) 29438 E: greville.cross@outlook.com

CROSS, James Stuart. b 36. Magd Coll Ox BA 65 MA 71. Ripon Hall Ox 62. **d** 65 **p** 66. C Leckhampton SS Phil and Jas *Glouc* 65–66; CF 66–92; QHC 89–92; R Stretford St Pet *Man* 92–00; rtd 00; PtO *Heref* 11–16. *St Davids, Redbrook Road, Monmouth NP25 3LY* T/F: (01600) 715977 E: jimcross1@aol.com

CROSS, Jeremy Burkitt. b 45. St Pet Coll Ox BA 68 MA 71. Wycliffe Hall Ox 67. **d** 69 **p** 70. C Mildenhall *St E* 69–72; C Lindfield *Chich* 72–77; V Framfield 77–89; R St Leonards St Leon 89–01; R Birling, Addington, Ryarsh and Trottiscliffe *Roch* 01–10; rtd 10; PtO *Roch* 10–14. *Les Sapins Verts, Branla, 56140 Réminiac, France* T: (0033) 2 97 93 25 63 E: jandscross@aol.com

CROSS, Katie Louise. b 70. Ox Brookes Univ BA 08 Ches Univ MA 17. St Jo Coll Nottm 11. **d** 13 **p** 14. C Newton Tracey, Horwood, Alverdiscott etc *Ex* 13–16; R Brampford Speke, Cadbury, Newton St Cyres etc 16–21; R Alcester Minster *Cov* from 21. *St Nicholas' Rectory, Old Rectory Garden, Alcester B49 5DB* M: 07976-263514 E: rector@alcesterminster.org

CROSS, Kenneth James. b 69. Trin Coll Bris BA 09. **d** 09 **p** 10. C Alcombe *B & W* 09–12; R Old Cleeve, Leighland and Treborough 12–18; V Alcombe from 18. *The Vicarage, 34 Manor Road, Minehead TA24 6EJ* T: (01643) 819389 M: 07708-925800 E: kennethjcross@gmail.com

CROSS, Mrs Linda Ann. b 57. St Jo Coll Dur BA 79 Wye Coll Lon MSc 80. **d** 10 **p** 11. OLM Wye w Brook and Hastingleigh etc *Cant* 10–14; OLM Wye from 14. *Yew Tree House, The Street, Brook, Ashford TN25 5PF* T: (01233) 813360 E: lindacross1957@gmail.com

CROSS, Max David. b 68. **d** 14 **p** 15. C Sheet *Portsm* 14–18; R Bedhampton from 18. *The Rectory, Bidbury Lane, Havant PO9 3JG* M: 07590-608766 E: max@maxcross.com

CROSS, Canon Michael Anthony. b 45. Leeds Univ BA 67 MA 69. Coll of Resurr Mirfield 68. **d** 70 **p** 71. C Bloemfontein Cathl S Africa 70–73; C Adel *Ripon* 74–76; Chapl Birm Univ 76–81; V Chapel Allerton *Ripon* 81–92; V Headingley 92–04; AD 96–01; P-in-c Wetherby 04–10; Hon Can Ripon Cathl 06–10; rtd 11; PtO *York* from 11. *1 Angram Close, York YO30 5ZN* T: (01904) 347051 E: mikeanthonycross@gmail.com

CROSS, Mrs Rachel Beth. b 73. Ox Brookes Univ BA 95. STETS 06. **d** 09 **p** 11. C Ponteland *Newc* 09–10; C Benwell 10–13; NSM Kenton Ascension 14; TV Thame *Ox* from 14. *22 Stuart Way, Thame OX9 3WP* T: (01844) 212344 M: 07795-292280 E: rachel@thecrosses.f9.co.uk

CROSS, Stephanie (Stevie). b 53. Essex Univ BSc 74 Loughb Univ MSc 76 Bris Univ BA 01 Reading Univ PGCE 93. Trin Coll Bris 99. **d** 01 **p** 02. C Lytchett Minster *Sarum* 01–05; TV

Wheatley *Ox* 05–11; R Aston-le-Walls, Byfield, Boddington, Eydon etc *Pet* 11–20; rtd 20. *2 Parkfield Road, Rugby CV21 1EN* E: crossstevie@hotmail.com

CROSSEY, The Very Revd Nigel Nicholas. b 59. Cam Univ BA. **d** 84 **p** 85. C Drumglass w Moygashel *Arm* 84–87; I Magheraculmoney *Clogh* 87–93; CF 93–09; Chapl St Columba's Coll Dub 09–15; Dean Kilmore *K, E & A* from 15; I Kilmore w Ballintemple from 15. *The Deanery, Danesfort, Cavan, Republic of Ireland* T: (00353) (49) 433 1918 M: (00353) 86-067 2528 E: dean@kilmore.anglican.org *or* nncrossey@hotmail.com

CROSSLAND, Richard Henry. b 49. Ex Univ BA 72. S'wark Ord Course 91. **d** 94 **p** 96. NSM Surbiton St Andr and St Mark *S'wark* 94–95; NSM Linc Cathl 95–98; NSM Springline 10–14; NSM Owmby Gp 10–14; V Nettleham from 14; RD Lawres from 12. *The Vicarage, 2 Vicarage Lane, Nettleham, Lincoln LN2 2RH* T: (01522) 754752 E: rector@ash.church

CROSSLEY, Dennis Thomas. b 23. AKC 52 St Boniface Warminster. **d** 53 **p** 54. C Crofton Park St Hilda *S'wark* 53–56; C Beddington 56–59; C Talbot Village *Sarum* 59–62; R Finchampstead *Ox* 62–97; rtd 97; PtO *Ox* 97–19. *1 Larkswood Close, Sandhurst, Camberley GU47 8QJ* T: (01344) 751456 E: dtcrossley@web-hq.com

CROSSLEY, George John. b 57. Bradf Univ BA 81 PhD 84. NOC 91. **d** 94 **p** 95. C Balderstone *Man* 94–98; V Branston w Tatenhill *Lich* 98–02; RD Tutbury 00–02; Chapl Burton Hosps NHS Foundn Trust 04–16; P-in-c Burton St Chad *Lich* 09–19; V from 19; P-in-c Stretton w Claymills from 16. *St Chad's Vicarage, 113 Hunter Street, Burton-on-Trent DE14 2SS* T: (01283) 564044 M: 07976-979755 E: vicar@stchadsburton.org.uk

CROSSLEY, Jeremy. *See* CROSSLEY, William Jeremy Hugh

CROSSLEY, Joan Winifred. b 57. Sussex Univ BA 78 Leic Univ MA 80 Univ Coll Lon PhD 85. SAOMC 97. **d** 00 **p** 01. C Goldington *St Alb* 00–02; C Bedf St Mark 02–08; Asst Chapl Gt Ormond Street Hosp for Children NHS Trust 03–05; Asst Chapl Westmr Sch 08–10; PV Westmr Abbey 08–10; PtO *St Alb* 08–18; Chapl K Coll Sch Wimbledon from 10. *King's College School, Southside Common, London SW19 4TT* T: (020) 8255 5300 E: jwcrossley@aol.com *or* jwc@kcs.org.uk

CROSSLEY, John Eric. b 51. St Martin's Coll Lanc BA 92. Carl Dioc Tr Inst 92. **d** 94 **p** 95. C Westfield St Mary *Carl* 94–97; P-in-c Penrith w Newton Reigny and Plumpton Wall 97–02; Chapl Newton Rigg Coll of H&FE 97–02; TV Cartmel Peninsula *Carl* 02–09; rtd 09; PtO *Carl* from 10. *The Vicarage, Market Place, Dalton-in-Furness LA15 8AZ* E: rjoncros@aol.com

CROSSLEY, Kenneth Ernest. b 38. NEOC 01. **d** 03 **p** 04. NSM Ripon Cathl 03–14; *Leeds* from 14. *11 Station Drive, Ripon HG4 1JA* T: (01765) 692499 E: kennethecrossley@aol.com

CROSSLEY, Reuben Verity. b 74. Man Univ BSc 96 Leic Univ MSc 10. St Mellitus Coll BA 18. **d** 18 **p** 19. C Charles w Plymouth St Matthias *Ex* from 18. *St Gabriel's Vicarage, 1 Peverell Terrace, Plymouth PL3 4JJ* M: 07879-416233 E: reubencrossley@outlook.com

CROSSLEY, Canon Robert Scott. b 36. Lon Univ BSc 61 BD 68 PhD 75. ALCD 64. **d** 64 **p** 65. C Beckenham St Jo *Roch* 64–68; C Morden *S'wark* 68–72; Chapl Ridley Hall Cam 72–75; V Camberley St Paul *Guildf* 75–83; TR Surrey Heath 81–84; Hon Can Guildf Cathl 89–98; rtd 98; PtO *Guildf* 98–01 and from 07; Hon C Camberley St Mich Yorktown 01–07. *20 Highbury Crescent, Camberley GU15 1JZ* T: (01276) 500036 E: robertcrossley@ntlworld.com

CROSSLEY, Canon Ruth Joy. b 54. Cranmer Hall Dur 00. **d** 02 **p** 03. C Cartmel Peninsula *Carl* 02–06; P-in-c Levens 06–17; Bp's Adv for CME 06–17; P-in-c Dalton-in-Furness and Ireleth-with-Askam 17–19; V from 19; RD Furness from 19; Hon Can Carl Cathl from 13. *The Vicarage, Market Place, Dalton-in-Furness LA15 8AZ* E: vicar@daltonparish.co.uk

CROSSLEY, Preb William Jeremy Hugh. b 55. St Jo Coll Dur BA 76. Cranmer Hall Dur 81. **d** 84 **p** 85. C Gillingham St Mark *Roch* 84–87; C Ches Square St Mich w St Phil *Lon* 87–94; V Westminster St Jas the Less 94–00; R St Marg Lothbury and St Steph Coleman Street etc from 00; P-in-c St Edm the King and St Mary Woolnoth etc 11–17; AD The City 06–09; Dir Post-Ord Tr 06–15; Dir of Ords Two Cities Area 08–16; Preb St Paul's Cathl from 11. *74 Antill Road, London E3 5BP* T: (020) 7726 4878 E: jeremy@stml.org.uk

CROSSMAN, Maria Antoinette (Manette). b 64. ERMC 09. **d** 12 **p** 13. C Haverhill w Withersfield *St E* 12–15; C Haughley w Wetherden and Stowupland 15; V Gt Barton and Thurston 15–20; P-in-c Higham, Holton St Mary, Raydon and Stratford from 20. *The Rectory, Raydon, Ipswich IP7 5LH* M: 07947-737789 E: revmcrossman@gmail.com

CROSSMAN, Sharon Margaret Joan. b 65. DipCOT 87. Linc Th Coll BTh 93. **d** 93 **p** 94. Par Dn Chippenham St Andr w

Tytherton Lucas *Bris* 93–94; C 94–96; Chapl UWE 96–02; Hon C Almondsbury 97–98; Hon C Almondsbury and Olveston 98–02; Chapl Würzburg Univ Germany 02–03; TV Portishead *B & W* 03–10; V Highbridge 10–19; C The Huntspills and Mark 13–19; RD Axbridge 15–19; Chapl MU 05–19; Preb Wells Cathl *B & W* 17–19; Dioc Voc Co-ord *Sarum* 19–20; PtO *B & W* 20; P-in-c Beckington w Standerwick, Berkley, Rodden etc from 20. *The Rectory, 8 Church Street, Beckington, Frome BA11 6TG* T: (01373) 831680 E: ronniecrossman65@outlook.com

CROSTHWAITE, Howard Wellesley. b 37. St Cuth Soc Dur BA 59. St Steph Ho *Ox* 59. **d** 61 **p** 62. C Workington St Mich *Carl* 61–63; Grenada 63–64; C Barnsley St Mary *Wakef* 64–68; V Milnsbridge 68–70; V Thurgoland 70–79; rtd 99; PtO *Sheff* from 08. *20 Lower Malton Road, Scawsby, Doncaster DN5 8SF* T: (01302) 811164 E: howard@yogadon.co.uk

CROTON, John Barry. b 43. **d** 09 **p** 10. NSM Reading Ch Ch *Ox* 09–13; PtO from 13. *35 Vine Crescent, Reading RG30 3LT* T: 0118-954 3134 M: 07704-858928 E: revjohnc@virginmedia.com

CROUCH, Daniel David. b 82. Ox Brookes Univ BA 09 Glos Univ MA 15. Trin Coll Bris 16. **d** 18 **p** 19. C Highbridge *B & W* from 18. *26 Hamley Close, Burnham-on-Sea TA8 1DS* M: 07890-569534 E: revdancrouch@gmail.com

CROUCH, Keith Matheson. Whitelands Coll Lon CertEd 71 Westhill Coll Birm BPhil 00. K Coll Lon AKC 70. **d** 72 **p** 73. C Hill *Birm* 72–75; C-in-c Woodgate Valley CD 75–77; V Bishop's Castle w Mainstone *Heref* 91–98; Vice-Prin WEMTC 98–04; TV Tenbury Wells 98–02; Public Preacher 02–04; Chapl Dorothy House Hospice Winsley 05–10; rtd 10; PtO *B & W* 05–11; *Heref* 12–15. *3 Julian Road, Ludlow SY8 1HA* T: (01584) 875567 E: keithandjoy@btinternet.com

CROUCHER, James Christopher William. b 84. Univ Coll Ox MChem 06. Oak Hill Th Coll BA 12. **d** 12 **p** 13. C Harold Wood *Chelmsf* 12–16; V Elburton *Ex* from 16. *The Vicarage, 3 Sherford Road, Plymouth PL9 8DQ* T: (01752) 547534 M: 07902-076783 E: james_croucher@yahoo.com

CROUCHER, Jonathan Edward. b 68. Trin Coll Cam BA 90 MA 93. SEITE 01. **d** 04 **p** 05. NSM Lee Gd Shep w St Pet *S'wark* 04–08; C Blackheath Park St Mich 08–12; P-in-c Gipsy Hill Ch Ch 12–13; V from 13; AD Lambeth S from 18; P-in-c W Dulwich Em from 21. *Christ Church Vicarage, 1 Highland Road, London SE19 1DP* T: (020) 8670 0799 M: 07766-072750 E: vicar@gipsyhill.org.uk

CROUCHER, Mrs Susan Rosemary. b 47. **d** 16 **p** 17. OLM Thundersley *Chelmsf* 16–20; PtO 20. *10 Douglas Road, Benfleet SS7 2HN* T: (01702) 555543 M: 07902-463829 E: scroucher@live.co.uk

CROUCHMAN, Eric Richard. b 30. Bps' Coll Cheshunt 64. **d** 66 **p** 67. C Ipswich H Trin *St E* 66–69; C Ipswich All Hallows 69–72; R Crowfield w Stonham Aspal and Mickfield 72–81; R Combs 81–90; RD Stowmarket 84–90; P-in-c Lydgate w Ousden and Cowlinge 90–95; R Wickhambrook w Lydgate, Ousden and Cowlinge 95–96; rtd 96; PtO *St E* from 97. *6 Mitre Close, Woolpit, Bury St Edmunds IP30 9SJ* T/F: (01359) 240070 E: ericthecleric@lineone.net

CROUD, Miss Helen Louise. b 84. Bournemouth Univ BA 12. Ripon Coll Cuddesdon 18. **d** 20 **p** 21. C Bridport *Sarum* from 20. *139 South Street, Bridport DT6 3PA* M: 07712-481835 E: helencroud84@gmail.com

CROW, Michael John. b 35. AKC 63. **d** 64 **p** 65. C Welwyn Garden City *St Alb* 64–67; C Sawbridgeworth 67–69; C Biscot 69–71; V Luton St Aug Limbury 71–79; TR Borehamwood 79–87; V Markyate Street 87–00; P-in-c Flamstead 00–06; rtd 00; PtO *Ex* from 00. *216 Pinhoe Road, Exeter EX4 7HH* T: (01392) 424804 M: 07926-704261 E: micthevic1935@gmail.com

CROWDER, George Timothy. b 74. Liv Univ MEng 96. Oak Hill Th Coll MTh 07. **d** 07 **p** 08. C Hartford *Ches* 07–11; V Over St Jo from 11. *St John's Vicarage, Delamere Street, Winsford CW7 2LY* T: (01606) 594651 E: gtcrowder@live.co.uk

CROWE, Anthony Murray. b 34. St Edm Hall Ox BA 58 MA 61. Westcott Ho Cam 57. **d** 59 **p** 60. C Stockingford *Cov* 59–62; C New Eltham All SS *S'wark* 62–66; V Clapham St Jo 66–73; R Charlton St Luke w H Trin 73–94; rtd 94; Sub-Chapl HM Pris Elmley 94–97; Sub-Chapl HM Pris Swaleside 94–99; PtO *Cant* 94–19. *4 South Lodge Close, Whitstable CT5 2AD* T: (01227) 273046 E: tonycrowe34@btinternet.com

CROWE, Brian John. b 57. Trin Hall Cam BA 78. LCTP 08. **d** 10 **p** 11. NSM Kendal St Thos *Carl* 10–15; NSM Crook 10–15; NSM Crosthwaite Kendal 10–15; NSM Cartmel Fell 10–15; NSM Winster 10–15; NSM Witherslack 10–15; NSM Helsington 10–15; 15; NSM Underbarrow 10–15; P-in-c 15; P-in-c Underbarrow w Helsington 15–17; rtd 17. *Middle Blakebank, Underbarrow, Kendal LA8 8HP* T: (015395) 68959 M: 07711-919572 E: brian.crowe@ymail.com

CROWE, Grant Norman. b 74. Keele Univ LLB 96. Cranmer Hall Dur 00. **d** 03 **p** 04. C Burton All SS w Ch Ch *Lich* 03–07; TV Cen Telford 07–15; Asst Chapl Utrecht w Zwolle *Eur* from 15. *Muiderslot 11, 3813 RR Amersfoort, The Netherlands* M: (0031) (06) 2997 2303 E: grantcrowe@ziggo.nl

CROWE, Canon John Yeomans. b 39. Keble Coll Ox BA 62 MA 66. Linc Th Coll 62. **d** 64 **p** 65. C Tettenhall Regis *Lich* 64–67; C Caversham *Ox* 67–71; V Hampton *Worc* 72–76; P-in-c Leek St Edw *Lich* 76–79; TR Leek 79–83; TR Leek and Meerbrook 83–87; RD Leek 82–87; TR Dorchester and V Warborough *Ox* 87–04; RD Aston and Cuddesdon 93–02; Hon Can Ch Ch 94–04; rtd 04; PtO *Heref* 08–16; *B & W* from 17. *16 Alexandra House, Midland Road, Bath BA2 3GD* T: (01225) 336839 E: johncrowemessages@gmail.com

CROWE, Rebecca Helena. See ROBERTS, Rebecca Helena

CROWHURST, Preb David Brian. b 40. Qu Coll Birm 77. **d** 80 **p** 81. NSM Ribbesford w Bewdley and Dowles *Worc* 80–82; Hon Chapl Birm Cathl 81–82; C Kidderminster St Jo *Worc* 82–83; C-in-c Wribbenhall 83–84; P-in-c 84–87; V Oswestry St Oswald *Lich* 87–94; P-in-c Oswestry H Trin 93–94; V Oswestry 94–08; P-in-c Rhydycroesau 90–91; R 91–08; RD Oswestry 95–01; Preb Lich Cathl 00–08; rtd 08; PtO *Heref* 08–20; *Lich* 18–20. *The Old Hall Coach House, Main Road, Dorrington, Shrewsbury SY5 7JD* T: (01743) 718049 M: 07885-021878 E: d.crowhurst@btinternet.com

CROWIE, Hermon John. b 41. Kelham Th Coll 61. **d** 69 **p** 73. C Sneinton St Cypr *S'well* 69; C Balderton 72–75; V Basford St Aid 75–78; R Everton and Mattersey w Clayworth 78–84; St Helena 84–89; Chapl HM Pris Nor 89–91; Chapl HM Pris Cant 91–02; Bulgaria from 02; PtO *Nor* from 15. *Nova Mahala 6191, Municipality Nikolaevo, Stara Zagora, Bulgaria* E: hermon.jc@hotmail.com

CROWLE, Sarah Ann. See BROUGH, Sarah Ann

CROWLEY, Mrs Jennifer Eileen. b 55. CITC 00. **d** 03 **p** 04. NSM Waterford w Killea, Drumcannon and Dunhill *C, F & O* 03–07; NSM New w Old Ross, Whitechurch, Fethard etc 07–10; Chapl Waterford Regional Hosp 10–17; rtd 17. *Glen, Stradbally, Kilmacthomas, Co Waterford, Republic of Ireland* T: (00353) (51) 293143 M: 87-780 0257 E: jcrowleyglen@gmail.com

CROWLEY, Melanie. b 55. **d** 10 **p** 11. NSM St Alb St Mich 10–13; TV Hitchin 13–16; TV Hitchin and St Paul's Walden from 16. *St Faith's Vicarage, 31 Meadowbank, Hitchin SG4 0HY* E: melanie.crowley@btinternet.com

CROWLEY, Thomas Philip Valentine. b 90. Wadh Coll Ox BA 12 LSE MSc 14. St Steph Ho Ox BA 18. **d** 19 **p** 20. C Eastbourne St Sav and St Pet *Chich* from 19. *4 Courland, 19 Grange Road, Eastbourne BN21 4HA* M: 07807-610034 E: father.thomas@yahoo.com

CROWN, Ola. b 42. **d** 06 **p** 07. NSM Walworth St Jo *S'wark* 06–17; PtO from 17. *23 Dawes House, Orb Street, London SE11 1RE* T: (020) 7708 5240 E: crownola665@yahoo.com

CROWTHER, Gordon Allan. b 63. Rhodes Univ BA 85 LLB 87 Spurgeon's Coll BD 94 St Jo Coll Dur MA. Cranmer Hall Dur 98. **d** 00 **p** 01. C Lancaster St Thos *Blackb* 00–03; Miss P Newcastle and Stoke *Lich* 03–08; C Kirstenhof H Spirit S Africa 09–20; Warden Lee Abbey from 20. *Garden Lodge, Lee Abbey Fellowship, Lee Abbey, Lynton EX35 6JJ* T: (01598) 754200 E: gordoncrowther@leeabbey.org.uk

CROWTHER, Mrs Sheila Ann. b 52. Homerton Coll Cam CertEd 74. Ripon Coll Cuddesdon 12. **d** 15 **p** 16. C Osney *Ox* 15–18; NSM Wolvercote and Wytham from 18; Chapl Ripon Coll Cuddesdon from 18. *15 Bullingdon Road, Oxford OX4 1QQ* T: (01865) 430704 M: 07774-254440 E: sacrowther@hotmail.com

CROWTHER-ALWYN, Benedict Mark. b 53. Kent Univ BA 74. Qu Coll Birm 74. **d** 77 **p** 78. C Fenny Stratford and Water Eaton *Ox* 77–80; C Moulsecoomb *Chich* 80–81; TV 81–83; R Glas St Serf and Baillieston *Glas* 83–87; R Bassingham *Linc* 87–90; V Aubourn w Haddington 87–90; V Carlton-le-Moorland w Stapleford 87–90; R Thurlby w Norton Disney 87–90; V Elmton *Derby* 90–03; P-in-c Matlock 03–05; R 05–14; R Matlock, Dethick, Lea and Holloway from 14. *The Rectory, 116 Church Street, Matlock DE4 3BZ* T: (01629) 582199 E: mcrowther-alwyn@tiscali.co.uk

CROYDON, Archdeacon of. See MALLETT, The Ven Marlene Rosemarie

CROYDON, Area Bishop of. See CLARK, The Rt Revd Jonathan Dunnett

CRUDDAS, Mrs Valerie Mary. b 52. Univ of Wales (Swansea) BSc 73 St Mark & St Jo Coll Lon PGCE 75. St Jo Coll Nottm 05 MA 10. **d** 07 **p** 08. NSM Leatherhead and Mickleham *Guildf* 07–11; TV Schorne *Ox* 11–19; rtd 19.

CRUISE, Brian John Alexander. Bris Univ BA 86 TCD BTh 88. **d** 88 **p** 89. C Lurgan Ch the Redeemer *D & D* 88–92;

I Kildress w Altedesert *Arm* 92–16; I Tullylish *D & D* from 16. *Tullylish Rectory, 100 Banbridge Road, Gilford, Craigavon BT63 6DL* T: (028) 3883 1298 E: b.cruise62@gmail.com

CRUMPLER, Peter George. b 56. ERMC. **d** 13 **p** 14. NSM Sandridge *St Alb* 13–18; SSMs' Officer St Alb Adnry from 17; Public Preacher 18–20; NSM St Alb St Paul from 20. *4 Belsize Close, St Albans AL4 9YD* T: (01727) 847760 E: peter@thecrumplers.co.uk

CRUMPTON, Colin. b 38. AKC 61 Sheff Univ Dip Leadership, Renewal & Miss Studies 97. **d** 64 **p** 65. C Billingham St Cuth *Dur* 64–66; C Shirley *Birm* 66–69; V Mossley *Ches* 69–75; Miss to Seamen 75–77; V Burslem St Paul *Lich* 77–82; V Edensor 82–97; V Llanrhaeadr-ym-Mochnant etc *St As* 97–00; Dir Accra Retreat Cen Ghana 00–01; rtd 02; Hon C Redmarley D'Abitot, Bromesberrow, Pauntley etc *Glouc* 02–03; PtO *Lich* 03–17; *Ches* 04–19; *Blackb* from 18. *5 Fosbrooke House, 8 Clifton Drive, Lytham St Annes FY8 5RQ* T: (01253) 667015 M: 07799-183971 E: colin.crumpton@virgin.net

CRUSE, John Jeremy. b 58. Univ of Wales (Lamp) BA 79 Hughes Hall Cam CertEd 87. Sarum & Wells Th Coll 81. **d** 82 **p** 83. C Newton St Pet *S & B* 82–84; P-in-c Newbridge-on-Wye and Llanfihangel Brynpabuan 84–86; PtO *Heref* 88–89; C Waltham H Cross *Chelmsf* 89–91; TV Yatton Moor *B & W* 91–00; V Shalford *Guildf* 00–18; TV Diss *Nor* from 18. *61 Roydon Road, Diss IP22 4LW* M: 07889-919928 E: john.cruse@disssteamministry.org.uk

CRUSE, Mrs Susan Elizabeth. b 51. Middx Univ BA 04. NTMTC 01. **d** 04 **p** 05. NSM Ingatestone w Fryerning *Chelmsf* 04–11; TV Halstead Area 11–16; rtd 16; PtO *Chelmsf* 16–17; Hon C Two Rivers from 17. *Goston Mount, Pottery Lane, Castle Hedingham, Halstead CO9 3EU* T: (01787) 462062 M: 07885-909837 E: sue.cruse@sky.com

CRUST, Mrs Erica Doreen. b 51. **d** 10 **p** 11. NSM Moulton *Linc* 10–14; NSM Mid Elloe Gp from 14. *3 St Guthlac's Close, Crowland, Peterborough PE6 0ES* T: (01733) 321077 M: 07751-323584 E: erica.crust@gmail.com

CRUTCHLEY, John Hamilton. b 62. Kingston Poly LLB 85 K Coll Lon MA 13. Trin Coll Bris 99. **d** 01 **p** 02. C Barnstaple *Ex* 01–06; R Ardingly *Chich* from 06. *The Rectory, Church Lane, Ardingly, Haywards Heath RH17 6UR* T: (01444) 892332 E: crutchley631@btinternet.com

CRYER, Gordon David. b 34. St D Coll Lamp BA 63. **d** 64 **p** 65. C Mortlake w E Sheen *S'wark* 64–67; C Godstone 67–70; Chapl St Dunstan's Abbey Sch Plymouth 71–02; R Stoke Damerel *Ex* 71–02; P-in-c Devonport St Aubyn 88–02; rtd 02; PtO *Truro* from 02. *9 St Stephens Road, Saltash PL12 4BG* T: (01752) 510436 E: gandvcryer@blueyonder.co.uk

CUBITT, Canon Paul. b 64. Sheff Univ BA 86. Cranmer Hall Dur 95. **d** 97 **p** 98. C Bromyard *Heref* 97–01; V Elloughton and Brough w Brantingham *York* 01–07; R Blofield w Hemblington *Nor* 07–14; RD Blofield 08–14; V N Walsham and Edingthorpe 14–18; V N Walsham, Edingthorpe, Worstead and Westwick 18–20; TR Dereham and Distr from 20; Hon Can Nor Cathl from 18. *The Vicarage, 1 Vicarage Meadows, Dereham NR19 1TW* E: revpcubitt@btinternet.com

CUFF, Gregor John. b 61. Keele Univ BSc 82 Liv Hope Univ MA 12 LTCL 07. Ridley Hall Cam 93. **d** 95 **p** 96. C Stanley *Liv* 95–99; V Waterloo Ch Ch and St Jo from 99; Hon Chapl Mersey Miss to Seafarers from 06. *The Vicarage, 22 Crosby Road South, Liverpool L22 1RQ* T/F: 0151-920 7791 E: gregor.cuff@btinternet.com

CUFF, Preb Pamela. b 47. MCSP 68. S Dios Minl Tr Scheme 89. **d** 92 **p** 94. NSM Nether Stowey w Over Stowey *B & W* 92–93; NSM Quantoxhead 93–07; NSM Quantock Coast 07–12; Asst Chapl Taunton Hosps 93–94; Asst Chapl Taunton and Somerset NHS Trust 94–05; Bp's Officer for Ord NSM (Taunton Adnry) *B & W* 06–09; PtO from 12; Preb Wells Cathl from 08. *Millands, Kilve, Bridgwater TA5 1EA* T: (01278) 741229 E: pam.cuff@hotmail.co.uk

CUFF, Simon Lloyd. b 88. Keble Coll Ox BA 09 MSt 10 DPhil 14. Ox Min Course 10. **d** 13 **p** 14. C Ealing Ch the Sav *Lon* 13–17; Tutor St Mellitus Coll from 17. *12 Linhope Street, London NW1 6HN* T: (020) 7052 0372 E: frsimon@ymail.com *or* simon.cuff@stmellitus.ac.uk

CULL, John. b 31. Oak Hill Th Coll 56. **d** 59 **p** 60. C Radipole *Sarum* 59–66; Chapl Mariners' Ch Glouc 66–70; R Woodchester *Glouc* 70–90; RD Stonehouse 85–89; V Walton St E 90–94; rtd 94; PtO *Glouc* 94–17. *Hillgrove Stables, Bear Hill, Woodchester, Stroud GL5 5DH* T: (01453) 872145

CULLEN, Canon John Austin. b 43. Auckland Univ BA 67 Otago Univ BD 76 Keble Coll Ox DPhil 86 FRSA 89. St Jo Coll Auckland 66. **d** 69 **p** 70. C Papatoetoe NZ 69–73; Assoc P Mt Albert St Luke 73–75; P-in-c 74; Hon C Remuera St Aiden 75–78; Asst Chapl Keble Coll Ox 79–82; PtO *Lon* 82–84; Chapl and Lect Worc Coll Ox 84–86; C St Botolph Aldgate w H Trin Minories *Lon* 86–87; Dir Inst of Chr Studies

87–91; Hon C St Marylebone All SS 87–91; Dir of Min Development *Win* 91–97 and 97–01; Hon Can Win Cathl 96–02; Sen Asst to Bp Lon 02–04; P-in-c St Geo-in-the-East w St Paul 03–04; V Palmers Green St Jo 05–12; rtd 12; PtO *Lon* from 14. *Southgate Beaumont, 15 Cannon Hill, London N14 7DJ* T: (020) 8350 5616 E: john.cullen1@virgin.net

CULLEN, Samantha Anne. b 72. NUI BA 93 Keele Univ MSc 96 Northumbria Univ PhD 04. Ox Min Course 14. **d** 17 **p** 18. C Petersfield *Portsm* 17–20; C Buriton 17–20; C Portsea St Mary from 20. *102A Copnor Road, Portsmouth PO3 5AL* E: revsamcullen@gmail.com

CULLENS, Lynne Susan. b 64. Man Univ BA 86. SNWTP 09. **d** 12 **p** 13. C Congleton *Ches* 12–15; NSM Sandbach Heath w Wheelock 15–16; P-in-c Crewe St Andr w St Jo 16–19; R Stockport and Brinnington from 19. *St Mary's Rectory, Gorsey Mount Street, Stockport SK1 4DU* M: 07544-350692 E: lynne.cullens@gmail.com

CULLIFORD, Jane Margaret. b 48. Lon Univ MB, BS 73. STETS 03. **d** 06 **p** 07. NSM Dorchester *Sarum* 06–14; NSM Dorchester and the Winterbournes from 14; Bp's Adv for Wholeness and Healing from 10. *8 Grosvenor Road, Dorchester DT1 2BB* T: (01305) 264360 E: janeculliford@aol.com

CULLIMORE, Jeremy Stuart. b 53. TD . Westcott Ho Cam. **d** 06 **p** 07. C New Sleaford *Linc* 06–10; P-in-c Linc St Pet-at-Gowts and St Andr 10–21; P-in-c Linc St Botolph 10–21; V Linc St Pet-at-Gowts w St Andr and St Botolph from 21; P-in-c Linc St Mary-le-Wigford w St Benedict etc from 10. *St Peter-at-Gowts Vicarage, 1 Sibthorpe Street, Lincoln LN5 7SP* T: (01522) 530256 M: 07733-114280 E: jscullimore@btinternet.com

CULLING, Elizabeth Ann. *See* HOARE, Elizabeth Ann

CULLINGWORTH, Anthony Robert. b 42. BSc. Ox NSM Course. **d** 83 **p** 84. NSM Slough *Ox* 83–99; NSM Denham 99–02; NSM Morton St Luke *Bradf* 02–04; PtO 04–14; *Leeds* from 14. *2 Thurleston Court, East Morton, Keighley BD20 5RG* T: (01535) 601187 E: thecullies@aol.com

CULLIS, Andrew Stanley Weldon. b 48. Hertf Coll Ox BA 69 LTh. St Jo Coll Nottm 70. **d** 73 **p** 74. C Reigate St Mary *S'wark* 73–78; C Yateley *Win* 78–82; V Dorking St Paul *Guildf* 82–00; RD Dorking 94–99; P-in-c Chilwell *S'well* 00–04; R Fisherton Anger *Sarum* 04–13; rtd 13; PtO *Sarum* 15–19. *76 Fernside Road, Poole BH15 2JL*

CULLWICK, Christopher John. b 53. Hull Univ BA 75. Wycliffe Hall Ox BA 80 MA 85. **d** 81 **p** 82. C Nottingham St Jude *S'well* 81–84; C York St Mich-le-Belfrey 84–87; TV Huntington 87–03; Ind Chapl 02–10; Ldr York Community Chapl 10–13; rtd 13; PtO *York* from 13. *1 Lastingham Terrace, York YO10 4BW* T: (01904) 764608 M: 07792-565805 E: chriscullwick@gmail.com

CULLY, Miss Elizabeth Faith. b 46. SRN 67 SCM 69 RGN 72. Trin Coll Bris BA 88. **d** 88 **p** 94. Par Dn Filton *Bris* 88–92; Par Dn Fishponds St Jo 92–94; C 94–95; P-in-c Brinsley w Underwood *S'well* 95–98; V 98–02; P-in-c Farnsfield 02–08; P-in-c Kirklington w Hockerton 02–08; P-in-c Bilsthorpe 02–08; P-in-c Eakring 02–08; P-in-c Maplebeck 02–08; P-in-c Winkburn 02–08; rtd 08; Hon C Salcombe and Malborough w S Huish *Ex* 08–16; PtO *D & D* from 17. *20 Seahaven Crescent, Groomsport, Bangor BT19 6PR* T: (028) 9146 6791 M: 07802-494260 E: e.faith.cully@gmail.com

CUMBERLAND, The Very Revd Barry John. b 44. Birm Univ BA 67 Worc Coll Ox DipEd 68. Trin Coll Singapore MDiv 88. **d** 88 **p** 89. NSM Westmr St Matt *Lon* 88–90; PtO 90–96; Philippines 90-96, 98-01 and from 03; Dean Manila 92–96; Chapl Stockholm w Gävle and Västerås *Eur* 96–98; P-in-c Las Palmas 01–03; rtd 09. *85A Aurora Pijuan Street, BFRV, Las Pinas City 1740, Metro Manila, Philippines* T: (0063) (2) 875 3528 E: barrycumberland@yahoo.co.uk

CUMBERLAND, John Allan. b 51. Chu Coll Cam BA 73 MA 78. WEMTC 07. **d** 10 **p** 11. NSM Wenlock *Heref* 10–20; rtd 20. *Priory Cottage, 5 The Bull Ring, Much Wenlock TF13 6HS* T: (01952) 727386 E: jacumberland@btinternet.com

CUMBERLEGE, Francis Richard. b 41. AKC 65. **d** 66 **p** 67. C Leigh Park St Fran CD *Portsm* 66–71; P-in-c Gona Papua New Guinea 71–75; R Popondetta 79–81; Adn N Papua 74–81; R Hastings St Clem and All SS *Chich* 81–86; V Broadwater Down 86–91; V Tunbridge Wells St Mark *Roch* 91–99; RD Tunbridge Wells 96–99; P-in-c Brockenhurst *Win* 99–03; V rtd 06; P-in-c Ashburnham w Penhurst *Chich* 09–12; PtO 12–17; *Win* from 14. *Kairos, 10 Forward Drive, Pennington, Lymington SO41 8GA* T: (01590) 719421 E: cumberlege@littleoaks.net

CUMBERLIDGE, Anthony Wynne. b 49. ACIB 75. Sarum & Wells Th Coll 79. **d** 82 **p** 83. C Llanrhos *St As* 82–85; R Llanfair Talhaearn and Llansannan etc 85–87; CF 87–04; P-in-c Lambourn and Eastbury and E Garston *Ox* 04–11; rtd 12. *17 Juniper Close, Bilsthorpe, Newark NG22 8UN* T: (01623) 871883

CUMBRAE, Provost of. *Vacant*

CUMMING, Miss Catriona Mary. b 82. York Univ BA 04 MA 05. Westcott Ho Cam 11. **d** 14 **p** 15. C Melton Mowbray *Leic* 14–17; Succ York Minster from 17. *Church House, 10-14 Ogleforth, York YO1 7JN* T: (01904) 559546 M: 07843-339982 E: succentor@yorkminster.org

CUMMING, Canon Nigel Patrick. b 42. St Jo Coll Nottm 73. **d** 75 **p** 76. C Castle Hall *Ches* 75–77; C Stalybridge H Trin and Ch Ch 77–78; C Tadley St Pet *Win* 78–82; R Overton w Laverstoke and Freefolk 82–07; RD Whitchurch 89–98; Hon Can Win Cathl 99–07; rtd 07; PtO *Win* from 08; *Sarum* from 09. *Pasture House, Whitsbury, Fordingbridge SP6 3QB* T: (01725) 518248 E: nigel.cumming@btinternet.com

CUMMING, Paul James. b 79. Cliff Coll BA 00. St Jo Coll Nottm 09. **d** 11 **p** 12. C Poynton *Ches* 11–14; V Cheadle All Hallows from 14. *All Hallows' Vicarage, 222 Councillor Lane, Cheadle SK8 2JG* T: 0161-478 8789 E: cumming-no-s@hotmail.co.uk *or* revpaul@live.co.uk

CUMMING, Susan Margaret. *See* FORSHAW, Susan Margaret

CUMMING-LATTEY, Mrs Susan Mary Ruth. b 47. Open Univ BA 77 SRN 69. STETS 00. **d** 03 **p** 04. NSM Ash Vale *Guildf* 03–07; NSM Crondall and Ewshot from 07; Chapl Phyllis Tuckwell Hospice Farnham from 12. *36A The Verne, Church Crookham, Fleet GU52 6LU* T: (01252) 621295 F: 815882 M: 07761-126354 E: suelattey@btinternet.com

CUMMINGS, Mrs Elizabeth. b 45. St Jo Coll Dur BA 84. NEOC 85. **d** 87 **p** 94. NSM Dur St Giles 87–89; Chapl HM Pris Dur 89–90; Chapl HM Rem Cen Low Newton 90–95; Chapl HM Pris Stocken 95–96; Chapl HM Pris Frankland 96–05; rtd 05; PtO *Dur* 05–21. *8 Bridgemere Drive, Framwellgate Moor, Durham DH1 5FG* T: 0191-383 0832

CUMMINGS, Canon William Alexander Vickery. b 38. Ch Ch Ox BA 62 MA 64. Wycliffe Hall Ox 61. **d** 64 **p** 65. C Leytonstone St Jo *Chelmsf* 64–67; C Writtle 67–71; R Stratton St Mary w Stratton St Michael *Nor* 71–73; R Wacton Magna w Parva 71–73; R Stratton St Mary w Stratton St Michael etc 73–91; RD Depwade 81–91; Hon Can Nor Cathl 90–91; V Battle *Chich* 91–04; Dean Battle 91–04; rtd 04; PtO *Win* from 13. *80 Samber Close, Lymington SO41 9LF* T: (01590) 610426

CUMMINS, Ashley Wighton. b 56. St Andr Univ BD 83. Coates Hall Edin 82. **d** 84 **p** 85. C Broughty Ferry *Bre* 84–87; P-in-c Dundee St Ninian 87–92; P-in-c Invergowrie 92–19; Chapl Angl Students Dundee Univ 92–07; rtd 19. *27 Errol Road, Invergowrie, Dundee DD2 5AG* T: (01382) 562525 E: ashleycummins@outlook.com

CUMMINS, Daphne Mary. *See* GREEN, Daphne Mary

CUMMINS, Nicholas Marshall. b 36. CITC 65. **d** 67 **p** 68. C Ballymena w Ballyclug *Conn* 67–70; C Belfast St Nic 70–73; I Buttevant Union *C, C & R* 73–78; I Mallow Union 78–83; I Kilmoe Union 83–96; Can Cork Cathl 90–96; Treas Cork Cathl 95–96; Preb Tymothan St Patr Cathl Dublin 95–01; Dean Killaloe and Clonfert *L & K* 96–01; Dean Kilfenora and Provost Kilmacduagh 96–01; I Killaloe w Stradbally 96–01; rtd 01; PtO *Chich* from 15. *13 Borough Hill, Petersfield GU32 3LQ* T: (01730) 269742

CUNLIFFE, Anne. b 48. CBDTI 01. **d** 04 **p** 05. OLM Poulton-le-Sands w Morecambe St Laur *Blackb* 04–07; NSM 04–14; rtd 14; PtO *Blackb* from 14. *14 Coniston Road, Morecambe LA4 5PS* T: (01524) 422509 E: revanne@gmail.com

CUNLIFFE, The Ven Christopher John. b 55. Ch Ox BA 77 MA 81 DPhil 81 Trin Coll Cam BA 82 MA 86 ARHistS 94. Westcott Ho Cam 80. **d** 83 **p** 84. C Chesterfield St Mary and All SS *Derby* 83–85; Chapl Linc Coll Ox 85–89; Chapl City Univ and Guildhall Sch of Music and Drama *Lon* 89–91; Voc Officer and Selection Sec ABM 91–97; Dir Professional Min *Lon* 97–03; Chapl to Bp Bradwell *Chelmsf* 04–06; Adn Derby 06–20; Can Res Derby Cathl 06–08; Dioc Dir of Ords 19–20; rtd 21. *Address temp unknown*

CUNLIFFE, Harold. b 28. St Aid Birkenhead 57. **d** 60 **p** 61. C Hindley All SS *Liv* 60–64; V Everton St Chad w Ch Ch 64–69; R Golborne 70–93; rtd 93; PtO *Liv* from 93. *51 Greenfields Crescent, Ashton-in-Makerfield, Wigan WN4 8QY* T: (01942) 202956 E: haroldcunliffe@sky.com

CUNLIFFE, The Ven Helen Margaret. b 54. St Hilda's Coll Ox BA 77 MA 78. Westcott Ho Cam 81. **dss** 83 **d** 87 **p** 94. Chesterfield St Mary and All SS *Derby* 83–85; Ox St Mary V w St Cross and St Pet 86–89; Par Dn 87–89; Chapl Nuff Coll Ox 86–89; Team Dn Clapham Team *S'wark* 89–94; TV 94–96; Can Res S'wark Cathl 96–03; Chapl Welcare 96–03; Adn St Alb 03–07; rtd 08. *Address temp unknown*

CUNLIFFE, Mrs Katherine Helen. b 79. Man Univ BMus 00 Sheff Univ MA 18 St Martin's Coll Lanc PGCE 07. Coll of Resurr Mirfield BA 15. **d** 15 **p** 16. C Manchester Gd Shep and St Barn *Man* 15–18; V Shaw from 18; V High Crompton and Thornham from 21. *Holy Trinity Vicarage,*

13 Church Road, Shaw, Oldham OL2 7AT M: 07548-295229 E: revkatycunliffe@gmail.com

CUNLIFFE, Peter Henry. b 54. Univ of Wales MA 93 SRN 77 RSCN 79 RCNT 83. Trin Coll Bris 92. **d** 94 **p** 95. C Carshalton Beeches *S'wark* 94–95; C Reigate St Mary 95–02; P-in-c Hemingford Grey *Ely* 02–04; V from 04; P-in-c Hemingford Abbots from 04. *The Vicarage, 6 Braggs Lane, Hemingford Grey, Huntingdon PE28 9BW* T: (01480) 394378 E: vicar@churchbytheriver.org.uk

CUNNINGHAM, Brian James. b 65. York Univ BA 88. Ripon Coll Cuddesdon BA 91. **d** 92 **p** 93. C Merrow *Guildf* 92–96; C Kennington St Jo w St Jas *S'wark* 96–99; Chapl Pangbourne Coll 99–11; Chapl Oundle Sch from 11. *Oundle School, New Street, Oundle, Peterborough PE8 4GH* T: (01832) 277122 E: bjc@oundleschool.org.uk

CUNNINGHAM, Wendy. b 42. SAOMC 01. **d** 04 **p** 05. NSM Hook Norton w Gt Rollright, Swerford etc *Ox* 04–19; rtd 19; PtO *Ox* from 20. *Homefield, Queen Street, Hook Norton, Banbury OX15 5PH* T: (01608) 737135 E: wendy@dewlands.me.uk

CUNNINGTON, Canon Andrew Thomas. b 56. Southn Univ BTh 86. Sarum & Wells Th Coll 82. **d** 85 **p** 86. C Ifield *Chich* 85–89; TV Haywards Heath St Wilfrid 89–94; V Midhurst 94–06; R Woolbeding 94–06; RD Midhurst 03–06; V Redhill St Matt *S'wark* from 06; Jt Dir of IME Croydon Area 09–13; AD Reigate 13–18; Hon Can S'wark Cathl from 15. *St Matthew's Vicarage, 27 Ridgeway Road, Redhill RH1 6PQ* T: (01737) 761568 E: andrew@stmatthews-redhill.org.uk

CUNNINGTON, Miss Averil. b 41. St Mary's Coll Chelt CertEd 61 Man Univ BA 68 MEd 73. NOC 93. **d** 95 **p** 96. Hd Mistress Counthill Sch Oldham 84–96; NSM Milnrow *Man* 95–98; NSM Hey 98–02; Lic Preacher 02–05; Tutor NOC 98–05; PtO *Heref* 05–10; *Man* from 10. *6 Summerhill View, Denshaw, Oldham OL3 5TB* E: averil.cunnington@zen.co.uk

CUNNINGTON, Howard James. b 56. Southn Univ BA 77 St Jo Coll Dur PGCE 78. Trin Coll Bris 90. **d** 92 **p** 93. C Ex St Leon w H Trin 92–96; V Sandown Ch Ch *Portsm* 96–04; V Lower Sandown St Jo 96–04; PtO from 04; *Ex* from 20. *2 Admiral Way, Exeter EX2 7GA* E: howard.cunnington@gmail.com

CUNNOLD, David Allen. b 36. St Boniface Warminster AKC 62. **d** 63 **p** 64. C Gillingham St Barn *Roch* 63–66; C Chilvers Coton w Astley *Cov* 66–69; C Banbury *Ox* 69–71; rtd 01. *14 Kirton Grove, Tettenhall, Wolverhampton WV6 8RX* T: (01902) 756008

CUPITT, Don. b 34. Trin Hall Cam BA 55 MA 58 Bris Univ Hon DLitt 84. Westcott Ho Cam 57. **d** 59 **p** 60. C Salford St Phil w St Steph *Man* 59–62; Vice-Prin Westcott Ho Cam 62–66; Dean Em Coll Cam 66–91; Asst Lect Div Cam Univ 68–73; Lect 73–96; rtd 96; Life Fell Em Coll Cam from 96. *Emmanuel College, Cambridge CB2 3AP* T: (01223) 334200

CURD, Preb Christine Veronica. b 51. Bris Univ BA 72 Leic Univ MSc 05. Oak Hill Th Coll 84 WMMTC 88. **d** 89 **p** 94. NSM Widecombe-in-the-Moor, Leusdon, Princetown etc *Ex* 89–93; NSM Bovey Tracey SS Pet, Paul and Thos w Hennock 94–97; Asst Chapl HM Pris Channings Wood 92–01; Chapl HM Pris Ex 01–10; Bp's Officer for Pris *Ex* 10–13; NSM Dawlish w Holcombe, Cofton and Starcross 13–20; Preb Ex Cathl 05–20; PtO from 20. *Address withheld by request* M: 07771-842334 E: prebchris2020@gmail.com

CURD, Clifford John Letsom. b 45. SRN RNT. Oak Hill Th Coll 84. **d** 86 **p** 87. C Stone Ch Ch *Lich* 86–89; TV Widecombe-in-the-Moor, Leusdon, Princetown etc *Ex* 89–93; P-in-c Ilsington 93–04; rtd 05. *Address withheld by request* M: 07881-442031

CURL, Roger William. b 50. BA BD DPhil. Oak Hill Th Coll. **d** 82 **p** 83. C Cromer *Nor* 82–86; C Sevenoaks St Nic *Roch* 86–88; V Fulham St Mary N End *Lon* 88–20; rtd 20. *7 Weybourne Hall, Weybourne, Holt NR25 7EX* T: (01263) 588278 E: revcurl@gmail.com

CURNEW, Brian Leslie. b 48. Qu Coll Ox BA 69 DPhil 77 MA 77. Ripon Coll Cuddesdon 77. **d** 79 **p** 80. C Sandhurst *Ox* 79–82; Tutor St Steph Ho Ox 82–87; V Fishponds St Mary *Bris* 87–94; TR Ludlow *Heref* 94–09; P-in-c Bitterley w Middleton, Stoke St Milborough etc 09; Preb Heref Cathl 02–09; P-in-c Headcorn *Cant* 09–11; P-in-c Sutton Valence w E Sutton and Chart Sutton 09–11; V Headcorn and The Suttons 11–14; rtd 14; PtO *Lon* from 15. *16 Richmond Road, London N11 2QR* M: 07540-441271 E: briancurnew@gmail.com

CURNOCK, Canon Karen Susan. b 50. Nottm Univ BTh 78. Linc Th Coll 74. **d** 95 **p** 97. NSM Graffoe Gp *Linc* 95–96; Dioc Sec *Sarum* 96–03; NSM Chalke Valley 96–03; V Buckland Newton, Cerne Abbas, Godmanstone etc 03–10; Can and Preb Sarum Cathl 02–10; RD Dorchester 06–09; rtd 10; PtO *Ex* from 11. *Stoneacre, Castle Hill, Seaton EX12 2QP* T: (01297) 24266 E: karen.curnock@gmail.com

CURNOW, Bronwyn Ellen. Ex Univ BA 05. St Padarn's Inst 16. **d** 17 **p** 18. C Glan Ithon *S & B* from 17. *16 Holcombe Drive, Llandrindod Wells LD1 6DN* T: (01597) 829133 M: 07719-854768 E: revbroncurnow@gmail.com

CURNOW, Terence Peter. b 37. Univ of Wales (Lamp) BA 62. **d** 63 **p** 64. C Llanishen and Lisvane *Llan* 63–71; Youth Chapl 67–71; Asst Chapl K Coll Taunton 71–74; Chapl Taunton Sch 74–84; Ho Master 84–98; PtO *B & W* 84–18; rtd 02. *19 Stonegallows, Taunton TA1 5JW* T: (01823) 330003 E: mai.curnow@googlemail.com

CURRALL, Canon James Edward Patrick. b 55. Man Univ BSc 76 Aber Univ PhD 81. TISEC 09. **d** 12 **p** 13. C Largs *Glas* 12–15; LtO *Mor* from 15; P-in-c Tain from 17; P-in-c Dornoch from 17; P-in-c Lairg from 17; P-in-c Ardgay from 17; P-in-c The Crask from 17; P-in-c Brora *Mor* from 19; P-in-c Tongue (St Mary-by-the-Cross) from 20; Can St Andr Cathl Inverness *Mor* from 20. *Kennic Cottage, Spinningdale, Ardgay IV24 3AD* T: (01862) 881737 M: 07989-383439 E: revjcurrall@mail.scot

CURRAM, Deborah Ann. b 62. Ripon Coll Cuddesdon 14. **d** 16 **p** 17. NSM Minchinhampton w Box and Amberley *Glouc* 16–18; NSM Rodborough, Woodchester and Brimscombe 18–19; C Hayling Is St Andr *Portsm* from 19. *29 Selsmore Road, Hayling Island PO11 9JZ* T: (023) 9246 2379 E: revdeborah01@gmail.com

CURRAN, John Henry. b 77. Nottm Univ BA 00. Wycliffe Hall Ox 00. **d** 02 **p** 03. C W Bridgford *S'well* 02–05; PtO 05–07; P-in-c Wollaton Park 07–11; V 11–21; Chapl Nottm Univ 07–11; P-in-c Moreton-in-Marsh w Batsford, Todenham etc *Glouc* from 21. *The Rectory, Bourton Road, Moreton-in-Marsh GL56 0BG*

CURRAN, The Ven Patrick Martin Stanley. b 56. K Coll (NS) BA 80 Southn Univ BTh 84. Chich Th Coll 80. **d** 84 **p** 85. C Heavitree w Ex St Paul 84–87; Bp's Chapl to Students *Bradf* 87–93; Chapl Bonn w Cologne *Eur* 93–00; Chapl Vienna from 00; Can Malta Cathl from 00; Adn E Adnry 02–15. *The British Embassy, Jaurèsgasse 12, A-1030 Vienna, Austria* T: (0043) (1) 714 8900 or 718 5902 E: office@christchurchvienna.org

CURRELL, Linda Anne. *See* SCOTT, Linda Anne

CURRER, Caroline Mary. b 49. Keele Univ BA 71 Warwick Univ PhD 86 Anglia Ruskin Univ MA 09 CQSW 71. EAMTC 02. **d** 04 **p** 05. NSM Stansted Mountfitchet w Birchanger and Farnham *Chelmsf* 04–09; P-in-c Poynings w Edburton, Newtimber and Pyecombe *Chich* 09–17; rtd 17; PtO *Chelmsf* 19–20; TV Saffron Walden and Villages from 20. *The Vicarage, Radwinter Road, Ashdon, Saffron Walden CB10 2ET* E: c.currer@btinternet.com

CURREY, Pauline Carol. *See* REES, Pauline Carol

CURRIE, Daniel Robert. b 71. Trin Coll Bris 07. **d** 09 **p** 10. C Gorleston St Andr *Nor* 09–12; C Marple All SS *Ches* 12–16; V from 16. *155 Church Lane, Marple, Stockport SK6 7LD* T: 0161-292 9305 E: revdcurrie@gmail.com

CURRIE, John Stuart. b 47. SEITE 94. **d** 97 **p** 98. C S Chatham H Trin *Roch* 97–01; TV 01–13; Dioc Ecum Officer 09–13; rtd 13; PtO *Roch* from 13; *Cant* from 14. *Pilgrim's House, Oxenden Street, Herne Bay CT6 8TD* T: (01227) 364842 M: 07814-670051 E: revjsc@gmail.com

CURRIE, Mrs Katherine Barbara. b 55. Huddersfield Univ BSc 01 York St Jo Univ BA 13 SRN 78. Yorks Min Course 12. **d** 14 **p** 15. NSM High Hoyland, Scissett and Clayton W *Leeds* from 14; P-in-c Skelmanthorpe from 20. *158 Blacker Lane, Netherton, Wakefield WF4 4EZ* T: (01924) 279295 M: 07949-850460 E: revkcurrie@icloud.com

CURRIE, Lesley Sarah. b 70. Nene Coll Northn BA 95 Herts Univ PGCE 97. All SS Cen for Miss & Min 14. **d** 14 **p** 15. C Marple All SS *Ches* from 14; RD Chadkirk from 19. *155 Church Lane, Marple, Stockport SK6 7LD* T: 0161-292 9305 E: dalcurries@gmail.com

CURRIE, Canon Stuart William. b 53. Hertf Coll Ox MA 79 Fitzw Coll Cam MA 85 Univ Coll Dur CertEd K Coll Lon PhD 11. Westcott Ho Cam 82. **d** 85 **p** 86. C Whitley Ch Ch *Ox* 85–89; TV Banbury 89–94; V Barbourne *Worc* 94–16; Bp's Chapl from 16; Hon Can Worc Cathl from 09. *The Old Palace, Deansway, Worcester WR1 2JE* T: (01905) 731599 E: bishopschaplain@cofe-worcester.org.uk

CURRIN, John. b 56. Keele Univ CertEd 78. St Jo Coll Nottm MA 93. **d** 93 **p** 94. C Eastwood *S'well* 93–97; P-in-c Matlock Bath and Cromford *Derby* 97–02; V 02–06; R Dibden *Win* 06–18; rtd 18; PtO *Win* from 19. *8 Velsheda Court, Hythe Marina Village, Hythe, Southampton SO45 6DW*

CURRY, Canon Bruce. b 39. Dur Univ BA 61. Wells Th Coll 61. **d** 63 **p** 64. C Shepton Mallet *B & W* 63–67; C Cheam *S'wark* 67–71; R W Walton *Ely* 71–78; V St Neots 78–94; P-in-c Everton w Tetworth 94–98; P-in-c Abbotsley 94–99; P-in-c Waresley 94–99; P-in-c Gt w Lt Gransden 98–99; R Gt Gransden and Abbotsley and Lt Gransden etc 99–04; RD

St Neots 90–02; Hon Can Ely Cathl 98–04; rtd 04; PtO *Ely* from 05. *10 Ravens Court, Ely CB6 3ED* T: (01353) 661494 E: brucecurry10@gmail.com

CURRY, Christopher James. b 90. Ox Univ BA 12 Univ Coll Lon MA 13 Dur Univ BA 21. St Mellitus Coll 18. d 21. C Brentford *Lon* from 21. *23 York Road, Brentford TW8 0QP* M: 07732-188063 E: chris@parishofbrentford.org.uk *or* c.j.curry@hotmail.co.uk

CURRY, George Robert. b 51. JP 90. Bede Coll Dur BA 72 Newc Univ MA 97. Cranmer Hall Dur Oak Hill Th Coll. d 76 p 77. C Denton Holme *Carl* 76–81; V Low Elswick *Newc* 81–06; P-in-c High Elswick St Paul 97–06; V Elswick from 06. *St Stephen's Vicarage, Clumber Street, Newcastle upon Tyne NE4 7ST* T: 0191-273 4680 E: g.r.curry@btinternet.com

CURRY, James Sebastian. b 63. Hatf Coll Dur BA 84. Ripon Coll Cuddesdon BTh 93. d 93 p 94. C Four Oaks *Birm* 93–96; C Erdington St Barn 96–99; TV Jarrow *Dur* 99–06; R Aboyne, Ballater and Braemar *Ab* 06–13; P-in-c Golcar *Wakef* 13–14; *Leeds* 14–17; P-in-c Longwood *Wakef* 13–14; *Leeds* 14–17; C Mansfield St Mark *S'well* from 17; C Mansfield SS Pet and Paul from 17. *The Vicarage, 112 Nottingham Road, Mansfield NG18 1BP* E: revjamescurry@btinternet.com

CURTIS, Adam John. b 90. Cardiff Univ BA 12. Oak Hill Th Coll MA 20. d 20. C Sidcup Ch Ch *Roch* from 20. *2 Ashly Court, 47 Station Road, Sidcup DA15 7DY* M: 07547-571097 E: adamjohncurtis@hotmail.co.uk

CURTIS, The Very Revd Anthony Gordon. b 74. Selw Coll Cam BTh 10 St Mary's Coll Dur PhD 19. Westcott Ho Cam 07. d 10 p 11. C Morpeth *Newc* 10–13; V Shiremoor 13–19; Dean Dunedin NZ from 19. *28 Rosebery Street, Belleknowes, Dunedin 9011, New Zealand* T: (0064) (3) 477 2336 M: (0064) 27-358 1998 E: tony.curtis@cantab.net

CURTIS, Colin. b 47. Open Univ BA 80 ALA 69. St Jo Coll Nottm 83. d 93 p 94. NSM Clarkston *Glas* 93–10; LtO from 12. *78 Auldhouse Road, Glasgow G43 1UR* T: 0141-569 4206 E: colin.curtis540@ntlworld.com

CURTIS, Mrs Jacqueline Elaine. b 60. Sarum & Wells Th Coll 87. d 90 p 94. Par Dn Bridport *Sarum* 90–94; C 94–95; TV Melbury 95–00; TV Maltby *Sheff* 00–02; TR 02–08; TR Crosslacon *Carl* 08–16; TR Chellington *St Alb* from 16. *The Rectory, 3 The Moor, Carlton, Bedford MK43 7JR* T: (01234) 720262 E: jecurtisx3@gmail.com *or* chellingtonteam@gmail.com

CURTIS, Jane Darwent. b 64. Leic Univ BA 86. Linc Th Coll BTh 93. d 93 p 94. Par Dn Oadby *Leic* 93–94; C 94–96; Chapl De Montfort Univ 96–03; C Leic H Spirit 96–97; TV 97–03; TV Gilmorton, Peatling Parva, Kimcote etc 03–09; Bp's Adv for Women's Min 04–09; V Whatborough Gp 09–17; Officer for IME 4-7 09–17; Bp's Adv for Women's Min 15–16; Hon Can Leic Cathl 06–17; V R Wootton Bassett *Sarum* from 17; RD Calne from 17. *St Bartholomew's Vicarage, Glebe Road, Royal Wootton Bassett, Swindon SN4 7DU* E: jane@chelmsworth.com

CURTIS, John Durston. b 43. Lich Th Coll 65. d 68 p 69. C Coseley Ch Ch *Lich* 68–71; C Sedgley All SS 71–74; CF 74–79; P-in-c Newton Valence *Win* 79–82; P-in-c Selborne 79–82; R Newton Valence, Selborne and E Tisted w Colemore 82–87; R Marchwood 87–09; AD Lyndhurst 05–08; PtO *Nor* from 09. *7 Pearce Road, Diss IP22 4YF* T: (01379) 640036 E: linda.john7@btinternet.com

CURTIS, Mrs Julia. b 67. Warwick Univ BSc 89 Anglia Ruskin Univ MA 13 MA 15 ACA 92. Westcott Ho Cam 13. d 15 p 16. C Creech St Michael and Ruishton w Thornfalcon *B & W* 15–18; P-in-c Teme Valley S *Worc* from 18. *The Rectory, Broadheath, Tenbury Wells WR15 8QW* T: (01886) 853286 M: 07908-925693 E: revjuliacurtis@gmail.com

CURTIS, Layton Richard. b 61. Leic Univ BSc 84 PGCE 85. Linc Th Coll BTh 93. d 93 p 94. C Knighton St Mary Magd *Leic* 93–96; C Leic St Phil 96–01; P-in-c Wigston Magna 01–12; P-in-c Haulton and Allexton, w Horninghold, Tugby etc 12–17; TR Cannings and Redhorn *Sarum* from 17. *St Bartholomew's Vicarage, Glebe Road, Royal Wootton Bassett, Swindon SN4 7DU* M: 07855-746041 E: richard@canred.org

CURTIS, Mrs Marian Ruth. b 54. Nottm Univ BA 75 CQSW 80. Trin Coll Bris 03. d 05 p 06. C Blackheath Park St Mich *S'wark* 05–08; Asst Chapl Salisbury NHS Foundn Trust 08–09; P-in-c Slindon, Eartham and Madehurst *Chich* 09–15; rtd 15; PtO *Sarum* 16–21. *Short Street Farm, 160 Short Street, Chapmanslade, Westbury BA13 4AA* T: (01373) 832654 E: mariancurtis@aol.com

CURTIS, Ronald Victor. b 47. SAOMC 98. d 01 p 02. NSM Shipton-under-Wychwood w Milton, Fifield etc Ox 01–05; P-in-c Stourbridge St Thos *Worc* 05–12; rtd 12; PtO Ox from 13; *Eur* from 19. *12 Waites Close, Aston, Bampton OX18 2ES* E: rev.ron@btinternet.com

CURTIS, Simon John. b 85. Trin Coll Bris 19. d 21. C Caddington *St Alb* from 21; C Farley Hill St Jo from 21. *47 Rotheram Avenue, Luton LU1 5PP* M: 07895-595384 E: simon.curtis1985@hotmail.co.uk

CURTIS, Mrs Susan Anne. b 51. Birm Univ CertEd 72 Open Univ BA 79. d 07 p 08. OLM Epsom Common Ch Ch *Guildf* 07–12; NSM 12–21; PtO from 21. *The Rye, 38C Woodlands Road, Epsom KT18 7HW* E: sacsac@ntlworld.com

CURTIS, Susannah Ruth. b 83. Jes Coll Cam BA 05 MA 09. Wycliffe Hall Ox MTh 10. d 08 p 09. C Preston-on-Tees and Longnewton *Dur* 08–12; C Stockton 08–12; C Billingham 12–13; P-in-c Doxford St Wilfrid 13–18; Chapl St Jo Coll Dur 13–18; PtO *Derby* 18–19; C Derby St Alkmund and St Werburgh from 19. *31 Mansfield Street, Derby DE1 3RJ* E: revsrcurtis@gmail.com

CURTIS, Thomas John. b 32. Pemb Coll Ox BA 55 MA 59 Lon Univ BD 58. Clifton Th Coll 55. d 58 p 59. C Wandsworth All SS *S'wark* 58–61; Chile 61–71; R Saxmundham *St E* 71–77; V Cheltenham St Mark *Glouc* 77–84; TR 84–86; V Chipping Norton *Ox* 86–95; rtd 95; Hon Dioc Rep SAMS St E 95–01; PtO *St E* 95–01; *Glouc* from 01; *Worc* 01–10. *60 Courtney Close, Tewkesbury GL20 5FB* T: (01684) 295298 E: curtistomjon@aol.com

CUSHING, Mrs Barbara Anne. b 51. Doncaster Coll of Educn CertEd 72 Sheff Univ BEd 73. Yorks Min Course 12. d 13 p 14. NSM Anston *Sheff* from 13. *17 Lindale Close, North Anston, Sheffield S25 4FD* T: (01909) 564905 M: 07854-728444 E: barbara_cush@hotmail.com

CUSHING, Gregory Douglas. b 84. Plymouth Univ BA 05 Cam Univ BTh 12. Ridley Hall Cam 09. d 12 p 13. C Wandsworth All SS *S'wark* 12–16; P-in-c Alfold and Loxwood *Guildf* 16–21; R from 21. *The Rectory, Vicarage Hill, Loxwood, Billingshurst RH14 0RG* T: (01403) 752320 *or* 753821 M: 07746-721504 E: revgregcushing@gmail.com

CUSHING, Sarah Louise. b 66. Ripon Coll Cuddesdon 19. d 21. C Warwick *Cov* from 21. *30 New Street, Stratford-upon-Avon CV37 6BX* M: 07950-827753 E: sarahlcushing@gmail.com

CUTCLIFFE, Canon Neil Robert. b 50. NUU BA 72 TCD BA 72. d 75 p 76. C Belfast St Mary *Conn* 75–78; C Lurgan Ch the Redeemer *D & D* 78–80; I Garrison w Slavin and Belleek *Clogh* 80–86; I Mossley *Conn* 86–16; Can Belf Cathl 07–16; rtd 16. *6 Ballymontenagh Road, Gracehill, Ballymena BT42 2QG* T: (028) 2587 8779 E: rathdune@hotmail.com

CUTHBERT, Canon John. b 52. Edin Univ BSc 76 PhD 80 Aber Univ MTh 05. Coates Hall Edin BD 92. d 92 p 93. Chapl St Mary's Cathl *Edin* 92–98; C Edin St Mary 92–98; P-in-c Forres *Mor* 98–03; R Arbroath *Bre* 04–14; R Auchmithie 04–14; Can St Paul's Cathl Dundee 09–14; P-in-c Inverness St Jo *Mor* 14–21; P-in-c Inverness St Mich 14–21. *Balnamara, 5 Point Road, North Kessock, Inverness IV1 3YB* T: (01463) 731471 M: 07929-555956 E: john2cuthbert@gmail.com

CUTHBERT, Mrs Penelope Jane. b 65. Collingwood Coll Dur BA 87 Ox Brookes Univ BA 12. Ox Min Course 09. d 12 p 13. C Reading St Agnes w St Paul and St Barn *Ox* 12–16; C Caversham Thameside and Mapledurham from 16. *St John's Vicarage, St John's Road, Caversham, Reading RG4 5AN* M: 07825-331810 E: penny_cuthbert@btinternet.com

CUTHBERT, Vernon John. Trin Coll Bris 02. d 04 p 05. C Alvaston *Derby* 04–08; P-in-c Cleadon *Dur* from 08; AD Jarrow 15–20; P-in-c Whitburn from 20. *The Vicarage, 5 Sunderland Road, Cleadon, Sunderland SR6 7UR* T: 0191-536 7147 E: vicar@cleadonallsaints.org *or* priest@whitburnparishchurch.co.uk

CUTHBERT, Victor. b 46. d 01 p 02. OLM Surbiton St Matt *S'wark* 01–11; PtO 11–21; rtd 21. *4 St Thomas Close, Surbiton KT6 7TU* T: (020) 8399 8722 E: victorcuthbert@btinternet.com

CUTHBERTSON, Canon Amanda. b 54. K Coll Lon BD 92 AKC 92 Open Univ PGCE 98 Lough Univ MA 00 ALCM 85 LLCM 87. EAMTC 98. d 00 p 01. C Northampton St Benedict *Pet* 00–03; V Wellingborough St Mark 03–17; Dioc Chapl MU 04–16; Can Pet Cathl 15–17; rtd 17; Bp's Adv for Healing Min *Pet* from 17; V Northampton Ch Ch from 17. *25 Glebe Road, Roade, Northampton NN7 2QH* T: (01604) 863488 M: 07525-257547 E: amandacuthbertson123@gmail.com

CUTLER, Robert Francis. b 37. Lon Univ BSc 57. Clifton Th Coll 62. d 64 p 65. C Peckham St Mary Magd *S'wark* 64–68; C Redhill H Trin 68–70; Travel Sec Inter-Coll Chr Fellowship of IVF 70–74; Hon C Selly Hill St Steph *Birm* 70–74; Interserve Internat Bangladesh 74–93; Internat Fellowship Evang Students 74–85; Bible Students Fellowship of Bangladesh 85–93; V Rochdale Deeplish St Luke *Man* 94–99; TV S Rochdale 00–02; rtd 02; PtO *St Alb* 03–19; *Pet* from 11. *10*

Troon Crescent, Wellingborough NN8 5WG T: (01933) 676322
E: robertcutler@btinternet.com
CUTLER, Roger Charles. b 49. Liv Univ BSc 70 Glas Univ
MPhil 98. Coll of Resurr Mirfield 86. **d** 88 **p** 89. C Walney
Is *Carl* 88–91; Chapl RN 91–98; PtO *Glas* 91–95; Hon C
Challoch w Newton Stewart 95–98; V Gosforth St Nic *Newc*
98–01; P-in-c St John Lee 01–04; R 05–08; P-in-c Warden
w Newbrough 01–04; V 05–08; R Kirkcudbright *Glas*
08–14; R Gatehouse of Fleet 08–14; rtd 14. *14 St John Street,
Creetown, Newton Stewart DG8 7JF* T: (01671) 820832
E: rogercutler49@gmail.com
CUTTELL, Jeffrey Charles. b 59. Birm Univ BSc 80 PhD 83
Sheff Univ MA 91. Trin Coll Bris 84. **d** 87 **p** 88. C
Normanton *Wakef* 87–91; V 91–95; Producer Relig Progr BBC
Radio Stoke 95–97; Presenter Relig Progr BBC 97–99; CF (TA)
97–06; R Astbury and Smallwood *Ches* 99–08; RD Congleton
04–08; Assoc Lect Th Univ of Wales (Cardiff) 01–06; Tutor
St Mich Coll Llan 01–06; Dean Derby 08–10; Chapl HM YOI
Werrington 10–11; R Astbury and Smallwood *Ches* 15–19;
Chapl HM YOI Werrington from 19; PtO *Ches* from 19; *Lich*
from 19. *HM Young Offender Institution, Werrington, Stoke-on-
Trent ST9 0DX* T: (01782) 463300
CUTTER, John Douglas. b 31. Lon Univ BD 61. Chich Th
Coll 56. **d** 59 **p** 60. C Blyth St Mary *Newc* 59–62; C Rugeley
Lich 62–65; V Rocester 65–73; V Shrewsbury St Giles 73–83;
R Yoxall and Dean's V Lich Cathl 83–91; rtd 91; PtO *Win*
from 91; Hon Chapl Win Cathl from 98. *Meadway, Mead
Road, Winchester SO23 9RF* T: (01962) 865784
CUTTING, The Ven Alastair Murray. b 60. Westhill Coll Birm
BEd 83 Heythrop Coll Lon MA 03. St Jo Coll Nottm 84. **d** 87
p 88. C Woodlands *Sheff* 87–88; C Wadsley 89–91; C Uxbridge
Lon 91–96; Chapl to the Nave and Uxbridge Town Cen

91–96; V Copthorne *Chich* 96–10; R Henfield w Shermanbury
and Woodmancote 10–13; Adn Lewisham and Greenwich
S'wark from 13; P-in-c Sydenham H Trin and St Aug 15–19.
1 Sydenham Park Road, London SE26 4DY M: 07736-676106
E: alastair.cutting@southwark.anglican.org
CUTTS, Canon David. b 52. Van Mildert Coll Dur BSc 73.
St Jo Coll Nottm BA 79. **d** 80 **p** 81. C Ipswich St Matt *St E*
80–82; Bp's Dom Chapl 82–85; R Coddenham w Gosbeck
and Hemingstone w Henley 85–94; RD Bosmere 92–94; V
Ipswich St Marg from 94; RD Ipswich 96–01; Hon Can St E
Cathl from 00. *St Margaret's Vicarage, 32 Constable Road,
Ipswich IP4 2UW* T: (01473) 253906 M: 07733-406552
E: david.cutts3@gmail.com
CUTTS, Elizabeth Joan Gabrielle. *See* STRICKLAND, Elizabeth
Joan Gabrielle
CYPRUS, Archdeacon of. *See* FUTCHER, Christopher David
CYRUS, Keyvan Dominic. b 74. Univ of Sistan & Baluchestan
BSc 98 Lon Sch of Th MA 11. Westcott Ho Cam 12. **d** 15
p 16. C Tividale *Lich* 15–18; Vice-Prin SWMTC from
18. *25 Eton Walk, Exeter EX4 1FD* T: (01392) 264404
E: fr.dominiccyrus@gmail.com
CZERNIAWSKA EDGCUMBE, Preb Irena Christine. b 59.
Trin Coll Ox BA 82. Oak Hill Th Coll 93. **d** 95 **p** 96.
NSM De Beauvoir Town St Pet *Lon* 95–99; Chapl Raines
Foundn Sch Tower Hamlets 99–04; NSM Bow Common
00–04; P-in-c Hoxton St Anne w St Columba 04–12; Min
Development Adv Stepney Area 04–07; Dean of Women's
Min Stepney Area 07–12; Dir Tr and Development Stepney
Area from 12; Preb St Paul's Cathl from 16. *24 Calabria
Road, London N5 1JA* T: (020) 7033 3446 *or* 3837 5238
E: irenaczerniawskaedgcumbe@hotmail.com

D

DABIN, Susan. *See* ADAMS, Susan
DABORN, Mark Henry. b 55. Magd Coll Cam BA 76 MA 80
Glos Univ BA 11 MRICS 82 QTS 01. WEMTC 99. **d** 05 **p** 06.
NSM Cleobury Mortimer w Hopton Wafers etc *Heref* 05–15;
P-in-c Stottesdon w Farlow, Cleeton St Mary etc 15–17; R
from 17; RD Bridgnorth from 17; Asst Dir of Ords from 19.
The Rectory, Stottesdon, Kidderminster DY14 8UE T: (01746)
718127 M: 07857-514909 E: mark.daborn@hotmail.co.uk
DABORN, Robert Francis. b 53. Keble Coll Ox BA 74 MA 78
Fitzw Coll Cam BA 77. Ridley Hall Cam 75. **d** 78 **p** 79. C
Mortlake w E Sheen *S'wark* 78–81; Chapl Collingwood
and Grey Coll *Dur* 82–83; V Lapley w Wheaton Aston
Lich 86–91; P-in-c Blymhill w Weston-under-Lizard 89–91;
P-in-c Tibberton w Bolas Magna and Waters Upton 91–99;
Shropshire Local Min Adv 91–99; P-in-c Childs Ercall and
Stoke upon Tern 92–95; Dir Local Min Development 99–05;
Dir Past Studies WEMTC 05–14; Vice-Prin 09–14; Preb Heref
Cathl 14; R Newcastle w Butterton *Lich* 14–18; rtd 18; PtO
Lich from 19. *20 Whiteway Drive, Bratton, Telford TF5 0DR*
E: robert.daborn@btinternet.com
DACK, Mrs Karen Ann. b 61. Univ of Otago MMin 13.
d 08 **p** 09. NZ 08–15; PtO *Win* 15–17; P-in-c Guernsey
St Matt 17–18; P-in-c Guernsey Ste Marie du Castel 17–18;
V Dargaville H Trin NZ 18–20; P-in-c St Maughen's w
Llangattock-vibon-Avel w Llanfihangel-ystern-Llewern
etc *Mon* from 20. *The Vicarage, Penallt, Monmouth
NP25 4SE* M: 07495-445807 E: karenann.nz@gmail.com
DACK, Timothy William. b 59. Didsbury Coll Man BTh 87
Newc Univ PGCE 93. **d** 05 **p** 05. V Tirau Co-operating NZ
05–12; PtO 11–15; R Guernsey St Sampson *Win* 15–18;
P-in-c Rockfield w Monmouth w Overmonnow etc *Mon* from
20. *The Vicarage, Penallt, Monmouth NP25 4SE* M: 07958-
022782   E: reverendtimothydack@gmail.com   *or*
vicar@monmouthparishes.org
DADD, Alan Edward. b 50. St Jo Coll Nottm 77. **d** 78 **p** 79. C
Bishopsworth *Bris* 78–81; V Springfield *Birm* 81–85; Chapl
Poly Cen Lon 85–86; V Hanger Lane St Ann 86–93; rtd 93;
PtO *Bris* 96–98; *Win* 10–20. *C14 Elizabeth Court, Grove Road,
Bournemouth BH1 3DU* E: al.e.dd@btinternet.com
DADD, Canon Peter Wallace. b 38. Sheff Univ BA 59. Qu
Coll Birm 59. **d** 61 **p** 62. C Grays Thurrock *Chelmsf* 61–65; C
Grantham St Wulfram *Linc* 65–70; C Grantham w Manthorpe

70–72; TV 72–73; V Haxey 73–90; RD Is of Axholme 82–90;
V Gainsborough All SS 90–98; Can and Preb Linc Cathl
91–08; P-in-c Flixborough w Burton upon Stather 98–00; V
00–08; rtd 08; PtO *S'well* 08–21; *Cant* 16–21. *11 Manor Farm
Rise, North Leverton, Retford DN22 0BH* T: (01427) 884191
E: peterdadd@tiscali.co.uk
DADSWELL, Canon David Ian. b 58. New Coll Ox BA 80
MA 83 Brunel Univ MPhil 97. Westcott Ho Cam 80. **d** 83
p 84. C W Derby St Mary *Liv* 83–87; Chapl Brunel Univ *Lon*
87–96; PtO 96–04; *Ox* 98–04; Hon C New Windsor 04–17;
Strategic Implementation Adv to Bp Linc 17–18; Dioc Sec
Linc from 18; Can Res Linc Cathl from 21. *1 St Giles Avenue,
Lincoln LN2 4PE* M: 07773-800731 E: d.dadswell@me.com
DADY (*formerly* **MARTIN**)**, Elizabeth Anne.** b 60. Sheff
Univ BMedSci 82. ERMC 05. **d** 09 **p** 10. C Gaywood *Nor*
09–14; R Blakeney w Cley, Wiveton, Glandford etc 14–18;
rtd 18; PtO *Nor* from 19. *3 The Sheltons, Barsham Road,
Great Snoring, Fakenham NR21 0HP* M: 07503-747484
E: reverend.libby@yahoo.co.uk
D'AETH, Mrs Emma Louise Alice. b 63. Portsm Univ BA 03.
STETS 04. **d** 07. NSM Portsea St Mary *Portsm* 07–11; PtO
from 11; *Chich* from 19; Chapl S Health NHS Foundn Trust
from 19; LtO *Win* from 19. *52 Belmont Street, Southsea
PO5 1ND* T: (023) 9286 2108 E: emmadaeth@yahoo.co.uk
DAFFERN, Canon Adrian Mark. b 68. St Jo Coll Dur BA 89
MA 06 Ox Univ MTh 15 FRCO 98 FRSA 99. St Steph Ho
Ox 90. **d** 92 **p** 93. C Lich St Chad 92–95; TV Stafford 95–00;
V Walsall Wood 00–03; Treas V Lich Cathl 97–03; Can
Res and Prec Cov Cathl 03–10; TR Blenheim *Ox* 10–17;
R Woodstock and Bladon 17–18; Asst Adn Dorchester
16–18; AD Woodstock 17–18; V Cambridge Gt St Mary w
St Mich *Ely* from 18; Fell Lucy Cavendish Coll Cam from
19; RD Cambridge N *Ely* from 20. *Great St Mary's Church,
St Mary's Passage, Cambridge CB2 3PQ* T: (01223) 747273
E: office@gsm.cam.ac.uk *or* vicar@gsm.cam.ac.uk
DAFFERN, Megan Isobel Jane. b 80. Ex Coll Ox BA 02 MA 06
DPhil 14 SS Coll Cam BA 05 MA 09. Westcott Ho Cam 03.
d 06 **p** 07. C Rugby *Cov* 06–09; Chapl Jes Coll Ox 09–19; LtO
Ox 09–19; Dir Ord and Voc *Ely* 19–21; Tutor ERMC from 20;
Tutor and Bye-Fell Lucy Cavendish Coll Cam from 21; NSM
Cambridge N *Ely* from 21. *Address temp unknown*

DAGGER, Ms Rose-Mary Anne. d 14 **p** 15. OLM Llandogo w Whitebrook Chpl and Tintern Parva *Mon* from 14. *Fox Cottage, Llandogo, Monmouth NP25 4TA* T: (01594) 530700 E: rm.a.dagger@icloud.com

DAGNALL, Canon Bernard. b 44. K Coll Lon BSc 65 AKC 65 Ox Univ BA 75 MA 78 CChem MRSC MSOSc 88 CSci 04. St Steph Ho Ox 72. **d** 75 **p** 76. C Stanningley St Thos *Ripon* 75–76; C Lightbowne *Man* 76–78; C-in-c Grahame Park St Aug CD *Lon* 78–84; V Earley St Nic *Ox* 84–91; Ind Chapl 85–91; TR N Huddersfield *Wakef* 91–93; TV Newbury *Ox* 93–09; Chapl W Berks Priority Care Services NHS Trust 93–01; Chapl Newbury and Community Primary Care Trust 01–06; Chapl Berks W Primary Care Trust 06–09; Superior Soc of Retreat Conductors 00–05; rtd 09; Dioc Adv for Min of Healing *Ox* 10–15; PtO from 10; *Lon* from 15; Hon Can Ho Ghana from 04. *10 Windsor Street, Headington, Oxford OX3 7AP* T: (01865) 751854 E: bernarddagnall@btinternet.com

DAHL, Madeleine Sara Martina. b 77. Skövde Univ MA 02 Uppsala Univ MTh 06. Past Inst Uppsala 06. **p** 07. C Vårgårda Sweden 07–09; C Österstund 09–15; C Chatham St Mary w St Jo *Roch* 15–19; C Chatham St Paul w All SS 15–19; C Vårgårda Sweden from 19. *Ornunga, Östergården 2b, 44793 Vårgårda, Sweden* M: 07469-246443 E: madeleine.dahl@outlook.com *or* madeleine.dahl@svenskakyrkan.se

DAINTREE, Canon Geoffrey Thomas. b 54. Bris Univ BSc 77. Trin Coll Bris 78. **d** 81 **p** 82. C Old Hill H Trin *Worc* 81–85; C Tunbridge Wells St Jo *Roch* 85–89; V Framfield *Chich* 89–00; RD Uckfield 96–00; V Eastbourne St Jo 00–09; Chs Relns Manager Chr Aid 09–17; rtd 17; PtO *Chich* from 09; Hon Can Cyangugu (Rwanda) from 97. *Wellstead, Caneheath, Polegate BN26 6SJ* T: (01323) 488110 M: 07921-722403 E: geoff.daintree@gmail.com

DAKIN (*née* HOLLETT), Mrs Catherine Elaine. b 53. Qu Eliz Coll Lon BSc 74. St Jo Coll Nottm 88. **d** 90 **p** 05. Par Dn Horley *S'wark* 90–93; NSM Heydon, Gt and Lt Chishill, Chrishall etc *Chelmsf* 93–97; NSM Gt and Lt Maplestead w Gestingthorpe 97–99; NSM Knights and Hospitallers Par 99–01; NSM Fulford w Hilderstone *Lich* 01–18. *29 The Flashes, Gnosall, Stafford ST20 0HL* T: (01785) 824340 M: 07971-101259

DAKIN, Preb Peter David. b 57. Wye Coll Lon BSc 79. St Jo Coll Nottm 91. **d** 91 **p** 92. NSM Southgate *Chich* 91–93; C Heydon, Gt and Lt Chishill, Chrishall etc *Chelmsf* 93–97; P-in-c Gt and Lt Maplestead w Gestingthorpe 97–99; P-in-c Alphamstone w Lamarsh and Pebmarsh 99; V Knights and Hospitallers Par 99–01; P-in-c Fulford w Hilderstone *Lich* 01–15; V 15–16; Rural Officer for Staffs 01–16; RD Stone 07–16; Preb Lich Cathl 16; rtd 16; PtO *Lich* 17–20. *29 The Flashes, Gnosall, Stafford ST20 0HL* T: (01785) 824340

DAKIN, Mrs Sally. b 58. SRN 79 SCM 82 RHV 85 K Coll Lon MSc 89 TCert 92 Win Univ MA 18. SAOMC 02. **d** 04 **p** 05. NSM Ruscombe and Twyford *Ox* 04–12; PtO *Win* from 12. *Wolvesey, Winchester SO23 9ND* T: (01962) 854050 F: 897088 E: sally.dakin@btinternet.com *or* sally.dakin@winchester.anglican.org

✠**DAKIN, The Rt Revd Dr Timothy John. b** 58. SS Mark & Jo Univ Coll Plymouth BA 86 Hon MEd 15 K Coll Lon MTh 87 Win Univ PhD 20. **d** 93 **p** 94 **c** 12. Prin Carlile Coll Kenya 93–00; C Nairobi Cathl 94–00; Gen Sec CMS 00–12; Gen Sec SAMS 09–12; Hon C Ruscombe and Twyford *Ox* 00–12; Can Th Cov Cathl 01–12; Bp Win 11–22; rtd 22; Visiting Prof Univ of St Mark and St Jo *Ex* from 20. *Address temp unkown*

DALAIS, Duncan John. b 56. St Paul's Coll Grahamstown. **d** 83 **p** 84. C Pinetown S Africa 83–87; C Chingford SS Pet and Paul *Chelmsf* 87–92; V Aldersbrook 92–02; P-in-c Leytonstone St Andr 02–14; V 14; P-in-c Leytonstone H Trin and St Aug Harrow Green 11–14; Asst Chapl Forest Healthcare NHS Trust Lon 02–09; rtd 14; PtO *Ely* 15–20. *The Cedars, 60 Mount Street, Diss IP22 4QQ* M: 07983-560245 E: duncan.dalais@virgin.net

DALBY, Mrs Deborah Anne. b 71. Leic Univ BSc 93. All SS Cen for Miss & Min 16. **d** 19 **p** 20. NSM Witton *Ches* 19–20; NSM Lostock Gralam 19–20; C Grange St Andr from 20. *7 St Michael's Close, Little Leigh, Northwich CW8 4SA* T: (01606) 891670 M: 07906-342145 E: revdeb19@btinternet.com

DALE, Charles William. b 49. **d** 02 **p** 03. OLM Uttoxeter Area *Lich* from 02. *Manor Court, Kingstone, Uttoxeter ST14 8QH* T: (01889) 500428

DALE, Canon Christine. b 62. Trin Coll Bris BA 94. **d** 94 **p** 95. C Thatcham *Ox* 94–98; TV Bracknell 98–02; R E Woodhay and Woolton Hill *Win* 02–09; R NW Hants from 09; RD Whitchurch 08–14; Hon Can Win Cathl from 17. *The Rectory, The Mount, Highclere, Newbury RG20 9QZ* T: (01635) 253323 E: cdale001@btinternet.com

DALE, John Anthony. b 42. Open Univ BSc 00. Qu Coll Birm 72. **d** 75 **p** 76. C Elmley Castle w Bricklehampton and Combertons *Worc* 75–81; P-in-c 81–83; R 83–88; Hon Can Worc Cathl 87–92; V Hallow 88–92; Dioc Registrar 92; P-in-c Michaelston-y-Fedw *Mon* 03–08; rtd 08; PtO *Ban* 15–20; C Willand, Uffculme, Kentisbeare etc *Ex* 15–20. *The Brae, Manse Road, Auldearn, Nairn IV12 5SX* E: jadale@onetel.com *or* revjohndale@googlemail.com

DALE, Mrs Joy. b 57. **d** 13 **p** 14. NSM Penn Fields *Lich* from 13. *17 Haden Hill, Wolverhampton WV3 9PT* T: (01902) 772239 E: steveandjoydale@blueyonder.co.uk

DALE, Martin Nicholas. b 55. Chelsea Coll Lon BSc 76 CPA 83. Wycliffe Hall Ox 99. **d** 01 **p** 02. C Stiffkey and Cockthorpe w Morston, Langham etc *Nor* 01–03; C Stiffkey and Bale 03–04; C Brinton, Briningham, Hunworth, Stody etc 01–04; P-in-c New Romney w Old Romney and Midley *Cant* 04–07; P-in-c St Mary's Bay w St Mary-in-the-Marsh etc 04–07; P-in-c Dymchurch w Burmarsh and Newchurch 05–07; P-in-c Upper Wreake *Leic* 07–10; P-in-c S Croxton Gp 07–10; P-in-c Burrough Hill Pars 07–10; V E Marshland *Ely* from 10; PtO *Eur* from 17. *The Vicarage, 37 Church Road, Tilney St Lawrence, King's Lynn PE34 4QQ* T: (01945) 880259 M: 07887-554761 E: fcbasle@aol.com

DALE (*née* LIVESEY), Mrs Rachel Elizabeth. b 67. Univ of Wales (Cardiff) BSc 89 MBA 96 Homerton Coll Cam BTh 09 Huddersfield Univ PGCE 99. Ridley Hall Cam 07. **d** 09 **p** 10. C Streetly *Lich* 09–12; R Watershed from 12. *The Rectory, Pinfold Lane, Wheaton Aston, Stafford ST19 9PD* T: (01785) 840395 M: 07977-310049 E: revracheldale@gmail.com *or* rachel.livesey@gmail.com

DALEY, David Michael. b 50. Oak Hill Th Coll BA 90. **d** 92 **p** 92. C Enfield Ch Ch Trent Park *Lon* 92–94; V Chitts Hill St Cuth 94–14; rtd 14. *65 Victoria Road, Bude EX23 8RH* T: (01288) 488546 E: ddaley24@btinternet.com

DALEY, Judith Hilda. b 54. Sheff Univ BA 94 Leeds Univ PhD 03. NOC 03. **d** 04 **p** 05. NSM Sheff St Leon Norwood from 04; Chapl Sheff Teaching Hosps NHS Foundn Trust from 02. *112 Broad Inge Crescent, Chapeltown, Sheffield S35 1RU* T: 0114-246 8824 *or* 271 1900 E: judith.daley@sth.nhs.uk *or* judith.daley@sheffield.anglican.org

DALGLISH, David John. b 45. Heriot-Watt Univ BSc 70 Open Univ BA 94 Edin Univ MBA 97. TISEC 02. **d** 08. NSM Melrose *Edin* 08–10; R Jedburgh 10–15; rtd 15; LtO *Edin* from 16. *Kirkbrae House, The Woll, Askirk, Selkirk TD7 4NY* T: (01750) 32293 M: 07858-140200 E: david_dalglish@btinternet.com

DALLAS, Lucy Joanne Clair. b 73. Kent Univ BA 95 Herts Univ PGCE 98. Ripon Coll Cuddesdon BA 11. **d** 12 **p** 13. C Welwyn *St Alb* 12–15; TV Elstree and Borehamwood 15–18; PtO from 18; Dir Past Studies ERMC from 18. *12 Crofts Path, Hemel Hempstead HP3 8HB* E: ljcdallas@gmail.com

DALLEN, Julia Anne. b 58. Matlock Coll of Educn TCert 79 Ex Univ BTh 10. SWMTC 07. **d** 10 **p** 11. NSM Brampford Speke, Cadbury, Newton St Cyres etc *Ex* 10–14; NSM Sark *Win* 14–17; NSM Brampford Speke, Cadbury, Newton St Cyres etc *Ex* from 19. *5 Prispen House, Prispen Drive, Silverton, Exeter EX5 4DR* M: 07936-282078 E: juliadallen@btinternet.com

DALLEY, Mrs Gail Margaret. b 53. Cranmer Hall Dur 05. **d** 07 **p** 08. NSM Pocklington Wold *York* 07–10; V Barmby Moor Gp 10–13; rtd 13; PtO *York* 14–19. *63 Algarth Rise, Pocklington, York YO42 2HX* T: (01759) 301920 E: gaildalley@outlook.com

DALLEY, Neil Michael. b 71. Reading Univ BA 92. Coll of Resurr Mirfield MA 16. **d** 16 **p** 17. C Leigh St Clem *Chelmsf* 16–20; TV Southend 20; V Westcliff St Alban and Southend St Mark from 21. *The Vicarage, 35 Avenue Road, Westcliff-on-Sea SS9 1DJ* M: 07947-363043 E: fr.neil.dalley@icloud.com

DALLISTON, The Very Revd Christopher Charles. b 56. Ox Univ BA Cam Univ MA. St Steph Ho Ox 81. **d** 84 **p** 85. C Halstead St Andr w H Trin and Greenstead Green *Chelmsf* 84–87; Bp's Dom Chapl 87–91; V Forest Gate St Edm 91–95; P-in-c Boston *Linc* 95–97; V 97–03; RD Holland E 97–03; Dean Newc 03–18; Dean Pet from 18. *The Deanery, 14 Minster Precincts, Peterborough PE1 1XX*

DALLISTON, Mrs Michelle Aleysha Caron. b 67. Qu Mary Coll Lon BSc 89 St Jo Coll Dur 10. Cranmer Hall Dur 08. **d** 10 **p** 11. C Gosforth St Nic *Newc* 10–13; C Newc St Gabr 13–14; C Hexham 14–15; TR Ch the King 15–18; C Higham Ferrers w Chelveston *Pet* 19; V from 19. *The Deanery, 14 Minster Precincts, Peterborough PE1 1XX* E: michelleacd@hotmail.co.uk

DALLY, Keith Richard. b 47. FCCA 77. St Jo Coll Nottm 80. **d** 82 **p** 83. C Southend St Sav Westcliff *Chelmsf* 82–85; Ind Chapl 85–93; C Southend 85–86; TV 86–92; C Harold Hill St Geo 92–93; Cen Co-ord Langham Place All So

Clubhouse *Lon* 97–02; PtO *Ox* 02–05; *Pet* 05–11; Hon C Northampton Em 11–13; P-in-c King's Beck *Nor* 13–18; R 18–21; rtd 21. *Goshen, 8 Bradley Close, Louth LN11 8YL* E: keithdally@btinternet.com

DALRIADA, Archdeacon of. *See* DUNDAS, The Ven Edward Paul

DALRYMPLE, Wendy Margaret. b 75. Coll of Resurr Mirfield. **d** 07 **p** 08. C Mirfield *Wakef* 07–10; Chapl Sir Robert Woodard Academy Lancing 10–12; P-in-c Alfold and Loxwood *Guildf* 12–15; R Loughborough All SS w H Trin *Leic* from 15; AD Akeley E 16–21. *The Rectory, 69 Westfield Drive, Loughborough LE11 3QL* T: (01509) 268362 E: priestwendy@btinternet.com

DALTON, Bertram Jeremy (Tod). b 32. ACIB 64. Sarum & Wells Th Coll 81. **d** 83 **p** 84. C Ringwood *Win* 83–86; R Norton sub Hamdon, W Chinnock, Chiselborough etc *B & W* 86–97; rtd 97; PtO *B & W* from 97. *Meadow Cottage, 8 Woodbarton, Milverton, Taunton TA4 1LU* T: (01823) 400302

DALTON, Darren Dean. b 78. Ripon Coll Cuddesdon 16. **d** 18 **p** 19. C Kinson and W Howe *Sarum* from 18. *1 Graycot Close, Bournemouth BH10 7BU* M: 07899-666561 E: ddalton103@googlemail.com

DALTON, Tod. *See* DALTON, Bertram Jeremy

DALTRY, Canon Paul Richard. b 56. St Jo Coll Nottm 90. **d** 92 **p** 93. C Ipswich St Matt *St E* 92–96; P-in-c Needham Market w Badley 96–05; RD Bosmere 01–05; R Ipswich St Helen, H Trin, and St Luke 05–09; Min for Ch and Community Engagement 09–17; Hon Can St E Cathl 10–17; P-in-c N Blackwater *Chelmsf* 17–19; rtd 19. *Brooklands, Chapels, Kirkby-in-Furness LA17 7XY* E: paul@daltry.co.uk

DALY, Ms Bernadette Theresa. b 45. TCD BTh 94. **d** 97 **p** 98. C Taney *D & G* 97–00 and 05–06; Dir Past Studies CITC 00–04; rtd 06. *27 Southmede, Balinteer Road, Dublin 16, D16 NK69, Republic of Ireland* T: (00353) (1) 294 8815 M: 86-241 9009 E: berdaly@live.com

DALY, Gary James. b 63. Wycliffe Hall Ox 07. **d** 09 **p** 10. C Muswell Hill St Jas w St Matt *Lon* 09–16; TR Broadwater *Chich* from 16. *8 Sompting Avenue, Worthing BN14 8HN* M: 07722-938757 E: gaz.daly@stmarysbroadwater.org

DALY, Jeffrey. b 50. Bris Univ BA 73 Jes Coll Cam PGCE 74 Fitzw Coll Cam BA 82 MA 86 Westmr Coll Ox MTh 03 Win Univ MTh 16. Ridley Hall Cam 80. **d** 83 **p** 84. C Tilehurst St Mich *Ox* 83–89; P-in-c Steventon w Milton 89–92; Asst Chapl Sherborne Sch 92–96; Chapl St Pet Sch York 96–11; rtd 11; PtO *Eur* from 07; *York* from 11. *3 Shotel Close, York YO30 5FY* T: (01904) 630142 E: fatherj.daly@cantab.net

DALY, Martin Jonathan. b 48. Woolwich Poly BSc 69. **d** 05 **p** 06. C Upton (Overchurch) *Ches* 05–13; rtd 13; PtO *Ches* from 13. *Fairfield Lodge, 1 Columbia Road, Prenton CH43 6TU* T: 0151-670 1461 *or* 677 1186 M: 07710-242241 E: martindaly1948@gmail.com

DANCE, Peter Patrick. b 31. Em Coll Saskatoon 66. **d** 69 **p** 69. R Mannville Canada 69–71; C Hednesford *Lich* 71–75; P-in-c Westcote Barton and Steeple Barton *Ox* 76–77; P-in-c Sandford St Martin 76–77; R Westcote Barton w Steeple Barton, Duns Tew etc 77–89; R Castle Douglas *Glas* 89–97; rtd 97. *Mannville, High Street, Adderbury, Banbury OX17 3NA* T: (01295) 811989

DAND, Andrew John. b 80. St Mellitus Coll. **d** 13 **p** 14. C Ealing St Steph Castle Hill *Lon* 13–17; V Hanwell St Mary from 17. *The Rectory, 91 Church Road, London W7 3BJ* T: (020) 8567 6185 E: andrew@stmaryshanwell.org.uk

DAND, Mrs Angela Jane. b 49. St Andr Univ BSc 70 Newc Univ PGCE 71. **d** 98 **p** 99. OLM Astley *Man* 98–06; OLM Astley, Tyldesley and Mosley Common 06–21; rtd 21; PtO *Man* from 21. *20 Acresfield, Astley, Tyldesley, Manchester M29 7NL* T: (01942) 879608 E: pandadand@btinternet.com

DAND, Mrs Susannah Elizabeth. b 86. Middx Univ BA 14 MA 18. St Mellitus Coll 16. **d** 18 **p** 19. C Hanwell St Thos *Lon* 18–20; C Hanwell St Mary 20–21; NSM from 21; Chapl Bp Ramsey Sch from 20. *91 Church Road, London W7 3BJ* E: susy.dand@gmail.com *or* susy@stmaryshanwell.org.uk

DANDO, Ms Elaine Vera. b 53. Coll of Resurr Mirfield 94 NOC 98. **d** 00 **p** 01. C Luddenden w Luddenden Foot *Wakef* 00–03; C Halifax 03–04; Lic to Offic 04–05; Chapl Univ Coll *Lon* 05–08; C St Pancras w St Jas and Ch Ch 05–08; C Northwood H Trin 08–10; rtd 10; PtO *Lon* 11–13; *Chich* from 13. *37 Wilderness Road, Hurstpierpoint, Hassocks BN6 9XD* T: (01273) 835277 E: evd.macrina@btinternet.com

DANDO, Stephen. b 49. Goldsmiths' Coll Lon TCert 70. Coll of Resurr Mirfield 81. **d** 83 **p** 84. C Wandsworth St Anne *S'wark* 83–87; V Stainland *Wakef* 87–99; V Illingworth 99–05; V Eastcote St Lawr *Lon* 05–13; PtO *Chich* from 14. *37 Wilderness Road, Hurstpierpoint, Hassocks BN6 9XD* T: (01273) 835277 E: revstephendando@hotmail.co.uk

DANE, John William. b 52. St Jo Coll Nottm 04. **d** 06 **p** 07. C Deddington w Barford, Clifton and Hempton *Ox* 06–09; Chapl Chich Univ 09–17; C Chich St Paul and Westhampnett 12–15; rtd 17. *15 Salthill Road, Chichester PO19 3QL* E: john@ausome.co.uk

DANES, Charles William. b 28. Chich Th Coll 54. **d** 56 **p** 57. C N Greenford All Hallows *Lon* 56–59; C Caversham *Ox* 59–63; V Walsgrave on Sowe *Cov* 63–65; P-in-c Hanworth All SS *Lon* 65–67; V 68–76; P-in-c Wick *Chich* 76–78; V Littlehampton St Jas 76–78; P-in-c Littlehampton St Mary 76–78; V W Worthing St Jo 78–87; Chapl Monte Carlo *Eur* 87–93; rtd 93; PtO *Chelmsf* from 93; *Eur* from 93. *31 Oakley Road, Braintree CM7 5QS* T: (01376) 324586

DANGERFIELD, Canon Andrew Keith. b 63. Univ of Wales (Ban) BD 87. St Steph Ho Ox 87. **d** 89 **p** 90. C St Marychurch *Ex* 89–93; C-in-c Grahame Park St Aug CD *Lon* 93–96; V Tottenham St Paul 96–06; P-in-c Edmonton St Mary w St Jo 98–04; AD E Haringey 00–05; V Kensal Green St Jo 06–12; Miss to Seafarers Chapl Yokohama Japan 12–18; Miss to Seafarers Chapl Aqaba Jordan 18–20; Miss to Seafarers Chapl Hong Kong from 20; Hon Can Cape Coast from 04. *The Mariners' Club, Container Port Road, Kwai Chung, Hong Kong* T: (00852) 9185 4842 E: andrew.dangerfield@mtsmail.org

DANGERFIELD, Miss Sarah Ann. b 66. Ripon Coll Cuddesdon 09. **d** 11 **p** 12. C Badgeworth, Shurdington and Witcombe w Bentham *Glouc* 11–15; P-in-c Fladbury, Hill and Moor, Wyre Piddle etc *Worc* from 15; C Abberton, The Flyfords, Naunton Beauchamp etc from 15; C Peopleton and White Ladies Aston w Churchill etc from 15; C Stoulton w Drake's Broughton and Pirton etc from 17; RD Pershore 18–21; AD Pershore and Evesham from 21. *The Rectory, Station Road, Fladbury, Pershore WR10 2QW* T: (01386) 861669 E: s.dangerfield150@btinternet.com

DANIEL, Canon Herrick Haynes. b 38. Open Univ BA 81. Trin Coll Bris 73. **d** 75 **p** 76. C Harlesden St Mark *Lon* 75–78; C Livesey *Blackb* 78–81; V Blackb St Barn 81–08; Hon Can Blackb Cathl 98–08; rtd 08; PtO *Blackb* from 08; *Eur* from 16. *40 Appleton Drive, Lancaster LA1 4QY* T: (01524) 389764 E: herrickdaniel@hotmail.co.uk

DANIEL, Mrs Joy. b 44. Gilmore Course 81 Oak Hill Th Coll 81. **dss** 84 **d** 87 **p** 94. Luton St Fran *St Alb* 84–02; Par Dn 87–94; C 94–02; P-in-c Woodside 02–10; rtd 10; PtO *St Alb* 10–17; Hon C Luton St Paul 17–18; PtO from 18. *22 Rowelfield, Luton LU2 9HN* E: joy.daniel@virginmedia.com

DANIEL, Pamela Olive. b 52. Middx Poly BEd 86 Brunel Univ MA 87 K Coll Lon MA 94 Westmr Coll Ox BTh 98 Cardiff Univ LLM 13. Wycliffe Hall Ox 04. **d** 06 **p** 07. C Kennington St Mark *S'wark* 06–10; P-in-c W Bromwich St Phil *Lich* 10–18. *54 Lytton Road, Oxford OX4 3PA* M: 07771-633035 E: p.daniel001@btinternet.com

DANIEL, Philip Sharman. b 62. Man Univ BA 83 Rob Coll Cam CertEd 84. Wycliffe Hall Ox 84. **d** 86 **p** 87. C Macclesfield Team *Ches* 86–89; C Cheadle 89–94; V Disley 94–07; TR Mid Trent *Lich* 07–18; RD Stafford 15–18; V Lt Aston from 18. *The Vicarage, 3 Walsall Road, Little Aston, Sutton Coldfield B74 3BD*

DANIEL, Rajinder Kumar. b 34. St Steph Coll Delhi 55 Westcott Ho Cam 61. **d** 63 **p** 64. C Purley St Barn *S'wark* 63–66; C Battersea St Pet 66–67; C N Harrow St Alb *Lon* 67–72; TV Beaconsfield *Ox* 72–75; V Smethwick St Matt w St Chad *Birm* 75–87; Dioc Adv on Black Min 87–92; Chapl Birm Gen Hosp 91–92; TR Braunstone *Leic* 92–01; rtd 01; USPG and R Arima St Jude Trinidad and Tobago 03–04. *508 Chester Road, Kingshurst, Birmingham B36 0LG* T: 0121-770 1066

DANIELL, Robert. b 37. **d** 87 **p** 88. C Camberwell St Giles w St Matt *S'wark* 90–92; V Lewisham St Swithun 92–07; rtd 07; PtO *S'wark* 10–16; *Roch* 12–18. *4 Glenhouse Road, London SE9 1JQ* T: (020) 8850 4594 E: r.daniell@btinternet.com

DANIELS, Ian Geoffrey. b 72. Univ of Wales (Ban) BEng 93. ERMC 09. **d** 12 **p** 13. NSM Ipswich St Aug *St E* from 12; Lead Min Lindbergh Road Community Ch from 20. *44 Lindbergh Road, Ipswich IP3 9QX* T: (01473) 719089 M: 07777-698353 E: iandaniels@btinternet.com

DANIELS, Preb John Wyn. b 60. Southn Univ BSc 82 PhD 87. Trin Coll Bris MA 92. **d** 92 **p** 93. C Roundhay St Edm *Ripon* 92–95; India 96; C Ambleside w Brathay *Carl* 97–01; Chapl St Martin's Coll Lanc 97–01; Res Can Ban Cathl 01–05; Min Development Officer *Bradf* 05–10; C Embsay w Eastby 05–10; C Skipton H Trin 05–10; Local Min Officer *Heref* 10–21; Warden of Readers 13–21; NSM Bishop's Castle w Mainstone, Lydbury N etc from 21; Preb Heref Cathl from 16. *6 Priory Gardens, Lower Galdeford, Ludlow SY8 1UP* T: (01584) 878276 E: jwd@phonecoop.coop

DANIELS, Lee Martin. b 61. Coll of Resurr Mirfield 99. **d** 01 **p** 02. C Toxteth Park St Agnes and St Pancras *Liv* 01–05; TV

Staveley and Barrow Hill *Derby* 05–10; P-in-c Blackb St Thos w St Jude 10–13; P-in-c Blackb St Mich w St Jo and H Trin 10–13; V N and E Blackb 13–17; V Hawes Side and Marton Moss from 17. *The Vicarage, Hawes Side Lane, Blackpool FY4 5AH* E: martindvvic@gmail.com

DANIELS, Philip John. b 70. Southn Univ BA 92 Reading Univ MA 93 PGCE 96. Ox Min Course 09. **d** 12 **p** 13. C Hullavington, Norton and Stanton St Quintin *Bris* 12–15; C Sherston Magna, Easton Grey, Luckington etc 12–15; P-in-c Ashley, Crudwell, Hankerton and Oaksey 15–16; R Braydon Brook 16–18. *Dyers Farm, Nethercott, Braunton EX33 1HT* M: 07896-742233 E: philjdaniels@talktalk.net

DANKS, Alan Adam. b 41. Essex Univ MA 01. Edin Th Coll 61. **d** 64 **p** 65. C Dumfries *Glas* 64–67; C Earl's Court St Cuth w St Matthias *Lon* 68–71; C St Steph Walbrook and St Swithun etc 71–74; C Brookfield St Mary 75–76; C Hendon St Mary 76–85. *327 Hanworth Road, Hampton TW12 3EJ* T: (020) 8941 6055

DANKS, Mark James. b 71. Qu Coll Birm. **d** 12 **p** 13. C Blakenall Heath *Lich* 12–16; Chapl HM Pris Brinsford 16–18; R Wednesbury St Bart, St Jas and St John *Lich* from 18. *The Vicarage, 4 Little Hill, Wednesbury WS10 9DE*

DANKS-FLOWER, Marilyn Clare. b 42. **d** 08 **p** 11. Chapl Barts and The Lon NHS Trust 89–10; NSM Egremont and Haile *Carl* 11–15; Chapl N Cumbria Integrated Care NHS Foundn Trust 11–21; PtO *Carl* 15–21. *39 Sheppard's College, London Road, Bromley BR1 1PF* M: 07967-369103 E: kajori1@gmail.com

DAPLYN, Timothy James. b 52. Ripon Coll Cuddesdon 92. **d** 94 **p** 95. C Southmead *Bris* 94–97; P-in-c Abbots Leigh w Leigh Woods 97–99; Dioc Communications Officer 97–99; R Clutton w Cameley *B & W* 99–04; RD Chew Magna 03–04; P-in-c E w W Harptree and Hinton Blewett 04–08; LtO *Mor* 09–10; R Poolewe 10–13; R Kishorn 10–13; P-in-c Lochalsh 10–13; rtd 13; PtO *B & W* from 19. *1 New Park House, Old Park Road, Clevedon BS21 7HU* M: 07747-464833 E: coillegillie@hotmail.com

DARBY, George. b 48. SWMTC 06. **d** 09 **p** 10. NSM Egloskerry, N Petherwin, Tremaine and Tresmere *Truro* 09–10; NSM Egloskerry, N Petherwin, Tremaine, Tresmere etc 10–12; NSM Lezant w Lawhitton and S Petherwin w Trewen 09–10; NSM Altarnon w Bolventor, Laneast and St Clether 10–11; P-in-c Slaidburn *Bradf* 12–14; *Leeds* 14–15; P-in-c Long Preston w Tosside 14–15; P-in-c Long Preston w Tosside *Bradf* 12–14; rtd 15; PtO *Truro* from 15. *7 Edymead Court, Tavistock Road, Launceston PL15 9EZ* T: (01566) 770850 E: gdandpd@btinternet.com

DARBY, Canon Nicholas Peter. b 50. Kent Univ BA 82 Surrey Univ MSc 02. Sarum & Wells Th Coll 71. **d** 74 **p** 75. C Walton-on-Thames *Guildf* 74–78; C Horsell 78–80; USA 82–84; Chapl Lon Univ 84–89; Chapl R Lon Hosp (Whitechapel) 90–91; V Kew St Phil and All SS w St Luke S'wark 91–04; Dean Gaborone Botswana 04–07; V Fenham St Jas and St Basil *Newc* 09–17; AD Newc W 11–17; Hon Can Newc Cathl 12–17; rtd 17; PtO *Newc* from 17; S'wark from 18. *3 Tersha Street, Richmond TW9 2LY*

DARBY, Preb Philip William. b 44. Bede Coll Dur TCert 66. Qu Coll Birm. **d** 70 **p** 71. C Kidderminster St Geo *Worc* 70–74; P-in-c Dudley St Jo 74–79; V 79–80; P-in-c Catshill 80–81; P-in-c Catshill and Dodford 81–82; V 82–88; V Ipplepen w Torbryan *Ex* 88–00; V Ipplepen, Torbryan and Denbury 01–02; RD Newton Abbot and Ipplepen 93–01; V Ashburton w Buckland in the Moor and Bickington 02–05; P-in-c Widecombe-in-the-Moor, Leusdon, Princetown etc 04–05; TR Ashburton, Bickington, Buckland in the Moor etc 05–10; Preb Ex Cathl 02–10; rtd 10. *3 Kellett Close, Ashburton, Newton Abbot TQ13 7FB* T: (01364) 652844 M: 07814-272198

DARBYSHIRE, Brian. b 48. TD 04. Oak Hill Th Coll BA 83. **d** 83 **p** 84. C Enfield St Jas *Lon* 83–86; R Slaidburn *Bradf* 86–92; V Gt Harwood St Jo *Blackb* 92–02; V Douglas St Ninian *S & M* 02–08; CF (TA) 90–04; V Bingara Australia 08–13; rtd 13; PtO Brisbane from 13. *27/91 Dorset Drive, Rochedale South QLD 4123, Australia* T: (0061) (7) 3423 2529 E: brian.darbyshire@bigpond.com

DARCH, John Henry. b 52. Univ of Wales (Lamp) BA 73 PhD 97 Lon Univ PGCE 74 MA 77 FRHistS 09 FHEA 04. Trin Coll Bris 80. **d** 82 **p** 83. C Meole Brace *Lich* 82–85; C Hoole *Ches* 85–88; V Hyde St Geo 88–99; P-in-c Godley cum Newton Green 89–93; RD Mottram 91–99; Lect St Jo Coll Nottm 99–06; Chapl 03–06; Public Preacher *S'well* 99–06; PtO *Derby* 03–06; Dir of Ords and Dir IME 4-7 *Blackb* 06–18; Hon C Mellor 11–13; rtd 18; PtO *Lich* from 18; *St As* from 18. *41 Swan Hill, Ellesmere SY12 0LZ* T: (01691) 624726 M: 07917-723972 E: johnhdarch@gmail.com

DARK, Nicholas John. b 62. Leic Univ BA 83 ACIB 92. CITC BTh 98. **d** 98 **p** 99. C Ballyholme *D & D* 98–05; I Magheragall

Conn from 05. *Magheragall Rectory, 70 Ballinderry Road, Lisburn BT28 2QS* T: (028) 9262 1273 E: magheragall@aol.com

DARKINS, Michael David William. b 93. R Holloway Coll Lon BA 15. Westcott Ho Cam BA 19. **d** 19 **p** 20. C Wantsum Gp *Cant* from 19. *Address withheld by request* E: revd.michaeldarkins@gmail.com

DARLEY, Canon Shaun Arthur Neilson. b 36. Dur Univ BA 61 Reading Univ MSc 75. Cranmer Hall Dur 61. **d** 63 **p** 64. C Luton w E Hyde *St Alb* 63–67; Chapl Bris Tech Coll 67–69; Chapl Bris Poly 69–92; Sen Chapl UWE 92–01; Lect 69–75; Sen Lect 75–01; Dir Cen for Performing Arts 85–02; Bp's Cathl Chapl *Bris* 69–76; Hon Can Bris Cathl 89–01; PtO *B & W* from 98; rtd 01; PtO *Bris* 02–06. *Church Paddock, Winscombe Hill, Bristol BS25 1DE* T: (01934) 843633 E: san.darley@btinternet.com

DARLING, Colin Patrick. QUB BA 84 TCD MTh 13. St Jo Coll Nottm. **d** 12 **p** 13. C Saintfield *D & D* 12–13; C Cregagh 13–16; I Killyleagh from 16. *34 Inishbeg, Killyleagh, Downpatrick BT30 9TR* T: (028) 4482 8231 M: 07925-672340 E: colin.darling@talktalk.net

DARLING, David Francis. b 55. K Coll Lon BSc 09 Heythrop Coll Lon MA 13. TISEC 93. **d** 96 **p** 97. SSF 88–05; Novice Guardian 99–05; NSM Edin St Ninian 96–98; Chapl W Gen Hosps NHS 96–98; Chapl Edin Sick Children's NHS Trust 96–98; Lic Preacher *Lon* 03–05; PtO from 15; Tutor Lon Cen for Spiritual Direction 16–19; PtO *Roch* from 19. *33 Sheppard's College, London Road, Bromley BR1 1PF* M: 07811-405835 E: davidfrancis.darling@gmail.com

✠**DARLING, The Rt Revd Edward Flewett.** b 33. TCD BA 55 MA 58. CITC. **d** 56 **p** 57 **c** 85. C Belfast St Luke *Conn* 56–59; C Orangefield *D & D* 59–62; C-in-c Carnalea 62–72; Chapl Ban Hosp 63–72; I Belfast Malone St Jo *Conn* 72–85; Min Can Belf Cathl 78–85; Chapl Ulster Independent Clinic 81–85; Bp L & K 85–00; rtd 00. *17 Queensfort Court, Carryduff, Belfast BT8 8NF* T: (028) 9081 7949 E: edwarddarling@hotmail.com

DARLING, John. b 47. Sarum & Wells Th Coll 76. **d** 79 **p** 80. NSM Trowbridge St Thos *Sarum* 79–82; NSM Trowbridge St Thos and W Ashton 82–92; NSM Atworth w Shaw and Whitley 07–13; NSM Melksham 01–13; NSM Broughton Gifford, Gt Chalfield and Holt 07–13; PtO 13–15. *43 Horse Road, Hilperton Marsh, Trowbridge BA14 7PF* T: (01225) 777803 E: revjohndarling@yahoo.co.uk

DARLINGTON, Paul Trevor. b 71. Imp Coll Lon BSc 92 K Coll Lon PGCE 93. Oak Hill Th Coll BA 99 MPhil 00. **d** 00 **p** 01. C Bispham *Blackb* 00–05; P-in-c Oswestry H Trin *Lich* 05–10; V from 10; RD Oswestry from 18. *Holy Trinity Vicarage, 29 Balmoral Crescent, Oswestry SY11 2XQ* T: (01691) 652184 E: paultrevordarlington@gmail.com

DARLISON, Geoffrey Stuart. b 49. MRTPI 80. St Jo Coll Nottm 89. **d** 91 **p** 92. C Horncastle w Low Toynton *Linc* 91–95; P-in-c Welton and Dunholme w Scothern 95–97; V 97–08; RD Lawres 07–08; P-in-c Thorpe Edge *Bradf* 08–14; P-in-c Greengates 08–14; rtd 14; PtO *Sheff* from 19. *3 Chestnut Road, Swallownest, Sheffield S26 4SJ*

DARMODY, Canon Richard Arthur. b 52. Lon Univ BD 90. Linc Th Coll MDiv 94. **d** 94 **p** 95. C Cherry Hinton St Jo *Ely* 94–97; I Belfast St Aid *Conn* 97–99; TR The Ramseys and Upwood *Ely* 99–10; R 10–20; RD St Ives 02–06; Asst Dir of Ords 16–20; Hon Can Ely Cathl 08–20; rtd 20; Asst Rtd Clergy Officer *Ely* from 20; PtO from 20; RD Ely from 20. *26 Henley Way, Ely CB7 4YJ* E: darmodyrichard@hotmail.com

DARRALL, Charles Geoffrey. b 32. Nottm Univ BA 55 MA 57. Qu Coll Birm 56. **d** 57 **p** 58. C Cockermouth All SS w Ch *Carl* 57–63; Chapl Dioc Youth Cen 63–95; V St John's in the Vale w Wythburn 63–95; P-in-c Threlkeld 85–95; rtd 96; PtO *Carl* 98–07. *Piper House, Naddle, Keswick CA12 4TF* T: (017687) 74500 E: geoff.darrall@btinternet.com

DARRALL, John Norman. b 34. Nottm Univ BA 57. Ripon Hall Ox 57. **d** 60 **p** 61. C Nottingham St Mary *S'well* 60–65; Chapl Nottm Children's Hosp 64–65; V Bole w Saundby and Sturton w Littleborough *S'well* 65–66; Chapl Oakham Sch 84–99; PtO *Leic* 01–13; *Pet* 05–18. *Grange Cottage, 69 Main Street, Cottesmore, Oakham LE15 7DH* T: (01572) 812443 E: johndarrall@gmail.com

DARRALL, Miss Laura Elizabeth. b 86. Ex Univ BA 07 R Cen Sch Speech & Drama MA 08 Sheff Univ BA 19. Coll of Resurr Mirfield 19. **d** 21. C Rustington *Chich* from 21. *23 Henry Avenue, Rustington, Littlehampton BN16 2PA* M: 07515-940639 E: laura.darrall@live.co.uk

DARRANT, Louis Peter. b 77. Aber Univ BD 00 Leeds Univ MA 03. Coll of Resurr Mirfield 01. **d** 03 **p** 04. C Kennington St Jo w St Jas *S'wark* 03–07; R Maldon St Mary w Mundon Chelmsf 07–15; C Wilton Place St Paul *Lon* 15–18; PtO *Chelmsf* from 15; *S'wark* 15–16; Chapl Costa Azahar *Eur* 18–20;

Chapl Málaga from 20. *Paseo Reding 21, 2D, 29016 Málaga, Spain* M: 07779-103826 E: louis.darrant@gmail.com

DART, Miss Andrea Elizabeth. b 47. Northd Coll of Educn TCert 68. Lindisfarne Regional Tr Partnership 12. d 14 p 15. NSM Stanley and S Moor *Dur* 14–17; rtd 17; PtO *Dur* from 17. *13 Tweed Terrace, Stanley DH9 6JQ* T: (01207) 237214 E: andrea.dart@btinternet.com

DART, John Peter. b 40. St Jo Coll Ox BA 62. Cuddesdon Coll 62. d 64 p 65. C W Hartlepool St Aid *Dur* 64–67; C Alverthorpe *Wakef* 67–70; Lic to Offic 70–79; rtd 05. *3 Springhill Avenue, Crofton, Wakefield WF4 1HA* T: (01924) 860374 E: mail@dart.eclipse.co.uk

DARVILL, Canon Christopher Mark. b 61. Ox Univ BA 83. St Steph Ho Ox 84. d 86 p 87. C Tottenham St Paul *Lon* 86–88; C Oystermouth *S & B* 88–90; Chapl Univ of Wales (Swansea) 90–94; Asst Dioc Warden of Ords from 92; V Llansamlet 94–17; V Newton St Pet from 17; Hon Can Brecon Cathl from 16. *The Vicarage, Mary Twill Lane, Mumbles, Swansea SA3 4RB* T: (01792) 219156

DARWENT, Thomas James. b 74. Wycliffe Hall Ox. d 07 p 08. C Claygate *Guildf* 07–11; C Guildf St Sav 11–16; V Camberley St Paul from 16. *The Vicarage, Sandy Lane, Camberley GU15 2AG* T: (01276) 700210

DASH, Mrs Janet Eleanor Gillian. b 47. SRN 69. Cant Sch of Min 89. d 93 p 94. C Morden *S'wark* 93–96; C S Croydon Em 96–98; P-in-c Borstal and Chapl HM Pris Cookham Wood 98–05; P-in-c Darenth *Roch* 05–10; rtd 10; PtO *Cant* 11–17; *York* from 17. *9 Horseman Avenue, York YO23 3UF* T: (01904) 289788 M: 07853-844509 E: jandash@hotmail.co.uk

DATTA, Adrian. b 66. STETS. d 13 p 14. NSM Guernsey W Par *Win* 13–16; PtO 16–17; R Guernsey St Pierre du Bois from 17. *The Rectory, Rue de l'Eglise, St Pierre du Bois, Guernsey GY7 9SB* E: adriandatta@icloud.com

DAUGHTERY, Stephen John. b 61. Kent Univ BSc 82. Trin Coll Bris BA 94. d 96 p 97. C Guildf Ch Ch 96–98; C Guildf Ch Ch w St Martha-on-the-Hill 98–03; R Southover *Chich* 03–17; P-in-c Lewes St Jo sub Castro and S Malling 14–17; R Trin in Lewes 18–21; P-in-c Bembridge *Portsm* from 21; AD Is of Wight from 21. *The Vicarage, Church Road, Bembridge PO35 5NA* E: steve@daughtery.plus.com

DAULMAN, John Henry. b 33. Lich Th Coll 60. d 62 p 63. C Monkseaton St Mary *Newc* 62–65; Min Can Newc Cathl 65–67; Chapl Crumpsall and Springfield Hosp 67–73; V Tyldesley w Shakerley *Man* 73–81; V Turton 81–00; rtd 00; PtO *Blackb* 01–14; *Man* 13–14. *17 Higher Bank Street, Withnell, Chorley PR6 8SF* T: (01254) 832597

DAUNTON-FEAR, Andrew. b 45. Univ of Tasmania BSc 64 Qu Coll Cam BA 67 MA 72 St Andr Univ BPhil 76 K Coll Lon PhD 00. Ridley Hall Cam 66. d 68 p 70. Lect Ridley Coll Melbourne Australia 68–70; C Epping w Thomastown 68–71; P-in-c Islington H Trin Cloudesley Square *Lon* 71–75; Hon C Islington St Mary 71–75; C Stoke Bishop *Bris* 76–79; R Thrapston *Pet* 79–89; R Barming *Roch* 89–03; Lect St Andr Th Sem Philippines 03–15; rtd 15; PtO *Bris* from 16. *17 Keys Avenue, Bristol BS7 0HQ* T: 0117-969 6694 M: 07532-154421 E: fear.no.evil70@gmail.com

DAVAGE, William Ernest Peter. b 50. MA 94. St Steph Ho Ox 89. d 91 p 92. C Eyres Monsell *Leic* 91–94; P Lib Pusey Ho 94–11; rtd 11; PtO *Lon* from 14. *7 Hampstead Square, London NW3 1AB* T: (020) 7209 5375 E: william.davage@stx.ox.ac.uk

DAVENPORT, Canon Ian Arthan. b 54. Linc Th Coll 85. d 87 p 88. C Ches H Trin 87–91; V Newton 91–97; V Oxton 97–10; RD Birkenhead 05–10; R Malpas and Threapwood 10–11; R Malpas and Threapwood and Bickerton 11–21; RD Malpas 14–21; Hon Can Ches Cathl 06–21; rtd 21; Chapl to The Queen from 15; PtO *Ches* from 21. *5 Ulverscroft, 25 Bidston Road, Prenton CH43 2JY* E: malpas.iandavenport@live.co.uk

DAVENPORT, Ms Sally Elizabeth. b 59. Lon Bible Coll BA 99. Ripon Coll Cuddesdon 99. d 01 p 02. C Bishop's Stortford St Mich *St Alb* 01–05; TV Bishop's Hatfield, Lemsford and N Mymms 05–10; P-in-c Fareham H Trin *Portsm* 11–15; TR 15–21; rtd 21; PtO *B & W* from 21. *St Peter's Cottage, 12 Horn Street, Nunney, Frome BA11 4NP* M: 07500-775926

DAVENPORT, Susan Jane. *See* MILLINCHIP, Susan Jane

DAVEY, Andrew John. b 57. Magd Coll Ox BA 78 MA 83. Wycliffe Hall Ox 80. d 83 p 84. C Bermondsey St Jas w Ch Ch *S'wark* 83–87; Chapl Trin Coll Cam 87–92; Pilsdon Community 94–04. *Kingswood, North Street, Axminster EX13 5QF* T: (01297) 33534

DAVEY, Andrew John. b 53. St Mich Coll Llan. d 77 p 78. C Gt Stanmore *Lon* 77–79; NSM Watford St Jo *St Alb* 87–92; C Potters Bar 92–95; P-in-c Clenchwarton *Ely* 95–96; P-in-c W Lynn 95–96; R Clenchwarton and W Lynn 96–19; rtd 19; PtO *Nor* from 19. *49 Queen's Road, Fakenham NR21 8BT* T: (01328) 856815 E: postmaster@andrewdavey.plus.com

DAVEY, Andrew Paul. b 61. Southn Univ BA 82 Sheff Univ DMinTh 98. Tamilnadu Th Sem 84 Westcott Ho Cam 85. d 87 p 88. C S'wark H Trin w St Matt 87–91; V Camberwell St Luke 91–96; Min Development Officer Woolwich Area Miss Team 96–98; Ho of Bps' Officer for UPAs 96–98; Asst Sec Abps' Coun Bd for Soc Resp 98–03; Nat Adv on Community and Urban Affairs 03–12; V Upper Tooting H Trin w St Aug *S'wark* 12–21; Hon Chapl S'wark Cathl 01–21; V Milton next Gravesend Ch Ch *Roch* from 21. *Christ Church Vicarage, 48 Old Road East, Gravesend DA12 1NR* T: (01474) 352643 E: vicar@christchurchgravesend.com

DAVEY, Christopher Mark. b 64. EN(G) 84 RGN 89. St Steph Ho Ox 92. d 95 p 96. C Leeds Belle Is St Jo and St Barn *Ripon* 95–97; C-in-c Grahame Park St Aug CD *Lon* 97–01; V St Alb St Mary Marshalswick 01–08; P-in-c Leavesden 08–12; V 12–13; P-in-c Coggeshall w Markshall *Chelmsf* 13–20; P-in-c Cressing w Stisted and Bradwell etc 15–20; R Coggeshall, Markshall, Cressing etc 20; RD Braintree 18–20; Hon Can Chelmsf Cathl 19–20; P-in-c Framlingham w Saxtead *St E* from 20. *The Rectory, St Michael's Close, Framlingham, Woodbridge IP13 9BJ*

DAVEY, Mrs Hilary Margaret. b 49. Bris Univ BSc 70. EAMTC 98. d 01 p 02. NSM Saffron Walden w Wendens Ambo, Littlebury etc *Chelmsf* 01–07; P-in-c Debden and Wimbish w Thunderley 07–11; TV Saffron Walden and Villages 12–17; rtd 17; PtO *Chelmsf* 17–19. *Barltrops, High Street, Debden, Saffron Walden CB11 3LE* T: (01799) 522616 E: hilarydavey@btopenworld.com

DAVEY, Julian Warwick. b 45. LRCPI 70 LRCSI 70. Qu Coll Birm 78. d 81 p 82. NSM Ipsley *Worc* 81–05; PtO from 05; *Cov* 05–19. *The Field House, Allimore Lane, Alcester B49 5PR* T: (01789) 764640 E: julianw.davey@yahoo.com *or* affgan1@yahoo.com

DAVEY, Kenneth William. b 41. Qu Coll Birm 84. d 86 p 87. C Baswich *Lich* 86–90; V Lostock Gralam *Ches* 90–96; P-in-c Thornton-le-Moors w Ince and Elton 96–07; rtd 07; PtO *Ches* from 08. *4 Firbank, Elton, Chester CH2 4LY* T: (01928) 726166 M: 07977-361059

DAVEY, Mark Sydney Henry. b 80. Wycliffe Hall Ox 10. d 13 p 14. C Herne Bay Ch Ch *Cant* 13–17; TV Morden *S'wark* from 17. *49 Camborne Road, Morden SM4 4JL*

DAVEY, Peter Francis. b 40. Trin Coll Cam BA 63 MA 68. Cuddesdon Coll 63. d 65 p 66. C Atherton *Man* 65–69; C Leesfield 69–72; V High Crompton 72–79; V Blackrod 79–89; P-in-c Ringley 89–91; V Ringley w Prestolee 91–95; P-in-c Dearnley 95–05; rtd 05; PtO *Man* 06–14. *73 Trimingham Drive, Bury BL8 1EP* T: 0161-964 9267 M: 07530-502228

DAVEY, Peter James. b 59. Bris Univ BSc 81 Loughb Univ MBA 91. Trin Coll Bris BA 00. d 00 p 01. C Long Eaton St Jo *Derby* 00–04; V Cotmanhay 04–20; RD Erewash 13–18; rtd 20. *21 Marygate, Pittenweem, Anstruther KY10 2LH* T: (01333) 311958 M: 07587-079265 E: revpete@outlook.com

DAVEY, Richard Henry. b 66. Man Univ BA 88 Nottm Univ PhD 06. Linc Th Coll BTh 93. d 93 p 94. C Parkstone St Pet w Branksea and St Osmund *Sarum* 93–96; Chapl and Min Can St E Cathl 96–99; Can Res S'well Minster 99–04; Chapl Nottm Trent Univ from 04; C Clifton from 04; C Nottingham St Pet and All SS from 10. *30 Pasture Lane, Sutton Bonington, Loughborough LE12 5PQ* E: rdavey1175@aol.com

DAVID, Brother. *See* JARDINE, David John

DAVID, Faith Caroline. *See* CLARINGBULL, Faith Caroline

DAVID, Gilbert. b 56. Karachi Univ BA 76. Ripon Coll Cuddesdon 08. d 11 p 12. C New Bury w Gt Lever *Man* 11–15; TV Darlaston and Moxley *Lich* from 15. *Moxley Vicarage, 5 Sutton Road, Wednesbury WS10 8SG* M: 07880-710122 E: gildavid2u@hotmail.com

DAVID, Kaushal. b 65. d 15 p 16. C Nantwich *Ches* 15–17; P-in-c Totternhoe, Stanbridge and Tilsworth *St Alb* 17–19; V from 19. *The Vicarage, Mill Road, Stanbridge, Leighton Buzzard LU7 9HX* T: (01525) 211864 *or* (01582) 662778 M: 07824-603592 E: kaushaldavid@hotmail.com

DAVID, Canon Kenith Andrew. b 39. Natal Univ BA(Theol) 64. Coll of Resurr Mirfield 64. d 66 p 67. C Harpenden St Nic *St Alb* 66–69; R Chatsworth Epiphany S Africa 69–71; P-in-c Southwick St Mich *Chich* 71–72; Th Educn Sec Chr Aid 72–75; Project Officer India and Bangladesh 76–81; Hon C Kingston All SS *S'wark* 72–76; Hon C Kingston All SS w St Jo 76–81; Lic to Offic Botswana 81–83; Hon C Geneva *Eur* 83–95; Co-ord Urban Rural Miss WCC 83–94; Can Lundi Zimbabwe from 93; V Hessle *York* 95–05; rtd 05; PtO *Cant* 05–11. *5 Randolph Close, Canterbury CT1 3AZ* T/F: (01227) 452009

DAVID, William John. b 57. Ban Univ BTh 07. d 04 p 05. OLM Eltham St Barn *S'wark* 04–07; NSM 07–09 and 11–15; C Toowoomba St Luke Australia 09–11; Chapl Lewisham and Greenwich NHS Trust from 14. *12 Tarnwood Park,*

London SE9 5NY T: (020) 8333 6338 M: 07929-644503 E: williamdavid10@aol.com

DAVID FRANCIS, Brother. *See* DARLING, David Francis

DAVIDGE-SMITH, Mrs Margaret Kathleen. b 53. CQSW 77. STETS 99. **d** 02 **p** 03. NSM E Acton St Dunstan w St Thos *Lon* 02–06; Asst Chapl Ealing Hosp NHS Trust 04–06; Asst Chapl Meadow House Hospice 04–06; Asst Chapl W Middx Univ Hosp NHS Trust 05–06; Asst Chapl W Lon Mental Health NHS Trust 05–06; Chapl Ealing Hosp NHS Trust 06–16; rtd 16; PtO *Lon* from 16. *36 Newburgh Road, London W3 6DQ* M: 07733-777450 E: mdavidge_s@hotmail.com *or* maggie.davidge-smith@london.anglican.org

DAVIDSON, Christopher John. b 45. St Luke's Coll Ex CertEd 67 St Martin's Coll Lanc BEd 74. EAMTC. **d** 91 **p** 92. NSM Taverham w Ringland *Nor* 91–93; Dir of Educn 87–93; P-in-c Whixley w Green Hammerton *Ripon* 93–96; RE Adv 93–96; Dioc Dir of Educn *Ex* 97–01; Assoc P Exminster and Kenn 97–01; R Quidenham Gp *Nor* 01–08; P-in-c Guiltcross 04–08; rtd 08; P-in-c Pyworthy, Pancrasweek and Bridgerule *Ex* 08–11; PtO *Nor* from 11; *St E* from 16. *2 The Old School, Hinderclay Road, Rickinghall, Diss IP22 1HD* T: (01379) 890465 E: chris.davidson@btinternet.com

DAVIDSON, Mrs Dawn Margaret. b 59. **d** 09 **p** 10. OLM Mulbarton w Bracon Ash, Hethel and Flordon *Nor* 09–14; TV Newton Flotman, Swainsthorpe, Tasburgh, etc 14–18; TR from 18. *The Rectory, The Street, Saxlingham Nethergate, Norwich NR15 1AJ* T: (01508) 498924 M: 07784-003432 E: dawndavidson@btinternet.com

DAVIDSON, Donald. b 52. TISEC 00. **d** 05 **p** 06. C W Highland Region *Arg* 05–15; rtd 15. *4 Kearan Road, Kinlochleven, Argyll PH50 4QU* T: (01855) 831444 E: donaldd@btinternet.com

DAVIDSON, Gillian. b 61. Newc Poly BA 84 Cumbria Univ BSc 03. Cumbria Chr Learning 18. **d** 20 **p** 21. NSM Cockermouth Area *Carl* from 20. *2 The Fallows, Cockermouth CA13 0ET* M: 07841-044404 E: gilly.fallows2@gmail.com

DAVIDSON, Trevor John. b 49. CertEd. Oak Hill Th Coll 80. **d** 85 **p** 86. C Drypool *York* 85–88; V Bessingby 88–97; V Carnaby 88–97; Chapl Bridlington and Distr Gen Hosp 88–94; Chapl E Yorks Community Healthcare NHS Trust 94–97; V Felling *Dur* 97–14; CUF Projects Officer 97–14; rtd 14; PtO *Dur* from 15. *10 Alder Grove, Seaham SR7 7RT* T: 0191-435 5685 M: 07447-772070 E: revtjd@gmail.com

DAVIE (née JONES), Canon Alyson Elizabeth. b 58. Ex Univ BA 86. Wycliffe Hall Ox 86. **d** 88 **p** 94. Par Dn Ipswich St Fran *St E* 88–92; PtO *Ox* 92–93; *St Alb* 93–94; NSM E Barnet 94–97; Asst Chapl Oak Hill Th Coll 94–96; P-in-c The Mundens w Sacombe *St Alb* 97–06; V St Paul's Cray St Barn *Roch* 06–14; P-in-c Meopham w Nurstead 14–19; R from 19; RD Cobham from 18; Hon Can Roch Cathl from 18. *The Rectory, Shipley Hills Road, Meopham, Gravesend DA13 0AD* T: (01474) 812068 E: alyson@stjohnsmeopham.co.uk

DAVIE, Peter Edward Sidney. b 36. LSE BSc 57 Birm Univ MA 73 K Coll Lon MPhil 78 Kent Univ PhD 90. Coll of Resurr Mirfield 57. **d** 60 **p** 61. C De Beauvoir Town St Pet *Lon* 60–63; C-in-c Godshill CD *Portsm* 63–67; R Upton St Leonards *Glouc* 67–73; Sen Lect Ch Ch Coll of HE Cant 73–98; Prin Lect Cant Ch Ch Univ Coll 98–01; rtd 01; Hon C Cant St Pet w St Alphege and St Marg etc 79–10; PtO 10–16; *Leeds* from 17. *Middle Cottage, Manor Heath Road, Halifax HX3 0EB* T: (01422) 751873 E: pedavie@dircon.co.uk *or* peteresdavie@talktalk.net

DAVIE, Canon Stephen Peter. b 52. S Bank Poly BA 75 Spurgeon's Coll PhD 03 MRTPI 77. Oak Hill Th Coll BA 93. **d** 93 **p** 94. C Luton Ch Ch *Roch* 93–97; R Cobham w Luddesdowne and Dode 97–04; P-in-c Horley *S'wark* 04–08; TR 08–12; P-in-c Tong *Bradf* 12–14; *Leeds* 14; AD N Bradford 14; Dir Bradf Sch of Min 14–18; Hon Can Bradf Cathl 13–14; *Leeds* 14–18; rtd 18; PtO *Sheff* 18–20. *93 The Village, Holme, Holmfirth HD9 2QG* T: (01484) 684973 M: 07918-654956

DAVIES, Adrian. *See* DAVIES, Glanmor Adrian

DAVIES, Adrian Paul. b 43. K Coll Lon. **d** 69 **p** 70. C Nottingham St Mary *S'well* 69–74; C Gt w Lt Billing *Pet* 74–75; P-in-c Marholm 75–82; R Castor 75; R Castor w Sutton and Upton 76–82; V Byker St Mich w St Lawr *Newc* 82–94; rtd 95. *27 Clougha Avenue, Halton, Lancaster LA2 6NR* T: (01524) 811141

DAVIES, Alan. *See* DAVIES, James Alan

DAVIES, Alan Douglas. b 49. ERMC 08. **d** 10 **p** 11. NSM Downham Market and Crimplesham w Stradsett *Ely* 10–19; NSM Downham Market and Stradsett 19–21; rtd 21; PtO *Ely* from 21. *The Lodge, Wallington Hall, Runcton Holme, King's Lynn PE33 0EP* T: (01553) 810675 E: fralandavies@hotmail.co.uk

DAVIES, Alastair John. b 56. Nottm Univ BA MTh. Westcott Ho Cam. **d** 84 **p** 85. C Eltham St Jo *S'wark* 84–87; C Dulwich St Barn 87–89; Chapl RAF 89–07;

P-in-c Lyneham w Bradenstoke *Sarum* 01–03; Sen Chapl R United Hosps Bath NHS Foundn Trust 07–17; rtd 17; PtO *Bris* from 17; *Eur* from 17; Spiritual Dir Cursillo *Bris* from 17. *8 Blicks Close, Hullavington, Chippenham SN14 6HQ* E: alastair.davies@icloud.com

DAVIES, Albert Brian. b 37. Worc Coll of Educn CertEd 60. Wycliffe Hall Ox 03. **d** 04 **p** 05. C Poitou-Charentes *Eur* 04–07; P-in-c The Vendée 07–10; Asst Chapl Aquitaine 11–12; rtd 13; PtO *Eur* from 16. *39 Rue Rempart Charles de Gaulle, Le Bourg Fontaines, 24320 Champagne et Fontaines, France* T: (0033) 2 51 62 96 32

DAVIES, Mrs Alison Margaret. b 57. Nottm Univ BA 78. STETS 96. **d** 99 **p** 00. NSM Win St Barn 99–04; PtO 04–07; *Nor* 07–10 and 13; Chapl S Lon Healthcare NHS Trust 10–13; PtO *St Alb* from 16. *Broadgate, Hillside Road, Leighton Buzzard LU7 3BU*

DAVIES, Mrs Allison Claire. b 65. Qu Coll Birm 12. **d** 15 **p** 16. NSM Redditch H Trin *Worc* 15–17; C 17–19; V Eckington from 19; V Defford w Besford from 19; C Overbury w Teddington, Alstone etc from 19; P-in-c Bredon w Bredon's Norton from 21; C Elmley Castle w Bricklehampton and Combertons from 21. *The Vicarage, Drakes Bridge Road, Eckington, Pershore WR10 3BN* T: (01386) 750203 E: eckingtonvicarage@hotmail.com

DAVIES, Andrew John. *See* GRACE, Andrew John

DAVIES, Anthony. *See* DAVIES, David Anthony

DAVIES, Anthony. *See* DAVIES, Vincent Anthony

DAVIES, Anthony Paul. b 56. JP 02. Univ of Wales (Swansea) BSc 76 CEng 85. St Mich Coll Llan 03. **d** 06 **p** 07. NSM Penllergaer *S & B* 06–07; NSM Gorseinon 07–12; PtO from 12; *B & W* from 15. *The Gate House, 1 Westend Court, Frome BA11 1ET* T: (01373) 473668 M: 07855-237866 E: anthonypdavies@yahoo.com

DAVIES, Barry Lewis. b 46. Boro Road Teacher Tr Coll CertEd 69 Lon Inst of Educn DipEd 84 MA 86. STETS 02. **d** 05 **p** 06. NSM Hardington Vale *B & W* 05–08; rtd 08; PtO *B & W* 09–13; *Bris* 10–15; Chapl Avon and Somerset Constabulary *B & W* from 10; Chapl Partis Coll Bath 10–13; NSM Mells w Buckland Dinham, Elm, Whatley etc *B & W* 13–19; PtO from 20. *3 The Lays, Goose Street, Beckington, Frome BA11 6RS* T: (01373) 831344 E: bandkdavies@msn.com

DAVIES, Beth. *See* DAVIES, Elizabeth

DAVIES, Sister Beverley. b 55. **d** 11 **p** 12. NSM Leic Presentation 11–14; PtO from 14; Chapl LOROS Hospice from 15; Chapl Qu Th Foundn Birm from 15. *St Matthew's House, 25 Kamloops Crescent, Leicester LE1 2HX* T: 0116-251 9158

DAVIES, Brian. *See* DAVIES, Albert Brian

DAVIES, Catharine Mary. *See* FURLONG, Catharine Mary

DAVIES, Mrs Catherine Olive Sarah Skeel. b 61. Univ of Wales (Cardiff) BA 84. WMMTC 03. **d** 06 **p** 07. NSM Wootton Wawen and Claverdon w Preston Bagot *Cov* 06–09; NSM Barford w Wasperton and Sherbourne and Hampton Lucy w Charlecote and Loxley 09–13; PtO 13–15; NSM Launde Abbey *Leic* 15–20; PtO *Pet* 15–20. *Address temp unknown* E: revcathydavies@aol.com

DAVIES, Ceri John. b 61. Univ of Wales (Lamp) BA 91 Univ of Wales (Abth) PGCE 92 Univ of Wales (Cardiff) BTh 00. St Mich Coll Llan 97. **d** 00 **p** 01. C Carmarthen St Dav *St D* 00–03; TV Llanelli 03–11; C Cynwyl Elfed w Newchurch and Trelech a'r Betws 11–14; PtO from 14. *79-80 Priory Street, Carmarthen SA31 1NU* T: (01267) 233976 E: cdavies465@btinternet.com

DAVIES, Christopher. *See* DAVIES, David Christopher

DAVIES, Christopher Edward. b 72. **d** 03 **p** 04. OLM Bilston *Lich* 03–18; TV Bloxwich from 18. *6 Cresswell Crescent, Walsall WS3 2UW* M: 07952-196204

DAVIES, Christopher John. b 55. St Alb Minl Tr Scheme 83. **d** 86 **p** 87. C Tooting All SS *S'wark* 86–90; V Malden St Jas 90–96; RD Kingston 92–96; TR Wimbledon 96–06; Hon Can S'wark Cathl 06; V Wymondham *Nor* 06–16; RD Humbleyard 08–15; rtd 16; C Foulsham, Guestwick, Stibbard, Themelthorpe etc *Nor* 17; C N Elmham, Billingford, Bintree, Guist etc 17; TV Heart of Norfolk from 17. *The Old Rectory, Deopham Road, Morley St Botolph, Wymondham NR18 9DB* M: 07702-865412 E: cjdoldrectory@gmail.com

DAVIES, Christopher Mark. b 76. Essex Univ BA 97 Sheff Univ BA 13 Southn Inst DipSW 02. Coll of Resurr Mirfield 11. **d** 13 **p** 14. C Gt Grimsby St Mary and St Jas *Linc* 13–16; R Loughton St Jo *Chelmsf* from 16. *St John's Rectory, Church Lane, Loughton IG10 1PD* E: cmdavies76@yahoo.co.uk

DAVIES, David Anthony. b 50. Thames Poly BSc 81 MRICS 84. Coll of Resurr Mirfield 85. **d** 88 **p** 89. C Stalybridge *Man* 88–91; C Swinton and Pendlebury 91–92 and 01–02; TV 92–01; V Tonge Moor from 02. *St Augustine's*

Vicarage, Redthorpe Close, Bolton BL2 2PQ T/F: (01204) 523899 M: 07866-359864 E: tony@davieses.co.uk

DAVIES, David Berwyn. b 42. St Mich Coll Llan 95. **d** 96 **p** 97. C Llanelli *St D* 96–98; I Llanerch Aeron w Ciliau Aeron and Dihewyd etc 98–07; rtd 07; PtO *St D* from 07. *56 Tyisha Road, Llanelli SA15 1RW* T: (01554) 774391 E: taddavid@aol.com

DAVIES, Canon David Christopher. b 52. Lon Univ BSc 73 UWE MSc 11. Coll of Resurr Mirfield 73. **d** 76 **p** 77. C Bethnal Green St Jo w St Simon *Lon* 76–78; C Bethnal Green St Jo w St Bart 78–80; C-in-c Portsea St Geo CD *Portsm* 80–81; V Portsea St Geo 81–87; Relig Affairs Producer Radio Victory 81–86; Chapl Ham Green Hosp Bris 87–94; Chapl Southmead Hosp Bris 87–94; Chapl Southmead Health Services NHS Trust 94–99; Chapl N Bris NHS Trust 99–05; Hd Spiritual and Past Care 05–13; Hd Spiritual and Past Care Univ Hosps Bris NHS Foundn Trust 05–13; PtO *B & W* 94–13; Hon Can Bris Cathl 99–13; rtd 13; Hd of Clinical Services Wessex Counselling and Psychotherapy 14–21; PtO *Bris* from 13. *28 Hortham Lane, Almondsbury, Bristol BS32 4JL* T: (01454) 616608

DAVIES, Canon David Jeremy Christopher. b 46. CCC Cam BA 68 MA 72. Westcott Ho Cam 68. **d** 71 **p** 72. C Stepney St Dunstan and All SS *Lon* 71–74; Chapl Qu Mary Coll 74–78; Chapl Univ of Wales (Cardiff) *Llan* 78–85; Can Res Sarum Cathl 85–12; rtd 12; PtO *Sarum* from 13; Chapl CCC Cam 19–20. *14 Shady Bower Close, Salisbury SP1 2RQ* M: 07713-324051 E: jeremy.davies1000@gmail.com

DAVIES, Canon David Michael Cole. b 44. St D Coll Lamp. **d** 68 **p** 69. C Carmarthen St Pet *St D* 68–72; R Dinas 72–77; V Ty-Croes w Saron 77–79; V Llanedi w Tycroes and Saron 80–90; RD Dyffryn Aman 85–90; V Dafen and Llwynhendy 90–94; V Dafen 94–08; Hon Can St D Cathl 00–08; rtd 08; PtO *St D* from 09. *30 Bro'r Dderwen, Clynderwen SA66 7NR* E: dcmcd@aol.com *or* revdmcd@btinternet.com

DAVIES, David Peter. b 47. **d** 13 **p** 14. NSM Worc City 13–14; NSM Worc St Nic and All SS w St Helen 14–15; NSM Claines St Jo from 15; NSM Worc St Geo w St Mary Magd from 15. *44 Battenhall Rise, Worcester WR5 2DE* T: (01905) 356714 E: peterdaviesworcs@waitrose.com

DAVIES, Canon Dewi Gwynfor. b 56. Univ of Wales (Abth) BD 92 MTh 98 RIBA 81.**d** 98 **p** 99. C Llangunnor w Cwmffrwd *St D* 98–99; P-in-c Elerch w Penrhyncoch w Capel Bangor and Goginan 99–00; P-in-c Cil-y-Cwm and Ystrad-ffin w Rhandir-mwyn etc 00–03; V Llanedi w Tycroes and Saron 03–09; V Pen-bre 09–19; AD Cydweli 15–18; P-in-c Bro Gwendraeth from 19; Hon Can St D Cathl from 18. *The Vicarage, Ar-y-bryn, Pembrey, Burry Port SA16 0AJ* T: (01554) 833766 E: frdewivicarage@btinternet.com

DAVIES, The Ven Dorrien Paul. b 64. Univ of Wales (Lamp) BA 95. Llan Dioc Tr Scheme 86. **d** 88 **p** 89. C Llanelli *St D* 88–91; V Llanfihangel Ystrad and Cilcennin w Trefilan etc 91–99; V St Dogmael's w Moylgrove and Monington w Meline 99–10; TV Dewisland 10–17; Can St D Cathl 07–17; Adn Carmarthen from 17; P-in-c St Clears w Llangynin and Llanddowror etc 18. *The New Vicarage, St Clears, Carmarthen SA33 4ED* T: (01994) 231611 M: 07384-631292 E: archdeacon.carmarthen@churchinwales.org.uk

DAVIES, Prof Douglas James. b 47. St Jo Coll Dur BA 69 St Pet Coll Ox MLitt 72 Nottm Univ PhD 80 Ox Univ DLitt 04 Uppsala Univ Hon DTh 98 FBA 17 FAcSS 09 FLSW 12. Cranmer Hall Dur 71. **d** 75 **p** 76. Lect Nottm Univ 75–97; Sen Lect 90–97; Hon C Wollaton *S'well* 75–83; Hon C Attenborough 83–85; Hon C E Leake 85–91; Hon C Daybrook 91–97; Prof RS Nottm Univ 93–97; Prin SS Hild and Bede Coll Dur 97–00; Prof Th Dur Univ from 97; Prof Study of Relig Dur Univ from 00; PtO *Dur* from 13. *Department of Theology and Religion, Abbey House, Palace Green, Durham DH1 3RS* T: 0191-375 7697 E: douglas.davies@durham.ac.uk

DAVIES, Canon Douglas Tudor. b 20. Univ of Wales (Ban) BA 44. Coll of Resurr Mirfield 44. **d** 46 **p** 47. C Swansea Ch Ch *S & B* 46–52; C Oystermouth 52–57; R Llangynllo and Bleddfa 57–63; C-in-c Treboeth CD 63–65; V Treboeth 65–90; RD Penderi 78–90; Hon Can Brecon Cathl 82–83; Can Brecon Cathl 83–90; rtd 90. *245A Swansea Road, Waunarlwydd, Swansea SA5 4SN* T: (01792) 879587

DAVIES, Edna Nansi Margaret. b 37. CBE . **d** 97 **p** 98. NSM Netherwent *Mon* 97–01; NSM Caerwent w Dinham and Llanfair Discoed etc 01–13; NSM Caerwent w Dinham and Llanvair Discoed etc 13–14; NSM Wentwood 14–17; rtd 17; PtO *Mon* from 17. *Junipers, Court House Road, LLanfair Discoed, Chepstow NP16 6LW* T: (01633) 400519 E: enm.davies@icloud.com

DAVIES, Edward Earl. b 40. Llan Dioc Tr Scheme 88. **d** 90 **p** 91. C Pontypridd St Cath w St Matt *Llan* 90–93; V Ferndale w Maerdy 93–00; V Cardiff Ch Ch Roath

Park 00–09; rtd 09; PtO *Llan* from 10. *4 St Augustine Road, Heath, Cardiff CF14 4BD* T: (029) 2061 0054 E: eeandsidavies@outlook.com

DAVIES, Edward Trevor. b 37. MRSC 62 MInstE 74 CEng 78. NOC 92. **d** 95 **p** 96. Hon Asst Chapl Countess of Chester Hosp NHS Foundn Trust 95–02; Chapl 02–05; NSM Waverton Ches 95–99; NSM Hargrave 99–00; C Bunbury and Tilstone Fearnall 00–02; NSM 02–03; PtO 05–10 and from 11; C Waverton w Aldford and Bruera 10–11; rtd 11. *Athergreen, 5 Allansford Avenue, Waverton, Chester CH3 7QH* T: (01244) 332106 E: etdavies1@btinternet.com

DAVIES, Canon Edward William Llewellyn. b 51. St Jo Coll Nottm BTh 77. **d** 78 **p** 79. C Southsea St Jude *Portsm* 78–81; C Alverstoke 81–84; R Abbas and Templecombe w Horsington *B & W* 84–89; PtO *Ches* 89–99; V Sutton St Jas 99–13; RD Macclesfield 05–12; Warden Foxhill Retreat and Conf Cen 13–15; Asst Warden of Readers 02–15; Hon Can Ches Cathl 10–15; rtd 15; PtO *Ches* from 15. *37 Minor Avenue, Lyme Green, Macclesfield SK11 0LQ* T: (01260) 253671 E: ewldavies@gmail.com

DAVIES, Eileen. *See* DAVIES, Rachel Hannah Eileen

DAVIES, Elizabeth. b 60. Trin Coll Carmarthen BA 04 PGCE 06. **d** 16 **p** 17. NSM Llandysul w Bangor Teifi and Llanfairollwyn etc *St D* 16–20; P-in-c Bro Aeron Mydr from 20; AD from 20. *Tynewydd, Gorrig Road, Llandysul SA44 4JP* T: (01559) 362850 M: 07901-716957 E: bethan@cd1340.f9.co.uk

DAVIES, Mrs Elizabeth Jean. b 39. Lon Univ MB, BS 63 MRCS 63 LRCP 63 DRCOG 65. Chich Th Coll 86. **d** 89 **p** 95. Par Dn Southwick St Mich *Chich* 89–91; Par Dn Littlehampton and Wick 91–95; C Seaford w Sutton 95–97; NSM E Preston w Kingston 97–04; rtd 99; P-in-c Everton and Mattersey w Clayworth *S'well* 04–05; PtO from 06. *16 Blackstope Lane, Retford DN22 6NF* T: (01777) 711513

DAVIES, Canon Emma Louise. b 67. St Andr Univ MA 89. Ripon Coll Cuddesdon 05. **d** 07 **p** 08. C Market Harborough and The Transfiguration etc *Leic* 07–10; TV Avon-Swift 10–21; Hon Can Leic Cathl 18–21; Can Res and Prec Leic Cathl from 21. *Leicester Cathedral, St Martin's House, 7 Peacock Lane, Leicester LE1 5PZ* E: emma.davies1@sky.com *or* emma.davies@leccofe.org

DAVIES, Mrs Felicity Ann. b 58. Wycliffe Hall Ox. **d** 11 **p** 12. C Wadhurst *Chich* 11–14; C Stonegate 11–14; C Tidebrook 11–14; R Ickenham *Lon* from 14. *St Giles's Rectory, 38 Swakeleys Road, Ickenham, Uxbridge UB10 8BE* T: (01895) 622970 E: fadavies58@gmail.com

DAVIES, Frances Elizabeth. b 38. BA CertEd. Moray Ord Course. **d** 95. Hon C Thurso *Mor* 95–12; Hon C Wick 95–12; PtO from 12. *22 Granville Crescent, Thurso, Caithness KW14 7NP* T: (01847) 892386 E: reallyfed@yahoo.co.uk

DAVIES, Gareth Clement. b 61. LSE BSc(Econ) 83 Open Univ LLB 03. Westcott Ho Cam 14. **d** 16 **p** 17. C Mortlake w E Sheen *S'wark* 16–18; C W Dulwich All SS 18–20; Chapl Lewisham and Greenwich NHS Trust from 20. *27 Maitland Road, London SE26 5NN* T: (020) 8676 0184 E: revd.gareth.davies@icloud.com

DAVIES, Gareth Rhys. b 51. Oak Hill Th Coll. **d** 83 **p** 84. C Gt Warley Ch Ch *Chelmsf* 83–86; C Oxhey All SS *St Alb* 86–90; C Aldridge *Lich* 90–99; V Colney Heath St Mark *St Alb* 99–00; V Sneyd Green *Lich* 00–16; Bp's Adv on Healing 09–15; rtd 16. *10 Durness Street, Thurso KW14 8BQ*

DAVIES, George William. b 51. Open Univ BA 74 MPhil 89 MCIPD. Sarum & Wells Th Coll 83. **d** 85 **p** 86. C Mansfield SS Pet and Paul *S'well* 85–89; Chapl Cen Notts HA 86–89; P-in-c Fobbing and Ind Chapl *Chelmsf* 89–96; Chapl Thurrock Lakeside Shopping Cen 93–96; R Mottingham St Andr w St Alban *S'wark* 96–04; V Lamorbey H Trin *Roch* 04–12; Chapl Rose Bruford Coll 04–12; rtd 12; PtO *S'well* 16–17. *106 Kirklington Road, Rufford Grange, Rainworth NG21 0JX* T: (01623) 490653 E: georgeandkatedavies@btinternet.com

DAVIES, Glanmor Adrian. b 51. St D Coll Lamp. **d** 73 **p** 75. C Llanstadwel *St D* 73–78; R Dinas w Llanllawer and Pontfaen w Morfil etc 78–84; V Lamphey w Hodgeston 84–85; V Lamphey w Hodgeston and Carew 85–03; V Borth and Eglwys-fach w Llangynfelyn 03–06; PtO from 16. *4 Somerset Place, Park Road, Tenby SA70 7NF* T: (01834) 843316 E: judymcg@hotmail.co.uk

✠**DAVIES, The Most Revd Glenn Naunton.** b 50. Sydney Univ BSc 72 Sheff Univ PhD 88. Westmr Th Sem (USA) BD 78 ThM 79. **d** 81 **p** 81 **c** 01. Australia 81–85; Hon C Fulwood *Sheff* 85–87; Hon C Lodge Moor St Luke 86–87; Lect Moore Th Coll Australia 87–95; R Miranda 95–01; Bp N Sydney 01–13; Abp from 13. *PO Box Q190, Queen Victoria Building, Sydney NSW 1230, Australia* T: (0061) (2) 9265 1555 F: 9261 1170 E: registry@sydney.anglican.asn.au

DAVIES, Glyndŵr George. b 36. Glouc Sch of Min 88. **d** 91 **p** 92. NSM Clodock and Longtown w Craswall, Llanveynoe etc *Heref* 91–02; rtd 02; PtO *Heref* 02–12. *White House Farm, Llanfihangel Crucorney, Abergavenny NP7 8HW* T: (01873) 890251

DAVIES, The Ven Graham James. b 35. Univ of Wales BD 72 St D Coll Lamp BA 56. St Mich Coll Llan 56 Episc Th Sch Cam Mass 58. **d** 59 **p** 60. C Johnston w Steynton *St D* 59–62; C Llangathen w Llanfihangel Cilfargen 62–64; Min Can St D Cathl 64–66; R Burton 66–71; R Hubberston 71–74; Hon C Lenham w Boughton Malherbe *Cant* 74–80; V Cwmdauddwr w St Harmon and Llanwrthwl *S & B* 80–86; V Cydweli and Llandyfaelog *St D* 86–97; Can St D Cathl 92–02; Adn St D 96–02; V Steynton 97–02; rtd 02. *16 Freshwater East Road, Lamphey, Pembroke SA71 5JX* T: (01646) 672272

DAVIES, Canon Henry Joseph. b 38. Univ of Wales (Cardiff) BSc 61. St Mich Coll Llan 75. **d** 76 **p** 77. C Griffithstown *Mon* 76–79; TV Cwmbran 79–85; V Newport St Andr 85–03; Can St Woolos Cathl 98–03; rtd 03; PtO *Mon* 03–11; P-in-c Bettws from 11. *14 Morden Road, Newport NP19 7EU* E: henry@bettws.org.uk *or* henry.d@ntlworld.com

DAVIES, Huw. *See* DAVIES, Peter Huw

DAVIES, Hywel John. b 45. Univ of Wales (Abth) BA 67 Univ of Wales (Ban) DipEd 68 Univ of Wales (Cardiff) MA 90 Univ of Wales (Ban) BTh 99. St Mich Coll Llan 94 Qu Coll Birm 96. **d** 97 **p** 98. Min Can Ban Cathl 97–98; C Llandudno 98–99; LtO *Llan* 99–03; NSM Canton Cardiff 03–04; P-in-c Llanarthne and Llanddarog *St D* 04–07; Chapl Coleg Sir Gâr 04–07; rtd 07; P-in-c Cardiff Dewi Sant *Llan* 08–10; PtO from 10; *Eur* from 17. *68 Glas y Gors, Cwmbach, Aberdare CF44 0BQ* T: (01685) 378457 E: hywel33@btinternet.com

DAVIES, Ian. b 45. Man Coll of Educn TCert 74 Open Univ BA 79. Carl Dioc Tr Inst 88. **d** 91 **p** 92. NSM Harraby *Carl* 91–95; C Barrow St Jo 95–96; P-in-c 96–00; P-in-c Beetham and Youth and Sch Support Officer 00–05; V Marown *S & M* 05–11; rtd 11; PtO *Dur* from 12. *10 Capulet Terrace, Sunderland SR2 8JL* T: 0191-514 3055 E: reviand@manx.net

DAVIES, Canon Ian. b 54. Sheff Hallam Univ BA 80 Univ of Wales (Cardiff) MSc(Econ) 86 MBA 92 Bris Univ PhD 01 Ox Univ BTh 06 CQSW 80. Wycliffe Hall Ox 02. **d** 04 **p** 05. C Swansea St Pet *S & B* 04–06; C Waunarllwydd 06–07; P-in-c 07–10; V 10–20; Hon Can Brecon Cathl 12–20; Dioc Dir of Ords and Dioc Dir of Min 12–20; Bp's Officer for Formation 18–20. *The New Vicarage, 59A Victoria Road, Waunarlwydd, Swansea SA5 4SY* M: 07779-145267 E: iandavies12@hotmail.com

DAVIES, Canon Ian Elliott. b 64. Univ of Wales (Ban) BD 85. Ridley Hall Cam 86. **d** 88 **p** 89. C Baglan *Llan* 88–90; C Skewen 90–96; C St Marylebone All SS *Lon* 96–01; R Hollywood St Thos USA from 02; Can Los Angeles from 14. *St Thomas's Church, 7501 Hollywood Boulevard, Hollywood CA 90046, USA* T: (001) (323) 876 2102 F: 876 7738 E: frdavies@saintthomashollywood.org

DAVIES, Mrs Jacqueline Ann. b 42. Bris Univ BA 64 CertEd 65 Univ of Wales (Lamp) MA 99. EMMTC 84 St As Minl Tr Course 97. **d** 98 **p** 99. NSM Llanfair DC, Derwen, Llanelidan and Efenechtyd *St As* 98–00; PtO 00–14; *Chich* 12–17; *B & W* 16–21. *2 Delphinium Drive, Langport TA10 9TN* T: (01458) 259300

DAVIES, James Alan. b 38. Lambeth STh 95. St Jo Coll Nottm. **d** 83 **p** 84. C Fletchamstead *Cov* 83–87; P-in-c Hartshill 87–89; V 89–93; V E Green 93–03; rtd 03; Hon C Mickleton, Willersey, Saintbury etc *Glouc* 04–05; PtO *Cov* 05–21. *5 Margetts Close, Kenilworth CV8 1EN* T: (01926) 854337 E: a.davies861@btinternet.com

DAVIES, James William. b 51. Trin Hall Cam BA 72 MA 76 St Jo Coll Dur BA 79. Cranmer Hall Dur 77. **d** 80 **p** 81. C Croydon Ch Ch Broad Green *Cant* 80–83; CMS 83–86; Chapl Bethany Sch Goudhurst 86–90; P-in-c Parkstone St Luke *Sarum* 90–00; Hon C Bournemouth St Andr *Win* 05–20; PtO *Sarum* from 05; rtd 20. *8 Newton Road, Swanage BH19 2DZ* T: (01929) 475770

DAVIES, Preb Jane Ann. b 58. Coll of Ripon & York St Jo MA 97. Aston Tr Scheme 91 WMMTC 93 NOC 94. **d** 96 **p** 97. NSM Heref S Wye 96–97; C 97–00; P-in-c Bishop's Frome w Castle Frome and Fromes Hill 00–08; P-in-c Acton Beauchamp and Evesbatch w Stanford Bishop 00–08; P-in-c Stoke Lacy, Moreton Jeffries w Much Cowarne etc 00–08; V Frome Valley 09–12; P-in-c Lugwardine w Bartestree, Weston Beggard etc 12; P-in-c Withington w Westhide 12; R Bartestree Cross 12–18; V Canon Pyon w King's Pyon, Birley and Wellington from 18; RD Leominster from 20; Preb Heref Cathl from 10. *The Vicarage, Brookside, Canon Pyon, Hereford HR4 8NY* T: (01432) 830581 E: trendy.rev2@btinternet.com

DAVIES, Jeffrey William. b 45. St Cath Coll Cam BA 66 MA 69 LLM 67 Liv Univ MTh 07 Solicitor 69. NOC 01. **d** 04 **p** 05.

NSM Ramsbottom and Edenfield *Man* 04–11; NSM Heaton Ch Ch w Halliwell St Marg 11–14; rtd 14; PtO *Man* from 14. *44 Higher Dunscar, Egerton, Bolton BL7 9TF* T/F: (01204) 412503 E: jeffdavies1@ntlworld.com

DAVIES, Jeremy. *See* DAVIES, David Jeremy Christopher

DAVIES, Joanna. b 65. St Mellitus Coll. **d** 10 **p** 11. C Onslow Square and S Kensington St Aug *Lon* 10–18; Managing Chapl HM Pris Pentonville from 18; PtO *Lon* from 18. *HM Prison Pentonville, Caledonian Road, London N7 8TT* T: (020) 7023 7217 E: jo.davies@justice.gov.uk

DAVIES, John. b 62. Univ of Wales (Cardiff) BA 88. Ridley Hall Cam 98. **d** 00 **p** 01. C Wavertree H Trin *Liv* 00–04; P-in-c W Derby Gd Shep 04–09; V 09–10; TV Okehampton w Inwardleigh, Bratton Clovelly etc *Ex* 10–11; TV Okehampton, Inwardleigh, Belstone, Sourton etc 12–13; V Whitegate w Lt Budworth *Ches* 13–14; R Cam Vale *B & W* 14–18; P-in-c Clapham-with-Keasden and Austwick *Leeds* 18–20; V from 20. *The Vicarage, Clapham Road, Austwick, Lancaster LA2 8BE* T: (01524) 805928 E: john.davies@leeds.anglican.org

DAVIES, John. *See* PAGE DAVIES, David John

DAVIES, John. *See* DAVIES, Kenneth John

✠**DAVIES, The Rt Revd John David Edward.** b 53. Southn Univ LLB 74 Univ of Wales (Cardiff) LLM 95 Univ of Wales (Trin St Dav) Hon DD 19 Swansea Univ Hon DLitt 19. St Mich Coll Llan 82. **d** 84 **p** 85 **c** 08. C Chepstow *Mon* 84–86; C-in-c Michaelston-y-Fedw and Rudry 86–89; R Bedwas and Rudry 89–95; V Maindee Newport 95–00; Dean Brecon *S & B* 00–08; V Brecon St Mary w Llanddew 00–08; P-in-c Cynog Honddu 05–08; Bp S & B 08–21; Abp Wales 17–21; rtd 21. *Oaklands, Dark Lane, Rhayader LD6 5DA* M: 07852-280918 E: jdedavies@outlook.com

✠**DAVIES, The Rt Revd John Dudley.** b 27. Trin Coll Cam BA 51 MA 63. Linc Th Coll 52. **d** 53 **p** 54 **c** 87. C Leeds Halton St Wilfrid *Ripon* 53–56; C Yeoville S Africa 57; R Evander 57–61; R Empangeni 61–63; Chapl Witwatersrand Univ 63–71; Sec Chapls in HE Gen Syn Bd of Educn 71–74; P-in-c Keele *Lich* 74–76; Chapl Keele Univ 74–76; Prin USPG Coll of the Ascension Selly Oak 76–81; Preb Lich Cathl 76–87; Can Res, Preb and Sacr St As Cathl 82–85; Dioc Missr 82–87; V Llanrhaeadr-ym-Mochnant, Llanarmon, Pennant etc 85–87; Suff Bp Shrewsbury *Lich* 87–92; rtd 94; PtO *Lich* 05–14; *St As* from 09. *Nyddfa, By-Pass Road, Gobowen, Oswestry SY11 3NG* T/F: (01691) 653434 E: davies.johnd@btinternet.com

DAVIES, John Gwylim. b 27. Ripon Hall Ox 67. **d** 70 **p** 71. C Ox St Mich 70–71; C Ox St Mich w St Martin and All SS 71–72; TV New Windsor 73–77; R Hagley *Worc* 77–83; TV Littleham w Exmouth *Ex* 83–92; Asst Dioc Stewardship Adv 83–92; rtd 92; PtO *Ex* from 92. *20 Gracey Court, Woodland Road, Broadclyst, Exeter EX5 3GA* E: daviesjg70@gmail.com

DAVIES, The Very Revd John Harverd. b 57. Keble Coll Ox BA 80 MA 84 CCC Cam MPhil 82 Lanc Univ PhD. Westcott Ho Cam 82. **d** 84 **p** 85. C Liv Our Lady and St Nic w St Anne 84–87; C Pet St Jo 87–90; Min Can Pet Cathl 88–90; V Anfield St Marg *Liv* 90–94; Chapl, Fell and Lect Keble Coll Ox 94–99; V Melbourne *Derby* 99–10; P-in-c Ticknall, Smisby and Stanton by Bridge etc 07–10; V Melbourne, Ticknall, Smisby and Stanton 10; Dioc Dir of Ords 00–09; Hon Can Derby Cathl 10; Dean Derby 10–16; Dean Wells *B & W* from 16. *The Dean's Lodging, 25 The Liberty, Wells BA5 2SZ* T: (01749) 670278 E: thedeanofwells@gmail.com

DAVIES, John Hugh Conwy. b 42. Bris Univ BSc 64 PhD 67 CEng 72 MICE 72. Linc Th Coll 84. **d** 86 **p** 87. C Limber Magna w Brocklesby *Linc* 86–89; R Wickenby Gp 89–94; R Denbigh *St As* 94–00; V Llanrhaeadr-ym-Mochnant etc 01–07; rtd 07; PtO *St As* 09–14; *B & W* 16–21. *2 Delphinium Drive, Langport TA10 9TN* T: (01458) 259300 E: jackiejohnlla@gmail.com

DAVIES, Canon John Hywel Morgan. b 45. St D Coll Lamp BA 71 LTh 73. **d** 73 **p** 74. C Milford Haven *St D* 73–77; V 89–11; R Castlemartin w Warren and Angle etc 77–82; R Walton W w Talbenny and Haroldston W 82–89; Can St D Cathl 03–11; rtd 11; PtO *St D* from 11. *6 Waterloo Road, Hakin, Milford Haven SA73 3PB* T: (01646) 692766

DAVIES, John Keith. b 33. St Mich Coll Llan 80. **d** 82 **p** 83. C Llanbadarn Fawr w Capel Bangor and Goginan *St D* 82–84; V Llandygwydd and Cenarth w Cilrhedyn etc 84–89; V Abergwili w Llanfihangel-uwch-Gwili etc 89–98; RD Carmarthen 93–98; rtd 98. *Tanyfron, 81 Hafod Cwnin, Carmarthen SA31 2AS* T: (01267) 223931 E: j50ked@yahoo.co.uk

✠**DAVIES, The Rt Revd John Stewart.** b 43. Univ of Wales BA 72 Qu Coll Cam MLitt 74. Westcott Ho Cam 72. **d** 74 **p** 75 **c** 99. C Hawarden *St As* 74–78; Tutor St Deiniol's Lib Hawarden 76–83; V Rhosymedre *St As* 78–87; Dir Dioc Minl Tr Course

83–93; Warden of Ords *St As* 83–91; Hon Can St As Cathl 86–91; V Mold 87–92; Adn St As 91–99; R Llandyrnog and Llangwyfan 92–99; Bp St As 99–08; rtd 09; PtO *St As* from 09. *17 Pont y Bedol, Llanrhaeadr, Denbigh LL16 4NF* T: (01745) 890899 E: johnstewartdavies@gmail.com

DAVIES, The Ven Jonathan Byron. b 69. Univ of Wales (Cardiff) BTh 95. St Mich Coll Llan 94. **d** 96 **p** 97. C Betws w Ammanford *St D* 96–99; Dioc Youth Chapl 96–99; C Newton St Pet *S & B* 99–00; P-in-c Swansea St Luke 03–05; V Manselton and Cwmbwrla 05–15; AD Penderi 12–15; Chapl Mid and W Wales Fire and Rescue Service 05–16; Can Res Brecon Cathl *S & B* from 15; V Llwynderw from 15; Adn Gower from 16. *The Vicarage, Fairwood Road, West Cross, Swansea SA3 5JP* T: (01792) 512747 E: archdeacon.gower@churchinwales.org.uk

DAVIES, Judith. b 54. Man Univ BA 75. WEMTC 97. **d** 00 **p** 01. C Harlescott *Lich* 00–04; Chapl Shrewsbury and Telford NHS Trust 04–05; Asst Chapl Severn Hospice Shrewsbury 05–06; PtO *Heref* 05–06; TV Wenlock 06–14; rtd 14; PtO *Lich* from 15. *3 Carnforth Close, Shrewsbury SY3 9QW* E: judydaviesrev@gmail.com

DAVIES, Prof Julia Mary. b 44. Ex Univ BA 65 FCIPD 00. **d** 04 **p** 05. OLM Deane *Man* 04–14; Hon Assoc Dioc Dir of Ords from 10; PtO from 15. *15 Newland Drive, Bolton BL5 1DS* T: (01204) 660260 M: 07966-528877

DAVIES, Julian Paul. b 70. UWE BA 98 Bris Univ PhD 03. Trin Coll Bris 18. **d** 20 **p** 21. C Timsbury w Priston, Camerton and Dunkerton *B & W* from 20. *3 Wakeford Way, Warmley, Bristol BS30 5HU* T: 0117-961 8195 E: julian.davies38@gmail.com

DAVIES, Justin Wyn. Cam Coll of Art & Tech BA 82. **d** 16 **p** 17. NSM Bishopston *S & B* 16–18; C SW Gower from 18. *The Rectory, Knelston, Reynoldston, Swansea SA3 1AR* M: 07881-501292 E: justindavies26@gmail.com

DAVIES, Mrs Karen Elizabeth. b 44. Univ of Wales (Abth) BA 66 Univ of Wales (Ban) MEd 85. **d** 11 **p** 12. OLM Criftins w Dudleston and Welsh Frankton *Lich* 11–16; rtd 16; PtO *Lich* 16–21; RD Ellesmere 15–17. *2 Cherry Drive, Ellesmere, SY12 9PF* T: (01691) 624917 M: 07787-324953 E: karendavies2000@gmail.com

DAVIES, Keith. *See* DAVIES, John Keith

DAVIES, Keith. *See* BERRY-DAVIES, Charles William Keith

DAVIES, Kenneth John. b 42. Ripon Coll Cuddesdon 79. **d** 80 **p** 81. C Buckingham *Ox* 80–83; V Birstall *Wakef* 83–91; TV Crookes St Thos *Sheff* 91–94; TR Huntington *York* 94–07; rtd 07; PtO *York* from 14. *18 Hall Rise, Haxby, York YO32 3LP* T: (01904) 768211

DAVIES, Canon Kevin Godfrey. b 62. Univ Coll Ox BA 84 MA 87. Trin Coll Bris BA 93. **d** 93 **p** 94. C Otley *Bradf* 93–97; P-in-c Scotby *Carl* 97–00; P-in-c Scotby and Cotehill w Cumwhinton 00–02; TR Langtree *Ox* from 02; P-in-c Whitchurch St Mary 02–03; AD Henley 11–16; Hon Can Ch Ch from 17. *The Rectory, Checkendon, Reading RG8 0SR* T: (01491) 680252

DAVIES, Lee. b 76. St Jo Coll Nottm 12. **d** 14 **p** 15. C Andover *Win* 14–17; P-in-c Knight's Enham 17–21; PtO from 21. *2 Red Cottages, East Anton, Andover SP11 6AA* E: revlee@daviestribe.co.uk

DAVIES, Leonard Hamblyn Kenneth. b 57. Birm Univ MA 03 Dur Univ MA 06. Sierra Leone Bible Coll 84. **d** 93 **p** 94. C St Geo Cathl Freetown Sierra Leone 93–96; C Freetown St Jo 96–98; P-in-c Freetown H Spirit 98–01; PtO *Worc* 01–02; *Birm* 02–03; *Chelmsf* 03–08; LtO 08–15; Asst Chapl E Lon Univ 08–09; Asst Chapl YMCA 09–10; C Forest Gate All SS *Chelmsf* 10–15; PtO from 15. *28B High Street, London SW19 2AB* T: (020) 8542 7957 M: 07834-971467 E: kendavies90@hotmail.com

DAVIES, Lynda. b 64. Cov Univ BA 87 CQSW 87 Leic Univ MA 09. ERMC 10. **d** 13 **p** 14. C Oundle w Ashton and Benefield w Glapthorn *Pet* 13–16; C Long Stanton w St Mich *Ely* 16–17; C Over 16–17; C Willingham 16–17; C Fen Drayton w Conington and Lolworth etc 16–17; P-in-c Cottenham 17–18; P-in-c Rampton 17–18; R Cottenham w Rampton from 18. *The Rectory, 6 High Street, Cottenham, Cambridge CB24 8SA* M: 07598-927416 E: revlyndadavies559@gmail.com

DAVIES, Mrs Margaret Adelaide. b 45. Weymouth Coll of Educn CertEd 67. S Dios Minl Tr Scheme 92. **d** 95 **p** 96. NSM Westbury *Sarum* 95–02; NSM White Horse 02–11; TV 07–11; rtd 11; PtO *Sarum* from 12. *20 The Knoll, Westbury BA13 3UB* T: (01373) 228671

✠**DAVIES, The Rt Revd Mark.** b 62. Leeds Univ BA 85. Coll of Resurr Mirfield 86. **d** 89 **p** 90 **c** 08. C Barnsley St Mary *Wakef* 89–95; R Hemsworth 95–06; Dioc Vocations Adv and Asst Dir of Ords 98–06; RD Pontefract 00–06; Hon Can Wakef Cathl 02–06; Adn Rochdale *Man* 06–08; Suff Bp Middleton from

08. *504 Manchester Road, Rochdale OL11 3HE* T: (01706) 358550 F: 354851 E: bishopmark@manchester.anglican.org

DAVIES, Martin. *See* DAVIES, William Martin

DAVIES, Canon Martyn John. b 60. Chich Th Coll 82. **d** 85 **p** 86. C Llantrisant *Llan* 85–87; C Whitchurch 87–90; V Porth w Trealaw 90–01; R Merthyr Tydfil St Dav 01–10; R Merthyr Tydfil St Dav and Abercanaid 10–12; AD Merthyr Tydfil 04–12; R Peterston-super-Ely w St Brides-super-Ely 12–19; P-in-c St Nicholas w Bonvilston and St George-super-Ely 12–19; C Pendoylan w Welsh St Donats 12–19; TR E Vale from 19; AD Vale of Glam from 12; Hon Can Llan Cathl from 16. *The Rectory, Peterston-super-Ely, Cardiff CF5 6LH* T: (01446) 760498 E: fr.martyn@sky.com

DAVIES, Michael. *See* DAVIES, David Michael Cole

DAVIES, Miss Moira Kathleen. b 41. Cant Sch of Min. **d** 88 **p** 94. Par Dn Walmer *Cant* 88–94; C 94–96; P-in-c Somercotes and Grainthorpe w Conisholme *Linc* 96–99; R 99–06; rtd 06; PtO *Linc* 15–18. *9 Amanda Drive, Louth LN11 0AZ* T: (01507) 609960 E: revmoirak@btinternet.com

DAVIES, Canon Mostyn David. b 37. AKC 64. **d** 65 **p** 66. C Corby St Columba *Pet* 65–69; Ind Chapl 69–03; P-in-c Pet St Barn 80–03; Can Pet Cathl 95–03; rtd 03; PtO *Pet* 03–17; *Linc* 17–20. *92 West End, Langtoft, Peterborough PE6 9LU* T: (01778) 342838 E: mostyn@mostyn.myzen.co.uk

DAVIES, Canon Myles Cooper. b 50. Sarum & Wells Th Coll 71. **d** 74 **p** 75. C W Derby St Mary *Liv* 74–77; C Seaforth 77–80; V 80–84; V Stanley 84–07; P-in-c Liv St Paul Stoneycroft 05–07; V Stanley w Stoneycroft St Paul 07–11; Chapl Rathbone Hosp *Liv* 84–91; Chapl N Mersey Community NHS Trust 92–05; Dioc Voc Adv *Liv* 94–05; Hon Can Liv Cathl 01–05; Can Res Liv Cathl 06–21; Prec 08–21; rtd 21; Chapl Liv Cathl from 21. *7 Cathedral Close, Liverpool L1 7BR* E: myles.davies@liverpoolcathedral.org.uk

DAVIES, Nicholas Duff. b 67. Sheff Univ BA 88 Edin Univ MTh 89 Anglia Ruskin Univ MA 09 FRSA 01. Westcott Ho Cam 06. **d** 08 **p** 09. C S Dulwich St Steph *S'wark* 08–12; TV S Cheltenham *Glouc* 12–16; TR from 16; Asst Chapl Glos Univ from 16; AD Cheltenham 17–18. *The Rectory, 80 Painswick Road, Cheltenham GL50 2EU* T: (01242) 321268 M: 07801-336144 E: nickduffdavies@gmail.com

DAVIES, Nicola Louise. b 69. STETS. **d** 14 **p** 15. NSM Fordingbridge and Hyde and Breamore etc *Win* 14–20; TV Axminster, All Saints, Axmouth, Chardstock etc *Ex* from 20; PtO *Win* from 20. *The Rectory, Rhode Lane, Uplyme, Lyme Regis DT7 3TX* T: (01297) 792177 E: daviesnicky@live.co.uk

DAVIES, Canon Nigel Lawrence. b 55. Lanc Univ BEd 77. Sarum & Wells Th Coll 84. **d** 87 **p** 88. C Heywood St Luke w All So *Man* 87–91; V Burneside *Carl* 91–07; P-in-c Crosscrake 04–06; P-in-c Skelsmergh w Selside and Longsleddale 06–07; TR Beacon TM 07–20; RD Kendal 03–08; Hon Can Carl Cathl 06–20; rtd 20; V of the Close Sarum Cathl from 20. *68A The Close, Salisbury SP1 2EL*

DAVIES, Noel Paul. b 47. Chich Th Coll 83. **d** 85 **p** 86. C Milford Haven *St D* 85–89; R Jeffreyston w Reynoldston and E Williamston etc 89–09; R Jeffreyston w Reynoldston and Loveston etc 09–12; rtd 12; PtO *St D* from 12. *Hungerford Farm, Loveston, Kilgetty SA68 0NY*

DAVIES, Mrs Pamela Elizabeth. b 55. Oak Hill Th Coll 09. **d** 11 **p** 12. C Berechurch St Marg w St Mich *Chelmsf* 11–15; R Sundridge w Ide Hill and Toys Hill *Roch* from 15. *Sundridge Rectory, Chevening Road, Sundridge, Sevenoaks TN14 6AB* T: (01959) 467223

DAVIES, Canon Patricia Elizabeth. b 36. Westf Coll Lon BA 58 Hughes Hall Cam CertEd 59 Leeds Univ MA 74. NEOC 83. **dss** 86 **d** 87 **p** 94. Killingworth *Newc* 86–90; Hon C 87–90; Hon C Newc H Cross 91–96; NSM Newc Epiphany 96–99; NSM Gosforth St Hugh 99–00; P-in-c 01; Hon Can Newc Cathl 00–01; rtd 01; PtO *York* from 01. *Applegarth, Middlewood Lane, Fylingthorpe, Whitby YO22 4TT* T: (01947) 881175

DAVIES, Patrick Charles Steven. b 59. Leeds Univ BA 99 Man Univ MA 13 RGN 86 RMN 92 RHV 94. Coll of Resurr Mirfield 97. **d** 99 **p** 00. C Reddish *Man* 99–04; P-in-c Withington St Crispin 04–18; R from 18. *296 Wilbraham Road, Manchester M21 0UU* T: 0161-282 8514 M: 07967-385357 E: fr.patrick@ntlworld.com

DAVIES, Patrick John Lyndon. b 86. Falmouth Univ BA 07. Trin Coll Bris BA 20. **d** 20 **p** 21. C Oxshott *Guildf* from 20. *St Andrew's Church, Oakshade Road, Oxshott, Leatherhead KT22 0LE* M: 07988-894397 E: pjld@me.com

DAVIES, Paul. b 80. City Univ BSc 05. SEITE BA 16. **d** 16 **p** 17. C Bexleyheath Ch Ch *Roch* 16–18; C Barnehurst 18–19; NSM 19–20; PtO from 20. *36 Horsham Road, Bexleyheath DA6 7HP* M: 07582-914056 E: revpauldavies@outlook.com

DAVIES, Paul. *See* DAVIES, Richard Paul

DAVIES, Paul Lloyd. b 46. Bris Univ LLB 68 Solicitor 71. Trin Coll Carmarthen 84. **d** 87 **p** 88. NSM Newport w Cilgwyn and Dinas w Llanllawer *St D* 87–97; P-in-c Mathry w St Edren's and Grandston etc 97–01; V 01–08; rtd 08; PtO *St D* from 09. *Treetops, Osborn Park, Neyland, Milford Haven SA73 1SX* T: (01646) 602919 E: revpaullloyddavies@gmail.com

DAVIES, Paul Martin. b 35. Lon Univ BD 75. Sarum & Wells Th Coll 75. **d** 75 **p** 76. C Walthamstow St Mary w St Steph *Chelmsf* 75–79; Kenya 79–86; R Leven w Catwick *York* 86–95; RD N Holderness 90–95; rtd 95; PtO *York* from 95. *48 All Saints Court, Market Weighton, York YO43 3NT*

DAVIES, Paul Scott. b 59. Cranmer Hall Dur 85. **d** 88 **p** 89. C New Addington *S'wark* 88–91; C Croydon H Sav 91–94; P-in-c Norton in the Moors *Lich* 94–99; R 99–03; V Sunbury *Lon* 03–15; Sen P Doha Epiphany Qatar 15–19; P-in-c Bedford All SS *St Alb* from 19. *All Saints' Vicarage, 1 Cutcliffe Place, Bedford MK40 4DF* E: paul@zippor.com

DAVIES, Paul Trevor. b 85. Oak Hill Th Coll 16. **d** 19 **p** 20. C Whittle-le-Woods *Blackb* from 19. *16 Carr Meadow, Bamber Bridge, Preston PR5 8HS* M: 07934-112146 E: revptd@gmail.com

DAVIES, Peter Huw. b 57. Crewe & Alsager Coll BEd 79. Wycliffe Hall Ox 87. **d** 89 **p** 90. C Moreton *Ches* 89–93; V Weston-super-Mare St Paul *B & W* 93–05; P-in-c Chesham Bois *Ox* 05–08; R 08–13; R Sandy *St Alb* from 13. *The Rectory, 34 High Street, Sandy SG19 1AQ* T: (01767) 682499

DAVIES, Preb Peter Timothy William. b 50. Leeds Univ BSc 74. Oak Hill Th Coll 75. **d** 78 **p** 79. C Kingston Hill St Paul *S'wark* 78–81; C Hove Bp Hannington Memorial Ch *Chich* 81–88; V Audley *Lich* 88–15; P-in-c Alsagers Bank 06–15; P-in-c Talke 13–15; Preb Lich Cathl 13–15; rtd 15; PtO Lich from 16. *174 Cheadle Road, Cheddleton, Leek ST13 7BD* T: (01538) 528349

DAVIES, Canon Philip James. b 58. UEA BA 79 Keswick Hall Coll PGCE 80 K Coll Lon MA 92. Ridley Hall Cam 86. **d** 89 **p** 90. C Rainham *Roch* 89–90; C Gravesend St Geo and Rosherville 90–95; V 95–98; Dioc Schs Development Officer Pet 98–13; P-in-c King's Cliffe 98–10; C Bulwick, Blatherwycke w Harringworth and Laxton 07–10; R King's Cliffe, Bulwick and Blatherwycke etc 10–17; C Ketton, Collyweston, Easton-on-the-Hill and Tinwell 13–17; V King's Cliffe, Bulwick and Blatherwycke, Collyweston etc from 17; Can Pet Cathl from 18. *The Rectory, 3 Hall Yard, King's Cliffe, Peterborough PE8 6XQ* T: (01780) 470314 E: philip.davies1605@gmail.com

DAVIES, Philip Simon. b 65. Trin Coll Ox BA 87 MA 91. Aston Tr Scheme 93 Ridley Hall Cam 95. **d** 97 **p** 98. C Burntwood *Lich* 97–00; TV Cheswardine, Childs Ercall, Hales, Hinstock etc 00–03; TR 03–04; P-in-c Olney *Ox* 04–08; P-in-c Banbury St Hugh 08–12; PtO from 12. *5 Kedleston Rise, Banbury OX16 9TX* T: (01295) 255744 E: revdavies@btinternet.com

DAVIES, Canon Philip Wyn. b 50. Univ of Wales BA 72 MA 82 BD 96. St D Dioc Tr Course 93 St Mich Coll Llan 94. **d** 96 **p** 97. C Llandysul *St D* 96–98; V Tregaron w Ystrad Meurig and Strata Florida 98–14; P-in-c Blaenpennal 01–07; V 07–14; V Tregaron Gp 14–20; Dioc Archivist 04–20; AD Lampeter and Ultra-Aeron 11–20; Can St D Cathl 07–20; PtO from 20. *Pengerwyn, Llangrannog, Llandysul SA44 6SD* E: philipwyn@btinternet.com

DAVIES, The Ven Rachel Hannah Eileen. b 64. Ban Univ BTh 08. St Mich Coll Llan 01. **d** 04 **p** 05. NSM Lampeter and Llanddewibrefi Gp *St D* 04–06; NSM Bro Teifi Sarn Helen 06–08; P-in-c Llanerch Aeron w Ciliau Aeron and Dihewyd etc 08–19; Dioc Adv on Rural Matters 05–19; Hon Can St D Cathl 12–14; Can St D Cathl 14–19; Adn Cardigan from 19. *The Vicarage, Llanllwni, Pencader SA39 9DR* T: (01559) 395775 M: 07814-272998 E: eileengwndwn@yahoo.co.uk *or* archdeacon.cardigan@churchinwales.org.uk

DAVIES, Reginald Charles. b 33. Hull Univ MA 93 Birm Univ MPh 09. Tyndale Hall Bris 58. **d** 64 **p** 65. C Heywood St Jas *Man* 64–66; C Drypool St Columba w St Andr and St Pet *York* 66–69; V Denaby Main *Sheff* 69–20; rtd 20. *Address temp unknown* E: ailsa.reg@hotmail.co.uk

DAVIES, Rhiannon Mary Morgan. *See* JOHNSON, Rhiannon Mary Morgan

DAVIES, Richard Martin. b 56. Qu Coll Birm 19. **d** 20 **p** 21. NSM Budbrooke *Cov* from 20. *51 Arras Boulevard, Hampton Magna, Warwick CV35 8TT* T: (01926) 498377 M: 07768-725755 E: revdmartindavies@outlook.com

DAVIES, Richard Paul. b 48. Wycliffe Hall Ox 72. **d** 75 **p** 76. C Everton St Sav w St Cuth *Liv* 75–78; Chapl Aast Basingstoke Distr Hosp 78–80; TV Basingstoke *Win* 80–85; V Southampton Thornhill St Chris 85–94; V Eastleigh 94–13; rtd 13; PtO *Win* 14–18; *Sarum* from 14. *1 Woodcock*

Gardens, Warminster BA12 9JH T: (01985) 300606 E: rp.davies@yahoo.co.uk

DAVIES, The Ven Richard Paul. b 73. Univ of Wales (Lamp) BA 94 Ox Univ MTh 98. Ripon Coll Cuddesdon 94. **d** 97 **p** 98. Min Can St D Cathl 97–01; Succ 01–06; TV Dewisland *St D* 01–06; V Burry Port and Pwll 06–12; Dioc Ecum Officer 02–06; OCM 05–07; Dioc Warden Ords *St D* 11–12; Adn Ban 12–17; R Llanfair Mathafarn Eithaf w Llanbedrgoch etc 12–14; Adn Surrey *Guildf* from 17. *Archdeacon's House, Lime Grove, West Clandon, Guildford GU4 7UT* T: (01483) 212663 *or* 790366 E: archdeacon.surrey@cofeguildford.org.uk

DAVIES, Robert Emlyn. b 56. N Staffs Poly BA 79. Coll of Resurr Mirfield 83. **d** 86 **p** 87. C Cardiff St Jo *Llan* 86–90; V Cwmparc 90–97; V Aberdare from 97; AD Cynon Valley 02–08. *13 Tan y Bryn Gardens, Llwydcoed, Aberdare CF44 0TQ* T: (01685) 884769

DAVIES, Roger Charles. b 46. Univ of Wales BD 72. St Mich Coll Llan 67. **d** 73 **p** 74. C Llanfabon *Llan* 73–75; C Llanblethian w Cowbridge and Llandough etc 75–78; CF 78–84; TV Halesworth w Linstead, Chediston, Holton etc *St E* 84–87; R Claydon and Barham 87–91; R Lavant and Chapl Lavant Ho Sch 91–94; TV Gt Aycliffe and Chilton *Dur* 04–08; P-in-c Wheatley Hill and Wingate w Hutton Henry 08–13; rtd 13; PtO *Dur* 13–17 and from 19; Hon C Blackhall, Castle Eden and Monkhesleden 17–19. *19 Taylor Grove, Wingate TS28 5PA* M: 07866-649300 E: r876davies@btinternet.com

DAVIES, Mrs Sally Jane. b 63. Linc Coll Ox BA 86. Trin Coll Bris BA 92. **d** 92 **p** 94. C E Molesey St Paul *Guildf* 92–96; C Chalfont St Peter *Ox* 96–99; Chapl RN Coll Greenwich and Trin Coll of Music 99–06; Hon C Greenwich St Alfege *S'wark* 99–06; P-in-c Shamley Green *Guildf* 06–11; V from 11. *The Vicarage, Church Hill, Shamley Green, Guildford GU5 0UD* T: (01483) 892030 E: vicar@shamleygreen.net

DAVIES (née Goddard), Mrs Sara Jayne. b 65. Liv Univ BSc 87 Sheff Univ MMedSc 92. Linc Sch of Th and Min 17. **d** 19 **p** 20. NSM Graffoe Gp *Linc* from 19. *31 Priory Road, Ruskington, Sleaford NG34 9DJ* T: (01526) 834490 M: 07768-706952 E: saraj65@btinternet.com

DAVIES, Canon Sarah Isabella. b 39. Llan Dioc Tr Scheme 87. **d** 91 **p** 97. NSM Pontypridd St Cath w St Matt *Llan* 91–93; C Ferndale w Maerdy 93–00; Chapl Univ Hosp of Wales and Llandough NHS Trust 98–00; Chapl Pontypridd and Rhondda NHS Trust 98–00; C Cardiff Ch Ch Roath Park *Llan* 00–09; Dioc Child Protection Officer 02–09; Hon Can Llan Cathl 06–09; rtd 09; PtO *Llan* from 10. *4 St Augustine Road, Heath, Cardiff CF14 4BD* T: (029) 2061 0054 E: sallydavies@outlook.com

DAVIES, Scott Lee. b 73. St Jo Coll Nottm. **d** 06 **p** 07. C Childwall All SS *Liv* 06–10; V Carr Mill from 10. *St David's Vicarage, 27 Eskdale Avenue, St Helens WA11 7EN* T: (01744) 732330 E: vicar.stdavids@uwclub.net

DAVIES, Stephen. b 56. Nottm Univ BSc 77. Wycliffe Hall Ox 01. **d** 03 **p** 04. C Crawley and Littleton and Sparsholt w Lainston *Win* 03–07; V Heacham *Nor* 07–13; RD Heacham and Rising 11–13; Min Abbeydale Ch Ch LEP *Glouc* 13–18; rtd 18; PtO *St Alb* from 19. *Broadgate, Hillside Road, Leighton Buzzard LU7 3BU* E: revdstevedavies@gmail.com

DAVIES, Stephen John. b 55. Bp Otter Coll Chich BA 01 IEng 77 CEng 82. St Steph Ho Ox 96. **d** 98 **p** 99. C Leigh Park and Warren Park *Portsm* 98–02; C Durrington *Chich* 02–05; P-in-c Earnley and E Wittering 05–08; R from 08; Chapl Chich Cathl 02–19; Chapl W Sussex Police from 00. *The Rectory, Church Road, East Wittering, Chichester PO20 8PS* T: (01243) 672260 M: 07899-948493 E: frsteve@btinternet.com

DAVIES, Mrs Susan Anne. b 48. N Co Coll Newc CertEd 69. St Mich Coll Llan 98. **d** 01 **p** 02. NSM Monmouth w Overmonnow etc *Mon* 01–05; NSM Goetre w Llanover 05; TV Rossendale Middle Valley *Man* 05–13; Dioc Rural Officer 07–13; AD Rossendale 08–13; rtd 13; PtO *Sheff* from 13. *10 Grange Mews, Wickersley, Rotherham S66 1YA* T: (01709) 207098 E: susannannedavies@aol.com

DAVIES, Taffy. *See* DAVIES, Edward William Llewellyn

DAVIES, Canon Timothy Robert. b 64. Bradf Univ BSc 87. Wycliffe Hall Ox BTh 93. **d** 93 **p** 94. C Eynsham and Cassington *Ox* 93–97; C Fulwood *Sheff* 97–03; Crosslinks Assoc Ch Ch Cen from 03; Hon Can Nairobi Cathl from 08. *Egerton Hall, Fitzwilliam Street, Sheffield S1 4JR* T: 0114-273 9750 E: tim.davies@christchurchcentral.co.uk

DAVIES, Trevor. *See* DAVIES, Edward Trevor

DAVIES, The Ven Vincent Anthony (Tony). b 46. Brasted Th Coll 69 St Mich Coll Llan 71. **d** 73 **p** 74. C Owton Manor CD *Dur* 73–76; C Wandsworth St Faith *S'wark* 76–78; P-in-c 78–81; V Walworth St Jo 81–94; RD S'wark and Newington 88–93; Adn Croydon 94–11; Bp's Adv for Hosp Chapl 00–11; P-in-c Sutton New Town St Barn 04–06; rtd 11;

PtO *S'wark* from 11; *Chich* from 12. *1 High Beeches, Worthing BN11 4TJ* M: 07946-640288 E: v.a.davies@hotmail.co.uk

DAVIES, Wayne Matthew. b 71. CGH 18. d 21. C Ludlow *Heref* from 21. *St Giles Vicarage, Sheet Road, Ludlow SY8 1LR* M: 07545-438892 E: wayne.davies@hereford.anglican.org *or* wayne@wsmen.co.uk

DAVIES, William Martin. b 56. Univ of Wales (Cardiff) BSc 78. Wycliffe Hall Ox 78. d 81 p 82. C Gabalfa *Llan* 81–84; P-in-c Beguildy and Heyope *S & B* 84–85; V 85–87; V Swansea St Thos and Kilvey 87–93; V Belmont *Lon* 93–03; Asst Chapl Miss to Seafarers 87–03; Area Co-ord Leprosy Miss for Wales 04–07; Area Co-ord Lon and Essex 07–11; V Harefield *Lon* from 11. *The Vicarage, 28 Countess Close, Harefield, Uxbridge UB9 6DL* T: (01895) 825960 M: 07050-042586 E: office@stmarys-harefield.org.uk *or* martin@stmarys-harefield.org.uk

DAVIES-COLE, Charles Sylester. b 38. New Coll Dur BA BD. Edin Th Coll 66. d 66. Hon C Edin Old St Paul 66–13; Prin Teacher Jas Gillespie's High Sch 82–03; LtO *Edin* from 14. *121 Mayburn Avenue, Loanhead EH20 9ER* T: 0131-440 4190

DAVIES-HANNEN, Robert John. b 65. W Glam Inst of HE BEd 89. St Mich Coll Llan BTh 92. d 92 p 93. C Gorseinon *S & B* 92–95; P-in-c Swansea St Luke 95–02; V Llangyfelach 02–17; V Sketty from 17. *The Vicarage, De La Beche Road, Sketty, Swansea SA2 9AR* T: (01792) 774120 E: rdhannen@gmail.com

DAVIES-JAMES, Mrs Roxana Ruth de la Tour. b 56. d 05 p 06. OLM Cusop w Blakemere, Bredwardine w Brobury etc *Heref* 05–11; P-in-c Magnis Gp from 11; Dioc Chapl MU 09–13. *8 Hillside View, Credenhill, Hereford HR4 7FD* T: (01432) 760443 M: 07870-929040 E: rana.james@virgin.net

DAVILL, Robin William. b 51. SS Paul & Mary Coll Cheltenham CertEd 73 BEd 74 Leic Univ MA 79. Westcott Ho Cam 86. d 88 p 89. C Broughton *Blackb* 88–91; C Howden *York* 91–93; NSM Crayke w Brandsby and Yearsley 93–97; P-in-c 97–03; P-in-c Thirkleby w Kilburn and Bagby 03–09; P-in-c Topcliffe, Baldersby w Dishforth, Dalton etc 09–12; rtd 12; PtO *York* from 12. *Leyland House, 44 Uppleby, Easingwold, York YO61 3BB* T: (01347) 823472 E: robin@davill.eclipse.co.uk

DAVIS, Alan. b 34. Birm Univ BSc 56. Ox NSM Course. d 75 p 76. NSM Chesham St Mary *Ox* 75–80; NSM Gt Chesham 80–00; rtd 00; PtO *Ox* 00–19. *18 Wood Cutters Way, Chapel-en-le-Frith, High Peak SK23 9TQ* T: (01298) 816494

DAVIS, Alan John. b 33. St Alb Minl Tr Scheme 77. d 80 p 81. NSM Goldington *St Alb* 80–84; C Bendchill *Man* 84–86; R Gt Chart Chart 86–02; rtd 02; PtO *Cant* from 02. *8 Roberts Road, Greatstone, New Romney TN28 8RL* T: (01797) 361917 E: alanandpat.davis@yahoo.com

DAVIS, Preb Andrew Fisher. b 46. St Chad's Coll Dur BA 67 K Coll Lon MA 99 MPhil 06. St Steph Ho Ox 68. d 70 p 71. C Beckenham St Jas *Roch* 70–74; C Kensington St Mary Abbots w St Geo *Lon* 74–80; V Sudbury St Andr 80–90; AD Brent 85–90; V Ealing Ch the Sav 90–16; Preb St Paul's Cathl 07–16; rtd 16. *The End House, 17 Weavering Close, Rochester ME2 4RQ* T: (01634) 786144 M: 07973-176445 E: fr.a@btopenworld.com

DAVIS, Andrew George. b 63. Bath Univ BSc Edin Univ BD. Edin Th Coll. d 89 p 90. C Alverstoke *Portsm* 89–92; C Portsea N End St Mark 92–96; Bp's Dom Chapl 96–98; R Bishop's Waltham and Upham 98–07; V Gosport H Trin 07–20; V Gosport Ch Ch 07–20; AD Gosport 14–15; P-in-c Bramley and Grafham *Guildf* from 20. *The Vicarage, 1 Birtley Rise, Bramley, Guildford GU5 0HZ* E: revd.andydavis@gmail.com

DAVIS, Anne. *See* DAVIS, Maureen Anne

DAVIS, Canon Bernard Rex. b 33. OAM 05. Sydney Univ BA 55 Gen Th Sem (NY) MDiv 60 Newc Univ MA 67 FRSA 87. Coll of Resurr Mirfield 55. d 57 p 58. C Guildf St Nic 57–59; USA 59–61; R Wickham Australia 62–66; Studies Sec ACC 66–68; Exec Sec Unit 3 WCC Geneva 68–77; Warden Edw K Ho 77–03; Can Res and Subdean Linc Cathl 77–03; PtO *S'well* 01–03; rtd 03; PtO *Lon* from 06; *Eur* from 06. *425 Bromyard House, Bromyard Avenue, London W3 7BY* T: (020) 8743 0181 E: subdean@aol.com

DAVIS, Canon Brian. b 40. AKC 69 BD 69. St Aug Coll Cant 69. d 70 p 71. C Humberstone *Leic* 70–73; C Kirby Muxloe 73–74; V Countesthorpe w Foston 74–91; RD Guthlaxton I 90–91; V Hinckley St Mary 91–10; RD Sparkenhoe W 92–02; Hon Can Leic Cathl 94–10; Bp's Adv for Wholeness and Healing 04–10; rtd 10; PtO *Leic* 10–13 and from 21; P-in-c Gaulby 13–21. *62 Lubenham Hill, Market Harborough LE16 9DQ* T: (01858) 431843 E: revbdavis@aol.com

DAVIS, Mrs Bryony Elizabeth. b 64. Ban Univ BTh 09 DipCOT 86. EAMTC 99. d 02 p 03. C Beccles St Mich *St E* 02–05; P-in-c Ottershaw *Guildf* 05–08; rtd 08; Chapl HM

Pris Bronzefield 10–18; Methodist Min from 10; PtO *Guildf* 11–18; Chapl HM Pris Leyhill from 18. *HM Prison Leyhill, Wootton-under-Edge, Gloucester GL12 8BT* T: (01454) 264000 E: bryony@tiscali.co.uk

DAVIS, Christopher James. b 63. Worc Coll Ox BA 85. Cranmer Hall Dur 88. d 91 p 92. C Margate H Trin *Cant* 91–94; C Cambridge H Sepulchre *Ely* 94–00; C Wimbledon Em Ridgway Prop Chpl *S'wark* 00–04; R Tooting Graveney St Nic from 04. *The Rectory, 20A Rectory Lane, London SW17 9QJ* T: (020) 8672 7691

DAVIS, Clinton Ernest Newman. b 46. Solicitor 71. Wycliffe Hall Ox 78. d 80 p 81. C Margate H Trin *Cant* 80–84; C St Laur in Thanet 84–87; V Sandgate St Paul 87–92; P-in-c Folkestone St Geo 92; V Sandgate St Paul w Folkestone St Geo 92–97; Chapl HM Pris Standford Hill 97–08; rtd 08; PtO *Cant* from 08. *Springfield, 39 Ashford Road, Maidstone ME14 5DP* T: (01622) 682330 E: clintonendavis@btinternet.com

DAVIS, Colin Anthony John. b 65. St Jo Coll Nottm. d 99 p 00. C Bletchley *Ox* 99–02; C S Molton w Nymet St George, High Bray etc *Ex* 02–03; TV 03–10; I Carrowdore w Millisle *D & D* from 10. *15 Kilbright Road, Carrowdore, Newtownards BT22 2HQ* T: (028) 9186 1802 M: 07768-781357 E: revcol23@btinternet.com

DAVIS, Canon Edward Gabriel Anastasius. b 75. R Holloway Coll Lon BA 97. Trin Coll Bris BA 02. d 03 p 04. C Boldmere *Birm* 03–06; Chapl Aston Univ 06; Chapl Bris Univ from 07; NSM Inner Ring Partnership from 07; Hon Can Bris Cathl from 17. *67 Waverley Road, Bristol BS6 6ET* T: 0117-942 5390 E: ed.davis@bris.ac.uk

DAVIS, Mrs Elizabeth Jane. b 42. S'wark Ord Course 91. d 94 p 95. NSM Plaistow St Mary *Roch* 94–99; NSM Bromley St Andr from 99. *11 Park Avenue, Bromley BR1 4EF* T: (020) 8460 4672 E: elizabeth.irwin.davis@gmail.com

DAVIS (née GENT), Emily Louise. b 88. Cant Ch Ch Univ BA 10. St Steph Ho Ox BA 13. d 14 p 15. C Bishop's Stortford St Mich *St Alb* 14–17; C Easthampstead *Ox* 17–20; NSM Huntingdon *Ely* from 20; Chapl NW Anglia NHS Foundn Trust from 21. *1 The Wales East, Huntingdon PE29 3AP* M: 07464-292353 E: rev.emilyldavis@gmail.com

DAVIS, Felicity Ann. *See* SMITH, Felicity Ann

DAVIS, Geoffrey. *See* DAVIS, Ronald Geoffrey

DAVIS, George Shaun. b 75. Middx Univ BA 01 Lon Inst of Educn PGCE 02 Leeds Univ BA 10. Coll of Resurr Mirfield 08. d 10 p 11. C W Bromwich All SS *Lich* 10–14; TV Worc SE 14–18; TV N Cheltenham *Glouc* from 18. *The Rectory, Rectory Lane, Swindon Village, Cheltenham GL51 9RD* E: fr.georgedavis@hotmail.com

DAVIS, Canon Herbert Roger. b 36. Kelham Th Coll 60. d 65 p 66. C Barkingside St Fran *Chelmsf* 65–69; C Harpenden St Nic *St Alb* 69–73; P-in-c Eaton Bray 73–75; P-in-c Eaton Bray w Edlesborough 75; V 75–81; RD Dunstable 77–81; R Gt Berkhamsted 81–95; Hon Can St Alb 93–95; rtd 99. *5 St Thomas Terrace, St Thomas Street, Wells BA5 2XG* T: (01749) 677195

DAVIS, Mrs Jacqueline. b 47. Cant Ch Ch Univ Coll BA 01. d 05 p 06. OLM Upchurch w Lower Halstow *Cant* 05–13; NSM The Six 13–14. *Mill House, The Street, Lower Halstow, Sittingbourne ME9 7DY* T: (01795) 842557 E: revjackytd@gmail.com

DAVIS, Jennifer Anne Stanway. b 38. SWMTC 04. d 05 p 06. NSM Cullompton, Willand, Uffculme, Kentisbeare etc *Ex* 06–08; rtd 08; PtO *B & W* from 09; *Sarum* from 11. *36 Church Acre, Bradford-on-Avon BA15 1RL* T: (01225) 866479

DAVIS, Mrs Jessica Hazel. b 80. St Mellitus Coll BA 18. d 18 p 19. C Brunswick *Man* 18–21; P-in-c Birstall Leeds from 21. *The Vicarage, Kings Drive, Birstall, Batley WF17 9JJ* E: revjessdavis@gmail.com

DAVIS, Mrs Joanna Helen. b 82. Ex Univ BA 04 K Coll Lon PGCE 05. St Jo Coll Nottm MTh 10. d 10 p 11. C Inglewood Gp *Carl* 10–14; Chapl Milton Abbey Sch *Dorset* 14–19; Chapl Bryanston Sch from 19. *Woodlands, The Drive, Bryanston, Blandford Forum DT11 0PS* T: (01258) 452411 E: joannahelendavis@hotmail.com

DAVIS, John George. b 65. Roehampton Inst BSc 87 S Glam Inst HE PGCE 88. St Steph Ho Ox BTh 96. d 96 p 97. C Newton Nottage *Llan* 96–00; V Tredegar *Mon* 00–18; TR Whitchurch *Llan* from 18. *The Rectory, 6 Penlline Road, Cardiff CF14 2AD* T: (029) 2062 6072 E: stgandj@gmail.com

DAVIS, John James. b 48. MBE 08. Keele Univ MA 93 Staffs Univ PGCE 98. Qu Coll Birm BA 05. d 05 p 06. NSM Baswich *Lich* 05–08; NSM Bradeley, Church Eaton, Derrington and Haughton 08–09; NSM Stafford 09–13; NSM Stafford St Mary and Marston 13–18; NSM Stafford St Chad 13–18; RD Stafford 11–15; CF (ACF) 06–09; Chapl Abbots Bromley Sch

13; PtO *Lich* from 18. *Stockton Croft, 87 Weeping Cross, Stafford ST17 0DQ* T: (01785) 661382 E: john_davis19@sky.com

DAVIS, Miss Judith Alison. b 88. Cam Univ BTh 11 Sheff Univ MA 14. Ridley Hall Cam 08. **d** 11 **p** 12. C Doncaster St Geo *Sheff* 11–14; P-in-c Hathersage w Bamford and Derwent and Grindleford *Derby* 14–17; R 17–19; Adv for Women in Min 18–19. *24 Roe Lane, Southport PR9 9DX* E: jude.davis@churcharmy.org

DAVIS, Mrs Kathleen Mary. b 37. Derby Coll of Educn TCert 58. **d** 07 **p** 08. OLM Morley *Wakef* 07–14; *Leeds* from 14. *13 New Park Street, Morley, Leeds LS27 0PT* T: 0113-253 4521

DAVIS, Lloyd Martin. b 88. Cant Ch Ch Univ BA 11 Dur Univ MA 20. Ridley Hall Cam 17. **d** 19 **p** 20. C Huntingdon *Ely* from 19. *1 The Walks East, Huntingdon PE29 3AP* T: (01480) 536813 M: 07458-303047 E: lloyd@huntingdonparish.org

DAVIS, Mrs Lucy Frances. b 72. Keble Coll Ox BA 93 Lon Inst of Educn PGCE 94. ERMC 09. **d** 12 **p** 13. NSM Redbourn *St Alb* 12–15; V Flitwick 15–21; V Bedford St Andr from 21. *The Vicarage, 1 St Edmond Road, Bedford MK40 2NQ* M: 07803-357891 E: vicar@standrewsbedford.org

DAVIS, Margaret Ann. b 59. Kingston Poly BA 81 Liv Univ MSc 93 RGN 85. Westcott Ho Cam 06. **d** 08 **p** 09. C Abbots Langley *St Alb* 08–11; P-in-c Clavering and Langley w Arkesden etc *Chelmsf* 11–13; V Clavering w Langley, Arkesden etc from 13; RD Saffron Walden 20–21. *The Vicarage, 54 Pelham Road, Clavering, Saffron Walden CB11 4PQ* T: (01799) 550703 E: m.davis.sasha@gmail.com

DAVIS, Martin John. b 59. Van Mildert Coll Dur BSc 80 K Coll Lon MA 11. Ox Min Course 07. **d** 09 **p** 10. C Colnbrook and Datchet *Ox* 09–13; PtO 14–15; TV Kidlington w Hampton Poyle from 15. *St John's Vicarage, 16 Broadway, Kidlington OX5 1EF* T: (01865) 421316 M: 07909-976637 E: martindavis26@tiscali.co.uk

DAVIS, Matthew Peter. **d** 18 **p** 19. C Cyncoed *Mon* 18–21; Min Area Ldr Tredegar from 21. *Address temp unknown* M: 07535-812191 E: mattdavisciw@gmail.com

DAVIS, Matthew William. b 82. Rob Coll Cam BA 06 MA 09 MSci 06 PhD 11 MInstP. Oak Hill Th Coll BA 16. **d** 16 **p** 17. C Toxteth St Philemon w St Gabr and St Cleopas *Liv* 16–17; C Aigburth 17–20; V Formby St Luke from 20. *St Luke's Vicarage, St Luke's Church Road, Formby, Liverpool L37 2DF* T: (01704) 871439 M: 07989-846871 E: revmattdavis@gmail.com

DAVIS, Maureen Anne. b 59. St Hilda's Coll Ox BA 80 MA 84. NOC 96. **d** 99 **p** 00. NSM Plemstall w Guilden Sutton *Ches* 99–01; C Ches St Mary 01–03; R Woodchurch 03–16; Hon Can Ches Cathl 11–16; V Northampton St Benedict *Pet* 16–21; rtd 21. *Address temp unknown* M: 07974-816390 E: marianne2june@gmail.com

DAVIS, Miriam Ruth Bowater. b 53. Cam Univ BA 75 York Univ MA 78 Man Univ PGCE 79. CGH 20. **d** 21. OLM Hucclecote *Glouc* from 21. *19C Dinglewell, Hucclecote, Gloucester GL3 3HW* T: (01452) 621950 M: 07964-825869 E: miriam.davis@omfmail.com

DAVIS, Nicholas Anthony Wylie. b 56. Univ of Wales (Lamp) BA 80. Chich Th Coll 82. **d** 84 **p** 85. C N Lambeth *S'wark* 84–88; TV Catford (Southend) and Downham 88–94; V Camberwell St Phil and St Mark 94–04; V Shrub End *Chelmsf* 04–19; rtd 19. *27 Cecil Road, Northampton NN2 6PG* E: nicholasdavis676@btinternet.com

DAVIS, Nicholas Edward. b 75. Univ of Wales (Ban) BD 96. Coll of Resurr Mirfield 98. **d** 00 **p** 01. C Darwen St Cuth w Tockholes St Steph *Blackb* 00–05; P-in-c Tarleton 05–11; P-in-c Rufford 07–11; P-in-c Rufford and Tarleton 11–12; R 12–16; P-in-c Hesketh w Becconsall 07–16; P-in-c Darwen St Cuth w Tockholes St Steph from 16. *St Cuthbert's Vicarage, 21 The Meadows, Darwen BB3 0PF* T: (01254) 701360 E: httarleton@hotmail.com or darwen.tockholes.priest@gmail.com

DAVIS, Canon Norman. b 38. Oak Hill Th Coll 77. **d** 79 **p** 80. C Walton *St E* 79–82; P-in-c Grundisburgh w Burgh 82–91; P-in-c Bredfield w Boulge 86–91; R Boulge w Burgh and Grundisburgh 91–03; P-in-c Ufford w Bredfield and Hasketon 01–03; R Boulge w Burgh, Grundisburgh and Hasketon 03–04; RD Woodbridge 90–96; Hon Can St E Cathl 01–04; rtd 04; PtO *St E* 04–19. *The Randalls, Front Street, Orford, Woodbridge IP12 2LN* T: (01394) 459449 E: n.l.davis@btinternet.com

DAVIS, Norman John. b 41. Oak Hill Th Coll 63. **d** 66 **p** 67. C Wellington w Eyton *Lich* 66–70; C Higher Openshaw *Man* 70–72; R S Levenshulme 72–79; P-in-c Berrow w Pendock and Eldersfield *Worc* 79–81; V 81–87; R Churchill-in-Halfshire w Blakedown and Broome 87–07; rtd 07; PtO *Worc* from 08. *48 Waterside Grange, Kidderminster DY10 2LA* T: (01562) 750079 M: 07792-119278 E: norsue16@yahoo.co.uk

DAVIS, Peter Thomas. b 61. Flinders Univ Aus BTh 87 MThSt 02. St Barn Coll Adelaide 83. **d** 87 **p** 87. C Modbury and Dioc Youth Chapl Adelaide Australia 87–89; C Port Lincoln 89–91; TV Gt and Lt Coates w Bradley *Linc* 91–92; Dioc Youth Officer Adelaide Australia 92–94; P-in-c Parafield Gardens St Barbara 94–98; R Elizabeth H Cross 98–01; Chapl Anglicare S 98–01; V Satley, Stanley and Tow Law *Dur* 01–04. *5 Mercury Court, 4 Eversholt Street, London NW1 1BR* M: 07795-417337 E: montedog2000@yahoo.co.uk

DAVIS, Rex. *See* DAVIS, Bernard Rex

DAVIS, Roger. *See* DAVIS, Herbert Roger

DAVIS, Ronald Geoffrey. b 47. St Jo Coll Nottm 79. **d** 81 **p** 81. C Maidstone St Luke *Cant* 81–84; P-in-c Lostwithiel *Truro* 84–86; P-in-c Lanhydrock 84–86; Asst Dioc Youth Officer 84–86; P-in-c Boughton Monchelsea *Cant* 86–88; V 88–15; Six Preacher Cant Cathl 94–99; C-in-c Parkwood CD 95–98; AD N Downs 99–02; rtd 15; PtO *Cant* from 15; *Truro* from 16. *3 The Links, Falmouth TR11 5UJ* T: (01326) 619468 M: 07802-422991

DAVIS, Royston Grandfield. b 33. Sarum & Wells Th Coll 86. **d** 88 **p** 89. C Cainscross w Selsley *Glouc* 88–90; TV Hugglescote w Donington, Ellistown and Snibston *Leic* 90–93; P-in-c Gilmorton w Peatling Parva and Kimcote etc 93–95; R Ogwell and Denbury *Ex* 95–99; rtd 00; OSB from 00. *22 Lock House, Keeper Close, Taunton TA1 1AX* T: (01823) 974467 E: royston.davis@prcdtr.org.uk

DAVIS, Ruth Elizabeth. *See* TAIT, Ruth Elizabeth

DAVIS, Simon Charles. b 63. Plymouth Poly BSc 86 Univ of Wales (Lamp) MTh 08 MIET. Trin Coll Bris BA 92. **d** 92 **p** 93. C Bollington St Jo *Ches* 92–96; P-in-c Abbots Bromley w Blithfield *Lich* 96–10; P-in-c Colton, Colwich and Gt Haywood 05–10; R Abbots Bromley, Blithfield, Colton, Colwich etc from 11; RD Rugeley from 15. *The Vicarage, Market Place, Abbots Bromley, Rugeley WS15 3BP* T: (01283) 840242 E: revdsimon@gmail.com

DAVIS, Susan Elizabeth Mary. *See* CLARKE, Susan Elizabeth Mary

DAVIS, Terence Lionel. b 46. FCA 72. **d** 16 **p** 17. NSM Llanilar w Rhostie and Llangwyryfon etc *St D* 16–20; NSM Bro Wyre from 20. *Felinpontfaen, Llangwyryfon, Aberystwyth SY23 4HA* T: (01974) 241653 E: terryd147@hotmail.co.uk

DAVIS, Thomas Henry. b 60. OLM course 97 Coll of Resurr Mirfield 05. **d** 99 **p** 00. OLM Sudbury and Chilton *St E* 99–03; NSM Preston St Jo and St Geo *Blackb* 03–05; C Torrisholme 05–08; C Blackpool St Steph 08–09; PtO 09–10; C Morecambe St Barn 10–12; V 12–17; V Douglas St Matt *S & M* 17–19; V Hollinwood and Limeside *Man* from 19. *St Margaret's Vicarage, Chapel Road, Oldham OL8 4QQ* T: 0161-681 4541 M: 07854-770360 E: father.tom@live.co.uk

DAVIS, Timothy Alwyn. b 74. Trin Coll Bris BTh. **d** 01 **p** 02. C Crich and S Wingfield *Derby* 01–05; V Leyton St Mary w St Edw and St Luke *Chelmsf* 05–10; V Clifton w Newton and Brownsover *Cov* 10–18; TV Dunstable *St Alb* from 18; Chapl All SS Academy Dunstable from 18; Chapl Manshead Academy Luton from 18. *St Fremund's Vicarage, 20 Friars Walk, Dunstable LU6 3JA* T: (01582) 477401 E: revd.timdavis@yahoo.co.uk

DAVIS, Mrs Yvonne Annie. b 30. CQSW 75. **d** 96 **p** 97. OLM Purley St Barn *S'wark* 96–00; PtO from 00. *8 Meadow Hill, Purley CR8 3HL* T: (020) 3441 9348 E: yvonnea.davis@talktalk.net

DAVISON, Canon Andrew Paul. b 74. Mert Coll Ox BA 96 MA 99 DPhil 00 CCC Cam BA 02 MA 08 PhD 13. Westcott Ho Cam 00 Ven English Coll Rome 02. **d** 03 **p** 04. C Bellingham St Dunstan *S'wark* 03–06; Tutor and Fell St Steph Ho Ox 06–10; Jun Chapl Mert Coll Ox 06–10; Tutor Westcott Ho Cam 10–14; Lect Div Cam Univ from 14; Fell CCC Cam from 14; Dean of Chpl from 19; Hon Can St Alb 15–21. *Faculty of Divinity, West Road, Cambridge CB3 9BS* T: (01223) 763027 E: apd31@cam.ac.uk

DAVISON, Deborah Karin Mary. b 56. Ex Univ BA 79 SRN 83 RHV 85. Ripon Coll Cuddesdon 09. **d** 11 **p** 12. C Boyne Hill *Ox* 11–13; C Wokingham St Paul 13–15; C Newbury St Geo and St Jo 15–19; R Paisley H Trin and St Barn *Glas* from 19; R Glas Gd Shep from 19. *31 Westfield Drive, Glasgow G52 2SG* M: 07833-935901

✠**DAVISON, The Rt Revd George Thomas William.** b 65. St Andr Univ BD 88. Oak Hill Th Coll 88 CITC BTh 92. **d** 92 **p** 93 **c** 20. C Portadown St Mark *Arm* 92–95; I Kinawley w H Trin *K, E & A* 95–09; Dir of Ords 97–09; Preb Kilmore Cathl 02–03; adn Kilmore 03–09; I Carrickfergus *Conn* 09–20; Adn Belfast 13–20; Bp Conn from 20. *Bishop's House, 27 Grange Road, Doagh, Ballyclare BT39 0RQ* T: (028) 9082 8870 E: bishop@connor.anglican.org

DAVISON, Philip Anthony. b 66. Magd Coll Cam BA 88 MA 93. Cuddesdon Coll BA 98. **d** 98 **p** 99. C Lancaster St Mary w St John and St Anne *Blackb* 98–02; P-in-c Feniscowles

02–08; R Finchley St Mary *Lon* from 08; Warden of Readers Edmonton Area from 17. *St Mary's Rectory, Rectory Close, London N3 1TS* T: (020) 8346 4600 *or* 8248 3818 F: 8248 3818 E: rector@stmaryatfinchley.org.uk

DAVISON, Canon Richard Ireland. b 42. St Chad's Coll Dur BSc 63. Linc Th Coll 64. **d** 66 **p** 67. C Cockerton *Dur* 66–70; C Houghton le Spring 70–73; V Heworth St Alb 73–80; Ascension Is 80–82; V Dunston *Dur* 82–85; V Bishopwearmouth Ch Ch 85–98; AD Wearmouth 94–99; P-in-c Dur St Giles 99–00; V 00–08; P-in-c Shadforth and Sherburn 03–08; Hon Can Dur Cathl 97–08; AD Dur 06–08; rtd 08; PtO Dur from 08. *16 Loraine Crescent, Darlington DL1 5TF* T: (01325) 486999 E: ridavison@hotmail.co.uk

DAVY, Mrs Helen Mary. b 44. **d** 05 **p** 06. OLM Kirton w Falkenham *St E* 05–06; OLM Nacton and Levington w Bucklesham etc 06–13; NSM 13–15; PtO from 15. *9 Roman Way, Felixstowe IP11 9NJ* T: (01394) 270703

DAVY, Martin Edward. b 82. Hull Univ LLB 03 Nottm Trent Univ LLM 05. Oak Hill Th Coll BA 16. **d** 16 **p** 17. C Morden *S'wark* 16–19; V Theale *Ox* from 19. *The Rectory, Englefield Road, Theale, Reading RG7 5AS* M: 07306-618147 E: martindavy@holytrinitytheale.org.uk

DAVY, Peter Geoffrey. b 31. St Pet Coll Saltley TCert 54. SWMTC 93. **d** 94 **p** 94. NSM St Columb Minor and St Colan *Truro* 94–99; rtd 99; PtO *Truro* from 00. *9 Tredour Road, Newquay TR7 2EY* T: (01637) 872241 E: gdavy9@googlemail.com

DAVYS, Mark Andrew. b 66. St Cath Coll Ox BA 87 MA 97 Keele Univ MA 01 Qu Coll Birm BA 04 Solicitor 90. WMMTC 01. **d** 04 **p** 05. NSM Colton, Colwich and St Haywood *Lich* 04–10; NSM Abbots Bromley, Blithfield, Colton, Colwich etc from 11. *Deer's Leap, Meadow Lane, Little Haywood, Stafford ST18 0TT* T: (01889) 883722 E: revmdavys@gmail.com

DAW, Geoffrey Martin. b 57. Oak Hill Th Coll 81. **d** 84 **p** 85. C Hollington St Leon *Chich* 84–87; C Seaford w Sutton 87–90; V Iford w Kingston and Rodmell 90–13; V Iford w Kingston and Rodmell and Southease from 13; RD Lewes and Seaford 08–17. *The Rectory, 14 Lockitt Way, Kingston, Lewes BN7 3LG* T: (01273) 473665 E: geoffrey.daw@btinternet.com

DAW, Nicholas William. b 69. **d** 13 **p** 14. NSM Worc SE 13–16; NSM Worc St Wulstan 16–17. *21 Oak Avenue, Worcester WR4 9UG* T: (01905) 745645 E: revdnickdaw@gmail.com

DAWES, Mrs Helen Elizabeth. b 74. Trin Coll Cam BA 96 MA 00. Westcott Ho Cam 99. **d** 02 **p** 03. C Chesterton St Andr *Ely* 02–05; P-in-c Sandon, Wallington and Rushden w Clothall *St Alb* 05–09; Dep Public Affairs Sec to Abp Cant 09–13; Abp's Soc and Public Affairs Adv 13–15; TR Shaftesbury *Sarum* 15–21; Dean of Women's Min 16–21; Prin Westcott Ho Cam from 21. *Westcott House, Jesus Lane, Cambridge CB5 8BP* T: (01223) 741000 E: principal@westcott.cam.ac.uk

DAWES, Hugh William. b 48. Univ Coll Ox BA 71 MA 76. Cuddesdon Coll 71. **d** 74 **p** 75. C Purley St Mark *S'wark* 74–77; Chapl G&C Coll Cam 77–82; Chapl Em Coll Cam 82–87; V Cambridge St Jas *Ely* 87–00; Dir Focus Chr Inst Cambridge 87–00; V N Dulwich St Faith *S'wark* 00–10; rtd 10; PtO *S'wark* from 10; *Guildf* 11–20. *8 The Wells, Lower Street, Haslemere GU27 2PA* T: (01428) 652466 E: jill@jericho-road.org

DAWKES, Peter. b 31. Roch Th Coll 64. **d** 66 **p** 67. C Newbold w Dunston *Derby* 66–69; C Buxton 69–72; V Somercotes 72–93; rtd 93; Hon C Kenton, Mamhead, Powderham, Cofton and Starcross *Ex* 93–14; PtO 14–21. *115 Exeter Road, Dawlish EX7 0AN* T: (01626) 862593

DAWKIN, Peter William. b 60. Nottm Univ BTh 88 Open Univ BA 91. St Jo Coll Nottm 85. **d** 88 **p** 89. C Birkdale St Jo *Liv* 88–91; C Netherton 91–93; V Liv Ch Ch Norris Green 93–03; Assoc Min Wigan Deaneries 03–06; V Hough Green St Basil and All SS from 06. *339 Ditchfield Road, Widnes WA8 8XR* T: 0151-420 4963 M: 07852-484802 E: peter.dawkin@btinternet.com

DAWKINS (*née* LEWIS-MORRIS), **Mrs Catherine Mary.** b 76. St Hilda's Coll Ox MA 98 Qu Mary Coll Lon MSc 01 Peterho Cam BA 08. Ridley Hall Cam 06. **d** 10 **p** 11. C Aden Yemen 10–11; C Dubai UAE 11–12; PtO *S'wark* 12–15; LtO from 15; PtO *Chich* from 17; Hon Min Can S'wark Cathl 15–17. *41 Harestone Hill, Caterham CR3 6SG* E: catherinemarydawkins@gmail.com

DAWKINS, Ms Jennifer Claire. b 76. Nottm Univ BA 97 SOAS Lon MSc 05 Wolfs Coll Cam BTh 13. Ridley Hall Cam 11. **d** 13 **p** 14. C Peckham All SS *S'wark* from 13. *18 Martock Court, Consort Road, London SE15 2PL* M: 07773-963198 E: jennydawkins@hotmail.com *or* jenny.dawkins@allsaintspeckham.org.uk

DAWKINS, John Haswell. b 47. MBIM 81. NEOC 98. **d** 01 **p** 02. NSM Barmby Moor Gp *York* 01–11; PtO from 17. *Norton Grove Lodge, Scarborough Road, Norton, Malton YO17 8AE*

DAWKINS, Michael Howard. b 44. Bris Univ BTh 68 Man Univ MA 96. Tyndale Hall Bris 67. **d** 69 **p** 69. C Drypool St Columba w St Andr and St Pet *York* 69–73; CF 74–80; P-in-c Bulford *Sarum* 80–81; P-in-c Figheldean w Milston 80–81; R Meriden *Cov* 85–09; rtd 09. *60 Wassell Road, Wollescote, Stourbridge DY9 9DB* T: (01384) 893299 M: 07854-833460 E: mhdawkins@aol.com

DAWKINS, Nigel Jonathan. b 72. St Jo Coll Ox BA 94 MA 97 Univ Coll Lon MSc 97 Peterho Cam BA 05 MA 07. Westcott Ho Cam 03. **d** 06 **p** 07. C Caterham *S'wark* 06–09; Chapl Aden Ch Ch and Yemen 09–11; Chapl Miss to Seafarers Dubai and UAE 11–12; PtO *S'wark* 12–13; Min Can and Sacr St Paul's Cathl *Lon* 13–14; PtO *S'wark* 15–16; NSM Caterham 16–17. *41 Harestone Hill, Caterham CR3 6SG* E: nigeldawkins@gmail.com

DAWKINS, Staffan Anthony. b 69. SEITE 12. **d** 15 **p** 16. C Stanground and Farcet *Ely* 15–17; C Whittlesey, Pondersbridge and Coates 17–18; V Tottenham St Paul *Lon* from 18. *St Paul's Vicarage, 60 Park Lane, London N17 0JR* M: 07481-861817 E: staffan.dawkins@gmail.com

DAWN, Maggi Eleanor. b 59. Fitzw Coll Cam MA 96 Selw Coll Cam PhD 02. Ridley Hall Cam 96. **d** 99 **p** 00. C Ely 99–01; Chapl K Coll Cam 01–03; Chapl and Fell Rob Coll Cam 03–11; Assoc Dean and Prof Yale Div Sch USA 11–19; Prin St Mary's Coll Dur from 19; Prof Th Dur Univ from 19; PtO *Dur* from 21. *St Mary's College, Elvet Hill Road, Durham DH1 3LR* E: maggi.dawn@durham.ac.uk

DAWSON, Alan David Hough. b 67. St Jo Coll Dur BA 09 ACIB 92. Cranmer Hall Dur 07. **d** 09 **p** 10. C Hale and Ashley *Ches* 09–13; V Neston from 13. *The Vicarage, High Street, Neston CH64 9TZ* T: 0151-353 1000 M: 07919-278104 E: alan.dawson21@btinternet.com

DAWSON, Andrew. See DAWSON, William James Andrew

DAWSON, Andrew. See DAWSON, Francis Andrew Oliver Duff

DAWSON, Miss Anne. b 54. Nottm Univ BA 76 Hull Coll of Educn PGCE 77. NEOC 03. **d** 06 **p** 07. NSM Market Weighton *York* 06–09; P-in-c Sigglesthorne w Nunkeeling and Bewholme 10–11; rtd 11; PtO *York* 11–21. *23 Sloe Lane, Beverley HU17 8ND* T: (01482) 862940 E: andaw@andaw.karoo.co.uk

DAWSON, Barry. b 38. Oak Hill Th Coll 63. **d** 66 **p** 67. C Fulham St Mary N End *Lon* 66–69; C St Marylebone All So w SS Pet and Jo 69–73; Bp's Chapl *Nor* 73–76; Gen Sec CEMS 76–81; V Rye Park St Cuth *St Alb* 81–89; V Attenborough *S'well* 89–98; rtd 98; PtO *S'well* 98–14. *27 Orlando Drive, Carlton, Nottingham NG4 3FN*

DAWSON, Canon Brian. b 33. Leeds Univ BA 54 Man Univ MA 84 Newc Univ MPhil 01. Coll of Resurr Mirfield 56. **d** 58 **p** 59. C Hollinwood *Man* 58–62; C Rawmarsh w Parkgate *Sheff* 62–63; V Royton St Anne *Man* 63–75; V Urswick *Carl* 75–86; V Bardsea 75–86; R Skelton and Hutton-in-the-Forest w Ivegill 86–98; RD Penrith 91–96; Hon Can Carl Cathl 94–98; rtd 98; PtO *Carl* from 98. *Apple Croft, High Hesket, Carlisle CA4 0HS* T: (016974) 73069 E: b.dawson324@btinternet.com

DAWSON, Miss Claire Louise. b 68. Nottm Poly BA 92 CQSW 92 Nottm Univ MA 04. EMMTC 01. **d** 04 **p** 05. C Mansfield Woodhouse *S'well* 04–05; C Sutton in Ashfield St Mary 05–08; C Orrell Hey St Jo and St Jas *Liv* 08–11; P-in-c 11–17; P-in-c Litherland St Phil 15–17; V Sheff St Mary Bramall Lane from 17; P-in-c Endcliffe from 17. *St Mary's Vicarage, 42 Charlotte Road, Sheffield S1 4TL* T: 0114-272 4987 E: cdawson@blueyonder.co.uk

DAWSON, Ms Cordella. Birkbeck Coll Lon LLB 02. St Aug Coll of Th 16. **d** 18 **p** 19. C Croydon Woodside *S'wark* from 18. *101 Albert Road, London SE25 4JE* M: 07702-616008 E: curate.woodside@gmail.com

DAWSON, David. b 57. TISEC 99. **d** 99 **p** 00. NSM Kirkwall *Ab* from 99; P-in-c 05–10; R from 10. *St Olaf's Rectory, Dundas Crescent, Kirkwall, Orkney KW15 1JQ* T: (01856) 872024 M: 07881-932657 E: ddawson572@gmail.com

DAWSON, Francis Andrew Oliver Duff. b 48. Keble Coll Ox BA 70 MA 74. St Jo Coll Nottm 74. **d** 76 **p** 77. C Billericay St Mary *Chelmsf* 76–77; C Billericay and Lt Burstead 77–80; C Childwall All SS *Liv* 80–84; Chapl St Kath Coll 80–84; V Shevington *Blackb* 84–97; Internat Officer and Team Ldr for Evang Affairs *Man* 97–03; P-in-c Werneth 03–14; rtd 14; PtO *Ches* from 14; *Man* from 14. *3 Woodside Drive, Hyde SK14 5QB* T: 0161-368 2129 E: andrewdawson51@hotmail.com

DAWSON, The Ven Hilary Joan. b 64. Univ of Wales (Lamp) BA 85 UWE PGCE 89 Ex Univ MA 08. SWMTC 05. **d** 08 **p** 09. C Thorverton, Cadbury, Upton Pyne etc *Ex* 08–10; C Brampford

Speke, Cadbury, Newton St Cyres etc 10–11; P-in-c Colyton, Musbury, Southleigh and Branscombe 11–15; R 15–19; Preb Ex Cathl 17–19; Adn Glouc from 19; Can Res Glouc Cathl from 19. *9 College Green, Gloucester GL1 2LX* T: (01452) 835555   E: hilary.dawson2@btinternet.com   *or* archdglos@glosdioc.org.uk

DAWSON, John William Arthur. b 43. EMMTC. d 95 p 96. NSM Breedon cum Isley Walton and Worthington *Leic* 95–05; NSM Ashby-de-la-Zouch and Breedon on the Hill 05–16; PtO 16–17; Chapl E Midl Airport 17–21; PtO *Win* from 21. *1 Croft Road, Oakley, Basingstoke RG23 7LA* T: (01256) 541677   M: 07541-284350 E: revjohndawson@gmail.com

DAWSON, Miss Mary. b 51. Loughb Coll ALA 73. EMMTC 85. d 90 p 94. Par Dn Braunstone *Leic* 90–92; Par Dn Shrewsbury H Cross *Lich* 92–94; C 94–95; P-in-c Glentworth Gp *Linc* 95–97; V 97–10; rtd 10; PtO *Linc* from 11. *20 Newbolt Close, Caistor, Market Rasen LN7 6NY* T: (01472) 859802 E: fenellacoughdrop@btinternet.com

DAWSON, Neil. b 49. Ripon Hall Ox 71. d 74 p 75. C Putney St Mary *S'wark* 74–78; C Camberwell St Giles 78–80; TV N Lambeth 84–86; V E Dulwich St Clem 86; V Dulwich St Clem w St Pet 86–89; Hon C Wilton Place St Paul *Lon* 92–06; P-in-c Madeira *Eur* 06–14; rtd 14; PtO *S'wark* from 15; *Eur* 15–20. *18 The High, Streatham High Road, London SW16 1HE* T: (020) 8769 9408 E: neildawson1949@gmail.com

DAWSON, Nicholas Anthony. b 52. St Jo Coll Nottm 88. d 90 p 91. C Mortomley St Sav High Green *Sheff* 90–95; V Owlerton 95–20; P-in-c Hillsborough and Wadsley Bridge 06–09; rtd 20. *40 Laird Avenue, Sheffield S6 4BU*

DAWSON, Canon Norman William. b 41. MBE 99. K Coll Lon BD 63 AKC 63. d 65 p 66. C Salford St Phil w St Steph *Man* 65–68; C Heaton Ch Ch 68–70; R Longsight St Jo 70–75; R Longsight St Jo w St Cypr 75–82; R Withington St Paul 82–99; Chapl Christie Hosp Man 81–91; AD Withington *Man* 91–99; P-in-c Davyhulme St Mary 99–04; Hon Can Man Cathl 98–04; rtd 04; PtO *Blackb* from 04; *Man* 04–12. *Well House, Lowgill, Lancaster LA2 8RA* T: (01524) 262936 E: ann@hindburn.com

DAWSON, Canon Paul Christopher Owen. b 61. Leeds Univ BA 82. Ripon Coll Cuddesdon 83. d 85 p 86. C Dovecot *Liv* 85–89; V Westbrook St Phil 89–94; Bp's Dom Chapl 94–98; V Witton *Ches* 98–06; R Ches St Mary 06–19; RD Ches 14–18; V Whitegate w Lt Budworth from 19; Hon Can Ches Cathl from 17. *The Vicarage, Cinderhill, Whitegate, Northwich CW8 2BH* T: (01606) 301563 E: paulcodawson@outlook.com

DAWSON, Paul Richard. b 67. Bris Univ BSc 89. Oak Hill Th Coll 99. d 01 p 02. C Wimbledon Em Ridgway Prop Chpl *S'wark* 01–09; V Chelsea St Jo w St Andr *Lon* from 09. *The Vicarage, 43 Park Walk, London SW10 0AU* T: (020) 7352 1675 E: paul@standrewschelsea.org

DAWSON, Peter John. b 44. Local Minl Tr Course. d 06 p 07. NSM Heckmondwike *Wakef* 06–12; NSM Liversedge w Hightown 06–12; NSM Roberttown w Hartshead 06–12; NSM Heckmondwike (w Norristhorpe) and Liversedge 12–14; NSM Hartshead, Hightown, Roberttown and Scholes 12–14; rtd 14; PtO *Leeds* from 14. *Address temp unknown* E: manxpeter@yahoo.co.uk

DAWSON, Ruth Adelaide. b 44. d 15 p 16. NSM Heighington and Darlington St Matt and St Luke *Dur* 15–21; PtO from 21. *27 Wilton Court, Greenfields, Newton Aycliffe DL5 7PU* T: (01325) 321729   M: 07786-154638

DAWSON, Ms Sarah. b 70. d 15 p 16. C Mitcham St Barn *S'wark* 15–19; P-in-c Camberwell St Geo 19–21; V from 21. *St George's Vicarage, 115 Wells Way, London SE5 7SZ* M: 07421-136431 E: vicar.stgeorgescamberwell@outlook.com

DAWSON, Stephen Charles. b 62. LCTP 08. d 10 p 11. C Bentham *Bradf* 10–13; P-in-c Langcliffe w Stainforth and Horton 13–14; *Leeds* from 14; C Settle *Bradf* 13–14; *Leeds* from 14; C Giggleswick and Rathmell w Wigglesworth *Bradf* 13–14; *Leeds* from 14; AD Bowland and Ewecross 17–19; PtO *Blackb* 12–14. *The Vicarage, Bankwell Road, Giggleswick, Settle BD24 0AP* E: scudawson@hotmail.com

DAWSON (formerly CORY), Mrs Valerie Ann. b 44. CertEd 65 Nottm Univ BEd 85. EMMTC. d 88 p 94. Area Sec CMS Linc and Pet 87–91; NSM Grantham *Linc* 88–91; Par Dn Ealing St Mary *Lon* 91–94; Chapl NW Lon Poly 91–92; Chapl Thames Valley Univ 92–96; C Ealing St Mary 94–96; Chapl Birm Cathl 96–99; C Surbiton St Andr and St Mark *S'wark* 99–08; rtd 08. *15A Greengate Close, Chesterfield S40 3SJ* T: (01246) 550445

DAWSON, Canon William James Andrew. b 48. TCD MA 72. CITC 88. d 88 p 89. NSM Killyman *Arm* 88–91; NSM Pomeroy 91–13; NSM Derryloran from 14; Can Arm Cathl from 98; Preb 98–01. *Tamlaght House, 29 Bridgend*

Road, Cookstown BT80 0AB T: (028) 8673 7151 *or* 8676 2227 F: 8676 2227 E: wjadawson@gmail.com

DAWSON-CAMPBELL, Olive Sheila. b 37. ACIB 70. WEMTC 99. d 00 p 01. OLM Longden and Annscroft w Pulverbatch *Heref* 00–07; rtd 07; PtO *Heref* 07–20; *Lich* 19–20. *70 The Coppice, Holyhead Road, Bicton, Shrewsbury SY3 8DT* T: (01743) 344302

DAWSON-JONES, Garry Alan. b 66. Cliff Coll MA 02. Yorks Min Course 11. d 12 p 13. C Hackenthorpe *Sheff* 12–15; R Warboys w Broughton and Bury w Wistow *Ely* from 15. *The Rectory, 1 Oaklands, Warboys, Huntingdon PE28 2XH* T: (01487) 824612 M: 07976-382681 E: rector@4parishes.org

DAWSWELL, Jonathan Andrew. b 65. Jes Coll Cam BA 86. Wycliffe Hall Ox BA 91. d 92 p 93. C Childwall All SS *Liv* 92–96; C Leyland St Andr *Blackb* 96–99; V Knypersley *Lich* 99–09; P-in-c Biddulph Moor 05–09; R Biddulph Moor and Knypersley 09–11; V Westlands St Andr from 11; RD Newcastle from 20. *St Andrew's Vicarage, 50 Kingsway West, Newcastle ST5 3PU* T: (01782) 619594 E: ja.dawswell@gmail.com

DAWTRY, The Ven Anne Frances. b 57. Westf Coll Lon BA 79 PhD 85. Ripon Coll Cuddesdon 91. d 93 p 94. C Corfe Mullen *Sarum* 93–96; C Parkstone St Pet w Branksea and St Osmund 96–97; Chapl Bournemouth Univ and Bournemouth and Poole Coll of FE 97–99; Prin OLM and Integrated Tr 99–03; Dir Tr and Prin Dioc OLM Scheme *Man* 03–06; Course Dir SNWTP 06–08; C Chorlton-cum-Hardy St Werburgh 06–08; P-in-c 08–09; R 09–11; Hon Can Man Cathl 06–11; Adn Halifax *Wakef* 11–14; *Leeds* 14–21; Warden of Readers *Wakef* 12–14; *Leeds* 14–19; Hon Can Wakef Cathl 11–21; Hon Can Bradf Cathl 15–21; Hon Can Ripon Cathl 15–21; rtd 21. *89 Rutland Avenue, Poulton-le-Fylde FY6 7RX* M: 07927-101502

DAY, Andrew Christopher. b 62. Lindisfarne Regional Tr Partnership 16. d 18 p 19. NSM Cambridge Gt St Mary w St Mich *Ely* from 18. *Address temp unknown*

DAY, Canon Charles Ian. b 48. Univ of Wales (Ban) BA 72. St Mich Coll Llan 73. d 75 p 76. C Llanrhos *St As* 75–79; V Mochdre 79–83; CF 80–91; V Minera *St As* 83–92; Dioc Soc Resp Officer 89–94; V Mold 92–11; AD 03–11; V Rhuddlan and Bodelwyddan 11–16; I Aber-Morfa Miss Area 17–18; AD St As 15–18; Hon Can St As Cathl 14–18; rtd 18; PtO *St As* from 18. *2 Ffordd Craiglun, Kinmel Bay, Rhyl LL18 5JL* T: (01745) 339050 M: 07977-001692 E: revian@spamex.com

DAY, Christine Audrey. b 63. K Alfred's Coll Win BTh 01 Univ of Wales (Lamp) MA(Theol) 06. STETS 02. d 04 p 05. NSM N Stoneham *Win* 04–08; NSM Swaythling 08–14; Chapl Southn Univ 11–14; Chapl Win Univ from 14. *The University of Winchester, Sparkford Road, Winchester SO22 4NR* T: (01962) 827246 M: 07580-968215 E: revchrisday@gmail.com *or* chaplaincy@winchester.ac.uk

DAY, Canon Colin Michael. b 40. Lon Univ BSc 62 AKC 62 Em Coll Cam BA 66 MA 71. Ridley Hall Cam 65. d 67 p 68. C Heworth w Peasholme St Cuth *York* 67–70; C Ox St Clem 70–76; V Kidsgrove *Lich* 76–86; Exec Officer Angl Evang Assembly and C of E Coun 86–90; Adv on Miss and Evang *Sarum* 90–95; P-in-c Branksome Park All SS 95–01; V 01–05; Can and Preb Sarum Cathl 94–05; Dioc Tr in Evang 95–05; rtd 05; PtO *Win* from 13. *113 Archery Grove, Southampton SO19 9ET* T: (023) 8043 9854 E: colin@ncd-uk.com

DAY, David John. b 44. CEng 72 MICE 72. Trin Coll Bris. d 90 p 91. C Stratton St Margaret w S Marston etc *Bris* 90–94; PtO from 95; Manager SA Addictions Rehab Cen Highworth 98–09; rtd 09. *62 Eastern Avenue, Swindon SN3 1AD* T: (01793) 524766 E: davidjday1@hotmail.com

DAY, David Vivian. b 36. Lon Univ BA 57 Nottm Univ MEd 73 MTh 77. d 99 p 00. NSM Dur St Nic 99–07; rtd 07; PtO *Dur* from 07. *35 Orchard Drive, Durham DH1 1LA* T: 0191-386 6909

DAY, Canon David William. b 37. St Andr Univ MA 58 BD 61 CertEd 73. St And Dioc Tr Course 74. d 76 p 77. C St Andrews All SS *St And* 76–77; P-in-c Dundee St Ninian *Bre* 77–84; Itinerant Priest *Arg* 84–02; R Duror 84–02; P-in-c Kentallen 84–02; P-in-c Kinlochleven 84–02; P-in-c Kinlochmoidart 84–96; P-in-c Lochbuie 84–96; P-in-c Portnacrois 84–02; P-in-c Strontian 84–96; Can St Jo Cathl Oban 89–02; rtd 02; Hon Can Cumbrae *Arg* from 02; LtO from 02; Hon C St Andrews All SS *St And* from 03. *10 Doocot Road, St Andrews KY16 8QP* T: (01334) 476991 E: arkvillewest@gmail.com

DAY, George Chester. b 45. Ex Univ BA 66 Lon Univ BD 70. Clifton Th Coll 67. d 71 p 72. C Reading St Jo *Ox* 71–75; C Morden *S'wark* 75–81; Sec for Voc and Min CPAS 81–83; Hon C Bromley Ch Ch *Roch* 83–86; V St Paul's Cray St Barn 86–05; RD Orpington 01–05; V Joydens Wood St Barn 05–10; rtd 10;

PtO *Ex* from 11. *5 Abbey Grange Close, Buckfast, Buckfastleigh TQ11 0EU* T: (01364) 643912

DAY, Mrs Janet. b 57. MAAT 11. St Mich Coll Llan 13. **d** 19 **p** 20. OLM Buallt *S & B* from 19. *3 Daffodil Wood, Builth Wells LD2 3LE* T: (01982) 553623 M: 07754-703709 E: revjanetday@gmail.com

DAY, Jennifer Ann. *See* BRADSHAW, Jennifer Ann

DAY, John Kenneth. b 58. Hull Univ BA 85. Cranmer Hall Dur 85. **d** 87 **p** 88. C Thornbury *Bradf* 87–90; V 90–96; V Whitkirk *Ripon* 96–01; V Fendalton NZ 01–15; Miss Strategy Development Officer *York* from 16; Asst Chapl to Abp from 16; P-in-c York St Chad 16–21; C from 21; C York St Clem w St Mary Bishophill from 20; C Bishopthorpe from 21. *St Chad's Vicarage, 36 Campleshon Road, York YO23 1EY* T: (01904) 689634

DAY, Mrs Judith Mollie. b 43. Warwick Univ BPhil 95 SRN 64 Lady Spencer Chu Coll of Educn CertEd 74. **d** 15 **p** 16. NSM Brecon St Mary *S & B* from 15. *Maes yr Haf, Pentrefelin, Sennybridge, Brecon LD3 8TT* T: (01874) 638307 E: judyday.jd@gmail.com

DAY, Martyn John. b 69. Univ Coll Lon BSc 90. St Jo Coll Nottm 07. **d** 09 **p** 10. C Horwich and Rivington *Man* 09–12; C Blackrod 11–12; V Epsom St Geo NZ 12–15; P Asst to Bp Auckland 15–16; C Blockhouse Bay 17–19; PtO Auckland from 19. *24A Liverpool Street, Epsom, Auckland 1023, New Zealand* T: (0064) (9) 948 7427 E: martyn.day9@gmail.com

DAY, Canon Mary Elizabeth. b 57. Leic Poly BEd 79. St Jo Coll Nottm 93. **d** 93 **p** 94. C Newbarns w Hawcoat *Carl* 93–98; P-in-c Allonby 98–03; P-in-c Cross Canonby 98–03; P-in-c Dearham 02–03; V Allonby, Cross Canonby and Dearham from 03; Adv for Women in Min from 07; RD Solway 08–11; Hon Can Carl Cathl from 08. *The Vicarage, Crosscanonby, Maryport CA15 6SJ* T: (01900) 814192 E: vicarmary@talktalk.net

DAY, Paul Geoffrey. b 56. St Pet Coll Ox BA 77. St Jo Coll Nottm 87. **d** 89 **p** 90. C Mildmay Grove St Jude and St Paul *Lon* 89–92; C Loughborough Em *Leic* 92–95; TV Loughborough Em and St Mary in Charnwood 95–98; PtO *Birm* 15–17; C Shirley 17–20; V from 20. *18 Whitney Lane, Solihull B91 3LS* T: 0121-537 9672 M: 07545-615924 E: pgday@hotmail.co.uk

DAY, Paul Geoffrey. b 51. Dur Univ BEd 75. Trin Coll Bris 76. **d** 78 **p** 79. C Roxeth Ch Ch *Lon* 78–82; TV Barking St Marg w St Patr *Chelmsf* 82–87; V Barrow St Mark *Carl* 87–00; V Eccleston St Luke *Liv* 00–07; TV Eccleston 07–13; rtd 13. *2 St Paul's Villas, King Street, Acrefair, Wrexham LL14 3RW* E: paulgday@btinternet.com

DAY, Peter. b 50. BPharm 71. Coll of Resurr Mirfield 85. **d** 87 **p** 88. C Eastcote St Lawr *Lon* 87–91; C Wembley Park St Aug 91–94; V Glen Parva and S Wigston *Leic* 94–14; C Wigston from 14; rtd 15; PtO *Nor* from 16. *2A Eastfields Close, Gaywood, King's Lynn PE30 4HQ* T: (01553) 676158 E: peterday260@gmail.com

DAY, Peter Andrew. b 67. Westmr Coll Ox BTh 98 Bris Univ PhD 03. Ripon Coll Cuddesdon 07. **d** 10 **p** 11. C Wokingham St Paul *Ox* 10–13; P-in-c Reading Ch Ch 13–15; V from 15. *Christ Church Vicarage, Vicarage Road, Reading RG2 7AJ* T: 0118-931 3468 M: 07702-043857 E: fr.peterday@virginmedia.com

DAY, Miss Sally Ann. b 43. **d** 07 **p** 08. OLM Shifnal and Sheriffhales *Lich* 07–16; OLM Shifnal, Sheriffhales and Tong 16–18; PtO 18–21. *Mount Pleasant, 11 Cherry Tree Hill, Coalbrookdale, Telford TF8 7EF* T/F: (01952) 433213 M: 07831-101361 E: sallyannday@hotmail.com

DAY, Stephen Michael. b 60. Down Coll Cam BA 82 MA 85 Open Univ BA 00. Ridley Hall Cam 02. **d** 05 **p** 06. C Waltham H Cross *Chelmsf* 05–09; TV Papworth *Ely* from 09. *The Rectory, 32 High Street, Bourn, Cambridge CB23 2SQ* T: (01954) 264226 E: revdsmday@cantab.net *or* stephen.day@elydiocese.org

DAY, Timothy Robert. b 63. WMMTC 07. **d** 10 **p** 11. NSM Leic H Apostles 10–14; TV Fosse Team from 14. *St Michael's Vicarage, 828 Melton Road, Thurmaston, Leicester LE4 8BE* T: 0116-348 6896 M: 07976-186546 E: revtimday.fosseteam@gmail.com

DAY, Trevor Martin. b 51. STETS 09. **d** 12 **p** 13. NSM Highworth w Sevenhampton and Inglesham etc *Bris* 12–15; NSM Broad Blunsdon 12–15; NSM W Swindon and the Lydiards 15–18; NSM W Swindon and Lydiard Tregoze from 18; Min Can Bris Cathl from 15. *23 Melfort Close, Sparcells, Swindon SN5 5FG* T: (01793) 875373 M: 07918-125826 E: trevor.day@btinternet.com

DAY, William Charles. b 47. Portsm Poly BEd 86. Ripon Coll Cuddesdon 88. **d** 90 **p** 91. C Bishop's Waltham *Portsm* 90–93; P-in-c Greatham w Empshott and Hawkley w Prior's Dean 93–95; R 95–98; V Titchfield 98–09; RD Fareham 04–08;

C-in-c Whiteley CD 08–09; rtd 09; PtO *Portsm* from 09. *19 Peter's Road, Locks Heath, Southampton SO31 6EB* T: (01489) 564035 E: revbillday@btinternet.com

DAY, William George. b 45. SNWTP 14. **d** 14 **p** 15. OLM Derby St Barn 14–18; PtO from 18. *2 Whenby Close, Mickleover, Derby DE3 0RQ* T: (01332) 518449 E: wwgday@btinternet.com

DAYKIN, Canon Timothy Elwin. b 54. R Holloway Coll Lon BSc 75 St Jo Coll Dur MA 81 K Coll Lon MPhil 93 MEHS 89. Cranmer Hall Dur 75. **d** 78 **p** 79. C Bourne *Guildf* 78–81; Chapl K Alfred Coll *Win* 82–87; C-in-c Valley Park CD 87–91; V Valley Park 91–92; P-in-c Fordingbridge 92–98; V 98–01; P-in-c Hale w S Charford 94–01; P-in-c Breamore 99–01; TR Fordingbridge and Breamore and Hale etc 01–05; TV Southampton (City Cen) 05–14; PtO from 14; *Nor* from 16; *Sarum* from 19; Producer/Presenter Relig Progr BBC Radio Solent 05–20; Can and Preb Sarum Cathl from 19. *5 Westgrove, Fordingbridge SP6 1LS* E: tim@fordingbridge.com

DAYNES, Andrew John. b 47. Jes Coll Cam BA 69 MA 73. Westcott Ho Cam 69. **d** 72 **p** 73. C Radlett *St Alb* 72–76; Chapl St Alb Abbey 76–80; Chapl Bryanston Sch 80–08; rtd 08; PtO *B & W* from 09. *Romneya, Claycastle, Haselbury Plucknett, Crewkerne TA18 7PE* T: (01460) 78971 M: 07580-003822 E: hilandandy@gmail.com

DAYNES, Rebecca Elizabeth. b 81. St Mellitus Coll BA 20. **d** 20 **p** 21. NSM Hanley Road *Lon* from 20. *10 Florence Road, London N4 4BU* E: bex.daynes@stsaviours.church

DAZELEY, Mrs Lorna. b 31. CertEd 53 New Hall Cam BA 82 MA 86. EAMTC 82. **dss** 84 **d** 87 **p** 94. Chesterton St Andr *Ely* 84–97; C 87–97; rtd 97; PtO *Ely* from 01. *Chesterton House, Church Street, Chesterton, Cambridge CB4 1DT* T: (01223) 356243 E: lorna.dazeley@gmail.com

DE ALMEIDA FEITAL, Peterson. b 75. Cliff Coll BA 05 MA 09. Ridley Hall Cam 09. **d** 11 **p** 12. C Muswell Hill St Jas w St Matt *Lon* 11–14; LtO from 15; Missr to the Arts from 15; PtO *Ox* 15–20. *4 Dollings Yard, 3 Bellingdon Road, Chesham HP5 2HA* M: 07889-463333 E: petersonfeital@hotmail.com

DE ANDRADE LIMA, Luiz Henrique. b 80. Trin Coll Bris BA 14. **d** 14 **p** 15. C Worksop St Anne *S'well* 14–17; C Norton Cuckney 14–17; V Worksop Ch Ch and Shireoaks from 17. *34 Boscombe Road, Worksop S81 7SB* T: (01909) 530127 M: 07989-674364 E: revluizlima@outlook.com

DE BERRY, Robert Delatour. b 42. Qu Coll Cam BA 64 MA 68. Ridley Hall Cam 65. **d** 67 **p** 68. C Bradf Cathl 67–70; Youth Worker CMS Uganda 71–75; V Attercliffe *Sheff* 75–83; V W Kilburn St Luke w St Simon and St Jude *Lon* 83–97; Gen Sec Mid-Africa Min (CMS) 97–99; P-in-c Kennington St Mark *S'wark* 99–01; V 01–08; rtd 08; PtO *Sarum* from 10. *27 Cossor Road, Pewsey SN9 5HX* T: (01672) 562907 E: robertdeberry@btinternet.com *or* robertdeberry42@gmail.com

de BOURCIER, Miss Katherine Elizabeth. b 71. Clare Coll Cam BA 92. St Mellitus Coll BA 12. **d** 12 **p** 13. C Gt Baddow *Chelmsf* 12–15; P-in-c Halstead Area from 15. *The Rectory, Parsonage Street, Halstead CO9 2LD* T: (01787) 472171 E: halsteadrector@gmail.com

DE CHAIR LADD, Anne. *See* LADD, Anne de Chair

de GARIS, Canon Jean Helier Thomson. b 60. K Alfred's Coll Win BA 82 PGCE 83. Sarum & Wells Th Coll BTh 93. **d** 93 **p** 94. C Chandler's Ford *Win* 93–98; P-in-c Lytchett Minster *Sarum* 98–10; TR The Lytchetts and Upton 10–19; RD Poole and N Bournemouth 09–16; V Salisbury St Fran and Stratford sub Castle from 19; Can and Preb Sarum Cathl from 14. *The Vicarage, 52 Park Lane, Salisbury SP1 3NP* T: (01722) 334214 M: 07760-224424 E: jeandegaris@st-francischurch.org.uk

DE GARIS, Juliette Elizabeth Charmaine. *See* ROBILLIARD, Juliette Elizabeth Charmaine

de GAY, Sandra Jane. b 66. Open Univ PhD 98 Leeds Univ MA 10. NOC. **d** 08 **p** 09. NSM Potternewton *Ripon* 08–14; *Leeds* 14–16; NSM Potternewton w Lt London from 16. *48 Vesper Way, Leeds LS5 3LN* T: 0113-258 2673 E: jane.degay@leeds.anglican.org

de GRUCHY, Heidi-Maria. Cardiff Univ BTh 12. St Mich Coll Llan 08. **d** 10 **p** 11. C Bedwellty w New Tredegar *Mon* 10–12; C Bassaleg 12–14; C Tredegar 14–16; P-in-c Goodna Australia 16–18; C St Ishmael's w Llan-saint and Ferryside *St D* 18–19; P-in-c Bro Cydweli from 19. *The Vicarage, Water Street, Ferryside SA17 5RT* T: (01267) 267559 E: heididegruchy@hotmail.co.uk

DE GRUYTHER, Mrs Heather Louise. b 79. Glos Univ BA 04. Ripon Coll Cuddesdon BA 19. **d** 19 **p** 20. C Glouc St Paul and St Steph from 19. *126 Fieldcourt Gardens, Quedgeley, Gloucester GL2 4TZ* T: (01452) 535970 E: revheatherdg@gmail.com

de JONGE, Elaine Irene. b 73. Sussex Univ BA 96. WMMTC 06. **d** 09 **p** 10. C Smestow Vale *Lich* 09–13; C Tettenhall Wood and Perton 13; Spiritual Care Co-ord and Chapl Compton

Care from 13. *Compton Care, Compton Hall, 4 Compton Road West, Wolverhampton WV3 9DH* T: (01902) 774554 E: spiritualcare@comptoncare.org.uk

de la HOYDE, Canon Denys Ralph Hart. b 33. G&C Coll Cam BA 57 MA 61. Westcott Ho Cam 57. **d** 59 **p** 60. C Moss Side Ch Ch *Man* 59–60; Chapl G&C Coll Cam 60–64; P-in-c Naini Tal etc India 64–68; C Eltham H Trin *S'wark* 68–69; Chapl Bromsgrove Sch 69–71; Asst Master Harrogate High Sch 71–78; Lic to Offic *Ripon* 71–78; V Pool w Arthington 86–98; Dioc Dir of Ords 86–98; Hon Can Ripon Cathl 92–98; rtd 98; PtO *Ripon* 00–14; *Leeds* from 14. *36 Hookstone Chase, Harrogate HG2 7HS* T: (01423) 548146 E: denys.delahoyde@ntlworld.com

de la MOUETTE, Norman Harry. b 39. Southn Univ BEd 73 MA 98. Sarum & Wells Th Coll 76. **d** 79 **p** 80. NSM Win St Lawr and St Maurice w St Swithun 79–99; Deputation Appeals Org CECS Win and Portsm 83–96; Chapl St Jo Win Charity 96–99; NSM Win St Lawr and St Maurice w St Swithun 99–04; rtd 04; PtO *Win* from 04. *146 Greenhill Road, Winchester SO22 5DR* T: (01962) 853191 E: norman.delamouette@yahoo.co.uk

DE LYON, Hilary Barbara. b 56. **d** 13 **p** 14. NSM Swaffham and Sporle *Nor* 13–21; NSM Launditch and the Upper Nar from 21. *Woodford Lodge, Tittleshall, King's Lynn PE32 2PF* T: (01328) 700066 E: delyonhilary@gmail.com

de MATTOS, Dominic James. b 63. St Aug Coll of Th 16. **d** 19 **p** 20. C Southborough St Thos *Roch* from 19. *19 Streamside, Tonbridge TN10 3PU* M: 07851-095264 E: revdomdem@gmail.com

de MELLO, Bridget Dorothea. *See* DEUCHAR de MELLO, Bridget Dorothea

de POMERAI, David Ian Morcamp. b 50. Edin Univ BSc 72 Univ Coll Lon PhD 75. EMMTC 90. **d** 93 **p** 94. NSM Sutton in Ashfield St Mary *S'well* 93–96; NSM Clifton 96–02; NSM Walton-on-Trent w Croxall, Rosliston etc *Derby* 02–13; LtO 13–15; rtd 15; LtO *Edin* from 16. *141/1 Comely Bank Road, Edinburgh EH4 1BH* T: 0131-332 4743

de QUIDT, Mrs Fiona Margaret Munro. b 53. St Andr Univ MTheol 76. NTMTC 97. **d** 00 **p** 01. NSM Kingston Hill St Paul *S'wark* from 00. *10 Norbiton Avenue, Kingston-upon-Thames KT1 3QS* T: (020) 8541 4700 E: revfiona.dequidt@btopenworld.com

de QUIDT, Canon Marion Elizabeth. b 59. Girton Coll Cam MPhil 83 MA 85 PhD 86. STETS 09. **d** 11 **p** 12. C Fetcham *Guildf* 11–15; P-in-c Whitewater *Win* 15–19; R from 19; AD Odiham from 17; Hon Can Win Cathl from 20. *The Vicarage, London Road, Hook RG27 9EG* T: (01256) 760169 M: 07866-304516 E: mariondequidt@whitewaterchurches.co.uk *or* marion.dequidt@gmail.com

DE ROBECK, Fiona Caroline. *See* GIBBS, Fiona Caroline

DE SALIS, Mary. *See* FANE DE SALIS, Mary

DE SAUSMAREZ, Canon John Havilland Russell. b 26. Lambeth MA 81 Wells Th Coll 54. **d** 56 **p** 57. C N Lynn w St Marg and St Nic *Nor* 56–58; C Hythe *Cant* 58–61; V Maidstone St Martin 61–68; V St Peter-in-Thanet 68–81; RD Thanet 74–81; Hon Can Cant Cathl 81–94; Hon Can Res Cant Cathl 81–94; rtd 94; PtO *Cant* 94–12. *6 Chantry Court, St Radigunds Street, Canterbury CT1 2AD* T: (01227) 458868

DE SILVA, David Ebenezer Sunil. b 48. **d** 72 **p** 73. Sri Lanka 72–84; C Elm Park St Nic Hornchurch *Chelmsf* 84–87; R Mistley w Manningtree and Bradfield 87–90; TR Stanground and Farcet *Ely* 90–01; V Stanground 01–05; rtd 05. *2 Fenmere Walk, Hampton Centre, Peterborough PE7 8GW* E: desdesilva84@gmail.com

DE SMET, Andrew Charles. b 58. Ex Univ BSc 79 Southn Univ BTh 88. Sarum & Wells Th Coll 85. **d** 88 **p** 89. C Portsea St Mary *Portsm* 88–93; R Shipston-on-Stour w Honington and Idlicote *Cov* 93–00; Warden Offa Retreat Ho and Dioc Spirituality Adv 00–07; P-in-c Kirkdale w Harome, Nunnington and Pockley *York* 07–14; V 14–17; Abp's Adv and Co-ord of Past Care from 07. *Egroms, 23 Tower Street, Flamborough, Bridlington YO15 1PD* M: 07583-279459 E: andrewdesmet@btinternet.com

DE SOUZA, Josias Pereira. b 75. Seminário Anglicano de Estudos Teológicos BA 00. **d** 04 **p** 05. Brazil 04–16; C Dover Town *Cant* from 16. *3 Monastery Avenue, Dover CT16 1AB* T: (01304) 275764 M: 07599-861598 E: josiasjunior@hotmail.com

de VIAL, Raymond Michael. b 39. Oak Hill Th Coll 77. **d** 80 **p** 81. NSM Beckenham St Jo *Roch* 80–84; C Morden *S'wark* 84–88; TV 88–94; V Kingston Hill St Paul 94–04; rtd 04; PtO *S'wark* 04–05; *Carl* from 05. *39 Helme Drive, Kendal LA9 7JB* T: (01539) 729396 E: revray@btinternet.com

DE VRIES-SYTSMA, Mrs Dorothee Joanne (Dorienke). b 62. ERMC 18. **d** 20 **p** 21. NSM Arnhem *Eur* from 20. *Backerstraat 47, 6861 XS Oosterbeek, The Netherlands* T: (0031) (26) 333 3182 M: (0031) 61-951 8500 E: curate@arnhemnijmegenchaplaincy.nl

de WAAL, Victor Alexander. b 29. Pemb Coll Cam BA 49 MA 53 Nottm Univ Hon DD 83. Ely Th Coll 50. **d** 52 **p** 53. C Isleworth St Mary *Lon* 52–56; Chapl Ely Th Coll 56–59; Chapl K Coll Cam 59–63; Hon C Nottingham St Mary *S'well* 63–69; Chapl Nottm Univ 63–69; Can Res and Chan Linc Cathl 69–76; Dean Cant 76–86; PtO *Heref* 88–99; rtd 90; Chapl Soc of Sacred Cross Tymawr 90–00; LtO *Mon* 90–02; PtO 02–08. *6 St James Close, Bishop Street, London N1 8PH* T: (020) 7354 2741

DEACON, Mrs Selina Frances. b 52. SRN 74. Ripon Coll Cuddesdon 01. **d** 03 **p** 04. C White Horse *Sarum* 03–07; P-in-c Studley 07–12; V 12–17; rtd 17; PtO *Sarum* 18–19; Hon C Salisbury St Thos and St Edm from 19. *51 St Mark's Road, Salisbury SP1 3AY* M: 07867-521909 E: selinadeacon@gmail.com

DEACON, Susan. b 47. **d** 14 **p** 15. OLM Springline *Linc* from 14; OLM Owmby Gp from 14. *Parsonage Lodge, High Street, Scampton, Lincoln LN1 2SE* T: (01522) 730167 E: susan.deacon3@btinternet.com

DEADMAN, Hugo Charles. b 67. Wadh Coll Ox BA 89 Birkbeck Coll Lon MA 94. Ripon Coll Cuddesdon 16. **d** 19 **p** 20. C Milton *Portsm* from 19. *102B Copnor Road, Portsmouth PO3 5AL* M: 07947-127349 E: hugo@hdeadman.myzen.co.uk

DEADMAN, Richard George Spencer. b 63. Ex Univ BA 85. Coll of Resurr Mirfield 86. **d** 88 **p** 89. C Grangetown *York* 88–91; P-in-c 91–93; V 93–96; V Wallsend St Luke *Newc* 96–01; V Newc St Phil and St Aug and St Matt w St Mary from 01. *St Matthew's Vicarage, 10 Winchester Terrace, Newcastle upon Tyne NE4 6EH* T: 0191-232 9039 E: richardgsd@aol.com

DEAKIN, Caroline Sarah Ann. b 73. Trin Coll Bris 16. **d** 18 **p** 19. C Bath St Mich Without *B & W* 18–21; P-in-c Milton and Kewstoke from 21. *The Vicarage, Baytree Road, Weston-super-Mare BS22 8HG* M: 07951-132629 E: caroline.sa.deakin@gmail.com

DEAKIN, Christopher Harold. b 49. ARMCM 72. Qu Coll Birm 02. **d** 04 **p** 05. C Wrockwardine Deanery *Lich* 04–07; P-in-c Bicton, Montford w Shrawardine and Fitz 07–14; P-in-c Leaton and Albrighton w Battlefield 07–14; P-in-c Hargrave *Ches* 14–19; V 19–21; rtd 21. *20 Westbury Road, Cleethorpes DN35 0QE* E: revdeakin@gmail.com

DEAKIN, John David. b 58. Qu Coll Birm BA 03. **d** 03 **p** 04. C Blakenall Heath *Lich* 03–07; TV Willenhall H Trin 07–11; TV Bentley Em and Willenhall H Trin 11–15; TR 15–19; rtd 20; PtO *Lich* from 20; Chapl R Wolv NHS Trust from 20. *1A Broad Lane North, Willenhall WV12 5UH* M: 07802-762715

DEAKIN, Kirsty Hayley. *See* SCREETON, Kirsty Hayley

DEAKIN, Paul David. b 62. Sheff Univ BA 13. Coll of Resurr Mirfield 11. **d** 13 **p** 14. C Bramhall *Ches* 13–14; C Hale and Ashley 14–16; V Knutsford St Cross from 16. *St Cross Vicarage, Mobberley Road, Knutsford WA16 8EL* T: (01565) 640702 M: 07813-368845 E: revdpauldeakin@gmail.com

DEALL, Stephen Charles. b 69. Oak Hill Th Coll 15. **d** 17 **p** 18. C Abbots Bromley, Blithfield, Colton, Colwich etc *Lich* 17–20; R Bradwell *Nor* from 20. *The Rectory, Church Walk, Bradwell, Great Yarmouth NR31 8QQ* T: (01493) 663219 E: revstevedeall@gmail.com

DEAMER, Mrs Carylle. b 40. SAOMC 96. **d** 99 **p** 00. OLM Riverside *Ox* 99–05; rtd 05; PtO *Ox* 05–08; *B & W* from 09. *7 Coombe Close, Castle Cary BA7 7HJ* T: (01963) 359243 E: rev.carylle@deamer.me.uk

DEAN, Antonia Jane. *See* LYNN, Antonia Jane

DEAN, Benjamin Timothy Frederic. b 70. Lon Bible Coll BA 93 K Coll Lon MA 94 Selw Coll Cam MPhil 02 PhD 06. Ridley Hall Cam 04. **d** 07. C Georgeham *Ex* 07–08; Lect Geo Whitefield Coll S Africa from 08. *George Whitefield College, PO Box 64, Muizenberg, 7950 South Africa* T: (0027) (21) 788 1652 E: btfd@mac.com

DEAN, Hazel Michaela. b 48. **d** 14 **p** 15. OLM Long Sutton w Lutton etc *Linc* from 14. *Milldean Cottage, Broadgate, Sutton St James, Spalding PE12 0EL* T: (01945) 440347 E: hazel-makaila.dean@sky.com

DEAN, Jonathan Charles. b 57. St Cath Coll Cam MA 83. NEOC 04. **d** 07 **p** 08. NSM Gt Ayton w Easby and Newton under Roseberry *York* from 07. *The White House, 2 Dikes Lane, Great Ayton, Middlesbrough TS9 6HJ* T: (01642) 722649 E: jondean@cantab.net

DEAN, Kathryn Ann. b 54. **d** 19. NSM Middlesbrough St Oswald and St Chad *York* from 19. *7 North Wood, Middlesbrough TS5 7LL* E: kath.dean@hotmail.com

DEAN, Mrs Linda Louise. b 39. **d** 04 **p** 05. NSM Primrose Hill St Mary w Avenue Road St Paul *Lon* 04–13. *52 Lanchester Road, London N6 4TA* T: (020) 8883 5417

DEAN, Lucas John William. b 57. St Jo Coll Nottm 05. **d** 07 **p** 08. C St Laur in Thanet *Cant* 07–11; V Hollington St Jo *Chich* from 11. *The Vicarage, 94 Lower Glen Road, St Leonards-on-Sea TN37 7AR* T: (01424) 751103 M: 07712-834472 E: ljwdean@hotmail.com

DEAN, Lynne. b 66. Cumbria Coll of Art & Design BA 02 Dur Univ BA 21 Northumbria Univ PGCE 07. Lindisfarne Coll of Th 19. **d** 21. NSM Reepham, Hackford w Whitwell, Kerdiston etc *Nor* 11–17; P-in-c Wensum Benefice 16–17; Hon Can Nor Cathl 16–17; rtd 17; PtO *Guildf* 18–21. *10 Henchley Dene, Guildford GU4 7BH* T: (01483) 562776 E: margaretdean@cnet.org

DEAN, Canon Margaret Heath. b 50. Newton Park Coll Bris BEd 72. STETS 05. **d** 07 **p** 08. C Farncombe *Guildf* 07–11; R Reepham, Hackford w Whitwell, Kerdiston etc *Nor* 11–17; P-in-c Wensum Benefice 16–17; Hon Can Nor Cathl 16–17; rtd 17; PtO *Guildf* 18–21. *10 Henchley Dene, Guildford GU4 7BH* T: (01483) 562776 E: margaretdean@cnet.org

DEAN, Simon Christopher. b 82. Dur Univ BA 18. St Mellitus Coll 17. **d** 19 **p** 20. C Bottesford w Ashby *Linc* from 19. *10 Old School Lane, Bottesford, Scunthorpe DN16 3RD* E: revdsimondean@gmail.com

DEAN, Timothy Charles Painter. b 50. STETS MA 08. **d** 07 **p** 08. NSM Godalming *Guildf* 07–11; CMD Officer *Nor* 11–15; NSM Reepham, Hackford w Whitwell, Kerdiston etc 11–17; NSM Wensum Benefice 16–17; NSM Lyng, Sparham, Elsing, Bylaugh, Bawdeswell etc 16–17; RD Sparham 14–17; rtd 17; PtO *Chelmsf* from 20. *10 Henchley Dene, Guildford GU4 7BH* T: (01483) 562776 E: timdean@cnet.org

DEAN, Trevor Stephen. b 58. Lon Hosp MB, BS 81. Trin Coll Bris BA 03. **d** 10 **p** 11. NSM Nailsea H Trin *B & W* from 10. *3 Ilminster Close, Nailsea, Bristol BS48 4YU* T: (01275) 851218 M: 07905-757649 E: trevor.dean@blueyonder.co.uk

DEAN-REVILL, David Frank. b 68. Univ Coll Ches BA 06. NOC 03. **d** 06 **p** 07. C Dinnington w Laughton and Throapham *Sheff* 06–09; P-in-c Shiregreen from 09. *The Vicarage, 510 Bellhouse Road, Sheffield S5 0RG* T: 0114-245 6526 E: davidrevill@hotmail.com

DEANE, Nicholas Talbot Bryan. b 46. Bris Univ BA 69. Clifton Th Coll 70. **d** 72 **p** 73. C Accrington Ch Ch *Blackb* 72–75; OMF Korea 75–89; P-in-c Newburgh *Liv* 90–93; P-in-c Westhead 90–93; V Newburgh w Westhead 93–97; R Chadwell *Chelmsf* 97–11; rtd 11; C Waverton w Aldford and Bruera *Ches* 11–15; PtO *S'well* from 16. *1 Patient Close, Chilwell, Beeston, Nottingham NG9 4HA* T: 0115-922 2926 M: 07712-153882 E: nicholasdeane7@gmail.com

DEANE, Robert William. b 52. CITC. **d** 85 **p** 86. C Raheny w Coolock *D & G* 85–88; I Clonsast w Rathangan, Thomastown etc *M & K* 88–00; Can Kildare Cathl 97–00; Can Meath Cathl 98–00; I Swords w Donabate and Kilsallaghan *D & G* 00–18; Can Ch Ch Cathl Dublin 08–18; rtd 18. *209 St Werburghs, Malahide Road, Swords, Co Dublin, K67 VRX4, Republic of Ireland* T: (00353) (1) 840 4282 M: 87-346 1342

DEANE, Stuart William. b 45. Sarum & Wells Th Coll 86. **d** 88 **p** 89. C Bromyard *Heref* 88–92; V Astley, Clive, Grinshill and Hadnall *Lich* 92–98; TV Cen Telford 98–00; TR 00–05; rtd 05; PtO *Heref* from 07. *38 Crest Court, Hereford HR4 9QD* T: (01432) 351937

DEANS, Bruce Gibson. b 64. MCIBS 86. Wycliffe Hall Ox 02. **d** 04 **p** 05. C Hartley Wintney, Elvetham, Winchfield etc *Win* 04–08; R Shedfield and Wickham *Portsm* 08–15; P-in-c Fareham St Jo 15–18; V from 18. *3A Upper St Michael's Grove, Fareham PO14 1DN* T: (01329) 281544

DEANS, Robert. b 58. Stirling Univ BA 82 Edin Univ MSc 83 Anglia Ruskin Univ MA 12. ERMC 09. **d** 12 **p** 13. NSM Pet St Jo 12–17; Chapl HM Pris Peterborough 17; PtO *York* from 19. *Hill View, Egton, Whitby YO21 1UT* E: robdeans@outlook.com

DEAR, Graham Frederick. b 44. St Luke's Coll Ex CertEd 66. Wycliffe Hall Ox 67. **d** 70 **p** 71. C Chigwell *Chelmsf* 70–73; C Chingford SS Pet and Paul 73–75; V Southchurch Ch Ch 75–82; CF 82–89; P-in-c The Cowtons *Ripon* 89–94; RE Adv 89–94; V Startforth and Bowes and Rokeby w Brignall 94–97; Chapl HM Pris Garth 97–01; rtd 09; PtO *Ripon* 01–14; *Leeds* from 14. *1 The Old Wynd, Bellerby, Leyburn DL8 5QJ* T: (01969) 623960

DEAR, Neil Douglas Gauntlett. b 35. Linc Th Coll 87. **d** 89 **p** 90. C Framlingham w Saxtead *St E* 89–92; P-in-c Eyke w Bromeswell, Rendlesham, Tunstall etc 92–98; Chapl Local Health Partnerships NHS Trust 98–02; Chapl Cen Suffolk Primary Care Trust 02–05; P-in-c Worlingworth, Southolt, Tannington, Bedfield etc *St E* 02–05; rtd 05; PtO *St E* 05–20. *Peacehaven, Duke Street, Stanton, Bury St Edmunds IP31 2AB* T: (01359) 252001

DEAR, Virginia Anne. b 65. Westcott Ho Cam. **d** 13 **p** 14. C Hertford *St Alb* 13–16; R St Ippolyts w Gt and Lt Wymondley from 16. *The Vicarage, Stevenage Road, St Ippolyts, Hitchin SG4 7PE* T: (01462) 237032 E: revginni@gmail.com

DEARDEN, Geoffrey. b 36. Salford Univ MSc 74. CBDTI 05. **d** 06 **p** 07. NSM Hurst Green and Mitton *Bradf* 06–10; PtO 10–14; *Leeds* 14–16; *Blackb* from 15. *14 Church Close, Waddington, Clitheroe BB7 3HX* T: (01200) 427380 E: geoffandann@btinternet.com

DEARDEN, Canon Philip Harold. b 43. AKC 65. **d** 66 **p** 67. C Haslingden w Haslingden Grane *Blackb* 66–69; C Burnley St Pet 69–71; V Langho Billington 71–78; TR Darwen St Pet w Hoddlesden 78–91; RD Darwen 86–91; V Altham w Clayton le Moors 91–97; RD Accrington 95–97; V Clitheroe St Mary 97–08; Hon Can Blackb Cathl 96–08; rtd 08; PtO *Blackb* 08–14; *Carl* 11–16. *20 South Park, Lincoln LN5 8EP* T: (01522) 533210

DEARMER, Juliet. See WOOLLCOMBE, Juliet

DEARNLEY, Ms Helen Elizabeth Booker. b 77. De Montfort Univ LLB 98 Cam Univ BTh 02 MSt 19 York St Jo Univ MA 09. Westcott Ho Cam 99. **d** 02 **p** 03. C Knighton St Mary Magd *Leic* 02–06; Co-ord Chapl HM Pris Leic 06–13; Adv Prison Chapl HQ 13–18; Angl Adv from 19; PtO *Leic* from 20. *HMPPS Chaplaincy HQ, Post Points 8.34-8.37, Ministry of Justice, 102 Petty France, London SW1H 9AJ* M: 07891-121388 E: helen.dearnley@justice.gov.uk

DEARNLEY, Mark Christopher. b 59. Cranmer Hall Dur 84. **d** 87 **p** 88. C Purley Ch Ch *S'wark* 87–91; C Addiscombe St Mary 91–93; C Addiscombe St Mary Magd w St Martin 93–94; V Hook 94–02; R Wendover and Halton *Ox* 02–16; AD Wendover 04–16; Hon Can Ch Ch 14–16; V St Alb St Pet from 16. *The Vicarage, 35 Hall Place Gardens, St Albans AL1 3SB* T: (01727) 851464 M: 07769-960447 E: mark.dearnley@btinternet.com

DEAS, Leonard Stephen. b 52. New Coll Ox BA 75 CertEd 76 MA 78. St Mich Coll Llan 81. **d** 82 **p** 83. C Dowlais *Llan* 82–84; Chapl St Mich Coll Llan 84–85; Chapl Univ of Wales (Cardiff) *Llan* 85–86; V Newbridge *Mon* 86–93; Can Res St Woolos Cathl 92–96; Master Charterhouse Hull 96–17; rtd 17. *98 Walkergate, Beverley HU17 9BT* T: (01482) 861399 E: dysgamyser@hotmail.co.uk

DEAVES, Peter. b 76. Sheff Univ BA 97. Ridley Hall Cam 14. **d** 16 **p** 17. C Rudgwick *Chich* 16–20; R Sissinghurst w Frittenden *Cant* from 20. *Oakleaves, The Rectory, Frittenden, Cranbrook TN17 2DD* T: (01580) 852275 M: 07900-185591 E: peterevd@gmail.com

DEBNEY, Nicholas Johnathan. b 72. SWMTC 10. **d** 13 **p** 14. C Dartmouth and Dittisham *Ex* 13–17; TV Newton Abbot from 17; P-in-c Bovey Tracey St Jo w Heathfield from 19. *St Luke's Vicarage, 10 Laburnum Road, Newton Abbot TQ12 4LQ* T: (01626) 334357 E: fr.debney@hotmail.co.uk

DEBOO, Canon Alan John. b 45. Qu Coll Cam BA 73 MA 77. Westcott Ho Cam 72. **d** 74 **p** 75. C Brackley St Pet w St Jas *Pet* 74–77; PtO *Sarum* 85–94; NSM Wexcombe 94–02; NSM Savernake 02–09 and 13–15; PtO from 15; Bp's Officer for NSMs 03–09; Bp's Adv for Assoc Min 09–15; Can and Preb Sarum Cathl from 05. *Mayzells Cottage, Collingbourne Kingston, Marlborough SN8 3SD* T: (01264) 850683 E: alandeboo@aol.com

DEBOYS, David Gordon. b 54. QUB BD 76 Wolfs Coll Ox MLitt. Ridley Hall Cam 90. **d** 92 **p** 93. C Ipswich St Aug *St E* 92–93; C Whitton and Thurleston w Akenham 93–95; R Hardwick *Ely* 95–00; R Toft w Caldecote and Childerley 95–00; V Cambridge St Jas 00–07; Dir Focus Chr Inst Cambridge 00–07; V Ealing St Barn *Lon* 07–12; C Tewkesbury w Walton Cardiff and Twyning *Glouc* 12–15; Dioc Worship Officer 12–15; TV Southampton (City Cen) *Win* 15–18; V Southampton St Mich 18–21; rtd 21. *Address withheld by request*

DEDMAN, Canon Roger James. b 45. Oak Hill Th Coll 68. **d** 71 **p** 72. C Gresley *Derby* 71–74; C Ipswich St Fran *St E* 74–79; P-in-c Bildeston w Wattisham 79–92; P-in-c Bramford 92–10; P-in-c Somersham w Flowton and Offton w Willisham 94–02; P-in-c Gt and Lt Blakenham w Baylham and Nettlestead 02–10; RD Bosmere 96–01 and 05–07; Hon Can St E Cathl 01–10; rtd 10; PtO *Bradf* 10–14; *Leeds* from 14; *St E* 10–17. *10 St Martin's Field, Otley LS21 2FN* E: rogerjdedman@gmail.com

DEEDES, Ms Rosemary Anne. b 66. Birm Univ BA 87 City Univ 90. Westcott Ho Cam 94. **d** 96 **p** 97. C St Botolph Aldgate w H Trin Minories *Lon* 96–99; Asst Chapl HM Pris Holloway 99–02; Chapl HM Pris Downview 02–10; Chapl HM Pris Is of Wight 10–15; Chapl Cov Univ from 15; Chapl Earl Mountbatten Hospice 17–20. *Address withheld by request* E: rosie.deedes@btinternet.com

DEEGAN, Arthur Charles. b 49. CertEd 71 Birm Univ BEd 86. Qu Coll Birm 86. **d** 88 **p** 89. C Leic St Jas 88–91; C Melton Gt Framland 91–92; TV 92–93; TV Melton Mowbray 93–96; R Barwell w Potters Marston and Stapleton 96–08; P-in-c Braunstone Town w Thorpe Astley 08–15; TR 15–18;

CF (TA) 95–15; rtd 18; PtO *Leic* from 19. *58 Amy Street, Leicester LE3 2FB* T: 0116-224 8346 E: ac.deegan@gmail.com

DEEGAN, Michael Joseph. b 54. Ripon Coll Cuddesdon. **d** 09 **p** 10. Dir Soc Justice and C Sarum Cathl 09–12; Warden Pilsdon Community 12–19; rtd 19; PtO *Sarum* from 20. *Flat 4 , 50 Peverell Avenue East, Poundbury, Dorchester DT1 3WE* M: 07502-216607 E: mdeegan01@aol.com

DEEMING, Paul Leyland. b 44. CA Tr Coll 65 CMS Tr Coll Selly Oak 70. **d** 80 **p** 80. CMS Pakistan 71–82; R E and W Horndon w Lt Warley *Chelmsf* 83–89; V Gt Ilford St Andr 89–01; Co-ord Chapl Heatherwood & Wexham Park Hosps NHS Foundn Trust 01–09; rtd 09. *10 Glenthorn Road, Bexhill-on-Sea TN39 3QH* T: (01424) 222287

DEERING, Stewart Clarke. b 87. Sheff Univ BEng 08. Oak Hill Th Coll 15. **d** 18 **p** 19. C Gleadless Valley *Sheff* from 18. *44 Warminster Crescent, Sheffield S8 9NW* M: 07813-733939 E: stewart.deering@gmail.com *or* stewart@hcgv.org.uk

DEETH, William Stanley. b 38. St Pet Coll Ox BA 59 MA 67. St Steph Ho Ox 66. **d** 68 **p** 69. C Eastbourne St Mary *Chich* 68–71; C Benwell St Jas *Newc* 71–75; C-in-c Byker St Martin CD 75–76; P-in-c Byker St Martin 76; V 76–89; P-in-c Bothal 89–91; R Bothal and Pegswood w Longhirst 91–94; rtd 94; PtO *Newc* 94–08; *Leeds* from 17. *2 All Saints Square, Ripon HG4 1FN* T: (01765) 690366 E: w.deeth@talktalk.net

DEGG, Miss Jennifer Margaret. b 39. Open Univ BA 85 Rolle Coll CertEd 64. NOC. **d** 06 **p** 07. NSM Saddleworth *Man* 06–09; PtO from 09. *2 Lowerfields, Dobcross, Oldham OL3 5NW* E: jennydegg@talktalk.net

DEHOOP, Brother Thomas Anthony. b 38. Bp's Univ Lennox BA 63 LTh 63. **d** 68 **p** 69. C Fort George w Painthills Canada 68–70; I Mistassini 70–72; R La Tuque 72–75; Assoc P Pierrefonds 75–79; SSF from 79; PtO *Sarum* 79–80; Hon C Toxteth St Marg *Liv* 80–85; Chapl Newsham Gen Hosp Liv 82–85; P-in-c Cambridge St Benedict *Ely* 85–88; V 88–92; PtO *Liv* 92–94; *Ely* 92–96; *Eur* from 94. *43 Balaam Street, London E13 8AQ* E: glasshamptonssf@franciscans.org.uk *or* thomasanthonyssf@franciscans.org.uk

DEIGHTON, Gary. b 61. Dundee Univ MA 83 Nottm Univ MA 89 Heythrop Coll Lon MA 11 PGCE 84. SWMTC 10. **d** 12 **p** 13. C Paignton St Jo, St Andr and St Boniface *Ex* 12–16; V Goodrington and Collaton St Mary from 16. *The Vicarage, 17 Seafields, Paignton TQ4 6NY* T: (01803) 843038 E: fr.gary@outlook.com

DEJA, Jonathan Joseph. b 87. Clare Coll Cam BA 08. Oak Hill Th Coll BA 16. **d** 16 **p** 17. C Harold Wood *Chelmsf* 16–19; C Moulton *Pet* from 19. *8 Cubleigh Close, Moulton, Northampton NN3 7BG* M: 07743-250432 E: jonniedeja@gmail.com *or* associatevicar@moultonchurch.co.uk

DEKKER, Denise Rosemary Irene. b 43. Th Ext Educn Coll 90. **d** 95 **p** 96. C Stutterheim S Africa 95–99; P-in-c 99–04; P-in-c Kokstad 04–09; PtO *Win* 09–11; P-in-c Guernsey St Andr 11–15; NSM Coventry Caludon *Cov* 15–18; rtd 18. *64 Waun Sidan, Pembrey, Burry Port SA16 0JY* M: 07850-995716 E: dekkerd1@hotmail.com

DEL PINO, Mrs Helena Mary Elizabeth. b 62. K Coll Lon LLB 85. Ox Min Course 13. **d** 16 **p** 18. NSM Pet H Spirit Bretton 16–20; V from 20. *17 Alexandra Road, Peterborough PE1 3DB* T: (01733) 310795 M: 07561-520989 E: revhelenadelpino@gmail.com

DELAFORCE, Stephen Robert. b 52. Middx Poly BSc 80 Cranfield Inst of Tech MSc 88 Nottm Univ MA 03 CEng MIMechE 83. EMMTC 04. **d** 07 **p** 08. NSM Woodhouse, Woodhouse Eaves and Swithland *Leic* 07–10; C Beaumont Leys 10–15; V Stocking Farm and Beaumont Leys 15–20; rtd 20; PtO *Leic* from 20. *10 Silverbirch Way, Loughborough LE11 2DH* E: steve.delaforce@gmail.com

DELAMERE, Isaac George. b 71. CITC BTh 02. **d** 02 **p** 03. C Newtownards *D & D* 02–05; I Narraghmore and Timolin w Castledermot etc *D & G* 05–14; I Tullamore w Durrow, Newtownfertullagh, Rahan etc *M & K* from 14; Can Meath from 18; Can Kildare Cathl from 18. *St Catherine's Rectory, Church Avenue, Tullamore, Co Offaly, Republic of Ireland* T: (00353) (57) 932 1731 M: 86-060 9241 E: revisaacdelamere@eircom.net *or* tullamore@meath.anglican.org

DELANEY, Anthony. b 65. St Jo Coll Nottm BTh 95. **d** 95 **p** 96. C Cullompton *Ex* 95–98; C Maidstone St Luke *Cant* 98–01; P-in-c W Horsley *Guildf* 01–03; R 03–08; PtO *Man* from 09. *99 Barlow Moor Road, Didsbury, Manchester M20 2GP* T: 0161-445 0446 M: 07881-902966 E: anthony@ivychurch.org

DELANEY, Janet. b 50. STETS. **d** 07 **p** 08. C Wootton Bassett *Sarum* 07–11; R Askerswell, Loders, Powerstock and Symondsbury 11–17; RD Lyme Bay 14–16; rtd 17; PtO *Win* from 17. *10 Doe Copse Way, New Milton BH25 5GB* T: (01425) 837746 E: jan.delaney@talktalk.net

DELANEY, The Ven Peter Anthony. b 39. MBE 01. AKC 65. **d** 66 **p** 67. C St Marylebone w H Trin *Lon* 66–70; Chapl Nat Heart Hosp Lon 66–70; Res Chapl Univ Ch Ch the K *Lon* 70–73; Can Res and Prec S'wark Cathl 73–77; V All Hallows by the Tower etc *Lon* 77–04; P-in-c St Kath Cree 98–02; Can Cyprus and the Gulf from 88; Preb St Paul's Cathl *Lon* 95–99; Adn Lon 99–09; P-in-c St Steph Walbrook and St Swithun etc 04–14; PtO from 14. *29 Portland Square, London E1W 2QR* T: (020) 7481 1786 E: padelaney@btinternet.com

DELAP, Canon Dana Lurkse. b 65. St Jo Coll Dur BA 87 MA 93 MATM 11. Cranmer Hall Dur 09. **d** 11 **p** 12. C Fenham St Jas and St Basil *Newc* 11–14; TV Vale and Cotswold Edge *Glouc* from 14; Hon Can Tamale Ghana from 16. *The Vicarage, High Street, Blockley, Moreton-in-Marsh GL56 9ES* T: (01386) 700676 M: 07952-096789 E: dana@delap.org.uk

DELFGOU, The Very Revd Jonathan Hawke. b 63. Aston Tr Scheme 89 Linc Th Coll BTh 94. **d** 94 **p** 95. C Greenstead *Chelmsf* 94–98; TV Wickford and Runwell 98–18; Chapl Southend Community Care Services NHS Trust 98–99; Chapl S Essex Mental Health & Community Care NHS Trust 00–06; Chapl S Essex Partnership Univ NHS Foundn Trust 06–17; Chapl Essex Partnership Univ NHS Foundn Trust 17–18; V Hadleigh, Layham and Shelley *St E* from 18; Dean Bocking from 18; RD Hadleigh from 21. *The Deanery, Church Street, Hadleigh, Ipswich IP7 5DT* E: delfgou@live.co.uk

DELIA, William Joshua James. b 92. St Steph Ho Ox 17. **d** 20 **p** 21. C W Worthing St Jo *Chich* from 20; C Worthing St Andr from 20. *The Vicarage, 56 The Boulevard, Worthing BN13 1LA* M: 07761-284226 E: wjjdelia@outlook.com

DELINGER, Ian Michael. b 70. Truman State Univ (USA) BSc 92 SS Coll Cam BTh 04. Westcott Ho Cam 01. **d** 04 **p** 05. C Chorlton-cum-Hardy St Clem *Man* 04–07; Chapl Ches Univ 08–16; R San Luis Obispo USA from 16. *St Stephen's Episcopal Church, 1344 Nipomo Street, San Luis Obispo CA 93401-3935, USA* T: (001) (805) 543 7212 F: 543 0744 E: fatherimd@aol.com

DELMEGE, Canon Andrew Mark. b 68. Essex Univ BA 91 Southn Univ MTh 98. SWMTC 94. **d** 97 **p** 98. C Kings Heath *Birm* 97–01; V Brandwood 01–20; Chapl to Deaf People 01–10; P-in-c Weoley Castle 10–14; Urban Estates Missr 18–20; Hon Can Birm Cathl 18–20; Can Res Birm Cathl from 20. *The Vicarage, 77 Doversley Road, Birmingham B14 6NN* T: 0121-693 0217 *or* 456 1535 *or* 246 6100 F: 246 6125 E: andydelmege@hotmail.com *or* canonmissioner@birminghamcathedral.com

DELVE, Eric David. b 42. Trin Coll Bris. **d** 89 **p** 90. NSM Bris St Matt and St Nath 89–92; P-in-c Kirkdale St Lawr *Liv* 93–96; V Maidstone St Luke *Cant* 96–12; AD Maidstone 93–02; Six Preacher Cant Cathl 99–09; rtd 13; PtO *Roch* 13–17; *B & W* from 19. *35 Manor Road, Weston-super-Mare BS23 2SU*

DELVES, Canon Anthony James. b 47. Birm Univ BSocSc 70 Hull Univ PhD 94. St Steph Ho Ox 83. **d** 85 **p** 86. C Cantley *Sheff* 85–90; V Goldthorpe w Hickleton 90–07; AD Wath 00–06; Hon Can Sheff Cathl 98–07; rtd 07; PtO *Sheff* 07–21; *Wakef* 07–14; *Leeds* from 14; *Chich* from 17. *3 Pelham Cottages, Pelham Yard, Seaford BN25 1PQ* T: (01323) 893695 E: ajdelves3@gmail.com

DELVES, Michelle Mary. b 67. Cranmer Hall Dur 16. **d** 18 **p** 19. C Stranton *Dur* from 18. *40 Browning Avenue, Hartlepool TS25 5PS*

DELVES (formerly MANHOOD), Canon Phyllis. b 32. Aston Tr Scheme 78 Qu Coll Birm 79. **dss** 82 **d** 87 **p** 94. Harwich *Chelmsf* 82–83; Dovercourt and Parkeston 83–85; Fawley *Win* 85–87; Par Dn 87–92; P-in-c Bournemouth St Aug 92–99; Hon Can Win Cathl 96–99; rtd 99; PtO *Win* from 01. *11 Rhyme Hall Mews, Fawley, Southampton SO45 1FX* T: (023) 8089 4450 E: phyllis.delves@sky.com

DELVES BROUGHTON, Simon Brian Hugo. b 33. Ex Coll Ox BA 56 MA 64. Kelham Th Coll 56. **d** 59 **p** 60. Ox Miss to Calcutta India 60–64; C Skirbeck St Nic *Linc* 64–67; Chapl Chittagong E Pakistan/Bangladesh 67–69; V St Thos Cathl Dhaka 69–74; V Northampton Ch Ch *Pet* 74–95; Chapl Northn Gen Hosp 77–87; rtd 95; PtO *Ox* 95–00. *71A Observatory Street, Oxford OX2 6EP* T: (01865) 515463

DEMAIN, Peter James. b 64. Salford Univ BA 85. SNWTP 07. **d** 10 **p** 11. OLM Middleton and Thornham *Man* from 10. *3 St Gabriel's Close, Rochdale OL11 2TG* T: (01706) 522985 M: 07747-398012 E: peterdemain@yahoo.co.uk

DEMERY, Rupert Edward Rodier. b 72. Trin Hall Cam BA 94 MA 01 BTh 01. Ridley Hall Cam 98. **d** 01 **p** 02. C New Borough and Leigh *Sarum* 01–05; Lower Chapl Eton Coll from 05. *Burnham Thorpe, Eton Wick Road, Eton College, Windsor SL4 6ET* T: (01753) 441629 M: 07801-825671 E: r.demery@etoncollege.org.uk

DEMETRI, Luke. b 92. Lanc Univ BA 13 Cumbria Univ PGCE 14. St Steph Ho Ox BA 20. **d** 21. C Croydon

St Mich w St Jas *S'wark* from 21. *Flat 3, St Michael's Court, 5 Poplar Walk, Croydon CR0 1UA* T: (020) 3609 4184 E: frlukedemetri@gmail.com

DEMPSEY, Oliver Jack. b 92. Newc Univ BA 15 MA 17 Trin Coll Cam BA 19. Westcott Ho Cam 17. d 20 p 21. C Cowgate *Newc* from 20; C Newbiggin Hall from 20. *31 Alnmouth Court, Newcastle upon Tyne NE5 3LG* T: 0191-435 8766 M: 07710-566423 E: fr.oliver.dempsey@outlook.com

DEMPSTER, Adrian. b 49. Newc Univ BSc 70. EMMTC 05. d 08 p 09. NSM Kirkby in Ashfield *S'well* 08–12; NSM Skegby w Teversal 12–17; NSM Selston from 17. *105 Nottingham Road, Selston, Nottingham NG16 6BU* T: (01773) 811846 F: 0115-950 4646 M: 07971-142829

DENBY, Canon Paul. b 47. NW Ord Course 73. d 76 p 77. C Stretford All SS *Man* 76–80; V Stalybridge 80–87; Chapl Tameside Gen Hosp 82–87; Dir of Ords *Man* 87–95; LNSM Officer 91–95; Hon Can Man Cathl 92–95; Bp's Dom Chapl 94–95; Can Admin and Prec Man Cathl 95–07; rtd 07; PtO *Man* 07–08 and from 12. *14 Cranberry Drive, Bolton BL3 3TB* T: (01204) 655157 *or* 0161-834 0490 E: paul@thedenbys.co.uk

DENCH, Canon Christopher David. b 62. RGN 83. Aston Tr Scheme 86 Sarum & Wells Th Coll 88. d 91 p 92. C Crayford *Roch* 91–94; P-in-c Leybourne 94–98; R 98–05; Dioc Lay Tr Adv 01–05; Tr Officer for CME 03–10; Min Development Officer 05–10; Bp's Officer for Min and Tr from 10; Hon Can Roch Cathl 11–18; Can Res Roch Cathl from 18. *Easter Garth, The Precinct, Rochester ME1 1SX* T: (01634) 560000 *or* (01732) 220245 M: 07961-433545 E: chris.dench@rochester.anglican.org

DENERLEY, John Keith Christopher. b 34. Qu Coll Ox BA 58 MA 61. St Steph Ho Ox 58. d 61 p 62. C Airedale w Fryston *Wakef* 61–64; Chapl Sarum Th Coll 64–68; Min Can Cov Cathl 68–76; Chapl Lanchester Poly 70–76; Chapl The Dorothy Kerin Trust Burrswood 76–85; V Trellech and Cwmcarvan *Mon* 85–86; V Penallt 85–86; V Penallt and Trellech 87–99; Chapl Ty Mawr Convent (Wales) 85–90; RD Monmouth *Mon* 93–99; rtd 99; PtO *Glouc* from 00. *Address temp unknown*

DENGATE, Richard Henry. b 39. Cant Sch of Min 82. d 85 p 86. NSM Wittersham w Stone and Ebony *Cant* 85; R Sandhurst w Newenden 90–01; rtd 01; PtO *Cant* from 01; Chich from 15. *Apuldram, Main Street, Peasemarsh, Rye TN31 6UL* T: (01797) 230980 E: rhdengate@btinternet.com

DENHAM, Anthony Christopher. b 43. Keble Coll Ox BA 65 MA 70. Oak Hill Th Coll 91. d 93 p 94. C Hythe *Cant* 93–97; V Haddenham w Cuddington, Kingsey etc *Ox* 97–08; rtd 08; PtO *Guildf* from 08. *3 The Larches, Woking GU21 4RE* T: (01483) 823310 E: a.chris.denham@gmail.com

DENHAM, Nicholas Philip. b 50. Salford Univ BSc 72 Dur Univ MA 10 Birm Univ CertEd 74. Wycliffe Hall Ox 87. d 89 p 90. C Bishopwearmouth St Gabr *Dur* 89–90; C Chester le Street 90–92; TV Rushden w Newton Bromswold *Pet* 92–95; R Teigh w Whissendine and Market Overton 95–02; P-in-c Greetham and Thistleton w Stretton and Clipsham 01–02; RD Rutland 01–02; TR Bedworth *Cov* 02–05; V Escomb *Dur* 05–08; R Etherley 05–08; V Witton Park 05–08; V Hamsterley and Witton-le-Wear 05–08; rtd 08; PtO *Ox* 09–14; *Ely* 14–19; *Derby* from 19. *1 Vicarage Close, Belper DE56 1TB*

DENHOLM, Robert Jack. b 31. Edin Th Coll 53. d 56 p 57. C Dundee St Mary Magd *Bre* 56–59; C Edin St Pet 59–61; R Bridge of Allan *St And* 61–69; Chapl Stirling Univ 67–69; R N Berwick *Edin* 69–80; R Gullane 76–80; R Edin St Mark 80–90; Can St Mary's Cathl 88–90; rtd 90. *20 St Vincent Court, 131 St Vincent Street, Broughty Ferry, Dundee DD5 2DA* T: (01382) 525400 E: jackdenholm@googlemail.com

DENIS LE SÈVE, Hilary. *See* LE SÈVE, Jane Hilary

DENISON, Canon Keith Malcolm. b 45. Down Coll Cam BA 67 MA 71 PhD 70. Westcott Ho Cam 70. d 71 p 72. C Chepstow *Mon* 71–72; C Bassaleg 72–75; Post-Ord Tr Officer 75–85; V Mathern and Mounton 75–80; V Mathern and Mounton w St Pierre 80–85; RD Chepstow 82–85; V Risca 85–91; V Goldcliffe and Whitson and Nash 91–96; Dioc Dir of Educn Monmouth 91–11; Hon Can St Woolos Cathl 91–94; Can St Woolos Cathl 94–11; Can Res St Woolos Cathl 96–11; rtd 11; PtO *Pet* from 12; *Linc* 18–21. *21 Melbourne Road, Stamford PE9 1UD* T: (01780) 751571 E: keith_denison@hotmail.com

DENISON, Philip. b 55. York Univ BA 77 CertEd. St Jo Coll Nottm 83. d 86 p 87. C Barnoldswick w Bracewell *Bradf* 86–88; P-in-c Basford St Leodegarius *S'well* 88–91; C Basford w Hyson Green 91–94; V Nether Stowey w Over Stowey *B & W* 94–04; R Aisholt, Enmore, Goathurst, Nether Stowey etc 05; RD Quantock 01–05; PtO 06–10; C Alfred Jewel 10–16; V Isle Valley from 16. *The Rectory, Broadway, Ilminster TA19 9RE* T: (01460) 259155 E: denisonphil15@hotmail.com

DENLEY, Adam Spencer. b 81. New Coll Dur BSc 06. Oak Hill Th Coll 14. d 16 p 17. C Southsea St Jude *Portsm* 16–21; V Folkestone St Jo *Cant* from 21. *St John's Vicarage, 4 Cornwallis Avenue, Folkestone CT19 5JA* M: 07985-749804 E: adam.denley@gmail.com *or* adam.denley@stjohnsfolkestone.org

DENLEY, Trevor Maurice. b 47. d 06 p 07. Partnership P E Bris 06–19; OLM Bris St Aid w St Geo 06–19; PtO from 19. *31 Dundridge Gardens, Bristol BS5 8SZ* T: 0117-961 4468 M: 07960-329127

DENNEN, Lyle. b 42. Harvard Univ LLB 67 Trin Coll Cam BA 70 MA 75. Cuddesdon Coll 70. d 72 p 73. C S Lambeth St Ann *S'wark* 72–75; C Richmond St Mary w St Matthias 75–78; P-in-c Kennington St Jo 78–79; V Kennington St Jo w St Jas 79–99; P-in-c Brixton Road Ch Ch 81–89; RD Brixton 90–99; Hon Can S'wark Cathl 99; Adn Hackney *Lon* 99–10; V St Andr Holborn 99–14; rtd 14; PtO *Lon* from 14. *1 Victoria Wharf, 46 Narrow Street, London E14 8DD* T: (020) 7353 3544 F: 7583 2750 E: lyle.dennen@hotmail.com

DENNER-BROWN, Sarah. *See* BROWN, Sarah Romilly Denner

DENNESS, Mrs Linda Christine. b 51. Portsm Dioc Tr Course 88. d 89 p 01. NSM Milton *Portsm* 89–93; Chapl Asst Portsm Hosps NHS Trust 89–91; NSM Portsea St Mary *Portsm* 93–96; NSM Wymering 96–06; P-in-c Cosham 06–09; P-in-c Wymering 07–09; PtO 09–10 and from 13; NSM Portsea N End St Mark 10–13. *19 Fourth Avenue, Cosham, Portsmouth PO6 3HX* T: (023) 9232 1583

DENNETT, Mrs Kirsty Ann. b 71. York Sch of Min BA 18 St Hild Coll 18. d 20 p 21. C Clifton *York* from 20. *1 Brougham Close, York YO30 5FX* M: 07403-438739 E: kdennett6@gmail.com

DENNIS, Barbara Christine. *See* HUME, Barbara Christine

DENNIS, David Alan. b 46. St Luke's Coll Ex BSc 90. d 05 p 06. OLM Alderholt *Sarum* 05–16; rtd 16; PtO *Sarum* 16–20. *18 Oak Road, Alderholt, Fordingbridge SP6 3BL* T: (01425) 655230 E: davidalan.dennis@btinternet.com

DENNIS, Miss Drucilla Lyn. b 49. Ox Univ BEd 71 Southn Univ MA(Ed) 82 Win Univ MA 10. S Dios Minl Tr Scheme 92. d 95 p 96. NSM Cowes H Trin and St Mary *Portsm* 95–01; TV Dorchester *Sarum* 01–08; Hon C Chale, Shorwell w Kingston and Brighstone and Brooke w Mottistone *Portsm* 08–11; Chapl Earl Mountbatten Hospice and Isle of Wight NHS Primary Care Trust 09–11; P-in-c Brading w Yaverland *Portsm* 11–16; rtd 16; PtO *Portsm* from 16. *40 Park Road, Cowes PO31 7LT* T: (01983) 297002 E: drucilladennis@hotmail.com

DENNIS, Canon Robert Franklin. b 51. St Paul's Coll Grahamstown 91. d 94 p 94. C Kuils River S Africa 94–96; C Matroosfontein 96–99; R Maitland 99–03; TR Bredasdorp 03–05; P-in-c Crumpsall *Man* 06–09; Min Can St Woolos Cathl *Mon* 09–11; P-in-c Llantilio Pertholey w Bettws Chpl etc 11–14; V Connah's Quay *St As* 14–16; TV Borderlands Miss Area 17; rtd 17; Chapl Pau *Eur* 17–20; PtO *St As* from 17; Hon Can Saldanha Bay S Africa from 14; PtO *Eur* from 17. *3 bis rue Pasteur, 64000 Pau, France* T: (0033) 5 59 30 91 84 E: rfd.stmark2@gmail.com

DENNIS, Samuel James. b 85. Peterho Cam BA 07. Westcott Ho Cam 08. d 11 p 12. C Catford (Southend) and Downham *S'wark* 11–16; P-in-c Croydon Woodside 16–18; V from 18. *St Luke's Vicarage, Portland Road, London SE25 4RB* T: (020) 8654 9841 M: 07940-576397 E: fr.sam.dennis@gmail.com

DENNIS, Timothy William. b 81. Southn Univ BSc 02. Wycliffe Hall Ox BA 19. d 19 p 20. C Winklebury and Worting *Win* from 19. *77 Camrose Way, Basingstoke RG21 3AW* M: 07734-663313 E: timwdennis@icloud.com

DENNIS, Canon Trevor John. b 45. St Jo Coll Cam BA 68 MA 71 PhD 74. Westcott Ho Cam 71. d 72 p 73. C Newport Pagnell *Ox* 72–74; Chapl Eton Coll 75–82; Tutor Sarum & Wells Th Coll 82–94; Vice-Prin 89–94; Can Res Ches Cathl 94–10; rtd 10; PtO *Ches* from 11. *11 Anne's Way, Chester CH4 7BA* T: (01244) 638441 E: trevordennis11@gmail.com

DENNISON, Philip Ian. b 52. Nottm Univ BTh 81. St Jo Coll Nottm 77. d 81 p 82. C Stalybridge H Trin and Ch Ch *Ches* 81–84; C Heswall 84–91; TV Bushbury *Lich* 91–04; V Shevington *Blackb* 04–17; rtd 17; PtO *York* from 18. *1 Algarth Rise, York YO31 1HD* E: joycedphilipid@gmail.com

DENNISS, Mrs Amanda Jane. b 57. Univ Coll Lon LLB 78. Oak Hill Th Coll 98 NTMTC 00. d 03 p 04. C Turnham Green Ch Ch *Lon* 03–06; PtO 06–08; C Westwood *Cov* 08–11; R Itchen Valley *Win* 15–18; PtO *Lon* from 13; *Win* 18–20; C Win Ch Ch from 20. *3C Longridge Road, London SW5 9SB* E: amandadenniss@gmail.com

DENNISTON, James Keith Stuart. b 49. Down Coll Cam MA 70 Barrister-at-Law 70. Oak Hill Th Coll DipEd 92. d 93 p 94. C Harborne Heath *Birm* 93–97; Chapl Lee Abbey 97–02; PtO *Ex* 02–03; TV Chippenham St Paul w Hardenhuish etc

Bris 03–07; PtO *Ex* from 07. *Rectory Cottage, King's Nympton, Umberleigh EX37 9SS* T: (01769) 581325

DENNISTON, Jennifer. b 58. Edin Univ BA 79. St Mellitus Coll 15. **d** 18 **p** 19. NSM Worcs W Rural *Worc* from 18. *Sapey Court Cottage, Clifton-on-Teme, Worcester WR6 6HE* T: (01886) 853280 M: 07783-432017 E: jendenniston@gmail.com

DENNO, Basil. b 52. Dundee Univ BSc 74. Oak Hill Th Coll BA 81. **d** 81 **p** 83. C Chaddesden St Mary *Derby* 81–83; Hon C 83–84; PtO from 08. *24 Macclesfield Old Road, Buxton SK17 6TY* T: (01298) 22193 E: lizziedenno@talk21.com

DENNO, Elizabeth Kate (Skye). b 79. Derby Univ BA 00 Ox Univ MA 19. St Jo Coll Nottm BA 08. **d** 08 **p** 09. C Dursley *Glouc* 08–12; TV Cowley St Jas *Ox* 12–17; V Marston w Elsfield from 17. *Marston Vicarage, Elsfield Road, Marston, Oxford OX3 0PR* T: (01865) 202988 M: 07720-768684 E: joskso@yahoo.co.uk *or* vicar@stnicholasmarston.org.uk

DENNY, Annita. b 46. **d** 13 **p** 15. NSM Budleigh Salterton, E Budleigh w Bicton etc *Ex* 13–17; NSM Sidmouth, Woolbrook, Salcombe Regis, Sidbury etc 17–20; PtO from 20. *119 Cotmaton Road, Sidmouth EX10 8XN* T: (01395) 512735

DENNY, Michael Thomas. b 47. Kelham Th Coll 68 St Jo Coll Nottm 71. **d** 73 **p** 74. C Gospel Lane St Mich *Birm* 73–77; P-in-c Frankley 77–82; R 82–07; rtd 07; PtO *Birm* 07–13; *Heref* from 08. *Orchard Cottage, Green Lane, Yarpole, Leominster HR6 0BE* T: (01568) 780874 E: revdenny1@btinternet.com

DENSMORE, Robert McCutchen. b 78. Amherst Coll (USA) BA 00 K Coll Lon MA 07. Duke Div Sch MDiv 16. **d** 16. C Upton *Ex* 16–20; R Bath St Sav w Swainswick and Woolley *B & W* from 20. *St Saviour's Rectory, Claremont Road, Bath BA1 6LX* M: 07852-335515 E: robert.densmore@gmail.com

DENT, Canon Christopher Mattinson. b 46. K Coll Lon BA 68 AKC 68 MTh 69 Jes Coll Cam BA 72 MA 76 New Coll Ox MA 76 DPhil 80. Westcott Ho Cam 70. **d** 72 **p** 73. C Chelsea St Luke *Lon* 72–76; Asst Chapl New Coll Ox 76–79; Fell Chapl and Dean Div 79–84; V Hollingbourne and Hucking w Leeds and Broomfield *Cant* 84–93; V Bedford St Andr *St Alb* 93–12; Hon Can St Alb 01–12; RD Bedford 05–10; rtd 12; PtO *Cant* from 13. *20 Ardent Avenue, Walmer, Deal CT14 7UE* T: (01304) 361624 E: cmdent@btinternet.com

DENT, Joseph Michael. b 73. Jes Coll Cam BA 94 MA 98. Wycliffe Hall Ox BTh 99. **d** 99 **p** 00. C Plymouth St Andr and Stonehouse *Ex* 99–03; C Sevenoaks St Nic *Roch* 03–13; TR Plymouth St Andr and Stonehouse *Ex* from 13. *St Andrew's Rectory, 13 Bainbridge Avenue, Plymouth PL3 5QZ* T: (01752) 211241 E: josephdent@gmail.com

DENT, Marie Penelope. b 46. K Coll Lon BA 88. Westcott Ho Cam 02. **d** 04 **p** 05. C N Walsham and Edingthorpe *Nor* 04–08; TV Redditch H Trin *Worc* 08–10; rtd 10; PtO *Nor* from 10. *1 Stirling Road, Norwich NR6 6GE* T: (01603) 487938 M: 07799-220357 E: mpd46@outlook.com

DENT, Michael Leslie. b 54. Leeds Univ BEd 76. St Steph Ho Ox 93. **d** 95 **p** 96. C Cockerton *Dur* 95–98; V Escomb 98–03; R Etherley 98–03; V Witton Park 98–03; Chapl Dur Constabulary 02–03; TR E Darlington 03–12; V Darlington St Jo 12–13; V Warkworth and Acklington *Newc* 13–17; rtd 17. *16 Dorchester Court, Marlborough Drive, Darlington DL1 5YD* E: mikedent54@gmail.com

DENT, Raymond William. b 47. TD 03. Open Univ BA 84 Birm Coll of Educn CertEd 68. Ridley Hall Cam 70. **d** 73 **p** 74. C Hyde St Geo *Ches* 73–76; C Eastham 76–79; TV E Runcorn w Halton 79–80; V Hallwood 80–83; V New Brighton Em 83–94; V Willaston 94–13; rtd 13; PtO *Ches* from 14. *32 Proctor Road, Wirral CH47 4BB* T: 0151-792 2022 E: raymondwdent@gmail.com

DENT, Stephen Edward. b 55. STETS 12. **d** 15 **p** 19. NSM Lee-on-the-Solent *Portsm* from 15. *St Faith's Church, Victoria Square, Lee-on-the-Solent PO13 9NF* M: 07722-902344 E: steve.e.dent@btinternet.com

DENTON, Peter Brian. b 37. Kelham Th Coll 57. **d** 62 **p** 63. C Ellesmere Port *Ches* 62–66; Chapl HM Borstal Hollesley Bay 66–69; CF 69–89; Warden Bridge Cen and C Hounslow H Trin w St Paul *Lon* 89–92; V Northolt Park St Barn 92–04; P-in-c Perivale 97–01; P-in-c N Greenford All Hallows 00–04; rtd 04; PtO *Ely* 05–10; *Pet* 05–10 and from 13; P-in-c Pet All SS 10–13; PtO *Ely* from 20. *52 Lornas Field, Hampton Hargate, Peterborough PE7 8AY* T: (01733) 552353 E: revddenton@aol.com

DENTON, Robert Gary. b 76. Leeds Univ BEng 99 PGCE 00. Trin Coll Bris BA 18. **d** 18 **p** 19. C Halton and Osmondthorpe *Leeds* from 18. *St Philip's Vicarage, Osmondthorpe Lane, Leeds LS9 9EF* M: 07402-052527 E: denton.robg@gmail.com

DENYER, Alan Frederick. b 31. Wycliffe Hall Ox 80. **d** 82 **p** 83. C Rodbourne Cheney *Bris* 82–84; P-in-c Garsdon w Lea and Cleverton 84–87; R Garsdon, Lea and Cleverton and Charlton 87–91; R Lydbury N w Hopesay and Edgton *Heref* 91–97; Asst Dioc Soc Resp Officer 91–97; rtd 97; Hon

C Long Preston w Tosside *Bradf* 97–02; PtO *Ripon* 03–14; *Leeds* from 14. *1 Old Deanery Close, St Marygate, Ripon HG4 1LZ* T: (01765) 602397 E: denyer1955@btinternet.com

DENYER, Christopher Richard Terence. b 79. Kent Univ BA 01 Cant Ch Ch Univ MA 05 PGCE 02. SEITE 13. **d** 15 **p** 16. C Bethersden w High Halden and Woodchurch *Cant* 15–18; P-in-c Stour Downs 18–20; V from 20; Jt AD Ashford from 21. *The Rectory, Church Road, Smeeth, Ashford TN25 6SA* M: 07702-584260 E: chrisdenyer1@sky.com

DENYER, Canon Paul Hugh. b 46. Lon Univ BA 68. Ripon Coll Cuddesdon 74. **d** 77 **p** 78. C Horfield H Trin *Bris* 77–82; TV Yate New Town 82–88; V Bris Lockleaze St Mary Magd w St Fran 88–95; Dioc Dir of Ords 95–02; R Warmley, Syston and Bitton 02–13; Hon Can Bris Cathl 99–13; rtd 13; PtO *Bris* from 13. *21 Westfield Close, Hanham, Bristol BS15 3SB* M: 07539-356222 E: paul.joanne4647@btinternet.com

DENYER, Samuel. b 74. Ripon Coll Cuddesdon 07. **d** 09 **p** 10. C Lostwithiel, St Winnow w St Nectan's Chpl etc *Truro* 09–12; C Lanreath, Pelynt and Bradoc 09–12; C Lanlivery 09–12; R Winnersh *Ox* 12–17; V Wells St Cuth w Wookey Hole *B & W* from 17; RD Shepton Mallet from 19. *3 Orchard Lea, Wells BA5 2LZ* T: (01749) 674613 M: 07443-418598 E: denyer.samuel@gmail.com

DEO, Paul Ernest. b 60. Coll of Ripon & York St Jo CertEd 81. St Jo Coll Nottm 95. **d** 97 **p** 98. C Tong *Bradf* 97–00; P-in-c Laisterdyke 00–02; V 02–07; C Baildon 07–12; V Heworth Ch Ch *York* from 12. *Christ Church Vicarage, 13 Lawnway, York YO31 1JD* T: (01904) 269054 E: pauldeo@sky.com

DERBY, Archdeacon of. *Vacant*

DERBY, Bishop of. *See* LANE, The Rt Revd Elizabeth Jane Holden

DERBY, Dean of. *See* ROBINSON, The Very Revd Peter John Alan

DERBYSHIRE, Philip Damien. b 50. Leic Poly LLB 71. Sarum & Wells Th Coll 80. **d** 82 **p** 83. C Chatham St Wm *Roch* 82–86; R Melfort Zimbabwe 86–88; TV Burnham w Dropmore, Hitcham and Taplow *Ox* 88–92; Chapl HM Pris Reading 92–97; Chapl HM Pris Holloway 97–00; Chapl HM Pris Bullingdon 00–04; C Buckingham *Ox* 04–11; AD 10–11; P-in-c Stewkley w Soulbury 11–12; TR Cottesloe 12–20; AD Mursley 14–19; rtd 20; PtO *Ox* from 21. *Rufaro Cottage, 20 Oxenhope Way, Broughton, Milton Keynes MK10 7AE* T: (01908) 633880 E: revphil16@gmail.com

DERLÉN, Mrs Eva Teresia Birgitta Andersdotter. b 75. Lund Univ Sweden MTheol 02. Westcott Ho Cam 02. **p** 03. Sweden 03–11; Hon C Prestwood and Gt Hampden *Ox* 12–19; NSM Swedish Ch from 19. *6-11 Harcourt Street, London W1H 4AG* E: chaplain@swedishchurch.com

DEROSAIRE, Leslie John. b 50. Univ of Wales BA 85 Univ of Wales Coll Newport MA 03. St Mich Coll Llan 01. **d** 04 **p** 05. NSM Govilon w Llanfoist w Llanellen *Mon* 04–07; NSM Llanddewi Rhydderch w Llangattock-juxta-Usk etc 07–09; P-in-c 09–11. *Elmgrove, Hereford Road, Mardy, Abergavenny NP7 6HU* T: (01873) 857256 E: derosaire@tiscali.co.uk

DeROY-JONES, Philip Antony. b 49. St Mich Coll Llan 92. **d** 92 **p** 93. C Neath w Llantwit *Llan* 92–95; V Caerau St Cynfelin 95–98; V Pontlottyn w Fochriw 98–14; rtd 14; PtO *Llan* from 14; *S & B* from 17. *Nyth Clyd, 36 Hoo Street, Neath SA11 2PA* T: (01639) 415304 E: fathertony@outlook.com

DERRICK, David John. b 46. Heythrop Coll Lon MA 08. S'wark Ord Course. **d** 84 **p** 85. NSM Angell Town St Jo S'wark 84–98; NSM St Mary le Strand w St Clem Danes *Lon* 86–93; PtO *Chelmsf* from 12. *Station View, Black Boy Lane, Wrabness, Manningtree CO11 2TL* T: (01255) 880125 E: daviddderrick3@btinternet.com

DERRICK, Mrs Dorothy Margaret. b 41. St Mary's Coll Chelt CertEd 63. Ox Min Course 89. **d** 92 **p** 94. NSM Gt Missenden w Ballinger and Lt Hampden *Ox* 92–98; P-in-c Drayton St Pet (Abingdon) 98–04; rtd 04; PtO *Carl* from 05. *Croft Cottage, 6 Milton Lane, Burgh-by-Sands, Carlisle CA5 6BG* T: (01228) 576860 E: dorothyderrick@btinternet.com

DERRIMAN, Canon Graham Scott. b 39. Bps' Coll Cheshunt 63. **d** 66 **p** 67. C Wandsworth St Mich *S'wark* 66–70; C Merton St Mary 70–74; P-in-c Earlsfield St Andr 74–79; V 79–81; V Camberwell St Luke 81–90; V Croydon St Aug 90–04; Voc Adv Croydon Adnry 93–04; RD Croydon Cen *S'wark* 95–04; Hon Can S'wark Cathl 01–04; rtd 04; PtO *S'wark* from 05. *15 Goodwood Close, Morden SM4 5AW* T: (020) 8648 1550 M: 07952-471515 E: gsd.24@virginmedia.com

DERRY AND RAPHOE, Bishop of. *See* FORSTER, The Rt Revd Andrew James

DERRY, Archdeacon of. *See* MILLER, The Ven Robert Stephen

DERRY, Dean of. *See* STEWART, The Very Revd Raymond John

DESBOROUGH, Mrs Margaret Maureen. b 63. S Bank Univ BSc 96 Goldsmiths' Coll Lon MA 00 PGCE 97. Yorks Min Course 13. **d** 15 **p** 16. NSM Skirlaugh, Catwick, Long Riston, Rise, Swine w Ellerby *York* 15–20; NSM Sigglesthorne w Nunkeeling and Bewholme 15–20; NSM Aldbrough, Mappleton w Goxhill and Withernwick 18–20; NSM Beeford w Frodingham and Foston 18–20; NSM Brandesburton and Leven 18–20; NSM Hornsea, Atwick and Skipsea 18–20. *Address temp unknown* M: 07941-494731 E: mo.desborough@gmail.com
DESBOROUGH, Paul. b 63. Regents Th Coll BA 99. Qu Foundn (Course) 15. **d** 17 **p** 18. C Boulton *Derby* 17–21; C Derby St Alkmund and St Werburgh 21; P-in-c Sinfin Moor from 21; Bp's Adv for New Housing from 21. *Address temp unknown* M: 07958-618507 E: revpaulcofe@gmail.com
DESCOMBES, Raymond Patrick Claude. b 51. Birkbeck Coll Lon BA 01. St Mellitus Coll 14. **d** 15 **p** 16. OLM Becontree S *Chelmsf* from 15. *129 Ballards Road, Dagenham RM10 9AR* M: 07918-050491 E: revraydescombes@gmail.com
DESERT, Thomas Denis. b 31. Bps' Coll Cheshunt 54. **d** 56 **p** 57. C Goldington *St Alb* 56–60; C-in-c Luton St Hugh Lewsey GD 60–63; C St Alb St Sav 63–65; C Cheshunt 65–68; V Bedford All SS 68–89; R Northill w Moggerhanger 89–96; rtd 96; PtO *St Alb* 96–13. *2 Phillpotts Avenue, Bedford MK40 3UJ* T: (01234) 211413 E: denisdesert@ntlworld.com
DESHPANDE, Lakshmi Anant. *See* JEFFREYS, Lakshmi Anant
DESICS, Robert Anthony. b 77. Bp Grosseteste Coll BA 99 Open Univ MA 00. St Jo Coll Nottm 99. **d** 01 **p** 02. C Potters Bar *St Alb* 01–04; C Rainham w Wennington *Chelmsf* 04–05; V Hemlington *York* 05–20; V S Thornaby from 20; CF from 18; PtO *Dur* from 19. *St Peter's Rectory, 14 White House Road, Thornaby, Stockton-on-Tees TS17 0AJ* E: rob_desics@hotmail.com
DESROCHES, Yvonne. b 58. Wilson Carlile Coll 13 Ridley Hall Cam 18. **d** 20 **p** 21. C Northampton Em *Pet* from 20. *13 Booth Lane North, Northampton NN3 6JE* M: 07989-023206 E: ydesroches050709@outlook.com
DESROSIERS, Jacques Thomas Maurice. b 55. Qu Univ Kingston Ontario BCom 77. S'wark Ord Course 91. **d** 94 **p** 95. NSM Benenden *Cant* 94–97; C Maidstone All SS and St Phil w Tovil 97–01; TV Pewsey and Swanborough *Sarum* 01–04; P-in-c Rolvenden *Cant* 04–10; P-in-c Newenden and Rolvenden 10–13; R Rother and Oxney 13–14; AD Tenterden 07–11; AD Romney and Tenterden 11–13; P-in-c Warminster St Denys and Upton Scudamore *Sarum* 14–17; R River Were 17–21; rtd 21. *5 Peacocke Way, Rye TN31 7FD* M: 07931-217458 E: jtmdesrosiers@gmail.com
d'ESTERRE, Mrs Jennifer Ann. b 48. Coll of St Matthias Bris BEd 77. WEMTC 01. **d** 04 **p** 05. NSM Sharpness, Purton, Brookend and Slimbridge *Glouc* 04–11; C Cromhall, Tortworth, Tytherington, Falfield etc 11–15; rtd 15; NSM Matson *Glouc* 15–17. *Gossington Cottage, Gossington, Slimbridge, Gloucester GL2 7DN* T: (01453) 890384 M: 077877-959439 E: revdjenny@gmail.com
DETTMER, The Ven Douglas James. b 64. Univ of Kansas BA 86 Yale Univ MDiv 90. Berkeley Div Sch 90. **d** 90 **p** 91. C Ilfracombe, Lee, Woolacombe, Bittadon etc *Ex* 90–94; Bp's Dom Chapl 94–98; P-in-c Thorverton, Cadbury, Upton Pyne etc 98–10; P-in-c Stoke Canon, Poltimore w Huxham and Rewe etc 06–10; R Brampford Speke, Cadbury, Newton St Cyres etc 10–15; Adn Totnes from 15; Preb Ex Cathl from 12. *Blue Hills, Bradley Road, Bovey Tracey, Newton Abbot TQ13 9EU* T: (01626) 832064 E: archdeacon.of.totnes@exeter.anglican.org
DEUCHAR, Canon Andrew Gilchrist. b 55. Southn Univ BTh 86. Sarum & Wells Th Coll 81. **d** 84 **p** 85. C Alnwick *Newc* 84–88; TV Heref St Martin w St Fran 88–90; Adv to Coun for Soc Resp Roch and *Cant* 90–94; Sec for Angl Communion Affairs 94–00; Hon Prov Can Cant Cathl 95–12; R Nottingham St Pet and St Jas S'well 00–02; R Nottingham St Pet and All SS 02–07; P-in-c Nottingham St Mary and St Cath 04–07; P-in-c Nottingham All SS, St Mary and St Pet 07–08; Chapl to The Queen 03–08; Dioc Audit Officer *Mor* 08–12; rtd 12. *Crosby House, Main Street West End, Chirnside, Duns TD11 3UG* M: 07861-769233
DEUCHAR de MELLO, Bridget Dorothea. b 55. Sussex Univ BA 77 Leic Univ PGCE 78. SEITE BA 08. **d** 08 **p** 09. NSM Gt Ilford St Luke *Chelmsf* 08–13; NSM Leytonstone H Trin and St Aug Harrow Green 13–19; PtO 19–21; NSM Gt Ilford St Luke from 21. *3 Lennox Gardens, Ilford IG1 3LF* E: demellobridget@gmail.com
DEVADASON, Jacob. b 61. Madras Bible Sem BTh Serampore Univ BTh Annamalai Univ MA United Th Coll Bangalore MTh. Tamilnadu Th Sem BD NOC. **d** 06 **p** 07. C Man Clayton St Cross w St Paul 06–09; TV Wythenshawe 09–13;

P-in-c Croydon Ch Ch S'wark 13–18; V 18; Interfaith Adv Croydon Area 13–18; V Heald Green St Cath *Ches* from 18. *The Vicarage, 217 Outwood Road, Heald Green, Cheadle SK8 3JS* M: 07814-845053 E: 2revjacob@gmail.com
DEVADASON, Mrs Jasmine. b 67. Kakatiya Univ India BA 91 Tamilnadu Th Sem BD 96 United Th Coll Bangalore MTh 99. SNWTP. **d** 08 **p** 09. C W Didsbury and Withington St Chris *Man* 08–11; PtO 12–14; NSM Heald Green St Cath *Ches* from 19. *The Vicarage, 217 Outwood Road, Heald Green, Cheadle SK8 3JS* M: 07515-726923 E: jasdevadason@yahoo.co.uk
DEVAL, Mrs Joan Margaret. b 38. Southlands Coll Lon TDip 58. SAOMC 95. **d** 98 **p** 99. OLM Chinnor, Sydenham, Aston Rowant and Crowell *Ox* 98–10; PtO from 10. *3 Orchard Way, Chinnor OX39 4UD* T: (01844) 353404
DEVALL, Elizabeth Jane. b 70. SNWTP. **d** 10 **p** 11. C Royton St Anne *Man* 10–13; C Heyside 12–13; P-in-c Hurst 13–18; V 18–21; V Heyside and Royton from 21. *St Anne's Vicarage, St Anne's Avenue, Royton, Oldham OL2 5AD* M: 07725-739506 E: revlizdevall@gmail.com
DEVAS, Thomas Christopher. b 86. Nottm Univ BSc 09. Wycliffe Hall Ox BTh 15. **d** 15 **p** 16. C Wollaton Park *S'well* 15–19; C Cornerstone Team *Leic* from 19. *16 Wadkins Way, Bushby, Leicester LE7 9NA* M: 07817-435483
DEVENISH, Nicholas Edward. b 64. Ridley Hall Cam 02. **d** 04 **p** 05. C Huntingdon *Ely* 04–07; C Farcet Hampton 07–12; TV Cartmel Peninsula *Carl* from 12. *The Vicarage, Priest Lane, Cartmel, Grange-over-Sands LA11 6PU* T: (015395) 36261 E: nickdevenish@mac.com *or* vicar.cartmel@virgin.net
DEVENNEY, Raymond Robert Wilmont. b 47. TCD BA 69 MA 73. CITC 70. **d** 70 **p** 71. C Ballymena w Ballyclug *Conn* 70–75; C Ballyholme *D & D* 75–81; I Killinchy w Kilmood and Tullynakill 81–00; I Drumbeg 00–12; rtd 12; PtO *Newc* from 18. *21 Thirlington Close, Newcastle upon Tyne NE5 4BN* T: 0191-271 2036 E: raydev@hotmail.com
DEVER, Paul. b 71. BSc. Wycliffe Hall Ox. **d** 06 **p** 07. C Fair Oak *Win* 06–10; TV Horwich and Rivington *Man* 10–12; Dioc Young Adults Missr 10–12; C Blackrod 11–12; C Howell Hill *Guildf* from 12. *18 Nonsuch Walk, Cheam SM2 7NG* T: (020) 8224 9838 M: 07726-302862 E: revpaul@gmail.com
DEVERAJ, Jacob Devadason. *See* DEVADASON, Jacob
DEVERELL, Clive David. b 61. Anglia Ruskin Univ BA 09. CA Tr Coll 83 ERMC 04. **d** 07 **p** 08. C Paston *Pet* 07–10; TV W Swindon and the Lydiards *Bris* 10–18; V W Swindon and Lydiard Tregoze from 18; AD Swindon 17–20. *26 The Bramptons, Shaw, Swindon SN5 5SL* T: (01793) 877111 E: clive.deverell@btinternet.com
DEVERELL, Canon William Robert Henry. b 61. CITC 88. St Jo Coll Nottm 90. **d** 92 **p** 93. C Agherton *Conn* 92–95; I Sixmilecross w Termonmaguirke *Arm* 95–99; I Tallaght *D & G* from 99; Can Ch Ch Cathl Dublin from 14. *St Maelruain's Rectory, 6 Sally Park, Firhouse Road, Tallaght, Dublin 24, Republic of Ireland* T: (00353) (1) 462 1044 *or* 462 6006 F: 462 1044 M: 86-803 0239 E: tallaghtparish@gmail.com
DEVEREUX, Canon John Swinnerton. b 32. Lon Univ BSc 53. Wells Th Coll. **d** 58 **p** 59. C Wigan St Mich *Liv* 58–60; C Goring-by-Sea *Chich* 60–69; Ind Chapl 69–97; Can and Preb Chich Cathl 90–97; rtd 97; PtO *Chich* from 97. *4 Pony Farm, Findon, Worthing BN14 0RS* T: (01903) 873638
DEVINE, Margaret Rose. b 50. Sunderland Poly BEd 76. NEOC 00. **d** 03 **p** 04. NSM E Boldon *Dur* 03–12; rtd 12; PtO *Dur* from 12; Hon Min Can Dur Cathl from 15. *13 Coniston Close, Belmont, Durham DH1 2UQ* M: 07708-222634 E: devinemargaret@gmail.com
DEVONISH, Clive Wayne. b 51. Ridley Hall Cam. **d** 96 **p** 97. C Meole Brace *Lich* 96–05; V Greenside *Dur* 05–15; rtd 15; Hon C Shrewsbury H Trin w St Julian *Lich* 16–18; P-in-c 19–20; PtO *Heref* 17–21. *Maranatha, 3 Dorricotts Place, Yockleton, Shrewsbury SY5 9PH* E: revclivedevo@gmail.com
DEW, Glyn. b 55. Worc Coll of Educn BEd 90. St Jo Coll Nottm MA 97. **d** 97 **p** 98. C Beoley *Worc* 97–01; TV Redditch, The Ridge 01–05; P-in-c Tardebigge 04–05; PtO from 05; *Birm* from 17. *21 Ashmead Drive, Cofton Hackett, Birmingham B45 8AA* E: glyndew@icloud.com
DEW, Canon Lindsay Charles. b 52. Wilson Carlile Coll 76 Cranmer Hall Dur 85. **d** 86 **p** 86. C Knottingley *Wakef* 86–89; V Batley St Thos 89–97; R Thornhill and Whitley Lower 97–09; RD Dewsbury 96–06; Hon Can Wakef Cathl 05–09; P-in-c Dunton w Wrestlingworth and Eyeworth *St Alb* 09–14; R 14–18; RD Biggleswade 11–18; Hon Can St Alb 16–18; rtd 18; PtO *St Alb* from 18; *Ely* from 20. *22 Angell's Meadow, Ashwell, Baldock SG7 5QS* T: (01462) 742165 M: 07545-878082 E: canon.lindsaydew@gmail.com
DEW, Martin John. b 49. CBDTI 00. **d** 04 **p** 05. NSM Natland *Carl* 04–09; NSM Shap w Swindale and Bampton w Mardale 09–13; rtd 13; PtO *Carl* from 13. *9 Burton*

Park, Burton, Carnforth LA6 1JB T: (01524) 781645 E: martindew23@live.co.uk

DEW, Maureen. b 51. Univ of Wales (Newport) MA 00. Qu Coll Birm BA 99. **d** 99 **p** 00. C Inkberrow w Cookhill and Kington w Dormston *Worc* 99–02; C Redditch, The Ridge 02–05; TV Redditch Ch the K 05–12; rtd 12; PtO *Worc* from 13; *Birm* from 18. *21 Ashmead Drive, Cofton Hackett, Birmingham B45 8AA* E: revmodew@btinternet.com

DEW, Robert David John. b 42. St Pet Coll Ox BA 63. St Steph Ho Ox 63. **d** 65 **p** 66. C Abington *Pet* 65–69; Chapl Tiffield Sch Northants 69–71; Ind Chapl *Pet* 71–79; Ind Chapl *Liv* 79–87; Sen Ind Missr 88–91; V Skelsmergh w Selside and Longsleddale *Carl* 91–06; Bp's Research Officer 91–95; Bp's Adv for CME 95–06; rtd 06; PtO *Carl* from 07. *Tither Crag Barn, Crook, Kendal LA8 8LE* T: (015395) 68680 E: bobdew68@gmail.com

DEWAR, Ian John James. b 61. Kingston Poly BA 83. Cranmer Hall Dur 89. **d** 92 **p** 93. C Blackb St Gabr 92–95; C Darwen St Cuth w Tockholes St Steph 95–97; V Appley Bridge 97–05; Chapl St Cath Hospice Preston 05–14; Chapl Univ Hosps of Morecambe Bay NHS Foundn Trust from 14. *Chaplain's Office, Royal Lancaster Infirmary, Ashton Road, Lancaster LA1 4RP* T: (01524) 65944 E: ian.dewar@mbht.nhs.uk

DEWAR, John. b 32. Chich Th Coll 58. **d** 61 **p** 62. C Leeds St Hilda *Ripon* 61–63; C Cross Green St Sav and St Hilda 63–65; C Cullercoats St Geo *Newc* 65–69; V Newsham 69–76; V Kenton Ascension 76–86; R Wallsend St Pet 86–92; V Longhorsley and Hebron 92–96; rtd 96; PtO *S'well* from 04. *51 Bonner Lane, Calverton, Nottingham NG14 6FU* T: 0115-965 2599 E: jandmedewar@ntlworld.com

DEWES, Canon Deborah Mary. b 59. Homerton Coll Cam BEd 81 St Jo Coll Dur BA 90 MA 93. Cranmer Hall Dur 88. **d** 92 **p** 94. C Stockton St Pet *Dur* 92–96; C Knowle *Birm* 96–03; C Bath Abbey w St Jas *B & W* 03–08; Chapl R United Hosp Bath NHS Trust 03–08; P-in-c Brislington St Luke *Bris* 08–14; V 14–21; P-in-c Upper Thames from 21; Hon Can Bris Cathl from 17. *The Vicarage, 14 Bath Road, Cricklade, Swindon SN6 6EY*

DEWEY, David Malcolm. b 43. Lon Univ BA 72 LSE MSc 87 Fitzw Coll Cam MPhil 94. Westcott Ho Cam 76. **d** 78 **p** 79. Sen Lect Middx Poly 72–92; Sen Lect Middx Univ 92–01; Hon C Enfield St Mich *Lon* 78–79; Hon C Bush Hill Park St Steph 79–84; Hon C Palmers Green St Jo 84–90; PtO 90–95; *St Alb* 95–98; Hon C Hertford All SS 98–01; P-in-c St Paul's Walden 01–08; rtd 08; PtO *St Alb* 09–21. *2 Church Meadow, Mundesley, Norwich NR11 8FB* T: (01263) 722162 M: 07813-439463 E: daviddewey8566@gmail.com

DEWEY, Peter Lewis. b 38. Wycliffe Hall Ox 69. **d** 71 **p** 72. C Hammersmith St Sav *Lon* 71–73; Chapl to Bp Kensington 73–75; C Isleworth All SS 75–81; TV Dorchester *Ox* 81–91; CF (TA) 86–91; Chapl Gordonstoun Sch 92–97; TR St Laur in Thanet *Cant* 97–03; rtd 03; P-in-c Sulhamstead Abbots and Bannister w Ufton Nervet *Ox* 03–10; Hon C 10–12; AD Bradfield 10–11; Chapl Allnutt's Hosp Goring Heath from 12. *Old School Cottage, Goring Heath, Reading RG8 7RR* T: (01491) 680261 M: 07784-912935 E: revpeterdewey@yahoo.co.uk

DEWEY, Sanford Dayton. b 44. Syracuse Univ AB 67 MA 72. Gen Th Sem (NY) MDiv 79. **d** 79 **p** 80. Assoc Chapl Roosevelt Hosp New York USA 80–81; Assoc Dir Relig Services 81–86; C St Mary le Bow w St Pancras Soper Lane etc *Lon* 87–92; C Hampstead St Steph w All Hallows 92–94; Co-Dir Hampstead Counselling Service 94–00; Dir from 00; NSM Hampstead Ch Ch *Lon* 94–96; Hon C Grosvenor Chpl from 96; Prov Past Consultant URC from 96; PtO *Lon* from 97. *B908 New Providence Wharf, 1 Fairmont Avenue, London E14 9PJ* E: daytondewey@gmail.com

DEWHIRST, Janice. b 50. EMMTC 99. **d** 02 **p** 03. NSM Forest Town *S'well* 02–04; NSM Mansfield SS Pet and Paul 04–06; P-in-c Ladybrook 06–09; rtd 09; PtO *S'well* from 18. *26 King Street, Mansfield Woodhouse, Mansfield NG19 9AU* T: (01623) 454471 E: revd.jan.d@ntlworld.com

DEWHURST, Russell James Edward. b 77. Magd Coll Ox MPhys 99 Selw Coll Cam BTh 03 Cardiff Univ LLM 10. Westcott Ho Cam 00. **d** 03 **p** 04. C Blewbury, Hagbourne and Upton *Ox* 03–05; P-in-c Ox St Frideswide w Binsey 05–09; Web Pastor i-church 05–07; Asst Chapl Ex Coll Ox 06–09; V Ewell *Guildf* 09–21. *The Butts, Monkmead Lane, West Chiltington, Pulborough RH20 2PE* E: rdewhurst@mac.com

DEWING, Robert Mark Eastwood. b 68. Bris Univ BA 90 PGCE 91. Ridley Hall Cam BA 98. **d** 99 **p** 00. C Alverstoke *Portsm* 99–03; V Sheet 03–11; AD Petersfield 09–11; Past Dir Lee Abbey 11–16; TR Portishead *B & W* from 16. *2 Brambling Lane, Portishead, Bristol BS20 7NN* T: (01275) 846592 M: 07923-484297 E: robdewing@gmail.com or rector@portisheadparish.co.uk

DEWING, William Arthur. b 52. NEOC 99. **d** 02 **p** 03. NSM Middlesbrough St Oswald *York* 02–06; NSM Stainton w Hilton 06–17; NSM Brookfield 14–17; NSM Osmotherley w Harlsey and Ingleby Arncliffe from 17; NSM Cowesby from 17; NSM Felixkirk w Boltby from 17; NSM Kirkby Knowle from 17; NSM Leake w Over and Nether Silton and Kepwick from 17. *Orchard House, Ingleby Arncliffe, Northallerton DL6 3LN* T: (01609) 882233 M: 07966-191640 E: bill@revd.me.uk

DEXTER, Canon Frank Robert. b 40. Cuddesdon Coll 66. **d** 68 **p** 69. C Newc H Cross 68–71; C Whorlton 71–73; V Pet Ch Carpenter 73–80; V High Elswick St Phil *Newc* 80–85; RD Newc W 81–85; V Newc St Geo 85–05; Hon Can Newc Cathl 94–05; P-in-c Newc St Hilda 95–98; rtd 05; PtO *Newc* from 05. *8 Tynedale Terrace, Hexham NE46 3JE* T: (01434) 601759

DEY, Canon Charles Gordon Norman. b 46. Lon Coll of Div. **d** 71 **p** 72. C Almondbury *Wakef* 71–76; V Mixenden 76–85; TR Tong *Bradf* 85–11; C Laisterdyke 08–11; Hon Can Bradf Cathl 00–11; rtd 11. *23 St Abbs Walk, Bradford BD6 1EP* E: gordondey1@gmail.com

DHANARAJ, Premraj Charles. See PREMRAJ, Dhanaraj Charles

DI CASTIGLIONE, James Alexander. b 81. St Jo Coll Nottm. **d** 08 **p** 09. C Mid-Sussex Network Ch *Chich* 08–12; Chapl Sir Robert Woodard Academy Lancing 12–13; R Chanctonbury *Chich* from 13. *The Rectory, Mill Lane, Ashington, Pulborough RH20 3BX* T: (01903) 893878 M: 07796-945662 E: jamesdicastiglione@me.com or james.dicas@chanctonbury.org.uk

DI CASTIGLIONE, Nigel Austin. b 57. St Jo Coll Dur BA 78. St Jo Coll Nottm MA 94. **d** 94 **p** 95. C Tamworth *Lich* 94–97; P-in-c Trentham 97–01; V 02–10; V Hanford 02–10; V Harborne Heath *Birm* 10–15; TR Papworth *Ely* from 15; P-in-c Conington 17–18; P-in-c Lolworth 18. *Elsworth Rectory, The Drift, Elsworth, Cambridge CB23 4JN* T: (01954) 267241 M: 07770-697240 E: nigel.dicastiglione@gmail.com

DI CHIARA, Miss Alessandra Maddalena. b 59. Univ of Wales (Swansea) BA 80. Wycliffe Hall Ox 00. **d** 02 **p** 03. C Hooton *Ches* 02–05; P-in-c Millbrook 05–15; P-in-c Micklehurst 14–15; C Douglas St Geo and All SS *S & M* 15–21; TR Onchan, Lonan and Laxey from 21. *62 Ballabrooie Way, Douglas, Isle of Man IM1 4HB* T: (01624) 679274

DI LEO, Paolo. b 62. Open Univ MBA 97 Dur Univ BA 18. ERMC 13. **d** 16 **p** 17. NSM Streatley *St Alb* 16–19; R Sharnbrook, Felmersham and Knotting w Souldrop from 19. *The Rectory, 81 High Street, Sharnbrook, Bedford MK44 1PE* T: (01234) 782000 M: 07968-606377 E: rev.pdileo@gmail.com

DIAKIESE, Guy Matumona. **d** 17 **p** 18. C The Hague *Eur* 17–21; Chapl Liège from 21. *Eglise Adventiste, 29 boulevard Frère-Orban, 4000 Liège, Belgium* T: (0032) (4) 6777 0340 E: guydiakiese@gmail.com or chaplain@englishchurch-liege.be

DIAMOND, Canon Michael Lawrence. b 37. St Jo Coll Dur BA 60 MA 74 Sussex Univ DPhil 84. ALCD 62. **d** 62 **p** 63. C Wandsworth St Mich *S'wark* 62–64; C Patcham *Chich* 64–69; R Hamsey 70–75; P-in-c Cambridge St Andr Less *Ely* 75–86; V 86–04; Hon Can Ely Cathl 94–04; RD Cambridge 96–04; rtd 04; PtO *S'well* 04–17; *Ely* from 17. *58 Desborough Road, Hartford, Huntingdon PE29 1SW*

DIAMOND, Capt Richard Geoffrey Colin. b 49. MBE 00. CA Tr Coll. **d** 93 **p** 93. Miss to Seafarers Kenya 90–01; rtd 01; PtO *Win* 02–21. *209A Priory Road, Southampton SO17 2LR* T: (023) 8067 8558 E: rgcdiamond@ic24.net

DIANA, Sister. See MORRISON, Diana Mary

DÍAZ BUTRÓN, Marcos Máximo. b 72. St Steph Ho Ox 06. **d** 08. C Wantage *Ox* 08–10; PtO 14–21; NSM Cowley St Jas from 21. *14 Milton Road, Oxford OX4 3EF* E: maxdiazbutron@yahoo.es

DIBB SMITH, John. b 29. Ex & Truro NSM Scheme 78. **d** 81 **p** 82. NSM Carbis Bay *Truro* 81–82; NSM Carbis Bay w Lelant 82–84; Warden Trelowarren Fellowship Helston 84–89; Chapl 89–91; NSM Halsetown *Truro* 91–97; rtd 98; PtO *Truro* 00–15. *Maple Cottage, Penstraze, Chacewater, Truro TR4 8GB* T: (01872) 560134

DIBBENS, Canon Hugh Richard. b 39. Lon Univ BA 63 MTh 67 St Pet Coll Ox BA 65 MA 74. Oak Hill Th Coll 60. **d** 67 **p** 68. C Holborn St Geo w H Trin and St Bart *Lon* 67–72; CMS 73–74; Japan 74–77; TR Chigwell *Chelmsf* 78–92; V Hornchurch St Andr 92–06; RD Havering 98–04; Hon Can Chelmsf Cathl 01–06; rtd 06; PtO *Chelmsf* from 07. *9 Stonehill Road, Roxwell, Chelmsford CM1 4PF* T: (01245) 248173 E: hrdibbens@gmail.com

DIBDEN, Alan Cyril. b 49. Hull Univ LLB 70 Fitzw Coll Cam BA 72 MA 76. Westcott Ho Cam 70 Virginia Th Sem 73. **d** 73 **p** 74. C Camberwell St Luke *S'wark* 73–77; TV Walworth 77–79; TV Langley Marish *Ox* 79–84; C Chalfont St Peter

84–90; TV Burnham w Dropmore, Hitcham and Taplow 90–08; V Taplow and Dropmore 08–15; rtd 15; PtO Ox from 15. *Russett Cottage, 228 Windsor Lane, Burnham SL1 7HN* M: 07900-824528 E: alan.dibden13@gmail.com

DICK, Canon Angela. b 62. Sheff Univ BA 92. St Jo Coll Nottm MA 94. **d** 96 **p** 97. C Mixenden *Wakef* 96–97; C Mount Pellon 97–99; P-in-c Bradshaw 99–00; P-in-c Holmfield 99–00; V Bradshaw and Holmfield 00–10; P-in-c Sowerby Bridge 10–11; V 11–14; *Leeds* from 14; Asst Dioc Dir of Ords *Wakef* 13–14; Asst Dir of Ords *Leeds* from 14; Hon Can Wakef Cathl from 10. *The Vicarage, 62 Park Road, Sowerby Bridge HX6 2BJ* T: (01422) 831253 E: angela.dick@leeds.anglican.org

DICK, Canon Caroline Ann. b 61. Nottm Univ BTh 88. Linc Th Coll 85. **d** 88 **p** 94. Par Dn Houghton le Spring *Dur* 88–93; Par Dn Hetton le Hole 93–94; C 94–96; Asst Chapl Sunderland Univ 94–98; C Harton 96–09; Development Officer Dioc Bd of Soc Resp 98–09; Adv for Women's Min 02–09; TV Dur N 09–16; TR from 16; Hon Can Dur Cathl from 03. *The Vicarage, 1A Church Parade, Sacriston, Durham DH7 6AD* M: 07947-741517 E: carolinedick@btinternet.com

DICK, Cecil Bates. b 42. TD 97. Selw Coll Cam BA 68 MA 72. EMMTC 73. **d** 76 **p** 78. NSM Cinderhill *S'well* 76–79; Chapl Dame Allan's Schs Newc 79–85; CF (TA) 84–99; C Gosforth All SS *Newc* 85–87; Chapl HM Pris Dur 88–89; Chapl HM Pris Hull 89–04; rtd 04; PtO *Newc* from 01; *York* from 04. *11 Juniper Chase, Beverley HU17 8GD* T: (01482) 862985

DICK, Malcolm Gordon (Mac). b 40. SWMTC 10. **d** 11 **p** 12. NSM Ottery St Mary, Alfington, W Hill, Tipton etc *Ex* 11–19; PtO from 19. *27 Beech Park, West Hill, Ottery St Mary EX11 1UJ* E: macdick1@aol.com

DICK, Canon Raymond Owen. b 53. Edin Univ BD 77. Edin Th Coll 73. **d** 77 **p** 78. C Glas St Mary 77–84; PtO *St Alb* 84–85; P-in-c Edin St Paul and St Geo 85; Edin St Phil 85–86; P-in-c Edin St Marg 85–87; TV Edin Old St Paul 87–88; R Hetton le Hole *Dur* 88–96; V Harton 96–13; P-in-c Cleadon Park 09–13; R The Boldons 13–19; AD Jarrow 14–15; Hon Can Dur Cathl 11–19; rtd 19. *The Vicarage, 1A Church Parade, Sacriston, Durham DH7 6AD* E: raymonddick53@gmail.com

DICKENS, Adam Paul. b 65. Man Univ BA 89 Nottm Univ MDiv 93. Linc Th Coll 91. **d** 93 **p** 94. C Pershore w Pinvin, Wick and Birlingham *Worc* 93–98; C Portsea St Mary *Portsm* 98–04; Pilsdon Community 04–12; Chapl Derby Univ from 14; Chapl Derby Cathl from 14. *1 Flamsteed Court, Kedleston Old Road, Derby DE22 1GA* T: (01332) 591878 E: adampdickens@hotmail.co.uk *or* a.dickens@derby.ac.uk

DICKENS, John Franklin. b 50. Birm Univ BEd 72 Leeds Univ MEd 82. St Mellitus Coll 12. **d** 13 **p** 14. OLM Maldon St Mary w Mundon *Chelmsf* 13–16; P-in-c from 16. *7 Viking Road, Maldon CM9 6JN* T: (01621) 858136 M: 07582-423219 E: johndickens129@btinternet.com

DICKENS, Timothy Richard John. b 45. Leeds Univ BSc 68. Westcott Ho Cam 68. **d** 71 **p** 72. C Meole Brace *Lich* 71–74; C-in-c Stamford Ch Ch CD *Linc* 74–80; V Anlaby St Pet *York* 80–91; V Egg Buckland *Ex* 91–10; P-in-c Estover 04–10; RD Plymouth Moorside 03–09; rtd 10. *52 Budshead Road, Plymouth PL5 2RA* T: (01752) 298570

DICKENSON, Charles Gordon. b 29. Bps' Coll Cheshunt 53. **d** 56 **p** 57. C Ellesmere Port *Ches* 56–61; R Egremont St Columba 61–68; V Latchford Ch Ch 68–74; P-in-c Hargrave 74–79; Bp's Chapl 75–79; V Birkenhead St Jas w St Bede 79–83; R Tilston and Shocklach 83–94; rtd 94; PtO *Ches* 94–14. *58 Kingsway, Crewe CW2 7ND* T: (01270) 560722

DICKENSON, Canon Robin Christopher Wildish. b 44. Lon Univ CertEd 67 Ex Univ BPhil 81 MA 98. SWMTC 94. **d** 97 **p** 98. NSM Week St Mary w Poundstock and Whitstone *Truro* 97–98; P-in-c 98–06; P-in-c St Gennys, Jacobstow w Warbstow and Treneglos 02–06; R Week St Mary Circle of Par 06–13; RD Stratton 05–11; Hon Can Truro Cathl 07–13; rtd 13; PtO *Truro* from 16. *Ranelagh, Week St Mary, Holsworthy EX22 6XA* T: (01288) 341016

DICKER, Jane Elizabeth Marie. b 64. Whitelands Coll Lon BA 87 Anglia Ruskin Univ MA 08 Greenwich Univ PGCE 11. Linc Th Coll 87. **d** 89 **p** 94. Par Dn Merton St Jas *S'wark* 89–93; C Littleham w Exmouth *Ex* 93–97; Chapl Plymouth Univ 93–97; Ecum Chapl for F&HE Grimsby *Linc* 97–02; Chapl Univ of Greenwich *Roch* 02–05; Chapl Kent Inst of Art and Design 02–04; Chapl Univ Coll for the Creative Arts *Roch* 05; Hon PV Roch Cathl 03–05; P-in-c Waltham Cross *St Alb* 05–08; TV Cheshunt 08–16; V W Bromwich All SS *Lich* 16–20; V W Bromwich All SS w St Mary and St Phil from 20. *7 Hopkins Drive, West Bromwich B71 3RR* T: 0121-588 5157 M: 07843-667971 E: mthr_jane@btinternet.com

DICKER, Mary Elizabeth. b 45. Girton Coll Cam BA 66 MA 70 Sheff Univ MSc 78. Cranmer Hall Dur 83. **dss** 85 **d** 87 **p** 94. Mortlake w E Sheen *S'wark* 85–88; Par Dn 87–88; Par Dn

Irlam *Man* 88–92; Par Dn Ashton Ch Ch 92–94; C 94–97; P-in-c Hopwood 97–98; TV Heywood 98–05; rtd 05; PtO *Man* from 05. *33 Waltham House, St John Street, Wirksworth, Matlock DE4 4DT* T: (01629) 820234

DICKIE, James Graham Wallace. b 50. Worc Coll Ox BA 72 MA BLitt 77. Westcott Ho Cam 78. **d** 81 **p** 82. C Bracknell *Ox* 81–84; LtO *Ely* 84–89; Chapl Trin Coll Cam 84–89; Chapl Clifton Coll Bris 89–96; Sen Chapl Marlborough Coll 96–10; rtd 10; PtO *Sarum* from 10. *Grey Gables, Easton Royal, Pewsey SN9 5LY* T: (01672) 810961

DICKIN, Patricia Margarita. *See* LENTON de DICKIN, Patricia Margarita

DICKINSON, Canon Anthony William. b 48. New Coll Ox BA 71 MA 74. Linc Th Coll 80. **d** 82 **p** 83. C Leavesden *St Alb* 82–86; TV Upton cum Chalvey *Ox* 86–94; P-in-c Terriers 94–99; V 99–18; Chapl Bucks New Univ 03–18; Hon Can Ch Ch *Ox* 05–18; Chapl Genova *Eur* from 18. *Via Goito 18/a, 16122 Genova, Italy* T: (0039) (10) 889 268 E: canontonyd@gmail.com

DICKINSON, David Charles. b 58. BA 79 Lanc Univ MA 97. CBDTI. **d** 99 **p** 00. NSM Ewood *Blackb* 99–04; NSM Blackb Redeemer 04–05; P-in-c Hoghton 05–12; V 12–13; PtO 13–15; NSM Hesketh w Becconsall from 16; R from 17. *1 Silverdale, Hesketh Bank, Preston PR4 6RZ* M: 07805-598256 E: dickinsonrev@aol.com

DICKINSON, Dyllis Annie. b 52. **d** 01 **p** 02. OLM Stalmine w Pilling *Blackb* 01–07; NSM 07–17; rtd 17; PtO *Blackb* from 18. *Springfield, Moss Side Lane, Stalmine, Poulton-le-Fylde FY6 0JP* T: (01253) 700011

DICKINSON, Gareth Lee. b 69. Ridley Hall Cam 06. **d** 08 **p** 09. C Bryanston Square St Mary w St Marylebone St Mark *Lon* 08–10; NSM Cheltenham H Trin and St Paul *Glouc* 10–19; PtO 19–20; V Maidstone St Luke *Cant* from 20. *St Luke's House, 16 St Luke's Road, Maidstone ME14 5AW* E: garethdickinson@stlukesmaidstone.org.uk

DICKINSON, The Very Revd the Hon Hugh Geoffrey. b 29. Trin Coll Ox BA 53 MA 56. Cuddesdon Coll 54. **d** 56 **p** 57. C Melksham *Sarum* 56–58; Chapl Trin Coll Cam 58–63; Chapl Win Coll 63–69; P-in-c Milverton *Cov* 69–77; V St Alb St Mich 77–86; Dean Sarum 86–96; rtd 96; PtO *Glouc* 96–18. *5 St Peter's Road, Cirencester GL7 1RE* T: (01285) 657710

DICKINSON, Paul John. b 66. Leic Univ BSc 88 Nottm Univ MA 89 Univ Coll Lon MSc 93 St Jo Coll Dur BA 18. Cranmer Hall Dur 15. **d** 18 **p** 19. C Brumby *Linc* 18–20; C Bishop Norton, Waddingham and Snitterby 20–21; NSM from 21; C Grayingham 20–21; NSM from 21; C Kirton in Lindsey w Manton 20–21; NSM from 21. *11 Kingsway, Scunthorpe DN17 1BL* M: 07730-385045

DICKINSON, Canon Robert Edward. b 47. Nottm Univ BTh 74. St Jo Coll Nottm 70. **d** 74 **p** 75. C Birm St Martin 74–78; P-in-c Liv St Bride w St Sav 78–81; TV St Luke in the City 81–86; Chapl Liv Poly 86–92; Chapl Liv Jo Moores Univ 92–08; Hon Can Liv Cathl 03–08; rtd 08. *3 Wightman Avenue, Newton-le-Willows WA12 0LS* T: (01925) 271124 E: bobdicko@blueyonder.co.uk

DICKINSON, Stephen Paul. b 54. SRN 75. NOC 85. **d** 88 **p** 89. NSM Purston cum S Featherstone *Wakef* 88–91; C Goldthorpe w Hickleton *Sheff* 91–94; V New Bentley 94–05; P-in-c Arksey 04–05; V New Bentley w Arksey from 05. *The Vicarage, Victoria Road, Bentley, Doncaster DN5 0EZ* T: (01302) 875266

DICKINSON, Victor Tester. b 48. Univ of Wales (Cardiff) BSc 70. St Steph Ho Ox 70. **d** 73 **p** 74. C Neath w Llantwit *Llan* 73–76; Asst Chapl Univ of Wales (Cardiff) 76–79; TV Willington *Newc* 79–86; V Kenton Ascension 86–97; V Lowick and Kyloe w Ancroft 97–18; R Ford and Etal 97–18; rtd 18. *48 St John Street, Whithorn, Newton Stewart DG8 8PF* T: (01988) 500343

DICKSON, Anthony Edward. b 59. Nottm Univ BTh 88. Linc Th Coll 85. **d** 88 **p** 89. C Portsea St Alb *Portsm* 88–91; C Cleobury Mortimer w Hopton Wafers *Heref* 91–94; R Fownhope w Mordiford, Brockhampton etc 94–99; PtO *B & W* 09–11; P-in-c Leigh upon Mendip w Stoke St Michael from 11; P-in-c Nunney and Witham Friary, Marston Bigot etc from 11. *The Rectory, High Street, Nunney, Frome BA11 4LZ* T: (01373) 837337 E: nunney.rectory@gmail.com

DICKSON (née TURPIN), Christine Lesley. b 63. Westcott Ho Cam. **d** 09 **p** 10. C Bredon w Bredon's Norton *Worc* 09–12; P-in-c Worc St Wulstan 12–14; Sen Chapl Dorothy House Hospice Winsley 15–16; Asst Chapl R United Hosps Bath NHS Foundn Trust 18–21; Chapl N Bris NHS Trust from 21; PtO *B & W* from 15; *Sarum* 15–20. *The Rectory, High Street, Nunney, Frome BA11 4LZ* T: (01373) 837337 M: 07511-522581 E: c.dickson22@icloud.com

DICKSON, Colin James. b 74. St Andr Univ MA 96 MPhil 00 Leeds Univ BA 01. Coll of Resurr Mirfield 99. **d** 02 **p** 03. C Tottenham St Paul *Lon* 02–05; C Croydon St Mich w St Jas *S'wark* 05–10; SSF from 10; PtO *Newc* from 15. *The Friary of St Francis, Alnmouth, Alnwick NE66 3NJ* E: josephemmanuelssf@franciscans.org.uk

DICKSON, Colin Patrick Gavin. b 56. d 96 p 97. C Grays Thurrock *Chelmsf* 96–00; V Glantawe *S & B* 00–16. *73 Webster Street, Treharris CF46 5HW* E: cdickson1@sky.com

DICKSON, Samuel Mervyn James. b 41. CITC. d 66 p 67. C Ballyholme *D & D* 66–70; C Knockbreda 70–75; I Clonallon w Warrenpoint 75–84; I Down H Trin w Hollymount 84–06; Bp's C Rathmullan 00–05; Bp's C Tyrella 00–06; Bp's C Loughinisland 01–06; Can Down Cathl 91–06; Treas Down Cathl 98–00; Prec Down Cathl 00–01; Chan Down Cathl 01–06; rtd 06. *Apartment 1, 40A Main Street, Dundrum, Newcastle BT33 0LY* T: (028) 4375 1112

DICKSON, Simon. b 90. Oak Hill Th Coll 17. d 20 p 21. C Fulham St Pet *Lon* from 20. *St Peter's Vicarage, St Peter's Terrace, London SW6 7JS* M: 07780-532127

DIDUK, Sergiy. b 74. Ukranian Nat Academy BA 08. St Jo Coll Nottm MA 11. d 11 p 12. C Hucknall Torkard *S'well* 11–15; C Hanworth All SS *Lon* 15–19; P-in-c from 19. *All Saints' Vicarage, Uxbridge Road, Feltham TW13 5EE* T: (020) 8894 9330 M: 07525-216850 E: sergius_nd99@hotmail.co.uk

DIETZ, Matthew Paul Richard. b 70. Magd Coll Cam MA 95. Wycliffe Hall Ox 05. d 07 p 08. C Win Ch Ch 07–08; C Throop 08–11; Chapl Monkton Combe Sch Bath 11–14; Chapl Taunton Sch 14–18; CF from 18. *c/o MOD Chaplains (Army)* T: (01264) 383430 F: 381824 M: 07751-454993 E: padredietz@gmail.com

DIFFEY, Margaret Elsie. b 39. MCSP. d 02 p 03. OLM Nor St Geo Tombland 02–10; rtd 10; PtO *Nor* from 10. *45 Welsford Road, Norwich NR4 6QB* T/F: (01603) 457248 E: maggiediffey@tiscali.co.uk

DIFFIN, Rosemary Gwendoline. MTh. St Jo Coll Nottm. d 12 p 13. C Drumglass w Moygashel *Arm* 12–13; C Seapatrick *D & D* 13–15; P-in-c Kilmore St Aid w St Sav *Arm* 15–16; I 16–21; I Kilcronaghan w Draperstown and Sixtowns *D & R* from 21. *12 Rectory Road, Tobermore, Magherafelt BT45 5QP* T: (028) 7962 7811 M: 07714-887977 E: rosemarydiffin@gmail.com

DIGGLE, Judith Margaret. *See* BROWN, Judith Margaret

DIGGLE, Richard James. b 47. Lon Inst BA 69 Man Poly CertEd 73. d 01 p 02. OLM Chorlton-cum-Hardy St Werburgh *Man* 01–05; NSM Bickerton, Bickley, Harthill and Burwardsley *Ches* 05–08; V Antrobus, Aston by Sutton, Lt Leigh etc 08–12; P-in-c Bickley from 12. *Ebnal House, Ebnal Lane, Malpas SY14 8DL* T: (01948) 820885 M: 07749-849783 E: diggle163@btinternet.com *or* rdiggle50@gmail.com

DIGGORY, Mrs Susan Jane. b 51. SEITE BA 09. d 09 p 10. NSM Tunbridge Wells St Mark *Roch* 09–14; V Crockham Hill H Trin 14–21; rtd 21. *3 Lynwood, Groombridge, Tunbridge Wells TN3 9LX* M: 07799-892583 E: sue.diggory@outlook.com

DIGMAN (née BUTTERFIELD), Mrs Amanda Helen. b 73. Derby Univ BA 96 Ches Univ MTh 15. St Jo Coll Nottm 07. d 09 p 10. C Sutton in Ashfield St Mary *S'well* 09–12; C Huthwaite 09–10; P-in-c Carlton 12–21; P-in-c Colwick 12–21; R Birstall and Wanlip *Leic* from 21. *Address temp unknown* M: 07803-625049 E: revamandadigman@me.com

DIGNUM, Keith Anthony. d 08 p 09. OLM Coltishall w Gt Hautbois, Frettenham etc *Nor* from 08. *Mill House, 4 Newton Road, Hainford, Norwich NR10 3LZ* T: (01603) 710397 E: kdignum@googlemail.com

DILKES, Nigel Bruce. b 58. Univ of Wales (Ban) BSc 97 Lanc Univ PhD 01. Ridley Hall Cam 03. d 05 p 06. C Llandudno *Ban* 05–07; C Holyhead 07–09; TV Barnstaple *Ex* 09–17; V Pilton w Ashford 17–20. *Aysgarth, 9 Sutton Close, Sutton Poyntz, Weymouth DT3 6LJ* E: nigeldilkes@aol.com

✠**DILL, The Rt Revd Nicholas Bayard Botolf.** b 63. Toronto Univ BA 86 Lon Univ LLB 89 Barrister 91. Wycliffe Hall Ox 96. d 98 p 99 c 13. C Lindfield *Chich* 98–05; R Pembroke St Jo Bermuda 05–13; Bp Bermuda from 13. *Diocesan Office, PO Box HM 769, Hamilton HM CX, Bermuda* T: (001) (441) 292 6987 F: 292 5421 E: bishop@anglican.bm

DILL, Peter Winston. b 41. ACP 66 K Coll Lon BD 72 AKC 72. St Aug Coll Cant 72. d 73 p 74. C Warsop *S'well* 73–75; C Rhyl w St Ann *St As* 75–77; C Oxton *Ches* 77–78; V Newton in Mottram 78–82; P-in-c Shelton and Oxon *Lich* 82–84; V 84–87; Chapl Clifton Coll Bris 87–00; C Thorverton, Cadbury, Upton Pyne etc *Ex* 00–01; PtO *Bris* 02–03; Past Co-ord St Monica Trust Westbury Fields 03–06; rtd 06; PtO *Bris* from 07. *85B Pembroke Road, Clifton, Bristol BS8 3EB* T: 0117-973 9769

DILLINGHAM, Canon Robert Paul. b 64. St Mellitus Coll. d 12 p 13. NSM Crowborough *Chich* from 12; Par Development Officer 16–18; Dep Dir for Apostolic Life from 18; Can and Preb Chich Cathl from 21. *Thornton, Crowborough Hill, Crowborough TN6 2SE* T: (01892) 660038 M: 07778-447434 E: rob.dillingham@allsaintscrowborough.org *or* rob.dillingham@chichester.anglican.org

DILLON, Gerard Francis. d 14 p 15. C Glenrothes *St And* from 14. *18 Sappi Road, Glenrothes KY7 6ZJ* T: (01592) 612602 E: gerryd74@gmail.com

DILWORTH, Anthony. b 41. St Deiniol's Hawarden 87. d 90 p 91. NSM Gt Saughall *Ches* 90–93; P-in-c Cwmcarn *Mon* 93–95; V 95–98; V Abercarn and Cwmcarn 99–01; TV Upholland *Liv* 01–06; rtd 06; PtO *St As* 09–10 and from 12; P-in-c Llansilin w Llangadwaladr and Llangedwyn 10–12. *4 Maes Owain, Glyndyfrdwy, Corwen LL21 9HF* T: (01490) 430586 M: 07773-389179 E: anthonydilworth536@btinternet.com

DIMES, Stuart Christopher Laurence. b 60. Warwick Univ BSc 81. St Jo Coll Nottm 99. d 01 p 02. C Branksome St Clem *Sarum* 01–05; P-in-c W Heath *Birm* 05–10; V 10–17; R Hampton-in-Arden w Bickenhill from 17; P-in-c Barston from 17. *The Vicarage, High Street, Hampton-in-Arden, Solihull B92 0AE* T: (01675) 442339 E: revsdimes@live.com

DIMOND, Mark James. b 68. Kent Univ BA 90 St Ant Coll Ox MPhil 93 Univ of Wales (Swansea) DPhil 04 Cardiff Univ DipEd 06. St Mich Coll Llan 09. d 11 p 12. C Penarth All SS *Llan* 11–14; Chapl to Abp Wales 14–17; Can Res St Woolos Cathl *Mon* 17–19; PtO *Eur* 19–21; TR King's Lynn St Marg w St Nic *Nor* from 21. *St Margaret's Vicarage, St Margaret's Place, King's Lynn PE30 5DL* E: mark.dimond@talk21.com

DIN, Munawar. b 67. Punjab Univ MSc 92 Azad Jammu and Kashmir Univ MBA 96. Cranmer Hall Dur 15. d 17 p 18. C Blackb Ch Ch w St Matt 17–21; V Brierfield from 21; V Burnley St Cuth from 21. *St Cuthbert's Vicarage, Barbon Street, Burnley BB10 1TS* M: 07728-373209 E: din5munawar@gmail.com

DINELEY, Margaret Anne. b 44. d 15 p 15. NSM Lochgelly *St And* from 15. *2 Dreghorn Park, Edinburgh EH13 9PH* E: margaret.dineley@gmail.com

DINES, Miss Rachael Irene Elizabeth. b 68. St Paul's Coll Chelt BEd 92. Cranmer Hall Dur 14. d 16 p 17. C N Walsham and Edingthorpe *Nor* 16–18; C N Walsham, Edingthorpe, Worstead and Westwick 18–19; P-in-c Hunstanton St Edm w Ringstead 19–20; P-in-c Hunstanton St Mary w Ringstead Parva etc 19–20; TR Hunstanton and Saxon Shore from 20. *St Mary's Rectory, Church Road, Old Hunstanton, Hunstanton PE36 6JS* T: (01485) 535936 M: 07763-211901 E: revd.rachael.dines@hotmail.com

DINGWALL-JONES, Christopher Lawrence. b 88. St Hugh's Coll Ox BA 11 Edin Univ MSc 11 Kent Univ PhD 15. St Steph Ho Ox BA 17. d 18 p 19. C Fleetwood St Pet and St Dav *Blackb* 18–21; Chapl Jes Coll Ox from 21. *3 Moberly Close, Oxford OX4 1HX* M: 07914-829793 E: fr.chrisdj@gmail.com

DINNEN, John Frederick. b 42. TCD BA 65 BD 72 QUB MTh 91. CITC. d 66 p 67. C Belfast All SS *Conn* 66–68; ICM Dub 69–71; C Carnmoney *Conn* 71–73; Asst Dean of Residences QUB 73–74; Dean 74–84; I Hillsborough *D & D* 84–07; Preb Down Cathl 93–96; Dir of Ords 96–98; Dean Down 96–06; rtd 08; PtO *Eur* from 18. *74 Demesne Road, Ballynahinch BT24 8NS* T: (028) 4481 1148 E: jdinnen@btinternet.com

DINNEN, Mrs Judith Margaret. b 48. Open Univ BA 87 Univ of Wales (Cardiff) MA 00 Goldsmiths' Coll Lon TCert 71. WEMTC 01. d 05 p 06. NSM Madley w Tyberton, Peterchurch, Vowchurch etc *Heref* 05–18; PtO from 19. *The Hawthorns, Madley, Hereford HR2 9LU* T: (01981) 251866 E: judy@dinnen.plus.com

DINSMORE, Stephen Ralph. b 56. Wye Coll Lon BSc 78 Man Univ MA 06. Cranmer Hall Dur 82. d 85 p 86. C Haughton le Skerne *Dur* 85–88; C Edgware *Lon* 88–93; V Plymouth St Jude *Ex* 93–05; RD Plymouth Sutton 96–01; Dioc Adv for Miss and Par Development *Chelmsf* 05–07; Hon C Cranham Park 05–07; Nat Dir SOMA UK from 07. *SOMA UK, PO Box 69, Merriott TA18 9AP* T: (01460) 279737 E: stephen.dinsmore@somauk.org

DINWIDDY SMITH, Emma Ruth. b 67. St Hugh's Coll Ox BA 89 MA 10 Ox Brookes Univ MA 10. Ripon Coll Cuddesdon 08. d 10 p 11. C Hampstead St Jo *Lon* 10–13; C Chelsea St Luke and Ch Ch 13–19; AD Chelsea 17–19; V Kensington St Mary Abbots from 19. *St Mary Abbots Parish Office, Vicarage Gate, London W8 4HN* T: (020) 7937 2419

DIPLOCK, Susan Elizabeth. b 47. Birm Univ BA 69 Lon Inst of Educn MA 99. St Mellitus Coll 16. d 17 p 18. NSM Walthamstow St Pet *Chelmsf* from 17. *8 Ravenswood Road, London E17 9LY* T: (020) 8923 4455 M: 07710-211176 E: diplock@diplock.demon.co.uk

DISLEY, Mrs Edith Jennifer. b 51. Sheff Univ BSc 72 Man Univ BD 79. NOC 99. d 01 p 02. NSM Man Victoria Park 01–10; NSM Withington St Paul 02–10; NSM Wythenshawe 10–12; P-in-c Leesfield 12–15; V 15–20; rtd

20; PtO *Man* from 20. *2 Wild Street, Shaw, Oldham OL2 8QJ* E: edithdisley@hotmail.com

DITCH, David John. b 45. St Cath Coll Cam BA 67 MA 70 Leeds Univ PGCE 68. WMMTC 88. **d** 91 **p** 92. C Biddulph *Lich* 91–94; V Hednesford 94–02; V Chasetown 02–08; rtd 09; PtO *Derby* from 09. *6 Redwing Croft, Derby DE23 1WF* T: (01332) 271767

DITCHBURN, Hazel. b 44. NEOC 82. **dss** 84 **d** 87 **p** 94. Scotswood *Newc* 84–86; Ind Chapl *Dur* 86–95; TV Gateshead 95–98; AD 92–98; P-in-c Stella 98–04; P-in-c Swalwell 01–04; R Blaydon and Swalwell 04–06; AD Gateshead W 98–00; Hon Can Dur Cathl 94–06; rtd 06; P-in-c Freshwater Australia 06–09; PtO *Newc* from 09. *2 Woburn Way, Westerhope, Newcastle upon Tyne NE5 5JD* T: 0191-286 0553

DITCHFIELD, Timothy Frederick. b 61. CCC Cam BA 83. Cranmer Hall Dur 85. **d** 88 **p** 89. C Accrington St Jo *Blackb* 88–89; C Accrington St Jo w Huncoat 89–91; C Whittle-le-Woods 91–95; Chapl K Coll Lon from 95; NSM St Mary le Strand w St Clem Danes *Lon* 17–20. *King's College, Strand, London WC2R 2LS* T: (020) 7848 2373 F: 7848 2344 E: tim.ditchfield@kcl.ac.uk

DIX, Edward Joseph. b 77. Goldsmiths' Coll Lon BMus 00. Wycliffe Hall Ox BTh 09. **d** 09 **p** 10. C Shadwell St Paul w Ratcliffe St Jas *Lon* 09–13; C Is of Dogs Ch Ch and St Jo w St Luke from 13. *170 Wheat Sheaf Close, London E14 9UZ* T: (020) 7515 5772 M: 07899-075935 E: edjdix@gmail.com *or* ed@stlukesmillwall.org

DIXON, Ms Anne Elizabeth. b 56. Leeds Univ LLB 77 Solicitor 80. Westcott Ho Cam. **d** 01 **p** 02. C Guildf H Trin w St Mary 01–05; Chapl HM Pris Bullwood Hall 06–09; Chapl HM Pris Send from 09; PtO *Guildf* from 05; *Blackb* from 10; S'wark 14–17; Ox 15–20; Chapl CSC 14–20. *HM Prison Send, Ripley Road, Send, Woking GU23 7LJ* T: (01483) 471000 M: 07973-542467

DIXON, Bruce Richard. b 42. Lon Univ BScEng 63. Sarum Th Coll 66. **d** 68 **p** 69. C Walton St Mary *Liv* 68–70; C Harnham *Sarum* 70–73; C Streatham St Leon *S'wark* 73–77; R Thurcaston *Leic* 77–83; R Cranborne w Boveridge, Edmondsham etc *Sarum* 83–02; rtd 07; PtO *Sarum* 16–21. *20 Cypress Road, Charlton Down, Dorchester DT2 9FF* E: bandk2d@hotmail.com

DIXON, Bryan Stanley. b 61. St Jo Coll Nottm BTh 93. **d** 93 **p** 94. C Beverley Minster *York* 93–96; C Kingston upon Hull St Aid Southcoates 96–97; Asst Chapl HM Pris Dur 97–98; R Mid Marsh Gp *Linc* 98–03; R Brandesburton and Leven w Catwick *York* 03–10; P-in-c Patrick Brompton and Hunton *Ripon* 10–14; *Leeds* 14–16; P-in-c Crakehall *Ripon* 10–14; *Leeds* 14–16; P-in-c Hornby *Ripon* 10–14; *Leeds* 14–16; AD Wensley *Ripon* 11–13; P-in-c Spennithorne w Finghall and Hauxwell 12–14; *Leeds* 14–16; R Middle Rasen Gp *Linc* from 16. *The Rectory, North Street, Middle Rasen, Market Rasen LN8 3TS* T: (01673) 842759 E: rev.bryan@icloud.com

DIXON, Campbell Boyd. MBE. Ulster Univ MA. **d** 07 **p** 08. NSM Jordanstown *Conn* 07–11; C Belf Cathl 11–16; P-in-c Belfast St Mark *Conn* 16–19; rtd 20. *10 Meadowbank, Newtownabbey BT37 0UP* T: (028) 9059 9880 M: 07879-427980 E: campbelldixon@hotmail.co.uk

DIXON, Charles William. b 41. NW Ord Course 78. **d** 81 **p** 82. C Almondbury *Wakef* 81–82; C Almondbury w Farnley Tyas 82–84; P-in-c Shelley 84–88; P-in-c Shepley 84–88; V Shelley and Shepley 88–89; V Ripponden 89–94; V Barkisland w W Scammonden 89–94; P-in-c Thornes 94–98; Chapl among Deaf People *Chelmsf* 98–06; rtd 06; Chapl among Deaf People *Ely* 06–10; PtO 10–19. *Address temp unknown* M: 07749-702924 E: chasd41@gmail.com

DIXON, David Hugh. b 40. Chich Th Coll 90. **d** 92 **p** 93. C Launceston *Truro* 92–95; TV Probus, Ladock and Grampound w Creed and St Erme 95–06; rtd 06; PtO *Ex* 08–21. *1 Rectory Close, Old Village, Willand, Cullompton EX15 2RH* T: (01884) 839984

DIXON, David Michael. b 58. Preston Poly BA 82 Barrister 83. Coll of Resurr Mirfield BA 98. **d** 98 **p** 99. C Goldthorpe w Hickleton *Sheff* 98–01; P-in-c W Kirby St Andr *Ches* 01–07; V 07–10; P-in-c Scarborough St Martin *York* 10–12; V from 12; P-in-c Scarborough St Sav w All SS 10–12; V from 12. *St Martin's Vicarage, Craven Street, Scarborough YO11 2BY* T: (01723) 363828 E: frdavidstmart@gmail.com

DIXON, Edward Michael. b 42. St Chad's Coll Dur BA 64 Newc Univ MA 93. **d** 66 **p** 67. C Hartlepool H Trin *Dur* 66–70; C Howden *York* 70–73; Chapl HM Pris Liv 73; Chapl HM Pris Onley 74–82; Chapl HM Pris Frankland 82–87; Chapl HM Pris Dur 87–97; Chapl HM Pris Acklington 97–98; Asst Chapl 98–02; P-in-c Shilbottle *Newc* 98–07; P-in-c Chevington 03–07; rtd 07; PtO *Dur* from 07; *Newc* from 18. *2 Crowley Place, Newton Aycliffe DL5 4JH* T: (01325) 312872 M: 07922-471448 E: dixon4474@gmail.com

DIXON, John Kenneth. b 40. Linc Th Coll 79. **d** 81 **p** 82. C Goldington *St Alb* 81–85; V Cardington 85–94; RD Elstow 89–94; R Clifton 94–95; P-in-c Southill 94–95; R Clifton and Southill 95–05; RD Shefford 95–01; rtd 05. *7 Milton Fields, Brixham TQ5 0BH* T: (01803) 854396

DIXON, John Scarth. b 69. Aber Univ MA 92. Westcott Ho Cam 95. **d** 98 **p** 99. C Walney Is *Carl* 98–01; R Harrington 01–06; V Hawkshead and Low Wray w Sawrey and Rusland etc from 06. *The Vicarage, Vicarage Lane, Hawkshead, Ambleside LA22 0PD* T: (015394) 36301 E: jjcedixon@btinternet.com

DIXON, Kenneth. *See* DIXON, John Kenneth

DIXON, Canon Kerry John. b 59. Wilson Carlile Coll 84. **d** 13 **p** 14. LtO *Bre* 13–14; P Missr from 14; P-in-c Dundee St Luke from 14; Can St Paul's Cathl Dundee from 17. *6 Dudhope Street, Dundee DD1 1JU* T: (01382) 523911 M: 07711-410017 E: kerry.dixon@churcharmy.org

DIXON, Lorraine. b 65. Leeds Univ BA 96. Qu Coll Birm BD 98. **d** 98 **p** 99. C Potternewton *Ripon* 98–01; Chapl Ches Univ 01–05; Min Can Ches Cathl 04–05; Deanery Missr to Young Adults Yardley & Bordsley *Birm* 05–12; PtO from 13. E: l.dixon65@btopenworld.com

DIXON, Margaret Innes Goodwin. b 58. Reading Univ BA 01. Ox Min Course 08. **d** 11 **p** 12. NSM Ellesborough, The Kimbles and Stoke Mandeville *Ox* 11–14; C N Leigh 14–17; V from 17; C Cogges and S Leigh 14–17. *The Vicarage, New Yatt Road, North Leigh, Witney OX29 6TT* T: (01993) 880095 M: 07773-017636 E: rev.margaret.dixon@btinternet.com

DIXON, Michael. *See* DIXON, Edward Michael

DIXON, Canon Peter. b 36. Qu Coll Ox BA 58 MA 62 Birm Univ BD 65 PhD 75. Qu Coll Birm. **d** 60 **p** 61. C Mountain Ash *Llan* 60–63; C Penrhiwceiber w Matthewstown and Ynysboeth 63–68; P-in-c 68–70; V Bronllys w Llanfilo *S & B* 70–02; Bp's Chapl for Readers 80–02; Bp's Chapl for Th Educn 83–02; Warden of Readers 92–02; RD Hay 90–02; Can Res Brecon Cathl 98–02; rtd 02. *22 The Caerpound, Hay-on-Wye, Hereford HR3 5DU* T: (01497) 820775

DIXON, Peter. b 70. Ex Univ BTh 08. SWMTC 04. **d** 07 **p** 08. C Redruth w Lanner and Treleigh *Truro* 07–10; V Wisborough Green *Chich* 10–13; P-in-c Lanteglos by Camelford w Advent *Truro* 13–15; P-in-c St Teath 13–15; CF from 15. *c/o MOD Chaplains (Army)* T: (01264) 383430 F: 381824

DIXON, Peter David. b 48. Edin Univ BSc 71 MIMechE. Edin Dioc NSM Course 75. **d** 79 **p** 80. NSM Prestonpans *Edin* 79–89; NSM Musselburgh 79–89; NSM Wester Hailes St Luke 90; P-in-c Edin St Barn from 91. *8 Oswald Terrace, Prestonpans EH32 9EG* T: (01875) 812985

DIXON, Philip. b 48. Leeds Univ BSc 69 Open Univ BA 91. St Jo Coll Nottm 77. **d** 80 **p** 81. C Soundwell *Bris* 80–82; C Stoke Bishop 82–84; TV Hemel Hempstead *St Alb* 84–85; Chapl Westonbirt Sch 85–11; rtd 11; PtO *Bris* from 86. *27 Downfield Lodge, Downfield Road, Bristol BS8 2TQ* T: 0117-373 8528 E: pdnovenove@yahoo.com

DIXON, Philip Roger. b 54. CCC Ox BA 77 MA 80. Oak Hill Th Coll BA 80. **d** 80 **p** 81. C Droylsden St Mary *Man* 80–84; TV Rochdale 84–91; V Audenshaw St Steph 91–21; C Denton Ch Ch 13–21; C Denton St Lawr 13–21; C Haughton St Anne 13–21; AD Ashton-under-Lyne 03–08 and 16–21; rtd 21. *42 Adlington Road, Stockport SK4 5LT* M: 07519-034686 E: revrogerdixon@outlook.com

DIXON, Robert. b 50. Univ of Wales (Lamp) BA 80 Sussex Univ MA 04. Chich Th Coll 80. **d** 81 **p** 82. C Maidstone St Martin *Cant* 81–84; Chapl HM Youth Cust Cen Dover 84–88; C All Hallows by the Tower etc *Lon* 88–90; P-in-c Southwick H Trin *Dur* 90–97; R 97; R Etchingham *Chich* 97–10; V Hurst Green 97–10; V Bedford Leigh *Man* 10–19; rtd 19. *65 Church Lane, South Bersted, Bognor Regis PO22 9QA* M: 07779-121169 E: lancsrob@aol.com

DIXON, Stephen. b 65. York St Jo Univ MA 07. Lindisfarne Regional Tr Partnership 13. **d** 15 **p** 16. C Gosforth All SS *Newc* 15–18; V Tynemouth Priory from 18. *1 Crossway, North Shields NE30 2LB* E: s.c.dixon@hotmail.co.uk

DIXON, Stephen William. b 53. Nottm Univ BA 75 Liv Univ MTh 00 Ches Univ DProf 12 Man Metrop Univ PGCE 88. NOC 96. **d** 99 **p** 00. NSM Meltham *Wakef* 99–02; Upper Holme Valley *Leeds* from 02; Children's Officer *Man* 01–15. *83 Totties, Holmfirth HD9 1UJ* T: (01484) 687376 E: familymasondixon@uwclub.net

DIXON, Mrs Teresa Mary. b 61. Southn Univ BSc 82 Ball Coll Ox PGCE 83. EAMTC 99. **d** 02 **p** 03. NSM Sutton and Witcham w Mepal *Ely* 02–04; C Littleport 04–06; NSM Witchford w Wentworth 06–19; PtO from 19. *Ash Tree Farm, Furlong Drove, Little Downham, Ely CB6 2EW* T: (01353) 699552 E: revteresa@gmail.com

DIXON, Tina Ann. b 51. Liv Univ MB, ChB 74 MRCP 79 FRCP 97. St Mellitus Coll 17. **d** 18 **p** 19.

NSM Oxton *Ches* from 18. *48 Birch Road, Prenton CH43 5UA* T: 0151-653 3256 E: dixon.tina51@gmail.com *or* tina.dixon@oxtonstsaviour.co.uk

DNISTRIANSKYJ, Stefan Mykola. b 61. Leic Univ BSc 82 Ches Coll of HE BTh 02. NOC 99. **d** 02 **p** 03. C Halliwell St Luke *Man* 02–06; TV New Bury w Gt Lever 06–09; P-in-c Anchorsholme *Blackb* 09–12; V 12–18; V Wrightington from 18. *The Vicarage, 92 Church Lane, Wrightington, Wigan WN6 9SP* M: 07445-445824 E: dnists@gmail.com

DOARKS, Andrew John. b 68. Leic Univ BA 91 De Montfort Univ MSc 92. St Mellitus Coll BA 08. **d** 11 **p** 12. C Brislington St Luke *Bris* 11–14; C Bedminster 14–20; P-in-c Bedminster St Mich 18–20; R Ashton from 20. *Bedminster Rectory, 287 North Street, Bedminster, Bristol BS3 1JP* T: 0117-963 9121 M: 07970-495654 E: adoarks@gmail.com

DOBBIE, Charles William Granville. b 49. OBE 92. Wycliffe Hall Ox 94. **d** 96 **p** 97. C Morriston *S & B* 96–00; Asst Chapl Morriston Hosp/Ysbyty Treforys NHS Trust 97–98; Asst Chapl Swansea NHS Trust 99–00; V Lyonsdown H Trin *St Alb* 00–21; rtd 21. *10 Wildcroft Manor, Wildcroft Road, London SW15 3TS* T: (020) 3016 7260

DOBBIN, Canon Charles Philip. b 51. MBE 14. Jes Coll Cam BA 73 MA 77 Oriel Coll Ox BA 75 MA 88 Birm Univ MPhil 04. St Steph Ho Ox 74. **d** 76 **p** 77. C New Addington *Cant* 76–79; C Melton Mowbray w Thorpe Arnold *Leic* 79–83; V Loughb Gd Shep 83–89; V Ashby-de-la-Zouch St Helen w Coleorton 89–00; RD Akeley W 93–00; Hon Can Leic Cathl 94–00; TR Moor Allerton *Ripon* 00–09; TR Moor Allerton and Shadwell 09–16; Dioc Interfaith Relns Officer 09–15; P-in-c Leeds City 14–15; PtO *Leic* from 17. *3 Outwoods Avenue, Loughborough LE11 3LP* E: cdobbin@aol.com

DOBBIN, Harold John. b 47. Liv Univ BSc 69. St Steph Ho Ox 70. **d** 73 **p** 74. C Newbold w Dunston *Derby* 73–77; C Leckhampton SS Phil and Jas w Cheltenham St Jas *Glouc* 77–80; V Hebburn St Cuth *Dur* 80–86; R Barlborough *Derby* 86–95; P-in-c Alfreton 95–00; V 00–04; RD 02–04; P-in-c Clifton 04–08; P-in-c Norbury w Snelston 04–08; rtd 08. *21 Dale Close, Fritchley, Belper DE56 2HZ* T: (01773) 857002 E: harolddobbin@yahoo.co.uk

DOBBINS, Lorraine Sharon. b 72. Ripon Coll Cuddesdon BTh 01. **d** 01 **p** 02. C Talbot Village *Sarum* 01–05; TV Preston w Sutton Poyntz, Littlemoor etc 05–15; TV Weymouth Ridgeway 15–19; V Warminster Ch Ch from 19; Asst Dioc Dir of Ords from 13. *The Vicarage, 13 Avon Road, Warminster BA12 9PR* E: vicarlorraine@gmail.com

DOBBS, Michael John. b 48. Linc Th Coll 74. **d** 77 **p** 78. C Warsop *S'well* 77–82; V Worksop St Paul 82–89; P-in-c Mansfield St Mark 89–03; V Kirk Hallam *Derby* 03–05; rtd 05; PtO *S'well* 06–21; *Derby* 13–18. *Address withheld by request* E: mjdobbs2@gmail.com

DOBELL (née PRICE), Mrs Alison Jane. b 63. Open Univ BA 98. Aston Tr Scheme 91 Westcott Ho Cam 93. **d** 95 **p** 96. C Upper Norwood All SS *S'wark* 95–99; V Mitcham St Barn 99–07; Chapl St Jo Win Charity from 11. *74 Radway Road, Southampton SO15 7PJ* T: (023) 8077 3631 E: alisonjane.price@btinternet.com

DOBLE, Dominic Julian Anderson. b 71. Wye Coll Lon BSc 92 Univ of Wales (Ban) MSc 99 Leeds Univ BA 10. Coll of Resurr Mirfield 08. **d** 10 **p** 11. C Crediton, Shobrooke and Sandford etc *Ex* 10–14; R Watercombe *Sarum* 14–21; TR Blyth Valley *St E* from 21; P-in-c Heveningham from 21. *11 Highfield Road, Halesworth IP19 8SJ* M: 07743-554955 E: dominic.doble@phonecoop.coop

DOBLE, Mrs Maureen Mary Thompson. b 44. RGN 65. S Dios Minl Tr Scheme 90. **d** 93 **p** 94. NSM Kingston St Mary w Broomfield etc *B & W* 93–07; Chapl Taunton and Somerset NHS Foundn Trust 03–07; rtd 07; PtO *B & W* from 07. *Rosebank, Lyngford Lane, Taunton TA2 7LL* T: (01823) 286772 E: rosebank@maureendoble.co.uk

DOBLE, Peter. b 29. Univ of Wales (Cardiff) BA 51 Fitzw Coll Cam BA 54 MA 58 St Edm Hall Ox MA 68 Leeds Univ PhD 92. Wesley Ho Cam 52. **d** 55 **p** 58. In Ch of S India 55–60; In Methodist Ch 60–64; Hd of RE Qu Mary Sch Lytham St Annes *Blackb* 64–67; Lect RS Culham Coll Abingdon *Ox* 67–69; Sen Lect 69–74; Prin Lect and Hd Relig Studies 74–80; PtO *York* 80–17; Dir York RE Cen 80–94; Sen Fell Th and RS Leeds Univ *Ripon* 95–98; Hon Lect from 98. *6 Witham Drive, Huntington, York YO32 9YD* T: (01904) 761288 E: peter.doble@btinternet.com

DOBRZYNSKI, Adam Andrzej. b 75. Catholic Univ of Lublin MPhil 01 Ivan Franko Nat Univ Lviv PhD 18. Pontifical Academy of Th Krakow MTS 06 LTh 07. **d** 07 **p** 07. C Ealing St Pet Mt Park *Lon* from 19. *St Peter's Church, Mount Park Road, London W5 2RU* T: (020) 8997 3655 M: 07453-619591 E: a.a.dobrzynski@gmail.com

DOBSON, Canon Catherine Heather. b 71. ERMC. **d** 09 **p** 10. NSM Broughton w Loddington and Cransley etc *Pet* 09–11; C 11–14; C Rothwell w Orton, Rushton w Glendon and Pipewell 11–14; R Bacton, Happisburgh, Hempstead w Eccles etc *Nor* from 14; RD St Benet from 19; Hon Can Nor Cathl from 20; Chapter Can Nor Cathl from 21. *The Rectory, The Hill, Happisburgh, Norwich NR12 0PW* T: (01692) 650359 E: revcdobson@live.com

DOBSON, Christopher John. b 62. Univ of Wales (Abth) BA 83. Wycliffe Hall Ox BA 88. **d** 89 **p** 90. C Biggin Hill *Roch* 89–92; C Tunbridge Wells St Jas w St Phil 92–95; USPG 95–99; V Harare All So Zimbabwe 96–99; V Paddock Wood *Roch* 00–08; Ecum and Global Adv *Bris* from 08; Hon C Downend from 09; Hd of Licensed Lay Min Formation Tr 18–21; Dioc Chapl MU from 19. *23 Ducie Road, Staple Hill, Bristol BS16 5JZ* M: 07904-831829 E: chris.j.dobson@gmail.com *or* chris.dobson@bristoldiocese.org

DOBSON, Mrs Elspeth Judith. b 53. Newc Univ CertEd 75 BPhil 88 MPhil 95. Lindisfarne Regional Tr Partnership 09. **d** 17 **p** 18. NSM Doddington, Ilderton, Kirknewton and Wooler *Newc* from 17. *The Crossings, Yeavering, Kirknewton, Wooler NE71 6HG* T: (01668) 216098 M: 07778-465527

DOBSON, Geoffrey Norman. b 46. Leeds Univ CertEd 68 Open Univ BA 77 MA 05 ACP 70. Wells Th Coll 71. **d** 74 **p** 75. C Wanstead H Trin Hermon Hill *Chelmsf* 74–76; Colchester Adnry Youth Chapl 76–78; C Halstead St Andr w H Trin and Greenstead Green *Chelmsf* 76–78; Asst Dir Educn (Youth) *Carl* 78–82; P-in-c Kirkandrews-on-Eden w Beaumont and Grinsdale 78–82; V Illingworth *Wakef* 82–86; V Roxton w Gt Barford *St Alb* 86–93; Chapl N Man Health Care NHS Trust 93–98; P-in-c Newton Heath 97–98; P-in-c Alconbury cum Weston *Ely* 98–00; P-in-c Buckworth 98–00; P-in-c Gt w Lt Stukeley 98–00; PtO from 02. *30 Lees Lane, Southoe, St Neots PE19 5YG* T: (01480) 475474 E: geoffreyndobson@aol.com

DOBSON, Mrs Joanna Jane Louise. b 61. Coll of Ripon & York St Jo BEd 83. NEOC 98. **d** 01 **p** 02. NSM Scalby *York* 01–04; V Bridlington Em 04–08; P-in-c Skipsea w Ulrome and Barmston w Fraisthorpe 04–08; Pioneer Min Retford Deanery *S'well* 08–10; P-in-c Mitford and Hebron *Newc* 10–16; P-in-c Ulgham 16–21; P-in-c Widdrington 16–21; rtd 21. *56 Wheatall Drive, Sunderland SR6 7HQ* M: 07828-181506 E: joannajldobson@yahoo.com

DOBSON, The Very Revd John Richard. b 64. Van Mildert Coll *Dur* BA 87. Ripon Coll Cuddesdon 87. **d** 89 **p** 90. C Benfieldside *Dur* 89–92; C Darlington St Cuth 92–96; C-in-c Blackwell All SS and Salutation CD 96–98; V Blackwell All SS and Salutation 98–14; P-in-c Coniscliffe 04–14; AD Darlington 01–14; Hon Can Dur Cathl 08–14; Dean Ripon Leeds from 14; V Ripon Cathl Benefice from 14. *Minster House, Bedern Bank, Ripon HG4 1PE* T: (01765) 602609 E: j.dobson991@btinternet.com

DOBSON, Judith. *See* DOBSON, Elspeth Judith

DOBSON, Michael William. b 66. Man Univ BA 89 Sussex Univ MSc 91 Open Univ PhD 99 FRSA 95. Regent Coll Vancouver MDiv 11. **d** 11 **p** 12. In Angl Network in Canada 11–14; R Maadi Egypt 14–19; C Pimlico St Gabr *Lon* 19–21; P-in-c Hanworth St Geo from 21; C Ashford St Matt from 21; C Stanwell from 21. *7 Arlington Road, Teddington TW11 8NL* E: mike.w.dobson@gmail.com

DOBSON, Owen James. b 83. Ex Univ BA 04 Cam Univ MPhil 14. Westcott Ho Cam 08. **d** 10 **p** 11. C St John's Wood *Lon* 10–14; C Paddington St Jas from 14. *61 Pembroke House, Hallfield Estate, London W2 6HQ* T: (020) 7706 1248 M: 07891-890837 E: owenjamesdobson@hotmail.com *or* owen@stjamespaddington.org.uk

DOBSON, Canon Peter David. b 88. St Andr Univ MTheol 10 Jes Coll Cam MPhil 11. Westcott Ho Cam 10. **d** 12 **p** 13. C Ch the King *Newc* 12–16; V Monkseaton St Pet 16–19; Can Res Newc Cathl from 19. *Cathedral House, 42 Mosley Street, Newcastle upon Tyne NE1 1DF* T: 0191-232 1939 M: 07940-706123 E: peterdobsonuk@yahoo.co.uk *or* peter.dobson@newcastlecathedral.org.uk

DOBSON, Philip Albert. b 52. Lanc Univ BA 73 CertEd 74. Trin Coll Bris 89. **d** 89 **p** 90. C Grenoside *Sheff* 89–92; C Cove St Jo *Guildf* 92–93; TV 93–96; V Camberley St Martin Old Dean 96–07; TR Bushbury *Lich* 07–13; rtd 13; PtO *Man* from 14. *134 Old Moat Lane, Manchester M20 1DE* T: 0161-283 9697 E: philip297dobson.home@gmail.com

DOCKREE, Peter Martin. b 74. Keele Univ BA 96 Ox Univ MSc 00. Ox Min Course 07. **d** 10 **p** 11. C Wolverton *Ox* 10–14; V Swaythling *Win* from 14. *The Vicarage, 357 Burgess Road, Southampton SO16 3BD* T: (023) 8055 4231 M: 07972-439865 E: peter.dockree@outlook.com

DODD, Canon Andrew Patrick. b 68. Hatf Poly BEng 91 Selw Coll Cam BTh 00. Westcott Ho Cam 97. **d** 00 **p** 01.

C New Addington *S'wark* 00–04; R Newington St Mary 04–11; AD S'wark and Newington 07–11; P-in-c Gt Grimsby St Mary and St Jas *Linc* 11–13; TR 13–20; AD Grimsby and Cleethorpes 11–20; Can and Preb Linc Cathl 12–20; Can Res Cant Cathl from 20. *22 The Precincts, Canterbury CT1 2EP* M: 07963-557897 E: andrew@vincerdodd.co.uk *or* andrew.dodd@canterbury-cathedral.org

DODD, Miss Denise Kate. b 72. Cranmer Hall Dur 07. d 09 p 10. C Porchester *S'well* 09–14; Bp's Dom Chapl *Dur* from 14; Hon Min Can Dur Cathl from 16. *Auckland Castle, Bishop Auckland DL14 7NR* T: (01388) 602576 F: 605264 E: denisekdodd@yahoo.co.uk *or* denise.dodd@durham.anglican.org

DODD, Graham Michael. b 38. St Jo Coll York CertEd 61 Hull Coll of Educn DipEd 67. NOC 93. d 96 p 97. NSM Golcar *Wakef* 96–99; NSM N Huddersfield 99–02; rtd 02; PtO *Wakef* 02–14; *Leeds* from 14. *9 Broombank, Huddersfield HD2 2DJ* T: (01484) 539832 *or* 687376 E: mikedodd184@btinternet.com

DODD, Michael Christopher. b 33. Ch Coll Cam BA 55 MA 59. Ridley Hall Cam 57. d 59 p 60. C Stechford *Birm* 59–62; V Quinton Road W St Boniface 62–72; TV Paston *Pet* 72–77; TR Hodge Hill *Birm* 77–89; rtd 90; PtO *Birm* from 90. *39 Regency Gardens, Birmingham B14 4JS* T: 0121-474 6945

DODD, Canon Peter Curwen. b 33. St Jo Coll Cam BA 57 FRSA 93. Linc Th Coll 58 Wm Temple Coll Rugby 59. d 60 p 61. C Eastwood *Sheff* 60–63; Ind Chapl 63–67; Ind Chapl *Newc* 67–98; RD Newc E 78–83 and 92–95; Hon Can Newc Cathl 82–98; rtd 98; PtO *Newc* from 98. *Glenesk, 26 The Oval, Benton, Newcastle upon Tyne NE12 9PP* T: 0191-266 1293

DODDS, Barry. *See* DODDS, Norman Barry

DODDS, Canon Graham Michael. b 58. Liv Univ MA 01 Bris Univ PhD 08 LTCL 80 GTCL 80 York Univ PGCE 81. Trin Coll Bris 84. d 84 p 85. C Reigate St Mary *S'wark* 84–91; P-in-c Bath Walcot *B & W* 91–93; R 93–96; Dir Reader Studies 96–18; Lay Tr Adv 96–01; Asst Dir Min Development 01–04; Prin Sch of Formation *B & W* 04–09; Dir of Learning Communities 10–18; Preb Wells Cathl 03–10; Can Res and Treas Wells Cathl 10–18; Bps' Chapl 18–21. *2 The Canaries Path, Shepton Mallet BA4 4FP* T: (01749) 672341 M: 07702-658687 E: gdcanaries@gmail.com

DODDS, Linda. b 54. d 08 p 09. OLM Bishop Auckland Woodhouse Close CD *Dur* 08–15; rtd 15; PtO *Dur* from 15. *30 Low Etherley, Bishop Auckland DL14 0EU* T: (01388) 832756 E: reverend.linda@yahoo.co.uk

DODDS, Canon Norman Barry. b 43. Open Univ BA. CITC 73. d 76 p 77. C Ballynafeigh St Jude *D & D* 76–80; I Belfast St Mich *Conn* 80–14; Chapl HM Pris Belfast 84–14; Can Belf Cathl 98–14; Adn Belfast *Conn* 07–13; rtd 14. *85 Bangor Road, Newtownards BT23 7BZ* T: (028) 9107 1347 M: 07763-935160 E: doddscavehill@yahoo.com

DODGSON, David. b 46. d 13 p 14. NSM Sandal St Cath *Leeds* 13–18; NSM Wakefield St Andr and St Mary and Belle Vue from 18. *St Catherine's Church, Doncaster Road, Belle Vue, Wakefield WF1 5HL* M: 07508-053587

DODGSON, Geoffrey John. b 51. Lon Univ BSc 73. ERMC 19. d 20 p 21. NSM Papworth *Ely* from 20. *Lavenders, 12 Cootes Lane, Fen Drayton, Cambridge CB24 4SL* T: (01954) 231662 M: 07710-379561 E: geoff@dodgson.info

DODHIA, Hitesh Kishorilal. b 57. Cranmer Hall Dur 85. d 88 p 89. C Leamington Priors All SS *Cov* 88–91; Asst Chapl HM YOI Glen Parva 91–92; Chapl 94–98; Chapl HM Pris Roch 92–94; The Mount 98–01. *Address temp unknown* M: 07546-033740 E: hiteshdodhia@yahoo.com

DODSON, Canon Gordon. b 31. Em Coll Cam BA 54 MA 58 LLB 55 LLM 01 Barrister 56. Ridley Hall Cam 57. d 59 p 60. C Belhus Park *Chelmsf* 59–60; C Barking St Marg 60–63; CMS 63–67; C New Malden and Coombe *S'wark* 67–69; V Snettisham *Nor* 69–81; RD Heacham and Rising 76–81; P-in-c Reepham and Hackford w Whitwell and Kerdiston 81–83; P-in-c Salle 81–83; P-in-c Thurning w Wood Dalling 81–83; R Reepham, Hackford w Whitwell, Kerdiston etc 83–94; Hon Can Nor Cathl 85–94; rtd 94; PtO *Nor* from 94. *Poppygate, 2 The Loke, Cromer NR27 9DH* T: (01263) 511811 E: dodlerpg@btinternet.com

DODWELL, Andrew James. b 75. Man Univ BSc 96 MSc 98. SWMTC 06. d 08 p 09. C Barnstaple *Ex* 08–17; V Newport and Bishops Tawton 17–20; RD Barnstaple 18–20; C Heref St Pet w St Owen and St Jas from 20. *1 Holme Lacy Road, Hereford HR2 6DD* E: revdodwell@gmail.com

DOE, Laura Elizabeth. b 88. UEA BA 10. Trin Coll Bris BA 18. d 19 p 20. C Bedminster *Bris* from 19. *St Anne's Vicaraage, 75 Greenbank Road, Greenbank, Bristol BS5 6HD* M: 07717-790871 E: lauraedoe@gmail.com

DOE, Martin Charles. b 54. Lon Univ BSc(Econ) 75 PGCE 87 MA 95. St Steph Ho Ox 89. d 91 p 92. C Portsea St Mary *Portsm* 91–94; Chapl Abbey Grange High Sch 94–00; Sen Angl Chapl Scarborough and NE Yorks Healthcare NHS Trust 00–14; Sen Chapl York Teaching Hosp NHS Foundn Trust 14–16; rtd 16; PtO *York* from 16. *5 Back Lane, Wigginton, York YO32 2ZH* E: revdmdoe91@btinternet.com

✠**DOE, The Rt Revd Michael David.** b 47. St Jo Coll Dur BA 69 Bath Univ Hon LLD 02. Ripon Hall Ox 69. d 72 p 73 c 94. C St Helier *S'wark* 72–76; Hon C 76–81; Youth Sec BCC 76–81; C-in-c Blackbird Leys CD *Ox* 81–88; V Blackbird Leys 88–89; RD Cowley 86–89; Soc Resp Adv *Portsm* 89–94; Can Res Portsm Cathl 89–94; Suff Bp Swindon *Bris* 94–04; Gen Sec USPG 04–11; rtd 11; Preacher Gray's Inn from 11; Asst Bp S'wark from 04. *405 West Carriage House, Royal Carriage Mews, London SE18 6GA* T: (020) 3259 3841 E: michaeldd@btinternet.com *or* michael.doe@graysinn.org.uk

DOE, Mrs Priscilla Sophia. b 41. LRAM 61. SEITE 97. d 00 p 01. NSM Maidstone All SS and St Phil w Tovil *Cant* 00–11; PtO from 11. *Mount St Laurence, High Street, Cranbrook TN17 3EW* T: (01580) 712330

DOERING, Monika Sigrid. b 72. Heidelberg Univ MA 00. St Steph Ho Ox BA 17. d 17 p 18. C W Barnsley *Leeds* 17–21; Chapl Nottm Univ Hosp NHS Trust from 21. *Nottingham University Hospitals Trust, Queens Medical Centre, Derby Road, Nottingham NG7 2UH* M: 07719-934327 E: monikadoering72@gmail.com

DOERR, Mrs Anne. b 55. Man Univ BA 76 Cant Ch Ch Univ BA 12. SEITE 06. d 09 p 10. NSM Belmont *S'wark* 09–13; NSM St Helier from 13; Chapl R Marsden NHS Foundn Trust from 14; PtO *Lon* from 20. *14 Central Way, Carshalton SM5 3NF* T: (020) 8669 2494 M: 07811-908731 E: aedoerr@btinternet.com *or* anne.doerr@rmh.nhs.uk

DOHERTY, Mrs Christine. b 46. SEN 72. STETS 97. d 00 p 01. NSM Framfield *Chich* 00–03; C Seaford w Sutton 03–11; rtd 11; PtO *Chich* 12–17. *27 Hawth Park Road, Seaford BN25 2RF* T: (01323) 351243 E: chris.doh@tiscali.co.uk

DOHERTY, Sean William. d 07 p 08. C Cricklewood St Gabr and St Mich *Lon* 07–10; Lect St Paul's Th Cen 08–10; Tutor St Mellitus Coll 10–19; Prin Trin Coll Bris from 19; LtO *Bris* from 20. *129 Reedley Road, Bristol BS9 1BE* T: 0117-968 2803 M: 07710-515800 E: principal@trinitycollegebristol.ac.uk

DOHERTY, Thomas Alexander. b 48. Chich Th Coll 73. d 76 p 77. V Choral Derry Cathl *D & R* 76–79; C Llandaff w Capel Llanilltern *Llan* 79–80; PV Llan Cathl 80–84; V Penmark w Porthkerry 84–90; R Merthyr Dyfan 90–02; V Margam 02–15; rtd 15; PtO *Llan* from 15. *Riverside Bungalow, 2 Library Lane, Port Talbot SA13 1LQ*

DOICK, Paul Stephen James. b 70. Chich Univ BA 10. Ripon Coll Cuddesdon 03. d 05 p 06. C Hove *Chich* 05–09; TV 09–10; V Hove St Jo 10–14; R Henfield w Shermanbury and Woodmancote from 14; RD Hurst from 18. *Henfield Vicarage, Church Lane, Henfield BN5 9NY* T: (01273) 492017 M: 07742-868602 E: p.doick@btinternet.com

DOIDGE, Charles William. b 44. Univ Coll Lon BSc 65 MSc 67 PhD 72. EMMTC 93. d 93 p 94. NSM Blaby *Leic* 93–96; P-in-c Willoughby Waterleys, Peatling Magna etc 96–04; rtd 04. *21 Brunel Mews, Solsbro Road, Torquay TQ2 6QA* T: (01803) 690548 E: doidge@dmu.ac.uk *or* charlesdoidge@talktalk.net

DOIDGE, Valerie Gladys. b 49. STETS 98. d 01 p 02. C St Leonards St Ethelburga *Chich* 01–07; C Hollington St Leon 07–12; rtd 12; PtO *Chich* from 17. *6 Collinswood Drive, St Leonards-on-Sea TN38 0NU* T: (01424) 425651 E: val.doidge@outlook.com

DOIG, Allan George. b 51. Univ of BC BA 69 K Coll Cam BA 73 MA 80 PhD 82 FSA 98 FRHistS 15. Ripon Coll Cuddesdon 86. d 88 p 89. C Abingdon *Ox* 88–91; Chapl LMH Ox 91–19; Fell 96–19; Select Preacher Ox 95–96; rtd 19; PtO *Ox* from 19. *The Priory, Hudson Street, Deddington, Banbury OX15 0SW* M: 07595-003240

DOLBY, Mrs Christine Teresa. b 54. Nottm Univ MA 01 SRN 80. EMMTC 98. d 01 p 02. C Cropwell Bishop w Colston Bassett, Granby etc *S'well* 01–05; P-in-c Ancaster Wilsford Gp *Linc* 05–08; Chapl Qu Medical Cen Nottm Univ Hosp NHS Trust 08–15; Hd Spiritual and Past Care Nottm Univ Hosp NHS Trust 15–18; rtd 18; Hon C Fosse Team *Leic* from 18. *Hall Lodge, 66 Kneeton Road, East Bridgford, Nottingham NG13 8PJ* T: (01949) 829090 M: 07464-547654 E: c.dolby263@btinternet.com

DOLL, Canon Peter Michael. b 62. Yale Univ BA 84 Ch Ch Ox DPhil 89. Cuddesdon Coll BA 94. d 95 p 96. C Cowley St Jo *Ox* 95–99; Chapl Worc Coll Ox 98–02; TV Abingdon Ox 02–09; Can Res Nor Cathl from 09. *56 The Close, Norwich NR1 4EG* T: (01603) 218336 E: canonlibrarian@cathedral.org.uk

DOLLERY, Anne Mary Elizabeth. b 55. Hull Univ BA 78. Ridley Hall Cam 02. **d** 04 **p** 05. C Thundersley *Chelmsf* 04–09; V Walthamstow St Andr 09–15; V Feltham *Lon* from 15. *The Vicarage, St Elmo, Cardinal Road, Feltham TW13 5AL* T: (020) 8890 8347 E: annedollery@yahoo.co.uk

DOLMAN, Derek Alfred George Gerrit. b 40. ALCD 64. **d** 65 **p** 66. C St Alb St Paul 65–68; C Bishopwearmouth St Gabr *Dur* 68–72; R Jarrow Grange 72–80; V New Catton St Luke *Nor* 80–98; V New Catton St Luke w St Aug 98–00; R S Croxton Gp *Leic* 00–06; rtd 06; PtO *Leic* 06–12; *Derby* 07–18; *Lich* 07–12. *17 Kestrel Way, Burton-on-Trent DE15 0DJ* T: (01283) 845330 E: derekdolman@uwclub.net

DOLMAN, William Frederick Gerrit. b 42. JP. K Coll Lon MB, BS 65 Lon Univ LLB 87 MRCS 65 LRCP 65. SEITE 04. **d** 06 **p** 07. NSM Beckley and Peasmarsh *Chich* 06–14; rtd 15; PtO *Chich* from 15. *Little Bellhurst Cottage, Hobbs Lane, Beckley, Rye TN31 6TT* T: (01797) 260203 E: hmcwd@aol.com

DOLPHIN, Mrs Kirstie. b 59. Ripon Coll Cuddesdon 13. **d** 16 **p** 17. NSM Reading St Matt *Ox* 16–20; P-in-c Reading St Agnes w St Paul and St Barn from 20. *St Matthew's Vicarage, 205 Southcote Lane, Reading RG30 3AX* T: 0118-954 7964 *or* 08444-771754 M: 07710-225413 E: kirstie.dolphin@st-matts.org.uk

DOMINIAK, Paul Anthony. b 78. Univ of the S (USA) BA 05 SS Coll Cam BA 07 MPhil 08 Dur Univ PhD 18. Westcott Ho Cam 05. **d** 08 **p** 09. C Ingleby Barwick *York* 08–11; Chapl Trin Coll Cam 11–15; Dean of Chapl Jes Coll Cam 15–19; Asst Dir of Ords *Ely* 16–19; Tutor Westcott Ho Cam 17–19; Vice-Prin from 19. *Westcott House, Jesus Lane, Cambridge CB5 8BP* T: (01223) 272975 E: pad39@cam.ac.uk

DOMINIC MARK, Brother. *See* IND, Dominic Mark

DOMINY, Canon Peter John. b 36. Qu Coll Ox BA 60 MA 64 Aber Univ MLitt 83 Ex Univ PhD 11. Oak Hill Th Coll 60. **d** 62 **p** 63. C Bedworth *Cov* 62–66; Nigeria 67–84; Sudan United Miss 67-72; V Jos St Piran 72–84; R Broadwater St Mary *Chich* 84–92; TR Broadwater 92–98; P-in-c Danehill 98–99; V 99–03; Can and Preb Chich Cathl 93–03; RD Uckfield 00–03; rtd 03; PtO *Sarum* from 03. *32 Bedwin Street, Salisbury SP1 3UT* T: (01722) 238635 E: peterd@uwclub.net

DOMMETT, Simon Paul. b 58. Warwick Univ BSc 79. St Jo Coll Nottm MA 99. **d** 99 **p** 00. C Weston Favell *Pet* 99–02; P-in-c Gt w Lt Harrowden and Orlingbury 02–06; P-in-c Isham w Pytchley 05–06; R Gt w Lt Harrowden and Orlingbury and Isham etc 06–12; R Aynho and Croughton w Evenley etc 12–18; RD Brackley 13–18; P-in-c Goldington *St Alb* 18–19; V from 19. *St Mary's Vicarage, Church Lane, Bedford MK41 0AP* E: the.revd.simon@gmail.com

DOMONEY, Canon Lynette May (Lyndy). b 44. Th Ext Educn Coll 90. **d** 92 **p** 93. S Africa 92–06; P-in-c Kessingland, Gisleham and Rushmere *Nor* 06–08; R 08–14; rtd 14; PtO *Nor* from 15. *25 Victory Court, Diss IP22 4GN* T: (01379) 650445 E: l.domoney@btinternet.com

DONAGHEY, Thomas Alfred. b 67. Trin Coll Bris 06. **d** 08 **p** 09. C Whittle-le-Woods *Blackb* 08–13; V Baxenden 13–20. *Address temp unknown* M: 07974-457544 E: tdonaghey@hotmail.com

DONALD, Dennis Curzon. b 38. Oak Hill Th Coll 68. **d** 70 **p** 71. C Carl St Jo 70–73; LtO 73–77; Warden Blaithwaite Ho Chr Conf Cen Wigton 73–90; Chapl Cumberland Infirmary 85–92; Chapl Eden Valley Hospice Carl 92–98; rtd 98; PtO *Carl* 77–13. *5 The Old Bakery, Gretna DG16 5FZ* T: (01461) 338053

DONALD, Mrs Philippa Jane. b 58. Bath Univ BA 79 Moray Ho Edin DipEd 80. WEMTC 08. **d** 11 **p** 12. NSM Churchdown St Jo and Innsworth *Glouc* 11–15; NSM Twigworth, Down Hatherley, Norton, The Leigh etc from 15. *8 Seabrook Road, Gloucester GL1 3JH* T: (01452) 528569 E: talk2philippa@hotmail.com

DONALD, Robert Francis. b 49. St Jo Coll Nottm BTh 75 LTh. **d** 75 **p** 76. C New Barnet St Jas *St Alb* 75–79; C St Alb St Paul 79–86; C St Alb St Mary Marshalswick 86–87; Dir Chr Alliance Housing Assn Ltd 87–98; LtO *St Alb* 87–19; PtO from 19. *24 Meadowcroft, St Albans AL1 1UD* T: (01727) 841647 M: 07973-208289

DONALD, Rosemary Anne. b 52. STETS 99. **d** 02 **p** 03. NSM Blendworth w Chalton w Idsworth *Portsm* 02–07; P-in-c 07–18; rtd 18; PtO *Portsm* from 18. *1A Havant Road, Horndean, Waterlooville PO8 0DB* T: (023) 9259 2121 E: rosemary.donald3@gmail.com

DONALD, Steven. b 55. CertEd 76 Hull Univ MA 99. Oak Hill Th Coll BA 88. **d** 88 **p** 89. C Cheadle All Hallows *Ches* 88–91; C Ardsley *Sheff* 91; V Kendray 92–99; P-in-c Chadderton Ch Ch *Man* 99–03; V 03–05; V Carl St Jo from 05. *St John's Vicarage, London Road, Carlisle CA1 2QQ* T: (01228) 521601 E: stevedon1@aol.com

DONALDSON, Alastair Philip. b 82. Sheff Hallam Univ BSc 04. CITC MTh 15. **d** 14 **p** 15. Fivemiletown *Clogh* 14–15; Bp's C Roscommon Gp *K, E & A* 15–18; I Kinawley w H Trin from 18. *The Rectory, 146 Main Street, Derrylin, Enniskillen BT92 9PD* T: (028) 6774 8994 M: 07737-865326 E: alastairdonaldson82@gmail.com

DONALDSON, Aron William Francis. b 92. Essex Univ BA 15. Wycliffe Hall Ox 16. **d** 19 **p** 20. C Corby Glen *Linc* 19–20; C Corby Glen Par from 20. *42 St John's Drive, Corby Glen, Grantham NG33 4NG*

DONALDSON, Miss Elizabeth Anne. b 55. Univ of Wales (Ban) BSc 76 Surrey Univ MSc 80 Nottm Univ BA 82. St Jo Coll Nottm 80. **dss** 83 **d** 87 **p** 94. Guildf Ch Ch 83–86; Cuddington 86–90; C 87–90; C Keresley and Coundon *Cov* 90–99; V Gt Amwell w St Margaret's and Stanstead Abbots *St Alb* 00–19; rtd 19; PtO *Chelmsf* from 20. *3 The Hill, Harlow CM17 0BH* E: annedonaldson55@gmail.com

DONALDSON, Mrs Janet Elizabeth. b 53. GTCL 74 Whitelands Coll Lon CertEd 75. EAMTC 95. **d** 98 **p** 99. NSM Tolleshunt Knights w Tiptree and Gt Braxted *Chelmsf* 98–02; V Knights and Hospitallers Par 02–11; P-in-c Deeping St James *Linc* 11–13; P-in-c Welford w Sibbertoft and Marston Trussell *Pet* 13–16; V 16–18; rtd 18. *11 Haddonian Road, Market Harborough LE16 9GD* E: rev.janet@donaldsonfamily.org.uk

DONALDSON, Malcolm Alexander. b 48. Cranmer Hall Dur 84. **d** 86 **p** 87. C Heworth H Trin *York* 86–89; Chapl York Distr Hosp 86–89; C Marfleet *York* 89–90; TV 90–96; R Collyhurst *Man* 96–05; rtd 05. *12 Clove Court, Tweedmouth, Berwick-upon-Tweed TD15 2FJ*

DONALDSON, Canon Roger Francis. b 50. Jes Coll Ox BA 71 MA 75. Westcott Ho Cam 72. **d** 74 **p** 75. C Mold *St As* 74–78; V Denio w Abererch *Ban* 78–95; TR Llanbeblig w Caernarfon and Betws Garmon etc 95–20; AD Arfon 04–09; Hon Can Ban Cathl 04–20; PtO from 20. *4 Trevelyan Terrace, High Street, Bangor LL57 1AX*

DONALDSON, William Richard. b 56. St Cath Coll Cam BA 78 MA 81. Ridley Hall Cam 79. **d** 82 **p** 83. C Everton St Sav w St Cuth *Liv* 82–85; C Reigate St Mary *S'wark* 85–89; V Easton H Trin w St Gabr and St Lawr and St Jude *Bris* 89–99; V W Ealing St Jo w St Jas *Lon* 99–07; Dir of Ords Willesden Area 06–07; Dir Chr Leadership Wycliffe Hall Ox 07–12; Course Dir Part-Time Tr 12–13; Chapl St Edm Hall Ox 13–19; C Ox St Aldate 12–19; AD Ox 15–19; Dioc Dir for New Congregations from 19; PtO from 19. *Church House, Langford Locks, Kidlington, Oxford OX5 1GF* T: (01865) 279021 M: 07745-363540

DONCASTER, Archdeacon of. *See* IQBAL, The Ven Javaid

DONCASTER, Suffragan Bishop of. *See* JELLEY, The Rt Revd Sophie Rebecca

DONE, Nigel Anthony. b 68. Wye Coll Lon BSc 89 St Jo Coll Dur BA 98. Cranmer Hall Dur. **d** 98 **p** 99. C Pilton w Croscombe, N Wootton and Dinder *B & W* 98–02; R Hardington Vale 02–12; V Ilminster and Whitelackington 12–18; RD Ilminster 17–18; Dioc Dir of Ords *Sarum* from 18; Co-ord of IME from 18. *Church House, Crane Street, Salisbury SP1 2QB* E: nigel.done@btinternet.com

DONE, Roy Edward. b 46. **d** 11. NSM Bain Valley Gp *Linc* from 11. *43 Park Lane, Coningsby, Lincoln LN4 4SW* T: (01526) 343013 E: roy.done@btinternet.com

DONEGAN-CROSS, Guy William. b 68. St Aid Coll Dur BA 90. Trin Coll Bris BA 98. **d** 99 **p** 00. C Swindon Ch Ch *Bris* 99–03; V Saltburn-by-the-Sea *York* 03–10; V Harrogate St Mark *Ripon* 10–14; Leeds 14–19; Hon Can Ripon Cathl 17–19; Dir Learning for Discipleship and Miss *Birm* from 19. *Christchurch Vicarage, 28 Burney Lane, Birmingham B8 2AS* E: guydonegancross@yahoo.co.uk *or* guydc@cofebirmingham.com

DONEGAN-CROSS, Ruth Katherine. b 68. Dur Univ BA 90 Sheff Univ BA 16. Yorks Min Course 13. **d** 16 **p** 17. C Bilton *Leeds* 16–20; V Ward End w Bordesley Green *Birm* from 20. *Christchurch Vicarage, 28 Burney Lane, Birmingham B8 2AS* M: 07588-813343 E: rev.ruthccwe@gmail.com

DONEY, Malcolm Charles. b 50. Lon Univ BA 71 Middx Univ BA 05. NTMTC 02. **d** 05 **p** 06. NSM Tufnell Park St Geo and All SS *Lon* 05–07; NSM W Holloway St Luke 07–12; NSM All Hallows Lon Wall 07–12; PtO *St E* from 10. *The Birdhouse, Old Angel Lane, Blythburgh, Halesworth IP19 9JW* T: (01502) 478229 E: malcolmdoney@me.com

DONKERSLEY, Mrs Christine Mary. b 44. K Alfred's Coll Win CertEd 65. STETS 98. **d** 01 **p** 02. NSM Baltonsborough w Butleigh, W Bradley etc *B & W* 01–06; P-in-c Fosse Trinity 06–13; rtd 13; PtO *B & W* 13–19. *7 Turnpike, Honiton EX14 2HX* M: 07866-531917 E: cm.donkersley@btinternet.com

DONKIN, Canon Robert. b 50. St Mich Coll Llan 71. **d** 74 **p** 75. C Mountain Ash *Llan* 74–77; C Coity w Nolton

77–79; V Oakwood 79–84; V Aberaman and Abercwmboi 84–91; V Aberaman and Abercwmboi w Cwmaman 91–99; R Penarth w Lavernock 99–04; R Penarth and Llandough 04–08; AD Penarth and Barry 04–08; R Caerphilly 08–14; AD 10–14; AD Merthyr Tydfil and Caerphilly 12–14; Hon Can Llan Cathl 06–14; rtd 14; PtO *Llan* from 14. *4 Heol-y-Gelli, Aberdare CF44 6LN* T: (01685) 884645 E: robert.donkin@hotmail.com

DONMALL, Michael Charles. b 53. Univ Coll Lon BSc 75 PhD 84 K Coll Lon PGCE 80 FFPH 06. Yorks Min Course 12. **d** 14 **p** 15. NSM Saddleworth *Man* from 14. *7 Higher Arthurs, Greenfield, Oldham OL3 7BE* T: (01457) 870427 E: michaeldonmall@cofeinsaddleworth.org.uk

DONNELL (née Wilkinson), Gemma Louise. b 88. Lanc Univ BA 06. Ripon Coll Cuddesdon BA 18. **d** 18 **p** 19. C Finchampstead and California *Ox* 18–21; R Moreton, Woodsford and Crossways w Tincleton *Sarum* from 21. *The Rectory, 17 Warmwell Road, Crossways, Dorchester DT2 8BS* M: 07809-376352 E: revdonnell@outlook.com

DONNELLY, Juliet Ann. See EVANS, Juliet Ann

DONNELLY, Nigel Mark. b 58. Wycliffe Hall Ox 15. **d** 17 **p** 18. C Oundle w Ashton and Benefield w Glapthorn *Pet* 17–20; P-in-c Salcey from 20. *18 Hartwell Road, Roade, Northampton NN7 2NT* T: (01604) 378557 E: vicar.salceybenefice@gmail.com

DONNELLY, Trevor Alfred. b 71. K Coll Lon BA 93 AKC 93. Cuddesdon Coll 94. **d** 97 **p** 98. C Southgate Ch Ch *Lon* 97–01; V Hinchley Wood *Guildf* 01–05; Sen Chapl Medway Secure Tr Cen 06–09; TV Deptford St Jo w H Trin and Ascension *S'wark* 09–17. *20 London Road, Stone, Dartford DA2 6DJ* E: trevordonnelly@mac.com

DONOGHUE, William Noel. b 80. Goldsmiths' Coll Lon BA 06. Trin Coll Bris MA 15. **d** 15 **p** 16. C Willowfield *D & D* 15–19; V Leyton St Cath and St Paul *Chelmsf* from 19. *The Vicarage, 2B Fairlop Road, London E11 1BL* T: (020) 8558 4607 M: 07719-754849 E: bill.donoghue@thecornerstone.org.uk

DONOVAN, Patrick James. b 89. Goldsmiths' Coll Lon BA 13. Trin Coll Bris 18. **d** 21. C Chanctonbury *Chich* from 21. *Address withheld by request* M: 07816-756147 E: paddyjamesdonovan@gmail.com *or* paddy.donovan@chanctonbury.org.uk

DONOVAN, Mrs Rosalind Margaret. b 48. Birm Univ LLB 69 Bedf Coll Lon DASS 73. SAOMC 95. **d** 98 **p** 99. NSM Seer Green and Jordans *Ox* 98–03; P-in-c Wexham 03–13; rtd 13; PtO *Ox* 14–15; *S'well* from 16. *10 Westerham Road, Ruddington, Nottingham NG11 6DP* T: 0115-989 9448 M: 07985-043893 E: rev.ros.donovan@gmail.com

DONOVAN, Mrs Rosemary Ann. b 71. La Sainte Union Coll BTh 92 Birm Univ PGCE 93. Qu Coll Birm MA 01. **d** 01 **p** 02. C Kings Heath *Birm* 01–04; C Moseley St Mary and St Anne 04–11; V Epsom Common Ch Ch *Guildf* from 11; AD Epsom from 20; Bp's Adv for Women's Min from 16. *Christ Church Vicarage, 20 Christ Church Road, Epsom KT19 8NE* T: (01372) 720302 E: vicar@christchurchepsom.org.uk

DONSON, Miss Helen Cripps. b 32. Somerville Coll Ox DipEd 55 MA 58. Dalton Ho Bris 58 Gilmore Ho 69. **dss** 79 **d** 87. Staines St Pet *Lon* 80–83; Staines St Mary and St Pet 83–90; Par Dn 87–90; Par Dn Herne Bay Ch Ch *Cant* 90–92; rtd 93; Hon Par Dn Bexhill St Aug *Chich* 93–97; PtO 97–07. *Flat 27, Manormead, Tilford Road, Hindhead GU26 6RA* T: (01428) 601527

DONSON, Margaret Christine. See BARROW, Margaret Christine

DOODES, Peter John. b 45. STETS 98. **d** 01. NSM Ninfield and Hooe *Chich* 01–02; NSM Hastings H Trin 02–07; PtO *Roch* 09–14; *Chich* from 15. *Catslide, The Common, Hooe, Battle TN33 9ET* T: (01424) 892329 M: 07718-302115 E: pjdoodes@hotmail.com

DOOGAN, Canon Simon Edward. b 70. Univ of Wales (Abth) LLB 92 Univ of Wales (Cardiff) LLM 01 TCD BTh 97. CITC 94. **d** 97 **p** 98. C Cregagh *D & D* 97–01; Dom Chapl to Bp Horsham *Chich* 01–04; I Aghalee *D & D* 04–08; I Ballyholme from 08; Dioc Registrar from 07; Can St Patr Cathl Dublin from 11. *Ballyholme Rectory, 3 Ward Avenue, Bangor BT20 5JW* T: (028) 9127 4901 *or* 9127 4912 F: 9146 6357 E: simon_doogan@hotmail.com

DOOLAN, Alison Ruth. b 59. Homerton Coll Cam BEd 93. Yorks Min Course 13. **d** 15 **p** 16. NSM Beverley St Mary *York* 15–20; PtO from 20. *25 Melrose Park, Beverley HU17 8JL* T: (01482) 864707 E: alidoolan@gmail.com

DOOLAN, Benjamin. b 87. Sheff Univ BA 08 Anglia Ruskin Univ MA 13. Ridley Hall Cam 11. **d** 13 **p** 14. C York St Mich-le-Belfrey 13–18; C Newc Cathl from 19; Master Newc St Thos Prop Chpl from 19. *9 Chester Crescent, Newcastle upon Tyne NE2 1DH* M: 07849-024523 E: ben@stthomas.church

DOOLAN, Canon Leonard Wallace. b 57. St Andr Univ MA 79 Ox Univ BA 82 MA 88. Ripon Coll Cuddesdon 80. **d** 83 **p** 84. C High Wycombe *Ox* 83–85; C Bladon w Woodstock 85–88; C Wootton by Woodstock 85–88; P-in-c 88–90; C Kiddington w Asterleigh 85–88; P-in-c 88–90; P-in-c Glympton 88–90; R Wootton w Glympton and Kiddington 90–91; TR Halesworth w Linstead, Chediston, Holton etc *St E* 91–98; RD Halesworth 95–98; TR Ifield *Chich* 98–08; V Cirencester *Glouc* 08–17; AD 11–15; Hon Can Glouc Cathl 12–17; Chapl Gtr Athens *Eur* from 17; Hon Can Douala Cameroon from 09. *St Paul, 27 Philellinon Street, Athens, Greece* E: anglican@otenet.gr

DOOLEY, Peter Martin. b 51. UEA BSc 72 Leic Univ PhD 77 Salford Univ DBA 96. St Mellitus Coll 18. **d** 19 **p** 20. NSM Cheadle *Ches* 19–20; NSM Heald Green St Cath from 20. *48 Chorlton Drive, Cheadle SK8 2BG* T: 0161-491 1816 E: pm.dooley@ntlworld.com

DOORE, Sandra Patricia. b 61. **d** 16 **p** 17. C Gateacre *Liv* 16–18; TV from 18. *St Mark's Vicarage, Cranwell Road, Liverpool L25 1NZ* E: sandra.doore25@gmail.com

DOORES, Jennifer Mary. See McKENZIE, Jennifer Mary

DOORES, Canon Peter George Herbert. b 46. Hull Univ BSc 67 Birm Univ PGCE 68. Linc Th Coll 92. **d** 92 **p** 93. C N Stoneham *Win* 92–96; V St Leonards and St Ives 96–03; P-in-c Alton St Lawr 03–09; V Alton 10–13; Hon Can Win Cathl 09–13; rtd 13; PtO *Win* from 13. *5 Cranford Gardens, Chandler's Ford, Eastleigh SO53 1PU* T: (023) 8025 3778 E: peterdoores@lineone.net *or* peter@doores.myzen.co.uk

DORAGH (née ELLIOTT), Mrs Sonya Jacqueline. b 72. Ox Brookes Univ BA 95. Trin Coll Bris MA 12. **d** 12 **p** 13. C Much Woolton *Liv* 12–16; TV Eccleston from 16. *Christchurch Vicarage, 34 Church Lane, Eccleston, St Helens WA10 5AD* T: (01744) 22698 M: 07852-244537 E: sonya@doragh.co.uk

DORAN, Clive. b 58. St Jo Coll Nottm 99. **d** 01 **p** 02. C Maghull *Liv* 01–05; V Huyton St Geo 05–13; TV Parr 13–16; TR from 16; Bp's Adv on Children and Communion from 06. *St Paul's Vicarage, 75 Chain Lane, St Helens WA11 9QF* T: (01744) 734335 E: revclivedoran@yahoo.co.uk

DORAN, Edward Roy. b 47. St Jo Coll Nottm. **d** 85 **p** 86. C Roby *Liv* 85–88; V Ravenhead 88–07; TV Eccleston 07–09; V Knotty Ash St Jo 09–16; rtd 16; PtO *Liv* from 17. *5 Moor Close, Southport PR8 3PA* T: (01704) 572387

DORBER, The Very Revd Adrian John. b 52. St Jo Coll Dur BA 74 K Coll Lon MTh 91. Westcott Ho Cam 76. **d** 79 **p** 80. C Easthampstead *Ox* 79–85; P-in-c Emmer Green 85–88; Chapl Portsm Poly 88–92; Chapl Portsm Univ 92–97; Lect 91–97; Public Orator 92–97; Hon Chapl Portsm Cathl 92–97; P-in-c Brancepeth *Dur* 97–01; Dir Min and Tr 97–05; Hon Can Dur Cathl 97–05; Dean Lich from 05. *The Deanery, 16 The Close, Lichfield WS13 7LD* T: (01543) 306250 F: 306109 E: adrian.dorber@lichfield-cathedral.org

DORCHESTER, Archdeacon of. See FRENCH, The Ven Judith Karen

DORCHESTER, Area Bishop of. See COLLINS, The Rt Revd Gavin Andrew

DORÉ, Eric George. b 47. S Dios Minl Tr Scheme 87. **d** 90 **p** 91. NSM Hove Bp Hannington Memorial Ch *Chich* 90–92; C Burgess Hill St Andr 92–95; R Frant w Eridge 95–00; V Framfield 00–07; rtd 07; PtO *St E* from 08. *Oak House, 86A Southwold Road, Wrentham, Beccles NR34 7JF* T: (01502) 675777 E: eric@ericdore.plus.com

DOREY, Miss Alison. b 77. Sheff Univ BA 98 Sheff Hallam Univ PGCE 01 St Jo Coll Dur MA 08. Cranmer Hall Dur 05. **d** 07 **p** 08. C Askern *Sheff* 07–11; Miss Development Co-ord N Sheff Estates 11–17; Dir Tr Fresh Expressions 15–19; PtO from 20. *85 Malton Street, Sheffield S4 7EA* T: 0114-272 6855 E: alidorey1@gmail.com

DOREY, Trevor Eric. b 30. ACIS 53. S Dios Minl Tr Scheme 87. **d** 90 **p** 91. NSM E Woodhay and Woolton Hill *Win* 90–96; P-in-c Manaccan w St Anthony-in-Meneage and St Martin *Truro* 96–99; rtd 99; PtO *Sarum* 01–05; *Ox* 07–17. *6 Marshall Court, Speen Lane, Newbury RG14 1RY* T: (01635) 551956 E: tandvdorey@btinternet.com

⊕**DORGU, The Rt Revd Woyin Karowei.** b 58. MB, BS 85. Lon Bible Coll BA 93 Oak Hill Th Coll 93. **d** 95 **p** 96 **c** 17. C Tollington *Lon* 95–98; C Upper Holloway 98–00; TV 00–12; V 12–17; Preb St Paul's Cathl 16–17; Area Bp Woolwich *S'wark* from 17. *37 South Road, London SE23 2UJ* T: (020) 7939 9400 E: wdorgu@yahoo.com *or* bishop.karowei@southwark.anglican.org

DORKING, Archdeacon of. See BREADMORE, The Ven Martin Christopher

DORKING, Suffragan Bishop of. See WELLS, The Rt Revd Joanne Caladine Bailey

DORLING, Philip Julian. b 69. Edin Univ BSc 91. Ripon Coll Cuddesdon BTh 08. **d** 05 **p** 06. C Ulverston St Mary w H Trin

Carl 05–09; C Furness Deanery 09; R Vryheid St Pet S Africa 10–12; R Inglewood Gp *Carl* 13–19; Lead Chapl Scargill Ho 19–20; R Seatallan *Carl* from 20. *The Rectory, Gosforth, Seascale CA20 1AZ* M: 07500-239684 E: philipdorling7@gmail.com

DORMANDY, Michael Peter. b 84. New Coll Ox BA 07 Ox Univ BA 15 Keble Coll Ox MSt 16 Chr Coll Cam PhD 20. Wycliffe Hall Ox 13. **d** 21. Lect Ripon Coll Cuddesdon from 20; C Albury w Tiddington etc *Ox* from 21. *Ripon College, Cuddesdon, Oxford OX44 9EX* M: 07739-550558 E: michael.dormandy@gmail.com

DORMANDY, Richard Paul. b 59. Univ Coll Lon BA 81 St Edm Ho Cam BA 88. Ridley Hall Cam 86. **d** 89 **p** 90. C Sydenham H Trin *S'wark* 89–93; V 93–01; V Westminster St Jas the Less *Lon* 01–09; V Tulse Hill H Trin and St Matthias *S'wark* from 09. *Holy Trinity Vicarage, 49 Trinity Rise, London SW2 2QP* T: (020) 8674 6721 M: 07960-170851 E: richard@dormandy.co.uk *or* richard.dormandy@htth.org.uk

DORMOR, Duncan James. b 67. Magd Coll Ox BA 88 Lon Univ MSc 89. Ripon Coll Cuddesdon BA 94. **d** 95 **p** 96. C Wolverhampton *Lich* 95–98; Chapl St Jo Coll Cam 98–02; Fell and Dean 02–18; Chief Exec Officer USPG from 18; Public Preacher *S'wark* from 18. *USPG, Rise House, 5 Trinity Street, London SE1 1DB* T: (020) 7921 2200 E: duncand@uspg.org.uk

DORMOR, Preb Duncan Stephen. b 36. St Edm Hall Ox BA 60. Cuddesdon Coll 60. **d** 62 **p** 63. C Headington *Ox* 62–66; USA 66–72; R Hertford St Andr *St Alb* 72–88; RD Hertford 77–83; TR Tenbury Wells *Heref* 88–01; R Burford I, Nash and Boraston 88–01; R Whitton w Greete and Hope Bagot 88–01; R Burford III w Lt Heref 88–01; V Tenbury St Mich 94–01; RD Ludlow 96–01; Preb Heref Cathl 99–02; C Tenbury Wells 01–02; C Burford I, Nash and Boraston 01–02; C Whitton w Greete and Hope Bagot 01–02; C Burford III w Lt Heref 01–02; C Tenbury St Mich 01–02; rtd 02; PtO *Heref* 02–14; *Chelmsf* from 15. *30 Queen Anne Road, West Mersea, Colchester CO5 8BB*

DORNAN, Michael Paul. CITC. **d** 09 **p** 10. C Hillsborough *D & D* 09–14; I Desertmartin w Termoneeny *D & R* 14–20; rtd 20. *Box 15, Pyrgos/Kalo Chorio, Lasithi 72100, Crete, Greece* M: 07858-597416 E: mikedornan@gmail.com

DORRIAN, Adrian Terence Warren. b 82. QUB BA 03 MTh 09 TCD BTh 06. CITC 04. **d** 06 **p** 07. C Newtownards *D & D* 06–09; I Belfast St Pet and St Jas *Conn* 09–12; I Dundela St Mark *D & D* 12–15; C Lecale Gp 15–19; V from 19; Min Can Down Cathl from 16. *40 English Street, Downpatrick BT30 6AB* T: (028) 4461 7469 M: 07760-664337 E: adriandorrian@gmail.com *or* revadriandorrian@icloud.com

DORRINGTON, Brian Goodwin. b 32. Leeds Univ CertEd 55. St Deiniol's Hawarden 65. **d** 66 **p** 67. C Poynton *Ches* 66–71; PtO *Truro* 71–78; Hd Master Veryan Sch Truro 71–84; Hon C Veryan *Truro* 78–83; Hon C Veryan w Ruan Lanihorne 83–84; C N Petherwin 84–87; C Boyton w N Tamerton 84–87; TV Bolventor 87–90; R Kilkhampton w Morwenstow 90–97; RD Stratton 92–97; rtd 97; PtO *Truro* 00–16. *Southcroft, 18 Elm Drive, Bude EX23 8EZ* T: (01288) 352467

DORSET, Archdeacon of. *See* MACROW WOOD, The Ven Antony Charles

DORSETT, Mark Richard. b 63. Univ of Wales (Lamp) BA 84 MTh 86 Birm Univ PhD 90. Ripon Coll Cuddesdon 91. **d** 93 **p** 94. C Yardley St Edburgha *Birm* 93–96; Chapl K Sch Worc from 96; Min Can Worc Cathl from 96. *12A College Green, Worcester WR1 2LH* T: (01905) 25837

DOSSOR, Timothy Charles. b 70. Birm Univ BEng 94. Ridley Hall Cam BTh 99. **d** 99 **p** 00. C Ipswich St Jo *St E* 99–03; Asst Ldr Iwerne Holidays Titus Trust from 03; PtO *Ox* 08–19; C Ox St Ebbe w H Trin and St Pet from 19. *31 Southdale Road, Oxford OX2 7SE* T: (01865) 553226 *or* 310513 M: 07748-184503 E: tim@dossor.org

DOTCHIN, Canon Andrew Steward. b 56. Federal Th Coll S Africa. **d** 84 **p** 85. C Standerton w Evender S Africa 84–87; Asst P St Martin's-in-the-Veld 87–89; R Belgravia St Jo the Divine 89–94; Chapl St Martin's Sch Rosettenville 94–01; TV Blyth Valley *St E* 01–04; P-in-c Whitton and Thurlston w Akenham 04–09; R 09–15; P-in-c Felixstowe St Jo 15–20; V from 20; RD Colneys from 15; Hon Can St E Cathl from 20. *The New Vicarage, 54 Princes Road, Felixstowe IP11 7PL* M: 07814-949828 E: revdotchin@gmail.com

DOTCHIN, Canon Joan Marie. b 47. NEOC 84. **d** 87 **p** 94. C Newc St Gabr 87–92; Team Dn Willington 92–94; TV 94–95; TR 95–03; V Fenham St Jas and St Basil 03–08; Hon Can Newc Cathl 01–08; rtd 08; PtO *Newc* from 08. *12 St Aidan's Court, Mariners Lane, North Shields NE30 2SE*

DOUBLE, Richard Sydney (Brother Samuel). b 47. K Coll Lon BD 69 AKC 69. St Aug Coll Cant 69. **d** 70 **p** 71. C Walton St Mary *Liv* 70–74; SSF from 75; Guardian Hilfield

Friary Dorchester 92–01; Min Prov SSF 02–12; Can and Preb Sarum Cathl 95–01 and from 09; V Cambridge St Benedict *Ely* 01–05; PtO *Chelmsf* from 18; *Eur* from 19. *The House of Divine Compassion, 42 Balaam Street, London E13 8AQ* E: samuelssf@franciscans.org.uk

DOUBTFIRE, Canon Barbara. b 39. LMH Ox BA 61 MA 65. **d** 91 **p** 94. Par Development Adv *Ox* 88–04; NSM Kidlington w Hampton Poyle 91–04; Hon Can Ch Ch 98–04; rtd 04; PtO *Ox* from 05. *6 Meadow Walk, Woodstock OX20 1NR* T: (01993) 812095 E: spidir@oxford.anglican.org

DOUGAL, Stephen George. b 62. FICS. **d** 06 **p** 07. OLM Lyminge w Paddlesworth, Stanford w Postling etc *Cant* 06–19; OLM Elham Valley from 20. *Bereforstal Farm Bungalow, Canterbury Road, Elham, Canterbury CT4 6UE* T: (01303) 840750

DOUGHTY, The Ven Andrew William. b 56. K Coll Lon BD AKC. Westcott Ho Cam 80. **d** 82 **p** 83. C Alton St Lawr *Win* 82–85; TV Basingstoke 85–91; V Chilworth w N Baddesley 91–95; R Warwick St Mary V Bermuda from 95; Adn Bermuda from 04. *PO Box WK 530, Warwick WK BX, Bermuda* T: (001) (441) 236 5744 F: 236 3667 E: adoughty@ibl.bm

DOUGLAS, Ann Patricia. b 49. Lon Univ CertEd 71. Oak Hill NSM Course 85. **d** 88 **p** 94. Par Dn Chorleywood Ch Ch *St Alb* 88–94; V Oxhey All SS 94–02; TR Woodley *Ox* 02–06; rtd 06; Development Officer Li Tim-Oi Foundn 06–09; Outreach Co-ord Refresh Weymouth and Portland *Sarum* 10–17; PtO 07–20. *20 Passage Close, Weymouth DT4 9GE* T: (01305) 788310 M: 07809-467717 E: annidouglas@gmail.com

DOUGLAS, Anthony Victor. b 51. St Jo Coll Nottm 74. **d** 76 **p** 77. C Gt Crosby St Luke *Liv* 76–79; TV Fazakerley Em 79–84; TR Speke St Aid 84–90; TR Gt and Lt Coates w Bradley *Linc* 90–97; TR E Ham w Upton Park and Forest Gate *Chelmsf* 97–02; R Holkham w Egmere w Warham etc *Nor* 02–12; Managing Chapl HM Pris Holme Ho 12–16; rtd 16; PtO *Nor* from 16. *9 Ashburton Close, Wells-next-the-Sea NR23 1QG* T: (01328) 712121 E: anthony.douglas123@btinternet.com

DOUGLAS, Caroline Emelia Aldridge (Kate). b 64. City Univ Lon MBA 97. ERMC 19. **d** 21. NSM Stevenage St Hugh and St Jo *St Alb* from 21. *17 School Lane, Welwyn AL6 9PQ* T: (01438) 840420 M: 07775-020796 E: katedouglas751@btinternet.com

DOUGLAS, Gavin Allan. b 52. OBE 00. Cardiff Univ BTh 08. St Mich Coll Llan 03. **d** 05 **p** 06. C Week St Mary Circle of Par *Truro* 05–08; R Castle Bromwich SS Mary and Marg *Birm* 08–16; rtd 16; PtO *Llan* from 13. *18 Cilgant y Meillion, Rhoose, Barry CF62 3LH* E: gavinadouglas@yahoo.co.uk

DOUGLAS, Jonathan William Dixon. b 75. QUB BSc 96 K Coll Lon MA 01 Spurgeon's Coll MTh 09. **d** 11 **p** 12. C Spitalfields Ch Ch w All SS *Lon* 11–14; C Northwood Em 15–18; V Swanley St Paul *Roch* from 18. *The Vicarage, Rowhill Road, Swanley BR8 7RL* T: (01322) 662320 M: 07799-072845 E: revjohnnydouglas@gmail.com *or* office@stph.org.uk

DOUGLAS, Maureen Eleanor. b 43. Open Univ BA 87 Worc Coll of Educn CertEd 65. SWMTC 10. **d** 12. NSM Littleham w Exmouth *Ex* 12–13; NSM Littleham-cum-Exmouth w Lympstone 13–18; PtO from 18. *8A Elwyn Road, Exmouth EX8 2EL* T: (01395) 225963 E: medouglas@uwclub.net

DOUGLAS, Michael Williamson. b 51. Birm Univ BSc 72 Liv Univ PGCE 74. Trin Coll Bris 00. **d** 02 **p** 03. C Macclesfield Team *Ches* 02–06; TV Hawarden *St As* 06–10; PtO *Ches* from 17. *46 Far Meadow Lane, Wirral CH61 4XW* T: 0151-648 4071 E: mikedougie@yahoo.co.uk

DOUGLAS, Pamela Jean. *See* WELCH, Pamela Jean

DOUGLAS, Patrick John. b 62. Ox Brookes Univ BA 05. St Mellitus Coll BA 13. **d** 13 **p** 14. C Walbrook Epiphany *Derby* 13–17; P-in-c Newhall from 17; C Swadlincote and Hartshorne from 20. *8 Breadsall Close, Newhall, Swadlincote DE11 0QJ* M: 07968-503447 E: patrickdouglas62@gmail.com

DOUGLAS, Richard Norman Henry. b 37. SAOMC 94. **d** 97 **p** 98. NSM Watercombe *Sarum* 97–02; PtO 02–04; *Ox* 04–06; NSM Grove 06–07; rtd 07; PtO *Ox* 07–16. *36 Mallard Court, West Mills, Newbury RG14 5HL* T: (01635) 741613 E: dickandnan@talktalk.net

DOUGLAS LANE, Charles Simon Pellew. b 47. BNC Ox MA 71 MCIPD 79. Oak Hill Th Coll 91. **d** 94 **p** 95. C Whitton St Aug *Lon* 94–97; P-in-c Hounslow W Gd Shep 97–02; V 02–05; TV Riverside *Ox* 05–08; V Horton and Wraysbury 08–13; rtd 13; PtO *Ox* from 13; *Lon* from 13. *1 Magnolia Villas, 30A Belgrade Road, Hampton TW12 2AZ* T: (020) 8941 5027 E: simonsdl14@gmail.com

DOUGLASS, Kieran Christopher. b 89. **d** 16 **p** 17. C Histon *Ely* 16–20; C Impington 16–20; Min Glouc Docks Mariners' Ch from 21. *123 Longford Lane, Gloucester GL2 9HD* T: (01452) 540307 E: kieran@marinersgloucester.org.uk

DOUGLASS, Michael Crone. b 49. Open Univ BA 96. NEOC 02. d 05 p 06. NSM Gosforth St Nic *Newc* 05–19; PtO from 19. *44 Regent Road, Newcastle upon Tyne NE3 1ED* T/F: 0191-285 0977 E: m.douglass@blueyonder.co.uk

DOUGLASS, Preb Philip. b 48. Open Univ BA 88. St Steph Ho Ox 87. d 89 p 90. C Peterlee *Dur* 89–92; V Crowan w Godolphin *Truro* 92–97; V Crowan and Treslothan 98–13; P-in-c Penponds 01–13; Preb St Endellion 02–13; rtd 13. *31 Bay View Terrace, Hayle TR27 4JY* T: (01736) 753382

DOULL, Canon Iain Sinclair. b 43. St Mich Coll Llan 86. d 88 p 89. C Malpas *Mon* 88–91; P-in-c Newport All SS 91–98; V 98–02; V Newport Ch Ch 02–12; Hon Can St Woolos Cathl 11–12; rtd 12. *Ty'r Ydlan, Fachelich, St Davids, Haverfordwest SA62 6QL*

DOULTON, Roderick John. b 55. Oak Hill Th Coll 91. d 93 p 94. C Hoddesdon *St Alb* 93–96; P-in-c Caldecote All SS 96–98; P-in-c Old Warden 97–98; V Caldecote, Northill and Old Warden 98–99; TV Macclesfield Team *Ches* 99–07; Chapl W Park Hosp Macclesfield 99–07; P-in-c Heydon, Gt and Lt Chishill, Chrishall etc *Chelmsf* 07–08; PtO *Ely* 14–19; *Lich* from 20. *Darwin Oaks, Grange Road, Bronington, Whitchurch SY13 3HL* E: roddoulton@btinternet.com

DOVE, Giles Wilfred. b 62. St Andr Univ MA 85 MPhil 88 Glas Univ BD 08 FSAScot FRSA. TISEC 03. d 05 p 06. NSM Dunblane *St And* 05–07; Chapl Glenalmond Coll 07–19; Chapl Glamis Castle from 19; PtO *St And* from 19; *Edin* from 19. *South Eden, 8A High Road, Strathkinness, St Andrews KY16 9XY* E: gileswdove@gmail.com

DOVE, Ms Jacqueline McClintock. b 65. Natal Univ BSSc 86 DipEd 89 UEA MA 95. Ripon Coll Cuddesdon 15. d 17 p 18. C Schorne *Ox* 17–20; C Buckingham 20–21; R Blackthorn Chase from 21. *The Rectory, Chapel Lane, Thornborough, Buckingham MK18 2DJ* M: 07775-387271 E: jacquelineleach.dove@gmail.com

DOVE, Lionel John. b 38. d 06 p 07. OLM N Bradley, Southwick, Heywood and Steeple Ashton *Sarum* 06–13; PtO 13–20. *Chobham Cottage, Acreshot Lane, Steeple Ashton, Trowbridge BA14 6HD* T: (01380) 870013

DOVER, Suffragan Bishop of. *See* HUDSON WILKIN, The Rt Revd Rose Josephine

DOVEY, Andrew Michael Stanley. b 59. SEITE 00. d 06 p 07. NSM Selsdon St Jo w St Fran *S'wark* 06–10; PtO 10–14; NSM Shirley St Geo 14–19; C 19–20; NSM Shirley St Jo 14–19; C 19–20; Chapl Croydon Health Services NHS Trust 15–18; Lead Chapl from 18. *6 Stokes Road, Croydon CR0 7SD* T: (020) 8656 9911 or 8401 3105 M: 07527-818816 E: andy.dovey@me.com

DOW, Canon Andrew John Morrison. b 46. Univ Coll Ox BA 67 MA 71. Oak Hill Coll 69. d 71 p 72. C Watford St Luke *St Alb* 71–74; C Chadderton Ch Ch *Man* 75–78; V Leamington Priors St Paul *Cov* 78–88; V Knowle *Birm* 88–97; RD Solihull 95–97; V Clifton Ch Ch w Em *Bris* 97–04; P-in-c Cheltenham St Mary, St Matt, St Paul and H Trin *Glouc* 04–07; R Cheltenham St Mary w St Matt 07–10; AD Cheltenham 06–10; Hon Can Glouc Cathl 08–10; rtd 10; PtO *Cov* from 10; *Glouc* from 21. *7 Bluebell Close, Moreton-in-Marsh GL56 9PW* E: andrewdow451@btinternet.com

⊕**DOW, The Rt Revd Geoffrey Graham.** b 42. Qu Coll Ox BA 63 MA 68 BSc 65 MSc 81 Nottm Univ MPhil 82. Clifton Th Coll 66. d 67 p 68 c 92. C Tonbridge SS Pet and Paul *Roch* 67–72; Chapl St Jo Coll Ox 72–75; Lect St Jo Coll Nottm 75–81; V Cov H Trin 81–92; Can Th Cov Cathl 88–92; Area Bp Willesden *Lon* 92–00; Bp Carl 00–09; rtd 09; Hon Asst Bp Ches from 09; Hon Asst Bp Man from 11. *34 Kimberley Avenue, Romiley, Stockport SK6 4AB* T: 0161-494 9148 E: graham@gdow.co.uk

DOW, Keir Thomas McNeill. b 76. Ex Univ BEd 00. ERMC 18. d 20 p 21. C King's Cliffe, Bulwick and Blatherwycke, Collyweston etc *Pet* from 20. *The Rectory, 38 West Street, Easton on the Hill, Stamford PE9 3LS* E: keir.dow@kingscliffe.church

DOWD, Garfield George. b 60. QUB BSc. d 86 p 87. C Monkstown *D & G* 86–90; I Carlow w Urglin and Staplestown C, F & O 90–05; Can Ossory Cathl 96–05; I Glenageary *D & G* from 05. *St Paul's Vicarage, Silchester Road, Glenageary, Co Dublin, Republic of Ireland* T/F: (00353) (1) 280 1616 M: 87-926 6558 E: glenageary@dublin.anglican.org

DOWDING, Ms Clare Alice Elizabeth. b 74. Ch Ch Coll Cant BA 98 Greenwich Univ PGCE 99. Westcott Ho Cam BA 02. d 03 p 05. USA 03–04; C Longsight St Luke *Man* 04–07; Chapl Man HE Institutions 07–11; R Earlham *Nor* 11–14; R St Marylebone St Paul *Lon* from 14; Dean of Women's Min Two Cities Area 16–20; AD Westmr St Marylebone from 19. *St Paul's House, 9 Rossmore Road, London NW1 6NJ* T: (020) 7262 9443 or 7724 8517 M: 07970-661534 E: caedowding@gmail.com

DOWDING, Canon Edward Brinley. b 47. St Mich Coll Llan 70 St D Coll Lamp BA 71. d 72 p 73. C Canton St Cath *Llan* 72–75; C Aberdare 75–78; V Aberavon H Trin 78–85; R Sully 85–13; R Wenvoe and St Lythans 10–13; RD Penarth and Barry 98–04; Hon Can Llan Cathl 11–13; rtd 13; PtO *Llan* from 13. *10 Clos Tawe, Barry CF62 7BN* T: (01446) 737180 E: edward.dowding@btinternet.com

DOWDING, Mrs Elizabeth Jean. b 43. Bath Coll of HE TCert 67. SAOMC 00. d 04 p 05. NSM Goring w S Stoke *Ox* 04–07; NSM Goring and Streatley w S Stoke from 07. *30 Milldown Avenue, Goring, Reading RG8 0AS* T: (01491) 873140 E: elizdowding@aol.com

DOWDING, Jeremy Charles. b 51. St Steph Ho Ox 89. d 91 p 92. C Newport St Steph and H Trin *Mon* 91–94; C Risca 94–96; P-in-c Whitleigh *Ex* 96–05; P-in-c Thorpe-le-Soken *Chelmsf* 05–17; V 17–19; P-in-c Weeley and Lt Clacton 17–19; rtd 19; PtO *S & B* from 19; *Mon* from 20. *16 Cwmbeth Close, Crickhowell NP8 1DX* T: (01873) 598385 M: 07815-773262

DOWDLE, Canon Cynthia. b 48. OBE 15. Cranmer Hall Dur 88. d 90 p 94. C Allerton *Liv* 90–94; TR Halewood 94–00; V Knowsley 00–11; Hd Spiritual Care Adelaide Ho Probation Hostel 11–15; Dean of Women's Min 01–15; Hon Can Liv Cathl 01–10; Can Res Liv Cathl 10–15; rtd 16; PtO *Liv* from 16. *24 Borromeo Close, Liverpool L17 7DS* T: 0151-384 1887 E: cynthiadowdle@hotmail.com

DOWDY, Simon Mark Christopher. b 67. Trin Hall Cam BA 89 MA 93. Wycliffe Hall Ox 93. d 96 p 97. C Beckenham Ch Ch *Roch* 96–00; C St Helen Bishopsgate w St Andr Undershaft etc *Lon* 00–05; P-in-c St Botolph without Aldersgate 02–21; Min Dulwich Grace Ch BMO *S'wark* from 21. *45 Woodwarde Road, London SE22 8UN* T: (020) 8299 1631

DOWER, Frances Helen. b 45. Lon Univ MB, BS 69. d 09 p 10. OLM Kirkwhelpington, Kirkharle, Kirkheaton and Cambo *Newc* 09–14; NSM 14–15; PtO from 15. *Cambo House, Front Row, Cambo, Morpeth NE61 4AY* T: (01670) 774297 E: frances.dower@dower.org.uk

DOWIE, Winifred Brenda McIntosh. b 57. Callendar Park Coll of Educn Falkirk DipEd 78. Trin Coll Bris BA 91. d 92 p 94. Par Dn Downend *Bris* 92–94; C 94–95; Chapl Asst Southmead Health Services NHS Trust 95–98; Chapl St Pet Hospice Bris 98–13; Hon Can Bris Cathl 02–13; Chapl Glos Hosps NHS Foundn Trust 13–16; Chapl N Bris NHS Trust from 16; Chapl Univ Hosps Bris NHS Foundn Trust 16–17; PtO *Bris* from 16. *Spiritual and Pastoral Care, The Chaplaincy, Gate 30, The Brunel Building, Southmead Hospital, Southmead Road, Westbury-on-Trym, Bristol BS10 5NB* T: 0117-414 3707 or 342 6795 E: brenda.dowie@nbt.nhs.uk

DOWLAND, Martin John. b 48. Lon Univ BD 70 Southn Univ PGCE 71. Wycliffe Hall Ox 75. d 77 p 78. C Jesmond Clayton Memorial *Newc* 77–80; C Chadderton Ch Ch *Man* 80–85; R Haughton St Mary 85–14; rtd 14; PtO *Derby* from 15; *Man* from 15; *Ches* from 19. *11 Overdale Drive, Glossop SK13 6GA* E: m.dowland@ntlworld.com

DOWLAND-OWEN, Edward Farrington. *See* OWEN, Edward Farrington

DOWLAND-PILLINGER, Catherine Louise. b 60. New Hall Cam BA 82 MA 86 PhD 89. SEITE 05. d 08 p 09. C Addington *S'wark* 08–12; PtO 12–13; Chapl S'wark Cathl 13; TV Caterham from 13. *The Rectory, Station Road, Woldingham, Caterham CR3 7DD* T: (01883) 652192 M: 07768-065301 E: rev.catherine1@gmail.com

DOWLEN, Isabella McBeath. b 45. Man Univ CertEd 86 Edin Univ MTh 06 RGN 67 SCM 68 HVCert 69. STETS 96. d 99 p 01. NSM Branksome St Clem *Sarum* 99–04; NSM Clarkston *Glas* 04–06; P-in-c Glas St Oswald 06–08; R Pittenweem *St And* 10–14; R Elie and Earlsferry 10–14; rtd 14; LtO *Edin* from 15; PtO *Glas* from 16. *45 The Quarryknowes, Bo'ness EH51 0QJ* T: (01506) 826610 M: 07974-084657 E: isabel.dowlen@gmail.com

DOWLER, The Ven Robert Edward Mackenzie. b 67. Ch Ch Ox BA 89 Selw Coll Cam BA 93 Dur Univ PhD 07. Westcott Ho Cam 91. d 94 p 95. C Southgate Ch Ch *Lon* 94–97; C Somers Town 97–01; Tutor and Dir Past Th St Steph Ho Ox 01–09; Vice Prin 03–09; Asst Chapl Malvern Coll 09; V Clay Hill St Jo and St Luke *Lon* 10–16; CME Officer Edmonton Area 13–16; Adn Hastings *Chich* from 16; P-in-c Crowborough St Jo from 20. *Beechmount, Beacon Road, Crowborough TN6 1UQ* T: (01892) 611561 or (01273) 425040 M: 07990-675242 E: archhastings@chichester.anglican.org

DOWLEY, Mrs Ruth Ada. b 49. St Mellitus Coll 13. d 14 p 15. OLM Becontree St Cedd *Chelmsf* 14–17; NSM from 17. *68 Malvern Drive, Ilford IG3 9DW* T: (020) 8597 1988 M: 07817-163203 E: ruthdowley@hotmail.com

DOWLING, Donald Edward. b 43. St Andr Univ MA 66. Cranmer Hall Dur. d 74 p 75. C Thame w Towersey *Ox*

74–77; C Norton *St Alb* 77–80; V Wilbury 81–99; V Stevenage St Nic and Graveley 99–10; rtd 10; PtO *St Alb* from 10. *56 Caslon Way, Letchworth Garden City SG6 4QL* T: (01462) 678934 E: rev.don68@gmail.com

DOWLING, Graham Paul. b 62. NTMTC BA 09. **d** 09 **p** 10. C Rainham w Wennington *Chelmsf* 09–13; TV Barking 13–16; V Barking St Patr 17–18; Rural Adv Colchester Area 18–19; NSM Witham and Villages 18–19; PtO from 19; Chapl Dioc Retreat Ho 17–19; C Goole *Sheff* from 20. *54 Thorntree Lane, Goole DN14 6LW* M: 07889-286308 E: revgpd@btinternet.com *or* graham@stjohnsgoole.org.uk

DOWLING, Canon Kingsley Avery Paul. b 60. Open Univ BA. Aston Tr Scheme 93 Ripon Coll Cuddesdon 95. **d** 97 **p** 98. C Headingley *Ripon* 97–99; C Far Headingley St Chad 99–01; V Wortley-de-Leeds 01–13; P-in-c Farnley 10–13; AD Armley 08–13; R Wortley and Farnley *Leeds* 13–15; V Meanwood 15–18; Hon Can Ripon Cathl 13–18; rtd 18. *70 Eaton Hill, Leeds LS16 6SE* M: 07810-212127 E: kingsley.dowling@hotmail.co.uk

DOWLING, Tracy Anne. b 59. SEITE 08. **d** 11 **p** 12. NSM Merton Priory *S'wark* 11–14; Chapl Dundee St Paul *Bre* 14–16; Hon Chapl Abertay Univ 14–16; P-in-c Auchterarder *St And* from 16; P-in-c Muthill from 16. *St Kessog's Rectory, High Street, Auchterarder PH3 1AD* T: (01764) 662525 M: 07788-239798 E: tadowling@btinternet.com

DOWMAN, Canon Jonathan Robert. b 76. Westmr Coll Ox BEd 00. Trin Coll Bris 04. **d** 07 **p** 08. C Anglesey Gp *Ely* 07–10; Deanery Missr *Birm* 10–14; Pioneer Development Worker *Leic* from 14; PtO from 15; Hon Can Leic Cathl from 19. *St Martin's House, 7 Peacock Lane, Leicester LE1 5PZ* E: jonathandowman@icloud.com *or* jonathan.dowman@leccofe.org

DOWMAN, Peter Robert. b 52. City Univ BSc 76. Wycliffe Hall Ox 82. **d** 84 **p** 85. C Cheltenham Ch Ch *Glouc* 84–87; C Danbury *Chelmsf* 87–90; R Woodham Ferrers and Bicknacre 90–95; Consultant E England CPAS 00–03; R Warboys w Broughton and Bury w Wistow *Ely* 03–14; rtd 14; PtO *Ely* from 16. *9 Peregrine Street, Hampton Vale, Peterborough PE7 8LH* T: (01733) 288865 E: peterdowman@me.com

DOWN, Andrew Stuart. b 77. Ex Univ BSc 99. Ripon Coll Cuddesdon BTh 14. **d** 14 **p** 15. C Ex St Jas 14–18; R Ipplepen w Torbryan, Denbury, Broadhempston and Woodland from 18. *The Rectory, Paternoster Lane, Ipplepen, Newton Abbot TQ12 5RY* M: 07443-458487 E: rev.andrewdown@gmail.com

DOWN, Edward William. b 91. Jes Coll Ox MChem 13. Trin Coll Bris MA 17. **d** 17 **p** 18. C St Jas in the City *Liv* 17–20; Min Hamilton CD *Leic* from 20. *2 Cransley Close, Hamilton, Leicester LE5 1QQ* M: 07541-904644 E: rev.ed.down@gmail.com

DOWN, Martin John. b 40. Jes Coll Cam BA 62 MA 68. Westcott Ho Cam 63. **d** 65 **p** 66. C Bury St Mary *Man* 65–68; C Leigh St Mary 68–70; R Fiskerton *Linc* 70–75; V Irnham w Corby 75–79; RD Beltisloe 76–84; P-in-c Swayfield and Creeton w Swinstead 78–79; V Corby Glen 79–84; Good News Trust 84–88; PtO *Linc* 84–88; *Pet* 86–88; P-in-c Ashill w Saham Toney *Nor* 88–94; R 94–00; C Watton w Carbrooke and Ovington 00–05; rtd 05; PtO *Nor* 05–12; *Ox* from 12. *36 Beechgate, Witney OX28 4JL* T: (01993) 709743

DOWN, The Ven Philip Roy. b 53. Hull Univ MA 93. Melbourne Coll of Div BTh 82 MTh 88. **d** 89 **p** 89. C Gt Grimsby St Mary and St Jas *Linc* 89–91; TV 91–95; R Hackington *Cant* 95–02; AD Cant 99–02; Adn Maidstone 02–11; Adn Ashford 11–17; rtd 17; PtO *Sarum* from 18. *4 Gooselands, Westbury BA13 3UQ* T: (01373) 822009

✠**DOWN, The Rt Revd William John Denbigh.** b 34. St Jo Coll Cam BA 57 MA 61 FNI 91. Ridley Hall Cam 57. **d** 59 **p** 60 **c** 90. C Fisherton Anger *Sarum* 59–63; Miss to Seamen 63–90; Australia 71–74; Dep Gen Sec Miss to Seamen 75; Gen Sec 76–90; Hon C Gt Stanmore *Lon* 75–90; Chapl St Mich Paternoster Royal 76–90; PtO *St Alb* 78–90; Hon Can Gib Cathl *Eur* 85–90; Hon Can Kobe Japan from 87; Bp Bermuda 90–95; Asst Bp Leic 95–01; P-in-c Humberstone 95–01; P-in-c Thurnby Lodge 01; rtd 01; Hon Asst Bp Ox 01–21. *54 Dark Lane, Witney OX28 6LX* T: (01993) 706615 E: bishbill@aol.com

DOWN AND DROMORE, Bishop of. *See* MACCLAY, The Rt Revd David Alexander

DOWN, Archdeacon of. *See* HIGGINS, The Ven Kenneth

DOWN, Dean of. *See* HULL, The Very Revd Thomas Henry

DOWNER, Barry Michael. b 58. STETS 99. **d** 02 **p** 07. NSM Lake and Shanklin St Sav *Portsm* 02–05; NSM Bonchurch, Ventnor H Trin and Ventnor St Cath 05–08; NSM Oakfield St Jo 09–14; NSM Brading w Yaverland 14; PtO from 16. *44 Landguard Road, Shanklin PO37 7JX* T: (01983) 867150

DOWNES, Andrew. b 83. St Mellitus Coll 19. **d** 21. *Address temp unknown* M: 07917-167574 E: mrdownes@hotmail.com

DOWNES, Andrew Victor John. b 65. STETS 10. **d** 13 **p** 14. C Chiswick St Nic w St Mary *Lon* 13–16; V Sunbury from 16. *The Vicarage, Thames Street, Sunbury-on-Thames TW16 6AA* T: (01932) 779431 *or* 785448 M: 07939-290265 E: andrewvjd@gmail.com *or* vicar@stmarys-sunbury.org

DOWNEY, Jocelyn Stewart. b 69. Surrey Univ BSc 92 Lon Univ PhD 98 St Edm Coll Cam MPhil 14 Ch Coll Cam BTh 13. Ridley Hall Cam 11. **d** 14 **p** 15. C Bermondsey St Jas and St Anne *S'wark* 14–17; Miss Without Borders (UK) Ltd from 17. *Mission Without Borders, 175 Tower Bridge Road, London SE1 2AG* T: (020) 7940 1370

DOWNEY, Canon John Stewart. b 38. QUB CertEd 60 Open Univ BA 76. Oak Hill Th Coll 63. **d** 66 **p** 67. C Londonderry St Aug *D & R* 66–71; I Dungiven w Bovevagh 71–82; Bp's Dom Chapl 75–82; V Bishopwearmouth St Gabr *Dur* 82–91; V New Malden and Coombe *S'wark* 91–06; Hon Can S'wark Cathl 97–06; rtd 06; PtO *S'wark* from 08; *Newc* 18–21. *171 Kenton Road, Newcastle upon Tyne NE3 4NR* T: 0191-597 2892 E: sdowney@mwbuk.org

DOWNEY, Olivia Margaret Grace. **d** 14 **p** 15. Aughaval w Achill, Knappagh, Dugort etc *T, K & A* 14–15; C Enniskillen Clogh 15–18; I Clogh w Errigal Portclare from 18. *The Rectory, 10 Augher Road, Clogher BT76 0AD* M: 07792-728495 E: odowney@clogher.anglican.org

DOWNHAM, Canon Peter Norwell. b 31. Man Univ BA 52. Ridley Hall Cam 54. **d** 56 **p** 57. C Cheadle *Ches* 56–62; V Rawtenstall St Mary *Man* 62–68; Chapl Rossendale Gen Hosp 62–68; V Denton Holme *Carl* 68–79; V Reading Greyfriars *Ox* 79–95; Hon Can Ch Ch 90–95; rtd 95; Hon C Cotehill and Cumwhinton *Carl* 95–00; PtO 98–07; *Ox* from 07. *17 Grange Close, Goring, Reading RG8 9DY* T: (01491) 875983 E: pndow@tiscali.co.uk

DOWNHAM, Simon Garrod. b 61. K Coll Lon LLB 84 Solicitor 87. Wycliffe Hall Ox BA 93. **d** 94 **p** 95. C Brompton H Trin w Onslow Square St Paul *Lon* 94–99; P-in-c Hammersmith St Paul 00–06; V from 06; P-in-c Fulham St Mary N End from 21. *14 Lena Gardens, London W6 7PZ* T: (020) 7603 9662 *or* 8748 3855 E: simon.downham@sph.org

DOWNING, Francis Gerald. b 35. Qu Coll Ox BA 56 MA 60. Linc Th Coll. **d** 58 **p** 59. C Filwood Park CD *Bris* 58–60; Tutor Linc Th Coll 60–64; V Unsworth *Man* 64–80; Tutor NOC 80–82; Vice-Prin 82–90; V Bolton SS Simon and Jude *Man* 90–97; rtd 97; PtO *Blackb* 97–20. *33 Westhoughton Road, Chorley PR7 4EU* T: (01257) 474240

DOWNS, Caroline Rebecca. b 58. UWIST BA 80 Univ of Wales (Cardiff) PGCE 81. St Mich Coll Llan 98. **d** 02 **p** 03. C Roath *Llan* 02–07; P-in-c Cathays from 07; Warden of Readers from 14; Asst Dir of Voc from 15. *6 Newminster Road, Roath, Cardiff CF23 5AP* T: (029) 2049 5699 E: carolinerebecca.downs@btinternet.com

DOWNS, John Alfred. b 58. Leic Univ BSc 79 PGCE 80 CBiol 80 MRSB 80. EMMTC 90. **d** 93 **p** 94. NSM Barlestone *Leic* 93–96; NSM Markfield, Thornton, Bagworth and Stanton etc 96–11; NSM Newbold de Verdun, Barlestone and Kirkby Mallory 11–21; NSM Newbold De Verdun, Barlestone, Kirkby Mallory and Peckleton from 21; PtO *Cov* 13–15. *29 Meadow Road, Barlestone, Nuneaton CV13 0JG* T: (01455) 290195 E: revjohndowns@hotmail.co.uk

DOWNS, Canon Lynsay Marie. b 75. Hull Univ BA 98. Ripon Coll Cuddesdon BTh 05. **d** 05 **p** 06. C Tettenhall Wood and Perton *Lich* 05–09; TV Brereton and Rugeley 09–13; R Penicuik *Edin* 13–18; R W Linton 13–18; R Banchory *Ab* from 18; Can Ch Ch Cathl Connecticut USA from 19. *The Rectory, High Street, Banchory AB31 5TB*

DOWSETT, Andrew Christopher. b 72. Sheff Univ BA 95 PhD 99. St Jo Coll Nottm 07. **d** 09 **p** 10. C Clubmoor *Liv* 09–11; C Birkdale St Jas and Birkdale St Pet 11–13; Min Sunderland Minster *Dur* 13–17; Min P from 17. *St Nicholas' Vicarage, 200 Queen Alexandra Road, Sunderland SR3 1XQ* T: 0191-551 1209 M: 07783-760012 E: andrew@dowsetts.net *or* minsterpriest@sunderlandminster.org

DOWSETT, Ian Peter. b 71. Liv Univ BA 95 Lon Inst of Educn PGCE 96. Wycliffe Hall Ox BA 01. **d** 02 **p** 03. C Kensington St Helen w H Trin *Lon* 02–09; V S Harrow St Paul from 09; AD Harrow 16–21. *St Paul's Vicarage, Findon Close, Harrow HA2 8NJ* T: (020) 8864 0362 M: 07908-517934 E: iandowsett@stpaulsharrow.org.uk

DOWSON, Ruth Helen. b 59. Sheff Univ BA 81 MA 12 Bradf Univ MBA 85 Leeds Metrop Univ PGCE 09. Yorks Min Course 09. **d** 12 **p** 13. C Clayton *Leeds* 12–15; C Bingley All SS from 15; Chapl Leeds Beckett Univ from 18. *2 Irving Terrace, Clayton, Bradford BD14 6LA* M: 07971-189599 E: r.dowson@leedsbeckett.ac.uk *or* ruth@dowson.com

DOWSON, Simon Paul. b 63. Bris Univ BSc 85 Cam Univ PGCE 89. Cranmer Hall Dur 95. **d** 97 **p** 98. C Bradf St Aug Undercliffe 97–99; C Werrington *Pet* 99–04; V Skirbeck H Trin *Linc* 04–14; RD Holland 13–14; TR Bilton *Leeds* from 14. *Bilton Vicarage, Bilton Lane, Harrogate HG1 3DT* T: (01423) 561030 E: simon.dowson@leeds.anglican.org

DOXSEY, Canon Roy Desmond. b 41. St D Coll Lamp 64. **d** 67 **p** 68. C Pembroke St Mary w St Mich *St D* 67–70; C Milford Haven 70–73; C Loughton *Ox* 73–75; Chapl Llandovery Coll 75–81 and 92–96; Zambia 81–86; Chapl Epsom Coll 86–92; V Roath St German *Llan* 96–11; Hon Can Llan Cathl 09–11; PtO from 12; *St D* from 12. *St Anne's Clergy House, 3 Snipe Street, Cardiff CF24 3RB* T: (029) 2048 9313

DOYE, Andrew Peter Charles. b 64. BNC Ox BA 85. Trin Coll Bris BA 93. **d** 93 **p** 94. C Surbiton St Matt *S'wark* 93–96; C Bourne *Guildf* 96–99; C The Bourne and Tilford 99–00; R Wheathampstead *St Alb* 00–09; RD 06–08; PtO 15–17; R Westbourne *Chich* from 17. *The Rectory, Westbourne Road, Westbourne, Emsworth PO10 8UL* T: (01243) 372867 E: westbournechirector@outlook.com

DOYLE, Andrew Michael. b 63. K Coll Lon BD 85 AKC 85. Ripon Coll Cuddesdon 86. **d** 88 **p** 89. C Lytchett Minster *Sarum* 88–92; TV Kirkby *Liv* 92–97; V Rotherhithe H Trin *S'wark* from 97; AD Bermondsey 00–08. *Holy Trinity Vicarage, Bryan Road, London SE16 5HF* T: (020) 7237 4098 E: andrewdoyle763@btinternet.com

DOYLE, Edward Michael. b 70. St Mich Coll Llan BTh 93. **d** 94 **p** 95. C Sketty *S & B* 94–96; C Llwynderw 96–00; R Rogate w Terwick and Trotton w Chithurst *Chich* from 00. *The Vicarage, Fyning Lane, Rogate, Petersfield GU31 5EE* T: (01730) 821576 E: edwarddoyle@uwclub.net

DOYLE, Michael Christopher. b 64. St Jo Coll Nottm 06. **d** 08 **p** 09. C Ashbourne St Oswald w Mapleton *Derby* 08–12; R N Beltisloe Gp *Linc* 12–16; P-in-c Devonport St Boniface *Ex* 17–20; P-in-c Weston Mill 17–20; V Devonport St Boniface and St Philip from 20. *The Vicarage, 1 Normandy Way, Plymouth PL5 1SW* T: (01752) 368895 E: mike_c_doyle@hotmail.co.uk

DOYLE, Nigel Paul. b 55. Ban Univ BTh 07 MHort(RHS) 82 MCIPS 10. St Mich Coll Llan 00. **d** 03 **p** 04. NSM Landore w Treboeth *S & B* 03–09; NSM Gower Deanery 09–15; NSM Gtr Gower *S & B* 16–21; V N Gower from 21; R SW Gower from 21; V Three Cliffs from 21. *3 Ael-y-Bryn, Penclawdd, Swansea SA4 3LF* T: (01792) 850659 E: tadnigel@yahoo.co.uk

DOYLE, Robin Alfred. b 43. Dur Univ BA 65. Westcott Ho Cam 66. **d** 68 **p** 69. C Edgbaston St Geo *Birm* 68–70; C Erdington St Barn 70–73; P-in-c Oldbury 73–81; R Maker w Rame *Truro* 81–11; rtd 11; PtO *Truro* 14–21. *9 Camperknowle Close, Millbrook, Torpoint PL10 1QB* T: (01752) 822302

DOYLE, Mrs Tracey Elizabeth. b 58. Open Univ BA 00. SAOMC 94. **d** 97 **p** 98. OLM Winslow w Gt Horwood and Addington *Ox* 97–99; C 00–04; P-in-c Ivinghoe w Pitstone and Slapton 04–08; V Ivinghoe w Pitstone and Slapton and Marsworth 08–14; NSM Newton Tracey, Horwood, Alverdiscott etc *Ex* 16–18 and from 19; C 18–19; RD Torrington from 20. *Stables Cottage, Nethergrove, High Bickington, Umberleigh EX37 9BQ* M: 07814-538208 E: revtracey@btinternet.com

DOYLE-BRETT, Mrs Jacqueline Margaret. b 62. Hull Univ BA 99 PGCE 00 Sheff Univ MA 13. Yorks Min Course 11. **d** 13 **p** 14. C Tadcaster *York* 13–16; V York St Luke 16–21; P-in-c Derwent Ings from 21. *The Rectory, 3 Charter Lane, Wheldrake, York YO19 6AW* M: 07793-545755 E: jackiemdb@gmail.com

DRACKLEY, John Oldham. b 36. Em Coll Cam BA 57 MA 61. Wells Th Coll 57. **d** 59 **p** 60. C Eckington *Derby* 59–62; C Lee Gd Shep w St Pet *S'wark* 62–63; C Derby St Thos 63–67; C Matlock and Tansley 67–77; P-in-c Radbourne 77–82; P-in-c Dalbury, Long Lane and Trusley 77–82; P-in-c Longford 77–82; Sec Dioc Cttee for Care of Chs 82–98; rtd 95; PtO *Derby* 98–16. *26 Highfield Drive, Matlock DE4 3FZ* T: (01629) 55902

DRACUP, John Stuart. b 75. Cranmer Hall Dur 13. **d** 15 **p** 16. C Coley *Leeds* 15–18; V Meltham from 18. *The Vicarage, 150 Huddersfield Road, Meltham, Holmfirth HD9 4AL* M: 07983-937132 E: revjohndracup@gmail.com

DRAIN, Walter. b 39. JP 75. Open Univ BA 76 Ches Univ Hon BEd 19 ACP 66. NW Ord Course 76. **d** 79 **p** 80. NSM Cheadle *Ches* 79–81; C 81–84; V Chatburn *Blackb* 84–02; Sub Chapl HM Pris Preston 94–02; rtd 02. PtO *Blackb* from 02. *Angels, 28 The Croft, Euxton, Chorley PR7 6LH* T: (01257) 249646 E: walterdrain@btinternet.com

DRAIN, William. b 84. Liv Hope Univ BDes 05 Edge Hill Univ PGCE 06. St Mellitus Coll BA 18. **d** 18 **p** 19. C Romiley *Ches* from 18. *21 Guywood Lane, Romiley, Stockport*

SK6 4AN M: 07525-782787 E: will.drain1@gmail.com *or* will@stchadsromiley.co.uk

DRAISEY, Damon Allan. STETS 10. **d** 13 **p** 14. C Warblington w Emsworth *Portsm* 13–18; V S Downs Gateway Churches *Win* from 18. *Holy Trinity Church Centre, 154 Main Road, Colden Common, Winchester SO21 1TJ* T: (01962) 711216 M: 07906-346498

DRAKE, Graham. b 46. Linc Th Coll 81. **d** 83 **p** 85. C Alford w Rigsby *Linc* 83–84; PtO *Wakef* 84–85; Hon C Purston cum S Featherstone 85–89; NSM Castleford All SS 89–92; C Cudworth 92–95; rtd 11. *8A Broomhill, Castleford WF10 4QP* T: (01977) 518407

DRAKE, Canon Graham Rae. b 45. Fitzw Coll Cam BA 68 MA 72. Qu Coll Birm 70. **d** 73 **p** 74. C New Windsor *Ox* 73–77; TV 77–78; P-in-c Bath Ascension *B & W* 78–81; TV Bath Twerton-on-Avon 81–86; P-in-c Buxton w Oxnead *Nor* 86–90; P-in-c Lammas w Lt Hautbois 86–90; R Buxton w Oxnead, Lammas and Brampton 90–95; RD Ingworth 88–94; P-in-c Cockley Cley w Gooderstone 95–01; P-in-c Gt and Lt Cressingham w Threxton 95–01; P-in-c Didlington 95–01; P-in-c Hilborough w Bodney 95–01; P-in-c Oxborough w Foulden and Caldecote 95–01; P-in-c Mundford w Lynford 99–01; P-in-c Ickburgh w Langford 99–01; P-in-c Cranwich 99–01; V Thorpe St Matt 01–10; Chapl NW Anglia Healthcare NHS Trust 96–99; Hon Can Nor Cathl 99–10; Chapter Can Nor Cathl 02–05; rtd 10; PtO *Nor* from 10. *13 Needham Place, St Stephen's Square, Norwich NR1 3SD* T: (01603) 886084 E: grahamrdrake@btinternet.com

DRAKE, Jonathan Charles. b 81. Down Coll Cam MEng 03 MA 05. Wycliffe Hall Ox BA 11. **d** 12 **p** 13. C Wargrave w Knowl Hill *Ox* 12–16; C Maidenhead St Andr and St Mary from 16. *1 Hemsdale, Maidenhead SL6 6SL* T: (01628) 638866 M: 07715-123856 E: jon.drake1981@gmail.com

DRAKE, Leslie Sargent. b 47. Boston Univ BA 69 MTh 72 Hull Univ BPhil 74 Anglia Poly Univ MSc 93. Coll of Resurr Mirfield 78. **d** 78 **p** 79. C Oldham *Man* 78–81; TV Rochdale 81–83; V Palmers Green St Jo *Lon* 83–89; St Mary's Sch Cheshunt 89–91; Hd RE St Mary's Sch Hendon 91–99; TV Wimbledon *S'wark* 99–03; V Clay Hill St Jo and St Luke *Lon* 03–09; V Aiken St Aug USA 09–12; V S Benfleet *Chelmsf* 12–20; rtd 20; PtO *Lon* from 20. *15 Edinburgh Close, Ickenham, Uxbridge UB10 8RA* E: frldrake@hotmail.co.uk

DRAKE, Nicholas James. b 78. St Chad's Coll Dur BA 00 K Coll Lon MA 08. St Mellitus Coll 13. **d** 17 **p** 18. C Birm St Luke from 17. *12 Emerson Road, Birmingham B17 9LT* M: 07738-007005 *or* 07778-882802 E: nick.drake@gasstreet.org

DRAKE-SMITH, Ms Jacqueline Ann. b 59. Ripon Coll Cuddesdon BTh 18. **d** 14 **p** 15. C Merrow *Guildf* 14–18; V Wrecclesham from 18. *The Vicarage, 2 Kings Lane, Wrecclesham, Farnham GU10 4QB* T: (01252) 716431 M: 07806-775974 E: jackieds8@hotmail.com

DRAPER, Charles James. b 59. Dur Univ BSc 80 Cam Univ BA 86. Ridley Hall Cam 84. **d** 87 **p** 88. C Wareham *Sarum* 87–90; C Maltby *Sheff* 90–93; R The Claydons *Ox* 93–99; R Chinnor w Emmington and Sydenham etc 99–02; P-in-c Gt Faringdon w Lt Coxwell 02–07; V 07–15; AD Vale of White Horse 13–15; V Wolvercote and Wytham 15–20; rtd 20; PtO *Ox* from 21. *5 Ashfield Close, East Hanney, Wantage OX12 0HW* E: charlesdraper@btinternet.com

DRAPER, Derek Vincent. b 38. Linc Th Coll 65. **d** 68 **p** 69. C Orpington All SS *Roch* 68–72; C Bramley *Guildf* 72–74; Min Kempston Transfiguration CD *St Alb* 74–79; V Kempston Transfiguration 79–84; RD Bedford 79–84; V Bromham w Oakley 84–88; P-in-c Stagsden 84–88; V Bromham w Oakley and Stagsden 88–03; RD Elstow 00–02; Chapl Bromham Hosp 84–03; rtd 03; PtO *Ely* from 03; *St Alb* from 03. *142 Wixams Retirement Village, Bedford Road, Wixams, Bedford MK42 6EB* T: (01234) 981142 E: drapers24@outlook.com

DRAPER, Elizabeth Ann. *See* BRADLEY, Elizabeth Ann

DRAPER, Ivan Thomas. b 32. Aber Univ MB, ChB 56 FRCP FRCPGlas. St Jo Coll Nottm 87. **d** 90 **p** 91. NSM Glas St Bride 90–06; P-in-c 96–99; LtO from 06. *13/1 Whistlefield Court, 2 Canniesburn Road, Bearsden, Glasgow G61 1PX* T: 0141-943 0954 E: muriel.draper@gmail.com

DRAPER, Canon John William. b 54. Win Univ MA 13. Qu Coll Birm 88. **d** 90 **p** 91. C Stepney St Dunstan and All SS *Lon* 90–94; C Leigh Park and Warren Park *Portsm* 94–96; R Rowner 96–19; V Bridgemary 04–08; AD Gosport 09–14; Hon Can Portsm Cathl 13–19; PtO *Eur* from 18. *1 Ladram Road, Gosport PO12 2RH*

DRAPER, Canon Martin Paul. b 50. OBE 98. Birm Univ BA 72 Southn Univ BTh 79. Chich Th Coll 72. **d** 75 **p** 76. C Primrose Hill St Mary w Avenue Road St Paul *Lon* 75–78; C Westmr St Matt 79–84; Chapl Paris St Geo *Eur* 84–02; Adn France 94–02; Can Gib Cathl 94–02; PtO from 02;

Lon from 10. *112 Bolanachi Building, Enid Street, London SE16 3EX* T: (020) 7740 1891

DRAPER, Patrick Hugh. b 43. S Dios Minl Tr Scheme 91. **d** 94 **p** 95. NSM Boscombe St Jo *Win* 94–99; P-in-c Southbourne St Chris 99–02; rtd 02; PtO from *Win* 04–14. *82 Tuckton Road, Bournemouth BH6 3HT* T: (01202) 420190

DRAPER (née TRIMMER), Mrs Penelope Marynice. b 65. STETS 01. **d** 04 **p** 05. C Talbot Village *Sarum* 04–08; TV Dunstable *St Alb* 08–16; TV N Poole Ecum Team *Sarum* 16; V Oakdale from 17. *St George's Rectory, 99 Darby's Lane, Poole BH15 3EU* T: (01202) 660612　M: 07842-317204 E: penny.draper1@outlook.com

DRAPER, Peter Raymond. b 57. Leeds Poly BSc 86 Leeds Univ CertEd 88 Hull Univ PhD 94 SRN 80. NEOC 01. **d** 04 **p** 05. NSM S Cave and Ellerker w Broomfleet *York* from 04. *122 The Stray, South Cave, Brough HU15 2AL* T: (01430) 425486　M: 07956-531002 E: p.r.draper@hull.ac.uk

DRAPER, Mrs Sylvia Edith. b 39. ARCM 60. NOC 86. **d** 89 **p** 94. C Aughton St Mich *Liv* 89–92; Par Dn Wigan St Jas w St Thos 92–94; Asst Chapl Wigan and Leigh Health Services NHS Trust 92–97; C Wigan St Jas w St Thos *Liv* 94–97; TV Walton-on-the-Hill 97–02; rtd 02; PtO *Liv* from 03. *6 Brookfield Lane, Aughton, Ormskirk L39 6SP* T: (01695) 422138

DRAX, Elizabeth Margaret. *See* ANSON, Elizabeth Margaret

DRAY, John. b 66. St Chad's Coll Dur BSc 87. St Steph Ho Ox BTh 95. **d** 95 **p** 96. C Byker St Ant *Newc* 95–98; C Cullercoats St Geo 98–01; P-in-c Platt *Roch* 01–05; Chapl to the Deaf 01–05. *14 Heol Fach, Caerbryn, Ammanford SA18 3DJ* E: john@flirdy.co.uk

DRAYCOTT, John Edward. b 54. EMMTC 99. **d** 01 **p** 02. C Calverton, Epperstone, Gonalston and Oxton *S'well* 01–05; TV Parr *Liv* 05–13; P-in-c E Scarsdale *Derby* 13–15; TR from 15. *The Rectory, Rectory Road, Upper Langwith, Mansfield NG20 9RE* T: (01623) 618972 E: john.draycott@sky.com

DRAYCOTT, Tina. *See* FOX, Tina

✠**DRAYSON, The Rt Revd Nicholas James Quested.** b 53. Keble Coll Ox BA 75 MA 83. Wycliffe Hall Ox 82. **d** 79 **p** 79 **c** 09. SAMS Argentina 79–82; 92–00; Pastor Tartagal and Chapl to Chorote Indians 79–82; P-in-c Seville Ascension Spain 83–91; Adn Andalucia 89–91; Translations Co-ord 92-98; Pastor Salta St Andr 98–00; C Beverley Minster *York* 00–09; Suff Bp N Argentina 09–11; Dioc Bp N Argentina from 11; PtO *York* from 20. *Abraham Cornejo 120, 4400 Salta, Argentina* T: (0054) (387) 578 7988 E: nicobispo@gmail.com

DRAYTON, James Edward. b 30. St Deiniol's Hawarden 81. **d** 84 **p** 86. Hon C Heald Green St Cath *Ches* 84–88; C Bollington St Jo 88–92; P-in-c Lt Leigh and Lower Whitley 92–96; P-in-c Aston by Sutton 92–96; P-in-c Antrobus 92–96; rtd 96; PtO *York* from 96. *64 Plaxton Court, Scarborough YO12 6QT* T: (01723) 372377

DREDGE, David John. b 32. Cranmer Hall Dur 69. **d** 71 **p** 72. C Goole *Sheff* 71–74; P-in-c Eastoft 74–77; V Whitgift w Adlingfleet 74–77; V Whitgift w Adlingfleet and Eastoft 77–78; V Walkley 78–81; TV Bicester w Bucknell, Caversfield and Launton *Ox* 81–86; V N Brickhill and Putnoe *St Alb* 86–90; P-in-c Sarratt 90–95; rtd 95; PtO *Lich* 95–14. *19 Waterdale, Wombourne, Wolverhampton WV5 0DH* T: (01902) 897467

DREDGE, David Julian. b 36. Sheff Univ BA 59 ALA 74. Cranmer Hall Dur 61 Ban Ord Course 85. **d** 87 **p** 88. NSM Dwygyfylchi *Ban* 87–92; R Llanllechid 92–97; rtd 97; PtO *Ban* from 97. *Westfield, Treforris Road, Penmaenmawr LL34 6RH* T: (01492) 623439　F: 0870-056 7258　M: 07721-941861 E: davidjuliandredge@gmail.com

DREVER, Helen. b 66. Plymouth Univ BA 06 Sarum Coll MA 14. Ripon Coll Cuddesdon 14. **d** 16 **p** 17. C Crediton, Shobrooke and Sandford etc *Ex* 16–20; V Alham Vale *B & W* from 20. *The Vicarage, Church Lane, Evercreech, Shepton Mallet BA4 6HU* E: vicar@alhamvale.plus.com

DREW, Daniel Alexander Blair. b 86. Ox Brookes Univ BA 08. St Mellitus Coll BA 14 MA 16. **d** 16 **p** 17. C Hitchin and St Paul's Walden *St Alb* 16–19; Australia from 19. *1/30A The Crescent, Dee Why NSW 2099, Australia* M: 07738-553264 E: blairdrew@yahoo.com

DREW, Gerald Arthur. b 36. Bps' Coll Cheshunt 59. **d** 61 **p** 62. C Lyonsdown H Trin *St Alb* 61–67; C Tring 67–71; R Bramfield w Stapleford and Waterford 71–78; V Langleybury St Paul 78–90; P-in-c Hormead, Wyddial, Anstey, Brent Pelham etc 90–95; R 95–01; rtd 01; PtO *St Alb* 01–17; *St E* 01–20. *33 The Glebe, Lavenham, Sudbury CO10 9SN* T: (01787) 248133

DREW (née ROY), Mrs Jennifer Pearl. b 53. SRN 75 CSS 91. Cranmer Hall Dur. **d** 01 **p** 02. C Hebburn St Jo and Jarrow Grange *Dur* 01–05; NSM Broom Leys *Leic* 05–08; PtO 08–11; NSM Loughborough Em and St Mary in Charnwood 11–14; PtO from 14. *5 Balmoral Road, Coalville LE67 4PE* T: (01530) 836329 E: revjen03@hotmail.co.uk

DREW, Jo Ann. b 57. Ripon Coll Cuddesdon 09. **d** 11 **p** 12. C Milton next Gravesend Ch Ch *Roch* 11–14; PtO *Blackb* 15–20; Chapl Burrswood Chr Hosp *Roch* 16–17; PtO from 17. *Address temp unknown* E: revjodrew@btinternet.com

DREW, Canon Rosemary. b 43. SRN 64. EAMTC 90. **d** 93 **p** 94. NSM Gt Dunmow *Chelmsf* 93–96; NSM Gt Dunmow and Barnston 96–11; Hon Can Chelmsf Cathl 01–11; rtd 11; Area Adv for Healing and Deliverance Min *Chelmsf* from 04; PtO from 13. *The Bowling Green, 8 The Downs, Dunmow CM6 1DT* T/F: (01371) 872662 E: rose.drew@btinternet.com

DREW, Simon Mark. b 68. Liv Univ BEng 89　CEng 94 MICE 94. St Jo Coll Nottm MA 98. **d** 99 **p** 00. C Torquay St Matthias, St Mark and H Trin *Ex* 99–03; V Marshfield w Cold Ashton and Tormarton etc *Bris* 03–11; V Middlewich w Byley *Ches* from 11; RD Middlewich from 12. *The Rectory, Poplar Fell, Nantwich Road, Middlewich CW10 9HG* T: (01606) 833440 E: revsdrew@btinternet.com or simon.drew@middlewichparishchurch.org.uk

DREWETT, Mrs Susan. b 56. **d** 06 **p** 07. NSM Bemerton *Sarum* 06–18; rtd 18; PtO *Sarum* from 19. *Melford House, 36 Bulford Road, Durrington, Salisbury SP4 8DJ* T: (01980) 652751 E: rev.susandrewett@btinternet.com

DREYER, Rodney Granville. b 55. Lon Univ MPhil 91 AKC 91. St Paul's Coll Grahamstown 79. **d** 81 **p** 82. S Africa 81–84; NSM Headstone St Geo *Lon* 84–86; NSM Northolt St Mary 86–87; C Portsea St Mary *Portsm* 87–90; V Sudbury St Andr *Lon* 90–94; Adn W and S Free State S Africa 94–95; V Hawkhurst *Cant* from 98; AD Weald from 20. *The Vicarage, Moor Hill Road, Hawkhurst, Cranbrook TN18 4QB* T: (01580) 753397 E: rodneydreyer@sky.com

DRING (née PETTY), Alicia Christina Margaret. b 64. Wycliffe Hall Ox 01. **d** 03 **p** 04. C Ockbrook *Derby* 03–07; P-in-c Sawley 07–10; R 10–13; V Littleover from 13; P-in-c Blagreaves from 19; Dean of Women's Min 11–13. *The Vicarage, 35 Church Street, Littleover, Derby DE23 6GF* T: (01332) 767802　M: 07944-626773 E: alicia.dring@gmail.com

DRINKWATER, Maximillian Luke Darryl. b 90. Jes Coll Cam BA 12 MA 16. Westcott Ho Cam 13. **d** 16 **p** 17. C Newmarket St Mary w Exning St Agnes *St E* 16–20; P-in-c Haverhill w Withersfield from 20. *The Rectory, 10 Hopton Rise, Haverhill CB9 7FS* M: 07989-779493 E: mlddrinkwater@cantab.net

DRISCOLL, Canon David. b 42. Lon Univ BSc 64. Linc Th Coll 68. **d** 71 **p** 72. C Walthamstow St Jo *Chelmsf* 71–76; Chapl NE Lon Poly 71–79; C-in-c Plaistow St Mary 76–79; P-in-c Stratford St Jo and Ch Ch w Forest Gate St Jas 79–89; V Theydon Bois 89–01; RD Epping Forest 92–00; Hon Can Chelmsf Cathl 01; C All Hallows by the Tower etc *Lon* 01–07; rtd 07; Educn Tutor R Foundn of St Kath in Ratcliffe 05–10; Exec Officer Miss in London's Economy 07–10; PtO *Chelmsf* 07–10; *Lon* 07–10; *Sarum* from 11; *B & W* from 11. *24 Baileys Barn, Bradford-on-Avon BA15 1BX* T: (01225) 865314 E: david_driscoll@btopenworld.com

DRISCOLL, Raymond Donald Charles. b 78. St Mellitus Coll 14. **d** 17 **p** 18. C Stoke Hill *Guildf* 17–20; TV Forton and Gosport *Portsm* from 20. *9 Britannia Way, Gosport PO12 4FZ* M: 07597-692683 E: raydriscoll78@gmail.com

DRIVER, Arthur John Roberts. b 44. SS Coll Cam MA 70 FCIPA 73. Linc Th Coll 73. **d** 76 **p** 77. C S'wark H Trin w St Matt 76–80; TV N Lambeth 80–85; CMS Sri Lanka 86–92; V Putney St Marg *S'wark* 92–97; V Streatham St Paul 97–09; rtd 09; PtO *Chelmsf* from 09. *91 Ernest Road, Wivenhoe, Colchester CO7 9LJ* T: (01206) 822135 E: ajrdriver@gmail.com

DRIVER, Bruce Leslie. b 42. Lon Univ LLB 73. Linc Th Coll 76. **d** 78 **p** 79. C Dunstable *St Alb* 78–81; TV 81–86; V Rickmansworth 86–98; RD 91–98; V Northwood Hills St Edm *Lon* 98–08; rtd 08; PtO *Roch* from 09; S'wark from 12. *7 Bromley College, London Road, Bromley BR1 1PE* T: (020) 8290 0366 E: brucedriver@gmx.com

DRIVER, Daniel John. b 93. Dur Univ BA 17. Ridley Hall Cam 14. **d** 17 **p** 19. C Gateshead St Geo *Dur* 17–18; C Cambridge St Barn *Ely* from 18. *122 Ditton Lane, Fen Ditton, Cambridge CB5 8SS* M: 07929-972152 E: danny.driver@ctrbarnwell.org

DRIVER, Gordon Geoffrey. b 32. Garnett Coll Lon Dip Teaching 59. Trin Coll Bris. **d** 95 **p** 96. NSM Radipole and Melcombe Regis *Sarum* 95–03; rtd 03; PtO *Sarum* 03–17. *11 Greenway Close, Weymouth DT3 5BQ* T: (01305) 814523

DRIVER (née FRENCH), Janet Mary. Leeds Univ BA 65 PGCE 66 Surrey Univ BA 98. Linc Th Coll 74. **dss** 80 **d** 92 **p** 94. St Paul's Cathl *Lon* 80–82; N Lambeth *S'wark* 80–85; CMS Sri Lanka 86–92; NSM Putney St Marg *S'wark* 92–97; Hon C Streatham St Paul 97–09; rtd 09; PtO *Chelmsf* from 11. *Address withheld by request* E: janet@janetdriver.co.uk

DRIVER, Jennifer. b 63. Kent Univ BA. SEITE 05. **d** 08 **p** 09. NSM Farnborough *Roch* 08–13; NSM Orpington All SS 13–18; rtd 18; PtO *Roch* from 18. *3 Starts Hill Road,*

Orpington BR6 7AR T: (01689) 858766 M: 07599-957969 E: jen.driver63@gmail.com

DRIVER, John. *See* DRIVER, Arthur John Roberts

DRIVER, The Ven Penelope May. b 52. NOC. d 87 p 94. Dioc Youth Adv *Newc* 86–88; C Cullercoats St Geo 87–88; Youth Chapl *Ripon* 88–96; Dioc Adv on Women's Min 91–06; Assoc Dir of Ords 96–98; Dioc Dir of Ords 98–06; Min Can Ripon Cathl 96–06; Hon Can Ripon Cathl 98–06; Adn Ex 06–12; P-in-c Dawlish 09–10; Adn Westmorland and Furness *Carl* 12–17; rtd 17. *32 Priory Crescent, Grange-over-Sands LA11 7BL* E: pennydriver52@gmail.com

DRIVER, Roger John. b 64. Liv Univ MA 08. Trin Coll Bris BA 88. d 90 p 91. C Much Woolton *Liv* 90–93; C Fazakerley Em 93–94; TV 94–00; P-in-c Bootle St Matt 00–03; P-in-c Bootle St Leon 00–03; P-in-c Litherland St Andr 00–03; TR Bootle 04–16; AD 07–16; Hon Can Liv Cathl 07–16; R Bath St Mich Without *B & W* from 16. *The Rectory, 71 Priory Close, Bath BA2 5AP* T: (01225) 833512 M: 07976-419981 E: rogerdriver@btinternet.com

DROBIG, Marion. *See* WOOD, Marion

DROMORE, Archdeacon of. *See* WEST, The Ven Thomas Roderic

DROMORE, Dean of. *See* WILSON, The Very Revd Samuel Geoffrey

DROWLEY, Arthur. b 28. Oak Hill Th Coll 54. d 56 p 57. C Longfleet *Sarum* 56–59; C Wallington *S'wark* 59–62; V Taunton St Jas *B & W* 62–73; RD Taunton N 72–73; V Rodbourne Cheney *Bris* 73–87; R Bigbury, Ringmore and Kingston *Ex* 87–94; rtd 94; PtO *Ex* 95–02; *Man* 03–08; *Lich* 05–19. *4 Inglis Road, Park Hall, Oswestry SY11 4AN* T: (01691) 671994

DRUMMOND, Matthew James. b 77. Roehampton Inst BSc 98 Birkbeck Coll Lon MSc. Westcott Ho Cam 12. d 14 p 15. C Limpsfield and Tatsfield *S'wark* 14–17; C Addington 17–19; TV Mardyke *Chelmsf* from 19. *All Saints' Vicarage, 121 Foyle Drive, South Ockendon RM15 5HF* E: revd.matt.drummond@gmail.com *or* purfleetvicar@gmail.com

DRUMMOND, Terence. b 50. d 16. NSM Norbury St Phil *S'wark* 16–20. *49 Throstle Nest Close, Otley LS21 2RR* E: terry.drummond@hotmail.com

DRURY, Anthony Desmond. b 42. NOC. d 99 p 00. NSM New Ferry *Ches* 99–15; rtd 15; PtO *Ches* from 15. *61 Church Road, Bebington, Wirral CH63 3DZ* T: 0151-334 4797 E: des88@talktalk.net

DRURY, Benjamin Guy. b 84. Worc Coll Ox BA 05 MA 11 MPhil 07. St Steph Ho Ox BA 13. d 14 p 16. C Stony Stratford w Calverton *Ox* 14–16; C S Hinksey 16–19; P-in-c Prittlewell St Luke *Chelmsf* from 19. *St Luke's Vicarage, St Luke's Road, Southend-on-Sea SS2 4AB* E: benjamin.drury@gmail.com

DRURY, Caroline Norah. *See* BURNETT, Caroline Norah

DRURY, Desmond. *See* DRURY, Anthony Desmond

DRURY, The Very Revd John Henry. b 36. Trin Hall Cam MA 66. Westcott Ho Cam 61. d 63 p 64. C St John's Wood *Lon* 63–66; Chapl Down Coll Cam 66–69; Chapl Ex Coll Ox 69–73; Can Res Nor Cathl 73–79; Vice-Dean 78–79; Lect Sussex Univ 79–81; Dean K Coll Cam 81–91; Dean Ch Ch Ox 91–03; rtd 03; Chapl and Fell All So Coll Ox from 03. *All Souls College, Oxford OX1 4AL* T: (01865) 279379 F: 279299

DRURY, Michael Dru. b 31. Trin Coll Ox BA 55 MA 59. Wycliffe Hall Ox. d 58 p 59. C Fulham St Mary N End *Lon* 58–62; C Blackheath St Jo *S'wark* 62–64; Chapl and Asst Master Canford Sch 64–80; Chapl and Teacher Fernhill Manor Sch New Milton 80–81; P-in-c Stowe *Ox* 82–92; Asst Master Stowe Sch 82–92; R Rampton w Laneham, Treswell, Cottam and Stokeham *S'well* 92–96; rtd 96; PtO *Sarum* 96–19. *Tanfield, Giddylake, Wimborne BH21 2QT* T: (01202) 881246 E: michaeldrury@talktalk.net

DRURY, Valerie Doreen. b 40. Univ of Wales (Cardiff) BA 62 K Coll Lon PGCE 63 MBATOD 80. Oak Hill Th Coll 85. d 87 p 94. NSM Becontree St Alb *Chelmsf* 87–89; NSM Becontree S 89–02; rtd 02; PtO *Chelmsf* from 02. *37 Blunts Hall Road, Witham CM8 1ES* T: (01376) 517330

DRYDEN, Barry Frederick. b 44. Ches Coll of HE BTh 00. NOC 97. d 00 p 01. C Formby St Pet *Liv* 00–03; V Woolston 03–10; rtd 10; PtO *Leic* 13–21; *Eur* from 17. *5 Briton Lodge Close, Moira, Swadlincote DE12 6DD* T: (01283) 550920 E: revbarrydryden@btinternet.com

DRYDEN, Martin John. b 57. Loughb Univ BA 80 Univ of Wales (Lamp) MA 09. STETS 05. d 09 p 10. NSM Jersey St Clem *Win* from 09. *Mont Ubé House, La rue de la Blinerie, St Clement, Jersey JE2 6QT* T: (01534) 874668 M: 07797-729525

DRYER, Richard Jonathan. b 75. d 14 p 15. NSM Wimbledon Em Ridgway Prop Chpl *S'wark* 14–18; PtO

from 18; V Paddington St Steph w St Luke *Lon* from 19. *25 Talbot Road, London W2 5JF* T: (020) 7221 9329 E: richard.dryer@ststephens.london

D'SILVA, David Paul. b 90. St Steph Ho Ox. d 16 p 17. C Edlington and Hexthorpe *Sheff* 16–18; C Doncaster St Leon and St Jude 18–20; P-in-c from 20. *The Vicarage, Barnsley Road, Doncaster DN5 8QE* T: (01302) 971841 M: 07507-730569 E: fr.david.dsilva@gmail.com

D'SOUZA, Derek Emile. b 54. Trin Coll Bris. d 07 p 08. C Edgbaston St Germain *Birm* 07–11; P-in-c Prince's Park *Roch* 11–18; PtO *Lich* from 19. *23 Hilary Drive, Wolverhampton WV3 7NJ* E: helennderek@yahoo.co.uk

du BOULAY, Sarah Elizabeth. *See* HOUSSEMAYNE du BOULAY, Sarah Elizabeth

du ROCHER, Jacqueline. b 56. d 17 p 18. C Dalkeith *Edin* from 17; C Lasswade from 17. *46 Burnside Road, Gorebridge EH23 4ET*

du SAIRE, Canon Michele Marie. b 55. Leeds Poly BSc 78. ERMC 06. d 09 p 10. C Leavesden *St Alb* 09–13; R Sarratt and Chipperfield from 13; Hon Can St Alb from 18. *The New Vicarage, The Street, Chipperfield, Kings Langley WD4 9BJ* T: (01923) 265848 E: micheledusairehcstp@gmail.com

DUBLIN (Christ Church), Dean of. *See* DUNNE, The Very Revd Dermot Patrick Martin

DUBLIN, Archbishop of, and Bishop of Glendalough. *See* JACKSON, The Most Revd Michael Geoffrey St Aubyn

DUBLIN, Archdeacon of. *See* PIERPOINT, The Ven David Alfred

DUBREUIL, Yann. b 70. Birm Univ BA 04. Wycliffe Hall Ox 05. d 07 p 08. C Four Marks *Win* 07–11; R Bentley, Binsted and Froyle from 11. *Holy Cross Vicarage, Church Street, Binsted, Alton GU34 4NX* T: (01420) 23339 M: 07777-684533 E: yann@benbinfro.org

DUCE, Ms Catherine Veronica. b 81. Newc Univ BA 04 MA 05 Heythrop Coll Lon MA 11 Fitzw Coll Cam BTh 14. Westcott Ho Cam 12. d 15 p 16. C Westmr St Steph w St Jo *Lon* 15–19; C St Martin-in-the-Fields from 19. *11 Woodland Road, London N11 1PN* M: 07948-980024 E: catherine.duce@smitf.org

DUCKERS, Miss Linda Jean. b 62. Univ of Wales (Abth) BSc 84 PGCE 85 Rob Coll Cam BTh 06. Ridley Hall Cam 04. d 06 p 07. C Leek and Meerbrook *Lich* 06–10; TV Warwick *Cov* from 10. *St Nicholas' Vicarage, 184 Myton Road, Warwick CV34 6PS* T: (01926) 496209 E: linda.duckers@gmail.com *or* linda.stnicswarwick@gmail.com

DUCKERS, Paul Gerrard. b 42. Qu Coll Birm 07. d 09 p 10. NSM Sutton Coldfield H Trin *Birm* 09–12; PtO from 12. *5 Moor Meadow Road, Sutton Coldfield B75 6BU* T: 0121-378 1835 E: paulduckers@talktalk.net

DUCKETT, Canon Brian John. b 45. ALCD 70. d 70 p 71. C S Lambeth St Steph *S'wark* 70–73; C Norwood St Luke 73–75; C Bushbury *Lich* 75–77; TV 77–79; V Dover St Martin *Cant* 79–92; TR Swindon Dorcan *Bris* 92–00; RD Highworth 95–99; V Clifton H Trin, St Andr and St Pet 00–09; Vulnerable Adults Policy Officer 07–09; Hon Can Bris Cathl 98–09; rtd 09; PtO *Chich* from 14. *52 The Fieldings, Southwater, Horsham RH13 9LZ* T: (01403) 733417

DUCKETT, Edward. b 36. Keble Coll Ox BA 59 MA 61 Portsm Poly CQSW 72. Cuddesdon Coll 59. d 61 p 62. C Portsea St Cuth *Portsm* 61–65; C Rotherham *Sheff* 65–68; LtO *Portsm* 68–69; Hon Chapl Portsm Cathl 69–75; PtO *Ely* 75–82; R Rampton 82–89; R Willingham 82–89; RD N Stowe 83–89; P-in-c Ramsey 89–90; P-in-c Upwood w Gt and Lt Raveley 89–90; TR The Ramseys and Upwood 90–92; RD St Ives 89–92; P-in-c Bassingbourn 93–95; V 95–96; P-in-c Whaddon 93–95; V 95–96; rtd 96. *3 Lancing Close, Battenhall, Worcester WR5 2HT* T: (01905) 357607

DUCKETT, Ms Helen Lorraine. b 71. Keble Coll Ox BA 92 Sheff Univ MA 94 Birm Univ MPhil 98. Qu Coll Birm 95. d 98 p 99. C Cannock *Lich* 98–01; TV Wednesfield 01–10; TV Cen Wolverhampton 10–14; Chapl K Sch Wolv 15–18; TV Bentley Em and Willenhall H Trin *Lich* from 16. *167 Coleman Avenue, Wolverhampton WV11 3RU* T: (01902) 258862 E: revhelen.duckett@gmail.com

DUCKETT, John Dollings. b 41. Nottm Univ BA 62 BTh 81. Linc Th Coll 79. d 81 p 82. C Boston *Linc* 81–84; V Baston 84–86; V Langtoft Gp 86–88; V Sutterton and Wigtoft 88–89; R Sutterton w Fosdyke and Algarkirk 89–92; P-in-c Chapel St Leonards w Hogsthorpe 92–97; V 97–00; V Bracebridge 00–06; rtd 06; PtO *Linc* 15–18. *Old Post Office, Faldingworth Road, Spridlington, Market Rasen LN8 2DF* T: (01673) 860116

DUCKETT, Keith Alexander. b 69. Worc Coll of HE BA 93. Qu Coll Birm BD 97 MA 98. d 98 p 99. C Willenhall H Trin *Lich* 98–01; TV Blakenall Heath 01–03; Asst Chapl Sandwell and W Birm Hosps NHS Trust 03–06; Chapl 06–13; Chapl K Sch Wolv 12–15; Spiritual Care Lead John Taylor

Hospice Birm 13; Chapl Karis Neighbour Scheme 15–16; C Oxley and Wednesfield St Greg *Lich* 15–16; Chapl Walsall Healthcare NHS Trust 16–19; PtO *Birm* 16–17; *Lich* from 19. *Walsall Palliative Care Centre, Goscote Lane, Walsall WS3 1SJ* M: 07972-525140 E: keith.duckett@sky.com

DUCKETT, The Very Revd Lee Christopher James. b 67. Wycliffe Hall Ox BTh 04. d 04 p 05. C Cranham Park *Chelmsf* 04–08; C Purley Ch Ch *S'wark* 08–12; V Ore Ch Ch *Chich* 12–19; V Battle from 19; Dean Battle from 19. *The Deanery, Caldbec Hill, Battle TN33 0JY* M: 07586-030299 E: dean@stmarysbattle.org.uk

DUCKETT, Matthew Robert. b 64. UEA BSc 85 PGCE 88. NTMTC BA 09. d 09 p 10. NSM Old St Pancras *Lon* 09–13; P-in-c Friern Barnet St Pet le Poer 13–18; P-in-c Colindale St Matthias from 18. *St Matthias' Vicarage, 48 Rushgrove Avenue, London NW9 6QY* E: matthew_duckett@yahoo.co.uk

DUCKETT, Raphael Thomas Marie James. b 65. N Staffs Poly BA 87. Cranmer Hall Dur 01. d 03 p 04. C Madeley *Heref* 03–06; V Bradley St Martin *Lich* 06–19; Chapl RN from 19. *Royal Naval Chaplaincy Service Headquarters, Tanner Building, HMS Excellent, Whale Island, Portsmouth PO2 8ER* T: 0300-157 7544 E: revraphael@blueyonder.co.uk

DUCKWORTH, Angela Denise. *See* WATTS, Angela Denise

DUCKWORTH, Annette Jacqueline. b 54. Univ of Wales (Ban) BSc 75 PGCE 76. d 00 p 01. OLM Moxley *Lich* 00–14; OLM Darlaston and Moxley from 14; Chapl Blue Coat Comp Sch Walsall 07–10. *1 Sutton Road, Wednesbury WS10 8SG* E: annette.duckworth@hotmail.com

DUCKWORTH, Brian George. b 47. Edin Th Coll 85. d 87 p 88. C Sutton in Ashfield St Mary *S'well* 87–95; C Sutton in Ashfield St Mich 89–95; P-in-c 95–98; TV Hucknall Torkard 98–03; R S Ockendon and Belhus Park *Chelmsf* 03–12; rtd 12; PtO *Cant* from 13. *24 Aspen Drive, Whitfield, Dover CT16 2EX* T: (01304) 827239 E: brian288@btinternet.com

DUDDLES (formerly MOORES), Samantha Jane. b 73. Man Metrop Univ BEd 96 Southn Univ MSc 01. Ripon Coll Cuddesdon. d 12 p 14. C Upper Dever *Win* 12–16; TV Portsea N End St Mark *Portsm* from 16. *St Peter's Vicarage, Playfair Road, Southsea PO5 1EQ* T: (023) 9307 0133 M: 07740-505271 E: samduddles@gmail.com

DUDGEON, Christopher Patrick. b 63. Portsm Poly BSc 86 Univ Coll Lon MSc 87. St Mellitus Coll 16. d 18 p 19. NSM N Hants Downs *Win* from 18. *43 High Street, Odiham, Hook RG29 1LF* T: (01256) 702918 M: 07810-544495 E: chrisdudgeon90@gmail.com

DUDLEY (formerly MORTIMER), Mrs Elizabeth Anne. b 69. RGN 92. Ripon Coll Cuddesdon 05. d 07 p 08. C Minehead *B & W* 07–10; P-in-c Castle Cary and Ansford 10–20; RD Bruton and Cary 16–20; V Frome Ch Ch w St Mary from 20. *The Vicarage, 73 Weymouth Road, Frome BA11 1HJ* E: revlizdudley@gmail.com

DUDLEY, Mrs Janet Carr. b 36. EMMTC 86. d 89 p 94. NSM Countesthorpe w Foston *Leic* 89–94; NSM Arnesby w Shearsby and Bruntingthorpe 94–01; rtd 01; PtO *Leic* 01–02 and from 10; NSM Market Harborough and The Transfiguration etc 02–10. *13 The Broadway, Market Harborough LE16 7LZ* T: (01858) 467619

DUDLEY, John Donald Swanborough. b 34. Ox Univ BTh 95. SAOMC 96. d 97 p 98. NSM Emmer Green *Ox* 97–02; PtO from 02. *26 Russet Glade, Emmer Green, Reading RG4 8UJ* T/F: 0118-954 6664

DUDLEY, Ms Josephine. b 52. ERMC 04. d 06 p 07. NSM Tolleshunt Knights w Tiptree and Gt Braxted *Chelmsf* 06–11; P-in-c Lonan *S & M* 11–14; P-in-c Laxey 11–14; TV Onchan, Lonan and Laxey from 14. *The Vicarage, 56 Ard Reayrt, Ramsey Road, Laxey, Isle of Man IM4 7QQ* T: (01624) 861989 M: 07054-431790 E: jodudley56@gmail.com

DUDLEY, Martin Raymond. b 53. K Coll Lon BD 77 AKC 77 MTh 78 PhD 94 City Univ MSc 07 Hon DArts 14 FRHistS 95 FSA 97. St Mich Coll Llan 78. d 79 p 80. C Whitchurch *Llan* 79–83; V Weston *St Alb* 83–88; P-in-c Ardeley 87–88; V Owlsmoor *Ox* 88–95; Lect Simon of Cyrene Th Inst 92–95; R Smithfield St Bart Gt *Lon* 95–15; P-in-c St Bart Less 12–15; R Smithfield Gt St Bart 15–16; rtd 17; Hon Research Fell Qu Foundn Birm from 17. *Apartment 20, 21 Newhall Hill, Birmingham B1 3JA* M: 07957-246461 E: drmrdudley@gmail.com

DUDLEY, Wendy Elizabeth. *See* KEAY, Wendy Elizabeth

DUDLEY, Archdeacon of. *See* GROARKE, The Ven Nicola Jane

DUDLEY, Suffragan Bishop of. *See* GORICK, The Rt Revd Martin Charles William

DUDLEY-SMITH, James. b 66. Fitzw Coll Cam BA 89 MA 92. Wycliffe Hall Ox BTh 94. d 97 p 98. C New Borough and Leigh *Sarum* 97–01; C Hove Bp Hannington Memorial Ch *Chich* 01–06; R Yeovil w Kingston Pitney *B & W* from

06; RD Yeovil 15–21. *The Rectory, 41 The Park, Yeovil BA20 1DG* T: (01935) 475352 E: jamesds100@outlook.com

⌖**DUDLEY-SMITH, The Rt Revd Timothy.** b 26. OBE 03. Pemb Coll Cam BA 47 MA 51 Lambeth MLitt 91 Dur Univ Hon DD 09. Ridley Hall Cam 48. d 50 p 51 c 81. C Erith St Paul *Roch* 50–53; LtO *S'wark* 53–62; Hd of Cam Univ Miss Bermondsey 53–55; Chapl 55–60; Ed Sec Evang Alliance and Ed Crusade 55–59; Asst Sec CPAS 59–65; Gen Sec 65–73; Adn Nor 73–81; Suff Bp Thetford 81–91; rtd 92; PtO *Sarum* from 12. *38 The Eights Marina, Mariner's Way, Cambridge CB4 1ZA* T: (01223) 360149

DUERDEN, Martin James. b 55. Liv Poly BA 77. Oak Hill Th Coll 86. d 88 p 89. C Tunbridge Wells St Jas *Roch* 88–92; V Southport SS Simon and Jude *Liv* 92–98; P-in-c Maghull 98–02; TR 02–07; P-in-c Marsh Green w Newtown 07; V 08–13; V Salesbury *Blackb* 13–20; Hon C Langho Billington 13–16; rtd 20. *42 Eagle Crescent, Rainford, St Helens WA11 8BG* E: martinduerden@hotmail.com

DUERR, Robert Kenneth. b 54. Univ of S California BMus 77 MMus 80. Ridley Hall Cam 04. d 04 p 06. NSM Cambridge Gt St Mary w St Mich *Ely* 04–05; C Marton-in-Cleveland *York* 06–07; C Scarborough St Martin and Scarborough St Sav w All SS 07–10. *258 Christiana Street, North Tonawanda NY 14120, USA* M: (001) (904) 671 2916 E: robert@robertduerr.com

DUFF, Alison. *See* FINCH, Alison

DUFF, Andrew John. b 57. Open Univ BSc 07. Sarum & Wells Th Coll 92. d 92 p 93. C Banbury *Ox* 92–95; C Bracknell 95–96; TV 96–98; CF 98–04; Chapl RN 04–12; rtd 12; PtO *Worc* from 12; *Glas* from 17. *50 Alyssum Crescent, Motherwell ML1 1DF*

DUFF, Miss Emma Cameron. b 73. St Andr Univ MA 95 Solicitor 99. Qu Coll Birm 12. d 14 p 15. C Willington *Newc* 14–18; C Wallsend St Jo 18–19; P-in-c from 19. *2 Burlington Court, Wallsend NE28 9YH* T: 0191-257 2405 E: revdemmaduff@gmail.com

DUFF, Jeremy. b 71. MA DPhil. d 06 p 07. NSM Toxteth St Philemon w St Gabr and St Cleopas *Liv* 06–10; Dir Lifelong Learning and Can Liv Cathl 04–10; TV S Widnes *Liv* 10–16; Prin St Padarn's Inst from 16. *St Michael's Centre, 54 Cardiff Road, Llandaff, Cardiff CF5 2YJ* T: (029) 2056 3379 E: jeremy.duff@stpadarns.ac.uk

⌖**DUFF, The Rt Revd Jillian Louise Calland.** b 72. Ch Coll Cam BA 93 MA 97 Worc Coll Ox DPhil 96. Wycliffe Hall Ox BA 02 MA 06. d 03 p 04 c 18. C Litherland St Phil *Liv* 03–05; Lic to Adn Liv 05–11; Chapl Liv Coll 09–16; Dir Tr for IME 2 and Dioc Voc Adv *Liv* 11–18; Dir St Mellitus NW 13–18; Suff Bp Lancaster *Blackb* from 18; PtO *Liv* from 13; *Ches* 17–18; *St As* from 18. *6 Marford Heights, Wrexham LL12 8TJ* E: jillduff@btinternet.com *or* bishop.lancaster@blackburn.anglican.org

DUFF, John Alexander. b 57. York Univ BA 78. EMMTC 91. d 94 p 95. NSM Linc St Geo Swallowbeck 94–00; PtO *Ripon* 02–03; C Harrogate St Mark 03–14; *Leeds* from 14. *1 Butterbur Way, Harrogate HG3 2XH* T: (01423) 549987 M: 07900-364958 E: ffudnhoj@hotmail.com

DUFF, Michael Ian. b 63. Ox Univ BA 85. Trin Coll Bris BA 98 MA 99. d 99 p 00. C Southsea St Jude *Portsm* 99–03; CMS Bandung Indonesia 03–07; V Southsea St Jude *Portsm* 07–19; Hon Can Portsm Cathl 17–19; Patr Sec CPAS from 19; PtO *Cov* 19–21; LtO from 21. *CPAS, Unit 3, Sovereign Court 1, Sir William Lyons Road, University of Warwick Science Park, Coventry CV4 7EZ* T: 0300-123 0780 E: mduff@cpas.org.uk

DUFF, Timothy Cameron. b 40. G&C Coll Cam BA 62 LLM 63 MA 66 Solicitor 65. NEOC 90. d 93 p 94. NSM Tynemouth Priory *Newc* 93–96; NSM N Shields 96–05; TV 00–05; rtd 05; PtO *Newc* from 05. *24A Percy Gardens, Tynemouth, North Shields NE30 4HQ* T: 0191-257 1463 E: timothy@timothyduff.co.uk

DUFFELL, Lucy Margaret. *See* GARDNER, Lucy Margaret

DUFFETT-SMITH, Ms Patricia Mary. Lon Univ BPharm 76 Anglia Poly Univ MA 99 MRPharmS 77. EAMTC 94. d 97 p 98. NSM Haddenham and Wilburton *Ely* 97–00; Asst Chapl Hinchingbrooke Health Care NHS Trust 99–17; Asst Chapl NW Anglia NHS Foundn Trust from 17. *Address withheld by request* M: 07788-668900 E: trishads@gmail.com *or* trishads@googlemail.com

DUFFIELD, Ian Keith. b 47. K Coll Lon BD 71 AKC 71 MTh 73 NY Th Sem DMin 84. St Aug Coll Cant 72. d 73 p 74. C Broxbourne *St Alb* 73–77; C Harpenden St Nic 77–81; TV Sheff Manor 81–87; V Walkley 87–02; V Sheff St Leon Norwood 02–13; rtd 13; PtO *Sheff* from 14. *17 Springwell Drive, Beighton, Sheffield S20 1XA*

DUFFIELD, Ronald Bertram Charles. b 26. Hull Univ Coll BA 49 TCert 50. Sarum & Wells Th Coll 91. d 92 p 93. NSM E Knoyle, Semley and Sedgehill *Sarum* 92–94; P-in-c 94–95; rtd

95; PtO *York* 95–99 and from 01; P-in-c Isfield *Chich* 99–01. *8 Beechdale, Cottingham HU16 4RH* T: (01482) 845086

DUFFUS, Barbara Rose. *See* HOBBS, Barbara Rose

DUFFY, Jennifer-Anne Lesley. b 71. Qu Foundn Birm 16. d 19 p 20. NSM Empingham, Edith Weston, Lyndon, Manton etc *Pet* from 19. *Lavender Cottage, 2 Water Lane, Ashwell, Oakham LE15 7LS* M: 07507-442539 E: curate.rwb@gmail.com

DUGDALE, Angela Marion. b 33. DL 92 MBE 06. ARCM 52 GRSM 54 UEA Hon MA 89. d 97 p 98. OLM Weybourne Gp *Nor* 97–03; rtd 03; PtO *Nor* from 03. *The Old Carpenter's Shop, Kelling, Holt NR25 7EL* T: (01263) 588389 F: 588594

DUGMORE, The Ven Barry John. b 61. STETS. d 01 p 02. C Cowplain *Portsm* 01–04; C-in-c Whiteley CD and Dioc Ecum Officer 04–07; P-in-c Tiverton St Geo and St Paul *Ex* 07–15; RD Tiverton and Cullompton 12–15; Dioc Miss Enabler 15–19; Adn Warwick *Cov* from 19. *Cathedral and Diocesan Office, 1 Hill Top, Coventry CV1 5AB* T: (024) 7652 1337 E: b.dugmore@ukgateway.net

DUGUID, Alison Audrey. b 52. STETS 99. d 02 p 03. C Appledore w Brookland, Fairfield, Brenzett etc *Cant* 02–06; P-in-c The Brents and Davington w Oare and Luddenham 06–12; P-in-c Eastling w Ospringe and Stalisfield w Otterden 06–12; V Marden 12–20; Dir Dioc Poverty and Hope Appeal 07–20; AD Weald 14–16; rtd 20. *Address temp unknown* E: ali@dogooders.co.uk

DUKE, David Malcolm. b 40. Ch Ch Ox BA 61 MA 65 Newc Poly MPhil 80 CQSW 81. Cuddesdon Coll 63. d 65 p 66. C Sunderland Pennywell St Thos *Dur* 65–68; C Dur St Oswald 68–70; C Harton 70–74; PtO 85–96; Hon C Hedworth 96–13; PtO from 13. *43 Coquet Street, Jarrow NE32 5SW* T: 0191-430 1200 M: 07887-383000 E: david.duke@sky.com

DUKE, Miss Judith Mary. b 47. Leeds Univ LLB 68. Cranmer Hall Dur 03. d 04 p 05. NSM Buckrose Carrs *York* 04–07; R 07–12; rtd 12; PtO *York* from 13. *13 Sledgate Garth, Rillington, Malton YO17 8JS* T: (01944) 758408 E: judithduke347@btinternet.com

DULFER, John Guidi. b 37. Lich Th Coll 62. d 64 p 65. C Fenny Stratford and Water Eaton *Ox* 64–67; C Cheshunt *St Alb* 67–68; C Kennington Cross St Anselm *S'wark* 68–73; C N Lambeth 74–76; P-in-c Kensington St Phil Earl's Court *Lon* 76–79; V 79–84; V Jersey City St Jo & Jersey City St Matt USA 84–85; R New York Resurr 00–01; P-in-c Castleton 02–06. *3700 Galt Ocean Drive Apt 607, Fort Lauderdale FL 33308, USA* T: (001) 91-7658 4512 E: johndulfer@hotmail.com

DULLEY, Priscilla Mary. b 72. St Aug Coll of Th 14. d 17 p 18. C Hythe *Cant* 17–20; C Cliftonville from 20. *18 Devonshire Gardens, Margate CT9 3AF* E: revprudulley@gmail.com

DUMAT, Mrs Jennifer. b 42. ARCM 62. Qu Coll Birm 80 EMMTC 82. dss 83 d 87 p 94. Chapl Asst Pilgrim Hosp Boston 83–94; P-in-c Friskney *Linc* 94–04; rtd 04; PtO *Linc* 16–19. *11 Sea Lane, Butterwick, Boston PE22 0EY* T: (01205) 760883

DUMBRECK, Geoffrey James William. b 84. Peterho Cam BA 05 MA 09 MPhil 06 PhD 10. Ripon Coll Cuddesdon MTh 13. d 13 p 14. C Cambridge Ascension *Ely* 13–17; Asst Chapl Peterho Cam 15–19; Acting Dean 17–18; V S Croydon St Pet and St Aug *S'wark* from 19. *20 Haling Park Road, South Croydon CR2 6NE* T: (020) 8688 4715 M: 07727-968985 E: geoff.dumbreck@gmail.com

DUNCAN, Mrs Amanda Jayne. b 58. Balls Park Coll Hertford BEd 79. ERMC 08. d 11 p 12. C Harpenden St Jo *St Alb* 11–15; TV Bishop's Hatfield, Lemsford and N Mymms 15–18; V High Cross from 18; V Thundridge from 18. *St Mary's House, Church Lane, Stapleford, Hertford SG14 3NB* T: (01992) 731904 M: 07506-715026 E: amanda.duncan2387@gmail.com

DUNCAN, Canon Bruce. b 38. MBE 93. Leeds Univ BA 60 FRSA. Cuddesdon Coll 65. d 67 p 68. C Armley St Bart *Ripon* 67–69; Dir Children's Relief Internat 69–71; Hon C Cambridge St Mary Less *Ely* 69–70; Chapl OHP and St Hilda's Sch Whitby 70–71; Chapl Vienna w Budapest and Prague *Eur* 71–75; V Crediton *Ex* 75–82; R Crediton and Shobrooke 82–86; RD Cadbury 76–81 and 84–86; Can Res Man Cathl 86–95; Prin Sarum Coll and Can and Preb Sarum Cathl 95–02; rtd 02; Chapl Ex Univ 03–04; PtO 02–08; *Sarum* from 08; *Eur* from 10; Hon C Salisbury St Martin and Laverstock *Sarum* 10–13; Hon C Salisbury St Martin 13–15. *92 Harnham Road, Salisbury SP2 8JW* T: (01722) 502227 M: 07851-737230 E: canon.duncan@gmail.com

DUNCAN, Christopher Robin. b 41. AKC 71. d 72 p 73. C Allington *Cant* 72–73; C Allington and Maidstone St Pet 73–77; P-in-c Wittersham 77–82; R Wittersham w Stone and Ebony 82–85; V Chilham 85–92; P-in-c Challock w Molash 87–92; V Chilham w Challock and Molash 92–11; RD W Bridge 92–95 and 02–03; rtd 12; PtO *Cant* 12–21. *173*

Shalmsford Street, Chartham, Canterbury CT4 7QP T: (01227) 733813 E: rev.chris.duncan@gmail.com

DUNCAN, Colin Richard. b 34. SS Coll Cam BA 58 MA 60. Ripon Coll Cuddesdon 83. d 85 p 86. C Stafford *Lich* 85–89; C Wednesfield 89–90; TV 90–99; rtd 99; PtO *Glouc* 99–16; *B & W* 13–18. *92 Kingfisher Road, Portishead, Bristol BS20 7QD* T: (01275) 818607 M: 07891-528295 E: duncan.firtree@tiscali.co.uk

✠**DUNCAN, The Rt Revd Gregor Duthie.** b 50. Glas Univ MA 72 Clare Coll Cam PhD 77 Oriel Coll Ox BA 83. Ripon Coll Cuddesdon 81. d 83 p 84 c 10. C Oakham, Hambleton, Egleton, Braunston and Brooke *Pet* 83–86; Chapl Birm Univ 86–89; R Largs *Glas* 89–99; Dean Glas 96–10; R Glas St Ninian 99–10; Bp Glas 10–18; rtd 18; LtO *Glas* from 18. *3 Golf Road, Rutherglen, Glasgow G73 4JW*

DUNCAN, The Ven John Finch. b 33. Univ Coll Ox BA 57 MA 63. Cuddesdon Coll 57. d 59 p 60. C S Bank *York* 59–61; SSF 61–62; C Birm St Pet 62–65; Chapl Birm Univ 65–76; V Kings Heath 76–85; Hon Can Birm Cathl 83–85; Adn Birm 85–01; rtd 01; PtO *Birm* 01–18; *Pet* from 01. *66 Glebe Rise, King's Sutton, Banbury OX17 3PH* T: (01295) 812641 E: jfduncan66@gmail.com

DUNCAN, Richard William. b 87. Ch Coll Cam BA 09. Wycliffe Hall Ox BTh 15. d 16 p 17. C Moulton *Pet* 16–19; V Brackley St Pet w St Jas from 19. *The Vicarage, Old Town, Brackley NN13 7BZ* T: (01280) 702767 M: 07985-315034 E: richduncan100@gmail.com *or* brackleyvicar@gmail.com

DUNCAN, Thomas James. b 37. d 97 p 98. NSM Poplar *Lon* 97–17; PtO from 17. *1 Chardwell Close, London E6 5RR* T: (020) 7538 9198 *or* 7476 6465 M: 07732-666434 E: duncant1@sky.com

DUNCANSON, Derek James. b 47. TD 93. AKC 69 Open Univ BA 80 Lon Univ MA(Ed) 93 FCollP 94. St Aug Coll Cant 69. d 70 p 71. C Norbury St Oswald *Cant* 70–72; CF (TAVR) 71–76 and 79–95; C Woodham *Guildf* 72–76; CF 76–79; V Burneside *Carl* 79–84; R Coppull St Jo *Blackb* 84–86; Chapl Bloxham Sch 86–99; V Pet St Mary Boongate 99–04; RD Pet 01–04; Chapl Pet Regional Coll 00–04; Chapl Heathfield Sch Ascot 04–08; rtd 08; PtO *Cant* from 08. *Old Forge Cottage, 235 Canterbury Road, Birchington CT7 9TB* T: (01843) 843289 E: dmduncanson@btinternet.com

DUNCOMBE, Maureen Barbara. *See* WHITE, Maureen Barbara

DUNDAS, The Ven Edward Paul. b 67. NUU BSc 88. TCD Div Sch BTh 91. d 91 p 92. C Portadown St Mark *Arm* 91–95; I Ardtrea w Desertcreat 95–00; Dioc Youth Adv to Abp Armagh 99–00; I Belfast St Aid *Conn* 00–05; I Lisburn Ch Ch from 05; Adn Dalriada from 18. *Christ Church Rectory, 27 Hillsborough Road, Lisburn BT28 1JL* T: (028) 9266 2163 *or* 9267 3271 M: 07740-589465 E: paul_dundas@yahoo.com

DUNDAS, Gary Walter. b 56. EMMTC 04. d 07 p 08. NSM Stanton-by-Dale w Dale Abbey and Risley *Derby* 07–14; NSM Wilne and Draycott w Breaston from 14. *17-19 Victoria Road, Draycott, Derby DE72 3PS* T: (01332) 872893 F: 875371 M: 07971-783083 E: gwdundas@aol.com

DUNDEE, Provost of. *See* THOMSON, The Very Revd Elizabeth Jane

DUNGAN, Hilary Anne. b 46. TCD BA 98 ARCM 68. CITC 98. d 00 p 01. C Arm St Mark 00–03; I Maryborough w Dysart Enos and Ballyfin *C, F & O* 03–11; Chapl Midlands and Portlaoise Pris 03–11; Chapl Midland Regional Hosp Portlaoise 03–11; rtd 11. *46 The Drive, Woodbrook Glen, Bray, Co Dublin, Republic of Ireland* T: (00353) (1) 200 5959 M: 087-6418125 E: hildungan@gmail.com

DUNGAN, Ivan Francis. b 49. CITC 06. d 09 p 10. NSM Bunclody w Kildavin, Clonegal and Kilrush *C, F & O* 09–14; NSM Ferns w Kilbride, Toombe, Kilcormack etc 14–16; P-in-c New w Old Ross, Whitechurch, Fethard etc 16–19; rtd 19. *Brookhaven, Lower Southknock, New Ross, Co Wexford, Republic of Ireland* T: (00353) (51) 422281 E: ivandungan@gmail.com

DUNHAM, Angela Mary. *See* CHEESEMAN, Angela Mary

DUNK, Carol Ann. b 65. EMMTC 08. d 11 p 13. NSM Retford Area *S'well* 11–12; NSM Tuxford w Weston, Markham Clinton etc 12–15; NSM Ollerton w Boughton from 15; C Fleet *Guildf* 16–20; C Easthampstead *Ox* from 20. *16 Blackcap Lane, Bracknell RG12 8AA* M: 07896-945636 E: revcaroldunk@gmail.com

DUNK, Carolyn Margaret. b 55. Wycliffe Hall Ox 04. d 06 p 07. C Uxbridge *Lon* 06–09; C W Ealing St Jo w St Jas 09–19; C Patcham *Chich* from 19. *32 Fairview Rise, Brighton BN1 5GL* M: 07554-343403 E: revcazdunk@gmail.com

DUNK, Michael John. b 43. Oak Hill Th Coll BA 82. d 82 p 83. C Northampton All SS w St Kath *Pet* 82–86; Ind Chapl *Birm* 86–96; P-in-c Warley Woods 96; V 96–08; AD Warley

01–06; rtd 08; Hon C Shepshed and Oaks in Charnwood *Leic* 08–10; PtO *Birm* 11–14; *Guildf* from 15. *Glenesk, Church Street, Ewell, Epsom KT17 2AQ* T: (020) 3609 8013 E: michael.dunk@talk21.com

DUNKLEY, Canon Christopher. b 52. Edin Univ MA 74 Ox Univ BA 77 MA 81. St Steph Ho Ox 75. **d** 78 **p** 79. C Newbold w Dunston *Derby* 78–82; C Chesterfield St Mary and All SS 82; Chapl Leic Univ 82–85; TV Leic Ascension 85–92; Chapl Leics Hospice 85–87; V Leic St Aid 92–97; V Holbrooks *Cov* 97–16; Hon Can Cov Cathl 07–16; rtd 16. *79 Trueway Drive South, Shepshed, Loughborough LE12 9DY*

DUNLOP, Andrew James. b 76. Collingwood Coll Dur BSc 97 MA 16 PGCE 98. Wycliffe Hall Ox BTh 07. **d** 07 **p** 08. C Plymouth St Andr and Stonehouse *Ex* 07–10; Pioneer Min Gtr Northampton Deanery *Pet* 10–15; TV Duston 15; Tutor Cranmer Hall Dur 15–18; P Missr E Dur Miss Project 15–18; Tutor Ridley Hall Cam from 18. *Ridley Hall, Ridley Hall Road, Cambridge CB3 9HG* T: (01223) 741074 E: ajd232@cam.ac.uk

DUNLOP, Mrs Anne Cecilia. b 50. **d** 14 **p** 15. NSM Ex St Thos and Em 14–17; PV Ex Cathl 17; PtO *Chich* 18–20; P-in-c Hamsey from 20; P-in-c Plumpton w E Chiltington cum Novington from 21. *The Rectory, Offham, Lewes BN7 3PX* T: (01273) 474356 M: 07929-571522 E: revannedunlop@gmail.com

DUNLOP, Brian Kenneth Charles. b 49. Ex Univ BSc 73. WEMTC 07. **d** 10 **p** 11. NSM S Cheltenham *Glouc* 10–19; rtd 19; PtO *Glouc* from 20. *31 Pickering Road, Cheltenham GL53 0LF* T: (01242) 580731 E: dogcollar@quinweb.net

DUNLOP, Mrs Frances Jane. b 57. New Hall Cam MA 82 ACA 84. STETS 06. **d** 09 **p** 10. NSM Clarendon *Sarum* 09–21; TV from 21. *Little Paddock, Romsey Road, Whiteparish, Salisbury SP5 2SD* T: (01794) 884793 M: 07795-836653 E: fjdunlop@hotmail.com

DUNLOP, Jennifer Mary. b 51. Hull Univ LLB 72 Solicitor 73. Yorks Min Course 13. **d** 15 **p** 16. NSM Dukinfield St Mark *Ches* from 15. *180A Dowson Road, Hyde SK14 5BW* T: 0161-368 2149 E: revjenny15@gmail.com

DUNLOP, Neil Stuart. b 78. Qu Coll Birm. **d** 10 **p** 11. C Lighthorne *Cov* 10–12; C Newbold Pacey w Moreton Morrell 10–12; C Chesterton 10–12; Chapl N Warks and Hinckley Coll of FE 13–16; C Arden Marches *Cov* 13–16; R Alveley and Quatt *Heref* from 16. *The Rectory, Alveley, Bridgnorth WV15 6ND* T: (01746) 780882 E: nsdunlop@gmail.com

DUNLOP, Peter John. b 44. TCD BA 68 MA 72 Dur Univ CertEd 71. Cranmer Hall Dur. **d** 71 **p** 72. C Barking St Marg w St Patr *Chelmsf* 71–75; C Gt Malvern Ch Ch *Worc* 75–78; Chapl K Sch Tynemouth 78–89; V Monkseaton St Pet *Newc* 90–96; rtd 96; PtO *Newc* from 96. *19 Cliftonville Gardens, Whitley Bay NE26 1QJ* T: 0191-251 0983

DUNN, Canon Alastair Matthew Crusoe. b 40. Lon Univ LLB 64 AKC 64 Barrister-at-Law (Gray's Inn) 65. Wycliffe Hall Ox 78. **d** 80 **p** 81. C Yardley St Edburgha *Birm* 80–83; R Bishop's Sutton and Ropley and W Tisted *Win* 83–90; V Milford 90–04; Hon Can Win Cathl 03–04; C Harrogate St Mark *Ripon* 04–05; Hon C 05–07; rtd 05; PtO *York* from 08. *13 Littlefield Close, Nether Poppleton, York YO26 6HX* T: (01904) 798487 E: asdunn@talk21.com

DUNN, Canon David Michael. b 47. AKC 70. St Aug Coll Cant 70. **d** 71 **p** 72. C Padgate *Liv* 71–74; C Halliwell St Marg *Man* 74–76; V Lever Bridge 76–84; V Bradshaw 84–01; TR Turton Moorland 01–12; Hon Can Man Cathl 12; rtd 12; PtO *Man* from 13. *1 Tottington Fold, Bolton BL2 4DX* T: (01204) 307199

DUNN, Derek William Robert. b 48. Open Univ BA 81 MA 01 Stranmillis Coll CertEd 70 AMusTCL 74 LTCL 75. **d** 85 **p** 87. Aux Min Carnalea *D & D* 85–97; Aux Min Bangor Abbey 97–05; C Ballymena w Ballyclug *Conn* 05–09; Bp's C Acton and Drumbanagher *Arm* from 09; V Choral Arm Cathl from 14. *Address temp unknown* M: 07745-584434 E: dwrdunn@gmail.com

DUNN, Florence Patricia. b 37. Ches Coll of HE BTh 02. NOC 99. **d** 02 **p** 03. NSM Basford *Lich* 02–17; PtO 18–21. *213 Newcastle Road, Trent Vale, Stoke-on-Trent ST4 6PU* T: (01782) 846417

DUNN, Graham Stuart. b 77. K Coll Lon BA 99 MA 00 AKC 99 Cam Univ BTh 21. Westcott Ho Cam 19. **d** 21. C Hampstead St Jo *Lon* from 21. *10A Dennington Park Mansions, 267-279 West End Lane, London NW6 1QR* E: grahamdunn77@hotmail.co.uk

DUNN, John Frederick. b 44. Trin Coll Bris 71. **d** 74 **p** 75. C Carl St Jo 74–77; C Tooting Graveney St Nic *S'wark* 77–82; V Attleborough *Cov* 85; PtO *Cant* 86–02; V Tipton St Martin and St Paul *Lich* 02–14; rtd 14. *16 School Crescent, Godshill, Ventnor PO38 3JL*

DUNN, Julian. b 46. Open Univ BA 83. K Coll Lon 67 St Aug Coll Cant 70. **d** 71 **p** 72. C Hanworth All Saints *Lon* 71–74; C Kidlington *Ox* 74–76; C-in-c Cleethorpes St Fran CD *Linc* 76–77; TV Cleethorpes 77–85; Chapl Friarage and Distr Hosp Northallerton 85–88; Chapl Broadmoor Hosp Crowthorne 88; Ind Chapl *York* 88–89; P-in-c Micklefield 88–89; PtO *Ox* from 95; rtd 11. *timbles brewery (sic), 1 Lewington Close, Great Haseley, Oxford OX44 7LS* T: (01844) 279687 E: eisendora@aol.com

DUNN (née LEE), Mrs Mary Elizabeth. b 49. Open Univ BA 81 Bp Grosseteste Coll CertEd 78. St Mich Coll Llan 08. **d** 09 **p** 10. NSM Malpas *Mon* 09–11; NSM Llanfair Caereinion, Llanllugan and Manafon *St As* 11–16; rtd 16; PtO *St D* from 17; *Llan* from 17; *S & B* from 17. *100 Parc Gilbertson, Gelligron, Pontardawe, Swansea SA8 4PU* T: (01792) 862143 E: ourmarylou@gmail.com

DUNN, Michael Henry James. b 34. Em Coll Cam BA 56 MA 62. Cuddesdon Coll 57 and 62. **d** 62 **p** 63. C Chatham St Steph *Roch* 62–66; C Bromley SS Pet and Paul 66–70; V Roch St Justus 70–83; P-in-c Malvern Wells and Wyche *Worc* 83–85; P-in-c Lt Malvern, Malvern Wells and Wyche 85–97; rtd 97; PtO *Worc* from 97. *253 Oldbury Road, Worcester WR2 6JT* T: (01905) 429938

DUNN, Pat. See DUNN, Florence Patricia

DUNN, Paul James Hugh. b 55. Lon Univ BD 80 MSc 08 Plymouth Univ MA 04 Greenwich Univ DMin 93. Ripon Coll Cuddesdon. **d** 83 **p** 84. C Wandsworth St Paul *S'wark* 83–87; C Richmond St Mary w St Matthias and St Jo 88–92; TV Wimbledon 92–98; V Ham St Rich 98–17. *Address temp unknown* E: pjhdunn@gmail.com

DUNN, Sharon Louise. See GOBLE, Sharon Louise

DUNN, Simon David. b 69. Trin Coll Bris BA 08. **d** 08 **p** 09. C Stoke Gifford *Bris* 08–11; TV Chippenham St Paul w Hardenhuish etc 11–14; P-in-c from 14; TV Kington St Michael 11–14. *Damsan House, Old Hardenhuish Lane, Chippenham SN14 6HH* T: (01249) 324944 M: 07904-733141 E: simon_dunn@hotmail.co.uk

DUNN, Canon Struan Huthwaite. b 43. Ch Coll Hobart 66 Moore Th Coll Sydney ThL 68 Clifton Th Coll 68. **d** 70 **p** 71. C Orpington Ch Ch *Roch* 70–74; C Cheltenham St Mary *Glouc* 74–76; C Welling *Roch* 76–79; Chapl Barcelona w Casteldefels *Eur* 79–83; R Addington w Trottiscliffe *Roch* 83–89; P-in-c Ryarsh w Birling 83–89; P-in-c S Gillingham 89–90; TR 90–96; R/D Gillingham 91–96; R Meopham w Nurstead 96–08; Hon Can Roch Cathl 97–08; rtd 08; Chapl HM Pris Standford Hill 09–18; PtO *Cant* from 08; *Roch* from 08. *18 Blenheim Avenue, Faversham ME13 8NR* T: (01795) 531700 E: struanhdunn@talktalk.net

DUNNAN, Donald Stuart. b 59. Harvard Univ AB 80 AM 81 Ch Ch Ox BA 85 MA 90 DPhil 91. Gen Th Sem (NY) 86. **d** 86 **p** 87. USA 86–87; Lib Pusey Ho 87–89; LtO *Ox* 87–92; PtO *Cant* 87–92; Chapl Linc Coll Ox 90–92; USA from 92. *St James School, 17641 College Road, St James MD 21781-9900, USA* E: dsdunnan@stjames.edu

DUNNE, The Very Revd Dermot Patrick Martin. b 59. Dub City Univ BA 04 MA 12. St Patr Coll Maynooth 78 CITC 98. **d** 83 **p** 84. In RC Ch 83–95; Dean's V Ch Ch Cathl Dublin *D & G* 99–01; I Crosspatrick Gp *C, F & O* 01–08; Prec Ferns Cathl 04–08; Adn Ferns 07–08; Dean Ch Ch Cathl Dublin *D & G* from 08. *Christ Church Deanery, Werburgh Street, Dublin 8, D08 WTC0, Republic of Ireland* T: (00353) (1) 677 8099 F: 679 8991 M: 87-986 5073 E: dean@christchurch.ie

DUNNE, Kevin Headley. b 43. Cranmer Hall Dur 85. **d** 87 **p** 88. C Chester le Street *Dur* 87–90; V S Hetton w Haswell 90–94; P-in-c Oxclose 94–02; R Chester le Street 02–08; AD Chester-le-Street 97–02 and 04–08; rtd 08; Chapl Sherburn Hosp Dur 09–13; PtO *Dur* from 13; *Eur* from 15. *7 Fir Tree Close, Durham DH1 1DT* T: 0191-375 0397 E: revdunne@btopenworld.com

DUNNE, The Very Revd Nigel Kenneth. b 66. TCD BA 88 BTh 90 MA 00 MPhil 00. **d** 90 **p** 91. C Dublin St Bart w Leeson Park *D & G* 90–93; C Taney 93–95; I Blessington w Kilbride, Ballymore Eustace etc 95–03; Can Ch Ch Cathl Dublin 01–03; I Bandon Union *C, C & R* 03–07; Dean Cork from 07; I Cork St Fin Barre's Union from 07. *The Deanery, Gilabbey Street, Cork, Republic of Ireland* T: (00353) (21) 431 8073 E: dean@cork.anglican.org

DUNNETT, Canon John Frederick. b 58. SS Coll Cam MA 84 Worc Coll Ox MSc 83 CQSW 82. Trin Coll Bris BA 87. **d** 88 **p** 89. C Kirkheaton *Wakef* 88–93; V Cranham Park *Chelmsf* 93–06; Public Preacher from 06; Gen Dir CPAS from 06; Hon Can Chelmsf Cathl from 20. *39 Crescent Road, Warley, Brentwood CM14 5JR* T: (01277) 221419 or (01926) 458427 E: jd@johndunnett.co.uk *or* jdunnett@cpas.org.uk

DUNNETT, Keith Owen. b 66. Cranfield Inst of Tech BSc 87. Trin Coll Bris BA 00. **d** 00 **p** 01. C Walton and Trimley *St E*

00–03; V Clayton *Bradf* 03–11; C Abingdon *Ox* 11–13; C N Abingdon 13–18; V from 18. *33 North Avenue, Abingdon OX14 1QW* M: 07974-081354 E: keith@cca.uk.net

DUNNETT, Nigella. *See* YOUNGS-DUNNETT, Elizabeth Nigella

DUNNETT, Robert Curtis. b 31. SS Coll Cam BA 54 MA 58. Oak Hill Th Coll 56. **d** 58 **p** 59. C Markfield *Leic* 58–60; C Bucknall and Bagnall *Lich* 60–73; Chapl and Tutor Birm Bible Inst 72–79; Vice-Prin 84–92; Hon Vice-Prin 92–05; PtO *Birm* 72–16; *Truro* from 16. *Potters Garden, Polcoverack Lane, Coverack, Helston TR12 6TD* T: (01362) 280964 E: dunnett670@btinternet.com

DUNNING, Adam Jonathan. b 73. Regent's Park Coll Ox BA 95 MA 99 Birm Univ PhD 00 Wolv Univ CertEd 05. Westcott Ho Cam 97. **d** 99 **p** 00. C Evesham w Norton and Lenchwick *Worc* 99–02; C Hamstead St Paul *Birm* 02–03; Hon C Moseley St Mary and Moseley St Anne 03–05; P-in-c The Ortons, Alwalton and Chesterton *Ely* 06–10; V Orton Longueville w Bottlebridge 10–11; Sen Chapl Cheltenham Coll from 11. *4 Waterfield Close, Cheltenham GL53 7NL* T: (01242) 228774 M: 07970-503909 E: a.dunning@cheltenhamcollege.org

DUNNINGS, Reuben Edward. b 36. Clifton Th Coll 62. **d** 66 **p** 67. C Longfleet *Sarum* 66–70; C Melksham 70–73; TV 73–78; R Broughton Gifford w Gt Chalfield 78–84; V Holt St Kath 78–84; R Broughton Gifford, Gt Chalfield and Holt 85–86; V Salisbury St Fran 86–99; P-in-c Stratford sub Castle 98–99; V Salisbury St Fran and Stratford sub Castle 99–01; rtd 01; PtO *Sarum* from 01. *11 Cornbrash Rise, Hilperton, Trowbridge BA14 7TS* T: (01225) 768834 E: reubendunnings@talktalk.net

DUNSETH, George William. b 52. Multnomah Sch of the Bible Oregon BRE 79. Oak Hill Th Coll BA 85. **d** 85 **p** 86. C Cheadle All Hallows *Ches* 85–88; C New Borough and Leigh *Sarum* 88–91; V Thurnby w Stoughton *Leic* 91–06; PtO 07–08; P-in-c Leic St Leon CD 08–14; rtd 14. *33 Nutfield Road, Leicester LE3 1AN* E: george.dunseth@sky.com

DUNSTAN, The Very Revd Gregory John Orchard. b 50. Cam Univ MA 75 TCD BTh 90. CITC 87. **d** 90 **p** 91. C Ballymena w Ballyclug *Conn* 90–93; I Belfast St Matt 93–11; Preb Swords St Patr Cathl Dublin 07–11; Dean Arm and Keeper of Public Lib from 11. *The Deanery, Library House, 43 Abbey Street, Armagh BT61 7DY* T: (028) 3751 8447 or 3752 3142 M: 07986-327333 E: dean@armagh.anglican.org

DUNSTAN, Kenneth Ian. b 40. Goldsmiths' Coll Lon BEd 71 ACP. Oak Hill NSM Course 86. **d** 88 **p** 89. NSM Creeksea w Althorne, Latchingdon and N Fambridge *Chelmsf* 88–94; P-in-c Woodham Mortimer w Hazeleigh 94–98; P-in-c Woodham Walter 94–98; NSM Bradwell on Sea 99–05; rtd 05; PtO *Chelmsf* 05–13; P-in-c Mayland 13–15. *35 Ely Close, Southminster CM0 7AQ* T: (01621) 772199 E: kandk@uwclub.net

DUNSTAN, Mark Philip. b 70. Middx Univ BSc 93. Oak Hill Th Coll BA 03. **d** 03 **p** 04. C Stranton *Dur* 03–06; P-in-c Hunsdon w Widford and Wareside *St Alb* 06–15; R from 15; RD Hertford and Ware from 21. *The Rectory, Acorn Street, Hunsdon, Ware SG12 8PB* T: (01920) 877276 E: dunstan_mark@hotmail.com

DUNSTAN-MEADOWS, Victor Richard. b 63. Chich Th Coll BTh 90. **d** 90 **p** 91. C Clacton St Jas *Chelmsf* 90–93; C Stansted Mountfitchet 93–95; CF 95–00; Chapl RAF 00–10; P-in-c Up Hatherley *Glouc* 10–13; V 13–18. *Address withheld by request* M: 07712-050629 E: rev.rdm@gmail.com

DUNTHORNE, Paul. b 63. K Coll Lon LLB 85 St Jo Coll Dur BA 96 Dur Univ MA 98. Cranmer Hall Dur 88. **d** 91 **p** 92. C Heacham and Sedgeford *Nor* 91–95; C Eastbourne H Trin *Chich* 95–98; P-in-c Preston and Ridlington w Wing and Pilton *Pet* 98–00; Local Min Officer 98–00; CME Officer *Heref* 00–06; TR Ledbury 06–14; Preb Heref Cathl 12–14; Miss and Tr Adv Win Sch of Miss 14–18; Dean Lic Min Tr 18–20; Prin IME 1 Cumbria Chr Learning *Carl* 20–21; Cen Lead Tutor Em Th Coll from 21. *11 Crocus Avenue, Penrith CA11 8FE* M: 07896-004428 E: paul.dunthorne@emmanueltheologicalcollege.org.uk

DUNTON, Stephen. b 72. Birm Univ BA 93 Paisley Univ PGCE 94. St Mary's RC Sem Birm 07 Ripon Coll Cuddesdon 18. **d** 11 **p** 19. C Pershore w Pinvin, Wick and Birlingham *Worc* from 19. *8 Hanson Way, Pershore WR10 1QW*

DUNWICH, Suffragan Bishop of. *See* HARRISON, The Rt Revd Michael Robert

DUNWOODY, Stephen John Herbert. b 71. Glam Univ BA 92. St Steph Ho Ox BTh 96. **d** 96 **p** 97. C Skewen *Llan* 96–98; C Roath 98–99; C Stanley *Liv* 99–02; TV Colyton, Southleigh, Offwell, Widworthy etc *Ex* 02–03; V Offwell, Northleigh, Farway, Cotleigh etc 03–05; CF from 05; Chapl Guards Chpl Lon 16–19. *c/o MOD Chaplains (Army)* T: (01264)

383430 F: 381824 E: stephendunwoody@hotmail.com *or* stephen.dunwoody954@mod.gov.uk

DUNWOODY, Thomas Herbert Williamson. b 35. TCD BA 58 MA 64. TCD Div Sch Div Test 59. **d** 59 **p** 60. C Newcastle *D & D* 59–61; Asst Missr Ballymacarrett St Martin 61–63; C Lurgan Ch the Redeemer 63–66; I Ardglass w Dunsford 66–74; OCM 66–74; V Urmston *Man* 74–85; I Wexford w Ardcolm and Killurin *C, F & O* 85–93; Can Ferns Cathl 88–93; I Newry *D & D* 93–02; rtd 02. *36 Godfrey Avenue, Bangor BT20 5LS* T: (028) 9145 3918 E: thw_d@tiscali.co.uk

DÜNZKOFER, Markus. b 69. Edin Univ MTh 94. Seabury-Western Th Sem MDiv 98. **d** 99 **p** 99. C Evanston St Matt USA 99–04; R Vancouver St Paul Canada 04–12; R Edin St Jo from 13. *1 Ainslie Place, Edinburgh EH3 6AR* T: 0131-225 5004 *or* 229 7565 M: 07962-536817 E: office@stjohns-edinburgh.org.uk *or* mduenz@gmail.com

DUPRÉ, Robin Charles. b 50. Nottm Univ BA 72 Worc Coll of Educn PGCE 76. SWMTC 08. **d** 11 **p** 12. NSM Jersey Grouville Win 11–18; PtO from 18. *Le Picachon, 4 Le Clos Royale, La Rue de la Ville es Renauds, Grouville, Jersey JE3 9DF* T: (01534) 856378 M: 07829-936250 E: dupre@freeuk.com

DUPREE, Hugh Douglas. b 50. Univ of the South (USA) BA 72 Virginia Th Sem MDiv 75 Ch Ch Ox MA 86 Ball Coll Ox DPhil 88. **d** 75 **p** 76. USA 75–80; Hon C Ox St Mich w St Martin and All SS 80–87; Asst Chapl Ball Coll Ox 84–87; Chapl 87–14; Dean 07–14; Chapl HM Pris Ox 88–97; rtd 14; R Bp's Inst for Min Florida USA from 15. *Diocesan House, 325 N Market Street, Jacksonville , Florida 32202 USA* T: (001) (904) 356 1328 M: 904-504-7042 E: ddupree@diocesefl.org

DURAND, Noel Douglas. b 33. Jes Coll Cam BA 57 MA 61 BD 76. Westcott Ho Cam 72. **d** 74 **p** 75. C Eaton *Nor* 74–78; V Cumnor *Ox* 78–01; rtd 01; PtO *Nor* from 01. *74 Amderley Drive, Norwich NR4 6JH* T: (01603) 501764 E: douglas.ismene@gmail.com

DURAND, Canon Stella Evelyn Brigid, Lady. b 42. TCD BA 64 Sorbonne Univ Paris DèS 65 UCD MLitt 04 NUI PhD 12. CITC BTh 99. **d** 00. C Kiltegan w Hacketstown, Clonmore and Moyne *C, F & O* 00–03; 103–17; Can Ossory Cathl 14–17; rtd 17. *Lisnalurg House, Sligo, Co Sligo, F91 XD30, Republic of Ireland* T: (00353) (71) 914 5819 E: stelladurand@gmail.com

DURANT, Lucas Crain. b 85. Wheaton Coll Illinois BA 07 Leuven Univ Belgium MA 08. Wycliffe Hall Ox 15. **d** 15 **p** 16. C Wootton *St Alb* 15–19; P-in-c Resurrection Hong Kong from 19. *5 Well Do Villas, Wong Chuk Wan Village, Tai Mong Tsai Road, Sai Kung, NT, Hong Kong, China* M: (00852) 8481 2116 E: lucas.durant@gmail.com

DURANT, Samuel John. b 85. Univ Coll Lon LLB 06. Wycliffe Hall Ox 12. **d** 15 **p** 16. C Linc St Pet in Eastgate 15–19; R Skellingthorpe w Doddington from 19. *The Rectory, Vicarage Drive, Skellingthorpe, Lincoln LN6 5UY* E: sam@stlawrenceskellingthorpe.co.uk

DURANT, William John Nicholls. b 55. K Coll Lon BA 76 Southn Univ PGCE 11. St Jo Coll Nottm 77. **d** 80 **p** 81. C Norwood St Luke *S'wark* 80–83; C Morden 83–88; TV 88–92; V Frindsbury w Upnor *Roch* 92–00; CF 00–13; V Vale *Ox* from 13; AD Wantage from 20. *The Vicarage, Main Street, Grove, Wantage OX12 7LQ* T: (01235) 766484 E: vicar@valebenefice.org.uk

DURANT-STEVENSEN, Mrs Helen Mary. b 53. Saffron Walden Coll TCert 74. Trin Coll Bris BA 04. **d** 04 **p** 05. C S Croydon Em *S'wark* 04–08; C New Malden and Coombe 08–18; AD Kingston 16–18; rtd 18; PtO *Sarum* from 19. *7 Caspian Gardens, Westbury BA13 3GP*

DURBIN, James. b 70. Victoria Univ Wellington BA 93 MA 96 Ches Univ MA 18. Oak Hill Th Coll BA 13. **d** 13 **p** 14. C Barnston *Ches* 13–16; C Waverton w Aldford and Bruera 16–17; PtO 17; CF from 17. *c/o MOD Chaplains (Army)* T: (01362) 627972 M: 07411-226948 E: durbin1970@gmail.com

DURBIN, Roger. b 41. Bris Sch of Min 83. **d** 85 **p** 86. NSM Bedminster *Bris* 85–91; NSM Henbury 91–94; NSM Clifton All SS w St Jo 94–11; PtO from 11. *13 Charbury Walk, Bristol BS11 9UU* T: 0117-985 8404

DURDANT-HOLLAMBY, Samuel. b 88. Ches Univ BA 10. St Mellitus Coll BA 19. **d** 20 **p** 21. C Hoole *Ches* –20 and from 20. *23 Linden Grove, Chester CH2 3JU* M: 07908-232049 E: sd-h@live.com

DURHAM, Miss Bethany Helen. b 58. Cranmer Hall Dur 86. **d** 89 **p** 94. C Newark *S'well* 89–93; rtd 93; PtO *S'well* 93–14. *c/o Crockford, Church House, 27 Great Smith Street, London SW1P 3AZ*

DURHAM, Mrs Eleanore Jane. b 62. St Andr Univ MTheol 84 Liv Hope Univ PhD 17. Trin Coll Bris MA 01. **d** 01 **p** 02. C Childwall All SS *Liv* 01–05; P-in-c Hunts Cross 05–12; TV Halewood and Hunts Cross 12–18; P-in-c Wheathill Priory Gp *B & W* from 18. *The Rectory, Church Street, Keinton Mandeville,*

Somerton TA11 6ER T: (01458) 223417 M: 07421-700242 E: rev.jane.durham@gmail.com

DURHAM, Archdeacon of. *See* WILKINSON, The Ven Elizabeth Mary

DURHAM, Bishop of. *See* BUTLER, The Rt Revd Paul Roger

DURHAM, Dean of. *See* TREMLETT, The Very Revd Andrew

DURIE, David James. b 63. Cen Lancs Univ BA 93 St Martin's Coll Lanc MA 99. CBDTI 97. **d** 99 **p** 00. C Briercliffe *Blackb* 99–01; P-in-c Edin St Dav 02–13. *20 Brucehaven Crescent, Limekilns, Dunfermline KY11 3JJ* T: (01890) 781542 E: patricia.durie@btinternet.com

DURING, Arthur Christopher. b 59. Sierra Leone Th Hall 80. **d** 83 **p** 85. C Freetown H Trin Sierra Leone 83–85; C St Geo Cathl 85–86; PtO *S'wark* 00–05. *22 Challice Way, London SW2 3RD* T: (020) 8671 7678 E: aduring@hotmail.co.uk

DURKIN, Anthony Michael. b 45. Sarum & Wells Th Coll 87. **d** 89 **p** 90. C Faversham *Cant* 89–92; V St Margarets-at-Cliffe w Westcliffe etc 92–09; rtd 09; PtO *Sarum* 10–20. *Church Cottage, Leigh, Sherborne DT9 6HL* T: (01935) 872117 E: anthonyd916@btinternet.com

DURKIN, Mrs Derath May. b 52. N Staffs Poly LLB 87. SAOMC 01. **d** 02 **p** 03. C Harlington Ch Ch CD *Lon* 02–06; TV Brentford 06–14; rtd 14; PtO *Truro* from 14. *35 Fore Street, Newlyn, Penzance TR18 5JP* T: (01736) 369176 M: 07962-168440 E: derath@btinternet.com

DURLEY, Jonathan Richard Hall. b 66. Wolv Univ BA 97 Ch Ch Coll Cant MA 01. S Wales Ord Course 04. **d** 05 **p** 06. C Canton Cardiff *Llan* 05–07; C Newton Nottage 07–10; P-in-c Kenfig Hill from 10. *The Vicarage, 5 Redman Close, Kenfig Hill, Bridgend CF33 6BF* T: (01656) 670148 E: fatherjon@btinternet.com

DURNDELL, Miss Irene Frances. b 43. Trin Coll Bris 84. **dss** 86 **d** 87 **p** 94. Erith Ch Ch *Roch* 86–93; Par Dn 87–93; Par Dn Erith St Paul 93–94; C 94–98; Asst Dir of Tr 93–98; V Falconwood 98–07; rtd 07; PtO *Chich* 12–17. *17A Buxton Drive, Bexhill-on-Sea TN39 4BA* T: (01424) 810477

DURNFORD, Canon Catherine Margaret. b 36. St Mary's Coll Dur BA 57. Gilmore Course 78 NW Ord Course 77. **d** 87 **p** 94. Area Sec USPG York and Ripon 82–89; Par Dn Whitby *York* 89–92; Par Dn Redcar 92–94; C Selby Abbey 94–97; V New Marske and Wilton 97–03; Can and Preb York Minster 01–03; rtd 03; PtO *York* from 03. *18 Canongate, Cottingham HU16 4DG* T: (01482) 844868 E: cmdurnford@gmail.com

DUROSE, Harry William. b 54. **d** 14 **p** 15. OLM Stoke-upon-Trent and Fenton *Lich* from 14. *48 Lime Street, Stoke-on-Trent ST4 4EF* T: (01782) 863956 E: badger_bill1954@yahoo.co.uk

DURRAN, Ms Margaret. Surrey Univ MSc 96 Lady Spencer Chu Coll of Educn CertEd 70. S'wark Ord Course 88. **d** 91 **p** 94. Par Dn Brixton St Matt *S'wark* 91–94; C Streatham St Leon 94–95; V Walworth St Chris 95–99; Hon C S'wark St Geo w St Alphege and St Jude 99–09; Hist Churches Project Officer *Lon* 99–07; rtd 08; PtO *Ox* from 09. *8 Bath Terrace, Victoria Road, Bicester OX26 6PR* M: 07739-988742

DURRANS, Mrs Janet. b 58. Westcott Ho Cam 09. **d** 11 **p** 12. C Chislehurst St Nic *Roch* 11–16; P-in-c St Peter-in-Thanet *Cant* 16–18; V from 18. *St Peter's Vicarage, 14 Vicarage Street, Broadstairs CT10 2SG* T: (01843) 869169 M: 07585-660621 E: revjandurrans@gmail.com

DURRANT, James Mark. b 89. York Univ BSc 11. Cranmer Hall Dur BA 16. **d** 16 **p** 17. C Derby St Alkmund and St Werburgh 16–19 and from 20; C Derby Cathl 19–20; P-in-c Derby St Paul from 20. *6 Old Chester Road, Derby DE1 3SA* E: jamesdurrant@sky.com *or* james@stalkmunds.org.uk *or* stpaulschestergreen@gmail.com

DURRANT, Melvyn Richard Bloomfield. b 59. Leeds Univ BA 82 St Luke's Coll Ex PGCE 86. Trin Coll Bris 01. **d** 03 **p** 04. C Watercombe *Sarum* 03–06; C Moreton and Woodsford w Tincleton 03–06; P-in-c Sixpenny Handley w Gussage St Andrew etc 06–18; C Chase 06–18; rtd 18. *1 Knole Court, Knole Road, Bexhill-on-Sea TN40 1LN* E: mdurrant22@icloud.com

DURRANT, Simon James. b 82. R Academy of Music BMus 04 LRAM 03. Trin Coll Bris BA 11. **d** 12 **p** 13. C Tiverton St Geo and St Paul *Ex* 12–16; V Roxeth *Lon* from 16. *Christ Church Vicarage, Roxeth Hill, Harrow HA2 0JN* T: (020) 8423 3168 M: 07898-350791 E: simondurrant7@me.com

DURSTON, Canon David Michael Karl. b 36. Em Coll Cam BA 60 MA 64. Clifton Th Coll 61. **d** 63 **p** 64. C Wednesfield Heath *Lich* 63–66; Project Officer Grubb Inst 67–78; Ind Chapl *Lich* 78–84; P-in-c W Bromwich St Paul 78–82; V 82–84; Adult Educn Officer 84–92; Preb Lich Cathl 89–92; Can Res and Chan Sarum Cathl 92–03; Can and Preb Sarum Cathl 03–06; TR Wylye and Till Valley 03–06; rtd 06; PtO *Sarum* from 06. *26 Mill Road, Salisbury SP2 7RZ* T: (01722) 334017 E: david.durston36@btinternet.com

DURUEKE, Collins. b 71. St Mellitus Coll 12. **d** 12 **p** 17. PtO *S'wark* 15–17; NSM Camberwell St Luke from 17. *83 Dawes House, Orb Street, London SE17 1RD* T: (020) 3561 6910 M: 07862-285672 E: collinsdurueke@yahoo.com

DURWARD, Rosemary. b 58. **d** 10 **p** 11. NSM Notting Hill St Jo *Lon* 10–12; PtO *Win* from 14; Hon Chapl Win Cathl 14–19; PtO *Guildf* 17–18; NSM E Horsley from 18. *Address withheld by request* E: rose@easthorsleychurch.org.uk

DUSSEK, Canon Jeremy Neil James Christopher. b 70. St Jo Coll Dur BA 92. Westcott Ho Cam 96. **d** 97 **p** 98. C Whickham *Dur* 97–00; C Fareham H Trin *Portsm* 00–01; TV 01–07; V Moseley St Mary and St Anne *Birm* 07–14; Can Res Ches Cathl from 14. *9 Abbey Street, Chester CH1 2JF* T: (01244) 500967 E: canon.precentor@chestercathedral.com

DUTHIE, Elliot Malcolm. b 31. Clifton Th Coll 63. **d** 66 **p** 67. C Eccleston St Luke *Liv* 66–69; Malaysia 70–75; P-in-c Bootle St Leon *Liv* 76–78; V 78–81; V Charlton Kings H Apostles *Glouc* 81–94; rtd 94; PtO *Glouc* 94–00; Ex 02–05; *Derby* 06–18. *25 De Ferrers Court, Tamworth Street, Duffield, Belper DE56 4HL* T: (01332) 843630 E: emduthie@btinternet.com

DUTTON, Antony John. b 82. Newc Univ BA 04 Liv Univ MTh 08 Ches Univ PGCE 08. Ripon Coll Cuddesdon BA 11 MSt 12. **d** 12 **p** 13. C Malpas and Threapwood and Bickerton *Ches* 12–14; V Gt Sutton from 14. *15 The Paddock, Great Sutton, Ellesmere Port CH66 2NN* T: 0151-339 9916 M: 07976-819114 E: ant_sjd@hotmail.com

DUTTON, Leonard Arthur. b 35. Bps' Coll Cheshunt 63. **d** 66 **p** 67. C Knighton St Jo *Leic* 66–70; C Chilvers Coton w Astley Cov 70–73; R Hathern *Leic* 73–79; V Ashby-de-la-Zouch H Trin 79–04; rtd 04; PtO *Leic* 04–16. *8 Merganser Way, Coalville LE67 4QA* T: (01530) 815420 E: lenmeg@uwclub.net

DUTTON, Sandra Rosemary. b 50. Ripon Coll Cuddesdon 03. **d** 04 **p** 05. NSM Chatham St Steph *Roch* 04–08; TV Hartshill, Penkhull and Trent Vale *Lich* 08–12; TR 12–13; R 13–14; P-in-c Rackheath and Salhouse *Nor* 14–17; rtd 17; PtO *Nor* from 17. *12 Blackthorn Close, Diss IP22 4ZA* T: (01379) 309012 E: sandydutton@hotmail.com

DUXBURY, Brian. b 59. **d** 13 **p** 14. NSM Drighlington *Wakef* 13–14; NSM Gildersome 13–14; Drighlington and Gildersome *Leeds* from 14. *27 Highfield Drive, Gildersome, Morley, Leeds LS27 7DW* T: 0113-252 6949 E: briandux@f2s.com

DUXBURY, Clive Robert. b 49. Open Univ BA(ThM) 06. St Jo Coll Nottm 90. **d** 92 **p** 93. C Horwich and Rivington *Man* 92–96; P-in-c Bury St Paul and Bury Ch King 98–00; P-in-c Freethorpe, Wickhampton, Halvergate w Tunstall *Nor* 00–02; P-in-c Reedham w Cantley w Limpenhoe and Southwood 00–02; R Freethorpe, Wickhampton, Halvergate etc 02–05; RD Blofield 04–05; R High Ongar w Norton Mandeville *Chelmsf* 05–08; Chapl HM Pris Everthorpe 08–14; Hon C Elloughton and Brough w Brantingham *York* 11–14; rtd 14; P-in-c S Rodings *Chelmsf* 14–17. *33 Mayfield Avenue, Holme, Carnforth LA6 1PT* T: (01524) 935261 M: 07368-565563 E: crduxbury1@sky.com

DWYER, James Richard. b 86. K Coll Lon BA 10 AKC 10. Wycliffe Hall Ox MTh 18. **d** 18 **p** 19. C Ox St Andr from 18. *5 Squitchey Lane, Oxford OX2 7LD* M: 07885-257932 E: jamesd522@gmail.com

DYAS, Stuart Edwin. b 46. Lon Univ BSc 67. Ridley Hall Cam 78. **d** 80 **p** 81. C Bath Weston St Jo w Kelston *B & W* 80–83; C Tunbridge Wells St Jas *Roch* 83–90; V Nottingham St Jude *S'well* 90–99; AD Nottingham Cen 93–98; V Long Eaton St Jo *Derby* 99–05; rtd 05; PtO *Derby* 05–15; *S'well* 14–15; *York* from 15. *50 Meadlands, York YO31 0NS* T: (01904) 427964

DYAS, Sylvia Denise (Dee). b 51. Bedf Coll Lon BA 72 Nottm Univ PhD 99. St Jo Coll Nottm MA 00. **d** 00 **p** 01. Dir Cen for Study of Christianity and Culture *York* from 99; Tutor St Jo Coll Nottm 00–12; PtO *Derby* 00–04; *S'well* 12–15; *York* from 15. *50 Meadlands, York YO31 0NS* T: (01904) 427964 E: dee.dyas@york.ac.uk

DYBALL, Rebecca Mary. b 82. Ridley Hall Cam 15. **d** 17 **p** 18. C The Ramseys and Upwood *Ely* 17–19; P-in-c Sawtry and Glatton 19; V Sawtry, Glatton and Holme w Conington from 20. *The Rectory, Church Causeway, Sawtry, Huntingdon PE28 5TD* M: 07484-234961 E: beckycurate@gmail.com

DYBLE, Ian Hugh. b 64. Anglia Poly LLB 85 Leic Univ MSc 98. Ridley Hall Cam 08. **d** 10 **p** 11. C Onslow Square and S Kensington St Aug *Lon* 10–13; P-in-c Heigham St Thos *Nor* 13–17; C Nor Lakenham St Alb and St Mark 15–17; P-in-c Heigham St Barn w St Bart 17; V The Mitre Benefice 17–20; RD Nor S 16–19; C Earlham 18–20; C Costessey 19–20; P-in-c Weybourne Gp from 20; Dioc Dir Ch Revitalisation from 19. *17 Back Lane, Blakeney, Holt NR25 7NP* M: 07884-037637 E: reviandyble@gmail.com

DYE, Mrs Margaret Mary. b 48. NOC 95. **d** 98 **p** 99. C Morley St Pet w Churwell *Wakef* 98–02; TV Morley 02–08; TR 08–13;

rtd 13; PtO *York* from 13. *5 Church Lane, Hutton, Driffield YO25 9PS* T: (01377) 271953 E: thedyes5@btinternet.com

DYE, Mervyn John. b 53. **d** 18 **p** 19. NSM Ipswich St Mary at Stoke w St Pet and St Fran *St E* 18–21; NSM Ipswich St Pet Stoke Park from 21. *Address withheld by request* T: (01473) 601750 M: 07982-236074 E: revmerv@switmparish.org.uk

DYER, Adrian Louis. b 67. Cant Univ (NZ) BA 02 Auckland Univ BTheol 03. **d** 04 **p** 05. C Methven NZ 04–06; V Ellesmere 06–09; Chapl RAF from 09. *Chaplaincy Services (RAF), HQ Air Command, RAF High Wycombe HP14 4UE* T: (01494) 496800

⌖**DYER, The Rt Revd Anne Catherine.** b 57. St Anne's Coll Ox MA 80 Lon Univ MTh 89. Wycliffe Hall Ox 84. **d** 87 **p** 94 **c** 18. NSM Beckenham St Jo *Roch* 87–88; NSM Beckenham St Geo 88–89; Hon Par Dn Luton Ch Ch 89–94; Chapl for Evang 93–98; NSM Istead Rise 94–98; Min Development Officer 98–04; Hon Can Roch Cathl 00–04; Warden Cranmer Hall Dur 05–11; Hon Can Dur Cathl 08–11; R Haddington *Edin* 11–18; Bp Ab from 18. *Ashley House, Ashley Gardens, Aberdeen AB10 6RQ* T: (01224) 208142 E: bishop@aberdeen.anglican.org

DYER, Ms Catherine Jane. b 46. Westf Coll Lon BA 68. Ox NSM Course 85. **d** 88 **p** 94. NSM Wokingham All SS *Ox* 88–90; C 90–95; TV W Slough 95–01; P-in-c Linslade 01–07; AD Mursley 03–06; rtd 07; PtO *Sarum* from 15. *45 Shady Bower, Salisbury SP1 2RG* T: (01722) 502781 E: catherine.dyer46@hotmail.co.uk

DYER, Canon Christine Anne. b 53. Nottm Univ BEd 75 MA 97. EMMTC 81. **dss** 84 **d** 87 **p** 94. Mickleover St Jo *Derby* 85–90; Par Dn 87–90; Dioc Voc Adv 86–90; Par Educn Adv 90–98; Dioc Youth Officer 91–98; P-in-c Morton and Stonebroom 98–99; P-in-c Shirland 98–99; R Morton and Stonebroom w Shirland 99–06; P-in-c Allestree 06–10; P-in-c Darley Abbey 06–10; V Allestree St Edm and Darley Abbey 10–15; Hon Can Derby Cathl 02–15; rtd 15; PtO *Derby* from 15. *22 Phildock Wood Road, Derby DE22 4PH* E: c.a.dyer.t21@btinternet.com *or* c.a.dyer@talk21.com

DYER, Fraser Colin. b 65. SEITE. **d** 09 **p** 10. C De Beauvoir Town St Pet *Lon* 09–12; P-in-c S Lambeth St Anne and All SS *S'wark* 12–17; V from 17. *The Vicarage, 179 Fentiman Road, London SW8 1JY* T: (020) 7735 3191 E: revdfraserdyer@gmail.com

DYER, Mrs Gillian Marie. b 50. Sheff Univ BA 71 Leic Univ PGCE 72. S Dios Minl Tr Scheme 81. **dss** 84 **d** 87 **p** 94. Witney *Ox* 84–85; Carl St Cuth w St Mary 86–89; Par Dn 87–89; Dioc Communications Officer 86–89; Par Dn Kirkbride w Newton Arlosh 89–91; Par Dn Carl H Trin and St Barn 91–94; TV 94–97; P-in-c Arbroath *Bre* 01–03; P-in-c Lower Darwen St Jas *Blackb* 03–10; P-in-c Whalley 10–12; P-in-c Sabden and Pendleton 10–12; V W Pendleside 12–15; PtO 15–17; *York* from 20. *19 Fountains Road, Northallerton DL6 1QR* T: (01609) 774944 E: revvygilly141@btinternet.com

DYER, Janet. b 35. LNSM course 77. **dss** 85 **d** 86 **p** 94. Balerno *Edin* 85–86; NSM 86–93; Chapl Edin R Infirmary 88–93; Dn-in-c Roslin (Rosslyn Chpl) *Edin* 93–94; P-in-c 94–97; NSM Livingston LEP 97–00; Chapl Livingstone St Jo Hosp 97–00; NSM Dalmahoy *Edin* 02–11; LtO from 11. *499 Lanark Road West, Balerno EH14 7AL* T: 0131-449 3767 E: jdyer499@googlemail.com

DYER, Mrs Joanne. b 69. Cov Univ BA 99 FCIPD. Qu Foundn Birm 15. **d** 17 **p** 18. C Woodfield *Leic* 17–20; C Whitwick, Thringstone and Swannington 20–21; R All So N Warks *Birm* from 21. *The New Vicarage, 132 Main Road, Austrey, Atherstone CV9 3EB* M: 07803-295282 E: jdyer269@btinternet.com

DYER, Mrs Kay. b 49. Open Univ BA 80. Qu Foundn Birm 14. **d** 15 **p** 16. NSM Shottery St Andr *Cov* 15–18; NSM Stratford-upon-Avon, Luddington etc from 18. *6 Sycamore Close, Stratford-upon-Avon CV37 0DZ* T: (01789) 298299 M: 07857-821168 E: revkaydyer@gmail.com

DYER, Ronald Whitfield. b 29. Solicitor 51. Guildf Dioc Min Course 91. **d** 95 **p** 96. NSM Fleet *Guildf* 95–99; rtd 99; PtO *Guildf* 99–17. *7 Dukes Mead, Fleet GU51 4HA* T: (01252) 621457

DYER, Stephen Roger. b 57. Brunel Univ BSc. Wycliffe Hall Ox 83. **d** 86 **p** 87. C Beckenham St Jo *Roch* 86–89; C Luton Ch Ch 89–94; V Istead Rise 94–01; V Frindsbury w Upnor 01–04; Hon C Easington, Easington Colliery and S Hetton *Dur* 05–09. *Ashley House, 16 Ashley Gardens, Aberdeen AB10 6RQ* T: (01224) 208142

DYER, Terence Neville. b 50. Sheff Univ BEng 71 Leic Univ PGCE 72 Open Univ MA 96. Carl Dioc Tr Course 86. **d** 89 **p** 90. NSM Kirkbride w Newton Arlosh *Carl* 89–91; NSM Carl H Trin and St Barn 91–97; NSM Arbroath *Bre* 01; P-in-c Monifieth 01–03; P-in-c Over Darwen St Jas *Blackb* 03–13; C Darwen St Pet w Hoddlesden 08–10; P-in-c Hoddlesden 10–13; V Over Darwen St Jas and Hoddlesden 13–16; rtd 16; PtO *Blackb* 16–17; P-in-c Cawood w Ryther and Wistow *York* 17–19; PtO from 20. *19 Fountains Road, Northallerton DL6 1QR* M: 07919-543475 E: terry255dyer@btinternet.com

DYKE, The Very Revd Elizabeth Muriel. b 55. St Mary's Coll Dur BSc 77 St Martin's Coll Lanc PGCE 78. Oak Hill Th Coll 92. **d** 94 **p** 95. C High Wycombe *Ox* 94–95; C W Wycombe w Bledlow Ridge, Bradenham and Radnage 95–97; TV Bedworth *Cov* 97–02; V Dunchurch 02–09; R Kidman Park and Mile End Australia 09–14; Adn Sturt 13–14; R Queanbeyan and Distr 14–18; Adn Queanbeyan, Monaro and Alpine Region 14–18; Dean Bendigo from 18. *38 Mafeking Street South, Kennington VA 3550, Australia* M: (0061) 40-950 4740 E: dean@bendigoanglican.org.au

DYKE, Kevin Robert. b 59. Sheff Univ BA 13. Coll of Resurr Mirfield 11. **d** 13 **p** 14. C Gainsborough and Morton *Linc* 13–16; TR Bottesford w Ashby from 16. *The Vicarage, St Paul's Road, Scunthorpe DN16 3DL* T: (01724) 852079 M: 07814-260467

DYKES, John Edward. b 33. Trin Coll Bris 82. **d** 84 **p** 85. C Rushden w Newton Bromswold *Pet* 84–87; R Heanton Punchardon w Marwood *Ex* 87–97; rtd 97; PtO *Guildf* 98–01; B & W from 02. *42 Ashley Road, Taunton TA1 5BP* T: (01823) 282507 E: johnvickydykes@gmail.com

DYKES, Mrs Katrina Mary. b 66. Trin Coll Bris BA 90. Guildf Dioc Min Course 03. **d** 04 **p** 05. NSM Windlesham *Guildf* 04–07; Chapl St Swithun's Sch Win 08–16; P-in-c Abbotts Ann and Upper Clatford and Goodworth Clatford *Win* 16–21; R Carlford *St E* from 21. *The Rectory, Woodbridge Road, Grundisburgh, Woodbridge IP13 6UF* M: 07922-153765 E: katrina@carlfordchurches.org

DYKES, Philip John. b 61. Loughb Univ BSc 83. Trin Coll Bris 88. **d** 91 **p** 92. C Morden *S'wark* 91–95; C St Helier 95–98; TV Camberley St Paul *Guildf* 98–99; V Camberley Heatherside 99–08; Chapl Win Univ 08–11; Dioc Adult Discipleship Adv *Win* 11–14; Evang Ch Growth and Fresh Expressions Adv 14–19; Ch Growth Missr from 19. *The Diocesan Office, Wolvesey Palace, Winchester SO23 9ND* T: (01962) 737354 E: phil.dykes@winchester.anglican.org

DYSON, Mrs Clare Louise. b 63. WMMTC 02. **d** 05 **p** 06. C Tupsley w Hampton Bishop *Heref* 05–08; P-in-c Kingstone w Clehonger, Eaton Bishop etc 08–10; R Cagebrook 10–14; NSM Cheltenham St Mary w St Matt and St Luke *Glouc* from 14. *7 Apple Orchard, Prestbury, Cheltenham GL52 3EH* E: clared@stmstm.org.uk

DYSON, Mrs Debra Anne. b 62. **d** 08 **p** 09. C Lich St Mich w St Mary and Wall 08–11; V Wigginton from 11; RD Tamworth 14–20. *The Vicarage, Comberford Lane, Wigginton, Tamworth B79 9DT* T: (01827) 690380 E: debdyson@btinternet.com

DYSON, Peter Whiteley. b 51. Man Univ BA 73 LLB 75. Qu Coll Birm 77. **d** 81 **p** 82. C Swindon Ch Ch *Bris* 81–84; P-in-c Brislington St Luke 84–91; V Bourne *Guildf* 91–92; PtO 02–04; P-in-c Herriard w Winslade and Long Sutton etc *Win* 04–08; P-in-c Newnham w Nately Scures w Mapledurwell etc 04–08; R N Hants Downs 08–16; RD Odiham 11–16; R Jersey St Sav 16–20; PtO *Win* from 21. *94 Grove Road, Chichester PO19 8AR* M: 07780-653588 E: pwdyson@btinternet.com

DYSON, Steven John. b 79. Univ of Wales (Ban) BSc 00. Trin Coll Bris BA 11. **d** 11 **p** 12. C Broadclyst, Clyst Honiton, Pinhoe, Rockbeare etc *Ex* 11–16; V Biddulph *Lich* 16–20; C Kingswood *Bris* from 20; C Hanham from 20. *The Vicarage, 30 Church Road, Hanham, Bristol BS15 3AE* M: 07753-383758 E: revstevedyson@gmail.com

DYTHAM, Linda Alison. b 52. STETS 02. **d** 05 **p** 06. NSM Savernake *Sarum* 05–14; PtO from 14; Chapl Fitzwarren Ho and Standon Lodge from 07. *10 Home Farm Close, Heddington, Calne SN11 0RH* T: (01380) 859571 M: 07921-123422 E: ladytham@btinternet.com

E

EADE, John Christopher. b 45. Ch Coll Cam BA 68 MA 72. Linc Th Coll 68. **d** 70 **p** 71. C Portsea N End St Mark *Portsm* 70–73; C Henleaze *Bris* 73–77; V Slad *Glouc* 77–82; V N Bradley, Southwick and Heywood *Sarum* 82–91; R Fovant, Sutton Mandeville and Teffont Evias etc 91–08; C Nadder Valley 06–08; TR 08–11; rtd 11; PtO *Sarum* 15–20. *Odd Acre, Ryall Road, Ryall, Bridport DT6 6EG* T: (01297) 489633 E: john@thames.me.uk

EADES, David Julian John. b 74. Univ of Wales BA 95 St Jo Coll Dur BA 99. Cranmer Hall Dur. **d** 00 **p** 01. C Walbrook Epiphany *Derby* 00–04; Chapl Essex Univ *Chelmsf* 04–06; PtO *Ox* 16–17. *62 Headingley Avenue, Leeds LS6 3ER* M: 07926-649602 E: julian_eades@yahoo.co.uk

EADON, Benjamin Myles. b 85. Univ Coll Dur BA 07 Clare Coll Cam BA 10 MA 14. Westcott Ho Cam 08. **d** 11 **p** 12. C Sunderland St Chad *Dur* 11–15; C Durrington *Chich* 15–16; P-in-c 16–19; V 19–20; V Brighton St Bart from 20; CMP from 14. *St Bartholomew's Church, Ann Street, Brighton BN1 4GP* T: (01273) 620491 E: ben.eadon@btinternet.com

EADY, Timothy William. b 57. Open Univ BA. Cranmer Hall Dur 82. **d** 85 **p** 86. C Boulton *Derby* 85–88; C Portchester *Portsm* 88–92; R Brighstone and Brooke w Mottistone 92–07; Relig Progr Adv Ocean Sound Radio 88–07; V Iver *Ox* 07–12; V Bangkok Ch Ch Thailand 12–19; C Penn Fields *Lich* from 19. *100 Bellencroft Gardens, Wolverhampton WV3 8DU* E: timothy_eady@me.com

EAGER, Ms Rosemary Anne McDowall. b 65. St Andr Univ MA 87 Strathclyde Univ 88. Ridley Hall Cam 92. **d** 95 **p** 96. C Walthamstow St Mary w St Steph *Chelmsf* 95–97; C Walthamstow 97–01; TV Bushbury *Lich* 01–05; PtO 05–07. *37 Park Dale East, Wolverhampton WV1 4TD* T: (01902) 710340 *or* 553945 E: revdrosie@yahoo.co.uk

✠**EAGLES, The Rt Revd Peter Andrew.** b 59. K Coll Lon BA 82 AKC 82 Ox Univ BA 88. St Steph Ho Ox 86. **d** 89 **p** 90 **c** 17. C Ruislip St Martin *Lon* 89–92; CF 92–17; Chapl Guards Chpl Lon 07–08; Asst Chapl Gen 08–17; Adn for the Army 11–17; Can and Preb Sarum Cathl 15–17; Bp S & M from 17. *Thie yn Aspick, 4 The Falls, Tromode Road, Cronkbourne, Isle of Man IM4 4PZ* T: (01624) 622108 E: bishop@sodoranndman.im

EAGLES, Thomas Ross. b 79. Southn Univ BSc 00 Dur Univ BA 17. St Mellitus Coll 14. **d** 17 **p** 18. C Cov St Mark Swanswell CD 17–21; P-in-c The Mitre Benefice *Nor* from 21. *St Thomas's Vicarage, 77 Edinburgh Street, Norwich NR2 3RL*

EALES, Canon Howard Bernard. b 46. Sarum & Wells Th Coll 73. **d** 76 **p** 77. C Timperley *Ches* 76–78; C Stockport St Thos 78–82; V Wythenshawe Wm Temple Ch *Man* 82–95; V Cheadle Hulme All SS *Ches* 95–11; RD Cheadle 02–09; Hon Can Ches Cathl 06–11; rtd 11; PtO *Ches* from 11. *8 Taxmere Close, Sandbach CW11 1WT* T: (01270) 763965 E: hbe.rev@gmail.com

EAMAN, Michael Leslie. b 47. Ridley Hall Cam 87. **d** 89 **p** 90. C Wharton *Ches* 89–93; V Buglawton 93–98; TV Congleton 98–10; rtd 10; Hon C Alcester and Arrow w Oversley and Weethley *Cov* 10–13; Hon C Kinwarton w Gt Alne and Haselor 10–13; P-in-c Potters Green 13–17; V from 17. *St Philip's Vicarage, Ringwood Highway, Coventry CV2 2GF* T: (024) 7661 2973 E: mikeeaman@virginmedia.com

EAMES, David John. b 80. Liv Hope Univ Coll BA 01 MA 04 St Jo Coll Dur MA 08. Cranmer Hall Dur 06. **d** 08 **p** 09. C Brigg, Wrawby and Cadney cum Howsham *Linc* 08–11; P-in-c Broughton from 11; P-in-c Scawby, Redbourne and Hibaldstow from 11. *St Hybald's Vicarage, Vicarage Lane, Scawby, Brigg DN20 9LX* T: (01652) 600860

EAMES (née WAKEHAM), Mrs Ellen Liesel. b 82. York Univ BA 04 CCC Cam BA 08. Westcott Ho Cam 06. **d** 09 **p** 10. C Frodingham *Linc* 09–12; Chapl St Gabr Coll Camberwell 12–18; Hon C Kennington St Jo w St Jas *S'wark* 12–19; PtO *Roch* 18–19; P-in-c Walworth St Chris *S'wark* from 19. *45 Aldbridge Street, London SE17 2RG* M: 07419-121950 E: mother.ellen@stchristopherswalworth.org.uk

EARDLEY, John. b 38. Ch Coll Cam BA 61 MA 12. Ridley Hall Cam 60. **d** 62 **p** 63. C Barnston *Ches* 62–65; C Wilmslow 65–67; V Hollingworth 67–75; V Leasowe 75–91; Chapl Leasowe Hosp 75–82; Chapl Arrowe Park Hosp Wirral 82–86; RD Wallasey *Ches* 86–91; V Church Hulme 91–03; Chapl Cranage Hall Hosp 91–03; rtd 03; PtO *Ches* from 03. *7 Banks Road, Heswall, Wirral CH60 9JS* T: 0151-342 9537 E: johneardley@talktalk.net

EARDLEY, Canon John Barry. b 35. MBE 97. MEd 87. AKC 62. **d** 63 **p** 64. C Merton St Jas *S'wark* 63–66; C St Helier 66–69;

C Bilton *Cov* 69–70; C Canley CD 70–74; P-in-c Church Lawford w Newnham Regis 74–80; P-in-c Leamington Hastings and Birdingbury 82–88; Dioc Educn Officer 82–00; Hon Can Cov Cathl 87–00; rtd 01; PtO *Cov* from 01. *8 Margetts Close, Kenilworth CV8 1EN* T: (01926) 748313 E: johnbarry.eardley@ntlworld.com

EARDLEY, Robert Bradford. b 44. St Alb Minl Tr Scheme 90. **d** 93 **p** 94. NSM Digswell and Panshanger *St Alb* 93–96; NSM Wheathampstead 97–98; NSM Tewin 98–05; P-in-c 98–04; rtd 05; PtO *St Alb* 05–07; *Sarum* from 06. *Bridge Cottage, Martin, Fordingbridge SP6 3LD* T: (01725) 519423 M: 07941-345895 E: rob.eardley@hotmail.co.uk

EAREY, Mark Robert. b 65. Loughb Univ BSc 87 St Jo Coll Dur BA 91. Cranmer Hall Dur 88. **d** 91 **p** 92. C Glen Parva and S Wigston *Leic* 91–94; C Luton Ch Ch *Roch* 94–97; Praxis Nat Educn Officer Sarum Coll 97–02; TR Morley *Wakef* 02–07; Tutor Qu Foundn Birm from 07; PtO *Birm* from 09. *The Queen's Foundation, Somerset Road, Edgbaston, Birmingham B15 2QH* T: 0121-452 2667 E: m.earey@queens.ac.uk

EARIS, Canon Stanley Derek. b 50. Univ Coll Dur BA 71 BCL 80. Ripon Hall Ox BA 73 MA 80. **d** 74 **p** 75. C Sutton St Jas and Wawne *York* 74–77; C Acomb St Steph and St Aid 77–81; V Skelmanthorpe *Wakef* 81–87; R Market Deeping *Linc* 87–02; V N Walsham and Edingthorpe *Nor* 02–13; C Bacton w Edingthorpe w Witton and Ridlington 04–07; Hon Can Nor Cathl 10–13; rtd 13; C York St Olave w St Giles 13–21; C York St Denys 13–21; C York St Helen w St Martin 13–21; C York All SS Pavement w St Crux and St Mich 13–21; PtO from 21. *49 St John Street, York YO31 7QR* T: (01904) 654767 E: dereke569@gmail.com

EARL (formerly LAMB), Mrs Alison. b 60. Ches Coll of HE BTh 04. NOC 01. **d** 04 **p** 05. C Rossington *Sheff* 04–08; V Worsbrough w Elsecar 08–18; V Tickhill w Stainton 18–21; rtd 21. *Lavender Cottage, 27A Rosevear Road, Bugle, St Austell PL26 8PJ* T: (01726) 850587 E: alison.lamb6@btinternet.com

EARL, Andrew John. b 61. Huddersfield Univ CertEd 01 Ches Coll of HE BTh 04. NOC. **d** 04 **p** 05. NSM Barnsley St Mary *Wakef* 04–08; NSM S Kirkby 08–09; Chapl W Yorks Police 04–09; CF 09–21; Asst Dioc Safeguarding Adv *Truro* from 21; CF (R of O) from 21. *Lavender Cottage, 27A Rosevear Road, Bugle, St Austell PL26 8PJ* M: 07557-362130 E: padreearl@hotmail.co.uk *or* andy.earl@truro.anglican.org

EARL, Simon Robert. b 50. Culham Coll of Educn CertEd 71 Open Univ BA 82. Linc Th Coll 94. **d** 96 **p** 97. C Bexhill St Aug *Chich* 96–99; R Ninfield 99–15; V Hooe 99–15; rtd 15; PtO *Chich* 15–19; TV Bexhill St Pet 19–20; PtO from 20. *6 Frant Avenue, Bexhill-on-Sea TN39 4NG* T: (01424) 842179 E: srearl@btinternet.com

EARL, Stephen Geoffrey Franklyn. b 53. Lon Univ BA 76 Goldsmiths' Coll Lon PGCE 77. Ridley Hall Cam 91. **d** 93 **p** 94. C Sawston *Ely* 93–96; V Burwell w Reach 96–10; RD Fordham and Quy 02–10; Hon Can Ely Cathl 07–10; P-in-c Lavenham w Preston *St E* 10–12; R from 12; RD Lavenham 12–17. *The Rectory, Church Street, Lavenham, Sudbury CO10 9SA* T/F: (01787) 247244 E: earls2222@btinternet.com

EARLE, Mrs Sylvia. b 51. St Aid Coll Dur BA 72. Cranmer Hall Dur 05. **d** 07 **p** 08. C Whitkirk *Ripon* 07–11; P-in-c Collingham w Harewood *Leeds* 12–14; P-in-c Spofforth w Kirk Deighton *Ripon* 12–14; *Leeds* 14–21; rtd 21; PtO *Leeds* from 21. *Punchbowl House, Preston under Scar, Leyburn DL8 4AJ*

EARLEY, Stephen John. b 48. Trin Coll Bris 91. **d** 93 **p** 94. C Stroud H Trin *Glouc* 93–98; C Leckhampton SS Phil and Jas w Cheltenham St Jas 98–02; V Nailsworth w Shortwood, Horsley etc 02–13; rtd 13; PtO *Glouc* from 14. *17 Whitecroft, Nailsworth, Stroud GL6 0NS* T: (01453) 836679 E: stevearl@earleys.f9.co.uk *or* stevejearley@gmail.com

EARLL, Miss Victoria Jane. b 79. R Holloway Coll Lon BSc 01. Cranmer Hall Dur 18. **d** 20 **p** 21. C York St Mich-le-Belfrey from 20. *Address withheld by request* E: revvickyearll@gmail.com

EARNEY, Preb Graham Howard. b 45. AKC 67. **d** 68 **p** 69. C Auckland St Helen *Dur* 68–72; C Corsenside *Newc* 72–76; P-in-c 76–79; TV Willington 79–83; TR 83–87; Dioc Soc Resp Officer *B & W* 87–95; Dir Bp Mascall Cen *Heref* 95–02; Hon TV Ludlow, Ludford, Ashford Carbonell etc 95–02; Dioc Development Rep 96–02; Local Min Officer 02–10; RD Condover 03–06; Preb Heref Cathl 02–10; rtd

10; PtO *Heref* from 10. *The Coppice, Castle Pulverbatch, Pulverbatch, Shrewsbury SY5 8DS* T: (01743) 718930 E: gandsearney@btinternet.com

EARNGEY, Mark Edward. b 80. Univ of NSW BSc 03. Moore Th Coll Sydney BD 11. d 12. C Toongabbie Australia 12–14; PtO *Ox* 15–18. *2 Court Place Gardens, Iffley, Oxford OX4 4EW* M: 07943-910520 E: mark.earngey@theology.ox.ac.uk

EARNSHAW, Simon James. b 79. Newc Univ BDS 03. St Mellitus Coll 19. d 21. C Clayton w Keymer *Chich* from 21. *Address temp unknown* M: 07596-485157 E: simonjearnshaw@outlook.com

EARWICKER, Matthew Charles. b 77. St Jo Coll Ox BA 00 MA 03. Ridley Hall Cam 12. d 14 p 15. C Salisbury St Mark and Laverstock *Sarum* 14–18; R Oldbury from 18. *The Rectory, The Street, Cherhill, Calne SN11 8XR* T: (01249) 821329 E: mattearwicker@gmail.com

EASEMAN, Robert Leslie. b 44. d 00 p 01. OLM Hunstanton St Mary w Ringstead Parva etc *Nor* 00–09; rtd 09; PtO *Nor* from 09. *5 Lighthouse Close, Hunstanton PE36 6EL* T/F: (01485) 535258 M: 07941-323218 E: rleaseman@gmail.com

EAST, Bryan Victor. b 46. Oak Hill Th Coll 91. d 93 p 94. C Waltham Cross *St Alb* 93–96; C Wotton St Mary *Glouc* 96–99; V Humberston *Linc* 99–12; rtd 12; PtO *Glouc* 15–18. *8 Ashway Court, Stroud GL5 4LL* T: (01453) 767261 E: bryan.east.be@gmail.com

EAST, Mark Richard. b 57. Trin Coll Bris BA 89. d 89 p 90. C Dalton-in-Furness *Carl* 89–93; TV Bucknall and Bagnall *Lich* 93–00; P-in-c Church Coniston *Carl* 00–12; P-in-c Torver 00–12; P-in-c Haughton le Skerne *Dur* 12–15; R from 15; P-in-c Sadberge 14–15; R from 15; AD Darlington from 19. *7 St Andrew's Close, Darlington DL1 2EB* T: (01325) 492993 E: east793@btinternet.com *or* revmark@standrewshaughton.org.uk

EAST, Martin James. b 47. STETS. d 10 p 11. NSM N Hants Downs *Win* 10–13; PtO from 13. *South Lodge, 112 London Road, Holybourne, Alton GU34 4EW* T: (01420) 549595 M: 07928-423762 E: martineast@btinternet.com

EAST, Peter Alan. See OSTLI-EAST, Peter Alan

EAST, Canon Richard Kenneth. b 47. Oak Hill Th Coll 86. d 88 p 89. C Necton w Holme Hale *Nor* 88–92; R Garsdon, Lea and Cleverton and Charlton *Bris* 92–12; C Gt Somerford, Lt Somerford, Seagry, Corston etc 10–12; C Brinkworth w Dauntsey 10–12; RD Malmesbury 93–99; Hon Can Bris Cathl 10–12; rtd 12; PtO *Sarum* from 13. *6 Ryeland Way, Trowbridge BA14 7SH* T: (01225) 282902 E: richardeast@homecall.co.uk

EAST, Stuart Michael. b 50. Chich Th Coll 86. d 88 p 89. C Middlesbrough St Martin *York* 88–93; R Upper Ryedale 92–97; V Macclesfield St Paul *Ches* 97–01; C Maidstone St Luke *Cant* 01–03; R Peopleton and White Ladies Aston w Churchill etc *Worc* 03–10; V Nunthorpe *York* 10–12; rtd 12; PtO *York* from 17. *12 Avon Drive, Guisborough TS14 8AX* M: 07754-244929

EAST RIDING, Archdeacon of. See BROOM, The Ven Andrew Clifford

EASTELL, Jane Rosamund. b 47. Sheff Univ BA 68 Univ of Wales (Lamp) MA 08 RIBA 73. Trin Coll Bris BA 99. d 99 p 00. C Backwell w Chelvey and Brockley *B & W* 99–03; C Chew Stoke w Nempnett Thrubwell 03–08; C Chew Magna w Dundry and Norton Malreward 03–08; Hon C Taunton St Jo 09–13; P-in-c 13–14; Hon C Taunton St Mary and St Jo from 14; Dioc Adv in Prayer and Spirituality 04–16. *19 King's Square, Taunton TA1 3FN* T: (01823) 321069 E: jane.eastell458@btinternet.com

EASTER, Canon Ann Rosemarie. SRN 68 Univ of E Lon MBA 94. Gilmore Ho 78. dss 80 d 87 p 94. Stratford St Jo and Ch Ch w Forest Gate St Jas *Chelmsf* 80–89; Par Dn 87–89; Chapl Asst Newham Gen Hosp 80–89; PtO *Chelmsf* 89–08; Chief Exec Officer The Renewal Programme 95–15; AD Newham 97–07; NSM W Ham 08–10; NSM E Ham H Trin from 11; Hon Can Chelmsf Cathl from 00; Chapl to The Queen 07–17. *67 Disraeli Road, London E7 9JU* T: (020) 8555 6337 M: 07889-799290 E: anneaster5@gmail.com

EASTOE, Canon Robin Howard Spenser. b 53. Lon Univ BD 75 AKC 75. Coll of Resurr Mirfield 77. d 78 p 79. C Gt Ilford St Mary *Chelmsf* 78–81; C Walthamstow St Sav 81–84; V Barkingside St Fran 84–92; V Leigh-on-Sea St Marg 92–08; RD Hadleigh 00–08; Chapl Southend Health Care NHS Trust 96–08; Hon Can Chelmsf Cathl 06–08; P-in-c Heavitree and St Mary Steps *Ex* 08–14; TR 14–20; RD Christianity 12–18; Preb Ex Cathl 16–20; rtd 20; PtO *Ex* from 20. *170 Summerway, Exeter EX4 8DA* M: 07813-289932 E: theeastoes@btinternet.com

EASTON, Canon Christopher Richard Alexander. b 60. TCD BA 81. d 84 p 85. C Belfast St Donard *D & D* 84–89; I Inishmacsaint *Clogh* 89–95; I Magheralin w Dollingstown *D & D* 95–01; I Coleraine *Conn* 01–09; P-in-c Belfast

Whiterock 09–14; I Armoy w Loughguile and Drumtullagh from 14; Can Conn Cathl from 16. *The Rectory, 181 Glenshesk Road, Armoy, Ballymoney BT53 8RJ* T: (028) 2075 1565 E: stpat@btinternet.com

EASTON, Donald Fyfe. b 48. St Edm Hall Ox BA 69 MA 85 Nottm Univ CertEd 70 Univ Coll Lon MA 76 PhD 90 Clare Hall Cam MA 85. Westcott Ho Cam 89. d 90 p 91. NSM Fulham St Andr *Lon* 90–97; Lic Preacher from 97. *12 Weltje Road, London W6 9TG* T: (020) 8741 0233 E: donaldfeaston@hotmail.com

EASTON, Robert Paul Stephen. b 62. Bris Univ BA 84. St Steph Ho Ox BTh 00. d 00 p 01. C Stoke Newington St Mary *Lon* 00–03; Chapl Brighton Coll 03–19; Chapl Highgate Sch *Lon* from 19. *Highgate School, North Road, London N6 4AY* T: (020) 8340 1524 M: 07793-417431 E: roberteaston1@onetel.com

EASTWOOD, David Dean. b 54. Newc Univ LLB 77. Ridley Hall Cam 06. d 08 p 09. C Westbrook St Phil *Liv* 08–10; P-in-c St Helens St Helen 10; TR St Helens Town Cen 10–18; AD St Helens 14–18; Hon Can Liv Cathl 14–18; rtd 18; P-in-c Sheff St Jo from 19. *Kairos, 199 Twentywell Lane, Sheffield S17 4QB* T: 0114-236 7496 M: 07785-542594 E: davideastwood86@gmail.com

EASTWOOD, Canon Janet. b 54. Wycliffe Hall Ox 83. dss 86 d 87 p 94. Ainsdale *Liv* 86–90; Par Dn 87–90; Team Dn Kirkby Lonsdale *Carl* 90–94; TV 94–95; Dioc Youth Officer 90–94; R Wavertree H Trin *Liv* 95–18; P-in-c Wavertree St Thos 95–97; Hon Can Liv Cathl 06–18; Chapl Blue Coat Sch Liv 96–18; rtd 18. *Wavertree Rectory, Hunters Lane, Liverpool L15 8HL* T: 0151-733 2172

EASTWOOD, Mrs Nicola Jane. b 63. d 11 p 12. C Upton (Overchurch) *Ches* 11–18; V from 18. *20 Church Road, Upton, Wirral CH49 6JZ* E: nikkieastwood@gmail.com *or* nikki@stm-upton.org.uk

EATOCK, John. b 45. Lanc Univ MA 82. Lich Th Coll 67. d 70 p 71. C Crumpsall St Mary *Man* 70–73; C Atherton 73–74; C Ribbleton *Blackb* 74–77; V Ingol 77–83; V Laneside 83–92; RD Accrington 90–92; PtO 92–08; *Truro* from 08. *29 Wellington Road, Camborne TR14 7LH* T: (01209) 714899 E: john.eatock@tiscali.co.uk

EATON, Benjamin. See EATON, Oscar Benjamin

EATON, David Andrew. b 58. MBE 06. Man Univ BSc 79 ACA 83 FCA. Trin Coll Bris BA 89. d 89 p 90. C Barking St Marg w St Patr *Chelmsf* 89–92; C Billericay and Lt Burstead 92–95; P-in-c Vange 95–05; TV Sole Bay *St E* 05–10; CF (VR) from 94; rtd 10; PtO *St E* from 10. *The Cedars, School Lane, Great Barton, Bury St Edmunds IP31 2RQ* T: (01284) 787718 M: 07841-215182 E: davidaeaton@lineone.net

EATON, Canon David John. b 45. Nottm Univ LTh BTh 74. St Jo Coll Nottm 70. d 74 p 75. C Headley All SS *Guildf* 74–77; Ind Chapl *Worc* 77–82; TV Halesowen 80–82; V Rowledge *Guildf* 82–89; V Leatherhead 89–01; R Leatherhead and Mickleham 01–09; RD Leatherhead 93–98; Hon Can Guildf Cathl 02–09; rtd 09; PtO *Guildf* from 10; S'wark from 09. *Two Way House, Wheelers Lane, Brockham, Betchworth RH3 7LA* T: (01737) 843915 E: rev_davideaton@hotmail.com

✠EATON, The Rt Revd Derek Lionel. b 41. MA 78. Trin Coll Bris. d 71 p 71 c 90. C Barton Hill St Luke w Ch Ch *Bris* 71–72; Chapl Br Emb Tunisia 72–78; Provost All SS Cathl Cairo 78–83; Chapl Br Emb Egypt 78–83; Hon Can All SS Cathl Cairo 85; Assoc P Papanui St Paul NZ 84; V Sumner-Redcliffs 85–90; Bp Nelson 90–06; rtd 06. *67 Grove Street, The Wood, Nelson 7010, New Zealand* T: (0064) (3) 545 6998 E: eaton.d.a@gmail.com

EATON (née CRAIG), Mrs Julie Elizabeth. b 57. Open Univ BA 08 Essex Univ MA 13. Trin Coll Bris 87. d 89 p 94. Par Dn Gt Ilford St Andr *Chelmsf* 89–92; NSM Billericay and Lt Burstead 92–95; C 95–96; TV 96–01; Chapl Thameside Community Healthcare NHS Trust 92–95; PtO *Chelmsf* 01–05; TV Sole Bay *St E* 05–10. *The Cedars, School Lane, Great Barton, Bury St Edmunds IP31 2RQ* T: (01284) 787718 E: julie@parkgates.plus.com

EATON, Mrs Margaret Anne. b 44. Ab Dioc Tr Course 82. dss 84 d 86 p 94. NSM Ellon and Cruden Bay *Ab* 84–95; C Bridge of Don 95–00; Co-ord Scottish Episc Renewal Fellowship 00–04; C Ellon *Ab* 01–03; C Elgin w Lossiemouth *Mor* 03–04 and 06–10; C Aberlour and Dufftown 06–10; LtO from 11. *Grianach, Tom-na-Muidh Road, Dufftown, Keith AB55 4AT* T: (01340) 821478 E: maggie-e@hotmail.co.uk

EATON, Canon Oscar Benjamin. b 37. Puerto Rico Th Coll STB 66. d 66 p 67. Ecuador 66–69; C Wandsworth St Anne S'wark 69–71; C Aldrington *Chich* 71–73; TV Littleham w Exmouth *Ex* 74–79; R Alphington 79–84; Chapl Barcelona w Casteldefels *Eur* 84–87; Chapl Barcelona 88; Chapl Maisons-Laffitte 88–02; P-in-c St Raphaël 02–10; Can Malta Cathl

96–10. *Flat 2, 104 Skipton Road, Ilkley LS29 9HE* T: (01943) 607205 E: beneatonsenior@gmail.com

✠**EATON, The Rt Revd Peter David.** b 58. K Coll Lon BA 82 AKC 82 Qu Coll Cam BA 85 MA 89 Magd Coll Ox MA 90. Westcott Ho Cam 83. **d** 86 **p** 87 **c** 15. C Maidstone All SS and St Phil w Tovil *Cant* 86–89; Fells' Chapl Magd Coll Ox 89–91; LtO *Ox* 89–06; PtO 14–19; Assoc R Salt Lake City St Paul USA 91–95; R Lancaster St Jas Penn 95–01; Hon Can Th Utah 91–01; Dean St Jo Cathl Denver 02–15; Adjunct Angl Studies Iliff Sem Denver 05–15; Coadjutor Bp SE Florida 15–16; Bp SE Florida from 16. *The Diocese of Southeast Florida, 555 NE 15th Street, Suite 934B, Miami FL 33132, USA* T: (001) (305) 373 0881 F: 375 8054 E: bishop@diosef.org

EATON, Miss Phyllis Mary. b 42. Qu Eliz Coll Lon BSc 63 UNISA BA 79 SRD. WMMTC 87. **d** 90 **p** 94. NSM Washwood Heath *Birm* 90–91; NSM Edgbaston SS Mary and Ambrose 91–95; PtO 95–05; NSM Oldbury, Langley and Londonderry 05–13; PtO from 13. *7 Milton Court, Sandon Road, Smethwick B66 4AD* T: 0121-420 3488 E: phyllis.eaton@btinternet.com

EAVES, Alan Charles. b 37. Tyndale Hall Bris 62. **d** 65 **p** 66. C Southport SS Simon and Jude *Liv* 65–66; C Eccleston Ch Ch 66–70; V Earlestown 70–79; V Orpington Ch Ch *Roch* 79–02; rtd 02; PtO *Ely* 03–21. *4 Chervil Close, Folksworth, Peterborough PE7 3SZ* T: (01733) 241464. M: 07904-357476

EBBSFLEET, Suffragan Bishop of (Provincial Episcopal Visitor). *Vacant*

EBELING, Mrs Barbara. b 44. Hull Univ BA 67. St Alb Minl Tr Scheme 87. **d** 94 **p** 95. C Stevenage St Hugh and St Jo *St Alb* 94–99; R Riversmeet 99–08; rtd 08; PtO *St Alb* 08–09; *Chelmsf* 09–13; V High Cross *St Alb* 10–13; V Thundridge 10–13. *7 Wicklands Road, Hunsdon, Ware SG12 8PD* T: (01279) 842086 E: barbara.ebeling@sky.com

ECCLES, Miss Helen Elizabeth. b 80. Liv Univ BA 01 Ches Coll of HE PGCE 02. St Mellitus Coll 18. **d** 20. NSM Knutsford St Jo and Toft *Ches* from 20. *4 Riddings Lane, Hartford, Northwich CW8 1NB* M: 07714-582261 E: heeccles@yahoo.co.uk

ECCLESTON, Mrs Frances Mary. b 61. Jes Coll Cam BA 83 York St Jo Coll MA 05 CQSW 88. NOC 00. **d** 03 **p** 04. C Ranmoor *Sheff* 03–06; C Sheff St Leon Norwood 06–09; P-in-c Crosspool 09–14; V 14–16; Dioc Ecum Officer 10–14; Bp's Adv in Past Care and Reconciliation 14–16; TR Aston cum Aughton w Swallownest and Ulley 16–19; Bp's Interim Min 19–20; AD Laughton 16–20; P-in-c Whaley Bridge *Ches* 20–21; R from 21. *46 Buxton Road, Whaley Bridge, High Peak SK23 7JE* T: (01663) 732724 M: 07554-240762 E: revfrances.whaley@gmail.com

ECCLESTONE, Canon Gary Edward. b 73. Ex Univ BA 95 PGCE 96. Cuddesdon Coll BTh 99. **d** 99 **p** 00. C Salisbury St Martin and Laverstock *Sarum* 99–03; P-in-c Hanslope w Castlethorpe *Ox* 03–09; V from 09; AD Newport from 17; Hon Can Ho Ghana from 14. *The Vicarage, Park Road, Hanslope, Milton Keynes MK19 7LT* T: (01908) 337936

ECKERSLEY, Mrs Nancy Elizabeth. b 50. York Univ BA 72 Leeds Univ CertEd 73. NEOC 86. **d** 89 **p** 94. C Clifton *York* 89–00; Chapl York Distr Hosp 90–93; Lay Tr Officer *York* 93–00; V Heslington 00–11; rtd 11; PtO *York* from 12. *14 Church Close, Flamborough, Bridlington YO15 1AF* T: (01262) 850515 E: revnance@yahoo.co.uk

ECKHARD, Robert Leo Michael. b 60. Middx Poly BA 87 Open Univ MA 96 La Sainte Union Coll PGCE 88. NTMTC BA 05. **d** 05 **p** 06. C Ealing St Paul *Lon* 05–08; C Hounslow H Trin w St Paul and St Mary 08–10; PtO from 14. *23 Ellerman Avenue, Twickenham TW2 6AA* M: 07985-003057 E: bob.eckhard50@gmail.com

EDDLESTON, Audrey Suzanne. b 65. Hull Univ BA 87 Ches Univ MA 19 Lon Inst of Educn PGCE 88. All SS Cen for Miss & Min 14. **d** 17 **p** 18. C Timperley *Ches* 17–20; C Crewe St Andr w St Jo from 21; C Crewe All SS and St Paul w St Pet from 21. *All Saints' Vicarage, 79 Stewart Street, Crewe CW2 8LX* M: 07723-157929 E: revdsuzie@outlook.com

EDDY, Paul Anthony. b 67. St Jo Coll Nottm 07. **d** 09 **p** 10. C Grove *Ox* 09–12; V Stanford in the Vale w Goosey and Hatford from 13; Dioc Missr from 11. *The Vicarage, 24 Church Green, Stanford in the Vale, Faringdon SN7 8HU* T: (01367) 710267 M: 07958-905716 E: paul@pauleddy.uk

EDEN, Lewis Scott. b 94. Robert Gordon Univ Aber BSC 16 Dur Univ BA 21. Cranmer Hall Dur 18. **d** 21. C Crediton, Shobrooke and Sandford etc *Ex* from 21. *50 Beech Park, Crediton EX17 1HW* M: 07731-833532 E: lewis.s.eden@gmail.com

EDEN-JONES, Mrs Sarah Rachel. b 72. St Hilda's Coll Ox BA 93 MA 98. St Mellitus Coll 13. **d** 16 **p** 17. C Reading Greyfriars *Ox* 16–20; C Reading St Jo 20–21; C Gt Marlow w Marlow Bottom, Lt Marlow and Bisham from 21. *33 Highdown Hill*

Road, Emmer Green, Reading RG4 8QR M: 07703-835704 E: sedenjones@gmail.com

EDGAR, David. b 59. Newc Univ BA 81. Linc Th Coll BTh 86. **d** 86 **p** 87. C Wednesbury St Paul Wood Green *Lich* 86–91; V Winterton Gp *Linc* 91–00; Chapl De Montford Univ *St Alb* 00–02; Chapl Linc Univ *York* 02–06; C Linc St Swithin 00–01; P-in-c 01–14; P-in-c Linc All SS 06–15; Chapl N Lincs Coll 00–15. *26 Holmfield, Fiskerton, Lincoln LN3 4GD*

EDGAR, Ian Henry. b 78. Huron Coll Ontario MDiv 18. **d** 18 **p** 19. C Durrington *Chich* from 18; C Maybridge and W Tarring from 18. *26 Vancouver Close, Worthing BN13 2SH* T: (01903) 694635 M: 07586-477191 E: st.kieran.st.luke@gmail.com *or* fr.ianedgar@gmail.com

EDGAR, Orion Burns. b 81. Nottm Univ BA 03 MA 07 PhD 12. Westcott Ho Cam 14. **d** 16 **p** 17. C Pershore w Pinvin, Wick and Birlingham *Worc* 16–17; C Malvern H Trin and St Jas 17–19; Chapl R Holloway and Bedf New Coll *Guildf* from 19. *10 Willow Walk, Englefield Green, Egham TW20 0DQ* M: 07421-354837 E: orion.edgar@rhul.ac.uk

EDGCUMBE, Irena Christine. *See* CZERNIAWSKA EDGCUMBE, Irena Christine

EDGE, Darren. b 69. Man Metrop Univ BEd 99 Newman Univ MA 17 Staffs Univ PGCE 06. SNWTP 10. **d** 13 **p** 14. C Werrington and Wetley Rocks *Lich* 13–17; Dir Progress Blythe Bridge High Sch 14–15; PtO *Lich* 18–19 and from 21; TV Bucknall 19–21; Chapl Denstone Coll Uttoxeter from 21. *Sandy Lodge, Cheddleton Road, Leek ST13 5QZ* M: 07940-555540 E: d.s.edge@hotmail.co.uk

EDGE, Michael MacLeod. b 45. St Andr Univ BSc 68 Qu Coll Cam BA 70 MA 74. Westcott Ho Cam 68. **d** 72 **p** 73. C Allerton *Liv* 72–76; R Bretherton *Blackb* 76–82; P-in-c Kilpeck *Heref* 82–84; P-in-c St Devereux w Wormbridge 82–84; TR Ewyas Harold w Dulas, Kenderchurch etc 82–93; RD Abbeydore 84–90; V Enfield St Andr *Lon* 93–13; rtd 13; PtO *St E* from 15. *19 Abbeyfields, Bury St Edmunds IP33 1AQ* T: (01284) 724178 E: michaeledge@cantab.net

EDGE, Philip John. b 54. Ripon Coll Cuddesdon 77. **d** 80 **p** 81. C N Harrow St Alb *Lon* 80–83; C St Giles Cripplegate w St Bart Moor Lane etc 83–86; P-in-c Belmont 86–88; V 88–92; V Ellesmere and Welsh Frankton *Lich* 92–97; V Ellesmere 97–19; RD 10–13; rtd 19. *127 Ellesmere Road, Shrewsbury SY1 2RA* T: (01743) 622842 E: philipedge@talktalk.net

EDGE, Stephen Paul. b 62. Westfield Ho Cam 00 Lindisfarne Coll of Th 20. **d** 21. NSM Hartlepool St Hilda *Dur* from 21. *The Vicarage, Melbury Street, Seaham SR7 7NF* M: 07909-968197 E: revsteve1508@outlook.com

EDGE, Timothy Peter. b 55. Brighton Poly BSc 80 K Coll Lon MA 10 St Jo Coll Dur DThM 20 CEng 85 MIET 85 FRAS 80. Westcott Ho Cam 85. **d** 88 **p** 89. C Norton *Ches* 88–91; C Bedworth *Cov* 91–96; TV Witney *Ox* 96–02; Asst Chapl HM Pris Bullingdon 02–04; Chapl 04–09; NSM Cogges and S Leigh *Ox* 03–11; PtO 11–20; *Chich* from 20. *53 Westbourne Gardens, Hove BN3 5PN* T: (01273) 227489 E: tim.edge@talk21.com

EDGERTON, Ms Hilary Ann. b 66. R Holloway & Bedf New Coll Lon BSc 88. Wycliffe Hall Ox BTh 93. **d** 93 **p** 94. Par Dn S Cave and Ellerker w Broomfleet *York* 93–94; C 94–97; TV Howden 97–00; V Hayfield and Chinley w Buxworth *Derby* 00–16; Chapl HM Pris Buckley Hall from 16; Hon C Saddleworth *Man* from 16. *HM Prison Buckley Hall, Buckley Farm Lane, Rochdale OL12 9DP* T: (01706) 514300 M: 07407-400261 E: hedgerton356@btinternet.com

EDIE, Jennifer Mary. b 40. Edin Univ MA 62 Hong Kong Univ PGCE 77. **d** 03 **p** 04. NSM Eyemouth *Edin* 03–09; P-in-c 06–09; rtd 09; LtO *Edin* from 09. *12 Barefoots Avenue, Eyemouth TD14 5JH* T: (018907) 50169 E: rev.jennifer@gmail.com

EDINBOROUGH, David. b 36. Nottm Univ BA 58 MEd 74. EMMTC 79. **d** 82 **p** 83. NSM Bramcote *S'well* 82–01; P-in-c 94–01; Dioc Officer for NSMs 89–94; rtd 01; PtO *S'well* 01–02; P-in-c Radford St Pet 02–04; PtO from 04; Bp's Chapl for Rtd Clergy 09–16. *105A Derby Road, Beeston, Nottingham NG9 3GZ* T: 0115-925 1066 E: david.edinborough@btopenworld.com *or* david.edinborough@googlemail.com

EDINBURGH, Bishop of. *See* ARMES, The Rt Revd John Andrew

EDINBURGH, Dean of. *See* BURBERRY, The Very Revd Frances Sheila

EDINBURGH, Provost of. *See* CONWAY, The Very Revd John Arthur

EDMANS, Mrs Jennifer. b 56. **d** 07 **p** 08. OLM Bernwode *Ox* 07–10; C from 10. *2 The Bungalow, Coldharbour Farm, Brill, Aylesbury HP18 9UA* T: (01844) 237855 M: 07808-347276 E: jennyedmans@aol.com

EDMEADS, Andrew. b 53. Linc Th Coll 84. **d** 86 **p** 87. C Sholing *Win* 86–89; R Knights Enham 89–97; rtd 97; PtO *Win* 97–13; Chapl St Mich Hospice Basingstoke 00–12; Chapl Naomi Ho Hospice 13–19; PtO *Win* from 19. *10 Altona Gardens, Andover SP10 4LG* T: (01264) 391464

EDMONDS (née HARRIS), Canon Catherine Elizabeth. b 52. Leic Coll of Educn CertEd 73 ACP 79. S Dios Minl Tr Scheme 91. **d** 95 **p** 96. NSM Basing *Win* 95–99; C Yeovil H Trin w Barwick *B & W* 99–01; Chapl Coll of SS Mark and Jo Plymouth *Ex* 01–06; TV Ottery St Mary, Alfington, W Hill, Tipton etc 06–17; C Broadhembury, Payhembury and Plymtree 09–16; Dioc Youth Adv 06–17; RD Ottery 14–17; rtd 17; Hon C Axminster, Chardstock, All Saints etc *Ex* 18–20; Hon C Axminster, All Saints, Axmouth, Chardstock etc from 20; RD Honiton from 19; Can Res Ex Cathl from 19. *Woodfield, Sidmouth Road, Lyme Regis DT7 3ES* T: (01297) 444465 E: cateedmonds@aol.com

EDMONDS, Clive Alway. b 42. ACII. S'wark Ord Course 78. **d** 81 **p** 82. C Horsell *Guildf* 81–85; R Bisley and W End 85–92; RD Surrey Heath 90–92; R Haslemere 92–00; Chapl Wispers Sch Haslemere 92–00; P-in-c Westbury-on-Severn w Flaxley and Blaisdon *Glouc* 00–02; V Westbury-on-Severn w Flaxley, Blaisdon etc 03–06; rtd 06; PtO *Heref* from 07; *Glouc* from 17. *3 Church Road, Longhope GL17 0LH* T: (01452) 831545 E: alwayedmonds@hotmail.com

EDMONDS, Michelle Kay. b 70. S Bank Univ BSc 98. Ripon Coll Cuddesdon BTh 08. **d** 06 **p** 07. C Croydon St Matt S'wark 06–09; TV Warlingham w Chelsham and Farleigh 09–16; TR from 16; Asst Dir of Ords Croydon Area from 13; AD Tandridge from 20. *The Vicarage, 2 Chelsham Road, Warlingham CR6 9EQ* T: (01883) 623011 M: 07799-713957 E: revmichelle@btinternet.com

EDMONDS (née MAGUIRE), Ms Sarah Alison. b 65. Univ Coll Lon BSc 87 South Univ MSc 93. STETS 95. **d** 98 **p** 99. C Warwick St Paul *Cov* 98–02; P-in-c Hampton Lucy w Charlecote and Loxley 02–06; PtO 12–14; Hon C Ilmington w Stretton-on-Fosse etc 14–17; Hon C Tredington and Darlingscott 14–17; R Shipston-on-Stour w Honington and Idlicote from 17; AD Shipston from 19. *The Rectory, 8 Glen Close, Shipston-on-Stour CV36 4ED* T: (01608) 661210 E: sarah_edmonds@btconnect.com

EDMONDS, Stephen Harry James. b 77. SS Hild & Bede Coll Dur BA 99 Leeds Univ MA 08. Coll of Resurr Mirfield 06. **d** 08 **p** 09. C Hendon *Dur* 08–12; V Edlington and Hexthorpe *Sheff* 12–21; Assoc Adn Doncaster from 21. *The Vicarage, 17 Heaton Gardens, Edlington, Doncaster DN12 1SY* T: (01709) 858358 M: 07882-443025 E: fr.s.edmonds@gmail.com

EDMONDS, Stephen Philip Augustine. Kent Univ BA 05 Heythrop Coll Lon MA 10 Selwyn Coll Cam PhD 16. Westcott Ho Cam 10. **d** 15 **p** 16. C Sydenham St Bart S'wark 15–19; TV Wimbledon from 19. *St Saviour's Vicarage, Church Walk, London SW20 9DL* M: 07746-294479 E: vicar@sedmonds.co.uk

EDMONDS, Tony Ernest. b 50. R Holloway Coll Lon BSc 71 Imp Coll Lon MSc 73 PhD 75 Nottm Univ MA 05. EMMTC 02. **d** 05 **p** 06. NSM Barrow upon Soar w Walton le Wolds *Leic* 05–10; TV Kegworth, Hathern, Long Whatton, Diseworth etc 10–16; Warden of Readers 10–13; AD Akeley E 11–16; rtd 16; PtO *Sarum* from 17. *Varhn, Agglestone Road, Studland, Swanage BH19 3BZ* T: (01929) 450097 M: 07837-009147 E: t.e.edmonds@btconnect.com

✠**EDMONDSON, The Rt Revd Christopher Paul.** b 50. St Jo Coll Dur BA 71 MA 81. Cranmer Hall Dur 71. **d** 73 **p** 74 **c** 08. C Kirkheaton *Wakef* 73–79; V Ovenden 79–86; Bp's Adv on Evang 81–86; Dioc Officer for Evang *Carl* 86–92; P-in-c Bampton w Mardale 86–92; V Shipley St Pet *Bradf* 92–02; Warden Lee Abbey 02–08; Suff Bp Bolton *Man* 08–16; rtd 16; Hon Asst Bp Leeds from 17. *16 Cavalier Drive, Apperley Bridge, Bradford BD10 0UF* T: (01274) 284031 E: chris.edmondson@me.com

EDMONDSON, David Philip Thomas. b 92. St Mellitus Coll BA 14. Trin Coll Bris 18. **d** 20 **p** 21. C Walthamstow *Chelmsf* from 20. *St Gabriel's Vicarage, 17 Shernall Street, London E17 3EU* M: 07927-412963 E: dptedmondson@gmail.com

EDMONDSON, Canon John James William. b 55. St Jo Coll Dur BA 83 MA 91 PhD 04. Cranmer Hall Dur 80. **d** 83 **p** 84. C Gee Cross *Ches* 83–86; C Camberley St Paul *Guildf* 86–88; TV 88–90; Chapl Elmhurst Ballet Sch 86–90; V Foxton w Gumley and Laughton and Lubenham *Leic* 90–94; R Bexhill St Mark *Chich* 94–05; V Battle 05–18; Dean Battle 05–18; P-in-c Sedlescombe w Whatlington 05–08; Dioc Voc Adv 98–02; Asst Dir of Ords 02–05; RD Battle and Bexhill 13–15; Can and Preb Chich Cathl 14–18; rtd 18; PtO *Nor* from 19. *Inglenooks, 49-53 Damgate Street, Wymondham NR18 0BG*

EDMONTON, Area Bishop of. See WICKHAM, The Rt Revd Robert James

EDMUNDS, Andrew Charles. b 57. Whitelands Coll Lon BEd 80 CQSW 84. Oak Hill NSM Course 87. **d** 89 **p** 90. NSM Hawkwell *Chelmsf* 89–95; C Torquay St Matthias, St Mark and H Trin *Ex* 95–97; V Ripley *Derby* 97–09; RD Heanor 06–09; PtO 09–11; R Yateley *Win* 11–19; rtd 19; PtO *Chich* from 19; *Portsm* from 21. *36 Durford Road, Petersfield GU31 4HA* M: 07715-377225 E: a.edmunds@me.com

EDMUNDS, Gary James William. b 56. K Coll Lon BD 78 RGN 89. STETS 12. **d** 15 **p** 16. NSM Norton sub Hamdon, W Chinnock, Chiselborough etc *B & W* 15–17; NSM Ham Hill Villages from 17; Chapl Taunton and Somerset NHS Foundn Trust from 17. *Hamdon Vale, West Street, Stoke-sub-Hamdon TA14 6QG* M: 07738-197880 E: gary.edmunds@hotmail.co.uk

EDMUNDSON, Susan Sharon. b 51. St Mellitus Coll 16. **d** 17 **p** 18. NSM Downham w S Hanningfield and Ramsden Bellhouse *Chelmsf* 17–21; NSM E Hanningfield from 21. *19 Westerings, Danbury, Chelmsford CM3 4ND* T: (01245) 224181 E: suzy.edmundson@btinternet.com

EDSON, The Ven Michael. b 42. Birm Univ BSc 64 Leeds Univ BA 71. Coll of Resurr Mirfield 69. **d** 72 **p** 73. C Barnstaple St Pet w H Trin *Ex* 72–77; TV Barnstaple and Goodleigh 77–79; TV Barnstaple, Goodleigh and Landkey 79–82; V Roxbourne St Andr *Lon* 82–89; AD Harrow 85–89; P-in-c S Harrow St Paul 86–89; Warden Lee Abbey 89–94; LtO *Ex* 89–94; Adn Leic 94–02; Bp's Insp of Par Registers and Records 94–02; TR Bideford, Northam, Westward Ho!, Appledore etc *Ex* 02–09; rtd 09; PtO *Leeds* from 19. *11 Belmont Road, Ilkley LS29 8PE* T: (01943) 969874 E: ven.mike.edson@gmail.com

EDWARDS, Adam Peter Michael. b 78. Birm Univ BA 01 Newman Univ MA 20. Qu Foundn (Course) 15. **d** 17 **p** 18. NSM Ettingshall *Lich* from 17; Dir Transforming Communities from 21. *35 Cherrington Gardens, Wolverhampton WV6 8AJ* M: 07523-907180 E: father.adam@hotmail.com

EDWARDS, Aiden James Alexander. b 82. Sheff Univ BA 17. Coll of Resurr Mirfield 14. **d** 17 **p** 18. C St Annes St Anne *Blackb* 17–20; V Burnley St Andr w St Marg and St Jas from 20. *St Andrew with St Margaret's Vicarage, 230 Barden Lane, Burnley BB10 1JD* T: (01282) 429723 M: 07758-919144 E: vicarofburnleystandrew@outlook.com

EDWARDS, Canon Aled. b 55. OBE 06. Univ of Wales (Lamp) BA 77. Trin Coll Bris 77. **d** 79 **p** 80. C Glanogwen *Ban* 79–82; V Llandinorwig w Penisa'r-waen 82–85; R Botwnnog 85–93; V Cardiff Dewi Sant *Llan* 93–99; Nat Assembly Liaison Officer from 99; Hon Chapl Llan Cathl from 99; Metrop Can Llan Cathl from 14. *20 Hilltop Avenue, Cilfynydd, Pontypridd CF37 4HZ* T: (01443) 407310

EDWARDS, Allen John. b 50. Univ of Wales (Cardiff) BSc 72 Imp Coll Lon PhD 81 York St Jo Univ MA 16 CEng 81 EurIng 88 FIMechE 93 FNucI 95 MCMI 95 MAPM 95. SAOMC 00. **d** 02 **p** 03. NSM Didcot All SS *Ox* 02–11; PtO *Eur* from 10; *Sarum* 12; NSM Warminster Ch Ch from 12. *10 Southdown Way, Warminster BA12 8FP* E: allen.edwards@btinternet.com

EDWARDS, Canon Andrew David. b 42. Tyndale Hall Bris 67. **d** 70 **p** 71. C Blackpool Ch Ch *Blackb* 70–73; C W Teignmouth *Ex* 73–76; P-in-c Ilfracombe SS Phil and Jas 76–85; C-in-c Lundy Is 79–89; V Ilfracombe SS Phil and Jas w W Down 85–89; TV Canford Magna *Sarum* 89–98; R Moresby *Carl* 98–07; RD Calder 02–07; Hon Can Carl Cathl 05–07; rtd 07; PtO *Carl* 07–14. *21 Grovelands Road, Headington, Oxford OX3 8HZ* T: (01865) 751591 E: a.edwards432@btinternet.com

EDWARDS, Andrew James. b 54. York Univ BA 76. Wycliffe Hall Ox 77. **d** 80 **p** 81. C Beckenham St Jo *Roch* 80–83; C Luton Ch Ch 83–87; V Skelmersdale Ch at Cen *Liv* 87–95; V Netherton 95–02; V Southport St Phil and St Paul 02–11; C Southport All SS 03–11; V W Derby Gd Shep 11–19; NSM Liv Cathl from 19. *4 Christchurch Close, Liverpool L11 3EN* T: 0151-474 1444 E: andrew@ajedwards.me.uk

EDWARDS, Andrew Jonathan Hugo (Joe). b 56. Ex Univ BA 78. Sarum & Wells Th Coll BTh 93. **d** 93 **p** 94. C Honiton, Gittisham, Combe Raleigh, Monkton etc *Ex* 93–97; P-in-c Queen Thorne *Sarum* 97–01; Chapl Clayesmore Sch Blandford 01–10; P-in-c Bridge Par *Sarum* 11–18; Chapl Qu Eliz Sch Wimborne 11–12; P-in-c Spetisbury w Charlton Marshall etc *Sarum* 13–18; rtd 18. *Church Farmhouse, Stourton Caundle, Sturminster Newton DT10 2JN*

EDWARDS, Anita Carolyn. See COLPUS, Anita Carolyn

EDWARDS, Canon Anne Joan. b 67. Lanc Univ BA 89 Liv Univ MTh 05 Salford Univ BSc 08. NOC 97. **d** 00 **p** 01. C Elton All SS *Man* 00–04; Chapl Bolton Hosps NHS Trust 02–04; Chapl and Spiritual Care Manager Wrightington, Wigan and Leigh Teaching Hosps NHS Foundn Trust from 04; Bp's Adv for Healthcare Chapl *Man* from 15; LtO *Blackb* from 10; Hon Can Man Cathl from 15. *9 Stocks Courts, 2*

Harriet Street, Worsley, Manchester M28 3JW T: (01942) 822324 E: anne.j.edwards@wwl.nhs.uk *or* anne@sajm.net

EDWARDS, Canon Arthur John. b 42. Qu Mary Coll Lon BA 64 MPhil 66 Cardiff Univ PhD 16. St Mich Coll Llan 66. d 68 p 69. C Newport St Woolos *Mon* 68–71; V Llantarnam 71–74; Chapl Bp of Llan High Sch 74–78; V Griffithstown *Mon* 78–86; Dioc Dir RE 86–91; TR Cwmbran 86–95; Hon Can St Woolos Cathl 88–91; Can St Woolos Cathl 91–12; V Caerleon 95–02; V Caerleon w Llanhennock 02–09; V Caerleon and Llanfrechfa 09–12; AD Newport 98–09; rtd 12; P-in-c Mynyddislwyn *Mon* 12–14; PtO from 14. *31 Candwr Park, Ponthir, Newport NP18 1HL* T: (01633) 430768 E: aandcedwards@talk21.com

EDWARDS, Benjamin John. b 78. Westcott Ho Cam 16. d 18 p 19. C Beccles St Mich and St Luke *St E* 18–20; C St E Cathl Distr 20–21; V Gt Barton and Thurston from 21. *The Vicarage, Church Road, Great Barton, Bury St Edmunds IP31 2QR* E: revdbenjaminedwards@gmail.com

EDWARDS, Carl Flynn. b 63. Cranmer Hall Dur 03. d 05 p 06. C Scartho *Linc* 05–09; P-in-c Fairfield *Derby* 09–18; C Buxton w Burbage and King Sterndale 09–12; P-in-c Peak Forest and Dove Holes 12–18; V Fairfield, Peak Forest and Dove Holes from 18. *Fairfield Vicarage, Cherry Tree Drive, Fairfield, Buxton SK17 7JN* T: (01298) 23629 E: revcarl@live.co.uk

EDWARDS, Miss Carol Rosemary. b 46. Trin Coll Bris 74. dss 81 d 87 p 94. Hengrove *Bris* 81–82; Filton 82–85; Brislington St Chris 85–99; Dn-in-c 87–94; P-in-c 94–99; P-in-c Brislington St Chris and St Cuth 99–00; Hon Can Bris Cathl 93–00; P-in-c California *Ox* 00–10; rtd 10; PtO *B & W* from 11. *44 Godwin Drive, Nailsea, Bristol BS48 2XF* T: (01275) 858168 M: 07879-536218 E: carol.edwards858@gmail.com

EDWARDS, Christopher Alban. b 27. Hertf Coll Ox. Th Ext Educn Coll. d 89 p 92. C Pietersburg Ch Ch S Africa 89; C Montagu 90–96; C Harare Cathl Zimbabwe 96–01; PtO *Ripon* 01; *York* 01–19. *1 Hastings House, Holyrood Lane, Ledsham, South Milford, Leeds LS25 5LL* T: (01977) 682117 M: 07780-543114 E: chrisalban@btopenworld.com

EDWARDS, Christopher David. b 72. Peterho Cam BA 93. Oak Hill Th Coll BA 18. d 18 p 19. C Lt Heath *St Alb* 18–21; C Oakwood St Thos Trent Park *Lon* from 21. *2 Chalk Lane, Cockfosters, Barnet EN4 9JQ*

EDWARDS, David Arthur. b 26. Wadh Coll Ox BA 50 MA 51 Edin Univ PhD 98. Wycliffe Hall Ox 50. d 52 p 53. C Barlow Moor *Man* 52–55; Liv Sec SCM 55–58; Chapl Liv Univ 55–58; R Burnage St Nic *Man* 58–65; V Yardley St Edburgha *Birm* 65–73; Org Sec CECS Blackb, Carl and Man 73–78; R Man Resurr 78–81; V Lorton and Loweswater w Buttermere *Carl* 81–87; USPG 87–92; Malaysia 87–92; rtd 92; PtO *Carl* 00–16. *46 Wainwright Court, Webb View, Kendal LA9 4TE* T: (01539) 739297

EDWARDS, The Most Revd David John. b 60. Loughb Univ BA 81 Homerton Coll Cam PGCE 82 Kent Univ MA 95 Wycliffe Coll Toronto DD 15. CA Tr Coll 86 EAMTC 94. d 95 p 96. C High Ongar w Norton Mandeville *Chelmsf* 95–98; Prin Taylor Coll Saint John Canada 98–07; P-in-c Saint John St Jas 98–01; R Saint John St Mark 01–11; Adn Saint John 08–11; Adn St Andrews 11–14; Par Development Officer 11–14; Bp Fredericton from 14; Abp and Metrop Prov of Canada from 20. *151 Norfolk Drive, Fredericton NB E3B 4W1, Canada* T: (001) (506) 459 1801 E: dedwards@diofton.ca

EDWARDS, Diana Clare. b 56. Nottm Univ BTh 86 SRN 77 RSCN 81. Linc Th Coll 83. dss 86 d 87 p 94. S Wimbledon H Trin and St Pet *S'wark* 86–90; Par Dn 87–90; Par Dn Lingfield and Crowhurst 90–94; C 94–95; Chapl St Piers Hosp Sch Lingfield 90–95; R Bletchingley *S'wark* 95–04; RD Godstone 98–04; Hon Can S'wark Cathl 01–04; Dean of Women's Min 03–04; Can Res Cant Cathl 04–18; R Drybrook, Lydbrook and Ruardean *Glouc* from 18. *The Rectory, High Street, Ruardean GL17 9US* T: (01594) 726318 E: revclareedwards@gmail.com

EDWARDS (née SMITH), Mrs Dorothea Violet (Thea). b 93. Warwick Univ BA 16. Trin Coll Bris BA 19. d 19 p 20. C Woking Ch Ch *Guildf* from 19. *4 Orchard Drive, Woking GU21 4BN* M: 07845-232393 E: thea.smith@rocketmail.com

EDWARDS, Gary Nord. St Mellitus Coll 17. d 19 p 20. OLM Ashingdon w S Fambridge, Canewdon and Paglesham *Chelmsf* from 19. *54 Durham Road, Southend-on-Sea SS2 4LU* T: (01702) 611777 E: gary-st.andrews@outlook.com

EDWARDS, Graham Charles. b 40. Qu Coll Birm 80. d 82 p 83. C Baswich *Lich* 82–86; C Tamworth 86–88; R Hertford St Andr *St Alb* 88–05; RD Hertford and Ware 96–99; rtd 05; PtO *Lich* 06–17. *2 The Old Forge, Main Road, Great Haywood, Stafford ST18 0RZ* T: (01889) 882868

EDWARDS, Guy. *See* EDWARDS, Jonathan Guy

EDWARDS, Helen. *See* HINGLEY, Helen

EDWARDS (née BENNETT), Canon Helen Anne. b 69. Coll of Ripon & York St Jo BEd 91 Bris Univ BA 01. Trin Coll Bris 99. d 01 p 02. C Beverley Minster *York* 01–05; P-in-c Liv Ch Ch Norris Green 05–09; V from 09; Hon Can Liv Cathl from 13. *4 Christchurch Close, Liverpool L11 3EN* T: 0151-474 1444 E: helenedwards@ymail.com

EDWARDS, Helen Glynne. *See* WEBB, Helen Glynne

EDWARDS, Canon Henry Victor. b 48. AKC 71 Open Univ BA 85 Middx Univ MSc 00. St Aug Coll Cant 72. d 73 p 74. C W Leigh CD *Portsm* 73–77; V Cosham 77–84; V Reydon *St E* 84–86; V Blythburgh w Reydon 86–96; Chapl St Felix Sch Southwold 86–96; Chapl Blythburgh Hosp 86–96; P-in-c Campsea Ashe w Marlesford, Parham and Hacheston *St E* 96–00; R 00–14; P-in-c Brandeston w Kettleburgh and Easton 07–14; Hon Can St E Cathl 00–14; rtd 14; PtO *St E* from 14; Dioc Advr for Counselling and Past Care 96–17. *Dunwich View, The Green, Walberswick, Southwold IP18 6TP* T: (01502) 722928 M: 07748-986022 E: harry@psalm23.demon.co.uk

EDWARDS, Canon James Frederick. b 36. ALCD 62. d 62 p 63. C Kenwyn *Truro* 62–68; V Tuckingmill 68–76; V St Columb Minor and St Colan 76–01; RD Pydar 84–93; Hon Can Truro Cathl 92–01; rtd 01; PtO *Truro* 01–21. *45 Tretherras Road, Newquay TR7 2TF* T: (01637) 870967

EDWARDS, Jane. *See* EDWARDS, Wendy Jane

EDWARDS, Janet Margaret. b 41. TCert 62 Lon Bible Coll BD 73. WEMTC 98. d 01 p 02. NSM Coalbrookdale, Iron-Bridge and Lt Wenlock *Heref* 01–10; PtO from 10. *2 Madeley Wood View, Madeley, Telford TF7 5YF* T: (01952) 583254

EDWARDS, Mrs Jill Kathleen. b 48. Man Univ BA 69 CQSW 72. S'wark Ord Course 90. d 93 p 95. NSM Grays Thurrock and Ind Chapl *Chelmsf* 93–07; Asst Dioc Soc Resp Officer *Truro* 07–19; Public Preacher 07–08; P-in-c Gerrans w St Anthony-in-Roseland and Philleigh 08–19; rtd 19; PtO *Truro* from 19. *Trelowen, Rosevine, Portscatho, Truro TR2 5EW* T: (01872) 580117 E: jill@jilledwards.com

EDWARDS, Joe. *See* EDWARDS, Andrew Jonathan Hugo

EDWARDS, Joel Kim. b 69. Oak Hill Th Coll BA 02. d 09 p 10. NSM Leyton Ch Ch *Chelmsf* 09–14; PtO 14–15; P-in-c Dagenham 15–18; V from 18. *The Vicarage, Church Lane, Dagenham RM10 9UL* T: (020) 8215 2962 M: 07903-516456 E: joel.dagenham@gmail.com

EDWARDS, Canon John Ralph. b 50. Bris Univ BSc 71 FCA 74. SAOMC 98. d 01 p 02. NSM California *Ox* 01–06; NSM Finchampstead 06–11; NSM Finchampstead and California 11–20; Hon Can Ch Ch 13–20; rtd 20; PtO *Ox* from 20. *Green Hedges, 25 St John's Street, Crowthorne RG45 7NJ* T: (01344) 774586 F: 774056 M: 07850-602488

EDWARDS, Jonathan Guy. b 63. Bris Univ BA 85 Fitzw Coll Cam BA 93 MA 95 Sarum Coll MA 16. Ridley Hall Cam 91. d 94 p 95. C Preston Plucknett *B & W* 94–98; C Clevedon St Andr and Ch Ch 98–02; V Farrington Gurney 02–06; V Paulton 02–06; P-in-c High Littleton 05–06; V Paulton w Farrington Gurney and High Littleton 07–18; R Bushey *St Alb* from 18. *The Rectory, High Street, Bushey WD23 1BD* T: (020) 8950 1546 M: 07837-672481 E: rector@busheyparish.org

EDWARDS, Judith Sarah. *See* McARTHUR-EDWARDS, Judith Sarah

EDWARDS (née EVANS), Mrs Linda Mary. b 49. Univ of Wales (Cardiff) BA 71 K Coll Lon BD 74 AKC 74. Yale Div Sch STM 76. dss 76 d 80 p 99. Llanishen and Lisvane *Llan* 76–78; Wrexham *St As* 78–80; C 80–82; Chapl Maudsley Hosp Lon 82–84; Chapl Bethlem R Hosp Beckenham 82–84; Chapl Lon Univ 84–87; NSM Llanfair-pwll and Llanddaniel-fab etc *Ban* 99–03; P-in-c Llangynog *St As* 03–06; C Llanrhaeadr ym Mochnant etc 07–10; rtd 10; PtO *St As* from 14. *15 The Meadows, Llandudno Junction LL31 9LP* T: (01492) 585063 M: 07791-467102 E: lindamaryedwards@yahoo.co.uk

EDWARDS, Lynda. *See* LILLEY, Lynda Jane

EDWARDS, Malcolm Ralph. b 27. Man Univ 49. Cranmer Hall Dur 57. d 59 p 60. C Withington St Paul *Man* 59–62; C Chadderton Em 62–64; R Longsight St Jo 64–70; V Halliwell St Thos 70–81; V Milnrow 81–92; rtd 92; PtO *Man* from 92. *20 Upper Lees Drive, Westhoughton, Bolton BL5 3UE* T: (01942) 813279 M: 07791-294680 E: revmr.edwards@virgin.net

EDWARDS, Mark Anthony. b 61. MBE 10. Cranmer Hall Dur 91. d 95 p 97. C Ulverston St Mary w H Trin *Carl* 95–97; C Barrow St Jo 97–00; TV Barrow St Matt 00–08; TV Ch the King *Newc* from 08; Chapl Northumbria Police 08–12. *The Vicarage, 2 East Acres, Dinnington, Newcastle upon Tyne NE13 7NA* T: (01661) 872320 E: haydenfox9411@gmail.com

EDWARDS, Mark John. b 66. St Aug Coll Cant 18. d 21. C Gravesend St Geo *Roch* from 21. *28 The*

Sandpipers, Gravesend DA12 5QB M: 07801-550812
E: revmarkedwards@outlook.com

EDWARDS, Mrs Mary. b 47. St Jo Coll York CertEd 69 Birkbeck Coll Lon BSc 74 New Coll Edin BD 93. S Dios Minl Tr Scheme 96. **d** 96 **p** 97. NSM Avon Valley *Sarum* 96–00; TV Wexcombe 00–02; TV Savernake 02–12; RD Pewsey 10–12; rtd 12; LtO *Edin* from 16. *The Coach House, Glenmayne, Galashiels TD1 3NR* T: (01896) 668383 E: mary_avonvalley@hotmail.com

EDWARDS, Nicholas James. b 83. Leic Univ BA 05. Wycliffe Hall Ox BA 20. **d** 20. C Moulton *Pet* from 20. *3 High Street, Moulton, Northampton NN3 7SR* T: (01604) 494698 E: nicholasedwards@hotmail.com *or* n.edwards@moultonchurch.co.uk

EDWARDS, Preb Nicholas John. b 53. UEA BA 75 Fitzw Coll Cam BA 77 MA 80. Westcott Ho Cam 75. **d** 78 **p** 79. C Kirkby *Liv* 78–81; V Cantril Farm 81–87; V Hale 87–94; R Chingford SS Pet and Paul *Chelmsf* 94–04; R Colyton, Musbury, Southleigh and Branscombe *Ex* 04–10; P-in-c Ex St Thos and Em 10–17; Preb Ex Cathl 13–17; rtd 17; PtO *Guildf* from 18. *2 Lawn Road, Guildford GU2 4DE* M: 07826-545315 E: fr.nicholasedwards@virginmedia.com

EDWARDS, Mrs Nita Mary. b 50. Univ of Wales (Ban) BD 72 Nottm Univ PGCE 73. Cranmer Hall Dur 93. **d** 93 **p** 94. C Ormesby *York* 93–95; C Billingham St Aid *Dur* 95–97; V 97–02; V Clayton *Lich* 02–17; rtd 17; PtO *St As* from 17; *Lich* 19–21. *13 T Gwylfa, Sandy Lane, Prestatyn LL19 7SB* T: (01745) 852106 E: nita.edwards@ntlworld.com

EDWARDS, Owen David. b 86. Ban Univ BA 07 Glyndŵr Univ PhD 15. St Seiriol Cen 12. **d** 16 **p** 18. C Carbonear Canada 16; C Prestwich St Mary *Man* 18–19; C Kersal Moor 19–21; R Brede w Udimore and Beckley and Peasmarsh *Chich* from 21. *The Rectory, Brede Hill, Brede, Rye TN31 6HG* T: (01424) 882201 M: 07512-760823 E: owen.edwards2@btinternet.com

EDWARDS, Peter Daniel. b 81. St Aid Coll Dur BA 02 Peterho Cam BA 09 MA 14. Ridley Hall Cam 07. **d** 10 **p** 11. C Gt Malvern St Mary *Worc* 10–14; P-in-c Walton le Soken *Chelmsf* from 15. *The Vicarage, Martello Road, Walton on the Naze CO14 8BP* T: (01255) 675351 E: peter.edwards@allsaintswalton.co.uk

EDWARDS, Peter Richard Henderson. b 65. Nottm Univ BA 86. St Steph Ho Ox 03. **d** 05 **p** 06. C Uppingham w Ayston and Wardley w Belton *Pet* 05–08; TV Bridport *Sarum* 08–13; P-in-c Bath Bathwick *B & W* 13–17; R from 17. *The Rectory, Sham Castle Lane, Bath BA2 6JL* T: (01225) 447450 M: 07776-227555 E: frpeteredwards@sky.com

EDWARDS, Phillip Gregory. b 52. Lon Univ BSc 73 ARCS 73 MSOSc 90. Qu Coll Birm 78. **d** 81 **p** 82. C Lillington *Cov* 81–85; P-in-c Cov St Alb 85–86; TV Cov E 86–01; C Bury St Paul and Bury Ch King *Man* 01–03; Chapl Bolton Univ 03–15; C Westhoughton and Wingates 04–05; C Leverhulme 05–07; Lic Preacher from 11; PtO *Ches* from 19. *14 Howey Lane, Congleton CW12 4AE* E: philgedwards@outlook.com

EDWARDS, Robert James. b 52. Chich Univ BA 07. Cranmer Hall Dur 01. **d** 03 **p** 04. C Broadwater *Chich* 03–08; TV S Crawley 08–20; rtd 20. *13 Acacia Avenue, Ashill, Thetford IP25 7AR* E: rev.robedwards@outlook.com

EDWARDS, Roger Brian. b 41. Sarum & Wells Th Coll 87. **d** 89 **p** 90. C Wellington and Distr *B & W* 89–92; V Hursley and Ampfield *Win* 92–06; rtd 06; PtO *Win* from 06. *34 Heatherstone Avenue, Dibden Purlieu, Southampton SO45 4LH* T: (023) 8087 9689

EDWARDS, Canon Rowland Thomas. b 62. Univ of Wales BTh 91. St Mich Coll Llan 85. **d** 88 **p** 89. C Llangiwg *S & B* 88–90; C Morriston 90–91; V Llangorse, Cathedine, Llanfihangel Tallyllyn etc 91–01; V Llyn Safaddan 01–06; V Talgarth w Bronllys w Llanfilo from 06; AD Hay 02–15; AD Gtr Brecon 16–17; Can Res Brecon Cathl from 08. *The Vicarage, Bronllys, Brecon LD3 0HS* T: (01874) 711200 E: rowlbar@talktalk.net

EDWARDS, Canon Ruth Blanche. b 39. Girton Coll Cam BA 61 MA 65 PhD 68 Aber Coll of Educn PGCE 75. Ab Dioc Tr Course 77. **d** 87 **p** 94. Lect Aber Univ *Ab* 77–90; Sen Lect 90–96; NSM Aberdeen St Jas 87–88; NSM Aberdeen St Jo 88–96; Lect Ripon Coll Cuddesdon 96–99; Hon Can St Andr Cathl *Ab* from 97; rtd 00; NSM Aberdeen St Jas *Ab* from 00; P-in-c 12–13. *99 Queen's Den, Aberdeen AB15 8BN* T: (01224) 312688

EDWARDS, Scott. b 71. Wolv Univ LLB 93 St Jo Coll Dur BA 00. Cranmer Hall Dur 97. **d** 00 **p** 01. C Halas *Worc* 00–03; V Frimley Green and Mytchett *Guildf* 03–12; V Chessington from 12. *The Vicarage, 1 Garrison Lane, Chessington KT9 2LB* T: (020) 8397 3016 E: scott_edwards@btinternet.com

EDWARDS, Stephen. b 44. S'wark Ord Course. **d** 82 **p** 83. C Benhilton *S'wark* 82–86; P-in-c Clapham Ch Ch and St Jo 86–87; TV Clapham Team 87–94; Chapl HM Pris Wormwood Scrubs 94–96; Chapl HM Pris Maidstone 96–01; Chapl HM Pris Wandsworth 01–04; rtd 04; PtO *S'wark* from 04. *12 Bucharest Road, London SW18 3AR* T: (020) 8870 1991

EDWARDS, Canon Stephen Michael. b 72. Lanc Univ BSc 93 Anglia Poly Univ MA 99 Man Univ DPT 16. Westcott Ho Cam 93. **d** 96 **p** 97. C Colwyn Bay *St As* 96–99; P-in-c Brynymaen 99–02; P-in-c Birch-in-Rusholme St Agnes w Longsight St Jo etc *Man* 02–12; R 12; TR Wythenshawe 12–19; AD Withington 13–19; Can Res Worc Cathl from 19. *2 College Green, Worcester WR1 2LH* E: revdstephenedwards@yahoo.co.uk

EDWARDS, Mrs Susan. b 54. R Holloway Coll Lon BSc 75 SS Hild & Bede Coll Dur PGCE 76. Qu Coll Birm 78. dss 81 **d** 87 **p** 94. Lillington *Cov* 81–85; Cov E 85–01; Par Dn 87–94; C 94–01; P-in-c Woolfold *Man* 01–07; TV Leverhulme 07–12; TR 12–18; rtd 18; PtO *Ches* from 19. *14 Howey Lane, Congleton CW12 4AE* M: 07982-674902 E: sedwards327@outlook.com

EDWARDS, Mrs Susan Diane. b 48. St Alb Minl Tr Scheme 86 Cranmer Hall Dur 91. **d** 92 **p** 94. Par Dn Borehamwood *St Alb* 92–94; C 94–96; V Arlesey w Astwick 96–13; rtd 13; PtO *Ches* from 14. *31 School Road, Meadowbank, Winsford CW7 2PG* T: (01606) 559458 E: susan.d.edwards@ntlworld.com *or* granny.s@outlook.com

EDWARDS, Thea. *See* SMITH, Dorothea Violet

EDWARDS, Timothy Mark. b 79. St Aid Coll Dur BA 00. Oak Hill Th Coll MA 12. **d** 12 **p** 13. C Eden, Gelt and Irthing *Carl* 12–17; R Knockholt w Halstead *Roch* from 17. *The Rectory, Church Road, Halstead, Sevenoaks TN14 7HQ* T: (01959) 532133 M: 07980-826365 E: rev.tim.edwards@btinternet.com

EDWARDS, Wendy Jane. b 49. Kent Univ BA 07 Cant Ch Ch Univ MA 12 Bingley Coll of Educn CertEd 71. SEITE 03. **d** 06 **p** 07. C Riverhead w Dunton Green *Roch* 06–11; P-in-c Belvedere All SS 11–12; V 12–18; rtd 18; PtO *Roch* from 19; Bp's Adv for Rtd Clergy from 20. *23 The Boundary, Langton Green, Tunbridge Wells TN3 0YA* T: (01892) 519227 E: revjaneedwards@btinternet.com

EDY, Robert James. b 48. Southn Univ BA 70 CertEd 71. Ox Min Course 90. **d** 93 **p** 94. Dep Hd Master Henry Box Sch Witney 90–08; NSM Ducklington *Ox* 93–99; P-in-c 99–13; R 13–15; PtO from 15; Chapl Rendcomb Coll Cirencester from 15. *The Rectory Cottage, Rendcomb, Cirencester GL7 7EZ* T: (01285) 831391 E: bobedy21@gmail.com

EGAR, Canon Judith Anne. b 57. Somerville Coll Ox BA 79 MA 84 Solicitor 83. STETS 01. **d** 04 **p** 05. NSM Brighton St Nic *Chich* 04–07; LtO 09–15; NSM Lewes St Anne and St Mich and St Thos etc from 15; PtO *Lon* 08–10; RD Lewes and Seaford *Chich* 17–21; Can and Preb Chich Cathl from 19. *15 St Peter's Place, Lewes BN7 1YP*

EGERTON, George. b 28. S'wark Ord Course 70. **d** 73 **p** 74. NSM Shere *Guildf* 73–94; PtO 94–17. *Weyside, Lower Street, Shere, Guildford GU5 9HX* T: (01483) 202549

EGERTON, Mrs Susan Doreen. b 52. MCSP 75. **d** 09 **p** 10. OLM Surrey Weald *Guildf* 09–15; rtd 15; PtO *Nor* from 16. *High Walls, Workhouse Road, Smallburgh, Norwich NR12 9NL* T: (01692) 536081 E: sueegerton@aol.com

EGGERTSEN, Jacob Harold. b 85. Newc Univ BA 08. Oak Hill Th Coll MTheol 19. **d** 19 **p** 20. C Banbury St Paul *Ox* from 19. *10 Hardwick Park, Banbury OX16 1YD* M: 07890-620541 E: jakeeggertsen@hotmail.com

EGGLESTON, Hugh Patrick. b 60. LSE BSc(Econ) 82 Leeds Univ BA 10. Coll of Resurr Mirfield 08. **d** 10 **p** 11. C E Dulwich St Jo *S'wark* 10–14; TR Thamesmead from 14; Ecum Adv Woolwich Area from 17. *Thamesmead Rectory, 22 Manor Close, London SE28 8EY* T: (020) 8312 0731 M: 07788-563253 E: peggleston@ymail.com

EGGLETON, Michael John. b 50. SAOMC 96 ERMC 06. **d** 07 **p** 08. NSM Northchurch and Wigginton *St Alb* from 07. *St Bartholomew's Vicarage, Vicarage Road, Wigginton, Tring HP23 6DZ* T: (01442) 823273 M: 07962-145398 E: mikeeggleton7@btopenworld.com

EGHTEDARIAN, Mohammad Reza. b 76. Wycliffe Hall Ox 12. **d** 15 **p** 16. C Liv Cathl 15–18; Chapl Ankara *Eur* 18–19; Intercultural Pioneer Min *Leic* from 20. *Parish Office, St Peter's Centre, Wigston Road, Oadby, Leicester LE2 5QE* T: 0116-272 0080 M: 07709-903764

EGLIN, Ian Charles. b 55. St Jo Coll Dur BA 76. Coll of Resurr Mirfield 77. **d** 79 **p** 80. C Cov St Mary 79–83; TV Kingsthorpe w Northampton St Dav *Pet* 83–87; P-in-c Pitsford w Boughton 85–87; Chapl RN 87–03; V Ipplepen, Torbryan and Denbury *Ex* 03–12; RD Newton Abbot and Ipplepen 07–12; rtd 12; Dioc Chapl MU *Ex* 13–16; PtO *Eur* from 12; *Ex* from 13.

27 Riverside Walk, Yealmpton, Plymouth PL8 2LU T: (01752) 881996 E: ian@eglins.co.uk

EJIMOFO, Beverley Marlene. RGN 83 RHV 88. St Aug Coll of Th 18. **d** 20. NSM Shortlands *Roch* 20–21; NSM Beckenham St Geo and St Barn from 21. *Address withheld by request* M: 07960-881805 E: bejimofo@gmail.com

EJINKONYE, Prorenata Emeka. b 52. **d** 08 **p** 09. OLM Victoria Docks St Luke *Chelmsf* 08–10; NSM 10–20; NSM N Woolwich w Silvertown from 20. *26 Boreham Avenue, London E16 3AG* T: (020) 3538 5076 E: emeka12@hotmail.com

EKE, Mrs Helen Margo. b 72. Linc Sch of Th and Min 15. **d** 20 **p** 21. NSM Carr Dyke Gp *Linc* from 20. *6 The Elms, Kirkby-on-Bain, Woodhall Spa LN10 6YP* T: (01526) 354231 M: 07736-780131 E: heleneke@hotmail.co.uk

EKIN, Tom Croker. b 29. Linc Th Coll 59. **d** 60 **p** 61. C Leamington Priors All SS *Cov* 60–63; R Ilmington w Stretton-on-Fosse 63–72; S Africa 72–77; R Moreton-in-Marsh w Batsford *Glouc* 77–83; R Moreton-in-Marsh w Batsford, Todenham etc 83–94; rtd 95; Hon C Theale and Englefield *Ox* 94–04. *6 Old Bell Court, Wrington, Bristol BS40 5QH* T: (01934) 862398

ELBOURNE, Keith Marshall. b 46. Nottm Univ BTh 74 Lon Univ BD 76. St Jo Coll Nottm 70. **d** 74 **p** 75. C Romford Gd Shep *Chelmsf* 74–78; C Victoria Docks St Luke 78–81; P-in-c 81–92; V Walthamstow St Pet 92–02; TR Tettenhall Wood and Perton *Lich* 02–10; rtd 10; PtO *Lich* from 10. *11 Windsor Gardens, Codsall, Wolverhampton WV8 2EX*

ELBOURNE, Timothy. b 60. Selw Coll Cam BA 81 MA 85 PGCE 82. Westcott Ho Cam 84. **d** 86 **p** 87. C Tottenham H Trin *Lon* 86–88; Chapl York Univ 88–94; P-in-c Thorp Arch w Walton 94–98; Dir of Educn *Ely* 98–12; Hon Can Ely Cathl 99–12; Dir of Educn *Chelmsf* from 13; Public Preacher from 13. *10 Sherwood Way, Feering, Colchester CO5 9LJ* T: (01245) 294400 F: 294477 Pager: (04325) 320796 E: telbourne@chelmsford.anglican.org

ELCOCK, Jonathan. b 64. Westcott Ho Cam 07. **d** 09 **p** 11. C Aberavon *Llan* 09; C Salford All SS *Man* 10–13; R Failsworth St Jo 13–19; Admin Sydney St Jas Australia from 20. *Address withheld by request* E: oldsalopian@hotmail.com

ELDER, Andrew John. b 49. Sunderland Poly BSc 72 MSc 76. NEOC 91. **d** 94 **p** 95. NSM Wallsend St Luke *Newc* 94–02; NSM Wallsend St Pet and St Luke 02–03; C Monkseaton St Pet 03–06; V Blyth St Mary 06–19; Hon C Cowpen 18–19; rtd 19; PtO *Newc* from 19. *51 Rowantree Road, Newcastle upon Tyne NE6 4TE* E: andy.elder@btinternet.com

ELDER, Nicholas John. b 51. Hatf Poly BA 73. Cuddesdon Coll 73. **d** 76 **p** 77. C Mill End and Heronsgate w W Hyde *St Alb* 76–79; TV Borehamwood 79–85; V Bedford St Mich 85–90; V Bedford All SS 90–00; V Camberwell St Geo *S'wark* 00–17; Warden Trin Coll Cen Camberwell 00–17; rtd 17. *28 Cardigan Street, Ipswich IP1 3PF* E: 1nicholaselder@gmail.com

ELDERGILL, Sharon Alice. b 62. **d** 13 **p** 14. NSM Burnham *B & W* from 13. *11 George Street, Burnham-on-Sea TA8 1BA* M: 07725-621437 E: sharon.eldergill@gmail.com

ELDRIDGE, John Frederick. b 48. Loughb Univ BSc 70 Golden Gate Sem (USA) MDiv 83 Fuller Th Sem California DMin 96. Oak Hill Th Coll 90. **d** 92 **p** 93. C Maidstone St Luke *Cant* 92–97; Min Prince's Park CD *Roch* 97–02; P-in-c Wickham Market w Pettistree *St E* 02–07; V 07–18; rtd 18. *23 Broad Road, Wickham Market, Woodbridge IP13 0RJ* M: 07835-733413 E: jeldridge@supanet.com

ELDRIDGE, John Kenneth Tristan. b 59. St Steph Ho Ox 90. **d** 92 **p** 93. C Brighton Resurr *Chich* 92–96; C Hangleton 96–98; TR Moulsecoomb 98–05; V W Worthing St Jo 05–19; P-in-c Worthing St Andr 18–19; V Hove St Barn and St Agnes from 19; V Hove St Phil from 19; Chapl Sussex Beacon Hospice from 00. *St Barnabas' Vicarage, 88 Sackville Road, Hove BN3 3HE* E: frjohn@live.co.uk

ELDRIDGE, Prof Sandra Mary. b 57. Ox Univ BA 76 LSHTM MSc 82 PhD 05 FRCGP (Hon). St Mellitus Coll 16. **d** 18 **p** 20. NSM W Ham St Matt *Chelmsf* from 18. *41 Hampton Road, London E7 0PD* M: 07421-768343

ELDRIDGE, Stephen William. b 50. Open Univ BA 98. Chich Th Coll 87. **d** 89 **p** 90. C Stroud and Uplands w Slad *Glouc* 89–92; C Glouc St Mary de Crypt w St Jo and Ch Ch 92–95; C Glouc St Mary de Lode and St Nic 92–95; Bp's Chapl 92–93; P-in-c Kingswood w Alderley and Hillesley 95–00; P-in-c Cheltenham St Pet 00–08; TV N Cheltenham 08–16; rtd 16; PtO *Glouc* from 17. *38 Stanwick Gardens, Cheltenham GL51 9LF* T: (01242) 321325 E: stephen.stanwick@outlook.com

ELEYAE, Mrs Adeola Winifred. b 63. Lagos Univ LLB 85 LLM 90 Bris Univ LLM 13. St Mellitus Coll 11. **d** 14 **p** 15. NSM E Ham St Paul *Chelmsf* 14–16; C Walthamstow 16–18; TV 18–19; V Goodmayes All SS from 19; Bp's Equality Adv from 19. *The Vicarage, 38 Broomhill Road, Ilford IG3 9SJ* T: (020)

8599 2052 M: 07484-193147 E: aweleyae333@gmail.com *or* asgvicar@gmail.com *or* aeleyae@chelmsford.anglican.org

ELFICK, Brian Richard. b 76. Ex Coll Ox BA 98 Selw Coll Cam BA 04 MPhil 05. Ridley Hall Cam 02. **d** 06 **p** 07. C Cambridge H Sepulchre *Ely* 06–12; TR Toxteth St Philemon w St Gabr and St Cleopas *Liv* 12–18; R Toxteth St Philemon from 19. *The Vicarage, 40 Devonshire Road, Toxteth L8 3TZ* T: 0151-222 0814

ELFORD, Keith Anthony. b 59. Em Coll Cam BA 80 MA 84. Wycliffe Hall *Ox* 87. **d** 90 **p** 91. C Chertsey *Guildf* 90–94; P-in-c Ockham w Hatchford 94–98; Bp's Chapl 94–98; PtO 98–00; LtO from 01; P-in-c W Byfleet from 21; Progr Ldr Sarum Coll from 20. *15 Canford Drive, Addlestone KT15 2HH* M: 07771-920976 E: keith@elfordconsulting.co.uk

ELFORD, Canon Robert John. b 39. Man Univ MA 71 Ex Univ PhD 74. Brasted Th Coll 64 Ridley Hall Cam 66. **d** 68 **p** 69. C Denton St Lawr *Man* 68–71; P-in-c Gwinear *Truro* 71–74; R Phillack w Gwithian and Gwinear 74–78; Lect Man Univ 78–87; Hon C Withington St Paul *Man* 79–83; Warden St Anselm Hall 82–87; LtO *Man* 84–87; Pro-R Liv Inst of HE 88–99; Can Th Liv Cathl 92–04; rtd 04. *The Penthouse, 120 The Cliff, Wallasey CH45 2NW*

ELFRED, Michael William. b 48. BA 76 MPhil. Linc Th Coll 77. **d** 79 **p** 80. C Boultham *Linc* 79–82; C Croydon H Sav *Cant* 82–84; C Upper Norwood All SS *S'wark* 84–88; V Sanderstead St Mary 88–01; P-in-c Tadworth 01–11; V 11–16; rtd 16; PtO *S'wark* from 17. *Gadbrook, Wonham Lane, Betchworth RH3 7AD* M: 07931-463661

ELGAR, Richard John. b 50. Charing Cross Hosp Medical Sch MB, BS 73 LRCP 73 MRCS 73 MRCGP 80. St Jo Coll Nottm 92. **d** 92 **p** 93. NSM Derby St Alkmund and St Werburgh 92–96; P-in-c Derby St Barn 96–01; V 01–08; RD Derby N 05–06; rtd 08; PtO *Derby* 08–18. *38 Holborn Drive, Derby DE22 4DX* T: (01332) 344895 *or* 342553 E: relgar1015@aol.com

ELIZABETH, Sister. *See* HEATON, Elizabeth Ann

ELKINGTON, The Ven Audrey Anne. b 57. St Cath Coll Ox BA 80 UEA PhD 83. St Jo Coll Nottm 85 EAMTC 86. **dss** 88 **d** 92 **p** 94. Monkseaton St Mary *Newc* 88–91; Ponteland 91–92; C 92–93; C Prudhoe 93–02; RD Corbridge 99–02; Bp's Adv for Women in Min 01–11; Bp's Chapl 02–11; Dir of Ords 02–11; Hon Can Newc Cathl 06–11; Adn Bodmin *Truro* 11–21; RD Trigg Major 16–19; rtd 21. *86 Abbots Way, North Shields NE29 8LX* M: 07766-822872

ELKINGTON, Canon David John. b 51. Nottm Univ BTh 76 Leic Univ MEd 81 Dur Univ MATM 05. St Jo Coll Nottm 73. **d** 76 **p** 77. C Leic Martyrs 76–78; C Kirby Muxloe 78–80; Asst Chapl Leic Univ 80–82; Hon C Leic H Spirit 82; Chapl UEA *Nor* 82–88; TV Newc Epiphany 88–91; TR 91–93; P-in-c Prudhoe 93–98; V 98–02; Can Res Newc Cathl 02–11; C St Tudy w St Mabyn and Michaelstow *Truro* 11–16; C Bodmin w Lanhydrock and Lanivet 11–16; RD Trigg Minor and Bodmin 13–16; rtd 16; PtO *Truro* from 16. *86 Abbots Way, North Shields NE29 8LX* E: djelk@btinternet.com

ELKINS, Mrs Joy Kathleen. b 45. S Tr Scheme 93. **d** 96 **p** 97. NSM Corfe Mullen *Sarum* 96–03; NSM W Byfleet *Guildf* 03–08; C 08–14; rtd 14; PtO *Nor* from 14. *4 The Lawn, Fakenham NR21 8DT* T: (01328) 855075 E: joyelkins@btinternet.com

ELKINS, Canon Patrick Charles. b 34. St Chad's Coll Dur BA 57 DipEd 58. **d** 60 **p** 61. C Moordown *Win* 60–63; C Basingstoke 64–67; V Bransgore 67–04; Hon Can Win Cathl 89–04; rtd 04; PtO *Win* 04–19. *1 Tyrrells Court, Bransgore, Christchurch BH23 8BU* T: (01425) 673103

ELKS, Roger Mark. b 60. Imp Coll Lon BSc 83. Wycliffe Hall Ox 89. **d** 92 **p** 93. C St Austell *Truro* 92–95; V Carbis Bay w Lelant 95–01; I Holywood *D & D* 01–15; TV Appledore, Northam and Westward Ho! *Ex* from 19; C Abbotsham from 19. *7 Shepherds Meadow, Abbotsham, Bideford EX39 5BP* M: 07954-406680 E: vicarroger@gmail.com

ELLEM, Peter Keith. b 58. Nottm Univ BTh 90 Leeds Univ MA 99 CQSW. St Jo Coll Nottm 87. **d** 90 **p** 91. C Islington St Mary *Lon* 90–94; C Leeds St Geo *Ripon* 94–99; R Yagoona Australia 00–08; Chapl Westmead Hosp from 08. *46 Archibald Street, Padstow NSW 2211, Australia* T: (0061) (2) 9771 9369 *or* 9845 6038 E: prellem@yahoo.com.au

ELLERY, Ian Martyn William. b 56. K Coll Lon BD AKC. Chich Th Coll. **d** 82 **p** 83. C Hornsey St Mary w St Geo *Lon* 82–85; V Choral York Minster 85–89; Subchanter 86–89; R Patrington w Hollym, Welwick and Winestead 89–97; TR Howden 97–05; RD 97–02; P-in-c Cawood w Ryther and Wistow 05–11; R 11–16; rtd 16. *Address temp unknown* E: ianmwellery@hotmail.co.uk

ELLETSON, Annabelle. b 58. Heref Coll of Arts BA 09. St Padarn's Inst 19. **d** 20 **p** 21. C Vale of Gwrynne *S & B*

from 20. *The Mill, Llanbedr, Crickhowell NP8 1SY* T: (01873) 811330 M: 07740-537694 E: a.elletson@me.com

ELLIN, Lindsey Jane. *See* GOODHEW, Lindsey Jane Ellin

ELLINGHAM, Fiona Madeleine. b 66. d 16 p 17. OLM Howell Hill *Guildf* 16–18; OLM Nork w Burgh Heath 18–21; P-in-c Ewell St Fran from 21. *3 Winkworth Road, Banstead SM7 2QJ* T: (01737) 212920 E: fiona.ellingham66@gmail.com

ELLINGTON, Mrs Joanna Elisabeth. b 68. Leeds Univ BSc 89. Ripon Coll Cuddesdon. d 14 p 15. OLM The Cookhams *Ox* 14–18; NSM Furze Platt from 18. *Frith Coppice, Church Road, Cookham, Maidenhead SL6 9UH* E: revjo.ellington@gmail.com

ELLIOT, William Brunton. b 41. Edin Dioc NSM Course 81. d 84 p 85. NSM Lasswade *Edin* 84–92; NSM Dalkeith 84–92; Assoc P Edin St Pet 92–94; R Selkirk 94–06; rtd 06; LtO *Edin* from 06. *157 Newbattle Abbey Crescent, Dalkeith EH22 3LR* T: 0131-663 1369 E: bille157@aol.com *or* billelsie@aol.com

ELLIOT-NEWMAN, Christopher Guy. b 43. Bede Coll Dur TCert 67 Hull Univ BTh 83 MEd 87. Westcott Ho Cam 67. d 70 p 71. C Ditton St Mich *Liv* 70–73; C Hazlemere *Ox* 73–77; R Stockton-the-Forest w Holtby and Warthill *York* 77–87; Dir of Educn *Cant* 87–94; P-in-c Warden w Newbrough *Newc* 99–01; PtO 95–99 and from 02. *63 Keepers Road, Devizes SN10 2FP* M: 07951-471189 E: christopher@firststandardltd.co.uk

ELLIOTT, Anne. *See* ELLIOTT, Elizabeth Anne

ELLIOTT, Mrs Antonia. b 66. St Mellitus Coll BA 14. d 14 p 15. C N Farnborough *Guildf* 14–17; C Finchampstead and California *Ox* from 18. *2 Oak Drive, Aborfield Green, Reading RG2 9GJ* M: 07871-047490 E: toniaelliott3@gmail.com

ELLIOTT, Ben. *See* ELLIOTT, William Henry Venn

ELLIOTT, Canon Brian. b 49. Dur Univ BA 73. Coll of Resurr Mirfield 73. d 75 p 76. C Nunthorpe *York* 75–77; CF 77–09; Dep Asst Chapl Gen 96–09; rtd 09; PtO Cyprus and the Gulf from 09; OCM from 09; Hon Can St Paul's Cathl Nicosia from 18. *St Paul's Cathedral, PO Box 22014, 1516 Nicosia, Cyprus* E: brian@newpost.org

ELLIOTT, Christopher John. b 44. Sarum Th Coll 66. d 69 p 70. C Walthamstow St Pet *Chelmsf* 69–71; C Witham 71–74; P-in-c Gt and Lt Bentley 74–80; R Colchester Ch Ch w St Mary V 80–85; R Sible Hedingham 85–93; V Leigh-on-Sea St Aid 93–98; P-in-c Thornton Gp *Linc* 98–01; RD Horncastle 98–01; P-in-c Gt Leighs *Chelmsf* 01–05; P-in-c Lt Leighs 01–05; P-in-c Lt Waltham 01–05; R Gt and Lt Leighs and Lt Waltham 05–06; RD Chelmsf N 04–06; rtd 06; PtO *Chelmsf* 06–10; P-in-c Middleton-in-Teesdale w Forest and Frith *Dur* 10–13; P-in-c Eggleston 10–13; PtO *St E* 14–18; *Chelmsf* from 18. *36 The Croft, Great Yeldham, Halstead CO9 4JD* M: 07899-905698 E: revchriselliott@gmail.com

ELLIOTT, Elizabeth Anne. b 52. Lon Bible Coll BA 03 Win Univ MA 13. STETS 09. d 11 p 12. NSM Pennington *Win* 11–20; NSM Hordle from 20. *19 Heron Close, Sway, Lymington SO41 6ET* M: 07553-552540 E: anne19elliott@gmail.com

ELLIOTT, Eveline Mary. *See* HALL, Eveline Mary

ELLIOTT, Ian Peter. b 58. d 16 p 17. OLM Barkingside St Laur *Chelmsf* 16–20; NSM Stebbing and Lindsell w Gt and Lt Saling from 20. *11 Ploughmans Way, Stebbing, Dunmow CM6 3XJ* E: ian7.elliott@gmail.com

ELLIOTT, Jane. b 49. d 08 p 09. NSM Hatcham St Cath *S'wark* from 08. *13 Seymour Gardens, London SE4 2DN* T: (020) 7277 7968 E: elliottj139@gmail.com

ELLIOTT, Mrs Joanna Margaret. b 64. Bris Univ BA 85. STETS 03. d 06 p 07. NSM Haywards Heath St Wilfrid *Chich* from 06; Chapl Brighton and Sussex Univ Hosps NHS Trust 10–19; Lead Chapl from 19. *20 Courtlands, Haywards Heath RH16 4JD* T: (01444) 413799 M: 07710-273299 E: joanna@ctsn.co.uk

ELLIOTT, John Andrew. b 44. ACIB 68. SAOMC 95. d 98 p 99. NSM Bedgrove *Ox* 98–01; C Modbury, Bigbury, Ringmore w Kingston etc *Ex* 01–09; rtd 09; PtO *Ex* from 10. *Little Cumery, Aveton Gifford, Kingsbridge TQ7 4NN* T: (01548) 830688 M: 07764-523243 E: jaandpelliott@outlook.com

ELLIOTT, Kathryn Georgina. b 50. d 08 p 17. NSM Manston *Ripon* 08–12; NSM Holbeck 12–14; *Leeds* 14–20; PtO 20–21. *2 Maypole Mews, Barwick in Elmet, Leeds LS15 4PE* T: 0113-281 2761 M: 07597-078567

ELLIOTT (née JUTSUM), Mrs Linda Mary. b 56. St Pet Coll Birm CertEd 77. WMMTC 92. d 95 p 96. NSM Longthorpe *Pet* 95–99; P-in-c Etton w Helpston and Maxey 99–04; Chapl Thorpe Hall Hospice 04–09; PtO *Pet* from 09; *Linc* 17–20. *42 Frognall, Deeping St James, Peterborough PE6 8RR* T: (01778) 219167 E: revlinda.elliott@gmail.com

ELLIOTT, Marilyn Elizabeth. b 53. Ex Univ BTh 10. SWMTC 05. d 08 p 09. C Stoke Climsland *Truro* 08–13; C Linkinhorne 08–13; P-in-c Lanreath, Pelynt and Bradoc 13–16; R

Lanreath and Pelynt 16–18; C Lanteglos by Fowey 13–15; P-in-c 15–18; C Talland 13–15; P-in-c 15–18; C Lansallos 13–15; P-in-c 15–18; R Trelawny 18–20; rtd 20. *27 Courtlands Road, Tavistock PL19 0EF* E: marilynelliottm@btinternet.com

ELLIOTT, Mary. *See* HALL, Eveline Mary

ELLIOTT, Canon Maurice John. b 65. St Andr Univ MA 87 TCD BTh 92 MPhil 93 QUB PhD 01. CITC 89. d 93 p 94. C Coleraine *Conn* 93–98; I Greenisland 98–02; I Lurgan Ch the Redeemer *D & D* 02–08; Dir Ch of Ireland Th Inst from 08; Can Ch Ch Cathl Dublin *D & G* from 15. *7 Coolgraney, Nutgrove Park, Clonskeagh, Dublin 14, Republic of Ireland* T: (00353) (1) 260 5737 *or* 492 3506 F: 492 3082 M: 87-968 5218 E: mauriceelliott@theologicalinstitute.ie

ELLIOTT, Michael James. b 58. Westmr Coll Ox MTh 96 Nottm Trent Univ PGCE 98. St Jo Coll Nottm LTh 83. d 83 p 84. C Pontypridd St Cath *Llan* 83–86; C Leamington Priors St Paul *Cov* 86–89; Chapl RAF 89–06 and 07–14; Chapl Kimbolton Sch 06–07; Chapl RAuxAF from 14; PtO *Ely* from 15; *Eur* from 17. *Chaplaincy Services (RAF), HQ Air Command, RAF High Wycombe HP14 4UE* T: (01494) 496800 F: 496343 E: elliott.michael50@yahoo.com

ELLIOTT, Neil Raymond. b 78. Trin Coll Bris 13. d 15 p 16. C Whalley Range St Edm and Moss Side etc *Man* 15–19; P-in-c Collyhurst from 19; P-in-c Harpurhey from 19. *Christ Church Rectory, 95 Church Lane, Manchester M9 5BG* E: revneilelliott@gmail.com

ELLIOTT, Nigel Harvey. b 55. St Jo Coll Nottm 90. d 92 p 93. C Radcliffe *Man* 92–95; V Kilnhurst *Sheff* 95–08; R Wombwell 08–14; AD Wath 06–11; P-in-c Sinfin *Derby* 14–20; V 20–21; rtd 21. *161 Loughborough Road, Mountsorrel, Loughborough LE12 7AR* T: (01509) 415100 E: sinfinvicar14@gmail.com

ELLIOTT, The Ven Peter. b 41. Hertf Coll Ox BA 63 MA 68. Linc Th Coll 63. d 65 p 66. C Gosforth All SS *Newc* 65–68; C Balkwell 68–72; V High Elswick St Phil 72–80; V N Gosforth 80–87; V Embleton w Rennington and Rock 87–93; RD Alnwick 89–93; Hon Can Newc Cathl 90–93; Adn Northd and Can Res Newc Cathl 93–05; rtd 05; PtO *Newc* 05–21. *56 King Street, Seahouses NE68 7XS* T: (01665) 721133

ELLIOTT, Rebecca Caroline. b 73. Qu Foundn Birm 15. d 17 p 18. C Worcs W Rural *Worc* 17–21; V Malvern H Trin and St Jas from 21. *Holy Trinity Vicarage, 2 North Malvern Road, Malvern WR14 4LR* T: (01684) 573559 E: revrebeccaelliott@btinternet.com

ELLIOTT, Richard David Clive. b 53. Portsm Poly BSc 74 MICE 79 MIStructE. STETS 03. d 06 p 07. NSM Sway *Win* 06–17; NSM Boldre w S Baddesley from 17. *19 Heron Close, Sway, Lymington SO41 6ET* T: (01590) 683778 M: 07836-760150 E: richard.elliott@uwclub.net

ELLIOTT, Simon Mark. b 76. Liv Hope Univ Coll BA 97. Ridley Hall Cam 05. d 08 p 09. C Gt Crosby St Luke *Liv* 08–12; C Netherton 12–14; TV 14–17; TV Netherton and Sefton 17–19; TV Maghull and Melling from 19. *23 Green Link, Liverpool L31 8DW* T: 0151-531 6622 E: revsielliott@gmail.com

ELLIOTT, Simon Richard James. b 66. Lon Univ BSc 88. Cranmer Hall Dur BA 95. d 95 p 96. C Hendon St Paul Mill Hill *Lon* 95–99; V Hull St Martin w Transfiguration *York* 99–17; V Hutton Cranswick w Skerne, Watton and Beswick from 17; V Nafferton w Wansford from 17. *5 Howl Lane, Hutton, Driffield YO25 9QA* T: (01377) 271592 M: 07958-398307 E: elliottrev66@gmail.com

ELLIOTT, Sonya Jacqueline. *See* DORAGH, Sonya Jacqueline

ELLIOTT, Stuart. b 75. Univ of Wales (Ban) BTh 98 MTh 00. St Mich Coll Llan 05. d 07 p 08. C Holywell *St As* 07–10; V Llanasa and Ffynnongroew 10–15; P-in-c Betws-y-Coed and Capel Curig w Penmachno etc *Ban* 15–16; P-in-c Bro Gwydyr from 16. *The Vicarage, Vicarage Road, Betws-y-Coed LL24 0AD* T: (01690) 710313 E: rev@stubiedoo.co.uk

ELLIOTT, William Henry Venn (Ben). b 34. K Coll Cam BA 55 MA 59. Wells Th Coll 59. d 61 p 62. C Almondbury *Wakef* 61–66; V Bramshaw *Sarum* 66–81; P-in-c Landford w Plaitford 77–81; V Mere w W Knoyle and Maiden Bradley 81–99; rtd 99. *3 St George's Close, Salisbury SP2 8HA* T: (01722) 338409

ELLIOTT DE RIVEROL, Mrs Jennifer Kathleen. b 52. UEA MA 88 St Pet Coll Birm CertEd 75. ERMC 09. d 11 p 12. C Puerto de la Cruz Tenerife *Eur* 11–17; R Brinton, Briningham, Hunworth, Stody etc *Nor* 17–20; rtd 20; PtO *Nor* from 20. *2A Cyprus Road, Attleborough NR17 2EF* M: 07591-609397 E: revderiv@gmail.com

ELLIS, Anthony. *See* ELLIS, John Anthony

ELLIS, Brian Eric James. b 50. STETS 05. d 08 p 09. NSM Preston w Sutton Poyntz, Littlemoor etc *Sarum* 08–15; NSM Bincombe w Broadwey, Upwey and Buckland Ripers 12–15; NSM Weymouth Ridgeway 15–19; rtd 19; PtO *Sarum* from 19. *9 Windermere Crescent, Weymouth DT3 5HG* T: (01305) 549651 M: 07533-941686 E: brian-ellis@talktalk.net *or* brian9ellis@outlook.com

ELLIS, Canon Bryan Stuart. b 31. Qu Coll Cam BA 54 MA 58. Ridley Hall Cam 55. **d** 57 **p** 58. C Ramsgate St Luke *Cant* 57–59; C Herne Bay Ch Ch 59–62; V Burmantofts St Steph and St Agnes *Ripon* 62–81; RD Wakef 81–96; V Wakef St Andr and St Mary 81–00; Hon Can Wakef Cathl 89–00; rtd 00; PtO *Ripon* 01–14; *Leeds* from 14. *302 Oakwood Lane, Leeds LS8 3LE* T: 0113-240 3122

ELLIS, Charles Harold. b 50. NOC 78. **d** 81 **p** 82. C Davyhulme St Mary *Man* 81–85; V Tonge w Alkrington 85–91; P-in-c Radcliffe St Thos and St Jo 91; P-in-c Radcliffe St Mary 91; TR Radcliffe 91–99; AD Radcliffe and Prestwich 96–99; P-in-c Newchurch 99–00; TR Rossendale Middle Valley 00–04; AD Rossendale 00–04; V Ingleton w Chapel le Dale *Bradf* 04–14; TV Bentham, Burton-in-Lonsdale, Chapel-le-Dale etc *Leeds* 14–15; rtd 15. *2 Dallam Chase, Milnthorpe LA7 7DW* T: (015395) 62262 E: chasellis@btinternet.com

ELLIS, Christopher Duncan. b 67. Anglia Ruskin Univ BA 09. ERMC 05. **d** 08 **p** 09. C Thorpe St Andr *Nor* 08–11; V Thorpe St Matt 11–15; R Thurton w Ashby St Mary, Bergh Apton etc from 15; Hon PV Nor Cathl from 14. *The Rectory, 29 Ashby Road, Thurton, Norwich NR14 6AX* T: (01508) 484174 E: chris.ellis23@btinternet.com

ELLIS, Canon David Craven. b 34. Man Univ BA 56 MA 57. St Aid Birkenhead 59. **d** 61 **p** 62. C Gt Crosby St Luke *Liv* 61–65; Hong Kong 65–69; P-in-c Sawrey *Carl* 69–74; Dioc Youth Officer 69–74; V Halifax St Aug *Wakef* 74–84; R Greystoke, Matterdale and Mungrisdale *Carl* 84–87; R Watermillock 84–87; TR Greystoke, Matterdale, Mungrisdale etc 88–91; RD Penrith 87–91; TR Carl H Trin and St Barn 91–96; Hon Can Carl Cathl 91–96; rtd 96; PtO *Carl* 97–02 and 04–13; *Cov* 13–15; NSM Cartmel Peninsula *Carl* 02–04. *44 Cherry Orchard, Stratford-upon-Avon CV37 9AP* T: (01789) 269409 E: dandbellis4@btinternet.com

ELLIS, Emma Louise. b 79. Coll of Ripon & York St Jo BA 00 Heythrop Coll Lon MTh 03. Ridley Hall Cam 05. **d** 07 **p** 08. C Addiscombe St Mary Magd w St Martin *S'wark* 07–10; TV Limpsfield and Tatsfield 10–15; Dioc Discipleship and Voc Missr 15–17; NSM S Croydon Em 15–16; NSM Sanderstead 16–17; Dioc Voc Adv 12–17; V Lilliput *Sarum* from 17; Asst Dioc Dir of Ords from 16. *The Vicarage, 55 Lilliput Road, Poole BH14 8JX* T: (01202) 708567 E: vicar.lilliput@gmail.com

ELLIS, Hugh William. b 54. Sussex Univ BSc 76. Ridley Hall Cam 88. **d** 90 **p** 91. C Reading St Jo *Ox* 90–93; P-in-c Bradfield and Stanford Dingley 93–97; R 97–03; TR Langport Area *B & W* 03–12; TR High Wycombe *Ox* from 12. *The Vicarage, 6 Priory Avenue, High Wycombe HP13 6SH* T: (01494) 527526 E: hughellis4@gmail.com

ELLIS, Ian Morton. b 52. QUB BD 75 MTh 82 TCD PhD 89. CITC. **d** 77 **p** 78. C Portadown St Columba *Arm* 77–79; C Arm St Mark w Aghavilly 79–85; Chapl Arm R Sch 79–85; Hon V Choral Arm Cathl 82–93; I Mullavilly 85–93; Dom Chapl to Abp Arm 86–93; Tutor for Aux Min (Arm) 90–93; Dioc Adv on Ecum 92–93; I Newcastle *D & D* 93–20; Ed *The Church of Ireland Gazette* 01–17; Hon Sec Gen Syn Ch of Ireland 05–09; Can Belf Cathl 00–03; Preb Newcastle St Patr Cathl Dublin 01–20; rtd 20. *19 Drumnacanvy Lodge, Portadown, Craigavon BT63 5XY* M: 07930-256564 E: ian.m.ellis@btinternet.com

✠**ELLIS, The Rt Revd Ian William.** b 57. QUB BSc 78 CertEd 79 EdD 13 TCD BTh 89. CITC 86. **d** 89 **p** 90 **c** 21. C Arm St Mark 89–91; I Loughgall w Grange 91–02; Sec Gen Syn Bd of Educn 02–15; I Rossorry *Clogh* 15–21; Preb St Patr Cathl Dublin 15–21; Bp Clogh from 21. *The See House, Ballagh Road, Fivemiletown BT75 0QP* T: (028) 8952 2461 E: bishop@clogher.anglican.org

ELLIS, Jenny Susan. b 56. Bp Grosseteste Coll BEd 80. STETS 08. **d** 11 **p** 12. NSM Martock w Ash *B & W* 11–12; PtO *Ox* 13–17; NSM W Wycombe w Bledlow Ridge, Bradenham and Radnage from 17. *The Vicarage, 6 Priory Avenue, High Wycombe HP13 6SH* T: (01494) 444883 E: ellisjene@aol.com

ELLIS, John Anthony. b 47. Open Univ BA 80. Coll of Resurr Mirfield 70. **d** 72 **p** 73. C Sketty *S & B* 72–75; C Duston *Pet* 75–80; R Lichborough w Maidford and Farthingstone 80–85; V Stratfield Mortimer *Ox* 85–98; P-in-c Mortimer W End w Padworth 85–98; TR Kidlington w Hampton Poyle 98–12; AD Ox 04–12; Hon Can Ch Ch 07–12; rtd 13; PtO *Heref* from 13. *The Skirrid, Ullingswick, Hereford HR1 3JG* T: (01432) 820759 E: janthonychurchkid@gmail.com

ELLIS, John Franklin. b 34. Leeds Univ BA 58. Linc Th Coll 58. **d** 60 **p** 61. C Ladybarn *Man* 60–63; C Stockport St Geo *Ches* 63–66; V High Lane 66–81; V Chelford w Lower Withington 81–99; rtd 99; PtO *Ches* from 00. *3 Millers Croft, Adlington Street, Macclesfield SK10 1BD*

ELLIS, Canon John Keith Randolph. b 44. Univ of Wales MEd 96 Ban Univ PhD 10 Man Univ CertEd 66. Westcott Ho Cam 98. **d** 01 **p** 02. C Glanogwen w St Ann's w Llanllechid *Ban* 01–04; Min Can Ban Cathl 04–09; rtd 09; LtO *Ban* 09–20; PtO from 20; Cathl High Street Chapl 12–19; Hon Can Ban Cathl from 12. *Glan Arthur, Penisarwaun, Caernarfon LL55 3PW* T: (01286) 871421 M: 07518-748825 E: randolphellis@hotmail.co.uk

ELLIS, The Ven John Raymond. b 63. St Steph Ho Ox 95. **d** 97 **p** 98. C Clare w Poslingford, Cavendish etc *St E* 97–00; P-in-c Bury St Edmunds St Jo 00–02; P-in-c Bury St Edmunds St Geo 00–02; TV Bury St Edmunds All SS w St Jo and St Geo 02–04; Chapl RAF 04–18; Chapl-in-Chief RAF from 18; Can and Preb Linc Cathl from 18. *Chaplaincy Services (RAF), HQ Air Command, RAF High Wycombe HP14 4UE* T: (01494) 493802 F: 496343 E: john.ellis932@mod.gov.uk

ELLIS, John Roland. b 32. Wells Th Coll 67. **d** 69 **p** 70. C Kettering SS Pet and Paul 69–71; C Kingsthorpe 71–73; TV 73; TV Kingsthorpe w Northampton St Dav 73–74; TV Ebbw Vale *Mon* 74–76; V Llanddewi Rhydderch w Llanvapley etc 76–83; Miss to Seamen 79–86; V New Tredegar *Mon* 83–86; V Llanelli *S & B* 86–98; RD Crickhowell 91–98; rtd 99; P-in-c Rockfield and St Maughen's w Llangattock etc *Mon* 99–05; Hon C Rockfield and Dingestow Gp 05–07; PtO from 12. *Address temp unknown* E: revjohn32@gmail.com

ELLIS, Canon John Wadsworth. b 42. MBE 98. TCD BA 64. **d** 66 **p** 67. C Lisburn Ch Ch Cathl *Conn* 66–69; C Norbiton *S'wark* 69–72; C New Clee *Linc* 72–85; V 85–11; RD Grimsby and Cleethorpes 94–99; Can and Preb Linc Cathl 98–11; rtd 11; PtO *Linc* 17–20. *9 Abbots Way, Grimsby DN32 0HB*

ELLIS, Kevin Stuart. b 67. Newc Univ BA 91 Lon Bible Coll PhD 97. Qu Coll Birm 99. **d** 01 **p** 02. C Matson *Glouc* 01–04; TV Maryport, Netherton and Flimby *Carl* 04–07; TR 07–09; V Bartley Green *Birm* 09–14; V Bro Cybi *Ban* 14–17; R Bro Eleth from 17. *The Rectory, Bull Bay Road, Amlwch LL68 9EA* T: (01407) 831525 M: 07535-557632 E: parchkevinellis@gmail.com

ELLIS, Sister Lilian. b 44. Keswick Hall Coll TCert 66. Oak Hill Th Coll 95. **d** 96 **p** 97. C Vange *Chelmsf* 96–00; C Pitsea w Nevendon 00–02; rtd 02; PtO *Chelmsf* 02–16; *Liv* from 16. *90 Moss Road, Southport PR8 4JQ* T: (01704) 565289 E: lilian.ellis@btinternet.com

ELLIS, Louise. *See* ELLIS, Emma Louise

ELLIS, Preb Mark Durant. b 39. Ex Univ BA 62. Cuddesdon Coll 62. **d** 64 **p** 65. C Lyngford *B & W* 64–67; V Weston-super-Mare St Andr Bournville 67–76; TV Yeovil 76–88; V Yeovil St Mich 88–09; Preb Wells Cathl 90–09; RD Yeovil 94–04; rtd 09; Hon C Bruton and Distr *B & W* 09–17; Hon C Bruton, Brewham, Pitcombe and Shepton Montague 17–20; Hon C Alham Vale 17–20; PtO from 21. *Orchard Barn, 34 Burfitt Road, Ansford, Castle Cary BA7 7FP*

ELLIS, Michael Edward. b 45. St Cath Coll Ox BA 67 MA 70 MSc 68 BM. Bath 72 Glos Univ BA 11 FRCP 92 FACP 05. St Steph Ho Ox 09. **d** 10 **p** 11. C Paphos Cyprus 10–12; PtO Cyprus and the Gulf from 12; PtO *Ex* from 13. *Lantern House, Maristow House, Roborough, Plymouth PL6 7BZ* T: (01752) 724178 E: mikeedwardellis@gmail.com

ELLIS, Paul. b 49. **d** 07 **p** 08. NSM Wakef St Jo 07–14; *Leeds* from 14. *98 Bradford Road, Wakefield WF1 2AH* T: (01924) 367976

ELLIS, Paul. b 56. Aston Tr Scheme 88 Trin Coll Bris 92. **d** 92 **p** 93. C Pennington *Man* 92–96; TV Deane 96–06; P-in-c Grassendale *Liv* 06–14; V from 14; P-in-c Liv All So Springwood 11–14; V from 14. *The Vicarage, 22 Eaton Road, Cressington, Liverpool L19 0PW* T: 0151-427 1474 E: rev.paul.ellis@gmail.com

ELLIS, Peter Andrew. b 46. St D Coll Lamp 65. **d** 69 **p** 70. C Milford Haven *St D* 69–71; R Walwyn's Castle w Robeston W 71–74; Miss to Seafarers 74–11; Hong Kong 74–75 and 92–11; Singapore 75–82; The Tees and Hartlepool 82–92; rtd 11; PtO *York* from 13. *The Forge, Home Farm, Hutton Village Road, Guisborough TS14 8EL* T: (01287) 348371 E: ellishongkong@gmail.com

ELLIS, Randolph. *See* ELLIS, John Keith Randolph

ELLIS, Richard. b 47. **d** 02 **p** 03. OLM Leiston *St E* 02–13; NSM 13–17; rtd 17; PtO *St E* from 17. *9 Kings Road, Leiston IP16 4DA* T: (01728) 832168 M: 07759-349057 E: skinny.elephant@hotmail.co.uk

ELLIS, Robert Albert. b 48. K Coll Lon BD 70 AKC 70. St Aug Coll Cant 70. **d** 72 **p** 73. C Liv Our Lady and St Nic w St Anne 72–76; P-in-c Meerbrook *Lich* 76–80; Producer Relig Progr BBC Radio Stoke 76–80; V Highgate All SS *Lon* 80–81; P-in-c Longdon *Lich* 81–87; Dioc Communications Officer 81–01; Chapl Palma de Mallorca *Eur* 01–11; rtd 11; PtO *Lich* from 11; *Eur* 16–21. *The Pump House, Jacks Lane, Marchington, Uttoxeter ST14 8LW* T: (01283) 820732 E: robertellis1948@gmail.com

ELLIS, Susannah Margaret. b 44. Open Univ BA 82 New Coll Dur CertEd 88. EAMTC 93. **d** 96 **p** 97. NSM S Elmham and

Ilketshall *St E* 96–98; Warden Quiet Waters Chr Retreat Ho 96–98; C Worlingham w Barnby and N Cove *St E* 98–01; C Beccles St Mich 98–01; P-in-c Worlingham w Barnby and N Cove 01–03; R 03–14; rtd 14; P-in-c Worlingham w Barnby and N Cove *St E* 14–15; PtO *Nor* from 15; *St E* from 15. *97 High Road, Gorleston, Great Yarmouth NR31 0PE* T: (01493) 604512

✠**ELLIS, The Rt Revd Timothy William.** b 53. AKC 75 York Univ DPhil 98. St Aug Coll Cant 75. **d** 76 **p** 77 **c** 06. C Old Trafford St Jo *Man* 76–80; V Pendleton St Thos 80–87; Chapl Salford Coll of Tech 80–87; V Sheff St Leon Norwood 87–01; P-in-c Shiregreen St Hilda 94–01; RD Ecclesfield 94–99; Hon Can Sheff Cathl 00–01; Adn Stow *Linc* 01–06; Suff Bp Grantham 06–13; Dean Stamford 05–11; Can and Preb Linc Cathl 01–13; rtd 13; Hon Asst Bp Linc from 13; Hon Asst Bp Sheff from 14; Hon Asst Bp Derby from 15. *8 Mason Grove, Sheffield S13 8LL* E: fatherowl@gmail.com

ELLIS, William David. b 92. Reading Univ BA 13 York Univ MA 15 Trin Hall Cam BA 19. Ridley Hall Cam 17. **d** 20 **p** 21. C Whitby w Ruswarp *York* from 20. *16 Swallow Crescent, Whitby YO22 4QR* E: will_ellis2@hotmail.com

ELLISDON, Canon Patrick Leon Shane. b 61. St Jo Coll Nottm 99. **d** 01 **p** 02. C Margate St Phil *Cant* 01–04; P-in-c Cliftonville 04–14; V from 14; Hon Can Cant Cathl from 14. *54 Bromstone Road, Broadstairs CT10 2HT* M: 07932-734932 E: stpaulscliftville@btinternet.com or pellisdon@diocant.org

ELLISON, John. b 37. FCA 64. Qu Coll Birm. **d** 04 **p** 05. NSM Northanger *Win* 04–07; PtO 07–21. *High Candovers, Hartley Mauditt, Alton GU34 3BP* T: (01420) 511346 E: revjohnellison@hotmail.com

ELLISON, Mrs Margaret Helen. b 50. Edin Univ BSc 77 Leeds Univ BA 09 RN 72. Yorks Min Course 07. **d** 09 **p** 10. NSM York St Hilda and York St Lawr w St Nic 09–13; PtO 13–15; NSM Stamford Bridge Gp 15–20; rtd 20; PtO *York* from 20. *17 Foresters Walk, Stamford Bridge, York YO41 1BB* T: (01759) 372696 E: maggs.ellison@gmail.com

ELLISON, Ms Sandra Anne. b 53. Anglia Poly Univ BA 96 RMN 74. EAMTC 99. **d** 02 **p** 03. C Hunstanton St Mary w Ringstead Parva etc *Nor* 02–05; R Ashmanhaugh, Barton Turf etc 05–15; rtd 15; PtO *Nor* from 15. *5 Howards Close, Old Hunstanton, Hunstanton PE36 6HR* T: (01485) 298852 E: sandraellison@homecall.co.uk

ELLISON, Simon John. b 51. SEITE 99. **d** 02 **p** 03. NSM Caterham *S'wark* 02–08; Asst Chapl Newcastle upon Tyne Hosps NHS Foundn Trust 08–09; Chapl Epsom and St Helier Univ Hosps NHS Trust 09–19; rtd 19; PtO *S'wark* 09–14; NSM Caterham 14–19. *24 Bunce Drive, Caterham CR3 5FF* T: (01883) 336671 E: father.simon@icloud.com

ELLISTON, John Ernest Nicholas. b 37. ALCD 61. **d** 61 **p** 62. C Gipsy Hill Ch Ch *S'wark* 61–64; C Whitton and Thurleston w Akenham *St E* 64–68; P-in-c New Clee *Linc* 68–71; V 75–76; V Grimsby St Steph 71–75; P-in-c Mildenhall *St E* 77–79; RD 81–84; R Barton Mills, Beck Row w Kenny Hill etc 80–84; V Ipswich St Aug 84–96; Chapl St Eliz Hospice Ipswich 93–96; R Guernsey St Peter Port *Win* 96–02; Chapl Princess Eliz Hosp Guernsey 98–02; Chapl Guernsey Police 99–02; rtd 02; PtO *St E* 03–20. *27 Wyvern Road, Ipswich IP3 9TJ* T: (01473) 726617 E: helenjohnelliston@talktalk.net

ELLOR, Preb Michael Keith. b 52. St Jo Coll Nottm 92. **d** 94 **p** 95. C Stafford St Jo and Tixall w Ingestre *Lich* 94–97; TV Bucknall and Bagnall 97–03; TR Bucknall 03–09; RD Stoke 02–06; V Branston 09–17; Local Min Adv (Stafford) 09–14; Local Par Development Adv Stafford Area 10–14; P-in-c Burton All SS w Ch Ch 14–17; Preb Lich Cathl 09–17; rtd 17; PtO *S & B* from 17. *28 Cae Folland, Penclawdd, Swansea SA4 3YJ* T: (01792) 852782 E: michael.ellor@btinternet.com

ELLSON, Montague Edward. b 33. Birm Univ BA 56 Cam Univ CertEd 67 Univ of Wales (Lamp) MA 08. EAMTC 84. **d** 87 **p** 88. Hon C Freethorpe w Wickhampton, Halvergate etc *Nor* 87–90; C Gaywood, Bawsey and Mintlyn 90–92; Miss to Seafarers from 90; R Pulham *Nor* 92–94; P-in-c Starston 93–94; R Pulham Market, Pulham St Mary and Starston 94–97; Dioc NSM Officer 94–97; RD Redenhall 95–97; rtd 97; PtO *Nor* from 97. *Barn Cottage, Neatishead Road, Horning, Norwich NR12 8LB* T: (01692) 630251 E: revmonty@btinternet.com

ELLSWORTH, Lida Elizabeth. b 48. Columbia Univ (NY) BA 70 Girton Coll Cam PhD 76. EMMTC 85. **d** 88 **p** 94. NSM Bakewell *Derby* 88–07; PtO 07–11; NSM Longstone, Curbar and Stony Middleton 11–18; rtd 18; PtO *Derby* from 18. *Apple Croft, Granby Gardens, Bakewell DE45 1ET* T/F: (01629) 814255 E: lidaellsworth@john-lewis.com

ELLWOOD, Keith Brian. b 36. Curwen Coll Lon BA 58 MMus 65 Bede Coll Dur CertEd 59 Hon DD 99 AIGCM 58 FRSA 64 ACP 66 FCollP 83. Bps' Coll Cheshunt 64. **d** 64 **p** 65. Asst Master R Wanstead Sch 60–66; Chapl 64–66;

C Wanstead St Mary *Chelmsf* 64–66; CF 66–70; OCM 70–71 and 76–79; Chapl St Paul's Coll Hong Kong 70–71; P-in-c Bicknoller *B & W* 71–73; Chapl Roedean Sch Brighton 73–76; PtO *B & W* 74–79; Chapl Windsor Boys' Sch Hamm W Germany 76–79; Chapl Trin Coll Glenalmond 79–81; Hd Master St Chris Sch Burnham-on-Sea 82–86; Hon C Burnham *B & W* 82–86; R Staple Fitzpaine, Orchard Portman, Thurlbear etc 86–89; P-in-c Hugill and Dioc Educn Adv *Carl* 89–93; P-in-c Coldwaltham and Hardham *Chich* 93–95; rtd 96; PtO *Chich* 96–04; *Sheff* 04–17. *2 Lindrick Close, Doncaster DN4 7JL*

ELMAN, Simon Laurie. b 57. NTMTC. **d** 99 **p** 00. C Loughton St Jo *Chelmsf* 99–01; C Tye Green w Netteswell 01–07; PtO from 08. *26 Pakes Way, Theydon Bois, Epping CM16 7NA* T: (01992) 813057 E: simon.elman@btinternet.com

ELMES, Amanda Jane. b 53. Lon Univ BDS 76 RCS LDS 77 Herts Univ PhD 04. ERMC 06. **d** 08 **p** 09. NSM W w E Mersea *Chelmsf* 08–10; NSM W w E Mersea, Peldon, Gt and Lt Wigborough 10–14; P-in-c Langham w Boxted 14–21; P-in-c W Bergholt and Gt Horkesley 14–21; C Colchester St Mich Myland 18–21; C Colchester St Luke 18–21; C Wormingford, Mt Bures and Lt Horkesley 18–21; rtd 21; PtO *Chelmsf* from 21. *5 Lockhart Avenue, Colchester CO3 3QU* E: revmandyelmes@btinternet.com

ELMES, The Ven Ruth Katherine. b 65. TCD BTh 09 RGN 83. CITC 06. **d** 09 **p** 10. C Stillorgan w Blackrock *D & G* 09–12; I Crosspatrick Gp *C, F & O* from 12; Can Ferns Cathl 17–18; Adn Ossory and Leighlin from 18. *The Rectory, Churchlands, Tinahely, Co Wicklow, Republic of Ireland* T: (00353) (402) 28922 M: 86-062 1009 E: relmes@eircom.net

ELMS, Christian Grant. b 71. Salford Univ BSc 04. Trin Coll Bris 07. **d** 09 **p** 10. C Pennington *Man* 09–12; TV Worle *B & W* from 12. *Church Cottage, 2A St Marks Road, Weston-super-Mare BS22 7PW* T: (01934) 515438 M: 07796-988907 E: chriselms1@gmail.com

ELOFF, Robert Craig. b 77. St Mellitus Coll BA 20. **d** 20 **p** 21. C Lower Broughton Ascension *Man* from 20; C Salford St Paul w Ch Ch 20–21; C Bedford Leigh from 21. *22 Kenwood Avenue, Leigh WN7 2LN* T: 0161-374 0236 M: 07879-842082 E: rceloff@outlook.com

ELPHICK, Robin Howard. b 37. ALCD 63. **d** 64 **p** 65. C Clapham Common St Barn *S'wark* 64–67; C Woking St Pet *Guildf* 67–71; R Rollesby w Burgh w Billockby *Nor* 71–80; P-in-c Ashby w Oby, Thurne and Clippesby 79–80; R Rollesby w Burgh w Billockby w Ashby w Oby etc 80–84; R Frinton *Chelmsf* 84–94; R W w E Mersea 94–02; R Peldon w Gt and Lt Wigborough 94–02; rtd 02; PtO *Nor* from 02. *5 Coralie Court, Westfield View, Norwich NR4 7FJ* T: (01603) 508061 E: robinelphick@btinternet.com

ELPHICK, Canon Vivien Margaret. b 53. Kent Univ BA 74 Solicitor 77. Trin Coll Bris BA 90. **d** 90 **p** 94. C Oulton Broad *Nor* 90–94; P-in-c Burlingham St Edmund w Lingwood, Strumpshaw etc 94–06; RD Blofield 98–04; Hon Can Nor Cathl 03–06; P-in-c Measham *Leic* 06–08; P-in-c Packington w Normanton-le-Heath 06–08; P-in-c Donisthorpe and Moira w Stretton-en-le-Field 06–08; TR Woodfield 08–21; AD NW Leics 11–20; Hon Can Leic Cathl 16–21; rtd 21. *11 Regent Road, Skipton BD23 1AT*

ELPHIN AND ARDAGH, Dean of. *See* WILLIAMS, The Very Revd Arfon

ELSDON, Mrs Janice Margaret. b 49. CITC 92. **d** 95 **p** 96. NSM Cloughfern *Conn* 95–99; NSM Ahoghill w Portglenone 99–02; NSM Belfast St Thos 02–05; LtO 05–08; NSM Belfast St Bart 08–13; NSM Belfast St Anne from 13. *128 Station Road, Greenisland, Carrickfergus BT38 8UW* T: (028) 9085 1963 E: janice@belfastcathedral.org

ELSDON, Ronald. b 44. St Jo Coll Cam BA 66 Trin Hall Cam PhD 69 K Coll Lon BD 86 Milltown Inst Dub PhD. CITC 97. **d** 99 **p** 00. C Ballymena w Ballyclug *Conn* 99–02; I Belfast St Bart 02–13; rtd 13. *128 Station Road, Greenisland, Carrickfergus BT38 8UW* T: (028) 9085 1963

ELSMORE, The Ven Guy Charles. b 66. Edin Univ BSc 88. Ridley Hall Cam 93. **d** 93 **p** 94. C Huyton St Mich *Liv* 93–98; V Hough Green St Basil and All SS 98–05; AD Widnes and Hon Can Liv Cathl 03–05; P-in-c St Luke in the City 05–10; TR 10–16; AD Toxteth and Wavertree 14–16; Hon Can Liv Cathl 14–16; Adn Buckingham *Ox* from 16. *Archdeacon's House, Stone, Aylesbury HP17 8RZ* T: (01865) 208266 E: archdeacon.buckingham@oxford.anglican.org

ELSOM, Neil. b 67. St Hild Coll 17. **d** 19 **p** 20. NSM Greasbrough *Sheff* from 19; Chapl Methodist Homes for the Aged from 21. *32 Whitehall Road, Rotherham S61 4JD* T: (01709) 324906 M: 07931-626988 E: elsom9@blueyonder.co.uk

ELSON, Alison Judith. b 66. Ch Ch Coll Cant BEd 89. SEITE 13. **d** 16 **p** 17. NSM Chipstead *S'wark* 16–19; NSM

Reigate St Luke from 19. *4 Broadhurst Gardens, Reigate RH2 8AW* E: curate@smchipstead.org

ELSTOB, Stephen William. b 57. Sarum & Wells Th Coll. **d** 86 **p** 87. C Sunderland Springwell w Thorney Close *Dur* 86–88; C Upholland *Liv* 88–89; TV 89–96; V Cinnamon Brow 96–07; TV N Wearside *Dur* 07–11; TR 11–20; rtd 20. *Address temp unknown* E: steveelstob182@gmail.com

ELSTON, James Ian. b 70. City Univ BSc 95. SEITE 01. **d** 04 **p** 05. NSM Old St Pancras *Lon* 04–12; TV 12–15; TR from 15. *23 Albert Street, London NW1 7LU* T: (020) 7424 0724 E: fr.jameselston@gmail.com

ELSTON, Jillian Frances. b 68. St Mellitus Coll 19. **d** 21. C Lymm *Ches* from 21. *30 Cromwell Road, Bramhall, Stockport SK7 1DA* M: 07963-906740 E: jillian.elston@icloud.com

ELSTON, Philip Herbert. b 35. RD 80 and Bar 90. Leeds Univ MA 76 K Coll Lon AKC 63 Leic Coll of Educn CertEd 67. St Boniface Warminster 63. **d** 64 **p** 65. C Thurnby Lodge *Leic* 64–66; Hon C 66–67; Chapl RNR 67–90; Chapl Malosa Sch Malawi 68–75; Hon C Far Headingley St Chad *Ripon* 75–79; V Knowl Hill w Littlewick *Ox* 79–84; Chapl RN Sch Haslemere 85–89; C Felpham w Middleton *Chich* 89–90; Asst S Regional Dir Miss to Seamen 91–93; Dep S Regional Dir 93–97; S Regional Dir 97–00; PtO *Win* 93–14; *Cant* 94–00; *Chich* from 97; Corps Chapl Sea Cadet Corps 83–95; rtd 00; Hon C Witchampton, Stanbridge and Long Crichel etc *Sarum* 00–04; Hon Chapl Miss to Seafarers from 00. *55A Queens Close, West Moors, Ferndown BH22 0HN* T: (01202) 854679 E: dee.elston1@btinternet.com

ELSTON, Vanessa Jane. b 64. Ex Univ BA 86 Goldsmiths' Coll Lon PGCE 99. St Aug Coll of Th 15. **d** 18 **p** 19. C S Lambeth St Anne and All SS *S'wark* from 18; C Battersea Fields from 18. *The Vicarage, 11 Patmore Street, London SW8 4JD* M: 07419-835197 E: vanessa@vanessae.force9.co.uk

ELTRINGHAM, Canon Anna. b 74. St Jo Coll Dur BA 96. SEITE 05. **d** 08 **p** 09. C S Norwood H Innocents *S'wark* 08–14; TV Oxted 14–19; TR from 19; Dean of Women's Min from 17; Hon Can S'wark Cathl from 20; Chapl to The Queen from 20. *The Vicarage, 14 Oast Road, Oxted RH8 9DU* T: (01883) 712674 M: 07826-524038 E: revd.anna@gmail.com

ELTRINGHAM, Mrs Fiona Ann. b 48. Bp Grosseteste Coll CertEd 69. NEOC 86. **d** 89 **p** 94. Par Dn Willington *Newc* 89–92; Chapl HM YOI Castington 92–95; Chapl HM Pris Dur 95–07; rtd 07; PtO *Dur* from 07. *Granary Cottage, Stockley House Farm, Oakenshaw, Crook DL15 0TJ* T: (01388) 746058 E: davefi122@btinternet.com

ELVERSON, Ronald Peter Charles. b 50. St Edm Hall Ox BA 73 MA 86. St Jo Coll Nottm 84. **d** 86 **p** 87. C Whitnash *Cov* 86–90; V Dunchurch 90–01; R Dersingham w Anmer and Shernborne *Nor* 01–05; P-in-c Ore Ch Ch *Chich* 05–08; V 08–11; rtd 11; PtO *Pet* from 12. *7 Cheltenham Close, Rushden NN10 0NY* T: (01933) 355716 E: ronelverson@hotmail.co.uk

ELVIDGE, Mrs Joanna. b 55. FCIPD 84. STETS BA 06. **d** 06 **p** 07. NSM Horsham *Chich* 06–14; P-in-c Hythe *Win* 14–18; V 18–20; rtd 20. *2 Garden Cottages, Forest Grange, Horsham RH13 6HX* E: joanna.elvidge@btinternet.com

ELVIN, Jonathan Paul Alistair. b 65. Bris Univ BSc 90 Fitzw Coll Cam BA 94 MA 00. Ridley Hall Cam 92. **d** 95 **p** 96. C Gravesend St Geo *Roch* 95–98; C Ex St Leon w H Trin 98–07; Min Ex Trin CD 07–13; V Ex H Trin from 13. *23 Couper Meadows, Exeter EX2 7TF* T: (01392) 363627 E: jonny@trinityexeter.com

ELWIS, Malcolm John. b 42. Melbourne Univ DipEd 74 ACT ThL 74. St Jo Coll Morpeth 69. **d** 70 **p** 72. C Bentleigh St Jo Australia 70–72; C St Paul's Cathl Sale 72–73; PtO Melbourne 73–80; PtO *Chich* from 80; Chapl Eastbourne and Co Healthcare NHS Trust 88–93 and 93–02; Chapl E Sussex Co Healthcare NHS Trust 02–06; Chapl Sussex Partnership NHS Foundn Trust 06–13; Sub Chapl HM Pris Lewes 92–04; Chapl 04–06; rtd 13. *Adams Barn, 85 Church Street, Willingdon, Eastbourne BN22 0HS* T: (01323) 903102 E: malcolmelwis21@hotmail.co.uk

ELWOOD, Callum Timothy. b 96. Wycliffe Hall Ox MTh 20. **d** 20 **p** 21. C Limehouse *Lon* from 20. *Flat 2, 135 Three Colt Street, London E14 8AP* E: callum.elwood@gmail.com

ELWOOD, Mrs Claire Siobhan. b 69. RGN 91. St Hild Coll BA 19. **d** 19 **p** 20. C Dur St Nic from 19. *20 Dickens Wynd, Durham DH1 3QY* M: 07751-358546 E: elwoodc42@gmail.com

ELY, Nigel Patrick. b 62. Thames Poly BA 83 Southn Univ BTh 92 Birm Univ MA 01. Chich Th Coll 89. **d** 92 **p** 93. C Rustington *Chich* 92–93; C Bexhill St Pet 93–96; Chapl St Geo Post 16 Cen *Birm* 96–99; PtO 02–06; *Lich* 11–13; Asst Chapl R Wolv NHS Trust 13–17; PtO *Birm* 14–17; C W Bromwich All SS *Lich* 15–19; C W Bromwich St Andr w Ch Ch 17–19; Chapl HM Pris Humber from 19. *HM Prison*

Humber, The Wolds, Everthorpe, Brough HU15 2JZ T: (01430) 273000 E: nigel_stgeorge@excite.com

ELY, Bishop of. *See* CONWAY, The Rt Revd Stephen David

ELY, Dean of. *See* BONNEY, The Very Revd Mark Philip John

EMBLIN, Canon Richard John. b 48. BEd 71 MA 81. S Dios Minl Tr Scheme 83. **d** 86 **p** 87. C S w N Hayling *Portsm* 86–89; P-in-c Wootton 89–95; V Cowes H Trin and St Mary 95–13; RD W Wight 01–07; Hon Can Portsm Cathl 05–13; rtd 13; PtO *Win* from 14. *125 Sandy Lane, St Ives, Ringwood BH24 2LQ* T: (01425) 482742 E: remblin@yahoo.com

EMERSON, Arthur Edward Richard. b 24. Lich Th Coll 69. **d** 72 **p** 73. C Barton upon Humber *Linc* 72–74; V Chapel St Leonards 75–88; P-in-c Hogsthorpe 77–88; V Chapel St Leonards w Hogsthorpe 88–91; rtd 91; PtO *Linc* 91–09; *Liv* from 16. *119 Folkestone Road, Southport PR8 5PH* T: (01704) 514778

EMERSON, Mrs Jan Vivien. b 44. S Dios Minl Tr Scheme 89. **d** 92 **p** 95. NSM Chich St Paul and St Pet 92–94; NSM Bosham 94–02; Asst Chapl R W Sussex NHS Trust 02–07; PtO *Chich* from 07. *Flete Cottage, Critchfield Road, Bosham, Chichester PO18 8HH* T: (01243) 574948 E: janvemerson@aol.com

✠**EMERTON, The Rt Revd Andrew Neil.** b 72. York Univ BSc 93 Qu Coll Ox DPhil 96 Down Coll Cam BTh 05. Ridley Hall Cam 02. **d** 05 **p** 06 **c** 20. C Brompton H Trin w Onslow Square St Paul *Lon* 05–07; Asst Dean St Mellitus Coll 08–16; Dean 16–20; Dir St Paul's Th Cen 08–20; PtO *Chelmsf* 08–20; Suff Bp Sherwood *S'well* from 20. *Diocese of Southwell and Nottingham, Jubilee House, Westgate, Southwell NG25 0JH* T: (01636) 819133 E: bishop.sherwood@southwell.anglican.org

EMERY, David John. b 37. Dur Univ BA 59. Chich Th Coll 63. **d** 65 **p** 66. C Upholland *Liv* 65–68; C Gt Crosby St Faith 68–70; V Warrington St Barn 70–73; rtd 02; PtO *Ches* 03–04. *86 Ullswater, Macclesfield SK11 7YP* T: (01625) 501179 E: d.emery433@btinternet.com

EMERY, Karen Maureen. *See* BECK, Karen Maureen

EMERY, Sandra Faith. b 50. **d** 10 **p** 11. NSM Minchinhampton w Box and Amberley *Glouc* 10–20; rtd 20; PtO *Glouc* from 21. *The Old Carriage House, Edge, Stroud GL6 6PQ* T: (01452) 814148 E: emery31@btinternet.com

EMINSON, Mark Franklin. b 79. Mert Coll Ox BA 01 MSt 03 MA 06 Trin Coll Cam BA 07. Westcott Ho Cam 05. **d** 08 **p** 09. C E Grinstead St Swithun *Chich* 08–12; V Pagham 12–19; TR Merton Priory *S'wark* from 19. *Holy Trinity Vicarage, 1 Trinity Road, London SW19 8QT* T: (020) 8542 2313 E: eminson.mark@gmail.com

EMMANUEL, Rufin. b 63. Punjab Univ BA 87. Nat Catholic Inst of Th Pakistan 89. **d** 96 **p** 96. In RC Ch 96–09; Chapl Mid-Essex Hosp Services NHS Trust 09–11; Chapl Lewisham Healthcare NHS Trust 12–14; Chapl Lewisham and Greenwich NHS Trust 14–20; Chapl W Suffolk NHS Foundn Trust from 20. *8 Mendip Place, Chelmsford CM1 2WT* T: (01245) 357579 M: 07583-087984 E: rufi49@hotmail.com *or* rufin.emmanuel@nhs.net

EMMETT, Kerry Charles. b 46. St Jo Coll Dur BA 68. St Jo Coll Nottm 71. **d** 73 **p** 74. C Attenborough w Chilwell *S'well* 73–75; C Chilwell 75–76; C Wembley St Jo *Lon* 76–79; V Hanworth St Rich 79–89; R Ravenstone and Swannington *Leic* 89–04; RD Akeley S 97–03; P-in-c Mountsorrel Ch Ch and St Pet 04–13; rtd 13; PtO *Leic* 13–21. *1 Chamberlain's Field, Birstall, Leicester LE4 3LD* T: 0116-319 4736

EMMETT, David Eugene. b 41. St Chad's Coll Dur BA 63. **d** 66 **p** 67. C Bingley H Trin *Bradf* 66–69; C Anfield St Marg *Liv* 69–70; C Kirkby 70–75; Chapl Newc Poly 75–78; Hon C Toxteth Park St Marg *Liv* 78–80; TV Upholland 80–88; V Southfields St Barn *S'wark* 88–99; TV Liv Our Lady and St Nic w St Anne 99–06; rtd 06; PtO *Liv* from 16; *Eur* from 16. *6A Eastern Drive, Liverpool L19 0NB* T: 0151-281 5493 E: davidemmott@mac.com

EMMOTT, Douglas Brenton. b 45. K Coll Lon BD 78 AKC 78 York Univ MA 97. Linc Th Coll 79. **d** 80 **p** 81. C Kingston upon Hull St Alb *York* 80–83; V Scarborough St Sav w All SS 83–91; V York St Chad 91–99; V Leeds All So *Ripon* 99–07; rtd 07. *Le Moulin de Vernay, 72500 Dissay-sous-Courcillon, France* T: (0033) 2 43 46 53 82 M: 6 37 79 26 45 E: douglas.emmott@mac.com

EMMOTT, John Charles Lionel. b 32. SEITE 96. **d** 96 **p** 97. NSM Tenterden St Mich *Cant* 96–02; rtd 02; PtO *Cant* from 02. *58 Grange Crescent, St Michaels, Tenterden TN30 6DZ* T: (01580) 762092 E: emmottjandc@gmail.com

EMPEY, Clement Adrian. b 42. TCD BA 64 MA 68 PhD 71. CITC. **d** 74 **p** 75. C Dublin St Ann *D&G* 75–76; I Kells-Inistioge Gp *C,F&O* 76–84; I Clane w Donadea and Coolcarragan *M&K* 84–88; Hon Chapl Miss to Seafarers from 88; Sen Chapl Miss to Seamen (Irish Republic) 97–08; I Dublin St Ann and St Steph *D&G* 88–01; Preb Tassagard

St Patr Cathl Dublin 82–89; Treas St Patr Cathl Dublin 89–91; Chan St Patr Cathl Dublin 91–96; Prec St Patr Cathl Dublin 96–01; Chapl Rotunda Hosp 98–08; Prin CITC 01–08; Prec Ch Ch Cathl Dublin *D & G* 01–08; rtd 08. *5 Callenders Mill, Simmonstown Manor, Celbridge, Co Kildare, W23 RP48, Republic of Ireland* T: (00353) (1) 503 7797 M: 87-902 2169 E: adrianempey@gmail.com

✠**EMPEY, The Rt Revd Walton Newcome Francis.** b 34. TCD BA 57 Hon FGCM 02. K Coll (NS) BD 68. **d** 58 **p** 59 **c** 81. C Glenageary *D & G* 58–60; Bp's C Grand Falls New Brunswick Canada 60–63; I Madawaska 63–66; I Stradbally *C, F & O* 66–71; Dean Limerick *L & K* 71–81; I Limerick St Mich 71–81; Preb Taney St Patr Cathl Dublin 73–81; Bp L & K 81–85; Bp M & K 85–96; Abp Dublin *D & G* 96–02; Preb Cualaun St Patr Cathl Dublin 96–02; rtd 02. *Rathmore Lodge, Rathmore, Tullow, Co Carlow, Republic of Ireland* T: (00353) (59) 916 1891 E: louempey@hotmail.com

EMTAGE, Miss Susan Raymond. b 34. St Mich Ho Ox 63. dss 79 **d** 87 **p** 94. SW Area Sec CPAS Women's Action 75–82; Leic St Chris 82–86; Bramerton w Surlingham *Nor* 86–88; C 87–88; C Rockland St Mary w Hellington, Bramerton etc 88–89; Par Dn W Bromwich St Jas and St Paul 89–94; C 94; rtd 94; Hon C Stapleton *Bris* 96–04; PtO *Glouc* 14–17. *23 Capel Court, The Burgage, Prestbury, Cheltenham GL52 3EL* T: (01242) 577535

ENDALL, Peter John. b 38. Linc Th Coll 83. **d** 85 **p** 86. C Burley in Wharfedale *Bradf* 85–88; V Thwaites Brow 88–03; RD S Craven 96–02; rtd 03; Hon C Tamworth *Lich* 04–08; PtO 08–15; *Leic* 09–15; *Blackb* 15–20. *21 Fosbrooke House, 8 Clifton Drive, Lytham St Annes FY8 5RQ* T: (01253) 667027 E: cpendall.red@outlook.com

ENDICOTT, Michael John. b 45. **d** 97. NSM Pontnewydd *Mon* 97; NSM Well Chr Healing Cen from 97. *41 Acer Way, Monmouth NP25 5UQ*

ENEVER, Canon Rosemary Alice Delande. b 45. Oak Hill Th Coll 86. **d** 88 **p** 94. NSM Gt Ilford St Jo *Chelmsf* 88–94; TV Waltham H Cross 94–02; Asst Area Dean Epping Forest 00–01; V Gt Ilford St Andr 02–10; RD Redbridge 06–08; Hon Can Chelmsf Cathl 06–10; rtd 10; PtO *Ex* from 12. *16 Honeylands Drive, Exeter EX4 8QP* T: (01392) 420057 E: rosemaryenever@gmail.com

ENEVER, Vivian John. b 61. Collingwood Coll Dur BA 82 Cam Univ PGCE 85 Man Univ BPhil 97. Westcott Ho Cam 88. **d** 91 **p** 92. C Gt Crosby St Faith *Liv* 91–95; C Cantril Farm 95–97; TV Halas *Worc* 97–03; TR Newark w Coddington *S'well* 03–13; R Queen Thorne *Sarum* 13–18; RD Sherborne 14–18; rtd 18. *Banksia, High Street, Queen Camel, Yeovil BA22 7NH* T: (01935) 851552 E: banksia2018@gmail.com

ENGA, Mrs Charis Amelia. b 84. Dur Univ BA 05. St Mellitus Coll 10. **d** 12 **p** 13. C Highbury Ch Ch w St Jo and St Sav *Lon* 12–16; P-in-c Stoke Newington St Andr from 16. *St Andrew's Vicarage, 106 Bethune Road, London N16 5DU* M: 07584-622091 E: revcharisenga@gmail.com

ENGEHAM, Leigh Michael. b 81. St Aug Coll Cant 19. **d** 21. C S Lambeth St Anne and All SS *S'wark* from 21. *23 Mardyke House, Crosslet Street, London SE17 1HH* E: l.engeham@gmail.com

ENGEL, Jeffrey Davis. b 38. Man Univ BA 59 Liv Univ PGCE 60 Aston Univ MSc 82 FCP 83. St Deiniol's Hawarden 86. **d** 89 **p** 90. NSM Formby St Pet *Liv* 89–92; C Prescot 92–94; P-in-c Hale 94–03; Dioc Adv for Past Care and Counselling 94–03; rtd 04; Chapl MU from 05; PtO *Liv* from 16. *Church View, West Street, Prescot L34 1LQ*

ENGELSEN, Christopher James. b 57. Nottm Univ BTh 86. Linc Th Coll 83. **d** 86 **p** 87. C Sprowston *Nor* 86–89; C High Harrogate Ch Ch *Ripon* 89–92; TV Seacroft 92–95; P-in-c Foulsham w Hindolveston and Guestwick *Nor* 95–01; P-in-c Hevingham w Hainford and Stratton Strawless 01–05; R Coltishall w Gt Hautbois, Frettenham etc from 05. *The Rectory, Rectory Road, Coltishall, Norwich NR12 7HL* T: (01603) 737255 M: 07399-403406 E: engelsen@btinternet.com

ENGH, Dwayne Darcy. b 72. Calgary Univ BMus 97 BEd 99 K Coll Lon MA 10 Wolfs Coll Cam BTh 15. Westcott Ho Cam 13. **d** 15 **p** 16. C Cov St Mary 15–18; V 18–21; Min Development Officer *Derby* from 21. *Derby Church House, 1 Full Street, Derby DE1 3DR* M: 07425-606421

ENGLAND, Mrs Elizabeth Anne. b 73. Qu Coll Birm BA 15. **d** 15 **p** 16. C Codsall *Lich* 15–19; TR Buxton w Burbage and King Sterndale *Derby* from 19. *7 Lismore Park, Buxton SK17 9AU* T: (01298) 212667 M: 07930-264857 E: reverendlizengland@gmail.com

ENGLAND, Richard Alan. b 74. Sheff Univ BA 97 Dur Univ MA 07. Wycliffe Hall Ox 06. **d** 08 **p** 09. C Whitfield *Derby* 08–13; C Gillingham St Mark *Roch* 13–16; V Crofton *Portsm* from 16; TR Bridgemary, Elson and Rowner from 21. *The*

Vicarage, 40 Vicarage Lane, Fareham PO14 2JX T: (01329) 661154 E: richard@croftonparish.org.uk

ENGLAND-SIMON, Haydn Henry. b 57. Llan Dioc Tr Scheme 92. **d** 96 **p** 97. NSM Penydarren *Llan* 96–97; C Caerphilly 97–01; V Pentre 01–07; V Ystradyfodwg from 07; AD Rhondda 11–18. *The Vicarage, St David's Close, Pentre CF41 7AX* T: (01443) 433651

ENGLER, Mrs Margaret Dorothy. b 44. Lon Univ TCert 77. S'wark Ord Course 90. **d** 93 **p** 94. NSM Harlesden All So *Lon* 93–97; Dep Chapl HM Pris Wandsworth 97; Acting Chapl HM Pris Wormwood Scrubs 97–98; Chapl HM Pris High Down 98–04; rtd 04; PtO *Lon* 04–07 and from 13; NSM Harlesden All So 07–13; PtO *S'wark* from 18. *35 Sheppard's Colleges, London Road, Bromley BR1 1PE* T: (020) 8466 9384 M: 07929-300048 E: margaretengler@waitrose.com

ENGLISH, Dana Leigh. **d** 12 **p** 13. C Rome *Eur* 12–18; NSM Holland Park *Lon* from 19. *25 Farmer Street, London W8 7SN* E: dlenglish@aya.yale.edu

ENGLISH, Helen Margaret (Sister Helen Julian). b 55. Newc Poly BA 76. Ripon Coll Cuddesdon 12. **d** 13. NSM Hanborough and Freeland Ox 13–14; NSM Edwinstowe *S'well* 14–17; NSM Clipstone 14–17; NSM Perlethorpe 14–17; Min Gen CSF from 12; PtO *Dur* from 17. *Address withheld by request* T: (01325) 462954 E: helenjuliancsf@franciscans.org.uk

ENGLISH, Philip Trevor. b 37. Dur Univ BSc 60 FLIA 81 MITPA 84. Cranmer Hall Dur 60. **d** 62 **p** 63. C Hull Green Ascension *Birm* 62–66; Chapl St Jo Cathl Hong Kong 66–67; V Dorridge *Birm* 67–72; PtO *Ox* from 04. *Churchlands, Appletree Road, Chipping Warden, Banbury OX17 1LN* T: (01295) 660222 F: 660725 M: 07831-446421 E: pteifs@aol.com

ENNION, Peter. b 56. Aston Tr Scheme 85 Coll of Resurr Mirfield 87. **d** 89 **p** 90. C Middlewich w Byley *Ches* 89–91; C Aylestone St Andr w St Jas *Leic* 91–92; C Coppenhall *Ches* 92–94; P-in-c Newton in Mottram 94–99; P-in-c Tranmere St Paul w St Luke 99–04; V Torrisholme *Blackb* 04–11; P-in-c Blackpool St Mary 11–13; V 13–19; V Blackpool H Cross 13–19; rtd 19; PtO *Blackb* 19–20; P-in-c Barthomley *Ches* from 20. *The Rectory, Rushy Lane, Barthomley, Crewe CW2 5PE* E: ennionpeter@gmail.com

ENNIS, Mrs Lesley. b 47. Bp Lonsdale Coll CertEd 68 Open Univ BA 84. OLM course 97. **d** 99 **p** 00. NSM Sowerby *Wakef* 99–13; NSM Norland 09–13; NSM Ryburn 13–14; *Leeds* 14–17; rtd 17; PtO *Leeds* from 17. *26 Springfield, Sowerby Bridge HX6 1AD* T: (01422) 832747 M: 07479-290340 E: lesleyennis@hotmail.co.uk

ENNIS, Martin Michael. b 58. Man Univ BSc 80 MCollP 84. Sarum & Wells Th Coll 87. **d** 89 **p** 90. C Newquay *Truro* 89–92; C Tewkesbury w Walton Cardiff *Glouc* 92–95; P-in-c Brockworth 95–96; V 96–03; Hon C Wotton St Mary 09–10; V Tividale *Lich* from 10; P-in-c Wednesbury St Jas and St Jo 14–17; RD Wednesbury from 16. *26 View Point, Tividale, Oldbury B69 1UU* T: (01384) 257888 E: frmennis@gmail.com

ENOCH, William Frederick Palmer. b 30. EMMTC 76. **d** 79 **p** 80. NSM Ilkeston St Mary *Derby* 79–85; P-in-c Ilkeston H Trin 85–95; rtd 95; PtO *Derby* 95–13. *82 Derby Road, Ilkeston DE7 5EZ* T: 0115-944 3003

ENTICOTT, Ian Peter. b 59. Sheff Univ BA 82 St Jo Coll Dur MA 00. Cranmer Hall Dur 97. **d** 99 **p** 00. C Higher Bebington *Ches* 99–02; P-in-c Kelsall 02–10; Dir African Pastors' Fellowship 10–14; PtO *Cov* 10–14; V Accrington St Jas and St Paul *Blackb* 14–20; P-in-c Accrington Ch Ch 19–20; AD Accrington 16–20; R Congleton *Ches* from 20. *The Rectory, 2 Hartley Gardens, Congleton CW12 3WA* T: (01260) 409039 M: 07941-389621 E: ian.enticott@dunelm.org.uk *or* rector@congletonparish.org.uk

ENTWISLE, George Barry. b 43. St Jo Coll Ox BA 66 MA 72 Massey Univ (NZ) MEd 99. Linc Th Coll 73. **d** 75 **p** 76. C Rawmarsh w Parkgate *Sheff* 75–78; C Ashburton NZ 78–80; V Upper Clutha 80–84; V Gore 84–94; Can St Paul's Cathl Dunedin 87–94; Hon C Upper Clutha 01–06; rtd 08. *5 Bruce Street, Cromwell 9310, New Zealand* T/F: (0064) (3) 445 1797 M: 27-426 5539 E: b.entwisle@xtra.co.nz

ENTWISTLE, Christopher John. b 47. NOC 79. **d** 82 **p** 83. NSM Colne H Trin *Blackb* 82–84; C Poulton-le-Fylde 84–87; V Blackpool St Paul 87–96; RD Blackpool 94–96; P-in-c Overton 96–01; V Ashton-on-Ribble St Andr 01–06; TV W Preston 06–10; AD Preston 04–09; rtd 10; PtO *Blackb* 10–21. *9 Chatsworth Avenue, Warton, Preston PR4 1BQ* T: (01772) 462742

ENTWISTLE, Frank Roland. b 37. Dur Univ BA 59. Cranmer Hall Dur 59. **d** 61 **p** 62. C Harborne Heath *Birm* 61–65; S Area Sec BCMS 65–66; Educn Sec 66–73; Hon C Wallington *S'wark* 68–73; UCCF 73–02; Hon C Ware Ch Ch *St Alb* 73–76; Hon C Leic H Trin w St Jo 76–02; rtd 02; PtO *Ex* from 14. *50*

Redlands Road, Fremington, Barnstaple EX31 2NY T: (01271) 342449

ENWEREM, Christopher Onyemaechi. b 75. St Jo Coll Nottm BA 15 MA 17. **d** 16 **p** 17. C Dudley Wood and Cradley Heath *Worc* 16–20; P-in-c Tipton St Matt w St Martin and St Paul *Lich* 20–21. *Address temp unknown* M: 07773-719434 E: c.enwerem@outlook.com

ENWEREM, Foluso Olusegun Adedoyin. b 72. Leeds Univ BA 96 MA 97. Qu Foundn Birm 17. **d** 20 **p** 21. C Dudley *Worc* from 20. *St Barnabas' Vicarage, Middlepark Road, Dudley DY1 2LD* T: (01384) 886165 M: 07896-881838 E: f.enwerem@outlook.com

ENWUCHOLA, The Ven Benjamin Ameh. b 56. Lon Bible Coll BA 94. **d** 95 **p** 98. NSM S Tottenham St Ann *Lon* 96–99; NSM W Kilburn St Luke w St Simon and St Jude 99–13; NSM W Kilburn St Luke and Harrow Road Em 13–16; Chapl Nigerian Congregation 99–16; Asst Gen Sec Ch of Nigeria from 16; Hon Can Ondo from 02. *24 Douala Street, Wuse Zone 5, Abuja, Nigeria* T: (00234) (9) 523 6950 E: benwuchola@yahoo.co.uk

EPPS, Christopher Derek. b 54. ACII 79. Linc Th Coll 95. **d** 95 **p** 96. C Clevedon St Jo *B & W* 95–98; R St John w Millbrook *Truro* 98–03; P-in-c Truro St Geo and St Jo 03–15; P-in-c Truro St Paul and St Clem 03–12; C 12–15; V Truro St Paul, St Geo and St Jo 15–18; rtd 19; PtO *Truro* from 19. *1 Penwethers Close, Truro TR1 3FS* E: frcdepps@gmail.com

EPPS, Gerald Ralph. b 31. Open Univ BA 79. Oak Hill Th Coll 52 K Coll Lon 54. **d** 57 **p** 58. C Slade Green *Roch* 57–60; V Freethorpe w Wickhampton *Nor* 60–70; P-in-c Halvergate w Tunstall 62–67; V 67–70; R Pulham St Mary Magd 70–80; P-in-c Alburgh 76–77; P-in-c Denton 76–77; P-in-c Pulham St Mary V 76–80; R Pulham 80–91; rtd 91; PtO *Nor* from 91. *10 Lime Close, Harleston IP20 9DG* T: (01379) 854532

EPPS (formerly REEVE), Mrs Sally Ann. b 55. SEITE 07. **d** 10 **p** 11. C Ringmer *Chich* 10–14; P-in-c Burwash 14–15; R Burwash, Burwash Weald and Etchingham 15–20; rtd 20. *The Rectory, Rectory Close, Etchingham Road, Burwash, Etchingham TN19 7BH* T: (01435) 882301 E: sallyaepps@btinternet.com

EPTON, John Alan. b 47. EMMTC 08. **d** 10 **p** 11. NSM Morton and Stonebroom w Shirland *Derby* from 10. *Phare, 22 Fernwood Close, Shirland, Alfreton DE55 6BW* T: (01773) 834153

ERLANDSON, Gareth Leslie. b 84. St Cuth Soc Dur BA 05. St Padarn's Inst 16. **d** 19 **p** 20. C Borderlands Miss Area *St As* from 19. *11 Bron yr Eglwys, Mynydd Isa, Mold CH7 6YQ* T: (01352) 756392 M: 07731-827988 E: curate@hopeparishchurch.org

ERLEBACH, Jonathan Bartholomew (Bart). b 77. York Univ BSc 99. Oak Hill Th Coll BA 05. **d** 05 **p** 06. C Hove Bp Hannington Memorial Ch *Chich* 05–09; C Surbiton Hill Ch Ch *S'wark* from 09. *181 Elgar Avenue, Surbiton KT5 9JX* T: (020) 8399 1503 M: 07714-379836 E: bart@emmanueltolworth.org.uk

ERLEWYN-LAJEUNESSE, Michel David Siva. b 68. Univ Coll of Swansea BSc 89 Imp Coll Lon MB, BS 95 Southn Univ DM 04 FRCPCH 11. Sarum Coll 16. **d** 21. NSM Romsey *Win* from 21. *The Warren, Stockbridge Road, Timsbury, Romsey SO51 0NF* T: (01794) 367675 M: 07471-125159 E: michlajeunesse@icloud.com

✠**ERNEST, The Most Revd Gerald James Ian.** b 54. Madras Univ BCom 79. St Paul's Th Coll Mauritius. **p** 85 **c** 01. Bp Mauritius 01–19; Abp Indian Ocean 06–17; Dir Angl Cen Rome from 19. *Palazzo Doria Pamphilj, Piazza del Collegio Romano 2, 00186 Rome, Italy* T: (0039) (06) 678 0302 E: director@anglicancentre.it

ERREY, Rosalind Elisabeth. See RUTHERFORD, Rosalind Elisabeth

ERRIDGE, David John. b 45. Tyndale Hall Bris 66. **d** 69 **p** 70. C Bootle St Matt *Liv* 69–72; C Horwich H Trin *Man* 72–77; R Blackley St Andr 77–00; All N Man 85–94; V Acomb St Steph and St Aid *York* 00–10; rtd 10; PtO *York* from 11. *51 Barlow Street, Acomb, York YO26 5HS* T: (01904) 797614 M: 07387-566374 E: davidandsusan51@hotmail.co.uk

ERRIDGE, Timothy John. b 65. Wye Coll Lon BSc 86 Croydon Coll CertEd 90. St Jo Coll Nottm 08. **d** 10 **p** 11. C Congresbury w Puxton and Hewish St Ann *B & W* 10–14; P-in-c Bleadon 14–16; P-in-c Weston-super-Mare St Andr Bournville 14–16; R Bleadon and Bournville from 16. *The Rectory, 14 Coronation Road, Bleadon, Weston-super-Mare BS24 0PG* T: (01934) 815404 E: revtimerridge@gmail.com

ERRINGTON, Mrs Sarah. b 67. UEA BA 90. Wycliffe Hall Ox BTh 94. **d** 97 **p** 98. C Gateacre *Liv* 97–02; TV Halewood 02–10; TV Wrexham *St As* from 10. *The Vicarage, 160 Borras Road, Wrexham LL13 9ER* T: (01978) 266018 E: vicarstjohnswxm@gmail.com

ERSKINE, Belinda Mary. b 63. CGH 16. **d** 20 **p** 21. C Coleford, Staunton, Newland, Redbrook etc *Glouc* from 20. *Bell's Old Grammar School, Newland, Coleford GL16 8NW* T: (01594) 835744 M: 07881-614636 E: erskinebea@gmail.com

ERVING, Christel Estelle Ann. See LANGDON-GRIFFITHS, Christel Estelle Ann

ESAU, John Owen. b 39. St Mich Coll Llan 93. **d** 95 **p** 96. Min Can St D Cathl 95–97; V Llanpumsaint w Llanllawddog 97–01; V Cydweli and Llandyfaelog 01–03; R Aberporth w Tremain w Blaenporth and Betws Ifan 03–04; rtd 04. *Nursery Cottage, 14 Grove Place, Cardiff CF14 4QS* T: (029) 2061 2190

ESCOTT, Mark David. b 81. Lon Bible Coll BA 01 Liv Hope Univ Coll PGCE 03. ERMC 18. **d** 21. C Cheshunt *St Alb* from 21. *4A Goffs Lane, Goffs Oak, Waltham Cross EN7 5EF* T: (01992) 445821 M: 07734-525715 E: teachermarkescott@hotmail.com

ESDAILE, Canon Adrian George Kennedy. b 35. Mert Coll Ox BA 57 MA 61. Wells Th Coll 59. **d** 61 **p** 62. C St Helier *S'wark* 61–64; C Wimbledon 64–68; V Hackbridge and N Beddington 68–80; RD Sutton 76–80; TR Chipping Barnet w Arkley *St Alb* 80–01; RD Barnet 89–94; Hon Can St Alb 94–01; rtd 01; PtO *S'wark* 01–16; *Guildf* from 02. *29 Hereford Close, Epsom KT18 5DZ* T/F: (01372) 723770 E: esdaileadrian@yahoo.co.uk

ESPIN-BRADLEY, Richard John. b 61. Lanc Univ BSc 84. Oak Hill Th Coll 93. **d** 95 **p** 96. C Brundall w Braydeston and Postwick *Nor* 95–98; C St Helier *S'wark* 98–02; V Wolverhampton St Luke *Lich* from 02; PtO *Eur* from 19. *St Luke's Vicarage, 122 Goldthorn Hill, Wolverhampton WV2 3HU* T: (01902) 340261 E: vicar@stlukeswolverhampton.org or richard.eb@outlook.com

ESSEX, Mary Rose. b 50. **d** 02 **p** 03. NSM E and W Leake, Stanford-on-Soar, Rempstone etc *S'well* 02–08; P-in-c Kirkby Woodhouse 08–15; rtd 15; PtO *S'well* from 16. *1A Bley Avenue, East Leake, Loughborough LE12 6NX* T: (01509) 856521 E: rev.maryessex@btopenworld.com

ESTALL, John William. b 81. Moorlands Coll BA 04. Ripon Coll Cuddesdon 14. **d** 16 **p** 17. C Washington *Dur* 16–20; P-in-c Lumley from 20; P-in-c E Rainton from 20; P-in-c W Rainton from 20; P-in-c Chilton Moor from 20. *Christ Church Vicarage, Great Lumley, Chester le Street DH3 4ER* M: 07525-478336 E: revjestall@gmail.com

ETCHELL, Diane. b 54. St Hild Coll 16. **d** 18 **p** 19. NSM Greasbrough *Sheff* from 18. *35 Allendale Road, Rotherham S65 3BY* E: st.mary.curate@gmail.com

ETCHES, Haigh David. b 45. St Jo Coll Dur BA 71. Cranmer Hall Dur. **d** 73 **p** 74. C Whitnash *Cov* 73–77; C Wallingford w Crowmarsh Gifford etc *Ox* 77–83; P-in-c Bearwood 83–86; R 86–11; rtd 11; PtO *Heref* from 12. *Silver Birches, 6 Chelmick Drive, Church Stretton SY6 7BP* T: (01694) 723266 E: haigh.etches@gmail.com

ETHERIDGE, Alastair. b 60. **d** 10 **p** 11. NSM Woking Ch Ch *Guildf* 10–15; NSM Fisherton Anger *Sarum* from 15. *18 Angler Road, Salisbury SP2 9PB* E: ali@wearestpauls.church

ETHERIDGE, Canon Richard Thomas. b 32. Lon Univ BD 62. ALCD 61. **d** 62 **p** 63. C Wilmington *Roch* 62–65; C Rainham 65–69; V Langley St Jo *Birm* 69–01; P-in-c Oldbury 83–01; P-in-c Langley St Mich 95–01; Hon Can Birm Cathl 97–01; rtd 01; PtO *Birm* 01–12; *Worc* from 02. *23 Scobell Close, Pershore, Worcester WR10 1QJ* T: (01386) 554745

ETHERINGTON (née SMITH), Mrs Elizabeth Anne. b 68. Keele Univ BA 95. Ridley Hall Cam 04. **d** 06 **p** 07. C E Twickenham St Steph *Lon* 06–11; C Hounslow H Trin w St Paul and St Mary 12–15; V Hounslow St Paul and Gd Shep 15–17; V Farnborough St Pet *Guildf* from 19. *The Rectory, 66 Church Avenue, Farnborough GU14 7AP* T: (01252) 513111 M: 07903-112082 E: libbyetherington@hotmail.com

ETHERINGTON, Mrs Ferial Mary Gould. b 44. Open Univ BA. St Alb Minl Tr Scheme 86. **d** 93 **p** 94. NSM Luton St Chris Round Green *St Alb* 93–04; Selection Sec and Co-ord for OLM Min Division 97–04; rtd 04; PtO *Carl* 04–10; Dioc Min Review Officer 05–11; TV Cartmel Peninsula 10–14; PtO from 14. *North View, Durdar, Carlisle CA2 4TX* T: (01228) 599658 E: ferial.etherington@btinternet.com

ETHERINGTON, Robert Barry. b 37. Man Univ BA 62. Linc Th Coll 62. **d** 64 **p** 65. C Linc St Jo 64–67; C Frodingham 67–69; V Reepham 69–78; Ind Chapl 70–78; Ind Chapl *St Alb* 78–88; V Luton St Chris Round Green 88–04; RD Luton 98–02; rtd 04; PtO *Carl* 05–19. *North View, Durdar, Carlisle CA2 4TX* T: (01228) 599658 E: revdbarry@btinternet.com

ETHERTON, Christopher Charles. b 47. UMIST BSc 68. STETS 04. **d** 07 **p** 08. NSM Lower Sandown St Jo and Sandown Ch Ch *Portsm* 07–10; P-in-c Binstead 10–14; P-in-c Havenstreet St Pet 10–14; NSM Bourton-on-the-Water w Clapton etc *Glouc* 14–19; rtd 19. *9 Parkers Close,*

Faringdon SN7 7BD T: (01367) 242884 M: 07906-238368 E: etherton473@btinternet.com

EUROPE, Bishop of Gibraltar in. *See* INNES, The Rt Revd Robert Neil

EUROPE, Suffragan Bishop in. *See* HAMID, The Rt Revd David

EVANS, Adrian John. b 81. St Jo Coll Nottm BA 13. d 13 p 14. C Walmley *Birm* 13–19; V from 19. *The Vicarage, 4 Walmley Road, Sutton Coldfield B76 1QN* T: 0121-313 0413 M: 07961-375769 E: adrianevans007@gmail.com *or* ade@stjw.org.uk

EVANS, Miss Alison Jane. b 66. Sheff Univ BSc 87 Bris Univ PGCE 93. Trin Coll Bris BA 04. d 04 p 05. C Finham *Cov* 04–08; V Cov St Geo 08–17; AD Cov N 15–17; V Attleborough from 17. *The Vicarage, 5 Fifield Close, Nuneaton CV11 4TS* T: (024) 7673 6002 E: htavicar1@gmail.com

EVANS, Alun John. b 86. Univ of Wales (Abth) BA 07 Univ of Wales (Lamp) MTh 09 Abth Univ PGCE 10. St Mich Coll Llan 13. d 16 p 17. C Haverfordwest *St D* 16–18; C Llanbadarn Fawr and Elerch and Penrhyncoch etc 18–20; P-in-c Bro Wyre from 20. *The Vicarage, Llanilar, Aberystwyth SY23 4PD* T: (01974) 241052 M: 07949-826270 E: rev.alun@outlook.com

EVANS, Mrs Amanda Jane. b 66. Southn Univ BA 88 QTS 04. Ripon Coll Cuddesdon 13. d 16 p 17. C Mabe *Truro* 16–20; P-in-c Mylor w Flushing from 20; C St Gluvias 20–21; P-in-c from 21. *The Vicarage, Driftwood, Pellew Road, Falmouth TR11 2NS* M: 07544-527649 E: rev.amanda.evans@outlook.com

EVANS, Andrew. b 57. Southn Univ BEd 80. S Dios Minl Tr Scheme 88. d 91 p 92. NSM Cricklade w Latton *Bris* 91–97; C Yatton Keynell 97–99; TV By Brook 99–00; R Hullavington, Norton and Stanton St Quintin 00–09; P-in-c Sherston Magna, Easton Grey, Luckington etc 06–09; Bp's Adv for Rural Min 00–09; Hon Can Bris Cathl 05–09; AD N Wilts 06–09; TR Bridport *Sarum* 09–17; V Ashton-on-Ribble St Mich and All Angels w Preston St Mark *Blackb* from 17; OCM from 00. *St Michael's Vicarage, 2 Egerton Road, Ashton-on-Ribble, Preston PR2 1AJ* T: (01772) 726157 M: 07931-616329 E: canonandrewevans@gmail.com

EVANS, Andrew. *See* EVANS, John Andrew

EVANS, Canon Andrew Eric. b 58. Sheff Univ LLB 80 Solicitor 83. Trin Coll Bris 01. d 03 p 04. C Gt Bookham *Guildf* 03–06; P-in-c Broughton Gifford, Gt Chalfield and Holt *Sarum* 06–14; R from 14; C Atworth w Shaw and Whitley from 07; C Melksham 07–10; TR 10–14; RD Bradford from 08; Can and Preb Sarum Cathl from 19. *The Rectory, Ham Green, Holt, Trowbridge BA14 7PZ* T: (01225) 782289 E: goodevansitsandrew@gmail.com

EVANS, Mrs Anna Rachel. b 77. Brunel Univ BA 00. St Mellitus Coll 16. d 19 p 20. C Hampton Wick *Lon* from 19. *16 Arlington Road, Ashford TW15 2LS*

EVANS, Anne. b 47. Ches Coll of HE MTh 99. d 05 p 06. OLM Broughton *Lich* 05–17; OLM Myddle 05–17; OLM Loppington w Newtown 05–17; rtd 17; PtO *Lich* 17–21. *The Fields, Welshampton, Ellesmere SY12 0NP* T: (01948) 710206

EVANS, Canon Anthony Nigel. b 53. Nottm Univ BA 74 Fitzw Coll Cam BA 76. Westcott Ho Cam 74. d 77 p 78. C Sneinton St Cypr *S'well* 77–80; C Worksop Priory 80–83; V Nottingham St Geo w St Jo 83–88; R Ordsall 88–95; P-in-c Sutton in Ashfield St Mary 95–07; AD Newstead 04–11; P-in-c Edwinstowe 11–17; P-in-c Perlethorpe 11–17; P-in-c Clipstone 11–17; rtd 17; Warden Sacrista Prebend Retreat Ho *S'well* from 18; PtO from 18. *8 The Fields, Rainworth, Mansfield NG21 0GY* E: vicarfcep@btinternet.com

EVANS, Ashley Francis. b 58. Birm Univ BA 79. WEMTC 00. d 03 p 04. C Kington w Huntington, Old Radnor, Kinnerton etc *Heref* 03–07; P-in-c Evyas Harold w Dulas, Kenderchurch etc 07–10; R 11–17; RD Abbeydore 09–14; V Ticehurst and Flimwell *Chich* from 17. *The Vicarage, Church Street, Ticehurst, Wadhurst TN5 7AB* T: (01580) 200316 M: 07763-070177 E: revd@penandashley.co.uk

EVANS, Brian. b 34. Open Univ BA 86. St Deiniol's Hawarden 70. d 71 p 72. C Porthkerry *Llan* 71–72; C Barry All SS 72–75; V Abercynon 75–82; V Pendoylan w Welsh St Donats 82–87; R Maentwrog w Trawsfynydd *Ban* 87–99; rtd 99; PtO *Ban* 99–14 and from 16. *Madryn, 46 Glan Ysgethin, Talybont LL43 2BB* T: (01341) 247965

EVANS, Mrs Christine Elizabeth. b 54. RGN 75 RMHN 77. STETS. d 12 p 13. NSM Hanham *Bris* 12–17 and from 18; NSM Kingswood from 12; P-in-c 17–18. *3 Teewell Hill, Bristol BS16 5PA* T: 0117-957 0731 E: se007a4909_2@blueyonder.co.uk

EVANS, Christopher Idris. b 51. Chich Th Coll 74. d 77 p 78. C Gelligaer *Llan* 77–80; C St Andrews Major w Michaelston-le-Pit 80–81; V Llangeinor 81–87; V Watling

w Pyrton and Shirburn *Ox* 87–97; R Icknield 97–16; rtd 16; PtO *Ox* from 17. *40 Croft Road, Wallingford OX10 0HH* E: c.idris.evans@gmail.com

EVANS, Christopher Jonathan. b 43. AKC 67 and 88. d 68 p 69. C Wednesfield St Thos *Lich* 68–71; C Dorridge *Birm* 71–74; V Marston Green 74–81; V Acocks Green 81–86; RD Yardley 84–86; V Hill 86–88; Area Officer COPEC Housing Trust 88–91; V Harborne St Pet *Birm* 91–08; rtd 08; PtO *Heref* 08–18. *3 Manor Road, Great Bedwyn, Marlborough SN8 3UF* E: s.evans761@btinternet.com

EVANS, Clive Roger. b 59. Worc Coll Ox BA 80 MA 84 Barrister (Middle Temple) 89. St Jo Coll Nottm 94. d 94 p 95. C Barton Seagrave w Warkton *Pet* 94–97; V Long Buckby w Watford 97–11; P-in-c W Haddon w Winwick and Ravensthorpe 03–11; V Long Buckby w Watford and W Haddon w Winwick 11–13; RD Brixworth 01–09; Can Pet Cathl 09–13; V Bromyard and Stoke Lacy *Heref* from 13; RD Bromyard from 17. *The Vicarage, 28 Church Lane, Bromyard HR7 4DZ* T: (01885) 788275 E: cliver.evans@tiscali.co.uk

EVANS, Canon Colin Rex. b 24. Reading Univ BA 49. Linc Th Coll. d 57 p 58. C Boultham *Linc* 57–59; C Linc St Nic w St Jo Newport 59–62; V Linc St Mary-le-Wigford w St Martin 62–66; P-in-c Linc St Faith 63–66; R Bassingham 66–74; V Aubourn w Haddington 66–74; V Carlton-le-Moorland w Stapleford 66–74; R Skinnand 66–74; R Thurlby w Norton Disney 66–74; RD Graffoe 69–74; RD Elloe E 74–89; Can and Preb Linc Cathl 74–89; V Holbeach 74–89; rtd 90; Hon C Dawlish *Ex* 90–97; RD Kenn 95–97; PtO 97–20. *Address temp unknown* E: canoncrevans@gmail.com

EVANS, Daniel Barri. b 70. St Steph Ho Ox 01. d 03 p 04. C Weymouth H Trin *Sarum* 03–07; V Llwynderw *S & B* 07–15; TV Hawarden *St As* from 15; TV Borderlands Miss Area from 17. *Address temp unknown* M: 07948-692927 E: revdannyevans@sky.com

EVANS, Miss Daphne Gillian. b 41. Bible Tr Inst Glas 67 Trin Coll Bris IDC 75. dss 83 d 87. Wenlock *Heref* 83–88; Team Dn 87–88; rtd 88. *3 Jean Lawrie Court, St Boswells, Melrose TD6 0BF* E: revevborders@gmail.com

EVANS, David. b 37. Open Univ BA 73 FRSA 95. St Mich Coll Llan 65. d 67 p 68. C Swansea St Pet *S & B* 67–70; C St Austell *Truro* 70–75; R Purley *Ox* 75–90; RD Bradfield 85–90; R Bryanston Square St Mary w St Marylebone St Mark *Lon* 90–99; P-in-c St Marylebone Ch Ch 90–91; R Nuthurst and Mannings Heath *Chich* 99–07; P-in-c 07–11; rtd 11; PtO *Chich* 12–17; S'wark from 15. *Flat 3, 4 Hardwicke Road, Reigate RH2 9AG* T: (01737) 479296 E: devans1662@gmail.com

EVANS, Canon David. b 37. Keble Coll Ox BA 60 MA 65 Lon Univ BD 64. Wells Th Coll 62. d 64 p 65. Min Can Brecon Cathl *S & B* 64–68; C Brecon w Battle 64–68; C Swansea St Mary and H Trin 68–71; Chapl Univ of Wales (Swansea) 68–71; Bp's Chapl for Samaritan and Soc Work *Birm* 71–75; Jt Gen Sec Samaritans 75–84; Gen Sec 84–89; R Heyford w Stowe Nine Churches *Pet* 89–96; R Heyford w Stowe Nine Churches and Flore etc 96–01; Chapl Northants Police 89–01; RD Daventry *Pet* 96–00; Can Pet Cathl 97–01; rtd 01; PtO *Ex* 01–17. *3 Elm Close, Tutshill, Chepstow NP16 7DA* T: (01291) 630398

EVANS, David Burton. b 35. Open Univ BA 87 Goldsmiths' Coll Lon BMus 93. K Coll Lon 58 Edin Th Coll 60. d 62 p 63. C Leeds St Hilda *Ripon* 62–63; C Cross Green St Sav and St Hilda 63–67; Min Can Dur Cathl 67–71; PV Chich Cathl 71–74; Chapl Prebendal Sch *Chich* 71–74; R Lynch w Iping Marsh *Chich* 74–79; V Easebourne 79–86; Chapl K Edw VII Hosp Midhurst 77–86; R St Mich Cornhill w St Pet le Poer etc *Lon* 86–96; rtd 96; Pau *Eur* 96–01; PtO from 05. *128 Little Breach, Chichester PO19 5UA* T: (01243) 773266 M: 07795-662991 E: evtherev@virginmedia.com

EVANS, David Elwyn. b 43. St Mich Coll Llan 71. d 73 p 74. C Llandybie *St D* 73–75; C Llanelli 75–78; V Tre-lech a'r Betws w Abernant and Llanwinio 78–02; rtd 02. *8 Ger y Llan, The Parade, Carmarthen SA31 1LY*

EVANS, David Julian James. b 65. Rob Coll Cam BA 87. Westcott Ho Cam 03. d 05 p 06. C W Hackney St Barn *Lon* 05–08; C St John-at-Hackney 08–10; V Walworth St Chris *S'wark* 10–18; Warden Pemb Coll Miss Walworth 10–18; PtO from 19; *Lon* from 21. *33C Aquinas Street, London SE1 8AD* E: davidjjevans@me.com

EVANS, David Meurig Ashton. b 56. Univ of Wales (Cardiff) BSc 78 PhD 82 Lon Bible Coll BA 90. SEITE 12. d 13 p 14. C Lewisham St Mary *S'wark* 13–16; TR Brereton and Rugeley w Armitage *Lich* from 16. *20 Church Street, Rugeley WS15 2AB* M: 07919-416900 E: davidmaevans1@gmail.com

EVANS, Capt David Raymond. b 48. d 11 p 12. C Dale and St Brides w Marloes etc *St D* 11–14; PtO *B & W*

from 20. *Address withheld by request*　M: 07814-699336 E: landevans79@aol.com

EVANS, David Richard. b 47. St Steph Ho Ox 68. **d** 72 **p** 73. C Cardiff St Jo *Llan* 72–76; PV Llan Cathl 76–80; V Cleeve Prior and The Littletons *Worc* 80–12; rtd 12. *Stone Barn, Main Street, Evesham WR11 8LG* T: (01789) 772299 E: father.richard@hotmail.co.uk

⛪**EVANS, The Rt Revd David Richard John.** b 38. G&C Coll Cam BA 63 MA 66. Clifton Th Coll 63. **d** 65 **p** 66 **c** 78. C Enfield Ch Ch Trent Park *Lon* 65–68; SAMS Argentina 69–77; Peru 77–88; Bp Peru 78–88; Bp Bolivia 82–88; Asst Bp Bradf 88–93; Gen Sec SAMS 93–03; Hon Asst Bp Chich 94–97; Hon Asst Bp Roch 95–97; Hon Asst Bp Birm 97–03; rtd 03; Hon Asst Bp Cov from 03; Hon C Alderminster and Halford 03–07; Hon C Butlers Marston and the Pillertons w Ettington 03–07; Hon C Stourdene Gp 07–10. *30 Charles Street, Warwick CV34 5LQ* T: (01926) 258791 E: bishopdrjevans@talktalk.net

EVANS, David Russell. b 36. Liv Univ BA 57. Ripon Hall Ox 59. **d** 61 **p** 62. C Netherton CD *Liv* 61–65; Chapl Canon Slade Sch Bolton 65–93; Lic Preacher *Man* 65–09; PtO from 09. *2 Rushford Grove, Bolton BL1 8TD* T: (01204) 592981 E: revvyevvy@gmail.com

EVANS, Canon Derek. b 45. St D Coll Lamp. **d** 68 **p** 69. C Pembroke Dock *St D* 68–74; V Ambleston, St Dogwells, Walton E and Llysyfran 74–77; V Wiston w Ambleston, St Dogwells and Walton E 78–81; V Wiston w Ambleston, St Dogwells, Walton E etc 81–85; R Haverfordwest St Mary and St Thos w Haroldston 85–09; Dep Dioc Dir of Educn 92–97; Dir 97–09; Can St D Cathl 99–09; RD Roose 00–04; rtd 09; PtO *St D* from 09. *Thimble Cottage, 10 Milford Road, Haverfordwest SA61 1PJ* T: (01437) 765655

EVANS, Mrs Dorothi Madogwen Parry. **d** 16 **p** 17. NSM Corwen w Llangar w Glyndyfrdwy etc *St As* 16–17; NSM Valle Crucis Miss Area from 18. *Fron Heulog, 17 Ffrydan Road, Bala LL23 7RY* T: (01678) 520496 E: fronheulog@yahoo.co.uk

EVANS, Canon Edward John. b 47. St Mich Coll Llan 67. **d** 71 **p** 72. C Llantwit Fardre *Llan* 71–77; R Eglwysilan 77–88; V Laleston w Tythegston and Merthyr Mawr 88–09; V Laleston and Merthyr Mawr 09–13; V Laleston and Merthyr Mawr w Penyfai 13–15; RD Bridgend 94–04; AD 12–15; Hon Can Llan Cathl 07–15; rtd 15. *15 St Andrews Road, Bridgend CF31 1RX* T: (01656) 655511 M: 07968-044583 E: ejevans972@btinternet.com

EVANS, Elaine. *See* EVANS, Jennifer Elaine.

EVANS, Elwyn David. b 36. Keble Coll Ox BA 58 MA 62. St Steph Ho Ox 58 St Mich Coll Llan 60. **d** 61 **p** 62. C Aberystwyth H Trin *St D* 61–63; C Llanelli St Paul 63–66; C Roath St German *Llan* 66–69; V Crynant 69–78; R Llanilid w Pencoed 79–95; rtd 95; PtO *Llan* from 95; *S & B* 95–14. *15 St Andrew's Road, Bridgend CF31 1RX* T: (01656) 655511 E: ejevans912@btinternet.com

EVANS, Canon Freda Christine. b 48. MBE 89. NTMTC 96. **d** 99 **p** 00. C Hampton Hill *Lon* 99–02; V Kingshurst *Birm* 02–08; TR Erdington 08–16; V Erdington St Barn 16–19; Hon Can Birm Cathl 14–19; rtd 19. *Address withheld by request*　M: 07957-666002 E: freda@fredaevans.co.uk

EVANS, Mrs Freda Mary Ann (Frieda). b 54. St D Coll Lamp 95. **d** 00 **p** 05. OLM Malpas *Mon* 00–09; NSM Caerleon and Llanfrechfa 09–13; NSM Cwmbran from 13. *3 The Firs, Malpas, Newport NP20 6YD* T: (01633) 850600 E: revfrieda@btinternet.com

EVANS, Canon Frederick John Margam. b 31. Magd Coll Ox BA 53 MA 57. St Mich Coll Llan 53. **d** 54 **p** 55. C New Tredegar *Mon* 54–58; C Chepstow 58–60; Asst Chapl United Sheff Hosps 60–62; Chapl Brookwood Hosp Woking 62–70; V Crookham *Guildf* 70–98; RD Aldershot 78–83; Hon Can Guildf Cathl 89–98; rtd 98; PtO *Guildf* from 98. *4 Radford Close, Farnham GU9 9AB* T/F: (01252) 710594 E: johnjunee@btinternet.com

EVANS, Genevieve Sarah. b 62. Univ of Wales (Cardiff) BA 04. St Mich Coll Llan 02. **d** 04 **p** 05. C Whalley Range St Edm and Moss Side etc *Man* 04–08; V Walsall Pleck and Bescot *Lich* 08–16; C Walsall St Matt 08–16; C Walsall St Paul 08–16; V Oxley and Wednesfield St Greg 16–19; R Comrie *St And* from 19; R Crieff from 19; R Killin from 19; R Lochearnhead from 19. *Strathearn Rectory, 3B Galvelmore Street, Crieff PH7 4DN* T: (01764) 656222 E: rev.gen@btinternet.com

EVANS, Geoffrey David. b 44. K Coll Lon BD 69 AKC 69 Ex Univ PGCE 74. St Aug Coll Cant 69. **d** 70 **p** 71. C Lawrence Weston *Bris* 70–73; Chapl Grenville Coll Bideford 74–79; Chapl Eastbourne Coll 79–82; Chapl Taunton and Somerset Hosp 83–91; Chapl Musgrove Park Hosp 83–91; Chapl Taunton Sch 92–04; rtd 09. *10 Chaucer Road, Bath BA2 4QU* E: suecebath@gmail.com

EVANS, Mrs Gillian. b 39. Imp Coll Lon BSc 61. Mon Dioc Tr Scheme 84. **d** 88 **p** 94. NSM Penallt and Trellech *Mon* 88–89; NSM Overmonnow w Wonastow and Michel Troy 89–92; Dioc Ecum Officer and C Ludlow, Ludford, Ashford Carbonell etc *Heref* 92–95; Pakistan 95–96; PtO *Heref* 96–06; Hon C Dawlish *Ex* 97–98; TV Golden Cap Team *Sarum* 98–01; rtd 01; PtO *Cov* 01–06; *Mon* 01–06; Hon C Wolford w Burmington *Cov* 06–08; Hon C Cherington w Stourton 06–08; Hon C Barcheston 06–08; Hon C Long Compton, Whichford and Barton-on-the-Heath 06–08; Hon C S Warks Seven Gp 08–16; PtO 16–20. *8 Grange Park, Stratford-upon-Avon CV37 6XH* T: (01789) 269421

EVANS, Canon Glyn. b 59. Nene Coll Northn BA 80 Leic Univ BA 80 Ch Ch Coll Cant CertEd 82 Kent Univ PGCE 82. Qu Coll Birm 85. **d** 88 **p** 89. C Denton *Newc* 88–92; V Choppington 92–97; P-in-c Longhorsley and Hebron 97–01; Chapl HM Pris Acklington 97–01; P-in-c Newc St Andr and St Luke 01–17; City Cen Chapl 01–17; Chapl Northumbria Police from 11; Chapl to the Deaf from 16; TR N Shields from 17; Hon Can Newc Cathl from 11. *Christ Church Vicarage, 26 Cleveland Road, North Shields NE29 0NG* T: 0191-258 6653 E: office@northshieldsparish.org

EVANS, Canon Glyn Peter. b 54. Leeds Univ BA 75. Ripon Coll Cuddesdon 76. **d** 77 **p** 78. C Binley *Cov* 77–80; C Clifton upon Dunsmore w Brownsover 80–84; P-in-c Lacock w Bowden Hill *Bris* 84–89; P-in-c Lt Compton w Chastleton, Cornwell etc *Ox* 89–00; Agric Chapl 89–00; Dioc Rural Officer 00–19; Hon Can Ch Ch 05–19; rtd 19; PtO *Cov* 16–21; *Ox* from 19. *Chelmscote Cottage, Brailes, Banbury OX15 5JJ* T: (01608) 686749 M: 07581-491713

EVANS, Canon Gwyneth Mary. b 43. Gilmore Ho 69 Linc Th Coll 70. dss 74 **d** 87 **p** 94. Stamford Hill St Thos *Lon* 74–79; Chapl Asst R Free Hosp Lon 79–89; Chapl Salisbury Health Care NHS Trust 89–01; Can and Preb Sarum Cathl 96–01; rtd 01; PtO *Sarum* from 01. *39 The Close, Salisbury SP1 2EL* T: (01722) 412546 E: gwyneth175@btinternet.com

EVANS, Ms Heather Rhiannon. **d** 14 **p** 15. NSM Llanbadarn Fawr and Elerch and Penrhyncoch etc *St D* 14–19; NSM Bro Padarn from 19. *The Vicarage, Llanbadarn Fawr, Aberystwyth SY23 3TT* T: (01970) 624638 E: heather.melindwr@live.co.uk

EVANS, Hilary Margaret. b 49. Redland Coll of Educn TDip 71 Ches Coll of HE BTh 97. NOC 94. **d** 97 **p** 98. C Heald Green St Cath *Ches* 97–00; P-in-c Davyhulme Ch Ch *Man* 00–03; P-in-c Blackley St Pet 03–09; AD N Man 06–08; rtd 09; Hon C SW Gower *S & B* 09–14; PtO from 14. *10 Meadow Croft, Southgate, Swansea SA3 2DF* T: (01792) 234230

EVANS, Ian David. b 61. Qu Coll Birm 13. **d** 15 **p** 16. NSM Ipsley *Worc* 15–20; TV from 20. *27 Belmont Close, Redditch B97 5AW* T: (01905) 571243 *or* (01527) 404522 E: ianevans223@gmail.com

EVANS, Mrs Jane. b 59. W Midl Coll of Educn BEd 81. **d** 03 **p** 04. OLM Lilleshall and Muxton *Lich* from 03. *5 Collett Way, Priorslee, Telford TF2 9SL* T: (01952) 291340 E: rev.jane@outlook.com

EVANS, Mrs Jennifer. b 41. Ilkley Coll DipEd 62. Sarum Th Coll 88. **d** 88 **p** 08. Par Dn Bramshott and Liphook *Portsm* 88–92; Par Dn Whippingham w E Cowes 92–95; Par Dn Sarisbury 95–05; Hon C Llawhaden w Bletherston and Llanycefn *St D* 08–10; Hon C Slebech and Uzmaston w Boulston 08; Hon C Uzmaston 08–10; Hon C Chaffcombe, Cricket Malherbie etc *B & W* 10–19. *Balm of Gilead, 19 Middle Green, Beaminster DT8 3SJ* M: 07932-746883 E: jennie.honeycombs@virgin.net

EVANS, Jennifer Elaine. b 59. Wolv Univ BA 92. Qu Coll Birm 00. **d** 02 **p** 03. C Stafford St Jo and Tixall w Ingestre *Lich* 02–06; TV Stafford 06–13; V Stafford St Bertelin and Whitgreave St Jo from 13; Dean's PV Lich Cathl from 17. *St Bertelin's Vicarage, 36 Holmcroft Road, Stafford ST16 1JF* T: (01785) 252874 E: elaine.dowevans@gmail.com

EVANS, Mrs Jennifer Mary. **d** 17. NSM Bro Cyfeiliog and Mawddwy *Ban* from 17. *Dolau, Llanbrynmair SY19 7DL* T: (01650) 521660 E: jenevans399@btinternet.com

EVANS, Jill. *See* EVANS, Gillian.

EVANS, Mrs Joan. b 36. Nor Tr Coll TCert 57 UEA BEd 94. **d** 02 **p** 03. OLM Loddon, Sisland, Chedgrave, Hardley and Langley Nor 02–06; rtd 06; PtO *Nor* from 06. *13 Drury Lane, Loddon, Norwich NR14 6LB* T: (01508) 528656 E: joanevans936@btinternet.com

EVANS, John. *See* EVANS, Frederick John Margam.

EVANS, John Andrew. b 53. Hull Univ BSc 74 Univ of Wales MSc 75 Bris Univ BA 96. Trin Coll Bris 94. **d** 96 **p** 97. C Walton H Trin *Ox* 96–98; C Caversham St Pet and Mapledurham etc 98–01; R Bradford Abbas and Thornford w Beer Hackett *Sarum* 01–09; V N Hayes St Nic *Lon* from 09. *St Nicholas'*

Vicarage, Raynton Drive, Hayes UB4 8BG T: (020) 8573 4122 M: 07725-805437 E: j_andrew_evans@btconnect.com

EVANS, John David Vincent. b 41. CQSW 78. Lich Th Coll 66. **d** 68 **p** 70. C Kingsthorpe *Pet* 68–69; C Corby Epiphany w St Jo 69–72; Bp's Adv in Children's Work 72–74; Probation Officer 74–90; PtO *Pet* 88–90; R Greens Norton w Bradden and Lichborough 90–96; V Northampton Ch Ch 96–06; rtd 06; PtO *Pet* from 06. *Ivy Cottage, Creaton Road, Hollowell, Northampton NN6 8RP* T: (01604) 211372 E: johnevanssr203@gmail.com

EVANS, John Laurie. b 34. Pretoria Univ BSc 54 Imp Coll Lon BSc 55 Rhodes Univ BA 59. Ripon Coll Cuddesdon 84. **d** 86 **p** 87. C Bruton and Distr *B & W* 86–89; P-in-c Ambrosden w Merton and Piddington *Ox* 89–91; C Pet St Mary Boongate 91–93; V Michael *S & M* 93–96; R Ballaugh 93–96; rtd 96; Chapl Allnutt's Hosp Goring Heath 96–99; P-in-c Fochabers *Mor* 99–00; P-in-c Strathnairn St Paul 00–03; TV Langtree *Ox* 03–07; Hon C Kelso *Edin* 07–12; PtO from 12; *Newc* from 12. *2 Pressen Farm Cottage, Cornhill-on-Tweed TD12 4RS* T: (01890) 850309 M: 07909-986369 E: jonevansscotland@btinternet.com

EVANS, John Miles. b 39. Yale Univ BA 61 JD 67 St Cath Coll Cam BA 64 MA 68. NY Th Sem MDiv 93. **d** 95 **p** 95. Chapl St Jo Cath Oban *Arg* 95–97; Interim R Lynbrook Ch Ch USA 98–99; R Davidsonville All Hallows 99–05. *PO Box 1272, Portsmouth NH 03802-1272, USA* E: johnmilesevans@comcast.net

EVANS, John Rhys. b 45. Hull Univ BSc 66. Sarum & Wells Th Coll 77. **d** 79 **p** 80. C Alton St Lawr *Win* 79–82; C Tadley St Pet 82–85; V Colden 85–91; V Bitterne Park 91–01; C Ringwood 01–11; Chapl R Bournemouth and Christchurch Hosps NHS Foundn Trust 01–11; rtd 11; PtO *Glouc* from 14. *The Cottage, Alderley, Wotton-under-Edge GL12 7QT* T: (01453) 845320 E: johnrhysevans@yahoo.co.uk

EVANS, John Stuart. b 57. Univ of Wales (Abth) BA 78 Bretton Hall Coll PGCE 81. Trin Coll Bris BA 98. **d** 98 **p** 99. C Connah's Quay *St As* 98–02; V Rhosllannerchrugog 02–10; AD Llangollen 05–10; R Ruthin w Llanrhydd and Llanfwrog 10–16; TV Dyffryn Clwyd Miss Area from 17. *The Cloisters, School Road, Ruthin LL15 1BL* T: (01824) 702068 E: cymrostu@gmail.com

EVANS, Canon John Thomas. b 43. St Mich Coll Llan 66. **d** 67 **p** 68. C Connah's Quay *St As* 67–71; C Llanrhos 71–74; Chapl Rainhill Hosp Liv 74–78; TV Wrexham *St As* 78–83; V Holywell 83–96; RD 95–96; V Colwyn Bay 96–99; V Colwyn Bay w Brynymaen 99–02; RD Rhos 00–02; R Caerwys and Bodfari 02–08; Can Cursal St As Cathl 96–08; rtd 08; PtO *St As* from 09. *4 Durham Drive, Prestatyn LL19 8DX* M: 07905-861174 E: johnbethevans@btinternet.com

✠**EVANS, The Rt Revd John Wyn.** b 46. FSA 88 FRHistS 94 Univ of Wales (Cardiff) BA 68 BD 71. St Mich Coll Llan 68. **d** 71 **p** 72 **c** 08. C St D Cathl 71–72; Min Can St D Cathl 72–75; PtO *Ox* 75–77; Dioc Archivist *St D* 76–82; R Llanfallteg w Clunderwen and Castell Dwyran etc 77–82; Warden of Ords 78–83; Dioc Dir of Educn 82–92; Chapl Trin Coll Carmarthen 82–90; Dean of Chpl 90–94; Hd Th and RS 91–94; Hon Can St D Cathl 88–90; Can St D Cathl 90–94; Dean St D 94–08; V St D Cathl 94–01; TR Dewisland 01–08; Bp St D 08–16; rtd 16; PtO *St D* from 16; *S & B* from 16. *12 Ffordd Caerfai, St Davids, Haverfordwest SA62 6QT* T: (01437) 729402

EVANS, Jonathan Alan. b 53. Fitzw Coll Cam BA 75 PGCE 77 MA 79. St Jo Coll Nottm MA 95. **d** 95 **p** 96. C Drypool *York* 95–98; V Beverley St Nic 98–12; V Rye Park St Cuth *St Alb* 12–18; rtd 18; PtO *Glouc* from 19. *38 Furlong Road, Gloucester GL1 4UT* M: 07908-059084 E: jonathanaevans@icloud.com

EVANS, Jonathan Edward. b 69. QC 14. Oriel Coll Ox MA 91. Ripon Coll Cuddesdon 16. **d** 18 **p** 19. C Christchurch *Win* 18–21; P-in-c Bruton, Brewham, Pitcombe and Shepton Montague *B & W* 21; R from 21. *8 Wellesley Green, Bruton BA10 0DU* E: revjonevans@gmail.com *or* rector@stmarysbruton.org

EVANS, Mrs Judith Ann. b 55. SEITE 99. **d** 02 **p** 03. C Crayford *Roch* 02–06; P-in-c Kells *Carl* 06–13; Chapl N Cumbria Univ Hosps NHS Trust 06–13; V Northampton St Alb *Pet* from 13. *St Alban's Vicarage, Broadmead Avenue, Northampton NN3 2RA* T: (01604) 407074 M: 07929-978523 E: revdjudyevans@btinternet.com

EVANS, Ms Juliet Ann. b 70. K Coll Lon BD 92 AKC 92 PGCE 93. Ripon Coll Cuddesdon 01. **d** 05 **p** 06. C Bexley St Jo *Roch* 05–07; C Sidcup St Jo 07–08; Chapl Bp Justus C of E Sch Bromley 09–15; Chapl Trin Sch Lewisham from 15; P-in-c Lewisham St Swithun *S'wark* from 17. *St Swithun's Vicarage, 191 Hither Green Lane, London SE13 6QE* M: 07955-229351 E: julietaevans@icloud.com

EVANS, Kathryn Louise. b 63. Birm Univ MHSc 96 Ches Univ MA 17 RGN 86 RM 88. St Jo Coll Nottm 12. **d** 14 **p** 15. C Blackheath *Birm* 14–17; V Oldbury, Langley and Londonderry 17–20; P-in-c Estuary and Mountain Miss Area *St As* from 20. *The Vicarage, St Mary's Court, Whitford Road, Whitford, Holywell CH8 9AG* T: (01745) 799200 M: 07568-555585 E: kathrynevans@cinw.org.uk

EVANS, Mrs Kathryn Ruth. b 77. Sydney Univ BA 99 MTeach 01. Qu Foundn Birm 16. **d** 19 **p** 20. C Brington w Whilton and Norton etc *Pet* from 19.

EVANS, Canon Keith. b 57. Trin Coll Carmarthen CertEd 81 BEd 82. St D Coll Lamp BA 84 Sarum & Wells Th Coll 84. **d** 85 **p** 86. C Swansea St Thos and Kilvey *S & B* 85–87; C Gorseinon 87–89; V Oxwich w Penmaen and Nicholaston 89–94; Dir Post-Ord Tr from 93; R Ystradgynlais 94–98; V Oystermouth from 98; Hon Can Brecon Cathl from 04. *The Vicarage, 9 Western Close, Mumbles, Swansea SA3 4HF* T: (01792) 369971 E: revkeithevans@talktalk.net

EVANS, Kevin Stuart. b 56. Bris Poly CQSW 80. Qu Coll Birm 93. **d** 95 **p** 96. C Madeley *Heref* 95–98; P-in-c Wombridge *Lich* from 98; TV Cen Telford 05–14; C St Georges' from 14. *Wombridge Vicarage, Wombridge Road, Telford TF2 6HT* T: (01952) 613334 E: wombridgechurch@hotmail.com

EVANS, Mrs Linda Joyce. b 54. Trin Coll Bris BA 06. **d** 06 **p** 07. NSM Weston super Mare Ch Ch and Em *B & W* 06–10; P-in-c Dale and St Brides w Marloes *St D* 10–11; P-in-c Herbrandston and Hasguard w St Ishmael's etc 10–11; P-in-c Dale and St Brides w Marloes etc 11–14; rtd 14; Chapl Weston Area Health NHS Trust from 20; PtO *Bris* from 21. *Weston General Hospital, Grange Road, Uphill, Weston-super-Mare BS23 4TQ* E: landevans54@aol.com

EVANS, Linda Mary. *See* EDWARDS, Linda Mary

EVANS, Lloyd Russell. b 59. K Coll Lon BSc 81 York Univ MA 97. **d** 15 **p** 16. NSM Talgarth w Bronllys w Llanfilo *S & B* 15–18; PtO *Dur* 17–20; C Lynesack from 20; C Cockfield from 20; C Evenwood from 20; PtO *Leeds* 20–21. *Denholme, Pinfold Lane, Butterknowle, Bishop Auckland DL13 5PS* T: (01388) 710394 E: l.evans758@btinternet.com

EVANS, Ms Margaret Elizabeth. b 48. Leeds Univ BA 69 Lon Inst of Educn CertEd 70. Oak Hill Th Coll 91. **d** 94 **p** 95. NSM Canonbury St Steph *Lon* 94–19; PtO from 19. *9 Compton Terrace, London N1 2UN* T: (020) 7359 4343

EVANS, Margaret Rose. b 48. **d** 12. NSM Ensbury Park *Sarum* 12–18; PtO from 18. *179 Redhill Drive, Bournemouth BH10 6AH* T: (01202) 513154

EVANS, Ms Marina Anne. b 58. **d** 14 **p** 15. NSM Pembroke Dock *St D* 14–20; NSM S W Pembrokeshire from 20. *43 Arthur Street, Pembroke Dock SA72 6EN* M: 07701-339490 E: rev.marina.evans@hotmail.com

EVANS, Martin Lonsdale. b 69. Man Univ BA 91. Ripon Coll Cuddesdon 93. **d** 95 **p** 96. C Morpeth *Newc* 95–98; Chapl RN from 98. *Royal Naval Chaplaincy Service Headquarters, Tanner Building, HMS Excellent, Whale Island, Portsmouth PO2 8ER* T: 0300-157 7544 E: padrecdo@aol.com

EVANS, Martyn Hywel. b 63. Univ of Wales (Cardiff) BScEcon 86 Glam Univ MBA 99. St Mich Coll Llan 10. **d** 12 **p** 13. C Tredegar *Mon* 12–14; C Lower Islwyn 14–15; P-in-c Lower Islwyn Min Area 15–19; V Llangynwyd w Maesteg *Llan* from 19. *18 Llynfi Court, Maesteg CF34 9NJ* T: (01656) 718449 E: revmhe@gmail.com

EVANS, Matthew Scott. b 72. Grey Coll Dur BA 93. Cranmer Hall Dur 96. **d** 98 **p** 99. C Fountains Gp *Ripon* 98–03; P-in-c Dacre w Hartwith and Darley w Thornthwaite 03–15; Jt AD Ripon 09–11; AD 11–14; P-in-c Dacre w Hartwith and Darley w Thornthwaite *Leeds* from 14; V High Harrogate Ch Ch from 15. *Christ Church Vicarage, 11 St Hilda's Road, Harrogate HG2 8JX* T: (01423) 530750 E: christchurch01@btconnect.com

EVANS, Merewyn Abigail. *See* SMITH, Merewyn Abigail

EVANS, Michael John. b 53. **d** 00 **p** 01. OLM Longnor, Quarnford and Sheen *Lich* 00–04; OLM Ipstones w Berkhamsytch and Onecote w Bradnop 04–11; P-in-c 11–15; V Butterton, Ipstones-w-Berkhamsytch etc 15–20; RD Alstonfield 16–20; rtd 20. *Address temp unknown* E: revdmjevans@gmail.com

EVANS, Preb Neil Robert. b 54. Lon Univ MA 93 K Coll Lon DMin 10. Coll of Resurr Mirfield. **d** 84 **p** 85. C Bethnal Green St Jo w St Bart *Lon* 84–86; C St Jo on Bethnal Green 87–88; P-in-c Stoke Newington Common St Mich 88–95; V 95–98; V Twickenham All Hallows 98–05; Kensington Area CME Officer 98–05; Par Min Development Adv Willesden Area 05–07; Area Dir Tr and Development 07–13; Dir Tr and Development Two Cities Area 13–19; Dioc Dir of Min from 07; Preb St Paul's Cathl from 18.

23 St Albans Avenue, London W4 5LL T: (020) 8987 7332
E: neil.evans@london.anglican.org

EVANS, Nicholas Anthony Paul. b 60. Sheff Univ BA 81 Liv Univ PGCE 86. Qu Coll Birm 81. **d** 84 **p** 87. C Ludlow *Heref* 84–85; C Sunbury *Lon* 86–92; Hd RE Guildf Co Sch 93–99; NSM Crookham *Guildf* 94–99; CF 99–02; V Shenley Green *Birm* 02–15; R Newport Pagnell w Lathbury and Moulsoe *Ox* from 15. *The Rectory, 81 High Street, Newport Pagnell MK16 8AB* T: (01908) 611145 M: 07769-550204 E: nickevans49@btinternet.com

EVANS, Nigel William Reid. b 70. Sheff Hallam Univ BEd 96. Ridley Hall Cam BTh 01. **d** 01 **p** 02. C Ossett and Gawthorpe *Wakef* 01–05; V Loddon, Sisland, Chedgrave, Hardley and Langley *Nor* 05–10; RD Loddon 06–10; TR Bucknall *Lich* 10–18; RD Stoke 14–17; RD Stoke N 16–17; RD Stoke-on-Trent 17–18. *Address temp unknown*

EVANS, The Ven Patrick Alexander Sidney. b 43. Linc Th Coll 70. **d** 73 **p** 74. C Lyonsdown H Trin *St Alb* 73–76; C Royston 76–78; V Gt Gaddesden 78–82; V Tenterden St Mildred w Smallhythe *Cant* 82–89; Adn Maidstone 89–02; Hon Can Cant Cathl 89–02; Dir of Ords 89–93; Adn Cant and Can Res Cant Cathl 02–07; rtd 07; PtO *Truro* from 16; *Sarum* from 20. *Cranleigh Cottage, 2 Abbot Close, Beaminster DT8 3FE* T: (01308) 862367 E: patrickevans120@hotmail.co.uk

EVANS, Paul David. b 54. Pemb Coll Cam BA 75 MA 79 Dur Univ BA 18 Lon Inst of Educn PGCE 76. SWMTC 11. **d** 14 **p** 15. NSM Cockington *Ex* from 14; NSM Torre All SS 14–16. *3 Hermosa, Higher Woodfield Road, Torquay TQ1 2LB* T: (01803) 215462 E: revpaulevans@gmail.com

EVANS, Peter Anthony. b 36. Imp Coll Lon BScEng 57. St Steph Ho Ox 58. **d** 60 **p** 61. C Surbiton St Mark *S'wark* 60–63; Asst Chapl Lon Univ 63–64; C S Kensington St Luke 64–68; C Surbiton St Andr and St Mark *S'wark* 68–69; C Loughton St Jo *Chelmsf* 69–74; P-in-c Becontree St Geo 74–82; PtO 82–89; NSM Romford St Alb 89–93; NSM Coopersale 93–95; NSM Epping Distr 95–96; rtd 97; PtO *Chelmsf* from 97. *6 Woodhall Crescent, Hornchurch RM11 3NN* T: (01708) 702668

EVANS, Peter Gerald. b 41. Man Univ BA 71. AKC 65. **d** 65 **p** 66. C Kidbrooke St Jas *S'wark* 65–68; C Fallowfield *Man* 68–71; C Brockley Hill St Sav *S'wark* 71–73; P-in-c Colchester St Botolph w H Trin and St Giles *Chelmsf* 74–79; V 79–92; PtO from 93. *97 Northgate Street, Colchester CO1 1EY* T: (01206) 543297 E: p555evans@yahoo.com

EVANS, Richard. *See* EVANS, David Richard

EVANS, Richard Gregory. b 50. St Mich Coll Llan 69. **d** 73 **p** 74. C Oystermouth *S & B* 73–76; C Clydach 76–79; CF(V) 78–81; V Llanddew and Talachddu *S & B* 79–83; Youth Chapl 79–83; Hon Min Can Brecon Cathl 79–83; Chapl Huntley Sch NZ 83–87; Chapl Nga Tawa Sch 83–90; Chapl Wanganui Sch 90–15; rtd 15. *5 Marshall Avenue, Wanganui East, Wanganui 4500, New Zealand* T: (0064) (6) 343 5434 M: (0064) 21-249 0860 E: rgevans@xtra.co.nz

EVANS, Richard Trevor. b 33. Jes Coll Ox MA 58 DipEd 58. St And Dioc Tr Course 73. **d** 76 **p** 76. NSM Leven *St And* 76–95; NSM St Andrews St Andr from 95. *33 Huntingtower Park, Whinnyknowe, Glenrothes KY6 3QF* T: (01592) 741670 E: revans9973@blueyonder.co.uk

EVANS, Robert. *See* EVANS, Simon Robert

EVANS, Robert Arnold Hughes. b 90. Ridley Hall Cam 12. **d** 15 **p** 16. C Cambridge St Andr Less *Ely* from 15. *Christ Church, Christchurch Street, Cambridge CB1 1HT* T: (01223) 750450 E: rob.evans@christchurchcambridge.org.uk

EVANS, Robert Charles. b 55. K Coll Lon BA 77 AKC 77 MA 78 MTh 89 Qu Coll Cam BA 80 MA 83 K Coll Lon CertEd 85 Qu Coll Ox DPhil 13. Westcott Ho Cam 79. **d** 81 **p** 87. C St Breoke *Truro* 81–83; C St Columb Minor and St Colan 83–84; Chapl Rob Coll Cam 87–92; Lect Ches Univ from 92. *University of Chester, Parkgate Road, Chester CH1 4BJ* T: (01244) 510000 E: r.evans@chester.ac.uk

EVANS, Robert George Roger. b 49. Cam Univ MA. Trin Coll Bris 74. **d** 77 **p** 78. C Bispham *Blackb* 77–80; C Chadwell *Chelmsf* 80–84; V Ardsley *Sheff* 84–09; P-in-c Kendray 04–09; Chapl Barnsley Community & Priority Services NHS Trust 98–00; rtd 09; PtO *Sheff* from 11. *73 High Street, Wombwell, Barnsley S73 8HS* T: (01226) 345635 E: rgrevans@gmail.com

EVANS, Robert Stanley. b 51. Univ of Wales (Lamp) BA 72 Univ of Wales (Cardiff) PGCE 73. St Mich Coll Llan 90. **d** 92 **p** 93. C Penarth All SS *Llan* 92–95; R Gelligaer 95–99; V Roath 99–04; R Coychurch, Llangan and St Mary Hill 04–06; rtd 06. *Ty Tudful, 5 Cook Road, Barry CF62 9HD* T: (01446) 420011 E: revrobertevans@hotmail.com

EVANS, Rupert Alexander. b 81. St Cath Coll Cam BA 02. Wycliffe Hall Ox MTh 10. **d** 10 **p** 11. C Crowborough *Chich* 10–14; Team Ldr Titus Trust from 14; PtO *S'wark* from 19.

LDN Holidays, 21 Fleet Street, London EC4Y 1AA T: (020) 3617 1606 E: rupertaevans@gmail.com

EVANS, Mrs Sarah Rosemary. b 64. Trevelyan Coll Dur BA 85. STETS 05. **d** 08 **p** 09. NSM Hullavington, Norton and Stanton St Quintin *Bris* 08–12; NSM Sherston Magna, Easton Grey, Luckington etc 08–12; NSM By Brook 12–17; Min Can Bris Cathl from 17. *Ashdown, Littleton Drew, Chippenham SN14 7NA* T: (01249) 782885 E: rev.sarahevans@gmail.com

EVANS, Selina Ann. b 62. ERMC 18. **d** 19 **p** 20. NSM Digswell *St Alb* from 19. *The Haven, Rabley Heath, Welwyn AL6 9UG* T: (01438) 813909 M: 07754-772445 E: saevans256@gmail.com

EVANS, Canon Simon. b 55. Newc Univ BA 77 Heythrop Coll Lon MA 06. St Steph Ho Ox 78. **d** 80 **p** 81. C Pet St Jude 80–84; Chapl Asst Pet Distr Hosp 80–84; C Wantage *Ox* 84–87; V W Leigh *Portsm* 87–96; Chapl E Hants Primary Care Trust 88–96; V Ruislip St Martin *Lon* 96–21; AD Hillingdon 08–13; rtd 21; Can Wiawso Ghana from 08. *Wagtail Cottage, 11 High Street, Hindon, Salisbury SP3 6DR* T: (01747) 820613 M: 07818-428463 E: frsimonevans@outlook.com

EVANS, Simon Andrew. b 59. Sarum & Wells Th Coll 81. **d** 84 **p** 85. C Norbury St Steph and Thornton Heath *S'wark* 84–88; C Putney St Mary 88–92; P-in-c Telford Park St Thos 92–94; V 94–04; V Ensbury Park *Sarum* from 04; Chapl Dorset Police from 06. *St Thomas's Vicarage, 42 Coombe Avenue, Bournemouth BH10 5AE* T: (01202) 519735 E: simon@evansonline.info *or* vicar@ensburypark.org.uk

EVANS, Simon Robert. b 58. Reading Univ BSc 79. NOC 99. **d** 02 **p** 03. C Pudsey St Lawr and St Paul *Bradf* 02–04; P-in-c Low Moor 04–05; TV Oakenshaw, Wyke and Low Moor 06–07; TR 07–10; P-in-c Harden and Wilsden 10–13; P-in-c Denholme 10–13; P-in-c Cullingworth 10–13; TR Harden and Wilsden, Cullingworth and Denholme 13–14; *Leeds* 14–17; V Heeley *Sheff* 17–21; V Heeley w Arbourthorne and Norfolk Park from 21. *Heeley Vicarage, 151 Gleadless Road, Sheffield S2 3AE* T: 0114-255 7718 E: vicarbob999@gmail.com

EVANS, Stanley George. b 43. CITC 00. **d** 03 **p** 04. Aux Min Killaloe w Stradbally *L & K* 03–04; P-in-c Killarney w Aghadoe and Muckross 04–05; Aux Min Leighlin w Grange Sylvae, Shankill etc *C, F & O* 05–09; PtO *L & K* 09–13; P-in-c Omey w Ballynakill, Errislannan and Roundstone *T, K & A* 13–19; Can Tuam Cathl 16–19; Can Killala Cathl 16–19; Chapl Lanzarote *Eur* from 19. *Calle los Sabandeños 37, 35510 Puerto del Carmen, Lanzarote, Canary Islands, Spain* T: (0034) 928 514 241 E: revdstanevans@gmail.com

EVANS, Stephen Gary. b 66. ERMC 16. **d** 19 **p** 20. NSM Somersham w Pidley and Oldhurst and Woodhurst *Ely* from 19. *4 Clark Drive, St Ives PE27 6AD* E: gevans8@btinternet.com

EVANS, Stephen John. b 60. Dartmouth RN Coll 81 St Steph Ho Ox BA 85 MA 89 Aber Univ MPhil 94 DHC 17. **d** 86 **p** 87. Prec St Andr Cathl Inverness *Mor* 86–89; R Montrose *Bre* 89–91; P-in-c Inverbervie 89–91; Miss to Seamen 89–91; V Northampton St Paul *Pet* 91–98; CME Officer 94–00; Liturg Officer 96–03; P-in-c Ecton and Warden Ecton Ho 98–00; R Uppingham w Ayston and Wardley w Belton *Pet* 00–10; Can Pet Cathl 03–10; RD Rutland 03–10; R St Marylebone w H Trin *Lon* from 10. *21 Beaumont Street, London W1G 6DQ* T: (020) 7935 8965 E: rector@stmarylebone.org

EVANS, Steven Edward. b 52. CBDTI 97. **d** 00 **p** 01. NSM Caton w Littledale *Blackb* 00–05; NSM Hornby w Claughton and Whittington etc 05–06; NSM Slyne w Hest and Halton w Aughton 06–08; PtO from 08. *Old Bank House, Farleton, Lancaster LA2 9LF* T: (01524) 222034 M: 07808-795528

EVANS, Stuart. *See* EVANS, John Stuart

EVANS, Ms Susan Mary. b 55. St Jo Coll Dur BA 76 CertEd 77 Nottm Univ BCombStuds 84. Linc Th Coll 81. **dss** 84 **d** 87 **p** 94. Weaste *Man* 84–88; Par Dn 87–88; Par Dn Longsight St Luke 88–92; Par Dn Claydon and Barham *St E* 92–94; C 94–99; P-in-c Coddenham w Gosbeck and Hemingstone w Henley 95–99; Chapl HM YOI Hollesley Bay Colony 99–02; NSM Henley, Claydon and Barham *St E* 02–06; Chapl HM Pris Whatton 06–09; P-in-c Castle Bytham w Creeton *Linc* 10–14; PtO 16–19; Chapl Lincs Partnership NHS Foundn Trust 17–20; rtd 20. *8 Abbey Road, Bardney, Lincoln LN3 5XA* T: (01526) 397101 E: broadbentevans@btinternet.com

EVANS, Terence Robert. b 45. NOC 82. **d** 85 **p** 86. C Warrington St Elphin *Liv* 85–88; V Cantril Farm 88–94; V Rainhill 94–03; R Odd Rode *Ches* 03–10; rtd 10; PtO *Ches* from 10. *11 Harpur Crescent, Alsager, Stoke-on-Trent ST7 2SX* T: (01270) 878209 E: evans338@mac.com *or* evans338@btinternet.com

EVANS, Timothy Simon. b 57. York Univ BA 79 Sussex Univ MA 81 Fitzw Coll Cam BA 85 MA 88. Ridley Hall Cam 83. **d** 87 **p** 88. C Whitton St Aug *Lon* 87–90; C Ealing St Steph Castle Hill 90–93; P-in-c Shireshead *Blackb* 93–97; Asst Chapl

Lanc Univ 93–97; Vice Prin LCTP 97–09; P-in-c Natland *Carl* 97–09; C Old Hutton and New Hutton 06–09; RD Kendal 00–03; Hon Can Carl Cathl 00–09; Dir Past Studies and Tutor Yorks Min Course 09–15; Dir Studies (Initial Tr) *Man* 15–18; Tr Officer CMD and IME 4-7 from 18; Lic Preacher from 15; PtO *Blackb* from 09. *Church House, 90 Deansgate, Manchester M3 2GH* T: 0161-828 1452 M: 07553-371165 E: timevans@manchester.anglican.org

EVANS, Mrs Wendy Nicola. b 59. St Jo Coll Dur BA 11. Cranmer Hall Dur 09. **d** 11 **p** 12. C Oulton Broad *Nor* 11–14; TV Diss 14–18; rtd 18; PtO *Nor* from 18. *5 Goshawk Way, Thetford IP24 3HX* M: 07971-082603 E: revwendi@icloud.com

EVANS, Wyn. See EVANS, John Wyn

EVANS-HILLS, Ms Bonnie Jean. b 57. Westcott Ho Cam. **d** 09 **p** 10. C Leic Resurr 09–10; C Oadby 10–14; Bp's Interfaith Adv 12–14; Dioc Interfaith Adv *St Alb* 14–20; P-in-c Kimpton w Ayot St Lawrence 14–15; R 15–18; P-in-c Leven *St And* from 20; PtO *Liv* from 19. *Address withheld by request* M: 07548-687504 E: bonnie.evans-hills@hotmail.co.uk

EVASON, Stuart Anthony. b 44. Salford Univ BSc. Chich Th Coll 79. **d** 81 **p** 82. C Heref St Martin 81–85; TV Cleethorpes *Linc* 85–87; TV Howden *York* 87–92; V Heywood St Jas *Man* 92–03; P-in-c Barrow St Jas *Carl* 03–10; TR Barrow St Matt 06–09; rtd 10; PtO *Man* from 10. *17 Drake Hall, Westhoughton, Bolton BL5 2RA* T: (01942) 810128 E: s.evason@gmail.com

EVE, David Charles Leonard. b 45. AKC 74. St Aug Coll Cant 74. **d** 75 **p** 76. C Hall Green Ascension *Birm* 75–79; TV Kings Norton 79–84; V Rowley Regis 84–93; PtO *Heref* 94–98 and from 01; NSM Hallow and Grimley w Holt *Worc* 98–05; PtO from 05. *14 Orchard End, Cleobury Mortimer, Kidderminster DY14 8BA* T: (01299) 270510 E: gabrielle.davideve@btinternet.com

EVE, Gary Henry. b 68. SWMTC 12. **d** 15 **p** 16. NSM St Germans *Truro* 15–17; NSM Lanteglos by Fowey 17–18; NSM Lansallos 17–18; NSM Talland 17–18; NSM Lanreath and Pelynt 17–18; NSM Trelawny 18–19. *The Vicarage, 4 Ocean View, Polruan, Fowey PL23 1QJ* T: (01726) 870568 E: revgaryeve@gmail.com

EVE, Hilary Anne. See FIFE, Hilary Anne

EVELEIGH, Raymond. b 36. Univ of Wales (Cardiff) BSc 58. NW Ord Course 73. **d** 76 **p** 77. NSM S Cave and Ellerker w Broomfleet *York* 76–79; P-in-c Kingston upon Hull St Mary 79–82; Chapl Hull Coll of FE 79–01; V Anlaby Common St Mark *York* 82–94; V Langtoft w Foxholes, Butterwick, Cottam etc 94–01; rtd 01; PtO *York* from 04. *Pasture Lodge, West End, Kilham, Driffield YO25 4RR* T: (01262) 420060 E: rev@revray.co.uk

EVENS, Jonathan Adrian Harvey. b 63. Middx Poly BA 84 Middx Univ BA 03 ACIPD 90. NTMTC 00. **d** 03 **p** 04. C Barking St Marg w St Patr *Chelmsf* 03–06; V Gt Ilford St Jo 06–15; P-in-c St Steph Walbrook and St Swithun etc *Lon* 15–18; C St Martin-in-the-Fields from 15. *St Martin-in-the-Fields, 5 St Martin's Place, London WC2N 4JH* T: (020) 7766 1100 E: jonathan.evens@smitf.org

EVENS, Robert Alan. b 51. **d** 00 **p** 01. NSM Sharnbrook and Knotting w Souldrop *St Alb* 00–03; P-in-c Wymington w Podington 03–05; R Sharnbrook, Felmersham and Knotting w Souldrop 05–15; RD Sharnbrook 12–15; R Ashwell w Hinxworth and Newnham 15–21; rtd 20; PtO *St Alb* from 21. *Library Cottage, Merchant Taylors Close, Ashwell, Baldock SG7 5LF* E: robert.evens@lineone.net

✠EVENS, The Rt Revd Robert John Scott. b 47. ACIB 74. Trin Coll Bris 74. **d** 77 **p** 78 **c** 04. C Southsea St Simon *Portsm* 77–79; C Portchester 79–83; V Locks Heath 83–96; RD Fareham 93–96; Adn Bath and Preb Wells Cathl *B & W* 96–04; Suff Bp Crediton *Ex* 04–12; rtd 12; Hon Asst Bp Glouc from 13; Hon Asst Bp Bris 13–18. *30 Highland Road, Charlton Kings, Cheltenham GL53 9LT* T: (01242) 251411 E: robertevens@hotmail.co.uk

EVERARD, Stephen Russell. b 54. Sarum Coll 13. **d** 16 **p** 17. NSM N Mundham w Hunston and Merston *Chich* from 16. *The Chestnuts, 30 The Drive, Emsworth PO10 8JP* T: (01243) 375858 E: jsne@talktalk.net

EVEREST, Canon John Cleland. b 45. Sarum Th Coll 66. **d** 68 **p** 69. C Moulsecoomb *Chich* 68–71; C Easthampstead *Ox* 71–74; C Southwick St Mich *Chich* 74–77; Dioc Soc Services Adv *Worc* 77–84; Ind Chapl 84–93; R Worc City St Paul and Old St Martin etc 84–93; RD Worc E 89–93; TR Halas 93–10; RD Dudley 95–98; Hon Can Worc Cathl 90–10; rtd 10; PtO *Worc* from 10. *18 Tunnel Hill, Worcester WR4 9RP* T: (01905) 723305 E: everestjc45@gmail.com

EVERETT, Alan Neil. b 57. St Cath Coll Ox BA 79 DPhil 96 SS Coll Cam BA 84. Westcott Ho Cam 82. **d** 85 **p** 86. C Hindley All SS *Liv* 85–88; Chapl Qu Mary Coll *Lon* 88–91; V S Hackney St Mich w Haggerston St Paul 94–10; V Notting Dale St Clem w St Mark and St Jas 10–19; Preb St Paul's Cathl 18–19; V

W Dulwich All SS *S'wark* from 19. *All Saints' Vicarage, 165 Rosendale Road, London SE21 8LN* T: (020) 8676 4550 E: alan@n16.org.uk or alan.everett@all-saints.org.uk

EVERETT, Anthony William. b 60. S Bank Poly BA 82. Oak Hill Th Coll BA 89. **d** 89 **p** 90. C Hailsham *Chich* 89–92; C New Malden and Coombe *S'wark* 92–97; V Streatham Park St Alb 97–02; V Herne Bay Ch Ch *Cant* from 02; Asst Dir of Ords 05–09; Jt AD Reculver 12–13; AD 15–19. *Christ Church Vicarage, 38 Beltinge Road, Herne Bay CT6 6BU* T: (01227) 374906 or 366640 E: vicar@parishofhernebay.org.uk

EVERETT, Mrs Christine Mary. b 46. St Osyth Coll of Educn CertEd 67. Westcott Ho Cam 90. **d** 92 **p** 94. Par Dn Ipswich St Fran *St E* 92–94; C 94–95; C Gt and Lt Bealings w Playford and Culpho 96; P-in-c 96–02; P-in-c The Creetings and Earl Stonham w Stonham Parva 02–11; rtd 11; PtO *St E* 11–17; *St D* from 17. *72 Charles Thomas Avenue, Pembroke Dock SA72 6UR* T: (01646) 684522 M: 07980-023236 E: c.everett65@btinternet.com

EVERETT, Colin Gerald Grant. b 44. Open Univ BA 77 Keswick Hall Coll CertEd. Ripon Coll Cuddesdon 79. **d** 81 **p** 82. C Aston cum Aughton *Sheff* 81–84; R Fornham All SS and Fornham St Martin w Timworth *St E* 84–92; P-in-c Old Newton w Stowupland 92–94; C Ipswich All Hallows 94–95; TV Ipswich St Fran 95–97; TV Ipswich St Mary at Stoke w St Pet and St Fran 97–09; rtd 09; PtO *St E* 09–17; *St D* from 17. *72 Charles Thomas Avenue, Pembroke Dock SA72 6UR* T: (01646) 684522 E: revcolin@btinternet.com

EVERETT, David John. b 51. Leeds Univ BA 07. NOC 04. **d** 07 **p** 08. NSM Moor Allerton and Shadwell *Ripon* 07–11; V Market Weighton *York* 11–17; R Goodmanham 11–17; V Sancton 11–17; rtd 17; PtO *St E* 18–21; TV Forest Heath from 21. *24 Oxford Close, Mildenhall, Bury St Edmunds IP28 7RP* T: (01638) 718801 E: david.j.everett24@gmail.com

EVERETT, Nevsky James. b 89. G&C Coll Cam BA 10. Westcott Ho Cam 10. **d** 13 **p** 14. C Norton *St Alb* 13–16; Chapl Keble Coll Ox from 16. *Keble College, Parks Road, Oxford OX1 3PG* T: (01865) 272725 M: 07791-910050 E: nevsky.everett@hotmail.co.uk or chaplain@keble.ox.ac.uk

EVERETT, Robert Henry. b 60. Em Coll Cam BA 82 MA 86 Ox Univ BA 85 MA 90 Ex Univ MPhil 95. St Steph Ho Ox 83. **d** 86 **p** 87. C Ex St Thos and Em 86–88; C Plymstock 88–91; R St Dominic, Landulph and St Mellion w Pillaton *Truro* 91–96; P-in-c Reading All SS *Ox* 96–98; V 98–07; P-in-c Paddington St Mary Magd *Lon* 07–09; P-in-c Paddington St Pet 07–09; V Paddington St Mary Magd and St Pet from 09. *The Vicarage, 2 Rowington Close, London W2 5TF* T: (020) 7289 1818 or 7289 2011 E: frhenry@yahoo.co.uk

EVERETT, Canon Simon Francis. b 58. Oak Hill Th Coll BA 89. **d** 89 **p** 90. C Wroughton *Bris* 89–93; TV Wexcombe *Sarum* 93–98; P-in-c The Iwernes, Sutton Waldron and Fontmell Magna 98–01; V Iwerne Valley 01–14; RD Milton and Blandford 01–13; TR Wareham from 14; RD Purbeck from 16; Can and Preb Sarum Cathl from 09. *The Rectory, 22 Worgret Road, Wareham BH20 4PN* T: (01929) 289236 M: 07879-658112 E: reveverett@btinternet.com

EVERETT-ALLEN, Canon Clive. b 47. AKC 70. St Aug Coll Cant 69. **d** 70 **p** 71. C Minera *St As* 70–72; C Hatcham St Cath *S'wark* 72–75; TV Beaconsfield *Ox* 75–83; R Southwick St Mich *Chich* 83–98; V E Grinstead St Swithun 98–15; RD E Grinstead 05–10; Can and Preb Chich Cathl 98–15; rtd 15; PtO *York* from 15. *2 Keble Park Crescent, Bishopthorpe, York YO23 2SY* T: (01904) 593969 E: cliveeval@gmail.com

EVERINGHAM, Miss Georgina Wendy. b 32. Tyndale Hall Bris BA 57. **d** 58 **p** 59. C Broadwater St Mary *Chich* 58–61; V Shipton Bellinger w S Tidworth *Win* 61–70; V Bournemouth St Paul 70–84; V Throop 84–95; rtd 95; PtO *Worc* from 96. *3 Harlech Close, Berkeley Alford, Worcester WR4 0JU* T: (01905) 758631 M: 07940-851495 E: georgina@wordoflife.uk.com

EVERITT, Anthony David. b 64. Ex Univ BA 85 ACA 88. STETS 09. **d** 12 **p** 13. NSM Knowle St Martin *Bris* 12–17; NSM Knowle H Nativity 17–18; NSM Bris St Mary Redcliffe w Temple etc from 18. *23 Dunford Road, Bristol BS3 4PN* T: 0117-966 0563 M: 07792-330836

EVERITT, Mrs Jane. b 57. St Jo Coll Nottm 08. **d** 10 **p** 11. C Poulton Carleton and Singleton *Blackb* 10–14; TR Launceston *Truro* 14–18; P-in-c Long Itchington and Marton *Cov* 18–21; rtd 21. *389 Fleetwood Road, Fleetwood FY7 8HL* M: 07923116962 E: revdjane@theeveritts.co.uk

EVERITT, Mark. b 34. Linc Coll Ox BA 58 MA 62. Wells Th Coll. **d** 60 **p** 61. C Hangleton *Chich* 60–63; Chapl Mert Coll Ox 63–02; rtd 02. *48 Annandale Avenue, Bognor Regis PO21 2EX* T: (01243) 823852 E: markeveritt934@btinternet.com

EVERITT, The Ven Michael John. b 68. K Coll Lon BD 90 AKC 90. Qu Coll Birm 90 English Coll Rome 91. **d** 92 **p** 93. C Cleveleys *Blackb* 92–95; Succ Bloemfontein Cathl S Africa

95–98; Prec 96–98; Chapl and Asst Lect Univ of Orange Free State 96–98; Sen Chapl St Martin's Coll *Blackb* 98–02; Asst Dir of Ords 00–02; R Standish 02–11; P-in-c Appley Bridge 06–09; AD Chorley 04–11; Hon Can Blackb Cathl 10–11; Adn Lancaster 11–19; R Preston St Jo and St Geo 18–19; Can Res Dur Cathl from 19. *15 The College, Durham DH1 3EQ* T: 0191-384 0164 M: 07715-490144 E: michael.everitt@durhamcathedral.co.uk

EVERITT, William Frank James. b 38. Dur Univ BA 68 FCA 63. Cranmer Hall Dur 65. d 69 p 70. C Leic St Phil 69–73; P-in-c Prestwold w Hoton 73–77; R Settrington w N Grimston and Wharram *York* 77–84; RD Buckrose 80–84; V Cheltenham St Pet *Glouc* 84–99; rtd 99; PtO *Ripon* 03–14; *Leeds* 14–16. *27 Lark Hill Crescent, Ripon HG4 2HN* T: (01765) 603683

EVERSLEY (formerly HUNTE), Canon Roxanne Fay. b 60. Gama Filho Univ Brazil BSc 93 Huron Univ MBA 94 Leeds Univ BA 08. Coll of Resurr Mirfield 07. d 09 p 10. C Newington St Mary *S'wark* 09–13; P-in-c S Norwood St Mark 15–18; V S Norwood H Innocents 13–18; P-in-c S Norwood St Mark 15–18; V S Norwood H Innocents and St Mark from 18; Dioc Minority Ethnic Voc Champion from 16; Dir of Ords Croydon Area from 21; Hon Can S'wark Cathl from 17. *The Vicarage, 192A Selhurst Road, London SE25 6XX* T: (020) 8916 1830 M: 07747-896779 E: mtrroxanne@gmail.com

EVETTS-SECKER, Ms Josephine. b 42. Univ Coll Lon BA 63 MPhil 65. Coll of Resurr Mirfield 06. d 07 p 08. NSM Hinderwell, Roxby and Staithes etc *York* 07–12; PtO from 12. *Lydgate, Victoria Square, Lythe, Whitby YO21 3RW* T/F: (01947) 893338 M: 07901-273411 E: revj@evetts-secker.co.uk

EWBANK, Canon Robin Alan. b 42. Ex Coll Ox BA 64 MA 88 Lon Univ BD 68. Clifton Th Coll 66. d 69 p 70. C Woodford Wells *Chelmsf* 69–72; Warden Cam Univ Miss Bermondsey 72–76; TV Sutton St Jas and Wawne *York* 76–82; R Bramshott *Portsm* 82–91; R Bramshott and Liphook 91–99; Hon Can Koforidua from 96; P-in-c Hartley Wintney, Elvetham, Winchfield etc *Win* 99–02; V 02–12; RD Odiham 04–11; rtd 12; Hon C Northanger *Win* 12–17; PtO *B & W* from 17. *Berry Farmhouse, Long Load, Langport TA10 9JX* E: robin.ewbank@gmail.com

EWEN, Keith John McGregor. b 43. Sarum & Wells Th Coll 77. d 79 p 80. C Kington w Huntington *Heref* 79–82; C Kington w Huntington, Old Radnor, Kinnerton etc 82–83; P-in-c Culmington w Onibury 83–89; P-in-c Bromfield 83–89; P-in-c Stanton Lacy 83–89; R Culmington w Onibury, Bromfield etc 90–01; R Llangenni and Llanbedr Ystrad Yw w Patricio *S & B* 01–08; rtd 08. *Ty Goleuddydd, 5 Goylands Close, Llandrindod Wells LD1 5RB* T: (01597) 825183

EWER, Edward Sydney John (Jonathan). b 36. Univ of New England BA 69 Lanc Univ MPhil 91 Ch Div Sch of the Pacific (USA) DMin 02. St Mich Th Coll Crafers ThL 63. d 62 p 63. Australia 62–83; SSM from 68; PtO *Blackb* 83–84; LtO *Dur* 84–98; Prior SSM Priory Dur 85–98; Dioc Dir of Ords *Dur* 94–98; PtO *S'wark* 00–05; Hon C Pimlico St Mary Bourne Street *Lon* 05–06; PtO 06–09; *Ox* from 09; *S'wark* 16–17. *3 Lawnsmead Gardens, Newport Pagnell MK16 8AY* M: 07915-377554 E: j_ewer@yahoo.com

EWINGTON, John. b 43. MRICS 65. Chich Th Coll 74. d 78 p 79. C Walthamstow St Jo *Chelmsf* 78–81; Papua New Guinea 81–87; V Southend St Sav Westcliff *Chelmsf* 87–96; TV Bideford, Northam, Westward Ho!, Appledore etc *Ex* 96–11; rtd 11. *The Ingle, Newland, Landkey, Barnstaple EX32 0LZ* T: (01271) 830949 E: jewington200@gmail.com

EWINS, Tiffany-Alice Letitia. b 74. Mansf Coll Ox BA 97. St Mellitus Coll MA 13. d 13 p 14. C Brixton St Paul w St Sav *S'wark* 13–16; PtO 16–17; P-in-c Battersea St Mich 17–20; V from 20. *St Michael's Church, Cobham Close, London SW11 6AY* T: (020) 7924 3450 M: 07970-259580 E: tiffewins@gmail.com *or* tewins@smwc.online

EXCELL, Bernadette Yasmin Carey. b 67. St Aug Coll of Th BA 19. d 19 p 20. C Balham St Mary and St Jo *S'wark* from

19. *42 Balham Park Road, London SW12 8DU* T: (020) 8675 3278 M: 07502-411918 E: curate@stmarybalham.org.uk

EXCELL, Robin Stanley. b 41. AKC 64. St Boniface Warminster 64. d 65 p 66. C Ipswich St Mary Stoke *St E* 65–68; C Melton Mowbray w Thorpe Arnold *Leic* 68–70; TV 70–71; R Gt and Lt Blakenham w Baylham *St E* 71–76; R Gt and Lt Blakenham w Baylham and Nettlestead 76–86; RD Bosmere 84–86; NSM Sproughton w Burstall 91–94; R Rattlesden w Thorpe Morieux, Brettenham etc 94–05; rtd 05; PtO *St E* 05–20. *Hollywater, Upper Street, Baylham, Ipswich IP6 8JR* T: (01473) 830228 E: robin.excell@btinternet.com

EXELL, Ernest William Carter. b 28. Qu Coll Cam BA 52 MA 53. Tyndale Hall Bris 49. d 52 p 53. C Sydenham H Trin *S'wark* 52–54; C E Ham St Paul *Chelmsf* 54–57; Uganda 57–65; Tanzania 66–70; R Abbess and Beauchamp Roding *Chelmsf* 70–71; P-in-c White Roding w Morrell Roding 70–71; R Abbess Roding, Beauchamp Roding and White Roding 71–94; RD Roding 75–79; rtd 94; PtO *St E* 94–19. *8 Ickworth Drive, Bury St Edmunds IP33 3PX* T: (01284) 724726

EXELL, Michael Andrew John. b 45. FHCIMA MRIPHH 67 MICA 70. Sarum & Wells Th Coll 87. d 89 p 90. C Ryde H Trin *Portsm* 89–93; C Swanmore St Mich w Havenstreet 89–92; C Swanmore St Mich 92–93; P-in-c Carisbrooke St Mary 93–99; V 99–10; P-in-c Carisbrooke St Nic 93–99; V 99–10; Chapl Trin C of E Middle Sch 00–08; Chapl Ch the K Coll 08–20; PtO *Portsm* from 10. *3 Glossop Close, East Cowes PO32 6PD* T: (01983) 293686 E: mikeexell@aol.com

EXETER, Archdeacon of. *See* BEANE, The Ven Andrew Mark

EXETER, Bishop of. *See* ATWELL, The Rt Revd Robert Ronald

EXETER, Dean of. *See* GREENER, The Very Revd Jonathan Desmond Francis

EXON, Helier John Philip. b 44. MBE 87. BSc 70 CEng 87 MIET 87. STETS 96. d 99 p 00. NSM Milton Abbas, Hilton w Cheselbourne etc *Sarum* 99–05; NSM Piddletrenthide w Plush, Alton Pancras etc 02–05; NSM Piddle Valley, Hilton, Cheselbourne etc 05–14; rtd 14; PtO *Sarum* 14–19. *The Monk's House, Hilton, Blandford Forum DT11 0DG* T: (01258) 881732 M: 07785-117773 E: helier@exon.me.uk *or* helier.exon@salisbury.anglican.org

EYEONS, Keith James. b 70. Clare Coll Cam BA 92 MA 96 Down Coll Cam PhD 10 Lon Inst of Educn PGCE 95. St Jo Coll Nottm MA(MM) 03. d 01 p 02. C Iffley *Ox* 01–03; Chapl Down Coll Cam from 03. *Downing College, Cambridge CB2 1DQ* T: (01223) 334810 E: kje11@cam.ac.uk

EYLES, Anthony John. b 34. Bris Univ BSc 57. Sarum Th Coll 61. d 63 p 64. C Wellington w W Buckland *B & W* 63–67; C Wilton 67–74; Ind Chapl *Dur* 74–85; Ind Chapl *Worc* 85–90; P-in-c Bickenhill w Elmdon *Birm* 90; P-in-c Bickenhill 90–00; Chapl Birm Airport 90–00; rtd 00; PtO *Ex* 00–19. *5 Kersbrook Lane, Kersbrook, Budleigh Salterton EX9 7AD* T: (01395) 446084

EYNON, John Kenneth. b 56. Nottm Univ BA 77 BArch 80. d 96 p 97. OLM Croydon Ch Ch *S'wark* 96–05. *21 Rye Close, Saltdean, Brighton BN2 8PP* T: (01273) 308397 M: 07702-126362 E: johneynon@me.com

EYRE, Canon Richard Stuart. b 48. Bris Univ BEd 81 Nottm Univ MTh 86. Linc Th Coll 74. d 77 p 78. C Henbury *Bris* 77–81; C Bedminster 81–82; TV 82–84; Chapl Bp Grosseteste Coll Linc 84–95; Sen Tutor 89–95; P-in-c Long Bennington w Foston *Linc* 95; P-in-c Saxonwell 95–97; R 97–01; RD Grantham 96–01; TR Hykeham 01–13; R 13; RD Graffoe 02–09; Can and Preb Linc Cathl 03–13; rtd 13; PtO *Linc* 17–20. *20 Quintin Close, Bracebridge Heath, Lincoln LN4 2LW* E: richard.eyre3@ntlworld.com

EZAT, Timothy. b 83. Wycliffe Hall Ox BTh 12. d 12 p 13. C Eastbourne All SS *Chich* 12–14; C Eastbourne St Mary 14–17; V Langney 17–20. *Address temp unknown* M: 07809-679421 E: timothy.ezat@gmail.com

EZE, Geoffrey Ejike. b 73. Trin Coll Bris 06. d 08 p 09. C Gt Ilford St Jo *Chelmsf* 08–12; TV Stoke-upon-Trent and Fenton *Lich* from 12. *23 Mere Side Close, Stoke-on-Trent ST1 5GH* T: (01782) 265129 E: geoffrey.e.eze@gmail.com

F

FABRIKANT-BURKE, Olga. b 88. Ridley Hall Cam 13. d 20 p 21. NSM Cambridge St Benedict *Ely* from 20; Chapl Trin Coll Cam from 20. *7 Green Street, Cambridge CB2 3JU* T: (01223) 338472 E: olgafabrikantburke@icloud.com

FACCINI (*née* **LEGG**), **Sandra Christine.** b 55. Surrey Univ BSc 78 PhD 82 Univ of Wales (Ban) BTh 07. d 04 p 05. OLM Howell Hill w Burgh Heath *Guildf* 04–09; P-in-c Ottershaw 09–14; V from 14; AD Runnymede 16–20. *50 Slade Road, Ottershaw, Chertsey KT16 0HZ* T: (01932) 873160 M: 07743-675633 E: sandrafster@gmail.com

FACEY, Miss Jane. b 54. EMMTC 05. d 07 p 08. NSM W Hallam and Mapperley w Stanley *Derby* 07–11; V Chellaston from 11. *The Vicarage, Yews Drive, Chellaston, Derby DE73 6UT* T: (01332) 704835 E: bjfacey@btinternet.com

FAGAN, Jeremy David. b 75. Qu Coll Ox BA 98. Wycliffe Hall Ox 99. d 01 p 02. C Chell *Lich* 01–04; TV Kirkby *Liv* 04–12; TR from 12. *27 Shakespeare Avenue, Liverpool L32 9SH* T: 0151-547 2133 E: faganj@mac.com

FAGBEMI, Preb Olubunmi Ayobami (Bunmi). b 57. Lagos Univ LLB 78 LSE LLM 81 Qu Mary Coll Lon PhD 91 Solicitor 79. Ripon Coll Cuddesdon 95. d 97 p 98. C Enfield St Andr *Lon* 97–01; V Tottenham H Trin from 01; AD E Haringey 11–16; Preb St Paul's Cathl from 20. *Holy Trinity Vicarage, Philip Lane, London N15 4GZ* T: (020) 8801 3021 E: bunmif@btinternet.com

✠**FAGBEMI, The Rt Revd Stephen Ayodeji Akinwale.** b 67. St Jo Coll Nottm BTh 96 Kent Univ PhD 04. Immanuel Coll Ibadan 87. d 90 p 91 c 17. C Iyere St Jo Nigeria 90–91; C Owo St Patr 91–92; P-in-c Wakajaye-Etile Ch Ch 92–93; V Emure-Ile St Sav 96–00; Can Owo from 99; PtO *Cant* 00–03; Hon C Murston w Bapchild and Tonge 03–05; Co-ord Chapl Sunderland Univ *Dur* 05–11; Hon C Sunderland Minster 05–11; Dean Abp Vining Coll of Th Nigeria 11–16; Gen Sec Ch of Nigeria 16–17; Bp Owo from 17. *Anglican Bishopscourt, PO Box 472, Owo, Ondo State, Nigeria* M: (00234) 803-695 6811 E: saaf95@hotmail.com *or* saaf90@yahoo.co.uk

FAGERSON, Joseph Leonard Ladd. b 35. Harvard Univ BA 57. Ridley Hall Cam 61. d 63 p 64. C Tonbridge SS Pet and Paul *Roch* 63–67; Afghanistan 67–74; P-in-c Marbury *Ches* 74–75; P-in-c Kinloch Rannoch *St And* 75–00; Chapl Rannoch Sch 75–00; rtd 00; Hon C Killin *St And* 00–12; PtO from 12. *Westgarth, Tomnacroich, Fortingall, Aberfeldy PH15 2LJ* T: (01887) 830569 E: laddandthea@gmail.com

FAHIE, Mrs Stephanie Bridget. b 48. St Jo Coll Nottm 85. d 87 p 94. Par Dn Leic St Chris 87–90; Chapl Scargill Ho 90–95; P-in-c Hickling w Kinoulton and Broughton Sulney *S'well* 95–00; R 00–10; rtd 11; PtO *Lich* from 12. *61 Monkmoor Avenue, Shrewsbury SY2 5ED* T: (01743) 588307 E: steph.fahie@gmail.com

FAINT, Paul Edward. b 38. Qu Coll Birm 85. d 87 p 88. C Cradley *Worc* 87–90; V Hanley Castle, Hanley Swan and Welland 90–94; V Northwood H Trin *Lon* 94–97; Miss to Seafarers from 97; Chapl Larnaca Cyprus 97–01; rtd 01; PtO *Ox* 01–20; Hon Chapl Miss to Seafarers from 02. *17 Priory Orchard, Wantage OX12 9EL* T: (01235) 772297 E: thefaints@sky.com

FAIRALL, Hannah Marie. *See* MEARS, Hannah Marie

FAIRBAIRN, Andrew Graham. b 48. SEITE 06. d 09 p 10. NSM Surbiton Hill Ch Ch *S'wark* 09–12; NSM High Ongar w Norton Mandeville *Chelmsf* 13–17; rtd 17; PtO *Chelmsf* 17–19; *Win* from 19. *1 The Ferns, New Milton BH25 5WW* T: (01425) 619007 M: 07789-992843 E: gandlfairbairn@btinternet.com

FAIRBAIRN, Francis Stephen. b 41. d 98 p 99. OLM Orrell *Liv* 98–13; rtd 13; PtO *Liv* from 16. *27 Greenslate Road, Billinge, Wigan WN5 7BQ* T: (01695) 623127 *or* (01722) 812176 F: 815398

FAIRBAIRN, John Alan. b 46. Trin Coll Cam BA 67 MA 72. Wycliffe Hall Ox 84. d 86 p 87. C Boscombe St Jo *Win* 86–89; C Edgware *Lon* 89–95; R Gunton St Pet *Nor* 95–11; Chapl Jas Paget Healthcare NHS Trust 96–08; rtd 11; PtO *Win* from 11. *28 Clifton Road, Bournemouth BH6 3PA* T: (01202) 424466 E: jfairbairn2017@gmail.com

FAIRBAIRN, Mrs Stella Rosamund. b 30. Bris Univ CertEd 51 De Montfort Univ BA 13. d 87 p 94. NSM Banbury *Ox* 87–99; PtO *Pet* 88–94; *Ox* from 99. *Hillside, Overthorpe, Banbury OX17 2AF* T: (01295) 710648

FAIRBAIRN, Stephen. *See* FAIRBAIRN, Francis Stephen

FAIRBAIRN, William James. b 89. Cardiff Univ BSc 10. St Mellitus Coll BA 17. d 17 p 18. C Bitterne Park *Win*

17–20; V Redland *Bris* from 20. *151 Redland Road, Bristol BS6 6YE* T: 0117-946 4690 E: info@redland.org.uk

FAIRBANK, Brian Douglas Seeley. b 53. AKC 75. St Steph Ho Ox 77. d 78 p 79. C Newton Aycliffe *Dur* 78–81; C Stocking Farm *Leic* 81–84; TV Ratby cum Groby 84–91; P-in-c Ottringham w Keyingham, Ottringham etc *York* 91–04; R Bramfield, Stapleford, Waterford etc *St Alb* 04–12; R Culworth w Sulgrave and Thorpe Mandeville etc *Pet* 12–20; rtd 20. *Address temp unknown* E: brianfairbank487@btinternet.com

FAIRCLOUGH, Miss Amanda Ann Catherine. b 68. Man Univ BSc 89. St Jo Coll Nottm 06 SNWTP 08. d 10 p 11. NSM Orford St Marg *Liv* 10–14; NSM Warrington E 14–17; P-in-c W Highland Region *Arg* from 17. *St Mary's Rectory, Glencoe, Ballachulish PH49 4HP* T: (01855) 811633 M: 07788-101178 E: a.fairclough@amandafairclough.co.uk

FAIRCLOUGH, Clive Anthony. b 54. TISEC 01. d 04 p 05. C Nadder Valley *Sarum* 04–08; R Abberton, The Flyfords, Naunton Beauchamp etc *Worc* 08–14; P-in-c Fladbury, Hill and Moor, Wyre Piddle etc 11–14; C Peopleton and White Ladies Aston w Churchill etc 11–14; Chapl Moscow *Eur* 14–17; P-in-c Mells w Buckland Dinham, Elm, Whatley etc *B & W* 17–18; R from 18. *The Rectory, Gay Street, Mells, Frome BA11 3PT* T: (01373) 673431 E: cliveatmellsgroup@gmail.com

FAIRCLOUGH, John Frederick. b 40. St Jo Coll Dur BA 63 MA 68 Keele Univ DASE 73 MBIM. Coll of Resurr Mirfield 81. d 83 p 84. C Horninglow *Lich* 83–87; V Skerton St Luke *Blackb* 87–94; V Thornton-le-Fylde 94–00; rtd 00; PtO *Blackb* 01–14. *18 Crosfield Avenue, Summerseat, Bury BL9 5NX* T: (01706) 825664

FAIREY, Michael. b 51. NEOC. d 08 p 10. NSM York St Hilda 08–12; PtO from 12. *10 Mallard Close, York YO10 3BS* T: (01904) 399655 E: mike@fairey-consulting.com

FAIRHURST, Rosemary Anne. b 63. Newnham Coll Cam BA 85 MA 85 Heythrop Coll Lon MTh 97 Lon Inst of Educn PGCE 86. Wycliffe Hall Ox MA 92. d 93 p 94. C Hackney Marsh *Lon* 93–97; C Islington St Mary 97–02; Dir Miss and Min Ripon Coll Cuddesdon 02–06; Organizational Analyst Grubb Inst 07–12; C St Martin-in-the-Fields *Lon* 98–12; PtO 12–14; Can Res and Chan Leic Cathl 14–18; V Bradf St Aug and St Clem *Leeds* from 18. *100 Harrogate Street, Bradford BD3 0LE* M: 07766-451316 E: rosy.fairhurst@leeds.anglican.org

FAIRHURST, Mrs Susan Mary. b 55. GBSM 80. Qu Coll Birm 12. d 14 p 15. NSM Lillington and Old Milverton *Cov* from 14. *23 Brese Avenue, Warwick CV34 4TS* T: (01926) 735254 M: 07906-610376 E: sue@fairhursts.me.uk

FAIRLAMB, Neil. b 49. Univ of Wales (Ban) BA 71 Jes Coll Ox BPhil 73 Univ of Wales (Abth) MTh 00 Pemb Coll Cam CertEd 74. S'wark Ord Course 90. d 93 p 94. NSM Dulwich St Barn *S'wark* 93–95; P-in-c Elerch w Penrhyncoch w Capel Bangor and Goginan *St D* 95–96; V 96–98; R Arthog w Fairbourne w Llangelynnin w Rhoslefain *Ban* 98–03; R Beaumaris 03–11; R Beaumaris w Llanddona and Llaniestyn 11–15; V Bro Seiriol 15–19; rtd 19; Hon C The Bourne and Tilford *Guildf* from 19. *All Saints' Vicarage, Tilford Road, Tilford, Farnham GU10 2DA* E: fairlamb49@gmail.com

FAIRLESS, Elizabeth Jane. *See* JONES, Elizabeth Jane

FAIRWEATHER, Colin Malcolm. b 72. Rob Coll Cam BA 94 MA 95. Ridley Hall Cam 14. d 16 p 17. C Braintree St Paul *Chelmsf* 16–21; P-in-c Stansted Mountfitchet w Birchanger and Farnham from 21; P-in-c Takeley w Lt Canfield from 21. *St John's Rectory, 5 St John's Road, Stansted CM24 8JP* T: (01279) 816721 M: 07791-188296 E: revdrcolinfairweather@gmail.com

FAIRWEATHER, John. b 39. K Coll Lon AKC 66 BD 72. d 67 p 68. C Plymouth St Jas Ham *Ex* 67–69; C Townstal w St Sav and St Petrox w St Barn 69–73; R Corringham w Springthorpe *Linc* 73–76; P-in-c Blyborough 76–78; P-in-c Heapham 76–78; P-in-c Willoughton 76–78; V Pinchbeck 78–82; V Exwick *Ex* 82–04; rtd 04; PtO *B & W* from 19. *52 Woodman's Crescent, Honiton EX14 2DY* T: (01404) 549711 E: john.fairweather6@btinternet.com

FAIRWEATHER, Sally Helen. *See* ROSS, Sally Helen

FALASCHI-RAY, Sonia Ofelia. Surrey Univ BSc 79 Wolfs Coll Cam BA 02 MA 06 CEng 86. Ridley Hall Cam 03. d 05 p 06. NSM Fowlmere, Foxton, Shepreth and Thriplow *Ely* 05–09; PtO from 09; *St Alb* from 09. *27 Church Lane, Barkway, Royston SG8 8EJ* T: (01763) 849057 M: 07747-844265 E: sonia@falaschi-ray.co.uk

FALCONER, Ian Geoffrey. b 40. BNC Ox BA 62 Newc Univ MA 93. Cuddesdon Coll 62. **d** 64 **p** 65. C Chiswick St Nic w St Mary *Lon* 64–68; C-in-c Hounslow Gd Shep Beavers Lane CD 68–76; P-in-c Hammersmith St Matt 76–84; P-in-c Byker St Silas *Newc* 84–93; V 93–95; P-in-c Newc St Phil and St Aug 95–98; P-in-c Newc St Matt w St Mary 95–98; P-in-c Newc St Phil and St Aug and St Matt w St Mary 98–00; V Seghill 00–06; rtd 06. *70 Lowgates, Staveley, Chesterfield S43 3TU* T: (01246) 471913 E: frianfalc@yahoo.co.uk

FALKINGHAM (née MOORE), Mrs Caroline Judith. b 57. Coll of Ripon & York St Jo BA 78 Leeds Univ MA 07. NOC 05. **d** 07 **p** 08. C Bilton *Ripon* 07–11; NSM Fountains Gp 11–12; R 12–14; *Leeds* 14–18; rtd 18; PtO *Leeds* 19–21. *111 Kirkby Road, Ripon HG4 2HH* E: carolinefalkingham@talktalk.net

FALKNER, Jonathan Michael Shepherd. b 47. Open Univ BA 74 Leeds Univ MPhil 02. Cranmer Hall Dur. **d** 79 **p** 80. C Penrith w Newton Reigny *Carl* 79–81; C Penrith w Newton Reigny and Plumpton Wall 81–82; C Dalton-in-Furness 82–84; V Clifton 84–90; P-in-c Dean 85–89; R 89–90; P-in-c Rumburgh w S Elmham w the Ilketshalls *St E* 90–92; R S Elmham and Ilketshall 92–99; RD Beccles and S Elmham 94–99; Hon Can St E Cathl 98–99; P-in-c W Newton and Bromfield w Waverton *Carl* 99–02; P-in-c Holme Cultram St Mary 00–02; P-in-c Holme Cultram St Cuth 00–02; TR Solway Plain 02–05; P-in-c Gosforth w Nether Wasdale and Wasdale Head 05–12; P-in-c Beckermet St Jo and St Bridget w Ponsonby 12; rtd 12; PtO *Carl* from 13. *22 Whole House Road, Seascale CA20 1QY* T: (019467) 21852 E: falcon626@btinternet.com

FALLA, Eric. b 60. **d** 18 **p** 19. NSM Whitton and Thurleston w Akenham *St E* 18–19; NSM E Bergholt and Brantham 19–21; P-in-c Bramford w Lt Blakenham, Baylham and Nettlestead from 21. *The Vicarage, Vicarage Lane, Bramford, Ipswich IP8 4AE* T: (01473) 484676 M: 07540-359993 E: eric.falla@yahoo.com

FALLA, Miles. b 43. MCIM. EAMTC 93. **d** 96 **p** 97. NSM Buckden *Ely* 96–98; P-in-c Gretton w Rockingham *Pet* 98–99; V Gretton w Rockingham and Cottingham w E Carlton 99–04; RD Corby 01–02; rtd 04; PtO *Ely* from 05. *Bowlings, Silver Street, Buckden, St Neots PE19 5TS* T: (01480) 811335 E: miles@falla.ndo.co.uk

FALLOWS, Stuart Adrian. b 50. Moray Ho Edin 75. **d** 78 **p** 79. Hon C Forres w Nairn *Mor* 78–81; Hon C Elgin w Lossiemouth 81–86; Hon Dioc Chapl 86; C Brighton St Geo w St Anne and St Mark *Chich* 86–89; V Wivelsfield 89–98; P-in-c Kieth, Huntly and Aberchirder *Mor* 98–02; P-in-c Ringwould w Kingsdown *Cant* 02–04; R Ringwould w Kingsdown and Ripple etc 05–09; R W Highland Region *Arg* 09–15; rtd 15; PtO *Arg* from 16. *Duncroft, 25 Murray Crescent, Lamlash, Isle of Arran KA27 8NS* T: (01855) 811987 E: afallows222@aol.com

FALVEY, Mrs Imogen Rosalind. b 62. Somerville Coll Ox BA 84 MA 89 Solicitor 88. ERMC 11. **d** 14 **p** 15. NSM Sawtry and Glatton *Ely* 14–17; NSM The Ortons 17–18; P-in-c from 18. *The New Rectory, 2A The Village, Orton Longueville, Peterborough PE2 7DN* T: (01733) 247329 E: revimogen@gmail.com

FANCOURT, Graeme. b 77. St Jo Coll Dur BA 00 DThM 11. Ripon Coll Cuddesdon 09. **d** 10 **p** 11. C Caversham Thameside and Mapledurham *Ox* 10–13; P-in-c Reading St Luke w St Bart 13–14; V 14–19; C Reading St Mary the Virgin from 19; AD Reading from 17. *The Vicarage, 50 London Road, Reading RG1 5AS* T: 0118-966 6389 E: fancourt@gmail.com

FANE DE SALIS, Mrs Mary. b 88. **d** 14 **p** 15. C Clothall, Rushden, Sandon, Wallington and Weston *St Alb* 14–17; R Holwell, Ickleford and Pirton from 17. *The Vicarage, 9 Crabtree Lane, Pirton, Hitchin SG5 3QE* T: (01462) 712230 M: 07866-890402 E: marydesalis@hotmail.com

FANTHORPE, Robert Lionel. b 35. Open Univ BA 80 CertEd 63 FCMI 81 FCP 90. Llan Dioc Tr Scheme. **d** 87 **p** 88. NSM Roath St German *Llan* 87–00; LtO 00–09. *Rivendell, 48 Claude Road, Roath, Cardiff CF24 3QA* T: (029) 2049 8368 F: 2049 6832 M: 07895-946123 E: fanthorpe@aol.com

FARADAY, John. b 49. Leeds Univ BSc 71 MICE 78. Oak Hill Th Coll 81. **d** 83 **p** 84. C Sutton *Liv* 83–86; C Rainhill and Chapl Whiston Hosp 86–89; V Over Darwen St Jas *Blackb* 89–02; TR S Rochdale *Man* 02–08; TR Gorton and Abbey Hey 08–15; rtd 15; PtO *Man* from 15. *1 Magpie Lane, Oldham OL4 5PB* E: john.faraday@sky.com

FARAGHER, James Philip. b 77. St Jo Coll Nottm 12. **d** 14 **p** 15. C St Alb St Paul 14–17; V Coney Hill *Glouc* from 17. *St Oswald's Vicarage, Coney Hill Road, Gloucester GL4 4LX* T: (01452) 690750 M: 07800-908396 E: jamesfaragher@yahoo.co.uk *or* vicar@stoswaldconeyhill.com

FARAH, The Ven Mones Anton. b 64. Trin Coll Bris BA 88. **d** 88 **p** 89. C Aberystwyth *St D* 88–91; Chapl St D Coll Lamp 91–98; TV Gt Baddow *Chelmsf* 98–14; P-in-c Aberystwyth *St D* 14–19; Can St D Cathl from 18; Adn for New Ch Communities from 18. *The Rectory, 7 Laura Place, Aberystwyth SY23 2AU* T: (01970) 617184 E: archdeacon.farah@churchinwales.org.uk

FARDELL, Rebecca Susan. b 70. Reading Univ BA 92 Leic Univ MA 94 Qu Coll Cam PGCE 93. Ridley Hall Cam 11. **d** 13 **p** 14. C Itchen Valley *Win* 13–17; V Sunnyside w Bourne End *St Alb* from 17. *The Vicarage, Ivy House Lane, Berkhamsted HP4 2PP* T: (01442) 865100 E: rebecca@sunnysidechurch.org.uk *or* vicar@sunnysidechurch.org.uk

FARLEY, Claire Louise. *See* McCLELLAND, Claire Louise

FARLEY, David Stuart. b 53. Univ Coll Dur BA 75 Westmr Coll Ox MTh 00. St Jo Coll Nottm. **d** 84 **p** 85. C Bath Weston All SS w N Stoke *B & W* 84–87; Chapl Scargill Ho 87–90; Min Hedge End N CD *Win* 90–94; V Hedge End St Luke 94–00; Dep Chapl HM Pris Belmarsh 00; Chapl HM Pris Shrewsbury 00–13; Chapl HM Pris Featherstone 13–16; rtd 16; PtO *Lich* from 16. *c/o Athlone House, 68 London Road, Shrewsbury SY2 6PG* E: dfarley3@hotmail.co.uk

FARLEY, Ian David. b 56. Linc Coll Ox BA 78 MA 87 Dur Univ PhD 88. Cranmer Hall Dur 84. **d** 87 **p** 88. C Thorpe Acre w Dishley *Leic* 87–92; V S Lambeth St Steph *S'wark* 92–99; V Bacton w Edingthorpe w Witton and Ridlington *Nor* 99–03; Ind Chapl 99–03; TR Buckhurst Hill *Chelmsf* from 03. *St John's Rectory, High Road, Buckhurst Hill IG9 5RX* T: (020) 8504 1931 E: parish-office@buckhursthill.free-online.co.uk *or* ian.farley@sjbh.org.uk

FARLEY, James Trevor. b 37. IEng MIET FRSA. EMMTC 80. **d** 82 **p** 83. NSM Grantham St Wulfram *Linc* from 82; PtO *Leic* 14–20. *Highfield Cottage, Station Road, Bottesford, Nottingham NG13 0EN* T/F: (01949) 843860 M: 07768-360592 E: jimfarley@talktalk.net

FARLEY-MOORE, Canon Peter James. b 72. Sheff Univ BA 94 UEA MA 00. Ridley Hall Cam. **d** 00 **p** 01. C Chapeltown *Sheff* 00–03; Miss Cell Adv CMS 04–05; Asst Min Kowloon St Andr Hong Kong 05–07; V Blackheath St Jo *S'wark* 07–14; TR Deptford St Jo w H Trin and Ascension 14–21; AD Deptford 16–21; Can Res Wakef Cathl *Leeds* from 21; Hon Can Mara Tanzania from 16. *3 Cathedral Close, Wakefield WF1 2DP* E: farleymoore@hotmail.com *or* missioner@wakefield-cathedral.org.uk

FARMAN, Joanne Margaret. b 46. Birkbeck Coll Lon BA 81 Leeds Univ MA 08 Southlands Coll Lon PGCE 82. SEITE 97. **d** 00 **p** 01. NSM Limpsfield and Titsey *S'wark* 00–04; Chapl St Geo Healthcare NHS Trust Lon 00–10; Lead Chapl R Hosp for Neuro-Disability 04–05; PtO *S'wark* 10–16; *Nor* from 16; *Roch* 12–16. *53B Colney Lane, Cringleford, Norwich NR4 7RG* T: (01603) 508380 E: joannefarman086@btinternet.com

FARMAN, Robert Joseph. b 54. Ridley Hall Cam 86. **d** 88 **p** 89. C Sutton St Nic *S'wark* 88–90; C Cheam Common St Phil 90–92; R Wootton w Glympton and Kiddington *Ox* 92–00; TV Kings Norton *Birm* 00–04; Chapl St Mary's Hospice 04–12; Chapl R Orthopaedic Hosp NHS Trust 05–06; Chapl Birm and Solihull Mental Health Trust 06–07; rtd 12; PtO *Birm* from 19. *121 The Hemisphere, 15 The Boulevard, Birmingham B5 7SU* M: 07766-054137 E: rjfarman@icloud.com

FARMER, Andrew. b 62. Birm Univ BSc 84 Bath Univ MBA 07 Ches Univ PGCE 12. SWMTC 14. **d** 17 **p** 19. C Buckland Monachorum *Ex* from 17. *Fernleigh, The Crescent, Crapstone, Yelverton PL20 7PS* T: (01822) 859328 M: 07500-948452 E: andrew.farmer99@btinternet.com

FARMER, Mrs Anne Louise. b 61. Warwick Univ BEd 84. Trin Coll Bris 04. **d** 06 **p** 07. C Stoke Bishop *Bris* 06–09; TV Worle *B & W* 09–17; P-in-c E Molesey *Guildf* 17–18; V E Molesey St Paul from 18. *101 Palace Road, East Molesey KT8 9DU* T: (020) 3566 5715 E: alf@rev21.co.uk *or* stpaulmolesey@gmail.com

FARMER, Diane Marcia (Diana). b 61. Warwick Univ BSc 82 PGCE 83. WMMTC 97 Cranmer Hall Dur 00. **d** 01 **p** 02. C Allesley Park and Whoberley *Cov* 01–05; Hd Tr and Development Rethink from 05; Hon C Pensnett *Worc* 05–07; PtO 07–09; Hon C Wollaston 09–17; Hon C Norton and Wollaston from 17. *13 Rectory Street, Stourbridge DY8 5QT* T: (01384) 295205

FARMER, Robert James. b 65. WMMTC 03. **d** 06 **p** 07. C Lich St Chad 06–10; C Longdon 08–10; P-in-c Longdon and C Heath Hayes 10–11; V Shelfield and High Heath 11–17; TR Worc SE 17–19; TV from 19. *33 Aconbury Close, Worcester WR5 1JD* E: revdrobfarmer@gmail.com

FARMER, Robert John Thayer. b 62. Kent Univ BA 84. St Steph Ho Ox 91. **d** 93 **p** 94. C Leigh St Clem

Chelmsf 93–96; P-in-c Wellingborough St Mary *Pet* 96–00; V from 00; Chapl Northants Healthcare NHS Foundn Trust from 99. *St Mary's Vicarage, 193 Midland Road, Wellingborough NN8 1NG* T: (01933) 225626 E: vicar@stmarywellingborough.org.uk

FARNHAM, Douglas John. b 30. SS Mark & Jo Univ Coll Plymouth TCert 52 Ex Univ MEd 75. S Dios Minl Tr Scheme 80. **d** 83 **p** 84. Lect Bp Otter Coll Chich 70–78; Sen Lect W Sussex Inst of HE 78–92; NSM Barnham and Eastergate *Chich* 83–85; NSM Aldingbourne, Barnham and Eastergate 85–92; R 92–96; rtd 96; PtO *Chich* from 96. *12 Summersdale Court, The Drive, Chichester PO19 5RF* T: (01243) 532251

FARNHAM, Mrs Rachael Theresa. b 87. Dur Univ BA 18. Ridley Hall Cam 15. **d** 18 **p** 19. C Bayston Hill *Lich* 18–21; Chapl HM Pris Frankland from 21. *HM Prison Frankland, Brasside, Durham DH1 5YD* T: 0191-376 5000

FARNWORTH, Ms Joanna Helen. b 66. Jes Coll Cam BA 88 MA 92. St Jo Coll Nottm BTh 98 MA 99. **d** 99 **p** 00. C Middleton w Thornham *Man* 99–03; TV Ashton 03–11; P-in-c Droylsden St Martin 11–16; R Droylsden St Andr and St Martin from 16; Dioc Ecum Officer from 16. *St James's Vicarage, Westbury Street, Ashton-under-Lyne OL6 9NL* T: 0161-330 4925 E: revdjofarnworth@gmail.com

FARNWORTH, Roger. b 60. Man Univ BSc 81. St Jo Coll Nottm MA 99. **d** 99 **p** 00. C Tonge w Alkrington *Man* 99–03; TV Ashton 03–05; TR from 05; AD Ashton-under-Lyne 08–16; Borough Dean Tameside from 18. *St James's Vicarage, Westbury Street, Ashton-under-Lyne OL6 9NL* T: 0161-330 2771 E: rogerfarnworth@aol.com

FARNWORTH, Russell. b 60. Lon Bible Coll BA 82 Nottm Univ MTh 85. St Jo Coll Nottm 81. **d** 84 **p** 85. C Blackpool St Jo *Blackb* 84–87; TV Darwen St Pet w Hoddlesden 87–91; V Kidsgrove *Lich* 91–02; Chief Exec Officer Trans World Radio UK from 03. *28 Kingsway East, Newcastle ST5 3PZ* T: (01782) 637130 E: rfarnworth@twr.org.uk

FARQUHAR, Iain. b 45. **d** 05 **p** 06. OLM Catford St Laur *S'wark* 05–15; PtO from 15. *18 Birkhall Road, London SE6 1TE* T: (020) 8698 7438 E: iainfarquhar@googlemail.com

FARQUHAR, Preb Patricia Ann. b 42. dss 78 **d** 87 **p** 94. S Hackney St Jo w Ch Ch *Lon* 80–01; Par Dn 87–94; C 94–01; Preb St Paul's Cathl 97–01; rtd 01; PtO *Nor* from 15. *8 Holme Terrace, Bishopgate, Norwich NR1 4EJ* T: (01603) 610112

FARQUHARSON, The Very Revd Hunter Buchanan. b 58. ALAM LLAM. Edin Th Coll 85. **d** 88 **p** 89. C Dunfermline *St And* 88–91; R Glenrothes 91–97; R Leven 95–97; R Dunfermline 97–99; Provost St Ninian's Cathl Perth from 99; R Perth St Ninian from 99. *St Ninian's Cathedral, North Methven Street, Perth PH1 5PP* T: (01738) 632053 E: huntfar@gmail.com *or* provost@perthcathedral.co.uk

FARR, John. *See* FARR, William John

FARR, Mrs Nicola. b 68. St Mellitus Coll 18. **d** 20 **p** 21. C Launceston *Truro* from 20; C Moorland Gp from 21; C Egloskerry, N Petherwin, Tremaine, Tresmere etc from 21. *2 Church Lea, Launceston PL15 8QZ* M: 07932-657171 E: revnfarr@icloud.com

FARR, Richard William. b 55. Ridley Hall Cam. **d** 83 **p** 84. C Enfield Ch Ch Trent Park *Lon* 83–87; C Eastbourne H Trin *Chich* 87–90; P-in-c Henham and Elsenham w Ugley *Chelmsf* 90–91; V 91–09; C Tunbridge Wells St Jo *Roch* 09–21; rtd 21; Past Adv to Bp Maidstone from 20; PtO *Ox* from 21. *21 Littlebrook Meadow, Shipton-under-Wychwood, Chipping Norton OX7 6EL* M: 07871-657920 E: rwf.shipton@gmail.com

FARR, William John. b 66. QUB BTh 05 MTh 07. **d** 08 **p** 09. NSM Muckamore and Killead w Gartree *Conn* 08–11; P-in-c Stoneyford from 11. *1 Ballyvannon Road, Ballinderry Upper, Lisburn BT28 2LB* T: (028) 9442 2158 M: 07808-399579 E: j20far@hotmail.com

FARRAN, Canon George Orman. b 35. Worc Coll Ox BA 58 MA 62. Wycliffe Hall Ox 58. **d** 60 **p** 61. C Tyldesley w Shakerley *Man* 60–62; Tutor Wycliffe Hall Ox 62–64; V Netherton *Liv* 64–73; R Sefton 69–73; R Credenhill w Brinsop, Mansel Lacey, Yazor etc *Heref* 73–83; RD Heref Rural 81–83; R Ditcheat w E Pennard and Pylle *B & W* 83–94; Dir of Ords 86–89; Can and Chan Wells Cathl 85–97; rtd 97; PtO *B & W* 97–19. *6 The Empire, Grand Parade, Bath BA2 4DF* T: (01225) 339365 E: george.farran@btinternet.com

FARRANT, Canon Martyn John. b 38. AKC 61. **d** 62 **p** 63. C Hampton St Mary *Lon* 62–65; C Shere *Guildf* 65–67; V Stoneleigh 67–75; V Addlestone 75–83; V Dorking w Ranmore 83–98; RD Dorking 89–94; Hon Can Guildf Cathl 96–98; rtd 98; Chapl Phyllis Tuckwell Hospice Farnham 98–01; PtO *Guildf* 98–17. *42 Hampstead Road, Dorking RH4 3AE* T: (01306) 740916 E: mandrfarrant@talktalk.net *or* martyn.farrant@gmail.com

FARRAR, Ruth. b 43. Matlock Coll of Educn CertEd 64. **d** 04 **p** 05. OLM Leesfield *Man* 04–13; rtd 13; PtO *Man* from 13.

Belvoir, 43 Coverhill Road, Grotton, Oldham OL4 5RE T: 0161-633 0374 M: 07894-466401 E: revruthfarrar@gmail.com

FARRELL, Mrs Joanna Susan Elizabeth. b 53. Southn Univ LLB 95. STETS 03. **d** 06 **p** 07. NSM Steep and Froxfield w Privett *Portsm* 06–16; Asst Chapl Portsm Hosps NHS Trust 11–14; PtO *Portsm* from 16. *Hurst Farm Cottage, Hurst Lane, Privett, Alton GU34 3PL* T: (01730) 828450 E: joanna@hfc.myzen.co.uk

FARRELL, Ms Katherine Lucy Anne. b 61. Westcott Ho Cam 00. **d** 02 **p** 03. C Forest Gate Em w Upton Cross *Chelmsf* 02–03; C Lt Ilford St Mich 03–07; V Bellingham St Dunstan *S'wark* 07–11; C Croydon St Jo 11–13; PtO 13–15; TV Gt Grimsby St Mary and St Jas *Linc* from 15. *62A Brighowgate, Grimsby DN32 0QW* M: 07904-653180 E: k.farrell916@btinternet.com

FARRELL, Lindsey Elaine. b 79. QUB BA 00. CITI 15. **d** 17 **p** 18. Rossorry *Clogh* 17–18; Bp's C Inver w Mountcharles, Killaghtee and Killybegs *D & R* from 18. *The Rectory, Inver, Co Donegal, Republic of Ireland* T: (00353) (74) 973 6013 M: 87-360 0896 E: lfarrell9@tcd.ie

FARRELL, Ms Margaret Ruth. b 57. Linc Inst Melbourne BAppSc(OT) 78. **d** 02 **p** 03. C Bury St Edmunds All SS w St Jo and St Geo *St E* 02–06; P-in-c Woolpit w Drinkstone 06–08; R from 08. *The Rectory, Rectory Lane, Woolpit, Bury St Edmunds IP30 9QP* T: (01359) 242244 E: ruthfarrell391@gmail.com

FARRELL, Peter Godfrey Paul. b 39. Sarum & Wells Th Coll 72. **d** 74 **p** 75. C St Just in Roseland *Truro* 74–77; C Kenwyn 77–80; V Knighton St Jo *Leic* 80–86; TR Clarendon Park St Jo w Knighton St Mich 86–89; V Woodham *Guildf* 89–99; V Wells St Cuth w Wookey Hole *B & W* 99–09; rtd 09; P-in-c E w W Harptree and Hinton Blewett *B & W* 09–12; PtO from 15. *Close Cottage, 1 Great Gardens, Gaol Lane, Shepton Mallet BA4 5LF* T: (01749) 345443 E: pgpfvic@gmail.com

FARRELL, Robert Edward. b 54. Univ of Wales (Abth) BA 74 Jes Coll Ox BA 77 MA 81. Qu Coll Birm 85. **d** 86 **p** 87. C Llanrhos *St As* 86–88; C Prestwich St Marg *Man* 89–91; V Moulsham St Luke *Chelmsf* 91–98; V Thorpe Bay 98–08; R Ardleigh and The Bromleys 08–13; rtd 13; PtO *Carnt* 14–17. *Villa Derwen, 135 London Road, Temple Ewell, Dover CT16 3BY* E: robert_farrell21@hotmail.com

FARRELL, Preb Ronald Anthony. b 57. Edin Univ BD 84 Birm Univ MA 86. Qu Coll Birm 84. **d** 86 **p** 87. C Shard End *Birm* 86–87; C Shirley 87–89; Bp's Officer for Schs and Young People 89–93; V Kingstanding St Mark 93–01; TR Swinton and Pendlebury *Man* 01–05; P-in-c Lower Broughton Ascension 02–05; V W Bromwich St Fran *Lich* from 05; V W Bromwich St Pet 17–18; RD W Bromwich from 17; Preb Lich Cathl from 20. *Friar Park Vicarage, Freeman Road, Wednesbury WS10 0HJ* T: 0121-556 5823 E: father.ron@btinternet.com

FARRELL, Stephen Andrew. b 84. Jes Coll Ox BA 05 MA 10 Cardiff Univ LLM 15. CITC BTh 08. **d** 08 **p** 09. C Taney *D & G* 08–11; I Dublin Zion Ch from 11; Prov and Dioc Registrar from 12. *Zion Rectory, 18 Bushy Park Road, Rathgar, Dublin 6, Republic of Ireland* T: (00353) (1) 492 2365 *or* 406 4730 E: zion@dublin.anglican.org

FARRELL, Thomas Stanley. b 32. Lon Univ BD 71. Ridley Hall Cam 69. **d** 71 **p** 72. C Much Woolton *Liv* 71–73; C Gt Sankey 73–74; Asst Chapl Dulwich Coll 74–76; Chapl 76–81; P-in-c Wonersh *Guildf* 81–86; V 86–90; RD Cranleigh 87–90; R St Marg Lothbury and St Steph Coleman Street etc *Lon* 90–00; P-in-c St Botolph without Aldersgate 90–97; rtd 00; Hon C Burford w Fulbrook, Taynton, Asthall etc *Ox* 00–04; PtO from 04. *17 Ridgeway Court, Cholsey, Wallingford OX10 9GU* T: (01491) 599433 E: tomfarrell@uwclub.net

FARRER, Canon Carol Elizabeth. b 47. Open Univ BA 88. Cranmer Hall Dur 81. dss 83 **d** 87 **p** 94. Newbarns w Hawcoat *Carl* 83–86; Egremont and Haile 86–91; Par Dn 87–91; Team Dn Penrith w Newton Reigny and Plumpton Wall 91–94; TV 94–01; Dioc Lay Min Adv 87–88; Assoc Dir of Ords 88–97; 97–00; Dioc OLM Officer 00–05; TV S Barrow 01–07; Hon Can Carl Cathl 01–07; rtd 08; PtO *St As* from 09. *3 Marlow Terrace, Mold CH7 1HH* T: (01352) 756011 E: carolfarrer@hotmail.com

FARRIMOND, Sarah Lucy. b 67. Hertf Coll Ox BA 89 Leeds Univ BA 99 Dur Univ PhD 09. Qu Coll Birm 12. **d** 14 **p** 15. C Birkby and Birchencliffe *Leeds* 14–18; R High Hoyland, Scissett and Clayton W from 18; Clergy Development Officer Huddersfield Area from 18. *The Rectory, 19 Church Lane, Clayton West, Huddersfield HD8 9LY* T: (01484) 900025 M: 07943-738638 E: revsarahfarrimond@yahoo.co.uk

FARRINGTON, Canon Christine Marion. b 42. Birkbeck Coll Lon BA 65 Nottm Univ DASS 66 Middx Poly MA 75. St Alb Minl Tr Scheme 79. dss 82 **d** 87 **p** 94. Redbourn *St Alb* 82–87; Dir Past Studies Linc Th Coll 86–87; HM Pris Linc 86–87; Dir Sarum Chr Cen 87–93; Dn Sarum Cathl 87–93; Co-Dir of Ords and Dir of Women's Min *Ely* 93–02; Hon Can Ely Cathl 93–02; C Cambridge Gt St Mary w St Mich 93–96; V Cambridge St Mark 96–02; Chapl Wolfs Coll Cam 97–02; rtd 02; PtO *St Alb* 97–04; RD Wheathampstead 04–07; Chapl to The Queen 98–12. *4 Pondesmeade, Redbourn, St Albans AL3 7LD* E: canon.cmf@tiscali.co.uk

FARROW, Elizabeth Maura. b 43. Edin Th Coll. **d** 91 **p** 96. NSM Glas H Cross 91–96; TV Bearsden w Milngavie 96–00 and 03–05; Asst P Sanibel USA 06–11; LtO *Glas* from 08. *5 Campsie Road, Strathblane G63 9AB* T: (01360) 770936 E: liz.farrow@gmail.com

FARROW, Ian Edmund Dennett. b 38. S'wark Ord Course 70. **d** 72 **p** 73. C Tunbridge Wells St Jo *Roch* 72–78; Chapl N Cambs Gen Hosp Gp 78–92; P-in-c Walsoken *Ely* 78–80; R 80–92; V Bisley, Oakridge, Miserden and Edgeworth *Glouc* 92–04; rtd 04; PtO *Ox* 18–20. *Wellspring, Brook Lane, Stonesfield, Witney OX29 8PR* T: (01993) 891293

FARROW, Canon Keith. b 59. Leeds Univ BA 05 RMN 91. NOC 02. **d** 05 **p** 06. C Sprotbrough *Sheff* 05–07; C Hillsborough and Wadsley Bridge 07–09; P-in-c 09–11; V 11–14; Dir IME 4-7 12–14; Can Missr Sheff Cathl from 14; Vice Dean from 19. *62 Kingfield Road, Sheffield S11 9AU* T: 0114-263 6065 E: keith.farrow@sheffield-cathedral.org.uk

FARROW, Peter Maurice. b 44. St Chad's Coll Dur BSc 65. **d** 68 **p** 69. C Gt Yarmouth *Nor* 68–71; C N Lynn w St Marg and St Nic 71–75; P-in-c Sculthorpe w Dunton and Doughton 75–77; PtO 78–89; TV Lowestoft and Kirkley 89–94; Ind Miss 89–94; Sen Ind Chapl 94–99; TV Gaywood 95–02; P-in-c Mundford w Lynford, Cranwich and Ickburgh w Langford 02–09; rtd 09; PtO *Nor* from 09. *21 Clifford Drive, Lowestoft NR33 9EX* T: (01502) 521817 E: farrpm@btinternet.com

FARTHING, Paul Andrew. b 58. McGill Univ Montreal BA 80 STM 82. Montreal Dioc Th Coll. **d** 83 **p** 84. C Montreal W St Phil Canada 83–85; R Montreal St Jo Divine 85–96; R Montreal St Jo Ev 96–99; P-in-c Burton *Lich* 99–05; V Burton St Aid and St Paul 05–13; PV Lich Cathl 12–13; V Chislehurst Annunciation *Roch* from 13. *The Vicarage, 2 Foxhome Close, Chislehurst BR7 5XT* T: (020) 8467 3606 E: pafarthing@fmail.co.uk *or* annunciation.chislehurst@gmail.com

FASS, Michael John. b 44. Trin Coll Cam MA 75. Edin Dioc NSM Course 89. **d** 95 **p** 95. NSM Penicuik *Edin* 95–97; NSM W Linton 95–97; NSM Roslin (Rosslyn Chpl) 97–06; Bp's Officer for Min 03–09; LtO 06–17; PtO from 17; *Heref* from 08. *Old Gore Coach House, Old Gore, Ross-on-Wye HR9 7QT* T: (01989) 780339

FAULDS, Ian Craig. b 48. **d** 03 **p** 04. NSM Maughold *S & M* 03–12; NSM Maughold and S Ramsey 12–13; PtO 13–14; Min Can and Prec St German's Cathl 14–19; R Ch Ch Cathl and the Falkland Is from 19. *The Deanery, 17 Ross Road, Stanley, Falkland Islands FIQQ 1ZZ* T: (00500) 21100 E: ian.faulds@gmail.com

FAULKNER, Mrs Anne Elizabeth. b 38. Bp Otter Coll BA 58. **d** 00 **p** 01. NSM Aylesbury *Ox* 00–04; Chapl to Bp Buckingham 02–04; rtd 04; Hon C Wroxall *Portsm* 04–05; P-in-c 05–11; P-in-c St Lawrence 08–10; Hon C N Swindon St Andr *Bris* 11–17; PtO *Win* 17–19; Hon C Fawley 19–21; PtO *Sarum* from 21. *39 Clarendon Road, Southampton SO16 4GB* T: (023) 8051 2272 E: aefaulkner77@gmail.com

FAULKNER, Brian Thomas. b 48. S Dios Minl Tr Scheme. **d** 84 **p** 85. C W Leigh *Portsm* 84–88; R Foulsham w Hindolveston and Guestwick *Nor* 88–93; P-in-c Erpingham w Calthorpe, Ingworth, Aldborough etc 93–94; R 94–13; RD Ingworth 10–13; rtd 13; PtO *Nor* 14–15; Hon C Barningham w Matlaske w Baconsthorpe etc 15–16; Hon C Lt Barningham, Blickling, Edgefield etc 15–16; PtO 16–20; P-in-c Erpingham w Calthorpe, Ingworth, Aldborough etc 20. *Oak Tree Cottage, Cherrytree Road, Plumstead, Norwich NR11 7LQ* T: (01263) 577868 E: brianfaulkner@btinternet.com

FAULKNER, Bruce Stephen. b 63. Trin Coll Bris BA 97 St Jo Coll Dur MA 08. Cranmer Hall Dur 06. **d** 08 **p** 09. C Somerton w Compton Dundon, the Charltons etc *B & W* 08–12; P-in-c Ilchester w Northover, Limington, Yeovilton etc 12–17; R from 17; RD Ivelchester from 13. *3 The Paddocks, West Street, Ilchester, Yeovil BA22 8PS* T: (01935) 849441 M: 07796-283766 E: bsfaulkner1@aol.com *or* ilchestervicar@aol.com

FAULKNER, Mrs Catherine Evelyn. b 43. Man Poly RHV 82. **d** 01 **p** 02. OLM Urmston *Man* 01–11; P-in-c 11–14; NSM Davyhulme Ch Ch 13–14; rtd 14; PtO *Man* from 14. *5 Barnfield, Urmston, Manchester M41 9EW* T: 0161-748 3226 E: catherine.faulkner@ntlworld.com

FAULKNER, Henry Odin. b 35. G&C Coll Cam BA 56 MA 59. St Jo Coll Nottm 70. **d** 74 **p** 75. C Heigham H Trin *Nor* 74–76; C Heeley *Sheff* 76–80; TV Netherthorpe 80–84; PtO

St Alb 84–20. *69 Holywell Hill, St Albans AL1 1HF* T: (01727) 854177 M: 07719-642479 E: henry.faulkner@ntlworld.com

FAULKNER, Iain Stuart. **d** 12 **p** 14. NSM Balham St Mary and St Jo *S'wark* 12–17; P-in-c S Wimbledon St Andr 17; NSM Stockwell St Andr and St Mich 18–20; PtO from 21. *25 Whinfell Road, Chesterfield S41 8BF* M: 07432-678139 E: iainsfaulkner@hotmail.com

FAULKNER (née RITCHIE), Ms June. b 41. UCD BA 64. **d** 05 **p** 06. OLM New Windsor *Ox* 05–11; PtO from 11. *69 Springfield Road, Windsor SL4 3PR* T: (01753) 622808 E: j.faulkner0406@gmail.com

FAULKNER, Margaret Evelyn. *See* WHITFORD, Margaret Evelyn

FAULKNER, Martin Trevor. b 62. Salford Univ BSc 83 Bretton Hall Coll PGCE 88 Leeds Univ BA 10 Sheff Univ MA 12. Coll of Resurr Mirfield 09. **d** 11 **p** 12. C Spilsby Gp *Linc* 11–14; C Bolingbroke Deanery 14–15; V S Holderness Coast *York* from 15. *28 Park Avenue, Withernsea HU19 2JU* T: (01964) 615060 M: 07908-703484 E: rev.martin@hotmail.co.uk

FAULKNER, Peter Graham. b 47. Lon Univ CertEd 69. Oak Hill Th Coll BA 87. **d** 82 **p** 83. C Crofton *Portsm* 87–89; R Mid Marsh Gp *Linc* 89–98; V S Cave and Ellerker w Broomfleet *York* 98–13; P-in-c N Cave w Cliffe 09–12; P-in-c Hotham 09–12; RD Howden 05–10; rtd 13; PtO *Linc* 16–19; *Eur* from 18. *9 Hurn Close, Ruskington, Sleaford NG34 9FE* T: (01526) 832184 E: faulkner47peter@gmail.com

FAULKNER, Robert Sonny. b 59. ACMA 98 FCCA 13. Ripon Coll Cuddesdon 15. **d** 17 **p** 18. C Clapham Ch Ch and St Jo *S'wark* 17–21; V Angell Town St Jo from 21. *49 Voltaire Road, London SW4 6DD* M: 07377-449607 E: robertsofaulkner@gmail.com

FAULKNER, Ms Susan Ann. b 70. Lanc Univ BA 96. Ripon Coll Cuddesdon 97. **d** 99 **p** 00. C Scotswood *Newc* 99–03; P-in-c Byker St Silas 03–10; P-in-c Badby w Newham and Charwelton w Fawsley etc *Pet* 10–12; R 12–19; V Dallington and St James from 19. *The Vicarage, 24A High Street, Silverstone, Towcester NN12 8US* T: (01327) 858018 M: 07786-265422 E: revsuefaulkner@aol.com

FAULKS, David William. b 45. EMMTC 82. **d** 86 **p** 87. C Market Harborough *Leic* 86–88; C Wootton Bassett *Sarum* 88–90; R Clipston w Naseby and Haselbech w Kelmarsh *Pet* 90–13; rtd 13; PtO *Leic* from 14. *7 Pochin Drive, Market Harborough LE16 7LP* E: david.faulks@btinternet.com

FAULKS, Simon George. b 73. Moorlands Th Coll BA 99. St Jo Coll Nottm 09. **d** 11 **p** 12. C Warminster Ch Ch *Sarum* 11–15; V Newton Longville, Mursley, Swanbourne etc *Ox* from 15. *The Rectory, 7 Main Street, Mursley, Milton Keynes MK17 0RT* T: (01296) 728531 M: 07795-154222 E: revsimon@notashamed.co.uk

FAULL, Janet Dorothy. b 60. SS Paul & Mary Coll Cheltenham PGCE 86 LGSM 82. WEMTC 05. **d** 08 **p** 09. C Cheltenham Ch Ch *Glouc* 08–12; V Tuffley 12–19; AD Glouc City 15–19; Hon Can Glouc Cathl 18–19; R Hook Norton w Gt Rollright, Swerford etc *Ox* from 19. *The Rectory, 2 Rectory Road, Hook Norton, Banbury OX15 5QQ* M: 07986-650459 E: rector@hooknortonbenefice.org.uk

✠**FAULL, The Rt Revd Vivienne Frances.** b 55. St Hilda's Coll Ox BA 77 MA 82 Clare Coll Cam MA 90. St Jo Coll Nottm BA 81. **dss** 82 **d** 87 **p** 94 **c** 18. Mossley Hill St Matt and St Jas *Liv* 82–85; Chapl Clare Coll Cam 85–90; Chapl Glouc Cathl 90–94; Can Res Cov Cathl 94–00; Vice-Provost 95–00; Provost Leic 00–02; Dean Leic 02–12; Dean York 12–18; Bp Bris from 18. *Bishop's Office, Church Lane, Winterbourne, Bristol BS36 1SG* T: (01454) 777728

FAULTLESS, Mrs Patricia Doreen. b 53. **d** 05 **p** 06. OLM Glascote and Stonydelph *Lich* from 05. *40 Stephenson Close, Glascote, Tamworth B77 2DQ* T: (01827) 287171 M: 07980-434897 E: patriciafaultless@gmail.com

FAUX, Steven Paul. b 58. UEA BA 79. Trin Coll Bris BA 07. **d** 07 **p** 08. C Bath St Mich w St Paul *B & W* 07–14; PtO from 14; C Redland *Bris* from 16. *Fleetlands, Weston Park, Bath BA1 4AL* T: (01225) 313145 E: steven@stevenfaux.com

FAWCETT, Mrs Diane Elizabeth. b 49. Cant Univ (NZ) BA 72 Kent Univ MA 03. Westcott Ho Cam 03. **d** 04 **p** 05. C Egerton w Pluckley *Cant* 04–08; PtO 08–10; P-in-c St Margarets-at-Cliffe w Westcliffe etc 10–19; rtd 19; PtO *Cant* from 20. *8 Luxmoore House, 75 New Dover Road, Canterbury CT1 3DZ* T: (01227) 760593 E: fawcett38@hotmail.com

FAWCETT, Mrs Joanna Mary. b 45. SRN 67 SCM 69. EAMTC 01. **d** 04 **p** 05. NSM Blakeney w Cley, Wiveton, Glandford etc *Nor* 04–12; PtO from 12. *14 The Cornfield, Langham, Holt NR25 7DQ* T: (01328) 830415 E: jofawcett@btinternet.com

FAWCETT, Laura Joy. *See* LUZ, Laura Joy

FAWCETT, Timothy John. b 44. K Coll Lon BD 66 AKC 67 PhD 71. St Boniface Warminster 66. **d** 67 **p** 68. C Blackpool St Steph *Blackb* 67–70; Hon C St Marylebone All SS *Lon*

68–70; C Southgate St Mich 70–72; Sacr Dur Cathl 72–75; V Wheatley Hill 75–79; V Torrisholme *Blackb* 79–84; V Thaxted *Chelmsf* 84–89; NSM Holt Deanery *Nor* 89–06; C Stiffkey and Bale 06–09; rtd 09; PtO *Nor* from 09. *Dowitchers, 14 The Cornfield, Langham, Holt NR25 7DQ* T: (01328) 830415 E: tjfawcett@btinternet.com

FAWNS, Canon Lynne. b 56. Thames Valley Univ BA 95. NTMTC 97. **d** 00 **p** 01. C Hillingdon All SS *Lon* 00–03; V London Colney *St Alb* 03–18; Hon Can St Alb 17–18; rtd 18. *Rowanlea, 55 Hull Road, Cottingham HU16 4PN*

FAYERS, Canon Robert Stanley. b 48. St Steph Ho Ox 82. **d** 84 **p** 85. C Deptford St Paul *S'wark* 84–88; V Beckenham St Mich w St Aug *Roch* 88–00; V Brighton St Mich *Chich* 00–11; P-in-c Brighton St Paul 06–11; V Brighton St Mich and St Paul 11–14; Can and Preb Chich Cathl 12–14; rtd 14; PtO *Nor* from 15; *Chich* from 15; *Ely* from 19. *Grampus House, 32 Pilot Street, King's Lynn PE30 1QL* M: 07706-067496 E: rsfayers@gmail.com

FAYLE, David Charles Wilfred. b 51. Sarum & Wells Th Coll. **d** 83 **p** 84. C Parkstone St Pet w Branksea and St Osmund *Sarum* 83–87; TV Dorchester 87–96; P-in-c Taunton All SS *B & W* 96–97; V 97–18; rtd 18. *Flat 2, 7 Fortfield Terrace, Sidmouth EX10 8HT* E: davidfayle@btinternet.com

FAZZANI, Keith. b 47. Portsm Poly BSc 70. Cant Sch of Min 93. **d** 96 **p** 97. NSM Appledore w Brookland, Fairfield, Brenzett etc *Cant* 96–01 and 05–13; Chapl Team Ldr E Kent Hosps Univ NHS Foundn Trust 01–12; rtd 13; PtO *Cant* 13–16. *Oakhouse Farm, Appledore, Ashford TN26 2BB* T: (01233) 758322 E: kfazzani@btinternet.com

FEAK, Christopher Martin. b 52. Keele Univ BA 75. Trin Coll Bris 92. **d** 94 **p** 95. C Handsworth St Mary *Birm* 94–97; P-in-c Perry Common 97–00; V 00–05; AD Aston 01–05; P-in-c Sandown Ch Ch *Portsm* 05–15; P-in-c Lower Sandown St Jo 05–15; AD E Wight 12–14; P-in-c Towyn *St As* 15–16; TV Aber-Morfa Miss Area 17–19; rtd 19. *Meredith Cottage, 12 Bodlondeb Castle, Bodlondeb Hill, Llandudno LL30 2HY* M: 07593-804539 E: cfeak173@gmail.com

FEARNLEY, Andrew Anthony. b 84. Nottm Univ BA 06. Oak Hill Th Coll MTh 13. **d** 13. C Sevenoaks St Nic *Roch* 13–17; C Fulwood *Sheff* from 17. *50 Brooklands Crescent, Sheffield S10 4GG* M: 07709-448080 E: andyfearnley1@gmail.com

FEARNLEY, Jeffrey Malcolm. b 46. Newc Univ BSc 69. St Jo Coll Nottm 90. **d** 92 **p** 93. C Bispham *Blackb* 92–95; C Bolton w Ireby and Uldale *Carl* 95–00; TV Binsey 00–02; C 02–07; rtd 07; PtO *Blackb* from 07. *32 Chestnut Court, Leyland PR25 3GN* T: (01772) 458696

FEARNSIDE, Mary Ingrid. b 44. **d** 98 **p** 99. OLM Shelton and Oxon *Lich* 98–08; Chapl Uplands Care Home 08–14; Chapl R Shrewsbury Hosps NHS Trust 98–04; Chapl Shrewsbury and Telford Hosp NHS Trust from 04; PtO *Lich* 11–21. *23 Eastwood Road, Shrewsbury SY3 8YJ* T: (01743) 353290 E: revmfearnside1@btinternet.com

FEARON, Mrs Irene. b 51. CBDTI 00. **d** 03 **p** 04. NSM Maryport, Netherton and Flimby *Carl* 03–08; NSM Camerton, Seaton and W Seaton from 08. *Kirkborough Lodge, Ellenborough, Maryport CA15 7RD* T: (01900) 813108 E: irene@kirklodge.com

FEASTER, Mrs Sarah Catherine. b 67. St Hugh's Coll Ox BA 89 Sheff Univ BA 13. Yorks Min Course 10. **d** 13 **p** 14. C Manston *Ripon* 13–14; Leeds 14–17; V Gt and Lt Ouseburn w Marton cum Grafton etc from 17. *The Vicarage, Main Street, Great Ouseburn, York YO26 9RQ* T: (01423) 330928 E: sarahfeaster@btinternet.com or gtouseburnvicarage@hotmail.com

FEATHER (formerly HESELTINE), Mrs Barbara Joan. b 42. Keele Univ BA 65. S'wark Ord Course 85. **d** 88 **p** 94. NSM Addington *S'wark* 88–98; PtO *Truro* 98–02; NSM Feock 02–13; rtd 13; PtO *Truro* from 16. *The Grange House, Feock, Truro TR3 6RG* T: (01872) 865497 M: 07767-264060 E: barbarafeather42@gmail.com

FEATHERSTON, Margery. *See* GRANGE, Alice Margery

FEATHERSTON, Nigel Havelock. b 56. SCRTP 15. **d** 17 **p** 18. OLM Wychert Vale *Ox* from 17. *Greenwood, New Road, Dinton, Aylesbury HP17 8UT* E: nfeatherston@btinternet.com

FEATHERSTONE (née HOWETT), Mrs Amanda Jane. b 68. Reading Univ BA 91 Birm Univ MPhil 08 Cam Univ BTh 11. Ridley Hall Cam 09. **d** 11 **p** 12. C Boldmere *Birm* 11–15; C Birm St Luke 15–19; V Wythall from 19. *15 Hawthorne Drive, Hollywood, Birmingham B47 5QT* T: (01564) 823248 E: churchoffice@wythallchurch.net

FEATHERSTONE, Gray. b 42. Stellenbosch Univ BA 62 LLB 64. Cuddesdon Coll 65. **d** 67 **p** 68. C Woodstock S Africa 67–70; Asst Master Waterford Sch Swaziland 70–72; P-in-c Maputo St Steph and St Lawr Mozambique 73–76; Miss to Seamen 73–80; V Upper Clapton St Matt *Lon* 80–83; V Stamford Hill St Thos 80–89; Chr Aid Area Sec (N & W Lon) 89–06; Chr Aid

Area Sec (Lon) 06–07; rtd 07; PtO *Lon* 97–18. *20 Richmond Road, London N2 7JT* T: (020) 3602 2788

FEATHERSTONE, Jonathan Mark. b 88. Regent's Park Coll Ox BA 10. Ridley Hall Cam MA 17. **d** 17 **p** 18. C Enfield Ch Ch Trent Park *Lon* from 17. *13 Wilton Road, Cockfosters, Barnet EN4 9DX* T: (020) 8449 0556 M: 07903-309440 E: featherstone.jon@gmail.com

FEATHERSTONE, Robert Leslie. b 54. Leeds Univ MA 04 LLCM 74 Lon Univ CertEd 75. Chich Th Coll 84. **d** 86 **p** 87. C Crayford *Roch* 86–89; V Belvedere St Aug 89–94; V Crowborough St Jo *Chich* 94–01; P-in-c New Brompton St Luke *Roch* 01–06; Hon Succ Roch Cathl 03–06; PtO 07–08; P-in-c Hastings St Clem and All SS *Chich* 09–16; TV Bexhill St Pet 16–18; rtd 18. *St Michael's House, 23 Glassenbury Drive, Bexhill-on-Sea TN40 2NY* T: (01424) 576826 M: 07878-237312 E: frrobertf@live.co.uk

FEAVER, Nigel Conway McDonald. b 51. Leeds Univ BA 73 Brunel Univ MA 76 CQSW 76. Ripon Coll Cuddesdon 03. **d** 05 **p** 06. C Oxton *Ches* 05–08; R Wincanton *B & W* 08–18; R Pen Selwood 08–18; rtd 18. *Carisbrooke, Blandford Road, Sturminster Marshall, Wimborne BH21 4AG* E: revnigelfeaver@gmail.com

FEENEY, Damian Prescott Anthony. b 62. Grey Coll Dur BA 83 PGCE 84 ALCM 81. Chich Th Coll BTh 94. **d** 94 **p** 95. C Harrogate St Wilfrid *Ripon* 94–96; C Preston St Jo and St Geo *Blackb* 96–99; Bp's Miss P to Longsands 99–01; TR Ribbleton 01–04; V Woodplumpton 04–09; Vice-Prin St Steph Ho Ox 09–15; V Ettingshall *Lich* from 15; PtO *Ox* 12–15. *Holy Trinity Vicarage, Farrington Road, Wolverhampton WV4 6QH* T: (01902) 478679 M: 07949-570387 E: ettingshall.priest@gmail.com

FEENEY, Miss Rebecca Anne Mary. b 89. Cardiff Univ BMus 11. St Steph Ho Ox BA 17. **d** 18 **p** 19. C Standish *Blackb* from 18. *89 Woodhurst Drive, Standish, Wigan WN6 0RW* M: 07970-557801 E: revd.ramfeeney@gmail.com

FEIST, Canon Nicholas James. b 45. Solicitor 70. St Jo Coll Nottm. **d** 76 **p** 77. C Didsbury St Jas *Man* 76–80; TV Didsbury St Jas and Em 80; V Friarmere 80–88; R Middleton 88–94; TR Middleton w Thornham 94–10; R Middleton and Thornham 10–14; AD Heywood and Middleton 99–07; Hon Can Man Cathl 98–14; rtd 14; PtO *Man* from 14; *Ches* from 15. *86 Rossendale Road, Heald Green, Cheadle SK8 3HF* T: 0161-286 9440 M: 07808-159339 E: njfeist@gmail.com

FEITAL, Peterson. *See* DE ALMEIDA FEITAL, Peterson

FELIX, David Rhys. b 55. Univ of Wales (Cardiff) LLB 76 Solicitor 81. Ripon Coll Cuddesdon 83. **d** 86 **p** 87. C Bromborough *Ches* 86–89; V Grange St Andr 89–99; Chapl Halton Gen Hosp NHS Trust 95–99; P-in-c Runcorn H Trin *Ches* 96–99; RD Frodsham 98–99; V Daresbury 99–21; Sen Ind Chapl 00–21; Hon Can Ches Cathl 06–21; rtd 21. *7 Milton Green, Wirral CH61 7YQ* M: 07778-859935 E: david.felix@btinternet.com

FELL, Canon Alan William. b 46. Ball Coll Ox BA 69. Coll of Resurr Mirfield 68. **d** 71 **p** 72. C Woodchurch *Ches* 71–74; C Man Clayton St Cross w St Paul 74–75; C Prestwich St Marg 75–77; V Hyde St Thos *Ches* 77–80; R Tattenhall and Handley 80–86; V Sedbergh, Cautley and Garsdale *Bradf* 86–12; Hon C Firbank, Howgill and Killington 86–06; P-in-c 06–12; Hon Can Bradf Cathl 96–12; RD Ewecross 00–05; rtd 12; PtO *Lich* 13–21. *The Wharfinger's House, Maesbury Marsh, Oswestry SY10 8JB* M: 07825-774588 E: fells.maesbury@gmail.com

FELL, David Edward. b 61. Bradf Univ BSc 84 Brunel Univ BA 05. ERMC 05. **d** 07 **p** 08. C Wootton *St Alb* 07–11; TV Barnsbury *Lon* from 11. *2 Brooksby Street, London N1 1HA* T: (020) 7697 4400 M: 07989-203429 E: ted_fell@hotmail.com

FELLOWS, Canon Grant. b 56. K Coll Lon BD 77 AKC 77. Coll of Resurr Mirfield 79. **d** 80 **p** 81. C Addington *Cant* 80–84; C S Gillingham *Roch* 84–86; V Heath and Reach *St Alb* 86–94; V Radlett 94–03; RD Aldenham 98–03; V Leighton Buzzard w Eggington, Hockliffe etc 03–05; TR Billington, Egginton, Hockliffe etc 06–08; TR Ouzel Valley 08–18; Hon Can St Alb 12–18; rtd 18; PtO *St Alb* from 18; *Ely* from 19; RD St Neots 19–20. *8 Radland Close, St Neots PE19 6BQ* E: rev.grant.fellows@gmail.com

FELLOWS, Ian Christopher. b 73. Univ Coll Ox BA 94 MA 98 St Jo Coll Dur BA 99. Cranmer Hall Dur 96. **d** 99 **p** 00. C Bucknall and Bagnall *Lich* 99–03; TV Broughton *Man* 03–07; P-in-c Blackley St Andr 07–16; TV Wythenshawe 16–21; TR from 21. *St Luke's Vicarage, Brownley Road, Manchester M22 4PT* T: 0161-998 2071 E: pointlessvicar@gmail.com

FELLOWS, Canon John Michael. b 46. Oriel Coll Ox MA 77. Coll of Resurr Mirfield 74. **d** 77 **p** 78. C Kings Heath *Birm* 77–80; TV E Ham w Upton Park and Forest Gate *Chelmsf* 80–85; P-in-c Wormingford 85–90; P-in-c Mt Bures 85–90; P-in-c Lt Horkesley 85–90; V Wormingford, Mt

Bures and Lt Horkesley 90; R Compton w Shackleford and Peper Harow *Guildf* 90–12; RD Godalming 07–12; Chapl Prior's Field Sch 90–12; Hon Can Guildf Cathl 12; rtd 12; Hon C Balsham, Weston Colville, W Wickham etc *Ely* 12–16; Hon C Gt w Lt Abington 12–16; Hon C Hildersham 12–16; PtO *Nor* from 16; *St E* from 17. *29 Upper Olland Street, Bungay NR35 1BE* T: (01986) 894414 E: j.fellows321@btinternet.com

FELLOWS, Lesley June. *See* CRAWLEY, Lesley June

FELLOWS, Mrs Susan Elizabeth. b 46. ATCL 65 LTCL 66 GTCL 67. SAOMC 99. **d** 02 **p** 03. NSM Weston Turville *Ox* from 02. *65 Craigwell Avenue, Aylesbury HP21 7AG* T: (01296) 424982 M: 07712-226999 E: susan.sefellows@btinternet.com

FELTHAM, Keith. b 40. **d** 75 **p** 76. In Bapt Ch 66–75; C Plympton St Mary *Ex* 75–79; TV Northam w Westward Ho! and Appledore 79–82; TR Lynton, Brendon, Countisbury, Lynmouth etc 82–85; P-in-c Bickleigh (Plymouth) 85–86; TR 86–91; Chapl R Bournemouth Gen Hosp 91–95; P-in-c Whimple, Talaton and Clyst St Lawr *Ex* 95–00; rtd 00; PtO *Ex* 00–14. *18 Oakland Walk, Dawlish EX7 9RS* T: (01626) 438663 E: keithfeltham@icloud.com

FENBY, Andrew Robert. b 66. Loughb Univ BSc 88. St Steph Ho Ox 03. **d** 05 **p** 06. C Leigh-on-Sea St Marg *Chelmsf* 05–09; V Barkingside St Fran 09–14; R Beddington *S'wark* from 14. *The Rectory, 18 Bloxworth Close, Wallington SM6 7NL* T: (020) 8647 1973 E: frandrew@me.com

FENBY, Canon Sarah Louise. b 66. Kent Univ BA 88 Lon Bible Coll BA 96. Trin Coll Bris MA 00. **d** 00 **p** 01. C Stoke Gifford *Bris* 00–04; C S Croydon Em *S'wark* 04–10; Min Selsdon St Fran CD 07–10; P-in-c Woolaston w Alvington and Aylburton *Glouc* 10–18; P-in-c Lydney 10–18; Voc and Tr Officer *Worc* 18–19; Can Res Ches Cathl and Dioc Dir of Voc from 19. *Church House, 5500 Daresbury Park, Daresbury, Warrington WA4 4GE* T: (01928) 718834 M: 07714-587250 E: ddv@chester.anglican.org

FENNELL (*née* PAVYER), **Mrs Jennifer Elizabeth.** b 75. Ex Univ BSc 96 Cam Univ BTh 02 Lon Univ MA 05. Westcott Ho Cam 99. **d** 02 **p** 03. C Stevenage St Andr and St Geo *St Alb* 02–05; C Harpenden St Nic 05–10; P-in-c Welwyn Garden City 10–14; V from 14; RD Welwyn Hatfield from 17. *The Vicarage, 48 Parkway, Welwyn Garden City AL8 6HH* T: (01707) 320960 E: jennyfennell@virginmedia.com

FENNELL, Julian. b 56. Dioc OLM tr scheme. **d** 08 **p** 09. OLM Ipswich St Mary at Stoke w St Pet and St Fran *St E* 08–13; NSM 13–14; C Bramford 14–18; C Gt and Lt Blakenham w Baylham and Nettlestead 14–18; TV Ipswich St Mary at Stoke w St Pet and St Fran 18–20; rtd 20. *70 Wellesley Road, Ipswich IP4 1PH* T: (01473) 218771 M: 07449-972663 E: julianfennell@hotmail.co.uk

FENNEMORE, Catherine Edwina. b 63. RGN 85. Sarum Coll 13. **d** 16 **p** 17. NSM W Leigh *Portsm* 16–19; PtO *Win* from 19. *Woodside, Christmas Hill, South Wonston, Winchester SO21 3ES* T: (01962) 883668 E: cefennemore@gmail.com

FENNEMORE, Canon Nicholas Paul. b 53. Wycliffe Hall Ox 76. **d** 79 **p** 80. C N Mymms *St Alb* 79–82; C Chipping Barnet w Arkley 82–83; TV 83–84; TV Preston w Sutton Poyntz, Littlemoor etc *Sarum* 84–86; Chapl St Helier Hosp Carshalton 86–90; Chapl Jo Radcliffe Hosp Ox 90–94; Chapl Ox Radcliffe Hosp NHS Trust 94–96; Sen Chapl Ox Radcliffe Hosps NHS Trust 96–06; Hon Can Ch Ch *Ox* 03–06; Hd Chapl Services Portsm Hosps NHS Trust 06–11; Dioc Adv for Healing *Portsm* 08–11; Chapl Martlets Hospice Hove 11–12; Lead Chapl St Wilfrid's Hospice Chich 12–14; Hd of Chapl S Health NHS Foundn Trust 14–20; P-in-c Soberton w Newtown *Portsm* 17–18; Lead Chapl Win City Cen Chapl from 20; Cathl Chapl and Min Can Win Cathl from 18; PtO *Chich* from 14; *Portsm* from 11. *Woodside, Christmas Hill, South Wonston, Winchester SO21 3ES* T: (01962) 883668 M: 07919-547508 E: canonfennemore@btinternet.com *or* nick.fennemore@winchester-cathedral.org.uk

FENSOME, Canon Anthony David. b 49. Open Univ BA 89. Sarum & Wells Th Coll 82. **d** 84 **p** 85. C Gtr Corsham *Bris* 84–88; P-in-c Lyddington w Wanborough 88–91; P-in-c Bishopstone w Hinton Parva 88–91; P-in-c Lyddington and Wanborough and Bishopstone etc 91; V 91–93; V Chippenham St Pet 93–08; RD Chippenham 94–99; AD 06–08; Hon Can Bris Cathl 98–08; rtd 08. *42 Francis Crescent, Tiverton EX16 4EP* T: (01884) 256611 E: tonyfens@aol.com

FENSOME, Grant Lewis. b 91. Trin Coll Bris BA 17. **d** 17 **p** 18. C Broxbourne w Wormley *St Alb* 17–21; V Basildon w Aldworth and Ashampstead *Ox* from 21. *The Vicarage, Upper Basildon, Reading RG8 8LS* T: (01491) 671555 E: revgrantfensome@gmail.com *or* grant@thebenefice.org

FENTIMAN, David Frank. b 43. RIBA 74 Roehampton Inst PGCE 94. S Dios Minl Tr Scheme 90. **d** 93 **p** 94. NSM Hastings

St Clem and All SS *Chich* 93–98; P-in-c Blacklands Hastings Ch Ch and St Andr 98–01; V 01–05; rtd 05; PtO *Chich* from 15. *4 Barnfield Close, Hastings TN34 1TS* T: (01424) 421821

FENTON, Allison Jane. b 66. Grey Coll Dur BA 87 St Jo Coll Dur MATM 08 Dur Univ DThM 17 PGCE 90. Cranmer Hall Dur 06. **d** 08 **p** 09. C Newc St Geo and St Hilda 08–10; C Newc Ch Ch w St Ann 10–12; P-in-c Scotswood 12–14; NSM Dur St Giles 14–17; NSM Shadforth and Sherburn 14–17; Vice Prin IME *Carl* 17–20; Tutor for Angl Admissions Qu Foundn Birm from 21; PtO *Birm* from 21. *The Queen's Foundation, Somerset Road, Edgbaston, Birmingham B15 2QH* T: 0121-454 1527 E: allisonjfenton@gmail.com *or* fentona@queens.ac.uk

FENTON, Barry Dominic. b 59. Leeds Univ BA 85. Coll of Resurr Mirfield 85. **d** 87 **p** 88. C Leigh Park *Portsm* 87–90; Chapl and Prec Portsm Cathl 90–95; Min Can and Prec Westmr Abbey 95–02; Chapl N Middx Hosp NHS Trust 02–04; Lead Chapl 04–16; P-in-c Broadstairs *Cant* 16–18; R from 18; Min Can Cant Cathl from 17; PV Westmr Abbey from 04. *The Rectory, Nelson Place, Broadstairs CT10 1HQ* T: (01843) 862921 M: 07846-629455 E: dominic.fenton11@btinternet.com

FENTON, David Frank. b 43. Open Univ BA 79 Matlock Coll of Educn CertEd 67. Wycliffe Hall Ox 07. **d** 08 **p** 09. NSM Win Ch 08–12; PtO from 12. *5 Glenwood Avenue, Southampton SO16 3PY* T: (023) 8076 9574 M: 07967-419169 E: dave.fenton1@btinternet.com

FENTON, Geoffrey Eric Crosland. b 54. St Jo Coll Ox BA 75 MSc 76. WEMTC 98. **d** 01 **p** 02. NSM Wedmore w Theale and Blackford *B & W* 01–05; NSM Greinton and W Poldens 05–08; C Mark w Allerton 08–10; P-in-c 10–11; TV Ashburton, Bickington, Buckland in the Moor etc *Ex* from 11. *The Vicarage, Widecombe-in-the-Moor, Newton Abbot TQ13 7TF* T: (01364) 621334 E: geoffrey.fenton@wildyeast.co.uk

FENTON, Heather. b 48. Trin Coll Bris. **d** 87 **p** 97. C Corwen and Llangar *St As* 87–89; C Corwen and Llangar w Gwyddelwern and Llawrybetws 89–98; Dioc Rural Min Co-ord 87–98; LtO 98–01; C Deanery of Penllyn 01–03; P-in-c Bryneglwys 03–11; P-in-c Gwyddelwern 09–11; AD Penllyn and Edeirnion 10–12; Ed The Reader 07–17; Dioc Rural Officer *St As* 08–21; PtO from 13. *7 Llys Trewithan, St Asaph LL17 0DJ* T: (01745) 583535 E: rev.heather@outlook.com

FENTON, Keith John. b 54. Coll of Resurr Mirfield 01. **d** 03 **p** 04. C St Annes St Anne *Blackb* 03–07; TV Ribbleton 07–12; C 12–14; R from 14. *140 Teil Green, Fulwood, Preston PR2 9PE* T: (01772) 791147 M: 07773-630784 E: keithjfenton@yahoo.co.uk *or* parishofribbleton@gmail.com

FENTON, Michael John. b 42. Linc Th Coll 67. **d** 69 **p** 70. C Guiseley *Bradf* 69–72; C Heswall *Ches* 72–75; TV Birkenhead Priory 75–81; V Alvanley 81–91; Chapl Crossley Hosp Cheshire 82–91; V Holbrook and Lt Eaton *Derby* 91–03; V Allenton and Shelton Lock 03–07; rtd 07; PtO *Derby* 07–18. *11 Nethercroft Lane, Danesmoor, Chesterfield S45 9DE* T: (01246) 250071 E: michaeljfenton@yahoo.co.uk

FENTON, Canon Nicola Jane. b 70. York Univ BSc 91 Leeds Univ PGCE 94 St Jo Coll Dur BA 12. Cranmer Hall Dur 10. **d** 12 **p** 13. C Nottingham St Ann w Em *S'well* 12–16; P-in-c Hazelwood, Holbrook and Milford *Derby* 16–21; Bp's Asst Chapl 16–21; Bp's Chapl from 21; Can Res Derby Cathl from 21; Spiritual Dir Adv from 18. *Bishop's Office, 6 King Street, Duffield, Belper DE56 4EU* T: (01332) 840132 M: 07811-957913 E: nicky.fenton@bishopofderby.org

FENTON, Miss Penelope Ann. b 41. Leic Univ BSc 64. Cant Sch of Min 92. **d** 95 **p** 96. NSM Eastling w Ospringe and Stalisfield w Otterden *Cant* 95–00; P-in-c 00–05; Asst to Bp's Officer for NSM 99–05; rtd 05; PtO *Cant* 05–08. *9 Brogdale Road, Faversham ME13 8SX* T: (01795) 536366 E: penny.fenton@lineone.net

FENTON, Canon Vincent Thompson. b 52. Cranmer Hall Dur 94. **d** 96 **p** 97. C Heworth St Mary *Dur* 96–99; C-in-c Bishop Auckland Woodhouse Close CD 99–06; Chapl S Durham Healthcare NHS Trust 01–02; Chapl Co Durham and Darlington Acute Hosps NHS Trust 02–05; P-in-c Crook *Dur* 06–16; V 16–19; AD Stanhope 07–18; Hon Can Dur Cathl from 16; rtd 19; PtO *Dur* from 20. *40 Bridge Street, Howden le Wear, Crook DL15 8EX* E: vicfenton@gmail.com

FENWICK, Canon Malcolm Frank. b 38. Cranmer Hall Dur 62. **d** 65 **p** 66. C Tynemouth Cullercoats St Paul *Newc* 65–68; C Bywell 68–73; V Alnmouth 73–75; CF (TAVR) 73–83; V Lesbury w Alnmouth *Newc* 75–80; V Delaval 80–91; RD Bedlington 83–88; V Riding Mill 91–01; P-in-c Whittonstall 91–01; Chapl Shepherd's Dene Retreat Ho from 91; RD Corbridge *Newc* 93–99; P-in-c Slaley 97–99; P-in-c Healey 99–01; Hon Can Newc Cathl 97–01; rtd 01; PtO *Newc* 01–19.

21 Welburn Close, Ovingham, Prudhoe NE42 6BD T: (01661) 835565

✠**FENWICK, The Rt Revd Richard David.** b 43. Univ of Wales (Lamp) BA 66 MA 86 TCD MusB 79 MA 92 Univ of Wales (Lamp) PhD 95 FLCM 68 FTCL 76 Hon FGCM 04. Ridley Hall Cam 66. **d** 68 **p** 69 **c** 11. C Skewen *Llan* 68–72; C Penarth w Lavernock 72–74; PV, Succ and Sacr Roch Cathl 74–78; Min Can St Paul's Cathl *Lon* 78–83; Succ 79–83; Warden Coll Min Cans *Lon* 81–83; PV Westmr Abbey 83–90; V Ruislip St Martin *Lon* 83–90; Can Res and Prec Guildf Cathl 90–97; Sub-Dean 96–97; Dean Mon 97–11; V Newport St Woolos 97–11; Warden Guild of Ch Musicians 98–11; Bp St Helena 11–18; rtd 18; PtO *Llan* from 18; *Eur* from 07. *St Anne's, 1 Insole Close, Cardiff CF5 2HQ* T: (029) 2021 9291 E: richard.d.fenwick@gmail.com

FERGUSON, Aean Michael O'Shaun. b 39. CITC 87. **d** 90 **p** 91. NSM Kilmallock w Kilflynn, Kilfinane, Knockaney etc *L & K* 90; NSM Killaloe w Stradbally 90–94; NSM Adare and Kilmallock w Kilpeacon, Croom etc 94–97; C Killala w Dunfeeny, Crossmolina, Kilmoremoy etc *T, K & A* 97–00; I Skreen w Kilmacshalgan and Dromard 00–08; Can Killala Cathl 05–08; rtd 08; Dioc Information Officer *T, K & A* 04–09. *Rathlee, Easkey, Co Sligo, Republic of Ireland* T: (00353) (96) 49865 M: 87-812 1020 E: amferguson@yahoo.com

FERGUSON, Caroline Maria. b 64. Sunderland Univ BA 08. Lindisfarne Regional Tr Partnership 10. **d** 13 **p** 14. NSM Darlington St Mark w St Paul *Dur* 13–17; PtO from 18. *19 Wallington Drive, Darlington DL1 2FA* M: 07816-154355 E: caroline.ferguson@ntlworld.com

FERGUSON, Jane Louise. *See* PLACKETT-FERGUSON, Jane Louise

FERGUSON, John Rudland. b 87. Derby Univ BSc 09. Qu Foundn Birm 18. **d** 21. NSM Derby St Barn from 21. *18 Manor School View, Overseal, Swadlincote DE12 6LN* M: 07803-511027 E: john@jfnetworks.uk

FERGUSON, Mrs Kathleen. b 46. LMH Ox BA 68 MA 72 ALA 76. St As Minl Tr Course 86. **d** 88 **p** 97. NSM Llanidloes w Llangurig *Ban* 88–01; P-in-c Llanidloes w Trefeglwys w Penstrowed 01–02; V 02–04; AD Arwystli 02–04; NSM Shelswell *Ox* 04–07; rtd 07; PtO *Ban* from 07. *Trawsnant, 18 Maes Trannon, Trefeglwys, Caersws SY17 5QX* T: (01686) 430666 E: kathy@oerle.co.uk

FERGUSON (née PASTERFIELD), Laura Sophia. b 85. Univ of the Arts Lon BA 07 Rob Coll Cam BTh 13. Ridley Hall Cam 11. **d** 13 **p** 14. C Liv All SS 13–16; PtO *Bris* 17–19; TV St Luke in the City *Liv* from 20. *7 Crossley Drive, Liverpool L15 8AJ* M: 07557-501582 E: laurasophiaferguson@gmail.com

FERGUSON, Michael Gary. b 89. Trin Coll Bris 16. **d** 19 **p** 20. C Sutton *Liv* 19–21; C Aigburth from 21. *7 Crossley Drive, Liverpool L15 8AJ* M: 07535-497830 E: fergiebromik@gmail.com

✠**FERGUSON, The Rt Revd Paul John.** b 55. New Coll Ox BA 76 MA 80 K Coll Cam BA 84 MA 88 FRCO 75. Westcott Ho Cam 82. **d** 85 **p** 86 **c** 14. C Ches St Mary 85–88; Sacr and Chapl Westmr Abbey 88–92; Prec 92–95; Can Res and Prec York Minster 95–01; Adn Cleveland 01–14; Warden of Readers 04–14; Suff Bp Whitby from 14; Can and Preb York Minster from 01; Asst Bp S & M from 18. *21 Thornton Road, Stainton, Middlesbrough TS8 9DS* T: (01642) 593273 E: bishopofwhitby@yorkdiocese.org

FERGUSON, Paul Stephen. b 80. Trin Hall Cam BA 02 MA 05. St Mellitus Coll BA 16. **d** 16 **p** 17. C Onslow Square and S Kensington St Aug *Lon* 16–19; V Bath Odd Down w Combe Hay B & W from 19. *39 Frome Road, Bath BA2 2QF* M: 07778-597491

FERGUSON, Peter Armstrong. **d** 10 **p** 11. C Carrickfergus *Conn* 10–15; I Derg w Termonamongan *D & R* from 15. *The Rectory, 13 Strabane Road, Castlederg BT81 7HZ* T: (028) 8167 9433 E: peteferg50@hotmail.com *or* derg@derry.anglican.org

FERGUSON, Raymond. *See* FERGUSON, Wallace Raymond

FERGUSON, Robert Garnett Allen. b 48. Leeds Univ LLB 70 Clare Coll Cam. Cuddesdon Coll 71. **d** 73 **p** 74. C Wakef Cathl 73–76; V Lupset 76–83; Chapl Cheltenham Coll 83–87; Sen Chapl Win Coll 87–05; PtO *S & M* from 09; *Eur* from 16. *Follaton, Highfield Drive, Baldrine, Isle of Man IM4 6EE*

FERGUSON, Robin Sinclair. b 31. Worc Coll Ox BA 53 MA 57 Lon Univ CertEd 63. ALCD 55 Wycliffe Coll Toronto 55. **d** 57 **p** 58. C Brompton H Trin *Lon* 57–60; C Brixton St Matt *S'wark* 60–63; Hon C Framlingham w Saxtead *St E* 63–65; Hon C Haverhill 65–67; Chapl St Mary's Sch Richmond 67–75; C Richmond St Mary w St Matthias *S'wark* 68–76; P-in-c Shilling Okeford *Sarum* 76–87; Chapl Croft Ho Sch Shillingstone 76–87; R Milton Abbas, Hilton

w Cheselbourne etc *Sarum* 87–96; rtd 96; PtO *Sarum* from 98. *Durnovaria, East Walls, Wareham BH20 4NJ* T: (01929) 551340 E: revrob@btinternet.com

FERGUSON, Ronald Leslie. b 36. Open Univ BA 86 BA 89. Chich Th Coll 65. **d** 68 **p** 69. C Toxteth Park St Marg *Liv* 68–72; C Oakham w Hambleton and Egleton *Pet* 72–74; Asst Chapl The Dorothy Kerin Trust Burrswood 74–76; V Castleside *Dur* 76–96; C Washington 96–99; P-in-c Eighton Banks 99–06; Chapl Gateshead Health NHS Trust 96–06; rtd 06; PtO *Dur* 07–18. *2 Lapwing Court, Burnopfield, Newcastle upon Tyne NE16 6LP* T: (01207) 271559 E: ronald.ferguson@mac.com

FERGUSON (née PAMPLIN), Mrs Samantha Jane. b 71. St Andr Univ MTheol 06. TISEC 06. **d** 08 **p** 09. C Aberdeen St Pet *Ab* 08–10; C Aberdeen St Jo 08–10; P-in-c Aberdeen St Ninian 10–14; Chapl Aber Univ 11–14; Chapl NHS Grampian 12–13; R Montrose *Bre* 14–17; R Inverbervie 14–17; R Pittenweem *St And* 17–18; R Elie and Earlsferry 17–18; Asst Chapl St Andr Univ from 19. *3 Silverdyke Gardens, Cellardyke, Anstruther KY10 3FH* T: (01333) 313798 M: 07971-231709 E: revsamferguson@gmail.com

FERGUSON, Wallace Raymond. b 47. Qu Coll Birm BTheol CITC 76. **d** 78 **p** 79. C Lurgan Ch the Redeemer *D & D* 78–80; I Newtownards w Movilla Abbey 80–84; I Mullabrack w Markethill and Kilcluney *Arm* 84–00; I Carnteel and Crilly 00–05; Hon V Choral Arm Cathl 86–05; Dioc Chapl to Rtd Clergy 92–05; Dean Kilmore *K, E & A* 05–14; I Kilmore w Ballintemple 05–14; All-Ireland Chapl MU 12–14; rtd 14. *81 Drumady Road, Stralustin, Newtownbutler, Enniskillen BT92 6NP* T: (028) 6775 1386 E: deanraymondferguson@gmail.com

FERGUSON, Mrs Zoë Marie. b 75. ERMC 09. **d** 12 **p** 13. C Trunch *Nor* 12–14; C Gaywood 14–16; P-in-c Mundford w Lynford 16–19; C Hilborough w Bodney 16–17; P-in-c 17–19; C Oxborough w Foulden and Caldecote 16–17; P-in-c 17–19. *Address temp unknown* M: 07767-878721 E: revzoe@hotmail.co.uk

FERGUSON-STUART, Hamish. b 51. Open Univ BA 92 Cardiff Univ MTh 10 RGN. **d** 99 **p** 00. OLM Burton St Chad *Lich* 99–05; Asst Chapl Rotherham NHS Foundn Trust 05–16; rtd 16; PtO *Lich* from 16. *210 Derby Road, Burton-on-Trent DE14 1RN* T: (01283) 510447 E: jacobus-senior@talk21.com

FERGUSSON, Norma. b 52. St Hilda's Coll Ox BA 73 MA 83. Sarum Coll 08. **d** 11 **p** 12. NSM Rowde and Bromham *Sarum* 11–14; NSM Shrivenham and Ashbury *Ox* 14–19; V from 19; PtO *Sarum* 14–20. *St Andrew's Vicarage, High Street, Shrivenham, Swindon SN6 8AN* M: 07799-545035 E: rev.n.fergusson@btinternet.com

FERMER, Richard Malcolm. b 71. St Pet Coll Ox BA 94 K Coll Lon MA 95 PhD 02 Surrey Univ PGCE 96. Coll of Resurr Mirfield 00. **d** 02 **p** 03. C Palmers Green St Jo *Lon* 02–05; USPG Brazil 05–09; Asst Chapl Paris St Geo *Eur* 09–12; P-in-c Grosvenor Chpl *Lon* from 12. *24 South Audley Street, London W1K 2PA* T: (020) 7499 1684 E: richard.fermer@grosvenorchapel.org.uk

FERN, John. b 36. Nottm Univ BA 57 MA 88. Coll of Resurr Mirfield 57. **d** 59 **p** 60. C Carlton *S'well* 59–61; C Hucknall Torkard 61–68; V Rainworth 68–97; rtd 97; PtO *S'well* 03–11. *4 Fosbrooke House, 8 Clifton Drive, Lytham St Annes FY8 5RQ*

FERNANDES, José Augusto dos Santos (Joseph). b 70. Lisbon Univ BA 95. Ripon Coll Cuddesdon BTh 15. **d** 15 **p** 16. C Horton and Wraysbury *Ox* 15–18; V Ashford St Hilda *Lon* from 18; AD Spelthorne from 20. *St Hilda's Vicarage, 8 Station Crescent, Ashford TW15 3HH* T: (01784) 245712 M: 07999-053433 E: joaufer@hotmail.com

FERNANDES, Sheila Maud. b 45. Punjab Univ MB, BS 69. NTMTC 05. **d** 08 **p** 09. NSM Leyton Em *Chelmsf* 08–12; NSM Tye Green w Netteswell 12–15; rtd 15; PtO *Chelmsf* from 15. *19 Wedgewood Drive, Harlow CM17 9PX* T: (01279) 629791

FERNÁNDEZ, Hugo. *See* ADÁN FERNÁNDEZ, Hugo Federico

FERNANDEZ, Mrs Valerie Anne. b 48. WMMTC 03. **d** 05 **p** 06. C Mile Cross *Nor* 05–08; P-in-c Doddington w Benwick and Wimblington *Ely* 08–11; rtd 11; PtO *Llan* from 11. *51 Glyn Bedw, Llanbradach, Caerphilly CF83 3PF* T: (029) 2088 2725 E: revval@btinternet.com

FERNANDEZ-SMAL, Manuel Lorenzo. b 68. Louvain Univ BA 92 MA 97 STL 97. **d** 97 **p** 97. C Battersea St Mary *S'wark* 04–08; V Malden St Jas 08–17; P-in-c Battersea St Luke 17–19; V from 19. *52 Thurleigh Road, London SW12 8UD* T: (020) 8673 6506 *or* 8772 0463 M: 07780-914434 E: lorenzo.fernandez@mac.com

FERNANDO, Joy. *See* FERNANDO, Susan Joy

FERNANDO, Percy Sriyananda. b 49. St And Dioc Tr Course 85. **d** 88 **p** 89. NSM Blairgowrie *St And* 88–93; NSM Alyth and Coupar Angus 89–93. *Gowrie Cottage, Perth Road, Blairgowrie PH10 6QB* E: percyf@hotmail.com

FERNANDO, Mrs Susan Joy. b 50. Nottm Univ CertEd 77 BEd 78. Linc Th Coll 83. **dss** 85 **d** 87 **p** 20. Kingsbury H Innocents *Lon* 85–88; Par Dn 87–88; Par Dn Harmondsworth 88–91; PtO *Guildf* 91–92 and 93–94; C Frimley 92–93; Chapl Grove Sch Hindhead 92–94; PtO *Nor* from 20. *12A Bells Park, Lynn Road, Swaffham PE37 7BN* T: (01760) 725938 M: 07905-039201 E: joy.fernando@live.co.uk

FERNELEY, Alastair John. b 69. Roehampton Inst BA 93 K Coll Lon MA 94 Birm Univ MPhil 98 St Jo Coll Dur MA 02. Cranmer Hall Dur 00. **d** 02 **p** 03. C Skipton Ch Ch *Bradf* 02–05; P-in-c Scalby *York* 05–14; V 14–16; P-in-c Scarborough St Luke 05–14; V 14–16; V Ravenscar and Staintondale 14–16; V Hackness w Harwood Dale 14–16; V Dacre w Hartwith and Darley w Thornthwaite *Leeds* from 16. *The Vicarage, Dacre Banks, Harrogate HG3 4ED* T: (01423) 780262 E: irreverend@btinternet.com

FERNS, Canon Stephen Antony Dunbar. b 61. St Chad's Coll Dur 84 MA 94. Ripon Coll Cuddesdon BA 87 MA 91. **d** 88 **p** 89. C Billingham St Cuth *Dur* 88–90; Chapl Dur Univ 91; Chapl Van Mildert and Trevelyan Colls Dur 91–95; V Norton St Mary 95–97; Bp's Dom Chapl *Blackb* 97–01; Voc Officer and Selection Sec Min Division 01–06; Sen Selection Sec 06–15; Sen Chapl to Bp Chich from 15; Can Res and Treas Chich Cathl 16–21; Can and Preb Chich Cathl from 21; PtO *Lon* 04–14. *The Palace, Chichester PO19 1PY* T: (01243) 782161 E: stephen.ferns@chichester.anglican.org

FERNS, Archdeacon of. *See* GRAY, The Ven Robert James

FERNS, Dean of. *See* MOONEY, The Very Revd Paul Gerard

FERNYHOUGH, Timothy John Edward. b 60. Leeds Univ BA 81. Linc Th Coll 81. **d** 83 **p** 84. C Daventry *Pet* 83–86; Chapl Tonbridge Sch 86–92; Chapl Dur Sch 92–02; Hd RS and Asst Chapl Radley Coll 02–17; R Lambfold *Pet* 17–20; rtd 20. *Address temp unknown* E: revtjef@gmail.com

FERRAR, Andrew Nicholas. b 46. Em Coll Cam MA 70 Liv Univ PhD 70. **d** 06 **p** 07. NSM St Alb St Sav from 06. *2 Tiberius Square, St Albans AL3 4GE* T: (01727) 685903 E: priest.stsaviours@gmail.com

FERRIER, Malcolm. b 38. Brasted Th Coll 65 St Mich Coll Llan 67. **d** 69 **p** 70. C Solihull *Birm* 69–73; C E Grinstead St Swithun *Chich* 73–75; V Saltley *Birm* 75–82; V Waterlooville *Portsm* 82–03; rtd 03. *44 Woodcock Gardens, Warminster BA12 9JG* T: (01985) 211344

FERRIS, Amanda Jane. b 61. RGN 83. SAOMC 00. **d** 03 **p** 04. NSM Letchworth St Paul w Willian *St Alb* from 03; Chapl E and N Herts NHS Trust 07–12; Chapl Milton Keynes Univ Hosp NHS Foundn Trust from 12; Spiritual Care Co-ord Garden Ho Hospice Letchworth from 18. *Rivendell, 33B Stotfold Road, Arlesey SG15 6XL* T: (01462) 834627 *or* (01908) 660033 M: 07780-670651 E: amanda.ferris@btinternet.com

FERRIS, Christopher. b 77. Univ of Wales (Lamp) BA 98. Trin Coll Bris 02. **d** 04 **p** 05. C Tunbridge Wells St Mark *Roch* 04–07; TV S Gillingham 07–11; C St John-at-Hackney *Lon* 11–14; Chapl Hackney Free and Paroch Sch 11–14; TR Chipping Barnet *St Alb* 14–19; PtO from 20. *16 The Ryde, Hatfield AL9 5DH* M: 07910-077885 E: frchris@ymail.com

FERRITER, Felicity Eunicé Myfanwy. b 54. Sheff Univ BA 76 Nottm Univ MA 98. EMMTC 95. **d** 98 **p** 99. NSM Retford S'well 98–03; Asst Chapl Rampton Hosp Retford 99–01; Asst Chapl Notts Healthcare NHS Trust 01–02; Chapl 02–03; Asst to AD Retford 03–04; C Rampton w Laneham, Treswell, Cottam and Stokeham S'well 04–11; C N and S Leverton 04–11; TV Retford Area 11–14; rtd 14; PtO S'well 16–19. *The Gables, Treswell Road, Rampton, Retford DN22 0HU* T: (01777) 248580   E: felicityemferriter@btinternet.com *or* felicity.ferriter@btinternet.com

FERRY, David Henry John. b 53. TCD BTh 88. **d** 88 **p** 89. C Enniskillen *Clogh* 88–90; I Leckpatrick w Dunnalong *D & R* 90–01; I Donagheady 01–12; I Balteagh w Carrick 12–19; I Tamlaghtard w Aghanloo 12–19; Bp's Dom Chapl 96–19; Can Derry Cathl 05–19; rtd 19. *15 Thorndale, Limavady BT49 0ST* M: 07813-983772 E: hdjferry@hotmail.com

FERRY, Malcolm Ronald Keith. b 66. QUB BEd 88. CITC BTh 96. **d** 96 **p** 97. C Agherton *Conn* 96–99; I Kilwaughter w Cairncastle and Craigy Hill 99–03; I Castlerock w Dunboe and Fermoyle *D & R* 03–08; I Clooney w Strathfoyle 08–14; I Londonderry St Aug 14–19; Can Derry Cathl 16–19; I Agherton *Conn* from 19. *59 Strand Road, Portstewart BT55 7LU* T: (028) 7083 3277 E: weechurch@btinternet.com

FERWERDA, Ms Ilse. b 71. Westmr Univ BSc 00 RGN 93. Qu Foundn Birm 13 WEMTC 14. **d** 16 **p** 17. C Northleach w Hampnett and Farmington etc *Glouc* 16–19; P-in-c Deerhurst and Apperley w Forthampton etc from 19. *The Vicarage, 1 The Green, Apperley, Gloucester GL19 4DQ* T: (01452) 780546 *or* 780880 E: revferwerda@gmail.com

FESSEY, Mrs Annis Irene. b 40. St Mary's Coll Chelt CertEd 60. Ripon Coll Cuddesdon 88. **d** 90 **p** 94. Par Dn

Bris St Andr Hartcliffe 90–94; C The Lydiards 94–95; C Penhill 95–00; rtd 00; PtO *Bris* 00–03; *Portsm* from 03. *Tintern, 17 Mayfield Road, Ryde PO33 3PR* T: (01983) 616466 E: annisfessey@gmail.com

FEWINGS, Peter Trenchard. b 53. WEMTC 12. **d** 14 **p** 15. NSM Sodbury Vale *Glouc* 14–15; NSM Charfield and Kingswood w Wickwar etc 15–17; NSM Sodbury Vale 17–19; NSM Lower Cam w Coaley from 19. *8 Highlands Drive, North Nibley, Dursley GL11 6DX* T: (01453) 436703 E: ptfewings@gmail.com

FEWKES, Jeffrey Preston. b 47. Derby Univ MA 99 DMin 04. Wycliffe Hall Ox 72. **d** 75 **p** 76. C Chester le Street *Dur* 75–78; C Kennington St Mark *S'wark* 78–81; V Bulwell St Jo *S'well* 81–98; V Stapleford 98–02; Victim Support Nottinghamshire 02–12; rtd 12; PtO *Derby* from 06. *3 Monks Close, Ilkeston DE7 5EY* T: 0115-930 2482 E: j.fewkes@btopenworld.com

FFRENCH (née WILLIAMS), Mrs Janet Patricia (Trish). b 59. Bradf Univ BTech 81. Trin Coll Bris BA 02. **d** 02 **p** 03. C Quinton Road W St Boniface *Birm* 02–05; C Mamble w Bayton, Rock w Heightington etc *Worc* 05–07; C Elmsett w Aldham, Hintlesham, Chattisham etc *St E* 07–17; C Horsmonden *Roch* from 17. *The Rectory, Goudhurst Road, Horsmonden, Tonbridge TN12 8JU* T: (01892) 732055 E: revsffrench@gmail.com

FFRENCH, Timothy Edward. b 58. Ball Coll Ox MA 86. Trin Coll Bris BA 01 MA 03. **d** 03 **p** 04. C Pedmore *Worc* 03–07; R Elmsett w Aldham, Hintlesham, Chattisham etc *St E* 07–17; R Horsmonden *Roch* from 17. *The Rectory, Goudhurst Road, Horsmonden, Tonbridge TN12 8JU* T: (01892) 732055 E: revsffrench@gmail.com

FFRENCH-HODGES, Christina Caroline. b 64. RGN 86. Aston Tr Scheme 94. **d** 99 **p** 00. C Castle Church *Lich* 99–02; C Rugby Cov 02–03; TV 03–05; PtO *Sheff* 06–07; NSM Arbourthorne and Norfolk Park 07–14; P-in-c Sheff St Jo 14–16; PtO 16–20. *All Hallows, Church Lane, High Hoyland, Barnsley S75 4BJ* M: 07850-660513 E: tinachodges@gmail.com

FFRENCH-HODGES, Jasper Tor. *See* HODGES, Jasper Tor

FIDDIAN-GREEN, Anthony Brian. b 39. Sussex Univ MA 88 Birm Univ CertEd 60 ACP 66. Bps' Coll Cheshunt 62. **d** 64 **p** 65. C Batheaston w St Cath *B & W* 64–67; Chapl Aiglon Coll and Chapl Villars *Eur* 67–71; Hd Master Battisborough Sch Holbeton 71–81; Chapl R Gr Sch Worc 81–83; Hd Master Frewen Coll Rye 83–96; P-in-c New Groombridge *Chich* 97–11; rtd 11; PtO *Chich* from 16. *21 Chatham Green, Eastbourne BN23 5PQ* T: (01323) 478533 E: revtfg@googlemail.com

FIDDYMENT, Alan John. b 40. Cant Sch of Min 91. **d** 94 **p** 95. NSM Chatham St Wm *Roch* 94–96; NSM Spalding St Mary and St Nic *Linc* 96–99; R Barkston and Hough Gp 99–07; rtd 07; PtO *Linc* from 07; *Pet* from 14. *5 Ascot Close, Spalding PE11 3BZ* T: (01775) 712837 M: 07706-367387 E: alan.fiddyment@gmail.com

FIDLER, John Harvey. b 49. Hatf Poly BSc 72. St Alb Minl Tr Scheme 84. **d** 87 **p** 88. NSM Royston *St Alb* from 87; PtO *Ely* 00–14. *8 Stamford Avenue, Royston SG8 7DD* T: (01763) 241886

FIELD, David Hibberd. b 36. K Coll Cam BA 58. Oak Hill Th Coll 58. **d** 60 **p** 61. C Aldershot H Trin *Guildf* 60–63; C Margate H Trin *Cant* 63–66; Sec Th Students Fellowship 66–68; Tutor Oak Hill Th Coll 68–93; Vice Prin 79–93; Dean Minl Tr Course 88–93; Dir Professional Min Div CPAS 94–00; Patr Sec CPAS 94–00; PtO *Cov* 94–07; rtd 00. *25 Field Barn Road, Hampton Magna, Warwick CV35 8RX* T: (01926) 410291 E: d.field@sky.com

FIELD, The Very Revd Gerald Gordon. b 54. K Coll Lon BD 75 AKC 75. Coll of Resurr Mirfield 76. **d** 77 **p** 78. C Broughton *Blackb* 77–79; C Blackpool St Steph 79–82; V Skerton St Luke 82–86; NSM Westleigh St Pet *Man* 92–93; V Shap w Swindale and Bampton w Mardale *Carl* 93–97; P-in-c Netherton 97; V 98–01; I Tullamore w Durrow, Newtownfertullagh, Rahan etc *M & K* 01–14; Can Meath 10–14; Can Kildare Cathl 10–14; Dean Cashel *C, F & O* from 14; I Cashel w Magorban, Tipperary, Clonbeg etc from 14. *Address temp unknown* M: 87-908 3821

FIELD, James Lewis. b 46. Open Univ BSc 96. SEITE 94. **d** 97 **p** 98. NSM Chatham St Mary w St Jo *Roch* 97–00; R Gravesend H Family w Ifield 00–08; P-in-c New Romney w Old Romney and Midley *Cant* 08–12; R Romney Marsh 12–14; rtd 14. *14 York Road, Littlehampton BN17 6EN* T: (01903) 713601 M: 07591-497378 E: revjamesfield@gmail.com

FIELD, Jeremy Mark. b 75. St Jo Coll Dur BA 96. Ridley Hall Cam 10. **d** 10 **p** 11. C Onslow Square and S Kensington St Aug *Lon* 10–13; C Teddington St Mark and Hampton Wick 13–17; V Hampton Wick from 17. *198 Broom Road, Teddington TW11 9PQ* T: (020) 8977 7733 M: 07767-784011 E: jerryfield@hotmail.com *or* jerry@stjohnshamptonwick.org

FIELD, Martin Richard. b 55. Keswick Hall Coll CertEd 76 Leic Univ MA 87. St Jo Coll Nottm BTh 82. **d** 82 **p** 83. C Gaywood, Bawsey and Mintlyn *Nor* 82–85; PtO *Leic* 85–87; Hon C S'well Minster 87–88; Hon C Stand *Man* 88–89; Dioc Press and Communications Officer 88–91; CUF 91–95; PtO *Cant* 96–99; Fundraising and Campaigns Dir Children's Soc 04–09; UK Dir of Fundraising Barnardo's 09–12; Dir Br Liver Trust 12–13; Dir Alabaré Chr Care Centres 15–17; Dir R Hosp Chelsea from 17; PtO *Sarum* 13–18; *Lon* from 20. *40 Elm Grove Road, Salisbury SP1 1JW* T: (01722) 502910 *or* (020) 7881 5334 M: 07902-394242 E: martin@fieldfamily.me.uk

FIELD, Preb Olwen Joyce. b 53. St Jo Coll Nottm 86. **d** 88 **p** 94. Par Dn Kensal Rise St Mark and St Martin *Lon* 88–91; Par Dn Northwood H Trin 91–94; C 94–95; Chapl Mt Vernon Hosp 91–99; P-in-c W Drayton 99–03; V 03–12; V Preston 12–20; Dean of Women's Min Willesden Area 01–03; AD Hillingdon 03–08; Dir of Ords Willesden Area 09–20; Preb St Paul's Cathl 10–20; rtd 20. *63 Beech Road, Saxmundham IP17 1FQ* M: 07901-563426 E: olwenfield123@btinternet.com

FIELD, Richard Colin. b 33. St Cath Soc Ox BA 54 MA 63. Clifton Th Coll 63. **d** 65 **p** 66. C Highbury Ch Ch *Lon* 65–70; V Hanger Lane St Ann 70–85; V Leytonstone St Jo *Chelmsf* 85–98; rtd 98; PtO *Chich* from 99. *3 St Thomas Court, Cliffe High Street, Lewes BN7 2AW* T: (01273) 472884 E: richard.field3@btinternet.com

FIELD, The Ven Susan Elizabeth. b 59. York Univ BA 80 Birm Univ CertEd 81 Ox Univ MTh 98. Qu Coll Birm 84. **d** 87 **p** 94. C Coleshill *Birm* 87–90; Chapl Loughb Univ *Leic* 91–98; TV Loughborough Em and St Mary in Charnwood 98–14; V Nanpantan St Mary in Charnwood 15–18; Dir Post-Ord Tr 95–04; Bp's Adv for Women's Min 97–04; Dioc Dir of Ords 04–18; Hon Can Leic Cathl 04–18; Adn Cov from 18; Chapl to The Queen from 17. *Cathedral and Diocesan Offices, 1 Hill Top, Coventry CV1 5AB* T: (024) 7652 1337 *or* 7669 7607 M: 07885-714829 E: sue.field@coventry.anglican.org

FIELDEN, Elizabeth Ann. b 42. TCert 63. **d** 99 **p** 00. OLM Broughton Gifford, Gt Chalfield and Holt *Sarum* 99–12; OLM Atworth w Shaw and Whitley 07–12; OLM Melksham 07–12; rtd 12; PtO *Sarum* from 12. *19 The Street, Broughton Gifford, Melksham SN12 8PW* T: (01255) 782509 E: fieldenann@gmail.com

FIELDEN, Henry Nicholas. b 70. Southn Univ BSc 92. Ripon Coll Cuddesdon 19. **d** 21. C Bodicote *Ox* from 21. *47 Orwell Drive, Didcot OX11 7RX* M: 07909-560833 E: henrynf11@gmail.com

FIELDEN, Hugh. b 66. BNC Ox BA 88 Birm Univ PGCE 90. Qu Coll Birm 91. **d** 93 **p** 94. C Sholing *Win* 93–97; TV Bramley *Ripon* 97–02; TV Bingley All SS *Bradf* 02–07; P-in-c Earby 07; P-in-c Kelbrook 07; V Earby w Kelbrook 08–14; *Leeds* from 14. *The Vicarage, 40 Brookfield Way, Earby, Barnoldswick BB18 6YQ* T: (01282) 844877 E: hugh.fielden@leeds.anglican.org *or* hugh@fielden.me.uk

FIELDEN, Mrs Janice Winifred. b 46. Warwick Univ BEd 82 MEd 89. SAOMC 99. **d** 02 **p** 03. NSM Chipping Norton *Ox* 02–05; NSM Charlbury w Shorthampton from 05; AD Chipping Norton 12–15. *11 Broad Field Road, Yarnton, Kidlington OX5 1UL* T: (01608) 842072 E: jan@charlburychurch.uk

FIELDER, Joseph Neil. b 67. Univ of Wales BSc 89. Wycliffe Hall Ox 93. **d** 96 **p** 97. C Cheadle All Hallows *Ches* 96–00; V Preston St Steph *Blackb* 00–09; P-in-c Baxenden 09–12; Supernumerary P Blackb and Darwen Deanery 12–13; Chapl Bradf Teaching Hosps NHS Foundn Trust 13–20; Chapl Walsall Healthcare NHS Trust from 20. *Walsall Healthcare NHS Trust, Manor Hospital, Moat Road, Walsall WS2 9PS* T: (01922) 721172 M: 07944-182058

FIELDING, Joanna. *See* BAXTER FIELDING, Joanna Nicola

FIELDING, Robert David. b 67. Liv Univ BA 89 St Jo Coll Dur BA 08. Cranmer Hall Dur 07. **d** 08 **p** 09. C Formby St Pet *Liv* 08–10; Chapl Mersey Care NHS Trust 10–14; PtO *Blackb* 14–15; P-in-c Read and Simonstone 15–21; Chapl Man Univ NHS Foundn Trust from 19. *Manchester University NHS Foundation Trust, Cobbett House, Manchester Royal Infirmary, Oxford Road, Manchester M13 9WL* M: 07951-173434 E: robertdfielding@gmail.com

FIELDING, Canon Stephen Aubrey. b 67. Ulster Univ BSc 89 TCD BTh 93. CITC 90. **d** 93 **p** 94. C Bangor Abbey *D & D* 93–97; I Templepatrick w Donegore *Conn* 97–07; I Agherton 07–18; I Belfast Malone St Jo from 18; Can Belf Cathl from 18. *St John's Rectory, 86 Maryville Park, Belfast BT9 6LQ* T: (028) 9066 6644 *or* 9066 7861 E: malone@connor.anglican.org *or* secstjohns@btconnect.com

FIELDING, Canon Stephen Lister. b 52. Ch Ch Ox BA 73 MA 77 Barrister 74. SAOMC 04. **d** 07 **p** 08. NSM Welwyn *St Alb* 07–11; TV Albury, Braughing, Furneux Pelham, Lt

Hadham etc 11–14; Can Res Cov Cathl 14–16; C Kensington St Mary Abbots *Lon* 16–19; TV Hitchin and St Paul's Walden *St Alb* from 19. *The Vicarage, Bendish Lane, Whitwell, Hitchin SG4 8HX* M: 07760-287614 E: slfielding@hotmail.com

FIELDSEND, John Henry. b 31. BEM 20. Nottm Univ BSc 54 Lon Univ BD 61. Lon Coll of Div ALCD 59. **d** 61 **p** 62. C Pennington *Man* 61–64; C Didsbury Ch Ch 64–66; P-in-c Bayston Hill *Lich* 66–67; V 67–88; UK Dir CMJ 89–91; Dir and Min at Large CMJ 91–96; rtd 96; PtO *St Alb* 96–00; *Ox* 01–18. *58 Cedar Crescent, Thame OX9 2AU* T: (01844) 212559 E: jandefieldsend@btinternet.com

FIELDSON, Canon Robert Steven. b 56. Qu Coll Cam BA 78 MA 81 Wye Coll Lon MSc 79. St Jo Coll Nottm BA 86. **d** 87 **p** 88. C Walmley *Birm* 87–90; Chapl Protestant Ch in Oman 90–95; P-in-c Cofton Hackett w Barnt Green *Birm* 95–98; V 98–21; AD Kings Norton 00–06 and 16–20; Co-AD Kings Norton, Moseley and Shirley 20–21; Hon Can Birm Cathl 14–21; rtd 21; PtO *Birm* from 21. *6 Gonerby Court, Gonerby Hill Foot, Grantham NG31 8HT* E: rob@fieldson.co.uk

FIFE (née EVE), Hilary Anne. b 57. Lon Univ BEd 80. Ripon Coll Cuddesdon 89. **d** 91 **p** 94. Par Dn Coulsdon St Andr S'wark 91–94; C 94–95; Chapl Croydon Coll 92–94; Chapl Harestone Marie Curie Cen Caterham 94–98; Asst Chapl Mayday Healthcare NHS Trust Thornton Heath 94–02; Sen Chapl 02–10; Sen Chapl Croydon Health Services NHS Trust 10–18; Hon C Shirley St Geo *S'wark* from 08. *19 Greenview Avenue, Croydon CR0 7QW* T: (020) 8654 8685 *or* 8401 3105 E: hilary.fife@croydonhealth.nhs.uk *or* h.fife@nhs.uk *or* thefifes19@gmail.com

FIFE, Janet Heather. b 53. Sussex Univ BA 77 Man Univ MPhil 98. Wycliffe Hall Ox 84. **d** 87 **p** 94. Chapl Bradf Cathl 87–89; Par Dn York St Mich-le-Belfrey 89–92; Chapl Salford Univ *Man* 92–00; Hon TV Pendleton St Thos w Charlestown 92–95; Hon TV Pendleton 95–96; V Upton Priory *Ches* 00–10; P-in-c Marske in Cleveland *York* 10–14; rtd 14; PtO *York* 15–19. *12 Waterstead Crescent, Whitby YO21 1PY* T: (01947) 459604 E: jhfife@icloud.com

FIFE, Mrs Miriam Ann. b 64. ERMC 14. **d** 17 **p** 18. C Launditch and the Upper Nar *Nor* from 17. *The Rectory, Great Dunham, King's Lynn PE32 2LQ* E: miriam.fife@btinternet.com

FIGG, Robin Arthur Rex. b 62. RN Eng Coll Plymouth BScEng 84 Leeds Univ MA 13. Westcott Ho Cam 91. **d** 94 **p** 95. C Old Cleeve, Leighland and Treborough *B & W* 94–97; C Gt Berkhamsted *St Alb* 97–01; V Kildwick *Bradf* 01–14; *Leeds* 14–17; V Warton St Oswald w Yealand Conyers *Blackb* from 17. *The Vicarage, 92 Main Street, Warton, Carnforth LA5 9PG* T: (01524) 732946 E: vicarwby@outlook.com

FIKSEAUNET, Mrs Torhild Holen. b 81. Norwegian Univ of Science and Tech MTech 07 Oslo Univ BA 14. ERMC 16. **d** 19 **p** 20. C Heathfield *Chich* from 19. *The Vicarage, Old Heathfield, Heathfield TN21 9AB* T: (01435) 862687 M: 07587-295676 E: torhild.fikseaunet@yahoo.no

FILES, Ian James. b 54. Loughb Univ BSc 76. Chich Th Coll 85. **d** 87 **p** 88. C Prestwich St Mary *Man* 87–89; C Man Clayton St Cross w St Paul 89–91; PtO *Blackb* from 12. *16 Stanah Gardens, Thornton-Cleveleys FY5 5JH* T: (01253) 854482 M: 07578-547081 E: ianfiles691@btinternet.com

FILIPE LOPES, Marco Gonzaga. b 73. St Mellitus Coll MA 19. **d** 19 **p** 20. C E Ham H Trin *Chelmsf* from 19; C Plaistow St Martin from 21. *34 St Martin's Avenue, London E6 3DX* M: 07506-926443 E: rev.marco.lopes@gmail.com

FILLERY, Paul Leslie. b 61. Ex Univ BTh 14. SWMTC 08. **d** 11 **p** 12. C Crediton, Shobrooke and Sandford etc *Ex* 11–21; NSM 11–16; V Martock w Kingsbury Episcopi and Ash *B & W* from 21. *The Vicarage, 1 New Street, Long Sutton, Langport TA10 9JW*

FILLERY, William Robert. b 42. Univ of Wales (Swansea) BA 65 St D Coll Lamp BD 69 PGCE 72 Surrey Univ MA 96. Bp Burgess Hall Lamp 65. **d** 68 **p** 69. C Llangyfelach *S & B* 68–71; C Morriston 71–72; LtO *Ox* 73–76; Chapl Windsor Girls's Sch Hamm W Germany 76–81; OCM 79–81; Chapl Reed's Sch Cobham 81–86; V Oxshott *Guildf* 86–89; P-in-c Seale 89–91; P-in-c Puttenham and Wanborough 89–91; Hd RE Streatham Hill & Clapham Sch for Girls 91–03; V Llanybydder and Llanwenog w Llanllwni *St D* 03–10; rtd 10; PtO *St D* from 10. *Afon Del, Falcondale Drive, Lampeter SA48 7SB* T: (01570) 421425 M: 07792-958431 E: fillerybill@gmail.com

FILMER, Paul James. b 58. Open Univ BA 88. Aston Tr Scheme 93 Oak Hill Th Coll 95. **d** 97 **p** 98. C Petham and Waltham w Lower Hardres etc *Cant* 97–00; P-in-c Patrixbourne w Bridge and Bekesbourne 00–06; P-in-c Lower Hardres w Nackington 00–06; Chapl Univ of Greenwich *Roch* 06–09; Chapl Univ for the Creative Arts 06–09; V Yalding w Collier Street 09–15; Chapl Kenward Trust 11–15; PtO *Roch* 16–19; V Prince's Park from 19.

6 Thrush Close, Chatham ME5 7TG   M: 07951-773426
E: vicarchristtheking@gmail.com

FILTNESS, Trevor Moshe. b 50. MNI MInstD. STETS 05.
d 08 p 09. NSM Farlington *Portsm* 08–11; NSM Rowlands
Castle 11–13; P-in-c 13–18; rtd 18. *24 Orchard Road, Brixton,
Plymouth PL8 2FE*   M: 07785-568056 E: trevor@filtness.org

FINCH, Alan James. b 51. d 06 p 07. OLM Orrell Hey St Jo
and St Jas *Liv* 06–15; NSM Litherland St Phil 15–18; NSM
Litherland and Orrell Hey from 19. *1 Kirkstone Road North,
Liverpool L21 7NP*   T: 0151-928 3919

FINCH, Mrs Alison. b 59. SEN 79. Sarum & Wells Th Coll 90.
d 92 p 94. Par Dn Banbury *Ox* 92–94; C 94–95; C Wokingham
All SS 95–98; C Binfield 98–99; C St Peter-in-Thanet *Cant*
99–02; R Kirkwall and P-in-c Stromness *Ab* 02–05; Ind Chapl
and C Colchester St Pet and St Botolph *Chelmsf* 05–13; TV
High Wycombe *Ox* 13–18; rtd 18; NSM Seaton and Beer *Ex*
from 20. *Address temp unknown*   M: 07762-744977

FINCH, Canon David Walter. b 40. Cam Univ MA 74
FIBMS 69. Ridley Hall Cam. d 91 p 92. C Ixworth and
Bardwell *St E* 91–92; C Blackbourne 92–94; P-in-c Stoke
by Nayland w Leavenheath 94–00; P-in-c Polstead 95–00;
P-in-c Fressingfield, Mendham, Metfield, Weybread etc
00–08; C Hoxne w Denham, Syleham and Wingfield
06–08; RD Hoxne 00–07; Hon Can St E Cathl 05–08;
rtd 08; PtO *St E* 08–21; LtO *Ab* 08–12; Hon C Cen
Buchan 10–12; Dioc Retirement Officer *St E* from 15. *3
Fleetwood Avenue, Felixstowe IP11 9HR*   T: (01394) 277061
E: canondavidfinch@btinternet.com

FINCH, Frank. b 33. Qu Coll Birm 72. d 74 p 75. C Bilston
St Leon *Lich* 74–78; R Sudbury and Somersal Herbert *Derby*
78–87; Chapl HM Pris Sudbury 78–87; HM Det Cen Foston
Hall 80–87; V Lilleshall and Sheriffhales *Lich* 87–90; R The
Ridwares and Kings Bromley 90–98; rtd 98; PtO *Lich* 00–21.
11 Ferrers Road, Yoxall, Burton-on-Trent DE13 8PS   T: (01543)
472065

FINCH, Jeffrey Walter. b 45. Man Univ BA(Econ) 66 Liv
Univ DASE 80. Linc Th Coll 82. d 84 p 85. C Briercliffe
Blackb 84–87; P-in-c Brindle and Asst Dir of Educn 87–93;
V Laneside 93–00; TV Fellside Team 00–08; TR 08–14; rtd
14; PtO *Blackb* from 14. *21 Cock Robin Lane, Catterall, Preston
PR3 1YL*   T: (01995) 601171 E: jeffinch187@yahoo.com

FINCH, Morag Anne Hamilton. b 64. EAMTC 97. d 00 p 01. C
Cranham *Chelmsf* 00–05; V Gidea Park 05–13; V Shortlands
Roch 13–18; NSM Leiston *St E* from 18; Chapl St Eliz Hospice
Ipswich from 19. *The Vicarage, Church Road, Leiston IP16 4HG*
E: revfinch@btinternet.com

FINCH, Paul William. b 50. Oak Hill Th Coll Lon Bible
Coll. d 75 p 76. C Hoole *Ches* 75–78; C Charlesworth
Derby 78–87; C Charlesworth and Dinting Vale 87–88; TV
Radipole and Melcombe Regis *Sarum* 88–01; V Malvern
St Andr and Malvern Wells and Wyche *Worc* 01–14; TR
Malvern Chase 14–15; rtd 15. *Address withheld by request*
E: paulwfinch@gmail.com

FINCH, Richard William. b 62. Glos Univ MA 16. Westcott
Ho Cam 95. d 97 p 98. C Saffron Walden w Wendens Ambo
and Littlebury *Chelmsf* 97–00; C Elm Park St Nic Hornchurch
00–01; V 01–10; Chapl and Faith Support Officer Forest
YMCA 10–15; Hon C Gidea Park *Chelmsf* 11–13; Public
Preacher 13–18; NSM Shortlands *Roch* 13–18; P-in-c Leiston
St E from 18. *The Vicarage, Church Road, Leiston IP16 4HG*
E: rich.w.finch@gmail.com

FINCH, Miss Rosemary Ann. b 39. Leeds Univ CertEd 60.
d 93 p 94. OLM S Elmham and Ilketshall *St E* 93–00; Asst
Chapl Ipswich Hosp NHS Trust 00–11; rtd 11; PtO *St E*
11–15; *Glouc* from 14. *Grace House, 15 Weston Park, Weston
under Penyard, Ross-on-Wye HR9 7FR*   T: (01989) 565019
E: revrosie.finch@btinternet.com

FINCH, Canon Stanley James. b 31. Mert Coll Ox BA 55
MA 58. Wells Th Coll 55. d 57 p 58. C Lancaster St Mary
Blackb 57–61; C Leeds St Pet *Ripon* 61–65; V Habergham
All SS *Blackb* 65–73; V S Shore H Trin 73–84; V Broughton
84–98; RD Preston 86–92; Hon Can Blackb Cathl 91–98; rtd
98; P-in-c Alderton, Gt Washbourne, Dumbleton etc *Glouc*
98–02; PtO from 02. *14 Bellflower Road, Walton Cardiff,
Tewkesbury GL20 7SB*   T: (01684) 850544

FINCH, Stephen James. b 91. Univ of Wales (Trin St Dav) BA 14.
Oak Hill Th Coll 18. d 20 p 21. C Hawkwell *Chelmsf* from 20.
The Vicarage, 6A Silvertree Close, Hockley SS5 4SP   M: 07795-
434015 E: steve.finch@hawkwellparishchurch.org

FINCHAM, Nicholas Charles. b 56. St Jo Coll Dur BA 78
MA 80. Westcott Ho Cam 80 Bossey Ecum Inst Geneva 81.
d 82 p 83. C Seaham w Seaham Harbour *Dur* 82–85; C
Lydney w Aylburton *Glouc* 85–87; C Isleworth All SS *Lon*
87–95; P-in-c Chiswick St Mich 95–10; rtd 10; PtO *Chich*
from 16. *7 Harding Avenue, Eastbourne BN22 8PH*   T: (01323)
638273 E: nicholas.fincham@talk21.com

FINDLAY, James. b 68. Bp Otter Coll BA 90 Westmr Coll Ox
PGCE 92. Wycliffe Hall Ox 02. d 04 p 05. C Gillingham
St Mark *Roch* 04–07; P-in-c Salisbury St Mark *Sarum*
07–13; V Salisbury St Mark and Laverstock 13–17; Asst
Dioc Dir of Ords 13–17; P-in-c Throop *Win* from 17. *1
Chesildene Avenue, Bournemouth BH8 0AZ*   T: (01202)
525525   M: 07854-510569 E: office@stpaulsthroop.com *or*
vicarjimfindlay@gmail.com

FINDLAYSON, Roy. b 44. Man Univ MA 89 CQSW 69. Sarum
& Wells Th Coll 80. d 82 p 83. C Benwell St Jas *Newc* 82–83;
Hon C 83–85; C Morpeth 85–88; C N Gosforth 88; TV Ch
the King 88–94; V Newc St Fran 94–98; Asst Chapl Newcastle
upon Tyne Hosps NHS Trust 98–06; Chapl Marie Curie Cen
Newc 98–06; rtd 06. *6A Hawthorn Mews, Newcastle upon Tyne
NE3 4DA* E: findlayson44@icloud.com

FINDLEY, Peter. b 55. Trin Coll Ox BA 77 MA 80 Barrister-
at-Law (Gray's Inn) 78. Trin Coll Bris 90. d 92 p 93. C
Yateley *Win* 92–97; V Westwood *Cov* 97–14; P-in-c Canley
09–14; Sen Miss P Philadelphia St Thos *Sheff* 14–20; rtd
20. *30 Victoria Road, Sheffield S10 2DL*   T: 0114-214 9560
E: peterfindley@outlook.com

FINDON, John Charles. b 50. Keble Coll Ox BA 71
MA 75 DPhil 79. Ripon Coll Cuddesdon. d 77 p 78.
C Middleton *Man* 77–80; Lect Bolton St Pet 80–83; V
Astley 83–91; V Baguley 91–98; P-in-c Bury St Mary
98–05; R 05–17; rtd 17; PtO *Ox* from 17. *78 Oxford
Road, Littlemore, Oxford OX4 4PE*   T: (01865) 424356
E: john.findon@virginmedia.com

FINK-JENSEN, Thomas Karel. b 86. Ede Chr Coll BEd 11.
Wycliffe Hall Ox BA 18. d 19. C Lancing St Mich *Chich*
from 19. *1 Annington Gardens, Shoreham-by-Sea BN43 5GS*
E: revthomasfj@gmail.com

FINLAY, Alison Mary. *See* CAW, Alison Mary

FINLAY, Canon Hueston Edward. b 64. TCD BA 85 BAI 85
BTh 89 MA 92 Cam Univ MA 98 Lon Univ PhD 98. CITC 86.
d 89 p 90. C Kilkenny w Aghour and Kilmanagh *C, F & O*
89–92; Bp's Dom Chapl 89–92; Bp's V and Lib Kilkenny
Cathl 90–92; Chapl Girton Coll Cam 92–95; C Cambridge
Gt St Mary w St Mich *Ely* 92–95; Chapl and Fell Magd Coll
Cam 95–99; Dean of Chpl 99–04; Can Windsor from 04;
Treas St Patr Cathl Dublin 11–16. *8 The Cloisters, Windsor
Castle, Windsor SL4 1NJ*   T: (01753) 867094 F: 833806

FINLAY, Malcolm Armstrong. b 85. Univ Coll Lon
BSc 10. Wycliffe Hall Ox BTh 13. d 13 p 14. C Southall
Green St Jo *Lon* 13–16; C Broxbourne w Wormley
St Alb 16–19; PtO *Lon* 16–19; LtO from 19. *69
Southdown Crescent, Harrow HA2 0QT*   M: 07460-866562
E: rev.malcolm.finlay@gmail.com

FINLAY, Canon Michael Stanley. b 45. NOC 78. d 81 p 82.
C Padgate *Liv* 81–85; V Newton-le-Willows 85–90; V
Orford St Marg 90–98; P-in-c Warrington St Elphin 98–00;
R 00–11; Hon Can Liv Cathl 07–11; rtd 11; PtO *Ches* from
12. *40 Chatteris Park, Runcorn WA7 1XE*   T: (01928) 579354
E: finlay289@btinternet.com

FINLAY, Nicholas. b 47. Regent Coll Vancouver MCS 00. St Jo
Coll Nottm 01. d 02 p 03. C Haydock St Mark *Liv* 02–03; C
Bootle 03–04; Lic to Adn Warrington 04–05; V Sittingbourne
St Mary and St Mich *Cant* 05–09; rtd 09; C Upper Ithon
Valley and Lower Ithon Valley *S & B* 09–12; PtO *St D* from
11; *S & B* from 12; *Heref* 12–16; *Lich* 13–19; *Blackb* from
19; *Eur* 19–20; Chapl Grenoble from 21. *Eglise Anglicane,
14 rue Gérard Philipe, 38100 Grenoble, France*   T: (0033)
476545085   M: 07771-688812E: nick.finlay047@gmail.com
or chaplain@grenoblechurch.org

FINLAYSON, Mrs Gladys Victoria. b 49. TCert 67. ERMC 05.
d 09 p 10. NSM Luton St Anne w St Chris *St Alb* 09–11; PtO
from 11. *St Andrew's Vicarage, 11 Blenheim Crescent, Luton
LU3 1HA*   T: (01582) 732380 E: gladysfinlayson@sky.com

FINLAYSON, Grantley Adrian. b 55. Wilson Carlile Coll 74
Chich Th Coll 87. d 89 p 90. C Watford St Mich *St Alb* 89–92;
TV W Slough *Ox* 92–97; Dioc Officer for Race Relations
Glouc 97–02; V Luton St Andr *St Alb* from 02. *St Andrew's
Vicarage, 11 Blenheim Crescent, Luton LU3 1HA*   T: (01582)
732380   M: 07488-253848 E: grantleyfinlayson11@sky.com

FINLINSON, Paul. b 58. St Chad's Coll Dur BA 79 St Martin's
Coll Lanc PGCE 81. Carl Dioc Tr Course 86. d 89 p 90.
NSM Kirkby Lonsdale *Carl* 89–99; Chapl Worksop Coll
Notts 99–19; Chapl Ranby Ho Sch Retford 11–19; PtO
Blackb 95–19; *Carl* 14–19; *Eur* from 19; *York* from 19.
32 Sherwood Drive, Thorpe Willoughby, Selby YO8 9TN
E: p.finlinson@outlook.com

FINN, Andrew David. b 79. Cant Ch Ch Univ Coll BA 00
PGCE 01 Glos Univ MA 14. Ridley Hall Cam 13. d 15 p 16.
C Ingatestone w Fryerning *Chelmsf* 15–17; C Margaretting
w Mountnessing and Buttsbury 15–17; C Gt Baddow
17–18; P-in-c Southsea St Simon *Portsm* 18–20; TV W

Sevenoaks *Roch* from 21. *St Mary's Vicarage, The Glebe Field, Shoreham Lane, Sevenoaks TN13 3DR* T: (01732) 669454 E: revandyfinn@outlook.com

FINN, Ms Frances Anne. b 72. Trin Coll Bris BA 94 MA 20. **d** 20 **p** 21. C Nottingham St Nic *S'well* from 20. *The Nurseries, 1 Lambley Road, Lowdham, Nottingham NG14 7AZ* E: franbmail@btinternet.com

FINN, Gordon Frederick. b 33. Dur Univ BA 60. Ely Th Coll 60. **d** 62 **p** 63. C Kingswinford St Mary *Lich* 62–65; C Northampton St Mary *Pet* 65–67; Chapl Barnsley Hall Hosp Bromsgrove 67–71; Chapl Lea Hosp Bromsgrove 67–71; C Swanage *Sarum* 71–73; P-in-c Ford End *Chelmsf* 73–79; V S Shields St Oswin *Dur* 79–98; rtd 98. *58 Hutton Lane, Guisborough TS14 8AW* T: (01287) 619132

FINN, Canon Ian Michael. b 58. AKC. Chich Th Coll 81. **d** 82 **p** 83. C Habergham All SS *Blackb* 82–83; C W Burnley All SS 83–85; C Torrisholme 85–87; V Lancaster Ch Ch w St Jo and St Anne 87–91; P-in-c Tillingham and Dengie w Asheldham *Chelmsf* 91–97; Chapl R Gr Sch Worc 97–99; P-in-c Denston w Stradishall and Stansfield *St E* 99–01; P-in-c Wickhambrook w Lydgate, Ousden and Cowlinge 00–01; R Bansfield 02–07; V Haverhill w Withersfield 07–19; RD Clare 06–17; Hon Can St E Cathl 11–19; rtd 19. *Huggens College, College Road, Northfleet, Gravesend DA11 9DL* E: ian.finn1@btinternet.com

FINN, Mrs Jane Lisa. b 65. Open Univ BSc 14. Coll of Resurr Mirfield BA 18. **d** 18 **p** 19. C Halifax w Siddal *Leeds* from 18. *41 Gibraltar Road, Halifax HX1 4HE* T: (01422) 355436 E: j.finn@halifaxminster.org.uk

FINN, Miss Sheila. b 30. LMH Ox BA 68 MA 69. Gilmore Ho 68. **dss** 78 **d** 87 **p** 94. Tettenhall Wood *Lich* 78–86; Dioc Ecum Officer 86–95; The Ridwares and Kings Bromley 86–87; Par Dn 87–94; C 94–95; rtd 95; PtO *Lich* 97–21. *56 Pencric, Tildesley Close, Penkridge, Stafford ST19 5FG*

FINNEMORE, James Christopher. b 59. Pemb Coll Cam BA 81 MA 85. Coll of Resurr Mirfield. **d** 85 **p** 86. C Manston *Ripon* 85–88; C Hessle *York* 88–92; R Bishop Wilton w Full Sutton, Kirby Underdale etc 92–99; R Garrowby Hill 99–16; RD S Wold 07–12; PtO *Ox* from 17; *B & W* 16–20; *York* 16–19. *2 Carey Close, Oxford OX2 8HX* T: (01865) 558480 E: j.c.finnemore@btinternet.com

FINNEMORE, Thomas John. b 79. Hull Univ BA 01. Wycliffe Hall Ox 05. **d** 07 **p** 08. C Crookes St Thos *Sheff* 07–11 and 16–21; TR from 21; C Cambridge St Barn *Ely* 11–16. *18A Hallamgate Road, Sheffield S10 5BT* E: admin@stcsheffield.org

FINNERTY, Cynthia Ann. b 46. **d** 05 **p** 06. OLM E Greenwich *S'wark* 05–16; PtO from 16. *33 Ruthin Road, London SE3 7SJ* T: (020) 8858 2883 E: cynthiafin@hotmail.com

✠**FINNEY, The Rt Revd John Thornley.** b 32. Hertf Coll Ox BA 55. Wycliffe Hall Ox 56. **d** 58 **p** 59 **c** 93. C Highfield *Ox* 58–61; C Weston Turville 61–65; R Tollerton *S'well* 65–71; V Aspley 71–80; Bp's Adv on Evang 80–89; Bp's Research Officer 88–89; Hon Can S'well Minster 84–89; Officer for Decade of Evang in C of E 90–93; Suff Bp Pontefract *Wakef* 93–98; rtd 98; Hon Asst Bp S'well and Nottm from 98. *Greenacre, Crow Lane, South Muskham, Newark NG23 6DZ* T/F: (01636) 679791 E: john.finney2@talktalk.net

FIRBANK, Michael John. b 73. R Holloway Coll Lon BA 94 St Mary's Coll Twickenham PGCE 94. St Jo Coll Nottm MTh 05. **d** 05 **p** 06. C St Illogan *Truro* 05–07; P-in-c Camborne 07–13; P-in-c Tuckingmill 12–13; R Camborne and Tuckingmill 13–14; V Gresley *Derby* from 14; AD Mercia from 21. *The Vicarage, 120 Church Street, Church Gresley, Swadlincote DE11 9NR* T: (01283) 208947 M: 07814-033183 E: mjfirbank@hotmail.com

FIRMIN, Paul Gregory. b 57. Win Univ MA 11 ACIB 80. Trin Coll Bris BA 87. **d** 87 **p** 88. C Swindon Ch Ch *Bris* 87–91; V Shrewsbury H Trin w St Julian *Lich* 91–99; V Astley, Clive, Grinshill and Hadnall 99–01; V Southampton St Mary Extra *Win* 01–10; V Shrewsbury H Cross *Lich* 10–18; rtd 18; PtO *Lich* from 19. *Police House, Railway Road, Brymbo, Wrexham LL11 5EA* E: nimrifs@sky.com

FIRMSTONE, Ian Harry. b 44. Qu Coll Birm. **d** 82 **p** 83. C Warminster St Denys *Sarum* 82–84; C N Stoneham *Win* 84–88; R Freemantle 88–90; V Littleport *Ely* 90–91; TV Stanground and Farcet 91–97; P-in-c Holme w Conington 95–96; rtd 97; PtO *Worc* from 12; *Birm* 15–18. *Cotswold Cottage, School Lane, Alvechurch, Birmingham B48 7SA* T: 0121-445 1318 E: ianfirmstone@gmail.com

FIRTH, Mrs Ann Neswyn. b 40. St As Minl Tr Course 95. **d** 98 **p** 99. NSM Llanidloes w Llangurig *Ban* 98–05; LtO 05–11; PtO 11–18. *Springfield, Westgate Street, Llanidloes SY18 6HJ* T: (01686) 413098

FIRTH, Christopher John Kingsley. b 37. St Mich Coll Llan. **d** 66 **p** 67. C Sutton in Ashfield St Mary *S'well* 66–70; V Langold 70–74; C Falmouth K Chas *Truro* 74–77; P-in-c Mabe

77–81; V 81–95; RD Carnmarth S 90–94; rtd 99. *1 Boscawen, Cliff Road, Falmouth TR11 4AW* T: (01326) 316734

FIRTH, Geoffrey David. b 74. Lincs & Humberside Univ BA 96. Oak Hill Th Coll BA 08. **d** 06 **p** 07. C Poynton *Ches* 06–10; Chapl RAF from 10. *Chaplaincy Services (RAF), HQ Air Command, RAF High Wycombe HP14 4UE* T: (01494) 496800 E: geoffrey.firth485@mod.gov.uk *or* geoffreyfirth@gmail.com

FIRTH, Mrs Jennifer Anne. b 52. Goldsmiths' Coll Lon BMus 75 Kingston Poly PGCE 83. **d** 07 **p** 08. OLM Dorking St Paul *Guildf* from 07. *33 Downsview Gardens, Dorking RH4 2DX* T: (01306) 887051 M: 07970-102987 E: jennyafirth@aol.com *or* jenny@stpaulsdorking.org.uk

FIRTH, Matthew Paul. b 83. Magd Coll Cam BA 04 MA 08. Wycliffe Hall Ox BTh 09. **d** 09 **p** 10. C Triangle, St Matt and All SS *St E* 09–12; Chapl Cumbria Univ *Carl* 12–17; 18-30 Pioneer Min 12–17; P-in-c Darlington St Cuth *Dur* 18–20; P-in-c Darlington H Trin 18–20. *Address temp unknown* M: 07932-482929 E: mpf1983@hotmail.com

FIRTH, Neswyn. *See* FIRTH, Ann Neswyn

✠**FIRTH, The Rt Revd Peter James.** b 29. Em Coll Cam BA 52 MA 63. St Steph Ho Ox 53. **d** 55 **p** 56 **c** 83. C Barbourne *Worc* 55–58; C Malvern Link St Matthias 58–62; R Abbey Hey *Man* 62–66; Asst Network Relig Broadcasting BBC Man 66–67; Sen Producer/Org Relig Progr TV & Radio BBC Bris 67–83; Hon Can Bris Cathl 74–83; Suff Bp Malmesbury 83–94; Angl Adv HTV West 84–94; rtd 94; Hon Asst Bp Glouc from 03; Hon Asst Bp Bris from 09. *Mill House, Silk Mill Lane, Winchcombe, Cheltenham GL54 5HZ* T: (01242) 603669

FIRTH, Peter William Simpson. b 39. SEITE 99. **d** 11. NSM New Romney w Old Romney and Midley *Cant* 11–12; NSM Romney Marsh 12–14; rtd 14; PtO *Cant* 15–16. *114 Leonard Road, Greatstone, New Romney TN28 8RZ* T: (01797) 367296 E: firth166@btinternet.com

FIRTH, Canon Rachel Naomi. b 73. Huddersfield Univ BA 97 Leeds Univ BA 08 Sheff Univ MA 12. NOC 05. **d** 08 **p** 09. C Halifax *Wakef* 08–11; V Lindley 11–14; *Leeds* 14–20; V Huddersfield St Pet from 20; Adv for Women's Min Huddersfield Area from 15; AD Huddersfield from 19; Jt AD Kirkburton 19; Hon Can Wakef Cathl from 19. *The Vicarage, 59 Lightridge Road, Huddersfield HD2 2HF* T: (01484) 427964 E: rachel.firth@leeds.anglican.org

FIRTH, Richard Geoffrey. b 48. **d** 06 **p** 07. OLM Dur St Marg and Neville's Cross St Jo 06–08; PtO *York* from 08. *6 Vicarage Close, Seamer, Scarborough YO12 4QS* T: (01723) 867957 E: afirth9819@aol.com

FISH, Jacqueline Wendy. b 42. NTMTC 02. **d** 04 **p** 05. NSM Enfield Chase St Mary *Lon* 04–19; PtO from 19. *52 Waverley Road, Enfield EN2 7AQ* T: (020) 8366 2235 E: jacquiefishie@aol.com

FISH, Michael. b 61. Lanc Univ BA 05. CBDTI 01. **d** 04 **p** 05. NSM Blackb St Mich w St Jo and H Trin 04–07; NSM Blackb St Thos w St Jude 04–07; P-in-c Cen Buchan *Ab* 07–08; P-in-c Shrewsbury All SS w St Mich *Lich* 08–16; TV Swinton and Pendlebury *Man* 16–18; V Blackfordby and Woodville *Leic* 18–21; V Blackpool H Cross *Blackb* from 21. *Holy Cross Vicarage, 388 Central Drive, Blackpool FY1 6LA* M: 07867-760110 E: fr.michaelfish@btinternet.com

FISH, Thomas Ronald Huxley. b 59. Chu Coll Cam BA 81. Oak Hill Th Coll 11. **d** 13 **p** 14. C The Lye and Stambermill *Worc* 13–19; TV Wednesfield *Lich* from 19. *The Vicarage, St Albans House, Griffiths Drive, Wolverhampton WV11 2LJ* T: (01902) 732317 M: 07841-382773 E: revtomfish@gmail.com

FISHER, Ms Alexandria Compton. b 53. Glas Univ MA 75. St Mellitus Coll 14. **d** 17 **p** 18. NSM Wilmslow *Ches* 17–18; C Brereton 18–20; V from 20. *The Rectory, Brereton Park, Brereton, Sandbach CW11 1RY* T: (01477) 533263 M: 07456-433103 E: fishersandi123@gmail.com

FISHER, Mrs Alison. b 48. Cranmer Hall Dur 04. **d** 05 **p** 06. NSM The Thorntons and The Otteringtons *York* 05–11; rtd 11; PtO *York* 11–20. *31 Church Close, Marske-by-the-Sea, Redcar TS11 7AW* T: (01642) 488682 E: ali.fisher913@btinternet.com

FISHER, Andrew John. b 72. St Jo Coll Nottm BA 02 St Mich Coll Llan MTh 13. **d** 02 **p** 03. C Ilkeston St Jo *Derby* 02–05; P-in-c Hodge Hill *Birm* 05–08; Chapl Worcs Acute Hosps NHS Trust 08–13; V Wood End *Cov* 13–17; R Bulwell St Mary *S'well* from 17. *The Rectory, Station Road, Bulwell, Nottingham NG6 9AA* T: 0115-975 5358 E: a.j.fisher@outlook.com

FISHER, Brian Robert. b 36. **d** 02 **p** 03. OLM Sole Bay *St E* 02–07; rtd 07; PtO *St E* 07–20. *Green Gates, The Street, Walberswick, Southwold IP18 6UH* T: (01502) 723023 M: 07766-216111 E: fishell@btopenworld.com

FISHER, David Benjamin. b 52. Bp Lonsdale Coll CertEd 74. Chich Th Coll 75. **d** 78 **p** 79. C Dovecot *Liv* 78–81; C Weymouth St Paul *Sarum* 81–82; R Lower Broughton Ascension *Man* 82–86; PtO *S'well* 10–14; *Derby* 14–15;

P-in-c Salisbury St Martin *Sarum* 15–18; V from 18. *The Rectory, 42 Tollgate Road, Salisbury SP1 2JJ* T: (01722) 320033 M: 07734-200314 E: benevans002@mac.com

FISHER, David Stephen. b 66. Ripon Coll Cuddesdon BTh 98. d 98 p 99. C Stockport SW *Ches* 98–01; V Gatley 01–06; V Gt Sutton 06–13; RD Wirral S 11–13; Can and Prec Ban Cathl 13–18; Hon C Bro Deiniol 16–18; P-in-c Carshalton *S'wark* 18–19; R from 19; PtO *Ches* 13–18. *The Rectory, 10 Beeches Avenue, Carshalton SM5 3LW* M: 07793-976292 E: daifisher@aol.com *or* canon.daifisher@icloud.com *or* rectorofcarshalton@gmail.com

FISHER, Eric Henry George. b 48. NTMTC 94. d 97 p 98. NSM Heydon, Gt and Lt Chishill, Chrishall etc *Chelmsf* 97–03; P-in-c Gt Oakley w Wix and Wrabness 03–08; rtd 08; PtO *Chelmsf* 09–15; *St E* from 09. *Sheldon, 12 Joseph Close, Hadleigh, Ipswich IP7 5FH* T: (01473) 832626 E: eric.fisher@ukgateway.net

FISHER, Eric William. b 30. Birm Univ BA 53. Coll of Resurr Mirfield 70. d 72 p 73. C Styvechale *Cov* 72–75; C Chesterfield St Mary and All SS *Derby* 75–78; Chapl Buxton Hosps 78–84; TV Buxton w Burbage and King Sterndale *Derby* 78–84; R Shirland 84–89; V Sheff St Matt 89–95; rtd 95; PtO *Lich* 95–15. *6 Hickstead Row, Main Road, Betley, Crewe CW3 9AB* T: (01270) 820653

FISHER, George Arnold. b 54. Lon Univ BD 75. NOC 81. d 84 p 85. C Conisbrough *Sheff* 84–92; V Blackpool St Thos *Blackb* 92–07; Dir Par Miss *Lich* 93–19; Hon C Walsall St Matt 07–19; rtd 19. *14 Lowther Close, Eastbourne BN23 8EZ* M: 07579-058653

FISHER, Gordon. b 44. NW Ord Course 74. d 77 p 78. NSM Airedale w Fryston *Wakef* 77–81; C Barkisland w W Scammonden 81–84; C Ripponden 81–84; V Sutton St Mich *York* 84–87; V Marton-in-Cleveland 87–96; R Kettering SS Pet and Paul 96–02; rtd 02. *8 Mount Pleasant Avenue, Marske-by-the-Sea, Redcar TS11 7BW* T: (01642) 489489

FISHER, Ian St John. b 59. Down Coll Cam BA 80 MA 84 Leic Univ PhD 84. St Steph Ho Ox BA 88. d 88 p 89. C Colwall w Upper Colwall and Coddington *Heref* 88–91; Chapl Surrey Univ *Guildf* 92–97; V Hurst *Man* 97–04; V N Shoebury *Chelmsf* 04–15; rtd 15; PtO *Chelmsf* 15–17; TV Linton *Ely* from 17. *The Camps Vicarage, Park Lane, Castle Camps, Cambridge CB21 4SR* T: (01799) 585977 E: ian.fisher@btconnect.com *or* ian59fisher@btinternet.com

FISHER, Mrs Joan. b 52. d 00 p 01. NSM Blackpool St Mark *Blackb* 00–04; NSM Blackpool St Thos 04–07; C Aldridge *Lich* 08–14; rtd 14; PtO *Lich* 17–20. *14 Lowther Close, Eastbourne BN23 8EZ*

FISHER, John. b 62. d 16 p 17. C Darton w Staincross and Mapplewell *Leeds* 16–19; P-in-c Ebchester *Dur* from 19; P-in-c Hamsterley and Witton-le-Wear from 19; P-in-c Leadgate from 19; P-in-c Medomsley from 19. *The New Rectory, Shaw Lane, Consett DH8 0PY* T: (01207) 774218 M: 07949-920170 E: revjohnfisher@gmail.com

FISHER, John Andrew. b 63. Bath Univ BSc 85 MA 97. Wycliffe Hall Ox BA 93. d 94 p 95. C Rayleigh *Chelmsf* 94–98; V Burton Joyce w Bulcote and Stoke Bardolph *S'well* 98–09; AD Gedling 00–05; Regional Leadership Adv (Midl) CPAS 09–11; Patr Sec 11–19; PtO *Sheff* 10–13; *York* 10–15; Dioc Dir of Ords *Ex* from 19. *The Bishop's Office, Palace Gate House, Palace Gate, Exeter EX1 1HX* T: (01392) 477702 E: john.fisher@exeter.anglican.org

FISHER, Mark Simon. b 52. K Coll Lon BD 76 AKC 76 Trin Coll Ox MA 82 DPhil 83. Kelham Th Coll 70 Perkins Sch of Th (USA) 76. d 78 p 78. SSF 78–80; Hon C Victoria Docks Ascension *Chelmsf* 78–79; LtO *Eur* 78–80; LtO *Lon* 78–80; LtO *Ox* 78–87; Chapl LMH Ox 80–86; R Glas St Matt 87–89; Hon Asst P W Derby St Jo *Liv* 97–05. *29A Rodney Street, Liverpool L1 9EH* T: 0151-707 9748

FISHER, Mary Christine. b 43. Bris Univ BA 64. LCTP 07. d 08 p 09. NSM Heaton St Barn *Bradf* 08–13; PtO 13–14; *Leeds* from 14. *423 Toller Lane, Bradford BD9 5NN* T: (01274) 541238

FISHER, Canon Michael Harry. b 39. Ex Univ BA 61. St Steph Ho Ox 61. d 63 p 64. C Wolverhampton St Pet *Lich* 63–67; C Newquay *Truro* 67–70; V Newlyn St Pet 70–75; P-in-c Launceston St Steph w St Thos 75–82; V Carbis Bay w Lelant 82–95; V Newquay 95–99; Hon Can Truro Cathl 85–99; RD Penwith 88–93; Chapl Costa del Sol W *Eur* 99–00; rtd 00; PtO *Truro* from 00; *Eur* 04–17. *Chymedda, Southway, Windmill, Padstow PL28 8RN* T: (01841) 521544 M: 07970-865049 E: mfisher39@aol.com

FISHER, Nicholas. b 48. Newc Univ BA 71 MLitt 87 Man Univ MA 98 Leeds Univ PhD 04 Birm Univ BA 09 Lambeth PhD 18. Qu Coll Birm 06. d 08 p 09. NSM Northleach w Hampnett and Farmington etc *Glouc* 08–13; P-in-c Sherborne, Windrush, the Barringtons etc 13–16; V 16–19; Dioc NSM

Officer 13–19; rtd 19; PtO *Eur* from 19. *Providence House, High Street, Northleach, Cheltenham GL54 3EU* T: (01451) 861195 E: nick@5fishers.co.uk

FISHER, Paul Vincent. b 43. Worc Coll Ox BA 66 MA 70 ARCM 73. Qu Coll Birm. d 70 p 71. C Redditch St Steph *Worc* 70–73; C Chorlton upon Medlock *Man* 73–79; Chapl Man Univ 73–79; Exec Sec Community Affairs Division BCC 79–81; Asst Dir of Tr and Dir of Lay Tr *Carl* 81–86; P-in-c Raughton Head w Gatesgill 81–85; Lay Tr Team Ldr *S'wark* 86–90; Dir of Tr 90–94; V Kingswood 94–00; rtd 00; *Leeds* 14–16 and 20–21. *3 Buxton Park, Langcliffe, Settle BD24 9NQ* T: (01729) 824058 E: paul.v.fisher@btconnect.com

FISHER, Canon Peter Timothy. b 44. Dur Univ BA 68 MA 75. Cuddesdon Coll 68. d 70 p 71. C Bedford St Andr *St Alb* 70–74; Chapl Surrey Univ *Guildf* 74–78; Sub-Warden Linc Th Coll 78–83; R Houghton le Spring *Dur* 83–94; RD Houghton 87–92; Prin Qu Coll Birm 94–02; V Maney *Birm* 02–10; Hon Can Birm Cathl 00–10; rtd 10; PtO *Leeds* from 17. *Eden, Unicorn View, Bowes, Barnard Castle DL12 9HW* T: (01833) 628001

FISHER, Richard John. b 60. K Coll Lon BA 82 AKC 82 Selw Coll Cam BA 87 MA 95. Ridley Hall Cam 85. d 88 p 89. C Woodley St Jo the Ev *Ox* 88–91; C Acomb St Steph and St Aid *York* 91–95; Chapl Preston Acute Hosps NHS Trust 98–02; Chapl Lancs Teaching Hosps NHS Trust 02–06; PtO *Blackb* 08–09; NSM Rufford and Tarleton 09; C Loughton St Jo *Chelmsf* 09–18; TV Smestow Vale *Lich* from 18. *The Vicarage, School Road, Trysull, Wolverhampton WV5 7HR* T: (01902) 476843 E: vicarage@trysullchurch.org.uk

FISHER, Sandi. *See* FISHER, Alexandria Compton

FISHER, Mrs Sheila Janet. b 50. WEMTC 01. d 04 p 05. NSM Cam w Stinchcombe *Glouc* 04–11; NSM Thornbury and Oldbury-on-Severn w Shepperdine 11–15; rtd 15; PtO *Glouc* from 16. *Court Hayes, Rockhampton, Berkeley GL13 9DU* T: (01454) 269700 E: ashmead.fishers@btinternet.com

FISHER, The Ven Simon John Plumley. b 80. St Jo Coll Dur BA 01. Ripon Coll Cuddesdon BA 04. d 05 p 06. C Bath Bathwick *B & W* 05–09; P-in-c Brigstock w Stanion and Lowick and Sudborough *Pet* 09–11; P-in-c Weldon w Deene 09–11; V W Derby St Jo *Liv* 11–20; Hon Can Liv Cathl 19–20; Adn St Helens and Warrington from 20. *The Vicarage, 685 West Derby Road, Liverpool L13 0BH* T: 0151-228 2023 M: 07525-617067 E: frsimonfisher@gmail.com

FISHER, Stephen Newson. b 46. Univ of Wales (Swansea) BSc 67 CEng 82 MIET 82. Linc Th Coll 84. d 86 p 87. C Nunthorpe *York* 86–89; P-in-c Middlesbrough St Oswald 89–90; V 90–94; V Redcar 94–02; P-in-c The Thorntons and The Otteringtons 02–11; Chapl N Yorks Police 01–11; PtO *Bradf* 02–11; rtd 11; PtO *York* from 11. *31 Church Close, Marske-by-the-Sea, Redcar TS11 7AW* T: (01642) 488682 E: stephen.fisher913@btinternet.com

FISHER, Stuart Frederick. b 48. d 11 p 12. OLM Swindon Dorcan *Bris* from 11; Chapl Swindon Coll from 16; PtO *Ox* 15–17 and from 18. *30 Blakeney Avenue, Swindon SN3 3NL* T: (01793) 497169 M: 07774-205640 E: revsffisher@btinternet.com

FISHER, Susan. b 49. Yorks Min Course 09. d 11. NSM Gomersal *Wakef* 11–12; NSM Griffin, Mango Hill and North Lakes Australia 12–13; C Culburra Beach, Callala and Currarong, NSW from 14. *21 Stott Crescent, Callala Bay, NSW 2540, Australia* T: (0061) (02) 8886 6684 M: 40-681 5449 E: sue@culburraanglican.asn.au

FISHER, Susan Alexandra. *See* NORTON, Susan Alexandra

FISHER, Thomas Ruggles. b 20. Cranmer Hall Dur 58. d 60 p 61. C Melton Mowbray w Thorpe Arnold *Leic* 60–63; R Husbands Bosworth 63–74; R Husbands Bosworth w Mowsley and Knaptoft etc 74–82; PtO 82–96; *Pet* 83–04; rtd 85. *12 The Dell, Oakham LE15 6JG* T: (01572) 757630 E: rugglesfisher@outlook.com

FISHER-BAILEY, Mrs Carol. b 56. d 96 p 97. C Eccleshill *Bradf* 96–99; TV Sutton St Jas and Wawne *York* 99–12; V Wawne 12; V Keyingham w Ottringham and Sunk Island 12–14; V Easington w Skeffling, Keyingham, Ottringham etc 14–19; R Lockington and Lund and Scorborough w Leconfield from 19. *Rectory House, 41 Church Lane, Lockington, Driffield YO25 9SU* E: ladyvicar@gmail.com

FISHLOCK, Christopher Douglas. b 70. Anglia Poly BA 91. Oak Hill Th Coll BA 06. d 07. C St Helen Bishopsgate w St Andr Undershaft etc *Lon* 07–12; C St Andr-by-the-Wardrobe w St Ann, Blackfriars and St Martin Ludgate from 12. *St Nicholas Cole Abbey, 114 Queen Victoria Street, London EC4V 4BJ* T: (020) 7248 5213 E: cfishlock@stnickstalks.org *or* chris@stnickschurch.org.uk

FISHWICK, Raymond Allen. b 42. St Fran Coll Brisbane 93 N Queensland Coll of Min ACP 96. **d** 91 **p** 92. P-in-c Charters Towers Australia 92–94; R 94–97; P-in-c Worthen *Heref* 98–02; P-in-c Hope w Shelve 98–02; P-in-c Middleton 98–02; P-in-c Weipa Australia 02–04; P-in-c Innisfail 04–08; CF 02–08; rtd 08. *217 Edward Road, Geraldton WA 6530, Australia* T: (0061) (8) 9921 5537 E: rfi64412@bigpond.net.au

FISKE, Paul Francis Brading. b 45. St Jo Coll Dur BA 68 PhD 72. Wycliffe Hall Ox 72. **d** 73 **p** 74. C Sutton *Liv* 73–76; TV Cheltenham St Mary, St Matt, St Paul and H Trin *Glouc* 76–80; C-in-c Hartplain CD *Portsm* 80–84; Hd of Miss UK CMJ 84–86; Hon C Edgware *Lon* 84–86; R Broughton Gifford, Gt Chalfield and Holt *Sarum* 86–95; TV Bourne Valley 95–97; Adv Chr Action 95–97; P-in-c Princes Risborough w Ilmer *Ox* 97–98; TR Risborough 98–08; rtd 08; PtO *Cov* 09–17; *Roch* from 17. *106 Ralph Perring Court, Stone Park Avenue, Beckenham BR3 3LX* M: 07969-112305 E: revpaulfiske@gmail.com

FISKEAUNET, Torhild Holen. *See* FIKSEAUNET, Torhild Holen

FITCH, Capt Alan John. b 45. Open Univ BA 82 Warwick Univ MA 84. Wilson Carlile Coll 64 Qu Coll Birm 92. **d** 92 **p** 93. CA from 66; C Glouc St Jas and All SS 92–97; NSM Wotton St Mary 93–97; V Douglas All SS and St Thos *S & M* 97–02; Chapl HM Pris Is of Man 97–02; TR Walbrook Epiphany *Derby* 02–09; rtd 09; PtO *Derby* from 09; Dioc Adv on Racial Justice from 02. *16 Nether Slade Road, Ilkeston DE7 8ET* T: 0115-930 5768 E: iom123@btinternet.com or alaniomfitch@gmail.com

FITTER, Matthew Douglas. b 59. City of Lon Poly BSc 81. Trin Coll Bris MA 03. **d** 03 **p** 04. C Purley Ch Ch *S'wark* 03–07; C Beckenham Ch Ch *Roch* 07–10; TR Anerley from 10; P-in-c Penge St Jo 13–17. *The Vicarage, 234 Anerley Road, London SE20 8TJ* T: (020) 8249 5330 E: matthewfitter@hotmail.com

FITTER, Mrs Ruth Patricia. b 69. Chelt & Glouc Coll of HE BEd 99. WEMTC 08. **d** 11 **p** 12. C S Cheltenham *Glouc* 11–14; V Glouc St Paul and St Steph from 14; AD Glouc City from 20. *84 Frampton Road, Gloucester GL1 5QB* T: (01452) 500537 M: 07553-758063 E: ruthfitter1@gmail.com or ruthfitter@paulstephenglos.org.uk

FITZGERALD, Elizabeth Anne. **d** 15 **p** 17. Donagheady *D & R* 15–17; C Gweedore, Carrickfin and Templecrone from 17. *The Rectory, Bunbeg, Co Donegal, Republic of Ireland* T: (00353) (74) 953 1043 M: 07771-728227 E: ea.fitzgerald1@btinternet.com

FITZGERALD, Miss Melanie Anne. b 52. Sheff Univ BMus 75. Westcott Ho Cam 96. **d** 98 **p** 99. C Rotherham *Sheff* 98–01; C Stannington 01–02; P-in-c Walkley 02–05; V 05–20; rtd 20; PtO *Sheff* from 21. *45 Pot House Lane, Stocksbridge, Sheffield S36 1ES* E: m.a.fitzgerald@icloud.com

FITZGERALD, Sarah. b 65. DipCOT 87. St Jo Coll Nottm 06. **d** 08 **p** 09. C Folkestone Trin *Cant* 08–12; TV Gt Marlow w Marlow Bottom, Lt Marlow and Bisham *Ox* from 12. *The Vicarage, 18 Oak Tree Road, Marlow SL7 3EE* T: (01628) 481167 E: sarah.fitzgerald@4u-team.org

FITZGERALD CLARK, Mrs Diane Catherine. b 54. Rhode Is Univ BA 76. Gen Th Sem NY MDiv 86. **d** 86 **p** 87. USA 86–95; NSM Hampstead Em W End *Lon* 96–99; Chapl St Alb High Sch for Girls from 98; Assoc Min St Alb Abbey from 98. *13 Eleanor Avenue, St Albans AL3 5TA* T: (01727) 860099 E: dfc@stahs.org.uk

FITZGIBBON, Kevin Peter. b 49. St Jo Coll Nottm BTh 81. **d** 81 **p** 82. C Corby St Columba *Pet* 81–85; V Newborough 85–99; V Eaton Socon *St Alb* 99–07; Min Consultant CPAS from 07; P-in-c Doddington w Benwick and Wimblington 11–15; rtd 15; PtO *Ely* from 15; *Pet* from 15. *127 High Street, Eye, Peterborough PE6 7UX* T: (01733) 221530 E: k.fitzgibbon@care4free.net

FITZHARRIS, The Ven Robert Aidan. b 46. Sheff Univ BDS 71. Linc Th Coll 87. **d** 89 **p** 90. C Dinnington *Sheff* 89–92; V Bentley 92–01; RD Adwick 95–01; Hon Can Sheff Cathl 98–01; Adn Doncaster 01–11; rtd 12; PtO *Sheff* from 12. *Amberley, Old Bawtry Road, Finningley, Doncaster DN9 3BY* T: (01302) 773220 M: 07767-355357 E: lesleyfitzharris@waitrose.com

FITZMAURICE, Arthur William John. b 65. Leeds Univ BA 99 Heythrop Coll Lon MA 04 K Coll Lon PhD 14 Lon Inst of Educn PGCE 92 AGSM 89. Coll of Resurr Mirfield 97. **d** 99 **p** 00. C Spondon *Derby* 99–02; P-in-c Emscote *Cov* 02–03; TV Warwick 03–15; Dir of Ords *Worc* from 15. *16 Lowesmoor Wharf, Lowesmoor, Worcester WR1 2RS* T: (01905) 732814 E: jfitzmaurice@cofe-worcester.org.uk

FITZPATRICK, Paul Kevin. b 60. Open Univ BA 99 Univ of Wales (Lamp) MTh 05 Univ of Wales (Cardiff) PhD 11 Robert Gordon Univ Aber MSc 17 Plymouth Univ PGCE 07 FHEA 09 CPsychol 17. Cuddesdon Coll 96. **d** 98 **p** 99. C Okehampton w Inwardleigh, Bratton Clovelly etc *Ex* 98–02; P-in-c Whipton 02–04; V 04–07; RD Christianity 05–06; Co-ord Chapl Cardiff Metrop Univ *Llan* from 07; PtO from 13; *Ex* from 21. *Great Knowle House, Pyworthy, Holsworthy EX22 6JY* M: 07917-818524 E: pfitzpatrick1@cardiffmet.ac.uk or winterbirder@outlook.com

FITZPATRICK, Paul Thomas. b 67. Coll of Resurr Mirfield 17. **d** 19 **p** 20. C S Beddington and Roundshaw *S'wark* from 19. *32 Waterer Rise, Wallington SM6 9DN* E: fr.paul.fitzpatrick@gmail.com

FITZSIMONS, Canon Kathryn Anne. b 57. Bedf Coll of Educn CertEd 78. NEOC 87. **d** 90 **p** 13. NSM Bilton *Ripon* 90–01; Soc Resp Development Officer Richmond Adnry 92–99; Urban Min Officer *Ripon* 99–14; P-in-c Leeds Gipton Epiphany 14 and 14–16; P-in-c Roundhay St Jo 15–16; V Gipton and Oakwood from 16; AD Allerton from 16; Hon Can Ripon Cathl from 04. *Epiphany Vicarage, 227 Beech Lane, Leeds LS9 6SW* T: 0113-225 6702 E: kathrynfitzsimons@hotmail.com

FLACH (*née* ROLLINS), **Canon Deborah Mary Rollins.** b 54. Sarum & Wells Th Coll 88. **d** 94 **p** 97. C Chantilly *Eur* 94–96; C Maisons-Laffitte 96–04; Asst Chapl 04–07; P-in-c Lille from 07; Can Gib Cathl from 07. *Christ Church, 14 rue Lyderic, 59000 Lille, France* T/F: (0033) 3 28 52 66 36 E: debbieflach@gmail.com or chaplain@christchurchlille.fr

FLACK, Miss Heather Margaret. b 47. **d** 95 **p** 96. C Shenley Green *Birm* 95–00; TV Kings Norton 00–07; rtd 07; PtO *Birm* from 07; *Worc* from 08. *23 Stourport Road, Bewdley DY12 1BB* T: (01299) 400691 E: hm.flack@btinternet.com

✠**FLACK, The Rt Revd John Robert.** b 42. Leeds Univ BA 64. Coll of Resurr Mirfield 64. **d** 66 **p** 67 **c** 97. C Armley St Bart *Ripon* 66–69; C Northampton St Mary *Pet* 69–72; V Chapelthorpe *Wakef* 72–81; V Ripponden and Barkisland w W Scammonden 81–85; Chapl Rishworth Sch Ripponden 81–85; V Brighouse *Wakef* 85–88; TR Brighouse St Martin 88–92; RD Brighouse and Elland 86–92; Hon Can Wakef Cathl 89–92; Adn Pontefract 92–97; Suff Bp Huntingdon and Hon Can Ely Cathl 97–03; Abp's Rep H See and Dir Angl Cen Rome 03–08; P-in-c Nassington w Yarwell and Woodnewton w Apethorpe *Pet* 08–12; Can Pet Cathl 04–12; Hon Asst Bp Pet 03–17; Hon Asst Bp Eur from 03; PtO *Ely* 03–17; Hon Asst Bp Ely 13–17; Hon Asst Bp Leeds from 17; Bp's Adv for Healing Min *Pet* 14–17; PtO *Linc* 16–19. *6 Oakhall Park, Crigglestone, Wakefield WF4 3HG* T: (01924) 259073 M: 07810-714056 E: flackjohn499@gmail.com

FLAGG, David Michael. b 50. CCC Cam BA 71 MA 75. St Jo Coll Nottm BA 76. **d** 77 **p** 78. C Hollington St Leon *Chich* 77–80; C Woodley St Jo the Ev *Ox* 80–86; Chapl The Dorothy Kerin Trust Burrswood 86–94; R Knockholt w Halstead *Roch* 94–99; Dir Chapl Services Mildmay UK 99–02; Hd Chapl Services Qu Eliz Hosp NHS Trust 02–11; Hd Chapl Services S Lon Healthcare NHS Trust 11–13; rtd 13; Chapl Burrswood Chr Hosp *Roch* 13–16; PtO *S'wark* from 13; *Roch* from 17. *61 Church Street, Edenbridge TN8 5BQ* T: (01732) 866058 M: 07910-141862 E: david.pastoral@mail.com

FLAHERTY, Jane Venitia. *See* ANDERSON, Jane Venitia

FLAHERTY, Miss Mandy Carol. b 63. Ches Coll of HE BA 86 Leic Univ PGCE 87. St Jo Coll Nottm MTh 04. **d** 04 **p** 05. C Oadby *Leic* 04–08; PtO *Ely* 09–10; NSM Alconbury cum Weston 10–14; NSM N Leightonstone 14–17; C 17–19; P-in-c 19; R from 19; Chapl K Sch Pet 14–19. *The Vicarage, Church Way, Alconbury, Huntingdon PE28 4DX* T: (01480) 896541 M: 07593-311568 E: rector@norleigh.org.uk

FLANAGAN, James. **d** 17 **p** 18. C Pen-bre *St D* 17–20; P-in-c Bro Lliedi from 20. *35 Stryd Y Maswr, Llanelli SA15 4DX* E: jimflanagan1662@gmail.com or frjimflanagan@gmail.com

FLANAGAN, Kevin Joseph. b 60. Middx Poly BA 87 Newman Coll Birm PGCE 80. St Jo Coll Nottm 04. **d** 06 **p** 07. C Allesley Park and Whoberley *Cov* 06–09; V Wolston and Church Lawford from 09. *The Vicarage, Brook Street, Wolston, Coventry CV8 3HD* T: (024) 7654 0778 or 7654 2722 E: vicar@wolston.net

FLANAGAN (*née* MALCOLM), **Mrs Mercia Alana.** b 54. St Andr Univ MA 77 TCD MPhil 03. S'wark Ord Course 84. **d** 87 **p** 94. C Dartford Ch Ch *Roch* 87–91; Par Dn Stockport St Geo Ches 91–94; C Jordanstown *Conn* 95–99; Chapl Ulster Univ 95–03; I Carnmoney *Conn* 03–18; C Ballyholme *D & D* 18–19; rtd 19. *95 Silverbirch Road, Bangor BT19 6FA* T: (028) 9147 9816 M: 07773-558326 E: merciaflanagan1@gmail.com

FLASHMAN (*née* WALLACE), **Sarah Louise.** b 63. Wycliffe Hall Ox MTh 18 RGN 85. STETS BA 13. **d** 13 **p** 14. NSM Southbourne w W Thorney *Chich* 13–16; PtO *Ox* 16–18; Chapl Wycliffe Hall Ox from 18; C Wolvercote and Wytham *Ox* 19–21; LtO from 21. *The Rectory, 27 Church Street, Quainton, Aylesbury HP22 4AW* T: (01296) 655237 M: 07443-637432 E: sarah@ontheboxmission.com

FLASHMAN, Stephen Trevor. b 49. Spurgeon's Coll Lon 69. **d** 08 **p** 10. NSM Chich St Paul and Westhampnett 08–16; NSM Schorne *Ox* from 16. *The Rectory, 27 Church Street, Quainton, Aylesbury HP22 4AW* T: (01296) 655237 M: 07950-000910 E: steve@ontheboxmission.com

FLATT, Lynn Patricia. b 47. Univ of Wales (Ban) BA 73 Birm Univ MSocSc 75 Ex Univ DipSW 79 RGN 68. SWMTC 12. **d** 14 **p** 15. NSM S Molton w Nymet St George, High Bray etc *Ex* 14–16; NSM S Molton w Nymet St George, Chittlehamholt etc 16–20; PtO from 20. *1 Widgery Drive, South Molton EX36 4DP* T: (01769) 572076 E: lynnflatt@btinternet.com

FLATT, Stephen Joseph. b 57. Cardiff Univ MTh 10 SRN 79 RSCN 81. Sarum & Wells Th Coll 92. **d** 92 **p** 93. C Limpsfield and Titsey *S'wark* 92–96; TV Pewsey *Sarum* 96–97; Staff Nurse R Free Hampstead NHS Trust 97–99; Charge Nurse 99–00; Asst Chapl Univ Coll Lon Hosps NHS Trust 00–01; Chapl 01–03; PtO *S'wark* 98–99; NSM Clapham H Trin and St Pet 99–02; Lead Chapl St Mary's NHS Trust Paddington 03–10; Hd Spiritual and Past Care Imp Coll Healthcare NHS Trust 10–13; Clinical Service Manager W Middx Univ Hosp NHS Trust 13–14; Assoc Dir Nursing Barts Health NHS Trust 14–19; NSM St Marylebone Annunciation Bryanston Street *Lon* 14–19; Hd of Quality Governance Poole Hosp NHS Foundn Trust 19–20; Univ Hosps Dorset NHS Foundn Trust from 20; NSM Branksome St Aldhelm *Sarum* from 19. *12 Sunset Lodge, 30-32 The Avenue, Poole BH13 6HG* M: 07956-278565

FLATTERS, Clive Andrew. b 56. Sarum & Wells Th Coll 83. **d** 86 **p** 88. C Weston Favell *Pet* 86–87; C Old Brumby *Linc* 88–91; C Syston *Leic* 91–93; TV 93–99; V Knottingley *Wakef* 99–02; TR Knottingley and Kellington w Whitley 02–14; Leeds from 14. *The Vicarage, Chapel Street, Knottingley WF11 9AN* T: (01977) 672267

FLAVELL, Paul William Deran. b 44. St Mich Coll Llan 67. **d** 68 **p** 69. C W Cairns Australia 68–71; C Blaenavon w Capel Newydd *Mon* 71–74; V Ynysddu 74–84; R Llanaber w Caerdeon *Ban* 84–00; V Llanstadwel *St D* 00–10; rtd 10; PtO *St As* from 10; *Ban* from 10. *7 Park Grove, Abergele LL22 7NE* T: (01745) 823668 E: fish.foulkes1811@btinternet.com

FLEET, Daniel James Russell. b 60. Wye Coll Lon BSc 84 Keele Univ PGCE 02. St Jo Coll Nottm 86. **d** 89 **p** 90. C Boldmere *Birm* 89–92; C Caverswall and Weston Coyney w Dilhorne *Lich* 92–95; V Alton w Bradley-le-Moors and Oakamoor w Cotton 95–01; rtd 01; PtO *Lich* 01–10. *124 Byrds Lane, Uttoxeter ST14 7NB* T: (01889) 560214 E: danielfleet@btinternet.com

FLEMING (formerly LOOKER), Miss Clare Margaret. b 55. Liv Univ CertEd 78. Westcott Ho Cam 85. **d** 87 **p** 02. Par Dn Prestwood and Gt Hampden *Ox* 87–90; Hon C Olney w Emberton 90–92; Hon C Blunham, Gt Barford, Roxton and Tempsford etc *St Alb* 01–03; P-in-c Welford w Sibbertoft and Marston Trussell *Pet* 03–04; PtO *St Alb* 04–05; Hon C Wilden w Colmworth and Ravensden 05–08; PtO *Ely* 11–16; *St E* from 12. *4 Long Meadow Walk, Carlton Colville, Lowestoft NR33 8LR* M: 07516-939693 E: fleming.clare@yahoo.co.uk

FLEMING, The Ven David. b 37. Kelham Th Coll 58. **d** 63 **p** 64. C Walton St Marg Belmont Road *Liv* 63–67; Chapl HM Borstal Gaynes Hall 68–76; V Gt Staughton *Ely* 68–76; RD St Neots 72–76; V Whittlesey 76–85; RD March 77–82; Hon Can Ely Cathl 82–01; P-in-c Ponds Bridge 83–85; Adn Wisbech 84–93; V Wisbech St Mary 85–89; Chapl Gen of Pris 93–01; Chapl to The Queen 95–07; PtO *Ely* from 01. *Fair Haven, 123 Wisbech Road, Littleport, Ely CB6 1JJ* T: (01353) 862498 E: davidfleming@hotmail.com

FLEMING, Elizabeth Julie. b 57. Westhill Coll Birm CertEd 79 Ches Coll of HE BTh 00. NOC 97. **d** 00 **p** 01. C Widnes St Jo *Liv* 00–03; P-in-c Walton Breck Ch Ch 03–04; V Walton Breck 04–08; V Becontree St Mary *Chelmsf* 08–17; Ad Barking and Dagenham 13–17; Hon Can Chelmsf Cathl 15–17; TR Worle *B & W* 17–19; rtd 19; PtO *Leeds* 20–21. *53 Wheathead Lane, Keighley BD22 6NL* E: lizjuliefleming@gmail.com

FLEMING, George. b 39. CITC. **d** 78 **p** 79. C Donaghcloney w Waringstown *D & D* 78–80; C Newtownards 80; I Movilla 80; C Heref St Pet w St Owen and St Jas 80–85; V Holmer w Huntington 85–96; P-in-c Worfield 96–98; V 98–04; rtd 04; PtO *Truro* 05–08; *Bris* 08–19; *Lich* 19–21. *11 Sherbrook Road, Cannock WS11 1HJ* T: (01543) 502857

FLEMING, Ian James. b 87. Man Univ BA 09. All SS Cen for Miss & Min 17. **d** 20 **p** 21. C Holcombe and Hawkshaw *Man* from 20. *16 Maple Grove, Ramsbottom, Bury BL0 0AN* M: 07543-213743 E: injflmng@gmail.com *or* ian@holcombehawkshaw.org

FLEMING, Canon Kathryn Claire. b 60. Trin Coll Cam BA 82 MA 91 Montessori TDip 92. WEMTC 01. **d** 04 **p** 05. C Charlton Kings St Mary *Glouc* 04–08; P-in-c Cainscross w Selsley 08–13; TV Stroud Team 13–14;

Can Res Cov Cathl from 14. *Coventry Cathedral, 1 Hill Top, Coventry CV1 5AB* T: (024) 7652 1200 F: 7652 1220 E: kathryn.fleming@coventrycathedral.org.uk

FLEMING, Victoria Rosalie. b 58. WEMTC 01. **d** 04 **p** 05. NSM St Breoke and Egloshayle *Truro* 04–08; TV Stratton St Margaret w S Marston etc *Bris* 08–11; P-in-c 11–19; V Cannock and Huntington *Lich* from 19; V Hatherton from 19. *11 Sherbrook Road, Cannock WS11 1HJ* T: (01543) 502857 E: vicky.fleming981@btinternet.com

FLEMING, William Edward Charlton. b 29. TCD BA 51 MA 65. CITC 52. **d** 52 **p** 53. C Dublin Santry *D & G* 52–56; C Arm St Mark w Aghavilly 56–61; I Tartaraghan 61–80; Prov Registrar 79–96; I Tartaraghan w Diamond 80–96; Can Arm Cathl 88–92; Treas Arm Cathl 88–92; Chan Arm Cathl 92–96; rtd 96. *65 Annareagh Road, Drumorgan, Richhill, Armagh BT61 9JT* T: (028) 3887 9612

FLENLEY, Benjamin Robert Glanville. b 50. Sarum & Wells Th Coll 86. **d** 88 **p** 89. C Eastleigh *Win* 88–92; V Micheldever and E Stratton, Woodmancote etc 92–03; R Bentworth, Lasham, Medstead and Shalden 03–15; rtd 15; Hon C Quantock Towers *B & W* 15–20; RD Quantock 17–20 . *74 Bruce Avenue, Worthing BN11 5LA* E: flenbenley@btinternet.com

FLENLEY, Kathryn Alison. b 51. STETS. **d** 12 **p** 13. NSM Bentworth, Lasham, Medstead and Shalden *Win* 12–15; PtO *B & W* 15–17; C Watchet and Williton 17–20; Asst Dir of Ords 19–20; rtd 21. *74 Bruce Avenue, Worthing BN11 5LA* E: kathryn.flenley@btinternet.com

FLETCHER, Canon Angela. b 59. EMMTC 04. **d** 07 **p** 08. C Edwinstowe and Perlethorpe *S'well* 07–10; P-in-c Warsop 10–11; R from 11; AD Mansfield 15–19; Hon Can S'well Minster from 21. *The Rectory, Church Road, Warsop, Mansfield NG20 0SL* T: (01623) 843290 E: rector@warsopparishchurch.org.uk

FLETCHER, Anthony. *See* FLETCHER, James Anthony

FLETCHER, Anthony Peter Reeves. b 46. Bede Coll Dur CertEd Nottm Univ BTh 78. Ridley Hall Cam 71. **d** 74 **p** 75. C Luton St Mary *St Alb* 74–78; Chapl RAF 78–00; P-in-c Lyneham w Bradenstoke *Sarum* 98–99; P-in-c Kyrenia St Andr and Chapl N Cyprus 00–04; P-in-c Lyneham w Bradenstoke *Sarum* 04–07; rtd 07; PtO *Bris* from 08; *Glouc* 14–20. *Glentworth House, Giles Avenue, Cricklade, Swindon SN6 6HS* T: (01793) 751333

FLETCHER, Barbara. b 41. ALAM 79. WMMTC 93. **d** 96 **p** 97. NSM Smethwick *Birm* 96–97; C 97–02; rtd 02; PtO *Birm* from 02; *Worc* from 12. *231 Abbey Road, Smethwick B67 5NN* T: 0121-429 9354 E: bfletcher@talktalk.net

FLETCHER, Bryce Clifford. b 45. ACIB. Cranmer Hall Dur. **d** 08 **p** 09. NSM Arle Valley *Win* 08–14; rtd 14; PtO *Win* from 14. *Camellia Cottage, Church Street, Ropley, Alresford SO24 0DS* E: bryce@newalresford.plus.com

FLETCHER, Christopher Ian. b 43. BSc PhD. Glouc Sch of Min. **d** 89 **p** 90. C Tenbury Wells *Heref* 89–93; R Bredenbury 93–09; RD Bromyard 99–05; rtd 09; PtO *Heref* from 10. *12 Geoffrey Avenue, Hereford HR1 1BZ* T: (01432) 273149

✠**FLETCHER, The Rt Revd Colin William.** b 50. OBE 00. Trin Coll Ox BA 72 MA 76. Wycliffe Hall Ox 72. **d** 75 **p** 76 **c** 00. C Shipley St Pet *Bradf* 75–79; Tutor Wycliffe Hall Ox 79–84; Hon C Ox St Andr 79–84; V Margate H Trin *Cant* 84–93; RD Thanet 88–93; Abp's Chapl 93–00; Area Bp Dorchester *Ox* 00–20; rtd 20; Hon Asst Bp Ox from 21; Hon Can Dallas from 93. *34 Park Street, Bladon, Woodstock OX20 1RW*

FLETCHER, David Clare Molyneux. b 32. Worc Coll Ox BA 55 MA 59. Wycliffe Hall Ox 56. **d** 58 **p** 59. C Islington St Mary *Lon* 58–62; Hon C 62–83; Field Worker Scripture Union 62–86; R Ox St Ebbe w H Trin and St Pet 86–98; rtd 98; PtO *Ox* 06–18. *49 Erdington House, Cresswell Close, Yarnton, Kidlington OX5 1FZ* T: (01865) 579360 E: sanddfletcher@gmail.com

FLETCHER, David Mark. b 56. Chich Th Coll 84. **d** 87 **p** 88. C Taunton St Andr *B & W* 87–91; P-in-c Chard, Furnham w Chaffcombe, Knowle St Giles etc 91–95; P-in-c Tiverton St Andr *Ex* 95–11; RD Tiverton 02–08; Chapl Mid Devon Primary Care Trust 95–11; C Barnstaple *Ex* 11–17; V Barnstaple St Pet and St Mary from 17. *The Vicarage, Sowden Lane, Barnstaple EX32 8BU* T: (01271) 373837 E: davidfletcher56@btinternet.com

FLETCHER, Capt Frank. b 40. Wilson Carlile Coll 71 EAMTC 94. **d** 96 **p** 96. Asst Chapl HM Pris Highpoint 90–97; Chapl HM Pris Wealstun 97–05; rtd 05; PtO *York* 05–20. *3 Pear Tree Close, Huntington, York YO32 9QZ* T: (01904) 765181 E: frank.fletcher2018@gmail.com

FLETCHER, Gordon Wolfe (Robin). b 31. Edin Th Coll. **d** 62 **p** 63. C Eston *York* 62–65; C Harton Colliery *Dur* 65–68; V Pelton 68–81; V Ryhope 81–96; rtd 96; PtO *Dur* from 04. *23 Swinburne Road, Darlington DL3 7TD* T: (01325) 265994 E: gordon.fletcher@btinternet.com

FLETCHER, Ian Paul. b 76. d 09 p 10. C Holdenhurst and Iford *Win* 09–13; P-in-c Eastleigh 14–19; V from 19. *Eastleigh Vicarage, 1 Cedar Road, Eastleigh SO50 9NR* T: (023) 8065 2295 E: ianpaulfletcher@gmail.com *or* ian@eastleighparish.com

FLETCHER, James Anthony. b 36. St Edm Hall Ox BA 60 MA 66. St Steph Ho Ox 60. d 62 p 63. C Streatham St Pet *S'wark* 62–65; C Hobs Moat CD *Birm* 65–66; C Hobs Moat 67–68; C Cowley St Jo *Ox* 68–77; V Hanworth All SS *Lon* 77–02; P-in-c Hanworth St Geo 89–91; rtd 02; PtO *Cant* from 02. *19 Strand Street, Sandwich CT13 9DX* T: (01304) 620506 E: franthonyfletcher@tiscali.co.uk

FLETCHER, James Arthur. b 71. Reading Univ BA 99. Trin Coll Bris 03. d 05 p 06. C Bexleyheath Ch Ch *Roch* 05–08; R Fawkham and Hartley 08–19; RD Cobham 13–18; R Gravesend St Geo from 19. *54 The Avenue, Gravesend DA11 0LX* T: (01474) 534965

FLETCHER, James John Gareth. b 79. Aber Univ MA 02 Selw Coll Cam BA 08 MA. Ridley Hall Cam 06. d 09 p 10. C Tooting Graveney St Nic *S'wark* 09–13; C Ox St Ebbe w H Trin and St Pet 13–18; V Summerstown *S'wark* from 18. *46 Wimbledon Road, London SW17 0UQ* T: (020) 8946 9853 E: jjgfletcher38@gmail.com

FLETCHER, Miss Janet. b 59. Lanc Univ MA 07. Cranmer Hall Dur 98. d 00 p 01. C Ainsdale *Liv* 00–04; TV Walton-on-the-Hill 04–09; Hon Chapl Liv Cathl 04–09; C Prescot 09–11; TV Bangor *Ban* 11–14; TV Bro Deiniol 14–15; Spirituality Officer 15–21; Spirituality and Min Officer from 21; C Bro Ystumanner 15–18; C Bro Enlli from 18. *9 Morfa Road, Llandudno LL30 2BS* T: (01492) 874947

FLETCHER, Jeremy James. b 60. Dur Univ BA 81. St Jo Coll Nottm 85. d 88 p 89. C Stranton *Dur* 88–91; C Nottingham St Nic *S'well* 91–94; P-in-c Skegby 94–00; P-in-c Teversal 96–00; Bp's Dom Chapl 00–02; Can Res and Prec York Minster 02–09; V Beverley Minster 09–17; P-in-c Routh 09–17; RD Beverley 12–17; V Hampstead St Jo *Lon* from 17. *St John's Vicarage, 14 Church Row, London NW3 6UU* T: (020) 7794 5808 E: jeremy@jjfletcher.co.uk *or* vestry@hampsteadparishchurch.org.uk

FLETCHER, Canon John Alan Alfred. b 33. Oak Hill Th Coll 58. d 61 p 62. C Erith St Paul *Roch* 61–64; C Rushden *Pet* 64–67; R Hollington St Leon *Chich* 67–86; V Chadwell Heath *Chelmsf* 86–00; RD Barking and Dagenham 91–00; Chapl Chadwell Heath Hosp Romford 86–93; Chapl Redbridge Health Care NHS Trust 93–00; Hon Can Chelmsf Cathl 99–00; rtd 00; PtO *Chich* from 01. *41 Parkstone Road, Hastings TN34 2NR* T: (01424) 712345 M: 07860-128912 E: jaaf@btinternet.com

FLETCHER, Linden Elisabeth. b 50. Lon Univ BEd 73 MA 80. St Jo Coll Nottm 87. d 89 p 94. C Fakenham w Alethorpe *Nor* 89–93; C Cumnor *Ox* 93–02; P-in-c Ringshall w Battisford, Barking w Darmsden etc *St E* 02–08; P-in-c Somersham w Flowton and Offton w Willisham 02–08; V Llanfair Caereinion, Llanllugan and Manafon *St As* 08–11; rtd 11. *Tanrallt, Cwrtnewydd, Llanybydder SA40 9YJ*

FLETCHER, Martin. b 60. Bradf Univ BEng 83 CEng MIMechE. Ripon Coll Cuddesdon. d 00 p 01. C Oatlands *Guildf* 00–04; R Tolleshunt Knights w Tiptree and Gt Braxted *Chelmsf* 04–10; V Hersham *Guildf* 10–18; R Richmond w Hudswell and Downholme and Marske *Leeds* from 18; AD Richmond from 19. *The Rectory, Church Wynd, Richmond DL10 7AQ* T: (01748) 821241 E: martin.fletcher@leeds.anglican.org

FLETCHER, Martin James. b 48. Ex Univ BA 03 MIFA 89. SWMTC 99. d 02 p 03. NSM Wolborough and Ogwell *Ex* 02–05; NSM Chudleigh w Chudleigh Knighton and Trusham from 05. *11 Troarn Way, Chudleigh, Newton Abbot TQ13 0PP* T: (01626) 853998 E: m.fletcher@uwclub.net

FLETCHER, Paul Gordon MacGregor. b 61. St Andr Univ MTheol 84. Edin Th Coll 84. d 86 p 87. C Cumbernauld *Glas* 86–89; C-in-c Glas H Cross 89–93; P-in-c Bearsden w Milngavie 93–99; R Clarkston 99–07; LtO *Arg* 08–10; R E Kilbride *Glas* from 10. *6 Kelvin Crescent, East Kilbride, Glasgow G75 0TY* T: (01355) 224895 E: paulmcgregorfletcher@hotmail.com

FLETCHER, Robert Alexander. b 52. Ridley Hall Cam. d 84 p 85. C Chalfont St Peter *Ox* 84–88; C Bushey *St Alb* 88–93; TV Digswell and Panshanger 93–00; P-in-c Aldenham 00–05; TV Aldenham, Radlett and Shenley from 05. *The Vicarage, Church Lane, Aldenham, Watford WD25 8BE* T/F: (01923) 854209

FLETCHER, Robin. *See* FLETCHER, Gordon Wolfe

FLETCHER, Mrs Sheila Elizabeth. b 35. Nottm Univ BA 57 CertEd 58. NEOC 84. d 87 p 94. NSM Dringhouses *York* 87–90; Par Dn 90–94; C 94–97; P-in-c Sutton on the Forest 97–02; rtd 02; PtO *York* 02–15. *Mulberry Court Nursing Home, Clifton Park Avenue, York YO30 5PD* E: sheeliz@tiscali.co.uk

FLETCHER, Stephen. b 57. Man Univ BA 79 MA 84. St Jo Coll Nottm 82. d 84 p 85. C Didsbury St Jas and Em *Man* 84–88; R Kersal Moor 88–01; TR Horwich and Rivington 01–20; C Blackrod 11–16; rtd 20; PtO *Blackb* from 21. *15 Foundry Close, Leyland PR25 3RA*

FLETCHER, Stephen William. b 62. Wolv Poly BA 84. Qu Coll Birm 85. d 88 p 89. C Rainham *Roch* 88–91; C Shottery St Andr *Cov* 91–97; Min Bishopton St Pet 91–97; V Llanrumney *Mon* 97–02; V Adderbury w Milton *Ox* 02–18; Hon C Ilmington w Stretton-on-Fosse etc *Cov* 18–20; C 20–21; Hon C Tredington and Darlingscott 18–20; C 20–21. *Tredington Rectory, Tredington, Shipston-on-Stour CV36 4NG* M: 07714-171143 E: revfletcher24@gmail.com

FLETCHER, Steven John Carylon. b 60. NCTJ 83. Aston Tr Scheme 89 Ripon Coll Cuddesdon 89. d 92 p 15. C Newquay *Truro* 92–93; NSM St Stythians w Perranarworthal and Gwennap 15–20; NSM Chacewater w St Day and Carharrack 15–20; NSM Feock 15–20; NSM Devoran 15–20. *5 Scorrier Street, St Day, Redruth TR16 5LH* T: (01209) 822584 E: steven.fletcher@btinternet.com

FLETCHER, Timothy John. b 63. Sheff Univ BA 88 St Jo Coll Dur MA 04. Cranmer Hall Dur 01. d 03 p 04. C Four Marks *Win* 03–06; V Walton le Soken *Chelmsf* 06–14; P-in-c Stannington Sheff 14–21; Dir IME 4-7 from 14. *The Vicarage, 214 Oldfield Road, Stannington, Sheffield S6 6DY* T: 0114-234 9247 E: tim906fletcher@btinternet.com

FLETCHER, Victor James Daniel. b 56. d 12 p 13. OLM Holcombe and Hawkshaw *Man* from 12. *32 Moor Way, Hawkshaw, Bury BL8 4LF* T: (01204) 882750 M: 07977-668836 E: vic@equilibriumarchitects.co.uk

FLEWKER, David William. b 53. Birm Univ BA 75. Wycliffe Hall Ox 76. d 78 p 79. C Netherton *Liv* 78–82; C Prescot 82–84; V Seaforth 84–88; TV Whitstable *Cant* 88–96; Miss to Seamen 88–96; V Bethersden w High Halden *Cant* 96–08; Asst Dir of Ords 02–06; P-in-c Deal St Leon w St Rich and Sholden etc 08–13; R 13–19; rtd 19. *24 Scholars Close, Deal CT14 9FA*

FLIGHT, Michael John. b 41. Sarum Th Coll 68. d 71 p 72. C Wimborne Minster *Sarum* 71–75; R Tarrant Gunville, Tarrant Hinton etc 75–78; P-in-c Tarrant Rushton, Tarrant Rawston etc 77–78; R Tarrant Valley 78–80; V Westbury 80–00; RD Heytesbury 83–87 and 96–00; R Broad Town, Clyffe Pypard, Hilmarton etc 00–07; RD Calne 03–06; rtd 07; PtO *Sarum* from 09. *11 Nursteed Close, Devizes SN10 3EU* T: (01380) 738493 E: michael@flightfamily.co.uk

FLINT, Howard Michael. b 59. Edge Hill Coll of HE BEd 81. Cranmer Hall Dur 95. d 97 p 98. C Chipping Campden w Ebrington *Glouc* 97–00; V Upper Wreake *Leic* 00–06; RD Framland 02–06; V Tunbridge Wells H Trin w Ch Ch *Roch* 06–16; V St Austell *Truro* from 16; RD from 19. *12 North Hill Park, St Austell PL25 4BJ* T: (01726) 64005 M: 07413-286491 E: rev4howard@hotmail.com *or* staustellparish@gmail.com

FLINT, Mrs Marie Louise. b 76. UMIST BSc 98 Bolton Univ PGCE 05. All SS Cen for Miss & Min 97. d 20 p 21. C Stockport and Brinnington *Ches* from 20. *7 Offerton Lane, Stockport SK2 5AA* M: 07780-964365 E: marie_flint@tiscali.co.uk

FLINT, Nicholas Angus. b 60. Chich Th Coll 84. d 87 p 88. C Aldwick *Chich* 87–91; Bp's Asst Chapl for the Homeless *Lon* 91–92; R Rusper *Chich* from 96. *The Rectory, High Street, Rusper, Horsham RH12 4PX* T: (01293) 871251

FLINT, Simon Paul. b 67. Trin Coll Bris 11. d 13 p 14. C Bath Weston All SS w N Stoke and Langridge *B & W* 13–16; C Streetsville Canada from 16. *69 Queen Street S, Mississauga ON L5M 1K5, Canada* M: 07864-910953 E: simonfredflint@gmail.com

FLINT, Tobias John Barnaby. b 76. Ex Univ BA 99. Wycliffe Hall Ox BA 08. d 08 p 09. C Brompton H Trin w Onslow Square St Paul *Lon* 08–11; C Onslow Square and S Kensington St Aug 11–18; C-in-c Bristol St Nic *Bris* from 18. *41 Lilymead Avenue, Bristol BS4 2BY* M: 07967-435080 E: toby@stnicholasbristol.org

FLINTHAM, Alan Jenkinson. b 45. Leeds Univ BSc 66 PGCE 67 MEd 74 Liv Univ PhD 09. EMMTC 98. d 00 p 01. NSM Melbourne *Derby* 00–10; NSM Melbourne, Ticknall, Smisby and Stanton 10–15; rtd 15; PtO *Derby* from 15; Chapl Derby Cathl from 18. *50 Burlington Way, Mickleover, Derby DE3 9BD* T: (01332) 512293 M: 07771-631370 E: alan@flintham.org.uk

FLINTOFT, Canon Ian Hugh. b 74. Pemb Coll Cam BA 97 MA 99 MPhil 98. Westcott Ho Cam 01. d 04 p 05. C Newc St Geo 04–06; C Newc St Geo and St Hilda 06–07; C Ch the King 07–08; TV 08–11; Bp's Chapl and Dioc Dir of Ords 11–17; Dir Discipleship and Min for Miss 17–19; NSM Cowgate 17–19; V Newsham and Horton from 19; P-in-c Cowpen from 20; Hon Can Newc Cathl from 14. *St Bede's Vicarage,*

96 Newcastle Road, Blyth NE24 4AS T: (01670) 364542
E: ianflintoft@hotmail.com

FLINTOFT-CHAPMAN, Mrs Margaret. b 47. Leeds Univ BA 68. NTMTC 03. **d** 05 **p** 06. NSM Barkingside St Cedd *Chelmsf* 05–12; NSM Barkingside H Trin 12–16; rtd 16. *84 Roding Lane North, Woodford Green IG8 8NG* T: (020) 8504 6750

FLIPSE, Miss Adriana Maria (Marja). b 82. Leiden Univ MA 05. St Mich Coll Llan 07. **d** 08 **p** 09. C Roath *Llan* 08–11; C Newton Nottage 11–14; TV Whitchurch 14–20; The Netherlands from 20. *Die Kloosterkerk, Lange Voorhout 4, 2514 ED Den Haag, The Netherlands* E: marfli@zeelandnet.nl

FLITCROFT, Jonathan Frederick. b 62. Leeds Univ BA 85. Qu Coll Birm 13. **d** 15 **p** 16. C Four Oaks *Birm* 15–18; R Old Swinford Stourbridge *Worc* from 19. *The Rectory, Rectory Road, Stourbridge DY8 2HA* M: 07905-975601 E: johnflit@hotmail.co.uk

FLOATE, Miss Rhona Cameron. b 59. Univ of Wales (Cardiff) BA 80. Trin Coll Bris 01. **d** 03 **p** 04. C Lighthorne *Cov* 03–07; C Chesterton 03–07; C Newbold Pacey w Moreton Morrell 03–07; P-in-c Wool and E Stoke *Sarum* 07–15; R 15–16; RD Purbeck 15–16; P-in-c White Horse 16–19; TV Whitton from 19. *The Vicarage, Back Lane, Aldbourne, Marlborough SN8 2BP* E: rhonafloate@aol.com

FLOCKHART, Mrs Ruth. b 56. TISEC 96. **d** 99 **p** 00. NSM Strathpeffer *Mor* 99–21; NSM Dingwall 99–21; rtd 21. *Kilmuir Farm Cottage, North Kessock, Inverness IV1 3ZG* T: (01463) 731580 E: kilmuirseabreeze@btinternet.com

FLOOD, Emma Louise. See ANTOINE, Emma Louise

FLOOD, Mrs Jean Anne. b 51. BEM 11. Liv Hope Univ MEd 00 Liv Univ CertEd 95. NOC 06. **d** 08 **p** 09. NSM Fazakerley Em *Liv* 08–11; Co-ord Miss in the Economy 11–16; NSM Walton-on-the-Hill 11–16; TV 16–19; rtd 19. *Address temp unknown* M: 07932-305963 E: revjflood@hotmail.com

FLOOD, Kenneth. b 75. St Chad's Coll Dur BSc 96. St Steph Ho Ox BTh 01. **d** 01 **p** 02. C Hulme Ascension *Man* 01–05; CP Wokingham St Paul *Ox* 05–08; P-in-c Chorlton-cum-Hardy St Clem *Man* 08–09; R from 09; AD Hulme 13–16. *The Rectory, 6 Edge Lane, Manchester M21 9JF* T: 0161-881 3063 E: ken@mightyflood.org.uk

FLOOD, Nicholas Roger. b 42. FCA. Ripon Hall Ox 71. **d** 92 **p** 93. NSM Romsey *Win* 92–94; Chapl Win and Eastleigh Healthcare NHS Trust 94–08; rtd 08; PtO *Win* from 09. *The Sanctuary, Salisbury Road, Plaitford, Romsey SO51 6EE* T: (01794) 323731

FLORANCE, James Andrew Vernon. b 44. MCIOB. Linc Th Coll 84. **d** 86 **p** 87. C Lt Ilford St Mich *Chelmsf* 86–90; TV Becontree S 90–93; R Orsett and Bulphan and Horndon on the Hill 93–97; P-in-c Liscard St Mary w St Columba *Ches* 97–02; RD Wallasey 99–02; Chapl St D Foundn Hospice Care Newport 02–03; P-in-c Abersychan and Garndiffaith *Mon* 03–08; rtd 08; PtO *Heref* 08–10; *Mon* 08–10; *St E* 10–20. *54 Laxfield Way, Lowestoft NR33 7HH* T: (01502) 511783 E: jandp2florance@gmail.com

FLORANCE (née WAINWRIGHT), Mrs Pauline Barbara. b 40. Edge Hill Coll of HE CertEd 60. St Deiniol's Hawarden 83. **dss** 84 **d** 87 **p** 94. New Ferry *Ches* 84–90; Par Dn 87–90; Par Dn Hallwood 90–94; C 94–00; rtd 00; PtO *Ches* 00–03; *Mon* 04–08; *Heref* 08–10; Bp's Adv in Past Care and Counselling *Mon* 07–10; PtO *St E* 10–20. *54 Laxfield Way, Lowestoft NR33 7HH* T: (01502) 511783 E: paulineb.florance@gmail.com

FLORY, John Richard. b 35. Clare Coll Cam BA 59 MA 63. Westcott Ho Cam 69. **d** 71 **p** 72. C Shirehampton *Bris* 71–74; V Patchway 74–82; R Lydiard Millicent w Lydiard Tregoz 82–86; TR The Lydiards 86–93; R Box w Hazlebury and Ditteridge 93–01; rtd 01; PtO *Derby* from 02. *3 Fir Close, Poynton, Stockport SK12 1PD* E: jeanmaryflory@gmail.com

FLOWER, Roger Edward. b 45. AKC 68. **d** 69 **p** 70. C Gt Stanmore *Lon* 69–72; C Wells St Cuth w Coxley and Wookey Hole *B & W* 72–77; V Tatworth 77–82; V-in-c Taunton St Andr 82–84; V 84–96; RD Taunton 90–96; Preb Wells Cathl 92–96; V Dartmouth *Ex* 96–99; rtd 10. *6 Trinity Close, Burnham-on-Sea TA8 2HH* T: (01278) 788614 E: rogerflower@talktalk.net

FLOWERDAY, Andrew Leslie. b 53. Imp Coll Lon BSc 75. St Jo Coll Nottm. **d** 90 **p** 91. C Farnborough *Guildf* 90–95; TV Morden *S'wark* 95–12; V Patcham *Chich* from 12. *All Saints' Vicarage, 12 Church Hill, Brighton BN1 8YE* T: (01273) 552157   E: vicar.allsaintspatcham@gmail.com   *or* fleurjour@tiscali.co.uk

FLOWERDEW, Martin James. b 56. Herts Coll CertEd 78 Pemb Coll Cam BEd 79. Sarum & Wells Th Coll 89. **d** 91 **p** 92. C Leagrave *St Alb* 91–95; C Radlett 95–99; TV Wilford Peninsula *St E* 99–01; V St Osyth *Chelmsf* 01–09; V Hoylake *Ches* 09–12; V Foremark and Repton w Newton Solney *Derby* from 12. *St Wystan's Vicarage,*

Willington Road, Repton, Derby DE65 6FH T: (01283) 619686 E: thevicarofrepton@gmail.com

FLYNN, Anna Therese. See LINDLEY, Anna Therese

FLYNN, Mrs Diane Mary. b 62. Yorks Min Course. **d** 09 **p** 10. C Roundhay St Edm *Ripon* 09–13; TV Kippax w Allerton Bywater 13–14; *Leeds* 14–16; TV Allerton Bywater, Kippax and Swillington from 16. *St Mary's Rectory, Wakefield Road, Swillington, Leeds LS26 8DS* T: 0113-286 4607 E: revdianeflynn@btinternet.com

FLYNN, Peter Murray. b 35. Oak Hill Th Coll 76. **d** 79 **p** 80. NSM Finchley St Mary *Lon* 79–83; NSM Mill Hill Jo Keble Ch 84–86; C Mill End and Heronsgate w W Hyde *St Alb* 86–92; V Chessington *Guildf* 92–05; rtd 05; PtO *Roch* from 05. *16 The Street, Plaxtol, Sevenoaks TN15 0QQ* T: (01732) 811304 E: revpeterflynn@yahoo.co.uk

FOBISTER, Mrs Wendy Irene. b 44. Lon Inst of Educn TCert 65. **d** 07 **p** 08. OLM Charminster and Stinsford *Sarum* 07–11; NSM 11–15; PtO 15–17. *44 Meadow View, Charminster, Dorchester DT2 9RE* T: (01305) 251681 E: wenfob@gmail.com

FODEN, Canon Janice Margaret. b 54. Sheff Univ BA 76 Sheff City Poly PGCE 77. NOC 98. **d** 01 **p** 02. NSM Kimberworth Park *Sheff* 01–05; P-in-c Barnby Dun 05–13; R Armthorpe from 13; AD Doncaster 10–18; Hon Can Sheff Cathl from 21. *The Rectory, Church Street, Armthorpe, Doncaster DN3 3AD* T: (01302) 831231 E: janfoden@hotmail.com *or* jan.foden@sheffield.anglican.org

FODEN-CURRIE, Mary Agnes. b 43. Bp Grosseteste Coll BEd 64. St Jo Coll Nottm MA 97. **d** 98 **p** 99. NSM Skegby *S'well* 98–02; NSM Skegby w Teversal 02–03; rtd 03; PtO *S'well* from 03. *40 Harvey Road, Mansfield NG18 4ES* T: (01623) 479838 E: revmaryfodencurrie@gmail.com

FOGDEN, Canon Elizabeth Sally. b 40. MBE 04. MCSP 61. Qu Coll Birm 76. **dss** 78 **d** 87 **p** 94. Chevington w Hargrave and Whepstead w Brockley *St E* 78–84; Honington w Sapiston and Troston 84–92; Par Dn 87–92; Par Dn Euston w Barnham, Elvedon and Fakenham Magna 90–92; Team Dn Blackbourne 92–94; TV 94–06; Chapl Center Parc Elvedon from 90; Dioc Adv for Women's Min *St E* 90–06; Hon Can St E Cathl 92–06; rtd 06; PtO *St E* 06–21; *Nor* from 19. *Meadow Farm, Coney Weston Road, Sapiston, Bury St Edmunds IP31 1RX* T: (01359) 268923 M: 07860-101980 E: sallyfogden@btinternet.com

FOGDEN, Mrs Patricia Lily Margaret. b 51. SRN 73. **d** 03 **p** 04. OLM Orlestone w Snave and Ruckinge w Warehorne etc *Cant* 03–10; NSM 10–11; NSM Appledore w Brookland, Fairfield, Brenzett etc 11–13; NSM Wittersham w Stone and Ebony 11–13; C Rother and Oxney 13–16; C Tenterden and Smallhythe 13–16; TV Tenterden, Rother and Oxney 16–21; rtd 21; PtO *Eur* from 10. *Harewood, Wye Street, Joyce, Ashford TN26 2QH* T: (01233) 733862 M: 07885-285736 E: patricia.fogden@btinternet.com

FOGG, Mrs Margaret. b 37. CBDTI 04. **d** 05 **p** 06. NSM Allonby, Cross Canonby and Dearham *Carl* 05–08; rtd 08; PtO *Carl* 08–20. *Green Pastures, 59 Sycamore Road, Maryport CA15 7AE* T: (01900) 816203 E: margaretfogg@talktalk.net

FOLEY, Geoffrey Evan. b 30. Univ of New England BA 71 DipEd 73 MEd 79. St Jo Coll Morpeth 51. **d** 53 **p** 54. C Murwillumbah Australia 53–59; R Mallanganee 59–65; R Woodburn 65–72; P-in-c Lismore 84–85; P-in-c Bangalow 87–88; P-in-c Alstonville 88–89; PtO *S'wark* 90–91; Chapl Hamburg *Eur* 91; C Stoke-upon-Trent *Lich* 91; rtd 93; Perm to Offic Grafton Australia from 93; Dioc Archivist from 97. *25 Caroona Village, 65 Rous Road, Goonellabah NSW 2480, Australia* M: (0061) 41-452 8023 E: gefoley@bigpond.net.au

FOLKARD, Oliver Goring. b 41. Nottm Univ BA 63. Lich Th Coll 64. **d** 66 **p** 67. C Carlton *S'well* 66–67; C Worksop Priory 67–68; C Brewood *Lich* 68–71; C Folkingham w Laughton *Linc* 72–75; P-in-c Gedney Hill 76–77; V 77–84; V Whaplode Drove 76–84; V Sutton St Mary 84–94; RD Elloe E 89–94; P-in-c Scotter w E Ferry 94–99; R 99–06; R Scotton w Northorpe 99–06; rtd 06; PtO *Nor* from 06. *1 Barons Close, Fakenham NR21 8BE* T: (01328) 851468

FOLKES, Arwen Mary Caroline. b 76. Dur Univ BA 16 MA 19. Westcott Ho Cam 13. **d** 16 **p** 17. C St Just-in-Roseland and St Mawes *Truro* 16–19; R E Blatchington and Bishopstone *Chich* from 19. *The Rectory, 86 Belgrave Road, Seaford BN25 2HE* T: (01323) 892964 E: rectoryebb@gmail.com

FOLKS, Peter William John. b 30. FRCO 56 ARCM. Launde Abbey 72. **d** 72 **p** 73. C Leic St Aid 72–76; V Newfoundpool 76–84; V Whetstone 84–94; rtd 94; PtO *Leic* 94–20. *4 Beaufort Close, Desford, Leicester LE9 9HS* T: (01455) 828090 E: peterfolks@hotmail.com

FOLLAND, Mrs Teresa Lorraine. b 61. SWMTC 13. **d** 16 **p** 17. C Launceston *Truro* 16–19; P-in-c N Kernow 19–21; P-in-c Kilkhampton w Morwenstow 19–21; P-in-c Poughill

19–21; R N Kernow from 21. *5 Cormorant Close, Bude EX23 8FJ* M: 07932-385995 E: teresa.folland@gmail.com

FOLLETT, Jeremy Mark. b 60. Jes Coll Cam BA 82 K Coll Lon DThMin 20. St Jo Coll Nottm 90. **d** 91 **p** 92. C Newark *S'well* 91–95; C Hellesdon *Nor* 95–01; V St Alb Ch Ch from 01. *Christ Church Vicarage, 5 High Oaks, St Albans AL3 6DJ* T: (01727) 859806 E: vicar@ccstalbans.org.uk

FOLLETT, Samuel Joseph. b 90. Nottm Univ BSc 13. Ridley Hall Cam 13. **d** 16 **p** 17. C Onslow Square and S Kensington St Aug *Lon* from 16. *1 Osten Mews, London SW7 4HW* M: 07412-555039 E: sam.follett@gmail.com

FOLLIN, Michael Stuart. b 62. UMIST BSc 84. St Jo Coll Nottm MTh 02. **d** 02 **p** 03. C Aughton Ch Ch *Liv* 02–06; TV Maghull 06–09; TV Maghull and Melling 09–17; V Werrington and Wetley Rocks *Lich* from 17; RD Cheadle from 18. *360 Ash Bank Road, Werrington, Stoke-on-Trent ST9 0JS* T: (01782) 302954 M: 07817-909525 E: michael.follin@gmail.com *or* vicar.wwr@gmail.com

FONTAINE, Mrs Marion Elizabeth. b 39. RN 61 RM 62. SAOMC 96. **d** 99 **p** 00. OLM Thatcham *Ox* from 99. *24 Ferndale Court, Thatcham RG19 4PW* T: (01635) 827746

FOOT, Canon Adam Julian David. b 58. Thames Poly BSc 80 Garnett Coll Lon CertEd 87. Trin Coll Bris 93. **d** 97 **p** 98. C Luton Ch Ch *Roch* 97–00; V Welling from 00; P-in-c Erith St Jo from 20; AD Erith from 17; Hon Can Roch Cathl from 21. *St John's Vicarage, Danson Lane, Welling DA16 2BQ* T: (020) 8303 1107 E: vicar@stjohnswelling.org.uk *or* adam_foot@lineone.net

FOOT, Daniel Henry Paris. b 46. Peterho Cam BA 67 MA 74 Didsbury Coll Man CertEd 69. Ridley Hall Cam 77. **d** 79 **p** 80. C Werrington *Pet* 79–82; P-in-c Cranford w Grafton Underwood 82; R Cranford w Grafton Underwood and Twywell 83–18; P-in-c Slipton 94–18; rtd 18. *27 Grosvenor Road, Barton Seagrave, Kettering NN15 6TF* E: katinafoot@gmail.com

FOOT, Daniel James. b 87. Trin Coll Bris 12. **d** 15 **p** 16. C Sandy *St Alb* 15–18; R Guernsey St Martin *Win* from 18. *The Rectory, La Grande Rue, St Martin, Guernsey GY4 6RR* T: (01481) 238303 E: danieljamesfoot@yahoo.co.uk

FOOT, Elizabeth Victoria Anne. b 55. St Mich Coll Sarum BEd 77 Win Univ MA 19. Trin Coll Bris BA 04. **d** 04 **p** 05. C Linkinhorne and Stoke Climsland *Truro* 04–07; C Godrevy 07–08; TV 08–11; P-in-c Zennor from 11; P-in-c Towednack from 11; C Halsetown 11–15. *The Vicarage, Nancledra, Penzance TR20 8LQ* T: (01736) 741488 E: guenolesenara@hotmail.co.uk

FOOT, Jeremy Michael. b 67. Qu Mary Coll Lon BSc 88. St Mellitus Coll 07. **d** 10 **p** 11. NSM Enfield St Jas *Lon* 10–17; NSM Bush Hill Park St Mark from 17; NSM Bush Hill Park St Steph from 17. *24 St Andrews Road, Enfield EN1 3UB* T: (020) 8366 1456 M: 07725-474769 E: jeremy@thefeet.net *or* revjeremyfoot@gmail.com

FOOT, Joachim Paul Winwaloe. b 85. Collingwood Coll Dur BA 08 K Coll Lon MA 12. Westcott Ho Cam 13. **d** 15 **p** 16. C Duloe, Herodsfoot, Morval and St Pinnock *Truro* 15–17; C Looe and Morval 17–18; TR Probus, Ladock and Grampound w Creed and St Erme from 18. *The Sanctuary, Wagg Lane, Probus, Truro TR2 4JX* E: jpwfoot@outlook.com *or* rector@probusteam.com

FOOT, Keith George. b 45. Surrey Univ BSc 70 Lon Univ PhD 73 MRSC CChem. NTMTC 96. **d** 99 **p** 00. C New Thundersley *Chelmsf* 99–03; Min Prince's Park CD *Roch* 03–07; V Prince's Park 07–10; rtd 10; PtO *Roch* from 10. *51 Elmshurst Gardens, Tonbridge TN10 3QT* T: (01732) 365185 E: rev.keith.foot@btinternet.com

FOOT, Lynda. b 43. Reading Univ BEd 75 Loughb Univ MSc 82 Nottm Univ MA 00. EMMTC 97. **d** 00 **p** 01. NSM Coalville and Bardon Hill *Leic* 00–03; NSM Hickling w Kinoulton and Broughton Sulney *S'well* 04–05; NSM Bingham 05–08; rtd 08; PtO *S'well* 08–21; *Leic* from 20. *24 Worcester Road, Leicester LE2 8HY* T: 0116-283 0330 E: lyndafoot@btinternet.com

FOOT, Prof Sarah Rosamund Irvine. b 61. Newnham Coll Cam BA 84 MA 87 PhD 90. Ox Min Course 17. **d** 17 **p** 17. Regius Prof Ecclesiastical Hist Ox Univ from 07; Can Res Ch Ch *Ox* from 17; NSM Ch Ch *Ox* 17–19. *Christ Church, Oxford OX1 1DP* T: (01865) 286078 E: sarah.foot@chch.ox.ac.uk

✠**FOOTTIT, The Rt Revd Anthony Charles.** b 35. K Coll Cam BA 57 MA 70. Cuddesdon Coll 59. **d** 61 **p** 62 **c** 99. C Wymondham *Nor* 61–64; C Blakeney w Lt Langham 64–67; P-in-c Hindringham w Binham and Cockthorpe 67–71; P-in-c Yarlington *B & W* 71–75; R N Cadbury 71–75; P-in-c S Cadbury w Sutton Montis 75; TR Camelot Par 76–81; RD Cary 79–81; Dioc Missr *Linc* 81–87; Can and Preb Linc Cathl 86–87; Dioc Rural Officer *Nor* 87; Adn Lynn 87–99; Suff Bp Lynn 99–03; rtd 03; Hon Asst Bp Nor from 04; Dioc

Environmental Officer 04–09. *1 The Dial, Reepham, Norwich NR10 4LX* T: (01603) 870340 E: acfoottit@hotmail.com

FORAN, Andrew John. b 55. Aston Tr Scheme 84 Linc Th Coll 86. **d** 88 **p** 89. C Epping St Jo *Chelmsf* 88–92; TV Canvey Is 92–97; C Dorking w Ranmore *Guildf* 97–99; Chapl HM Pris Send 97–09; Chapl HM Pris Bullingdon 09–18; PtO *Ox* from 18. *Address withheld by request* M: 07753-677470 E: andrew.foran01@gmail.com

FORBES, Mrs Angela Laura. b 47. Ox Min Course 91. **d** 94 **p** 96. NSM Cowley St Jo *Ox* 94–04; PtO from 04. *6 Elm Crescent, Charlbury, Chipping Norton OX7 3PZ* T: (01608) 819121

FORBES, Benjamin John. b 93. **d** 20 **p** 21. C Deal St Geo *Cant* from 20. *37 Nelson Street, Deal CT14 6DR*

FORBES, Elizabeth Karen. *See* FORBES STONE, Elizabeth Karen

FORBES, Canon Graham John Thompson. b 51. CBE 04. Aber Univ MA 73 Edin Univ BD 76. Edin Th Coll 73. **d** 76 **p** 77. C Edin Old St Paul 76–82; Can St Ninian's Cathl Perth *St And* 82–90; R Stanley 82–88; Provost St Ninian's Cathl Perth 82–90; R Perth St Ninian 82–90; Provost St Mary's Cathl *Edin* 90–17; R Edin St Mary 90–17; rtd 17; Hon Can St Mary's Cathl *Edin* from 19. *The Priory, 18 Priory Court, Pittenweem, Anstruther KY10 2LJ* T: (01333) 312061 M: 07711-199297 E: gjtforbes@outlook.com

FORBES, Iain William. b 56. Ex Univ BA 81. Chich Th Coll 83. **d** 85 **p** 86. C Upper Norwood St Jo *S'wark* 85–88; C Lewisham St Mary 88–90; Chapl St Martin's Coll of Educn *Blackb* 90–94; P-in-c Woodplumpton 94–99; Dioc Voc Adv 94–99; V Woodham *Guildf* from 99. *The Vicarage, 25 Woodham Waye, Woking GU21 5SW* T: (01483) 762857 E: fatheriainforbes@aol.com

FORBES, Canon Joyce Brinella. b 52. **d** 03 **p** 04. OLM Norbury St Steph and Thornton Heath *S'wark* from 03; Hon Can S'wark Cathl from 14. *36 Dalmeny Avenue, London SW16 4RT* T: (020) 8240 0283 *or* 7525 7982 E: petnard36@aol.com

FORBES, Moira Ruth. b 76. Birm Univ BA 99. Ridley Hall Cam 02. **d** 04 **p** 05. C Welling *Roch* 04–08; NSM Aldershot H Trin *Guildf* 09–12; PtO 13–15; V Hazelwell *Birm* from 15. *St Mary Magdalen's Vicarage, 316 Vicarage Road, Kings Heath, Birmingham B14 7NN* T: 0121-444 4469 E: hazelwellvicar@gmail.com

FORBES, Patrick. b 38. Open Univ BA 82. Linc Th Coll 64. **d** 66 **p** 67. C Yeovil *B & W* 66–69; C Plumstead Wm Temple Ch Abbey Wood CD *S'wark* 69–70; Thamesmead Ecum Gp 70–73; TV Thamesmead *S'wark* 73–78; Dioc Communications Officer *St Alb* 78–90; P-in-c Offley w Lilley 78–82; Info Officer Communications Dept Ch Ho Lon 91–95; Press Officer Miss to Seamen 95–99; rtd 99; PtO *St Alb* from 04. *18 Francis Road, Hinxworth, Baldock SG7 5HL* T: (01462) 742015 E: patrickforbes06@gmail.com

FORBES, Raymond John. b 34. ALCD 58. **d** 58 **p** 59. C Wandsworth St Steph *S'wark* 58–61; C Kewstoke *B & W* 61–63; V Fordcombe *Roch* 63–73; R Ashurst 64–73; P-in-c Morden w Almer and Charborough *Sarum* 73–76; P-in-c Bloxworth 73–76; V Red Post 76–84; P-in-c Hamworthy 84–92; P-in-c Symondsbury and Chideock 92–96; rtd 96; PtO *Sarum* 96–19. *3 Shelley Court, Library Road, Ferndown BH22 9JZ* T: (01202) 897567

FORBES, Stuart. b 33. Lon Univ BD 59. Oak Hill Th Coll 56. **d** 61 **p** 62. C Halliwell St Pet *Man* 61–64; P-in-c Wicker w Neepsend *Sheff* 64–69; V Stainforth 69–77; V Salterhebble All SS *Wakef* 77–89; V Toxteth Park St Mich w St Andr *Liv* 89–98; rtd 98; PtO *Lich* 00–19. *29 Firbeck Gardens, Wildwood, Stafford ST17 4QR* T: (01785) 663658

FORBES, Susan Margaret. *See* VAN BEVEREN, Susan Margaret

FORBES STONE, Elizabeth Karen (Buff). b 61. Birm Univ MB, ChB 85 MRCGP 89. Ridley Hall Cam BA 99. **d** 00 **p** 01. C Brentford *Lon* 00–02; C Shaw cum Donnington *Ox* 02–08; Chapl R Berks NHS Foundn Trust 09–10; PtO *Cov* 10–12; C Cov St Fran N Radford 12–16; Min Stoke Aldermoor CD 16–19; V Stoke Aldermoor and New Century Park from 19; AD Cov E from 19. *55 Cotswold Drive, Coventry CV3 6EZ* T: (024) 7641 9831 M: 07954-652824 E: buff@dandb.org.uk

FORD, Adam. b 40. Lanc Univ MA 72 K Coll Lon BD 63 AKC 63. **d** 65 **p** 65. C Cirencester *Glouc* 65–70; V Hebden Bridge *Wakef* 70–76; Chapl St Paul's Girls' Sch Hammersmith 77–01; LtO *Lon* 77–98; P in O 84–91; rtd 05; PtO *Chich* from 13. *Bramble, Weaver's Lane, Alfriston BN26 5TH* E: adamfordspgs@hotmail.com

FORD, Alun James. b 73. Ex Univ BA 94 MA 96 Man Univ PhD 09 St Jo Coll Cam BA 11. Westcott Ho Cam 08. **d** 11 **p** 12. C Newc St Geo and St Hilda 11–14; V Sugley 14–17; P-in-c Fen Ditton *Ely* 17–20; P-in-c Horningsea 17–20;

P-in-c Teversham 17–20; Bp's Chapl *S'wark* from 20; Hon Min Can *S'wark* Cathl from 20; PtO *Lon* from 20. *Bishop's House, 38 Tooting Bec Gardens, London SW16 1QZ* T: (020) 8769 3256 E: alun.ford@southwark.anglican.org

FORD, The Very Revd Amanda Kirstine. b 61. Middx Univ BA 83 Open Univ MA 97 Ox Univ BTh 04 Nottm Univ MA 07 PhD 12. St Steph Ho Ox 98. **d** 00 **p** 01. C Leic Resurr 00–05; P-in-c Beaumont Leys 05–09; V 09–14; P-in-c Stocking Farm 11–14; AD City of Leic 11–14; Dioc CUF Officer 04–14; Hon Can Leic Cathl 13–14; Can Res and Chan S'wark Cathl 14–20; Dir Minl Educn 14–20; Dir Min Division Abps' Coun 18–19; Dean Bris from 20. *The Deanery, 20 Charlotte Street, Bristol BS1 5PZ* E: mandyford@btinternet.com *or* dean@bristol-cathedral.co.uk

FORD, Anthony. b 60. Oak Hill Th Coll 06. **d** 08 **p** 09. C Chadderton Ch Ch *Man* 08–11; P-in-c Balderstone 11–13; V 13–18; P-in-c Barrow St Mark *Carl* from 18. *St Mark's Vicarage, Rawlinson Street, Barrow-in-Furness LA14 1BX* T: (01229) 820405 M: 07816-596878 E: tonyford227@btinternet.com

FORD, Mrs Avril Celia. b 43. St Mary's Coll Dur BSc 64 Chelsea Coll Lon PGCE 65. **d** 92 **p** 94. OLM Horncastle w Low Toynton *Linc* 92–98; NSM 98–06; OLM High Toynton 92–98; NSM 98–06; OLM Greetham w Ashby Puerorum 92–98; NSM 98–06; OLM Horncastle Gp 06–16; PtO from 16. *Frolic, Reindeer Close, Horncastle LN9 5AA* T: (01507) 526234 *or* 525600 E: avrilford@btinternet.com

FORD, Brian. b 40. OBE 89. Imp Coll Lon BSc 62 Nottm Univ MSc 66 PhD 74 Ox Univ MA 74 CMath FIMA ARCS. SAOMC 96. **d** 99 **p** 00. NSM Witney *Ox* 99–02; NSM Forest Edge 02–15; rtd 15; PtO *Ox* from 15. *Ramsden Farmhouse, Ramsden, Oxford OX7 3AU* T: (01993) 868343 F: 868322 E: brianford2809@gmail.com

FORD, Carol Mary. See BARRETT FORD, Carol Mary

FORD (née HARRISON-WATSON), Mrs Carole. b 44. Reading Univ BSc 66 St Martin's Coll Lanc PGCE 79. Carl Dioc Tr Inst 92. **d** 95 **p** 96. NSM Windermere St Martin *Carl* 95–98; NSM Borrowdale 98–01; NSM Thornthwaite cum Braithwaite, Newlands etc 01–05; rtd 05; PtO *Carl* from 05. *4 Woodlands Drive, Allithwaite, Grange-over-Sands LA11 7PZ*

FORD, Canon Christopher Simon. b 51. Leeds Univ MPhil 86 PhD 91. AKC 74. **d** 75 **p** 76. C Wythenshawe Wm Temple Ch *Man* 75–77; C New Bury 77–80; R Old Trafford St Jo 80–94; R Moston St Jo 94–05; P-in-c Davyhulme St Mary 05–09; V from 09; AD N Man 94–00; Hon Can Man Cathl from 04; Borough Dean Trafford from 11; AD Stretford 19–21. *St Mary's Vicarage, 13 Vicarage Road, Urmston, Manchester M41 5TP* T: 0161-748 2210 E: christopher.ford5@btinternet.com

FORD, David John. b 38. Lon Coll of Div BD 68. **d** 69 **p** 70. C Blackheath St Jo *S'wark* 69–71; C Westlands St Andr *Lich* 71–75; V Sheff St Steph w St Phil and St Ann 75–77; R Netherthorpe 77–80; TR 80–84; R Thrybergh 82–84; R Thrybergh w Hooton Roberts 84–94; Ind Chapl 86–87; TV Parkham, Alwington, Buckland Brewer etc *Ex* 94–01; rtd 03; Hon C Knaresborough *Ripon* 01–05; PtO *York* 07–16. *19 Broom Drive, Rotherham S60 3NS* T: (01709) 641375

FORD, David Stuart. b 61. City of Lon Poly BA 82 Qu Coll Birm MA 09. WMMTC 06. **d** 09 **p** 10. C Bramhope and Ireland Wood *Ripon* 09–10; C Leeds City 10–11; Chapl Chapl Abbey Grange High Sch 09–11; TV Hucknall Torkard *S'well* 11–14; Chapl Nat C of E Academy Hucknall 11–14; P-in-c Northleach w Hampnett and Farmington etc *Glouc* 14–16; R 16–19; TR Bromsgrove *Worc* from 19; V Dodford from 19. *The Vicarage, 15 Finstall Road, Bromsgrove B60 2EA* T: (01527) 873831 M: 07973-412625 E: revdavidford@googlemail.com

FORD, Mrs Deborah Perrin. b 59. Leeds Univ BA 81 Birm Univ MSocSc 85 Univ of Wales (Ban) BTh CQSW 85. EAMTC 00. **d** 03 **p** 04. NSM Cambridge St Benedict *Ely* 03–12; NSM Cambridge St Jas from 12; Chapl Cam Univ Hosps NHS Foundn Trust from 03; Bp's Adv for Healthcare Chapl *Ely* from 16. *102 Millington Lane, Cambridge CB3 9HA* T: (01223) 329321 *or* 363113 E: deborahford@gmail.com

FORD, Mrs Gaynor. b 47. Univ of Wales (Lamp) BA 99. **d** 17 **p** 18. NSM Dale and St Brides w Marloes and Hasguard w St Ishmael's St D 17–19; NSM Roose from 19. *4 Pond Meadow, Steynton, Milford Haven SA73 1HB* T: (01646) 693452 E: gaynorford2846@btinternet.com

FORD, Canon Henry Malcolm. b 33. Em Coll Cam BA 54 MA 58. Ely Th Coll 58. **d** 59 **p** 69. C Ipswich St Matt *St E* 59–61; Hon C Bury St Edmunds St Jo 66–76; Hon C Hawstead and Nowton w Stanningfield etc 76–89; Hon Can St E Cathl 86–97; Hon Cockfield w Bradfield St Clare, Felsham etc 89–98; PtO 09–19. *Thatch on the Green, Cross Green, Cockfield, Bury St Edmunds IP30 0LG* T: (01284) 828479

FORD, John. See FORD, William John

⊠**FORD, The Rt Revd John Frank.** b 52. Chich Univ MA 04. Chich Th Coll 76. **d** 79 **p** 80 **c** 05. C Forest Hill Ch Ch *S'wark* 79–82; V Lee St Aug 82–91; V Lower Beeding and Dom Chapl to Bp Horsham *Chich* 91–94; Dioc Missr 94–00; Can and Preb Chich Cathl 97–00; Can Res and Prec Chich Cathl 00–05; Suff Bp Plymouth *Ex* 05–13; Asst Bp Truro 11–13; Bp The Murray Australia 13–19; rtd 19. *Address temp unknown*

FORD, Jonathan Laurence. See ALDERTON-FORD, Jonathan Laurence

FORD, Mrs Kimberley Kaye. b 65. St Jo Coll Nottm 09. **d** 11 **p** 12. C Market Harborough and The Transfiguration etc *Leic* 11–14; P-in-c Glen Magna cum Stretton Magna etc 14–19; TV Oadby from 19; Warden Past Assts from 18. *St Cuthbert's Vicarage, Church Road, Great Glen, Leicester LE8 9FE* T: 0116-259 2238 E: kimberleykford@aim.com

FORD, Nancy Celia. b 48. Open Univ BA 02 FCIPD 00. STETS 98. **d** 01 **p** 02. NSM Crookham *Guildf* 01–04; NSM Aldershot St Mich 04–07; Asst Dioc Dir of Ords 04–05; Bp's Chapl 05–10; Min Can Guildf Cathl 07–14; rtd 14; PtO *Chich* from 14. *40 Orchard Avenue, Worthing BN14 7QB* T: (01903) 411523 E: nancyc.ford@sky.com

FORD, Peter. b 46. York Univ MA 96 Bede Coll Dur TCert 72 ACP 75. Linc Th Coll 76. **d** 78 **p** 79. OGS from 72; C Hartlepool H Trin *Dur* 78–81; Dioc Youth Officer *Wakef* 81–84; C Mirfield Eastthorpe St Paul 82–84; C Upper Hopton 82–84; V Dodworth 84–88; Chapl and Hd RS Rishworth Sch Ripponden 88–97; Ho Master 94–97; P-in-c Accrington St Mary *Blackb* 97–99; C Torrisholme 99–01; V Warton St Paul 01–08; Dioc Ecum Officer 01–08; Germany 08–09; P-in-c Las Palmas *Eur* 09–13; P-in-c Oporto 13; rtd 13; Port Chapl Miss to Seafarers and Asst Chapl Gib Cathl *Eur* 16–17; P-in-c Lanzarote 17–18; PtO from 18; *York* from 21. *32 Dulverton Hall, Esplanade, Scarborough YO11 2AR* T: (01723) 354211 M: 07506-702713 E: pford@ogs.net *or* peter.ford75@yahoo.co.uk

FORD, Canon Peter Hugh. b 43. St Cath Coll Cam BA 65 MA 69. Cuddesdon Coll 65. **d** 67 **p** 68. C Is of Dogs Ch Ch and St Jo w St Luke *Lon* 67–70; C Tillsonburg St Jo Canada 70–71; St Catherine's St Thos 71–73; P-in-c Thorold South Resurr 71–73; R Port Colborne St Brendan 73–78; R Milton Grace Ch 78–80; Can Pastor Ch Ch Cathl Hamilton 80–86; Adn Lincoln 86–91; R Niagara-on-the-Lake St Mark 86–91; Hon Chapl Niagara from 91; Hon C Montserrat St Geo Canada 91; R Saba 92–98; PtO *Chich* 98–99; V Newchurch and Arreton *Portsm* 99–07; rtd 07; PtO *Portsm* from 15. *11 Vokins Rise, Esplanade, Ryde PO33 2AX* T: (01983) 568286 E: islandpeter@btinternet.com

FORD, Philippa. b 65. RVC (Lon) BVetMed 90. St Mellitus Coll MA 18. **d** 16 **p** 17. C Burpham *Guildf* 16–17; C Guildf All SS 17–19; C Woking Ch Ch 19–21; V Camberley St Mich Yorktown from 21. *The Vicarage, 286 London Road, Camberley GU15 3JP* M: 07814-847436

FORD, Mrs Rachel Joy. b 83. York Univ BA 04 York St Jo Univ PGCE 05. St Hild Coll 16. **d** 19 **p** 21. C Abbeylands *Leeds* from 19. *The Vicarage, 1 Scotland Close, Horsforth, Leeds LS18 5SG* T: 0113-258 1719 E: rachel.ford@leeds.anglican.org

FORD, Richard. b 47. Grey Coll Dur BA 69 PGCE 70 FRSA 94. SEITE 06. **d** 09 **p** 10. NSM Sanderstead *S'wark* 09–15; NSM W Wickham St Fran and St Mary 15–17; NSM W Wickham St Jo 15–17; PtO from 17. *7 Sylvan Way, West Wickham BR4 9HA* T: (020) 8289 2432 M: 07706-998272 E: richard.ford73@ntlworld.com

FORD, Richard Graham. b 39. AKC 65 Open Univ BA 96. **d** 66 **p** 67. C Morpeth *Newc* 66–71; C Fordingbridge w Ibsley *Win* 71–73; TV Whorlton *Newc* 73–80; Chapl RNR 75–92; V Choppington *Newc* 80–92; V Tynemouth Priory 92–04; rtd 04; PtO *S'well* from 16. *13 St Mary's Drive, Edwinstowe, Mansfield NG21 9LY* T: (01623) 824985 E: richardford43@btinternet.com

FORD, Roger James. b 33. Sarum & Wells Th Coll 81. **d** 83 **p** 84. C Sidcup St Jo Roch 83–86; V Darenth 86–98; rtd 98; PtO *Cov* 02–04. *21 Hawthorn Way, Shipston-on-Stour CV36 4FD* T: (01608) 664875 E: roger585413@gmail.com

FORD, Roger Lindsay. b 47. Ex Univ LLB 68. Llan Dioc Tr Scheme 87. **d** 91 **p** 92. NSM Fairwater *Llan* 91–96; NSM Llandaff 96–01; NSM Arthog w Fairbourne w Llangelynnin w Rhoslefain *Ban* 12–14; NSM Bro Cymer from 14. *The Rectory, Llwyngwril LL37 2JB* T: (01341) 250888 E: lindsayrectory@hotmail.co.uk

FORD, Mrs Shirley Elsworth. b 40. AIMLS 67. Sarum & Wells Th Coll 89. **d** 91 **p** 94. C Farnham *Guildf* 91–96; V Wrecclesham 96–04; rtd 04; PtO *Chich* from 05. *19 St Luke's Terrace, Brighton BN2 9ZE* T: (01273) 674061

FORD, Canon William John. b 50. Linc Th Coll 89. **d** 91 **p** 92. C Marton-in-Cleveland *York* 91–94; V Whorlton w Carlton and Faceby 94–02; P-in-c Stainton w Hilton 02–12; P-in-c Brookfield 11–12; R Yarm 12–19; P-in-c Crathorne 17–19; P-in-c Kirklevington w Picton, and High and Low Worsall 17–19; P-in-c Rudby in Cleveland w Middleton 17–19; P-in-c Whorlton w Carlton and Faceby 18–19; R Yarm w Kirklevington, Picton and Worsall 19–20; RD Stokesley 03–20; Can and Preb York Minster 13–20; rtd 20; Hon Can False Bay S Africa from 19; PtO *York* from 20. *21 Swainston Close, Middlesbrough TS5 8SF* T: (01642) 837171 E: revjohnford@sky.com

FORDE, The Ven Barry George. d 07 **p** 08. C Coleraine *Conn* 07–10; Chapl and Dean of Residence QUB from 10; Adn Belfast *Conn* from 20. *22 Elmwood Avenue, Belfast BT9 6AY* T: (028) 9573 5980 *or* 9066 7754 E: barryforde74@gmail.com

FORDE, The Very Revd Stephen Bernard. b 61. Edin Univ BSc. TCD Div Sch. **d** 86 **p** 87. C Belfast St Mary w H Redeemer *Conn* 86–89; Chapl QUB 89–95; Min Can Belf Cathl 89–91; Bp's Dom Chapl *Conn* 90–95; I Dublin Booterstown *D & G* 95–99; Dean of Res UCD 95–99; I Larne and Inver *Conn* 99–18; I Glynn w Raloo 99–18; Adn Dalriada 06–18; Dean Belf from 18. *The Deanery, 5 Deramore Drive, Belfast BT9 5JQ* T: (028) 9066 0980 *or* 9032 8332 E: stephenforde@btinternet.com *or* dean@belfastcathedral.org

FORDHAM, Richard George. b 34. AIMarE 60 TEng(CEI) 71 FBIM 74. **d** 91 **p** 92. NSM Cookham *Ox* 91–94; NSM Hedsor and Bourne End 94–01; PtO 01–03; *Ely* from 03. *6 Sorrel Way, Downham Market PE38 9UD* T: (01366) 384271 E: richardfordham939@btinternet.com

FORDYCE, Andrew Ian. b 70. MBE 21. K Alfred's Coll Win BA 94 Southn Univ PGCE 96. Trin Coll Bris BA 03. **d** 03 **p** 04. C Bramshott and Liphook *Portsm* 03–07; V Berechurch St Marg w St Mich *Chelmsf* 07–19; V Tenpenny Villages from 19. *The Rectory, St Andrew's Close, Alresford, Colchester CO7 8BL* M: 07790-543304 E: revdyce@gmail.com

FOREMAN, Mrs Jennifer Ruth. b 90. York Univ BA 11 St Jo Coll Dur BA 17. Cranmer Hall Dur 14. **d** 17 **p** 18. C Kingston upon Hull St Nic *York* from 17. *5 Gemsbok Way, Hull HU4 6UF* M: 07768-593395 E: jenni.r.foreman@gmail.com

FOREMAN, Canon Patrick Brian. b 41. CertEd. St Jo Coll Nottm 77. **d** 79 **p** 80. C Gainsborough All SS *Linc* 79–83; V Thornton St Jas *Bradf* 83–91; R Hevingham w Hainford and Stratton Strawless *Nor* 91–99; RD Ingworth 94–99; V Heacham 99–06; Hon Can Nor Cathl 03–06; rtd 06; PtO *Nor* from 06; Bp's Officer for Rtd Clergy and Widows 08–15. *Seorah, 7 Mallard Close, Fakenham NR21 8PU* T: (01328) 853691 E: patrick@pandmforeman.eclipse.co.uk

FOREMAN, Mrs Penelope. b 47. Lon Inst of Educn TCert 68 Ch Ch Coll Cant BEd 90 MA 93. SEITE 04. **d** 06 **p** 07. NSM Roch St Justus 06–15; P-in-c Chatham St Mary w St Jo 15–17; AD Roch 14–17; rtd 17. *28 Kingsway, Chatham ME5 7HT* T: (01634) 571220 E: penny.foreman@btinternet.com

FOREMAN, Timothy. b 56. K Coll Lon BD 77. SEITE 97. **d** 99 **p** 00. C Camberwell St Giles w St Matt *S'wark* 99–02; R Buckland-in-Dover *Cant* 02–13; Hon Min Can Cant Cathl 04–13; V Walker *Newc* 13–18; P-in-c Eastchurch w Leysdown and Harty *Cant* 18–20; PtO from 20. *1 Redan Place, Marine Parade, Sheerness ME12 2AA* E: fr.timforeman@gmail.com

FOREMAN, Vanessa Jane. See LAWRENCE, Vanessa Jane

FORESHEW-CAIN, Andrew David. b 63. Aber Univ BSc 86. Ripon Coll Cuddesdon BA 89. **d** 90 **p** 91. C Walworth St Jo *S'wark* 90–94; Bp's Dom Chapl *Ox* 94–98; P-in-c Kilburn St Mary w All So *Lon* 98–01; P-in-c W Hampstead St Jas 98–01; V Kilburn St Mary w All So and W Hampstead St Jas 01–17; AD N Camden 07–14; Chapl LMH Ox from 19. *Lady Margaret Hall, Norham Gardens, Oxford OX2 6QA* T: (01865) 274300 E: andynw6@icloud.com *or* andrew.foreshew-cain@lmh.ox.ac.uk

FORMAN, Alastair Gordon. b 48. St Jo Coll Nottm 78. **d** 80 **p** 81. C Pennycross *Ex* 80–83; C Woking St Jo *Guildf* 83–88; V Luton Lewsey St Hugh *St Alb* 88–95; P-in-c Jersey Millbrook St Matt *Win* 95–01; P-in-c Jersey St Lawr 95–01; PtO 14–16; C Bishopsnympton, Rose Ash, Mariansleigh etc *Ex* 15–16; C S Molton w Nymet St George, High Bray etc 15–16; TV Bishopsnympton, Charles, E Anstey, High Bray etc from 16. *East Rock Barn, Bishops Nympton, South Molton EX36 4PL* T: (01769) 551719 M: 07776-144540 E: alastair.forman@gmail.com

FORMAN, Deborah Jayne. b 56. LMH Ox BA 78 MA 83 PGCE 79 Lambeth STh 07. STETS 05. **d** 08 **p** 09. C Churchdown St Jo and Innsworth *Glouc* 09–11; P-in-c Pebworth, Dorsington, Honeybourne etc 11–14; C Quinton and Welford w Weston 11–14; TV Vale and

Cotswold Edge 14–16; V Addington *S'wark* from 16; Dir Ords Croydon Area from 17. *The Vicarage, Spout Hill, Croydon CR0 5AN* T: (01689) 847092 M: 07985-943371 E: deborah.forman2@btinternet.com

FORRER, Michael Dennett Cuthbert. b 34. St Pet Hall Ox BA 59 MA 63. Wycliffe Hall Ox 59. **d** 60 **p** 61. C Westwood *Cov* 60–63; C Cov Cathl 63–71; Ind Chapl 63–69; Sen Ind Chapl 69–71; Hon C All Hallows by the Tower etc *Lon* 76–99; Asst P Bangkok Ch Ch Thailand 81–89; PtO *Sarum* 99–01; *Ox* 01–02 and from 11; Hon C Sonning 02–11; rtd 04. *36 Ravensbourne Drive, Woodley, Reading RG5 4LJ* T: 0118-996 8050 M: 07899-926020 E: majing3008@gmail.com

FORREST, Antony William. b 60. Imp Coll Lon BSc 82 Sussex Univ PGCE 83 Leic Univ MBA 06 Win Univ MA 12 ARCS 82 FCollP 08. STETS 08. **d** 11 **p** 12. C Portsea N End St Mark *Portsm* 11–15; Chapl Portsm Coll 12–15; R Meon Bridge *Portsm* from 15; C Soberton, Newtown and Hambledon from 19. *The Rectory, Rectory Lane, Meonstoke, Southampton SO32 3NF* T: (01489) 877422

FORREST, Michael Barry Eric. b 38. Lon Univ BA 87 MA 89. NZ Bd of Th Studies LTh 62 Chich Th Coll 64. **d** 66 **p** 67. C Beckenham St Jas *Roch* 66–70; P-in-c Cape Vogel Papua New Guinea 70–73; P-in-c Alotau 74; R Lae 74–76; C Altarnon and Bolventor *Truro* 76–78; TV N w Altarnon, Bolventor and Lewannick 78–79; R St Martin w E and W Looe 79–84; V Kensington St Phil Earl's Court *Lon* 84–04; rtd 04; PtO *Chich* from 04. *12 Riley Road, Brighton BN2 4AH* T: (01273) 690231 E: mbe.forrest@gmail.com

FORREST, Canon Robin Whyte. b 33. Edin Th Coll 58. **d** 61 **p** 62. C Glas St Mary 61–66; R Renfrew 66–70; R Motherwell 70–79; R Wishaw 75–79; R Forres *Mor* 79–98; R Nairn 79–92; Can St Andr Cathl Inverness 88–98; Hon Can St Andr Cathl Inverness from 98; Syn Clerk 91–92; Dean Mor 92–98; rtd 98. *Landeck, Cummingston, Elgin IV30 5XY* T/F: (01343) 835539 E: robin.forrest33@btinternet.com

FORREST (*née* Dinwiddy), **Sarah Louise.** b 72. Charing Cross Hosp Medical Sch MB, BS 97 MRCGP 07. ERMC 14. **d** 17 **p** 18. C Bishop's Stortford *St Alb* 17–20; P-in-c Gt Amwell w St Margaret's and Stanstead Abbots from 20. *The Vicarage, 25 Hoddesdon Road, Stanstead Abbotts, Ware SG12 8EG* M: 07488-914972 E: sarahforrest23@icloud.com *or* vicar@3churches.net

FORREST-REDFERN, Mrs Susan Michéle. b 57. S Bank Poly BEd 86. St Jo Coll Nottm 01. **d** 03 **p** 04. C Lostock St Thos and St Jo *Man* 03–06; C Bolton St Bede 05–06; Ch/Sch Missr E Bolton 06–15; C Tonge Fold 07–10; Chapl St Cath Academy Bolton 11–15; TV Morley *Leeds* from 15. *4 Lewisham Street, Morley, Leeds LS27 0LA* T: 0113-252 3783 M: 07738-407852 E: revsuefr@yahoo.co.uk

FORRESTER, Brenda Rose. b 72. Newc Univ BSc 93 Dur Univ MA 02. Lindisfarne Regional Tr Partnership 15. **d** 18 **p** 19. NSM Washington *Dur* from 18. *113 Rydal Road, Chester le Street DH2 3DS* T: 0191-387 3993 M: 07988-320368 E: forresterbrenda06@gmail.com

FORRESTER, Ian Michael. b 56. Chich Th Coll. **d** 82 **p** 83. C Leigh-on-Sea St Marg *Chelmsf* 82–84; Min Can, Succ and Dean's V Windsor 84–86; Prec and Chapl Chelmsf Cathl 86–91; Chapl Lancing Coll 91–99; P-in-c Boxgrove *Chich* 99–20; V from 20; Dioc Liturgy and Music Consultant from 95. *The Vicarage, Boxgrove, Chichester PO18 0ED* T: (01243) 774045 E: revdianforrester@hotmail.com

FORRESTER, James Oliphant. b 50. SS Coll Cam BA 72 MA 76. Wycliffe Hall Ox 73. **d** 76 **p** 77. C Hull St Jo Newland *York* 76–80; C Fulwood *Sheff* 80–87; V Lodge Moor St Luke 87–90; V Ecclesfield 90–01; AD 99–01; P-in-c Kingston upon Hull H Trin *York* 01–02; V and Lect 02–09; V Longnor, Quarnford and Sheen *Lich* 09–16; RD Alstonfield 12–16; rtd 16; PtO *Heref* from 17. *4 Mortimer Drive, Orleton, Ludlow SY8 4JW* E: james@forres50.plus.com

FORRESTER, Robin William. b 43. Kent Univ MA 84 Aston Univ MSc 90. All Nations Chr Coll 64. **d** 04 **p** 05. NSM Wharton *Ches* 04–11; P-in-c Moulton 06–11; rtd 11; PtO *Ches* from 11. *27 Leven Avenue, Winsford CW7 3TA* T: (01606) 215248 E: robinforrester@sky.com

FORSDIKE, Alan William. b 55. **d** 05 **p** 06. NSM Westerfield and Tuddenham w Witnesham *St E* 05–19; P-in-c 17–19; Chapl Inspiring Ipswich project from 19. *Hill House, 2 Henley Road, Ipswich IP1 3SF* T: (01473) 252904 E: alan@wtandw.org.uk *or* alan.forsdike@btinternet.com

FORSE, Reginald Austin. b 43. Oak Hill Th Coll 77. **d** 79 **p** 80. C Crofton *Portsm* 79–84; NSM Gosport Ch Ch 91–96; NSM Alverstoke 96–13; PtO from 13. *40 Osprey Gardens, Lee-on-the-Solent PO13 8LJ* T: (023) 9255 3395 E: regforse@yahoo.co.uk

FORSHAW, David Oliver. b 27. Trin Coll Cam BA 50 MA 52. Qu Coll Birm. **d** 53 **p** 54. C Glen Parva and S Wigston *Leic* 53–55; Singapore 55–59; V Heptonstall *Wakef* 59–66; V

Whitehaven St Nic *Carl* 66–76; P-in-c Whitehaven Ch Ch w H Trin 73–76; V Benchill *Man* 76–89; C Elton All SS 89–92; rtd 92; PtO *Carl* 92–18. *The College of St Barnabas, Blackberry Lane, Lingfield RH7 6NJ*

FORSHAW, Mrs Frances Ann. b 52. Edin Univ BSc 74 Glas Univ MN 91 RGN 76 SCM 78. Moray Ord Course 91. **d** 98 **p** 02. NSM Elgin w Lossiemouth *Mor* 98–01; NSM Perth St Jo *St And* 01–05; P-in-c Pitlochry and Kilmaveonaig 05–09; NSM St Ninian's Cathl Perth 09–10; Miss P Fochabers *Mor* 10–15; rtd 15; PtO *St And* from 17. *Sunhaven, Caputh, Perth PH1 4JL* E: francesforshaw1@gmail.com

FORSHAW, Mrs Susan Margaret. b 47. Man Univ BSc 68 Makerere Univ Kampala DipEd 69. EMMTC 82. **dss** 82 **d** 87 **p** 95. Cinderhill *S'well* 82–85; Dioc Adv in Adult Educn 85–92; Par Dn Nottingham St Mary and St Cath 93–95; Lect 95–97; Asst Chapl Qu Medical Cen Nottm Univ Hosp NHS Trust 97–03; Sen Chapl 03–07; rtd 07; PtO *Leic* from 08. *33 Upton Close, Millers Reach, Castle Donington, Derby DE74 2GN* T: (01332) 858267 E: susanforshaw@talktalk.net

FORSTER, Alistair Marcus. b 66. Ch Ch Coll Cant BA 90. St Aug Coll of Th 15. **d** 18 **p** 19. C Norbury St Oswald *S'wark* from 18. *The Vicarage, 23 St Paul's Road, Thornton Heath CR7 8NB* M: 07710-405187 E: alistair.forster101@gmail.com

✠**FORSTER, The Rt Revd Andrew James.** b 67. QUB BA 89. CITC BTh 92. **d** 92 **p** 93 **c** 19. C Willowfield *D & D* 92–95; Dean of Res QUB 95–02; C of I Adv Downtown Radio Newtownards 96–02; I Drumcliffe w Lissadell and Munninane *K, E & A* 02–07; Adn Elphin and Ardagh 02–07; I Drumglass w Moygashel *Arm* 07–19; Adn Ardboe 15–19; Bp D & R from 19. *The See House, 112 Culmore Road, Londonderry BT48 8JF* T: (028) 7135 1206 E: bishop@derry.anglican.org

FORSTER, Gregory Stuart. b 47. Worc Coll Ox BA 69 MA 73. Wycliffe Hall Ox 69. **d** 72 **p** 73. C Bath Walcot *B & W* 72–74; C Bolton Em *Man* 74–76; C Bolton St Paul w Em 77–79; R Northenden 79–15; rtd 15; PtO *Heref* from 16. *43 Essex Road, Church Stretton SY6 6AY*

FORSTER, Jonathan William. b 82. St Mellitus Coll 15. **d** 18 **p** 19. C Huyton Quarry *Liv* 18–21; C 4Saints Team from 21. *Address withheld by request* E: revjontyforster@gmail.com

FORSTER, The Very Revd Thomas Shane. b 72. QUB BA 93 TCD MPhil 95. CITC BTh 93. **d** 96 **p** 97. C Drumglass w Moygashel *Arm* 96–99; I Donaghmore w Donaghmore Upper 99–06; I Ballymore from 06; Dom Chapl to Abp *Arm* 97–06; Sen Dom Chapl 06–13; Exec Chapl from 13; Hon V Choral Arm Cathl 97–07; Dioc Communications Officer 02–09; Asst Dioc and Prov Registrar from 09; Dean Arm and Keeper of Public Lib from 21; Can St Patr Cathl Dublin from 14. *Ballymore Rectory, 10 Glebe Hill Road, Tandragee, Craigavon BT62 2DP* T: (028) 3884 0224 E: ballymore@armagh.anglican.org*or*dean@stpatricks-cathedral.org *or* executivechaplain@armagh.anglican.org

FORSTER, William. b 50. NOC 92. **d** 95 **p** 96. C Ashton-in-Makerfield St Thos *Liv* 95–00; TR Fazakerley Em 00–08; TV Eccleston 08–15; rtd 15; PtO *Liv* from 16. *7 Sunningdale Close, Liverpool L36 4QF* T: 0151-482 6623 E: william.forster1@btopenworld.com

FORSYTH, John Warren. b 38. Univ of W Aus BA 62 Princeton Th Sem DMin 98. St Mich Th Coll Crafers 65. **d** 65 **p** 66. C Busselton Australia 65–68; R Kondinin 68–72; C Warwick St Mary *Cov* 72–74; C Edin St Pet 74–76; R E Fremantle and Palmyra Australia 76–79; Chapl Abp Perth 79–82; Warden Wollaston 79–82; R Midland 82–89; Sen Angl Chapl R Perth Hosp 89–06; rtd 06; Perm to Offic Dio Perth Australia from 06. *40B Cookham Road, Lathlain WA 6100, Australia* T: (0061) (8) 9472 1893 M: 89-472 1893 E: forsyth@iinet.net.au

FORTNUM, Brian Charles Henry. b 48. Hertf Coll Ox MA Imp Coll Lon MSc. Wycliffe Hall Ox 82. **d** 84 **p** 85. C Tonbridge St Steph *Roch* 84–87; V Shorne 87–94; P-in-c Speldhurst w Groombridge and Ashurst 94–98; R 98–01; V Tunbridge Wells St Mark 01–12; rtd 12; PtO *Roch* from 13. *27 Ames Way, Kings Hill, West Malling ME19 4HT* E: brian.fortnum@btinternet.com

FORWARD, Canon Eric Toby. b 50. Nottm Univ BEd 72 Hull Univ MA 93. Cuddesdon Coll 74. **d** 77 **p** 78. C Forest Hill Ch Ch *S'wark* 77–80; Chapl Goldsmiths' Coll Lon 80–84; Chapl Westwood Ho Sch Pet 84–86; V Brighton St Aug and St Sav *Chich* 86–90; PtO *York* 90–95; V Kingston upon Hull St Alb 95–05; Can Res and Prec Liv Cathl 05–07; rtd 07. *2 Kingsway, Liverpool L22 4RQ* T: 0151-928 0681 E: toby.forward@blueyonder.co.uk

FORWARD, Miss Frances Mary. b 43. Bp Otter Coll Chich TCert 64. SEITE 96. **d** 99 **p** 00. NSM Ham St Andr *S'wark* 99–09; NSM Ham St Rich 09–13; NSM Petersham 09–13; PtO from 13. *66 Tudor Drive, Kingston upon Thames KT2 5QF* T: (020) 8546 1833

FORWARD, James Richard Wesley. b 93. Oak Hill Th Coll BA 20. **d** 20 **p** 21. C Gerrards Cross and Fulmer *Ox* from 20. *7 Gaviots Close, Gerrards Cross SL9 7EJ* M: 07905-363714 E: forwardjames@yahoo.com

FORWARD, Toby. *See* FORWARD, Eric Toby

FOSS, David Blair. b 44. Bris Univ BA 65 Dur Univ MA 66 Fitzw Coll Cam BA 68 MA 72 K Coll Lon PhD 86. St Chad's Coll Dur 68. **d** 69 **p** 70. C Barnard Castle *Dur* 69–72; Sierra Leone 72–74; Chapl St Jo Coll York 74–75; Chapl Ch Ch Coll of HE Cant 75–80; Chapl Elmslie Girls' Sch Blackpool 80–83; Tutor Coll of Resurr Mirfield 83–88; V Battyeford *Wakef* 88–99; V Ryde All SS *Portsm* 99–01; TR Rochdale *Man* 01–09; R 09–10; rtd 10; PtO *Man* 10–19. *11 Sims Close, Ramsbottom, Bury BL0 9NT* T: (01706) 828248

FOSS, Esther Rose. b 79. Regent's Park Coll Ox BA 00 MA 04 Clare Hall Cam MPhil 04 Univ of Wales (Trin St Dav) MA 12. Westcott Ho Cam 03. **d** 05 **p** 06. C Altrincham St Geo *Ches* 05–07; C Bramhall 07–09; TV Knaresborough *Ripon* 09–14; Leeds 14–15; P-in-c Coulsdon St Andr *S'wark* 15–18; V from 18; Women's Min Adv Croydon Area from 20; Dioc Chapl MU from 17. *St Andrew's Vicarage, Julien Road, Coulsdon CR5 2DN* T: (020) 3620 1885 E: esther.foss@live.co.uk *or* standrewsvicar@yahoo.co.uk

FOSSETT, Michael Charles Sinclair. b 30. Dur Univ BSc 54 CEng 59 MIMechE 59. NEOC 82. **d** 90 **p** 91. NSM Nether w Upper Poppleton *York* 90–19; PtO 19–21. *20 Fairway Drive, Upper Poppleton, York YO26 6HE* T: (01904) 794712 E: michael_fossett@hotmail.com

FOSSEY (*née* HIRST), Margaret. b 52. Huddersfield Univ BA 96. NOC 06. **d** 09 **p** 10. NSM Birkby and Birchencliffe *Leeds* 09–16; NSM Almondbury w Farnley Tyas 16–20; rtd 21; PtO *Leeds* 21. *103 Kirkstone Avenue, Dalton, Huddersfield HD5 9ES* T: (01484) 301242 E: m.fossey@ntlworld.com

FOSTEKEW, Canon Dean James Benedict. b 63. Bulmershe Coll of HE BEd 86. Chich Th Coll 89. **d** 92 **p** 93. C Boyne Hill *Ox* 92–95; P-in-c Lockerbie and Annan *Glas* 95–97; P-in-c Dalmahoy *Edin* 97–02; TV Edin St Mary 02–09; R Edin Gd Shep from 09; Dioc Miss 21 Co-ord 97–11; Prov Miss 21 Co-ord 01–11; Bp's Chapl from 13; Can St Mary's Cathl from 15. *The Rectory, 9 Upper Coltbridge Terrace, Edinburgh EH12 6AD* T: 0131-346 4127 M: 07968-099470 E: therector@uwclub.net

FOSTER, Antony John. b 39. Down Coll Cam BA 61 MA 65. Ridley Hall Cam 63. **d** 66 **p** 67. C Sandal St Helen *Wakef* 66–69; Uganda 69–74; V Mount Pellon *Wakef* 74–92; rtd 92; PtO *Wakef* 92–14; *Leeds* from 14. *32 Savile Drive, Halifax HX1 2EU* T: (01422) 344152

✠**FOSTER, The Rt Revd Christopher Richard James.** b 53. Univ Coll Dur BA 75 Man Univ MA 77 Trin Hall Cam BA 79 MA 83 Wadh Coll Ox MA 83. Westcott Ho Cam 78. **d** 80 **p** 81 **c** 01. C Tettenhall Regis *Lich* 80–82; Chapl Wadh Coll Ox 82–86; C Ox St Mary V w St Cross and St Pet 82–86; V Southgate Ch Ch *Lon* 86–94; CME Officer 88–94; Can Res and Sub-Dean St Alb 94–01; Suff Bp Hertford 01–10; Bp Portsm 10–21; rtd 21; PtO *B & W* from 21. *St Peter's Cottage, 12 Horn Street, Nunney, Frome BA11 4NP* E: bishopchrisfoster@gmail.com

FOSTER, Canon David Brereton. b 55. Selw Coll Cam BA 77 MA 81 Ox Univ BA 80. Wycliffe Hall Ox 78. **d** 81 **p** 82. C Luton St Mary *St Alb* 81–84; C Douglas St Geo and St Barn *S & M* 84–87; V S Ramsey St Paul 87–91; Dir Dioc Tr Inst 88–91; Asst Dir Buckingham Adnry Chr Tr Progr *Ox* 91–95; Dir 95–97; C W Wycombe w Bledlow Ridge, Bradenham and Radnage 91–97; TV High Wycombe 97–07; Tr Officer CME and Laity Development *Man* 07–12; Bp's Officer for Ord and Initial Tr *Nor* 12–21; Hon Can Nor Cathl 17–21; rtd 21. *Address temp unknown* E: davidfoster@runbox.com

FOSTER, Edward Philip John. b 49. Trin Hall Cam BA 70 MA 74. Ridley Hall Cam 76. **d** 79 **p** 80. C Finchley Ch Ch *Lon* 79–82; C Marple All SS *Ches* 82–86; P-in-c Cambridge St Matt *Ely* 86–90; V 90–07; rtd 07. *1 Barnfield, Common Lane, Hemingford Abbots, Huntingdon PE28 9AX* T: (01480) 399098

FOSTER, Frances Elizabeth. *See* TYLER, Frances Elizabeth

FOSTER, Canon Gareth Glynne. b 44. Open Univ BA. Chich Th Coll 66. **d** 69 **p** 70. C Fairwater *Llan* 69–71; C Merthyr Tydfil and Cyfarthfa 71–76; TV 76–87; P-in-c Abercanaid and Dioc Soc Resp Officer 87–10; Exec Officer Dioc Bd Soc Resp 95–10; Can Llan Cathl 00–10; rtd 10; PtO *Llan* 12–18. *19 The Walk, Merthyr Tydfil CF47 8RW* T: (01685) 722375 M: 07850-823038

FOSTER, Gavin Richard. b 76. Regent's Park Coll Ox BA 97 MA 01 Cardiff Univ LLM 13 Barrister-at-Law (Gray's Inn) 98. Wycliffe Hall Ox BTh 09. **d** 09 **p** 10. C Radipole and Melcombe Regis *Sarum* 09–12; Bp's Dom Chapl *Win* 12–16; V Locks Heath *Portsm* 16–20; PtO from 20; Dep Registrar *Win* from 20; Dep Registrar *Sarum* from

20. *Batt Broadbent Solicitors LLP, Minster Chambers, 42-44 Castle Street, Salisbury SP1 3TX* T: (01722) 432390 E: gavin.foster@battbroadbent.co.uk

FOSTER, Mrs Gemma Michelle Hope. b 81. Lon Sch of Th BA 04 K Coll Lon MA 13. St Mellitus Coll 13. **d** 15 **p** 16. C Letchworth St Paul w Willian *St Alb* 15–19; P-in-c Cove St Jo *Guildf* 19–20; R from 20. *Fircroft, 21 St John's Road, Farnborough GU14 9RL* M: 07775-761518 E: revgemmafoster@gmail.com

FOSTER, Mrs Geraldine. b 55. RGN 77. SAOMC 00. **d** 03 **p** 04. C Flackwell Heath *Ox* 03–07; C Ashton-upon-Mersey St Mary Magd *Ches* 07–12; PtO *Nor* 12–13; C Wroxham w Hoveton and Belaugh 13–14; V Watton 14–21; C Gt and Lt Cressingham w Threxton 14–21; rtd 21. *Address temp unknown* M: 07730-586839 E: gerryfoster@runbox.com

FOSTER, Mrs Gillian Susan. b 62. Leeds Univ BA 09. NOC 06. **d** 09 **p** 10. C Frankby w Greasby *Ches* 09–13; C Ellesmere Port from 13. *4 Deeside Close, Whitby, Ellesmere Port CH65 6TH* T: 0151-356 2202 M: 07970-522365 E: revgill52@gmail.com

FOSTER, Canon Graham Paul. b 66. Univ of W Aus BSc 86 DipEd 87 BEd 88 Murdoch Univ Aus BD 99 Qu Coll Ox MSt 00 DPhil 02. **d** 04 **p** 05. Lect NT Edin Univ from 03; NSM Edin St Mary from 04; Hon Can St Mary's Cathl from 16. *University of Edinburgh School of Divinity, New College, Mound Place, Edinburgh EH1 2LX* T: 0131-650 8917 E: paul.foster@ed.ac.uk

FOSTER, Mrs Jessica Beatrice. b 70. Birm Univ BA 91 Newman Univ MA 15. WEMTC 12. **d** 15. C Hall Green St Pet *Birm* 15–18; PtO from 19; Tutor Qu Foundn Birm 17–20; Bp's Dom Chapl *Birm* from 20. *Address temp unknown* T: 0121-427 1163 M: 07817-853452 E: jessbfoster3@gmail.com

FOSTER, Mrs Joan Alison. b 46. ARMCM 67. NOC 95. **d** 98 **p** 99. NSM Blundellsands St Nic *Liv* 98–02; Asst Chapl Southport and Ormskirk Hosp NHS Trust 98–02; V N Harrow St Alb 02–16; rtd 16; PtO *Lon* from 17. *Arden Cottage, 12 Chapel Lane, Pinner HA5 1AB* T: (020) 8868 7589 M: 07713-819012 E: revjoanfoster@yahoo.co.uk

FOSTER, Leslie. b 49. Linc Th Coll 89. **d** 91 **p** 92. C Coseley Ch Ch *Lich* 91–93; C Coseley Ch Ch *Worc* 93–95; V Firbank, Howgill and Killington *Bradf* 95–00; Hon C Sedbergh, Cautley and Garsdale 95–00; Dioc Rural Adv 96–00; P-in-c Ruyton XI Towns w Gt and Lt Ness *Lich* 00–10; V Ellesmere 08–10; rtd 14. *1 Cambridge Court, Ellesmere SY12 0FN*

FOSTER, Luke Richard. b 78. St Anne's Coll Ox MA 00. Oak Hill Th Coll MTh 11. **d** 11 **p** 12. C Banbury St Paul *Ox* 11–15; Chile from 15. *2 Blenheim Court, High Street, Eynsham, Witney OX29 4NU*

FOSTER, Marianne Sarah. b 77. UWE DipSW 00. SCTEI 18. **d** 21. C Win Ch Ch from 21; C Stanmore from 21. *146A Olivers Battery Road South, Winchester SO22 4LF* M: 07980-837856

FOSTER, Michael John. b 52. St Steph Ho Ox 76. **d** 79 **p** 80. C Wood Green St Mich *Lon* 79–82; TV Clifton *S'well* 82–85; P-in-c Aylesbury *Ox* 85–87; Dep Warden Durning Hall Chr Community Cen 87–89; V Lydbrook *Glouc* 89–97; R Hemsby, Winterton, E and W Somerton and Horsey *Nor* 97–99; P-in-c Tarrant Valley *Sarum* 99–01; P-in-c Tollard Royal w Farnham, Gussage St Michael etc 99–01; R Chase 01–20; C Sixpenny Handley w Gussage St Andrew etc 06–20; rtd 20. *Address temp unknown*

FOSTER, Paul. b 60. MAAT 80. Oak Hill Th Coll 91. **d** 93 **p** 94. C New Clee *Linc* 93–96; P-in-c Aldington w Bonnington and Bilsington *Cant* 96–02; P-in-c Sellindge w Monks Horton and Stowting etc 00–02; Chapl HM Pris Aldington 96–02; Chapl HM YOI Feltham 02–10; Chapl HM Pris Whitemoor from 10. *HM Prison, Whitemoor, Longhill Road, March PE15 0PR* T: (01354) 602350 E: pfozzy@hotmail.com *or* paul.foster01@justice.gov.uk

FOSTER, Paul. *See* FOSTER, Graham Paul

FOSTER, Philip. *See* FOSTER, Edward Philip John

FOSTER, Simon John Darby. b 57. Qu Mary Coll Lon BSc 78. Wycliffe Hall Ox 85. **d** 88 **p** 89. C Bedgrove *Ox* 88–92; C Glyncorrwg w Afan Vale and Cymmer Afan *Llan* 92–94; R Breedon cum Isley Walton and Worthington *Leic* 94–98; R Anstey 98–06; R Anstey and Thurcaston w Cropston 06–10; V Croydon St Matt *S'wark* from 10; P-in-c Croydon St Andr 17–18; AD Croydon Cen from 18. *The Vicarage, 7 Brownlow Road, Croydon CR0 5JT* T: (020) 8688 5055 *or* 8681 3147 E: revsimon@stmatthew.org.uk

FOSTER, Stephen. b 80. St Anne's Coll Ox BA 02 MA 11 Selw Coll Cam BTh 13 MPhil 14. Ridley Hall Cam 10. **d** 14 **p** 15. C Onslow Square and S Kensington St Aug *Lon* 14–21; R Ox St Aldate from 21. *St Aldates Parish Centre,*

40 Pembroke Street, Oxford OX1 1BP T: (01865) 254800 E: office@staldates.org.uk

FOSTER, Stephen. b 47. Leeds Univ CertEd 69. NEOC 83. **d** 86 **p** 87. NSM Kingston upon Hull St Nic *York* 86–87; NSM Aldbrough, Mappleton w Goxhill and Withernwick 87–98; TV Howden 98–05; RD 02–05; Chapl HM Pris Wolds 03–05; rtd 05; PtO *York* from 05; Chapl Costa Blanca *Eur* 13–16; PtO from 16; Chapl OHP 17–19. *Wycliffe, Victoria Terrace, Robin Hoods Bay, Whitby YO22 4RJ* T: (01947) 880055 M: 07791-547727 E: tuftyclubbadge@gmail.com

FOSTER, Canon Stephen Arthur. b 54. Lon Univ BMus 75 BA 78 Potchefstroom Univ PhD 98. Coll of Resurr Mirfield 75. **d** 78 **p** 79. C Ches H Trin 78–82; C Tranmere St Paul w St Luke 82–83; V Grange St Andr 83–88; V Cheadle Hulme All SS 88–94; P-in-c Stockport St Matt 94–00; Asst Dir of Ords 96–04; V Sale St Anne 00–04; Can Res Leic Cathl 04–10; Prec Leic Cathl 04–10; Chapl Leic Univ 10–19; Hon Can Leic Cathl 11–19; rtd 19; PtO *Leic* from 19. *6 Pine Tree Avenue, Leicester LE5 1AJ* E: safpta6@gmail.com

FOSTER, Steven Francis. b 55. Lon Univ BD 76 AKC 76 Open Univ BA 91 FRSA 90. Coll of Resurr Mirfield 77. **d** 78 **p** 79. C Romford St Edw *Chelmsf* 78–80; C Leigh St Clem 80–83; Ed Mayhew McCrimmon Publishers 84–86; Hon C Southend *Chelmsf* 85–86; P-in-c Sandon 86–90; R 90–91; R Wanstead St Mary 91–93; R Wanstead St Mary w Ch Ch 93–00; PtO 00–05; Asst to Master R Foundn of St Kath in Ratcliffe 04–05; P-in-c Brighton Annunciation *Chich* 05–09; rtd 10; PtO *Chich* from 11. *55 Farm Road, Hove BN3 1FD* T: (01273) 206478 M: 07901-554866 E: stevenffoster@aol.com

FOSTER, Stuart Jack. b 47. Oak Hill Th Coll BA 80 Lambeth STh 86. **d** 80 **p** 81. C Worting *Win* 80–84; C-in-c Kempshott CD 84–88; R Hook 88–95; Chapl and Warden Bp Grosseteste Coll Linc 95–99; R Kirton in Lindsey w Manton *Linc* 99–05; R Grayingham 99–05; P-in-c Vale of Belvoir *Leic* 05–09; OCM 99–04; Chapl ATC 04–09; rtd 09; PtO *Leic* 10–20; Linc 16–19. *Temple Chase, 3 Pingle Lane, Wellingore, Lincoln LN5 0JR* M: 07885-701876 E: rafikimusoma@gmail.com

FOSTER, Susan. b 58. Nottm Univ BMedSci 80 BM, BS 82. WEMTC 00. **d** 03 **p** 05. NSM Tenbury *Heref* from 03; Chapl Kemp Hospice Kidderminster from 07. *Little Oaks Cottage, Hope Bagot, Ludlow SY8 3AE* T: (01584) 891092

FOSTER, Susan Anne. b 53. Trin Coll Bris BA 97. **d** 98 **p** 99. C Watton w Carbrooke and Ovington *Nor* 98–02; Min S Wonston CD *Win* 02–07; P-in-c Micheldever and E Stratton, Woodmancote etc 05–07; V Upper Dever 07–16; rtd 16; PtO *Chich* from 16. *10 Ham Way, Worthing BN11 2QH*

FOSTER, Mrs Susan Doreen. b 58. Win Sch of Art BA 02 Anglia Ruskin Univ MA 13. Coll of Resurr Mirfield 15. **d** 16 **p** 17. C Hadleigh, Layham and Shelley *St E* 16–19; V Rushmere from 19. *The Vicarage, 253 Colchester Road, Ipswich IP4 4SH* T: (01473) 270976 M: 07415-175745 E: revd.susanfoster@gmail.com

FOTHERGILL, Richard Patrick. b 61. Newc Univ BA 83. Trin Coll Bris 91. **d** 95 **p** 96. C E Twickenham St Steph *Lon* 95–97; Assoc R Kirstenhof S Africa 97–04; Network Miss P *Bris* 04–06; Hon C Peasedown St John w Wellow and Foxcote etc *B & W* 08–15; PtO *Bris* 07–15; Ox 12–17; *B & W* 16–19; Carl from 20. *Copper Jon, Town Head, Troutbeck, Windermere LA23 1PP* M: 07835-263706 E: richard@thefillingstation.org.uk

FOUHY, Giles. b 71. Oak Hill Th Coll. **d** 07 **p** 08. C Shoreditch St Leon w St Mich *Lon* 07–13; C W Hackney 13–19. *16 Albion Drive, London E8 4ET* T: (020) 7249 7119 E: gilesfouhy@hotmail.com

FOULDS, Samuel Richard. b 89. St Mellitus Coll BA 18. **d** 18 **p** 19. C Rusholme H Trin *Man* from 18. *2 Aldwych Avenue, Manchester M14 5NL* M: 07874-293776 E: sam-foulds@hotmail.co.uk

FOULGER, Jeffrey William. b 65. St Aug Coll of Th 15. **d** 17 **p** 18. NSM Beckenham St Barn *Roch* 17–18; NSM Beckenham St Geo and St Barn 18–19; NSM New Beckenham St Paul 19–20; NSM Beckenham St Jo from 20. *1 Tudor Gardens, West Wickham BR4 9LX*

FOULGER, Wendy. b 43. St D Coll Lamp BA 90. St Jo Coll Nottm 04. **d** 11 **p** 12. NSM Cil-y-Cwm and Ystrad-ffin w Rhandir-mwyn etc *St D* 11–12; NSM Winchcombe *Glouc* 16–17; rtd 17; PtO *Glouc* from 17. *20 Gilders Paddock, Bishops Cleeve, Cheltenham GL52 8UJ* T: (01242) 679956 E: defldo6@aol.com

FOULGER, William John. b 86. St Andr Univ MTheol 08 Princeton Th Sem MA 10. Cranmer Hall Dur 13. **d** 16 **p** 17. C Lenton Abbey *S'well* 16–19; Dir Miss and Evang Cranmer Hall Dur from 19. *Cranmer Hall, St John's College, 3 South Bailey, Durham DH1 3RJ* M: 07429-325566 E: foulger@me.com

FOULKES, Simon. b 58. Ox Poly BA 81. Oak Hill Th Coll BA 89. **d** 89 **p** 90. C St Austell *Truro* 89–92; C Boscombe

St Jo *Win* 92–94; P-in-c Portswood St Denys 94–99; Par Evang Adv *Wakef* 99–04; TR Almondbury w Farnley Tyas 02–05; PtO *Cant* 07–09; P-in-c Bethersden w High Halden 09–11; Asst Dir of Educn 11–16; PtO 16–19. *53 Littlestone Road, Littlestone, New Romney TN28 8LN* T: (01797) 364517 E: vicar@idnet.co.uk

FOUNTAIN, Jacqueline. b 64. Warwick Univ 1985 PGCE 86. St Mellitus Coll BA 20. **d** 20 **p** 21. C Newbury St Nic and Speen *Ox* from 20. *10 Braunfels Walk, Newbury RG14 5NQ* M: 07948-047554 E: pandjfountain@gmail.com

FOUNTAIN, John Stephen. b 43. Solicitor 80. LNSM course 91. **d** 93 **p** 94. NSM Nacton and Levington w Bucklesham and Foxhall *St E* 93–03; NSM Taddington, Chelmorton and Monyash etc *Derby* 03–13; Chapl Derbyshire Constabulary 13–18; PtO *Derby* from 13. *Willow Barns, Stonewell Lane, Hartington, Buxton SK17 0AH* E: johnfountain@fastmail.fm

FOUNTAIN, Preb Stephanie Ann Cecilia. b 58. Lon Univ BMus 81 Heythrop Coll Lon MA 06 Roehampton Inst PGCE 88. Westcott Ho Cam 00. **d** 02 **p** 03. C Tadworth *S'wark* 02–06; TV Boston *Linc* 07–10; P-in-c Bishop's Castle w Mainstone, Lydbury N etc *Heref* from 10; P-in-c Churchstoke w Hyssington and Sarn from 10; RD Clun Forest from 16; Asst Adn Ludlow 20–21; Preb Heref Cathl from 20. *The Vicarage, Church Lane, Bishops Castle SY9 5AF* T: (01588) 630324 E: stephaniefountain@yahoo.co.uk

FOUTS, Arthur Guy. b 44. Washington Univ BA 72 Seabury-Western Th Sem DMin 98. Ridley Hall Cam 78. **d** 81 **p** 82. C Alperton *Lon* 81–84; R Pinxton *Derby* 84–87; R Dublin St Patr USA 88–89; Pastor Warren St Mark 90–91; R Silver Spring St Mary Magd 91–99; Chapl St Andr Sch 99–00; P-in-c Point of Rocks St Paul 01–08. *603 Ramapo Avenue, Pompton Lakes NJ 07442, USA* T: (001) (973) 513 9810 E: rubberduck301@yahoo.com

FOWELL, Preb Graham Charles. b 48. Southn Univ BTh 85. Chich Th Coll 79. **d** 82 **p** 83. C Clayton *Lich* 82–86; C Uttoxeter w Bramshall 86–90; V Oxley 90–95; P-in-c Shifnal 95–07; V Shifnal and Sheriffhales 07–08; RD Edgmond and Shifnal 06–08; TR Stafford 08–13; V Stafford St Mary and Marston 13–14; V Stafford St Chad 13–14; Preb Lich Cathl 08–14; rtd 14; PtO *Lich* 14–15; Hon C Fenton 15–16; Hon C Wolstanton 16–17; Hon C Basford 16–17; PtO from 17; Bp's Officer for Rtd Clergy from 18. *2 The Millway, Swynnerton, Stone ST15 0PN* T: (01782) 796153 E: email@grahamisobel.plus.com

FOWLER, Canon Colin. b 40. Linc Th Coll 80. **d** 82 **p** 83. C Barbourne *Worc* 82–85; TV Worc St Martin w St Pet, St Mark etc 85–86; TV Worc SE 86–92; P-in-c Moulton *Linc* 92–95; Chapl Puerto de la Cruz Tenerife *Eur* 95–01; Hon Can Madrid Cathl from 99; R Tangmere and Oving *Chich* 01–05; rtd 05; PtO *Nor* from 07. *10 Drakes Heath, Lowestoft NR32 2QQ* T: (01502) 564707

FOWLER, Canon David Mallory. b 51. Ian Ramsey Coll Brasted 74 Trin Coll Bris 75. **d** 78 **p** 79. C Rainhill *Liv* 78–81; C Houghton *Carl* 81–84; P-in-c Grayrigg 84–89; P-in-c Old Hutton w New Hutton 84–89; V Kirkoswald, Renwick and Ainstable 89–99; P-in-c St Salkeld w Lazonby 98–99; R Kirkoswald, Renwick w Croglin, Gt Salkeld etc 00–17; RD Penrith 99–06; Hon Can Carl Cathl 99–17; rtd 17; PtO *Carl* from 17; *Dur* from 18. *High Burnt Hills, Lanehead, Bishop Auckland DL13 1AJ* T: (01388) 537996 E: revdmf@btinternet.com

FOWLER, Mrs Janice Karen Brenda. b 56. Middx Univ BA 97. Oak Hill Th Coll 91. **d** 93 **p** 94. NSM Walton *St E* 93–96; Chapl Ipswich Hosp NHS Trust 94–00; NSM Combs *St E* 96–98; NSM Combs and Lt Finborough 98–00; C 00–04; P-in-c 04; C S Hartismere 04–07; PtO *Lich* 08–09; C Lich St Chad 09–10; P-in-c Worlingworth, Southolt, Tannington, Bedfield etc *St E* 10–11; NSM S Hartismere 11–13; PtO 13–17; Chapl Havebury Housing Partnership 13–18; Chapl HM Pris Highpoint 14–18; V Alderney *Win* from 18. *Address withheld by request*

FOWLER, Mrs Jean Elsie. b 52. **d** 19. NSM Bridlington Priory *York* from 19. *3 Omega Road, Bridlington YO16 6RJ* T: (01262) 673019 M: 07971-914381 E: email@jeanfowler.plus.com

FOWLER, John Thomas. b 42. EAMTC. **d** 01 **p** 02. NSM Stoke by Nayland w Leavenheath and Polstead *St E* 01–11; rtd 11; PtO *St E* from 11. *Warners, Thorington Street, Stoke by Nayland, Colchester CO6 4SP* T/F: (01206) 337229 E: twam.johnf@gmail.com

FOWLER, Josephine Margaret. b 47. Worc Coll of Educn TCert 69 BEd 70. **d** 12 **p** 12. OLM Oulton Broad *Nor* 12–19; PtO from 19. *1 Swonnells Court, Lowestoft NR32 3PY* T: (01502) 572302 E: josephinefowler@talktalk.net

FOWLER, Margaret Joan. b 47. St Mellitus Coll 06. **d** 14 **p** 15. OLM Billericay and Lt Burstead *Chelmsf* 14–17; NSM from 17. *4 Chestwood Close, Billericay*

CM12 0PB T: (01277)　　630144　　M: 07974-720510 E: margaret.fowler@billericaychurches.org

FOWLER, Rachel Mary. b 56. Linc Sch of Th and Min 15. **d** 17 **p** 18. NSM Waltham Gp *Linc* from 17. *80 Cheapside, Waltham, Grimsby DN37 0HW* E: rachel_m_fowler@hotmail.co.uk

FOWLER, Robert Charles Matthew. b 82. Wycliffe Hall Ox BTh 16. **d** 16. C Charles w Plymouth St Matthias *Ex* 16–20; Pioneer Min from 20. *32 Lancaster Gardens, Plymouth PL5 4AA* M: 07890-262863 E: robcharliefowler@hotmail.co.uk

FOX, Mrs Carole Ann. b 36. TISEC 98. **d** 99 **p** 00. NSM Ellon *Ab* from 99. *6 McDonald Drive, Ellon AB41 8BD* E: charlesandcarole@btinternet.com

FOX, Christopher. b 79. UWE BSc 01. Trin Coll Bris BA 10. **d** 11 **p** 12. C Ealing St Paul *Lon* from 11. *2 Nightingale Road, London W7 1DG* M: 07974-320324 E: chrispfox@gmail.com *or* chris@stpaulsealing.com

FOX, Colin George. b 46. TD . Sarum & Wells Th Coll 73. **d** 75 **p** 76. C N Hammersmith St Kath *Lon* 75–79; CF (TA) 76–90; C Heston *Lon* 79–81; TV Marlborough *Sarum* 81–90; P-in-c Pewsey 90–91; TR 91–98; TR Pewsey and Swanborough 98–03; Chapl Pewsey Hosp 90–95; P-in-c Avon Valley *Sarum* 03–11; C Durrington 08–11; rtd 11; PtO *Sarum* from 12. *The Pightle, The Street, Teffont, Salisbury SP3 5QP* T: (01722) 716010 E: colingeorgefox@gmail.com

FOX, Canon Ian James. b 44. Selw Coll Cam BA 66 MA 70. Linc Th Coll 66. **d** 68 **p** 69. C Salford St Phil w St Steph *Man* 68–71; C Kirkleatham *York* 71–73; TV Redcar w Kirkleatham 73–77; V Bury St Pet *Man* 77–85; V Northallerton w Kirby Sigston *York* 85–03; RD Northallerton 85–91; Chapl Friarage and Distr Hosp Northallerton 88–91; Chapl Northallerton Health Services NHS Trust 92–03; P-in-c Barlby and Riccall *York* 03–09; P-in-c Hemingbrough 06–09; rtd 09; Can and Preb York Minster 95–18; PtO 10–20. *21 Springfield Close, Thirsk YO7 1FH* T: (01845) 526889 E: ianfox321@btinternet.com

FOX, Preb Jacqueline Frederica. b 43. Ripon Coll of Educn CertEd 66 Leeds Univ BEd 74 MEd 84 HonRCM 85. S Dios Minl Tr Scheme 83. **dss** 85 **d** 87 **p** 94. RCM 64–85; Dioc FE Officer 87–96; Hon C Acton St Mary 87–96; R 96–08; Dean of Women's Min 96–08; Dir of Ords Willesden Area 01–08; Preb St Paul's Cathl 01–08; rtd 08; PtO *Leeds* from 17. *52 North Street, Ripon HG4 1EN* T: (01765) 603698 E: jackie@actonfox.co.uk

FOX, Mrs Jane. b 47. Open Univ BA 91 Bp Otter Coll Chich CertEd 75 ALA 70. S Dios Minl Tr Scheme 92. **d** 95 **p** 96. NSM W Blatchington *Chich* 95–98; C Peacehaven and Telscombe Cliffs 98–01; C Telscombe w Piddinghoe and Southease 98–01; TV Hitchin *St Alb* 01–08; P-in-c Harrold and Carlton w Chellington 08–15; rtd 15; PtO *St Alb* from 16. *14 Bedford Road, Barton-le-Clay, Bedford MK45 4JU* T: (01582) 882350 E: jandjsmfox@gmail.com

FOX (née COULDRIDGE), Mrs Janice Evelyn. b 49. Bognor Regis Coll of Educn CertEd 71. Glouc Sch of Min 89. **d** 92 **p** 94. C Tupsley w Hampton Bishop *Heref* 92–96; P-in-c Orleton w Brimfield 96–01; Dioc Ecum Officer 96–01; TV Worc SE 01–05; rtd 05; PtO *Worc* from 05. *Address temp unknown* E: janfox2@gmail.com

FOX, June Kathryn. b 51. York St Jo Univ BA 11. St Hild Coll 18. **d** 19. NSM Woodhouse St Jas *Sheff* from 19. *12 Delves Avenue, Sheffield S12 4AB* T: 0114-248 8808 M: 07855-240978 E: junekfox@mail.com

FOX, Leonard. b 41. AKC 66. **d** 67 **p** 68. C Salford Stowell Memorial *Man* 67–68; C Hulme St Phil 68–72; C Portsea All SS w St Jo Rudmore *Portsm* 72–75; V Oakfield St Jo 75–92; P-in-c Portsea All SS 92–06; V 06; Dir All SS Urban Miss Cen 92–06; rtd 06; PtO *Portsm* from 07. *Middle Reach, Ashlake Farm Lane, Wootton Bridge, Ryde PO33 4LF* T: (01983) 880138 E: lenfox127@talktalk.net

FOX, Linda Margaret. b 58. **d** 08 **p** 09. NSM S Croydon St Pet and St Aug *S'wark* 08–19; NSM Croydon St Matt from 19. *67 Kingsdown Avenue, South Croydon CR2 6QJ* M: 07736-708828

FOX, Michael Adrian Orme. b 47. Bris Univ BSc 68 PhD 72. WMMTC 01. **d** 04 **p** 05. NSM Codsall *Lich* 04–19; Ind Chapl Black Country Urban Ind Miss 04–12; PtO 19–20; rtd 21. *1 Windsor Gardens, Codsall, Wolverhampton WV8 2EX* T: (01902) 843442 E: mike@maofox.me.uk

FOX, Michael Frederick. b 58. St Pet Coll Ox BA 80 Birm Univ PhD 19. All SS Cen for Miss & Min 12. **d** 14 **p** 15. NSM Bollington *Ches* 14–16; P-in-c Macclesfield St Paul 16–21; Chapl to Bp Stockport 16–19; Asst Dir of Ords 18–21; Dioc Dir of Ords and IME 2 *Nor* from 21. *Diocesan House, 109 Dereham Road, Easton, Norwich NR9 5ES* T: (01603) 882337 M: 07714-216665 E: therevdfox@gmail.com

FOX, The Ven Michael John. b 42. Hull Univ BSc 63. Coll of Resurr Mirfield 64. **d** 66 **p** 67. C Becontree St Elisabeth *Chelmsf* 66–70; C Wanstead H Trin Hermon Hill 70–72; V

Victoria Docks Ascension 72–76; V Chelmsf All SS 76–88; P-in-c Chelmsf Ascension 85–88; RD Chelmsf 86–88; R Colchester St Jas, All SS, St Nic and St Runwald 88–93; Hon Can Chelmsf Cathl 91–93; Adn Harlow 93–95; Adn W Ham 95–07; rtd 07; PtO *Chelmsf* from 08. *17A Northgate Street, Colchester CO1 1EZ* T: (01206) 710701 E: michael.fox510@ntlworld.com

FOX, Michael John Holland. b 41. Lon Univ BD 68. Oak Hill Th Coll 64. **d** 69 **p** 70. C Reigate St Mary *S'wark* 69–73; NSM 76–01; C Guildf St Sav 73–76; Asst Chapl Reigate Gr Sch 76–81; Chapl 81–01; NSM Reigate St Pet CD *S'wark* 96–01; P-in-c Reigate St Luke w Doversgreen 01–09; rtd 09; PtO *S'wark* from 09. *71 Blackborough Road, Reigate RH2 7BU* T: (01737) 226616 M: 07511-752796 E: mikejh.fox60@gmail.com

✠**FOX, The Rt Revd Peter John.** b 52. AKC 74. St Aug Coll Cant 74. **d** 75 **p** 76 **c** 02. C Wymondham *Nor* 75–79; Miss P Papua New Guinea 79–85; R Gerehu 80–85; Dioc Sec Port Moresby 84–85; P-in-c E w W Rudham *Nor* 85–88; P-in-c Syderstone w Barmer and Bagthorpe 85–88; P-in-c Tatterford 85–88; P-in-c Tattersett 85–88; P-in-c Houghton 85–88; R Coxford Gp 88–89; TR Lynton, Brendon, Countisbury, Lynmouth etc *Ex* 89–95; RD Shirwell 92–95; P-in-c Harpsden *Ox* 95–02; Gen Sec Melanesian Miss 95–02; Bp Port Moresby Papua New Guinea 02–06; Hon Asst Bp Nor from 06; P-in-c Nor Lakenham St Jo and All SS and Tuckswood 06–07; V 07–17; rtd 17; Hon Asst Bp Leic from 18; Bp's Adv for Healing and Deliverance from 18. *19 Cordwell Close, Castle Donington, Derby DE74 2JL* E: peterandangiefox@yahoo.co.uk

FOX, Raymond. b 46. QUB BSc 69. CITC 71. **d** 71 **p** 72. C Holywood *D & D* 71–75; C Min Can Down Cathl 75–78; I Killinchy w Kilmood and Tullynakill 78–81; I Belfast St Mary *Conn* 81–88; I Killaney w Carryduff *D & D* 88–02; Can Down Cathl 98–02; Chapter Clerk and V Choral Belf Cathl 00–02; I Donegal w Killymard, Lough Eske and Laghey *D & R* 02–10; Can Raphoe Cathl 09–10; rtd 10. *14 St Helens Court, High Street, Holywood BT18 9SS* T: (028) 9042 4560 M: 07511-752160 E: canonfox@btinternet.com

FOX, Robert. b 54. Man Univ BEd 76. NOC 89. **d** 91 **p** 92. NSM Stalybridge *Man* 91; NSM Ashton 91–16; PtO *Newc* from 18. *22 Queensbury Gate, Newcastle upon Tyne NE12 8JW* E: rob.fox36@gmail.com

FOX, Canon Sidney. b 47. Nottm Univ BTh 79 PhD 93. Linc Th Coll 75. **d** 79 **p** 80. C Middlesbrough St Oswald *York* 79–81; P-in-c 81–86; V 86–87; V Newby 87–92; R Brechin and Tarfside *Bre* 92–05; P-in-c Auchmithie 92–00; Can St Paul's Cathl Dundee 98–05; V Broughton *Blackb* 05–13; rtd 13; PtO *York* from 13. *15 Rawson Way, Hornsea HU18 1DH* E: revsfox@yahoo.co.uk

FOX, Timothy William Bertram. b 37. CCC Cam BA 61. Qu Coll Birm 66. **d** 68 **p** 69. C Cannock *Lich* 68–72; C Bilston St Leon 72–75; V Essington 75–81; R Buildwas and Leighton w Eaton Constantine etc 81–92; RD Wrockwardine 88–92; R Bradeley, Church Eaton and Moreton 92–04; rtd 04; Hon C Hanbury, Newborough, Rangemore and Tutbury *Lich* 04–08; PtO *Bradf* 09–14; *Leeds* from 14. *40 Lakeber Avenue, High Bentham, Lancaster LA2 7JN* T: (01524) 262575 E: wenningfoxes@btinternet.com

FOX (née DRAYCOTT), Tina. b 57. Win Univ BA 11. STETS 08. **d** 11 **p** 12. OLM Avon River *Sarum* 11–17; NSM Nadder Valley from 17. *The Pightle, The Street, Teffont, Salisbury SP3 5QP* T: (01722) 716010 M: 07747-033585

FOXWOOD, Hugo Charles Amory. b 73. Bris Univ BA 95. St Mellitus Coll BA 18. **d** 18 **p** 19. C E Twickenham St Steph *Lon* 18–21; V Norbiton *S'wark* from 21. *St Peter's Church, London Road, Kingston upon Thames KT2 6QL* T: (020) 8546 3212 M: 07931-578068

FOY, Malcolm Stuart. b 48. Univ of Wales (Lamp) BA 71 Magd Coll Cam CertEd 72 K Coll Lon MA 89 ACP 80 FCollP FRSA. Ox NSM Course 84. **d** 87 **p** 88. NSM Tilehurst St Mich *Ox* 87–90; C Ireland Wood *Ripon* 90–96; Adv RE Leeds Adnry 90–96; Dir Educn *Bradf* 96–99; C Otley 99; PtO 00–05; Hon C Keighley All SS 05–14; *Leeds* 14–16; Hon C Keighley from 16. *45 The Chase, Keighley BD20 6HU* T: (01535) 665112

FOY, Matthew John. b 81. Sheff Univ BA 04 Solicitor 07. Oak Hill Th Coll 13. **d** 16 **p** 17. C S Tottenham St Ann *Lon* 16–17; C Muswell Hill Grace Ch 17–19; P-in-c Silverhill St Matt *Chich* from 19; P-in-c St Leonards St Ethelburga and St Leon from 19. *81A Filsham Road, St Leonards-on-Sea TN38 0PE* T: (01424) 432679 M: 07752-787139 E: matthew@stmatts.co.uk *or* matthew@stethelburga.org.uk *or* matthew.foy@btinternet.com

FOY, Peter James. b 59. **d** 08 **p** 09. NSM Warminster Ch Ch *Sarum* 08–15; Ind Chapl *St E* from 16. *2 Orford Road, Felixstowe IP11 2DY* M: 07557-922065 E: revpfoy@gmail.com

FRAIS, Jonathan Jeremy. b 65. Kingston Poly LLB 87. Oak Hill Th Coll BA 92. **d** 92 **p** 93. C Orpington Ch Ch *Roch* 92–96; Asst Chapl Moscow *Eur* 96–99; Chapl Kiev 99–05; R Bexhill St Mark *Chich* from 05; RD Battle and Bexhill from 15. *St Mark's Rectory, 11 Coverdale Avenue, Bexhill-on-Sea TN39 4TY* T/F: (01424) 843733 E: frais@tiscali.co.uk

FRAMPTON, Miss Marcia Ellen. b 36. SRN 65 SCM 66. Ripon Coll Cuddesdon 86. **d** 88 **p** 95. Par Dn Paston *Pet* 88–89; Par Dn Burford w Fulbrook and Taynton *Ox* 90–92; Par Dn Witney 92–93; NSM Heref S Wye 94–01; rtd 01; PtO *Heref* 02–17. *18 Brook Farm Court, Belmont, Hereford HR2 7TZ* T: (01432) 509007 E: revmframpton@talktalk.net

FRAMPTON, Mrs Ruth. b 57. SWMTC 12. **d** 15 **p** 16. C Salcombe and Malborough w S Huish *Ex* 15–19; P-in-c Christow, Ashton, Bridford, Dunchideock etc 19–21; V from 21. *The Rectory, Dry Lane, Christow, Exeter EX6 7PE* T: (01647) 253164 E: tvhhrectory@yahoo.com

FRAMPTON, Samuel Francis. b 92. Dur Univ BA 18. Westcott Ho Cam 15. **d** 18 **p** 19. C Mill End and Heronsgate w W Hyde *St Alb* 18–21; V Oxhey St Matt from 21. *St Matthew's Vicarage, St Matthew's Close, Watford WD19 4ST* M: 07881-293543 E: frsamframpton@gmail.com

FRANCE, Canon Charles Malcolm. b 48. Westmr Coll Ox BTh 01 ACA 71 FCA 76. EAMTC 94. **d** 97 **p** 98. C Gt Grimsby St Mary and St Jas *Linc* 97–02; P-in-c Skegness and Winthorpe 02–04; P-in-c Ingoldmells w Addlethorpe 02–04; R Skegness Gp 04–14; Can and Preb Linc Cathl 14–18; rtd 14; PtO *Nor* from 15; *Linc* 17–20; *Eur* from 19. *7 High View Park, Cromer NR27 0HQ* T: (01263) 512861 E: malcolmfrance@aol.com

FRANCE (née PIERCY), Mrs Elizabeth Claire. b 66. Qu Mary Coll Lon BSc 87. Wycliffe Hall Ox 97. **d** 99 **p** 00. C Dronfield w Holmesfield *Derby* 99–03; V Allestree 03–05; P-in-c Etchingham *Chich* 11–12; PtO *Lon* 13–18; Chapl W Lon Univ from 18. *West London University, St Mary's Road, London W5 5RF* T: (020) 8231 2365 E: lizfrance@btinternet.com *or* liz.france@uwl.ac.uk

FRANCE, Evan Norman Lougher. b 52. Jes Coll Cam BA 74 MA 78. Wycliffe Hall Ox 76. **d** 79 **p** 80. C Hall Green Ascension *Birm* 79–82; CMS 82–84; C Bexhill St Pet *Chich* 84–87; V Westfield 87–11; R Buxted and Hadlow Down 11–15; rtd 15; PtO *Chich* from 17. *17 Lansdowne Way, Bexhill-on-Sea TN40 2UJ* E: enlfrance@gmail.com

FRANCE, Geoffrey. b 37. S Dios Minl Tr Scheme 87. **d** 90 **p** 91. NSM Uckfield *Chich* 90–92; C 92–94; R Warbleton and Bodle Street Green 94–02; rtd 02; PtO *Chich* from 15. *3 Osborne House, Rushlake Green, Heathfield TN21 9QL* T: (01435) 830309

FRANCE, Malcolm. *See* FRANCE, Charles Malcolm

FRANCE, Stephen Mark. b 66. Wycliffe Hall Ox BTh 00. **d** 00 **p** 01. C Newbold w Dunston *Derby* 00–03; P-in-c Darley Abbey 03–05; Dioc Duty Press Officer 03–04; P-in-c Burwash *Chich* 05–06; R 06–12; R Brondesbury Ch Ch and St Laur *Lon* 12–19; rtd 20. *46 Fernlea Road, London SW12 9RN* M: 07379-216047 E: revfrance@btinternet.com

FRANCE, William Michael. b 43. Sydney Univ BA 68 Lon Univ BD 72 Chas Sturt Univ NSW MEd 96. Moore Th Coll Sydney LTh 70. **d** 73 **p** 73. C Turramurra Australia 73–75; C Barton Seagrave w Warkton *Pet* 76–78; R Dundas Australia 79–82; Chapl The K Sch 83–94; Chapl Sydney C of E Girls' Gr Sch 94–99; Assoc Chapl St Andr Cathl Sch 99–04; R Murchison 04–08; rtd 08. *6 Wesson Road, West Pennant Hills NSW 2125, Australia* T: (0061) (2) 9945 0939 E: billandjackie@optusnet.com.au

FRANCE, Archdeacon of. *See* HOOPER, The Ven Peter George

FRANCES ANNE, Sister. *See* COCKER, Frances Rymer

FRANCIS, Mrs Coral Elizabeth. b 73. Portsm Univ BA 95. Wycliffe Hall Ox BA 21. **d** 21. C Minchinhampton w Box and Amberley *Glouc* from 21. *The Rectory, Walkley Hill, Stroud GL5 3TX* T: (01453) 759680 E: coral.phoenix@gmail.com

FRANCIS, David Carpenter. b 45. Southn Univ BSc 66 Loughb Univ MSc 71 Sussex Univ MA 83. Westcott Ho Cam 85. **d** 87 **p** 88. C Ealing St Mary *Lon* 87–90; Chapl Ealing Coll of HE 87–90; Chapl Clayponds Hosp Ealing 88–90; P-in-c Wembley St Jo *Lon* 90–93; Chapl Wembley Hosp 90–93; V Platt *Roch* 93–01; Post Ord Tr Officer 93–98; RD Shoreham 99–01; R Stow on the Wold, Condicote and The Swells *Glouc* 01–11; AD Stow 04–09; rtd 11; PtO *Ex* from 12; RD Cadbury 18–20. *East Forches, Alexandra Road, Crediton EX17 2DH* T: (01363) 776606 M: 07799-410370 E: stowrector@yahoo.co.uk

FRANCIS, Canon James More MacLeod. b 44. Edin Univ MA 65 BD 68 PhD 74 Yale Univ STM 69. New Coll Edin 65. **d** 87 **p** 87. Sen Lect RS Sunderland Univ *Dur* 82–03; NSM Sunderland St Chad 87–98; TV Sunderland 98–07; NSM Sunderland Minster 07–09; Tutor NEOC 89–98; Bp's Adv for NSM *Dur* 99–10; Prin Dioc OLM Course 02–09; Hon Can Dur Cathl 00–10; rtd 10; PtO *Dur* 14–19. *11*

Heatherdale Crescent, Durham DH1 2AP T: 0191-386 6623 E: jamesfrancis@mac.com

FRANCIS, James Stephen. b 66. K Coll Lon MA 17 FInstD 97 FRSA 99. SEITE 95. **d** 99 **p** 07. NSM St Botolph Aldgate w H Trin Minories *Lon* 99–02; NSM Soho St Anne w St Thos and St Pet 02–05; Chapl RNR 05–07; NSM St Mary le Strand w St Clem Danes *Lon* 07; Chapl RN from 07. *Royal Naval Chaplaincy Service Headquarters, Tanner Building, HMS Excellent, Whale Island, Portsmouth PO2 8ER* T: 0300-157 7544 M: 07961-123811 E: james.francis118@hotmail.co.uk

FRANCIS, Jennifer Anne Harrison. b 45. JP . Southn Univ BSc 67 Brunel Univ MA 74 CQSW 73. WEMTC 07. **d** 07 **p** 08. NSM Stow on the Wold, Condicote and The Swells *Glouc* 07–11; rtd 11; PtO *Ex* from 12. *East Forches, Alexandra Road, Crediton EX17 2DH* T: (01363) 776606 M: 07881-953769 E: jennyfrancis1@btinternet.com

FRANCIS, Jeremy Montgomery. b 31. BNC Ox BA 53 MA 56. Glouc Sch of Min 84. **d** 87 **p** 88. NSM Chedworth, Yanworth and Stowell, Coln Rogers etc *Glouc* 87–90; NSM Coates, Rodmarton and Sapperton etc 90–01; NSM Daglingworth w the Duntisbournes and Winstone 95–97; NSM Brimpsfield w Birdlip, Syde, Daglingworth etc 97–00; PtO from 01. *Old Barnfield, Duntisbourne Leer, Cirencester GL7 7AS* T: (01285) 821370

FRANCIS, John. b 56. Bris Poly BA 78 MCIH 81. **d** 98 **p** 99. OLM Hatcham Park All SS *S'wark* from 98. *4A Hatcham Park Mews, London SE14 5QA* T: (020) 7358 1769 M: 07703-567214 E: johnfrancis878@btinternet.com

FRANCIS, The Ven Julian Montgomery. b 60. Selw Coll Cam BA 83 MA 83. S'wark Ord Course 88. **d** 91 **p** 92. C S Wimbledon H Trin and St Pet *S'wark* 91–95; V Cottingley *Bradf* 95–99; Minority Ethnic Angl Concerns Officer *Lich* 99–02; C W Bromwich St Andr w Ch Ch 99–02; TR Coventry Caludon *Cov* 02–08; Nat Tr Co-ord for Minority Ethnic Anglicans 08–11; V Edgbaston St Geo *Birm* 11–19; Bp's Ecum Adv 18–19; Adn Walsall *Lich* from 19. *1 Three Spires House, Station Road, Lichfield WS13 6HX* T: (01543) 622590 M: 07950-309554 E: archdeacon.walsall@lichfield.anglican.org

FRANCIS, Miss Katherine Jane. b 67. St Jo Coll Dur BA 08 RGN 88 RM 92. Cranmer Hall Dur 06. **d** 08 **p** 09. C Sprotbrough *Sheff* 08–10; Chapl Newcastle upon Tyne Hosps NHS Foundn Trust 10–16; Chapl Marie Curie Cen Newc from 16. *Marie Curie Cancer Care, Marie Curie Drive, Newcastle upon Tyne NE4 6SS* T: 0191-219 1000

FRANCIS, Kenneth Charles. b 22. Oak Hill Th Coll 46. **d** 50 **p** 51. C Wandsworth All SS *S'wark* 50–53; V Deptford St Nic w Ch Ch 53–61; V Summerstown 61–77; R Cratfield w Heveningham and Ubbeston etc *St E* 77–87; rtd 87; PtO *Truro* 87–14. *Wheal Alfred, Chapel Hill, Bolingey, Perranporth TR6 0DQ* T: (01872) 571317

FRANCIS, Kevin. b 52. Glas Univ MA 83 PhD 88. TISEC 08. **d** 11 **p** 12. Hon C Glas St Bride 11–15; R from 15; Hon Chapl Glas Univ 07–20. *St Bride's Rectory, Flat 1/1, 25 Queensborough Gardens, Glasgow G12 9QP* T: 0141-334 1401 E: rev.kevinfrancis@gmail.com

FRANCIS, Prof Leslie John. b 47. Pemb Coll Ox BA 70 MA 74 BD 90 DD 01 Nottm Univ MTh 76 Qu Coll Cam PhD 76 ScD 97 Lon Univ MSc 77 Univ of Wales (Ban) DLitt 07 FBPsS 88 FCP 94 FAcSS 14. Westcott Ho Cam 70. **d** 73 **p** 74. C Haverhill *St E* 73–77; P-in-c Gt Bradley 78–82; Hon C Gt w Lt Wratting 79–82; Research Officer Culham Coll Inst 82–88; P-in-c N Cerney w Bagendon *Glouc* 82–85; PtO 85–95; Fell Trin Coll Carmarthen 89–99; Dean of Chpl 95–99; Prof Th Univ of Wales (Lamp) 92–99; Prof Practical Th Univ of Wales (Ban) 99–07; Prof Religions and Educn Warw Univ *Cov* 07–19; Prof Religions and Psychology from 20; PtO *Ox* 95–01; *Ban* 99–06; Hon C Llanfair-pwll and Llanddaniel-fab etc 06–12; Hon C Seintiau Braint a Chefni 12–14; Hon C Bro Dwynwen 15–17; Hon Can St D Cathl 98–99; Hon Can and Can Th Ban Cathl 06–16; Cursal Can 11–12; Treas 12–16; Hon Can Man Cathl from 16; Can Th St Jo Cathl Newfoundland 17–19; Hon Can E Newfoundland and Labrador from 19; Can Th Liv Cathl from 19; PtO *D & G* from 18; *St As* from 20. *Llys Onnen, Abergwyngregyn, Llanfairfechan LL33 0LD* T: (01248) 681877 E: leslie.francis@warwick.ac.uk

FRANCIS, Mark Simon. b 77. Dur Univ BSc 98. Oak Hill Th Coll BA 10. **d** 10 **p** 11. C Egham *Guildf* 10–13; P-in-c Felbridge *S'wark* 13–16; V from 16. *The Vicarage, 8 The Glebe, Felbridge, East Grinstead RH19 2QT* T: (01342) 321524 M: 07774-324934 E: mark8sjf@gmail.com

FRANCIS, Martin Rufus. b 37. Pemb Coll Ox BA 60 MA 64. Linc Th Coll 60. **d** 63 **p** 64. C W Hartlepool St Paul *Dur* 63–67; C Yeovil St Jo w Preston Plucknett *B & W* 67–69; Chapl Tonbridge Sch 69–83; Chapl and Dep Hd St Jo Sch Leatherhead 83–94; R Herstmonceux and Wartling *Chich* 94–01; rtd 01; PtO *Sarum* 02–18. *4 Abbots Way,*

Sherborne DT9 6DT E: venetiakfrancis@hotmail.co.uk *or* mrufus37@hotmail.com

FRANCIS, Canon Paul Edward. b 52. Southn Univ BTh 84. Sarum & Wells Th Coll 78. **d** 81 **p** 82. C Biggin Hill *Roch* 81–85; R Fawkham and Hartley 85–90; V Aylesford 90–99; V Riverhead w Dunton Green 99–11; Chapl Dioc Assn of Readers 01–11; RD Sevenoaks 05–11; R Beckenham St Geo 11–15; Hon Can Roch Cathl 10–15; Can Res Roch Cathl 15–17; rtd 17; PtO *Cant* 18–21. *5 Russet Row, Grove Road, Preston, Canterbury CT3 1FS*

FRANCIS, Peter Alan. b 73. Wycliffe Hall Ox. **d** 09 **p** 10. C Horsham *Chich* 09–13; P-in-c Woodchester and Brimscombe *Glouc* 13–18; P-in-c Rodborough 16–18; R Rodborough, Woodchester and Brimscombe from 18. *The Rectory, Walkley Hill, Stroud GL5 3TX* T: (01453) 752659 E: peterfrancis777@gmail.com

FRANCIS, Peter Brereton. b 53. St Andr Univ MTheol 77. Qu Coll Birm 77. **d** 78 **p** 79. C Hagley *Worc* 78–81; Chapl Qu Mary Coll *Lon* 81–87; R Ayr *Glas* 87–92; Miss to Seamen 87–92; Provost St Mary's Cathl *Glas* 92–96; R Glas St Mary 92–96; Warden and Lib Gladstone's Lib Hawarden from 97; Visiting Prof Glyndŵr Univ from 09. *Gladstone's Library, Church Lane, Hawarden, Deeside CH5 3DF* T: (01244) 532350 E: peter.francis@gladlib.org

FRANCIS, Peter Philip. b 48. St Jo Coll Dur BA 73. Wycliffe Hall Ox 73. **d** 75 **p** 76. C Folkestone St Jo *Cant* 75–78; C Morden *S'wark* 78–83; P-in-c Barford St Martin, Dinton, Baverstock etc *Sarum* 83–88; P-in-c Fovant, Sutton Mandeville and Teffont Evias etc 83–86; R Newick *Chich* 88–14; rtd 14; PtO *Chich* from 15. *12 Downland Copse, Uckfield TN22 1SX* T: (01825) 763557 E: pandnfrancis@btinternet.com

FRANCIS, Mrs Sharon Edwina. b 57. Westmr Coll Ox BTh 99 Heythrop Coll Lon MA 11. SEITE 98. **d** 08 **p** 09. NSM Langton Green *Roch* 08–12; P-in-c New Groombridge *Chich* 12–18; V 18–21; RD Rotherfield 18–21; rtd 21. *East Hill House, 3 East Hill, Tenterden TN30 6RL* M: 07527-396403

FRANCIS, Canon Younis. b 66. **d** 95 **p** 95. C Addington *S'wark* 05–07; TV Cheam 07–11; P-in-c Norbury St Phil 11–16; V 16–21; R Selsdon St Jo w St Fran from 21; Hon Can S'wark Cathl from 17. *St John's Rectory, Upper Selsdon Road, South Croydon CR2 8DD* M: 07504-721294 E: revd.younis@gmail.com

✠**FRANCIS-DEHQANI, The Rt Revd Gulnar Eleanor (Guli).** b 66. Nottm Univ BA 89 Bris Univ MA 94 PhD 99. SEITE 95. **d** 98 **p** 99 **c** 17. C Mortlake w E Sheen *S'wark* 98–02; Chapl R Academy of Music *Lon* 02–04; Chapl St Marylebone C of E Sch 02–04; PtO *Pet* 04–11; C Tr Officer 11–17; Adv in Women's Min 12–17; Can Pet Cathl 16–17; Suff Bp Loughborough *Leic* 17–21; Bp Chelmsf from 21. *Bishopscourt, Main Road, Margaretting, Ingatestone CM4 0HD* T: (01277) 352001 E: bishopscourt@chelmsford.anglican.org

FRANCIS-DEHQANI, Canon Lee Thomas. b 67. Nottm Univ BA 89. Sarum & Wells Th Coll 92 Trin Coll Bris BA 95. **d** 95 **p** 96. C Putney St Mary *S'wark* 95–98; TV Richmond St Mary w St Matthias and St Jo 98–04; P-in-c Oakham, Hambleton, Egleton, Braunston and Brooke *Pet* 04–10; P-in-c Langham 04–10; C Teigh w Whissendine and Market Overton 04–10; C Cottesmore and Barrow w Ashwell and Burley 04–10; TR Oakham, Ashwell, Braunston, Brooke, Egleton etc 11–18; RD Rutland 10–18; Can Pet Cathl 10–18; TR Fosse Team *Leic* 18–20; P-in-c 20–21. *Bishopscourt, Main Road, Margaretting, Ingatestone CM4 0HD* M: 07827-668169 E: leet.fd@gmail.com

FRANCK, Mrs Janet. b 53. MCSP 75. **d** 14 **p** 15. OLM Egham Hythe *Guildf* from 14. *56 Hazel Grove, Staines TW18 1JL* T: (01784) 465879 E: janetf56@aol.com

FRANK, Garreth Edward Arthur. b 90. York Univ BA 12 St Jo Coll Dur BATM 17. Cranmer Hall Dur 14. **d** 17 **p** 18. C Nottingham St Nic *S'well* from 17. *The Penthouse, The Courtyard, 10 Castle Gate, Nottingham NG1 7AS* M: 07554-641607 E: garretheafrank@gmail.com

FRANK, Penelope Edith. b 45. WMMTC 96. **d** 99 **p** 00. NSM Edgbaston St Geo *Birm* 99–02; PtO *Cov* 03–04; NSM Stoneleigh w Ashow 04–10; CPAS 87–06; rtd 06; Asst Chapl Vevey w Château d'Oex *Eur* 10–12; PtO *Cov* 15–20; *Glouc* 16–20. *9 Langham Court, Grand Avenue, Worthing BN11 5BW*

FRANK, Canon Richard Patrick Harry. b 40. St Chad's Coll Dur BA 66. **d** 68 **p** 69. C Darlington H Trin *Dur* 68–72; C Monkwearmouth St Andr 72–74; C-in-c Harlow Green CD 74–79; R Skelton and Hutton-in-the-Forest w Ivegill *Carl* 79–86; V Carl St Luke Morton 86–92; RD Carl 88–89; P-in-c Thursby 89–90; P-in-c Kirkbride w Newton Arlosh 89–92; TR Greystoke, Matterdale, Mungrisdale etc 92–98; P-in-c Patterdale 95–98; TR Gd Shep TM 98–99; RD Penrith 96–99; Hon Can Carl Cathl 97–99; rtd 99; PtO *Carl*

00–02; *York* from 02. *8 Taylors Rise, Walkington, Beverley HU17 8SF* T: (01482) 872262 E: taylors@taylors.karoo.co.uk

FRANK, The Ven Richard Stephen. b 70. Keble Coll Ox MEng 93 Fitzw Coll Cam MA 98. Ridley Hall Cam 96. **d** 99 **p** 00. C Cranham Park *Chelmsf* 99–04; P-in-c St Margaret's-on-Thames *Lon* 05–11; V 11–20; AD Hounslow 15–20; Adn Middx from 20; P-in-c Hanworth St Geo 20–21. *289 St Margarets Road, Twickenham TW1 1PN* M: 07931-533581 E: archdeacon.middlesex@london.anglican.org

FRANKLAND, Angela Tara. b 69. Lon Bible Coll BA 96 MA 98. EAMTC 97. **d** 99 **p** 00. C Hornchurch St Andr *Chelmsf* 99–03; TV Wickford and Runwell 03–11; P-in-c Aveley and Purfleet 11–13; TR Mardyke from 13. *The Vicarage, Mill Road, Aveley, South Ockendon RM15 4SR* T: (01708) 891471 E: tfrankland@sky.com

FRANKLIN, Bryony Dean. b 69. Bath Univ BPharm 89 Sch of Pharmacy Lon MSc 93 PhD 99 FRPharmS 13. St Mellitus Coll BA 19. **d** 19 **p** 20. NSM W Acton St Martin *Lon* from 19. *4 King Edwards Gardens, London W3 9RG* E: bryonyfranklin@gmail.com

FRANKLIN, David John. b 67. Selw Coll Cam BA 88 MA 92. St Jo Coll Nottm MTh 06. **d** 06 **p** 07. C Windermere St Martin *Carl* 06–10; Hon C Bramley *Sheff* 10–12; V Askern from 12. *The Vicarage, Church Street, Askern, Doncaster DN6 0PH* T: (01302) 708081 E: david.franklin@sheffield.anglican.org

FRANKLIN, Dianne Mary. *See* COX, Dianne Mary

FRANKLIN (formerly WILKES), Mrs Elizabeth Ann. b 76. St Jo Coll Dur BA 97 UEA MA 01. **d** 13 **p** 14. C Blackheath Park St Mich *S'wark* 13–17; PtO *S'well* from 17; Chapl Sherwood Forest Hosps NHS Foundn Trust from 19. *Christ Church Vicarage, Boundary Road, Newark NG24 4AJ* T: (01636) 611345 E: liz.franklin@outlook.com

FRANKLIN, Jamie Andrew. b 87. Kent Univ BA 08 MA 09 K Coll Lon MA 15. Ripon Coll Cuddesdon 17. **d** 19. C Nottingham St Geo w St Jo *S'well* from 19. *7 Chancery Court, Wilford, Nottingham NG11 7EQ* M: 07883-184934 E: jamieandrewfranklin@gmail.com

FRANKLIN, Mrs Janet. b 67. Selw Coll Cam VetMB 91 MA 92 Cumbria Univ BA 10 Sheff Univ MA 17. LCTP 06. **d** 10 **p** 11. C Maltby and Thurcroft *Sheff* 10–13; P-in-c Stainforth 13–18; PtO from 18. *The Vicarage, Church Street, Askern, Doncaster DN6 0PH* T: (01302) 708081 E: janet.franklin@sheffield.anglican.org *or* janetfranklin3@hotmail.com

FRANKLIN, Mrs Karen Anne. b 74. Moorlands Coll BA 18 Open Univ DipSW 03. Sarum Coll MA 20. **d** 20 **p** 21. C Canford Magna *Sarum* from 20. *174 Lynwood Drive, Wimborne BH21 1UU* M: 07793-466316 E: neilandkarenfranklin99@gmail.com

FRANKLIN, Miss Ola. b 55. Balls Park Coll Hertford CertEd 76 Open Univ BA 92 Birkbeck Coll Lon MA 95. NTMTC BA 09. **d** 09 **p** 10. C Harlow St Mary and St Hugh w St Jo the Bapt *Chelmsf* 09–13; PtO 13–14; V Woodford Bridge from 14. *St Paul's Vicarage, 4 Cross Road, Woodford Green IG8 8BS* T: (020) 8506 0662 E: ofrank@btinternet.com

FRANKLIN, Paul Steven. b 78. Portsm Univ BSc 01 Brighton Univ PGCE 02 Kent Univ MA 07. Wycliffe Hall Ox 11. **d** 13 **p** 14. NSM Kidbrooke St Nic *S'wark* 13–17; TV Newark w Coddington *S'well* 17; V Newark Ch Ch from 18. *Christ Church Vicarage, Boundary Road, Newark NG24 4AJ* T: (01636) 611345 E: rev.p.franklin@gmail.com

FRANKLIN, Canon Richard Charles Henry. b 48. Ch Ch Coll Cant CertEd 70 Heythrop Coll Lon MA 08. Sarum & Wells Th Coll 75. **d** 78 **p** 79. C Pershore w Pinvin, Wick and Birlingham *Worc* 78–80; Educn Chapl 80–85; V Wollescote 85–92; V Fareham SS Pet and Paul *Portsm* 92–98; V Luton All SS w St Pet St Alb 98–12; RD Luton 02–07; Hon Can St Alb 09–12; rtd 19; PtO *Glouc* from 13. *Baldwin's Oak, Castle Tump, Newent GL18 1LS* T: (01531) 890289 E: richardfranklin@mail2world.com

FRANKLIN, Canon Richard Heighway. b 54. Southn Univ BA 75 MPhil 83. Sarum & Wells Th Coll 75. **d** 78 **p** 79. C Thame w Towersey *Ox* 78–81; Asst Chapl Southn Univ *Win* 81–83; Dir of Studies Chich Th Coll 83–89; P-in-c Stalbridge *Sarum* 89–94; V Weymouth H Trin 94–16; Can and Preb Sarum Cathl 02–16; RD Weymouth 04–08; rtd 16; PtO *Sarum* 16–21. *3 d'Urberville Close, Dorchester DT1 2JT* E: richardfranklin@iname.com

FRANKLIN (née WESTMACOTT), Mrs Rosemary Margaret. b 41. WEMTC 03. **d** 05 **p** 06. NSM Cirencester *Glouc* 05–13; rtd 13; PtO *Glouc* from 17. *Waterton Farm House, Ampney Crucis, Cirencester GL7 5RR* T: (01285) 654282 E: revrmf@btinternet.com

FRANKLIN, Roxanne Fay. *See* EVERSLEY, Roxanne Fay

FRANKLIN, Preb Simon George. b 54. Bris Univ BA 75. Ridley Hall Cam 77. **d** 79 **p** 80. C Woodmansterne *S'wark* 79–83; C St Peter-in-Thanet *Cant* 83–86; R Woodchurch 86–96; P-in-c Ottery St Mary, Alfington, W Hill, Tipton etc *Ex* 96–99; TR 99–12; P-in-c Feniton and Escot 07–12; P-in-c Moretonhampstead, Manaton, N Bovey and Lustleigh 12–15; R 15–19; RD Moreton 15–19; Preb Ex Cathl 07–19; rtd 19. *2 Lanveoc Way, Modbury, Ivybridge PL21 0FW* E: safranklin@btinternet.com

FRANKLIN, Stephen Alaric. b 58. Lon Univ BD 87. Sarum & Wells Th Coll 87. **d** 89 **p** 90. C Chenies and Lt Chalfont, Latimer and Flaunden *Ox* 89–93; CF 93–18; V Crookham *Guildf* from 18. *14 Gally Hill Road, Church Crookham, Fleet GU52 6LH* T: (01252) 617130

FRANKUM, Matthew David Hyatt. b 65. Leic Poly BSc 87 Univ of Wales MA 13. Trin Coll Bris 97. **d** 99 **p** 00. C Bath St Luke *B & W* 99–03; TV Worle 03–08; P-in-c Bath St Luke 08–16; V from 16; RD Bath 18–20; Asst Dir of Ords from 20. *St Luke's Vicarage, Hatfield Road, Bath BA2 2BD* T: (01225) 311904 E: matthew@stlukesbath.com

FRANSELLA, Cortland Lucas. b 48. Trin Hall Cam BA 70 MA 74 Heythrop Coll Lon MA 00 Open Univ BSc 05 MSc 11. NTMTC 95. **d** 98 **p** 99. NSM Palmers Green St Jo *Lon* 98–03 and 09–12; NSM Hornsey St Mary w St Geo 03–08; PtO from 08; Asst Chapl to Abp *Cant* 11–12 and 20–21; Lambeth Awards Officer from 14; Asst P Chpl R St Pet-ad-Vincula at HM Tower of Lon from 12; Dep P in O from 19. *17 Warner Road, London N8 7HB* T: (020) 8340 7706 E: fransella@btinternet.com *or* cortland.fransella@lambethpalace.org

FRANZ, Kevin Gerhard. b 53. Edin Univ MA 74 BD 79 PhD 92. Edin Th Coll 76. **d** 79 **p** 80. C Edin St Martin 79–83; R Selkirk 83–90; Provost St Ninian's Cathl and R Perth St Ninian *St And* 90–99; Gen Sec Action of Churches Together in Scotland 99–07; Hon Can St Ninian's Cathl Perth *St And* 00–05. *14 Comely Bank, Perth PH2 7HU* E: kgfranz53@gmail.com

FRASER, Alan Richard. b 69. Leeds Univ BA 91 MA 94. WMMTC 04. **d** 07 **p** 08. NSM Gravelly Hill *Birm* 07–16; PtO from 16. *41 Hobhouse Close, Birmingham B42 1HB* T: 0121-358 7576 E: alan-fraser2@sky.com

FRASER, Andrew Thomas. b 52. Newc Univ Aus BA 81. St Jo Coll (NSW) ThL 79. **d** 81 **p** 82. Australia 81–87; C Prestbury *Glouc* 87–91; C Wotton St Mary 91–92; PtO from 19. *79 Victoria Street, Gloucester GL1 4EP* M: 07887-605747 E: andyinglos@live.co.uk

FRASER, Ann. *See* FRASER, Elizabeth Ann

FRASER, Charles Ian Alexander. b 68. Ex Univ BA Cam Univ PGCE Open Univ MA MCMI. ERMC. **d** 10 **p** 11. NSM Cherry Hinton St Jo *Ely* 10–13; NSM Lordsbridge from 13; Asst Master The Leys School from 10. *The Leys School, Fen Causeway, Cambridge CB2 7AD* T: (01223) 264974 *or* 508916 M: 07889-019157 E: ciaf@theleys.net *or* revd.charlesfraser@gmail.com *or* charlesfraser@lordsbridge.org

FRASER, Canon Christine Nancy. b 61. TISEC 98. **d** 02 **p** 03. NSM St Ninian's Cathl Perth *St And* 02–13; Chapl Perth High Sch 09–13; R Kirkcaldy *St And* from 13; R Kinghorn from 13; Can St Ninian's Cathl Perth from 19. *1 Longbraes Garden, Kirkcaldy KY2 5YJ* T: (01592) 204208 E: cnfraser@btinternet.com

FRASER, Darren Anthony. b 71. Wilson Carlile Coll 02. **d** 08 **p** 09. C Bucknall *Lich* 08–12; R Biddulph Moor and Knypersley from 12. *St John's Vicarage, 62 Park Lane, Knypersley, Stoke-on-Trent ST8 7AU* T: (01782) 512240 M: 07766-198455 E: rev.dfraser@gmail.com

FRASER, Duncan Piers. b 71. Bris Univ BA 93 Ch Ch Coll Cant PGCE 94. Wycliffe Hall Ox 11. **d** 13 **p** 14. C Eastbourne H Trin *Chich* 13–15; C Eastbourne All SS 15–17; V Eynsham and Cassington *Ox* from 17. *45 Acre End Street, Eynsham, Witney OX29 4PF* T: (01865) 682399 M: 07810-324088 E: duncanpfraser@gmail.com

FRASER, Elizabeth Ann. b 44. SRN 65. **d** 07 **p** 08. OLM Witley *Guildf* 07–14; PtO from 14. *Oakwood, Petworth Road, Milford, Godalming GU8 5BS* T: (01483) 417190 M: 07966-513450 E: revann@allsaintswitley.org.uk

FRASER, Helen Jane. b 77. Man Univ LLB 98. Trin Coll Bris BA 11. **d** 11 **p** 12. C Chipstead *S'wark* 11–14; C Reigate St Mary 14–19; NSM from 19; Hd of Voc Nat Min Team Abps' Coun from 19. *National Ministry Team, Church House, 27 Great Smith Street, London SW1P 3AZ* T: (020) 7898 1393 E: helen.fraser@churchofengland.org

FRASER, Canon Jane Alicia. b 44. Man Univ BA. Glouc Sch of Min 86. **d** 89 **p** 94. NSM Upton on Severn *Worc* 89–00; NSM Ripple, Earls Croome w Hill Croome and Strensham 97–00; Faith Adv Dept of Health's Adv Gp on Teenage Pregnancy 00–20; NSM Upton-on-Severn, Ripple, Earls Croome etc *Worc* 00–14; Hon Can Worc Cathl 05–14; PtO

FRASER, Canon Jeremy Stuart. b 58. d 08 p 09. C E Greenwich *S'wark* 08–13; P-in-c Stratford St Paul and St Jas *Chelmsf* 13–15; V 15–18; P-in-c Forest Gate All SS from 16; AD Newham 15–19; Miss and Development Adv Bradwell Area from 18; V N Woolwich w Silvertown from 19; Hon Can Chelmsf Cathl from 15. *7 Duchess Drive, London E13 8FE* T: (020) 7473 5670 M: 07970-139881 E: jeremy@fraserwireless.co.uk *or* jfraser@chelmsford.anglican.org

FRASER, Juliet. d 16 p 17. C Rhyl w St Ann *St As* 16; C Aber-Morfa Miss Area 17–18; C Aberconwy Miss Area from 18. *The Rectory, 16 Y Bryn, Glan Conwy, Colwyn Bay LL28 5NJ* E: juliet@parishofrhyl.co.uk *or* squirt5@clive.co.uk

FRASER, Mark Adrian. b 69. Warwick Univ BSc 90 Birm Univ MSc 91. St Jo Coll Nottm MTh 04. d 05 p 06. C Astley Bridge *Man* 05–08; P-in-c Gamston and Bridgford *S'well* 08–11; V from 11; P-in-c Edwalton from 14; AD W Bingham 17–19. *10 Scafell Close, West Bridgford, Nottingham NG2 6RJ* T: 0115-982 2834 M: 07963-397688 E: mark@st-lukes-gamston.org *or* fraser5mark@gmail.com

FRASER, Simon Bernard Lovat. b 52. d 17 p 18. C Egham *Guildf* from 17. *5 Magnolia View, 77 Worple Road, Staines-upon-Thames TW18 1HJ*

FRASER-SMITH, Keith Montague. b 48. St Jo Coll Dur BA 70. Trin Coll Bris. d 73 p 74. C Bishopsworth *Bris* 73–75; CMS 76–84; Egypt 76–80; Jerusalem 80–84; Asst Chapl Marseille w St Raphaël, Aix-en-Provence etc *Eur* 84–90; Media Dir Arab World Min 84–92; E Area Dir 92–97; Dep Internat Dir 97–98; NSM Worthing Ch the King *Chich* 90–93; Cyprus 93–97; NSM Tranmere St Cath *Ches* 97–98; P-in-c Barnton 98–03; Dir Global Mobilisation Arab World Min 03–10; Min Ldr UK 10–13; rtd 13; PtO *Ches* 03–15; *Leeds* from 17. *8 Cockshott Close, Leeds LS12 2RJ* T: 0113-450 1844 E: kieth.fraser-smith@tiscali.co.uk

FRAY, Bernard Herbert. b 44. Open Univ BA 73 Worc Coll of Educn CertEd 65 LTCL 67. Cranmer Hall Dur 02. d 03 p 04. NSM Long Marston *York* 03–06; NSM Rufforth w Moor Monkton and Hessay 03–06; NSM Healaugh w Wighill, Bilbrough and Askham Richard 03–06; NSM Tockwith and Bilton w Bickerton 03–06; P-in-c Aberford w Micklefield 06–11; rtd 11; PtO *York* 11–19; *Lon* from 19; *Roch* from 16. *31 Bromley College, London Road, Bromley BR1 1PE* T: (020) 3539 7650 M: 07967-232535 E: fraybernard985@gmail.com

FRAY, Vernon Francis. b 41. FCIOB 79. S'wark Ord Course 91. d 94 p 95. NSM Heston *Lon* 94–96; NSM Twickenham All Hallows 96–02; NSM Teddington St Mark and Hampton Wick 02–08; NSM Whitton SS Phil and Jas 08–11; PtO from 11; *S'wark* from 15. *1 Cavalier Court, 14 St Mark's Road, Teddington TW11 9DY* T: (020) 8614 1914 M: 07958-751915 E: v.fray@btinternet.com

FRAYLING, The Very Revd Nicholas Arthur. b 44. Ex Univ BA 69 Liv Univ Hon LLD 01. Cuddesdon Coll 69. d 71 p 72. C Peckham St Jo *S'wark* 71–74; V Tooting All SS 74–83; Can Res and Prec Liv Cathl 83–87; R Liv Our Lady and St Nic w St Anne 87–90; TR 90–02; Hon Can Liv Cathl 89–02; Dean Chich 02–14; rtd 14; PtO *Portsm* from 14. *Flat 5, 27 South Parade, Southsea PO5 2JF* T: (023) 9281 7041 E: nicholasfrayling@gmail.com

FRAYNE, The Very Revd David. b 34. St Edm Hall Ox BA 58 MA 62. Qu Coll Birm 58. d 60 p 61. C E Wickham *S'wark* 60–63; C Lewisham St Jo Southend 63–67; V N Sheen St Phil and All SS 67–73; R Caterham 73–83; RD 80–83; Hon Can S'wark Cathl 82–83; V Bris St Mary Redcliffe w Temple etc 83–92; RD Bedminster 86–92; Hon Can Bris Cathl 91–92; Provost Blackb 92–00; Dean Blackb 00–01; rtd 01; PtO *Sarum* 02–13; *B & W* from 12. *30 Coleridge Vale Road South, Clevedon BS21 6PB* T: (01275) 873799 M: 07788-795698 E: davidfrayne666@btinternet.com

FRAZER, Ian Martin. b 44. QUB BTh. d 91 p 93. LtO *D & D* 91–98; Aux Min Orangefield w Moneyreagh 98–04; Aux Min Ballymacarrett 04–09; NSM Belfast St Geo *Conn* from 09. *The Stacks, 14B Deramore Park South, Belfast BT9 5JY* E: genie.frazer@gmail.com

FREAR, Canon Philip Scott. b 45. Univ of Wales (Lamp) BA 66. Bris & Glouc Tr Course 77. d 80 p 81. Hon C Purton *Bris* 80–81; C Rodbourne Cheney 81–85; V Hengrove 85–95; V Braddan *S & M* 95–12; Chapl Isle of Man Dept of Health and Social Security 98–12; Can St German's Cathl *S & M* 04–12; rtd 12. *37 Hutchinson Square, Douglas, Isle of Man IM2 4HW* T: (01624) 615066 E: philipfrear@yahoo.com

FREARSON, Andrew Richard. b 57. Wolv Univ BA 80. Wycliffe Hall Ox. d 83 p 84. C Acocks Green *Birm* 83–86; C Moseley St Mary 86–89; P-in-c Holme *Blackb* 89–96; P-in-c Norcross Ch Ch USA 97–06; TV Bracknell *Ox* 06–10; R Dollar *St And*

10–18; PtO *Glouc* from 19. *10 Lancaster Road, Brockworth, Gloucester GL3 4FN* E: andrewfrearsontron@hotmail.co.uk

FREATHY, Nigel Howard. b 46. Lon Univ BA 68 CertEd. Sarum & Wells Th Coll 79. d 81 p 82. C Crediton *Ex* 81–82; C Crediton and Shobrooke 82–84; TV Ex St Thos and Em 84–86; V Beer and Branscombe 86–01; P-in-c Stockland, Dalwood, Kilmington and Shute 01–03; V Kilmington, Stockland, Dalwood, Yarcombe etc 03–08; RD Honiton 96–99; rtd 08; PtO *Ex* from 01. *7 Hawksdown View, Seaton EX12 2BJ* T: (01297) 22303 E: nigelfreathy@hotmail.co.uk

FREDERICK, David George. b 68. Birm Univ BSc 92. Ridley Hall Cam 08. d 10 p 11. C Cromer *Nor* 10–13; Pioneer Min *Ex* from 13. *26 Thompson Road, Exeter EX1 2UB* M: 07766-051948 E: dgfrederick@hotmail.com

FREDERICK, John Bassett Moore. b 30. Princeton Univ BA 51 Birm Univ PhD 73. Gen Th Sem (NY) MDiv 54. d 54 p 55. C Cheshire St Pet USA 54–56; C All Hallows Barking *Lon* 56–58; C Ox SS Phil and Jas 58–60; R New Haven St Jo USA 61–71; R Bletchingley *S'wark* 74–95; Reigate Adnry Ecum Officer 90–95; RD Godstone 92–95; rtd 95. *32 Chestnut Street, Princeton NJ 08542-3806, USA* T: (001) (609) 924 7590 F: 924 1694 E: jf9642@netscape.net

FREDRIKSEN, Martin. b 47. St Chad's Coll Dur BA 69 Univ of Wales (Lamp) MA 03. d 70 p 71. C Bideford *Ex* 70–73; C Guildf St Nic 73–76; R Cossington *B & W* 76–82; V Woolavington 76–82; Asst Chapl K Coll Taunton 82–84; C Bp's Hatfield *St Alb* 84–94; P-in-c Broadstone *Sarum* 94; V 94–12; rtd 12; PtO *Sarum* 12–21; *Heref* from 21. *5 Millbrook Gardens, Lea, Ross-on-Wye HR9 7LA* E: fr.fred04@gmail.com

FREELAND, Nicolas John Michell. b 65. FNMSM 99 FCMI 10. STETS 07. d 10 p 11. NSM Jersey St Pet *Win* 10–13; C 13–15; C Jersey St Brelade 15–16; R Swanbourne w Mt Claremont Australia 16–18; R S Perth from 18. *3/9 Ridge Street, South Perth WA 6151, Australia* E: fr.nick@me.com

FREELAND, Paul William. b 77. Brunel Univ BSc 99. St Mellitus Coll 17. d 19 p 20. C Swindon St Aug *Bris* from 19. *80 Queen Elizabeth Drive, Swindon SN25 1UE* M: 07736-928126 E: paulwfreeland@gmail.com

FREEMAN, Anthony John Curtis. b 46. Ex Coll Ox BA 68 MA 72. Cuddesdon Coll 70. d 72 p 73. C Worc St Martin 72–74; C Worc St Martin w St Pet 74–75; Bp's Dom Chapl *Chich* 75–78; C-in-c Parklands St Wilfrid CD 78–82; V Durrington 82–89; P-in-c Staplefield Common 89–94; Bp's Adv on CME 89–93; Asst Dir of Ords 89–93; PtO from 13. *6 Winchester Drive, Chichester PO19 5DE* T: (01243) 783136 E: anthony.jcs@gmail.com

FREEMAN, Daniel James. b 88. Cam Univ BA 09 VetMB 12. Oak Hill Th Coll BA 20. d 20 p 21. C Preston Risen Lord *Blackb* from 20. *550 New Hall Lane, Preston PR1 4TE* M: 07917-758891 E: dan@the-freemans.net

FREEMAN, Mrs Dorothy Lloyd (Dee). b 54. Lon Inst of Educn BEd 76 Nottm Univ MA 11. EMMTC 06. d 09 p 10. NSM Linc St Geo Swallowbeck 09–16; R Withamside from 16. *The Rectory, 11 Torgate Lane, Bassingham, Lincoln LN5 9HF* T: (01522) 788383 M: 07792-780683 E: revdee@withamsidechurches.org.uk

FREEMAN, Gordon Bertie. b 37. CITC BTh 95. d 95 p 96. C Lecale Gp *D & D* 95–98; I Ardara w Glencolumbkille, Inniskeel etc *D & R* 98–07; Bp's Dom Chapl 06–07; rtd 07. *3 Leyland Meadow, Ballycastle BT54 6JX* T: (028) 2076 8458 E: gordon.freeman2@btinternet.com

FREEMAN, Jane. b 54. Dur Univ BA 75 PhD 80. Qu Coll Birm BD 00. d 00 p 01. C Waterloo St Jo w St Andr *S'wark* 00–03; TV E Ham w Upton Park and Forest Gate *Chelmsf* 03–11; TR Wickford and Runwell 11–19; RD Basildon 16–19; Hon Can Chelmsf Cathl 09–19; rtd 19. *25 Foundry Street, Kingswinford DY6 9BB* M: 07702-922818 E: canjanefree@gmail.com

FREEMAN, Mrs Karen Lynn. b 62. San Diego State Univ USA BS 86 Leeds Univ BA 09. NOC 06. d 09 p 10. C New Brighton St Jas w Em *Ches* 09–12; P-in-c Birkenhead Ch Ch 13–18. *12510 Dennis Court, Auburn CA 95603, USA* E: k.freeman62@gmail.com

FREEMAN, Preb Karl Fredrick. b 57. MBE 15. St Luke's Coll Ex BEd 80. d 90 p 91. C Plymouth St Andr w St Paul and St Geo *Ex* 90–95; TV Plymouth St Andr and Stonehouse 95–96; Chapl Coll of SS Mark and Jo Plymouth 96–01; TR Plymouth Em w St Paul from 01; Preb Ex Cathl from 14; RD Plymouth City 15–17. *The Rectory, 9 Seymour Drive, Plymouth PL3 5BG* T: (01752) 248601 *or* 260317 E: karldesk@blueyonder.co.uk

FREEMAN, Keith Ian. b 66. St Jo Coll Nottm 10. d 12 p 13. C Shelley and Shepley *Leeds* 12–15; C W Barnsley 15–20; TR Castleford from 20. *The Rectory, 15 Barnes Road, Castleford WF10 5AA* M: 07958-328289 E: keithfreeman66@hotmail.com *or* keith.freeman@leeds.anglican.org

FREEMAN, Malcolm Robin. b 48. Master Mariner 78. St And NSM Tr Scheme 85. **d** 88 **p** 89. NSM Kirkcaldy *St And* 88–94; NSM Westbury *Sarum* 99–02; R Tidworth, Ludgershall and Faberstown 02–13; rtd 13; PtO *Win* from 14. *26 Home Farm Gardens, Charlton, Andover SP10 4AX* M: 07810-862740 E: fgmastermariner@gmail.com

FREEMAN, Martin. *See* FREEMAN, Philip Martin

FREEMAN, Michael Charles. b 36. Magd Coll Cam BA 61 MA 68 Lon Univ BD 69 PhD 93. Clifton Th Coll 67. **d** 69 **p** 70. C Bedworth *Cov* 69–72; C Morden *S'wark* 72–77; P-in-c Westcombe Park St Geo 77–85; V Kingston Vale St Jo 85–94; rtd 99; PtO *B & W* from 11. *6 Wristland Road, Watchet TA23 0DH* T: (01984) 634378 E: freemmic@talktalk.net

FREEMAN, Michael Curtis. b 51. Lanc Univ BA 72 Liv Hope Univ Coll MA 96 PhD 05. Cuddesdon Coll 72. **d** 75 **p** 76. C Walton St Mary *Liv* 75–78; C Hednesford *Lich* 78–81; TV Solihull *Birm* 81–86; V Yardley Wood 86–90; V Farnworth *Liv* 90–03; AD Widnes 02–03; P-in-c Blundellsands St Mich 03–12; V 12; P-in-c Thornton and Crosby 05–12; rtd 12; PtO *Liv* from 16. *5 Lincoln Crescent, Bootle L20 7EB* E: michael.freeman6@mypostoffice.co.uk

FREEMAN, Preb Michael Raymond. b 58. Chu Coll Cam BA 80 MA 84 Ox Univ BA 87. St Steph Ho Ox 85. **d** 88 **p** 89. C Clifton All SS w St Jo *Bris* 88–92; TV Elland *Wakef* 92–01; V Horninglow *Lich* from 01; RD Tutbury from 10; Preb Lich Cathl from 16. *Horninglow Vicarage, 14 Rolleston Road, Burton-on-Trent DE13 0JZ* T: (01283) 568613 E: freeman.burton@googlemail.com

FREEMAN, Peter Cameron Jessett. b 41. **d** 05 **p** 06. OLM Sturry w Fordwich and Westbere w Hersden *Cant* 05–11; rtd 11; PtO *Cant* from 11. *29 Cedar Road, Sturry, Canterbury CT2 0HZ*

FREEMAN, Philip Martin. b 54. Westcott Ho Cam 76. **d** 79 **p** 80. C Stanley *Liv* 79–82; C Bromborough *Ches* 82–84; V Runcorn H Trin 84–91; Chapl Halton Gen Hosp 84–91; R Ashton-upon-Mersey St Martin *Ches* 91–96; SSF 96–06; PtO *Sarum* 96–99; Asst Chapl HM Pris Birm 98–99; PtO *Lon* 99–02; *Ely* 02–05; Chapl Barts and The Lon NHS Trust 00–02 and 05–08; Chapl Guy's and St Thos' NHS Foundn Trust 05–08; PtO *S'wark* 05–08; Chapl Univ Coll Lon Hosps NHS Foundn Trust 08–16; Hon C Smithfield St Bart Gt *Lon* 06–08; rtd 16; PtO *Lon* from 16; *S'wark* from 16. *18 Foxley Gardens, Purley CR8 2DQ* T: (020) 3302 3099 M: 07985-512436 E: pmfreeman3@gmail.com

FREEMAN, Richard Alan. b 52. Ripon Coll Cuddesdon. **d** 83 **p** 84. C Crayford *Roch* 83–86; V Slade Green 86–94; R Eynsford w Farningham and Lullingstone 94–01; P-in-c Shoreham 01–12; V 12–15; Chapl St Mich Sch Otford 01–15; R Bradworthy, Sutcombe, Putford etc *Ex* 15; R Bradworthy, Sutcombe etc 15–20; R Bradworthy, Sutcombe, Putford etc from 20; RD Holsworthy from 19. *The New Rectory, St Peters Well Lane, Bradworthy, Holsworthy EX22 7TG* T: (01409) 241315 E: ricktherec@aol.com

✠**FREEMAN, The Rt Revd Robert John.** b 52. St Jo Coll Dur BSc 74 Fitzw Coll Cam BA 76 MA. Ridley Hall Cam 74. **d** 77 **p** 78 **c** 11. C Blackpool St Jo *Blackb* 77–81; TV Chigwell *Chelmsf* 81–85; V Leic Martyrs 85–99; Hon Can Leic Cathl 94–03; RD Christianity S 95–98; Nat Adv in Evang 99–03; LtO *Leic* 99–03; Adn Halifax *Wakef* 03–11; Suff Bp Penrith *Carl* 11–18; rtd 18; Hon Asst Bp Leic from 18. *40 Eastfield Road, Leicester LE3 6FE* E: frmnfrmn@gmail.com

FREEMAN, Rosemary. b 47. **d** 03 **p** 04. NSM Madeley *Heref* 03–17; PtO from 17. *5 Rowley Close, Madeley, Telford TF7 5RR* T: (01952) 583460 E: rosemary_freeman@sky.com

FREEMAN, Simon Thomas Allan. b 69. Univ of Wales (Trin St Dav) BTh 18. St Padarn's Inst 15. **d** 18 **p** 19. C Bro Gwydyr *Ban* 18–21; TR Llantrisant *Llan* from 21. *The Vicarage, Brynna Road, Brynna, Pontyclun CF72 9QE* T: (01443) 286674 E: revsimonfreeman18@gmail.com

FREESTONE, Anne Elizabeth. b 52. Bp Otter Coll Chich CertEd 73 Coll of Ripon & York St Jo MA 00. NEOC 04. **d** 07 **p** 08. NSM Middleton-in-Teesdale w Forest and Frith *Dur* 07–11; PtO from 11; *Leeds* from 14; Chapl Castle Howard 15–18; PtO *York* from 18; *Ches* from 19. *5 Tedder Road, York YO24 3JD* M: 07939-964011 E: annefreestone123@gmail.com

FREETH, Barry James. b 35. Birm Univ BA 60. Tyndale Hall Bris 60. **d** 62 **p** 64. C Selly Hill St Steph *Birm* 62–63; C Birm St Jo Ladywood 63–71; Chapl RAF 71–75; P-in-c Crudwell w Ashley *Bris* 75–81; P-in-c Lanreath *Truro* 81–84; R 84–87; P-in-c Pelynt 81–84; V 84–87; R Harvington and Norton and Lenchwick *Worc* 87–93; V Ramsden, Finstock and Fawler, Leafield etc *Ox* 93–99; rtd 99; PtO *Derby* 99–03; *Ox* 08–12. *16 Broad Meadow, Leonard Stanley, Stonehouse GL10 3PG* T: (01453) 823890

FREETH, Mrs Patricia. b 48. Wycliffe Hall Ox BTh 95. **d** 95 **p** 96. NSM Ramsden, Finstock and Fawler, Leafield etc *Ox* 95–99; TV Burbage and King Sterndale *Derby* 99–03; V Shires' Edge *Ox* 03–12; AD Deddington 10–12; rtd 12; PtO *Glouc* from 13; AD Stroud 18–19. *16 Broad Meadow, Leonard Stanley, Stonehouse GL10 3PG* T: (01453) 827154 M: 07599-984735 E: revpfreeth@gmail.com

FREMMER, Ludger. b 56. Ridley Hall Cam 02. **d** 04 **p** 05. C Mattishall w Mattishall Burgh, Welborne etc *Nor* 04–07; P-in-c Kibworth and Smeeton Westerby and Saddington *Leic* 07–17; R from 17. *The Rectory, 25 Church Road, Kibworth, Leicester LE8 0NB* T: 0116-279 2294 *or* 279 6577 M: 07753-213145 E: ludger.fremmer@gmail.com *or* wilfs.kibworth@gmail.com

FRENCH, Alexander James Watkins. b 70. Univ of Wales (Ban) BA 92 Univ Coll Worc PGCE 93. Qu Foundn Birm 13. **d** 16 **p** 17. C Old Swinford Stourbridge *Worc* 16–20; P-in-c Yardley St Cypr Hay Mill *Birm* from 20; P-in-c S Yardley St Mich from 20. *The Vicarage, 60 Yew Tree Lane, Yardley, Birmingham B26 1AP* M: 07745-780629 E: ajwfrench@yahoo.co.uk

FRENCH, Mrs Christine. b 68. Nottm Trent Univ PGCE 05. EMMTC MA 08. **d** 09 **p** 10. C Keyworth and Stanton-on-the-Wolds and Bunny etc *S'well* 09–13; P-in-c Norwell w Ossington, Cromwell and Caunton 13–14; P-in-c Kirk Hallam *Derby* from 14; C Ilkeston St Jo from 15. *The Vicarage, 71 Ladywood Road, Ilkeston DE7 4NF* T: 0115-783 1793 E: revchristine@outlook.com

FRENCH, Canon Clive Anthony. b 43. AKC 70. St Aug Coll Cant 70. **d** 71 **p** 72. C Monkseaton St Mary *Newc* 71–73; Dioc Youth Adv 73–76; Chapl RN 76–77; Dir of Ords RN 85–90; Chapl RN Coll Greenwich 95–97; R Cheam *S'wark* 97–06; TR Catford (Southend) and Downham 06–09; Hon Can *S'wark* Cathl 08–09; rtd 09; PtO *S'wark* 10 and 14–17; *Eur* from 18. *17 Kingslea, Leatherhead KT22 7SN* T: (01372) 375418

FRENCH, Daniel Alain. b 68. Kent Univ BSc 91. St Jo Sem Wonersh BTh 97. **d** 97 **p** 98. In RC Ch 97–01; C Aberdeen St Clem *Ab* 02–03; C Aberdeen St Mary 02–03; P-in-c Aberdeen St Clem 03–08; Chapl Robert Gordon Univ 04–08; V Malborough, Salcombe and S Huish *Ex* from 08; RD Woodleigh 12–16. *The Vicarage, Devon Road, Salcombe TQ8 8HJ* T: (01548) 842853 *or* 842626 E: cybervicar@gmail.com

FRENCH, Derek John. b 47. Man Univ BA 03. Ripon Coll Cuddesdon 93. **d** 95 **p** 96. C Stand *Man* 95–98; TV E Farnworth and Kearsley 98–00; P-in-c Halliwell St Marg 00–09; P-in-c Ringley w Prestolee 06–09; P-in-c Elton St Steph 09–11; V 11–15; rtd 15; PtO *Blackb* 15–21. *22 Links Road, Knott End-on-Sea, Poulton-le-Fylde FY6 0DG* T: (01253) 812006 E: revdelboy@gmail.com

FRENCH, George Leslie. b 47. AIFST NE Lon Poly BSc 70. S'wark Ord Course 86. **d** 89 **p** 90. NSM Reading St Barn *Ox* 89–99. *Hawthorne House, 2 Cutbush Close, Lower Earley, Reading RG6 4XA* T: 0118-986 1886

FRENCH, Janet Mary. *See* DRIVER, Janet Mary

FRENCH, Jonathan David Seabrook. b 60. Westcott Ho Cam 84. **d** 87 **p** 88. C Loughton St Jo *Chelmsf* 87–90; Chapl St Bede's Ch for the Deaf Clapham 90–92; C Richmond St Mary w St Matthias and St Jo *S'wark* 92–95; TV 96–03; V Downham St Barn 03–10; Chapl RAD 92–03; Dioc Adv for Min of Deaf and Disabled People *S'wark* 03–10; R Southwick *Chich* from 10. *The Rectory, 22 Church Lane, Southwick, Brighton BN42 4GB* T: (01273) 592389 E: jo.nathan@btinternet.com

FRENCH, Mrs Joy Elizabeth. b 75. Sheff Univ BA 98 MA 17. St Hild Coll 14. **d** 17 **p** 18. C Owlerton *Sheff* 17–21; P-in-c from 21. *St Mark's Vicarage, 19 Graven Close, Grenoside, Sheffield S35 8QT* M: 07496-531257 E: joyfrench@hotmail.co.uk *or* joy@stjb.org.uk

FRENCH, The Ven Judith Karen. b 60. St D Coll Lamp BA 89. St Steph Ho Ox 89. **d** 91 **p** 94. Par Dn Botley *Portsm* 91–94; C Bilton *Cov* 94–97; V Charlbury w Shorthampton *Ox* 97–14; AD Chipping Norton 07–12; Hon Can Ch 12–14; Adn Dorchester from 14. *11 Broad Field Road, Yarnton, Kidlington OX5 1UL* T: (01865) 208245 M: 07460-888482 E: archdeacon.dorchester@oxford.anglican.org

FRENCH, Julia. b 63. **d** 06 **p** 07. NSM Plympton St Maurice *Ex* 06–09; NSM Yealmpton and Brixton 09–15; Chapl Plymouth Hosps NHS Trust 09–15; PtO *B & W* 15–16; Chapl Taunton and Somerset NHS Foundn Trust 16–18; Lead Chapl 18–20; Lead Chapl Somerset NHS Foundn Trust from 20; Public Preacher *B & W* 16–18; NSM Taunton St Mary and St Jo from 17. *16 Northfield Road, Taunton TA1 1XE* T: (01823) 710798 E: julia.m.french@gmail.com

FRENCH, Michael John. b 37. WEMTC 92. **d** 95 **p** 96. OLM Cheltenham St Pet *Glouc* 95–01; NSM 01–08; NSM N Cheltenham 08–09; PtO from 09. *8 Alexandria*

Walk, Cheltenham GL52 5LG T: (01242) 236661 E: mike.french@northchelt.org.uk

FRENCH, Peter Robert. b 65. Man Univ BTh 87. Qu Coll Birm 88. **d** 90 **p** 91. C Unsworth *Man* 90–93; C Bury Ch King w H Trin 93–95; V Bury Ch King 95–98; V Handsworth St Andr *Birm* 98–06; Sch Support Officer 06–18; PtO from 18. *Address temp unknown*

FRENCH, Richard John. b 34. Open Univ BA 82. Tyndale Hall Bris 62. **d** 64 **p** 65. C Rustington *Chich* 64–68; C Walton H Trin *Ox* 68–72; V Grove 72–99; rtd 99; PtO *Chich* from 01. *5 Green Meadows, The Welkin, Haywards Heath RH16 2PE* T: (01444) 487842

FRENCH, Stephen Robert James. b 52. St Jo Coll Nottm. **d** 87 **p** 88. C Chell *Lich* 87–91; TV 91–94; V Wednesfield Heath 94–01; TV Hemel Hempstead *St Alb* 01–06; P-in-c Bugbrooke w Rothersthorpe *Pet* 06–10; P-in-c Kislingbury and Harpole 06–10; R Bugbrooke, Harpole, Kislingbury etc from 10. *The Rectory, Church Lane, Bugbrooke, Northampton NN7 3PB* T: (01604) 831621 E: srjfrench@hotmail.co.uk

FRENCH, William Stephen. b 49. STETS 07. **d** 10 **p** 11. NSM Verwood *Sarum* 10–16; NSM Wimborne Minster and the N Villages 16–19; rtd 19; PtO *Sarum* from 19. *Hollow Tree House, Chalbury, Wimborne BH21 7ER* T: (01258) 841061 M: 07771-560128 E: william.french4@btinternet.com

FRETT, Daniel Calvin. b 60. Univ of S Carolina 85. NTMTC 95 Oak Hill Th Coll BA 99. **d** 98 **p** 99. NSM Clerkenwell St Jas and St Jo w St Pet *Lon* 98–00; NSM Chelsea St Jo w St Andr 00–05; NSM Tulse Hill H Trin and St Matthias *S'wark* 05–08; NSM Cranleigh *Guildf* 09–16; PtO *Mon* 16–20; TR Caldicot from 20. *St Mary's Rectory, 39 Church Road, Caldicot NP26 4HN* M: 07966-196852 E: dfrett@mac.com or danfrett@gmail.com

FREYHAN, Daniel Jonathan. b 83. Oriel Coll Ox MMath 06. Oak Hill Th Coll BA 14. **d** 14 **p** 15. C Stevenage St Nic and Graveley *St Alb* 14–17; V Prudhoe *Newc* from 17. *The Vicarage, 5 Kepwell Court, Prudhoe NE42 5PE* T: (01661) 836059 E: vicar@prudhoeparishchurch.org.uk

FRIARS, Ian Malcolm George. b 50. Sarum & Wells Th Coll 83. **d** 85 **p** 86. C Norton *St Alb* 85–88; C Ramsey *Ely* 88–90; TV The Ramseys and Upwood 90–93; P-in-c Cottenham 93–94; R 94–01; P-in-c Long Melford *St E* 01–02; R Chadbrook 02–13; rtd 13; PtO *Ely* from 12; *St Alb* from 13; *St E* from 13; *Eur* from 17. *Clanjenian, 3A Swan Street, Ashwell, Baldock SG7 5NY* T: (01462) 742441 E: ianmgfriars@gmail.com

FRICKER, Oliver Samuel George. b 89. Fitzw Coll Cam BA 11 MA 15 Dur Univ MA 21. St Mellitus Coll 18. **d** 21. C Hampreston *Sarum* from 21. *19 Canford Bottom, Wimborne BH21 2HA* M: 07815-501342 E: olifricker@gmail.com

FRIDD, Nicholas Timothy. b 53. Ch Ch Ox BA 74 MA 78. STETS 05. **d** 08 **p** 09. NSM Wells St Thos w Horrington *B & W* from 08. *The Old Bakery, 30 St Thomas Street, Wells BA5 2UX* T: (01749) 679832 M: 07831-209240 E: wellscottages@btconnect.com

FRIEDRICH, Robert Edmund. b 48. Houghton Coll (USA) BA 70 Gordon-Conwell Th Sem MDiv 74 DMin 96. Gen Th Sem NY 86. **d** 86 **p** 86. C Westfield Atonement USA 86–88; R Penfield 88–92; R Newport Epiphany 92–97; Meriden All SS 99–02; W Haven St Jo 04; Las Vegas Grace in the Desert 04–06; Olean 06–07; PtO *St As* from 15; *Ban* from 15. *Polyanna Cottage, Castle Street, Conwy LL32 8AY* E: bobfriedrich@gmail.com

FRIENDSHIP, Roger Geoffrey (John-Francis). b 46. ACII 72. WMMTC 90. **d** 93 **p** 94. SSF 76–02; NSM Harborne St Faith and St Laur *Birm* 93–94; Asst Novice Guardian Hilfield Friary Dorchester 94–97; Novice Guardian 97–99; Gen Sec SSF 99–01; C Clerkenwell H Redeemer and St Mark *Lon* 00–01; R Romford St Andr *Chelmsf* 01–11; rtd 11; PtO *S'wark* from 12; *Chelmsf* from 15. *22 The Old Fire Station, Eaglesfield Road, London SE18 3BT* T: (020) 3583 9312 M: 07808-500717 E: jff2209@yahoo.com

FRIGGENS, Canon Maurice Anthony. b 40. Sheff Univ BA 65. Westcott Ho Cam 65. **d** 67 **p** 68. C Stocksbridge *Sheff* 67–70; C St Buryan, St Levan and Sennen *Truro* 70–72; R 72–84; RD Penwith 82–84; R St Columb Major w St Wenn 84–91; Dioc Dir of Ords 87–93; Hon Can Truro Cathl 87–00; V St Cleer 91–00; rtd 00; PtO *Ban* from 00; *Eur* from 01. *T Cernyw, Rhiw, Pwllheli LL53 8AF* T: (01758) 780365

FRISWELL, Caroline Anne. b 52. St Mary's Coll Chelt BEd 78 Sunderland Poly MA 90 Dur Univ PhD 99. Cranmer Hall Dur 06. **d** 09 **p** 10. NSM Greenside *Dur* 09–12; P-in-c Byers Green 12–19; rtd 19; PtO *Dur* from 20. *Westholme, Durham Moor, Durham DH1 5AH* E: caroline.friswell@btinternet.com

FRITH, Canon Christopher John Cokayne. b 44. Ex Coll Ox BA 65 MA 69. Ridley Hall Cam 66. **d** 68 **p** 69. C Crookes St Thos *Sheff* 68–71; C Rusholme H Trin *Man* 71–74; R Haughton St Mary 74–85; R Brampton St Thos *Derby* 85–02; V Alvaston 02–09; Hon Can Derby Cathl 99–09; rtd 09; PtO *Worc* from 10. *Cover Point, Back Lane, Bredon, Tewkesbury GL20 7LH* T: (01684) 773164

FRITH, Mrs Gillian. b 43. EAMTC 99. **d** 02 **p** 03. NSM Chipping Ongar w Shelley *Chelmsf* 02–06; P-in-c Doddinghurst 06–13; rtd 13; PtO *Chelmsf* 14–17. *29 Windmill Fields, Coggeshall, Colchester CO6 1PJ* T: (01376) 566815 M: 07890-376779 E: frithgill29@gmail.com

FRITH, Jonathan Paul (Jonty). b 72. Jes Coll Cam BA 94 MA 97. Wycliffe Hall Ox 95. **d** 97 **p** 98. C Houghton *Carl* 97–00; Chapl Cranleigh Sch Surrey 00–04; C Crowborough *Chich* 04–15; R Bathampton w Claverton *B & W* from 15. *The Vicarage, Bathampton Lane, Bathampton, Bath BA2 6SW* T: (01225) 338055 E: jontyfrith@gmail.com

FRITH, Canon Richard John. b 77. Warwick Univ BA 98 Sheff Univ MA 99 Trin Hall Cam PhD 04. Ripon Coll Cuddesdon BA 10. **d** 11 **p** 12. C Ox St Mary Magd 11–14; V Halifax H Trin and St Jude *Leeds* 14–19; Can Res S'well Minster from 19. *2 Vicars Close, Southwell NG25 0HP* M: 07754-524206 E: richard.frith@ymail.com or precentor@southwellminster.org.uk

✠**FRITH, The Rt Revd Richard Michael Cokayne.** b 49. Fitzw Coll Cam BA 72 MA 76. St Jo Coll Nottm 72. **d** 74 **p** 75 **c** 98. C Mortlake w E Sheen *S'wark* 74–78; TV Thamesmead 78–83; TR Keynsham *B & W* 83–92; Preb Wells Cathl 91–98; Adn Taunton 92–98; Suff Bp Hull *York* 98–14; Bp Heref 14–19; rtd 19; PtO *York* from 20. *64 Oakland Avenue, York YO31 1DF*

FRITZE-SHANKS, Miss Annette. Sydney Univ BA 86 DipEd 87 LLB 89 Solicitor. SEITE 01. **d** 04 **p** 05. NSM Kilburn St Mary w All So and W Hampstead St Jas *Lon* 04–08; PtO 08–10; NSM Hampstead Em W End from 10. *13 Elm Grove, London NW2 3AE* M: 07771-544201 E: afritze-shanks@btconnect.com

FROGGATT, Peter Michael. b 65. St Hild Coll Dur BA 86 PGCE 88. Wycliffe Hall Ox BTh 95. **d** 95 **p** 96. C Bebington *Ches* 95–00; V Rock Ferry 00–11; RD Birkenhead 10–11; V Barnston 11–21; RD Wirral N 15–20; Dir of Outreach from 21. *Church House, 5500 Daresbury Park, Daresbury, Warrington WA4 4GE* T: (01928) 718834 E: peter@froggatt.org.uk or peter.froggat@chester.anglican.org

FROOM, Ian Leonard John. b 42. Sarum Th Coll 69. **d** 71 **p** 72. C Gillingham and Fifehead Magdalen *Sarum* 71–75; C Parkstone St Pet w Branksea and St Osmund 75–78; V Sedgley St Mary *Lich* 78–85; TV Weston-super-Mare Cen Par *B & W* 85–94; PtO 94–97; V Truro St Geo and St Jo 97–03; rtd 03; PtO *Truro* from 03. *11 Marlborough Crescent, Falmouth TR11 2RJ* T: (01326) 311760 E: sea2firechap@yahoo.co.uk

FROST, Christopher Dominic. b 83. Abth Univ BA 05 Cardiff Univ BTh 15. St Mich Coll Llan 12. **d** 15 **p** 16. C Cardigan w Mwnt and Y Ferwig w Llangoedmor *St D* 15–17; C Aberporth w Blaenporth w Betws Ifan 17–18; P-in-c Bro Teifi from 18. *Bronwydd, Parc y Plas, Aberporth, Cardigan SA43 2BJ* M: 07432-692179 E: christopher_dominic_frost@yahoo.co.uk

FROST, David John. b 48. **d** 86 **p** 87. Hon C Upper Norwood All SS *S'wark* 86–89; C Battersea St Luke 90–94; V Shirley St Geo 94–12; rtd 12; PtO *S'wark* from 12; *Cant* from 12. *19 Reculver Avenue, Birchington CT7 9NT* T: (01843) 844511 E: revdfrost1@gmail.com

FROST, Canon David Richard. b 54. Ridley Hall Cam 84. **d** 86 **p** 87. C Burgess Hill St Andr *Chich* 86–90; TV Rye 90–94; V Bexhill St Steph 94–10; RD Battle and Bexhill 06–10; TR Rye 10–20; RD 11–18; Can and Preb Chich Cathl 10–20; rtd 21. *68 Marley Road, Rye TN31 7BD* M: 07970-746545 E: david@drfrost.org.uk

FROST, Derek Charles. b 47. Lich Th Coll 69. **d** 71 **p** 72. C Woodley St Jo the Ev *Ox* 71–76; V Bampton w Clanfield 76–81; V Minster Lovell and Brize Norton 81–88; TV Upper Kennet *Sarum* 88–92; P-in-c Seend and Bulkington 92–97; P-in-c Seend, Bulkington and Poulshot 95–97; V 97–01; V Derry Hill w Bremhill and Foxham 01–10; rtd 10; PtO *Sarum* from 10. *Longhope Cottage, 93 North Street, Calne SN11 0HJ* T: (01249) 811565

FROST, The Ven George. b 35. Dur Univ BA 56 MA 61. Linc Th Coll 57. **d** 60 **p** 61. C Barking St Marg *Chelmsf* 60–64; C-in-c Marks Gate CD 64–70; V Tipton St Matt *Lich* 70–77; V Penn 77–87; RD Trysull 84–87; Preb Lich Cathl 85–87; Adn Salop 87–98; V Tong 87–98; P-in-c Donington 97–98; Adn Lich and Can Res and Treas Lich Cathl 98–00; rtd 00; PtO *Lich* 00–21. *23 Darnford Lane, Lichfield WS14 9RW* T: (01543) 415109 E: frost151@btinternet.com

FROST, George Irving. b 95. Aber Univ MA 17. Cranmer Hall Dur 19. **d** 21. C Silverstone and Abthorpe w Slapton etc *Pet* from 21. *33 Murswell Lane, Silverstone, Towcester NN12 8UT* T: (01327) 857827 E: rev@gfrost.name

FROST, Mrs Jane Helena. b 59. St Aid Coll Dur BA 81 Newc Univ PGCE 82. SWMTC 12. **d** 15 **p** 16. C Totnes w Bridgetown, Berry Pomeroy etc *Ex* 15–19; TV Teignmouth, Ideford w Luton, Ashcombe etc from 19. *The Vicarage, 3 Moors Park, Bishopsteignton, Teignmouth TQ14 9RH* T: (01626) 870288 E: revjanefrost@gmail.com

✠**FROST, The Rt Revd Jonathan Hugh.** b 64. Aber Univ BD 88 Nottm Univ MTh 99 Surrey Univ DUniv 12 MSSTh 91. Ridley Hall Cam 91. **d** 93 **p** 94 **c** 10. C W Bridgford *S'well* 93–97; Police Chapl Trent Division 94–97; R Ash *Guildf* 97–02; Tutor Local Min Progr 99–10; Can Res Guildf Cathl 02–10; Chapl Surrey Univ 02–10; Co-ord Chapl 08–10; Bp's Adv Inter-Faith Relns *Guildf* 07–10; Suff Bp Southampton *Win* 10–19; Hon Asst Bp Portsm 16–19; Dean York from 19; Hon Asst Bp York from 19; PtO *Portsm* from 16. *The Deanery, Dean's Park, York YO1 7JQ* T: (01904) 557202 E: dean@yorkminster.org

FROST, Linda May. b 59. CITC MTh 14. **d** 13 **p** 14. Howth *D & G* 13–14; Bp's C Mohill w Farnaught, Aughavas, Oughteragh etc *K, E & A* 14–17; I from 17. *Corbo, Kilrooskey, Co Roscommon, F42 E671, Republic of Ireland* M: (00353) 86-601 0895 E: welcomefrost@iol.ie

FROST, Michael John. b 42. Westmr Coll Ox TCert 64. **d** 95 **p** 96. OLM Harwood *Man* 95–12; rtd 12; PtO *Man* from 12. *86 Harden Drive, Harwood, Bolton BL2 5BX* T: (01204) 418596 E: revmikefrost@live.co.uk

FROST, Michelle. b 68. Qu Foundn Birm 17. **d** 20 **p** 21. C Irthlingborough, Gt Addington, Lt Addington etc *Pet* from 20. *64 Torksey Close, Corby NN18 9PL* E: revd.michelle@nenecrossings.org.uk

FROST, Paul William. b 75. Sheff Univ BA 97 Ox Univ PGCE 98. Wycliffe Hall Ox MTh 08. **d** 08 **p** 09. C Kettering Ch the King *Pet* 08–12; P-in-c Corby St Jo w Epiphany 12–17; R from 17; P-in-c Gretton w Rockingham and Cottingham w E Carlton from 20. *16 Streather Drive, Corby NN17 1TN* M: 07979-547279 E: frost.pw@gmail.com

FROST, Richard John. b 49. Ch Ch Coll Cant CertEd 71 BA 00. SWMTC 95. **d** 97 **p** 98. NSM Bideford, Northam, Westward Ho!, Appledore etc *Ex* 97–00; C 00–03; TV 03–09; rtd 09; PtO *Ex* from 10; Chapl Kyrenia St Andr Cyprus 11–13; PtO *St E* from 15; *Eur* 10–19 and from 20; Chapl Málaga 19–20. *Cana, 2 Tarka Falls, Old Barnstaple Road, Bideford EX39 4FL* E: richardjohnfrost@hotmail.co.uk

FROST, Stanley. b 37. Univ of Wales BSc 61 Liv Univ MSc 65 PhD 68 CBiol 66 MRSB 66 FAEB 82. NOC 79. **d** 82 **p** 83. NSM Lower Kersal *Man* 82–87; NSM Patricroft 87–89; NSM Convenor 87–95; Lic Preacher 89–03; P-in-c Pittenweem and Elie and Earlsferry *St And* 03–04; rtd 04; PtO *Derby* 04–18. *25 Somersall Park Road, Chesterfield S40 3LD* T: (01246) 567184 E: stan.frost@homecall.co.uk

FROSTICK, Paul Andrew. b 52. Stockwell Coll of Educn CertEd 73. Ripon Hall Ox 74. **d** 77 **p** 78. C Shepton Mallet *B & W* 77–80; TV Barton Mills, Beck Row w Kenny Hill etc *St E* 80–85; TV Mildenhall 85–86; TV Raveningham *Nor* 86–89; V Bottisham and P-in-c Lode and Longmeadow *Ely* 89–90; V Bottisham and Lode w Long Meadow 90–94; Hd RE Brittons Sch Romford 94–97; Hd RE The Grove Sch St Leonards 97–00; rtd 00; Assoc P Bexhill St Aug *Chich* 99–14; PtO 14–17; P-in-c Hooe from 17; P-in-c Ninfield from 17. *18 The Ridings, Bexhill-on-Sea TN39 5HU* T: (01424) 218126 M: 07713-243427 E: paul.frostick@sky.com

FROUD, Andrew William. b 65. Mansf Coll Ox BA 87 St Cath Coll Cam MPhil 92. Westcott Ho Cam 90. **d** 93 **p** 94. C Almondbury w Farnley Tyas *Wakef* 93–96; P-in-c Wootton *Portsm* 96–00; R 00–01; V Thornton-le-Fylde *Blackb* 01–05; Chapl St Geo C of E Sch Blackpool 05–09; P-in-c Clitheroe St Mary 09–13; V 13–17; P-in-c Chatburn and Downham 14–17; V Clitheroe St Mary and St Paul, Chatburn and Downham from 18. *The Vicarage, Church Street, Clitheroe BB7 2DD* T: (01253) 764467 E: andyfroud@gmail.com

FROUDE (née WOOLCOCK), The Ven Christine Ann. b 47. ACIB 73. S Dios Minl Tr Scheme 92. **d** 95 **p** 96. NSM Stoke Bishop *Bris* 95–99; Chapl United Bris Healthcare NHS Trust 99–01; P-in-c Shirehampton *Bris* 01–11; Dean of Women's Min 00–11; Hon Can Bris Cathl 01–11; Adn Malmesbury 11–18; Adn Bris 12–18; rtd 18; PtO *Bris* from 19. *24 Waterloo Street, Clifton, Bristol BS8 4BT* E: christine.froude@bristoldiocese.org

FRUEHWIRTH, Robert Alan. b 69. **d** 97 **p** 97. PtO *Nor* 11–13; Dir Julian Cen 13–15; C Nor St Pet Mancroft w St Jo Maddermarket 13–15; USA from 15. *302 Chesapeake Way, Chapel Hill NC 27516, USA* M: (001) (540) 406 3304 E: r.fruehwirth@icloud.com

FRY, Alison Jacquelyn (Sister Alison). b 65. Newnham Coll Cam BA 86 MA 90 Hertf Coll Ox DPhil 90 St Jo Coll Dur BA 95. Cranmer Hall Dur 93. **d** 96 **p** 97. C Milton

B & W 96–00; V Batheaston w St Cath 00–12; OSB from 12; PtO *Worc* from 12. *Mucknell Abbey, Mucknell Farm Lane, Soulton, Worcester WR7 4RB* T: (01905) 345900 E: revajfry@gmail.com

FRY, Canon Barry James. b 49. K Alfred's Coll Win MA 03 Win Univ PhD 15 ACIB. Ripon Coll Cuddesdon 81. **d** 83 **p** 84. C Highcliffe w Hinton Admiral *Win* 83–87; V Southampton St Barn 87–19; rtd 19; Hon Can Ruvuma Cathl Tanzania from 02. *3 Sway Road, Brockenhurst SO42 7SH* T: (01590) 622486

FRY, David William. b 51. St Jo Coll Nottm. **d** 08 **p** 09. C Heeley and Gleadless Valley *Sheff* 08–10 and 12; V Ardsley 10–12; V Heeley 12–16; AD Attercliffe 13–16; rtd 16; PtO *Sheff* from 20. *9 Ashfield Close, Sheffield S12 2QU*

FRY, John Edward. b 80. Univ of Wales (Swansea) BSc 01 PGCE 03. Wycliffe Hall Ox BTh 13. **d** 13 **p** 14. C Theydon Bois and Theydon Garnon *Chelmsf* 13–16; V 16–17; C Theydon Par from 17. *The Vicarage, 2 Piercing Hill, Theydon Bois, Epping CM16 7JN* T: (01992) 812744 M: 07719-469029 E: revjefry@gmail.com

FRY, Lynn Jane. b 60. **d** 03 **p** 04. OLM E w W Harling, Bridgham w Roudham, Larling etc *Nor* 03–19; Papua New Guinea 15 and 17–18; C Three Valleys *Sarum* from 20. *Society of St Francis, The Friary, Hilfield, Dorchester DT2 7BE* M: 07554-930054 E: lynnandtony@outlook.com

FRY, Nigel Edward. b 57. St Jo Coll Nottm 91. **d** 93 **p** 94. C Wellingborough All Hallows *Pet* 93–96; R Peakirk w Glinton and Northborough 96–05; V Pet Ch Carpenter 05–16; TV Barby w Kilsby 16; TV Daventry from 16. *4 Emery Road, Malt Mill Green, Kilsby, Rugby CV23 8YY* M: 07854-810588 E: enfrys@gmail.com

FRY, Roger Joseph Hamilton. b 29. Em Coll Cam BA 52 MA 56. Clifton Th Coll 52. **d** 54 **p** 55. C Walcot *B & W* 54–57; C Gresley *Derby* 57–61; P-in-c Bowling St Bart and St Luke *Bradf* 61–65; V Bowling St Jo 61–87; V Ingleton w Chapel le Dale 87–95; rtd 95; PtO *Bradf* 95–14; *Leeds* from 14. *5 Margerison Crescent, Ilkley LS29 8QZ* T: (01943) 608738 E: rjhfry@gmail.com

FRYDAY, Canon Barbara Yvonne. b 47. Ch of Ireland Tr Coll TCert 67. CITC 90. **d** 92 **p** 93. NSM Cashel w Magorban, Tipperary, Clonbeg etc *C, F & O* 93–96; C Kilcooley w Littleon, Crohane and Fertagh 96–99; I 99–07; I Clonmel w Innislounagh, Tullaghmelan etc from 07; Can Ossory Cathl from 03; Warden of Readers from 08. *Address temp unknown* M: (00353) 86-275 0735 E: frydayb@gmail.com

FRYER, Alison Jane. *See* BOWNASS, Alison Jane

FRYER, Cora Lynette. *See* YARRIEN, Cora Lynette

FRYER, Mrs Jenifer Anne. b 43. NOC 89. **d** 92 **p** 94. Par On Ecclesfield *Sheff* 92–94; C 94–95; Asst Chapl Cen Sheff Univ Hosps NHS Trust 93–96; Chapl Weston Park Hosp Sheff 94–96; Chapl Asst N Gen Hosp NHS Trust Sheff 96–04; Chapl Asst Sheff Teaching Hosps NHS Foundn Trust 04–07; rtd 07; PtO *Sheff* from 07. *5 Nursery Drive, Ecclesfield, Sheffield S35 9XU* T: 0114-246 1027 E: jeni_fryer@talktalk.net

FRYER, Michael Andrew. b 56. St Jo Coll Nottm 88. **d** 90 **p** 91. C Hull St Martin w Transfiguration *York* 90–95; V Kingston upon Hull St Aid Southcoates 95–14; AD E Hull 06–13; P-in-c Elloughton and Brough w Brantingham 14–16; V from 16. *55 Stockbridge Park, Elloughton, Brough HU15 1JQ* T: (01482) 667431 E: mickfryer55@gmail.com

FRYER, Mrs Suzanne Elizabeth. b 75. Sheff Univ BMus 96 Bretton Hall Coll PGCE 97. St Mellitus Coll BA 18. **d** 18 **p** 19. C Grays Thurrock *Chelmsf* from 18. *19 Martello Close, Grays RM17 6FL* T: (01375) 370884 E: revdsuziefryer@gmail.com *or* rev.suzie@gttm.org

FRYER-SPEDDING, Mrs Clare Caroline. b 47. St Aid Coll Dur BA. LCTP 06. **d** 09 **p** 10. NSM Binsey *Carl* from 09. *West Mirehouse, Underskiddaw, Keswick CA12 4QE* E: cfs@mirehouse.com

FRYMANN, Mrs Janet Elizabeth. b 57. St Jo Coll Nottm BA 12. **d** 12 **p** 13. C N Wingfield, Clay Cross and Pilsley *Derby* 12–15; P-in-c Roughton and Felbrigg, Metton, Sustead etc *Nor* 15–17; R 17–20; rtd 20. *Address temp unknown* M: 07766-712545 E: rev.roughton@gmail.com

FUDGER, David John. b 53. Sheff Univ MMin 96. K Coll Lon 73 Coll of Resurr Mirfield 76. **d** 77 **p** 78. C Sutton in Ashfield St Mary *S'well* 77–80; P-in-c Duston *Pet* 80–82; V Radford All So w Ch Ch and St Mich *S'well* 82–91; Min Bermondsey St Hugh CD *S'wark* 91–97; P-in-c Blackheath Ascension 97–04; Hon Chapl S'wark Cathl 91–01; P-in-c Mansfield SS Pet and Paul *S'well* 04–11; V 11–17; P-in-c Mansfield St Mark 12–14; V 14–17; rtd 17; PtO *S'well* from 18. *Gardeners Cottage, Sherwood Grange, Mansfield NG18 2EJ* E: revfudger@mistral.co.uk

FUDGER, Michael Lloyd. b 55. K Coll Lon BD 77 AKC 77. Coll of Resurr Mirfield 77. **d** 78 **p** 79. C Weston Favell *Pet*

78–82; C Pet H Spirit Bretton 82–84; V Irchester 84–90; TV Darnall-cum-Attercliffe *Sheff* 90–96; TV Attercliffe, Darnall and Tinsley 96–97; TR 97–03; TR Attercliffe and Darnall 03–05; V 05–06; Chapl Nine o'Clock Community 04–06; RD Attercliffe 91–96; Hon Can Sheff Cathl 00–06; R Bedford St Pet w St Cuth *St Alb* 06–16; rtd 16. *64 The Promenade, Peacehaven BN10 8NH* E: fudgerm@yahoo.co.uk

FUERTE, Antonio. *See* GARCIA FUERTE, Antonio

FUHRI, Tessa Jane. *See* NISBET, Tessa Jane

FULFORD, Alison Jane. b 79. CCC Cam BA 00 MA 04. Ridley Hall Cam 01. **d** 04 **p** 05. C Old Catton *Nor* 04–07; Hon Chapl St Jo Coll Nottm 08–11; P-in-c Hickling w Kinoulton and Broughton Sulney *S'well* 11–13; R 13–14; P-in-c Baddiley and Wrenbury w Burleydam *Ches* 14–20; V Wybunbury and Audlem w Doddington from 20; Dean of Women in Min 15–18; RD Nantwich from 20. *105 McKelvey Way, Audlem, Crewe CW5 8EY* T: (01270) 740782 E: revalisonfulford@hotmail.co.uk

FULFORD, Susan Yvonne. b 61. **d** 03. OLM Pemberton St Mark Newtown *Liv* 03–07; OLM Marsh Green w Newtown 08–14; OLM Newtown 14–19; OLM Wigan 20–21; TV from 21. *13 Mitchell Street, Wigan WN5 9BY* T: (01942) 242369 E: sueandmike2003@yahoo.co.uk *or* ahl.south@churchwigan.org

FULHAM, Suffragan Bishop of. *See* BAKER, The Rt Revd Jonathan Mark Richard

FULKER, Lois Valerie. b 42. Keele Univ BA 64. Cranmer Hall Dur 03. **d** 04 **p** 05. NSM Egremont and Haile *Carl* 04–08; rtd 08; PtO *Carl* 08–13. *3 Mill Farm, Calderbridge, Seascale CA20 1DN* T: (01946) 841475

FULLAGAR, Michael Nelson. b 35. SS Coll Cam BA 57 MA 61. Chich Th Coll 57. **d** 59 **p** 60. C Camberwell St Giles *S'wark* 59–61; C Northolt Park St Barn *Lon* 61–64; C Hythe *Cant* 64–66; R Chipata Zambia 66–70; P-in-c Livingstone 70–75; P-in-c Chingola 75–78; R Freemantle *Win* 78–87; Buckingham Deanery Health Chapl and P-in-c Westbury w Turweston, Shalstone and Biddlesden *Ox* 87–94; Chapl S Bucks NHS Trust 94–96; rtd 96; P-in-c Burwash Weald *Chich* 97–04; PtO from 04. *1 Roffrey Avenue, Eastbourne BN22 0AE* T: (01323) 503212 E: michaelfullagar@aol.com

FULLALOVE, Brenda Hurst. *See* CRASTON, Brenda Hurst

FULLARTON, Mrs Heather Mary. b 42. Whitelands Coll Lon TCert 63. Qu Coll Birm 90. **d** 92 **p** 94. Par Dn Colwich w Gt Haywood *Lich* 92–94; C 94–97; P-in-c Swindon and Himley 97–01; V Prees and Fauls 01–02; rtd 02; PtO *Sarum* 03–19. *26 Drovers, Sturminster Newton DT10 1QY* T: (01258) 269072 M: 07741-403539 E: heatherfullarton74@gmail.com

FULLER, Alison Jane. *See* COZENS, Alison Jane

FULLER, Christopher John. b 53. Chich Th Coll 85. **d** 87 **p** 88. C Swinton and Pendlebury *Man* 87–90; C Chiswick St Nic w St Mary *Lon* 90–92; V Hounslow W Gd Shep 92–96; V Stoke Newington St Faith, St Matthias and All SS 96–05; V Enfield St Geo 05–13; P-in-c S Shields St Hilda w St Thos *Dur* 13–18; Chapl Miss to Seafarers 13–15; rtd 18. *Address withheld by request*

FULLER, Canon Graham Drowley. b 33. AKC 58. **d** 59 **p** 60. C E Grinstead St Swithun *Chich* 59–62; C Coulsdon St Andr *S'wark* 62–64; Chapl RN 64–68; V Battersea St Luke *S'wark* 68–75; V S Stoneham *Win* 75–90; R Eversley 90–96; Bp's Ecum Officer 84–95; Hon Can Win Cathl 93–96; rtd 96; PtO *Portsm* from 03. *Brookside Dairy, Nunnery Lane, Newport PO30 1YR* T: (01983) 525976 E: teasel@brooksidedairy.co.uk

FULLER, Ian David. b 60. St Mellitus Coll 16. **d** 17 **p** 18. OLM Springfield H Trin *Chelmsf* from 17. *8 Jasmine Close, Chelmsford CM1 6XL* T: (01245) 465777 E: iandavidfuller@gmail.com

FULLER, Canon John James. b 38. SS Coll Cam BA 63 MA 66. Chich Th Coll 63 Union Th Sem (NY) STM 64. **d** 65 **p** 66. C Westmr St Steph w St Jo *Lon* 65–71; Tutor Cuddesdon Coll 71–75; Tutor Ripon Coll Cuddesdon 75–77; Prin S Dios Minl Tr Scheme 77–96; Can and Preb Sarum Cathl 83–96; V Wheatley w Forest Hill and Stanton St John *Ox* 96–97; TR Wheatley 97–03; rtd 03; PtO *Sarum* 13–21. *11 Ratcliffs Garden, Shaftesbury SP7 8HJ* T: (01747) 850079

FULLER, Mark Joseph Tobias. b 82. Ridley Hall Cam 12. **d** 15 **p** 16. C Yaxley and Holme w Conington *Ely* 15–17; TV Portishead *B & W* from 17. *25 Lambourne Way, Portishead, Bristol BS20 7LQ* M: 07766-310509 E: markfuller952@btinternet.com *or* pilgrim@portisheadparish.co.uk

FULLER, Matthew John. b 74. Birm Univ BA 95 PGCE 96. Oak Hill Th Coll BA 05. **d** 05 **p** 06. C St Helen Bishopsgate w St Andr Undershaft etc *Lon* 05–19; V Down Street Ch Ch from 19. *54 Monkton Street, London SE11 4TX* T: (020) 7735 2494 M: 07903-045667

FULLER, Michael George. b 46. Chich Th Coll 90. **d** 92 **p** 93. C Fulham All SS *Lon* 92–94; C Kensington St Mary Abbots w St Geo 94–06; V Holland Park 06–12; Dir Post-Ord Tr Kensington Area 94–99; Bp Kensington's Liaison Officer to Metrop Police *Lon* 99–12; rtd 12; R Vancouver St Jo Shaughnessy Canada 12–15; PtO *Lon* 15–16; Hon C St Marylebone St Cypr from 16. *21 Mordern House, Harewood Avenue, London NW1 6NR* T: (020) 3536 6357 M: 07495-726006 E: michaelfuller1946@gmail.com

FULLER, Canon Michael Jeremy. b 63. Worc Coll Ox BA 85 MA 89 DPhil 89 Qu Coll Cam BA 91. Westcott Ho Cam 89. **d** 92 **p** 93. C High Wycombe *Ox* 92–95; C Edin St Jo 95–00; Prin TISEC 00–02; IME Officer 02–14; Pantonian Prof 00–14; Can St Mary's Cathl *Edin* 00–14; Hon Can St Mary's Cathl from 14; Teaching Fell Edin Univ 14–18; Sen Teaching Fell 18–21; Lect from 21; Hon Research Fell Glas Univ 08–18. *28 Blackford Avenue, Edinburgh EH9 2PH* T: 0131-667 7273 E: michael.fuller@ed.ac.uk

FULLER (formerly MCCULLOCK), Mrs Patricia Ann. b 46. EMMTC 87. **d** 90 **p** 94. C Bottesford w Ashby *Linc* 90–95; P-in-c Wragby 95–98; Chapl N Lincs Coll of FE 95–98; Ind Chapl 98–01; rtd 01; PtO *Linc* 01–11; NSM Marden w Preston Grange and Billy Mill *Newc* 12–13; PtO from 14. *1 Orchard Close, Morpeth NE61 1XE* T: (01670) 519800 E: pat.fuller25@gmail.com

FULLER, Canon Terence James. b 30. Bris Univ BA 55. Clifton Th Coll 55. **d** 56 **p** 57. C Uphill *B & W* 56–60; V Islington St Jude Mildmay Park *Lon* 60–67; V Southgate *Chich* 67–80; R Stoke Climsland *Truro* 80–85; RD Trigg Major 85–91; P-in-c Lezant w Lawhitton and S Petherwin w Trewen 93–95; Hon Can Truro Cathl 94–96; rtd 96; PtO *Truro* 96–15. *9 Westover Road, Callington PL17 7EW* T: (01579) 384958

FULLERTON, Hamish John Neville. b 45. Ball Coll Ox BA 68 MA 73. S'wark Ord Course 76. **d** 79 **p** 80. Hd English Abp Tenison's Sch Kennington 79–88; Hon C Clapham Old Town *S'wark* 79–82; PtO 82–89; Hon C Brixton Road Ch Ch 89–91; C Streatham Ch Ch 91–96; C Purley St Mark 96–98; Asst P Tooting St Aug 98–01; PtO from 03. *Flat 4, 21 Offerton Road, London SW4 0DJ* T: (020) 7622 7890

FULLJAMES, Mrs Janet Kathleen Doris. b 43. Open Univ BA 79 Birm Univ MA 93. Qu Coll Birm 85. **d** 87 **p** 94. Par Dn Harborne St Pet *Birm* 87–93; Par Dn Smethwick SS Steph and Mich 93–94; C 94–95; C Smethwick Resurr 95–98; P-in-c Dudley St Thos and St Luke *Worc* 98–04; P-in-c Dudley St Jo 98–04; rtd 04; PtO *B & W* from 04. *12 Obridge Road, Taunton TA2 7PX* T: (01823) 333585 E: fullj9@gmail.com

FULTON, Miss Ann Elizabeth. b 47. SWMTC 01. **d** 04 **p** 05. NSM Kingston St Mary w Broomfield etc *B & W* 04–11; NSM W Monkton 10–11; NSM W Monkton w Kingston St Mary, Broomfield etc 11–14; Chapl St Marg Hospice Taunton from 14; PtO *B & W* 14–16; LtO from 16. *St Margaret's Somerset Hospice, Heron Drive, Bishops Hull, Taunton TA1 5HA* T: (01823) 259394 M: 07765-925236 E: annfulton29@yahoo.co.uk *or* ann.fulton@st-margarets-hospice.org.uk

FULTON, John William. b 49. Ex Coll Ox BA 71 BPhil 72 MA 75 MPhil 79. Wycliffe Hall Ox 72. **d** 76 **p** 77. C Bexleyheath Ch Ch *Roch* 76–79; C Ealing Dean St Jo *Lon* 79–83; V Aldborough Hatch *Chelmsf* 83–87; Chapl Chantilly *Eur* 87–90; R Hepworth, Hinderclay, Wattisfield and Thelnetham *St E* 90–14; RD Ixworth 09–14; rtd 15; PtO *St E* from 15; *Eur* from 18. *11 Chancellery Mews, Bury St Edmunds IP33 3AB* T: (01284) 765744 E: jwfulton@btinternet.com

FUNNELL, Preb Norman Richard James. b 40. Univ of Wales (Lamp) BA 64. Ripon Hall Ox 64. **d** 66 **p** 67. C Hackney *Lon* 66–70; Hon C 71–85; TV 85–93; R S Hackney St Jo w Ch Ch 93–08; Chapl St Joseph's Hospice Hackney 93–08; Preb St Paul's Cathl *Lon* 05–08; rtd 08; PtO *Truro* from 14. *37 Brunel Quays, Great Western Village, Lostwithiel PL22 0JB* T: (01208) 873867 M: 07966-238934 E: jamesfunnell@btinternet.com

FURBER, Mrs Jennifer Margaret. b 50. WEMTC 98. **d** 01 **p** 02. NSM Malvern Link w Cowleigh *Worc* 01–08; rtd 09; PtO *Win* from 09. *3 Ravenswood, 23 Wimborne Road, Bournemouth BH2 6LZ* T: (01202) 296886 E: jenny@furber.me.uk

FURBER, Peter. b 43. Ex Univ BA. Sarum & Wells Th Coll 83. **d** 85 **p** 86. C Stanmore *Win* 85–88; TV Basingstoke 88–95; C Ringwood 95–98; P-in-c Gt Malvern Ch Ch *Worc* 98–99; V 99–08; rtd 09; PtO *Win* from 09. *3 Ravenswood, 23 Wimborne Road, Bournemouth BH2 6LZ* T: (01202) 296886 E: peter@furber.me.uk

FURBER, Sarah Anne. *See* COAKLEY, Sarah Anne

FUREY, Scott Robert. b 87. Ch Coll Cam MA 14. Oak Hill Th Coll BA 18. **d** 18 **p** 19. C Mayfair Ch Ch *Lon* 18–19; C Down Street Ch Ch from 19. *Flat 1, 86 Wilberforce Road, London N4 2SR* M: 07729-067651 E: scott@christchurchmayfair.org

FURLONG, Andrew William Ussher. b 47. TCD BA 69 Jes Coll Cam BA 71. Westcott Ho Cam 70 CITC 72. **d** 72 **p** 73. C

Dundela St Mark *D & D* 72–76; C Dublin St Ann w St Mark and St Steph *D & G* 76–83; Zimbabwe 83–94; Adn W Harare 88–89; Can Harare 89–94; Asst Chapl Leeds Teaching Hosps NHS Trust 94–97; Dean Clonmacnoise *M & K* 97–02; I Trim and Athboy Gp 97–02; Prec Kildare Cathl 98–02. *12 Tubbermore Road, Dalkey, Co Dublin, Republic of Ireland* T: (00353) (1) 285 9817 E: awufurlong@gmail.com

FURLONG (*née* DAVIES), **Mrs Catharine Mary.** b 48. Philippa Fawcett Coll CertEd 73. EMMTC 85. **d** 88 **p** 95. C Spalding St Mary and St Nic *Linc* 88–92; Zimbabwe 92–94; C Gt w Lt Gidding and Steeple Gidding *Ely* 94–96; P-in-c 96–06; P-in-c Brington w Molesworth and Old Weston 96–06; P-in-c Leighton Bromswold 96–06; P-in-c Winwick 96–06; P-in-c Gt Gransden and Abbotsley and Lt Gransden etc 06–18; Asst Chapl Hinchingbrooke Health Care NHS Trust 06–17; rtd 18; PtO *Ely* from 18; *Eur* from 19; *Pet* 18–21; Hon C Warmington, Tansor and Cotterstock etc from 21. *36 St Peters Road, Oundle, Peterborough PE8 4NT* T: (01832) 272650 E: catharinemfurlong@tiscali.co.uk

FURNESS, Barry Keith. b 47. Open Univ BSc 93. **d** 04 **p** 05. OLM High Oak, Hingham and Scoulton w Wood Rising *Nor* 04–09; P-in-c Smallburgh w Dilham w Honing and Crostwight 09–11; R 11–15; rtd 15; PtO *Nor* from 15. *Church View, 6 Alderfen Way, Hoveton NR12 8GA* T: (01603) 782919 E: barry.furness6@btinternet.com

FURNESS, Christine Anne. b 51. Leic Coll of Educn CertEd 73 Open Univ BA 76 Man Univ MEd 84 PhD 91 Ches Coll of HE MTh 02. NOC 99. **d** 02 **p** 03. C Offerton *Ches* 02–06; V Brinnington w Portwood 06–12; rtd 13; PtO *Ches* 13–17; *Lich* 13–16 and from 18; *Heref* from 21. *8 Hyde Lane, Kinver, Stourbridge DY7 6AF* M: 07771-601615 E: anne@afurness.co.uk

FURNESS, Dominic John. b 53. Bris Univ BA 76. Ridley Hall Cam 82. **d** 84 **p** 85. C Downend *Bris* 84–88; V Stoke Hill *Guildf* 88–05; V Milford *Win* 05–19; AD Lyndhurst 08–13; rtd 19. *Red House Cottage, 88 Lower Road, Salisbury SP2 9NJ* E: dominic.furness@talktalk.net

FURNESS, Edward Joseph. b 41. S'wark Ord Course 74. **d** 77 **p** 78. NSM S Lambeth St Steph *S'wark* 77–81; Warden Mayflower Family Cen Canning Town *Chelmsf* 82–96; P-in-c Aston St Jas *Birm* 96–00; V 00–05; rtd 05; PtO *Birm* from 05. *304 New Oscott Village, 25 Fosseway Drive, Birmingham B23 5GP* T: 0121-377 5304

FURSE, Adrian Thomas. b 76. Bris Univ BA 99 Univ of Wales (Swansea) MA 01 Leeds Univ PhD 06. St Steph Ho Ox 08. **d** 10 **p** 11. C Wistow *Leic* 10–14; TV Dewisland *St D* 14–18; Min Can St D Cathl 14–18; P-in-c W Cemaes from 18. *The*

Vicarage, Maenclochog, Clynderwen SA66 7LD T: (01437) 532238 M: 07890-020849 E: adrian.t.furse@gmail.com

FUTCHER, Anne Elizabeth. b 57. Portsm Poly BA 78 Univ of Wales (Swansea) MEd 83 PGCE 80 Ox Univ BTh 19. Ripon Coll Cuddesdon 13. **d** 15 **p** 16. C Colyton, Musbury, Southleigh and Branscombe *Ex* 15–19; NSM Larnaca Cyprus from 19. *15 Odysseas Androutsou Street, Aradippou, 7104 Larnaca, Cyprus* M: 07551-007123 E: anne.futcher@cypgulf.org

FUTCHER, The Ven Christopher David. b 58. Edin Univ BD 80 Lon Univ MTh 04 K Coll Lon MA 11. Westcott Ho Cam 80. **d** 82 **p** 83. C Borehamwood *St Alb* 82–85; C Stevenage All SS Pin Green 85–88; V 88–96; V St Alb St Steph 96–00; R Harpenden St Nic 00–12; Adn *Ex* 12–19; Adn Cyprus and Chapl Larnaca Cyprus and the Gulf from 19. *15 Odysseas Androutsou Street, Aradippou, 7104 Larnaca, Cyprus* E: archdeacon.christopher@cypgulf.org

FUTERS, Michael Roger. b 58. Trin & All SS Coll Leeds BEd 80. St Jo Coll Nottm 82. **d** 85 **p** 86. C Narborough and Huncote *Leic* 85–87; C Spondon *Derby* 87–90; P-in-c Derby St Jas 90–95; TV Walbrook Epiphany 95–99; Hon C Derby St Mark 99–09; Community Development Officer Home Housing from 99; Hon C Chaddesden St Phil w Derby St Mark from 09. *3 St Pancras Way, Derby DE1 3TH* T: (01332) 203075 E: futersm@hotmail.com

FYFE, Mrs Deirdre Bettina. b 44. STETS 05. **d** 07 **p** 08. NSM S Petherton w The Seavingtons *B & W* 07–12; NSM Winsmoor 12–19; PtO from 19. *1 Waldock Barton, South Petherton TA13 5NZ* T: (01460) 241977 M: 07746-472445 E: dbfyfe@btinternet.com

FYFE, Stewart John. b 69. City Univ BSc 91. Ridley Hall Cam 03. **d** 05 **p** 06. C Barony of Burgh *Carl* 05–07 and 08–10; P-in-c Bolton 10–17; P-in-c Crosby Ravensworth 10–17; P-in-c Morland, Thrimby, Gt Strickland and Cliburn 10–17; R N Westmorland from 17; RD Appleby from 13; C Heart of Eden from 18; Asst Dir of Ords from 18. *The Vicarage, Morland, Penrith CA10 3AX* T: (01931) 714620 M: 07985-900477 E: rectornwparishes@gmail.com

FYFE-JAMIESON (*formerly* HENDERSON), **Lucy.** b 72. Wycliffe Hall Ox 18. **d** 20 **p** 21. C Cant All SS from 20. *Address withheld by request* M: 07970-489636 E: revlucyfj@gmail.com

FYSH, Leslie David. b 35. Glouc Sch of Min 88. **d** 91 **p** 92. NSM Stonehouse *Glouc* 91–95; Asst Chapl Wycliffe Coll Glos 91–95; NSM W Walton *Ely* 95–00; PtO 00–11; *Nor* 08–12; PV Ely Cathl 03–06; Sub-Warden Coll of St Barn Lingfield 14–16; PtO *Ely* 16–21. *3 King John House, Kings Walk, Wisbech PE13 1HU* T: (01945) 589616 E: revfysh@gmail.com

G

GABBADON, Kenneth Fitz Arthur. b 53. NOC 97. **d** 99 **p** 00. C Burnage St Marg *Man* 99–01; C Bury St Jo w St Mark 01–03; P-in-c Newton Heath 03–08; R 08–09; Chapl HM Pris Leeds 09–14; Chapl HM Pris Wealstun 14–18; rtd 18; P-in-c Clifford *York* from 09; P-in-c York All SS N Street 17–19. *The Vicarage, 19 Chapel Lane, Clifford, Wetherby LS23 6HU* T: (01937) 541165 M: 07808-762629 E: kgabba7036@aol.com

GABEL, Lee. b 75. Ripon Coll Cuddesdon 11. **d** 14 **p** 15. C Frodingham and New Brumby *Linc* 14–17; P-in-c Brocklesby Park 17–18; P-in-c N Wolds Gp 17–18; P-in-c Brocklesby Park, Croxton and North Wolds 18–19; R from 19. *The Vicarage, St Barnabas Road, Barnetby DN38 6JE* T: (01652) 680414 M: 07999-538824 E: leebbgabel@gmail.com

GABLE, Michael David. b 70. Poly of Wales BEng 92. St Mich Coll Llan BTh 95. **d** 95 **p** 96. C Newton Nottage *Llan* 95–99; V Aberavon H Trin 99–01; TV Aberavon 01–05; P-in-c Rhydyfelin w Graig 05–11; V Glyntaff, Rhydfelin and the Graig 11–15; TV Pontypridd from 15; AD from 11. *St John's Vicarage, 28 Llantrisant Road, Graig, Pontypridd CF37 1LW* T: (01443) 650336 M: 07561-313199 E: michaeldgable@gmail.com

GABOR, Balint Joseph. b 68. Heythrop Coll Lon MA 02. St Gerardus Th Coll Pannonhalma 91. **d** 96 **p** 97. In RC Ch 96–14; PtO *Lon* 15–16; Min Grahame Park St Aug CD from 16. *St Augustine's House, Great Field, London NW9 5SY* T: (020) 8205 1979 E: saintaugustinecolindale@gmail.com

GABRIEL (*formerly* MARTLEW), **Mrs Catherine Linda.** b 54. Bolton Inst of Educn BSc 84 Lon Inst of Educn MSc 85.

LCTP 09. **d** 12 **p** 15. NSM Chorley St Geo *Blackb* 12–17; NSM Standish from 17. *148 Appley Lane North, Appley Bridge, Wigan WN6 9DX* T: (01257) 253345 M: 07969-878655 E: smartlew@sky.com

GADD, Alan John. b 44. Imp Coll Lon BSc 65 PhD 69 Heythrop Coll Lon MA 07 FRMetS 67. S'wark Ord Course 68. **d** 71 **p** 72. Asst Chapl Lon Univ 71–72; PtO *S'wark* 73–91; C Battersea Park All SS 91–95; P-in-c 95–96; C Battersea Fields 96–05; rtd 05; PtO *S'wark* from 05. *24 Holmewood Gardens, London SW2 3RS* T: (020) 8678 8977 E: alangadd@yahoo.co.uk

GADD, Brian Hayward. b 33. Hatf Coll Dur BA 54 DipEd 55. Glouc Sch of Min 82. **d** 85 **p** 87. NSM Cleobury Mortimer w Hopton Wafers etc *Heref* 85–98; rtd 98; PtO *Heref* 99–12. *34 Lower Street, Cleobury Mortimer, Kidderminster DY14 8AB* T: (01299) 270758

GADD, Bryan Stephen Andrew. b 56. Dur Univ BA Ox Univ CertEd Univ of Qld MPhil Cen Qld Univ MLitt. Chich Th Coll. **d** 81 **p** 82. C Newlyn St Pet *Truro* 81–86; R St Mawgan w St Ervan and St Eval 86–90; Chapl Summer Fields Sch Ox 90–02; PtO *Truro* 90–00; Chapl Southport Sen Sch Australia 02–09; Sen Chapl Angl Ch Gr Sch from 09. *Anglican Church Grammar School, Oaklands Parade, East Brisbane QLD 4169, Australia* T: (0061) (7) 3896 2281 F: 3891 5976 E: bryan.gadd@churchie.com.au

GADSBY, Alison. *See* HOGGER-GADSBY, Alison

GADSBY, Julian Timothy David Moritz. b 74. K Coll Lon BA 96 AKC 96. Oak Hill Th Coll 02. d 04 p 05. C Chadwell *Chelmsf* 04–09; P-in-c Bucklebury w Marlston *Ox* from 09. *The Vicarage, Burdens Heath, Upper Bucklebury, Reading RG7 6SX* T: (01635) 866731 *or* 860220

GAFFIN, Jennifer Clare. b 78. Mansf Coll Ox BA 99 Man Univ MA 00 Win Univ PhD 06. Ripon Coll Cuddesdon 07. d 09 p 10. C Parkstone St Pet and St Osmund w Branksea *Sarum* 09–12; Bp's Dom Chapl *Portsm* 12–16; P-in-c N Hayling St Pet from 16; P-in-c S Hayling from 16; P-in-c Hayling Is St Andr from 16. *St Mary's Vicarage, 34 Church Road, Hayling Island PO11 0NT* T: (023) 9307 0178 M: 07855-024789 E: jennyhaylingvicar@hotmail.com *or* jennyhaylingisland@gmail.com

GAGE, Aëlla Rupert Fitzhardinge Berkeley. b 66. Bulmershe Coll of HE BEd 92. Oak Hill Th Coll 98. d 00 p 02. C Muswell Hill St Jas w St Matt *Lon* 00–05; C Hadley Wood St Paul Prop Chpl 05–08; C Highgate Australia 08–10; C Fordham *Chelmsf* 10–14; C Colchester St Pet and St Botolph 14–20; PtO from 20. *Address temp unknown* M: 07729-137504 E: aella.gage@gmail.com

GAGE, Alan William. b 52. Univ of Wales (Cardiff) BMus 72 PGCE 73 Bris Univ MEd 90. WEMTC 98. d 00 p 01. NSM Tuffley *Glouc* 00–08; NSM Hardwicke and Elmore w Longney 08–09; PtO 14–20. *Chadburn, 83 Dinglewell, Hucclecote, Gloucester GL3 3HT* T: (01452) 614892 E: curatealan@blueyonder.co.uk

GAGE, Jennifer Anne. b 50. Girton Coll Cam MA 75 Open Univ BA 85 PhD 05 Anglia Ruskin Univ DProf 19 Keele Univ PGCE 86. ERMC 07. d 09 p 10. NSM Three Rivers Gp *Ely* 09–15; NSM Haddenham 15–19; NSM Wilburton 15–19; NSM Witchford w Wentworth 15–19; Bp's Adv for Self-Supporting Min from 14; Min Can Ely Cathl from 19. *51 Henley Way, Ely CB7 4YH* M: 07515-732687 E: revd.jennygage@gmail.com

GAGE, Canon Robert Edward. b 47. Whitman Coll Washington BA 69. Cuddesdon Coll BA 75 MA 81. d 76 p 77. C Cheshunt *St Alb* 76–79; C Harpenden St Nic 79–81; V S Mymms 81–82; P-in-c Ridge 81–82; V S Mymms and Ridge 82–97; Prec and Can Res Wakef Cathl 97–05; Can Res Newc Cathl 05–09; rtd 09; PtO *Newc* from 09. *44 Warkworth Avenue, Whitley Bay NE26 3PS* E: robertgage1@yahoo.co.uk

GAGE, Timothy Arthur John. b 85. Ridley Hall Cam 13. d 16 p 17. C Hove Bp Hannington Memorial Ch *Chich* 16–20; R W Blatchington from 20. *The Rectory, 23 Windmill Close, Hove BN3 7LJ* T: (01273) 270427 M: 07910-938810 E: rector.westblatchington@gmail.com

GAGEN, Mrs Valerie Elizabeth. b 52. Ripon Coll of Educn BEd 75. NTMTC BA 10. d 10 p 11. NSM N Hinckford *Chelmsf* 10–14; NSM Pastrow *Win* 14–18; NSM Bury St Edmunds All SS w St Jo and St Geo *St E* 18–19; NSM Lark Valley 18–19; TV Lark Valley and N Bury from 19. *The Vicarage, 16A Anselm Avenue, Bury St Edmunds IP32 6JY* M: 07874-067371 E: valgagen@hotmail.com

GAINER, Canon Jeffrey. b 51. Jes Coll Ox BA 73 MA 77 Univ of Wales LLM 94. Wycliffe Hall Ox 74. d 77 p 78. C Baglan *Llan* 77–81; V Cwmbach 81–85; V Tonyrefail w Gilfach Goch and Llandyfodwg 85–87; Dir NT Studies and Dir Past Studies St Mich Coll Llan 87–92; V Meidrim and Llanboidy and Merthyr *St D* 92–21; P-in-c Abernant 07–18; AD St Clears 03–13; Cursal Can St D Cathl 11–21; PtO *Eur* from 19. *Address temp unknown* E: sieffremeidrim@googlemail.com

GAINES, Miss Atalie Clodia. b 78. Brighton Univ BA 00 Cam Univ BTh 14. Westcott Ho Cam 12. d 14 p 15. C Bedford St Andr *St Alb* 14–17; V Potters Bar K Chas from 17. *The Vicarage, 8 Dugdale Hill Lane, Potters Bar EN6 2DW* T: (01707) 661266

GAINSBOROUGH, Canon Jonathan Martin. b 66. SOAS Lon MA 91 MSc 95 PhD 01. STETS MA 10. d 10 p 11. NSM Barton Hill St Luke w Ch Ch and Moorfields *Bris* 10–13; P-in-c 13–16; Prof Development Politics Bris Univ 12–18; Can Th Bris Cathl 16–18; Dioc Soc Justice and Environmental Adv 17–18; Bp's Chapl *Bris* from 19; Can Res Bris Cathl from 19. *21 Cotham Lawn Road, Bristol BS6 6DS* T: (01454) 777728 E: bishop.chaplain@bristoldiocese.org

GAIR, Andrew Kennon. b 62. Westcott Ho Cam 88. d 91 p 92. C Clare w Poslingford, Cavendish etc *St E* 91–95; R Debden and Wimbish w Thunderley *Chelmsf* 95–06. *18-20 High Street, Wrentham, Beccles NR34 7HB*

✠**GAISFORD, The Rt Revd John Scott.** b 34. St Chad's Coll Dur BA 59 MA 76. d 60 p 61 c 94. C Audenshaw St Hilda *Man* 60–62; C Bramhall *Ches* 62–65; V Crewe St Andr 65–86; RD Nantwich 74–85; Hon Can Ches Cathl 80–86; Adn Macclesfield 86–94; Suff Bp Beverley (PEV) *York* 94–00; Asst Bp Ripon and Leeds 96–00; rtd 00; PtO *Ches* from 00; *Man* from 04. *5 Trevone Close, Knutsford WA16 9EJ* T: (01565) 633531 M: 07429-340155 E: jsandg.gaisford@gmail.com

GAIT, Canon David James. b 48. BNC Ox BA 71 BSc 72 MA 77 MSc 83. Ridley Hall Cam 71. d 74 p 75. C Litherland St Paul Hatton Hill *Liv* 74–77; C Farnworth 77–80; V Widnes St Jo 80–13; TV E Widnes 13; Chapl Widnes Maternity Hosp 86–90; AD Widnes *Liv* 07–13; Hon Can Liv Cathl 05–13; rtd 13. *Bryn Celyn, Betws Gwerfil Goch, Corwen LL21 9PP* T: (01490) 420759 E: dave.gait@btinternet.com

GAKURU, Griphus Stephen. b 59. Makerere Univ Kampala BSc 81 PGDE 83 Selw Coll Cam MPhil 92 PhD 95. Bp Tucker Coll Mukono BD 88. d 88 p 91. Uganda 89–91; Hon C Cambridge H Trin *Ely* 91–95; Chapl Selw Coll Cam 91–95; C Small Heath *Birm* 95–98; C Huyton St Mich *Liv* 98–01; P-in-c Brownswood Park *Lon* 01–03; PtO *St Alb* 03–05; P-in-c Stechford *Birm* 05–07; V 07–21; rtd 21. *51 Tollgate Road, Colney Heath, St Albans AL4 0PX* T: (01727) 826973 M: 07795-206034

GALANZINO, Diego. b 80. St Steph Ho Ox BTh 11. d 11 p 12. C St Ives *Truro* 11–15; C Halsetown 11–15; P-in-c Houghton Regis *St Alb* from 15. *Clergy House, Lowry Drive, Houghton Regis, Dunstable LU5 5SJ* T: (01582) 867246 E: frdiego@mail.com

GALBRAITH, Alexander Peter James. b 65. Qu Coll Ox BA 86 MA 90. Wycliffe Hall Ox 87. d 90 p 91. C Southport Em *Liv* 90–94; C Mossley Hill St Matt and St Jas 94–97; V Kew from 97; Chapl Southport and Ormskirk Hosp NHS Trust 97–11. *20 Markham Drive, Kew, Southport PR8 6XR* T: (01704) 547758 E: alexgalbraith20@hotmail.com

GALBRAITH, Canon Jane Alexandra. d 95 p 96. NSM Kildare w Kilmeague and Curragh *M & K* 95–97; NSM Newbridge w Carnalway and Kilcullen 97–99; C Limerick *L & K* 03–14; C Tralee w Kilmoyley, Ballymacelligott etc 14–15; I Roscrea w Kyle, Bourney and Corbally from 15; Can Limerick, Killaloe and Clonfert Cathls from 16. *St Cronan's Rectory, Rosemount, Roscrea, Co Tipperary, Republic of Ireland* T: (00353) (505) 21725 M: 87-382 5336 E: galbraithjane@gmail.com

GALBRAITH, John Angus Frame. b 44. Sarum Th Coll 68. d 71 p 72. C Richmond St Mary w St Matthias *S'wark* 71–74; Chapl W Lon Colls 74–79; R S'wark H Trin w St Matt 79–95; V New Addington 95–02; Asst Chapl HM Pris Wandsworth 02–04; Chapl 04–09; rtd 09; PtO *S'wark* from 09. *35 Joseph Hardcastle Close, London SE14 5RN* T: (020) 7635 3607 E: angus.galbraith@talktalk.net

GALE, Ms Charlotte. b 70. Leeds Univ BEng 92 Nottm Univ MA 00. St Jo Coll Nottm 98. d 01 p 02. C Whitnash *Cov* 01–05; P-in-c Potters Green 05–08; P-in-c Lillington and Old Milverton 08–14; V 14–17; C Leamington Spa H Trin 08–17; AD Warwick and Leamington 14–17; C St Clare in Cov Cathl 17–21. *6 Carthusian Road, Coventry CV3 6HA* T: (024) 7652 1200 E: charlotte.gale@sky.com

GALE, Colin Edward. b 49. Lon Univ PGCE 74. St Jo Coll Nottm BTh 73. d 79 p 80. C Hoole *Ches* 79–82; C Woodley St Jo the Ev *Ox* 82–87; V Clapham St Jas *S'wark* 87–96; V Sutton Ch Ch 96–05; R Burstow w Horne 05–14; rtd 14; PtO *Chich* from 16. *29 Kelmscott Way, Bognor Regis PO21 5DU* T: (01243) 870199 M: 07710-895463 E: revceg@aol.com

GALE, The Ven John. b 34. Univ of Wales (Lamp) 67. d 69 p 70. C Aberdare *Llan* 69–71; C Merthyr Dyfan 71–74; R Walmer St Sav S Africa 74–82; R Knysna St Geo 82–00; Adn Knysna 93–00; LtO *St D* from 00. *3 Connacht Way, Pembroke Dock SA72 6PB* T/F: (01646) 622219

GALE, Keith George. b 44. Bernard Gilpin Soc Dur 65 Bps' Coll Cheshunt 66 St Jo Coll Lusaka 68 Sarum Th Coll 69. d 70 p 71. C Sheff St Cuth 70–77; P-in-c Brightside All SS 72–77; C Birm St Martin 77–81; C Dwangwa Malawi 81–83; R Lilongwe St Pet 83–93; Adn Lilongwe 89–92; TV Sampford Peverell, Uplowman, Holcombe Rogus etc *Ex* 94–09; rtd 09; PtO *Ex* from 10. *101 Chapel Street, Tiverton EX16 6BU* T: (01884) 254346 E: keithgale101@gmail.com

GALE, Ms Lucille Catherine. b 67. Sarum & Wells Th Coll 92. d 94 p 95. C Welling *S'wark* 94–97; Chapl Greenwich Univ 97–00; V Welling 00–09; Officer Lay Min and Miss 09–14; Officer for Reader Tr 12–14; Dir of Ords *Chich* 14–16; V Shirley St Jo *S'wark* from 16. *49 Shirley Church Road, Croydon CR0 5EF* T: (020) 8654 1013 E: lugale2@zoho.com

GALES, Bernard Henry. b 27. Lon Univ BSc(Econ) 51 Open Univ BA 02. Wells Th Coll 62. d 64 p 65. C Sholing *Win* 64–67; C Fordingbridge w Ibsley 67–71; C S Molton w Nymet St George *Ex* 71–73; C Thelbridge 73–77; P-in-c 77–78; P-in-c Creacombe 77–78; P-in-c W w E Worlington 77–78; P-in-c Meshaw 77–78; P-in-c Witheridge 77–78; C Witheridge, Thelbridge, Creacombe, Meshaw etc 79–80; R Bow w Broad Nymet 80–93; V Colebrooke 80–93; R Zeal Monachorum 80–93; RD Cadbury 90–93; rtd 93; PtO *Ex* 93–21. *8 Old Rectory Gardens, Morchard Bishop, Crediton EX17 6PF* T: (01363) 877601 E: suebern.gales@btinternet.com

GALES, Simon Richard. b 59. Jes Coll Cam BA 81 MA 84 CEng 87 MICE 87. Wycliffe Hall Ox 91. d 93 p 94. C

Houghton *Carl* 93–97; V Lindow *Ches* from 97. *St John's Vicarage, 137 Knutsford Road, Wilmslow SK9 6EL* T: (01625) 583251 *or* 586329 E: simongales22@gmail.com

GALLACHER, Owen Thomas. b 85. Nottm Univ BA 07. Wycliffe Hall Ox BA 13. **d** 14 **p** 15. C Worc St Nic and All SS w St Helen from 14. *160 Bath Road, Worcester WR5 3EP* E: owen@allsaintsworcester.org.uk

GALLAGHER, Mrs Barbara Jean. b 53. Ex Univ BA 73 Coll of Ripon & York St Jo PGCE 76 Open Univ MA 99. **d** 08 **p** 09. OLM The Creetings and Earl Stonham w Stonham Parva *St E* 08–13; NSM 13–18; P-in-c Weedon Bec w Everdon and Dodford *Pet* from 18. *The Vicarage, Church Street, Weedon, Northampton NN7 4PL* T: (01327) 340585 E: barbarajg@btopenworld.com

GALLAGHER, Canon Ian. BTh. **d** 90 **p** 91. C Annagh w Drumgoon, Ashfield etc *K, E & A* 90–93; I Drumcliffe w Lissadell and Munninane 93–01; Can Elphin Cathl 97–01; Dioc Sec (Elphin and Ardagh) 97–01; Preb Mulhuddart St Patr Cathl Dublin 98–01; I Stillorgan w Blackrock *D & G* from 01. *The Rectory, St Brigid's Church Road, Stillorgan, Blackrock, Co Dublin, Republic of Ireland* T: (00353) (1) 288 1091 F: 278 1833 M: 86-811 9544 E: stillorgan@dublin.anglican.org

GALLAGHER, Ian Míceál. b 71. Oberlin Coll (USA) BMus 93 Duke Univ (USA) MA 95. Westcott Ho Cam 06. **d** 08 **p** 09. C Walton-on-the-Hill *Liv* 08–12; R Frankfurt am Main Ch the K Germany 12–14; V Enfield St Jas *Lon* from 14. *St James's Vicarage, 144 Hertford Road, Enfield EN3 5AY* T: (020) 8804 1966 E: ian.gallagher@stjameschurch.cc

GALLAGHER, Mrs Margaret. b 60. SRN 82 RM 84. Westcott Ho Cam 09. **d** 11 **p** 12. C Carrington *S'well* 11–14; V S and N Elmsall *Leeds* from 14; AD Pontefract from 18. *St Mary's Vicarage, Doncaster Road, South Elmsall, Pontefract WF9 2HS* T: (01977) 642861 E: revmgallagher@btinternet.com

GALLAGHER, Michael Collins Francis. b 48. St Jo Coll Dur BA 70. Sarum Th Coll 79. **d** 82 **p** 83. C Bridport *Sarum* 82–86; V Downton 86–01; RD Alderbury 93–99; R Crewkerne w Wayford *B & W* 01–07; R Wulfric Benefice 07–14; rtd 14; PtO *Heref* from 15. *Ridgeway, Woodleigh Road, Ledbury HR8 2BG* T: (01531) 635844 E: mcfgallagher@gmail.com

GALLAGHER, Neville Roy. b 45. K Coll Lon AKC 70 BD 76 Open Univ BA 97 Birm Univ CertEd 66. **d** 71 **p** 72. C Folkestone St Mary and St Eanswythe *Cant* 71–74; Hon C Sutton Valence w E Sutton and Chart Sutton 74–76; TV Cen Telford *Lich* 76–78; P-in-c Gt Mongeham *Cant* 78–80; P-in-c Ripple 78–80; R Gt Mongeham w Ripple and Sutton by Dover 80–83; V Kennington 83–88; Chapl and Dep Hd Bedgebury Sch Kent 88–05; P-in-c Appledore w Brookland, Fairfield, Brenzett etc *Cant* 05–11; P-in-c Woodchurch 06–11; P-in-c Wittersham w Stone and Ebony 08–11; AD Romney 08–10; rtd 11; PtO *Cant* from 11; *Chich* 16–20. *1 Church Cottages, Church Road, Kilndown, Cranbrook TN17 2SF* T: (01892) 890426 E: nrwg45@aol.com

GALLAGHER, Robert. b 43. St Chad's Coll Dur BSc 65. **d** 67 **p** 68. C Crosland Moor *Wakef* 67–69; C Huddersfield SS Pet and Paul 69–71; Chapl Huddersfield Poly 72–79; Min Coulby Newham LEP *York* 79–90; V Toxteth St Marg *Liv* 90–13; rtd 13. *36 Bridge Road, Mossley Hill, Liverpool L18 5EG* T: 0151-903 1189

GALLAGHER, Canon Stephen. b 58. Southn Univ BTh 89. Chich Th Coll 86. **d** 89 **p** 90. C S Shields All SS *Dur* 89–92; C Hartlepool St Paul and Chapl Hartlepool Gen Hosp 92–94; R Loftus and Carlin How w Skinningrove *York* 94–97; P-in-c Lower Beeding and Dioc Youth Officer *Chich* 97–09; Shrine P and Youth Missr Shrine of Our Lady of Walsingham 09–16; P-in-c Enfield SS Pet and Paul *Lon* 16–20; V from 20; AD Enfield from 20; Can St Helena from 10. *177 Ordnance Road, Enfield EN3 6AB* M: 07969-367421 E: ssppen3@virginmedia.com

GALLANT, Mrs Joanna-Sue Sheena. b 62. Heythrop Coll Lon MA 18. SAOMC 99. **d** 02 **p** 03. C Amersham on the Hill *Ox* 02–05; NSM Gt Missenden w Ballinger and Lt Hampden 06–10; NSM Chenies and Lt Chalfont, Latimer and Flaunden 10–12; Dir Pelagos Spirituality and Retreat Cen from 09; PtO *Ox* 15–19; TV High Wycombe from 19. *51 Wellesbourne Crescent, High Wycombe HP13 5HF* M: 07791-839756 E: teamvicar@terrierschurch.org.uk

GALLEY, Giles Christopher. b 32. Qu Coll Cam BA 56 MA 60. Linc Th Coll 56. **d** 58 **p** 59. C Gt Yarmouth *Nor* 58–62; C N Lynn w St Marg and St Nic 62–66; C Leeds St Pet *Ripon* 66–69; V N Hull St Mich *York* 70–79; V Strensall 79–00; RD Easingwold 82–97; rtd 00; PtO *York* 00–21. *19 St John's Road, Stamford Bridge, York YO41 1PH* T: (01759) 371592

✠**GALLIFORD, The Rt Revd David George.** b 25. Clare Coll Cam BA 49 MA 51. Westcott Ho Cam. **d** 51 **p** 52 **c** 75. C Newland St Jo *York* 51–54; C Eton w Boveney *Ox* 54–56; Min

Can Windsor 54–56; V Middlesbrough St Oswald *York* 56–61; R Bolton Percy 61–71; Dioc Adult Tr Officer 61–71; Can and Preb York Minster 69–70; Can Res and Treas York Minster 70–75; Suff Bp Hulme *Man* 75–84; Suff Bp Bolton 84–91; rtd 91; Hon Asst Bp York 95–11; PtO from 11. *Connaught Court, St Oswalds Road, York YO10 4FA* T: (01904) 626208 E: galliford2se@btinternet.com

GALLON, Mrs Audrey Kay. b 41. SEITE 94. **d** 97 **p** 98. NSM Gt Mongeham w Ripple and Sutton by Dover *Cant* 97–98; NSM Eastry and Northbourne w Tilmanstone etc 97–98; NSM Walmer 98–04; PtO 04–05; *Roch* 07–17. *12 Arne Close, Tonbridge TN10 4DH* T: (01732) 355633 E: audreygallon@talktalk.net

GALLOWAY, Canon Peter John. b 54. JP 89 OBE 96 LVO 19. Goldsmiths' Coll Lon BA 76 K Coll Lon PhD 87 Brunel Univ Hon DLitt 09 FSA 00 FRHistS 21. St Steph Ho Ox 80. **d** 83 **p** 84. C St John's Wood *Lon* 83–86; C St Giles-in-the-Fields 86–90; Warden of Readers (Lon Episc Area) 87–92; P-in-c Hampstead Em W End *Lon* 90–95; V 95–08; AD N Camden 02–07; Chapl to RVO and Qu Chpl of the Savoy 08–19; Hon Fell Goldsmiths' Coll Lon from 99; Hon Prof Brunel Univ *Lon* from 08; Dep P in O from 16; Can Chpls R 17–19; PtO *Lon* from 20. *Address withheld by request*

GALVIN, Mrs Linda Susan. b 59. Ox Min Course 13. **d** 15 **p** 16. NSM W End *Win* from 15. *11A Westbury Court, Hedge End, Southampton SO30 0HN* T: (01489) 788880

GAMBLE, Bronwen. *See* GAMBLE, Edana Bronwen

GAMBLE, Miss Dianne Elizabeth. b 71. Hull Univ BSc 92 PGCE 94. Cranmer Hall Dur 13. **d** 15 **p** 16. C Sowerby *Leeds* 15–19; C Sessay 15–19; C Thirkleby w Kilburn and Bagby 15–19; P-in-c Osmotherley w Harlsey and Ingleby Arncliffe from 19; P-in-c Cowesby from 19; P-in-c Felixkirk w Boltby from 19; P-in-c Kirkby Knowle from 19; P-in-c Leake w Over and Nether Silton and Kepwick from 19. *Leake Vicarage, Knayton, Thirsk YO7 4AZ* M: 07761-125748 E: 229club.dg@gmail.com

GAMBLE, Canon Edana Bronwen. b 56. Hull Univ BSc(Econ) 78 Nottm Univ MA 02 FCA 82. EMMTC 99. **d** 02 **p** 03. NSM Nuthall *S'well* 02–06; R Wiverton in the Vale 06–18; AD E Bingham 16–18; C Retford Area 18–19; R The Rivers from 19; Hon Can S'well Minster from 17. *The Rectory, Lincoln Road, East Markham, Newark NG22 0SH* T: (01777) 870848 E: brongamble@hotmail.com

GAMBLE, Kenneth Wesley. b 52. Ulster Univ BA 81. CITC 04. **d** 07 **p** 08. NSM Ballymacash *Conn* 07–17; NSM Derriaghy w Colin 17–20; rtd 21. *21 Dalboyne Park, Lisburn BT28 3BU* T: (028) 9267 7498 E: kengamble@btinternet.com

GAMBLE, Norman Edward Charles. b 50. TCD BA 72 PhD 78 HDipEd 73. CITC 76. **d** 79 **p** 80. C Bangor St Comgall *D & D* 79–83; I Dunleckney w Nurney, Lorum and Kiltennel *C, F & O* 83–90; Warden of Readers 84–90; P-in-c Leighlin w Grange Sylvae, Shankill etc 89–90; Can Leighlin Cathl 89–90; Preb Ossory Cathl 89–90; I Malahide w Balgriffin *D & G* 90–21; Abp's Dom Chapl 95–03; rtd 21. *14 Park Row, Belltree, Clongriffin, Dublin 13, D13 T0FR, Republic of Ireland* M: (00353) 86-815 3277 E: normanegamble@gmail.com

GAMBLE, Canon Robin Philip. b 53. Oak Hill Th Coll 74. **d** 77 **p** 78. C Laisterdyke *Bradf* 77–80; C York St Paul 80–82; V Bradf St Aug Undercliffe 82–95; Dioc Adv in Evang 93–01; Can Ev Man Cathl 01–08; P-in-c Idle *Bradf* 08–14; *Leeds* 14–18; Dioc Ev *Bradf* 08–14; *Leeds* 14–18; Bps' Adv for Church Growth from 18; Hon Can Bradf Cathl from 13. *25 Baker Street, Undercliffe, Bradford BD2 4NU* T: (01274) 635728 M: 07748-943541   E: robin.gamble@leeds.anglican.org   *or* robinp.gamble@gmail.com

GAMBLE, Ronald George. b 41. Cant Sch of Min 92. **d** 95 **p** 96. NSM Loose *Cant* 95–00; P-in-c Boxley w Detling 00–07; Chapl NHS Ambulance Trust 99–07; rtd 07; PtO *Cant* 07–19; *Roch* from 13. *18 Copper Tree Court, Maidstone ME15 9RW* T: (01622) 744455 E: r-gamble@sky.com

GAMBLE, Stanley Thomas Robert. b 82. QUB BA 03 MTh 05. CITC 05. **d** 07 **p** 08. C Knockbreda *D & D* 07–12; I Killinchy w Kilmood and Tullynakill from 12. *Killinchy Rectory, 11 Whiterock Road, Killinchy, Newtownards BT23 6PR* T: (028) 9754 1249 E: stanleygamble@gmail.com

GAMBLING, Paul Anthony. b 62. Middx Univ BA 06. NTMTC 03. **d** 06 **p** 07. C Warley Ch Ch and Gt Warley St Mary *Chelmsf* 06–10; TV Billericay and Lt Burstead 10–16; C Westcliff St Andr 16–19; P-in-c from 19; C Westcliff St Mich 16–19. *65 Electric Avenue, Westcliff-on-Sea SS0 9NN* M: 07821-201379 E: revpg@icloud.com

GAMLEN, Laurence William. b 59. STETS BA 07. **d** 07 **p** 08. NSM Chertsey, Lyne and Longcross *Guildf* 07–12; C from 12; Chapl Ashford and St Pet Hosps NHS Foundn Trust from 17. *The Vicarage, Lyne Lane, Lyne, Chertsey*

KT16 0AJ T: (01932) 872534 *or* 874405 M: 07939-094851 E: laurence@intermissio.com *or* laurence@lyneparish.org.uk

GAMMON, Elizabeth Angela Myfanwy. b 47. SWMTC 06. **d** 09 **p** 10. NSM Sidmouth, Woolbrook, Salcombe Regis, Sidbury etc *Ex* 09–12; P-in-c Burley Ville *Win* 12–21; rtd 21. *Tracey Mill, Tracey Road, Honiton EX14 3FA* E: revd.angie@gmail.com

GANDIYA, Leonard Farirayi (Lee). b 64. Cardiff Univ MTh 11. Gordon-Conwell Th Sem 90 Ridley Hall Cam 92. **d** 94 **p** 95. NSM Camberwell St Luke *S'wark* 94–95; C Lowestoft St Marg *Nor* 95–98; Dioc Rep for Black Anglican Concerns 96–98; CF 98–16; R King George St Paul USA from 16; Dioc Dir Young P Initiative from 20. *St Paul's Episcopal Church, 5486 St Paul's Road, King George VA 22485, USA* T: (001) (540) 663 3085 E: stpaulskgva@gmail.com

GANDON, Andrew James Robson. b 54. St Jo Coll Dur BA 76. Ridley Hall Cam 76. **d** 78 **p** 79. C Aston SS Pet and Paul *Birm* 78–82; CMS 82–95; Zaïre 82–88; Kenya 89–94; V Harefield *Lon* 95–10; Chapl R Brompton and Harefield NHS Trust 95–05; V Exhall *Cov* 10–18; rtd 18. *197 Bilford Road, Worcester WR3 8HL*

GANDON, James Noel. b 84. Leic Univ BSc 05. Trin Coll Bris BA 14. **d** 14 **p** 15. C Linc St Geo Swallowbeck 14–17; V Sneyd Green *Lich* from 17. *Sneyd Green Vicarage, 42 Granville Avenue, Stoke-on-Trent ST1 6BH* T: (01782) 363531 E: james@standrewssneydgreen.com

GANDY, Canon Nicholas John. b 53. Westf Coll Lon BSc 75 Reading Univ MSc 76 Ex Coll Ox PGCE 78 CBiol 79 MRSB. St Steph Ho Ox 86. **d** 88 **p** 89. C Crowthorne *Ox* 88–89; C Tilehurst St Mary 89–93; P-in-c Didcot St Pet 93–97; V 97–03; V Brackley St Pet w St Jas *Pet* 03–18; rtd 18; Past Care and Counselling Adv *Pet* from 18; Can Pet Cathl from 18; OGS from 96. *37 Debdale Road, Northampton NN3 2TR* E: nicholas.gandy@btinternet.com

GANE, Canon Christopher Paul. b 33. Qu Coll Cam BA 57 MA 61. Ridley Hall Cam 57. **d** 59 **p** 60. C Rainham *Chelmsf* 59–62; C Farnborough *Guildf* 62–64; V Erith St Paul *Roch* 64–71; V Ipswich St Marg *St E* 71–88; Hon Can St E Cathl 82–98; R Hopton, Market Weston, Barningham etc 88–98; rtd 98; PtO *St E* from 98. *5 Woodfields, Stradbroke, Eye IP21 5JQ* T: (01379) 388707 E: christopherpaulgane@gmail.com

GANN, Canon Anthony Michael. b 37. TCD BA 60 MA 64 BD 64. **d** 62 **p** 63. V Choral Derry Cathl *D & R* 62–66; Lesotho 66–74; Dioc Officer for Miss and Unity *Carl* 75–80; P-in-c Bampton and Mardale 75–80; TV Cen Telford *Lich* 80–89; TR Wolvercote w Summertown *Ox* 89–02; RD Ox 95–99; rtd 02; PtO *Worc* from 02. *Avalon, 84 Pickersleigh Road, Malvern WR14 2RS* T: (01684) 568114 E: connielightowler@agann.plus.com

GANN, John West. b 29. Ex Coll Ox BA 55 MA 59. Wells Th Coll 55. **d** 57 **p** 58. C Wendover *Ox* 57–59; C Walton St Mary *Liv* 59–62; R Didcot *Ox* 62–70; R Newbury St Nic 70–73; TR Newbury 73–78; V Twickenham St Mary *Lon* 78–87; Dir of Ords 81–87; TR Bridport *Sarum* 87–94; RD Lyme Bay 89–92; rtd 94; PtO *Glouc* from 94; *Bris* 96–04. *3 Buttercross Lane, Prestbury, Cheltenham GL52 5SF* T: (01242) 220787

GANNEY (née CHAMBERS), Mrs Rachel Jill. b 73. Hull Univ BSc 94 MSc 96 Selw Coll Cam BTh 04. Ridley Hall Cam 01. **d** 04 **p** 05. C Sutton St Jas and Wawne *York* 04–10; TV Plaistow and N Canning Town *Chelmsf* 10–14. *26 Pentreath Close, Fowey PL23 1ER* E: rachel@ganney.net

GANNON, James (Dub). b 75. W Sydney Univ BComm 98 BAppSc(Agric) 98. Moore Th Coll Sydney BTheol 08. **d** 10 **p** 11. NSM Henham and Elsenham w Ugley *Chelmsf* 10–13; P-in-c High and Gd Easter w Margaret Roding 13–17; P-in-c Gt Canfield w High Roding and Aythorpe Roding 13–17; Rural Evang Adv Colchester Area 13–17; TV W Tamworth Australia from 17. *16 Church Street, Tamworth NSW 2340, Australia* E: dub1994@hotmail.com

GANT, Canon Brian Leonard. b 45. Ox Univ MTh 01. K Coll Lon 72. **d** 73 **p** 74. C Hillmorton *Cov* 73–75; C Cov St Geo 76; P-in-c Maldon St Mary *Chelmsf* 76–79; R Muthill, Crieff and Comrie *St And* 79–81; V Walsall St Paul *Lich* 81–84; Chapl K Sch Worc and Min Can Worc Cathl 84–89; V Tunbridge Wells K Chas *Roch* 89–95; Hon Can Kumasi from 94; V Wymondham *Nor* 95–01; P-in-c York All SS St Street 01–03; TV Haxby and Wigginton 03–09; CME Officer York Adnry 01–07; rtd 09; PtO *York* 09–14; *Worc* from 14. *122 Henwick Road, Worcester WR2 5PB* T: (01905) 923933 M: 07944-286915 E: brianlgant@aol.com

GANT, Joanna Elizabeth. *See* NORTHEY, Joanna Elizabeth

GANT, Russell William. b 77. Suffolk Coll BA 02 St Jo Coll Dur BA 13. Cranmer Hall Dur 09. **d** 12 **p** 13. C Camberley St Paul *Guildf* 12–16; V Rowledge from 16. *The Vicarage,*

Church Lane, Rowledge, Farnham GU10 4EN T: (01252) 792402 M: 07414-631359 E: vicar@stjamesrowledge.org.uk

GANT, Trevor Malcolm. b 56. Leeds Univ BSc 97. NEOC 05. **d** 08 **p** 09. NSM York St Luke 08–16; NSM Skelton w Shipton and Newton on Ouse from 16; NSM Alne from 17; NSM Brafferton w Pilmoor, Myton-on-Swale etc from 17; NSM Coxwold and Husthwaite from 17; NSM Crayke w Brandsby and Yearsley from 17; NSM Easingwold w Raskelf from 17; NSM Stensall from 17; NSM Forest of Galtres from 17. *6 Lumley Road, York YO30 6DB* T: (01904) 654784 E: t.gant@st-peters.york.sch.uk

GARBUTT, Canon Mary Yvonne. b 45. Ridley Hall Cam 00. **d** 02 **p** 03. C Desborough, Brampton Ash, Dingley and Braybrooke *Pet* 02–05; P-in-c Arthingworth, Harrington w Oxendon and E Farndon 05–07; R 07–15; P-in-c 15–17; P-in-c Maidwell w Draughton, Lamport w Faxton 05–07; R 07–15; P-in-c 15–17; RD Brixworth 09–15; Can Pet Cathl 12–15; TV Daventry 17–20; RD 19–20; rtd 21. *27 Ropewalk Avenue, Leominster HR6 8LY* E: mygarbutt@gmail.com

GARCIA FUERTE, Antonio. b 77. St Damasus Univ Madrid BST 02 Anglia Ruskin Univ MA 15. Westcott Ho Cam 13. **d** 15 **p** 16. C Paddington St Jo w St Mich *Lon* 15–18; Asst Chapl St Chris Hospice Lon 18–19; C Dulwich St Barn *S'wark* 18–19; C S'wark H Trin w St Matt from 19. *89 Ambergate Street, London SE17 3RZ* M: 07939-997819 E: a.g.fuerte@gmail.com

GARDEN, Robert Andrew (Robin). b 26. Edin Univ BSc 49 Kent Univ MA 95 MInstP 58 FIMA 72. Cant Sch of Min 87. **d** 90 **p** 91. NSM Sandwich *Cant* 90–97; Chapl St Bart Hosp Sandwich 91–00; PtO *Cant* 97–15. *Naini, 164 St George's Road, Sandwich CT13 9LD* T: (01304) 612116

GARDINER, Mrs Anika. b 84. Ox Brookes Univ BA 08. Trin Coll Bris 13. **d** 16 **p** 17. C Warmley, Syston and Bitton *Bris* 16–19; TV Keynsham *B & W* from 19. *St Francis's Vicarage, Warwick Road, Keynsham, Bristol BS31 2PW* E: anikagardiner@keynshamparish.org.uk

GARDINER, Mrs Cathrine Leigh. b 64. STETS 05. **d** 08 **p** 09. C Bedminster *Bris* 08–11; TV Anerley *Roch* 11–15; P-in-c Filwood Park *Bris* 15–21; V from 21. *Christ Church Vicarage, 7 Petherton Road, Bristol BS14 9BP* T: 0117-953 1060 E: cathrinegardiner@gmail.com

GARDINER, David Andrew. b 81. Surrey Univ BA 03 Fitzw Coll Cam BTh 08. Westcott Ho Cam 05. **d** 08 **p** 09. C N Cheltenham *Glouc* 08–12; TV Richmond St Mary w St Matthias and St Jo *S'wark* 12–16; Bp's Chapl *Glouc* 16–19; R Lydney, Woolaston, Alvington and Aylburton from 19. *The Vicarage, 5 Raglan Gardens, Lydney GL15 5GZ* T: (01594) 842321 E: revd.david@lydneyparish.org.uk

GARDINER, Gerald. *See* GARDINER, William Gerald Henry

GARDINER (née SAYERS), Ms Karen Jane. b 69. Sheff Univ BMus 90 Heythrop Coll Lon MA 11. Ripon Coll Cuddesdon 00. **d** 02 **p** 03. C Dunstable *St Alb* 02–05; TV Elstree and Borehamwood 05–15; Hon C Escrick and Stillingfleet w Naburn *York* 15–19; Hon C Bubwith w Skipwith 15–19; V Aldborough w Boroughbridge and Roecliffe *Leeds* from 19. *The Vicarage, Church Lane, Boroughbridge, York YO51 9BA* T: (01423) 326518 E: karen.gardiner@leeds.anglican.org

GARDINER, Richard Allen. b 51. St Steph Ho Ox 12. **d** 13 **p** 14. C Bonn w Cologne *Eur* 13–17; Asst Chapl 17–20; Chapl from 20. *Auf dem Kälberhof 12, D-53797 Lohmar-Krahwinkel, Germany* T: (0049) (2247) 1472 M: (0049) 172-532 8025 E: richard.gardiner@web.de

GARDINER, Wendy Doreen. b 49. SRN 71. Trin Coll Bris 10. **d** 12 **p** 13. OLM Barton Hill St Luke w Ch Ch and Moorfields *Bris* from 12. *55 Whitehall Road, Bristol BS5 9BG* T: 0117-954 1645 M: 07902-318663 E: wdgardiner@btopenworld.com

GARDINER, Preb William Gerald Henry. b 46. Lon Univ BD 72. Oak Hill Th Coll 68. **d** 72 **p** 73. C Beckenham St Jo *Roch* 72–75; C Cheadle *Ches* 75–81; P-in-c Swynnerton *Lich* 81–83; P-in-c Tittensor 81–83; R Swynnerton and Tittensor 83–86; V Westlands St Andr 86–11; RD Newcastle 97–11; Preb Lich Cathl 05–11; rtd 11; PtO *Lich* 12–21. *4 The Lindens, Stone ST15 0BD* T: (01785) 286460 E: geraldgardiner@btopenworld.com

GARDNER, Andrew Neil. b 64. **d** 16 **p** 17. C Luton St Mary *St Alb* 16–19; TV Bishop's Hatfield, Lemsford and N Mymms from 19. *47 Heron Way, Hatfield AL10 8QT* M: 07581-292800

GARDNER, Benjamin James. b 84. St Jo Coll Dur BA 08. St Barn Th Cen 13. **d** 16 **p** 17. C Loughborough Em *Leic* 16–19; V Loughb Gd Shep from 19. *47 Brookfield Avenue, Loughborough LE11 3LN* M: 07454-836131 E: benjgardner@me.com

GARDNER, Brian Charles. b 46. FIBMS 71. **d** 04 **p** 05. OLM Bodicote *Ox* 04–16; PtO from 16. *11 Farm Way,*

Banbury OX16 9TB T: (01295) 253309 M: 07967-859457 E: bri.jen@btopenworld.com

GARDNER, Clive Bruce. b 67. Selw Coll Cam BA 89 MA 93. Wycliffe Hall Ox BA 95 MA 01. **d** 96 **p** 97. C Beverley Minster *York* 96–98; Bp's Dom Chapl *Liv* 98–01; V Cumnor *Ox* 01–06; TV Wimbledon *S'wark* from 11. *55 Alwyne Road, London SW19 7AE* T: (020) 8944 0184 E: clivegardner@outlook.com

GARDNER, Canon David. b 57. Oak Hill Th Coll BA 87. **d** 87 **p** 88. C Ogley Hay *Lich* 87–91; TV Mildenhall *St E* 91–98; P-in-c Woodbridge St Jo 98–00; V 00–03; V Woodbridge St Jo and Bredfield 03–12; P-in-c Ufford w Bredfield and Hasketon 01–03; Dir Miss from 12; Hon Can St E Cathl from 15. *St Nicholas Centre, 4 Cutler Street, Ipswich IP1 1UQ* T: (01473) 298500 F: 298501 E: dave.gardner@cofesuffolk.org

GARDNER, Elizabeth Mary. b 47. Nottm Univ BA 01. Trin Coll Bris 72 St Jo Coll Nottm 00. **d** 01 **p** 02. C Swindon Dorcan *Bris* 01–04; P-in-c Runcorn St Jo Weston *Ches* 04–09; V 09–13; rtd 13; PtO *Ches* from 13; Dioc Clergy Widows and Retirement Officer 07–10; Chapl Countess of Chester Hosp NHS Foundn Trust from 13. *69 Ford Road, Wirral CH49 0TD* T: 0151-792 5128 E: revbethgardner@gmail.com or bethgardner@nhs.net

GARDNER, Geoffrey Maurice. b 28. K Coll Lon BA 51 Lon Inst of Educn PGCE 52 Bris Univ DipEd 74. Cranmer Hall Dur. **d** 59 **p** 60. C Bowling St Jo *Bradf* 59–62; Nigeria 62–72; Hon C Bath St Luke *B & W* 72–73; PtO 73–90 and 94–99; NSM Bath Widcombe 90–94; rtd 94; PtO *Ex* from 99. *27 Gracey Court, Woodland Road, Broadclyst, Exeter EX5 3GA* T: (01392) 468553 E: 15geoffgardner@gmail.com

GARDNER, Mrs Helen Elizabeth. b 56. ERMC 05. **d** 08 **p** 09. C Sunnyside w Bourne End *St Alb* 08–12; V Totternhoe, Stanbridge and Tilsworth 12–16; rtd 16; PtO *St Alb* from 17; Chapl Bedford Hosp NHS Trust 20. *7 Great Blakelands, Marston Moretaine, Bedford MK43 0WY* E: helerevg@gmail.com

GARDNER, Helen Jane. b 39. Man Univ BSc 61 PGCE 62. WEMTC 93. **d** 96 **p** 97. NSM Stow on the Wold *Glouc* 96–00; NSM Stow on the Wold, Condicote and The Swells 00–02; NSM The Guitings, Cutsdean, Farmcote etc 03–04; PtO 04–07; NSM Stow on the Wold, Condicote and The Swells 07–12; rtd 12. *6 St Mary's Close, Lower Swell, Cheltenham GL54 1LJ* T: (01451) 832553 E: gardner269@btinternet.com

GARDNER, Ian Douglas. b 34. St Pet Hall Ox BA 58 MA 62. Oak Hill Th Coll 58. **d** 60 **p** 61. C Biddulph *Lich* 60–63; C Weston St Jo *B & W* 64; Nigeria 65–76; P-in-c Hurstbourne Tarrant and Faccombe *Win* 77–79; V Hurstbourne Tarrant, Faccombe, Vernham Dean etc 79–85; R Nursling and Rownhams 85–99; rtd 99; LtO *St D* from 99. *Wilderness Cottage, Haroldston Hill, Broad Haven, Haverfordwest SA62 3JP* T: (01437) 781592

GARDNER, Ian Norman. b 52. Open Univ BSc 96. WEMTC 03. **d** 05 **p** 06. NSM Dursley *Glouc* 05–18; NSM Dursley, Uley, Owlpen etc from 18. *9 Chestal Lodge, Chestal, Dursley GL11 5AA* T: (01453) 546895 M: 07960-287403 E: chestal@hotmail.com

GARDNER, Mrs Jacqueline Anne. b 49. WEMTC 95. **d** 98 **p** 99. NSM Fairford and Kempsford w Whelford *Glouc* 98–02; NSM Cirencester 02–05; PtO *Ox* 05–07; NSM Hanborough and Freeland 07–13; PtO 13–15; *Glouc* from 16. *11 Regency House, Humphris Place, Cheltenham GL53 7EW* T: (01242) 570264 E: jackiegardner@hotmail.com

GARDNER, Jacqueline Mary. b 71. St Hild Coll 16. **d** 18 **p** 19. NSM Adwick-le-Street w Skelbrooke *Sheff* from 18. *All Saints' Vicarage, 9 Great North Road, Woodlands, Doncaster DN6 7RB* T: (01302) 339618 M: 07827-918419

GARDNER, Jane. *See* GARDNER, Helen Jane

GARDNER, Jason Matthew. b 71. Loughb Univ BA 94 Lon Sch of Th BA 98. St Mellitus Coll 14. **d** 16 **p** 17. C W Harrow St Pet *Lon* 16–19; C Preston St Jo and St Geo *Blackb* 19–21; C Blackb St Aid, St Luke, St Mark and St Phil from 21. *St Francis's Vicarage, 1 St Francis Road, Blackburn BB2 2TZ* M: 07816-775916 E: gardnerjason42@gmail.com

GARDNER, Mrs Lorna Olive. b 54. **d** 14 **p** 15. NSM Blaydon and Swalwell *Dur* 14–20; NSM Blaydon from 21; NSM High Spen and Rowlands Gill from 21. *1 Kirkstone Close, Blaydon-on-Tyne NE21 6SY* T: 0191-414 5300 E: lornagardner6@gmail.com

GARDNER (née DUFFELL), Mrs Lucy Margaret. b 67. St Jo Coll Ox BA 90 MA 96. Ox Min Course 11. **d** 12 **p** 13. Tutor St Steph Ho Ox from 05; NSM Wheatley *Ox* 12–14; NSM Albury w Tiddington etc 14–16; PtO 16–21. *St Stephen's House, 16 Marston Street, Oxford OX4 1JX* T: (01865) 613500 E: lucy.gardner@ssho.ox.ac.uk

GARDNER, Mrs Marian Elizabeth. b 50. Ripon Coll of Educn DipEd 71. WMMTC 00. **d** 03 **p** 04. NSM Kirkleatham *York* 03–07; P-in-c Easington w Liverton 07–15; rtd 15; PtO *York* from 17. *37 Bennison Street, Guisborough TS14 6HY* M: 07736-350643 E: marian@thegardners.org.uk

GARDNER, Canon Mark Douglas. b 58. TCD BA 80 MA 83. **d** 83 **p** 84. C Ballymacarrett St Patr *D & D* 83–87; C Belfast St Steph w St Luke *Conn* 87–89; C Hendon and Sunderland *Dur* 89–90; TV Sunderland 90–95; I Dublin Santry w Glasnevin and Finglas *D & G* 95–01; PV and Chapter Clerk Ch Ch Cathl Dublin 96–10; Min Can St Patr Cathl Dublin 96; Treas V 96–01; Can Ch Cathl Dublin *D & G* from 08; V Dublin St Patr Cathl Gp 10–12; I Dublin St Cath and St Jas w St Audoen from 12; Preb Tipperkevin St Patr Cathl Dublin 10–12; Preb Maynooth from 12. *St Catherine's Rectory, 248 South Circular Road, Dolphin's Barn, Dublin D08 R6YC, Republic of Ireland* T: (00353) (1) 454 2274 M: 87-266 0228 E: markgardner300@gmail.com

GARDNER, Paul Douglas. b 50. K Coll Lon BA 72 AKC 72 Reformed Th Sem Mississippi MDiv 79 SS Coll Cam PhD 89. Ridley Hall Cam 79. **d** 80 **p** 81. C Cambridge St Martin *Ely* 80–83; Lect Oak Hill Th Coll 83–90; V Hartford *Ches* 90–03; RD Middlewich 94–99; Adn Ex 03–05; USA 05–17; rtd 17. *30 Archibald Road, Exeter EX1 1SA* E: p.d.g@att.net

GARDNER (née JAMES), Mrs Sandra Kay. b 66. Westcott Ho Cam 97. **d** 99 **p** 00. C Whittlesey, Pondersbridge and Coates *Ely* 99–02; R Leverington 02–04; V Southea w Murrow and Parson Drove 02–04; R Leverington, Newton and Tydd St Giles from 05. *The Rectory, 35 Gorefield Road, Leverington, Wisbech PE13 5AS* T: (01945) 581486 E: sandra.gardner952@btinternet.com

GARDNER, Stephen John. b 70. Southn Univ MEng 92. St Jo Coll Nottm 00. **d** 02 **p** 03. C Brinsworth w Catcliffe and Treeton *Sheff* 02–03; C Rivers Team 03–05; V Woodlands from 05; P-in-c Owston from 21; AD Adwick 11–15. *All Saints' Vicarage, 9 Great North Road, Woodlands, Doncaster DN6 7RB* T: (01302) 339618 M: 07740-200942 E: stephen@all-saints-church.net

GARDNER, Susan Carol. *See* CLARKE, Susan Carol

GARDOM, James Theodore Douglas. b 61. St Anne's Coll Ox BA 83 K Coll Lon PhD 92. Ripon Coll Cuddesdon 88. **d** 90 **p** 91. C Witney *Ox* 90–92; Dean of Studies Bp Gaul Coll Harare Zimbabwe 93–97; V Chesterton St Andr *Ely* 97–06; Dean Pemb Coll Cam from 06. *Pembroke College, Cambridge CB2 1RF* T: (01223) 338147 F: 338163 E: jtdg2@cam.ac.uk

GARFIELD, Diana Margaret. b 52. Leeds Poly BA 73 Anglia Poly Univ MA 02 Anglia Ruskin Univ PhD 12. St Mellitus Coll 16. **d** 17 **p** 18. OLM Broomfield *Chelmsf* from 17; OLM The Chignals w Mashbury from 21. *71 Pickwick Avenue, Chelmsford CM1 4UR* T: (01245) 443205 M: 07767-387959 E: dianagarfield@hotmail.com

GARLAND, Canon Michael. b 50. Sarum & Wells Th Coll 72. **d** 73 **p** 74. C Swansea St Thos and Kilvey *S & B* 73–76; C Boldmere *Birm* 76–79; V Kingshurst 79–88; P-in-c Curdworth w Castle Vale 88–90; R Curdworth 90–03; P-in-c Wishaw 99–00; V Charlton Kings St Mary *Glouc* 03–17; Hon Can Glouc Cathl 13–17; rtd 17; PtO *Glouc* from 18; AD Glouc City 19–20. *6 Whimbrel Road, Quedgeley, Gloucester GL2 4LJ* T: (01452) 720872 M: 07974-066929 E: michaelgarland368@btinternet.com

GARLICK, Preb Kathleen Beatrice. b 49. Leeds Univ BA 71 Birm Univ PGCE 72. Glouc Sch of Min 87. **d** 90 **p** 94. NSM Much Birch w Lt Birch, Much Dewchurch etc *Heref* 90–03; P-in-c 03–07; R Wormelow Hundred 07–09; Chapl Heref Sixth Form Coll 96–03; Chapl Heref Cathl 99–14; rtd 14; PtO *Heref* from 14; Chapl to The Queen 11–19. *Birch Lodge, Much Birch, Hereford HR2 8HT* T: (01981) 540666 M: 07812-995442 E: kaygarlick@hotmail.com

GARLICK, Canon Peter. b 34. AKC 57. **d** 58 **p** 59. C Swindon New Town *Bris* 58–63; St Kitts-Nevis 63–66; V Heyside *Man* 66–73; R Stretford All SS 73–79; RD Wootton *Pet* 79–88; V Duston 79–91; TR 91–94; Can Pet Cathl 85–94; rtd 94; PtO *Pet* 94–18. *75 Foxfields, 33 Latchet Lane, Upton, Northampton NN5 4GG* M: 07786-695939 E: petergarlick82@gmail.com

GARLICK, William Frederick. b 51. **d** 98 **p** 99. OLM Bermondsey St Jas w Ch Ch and St Crispin *S'wark* 98–06; PtO *Chich* 12–17. *33 Penfolds Place, Arundel BN18 9SA*

GARMAN, Mrs Elaine Christine. b 60. Newc Poly BA 82 Glas Caledonian Univ MBA 95 Glas Univ MPH 01 FFPH 07. TISEC 14. **d** 15 **p** 16. C Dunoon *Arg* 15–18; C Rothesay 15–18; Dioc Miss Enabler 17–18; R Forfar *St And* from 18. *St John's Rectory, 24 St James Road, Forfar DD8 1LG* T: (01307) 463440 M: 07733-151458 E: rector@stjohnsforfar.co.uk or revelainegarman@outlook.com

GARNELL, Paul Owen. b 81. ERMC 16. **d** 19 **p** 20. C Lordsbridge *Ely* from 19. *70 High Street, Coton, Cambridge CB23 7PL* M: 07761-454268 E: paulgarnell@hotmail.co.uk

GARNER, Alistair Ross. b 58. Pemb Coll Ox BA 81 MA 86. St Jo Coll Nottm 90. **d** 92 **p** 93. C Ashton-upon-Mersey St Mary Magd *Ches* 92–96; P-in-c Bredbury St Mark 96–01; V

01–09; Miss Growth Team Ldr *Roch* 09–12; TR Walkden and Lt Hulton *Man* 12–17; TR Eccles from 17. *12B Westminster Road, Eccles, Manchester M30 9EB* T: 0161-661 6861 E: rectoreccles@gmail.com

GARNER, Canon Carl. b 42. Rhodes Univ BA 62 Keble Coll Ox BA 65 MA 70. St Paul's Coll Grahamstown 66. **d** 67 **p** 68. C Pietersburg S Africa 67–71; R Louis Trichardt 71–75; Chapl St Paul's Coll Grahamstown 75–84; Dioc Missr *St Alb* 84–98; Can Res St Alb 84–98; P-in-c Digswell and Panshanger 98–06; TR 06–12; Hon Can St Alb 99–12; Jt RD Welwyn Hatfield 01–12; rtd 12; PtO *St Alb* from 12. *20 Howe Dell, Hatfield AL10 8BP*

GARNER, Mrs Carole. b 61. LCTP 05. **d** 08 **p** 09. NSM Oswaldtwistle St Paul *Blackb* 08–12; NSM Oswaldtwistle from 12. *17 Spinning Mill Close, Oswaldtwistle, Accrington BB5 4AB* E: carole.garner@blackburn.anglican.org

GARNER, Catherine Elizabeth. b 63. UWE BSc 02 PhD 07. Ripon Coll Cuddesdon 14. **d** 16 **p** 17. C E Meon *Portsm* 16–19; C W Meon and Warnford 16–19; C Langrish 16–19; R Backwell w Chelvey and Brockley *B & W* from 19. *The Rectory, 72 Church Lane, Backwell, Bristol BS48 3JJ* M: 07879-665767 E: revdrkatygarner@gmail.com

GARNER, David Henry. b 40. Trin Coll Bris 70. **d** 73 **p** 74. C Tunstead *Man* 73–75; C Fazeley *Lich* 76–78; V Sparkhill St Jo *Birm* 78–85; V Blackheath 85–01; Deanery P Warley Deanery 01–05; rtd 05; PtO *Birm* 05–22; Chapl Sandwell and W Birm Hosps NHS Trust from 06; PtO *Worc* from 06. *94 Honeybourne Road, Halesowen B63 3HD* T: 0121-550 2498 M: 07779-948333 E: davidhenrygarner@yahoo.co.uk

GARNER, John David. b 47. **d** 03. OLM Kirkdale St Lawr *Liv* 03–15; rtd 15; PtO *Liv* from 15. *10 Doon Close, Liverpool L4 1XW* T: 0151-284 0388 E: johngarner65@aol.com

GARNER, John Howard. b 45. Univ of Wales (Swansea) BSc 67 Univ of Wales (Ban) PhD 75. SWMTC 95. **d** 98 **p** 99. NSM Upton *Ex* from 98; Sen Chapl S Devon Healthcare NHS Foundn Trust 06–15. *Highgrove Lodge, Sunbury Hill, Upton, Torquay TQ1 3ED* T: (01803) 293640 *or* 654186

GARNER, Mark William John. b 50. Melbourne Univ BA 71 DipEd 73 PhD 86 Essex Univ MA 75 Aber Univ MTheol 08. TISEC 09. **d** 11. C Turriff *Ab* 11–12; Hd of Whitelands Coll Roehampton Univ *S'wark* 12–20; PtO 13–20; *Sarum* 15–20; rtd 20; LtO Ballarat Australia from 20. *201 Ripon Street South, Ballarat VA 3350, Australia* E: mark.garner@roehampton.ac.uk

GARNER, Canon Rodney George. b 48. Lon Univ BA 87 Hull Univ MPhil 96 Man Univ PhD 01 MCIPD 75. Qu Coll Birm 75. **d** 78 **p** 79. C Tranmere St Paul w St Luke *Ches* 78–81; V Eccleston St Thos *Liv* 81–90; P-in-c Sculcoates St Paul w Ch Ch and St Silas *York* 90–95; Lay Tr Officer (E Riding Adnry) 90–95; P-in-c Southport H Trin *Liv* 95–96; V 96–18; Dioc Th Consultant 95–18; Hon Can Liv Cathl 07–18; rtd 18. *15 Carisbrooke Drive, Southport PR9 7JD* M: 07754-812915 E: rgcfgarner@gmail.com

GARNER, Ross. *See* GARNER, Alistair Ross

GARNER, Mrs Selina Clare. b 69. Newnham Coll Cam BA 90 K Coll Lon PGCE 93. EAMTC 00. **d** 06 **p** 07. C Fulbourn *Ely* 06–09; C Gt Wilbraham 06–09; C Lt Wilbraham 06–09; C Cullompton, Willand, Uffculme, Kentisbeare etc *Ex* 09–15; C Willand, Uffculme, Kentisbeare etc 15–16; Pioneer Youth Min Tiverton and Cullompton Deanery from 09 and 14–16; TV Wellington and Distr *B & W* 16–21. *The Vicarage, 40 Chichester Road, Barnstaple EX32 9EH* E: selina@thegarners.me.uk

GARNER, Thomas Richard. b 43. K Coll Lon. **d** 69 **p** 70. C Tynemouth Ch Ch *Newc* 69–73; C Fenham St Jas and St Basil 73–76; V Hamstead St Bernard *Birm* 76–80; V Greytown NZ 80–87; V Levin 87–96; Can Wellington 96–99; V Upper Riccarton w Yaldhurst 99–06; P-in-c Carterton 06–08; rtd 08; PtO Wellington NZ from 08. *267 Chester Road, RD 1, Carterton 5791, New Zealand* T: (0064) (6) 379 9375 M: 21-214 8897 E: rgarner@ihug.co.nz

GARNETT, Alyson Susan. *See* PEBERDY, Alyson Susan

GARNETT, The Ven David Christopher. b 45. Nottm Univ BA 67 Fitzw Coll Cam BA 69 MA 73. Westcott Ho Cam 67. **d** 69 **p** 70. C Cottingham *York* 69–72; Chapl Selw Coll Cam 72–77; P-in-c Patterdale *Carl* 77–80; Dir of Ords 78–80; V Heald Green St Cath *Ches* 80–87; R Christleton 87–92; TR Ellesmere Port 92–96; Adn Chesterfield *Derby* 96–09; P-in-c Beeley and Edensor 07–10; Hon Can Derby Cathl 96–10; rtd 10; PtO *York* from 13. *Wayside, Goslipgate, Pickering YO18 8EQ* E: davidcgarnett@aol.co.uk

GARNETT, Preb Ralph Henry. b 28. Cuddesdon Coll 58. **d** 60 **p** 61. C Broseley w Benthall *Heref* 60–64; V Leintwardine 64–69; P-in-c Downton w Burrington and Aston and Elton 66–69; RD Ludlow 72–75; R Whitton w Greete and Hope Bagot 69–87; R Burford III w Lt Heref 69–87; P-in-c Burford I,

Nash and Boraston 72–74; R 74–87; V Tenbury Wells 69–74; TR 74–87; Preb Heref Cathl 82–93; P-in-c Fownhope 87–93; P-in-c Brockhampton w Fawley 87–93; RD Heref Rural 92–93; rtd 93; PtO *Heref* 93–12. *8 Butlers Place, Portsmouth Road, Milford, Godalming GU8 5EX*

GARNHAM, Laura Felicity. b 50. **d** 17 **p** 18. NSM Gt Oakley, Wix, Wrabness etc *Chelmsf* from 17. *1 Church Road, Wrabness, Manningtree CO11 2TG* E: landm.garnham@virgin.net

GARRARD, Mrs Christine Ann. b 51. Open Univ BA 86 LCST 75. EAMTC 87. **d** 90 **p** 94. Par Dn Kesgrave *St E* 90–94; C 94–96; V Ipswich All Hallows 96–02; R Higham, Holton St Mary, Raydon and Stratford 02–08; Asst Dioc Dir of Ords 03–08; Sen Chapl Burrswood Chr Hosp 08–14; rtd 14. *40 Oakbury Drive, Weymouth DT3 6JE* T: (01305) 833475 E: revdchris@aol.com

GARRARD, Mrs Elizabeth Helen. b 65. Dundee Univ BN 11 RGN 89. ERMC 09. **d** 11 **p** 12. OLM Broadside *Nor* 11–20; NSM Rockland St Mary w Hellington, Bramerton etc from 20; Chapl Norfolk Community Health and Care NHS Trust 14–16; Lead Chapl James Paget Univ Hosps NHS Foundn Trust 16; Lead Chapl Norfolk Community Health and Care NHS Trust from 16. *Colman Hospital, Priscilla Bacon Lodge, Unthank Road, Norwich NR2 2PJ* T: (01603) 255728 M: 07920-528282

GARRARD, Canon James Richard. b 65. Dur Univ BA 88 Keble Coll Ox DPhil 92 Leeds Univ MA 01 FRHistS 16. Westcott Ho Cam. **d** 94 **p** 95. C Elland *Wakef* 94–97; TV Brighouse and Clifton 98–01; P-in-c Balderstone *Blackb* 01–08; Warden of Readers 01–08; Can Res Ely Cathl from 08. *The Precentor's House, 32 High Street, Ely CB7 4JU* T: (01353) 660335 *or* 660300 F: 665658 E: j.garrard@elycathedral.org

GARRARD, Canon Nicholas James Havelock. b 62. Leeds Univ BA 83. Westcott Ho Cam 86. **d** 88 **p** 89. C Scotforth *Blackb* 88–91; C Eaton *Nor* 91–95; V Heigham St Thos 95–96; RD Nor S 03–06; R Broadside 06–20; RD Blofield 14–17; P-in-c Rockland St Mary w Hellington, Bramerton etc from 20; Bp's Officer for Chr Spirituality through Creative Arts from 20; Hon Can Nor Cathl from 14. *The Rectory, 2 Rectory Lane, Rockland St Mary, Norwich NR14 7EY* E: nickgarr39@aol.com

✠**GARRARD, The Rt Revd Richard.** b 37. K Coll Lon BD 60 AKC 60. **d** 61 **p** 62 **c** 94. C Woolwich St Mary w H Trin *S'wark* 61–66; C Cambridge Gt St Mary w St Mich *Ely* 66–68; Chapl Keswick Hall Coll of Educn 68–74; Prin Wilson Carlile Coll of Evang 74–79; Can Res and Chan S'wark Cathl 79–87; Dir of Tr 79–87; Can Res St E Cathl 87–94; Dioc Adv for CME 87–91; Adn Sudbury 91–94; Suff Bp Penrith *Carl* 94–01; Hon Can Carl Cathl 94–01; Abp's Rep H See and Dir Angl Cen Rome 01–03; Hon Asst Bp Eur from 01; rtd 03; PtO *Nor* from 03; Hon Asst Bp Nor from 03. *26 Carol Close, Stoke Holy Cross, Norwich NR14 8NN* T: (01508) 494165 E: garrard.r.a@gmail.com

GARRARD, Miss Valerie Mary. b 48. K Alfred's Coll Win TCert 69 St Paul's Coll Chelt BEd 84. **d** 03 **p** 04. OLM Wylye and Till Valley *Sarum* 03–11; rtd 18; PtO *Sarum* from 18. *Cowslip Cottage, Wylye Road, Hanging Langford, Salisbury SP3 4NW* T: (01722) 790739 E: vmgarrard@btinternet.com

GARRATT, Alan William. b 54. **d** 04 **p** 05. NSM Hazlemere *Ox* 04–08; TR Thame 08–19; AD Aston and Cuddesdon 13–17; rtd 19; PtO *Ox* from 20. *36 Eastfield Road, Princes Risborough HP27 0JA* E: alan.garratt@hotmail.co.uk

GARRATT, Roger Charles. b 50. St Jo Coll Dur BA 72. Cranmer Hall Dur 72. **d** 74 **p** 75. C Leamington Priors St Paul *Cov* 74–77; Chapl Emscote Lawn Sch Warw 77–99; Chapl and Dep Hd Arden Lawn Sch 77–00; TV Warwick *Cov* 02–08; rtd 08; PtO *Cov* 08–20. *8 Wasdale Close, Leamington Spa CV32 6NF* T: (01926) 335474 E: roger.garratt@btinternet.com

GARRETT, Clive Robert. b 54. Sheff Univ BA 75 PhD 80 Ex Univ PGCE 88. St Jo Coll Nottm MA 98. **d** 98 **p** 99. C Bath Weston St Jo w Kelston *B & W* 98–02; R Cov 02–19; rtd 19. *3 Wheatfield Avenue, Worcester WR5 3HA* E: clivepics@uwclub.net

GARRETT, Miss Elizabeth Clare. b 46. Trin Coll Bris. **d** 94 **p** 95. C Ewyas Harold w Dulas, Kenderchurch etc *Heref* 94–96; C Tupsley w Hampton Bishop 96–00; TV Uttoxeter Area *Lich* 00–05; P-in-c Gt Canfield w High Roding and Aythorpe Roding *Chelmsf* 05–11; rtd 11; PtO *Win* from 20. *10 Culverwell Gardens, Winchester SO23 9JG* M: 07790-878307 E: ecgarrett@btinternet.com

GARRETT, Geoffrey David. b 57. Oak Hill Th Coll 83. **d** 86 **p** 87. C Trentham *Lich* 86–90; V Rhodes *Man* 90–00; P-in-c Bardsley 00–05; V 05–08; V Watton *Nor* 08–13; P-in-c Gt and Lt Cressingham w Threxton 10–13; R Condover w Frodesley, Acton Burnell etc *Heref* from 13; RD Condover from 18. *The Rectory, Condover, Shrewsbury SY5 7AA* T: (01743) 872251 E: revgeoff@live.co.uk

GARRETT, Ian Lee. b 60. MCSP 81. Sarum & Wells Th Coll 86. **d** 89 **p** 90. C Maidstone St Martin *Cant* 89–95; P-in-c S Ashford St Fran 95–07; TV Bishopsworth and Bedminster Down *Bris* 07–13; P-in-c Brislington St Anne from 13; C Brislington St Chris and St Cuth 07–08; P-in-c Brislington St Cuth from 08. *35 Wick Crescent, Bristol BS4 4HG* T: 0117-971 0523 E: ianlgarrett@gmail.com

GARRETT (née KIRK), Natalie Roberta. b 71. Leeds Univ BA 93. Wycliffe Hall Ox 03. **d** 05 **p** 06. C Gipsy Hill Ch Ch *S'wark* 05–06; Hon C Burford w Fulbrook, Taynton, Asthall etc *Ox* 06–10; Hon C Twickenham Common H Trin *Lon* from 10. *Holy Trinity Vicarage, 1 Vicarage Road, Twickenham TW2 5TS* T: (020) 8898 1168

GARRETT, Timothy Michael. b 70. Univ of Wales (Abth) BA 91. Wycliffe Hall Ox BA 01. **d** 02 **p** 03. C Ox St Andr 02–06; C Burford w Fulbrook, Taynton, Asthall etc 06–10; V Twickenham Common H Trin *Lon* from 10; AD Hampton from 19. *Holy Trinity Vicarage, 1 Vicarage Road, Twickenham TW2 5TS* T: (020) 8898 1168 E: revgaz@hotmail.com

GARROD, Mrs Christine Anne. b 49. EAMTC. **d** 00 **p** 01. C N w S Wootton *Nor* 00–04; P-in-c Brinklow *Cov* 04–09; P-in-c Harborough Magna 04–09; P-in-c Monks Kirby w Pailton and Stretton-under-Fosse 04–09; P-in-c Churchover w Willey 04–09; R Gd and Lt Plumstead w Thorpe End and Witton *Nor* 09–14; rtd 14; PtO *Nor* from 14. *17 Philip Nurse Road, Dersingham, King's Lynn PE31 6WJ* T: (01485) 543078 E: cagarrod@hotmail.com

GARROW, Alan John Philip. b 67. Lon Bible Coll BA 90 Wycliffe Hall Ox MPhil 94 Jes Coll Ox DPhil 00. **d** 93 **p** 94. C Waltham H Cross *Chelmsf* 93–97; C Akeman *Ox* 00–04; Tutor SAOMC 00–04; Dir Studies 04–05; Dir Studies Ox Min Course 05–06; V Th Bath Abbey w St Jas *B & W* 06–14; PtO *Sheff* 14–16; V High Harrogate St Pet *Leeds* from 16. *St Peter's Vicarage, 13 Beech Grove, Harrogate HG2 0ET* T: (01423) 568218 M: 07761-017658 E: alan.garrow@gmail.com

GARSIDE, Geoffrey Malcolm. b 43. Huddersfield Poly CertEd Huddersfield Univ BEd. **d** 05 **p** 06. OLM Almondbury w Farnley Tyas *Wakef* 05–10; P-in-c Marsden 10–14; *Leeds* 14–15; rtd 15; PtO *Leeds* from 17. *16 Mountfield Avenue, Huddersfield HD5 8RD* E: ggarside@aol.com

GARSIDE, Melvin. b 42. NOC 85. **d** 88 **p** 89. C Lindley *Wakef* 88–91; C Shelf *Bradf* 91–93; V Lundwood *Wakef* 93–97; V Hanging Heaton 97–01; V Woodhouse and Bp's Adv in Racial Justice 01–05; rtd 05. *5 Hawthorne Close, Nether Poppleton, York YO26 6HP* M: 07803-250258 E: melgarside@melgarside.demon.co.uk

GARTHWAITE, Linda Petra. b 55. SWMTC 16. **d** 18 **p** 19. NSM Ludgvan, Marazion, St Hilary and Perranuthnoe *Truro* from 18. *Joyce's Farm, Higher Kenneggy, Rosudgeon, Penzance TR20 9AU* E: linda.garthwaite@kenneggycove.co.uk

GARTLAND, Christopher Michael. b 49. Man Univ BA 78 Leeds Univ MEd 99 Univ Coll Lon MSc 04. Coll of Resurr Mirfield 82. **d** 84 **p** 85. C Almondbury w Farnley Tyas *Wakef* 84–87; P-in-c Upperthong 87–89; TV Upper Holme Valley 89–91; Chapl Stanley Royd Hosp *Wakef* 91–94; Chapl Wakef HA (Mental Health Services) 91–95; Chapl Wakef and Pontefract Community NHS Trust 95–01; Hd Past/Spiritual Care SW Yorks Partnership NHS Foundn Trust from 02. *2 Weirside, Marsden, Huddersfield HD7 6BU* T: (01924) 327498 E: mike.gartland@swyt.nhs.uk or michaelgartland4@aol.com

GARTON, Mrs Anne-Marie. b 48. BA MSW CQSW. **d** 02 **p** 03. NSM Caterham *S'wark* 02–10 and from 14; PtO 10–14. *The Vicarage, 2 Churchview Close, Caterham CR3 6EZ* T: (01883) 343188 M: 07811-186526 E: anne-marie@garton.com

GARTON, Capt Jeremy. b 56. Wilson Carlile Coll 78 SEITE 94. **d** 96 **p** 97. C Clapham Team *S'wark* 96–00; P-in-c Caterham Valley 00–03; TV Caterham from 03. *The Vicarage, 2 Churchview Close, Caterham CR3 6EZ* T: (01883) 343188 F: (020) 7863 4120 E: jerry@garton.com

GARVIE, Mrs Anna-Lisa Karen. b 48. Luton Univ BA 99 Leeds Univ MA 05. St Alb Minl Tr Scheme 89. **d** 96 **p** 97. NSM Caddington *St Alb* 96–99; NSM St Paul's Walden 99–01; Chapl Chelsea and Westmr Hosp NHS Foundn Trust 98–01; Co-ord Chapl Hinchingbrooke Health Care NHS Trust 01–09; Chapl Thorpe Hall Hospice 09–12; Chapl NHS Borders 12–16; rtd 16; PtO *Ely* from 09; *St Alb* from 19. *3 The Stiles, Godmanchester, Huntingdon PE29 2JF*

GARWOOD, Simon Frederick. b 62. Reading Univ BA 85 Lon Univ PGCE 93 Birm Univ BD 99. Qu Coll Birm MA 00. **d** 00 **p** 01. C Chelmsf All SS 00–03; TV Witham 03–14; P-in-c Kelvedon and Feering from 14; AD Witham from 20. *The Vicarage, Church Street, Kelvedon, Colchester CO5 9AH* T: (01376) 573701 E: simongarwood@simonliz62.plus.com

GASCOIGNE, Philip. b 27. Oak Hill Th Coll. **d** 62 **p** 63. C Blackpool Ch Ch *Blackb* 62–65; V Bootle St Leon *Liv* 65–71;

Staff Evang CPAS 71–74; V St Helens St Mark *Liv* 74–77; V Blackpool Ch Ch *Blackb* 77–81; V Blackpool Ch Ch w All SS 81–97; rtd 98; PtO *Blackb* from 98. *18 Grange Road, Blackpool FY3 8EJ* T: (01253) 315607

GASKELL, Barrie Stuart. b 56. SNWTP 07. **d** 10 **p** 11. NSM Bolton St Pet *Man* 10–11; NSM Bolton St Pet w St Phil from 11; Chapl Bolton NHS Foundn Trust from 10; Chapl Gtr Man W Mental Health NHS Foundn Trust from 13; PtO *Liv* from 16. *1 Old Vicarage Mews, Westhoughton, Bolton BL5 2EQ* T: (01942) 818797 E: barrie.gaskell@gmw.nhs.uk

GASKELL, David. b 48. Lon Univ BD 76. Trin Coll Bris 72. **d** 76 **p** 77. C Eccleston Ch Ch *Liv* 76–80; C Rainhill 80–83; V Over Darwen St Jas *Blackb* 83–88; V Livesey 88–95; V Preston St Cuth 95–01; V Copp w Inskip 01–13; rtd 13; PtO *Blackb* from 13. *4 St James Gardens, Leyland PR26 7XA* T: (01772) 452045 E: dabberoarer@btinternet.com

GASKELL, Canon Ian Michael. b 51. Nottm Univ BTh 81. Linc Th Coll 77. **d** 81 **p** 82. C Wakef St Jo 81–83; Ind Chapl *Sheff* 83–86; V Cleckheaton St Luke and Whitechapel *Wakef* 86–93; V Birkenshaw w Hunsworth 93–98; RD Birstall 96–98; Can Res Wakef Cathl 98–05; Dioc Soc Resp Adv 98–06; V Chapelthorpe 06–14; *Leeds* 14; Hon Can Wakef Cathl 05–14; rtd 15; PtO *Leeds* from 17. *21 Old Royston Avenue, Royston, Barnsley S71 4FZ*

GASKELL, Marion Ingrid. b 52. Wilson Carlile Coll 74 NOC 96. **d** 99 **p** 00. C Thorpe Edge *Bradf* 99–02; TV Shelf w Buttershaw St Aid 02–04; TR 04–18; rtd 18; PtO *Leeds* from 18. *12 Mayfield Gardens, Ossett WF5 9PW* T: (01924) 276451

GASKELL, Peter John. b 70. Bris Univ MS 93 ChB 93. Oak Hill Th Coll BA 03. **d** 03 **p** 04. NSM Poulton Lancelyn H Trin *Ches* 03–07; NSM Rusholme H Trin *Man* from 09. *47 Linden Park, Manchester M19 2PQ* T: 0161-224 7493 M: 07769-682142 E: peter@glod.co.uk

GASPER (née COHEN), Mrs Janet Elizabeth. b 47. Birm Univ CertEd 70. WMMTC 93. **d** 96 **p** 97. NSM Leominster *Heref* 96–99; C Letton w Staunton, Byford, Mansel Gamage etc 99–01; Hon Chapl RAF 97–01; R Baxterley w Hurley and Wood End and Merevale etc *Birm* 01–13; P-in-c Kingsbury 04–13; rtd 13; P-in-c The Langtons and Shangton *Leic* 14–17; P-in-c Welham, Glooston and Cranoe and Stonton Wyville 14–17; PtO from 18. *21 Northfold Road, Leicester LE2 3YG* E: janet.gasper@hotmail.co.uk

GASSON, Mrs Siân. b 68. **d** 12 **p** 13. C Collyhurst *Man* 12–15; V Bryn *Liv* 15–19; V Dingle from 19. *St Cleopas' Vicarage, Beresford Road, Liverpool L8 4SG* E: siangasson@gmail.com

GASTON, Mrs Lydia Madeleine. b 79. St Andr Univ MA 03 Rob Coll Cam BTh 09. Ridley Hall Cam 06. **d** 09 **p** 10. C Erdington Ch the K *Birm* 09–14; V Yardley Wood from 14. *The Vicarage, School Road, Yardley Wood, Birmingham B14 4EP* T: 0121-430 8367 M: 07779-006178 E: lydgaston@hotmail.co.uk or christchurchyardleywood@outlook.com

GASTON, Raymond Gordon. b 62. Leeds Univ BA 94 Nottm Univ MTh 97. Linc Th Coll 94. **d** 96 **p** 97. C Leeds Gipton Epiphany *Ripon* 96–99; V Leeds St Marg and All Hallows 99–07; Tutor Qu Coll Birm 08–16; PtO *Birm* 14–17; TV Cen Wolverhampton *Lich* from 15; Interfaith Officer Wolverhampton Area from 16. *St Chad's Vicarage, Manlove Street, Wolverhampton WV3 0HG* T: (01902) 652633 M: 07751-155124 E: revdray@hotmail.co.uk

GATENBY, Canon Simon John Taylor. b 62. Nottm Univ BA 83. St Jo Coll Nottm 84. **d** 87 **p** 88. C Haughton St Mary *Man* 87–90; C Newburn *Newc* 90–93; P-in-c Brunswick *Man* 93–96; R from 96; AD Hulme 99–05; Hon Can Man Cathl from 13; Tutor Westcott Ho Cam from 05. *The Rectory, Hartfield Close, Brunswick, Manchester M13 9YX* T: 0161-273 2470 E: simon@brunswickchurch.org.uk

GATES, Alan Raymond. b 46. EAMTC 98. **d** 01 **p** 02. C W w E Mersea and Peldon w Gt and Lt Wigborough *Chelmsf* 01–05; P-in-c Gt Barton *St E* 05–12; P-in-c Thurston 12; V Gt Barton and Thurston 12–14; RD Thingoe 08–14; rtd 14; Hon C Langtree *Ox* 16–19; PtO from 19. *8 Waterside Drive, Purley on Thames, Reading RG8 8AQ* M: 07528-087733 E: pearleygates@outlook.com

GATES, Mrs Frances Margaret. b 44. STETS 01. **d** 04 **p** 05. NSM Portsea St Mary, Portsea St Geo and Portsea All SS *Portsm* 04–11; rtd 11; PtO *Portsm* from 11. *114 Kings Road, Southsea PO5 4DW* T: (023) 9282 0326 M: 07951-062226

GATES, John Richard. b 47. Oak Hill Th Coll 70. **d** 73 **p** 74. C Iver *Ox* 73–76; C Broadwater St Mary *Chich* 76–79; Dioc Youth Officer *Nor* 79–82; V Cosby *Leic* 82–86; Asst Chapl Bucharest w Sofia *Eur* 98–99; rtd 08; PtO *Leic* from 15. *697A Melton Road, Thurmaston, Leicester LE4 8ED* M: 07851-628100 E: evingtonuk368@gmail.com

GATES, Richard James. b 46. Oak Hill Th Coll BA 85. **d** 85 **p** 86. C Heald Green St Cath *Ches* 85–89; V Norton 89–98; V Bunbury and Tilstone Fearnall 98–11; rtd 12; PtO *Ches*

from 12; Chapl St Luke's Cheshire Hospice from 13. *Vicarage Cottage, Church Street, Tarvin, Chester CH3 8EB* T: (01829) 749134 M: 07715-178750 E: rickjgates@me.com

GATES, The Ven Simon Philip. b 60. St Andr Univ MA 82 St Jo Coll Dur BA 86. Cranmer Hall Dur 84. **d** 87 **p** 88. C Southall Green St Jo *Lon* 87–91; Assoc Min St Andr Ch Hong Kong 91–95; V Clapham Park St Steph *S'wark* 96–06; P-in-c Telford Park St Thos 05–06; V Telford Park 06–13; AD Lambeth S 06–13; Adn Lambeth from 13. *The Vicarage, 7 Hoadly Road, London SW16 1AE* T: (020) 8545 2440 E: simon.gates@southwark.anglican.org

GATFORD, The Ven Ian. b 40. AKC 65. **d** 67 **p** 68. C Clifton w Glapton *S'well* 67–71; TV Clifton 71–84; V Sherwood 75–84; Can Res Derby Cathl 84–99; Adn Derby and Hon Can Derby Cathl 93–05; rtd 05; PtO *Derby* from 05. *9 Poplar Nook, Allestree, Derby DE22 2DW* T: (01332) 557567

GATISS, Lee. b 72. New Coll Ox BA 96 MA 01 Westmr Th Sem Philadelphia ThM 09 Cam Univ PhD 14. Oak Hill Th Coll BA 00. **d** 01 **p** 02. C Barton Seagrave w Warkton *Pet* 01–04; C St Helen Bishopsgate w St Andr Undershaft etc *Lon* 04–09; PtO *Ely* from 11; Dir Ch Soc from 13. *Church Society, Ground Floor, Centre Block, Hille Business Estate, 132 St Albans Road, Watford WD24 4AE* T: (01923) 255410 F: 800362 E: director@churchsociety.org

GATLIFFE, David Spenser. b 45. Keble Coll Ox BA 67 Fitzw Coll Cam BA 69. Westcott Ho Cam 67. **d** 69 **p** 70. C Oxted *S'wark* 69–72; C Roehampton H Trin 72–75; C S Beddington St Mich 76–77; TV Clapham Old Town 78–87; P-in-c Clapham Ch Ch and St Jo 81–87; TV Clapham Team 87–89; V S Wimbledon H Trin and St Pet 89–01; Dir Reader Tr 93–01; R Lee St Marg *S'wark* 01–10; Ldr Post Ord Tr Woolwich Area 04–09; rtd 10; PtO *B & W* from 15. *47 Catherine Street, Frome BA11 1DA* T: (01373) 228757 M: 07527-424526 E: dgatliffe@yahoo.com

GATRILL, Canon Adrian Colin. b 60. Southn Univ BTh 82. Linc Th Coll 83. **d** 85 **p** 86. C W Bromwich St Andr *Lich* 85–88; C W Bromwich St Andr w Ch Ch 88–89; Chapl RAF 89–11; Dir of Ords 06–11; Sen Chapl Dur Constabulary from 11; PtO *St D* 90–95; *Ripon* 00–14; *Leeds* from 14; Hon Can Dur Cathl from 16. *Durham Constabulary Headquarters, Aykley Heads, Durham DH1 5TT* T: 0191-375 2361 E: adrian.gatrill@durham.police.uk

GAU, Justin Charles. b 65. Univ Coll Lon LLB 87 Down Coll Cam BTh 11. Westcott Ho Cam 09. **d** 11 **p** 12. Dep Chan *Linc* from 01; Dep Chan *B & W* from 11; Chan *Bris* from 11; Chan *St E* from 21; NSM S Hackney St Jo w Ch Ch *Lon* 11–15; NSM Brownswood Park 15–17; NSM W Hackney from 17. *27 Arlington Square, London N1 7DP* T: (020) 7353 0711 M: 07771-711114 E: j.gau@pumpcourtchambers.com *or* justin@stpaulswesthackney.org

GAUDION, Craig Simon. b 84. Univ of Wales BA 08 Birm Univ MA 10. Trin Coll Bris 16. **d** 18 **p** 19. C S Widnes *Liv* 18–21; C Widnes St Jo and St Paul from 21. *St Paul's Vicarage, Victoria Square, Widnes WA8 7QU* M: 07896-055484 E: craiggaudion@hotmail.co.uk

GAUGE, Canon Barrie Victor. b 41. St D Coll Lamp BA 62 Selw Coll Cam BA 64 MA 74 CQSW 81. Bp Burgess Hall Lamp. **d** 65 **p** 66. C Newtown w Llanllwchaiarn w Aberhafesp *St As* 65–68; C Prestatyn 68–73; R Bodfari and Dioc RE Adv 73–76; PtO *Ches* 76–84; V Birkenhead St Jas w St Bede 84–90; Dir of Resources 90–98; Hon Can Ches Cathl 94–98; C Lache cum Saltney 95–98; Par Development Adv *Derby* 98–06; Can Res Derby Cathl 99–06; Dioc Miss Adv 01–04; rtd 06; PtO *St As* from 09; *Ches* 10–14; *S & B* 11–14. *40 Saxon Street, Wrexham LL13 7BD* T: (01978) 353715 E: bgauge254@btinternet.com

GAUNT, Adam. b 79. St Jo Coll Dur BA 00 MA 02. St Steph Ho Ox 03. **d** 05 **p** 06. C Middlesbrough Ascension *York* 05–09; R Loftus and Carlin How w Skinningrove from 09. *The Rectory, 11 Micklow Lane, Loftus, Saltburn-by-the-Sea TS13 4JE* T: (01287) 644047 E: adamgaunt@btinternet.com

GAUNT (née COTTELL), Mrs Avril Jane. b 50. SRN 72 SCM 74. S Dios Minl Tr Scheme 92. **d** 95 **p** 97. NSM Yatton Moor *B & W* 95–96 and 97–02; NSM Bourne *Guildf* 96–97; Chapl N Bris NHS Trust 02–14; rtd 14; PtO *B & W* from 05. *Myrtle Cottage, Ham Lane, Kingston Seymour, Clevedon BS21 6XE* T: (01934) 832995

GAUNT, Rachel. *See* SHUTTLEWORTH, Rachel

GAUNTLETT, Gilbert Bernard. b 36. Oriel Coll Ox BA 59 MA 62. Wycliffe Hall Ox 59. **d** 61 **p** 62. C Maidenhead St Andr and St Mary *Ox* 61–64; C Ox St Ebbe w St Pet 64–68; R Nottingham St Nic *S'well* 68–72; Asst Master Leys High Sch Redditch 73–79; Asst Master Stourport High Sch 79–85; rtd 97. *The Tower, Brynygwin Isaf, Dolgellau LL40 1YA* T: (01341) 423481 E: gauntlett278@btinternet.com

GAUSDEN, Canon Peter James. b 32. Qu Coll Birm 57. **d** 60 **p** 61. C Battersea St Pet and Chapl S Lon Ind Miss

S'wark 60–63; C St Peter-in-Thanet *Cant* 63–68; V Sturry 68–74; R Sturry w Fordwich and Westbere w Hersden 74–97; Dioc Ecum Officer 91–96; Hon Can Cant Cathl 96–97; rtd 97; PtO *Portsm* 97–98; Hon C Wantsum Gp *Cant* 99–04; PtO from 04. *2 The Paddocks, Collards Close, Monkton, Ramsgate CT12 4JZ* T: (01843) 825374 E: peter.gausden374@btinternet.com

GAVIGAN, Canon Josephine Katherine. b 49. Univ Coll Chich BA 00. Sarum Th Coll 93. **d** 96. NSM Boxgrove *Chich* 96–00; C 00–03; Dn-in-c Maybridge 03–14; RD Worthing 05–10; Can and Preb Chich Cathl 07–14; rtd 14; PtO *Chich* from 15. *72 Navigation Drive, Yapton, Arundel BN18 0FS* M: 07760-277262

GAWNE-CAIN, John. b 38. G&C Coll Cam BA 61 MA 66 CEng MICE. Cuddesdon Coll 74. **d** 76 **p** 77. C Cowley St Jas *Ox* 76–80; P-in-c Ox St Giles 80–85; V Ox St Giles and SS Phil and Jas w St Marg 85–92; P-in-c Uffington w Woolstone and Baulking 92–93; P-in-c Shellingford 92–93; R Uffington, Shellingford, Woolstone and Baulking 93–03; rtd 03; PtO *Ox* 04–08; *Win* 10–14. *51 Chesil Lodge, Chesil Street, Winchester SO23 0AH* E: j.gawne-cain@ruralnet.org.uk

GAWTHROP-DORAN, Mrs Sheila Mary. b 37. Birm Univ CertEd. Dalton Ho Bris 68. **dss** 79 **d** 87. Halliwell St Paul *Man* 79–82; New Bury 82–89; Par Dn 87–89; Par Dn Tonge w Alkrington 89–94; rtd 94; PtO *York* 95–15. *35 Swarthdale, Haxby, York YO32 3NZ* T: (01904) 761247

GAWTHROPE, Julie Anne. b 57. **d** 10 **p** 11. C Cherry Hinton St Jo *Ely* 10–15; TV Albury, Braughing, Furneux Pelham, Lt Hadham etc *St Alb* 15–16; R Braughing, Furneux Pelham and Stocking Pelham from 16. *The Vicarage, 1 Pentlows, Braughing, Ware SG11 2QD* M: 07789-838084 E: julie.gawthrope@ntlworld.com

GAY, Adam Garcia Hugh. b 57. STETS 02. **d** 05 **p** 06. C Bitterne *Win* 05–09; V Hedge End St Luke 09–13; PtO from 13; *Portsm* from 13. *14 Sissinghurst Road, Fareham PO16 9YA* T: (01329) 237126 E: adamgay@totalise.co.uk

GAY, John Charles Nankervis. b 58. ERMC 03. **d** 06 **p** 07. C Wilton *B & W* 06–10; R Itchingfield w Slinfold *Chich* 10–14; TV Brixham w Churston Ferrers and Kingswear *Ex* from 14; PtO *Eur* from 17. *13 Warborough Road, Churston Ferrers, Brixham TQ5 0JY* T: (01803) 845692 E: revjohngay@gmail.com

GAY, John Dennis. b 43. St Pet Coll Ox BA 64 MA 68 DPhil 69 MSc 78. Ripon Hall Ox 64. **d** 67 **p** 68. C Paddington St Jas *Lon* 67–71; P-in-c 71–72; Chapl Culham Coll Abingdon 72–79; Lect Ox Univ 78–80; Dir Culham Inst 80–11; Research Fell Dept of Educn Ox Univ from 11; LtO *Ox* 72–15; PtO 15–18; Visiting Prof Win Univ from 14. *43A Bulmershe Road, Reading RG1 5RH* M: 07836-687452 E: john.gay@education.ox.ac.uk

GAY, Canon Perran Russell. b 59. St Cath Coll Cam BA 81 MA 85 Ex Univ PGCE 82 FRGS 97 Hon FGCM 15. Ripon Coll Cuddesdon BA 86 MA 14. **d** 87 **p** 88. C Bodmin w Lanhydrock and Lanivet *Truro* 87–90; Bp's Dom Chapl 90–94; Dioc Officer for Unity 90–94; Can Res and Chan Truro Cathl 94–15; Prec 01–15; Dir of Tr *Truro* 94–99; Chapl Epiphany Ho 06–15; Chapl Is of Scilly from 15. *The Chaplaincy, Church Road, St Mary's, Isles of Scilly TR21 0NA* T: (01720) 423911 E: perran@perrangay.com *or* chaplain@scilly.church

GAY, Stuart. b 66. Oak Hill Th Coll BA 94. **d** 00 **p** 01. C Sunningdale *Ox* 00–04; V Margate St Phil *Cant* from 04. *St Philip's Church, Summerfield Road, Cliftonville, Margate CT9 3JJ* T: (01843) 231825 E: vicarstphilips@btconnect.com

GAYFORD, John. b 37. Lon Univ BDS 61 MB, BS 65 MD 78 Nottm Univ MA 13 FDSRCS 64 FRCPsych 86 Heythrop Coll Lon MA 05 Univ of Wales (Lamp) MTh 09. St Jo Sem Wonersh 02. **d** 03 **p** 04. NSM E Grinstead St Mary *Chich* from 03; PtO *S'wark* from 13. *Third Acre, 217 Smallfield Road, Horley RH6 9LR* T: (01342) 842752

GAYLE, Steve Anthony. b 74. Univ of W Indies BA 03 Heythrop Coll Lon MA 09. Ripon Coll Cuddesdon 13. **d** 15 **p** 16. C S Hackney St Jo w Ch Ch *Lon* 15–18; V Stoke Newington Common St Mich from 18. *St Michael's Vicarage, 55 Fountayne Road, London N16 7ED* M: 07903-175038 E: steveagayle@yahoo.com

GAYLER, Canon Roger Kenneth. b 44. Lich Th Coll 68. **d** 70 **p** 71. C Chingford St Anne *Chelmsf* 70–75; P-in-c Marks Gate 75–81; V 81–14; RD Barking and Dagenham 04–13; Hon Can Chelmsf Cathl 01–14; rtd 14; PtO *Chelmsf* 14–19; V Lambourne w Abridge and Stapleford Abbotts *Chelmsf* 14–19; TV Vale of Roding 19–20; PtO from 21. *35 Lancaster Road, North Weald, Epping CM16 6JA* E: rogergayler@btinternet.com

GAYNOR, Christopher Thomas. b 68. **d** 08 **p** 09. C Banbury St Fran *Ox* 08–13; V from 13. *26 Meadowsweet Way, Banbury OX16 1WE* T: (01295) 271403 E: allrevedup@hotmail.co.uk

GAYNOR, Mrs Mieke Aaltjen Cornelia. b 43. UEA BA 79. St Jo Coll Nottm 02. **d** 03 **p** 04. NSM Hambleden Valley *Ox* 03–09; C Wollaton *S'well* 09–13; rtd 13; PtO *Ox* from 13. *5 Lodge Close, Marlow SL7 1RB* T: (01628) 487012 M: 07856-844554 E: mieke.gaynor@btopenworld.com

GAZE, The Ven Sally Ann. b 69. SS Coll Cam BA 91 MA 95 Birm Univ MPhil 98 PGCE 92. Qu Coll Birm 94. **d** 96 **p** 97. C Martley and Wichenford, Knightwick etc *Worc* 96–00; C Crickhowell w Cwmdu and Tretower *S & B* 00–02; TR Newton Flotman, Swainsthorpe, Tasburgh, etc *Nor* 02–17; Dioc Fresh Expressions Facilitator 09–17; Hon Can Nor Cathl 15–17; Dean for Rural Miss Consultancy *St E* 17–19; Adn for Rural Miss from 19; Can Res St E Cathl from 19. *The Cathedral Office, Abbey House, 30 Angel Hill, Bury St Edmunds IP33 1LS* T: (01284) 748720 E: archdeacon.sally@cofesuffolk.org

GBEBIKAN, Canon Angela Maria Abike. b 56. Lon Univ MA 07. Westcott Ho Cam 02. **d** 04 **p** 05. C Norbury St Steph and Thornton Heath *S'wark* 04–07; P-in-c S Beddington and Roundshaw 07–08; V from 08; Asst Dir of Ords and Adv in Women's Min Croydon Area from 13; AD Sutton from 18; Hon Can S'wark Cathl from 16. *St Michael's Vicarage, Milton Road, Wallington SM6 9RP* T: (020) 8647 1201 E: gbebikan@cantab.net

GBONDA, Egerton Joe Fode. b 67. Univ of Sierra Leone BSc 94 MSc 03 E Lon Univ MA Heythrop Coll Lon MA. **d** 06 **p** 08. Sierra Leone 06–09; PtO *S'wark* 10–12; NSM Deptford St Jo w H Trin and Ascension 12–14; NSM Bermondsey St Kath w St Bart from 14; P-in-c 20–21; V from 21; Chapl HM Pris High Down from 19. *HM Prison High Down, High Down Lane, Sutton SM2 5PJ* T: (020) 7147 6300 M: 07882-872830 E: father.egerton.gbonda@gmail.com

GEARY, John Martin. b 52. LRSC 77. **d** 08 **p** 09. OLM Heywood *Man* 08–10; OLM Heywood St Marg and Heap Bridge 10–13; NSM Bagillt *St As* 13–16; NSM Flint 13–16; P-in-c Middlestown *Leeds* from 17. *The Vicarage, 6 Coxley Dell, Horbury, Wakefield WF4 5LF* T: (01924) 629269 M: 07753-462460 E: john@johngeary.co.uk

GEARY, Mrs Paula June. b 48. NUI BSc 69 HDipEd 70. CITC 06. **d** 06 **p** 07. NSM Movidy Union *C, C & R* 06–12; NSM Cork St Ann's Union 12–20; rtd 20. *Lehenaghbeg Farm, Lehenaghbeg, Togher, Cork, Republic of Ireland* E: pjgeary650@hotmail.com

GEBAUER, George Gerhart. b 25. Sarum & Wells Th Coll 71. **d** 73 **p** 74. C Portsdown *Portsm* 73–78; V Purbrook 78–91; rtd 91; PtO *Portsm* from 91. *52 St John's Road, Locks Heath, Southampton SO31 6NF* T: (01489) 575172

GEDDES, Peter Henry. b 51. Trin Coll Bris 84. **d** 86 **p** 87. C Blackpool St Mark *Blackb* 86–88; C Barnston *Ches* 88–92; V Haslington w Crewe Green 92–04; V Partington and Carrington 04–16; rtd 16; PtO *Ches* from 17. *3 Elms Park, Thingwall, Wirral CH61 9PJ* T: 0151-648 9776 E: rev.peter.h.geddes@gmail.com

GEDGE, Richard John Anthony. b 70. Bath Univ BEng 92 CEng 96 MIMechE 96. St Jo Coll Nottm MTh 09. **d** 09 **p** 11. C Much Woolton *Liv* 09–16; C Halewood and Hunts Cross 17; C Liv Cathl 17–19. *4 Thackmore Way, Liverpool L19 4AE* T: 0151-427 9553 E: rjagedge@gmail.com

GEE, Anne Alison. b 43. OBE 99. Man Univ MB, ChB 66. STETS BA 01. **d** 01 **p** 02. NSM Canford Magna *Sarum* 01–06; NSM Horton, Chalbury, Hinton Martel and Holt St Jas 06–13; P-in-c 11–13; NSM Witchampton, Stanbridge and Long Crichel etc 06–13; P-in-c 11–13; rtd 13; PtO *Sarum* from 14; *Eur* from 16. *14 Merley Gardens, Wimborne BH21 1TB* T: (01202) 285819 E: a.gee@doctors.org.uk

GEERING, Preb Anthony Ernest. b 43. Columbia Pacific Univ BSc. Kelham Th Coll 62. **d** 68 **p** 69. C Cov St Mary 68–71; NZ 71–75; P-in-c Brinklow *Cov* 75–77; R 77–81; V Monks Kirby w Pailton and Stretton-under-Fosse 77–81; R Harborough Magna 77–81; V Pilton w Ashford *Ex* 81–86; P-in-c Shirwell w Loxhore 83–86; R Crediton and Shobrooke 86–01; P-in-c Sandford w Upton Hellions 00–01; R Crediton, Shobrooke and Sandford etc 01; RD Cadbury 93–97; R Chagford, Drewsteignton, Hittisleigh etc 01–09; P-in-c 09–10; RD Okehampton 02–05; Preb Ex Cathl 02–09; rtd 09. *20 Iter Park, Bow, Crediton EX17 6BY* T: (01363) 881263 E: prebant43@gmail.com

GEILESKEY, Mrs Sarah Jane. b 73. ERMC 17. **d** 19 **p** 20. C St E Cathl Distr from 19. *Corner Mill, Hill Road, Westley, Bury St Edmunds IP33 3TR* T: (01284) 748720 E: curate@stedscathedral.org

GEISOW, Hilary Patricia. b 46. Salford Univ BSc 67 Warwick Univ PhD 71 Nottm Univ PGCE 94. St Jo Coll Nottm 01. **d** 03 **p** 04. C Linc St Faith and St Martin w St Pet 03–06; P-in-c Colsterworth Gp 06–08; P-in-c Peakirk w Glinton and Northborough *Pet* 08–16; P-in-c Etton

w Helpston and Maxey 08–12; rtd 16; PtO *Linc* 17–20. *73 Queens Road, Bourne PE10 9DR* T: (01778) 425842 E: hilary.geisow@btinternet.com

GELDARD, Preb Mark Dundas. b 50. Liv Univ BA 71 Bris Univ MA 75. Trin Coll Bris 73. **d** 75 **p** 76. C Aughton Ch Ch *Liv* 75–78; Tutor Trin Coll Bris 78–84; V Fairfield *Liv* 84–88; Dioc Dir of Ords *Lich* 88–07; C Lich St Mich w St Mary and Wall 95–07; P-in-c Wigginton 07–08; V 08–11; Preb Lich Cathl 00–11; rtd 11; PtO *Chich* from 12. *10 Fitzalan Court, Rackham Road, Rustington, Littlehampton BN16 2LE* T: (01903) 786665 E: mark.geldard2@btinternet.com

GELL, The Ven Anne Elizabeth. b 63. St Hugh's Coll Ox BA 85 MA 01 R Free Hosp Sch of Medicine MB, BS 90 Surrey Univ BA 01. STETS 98. **d** 01 **p** 02. C Headley All SS *Guildf* 01–05; V Wrecclesham 05–17; AD Farnham 10–17; Hon Can Guildf Cathl 13–17; Adn Wells and Can Res Wells Cathl *B & W* from 17. *6 The Liberty, Wells BA5 2SU* T: (01749) 685147 E: annegell@lineone.net *or* adwells@bathwells.anglican.org

GELLI, Frank Julian. b 43. Birkbeck Coll Lon BA 78 K Coll Lon MTh 82. Ripon Coll Cuddesdon 84. **d** 86 **p** 87. C Chiswick St Nic w St Mary *Lon* 86–89; Chapl Ankara *Eur* 89–91; C Kensington St Mary Abbots w St Geo *Lon* 91–99; rtd 03. *58 Boston Gardens, Brentford TW8 9LP* T: (020) 8847 4533 E: numapomp@talk21.com

GELSTON, Anthony. b 35. Keble Coll Ox BA 57 MA 60 DD 85. Ridley Hall Cam 59. **d** 60 **p** 61. C Chipping Norton *Ox* 60–62; Lect Th Dur Univ 62–76; Sen Lect 76–88; Dean Div Faculty 77–79; Reader 89–95; LtO 62–95; rtd 95; PtO *Dur* from 95. *Lesbury, Hetton Road, Houghton le Spring DH5 8JW* T: 0191-584 2256 E: agelston35@btinternet.com

GEMMELL, Canon Ian William Young. b 52. ALAM. St Jo Coll Nottm LTh. **d** 77 **p** 78. C Old Hill H Trin *Worc* 77–81; C Selly Park St Steph and St Wulstan *Birm* 81–83; V Leic St Chris 83–93; RD Christianity S 92–93; P-in-c Gt Bowden w Welham, Glooston and Cranoe 93–02; P-in-c Church Langton w Tur Langton, Thorpe Langton etc 93–99; P-in-c Church Langton cum Tur Langton etc 99–02; R Gt Bowden w Welham, Glooston and Cranoe etc 02–06; RD Gartree I 97–06; Hon Can Leic Cathl 03–06; P-in-c Welford w Sibbertoft and Marston Trussell *Pet* 06–12; P-in-c Foxton w Gumley and Laughton *Leic* 12–17; rtd 17; Hon C Foxton w Gumley and Laughton *Leic* 17; PtO from 18. *2 Marriott Drive, Kibworth Harcourt, Leicester LE8 0JX* E: budgemmell@mac.com

GENDALL, Stephen Mark. b 63. **d** 89 **p** 90. Lundi St Apollos Zimbabwe 89–01; Youth Chapl 93–01; Can Cen Zimbabwe 00–01; V Lingfield and Crowhurst *S'wark* 01–12; Chapl Crowhurst Chr Healing Cen from 12. *Crowhurst Christian Healing Centre, The Old Rectory, Crowhurst, Battle TN33 9AD* T: (01424) 830204 M: 07752-063150

GENDERS, Canon Nigel Mark. b 65. Oak Hill Th Coll BA 92. **d** 92 **p** 93. C New Malden and Coombe *S'wark* 92–96; C Enfield Ch Ch Trent Park *Lon* 96–98; P-in-c Eastry and Northbourne w Tilmanstone etc *Cant* 98–03; P-in-c Woodnesborough w Worth and Staple 03–08; AD Sandwich 06–08; Min to Sandwich Secondary Schs 03–08; Dir of Educn *Cant* 08–12; C Margate H Trin 11–12; Hd of Sch Policy Bd of Educn and Dep Sec Nat Soc 12–14; Chief Educn Officer Abps' Coun from 14; PtO *Cant* from 12; Hon Can Cant Cathl from 20. *Church House, 27 Great Smith Street, London SW1P 3AZ* T: (020) 7898 1500 E: nigel.genders@churchofengland.org

GENOE, Simon Alfred. b 82. Stranmillis Coll BEd 06 TCD BTh 09. CITC 06. **d** 09 **p** 10. C Lisburn Ch Ch Cathl *Conn* 09–13; V 13–16; I Magheralin w Dollingstown *D & D* from 16. *12 New Forge Road, Magheralin, Craigavon BT67 0QJ* T: (028) 9261 1273 M: 07501-288941 E: simon.genoe@gmail.com

GENT, David Robert. b 71. Surrey Univ BSc 94. Qu Coll Birm BD 97. **d** 98 **p** 99. C Wotton-under-Edge w Ozleworth and N Nibley *Glouc* 98–02; Chapl Yeovil Coll and C Yeovil H Trin w Barwick *B & W* 02–08; Churches' Development officer for FE 07–08; P-in-c Martock w Ash *B & W* 08–14; P-in-c Kingsbury Episcopi w E Lambrook, Hambridge etc 13–14; V Martock w Kingsbury Episcopi and Ash 14–18; R Wrington w Butcombe and Burrington from 18; Asst Dir of Ords from 19. *The Rectory, 3 Alburys, Wrington, Bristol BS40 5NZ* T: (01934) 862348 E: david@rectory.org.uk

GENT, Emily Louise. *See* DAVIS, Emily Louise

GENT, Miss Susan Elizabeth. K Coll Lon LLB 78 Brunel Univ BA 95. Wycliffe Hall Ox MPhil 96. **d** 97 **p** 98. C Notting Hill St Jo and St Pet *Lon* 97–00; Chapl to City law firms 00–12; Hon Assoc P St Paul's Cathl 00–12; Dioc Visitor 01–12; P-in-c St Martin Ludgate 05–12; Tutor Trin Coll Bris from 12; Dioc Dir of Ords *Bris* from 20. *4 Worrall Mews, Clifton, Bristol BS8 2HF* T: 0117-968 2803 E: sue.gent@trinity-bris.ac.uk

GENTILELLA, Barbara Catherine. b 55. SEITE 05. **d** 08 **p** 09. NSM Shirley St Jo *S'wark* 08–12; NSM Addington from

12. *42 Devonshire Way, Croydon CR0 8BR* T: (020) 8777 4462 M: 07977-190155 E: bb2ke@sky.com

GENTRY, Michael John. b 66. St Steph Ho Ox BTh 95. **d** 98 **p** 99. C Bromley SS Pet and Paul *Roch* 98–02; V Langton Green 02–16; NSM Westerham 19–21; RD Sevenoaks 19–21; C Chelsfield w Green Street Green and Pratts Bottom from 21. *The Rectory, Skibbs Lane, Orpington BR6 7RH* T: (01689) 825749

GEOGHEGAN, Luke. b 62. SS Hild & Bede Coll Dur BA 83 Bedf Coll Lon MSc 87 CQSW 87 Bedfordshire Univ MA 13 FRSA 93. SAOMC 87. **d** 00 **p** 01. NSM Spitalfields Ch Ch w All SS *Lon* 00–03; NSM Gt Berkhamsted *St Alb* 03–05; NSM Gt Berkhamsted, Gt and Lt Gaddesden etc from 05; NSM Hemel Hempstead from 14; Warden Toynbee Hall 98–08; Visiting Prof Lon Metrop Univ 00–08; Chapl Ashridge Exec Educn from 08. *1 Clapton Terrace, London E5 9BW*

GEORGE, Alexander Robert. b 46. K Coll Lon BD 69 AKC 69. St Aug Coll Cant. **d** 70 **p** 71. C Newmarket St Mary w Exning St Agnes *St E* 70–74; C Swindon Ch Ch *Bris* 74–76; C Henbury 76–79; LtO 79–80; TV Oldland 80–88; C Ipswich St Aug *St E* 89; C Hadleigh w Layham and Shelley 89–90; P-in-c Assington 90–91; R Assington w Newton Green and Lt Cornard 91–00; P-in-c Hundon 00–03; Hon C 03–04; C Stour Valley 04–11; Dioc Moderator for Reader Tr 95–03; Asst Liturg Officer (Formation and Educn) 00–03; Nat Moderator for Reader Tr 04–08; rtd 11; PtO *St E* from 11. *103 Bixley Road, Ipswich IP3 8NP* T: (01473) 727351 E: alecrg@btinternet.com

GEORGE, Carole. b 64. St Mellitus Coll BA 19. **d** 18 **p** 19. NSM Sunbury *Lon* 18–21; R Shepperton from 21; PtO *Ox* from 19. *St Nicholas Rectory, Church Square, Shepperton TW17 9JY* M: 07786-880392 E: carolegeorge1@sky.com

GEORGE, David. b 64. Wycliffe Hall Ox 01. **d** 03 **p** 04. C Inkberrow w Cookhill and Kington w Dormston *Worc* 03–07; P-in-c Dudley St Jo 07–10; TV Kidderminster St Jo and H Innocents 10–16; P-in-c Cockington *Ex* from 16. *The Vicarage, 22 Monterey Close, Torquay TQ2 6QW* T: (01803) 391425 M: 07824-885561 E: revdavegeorge@gmail.com

GEORGE, Mrs Elizabeth Ann. b 33. Westf Coll Lon BA 56 Southn Univ MA 01. S Dios Minl Tr Scheme 84. **d** 87 **p** 94. NSM Basingstoke *Win* 87–05; PtO from 05. *71 Camrose Way, Basingstoke RG21 3AW* T: (01256) 464763 E: elizabethmgeorge@btinternet.com

GEORGE, Henderson Rudolph. b 44. Open Univ BA 80 Chelsea Coll Lon MEd 85. NTMTC BA 07. **d** 07 **p** 08. NSM Clapton St Jas *Lon* 07–11; NSM Enfield St Jas from 11. *12 Cowland Avenue, Enfield EN3 7DX* T: (020) 8804 9224 E: henderson.george@stjameschurch.cc *or* hendersonrgeorge@gmail.com

GEORGE, Nicholas Paul. b 58. St Steph Ho Ox 86. **d** 89 **p** 90. C Leeds St Aid *Ripon* 89–92; C Leeds Richmond Hill 92–96; Chapl Agnes Stewart C of E High Sch Leeds 93–96; V Leeds Halton St Wilfrid *Ripon* 96–02; V Camberwell St Giles w St Matt *S'wark* from 02. *St Giles's Vicarage, 200 Benhill Road, London SE5 7LL* T: (020) 7703 4504 M: 07771-603217 E: mail@nickgeorge.org

GEORGE-JONES, Canon Gwilym Ifor. b 26. K Coll (NS) 56. **d** 57 **p** 57. R Seaforth St Jas Canada 57–61; V Kirton in Lindsey *Linc* 61–71; R Grayingham 61–71; R Manton 61–71; V Alford w Rigsby 71–92; R Maltby 71–92; R Well 71–92; V Bilsby w Farlesthorpe 71–92; R Hannah cum Hagnaby w Markby 71–92; R Saleby w Beesby 71–92; RD Calcewaithe and Candleshoe 77–85 and 87–89; Can and Preb Linc Cathl 81–01; rtd 92. *42 Kelstern Road, Lincoln LN6 3NJ* T: (01522) 691896

GEORGE-ROGERS, Gillian Jean Richeldis. See WILLIAMS, Gillian Jean Richeldis

GERAERTS, Virginia Gwynneth. b 50. **d** 15 **p** 16. NSM Davenham *Ches* from 15. *The Old Coach House, 466 London Road, Davenham, Northwich CW9 8HW* T: (01606) 47111 M: 07709-049079 E: virginia_gray@hotmail.com

GERARD, Patrick Hoare. b 64. Man Univ BSc 86 MSc 88. Qu Coll Birm 04. **d** 06 **p** 07. C Solihull *Birm* 06–10; R Baddesley Clinton from 10; R Lapworth from 10; Bp's Adv for the Environment from 12. *The Rectory, Church Lane, Lapworth, Solihull B94 5NX* T: (01564) 782098 M: 07905-967930 E: patrick@gerard.net

GERD, Sister. See SWENSSON, Gerd Inger

GERMANY AND NORTHERN EUROPE, Archdeacon of. See NATHANIEL, The Ven Leslie Satianathan

GERRANS, Daniel. b 58. Em Coll Cam LLB 80 MA 83 Barrister-at-Law (Middle Temple) 81. SEITE 02. **d** 05 **p** 06. NSM De Beauvoir Town St Pet *Lon* 05–11; Chapl to Bp Stepney 07–11; V S Hackney St Mich w Haggerston St Paul from 11. *97 Lavender Grove, London E8 3LR* T: (020) 7249 2627 E: daniel.gerrans@xxiv.co.uk

GERRARD, The Ven David Keith Robin. b 39. St Edm Hall Ox BA 61. Linc Th Coll 61. **d** 63 **p** 64. C Stoke Newington St Olave *Lon* 63–66; C Primrose Hill St Mary w Avenue Road St Paul 66–69; V Newington St Paul *S'wark* 69–79; V Surbiton St Andr and St Mark 79–89; RD Kingston 84–88; Hon Can S'wark Cathl 85–89; Adn Wandsworth 89–04; rtd 05; PtO *Guildf* from 05; *S'wark* from 05. *15 Woodbourne Drive, Claygate, Esher KT10 0DR* T: (01372) 467295 E: david.gerrard@btinternet.com

GERRY, Brian John Rowland. b 38. Oak Hill Th Coll 69. **d** 71 **p** 72. C Hawkwell *Chelmsf* 71–74; C Battersea Park St Sav *S'wark* 74–77; C Battersea St Geo w St Andr 74–77; V Axmouth w Musbury *Ex* 77–86; R Upton 86–04; rtd 04. *49 Peasland Road, Torquay TQ2 8PA* T: (01803) 322788 E: gerry113@btinternet.com

GERRY, Ulric James. b 67. Bris Univ BEng 89. Wycliffe Hall Ox BA 96. **d** 97 **p** 98. C Hemel Hempstead *St Alb* 97–00; PtO 01–02; Crosslinks Tanzania 02–11; P-in-c Glas St Oswald 11–14; NSM Avondale Zimbabwe from 15. *20 Epping Road, Mount Pleasant, Harare, Zimbabwe* T: (00263) (77) 722 3432 E: ulricgerry@gmail.com

GETMAN, Elizabeth Jane. b 71. McGill Univ Montreal BA 94 Cape Town Univ MA 04 Kwazulu-Natal Univ PhD 15. **d** 07 **p** 08. C Hillcrest H Trin S Africa 07–09; C Pinetown St Jo 09–17; Chapl Durban Girls' Coll 09–12; NSM Ex St Thos and Em 18–20; Chapl Ex Hospiscare 18–20; Chapl Taunton Sch from 20. *2 Elmbarton Cottages, Staplegrove, Taunton TA2 6AN* T: (01823) 703751 M: 07748-438183 E: reveliza@gmail.com *or* eliza.getman@tauntonschool.co.uk

GHEORGHIU GOULD, Helen Elizabeth-Anne. b 65. Lanc Univ BA 87. St Mellitus Coll BA 10. **d** 10 **p** 11. C Epping Distr *Chelmsf* 10–14; C Nazeing 14–15; P-in-c 15–21; C Valle Crucis Miss Area *St As* from 21. *Address temp unknown* M: 07866-451744 E: h.gheorghiugould@btinternet.com

GHEST, Richard William Iliffe. b 31. Em Coll Cam BA 53 MA 57 Lon Univ BA 66. Wells Th Coll 53. **d** 55 **p** 56. C Weston-super-Mare St Jo *B & W* 55–57; India 58–63; C Holborn St Geo w H Trin and St Bart *Lon* 63–67; Ceylon 67–68; C Combe Down *B & W* 68–73; C Combe Down w Monkton Combe 73–74; R Tickenham 74–96; rtd 96. *120 Cottrell Road, Roath, Cardiff CF24 3EX* T: (029) 2048 1597

GIBAUT, Canon John St Helier. b 58. Toronto Univ BA 80. Trin Coll Toronto MDiv 84 ThD 94. **d** 84 **p** 84. P-in-c Mutton Bay Canada 84–87; C St Jas Cathl Toronto 87–94; Prof Th St Paul Univ Ottawa 94–07; Dir Faith and Order WCC 08–15; Dir Unity, Faith and Order Angl Communion Office 15–19; PtO *Lon* from 16; *Eur* from 16; Pres Thorneloe Univ Canada from 19. *Thorneloe University, 935 Ramsey Lake Road, Sudbury ON P3E 2C6, Canada* T: (001) (705) 673 1730 ext 101 *or* (705) 929 6784

GIBBENS, Gwyneth Andrea. b 52. Nottm Univ BA 73 PhD 78. WEMTC 07. **d** 10 **p** 11. NSM Kemble, Poole Keynes, Somerford Keynes etc *Glouc* 10–13; V Wotton St Mary 13–21; rtd 21. *1 The Gryphons, Pittville Circus Road, Cheltenham GL52 2GB* T: (01242) 221202 E: revgwynethgibbens@gmail.com

GIBBINS, Mrs Megan Ceinwen. b 59. Birm Univ MSc 03. St Jo Coll Nottm 12. **d** 14 **p** 15. C Selly Park Ch Ch *Birm* 14–18; R Ribbesford w Bewdley and Dowles and Wribbenhall *Worc* from 18. *57 Park Lane, Bewdley DY12 2HA* T: 0121-345 2277 M: 07896-499640 E: megan.gibbins@talk21.com

GIBBON, Matthew. b 79. Trin Coll Carmarthen BA 00. St Steph Ho Ox BTh 03. **d** 03 **p** 04. C Caerau w Ely *Llan* 03–05; C Aberavon 05–08; P-in-c Treharris, Trelewis and Bedlinog 08–11; P-in-c Treharris, Trelewis, Bedlinog and Llanfabon 11–16; P-in-c Aberaman and Cwmaman from 16. *St Margaret's Vicarage, Gladstone Street, Aberdare CF44 6SA* T: (01443) 410280 E: frmatthewgibbon@outlook.com

GIBBONS, David Austen. b 63. York Univ BSc 84. Ch Div Sch of Pacific 93 Ripon Coll Cuddesdon BA 94. **d** 94 **p** 95. C Ryde H Trin *Portsm* 94–97; C Swanmore St Mich 94–97; C Gosport Ch Ch 97–01; R Havant 01–08; R Barrington Hills USA from 08. *337 Ridge Road, Barrington IL 60010-2331, USA* T: (001) (847) 381 0596 E: dgibbons.stmarks@gmail.com

GIBBONS, Harvey Lloyd. b 62. Open Univ BA 12 York St Jo Univ MA 16. Ripon Coll Cuddesdon 97. **d** 99 **p** 00. C Verwood *Sarum* 99–00; C Gillingham 00–02; Dioc Voc Adv and P-in-c Upavon w Rushall and Charlton 02–07; R Warminster St Denys and Upton Scudamore 07–13; asst Dioc Dir of Ords 11–13; P-in-c Swindon All SS w St Barn *Bris* 13–18; P-in-c Swindon St Aug 13–18; V Oswestry *Lich* from 18; R Rhydycroesau from 18. *St Oswald's Vicarage, Penylan Lane, Oswestry SY11 2AJ* T: (01691) 662253 E: revdharvey@gmail.com

GIBBONS, Jayne Lisa. See LEWIS, Jayne Lisa

GIBBONS, The Ven Kenneth Harry. b 31. Man Univ BSc 52. Cuddesdon Coll 54. **d** 56 **p** 57. C Fleetwood St Pet *Blackb* 56–60; NE Sch Sec SCM 60–62; Hon C Leeds St Pet *Ripon* 60–62; C St Martin-in-the-Fields *Lon* 62–65; V New Addington *Cant* 65–70; V Portsea St Mary *Portsm* 70–81; RD Portsm 73–79; Hon Can Portsm Cathl 76–81; Dir Post-Ord Tr *Blackb* 81–83; Dir of Ords and Dir IME 4-7 82–90; Adn Lancaster 81–97; P-in-c Weeton 81–85; V St Michaels-on-Wyre 85–97; rtd 97; P-in-c St Magnus the Martyr w St Marg New Fish Street *Lon* 97–03; P-in-c St Clem Eastcheap w St Martin Orgar 99–08. *15 The Oaks, Taunton TA1 2QX* T: (01823) 271140 E: margyandken@btinternet.com

GIBBONS, Lissa Melanie. *See* SCOTT, Lissa Melanie

GIBBONS, Paul James. b 37. JP . Chich Th Coll 63. **d** 65 **p** 66. C Croydon St Mich *Cant* 65–72; V Maidstone St Mich 72–12; rtd 12. *19 Sterling Avenue, Maidstone ME16 0AY* T: (01622) 754812

GIBBONS, Ruth Banbury. b 91. York St Jo Univ BA 15. Cranmer Hall Dur 14. **d** 16 **p** 17. C Fulford *York* 16–18; C Dringhouses 18–21. *The Vicarage, 10 Clifton Crescent North, Rotherham S65 2AS* E: revdruthi@gmail.com

GIBBONS, Tobias Franklyn. b 89. Reading Univ BA 10 Ex Univ MA 11 St Jo Coll Dur BA 17. Cranmer Hall Dur 14. **d** 17 **p** 18. C York St Chad 17–21; C York St Clem w St Mary Bishophill 20–21; P-in-c Clifton St Jas *Sheff* from 21; C Whiston from 21; C Herringthorpe from 21. *The Vicarage, 10 Clifton Crescent North, Rotherham S65 2AS* M: 07507-524699 E: revtobygibbons@gmail.com

GIBBONS, Mrs Valerie Mary Lydele. b 49. St Aid Coll Dur BA 72 Solicitor 75. Wycliffe Hall Ox 98. **d** 03 **p** 04. OLM Cholsey and Moulsford Ox from 03. *Kilifi, Caps Lane, Cholsey, Wallingford OX10 9HF* T/F: (01491) 651377 E: val.gibbons@btinternet.com

GIBBONS, William Jacob. b 84. **d** 11 **p** 12. C E Carmarthen *St D* 11–12; C Carmarthen St Pet 12–13; P-in-c Newtown *Liv* 13–19; TR Wigan All SS 18–19; TV Wigan from 20. *22 Mabel Street, Wigan WN5 9EJ* E: willgibbons@hotmail.co.uk *or* hubleader.towncentre@churchwigan.org

GIBBS, Ann Margaret. b 59. **d** 17 **p** 18. NSM Porlock and Porlock Weir w Stoke Pero etc *B & W* 17–21; R from 21. *The Rectory, Parsons Street, Porlock, Minehead TA24 8QL* T: (01643) 863593

GIBBS, Mrs Claire Anne. b 76. York Univ BA 99 MA 01. Cranmer Hall Dur 12. **d** 13 **p** 14. C Evenwood *Dur* 13–17; C Cockfield 13–17; C Lynesack 13–17; P-in-c Stockton Country Par from 17. *The Rectory, Redmarshall, Stockton-on-Tees TS21 1ES* T: (01740) 631183 M: 07968-235688 E: protorevclaire@gmail.com

GIBBS, Colin Wilfred. b 39. Man Univ BA 62 Birm Univ CertEd 63. St Jo Coll Nottm 71. **d** 73 **p** 74. C Crowborough *Chich* 73–76; C Rodbourne Cheney *Bris* 76–77; C Bickenhill w Elmdon *Birm* 77–80; CF 80–96; Dir Ichthus Ho Homestay 96–06; Chapl Grenville Coll Bideford 99–02; P-in-c Cowden w Hammerwood *Chich* 06–10; PtO 12–17. *11 The Gorses, Bexhill-on-Sea TN39 3BE* T: (01424) 845299 E: fayandcolin@me.com

GIBBS, Donna Louise. b 66. Sarum Coll 14. **d** 17 **p** 18. C Ipswich St Mary at Stoke w St Pet and St Fran *St E* 17–20; TV N Lambeth *S'wark* from 20. *Address temp unknown* M: 07765-215661 E: donna.donnagibbs.gibbs@gmail.com

GIBBS (*née* DE ROBECK), Fiona Caroline. b 74. St Martin's Coll Lanc BA 96. St Jo Coll Nottm MA(TS) 99. **d** 00 **p** 01. C Bitterne *Win* 00–05; C Chandler's Ford 05–13; P-in-c Hedge End St Luke 13–19; V 19–20; AD Eastleigh 17–19; Hon Can Win Cathl 17–20. *Address temp unknown*

GIBBS, Mrs Fiorenza Silvia Elisabetta. b 49. SRN 71. St Alb Minl Tr Scheme 90. **d** 93 **p** 99. NSM Hitchin *St Alb* 93–96; NSM Pirton 97–99; Asst Chapl N Herts NHS Trust 99–00; Asst Chapl E and N Herts NHS Trust 00–02; Chapl 02–10; NSM Hitchin *St Alb* 10–16; NSM Hitchin and St Paul's Walden from 16. *12 Bunyon Close, Pirton, Hitchin SG5 3RE* T: (01462) 711846

GIBBS, Ian Edmund. b 47. Lon Univ BEd 69. St Steph Ho Ox 72. **d** 75 **p** 76. C Stony Stratford *Ox* 75–79; V Forest Town *S'well* 79–83; R Diddlebury w Munslow, Holdgate and Tugford *Heref* 83–12; R Abdon 83–12; rtd 12; PtO *Heref* from 12. *Dhustone Cottage, 10 High Street, Clee Hill, Ludlow SY8 3LZ* T: (01584) 890828

⌘**GIBBS, The Rt Revd Jonathan Robert.** b 61. Jes Coll Ox MA 89 Jes Coll Cam PhD 90. Ridley Hall Cam 84. **d** 89 **p** 90 **c** 14. C Stalybridge H Trin and Ch Ch *Ches* 89–92; Chapl Basle w Freiburg-im-Breisgau *Eur* 92–98; R Heswall *Ches* 98–14; Suff Bp Huddersfield *Leeds* from 14. *Stone Royd, 9 Valley Head, Huddersfield HD2 2DH* T: (01484) 900656 *or* 471801 E: bishop.jonathan@leeds.anglican.org

GIBBS, Marcus Timothy. b 73. UMIST BSc 95. Trin Coll Bris BA 10. **d** 10 **p** 11. C Northampton St Giles *Pet* 10–13; V Balham Hill Ascension *S'wark* from 13; Dir IME Kingston Area from 17; AD Tooting from 20. *5 Rossiter Road, London SW12 9RY* T: (020) 8675 8626 F: 8673 3796 E: marcus.gibbs@ascensionbalhamhill.org

GIBBS, Peter Winston. b 50. Ex Univ BA 72 CQSW 75. St Jo Coll Nottm. **d** 90 **p** 91. C Hampreston *Sarum* 90–94; P-in-c Ipswich St Matt *St E* 94–99; Assoc P Attenborough *S'well* 99–01; V Toton 01–08; TV N Poole Ecum Team *Sarum* 08–15; rtd 15; PtO *Sarum* from 16. *98 Weymouth Bay Avenue, Weymouth DT3 5AA* T: (01305) 570241

GIBBS, Canon Philip Roscoe. b 33. Codrington Coll Barbados 57. **d** 60 **p** 61. C St Jo Cathl Belize Br Honduras 61–63; P-in-c S Distr Miss 63–69; V Pomona St Matt 70–71; R Corozal Belize 71–74; Hon Can Belize from 71; V Stoke Newington Common St Mich *Lon* 74–87; R Johnsonville NZ 87–96; rtd 96. *13 Sim Street, Johnsonville 6037, New Zealand* T: (0064) (4) 478 2886 E: philip.g@actrix.gen.nz

GIBBS, Raymond George. b 55. NTMTC 94. **d** 97 **p** 98. NSM Becontree S *Chelmsf* 97–99; C Dedham 99–04; C Colchester St Mich Myland 04–08; P-in-c from 08; Area Youth Officer 04–08; C Colchester St Luke from 18; C Langham w Boxted from 18; C W Bergholt and Gt Horkesley from 18; C Wormingford, Mt Bures and Lt Horkesley from 18. *352 Mill Road, Mile End, Colchester CO4 5JF* T: (01206) 843926 E: raymond359gibbs@btinternet.com

GIBBS, Richard James. b 68. St Paul's Coll Chelt BSc 90. St Jo Coll Nottm MTh 01. **d** 01 **p** 02. C Southport Ch Ch *Liv* 01–05; Min Banks St Steph CD 05–12; C Southport St Phil and St Paul 12–16; P-in-c Elton *Ely* 16–20; V from 20; P-in-c Stilton w Denton and Caldecote etc 16–20; R from 20. *The Rectory, Church Street, Stilton, Peterborough PE7 3RF* T: (01733) 248701 E: stiltonvicar@hotmail.com

GIBBS, Stewart Henry. b 77. CCC Cam BA 98 MA PGCE 99 Anglia Poly Univ BTh 05. Ridley Hall Cam 02. **d** 05 **p** 06. C Grays North *Chelmsf* 05–10; R Hatfield Heath and Sheering 10–15; PtO 15–17; NSM Blackmore and Stondon Massey 17–18; P-in-c High Ongar w Norton Mandeville from 18. *The Vicarage, Church Street, Blackmore, Ingatestone CM4 0RN* T: (01277) 821464 *or* 366047 M: 07889-092559 E: parishoffice@parishofhighongar.org

GIBBS, William John Morris. b 71. Birm Univ BSc 94. Ripon Coll Cuddesdon BTh 00. **d** 00 **p** 01. C Staines St Mary and St Pet *Lon* 00–03; C Kensington St Mary Abbots w St Geo 03–06; V Redbourn *St Alb* from 06; RD Wheathampstead 10–15. *The Vicarage, 49 Church End, Redbourn, St Albans AL3 7DU* T: (01582) 791669

GIBLIN, Canon Brendan Anthony. b 64. K Coll Lon BD 86 AKC 93 Leeds Univ MA 95. Wycliffe Hall Ox 90. **d** 92 **p** 93. C Tadcaster w Newton Kyme *York* 92–96; R Stockton-on-the-Forest w Holtby and Warthill 96–02; P-in-c Middleham w Coverdale and E Witton etc *Ripon* 02–03; R 03–11; AD Wensley 10–11; P-in-c Wetherby 11–14; *Leeds* from 14; AD Harrogate 13–16; Hon Can Ripon Cathl from 19. *3 Lazenby Drive, Wetherby LS22 6WL* T: (01937) 520951 E: bgiblin@me.com

GIBRALTAR, Archdeacon of. *See* WALLER, The Ven David James

GIBRALTAR, Dean of. *See* TARRANT, The Very Revd Ian Denis

GIBSON, Catherine Snyder. b 39. Parson's Sch of Design (NY) 57. Ab Dioc Tr Course 81 Edin Th Coll 92. **d** 86 **p** 94. Colombia 86–87; NSM Aberdeen St Marg *Ab* 87–88; Dioc Hosp Chapl 88–92; C Aberdeen St Mary 93–94; Bp's Chapl for Tr and Educn 93–94; P-in-c Ballater 95–96; R 96–98; P-in-c Aboyne 95–96; R 96–98; P-in-c Braemar 95–97; Assoc P Fort Lauderdale USA 98–03; I Fermoy Union *C, C & R* 04–06; P-in-c Lugano *Eur* 06–07; P-in-c Dayton St Matt USA 09–10; Assoc P W Palm Beach 11–12; rtd 10; Dioc Supernumerary *Ab* 13–17; P-in-c Brechin *Bre* 17–18; Hon C Aberdeen St Jo *Ab* from 18. *65 Blenheim Place, Aberdeen AB25 2DZ* T: (01224) 611806 E: ecscanair@gmail.com

GIBSON, Charles Daniel. b 48. **d** 03 **p** 04. OLM Wisley w Pyrford *Guildf* 03–18; PtO from 18. *The Corner Cottage, Send Marsh Road, Ripley, Woking GU23 6JN* T: (01483) 225317 F: 223681

GIBSON, Colin Taylor. b 54. Trin Coll Cam BA 77. Oak Hill Th Coll 86. **d** 88 **p** 89. C Thrybergh w Hooton Roberts *Sheff* 88–91; P-in-c Tinsley 91–96; TV Attercliffe, Darnall and Tinsley 96–02; TR Walsall *Lich* 02–11; R Walsall St Matt 11–13; Hon C Walsall St Paul 05–13; Hon C Walsall Pleck and Bescot 05–13; V Horton and Wraysbury Ox from 13. *The Vicarage, 55 Welley Road, Wraysbury, Staines-upon-Thames TW19 5ER* T: (01784) 481258 E: vicar.hortonandwraysbury@gmail.com

GIBSON, The Ven Fiona Ruth. b 70. Homerton Coll Cam BEd 93. Oak Hill Th Coll MTh 11. **d** 11 **p** 12. C Bedford Ch St *Alb* 11–14; V Cople, Moggerhanger and Willington 14–21; Adn Ludlow *Heref* from 21; Preb Heref Cathl from 21. *The Archdeaconry, Corvedale Road, Halford, Craven Arms SY7 9BT* T: (01588) 673571 E: fiona.gibson@hereford.anglican.org

GIBSON, Canon Ian. b 48. Open Univ BA 85 Wolv Univ MSc 95 Liv Jo Moores Univ MA 09 FCIPD. S Dios Minl Tr Scheme 82. **d** 85 **p** 86. NSM Uckfield *Chich* 85–88; NSM Lt Horsted 85–88; NSM Isfield 85–88; V Fairwarp 88–93; P-in-c 94–00; NSM 00–04; V High Hurstwood 88–93; P-in-c 94–00; RD Uckfield 03–04; Bp's Dom Chapl and Research Asst 04–09; Acting Adn Lewes and Hastings 04–05; Episc V for Min and Bp's Sen Chapl 09–13; Can Res and Treas Chich Cathl 09–14; PtO *B & W* from 15; *Ex* from 15. *Windwhistle Down, Upton Lane, Seavington, Ilminster TA19 0PZ* T: (01460) 249566 M: 07843-672803 E: igchichester@gmail.com

GIBSON, James Campbell Ramsay. b 70. Southn Univ BEng 92 Cranfield Univ MSc 97 CEng 96 MIMechE 96. Trin Coll Bris 10. **d** 12 **p** 13. C Busbridge and Hambledon *Guildf* 12–16; V Hurdsfield *Ches* from 16. *197A Hurdsfield Road, Macclesfield SK10 2PX* T: (01625) 424587 E: jcrgibson@gmail.com *or* james@hthmacc.com

GIBSON, John Murray Hope. b 35. Dur Univ BA 58. Cranmer Hall Dur 58. **d** 60 **p** 61. C Chester le Street *Dur* 60–63; C Stockton 63–68; V Denton and Ingleton 68–75; V Swalwell 75–00; Chapl Dunston Hill Hosp Gateshead 80–93; Chapl Gateshead Health NHS Trust 94–99; rtd 00; PtO *Newc* from 01; *Dur* 01–13; *Glouc* from 14. *2 Cathedral Court, London Road, Gloucester GL1 3QE* T: (01452) 416397

GIBSON, Canon Noël Keith. b 22. MBE 89. Ch Coll Cam MA 48 Lon Univ BD 59. Coll of Resurr Mirfield 45. **d** 47 **p** 48. C S Elmsall *Wakef* 47–51; Antigua 51–56; Virgin Is 56–13; Can All SS Cathl 89–92; rtd 92. *College of St Barnabas, Blackberry Lane, Lingfield RH7 6NJ*

GIBSON, Canon Kenneth George Goudie. b 54. Glas Univ MA 83 Edin Univ BD 87 Strathclyde Univ PGCE 95. Edin Th Coll 83. **d** 88 **p** 89. C Glas St Marg 88–90; R E Kilbride 90–98; R Carnoustie *Bre* 98–07; PtO 08–14; P-in-c Monifieth 14–20; P-in-c Dundee St Mary Magd from 20; Can St Paul's Cathl Dundee from 19. *39 Durham Street, Monifieth, Dundee DD5 4PF* M: 07825-554419 E: kenneth.gibson1@btinternet.com

GIBSON, Laura Mary. *See* WILFORD, Laura Mary

GIBSON, Lynne Margaret. b 65. St Andr Univ MA 88 TCD BTh 10. CITC 08. **d** 10 **p** 11. C Dundela St Mark *D & D* 10–16; I Ballymacash *Conn* from 16. *St Mark's Rectory, 97 Antrim Road, Lisburn BT28 3EA* T: (028) 9266 2393 M: 07828-516799 E: lynnetigger@gmail.com *or* lynneballym@gmail.com

GIBSON, Nigel Stephen David. b 53. St Barn Coll Adelaide 84. **d** 87 **p** 87. C N Adelaide Ch Ch Australia 87–89; Lect Boston *Linc* 90–91; P-in-c Stamford St Mary and St Mich 91–92; P-in-c Stamford Baron 91–92; R Stamford St Mary and St Martin 92–98; PtO 98–00; V Kempston Transfiguration *St Alb* 00–04; Chapl Milan w Cadenabbia and Varese *Eur* 04–10; Chapl St Jo Cathl and P-in-c Pokfulam Em Hong Kong 10–16; P-in-c Lugano *Eur* 16–20. *Address temp unknown* E: frnigelgibson@gmail.com

GIBSON, Mrs Patricia Elizabeth. b 57. Nottm Univ MA 02. EMMTC 99. **d** 02 **p** 03. C Wigston Magna *Leic* 02–06; TV Gt Berkhamsted, Gt and Lt Gaddesden etc *St Alb* 06–10; Bp's Adv for Women in Min 07–10; PtO *B & W* from 21. *Combe, Luckwell Bridge, Wheddon Cross, Minehead TA24 7EJ* E: revteg1@gmail.com

GIBSON, Philip Nigel Scott. b 53. St Jo Coll Dur BA 78. Cranmer Hall Dur 79. **d** 79 **p** 80. C Yardley St Edburgha *Birm* 79–82; C Stratford-on-Avon w Bishopton *Cov* 82–84; Chapl SW Hosp Lon 84–91; Chapl St Thos Hosp Lon 84–91; Assoc P Newington St Paul *S'wark* 91–92; Chapl Charing Cross Hosp Lon 92–93; Chapl R Lon Hosp (Whitechapel) 93–94; Chapl Bedford Hosp NHS Trust 95–08. *Sillwood, 1 Wood Lane, Aspley Guise, Milton Keynes MK17 8EJ* E: philip.gibson912@btinternet.com

GIBSON, Samuel James. b 89. Birm Univ BA 11 MA 12 PhD 16. St Steph Ho Ox MTh 17. **d** 17 **p** 18. C Solihull *Birm* 17–20; V Edgbaston St Geo from 20. *3 Westbourne Road, Edgbaston B15 3TH* T: 0121-454 9929 E: vicar@stgeorgesedgbaston.org.uk

GIBSON, Timothy John. b 80. Ex Univ BA 01 MA 02 PhD 06. SWMTC 12. **d** 14 **p** 15. Dir Reader Tr and Lay Educn SWMTC from 11; NSM Isle Valley *B & W* 14–18; PtO from 18. *Wayside, Hare Lane, Broadway, Ilminster TA19 9LN* T: (01460) 54182 E: timjohngibson@hotmail.co.uk

GIDDINGS, Mrs Jacqueline Mary. b 44. St Aid Coll Dur BA 67. SWMTC 91. **d** 94 **p** 95. C Plympton St Mary

Ex 94–02; rtd 02; PtO *Ex* from 21. *15 Glenwood Drive, Roundswell, Barnstaple EX31 3GD* T: (01271) 346324 E: anthonygiddings@btinternet.com

GIFFORD, David Christopher. b 53. Lon Univ BEd 75 Sussex Univ MA 85 Ox Brookes Univ BA 11. Ripon Coll Cuddesdon 08. **d** 11 **p** 12. Chief Exec Coun of Chrs and Jews 06–14; NSM Benson *Ox* 11–14; R Port Glas 14–20; R Bridge of Weir 14–20; R Kilmacolm 14–20; rtd 20; PtO *Heref* from 21. *2 The Firs, Bosbury, Ledbury HR8 1PS* M: 07403-740185 E: dgdavid706@gmail.com

GIFFORD, Ms Elizabeth Ann. b 47. St Kath Coll Liv CertEd 72 Open Univ BSc 96. STETS 99. **d** 02 **p** 09. NSM Trowbridge H Trin *Sarum* 02–09; NSM Studley 09–16; PtO 17–18 and 20–21. *14 Innox Mill Close, Trowbridge BA14 9BA* T: (01225) 752756 M: 07903-269587

GIFFORD, Patricia Rose. b 47. **d** 10 **p** 11. NSM Glouc St Jas and All SS and Ch Ch 10–19; rtd 19; PtO *Glouc* from 20. *49 Ducie Street, Gloucester GL1 4NZ* T: (01452) 306746 E: patgifford@btopenworld.com

GILBERT, Anne Elizabeth. b 66. Liv Univ BA 88 Ches Univ MA 19 Bris Univ PGCE 89. All SS Cen for Miss & Min 15. **d** 18 **p** 19. C Dearnley, Wardle and Smallbridge *Man* 18–21; R Rochdale from 21; V Deeplish and Newbold from 21. *89 Clement Royds Street, Rochdale OL12 6PL* T: (01706) 346774 M: 07865-293827 E: revannegilbert@gmail.com

GILBERT, Anthony John David. b 54. Open Univ BA 91 LRSC 83 MRSC 01. Ripon Coll Cuddesdon 83. **d** 86 **p** 87. C Exning St Martin w Landwade *St E* 86–89; Chapl RAF 89–14; QHC 10–14; TR Three Valleys *Sarum* from 14; RD Sherborne from 18. *The Rectory, Church Road, Thornford, Sherborne DT9 6QE* T: (01935) 873044 M: 07810-760680 E: rector3valleys@gmail.com

GILBERT, Canon Barry. b 46. Leeds Univ BA 67. Coll of Resurr Mirfield 67. **d** 69 **p** 70. C Malvern Link w Cowleigh *Worc* 69–73; P-in-c Bromsgrove All SS 73–81; V 81–83; P-in-c Lower Mitton 83–88; V 88–92; V Stourport and Wilden 92–06; RD Stourport 93–00 and 02–06; P-in-c Brierley Hill 06–07; TR 07–11; Hon Can Worc Cathl 09–11; rtd 11; LtO *Glas* from 11. *Allandale, High Street, New Galloway, Castle Douglas DG7 3RL* T: (01644) 420665 E: barry_gilbert@talk21.com

GILBERT, Clive Franklyn. b 55. City of Liv Coll of HE CertEd 76 BEd 77. SEITE 01. **d** 02 **p** 03. C Paddock Wood *Roch* 02–06; V Dartford St Alb 06–11; V Watchet and Williton *B & W* 11–21; rtd 21. *15 Carthew Close, Liskeard PL14 3UQ*

GILBERT, Hilda. b 57. Lon S Bank Univ BSc 01 Spurgeon's Coll BD 11 RGN 82. St Mellitus Coll 13. **d** 14 **p** 15. NSM Leyton St Mary w St Edw and St Luke *Chelmsf* 14–18; NSM Walthamstow St Andr from 18. *13 Priory Avenue, London E17 7QP* T: (020) 8521 8048 M: 07946-407294 E: gilberhil@aol.com

GILBERT, Canon Howard Neil. b 73. Southn Univ BA 96. Ripon Coll Cuddesdon BTh 05. **d** 05 **p** 06. C Dulwich St Barn *S'wark* 05–08; C Cirencester *Glouc* 09–19; AD 15–18; R Minchinhampton w Box and Amberley from 19; Hon Can Glouc Cathl from 18. *The Rectory, Butt Street, Minchinhampton, Stroud GL6 9JP* T: (01453) 889004 M: 07887-800478 E: father.howard@gmail.com

GILBERT, Mark. *See* GILBERT, Philip Mark

GILBERT, Michael Victor. b 61. Dur Univ BA 84. Trin Coll Bris 92. **d** 94 **p** 95. C Chapeltown *Sheff* 94–97; V Brightside w Wincobank 97–07; Adult Educator Wilson Carlile Coll of Evang 07–12; R Baslow and Eyam *Derby* from 12. *The Rectory, Church Street, Eyam, Hope Valley S32 5QH* T: (01433) 639637 E: thegilberts@thegilberts.f9.co.uk *or* rector@eyamchurch.org

GILBERT, Patrick Andrew. b 71. New Sch (USA) BA 08. St Mellitus Coll 18. **d** 20 **p** 21. C Highertown and Baldhu *Truro* from 20. *17 Olivey Place, Bells Hill, Mylor Bridge, Falmouth TR11 5RX* M: 07706-415378 E: patrickgilbert5@icloud.com

GILBERT, Canon Philip Mark. b 62. Liv Univ BA 84. Coll of Resurr Mirfield 84. **d** 87 **p** 88. C Frodsham *Ches* 87–89; C Stockton Heath 89–92; R Tangmere and Oving *Chich* 92–01; Chapl Seaford Coll and P-in-c Graffham w Woolavington 01–09; P-in-c Chich St Wilfrid 09–10; V 10–15; Chapl Bp Luffa Sch Chich 09–15; RD Chich 11–15; P-in-c Petworth 15–16; R from 16; P-in-c Egdean 15–16; R from 16; RD Petworth from 16; Can and Preb Chich Cathl from 15. *The Rectory, Rectory Lane, Petworth GU28 0DB* T: (01798) 345278 M: 07810-004062 E: frmarkssc@msn.com

GILBERT, Raymond. b 34. AKC 61. **d** 62 **p** 63. C Newbold w Dunston *Derby* 62–66; PV and Succ S'wark Cathl 66–68; P-in-c Stuntney *Ely* 68–74; Prec and Sacr Ely Cathl 68–74; Min Can Cant Cathl 74–79; Hon Min Can from 79; P-in-c Patrixbourne w Bridge and Bekesbourne *Cant* 79–81; V 81–00; RD E Bridge 92–98; rtd 00; PtO *Cant* 09–16. *16 Green Acres, Eythorne, Dover CT15 4LX* T: (01304) 831485

GILBERT, Raymond Frederick. b 44. d 93 p 94. OLM Stowmarket *St E* 93–10; rtd 10; PtO *St E* from 10. *3 Violet Hill Road, Stowmarket IP14 1NE* T: (01449) 677700

GILBERT, Mrs Rebecca. b 76. Univ of Wales (Lamp) BA. Ridley Hall Cam. d 10 p 11. C Ely 10–13; C Three Rivers Gp 13–14; TV Lordsbridge 14–20; C Western Dales *Carl* from 20. *Address temp unknown* E: becgilb@gmail.com

GILBERT, Prof Robert John Crispin. b 74. Hatf Coll Dur BSc 95 Leic Univ PhD 99 Magd Coll Ox MA 05. Ripon Coll Cuddesdon 09. d 11 p 12. NSM Wolvercote and Wytham *Ox* 11–16; NSM Headington Quarry from 16; Fells' Chapl Magd Coll Ox from 14. *Magdalen College, High Street, Oxford OX1 4AU* T: (01865) 276070 E: gilbert@strubi.ox.ac.uk

GILBERT, Roger Charles. b 46. Ex Coll Ox BA 69 MA 74 Nottm Univ MEd 81. St Steph Ho Ox 69. d 71 p 72. NSM Bridgwater St Mary w Chilton Trinity *B & W* 71–74; NSM Rugeley *Lich* 74–81; NSM Cannock 81–83; NSM Wednesbury St Jas and St Jo 83–12; NSM Tividale 08–11; NSM W Bromwich St Pet 11–12; NSM Ettingshall 12–16; NSM Armitage 16; PtO 17–19 and from 21; NSM Wolverhampton St Martin and St Steph 19–21. *41 Stafford Road, Cannock WS11 4AF* T: (01543) 570531

GILBERT, Sean William. b 89. St Steph Ho Ox 12. d 15 p 16. C St Leonards Ch Ch and St Mary etc *Chich* 15–19; V S Norwood St Alb *S'wark* from 19. *6 Dagmar Road, London SE25 6HZ* M: 07535-445512 E: seanwgilbert@msn.com

GILBERTSON, The Ven Michael Robert. b 61. New Coll Ox BA 82 MA 92 St Jo Coll Dur BA 93 Dur Univ PhD 97. Cranmer Hall Dur. d 97 p 98. C Surbiton St Matt *S'wark* 97–00; V Stranton *Dur* 00–10; AD Hartlepool 02–10; Hon Can Dur Cathl 08–10; Adn Ches from 10; Chapter Can Ches Cathl from 17. *Church House, 5500 Daresbury Park, Daresbury, Warrington WA4 4GE* T: (01928) 718834 ext 253 M: 07921-040154 E: michael.gilbertson@chester.anglican.org

GILCHRIST, Gavin Frank. b 53. AKC 74. Coll of Resurr Mirfield 76. d 77 p 78. C Newbold w Dunston *Derby* 77–80; C Addlestone *Guildf* 80–84; V Blackpool St Mary *Blackb* 84–92; P-in-c Carl St Herbert w St Steph 92–97; V 97–01; V Tynemouth Cullercoats St Paul *Newc* 01–18; rtd 18. *1 Milton Close, Harrogate HG1 3NB* E: gg00217513@blueyonder.co.uk

GILDAY, Patrick Edward. b 84. Jes Coll Ox BA 05 MSt 07 DPhil 12 LRSM 02. Wycliffe Hall Ox BA 13. d 14 p 15. C Ascot Heath *Ox* 14–17; R Benson w Ewelme from 17. *Benson Vicarage, Church Road, Benson, Wallingford OX10 6SF* T: (01491) 201668

GILDER, James Bernard. b 85. JP 21. Magd Coll Cam BA 07 MA Middx Univ PGCE 11. Westcott Ho Cam 16. d 19 p 20. C Chingford St Edm *Chelmsf* from 19; Dioc Environmental Officer from 20. *44 Hurst Avenue, London E4 8DW* M: 07729-109638 E: jbgilder@hotmail.com

GILDERSLEVE, Paul. b 43. Lon Univ BD. Ridley Hall Cam. d 06 p 07. NSM Papworth *Ely* 06–17; PtO from 17. *Manor Farm, 14 Alms Hill, Bourn, Cambridge CB23 2SH* T: (01954) 713989 *or* 719318 E: paulg@miscom.co.uk

GILES, Andrew William. b 75. St Mellitus Coll 15. d 18 p 19. C Market Harborough and The Transfiguration etc *Leic* from 18. *49 Ashley Way, Market Harborough LE16 7XD* E: andy@harborough-anglican.org.uk

GILES, Anthony John. b 50. Aston Univ BSc 71 Surrey Univ MSc 78 Homerton Coll Cam PGCE 86 CEng 80 MIET 80. SAOMC 01. d 04 p 05. NSM Stevenage H Trin *St Alb* 04–09; NSM Norton 09–11; P-in-c High Wych and Gilston w Eastwick 11–15; R 15–17; RD Bishop's Stortford 14–17; rtd 17; PtO *St Alb* from 17. *8 Norton Road, Letchworth Garden City SG6 1AB* T: (01462) 620142 E: anthonyj.giles@ntlworld.com

GILES, Caroline Evelyn. See BECKETT, Caroline Evelyn

GILES, Christopher John. b 61. Westcott Ho Cam 14. d 16 p 17. C Pitsea w Nevendon *Chelmsf* 16–17; C Thorpe Bay 17–20; R Stourhead *St E* from 20. *The Rectory, Mill Road, Kedington, Haverhill CB9 7NN* T: (01440) 762901 E: stourheadbenefice@gmail.com

GILES, Canon Gordon John. b 66. Lanc Univ BA 88 Magd Coll Cam BA 95 MLitt 95 Middx Univ PhD 13. Ridley Hall Cam 92. d 95 p 96. C Chesterton Gd Shep *Ely* 95–98; Min Can and Succ St Paul's Cathl *Lon* 98–03; V Enfield Chase St Mary 03–20; Dir Post-Ord Tr Edmonton Area 08–19; Can Res Roch Cathl from 20. *The Chapter Office, Garth House, The Precinct, Rochester ME1 1SX* T: (01634) 843366 E: gordongiles@me.com

GILES, Graeme John. b 56. Linc Th Coll 82. d 85 p 86. C Prestbury *Glouc* 85–88; C Paulsgrove *Portsm* 88–96; V Friern Barnet St Pet le Poer *Lon* 96–04. *30A Vine Road, East Molesey KT8 9LF* M: 07981-708606 E: graeme@priest.com

GILES, Canon John Robert. b 36. Em Coll Cam BA 60 MA 65. Ripon Hall Ox 60. d 61 p 62. C Lowestoft St Marg *Nor* 61–65;

GILES, Peter Michael Osmaston. b 40. Solicitor 65. S Dios Minl Tr Scheme 85. d 88 p 89. Hon C Wootton Bassett *Sarum* 88–90; Lic to RD Calne 91–13; RD Calne 98–03; Chapl St Mary's Sch Calne 00–13; PtO *Sarum* from 14. *The Old Vicarage, Honeyhill, Royal Wootton Bassett, Swindon SN4 7DY* T: (01793) 852643 E: gilesoldvic@talk21.com

GILES, The Very Revd Richard Stephen. b 40. Newc Univ BA 63 MLitt 88 MRTPI 71. Cuddesdon Coll 64. d 65 p 66. C Higham Ferrers w Chelveston *Pet* 65–68; PtO *Ox* 69; C Oakengates *Lich* 70; C Stevenage St Geo *St Alb* 71–75; P-in-c Howdon Panns *Newc* 75–76; TV Willington 76–79; Bp's Adv for Planning *Pet* 79–87; V Pet St Jude 79–87; Par Development Officer *Wakef* 87–99; P-in-c Huddersfield St Thos 87–93; V 93–99; Hon Can Wakef Cathl 94–99; Can Th Wakef Cathl 98–99; Dean Philadelphia USA 99–08; rtd 08; PtO *Newc* from 09. *5 Lovaine Row, North Shields NE30 4HF* T: 0191-258 7621 E: tynegiles@talktalk.net

GILES, Sarah Jayne. See MORRIS, Sarah Jayne

GILES, Susan Jane. b 58. BSc. dss 83 d 92 p 94. Balsall Heath St Paul *Birm* 83–85; Asst Chapl Southmead Hosp Bris 86–90; Asst Chapl HM Rem Cen Pucklechurch 90–96; Asst Chapl HM Pris Bris 92–98; Chapl HM Pris Shepton Mallet 98–01; P-in-c Stockton H Trin *Dur* 01–09; P-in-c Stockton H Trin w St Mark 09–12; Chapl Ian Ramsey Sch Stockton 01–09; V Anglesey Gp *Ely* from 12; RD Fordham and Quy 17–20. *The Vicarage, 86 High Street, Bottisham, Cambridge CB5 9BA* T: (01223) 812726 E: suethevic@btinternet.com

GILES, Canon Timothy David. b 46. FCA 69. Oak Hill Th Coll 88. d 90 p 91. C Ipswich St Marg *St E* 90–94; C Reigate St Mary *S'wark* 94–99; P-in-c W Wickham St Jo 99–03; V 03–10; Hon Can Offa Nigeria from 06. *Lea Cottage, Hillhead Road, Kergilliack, Falmouth TR11 5PA* T: (01326) 377094

GILKES, Donald Martin. b 47. St Jo Coll Nottm 78. d 80 p 81. C Conisbrough *Sheff* 80–84; P-in-c Balne 84–86; P-in-c Hensall 84–86; TV Gt Snaith 86–88; V Whittle-le-Woods *Blackb* 88–02; V Normanton *Wakef* 02–12; rtd 12; PtO *Roch* from 12. *35 Tradescant Drive, Meopham, Gravesend DA13 0EL* E: don.gilkes1@gmail.com

GILKS, Canon Peter Martin. b 51. Nottm Univ BMus 72 SRN 77. Ripon Coll Cuddesdon 82. d 84 p 85. C Bitterne Park *Win* 84–87; TV Basingstoke 87–93; R Abbotts Ann and Upper Clatford and Goodworth Clatford 93–98; V Boyatt Wood 98–06; V Chilworth w N Baddesley 06–10; P-in-c Ampfield 08–10; V Ampfield, Chilworth and N Baddesley 10–15; TR Portway and Danebury 15–19; Hon Can Win Cathl 16–19; rtd 19; PtO *Win* 19–20; Ex from 20. *1 Bramble Lane, Crediton EX17 1DA* T: (01363) 777660 E: peter.gilks@ntlworld.com

GILL, Canon Alan Gordon. b 42. Sarum & Wells Th Coll 73. d 75 p 76. C Wimborne Minster *Sarum* 75–78; R Winterbourne Stickland and Turnworth etc 78–86; V Verwood 86–00; TR Gillingham 00–04; V Gillingham and Milton-on-Stour 04–08; Can and Preb Sarum Cathl 99–08; rtd 09; PtO *Sarum* from 09. *1 Cheshire Close, Salisbury SP2 9JT* T: (01722) 325239 E: erznmine1@gmail.com

GILL, Alec John. b 79. Trin Coll Bris 11. d 13 p 14. C Thatcham *Ox* 13–16; C Vale from 16. *The Vicarage, Winter Lane, West Hanney, Wantage OX12 0LF* M: 07954-433513 E: revalec@hotmail.co.uk

GILL, Mrs Carol Ann. b 42. Lady Mabel Coll TCert 71. NOC 96. d 99 p 00. NSM Hanging Heaton *Wakef* 99–07; P-in-c 02–07; rtd 07; PtO *Wakef* 08–14; *Leeds* from 14. *6 Queen's Crescent, Ossett WF5 8AU* T: (01924) 276821 M: 07946-038562

GILL, Daud. b 66. Punjab Univ BA 90. St Jo Coll Nottm 13. d 15 p 16. C Levenshulme *Man* 15–18; V Broadheath *Ches* from 18. *The Vicarage, Lindsell Road, West Timperley, Altrincham WA14 5NX* T: 0161-928 4820 M: 07513-913756 E: daudgill@hotmail.co.uk

GILL, David Alan. b 64. Coll of Resurr Mirfield 98. d 00 p 01. C Devizes St Jo w St Mary *Sarum* 00–04; P-in-c Brockworth *Glouc* 04–10; V 10–11; P-in-c Abenhall w Mitcheldean 11–17; R from 17; C Westbury-on-Severn w Flaxley, Blaisdon etc 11–17; C Huntley and Longhope, Churcham and Bulley 12–17. *The Rectory, The Stenders, Mitcheldean GL17 0HX* T: (01594) 542952 E: fr.d.gill@gmail.com

GILL, Preb David Brian Michael. b 55. Southn Univ BTh 88. Sarum & Wells Th Coll 83. d 86 p 87. C Honiton, Gittisham, Combe Raleigh, Monkton etc *Ex* 86–89; C Teignmouth, Ideford w Luton, Ashcombe etc 89–91; TV Ex St Thos and Em 91–05; RD Christianity 03–05; P-in-c Tamerton Foliot 05–17; C Southway 06–17; TR Tamerton Foliot and Southway from 17; RD Plymouth Moorside 09–15; RD Plymouth City 17–20; Preb Ex Cathl from 17. *The Vicarage, 53 Whitson Cross Lane, Tamerton Foliot, Plymouth PL5 4NT* T: (01752) 771033 E: dbmgill@tiscali.co.uk

GILL, Miss Helen Barbara. b 61. K Alfred's Coll Win BEd 87. Cranmer Hall Dur. **d** 99 **p** 00. C Newc St Gabr 99–04; P-in-c Tynemouth St Jo 04–17; V Byker St Silas from 17; P-in-c Byker St Mich w St Lawr from 20. *40 Heaton Grove, Newcastle upon Tyne NE6 5NP* T: 0191-276 5005 E: helenbarbara1999@hotmail.co.uk

GILL, Michael John. b 59. K Coll Lon BA 81 AKC 81 Univ of Wales (Cardiff) BD 85. St Mich Coll Llan 82. **d** 85 **p** 86. Min Can St Woolos Cathl *Mon* 85–90; Chapl St Woolos Hosp Newport 87–90; Succ Heref Cathl and C Heref St Jo 90–93; TV Ebbw Vale *Mon* 93–96; V Tonypandy w Clydach Vale *Llan* 96–09; R Cranford *Lon* from 09. *The Rectory, 34 High Street, Cranford, Hounslow TW5 9RG* T: (020) 8897 8836 E: fathermichaelgill@gmail.com

GILL, Paul Joseph. b 45. Melbourne Coll of Div MMin 07. Ridley Coll Melbourne 73. **d** 74 **p** 74. C Applecross Australia 74–76; C Birm St Martin 77–79; V Pype Hayes 79–89; Perm to Offic Perth Australia 89–93; R Perth St Paul 93–00; Sen Chapl HM Min of Justice 00–10; rtd 10; Hon C Heref S Wye 11–13; PtO from 13. *7 Camelot Close, Hereford HR4 9XH* T: (01432) 507146 M: 07765-660418 E: pandagill@talktalk.net *or* pandagill1@gmail.com

GILL, Peter Stephen. b 48. FCA 79. **d** 09 **p** 10. OLM Exning St Martin w Landwade *St E* 09–13; NSM 13–18; rtd 18; PtO *Ely* from 21. *11 Isinglass Close, Newmarket CB8 8HX* T: (01638) 660335 M: 07762-608031 E: petergill861@btinternet.com

GILL, Canon Robin Morton. b 44. K Coll Lon BD 66 AKC 66 Lon Univ PhD 69 Birm Univ MSocSc 72. **d** 68 **p** 69. C Rugby St Andr *Cov* 68–71; Papua New Guinea 71–72; Lect Th Edin Univ 72–86; Sen Lect 86–88; Assoc Dean Faculty of Div 85–88; P-in-c Edin SS Phil and Jas 73–75; P-in-c Ford *Newc* 75–87; P-in-c Coldstream *Edin* 87–92; Wm Leech Prof Applied Th Newc Univ 88–92; Mich Ramsey Prof Modern Th Kent Univ 92–11; Prof Th from 11; Hon Prov Can Cant Cathl from 92; AD N Downs 02–09; P-in-c Hollingbourne and Hucking w Leeds and Broomfield 03–11; Hon C 11–14; PtO from 14; Can Th *Eur* from 12; Ed *Theology* from 14; Acting Dean Gib *Eur* 17–20. *512 Royal Ocean Plaza, Gibraltar GX11 1AA* T: (00350) 200 67563 *or* (01227) 457762 E: r.gill@kent.ac.uk

GILL, Canon Ruth Montcrieff. b 48. CITC 01. **d** 04 **p** 05. NSM Cloughjordan w Borrisokane etc *L & K* 04–06; NSM Birr w Lorrha, Dorrha and Lockeen from 06; Can Limerick, Killaloe and Clonfert Cathls from 16. *Kilgolan House, Kilcormac, Birr, Co Offaly, Republic of Ireland* T: (00353) (57) 913 5341 M: 87-948 4402 E: ruth_gill40@outlook.ie

GILL, Miss Sandra Julie. b 67. N Riding Coll of Educn BEd 90 Rolle Coll MEd 01 Ex Univ BTh 08. SWMTC 03. **d** 06 **p** 07. NSM Kingsteignton and Teigngrace *Ex* from 06. *58 Furze Cap, Kingsteignton, Newton Abbot TQ12 3TF* T: (01626) 355287

GILL, Miss Sarah Siddique. b 77. Punjab Univ BA 96 MA 01. Qu Coll Birm 08. **d** 11 **p** 12. C Shipley St Paul *Bradf* 11–14; *Leeds* 14–15; C-in-c Bishop Auckland Woodhouse Close CD *Dur* 15–19; V Blackb St Steph and St Jas from 19. *St James's Vicarage, Cromer Place, Blackburn BB1 8EL* M: 07584-498390 E: sarah_siddique_gill@yahoo.co.uk

GILL, Simon David. b 66. Southn Univ BSc 87 PhD 91. St Jo Coll Nottm BTh 00. **d** 01 **p** 02. C Frinton *Chelmsf* 01–05; P-in-c Sudbury w Ballingdon and Brundon *St E* 05–19; RD Sudbury 16–19; P-in-c Long Stanton w St Mich *Ely* 19–21; P-in-c Over 19–21; P-in-c Swavesey 19–21; P-in-c Willingham 19–21; TR 5folds from 21. *The Vicarage, Horseware, Over, Cambridge CB24 5NX* E: simon@5folds.org.uk

GILL, Miss Susan Mary. b 62. Girton Coll Cam BA 84 MA 87 CPFA 91. Ripon Coll Cuddesdon 13. **d** 16 **p** 17. NSM Amersham *Ox* from 16. *137 Carver Hill Road, High Wycombe HP11 2UQ* T: (01494) 451485 M: 07779-575702 E: susangill01@gmail.com

GILL, Timothy Charles. b 66. Newc Univ BA 88 Jes Coll Cam MPhil 93 Leeds Univ PhD 08. Westcott Ho Cam 89. **d** 92 **p** 93. C N Hull St Mich *York* 92–96; P-in-c Sculcoates St Paul w Ch Ch and St Silas 96–98; P-in-c Hull St Mary Sculcoates 96–98; V York St Luke 98–02; R Adel *Ripon* 02–08; V Roby *Liv* 08–16; V Ecclesfield *Sheff* from 16. *The Vicarage, 230 The Wheel, Ecclesfield, Sheffield S35 9ZB* T: 0114-257 0002 M: 07853-293294 E: ttimgill@aol.com *or* tim.gill@sheffield.anglican.org

GILL, Preb Wilson Ernest. b 55. SAOMC. **d** 05 **p** 06. C Walton H Trin *Ox* 05–09; V Southall Em *Lon* from 09; Preb St Paul's Cathl from 20. *37 Dormers Wells Lane, Southall UB1 3HX* T: (020) 8843 9556 E: wilsongill37@gmail.com *or* vicar.ecs@gmail.com

GILLANDERS, Jill Margaret. b 56. St Hild Coll 16. **d** 18 **p** 19. NSM Thirsk *York* from 18. *Finkle Cottage, Little Thirkleby, Thirkleby, Thirsk YO7 2AZ* T: (01845) 501174

GILLARD, Canon David John. b 66. Lanc Univ PhD 20. Ridley Hall Cam 96. **d** 98 **p** 99. C Seaford w Sutton *Chich* 98–02; P-in-c Eastbourne St Elisabeth 02–06; V 06–21; RD Eastbourne 15–21; P-in-c Westham from 21; Can and Preb Chich Cathl from 19. *The Vicarage, 6 Rattle Road, Westham, Pevensey BN24 5DE* T: (01323) 762294

GILLARD, Linda Ann. b 53. York St Jo Univ BA 09. Yorks Min Course 15. **d** 17 **p** 19. NSM Marfleet *York* 17–18; NSM Kingston upon Hull St Alb from 18. *15 Rillington Avenue, Cottingham HU16 5HP* M: 07955-891226 E: linda.gillard@hey.nhs.uk *or* revlinz2609@gmail.com

GILLARD-FAULKNER, Mrs Sarah Kate. b 80. Coll of Ripon & York St Jo BA 01 Glos Univ PGCE 02. St Mich Coll Llan BTh 06. **d** 09. C Abertillery w Cwmtillery *Mon* 09–10; C Abertillery w Cwmtillery w Llanhilleth etc 10–12; PtO *Llan* 13–14; Dn and Sub-Prior Abergavenny St Mary w Llanwenarth Citra *Mon* 14–17; Bp's Chapl 14–17; Chapl HM Pris Onley from 17. *HM Prison Onley, Willoughby, Rugby CV23 8AP* T: (01788) 523400

GILLESPIE, Bridget Jane. b 62. St Hild Coll 17. **d** 19 **p** 20. NSM Kirkbymoorside w Gillamoor, Farndale etc *York* from 19. *Fir Tree House, High Lane, Beadlam, Nawton, York YO62 7SX*

GILLESPIE, Canon David Ivan. b 68. TCD BTh 01. CITC 98. **d** 01 **p** 02. C Agherton *Conn* 01–04; I Moy w Charlemont Arm 04–09; I Dublin St Ann and St Steph *D & G* from 09; Can Ch Ch Cathl Dublin from 14. *88 Mount Anville Wood, Lower Kilmacud Road, Dublin 14, Republic of Ireland* T: (00353) (1) 288 0663 *or* 676 7727 M: 86-026 7528 E: digillespie@eircom.net *or* vicar@stannschurch.ie

GILLESPIE, Jonathan Charles. b 64. NUU BSc 87 Cranfield Univ MSc 97 Oak Hill Th Coll BA 09 St Jo Coll Dur MA 17. Cranmer Hall Dur 14. **d** 16 **p** 17. C Windermere St Mary and Troutbeck *Carl* 16–20; P-in-c Stanmer w Falmer *Chich* 20–21; Asst Chapl Sussex Univ from 20. *St Laurence House, Park Street Falmer, Brighton BN1 9PG* M: 07951-922924 E: gillespie.jc@gmail.com *or* stlaurence.falmer@gmail.com

GILLESPIE, Michael David. b 41. EMMTC 86. **d** 89 **p** 90. NSM Countesthorpe w Foston *Leic* 16–18; NSM Four Saints 16–18; rtd 18; PtO *Leic* from 20. *3 Penfold Drive, Countesthorpe, Leicester LE8 3TP* T: 0116-278 1130 E: mick.gillespie@btinternet.com

GILLETT, Brian Alan Michael. b 42. MRICS 73. Chich Th Coll. **d** 82 **p** 83. C Tupsley *Heref* 82–86; R Kingstone w Clehonger, Eaton Bishop etc 86–97; V Baltonsborough w Butleigh, W Bradley etc *B & W* 97–09; Warden of Readers Wells Adnry 00–02; rtd 09; PtO *Bris* from 09; *B & W* from 15. *1 Barn Close, Somerton TA11 6PH* T: (01458) 272738 E: gillett546@btinternet.com *or* alary073@gmail.com

✠**GILLETT, The Rt Revd David Keith.** b 45. Leeds Univ BA 65 MPhil 68. Oak Hill Th Coll 66. **d** 68 **p** 69 **c** 99. C Watford St Luke *St Alb* 68–71; Sec Pathfinders and CYFA N Area 71–74; Lect St Jo Coll Nottm 74–79; Ch of Ireland Renewal Cen 79–82; V Luton Lewsey St Hugh *St Alb* 82–88; Prin Trin Coll Bris 88–99; Hon Can Bris Cathl 91–99; Suff Bp Bolton *Man* 99–08; rtd 08; Hon Asst Bp Nor from 08; Dioc Interfaith Adv 10–20; PtO from 13. *10 Burton Close, Diss IP22 4YJ* T: (01379) 640309 E: dkgillett@btinternet.com

GILLEY, Margaret Mary. b 54. St Andr Univ MTheol 76 Dur Univ PhD 97. NEOC 97. **d** 00 **p** 01. C Birtley *Dur* 00–03; P-in-c Stockton St Mark 03; V 03–09; V Elton 03–09; Assoc P Lanchester Deanery 09–11; V Bensham and Teams 11–20; rtd 20; PtO *Dur* from 20. *36 Albert Street, Durham DH1 4RJ* E: meg.gilley@btinternet.com

GILLHAM, Catherine Anne. b 73. Southn Univ BN 95. Trin Coll Bris BA 09. **d** 09 **p** 10. C Kempshott *Win* 09–13; CF from 13. *c/o MOD Chaplains (Army)* T: (01264) 383430 F: 381824 M: 07803-525602 E: catgillham@hotmail.com

GILLHAM, Martin John. b 45. Wilson Carlile Coll IDC 66 Qu Coll Birm 72. **d** 75 **p** 76. C Whitley Ch Ch *Ox* 75–78; TV Crowmarsh Gifford w Newnham Murren 78–79; TV Wallingford w Crowmarsh Gifford etc 79–83; V Kintbury w Avington 83–94; Dioc Lay Min Adv and Warden of Readers 89–97; P-in-c W Wycombe w Bledlow Ridge, Bradenham and Radnage 94–00; R 00; Prov Chapl Third Order SSF 95–99; P-in-c Norham and Duddo *Newc* 00–04; V 04–09; P-in-c Cornhill w Carham 00–09; P-in-c Branxton 00–09; AD Norham 05–09; rtd 09; PtO *Newc* 10–13; P-in-c Shilbottle 13–17; PtO from 17. *2 Duddo Farm Cottages, Duddo, Berwick-upon-Tweed TD15 2PS* T: (01890) 820533 E: martingillham@btinternet.com

GILLHAM, Mrs Patricia Anne. b 40. Wilson Carlile Coll IDC 66 Ox Min Course 90. **d** 93 **p** 94. Par Dn Kintbury w

Avington Ox 93–94; C 94–95; C W Wycombe w Bledlow Ridge, Bradenham and Radnage 95–00; rtd 00; PtO Newc from 00. *2 Duddo Farm Cottages, Duddo, Berwick-upon-Tweed TD15 2PS* T: (01890) 820533 E: gillysofduddo@gmail.com

GILLIAN, Patricia Julie. b 54. All SS Cen for Miss & Min 14. d 16 p 17. OLM Saddleworth *Man* from 16. *53 Burnedge Fold Road, Grasscroft, Oldham OL4 4EE* T: (01457) 870162 M: 07967-852149 E: patgillian54@gmail.com

GILLIBRAND, John Nigel. b 60. Ox Univ BA 82 MA 86 Lon Univ PGCE 83. St Steph Ho Ox BTh 87. d 88 p 89. C Dolgellau w Llanfachreth and Brithdir etc *Ban* 88–90; C Llanbeblig w Caernarfon and Betws Garmon etc 90–91; R Ffestiniog w Blaenau Ffestiniog 91–97; V Llandegfan w Llandysilio 97–02; Nat Co-ord (Wales) Nat Autistic Soc 02–04; P-in-c Llangeler w Pen-Boyr *St D* 04–10; V 10–16; V Llandeilo Tal-y-bont *S & B* from 16. *The Vicarage, 28 Bolgoed Road, Pontarddulais, Swansea SA4 8JE* T: (01792) 881965

GILLIBRAND, Margaret Ann Jane. b 43. d 01 p 02. OLM Deal St Leon and St Rich and Sholden *Cant* 01–04; PtO *Eur* 04–07; Asst Chapl Poitou-Charentes 07–09; NSM Whitstable *Cant* 11–13; rtd 13; PtO *Blackb* 14–17. *Address temp unknown* E: cornerstone161@yahoo.co.uk

GILLIES, Mrs Jennifer Susan. b 63. Westmr Coll Ox BEd 85. SNWTP 07. d 10 p 11. C Bidston *Ches* 10–13; R Bromborough from 13. *The Rectory, Mark Rake, Wirral CH62 2DH* T: 0151-201 9002 E: jennygillies@outlook.com

✠**GILLIES, The Rt Revd Robert Arthur.** b 51. Edin Univ BD 77 St Andr Univ PhD 91. Edin Th Coll 73. d 77 p 78 c 07. C Falkirk *Edin* 77–80; C Edin Ch Ch 80–84; Chapl Napier Tech Coll 80–84; Chapl Dundee Univ *Bre* 84–90; R St Andrews St Andr *St And* 91–07; Dioc Dir of Ords 96–07; Can St Ninian's Cathl Perth 97–07; Dean St Andr 07; Bp Ab 07–16; rtd 16; PtO *Ab* from 19. *4 Kilrymont Place, St Andrews KY16 8DH* T: (01334) 476738 E: ragillies1@gmail.com

GILLIES, Miss Sheila Jennifer. b 50. St Martin's Coll Lanc TCert 71. d 06 p 07. OLM Childwall All SS *Liv* from 06. *190 Thomas Drive, Liverpool L14 3LE* T: 0151-228 4304

GILLINGHAM, Michael John. b 46. Hull Univ MA 90. Chich Th Coll 68. d 71 p 72. C Llanharan w Peterston-super-Montem *Llan* 71–73; C Skewen 73–76; PtO 79–80; TV Kirkby *Liv* 76–77; Youth Chapl Woodchurch *Ches* 77–79; Sen Youth Worker (Bedfordshire) *St Alb* 80–83; PtO 80–83; TV Sheff Manor 83–88; R Frecheville 88–16; Chapl RNR 90–92; Chapl S Yorks Police *Sheff* 93–16; rtd 16; PtO *Sheff* from 16; *Derby* from 17. *14 Nethergreen Gardens, Killamarsh, Sheffield S21 1FX* T: 0114-327 7376 M: 07764-606456 E: mgillingham@talktalk.net

GILLINGHAM, Mrs Stephanie Ruth. b 60. W Lon Inst of HE CertEd 82 Open Univ BA 86 Man Univ MEd 06 Cliff Coll MA 15. NTMTC BA 09. d 09 p 10. C Galleywood Common *Chelmsf* from 09; P-in-c Widford 13–18; R from 18; C Moulsham St Jo from 13; C Moulsham St Luke from 13; Chapl Chelmsf Coll 13; Chapl amongst Deaf and Deaf-blind People *Chelmsf* from 19. *Widford Rectory, 3 Canuden Road, Chelmsford CM1 2SU* T: (01245) 477818 E: stephaniegillingham@hotmail.co.uk

GILLINGHAM, Prof Susan. b 51. St Jo Coll Nottm BTh 73 Keble Coll Ox PGCE 74 MA 80 DPhil 87 Ox Univ DD 15. d 18. C Ox St Barn and St Paul w St Thos from 18; Can Th Ex Cathl from 18. *43 Cranham Street, Oxford OX2 6DD* M: 07711-272076   E: susan.gillingham@worc.ox.ac.uk   *or* susan.gillingham@theology.ox.ac.uk

GILLINGS, The Ven Richard John. b 45. St Chad's Coll Dur BA 67. Linc Th Coll 68. d 70 p 71. C Altrincham St Geo *Ches* 70–75; P-in-c Stockport St Thos 75–77; R 77–83; P-in-c Stockport St Pet 78–83; TR Birkenhead Priory 83–93; V Bramhall 93–05; RD Birkenhead 85–93; Hon Can Ches Cathl 92–94; Adn Macclesfield 94–10; rtd 11; PtO Ches from 11; Hon C Rothiemurchus *Mor* from 11; Hon C Grantown-on-Spey from 11. *Culvardie, Deshar Road, Boat of Garten PH24 3BN* T: (01479) 831365 E: richard.gillings698@btinternet.com

GILLINGS, Mrs Ruth Elizabeth. b 63. d 12 p 15. NSM Atworth w Shaw and Whitley *Sarum* 12–18; Past Care Co-ord St Monica Trust Bris from 18; PtO *Bris* from 20. *St Monica Trust, Cote Lane, Bristol BS9 3UN* T: 0117-949 4000 E: ruthgillings@sky.com

✠**GILLION, The Rt Revd Alan Robert.** b 51. LRAM 73. Sarum & Wells Th Coll 81. d 83 p 84 c 14. C E Dereham *Nor* 83–86; C Richmond St Mary w St Matthias and St Jo *S'wark* 86–90; P-in-c Discovery Bay Ch Hong Kong 90–98; Chapl Shek Pik Pris 90–98; Bp Kensington's Officer for Evang *Lon* 98–01; P-in-c Upper Chelsea St Sav and St Simon 01–02; V 02–08; R Upper Chelsea H Trin 08–11; R Upper Chelsea H Trin and St Sav 11–14; AD Chelsea 04–11; Bp Riverina Australia 14–18; rtd 18; Hon Asst Bp Linc from 18; P-in-c Spalding St Jo w

Deeping St Nicholas 19–20; P-in-c Streatham Ch Ch *S'wark* 20–21; V from 21; Hon Asst Bp S'wark from 20. *Christchurch Vicarage, 3 Christchurch Road, London SW2 3ET* M: 07465-696419 E: robgillion@hotmail.com

GILLON, Patrick. b 51. WMMTC 05. d 08 p 09. NSM Kingstanding St Mark *Birm* 08–11; PtO *Lich* 11–14; NSM Small Heath *Birm* 12–13; Chapl HM Pris Birm from 13. *HM Prison Birmingham, Winson Green Road, Birmingham B18 4AS* T: 0121-598 8000 E: patrick_gillon2000@yahoo.co.uk

GILLUM, Thomas Alan. b 55. Ex Univ BSc 76. Cranmer Hall Dur 87. d 89 p 90. C Brompton H Trin w Onslow Square St Paul *Lon* 89–94; P-in-c Paddington St Steph w St Luke 94–04; P-in-c S Kensington St Jude 04–06; Warden Community of St Jude 06–11; P-in-c Isleworth St Jo 11–12; V 12–14; V Isleworth St Jo w St Mary 15–17; Bp's Dom Chapl *S'well* 17–18; V Nottingham St Mary Lace Market from 18. *20 Cavendish Road East, Nottingham NG7 1BB* T: 0115-958 2105 E: tom.gillum@stmarynotts.org

GILMARTIN, Frances. See CLARKE, Frances

GILMORE, David Samuel. b 70. Univ of Ulster BSc 92 QUB MSSc 95 Anglia Poly Univ MA 05 CQSW 92. EAMTC 01. d 03 p 04. C Basildon St Martin *Chelmsf* 03–04; C Danbury 04–08; R Soho St Anne w St Thos and St Pet *Lon* 08–10. *Address temp unknown* E: davidgilmore@btinternet.com

GILMORE, Canon Henry. b 51. Man Univ BA 72 TCD BD 82. CITC 75. d 75 p 76. C Arm St Mark w Aghavilly 75–78; C Dublin St Patr Cathl Gp *D & G* 78–81; I Stranorlar w Meenglas and Kilteevogue *D & R* 81–84; I Achill w Dugort, Castlebar and Turlough *T, K & A* 84–90; I Moville w Greencastle, Donagh, Cloncha etc *D & R* 91–11; I Tullyaughnish w Kilmacrennan and Killygarvan from 11; Can Raphoe Cathl from 01. *The Rectory, Ramelton, Letterkenny, Co Donegal, Republic of Ireland* T: (00353) (74) 915 1013 E: tkkgparishes@hotmail.com

GILMOUR, Miss Erin Victoria. b 81. Trin Coll Bris 17. d 19 p 20. C Reigate St Mary *S'wark* from 19. *3 St Clair Close, Reigate RH2 0QB* M: 07719-830624 E: erin.gilmour@live.co.uk

GILMOUR, Ian Hedley. b 57. Ex Univ LLB Lon Univ BD. Wycliffe Hall Ox 80. d 83 p 84. C Harold Wood *Chelmsf* 83–86; C Thame w Towersey Ox 86–91; V Streatham Vale H Redeemer *S'wark* from 91. *The Vicarage, Churchmore Road, London SW16 5UZ* T: (020) 8765 9923

GILPIN, Martin Leonard. b 49. Imp Coll Lon BSc 72 Magd Coll Ox DPhil 75. d 13 p 14. OLM Surrey Weald Guildf 13–19; PtO from 19. *Yendayar, Parkgate Road, Newdigate, Dorking RH5 5DX* T: (01306) 631485 E: martin.gilpin@btinternet.com

GILPIN, Canon Richard John. b 45. Lon Univ BSc 66. Wells Th Coll 67. d 70 p 71. C Davyhulme Ch Ch *Man* 70–71; Pastor Gustav Adolf Berlin EKD 74–77; R Heaton Norris Ch w All SS *Man* 77–83; R Chorlton-cum-Hardy St Clem 83–99; AD Hulme 95–99; V Norley, Crowton and Kingsley *Ches* 99–07; RD Frodsham 03–06; Hon Can Ches Cathl 04–06; rtd 07; PtO *Ches* from 08. *4 Smithy Close, Shocklach, Malpas SY14 7BX* T: (01829) 250413 E: dick@shocklach.plus.com

GILROY, Peter William. b 62. Univ of Wales (Ban) MTh 09. Ridley Hall Cam 09. d 11 p 12. C Stapleford *S'well* 11–14; TV Eccleston *Liv* 14–18; TV Binsey *Carl* from 18. *The Vicarage, Ireby, Wigton CA7 1EX* T: (016973) 71659 E: peterwgilroy@gmail.com

GIMSON, Francis Herbert. b 54. Reading Univ BSc 79. St Jo Coll Nottm 83. d 86 p 87. C Menston w Woodhead *Bradf* 86–89; C Barnoldswick w Bracewell 89–91; V Langleybury St Paul *St Alb* 91–02; P-in-c Downton *Sarum* 02–06; P-in-c Redlynch and Morgan's Vale 04–06; TR Forest and Avon 06–21; rtd 21. *Address temp unknown* E: fhg@jf1990.co.uk

GINEVER, Paul Michael John. b 49. AKC 71. d 72 p 73. C Davyhulme Ch Ch *Man* 72–75; Australia 76–77; C Tettenhall Wood *Lich* 77–80; C Halesowen *Worc* 80; TV 80–86; P-in-c Gt Malvern Ch Ch 86–98; V S Hayling *Portsm* 98–14; rtd 14; PtO *Portsm* from 15. *33 Cotton Road, Portsmouth PO3 6FL* T: (023) 9217 4692

GINGRICH, Dale Robert. b 64. Midland Lutheran Coll (USA) BSc 86 Lutheran Th Sem Gettysburg MDiv 93. EAMTC 03. d 04 p 05. NSM Shingay Gp *Ely* 04–08; TV Gaywood *Nor* 08–16; Dioc Ecum Officer 09–16; V Bloxham w Milcombe and S Newington Ox from 16. *St Mary's Vicarage, Church Street, Bloxham, Banbury OX15 4ET* T: (01295) 720252 M: 07982-627703 E: dalegingrich@hotmail.com

GINNELLY, Yvonne Anne. d 11 p 12. NSM Monkstown *D & G* 11–14; NSM Dublin St Ann and St Steph from 14. *Alexandra College, Milltown Road, Milltown, Dublin 6, Republic of Ireland* M: (00353) 87-699 8238 E: yvonneginelly@gmail.com

GINNO, Albert Charles. b 31. CA Tr Coll 51 Lon Coll of Div 66. d 68 p 69. C Kemp Town St Mark and St Matt *Chich* 68–72; P-in-c E Hoathly 72–83; V Westham 83–96; rtd 96; PtO *Chich* from 96. *106 Sorrel Drive, Eastbourne BN23 8BJ* T: (01323) 761479

GIRLING, Andrew Martin. b 40. Em Coll Cam BA 63 MA 67. Wycliffe Hall Ox 63. d 65 p 66. C Luton w E Hyde *St Alb* 65–69; Chapl Hull Univ *York* 69–75; V Dringhouses 75–00; Can and Preb York Minster 97–00; P-in-c Thurlestone w S Milton *Ex* 00–02; R Thurlestone, S Milton, W Alvington etc 02–08; rtd 08; PtO *Ex* from 08. *2 Mead Drive, Thurlestone, Kingsbridge TQ7 3TA*

GIRLING, Ian John. b 53. Oak Hill Th Coll 03. d 05 p 06. C Hubberston *St D* 05–08; TV Aberystwyth 08–17; rtd 17; PtO *St D* from 17; *B & W* from 17; *Eur* from 18. *22 Quantock Road, Weston-super-Mare BS23 4DT* T: (01934) 420411 E: iangirling@yahoo.co.uk

GIRLING, Stephen Paul. b 61. Southn Univ BSc 83. Trin Coll Bris BA 91. d 91 p 92. C Ogley Hay *Lich* 91–95; TV S Molton w Nymet St George, High Bray etc *Ex* 95–01; RD S Molton 97–01; V Crofton *Portsm* 01–15; RD Fareham 08–13; Hon Can Portsm Cathl 11–15; C Bath Abbey w St Jas *B & W* from 15; RD Bath from 20. *26 Castle Gardens, Bath BA2 2AN* T: (01225) 422462 E: spgirling@gmail.com or missioner@bathabbey.org

GIRLING, Canon Timothy Havelock. b 43. St Aid Birkenhead 63. d 67 p 68. C Wickford *Chelmsf* 67–70; C Luton w E Hyde *St Alb* 70–74; C Luton All SS w St Pet 74–80; Chapl Luton and Dunstable Hosp 74–80; R Northill w Moggerhanger *St Alb* 80–89; Chapl Glenfield Hosp NHS Trust Leic 89–00; Chapl Glenfrith Hosp 89–93; Chapl Univ Hosps Leic NHS Trust 00–04; Hon Can Leic Cathl 97–04; rtd 04; Chapl Leics Partnership NHS Trust from 04; PtO *Pet* 04–08; *Leic* 04–10; *Blackb* from 17. *5 Jefferson Close, Lancaster LA1 5EZ* T: (01524) 942113 M: 07947-026430 E: timothy.girling@gmail.com

GISBOURNE, Canon Michael Andrew. b 65. Leeds Univ BA 87 St Martin's Coll Lanc MA 09. St Jo Coll Nottm BTh 91. d 92 p 93. C Gateacre *Liv* 92–95; C Marton *Blackb* 95–98; V Freckleton 98–03; V Garstang St Thos 03–10; Chapl Cumbria Univ 10–11; V Scotforth 11–18; AD Lancaster and Morecambe 17–18; Can Res Ripon Cathl *Leeds* from 18. *St Wilfrid's House, Minster Close, Ripon HG4 1QP* T: (01765) 618536 E: canonmichael@riponcathedral.org.uk

GISBY, Mrs Vivien Barbara. b 56. Wolv Poly BSc 78 Leeds Univ BA 08. NOC 05. d 08 p 09. C Sutton St Jas *Ches* 08–14; V Runcorn St Jo Weston from 14; Warden of Past Workers from 11; Warden of Readers from 17. *St John's Vicarage, 225 Heath Road South, Weston, Runcorn WA7 4LY* T: (01928) 573798 E: vivien.gisby@btinternet.com

GISLESKOG, Catharina Irene Gunilla Margaretha Elizabeth Olsson. b 65. St Mellitus Coll 16. d 18 p 19. NSM Isleworth All SS *Lon* 18–20; NSM Hampton St Mary from 20. *28 Ashfield Road, London W3 7JJ* T: (020) 8740 8153 E: catharina.gisleskog@allsaints-isleworth.org

GISMONDI, Paul Arthur. b 55. Williams Coll Mass BA 77 Trin Hall Cam BTh 16. Westcott Ho Cam 14. d 16 p 17. NSM Sandringham w W Newton and Appleton etc *Nor* 16–20; NSM Upper Chelsea H Trin and St Sav *Lon* 16–19; PtO from 19; *Nor* from 20. *Ken Hill House, Lynn Road, Snettisham, King's Lynn PE31 7PG* T: (01485) 571111 M: 07770-500957 E: kenhillhouse@btinternet.com

GITTINS, Lawrence Bryn. b 66. Qu Mary Coll Lon BA 89 W Lon Inst of HE PGCE 90. Ripon Coll Cuddesdon 17. d 20 p 21. C Ludlow *Heref* from 20. *8-9 Mill Lane, Newcastle, Craven Arms SY7 8QN* T: (01588) 640829 M: 07786-625565 E: lawrence.gittins@talk21.com

GITTOES, Julie Anne. b 76. Trevelyan Coll Dur BA 98 Graduate Soc Dur MA 99 Selw Coll Cam PhD 04. Westcott Ho Cam 99. d 03 p 04. C Hampton Hill *Lon* 03–06; V Hampton All SS 06–12; Can Res Guildf Cathl 12–19; V Hendon St Mary and Ch Ch *Lon* from 19; AD Barnet from 20. *The Vicarage, 34 Parson Street, London NW4 1QR* M: 07702-151173 E: juliegittoes@gmail.com

GLADSTONE, Nicole Dominique Marie. b 72. St Hild Coll 18. d 21. NSM York All SS Pavement w St Crux and St Mich from 21; NSM York St Denys from 21; NSM York St Olave w St Giles from 21; NSM York St Helen w St Martin from 21. *Brownhills House, Holtby Lane, Holtby, York YO19 5XQ*

GLADSTONE, Canon Robert Michael. b 60. Ch Ox BA 82 MA 86. Wycliffe Hall Ox 92. d 94 p 95. C Trentham *Lich* 94–97; C Heigham H Trin *Nor* 97–01; V Rothley *Leic* from 01; AD Goscote from 06; Hon Can Leic Cathl from 10. *The Vicarage, 128 Hallfields Lane, Rothley, Leicester LE7 7NG* T: 0116-230 2241 E: rob.gladstone@btconnect.com

✠**GLADWIN, The Rt Revd John Warren.** b 42. Chu Coll Cam BA 65 MA 68. Cranmer Hall Dur. d 67 p 68 c 94. C Kirkheaton *Wakef* 67–71; Tutor St Jo Coll Dur 71–77; Dir Shaftesbury Project 77–82; Sec Gen Syn Bd for Soc Resp 82–88; Preb St Paul's Cathl *Lon* 84–88; Provost Sheff 88–94; Angl Adv Yorkshire TV 88–94; Bp Guildf 94–03; Bp Chelmsf 03–09; rtd 09; PtO *St Alb* from 10. *131A Marford Road, Wheathampstead, St Albans AL4 8NH* T: (01582) 834223 E: johnwgladwin@hotmail.com

GLADWIN, Thomas William. b 35. St Alb Minl Tr Scheme 78. d 81 p 82. NSM Hertford St Andr *St Alb* 81–82; NSM Digswell and Panshanger 82–86; C 86–96; rtd 96; PtO *St Alb* from 96. *99 Warren Way, Welwyn AL6 0DL* T: (01438) 714700

GLAISTER, James Richard. b 30. Oak Hill Th Coll 81. d 83 p 84. NSM Shrub End *Chelmsf* 83–85; NSM Lawshall w Shimplingthorne and Alpheton *St E* 85–87; NSM Lavenham 87–88; C Felixstowe St Jo 88–95; rtd 95; PtO *St E* 95–01; *Carl* 00–02; *Blackb* 02–05; *York* 20–21. *9 The Orchard, Fangfoss, York YO41 5SG*

GLAISYER, Canon Hugh. b 30. Oriel Coll Ox BA 51 MA 55. St Steph Ho Ox 51. d 56 p 56. C Tonge Moor *Man* 56–62; C Sidcup St Jo *Roch* 62–64; V Milton next Gravesend Ch Ch 64–81; RD Gravesend 74–81; V Hove All SS *Chich* 81–91; Can and Preb Chich Cathl 82–91; RD Hove 82–91; P-in-c Hove St Jo 87–91; Adn Lewes and Hastings 91–97; rtd 97; PtO *Chich* 97–03; LtO from 03. *Florence Villa, Hangleton Lane, Ferring, Worthing BN12 6PP* T/F: (01903) 244688 M: 07712-317118 E: h.glaisyer@virgin.net or exarch2005@gmail.com

GLANVILLE-SMITH, Canon Michael Raymond. b 38. Leeds Univ MA 95 AKC 61. d 62 p 63. C St Marylebone St Mark w St Luke *Lon* 62–64; C Penzance St Mary *Truro* 64–68; R Worc St Andr and All SS w St Helen 68–74; Dioc Youth Chapl 68–74; V Catshill 74–80; P-in-c Worc St Martin w St Pet 80–81; TR Worc St Martin w St Pet, St Mark etc 81–86; TR Worc SE 86–90; Hon Can Worc Cathl 83–90; Can Res Ripon Cathl 90–07; RD Ripon 96–97; rtd 07; PtO *Ripon* 13–14; *Leeds* from 14. *13 Ure Bank Terrace, Ripon HG4 1JG* T: (01765) 609428 M: 07792-014055 E: mglansmith@hotmail.com

GLASBY, Alan Langland. b 46. St Jo Coll Nottm 74. d 77 p 78. C Erith St Paul *Roch* 77–80; C Moor Allerton *Ripon* 80–81; TV 81–87; V Middleton St Mary 87–92; V Bilton 92–00; V Barton and Manfield and Cleasby w Stapleton 00–04; TR E Richmond 04–11; rtd 11; PtO *Ripon* 13–14; *Leeds* from 14. *23 Westwinn View, Leeds LS14 2HY* T: 0113-265 5992 M: 07970-712484 E: alanglasby@btinternet.com

GLASGOW AND GALLOWAY, Bishop of. See PEARSON, The Rt Revd Kevin

GLASGOW AND GALLOWAY, Dean of. See PRESTON, The Very Revd Reuben James

GLASGOW, Provost of. See HOLDSWORTH, The Very Revd Kelvin

GLASS, Caroline Mary. b 57. Southn Univ BSc 79 Open Univ MA(Ed) 01. Trin Coll Bris BA 06. d 06 p 07. C Redhill H Trin *S'wark* 06–10; V Tunbridge Wells St Luke *Roch* from 10. *St Luke's Vicarage, 158 Upper Grosvenor Road, Tunbridge Wells TN1 2EQ* T: (01892) 521374 M: 07910-066837 E: caroline.glass957@btinternet.com

GLASS, Mrs Yvonne Elizabeth. b 58. EMMTC 94. d 97 p 98. NSM Bingham *S'well* 97–00; Chapl Nottm City Hosp NHS Trust 00–11; rtd 11; PtO *Glas* from 12. *Coigach, Laurieston Road, Gatehouse of Fleet, Castle Douglas DG7 2BE* T: (01557) 814045 E: yvonne.glass58@hotmail.co.uk

GLASSPOOL, John Martin. b 59. Kent Univ BA 83 Heythrop Coll Lon MTh 95 Leeds Univ MA 05 RGN 87. Westcott Ho Cam 88. d 90 p 91. C Forest Gate Em w Upton Cross *Chelmsf* 90–93; P-in-c Theydon Garnon 93–95; Chapl St Marg Hosp Epping 93–99; TV Epping Distr *Chelmsf* 95–99; Asst Chapl R Free Hampstead NHS Trust 99–02; Chapl Surrey and Sussex Healthcare NHS Trust 02–18; rtd 19. *50 Talfourd Way, Redhill RH1 6GF* M: 07375-045390 E: glasspool59@gmail.com

GLEAVES, John. b 39. Alsager Coll of Educn CertEd 60 Westmr Coll Ox BTh 03. NOC 99. d 00 p 01. NSM Alsager St Mary *Ches* 00–03; P-in-c Alvanley 03–08; rtd 08; PtO *Ches* from 10. *46 Linley Grove, Alsager, Stoke-on-Trent ST7 2PS* T: (01270) 878169 E: rev.johngleaves@gmail.com

GLEDHILL, Alan. b 43. Lon Univ BSc(Econ) 73. NOC 81. d 84 p 85. C Knaresborough *Ripon* 84–87; P-in-c Easby 87–88; P-in-c Bolton on Swale 87–88; V Easby w Brompton on Swale and Bolton on Swale 88–96; Teacher St Fran Xavier Sch Richmond 96–08; PtO *Ripon* 96–08; rtd 08; Hon C Gilling and Kirkby Ravensworth *Ripon* 08–14; *Leeds* 14–18. *75 High Street, Gilling West, Richmond DL10 5JW* T: (01748) 824466 M: 07906-195390 E: gledhill356@btinternet.com

✠**GLEDHILL, The Rt Revd Jonathan Michael.** b 49. Keele Univ BA 72 Hon DUniv 07 Bris Univ MA 75. Trin Coll Bris 72. d 75 p 76 c 96. C Marple All SS *Ches* 75–78; C

Folkestone H Trin w Ch Ch *Cant* 78–83; V Cant St Mary Bredin 83–96; Tutor Cant Sch of Min 83–96; RD Cant 88–94; Hon Can Cant Cathl 92–96; Suff Bp Southampton *Win* 96–03; Bp Lich 03–15; rtd 15; PtO *Cant* 16–19. *16 Cherry Garden Road, Canterbury CT2 8EL* T: (01227) 765062 E: jonathan.gledhill68@gmail.com

GLEDHILL, Miss Rachael Elizabeth. b 93. Ch Ch Ox BA 15 MA 20 Pemb Coll Cam BA 19 K Coll Cam MPhil 20. Westcott Ho Cam 17 St Mellitus Coll 19. d 20 p 21. C Dulwich St Barn *S'wark* from 20. *70 Frankfurt Road, London SE24 9NY* M: 07447-419003 E: rachaelgledhill@hotmail.com

GLEGHORN, Timothy. b 69. York Univ BA 92. St Jo Coll Nottm 10. d 12 p 13. C Win Ch Ch 12–16; R Bath Walcot *B & W* from 17. *Swallowgate, Lansdown Road, Bath BA1 5TD* T: (01225) 423013 M: 07754-801151 E: tim@stswithinswalcot.org.uk

GLEN, Mrs Dawn Andrea. b 64. Liv Univ BA 86. Westcott Ho Cam 07. d 09 p 10. C Derby Cathl 09–11; C Kirk Langley 11–15; C Mackworth All SS 11–15; C Mugginton and Kedleston 11–15; C Brailsford w Shirley, Osmaston w Edlaston etc 15–16; PtO from 17; S'well from 16. *41 Letchworth Crescent, Beeston, Nottingham NG9 5LL* T: 0115-783 8103 E: revdawnglen@gmail.com

✠**GLENFIELD, The Rt Revd Samuel Ferran.** b 54. QUB BA 76 TCD MLitt 90 MA 94 Ox Univ MTh 99. Wycliffe Hall Ox 88. d 91 p 92 c 13. C Douglas Union w Frankfield *C, C & R* 91–94; I Rathcooney Union 94–96; I Kill *D & G* 96–12; I Hillsborough *D & D* 12–13; Bp K, E & A from 13. *The See House, Kilmore, Cavan, Republic of Ireland* T: (00353) (49) 437 1551 E: bishop@kilmore.anglican.org

GLENNY, Robert Michael. b 90. d 14 p 15. C Marston w Elsfield *Ox* 14–17; R Radley, Sunningwell and Kennington from 17. *The Vicarage, Kennington Road, Radley, Abingdon OX14 2JN* T: (01235) 554739 M: 07871-644811 E: robertglenny@gmail.com

GLEW, Mark Roy. b 78. Bris Univ BSc 99 ACA 03. Oak Hill Th Coll BA 12. d 13 p 14. C Rusholme H Trin *Man* 13–17; P-in-c Haughton St Mary 17–19; R from 19. *St Mary's Rectory, Meadow Lane, Denton, Manchester M34 7GD* T: 0161-336 4529 E: markglew@hotmail.com *or* smhg.church@virginmedia.com

GLIDDON, Andrew James. b 86. LSE BSc 09 Nottm Trent Univ LLB 11. Trin Coll Bris MA 17. d 17 p 18. C Luton Lewsey St Hugh *St Alb* 17–20; C Woodside Park St Barn *Lon* from 20. *610 High Road, London N12 0AA* M: 07746-212304 E: andrew@thegliddons.co.uk

GLITHERO, Mrs Helen Elizabeth. b 60. Nottm Univ BA 81 CQSW 83. Qu Coll Birm 11. d 14 p 15. NSM Highters Heath *Birm* 14–17; PtO from 17. *61 Stonerwood Avenue, Birmingham B28 0AX* T: 0121-778 3925 E: hglithero@btinternet.com *or* revdhelen@icloud.com

GLOSSOP, Jonathan Mark. b 55. Open Univ BA 91 Bradf Univ MA 93 Eaton Hall Coll of Educn CertEd 76. Linc Sch of Th and Min 10. d 14 p 15. OLM Immingham *Linc* from 14. *23 Pilgrims Way, Immingham DN40 2HD* T: (01469) 574522 E: jmseglossop@tiscali.co.uk

GLOUCESTER, Archdeacon of. See DAWSON, The Ven Hilary Joan

GLOUCESTER, Bishop of. See TREWEEK, The Rt Revd Rachel

GLOUCESTER, Dean of. See LAKE, The Very Revd Stephen David

GLOVER, Alan. b 47. SWMTC 96. d 99 p 00. NSM Bideford, Northam, Westward Ho!, Appledore etc *Ex* 99–17; NSM Bideford, Landcross, Littleham etc from 17. *West Fordlands, Heywood Road, Northam, Bideford EX39 3QA* T: (01237) 479542 E: alanglover2014@gmail.com

GLOVER, Clare-Jane. b 72. Leic Univ BSc 93 MB, ChB 96. Ripon Coll Cuddesdon 18. d 21. C Kettering SS Pet and Paul from 21; C Kettering All SS from 21. *7 Heritage Court, Kettering NN16 0DU* E: clarejane.glover@icloud.com

GLOVER, David Charles. b 66. St Jo Coll Dur BA 87 St Jo Coll Cam MPhil 91. Ridley Hall Cam 87. d 90 p 91. C Wath-upon-Dearne w Adwick-upon-Dearne *Sheff* 90–92; Chapl Hatf Coll Dur 92–00; P-in-c Dur St Marg 95–00; R Dur St Marg and Neville's Cross St Jo 00–05; P-in-c Washington 05–07; R 07–20; AD Chester-le-Street 08–18; AD Chester le Street and Houghton 18–20; Hon Can Dur Cathl 11–20; R Hexham *Newc* from 20; Chapl to The Queen from 17. *The Rectory, Eilansgate, Hexham NE46 3EW* T: (01434) 602031 M: 07886-289311 E: rector@hexhamabbey.org.uk

GLOVER, Mrs Diana Mary. b 50. Kent Univ BA 73 MA 75. SAOMC. d 01 p 02. C Aylesbury *Ox* 01–05; P-in-c Amersham on the Hill 05–08; V 08–15; rtd 15; PtO *Ox* from 15. *11 Hamilton Close, Bicester OX26 2HX* E: diana.glover@btinternet.com

GLOVER, Elisabeth Ann. b 53. Univ Coll Ches BTh 99. d 98 p 99. NSM Thurstaston *Ches* 98–99; C Stockton Heath 00–04; V Eastham from 04; RD Wirral S from 13. *The Vicarage, 29 Ferry Road, Eastham, Wirral CH62 0AJ* T: 0151-327 2182

GLOVER, Janet Mary. b 58. Natal Univ BSc 79 UED 80 Anglia Ruskin Univ MA 05. EAMTC 98. d 01 p 02. NSM Cambridge St Phil *Ely* 01–04; NSM Histon 04–14; NSM Impington 04–14; Hon Asst Dir of Ords 07–18 and from 20; NSM Deanery of N Stowe from 15. *139 Waterbeach Road, Landbeach, Cambridge CB25 9FA* T: (01223) 864931 E: janet@theglovers.name

GLOVER, Canon John. b 48. DL . Kelham Th Coll 67. d 71 p 72. C Foley Park *Worc* 71–75; TV Sutton *Liv* 75–79; P-in-c Churchill w Blakedown *Worc* 79–84; R 84–87; R Belbroughton w Fairfield and Clent 87–91; Chapl Children's Family Trust 91–13; NSM Flint St As 92–93; R Halkyn w Caerfallwch w Rhesycae 93–97; V Rhyl w St Ann 97–13; Can Cursal St As Cathl 02–08; Sacr 08–13; rtd 13; PtO *St As* from 15. *Bryn Oswald, James Park, Dyserth, Rhyl LL18 6AG* T: (01745) 571473 E: gloverjohn@btinternet.com

GLOVER, Canon Judith Rosalind. b 53. NEOC 93. d 95 p 96. C Glendale Gp *Newc* 95–99; P-in-c Alwinton w Holystone and Alnham 99–04; R Upper Coquetdale 04–09; R Alston Moor 09–13; V Beadnell 13–18; V N Sunderland 13–18; AD Bamburgh and Glendale 16–18; Hon Can Newc Cathl 10–18; rtd 18; PtO *Newc* from 18. *The Hemmel, Ellingham, Chathill NE67 5EU* T: (01665) 589628 E: judyglover432@btinternet.com

GLOVER, Richard John. b 47. Nottm Univ BTh 77. Linc Th Coll 73. d 77 p 78. C Barrow St Geo w St Luke *Carl* 77–79; C Netherton 79–80; P-in-c Addingham 80–83; P-in-c Edenhall w Langwathby and Culgaith 80–83; V Addingham, Edenhall, Langwathby and Culgaith 83–84; V Bishops Hull *B & W* 84–89; V Shilbottle *Newc* 89–96; V Whittingham and Edlingham w Bolton Chapel 96–00; P-in-c Barton, Pooley Bridge and Martindale *Carl* 00–04; Dioc Adv for Spiritual Direction and Healing 00–04; R Lower Swale *Ripon* 04–12; rtd 13; PtO *York* from 13. *45 Grovehill Road, Filey YO14 9NL*

GLOVER, Thomas Edward. b 85. Grey Coll Dur BA 06 Clare Coll Cam BA 09. Westcott Ho Cam 07. d 10 p 11. C Dur N 10–14; R Winlaton 14–18; AD Gateshead W 17–18; P-in-c Dur St Giles 18–21; P-in-c Shadforth and Sherburn 18–21. *Address temp unknown* M: 07711-576522 E: vicarofsgss@gmail.com

GLYN, Aneirin. b 75. St Hugh's Coll Ox MMath 98 DPhil 02. Oak Hill Th Coll MTh 09. d 09 p 10. C St Helen Bishopsgate w St Andr Undershaft etc *Lon* from 09; P-in-c St Benet Paul's Wharf from 11. *28 Sharon Gardens, London E9 7RX* T: (020) 7283 2231 M: 07905-288078 E: aneirin@gmail.com *or* a.glyn@st-helens.org.uk

GLYN-JONES, Alun. b 38. JP . CCC Cam BA 59 MA 63. Bps' Coll Cheshunt 60. d 61 p 62. C Portsea St Mary *Portsm* 61–65; Chapl Hampton Sch Middx 65–76; Hd Master Abp Tenison's Gr Sch Croydon 76–88; V Twickenham St Mary *Lon* 88–01; rtd 01; PtO *B & W* from 01; *Sarum* 01–20; *Eur* 01–14; *Bris* from 02. *2 Huntingdon Rise, Bradford-on-Avon BA15 1RJ* T: (01225) 866874 E: alunandchrisgj@gmail.com

GOALBY, George Christian. b 55. Leeds Univ BA 77. St Jo Coll Nottm 79. d 81 p 82. C Wakef St Andr and St Mary 81–84; Asst Chapl HM Pris Wakef 84–85; Chapl HM Youth Cust Cen Deerbolt 85–87; Chapl HM Pris Frankland 87–89; V Swinderby *Linc* 89–15; CF (ACF) 04–18; R Washingborough w Heighington and Canwick *Linc* from 15. *The Rectory, Church Hill, Washingborough, Lincoln LN4 1EJ* T: (01522) 800240 M: 07923-546599 E: george.goalby@btconnect.com

GOATCHER, Mrs Sara Jacoba Helena. b 46. Oak Hill NSM Course 86. d 89 p 94. NSM S Croydon Em *S'wark* 89–95; C 95–96; R Sutton St Nic 96–06; Asst Chapl Old Palace Sch Croydon 06–11; C Croydon St Jo *S'wark* 07–12; rtd 13; PtO *S'wark* from 13. *8 Hornchurch Hill, Whyteleafe CR3 0DA* T: (020) 8660 6198 M: 07785-230983 E: sara.goatcher@btinternet.com

GOATER, Canon Michael Robert. b 46. York Univ BA MA. NOC 89. d 92 p 93. C Norton *Sheff* 92–94; V Endcliffe 94–99; Chapl Sheff Ind Miss 94–95; Assoc Chapl Sheff Hallam Univ 95–99; Asst Post-Ord Tr Officer 95–99; Dioc Voc Officer 96–99; C Stratford-upon-Avon, Luddington etc *Cov* 99–02; P-in-c Gt Shelford *Ely* 02–11; RD Shelford 04–09; Hon Can Ely Cathl 10–11; rtd 11; Master St Nic Hosp Salisbury 11–16; PtO *Sarum* from 17. *17 Chiselbury Grove, Salisbury SP2 8EP* T: (01722) 331899 E: michael@mickthevic.org.uk

GOATLY, Ms Ruth Christine. b 50. Leic Univ LLB 72 Herts Univ MA 98 CQSW 74. Westcott Ho Cam 08. d 09 p 10. NSM Boxmoor St Jo *St Alb* 09–13; NSM St Alb St Mary Marshalswick 13–15; NSM St Alb St Luke 15–16; PtO 16–18; NSM Boxmoor St Jo 18–20; rtd 20; PtO *St Alb*

from 20. *30 Newgate Close, St Albans AL4 9JE* T: (01727) 751542 M: 07961-980158 E: ruthgoatly@hotmail.com

GOBBETT, Michael George Timothy. b 64. St Chad's Coll Dur BSc 86. St Steph Ho Ox BA 89 MA 98. **d** 90 **p** 91. C Hartlepool St Aid *Dur* 90–94; P-in-c Norton St Mich 94–95; V 95–05; TR Upper Skerne 05–16; TR Whitby w Ruswarp *York* from 16; AD Whitby from 17; CMP from 91. *The Rectory, Chubb Hill Road, Whitby YO21 1JP* T: (01947) 602590 E: michael.gobbett@btinternet.com

GOBEY, Ian Clifford. b 48. WEMTC 94. **d** 96 **p** 97. NSM Whiteshill and Randwick *Glouc* 96–00; NSM Painswick, Sheepscombe, Cranham, The Edge etc 00–07; P-in-c Westbury-on-Severn w Flaxley, Blaisdon etc 07–13; C Abenhall w Mitcheldean 11–13; C Huntley and Longhope, Churcham and Bulley 12–13; rtd 13; PtO *Glouc* from 13. *18 Blenheim Orchard, Shurdington, Cheltenham GL51 4TG* E: iangobey588@gmail.com

GOBLE, Clifford David. b 41. Oak Hill Th Coll 69. **d** 72 **p** 73. C Erith St Paul *Roch* 72–76; C Tunbridge Wells St Jas 76–79; R Southfleet 79–05; RD Gravesend 94–05; Hon Can Roch Cathl 99–05; rtd 05; PtO *Cant* from 06. *15 Martindown Road, Whitstable CT5 4PX* T: (01227) 263333 E: cliandjog@gmail.com

GOBLE (*née* **DUNN**), **Sharon Louise.** b 71. Univ of Wales (Swansea) BA 93 Fitzw Coll Cam BA 97 MA 01. Ridley Hall Cam 95. **d** 98 **p** 99. C Malpas *Mon* 98–01; C Cyncoed 01–02; R Heyford w Stowe Nine Churches and Flore etc *Pet* 02–04; PtO 04–08; Chapl Shakespeare Hospice 08–11; PtO *Cov* 08–13; P-in-c Stoneleigh w Ashow 13–17; R Stourdene Gp from 17. *The Rectory, Valenders Lane, Ilmington, Shipston-on-Stour CV36 4LB* T: (01608) 682282 M: 07799-220407 E: sharon.goble@btinternet.com

GODBOLD, Michelle Joanne. b 80. Bradf Univ BSc 01 BA 13. Linc Sch of Th and Min 09. **d** 13 **p** 14. C Boultham *Linc* 13–16; R Graffoe Gp from 16; Dioc Adv in Women's Min from 17. *The Rectory, 20 Temple Goring, Navenby, Lincoln LN5 0TX* T: (01522) 426723 E: michelle.godbold@hotmail.co.uk

GODDARD, Canon Andrew John. b 67. St Jo Coll Ox BA 88 MA 93 DPhil 96. Cranmer Hall Dur 94. **d** 96 **p** 97. C Cogges and S Leigh *Ox* 96–99; Tutor Wycliffe Hall Ox 99–08; Tutor Trin Coll Bris 08–18; PtO *Lon* 11–13; Hon C Westminster St Jas the Less from 13; Hon Can Win Cathl from 12. *56 Tachbrook Street, London SW1V 2NA* T: (020) 7834 1343 M: 07786-907946 E: goddardaj@gmail.com

GODDARD, Charles Anthony Ashton. b 54. Cam Univ MA 77. St Mellitus Coll. **d** 20 **p** 21. NSM W Wittering and Birdham w Itchenor *Chich* from 20. *Rookwood Lodge, Rookwood Road, West Wittering, Chichester PO20 8QL* T: (01243) 514518 M: 07860-530154 E: caagoddard@gmail.com

GODDARD, Canon Charles Douglas James. b 47. CITC 67. **d** 70 **p** 71. C Orangefield *D & D* 70–73; C Stormont 73–75; Miss to Seafarers from 75; Sen Chapl and Sec N Ireland 77–09; rtd 10; Can Belf Cathl from 05. *9 Governors Gate Manor, Hillsborough BT26 6FZ* T: (028) 9268 3592 E: cdjgoddard@gmail.com

GODDARD, Christopher. b 45. Sarum & Wells Th Coll 79. **d** 81 **p** 82. C Whitehaven *Carl* 81–83; C Barrow St Geo w St Luke 83–85; P-in-c Hayton St Mary 85–90; V Brigham 90–98; V Mosser 90–98; PtO 00–03; Hon C Cockermouth w Embleton and Wythop 03–05; TV Cockermouth Area 05–10; rtd 10; PtO *Carl* from 11. *5 Craig Drive, Whitehaven CA28 6JX* T: (01946) 328099 E: chrisgoddardmail@gmail.com

GODDARD, Derek George. b 38. St Martin's Coll Lanc BA 97 CEng FIMechE FIMarEST FCMI. Cranmer Hall Dur 94 CBDTI 95. **d** 97 **p** 98. NSM Windermere St Mary and Troutbeck *Carl* 97–01; P-in-c Leven Valley 01–06; P-in-c Palermo w Taormina *Eur* 06–09; PtO *Blackb* 09–10; P-in-c Overton 10–12; rtd 13; PtO *Blackb* 13–17; *Chich* from 16; *Eur* 09–21. *15 The Towpath, Yapton, Arundel BN18 0FW* E: d.d.goddard@hotmail.co.uk

GODDARD, Mrs Doris. b 48. St Mary's Coll Twickenham CertEd 70 Open Univ BA 80. S'wark Ord Course 93. **d** 96 **p** 97. Chapl John Nightingale Sch W Molesley 96–00; NSM Addlestone *Guildf* 96–98; NSM Botleys and Lyne 98–04; NSM Long Cross 98–04; NSM Chertsey, Lyne and Longcross 04–05; NSM Blackdown *B & W* 05–09; P-in-c Puriton and Pawlett 09–19; Chapl Bridgwater Hosp 15–19; rtd 20. *1 St Paul's Terrace, Easton, Wells BA5 1DX* E: rev.doris.goddard@btinternet.com

GODDARD, Douglas. See GODDARD, Charles Douglas James

GODDARD, Mrs Elaine Clare. b 53. K Alfred's Coll Win CertEd 78. WEMTC 96. **d** 99 **p** 00. C Leominster *Heref* 99–04; P-in-c St Weonards 04–07; R 07–15; RD Ross and Archenfield 07–13; rtd 15. *Little Bylets House, Pembridge, Leominster HR6 9HY* E: email@ecgoddard.co.uk

GODDARD, Elisabeth Ann. b 64. St Hugh's Coll Ox BA 89 MA 99. Cranmer Hall Dur 94. **d** 96 **p** 97. C Cogges and S Leigh *Ox* 96–99; Chapl Jes Coll Ox 99–04; Tutor Wycliffe Hall Ox 04–08; Hon C Ox St Andr 04–08; Hon C Stoke Bishop *Bris* 09–10; V Westminster St Jas the Less *Lon* from 10. *56 Tachbrook Street, London SW1V 2NA* T: (020) 7834 1343 E: goddardea@gmail.com

GODDARD, Canon Giles William. b 62. Clare Coll Cam MA 84 K Coll Lon MA 99 Goldsmiths' Coll Lon MA 10. S'wark Ord Course 92. **d** 95 **p** 96. C N Dulwich St Faith *S'wark* 95–98; R Walworth St Pet 98–09; AD S'wark and Newington 02–07; P-in-c Waterloo St Jo w St Andr 09–14; V from 14; Hon Can S'wark Cathl from 07. *St John's Vicarage, 1 Secker Street, London SE1 8UF* T: (020) 7633 9819 E: giles@stjohnswaterloo.org

GODDARD, Canon Harold Frederick. b 42. Keble Coll Ox BA 63 MA 69. Cuddesdon Coll 64. **d** 66 **p** 67. C Birm St Pet 66–70; Chapl Dudley Road Hosp Birm 66–70; Chapl HM Pris Birm 68–70; C Alverstoke *Portsm* 70–72; Chapl Gosport Cottage Hosp Portsm 70–72; Chapl HM Det Cen Haslar 70–72; P-in-c Portsea St Geo CD *Portsm* 72–76; Chapl Portsm Cathl 73–76; Asst Chapl Portsm Gr Sch 73–75; P-in-c Stoke Prior *Worc* 76–78; P-in-c Wychbold and Upton Warren 77–78; R Stoke Prior, Wychbold and Upton Warren 78–80; Chapl Forelands Orthopaedic Hosp Worc 77–80; Chapl R Marsden Hosp 80–83; R Martley and Wichenford *Worc* 83–88; P-in-c Knightwick w Doddenham, Broadwas and Cotheridge 85–88; R Martley and Wichenford, Knightwick etc 89–90; Bp's Adv on Min of Healing 84–99; Chapl St Richard's Hospice Worc 87–94; RD Martley and Worc W 88–90; Chapl Kidderminster Gen Hosp 90–92; P-in-c Hallow *Worc* 91–92; P-in-c Sedgeberrow w Hinton-on-the-Green 92–00; Chapl Evesham Hosp 93–00; Chapl Worcs Community Healthcare NHS Trust 97–00; Co-ord W Midl Healing Advisers 94–99; RD Evesham *Worc* 97–00; TR Kidderminster St Jo and H Innocents 00–08; Hon Can Worc Cathl 03–08; rtd 08; PtO *Worc* 08–15 and from 20; Hon C Gt Malvern Ch Ch 15–20; Dioc Chapl MU 11–16. *1 Springfield House, Como Road, Malvern WR14 2HS* T: (01684) 563350 M: 07768-106287 E: h.goddard@hotmail.com

GODDARD, Ms Marion. b 54. Sarum & Wells Th Coll 87. **d** 89 **p** 94. Par Dn Lewisham St Swithun *S'wark* 89–94; C 94–95; TV Thamesmead 96–04; rtd 04. *1 Hollows Close, Salisbury SP2 8JU* T: (01722) 338562

GODDARD, Matthew Francis. b 45. Kelham Th Coll 65. **d** 69 **p** 70. C Mansfield St Mark *S'well* 69–72; C Northolt Park St Barn *Lon* 72–78; P-in-c Acton Green St Pet 78–87; R Norwood St Mary 87–96. *27 Hounslow Avenue, Hounslow TW3 2DZ* T: (020) 8230 6591 E: mattandtrace@hotmail.com

GODDARD, Mrs Pamela Gay. b 53. LSE BSc(Econ) 74 CQSW 77. SAOMC 95 EAMTC 97. **d** 98 **p** 99. C New Catton St Luke w St Aug *Nor* 98–03; PtO 03–05; NSM Hamworthy *Sarum* 05–07; C Throop *Win* 07–08; C Hamworthy *Sarum* 08–17; rtd 17; PtO *Win* from 18. *180 Salisbury Road, Totton, Southampton SO40 3LQ* T: (023) 8206 0439 E: pam.goddard@gmail.com

GODDARD, Mrs Rosemary Joy. b 48. Philippa Fawcett Coll CertEd 69. EAMTC 00. **d** 03 **p** 04. C Linc St Nic w St Jo Newport 03–05; P-in-c Bicker 05–08; P-in-c Donington 08; P-in-c Fleet w Gedney 08–13; P-in-c Holbeach Marsh 08–13; rtd 13; PtO *Pet* 14–19; *Linc* 16–19. *9B Church Lane, Donington, Spalding PE11 4UD* T: (01775) 822398 M: 07740-203149 E: rogo9@btinternet.com

GODDARD, Stuart David. b 53. Cen Sch of Art Lon BA 76 Middx Poly PGCE 82. Trin Coll Bris 91. **d** 93 **p** 94. C Watling Valley *Ox* 93–97; P-in-c Bowthorpe *Nor* 97–00; TV 00–05; P-in-c Hamworthy *Sarum* 05–09; R 09–17; rtd 17; PtO *Win* from 18. *180 Salisbury Road, Totton, Southampton SO40 3LQ* T: (023) 8206 0439 E: goddard.stuart@gmail.com

GODDARD, Trevor Paul. b 63. NTMTC 03. **d** 06 **p** 07. NSM Kensal Rise St Mark and St Martin *Lon* 06–11; NSM Kensal Rise St Mark 11–13; P-in-c S Kenton from 13; C N Wembley St Cuth from 20. *194 Windermere Avenue, Wembley HA9 8QT* T: (020) 8908 2252 E: trevorgoddard@mac.com

GODDEN, Canon Peter David. b 47. Leeds Univ BA 69 MA 04 ARCO 70. Linc Th Coll 85. **d** 87 **p** 88. C Bearsted w Thurnham *Cant* 87–90; C Hykeham *Linc* 90–91; TV 91–95; P-in-c Linc St Pet-at-Gowts and St Andr 95–99; Hon PV Linc Cathl 90–99; R Armthorpe *Sheff* 99–00; R Owmby Gp *Linc* 00–12; RD Lawres 05–06 and 09–12; P-in-c Spring Line Gp 08–12; Can and Preb Linc Cathl 10–12; rtd 12; PtO *York* 13–16; *Nor* from 18. *7 Hampton Court, Nelson Street, King's Lynn PE30 5DX* T: (01553) 279954 E: petergoddenls@gmail.com

GODDEN, Peter James Howard. b 86. St Jo Coll Dur BA 08 Clare Coll Cam BA 13. Westcott Ho Cam 11. **d** 14 **p** 15. C Northwood H Trin *Lon* 14–17; V Clay Hill St Jo and St Luke

17–21; TV Risborough *Ox* from 21. *The Rectory, Mill Lane, Monks Risborough, Princes Risborough HP27 9JE* T: (01844) 274771 E: revpetergodden@outlook.com

GODDEN, Timothy Richard James. b 62. Univ Coll Lon BA 84. St Jo Coll Nottm 89. **d** 89 **p** 90. C Tulse Hill H Trin and St Matthias *S'wark* 89–93; TV Horsham *Chich* 93–01; TR Bishopsworth and Bedminster Down *Bris* from 01. *St Peter's Vicarage, 61 Fernsteed Road, Bristol BS13 8HE* T/F: 0117-964 2734 E: goddenfamily@blueyonder.co.uk

GODFREY, Ann Veronica. *See* MacKEITH, Ann Veronica

GODFREY, David Samuel George. b 35. CITC 64. **d** 66 **p** 67. C Londonderry Ch Ch *D & R* 66–68; I Tomregan w Drumlane *K, E & A* 68–72; I Cloonclare 72–79; I Templebreedy *C, C & R* 79–85; I Bray *D & G* 85–97; Can Ch Ch Cathl Dublin 95–97; Dean Kilmore *K, E & A* 97–04; I Kilmore w Ballintemple 97–04; Preb Mulhuddart St Patr Cathl Dublin 01–04; rtd 04. *37 Earlsfort Meadows, Earlsfort, Lucan, Co Dublin, Republic of Ireland* T: (00353) (1) 624 1906 M: 86-238 9686 E: godfreyd@tcd.ie *or* dsggodfrey@gmail.com

⌖**GODFREY, The Rt Revd Harold William.** b 48. AKC 71. St Aug Coll Cant 71. **d** 72 **p** 73 **c** 87. C Warsop *S'well* 72–75; TV Hucknall Torkard 75–86; Bp's Ecum Officer 81–82; United Soc 86–14; R and Adn Montevideo and Can Buenos Aires 86–88; Asst Bp Argentina and Uruguay 87–88; Bp Uruguay 88–98; Bp Peru 98–16; P-in-c Lastingham w Appleton-le-Moors, Rosedale etc *York* 16–17; V 17–20. *Address temp unknown* E: hwgodfrey@gmail.com

GODFREY, Jennifer Olwen. b 48. Hamilton Coll of Educn DipEd 70. TISEC 99. **d** 02 **p** 03. NSM Dalkeith *Edin* 02; NSM Lasswade from 02. *131 Newbattle Abbey Crescent, Dalkeith EH22 3LP* T: 0131-660 6145 M: 07812-923159 E: jennie.o.godfrey@googlemail.com

GODFREY, Kesari Freeda. *See* KESARI, Godfrey Freeda

GODFREY, Matthew Fenton. b 69. Univ Coll Dur BA 91 K Coll Lon MA 94. Ripon Coll Cuddesdon MTh 04. **d** 04 **p** 05. C Bodmin w Lanhydrock and Lanivet *Truro* 04–09; Chapl RN from 09. *Royal Naval Chaplaincy Service Headquarters, Tanner Building, HMS Excellent, Whale Island, Portsmouth PO2 8ER* T: 0300-157 7544 E: nitrogen_narcosis@hotmail.com

GODFREY, Michael. b 49. K Coll Lon BD 70 Wolv Univ PGCE 97. St Aug Coll Cant AKC 72. **d** 72 **p** 73. C Birtley *Dur* 72–75; Ind Chapl 76–79; TV Bilston *Lich* 79–86; TV Wolverhampton 86–93; Chapl Black Country Urban Ind Miss 79–86; Team Ldr 86–93; Preb Lich Cathl 87–93; PtO *Worc* 04–08; *Cov* 05–08; R Newport Pagnell w Lathbury and Moulsoe *Ox* 08–14; rtd 14; PtO *Cov* 15–21; *Worc* from 15. *2 Dugdale Avenue, Bidford-on-Avon, Alcester B50 4QE* T: (01789) 773022 E: rev.michael.godfrey@gmail.com *or* rector_08@btinternet.com

GODFREY, Michael James. b 50. Sheff Univ BEd 77. St Jo Coll Nottm 79. **d** 82 **p** 83. C Walton H Trin *Ox* 82–86; C Chadderton Ch Ch *Man* 86–91; V Woodlands *Sheff* 91–03; V Wythall *Birm* 03–11; TV Morley *Wakef* 11–14; *Leeds* 14–18; rtd 18. *26 Wye Road, Brockworth, Gloucester GL3 4PP*

GODFREY, The Very Revd Nigel Philip. b 51. Ripon Coll Cuddesdon BA 78 MA 84 Lon Guildhall Univ MBA 00 K Coll Lon MSc 09 MRTPI 76. Ripon Coll Cuddesdon 77. **d** 79 **p** 80. C Kennington St Jo w St Jas *S'wark* 79–89; Community of Ch the Servant 84–93; V Brixton Road Ch Ch *S'wark* 89–01; Prin OLM Scheme 01–07; Chapl *S'wark* Cathl 02–07; V German *S & M* 07–12; P-in-c Patrick 11–12; V W Coast from 12; Vice-Dean St German's Cathl 07–11; Dean St German's Cathl from 11; Dir Voc and Tr from 10. *The Deanery, Albany Road, Peel, Isle of Man IM5 1JS* T: (01624) 844830 E: dean@sodorandman.im

GODFREY, Mrs Patricia Ann. b 54. SEITE 01. **d** 04 **p** 05. NSM Dover St Mary *Cant* 04–14; NSM Dover Town 14–17; NSM Dover St Martin 14–17; rtd 17; PtO *Cant* from 17. *8 Longfield Road, Dover CT17 9QU* T: (01304) 206019 E: trishgodfrey8@yahoo.co.uk

GODFREY (née ROGERS), Canon Pauline Ann. b 58. LMH Ox BA 79 MA 83 Ox Univ Inst of Educn PGCE 80. S Dios Minl Tr Scheme 89. **d** 92 **p** 94. NSM Headley All SS *Guildf* 92–96; C 96–99; P-in-c Wyke 99–01; V 01–11; Past Tutor Local Min Progr 96–11; Dioc Voc Officer *Glouc* 11–18; Hd Discipleship and Voc and Dep Dir Dept Miss and Min from 18; Hon Can Glouc Cathl from 19. *3 Manston Way, Kingsway, Quedgeley, Gloucester GL2 2FB* T: (01452) 699803 *or* 835548 E: p.a.g@talktalk.net

GODFREY, Mrs Sarah Joy. b 64. Southn Univ BSc 85 Bath Univ PGCE 86. STETS 02. **d** 05 **p** 06. NSM Puddletown, Tolpuddle and Milborne w Dewlish *Sarum* 05–14; Asst Dioc Dir of Ords 11–14; V Milborne Port w Goathill etc *B & W* 14–21; Asst Dir of Ords 19–21; TV Golden Cap Team *Sarum*

from 21. *The Vicarage, 4 Dragons Hill, Lyme Regis DT7 3HW* E: revsjgodfrey@gmail.com

GODFREY, Canon Simon Henry Martin. b 55. TD 00. K Coll Lon BD 80 AKC 80. St Steph Ho Ox 80. **d** 81 **p** 82. C Kettering SS Pet and Paul 81–84; R Crick and Yelvertoft w Clay Coton and Lilbourne 84–89; V Northampton All SS w St Kath 89–98; R Northampton All SS w St Kath and St Pet 98–09; Sen Chapl Malta and Gozo *Eur* from 09; Can and Chan St Paul's Pro-Cathl Valletta from 09; CF (VR) from 88. *St Paul's Anglican Pro-Cathedral, Independence Square, Valletta VLT 1535, Malta GC* T: (00356) 2122 5714 F: 2122 5867 E: simonhmgodfrey@gmail.com

GODFREY, William. *See* GODFREY, Harold William

GODIN, Mrs Mary Louise. b 42. SRN 64 QN 66. Oak Hill NSM Course 89. **d** 92 **p** 94. NSM Surbiton Hill Ch Ch *S'wark* 92–03; Chapl Kingston and Distr Community NHS Trust 97–01; Team Chapl SW Lon and St George's Mental Health NHS Trust 01–03; Chapl Taunton and Somerset NHS Foundn Trust 03–11; C Beercrocombe w Curry Mallet, Hatch Beauchamp etc *B & W* 11–17; rtd 17; PtO *B & W* from 18. *The Stables, Capland Court, Capland Lane, Hatch Beauchamp, Taunton TA3 6TP* T: (01823) 480606 E: revmarygodin@gmail.com

GODLINGTON, Ian Denis. b 58. All SS Cen for Miss & Min 13. **d** 14 **p** 15. OLM Mickleover *Derby* from 14; Chapl Rolls-Royce Derby from 14. *46 Bren Way, Hilton, Derby DE65 5HP* T: (01283) 730832 M: 07788-417819 E: godlingtons46@gmail.com

GODSALL, Canon Andrew Paul. b 59. Birm Univ BA 81. Ripon Coll Cuddesdon 86. **d** 88 **p** 89. C Gt Stanmore *Lon* 88–91; C Ealing All SS 91–94; V Hillingdon All SS 94–01; Dir of Ords Willesden Area 99–01; Bp's Chapl and Asst *Ex* 01–06; Dioc Dir of Min 06–14; PV Ex Cathl 04–06; Can Res and Chan Ex Cathl 06–14; Miss Community Min Development Adv 14–17; Dioc Dir of Ords Admin from 17. *20 Newcourt Way, Exeter EX2 7SA* T: (01392) 294902 E: andrew.godsall@exeter.anglican.org

GODSALL, Peter. **d** 17 **p** 18. NSM Aberdare St Fagan *Llan* 17–20; P-in-c Hirwaun from 20. *Oaktree House, 60 Glan Road, Aberdare CF44 8BW* T: (01685) 883697 E: peteroaktree@aol.com

GODSALL, Canon Ralph Charles. b 48. Qu Coll Cam BA 71 MA 75. Cuddesdon Coll 73. **d** 75 **p** 76. C Sprowston *Nor* 75–78; Chapl Trin Coll Cam 78–84; V Hebden Bridge *Wakef* 84–93; V Westmr St Steph w St Jo *Lon* 93–01; Can Res Roch Cathl 01–08; rtd 08; PV Westmr Abbey from 08. *39 Vincent Square, London SW1P 2NP* T: (020) 7976 5899 M: 07786-959540 E: canonralph@hotmail.co.uk

GODSELL, Philip Winston. b 66. Cardiff Univ BTh 15 MTh 16. St Mich Coll Llan 13. **d** 15 **p** 16. C Cyncoed *Mon* 15–17; C Upper Torfaen 17–20; C Mid Torfaen from 20. *The Vicarage, Freeholdland Road, Pontnewynydd, Pontypool NP4 8LW* T: (01495) 759980 M: 07411-667301 E: frgodsell@gmail.com

GODSELL, Stephen Phillip. b 72. WEMTC 15. **d** 18 **p** 19. C Ashleworth, Corse, Hartpury, Hasfield etc *Glouc* 18–21; P-in-c Berkeley w Wick, Breadstone, Newport, Stone etc from 21. *The Vicarage, Church Lane, Berkeley GL13 9BN* M: 07752-463536 E: stevegodsell@gmail.com

GODSMARK, Susan Mary. **d** 14 **p** 15. OLM Gt Totham and Lt Totham w Goldhanger *Chelmsf* 14–18; NSM from 18; NSM N Blackwater from 20. *57 Mill Road, Great Totham, Maldon CM9 8DH* T: (01621) 891513 E: suegodsmark@aol.com

GODSON, Mark Rowland. b 61. K Coll Lon BD 83 AKC 83 CertEd 84. Linc Th Coll 84. **d** 86 **p** 87. C Hurst Green *S'wark* 86–88; C Fawley *Win* 88–90; TV Wimborne Minster and Holt *Sarum* 90–95; P-in-c Horton and Chalbury 90–93; P-in-c Vale of Allen 93–95; P-in-c Stalbridge 95–96; Chapl Forest Healthcare NHS Trust Lon 96–00; P-in-c Bicton, Montford w Shrawardine and Fitz *Lich* 00–06; Chapl Shropshire Co Primary Care Trust 01–06; TR Fordingbridge and Breamore and Hale etc *Win* 06–10; R 10–12; AD Christchurch 10–12; Dir Lon Cen for Spirituality 12–16; Hon C Abinger and Coldharbour and Wotton and Holmbury St Mary *Guildf* 16–18; P-in-c Ewyas Harold w Dulas, Kenderchurch etc *Heref* 18–21; R from 21; PtO *Lon* from 17. *The Rectory, Ewyas Harold, Hereford HR2 0EZ* T: (01981) 240079 E: mrkgdsn@gmail.com

GODWIN, Canon David Harold. b 45. Glos Univ BA 09. Kelham Th Coll 67. **d** 71 **p** 72. C Camberwell St Phil and St Mark *S'wark* 71–75; Asst Chapl The Lon Hosp (Whitechapel) 75–79; Chapl R E Sussex Hosp Hastings 79–86; Chapl Over Hosp Glouc 86–92; Chapl Glos R Hosp 86–94; Chapl Glos R Hosp NHS Trust 94–02; Chapl Glos Hosps NHS Foundn Trust 02–05; Hon Can Glouc Cathl 03–05; rtd 05; PtO *Glouc* 05–19; *Chelmsf* from 19. *3*

Fairlawn Drive, Woodford Green IG8 9AW   M: 07989-046118 E: davidhgodwin@live.co.uk

GODWIN, Canon Michael Francis Harold. b 35. Nottm Univ BSc 57. Ely Th Coll 59. **d** 61 **p** 62. C S Farnborough *Guildf* 61–65; V Epsom St Barn 66–85; V Bramley and Grafham 85–98; Hon Can Guildf Cathl 89–98; rtd 00; PtO *Chich* from 13. *14 Lemmington Way, Horsham RH12 5JG*   T: (01403) 273411

GOFF, Philip Francis Michael. b 52. K Coll Lon BD 73 AKC 73 FBS 00 FSA 08. St Aug Coll Cant 74. **d** 75 **p** 76. C Ruislip St Martin *Lon* 75–79; Chapl Aldenham Sch Herts 79–82; V Tokyngton St Mich *Lon* 82–89; In RC Ch 89–91; Primary Care Cllr NHS 91–98; PtO *Lon* 99–00; Chapl to Bp Edmonton 00–04; Asst Dir Post-Ord Tr Edmonton Area 03–06; P-in-c Highgate St Aug 04–14; V 14–15; AD W Haringey 11–14; rtd 15; PtO *Lon* 16–18. *51 Kingsmere, Benfleet SS7 3XN*   M: 07768-920506 E: phildress@blueyonder.co.uk

GOFTON, Canon William Alder. b 31. Dur Univ BA 54. Coll of Resurr Mirfield 59. **d** 61 **p** 62. C Benwell St Aid *Newc* 61–64; C N Gosforth 64–69; V Seaton Hirst 69–77; V Newc H Cross 77–89; RD Newc W 85–89; Hon Can Newc Cathl 88–96; R Bolam w Whalton and Hartburn w Meldon 89–96; P-in-c Nether Witton 89–95; V 95–96; Chapl Kirkley Hall Coll 90–96; rtd 96; PtO *Newc* from 96. *4 Crossfell, Ponteland, Newcastle upon Tyne NE20 9EA*   T: (01661) 820344 E: aggofton@yahoo.co.uk

GOGGIN, Philip Frederick de Jean. b 46. Rhodes Univ BA 66 Lon Univ MA 73 Keele Univ PhD 89 Leeds Univ MA 05. NOC 03. **d** 05 **p** 06. NSM Sandbach Heath w Wheelock *Ches* 05–07; P-in-c Leighton-cum-Minshull Vernon 07–11; V Leighton-cum-Minshull Vernon and Warmingham 11–20; rtd 20. *4 Valley Road, Wistaston, Crewe CW2 8JU*   E: gail.philip4@gmail.com

GOLD, Stephen Eric. b 67. St Mellitus Coll 12. **d** 15 **p** 16. C Hillmorton *Cov* 15–18; P-in-c from 18. *2 Maxwell Road, Houlton, Rugby CV23 1AH*   E: steve.gold2@me.com or steve@stjohnhillmorton.org.uk

GOLDBY, Miss Emma Lucy. b 73. Glos Univ BEd 97. Ripon Coll Cuddesdon 12. **d** 14 **p** 15. C Malvern H Trin and St Jas *Worc* 14–17; C Abberton, The Flyfords, Naunton Beauchamp etc from 17; C Fladbury, Hill and Moor, Wyre Piddle etc from 17; C Stoulton w Drake's Broughton and Pirton etc from 17; C Peopleton and White Ladies Aston w Churchill etc from 21. *The Rectory, 4 Manor Farm, Stoulton, Worcester WR7 4RS*   T: (01905) 840752 E: revdemmagoldby@gmail.com

GOLDENBERG, Ralph Maurice. b 45. City Univ FBCO 67 FBOA 67. Trin Coll Bris 88. **d** 90 **p** 91. C Kinson *Sarum* 90–93; C Edgware *Lon* 93–97; TV Roxeth 97–01; V Bayston Hill *Lich* 01–10; rtd 10; PtO *Sarum* 11–20. *2 Golf Links Road, Ferndown BH22 8BY*   T: (01202) 893131 E: r.goldenberg@btopenworld.com

GOLDER, Rebecca Marie. *See* ROGERS, Rebecca Marie

GOLDIE, Prof James Stuart. b 46. Edin Univ BEd 73 Hon MEd 00 Cairo Univ Hon PhD 06. Lon Coll of Div BDQ 67 BTh 70 ALCD 69. **d** 69 **p** 70. C Blackpool St Paul *Blackb* 69–70; C Gt Sankey *Liv* 70–73; C-in-c Penketh CD 70–73; Asst Chapl Greystone Heath Sch 70–73; Chapl Kilmarnock Academy 73–75; V Flixton St Jo *Man* 75–78; Chapl Friars Sch Man 75–78; V Skelmersdale St Paul *Liv* 78–80; Chapl Trin Sch Liv 78–80; Lect Man Bible Coll and Dir Man City Miss 80–83; Hon Prof Cam Univ from 81; Chapl Westbrook Hay Sch Hemel Hempstead 83–89; V Pennington w Lindal and Marton *Carl* 89–90; Chapl Queenswood Sch Herts 96–97; Hd Master Westcliff Prep Sch 97–03; V Red Sea Area (w ecum oversight) Egypt 04–12; Prin El Gouna Internat Sch 04–12; rtd 12. *23 Ffordd Naddyn, Glan Conway, Colwyn Bay LL28 4NH*   T: (01492) 593996

GOLDIE, Katrina Ruth. *See* SCOTT, Katrina Ruth

GOLDING, Neil Christopher. b 47. Warwick Univ BA 69. S'wark Ord Course 92. **d** 95 **p** 96. C Mitcham Ascension S'wark 95–00; P-in-c Croydon Woodside 00–05; V 05–15; rtd 15; PtO *Truro* from 15. *93 Retallick Meadows, St Austell PL25 3BZ*   T: (01726) 69261 E: rev_neil@btopenworld.com

GOLDING, The Ven Simon Jefferies. b 46. CBE 02. Brasted Place Coll 70. Linc Th Coll 72. **d** 74 **p** 75. C Wilton *York* 74–77; Chapl RN 77–97; Chapl of the Fleet 97–98 and 00–02; Adn for the RN 97–02; Dir Gen Naval Chapl Service 00–02; QHC 97–02; Hon Can Gib Cathl 97–02; rtd 02; PtO *Ripon* 02–11; Dioc Adv for NSM 08–11; Hon C E Richmond 11–14; Leeds 14–16; Hon C Wiske Benefice from 16. *Arlanza, Hornby Road, Appleton Wiske, Northallerton DL6 2AF*   T: (01609) 881185 E: golding@clannet.co.uk

GOLDING, Stephen. b 57. Keele Univ BA 79 CertEd 79 Lon Bible Coll BA 86 Heythrop Coll Lon MA 09. Cant Sch of

Min 93. **d** 95 **p** 96. NSM Ramsgate St Luke *Cant* 95–98; Chapl St Lawr Coll Ramsgate 95–98; Chapl Berkhamsted Sch Herts 98–10; Chapl Ch Hosp Horsham 10–19; Chapl Treloar Coll of FE from 19; PtO *Win* from 19. *5 Loader Close, Kings Worthy, Winchester SO23 7TF*

GOLDING, Trevor. b 58. Ridley Hall Cam 07. **d** 09 **p** 10. C Highbury Ch Ch w St Jo and St Sav *Lon* 09–12; V Ipswich St Aug *St E* 13–19; V Tollington Park *Lon* from 19. *St Mark's Vicarage, 1 Moray Road, London N4 3LD*   M: 07511-870694 E: revtrev@stmarksn4.com

GOLDINGAY, Prof John Edgar. b 42. Keble Coll Ox BA 64 Nottm Univ PhD 83 Lambeth DD 97. Clifton Th Coll 64. **d** 66 **p** 67. C Finchley Ch Ch *Lon* 66–69; Lect St Jo Coll Nottm 70–75; Dir Studies 76–79; Registrar 79–85; Vice-Prin 85–88; Prin 88–97; Prof OT Fuller Th Sem Pasadena 97–18. *4 Mill Stream House, Norfolk Street, Oxford OX1 1EB*   T: (01865) 244090 E: johngold@fuller.edu

GOLDRING, Mrs Philippa Elizabeth Vincent. b 58. Southn Univ LLB 79 Spurgeon's Coll BD 05. SEITE BA 10. **d** 10 **p** 11. C Wednesfield Heath *Lich* 10–14; PtO 14–15; Hon C Heath Town from 15. *571 Cannock Road, Wolverhampton WV10 0RH*   T: (01902) 731456 E: pippa.goldring@gmail.com

GOLDSMITH, Brian Derek. b 36. Leeds Univ BA 64. Coll of Resurr Mirfield 64. **d** 66 **p** 67. C Littlehampton St Mary *Chich* 66–69; C Guildf St Nic 69–73; V Aldershot St Aug 73–81; C-in-c Leigh Park St Clare CD *Portsm* 82–85; C Rowner 85–96; rtd 97; C Catherington and Clanfield *Portsm* 97–01; PtO *Win* 98–14. *27 White Dirt Lane, Catherington, Waterlooville PO8 0NB*   T: (023) 9259 9462

GOLDSMITH, Christine Ann. b 63. Qu Coll Newfoundland BTh 18. **d** 15 **p** 16. Cyprus 15–19; R Brant Broughton and Beckingham *Linc* from 19; R Leadenham from 19; R Welbourn from 19. *The Rectory, Church End Fulbeck Road, Leadenham, Lincoln LN5 0PX*   T: (01400) 679081   M: 07494-870701 E: rectorleadenham@gmail.com

✠**GOLDSMITH, The Rt Revd Christopher David.** b 54. York Univ BA 76 DPhil 79. NTMTC 97. **d** 00 **p** 01 **c** 13. NSM Pitsea w Nevendon *Chelmsf* 00–04; V Warley Ch Ch and Gt Warley St Mary 04–13; Suff Bp St Germans *Truro* 13–19; Dioc Warden of Readers 13–19; Dir Nat Min Team Abps' Coun from 19. *National Ministry Team, Church House, 27 Great Smith Street, London SW1P 3AZ*   T: (020) 7898 1403 E: chris.goldsmith@churchofengland.org

GOLDSMITH, Mrs Ellen Elizabeth. b 48. York Univ BA 77 Middx Univ BA 06. NTMTC 03. **d** 06 **p** 07. NSM Bentley Common, Kelvedon Hatch and Navestock *Chelmsf* 06–10; NSM Warley Ch Ch and Gt Warley St Mary 10–13; TV Probus, Ladock and Grampound w Creed and St Erme *Truro* 14–18; NSM 18–19; rtd 19. *Address temp unknown*   M: 07906-979321 E: ellen.goldsmith@btinternet.com

GOLDSMITH, Kathryn Jane Alexandra. b 78. K Alfred's Coll Win BTh 01 Univ Coll Lon BSc 11 Qu Mary Coll Lon MSc 14 Leeds Univ PhD 19 FRAS 11. Coll of Resurr Mirfield MA 19. **d** 19 **p** 20. C Chapelthorpe *Leeds* from 19; C Woolley from 19. *15 The Crimbles, Durkar, Wakefield WF4 3EX* E: kathryn.goldsmith@leeds.anglican.org

GOLDSMITH, Lesley Anne. DL 19. NTMTC 02. **d** 05 **p** 06. C E Ham w Upton Park and Forest Gate *Chelmsf* 05–08; V Chingford St Edm from 08. *St Edmund's Vicarage, Larkswood Road, London E4 9DS*   T: (020) 8529 5226 E: lesley.goldsmith@btinternet.com

GOLDSMITH, Canon Mary Louie. b 48. K Coll Lon BA 70 AKC 70. Qu Coll Birm 91. **d** 93 **p** 94. NSM Matlock Bank *Derby* 93–97; NSM Kirk Hallam 97–02; NSM Taddington, Chelmorton and Monyash etc 00–11; Hon Can Derby Cathl from 05. *9 Highfield Gardens, Highfield Road, Derby DE22 1HT*   T: (01332) 209392

GOLDSMITH, Mrs Pauline Anne. b 40. Linc Th Coll 82. dss 84 **d** 87 **p** 94. Waddington *Linc* 86–88; Par Dn 87–88; Par Dn Gt and Lt Coates w Bradley 88–94; TV 94–96; TV Kidderminster St Mary and All SS w Trimpley etc *Worc* 96–01; rtd 01; PtO *Derby* from 01; *Sheff* 01–14. *143 Ravencar Road, Eckington, Sheffield S21 4JR*   T: (01246) 430083 E: paulnstevgoldsmith@gmail.com

GOLDSMITH, Stephen. b 32. Edin Th Coll. **d** 76 **p** 77. SPCK Staff 53–97; Bookshops Regional Manager SPCK 87–97; NSM Penicuik *Edin* 76–81; NSM Linc St Nic w St Jo Newport 81–90; NSM Gt and Lt Coates w Bradley 90–96; NSM Kidderminster St Mary and All SS w Trimpley etc *Worc* 96–01; PtO *Derby* from 01; *Sheff* 01–14. *143 Ravencar Road, Eckington, Sheffield S21 4JR*   T: (01246) 430083

GOLDSTONE-CREASEY, Graham. b 51. Trent Poly BA 73. Cranmer Hall Dur 80. **d** 83 **p** 84. C Birstall and Wanlip *Leic* 83–87; C-in-c Wheatley Park St Paul CD *Sheff* 87–92; V Wheatley Park 92–95; P-in-c Gleadless Valley 95–98. *281*

Fleetwood Road North, Thornton-Cleveleys FY5 4LE T: (01253) 862668 E: grahamgc10@gmail.com

GOLDTHORP, Ms Ann Lesley. b 59. Qu Coll Birm 08. **d** 11 **p** 12. C Harbury and Ladbroke *Cov* 11–15; V Deddington w Barford, Clifton and Hempton *Ox* from 15. *The Vicarage, 1 Earls Close, Deddington OX15 0TJ* T: (01869) 336880 E: reverendannie@hotmail.com

GOLDTHORPE, Duncan Robert. b 70. Herts Univ BA 99. ERMC 15. **d** 18 **p** 19. C Bedford St Andr *St Alb* 18–21; P-in-c E Leightonstone *Ely* from 21. *The Rectory, 15 Church Road, Brampton, Huntingdon PE28 4PF* T: (01234) 268689

GOLDTHORPE, Ms Shirley. b 42. Linc Th Coll 70. **dss** 76 **d** 87 **p** 94. Thornhill Lees *Wakef* 76–78; Birkenshaw w Hunsworth 78–80; Batley St Thos 80–85; Batley All SS 80–85; Purlwell 80–92; Par Dn 87–88; Dn-in-c 88–92; Dn-in-c Horbury Junction 92–94; P-in-c 94–01; rtd 02; PtO *Wakef* 02–14; *Leeds* from 14. *10 Orchid View, Alverthorpe, Wakefield WF2 0FG* T: (01924) 383181 M: 07885-462837

GOLLEDGE, Canon Patricia Anne. b 55. Trin Coll Bris BA 00. **d** 00 **p** 01. C Pontypool *Mon* 00–03; TV 03–09; V Griffithstown 09–13; R and Min Area Ldr Panteg and Griffithstown 13–19; TV Bassaleg from 19; AD Pontypool 16–19; Can St Woolos Cathl from 17. *St John's Vicarage, 25 Wern Terrace, Rogerstone, Newport NP10 9FG* T: (01633) 897571 E: p.annegolledge55@btinternet.com

GOLLOP, Michael John. b 58. Keble Coll Ox BA 81 MA 85. St Mich Coll Llan BD 85. **d** 85 **p** 86. C Newport St Mark *Mon* 85–87; C Bassaleg 87–91; V St Hilary Greenway 91–93; V Itton and St Arvans w Penterry and Kilgwrrwg w Devauden from 93. *The Vicarage, Wyndcliffe View, St Arvans, Chepstow NP16 6ET* T: (01291) 622064 E: frmichael1@aol.com

GOLTON, Alan Victor. b 29. St Jo Coll Ox BA 51 MA 54 DPhil 54. **d** 85 **p** 86. NSM Barston *Birm* 85–95; P-in-c 87–95; rtd 95; PtO *Birm* 95–96; Hon C Grenoble *Eur* 97–00. *Chant du Matin, Les Michallons, 38250 St Nizier du Moucherotte, France* T: (0033) 4 76 53 43 77 E: avgolton@hotmail.com

GOMERSALL, Canon Ian Douglass. b 56. Birm Univ BSc 77 Fitzw Coll Cam BA 80 MA 85 Dur Univ MA 94. Westcott Ho Cam 78. **d** 81 **p** 82. C Darlington St Mark w St Paul *Dur* 81–84; C Barnard Castle w Whorlton 84–86; Chapl HM YOI Deerbolt 85–90; P-in-c Cockfield *Dur* 86–88; R 88–90; Dep Chapl HM Pris Wakef 90–91; Chapl HM Pris Full Sutton 91–97; P-in-c Kexby w Wilberfoss *York* 93–97; TV Man Whitworth 97–03; P-in-c Man Victoria Park 98–09; R from 09; Chapl Man Univ 97–03; Hon Chapl from 03; AD Ardwick Man 08–15; Hon Can Man Cathl from 11. *St Chrysostom's Rectory, 38 Park Range, Manchester M14 5HQ* T: 0161-224 6971 M: 07711-670225 E: ian.gomersall@btinternet.com

GOMERSALL, Richard. b 45. FCA 68. NOC 90. **d** 93 **p** 94. NSM Thurcroft *Sheff* 93–96; NSM Sheff St Matt 96–03; Ind Chapl 98–03; C-in-c Southey Green St Bernard CD 03–11. *Dale View House, 14 Wignall Avenue, Wickersley, Rotherham S66 2AX* T: (01709) 546441 F: 701900 E: fr.gomersall@btinternet.com

GOMM, Timothy Frank. b 64. St Jo Coll Nottm 00. **d** 02 **p** 03. C Kinson *Sarum* 02–04; C Heatherlands St Jo and Community Chapl Rossmore Community Coll 04–10; C Longfleet *Sarum* 10–11; TR Portland from 11. *St John's Vicarage, Ventnor Road, Portland DT5 1JE* T: (01305) 820103 E: rev.gomm@btinternet.com

GOMPERTZ, Adam Charles John. b 73. Trin Coll Bris 11. **d** 13 **p** 14. C Lt Aston *Lich* 13–16; C Kinnerley w Melverley, Knockin w Maesbrook and Maesbury 16–19; Pioneer Min from 19; PtO *Cov* from 19; *Ox* from 20. *Oxon Vicarage, Shelton Gardens, Bicton Heath, Shrewsbury SY3 5AG* M: 07917-248973 E: revagomp@gmail.com

GOMPERTZ, Mrs Charlotte. b 72. St Jo Coll Nottm 13. **d** 16 **p** 17. C Meole Brace *Lich* 16–19; V Shelton and Oxon from 19. *Oxon Vicarage, Shelton Gardens, Bicton Heath, Shrewsbury SY3 5AG* M: 07769-349052 E: chargomp@gmail.com

GONIN, Christopher Willett. b 33. Man Univ DACE 87 MBA 92. AKC 59. **d** 60 **p** 61. C Camberwell St Geo *S'wark* 60–64; C Stevenage H Trin *St Alb* 64–69; C Bletchley *Ox* 70–73; R Newington St Mary *S'wark* 73–76; PtO *Bris* 76–77; Hon C Horfield H Trin 77–89; Hon C City of Bris 89–91; V Milton Ernest *St Alb* 92–97; V Thurleigh 92–97; rtd 97; PtO *St E* from 99. *24 Booth Court, Handford Road, Ipswich IP1 2GD* T: (01473) 232732 E: c.gonin@btinternet.com

GONZALEZ PENA, Heller. b 72. **d** 11 **p** 12. C La Coruña H Cross Spain 11–12; R 12–15; C Port Glas 15–20; C Kilmacolm 15–20; C Bridge of Weir 15–20; R Dumbarton from 20. *St Augustine's Church, High Street, Dumbarton G82 1LL* T: 07496-841775 E: hellerg@hotmail.com

GOOCH, Michael Anthony. b 44. Nottm Coll of Educn TCert 66. Cant Sch of Min 90. **d** 93 **p** 94. NSM New Romney w Old Romney and Midley *Cant* 93–97; P-in-c Teynham w Lynsted and Kingsdown 97–08; Bp's Officer for NSM 98–03; rtd 08; PtO *Cant* from 08. *Little Owls, Tookey Road, New Romney TN28 8ET* T: (01797) 367858 E: manddgooch@hotmail.co.uk

GOOD, Andrew Ronald. b 60. Bris Univ BA 82. Linc Th Coll 83. **d** 85 **p** 86. C Epping St Jo *Chelmsf* 85–88; C Cheshunt *St Alb* 88–91; R Spixworth w Crostwick and Frettenham *Nor* 91–04; PtO 04–10; P-in-c Ashwellthorpe, Forncett, Fundenhall, Hapton etc 11–12; R Holkham w Egmere w Warham etc 12–14. *Ferrar House, Little Gidding, Huntingdon PE28 5RJ* E: andrewrgood@hotmail.com

GOOD, David Howard. b 42. Glouc Sch of Min 84. **d** 87 **p** 88. NSM Bromyard *Heref* 87–92; C Pontesbury I and II 92–95; P-in-c Ditton Priors w Neenton, Burwarton etc 95–98; R 98–02; rtd 02; PtO *Heref* from 02. *26 Farjeon Close, Ledbury HR8 2FU* T: (01531) 636474

GOOD, Preb John Hobart. b 43. Bps' Coll Cheshunt 66 Coll of Resurr Mirfield 68. **d** 69 **p** 70. C Ex St Jas 69–73; C Cockington 73–75; C Wolborough w Newton Abbot 75–78; P-in-c Exminster and Kenn 78–80; R 80–95; RD Kenn 89–95; TR Axminster, Chardstock, All Saints etc 95–09; Chapl All Hallows Sch Rousdon 98–99; Preb Ex Cathl 02–09; rtd 09; TV Dorchester *Sarum* 09–13; Hon C The Winterbournes and Compton Valence 09–13; PtO *Ex* from 13. *3 Home Farm Court, Deane Road, Stokeinteignhead, Newton Abbot TQ12 4QF* E: johngood1@outlook.com

✠**GOOD, The Rt Revd Kenneth Raymond.** b 52. TCD BA 74 Nottm Univ BA 76 NUI HDipEd 81 MEd 84. St Jo Coll Nottm 75. **d** 77 **p** 78 **c** 02. C Willowfield *D & D* 77–79; Chapl Ashton Sch Cork 79–84; I Dunganstown w Redcross and Conary *D & G* 84–90; I Lurgan Ch the Redeemer *D & D* 90–02; Adn Dromore 97–02; Bp D *&* D 02–19; rtd 19. *15 Woodhall, Moira, Craigavon BT67 0NG* M: 07734-111990 E: krgood15@gmail.com

GOOD, The Ven Kenneth Roy. b 41. K Coll Lon BD 66 AKC 66. **d** 67 **p** 68. C Stockton St Pet *Dur* 67–70; Chapl Antwerp Miss to Seamen *Eur* 70–74; Chapl Kobe Japan 74–79; Asst Gen Sec Miss to Seamen and Asst Chapl St Mich Paternoster Royal *Lon* 79–85; Hon Can Kobe from 85; V Nunthorpe *York* 85–93; RD Stokesley 90–93; Adn Richmond *Ripon* 93–06; rtd 06; PtO *York* 07–17; *Dur* from 10. *18 Fox Howe, Coulby Newham, Middlesbrough TS8 0RU* T: (01642) 594158 E: joken.good@ntlworld.com

GOOD, Stuart Eric Clifford. b 37. Wycliffe Hall Ox 63. **d** 64 **p** 65. C Walton H Trin *Ox* 64–66; C Nedlands Australia 66–67; R Mundaring 67–71; R Bassendean 71–78; R Como 78–85; Dir Chapl Services Angl Homes Inc 85–05; rtd 05. *135/27 Pearson Drive, Success WA 6164, Australia* M: (0061) 41-894 3337 E: sbargood@bigpond.net.au

GOODACRE, Canon David Leighton. b 36. AKC 59. **d** 60 **p** 61. C Stockton St Chad *Dur* 60–63; C Birtley 63–68; Chapl Sunderland Gen Hosp 69–74; P-in-c Ryhope *Dur* 75–81; V Ovingham *Newc* 81–01; Hon Can Newc Cathl 92–01; rtd 01; PtO *Newc* from 01. *9 Wilmington Close, Newcastle upon Tyne NE3 2SF* T: 0191-271 4382 E: david.goodacre29@sky.com

GOODACRE, Philip James. b 81. Ox Brookes Univ BA 04 Birm Univ MA 06 Anglia Ruskin Univ MA 13. Ridley Hall Cam 09. **d** 11 **p** 12. C Brightside w Wincobank *Sheff* 11–14; P-in-c Hillsborough and Wadsley Bridge from 14. *Christ Church Vicarage, 218 Fox Hill Road, Sheffield S6 1HJ* T: 0114-234 9376 E: philipgoodacre@gmail.com

GOODAIR, Jan. b 59. K Coll Lon BA 81 Leeds Univ PhD 02 Roehampton Inst PGCE 82. NEOC 97. **d** 00 **p** 01. NSM Tockwith and Bilton w Bickerton *York* 00–01; NSM York St Olave w St Giles 00–01; Chapl Harrogate Ladies' Coll 01–10; Chapl Haberdashers' Aske's Sch Elstree 10–15; Chapl Pocklington Sch 15–19; rtd 19; PtO *Leeds* 20–21. *19 Shaw Leys, Yeadon, Leeds LS19 7LA* M: 07846-621427 E: jan.goodair@hotmail.co.uk

GOODALL, Alice Elizabeth. b 58. Keele Univ BA 80. STETS 09. **d** 12 **p** 13. C St Bartholomew *Sarum* 12–16; R Shelswell *Ox* from 16. *The Rectory, Water Stratford Road, Finmere, Buckingham MK18 4AT* T: (01280) 848192 M: 07447-933140 E: alicegoodall313@gmail.com

GOODALL, Canon John William. b 45. Hull Univ BA 69. Ripon Hall Ox 69. **d** 71 **p** 72. C Loughborough Em *Leic* 71–74; C Dorchester *Ox* 74–75; TV 75–80; Tutor Sarum & Wells Th Coll 80–88; Vice Prin S Dios Minl Tr Scheme 80–88; P-in-c Gt Wishford *Sarum* 80–83; P-in-c Colehill 88–96; V 96–13; Dioc Dir of Readers 88–95; Can and Preb Sarum Cathl 07–13; rtd 13; PtO *Sarum* 13–22. *27 Fishers Close, Blandford Forum DT11 7EL* E: canongoodall@gmail.com

GOODALL, Peter Norman. b 56. City of Lon Poly BA 77. Win Sch of Miss 17. **d** 20 **p** 21. C Bitterne Park *Win* from 20. *The Poplars, 12 Midanbury Lane, Southampton SO18 4HP* M: 07403-331319 E: peter@ascensionsouthampton.co.uk

GOODBODY, Ruth Vivien. b 68. Surrey Univ BA 02. Wycliffe Hall Ox 96 STETS 00. **d** 02 **p** 03. C Bourne Valley *Sarum* 02–06; C Stebbing and Lindsell w Gt and Lt Saling *Chelmsf* 06–10; rtd 10; PtO *Chelmsf* from 12. *The Rectory, Old Vicarage Close, High Easter, Chelmsford CM1 4RW* T: (01245) 294421

GOODBODY, Steven John. b 70. Univ of Wales (Cardiff) BD 92. Wycliffe Hall Ox 00. **d** 02 **p** 03. C Tunbridge Wells St Jo *Roch* 02–05; C Ex St Leon w H Trin 05–10; TR Washfield, Stoodleigh, Withleigh etc 10–15; V Fremington 15–19. *19 Lane End Close, Instow, Bideford EX39 4LG* T: (01271) 861082 M: 07768-645172 E: stevegoodbody@btinternet.com

GOODBODY, Timothy Edward. b 66. York Univ BA 89. Wycliffe Hall Ox BTh 98. **d** 98 **p** 99. C Blandford Forum and Langton Long *Sarum* 98–02; NSM Bourne Valley 02–06; P-in-c Stebbing and Lindsell w Gt and Lt Saling *Chelmsf* 06–20; P-in-c Broxted w Chickney and Tilty etc 16–20; Dioc Dir of Ords from 20; NSM S Rodings from 20; NSM High Easter and Good Easter w Margaret Roding from 20; NSM Gt Canfield w High Roding and Aythorpe Roding from 20. *The Rectory, Old Vicarage Close, High Easter, Chelmsford CM1 4RW* T: (01245) 294421

GOODBURN, David Henry. b 41. S'wark Ord Course 73. **d** 76 **p** 77. NSM Enfield SS Pet and Paul *Lon* 76–82; PtO 83–85; NSM Potters Bar *St Alb* 85–88; Chapl RN 88–96; V Luton St Sav *St Alb* 96–09; rtd 09; PtO *St Alb* 09–20; *Cant* from 12; *Lon* 17–18. *Major's, Barrack Hill, Hythe CT21 4BZ* T: (01303) 262736

GOODDEN, John Maurice Phelips. b 34. Sarum & Wells Th Coll 70. **d** 72 **p** 75. C Weymouth H Trin *Sarum* 72–74; C Harlow New Town w Lt Parndon *Chelmsf* 74–78; Ind Chapl and Chapl Princess Alexandra Hosp Harlow 78–82; V Moulsham St Jo *Chelmsf* 86–90; R Chipstead and Adv Rural Min *S'wark* 90–04; rtd 04; PtO *B & W* from 05; *Sarum* 05–16. *7 Fitzjocelyn House, St John's Hospital, Chapel Court, Bath BA1 1SL* T: (01225) 444381 E: goodden@msn.com

GOODDEN, Stephanie Anne. See NADARAJAH, Stephanie Anne

GOODE, Allan William. b 50. St Mellitus Coll 16. **d** 17 **p** 18. NSM Birkenhead Ch Ch *Ches* from 17. *49 Birch Road, Prenton CH43 5UF* T: 0151-652 1304 E: twogoodes@hotmail.com

GOODE, Claire Elizabeth. b 60. Nottm Univ BSc 82. EMMTC 04. **d** 08 **p** 09. C S Notts Cluster of Par *S'well* 08–11; P-in-c Thurgarton w Hoveringham and Bleasby etc 11–14; P-in-c Rolleston w Fiskerton, Morton and Upton 11–14; V Nottingham St Andr 14–20; Chapl Launde Abbey *Leic* from 20. *Launde Abbey, Launde Road, Launde, Leicester LE7 9XB* T: (01572) 717254 E: revclairegoode@gmail.com

GOODE, John Laurence. b 48. W Cheshire Coll of Tech TEng 70 Federal Univ Minas Gerais Brazil Dip Teaching 78. Chich Th Coll 81. **d** 83 **p** 84. C Crewe St Andr *Ches* 83–86; USPG 87–94; Brazil 91–94; TV Latchford Ch Ch 00–20; P-in-c Latchford St Jas 15–18; rtd 20. *Address temp unknown* E: dida1@btopenworld.com

GOODE, Jonathan. b 67. St Martin's Coll Lanc BA 89. Qu Coll Birm. **d** 00 **p** 01. C Middleton St Mary *Ripon* 00–04; P-in-c Hartlepool St Hilda *Dur* 04–08; Chapl St Hilda's Sch 04–08; V Denton *Newc* 08–12; PtO 13–18; Chapl Northumberland, Tyne and Wear NHS Foundn Trust from 15. *St Mary's Vicarage, 77 Holywell Avenue, Whitley Bay NE26 3AG* T: 0191-280 3555 E: revjgoode@yahoo.com

GOODE, Michael Arthur John. b 40. K Coll Lon BD AKC 63. **d** 64 **p** 65. C Sunderland Springwell w Thorney Close *Dur* 64–68; C Solihull *Birm* 68–70; R Fladbury, Wyre Piddle and Moor *Worc* 70–75; P-in-c Foley Park 75–81; V 81–83; RD Kidderminster 81–83; TR Crawley *Chich* 83–93; TR Abingdon and V Shippon *Ox* 93–05; rtd 05; PtO *Worc* from 07. *13 Britannia Square, Worcester WR1 3DG* T: (01905) 616982 E: maj.goode@btinternet.com

GOODE, Canon Peter William Herbert. b 23. Oak Hill Th Coll 60. **d** 62 **p** 63. C Woodford Wells *Chelmsf* 62–65; V Harold Hill St Paul 65–76; V Gt Warley Ch Ch 76–93; RD Brentwood 89–93; Hon Can Chelmsf Cathl 90–93; rtd 93; PtO *St Alb* 93–18. *52 Slimmons Drive, St Albans AL4 9AP* T: (01727) 852166

GOODE, Canon Timothy. b 69. Huddersfield Poly BA 90 Roehampton Inst PGCE 91. Ripon Coll Cuddesdon 07. **d** 09 **p** 10. C Croydon St Jo *S'wark* 09–12; TV Caterham 12–18; R Lee St Marg from 18; Dioc Disability Adv from 13; Hon Can S'wark Cathl from 20. *St Margaret's Rectory, Brandram Road, London SE13 5EA* T: (020) 8318 5438 E: revtimgoode@gmail.com

GOODEY, Philip Julian Frank. b 61. Aston Tr Scheme 87 Trin Coll Bris 89. **d** 92 **p** 93. C Iver *Ox* 92–94; C Hornchurch St Andr *Chelmsf* 94–99; V Wickham Market w Pettistree *St E* 99–01; TR Parkham, Alwington, Buckland Brewer etc *Ex* 01–06; P-in-c Lundy Is 01–06; R Botley *Portsm* 06–11; V Curdridge 06–11; R Durley 06–11; TR Drypool *York* 11–15; V Boughton Monchelsea *Cant* from 15. *The Vicarage, Church Hill, Boughton Monchelsea, Maidstone ME17 4BU* T: (01622) 743321 E: phil.goodey@gmail.com

GOODFELLOW, Ian. b 37. St Cath Coll Cam BA 61 MA 65 Lon Univ PGCE 76 Dur Univ PhD 83. Wells Th Coll 61. **d** 63 **p** 64. C Dunstable *St Alb* 63–67; Chapl Haileybury Coll 67–71; Asst Chapl St Bede Coll Dur 71–74; Lect and Tutor 71–75; Sen Lect and Tutor SS Hild and Bede Coll Dur 75–78; Sen Cllr Open Univ (SW Region) 78–97; PtO *Ex* from 89. *Crosslea, 206 Whitchurch Road, Tavistock PL19 9DQ* T: (01822) 612069 E: ian1@waitrose.com

GOODFELLOW, Richard Oliver. b 76. Cumbria Coll of Art & Design BA 00. St Jo Coll Nottm 14. **d** 16 **p** 17. C Aspatria w Hayton and Gilcrux *Carl* 16–19; P-in-c Harraby from 19; P-in-c Upperby from 20. *St Elizabeth's Vicarage, Arnside Road, Carlisle CA1 3QA* T: (01228) 596427 M: 07720-784722 E: richard_goodfellow@yahoo.co.uk

GOODGER, The Very Revd Kenneth Andrew. b 67. Univ of Qld BA 96. St Fran Coll Brisbane BTh 97. **d** 93 **p** 96. C Milton Australia 93–96; C Caloundra 96–99; C Pimlico St Pet w Westmr Ch Ch *Lon* 99–02; R Moorooka and Salisbury Australia 02–06; R Caloundra 06–14; R Wangaratta and Dean H Trin Cathl from 14; V Gen Wangaratta 15-18 and from 20. *2 The Close, Wangaratta VIC 3677, Australia* T: (0061) (3) 5721 8292 E: kagoodger67@gmail.com

GOODHEW, David John. b 65. Collingwood Coll Dur BA 86 CCC Ox DPhil 92 St Jo Coll Dur BA 92. Cranmer Hall Dur 90. **d** 93 **p** 94. C Bedminster *Bris* 93–96; Chapl and Fell St Cath Coll Cam 96–01; V Fulford *York* 01–08; P-in-c York St Denys 01–04; Dir Minl Practice Cranmer Hall Dur 08–19; V Linthorpe *York* from 19; Visiting Fell St Jo Coll Dur from 19. *St Barnabas' Vicarage, 8 The Crescent, Middlesbrough TS5 6SQ* T: (01642) 817306 E: d.j.goodhew@durham.ac.uk *or* david@st-barnabas.net

GOODHEW, Lindsey Jane Ellin. b 66. UEA BA 87 St Jo Coll Dur BA 92. Cranmer Hall Dur 90. **d** 93 **p** 94. C Bishopsworth *Bris* 93–96; PtO *Ely* 96–97; Hon C Cambridge St Mark 97–01; PtO *York* 01–07; Hon C Fulford 07–08; PtO *Dur* 08–09; Hon C Dur St Nic 09–19; Hon C Linthorpe *York* from 19. *St Barnabas Church, 1A St Barnabas Road, Middlesbrough TS5 6JR* E: lindsey@st-barnabas.net

GOODING, Carole Jeanette. b 63. Ripon Coll Cuddesdon 18. **d** 21. NSM Eton w Eton Wick, Boveney and Dorney *Ox* from 21. *The Vicarage, Delaford Close, Iver SL0 9JX* T: (01753) 372298 E: revcarolegooding@gmail.com

GOODING, Ms Karen Ann. b 55. LRAM 76 ARCM 77. **d** 11 **p** 16. OLM Alford w Rigsby *Linc* 11–12; NSM Enfield St Mich *Lon* 12–15; Chapl All SS Academy Dunstable 15–16; PtO *Lon* 15–18; C Wantsum Gp *Cant* 16–20; P-in-c Westgate St Sav from 19. *6 Thanet Road, Westgate-on-Sea CT8 8PB* E: karenanngooding@gmail.com

GOODING, Paul David Buchanan. b 76. Pemb Coll Ox MA 98 Green Coll Ox PGCE 01. Ox Min Course 06. **d** 08. NSM Grove *Ox* 08–12; NSM Vale from 12; Asst Chapl Abingdon Sch from 10. *c/o Crockford, Church House, 27 Great Smith Street, London SW1P 3AZ* E: pdbgooding@hotmail.com

GOODING, Robert Henry. b 60. ACII 87. Trin Coll Bris 08. **d** 10 **p** 11. C Walton le Soken *Chelmsf* 10–13; V Iver Ox from 13. *St Peter's Church, 1 Thorney Lane North, Iver SL0 9JU* T: (01753) 652078 M: 07943-612205 E: rev.robert@goodingonline.co.uk

GOODISON, Miss Eleanor Mary. b 57. Leeds Univ BA 78. ERMC 11. **d** 14 **p** 15. NSM S Hartismere *St E* 14–17; NSM Athelington, Denham, Horham, Hoxne etc 17–20; P-in-c from 20. *Catelyn's House, Wingfield, Diss IP21 5QZ* T: (01379) 384181 M: 07876-143579 E: eleanor.goodison@gmail.com

GOODLAND, Michael Eric. b 53. WEMTC 97. **d** 97 **p** 98. NSM Ilminster and Distr *B & W* 97–02; NSM Crewkerne w Wayford 02–07; PtO *Truro* 07–10; P-in-c Lanreath, Pelynt and Bradoc 10–12; P-in-c St Germans 12–14; V 14–17; C Saltash 12–17; RD E Wivelshire 12–17; rtd 17; PtO *B & W* from 18. *5 Lower Meadow, Ilminster TA19 9DR* M: 07947-719487 E: michaelgoodland08@gmail.com

GOODMAN, Alice Abigail. b 58. Harvard Univ BA 80 Girton Coll Cam BA 82 MA 86 Boston Univ MDiv 97. Ripon Coll Cuddesdon 00. **d** 01 **p** 03. C Redditch, The Ridge *Worc* 01–02; C Kidderminster St Mary and All SS w Trimpley etc 02–06; Chapl Trin Coll Cam 06–11; R Fulbourn *Ely* from 11; V Gt Wilbraham from 11; R Lt Wilbraham from 11. *The Rectory, 2 Apthorpe Street, Fulbourn, Cambridge CB21 5EY* T: (01223) 880337 E: goodhill@appleinter.net

GOODMAN, Garry Gordon. b 52. **d** 09 **p** 10. OLM Bure Valley *Nor* 09–12; NSM Horsford, Felthorpe and Hevingham 12–19; rtd 19; PtO *Nor* from 19. *Heath Farm House, Coltishall Road, Buxton, Norwich NR10 5JD*   T: (01603)   279393 E: garry.goodman@btinternet.com

GOODMAN, John Dennis Julian. b 35. Sarum & Wells Th Coll 74. **d** 76 **p** 77. C Cotmanhay *Derby* 76–79; TV Old Brampton and Loundsley Green 79–86; R Finningley w Auckley *S'well* 86–96; rtd 96; PtO *Pet* 96–19. *8 Springfield, Wootton, Northampton NN4 6HB*   T: (01604)   706443 E: johndi.goodman@btinternet.com

GOODMAN, John Paul. b 84. Trin Coll Bris BA 13 MA 14. **d** 14 **p** 15. C Banbury St Fran *Ox* 14–17; R Chalfont St Peter from 17. *The Vicarage, 4 Austenway, Chalfont St Peter, Gerrards Cross SL9 8NW*   M: 07726-971772 E: goodmanjpf@gmail.com

GOODMAN, Brother Kevin Charles. b 54. Surrey Univ BA 06. STETS 03. **d** 06 **p** 07. NSM Buckland Newton, Cerne Abbas, Godmanstone etc *Sarum* 06–09; PtO *Cant* 09–10; C Cant St Dunstan w H Cross 10–17; C Cant St Dunstan, St Mildred and St Pet 17–20. *6 Eastbridge Hospital, High Street, Canterbury CT1 2BD* E: kevinssf@franciscans.org.uk

GOODMAN, Mrs Mairion Kim (Mars). b 73. Leeds Univ BA 95. Trin Coll Bris BA 03. **d** 05 **p** 06. NSM Redland Bris 05–10 and 13–15. *6 Willoughby Road, Horfield, Bristol BS7 8QX*   T: 0117-989 2597

GOODMAN, Mark Alexander Scott. b 61. Lanc Univ BA 84 Nottm Univ BTh 90 New Coll Edin MTh 97. Linc Th Coll 87. **d** 90 **p** 91. C Denton St Lawr *Man* 90–93; R Dalkeith and Lasswade *Edin* 93–06; Dioc Communications Officer 96–06; Can St Mary's Cathl and Syn Clerk 02–06; Chapl Stamford Sch from 06. *Stamford Endowed Schools, Brazenose House, St Paul's Street, Stamford PE9 2BE*   T: (01780) 750363   M: 07947-032739   E: mgoodman@ses.lincs.sch.uk

GOODMAN, Mrs Penelope Jane. b 52. ERMC 06. **d** 09 **p** 10. OLM Bure Valley *Nor* 09–12; NSM Horsford, Felthorpe and Hevingham 12–17; C Easton, Colton, Marlingford and Bawburgh 17–19; NSM from 19; Chapl to Dioc Staff from 19. *Heath Farm House, Coltishall Road, Buxton, Norwich NR10 5JD*   T: (01603)   279393 E: garry.goodman@btinternet.com

GOODMAN, Peter William. b 60. St Cath Coll Cam BA 82 Sheff Univ MPhil 98 PhD 11 Linc Univ PGCE 13. St Jo Coll Nottm 85. **d** 89 **p** 90. C Stapenhill w Cauldwell *Derby* 89–92; C Ovenden *Wakef* 92–94; P-in-c Halifax St Aug 94–98; Crosslinks Ethiopia 98–05; C Leic H Trin w St Jo 05–08; PtO 13–16; CMD Officer *Linc* 14–17; Asst Prin St Pet Coll and Dir CMD *Sheff* from 17. *Diocesan Church House, 95-99 Effingham Street, Rotherham S65 1BL*   T: (01709) 309100   M: 07387-260826 E: bill.goodman@sheffield.anglican.org

GOODMAN, Victor Terence. b 46. Liv Univ BSc 67 CEng 92 MBCS 74. EMMTC 82. **d** 85 **p** 86. NSM Barwell w Potters Marston and Stapleton *Leic* 85–89; NSM Croft and Stoney Stanton 89–94; P-in-c Whetstone 94–03; TV Hugglescote w Donington, Ellistown and Snibston 03–07; C Coalville w Bardon Hill and Ravenstone 07–10; rtd 10; PtO *Leic* 13–21. *21 New Inn Close, Broughton Astley, Leicester LE9 6SU*   T: (01455) 285410 E: victor.goodman1@btinternet.com

GOODMAN, Mrs Victoria Elizabeth Stuart. b 51. RGN 74. Trin Coll Bris. **d** 98 **p** 99. C Ilminster and Distr *B & W* 98–02; R Blagdon w Compton Martin and Ubley 02–10; Dioc Chapl MU 01–10; rtd 10; PtO *Sarum* from 12; *B & W* 13–18. *Underhill, Castle Hill Lane, Mere, Warminster BA12 6JB*   T: (01747) 860070 E: vickieplum51@btinternet.com

GOODMAN, William. *See* GOODMAN, Peter William

GOODRICH, The Very Revd Derek Hugh. b 27. Selw Coll Cam BA 48 MA 54. St Steph Ho Ox 50. **d** 52 **p** 53. C Willesden St Andr *Lon* 52–57; W Lodge St Sidwell Guyana 57–67; V Port Mourant 67–71; R New Amsterdam All SS 71–84; Adn Berlice 81–84; V Gen Dio Guyana 82–94; Dean Georgetown 84–93; P-in-c St Aloysius 93–00; rtd 00; PtO *S'wark* 03–14. *The College of St Barnabas, Blackberry Lane, Lingfield RH7 6NJ*   T: (01342) 872873

GOODRICH, Mrs Michelle Susan. b 69. All SS Cen for Miss & Min 13. **d** 16 **p** 17. C Prestbury *Ches* 16–18; P-in-c Alsager St Mary 18–20; V from 20. *The Vicarage, 37 Eaton Road, Alsager, Stoke-on-Trent ST7 2BQ*   M: 07562-723798 E: vicar@stmarysalsager.org

GOODRICH, Mrs Nancy Elisabeth. b 66. St Hilda's Coll Ox BA 88 MA 09 ACA 93. WMMTC 06. **d** 09 **p** 10. C St Annes St Thos *Blackb* 09–12; V Bolton-le-Sands 12–21; AD Tunstall 16–21; V Bollington *Ches* from 21. *19 Waterwheel Way, Bollington, Macclesfield SK10 5DJ*   M: 07974-250466 E: revnancygoodrich@gmail.com

GOODRICH, Canon Peter. b 36. Dur Univ BA 58. Cuddesdon Coll 60. **d** 62 **p** 63. C Walton St Jo *Liv* 62–66; C Prescot

66–68; V Anfield St Marg 68–72; V Gt Crosby St Faith 72–83; P-in-c Seaforth 76–80; RD Bootle 78–83; TR Upholland 83–94; R Halsall 94–02; Dir Dioc OLM Scheme 94–02; Hon Can Liv Cathl 89–02; rtd 03; PtO *Liv* from 03. *Dunelm, 16 Hillside Avenue, Ormskirk L39 4TD*   T: (01695) 573285

GOODRIDGE, Elizabeth Jane. b 57. SEITE 06. **d** 09 **p** 10. NSM S Beddington and Roundshaw *S'wark* 09–13; NSM Kenley from 13; NSM Purley St Barn from 13. *4 Gander Green Lane, Sutton SM1 2EJ*   T: (020) 8661 5343   M: 07788-755752 E: elizabeth.goodridge1@btinternet.com

GOODRIDGE, John Francis James. b 49. Open Univ BA 86. WEMTC 04. **d** 07 **p** 08. Partnership P E Bris 07–13; NSM Two Mile Hill St Mich 07–13; NSM Hanham 13–19; NSM Kingswood 13–19; PtO from 19. *153 Whittucks Road, Bristol BS15 3PY*   T: 0117-940 1508

GOODRIDGE, Paul Charles. b 54. Leic Univ MSc 98 MCIPD 88. **d** 04 **p** 05. OLM Cheam *S'wark* 04–08; C Beddington 08–10; R Godstone and Blindley Heath 10–14; PtO *Eur* 15–16; Chapl Bucharest w Sofia 16–19; rtd 19. *15 Poltova Street, Samovodene, Veliko Turnovo 5040, Bulgaria*

GOODRIDGE, Peter Warren. b 66. Liv Univ BA 87. Wycliffe Hall Ox 07. **d** 09 **p** 10. C Tonbridge SS Pet and Paul *Roch* 09–13; R Elmswell *St E* from 13. *The Rectory, Church Road, Elmswell, Bury St Edmunds IP30 9DY*   T: (01359) 240512 E: elmswellrector@gmail.com

GOODSON, Sally Louise. b 64. BSc. STETS. **d** 13 **p** 14. C Win St Bart and St Lawr w St Swithun 13–17; C Harpenden St Nic *St Alb* from 17. *86 Tuffnells Way, Harpenden AL5 3HG*   M: 07840-926507 E: sally.goodson21@gmail.com

GOODWIN, Canon Barry Frederick John. b 48. Birm Univ BSc 69 PhD 77. St Jo Coll Nottm 86. **d** 88 **p** 89. C Ware Ch Ch *St Alb* 88–91; P-in-c Stanstead Abbots 91–96; P-in-c Gt Amwell w St Marg 95–96; V Gt Amwell w St Margaret's and Stanstead Abbots 96–99; RD Hertford and Ware 96–99; V Clapham Park All SS *S'wark* 99–05; RD Clapham 02–05; Soc Resp (Par Development) Adv Croydon Adnry 05–11; Hon C Addiscombe St Mildred 09–11; Hon Can S'wark Cathl 11–13; Acting Adn Croydon 11–13; rtd 13; PtO *S'wark* from 13. *57 South Way, Croydon CR0 8RH*   M: 07967-917151 E: barry@bcgoodwin.me.uk

GOODWIN, Bruce William. b 64. Univ of W Aus BA 84 DipEd 85. Trin Coll Bris BA 09. **d** 09 **p** 10. C Thornbury and Oldbury-on-Severn w Shepperdine *Glouc* 09–12; Sen Chapl Glos Univ 12–17; V Oldland *Bris* from 17; P-in-c Longwell Green from 17. *St Anne's Vicarage, Grangeville Close, Longwell Green, Bristol BS30 9YJ*   T: (01454)   853213   M: 07720-772190 E: goodwins07@gmail.com

GOODWIN, Daphne Mary. b 35. Lon Univ MB, BS 60. STETS 94. **d** 97 **p** 98. NSM Ifield *Chich* 97–17; rtd 17; PtO *Chich* from 17. *1 Selbourne Close, Crawley RH10 3SA*   T: (01293) 612906 E: dapheter@aol.com

GOODWIN, Mrs Gillian Sheila. b 54. NOC MTh 99. **d** 99 **p** 00. C Penkridge *Lich* 99–02; TV Wrockwardine Deanery 02–15; rtd 15; PtO *Ches* from 16. *4 Gloucester Road, Hyde SK14 5JG*   T: 0161-368 6740 E: gillgoodwin61@gmail.com

GOODWIN, Mrs Josephine Anne. b 64. Ripon Coll Cuddesdon 09. **d** 12 **p** 13. C Stow on the Wold, Condicote and The Swells *Glouc* 12–16; C Cheltenham St Mark 16–17; Chapl Cheltenham Ladies' Coll from 17. *Rose Cottage, St Margaret's Road, Alderton, Tewkesbury GL20 8NN*   T: (01242)   620391   M: 07718-089099 E: revdjosie.goodwin@btinternet.com

GOODWIN, Michelle Amanda. b 79. UEA BSc 03 PhD 07 Middx Univ MA 21. St Mellitus Coll 18. **d** 21. C St Jas in the City *Liv* from 21. *10 Bethel Grove, Liverpool L17 2BJ*   M: 07717-005754   E: revmichellegoodwin@gmail.com   or drmichellegoodwin@gmail.com

GOODWIN, Stephen. b 58. Sheff Univ BA 80 Wolv Univ BSc 14. Cranmer Hall Dur 82. **d** 85 **p** 86. C Lytham St Cuth *Blackb* 85–87; C W Burnley All SS 88–90; TV Headley All SS *Guildf* 90–98; NSM Leek and Meerbrook *Lich* 98–03; Chapl Univ Hosp of N Staffs NHS Trust 03–08; Chapl Douglas Macmillan Hospice Blurton 08–17; PtO *Eur* from 17. *2 Lordshire Mews, Armshead Road, Werrington, Stoke-on-Trent ST9 0HJ*   T: (01782) 961242   M: 07496-816239 E: goodwinstephen22@gmail.com

GOODWIN, Mrs Susan Elizabeth. b 51. Leeds Poly BSc 74 Leeds Univ MSc 76. Cranmer Hall Dur 82. **dss** 84 **d** 87 **p** 94. Norton Woodseats St Chad *Sheff* 84–87; Par Dn 87; Chapl Scargill Ho 87–89; NSM W Burnley All SS *Blackb* 89–90; NSM Headley All SS *Guildf* 90–98; Past Asst Acorn Chr Healing Trust 91–93; P-in-c Wetley Rocks *Lich* 98–09; P-in-c Werrington 08–09; V Werrington and Wetley Rocks 09–16; RD Cheadle 14–16; rtd 16; PtO *Eur* from 18. *2*

Lordshire Mews, Armshead Road, Werrington, Stoke-on-Trent ST9 0HJ T: (01782) 302418 E: revsueg@gmail.com

GOODWIN-HUDSON, Anthony James Philip. b 76. **d** 14 **p** 15. C Appley Bridge and Parbold *Blackb* 14–16; C Leyland St Andr 16–18; PtO 18–20; Chapl St Lawr Coll Ramsgate from 19. *St Lawrence College, College Road, Ramsgate CT11 7AE* T: (01843) 808080 E: jg-h@hotmail.com

GOODWIN HUDSON, Brainerd Peter de Wirtz. b 34. K Coll Lon BD 57 AKC 57. Westcott Ho Cam 57. **d** 59 **p** 60. C Morden *S'wark* 59–60; Australia 61–65; Asst Sec CCCS 65–68; Chapl St Lawr Coll Ramsgate 68–74; Chapl Repton Sch Derby 74–94; Chapl Santiago Chile 94–01; rtd 99; Hon C Broadwell, Evenlode, Oddington, Adlestrop etc *Glouc* 02–06; PtO from 19. *10 Old Forge Close, Bledington, Chipping Norton OX7 6XW* T: (01608) 658002 E: petergoodwinhudson@gmail.com

GOODWINS, Christopher William Hedley. b 36. St Jo Coll Cam BA 58 MA 62. Linc Th Coll 62. **d** 64 **p** 65. C Lowestoft St Marg *Nor* 64–69; V Tamerton Foliot *Ex* 69–98; P-in-c Southway 78–82; rtd 98; P-in-c Isleham *Ely* 99–04; PtO from 05; *St E* 10–15. *102 The Causeway, Isleham, Ely CB7 5ST* T: (01638) 780284 E: cwhgoodwins@gmail.com

GOODYEAR, Benjamin. b 76. LSE BSc 98. Ridley Hall Cam 03. **d** 06 **p** 07. C Balham Hill Ascension *S'wark* 06–09; P-in-c Brixton St Paul w St Sav 09–13; V 13–18; V Herne Hill from 18. *1 Finsen Road, London SE5 9AX* T: (020) 7737 4978 M: 07866-774354 E: vicar@hernehillparish.org.uk

GOODYER, Canon Edward Arthur. b 42. Witwatersrand Univ BA 63 SS Coll Cam BA 67 MA 70 Rhodes Univ MTh 91. St Paul's Coll Grahamstown 68. **d** 68 **p** 69. C Rosebank S Africa 69; R Vanderbijlpark 71–72; Chapl St Jo Coll Houghton Estate 73–75; R Stellenbosch 76–84; Can Cape Town 80–84; R Bramley S Africa 84–87; Chapl St Andr Coll Grahamstown 88–92; P-in-c Sidbury 90–92; R Alverstoke *Portsm* 92–12; P-in-c Gosport Ch Ch 97–01; rtd 12; Chapl Huggens Coll Northfleet 12–19; PtO *Portsm* from 19; Hon Can Wusasa Nigeria from 99. *39 Burnt House Lane, Fareham PO14 2LP* M: 07952-194187 E: ego.lizg@gmail.com

GOOLJARY, Yousouf Azad. b 59. Ex Univ BSc 80 Man Poly PGCE 82. SEITE 07. **d** 10 **p** 11. C Greenwich St Alfege *S'wark* 10–13; C Becontree S *Chelmsf* 13–16; Chapl Dagenham Park C of E Sch 13–16; C Edin Ch Ch 16–18; R Edin St Martin 18–19. *15 Ardmillan Terrace, Edinburgh EH11 2JW* M: 07563-366811 E: revgooljary@aol.com

GORDON, Alan Williamson. b 53. Strathclyde Univ BA 75 MCIBS 79. Wycliffe Hall Ox 98. **d** 98 **p** 99. C Win Ch Ch 98–02; R King's Worthy 02–15; R Headbourne Worthy 02–15; RD Win 07–13; V Tamworth *Lich* 15–20; rtd 20; PtO *Lich* from 20. *6 Harington Close, Formby, Liverpool L37 1XP* T: (01704) 620224 E: worthyrector@gmail.com

GORDON, Canon Alexander Ronald. b 49. Nottm Univ BPharm 71. Coll of Resurr Mirfield 74. **d** 77 **p** 78. C Headingley *Ripon* 77–80; C Fareham SS Pet and Paul *Portsm* 80–83; V Cudworth *Wakef* 83–85; P-in-c Tain *Mor* 85–87; P-in-c Lairg Miss 87–01; P-in-c Brora *Mor* 88–01; P-in-c Dornoch 88–01; Dioc Dir of Ords 89–01; Can St Andr Cathl Inverness 95–01; Hon Can St Andr Cathl Inverness from 02; Chapl Strasbourg *Eur* 02–05; Provost St Andr Cathl Inverness *Mor* 05–14; Chapl Geneva *Eur* 14–19; PtO from 20. *12 Culpleasant Avenue, Tain IV19 1JS* T: (01862) 892617 M: 07485-257257 E: canonalexgordon@outlook.com

GORDON, Alexander Strathearn. b 77. Edin Univ MA 00. St Mellitus Coll BA 12. **d** 12 **p** 13. C Onslow Square and S Kensington St Aug *Lon* 12–16; R St John-at-Hackney 16–19; P-in-c Homerton St Luke 18–19; R Hackney from 19; P-in-c Leyton St Mary w St Edw and St Luke *Chelmsf* from 19; V Shoreditch St Leon w St Mich *Lon* from 20; C W Ham *Chelmsf* from 20. *The Rectory, 11 Clapton Square, London E5 8HP* T: (020) 8985 5374 ext 201 E: rector@stjohnathackney.org

GORDON, Anne. *See* LE BAS, Jennifer Anne

GORDON, Mrs Avis Patricia. b 52. Man Univ BA 73. **d** 08 **p** 09. NSM Clifton *Man* 08–20; PtO from 20; Assoc Dir of Ords from 15. *47 Agecroft Road West, Prestwich, Manchester M25 9RF* T: 0161-798 8018 M: 07544-058011 E: avis.1968@hotmail.co.uk

GORDON, Bruce Harold Clark. b 40. Edin Univ MTh 96. Cranmer Hall Dur 65. **d** 68 **p** 69. C Edin St Jas 68–71; C Blackheath St Jo *S'wark* 71–74; R Duns Edin 74–90; R Lanark w Douglas *Glas* 90–05; rtd 05; LtO *Edin* from 05. *52 Foxknowe Place, Livingston EH54 6TX* T: (01506) 418466 M: 07769-927195 E: bruehc.gordon@btinternet.com

GORDON, David John. b 65. Edin Th Coll 90. **d** 93 **p** 94. Chapl St Andr Cathl *Ab* 93–95; P-in-c Alexandria *Glas* 95–00; Chapl Vale of Leven Distr Gen Hosp 95–00; Chapl Christie Park

Primary Sch 95–00; Asst Chapl NE Lincs NHS Trust 00–01; Chapl Tayside Univ Hosps NHS Trust 01–06; Lead Chapl Acute Services NHS Tayside 06; Sen Staff Support Chapl 13–20; PtO *Bre* 13–20; Dioc Supernumerary from 20; P-in-c Invergowrie from 20; P-in-c Dundee St Paul 20–21; P-in-c Dundee St Salvador from 21. *20 Lintrathen Gardens, Dundee DD3 8EJ* M: 07311-070277 E: saintsalvadors@gmail.com *or* david.gordon@brechin.anglican.org

GORDON, Canon Jonathan Andrew. b 61. Keele Univ BA 83 MPhil 98 Southn Univ BTh 88 Southn Inst MPhil 04. Sarum & Wells Th Coll 84. **d** 87 **p** 88. C Wallingford w Crowmarsh Gifford etc *Ox* 87–91; C Tilehurst St Mich 91–93; TV Stoke-upon-Trent *Lich* 93–97; Chapl Southn Solent Univ *Win* 98–05; R Northchurch and Wigginton *St Alb* from 05; RD Berkhamsted from 14; Hon Can St Alb from 19. *St Mary's Rectory, 80 High Street, Northchurch, Berkhamsted HP4 3QW* T: (01442) 871547 E: revjagordon@googlemail.com

GORDON, Julia Kathryn. b 62. Dur Univ BA 17. SNWTP 15. **d** 17 **p** 18. OLM Harwood *Man* from 17. *163 Tottington Road, Bolton BL2 4DF* M: 07968-045893 E: dewhurst4@ntlworld.com

GORDON, Kristy. *See* PATTIMORE, Kristy

GORDON, Lee Veronica. b 65. Univ of Wales BSc 87 Lon Univ PhD 93 Nottm Univ PGCE 12. St Hild Coll 18. **d** 20 **p** 21. C Selston *S'well* from 20. *23 Westbourne Road, Underwood, Nottingham NG16 5EG* M: 07922-435598 E: jamieleegordon@live.co.uk

GORDON, Martin Lewis. b 73. Edin Univ MA 97 K Coll Lon MA 14. Wycliffe Hall Ox BA 09. **d** 10 **p** 11. C Stoke Gifford *Bris* 10–14; P-in-c Telford Park *S'wark* 14–15; V 15–20; V Gen Dio Goma Democratic Republic of Congo from 20. *Address temp unknown* E: martingordon2@gmail.com

GORDON, Mrs Pamela Anne. b 48. Brighton Coll of Educn CertEd 69 BEd 70. SAOMC 99. **d** 02 **p** 03. NSM Wargrave w Knowl Hill *Ox* 02–12; PtO from 12. *Rebeny, 2A Hawthorn Road, Caversham, Reading RG4 6LY* T: 0118-946 3727 M: 07714-256272 E: revpam.sdh@gmail.com

GORDON, Robert John. b 56. Edin Univ MA 81. Wycliffe Hall Ox 87. **d** 89 **p** 90. C Wilnecote *Lich* 89–91; C Bideford *Ex* 91–95; P-in-c Feniton, Buckerell and Escot 95–05; P-in-c Tiverton St Pet and Chevithorne w Cove 05–15; R 15–21; P-in-c Tiverton St Andr 11–21; RD Tiverton and Cullompton 15–17; C N Creedy from 21. *The Rectory, Withleigh, Tiverton EX16 8JQ* T: (01884) 250417 E: robert.j.gordon@btinternet.com

GORDON, The Very Revd Thomas William. b 57. QUB BEd 80 Univ of Ulster MA 86 TCD BTh 89. CITC 85. **d** 89 **p** 90. C Ballymacash *Conn* 89–91; Min Can Belf Cathl 91–95; Chapl and Tutor CITC 91–96; Dir Extra-Mural Studies 96–10; Lect Past Th and Liturgy 01–10; Consultant Dir Past Formation and NSM 06–09; PV Ch Ch Cathl Dublin *D & G* 96–10; Co-ord Relig Progr RTE 99–10; Dean Leighlin *C, F & O* from 10; I Leighlin w Grange Sylvae, Shankill etc from 10. *The Deanery, Old Leighlin, Co Carlow, Republic of Ireland* T: (00353) (59) 972 1570 M: 87-276 7562 E: dean.leighlin@gmail.com

GORDON CLARK, John Vincent Michael. b 29. FCA. S'wark Ord Course 73. **d** 76 **p** 77. NSM Guildf H Trin w St Mary 76–81; NSM Albury w St Martha 81–91; Dioc Chapl to MU 92–95; LtO 95–99; Hon C Guildf Cathl 91–99; PtO 99–12; Newc from 12. *Bethany, 250 Western Way, Ponteland, Newcastle upon Tyne NE20 9ND* T: (01661) 598052

GORDON-CUMMING, Henry Ian. b 28. Barrister-at-Law (Gray's Inn) 56. Oak Hill Th Coll 54. **d** 57 **p** 58. C Southsea St Jude *Portsm* 57–60; Chapl to Bp Ankole-Kigezi Uganda 61–65; Chapl Ntari Sch 65–67; V Virginia Water *Guildf* 68–78; R Busbridge 78–87; R Lynch w Iping Marsh and Milland *Chich* 87–94; rtd 94; PtO *Chich* from 94. *Bay Cottage, Brookside, Runcton, Chichester PO20 1PX* T: (01243) 783395

GORDON-TAYLOR, Benjamin Nicholas. b 69. St Jo Coll Dur BA 90 MA 92 Leeds Univ BA 94 Dur Univ PhD 08 FRSA 99. Coll of Resurr Mirfield 92. **d** 95 **p** 96. C Launceston *Truro* 95–97; C Northampton St Matt *Pet* 97–99; Fell and Chapl Univ Coll Dur 99–04; Lect and Tutor Coll of Resurr Mirfield from 05; Visiting Lect Leeds Univ from 05; Dir Mirfield Liturg Inst from 08; Dioc Liturg Adv *Eur* from 13; PtO *Leeds* from 08. *College of the Resurrection, Stocks Bank Road, Mirfield WF14 0BW* T: (01924) 490441 E: bgordon-taylor@mirfield.org.uk

GORE, Canon John Charles. b 29. Leeds Univ BA 52. Coll of Resurr Mirfield 54. **d** 54 **p** 55. C Middlesbrough St Jo the Ev *York* 54–59; N Rhodesia 59–64; Zambia 64–75; Can Lusaka 70–75; R Elland *Wakef* 75–84; TR 84–86; RD Brighouse and Elland 77–86; V Wembley Park St Aug *Lon* 86–95;

P-in-c Tokyngton St Mich 89–90; AD Brent 90–95; rtd 95; P-in-c Heptonstall *Wakef* 95–99; PtO *Bradf* 99–14; *Leeds* 14–19. *Address temp unknown*

GORHAM, Canon Andrew Arthur. b 51. Bris Univ BA 73 Birm Univ MA 87. Qu Coll Birm 77. **d** 79 **p** 80. C Plaistow St Mary *Roch* 79–82; Chapl Lanchester Poly *Cov* 82–87; TV Warwick 87–95; Chapl Birm Univ 95–00; Bp's Dom Chapl 00–11; Hon Can Birm Cathl 06–11; Master St Jo Hosp Lich 11–16; PtO *Cov* from 11; P-in-c Birm St Paul 18–20; PtO from 20. *St Paul's Church, St Paul's Square, Birmingham B3 1QZ* T: 0121-236 7858 E: andrewgorham@hotmail.co.uk *or* andrew.gorham@stpaulsjq.church

✠**GORHAM, The Rt Revd Karen Marisa.** b 64. Trin Coll Bris BA 95. **d** 95 **p** 96 **c** 16. C Northallerton w Kirby Sigston *York* 95–99; P-in-c Maidstone St Paul *Cant* 99–07; Asst Dir of Ords 02–07; AD Maidstone 03–07; Hon Can Cant Cathl 06–07; Adn Buckingham *Ox* 07–16; Area Bp Sherborne *Sarum* from 16; Hon Asst Bp Portsm from 19. *Sherborne House, Tower Hill, Iwerne Minster, Blandford Forum DT11 8NH* T: (01202) 659427 F: 691418 E: bishop.sherborne@salisbury.anglican.org

✠**GORICK, The Rt Revd Martin Charles William.** b 62. Selw Coll Cam BA 84 MA 88. Ripon Coll Cuddesdon 85. **d** 87 **p** 88 **c** 20. C Birtley *Dur* 87–91; Bp's Dom Chapl *Ox* 91–94; V Smethwick *Birm* 94–01; AD Warley 97–01; R Stratford-upon-Avon, Luddington etc *Cov* 01–13; Adn Ox and Can Res Ch Ch 13–20; Suff Bp Dudley *Worc* from 20. *The Rectory, Main Road, Bredon, Tewkesbury GL20 7LT* E: bishop.dudley@cofe-worcester.org.uk

GORRINGE, Edward George Alexander. b 63. TD . QUB BA 85 Strathclyde Univ MBA 00 FCMA 06. CITC 04. **d** 07 **p** 08. NSM Aghalee *D & D* 07–09; CF from 09; Dioc Sec *Dur* 18–20; PtO from 18. *c/o MOD Chaplains (Army)* T: (01264) 383430

GORRINGE, Prof Timothy Jervis. b 46. St Edm Hall Ox BA 69 MPhil 75 Ox Univ DD 92. Sarum Th Coll 69. **d** 72 **p** 73. C Chapel Allerton *Ripon* 72–75; C Ox St Mary V w St Cross and St Pet 76–78; India 79–86; Chapl St Jo Coll Ox 86–96; Reader St Andr Univ from 96; Prof Th Ex Univ from 99. *Venbridge House, Cheriton Bishop, Exeter EX6 6HD* T: (01392) 264242 E: t.j.gorringe@exeter.ac.uk

GORTON, Angela Deborah. *See* WYNNE, Angela Deborah

GORTON (née CARTER), Sarah Helen Buchanan. b 44. St Andr Univ BSc 65 DipEd 66. TISEC 93. **d** 96 **p** 98. NSM Lenzie *Glas* 96–01; P-in-c Alexandria 01–12; Chapl Gtr Glas and Clyde NHS 01–11; rtd 12. *Northbank Gardens, 6B Northbank Road, Kirkintilloch, Glasgow G66 1EZ* T: 0141-775 1204 E: shbgorton@btinternet.com

GORWOOD, Duncan Brian. b 73. JP . Huddersfield Univ BMus 95 Bretton Hall Coll PGCE 97. Ripon Coll Cuddesdon 17. **d** 19 **p** 20. C Horninglow *Lich* from 19. *62 Redhill Lane, Tutbury, Burton-on-Trent DE13 9JW* M: 07841-098465 E: revfrduncan@hotmail.com

GOSDEN, Angela. b 50. Ox Min Course 07. **d** 11 **p** 12. NSM Stanford in the Vale w Goosey and Hatford *Ox* 11–14; PtO 14–15; Chapl Gt Western Hosps NHS Foundn Trust from 15; PtO *Win* from 17; *Eur* from 17. *The Haven, 4 Garden Close, New Milton BH25 6NL* T: (01425) 629491 E: angela_gosden@btconnect.com

GOSDEN, Timothy John. b 50. Open Univ BA 86. Chich Th Coll 74. **d** 77 **p** 78. C Cant All SS 77–81; Asst Chapl Loughb Univ *Leic* 81–85; LtO *Cant* 85–87; Chapl Ch Ch Coll of HE Cant 85–87; Sen Chapl Hull Univ 87–94; V Taunton Lyngford *B & W* 94–98; V Harrow St Mary *Lon* 98–15; rtd 15; PtO *Lon* 15–16; *Nor* from 16. *24 Fletcher Close, Tunstead, Norwich NR12 8RA* T: (01603) 783973 E: fr.timgosden@gmail.com

GOSLER, Andrew Graham Gabriel. b 58. Aber Univ BSc 79 Reading Univ MSc 81 Wolfs Coll Ox DPhil 87 FLS 98 FRSB 16. Ox Min Course 15. **d** 18 **p** 19. NSM Marston w Elsfield *Ox* from 18. *Mansfield College, Mansfield Road, Oxford OX1 3TF* T: (01865) 761110 M: 07778-302488 E: andrew.gosler@zoo.ox.ac.uk

GOSLING, David. b 27. SAOMC 95. **d** 98 **p** 99. OLM High Wycombe *Ox* 98–03; PtO 02–09; *Nor* from 10. *18 Parsons Mead, Norwich NR4 6PG* T: (01603) 506025 E: greygoosedt@gmail.com

GOSLING, David Lagourie. b 39. Man Univ MSc 63 Fitzw Coll Cam MA 69 Lanc Univ PhD 74 MInstP 69 CPhys 84. Ridley Hall Cam 63. **d** 73 **p** 74. Hon C Lancaster St Mary *Blackb* 73–74; Hon C Kingston upon Hull St Matt w St Barn *York* 74–77; Hon C Cottingham 78–83; Asst Chapl Geneva *Eur* 84–89; C Cambridge Gt St Mary w St Mich *Ely* 89–90; C Dry Drayton 90–94; USPG India 95–99; PtO *York* from 95; *Ely* 01–17; Fell Clare Hall Cam from 01; Prin Edwardes Coll Peshawar Pakistan from 06. *Clare Hall, Herschel*

Road, Cambridge CB3 9AL T: (01223) 352450 F: 332333 E: dlg26@cam.ac.uk

GOSLING, Ms Dorothy Grace. b 57. St Martin's Coll Lanc BA 94 K Coll Lon MA 06. SNWTP 07. **d** 10 **p** 11. NSM Ches Cathl 10–14; Chapl Ches Univ 11–14; C Llanbedr DC, Llangynhafal, Llanychan etc. *St As* 14–16; V Llanasa and Ffynnongroew 16–17; I Bryn a Mor Miss Area 18–19; TV Wigan *Liv* from 19. *The Vicarage, 70 Belle Green Lane, Ince, Wigan WN2 2EP* M: 07976-274459 E: dotchka@icloud.com *or* hubleader.central@churchwigan.org

GOSLING, John William Fraser. b 34. St Jo Coll Dur BA 58 MA 71 Ex Univ PhD 78 Win Univ MA 12. Cranmer Hall Dur 58. **d** 60 **p** 61. C Plympton St Mary *Ex* 60–68; V Newport 68–78; Org Sec CECS St Alb and Ox 78–82; C Stratford sub Castle *Sarum* 83–86; Adv on CME 83–86; PtO 86–91 and 95–20; C Swindon Ch Ch *Bris* 91–95; rtd 95. *1 Wiley Terrace, Wilton, Salisbury SP2 0HN* T: (01722) 742788 E: jwfgosling@gmail.com

GOSNEY, The Ven Jeanette Margaret. b 58. Bath Univ BA 81 Univ Coll Ches MA 05 Nottm Univ PGCE 82. St Jo Coll Nottm BTh 93 MPhil 95. **d** 95 **p** 96. C Ipswich St Marg *St E* 95–98; Chapl Loughb Univ *Leic* 98; Sen Chapl 98–01; Tutor Trin Coll Bris 01–04; Chapl Repton Sch Derby 04–05; TV Albury, Braughing, Furneux Pelham, Lt Hadham etc *St Alb* 06–10; Par Development Officer 10–17; Bp's Min Officer *St E* 17–20; NSM Ipswich St Mary-le-Tower 18–20; Dioc Adv for Women's Min from 18; Adn Suffolk from 20. *St Nicholas Centre, 4 Cutler Street, Ipswich IP1 1UQ* T: (01473) 298500 M: 07710-479497 E: archdeacon.jeanette@cofesuffolk.org

GOSS, David James. b 52. Nottm Univ BCombStuds 83 York St Jo Univ MA 10. Linc Th Coll 80. **d** 83 **p** 84. C Wood Green St Mich w Bounds Green St Gabr etc *Lon* 83–86; TV Gleadless Valley *Sheff* 86–89; TR 89–95; V Wheatley Hills 95–15; V Wheatley Hills w Intake 15–21; rtd 21. *30 Cherry Tree Avenue, Ulverston LA12 9HE* T: (01229) 585414 E: davidjamesgoss@gmail.com

GOSS, Canon Kevin Ian. b 56. LRAM 75 LTCL 76 GRSM 77 LGSM 80 Hughes Hall Cam PGCE 78 Heythrop Coll Lon MA 08. S Dios Minl Tr Scheme 89. **d** 92 **p** 93. NSM Ardingly *Chich* 92–98; Asst Chapl Ardingly Coll 92–98; Min Can, Prec and Sacr Cant Cathl 98–03; P-in-c Hockerill *St Alb* 04–13; V 13–14; Chapl Herts Community NHS Trust 04–14; RD Bishop's Stortford *St Alb* 12–14; V Bedford St Paul from 14; Hon Can St Alb from 18. *St Paul's Vicarage, 12 The Embankment, Bedford MK40 3PD* T: (01234) 364638 E: vicarstpaulsbedfd@btinternet.com

GOSS, Michael John. b 37. Chich Th Coll 62. **d** 65 **p** 66. C Angell Town St Jo *S'wark* 65–68; C Catford St Laur 68–71; P-in-c Lewisham St Swithun 71–81; V Redhill St Jo 81–88; V Dudley St Thos and St Luke *Worc* 88–98; C Small Heath *Birm* 98–02; rtd 02; PtO *Birm* from 02. *8 Mayland Road, Birmingham B16 0NG* T: 0121-429 6022 E: michael.goss@tinyworld.co.uk

GOSTELOW (née THOMPSON), Mrs Ruth Jean. b 47. St Alb Minl Tr Scheme 85. **d** 90 **p** 94. Par Dn Stonebridge St Mich *Lon* 90–94; C Ealing St Paul 94–96; TV W Slough *Ox* 96–03; V New Haw *Guildf* 03–13; rtd 13; TV Rye *Chich* 16–20. *34 Oak Tree Court, Smallhythe Road, Tenterden TN30 7EQ* E: rev.ruth@btinternet.com

GOSWELL, Geoffrey. b 34. SS Paul & Mary Coll Cheltenham CertEd 68. Glouc Th Course 70. **d** 71 **p** 72. C Cheltenham Em *Glouc* 71–73; C Lydney w Aylburton 73–76; P-in-c Falfield w Rockhampton 76–79; Chapl HM Det Cen Eastwood Park 76–79; Area Sec CMS Ely 79–81; PtO *Linc* 79–86; *Pet* 79–86; Dep Regional Sec (UK) CMS 86–97; P-in-c Orton Waterville *Ely* 90–96; TV The Ortons, Alwalton and Chesterton 96–97; rtd 97; PtO *Pet* 01–07 and 11–16 and from 19. *8 Lapwing Close, Northampton NN4 0RT* T: (01604) 701572 E: g.goswell@hotmail.co.uk

GOTHARD, Mrs Anne Marie. b 51. STETS. **d** 00 **p** 11. NSM E Meon and Langrish *Portsm* 00–04; NSM Catherington and Clanfield from 04. *27 Green Lane, Clanfield, Waterlooville PO8 0JU* T: (023) 9259 6315 M: 07939-472796 E: rev_gothard@hotmail.com

GOTT, Stephen. b 61. St Jo Coll Nottm 92. **d** 94 **p** 95. C Mount Pellon *Wakef* 94–97; V Greetland and W Vale 97–06; TR Em TM 06–16; V Queensbury *Leeds* from 16. *The Vicarage, 7 Russell Hall Lane, Queensbury, Bradford BD13 2AJ* E: revdsgott@gmail.com

GOUGH, Andrew Stephen. b 60. Sarum & Wells Th Coll 83. **d** 86 **p** 87. C St Leonards Ch Ch and St Mary *Chich* 86–88; C Broseley w Benthall *Heref* 88–90; V Ketley and Oakengates *Lich* 90–93; TV Bickleigh (Plymouth) *Ex* 93; TV Bickleigh and Shaugh Prior 94; P-in-c St Day *Truro* 94–96; V Chacewater w St Day and Carharrack 96–09; P-in-c St Ives

09–16; P-in-c Halsetown 09–16; V St Ives and Halsetown 16–17; Hon Can Truro Cathl 14–17; V Weymouth H Trin *Sarum* from 17. *Holy Trinity Vicarage, 7 Glebe Close, Weymouth DT4 9RL* T: (01305) 760354 M: 07590-695515 E: goughfr@hotmail.com

GOUGH, Andrew Walter. b 55. Bris Univ BA 78. Trin Coll Bris 90. **d** 92 **p** 93. C Mossley Hill St Matt and St Jas *Liv* 92–94; V Wavertree H Trin 94–96; Chapl Warw Sch 96–18; Chapl Bp Wordsworth's Sch Salisbury 18–21; rtd 21; PtO *Sarum* from 21. *Address temp unknown*

GOUGH, Canon Colin Richard. b 47. St Chad's Coll Dur BA 69. Cuddesdon Coll 73. **d** 75 **p** 76. C Lich St Chad 75–78; C Codsall 78–84; V Wednesbury St Paul Wood Green 84–92; TR Tettenhall Wood 92–99; TR Tettenhall Wood and Perton 99–01; P-in-c Stannington *Newc* 01–10; Dioc Adv for CME 01–10; AD Morpeth 08–10; Hon Can Newc Cathl 06–10; rtd 10; PtO *Newc* from 10; Bp's Officer for Rtd Clergy 12–17. *44 Tyelaw Meadows, Shilbottle NE66 2JJ* T: (01665) 581100 E: canoncolin@gmail.com

GOUGH, David Norman. b 42. Oak Hill Th Coll 70. **d** 70 **p** 71. C Penn Fields *Lich* 70–73; C Stapenhill w Cauldwell *Derby* 73–77; V Heath 77–86; P-in-c Derby St Chad 86–95; TV Walbrook Epiphany 95–03; P-in-c Codnor and Loscoe 03–07; rtd 07. *4 Leche Croft, Belper DE56 0DD* E: heyhogough1@gmail.com

GOUGH, Derek William. b 31. Pemb Coll Cam BA 55 MA 59. St Steph Ho Ox 55. **d** 57 **p** 58. C E Finchley All SS *Lon* 57–60; C Roxbourne St Andr 60–66; V Edmonton St Mary w St Jo 66–98; rtd 98; PtO *Chelmsf* 98–07; *St Alb* 00–07. *5 Old Priory Farm, Deeping St James, Peterborough PE6 8PW* T: (01778) 341421 E: derek.gough.1952@pem.cam.ac.uk

GOUGH, Elizabeth. b 54. CBDTI 97. **d** 00 **p** 01. OLM Eden, Gelt and Irthing *Carl* 00–06; TV 06–14; rtd 14; PtO *Carl* from 14. *Brackenside Barn, Brampton CA8 2QX* T: (016977) 746252 E: elizabeth.gough3@btinternet.com

GOUGH, Canon Ernest Hubert. b 31. TCD BA 53 MA 57. TCD Div Sch Div Test 54. **d** 54 **p** 55. C Glenavy *Conn* 54–57; C Lisburn Ch Ch 57–61; P-in-c Belfast St Ninian 61–62; I 62–71; I Belfast St Bart 71–85; I Templepatrick w Donegore 85–97; Can Conn Cathl from 91; rtd 97. *The Caim, 15 Swilly Road, Portstewart BT55 7DJ* T: (028) 7083 3253

GOUGH, Frank Peter. b 32. Lon Coll of Div 66. **d** 68 **p** 69. C Weymouth St Mary *Sarum* 68–70; C Attenborough w Chilwell *S'well* 70–73; R Barrow *Ches* 73–77; P-in-c Summerstown *S'wark* 77–88; RD Tooting 80–88; Dioc Past Sec 88–93; Tutor and Chapl Whittington Coll Felbridge 93–98; rtd 98; PtO *Roch* 03–07; *S'wark* 13–16. *The College of St Barnabas, Blackberry Lane, Lingfield RH7 6NJ* M: 07970-199135 E: frank_gough@msn.com

GOUGH, The Ven Jonathan Robin Blanning. b 62. Univ of Wales (Lamp) BA 83 Westmr Coll Ox MTh 96 FRSA 03. St Steph Ho Ox 83. **d** 85 **p** 86. C Braunton *Ex* 85–86; C Matson *Glouc* 86–89; CF 89–01; Abp's Officer for Ecum *Cant* 01–05; Can Gib Cathl *Eur* 02–05; Hon Can Nicosia from 06; CF 05–08; Sen CF 08–19; Chapl R Memorial Chpl Sandhurst 08–11; Adn Richmond and Craven *Leeds* from 19; Warden of Readers from 19; PtO *Eur* from 05. *4 Appleby Way, Knaresborough HG5 9LX* T: (01423) 866717 E: jonathan.gough@leeds.anglican.org

GOUGH, Miss Lynda Elizabeth. b 54. SS Hild & Bede Coll Dur BA 94 RGN 83. Wycliffe Hall Ox 97. **d** 99 **p** 00. C Stranton *Dur* 99–03; V Spennymoor and Whitworth 03–11; C Darlington H Trin 11–16; AD Darlington 14–16; rtd 16. *19 Pentland Grove, Darlington DL3 8BA* T: (01325) 464799 E: lyndaegough@gmail.com

GOUGH, The Ven Martyn John. b 66. Univ of Wales (Cardiff) BTh 87 Univ of Wales (Lamp) MA 05 FRSA 04. St Steph Ho Ox 88. **d** 90 **p** 91. C Port Talbot St Theodore *Llan* 90–92; C Roath 92–94; Asst Chapl Milan w Genoa and Varese *Eur* 95–98; Chapl RN 98–14; Asst Dir of Ords 07–09; Dir of Ords 09–14; Voc Adv 07–14; Dir 09–14; Dep Chapl of the Fleet 14–17; Chapl of the Fleet and Adn for the RN 18–21; QHC 18–21; Hon Can Portsm Cathl 20–21; rtd 21; PtO *Sarum* from 21. *Address temp unknown* M: 07867-720570 E: martyngough@yahoo.com

GOUGH, Matthew James Charles. b 72. Hull Univ BA 94 MSW 98. Qu Coll Birm 17. **d** 19 **p** 20. C Knighton *Leic* from 19. *Knighton Parish Centre, Church Lane, Leicester LE2 3WG* T: 0116-270 2705 M: 07754-961997 E: revgough@gmail.com

GOUGH, Sally Elizabeth. b 56. St Hild Coll 16. **d** 18 **p** 19. NSM Thornton Dale w Allerston, Ebberston etc *York* from 18; NSM Upper Derwent from 21. *8 Westfield Terrace, Thornton-le-Dale, Pickering YO18 7SQ* E: theflyingphysio@hotmail.com

GOUGH, Stephen William Cyprian. b 50. Alberta Univ BSc 71. Cuddesdon Coll BA 80 MA. **d** 79 **p** 80. C Walton St Mary *Liv* 79–83; V New Springs 83–87; V Childwall St Dav 87–06; V Stoneycroft All SS 04–06; Co-ord Chapl HM Pris Risley 06–08; P-in-c Rainford *Liv* 08–11; V 11–13; TV Walton-on-the-Hill 13–16; rtd 16; PtO *Liv* from 17. *49 Grange Lane, Gateacre, Liverpool L25 4SA* T: 0151-421 1213 M: 07881-648037 E: gough_stephen@btopenworld.com

GOULD, Christine. b 52. **d** 10. NSM Darwen St Pet *Blackb* 10–14; rtd 14; PtO *Blackb* from 14. *15 Lamaleach Drive, Freckleton, Preston PR4 1AJ* T: (01772) 755746 E: b.gould@yahoo.com

GOULD, David Robert. b 59. Cov Poly BA 81. Cranmer Hall Dur 87. **d** 90 **p** 91. C Rugby *Cov* 90–93; CF 93–94; PtO *Cov* 01–05; TV Kings Norton *Birm* 05–08; V Smethwick Resurr from 08. *The Vicarage, 69 South Road, Smethwick, Warley B67 7BP* T: 0121-558 0373 M: 07787-199998 E: davidgould1@btinternet.com

GOULD, Gary David. b 57. ERMC 17. **d** 19. OLM Hempton and Pudding Norton *Nor* 19–20; OLM Walsingham, Houghton and Barsham 19–20; NSM Holt w High Kelling from 20. *23 Priory Crescent, Binham, Fakenham NR21 0DB* T: (01328) 830715 M: 07469-921999 E: garygould57@gmail.com

GOULD, Gerald. b 37. Wilson Carlile Coll 60 S Dios Minl Tr Scheme 84. **d** 86 **p** 87. CA from 62; C Hedge End St Jo *Win* 86–89; V St Goran w Caerhays *Truro* 89–93; P-in-c Crook Peak *B & W* 93–94; R 94–99; rtd 99; PtO *Ex* 99–09. *2 Nightingale Lawns, Cullompton EX15 1UB* T: (01884) 38105 E: g.sj.gould@amserve.com

GOULD, Helen Elizabeth-Anne. See GHEORGHIU GOULD, Helen Elizabeth-Anne

GOULD, Ms Janet. b 63. BEM 17. LTCL 85. Westcott Ho Cam 92. **d** 95 **p** 96. C Pet St Mary Boongate 95–98; C Fleet *Guildf* 98–04; C St Mellons *Mon* 04–05; P-in-c Glan Ely *Llan* from 06. *Church House, Grand Avenue, Cardiff CF5 2YJ* T: (029) 2067 9833 E: jan.gould2@btinternet.com

GOULD, Mark Fearnley. b 70. Southn Univ BEng 92 Ox Univ PGCE 93. St Mellitus Coll 19. **d** 21. C Gt Marlow w Marlow Bottom, Lt Marlow and Bisham *Ox* from 21. *7 Furze Platt Road, Maidenhead SL6 7ND* M: 07910-598977 E: mark_gould@tiscali.co.uk

GOULD, Mrs Pamela Rosemarie. b 41. **d** 01 **p** 02. NSM New Bilton *Cov* 01–03; Asst Chapl HM YOI Onley 01–03; NSM Clifton upon Dunsmore and Newton *Cov* 03–05; P-in-c 05–06; PtO 07–20. *19 Church Road, Church Lawford, Rugby CV23 9EG* T: (024) 7654 5745 E: revpamgould@aol.com

GOULD, Peter Richard. b 34. Univ of Wales BA 57. Qu Coll Birm. **d** 62 **p** 63. C Rothwell *Ripon* 62–68; Chapl Agnes Stewart C of E High Sch Leeds 65–68; V Allerton Bywater *Ripon* 68–73; Asst Master S'well Minster Gr Sch 73–76; Chapl Lic Victuallers' Sch Ascot 76–93; V Aberavon H Trin *Llan* 93–99; rtd 99. *Amber Cottage, 1 Load Lane, Weston Zoyland, Bridgwater TA7 0EQ* T: (01278) 691029

GOULD, Robert Ozburn. b 38. Williams Coll Mass BA 59 St Andr Univ PhD 63. **d** 78 **p** 83. NSM Edin St Columba 78–80; TV from 83; Hon Dioc Supernumerary 80–83; Hon Chapl Edin Univ 00–04. *80 Strathearn Road, Edinburgh EH9 2AF* T: 0131-447 8513 M: 07960-403872 E: bob@gould.ca

GOULD, Susan Judith. See MURRAY, Susan Judith

GOULDER, Canon Catherine Helen. b 44. Hull Univ BA 65 MA 67 Ox Univ DipEd 68. NEOC 96. **d** 98 **p** 99. NSM Sutton St Mich *York* 98–02; P-in-c N Cave w Cliffe 02–08; P-in-c Hotham 02–08; PtO from 08; Can and Preb York Minster from 05. *5 Bishops Croft, Beverley HU17 8JY* T: (01482) 880553 E: kategoulder@katgoulder.karoo.co.uk

GOULDING, Amanda. Win Univ BTh 01. STETS. **d** 07 **p** 08. NSM Upper Dever *Win* 07–08; NSM Win St Bart 08–10; NSM Win St Bart and St Lawr w St Swithun from 10. *St Lawrence Parish Office, Colebrook Street, Winchester SO23 9LH* T: (01962) 849434 E: threesaintswin@gmail.com

GOULDING, John Gilbert. b 29. Univ Coll Dur BA 54 MA 59. **d** 88 **p** 89. NSM Kemsing w Woodlands *Roch* 88–91; Hon Nat Moderator for Reader Tr ACCM 90-91; ABM 91–94; NSM Sevenoaks St Luke CD *Roch* 91–96; PtO 97–12. *Springwood, 50 Copperfields, Kemsing, Sevenoaks TN15 6QG* T: (01732) 762558 E: jonmar.611@btinternet.com

GOULDING, Nicolas John. b 56. Southn Univ BSc 78 PhD 82. NTMTC 94. **d** 97 **p** 98. NSM St Bart Less *Lon* 97–05; Chapl St Bart's and RLSMD Qu Mary and Westf Coll from 97; PtO *St Alb* 99–17; Dioc Adv on Faith and Science from 17; Public Preacher from 17. *5 Greatfield Close, Harpenden AL5 3HP* T: (01582) 461293 *or* (020) 7882 6128 F: 7982 6076 E: n.j.goulding@qmul.ac.uk

GOULDTHORPE, Rachel Carolyn. b 72. Bp Otter Coll 00. **d** 03 **p** 10. NSM Hove *Chich* 03–05; C Moulsecoomb 05–11; TV 11–12; V Bolsover *Derby* from 12. *The Vicarage, Church Street, Bolsover, Chesterfield S44 6HB* T: (01246) 824888 E: rachelgouldthorpe@gmail.com

GOULSTON, Jeremy Hugh. b 68. St Aid Coll Dur BA 90. Ripon Coll Cuddesdon 01. **d** 03 **p** 04. C Henfield w Shermanbury and Woodmancote *Chich* 03–07; TV Wallingford *Ox* 07–15; R Uffington, Shellingford, Woolstone and Baulking from 15. *The Vicarage, Broad Street, Uffington, Faringdon SN7 7RA* T: (01367) 821143 E: jgoulston@btinternet.com

GOUNDREY-SMITH, Stephen John. b 67. Brighton Poly BSc 88 City Univ MSc 94 Ex Univ PhD 21 MRPharmS 89 FFCI 17. Aston Tr Scheme 96 Wycliffe Hall Ox BTh 01. **d** 99 **p** 00. C Happisburgh, Walcott, Hempstead w Eccles etc *Nor* 99–01; PtO *Pet* 02–03; NSM Chenderit 03–08; PtO 09–11; P-in-c Chedworth, Yanworth and Stowell, Coln Rogers etc *Glouc* 10–16; R from 16; Hon C Northleach w Hampnett and Farmington etc 10–16; Hon C Sherborne, Windrush, the Barringtons etc 10–16. *The Vicarage, Cheap Street, Chedworth, Cheltenham GL54 4AA* T: (01285) 720392 M: 07971-524318 E: stephengoundreysmith@gmail.com

GOURDIE, Janice Elizabeth. *See* BROWN, Janice Elizabeth

GOURLAY, Wendy Elizabeth. b 50. DipOT 71. ERMC 08. **d** 11 **p** 12. NSM Boulge w Burgh, Grundisburgh and Hasketon *St E* 11–13; NSM Carlford 13–17; rtd 17; PtO *St E* from 17. *Tubric Cottage, The Street, Cretingham, Woodbridge IP13 7BL* T: (01728) 685335 E: rev.gourlay@gmail.com

GOURLEY, Malcolm James. b 37. MRPharmS 58. NEOC 94. **d** 98 **p** 98. NSM Gt Smeaton w Appleton Wiske and Birkby etc *Ripon* 98–00; NSM Ainderby Steeple w Yafforth and Kirby Wiske etc 00–02; NSM Herrington, Penshaw and Shiney Row *Dur* 02–07; rtd 07; PtO *Dur* 07–20. *Linden House, Lawn Drive, West Boldon, East Boldon NE36 0AZ* T: 0191-597 7548 E: malcolm.gourley@tombola.com

GOVAN, Kesh Rico. b 66. St Jo Coll Dur BA 96. Cranmer Hall Dur 93. **d** 96 **p** 97. C Astley Bridge *Man* 96–00; TV Walkden and Lt Hulton 00–04; I Blessington w Kilbride, Ballymore Eustace etc *D & G* 04–07; C Uttoxeter Area *Lich* 07–10; C Rocester and Croxden w Hollington 07–10; V 10–14; Chapl JCB Academy 10–14; R Nelson Bay Australia 14–16. *29 Tomaree Street, Nelson Bay NSW 2315, Australia* T: (0061) (2) 4981 1839 E: revkesh@sky.com *or* allsaint@nelsonbay.com

GOVENDER, The Very Revd Rogers Morgan. b 60. MBE 19. Natal Univ BTh 97. St Paul's Coll Grahamstown 83. **d** 85 **p** 86. C Overport Ch Ch S Africa 85–87; R Greyville St Mary 88–92; R Hayfields St Matt 93–98; Adn Pietermaritzburg 97–98; R Berea St Thos S Africa 99–00; P-in-c Didsbury Ch Ch *Man* 01–06; P-in-c Withington St Chris 03–06; AD Withington 04–06; Dean Man from 06; Borough Dean Man from 18. *1 Booth Clibborn Court, Salford M7 4PJ* T: 0161-792 2801 *or* 833 2220 F: 839 6218 E: dean@manchestercathedral.org

GOWDEY, Michael Cragg. b 32. Oriel Coll Ox BA 56 MA 58 Keele Univ CertEd 73. Qu Coll Birm. **d** 58 **p** 59. C Ashbourne w Mapleton and Clifton *Derby* 58–63; V Chellaston 63–69; Asst Chapl Ellesmere Coll 69–74; Chapl Trent Coll Nottm 74–81; Educn Chapl *Worc* 81–97; Chapl K Edw Sixth Form Coll Worc 81–97; rtd 97; P-in-c Beeley and Edensor *Derby* 97–02; PtO 02–18. *18 Moorhall Estate, Bakewell DE45 1FP* T: (01629) 814121 E: jandmgowdey@uwclub.net

GOWER, Denys Victor. b 33. Cant Sch of Min 85. **d** 87 **p** 88. NSM Gillingham H Trin *Roch* 87–91; NSM Gillingham St Aug 89–91; C Perry Street 91–93; P-in-c Wateringbury w Teston and W Farleigh 93–96; R 96–00; rtd 00; PtO *Roch* from 00; Ind Chapl from 02; PtO *Cant* 03–09; Hon Chapl Medway NHS Foundn Trust from 05; PV Roch Cathl from 07. *4 Locarno Avenue, Gillingham ME8 6ET* T: (01634) 375765 M: 07985-781161

GOWER, Nikolas John . b 88. Wycliffe Hall Ox BA 17. **d** 17 **p** 18. C Romsey *Win* 17–20; CF from 20. *c/o MOD Chaplains (Army)* T: (01264) 383430 M: 07967-766070 E: nikolasgower@icloud.com

GOWER, Miss Patricia Ann. b 44. Wilson Carlile Coll IDC 79 Sarum & Wells Th Coll 88. **d** 88 **p** 94. Chapl Bris Univ 88–91; Hon Par Dn Clifton St Paul 88–91; Par Dn Spondon *Derby* 91–94; C 94–95; P-in-c Hatton 95–98; Asst Chapl HM Pris Sudbury 95–98; Chapl 98–04; rtd 04; PtO *Derby* from 04. *19 Heronswood Drive, Spondon, Derby DE21 7AX* T: (01332) 671031

GOWER, Miss Paulette Rose-Mary de Garis. b 70. Plymouth Univ BEd 93 St Jo Coll Dur MA 08. Cranmer Hall Dur 01. **d** 03 **p** 04. C Shrewsbury St Geo w Greenfields *Lich* 03–07; TV Hawarden *St As* 07–14; V Gwersyllt 14–16; I Alyn Miss Area from 17; AD Alyn from 16. *The Vicarage, Old Mold Road, Gwersyllt, Wrexham LL11 4SB* T: (01978) 756391 E: paulettegower@gwersyllt.plus.com

GOWER, Canon Sarah Catherine. b 63. Ex Univ BA 84 Cam Univ BTh 09. Westcott Ho Cam 07. **d** 09 **p** 10. C St Neots *Ely* 09–13; C Eynesbury 13–13; Min Orton Goldhay LEP from 13; Jt RD Yaxley 16–19; RD from 19; P-in-c Alwalton and Chesterton from 21; Hon Can Ely Cathl from 20. *Christ Church House, 1 Benstead, Orton Goldhay, Peterborough PE2 5JJ* T: (01733) 394411 E: sarahcgower@btinternet.com

GOWER, Archdeacon of. *See* DAVIES, The Ven Jonathan Byron

GOWING, Wilfred Herbert. b 50. QUB BSc 72. NEOC 03. **d** 06 **p** 07. NSM Ripon H Trin 06–14; *Leeds* 14–20; PtO 20–21. *Littlemead, 20 Springfield Rise, Great Ouseburn, York YO26 9SE* T: (01423) 331177 F: 331178 E: wilfgowing@btinternet.com

GOWING-CUMBER, Alexander John. b 72. Fitzw Coll Cam MA 00 Moorlands Th Coll MA 94. Ridley Hall Cam 98. **d** 00 **p** 03. C Vange *Chelmsf* 00–02; C Rayleigh 02–05; TV Grays Thurrock 05–15; rtd 15; PtO *Chelmsf* from 15. *Trinity House, 5 Nevada Road, Canvey Island SS8 8EX* T: (01268) 698414 M: 07786-652286 E: fralexgc@aol.com

GOWLER, Simon Daniel Luke. b 60. Univ of Wales (Abth) LLB 83. All SS Cen for Miss & Min 16. **d** 18 **p** 19. NSM Knutsford St Cross *Ches* 18–21; V Rainow w Saltersford and Forest from 21. *The Vicarage, Pedley Hill, Rainow, Macclesfield SK10 5TZ* T: (01625) 572013 M: 07881-912681 E: simon.gowler@jobling-gowler.co.uk

GRACE, Canon Andrew John. b 54. Univ of Wales (Abth) BMus 76 St Martin's Coll Lanc PGCE 78 FRCO 75 FTCL 76 LRAM 75. Sarum & Wells Th Coll 79. **d** 81 **p** 82. C Tenby w Gumfreston *St D* 81–84; C Llanelli 84–86; V Monkton 86–91; V Fairfield *Derby* 91–96; P-in-c Barlborough 96–01; R Barlborough and Renishaw 01–03; V Pembroke Dock *St D* 03–04; TR Carew 04–08; TR Tenby 08–20; P-in-c Narberth and Tenby LMA from 20; AD Pembroke 13–16; Can St D Cathl from 12. *The Rectory, Church Park, Tenby SA70 7EE* T: (01834) 842068

GRACE, Capt David Leonard. b 55. Wilson Carlile Coll 89 Ripon Coll Cuddesdon 97. **d** 99 **p** 00. CA from 92; C St Leonards and St Ives *Win* 99–04; V 04–09; Chapl Basingstoke and N Hants NHS Foundn Trust 09–11; Chapl Hants Hosps NHS Foundn Trust 12–13; Chapl Weston Area Health NHS Trust 13–19; Chapl Univ Hosps Bris and Weston NHS Foundn Trust 20–21; PtO *B & W* from 20; *Bris* 20–21. *Address withheld by request* M: 07742-004644

GRACE, Miss Michelle Elizabeth. b 69. St Jo Coll Nottm BA 12. **d** 12 **p** 13. C Chell *Lich* 12–13; C Oswestry 13–17; TV Tring *St Alb* from 17. *The Vicarage, Station Road, Aldbury, Tring HP23 5RS* T: (01442) 851200

GRACIE, Canon Bryan John. b 45. MBE 06. Open Univ BA 81. AKC 67. **d** 68 **p** 69. C Whipton *Ex* 68–72; Chapl St Jo Sch Tiffield 72–73; Chapl HM Borstal Stoke Heath 74–78; Asst Chapl HM Pris Liv 74; Chapl HM Youth Cust Cen Feltham 78–85; Chapl HM Pris Birm 85–10; Hon Can Birm Cathl 05–10; rtd 10; PtO *Birm* from 10. *25 Mills Court, 263 Lichfield Road, Sutton Coldfield B74 2XH*

GRADY, Gary Brian. b 69. Bris Poly BA 92. WEMTC 10. **d** 13 **p** 14. C Cirencester *Glouc* 13–16; TV S Cheltenham from 16; AD Cheltenham from 18. *The Rectory, Kidnappers Lane, Cheltenham GL53 0NT* T: (01242) 242831 M: 07713-654074 E: garygrady@btinternet.com

GRAEME, Emma Jane. b 60. Southn Univ BA 00. Ripon Coll Cuddesdon 10. **d** 12 **p** 13. C E Grinstead St Swithun *Chich* 12–15; C New Fishbourne 15–17; R Beeding and Bramber w Botolphs 17–20; rtd 20. *Meadow Corner, The Street, Boxgrove, Chichester PO18 0DY* M: 07403-114365 E: estonham@yahoo.co.uk

GRAESSER, Adrian Stewart. b 42. Tyndale Hall Bris 63. **d** 67 **p** 68. C Nottingham St Jude *S'well* 67–69; C Slaithwaite w E Scammonden *Wakef* 69–72; CF 72–75; V Earl's Heaton *Wakef* 75–81; R Norton Fitzwarren *B & W* 81–86; R Bickenhill w Elmdon *Birm* 86–90; R Elmdon St Nic 90–00; P-in-c Dolton *Ex* 00–05; P-in-c Iddesleigh w Dowland 00–05; P-in-c Monkokehampton 00–05; RD Torrington 02–05; rtd 05; PtO *Worc* from 09; *Glouc* from 19. *31 Capel Court, The Burgage, Prestbury, Cheltenham GL52 3EL* T: (01242) 462600 E: adrian.graesser@sky.com

GRAHAM, Alan Robert. b 44. St Edm Hall Ox BA 67 MA 71. St Steph Ho Ox BA 70. **d** 70 **p** 71. C Clifton All SS *Bris* 70–74; C Tadley St Pet *Win* 74–77; P-in-c Upper Clatford w Goodworth Clatford 77–79; R Abbotts Ann and Upper Clatford and Goodworth Clatford 79–84; V Lyndhurst and Emery Down 84–92; P-in-c Over Wallop w Nether Wallop 92–02; rtd 02; PtO *Win* from 08. *8 Holmwood, The Rise, Brockenhurst SO42 7AF* T: (01590) 619338

GRAHAM, Alastair. *See* GRAHAM, Michael Alastair

GRAHAM, Alfred. b 34. Bris Univ BA 57. Tyndale Hall Bris. **d** 58 **p** 59. C Chaddesden St Mary *Derby* 58–61; C Bickenhill w Elmdon *Birm* 61–64; V Kirkdale St Lawr *Liv* 64–70; V Stapleford *S'well* 70–83; V Burton Joyce w Bulcote 83–95; V Burton Joyce w Bulcote and Stoke Bardolph 95–97; rtd 97; PtO *S'well* 03–11; *Blackb* 11–19. *16 Meadow View, Clitheroe BB7 2NT* T: (01200) 426805

GRAHAM, Canon Anthony Nigel. b 40. Univ of Wales (Abth) BA 62 CertEd 70. Ripon Hall Ox 62. **d** 64 **p** 65. C Heref H Trin 64–67; C Birm St Martin 67–69; C Selly Oak St Mary 71–75; V Edgbaston SS Mary and Ambrose 75–83; CMS Miss Partner Nigeria 84–88; Hon Can Jos from 88; V Highworth w Sevenhampton and Inglesham etc *Bris* 88–95; RD Highworth 93–95; P-in-c Coalpit Heath 95–99; V 99–00; rtd 00; PtO *Glouc* from 17. *19 Dormer Road, Cheltenham GL51 0AX*

GRAHAM, Benjamin Robert. b 85. **d** 16 **p** 17. C Wandsworth All SS *S'wark* 16–20; C Yeovil w Kingston Pitney *B & W* from 20. *9 Park Gardens, Yeovil BA20 1DW*

GRAHAM, Christopher John. b 55. EMMTC. **d** 03 **p** 04. NSM Ripley *Derby* 03–08; NSM Ilkeston St Jo 08–13; PtO from 13. *7 Derwent Drive, Merebrook Park, Whatstandwell, Matlock DE4 5PG* M: 07933-301562 E: revchrisg@hotmail.co.uk

GRAHAM, Clifton Gordon. b 53. ARCM 72 GRSM 74 FRCO 75 Coll of Ripon & York St Jo PGCE 76. St Steph Ho Ox 90. **d** 92 **p** 93. C Northfield *Birm* 92–93; C Perry Beeches 93–97; P-in-c S Yardley St Mich 97–00; V 00–06; Chapl Birm City Univ 06–10; Chapl Ex Univ 10–13; rtd 13; PtO *Ex* 13–19; *B & W* from 19; Chapl Wellington Sch Somerset from 19. *Springwell, 31 Olympian Way, Cullompton EX15 1GB* T: (01884) 32545 E: jgccgg@gmail.com

GRAHAM, David. *See* GRAHAM, George David

GRAHAM, Fiona Karen. *See* WHEATLEY, Fiona Karen

GRAHAM, Frederick Lawrence. b 35. TCD BA 65. CITC 66. **d** 66 **p** 67. C Belfast St Matt *Conn* 66–69; TV Chelmsley Wood *Birm* 69–73; Ch of Ireland Youth Officer 73–78; Bp's C Stoneyford *Conn* 78–88; Bp's C Fahan Lower and Upper *D & R* 88–91; Can Raphoe Cathl 90–01; I Donagheady 91–01; Can Derry Cathl 95–01; rtd 01. *14 Greenmount Gardens, Lisburn BT27 5HD* T: (028) 9258 2639 M: 07719-529989 E: freka1@virginmedia.com

GRAHAM, George David. b 42. Jes Coll Cam BA 64 MA 68. St Jo Coll Nottm LTh Lon Coll of Div 66. **d** 71 **p** 72. C Corby St Columba *Pet* 71–74; C Deptford St Jo *S'wark* 74–77; P-in-c Deptford St Pet 77–82; C-in-c Wheatley Park St Paul CD *Sheff* 82–87; TV Dunstable *St Alb* 87–92; V Bromley Common St Luke *Roch* 92–02; R Hayes 02–12; rtd 12; PtO *Roch* from 13. *129 Warren Road, Orpington BR6 6JE* T: (01689) 850656 E: gd.graham77@gmail.com

GRAHAM, Canon George Edgar. b 55. QUB BA 91. Sarum & Wells Th Coll 74 CITC 77. **d** 78 **p** 79. C Lisburn Ch Ch *Conn* 78–81; C Mossley 81–83; I Broomhedge 83–91; I Derriaghy w Colin 91–96; I Ballywillan 96–05; I Dunluce from 05; Can Conn Cathl from 05; Preb from 06; Prec from 16; Chan from 16. *Dunluce Rectory, 17 Priestland Road, Bushmills BT57 8QP* T: (028) 2073 1221 *or* 2073 0537 E: g.k.graham@btinternet.com *or* admindunluce@btconnect.com

GRAHAM, Harry John. b 52. Magd Coll Cam BA 75 MA 86. Trin Coll Bris BA 94. **d** 96 **p** 97. C Walkden and Lt Hulton *Man* 96–99; Chapl Salford Coll of Tech 96–99; P-in-c Edgeside *Man* 99–00; TV Rossendale Middle Valley 00–02; Gen Sec Miss Without Borders (UK) Ltd 02–08; Pres and CEO Miss Without Borders Internat 08–19; PtO *S'wark* 07–13; *Lon* 09–19 and from 20; NSM Edmonton St Aldhelm 19–20. *69 Eyre Court, 3-21 Finchley Road, London NW8 9TX* M: 07545-150863 E: harryjgraham67@outlook.com

GRAHAM, Mrs Heather Karen. b 62. Keele Univ BA 83. Ripon Coll Cuddesdon 13. **d** 16 **p** 17. NSM High Wycombe *Ox* 16–19; TV from 19. *5 Manor Gardens, High Wycombe HP13 5HD* T: (01494) 534315 M: 07876-292288 E: heather.graham@stjamesdownley.org.uk

GRAHAM, Ian Maxwell. b 50. CertEd 76. Chich Th Coll 86. **d** 88 **p** 89. C Middlesbrough St Thos *York* 88–90; C Stainton-in-Cleveland 90–93; V Hemlington 93–00; V Grangetown 00–14; rtd 14; PtO *York* 18–20. *19 Whitehouse Road, Thornaby, Stockton-on-Tees TS17 0AJ* T: (01642) 882323 E: ianmgraham50@gmail.com

GRAHAM, Kevin. *See* GRAHAM, Terence Kevin Declan

GRAHAM, Matthew John. b 78. Lon Guildhall Univ BSc 00. Oak Hill Th Coll BA 13. **d** 13 **p** 14. C Lt Heath *St Alb* 13–16; V Prenton *Ches* from 16. *The Vicarage, 1 Vicarage Close, Birkenhead CH42 8QX* T: 0151-608 1808

GRAHAM, Michael. b 51. CITC BTh 95. **d** 95 **p** 96. C Cork St Fin Barre's Union *C, C & R* 95–98; Min Can Cork Cathl 97–98; I Drogheda w Ardee, Collon and Termonfeckin

Arm 98–16; Ch of Ireland Internet Co-ord 99–05; I Kilsaran w Drumcar, Dunleer and Dunany *Arm* 07–16; rtd 16; PtO Cyprus and the Gulf from 16; PtO *Arm* from 20. *1 Laurel Mews, Thomas Street, Drogheda, Co Louth, A92 DWA4, Republic of Ireland* M: (00353) 89-255 1240 E: mgraham597@gmail.com

GRAHAM, Canon Michael Alastair. b 47. CITC 67. **d** 70 **p** 71. C Dublin Clontarf *D & G* 71–75; C Ox St Mich w St Martin and All SS 76–78; P-in-c Dublin Sandymount *D & G* 80–86; I Stillorgan w Blackrock 86–00; Mgt Consultant E Regional Health Authority Dub 00–09; I Mullingar, Portnashangan, Moyliscar, Kilbixy etc *M & K* from 09; Can Kildare Cathl from 18; Can Meath from 18. *The Rectory, Gaol Hill, Mullingar, Co Westmeath, Republic of Ireland* T: (00353) (44) 934 8376 M: 87-787 0985 E: agkilliney@hotmail.com

GRAHAM, Michael John. b 50. Birm Univ BSc 72 Loughb Univ MSc 78 Bris Univ MEd 89. Trin Coll Bris 15. **d** 17 **p** 18. OLM Woodbridge *Bris* from 17. *Crosthwaite, Barnes Green, Brinkworth, Chippenham SN15 5AG* T: (01666) 510441 E: mike.graham@btinternet.com

GRAHAM, Nigel. *See* GRAHAM, Anthony Nigel

✠**GRAHAM, The Rt Revd Olivia Josephine.** b 56. UEA BA 84. SAOMC 94. **d** 97 **p** 98 **c** 19. NSM Wheatley *Ox* 97–98; C Risborough 98–01; TV Burnham w Dropmore, Hitcham and Taplow 01–07; Par Development Adv 07–13; Hon Can Ch Ch 12–13; Adn Berks 13–19; Area Bp Reading from 19. *Bishop's House, Tidmarsh Lane, Tidmarsh, Reading RG8 8HA* T: 0118-984 1216 E: bishopreading@oxford.anglican.org

GRAHAM, Richard William. b 63. Poly of Wales BA 86 ACA 91. Trin Coll Bris 03. **d** 05 **p** 06. C Savernake *Sarum* 05–09; TV Hemel Hempstead *St Alb* from 09. *St Barnabas' Vicarage, Everest Way, Hemel Hempstead HP2 4HY* T: (01442) 253681 E: randmgraham@hotmail.com

GRAHAM, Rory Malise. b 75. Southn Univ BSc 97. Oak Hill Th Coll BA 12. **d** 12 **p** 13. C Hove Bp Hannington Memorial Ch *Chich* 12–16; C Hailsham from 16. *1 Barn Close, Hailsham BN27 1TL* T: (01323) 844502 E: rorygraham@hailshamchurch.org

GRAHAM, Roy Richard Arthur. b 39. Lon Univ BD 63 Open Univ BA 78 Dur Univ MA 92. ALCD 62. **d** 63 **p** 64. C Southsea St Jude *Portsm* 63–66; C Morden *S'wark* 66–70; V Tittensor *Lich* 70–79; R Hurworth *Dur* 79–02; R Dinsdale w Sockburn 79–02; rtd 02; PtO *Leeds* from 19. *Rose Cottage, Hackforth Road, Patrick Brompton, Bedale DL8 1JR* E: roygraham39@outlook.com

GRAHAM, Stephen Alan. b 78. QUB BA 99 MA 00 CCC Cam PGCE 01. St Steph Ho Ox. **d** 16 **p** 17. C Holt w High Kelling *Nor* 16–20; Chapl Milton Abbey Sch Dorset 20; Chapl Glenalmond Coll *St And* from 20. *Birnam House, Glenalmond College, Glenalmond, Perth PH1 3RY* M: 07856-071178 E: revdstephengraham@gmail.com

GRAHAM, Stig. *See* GRAHAM, William Stig

GRAHAM, Canon Terence Kevin Declan. b 67. NUI BSc 89 TCD BTh 02. CITC 99. **d** 02 **p** 03. C Knock *D & D* 02–05; I Carrowdore w Millisle 05–09; I Movilla 09–13; I Belfast St Bart *Conn* from 13; Can Belf Cathl from 19. *St Bartholomew's Rectory, 16 Mount Pleasant, Belfast BT9 5DS* T: (028) 9066 9995 M: 07964-663745 E: stbartholomew@connor.anglican.org

GRAHAM, William Stig. b 53. Newc Univ BSc 75. NEOC. **d** 99 **p** 00. C W Acklam *York* 99–02; Chapl Myton Hamlet Hospice 02–20; rtd 20; PtO *Cov* from 20. *2 Winyates Road, Lighthorne Heath, Leamington Spa CV33 9TU* T: (01926) 640811 E: stiggraham@netscape.net

GRAHAM-BROWN, John George Francis. b 34. CA 60. Wycliffe Hall Ox 60. **d** 63 **p** 64. C Darlington St Cuth *Dur* 63–67; C Rufforth w Moor Monkton and Hessay *York* 67–73; Sec York Dioc Redundant Chs Uses Cttee 69–89; Asst Sec DBF 73–84; Dioc Past Cttee *York* 73–89; Hon C York St Barn 73–85; P-in-c 85–92; TV Marfleet 92–99; rtd 99; PtO *St Alb* from 00. *40 Hunters Oak, Hemel Hempstead HP2 7SW* T: (01482) 402226 M: 07961-997089

GRAINGER, Ian. b 66. Cranmer Hall Dur 89. **d** 92 **p** 93. C Whitehaven *Carl* 92–94; C Walney Is 94–97; P-in-c Barrow St Aid 97–02; V Camerton, Seaton and W Seaton from 02; Dioc World Development Officer from 11. *The Vicarage, Ling Beck Park, Seaton, Workington CA14 1JQ* T: (01900) 602162 E: ian.grainger66@btinternet.com

GRAINGER, Michael Noel Howard. b 40. Trin Coll Carmarthen. **d** 91 **p** 92. NSM Haverfordwest St Martin w Lambston *St D* 91–95; V Maenclochog and New Moat etc 95–05; rtd 05. *14 Swallowdale, Swindon SN3 5AZ*

GRAINGER-SMITH, James Edward. b 71. Nottm Univ BA 92. St Jo Coll Nottm MA 02. **d** 02 **p** 03. C Hordle *Win* 02–07; R Beeford w Frodingham and Foston *York* from 07; P-in-c Brandesburton and Leven w Catwick 11–13;

V Brandesburton and Leven from 13; RD N Holderness 12–16. *The Rectory, 11 Glebe Gardens, Beeford, Driffield YO25 8BF* T: (01262) 488042 E: j.grainger-smith@sky.com

GRANDEY, Frederick Michael. b 56. St Jo Coll Ox MA 83 BM, BCh 84 Newc Univ MSc 98 MRCGP 90 FFPH 04. St Jo Coll Nottm 06. **d** 09 **p** 10. C Haxby and Wigginton *York* 09–13; P-in-c S Molton w Nymet St George, High Bray etc *Ex* 13–16; TR S Molton w Nymet St George, Chittlehamholt etc from 16. *The Rectory, Parsonage Lane, South Molton EX36 3AX* E: m.grandey@talk21.com

GRANGE (*née* FEATHERSTON), Mrs Alice Margery. b 55. Teesside Univ BA 97. NEOC. **d** 99 **p** 00. C Pickering w Lockton and Levisham *York* 99–02; TV Crosslacon *Carl* 02–07; P-in-c Middlesbrough St Agnes *York* 07–18; Chapl S Tees Hosps NHS Foundn Trust 07–18; rtd 18; PtO *York* 18–21. *25 Egton Close, Redcar TS10 4PG* M: 07359-161577 E: margery-grange@sky.com

GRANNER, Mrs Linda. b 52. Westmr Coll Ox BTh 00. WMMTC 01. **d** 03 **p** 04. NSM Bearwood *Birm* 03–06; C Edgbaston St Bart 06–08; C Edgbaston St Geo 06–08; P-in-c Hobs Moat from 08. *St Mary's House, 30 Hobs Meadow, Solihull B92 8PN* T: 0121-743 4955 E: l.granner@sky.com

GRANT, Andrew James. b 68. Cranmer Hall Dur 09. **d** 11 **p** 12. C Bramham *York* 11–15; V Marton-in-Cleveland 15–20; P-in-c Middlesbrough St Agnes 18–20; CF from 20. *c/o MOD Chaplains (Army)* T: (01264) 383430 M: 07519-423552

GRANT, Canon Andrew Richard. b 40. Univ of Wales BA 62. Chich Th Coll 63. **d** 65 **p** 66. C Kennington St Jo *S'wark* 65–68; Hon C 70–72; Hon C Stockwell Green St Andr 68–70; V Nunhead St Antony 72–79; TR N Lambeth 79–92; USPG Ghana 92–99; Hon Can Kumasi from 02; C Paddington St Jo w St Mich *Lon* 99–01; P-in-c Stockwell St Mich *S'wark* 01–03; P-in-c Stockwell St Andr and St Mich 03–04; V 04–09; rtd 09; PtO *S'wark* 09–13 and from 15. *48 Stannard Court, Culverley Road, London SE6 2LE* M: 07448-583179 E: argstockwell@hotmail.co.uk

GRANT, Antony Richard Charles. b 34. Ch Ch Ox BA 59 MA 64. Coll of Resurr Mirfield 72. **d** 74 **p** 75. C St John's Wood *Lon* 74–77; Novice CR 77–79; CR from 79; Lic to Offic *Wakef* 80–14; rtd 99; LtO *Leeds* from 14. *House of the Resurrection, Stocks Bank Road, Mirfield WF14 0BN* T: (01924) 483332 F: 490489 E: agrant@mirfield.org.uk

GRANT, Miss Frances Mary. b 52. Qu Coll Birm. **d** 12 **p** 13. NSM Etwall w Egginton *Derby* 12–18; NSM Brailsford w Shirley, Osmaston w Edlaston etc from 18; PtO *Lon* from 18. *177 Drewry Lane, Derby DE22 3QT* T: (01332) 364617 M: 07714-780668 E: franmgrant@gmail.com

GRANT, Canon Geoffrey Leslie. b 33. Trin Coll Cam BA 57 MA 61. Ridley Hall Cam 57. **d** 59 **p** 60. C Chelsea St Luke *Lon* 59–64; R Nacton w Levington *St E* 64–78; P-in-c Bucklesham w Brightwell and Foxhall 75–76; R Nacton and Levington w Bucklesham and Foxhall 78–06; P-in-c Kirton w Falkenham 96–06; R Nacton and Levington w Bucklesham etc 06–14; RD Colneys 86–11; Hon Can St E Cathl 94–14; Chapl Orwell Park Sch Nacton 64–14; rtd 14; PtO *St E* 14–19. *Daisy Chain, The Common, Lavenham, Sudbury CO10 9RL* T: (01787) 247343 E: geoffrey@john-lewis.com

GRANT, James Nikolas. b 78. Glas Univ MA 07 Anglia Ruskin Univ MA 11. Westcott Ho Cam 09. **d** 11 **p** 12. C Chorlton-cum-Hardy St Clem *Man* 11–14; C Worth, Pound Hill and Maidenhower *Chich* 15; C Old Shoreham and Kingston Buci 15–19; R from 19. *Kingston Buci Rectory, Rectory Road, Shoreham-by-Sea BN43 6EB* T: (01273) 979811 M: 07753-456210 E: frjames.grant@gmail.com

GRANT, Julia Rosalind Russell. *See* RUSSELL GRANT, Julia Rosalind

GRANT, Ms Kes. b 65. SEITE 00. **d** 03 **p** 04. NSM Eltham St Sav *S'wark* 03–09; C Bermondsey St Hugh CD 09–11; Chapl Lewisham Hosp NHS Trust 05–09; Chapl St Sav and St Olave's Sch Newington *S'wark* 09–11; Chapl St Aug Academy Maidstone 11–16; rtd 16; PtO *Cant* from 16. *The Vicarage, Wallis Avenue, Maidstone ME15 9JJ* M: 07579-058895 E: rebelrev7@gmail.com

GRANT, Canon Malcolm Etheridge. b 44. Edin Univ BSc 66 BD 69. Edin Th Coll 66. **d** 69 **p** 70. C St Mary's Cathl *Glas* 69–72; C Grantham w Manthorpe *Linc* 72; TV Grantham 72–78; P-in-c Invergordon St Ninian *Mor* 78–81; Provost St Mary's Cathl *Glas* 81–91; R Glas St Mary 81–91; Provost St Andr Cathl Inverness *Mor* 91–02; R Inverness St Andr 91–02; P-in-c Culloden St Mary-in-the-Fields 91–97; R Strathnairn St Paul 91–97; Hon Can St Andr Cathl Inverness from 02; V Eaton Bray w Edlesborough *St Alb* 02–09; RD Dunstable 04–09; rtd 09; PtO *St Alb* from 09; *Ox* 09–20. *13 Rock Lane, Leighton Buzzard LU7 2QQ* T: (01525) 372771 E: mandkgrant@btinternet.com

GRANT, Murray William. b 36. Chich Th Coll 64. **d** 66 **p** 67. C Stanley *Liv* 66–70; C Munster Square St Mary Magd *Lon* 70–74; C Westmr St Sav and St Jas Less 74–82; P-in-c Albany Street Ch Ch 82; P-in-c Hammersmith H Innocents 83–94; V 94–99; Chapl Naples w Sorrento, Capri and Bari *Eur* 99–03; rtd 04; PtO *Lon* 12–18. *12 Ashdown Crescent, London NW5 4QB* T: (020) 7419 2519 E: mwgrant@gmail.com

GRANT, Patrick Iain Douglas. b 67. K Alfred's Coll Win BA 88. Cuddesdon Coll BTh 93. **d** 96 **p** 97. C Croydon Woodside *S'wark* 96–99; V S Beddington and Roundshaw 99–07; R Perth St Jo *St And* 07–14; rtd 14. *42 Bonhard Road, Scone, Perth PH2 6QB* T: (01738) 259663 M: 07948-270941 E: patrickidgrant@gmail.com

GRANT, Richard. b 83. Leeds Univ BA 08. St Mellitus Coll MA 13. **d** 13 **p** 14. C Crookes St Thos *Sheff* 13–16; P-in-c Gateshead St Geo *Dur* from 16. *18 East Park Road, Gateshead NE9 5AX* T: 0191340 4844 M: 07474-903903 E: richgrantuk@gmail.com *or* rich.grant@gateshead.church

GRANT, Stuart Peter. b 64. Leeds Poly BSc 87 Leeds Univ BA 11. Yorks Min Course 08. **d** 12 **p** 13. NSM Gt and Lt Driffield *York* 12–17; V from 17; NSM Langtoft w Foxholes, Butterwick, Cottam etc 12–17; V from 17. *The Vicarage, Downe Street, Driffield YO25 6DX* T: (01377) 257712 M: 07795-560065 E: stuart@hastpace.co.uk

GRANT, William John. b 88. Dur Univ BA 19. Ridley Hall Cam 17. **d** 20 **p** 21. C Clayton *Leeds* from 20; C Allerton from 21; C Fairweather Green from 21. *36 Blackberry Way, Clayton, Bradford BD14 6NB* M: 07732-281271 E: revwillgrant@gmail.com

GRANTHAM, David George. b 70. **d** 07 **p** 08. C Bury St Edmunds Ch Ch *St E* 07–11; V Jersey All SS *Win* from 11; V Jersey St Simon from 11. *All Saints' Vicarage, Savile Street, St Helier, Jersey JE2 3XF* T: (01534) 768323 E: godistheguy@hotmail.com

GRANTHAM, Michael Paul. b 47. Linc Th Coll. **d** 84 **p** 85. C Gainsborough All SS *Linc* 84–87; R S Kelsey Gp 87–94; R Dunster, Carhampton and Withycombe w Rodhuish *B & W* 94–06; RD Exmoor 03–05; P-in-c Peakirk w Glinton and Northborough *Pet* 06–07; P-in-c Etton w Helpston and Maxey 06–07; rtd 07; PtO *Derby* 07–18; Hon C Albury w Tiddington etc *Ox* 13–16. *22 The Covert, Tattersall, Lincoln LN4 4GN* T: (01526) 344515 E: granthammichael@sky.com *or* michaelgrantham@tiscali.co.uk

GRANTHAM, Suffragan Bishop of. *See* CHAMBERLAIN, The Rt Revd Nicholas Alan

GRASBY, Derek. b 56. Bris Univ BA 80 MA 82. Wesley Coll Bris 77 EAMTC 95. **d** 95 **p** 96. C Harlescott *Lich* 95–96; C W Bromwich St Andr w Ch Ch 96–98; R Newton Heath *Man* 98–02; Chapl UWE *Bris* 02–03; R Farnley *Ripon* 03–09; rtd 09; PtO *Ripon* 10–13; *Nor* from 14. *9 Boundary Avenue, Norwich NR6 5HY* T: (01603) 291211 M: 07834-276382 E: derek.grasby@gmail.com

GRASHAM, Mrs Frances Mary. b 68. Roehampton Inst BA 89 Kingston Poly PGCE 90. Yorks Min Course 11. **d** 13 **p** 14. NSM Steeton *Bradf* 13–14; Leeds 14–16; NSM Newbridge w Carnalway and Kilcullen *M & K* 16–20; NSM Kildare w Kilmeague and Curragh 16–20; P-in-c Geashill w Killeigh and Ballycommon from 20; Chapl Defence Forces 16–20. *The Rectory, Ballydownan, Geashill, Co Offaly, R35 X4C0, Republic of Ireland* M: (00353) 83-826 3792 E: fran.grasham@gmail.com

GRASSKE, Christopher Karl. b 65. Ripon Coll Cuddesdon 12. **d** 14 **p** 15. C Chagford, Gidleigh, Throwleigh etc *Ex* 14–17; R Eggardon and Colmers *Sarum* from 17. *The Vicarage, Loders, Bridport DT6 3SA* T: (01308) 425161 E: cgrasske@outlook.com

GRATION, Phillip John. b 83. **d** 12 **p** 13. Chapl HM Pris Linc 12–15; C Linc St Pet-at-Gowts and St Andr 12–15; C Linc St Botolph 12–15; C Linc St Mary-le-Wigford w St Benedict etc 12–15; Chapl Ellesmere Coll from 15. *Ellesmere College, Ellesmere SY12 9AB* T: (01691) 622321 E: phillip.gration@ellesmere.com

GRATTON, Patricia Margaret. *See* MAGUIRE, Patricia Margaret

GRATTON, Richard James. **d** 21. C Llantrisant *Llan* from 21. *Address temp unknown* E: rickgratton@outlook.com

GRATY, Canon John Thomas. b 33. Univ Coll Ox BA 58 MA 60. Coll of Resurr Mirfield 58. **d** 60 **p** 61. C Cov St Mark 60–63; C Hitchin St Mary *St Alb* 63–67; R Cov St Alb 67–75; P-in-c Radway w Ratley 75–77; P-in-c Warmington w Shotteswell 75–77; RD Dassett Magna 76–78; R Warmington w Shotteswell and Radway w Ratley 77–84; Hon Can Cov Cathl 80–96; P-in-c Nuneaton St Mary 84–89; V 89–96; rtd 96; PtO *Cov* from 96. *10 Kendall Avenue, Stratford-upon-Avon CV37 6SG* T: (01789) 298856 E: gratyseniors@aol.com

GRAVELING, Hannah. *See* PATTON, Hannah

GRAVELL, Canon John Hilary. b 45. Univ of Wales (Abth) BA 65 DipEd 66. Bp Burgess Hall Lamp 66. **d** 68 **p** 69. C Aberystwyth *St D* 68–72; R Llangeitho w Blaenpennal 72–73; V Llangeitho, Blaenpennal and Betws Leucu 73–81; V Betws Leuci 73–81; V Llan-non 81–95; Can St D Cathl 92–09; V Llandybie 95–09; AD Dyffryn Aman 01–07; rtd 09; PtO *St D* from 09. *16 Stewart Drive, Ammanford SA18 3BH* T: (01269) 594366

GRAVER, John Michael William. b 40. **d** 21 **p** 21. PtO *Blackb* from 21. *4 Trinity Close, Padiham, Burnley BB2 7DG* T: (01282) 723580 M: 07940-897070 E: gravers@3strands.net

GRAVES, John Ivan. b 44. **d** 10 **p** 11. OLM Romney Deanery Romney Marsh *Cant* 10–17; PtO 15; *Sarum* 16–21. *22 Vicarage Road, Poole BH15 3AZ* E: gwthms44@gmail.com

GRAVES, Peter. b 33. EMMTC 78. **d** 81 **p** 82. NSM Roughey *Chich* 81–89; NSM Itchingfield w Slinfold 89–98; PtO *S'well* 98–18. *5 Fletcher Court, The Woodlands, Farnsfield, Newark NG22 8LY* T: (01623) 882987 E: gravesp1@btinternet.com

GRAY, Alison Jane. b 63. New Hall Cam MB, BChir 87 MA 89 Birm Univ MMedSc 01 MRCPsych 95 FRCPsych 15. Qu Coll Birm 07. **d** 10 **p** 11. NSM Malvern St Andr and Malvern Wells and Wyche *Worc* 10–14; NSM Gt Malvern St Mary 14–18; Hon C Munich Ascension Germany from 19; PtO *Worc* from 20; *Eur* from 20. *42 Wyche Road, Malvern WR14 4EG* T: (01684) 893637

GRAY, Andrew Stuart. b 70. LCTP. **d** 11 **p** 12. C Clitheroe St Jas *Blackb* 11–18; Faith Sharing Enabler *B & W* from 18. *Diocesan Office, The Old Deanery, Wells BA5 2UG* T: (01749) 670777

GRAY, Ms Ann. b 54. Newc Univ BEd 77. LCTP 09. **d** 12 **p** 13. NSM Lanercost, Walton, Gilsland and Nether Denton *Carl* 12–16; Chapl N Cumbria Integrated Care NHS Foundn Trust 16–20; Chapl Newc Univ from 20; P-in-c Kingston Park from 20. *12 Shannon Court, Newcastle upon Tyne NE3 2XF* E: a.gray147@btinternet.com

GRAY, Brett Christopher. b 71. Lon Bible Coll BA 95 Selw Coll Cam MPhil 04 PhD 15. Ridley Hall Cam 02. **d** 04 **p** 05. C Sunnyside w Bourne End *St Alb* 04–07; V St Alb St Mich 07–11; Asst Chapl Selw Coll Cam 11–15; Chapl and Fell SS Coll Cam from 15. *Sidney Sussex College, Cambridge CB2 3HU* T: (01223) 338837 M: 07795-580051 E: bcg24@cam.ac.uk *or* chaplain@sid.cam.ac.uk

GRAY, Ms Christine Angela (Kit). b 46. Nottm Univ BA 67 CertEd 68. Cranmer Hall Dur 71. **dss** 80 **d** 87 **p** 94. Rawthorpe *Wakef* 74–81; Chapl Nottm Univ *S'well* 81–88; C Rushmere *St E* 88–94; P-in-c Ringshall w Battisford, Barking w Darmsden etc 94–00; P-in-c Nayland w Wiston 00–10; rtd 10; PtO *St E* 10–15; *Chelmsf* from 12. *Address temp unknown*

GRAY, Dale Armitage. b 42. Edin Th Coll 62. **d** 92 **p** 93. Dioc Missr *Arg* 92–98; Chapl St Jo Cathl Oban 92–95; P-in-c Cumbrae (or Millport) 95–98; rtd 98; PtO *Edin* from 98. *The Dovecote, Duke Street, Coldstream TD12 4BN* T: (01890) 883247

GRAY, David. b 55. Oak Hill Th Coll. **d** 00 **p** 01. C Bestwood Em w St Mark *S'well* 00–04; P-in-c Bulwell St Jo 04–06; V 06–21; rtd 21. *Address temp unknown* E: davidgray72@hotmail.com

GRAY, David Cedric. b 53. RMN 77. **d** 97 **p** 98. OLM Gorton Em w St Jas *Man* 97–06; OLM Gorton and Abbey Hey 06–11. *Creoginity at St Francis Monastery, 89 Gorton Lane, Manchester M12 5WF* M: 07927-734419 E: rev.elation4.1@ntlworld.com

GRAY, David Michael. b 57. St Jo Coll Dur BA 99 ACIBS 80. CA Tr Coll 90 Cranmer Hall Dur 97. **d** 99 **p** 00. C Newc H Cross 99–02; V Long Benton St Mary 02–11; V Killingworth 11–19; TV Cramlington from 19. *119 Newlyn Drive, Cramlington NE23 1RP* T: (01670) 946017 M: 07540-620632 E: revdavegray@aol.com

GRAY, Canon Donald Clifford. b 30. TD 70 CBE 98. Liv Univ MPhil 81 Man Univ PhD 85 FRHistS 88 FSA 07. AKC 55. **d** 56 **p** 57. C Leigh St Mary *Man* 56–60; CF (TA) 58–67; V Westleigh St Pet *Man* 60–67; V Elton All SS 67–74; CF (TAVR) 67–77; QHC 74–77; R Liv Our Lady and St Nic w St Anne 74–87; RD Liv 75–81; Hon Can Liv Cathl 82–87; Chapl to The Queen 82–00; Can Westmr Abbey 87–98; I Westmr St Marg 87–98; Chapl to Speaker of Ho of Commons 87–98; rtd 98; PtO *Linc* from 98. *3 Barn Hill Mews, Stamford PE9 2GN* T: (01780) 765024

GRAY, Duncan Cowan. b 83. St Aug Coll of Th 15. **d** 18 **p** 19. NSM Hackney Wick St Mary of Eton w St Aug *Lon* from 18. *27 Powell Road, London E5 8DJ*

GRAY, Ms Elaine. b 62. Lindisfarne Regional Tr Partnership BA 20. **d** 20 **p** 21. NSM Hebburn St Jo *Dur* from 20; NSM Jarrow Grange from 20. *35 Breamish Street, Jarrow NE32 5SH* M: 07533-573922 E: elainegray2014@gmail.com

GRAY, James William. b 48. SAOMC. **d** 05 **p** 06. NSM Crich and S Wingfield *Derby* 05–15; PtO from 15. *Holmleigh, Market Place, Crich, Matlock DE4 5DD* T: (01773) 857921 E: jimlynda.gray@btopenworld.com

GRAY (née ROBERTS), Ms Jennifer. b 55. R Holloway Coll Lon BA 76 Somerville Coll Ox PGCE 77. SAOMC 00. **d** 03 **p** 04. C Welwyn Garden City *St Alb* 03–13; P-in-c Bramfield, Stapleford, Waterford etc 13–16; Min Aston St Mary CD 15–16; R Beane Valley from 16. *The Rectory, Church Lane, Watton-at-Stone, Hertford SG14 3RD* T: (01920) 830035 E: jennygrayrectory@gmail.com

GRAY, Joan. See BURKITT-GRAY, Joan Katherine

GRAY, John David Norman. b 38. Oak Hill Th Coll 84. **d** 86 **p** 87. C Portsdown *Portsm* 86–88; C Worthing St Geo *Chich* 88–91; TV Swanborough *Sarum* 91–98; rtd 98; PtO *Ex* 00–03; *Portsm* from 03. *15 Charminster Court, 46 Craneswater Park, Southsea PO4 0NU* T: (023) 9285 1299 E: johndngray@gmail.com

GRAY, Mrs Joy Dora. b 24. SRN 46 SCM 48. Gilmore Ho 79. **dss** 81 **d** 87 **p** 95. Newick *Chich* 81–94; Hon Par Dn 87–94; NSM Fletching 94–98; PtO from 98. *10 High Hurst Close, Newick, Lewes BN8 4NJ* T: (01825) 722965

GRAY, Julian Francis. b 64. Univ of Wales (Lamp) BA 86 MA 09. Coll of Resurr Mirfield 86. **d** 88 **p** 89. Min Can St Woolos Cathl *Mon* 88–91; C Bassaleg 91–93; V Overmonnow w Wonastow and Michel Troy 93–98; V King's Sutton and Newbottle and Charlton *Pet* 98–00; V Usk and Monkswood w Glascoed Chpl and Gwehelog *Mon* 00–03; V Usk and Gwehelog w Llantrisant w Llanllowell 03–14; P-in-c Llantilio Pertholey w Bettws Chpl etc from 14; AD Abergavenny from 20. *The Vicarage, 10 The Pines, Mardy, Abergavenny NP7 6HQ* T: (01873) 859881 E: mardyvicarage@yahoo.co.uk

GRAY, Lindsay Doreen. b 50. Open Univ BA 83 Leic Univ PhD 87. Coll of Resurr Mirfield 05. **d** 06 **p** 07. NSM Firbank, Howgill and Killington *Bradf* 06–09; NSM Sedbergh, Cautley and Garsdale 06–09; TV Egremont and Haile *Carl* 09–13; P-in-c Seascale and Drigg 13–16; Ind Chapl 09–16; rtd 16; Hon C Seascale and Drigg *Carl* 16; PtO *Bris* 18–19. *The Vicarage, The Banks, Seascale CA20 1QT* T: (019467) 28217 E: lgray782@btinternet.com

GRAY, The Ven Martin Clifford. b 44. Westcott Ho Cam 78. **d** 80 **p** 81. C Gaywood, Bawsey and Mintlyn *Nor* 80–84; V Sheringham 84–94; TR Lowestoft St Marg 94–99; Chapl Lothingland Hosp 95–99; RD Lothingland *Nor* 97–99; Adn Lynn 99–09; rtd 09; PtO *Nor* from 09; Acting Adn Stow and Lindsey *Linc* 15. *11 Chapel Lane, Hethersett, Norwich NR9 3JE* T: (01603) 812610 E: mandpgray11@btinternet.com

GRAY, Melvyn Dixon. b 38. Lon Univ BD 86 Dur Univ MA 89 PhD 07. NEOC 84. **d** 87 **p** 88. C Richmond w Hudswell *Ripon* 87–90; P-in-c Downholme and Marske 88–90; P-in-c Forcett and Aldbrough and Melsonby 90–91; R 91–00; R Mobberley *Ches* 00–04; rtd 04; PtO *Dur* from 04; *Ripon* 13–14; *Leeds* from 14. *51 The Orchard, Sedgefield, Stockton-on-Tees TS21 3AQ* T: (01740) 629069 E: melandanne@gray19.plus.com

GRAY, Natty. See GRAY, Renate Kathrina

GRAY, Mrs Patricia Linda. b 51. Univ of Wales (Swansea) BA 73 Ches Coll of HE BTh 02. NOC 99. **d** 02 **p** 03. C Glazebury w Hollinfare *Liv* 02–12; rtd 12; PtO *Liv* from 16. *14 Bollin Close, Culcheth, Warrington WA3 5DU* T: (01925) 763750 M: 07747-772345 E: pat.gray@bollinclose.uk

GRAY, Paul Alfred. b 41. BA. Sarum & Wells Th Coll. **d** 82 **p** 83. C Harpenden St Jo *St Alb* 82–85; TV Lynton, Brendon, Countisbury, Lynmouth etc *Ex* 85–86; rtd 06. *28 Baymead Meadow, North Petherton, Bridgwater TA6 6QW* T: (01278) 661258

GRAY, Penelope Jane. See GRAYSMITH, Penelope Jane

GRAY, Canon Philip Charles. b 67. Nottm Univ BA 91. St Steph Ho Ox 91. **d** 93 **p** 94. C Scarborough St Martin *York* 93–97; TV Leek and Meerbrook *Lich* 97–01; Bp's Dom Chapl *Blackb* 02–07; P-in-c Ilkley St Marg *Bradf* 07–12; V 12–14; *Leeds* 14–21; AD Ilkley 14–16; AD S Craven and Wharfedale 17–20; PtO 21; Hon Can Ho Ghana from 04. *Address temp unknown*

GRAY, Philip Thomas. Lon Univ BA 65. Chich Th Coll 66. **d** 68 **p** 69. C Leigh St Clem *Chelmsf* 68–74; V Mendlesham *St E* from 74; P-in-c Wickham Skeith 86–95; PtO *Nor* from 08. *The Vicarage, Mendlesham, Stowmarket IP14 5RS* T: (01449) 766359

GRAY, Renate Kathrina (Natty). b 52. SNWTP. **d** 13 **p** 14. OLM Deeplish and Newbold *Man* 13–18; NSM from 18; NSM Rochdale from 21. *669 Oldham Road, Rochdale OL16 4PE* T: (01706) 358550 M: 07577-825371 E: renate.gray@ntlworld.com *or* pabishopmark@manchester.anglican.org

GRAY, The Ven Robert James. b 70. TCD BA 92 HDipEd 93 MA 95 Irish Sch of Ecum MPhil 97. CITC 94. **d** 96 **p** 97. C Clooney w Strathfoyle *D & R* 96–99; I Ardamine w Kiltennel, Glascarrig etc *C, F & O* from 99; Treas Ferns Cathl from 04; Adn Ferns from 15; Adn Cashel, Waterford and Lismore from 15. *The Rectory, Knockroe, Courtown, Gorey, Co Wexford, Y25 NV02, Republic of Ireland* T: (00353) (53) 942 5423 M: 86-684 7621 E: ardamine@ferns.anglican.org

GRAY, Stephen James Norman. b 66. Lon Univ BA 89 Hughes Hall Cam PGCE 91. Ridley Hall Cam MA 00. **d** 00 **p** 01. C Cheltenham Ch Ch *Glouc* 00–03; Chapl RN 03–04; Chapl Sherborne Sch 04–10; Chapl Seaford Coll Petworth 10–13; P-in-c Graffham w Woolavington *Chich* 10–13; Chapl Bradfield Coll Berks 14–16; Conduct and Sen Chapl Eton Coll from 16. *3 Savile House, Eton College, Windsor SL4 6DW* T: (01753) 370864 E: s.gray@etoncollege.org.uk

GRAY, Mrs Susan Hazel. b 49. Kingston Univ BA 06. **d** 09 **p** 10. OLM Hersham *Guildf* 09–19; PtO from 19. *39 Misty's Field, Walton-on-Thames KT12 2BG* T: (01932) 242838 E: suehgray@btinternet.com or suegray@stpetershersham.com

GRAY, Mrs Trudy Ann Jennifer. b 48. Univ of Wales (Abth) BSc 69 Aston Univ MSc 72. **d** 05 **p** 06. NSM Gt Finborough w Onehouse, Harleston, Buxhall etc *St E* 05–10; NSM Upper Coquetdale *Newc* 10–13; rtd 13; PtO *Newc* from 13. *1 Greenside Avenue, Berwick-upon-Tweed TD15 1BZ* T: (01289) 331722 E: tajgrayfin@aol.com

GRAY, Mrs Ursula Mary. b 33. K Coll Lon BD 56 AKC 91 Univ of Wales (Lamp) MA 02. **d** 04 **p** 05. NSM Shaston *Sarum* 04–08; PtO 09; *Glouc* 16–21. *27 Townsend Court, Priory Way, Malmesbury SN16 0FB* T: (01666) 824851 E: umg@shaston.plus.com

GRAY-HAMMOND, Betsy. b 58. Ripon Coll Cuddesdon BA 10. **d** 10 **p** 11. C Brighton St Nic *Chich* 10–14; TV Moulsecoomb w Bevendean and Coldean from 14. *The Vicarage, Selham Drive, Brighton BN1 9EL* T: (01273) 601854 E: revbetsy@btinternet.com

GRAYSHON, Matthew Richard. b 47. St Jo Coll Nottm BTh 81. **d** 81 **p** 82. C Beverley Minster *York* 81–85; V Hallwood *Ches* 85–93; R Hanwell St Mary w St Chris *Lon* 93–16; rtd 16; Hon C Portway and Danebury *Win* from 16. *The Vicarage, Amport, Andover SP11 8BE* M: 07960-299434 E: revupmg@gmail.com

GRAYSHON, Paul Nicholas Walton. b 50. Cranmer Hall Dur 81. **d** 83 **p** 84. C Walkden Moor *Man* 83–87; V Radcliffe St Andr 87–07; P-in-c Matlock Bath and Cromford *Derby* 07–20; rtd 20; PtO *Sheff* from 21. *142 Rural Lane, Sheffield S6 4BL* M: 07421-740640 E: nickgrayshon@btopenworld.com

GRAYSMITH (née GRAY), Mrs Penelope Jane. b 63. SS Hild & Bede Coll Dur BA 85 Em Coll Cam MPhil 88. Westcott Ho Cam 86. **d** 89 **p** 94. Par Dn Evington *Leic* 89–92; Par Dn Cannock *Lich* 92–94; C 94–96; Chapl Asst Mid Staffs Gen Hosps NHS Trust 96–07; Hd Chapl Services Mid Staffs NHS Foundn Trust 07–12; Chapl Kath Ho Hospice Stafford 96–17; Chapl HM Pris Guernsey from 17. *HM Prison Guernsey, Les Nicolles, St Sampson, Guernsey GY2 4YF* T: (01481) 248376

GRAYSMITH, Peter Alexander. b 62. UEA BSc 83. Westcott Ho Cam 85. **d** 88 **p** 89. C Tettenhall Regis *Lich* 88–89; C Cannock 89–92; TV 92–99; V Rocester and Croxden w Hollington 99–01; V Baswich 01–16; Miss P Guernsey St Peter Port *Win* from 16; Miss P Guernsey St Jo from 16; Chapl Eliz Coll Guernsey from 16. *The Rectory, Cornet Street, St Peter Port, Guernsey GY1 1BZ* E: pgraysmith@elizabethcollege.gg

GRAYSON, Jane Elizabeth. b 71. **d** 07 **p** 08. OLM Moston St Mary *Man* 07–15; NSM Man Apostles w Miles Platting 15–18; PtO from 18. *296 St Mary's Road, Manchester M40 0BD* T: 0161-688 7073 E: janegrayson@aol.com

GRAYSON, Philip George. b 91. York St Jo Univ BA 12 St Jo Coll Dur MA 20. Cranmer Hall Dur 18. **d** 20 **p** 21. C Aberford w Micklefield *York* from 20; C Sherburn in Elmet w Saxton from 20. *1 Hastings House, Holyrood Lane, Ledsham, South Milford, Leeds LS25 5LL* T: (01977) 680234 E: philip.gg@live.co.uk

GRAYSON, Robin John. b 53. Mert Coll Ox BA 74 DPhil 78. Wycliffe Hall Ox 00. **d** 02 **p** 03. C Beaconsfield *Ox* 02–06; P-in-c Langley Marish 06–08; TR 08–21. *32 St Mary Street, Risca, Newport NP11 6GS* M: 07801-280475 E: r.j.grayson@btinternet.com

GREADY, Andrew John. b 63. Univ Coll Lon BSc 84 Newc Univ MA 93 Surrey Univ BSc 05. St Jo Coll Nottm 86. **d** 89 **p** 90. C Monkwearmouth St Andr *Dur* 89–92; C Bramley St Cath S Africa 92–96; R Sunninghill St Steph 96–99; Chapl St Pet Prep Sch 99; V Shottermill *Guildf* 00–06; Chapl Amesbury Sch 01–06; P-in-c Wynberg St Jo S Africa 06–08; R 08–12; Chapl W Prov Prep Sch 07–12;

Chapl The Hague *Eur* 13–18; V Clifton *York* from 18. *Clifton Vicarage, Clifton, York YO30 6BH* T: (01904) 656788 E: andrew.gready12@gmail.com

GREANY, Canon Richard Andrew Hugh. b 44. Qu Coll Ox BA 67 MA 83. Coll of Resurr Mirfield 67. **d** 69 **p** 70. C Hartlepool St Oswald *Dur* 69–72; C Clifton All SS *Bris* 72–75; Tutor Coll of Resurr Mirfield 75–78; V Whitworth w Spennymoor *Dur* 78–83; P-in-c Byers Green 78–79; Asst Prin St Alb Minl Tr Scheme 83–88; V Flamstead *St Alb* 83–88; V Hessle *York* 88–94; V Cambridge St Mary Less *Ely* 94–11; Dioc Spirituality Officer 99–06; Hon Can Ely Cathl 05–11; RD Cambridge S 06–11; rtd 11; Chapl Laslett's *Worc* 11–14; Hon C Worc City 11–14; PtO *York* 14–19; *Ox* 15–18; *Nor* from 18; Chantry P Shrine of Our Lady of Walsingham from 18. *8 Guild Street, Walsingham NR22 6BU* M: 07791-632976 E: andrewgreany@btinternet.com

GREAR, Hugh Massey. b 60. Bris Univ LLB 82. SEITE. **d** 00 **p** 01. C Warlingham w Chelsham and Farleigh *S'wark* 00–04; V Upper Tooting H Trin w St Aug 04–10; R Worplesdon *Guildf* 10–15; P-in-c Ockham w Hatchford and Downside 15–17; R 17–21; rtd 21. *Arctic Star, Port Werburgh, Vicarage Lane, Hoo, Rochester ME3 9TW* E: hugh.grear@sky.com

GREASLEY, James Kenneth. b 39. K Coll Lon BD 66 AKC 66. **d** 67 **p** 68. C Stoke upon Trent *Lich* 67–70; P-in-c Lusaka St Pet Zambia 70–76; V Gt Staughton *Ely* 76–81; Chapl HM Borstal Gaynes Hall 76–81; V Melbourn and Meldreth *Ely* 81–96; RD Shingay 82–96; R Chalfont St Peter *Ox* 96–04; rtd 04; PtO *Heref* from 05; *Sarum* from 19. *2 Bailey Mews, Old Sarum, Salisbury SP4 6FJ* T: (01722) 325017 E: jk.greasley@btinternet.com

GREATOREX, Mrs Susan Kathleen. b 58. St Hilda's Coll Ox BA 79 MA 04 Univ of Wales (Cardiff) PGCE 80. WEMTC 01. **d** 04 **p** 05. C Keynsham *B & W* 04–08; R Radstock w Writhlington 08–15; R Kilmersdon w Babington 08–15; V Lower Cam w Coaley *Glouc* 15–20; rtd 20. *The Vicarage, 99 Fairmead, Cam, Dursley GL11 5JU* T: (01543) 542547 E: susangreatorex@btinternet.com

GREATREX, Richard Quintin. b 65. K Coll Lon BD 86 Surrey Univ BA 02. STETS 99. **d** 02 **p** 03. NSM Westbury-on-Trym St Alb *Bris* 02–06; NSM Flax Bourton *B & W* 06–09; NSM Barrow Gurney 06–09; NSM Long Ashton w Barrow Gurney and Flax Bourton 09–21; R Chew Magna w Dundry, Norton Malreward etc from 21. *The Rectory, Tunbridge Close, Chew Magna, Bristol BS40 8SU* E: rqg@hotmail.co.uk

GREAVES, Kevin Adam Nathanael. b 65. Sheff Univ BA 13. Yorks Min Course 10. **d** 13 **p** 14. C Castleford *Wakef* 13–14; *Leeds* 14–16; V Chapelthorpe from 16; P-in-c Woolley from 19. *St James's Vicarage, 21 Stoney Lane, Chapelthorpe, Wakefield WF4 3JN* T: (01924) 256031 E: rev.kevingreaves@priest.com or kevin.greaves@leeds.anglican.org

GREAVES, Rachel Miriam Jane. See GREAVES-BROWN, Rachel Miriam Jane

GREAVES-BROWN, Andrew Paul. b 85. Trin Coll Bris 15. **d** 18 **p** 19. C Widford *Chelmsf* 18–21; C E Springfield from 21. *The Vicarage, 17 Ashton Place, Chelmsford CM2 6ST*

GREAVES-BROWN, Rachel Miriam Jane. b 86. Univ of the Arts Lon BA 08. Trin Coll Bris BA 18. **d** 18 **p** 19. C Highgate St Mich *Lon* 18–20; C Hendon St Mary and Ch Ch 20–21; C Hoxton St Jo w Ch Ch from 21. *Address withheld by request* E: rev.r.greaves@gmail.com

GREBE, Matthias. b 82. Tübingen Univ BA 07 Hughes Hall Cam MPhil 08 Ch Coll Cam PhD 12. Ridley Hall Cam 09. **d** 13 **p** 14. Asst Chapl Bonn w Cologne *Eur* 13–15; C Regent's Park St Mark *Lon* 15–17; C Cam St Edw *Ely* from 17; Adv Eur Ch Relns Coun for Chr Unity from 17; Chapl Westcott Ho Cam from 20. *15 Hillfield Road, Comberton, Cambridge CB23 7DB* M: 07387-092249 E: chaplain@westcott.cam.ac.uk or matthias.grebe@churchofengland.org

GREED, Frederick John. b 44. Trin Coll Bris 79. **d** 81 **p** 82. C Yateley *Win* 81–85; R Ore St Helen and St Barn *Chich* 85–95; R Street w Walton *B & W* 95–09; RD Glastonbury 08–09; rtd 09; PtO *B & W* from 09. *40 St Cleers Orchard, Somerton TA11 6QU* T: (01458) 272754 M: 07887-366698 E: john_greed@btinternet.com

GREEN, Adrian Paul. b 66. Trin Coll Bris 06. **d** 08 **p** 09. C Willowfield *D & D* 08–11; I Mt Merrion 11–21; Dir of Ords 15–21; Chapl Ibiza *Eur* from 21. *Capellania Anglicana, Apartado de Correos 838, 07830 Sant Josep (Illes Balears), Spain* T: (0034) 606 509 542 E: chaplainibiza11@gmail.com

GREEN, Preb Alan John Enrique. b 56. Worc Coll Ox BA 78 MA 83. Linc Th Coll 83. **d** 85 **p** 86. C Kirkby *Liv* 85–88; TV 88–94; Chapl Knowsley Community Coll 87–90; Chapl Worc Coll and C Ox St Giles and SS Phil and Jas w St Marg 94–98; TR St Jo on Bethnal Green *Lon* from 98; AD Tower Hamlets 06–12; Preb St Paul's Cathl from 10. *St John's Rectory,*

30 Victoria Park Square, London E2 9PB T/F: (020) 8980 1742 E: alan.green@virgin.net

GREEN, Alison Iola. b 58. Glas Univ MB, ChB 81 Lon Univ MSc 97 Anglia Ruskin Univ BA 13 MRCPCH 96. Westcott Ho Cam 11. **d** 13 **p** 14. C Chich Cathl 13–17; NSM Westbourne 17–18; Chapl Chich Univ from 17. *61 Southleigh Road, Havant PO9 2QQ* M: 07581-070669 E: iolag1@yahoo.com *or* alison.green@chi.ac.uk

GREEN, Alison Mary. b 51. Boro Road Teacher Tr Coll BEd 74 Wesley Coll Bris MA 03 Roehampton Univ PhD 07. STETS 02. **d** 04 **p** 05. NSM Bath St Barn w Englishcombe *B & W* 04–06; NSM Monmouth w Overmonnow etc *Mon* 06–13; NSM Bradford on Avon H Trin, Westwood and Wingfield *Sarum* from 14. *36 Budbury Close, Bradford-on-Avon BA15 1QG* T: (01225) 868259 E: alig9@btinternet.com

GREEN, Barrie. b 51. SS Coll Cam BA 72 MA 76. Wycliffe Hall Ox 75. **d** 78 **p** 79. C Castle Vale *Birm* 78–81; V W Heath 81–96; RD Kings Norton 87–95; TR Dronfield w Holmesfield *Derby* 96–09; P-in-c Bris St Paul's 09–15; rtd 15. *9 route de la Croix, 33220 Riocaud, France* E: barriegreen1951@gmail.com

GREEN, Benjamin Charles. b 83. Magd Coll Cam BA 04 MA 08. Wycliffe Hall Ox MTh 08. **d** 08 **p** 14. C Stockton *Dur* 08–09; C Arden Marches *Cov* 13–16; V Amington *Birm* 16–21; P-in-c Selly Park Ch Ch from 21. *16 Overmill Drive, Selly Park, Birmingham B29 7JL* M: 07985-490173 E: ben@rev.me.uk

GREEN, Brutus Zachary. b 78. Ex Univ BA 99 PhD 07 St Edm Coll Cam MPhil 04. Westcott Ho Cam 07. **d** 09 **p** 10. C Paddington St Jo w St Mich *Lon* 09–14; CF 14–18; P-in-c Putney St Marg *S'wark* 18–20; V from 20. *St Margaret's Vicarage, 46 Luttrell Avenue, London SW15 6PE* T: (020) 8355 2373 E: brutuszgreen@gmail.com

GREEN, Mrs Carol Amanda. b 64. Ex Univ BA 08. SWMTC 00. **d** 03 **p** 05. C Headingley Truro 03–07; TV Hale w Badshot Lea *Guildf* 07–12; P-in-c Mere w W Knoyle and Maiden Bradley *Sarum* 12–21; P-in-c Teignmouth, Ideford w Luton, Ashcombe etc *Ex* from 21. *St Michael's Rectory, 30 Dawlish Road, Teignmouth TQ14 8TG*

GREEN, Catherine Isabel. *See* HITCHENS, Catherine Isabel

GREEN, Christopher Martyn. b 58. New Coll Edin BD 80. Cranmer Hall Dur 82. **d** 83 **p** 84. C Virginia Water *Guildf* 83–87; C Bromley Ch Ch *Roch* 87–91; Study Asst the Proclamation Trust 91–92; C Surbiton Hill Ch Ch *S'wark* 92–00; Vice Prin Oak Hill Th Coll 00–13; PtO *Lon* 02–13; V Muswell Hill St Jas w St Matt from 14. *St James's Vicarage, 2 St James's Lane, London N10 3DB* T: (020) 8442 2900 *or* 8883 6277

GREEN, Daphne Mary. b 55. K Coll Cam BA 77 Bradf Univ MBA 91 Leeds Univ PhD 01 Lon Inst of Educn PGCE 79. NOC 95. **d** 98 **p** 99. C Headingley Ripon 98–02; Chapl Leeds Metrop Univ 00–02; R Stanningley St Thos 02–08; Abp's Chapl and Researcher *York* 08–21; Can and Preb York Minster 16–21; Chapl Geneva *Eur* from 21. *Holy Trinity, 14 bis rue du Mont Blanc, CH-1201 Geneva, Switzerland* M: 07796-084264 *or* (0041) 79-945 0605 E: chaplainhtc@gmail.com

GREEN, David Allen. b 61. Sheff City Poly BA 90. Cranmer Hall Dur 00. **d** 02 **p** 03. C Huyton St Geo *Liv* 02–06; TV Walkden and Lt Hulton *Man* 06–10; P-in-c Thorne *Sheff* 10–14; V 14–20; rtd 21; PtO *Sheff* from 21. *1 Lime Tree Walk, Denaby Main, Doncaster DN12 4TE* E: redrev@talktalk.net

GREEN, David Michael. b 62. Lanc Univ BSc 83. St Mellitus Coll BA 12. **d** 12 **p** 13. NSM Ruislip St Martin *Lon* 12–17; V Hatch End St Anselm from 17. *The Vicarage, 50 Cedar Drive, Pinner HA5 4DE* M: 07962-057767 E: fr.david@live.co.uk

GREEN, David Norman. b 37. Magd Coll Cam BA 60. Clifton Th Coll 60. **d** 62 **p** 63. C Islington St Mary *Lon* 62–65; C Burley *Ripon* 65–68; Kenya 69–80; P-in-c Brimscombe *Glouc* 81–90; R Woodchester and Brimscombe 90–96; P-in-c Coberley w Cowley 96–97; P-in-c Colesborne 96–97; P-in-c Coberley, Cowley, Colesbourne and Elkstone 97–04; Dioc Rural Adv 96–04; rtd 04; Tanzania 04–13; PtO *S'well* 13–21. *8 Cherrywood Gardens, Nottingham NG3 6LQ* T: 0115-950 2958 E: revdavidngreen@hotmail.com

GREEN, David Robert John. b 73. Sheff Univ BA 96 Anglia Ruskin Univ MA 12. Ridley Hall Cam 06. **d** 08 **p** 09. C Chatham St Phil and St Jas *Roch* 08–11; P-in-c W Malling w Offham 11–18; V from 18. *The Vicarage, 138 High Street, West Malling ME19 6NE* T: (01732) 842245 E: vicar@stmaryswestmalling.org.uk

GREEN, David William. b 53. CertEd 75 Nottm Univ BCombStuds 84. Linc Th Coll 81. **d** 84 **p** 85. C S Merstham *S'wark* 84–88; C Walton-on-Thames *Guildf* 88–91; V Gillingham H Trin and Chapl Lennox Wood Elderly People's Home *Roch* 91–99; V Strood St Nic w St Mary from 99; RD Strood 12–17. *18 Honeypot Close, Rochester ME2 3DU* T: (01634) 719052 E: revdavidgreen@blueyonder.co.uk

GREEN, Canon Denise Penelope. b 57. Bedf Coll of Educn BEd 80 MPhil 89 Nottm Univ MA 05. EMMTC 03. **d** 06 **p** 09. C Skirbeck H Trin *Linc* 06–10; P-in-c S Lawres Gp 10–14; R from 14; V Barlings from 14; Can and Preb Linc Cathl from 18. *The Vicarage, 14 Church Lane, Cherry Willingham, Lincoln LN3 4AB* T: (01522) 595596 M: 07812-006295 E: revdpg@virginmedia.com

GREEN, The Ven Duncan Jamie. b 52. Sarum & Wells Th Coll 82. **d** 84 **p** 85. C Uckfield *Chich* 84–87; Dioc Youth Officer *Chelmsf* 87–96; Warden and Chapl St Mark's Coll Res Cen 93–96; TR Saffron Walden w Wendens Ambo, Littlebury etc *Chelmsf* 96–07; RD Saffron Walden 05–07; C of E Olympic and Paralympic Co-ord 07–13; Hon Can Chelmsf Cathl 03–13; Adn Northolt *Lon* 13–19; P-in-c Ealing Common St Matt 16–17; rtd 19; PtO *St E* from 20; *Chelmsf* from 20. *Flints, Hawstead Lane, Sicklemere, Bury St Edmunds IP30 0BT* M: 07741-246521

GREEN, Edward Marcus. b 66. Mert Coll Ox BA 88 MA 92. Wycliffe Hall Ox 90. **d** 94 **p** 95. C Glyncorrwg w Afan Vale and Cymmer Afan *Llan* 94–96; C Aberystwyth *St D* 96–99; P-in-c Pontypridd St Cath *Llan* 00–01; V 01–11; PtO *Bradf* 11–13; R Steeple Aston w N Aston and Tackley *Ox* from 13; PtO *Eur* from 17. *The Rectory, Fir Lane, Steeple Aston, Bicester OX25 4SF* T: (01869) 340903 E: steeplerector@hotmail.co.uk

GREEN, Mrs Elizabeth Pauline Anne. b 29. Gilmore Ho 69. **dss** 76 **d** 87 **p** 94. Chorleywood Ch Ch *St Alb* 76–87; Par Dn 87–90; C Chipping Sodbury and Old Sodbury *Glouc* 90–95; Asst Dioc Missr 90–95; rtd 95; NSM Chipping Sodbury and Old Sodbury *Glouc* 95–99; PtO from 99; *Bris* from 99. *The Old House, The Common, Chipping Sodbury, Bristol BS37 6PX* T: (01454) 311936

GREEN, Ernest James. b 31. Pemb Coll Cam BA 55 MA 62. Linc Th Coll 55. **d** 57 **p** 58. C Rawmarsh w Parkgate *Sheff* 57–60; Sec Th Colls Dept SCM 60–62; Prec and Sacr Bris Cathl 62–65; Min Can 62–65; V Churchill *B & W* 65–78; RD Locking 72–78; V Burrington and Churchill 78–82; Preb Wells Cathl 81–82; V Ryde All SS *Portsm* 82–91; P-in-c Ryde H Trin 82–86; RD E Wight 83–88; TR Hempnall *Nor* 91–96; rtd 96; PtO *B & W* 97–07. *12 Monica Wills House, Cromwell Street, Bristol BS3 3NH* T: 0117-239 4257 E: revdern17@yahoo.co.uk

GREEN, Ms Fiona Jenifer. b 67. Rob Coll Cam BA 89 MA 93. Ridley Hall Cam 02. **d** 05 **p** 06. C Highbury Ch Ch w St Jo and St Sav *Lon* 05–08; C St Jo on Bethnal Green 08–12; Co-ord Reader Tr Stepney Area 08–12; Intern Programme Dir 12–19; Vice-Prin Ridley Hall Cam from 19. *Ridley Hall, Ridley Hall Road, Cambridge CB3 9HG* T: (01223) 741065 M: 07786-541559 E: fionajgreen@yahoo.co.uk *or* fjg32@cam.ac.uk

GREEN, Canon Fleur Estelle. b 72. Univ of Wales (Ban) BD 94. Ripon Coll Cuddesdon 95. **d** 97 **p** 98. C Blackpool St Jo *Blackb* 97–00; C Lancaster St Mary w St John and St Anne 00–03; P-in-c Blackb St Luke w St Phil 03–04; P-in-c Witton 03–04; V Blackb Christ the King 04–12; V Darwen St Pet from 12; AD Blackb and Darwen from 18; Asst Dir of Ords 06–12; Women's Min Adv from 11; Hon Can Blackb Cathl from 11. *The Rectory, St Peter's Close, Darwen BB3 2EA* T: (01254) 702411 E: chauntry1@live.co.uk

GREEN, Frank Gilbert. b 23. Kelham Th Coll 46. **d** 50 **p** 51. C Sheff St Cecilia Parson Cross 50–56; SSM from 52; C Nottingham St Geo w St Jo *S'well* 56–58; Basutoland 59–62; S Africa 62–69 and 84–88; Lesotho 69–84; PtO *Ox* 88–16; rtd 93. *Society of the Sacred Mission, Provincial Office, St Michael's Priory, The Well, Newport Road, Willen, Milton Keynes MK15 9AA*

GREEN, Gary Henry. b 64. Univ of Wales (Cardiff) BD 87. St Mich Coll Llan 93. **d** 95 **p** 96. C Baglan *Llan* 95–97; C Neath w Llantwit 97–01; TV Neath 01–02; V Llangiwg *S & B* from 02. *1 Clos yr Hen Ysgol, Pontardawe, Swansea SA8 4AZ* T: (01792) 862003 E: gary.green890@btinternet.com

GREEN, Gloria. *See* SHERBOURNE, Gloria

GREEN, Graham Herbert. b 53. City Univ BSc 74. Westcott Ho Cam 75. **d** 78 **p** 79. C Hatcham St Cath *S'wark* 78–82; C S Ashford Ch Ch *Cant* 82–88; V Cheriton All So w Newington 88–97; P-in-c Milton next Sittingbourne 97–02; V 02–06; PtO *Roch* 12–13; V Helsby and Dunham-on-the-Hill *Ches* 13–21; Dioc Adv in Spirituality 13–21; rtd 21. *Address temp unknown* M: 07988-850261 E: millett1006@btinternet.com

GREEN, Imogen Elizabeth. *See* VIBERT, Imogen Elizabeth

GREEN, Miss Jennifer Mary. b 55. SEN 78 SRN 81 RM 84. Trin Coll Bris 87. **d** 90 **p** 95. C Tong *Bradf* 90–93; Chapl Bradf Cathl 93; CMS Uganda 94–15; C Lt Horton *Leeds* 15–20; C Bankfoot and Bowling St Steph 15–20. *54 Eden Street, Carlisle CA3 9LH* E: jennykisoro@hotmail.com

GREEN, Jeremy Nigel. b 52. St Andr Univ MA. St Jo Coll Nottm 80. **d** 83 **p** 84. C Dorridge *Birm* 83–86; V Scrooby

S'well 86–94; V Bawtry w Austerfield and Misson 94–06; AD Bawtry 01–06; P-in-c Haxey *Linc* 06–12; V 12–18; P-in-c Owston 06–12; V 12–18; rtd 18. *6 Harvester Close, Epworth, Doncaster DN9 1QZ* E: jngreen@live.co.uk

GREEN, The Ven John. b 53. CB 10. Nottm Univ BCombStuds 83. Linc Th Coll 80. **d** 83 **p** 84. C Watford St Mich *St Alb* 83–86; C St Alb St Steph 86–91; Chapl RN 91–06; Chapl of the Fleet and Adn for the RN 06–10; QHC 06–10; Hon Can Portsm Cathl 06–10; PtO *Cov* 11–12; Adn *Cov* 12–17; C Cov St Mary 14–17; PtO *Birm* 12–16; rtd 17. *Tigh Callum, Culkein, Drumbeg, Lairg IV27 4NL* M: 07929-003361 E: venjgreen@gmail.com

GREEN, Canon John Francis Humphrey. b 44. Ex Univ BA 65 Heythrop Coll Lon MA 96. Westcott Ho Cam 91. **d** 93 **p** 94. C Tadworth *S'wark* 93–96; Chapl St Geo Sch Harpenden 96–01; P-in-c Flamstead *St Alb* 01–12; P-in-c Markyate Street 01–12; V Flamstead and Markyate Street 12–14; RD Wheathampstead 09–10; Hon Can St Alb 13–14; rtd 14; P-in-c Barlavington, Burton w Coates, Sutton and Bignor *Chich* from 14. *The Rectory, The Street, Sutton, Pulborough RH20 1PS* T: (01798) 869023 E: johnfhgreen@gmail.com

GREEN, Canon John Henry. b 44. K Coll Lon BD 72 AKC. **d** 73 **p** 74. C Tupsley *Heref* 73–77; Asst Chapl Newc Univ 77–79; V Stevenage St Hugh Chells *St Alb* 79–85; V St Jo in Bedwardine *Worc* 85–92; Dir of Ords 92–08; P-in-c Guarlford and Madresfield w Newland 92–99; C Fladbury w Wyre Piddle and Moor etc 99–08; P-in-c Bowbrook N 08–12; P-in-c Bowbrook S 08–12; Hon Can Worc Cathl 94–12; rtd 12; PtO *Worc* from 12. *25 Station Road, Alcester B49 5ET* T: (01789) 400213 M: 07778-585746 E: ddocropthorne@waitrose.com

GREEN, Jonathon Samuel McKibbin. b 58. LCTP 10. **d** 13 **p** 14. Gen Manager Rydal Hall *Carl* 07–16; NSM Windermere St Mary and Troutbeck 13–14; NSM Grasmere 14–16; NSM Rydal 14–16; Dir Foxhill Retreat and Conf Cen *Ches* from 16. *The Bungalow, Foxhill Conference Centre, Tarvin Road, Frodsham WA6 6XB* T: (01928) 733777 E: jsmamgreen@gmail.com *or* jonathon.green@chester.anglican.org

GREEN, Mrs Joy Elizabeth. b 53. Open Univ BA 00. SEITE 04. **d** 07 **p** 08. NSM Maidstone St Martin *Cant* 07–14; rtd 14; PtO *Cant* from 14. *50 Anglesey Avenue, Maidstone ME15 9SU* T: (01622) 741616 E: joy.green50@tiscali.co.uk

GREEN, Julia Ann. *See* CARTWRIGHT, Julia Ann

GREEN, Canon Karina Beverley. b 61. Ripon Coll Cuddesdon 87. **d** 90 **p** 94. C Lee-on-the-Solent *Portsm* 90–93; Dioc Youth Officer *Guildf* 94–99; Youth and Children's Work Adv *Portsm* 99–03; P-in-c Portsea St Geo 03–05; V 05–12; P-in-c W Leigh from 12; CME Officer 03–13; Jt AD Havant 14–20; Hon Can Portsm Cathl from 06. *St Alban's Vicarage, Martin Road, Havant PO9 5TE* T: (023) 9307 6871 E: canonkarina@talktalk.net

✠**GREEN, The Rt Revd Laurence Alexander.** b 45. K Coll Lon BD 68 AKC 68 NY Th Sem STM 69 DMin 82. St Aug Coll Cant 70. **d** 70 **p** 71 **c** 93. C Kingstanding St Mark *Birm* 70–73; V Erdington St Chad 73–83; Prin Aston Tr Scheme 83–89; Hon C Birchfield *Birm* 84–89; TR Poplar *Lon* 89–93; Area Bp Bradwell *Chelmsf* 93–11; rtd 11; Hon Asst Bp Chich from 11; Hon Asst Bp Roch from 18. *4 Rotherfield Avenue, Bexhill-on-Sea TN40 1SY* T: (01424) 217872 M: 07891-938647 E: mail@lauriegreen.org

GREEN, Mrs Linda Anne. b 60. Westcott Ho Cam 84. dss 86 **d** 87 **p** 94. Borehamwood *St Alb* 86–89; Par Dn 87–89; Par Dn Sheff St Cuth 89–90; Chapl Asst N Gen Hosp Sheff 89–91; Chapl 91–95; Chapl Qu Mary's Sidcup NHS Trust 96–05; P-in-c Crockenhill All So *Roch* 06–10; P-in-c Brasted 10–12; R 12–21; Chapl R Marsden NHS Foundn Trust from 21. *The Royal Marsden, Fulham Road, London SW3 6JJ* T: (020) 7808 2818 E: revlindagreen@aol.com

GREEN, Canon Linda Jeanne. b 50. R Holloway Coll Lon BSc 72 RGN 74 RCNT 79. SAOMC 01. **d** 04 **p** 05. C Headington Quarry *Ox* 04–09; P-in-c Banbury 09–13; R 13–15; Hon Can Ch Ch 14–15; rtd 15; PtO *Chich* from 15. *118 Marine Parade, Seaford BN25 2QR* M: 07455-074003 E: revlindagreen@gmail.com

GREEN, Malcolm Colin Robert. b 59. St Mellitus Coll 14. **d** 17 **p** 18. NSM St Mary-at-Latton *Chelmsf* from 17. *5 The Gowers, Harlow CM20 2JP* E: malcolm.green23@ntlworld.com

GREEN, Marcus. *See* GREEN, Edward Marcus

GREEN, Mark Richard. b 66. York Univ BA 87. All SS Cen for Miss & Min 14. **d** 17 **p** 18. NSM Witton *Ches* 17–19; P-in-c Moulton from 19. *15 Park Lane, Moulton, Northwich CW9 8QG* T: (01606) 557712 M: 07940-950311 E: mark@markrgreen.co.uk

GREEN, Martin Charles. b 59. Bris Univ BA 81 MPhil 86. Wycliffe Hall Ox 82. **d** 84 **p** 85. C Margate H Trin *Cant* 84–88; V Kingston upon Hull St Aid Southcoates *York*

88–94; P-in-c Bishop's Itchington *Cov* from 94; Dioc Children's Officer 94–05; P-in-c Radford Semele from 05; AD Southam from 16. *The Vicarage, 1 Manor Road, Bishop's Itchington, Southam CV47 2QJ* T: (01926) 613466 E: revmcg@kerrins.com

GREEN, Mrs Maureen. b 49. Avery Hill Coll CertEd 70 Lon Univ BEd 71. EAMTC 95. **d** 98 **p** 02. NSM Ipswich St Jo *St E* 98–10; Asst Chapl Ipswich Hosp NHS Trust 98–05; Asst Chapl Local Health Partnerships NHS Trust 98–02; Asst Chapl Cen Suffolk Primary Care Trust 02–05; PtO *Ox* 11–15; *St E* 15–19. *Church House, Lower Farm Road, Ringshall, Stowmarket IP14 2JE* T: (01473) 657472 E: maureengreen@talk21.com

GREEN, Michael Alan. b 78. St Mellitus Coll BA 19. **d** 19 **p** 20. C Brownhill *Leeds* from 19. *26 Burnley's Mill Road, Gomersal, Cleckheaton BD19 4PQ* T: (01274) 871570 M: 07403-069879 E: revmike@mailbox.org

GREEN, Nicholas. b 67. CA Tr Coll 98 Cranmer Hall Dur 07. **d** 08 **p** 09. CA from 01; C Marton-in-Cleveland *York* 08–11; C Brookfield 11–13; R Dunblane *St And* 13–18; V Walton St Jo *Derby* from 18. *6 Medlock Road, Chesterfield S40 3NH* T: (01246) 555881 E: greennick@live.co.uk

GREEN, Paul John. b 48. Sarum & Wells Th Coll 72. **d** 73 **p** 74. C Tuffley *Glouc* 73–76; C Prestbury 76–82; P-in-c Highnam w Lassington and Rudford 82–83; P-in-c Tibberton w Taynton 82–83; R Highnam, Lassington, Rudford, Tibberton etc 84–92; Hon Min Can Glouc Cathl 85–96; V Fairford 92–96; RD 93–96; rtd 96; PtO *Glouc* 98–17. *15 Roselle Drive, Brockworth, Gloucester GL3 4GG*

GREEN, Pauline. *See* GREEN, Elizabeth Pauline Anne

GREEN, Penny. *See* GREEN, Denise Penelope

GREEN, Peter. b 38. Ex Univ BSc 59. Sarum Th Coll 59. **d** 61 **p** 62. C Romford St Edw *Chelmsf* 61–66; Chapl Trin Coll Kandy Ceylon 66–70; V Darnall *Sheff* 71–80; TV Stantonbury *Ox* 80–87; TV Stantonbury and Willen 87–91; Dep Chapl HM Pris Belmarsh 91–92; Chapl HM Pris Woodhill 92–03; rtd 03; PtO *Ox* from 04; *St D* from 06. *34 North Twelfth Street, Milton Keynes MK9 3BT* T: (01908) 240634 M: 07437-473181 E: petergreen1938@icloud.com

GREEN, Peter Geoffrey. b 59. St Andr Univ MA 83 MLitt 20 Open Univ MA 01 PhD 10 BA 15. Coll of Resurr Mirfield 85. **d** 88 **p** 89. C Pershore w Pinvin, Wick and Birlingham *Worc* 88–91; V Dudley St Barn 91–99; V W Bromwich St Fran *Lich* 99–04; RD W Bromwich 02–04; Chapl Abbots Bromley Sch 04–12; P-in-c Hoar Cross w Newchurch *Lich* 07–12; Dean of Chpl and Chapl Bp Grosseteste Univ from 13; PV Linc Cathl from 15; PtO *Leeds* from 17. *Bishop Grosseteste University, Longdales Road, Lincoln LN1 3DY* T: (01522) 583607 E: peter.green@bishopg.ac.uk

GREEN, Peter Jamie. b 63. Aston Tr Scheme 87 Oak Hill Th Coll BA 93. **d** 93 **p** 94. C Brigg *Linc* 93–97; P-in-c Billinghay 97–01; V Carr Dyke Gp 01–02; R Kelsey Gp 02–09; P-in-c St Mark's Bermuda 09–12; R Old Brampton and Gt Barlow *Derby* 12–19; P-in-c Loundsley Green 12–19; V Abbey Gp *Linc* from 19. *The Vicarage, Church Lane, Ulceby DN39 6TB* M: 07858-413031 E: peter.green_99@tiscali.co.uk

GREEN, Philip Charles. b 53. NOC 91. **d** 94 **p** 95. C Southport Em *Liv* 94–98; P-in-c Crossens 98–03; TV N Meols 03–05; TR 05–18; AD 09–18; Hon Can Liv Cathl 09–18; rtd 18; PtO *Blackb* from 19. *45 Seacroft Crescent, Southport PR9 9FR* E: revphilgreen@talktalk.net

GREEN, Philip Stuart. b 69. Man Poly BA 90 Man Univ PGCE 91. ERMC 11. **d** 14 **p** 15. NSM London Colney *St Alb* from 14; Asst Chapl Aldenham Sch Herts from 17. *Aldenham School, Aldenham Road, Elstree, Borehamwood WD6 3AJ* T: (01923) 851636 M: 07934-335793 E: revphilipgreen@btinternet.com *or* psg@aldenham.com

GREEN, Richard Alistair. b 76. Ex Univ BA 97. St Steph Ho Ox BA 01. **d** 01 **p** 02. C Cockerton *Dur* 01–05; TV Ludlow *Heref* 05–13; Chapl Shropshire Co Primary Care Trust 05–13; V Aberdare St Fagan *Llan* from 13. *The Vicarage, 5 Redwood Court, Aberdare CF44 8RX* T: (01685) 881435 E: vicar.stfagans@btconnect.com

GREEN, Robert Henry. b 57. K Coll Lon BD 79. Wycliffe Hall Ox 81. **d** 83 **p** 84. C Norbury *Ches* 83–86 and 91–19; C Knutsford St Jo and Toft 86–88; PtO from 19. *122 Cavendish Road, Hazel Grove, Stockport SK7 6JH* T: (01625) 858680 E: rob.green122@btinternet.com

GREEN, Robert Leonard. b 44. Open Univ BA 98. Sarum & Wells Th Coll 82. **d** 84 **p** 85. C Battersea St Luke *S'wark* 84–89; CF 89–04; P-in-c Southwick w Boarhunt *Portsm* 05–16; PtO *Sarum* 16–21; *Win* 16–21. *5 Grouse Road, Old Sarum, Salisbury SP4 6GE* T: (01722) 321870 M: 07876-426384 E: robertgreen7@btinternet.com

GREEN, Robert Stanley. b 42. Dur Univ BA 65. Wells Th Coll 65. **d** 67 **p** 68. C Ashford *Cant* 67–73; R Otham 73–80; V

Bethersden w High Halden 80–87; R Winterbourne Stickland and Turnworth etc *Sarum* 87–99; R Monkton Farleigh, S Wraxall and Winsley 99–05; rtd 05; PtO *Sarum* from 06. *The Bungalow, Wootton Grove, Sherborne DT9 4DL* T: (01935) 817066 E: robertgreen@hotmail.com

GREEN, Robin. b 47. St As Minl Tr Course. **d** 06 **p** 07. NSM Llangystennin *St As* 06–09; NSM Rhos-Cystennin 09–11; rtd 11; PtO *St As* from 12; *Ban* from 15. *140 Queens Road, Llandudno LL30 1UE* T: (01492) 876451 E: robandjoy_@hotmail.com

GREEN, The Ven Roderick Ernest Alexander. b 74. Reading Univ BA 95 Brunel Univ MA 99. Wycliffe Hall Ox MTh 07. **d** 07 **p** 08. C Spitalfields Ch Ch w All SS *Lon* 07–11; C Shadwell St Paul w Ratcliffe St Jas 11–14; V W Harrow St Pet 14–21; Adn Llan from 21. *Llandaff Cathedral Administrative Office, Prebendal House, Llandaff, Cardiff CF5 2LA* M: 07957-247229 E: rodeagreen@gmail.com

GREEN, Rodney William. b 52. **d** 93 **p** 94. OLM Flixton St Jo *Man* from 93; PtO *Eur* from 16. *85 Arundel Avenue, Flixton, Manchester M41 6MG* T: 0161-748 7238

GREEN, Roger Thomas. b 43. Oak Hill Th Coll. **d** 79 **p** 80. C Paddock Wood *Roch* 79–83; R High Halstow w All Hallows and Hoo St Mary 83–89; Chapl HM Pris Brixton 89–90; Chapl HM Pris Standford Hill 90–94; Chapl HM Pris Swaleside 94–99; Chapl HM Pris Roch 99–03; Chapl HM Pris Blantyre Ho 03; Chapl HM Pris Brixton 03–06; rtd 06; PtO *Sarum* from 11. *86 Tatnam Road, Poole BH15 2DS* E: rogert.green@gmail.com

GREEN, Ruth. b 54. Pittsburgh Th Sem DMin 18 RGN 76. New Coll Edin BD 11. **d** 11 **p** 12. C Edin St Pet 11–14; R Edin St Dav 14–19; P-in-c Aberdeen St Jas *Ab* from 19. *95 Gray Street, Aberdeen AB10 6JH* M: 07941-552768 E: revruthstjames@hotmail.com

GREEN, Ruth Valerie. *See* JAGGER, Ruth Valerie

GREEN, Ryan Albert. b 77. Nottm Univ BA 99. St Steph Ho Ox MTh 05. **d** 05 **p** 06. C The Cookhams *Ox* 05–09; R Swanbourne w Mt Claremont Australia 09–17; V Hove All SS *Chich* from 17. *24 Denmark Villas, Hove BN3 3TE* T: (01273) 733331 E: rev_green@hotmail.co.uk or frryan@allsaintshove.org

GREEN, Samuel John McKibbin. *See* COWLING-GREEN, Samuel John McKibbin

GREEN, Sidney Leonard. b 44. K Coll Lon MTh 86 Montessori DipEd 84 Tabor Coll (Australia) ThD 13. Oak Hill Th Coll BD 72. **d** 72 **p** 73. C Skelmersdale St Paul *Liv* 72–74; C Denton Holme *Carl* 74–76; In Bapt Min 76–85; Chapl Qu Eliz Gr Sch Blackb 85–91; Chapl Epsom Coll 91–01; P-in-c Sway *Win* 01–03; V 03–04; rtd 04; Australia from 04; Asst Min Adelaide H Trin 05; R Adelaide St Luke 06; Chapl Kensington St Matt 07–12; Asst Min Adelaide St Jude from 12. *Bethany, 44/7 Sommer Place, Pasadena, Adelaide SA 5042, Australia* T: (0061) (8) 8277 7944 M: 43-989 5117 E: sidneygreen@adam.com.au

GREEN, Ms Stella Louise. b 61. Kent Univ BA 84 Cardiff Univ MTh 05 Anglia Ruskin Univ MA 16. St Mich Coll Llan 01. **d** 03 **p** 04. C Stamford Hill St Thos *Lon* 03–06; R Horsford, Felthorpe and Hevingham *Nor* 06–10; Chapl Norfolk and Nor Univ Hosps NHS Foundn Trust 10–18; Lead Chapl Qu Eliz Hosp King's Lynn NHS Foundn Trust from 18. *Chaplaincy Department, Queen Elizabeth Hospital, Gayton Road, King's Lynn PE30 4ET* T: (01553) 613441 E: stella.green@qehkl.nhs.uk or stella.green454@btinternet.com

GREEN, Stephen Gurner. b 62. Bath Univ BSc 83 Ken Univ MA 85 Cant Ch Ch Univ PhD 16. SCTEI 19. **d** 21. C W Horsley *Guildf* from 21. *70 Send Barns Lane, Send, Woking GU23 7BS* T: (01483) 223820 M: 07818-041294 E: steveandhelengreen@gmail.com

GREEN, Canon Steven Douglas. b 57. Univ of Wales BA 97. Sarum & Wells Th Coll 81. **d** 82 **p** 83. C Hawarden *St As* 82–86; V Mostyn 86–93; V Ffynnongroew 86–93; V Mostyn w Ffynnongroyw 93–99; R Trefnant w Tremeirchion 99–01; R Cefn w Trefnant w Tremeirchion 01–07; V Shotton 07–16; TV Borderlands Miss Area from 17; Warden of Readers from 10; Hon Can St As Cathl from 19. *The Vicarage, Chester Road East, Shotton, Deeside CH5 1QD* T: (01244) 836991 E: sdgreen1957@gmail.com

GREEN, The Very Revd Susan Denise. b 66. TCD BA 89 HDipEd 90. **d** 92 **p** 93. C Antrim All SS *Conn* 92–95; Dioc Youth Officer (Cashel) *C, F & O* 95–00; Chapl Adelaide and Meath Hosp Dublin 00–09; Chapl Kilkenny Coll *C, F & O* 10–18; Can Ossory Cathl 13–18; Dean Cloyne *C, K & R* from 18; I Cloyne Union from 18. *13 The Pinnacles, Midleton, Co Cork, Republic of Ireland* T: (00353) (21) 463 7913 E: s2011green@gmail.com

GREEN, Mrs Susan Margaret. b 54. Univ of Wales (Abth) BSc 75. SWMTC 92. **d** 95 **p** 96. NSM Wiveliscombe w Chipstable, Huish Champflower etc *B & W* 95–05; R Blackdown 05–14; C Trull w Angersleigh 05–14; rtd 14; PtO *B & W* from 15. *Stonehouse, Allenslade Close, Wiveliscombe, Taunton TA4 2BS* T: (01984) 623012 E: suegreen@summit.me.uk

GREEN, Susannah Ruth. *See* CURTIS, Susannah Ruth

GREEN, Canon Trevor Geoffrey Nash. b 45. BA. Oak Hill Th Coll 81. **d** 84 **p** 85. C Stalybridge H Trin and Ch Ch *Ches* 84–89; V 89–96; V Lache cum Saltney 96–10; Hon Can Ches Cathl 08–10; rtd 10; PtO *Ches* from 10; *Man* 13–18; *Derby* 15–18. *27 Winchester Road, Dukinfield SK16 5DH* T: 0161-304 7796 M: 07837-424038 E: trevlaine10@aol.co.uk

GREEN, Trevor Howard. b 37. Sarum & Wells Th Coll 72. **d** 74 **p** 75. C Bloxwich *Lich* 74–77; C Willenhall St Steph 77–79; P-in-c 79–80; V 80–82; V Essington 82–90; V Bishopswood and Brewood 90–02; P-in-c Coven 00–02; RD Penkridge 94–01; rtd 02; PtO *Lich* 02–19. *113 Stafford Street, Cannock WS12 2EN* T: (01543) 271159

GREEN, Mrs Veronica Gale. b 62. All SS Cen for Miss & Min 12. **d** 14 **p** 15. C Bunbury and Tilstone Fearnall *Ches* 14–15; C Marbury w Tushingham and Whitewell 15–17; P-in-c from 17. *The Vicarage, Marbury, Whitchurch SY13 4LN* T: (01948) 663758 M: 07928-792337 E: veronicarom838@aol.com

GREENALL, Canon Ronald Gilbert. b 41. St Aid Birkenhead 61. **d** 64 **p** 65. C Adlington *Blackb* 64–67; C Ribbleton 67–69; R Coppull St Jo 69–84; V Garstang St Thos 84–99; RD Garstang 89–96; Hon Can Blackb Cathl 95–99; rtd 99; PtO *Blackb* from 99. *40 Duckworth Drive, Catterall, Preston PR3 1YS* T: (01995) 606135 E: canon.ron@tiscali.co.uk

GREENAWAY-ROBBINS, Mark. b 72. Ox Univ BA 95. Qu Coll Birm 96. **d** 99 **p** 00. C Redruth w Lanner and Treleigh *Truro* 99–01; Consultant on Other Faiths 00–01; TV Whitchurch *Llan* 02–06; R Vancouver St Jas Canada 06–15; TR Eglwysilan and Caerphilly *Llan* from 15. *The Rectory, Rectory Close, Caerphilly CF83 1EQ* T: (029) 2085 1991 E: rector.rbec@gmail.com

GREENE, Colin John David. b 50. QUB BA 73 Fitzw Coll Cam MA 75 Nottm Univ PhD. St Jo Coll Nottm 78. **d** 80 **p** 81. NSM Sandiacre *Derby* 80–81; C Loughborough Em *Leic* 81–84; V Thorpe Acre w Dishley 84–89; Evang Tr Consultant Bible Soc 89–91; Tutor Trin Coll Bris 91–95; Th Consultant Bible Soc and Springdale Coll 95–96; Hd Th and Public Policy Bible Soc 96–03; Dean Th and Prof Seattle Pacific Univ USA 03–05; Prof Seattle Sch of Th and Psychology 05–08; Research Prof New York Th Sem from 11; Progr Ldr Sarum Coll 11–19; P-in-c Marnhull *Sarum* 11–13; R 13–15. *4 Old Manor Farm, Hinton Martell, Wimborne BH21 7HR* E: colin.greene@gmail.com

GREENE, Rachel Elizabeth. b 78. Virginia Univ BA 01 Peterho Cam MPhil 04 Cam Univ PhD 19. Westcott Ho Cam 05 Yale Div Sch 06. **d** 08 **p** 09. C Sturminster Newton, Hinton St Mary and Lydlinch *Sarum* 08–11; C Ox St Mary V w St Cross and St Pet 11–13; Chapl Trin Coll Cam 14–15; R Chiddingfold *Guildf* from 19. *The Rectory, Coxcombe Lane, Chiddingfold, Godalming GU8 4QA* T: (01428) 682008 E: rector.chiddingfold@gmail.com

GREENE, Richard Francis. b 47. TCD BAI 70 BA 70 MA 86 AMIMechE. CITC 03. **d** 06 **p** 07. NSM Waterford w Killea, Drumcannon and Dunhill *C, F & O* 06–10; NSM New w Old Ross, Whitechurch, Fethard etc 10–11; P-in-c 11–15. *Shallon, 2 Pleasant Avenue, Mount Pleasant, Waterford, Republic of Ireland* T: (00353) (51) 878477 M: 87-825 0418 E: rev.greene@gmail.com

GREENE, Valerie. b 45. Sheff Univ MA 04. Linc Th Coll 09. **d** 11 **p** 12. OLM Kirkby Laythorpe *Linc* from 11. *68 Church Lane, Kirkby-la-Thorpe, Sleaford NG34 9NU* T: (01529) 413148

GREENER, The Very Revd Jonathan Desmond Francis. b 61. Trin Coll Cam BA 83 MA 87. Coll of Resurr Mirfield 89. **d** 91 **p** 92. C S'wark H Trin w St Matt 91–94; Bp's Dom Chapl *Truro* 94–96; V Brighton Gd Shep Preston *Chich* 96–03; Adn Pontefract *Wakef* 03–07; Dean Wakef 07–17; Dean Ex from 17. *The Deanery, 10 Cathedral Close, Exeter EX1 1EZ* T: (01392) 255573 or 256730 E: jonathan.greener@exeter-cathedral.org.uk

GREENFIELD, Brian James. b 62. Liv Poly BSc 86 Leeds Univ PGCE 02. St Hild Coll 15. **d** 18 **p** 19. C Sutton w Cowling and Lothersdale *Leeds* from 18. *21 Walker Close, Glusburn, Keighley BD20 8PW* T: (01535) 637123 E: revd.brian.greenfield@gmail.com

GREENFIELD, Daniel James. b 82. Sheff Univ BA 03. St Mellitus Coll BA 18. **d** 18 **p** 19. C Crofton *Portsm*

from 18. *7 Darren Close, Fareham PO14 2LU* T: (01329) 661154 E: dan@croftonparish.org.uk

GREENFIELD, Diana Marion. b 71. NTMTC. d 10 p 11. C Glastonbury w Meare *B & W* from 10; C Street w Walton and Compton Dundon from 13; Adv on New Relig Movements etc from 15. *25 Brookfield Way, Street BA16 0UE* T: (01458) 446838 E: dmgreenfield@me.com

GREENFIELD, Mrs Judith Clare. b 81. Sheff Univ BA 02. St Mellitus Coll BA 17. d 18 p 19. C Crofton *Portsm* 18–20; TV Bridgemary, Elson and Rowner from 20. *7 Darren Close, Fareham PO14 2LU* T: (01329) 661154 E: jude@croftonparish.org.uk

GREENFIELD, Canon Martin Richard. b 54. Em Coll Cam MA 75. Wycliffe Hall Ox MA 78. d 79 p 80. C Enfield Ch Ch Trent Park *Lon* 79–83; CMS 84–94; Nigeria 85–94; Hon Can Aba from 89; C Langdon Hills *Chelmsf* 94–95; R Brampton *Ely* 95–13; RD Huntingdon 99–04; P-in-c Sanderstead *S'wark* from 13; PtO *Eur* from 17. *53 Glebe Hyrst, South Croydon CR2 9JJ* T: (020) 8657 1366 E: rector@sanderstead-parish.org.uk

GREENHALGH, Harry. b 54. d 11 p 13. NSM Winwick *Liv* 11–15; NSM Leigh St Mary *Man* 16–20; rtd 20. *Address withheld by request*

GREENHALGH, Canon Ian Frank. b 49. Wycliffe Hall Ox 74. d 77 p 78. C Parr *Liv* 77–80; V Wigan St Barn Marsh Green 80–84; Chapl RAF 84–04; V Clapham-with-Keasden and Austwick *Bradf* 04–14; Leeds 14–17; RD Ewecross *Bradf* 05–14; RD Bowland 14; AD Leeds 14–16; AD Ewecross 14–16; AD Bowland and Ewecross 17; Hon Can Bradf Cathl 11–17; rtd 17; PtO *Eur* from 16; AD Bowland and Ewecross Leeds from 21. *1 Riversdale, Giggleswick, Settle BD24 0AW* E: iangreenhalgh49@gmail.com

GREENHALGH, Jane. b 64. d 11 p 12. OLM New Bury w Gt Lever *Man* 11–14; TV 14–18; V Freckleton and Warton St Paul *Blackb* from 18. *The Vicarage, Church Road, Warton, Preston PR4 1BD* T: (01772) 631885 M: 07843-266881 E: jane.greenhalgh@hotmail.com *or* jane.greenhalgh@freckletonparishchurch.org.uk

GREENHALGH, Philip Adrian. b 52. Dur Univ MA 05. Ian Ramsey Coll Brasted 75 Wycliffe Hall Ox 76. d 79 p 80. C Gt Clacton *Chelmsf* 79–82; P-in-c Stalmine *Blackb* 82–86; Rep Leprosy Miss E Anglia 86–87; Area Org CECS 88–90; NSM Alston Team *Newc* 90–92; NSM Chulmleigh *Ex* 92–93; NSM Chawleigh w Cheldon 92–93; NSM Wembworthy w Eggesford 92–93; P-in-c Gilsland w Nether Denton *Carl* 93–95; V Millom 95–00; P-in-c Heatherycleugh *Dur* 00–04; P-in-c St John in Weardale 00–04; P-in-c Stanhope w Frosterley 02–04; P-in-c Eastgate w Rookhope 02–04; R Upper Weardale 04–07; AD Stanhope 00–07; R Bewcastle, Stapleton and Kirklinton etc *Carl* 07–12; RD Brampton 12–15; P-in-c Veryan w Ruan Lanihorne *Truro* 17–19; rtd 19. *Doctor Hill, Mickleton, Barnard Castle DL12 0JY* T: (01833) 640773

GREENHALGH, Mrs Rosalyn. b 61. S Bank Poly BSc 83. WEMTC 09. d 12 p 13. C Cheltenham St Mark *Glouc* 12–16; V Quinton, Welford, Weston and Marston Sicca from 16. *The Rectory, Church Lane, Welford on Avon, Stratford-upon-Avon CV37 8EL* M: 07581-235524 E: revdrosgreenhalgh@gmail.com

GREENHAM (née MORTIMER), Mrs Helen Teän. b 69. Leeds Univ BA 91 Univ of Wales (Swansea) PGCE 92. Ripon Coll Cuddesdon 06. d 08 p 09. C Bridgnorth, Tasley, Astley Abbotts, etc *Heref* 08–11; TV Solihull *Birm* from 11. *St Helen's House, 6 St Helen's Road, Solihull B91 2DA* T: 0121-704 2878 M: 07909-225546 E: helen.greenham@gmail.com

GREENHILL, Anthony David. b 39. Bris Univ BSc 59. Tyndale Hall Bris 61. d 63 p 64. C Southsea St Jude *Portsm* 63–65; India 65–78; C Kinson *Sarum* 78–81; V Girlington *Bradf* 81–97; C Platt Bridge *Liv* 97–00; rtd 00; PtO *Bradf* 01–05; *Man* 05–17. *65 Lymbridge Drive, Blackrod, Bolton BL6 5TH* T: (01204) 696509 E: green-hill@ntlworld.com

GREENHOUGH, Alan Kenneth. b 40. St D Coll Lamp. d 66 p 67. C Allestree *Derby* 66–70; C Ilkeston St Mary 70–73; V Bradwell 73–85; R Twyford w Guist w Bintry w Themelthorpe etc *Nor* 85–95; P-in-c Stibbard 94–95; R Twyford, Guist, Bintree, Themelthorpe etc 95–05; rtd 05; PtO *Linc* 17–20. *10 Newton Close, Metheringham, Lincoln LN4 3EQ* T: (01526) 328642

GREENHOUGH, Andrew Quentin. b 68. E Lon Poly BSc 89. Wycliffe Hall Ox BTh 94. d 94 p 95. C Partington and Carrington *Ches* 94–98; C Davenham 98–05; P-in-c Moulton 01–05; V New Ferry from 05. *St Mark's Vicarage, New Chester Road, Wirral CH62 1DG* T: 0151-645 2638 E: andy@macvicar.org.uk

GREENHOUGH, Arthur George. b 30. Fitzw Ho Cam BA 52 MA 56. Tyndale Hall Bris 55. d 57 p 58. C Wakef St Andr 57–63; R Birkin w Haddlesey *York* 63–85; RD Selby 77–84;

P-in-c Hambleton 84–85; R Haddlesey w Hambleton and Birkin 85–00; rtd 00; PtO *York* from 01. *4 Sandway Drive, Camblesforth, Selby YO8 8JX* T: (01757) 617347 E: rev.greenhough@btinternet.com

GREENHOUGH, Geoffrey Herman. b 36. Sheff Univ BA 57 Lon Univ BD 71. St Jo Coll Nottm 74. d 75 p 76. C Cheadle Hulme St Andr *Ches* 75–78; R Tilston and Shocklach 78–82; V Hyde St Geo 82–87; V Pott Shrigley 87–00; rtd 00; PtO *Ches* from 01. *9 Spey Close, Winsford CW7 3BP* T: (01606) 556275 E: ghgreenhough@uwclub.net

GREENIDGE-SILCOTT (formerly LARKIN), Mrs Karen Maria. b 74. Qu Coll Birm BA 08. d 08 p 09. C Coleshill and Maxstoke *Birm* 08–12; Chapl Lon City YMCA 12–16; NSM Southall Em 16–18; P-in-c N Greenford All Hallows from 18. *72 Horsenden Lane North, Greenford UB6 0PD* M: 07956-923653 E: karengsilcott@gmail.com

GREENLAND, Hazel. b 64. ERMC 14. d 17 p 18. C Colchester St Mich Myland *Chelmsf* from 17; C Colchester St Luke from 21; C Langham w Boxted from 21; C W Bergholt and Gt Horkesley from 21; C Wormingford, Mt Bures and Lt Horkesley from 21. *Myland Parish Hall, Mile End Road, Colchester CO4 5DY* T: (01206) 855040 E: hazel@mylandchurch.org.uk

GREENLAND, Martin. b 65. Warwick Univ BSc 87. Westcott Ho Cam 94. d 97 p 98. C Scarborough St Martin *York* 97–00; TV Bramley and Ravenfield w Hooton Roberts etc *Sheff* 00–04; V Ravenfield, Hooton Roberts and Braithwell 04–08; R Acle w Fishley, N Burlingham, Beighton w Moulton *Nor* 08–15; R Acle and Bure to Yare from 15; Jt RD Blofield from 17. *The Rectory, Norwich Road, Acle, Norwich NR13 3BU* T: (01493) 750393 E: rector@aclechurch.plus.com

GREENLAND, Paul Howard. b 59. Bath Univ BA 80 ACA 85. Trin Coll Bris 98. d 00 p 01. C Caverswall and Weston Coyney w Dilhorne *Lich* 00–03; P-in-c Chelmsf St Andr 03–05; V 05–20. *Address temp unknown* M: 07811-539328 E: paulhgreenland@care4free.net

GREENLAND, Robert James William. d 17 p 18. NSM Usk Min Area *Mon* from 17. *Model Farm, Wolvesnewton, Devauden, Chepstow NP16 6NZ* T: (01291) 650231 E: bob@deanery.info

GREENLAND, Roy Wilfrid. b 37. St Steph Ho Ox 71. d 73 p 74. C Wanstead St Mary *Chelmsf* 73–76; V Harlow St Mary Magd 76–83; P-in-c Huntingdon All SS w St Jo *Ely* 83–84; P-in-c Huntingdon St Barn 83–84; P-in-c Huntingdon St Mary w St Benedict 83–84; Bermuda 84–89; V Northampton St Alb *Pet* 89–92; R Waldron *Chich* 92–02; PtO *Pet* 05–07; Cov from 08. *7 Margetts Close, Kenilworth CV8 1EN* T: (01926) 852560

GREENMAN, David John. b 35. Lon Univ BA 59. Oak Hill Th Coll 57. d 61 p 62. C Wandsworth St Steph *S'wark* 61–63; C Bishopwearmouth St Gabr *Dur* 63–66; C-in-c Bedgrove CD *Ox* 66–74; P-in-c Macclesfield Ch Ch *Ches* 74–77; V 77–81; P-in-c Glouc All SS 81–85; V Glouc St Jas 81–85; V Bare *Blackb* 85–91; V Market Lavington and Easterton *Sarum* 91–99; rtd 99; PtO *Sarum* 00–13; Win from 00. *3 Bure Lane, Christchurch BH23 4DJ* T: (01425) 241034 E: davidjeangreenman@hotmail.co.uk

GREENMAN (née CHESTER), Mrs Irene Mary. b 51. Dioc OLM tr scheme 97. d 99 p 00. OLM Cornholme *Wakef* 99–00; OLM Cornholme and Walsden 00–11. *8 Glen View Street, Cornholme, Todmorden OL14 8LT* T/F: (01706) 817296 E: revgreenman@aol.com

GREENSLADE, Canon Gillian Carol. b 43. Leic Univ BA 64 Essex Univ MA 78 Nottm Univ PGCE 65. EAMTC 93. d 96 p 97. NSM Dovercourt and Parkeston w Harwich *Chelmsf* 96–00; NSM Colchester, New Town and The Hythe 00–02; R Broxted w Chickney and Tilty etc 02–08; Hon Can Chelmsf Cathl 07–08; rtd 08; Adv for Women's Min (Colchester Area) *Chelmsf* 05–08; PtO from 08. *15 The Grand, 6 The Esplanade, Frinton-on-Sea CO13 9DS* T: (01255) 676755 E: gcgreenslade@googlemail.com

GREENSLADE, Timothy Julian. b 63. St Jo Coll Ox BA 86. Oak Hill Th Coll BA 95. d 95 p 96. C Broadwater *Chich* 95–99; TV Radipole and Melcombe Regis *Sarum* 99–16; TR Melbury from 16. *The Vicarage, Tollerford Lane, Higher Frome Vauchurch, Dorchester DT2 0AT* T: (01300) 748675 E: the.greenslades@tiscali.co.uk

GREENSMITH, Mrs Sharon Suzanne. b 68. RGN 89. Qu Foundn Birm 12. d 14 p 15. NSM Clayton *Lich* 14–18; C Chesterton 18–21; V Briercliffe *Blackb* from 21. *St James's Vicarage, Church Street, Briercliffe, Burnley BB10 2HU* M: 07962-139947 E: sharon116@btinternet.com

GREENWAY, Gayle Kimberley. b 68. St Jo Coll Nottm 14. d 17 p 18. C Wolverhampton St Matt *Lich* 17–20; V Ogley Hay from 20. *37 New Road, Brownhills, Walsall WS8 6AT* M: 07545-657636 E: greenway.gayle@googlemail.com

GREENWAY, John. b 32. Bps' Coll Cheshunt 68 Qu Coll Birm 69. **d** 69 **p** 70. C Luton Ch Ch *St Alb* 69–74; C Pulloxhill w Flitton 75–76; P-in-c Marston Morteyne 76–79; P-in-c Lidlington 77–79; P-in-c Marston Morteyne w Lidlington 80–81; R 81–97; rtd 97; PtO *Portsm* 98–21. *73 Northmore Road, Locks Heath, Southampton SO31 6ZW* T: (01489) 886791

GREENWAY, John Michael. b 34. **d** 96 **p** 97. OLM Gt Yarmouth *Nor* 96–04; PtO from 04. *17 Hamilton Road, Great Yarmouth NR30 4ND* T: (01493) 853558 E: john.greenway3@ntlworld.com

GREENWELL, Christopher. b 49. Linc Th Coll 79. **d** 81 **p** 82. C Scarborough St Martin *York* 81–84; V S Bank 84–89; R Bolton by Bowland w Grindleton *Bradf* 89–92; V Nether Hoyland St Andr *Sheff* 92–96; V Kirkleatham *York* 96–07; rtd 07. *79 Hillshaw Park Way, Ripon HG4 1JU* T: (01765) 600467

GREENWELL, Canon Paul. b 60. Magd Coll Ox BA 81 MA 85. St Steph Ho Ox 82. **d** 85 **p** 86. C Hendon and Sunderland *Dur* 85–88; Min Can and Prec Ripon Cathl 88–93; Chapl Univ Coll of Ripon and York St Jo 88–93; V Hunslet St Mary *Ripon* 93–02; Chapl Harrogate and Distr NHS Foundn Trust 02–08; Chapl St Meh Hospice Harrogate 02–08; Convenor Dioc Adv Gp for Chr Healing *Ripon* 03–08; Can Res Ripon Cathl 08–17; Master Charterhouse Hull from 17; Chapl MU 09–14. *The Master's House, Charterhouse Lane, Hull HU2 8AF* T: (01482) 329307 E: master@thecharterhouse.karoo.co.uk

GREENWOOD, Caroline Elizabeth. b 63. Lanc Univ BSc 85 Open Univ BSc 96 Trent Poly PGCE 88. St Jo Coll Nottm MTh 14. **d** 14 **p** 15. C Hillock and Unsworth *Man* 14–16; C Prestwich St Marg 16–18; PtO from 18; V Warley and Halifax St Hilda *Leeds* from 18. *The Vicarage, 466 Burnley Road, Halifax HX2 7LW* T: (01422) 363623 M: 07771-858404 E: caroline.greenwood@leeds.anglican.org *or* rev.caroline14@gmail.com

GREENWOOD, Claire. *See* GREENWOOD, Helen Claire

GREENWOOD, David. *See* GREENWOOD, Norman David

GREENWOOD, Canon David Michael. b 57. and Bars CD 89. Univ of New Brunswick BBA 79 St Thos Aquinas Pontifical Univ Rome MA(Theol) 10 STL 14. Vancouver Sch of Th MDiv 95. **d** 95 **p** 96. C Nanaimo Canada 95–97; CF 97–08; PtO *Eur* 08–10; Course Resource Research Development Officer Forces Chapl Sch Canada 10–13; PtO *Eur* 13–15 and from 17; P-in-c Marseille w Aix-en-Provence and the Luberon 15–17; PtO Nova Scotia & Prince Edw Is Canada from 17; PtO Cen Florida USA from 17. *Suite 1201, 31 King's Wharf Place, Dartmouth NS B2Y 0C1, Canada* E: dmgcag1@msn.com

GREENWOOD, Elizabeth. *See* GREENWOOD, Margaret Elizabeth

GREENWOOD, Canon Gerald. b 33. Leeds Univ BA 57 Sheff Poly MSc 81 Surrey Univ Hon MA 93. Linc Th Coll 57. **d** 59 **p** 60. C Rotherham *Sheff* 59–62; V Elsecar 62–70; V Wales 70–77; P-in-c Thorpe Salvin 74–77; Dioc Sch Officer 77–84; P-in-c Bramley and Ravenfield 77–78; P-in-c Hooton Roberts 77–78; R 78–84; Hon Can Sheff Cathl 80–84; Dioc Dir of Educn 81–84; Hon Can S'wark Cathl 84–97; Dir of Educn 84–97; rtd 97; PtO *Cant* from 97. *Home Farm Cottage, Westmarsh, Canterbury CT3 2LW* T: (01304) 812160

GREENWOOD, Helen Claire. b 54. Cranmer Hall Dur 05. **d** 06 **p** 07. C Willington *Newc* 06–10; V Marden w Preston Grange 10–13; V Billy Mill 10–13; rtd 13; Hon C Barnoldswick w Bracewell *Bradf* 14; *Leeds* 14–18; PtO *Glouc* from 20. *27 Youngs Orchard, Abbeymead, Gloucester GL4 4RR* E: hcgreenwood@yahoo.com

GREENWOOD, Ian Richard. b 74. Liv Hope BEd 96. St Jo Coll Nottm MTh 09. **d** 09 **p** 10. C Burscough Bridge *Liv* 09–13; P-in-c Aigburth 13–14; V from 14. *St Anne's Vicarage, 389 Aigburth Road, Liverpool L17 6BH* T: 0151-727 1101 M: 07840-829956 E: reviangreenwood@gmail.com

GREENWOOD, James Peter. b 61. Univ Coll Lon BSc 83 St Jo Coll Dur BA 90 RIBA 87. Cranmer Hall Dur 88. **d** 91 **p** 92. C Belper *Derby* 91–94; CMS Pakistan 95–01; V Islamabad St Thos 00; V Silsden *Bradf* 01–09; Dioc Spirituality Adv 05–09; RD S Craven 07–09; P-in-c Gillingham and Milton-on-Stour *Sarum* 09–16; V 16–19; R Gillingham, Milton-on-Stour and Silton from 19. *The Rectory, High Street, Gillingham SP8 4AJ* T: (01747) 822435 *or* 821598

GREENWOOD, John Newton. b 44. St Chad's Coll Dur 69. **d** 70 **p** 71. C Hartlepool H Trin *Dur* 70–72; LtO 72–99; Hd Master Archibald Primary Sch Cleveland 84–97; Asst Chapl HM Pris Holme Ho 99–11; PtO *Dur* from 13. *1 Brae Head, Eaglescliffe, Stockton-on-Tees TS16 9HP* T: (01642) 783200

GREENWOOD, Leslie. b 37. Dur Univ BA 59. Cranmer Hall Dur. **d** 61 **p** 62. C Birstall *Wakef* 61–63; C Illingworth

64–70; Chapl H Trin Sch Halifax 64–89; V Charlestown *Wakef* 70–91; TV Upper Holme Valley 91–97; PtO 97–14; *Leeds* from 14; rtd 00. *2 Trenance Gardens, Greetland, Halifax HX4 8NN* T/F: (01422) 373926 E: kyandles@aol.com

GREENWOOD, Mrs Margaret Elizabeth. b 34. St Mary's Coll Chelt TCert 65 Surrey Univ MA 93. St Mich Ho Ox 60. **d** 00. NSM Shepperton *Lon* 00–01; NSM Whitton SS Phil and Jas 01–04; PtO from 04. *Bundoran Cottage, Vicarage Lane, Staines TW18 1UE* T: (01784) 458115 E: elizabethgreenwood@btinternet.com

GREENWOOD, Canon Michael Eric. b 44. Oak Hill Th Coll 78. **d** 80 **p** 81. C Clubmoor *Liv* 80–83; V Pemberton St Mark Newtown 83–94; V Grassendale 94–00; V Ashton-in-Makerfield St Thos 00–09; Hon Can Liv Cathl 08–09; rtd 09. *1 Fardon Close, Wigan WN3 6SN* T: (01942) 825670 E: mikeg09@btinternet.com

GREENWOOD, Norman David. b 52. Edin Univ BMus 74 Lon Univ BD 78 Nottm Univ MPhil 90. Oak Hill Th Coll 76. **d** 78 **p** 79. C Gorleston St Andr *Nor* 78–81; SAMS 81–83; C Cromer *Nor* 83–84; R Appleby Magna and Swepstone w Snarestone *Leic* 84–94; P-in-c Chesterfield H Trin *Derby* 94–95; P-in-c Chesterfield Ch Ch 94–95; R Chesterfield H Trin and Ch Ch 95–99; V S Ramsey St Paul *S & M* 99–12; Dir Voc and Tr 01–12; RD Ramsey 08–11; Chapl HM Pris Is of Man 05–12; Hon Can St German's Cathl *S & M* 09–12; Chapl St Pet Viña del Mar Chile 12–15; Chapl Rio de Janeiro Ch Ch Brazil 15–16; PtO *S & M* from 16; *Eur* 17–20. *24 St Paul's Mews, Ramsey, Isle of Man IM8 1EE* M: 07624-234414 E: davidgreenwood@manx.net

GREENWOOD, Peter. *See* GREENWOOD, James Peter

GREENWOOD, Canon Robin Patrick. b 47. St Chad's Coll Dur BA 68 MA 71 Birm Univ PhD 92. **d** 70 **p** 71. C Adel *Ripon* 70–73; Min Can and Succ Ripon Cathl 73–78; V Leeds Halton St Wilfrid 78–86; Dioc Can Res Glouc Cathl 86–95; Dioc Missr and Dir Lay and Post-Ord Tr 86–95; Dir of Min and Hon Can Chelmsf Cathl 95–00; Prov Officer for Min Ch in Wales 01–05; Hon C Canton St Jo *Llan* 02–05; V Monkseaton St Mary *Newc* 05–13; Visiting Fell St Jo Coll Dur from 12; rtd 13; PtO *Leeds* from 17; *Glouc* from 20. *27 Youngs Orchard, Abbeymead, Gloucester GL4 4RR* E: robingreenwood1@gmail.com

GREENWOOD, Sharon. b 44. **d** 07 **p** 08. NSM Welling *S'wark* 07–18; rtd 18; PtO *Cant* from 19. *Address temp unknown* E: sharon.greenwood44@tiscali.co.uk

GREENWOOD, Stella Jane. b 68. Teesside Poly BSc 90. All SS Cen for Miss & Min 15. **d** 17 **p** 18. NSM Swadlincote *Derby* 17–18; C 18–19; NSM Hartshorne and Bretby 17–18; C 18–19; C Swadlincote and Hartshorne 20–21; P-in-c Etwall w Egginton from 21; C Boylestone, Church Broughton, Dalbury, etc from 21. *Etwall Rectory, Rectory Court, Main Street, Etwall, Derby DE65 6LP* M: 07802-963817 E: greenwoodstella@yahoo.com

GREEVES, Roger Derrick. b 43. TCD BA 66 MA 70 Fitzw Coll Cam BA 68 MA 73. Westcott Ho Cam 98. **d** 98 **p** 99. In Methodist Ch 68–98; NSM Cam St Edw *Ely* 98–00; Chapl Oakington Immigration Reception Cen 00–01; Chapl Peterho Cam 00–01; Dean Clare Coll Cam 01–08; rtd 08; PtO *Ely* from 08; *Eur* from 15. *The Cart Lodge, 5 Home Farm, 89 High Street, Harston, Cambridge CB22 7PZ* T: (01223) 977988 M: 07817-032301 E: rdg20@cam.ac.uk

GREGG, David William Austin. b 37. Lon Univ BD 66 Bris Univ MA 69. Tyndale Hall Bris 63. **d** 68 **p** 69. C Barrow St Mark *Carl* 68–71; P-in-c Lindal w Marton 71–75; Communications Sec Gen Syn Bd for Miss and Unity 76–81; Prin Romsey Ho Coll Cam 81–83; V Haddenham w Cuddington, Kingsey etc *Ox* 88–96; P-in-c Newton Longville w Stoke Hammond and Whaddon 96–02; rtd 03; PtO *Carl* 03–19. *Lowick Farm House, Lowick Green, Ulverston LA12 8DX* T: (01229) 885258

GREGORY, Alan Paul Roy. b 55. K Coll Lon BD 77 MTh 78 Emory Univ Atlanta PhD 94 AKC 77. Ripon Coll Cuddesdon 78. **d** 79 **p** 80. C Walton-on-Thames *Guildf* 79–82; Lect Sarum & Wells Th Coll 82–88; Dir Studies 85–88; Assoc R Atlanta St Patr USA 88–94; R Athens Em 94–95; Assoc Prof Ch Hist Episc Th Sem of the SW 95–04; Academic Dean and Prof Ch Hist 04–12; P-in-c Stannington *Newc* 12–14; Dioc CMD Officer 12–14; Prin St Aug Coll of Th from 14; PtO *S'wark* 14–15; Public Preacher from 15. *St Augustine's College of Theology, 52 Swan Street, West Malling ME19 6JX* T: (01732) 252656 M: 07969-335562 E: principal@seite.co.uk *or* alan@scrivenersgloom.com

GREGORY, Andrew Forsythe. b 71. St Jo Coll Dur BA 92 Linc Coll Ox DPhil 01. Wycliffe Hall Ox BA 96 MA 00. **d** 97 **p** 98. C E Acton St Dunstan w St Thos *Lon* 97–99; Asst Chapl Keble Coll Ox 97–99; Chapl and Jun Research Fell Linc Coll Ox 99–03; Research Fell Keble Coll Ox 03–05; Chapl and Fell Univ Coll Ox from 05; LtO *Ox* from 08. *University College, High Street, Oxford OX1 4BH* T: (01865) 276663 E: andrew.gregory@theology.ox.ac.uk

GREGORY, **Anthony Lawrence.** b 43. Lon Univ BD 71. Tyndale Hall Bris 67. d 71 p 72. C Branksome St Clem *Sarum* 71–74; SAMS from 74; rtd 08. *Molina Campos 507, V Vega San Martin, San Martin de los Andes, Q8370 Neuquen, Argentina* T: (0054) (2972) 425191 E: anthmollie@gmail.com

GREGORY, **Brian.** b 43. BEM 14. Trin Coll Bris. d 82 p 83. C Burscough Bridge *Liv* 82–85; V Platt Bridge 85–92; V Ben Rhydding *Bradf* 92–06; rtd 06; PtO *Bradf* 07–14; *Leeds* 14–16; *Blackb* from 15. *6 Hawthorn Close, Hesketh Bank, Preston PR4 6EP* T: (01772) 812234 E: gregory.brian@btinternet.com

⚥GREGORY, **The Rt Revd Clive Malcolm.** b 61. Lanc Univ BA 84 Qu Coll Cam BA 87 MA 89 Warwick Univ Hon MA 99. Westcott Ho Cam 85. d 88 p 89 c 07. C Margate St Jo *Cant* 88–92; Chapl Warw Univ *Cov* 92–98; TR Cov E 98–07; Area Bp Wolverhampton *Lich* from 07. *61 Richmond Road, Wolverhampton WV3 9JH* T: (01902) 824503 F: 824504 E: bishop.wolverhampton@lichfield.anglican.org

GREGORY, **Ms Elizabeth Louise Annunciata.** b 83. UWE LLB 05 Univ of Wales (Swansea) MA 07 Lucy Cavendish Coll Cam BA 11. Westcott Ho Cam 09. d 12 p 13. C Sole Bay *St E* 12–15; R Filton *Bris* from 15. *The Rectory, Rectory Lane, Filton, Bristol BS34 7BE* T: 0117-979 1128 M: 07528-518968 E: elizabeth.gregory@talk21.com

GREGORY, **Hannah Joy.** b 80. Qu Foundn Birm 18. d 20. C Shipston-on-Stour w Honington and Idlicote *Cov* from 20. *3 Bosley Close, Shipston-on-Stour CV36 4QA* M: 07706-628722 E: curate@shipstonchurch.org

GREGORY, **Miss Mary Emma.** b 70. Durham Univ BA 92 St Jo Coll Dur BA 04 MA 06. Cranmer Hall Dur 02. d 05 p 06. C Hatfield *Sheff* 05–08; R Kirk Sandall and Edenthorpe 08–15; Dean of Women's Min 13–15; Hon Can Sheff Cathl 14–15; TR Ashby-de-la-Zouch and Breedon on the Hill *Leic* from 15; Dioc Miss Enabler from 20. *The Rectory, 4 Upper Packington Road, Ashby-de-la-Zouch LE65 1EF* T: (01530) 534672 M: 07734-052524 E: revmarygregory@aol.co.uk

GREGORY, **Peter.** b 35. Cranmer Hall Dur 59. d 62 p 63. C Pennington *Man* 62–65; C N Ferriby *York* 65–68; V Tonge Fold *Man* 68–72; V Hollym w Welwick and Holmpton *York* 72–77; P-in-c Foston w Flaxton 77–80; P-in-c Crambe w Whitwell and Huttons Ambo 77–80; R Whitwell w Crambe, Flaxton, Foston etc 81–94; rtd 94; PtO *York* 13–20. *6 High Terrace, Northallerton DL6 1BG* T: (01609) 776956

GREGORY, **Richard Branson.** b 33. Fitzw Ho Cam BA 58 MA 62. Sarum Th Coll 58 Ridley Hall Cam 59. d 60 p 61. C Sheff St Cuth 60–62; Asst Chapl Leeds Univ *Ripon* 62–64; V Yeadon St Jo *Bradf* 64–71; R Keighley 71–74; TR Keighley St Andr 74–82; Hon Can Bradf Cathl 71–82; RD S Craven 71–73 and 78–82; P-in-c Broadmayne, W Knighton, Owermoigne etc *Sarum* 82–85; R 85–98; rtd 98; PtO *Sarum* 98–18. *2 Huish Cottages, Sydling, Dorchester DT2 9NS* T: (01300) 341835

GREGORY, **Canon Stephen Simpson.** b 40. Nottm Univ BA 62 CertEd 63. St Steph Ho Ox. d 68 p 69. C Aldershot St Mich *Guildf* 68–71; Chapl St Mary's Sch Wantage 71–74; R Edgefield *Nor* 74–88; R Holt 74–94; R Holt w High Kelling 94–95; RD Holt 79–84 and 93–95; Hon Can Nor Cathl 94–95; V Prestbury *Glouc* 95–03; P-in-c Pittville All SS 99–03; TR Prestbury and All SS 03–06; RD Cheltenham 00–05; Hon Can Glouc Cathl 04–06; rtd 06; PtO *Nor* from 08; *Glouc* from 14. *Mulberry Cottage, Balfour Road, West Runton, Cromer NR27 9QJ* T: (01263) 838049

GREGORY-WITHAM, **Ms Katherine Fiona Marie.** b 90. Ches Univ BA 12. Cranmer Hall Dur BA 18. d 19 p 20. C Burnley St Matt w H Trin *Blackb* from 19. *229 Coal Clough Lane, Burnley BB11 4DL* E: kfmwitham@gmail.com

GREGSON (*née* ROBERTSON), **Fiona Jane Robertson.** b 76. Birm Univ BA 98 Lon Sch of Th PhD 14. Wycliffe Hall Ox BA 05 MA 10. d 06 p 07. C Aston SS Pet and Paul *Birm* 06–08; C Aston St Jas 06–08; C Nechells 06–08; C Aston and Nechells 08–10; P-in-c Girlington *Bradf* 10–13; V 13; C Manningham 10–12; PtO *Birm* 14–18; C Harborne Heath from 18. *18 Willow Avenue, Birmingham B17 8HD* M: 07958-494560 E: fionajanerobertson@yahoo.co.uk or fionagregson@stjohnsharborne.org

GREGSON, **Gillian Amy.** b 33. Westmr Coll Ox BTh 02 CQSW 78. d 98 p 99. OLM Coulsdon St Jo *S'wark* 98–05; PtO 05–18. *21 Canons Hill, Coulsdon CR5 1HB* T: (01737) 479689 E: gillgregson21@gmail.com

GREGSON, **Peter John.** b 36. Univ Coll Dur BSc 61. Ripon Hall Ox 61. d 63 p 64. C Radcliffe St Thos *Man* 63–65; C Baguley 65–67; Chapl RN 68–91; V Ashburton w Buckland in the Moor and Bickington *Ex* 91–01; RD Moreton 95–98;

rtd 01; PtO *Sarum* 01–11; *Blackb* 11–19. *26 Astley Road, Chorley PR7 1RR* T: (01257) 247999

GREIFF, **Andrew John.** b 64. Huddersfield Univ BA 98 Leeds Univ PGCE 99 St Jo Coll Dur BA 05. Cranmer Hall Dur 03. d 05 p 06. C Pudsey St Lawr and St Paul *Bradf* 05–08; P-in-c Thornton St Jas 08–12; P-in-c Fairweather Green 08–12; TV Shelf w Buttershaw St Aid 12–14; *Leeds* from 14. *80 Carr House Road, Halifax HX3 7RJ* T: (01274) 671576 or 676335 E: andrew.greiff667@gmail.com

GREIG, **George Malcolm.** b 28. CA 53 St Andr Univ BD 95. LNSM course 75. d 81 p 82. NSM Dundee St Mary Magd *Bre* 81–84; NSM Dundee St Jo 82–84; P-in-c Dundee St Ninian 84–85; Chapl St Paul's Cathl Dundee 85–98; rtd 98; Hon C Dundee St Salvador *Bre* 98–16; PtO from 16. *61 Charleston Drive, Dundee DD2 2HE* T: (01382) 566709 E: gmg28@btinternet.com

GREIG, **Martin David Sandford.** b 45. Bris Univ BSc 67. St Jo Coll Nottm 72. d 75 p 76. C Keresley and Coundon *Cov* 75–79; C Rugby 79–83; TV 83–86; V Cov St Geo 86–93; TV Southgate *Chich* 93–01; R Maresfield 01–06; P-in-c Nutley 01–06; rtd 06. *105 Sunnymead, Copplestone, Crediton EX17 5NB* T: (01363) 84679 E: mg@bodawen.org.uk

GREIG, **Michael Lawrie Dickson.** b 48. All Nations Chr Coll 78 St Jo Coll Nottm 94. d 96 p 97. C Hunningham *Cov* 96–00; C Wappenbury w Weston under Wetherley 96–00; C Offchurch 96–00; C Long Itchington and Marton 96–00; P-in-c Napton-on-the-Hill, Lower Shuckburgh etc 00–13; P-in-c Priors Hardwick, Priors Marston and Wormleighton 09–13; rtd 13; PtO *Cov* 13–18; *Ox* from 14. *Owl Cottage, 21 Lenborough Road, Buckingham MK18 1DH* T: (01280) 309025 E: michael.greig@hotmail.co.uk

GREIG, **Phil.** b 76. Ox Brookes Univ BA 02. Ridley Hall Cam 09. d 11 p 12. C Chartham *Cant* 11–14; C Cant All SS 14–19; P-in-c from 19; Asst Dir of Ords from 19. *Glebe House, Military Road, Canterbury CT1 1PA* T: (01227) 450669 M: 07411-936354 E: revphilgreig@me.com

GRENFELL, **James Christopher.** b 69. Qu Coll Ox BA 91 MA 96 MPhil 95 Ox Univ DPhil 00. Westcott Ho Cam 98. d 00 p 01. C Kirkby *Liv* 00–03; P-in-c Sheff Manor 03–06; TR 06–09; P-in-c Ranmoor 09–13; AD Hallam 12–13; PtO *Portsm* 13–16; Dir Portsm Pathway Ripon Coll Cuddesdon 16–20; Hon Can Portsm Cathl 19–20; Chapl Barts Health NHS Trust from 20. *63 Coborn Road, London E3 2DB* M: 07759-974332 E: jamescgrenfell@gmail.com or portsmouthpathway@rcc.ac.uk

⚥GRENFELL, **The Rt Revd Joanne Woolway.** b 72. Oriel Coll Ox BA 93 DPhil 97 Univ of BC MA 94. Westcott Ho Cam 98. d 00 p 01 c 19. C Kirkby *Liv* 00–03; Jt P-in-c Sheff Manor 03–06; Can Res Sheff Cathl 06–13; Dioc Dir of Ords 06–13; Dean of Women's Min 08–13; Adn Portsdown *Portsm* 13–19; Area Bp Stepney *Lon* from 19. *63 Coborn Road, London E3 2DB* M: 07936-043945

GRENHAM-THOMPSON, **Mrs Sharon Carmel.** b 66. Reading Univ LLB 87 Solicitor 92. Trin Coll Bris 94 SAOMC 96. d 98 p 00. C Buckingham *Ox* 98–00; C Milton Keynes 00–02; Miss Adv USPG Lon, Ox and St Alb 02–03; NSM Wilshamstead and Houghton Conquest *St Alb* 03–04; Chapl Oakhill Secure Tr Cen 04–05; PtO *St Alb* from 04; Asst Chapl HM Pris Woodhill 08–11; Chapl HM Pris Bedf 11–16; TV Watling Valley *Ox* from 16. *Address withheld by request* M: 07891-892550

GRESHAM, **Karen Louise.** *See* SMEETON, Karen Louise

GRETTON-DANN, **Judith Adrienne.** b 75. St Andr Univ MSci 97 PhD 01 Dur Univ MA 20. St Mich Coll Llan 12. d 14 p 15. NSM Chesterton Gd Shep *Ely* 14–19; PtO *Ox* from 20. *60 Mortimer Drive, Marston, Oxford OX3 0RU* M: 07900-523959

GREW, **Nicholas David.** b 52. Surrey Univ BSc 74 MSc 75. Wycliffe Hall Ox 93. d 95 p 96. C Biddulph *Lich* 95–99; P-in-c Knaphill *Guildf* 99–00; V Knaphill w Brookwood 00–15; V Luton St Fran *St Alb* 15–20; rtd 20; PtO *Win* from 21. *139 Bournemouth Road, Chandler's Ford, Eastleigh SO53 3HA* M: 07527-269373 E: nick1806grew@gmail.com

GREW, **Timothy Richard.** b 65. SS Coll Cam MA 88. WEMTC 03. d 06 p 07. NSM Cheltenham H Trin and St Paul *Glouc* 06–10; TV from 10. *208 Prestbury Road, Cheltenham GL52 3ER* T: (01242) 321473 E: tim.grew@trinitycheltenham.com

GREY, **Mrs Nicola Jane Francis.** b 61. d 13 p 14. C Burton St Chad *Lich* 13–16; Chapl HM YOI Werrington 16–18; Chapl HM Pris Drake Hall 16–18; R Cheadle w Freehay *Lich* from 18. *The Rectory, Church Street, Cheadle, Stoke-on-Trent ST10 1HU* T: (01538) 753337 E: rector@cheadlefreehay.org.uk

GREY, **Canon Roger Derrick Masson.** b 38. AKC 61. d 62 p 63. C Darlington H Trin *Dur* 62–63; C Bishopwearmouth

St Mich 63–67; V Mabe *Truro* 67–70; Dioc Youth Chapl 67–70; Youth Chapl *Glouc* 70–77; V Stroud H Trin 77–82; Dioc Can Res Glouc Cathl 82–03; Dir of Educn 82–94; Bp's Chapl 94–03; rtd 03; Clergy Widows' Officer (Glouc Adnry) *Glouc* from 03; PtO from 04. *12 Buckingham Close, Walton Cardiff, Tewkesbury GL20 7QB* T: (01684) 275742

GREY, Canon Stephen Bernard. b 56. Linc Th Coll 86. d 88 p 89. C Worsley *Man* 88–93; V Bamford 93–04; P-in-c Rochdale St Geo w St Alb 99–04; P-in-c Preesall *Blackb* 04–05; P-in-c Hambleton w Out Rawcliffe 04–05; V Waterside Par 05–10; P-in-c Garstang St Thos 10–13; V 13–17; TV Newton *Liv* from 17; AD Winwick from 17; Hon Can Liv Cathl from 17. *8 The Parchments, Newton-le-Willows WA12 0DY* M: 07910-854911 E: revstephengrey@gmail.com

GRIBBEN, John Gibson. b 44. K Coll Lon BD 75 QUB MTh 81. CITC 73. d 75 p 76. C Dunmurry *Conn* 75–78; CR from 79; Lic to Offic *Wakef* 83–14; rtd 09; LtO *Leeds* from 14. *House of the Resurrection, Stocks Bank Road, Mirfield WF14 0BN* T: (01924) 483339 E: jgribben@mirfield.org.uk

GRIBBIN, Canon Bernard Byron. b 35. Bradf Univ MPhil 84. St Aid Birkenhead 58. d 60 p 61. C Maghull *Liv* 60–63; C Prescot 63–65; V Denholme Gate *Bradf* 65–71; V Bankfoot 71–79; Dioc Stewardship Adv 79–86; Prec and Chapl Choral Ches Cathl 86–91; V Ringway 91–96; Dioc Tourism Officer 91–96; Hon Can Ches Cathl 91–96; rtd 96; PtO *Bradf* 96–14; *Leeds* from 14. *5 Heather Court, Ilkley LS29 9TZ* T: (01943) 816253 E: b.b.gribbin@btinternet.com

GRIBBLE, Malcolm George. b 44. Chu Coll Cam BA 67 MA 71. Linc Th Coll 79. d 81 p 82. C Farnborough *Roch* 81–84; V Bostall Heath 84–90; V Bexleyheath Ch Ch 90–02; P-in-c Hever, Four Elms and Mark Beech 02–06; R 06–09; rtd 10. *26 Neville Road, Tewkesbury GL20 5ED* T: (01684) 290641 E: mgg@myphone.coop

GRICE, Canon David Richard. b 32. Keble Coll Ox BA 55 MA 59. St Steph Ho Ox 55. d 57 p 58. C Leeds St Aid *Ripon* 57–61; C Middleton St Mary 61–62; V Woodlesford 62–69; V Leeds St Wilfrid 69–78; TR Seacroft 78–93; Hon Can Ripon Cathl 92–99; P-in-c Thorner 93–95; V 95–99; rtd 99; PtO *Ripon* 00–14; *Leeds* from 14. *15 Mead Road, Leeds LS15 9JR* T: 0113-260 4371

GRIER, Preb James Emerson. b 74. St Pet Coll Ox BA 95 MA 01. Wycliffe Hall Ox 96. d 98 p 99. C Ox St Andr 98–02; C Harborne Heath *Birm* 02–07; TV Pinhoe and Broadclyst *Ex* 07–12; Dioc Youth Adv 07–19; Dioc Miss Enabler from 19; Ldr Unlimited Ch 12–21; Deanery Fresh Expressions Officer from 21; Preb Ex Cathl from 20. *St Thomas's Rectory, 57 Cowick Street, Exeter EX4 1HR* M: 07825-610288 E: james.grier@exeter.anglican.org

GRIERSON, Peter Stanley. b 42. Lon Univ BD 68 Leeds Univ MPhil 74. Linc Th Coll 68. d 69 p 70. C Clitheroe St Mary *Blackb* 69–71; C Aston cum Aughton *Sheff* 71–74; V Preston St Jude w St Paul *Blackb* 74–81; V Blackb St Luke w St Phil 89–97; RD Blackb 91–97; V Burnley St Matt w H Trin 97–02; PtO *Bradf* 03–13; *Blackb* 13–19. *21 Fosbrooke House, 8 Clifton Drive, Lytham St Annes FY8 5RQ* T: (01253) 667014 E: olwen62@sky.com

GRIEVE, David Campbell. b 51. St Jo Coll Dur BA 74. Wycliffe Hall Ox 74. d 76 p 77. C Upton (Overchurch) *Ches* 76–80; C Selston *S'well* 80–82; V Pelton *Dur* 82–89; rtd 89; PtO *Dur* from 04. *The Old Rectory, The Village, Castle Eden, Hartlepool TS27 4SL* T: (01388) 718447 E: davidgrieve0@icloud.com

GRIEVE (née PIERSSENÉ), Canon Frances Jane. b 55. St Jo Coll Dur BA 76. Cranmer Hall Dur 99. d 01 p 02. C Barnard Castle w Whorlton *Dur* 01–05; P-in-c Cockfield 05–14; R 14–15; P-in-c Lynesack 05–14; V 14–15; P-in-c Evenwood 09–14; V 14–15; P-in-c Wheatley Hill, Thornley and Wingate w Hutton Henry 15–21; V from 21; V Haswell and Shotton from 10; Hon Can Dur Cathl from 10. *The Old Vicarage, The Village, Castle Eden, Hartlepool TS27 4SL* T: (01429) 835479 E: jane.grieve@durham.anglican.org

GRIFFIN, Andrew Norman. b 64. St Hild Coll 15. d 18 p 19. C Wakefield St Andr and St Mary and Belle Vue *Leeds* 18–21; C Ossett and Gawthorpe from 21; C S Ossett from 21. *Address temp unknown* M: 07799-645090 E: andrew.griffin@leeds.anglican.org

GRIFFIN, Christopher Donald. b 59. Reading Univ BA 80 CertEd 81. Wycliffe Hall Ox 82. d 85 p 86. C Gerrards Cross *Ox* 85–88; Chapl Felsted Sch 88–98; Chapl Sedbergh Sch 98–06; Ho Master 00–17. *39 Dial Hill Road, Clevedon BS21 7EL* E: chrisdgriffin1@outlook.com

GRIFFIN, David Philip. b 90. Oak Hill Th Coll BA 20. d 20 p 21. C Hailsham *Chich* from 20. *9 Riggers Way, Hailsham BN27 1FL* M: 07770-576170 E: davidpgriffin@outlook.com

GRIFFIN, Eugene Thomas. MTh FCCA. d 13 p 14. C Castleknock and Mulhuddart w Clonsilla *D & G* 14–18; Abp's Dom Chapl 15–18; I Dunboyne and Rathmolyon *M & K* from 18. *The Rectory, 1 The Close, Plunkett Hall, Dunboyne, Co Meath, A86 E167, Republic of Ireland* T: (00353) (1) 825 3288 M: 86-382 6646 E: eugenethomasgriffin@gmail.com

GRIFFIN, Canon Joseph William. b 48. St Mich Coll Llan 70. d 74 p 75. C Killay *S & B* 74–78; C Swansea St Thos and Kilvey 78–81; V Troedrhiwgarth *Llan* 81–91; V Llanrhidian w Llanmadoc and Cheriton *S & B* 91–99; RD Gower 94–99; V Swansea St Nic 99–04; RD Swansea 02–04; P-in-c SW Gower 04–05; R 05–15; AD Gower 11–14; Hon Can Brecon Cathl 98–01; Can Res 01–11; Can Treas 11–15; rtd 15; PtO *S & B* from 15. *25 Maes-y-Coed, Gorseinon, Swansea SA4 6RN* T: (01792) 410321 E: joe.griffin3@hotmail.co.uk

GRIFFIN, Judith. Wycliffe Hall Ox. d 12 p 12. C Onslow Square and S Kensington St Aug *Lon* 12–15; Chapl R Brompton and Harefield NHS Foundn Trust 15–16. *Address withheld by request*

GRIFFIN, Keith. b 66. Nottm Trent Univ BA 88. Cranmer Hall Dur BA 94. d 95 p 96. C Gedling *S'well* 95–98; V Barkingside St Geo *Chelmsf* 99–02; TV Upper Holme Valley *Wakef* 02–14; *Leeds* from 14. *The Vicarage, 3 Vicarage Meadows, Holmfirth HD9 1DZ* T: (01484) 682644 E: revdkg@tiscali.co.uk

GRIFFIN, Mark Richard. b 68. Trin Coll Bris BA 93. Westcott Ho Cam 94. d 96 p 97. C Walmer *Cant* 96–00; V Wingham w Elmstone and Preston w Stourmouth 00–07; V Sevenoaks St Luke *Roch* 07–17; RD Sevenoaks 11–16; Hon Can Roch Cathl 15–17; R Cant St Martin and St Paul from 17; AD Cant from 20. *The Rectory, 13 Ersham Road, Canterbury CT1 3AR* T: (01227) 768072 E: revd.mark.griffin@talk21.com

GRIFFIN, Niall Paul. b 37. TCD BA 61 Div Test 61. d 61 p 62. C Newtownards *D & D* 61–63; C Arm St Mark w Aghavilly 63–64; C Cross Roads Jamaica 64–66; C Lurgan Ch the Redeemer *D & D* 66–69; Chapl RAF 69–84; Missr Chr Renewal Cen *D & D* 84–89; Nat Dir (Ireland) SOMA UK 89–07; rtd 07. *7 Cloughmore Park, Rostrevor, Newry BT34 3AX* T/F: (028) 4173 8959 E: niallpgriffin@gmail.com

GRIFFIN, Nicholas Philip. b 84. Moorlands Coll BA 06 Ox Univ MTh 11 K Coll Lon PhD 19. Wycliffe Hall Ox 09. d 11 p 12. C Frome H Trin *B & W* 11–15; Chapl Univ of St Mark and St Jo *Ex* 15–18; Tutor St Mellitus Coll 18–21; NSM Blackdown *B & W* 18–21; V Wilton from 21. *Wilton Vicarage, Fons George, Taunton TA1 3JT* M: 07947-672547 E: ngriffin84@gmail.com

GRIFFIN, Patrick Matthew. b 90. Nottm Univ BA 12. Coll of Resurr Mirfield MA 15. d 17 p 18. C Basford *Lich* from 17; C Wolstanton from 17. *Wolstanton Vicarage, Knutton Road, Newcastle ST5 0HU* T: (01782) 922730 M: 07792-467190 E: pgriffin1990@hotmail.com

GRIFFISS, Canon Helen Mary. b 48. Univ of Wales (Ban) CertEd 69 K Alfred's Coll Win MA 98. STETS 97. d 00 p 01. Miss Adv USPG Bris, Sarum and Win 00–03; NSM Bransgore Win 00–03; C Milton 04–06; P-in-c Mudeford 06–09; V 09–17; rtd 17; Hon Can Win Cathl from 16; PtO from 17. *35A River Way, Christchurch BH23 2QQ* T: (01202) 474067 E: revhelengriffiss@gmail.com

GRIFFITH, Benedict Lloyd Thomas. b 64. Trin Coll Carmarthen BA 86. Ripon Coll Cuddesdon 04. d 06 p 07. C Kempston Transfiguration *St Alb* 06–09; V Upper Wye *S & B* 09–14; P-in-c Erwood Gp w Painscastle Gp 14–16; R Kington w Huntington, Old Radnor, Kinnerton etc *Heref* from 16. *The Vicarage, Church Road, Kington HR5 3AG* T: (01544) 230525 M: 07960-947137 E: vicar@kingtonparishes.org.uk

GRIFFITH, The Ven David Vaughan. b 36. St D Coll Lamp BA 60. Lich Th Coll 60. d 62 p 63. C Llanfairfechan *Ban* 62–66; C Dolgellau 66–70; R Llanfair Talhaiarn *St As* 70–82; R Llanfairtalhaiarn and Llansannan 82–85; P-in-c Llangernyw and Gwytherin 77–85; V Colwyn 85–98; Warden of Readers 91–99; Can Cursal St As Cathl 95–98; P-in-c Berriew and Manafon 98–99; V 99–02; Preb St As Cathl and Adn Montgomery 98–02; rtd 02; PtO *St As* from 09. *1 Bishop's Walk, St Asaph LL17 0SU* T: (01745) 582903

GRIFFITH, Canon John Vaughan. b 33. St D Coll Lamp 53. d 58 p 59. C Holyhead w Rhoscolyn *Ban* 58–63; R Maentwrog w Trawsfynydd 63–68; Chapl RAF 68–72; V Winnington *Ches* 72–76; V Northwich St Luke and H Trin 76–81; V Sandiway 81–98; Dioc Communications Officer 84–86; Ed Chester Diocesan News 84–92; Hon Can Ches Cathl 89–98; rtd 98; PtO *Ches* 99–14. *8 Abbey Lane, Hartford, Northwich CW8 1LX*

GRIFFITH, Justin David. b 48. Imp Coll Lon BScEng 74 Cranfield Inst of Tech MSc 89. NEOC 03. d 06 p 07. NSM N Ferriby *York* 06–09; NSM Broad Blunsdon *Bris* 10–14; NSM

Highworth w Sevenhampton and Inglesham etc 10–14; CF (ACF) 09–14; PtO Auckland NZ from 14. *1 Miro Street, New Lynn, Auckland 0600, New Zealand* T: (0064) (9) 282 3104 M: (0064) 21-0849 0906 E: justin@griffith.co.nz

GRIFFITH, Sandra. b 44. Open Univ BA 94. EAMTC 01. **d** 04 **p** 05. NSM The Ortons, Alwalton and Chesterton Ely 04–06; NSM Sawtry and Glatton 06–11; Asst Chapl Hinchingbrooke Health Care NHS Trust from 05. *14 Nene Way, Oundle, Peterborough PE8 4LR* M: 07450-470685 E: sandra@revgriffith.com

GRIFFITH, Stephen. *See* GRIFFITH, William Stephen

GRIFFITH, Steven Ellsworth. b 63. Univ of Wales BTh 91. St Steph Ho Ox 85. **d** 87 **p** 88. C Holyhead w Rhoscolyn w Llanfair-yn-Neubwll *Ban* 87–90; CF 90–08; Sen CF 08–13; PtO *S & B* 12–13; Min Can Brecon Cathl 13–15; PV Brecon Cathl from 15; P-in-c Brecon St Mary from 14; AD Gtr Brecon 17–20. *The Clergy House, Cathedral Close, Brecon LD3 9DP* T: (01874) 622044 M: 07540-609029 E: frstevengriffith@outlook.com

GRIFFITH, Mrs Wendy Margaret. b 41. **d** 01 **p** 02. NSM Sixpenny Handley w Gussage St Andrew etc *Sarum* 01–06; NSM Wimborne Minster 06–08; NSM Somerton w Compton Dundon, the Charltons etc *B & W* 08–14; NSM Ivelchester Deanery 14–16; PtO *B & W* from 17; *Sarum* from 18. *Homelea, 5 Church Walk, Cross Lane, Long Sutton, Langport TA10 9LR* T: (01458) 241771 M: 07720-942996 E: wendymgriffith@gmail.com

GRIFFITH, William Stephen. b 50. MBE 02. Univ of Wales (Ban) BA 71 FRAS 92. Westcott Ho Cam 71. **d** 73 **p** 74. C Llandudno *Ban* 73–76; C Calne and Blackland *Sarum* 76–78; P-in-c Broadwindsor w Burstock and Seaborough 78–79; TV Beaminster Area 79–81; PtO 81–83; Chapl St Pet Sch York 83–87; C Leeds St Pet *Ripon* 87; Chapl Bearwood Coll Wokingham 87–92; CMS Jordan 92–95; Sen Chapl Univ of Wales (Cardiff) *Llan* 95–96; Chapl Damascus 96–02; P-in-c Yerevan, Baku and Tbilisi *Eur* 03; V Denton *Newc* 04–08; TV Mortlake w E Sheen *S'wark* 09–15; rtd 15; PtO *York* from 15. *14 North Parade, York YO30 7AB* T: (01904) 626819 M: 07729-278294 E: haywales1@gmail.com

GRIFFITH-JONES, David Laugharne. b 79. Pemb Coll Cam MA 06. Wycliffe Hall Ox BTh 12. **d** 12 **p** 13. C Toxteth St Philemon w St Gabr and St Cleopas *Liv* 12–16; TR Drypool *York* from 16. *139 Laburnum Avenue, Garden Village, Hull HU8 8PA* T: (01482) 786553 M: 07775-563126 E: dave_gj@hotmail.com

GRIFFITH-JONES, Robin Guthrie. b 56. New Coll Ox BA 78 Ch Coll Cam BA 88. Westcott Ho Cam 86. **d** 89 **p** 90. C Cantril Farm *Liv* 89–92; Chapl Linc Coll Ox 92–99; Master of The Temple from 99. *The Master's House, Temple, London EC4Y 7BB* T: (020) 7353 8559 E: master@templechurch.com

GRIFFITHS, Ainsley. *See* GRIFFITHS, John Mark Ainsley

GRIFFITHS, Alan Charles. b 46. Dur Univ BA 67. Cranmer Hall Dur 66. **d** 69 **p** 70. C Leic H Apostles 69–72; pto *York* 73–77; V Lea Hall *Birm* 77–87; Asst Dir of Educn *Sheff* 87–92; V W Bessacarr 92–02; V Conisbrough 02–13; rtd 13; PtO *Sheff* 13–14; P-in-c Barnburgh w Melton on the Hill etc 14–16; PtO from 16. *356C Thorne Road, Doncaster DN2 5AN* T: (01302) 365164 E: alan.c.griffiths@btinternet.com

GRIFFITHS, Canon Andrew Taylor. b 68. Jes Coll Ox BA 92 MA 96. Cranmer Hall Dur 98. **d** 00 **p** 01. C Paris St Mich *Eur* 00–04; C Galleywood Common *Chelmsf* 04–05; V 05–17; C Moulsham St Luke 13–17; C Moulsham St Jo 13–17; C Widford 13–17; RD Chelmsf S 07–17; Chelmsf IME Co-ord and Bradwell Area CMD Adv from 17; Public Preacher *Chelmsf* from 17; Hon Can Chelmsf Cathl from 15. *Chelmsford Diocesan Board of Finance, 53 New Street, Chelmsford CM1 1AT* T: (01245) 294400 M: 07969-605059 E: agriffiths@chelmsford.anglican.org

GRIFFITHS, Beatrice Mary. b 29. Chelsea Coll Lon CertEd 60. Westcott Ho Cam 85. **dss** 86 **d** 87 **p** 94. W Bridgford *S'well* 86–87; NSM Wilford Hill 87–99; rtd 99; PtO *S'well* from 99. *7 Stella Avenue, Tollerton, Nottingham NG12 4EX* T: 0115-937 4155

GRIFFITHS, Benjamin David. b 78. Ches Univ MA 14. St Jo Coll Nottm BA 12. **d** 13 **p** 14. C Brampton St Thos *Derby* 13–16; V Newbold w Dunston 16–21; Asst Dir of Ords 18–21; Ord Voc Officer from 21. *Derby Church House, 1 Full Street, Derby DE1 3DR* T: (01332) 388650 M: 07813-285445 E: revbengriffiths@gmail.com

GRIFFITHS, Brian John. b 45. Brunel Univ PhD 82. **d** 05 **p** 06. OLM Iver Ox 05–14; PtO from 14; *Win* 11–15. *7 Benton Drive, Chinnor OX39 4DP* T: (01844) 355953

GRIFFITHS, Christopher Rhys. b 82. Leeds Univ BA 06 Anglia Ruskin Univ MA 14. Westcott Ho Cam 10. **d** 13 **p** 14. C Wimbledon *S'wark* 13–16; R Horringer *St E* 16–21; TV Mortlake w E Sheen *S'wark* from 21. *Christ*

Church Vicarage, 17 Sheen Gate Gardens, London SW14 7PD E: chrisgriffiths82@protonmail.com

GRIFFITHS, David Bruce. b 44. Sussex Univ BA 69 Hull Univ MA 83. Linc Th Coll. **d** 82 **p** 83. C Springfield All SS *Chelmsf* 82–84; TV Horwich *Man* 84–92; V Heaton Ch Ch 92–03; P-in-c Ainsworth 03–09; rtd 09; PtO *Man* from 09. *Woodford, Mill Lane, Horwich, Bolton BL6 6AQ* T: (01204) 469621 M: 07854-769119 E: dandbgriffiths@googlemail.com

GRIFFITHS, David John. b 53. St Jo Coll Nottm BTh 93. **d** 94 **p** 95. C Retford St Sav *S'well* 94–96; NSM Thwaites Brow *Bradf* 96–98; P-in-c Oakenshaw cum Woodlands 98–03; V Buttershaw St Paul 03–10; V Silsden 10–14; *Leeds* from 14; Asst Chapl Airedale NHS Foundn Trust from 96. *The Vicarage, Briggate, Silsden, Keighley BD20 9JS* T: (01535) 652204 E: david.griffiths@leeds.anglican.org

GRIFFITHS, David Mark. b 59. Kent Univ BA 80. Chich Th Coll 81. **d** 83 **p** 84. C Clydach *S & B* 83–84; C Llwynderw 84–88; V Swansea St Nic 88–98; Chapl Swansea Inst of HE 88–98; V Swansea St Gabr from 98; P-in-c Swansea St Barn from 17; Chapl Swansea NHS Trust from 98. *3 Trafalgar Place, Brynmill, Swansea SA2 0BU* T: (01792) 464011 E: mark.griffiths35@btinternet.com

GRIFFITHS, David Mark. b 41. Univ of Wales (Cardiff) BA 67 CertEd 71. St Mich Coll Llan 92. **d** 94 **p** 95. C Llwynderw *S & B* 94–96; R Llanbadarn Fawr, Llandegley and Llanfihangel etc 96–02; P-in-c Slebech and Uzmaston w Boulston *St D* 02–06; rtd 06; PtO *St D* from 06. *17 Catherine's Gate, Merlins Bridge, Haverfordwest SA61 1NB* T: (01437) 783950 M: 07811-647910 E: davidgriffiths41@mypostoffice.co.uk

GRIFFITHS, David Rowson Hopkin. b 38. Oak Hill Th Coll 59. **d** 62 **p** 63. C Barrow St Mark *Carl* 62–65; OMF Internat 66–09; Japan 66–88; Philippines 88–09; rtd 03. *4 Warwick Place, West Cross, Swansea SA3 5JG* T: (01792) 402885 E: david.griffiths@omfmail.com

GRIFFITHS, Dorothy Anastasia de Jaegher. b 55. **d** 14 **p** 15. NSM Cheltenham St Mary w St Matt and St Luke *Glouc* 14–16; NSM Charlton Kings St Mary 16–17; PtO from 17. *35 St Mary's Square, Gloucester GL1 2QT* T: (01452) 453429 E: anna.dejaegher.griffiths@gmail.com

GRIFFITHS, Ms Elizabeth Leigh. b 61. St Hugh's Coll Ox BA 83 MA 87 Warwick Univ PGCE 84. Ripon Coll Cuddesdon 96. **d** 98 **p** 99. C Bettws *Mon* 98–99; C Maindee Newport 99–01; TV Cen Swansea and Dioc Chapl Tertiary Educn *S & B* 01–03; C St Martin-in-the-Fields *Lon* 03–09; Dir Past Studies ERMC and Nor Dioc Min Course 09–10; Dir Past Studies and Vice Prin ERMC 10–11; V Cardiff City Par *Llan* 11–12; Dioc Dir of Ords 12; TV Basingstoke *Win* 14–17; Dir Tr Bridge Builders Min from 17; PtO *Bris* from 17. *16 Horse Fair Lane, Cricklade, Swindon SN6 6BN* T: (01793) 759080 M: 07710-179162 E: lizgriff999@btinternet.com

GRIFFITHS, Mrs Frances Karen Bernadette. b 62. St Mellitus Coll 17. **d** 19 **p** 20. C Kirkholt *Man* 19–21. *Address temp unknown* M: 07592-191504 E: griffclan2@gmail.com

GRIFFITHS, Garrie Charles. b 53. St Jo Coll Nottm. **d** 77 **p** 78. Canada 77–78; C Stalybridge H Trin and Ch Ch *Ches* 78–81; C Moreton 81–84; V Godley cum Newton Green 84–89; V Bayston Hill *Lich* 89–01; TR Mildenhall *St E* 01–04; V Hadfield *Derby* 04–10; RD Glossop 06–10; V Youlgreave, Middleton, Stanton-in-Peak etc 10–16; Spiritual Dir Adv 13–16; rtd 16. *8 Main Road, Martlesham, Woodbridge IP12 4SF*

GRIFFITHS, Gerald Brian. b 41. Open Univ BA 88. SEITE 97. **d** 00 **p** 01. NSM Cliftonville *Cant* 00–03; TV St Laur in Thanet 04–09; rtd 09; Chapl Costa Blanca *Eur* 10–12; PtO *Cant* from 13; *Eur* from 14. *11 Wellesley Court, Ramsgate CT11 8NU* T: (01843) 850229 E: gbgriffiths41@gmail.com

GRIFFITHS, Gordon John. b 31. Univ of Wales (Cardiff) BA 53. S'wark Ord Course 72. **d** 75 **p** 76. NSM Sutton St Nic *S'wark* 75–78; Asst Chapl Eastbourne Coll 78–81; PtO *Chich* from 81. *15 Buckhurst Close, Willingdon, Eastbourne BN20 9EF* T: (01323) 505547

GRIFFITHS, Griff. *See* GRIFFITHS, Stephen David

GRIFFITHS, Harvey Stephen. b 35. Linc Coll Ox BA 58 MA 62. Linc Th Coll 62. **d** 62 **p** 63. C Frodingham *Linc* 62–65; C Darlington St Cuth *Dur* 65–70; Chapl RN 70–92; P-in-c Southwick w Boarhunt *Portsm* 92–05; rtd 05; PtO *Portsm* from 05. *141 High Street, Lindfield, Haywards Heath RH16 2HT* T: (01444) 523114 E: harvey@griffithsonline.co.uk

GRIFFITHS, Hugh. b 44. Nottm Univ BEd 78. Clifton Th Coll 69. **d** 71 **p** 72. C Mansfield SS Pet and Paul *S'well* 71–77; NSM Stockport St Geo *Ches* 08–09; rtd 09; PtO *Ches* from 09. *1 Heath Crescent, Stockport SK2 6JN* T: 0161-285 9772 E: hugh.griffiths@norburychurch.org.uk

GRIFFITHS, James Brian. b 69. Man Univ BSocSci 92. Oak Hill Th Coll BA 13 MA 15. **d** 15 **p** 16. C Gabalfa *Llan* 15–19;

V Lisvane from 19. *The Vicarage, Green Gables, 2 Llwyn y Pia Road, Lisvane, Cardiff CF14 0SY* T: 07902-914374 E: j.b.griffiths69@gmail.com

GRIFFITHS, Jason Anthony. b 70. St Jo Coll Nottm 14. **d** 17 **p** 18. C Britwell *Ox* 17–21; V Northampton St Benedict *Pet* from 21. *St Benedict's Vicarage, 16 Sentinel Road, Northampton NN4 9UF* M: 07400-316603 E: griff205@gmail.com *or* vicar.griff@gmail.com

GRIFFITHS, John. b 57. Coll of Ripon & York St Jo BEd 83. LCTP 12. **d** 14 **p** 15. C Heart of Eden *Carl* 14–15; C Cockermouth Area from 15; V Garstang St Thos *Blackb* 18–21; rtd 21. *Address temp unknown* M: 07984-895722 E: johntherev@btinternet.com

GRIFFITHS, John Gareth. b 44. Lich Th Coll 68. **d** 71 **p** 72. C Shotton *St As* 71–73; C Rhyl w St Ann 73–76; V Llanasa 76–95; RD Holywell 89–95; V Rhuddlan 95–10; rtd 10; PtO *St As* from 10. *13 Llwyn Harlech, Bodelwyddan, Rhyl LL18 5WG* T: (01745) 539955 E: jg.griffiths@btinternet.com

GRIFFITHS, John Mark Ainsley. b 68. Man Univ BSc 90 MSc 91 PGCE 92 Nottm Univ PhD 15. Ripon Coll Cuddesdon Ba 97. **d** 98 **p** 99. Min Can Bangor *Ban* 98–01; P-in-c Denio w Abererch 01–02; V 02–05; Chapl Univ of Wales (Trin St Dav) 05–18; CMD Officer *St D* 05–18; Dir Faith, Order and Unity Ch in Wales from 18. *The Church in Wales, 2 Callaghan Square, Cardiff CF10 5BT* E: ainsleygriffiths@churchinwales.org.uk

GRIFFITHS, Mrs Linda Betty. b 48. Trin Coll Carmarthen CertEd 69 Gwent Coll of HE BEd 96 Open Univ MA 97. Mon Dioc Tr Scheme 05. **d** 06 **p** 11. NSM Newbridge *Mon* 06–10; NSM Risca 10–13; NSM Lower Islwyn 13–16; rtd 16; PtO *Mon* from 16. *19 Cromwell Road, Risca, Newport NP11 7AF* T: (01495) 270455 E: griff.l@btinternet.com

GRIFFITHS, Malcolm. b 47. St Alb Minl Tr Scheme. **d** 82 **p** 83. NSM Hemel Hempstead *St Alb* 82–86; C 86–87; TV Liskeard, St Keyne, St Pinnock, Morval etc *Truro* 87–96; V Landrake w St Erney and Botus Fleming 96–12; rtd 12. *12 Lowertown Close, Landrake, Saltash PL12 5DG*

GRIFFITHS, Margaret. *See* MacLACHLAN, Margaret

GRIFFITHS, Mrs Margarett. b 29. ATCL 47 LRAM 48. CA Tr Coll 50. **dss** 81 **d** 87. Hackington *Cant* 81–83; Ashford 84–89; Par Dn 87–89; rtd 89. *39 Newington Way, Craven Arms SY7 9PS* T: (01588) 673848

GRIFFITHS, Mark. b 68. JP . Nottm Univ PhD 09. St Jo Coll Nottm 04. **d** 07 **p** 08. C Stoke Poges *Ox* 07–10; P-in-c Warfield 10–16; Tutor St Padarn's Inst from 17; Hd Children, Young People and Family Min Development Ch in Wales from 17; Hd C and Lic Min Tr and Development from 18; PtO *Llan* from 17; *St As* from 19; *Ban* from 19; *St D* from 19; *Mon* from 19; *S & B* from 19. *83 Picca Close, Cardiff CF5 6XR* T: (029) 2056 3379 M: 07592-242303 E: mark.griffiths@stpadarns.ac.uk *or* revmarkgriff@hotmail.com

GRIFFITHS, Mark. *See* GRIFFITHS, David Mark

GRIFFITHS, Canon Martyn Robert. b 51. Nottm Univ BTh 74 St Martin's Coll Lanc PGCE 75. Kelham Th Coll 70. **d** 74 **p** 75. C Kings Heath *Birm* 74–77; C-in-c Elmdon Heath CD 77–79; TV Solihull 79–81; Asst Admin Shrine of Our Lady of Walsingham 81–85; V Oldham St Steph and All Martyrs *Man* 85–89; TR Swinton and Pendlebury 89–98; Hon Can Man Cathl 96–98; R Preston St Jo and St Geo *Blackb* 98–05; Hon Can Blackb Cathl 00–05; R Henley w Remenham *Ox* 05–18; rtd 18; PtO *Ox* from 18. *1 Southby Close, Cholsey, Wallingford OX10 9FQ* T: (01491) 659040 E: martynrgriffiths@btinternet.com

GRIFFITHS, Michael James. b 76. St Mellitus Coll BA 15. **d** 15 **p** 16. C Tadley Win 15–18; P-in-c E Win 18–21; R from 21. *All Saints' Rectory, 19 Petersfield Road, Winchester SO23 0JD* M: 07866-727146 E: vicar@eastwinchester.org

GRIFFITHS, Neil Timothy. b 62. Portsm Poly BSc 84 De Montfort Univ MSc 01. Qu Coll Birm 12. **d** 14 **p** 15. C Broom Leys *Leic* 14–18; P-in-c Colsterworth Gp *Linc* 18–20; V Colsterworth Par from 20. *The Rectory, 13A Back Lane, Colsterworth, Grantham NG33 5NJ* T: (01476) 860630 M: 07879-620041 E: neilgriffiths01@btinternet.com

GRIFFITHS, Neville. b 39. Univ of Wales BA 63. St D Coll Lamp LTh 66. **d** 66 **p** 67. C Newport St Mark *Mon* 66–68; C Cardiff St Jo *Llan* 68–70; Chapl Greystoke Coll Carl 70–76; C Greystoke w Matterdale Carl 70–75; TV Greystoke, Matterdale and Mungrisdale 75–76; Chapl Grey Coll Dur 76–81; C Croxdale *Dur* 76–81; R Didsbury Ch Ch *Man* 81–83; P-in-c Lowther and Askham *Carl* 83–84; R 84–88; V Guernsey St Matt *Win* 88–93; R Guernsey St Pierre du Bois 93–02; R Guernsey St Philippe de Torteval 93–02; Vice-Dean Guernsey 99–02; rtd 03; PtO *Dur* 02–20; *Eur* from 17. *6 Howlcroft Villas, Neville's Cross, Durham DH1 4DU* T: 0191-386 4778 E: griff.nevboy@yahoo.co.uk

GRIFFITHS, Nigel Timothy. b 64. Sheff Univ BSc 86 Imp Coll Lon PhD 90. Wycliffe Hall Ox 13. **d** 15 **p** 16. C

Southborough St Pet w Ch Ch and St Matt etc *Roch* 15–19; C Reigate St Mary *S'wark* from 19. *63 Chart Lane, Reigate RH2 7EA* M: 07879-427944 E: nigegriffiths@hotmail.com *or* nigel.griffiths@stmaryreigate.org

GRIFFITHS, Mrs Pamela Verley. d 07 **p** 10. NSM Ebbw Vale *Mon* 07–13; NSM Upper Ebbw Valleys from 13. *221 Marine Street, Cwm, Ebbw Vale NP23 7TA* T: (01495) 371819

GRIFFITHS, Paul Edward. b 48. St Jo Coll Nottm 86. **d** 88 **p** 89. C Ipswich St Andr *St E* 88–92; P-in-c Tollerton *S'well* 92–00; P-in-c Plumtree 95–97; Ind Chapl and Dioc Adv on Ind Soc 97–00; V Hellesdon *Nor* 00–13; rtd 13; PtO *Leic* 13–15; *St E* from 15. *111 Colneis Road, Felixstowe IP11 9LH* E: revgriffiths@btinternet.com

GRIFFITHS, Ms Paula Whitmore Llewellyn. b 49. LMH Ox BA 71 MA 75 Anglia Ruskin Univ BA 09. Westcott Ho Cam 08. **d** 09 **p** 10. NSM Saffron Walden and Villages *Chelmsf* 09–21; rtd 21; PtO *Chelmsf* from 21. *Greatford Cottage, Stocking Green, Radwinter, Saffron Walden CB10 2SS* E: paula.greatford@btinternet.com

GRIFFITHS, Richard Barré Maw. b 43. CCC Ox BA 65 MA 69 St Jo Coll Dur BA 71. Cranmer Hall Dur. **d** 71 **p** 72. C Fulwood *Sheff* 71–74; Hon C Sheff St Jo 74–76; Field Dept of Bibl Studies Sheff Univ 74–76; C Fulham St Matt *Lon* 76–78; P-in-c 78–83; R Chich St Pancras and St Jo 83–09; rtd 09. *24 Beechcroft, Humshaugh, Hexham NE46 4DN* E: richardgriff@clara.co.uk

GRIFFITHS, Prof Richard Mathias. b 35. K Coll Cam BA 57 MA 61 PhD 62 BNC Ox MA 66 FIL 91 FKC 95. Ox Min Course 89 SAOMC 96. **d** 97 **p** 98. Prof French K Coll Lon 90–00; NSM W Woodhay w Enborne, Hampstead Marshall etc *Ox* 97–00; NSM Llantrisant *Llan* 01–02; NSM Penarth and Llandough from 03. *Waltham House, Bradford Place, Penarth CF64 1AG* T: (029) 2070 7828 F: 2070 9699 E: richardgriffiths477@gmail.com

GRIFFITHS, The Ven Robert Herbert. b 53. Chich Th Coll 75. **d** 76 **p** 77. C Holywell *St As* 76–80; CF (TA) 79–87; P-in-c Gyffylliog *St As* 80–84; V Llanfair Dyffryn Clwyd 80–84; V Llanfair DC, Derwen, Llanelidan and Efenechtyd 84–88; Asst Dioc Youth Chapl 81–86; Dioc Youth Chapl 86–91; PV St As and Tremeirchion w Cefn 88–97; Chapl H M Stanley Hosp 88–97; Bp's Visitor and Dioc RE Adv *St As* 88–93; Chapl Glan Clwyd Distr Gen Hosp 93–97; V Llanrhos *St As* 97–09; TR Rhos-Cystennin 09–14; R Llandegla and Bryneglwys 14–18; Can St As Cathl 98–18; AD Llanrwst 01–09; Chapl NW Wales NHS Trust 97–18; Adn Wrexham *St As* 14–18; rtd 18; PtO *St As* from 18; *Ban* from 18. *Camelot, 26 St Anne's Gardens, Llandudno LL30 1SD* T: (01492) 584890 M: 07583-391214 E: venbob14@btinternet.com

GRIFFITHS, Robert James. b 52. Nottm Univ BTh 82. St Jo Coll Nottm 79. **d** 82 **p** 83. C Kettering St Andr *Pet* 82–85; C Collier Row St Jas and Havering-atte-Bower *Chelmsf* 86–89; R High Ongar w Norton Mandeville 89–97; R Ilmington w Stretton-on-Fosse etc *Cov* 97–99; V Newport *Chelmsf* 99–03; V Newport and Widdington 03–06; PtO *Ely* 09–10; R Horringer *St E* 10–15; rtd 15. *31 Castle View Gardens, Westham, Pevensey BN24 5HP* T: (01323) 461511 E: r.griffiths45@btinternet.com

GRIFFITHS, Roger Michael. b 47. Wycliffe Hall Ox 83. **d** 86 **p** 87. Min Can St D Cathl 86–88; V Pen-boyr 88–94; V Fishguard w Llanychar and Pontfaen w Morfil etc 94–03. *Nevern Cottage, 10 Feidr Gongol, Fishguard SA65 9BA* T: (01348) 218073

GRIFFITHS, Sarah. *See* BICK, Sarah

GRIFFITHS, Canon Shane Owen. b 63. Ripon Coll Cuddesdon 01. **d** 04 **p** 04. C Icknield *Ox* 04–07; P-in-c Mullion *Truro* 07–16; P-in-c Cury and Gunwalloe 07–16; V Mullion and Cury w Gunwalloe from 16; Hon Can Truro Cathl from 18. *The Vicarage, Nansmellyon Road, Mullion, Helston TR12 7DH* T: (01326) 240325 E: shaneowengriffiths@yahoo.co.uk

GRIFFITHS, The Ven Shirley Thelma. b 48. Univ of Wales (Ban) CertEd 69 Open Univ BA 83 Coll of Ripon & York St Jo MA 01. St Deiniol's Hawarden 79. **d** 82 **p** 95. NSM Dyserth and Trelawnyd and Cwm *St As* 82–91; RE Officer 89–95; Min Can St As Cathl 91–95; P-in-c The Cowtons *Ripon* 95–02; RE Adv 95–02; V Abergele *St As* 02–08; V Abergele and St George 08–10; Adn Wrexham 10–13; R Llandegla 10–11; V Bryneglwys 11; R Llandegla and Bryneglwys 11–13; rtd 13; PtO *Dur* from 14; *Eur* from 17. *The Gables, 22 Greenways, Sunnybrow, Crook DL15 0LX* T: (01388) 747035 E: shirleytgriffiths@gmail.com

GRIFFITHS, Simon Huw. b 82. Oak Hill Th Coll 18. **d** 21. C Preston All SS *Blackb* from 21. *2A Grosvenor Place, Ashton-on-Ribble, Preston PR2 1ED* M: 07779-572861 E: simongriffiths@gmail.com

GRIFFITHS, Canon Simon Mark. b 62. Ch Ch Coll Cant BA 84 Kent Univ MA 95. Chich Th Coll. d 87 p 88. C Cardiff St Jo Llan 87–91; Sub Chapl HM Pris Cardiff 87–91; Chapl and Succ Roch Cath 91–96; Chapl Univ Coll Chich 96–01; V Sheff St Matt 01–11; TR Cen Swansea S & B 11–16; Can Prec Truro Cathl from 16. *52 Daniell Road, Truro TR1 2DA* T: (01872) 450779 E: simongriffiths@trurocathedral.org.uk

GRIFFITHS, Stephen David (Griff). b 70. Oak Hill Th Coll BA 96 Trin Coll Bris. d 00 p 01. C Cranleigh *Guildf* 00–04; TV Thetford *Nor* 04–10; Chapl Cam Univ Hosps NHS Foundn Trust 10–17; Chapl W Suffolk NHS Foundn Trust from 17. *89 Sycamore Drive, Bury St Edmunds IP32 7PW* T: (01284) 712704 M: 07802-224140 E: revgriff70@gmail.com *or* stephen.griffiths@wsh.nhs.uk

GRIFFITHS, Stephen Mark. b 67. Nottm Univ BTh 93 PhD 00 K Coll Lon MA 01. St Jo Coll Nottm 90. d 93 p 94. C Glascote and Stonydelph *Lich* 93–96; P-in-c Stratford New Town St Paul *Chelmsf* 96–02; P-in-c Steeple Bumpstead and Helions Bumpstead 02–05; Tutor Ridley Hall Cam 01–09; TR Linton Ely 09–14; V Enfield St Andr *Lon* from 14. *Enfield Vicarage, 36 Silver Street, Enfield EN1 3EG* T: (020) 8363 8676 M: 07905-861234 E: steve.griffiths@london.anglican.org

GRIFFITHS, Stephen Robert. b 78. Oak Hill Th Coll BA 00 Anglia Poly Univ MA 05. Ridley Hall Cam 02. d 04 p 05. C Normanton *Derby* 04–08; P-in-c Moresby *Carl* 08–13; RD Calder 12–13; TR Cherwell Valley *Ox* 13–18; AD Bicester and Islip 14–18; TR Oakham, Ashwell, Braunston, Brooke, Egleton etc *Pet* from 18. *All Saints' Vicarage, 2 Vicarage Road, Oakham LE15 6EG* T: (01572) 724007 M: 07504-320597 E: steph78griff@hotmail.com

GRIFFITHS (née BANKS), Mrs Susan Angela. b 61. St Jo Coll Nottm BTh 94. d 94 p 95. C Ingrow w Hainworth *Bradf* 94–98; V Wyke 98–03; C Buttershaw St Paul 03–10; C Silsden 10–14; *Leeds* from 14; RD S Craven *Bradf* 10–14; AD Keighley *Leeds* 14–16. *The Vicarage, Briggate, Silsden, Keighley BD20 9JS* T: (01535) 652204 E: susan.griffiths@leeds.anglican.org

GRIFFITHS, Canon Sylvia Joy. b 50. Gipsy Hill Coll of Educn CertEd 71. St Jo Coll Nottm 85. dss 86 d 87 p 94. Woodthorpe *S'well* 86–90; Par Dn 87–90; Min Bestwood/ Rise Park LEP 90–94; Team Dn Bestwood 90–94; TR 94–99; P-in-c Sherwood 99–01; V 01–16; Hon Can S'well Minster 04–11; rtd 16; PtO *S'well* from 17. *2 Islay Close, Arnold, Nottingham NG5 8FL* T: 0115-920 8090 E: sylvia.griffiths1@outlook.com

GRIFFITHS, Timothy James. b 60. Edge Hill Coll of HE BEd 92. All SS Cen for Miss & Min 17. d 19 p 20. C Clubmoor *Liv* from 19. *37 Clinton Road, Liverpool L12 7HA* M: 07894-051153 E: tgriffiths30@sky.com

GRIFFITHS, Canon Tudor Francis Lloyd. b 54. Jes Coll Ox BA 76 MA 81 Wycliffe Hall Ox BA 78 MA 81 Leeds Univ PhD 99. Wycliffe Hall Ox 76. d 79 p 80. C Brecon w Battle S & B 79–81; Min Can Brecon Cathl 79–81; C Swansea St Mary w H Trin 81–83; R Llangattock and Llangynidr 83–88; CMS Uganda 89–95; C Newton St Pet S & B 96; Dioc Missr *Mon* 96–03; V Goldcliffe and Whitson and Nash 96–98; TV Magor 98–03; TR Hawarden *St As* 03–11; Can Cursal St As Cathl 05–08; Chan St As Cathl 08–11; R Cheltenham St Mary w St Matt *Glouc* 11–12; R Cheltenham St Mary w St Matt and St Luke 12–17; AD Cheltenham 11–17; Sen Interim Min 17–20; Hon Can Glouc Cathl 13–20; rtd 20. *5 Phoenix Drive, Chepstow NP16 5TJ* M: 07718-906066 E: tudor.griffiths1@gmail.com

GRIFFITHS, William Thomas Gordon. b 48. York Univ BA 70 Fitzw Coll Cam BA 79. Ridley Hall Cam 78. d 80 p 81. C Dulwich St Barn *S'wark* 80–83; C Egglescliffe *Dur* 83–85; Ind Chapl 85–90; V Stockton St Jas 90–98; NSM Leamington Hastings and Birdingbury *Cov* 98–03; NSM Grandborough w Willoughby and Flecknoe 98–03; NSM Leam Valley 03–06; PtO from 06. *24 Park Road, Rugby CV21 2QH* T: (01788) 547815 E: wtg.griffiths@btopenworld.com

GRIGG, Deborah Ann. b 56. R Holloway Coll Lon BA 79 Kingston Poly PGCE 80. SWMTC 09. d 12 p 14. C Liskeard and St Keyne *Truro* 12–13; C Bodmin w Lanhydrock and Lanivet 13–16; Public Preacher from 16; TV Redruth w Lanner and Treleigh 19–21. *Rose Vean, North Pool Road, Redruth TR15 3JQ* M: 07742-865618

GRIGG, Robin Harold. b 44. d 07 p 08. NSM St Mewan w Mevagissey and St Ewe *Truro* 07–15; Chapl R Cornwall Hosps Trust 07–11; PtO *Truro* from 15. *33 Tregolls Lodge, St Clements Hill, Truro TR1 1GW* E: robingrigg124@btinternet.com

GRIGG, Simon James. b 61. Warwick Univ BA 82 MA 83 Southn Univ BTh 90. Chich Th Coll 87. d 90 p 91. C Cowley St Jas *Ox* 90–94; C W Hampstead St Jas *Lon* 94–95; V Munster Square Ch Ch and St Mary Magd 95–06; R Covent Garden St Paul from 06. *Flat 4, 19 Bedford Street,*

London WC2E 9HP T: (020) 3509 9374 M: 07958-472568 E: simon.grigg@btopenworld.com

GRIGGS, Alan Peter. b 71. St Jo Coll Nottm. d 15 p 16. NSM Derby St Barn 15–18; NSM Fenny Bentley, Thorpe, Tissington, Parwich etc 18–20; PtO from 20; Agric Chapl from 21. *4 Ravenscourt Road, Derby DE22 4DL* T: (01332) 361534 M: 07804-735556 E: alandeut6@gmail.com

GRIGGS, Canon Alan Sheward. b 33. Trin Hall Cam BA 56 MA 60. Westcott Ho Cam 58. d 60 p 61. C Arnold *S'well* 60–63; Succ S'wark Cathl 63–66; Ind Chapl 66–71; C Leeds H Trin *Ripon* 71–81; V 81–90; Soc and Ind Adv 71–81; Hon Can Ripon Cathl 84–98; Soc Resp Officer 91–98; rtd 98; PtO *Ripon* 98–14; *Leeds* from 14. *7 Linden Court, Hollin Lane, Leeds LS16 5NB* T: 0113-275 8100 E: alangriggs3@gmail.com

GRIGGS, Mrs Anthea Mary. b 37. Homerton Coll Cam TCert 57 New Coll Edin BA 86. SAOMC. d 00 p 01. NSM Sunningdale *Ox* 00–05; LtO *Edin* from 06. *8/1 Rattray Drive, Edinburgh EH10 5TH* T: 0131-447 2448 E: antheagriggs@me.com

GRIGSON, Preb Richard John Stephen. b 60. Man Univ BA 83. Qu Coll Birm 86. d 88 p 89. C W Bromwich St Fran *Lich* 88–92; V Smallthorne 92–14; P-in-c Brown Edge 05–14; V Stafford St Mary and Marston from 14; V Stafford St Chad from 14; Preb Lich Cathl from 11. *The Vicarage, Victoria Terrace, Stafford ST16 3HA* T: (01785) 223600 E: richard.grigson@staffordchurches.uk

GRIMASON, The Very Revd Alistair John. b 57. CITC 76. d 79 p 80. C Belfast H Trin *Conn* 79–82; C Dublin Drumcondra w N Strand *D & G* 82–84; I Navan w Kentstown, Tara, Slane, Painestown etc *M & K* 84–91; Dioc Youth Officer (Meath) 90–94; Dioc Info Officer (Meath) 90–96; I Tullamore w Durrow, Newtownfertullagh, Rahan etc 91–00; Preb Tipper St Patr Cathl Dublin 92–00; Can Meath *M & K* 92–00; Chan Kildare Cathl 98–00; Dean Tuam *T, K & A* from 00; I Tuam w Cong and Aasleagh from 00; Dioc Communications Officer from 10; Dean Killala from 13; Dean Achonry from 13. *Deanery Place, Cong, Claremorris, Co Mayo, Republic of Ireland* T: (00353) (94) 954 6909 M: 85-282 1073 E: deantuam@yahoo.co.uk

GRIMLEY, The Very Revd Robert William. b 43. Ch Coll Cam BA 66 MA 70 Wadh Coll Ox BA 68 MA 76 UWE Hon DLitt 04 Bris Univ Hon LLD 09. Ripon Hall Ox 66. d 68 p 69. C Radlett *St Alb* 68–72; Chapl K Edw Sch Birm 72–84; Hon C Moseley St Mary *Birm* 72–84; V Edgbaston St Geo 84–97; Dean Bris 97–09; rtd 09; PtO *Ox* from 10. *88 Old High Street, Headington, Oxford OX3 9HW* T: (01865) 308219 E: robertgrimley88@gmail.com

GRIMSBY, Suffragan Bishop of. *See* COURT, The Rt Revd David Eric

GRIMSTER, Barry John. b 49. Ex Univ BA 70. Trin Coll Bris 72. d 74 p 75. C S Lambeth St Steph *S'wark* 74–77; C New Malden and Coombe 77–82; P-in-c Deptford St Jo 82–84; V Deptford St Jo w H Trin 84–89; V Woking St Pet *Guildf* 89–01; TR 02–13; rtd 13; PtO *Ex* 15–20. *16 Littlefield, Bishopsteignton, Teignmouth TQ14 9SG* T: (01626) 870921 E: bjgrimster@live.co.uk

GRIMWOOD, Canon David Walter. b 48. Lon Univ BA 70 K Coll Lon BD 73 AKC 73. d 74 p 75. C Newc St Geo 74–78; C Whorlton 78–80; TV Totton *Win* 80–93; Adv to Coun for Soc Resp Roch and *Cant* 93–02; Chief Exec Ch in Soc Roch and Cant 02–09; Hon Can Roch Cathl 97–09; PtO *Cant* from 09; Roch from 12. *56 Postley Road, Maidstone ME15 6TR* T: (01622) 764625 M: 07600-369681 E: dwgrimwood@gmail.com

GRINDROD (née UTTIN), Suzanne. b 72. Trin Coll Bris 09. d 11 p 12. C Lydney *Glouc* 11–15; P-in-c Ashchurch and Kemerton from 15. *14 Feltham Way, Tewkesbury GL20 5FQ* T: (01684) 293729 E: revsuttin@hotmail.co.uk

GRINDVOLL, Morten. b 92. Norwegian Sch of Th BA 14 Dur Univ MA 18. Westcott Ho Cam 15. d 17 p 18. C Ch the King *Newc* 17–18; TR Nord-Odal Norway from 19. *Granlivegen 451, 2210 Granli, Norway* T: (0047) 9570 9902 M: (0047) 4783 2010 E: morten.grindvoll@hotmail.com

GRINHAM, Julian Clive. b 39. Birkbeck Coll Lon BA 65. Oak Hill Th Coll 79. d 81 p 82. C Blackb Ch Ch w St Matt 81–83; Nat Sec Pathfinders CPAS 83–89; Dir CYPECS 89–94; V Normanton *Derby* 94–00; rtd 00; PtO Nor 01–17; Roch from 17. *104 Ralph Perring Court, Stone Park Avenue, Beckenham BR3 3LX* T: (020) 3105 2668 E: grinham@pobroadband.co.uk

GRINSTED, Richard Anthony. b 43. Leic Univ BSc 65. Oak Hill Th Coll 67. d 70 p 71. C Egham *Guildf* 70–73; C Woodford Wells *Chelmsf* 73–76; P-in-c Havering-atte-Bower 76–84; R Ditton *Roch* 84–94; R Chulmleigh *Ex* 94–96; R Chawleigh w Cheldon 94–96; R Wembworthy w Eggesford 94–96; R Chulmleigh, Chawleigh w Cheldon, Wembworthy etc 96–00; rtd 00. *Stone House, Village Road, Christow, Exeter EX6 7NF* T: (01647) 252653

GRISCOME, David. b 47. Oak Hill Th Coll BA 88 TCD Div Sch 89. **d** 89 **p** 90. C Glendermott *D & R* 89–91; I Clondehorkey w Cashel 91–95; I Mevagh w Glenalla 91–95; Bp's C Calry *K, E & A* 95–97; I 97–00; Dean Elphin and Ardagh 99–04; I Sligo w Knocknarea and Rosses Pt 99–04; PtO *Carol* 04–06; I Convoy w Monellan and Donaghmore *D & R* 06–13; Bp's Dom Chapl 07–13; rtd 13; Hon C Clondevaddock w Portsalon and Leatbeg *D & R* 16–21. *Keida's View, Cashel, Creeslough, Co Donegal, F92 T2W0, Republic of Ireland* E: keida@eircom.net *or* davidgriscome1@gmail.com

GROARKE, The Ven Nicola Jane. b 62. Lanc Univ BA 84. Ridley Hall Cam. **d** 00 **p** 01. C Balham Hill Ascension *S'wark* 00–08; V Canonbury St Steph *Lon* 08–14; Adn Dudley *Worc* from 14. *15 Worcester Road, Droitwich WR9 8AA* T/F: (01905) 773301 E: ngroarke@cofe-worcester.org.uk

GROOCOCK, Christopher John. b 59. Cardiff Univ MTh 12. St Jo Coll Nottm LTh 92. **d** 92 **p** 93. C Shawbury *Lich* 92–95; V Hengoed w Gobowen 95–00; CF 00–16; P-in-c Ashington *Newc* from 16. *Holy Sepulchre Vicarage, Wansbeck Road, Ashington NE63 8HZ* T: (01670) 813358 E: chrisgroocock@hotmail.com

GROOCOCK, Craig Ronald. Open Univ BA 11. WMMTC 03. **d** 05 **p** 06. C Kenilworth St Nic *Cov* 05–08; P-in-c Harbury and Ladbroke 08–19; AD Southam 11–15; V Shottery St Andr from 19. *St Andrew's Vicarage, Church Lane, Shottery, Stratford-upon-Avon CV37 9HQ* M: 07811-395169 E: kankudai43@aol.co.uk

GROOM, The Ven Susan Anne. b 63. Univ of Wales BA 85 Hughes Hall Cam MPhil 86 Lon Bible Coll MA 94 Open Univ MPhil 00 Dur Univ DThM 16. St Jo Coll Nottm 94. **d** 96 **p** 97. C Harefield *Lon* 96–99; C Eastcote St Lawr 99–01; P-in-c Yiewsley 01–03; V 03–07; Dir Lic Min Kensington Area 07–09; P-in-c Henlow and Langford *St Alb* 09–16; Asst Dir of Ords 09–11; Dir of Ords 11–16; Adn Wilts *Sarum* from 16; Can and Preb Sarum Cathl from 16. *Southbroom House, London Road, Devizes SN10 1LT* T: (01722) 438662 *or* (01380) 738097 E: adwilts@salisbury.anglican.org

GROOMBRIDGE, Jeremy Carl. b 55. CB 08. SEITE 13. **d** 15 **p** 16. NSM Sanderstead *S'wark* from 15. *Lothlorien, 7 Callow Field, Purley CR8 4DU* T: (020) 8668 7795 M: 07590-262866 E: jeremy@sanderstead-parish.org.uk

GROOMBRIDGE, Mrs Sonia Elizabeth. b 58. NTMTC. **d** 12 **p** 13. OLM Hornchurch St Andr *Chelmsf* 12–19; PtO from 19. *300 Goodwood Avenue, Hornchurch RM12 6DH* T: (01708) 440585 E: segroombridge@gmail.com

GROSSCURTH, Stephen. b 55. Sarum & Wells Th Coll 81. **d** 84 **p** 85. C Southport H Trin *Liv* 84–87; C Amblecote *Worc* 87–89; V Walton St Jo *Liv* 89–95; Chapl Univ Hosp of S Man NHS Foundn Trust 95–12; rtd 12. *68 Lincoln Close, Woolston, Warrington WA1 4LU* T: (01925) 821124

GROSSE, Anthony Charles Bain. b 30. Oak Hill Th Coll 58. **d** 61 **p** 62. C Chislehurst Ch Ch *Roch* 61–65; C Washfield *Ex* 65–71; TV Washfield, Stoodleigh, Withleigh etc 71–73; R Hemyock 73–86; P-in-c Clayhidon 76–86; R Hemyock w Culm Davy and Clayhidon 87–93; R Hemyock w Culm Davy, Clayhidon and Culmstock 93–96; rtd 96; PtO *Ex* 98–19. *8 Fore Street, Bampton, Tiverton EX16 9ND* T: (01398) 331981 E: tony.grosse@btinternet.com

GROSSE, Peter George. b 43. St Steph Ho Ox 02. **d** 03 **p** 04. NSM Reading St Matt *Ox* 03–06; NSM Tilehurst St Geo and St Mary 06–12; PtO from 12. *18 Rangewood Avenue, Reading RG30 3NN* T: 0118-959 4573 E: revdpetergrosse@talktalk.net

GROSSE, Canon Richard William. b 52. Mid Essex Tech Coll LLB 73 Solicitor 77. Ridley Hall Cam 86. **d** 88 **p** 89. C Soham *Ely* 88–91; C Bedale *Ripon* 91–93; C-in-c Thornton Watlass w Thornton Steward 91–93; V Barton and Manfield w Cleasby 93–95; V Barton and Manfield and Cleasby w Stapleton 95–99; R Keelby Gp *Linc* 99–04; R Callander *St And* 04–20; R Aberfoyle 04–20; Syn Clerk 15–20; Can St Ninian's Cathl Perth 15–20; rtd 20; Dioc Chapl to Rtd Clergy and Lay Readers *St And* from 20. *Oakbank, 14 Culbowie Crescent, Buchlyvie, Stirling FK8 3NH* T: (01360) 850012 E: richard_grosse@hotmail.com

GROSU, Iosif. b 60. Iasi Univ BTh 92. RC Inst Iasi. **d** 89 **p** 89. In RC Ch 89–93; C Darlington St Cuth *Dur* 96–99; C Stockton St Jo and Stockton St Jas 99–02; TV Ch the K 02–08; P-in-c Purston cum S Featherstone *Wakef* 08–09; P-in-c Featherstone 08–09; V 09–14; *Leeds* from 14. *St Thomas's House, 32 Victoria Street, Featherstone, Pontefract WF7 5EZ* T: (01977) 792280 E: iosifgrosu@btinternet.com

GROSVENOR, Royston Johannes Martin. b 47. K Coll Lon BD 70 AKC. **d** 71 **p** 72. C Pontesbury I and II *Heref* 71–75;

C Bishopston *Bris* 75–79; P-in-c Croydon St Pet S End *Cant* 79–81; V Croydon St Pet 81–84; V Croydon St Pet *S'wark* 85–87; R Merstham and Gatton 87–97; V Tidenham w Beachley and Lancaut *Glouc* 97–11; P-in-c St Briavels w Hewelsfield 05–11; AD Forest S 04–09; rtd 11; PtO *Bris* from 12; *B & W* from 14. *75 King's Drive, Bishopston, Bristol BS7 8JQ* T: 0117-924 7919 E: royston.grosvenor@hotmail.co.uk

GROVE, Lynn. b 43. Lon Univ MB, BS 67. Cranmer Hall Dur 03. **d** 04 **p** 05. NSM Pickering w Lockton and Levisham *York* 04–11; NSM Helmsley 12–17; NSM Upper Ryedale 12–17; rtd 17; PtO *York* from 18. *Hillcrest, Newton-on-Rawcliffe, Pickering YO18 8QA* T: (01751) 475928 E: revlynn625@gmail.com

GROVER, Helen Louise. b 66. ERMC 18. **d** 21. NSM Bradfield St Clare, Bradfield St George etc *St E* from 21. *Spring House, Cross End, Pebmarsh, Halstead CO9 2NU* T: (01787) 269223 M: 07775-434388 E: helengrover.pebmarsh@gmail.com

GROVER, Paul Anthony. b 53. St Mellitus Coll 15. **d** 17 **p** 18. C N Hinckford *Chelmsf* 17–21. *Spring House, Cross End, Pebmarsh, Halstead CO9 2NU* T: (01787) 269223 E: paulgrover.pebmarsh@gmail.com

GROVES, Caroline Anne. b 41. **d** 05 **p** 06. OLM Norbiton *S'wark* 05–11; PtO from 11; *Lon* from 15. *16 Beaufort Road, Kingston upon Thames KT1 2TQ* T: (020) 8549 1585 E: sicaro@blueyonder.co.uk

GROVES, Elizabeth Ann. b 36. Bp Otter Coll 94. **d** 97 **p** 09. NSM Soberton w Newtown *Portsm* 97–01; NSM Botley, Durley and Curdridge 01–06; NSM Wickham 06; NSM Shedfield and Wickham 07–12; rtd 12; PtO *Portsm* from 12. *54 Privett Road, Gosport PO12 3SU* T: (023) 9258 6168 E: rev.elizabeth@btinternet.com

GROVES, James Alan. b 32. CCC Cam BA 58 MA 62. Wells Th Coll 58. **d** 60 **p** 61. C Milton next Gravesend Ch Ch *Roch* 60–64; C Beckenham St Jas 64–66; V Orpington St Andr 66–98; rtd 98; PtO *Chich* from 98. *9 Wykeham Road, Hastings TN34 1UA* T: (01424) 200839

GROVES, Preb Jill. b 61. Univ Coll Lon BSc 82. St Jo Coll Nottm MA 93. **d** 93 **p** 94. C Tenbury Wells *Heref* 93–98; P-in-c Hope Bowdler w Eaton-under-Heywood 98–11; P-in-c Cardington 98–11; P-in-c Rushbury 98–11; Asst Chapl St Mich Hospice Hereford from 11; Preb Heref Cathl from 09. *St Michael's Hospice, Bartestree, Hereford HR1 4HA* T: (01432) 851000 E: jill@grovesfamily.org.uk

GROVES, Justin Simon John. b 69. Lon Bible Coll BA 93. Ridley Hall Cam 00. **d** 02 **p** 03. C Glouc St Cath 02–05; C Newport St Paul *Mon* 05–07; P-in-c 07–17; P-in-c Newport Maesglas St Paul w St Steph and H Trin from 17; AD Newport 16–21. *52 Oakfield Road, Newport NP20 4LX* T: (01633) 842317 E: justtherev@gmail.com

GROVES, Canon Peter John. b 70. New Coll Ox BA 92 MA 96 DPhil 96. Westcott Ho Cam 95. **d** 97 **p** 98. C Leigh-on-Sea St Marg *Chelmsf* 97–99; Lib Pusey Ho 99–01; Asst Chapl and Tutor Keble Coll Ox 01–02; Chapl and Fell BNC Ox 02–06; Hon C Ox St Mary Magd 01–04; P-in-c 05–13; V From 13; Hon Can Ch Ch from 16; Sen Research Fell Worc Coll Ox from 17; Asst Adn Ox from 18. *15 Beaumont Street, Oxford OX1 2NA* T: (01865) 247836 E: peter.groves@theology.ox.ac.uk

GROVES, Canon Philip Neil. b 62. Man Univ BA 84 Birm Univ PhD 10. St Jo Coll Nottm 86. **d** 88 **p** 89. C Holbeck *Ripon* 88–91; CMS 91–99; Lect St Phil Th Coll Kongwa Tanzania 93–98; Hon Can Mpwapwa from 98; TV Melton Mowbray *Leic* 99–05; Listening Process Facilitator on Human Sexuality Angl Communion 06–09; Project Dir for Continuing Indaba 09–16; PtO *Ox* 15–16; C Wychert Vale from 16. *7 Badgers Rise, Stone, Aylesbury HP17 8RR* T: (01296) 748390 M: 07875-438244 E: drphilgroves@gmail.com

GROVES, Robert John. b 42. Trin Coll Bris 74. **d** 76 **p** 77. C Norwood St Luke *S'wark* 76–79; P-in-c Clapham Park All SS 79–86; V Anerley *Roch* 86–95; TV Canford Magna *Sarum* 95–98; TR Tollington *Lon* 98–02; rtd 02; PtO *Cant* 02–09; *Roch* 02–15; *Chich* from 15. *23 Ramsay Hall, 9-13 Byron Road, Worthing BN11 3HN*

GRUBB, Greville Alexander (Alex). b 36. Saltley Tr Coll Birm CertEd 60. St Jo Coll Nottm 72. **d** 74 **p** 75. C Rushden w Newton Bromswold *Pet* 74–77; Chapl St D Coll Llandudno 77–89; Chapl Casterton Sch Lancs 90–96; rtd 96; PtO *Blackb* 96–11; *Bradf* 02–14; *Leeds* 14–16; *Chich* from 15. *5 Cambridge Lodge, 10 Southey Road, Worthing BN11 3HT* T: (01903) 368580

GRUMBALL, Kevin Shaun. b 56. St Steph Ho Ox. **d** 11 **p** 12. NSM Temple Grafton w Binton *Cov* 11–15; NSM Exhall w Wixford 11–15; NSM Salford Priors 11–15; NSM Heart of England 15–19; NSM Vale and Cotswold Edge *Glouc* from 19. *Stone Croft, Ardens Grafton, Alcester B49 6DR*

GRUNDY, Anthony Brian. b 36. Pemb Coll Cam BA 62 MA 87. Ridley Hall Cam 61. **d** 63 **p** 64. C Hatcham St Jas *S'wark* 63–66; C Margate H Trin *Cant* 66–68; C Brixton Hill St Sav *S'wark* 68–70; V Assington *St E* 70–76; TV Much Wenlock w Bourton *Heref* 76–81; TV Wenlock 81–82; TR 82–88; RD Condover 86–88; R Burghfield *Ox* 88–02; rtd 02; PtO *Chich* from 03. *18 Victoria Court, Henley-on-Thames RG9 1XG*

GRUNDY, Canon Christopher John. b 49. ACA 72 FCA 79. Trin Coll Bris 74. **d** 77 **p** 78. C Maidstone St Luke *Cant* 77–81; Argentina 81–82; Chile 82–84; PtO *Guildf* 84–95; C Seale 95; NSM Guildf Ch Ch w St Martha-on-the-Hill 96–99; C Shere, Albury and Chilworth 99–06; TV Drypool *York* 06–12; rtd 12; PtO *Guildf* from 16; Hon Can Wusasa Nigeria from 03. *The Lyttons, Elstead Road, Seale, Farnham GU10 1HZ* E: chris@grundy.org.uk

GRUNDY, Judith Michal Towers Mynors. b 54. Lady Spencer Chu Coll of Educn CertEd 76 Ox Univ BEd 77. Trin Coll Bris 85. **d** 93 **p** 94. NSM Kensal Rise St Mark and St Martin *Lon* 93–95; NSM Snettisham w Ingoldisthorpe and Fring *Nor* 95–04; R Denver and Ryston w Roxham etc *Ely* 04–19; rtd 19. *Address temp unknown*

GRUNDY, Canon Malcolm Leslie. b 44. Open Univ BA 76 Leeds Univ PhD 14. St Boniface Warminster AKC 68. **d** 69 **p** 70. C Doncaster St Geo *Sheff* 69–72; Ind Chapl 72–80; Dir of Educn *Lon* 80–86; TR Huntingdon *Ely* 86–91; Hon Can Ely Cathl 88–94; Dir Avec 91–94; Adn Craven *Bradf* 94–05; Dir Foundn for Ch Leadership 05–09; rtd 09; PtO *York* from 09. *11 Givendale Grove, York YO10 3QF* T: (01904) 422999 M: 07341-262045 E: mlgweg@gmail.com

GRUNDY, Paul. b 55. BD 77 AKC. Linc Th Coll 79. **d** 80 **p** 81. C Ryhope *Dur* 80–82; C Ferryhill 82–85; TV Cramlington *Newc* 85–87; TV Swinton and Pendlebury *Man* 87–90; V Wingate Grange *Dur* 90–95; R Willington and Sunnybrow 95–07; P-in-c Usworth 07–09; R 09–13; rtd 13; PtO *Dur* from 13. *14 Kellsway, Gateshead NE10 8NB* E: p-grundy@ntlworld.com

GRUNDY, Simon. b 80. St Jo Coll Dur BA 02. Cranmer Hall Dur 15. **d** 17 **p** 18. C Herrington, Penshaw and Shiney Row *Dur* 17–19; C Chester le Street 19–21; P-in-c Consett from 21. *Spring House, Knitsley Nook, Consett DH8 9EE* E: revsimongrundy@gmail.com

GRÜNEBERG, Keith Nigel. See BEECH-GRÜNEBERG, Keith Nigel

GRÜNEWALD, Gottfried Johannes. b 38. Loyola Univ Chicago MPS 92. Th Faculty Frankfurt 66. **d** 69 **p** 69. Denmark 70–95; C Dunbar *Edin* 95–97; R Dollar *St And* 98–05; rtd 05. *Teglparken 8, 8860 Ulstrup, Denmark* T: (0045) 864 6341 E: grunewald@email.dk

GRYLLS, Canon Catherine Anne. b 70. **d** 00 **p** 01. C Hall Green St Pet *Birm* 00–04; P-in-c Balsall Heath St Paul 04–07; P-in-c Edgbaston SS Mary and Ambrose 04–07; P-in-c Balsall Heath and Edgbaston SS Mary and Ambrose 07–08; V 08–16; PtO 16–17; AD Moseley 13–17; V Stirchley from 17; Warden of Readers from 17; AD Kings Norton, Moseley and Shirley 21; Hon Can Birm Cathl from 15. *18 Pineapple Grove, Birmingham B30 2TJ* T: 0121-443 1371 E: gryllsc@btinternet.com

GRYLLS, Canon Michael John. b 38. Qu Coll Cam BA 62 MA 66. Linc Th Coll 62. **d** 64 **p** 65. C Sheff Gillcar St Silas 64–67; C-in-c Dunscroft CD 67–70; V Herringthorpe 70–78; V Amport, Grateley, Monxton and Quarley *Win* 78–89; RD Andover 85–89; V Whitchurch w Tufton and Litchfield 89–03; Hon Can Win Cathl 01–03; rtd 03; PtO *Worc* from 04. *41 Church Street, Evesham WR11 1DY* T: (01386) 442086

GUBBINS, Andrew Martin. b 65. York Univ BA 86 Keele Univ 93. St Jo Coll Nottm LTh 93. **d** 96 **p** 97. C Harrogate St Mark *Ripon* 96–00; P-in-c Osmondthorpe St Phil 00–03; V Leeds All SS w Osmondthorpe 03–09; P-in-c Chippenham St Pet *Bris* from 09. *St Peter's Vicarage, 32 Lords Mead, Chippenham SN14 0LL* T: (01249) 448530 E: gubbinsrevs@sky.com

GUBBINS (née O'BRIEN), Mrs Mary Veronica. b 68. Leeds Univ BSc 90. St Jo Coll Nottm BTh 93. **d** 94 **p** 95. C Middleton St Mary *Ripon* 94–96; C Bilton 96–99; PtO 99–09; *Bris* 10–19; NSM By Brook 19–20; TV Gtr Corsham and Lacock from 20. *St Peter's Vicarage, 32 Lords Mead, Chippenham SN14 0LL* T: (01249) 448530

GUDGEON, Canon Michael John. b 40. Qu Coll Cam BA 63 MA 67. Chich Th Coll 65. **d** 66 **p** 67. C Kings Heath *Birm* 66–72; Asst Chapl K Edw Sch Birm 69–72; Chapl and Tutor Cuddesdon Coll 72–75; V Hawley H Trin *Guildf* 75–80; V Minley 75–80; Adult Educn Adv *Chich* 80–87; Can Res Portsm Cathl 87–90; Dioc Dir of Educn 87–90; V Hove St Thos *Chich* 90–93; TV Hove 93–94; Bp's Chapl *Eur* 94–98; Dir of Ords 94–97; Can Gib Cathl 96–06; P-in-c Worthing St Andr *Chich* 98–05; rtd 05; PtO *Chich* 15–21; *S'wark* from

16; *Roch* from 16; *Eur* from 18. *36 Ariel Court, Essenden Road, Belvedere DA17 5EG* E: michaelgudgeon@aol.com

GUERNSEY, Dean of. See BARKER, The Very Revd Timothy Reed

GUEST, Miss Alexandra Jodie. b 92. Heythrop Coll Lon BA 14 Dur Univ MA 17. Ridley Hall Cam 15. **d** 17 **p** 18. C Waltham H Cross *Chelmsf* 17–20; P-in-c Marks Gate from 20; P-in-c Romford Ascension Collier Row from 20. *15 Deer Park Way, Waltham Abbey EN9 3YN* T: (01992) 679332 M: 07393-203544 E: alexandrajguest@gmail.com

GUEST, David Andrew. b 61. Chich Th Coll BTh 92. **d** 92 **p** 93. C Prenton *Ches* 92–94; C Ches H Trin 94–97; Assoc P Douglas All SS and St Thos *S & M* 97–00; Dioc Communications Officer 97–00; Relig Adv Manx Radio 97–00; Bp's Dom Chapl *S & M* 98–00; Dioc Communications Officer *Chich* 00–09; C Hove 00–03; C Southwick 03–09; P-in-c Heathfield 09–13; V 13–16; TV Mortlake w E Sheen *S'wark* 16–20; V Otford *Roch* from 20. *The Vicarage, The Green, Otford, Sevenoaks TN14 5PD* T: (01959) 523185 E: otfordvicar@gmail.com

GUEST, Derek William. b 55. NOC 90. **d** 93 **p** 94. C Cheadle Hulme St Andr *Ches* 93–99; V 99–16; V Runcorn All SS w H Trin from 16; RD Frodsham from 18. *The Vicarage, 1 Highlands Road, Runcorn WA7 4PS* T: (01928) 572417 M: 07941-874259 E: revdguest@yahoo.co.uk

GUEST, Miss Elizabeth Judy. b 76. Qu Foundn Birm 16. **d** 18 **p** 19. C Oxhey All SS *St Alb* from 18. *14 The Hoe, Watford WD19 5AY* T: (020) 3270 0091 M: 07545-328187 E: lizzie_1976@hotmail.co.uk

GUEST, Ernest Anthony. b 64. NTMTC 99. **d** 02 **p** 03. C Gt Ilford St Jo *Chelmsf* 02–05; V Barkingside St Laur 05–13; P-in-c Tye Green w Netteswell 13–19; P-in-c Ashingdon w S Fambridge, Canewdon and Paglesham from 19. *35 Henry Crescent, Rochford SS4 1GU* T: (01702) 904558 M: 07810-516356 E: ernieguest@btinternet.com

GUEST, Canon Helen. b 54. Totley Thornbridge Coll CertEd 75 Nottm Univ MA 02. EMMTC 99. **d** 02 **p** 03. NSM Brimington *Derby* 02–05; C Hatton 05–07; P-in-c Killamarsh 07–13; C Barlborough and Renishaw 07–13; R Killamarsh and Renishaw from 13; RD Bolsover and Staveley 11–16; Hon Can Derby Cathl from 12. *The Rectory, Sheepcote Road, Killamarsh, Sheffield S21 1DU* T: 0114-248 2769 E: revsguest@btinternet.com *or* revshmguest@gmail.com

GUEST, Michael. b 52. EMMTC. **d** 99 **p** 00. NSM Heath *Derby* 99–07; NSM Killamarsh and Barlborough and Renishaw 07–13. *The Rectory, Sheepcote Road, Killamarsh, Sheffield S21 1DU* T: 0114-248 2769 E: revsguest@btinternet.com *or* revshmguest@gmail.com

GUEST, Mrs Sharon Michelle. b 62. St Jo Coll Nottm. **d** 12 **p** 13. C Chigwell and Chigwell Row *Chelmsf* 12–16; C Gt Parndon 16–19; C Rochford and Sutton w Shopland 19; C Gt Wakering w Foulness 19; C Barling w Lt Wakering 19; TV Roach Par from 19. *35 Henry Crescent, Rochford SS4 1GU* T: (01702) 904557 E: sharonguest07@btinternet.com

GUILDEA, Rebecca Ghislane. K Coll Lon BA 10 TCD MTh 17. **d** 16 **p** 17. Dublin Zion Ch *D & G* 16–17; NSM Greystones from 17. *64 Redford Park, Greystones, Co Wicklow, Republic of Ireland* M: (00353) 85-819 4377 E: rebeccaguildea@gmail.com

GUILDER, Matthew William Alan. b 87. Ches Univ BA 08 St Jo Coll Dur BA 20. Cranmer Hall Dur 17. **d** 20 **p** 21. C Lancaster St Thos *Blackb* from 20. *6 Beechwood Gardens, Lancaster LA1 4PH* M: 07828-903795 E: mattguilder@gmail.com

GUILDFORD, Bishop of. See WATSON, The Rt Revd Andrew John

GUILDFORD, Dean of. See GWILLIAMS, The Very Revd Dianna Lynn

GUILFORD, John Edward. b 50. S & M Dioc Tr Inst 94. **d** 99 **p** 00. OLM Lonan *S & M* 99–12; OLM Laxey 99–12; OLM Onchan, Lonan and Laxey 12–15; NSM Douglas St Geo and All SS 15–17; NSM Douglas St Ninian from 17. *14 Harbour View, Onchan, Isle of Man IM3 2AN* M: 07624-353475 E: revjohnnyg@manx.net

GUILIANO, Zachary Morgan. b 86. Evangel Univ (USA) BA 09 Harvard Univ MDiv 12 St Jo Coll Cam PhD 16. Westcott Ho Cam 15. **d** 17 **p** 18. C Cambridge St Benedict *Ely* 17–20; Asst Chapl Jes Coll Cam 19–20; Chapl St Edm Hall Ox from 20; LtO *Ox* from 20. *2A Crick Road, Oxford OX2 6QJ* M: 07986-816854 E: zachary.guiliano@seh.ox.ac.uk

GUILLE, The Very Revd John Arthur. b 49. Southn Univ BTh 79. Sarum & Wells Th Coll 73. **d** 76 **p** 77. C Chandler's Ford *Win* 76–80; P-in-c Bournemouth St Jo 80–84; P-in-c Bournemouth St Mich 83–84; V Bournemouth St Jo w St Mich 84–89; R Guernsey St Andr 89–99; Adn Win 99–07; Can Res Win Cathl 99–07; Dean S'well 07–14; rtd 14; PtO *Win* from 14. *Pelerins, La Planque Road, St Martin, Guernsey GY4 6TH* T: (01481) 237168

GUILLEBAUD, Mrs Jette Margaret (Maggie). b 48. Ex Univ BA 70 UWE Hon MA 98 Ox Univ BTh 08 FRSA 95. Ripon Coll Cuddesdon 03. d 05 p 06. NSM Sarum Cathl 05–12; Asst Chapl Sarum Coll 10–12; Chapl Ch Ho *Sarum* from 12. *178 The Close, Salisbury SP1 2EZ* T: (01722) 411922 M: 07985-576739 E: maggieguillebaud@gmail.com

GUILLEBAUD, Canon Margaret Jean. b 43. MBE 03. Edin Univ BSc 66. Cranmer Hall Dur 79. dss 80 d 87 p 94. New Malden and Coombe *S'wark* 80–84; Carlton Colville w Mutford and Rushmere *Nor* 84–91; Par Dn 87–91; Par Dn Rodbourne Cheney *Bris* 91–94; C 94–95; CMS Rwanda 95–08; rtd 08; PtO *Birm* from 08; Can Res Byumba 10–15; PtO *Sarum* from 21. *7 Poplar Road, Dorridge, Solihull B93 8DD* T: (01564) 770113 E: mguillebaud@gmail.com

GUILLEMIN, Thierry Jean-Louis. b 62. Coll of Resurr Mirfield 08. d 01 p 01. In RC Ch 01–07; PtO *Wakef* 08–09; C Heckmondwike 09–11; C Liversedge w Hightown 09–11; P-in-c Wibsey St Paul *Bradf* 11–14; Leeds 14–17; V from 17. *St Paul's Vicarage, 42A Wibsey Park Avenue, Bradford BD6 3QA* T: (01274) 676359 M: 07778-577008 E: t.guillemin@btinternet.com

GUINNESS, Alexander. *See* GUINNESS, Graham Alexander

GUINNESS, Christopher Paul. b 43. Lon Coll of Div 64. d 67 p 68. C Farnborough *Guildf* 67–70; C Tulse Hill H Trin *S'wark* 70–74; C Worting *Win* 74–78; P-in-c S Lambeth St Steph *S'wark* 78–89; V 89–91; RD Lambeth 86–90; C Ches Square St Mich w St Phil *Lon* 91–97; Living Waters Trust 98–00; Chapl Ealing Hosp NHS Trust 00–01; Chapl Hammersmith Hosps NHS Trust 01–08; Chapl Imp Coll Healthcare NHS Trust 08–10; rtd 10; PtO *Win* from 15. *Ashley Cottage, Station Road, Sway, Lymington SO41 6AA* T: (01590) 682463 E: christopherguinness@live.co.uk

GUINNESS, Canon Garry Grattan. b 40. Em Coll Cam BA 64 MA 68. Ridley Hall Cam 64. d 66 p 67. C Wallington *S'wark* 66–69; C St Marylebone All So w SS Pet and Jo *Lon* 69–72; P-in-c Clifton H Trin, St Andr and St Pet *Bris* 72–79; V Watford St Luke *St Alb* 79–90; TR Worthing Ch the King *Chich* 90–05; Hon Can Kigeme from 02; rtd 05; PtO *Sarum* from 05. *37 Stowell Crescent, Wareham BH20 4PT* T: (01929) 550215 E: gguinness@talktalk.net

GUINNESS, Graham Alexander. b 60. Edin Th Coll 82. d 85 p 86. Dioc Youth Chapl *Mor* 85–88; C Elgin w Lossiemouth 85–88; Asst P Glas St Ninian 88–90; R Tighnabruaich *Arg* 90–91 and 94–99; R Dunoon 90–99; Miss to Seamen 90–99; R Fort William *Arg* from 99. *St Andrew's Rectory, Parade Road, Fort William PH33 6BA* T/F: (01397) 702979 E: ftwilliam@argyll.anglican.org or alexinness@ymail.com

GUINNESS, Canon Peter Grattan. b 49. Man Univ BSc 71 CertEd 73. St Jo Coll Nottm 80. d 82 p 83. C Normanton *Wakef* 82–87; V Fletchamstead *Cov* 87–91; V Lancaster St Thos *Blackb* 91–10; Hon Can Blackb Cathl 04–10; P-in-c Gillingham St Mark *Roch* 10–14; rtd 14; PtO *Roch* from 15. *56 Malvern Road, Gillingham ME7 4BB* E: peter.guinness@yahoo.co.uk

GUINNESS, Sarah Helen. b 76. Cant Ch Ch Univ Coll BSc 98. STETS 11. d 14 p 15. C Buckhurst Hill *Chelmsf* 14–18; P-in-c Brentford *Lon* from 18; AD Hounslow 20–21. *The Rectory, 3 The Butts, Brentford TW8 8BJ* T: (020) 8568 7442 E: sarah.guinness@gmx.com

GUISE, John Christopher. b 29. Cheltenham & Glouc Coll of HE MA 94 MRPharmS 51. WMMTC 80. d 83 p 84. NSM Alfrick, Lulsley, Suckley, Leigh and Bransford *Worc* 83–94; NSM Martley and Wichenford, Knightwick etc 94–00; PtO from 00. *Marsh Cottage, Leigh, Worcester WR6 5LE* T: (01886) 832336

GUISE, Stephen. b 48. Win Sch of Art BA 75. Chich Th Coll 85. d 87 p 88. C Bexhill St Pet *Chich* 87–90; TV Haywards Heath St Wilfrid 90–94; V Kirdford 94–97; Chapl Community of Servants of the Cross 97–01; P-in-c Amberley w N Stoke and Parham, Wiggonholt etc *Chich* 99–07; TV Bridport *Sarum* 03–07; PtO *Chich* 07–09; P-in-c Sidlesham 09–21. *Address withheld by request* E: frstephenguise@gmail.com

GUITE, Ayodeji Malcolm. b 57. Pemb Coll Cam BA 80 MA 84 Newc Poly PGCE 82 Dur Univ PhD 93. Ridley Hall Cam 88. d 90 p 91. C Ely 90–93; TV Huntingdon 93–98; Chapl Anglia Poly Univ 98–03; Chapl Girton Coll Cam 03–20; Life Fell from 20; rtd 20; PtO *Ely* from 21. *Melrose Cottage, 1 Kimberley Road, North Walsham NR28 9DZ* E: mg320@cam.ac.uk

GUITE, Mrs Frances Clare. b 56. Leeds Univ BA 08. Coll of Resurr Mirfield 06. d 08 p 09. C Westleigh St Pet *Man* 08–11; C Westleigh St Paul 09–11; P-in-c Castleton Moor 11–16; V from 16; AD Heywood and Middleton 16–20. *St Martin's Vicarage, Vicarage Road North, Rochdale OL11 2TE* T: (01706) 632353 M: 07791-328624 E: francesguite@yahoo.co.uk

GUITE, Canon Margaret Ann. b 53. Girton Coll Cam BA 74 MA 78 St Jo Coll Dur PhD 81. Cranmer Hall Dur 75. dss 79 d 87 p 94. Warlingham w Chelsham and Farleigh *S'wark* 79–82; Cherry Hinton St Jo *Ely* 82–86; Tutor Westcott Ho Cam 82–90; Tutor Wesley Ho Cam 87–90; NSM Ely 90–93; NSM Chettisham 90–93; NSM Prickwillow 90–93; NSM Huntingdon 93–99; V Fenstanton 99–06; V Hilton 99–06; RD Huntingdon 05–06; P-in-c Cambridge St Mark 06–15; TR Linton 15–21; Hon Can Ely Cathl 04–21; rtd 21. *Melrose Cottage, 1 Kimberley Road, North Walsham NR28 9DZ* E: margaret.guite@icloud.com

GUIVER, George Paul Alfred. b 45. St Chad's Coll Dur BA 68. Cuddesdon Coll 71. d 73 p 74. C Mill End and Heronsgate w W Hyde *St Alb* 73–76; P-in-c Bishop's Frome *Heref* 76–82; P-in-c Castle Frome 76–82; P-in-c Acton Beauchamp and Evesbatch w Stanford Bishop 76–82; CR from 83; Superior CR 02–18; Lic to Offic *Wakef* 85–14; LtO *Leeds* from 14. *House of the Resurrection, Stocks Bank Road, Mirfield WF14 0BN* T: (01924) 483317 E: gguiver@mirfield.org.uk

GUIVER, Roger William Antony. b 53. Edin Univ MA 75 St Chad's Coll Dur BA 78. Coll of Resurr Mirfield. d 82 p 83. C Rekendyke *Dur* 82–85; Chapl Middlesbrough Gen Hosp 85–91; Chapl S Tees Acute Hosps NHS Trust 92–93; P-in-c Middlesbrough St Columba w St Paul *York* 85–94; V Acomb Moor 94–97; V Middlesbrough St Thos 97–00. *Swang Farm, Glaisdale, Whitby YO21 2QZ* T: (01947) 897210

GULL, William John. b 42. Ripon Hall Ox 63. d 65 p 66. C Worksop Priory *S'well* 65–69; C Newark St Mary 69–71; P-in-c Mansfield St Lawr 71–77; V 77–78; Chapl HM YOI Lowdham Grange 78–90; R Lambley *S'well* 78–91; V Sneinton St Cypr 91–99; rtd 99; PtO *S'well* 03–11. *37 Hazel Grove, Mapperley, Nottingham NG3 6DQ* T: 0115-920 8071 E: wjgull@btopenworld.com

GULLAND, Ian Robertson. b 77. Sheff Univ MEng 99 Univ of Florida MBA 02 Wycliffe Hall Ox MA 19. 14. d 17 p 18. C St Austell *Truro* 17–21; P-in-c Fowey 19–20; R Padstow, St Merryn and St Issey w St Petroc Minor from 21. *Address withheld by request* T: (01841) 534898 E: pmilbenefice1235@outlook.com

GULLAND, John Robertson. b 46. Open Univ BA 76 Chelsea Coll Lon MA 82 Avery Hill Coll CertEd 70 ACIB. Oak Hill Th Coll 88. d 90 p 91. NSM Woodside Park St Barn *Lon* 90–92; LtO *S & M* 91–09; NSM Castletown 92–09; Chapl K Wm's Coll Is of Man 92–09; P-in-c Corfu *Eur* 09–12; PtO *S & M* from 13; Dir Studies from 14; PtO *Eur* from 18. *3 Snaefell House, Promenade, Port Erin, Isle of Man IM9 6LE* T: (01624) 834548 E: gulland@talk21.com

GULLIDGE, Philip Michael Nowell. b 60. Univ of Wales (Swansea) BSc 82 Univ of Wales (Cardiff) BD 93. St Mich Coll Llan 90. d 93 p 94. C Neath w Llantwit *Llan* 93–97; V Treharris w Bedlinog 97–03; V Treharris, Trelewis and Bedlinog 04–08; V Llantwit Fardre 08–20; TV Llantrisant from 20. *The Vicarage, Church Village, Pontypridd CF38 1EP* T: (01443) 202538 E: philipgullidge@aol.com

GULLIFORD, Canon William Douglas FitzGerald. b 69. Selw Coll Cam BA 91 MA 95. Westcott Ho Cam. d 94 p 95. C Banstead *Guildf* 94–97; C Wilton Place St Paul *Lon* 97–00; Chapl Guildhall Sch of Music and Drama 97–01; P-in-c St Dunstan in the West 00–08; V 08–12; Gen Sec Angl and E Churches Assn 00–05; Bp's Chapl *Lon* 00–02; R St Mary le Strand w St Clem Danes 02–08; Bp's Chapl for E Orthodox Affairs 02–12; V Regent's Park St Mark from 12; Dioc Dir of Ords *Eur* from 03; Hon Can from 12; PtO from 03. *St Mark's Vicarage, 4 Regent's Park Road, London NW1 7TX* T: (020) 7485 6340 E: william.gulliford@london.anglican.org

GULLY, Mrs Carol Glenys. b 57. Coll of Ripon & York St Jo BEd 79. NOC 02. d 05 p 06. NSM Castleton Moor *Man* 05–09; NSM Kirkholt 09–10; Asst Chapl Pennine Acute Hosps NHS Trust 08–10; PtO *Portsm* 10–11; NSM Portsea St Cuth from 11; Asst Chapl Portsm Hosps NHS Trust 12–13; Chapl The Rowans Hospice from 13. *The Rectory, 27 Farlington Avenue, Cosham, Portsmouth PO6 1DF* T: (023) 9237 5145 or 9225 0001 E: revdcarolgully@gmail.com or carol.gully@rowanshospice.co.uk

GULLY, Canon Paul David. b 59. Shoreditch Coll Lon BEd 81. Trin Coll Bris BA 95. d 95 p 96. C Radcliffe *Man* 95–99; TV New Bury 99–05; V Oakenrod and Bamford 05–10; R Farlington *Portsm* from 10; Hon Can Ho Ghana from 17. *The Rectory, 27 Farlington Avenue, Cosham, Portsmouth PO6 1DF* T: (023) 9237 5145 E: paul@farlingtonparish.co.uk

GUMBEL, Jonathan Philip. b 82. Oriel Coll Ox BA 05. NTMTC 07. d 09 p 10. C Brighton St Pet *Chich* from 09. *9 St Peter's Place, Brighton BN1 4SA* T: (01273) 698182

GUMBEL, Nicholas Glyn Paul. b 55. Trin Coll Cam MA 76. Wycliffe Hall Ox MA 86. d 86 p 87. C Brompton H Trin w Onslow Square St Paul *Lon* 86–05; V 05–11; V Onslow Square and S Kensington St Aug from 11; V S Kensington St Luke from 21. *Holy Trinity Vicarage, 73 Princes Gate Mews, London SW7 2PP* T: (020) 7052 0263 *or* 7052 0264 F: 7589 3390 E: nicky.gumbel@htb.org.uk

GUNASEKERA, Nilanka Keith (Kit). b 72. Ridley Hall Cam 04. **d** 06 **p** 07. C Brentford *Lon* 06–09; P-in-c Clapham St Jas *S'wark* 09–20; V from 20. *The Vicarage, 8A West Road, London SW4 7DN* T: (020) 7652 0882 M: 07948-397114 E: kit.gunasekera2014@gmail.com

GUNDERSON, Ross. b 79. Westcott Ho Cam 13. **d** 15 **p** 16. C Dulwich St Barn *S'wark* 15–18; V Fulham St Etheldreda w St Clem *Lon* from 18; C Fulham All SS 18–19. *St Etheldreda's Vicarage, Doneraile Road, London SW6 6EL* T: (020) 7736 3809 M: 07962-274381 E: gunderson_ross@hotmail.com *or* vicar@stethsfulham.org

GUNN, Edward James. b 76. Dur Univ BA 08 BA 21. Lindisfarne Coll of Th 18. **d** 21. NSM Auckland St Helen *Dur* from 21. *60 Cinnamon Drive, Trimdon Station TS29 6NY* T: (01429) 881844 M: 07926-086537 E: edwardgunn76@outlook.com *or* st.helen.curate@gmail.com

GUNN, Jeffrey Thomas. b 47. St Chad's Coll Dur BA 77 Kent Univ MA 95. Coll of Resurr Mirfield 77. **d** 79 **p** 80. C Prestbury *Glouc* 79–82; P-in-c Coldham, Elm and Friday Bridge *Ely* 82–87; V Larkfield *Roch* 87–94; P-in-c Leybourne 87–94; V Petts Wood 94–99; Dean Ballarat Australia 99–04; V Eastbourne St Sav and St Pet *Chich* 05–15; RD Eastbourne 10–15; rtd 15; PtO *Glouc* from 16. *4 Victoria Circus, Tewkesbury GL20 5GF* T: (01684) 290972

GUNN-JOHNSON, The Ven David Allan. b 49. Lambeth STh 85 MA 95. St Steph Ho Ox 79. **d** 81 **p** 82. C Oxhey St Matt *St Alb* 81–84; C Cheshunt 84–88; TR Colyton, Southleigh, Offwell, Widworthy etc *Ex* 88–03; RD Honiton 90–96; Preb Ex Cathl 99–03; Adn Barnstaple 03–14; Warden of Readers 04–14; rtd 14; Hon PV Ex Cathl from 18. *12 Hylton Gardens, Exeter EX4 2QE* T: (01392) 496877 M: 07921-150428 E: dgunnjohnson549@btinternet.com

GUNNER, Canon Laurence François Pascal. b 36. Keble Coll Ox BA 59 MA 63. Wells Th Coll 59. **d** 61 **p** 62. C Charlton Kings St Mary *Glouc* 61–65; C Hemel Hempstead *St Alb* 65–69; Hd RE Adeyfield Secondary Modern Sch 67–69; Chapl Bloxham Sch 69–86; Chapl Tudor Hall Sch 70–84; Sen Chapl Marlborough Coll 86–96; Can Windsor 96–06; Can Steward 97–06; rtd 06; LtO *Mor* from 07; PtO *Eur* 05–20. *Contin Mains, Contin, Strathpeffer IV14 9ES* T/F: (01997) 421996 M: 07836-369729 E: laurence@gunner.co.uk

GUNNER, Canon Susanna Mary. b 58. St Jo Coll Dur BA 80 Anglia Ruskin Univ MA 10 SS Coll Cam PGCE 81. ERMC 05. **d** 08 **p** 09. Dioc Lay Development and Tr Co-ord *Nor* 07–16; C N Walsham and Edingthorpe 08–11; NSM 13–16; Bp's Chapl 16–19; Dioc Spirituality and Discipleship Adv from 19; Hon PV Nor Cathl 16–20; Hon Can Nor Cathl from 20; Chapl to The Queen from 20. *Diocesan House, 109 Dereham Road, Easton, Norwich NR9 5ES* T: 614172 *or* (01603) 880853 E: susanna.gunner@gmail.com *or* susanna.gunner@dioceseofnorwich.org

GUNSTONE, Peter Wilfrid. b 77. Leeds Univ BA 99 St Jo Coll Dur BA 18 MA 19. Cranmer Hall Dur 16. **d** 19 **p** 20. C Bradf City Cen Resource Ch *Leeds* from 19. *35 Scarborough Road, Shipley BD18 3DW* M: 07932-792373 E: petegunstone@gmail.com

GUNTER, Benjamin Luke William. b 65. Coll of Ripon & York St Jo BEd 89. Cranmer Hall Dur 15. **d** 17 **p** 18. C Norton juxta Malton *York* 17–21; P-in-c Stokesley w Seamer from 21. *The Rectory, Leven Close, Stokesley, Middlesbrough TS9 5AP* M: 07902-670311 E: revbengunter@gmail.com

GUNTER, Timothy Wilson. b 37. Leeds Univ BA 59 St Jo Coll Cam BA 62 MA 66. Ridley Hall Cam 59. **d** 62 **p** 63. C Beverley Minster *York* 62–65; C Hornsea and Goxhill 65–70; V Silsden *Bradf* 70–80; V Sunninghill *Ox* 80–03; rtd 03; PtO *Worc* from 04. *2 Hillstone Court, Victoria Road, Malvern WR14 2TE* T: (01684) 899377 E: gunters@gmail.com

GUNTON, Helen Louise. b 71. Lanc Univ BA 93. Sarum Coll MA 17. **d** 17 **p** 18. NSM Jersey St Ouen w St Geo *Win* 17–20; P-in-c Jersey Grouville from 20. *Grouville Rectory, La Rue a Don, Grouville, Jersey JE3 9GB* M: 07700-339356 E: hlgunton@gmail.com

GURD, Brian Charles (Simon). b 44. Sarum & Wells Th Coll 72. **d** 74 **p** 75. OSP from 67; LtO *Win* 74–82; Prior Alton Abbey 79–82; C Shepherd's Bush St Steph w St Thos *Lon* 82–84; NSM Willesborough *Cant* 85–87; V Bethersden w High Halden 87–95; R Etchingham and V Hurst Green *Chich* 95–97; V Langney 97–01; R Yarm *York* 01–10; rtd 10; PtO *Chich* 11–15; *Leeds* from 15. *27 Jubilee Road, Aiskew, Bedale DL8 1FD* T: (01677) 427440 E: simongurd@btinternet.com

GURNER (formerly RAVEN), Mrs Margaret Ann. b 54. Westmr Univ BSc 76 City Univ MSc 87 Anglia Ruskin Univ BA 08.

Ridley Hall Cam 03. **d** 05 **p** 06. C Woodhall Spa Gp *Linc* 05–08; P-in-c Cheveley *Ely* 08–12; P-in-c Wood Ditton w Saxon Street 08–12; P-in-c Kirtling 08–12; P-in-c Ashley w Silverley 08–12; rtd 12; PtO *B & W* 12–16; C Norton sub Hamdon, W Chinnock, Chiselborough etc 16–17; C Stoke sub Hamdon 16–17; C Odcombe, Brympton, Lufton and Montacute 16–17; C Ham Hill Villages from 17. *Parish Office, 1 Castle Street, Stoke-sub-Hamdon TA14 6RE* T: (01935) 824167 E: revgurner@btinternet.com

GURNEY, Canon Dennis Albert John. b 31. OBE 02. Lon Coll of Div. **d** 67 **p** 68. C Boscombe St Jo *Win* 67–70; V Hurstbourne Tarrant and Faccombe 70–77; R Jersey St Ouen w St Geo 77–84; Hon Chapl Miss to Seafarers from 84; Chapl ICS UAE 84–01; Can Bahrain from 98; rtd 01; PtO *Ex* from 02; *B & W* from 02. *3 Stevens Cross Close, Sidford, Sidmouth EX10 9QJ* T: (01395) 515362 M: 07789-111226 E: d.gurney123@btinternet.com

GURNEY, Jean Elizabeth. *See* MAYHEW, Jean Elizabeth

GURR, Mrs Mary Sandra. b 42. SAOMC 95. **d** 98 **p** 99. C Easthampstead *Ox* 98–02; TV High Wycombe 02–09; rtd 09; Chapl Pipers Corner Sch 04–17; Chapl to the Homeless *Ox* from 11. *12 Navigation Way, Oxford OX2 6XW* T: (01865) 552010 M: 07745-601046 E: mary.gurr1@btinternet.com

GURR, Stephen John. b 72. Kent Univ BA 94. Trin Coll Bris MLitt 97. **d** 97 **p** 98. C Ore St Helen and St Barn *Chich* 97–00; C Goring-by-Sea 00–03; V Findon w Clapham and Patching 03–06; Chapl St Barn Ho Worthing from 07; Chapl Chestnut Tree Ho Arundel from 07; PtO *Chich* from 07. *St Barnabas House, Titnore Lane, Worthing BN12 6NZ* T: (01903) 706374 E: stephen.gurr@stbh.org.uk

GUSSMAN, Canon Robert William Spencer Lockhart. b 50. Ch Ch Ox BA 72 MA 76. Coll of Resurr Mirfield BA 74. **d** 75 **p** 76. C Pinner *Lon* 75–79; C Northolt St Jos 79–81; P-in-c Sutton *Ely* 81–82; V 82–89; P-in-c Witcham w Mepal 81–82; R 82–89; RD Ely 86–89; V Alton St Lawr *Win* 89–02; Hon Can Win Cathl 99–02; rtd 02; PtO *Win* 02–10. *6A Patrick's Close, Liss GU33 7ER* T: (01730) 893545

GUTHRIE, Adrian Malcolm. b 57. Goldsmiths' Coll Lon BEd 80. Wycliffe Hall Ox 01. **d** 03 **p** 04. C Ickenham *Lon* 03–05; R 05–13; R Alcester Minster *Cov* 13–20; C Weddington and Caldecote from 20. *The Rectory, 49B Church Lane, Nuneaton CV10 0EX* E: revadrian@stjameswaddington.org.uk

GUTHRIE, Preb Nigel. b 60. Bris Univ BA 82 LRAM 78 ARCO 80 ARCM 81. Ripon Coll Cuddesdon BA 87 MA 91. **d** 88 **p** 89. C Cov St Jo 88–91; Chapl Cov Cathl 91–94; V Chellaston *Derby* 94–02; RD Melbourne 99–02; R Crediton, Shobrooke and Sandford etc *Ex* 02–18; RD Cadbury 13–18; V Ex St Dav from 18; Preb Ex Cathl from 10. *St David's Vicarage, 95 Howell Road, Exeter EX4 4LH* T: (01392) 660226 E: rev.guthrie@btinternet.com *or* vicar@stdavidschurchexeter.org.uk

GUTSELL, Canon David Leonard Nicholas. b 35. Sheff Univ BA 59. ALCD 61. **d** 61 **p** 62. C Clapham Common St Barn *S'wark* 61–65; V Upper Tulse Hill St Matthias 65–76; RD Clapham and Brixton 74–75; V Patcham *Chich* 76–93; Can and Preb Chich Cathl 89–00; V Polegate 93–00; rtd 00; C Peacehaven and Telscombe Cliffs *Chich* 01–05; C Southease 01–05; C Piddinghoe 01–05; PtO from 05. *6 Solway Avenue, Brighton BN1 8UJ* T: (01273) 554434 E: davidgutsell@gmail.com

GUTSELL, Eric Leslie. b 44. Goldsmiths' Coll Lon TCert 65. Ox NSM Course 79. **d** 82 **p** 83. NSM Gt Faringdon w Lt Coxwell *Ox* 82–88; NSM Shrivenham w Watchfield and Bourton 82–99; Asst Chapl HM Pris Wormwood Scrubs 99–00; Chapl HM Pris Coldingley 00–03; Chapl HM Pris Erlestoke 03–04; rtd 04; PtO *Ox* 05–18. *54 Folly View Road, Faringdon SN7 7DH* T: (01367) 240886 E: eric.gutsell@gmail.com

GUTTERIDGE, David Frank. b 39. Man Univ BSc 61 Lon Inst of Educn PGCE 62 DipEd 67 Birkbeck Coll Lon MSc 73. WMMTC 82. **d** 85 **p** 87. NSM Droitwich *Worc* 85–87; NSM Droitwich Spa 87–93; C Shrawley, Witley, Astley and Abberley 93–98; Chapl Abberley Hall Sch *Worc* 93–97; Dioc Tertiary Educn Officer *Worc* 97–99; NSM Ombersley w Doverdale 98–99; TV Malvern Link w Cowleigh 99–02; rtd 02; PtO *Worc* from 12. *34 Westward Road, Malvert WR14 1JU* T: (01886) 832627 M: 07962-129241 E: david@mlwc.co.uk

GUTTERIDGE, John. b 34. Oak Hill Th Coll 60. **d** 63 **p** 64. C Deptford St Luke *S'wark* 63–66; C Southgate *Chich* 66–70; P-in-c Brixton Road Ch Ch *S'wark* 70–73; P-in-c Manuden w Berden *Chelmsf* 73–76; Distr Sec (N Lon, Herts and Essex) BFBS 76–82; Hon C Walthamstow St Gabr *Chelmsf* 79–82; V 82–95; Chapl Thorpe Coombe Psycho-Geriatric Hosp 83–95; rtd 95; PtO *Chelmsf* 95–12. *52 Hatch Road, Pilgrims Hatch, Brentwood CM15 9PX* T: (01277) 375401

GUTTRIDGE, John William. b 54. Surrey Univ BSc 75 Cardiff Coll of Educn PGCE 76 MRSC 95. STETS 08. **d** 11

p 12. NSM Aisholt, Enmore, Goathurst, Nether Stowey etc *B & W* 11–15; PtO from 15. *Tresco, Creech Heathfield, Taunton TA3 5EH* T: (01823) 413611 M: 07813-350710 E: jwguttridge@hotmail.com

GUTWEIN, Martin. b 45. Hobart Coll (NY) BA 67. Episc Th Sch Cam Mass MA 69 MDiv 72. **d** 72 **p** 72. USA 72–78 and from 80; C Toxteth St Marg *Liv* 78–80; rtd 10; PtO *S'wark* from 16. *527 N 2nd Street, Camden NJ 08102-2101, USA* E: revgutwein@yahoo.com

GUY, Mrs Alison. b 43. CQSW 69. WMMTC 95. **d** 98 **p** 99. NSM Minchinhampton *Glouc* 98–04; C Bisley, Chalford, France Lynch, and Oakridge 04–08; PtO from 14. *7 Tooke Road, Minchinhampton, Stroud GL6 9DA* T: (01453) 883906 E: alisonguy@metronet.co.uk

GUY, Ian Towers. b 47. Newc Univ MB, BS 70 MSc 89 MRCGP. NEOC. **d** 83 **p** 84. NSM Saltburn-by-the-Sea *York* 83–88; NSM Skelton w Upleatham 88–92; PtO from 92. *14 North Terrace, Skelton-in-Cleveland, Saltburn-by-the-Sea TS12 2ES* T: (01287) 650309 M: 07092-298033 E: iantguy@mac.com

GUY, John Richard. *See* MORGAN-GUY, John Richard

GUY, Peter-John. b 71. Bournemouth Univ BA 93. Oak Hill Th Coll BA 03. **d** 03 **p** 04. C Eastbourne All So *Chich* 03–07; C Lindfield 07–11; V Horam from 11. *The Vicarage, Horebeech Lane, Horam, Heathfield TN21 0DT* T: (01435) 813372 E: pjgerdaguy@hotmail.com

GUY, Simon Edward Walrond. b 39. St Andr Univ MA 61. St D Coll Lamp LTh 67. **d** 67 **p** 68. C Bris St Mary Redcliffe w Temple etc 67–68; C Knowle St Martin 68–71; C Bishopston 71–75; V Westwood *Sarum* 75–81; TV Melksham 81–82; TV Wednesfield *Lich* 82–90; R Heaton Moor *Man* 90–02; P-in-c Heaton Norris Ch w All SS 99–01; TV Heatons 02–04; rtd 04. *1 Holley Close, Exminster, Exeter EX6 8SS* T: (01392) 823084 E: sewguy@supanet.com *or* sewguy@uwclub.net

GUYMER, Canon Raymond John. b 41. AKC 64. St Boniface Warminster. **d** 65 **p** 66. C W Bromwich All SS *Lich* 65–70; Chapl HM Pris Wormwood Scrubs 70–71 and 84–93; Chapl HM Borstal Portland 71–78; Chapl HM Youth Cust Cen Hollesley Bay Colony 78–84; Chapl HM Pris Win 93–01; Hon C Upper Itchen *Win* 02–06; Hon Can Win Cathl 99–06; rtd 06; PtO *Sarum* from 14. *39A Horse Road, Hilperton Marsh, Trowbridge BA14 7PF*

GUZEK, Mrs Bridget Louise. b 47. York Univ BA 70 Keswick Hall Coll PGCE 79. STETS 05. **d** 08 **p** 09. NSM E Clevedon w Clapton in Gordano etc *B & W* 08–12; P-in-c St Buryan, St Levan and Sennen *Truro* 12–13; C St Stythians w Perranarworthal and Gwennap 14–15; C Chacewater w St Day and Carharrack 14–15; C Feock 14–15; C Devoran 14–15; PtO *B & W* 15–16; *Truro* from 17. *4 Hendra Terrace, Stithians, Truro TR3 7AJ* M: 07985-977666 E: blguzek@gmail.com

GWALCHMAI, Mrs Alison Clare. b 63. N Lon Poly BA 84. **d** 16 **p** 17. NSM Bro Arwystli *Ban* 16–19; C 19–21; Min Area Ldr from 21. *1 Wesley Place, Llandinam SY17 5DW* T: (01686) 689142 M: 07789-860066 E: alisong@care4free.net *or* alisongwalch@gmail.com

GWILLIAMS, The Very Revd Dianna Lynn. b 57. California Univ BA 78 K Coll Lon MA 01. S'wark Ord Course 89. **d** 92 **p** 94. NSM Peckham St Sav *S'wark* 92–97; C Dulwich St Barn 97–99; V 99–13; P-in-c Peckham St Sav 07–11; AD Dulwich 05–12; Dean of Women's Min 09–12; Chapl Alleyn's Foundn Dulwich 99–13; Hon Can S'wark Cathl 06–13; Dean Guildf from 13. *The Deanery, Cathedral Close, Guildford GU2 7TL* T: (01483) 547860 F: 303350 E: dean@guildford-cathedral.org

GWILLIM, Allan John. b 51. Coll of Resurr Mirfield 87. **d** 89 **p** 90. C Skerton St Luke *Blackb* 89–94; P-in-c Ellel 94–98; V Fleetwood St Pet 98–06; V Leyland St Jas 06–08; V Ocker Hill *Lich* 08–16; RD Wednesbury 13–16; rtd 16; PtO *Worc* from 17; *Lich* from 17. *2 Little Holt Cottages, Quatt, Bridgnorth WV15 6QW* T: (01746) 780798 E: allan.gwillim@btinternet.com

GWINN, Brian Harvey. b 35. MIQA 75. St Alb Minl Tr Scheme 83. **d** 86 **p** 87. NSM Wheathampstead *St Alb* 86–88; Ind Chapl 88–95; RD Hatfield 93–95; P-in-c Watton at Stone 95–99; P-in-c Bramfield w Stapleford and Waterford 96–99; R Bramfield, Stapleford, Waterford etc 99–01; rtd 01; PtO *St Alb* from 01. *18 Kingfisher Close, Wheathampstead, St Albans AL4 8JJ* T: (01582) 629903 M: 07966-469754 E: gwinns@ntlworld.com

GWINNETT, Clifton Harry. b 57. Cranmer Hall Dur 08. **d** 10 **p** 11. C Golcar and Longwood *Wakef* 10–13; V Thornton St Jas *Bradf* 13–14; *Leeds* from 14. *The Vicarage, Thornton Road, Thornton, Bradford BD13 3AB* T: (01274) 830133 M: 07817-526342 E: harry@james4u.org

GWYN-THOMAS, James John. b 82. Ex Univ BA 03. Wycliffe Hall Ox BTh 13. **d** 13 **p** 14. C Leyland St Andr *Blackb* 13–17; Min Buckshaw Village Ch CD from 17. *1 Bridgewater Drive, Buckshaw Village, Chorley PR7 7EU* T: (01772) 453205 M: 07988-66360 E: jamesgwynthomas@gmail.com *or* james.gt@buckshawvillagechurch.org.uk

GWYNN, Mrs Fiona Jane. b 67. **d** 15 **p** 16. OLM Haslemere and Grayswood *Guildf* 15–20; NSM from 20. *The Gables, Park Close, Grayswood, Haslemere GU27 2DT* T: (01428) 654728 M: 07929-935179 E: revfigwynn@gmail.com

GWYNN, Canon Phillip John. b 57. Univ of Wales (Lamp) BA 87 MA 04. St Mich Coll Llan 87. **d** 89 **p** 90. C Clydach *S & B* 89–93; V Swansea St Thos and Kilvey 93–00; Hon Chapl Miss to Seafarers 93–00; V Tycoch *S & B* from 00; V Killay from 16; AD Clyne 12–15; Chapl Swansea NHS Trust 00–19; Hon Can Brecon Cathl *S & B* from 17. *68 Ffordd yr Olchfa, Sketty, Swansea SA2 7RF* T: (01792) 204758 M: 07946-351787 E: phillip@gwynn.org.uk

GWYNNE, Robert Durham. b 44. Qu Coll Birm 67. **d** 70 **p** 72. C N Hammersmith St Kath *Lon* 70–75; C Ramsey *Ely* 76–78; TV Old Brumby *Linc* 78–81; P-in-c Goxhill and Thornton Curtis 81–83; C Edmonton All SS w St Mich *Lon* 83–84; rtd 86. *127 Eastfield Road, Louth LN11 7AS* T: (01507) 600966

GWYTHER, Canon Geoffrey David. b 51. St D Coll Lamp. **d** 74 **p** 75. C Pembroke Dock *St D* 74–77; C Milford Haven 77–81; V Llawhaden w Bletherston and Llanycefn 81–88; R Prendergast w Rudbaxton 88–16; AD Daugleddau 01–12; Can St D Cathl 01–16; Treas 14–16; rtd 16; PtO *St D* from 18. *30 Gibbas Way, Pembroke SA71 5JA* T: (01646) 685591

GYLE, Alan Gordon. b 65. Aber Univ MA 87 Ox Univ BA 91 Univ of E Lon MA 09 FRSA 99. St Steph Ho Ox. **d** 92 **p** 93. C Acton Green *Lon* 92–94; Min Can, Succ and Dean's V Windsor 94–99; Chapl Imp Coll and R Coll of Art 99–04; P-in-c Wilton Place St Paul *Lon* 01–03; V from 03; PV Westmr Abbey from 07; Dir Development Two Cities Area *Lon* 08–12. *St Paul's Vicarage, 32 Wilton Place, London SW1X 8SH* T: (020) 7201 9990 *or* 7201 9999 F: 7201 9990 E: alan@stpaulsknightsbridge.org

GYLES, Canon Sonia. b 76. TCD BTh 01. CITC 98. **d** 01 **p** 02. C Taney *D & G* 01–04; I Dublin Sandford w Milltown from 04; Chan V St Patr Cathl Dublin 01–07; Can Ch Ch Cathl Dublin 07 from 17. *The Rectory, Sandford Close, Ranelagh, Dublin 6, Republic of Ireland* T: (00353) (1) 497 2983 E: sandford@dublin.anglican.org

H

HAARHOFF, Preb Robert Russell. b 46. St Paul's Coll Grahamstown 89 Th Ext Educn Coll 91. **d** 90 **p** 91. Harare Cathl Zimbabwe 91–94; I Makonde 94–02; P-in-c Astley, Clive, Grinshill and Hadnall *Lich* 02–17; RD Wem and Whitchurch 08–13; Preb Lich Cathl 11–17; rtd 17; PtO *Lich* 17–21. *25 Fismes Way, Wem, Shrewsbury SY4 5YD* T: (01939) 769325 E: rob.haarhoff@gmail.com

HABERSHON, Kenneth Willoughby. b 35. MBE 01. New Coll Ox BA 57 MA 60. Wycliffe Hall Ox 57. **d** 59

p 60. C Finchley Ch Ch *Lon* 59–66; Sec CYFA 66–74; CPAS Staff 74–90; Hon C Slaugham *Chich* 84–10; Hon C Slaugham and Staplefield Common from 10; Ldr Mayfield CYFA 90–00; rtd 00; Sec Patr Trust 90–07; Sec Peache Trustees 90–11. *Truckers Ghyll, Horsham Road, Handcross, Haywards Heath RH17 6DT* T: (01444) 400274 E: kandmhab@btopenworld.com

HABGOOD, Simon. *See* LAWRENCE, Simon Peter

HABGOOD, Stephen Roy. b 52. Open Univ MBA 95 Fitzw Coll Cam MSt 01. St Mich Coll Llan 75. **d** 77 **p** 78. C Whitchurch *Llan* 77–80; PtO *Worc* 85–91; *Lich* from 18. *16 Hugo Way, Loggerheads, Market Drayton TF9 4RP* T: (01630) 672656 M: 07403-242910

✠**HACKER, The Rt Revd George Lanyon.** b 28. Ex Coll Ox BA 52 MA 56. Cuddesdon Coll 52. **d** 54 **p** 55 **c** 79. C Bris St Mary Redcliffe w Temple 54–59; Chapl St Boniface Coll Warminster 59–64; V Bishopwearmouth Gd Shep *Dur* 64–71; R Tilehurst St Mich *Ox* 71–79; Suff Bp Penrith *Carl* 79–94; Hon Can Carl Cathl 79–94; Episc Adv for the Angl Young People's Assn 87–94; rtd 94; Hon Asst Bp Carl from 94. *Keld House, Milburn, Penrith CA10 1TW* T: (01768) 361506 E: bishhack@outlook.com

HACKER HUGHES, Katherine Lucy. b 60. York Univ BA 81. Westcott Ho Cam 90. **d** 92 **p** 94. Par Dn S Woodham Ferrers *Chelmsf* 92–94; C 94–95; NSM Maldon All SS w St Pet 95–98; Chapl Chelmsf Cathl 98–01; P-in-c Gt Waltham w Ford End 01–05; Adv relationship and family issues (Bradwell Area) 01–03; PtO 05–09; Chapl Mid-Essex Hosp Services NHS Trust 06–07; Chapl Farleigh Hospice 07–14; P-in-c Newington St Paul *S'wark* 14–19; V 19; C St Marylebone w H Trin *Lon* from 19; Dean of Women's Min Two Cities Area 20. *St Marylebone Parish Church, 17 Marylebone Road, London NW1 5LT* T: (020) 7935 7315 E: katyhh@hotmail.co.uk

HACKETT, Bryan Malcolm. b 66. Magd Coll Ox BA 88 MA 93 SS Coll Cam BA 92 MA 03. Westcott Ho Cam 90. **d** 93 **p** 94. C Willington *Newc* 93–97; TV Radcliffe *Man* 97–03; P-in-c Prestwich St Mary 03–13; C Prestwich St Marg 10–13; C Prestwich St Gabr 10–13; V Baguley 13–15; PtO *Carl* 15–16; P-in-c Portsea N End St Mark *Portsm* from 16; P-in-c Portsea St Sav 17–18; P-in-c Portsea Ascension 17–18; C from 20. *St Mark's Rectory, 3A Wadham Road, Portsmouth PO2 9ED* T: (023) 9265 5654 E: bryan.hackett@btinternet.com

HACKETT, Richard Anthony. b 77. Cov Univ BSc 00. Qu Foundn (Course) 15. **d** 18 **p** 19. C Old Hill H Trin *Worc* 18–20; C Darby End and Netherton 20–21; P-in-c from 21. *The Vicarage, Highbridge Road, Dudley DY2 0HT*

HACKETT, The Ven Ronald Glyndwr. b 47. Hatf Coll Dur BA 70. Cuddesdon Coll 70. **d** 72 **p** 73. C Pembroke St Mary w St Mich *St D* 72–75; C Bassaleg *Mon* 75–78; V Blaenavon w Capel Newydd 78–84; Chapl R Gwent Hosp 84–90; V Newport St Paul *Mon* 84–90; V Newport Ch Ch 90–01; Adn Mon 01–08; R Mamhilad and Llanfihangel Pontymoile 01–03; R Mamhilad w Monkswood and Glascoed Chapel 03–08; Adn Newport 08–12; rtd 12. *71 Castle Lea, Caldicot NP26 4PJ* T: (01291) 425353 E: glyndwr.hackett@btinternet.com

HACKETT, Victoria Anne. b 52. Open Univ BA 91 St Gabr Coll Lon CertEd 73. SEITE 97. **d** 00 **p** 01. NSM Earlsfield St Andr *S'wark* 00–14; PtO *St D* 14–19; NSM Lampeter from 19. *Gelli Aur, Bryn Road, Lampeter SA48 7EE* T: (01570) 421683 E: vhackett@outlook.com

HACKING, Philip Henry. b 31. St Pet Hall Ox BA 53 MA 57. Oak Hill Th Coll 53. **d** 55 **p** 56. C St Helens St Helen *Liv* 55–58; C-in-c Edin St Thos 59–68; V Fulwood *Sheff* 68–97; rtd 97; PtO *Sheff* 98–16. *61 Sefton Court, Sefton Road, Sheffield S10 3TP* T: 0114-230 4324

HACKING, Rodney Douglas. b 53. K Coll Lon BD 74 AKC 74 Man Univ MA 83. St Aug Coll Cant 75. **d** 76 **p** 78. C Byker St Mich *Newc* 76–77; C Eltham St Jo *S'wark* 77–79; Ind Chapl *Ripon* 80–85; R Upwell St Pet and Outwell *Ely* 85–88; Vice Prin S Dios Minl Tr Scheme 89–93; V Bolton-le-Sands *Blackb* 93–97; In Orthodox Ch 01–03; R The Wainfleet Gp *Linc* 03–06; rtd 06. *135 The Close, Salisbury SP1 2EY* T: (01722) 417289 E: rodhacking@btinternet.com

HACKING, Stuart Peter. b 60. St Pet Coll Ox BA 82 MA. Oak Hill Th Coll 83. **d** 85 **p** 86. C Shipley St Pet *Bradf* 85–88; C Darfield *Sheff* 88–91; V Thornton St Jas *Bradf* 91–00; P-in-c Frizinghall St Marg 00–12; Chapl Immanuel Coll from 00. *33 Cyprus Gardens, Idle, Bradford BD10 8JF* T: (01274) 616473 *or* 425900 E: stuart.hacking@btinternet.com

HACKL, Aileen Patricia. b 41. Wycliffe Hall Ox 00. **d** 01 **p** 02. C Vienna *Eur* 01–09; NSM 09–11; rtd 11. *Hardtmuthgasse 28/3/20, A-1100 Vienna, Austria* T/F: (0043) (1) 600 3083 E: aileen_hackl@hotmail.com

HACKNEY, Archdeacon of. Harvard Univ LLB 67 Trin Coll Cam BA 70 MA 75. Cuddesdon Coll 70. C S Lambeth St Ann *S'wark* 72–75; C Richmond St Mary w St Matthias 75–78; P-in-c Kennington St Jo 78–79; V Kennington St Jo w St Jas 79–99; P-in-c Brixton Road Ch Ch 81–89; RD Brixton 90–99; Hon Can S'wark Cathl 99; Adn Hackney *Lon* 99–10; V St Andr Holborn 99–14; rtd 14; PtO *Lon* from 14. *1 Victoria Wharf, 46 Narrow Street, London E14 8DD* T: (020) 7353 3544 F: 7583 2750 E: lyle.dennen@hotmail.com

HACKSHALL, Brian Leonard. b 33. K Coll Lon BD 53 AKC 53. **d** 57 **p** 58. C Portsea St Mary *Portsm* 57–62; C Westbury-on-Trym St Alb *Bris* 62–64; V Avonmouth St Andr 64–71; Miss to Seamen 71–79; C Crawley *Chich* 79; TV 79–98; Ind Chapl 89–98; rtd 98. *5 St Michael Street, Brecon LD3 9AB* T: (01874) 611319 E: b.hackshall319@btinternet.com

HACKWOOD, Canon Paul Colin. b 61. Huddersfield Poly BSc 84 Bradf Univ MBA 05. Qu Coll Birm 86. **d** 89 **p** 90. C Horton *Bradf* 89–93; Soc Resp Adv *St Alb* 93–97; V Thornbury *Bradf* 97–05; Adn Loughborough *Leic* 05–09; Can Res Leic Cathl 07–15; Exec Chair CUF from 15; PtO *Leic* from 15; Hon Can Leic Cathl from 15. *Church View Farmhouse, 4 St Mary's Close, Osgathorpe, Loughborough LE12 9SY* T: (01530) 223265 M: 07738-286428 E: paulhackwood@me.com

HADDEN, Timothy. b 48. Brighton Poly BSc 72 Surrey Univ MSc 75. **d** 05 **p** 06. OLM Watling Valley *Ox* 05–16; PtO from 16. *13 Weavers Lane, Oakridge Park, Milton Keynes MK14 6FQ* M: 07889-614386 E: tim.hadden@btinternet.com

HADDOCK, Malcolm George. b 27. Univ of Wales (Cardiff) BA 56 CertEd 73. St Deiniol's Hawarden 87. **d** 80 **p** 81. NSM Newport Ch Ch *Mon* 80–85; NSM Risca 85–87; C 87–89; C Caerleon 89–96; rtd 96; Lich *Mon* from 96. *48 Cambria Close, Caerleon, Newport NP18 1LF* T: (01633) 422960

HADDON-REECE (née STREETER), Mrs Christine Mary. b 50. St Jo Coll Nottm BTh 81 LTh 81. dss 83 **d** 87 **p** 94. Monkwearmouth St Andr *Dur* 83–85; Stranton 85–87; Par Dn 87–90; Par Dn Lastingham w Appleton-le-Moors, Rosedale etc *York* 90–94; C 94–97; V Topcliffe, Baldersby w Dishforth, Dalton etc 97–08; V Middle Esk Moor 08–15; rtd 16; PtO *York* 16–19 and from 21; Chapl York Minster from 17. *Thorgill House, Rosedale Abbey, Pickering YO18 8SE* T: (01751) 417401 E: c.haddonreece@gmail.com

HADDON-REECE, David. b 45. Liv Univ BEng 69 Bradf Univ MPhil 81 FRSA 72 CEng 77 MIEE 76. **d** 19. NSM Lastingham w Appleton-le-Moors, Rosedale etc *York* from 19; Chapl York Minster from 17. *Thorgill House, Rosedale Abbey, Pickering YO18 8SE* T: (01751) 417401 E: d.haddonreece@gmail.com

HADFIELD, Prof Brigid. b 50. Edin Univ LLB 72 QUB LLM 77 Essex Univ PhD 03. EAMTC 02. **d** 03 **p** 04. NSM Wivenhoe *Chelmsf* 03–06; NSM Shrub End 06–11; P-in-c Harston w Hauxton and Newton *Ely* 11–18; rtd 18; PtO *Ely* 18–19; *Chich* from 18. *6 Cornfield Road, Seaford BN25 1SW* E: bhadfield216@gmail.com

HADFIELD, Christopher John Andrew Chad. b 39. Jes Coll Cam BA 61. Wells Th Coll 63. **d** 65 **p** 66. C Wigton w Waverton *Carl* 65–68; Teacher Newlands Sch Seaford 70–06; LtO *Mor* from 92; PtO *Chich* from 96. *15 The Fridays, East Dean, Eastbourne BN20 0DH* T: (01323) 422050

HADFIELD, David William. b 53. Newc Univ BA 74 MA 76 PhD 83 Barrister 82 Solicitor 88. SEITE 10. **d** 13 **p** 14. NSM E Grinstead St Mary *Chich* from 13. *Highgate House, Tomtits Lane, Forest Row RH18 5AT* T: (01342) 823105 M: 07860-125001 E: revdhad@gmail.com

HADFIELD, Derek. b 34. **d** 01 **p** 02. OLM Folkestone H Trin w Ch Ch *Cant* 01–04; OLM Sandgate St Paul w Folkestone St Geo 01–04; rtd 04; PtO *Cant* 04–11; *York* from 11. *Mon Abri, South Duffield Road, Osgodby, Selby YO8 5HW* T: (01757) 705940 E: dhaddy1146@gmail.com

HADFIELD, Graham Francis. b 48. Bris Univ BSc 69. Cranmer Hall Dur 69. **d** 73 **p** 74. C Blackpool St Thos *Blackb* 73–76; CF 76–99; Asst Chapl Gen 99–04; QHC 02–04; P-in-c Nottingham St Jude *S'well* 04–11; V 11–12; rtd 12; PtO *Chelmsf* from 13; *Eur* from 17. *22 Coast Road, West Mersea, Colchester CO5 8LH* T: (01206) 382458

HADFIELD, Jonathan Benedict Philip John. b 43. Lon Univ BA 64 Jes Coll Cam BA 67 MA 72. Edin Th Coll 66. **d** 68 **p** 69. C Fort William *Arg* 68–70; Chapl K Sch Glouc and Hon Min Can Glouc Cathl 70–03; rtd 03. *36 Corsend Road, Hartpury, Gloucester GL19 3BP*

HADFIELD, Norman. b 39. Doncaster Coll of Educn TEng 78. St Mich Coll Llan 89 Llan Dioc Tr Scheme 83. **d** 86 **p** 87. NSM Ferndale w Maerdy *Llan* 86–90; C Llanblethian w Cowbridge and Llandough etc 90–92; V Resolven w Tonna 92–04; RD Neath 01–03; rtd 04; PtO *Llan* from 04. *42 Lakeside, Cwmdare, Aberdare CF44 8AX* T: (01685) 872764

HADJIOANNOU, John. b 56. Ch Coll Cam BA 78 MA 81. SAOMC 95. **d** 97 **p** 98. C Linslade *Ox* 97–00; V Kinsley w Wragby *Wakef* 00–14; *Leeds* from 14; P-in-c Felkirk *Wakef* 05–06. *Kinsley Vicarage, Wakefield Road, Fitzwilliam, Pontefract WF9 5BX* T: (01977) 610497 E: john@minster.co.uk

HADLEY, Adam Richard. b 82. York Univ BA 03 Essex Univ MA 05. Qu Foundn Birm 16. **d** 18 **p** 19. C Stourbridge St Thos *Worc* 18–21; P-in-c Kingswinford St Mary from 21. *The Vicarage, 15 Penzer Street, Kingswinford DY6 7AA* M: 07759-900947

HADLEY, Ann. *See* HADLEY, Elizabeth Ann

HADLEY, Charles Adrian. b 50. Trin Coll Cam BA 71 MA 75. Cuddesdon Coll 73. d 75 p 76. C Hadleigh w Layham and Shelley *St E* 75–78; C Bracknell *Ox* 78–82; R Blagdon w Compton Martin and Ubley *B & W* 82–92; RD Chew Magna 88–92; R Somerton w Compton Dundon, the Charltons etc 92–04; Chapl Ex Univ 04–10; Chemin Neuf Community Israel 10–15; Hon C Storrington *Chich* from 15. *28 Meadowside, Storrington, Pulborough RH20 4EG* T: (01903) 740787 E: charles.felicity@gmail.com

HADLEY, David Charles. b 42. d 02 p 03. NSM Kenley *S'wark* 02–13; NSM Purley St Barn 08–13; PtO from 13. *21 Park Road, Kenley CR8 5AQ* T: (020) 8763 6206

HADLEY, Preb Elizabeth Ann. b 33. St Jo Coll Nottm 80. dss 81 d 87 p 94. Aspley *S'well* 81–85; Stone St Mich w Aston St Sav *Lich* 85–92; Par Dn 87–92; P-in-c Myddle 92–97; R 97–99; P-in-c Broughton 92–97; V from 97; Dioc Voc Officer 92–99; Preb Lich Cathl 97–99; rtd 99; P-in-c Harvington *Worc* 99–00; PtO from 00. *6 Peninsula Road, Brockhill Village, Norton, Worcester WR5 2SE* T: (01905) 353710 E: revannhadley@gmail.com

HADLEY, Georgina Ann Lacy. b 53. De Montfort Univ BA 95 PGCE 96. Linc Sch of Th and Min 12. d 13 p 14. NSM Retford Area *S'well* 13–16; C Averham w Kelham from 16; C N and S Muskham from 16. *43 Great North Road, Sutton on Trent, Newark NG23 6PL* T: (01636) 821343 M: 07811-393920 E: georgie.hadley@yahoo.co.uk

HADLEY, James Thomas. b 78. ERMC 16. d 18 p 19. C Harpenden St Nic *St Alb* 18–21; Chapl Palermo w Taormina *Eur* from 21. *Via Severoli 10, 48018 Faenza, Italy*

HADLEY, Canon John Spencer Fairfax. b 47. Ch Ch Ox BA 70 MA 73. Coll of Resurr Mirfield BA 72. d 73 p 74. C Stoke Newington St Mary *Lon* 73–77; C High Wycombe *Ox* 77–81; TV 82–87; P-in-c Clifton St Paul *Bris* 87–91; Sen Chapl Bris Univ 87–91; Chapl Imengrave Hall Ecum Cen 91–94; Ecum Assoc Min Chelsea Methodist Ch 94–97; Hon C Chelsea St Luke and Ch Ch *Lon* 94–97; Chapl Westcott Ho Cam 97–02; P-in-c Horfield H Trin *Bris* 02–15; R 15–17; Hon Can Bris Cathl 12–17; rtd 17; Hon C Eastville St Anne w St Mark and St Thos *Bris* from 19. *14 Picton Street, Bristol BS6 5QA* T: 0117-944 6153

HADLEY, Stuart James. b 55. K Coll Lon BD 76 AKC 76. St Steph Ho Ox 77. d 78 p 79. C Mansfield St Mark *S'well* 78–82; V Cowbit *Linc* 82–86; PtO 86–88; NSM W w E Allington and Sedgebrook 88–95; NSM Saxonwell 95–96; NSM Woolsthorpe 88–95; NSM Harlaxton Gp 95–96; PtO 97–99; NSM Barkston and Hough Gp 99–17; P-in-c 17–18; P-in-c Caythorpe 17–18; R S Cliff Villages Gp from 18. *35 Wensleydale Close, Grantham NG31 8FH* T: (01476) 575854 M: 07398-390549 E: rectorsouthcliff@outlook.com

HADLEY-SPENCER, Miss Vanessa Victoria Iris. b 93. Herts Univ LLB 14 Cam Univ BTh 19. Westcott Ho 17. d 20 p 21. C Cheshunt *St Alb* from 20. *103 Northfield Road, Waltham Cross EN8 7RD* T: 07494-906930 *or* 07854-377951 E: vanessahadley@btinternet.com

HADLOW, Mrs Jennifer Lesley. b 48. d 01 p 02. OLM Reculver and Herne Bay St Bart and Hoath *Cant* 01–18; rtd 18; PtO *Cant* 18–21. *2 Hicks Forstal Cottages, Hicks Forstal Road, Hoath, Canterbury CT3 4NA* T: (01227) 711516

HAGAN, Matthew Henry. b 59. TCD MPhil 09. CITC. d 06 p 07. NSM Derryloran *Arm* 06–10; P-in-c Tynan w Middletown and Aghavilly 10–12; Bp's C 12–13; I from 13. *The Rectory, 16 Derryhaw Road, Tynan, Armagh BT60 4SS* T: (028) 3756 8619 M: 07778-038454 E: mhhagan@hotmail.com

HAGAN, Yvonne Joan Katherine. b 59. Yorks Min Course 14. d 17 p 18. NSM Mixenden and Illingworth *Leeds* from 17. *6 Roseberry Terrace, Halifax HX1 4AW*

HAGAN-DALL, David Edward. b 66. UEA BSc 88 PGCE 96. ERMC 10. d 13 p 14. C Lowestoft St Marg *Nor* 13–14; C Drayton 14–16; C Taverham 14–16; C Cawston w Booton and Brandiston etc 16–17; TV Aylsham and Distr 17–21; V Old Catton from 21. *1 Parkside Drive, Norwich NR6 7DP* M: 07880-660900 E: revdavepalmer@gmail.com

HAGENBUCH, Mrs Andrea. b 63. STETS 05. d 08 p 09. C Corfe Castle, Church Knowle, Kimmeridge etc *Sarum* 08–12; V Stour Vale 12–16; R Milngavie *Glas* from 16. *1 Westbourne Drive, Bearsden, Glasgow G61 4BD* T: 0141-942 0029 E: stephenhagenbuch@hotmail.com

HAGGAR, Emma Elizabeth. b 86. Trin Coll Bris 19. d 21. C Felixstowe SS Pet and Paul *St E* from 21. *67 Ferry Road, Old Felixstowe IP11 9LN* M: 07767-208400 E: revemma@oldfelixstoweparish.org.uk

HAGGIS, Richard. b 66. Ch Ch Ox BA 88 MA 95 Nottm Univ MA 95. Linc Th Coll. d 95 p 96. C Romford St Edw *Chelmsf* 95–98; Chapl Trin Coll Cam 98–00; C St Giles-in-the-Fields *Lon* 00–03; C Upper Chelsea H Trin 04–06. *Flat 5, 14-16 Mather Road, Barton-Upon-Bayswater, Oxford OX3 9PG* T: (01865) 750068 M: 07788-704044 E: rh.giles@btopenworld.com

HAGGIS, Timothy Robin. b 52. New Coll Ox BA 75 MA 79. St Jo Coll Nottm. d 82 p 83. C Chilwell *S'well* 82–86; TV Hucknall Torkard 86–94; Chapl Trent Coll Nottm 94–11; rtd 11. *86 Trowell Grove, Long Eaton, Nottingham NG10 4BB* T: 0115-972 9589 E: timhaggis@hotmail.co.uk

HAGON, Roger Charles. b 58. Nottm Univ BA 80. St Steph Ho Ox 82. d 85 p 86. C Charlton St Luke w H Trin *S'wark* 85–88; C St Helier 88–95; V Kenley 95–10; P-in-c Purley St Barn 01–10; V Addiscombe St Mildred from 10. *St Mildred's Vicarage, Sefton Road, Croydon CR0 7HR* T: (020) 8676 1569 E: vicar@stmildredschurch.org.uk

HAGUE, Canon David Hallett. b 59. Univ Coll Lon BScEng 81 MSc 82. Ridley Hall Cam 91. d 93 p 94. C Luton St Mary *St Alb* 93–96; V Stevenage St Pet Broadwater 96–09; P-in-c Romford Gd Shep *Chelmsf* 09–14; V from 14; AD Havering 14–18; Hon Can Chelmsf Cathl from 15. *Good Shepherd Vicarage, 97 Collier Row Lane, Romford RM5 3BA* T: (01708) 753395 E: vicargs@thegoodshepherd.co.uk

HAIG, Alistair Alexander Matthew. b 39. K Coll Lon BD 63 AKC 63. d 64 p 65. C Forest Gate St Edm *Chelmsf* 64–67; C Laindon w Basildon 67–71; V S Woodham Ferrers 71–78; P-in-c Bath H Trin *B & W* 78–83; R 83–89; R Bocking St Mary *Chelmsf* 89–95; Dean Bocking 89–95; rtd 00. *17 Maidenburgh Street, Colchester CO1 1UB* T: (01206) 530530 E: aam.haig@ntlworld.com

HAIG, Canon Andrew Livingstone. b 45. Keble Coll Ox BA 67. Coll of Resurr Mirfield 67. d 69 p 70. C Elton All SS *Man* 69–75; R Brantham *St E* 75–76; R Brantham w Stutton 76–82; RD Samford 81–82; P-in-c Haverhill 82; TR Haverhill w Withersfield, the Wrattings etc 82–90; RD Clare 84–87; Chapl Qu Eliz Hosp King's Lynn 90–10; Hon Can Nor Cathl 07–10; rtd 10; PtO *Nor* from 10; *Ely* from 13; *Eur* 17–20. *46 Elvington, King's Lynn PE30 4TA* T: (01553) 761389 E: bandahaig@yahoo.co.uk

HAIG, Canon Murray Nigel Francis. b 39. Univ of Wales (Lamp) BA 62. Kelham Th Coll 62. d 66 p 67. C Felixstowe St Jo *St E* 66–72; C Morpeth *Newc* 72–74; V Byker St Mich 74–79; V Byker St Mich w St Lawr 79–81; I Benwell St Jas 81–85; TR Benwell 85–91; TR Cramlington 91–97; P-in-c Alnwick 97–98; V 98–05; Hon Can Newc Cathl 95–05; rtd 05; PtO *Newc* from 05. *45 Castle Street, Warkworth, Morpeth NE65 0UN* M: 07801-495616 E: m.haig@hotmail.co.uk

HAIGH, Nicholas James. b 71. Sheff Univ BA 00 St Jo Coll Dur MA 04. Cranmer Hall Dur 02. d 04 p 05. C Bredbury St Mark *Ches* 04–06; P Missr Huddersfield *Wakef* 06–09; C Crookes St Thos *Sheff* 09–15; V Haydock St Mark *Liv* 15–17; Miss Chapl Lee Abbey from 17. *Lee Abbey, Lynton EX35 6JJ* T: (01598) 752621 E: nickhaigh@leeabbey.org.uk *or* missionpriest@gmail.com

HAIGH, Nicolas Peter. b 57. Teesside Poly BEd 84. Ripon Coll Cuddesdon 07. d 09 p 10. C Eastbourne St Mary *Chich* 09–12; P-in-c Fernhurst 12–14; V 14–16; V Fernhurst, Lynchmere and Camelsdale from 16. *The Vicarage, Church Road, Fernhurst, Haslemere GU27 3HZ* T: (01428) 652229 M: 07966-187349 E: nickhaigh95@hotmail.com

HAIGH, Richard Michael Fisher. b 30. Dur Univ BA 57. Cranmer Hall Dur 57. d 59 p 60. C Stanwix *Carl* 59–62; CMS India 63–67; 68–70; R Salford St Clem w St Cypr Ordsall *Man* 71–75; R Holcombe 75–85; V Unsworth 85–93; R Brough w Stainmore, Musgrave and Warcop *Carl* 93–97; rtd 97; PtO *Carl* 98–19. *21 Templand Park, Allithwaite, Grange-over-Sands LA11 7QS* T: (015395) 32312

HAIGH, Samuel Edward. b 85. Anglia Ruskin Univ BA 11. Ridley Hall Cam 08. d 11 p 12. C Wootton *St Alb* 11–14; TV Tollington *Lon* 14–18; C Onslow Square and S Kensington St Aug 18–19; R Preston St Jo and St Geo *Blackb* from 19. *The Rectory, 13 Ribblesdale Place, Preston PR1 3NA* T: (01772) 901313 M: 07429-022977 E: revhaigh@me.com

HAILES, Derek Arthur. b 38. Coll of Resurr Mirfield. d 82 p 83. C Sneinton St Cypr *S'well* 82–84; V Kneesall w Laxton 84–85; P-in-c Wellow 84–85; V Kneesall w Laxton and Wellow 85–88; V Sneinton St Steph w St Alb 88–95; P-in-c Bury H Trin *Man* 95–03; rtd 03; PtO *S'well* from 05. *14 Manor Road, Carlton, Nottingham NG4 3AY* T: 0115-987 3314 E: derek.hailes@hotmail.com

HAILS, Canon Brian. b 33. JP 71. ACMA 62 FCMA 76. NEOC 77. d 81 p 82. NSM Harton *Dur* 81–87; Ind Chapl 87–99; Hon Can Dur Cathl 93–99; TR Sunderland 96–99; rtd 99; PtO *Dur* from 99. *The Coach House, Church Lane, Whitburn, Sunderland SR6 7JL* T: 0191-529 5297 E: bhails@btinternet.com

HAINE, Mrs Joanne Elizabeth. b 78. Sarum Coll MA 20 RMN 00. St Jo Coll Nottm 13. d 15 p 16. C Dorchester and the Winterbournes *Sarum* 15–18; TV Radipole and

Melcombe Regis from 18. *The Vicarage, 74 Field Barn Drive, Weymouth DT4 0EF* T: (01305) 581399 M: 07530-255684 E: revjohaine@gmail.com *or* vicar@emmanuelwey.co.uk *or* vicar@stmarysweymouth.co.uk

HAINES, Andrew Philip. b 47. LSE BSc 68. Oak Hill Th Coll 84. **d** 87 **p** 88. C Enfield Ch Ch Trent Park *Lon* 87–91; V Hillmorton *Cov* 91–12; rtd 12; PtO *Cov* from 12. *69 Waverley Road, Kenilworth CV8 1JL* T: (01926) 855518 E: revaph@btinternet.com *or* andrew@haines.uk.com

HAINES, Fiona Elizabeth. b 56. Open Univ BA 95 York Univ MA 00. LCTP 14. **d** 16 **p** 17. NSM Freckleton and Warton St Paul *Blackb* from 16. *19 Derbe Road, Lytham St Annes FY8 1NJ* M: 07850-422566 E: fiona_haines@outlook.com

HAINSWORTH, Richard John. b 79. Jes Coll Cam BA 01 MA 03. St Mich Coll Llan 04. **d** 06 **p** 07. C Newtown w Llanllwchaiarn w Aberhafesp *St As* 06–07; C Llanllwchaiarn and Newtown w Aberhafesp 07–08; C Wrexham 08–09; TV 09–14; V Northop 14–16; TV Mold Miss Area 17–19; Dioc Dir for Exploring Faith from 14. *The Vicarage, Sychdyn Road, Northop, Mold CH7 6AW* T: (01352) 840842 M: 07886-117922 E: rich_hainsworth@yahoo.co.uk

HAIR, James Eric. b 48. Lon Univ BA 69 MPhil 92. St Steph Ho Ox 69. **d** 72 **p** 73. C Fishponds St Jo *Bris* 72–75; C Bushey *St Alb* 75–79; P-in-c Lake *Portsm* 79–81; V 81–88; P-in-c Shanklin St Sav 79–81; V 81–88; TV Totton *Win* 88–95; C Portchester *Portsm* 96–97; Community Mental Health Chapl Portsm Health Care NHS Trust 97–00; Community Portsm Hosps NHS Trust 01–02; Community Mental Health Chapl Hants Partnership NHS Trust 02–13; Chapl Team Ldr E Hants Primary Care Trust 99–13; Asst to RD Fareham *Portsm* 97–98 and 99; Dioc Adv for Mental Health from 12; PtO *Win* 09–14; *Portsm* from 16. *26 Bayly Avenue, Fareham PO16 9LD*

HAITH, James Rodney. b 69. Ex Univ BA. Ridley Hall Cam 02. **d** 04 **p** 05. C Brompton H Trin w Onslow Square St Paul *Lon* 04–11; C Onslow Square and S Kensington St Aug 11–12; C Holborn St Geo w H Trin and St Bart from 19. *13 Doughty Street, London WC1N 2PL* T: (020) 7430 2272 M: 07833-705271

HAKE, Darren Mark. b 73. Plymouth Univ BSc 00 Lanc Univ MRes 01 FGS 01. Wycliffe Hall Ox 09. **d** 11 **p** 12. C Wembdon *B & W* 11–14; PtO 14–18; C Peacehaven and Telscombe Cliffs w Piddinghoe etc *Chich* from 18. *79 Ambleside Avenue, Telscombe Cliffs, Peacehaven BN10 7LN* M: 07545-379112 E: revd.mark.hake@gmail.com

HAKE (*née* JACKSON), Mrs Ruth Victoria. b 75. MBE 11. Univ Coll Dur BA 99 Fitzw Coll Cam BA 01 MA 05. Ridley Hall Cam 99. **d** 02 **p** 03. C York St Mich-le-Belfrey 02–05; CF(V) 04–05; Chapl RAF from 05. *Chaplaincy Services (RAF), HQ Air Command, RAF High Wycombe HP14 4UE* T: (01494) 496500

HALDON-JONES, Mark Vincent. b 60. St Mich Coll Llan 81. **d** 84 **p** 85. C Whitchurch *Llan* 84–89; V Pwllgwaun w Llanddewi Rhondda 89–90; CF 90–19; P-in-c Folkestone St Pet *Cant* from 19; PtO *Lon* from 19. *St Peter's Vicarage, North Street, Folkestone CT19 6AL*

HALE, Antony Jolyon (Jon). b 56. Newc Univ BA 79 MRTPI 89. Sarum & Wells Th Coll 86. **d** 88 **p** 89. C Monkseaton St Mary *Newc* 88–92; P-in-c Tandridge *S'wark* 92–97; C Oxted 92–97; C Oxted and Tandridge *S'wark* V Crawley Down All SS *Chich* 98–16; R Alderley w Birtles *Ches* from 16. *St Mary's Rectory, Congleton Road, Nether Alderley, Macclesfield SK10 4TW* T: (01625) 586467 E: rector@alderleychurch.co.uk *or* aj@jckahale.co.uk

HALE, David Nigel James. b 43. SEITE 00. **d** 03 **p** 04. NSM Aylesham w Adisham *Cant* 03–12; NSM Nonington w Wymynswold and Goodnestone etc 03–12; NSM Canonry 12–13; rtd 14; PtO *Cant* from 14; Chapl Northbourne Park Sch from 14. *Chilton House, 43 The Street, Ash, Canterbury CT3 2EN* T: (01304) 813161 *or* (01843) 862991 E: halenigelval@hotmail.com

HALE, Eira Jayne. b 73. Sussex Univ BA 96 Leic Univ MSc 04. Qu Foundn Birm 18. **d** 21. C Warwick *Cov* from 21. *29 Rogers Way, Warwick CV34 6PY* M: 07837-064081 E: eirahale@gmail.com

HALE, Jon. *See* HALE, Antony Jolyon

HALE, Canon Keith John Edward. b 53. Sheff Poly BSc 75. St Jo Coll Nottm MA 94. **d** 91 **p** 92. C Greasbrough *Sheff* 91–94; P-in-c Tankersley 94–95; R Tankersley, Thurgoland and Wortley from 95; Ind Chapl 96–01; Bp's Rural Adv from 01; AD Tankersley 07–19; Hon Can Sheff Cathl from 10. *The Rectory, 9 Chapel Road, Tankersley, Barnsley S75 3AR* T: (01226) 744140 E: revkeith.hale@virgin.net

HALE (*née* McKAY), Mrs Margaret McLeish (Greta). b 37. RN 76. WEMTC 92. **d** 95 **p** 96. OLM Bream *Glouc* 95–01; NSM 01–04; NSM Newland and Redbrook w Clearwell 04–06; NSM Coleford, Staunton, Newland, Redbrook etc

06–13. *14 Meadow Walk, Sling, Coleford GL16 8LR* T: (01594) 832400 E: gretahale@hotmail.com

HALE, Nigel. *See* HALE, David Nigel James

HALE, Roger Anthony. b 41. MCIH 85. Brasted Th Coll 68 Oak Hill Th Coll 70. **d** 72 **p** 73. C Blackb Sav 72–75; C Burnley St Pet 75–77; Chapl Burnley Gen Hosp 75–77; V Fence in Pendle *Blackb* 77–82; Chapl Lancs Ind Miss 77–82; NSM Tottenham St Mary *Lon* 88–91; R Cheddington w Mentmore and Marsworth *Ox* 91–06; rtd 06; PtO *Ox* from 06. *9 Ridgeway Place, 8 Hale Road, Wendover, Aylesbury HP22 6BJ* E: rogertherector@yahoo.co.uk

HALE, Susan Mary. b 55. Dur Univ BA 77 Newman Coll Birm PGCE 96. Qu Foundn Birm 13. **d** 16 **p** 17. NSM Pennsett *Worc* 16–20; NSM Dudley from 20; PtO *Birm* from 16. *20 Links View, Halesowen B62 8SS* M: 07946-700236 E: revsuehale@gmail.com

HALE-HEIGHWAY, Catherine Anne. b 58. Lanc Univ BEd 79 Cumbria Univ BA 16. LCTP 10. **d** 12 **p** 13. NSM Colne and Villages *Blackb* 12–14; NSM Colne 14–18; C Clitheroe St Mary and St Paul, Chatburn and Downham from 18. *The Vicarage, St Paul's Street, Clitheroe BB7 2LS* T: (01200) 458019 E: revdcahale@gmail.com

HALES, Peter John. b 45. Open Univ BSc 02. ERMC 08. **d** 08 **p** 09. C Coutances *Eur* 08–09; P-in-c 09–14; PtO from 18. *4 rue le Mascaret, 50220 Précey, France* T: (0033) 2 33 58 86 76 F: 6 87 53 20 13 E: halesphx2@aol.com

HALEY, Thomas Arthur. b 52. NTMTC 98. **d** 98 **p** 99. NSM Old Ford St Paul and St Mark *Lon* 98–02; NSM Hackney Marsh 02–16; TV 07–16; PtO *Ox* from 17. *3 College Close, Thame OX9 2DQ* E: thaley2607@gmail.com

HALFORD, David John. b 47. JP 84. Didsbury Coll Man CertEd 69 Open Univ BA 75 DipEd 86 Man Univ MEd 79 ACP 72. **d** 96 **p** 97. OLM Royton St Anne *Man* 96–12; NSM Leesfield 12–17; rtd 17; PtO *Man* from 17. *33 Broadway, Royton, Oldham OL2 5DD* T: 0161-633 4650 M: 07966-178836 E: djhalford81@hotmail.com

HALFPENNY, Brian Norman. b 36. CB 90. St Jo Coll Ox BA 60 MA 64. Wells Th Coll 60. **d** 62 **p** 63. C Melksham *Sarum* 62–65; Chapl RAF 65–83; Sen Chapl RAF Coll Cranwell 82–83; Asst Chapl-in-Chief RAF 83–88; Chapl-in-Chief RAF 88–91; QHC 85–91; Can and Preb Linc Cathl 89–91; TR Redditch, The Ridge *Worc* 91–01; rtd 01; PtO *Glouc* 02–17. *80 Roman Way, Bourton-on-the-Water, Cheltenham GL54 2EW* T: (01451) 821589 E: bnhalfpenny@gmail.com

HALIFAX, Archdeacon of. *Vacant*

HALKES, Canon John Stanley. b 39. SWMTC 87. **d** 90 **p** 91. NSM St Buryan, St Levan and Sennen *Truro* 90–92; P-in-c Lanteglos by Fowey 92–04; P-in-c Lansallos 03–04; Hon Can Truro Cathl 03–08; rtd 04; PtO *Truro* from 16. *Creek Cottage, Lerryn, Lostwithiel PL22 0QB*

HALL, Canon Alfred Christopher. b 35. Trin Coll Ox BA 58 MA 61. Westcott Ho Cam 58. **d** 61 **p** 62. C Frecheville *Derby* 61–64; C Dronfield 64–67; V Smethwick St Matt *Birm* 67–70; V Smethwick St Matt w St Chad 70–75; Can Res Man Cathl 75–83; Hon Can Man Cathl 83–90; Dioc Adult Educn Officer 75–83; Dioc World Development Officer 76–88; V Bolton St Pet 83–90; Co-ord Chr Concern for One World *Ox* 90–00; LtO 90–00; rtd 01; Hon Can Ch Ch *Ox* 00–01; PtO from 01; Hon Sec Li Tim-Oi Foundn 93–17. *The Knowle, Philcote Street, Deddington, Banbury OX15 0TB* T: (01869) 338225 E: gaedoh@icloud.com

HALL, Andrew David. b 62. Mattersey Hall MA 09 St Jo Coll Dur MATM 12. Cranmer Hall Dur 10. **d** 12 **p** 13. C Brighouse and Clifton *Leeds* 12–15; R Burbage w Aston Flamville *Leic* from 15. *The Rectory, New Road, Burbage, Hinckley LE10 2AW* T: (01455) 230512 M: 07507-561216 E: 1andrewdavidhall@gmail.com

HALL, Andrew John. b 49. **d** 14 **p** 15. C Cheltenham St Mary w St Matt and St Luke *Glouc* 14–19; rtd 19; PtO *Glouc* from 19. *17 Carisbrooke Drive, Charlton Kings, Cheltenham GL52 6YA* T: (01242) 584711

HALL, Barry George. b 38. Solicitor 62. Oak Hill Th Coll 78. **d** 81 **p** 82. NSM Stock Harvard *Chelmsf* 81–90; NSM W Hanningfield 90–02; P-in-c 93–02; PtO from 02. *Harvard Cottage, Swan Lane, Stock, Ingatestone CM4 9BQ* T: (01277) 840387

HALL, Brian. b 59. Aston Tr Scheme 90 Oak Hill Th Coll 92. **d** 94 **p** 95. C Mansfield St Jo *S'well* 94–96; C Skegby 96–99; P-in-c Sutton in Ashfield St Mich 99–04; R Carlton-in-the-Willows 04–16; V Gorleston St Andr *Nor* from 16. *St Andrew's Vicarage, 16 Duke Road, Gorleston, Great Yarmouth NR31 6LL* T: (01493) 296950 E: revbhall@sky.com

HALL, Canon Brian Arthur. b 48. Ex Univ BEd 70. Cuddesdon Coll 73. **d** 75 **p** 76. C Hobs Moat *Birm* 75–79; V Smethwick 79–93; R Handsworth St Mary 93–13; AD Handsworth 99–05 and 06–08; Hon Can Birm Cathl 05–13; rtd 13;

PtO *Birm* from 13. *97 Perry Hill Road, Oldbury B68 0AH* E: brian.a.hall@btinternet.com

HALL, Mrs Carolyn Ruth. d 08 **p** 09. NSM Builth and Llanddewi'r Cwm w Llangynog etc *S & B* 08–11; NSM Builth Deanery 11–15; NSM Radnor and Builth *S & B* from 16. *Coedmor, Broadway, Llandrindod Wells LD1 5HT* T: (01597) 829637

HALL, Ms Christine Beryl. b 52. Southn Univ BSc 73 Leeds Univ MA 06. NTMTC BA 08. **d** 08 **p** 09. NSM Stepney St Dunstan and All SS *Lon* 08–13; NSM St Jo on Bethnal Green from 13; Chapl Guy's and St Thos' NHS Foundn Trust 08–11; Chapl Lon Fire Brigade 08–11. *15 Lidfield Road, London N16 9NA* T: (020) 7254 9185 E: christine.b.hall@btinternet.com

HALL, Canon Christine Mary. K Coll Lon BD 67 MPhil 86. **d** 87. NSM Bickley *Roch* 87–92; Vice-Prin Chich Th Coll 92–94; LtO *Chich* 95–03; Can and Preb Chich Cathl from 15; PtO *Portsm* from 15. *The Old School, East Marden, Chichester PO18 9JE* T: (01243) 535244 E: dcnchall@eastmarden.net

HALL, Christopher. *See* HALL, Alfred Christopher

HALL, Clive Richard. b 61. Lindisfarne Regional Tr Partnership 15. **d** 18 **p** 19. NSM Stranton *Dur* from 18. *10 Clarkson Court, Hartlepool TS25 5HP* T: (01429) 278504 M: 07804-530120 E: clive.hall7@ntlworld.com

HALL, Darryl Christopher. b 69. Cranmer Hall Dur 07. **d** 09 **p** 10. C Knaresborough *Ripon* 09–13; V Upper Nidderdale 13–14; *Leeds* from 14; AD Ripon 17–19. *The New Vicarage, New Church Street, Pateley Bridge, Harrogate HG3 5LQ* T: (01423) 711414 M: 07792-419982 E: horlix@aol.com

HALL, David Anthony. b 43. Reading Univ BA 66. Qu Coll Birm 79. **d** 81 **p** 82. C Norton *St Alb* 81–85; TV Hitchin 85–93; P-in-c Buckworth w Alconbury *Cov* 93; V 93–08; RD Alcester 05–08; rtd 08; PtO *Cov* from 09; *Worc* from 14. *1 Abbey Close, Alcester B49 5QW* T: (01789) 763252 E: davidahall@onetel.com

HALL, Canon David Martin. b 66. Greenwich Univ BA 89. Oak Hill Th Coll BA 00. **d** 00 **p** 01. C Bebington *Ches* 00–03; P-in-c Danehill *Chich* 03–05; V 05–12; RD Uckfield 11–12; V Chorleywood Ch Ch *St Alb* from 12; RD Rickmansworth 16–20; Hon Can St Alb from 19. *Christ Church Vicarage, Rickmansworth Road, Chorleywood, Rickmansworth WD3 5SG* T: (01923) 282149 *or* 284325 E: david.andmaryhall@tiscali.co.uk *or* david.hall@cccw.org.uk

HALL, Derek. *See* HALL, John Derek

HALL, Derek Guy. b 26. Tyndale Hall Bris 50. **d** 51 **p** 52. C Preston All SS *Blackb* 51–54; C Halliwell St Pet *Man* 54–56; C-in-c Buxton Trin Prop Chpl *Derby* 56–58; V Blackb St Jude 58–67; R Fazakerley *Liv* 67–74; TR 74–81; V Langdale *Carl* 81–86; rtd 86; PtO *Carl* 86–10. *14 Gale Park, Ambleside LA22 0BN* T: (01539) 433144

HALL, Diana Mary. b 76. Edin Univ MA 98 BD 14 LLB 00 St Aid Coll Dur MLitt 16. **d** 14 **p** 15. C St Andrews St Andr *St And* 14–17; R Dunbar *Edin* from 17. *St Anne's House, 1 Westgate, Dunbar EH42 1JL* E: rector@stannesdunbar.org.uk

HALL, Canon Elaine Chegwin. b 59. Liv Univ MTh 01 RGN 82. NOC 94. **d** 97 **p** 98. C Frankby w Greasby *Ches* 97–01; V Stretton and Appleton Thorn 01–13; RD Gt Budworth 03–10; V Stockport St Geo from 13; Hon Can Ches Cathl from 12. *17 Frewland Avenue, Stockport SK3 8TZ* T: 0161-456 9382 *or* 480 2453 E: petera.hall@care4free.net *or* vicar@stgeorgestockport.org.uk

HALL, Elizabeth. *See* SNOWDEN, Elizabeth

HALL (*née* Elliott***), Mrs Eveline Mary. b** 39. Bedf Coll Lon BA 60 Cam Univ 92 ALA 63. EAMTC 92. **d** 95 **p** 96. NSM Bury St Edmunds St Mary *St E* 95–07; NSM Lark Valley 97–07; rtd 07; PtO *St E* 07–17; *St And* from 17. *15 High Street, Elie, Leven KY9 1BY* T: (01333) 330216

HALL, Frances. *See* SHOESMITH, Judith Frances

HALL, Geoffrey Hedley. b 33. Bris Univ BA 55. St Steph Ho Ox 63. **d** 65 **p** 66. C Taunton H Trin *B & W* 65–67; CF 67–80; Sen CF 80–86; P-in-c Ambrosden w Arncot and Blackthorn *Ox* 72–75; V Barnsley St Edw *Wakef* 86–98; rtd 98; PtO *St And* from 98; *Bre* from 99. *Montana Villa, 39 Haston Crescent, Perth PH2 7XD* T: (01738) 636802 M: 07803-578499 E: geoffreyhall@blueyonder.co.uk

HALL, George Richard Wyndham. b 49. Ex Univ LLB 71. Wycliffe Hall Ox BA 74 MA 78. **d** 75 **p** 76. C Walton H Trin *Ox* 75–79; C Farnborough *Guildf* 79–84; Bp's Chapl *Nor* 84–87; R Saltford w Corston and Newton St Loe *B & W* 87–14; Chapl Bath Coll of HE 88–90; RD Chew Magna *B & W* 97–03; rtd 14; PtO *Carl* from 16. *45 Howard Park, Greystoke, Penrith CA11 0TU* T: (01768) 483394 E: revrichardhall45@gmail.com

HALL, Canon George Rumney. b 37. LVO 99 CVO 03. Westcott Ho Cam 60. **d** 62 **p** 63. C Camberwell St Phil *S'wark* 62–65; C Waltham Cross *St Alb* 65–67; R Buckenham

w Hassingham and Strumpshaw *Nor* 67–74; Chapl St Andr Hosp Thorpe 67–72; Chapl HM Pris Nor 72–74; V Wymondham *Nor* 74–87; RD Humbleyard 86–87; R Sandringham w W Newton 87–94; P-in-c Flitcham 87–94; P-in-c Wolferton w Babingley 87–94; R Sandringham w W Newton and Appleton etc 95–03; P-in-c Castle Rising 87–03; P-in-c Hillington 87–03; Hon Can Nor Cathl 87–03; RD Heacham and Rising 89–01; Dom Chapl to The Queen 87–03; Chapl to The Queen 89–07; rtd 03; PtO *Nor* from 03. *Town Farm Cottage, 95 Lynn Road, Great Bircham, King's Lynn PE31 6RJ* T: (01485) 576134 M: 07889-627940

HALL, Gillian Helen. b 60. Man Univ BA 81 Bris Univ MA 83 Dur Univ MA 20. St Mellitus Coll 18. **d** 20 **p** 21. NSM Cheadle All Hallows *Ches* from 20. *58 Warren Avenue, Cheadle SK8 1ND* T: 0161-428 9645 E: ghh@swissmail.org

HALL, Mrs Gillian Louise. b 45. Univ of Wales (Ban) MPhil 06. NOC 87. **d** 90 **p** 94. NSM Earby *Bradf* 90–96; NSM Gisburn 96–01; NSM Hellifield 96–01; PtO 01–02; Chapl Airedale NHS Trust 02–04; PtO *Bradf* 05–14; *Leeds* from 14. *Mitton House, Lothersdale, Keighley BD20 8HR* T: (01535) 636144 E: mittonhouse@dsl.pipex.com

HALL, Gillian Mary. b 58. Linc Sch of Th and Min. **d** 12 **p** 13. NSM Bilborough w Strelley *S'well* 12–15; NSM Bilborough and Strelley 15–19; NSM Kimberley and Nuthall 19–20; NSM Clifton from 20. *30 Parkside, Nottingham NG8 2NN* E: gillhall30@gmail.com

HALL (*née* JACKSON***), Hannah Louise. b** 81. St Cuth Soc Dur BA 04 St Jo Coll Dur MA 06. St Mellitus Coll 10. **d** 12 **p** 13. C Pitsmoor Ch Ch *Sheff* 12–15; V Nottingham St Sav *S'well* from 15. *St Saviour's Vicarage, Arkwright Walk, Nottingham NG2 2JU* M: 07702-163138 E: hannah3hall@gmail.com

HALL, Harry. b 41. Open Univ BA 93. Chich Th Coll 91. **d** 91 **p** 92. C Boston *Linc* 91–92; C Bourne 92–94; P-in-c Sutterton w Fosdyke and Algarkirk 94–97; R Sutterton, Fosdyke, Algarkirk and Wigtoft 97–99; V Barnsley St Edw *Wakef* 99–05; Chapl ATC 99–05; R Ardstraw w Baronscourt, Badoney Lower etc *D & R* 05–10; rtd 10; PtO *Linc* from 11. *18 Kings Road, Metheringham, Lincoln LN4 3HT* T: (01526) 320308 E: slk248@hotmail.com

HALL, Canon Hubert William Peter. b 35. Ely Th Coll 58. **d** 60 **p** 61. C Louth w Welton-le-Wold *Linc* 60–62; C Gt Grimsby St Jas 62–69; C Gt Grimsby St Mary and St Jas 69–71; Hon Chapl Miss to Seafarers 71–01; V Immingham *Linc* 71–01; RD Haverstoe 86–01; Can and Preb Linc Cathl 89–01; rtd 01; PtO *Linc* from 01. *6 Abbey Rise, Barrow-upon-Humber DN19 7TF* T: (01469) 531504 E: hwphall@gmail.com

HALL, Mrs Jane Daphne. b 60. Trent Poly BA 92 Solicitor 93. **d** 09 **p** 10. NSM Clopton w Otley, Swilland and Ashbocking *St E* 09–13; NSM Carlford 13–17; rtd 17. *Lark Rise, 230 Ferry Road, Felixstowe IP11 9RU* E: jane.d.pearse@gmail.com

HALL, Jeffrey Ernest. b 42. Linc Th Coll 73. **d** 75 **p** 76. C Brampton St Thos *Derby* 75–78; C Whittington and New Whittington 78–81; TV Riverside *Ox* 81–90; Ind Chapl Slough Deanery 81–89; R Anstey *Leic* 90–97; TR Hugglescote w Donington, Ellistown and Snibston 97–08; rtd 08; PtO *Sarum* 10–19; *B & W* from 17. *21 Woodsage Drive, Gillingham SP8 4UE* T: (01747) 823480 M: 07876-540343 E: jeffreyhall123@btinternet.com

HALL, Jennifer. *See* HALL, Margaret Jennifer

HALL, The Ven John Barrie. b 41. Sarum & Wells Th Coll 82. **d** 84 **p** 85. Chapl St Edward's Hosp Cheddleton 84–88; C Cheddleton *Lich* 84–88; V Rocester 88–94; V Rocester and Croxden w Hollington 94–98; RD Uttoxeter 91–98; Adn Salop 98–11; V Tong 98–11; P-in-c Donington 98–00; rtd 11; PtO *Lich* 11–13; Hon C Hanbury, Newborough, Rangemore and Tutbury 13; PtO 13–21. *16 Mill House Drive, Cheadle, Stoke-on-Trent ST10 1XL* T: (01538) 750628 E: j.hall182@btinternet.com

HALL, John Bruce. b 33. Covenant Th Sem St Louis MTh 80 DMin 85. ALCD 60. **d** 60 **p** 61. C Kingston upon Hull H Trin *York* 60–67; C Beverley Minster 67–68; V Clapham Park St Steph *S'wark* 68–76; R Tooting Graveney St Nic 76–03; rtd 03; PtO *S'wark* from 03; *Eur* from 04. *44 Mayford Road, London SW12 8SD* T: (020) 8673 6869 E: jbewhall@gmail.com

HALL, John Charles. b 46. Hull Univ BA 71 Spurgeon's Coll MTh 05. Ridley Hall Cam 71. **d** 73 **p** 74. C Bromley Common St Aug *Roch* 73–77; C Westbury-on-Trym St Alb *Bris* 78–80; Oman 80–82; C-in-c Bishop Auckland Woodhouse Close CD *Dur* 82–90; P-in-c Gt and Lt Glemham, Blaxhall etc *St E* 90–91; P-in-c Rodney Stoke w Draycott *B & W* 91–11; Dioc Ecum Officer 91–01; V Southmead *Bris* 01–11; rtd 11; PtO *B & W* 15–20; *Ex* from 21. *2 Church Path, Okehampton EX20 1LW* T: (01837) 53063 M: 07771-848412 E: sarasgarden@hotmail.co.uk

HALL, John Curtis. b 39. CEng 73 MIMechE 73. Coll of Resurr Mirfield 80. **d** 82 **p** 83. C Pet Ch Carpenter 82–86;

TV Heavitree w Ex St Paul 86–93; R Bow w Broad Nymet 93–04; V Colebrooke 93–04; R Zeal Monachorum 93–04; RD Cadbury 97–02; rtd 04. *37 Lawn Drive, Chudleigh, Newton Abbot TQ13 0LS* T: (01626) 853245

HALL, Canon John Derek. b 25. St Cuth Soc Dur BA 50. Linc Th Coll 50. **d** 52 **p** 53. C Redcar *York* 52–54; C Newland St Jo 54–57; V Boosbeck w Moorsholm 57–61; V Middlesbrough St Oswald 61–68; Chapl St Luke's Hosp Middlesbrough 61–67; V York St Chad 68–90; Chapl Bootham Park Hosp 68–85; Can and Preb York Minster 85–90; rtd 90; Chapl Castle Howard 90–02; PtO *York* 85–14. *25 Fairfields Drive, Skelton, York YO30 1YP* T: (01904) 470978

HALL, Canon John Edmund. b 49. Open Univ BA 84 Birm Univ MPhil 05 Warwick Univ PhD 06 CQSW 76. Trin Coll Bris BA 89. **d** 89 **p** 90. C Winchmore Hill St Paul *Lon* 89–92; V Edmonton St Aldhelm 92–01; Dir Soc Resp *Cov* 01–10; Dir Interfaith Relns and Dir St Phil Cen *Leic* 10–14; Hon Can Leic Cathl 10–14; rtd 14; Dioc Interfaith Adv *Ex* 15–19; PtO from 20. *7 Riverside View, Ottery St Mary EX11 1YA*

HALL, John Michael. b 47. BD. Oak Hill Th Coll 68. **d** 73 **p** 74. C Walthamstow St Mary w St Steph *Chelmsf* 73–76; C Rainham 76–79; P-in-c Woodham Mortimer w Hazeleigh 79–93; P-in-c Woodham Walter 79–93; Ind Chapl 79–93; R Fairstead w Terling and White Notley etc 93–13; RD Witham 01–07; rtd 13; PtO *Ely* from 14. *43 Northwold, Ely CB6 1BG* T: (01353) 969089 E: rev.johnhall@tiscali.co.uk

HALL, Canon John Michael. b 62. Leeds Univ BA. Coll of Resurr Mirfield 83. **d** 86 **p** 87. C Ribbleton *Blackb* 86–89; C Carnforth 89–92; V Lt Marsden 92–98; V Lt Marsden w Nelson St Mary 98; V Warton St Oswald w Yealand Conyers 98–08; AD Tunstall 05–08; P-in-c Fleetwood St Pet 08–11; V 11–14; P-in-c Fleetwood St Dav 08–14; V Fleetwood St Pet and St Dav from 14; Hon Can Bloemfontein Cathl from 01; Hon Can Blackb Cathl from 09. *The Vicarage, 49 Mount Road, Fleetwood FY7 6QZ* T: (01253) 876176 E: johnbloem@aol.com

HALL, The Very Revd John Robert. b 49. KCVO 19. St Chad's Coll Dur BA 71 FRSA 02 FSA 14 Hon FCollT 09 Roehampton Univ Hon DD 07 Ches Univ Hon DTheol 08 Westmr Univ Hon DLitt 14 Hull Univ Hon DLitt 16. Cuddesdon Coll 73. **d** 75 **p** 76. C Kennington St Jo *S'wark* 75–78; P-in-c S Wimbledon All SS 78–84; V Streatham St Pet 84–92; Dioc Dir of Educn *Blackb* 92–98; Hon Can Blackb Cathl 92–94 and 98–00; Can Res Blackb Cathl 94–98; Gen Sec Nat Soc 98–06; Gen Sec C of E Bd of Educn 98–02; Chief Educn Officer and Hd Educn Division Abps' Coun 03–06; Hon C S Norwood St Alb *S'wark* 03–06; Dean Westmr 06–19; rtd 19; Wiccamical Preb Chich Cathl from 18. *15 Little London, Chichester PO19 1NZ* T: (01243) 465618 M: 07973-418859 E: johnrhall1949@gmail.com

HALL, Canon John Terence Peter. b 67. St Jo Coll Dur BA 98. Cranmer Hall Dur. **d** 98 **p** 99. C Towcester w Easton Neston *Pet* 98–01; P-in-c Blakesley w Adstone and Maidford etc 01–07; P-in-c Lichborough 06–07; R Lambfold *Pet* 07–11; RD Towcester 09–11; P-in-c Irthlingborough 11–12; P-in-c Gt w Lt Addington and Woodford 11–12; R Irthlingborough, Gt Addington, Lt Addington etc from 13; Warden of Readers 14–19; Warden Lay Min Oakham Adnry from 19; Can Pet Cathl from 10. *The Rectory, 79 Finedon Road, Irthlingborough, Wellingborough NN9 5TY* T: (01933) 650278 E: canon.johnhall@gmail.com *or* fr.john@nenecrossings.org.uk

HALL, Jonathan. b 62. Ch Ch Coll Cant BA 83 MCIPD 94. STETS BTh 99. **d** 99 **p** 00. C Weymouth H Trin *Sarum* 99–03; R Whippingham w E Cowes *Portsm* 03–10; RD W Wight 07–10; Chapl Burrswood Chr Hosp *Roch* 10–16; V Aylesford 16–18; PtO *Portsm* 14–18; P-in-c Lower Sandown St Jo from 18; P-in-c Shanklin St Blasius from 18. *10 Elmbank Gardens, Sandown PO36 9SA* T: (01983) 402480 E: rev.jonathanhall@btinternet.com

HALL, Judith Frances. *See* SHOESMITH, Judith Frances

HALL, The Very Revd Kenneth Robert James. b 59. St Jo Coll Nottm 95. **d** 98 **p** 99. NSM Derryloran *Arm* 98–02; C Drumglass w Moygashel 02–03; C Brackaville w Donaghendry and Ballyclog 03–04; I 04–10; Dean Clogh from 10; I Enniskillen from 10. *St Macartin's Deanery, 13 Church Street, Enniskillen BT74 7DW* T: (028) 6632 2465 *or* 6632 2917 E: krjhall@btinternet.com

HALL, Liliana Miheala Nutu (Ela). b 70. Regents Th Coll BA 98 Sheff Univ PhD 04. St Hild Coll 18. **d** 19 **p** 20. NSM Endcliffe *Sheff* from 19; NSM Sheff St Mary Bramall Lane from 19. *16 Botanical Road, Sheffield S11 8RP* T: 0114-268 7002 M: 07595-087441 E: elanutuhall@gmail.com *or* l.m.nutu@sheffield.ac.uk

HALL, Mrs Linda Charlotte. b 50. Wall Hall Coll Aldenham CertEd 72. St Alb Minl Tr Scheme 85 Oak Hill Th Coll 91.

d 92 **p** 94. NSM St Alb St Steph 92–98; NSM Sandridge 98–99; C Ipswich All Hallows *St E* 99–00; PtO 01; TV Cwmbran *Mon* 01–08; P-in-c Maesglas and Duffryn 08–15; rtd 16; PtO *Mon* from 16. *32 Woodlands Park, Pontypool NP4 6UP* T: (01495) 760472 E: rev.linda.chall@gmail.com

HALL, Malcolm. b 67. Lindisfarne Regional Tr Partnership 15. **d** 18 **p** 19. NSM N Shields *Newc* 18–21; C from 21. *4 Allendale Crescent, Shiremoor, Newcastle upon Tyne NE27 0UE* T: 0191-295 4760 M: 07833-497208

HALL, Margaret Jennifer. b 44. Univ Coll Lon BSc 67 Brunel Univ MA 83. Trin Coll Bris 10. **d** 12 **p** 13. OLM Stoke Bishop *Bris* 12–20; NSM from 20. *Dial Cottage, 34 Julian Road, Bristol BS9 1JY* T: 0117-968 5959 E: mjenniferhall@btinternet.com

HALL, Mary. *See* HALL, Eveline Mary

HALL, Ms Melanie Jane. b 55. Ex Univ BA 78. Ripon Coll Cuddesdon 01. **d** 03 **p** 04. C Stepney St Dunstan and All SS *Lon* 03–06; rtd 06; PtO *Lon* 14–19. *Gramarye House, Bush Road, Spaxton, Bridgwater TA5 1BX* T: (01278) 671034 M: 07788-440078

HALL, Michael Alan. b 76. Univ of Wales (Lamp) BA 98. Ripon Coll Cuddesdon 99. **d** 01 **p** 02. C Wellington Ch Ch *Lich* 01–05; V Chelmsf All SS 05–14; P-in-c Gt Burstead w Ramsden Crays from 14. *The Vicarage, 111 Church Street, Billericay CM11 2TR* T: (01277) 632060 E: revd.michael@btinternet.com

HALL, Canon Michael Anthony. b 41. St Paul's Coll Grahamstown LTh 64. **d** 64 **p** 65. C E London St Alb S Africa 65–67; C Queenstown St Mich 67–69; R Port Elizabeth All SS 70–78; R E London All SS 78–81; R Queenstown St Mich w Tarkastad St Mary 81–91; Adn Aliwal N 81–01; R Barkly E St Steph 91–01; P-in-c Dordrecht St Aug 91–02; Hon Can Grahamstown from 01; P-in-c Lapford, Nymet Rowland and Coldridge *Ex* 01–03; TV N Creedy 03–11; rtd 11; PtO *Ex* from 02. *10 Blagdon Rise, Crediton EX17 1EN* T: (01363) 776574 M: 07751-798670 E: micksandhall@btopenworld.com

HALL, Nicholas Charles. b 56. **d** 86 **p** 87. C Hyde St Geo *Ches* 86–89; C Cheadle 89–91; NSM 91–11; PtO from 11. *58 Warren Avenue, Cheadle SK8 1ND* T: 0161-491 6758 F: 491 0285 E: kairosmedia@swissmail.org

HALL, Canon Nigel David. b 46. Univ of Wales (Cardiff) BA 67 BD 76 Lon Univ CertEd 68. St Mich Coll Llan 73. **d** 76 **p** 77. C Cardiff St Jo *Llan* 76–81; R Llanbadarn Fawr, Llandegley and Llanfihangel etc *S & B* 81–95; RD Maelienydd 89–95; V Builth and Llanddewi'r Cwm w Llangynog etc 95–11; Can Brecon Cathl 94–11; Prec Brecon Cathl 99–00; Treas Brecon Cathl 00–04; Dean Brecon Cathl 04–11; AD Builth 04–11; rtd 11; PtO *S & B* from 11. *Coedmor, Broadway, Llandrindod Wells LD1 5HT* T: (01597) 829637

HALL (née WANSTALL), Canon Noelle Margaret. b 53. Wolfs Coll Cam BEd 76. Sarum & Wells Th Coll 84. **dss** 86 **d** 87 **p** 94. Hythe *Cant* 86–89; Par Dn 87–89; Par Dn Reculver and Herne Bay St Bart 89–94; C 94–95; Dioc Adv in Women's Min 92–99; Asst Dir Post-Ord Tr 94–97; P-in-c Sittingbourne St Mary 95–00; P-in-c Bilean 07–09; P-in-c Cant All SS 14–16; AD Cant 05–11; Hon Can Cant Cathl 96–16; rtd 16; PtO *Cant* 17–19. *127 Rylands Road, Kennington, Ashford TN24 9LR* M: 07743-629975 E: nmhall1556@gmail.com

HALL, Peter. *See* HALL, Hubert William Peter

HALL, Canon Peter Douglas. b 60. Oak Hill Th Coll BA 92. **d** 92 **p** 93. C Bromyard *Heref* 92–96; C Dorridge *Birm* 96–01; V Fareham St Jo *Portsm* 01–13; P-in-c Crookhorn 13–18; C Purbrook 13–18; C Portsdown 13–18; Dean Pioneer Min 15–18; Dioc Dir Voc and Ord from 18; Hon Can Portsm Cathl from 15. *269 Hawthorn Crescent, Cosham, Portsmouth PO6 2TL* T: (023) 9221 0283 E: revpdhall@gmail.com *or* peter.hall@portsmouth.anglican.org

HALL, Philip Edward Robin. b 36. Oak Hill Th Coll 64. **d** 67 **p** 68. C Ware Ch Ch *St Alb* 67–70; C Rayleigh *Chelmsf* 70–73; R Leven w Catwick *York* 73–85; P-in-c Mayfield *Lich* 85–95; P-in-c Ilam w Blore Ray and Okeover 89–95; Res Min Canwell 95–01; Res Min Hints 95–01; Res Min Drayton Bassett 95–01; rtd 01; PtO *Sheff* 01–20; *Derby* 02–13. *22 Kings Court, 358 Manchester Road, Sheffield S10 5DQ* T: 0114-438 2564 E: per.hall13@uwclub.net

HALL, Richard. *See* HALL, George Richard Wyndham

HALL, Richard Alexander Bullock. b 71. Ex Univ BA 93 Edin Univ MTh 95 BD 98. TISEC 95. **d** 98 **p** 99. C Boxmoor St Jo *St Alb* 98–01; CF 01–09; Hon Min Can Ripon Cathl 06–09; P-in-c Kirkby Stephen w Mallerstang etc *Carl* 09–11; CF from 11. *c/o MOD Chaplains (Army)* T: (01264) 383430 F: 381824 E: richard.moonhall@btinternet.com

HALL, Robert Arthur. b 35. Lon Univ BSc 66. NW Ord Course 74. **d** 77 **p** 78. C York St Paul 77–79; R Elvington w Sutton on Derwent and E Cottingwith 79–82; Chapl Tiffield

Sch Northants 82–84; V Bessingby and Carnaby *York* 84–88; V Fulford 88–00; P-in-c York St Denys 97–00; rtd 00; PtO *York* 00–20. *11 Almond Grove, Filey YO14 9EH* T: (01723) 518355

HALL, Canon Robert Stainburn. b 72. Qu Coll Cam BA 93. St Steph Ho Ox 96. **d** 98 **p** 99. C Worc SE 98–01; TV Halas 01–10; P-in-c 10–15; TR from 15; Hon Can Worc Cathl from 17. *St Margaret's Vicarage, 55 Quarry Lane, Halesowen B63 4PD* T: 0121-550 8744

HALL, Canon Roger John. b 53. MBE 97. Linc Th Coll. **d** 84 **p** 85. C Shrewsbury St Giles w Sutton and Atcham *Lich* 84–87; CF 87–07; Warden Amport Ho 98–01; Chapl Guards Chpl Lon 01–03; Asst Chapl Gen 03–07; Dir Ords 98-02 and Warden of Readers 98–07; QHC 06–07; Dep P in O from 07; Chapl St Pet-ad-Vincula at HM Tower of Lon from 07; Can Chpls R from 12; Chapl Bacon's Coll from 07. *The Chaplain's Residence, HM Tower of London, London EC3N 4AB* T: (020) 3166 6796 E: roger.hall@hrp.org.uk

HALL, Mrs Rosalyn. b 58. NEOC 04. **d** 07 **p** 08. C Washington *Dur* 07–11; V Hartlepool H Trin from 11. *Holy Trinity Vicarage, Davison Drive, Hartlepool TS24 9BX* T: (01429) 869618 M: 07985-134577 E: rosalyn44@hotmail.com

HALL, Sandra June. b 58. Westcott Ho Cam. **d** 10 **p** 11. C Cuckfield *Chich* 10–15; P-in-c Itchingfield w Slinfold 15–16; R from 16. *The Rectory, The Street, Slinfold, Horsham RH13 0RR* T: (01403) 790197 M: 07817-056986

HALL, Sonia Winifred. *See* RUDD, Sonia Winifred

HALL, Stephen Philip. b 56. Ripon Coll Cuddesdon. **d** 84 **p** 85. C Camberwell St Giles S'wark 84–88; Chapl Brighton Poly *Chich* 88–92; TV Bicester w Bucknell, Caversfield and Launton *Ox* 92–02; Sub Chapl HM Pris Bullingdon 92–02; TV Southampton (City Cen) *Win* 02–12; V Lewisham St Mary S'wark from 12; AD E Lewisham from 17; Asst Dir of Ords Woolwich Area from 17; Chapl Colfe's Sch Lon from 15. *48 Lewisham Park, London SE13 6QZ* T: (020) 8690 2682

HALL, Prof Stuart George. b 28. New Coll Ox BA 52 MA 55 BD 72. Ripon Hall Ox 53. **d** 54 **p** 55. C Newark w Coddington S'well 54–58; Tutor Qu Coll Birm 58–62; Lect Th Nottm Univ 62–73; Sen Lect 73–78; Prof Ecclesiastical Hist K Coll Lon 78–90; PtO *St Alb* 80–86; S'wark 86–90; R Pittenweem *St And* 90–98; R Elie and Earlsferry 90–98; rtd 93. *Hopedene, 15 High Street, Elie, Leven KY9 1BY* T: (01333) 330216 E: s.hall579@btinternet.com

HALL, Timothy Patrick. b 65. Bucks Coll of Educn BSc 87 Oak Hill Th Coll BA 93. Trin Coll Bris 99. **d** 01 **p** 02. C Kingsnorth and Shadoxhurst *Cant* 01–04; P-in-c Crowfield w Stonham Aspal and Mickfield *St E* 04–12; P-in-c Coddenham w Gosbeck and Hemingstone w Henley 04–12; RD Bosmere 07–08; V W Sheppey *Cant* 12–18; Chief Exec Officer Through Faith Miss from 18; PtO *Ely* from 19. *14 Bowthorpe Road, Wisbech PE13 2DX* E: tim@throughfaithmissions.org

HALL, Timothy Robert. b 52. Dur Univ BA 74. St Jo Coll Nottm LTh 87. **d** 87 **p** 88. C Hawarden *St As* 87–89; Chapl St D Coll Llandudno from 90. *Woodpecker Cottage, St David's College, Llandudno LL30 1RD* T: (01492) 581224 M: 07887-874487 E: revtimhall@stdavidscollege.co.uk

HALL, William. b 34. Hull Univ BSc(Econ) 56. NEOC 89. **d** 92 **p** 93. NSM Bishopwearmouth St Nic *Dur* 92–01; rtd 01. *31 Nursery Road, Silksworth Lane, Sunderland SR3 1NT* T: 0191-528 4843

HALL-MATTHEWS, Preb John Cuthbert Berners. b 33. Univ of Qld BA 55 K Coll Lon PGCE 65. Coll of Resurr Mirfield 58. **d** 60 **p** 61. C Woodley St Jo the Ev *Ox* 60–63; CT Is of Dogs Ch Ch and St Jo w St Luke *Lon* 63–65; Asst Chapl Ch Hosp Horsham 65–72; Chapl R Hosp Sch Holbrook 72–75; V Tupsley *Heref* 75–90; P-in-c Hampton Bishop and Mordiford w Dormington 77–90; RD Heref City 84–90; Preb Heref Cathl 85–90; TR Wolverhampton *Lich* 90–98; TR Cen Wolverhampton 98–02; Preb Lich Cathl 01–02; rtd 02; PtO *Heref* 11–15; *Cov* 16–21. *26 Plover Close, Stratford-upon-Avon CV37 9EN* T: (01789) 414182 E: jotricia@btinternet.com

HALL-THOMPSON, Colin Lloyd. b 51. JP . TCD. **d** 84 **p** 85. C Dublin Rathfarnham *D & G* 84–86; Bp's C Clonmel Union *C, C & R* 86–91; Chapl Fort Mitchel Pris 86–91; Miss to Seafarers Chapl Port of Cork 86–89; I Kilbride *Conn* 91–03; I Ballymacarrett *D & D* 03–09; Hon Chapl Miss to Seafarers 91–09; Sen Chapl from 09. *7A Wilshere Drive, Belmont, Belfast BT4 2GP* T: (028) 9022 3910 *or* 9075 1131 M: 07984-571220 E: colin.hall-thompson@mtsmail.org

HALLAM, Mrs Janet Kay. b 59. EN(G) 79 RGN 01. STETS 05. **d** 08 **p** 13. NSM Newport St Jo *Portsm* 08–18; NSM Newport St Thos 08–18; Chapl Isle of Wight NHS Trust from 13. *Maranatha, 10 Broadwood Lane, Newport PO30 5NE* T: (01983) 529973 M: 07955-381319

HALLAM, Leslie. b 50. All SS Cen for Miss & Min 13. **d** 17 **p** 17. OLM Ramsbottom and Edenfield *Man* from 17. *25 Rochdale Road, Ramsbottom, Bury BL0 0JT* T: (01706) 823240 E: leshallam50@gmail.com

HALLAM, Mrs Marilyn. b 61. **d** 03 **p** 04. NSM Hayes *Roch* 03–19; PtO from 19. *83 Pickhurst Rise, West Wickham, Bromley BR4 0AE* T: (020) 8777 2246

HALLAM, Canon Nicholas Francis. b 48. Univ Coll Ox BA 71 MA 81 Glas Univ PhD 76 MB, ChB 81 FRCPath 00. Ox NSM Course 84. **d** 87 **p** 88. NSM Ox St Clem 87–93; NSM Balerno *Edin* 93–05; NSM Hawkshead and Low Wray w Sawrey and Rusland etc *Carl* from 06; NSM Ambleside w Brathay 06–10; NSM Loughrigg from 10; Hon Can Carl Cathl from 18. *Wetherlam, Hawkshead, Ambleside LA22 0NR* T: (01539) 436069 E: nick.hallam@uwclub.net

HALLAM, Stuart Peter. b 66. St Martin's Coll Lanc BA 92 Wolfs Coll Cam BTh 99. Westcott Ho Cam 96. **d** 99 **p** 00. C Battersea St Mary S'wark 99–02; Chapl RN 02–18; R Vancouver St Phil Canada from 18. *3691 West 27th Avenue, Vancouver BC V6S 1RS, Canada* E: revhallam@aol.com

✠**HALLATT, The Rt Revd David Marrison.** b 37. Southn Univ BA 59 St Cath Coll Ox BA 62 MA 66. Wycliffe Hall Ox 59. **d** 63 **p** 64 **c** 94. C Maghull *Liv* 63–67; PC Totley *Derby* 67–75; R Didsbury St Jas *Man* 75–80; R Barlow Moor 76–80; TR Didsbury St Jas and Em 80–89; Adn Halifax *Wakef* 89–94; Area Bp Shrewsbury *Lich* 94–01; Asst Bp Shrewsbury *Lich* 94–01; Asst Bp Sarum from 11; PtO *Win* 11–15. *10 St Nicholas Hospital, St Nicholas Road, Salisbury SP1 2SW* T: (01722) 413360 E: david.hallatt@btopenworld.com

HALLETT, Miss Caroline Morwenna. b 51. Nottm Univ BSc 72 PGCE 74 Univ of Wales (Ban) BTh 05. EAMTC 03. **d** 05 **p** 06. C Sole Bay *St E* 05–09; P-in-c Acton w Gt Waldingfield 09–20; V 20–21; rtd 21. *79 Dumbarton Road, Ipswich IP4 3JR* E: revhallett@yahoo.co.uk

HALLETT, Keith Philip. b 37. Tyndale Hall Bris 61. **d** 64 **p** 65. C Higher Openshaw *Man* 64–68; C Bushbury *Lich* 68–71; P-in-c Drayton Bassett 71–72; R 72–90; V Fazeley 71–90; P-in-c Hints 78–83; V 83–90; C-in-c Canwell CD 78–83; V Canwell 83–90; RD Tamworth 81–90; P-in-c Buckhurst Hill *Chelmsf* 90–93; TR 93–02; rtd 02; PtO *B & W* from 03. *46 Balmoral Way, Weston-super-Mare BS22 9AL* T: (01934) 413711 E: keithkph@talktalk.net

HALLETT, Peter. b 49. Bath Univ BSc 72. Oak Hill Th Coll. **d** 76 **p** 77. C Brinsworth w Catcliffe *Sheff* 76–79; P-in-c Doncaster St Jas 80–81; V 81–86; R Henstridge and Charlton Horethorne w Stowell *B & W* 86–07; P-in-c Abbas and Templecombe w Horsington 06–07; R Abbas and Templecombe, Henstridge and Horsington 07–17; rtd 17; PtO *Bris* from 18; *B & W* 18–19. *27 Atherston, Bristol BS30 8YB* T: 0117-961 6262 E: halatvic@gmail.com

HALLETT, Peter Duncan. b 43. CCC Cam BA 66 MA 68. Westcott Ho Cam 69. **d** 71 **p** 72. C Sawston *Ely* 71–73; C Lyndhurst and Emery Down *Win* 73–78; C Skegness and Winthorpe *Linc* 78–80; P-in-c Samlesbury *Blackb* 80–91; Asst Dir RE 80–00; C Leyland St Ambrose 91–94; V Lostock Hall 00–09; P-in-c Farington Moss 03–09; V Lostock Hall and Farington Moss 09; rtd 09; PtO *Blackb* from 09. *121 Pleasington Close, Blackburn BB2 1TU*

HALLETT, Stephen Jonathan. b 70. Trin Coll Bris BA 96. Ripon Coll Cuddesdon 17. **d** 19 **p** 20. C Water Eaton *Ox* from 19. *Water Eaton Church Centre, Drayton Road, Bletchley, Milton Keynes MK2 3RR* T: (01908) 630599 M: 07702-098719 E: mkstevehallett@gmail.com

HALLIDAY, Christopher Norton Robert. b 48. Bradf Univ PhD 99. NOC 82. **d** 85 **p** 86. C Davyhulme St Mary *Man* 85–87; Lect Bolton St Pet 87–90; I Rathdrum w Glenealy, Derralossary and Laragh *D & G* 90–00; R Valley Lee St Geo USA 00–05; PtO *Man* 07–08; TR Saddleworth 08–16; rtd 16; PtO *Man* from 16. *2A Gatehead Mews, Delph, Oldham OL3 5QA* E: frchristopher@waitrose.com

HALLIDAY, Mrs Diana Patricia. b 40. ALA 66. NOC 89. **d** 92 **p** 94. NSM Burley in Wharfedale *Bradf* 92–95; NSM Harden and Wilsden 95–97; P-in-c Cullingworth 97–05; Chapl Airedale NHS Foundn Trust 04–11; PtO *Bradf* 11–14; *Leeds* from 14. *8 Malham Court, Silsden, Keighley BD20 0QB* T: (01535) 656777 E: revdi.halliday@btinternet.com

HALLIDAY, Jean Douglas. b 47. NTMTC 99. **d** 01 **p** 02. NSM Forest Gate Em w Upton Cross *Chelmsf* 01–02; NSM E Ham w Upton Park and Forest Gate 02–05; NSM Becontree S 05–09; P-in-c Margaretting w Mountnessing and Buttsbury 09–13; Dioc Child Protection Adv 05–13; rtd 13; PtO *St E* 15–20; *Chelmsf* from 21. *112 McMillan Court, Godfreys Mews, Chelmsford CM2 0XE* T: (01245) 490566 E: jeanhalliday456@btinternet.com

HALLIDAY, Louisa Elizabeth. b 42. Open Univ BA 77 BA 94. STETS. **d** 00 **p** 01. NSM Wylye and Till Valley *Sarum* 00–09; rtd 09; PtO *Sarum* from 10. *Station House,*

Great Wishford, Salisbury SP2 0PA T: (01722) 790618
E: louisahalliday@rocketmail.com
HALLIDAY, Paula Patricia. *See* ROBINSON, Paula Patricia
✠**HALLIDAY, The Rt Revd Robert Taylor.** b 32. Glas Univ
MA 54 BD 57. Edin Th Coll 55. **d** 57 **p** 58 **c** 90. C St Andrews
St Andr *St And* 57–60; C Glas St Marg 60–63; Lect NT Edin Th
Coll 63–74; R Edin H Cross 63–83; Tutor Edin Univ 69–71;
Can St Mary's Cathl *Edin* 73–83; R St Andrews St Andr *St And*
83–90; Tutor St Andr Univ 84–90; Bp Bre 90–96; rtd 96; LtO
Edin from 97; NSM Edin Ch Ch 97–09; NSM Edin St Pet
09–18. *28 Forbes Road, Edinburgh EH10 4ED* T: 0131-221
1490
HALLIDIE SMITH, William. b 35. Pemb Coll Cam BA 58
MA 62. Coll of Resurr Mirfield 59. **d** 60 **p** 62. C Poplar *Lon*
60–67; rtd 00. *69 Park Road, Chilwell, Beeston, Nottingham
NG9 4DD* T: 0115-943 1896
HALLIGAN, Adrian Ronald. b 69. Ulster Univ MSc 96 PGCE 05.
CITC 06. **d** 11. NSM Antrim All SS *Conn* 11–14; NSM Skerry
w Rathcavan and Newtowncrommelin 14–18; NSM Craigs w
Dunaghy and Killagan from 18. *Craigs Rectory, 95 Hillmount
Road, Cullybackey, Ballymena BT42 1NZ* T: (028) 2588
0248 M: 07846-451932 E: adrian.halligan@sky.com
HALLISSEY, Catherine Jane. **d** 14 **p** 15. Kilternan *D & G*
14–15; C Taney 15–19; I Powerscourt w Kilbride
from 19. *Powerscourt Rectory, Enniskerry, Bray, Co
Wicklow, Republic of Ireland* M: (00353) 86-358 3104
E: cathyhallissey@hotmail.com
HALLIWELL, Christopher Eigil. b 57. Newc Univ BA 78. Trin
Coll Bris 89. **d** 91 **p** 92. C Mildenhall *St E* 91–94; R Wrentham
w Benacre, Covehithe, Frostenden etc 94–97; TV Sileby,
Cossington and Seagrave *Leic* 97–01; V Preston St Cuth
Blackb 01–12; V Grimsargh 12–17; Rural and Environmental
Officer 11–17; rtd 17; PtO *Blackb* 17–20. *14 Durham Avenue,
Lancaster LA1 4ED* E: chris.halliwell@btinternet.com
HALLIWELL, Ivor George. b 33. St Cath Coll Cam BA 57
MA 60. Wells Th Coll 58. **d** 60 **p** 60. C Hanworth St Geo *Lon*
60–62; C Willenhall *Cov* 62–65; C-in-c Whitley St Jas CD
65–68; V Whitley 68–72; V Corton *Nor* 72–77; P-in-c Hopton
72–74; V 74–77; Asst Chapl HM Pris Pentonville 77;
Chapl HM Pris Ex 77–83; Chapl HM Pris Wakef 83–85;
P-in-c Bickington *Ex* 85–87; P-in-c Ashburton w Buckland-
in-the-Moor 85–87; V Ashburton w Buckland in the Moor
and Bickington 87–90; Chapl HM Pris Channings Wood
90–97; LtO *Ex* 90–97; rtd 97; PtO *Ex* 97–19. *Anastasis, Lemon
Road, Bovey Tracey, Newton Abbot TQ13 9BQ* T: (01626)
834899 E: ivor@ivorhalliwell.com
HALLIWELL, Canon Michael Arthur. b 28. St Edm Hall Ox
BA 50 MA 53. Ely Th Coll 52. **d** 54 **p** 55. C Welling *S'wark*
54–57; C Bournemouth St Alb *Win* 57–59; Asst Gen Sec C of
E Coun on Foreign Relns 59–62; C St Dunstan in the West
Lon 60–62; Chapl Bonn w Cologne *Eur* 62–67; Chapl RAF
66–67; V Croydon St Andr *Cant* 67–71; R Jersey St Brelade
Win 71–96; Chapl HM Pris Jersey 75–80; Vice-Dean Jersey
Win 85–99; Tutor S Dios Minl Tr Scheme 92–96; rtd 96;
Hon C Jersey Grouville *Win* 96–99; Hon Can Win Cathl
98–99; PtO 99–21. *Flat 27, Manormead Supported Housing,
Tilford Road, Hindhead GU26 4RA* T: (01428) 601527
E: michaelandsusan@halliwell.info
HALLS, Canon Peter Ernest. b 38. Bris Univ BA 62. Tyndale
Hall Bris 59. **d** 64 **p** 65. C Blackb St Barn 64–67; C Bromley
Ch Ch *Roch* 67–70; V Halvergate w Tunstall *Nor* 70–79; V
Freethorpe w Wickhampton 71–79; P-in-c Beighton and
Moulton 77–79; V Tuckswood 79–90; RD Nor S 86–90;
R Brooke, Kirstead, Mundham w Seething and Thwaite
90–03; RD Depwade 91–97; rtd 03; Hon Can Nor
Cathl 99–03; rtd 03; PtO *Nor* from 03. *1 Church Farm Close,
Weston Longville, Norwich NR9 5JY* T: (01603) 880835
E: pandm.halls@gmail.com
HALLS, Simon David. b 71. Ripon Coll Cuddesdon 15. **d** 19
p 20. LtO *Bris* from 19. *14 The Circle, Swindon SN2 1QR*
HALLS, Susan Mary. *See* HEMSLEY HALLS, Susan Mary
HALLSWORTH, Peter Michael. b 59. Nottm Univ BSc 81
PGCE 82 York St Jo Univ MA 05. Wilson Carlile Coll 00.
d 12 **p** 13. C Bridlington Quay Ch Ch *York* 12–15; C Clifton
15–19; C Langley Mill and Aldercar *Derby* from 19. *The
Vicarage, Church Street, Horsley, Derby DE21 5BR* M: 07772-
549088 E: petermhallsworth@gmail.com
HALMSHAW, Caroline Elizabeth. b 65. St Mellitus Coll 15.
d 18 **p** 19. C Teddington St Mary w St Alb *Lon* from 18. *45
Bushy Park Road, Teddington TW11 9DQ*
HALMSHAW, Mrs Stella Mary. b 36. Brighton Coll of Educn
TCert 57. St Alb Minl Tr Scheme 81. **dss** 84 **d** 87 **p** 96. Radlett
St Alb 84–01; Par Dn 87–93; Hon C 93–01; Chapl Herts Univ
93–96; rtd 96; NSM Wittersham w Stone and Ebony *Cant*
01–12; PtO from 13. *Orchard Field House, Grove Lane, Iden,
Rye TN31 7PX* T: (01797) 280435 E: stellashaw@gmail.com

HALSALL, Graham. b 61. Sheff Univ BA 82 Westmr Coll
Ox PGCE 84. St Steph Ho Ox MTh 00. **d** 00 **p** 01. C
Preston St Jo and St Geo *Blackb* 00–02; C Torrisholme
02–04; P-in-c Bamber Bridge St Sav 04–12; V 12–21;
R Saxon Shoreline *Cant* from 21. *The Rectory, Cock
Lane, Hamstreet, Ashford TN26 2HU* T: (01233) 329072
E: rectorsaxonshoreline@gmail.com
HALSALL, Mrs Isobel Joan. b 47. Liv Univ CertEd 71. **d** 94
p 95. OLM Walshaw Ch Ch *Man* 94–05; NSM Cockermouth
Area *Carl* 05–13; rtd 13; PtO *Carl* from 13. *1 London Head,
Santon Bridge, Holmrook CA19 1UY*
HALSEY, David Mark. b 61. Qu Coll Cam BA 83 MA 87
Cranfield Inst of Tech PhD 87. ERMC 16. **d** 18 **p** 19. NSM
St Alb St Luke from 18. *32 Wordsworth Road, Harpenden
AL5 4AF* T: (01582) 462322 E: david.halsey@clara.co.uk
HALSEY, Brother John Walter Brooke. b 33. Cam Univ BA 57.
Westcott Ho Cam 61. **d** 61 **p** 62. C Stocksbridge *Sheff* 61–65;
Community of the Transfiguration Midlothian from 65; Ind
Chapl Edin 65–69. *The Hermitage, 70E Clerk Street, Loanhead
EH20 9RG* T: 0131-440 3028
HALSON, Bryan Richard. b 32. Jes Coll Cam BA 56 MA 60
Liv Univ MA 72 Geneva Univ 59. Ridley Hall Cam 57. **d** 59
p 60. C Coulsdon St Andr *S'wark* 59–62; LtO *Ches* 63–68;
Tutor St Aid Birkenhead 63–65; Sen Tutor 65–68; Vice-Prin
68–69; Lect Alsager Coll of Educn 69–72; Prin Lect Crewe
and Alsager Coll of HE 72–90; PtO *Ches* 97–18. *1 Victoria
Mill Drive, Willaston, Nantwich CW5 6RR* T: (01270) 652393
E: bbhalson@gmail.com
HALSTEAD, James. b 74. Nottm Univ BA 97. Oak Hill Th Coll
MTh 09. **d** 09 **p** 10. C Gee Cross *Ches* 09–12; V Mottram in
Longdendale 12–19; Prin Sch of Discipleship *S'well* from
19. *Jubilee House, Westgate, Southwell NG25 0JH* M: 07732-
083770 E: james.halstead@southwell.anglican.org
HALSTEAD, Stuart. NTMTC 02. **d** 05 **p** 06. C Houghton Regis
St Alb 05–08; C Kilburn St Aug w St Jo *Lon* 08–10; P-in-c Gt
Ilford St Alb *Chelmsf* 10–14; V 14–21. *Arnford Farm, Long
Preston, Skipton BD23 4QS* E: sh927b@hotmail.com
HAM, Mark Peter. b 65. Sheff Univ BA 86 Birkbeck Coll
Lon MSc 96. Ripon Coll Cuddesdon BA 15. **d** 14 **p** 15. C
Staplehurst *Cant* 14–15; C The Six 15–18; P-in-c Dartford
St Alb *Roch* 18–20; P-in-c Dartford St Edm 18–20;
P-in-c Birchington w Acol and Minnis Bay *Cant* from
20. *15 Minnis Road, Birchington CT7 9SE* T: (01843)
841117 M: 07790-430805 E: m.ham904@gmail.com
HAM, Robin Peter. b 84. St Aid Coll Dur BA 07. Oak Hill Th
Coll MA 15. **d** 15 **p** 16. C S Barrow *Carl* 15–21; P-in-c Barrow
St Paul from 21; Pioneer Min from 19. *St Paul's Vicarage, 353
Abbey Road, Barrow-in-Furness LA13 9JY* M: 07828-333106
E: robinpeterham@gmail.com
HAM-RICHE, Mrs Emma Louise. b 73. Univ of Wales (Abth)
BA 95 Surrey Univ PGCE 96. St Aug Coll of Th 17. **d** 19
p 20. C E Preston w Kingston *Chich* from 19. *20 The Ridings,
East Preston, Littlehampton BN16 2TN* M: 07720-709119
E: ehamriche@gmail.com
HAMBIDGE, John Robert. b 29. Birm Univ MA 02. Sarum Th
Coll. **d** 55 **p** 56. C Tynemouth H Trin W Town *Newc* 55–57;
C Middlesbrough St Jo the Ev *York* 58–63; C Clerkenwell
H Redeemer w St Phil *Lon* 63–64; C Richmond St Mary
w St Matthias *S'wark* 64–66; V Richmond St Jo 66–76; R
Swanscombe *Roch* 76–84; V Aberedw w Llandeilo Graban
and Llanbadarn etc *S & B* 84–91; P-in-c Sibson w Sheepy
and Ratcliffe Culey *Leic* 91–94; P-in-c Orton-on-the-Hill w
Twycross etc 92–94; R The Sheepy Gp 95–97; rtd 97; PtO *Lich*
99–18. *99 Elizabeth Drive, Tamworth B79 8DE* T: (01827)
61526 E: john@hambidge.com
HAMBLIN, Derek Gordon Hawthorn. b 35. SWMTC 94. **d** 96
p 97. NSM S Brent and Rattery *Ex* 96–01; Chapl Larnaca
Cyprus 01–02; Asst Chapl Dubai UAE 03–04; PtO *Ex* 04–19;
PtO Cyprus and the Gulf 04–12. *3 The Beeches, 2 Woodside
Road, Ferndown BH22 9LD* T: (01202) 911138 M: 07486-
912919 E: derekthecleric1@aol.com
HAMBLIN, Canon Karen Elizabeth. b 59. St Mary's Coll Dur
BA 80 Homerton Coll Cam PGCE 82. St Jo Coll Nottm 05.
d 07 **p** 08. C Long Eaton St Jo *Derby* 07–11; TV N Wingfield,
Clay Cross and Pilsley 11–16; P-in-c Brampton St Mark
from 16; C Chesterfield St Mary and All SS from 16; C
Chesterfield H Trin and Ch Ch from 16; C Chesterfield SS
Aug from 16; RD Chesterfield 15–18; AD NE Derbyshire
from 18; Hon Can Derby Cathl from 17. *1 Whitecotes
Lane, Chesterfield S40 3HJ* T: (01246) 913688 *or* (01332)
388699 M: 07432-705255 E: khnedeanery@gmail.com *or*
karen.hamblin@derby.anglican.org
HAMBLIN, Canon Roger Noel. b 42. Ripon Hall Ox 67. **d** 70
p 71. C Scotforth *Blackb* 70–73; C Altham w Clayton le Moors
73–76; V Cockerham w Winmarleigh 76–87; V Cockerham
w Winmarleigh and Glasson 87–00; P-in-c Wray w Tatham

and Tatham Fells 00–03; V E Lonsdale 03–09; Agric Chapl 01–09; Hon Can Blackb Cathl 04–09; rtd 09; PtO *Blackb* from 09. *Wycoller, School Lane, Pilling, Preston PR3 6AA*　T: (01253) 790555　E: rogerhamblin@yahoo.co.uk

HAMBLING, Paul Gary. b 73. St Steph Ho Ox 05. **d** 07 **p** 08. C Woodbridge St Mary *St E* 07–10; TV Merton Priory *S'wark* 10–15; R Melton and Ufford *St E* from 15. *Melton Rectory, Station Road, Melton, Woodbridge IP12 1PX*　T: (01394) 387491　E: rector.uffordmelton@gmail.com

HAMBORG, Canon Graham Richard. b 52. Bris Univ BSc 73 Nottm Univ BA 76 MTh 77 PhD 09. St Jo Coll Nottm 74. **d** 77 **p** 78. C Tile Cross *Birm* 77–80; C Upton cum Chalvey *Ox* 80–82; TV 82–86; V Ruscombe and Twyford 86–04; AD Sonning 03–04; CME Adv *Chelmsf* 04–12; Ord Min Development Adv 12–17; C Gt Baddow 04–17; Hon Can Chelmsf Cathl 12–17; rtd 17; PtO *Portsm* from 18. *3 Hatchlands, Huntsbottom Lane, Liss GU33 7EU*　E: revghamborg@hotmail.com

HAMBORG, Peter Graham. b 79. BMus 00. Trin Coll Bris BA 09. **d** 10 **p** 11. C Fulwood Ch Ch *Blackb* 10–14; V Lea from 14; V Preston Em from 14. *45 Abingdon Drive, Ashton-on-Ribble, Preston PR2 1EY*　T: (01772) 726987　M: 07771-993004　E: revpete@emmanuelpreston.org

HAMEEM, Samuel. b 77. **p** 17. NSM Kingsbury H Innocents *Lon* from 15. *458B Church Lane, London NW9 8UA*　M: 07481-753258　E: hameem_77@yahoo.com

HAMER, Irving David. b 59. **d** 84 **p** 85. C Newton Nottage *Llan* 84–88; C Roath 88–90; V Llansawel, Briton Ferry 90–00; V Roath St Martin from 00; Miss to Seafarers from 90. *St Martin's Vicarage, Strathnairn Stree, Roath, Cardiff CF24 3JL*　T: (029) 2048　2295　E: fr.irving.hamer@ntlworld.com *or* contact@stmartininroath.co.uk

HAMER, Mrs Jeanette Estelle. b 55. Wall Hall Coll Aldenham CertEd 76. SNWTP 10. **d** 12 **p** 13. NSM Douglas St Geo *S & M* 12–14; NSM W Coast from 14. *15 Faaie Ny Cabbal, Kirk Michael, Isle of Man IM6 2HS*　T/F: (01624) 877814　M: 07624-462251　E: manxmiffy55@gmail.com

HAMER, Penelope Ann. *See* WEST, Penelope Ann

HAMER, Canon Val. b 52. Leeds Univ BA 74. S'wark Ord Course 83. **dss** 86 **d** 87 **p** 94. Warlingham w Chelsham and Farleigh *S'wark* 86–88; Par Dn 87–88; Par Dn Caterham 88–94; C 94–96; RD 95–96; Sub Chapl HM Pris Wandsworth 88–95; V Addiscombe St Mildred *S'wark* 96–02; Ldr Post Ord Tr Croydon Area 94–99; Can Res and Chan Heref Cathl 02–08; Dioc Missr and P-in-c Coychurch, Llangan and St Mary Hill *Llan* 08–12; rtd 12; PtO *Chich* from 13. *Noddfa Fach, 126 West Hill Road, St Leonard's-on-Sea TN38 0AY*　T: (01424) 254564　E: val_hamer@hotmail.com

HAMES, Daniel Lewis. b 84. Leic Univ BSc 06. Wycliffe Hall Ox BA 11 MSt 12. **d** 15 **p** 16. NSM Ox St Aldate from 15. *17 Hogarth Place, Abingdon OX14 5LR*　E: danielhames@gmail.com *or* daniel.hames@staldates.org.uk

✠**HAMID, The Rt Revd David.** b 55. McMaster Univ Ontario BSc 78. Trin Coll Toronto MDiv 81 Hon DD 05. **d** 81 **p** 82 **c** 02. C Burlington St Chris Canada 81–83; R Burlington St Jo 83–87; Miss Co-ord Gen Syn of Angl Ch of Canada 87–96; Hon Can Santo Domingo 93–02; Dir Ecum Affairs ACC 96–02; Suff Bp Eur from 02; Hon Asst Bp Roch 03–11; Hon C Orpington St Andr 03–09. *14 Tufton Street, London SW1P 3QZ*　T: (020) 7898 1160　F: 7898 1166　E: david.hamid@churchofengland.org

HAMIL, Sheila. b 49. Northd Coll of Educn TCert 71. NEOC 92. **d** 95 **p** 98. NSM Wallsend St Luke *Newc* 95–97; NSM Long Benton St Mary 97–02; NSM Willington 02–06; rtd 06; PtO *Newc* from 06. *22 Askrigg Avenue, Wallsend NE28 9YA*　T: 0191-422 0423　E: sheilahamil@gmail.com

HAMILL-STEWART, Simon Francis. b 32. Pemb Coll Cam BA 56. NOC 77. **d** 80 **p** 81. NSM Neston *Ches* 80–83; C 83–86; V Over St Jo 86–00; Dioc Ecum Officer 92–00; rtd 00; PtO *Ches* 00–01 and from 04; C Middlewich w Byley 01–03. *87 Warmingham Lane, Middlewich CW10 0DJ*　T: (01606) 737329

HAMILTON, Graham. *See* HAMILTON, William Graham

HAMILTON, Janice Patricia. b 64. Ch Ch Coll Cant BEd 86. Ox Min Course 14. **d** 17 **p** 18. C Tidenham w Beachley and Lancaut *Glouc* 17–21; Pioneer Min from 21. *St Barnabas' Vicarage, 152 Alstone Lane, Cheltenham GL51 8HL*　M: 07749-130323　E: janice-hamilton@outlook.com

HAMILTON, John Hans Patrick. b 44. K Coll Lon BD 66 AKC 67　Lon　Univ　DipAdEd 76　FCMI 96.　St Boniface Warminster 66. **d** 67 **p** 68. C Cleobury Mortimer w Hopton Wafers *Heref* 67–69; C Sanderstead All SS *S'wark* 69–73; V Battersea St Mary-le-Park 73–75; PtO *Ely* 75–90; Dir of Educn *Derby* 90–95; P-in-c Cliddesden and Ellisfield w Farleigh Wallop etc *Win* 95–00; PtO 00–03; P-in-c Dungeon Hill and The Caundles w Folke and Holwell *Sarum* 03–07; TR Wylye

and Till Valley 07–11; rtd 11; PtO *Sarum* from 11. *Hillview, Duck Street, Tisbury, Salisbury SP3 6LJ*　T: (01722) 790117

HAMILTON, John Nicholas. b 49. Trin Coll Cam BA 71 MA 75. Ridley Hall Cam 72. **d** 75 **p** 76. C Ealing Dean St Jo *Lon* 75–79; C Stoughton *Guildf* 79–83; R Denton St Lawr *Man* 83–88; R The Sherbornes w Pamber *Win* 88–19; rtd 19; PtO *Ox* from 19. *54 Little Hivings, Chesham HP5 2LU*　E: jt77hamilton@waitrose.com

HAMILTON, Nigel John. *See* TABER-HAMILTON, Nigel John

HAMILTON, Canon Paul Stuart. b 69. Univ of Wales (Ban) BTh 02. EAMTC. **d** 02 **p** 03. C Hawkwell *Chelmsf* 02–06; V Ingrave St Nic and St Steph from 06; AD Brentwood 15–20; Hon Can Chelmsf Cathl from 15. *The Rectory, Thorndon Gate, Ingrave, Brentwood CM13 3RG*　T: (01277) 812452　E: psh@btinternet.com

HAMILTON, Reid Henry. b 56. **d** 98 **p** 98. C Kansas City St Paul USA 98–01; R Kent Ch Ch 01–04; Chapl Canterbury Ho Univ of Michigan 04–17; Chapl Algarve *Eur* from 18. *Casa São Vicente, Apartado 2135, 8100-070 Boliqueime, Portugal*　T: (00351) (289) 366720　M: (00351) 96-827 1889　E: stvincentsalgarve.east@gmail.com

HAMILTON, Sarah Louise. *See* BRUSH, Sarah Louise

HAMILTON, Sebastian John Marie. b 91. Coll of Resurr Mirfield BA 18. **d** 18 **p** 19. C Tewkesbury w Walton Cardiff and Twyning *Glouc* 18–21; C S Cheltenham from 21. *Flat 2, 24 St Stephen's Road, Cheltenham GL51 3AA*　E: fr.sjm.hamilton@gmail.com

HAMILTON, William Graham. b 63. New Coll Ox BA 86. Wycliffe Hall Ox BA 95. **d** 95 **p** 96. C Ivybridge w Harford *Ex* 95–99; V Bovey Tracey SS Pet, Paul and Thos w Hennock from 99. *The Vicarage, Coombe Cross, Bovey Tracey, Newton Abbot TQ13 9EP*　T: (01626) 833813　E: pptbovey@mac.com

HAMILTON, William Joseph Taylor. b 40. Univ Coll Ches MTh 00. **d** 97 **p** 98. NSM Ches 97–02; C Thurlestone, S Milton, W Alvington etc *Ex* 02–07; rtd 07; PtO *Ches* from 07. *51 Vincent Drive, Chester CH4 7RQ*　T: (01244) 428457　E: william-hamilton3@sky.com

HAMILTON-BOX, William Michael. b 90. Cant Ch Ch Univ BMus 13 MMus 15. St Steph Ho Ox BA 19. **d** 19 **p** 20. C Hammersmith St Luke *Lon* from 19. *1 Fielding Road, London W14 0LL*

HAMILTON-BROWN, James John. b 35. Lon Univ BSc 59. Ridley Hall Cam 59. **d** 61 **p** 62. C Attenborough w Bramcote *S'well* 61–67; V Bramcote 67–76; R and D Officer Abps' Coun on Evang 76–79; LtO *Sarum* 76–81 and 91–95; TR Dorchester 81–91; Sec Par and People 91–95; P-in-c Tarrant Valley *Sarum* 95–99; C Tollard Royal w Farnham, Gussage St Michael etc 99–00; rtd 00; PtO *Sarum* from 00. *April Cottage, West Street, Winterborne Stickland, Blandford Forum DT11 0NT*　T: (01258) 880627　E: jumperhb@btinternet.com

HAMILTON-GREY, Mrs Deborah. b 66. Birm Univ BA 99 MA 03 Sheff Univ BA 14. Coll of Resurr Mirfield 12. **d** 14 **p** 15. C Diss *Nor* 14–15; C Watton 15–17; V Ludham, Potter Heigham, Hickling and Catfield 17–19; PtO from 19. *51A Station Road, Sheringham NR26 8RG*　M: 07896-658373　E: deborah.hamiltongrey@gmail.com

HAMILTON-MANON, Phillipp Robert Christian. b 49. BA 88. St Steph Ho Ox 89. **d** 90 **p** 91. C Norton St Mary *Dur* 90–94; P-in-c Cleadon Park 94–95; V 95–97; TV Lewes All SS, St Anne, St Mich and St Thos *Chich* 97–00; R Lewes St Anne 00–10; R Lewes St Anne and St Mich and St Thos etc 10–12; rtd 12; PtO *Chich* from 13. *9 Belgrave Crescent, Seaford BN25 3AX*　E: phm1949@aol.com

HAMLET, Paul Manning. b 42. Open Univ BA 81 Ex Univ MEd 96 Univ of Wales (Lamp) MTh 04 PhD 12 Lambeth STh 84 FCollP 96. Kelham Th Coll 61. **d** 66 **p** 67. C Rumboldswyke *Chich* 66–69; C Ely 69–73; Hon C Ipswich St Bart *St E* 73–84; Chapl Wellington Sch Somerset 84–94; Chapl Ipswich Sch 94–02; CF (TAVR) 88–99; CF (ACF) 99–09; rtd 02; PtO *St E* from 02; *Chelmsf* from 18. *5 Wincanton Close, Ipswich IP4 3EE*　T: (01473) 724413　E: paul.hamlet@btopenworld.com

HAMLETT, David. b 50. All SS Cen for Miss & Min 13. **d** 15 **p** 16. OLM Wigan All SS *Liv* 15–19; TV Maghull and Melling from 19. *17 Woodedge, Ashton-in-Makerfield, Wigan WN4 9JY*　T: (01942) 740812　M: 07972-577801　E: dhamlett@blueyonder.co.uk

HAMLEY, Preb Isabelle Maryvonne. b 75. Orléans Univ BA 95 MA 96 Birm Univ BA 03 Ches Univ PhD 17. St Jo Coll Nottm 09. **d** 11 **p** 12. C W Bridgford *S'well* 11–12; C Wilford Hill 12–14; C Edwalton 14–17; Abp's Chapl *Cant* 17–20; Sec Ecum Relns and Th Coun for Chr Unity from 20; PtO *S'wark* from 17; *Lon* from 17; Preb St Paul's Cathl from 19. *Council for Christian Unity, Church House, 27 Great Smith Street, London SW1P 3AZ*　T: (020) 7898 1000　M: 07850-402321　E: isabelle.hamley@churchofengland.org

HAMMERSLEY, Susan. b 67. Nottm Univ BA 90. Ripon Coll Cuddesdon BA 07. **d** 07 **p** 08. C Ecclesfield *Sheff* 07–10; C Sheff St Mark Broomhill 10–15; V from 15; P-in-c Walkley from 21. *The Vicarage, 4 St Mark's Crescent, Sheffield S10 2SG* T: 0114-327 6908 *or* 266 0260 E: sue.hammersley@sheffield.anglican.org *or* sue@stmarkssheffield.co.uk

HAMMETT, The Ven Barry Keith. b 47. CB 06. Magd Coll Ox BA 71 MA 74. St Steph Ho Ox 71. **d** 74 **p** 75. C Plymouth St Pet *Ex* 74–77; Chapl RN 77–02; Chapl of the Fleet and Adn for the RN 02–06; Dir Gen Naval Chapl Service 02–06; Hon Can Portsm Cathl 02–06; Can Gib Cathl *Eur* 03–06; rtd 06; QHC 99–06; PtO *Portsm* 07–15; *Ox* from 15. *26 Penhurst Gardens, Chipping Norton OX7 5ED*

HAMMILL, Anthony Lawrence. b 71. Linc Coll Ox BA 92 MA 97 Univ Coll Lon MSc 95 Anglia Ruskin Univ MA 08 Fitzw Coll Cam MPhil 08. Ridley Hall Cam 05. **d** 08 **p** 09. C Chalk *Roch* 08–11; C Tonbridge SS Pet and Paul 11–18; CMD Officer from 18. *3 Andrews Close, Tunbridge Wells TN2 3PA* E: anthony.hammill@rochester.anglican.org

HAMMILL, Judith Anne. b 69. St Mellitus Coll 15. **d** 18 **p** 19. C Tunbridge Wells St Jas *Roch* from 18. *3 Andrews Close, Tunbridge Wells TN2 3PA*

HAMMOND, Andrew Charles Raphael. b 63. Clare Coll Cam BA 86 K Coll Cam MPhil 07 LRAM 91. Westcott Ho Cam 05. **d** 07 **p** 08. C St John's Wood *Lon* 07–09; Min Can and Succ St Paul's Cathl 09–12; V Willesden St Mary 12–15; Chapl K Coll Cam 15–19; Chapl St Jo Coll Cam from 20. *St John's College, Cambridge CB2 1TP* T: (01223) 338617 M: 07884-185207 E: andrewch007@hotmail.com *or* ach71@cam.ac.uk

HAMMOND, Mrs Barbara Watson. b 33. Lanc Univ MA 79 Bp Otter Coll TCert 53 ACP 70. S'wark Ord Course 89. **d** 92 **p** 94. NSM Upper Norwood St Jo *S'wark* 92–94; Hon C Spring Park All SS 94–97; PtO 97–02; *Portsm* from 98; *Chich* 12–17. *28 Church Path, Emsworth PO10 7DP* T: (01243) 370531 E: barbarawhammond@hotmail.com

HAMMOND, Carolyn John-Baptist. b 64. St Jo Coll Ox MA 90 Univ Coll Ox DPhil 93 CCC Cam BA 97 MA 02. Westcott Ho Cam 95. **d** 98 **p** 99. C Gamlingay w Hatley St George and E Hatley *Ely* 98–99; C Gamlingay and Everton 99–01; R 01–05; Dean G&C Coll Cam from 05. *Gonville and Caius College, Trinity Street, Cambridge CB2 1TA* T: (01223) 332400 F: 332336 E: cjbh2@cam.ac.uk *or* dean@cai.cam.ac.uk

HAMMOND, Kathryn Mary. b 49. LCTP 07. **d** 08 **p** 09. NSM Linton in Craven *Bradf* 08–11; NSM Burnsall w Rylstone 08–11; NSM Adbaston, High Offley, Knightley, Norbury and Woodseaves *Lich* 11–16; R 16–21; rtd 21; PtO *Cov* from 21. *Address temp unknown* E: rev.kathrynh@gmail.com

HAMMOND, Canon Lindsay John. b 57. Southn Univ BA 83. Sarum & Wells Th Coll 84. **d** 86 **p** 87. C Ashford *Cant* 86–90; V Appledore w Brookland, Fairfield, Brenzett etc 90–03; P-in-c Wittersham w Stone and Ebony 95–03; RD S Lympne 95–01; P-in-c Westwell and Hothfield 03–11; P-in-c Charing w Charing Heath and Lt Chart 06–11; AD Ashford 09–11; V Tenterden and Smallhythe 11–16; TR Tenterden, Rother and Oxney from 16; Hon Min Can Cant Cathl 93–08; Hon Can Cant Cathl from 08; AD Romney and Tenterden 13–19. *The Vicarage, Church Road, Tenterden TN30 6AT* T: (01580) 761591 *or* 765414 E: tentvic@gmail.com

HAMMOND, Martin James. b 62. St Jo Coll Nottm 03. **d** 05 **p** 06. C Walmley *Birm* 05–08; C Erdington 08–09; TV Bedworth *Cov* 09–18; Chapl Geo Eliot Hosp NHS Trust Nuneaton from 14. *The George Eliot Hospital NHS Trust, Lewes House, College Street, Nuneaton CV10 7DJ* T: (024) 7635 1351 E: revmartinh@btinternet.com

HAMMOND, Peter Clark. b 27. Linc Coll Ox BA 49 MA 53. Wells Th Coll 51. **d** 52 **p** 53. C Willesborough *Cant* 52–55; C Croydon St Jo 55–59; R Barham 60–66; V Walmer 66–85; V Rolvenden 85–89; rtd 89; PtO *Ely* 89–15. *19 Hardwick Street, Cambridge CB3 9JA* T: (01223) 467425

HAMNETT, Mrs Karen. b 63. All SS Cen for Miss & Min. **d** 16 **p** 17. OLM Middleton and Thornham *Man* from 16. *15 Cragg Road, Oldham OL1 2RX* M: 07759-286653 E: karenhamnett313@gmail.com

HAMPEL, Canon Michael Hans Joachim. b 67. Univ Coll Dur BA 89 St Chad's Coll Dur MA 02 FRSA 02. Westcott Ho Cam 90. **d** 93 **p** 94. C Whitworth w Spennymoor *Dur* 93–97; Min Can, Prec and Sacr Dur Cathl 97–02; Sen Tutor St Chad's Coll Dur 02–04; Can Res St E Cathl 04–11; Sub Dean 08–11; Can Res and Prec St Paul's Cathl *Lon* 11–18; Can Res Dur Cathl from 18. *7 The College, Durham DH1 3EQ* E: michael.hampel@durhamcathedral.co.uk

HAMPSON, Miss Judith Elizabeth. b 50. I M Marsh Coll of Physical Educn Liv BEd 72 Open Univ BA 89. Ripon Coll Cuddesdon 90. **d** 92 **p** 94. C Alnwick *Newc* 92–96; R Allendale

w Whitfield 96–05; V Haydon Bridge and Beltingham w Henshaw 05–13; rtd 13. *5 St Aidan's Terrace, Trimdon Station TS29 6BT* T: (01429) 551022 E: judithhmpsn19@gmail.com

HAMPSON, Michael John. b 67. Jes Coll Ox BA 88. Ripon Coll Cuddesdon 88. **d** 91 **p** 92. C W Burnley All SS *Blackb* 91–93; C Harlow St Mary Magd *Chelmsf* 93–00; V Church Langley 00–04; PtO *Blackb* 10–12; V Hornby w Claughton and Whittington etc from 12. *Station House, Arkholme, Carnforth LA6 1AZ* T: (015242) 21712 M: 07712-477003 E: michael.hampson.mobile@googlemail.com

HAMPSON, Michele Elizabeth. b 55. Univ Coll Lon MB, BS 79 Edin Univ MPhil 85. Ridley Hall Cam 15. **d** 17 **p** 18. NSM Lenton *S'well* from 17. *Address withheld by request* T: 0115-845 7985

HAMPSTEAD, Archdeacon of. See HAWKINS, The Ven John Edward Inskipp

HAMPTON, Alison Jean. b 61. St Mary's Coll Twickenham BA 98 Qu Foundn for Ecum Th Educn MA 11. SEITE 98. **d** 01 **p** 02. C Notting Dale St Clem w St Mark and St Jas *Lon* 01–04; P-in-c Burrough Hill Pars *Leic* 04–06; Chapl Brooksby Melton Coll 04–06; P-in-c Husbands Bosworth w Mowsley and Knaptoft etc *Leic* 06–09; P-in-c Arnesby w Shearsby and Bruntingthorpe 06–09; R Hexagon 09–10; PtO *Cov* 10–11; Chapl Shakespeare Hospice 11–13; Dominican Republic 13–15; V Millfield St Mark and Pallion St Luke *Dur* 15–19; P-in-c Wootton Wawen *Cov* from 20; P-in-c Claverdon w Preston Bagot from 20; C Aston Cantlow and Wilmcote w Billesley from 21. *The Vicarage, Stratford Road, Wootton Wawen, Henley-in-Arden B95 6BD* T: (01564) 792988 E: alijhampton@gmail.com

HAMPTON, Canon Carla Irene. b 47. ARCM 67 GRSM 68. NTMTC 96. **d** 99 **p** 00. Asst Chapl Mid-Essex Hosp Services NHS Trust 98–02; Chapl Team Ldr 02–04; NSM Chelmsf St Andr 99–04; NSM Gt and Lt Leighs and Lt Waltham 04–06; P-in-c Gt Waltham w Ford End 06–10; V 10–12; rtd 12; Hon C Springfield All SS *Chelmsf* 12–17; RD Chelmsf N 07–14; Hon Can Chelmsf Cathl 08–17; PtO *Nor* from 17; *Chelmsf* from 17. *14 Fairfield Close, Mundesley, Norwich NR11 8BZ* M: 07850-913452 E: revcarlahampton@gmail.com

HAMPTON, Canon John Waller. b 28. Linc Coll Ox BA 51 MA 58. Westcott Ho Cam 51. **d** 53 **p** 54. C Rugby St Andr *Cov* 53–56; Chapl St Paul's Sch Hammersmith 56–65; Chapl St Paul's Girls' Sch Hammersmith 60–65; V Gaydon w Chadshunt *Cov* 65–69; Fell Qu Coll Birm 75–76; P-in-c Wetton *Lich* St Nic 69–75; Fell Qu Coll Birm 75–76; P-in-c Alstonfield 76–82; P-in-c Sheen 76–80; RD Alstonfield 80–82; P-in-c Butterton 80–82; P-in-c Warslow and Elkstones 80–82; P-in-c Broadway *Worc* 82–91; V 91–93; RD Evesham 87–93; Hon Can Worc Cathl 88–93; rtd 93; PtO *Ab* from 93. *29 Midmar Gardens, Edinburgh EH10 6DY* T: 0131-447 3520

HAMPTON, Stephen William Peter. b 72. Magd Coll Cam BA 93 MA 97 Ex Coll Ox MSt 99 DPhil 02. Wycliffe Hall Ox BA 95 MA 98. **d** 96 **p** 97. C St Neots *Ely* 96–98; Chapl and Fell Ex Coll Ox 98–03; Sen Tutor St Jo Coll Dur 04–07; Hon Min Can Dur Cathl 05–07; Fell and Dean Peterho Cam from 07. *Peterhouse, Cambridge CB2 1RD* T: (01223) 338217 F: 337578 E: swph2@cam.ac.uk

HANAWAY, Peter Louis. b 47. Open Univ BA 85 Middx Univ BA 02. NTMTC 99. **d** 02 **p** 03. NSM Westmr St Matt *Lon* from 02; NSM St Mary le Strand w St Clem Danes from 17. *St Matthew's House, 20 Great Peter Street, London SW1P 2BU* T: (020) 7222 3704 M: 07947-722219 E: peter.hanaway@cwctv.com *or* fr.peter@stmw.org

HANCE, Mrs Joy. b 47. Balls Park Coll Hertford QTS 69. SAOMC 99. **d** 02 **p** 03. NSM Cherbury w Gainfield *Ox* 02–14; C Witney 14–20. *5 Plover Close, Stratford-upon-Avon CV37 9EN* M: 07752-187014 E: joysmail@talk21.com

HANCE, Mrs Marion. b 49. **d** 01 **p** 02. OLM Cheddington w Mentmore and Marsworth *Ox* 01–08; NSM Quantock Coast *B & W* 08–13; PtO from 13; rtd 13. *14 Parnell Way, Burnham-on-Sea TA8 2EG* T: (01278) 792082 E: marionhance@yahoo.co.uk

HANCE, Stephen John. b 66. Portsm Poly BSc 89 Nottm Univ BTh 92 MA 93. St Jo Coll Nottm 90. **d** 93 **p** 94. C Southsea St Jude *Portsm* 93–96; TV Tollington *Lon* 96–99; V Balham Hill Ascension *S'wark* 99–13; Can Res S'wark Cathl 13–17; Dean Derby 17–19; Nat Lead for Evang and Witness Abps' Coun from 19. *92 Greyhound Lane, London SW16 5RW* T: (020) 7898 1000 E: stephen.hance@btinternet.com *or* stephen.hance@churchofengland.org

HANCOCK, Christopher David. b 54. Qu Coll Ox BA 75 MA 80 St Jo Coll Dur BA 78 PhD 84. Cranmer Hall Dur. **d** 82 **p** 83. C Leic H Trin w St Jo 82–85; Chapl Magd Coll Cam 85–88; USA 88–94; V Cambridge H Trin *Ely* 94–02;

Dean Bradf 02–04. *3 College Farm Cottages, Garford, Abingdon OX13 5PF* T: (01865) 392804 E: chancock@btinternet.com

HANCOCK, Christopher Michael Jefferies. b 67. Ex Coll Ox MA 90 ACA 93. **d** 16 **p** 17. OLM Epsom St Martin *Guildf* 16–17; NSM Headley and Box Hill w Walton on the Hill from 17. *Cleaver House, Headley Common Road, Headley, Epsom KT18 6NR* T: (01372) 362386 M: 07901-715882 E: cmjhancock@gmail.com

HANCOCK, Dorothy Myfanwy. See WOFFENDEN, Dorothy Myfanwy

HANCOCK, Mrs Eleanor Mary Catherine. b 55. Huddersfield Univ CertEd 91. CBDTI. **d** 05 **p** 06. C Carl H Trin and St Barn 05–08; P-in-c 08–17; rtd 17. *111 Holmrook Road, Carlisle CA2 7TQ* T: (01228) 527106 M: 07763-482542 E: eleanor.hancock55@gmail.com

HANCOCK, Preb Frances Margaret. b 34. LMH Ox BA 56 MA 94. Gilmore Course IDC 81. **dss** 81 **d** 87 **p** 94. Isleworth All SS *Lon* 81–87; Team Deacon Ross w Brampton Abbotts, Bridstow and Peterstow *Heref* 87–93; rtd 94; Dioc Adv on Women in Min *Heref* 93–99; NSM Peterchurch w Vowchurch, Turnastone and Dorstone 93–00; NSM Madley w Tyberton, Peterchurch, Vowchurch etc 00–04; Preb Heref Cathl 96–99; PtO 06–19. *Flat 4, 102 East Street, Hereford HR1 2LW* T: (01981) 550457

HANCOCK, Miss Gillian. b 59. St Jo Coll Nottm 05. **d** 07 **p** 08. C Iffley *Ox* 07–11; Chapl Mary Ann Evans Hospice from 11; PtO *Cov* from 19. *Mary Ann Evans Hospice, Eliot Way, Nuneaton CV10 7QL* T: (024) 7686 5440 M: 07919-064612 E: gillhancock@btinternet.com *or* gill.hancock@geh.nhs.uk

HANCOCK, Mrs Helen Margaret. b 62. Rob Coll Cam MA 85. SEITE 06. **d** 09 **p** 10. NSM New Malden and Coombe *S'wark* 09–11; C Surbiton St Andr and St Mark 11–12; P-in-c Surbiton St Matt 12–14; TR 14–15; TR Tolworth, Hook and Surbiton from 15. *The Vicarage, 20A Kingsdowne Road, Surbiton KT6 6JZ* T: (020) 8942 6987 E: helenccnm@gmail.com *or* teamrector@tolworthtm.org

HANCOCK, Jill Catherine. b 72. Coll of Resurr Mirfield BA 18. **d** 18 **p** 19. C E Scarsdale *Derby* 18–21; P-in-c Chesterfield H Trin and Ch Ch from 21. *114 Horsehead Lane, Bolsover, Chesterfield S44 6XH* M: 07746-668257 E: jillhancock@outlook.com

HANCOCK, Canon John Clayton. b 36. Dur Univ BA 58. Cranmer Hall Dur. **d** 60 **p** 61. C Newbarns w Hawcoat *Carl* 60–65; V Church Coniston 65–76; R Torver 66–76; P-in-c Heversham 76–77; V 77–93; V Heversham and Milnthorpe 93–05; Hon Can Carl Cathl 98–05; rtd 05; P-in-c Levens *Carl* 04–06; PtO from 06. *Fairfield, Sandside, Milnthorpe LA7 7HW* T: (015395) 63659

HANCOCK, John Llewellyn. **d** 14 **p** 15. NSM Llanstadwel *St D* 14–16; NSM Llanstadwel and Burton and Rosemarket 16–19; NSM Roose from 19. *Mill House, Llanstadwell, Milford Haven SA73 1EG* T: (01646) 600610 E: john.hancock3@me.com

HANCOCK, John Martin. b 55. Ealing Coll of Educn BA 78. Wycliffe Hall Ox 97. **d** 99 **p** 00. C Bedford St Jo and St Leon *St Alb* 99–04; V Old Hill H Trin *Worc* 04–12; P-in-c Hengrove *Bris* 12–19; P-in-c Whitchurch 12–15; V Whitchurch St Nic 15–19; rtd 19. *40A Queen Alexandra Road, Salisbury SP2 9LN* E: martin@hancocks.plus.com

HANCOCK, Canon John Mervyn. b 38. St Jo Coll Dur BA 61 MA 70 Hertf Coll Ox BA 63 MA 66. Cranmer Hall Dur 63. **d** 64 **p** 65. C Bishopwearmouth St Gabr *Dur* 64–67; V Hebburn St Jo 67–87; RD Jarrow 83–92; V S Westoe 87–03; C-in-c S Shields St Aid w St Steph 92–95; Hon Can Dur Cathl 88–03; rtd 03; PtO *Dur* from 04. *9 Railway Cottages, Dubmire, Houghton le Spring DH4 6LE* T: 0191-385 7491 E: canonhancock21@talktalk.net

HANCOCK, Malcolm James. b 50. Leeds Univ MA 02 AGSM 73. Sarum & Wells Th Coll 85. **d** 87 **p** 88. C Sandhurst *Ox* 87–90; P-in-c Bradbourne and Brassington *Derby* 90–92; TV Wirksworth 92–95; V Tunbridge Wells K Chas *Roch* 95–02; R Beckenham St Geo 02–10; Asst Chapl Lewisham Healthcare NHS Trust 10–11; Chapl Lewisham and Greenwich NHS Trust 11–15; rtd 15. *3 Seymour Place, Totnes TQ9 5AY* T: (01803) 866147 E: malcolm.j.hancock@btinternet.com

HANCOCK, Martin. See HANCOCK, John Martin

HANCOCK, Mrs Mary. b 52. Imp Coll Lon BSc 73 ARCS 73. Ridley Hall Cam 04. **d** 07 **p** 08. C Fen Orchards *Ely* 07–11; P-in-c Witcham w Mepal 11–17; R from 17; P-in-c Sutton 11–17; V from 17. *The Vicarage, 7 Church Lane, Sutton, Ely CB6 2RQ* T: (01353) 778722 E: mhancock@waitrose.com

HANCOCK, Ms Mary Joy. b 40. Auckland Univ BA 61 Auckland Teachers' Coll PGCE 62 Man Univ CQSW 69. S'wark Ord Course 91. **d** 94 **p** 95. NSM Merton St Mary *S'wark* 94–01; NSM Colliers Wood Ch Ch 01–06; NSM Upper Tooting H Trin w St Aug 06–12; PtO 12–18. *55 Huntspill Street, London SW17 0AA* T: (020) 8946 8984

HANCOCK, Nigel John. b 35. K Coll Cam BA 63 MA 67. EAMTC 86. **d** 89 **p** 91. NSM Cambridge St Mary Less *Ely* 89–00; PV St Jo Coll Cam 95–99; PtO *Ely* 00–12. *5 Atherton Close, Cambridge CB4 2BE* T: (01223) 355828

HANCOCK, Preb Paul. b 43. AKC 66. **d** 67 **p** 68. C Wednesbury St Paul Wood Green *Lich* 67–70; C Rugeley 70–73; V Rickerscote 73–75; R Blisland w St Breward *Truro* 75–78; V Mansfield St Lawr *S'well* 78–82; P-in-c Charleton *Ex* 82–83; P-in-c E Portlemouth, S Pool and Chivelstone 82–83; R Charleton w Buckland Tout Saints etc 83–95; RD Woodleigh 88–95; P-in-c Plymouth Crownhill Ascension 95–99; V 99–09; Preb Ex Cathl 03–09; rtd 09; PtO *Ex* from 11. *27 Paddock Drive, Ivybridge PL21 0UB* T: (01752) 690655 E: hazelnut330@gmail.com

HANCOCK, Paul David. Oak Hill Th Coll. **d** 10 **p** 11. C Buxton Trin Prop Chpl *Derby* 10–14. *24 Bath Road, Buxton SK17 6HH* T: (01298) 23104 M: 07816-409476 E: paulhancock2001@hotmail.com

✠**HANCOCK, The Rt Revd Peter.** b 55. Selw Coll Cam BA 76 MA 79. Oak Hill Th Coll BA 80. **d** 80 **p** 81 **c** 10. C Portsdown *Portsm* 80–83; C Radipole and Melcombe Regis *Sarum* 83–87; V Cowplain *Portsm* 87–99; Adn The Meon 99–10; RD Havant 93–98; Hon Can Portsm Cathl 97–10; Dioc Dir Miss 03–06; Suff Bp Basingstoke *Win* 10–14; Bp B & W 14–21; rtd 21. *Lowers Edge, The Common, Cranleigh GU6 8SH* M: 07974-008134 E: phancock452@gmail.com

HANCOCK, Peter Thompson. b 31. G&C Coll Cam BA 54 MA 58. Ridley Hall Cam 54. **d** 56 **p** 57. C Beckenham Ch Ch *Roch* 56–59; Chapl St Lawr Coll Ramsgate 59–62; Chapl Stowe Sch 62–67; Asst Chapl and Lect Br Embassy Ch Paris *Eur* 67–70; V Walton H Trin *Ox* 70–80; Canada 80–84; V Northwood H Trin *Lon* 84–94; rtd 94; PtO *Ox* 99–07; *Guildf* 07–10. *High Lawns, Woodhouse Lane, Holmbury St Mary, Dorking RH5 6NN* T: (01483) 205430 E: suemhancock@gmail.com

HANCOCK, Mrs Rebecca Jane. b 72. St Jo Coll Nottm 14. **d** 17 **p** 18. C Bawtry w Austerfield, Misson, Everton and Mattersey *S'well* 17–20; V from 20. *The Vicarage, Martin Lane, Bawtry, Doncaster DN10 6NJ* E: revbeckyhancock@gmail.com

HANCOCK, Canon Richard Manuel Ashley. b 69. Linc Th Coll 94 Westcott Ho Cam 95. **d** 97 **p** 98. C Didcot St Pet *Ox* 97–00; P-in-c Shrivenham w Watchfield and Bourton 00–03; V Shrivenham and Ashbury 03–18; AD Vale of White Horse 05–12; Hon Can Ch Ch 12–18; P-in-c Sixpenny Handley w Gussage St Andrew etc *Sarum* from 18; Rural Field Officer (Dorset Adnry) from 18. *The Vicarage, 60 High Street, Sixpenny Handley, Salisbury SP5 5ND* T: (01725) 552608 E: canonrick@icloud.com

HANCOCK, Miss Sarah. b 80. Ches Univ BSc 01. Ridley Hall Cam 15. **d** 17 **p** 18. C Luton St Fran *St Alb* 17–21; V Cheadle Hulme All SS *Ches* from 21. *The Vicarage, 27 Church Road, Cheadle Hulme, Cheadle SK8 7JL* M: 07738-441486 E: revsarahhancock@icloud.com

HANCOCK, Canon Vittoria Ruth. b 74. Univ of Wales (Ban) BSc 95 BD 99 Dur Univ MA 19. Cranmer Hall Dur 91. **d** 01 **p** 02. C Llanberis w Llanrug *Ban* 01–03; C Llanberis, Llanrug and Llandinorwig 03–04; C Dolgellau w Llanfachreth and Brithdir etc 04–05; Chapl St As Cathl and Dioc Evang Officer 06–12; R Ballater *Ab* from 14; R Aboyne from 14; Dioc Dir Ords 14–19; Can St Andr Cathl from 18. *7 Invercauld Road, Ballater AB35 5RP* T: (013397) 55919 E: vittoriahancock@gmail.com

HANCOCKS, Graeme. b 58. Univ of Wales (Ban) BD 79 Oslo Univ 78. Oslo Univ Th Coll 79. **d** 81 **p** 82. C Denbigh and Nantglyn *St As* 81–84; Asst Chapl Oslo St Edm *Eur* 84–88; Chapl Stockholm 88–89; Chapl Marseille w St Raphaël, Aix-en-Provence etc 89; Chapl Gothenburg w Halmstad, Jönköping etc 90–93; Chapl Southn Univ Hosps NHS Trust 93–98; Chapl Trafford Healthcare NHS Trust 98–02; Chapl Leeds Teaching Hosps NHS Trust 02–09; rtd 09; PtO *Bradf* 09–14; *Leeds* 14–16. *7 Woodfield Road, Cullingworth, Bradford BD13 5JL* T: (01535) 271551

HANCOX, Ms Sarah Anne. b 85. Edin Univ BD 07. Cranmer Hall Dur 09. **d** 11 **p** 12. C Kirk Sandall and Edenthorpe *Sheff* 11–14; P-in-c Methley w Mickletown *Leeds* 14–15; P-in-c Oulton w Woodlesford 14–15; TV Rothwell, Lofthouse, Methley etc from 15. *The Rectory, Church Side, Methley, Leeds LS26 9BJ* E: hancoxsa@gmail.com

HAND, Michael. See HAND, Peter Michael

HAND, Michael Anthony (Tony). b 63. York Univ BA 84 DipCOT 88. St Jo Coll Nottm MA 95. **d** 95 **p** 96. C Lutterworth w Cotesbach *Leic* 95–98; C Lutterworth w Cotesbach and Bitteswell 99–01; V Acomb H Redeemer *York* 01–20; Chapl Manor Sch 01–20; P-in-c Scalby *York* from 20; P-in-c Hackness w Harwood Dale from 20. *1 Queen Elizabeth*

Drive, Scalby, Scarborough YO13 0SR T: (01723) 501305
E: revtonyhand@outlook.com

HAND, Canon Nigel Arthur. b 54. St Jo Coll Nottm. d 84
p 85. C Birm St Luke 84–88; C Walton H Trin *Ox* 88–89; TV
89–97; C Selly Park St Steph and St Wulstan *Birm* 97–04;
P-in-c Selly Park Ch Ch 04–08; AD Moseley 04–07; Can Res
Birm Cathl 08–19; rtd 19; PtO *Birm* from 19. *382 Hay Green
Lane, Birmingham B30 1SR* E: nigelhand@me.com

HAND, Peter Michael. b 42. Univ Coll Ox BA 63 Lon
Univ BSc 75. Sarum & Wells Th Coll 77. d 80 p 81. NSM
Shaston *Sarum* 80–81; C Tisbury 81–83; C Glastonbury
St Jo w Godney *B & W* 83–84; C Glastonbury w Meare, W
Pennard and Godney 84–87; V High Littleton 87–99; RD
Midsomer Norton 92–98; R Winford w Felton Common
Hill 99–07; Warden of Readers Bath Adnry 98–06; rtd 07;
TV Winchcombe *Glouc* 10–13; PtO from 17. *27 Stancombe
View, Winchcombe, Cheltenham GL54 5LE* T: (01242) 609575
E: anne_michael_hand@yahoo.co.uk

HAND, Philip Ronald. b 53. Spurgeon's Coll BA 78.
d 03 p 04. NSM Southampton (City Cen) *Win*
03–18; NSM Southampton St Mich from 18. *21 The
Greenwich, Gloucester Square, Southampton SO14 2GJ*
E: philhand@newporteducational.co.uk

HANDCOCK, Mrs Alison Dawn. d 15. C Preston
Plucknett *B & W* 15–19; PtO from 19. *Address withheld by
request* M: 07791-546435 E: rev.alisonh@yahoo.co.uk

✠**HANDFORD, The Rt Revd George Clive.** b 37. CMG 07.
Hatf Coll Dur BA 61. Qu Coll Birm 61. d 63 p 64 c 90. C
Mansfield SS Pet and Paul *S'well* 63–67; Lebanon 67–74; Dean
Jerusalem 74–78; UAE 78–83; Adn Gulf 78–83; V Kneesall w
Laxton *S'well* 83–84; P-in-c Wellow 83–84; RD Tuxford and
Norwell 83–84; Adn Nottingham 84–90; Suff Bp Warw *Cov*
90–96; Bp Cyprus and the Gulf 96–07; Pres Bp Episc Ch
Jerusalem and Middle E 02–07; rtd 07; Hon Asst Bp Ripon
and Leeds 07–14; Asst Bp Leeds from 14. *Wayside, 1 The
Terrace, Kirby Hill, Boroughbridge, York YO51 9DQ* T: (01423)
325406 E: cpdhandford@gmail.com

HANDFORTH, Canon Richard Brereton. b 31. St Pet Coll
Ox BA 55 MA 60. Westcott Ho Cam 63. d 64 p 65. C
Hornchurch St Andr *Chelmsf* 64–65; Warden St Steph Coll
Hong Kong 65–73; Chapl CMS Fellowship Ho Chislehurst
73–75; Hon C Chislehurst St Nic *Roch* 73–75; Home Educn
Sec CMS 75–83; V Biggin Hill *Roch* 83–88; Inter-change
Adv CMS 88–96; Hon C Plaistow St Mary *Roch* 95–04; Hon
Can Lagos from 95; rtd 96; PtO *Roch* from 01. *1 Bromley
College, London Road, Bromley BR1 1PE* T: (020) 8460 0238
E: r.handforth1@btinternet.com

HANDLEY, The Ven Anthony Michael. b 36. Selw Coll Cam
BA 60 MA 64. Chich Th Coll 60. d 62 p 63. C Thorpe
St Andr *Nor* 62–66; C Gaywood, Bawsey and Mintlyn
66–72; V Hellesdon 72–81; RD Nor N 80–81; Adn Nor
81–93; Adn Norfolk 93–02; rtd 02; PtO *Nor* from 02. *25
New Street, Sheringham NR26 8EE* T: (01263) 820928
E: amhandley@yahoo.co.uk

HANDLEY, Canon Dennis Francis. b 57. MIE 79 TEng(CEI) 80.
Coll of Resurr Mirfield 82. d 85 p 86. C Headingley *Ripon*
85–88; C Rothwell 88–92; V Liversedge *Wakef* 92–97; V
Ripponden and Barkisland w W Scammonden 97–06;
TR Almondbury w Farnley Tyas 06–14; Dioc Rural Officer
04–14; V Berwick H Trin and St Mary *Newc* from 14; Hon
Can Newc Cathl from 19. *The Vicarage, Parade, Berwick-upon-
Tweed TD15 1DF* T: (01289) 306136

HANDLEY, James William. b 74. Imp Coll Lon MEng 96
Leeds Univ PhD 04 Dur Univ BA 17. St Hild Coll 14.
d 17 p 18. NSM Harrogate St Mark *Leeds* from 17. *32
St Helens Road, Harrogate HG2 8LD* M: 07392-599699
E: revjameshandley@gmail.com

HANDLEY, John. b 38. Oak Hill Th Coll. d 83 p 84. C Witton
w Brundall and Braydeston *Nor* 83–86; R Reedham w
Cantley w Limpenhoe and Southwood 86–93; P-in-c E
w W Harling and Bridgham w Roudham 93–95; R E w W
Harling, Bridgham w Roudham, Larling etc 95–05; RD
Thetford and Rockland 95–98; rtd 05; PtO *Nor* from 05.
6 Barton Close, Swaffham PE37 7SB T: (01760) 336328
E: john.handley.home@hotmail.com

HANDLEY, Mrs Kathryn Emma. b 70. d 14 p 15. C Bredbury
St Mark *Ches* 14–16; P-in-c Stalybridge St Paul 16–21; V
from 21. *St Paul's Vicarage, Huddersfield Road, Stalybridge
SK15 2PT* T: 0161-338 2966 E: kehandley@btinternet.com

HANDLEY, Michael. *See* HANDLEY, Anthony Michael

HANDLEY, Timothy John. b 63. Glos Univ BTh 01. St Steph
Ho Ox 94. d 96 p 97. C St Marychurch *Ex* 96–98; PtO *Cant*
06–10; *Lon* 15–17; P-in-c St Jas Garlickhythe w St Mich
Queenhithe etc 17–21; R from 21. *35 Buckhurst Street,
London E1 5QT* T: (01227) 720765 M: 07912-583201
E: frtimhandley@gmail.com

HANDLEY MacMATH, Terence. b 59. Goldsmiths' Coll
Lon BA 80 K Coll Cam MA 98. Westcott Ho Cam 91.
d 94 p 95. NSM Southwold *St E* 94–95; PtO *St Alb* 96–99;
C St Alb St Pet 99–05; PtO 09–19; V Harrow Weald All SS
Lon 05–07; Chapl R Free Hampstead NHS Trust 07–09;
Chapl R Brompton and Harefield NHS Foundn Trust
09–16; rtd 16; PtO *Sarum* from 17. *c/o Church Times,
108 Golden Lane, London EC1Y 0TG* T: (020) 7776 1061
E: terencehandleymacmath@gmail.com

HANDY, Miss Laura Jane. b 82. Regents Th Coll BA 13.
St Mellitus Coll 13. d 15 p 16. C Droitwich Spa *Worc* 15–18;
TV 18–19; C Salwarpe and Hindlip w Martin Hussingtree
18–19; TV Droitwich, and Salwarpe and Hindlip w
Martin Hussingtree from 19. *7 College Green, Droitwich
WR9 8QY* M: 07921-524394 E: revlaurahandy@gmail.com

HANDY, Thomas. b 79. Ex Univ BA 02 Bris Univ PGCE 05. Trin
Coll Bris MA 09. d 09 p 10. C Shepton Mallet w Doulting
B & W 09–12; R S Petherton w The Seavingtons 12–14; C
Kingsbury Episcopi w E Lambrook, Hambridge etc 13–14; R
S Petherton w The Seavingtons and The Lambrooks 14–21.
Address temp unknown E: revdtomhandy@hotmail.com

HANFORD, Karen Anne. b 60. d 17 p 18. NSM Wollaton
S'well 17–21; NSM Stapleford from 21. *6 Beeston Fields Drive,
Beeston, Nottingham NG9 3DB*

HANFORD, Richard James. b 90. St Andr Univ MTheol 12.
Trin Coll Bris 16. d 18 p 19. C Worksop St Anne *S'well* from
18; C Norton Cuckney from 18. *129 Stubbing Lane, Worksop
S80 1NF* E: richard.hanford@btinternet.com

HANFORD, Canon William Richard. b 38. Keble Coll Ox
BA 60 MA 64 Lon Univ BD 66 Univ of Wales LLM 95.
St Steph Ho Ox 60. d 63 p 64. C Roath St Martin *Llan*
63–66; C Llantwit Major 67–68; PV Llan Cathl 68–72; Chapl
RN 72–76; Hon Chapl Gibraltar Cathl *Eur* 74–76; Hon C
Eastbourne St Sav and St Pet *Chich* 76–77; C Brighton St Pet
77–78; Can Res and Prec Guildf Cathl 78–83; Hon Can
Guildf Cathl 03–09; V Ewell 83–09; Tutor and Lect Chich Th
Coll 79–86; rtd 09; PtO *Guildf* 09–10; *Llan* from 09. *15 Austin
Avenue, Laleston, Bridgend CF32 0LG* T: (01656) 656892
E: wrhanford@btinternet.com

HANILY, Séan Jerome Keanspark. b 90. TCD BA 12 MA 15
MTh 18 FRAS 16 LLCM 17. CITI. d 17 p 18. Dublin
Rathfarnham *D & G* 17–18; C Drumragh w Mountfield
D & R 18–20; I Rathmichael *D & G* from 20. *Rathmichael
Rectory, Ferndale Road, Shankill, Dublin, D18 NK45, Republic
of Ireland* T: (00353) (1) 282 2803 M: 07597-364299
E: hanilys@tcd.ie

HANKEY, Miss Dorothy Mary. b 38. CertEd 65. Trin Coll
Bris 75. dss 78 d 87 p 94. Wigan St Jas w St Thos *Liv* 78–84;
Middleton *Man* 84–85; Litherland Ch Ch *Liv* 85–89; Par Dn
87–89; Par Dn Blackpool St Mark *Blackb* 89–94; C 94–95;
C Blackpool St Paul 95–98; rtd 98; PtO *Blackb* from 98. *89
Rutland Avenue, Poulton-le-Flyde FY6 7RX* T: (01253) 890635

HANKEY, Rupert Christopher Alers. b 60. Sheff Univ LLB 82.
Wilson Carlile Coll 86 St Jo Coll Nottm MTh 06. d 07 p 08. C
Bedford St Jo and St Leon *St Alb* 07–11; V Sidcup St Andr *Roch*
11–20; TV Billericay and Lt Burstead *Chelmsf* from 20. *The
Vicarage, 7A Horace Road, Billericay CM11 1AA* M: 07539-
319545 E: ruperth5@btinternet.com

HANKS, John Martin. b 57. St Chad's Coll Dur BA 80 Univ
of Wales (Cardiff) LLM 94 Selw Coll Cam PGCE 82. St Steph
Ho Ox 10. d 12. NSM Ox St Barn and St Paul 12–15;
NSM Ox St Thos 12–15; Chapl to Suff Bp Ebbsfleet (PEV)
Cant 12–13; PtO *York* 16–18; NSM York All SS N Street
from 18. *20 Ogleforth, York YO1 7JG* T: (01904) 731636
E: hanksj@gmail.com

HANLEY, Máirt Joseph. b 74. Univ Coll Ches BA 95. CITC
BTh 03. d 03 p 04. NSM Tralee w Kilmoyley, Ballymacelligott
etc *L & K* 03–11; Bp's C Kilcolman w Kiltallagh, Killorglin,
Knockane etc 11–15; I Baltinglass w Ballynure etc *C, F & O*
from 15. *The Rectory, Church Lane, Baltinglass, Co Wicklow,
W91 T8X6, Republic of Ireland* T: (00353) (59) 648
1321 M: 87-619 4733 E: baltinglassgroup@gmail.com

HANLON, Canon Thomas Kyle. b 72. QUB BA 94 TCD BTh 97.
d 97 p 98. C Bangor St Comgall *D & D* 97–00; I Dromore *Clogh*
00–06; I Fivemiletown from 06; Chapl to Bp Clogh 03–12;
Can Clogh Cathl from 16; Prec from 19. *St John's Rectory, 160
Ballagh Road, Fivemiletown BT75 0QP* T: (028) 8952 1030 *or*
8952 2422 E: fivemiletown@clogher.anglican.org

HANMER, Sister Phoebe Margaret. b 31. Edin Univ MA 54.
d 96 p 97. NSM Brakpan S Africa 96–00; NSM Actonville
00–03; PtO *Ox* 99–00; *Birm* 04–15; Ox from 16. *St Mary's
Convent, Denchworth Road, Wantage OX12 9AU* T: (01235)
763141

HANMER, Canon Richard John. b 38. Peterho Cam BA 61
MA 65. Linc Th Coll 62. d 64 p 65. C Sheff St Swithun 64–69;
Bp's Chapl *Nor* 69–73; V Cinderhill *S'well* 73–81; V Eaton *Nor*

81–94; Dioc Chapl MU 91–04; Hon Can Nor Cathl 93–94; Can Res Nor Cathl 94–04; P-in-c Nor St Mary in the Marsh 94–04; rtd 04; PtO Nor from 04. *18 Quebec Road, Dereham NR19 2DR* T: (01362) 655092 E: rj.hanmer@outlook.com

HANNA, Miss Elizabeth. b 50. QUB BA 73 Lon Bible Coll BA 79 Milltown Inst Dub MA 01. CITC 99. **d** 01 **p** 02. C Bangor Abbey *D & D* 01–04; I Magherally w Annaclone 04–08; I Belfast St Nic *Conn* 08–18; rtd 18. *9 Bignian Avenue, Kilkeel, Newry BT34 4NF* T: (028) 4176 5851 M: 07801-946909 E: hannamanor15@btinternet.com

HANNA, John. b 44. Lon Bible Coll BA 83. Westcott Ho Cam 86. **d** 87 **p** 88. C Denton Ch Ch *Man* 87–91; V Higher Walton *Blackb* 91–98; C Marple All SS *Ches* 98–02; TV Burrington, Chawleigh, Cheldon, Chulmleigh etc *Ex* 02–09; RD S Molton 03–09; rtd 09; PtO *S & B* 10–12 and from 16; P-in-c Beguildy and Heyope and Llangynllo and Bleddfa 12–16. *Victoria House, Victoria Road, Knighton LD7 1BD* T: (01547) 529296

HANNA, Patricia Elizabeth. *See* McKEE HANNA, Patricia Elizabeth

HANNA, Peter Thomas. b 45. ACII 66 GIFireE 75. CITC 85. **d** 88 **p** 89. Aux Min Cork St Fin Barre's Union *C, C & R* 88–95; Min Can Cork Cathl 92–03; Dioc Info Officer 94–95; Aux Min Cork St Luke Union 95–00; Aux Min Douglas Union w Frankfield 00 and 02–03 and 04–07; Aux Min Kinsale Union 00–02 and 03–04 and 10–20; Aux Min Fanlobbus Union 07–08; Aux Min Kinneigh Union 09; rtd 20. *Mount Windsor, Farnahoe, Inishannon, Co Cork, Republic of Ireland* T: (00353) (21) 477 5470 E: peterthanna@gmail.com

HANNA, Canon Robert Charles. b 49. Oak Hill Th Coll 75. **d** 77 **p** 78. C Coleraine *Conn* 77–82; I Convoy w Monellan and Donaghmore *D & R* 82–94; Can Raphoe Cathl 88–94; I Drumcliffe w Kilnasoolagh *L & K* 94–18; Can Limerick, Killaloe and Clonfert Cathls 00–18; Chan 04–18; rtd 18. *Seafield Cottage, Baile an tSagart, Tromara West, Quilty, Co Clare, V95 YOP4, Republic of Ireland* T: (00353) (65) 708 7965 M: 86-6216 7040 E: bobhanna@eircom.net

HANNAFIN (née Lewis), Angela Jane. b 69. Portsm Univ BA 92. St Jo Coll Nottm 13. **d** 15 **p** 16. C Uxbridge *Lon* from 15; P-in-c Bardsey *Leeds* 18–19; V from 19; Lay Tr Officer from 18. *The Vicarage, Woodacre Lane, Bardsey, Leeds LS17 9DX* M: 07860-824314 E: angelalewisjane@gmail.com

HANNAFORD, Prof Robert. b 53. Ex Univ BEd 76 MA 78 PhD 87. St Steph Ho Ox 78. **d** 80 **p** 81. C Ex St Jas 80–83; Chapl Ex Univ 83–88; Tutor St Steph Ho Ox 89–92; Sen Lect Cant Ch Ch Univ Coll 92–99; Prof Chr Th Univ Coll Chich 99–01; Hon C Bury w Houghton and Coldwaltham and Hardham *Chich* 99–01; Th Consultant Bp Horsham 99–01; Can and Preb Chich Cathl from 00; Prof Th St Martin's Coll Lanc 02–05; Dean of Faculty 05–07; Dean of Faculty Cumbria Univ *Carl* from 07; Hon C Tunstall w Melling and Leck *Blackb* 02–03; Hon C E Lonsdale 03–15; P-in-c Workington St Jo *Carl* 15–19; Dir Cumbria Chr Learning 18–20; Dioc Dir Minl Formation *Carl* from 20. *Cumbria Christian Learning, Church House, 19-24 Friargate, Penrith CA14 4DP* T: (01768) 807765 E: rhannaford@ucsm.ac.uk

HANNAH, Darrell Dale. b 62. Grand Canyon Univ BA 85 S Bapt Th Sem MDiv 89 Regent Coll Vancouver ThM 92 Magd Coll Cam PhD 96. WMMTC 00. **d** 03 **p** 03. NSM Edgbaston St Geo *Birm* 03–04; NSM Iffley *Ox* 04–07; NSM Earley St Pet 07–08; R Ascot Heath from 08; AD Bracknell 16–19. *All Saints' Rectory, London Road, Ascot SL5 8DQ* T: (01344) 621200 E: drddhannah@yahoo.co.uk

HANNAH, Kimberley Victoria. *See* WILLIAMS, Kimberley Victoria

HANNAM, Robert Stephen. b 46. CertEd 69. **d** 05 **p** 06. NSM Rastrick St Matt *Wakef* 05–08; NSM Rastrick 08–14; *Leeds* from 14. *33 Lyndhurst Road, Brighouse HD6 3RX* T: (01484) 716053 E: stephenr.hannam@btinternet.com

HANNEN, Robert John. *See* DAVIES-HANNEN, Robert John

HANNING, Christopher William Arthur. b 80. Edin Univ MA 04 MSc 05. Oak Hill Th Coll BA 16. **d** 18 **p** 19. C Blackheath St Jo *S'wark* from 18. *Flat A, 15 St John's Park, London SE3 7TD* M: 07743-828309 E: cwahanning@gmail.com

✠**HANNON, The Rt Revd Brian Desmond Anthony.** b 36. TCD BA 59 MA 62. TCD Div Sch Div Test 61. **d** 61 **p** 62 **c** 86. C Clooney *D & R* 61–64; I Desertmartin 64–69; I Londonderry Ch Ch 69–82; I Enniskillen *Clogh* 82–86; Preb Clogh Cathl 82–84; Dean Clogh 85–86; Bp Clogh 86–01; rtd 01. *Drumconnis Top, 202 Mullaghmeen Road, Ballinamallard, Enniskillen BT94 2DZ* T: (028) 6638 8557 F: 6638 8086

HANSCOMBE, Stephen John. b 63. Bp Grosseteste Coll BEd 84 Hughes Hall Cam MEd 05. Yorks Min Course BA 16. **d** 16 **p** 17. NSM Bedale and Leeming and Thornton Watlass *Leeds* 16–19; V Leyburn w Bellerby from 19. *The*

Vicarage, I'Anson Close, Leyburn DL8 5LF M: 07734-138431 E: stephen.hanscombe@leeds.anglican.org

HANSELL, Anupama. b 76. Pune Univ India BSc 97 Serampore Univ BD 03 Birm Univ MA 06. **d** 02 **p** 04. C Birm St Martin w Bordesley St Andr 04–08; Chapl Aston Univ 05–08; TV Coventry Caludon *Cov* 08–10; PtO *Nor* 10–11; C Bure Valley 11–13; PtO *Derby* 13–14; *Bris* 14–18; Chapl Univ Hosps Bris NHS Foundn Trust 16–18; PtO *Ox* from 19; Chapl St Edm Hall Ox 19–20. *Garras, Bradfield, Reading RG7 6AJ* E: revd.akh@btinternet.com

HANSELL, Peter Michael. b 76. Selw Coll Cam BA 97 MA 01 MPhil 99 PhD 02. Qu Coll Birm 03. **d** 05 **p** 06. C Moseley St Mary *Birm* 05–07; C Moseley St Mary and St Anne 07–09; Reader Initial Tr Adv *Cov* 09–10; R Bure Valley *Nor* 10–13; Chapl Trent Coll Nottm 13–14; Chapl Clifton Coll Bris 14–16; Chapl Bradfield Coll Berks from 16; PtO *Ox* from 16. *Bradfield College, Bradfield, Reading RG7 6AU* T: 0118-964 4776 M: 07825-714728 E: chaplain@bradfieldcollege.org.uk

HANSEN, Ernest Paul. b 46. Linc Th Coll 78. **d** 80 **p** 81. C Greenside *Dur* 80–83; rtd 11. *34 Riversley Road, Gloucester GL2 0QT* T: (01452) 415923 E: ernie.hansen46@gmail.com

HANSEN, James Edwin. b 41. Concordia Coll (USA) BSc 64 San Jose State Univ MA 71. Ch Div Sch of the Pacific (USA) MDiv 86. **d** 86 **p** 87. C Swansea St Pet *S & B* 86–87; C Sketty 87–89; C Hornchurch St Andr *Chelmsf* 89–91; P-in-c Chelmsf St Andr 91–94; USA from 94; rtd 06. *PO Box 7830, Brookings OR 97415-0370, USA* T: (001) (541) 412 9993 E: jimehansen@charter.net

HANSFORD, Ruth Patricia. b 68. K Coll Lon BSc 90 Surrey Univ MSc 96 Sch of Pharmacy Lon PhD 00. Trin Coll Bris BA 02. **d** 03 **p** 04. C Parkham, Alwington, Buckland Brewer etc *Ex* 03–07; P-in-c Hatherleigh, Meeth, Exbourne and Jacobstowe 07–11; TV Okehampton, Inwardleigh, Belstone, Sourton etc 12–18; RD Okehampton 12–16; V Bro Ystumanner *Ban* from 18. *Y Ficerdy, Ffynnon Arian, Tywyn LL36 9BF* T: (01654) 710255 E: maggiethecat@waitrose.com

HANSHAW, Eugene Edward. b 73. ERMC 13. **d** 16 **p** 17. C Chipping Barnet *St Alb* 16–19; TV Cheshunt from 19. *The Vicarage, Churchgate, Cheshunt, Waltham Cross EN8 9DY* M: 07795-195728 E: rev.eugene@outlook.com

HANSON, Barry James. b 70. Qld Univ of Tech DipEd 91 BEd 94 Lon Inst of Educn MA 03. Ripon Coll Cuddesdon 15. **d** 19. C Merrow *Guildf* 19–20; C Worplesdon from 20. *3 Southbury, Lawn Road, Guildford GU2 4DD* M: 07949-654988 E: revbarryhanson@outlook.com

HANSON, David John. b 59. All SS Cen for Miss & Min. **d** 14 **p** 15. C Chadderton Ch Ch *Man* 14–17; V Preston St Steph *Blackb* from 17. *6 Woodfield Close, Penwortham, Preston PR1 0SJ* E: djhanson59@gmail.com

HANSON, Edward William. b 51. Salem State Coll (USA) BA 73 Tufts Univ MA 78 Boston Coll PhD 92 Episc Div Sch MDiv 00. Ripon Coll Cuddesdon 00. **d** 01 **p** 02. C Linc St Botolph and Linc St Pet-at-Gowts and St Andr 01–04; P-in-c Orsett and Bulphan and Horndon on the Hill *Chelmsf* 04–06; R 06–14; RD Thurrock 08–11; rtd 14; PtO *Lon* from 15; *Eur* from 16. *14 Erncroft Way, Twickenham TW1 1DA* E: ed.hanson@alumni.tufts.edu

HANSON, James Andrew. b 77. BNC Ox MMath 99 MSc 01 Brunel Univ CMath 12 QTS 02 FIMA 14. St Mellitus Coll MA 21. **d** 21. C Alfold and Loxwood *Guildf* from 21. *8 Springbok Cottages, Springbok Estate, Alfold, Cranleigh GU6 8HT* M: 07770-403779 E: hansonjames@hotmail.com

HANSON, Michael Beaumont. b 49. Univ Coll Ox MA 70 PGCE 71. NOC 81. **d** 84 **p** 85. Chapl Leeds Gr Sch 84–99; Hon C Leeds St Geo *Ripon* 84–99; rtd 99; PtO *Carl* from 99. *5 The Crofts, Crosby, Maryport CA15 6SP* T: (01900) 816630 E: mikeandchristinehanson@sky.com

HANSON, Philip Arthur. b 46. Loughb Univ BTech 69 City Univ MSc 73 St Jo Coll Nottm MA 04 CEng 72 FRSA 96. Qu Coll Birm MA 12. **d** 12 **p** 13. NSM Claverdon w Preston Bagot *Cov* 12–16; PtO from 17. *Lion Hill Cottage, Station Road, Claverdon, Warwick CV35 8PE* T: (01926) 843421 M: 07879-400947 E: phil@philiphanson.net

HANSON, Robert Arthur. b 35. Keele Univ BA 57. St Steph Ho Ox 57 St Mich Coll Llan 59. **d** 60 **p** 61. C Longton St Mary and St Chad *Lich* 60–65; Chapl St Mary's Cathl Edin 65–69; R Glas St Matt 69–79; R Paisley H Trin 79–87; V Walsall St Andr *Lich* 87–93; PtO *Worc* 94–97; C Kentish Town Lon 97–01; Hon C 02–06; rtd 02; PtO *Lon* from 06. *7B Fraser Regnart Court, Southampton Road, London NW5 4HU* T: (020) 7284 3634 M: 07951-154384 E: bob.hanson@btinternet.com

HANWELL, David John. b 46. Leic Univ CertEd 74 UEA BEd 94. **d** 98 **p** 99. OLM Mundford w Lynford, Cranwich and Ickburgh w Langford *Nor* 98–04; OLM Cockley Cley w Gooderstone 99–04; P-in-c 04–13; OLM Gt and Lt Cressingham w Threxton 99–04; C 04–13; OLM Hilborough w Bodney

99–04; C 04–13; OLM Oxborough w Foulden and Caldecote 99–04; C 04–13; rtd 13; PtO *Nor* from 15. *Cherry Tree Cottage, Back Lane, Castle Acre, King's Lynn PE32 2AR* T: (01760) 755812 E: david.hanwell@btopenworld.com

HARALD, Claire Louise. b 76. St Mellitus Coll 16. **d** 19 **p** 20. C Norton *St Alb* from 19. *2 Common View, Letchworth Garden City SG6 1DA* M: 07739-515172 E: claire_harald@hotmail.com

HARBAGE, Matthew Michael. b 86. York Univ MMath 10 Cam Univ BTh 15. Westcott Ho Cam 12. **d** 15 **p** 16. C Louth *Linc* from 15; C Regent's Park St Mark *Lon* 18–20; V New Southgate St Paul from 20. *The Vicarage, 1 Woodland Road, London N11 1PN* T: (020) 8361 1946 E: mharbage@hotmail.com

HARBIDGE, The Ven Adrian Guy. b 48. St Jo Coll Dur BA 70. Cuddesdon Coll 73. **d** 75 **p** 76. C Romsey *Win* 75–80; V Bournemouth St Andr 80–86; V Chandler's Ford 86–99; RD Eastleigh 93–99; Adn Bournemouth 99–10; P-in-c Seale, Puttenham and Wanborough *Guildf* 10–15; R 15–16; rtd 17. *2 Tudor Cottages, 309 Catherington Lane, Waterlooville PO8 0TE* E: adriangharbidge@gmail.com

HARBORD, Canon Paul Geoffrey. b 56. JP 99. Keble Coll Ox BA 78 MA 86 Cardiff Univ LLM 11. Chich Th Coll 81. **d** 83 **p** 84. C Rawmarsh w Parkgate *Sheff* 83–86; C Doncaster St Geo 86–90; C-in-c St Edm Anchorage Lane CD 90–95; V Masbrough 95–03; Bp's Chapl from 03; Hon Can Sheff Cathl 07–20; Acting Dean and Can Res Sheff Cathl from 20. *4 Clarke Drive, Sheffield S10 2NS* T: 0114-263 6061 *or* 266 1932 M: 07898-485428 E: geoffrey.harbord@sheffield-cathedral.org.uk *or* geoffrey@bishopofsheffield.org.uk

HARBORD, Philip James. b 56. St Cath Coll Ox BA 77. Cranmer Hall Dur 78. **d** 80 **p** 81. C Enfield St Andr *Lon* 80–83; CMS Pakistan 84–88; C Clay Hill St Jo and St Luke *Lon* 88–91; Chapl Wexham Park Hosp Slough 91–92; Chapl Upton Hosp Slough 91–92; Chapl Heatherwood and Wexham Park Hosps NHS Trust 92–95; Chapl Leic Gen Hosp NHS Trust 95–98; Chapl Fosse Health NHS Trust 98–99; Chapl Leics and Rutland Healthcare NHS Trust 99–01; P-in-c Cosby *Leic* 01–07; P-in-c Whetstone 03–07; rtd 07; PtO *Leic* 15–18. *122 Durban Road, Grimsby DN32 8AY*

HARBRIDGE, Philip Charles Anthony. b 65. K Coll Lon LLB 88 AKC 88 Ch Coll Cam BA 98 MA 02. Westcott Ho Cam. **d** 99 **p** 00. C Hampton All SS *Lon* 99–02; Chapl Ch Coll Cam 02–07; Chapl Millfield Sch Somerset from 07. *Millfield School, Street BA16 0YD* T: (01458) 442291 E: pch@millfieldschool.com

HARCOURT, Canon Giles. b 36. Westcott Ho Cam 68. **d** 71 **p** 72. C Bishopwearmouth St Mich w St Hilda *Dur* 71–73; C Fishponds St Mary *Bris* 73–75; Bp's Dom Chapl *S'wark* 75–78; LtO 78–79; V S Wimbledon H Trin and St Pet 79–88; V Greenwich St Alfege 88–04; Hon Chapl RN Coll Greenwich 89–99; RD Greenwich Thameside *S'wark* 94–98; Boro Dean Greenwich 94–98; Hon Can S'wark Cathl 96–04; rtd 05; PtO *Chich* from 05. *1A Trinity Trees, Eastbourne BN21 3LA* T: (01323) 638790

HARCOURT, Canon Paul George. b 67. Em Coll Cam BA 88 MA 92. Wycliffe Hall Ox BA 91 MA 17. **d** 92 **p** 93. C Moreton *Ches* 92–95; C Woodford Wells *Chelmsf* 95–00; V from 00; P-in-c Barkingside St Cedd from 16; AD Redbridge 10–14; Nat Ldr New Wine from 16; Hon Can Chelmsf Cathl from 20. *All Saints' Vicarage, 4 Inmans Row, Woodford Green IG8 0NH* T: (020) 8504 0266 F: 8504 9640 E: paul@asww.org.uk *or* paul.harcourt@new-wine.org

HARCOURT-NORTON, Michael Clive. *See* NORTON, Michael Clive Harcourt

HARDACRE (née BROOKFIELD), Mrs Patricia Anne. b 50. St Mary's Coll Dur BA 72 St Jo Coll Dur MA 74. Cranmer Hall Dur. **dss** 84 **d** 87 **p** 94. Kingston upon Hull St Nic *York* 84–86; Acomb St Steph and St Aid 86–96; Par Dn 87–94; C 94–96; rtd 07; PtO *Blackb* from 07. *17 Fairfield Drive, Clitheroe BB7 2PE* T: (01200) 429341 E: annederekh@talktalk.net

HARDCASTLE, Ian Kenneth Dalton. b 56. Auckland Univ BE 78 ME 80. St Jo Coll Nottm MTh 04. **d** 04 **p** 05. C Denton Holme *Carl* 04–09; V Whangaparaoa Peninsular NZ from 09. *20 Rakino Avenue, Manly, Whangaparaoa 0930, New Zealand* T: (0064) (9) 424 0939 E: vicar@ststephenswgp.org.nz

HARDCASTLE, Nigel John. b 47. Reading Univ BSc 68. Qu Coll Birm. **d** 72 **p** 73. C Weoley Castle *Birm* 72–75; C Handsworth St Andr 75–78; V Garretts Green 78–86; Exec Sec Ch Computer Project BCC 86–89; R Emmer Green *Ox* 89–99; V Reading St Luke w St Bart 99–12; rtd 12; PtO *Ox* from 13. *67 Dunstall Close, Tilehurst, Reading RG31 5AY* T: 0118-943 1258 E: nigel.hardcastle@btinternet.com

HARDCASTLE, Roger Clive. b 52. Southn Univ BSc 73. Qu Coll Birm. **d** 78 **p** 79. C Walton St Mary *Liv* 78–82; V

Pemberton St Fran Kitt Green 82–94; TV Padgate 94–96; V Birchwood 96–06; rtd 06. *15 Ullswater Avenue, Orrell, Wigan WN5 8PF* T: (01942) 513568

HARDING, Alan. b 45. St Jo Coll Ox BA 67 MA 73 Pemb Coll Ox DPhil 92. Oak Hill NSM Course 89. **d** 93 **p** 94. NSM Lt Heath *St Alb* 93–99; P-in-c S Mymms and Ridge 99–05; PtO *St E* 05–08; NSM S Hartismere 08–13; PtO *St Alb* 05–20; *St E* from 13. *The Old Guildhall, Mill Street, Gislingham, Eye IP23 8JT* T: (01379) 783361 E: alansharon.harding@googlemail.com

HARDING, Canon Alec James. b 61. St Andr Univ MA 83 DTh. Cranmer Hall Dur 86. **d** 89 **p** 90. C Thirsk *York* 89–93; TV Heref St Martin w St Fran 93–95; TV Heref S Wye 95–00; V Barnard Castle w Whorlton *Dur* from 00; AD Barnard Castle from 03; Hon Can Dur Cathl from 11; PtO *Leeds* 20–21. *The Vicarage, Parson's Lonnen, Barnard Castle DL12 8ST* T: (01833) 637018 E: alec.harding@durham.anglican.org

HARDING, Mrs Allison Joan. b 65. Sheff Univ BA 96 Northumbria Univ BSc 04. Cranmer Hall Dur 11. **d** 13 **p** 14. C Benwell *Newc* 13–15; C Benwell and Scotswood 15–17; V Newburn from 17. *The Vicarage, High Street, Newburn, Newcastle upon Tyne NE15 8LQ* T: 0191-229 0522 E: revallisonharding@gmail.com

HARDING, Canon Brenda Kathleen. b 39. Bedf Coll Lon BA 60 K Coll Lon BD 62 Lon Inst of Educn PGCE 65. St Deiniol's Hawarden 91. **d** 92 **p** 94. NSM Lancaster Ch Ch *Blackb* 92–13; Acting Vice-Prin CBDTI 04–05; Hon Can Blackb Cathl 05–13; rtd 13; PtO *Blackb* from 13. *14 Ascot Close, Lancaster LA1 4LT* T: (01524) 66071 E: brendakharding@hotmail.com

HARDING, Canon Brian Edward. b 38. ALCD 65. **d** 65 **p** 66. C Chislehurst Ch Ch *Roch* 65–68; P-in-c Baxenden *Blackb* 68–70; V 70–88; V Douglas 88–07; Hon Can Blackb Cathl 96–07; rtd 07; PtO *S'wark* from 08. *8 Lon Eirlys, Prestatyn LL19 9JZ* T: (01745) 851615 E: bnbharding@tiscali.co.uk

HARDING, Carl Julius. b 64. St Jo Coll Dur BA 15. Cranmer Hall Dur 12. **d** 15 **p** 16. C Stanwix *Carl* 15–20; P-in-c S Barrow from 20. *98 Roose Road, Barrow-in-Furness LA13 9RL* M: 07961-862956 E: carljharding@gmail.com

HARDING, Mrs Christine Joan. b 54. St Mellitus Coll. **d** 11 **p** 12. NSM Chadwell Heath *Chelmsf* from 11. *69 Eric Road, Romford RM6 6JH* T: (020) 8599 6174 E: christine@romfordhardings.me.uk

HARDING, Derek Gordon Edward. b 50. Open Univ BA 89 MIAP 95. **d** 01 **p** 02. OLM Godstone and Blindley Heath *S'wark* 01–09; C Blenheim NZ 09; PtO Dio Nelson 10–15; 16–18; rtd 15; PtO *S'wark* 15–16. *27 Moran Street, Redwoodtown, Blenheim 7201, New Zealand* E: peripatetic.padre@gmail.com

HARDING, Mrs Elise. b 44. RGN 65. STETS 07. **d** 10 **p** 11. NSM Wimborne Minster *Sarum* 10–15; NSM Witchampton, Stanbridge and Long Crichel etc 15; NSM Horton, Chalbury, Hinton Martel and Holt St Jas 15; NSM Wimborne Minster and the N Villages 15–17; rtd 17; PtO *Sarum* from 17; *Eur* 11–21. *The Beaches, 22 Middlehill Road, Wimborne BH21 2SD* T: (01202) 884775 E: fur_elise_h@yahoo.co.uk

HARDING, Elizabeth. *See* BUNKER, Elizabeth

HARDING, James Alexander. b 78. Trin Coll Bris BA 11. **d** 11 **p** 12. C Fulham Ch Ch *Lon* 11–16; CF from 16. *c/o MOD Chaplains (Army)* T: (01264) 383430 F: 381824 M: 07956-222940 E: hardingjamesa@gmail.com

HARDING, James Owen Glyn. b 42. Sussex Univ BA 65. NEOC 04. **d** 06 **p** 07. NSM Acomb H Redeemer *York* 06–12; PtO from 12. *63 Station Road, Upper Poppleton, York YO26 6PZ* T: (01904) 784495 E: jim2sal65@yahoo.co.uk

HARDING, John Stuart Michael. b 45. St Jo Coll Nottm 79. **d** 81 **p** 82. C Clifton *S'well* 81–87; V Broxtowe 87–98; PtO *Chelmsf* 98–01; M & K 01–02; rtd 07. *Greystone Farm, 9 Liscable Road, Newtownstewart BT78 4EF* E: john@greystomefarming.org

HARDING, Lesley Anne. *See* ATKINS, Lesley Anne

HARDING, Mrs Mary Elizabeth. b 46. SRN 67. STETS 97. **d** 00 **p** 01. NSM Shaftesbury *Sarum* 00–13; Chapl Westmr Memorial Hosp Shaftesbury 02–13; rtd 13. *Greenacres, Boxfield Road, Axminster EX13 5LD* T: (01297) 32155

HARDING, Michael Anthony John. b 37. Brasted Th Coll 67 Sarum Th Coll 68. **d** 71 **p** 72. C Forest Hill Ch Ch *S'wark* 71–72; C Catford St Laur 72–74; C Leominster *Heref* 74–77; R Neenton and V Ditton Priors 77–86; P-in-c Aston Botterell w Wheathill and Loughton 77–86; P-in-c Burwarton w N Cleobury 77–86; R Ditton Priors w Neenton, Burwarton etc 86–94; V E Budleigh w Bicton and Otterton *Ex* 94–03; rtd 03; PtO *Sarum* 03–20; *Eur* from 04. *The Beaches, 22 Middlehill Road, Wimborne BH21 2SD* T: (01202) 884775 E: michaelharding@talktalk.net

HARDING, Preb Michael David. b 38. Man Univ BA 61. Lich Th Coll 61. **d** 63 **p** 64. C Hednesford *Lich* 63–67; C Blurton 67–70; V Newcastle St Paul 70–99; RD Newcastle 87–97; Preb

Lich Cathl 89–99; rtd 99; PtO *Lich* 00–21. *7 Staines Court, Stone ST15 8XF* T: (01785) 811737 E: church@mdharding.org.uk

HARDING, Peter Gordon. b 45. Lon Univ BA 70 Open Univ BA 88 MA 90. Cranmer Hall Dur 77. **d** 79 **p** 80. C Kirkheaton *Wakef* 79–82; NSM New Sleaford *Linc* 90–00. *77 The Drove, Sleaford NG34 7AS* T: (01529) 306055

HARDING, Canon Ren Elaine Lois. b 56. Glos Univ BA 05. Trin Coll Bris MA 07. **d** 07 **p** 08. C Rainham *Roch* 07–11; V Joydens Wood St Barn 11–18; TR Bexley from 18; Hon Can Roch Cathl from 21. *The Vicarage, 6 Tile Kiln Lane, Bexley DA5 2BB* T: (01322) 528923 M: 07836-644782 E: renharding@hotmail.co.uk

HARDING, Richard Warrington. b 60. Trin Coll Bris 05. **d** 07 **p** 08. C Broadway w Wickhamford *Worc* 07–09; C Old Hill H Trin 09–11; TV Ipsley 11–19; rtd 20. *Address withheld by request*

HARDING, Ruth Mary. b 68. Trin Coll Bris 18. **d** 21. C Frenchay and Stapleton *Bris* from 21. *17 North Devon Road, Bristol BS16 2EX* T: 0117-965 8375 M: 07922-193561 E: r.harding208@btinternet.com

HARDINGHAM, Canon Paul David. b 52. Lon Univ BSc 74 Fitzw Coll Cam BA 77. Ridley Hall Cam 75. **d** 78 **p** 79. C Cambridge St Martin *Ely* 78–81; C Jesmond Clayton Memorial *Newc* 81–88; C Harborne Heath *Birm* 88–91; R Ipswich St Matt *St E* 91–04; V Halliwell St Pet *Man* 04–21; Hon Can Man Cathl 19–21; rtd 21. *Address temp unknown*

HARDISTY, Gloria. b 62. **d** 10 **p** 11. NSM Thornton St Jas *Bradf* 10–14; *Leeds* from 14. *1 Wembley Avenue, Thornton, Bradford BD13 3BY* T: (01274) 833280 E: john-hardisty@sky.com

✠**HARDMAN, The Rt Revd Christine Elizabeth.** b 51. Lon Univ BSc(Econ) 73. St Alb Minl Tr Scheme 81. **dss** 84 **d** 87 **p** 94 **c** 15. Markyate Street *St Alb* 84–88; Par Dn *St Alb*; Tutor St Alb Minl Tr Scheme 88–91; Course Dir 91–96; C Markyate Street *St Alb* 94–96; V Stevenage H Trin 96–01; RD Stevenage 99–01; Adn Lewisham *S'wark* 01–08; Adn Lewisham and Greenwich 08–12; NSM S'wark Cathl 12–15; PtO *St Alb* 13–15; Bp Newc from 15. *The Bishop's House, 29 Moor Road South, Newcastle upon Tyne NE3 1PA* T: 0191-285 2220 E: bishop@newcastle.anglican.org

HARDMAN, Geoffrey James. b 41. Birm Univ BA 63. NOC 77. **d** 80 **p** 81. NSM Latchford St Jas *Ches* 80–93; NSM Haydock St Jas *Liv* 94–06; rtd 06; PtO *Ches* from 16; *Liv* from 16. *48 Denbury Avenue, Stockton Heath, Warrington WA4 2BW* T: (01925) 264064 E: geoffrey.hardman1@ntlworld.com

HARDMAN, Canon Peter George. b 35. Man Univ BSc 56. Ridley Hall Cam 58. **d** 60 **p** 61. C Oldham St Paul *Man* 60–63; NW England Area Sec SCM 63–64; NW England Area Sec CEM 64–67; Asst Chapl Marlborough Coll 67–72; Chapl 72–79; P-in-c Wareham *Sarum* 79–80; TR 80–00; Chapl Wareham Hosp 80–92; Chapl Dorset HealthCare University NHS Foundn Trust 92–00; Can and Preb Sarum Cathl 87–00; RD Purbeck 89–99; rtd 00; PtO *Sarum* from 00; *B & W* 02–14. *55 Palairet Close, Bradford-on-Avon BA15 1US* T: (01225) 867198 E: peterhardman3@gmail.com

HARDWICK, Christopher George. b 57. Open Univ BA 94 Birm Univ MA 96 PhD 00 ACIB 79. Ripon Coll Cuddesdon 90. **d** 92 **p** 93. C Worc SE 92–95; R Ripple, Earls Croome w Hill Croome and Strensham 95–00; R Upton-on-Severn, Ripple, Earls Croome etc 00–05; RD Upton 97–05; Hon Can Worc Cathl 03–05; Dean Truro 05–11; R Truro St Mary 05–11; P-in-c Pyworthy, Pancrasweek and Bridgerule *Ex* 11–15; P-in-c Tavistock and Gulworthy 15; V Tavistock, Gulworthy and Brent Tor 15–21; rtd 21. *1 Springfield Villas, Harrowbarrow, Callington PL17 8JQ* E: veryrevdchristhardwick@btinternet.com

HARDWICK, Mrs Daphne Anne. b 45. Reading Univ BA 97 SRN 67 SCM 69 HVCert 79. Trin Coll Bris 10. **d** 12 **p** 13. OLM Swindon Ch Ch *Bris* 12–20; NSM from 20. *6 St Margaret's Road, Swindon SN3 1RU* T: (01793) 693721 M: 07909-988464 E: daphne@christchurchswindon.co.uk

HARDWICK, Canon Graham John. b 42. Qu Coll Birm 68. **d** 70 **p** 71. C Watford St Mich *St Alb* 70–73; C N Mymms 73–75; Youth Officer Cov Cathl 75–81; Chapl Lanchester Poly 76–81; V Nuneaton St Nic 81–95; Ind Chapl and P-in-c New Bilton 95–07; Hon Can Cov Cathl 04–07; rtd 08; PtO *Cov* from 08. *150 Pytchley Road, Rugby CV22 5NG* T: (01788) 544011 F: 333256 E: revgjh@btinternet.com

HARDWICK, Canon Susan Frances. b 44. Warwick Univ BA 81. Qu Coll Birm 82. **dss** 85 **d** 87 **p** 94. Chilvers Coton w Astley *Cov* 85–91; C 87–91; Dioc Disabilities Officer 91–96; Chapl Hereward Coll 91–96; Chapl FE Colls *Cov* 94–09; Hon C New Bilton 96–98; FE Field Officer Team Co-ord (W Midl) 97–09; Chapl Rainsbrook Secure Tr Cen 99–09; Hon Can

Cov Cathl 04–09; rtd 09; PtO *Cov* from 09. *150 Pytchley Road, Rugby CV22 5NG* T: (01788) 544011 F: 333256

HARDY, Alison Jane. b 60. **d** 14 **p** 15. C Stratton and Launcells *Truro* 14–16; C Bude Haven and Marhamchurch 14–16; C N Kernow 16–18; C Kilkhampton w Morwenstow 16–18; C Launceston 18–21; TV from 21; P-in-c Moorland Gp from 21; P-in-c Egloskerry, N Petherwin, Tremaine, Tresmere etc from 21. *St Mary's Church Hall, Tower Street, Launceston PL15 8BQ* T: (01566) 785365 M: 07780-295752 E: reverendalisonhardy@gmail.com

HARDY, Ms Alison Jane. b 61. St Anne's Coll Ox BA 82 MA 96. NOC 92. **d** 95 **p** 96. C Flixton St Mich *Man* 95–98; Lect Bolton St Pet 98–00; P-in-c Irlam 00–05; R Stand 05–18; AD Radcliffe and Prestwich 13–18; P-in-c Embleton w Rennington and Rock *Newc* from 18; AD Alnwick from 18. *The Vicarage, Embleton, Alnwick NE66 3UW* E: revalisonhardy@gmail.com

HARDY, Anthony. b 36. **d** 86 **p** 87. NSM Malden St Jas *S'wark* 86–06; PtO 06–10. *48 Blake's Lane, New Malden KT3 6NR* T: (020) 8949 0703 E: aehardy@waitrose.com

HARDY, Anthony William. b 56. Man Univ BEd 79 MEd 86 Open Univ BSc 00. St Jo Coll Nottm LTh 88. **d** 88 **p** 89. C Pennington *Man* 88–91; V Eccleston St Luke *Liv* 91–00; Min Consultant CPAS 00–09; Dioc Evang *Liv* 00–02; Can Ev Man Cathl 09–14; R Whalley Range St Edm and Moss Side etc from 14; AD Hulme 16–21. *St Edmund's Rectory, 1 Range Road, Manchester M16 8FS* T: 0161-226 4554 E: tonybillhardy@gmail.com *or* stedsandstjames@gmail.com

HARDY, Christopher Richard. b 52. R Holloway Coll Lon BMus 77 Southn Univ BTh 90. Chich Th Coll 87. **d** 90 **p** 91. C Kenton *Lon* 90–95; V E Finchley All SS 95–19; rtd 19. *6 rue de l'eglise, 62770 Le Parcq, France* M: 07785-728272 E: amictus@gmail.com

HARDY, Miss Janet Frances. b 59. Newc Univ BA 81 CertEd 82. Trin Coll Bris 87. **d** 89 **p** 94. Par Dn Sheff St Paul 89–92; Team Dn Gt Snaith 92–94; TV 94–96; V Pitsmoor Ch Ch 96–01; V Thorpe Hesley 01–14; Dioc Ecum Officer 11–14; V Barmby Moor Gp *York* from 14. *The Vicarage, St Helen's Square, Barmby Moor, York YO42 4HF* T: (01759) 307042 E: rev.j.hardy@btinternet.com

HARDY, Jennifer. b 85. Liv Hope Univ BA 14 Middx Univ MA 19. St Mellitus Coll 19. **d** 21. C St Jas in the City *Liv* from 21. *18 Lady Chapel Close, Liverpool L1 7BZ* M: 07905-875944 E: jenniehardy5485@yahoo.co.uk

HARDY, John Christopher. b 61. St Jo Coll Dur BA 83 Dur Univ MA 95 New Coll Edin BD 92 Ox Univ MLitt 00. Aston Tr Scheme 87 Coates Hall Edin 89. **d** 92 **p** 93. C Walker *Newc* 92–95; Fell Chapl Magd Coll Ox 95–98; TV Benwell *Newc* 98–03; R Ashton Moor 03–08; R Newmarket St Mary w Exning St Agnes *St E* from 08; P-in-c Exning St Martin w Landwade from 18; RD Mildenhall 16–18. *The Rectory, 21 Hamilton Road, Newmarket CB8 0NY* T: (01638) 660729 E: jhardy153@btinternet.com

HARDY, Mrs Julie Anne. b 68. St Mellitus Coll BA 16. **d** 16 **p** 17. C Broomfield *Chelmsf* 16–20; P-in-c Bentley Common, Kelvedon Hatch and Navestock from 20. *The Rectory, 2 Church Road, Kelvedon Hatch, Brentwood CM14 5TJ* E: revjuliehardy@btinternet.com

HARDY, Lesley Ann. b 64. Sussex Univ BA 87 MA 88 Birm Univ PhD 99. St Aug Coll of Th 16. **d** 19 **p** 20. NSM Eastry and Woodnesborough *Cant* 19–20; C Barham Downs w Adisham from 20. *St Mary's House, 5 St Mary's Meadow, Wingham, Canterbury CT3 1DF* M: 07725-944553 E: revlesleyhardy@gmail.com

HARDY, Lesley Anne. b 53. Nottm Univ BA 75 St Luke's Coll Ex PGCE 76. **d** 05 **p** 06. OLM Lydd *Cant* 05–09; NSM Barham Downs 09–16; rtd 16; PtO *Cant* from 17. *Russets, Maidstone Road, Marden, Tonbridge TN12 9AE* M: 07752-517903

HARDY, Michael Henry. b 33. Qu Coll Birm 85. **d** 86 **p** 87. C Leic St Jas 86–88; R Arnesby w Shearsby and Bruntingthorpe 88–94; RD Guthlaxton I 91–94; TV Bradgate Team 94–99; rtd 99; PtO *Leic* 99–12; *Pet* from 99. *14 Dean's Street, Oakham LE15 6AF* T: (01572) 722591

HARDY, Miss Pauline. b 41. CertEd. Linc Th Coll 85. **d** 87 **p** 94. Par Dn Walsall Wood *Lich* 87–89; Par Dn Buckingham *Ox* 89–93; C Buckingham w Radclive cum Chackmore 93–97; C Nash w Thornton, Beachampton and Thornborough 96–97; C Buckingham 97–03; C Watling Valley 03–06; rtd 06. *32 Campbell Road, Plymouth PL9 8UE* E: pauline@revhardy.plus.com

HARDY, Sam Richard Ian. b 71. Wall Hall Coll Aldenham BEd 95 Open Univ MA 00. Wycliffe Hall Ox BTh 04. **d** 04. C Parr *Liv* 04–05. *Knarrside, Woodhead Road, Tintwistle, Glossop SK13 1JX* E: sam.hardy@tiscali.co.uk

HARDY, Stephen John Arundell. b 49. SEITE 95. **d** 97 **p** 98. NSM Marden *Cant* 97–00; P-in-c Lydd 00–09; AD Romney 03–08; P-in-c Barham w Bishopsbourne and Kingston 09–12;

C Nonington w Wymynswold and Goodnestone etc 11–12; P-in-c Barham Downs 12–16; AD E Bridge 11–16; AD W Bridge 11–14; rtd 16; PtO *Cant* from 17. *Russets, Maidstone Road, Marden, Tonbridge TN12 9AE* M: 07752-517903 E: stephenhardy1@mac.com

HARE, Christopher Sumner. b 49. Solicitor 73. WEMTC 92. d 95 p 96. NSM Saltford w Corston and Newton St Loe *B & W* 95–01; P-in-c Timsbury and Priston 01–10; R Timsbury w Priston, Camerton and Dunkerton 10–12; Bp's Officer for Ord NSM (Bath Adnry) 07–08; RD Midsomer Norton 07–12; rtd 12; PtO *B & W* from 12; Acting Adn Bath from 17. *Cuckoo Hill, 61 Packsaddle Way, Frome BA11 2RW* T: (01373) 469788 M: 07368-881336

HARE, David. b 46. Qu Coll Birm 81. d 83 p 83. SSF 67–94; Bp's Dom Chapl *Birm* 83–87; V Handsworth St Mich 87–97; R Newton Regis w Seckington and Shuttington 97–03; rtd 03; PtO *Birm* 03–12. *34 The Charters, Lichfield WS13 7LX* E: dandjhare7@gmail.com

HARE, Michael John. b 41. Lon Univ MD 71 Cam Univ MA 77. EAMTC 00. d 02 p 03. NSM E Leightonstone *Ely* 02–06; NSM Buckworth and Alconbury cum Weston 04–06; PtO *St E* 06–09; NSM Woodbridge St Mary 09–11; PtO from 11. *3 Estuary Reach, Old Maltings Approach, Melton, Woodbridge IP12 1FN* T: (01394) 387151 E: john.hare6@gmail.com

HARE, Richard William. b 66. Bris Univ BSc 88 PhD 94 St Jo Coll Dur BA 95 Heythrop Coll Lon MA 98. Cranmer Hall Dur 92. d 95 p 96. C Coulsdon St Jo *S'wark* 95–98; C Coventry Caludon *Cov* 98–99; TV 99–07; AD Cov E 01–07; TR Bedworth 07–16; AD Nuneaton 12–16; V Bridlington Em and Barmston w Fraisthorpe *York* from 16. *72 Cardigan Road, Bridlington YO15 3JT* M: 07871-194435 E: thehares@ic24.net

HARE (née CALDWELL), Mrs Sarah Louise. b 75. St Jo Coll Nottm 11. d 13 p 14. C Bishop's Castle w Mainstone, Lydbury N etc *Heref* 13–16; TV Wenlock 16–19; P-in-c Yaxley and Holme w Conington *Ely* 19; V Yaxley from 20. *The Vicarage, 43 Church Street, Yaxley, Peterborough PE7 3LH* M: 07709-056177 E: sarah.hare@aol.co.uk

HARES, David Ronald Walter. b 40. Qu Coll Cam BA 63 MA 67 CertEd. Westcott Ho Cam 64. d 66 p 67. C Cannock *Lich* 66–69; Chapl Pembroke Cam 69–72; Asst Master Chesterton Sch Cam 72–74; V Kesgrave *St E* 74–98; R Lt Barningham, Blickling, Edgefield etc *Nor* 98–05; rtd 05; PtO *Nor* from 05. *17 Trory Street, Norwich NR2 2RH* T: (01603) 626392 E: david.hares@gmail.com

HARFORD, Paul Roger. b 83. York Univ BA 04 Selw Coll Cam BA 09 MA 14. Ridley Hall Cam 07. d 10 p 11. C Stokesley w Seamer *York* 10–13; R Bishop Thornton, Burnt Yates, Markington etc *Ripon* 13–14; *Leeds* from 14. *The Vicarage, Westerns Lane, Markington, Harrogate HG3 3PB* T: (01765) 677123 E: paul@theunitedbenefice.org

HARFORD, Timothy William. b 58. Nottm Univ BTh 89. Linc Th Coll 86. d 89 p 90. C Minehead *B & W* 89–93; R Knebworth *St Alb* 93–03; Children's Soc 03–09; Hd Donor Care and Fund-raising Depaul UK 12–18; Dir Fund-raising and Communications USPG 14–18; PtO *Chich* 15–18; *S'wark* 16–18; R Poynings w Edburton, Newtimber and Pyecombe *Chich* from 18. *The Rectory, The Street, Poynings, Brighton BN45 7AQ* E: twharford@gmail.com

HARGER, Robin Charles Nicholas. b 49. BTh. Sarum & Wells Th Coll 78. d 81 p 82. C Charlton Kings St Mary *Glouc* 81–85; C Folkestone St Mary and St Eanswythe *Cant* 85–89; TV Langley and Parkfield *Man* 89–95; TV Bournemouth Town Cen *Win* 95–12; rtd 12; PtO *Win* from 17. *1 Northover Gardens, 5 Dunbar Road, Bournemouth BH3 7AZ* T: (01202) 318126 E: robin.cn.harger@gmail.com

HARGRAVE, Canon Alan Lewis. b 50. Birm Univ BSc 73 PhD 77. Ridley Hall Cam 87. d 89 p 90. C Cambridge H Trin w St Andr Gt *Ely* 89–92; C Cambridge H Trin 92–93; C-in-c Fen Ditton 93–94; V Cambridge H Cross 94–04; Can Res Ely Cathl 04–16; rtd 16; PtO *S'well* from 16. *16 Foxhollies Grove, Nottingham NG5 2NP*

HARGRAVE, Seamus Addison. b 94. St Andr Univ MTheol 12 MLitt 16. St Steph Ho Ox 19. d 21. C Narberth and Tenby LMA *St D* from 21. *16 Redstone Court, Narberth SA67 7EU* T: (01834) 860611 E: chantoflight@gmail.com

HARGRAVES, Mrs Christobel Mary Kathleen. b 58. Man Poly BSc 79 Open Univ MBA RGN 83. SAOMC 03. d 06 p 07. C Goring and Streatley w S Stoke *Ox* 06–09; R Shelswell 09–14; AD Bicester and Islip 13–14; PtO *S & B* from 15; *Heref* 15–20; NSM Church Stretton from 20. *Pye Corner, Llangunllo, Knighton LD7 1ST* T: (01547) 550311 E: hargraves391@btinternet.com

HARGRAVE, James David. b 44. K Coll Lon BA 66 PGCE 68 ALCM 89 LTCL 90. Coll of Resurr Mirfield 70. d 73 p 74. C Houghton le Spring *Dur* 73–77; C Gateshead St Cuth w

St Paul 77–79; V Trimdon 79–87; C-in-c Stockton Green Vale H Trin CD 87–94; V Hedon w Paull *York* 94–02; rtd 02; PtO *York* from 03. *1 The Avenue, Crescent Street, Cottingham HU16 5QT* T: (01482) 844297 E: j.hargr25@gmail.com

HARGREAVES, Andrew David. b 74. Homerton Coll Cam BEd 97. Trin Coll Bris BA 08. d 08 p 09. C Shirley *Win* 08–12; V Whitfield *Derby* 12–17; Miss Development Officer *Portsm* 17–20; P-in-c Portsea All SS from 20. *19 Herbert Road, Southsea PO4 0QA* T: (023) 9275 1545 E: andrew@harbourchurchportsmouth.org

HARGREAVES, David Andrew. b 58. St Jo Coll Cam BA 80 MA 84. All SS Cen for Miss & Min 18. d 20 p 21. NSM Barrowford and Newchurch-in-Pendle *Blackb* from 20. *Lakeside, Red Lane, Colne BB8 7JR* T: (01282) 865543 M: 07786-534050 E: da.hargreaves@virgin.net

HARGREAVES, John. b 43. St Jo Coll Nottm 86. d 88 p 89. C Werneth *Man* 88–91; TV Rochdale 91–96; C Man Gd Shep 96–97; PtO *Liv* 96–97; C Manchester Gd Shep and St Barn *Man* 97–98; rtd 98; PtO *Man* 06–08. *Water House, Wyebank, Bakewell DE45 1BH* M: 07922-004930 E: johnatbakewell@gmail.com

HARGREAVES, John Wilson. b 46. Aber Univ BScFor 67. Westcott Ho Cam 84. d 86 p 87. C Rugby *Cov* 86–90; TV Daventry, Ashby St Ledgers, Braunston etc *Pet* 90–97; Chapl Daventry Tertiary Coll 94–97; P-in-c Pinxton *Derby* 97–01; R 01–02; TR E Scarsdale 02–11; rtd 11; PtO *Leeds* from 17. *66 Bishopton Lane, Ripon HG4 2QN* T: (01765) 609413

HARGREAVES, Julia Gay. b 61. EMMTC 04. d 07 p 08. NSM Glenfield *Leic* 07–08; NSM Upper Soar 08–11; TV Bosworth and Sheepy Gp 11–19; C Nailstone and Carlton w Shackerstone 11–19; R Sheepy from 19. *The Rectory, Church Lane, Sheepy Magna, Atherstone CV9 3QS* T: (01827) 881389 E: julia.hargreaves@gmail.com

HARGREAVES, Ms Marise. b 60. Leeds Univ BA 81. Cranmer Hall Dur 82. dss 85 d 94 p 95. Yeadon St Jo *Bradf* 85–87; NSM Bradf St Clem 94–96; NSM Buttershaw St Paul 96–00; C Eccleshill 00–03; PtO 03–09; Chapl Univ Hosps of Derby and Burton NHS Foundn Trust from 09. *Chaplaincy, Royal Derby Hospital, Uttoxeter Road, Derby DE22 3NE* T: (01332) 340131 E: marise.hargreaves@nhs.net

HARGREAVES, Mark Kingston. b 63. Oriel Coll Ox BA 85 MA 89 Rob Coll Cam PhD 91 W Lon Inst of HE PGCE 86. Ridley Hall Cam 87. d 91 p 92. C Highbury Ch Ch w St Jo and St Sav *Lon* 91–94; C Ealing St Steph Castle Hill 94–97; C Notting Hill St Jo and St Pet 97–02; V Notting Hill St Pet 03–16; AD Kensington 06–11; R La Jolla USA from 16. *743 Prospect Street, La Jolla, CA 92037-4229, USA* T: (001) (858) 459 3421 E: mark@sjbts.org

HARKER, Harold Aidan. b 35. d 82 p 83. OSB from 53; C Reading St Giles *Ox* 82–83; LtO 83–87; C Halstead St Andr w H Trin and Greenstead Green *Chelmsf* 87–89; P-in-c Belchamp St Paul 89–97; R Belchamp Otten w Belchamp Walter and Bulmer etc 97–00; rtd 00; LtO *Chelmsf* from 00; PtO *Lon* 15–20. *38 Sheppard's College, London Road, Bromley BR1 1PE* T: (020) 8464 1206

HARKER, Ian. b 39. Dur Univ BA 61. Lich Th Coll Moray Ho Edin 66. d 63 p 64. C Knottingley *Wakef* 63–66; PtO 66–70; C Notting Hill *Lon* 70–75; Chapl Newc Univ 75–83; Master Newc St Thos Prop Chpl 75–83; PtO *Chelmsf* 99–01; C Plaistow and N Canning Town 01; C Loughton St Jo 01–02; V Leytonstone H Trin and St Aug Harrow Green 02–11; rtd 11; PtO *Chelmsf* 11–13; *Cant* from 14. *70 Sturry Hill, Canterbury CT2 0NH* T: (01227) 711247 E: harkatvic@aol.com or i.harker@aol.com

HARKER, Stephan John Innocent. b 47. Em Coll Cam BA 68 MA 72. Westcott Ho Cam 70. d 72 p 73. C Marton *Blackb* 72–76; C Preston St Matt 76–79; C Fleetwood St Pet 79–80; Sen Chapl Charterhouse Sch Godalming 81–07; Chapl 07–16; rtd 16; PtO *Blackb* from 16. *17 The Millrace, Damside Street, Lancaster LA1 1BL* T: (01524) 555740 M: 07850-915725 E: stephanjh@btinternet.com

HARKIN, Canon John Patrick. b 53. Oak Hill Th Coll 87. d 89 p 90. C Wisley w Pyrford *Guildf* 89–93; P-in-c Mickleham 93–98; Chapl Box Hill Sch Surrey 93–98; R Jersey St Ouen w St Geo *Win* 98–10; Vice-Dean Jersey 01–10; P-in-c Andover 10–11; V 11–18; RD 10–18; Hon Can Win Cathl 09–18; Hon C Leatherhead and Mickleham *Guildf* 18–20; Hon C Godalming 20–21; P-in-c from 21. *The Rectory, Westbrook Road, Godalming GU7 1ET* E: harkin12@btinternet.com

HARKIN, Terence James. b 46. Lon Bible Coll BA 82 New Coll Edin MTh 94. d 95 p 96. In Bapt Min 86–95; C Edin H Cross 95–96; C S Queensferry 95–96; P-in-c from 96; R Edin Clermiston Em 09–18; rtd 18; PtO *Newc* from 21. *6 Wellhead Close, South Queensferry EH30 9WA* T: 0131-319 1099 or 331 1958

HARKNETT, David Philip. b 74. St Pet Coll Ox BA 97. Oak Hill Th Coll BA 03. d 03 p 04. C Radipole and Melcombe Regis *Sarum* 03–07; TV Melbury 07–17; P-in-c Upper Wreake *Leic* from 17. *2 Carrfields Lane, Frisby on the Wreake, Melton Mowbray LE14 2NT* T: (01664) 434517 E: david.harknett@btinternet.com

HARKNETT, Mrs Helen. b 78. Loughb Univ BA 00. Westcott Ho Cam 14. d 16 p 17. C Clapham H Spirit *S'wark* 16–18; C Kennington St Jo w St Jas 18–20; P-in-c Camberwell St Phil and St Mark from 20. *60 Wix's Lane, London SW4 0AQ* M: 07557-093585 E: hhharknett@gmail.com

HARKNETT, Linda. b 48. Open Univ BA 81 Croydon Coll CertEd 92. SEITE 97. d 00 p 01. NSM Sutton St Nic *S'wark* 00–03; Chapl Epsom and St Helier NHS Trust 00–03; Chapl Whitelands Coll Roehampton Univ *S'wark* 03–07; Dioc FE and HE Chapl Officer 03–07; P-in-c Headley w Box Hill *Guildf* 07–16; rtd 16. *7 Bridge Place, Edinburgh EH3 5JJ* M: 07796-903167 E: lindaharknett@gmail.com

HARLAND, Brenda. b 53. d 08. NSM Thatcham *Ox* from 08. *St Mary's Church Office, Church Gate, Thatcham RG19 3PN* T: (01635) 862277 E: brenda.harland@ntlworld.com

HARLAND, Canon Harold William James. b 35. Hertf Coll Ox BA 59 MA 63. Clifton Th Coll 59. d 61 p 62. C Reigate St Mary *S'wark* 61–64; C Farnborough *Guildf* 64–68; V Walmley *Birm* 68–74; V Bromley Ch Ch *Roch* 74–86; V Folkestone St Jo *Cant* 86–00; Dir Post-Ord Tr 93–97; Hon Can Cant Cathl 94–00; rtd 00; PtO *Cant* from 00. *121 Station Road West, Canterbury CT2 8DE* T: (01227) 764699 E: harland672@btinternet.com

HARLE, Michael Richardson. b 58. BA 80 Man Univ MBM 91. d 11 p 12. NSM Claygate *Guildf* from 11. *1 The Green, Claygate, Esher KT10 0JL* T: (01372) 463898 M: 07788-160040

HARLEY, Mrs Carol Anne. b 46. d 00 p 01. OLM Tettenhall Wood and Perton *Lich* 00–19; PtO from 19. *27 Tyrley Close, Compton, Wolverhampton WV6 8AP* T: (01902) 755316

HARLEY, Christopher David. b 41. Selw Coll Cam BA 63 MA 69 Bris Univ PGCE 64 Columbia Bible Sem DMin 92 Utrecht Univ PhD 02. Clifton Th Coll 64. d 66 p 67. C Finchley Ch Ch *Lon* 66–69; Hon C 75–78; Ethiopia 70–75; Hd of UK Miss CMJ 75–78; Lect All Nations Chr Coll Ware 78–85; Prin 85–93; Chmn Lon Inst of Contemporary Christianity 88–89; Chmn CMJ 89–90; Crosslinks 93–06; Gen Dir OMF Internat 93–05; NSM Bromley Ch Ch *Roch* 93–96; NSM Singapore 96–06; rtd 06; PtO *Ex* from 06. *12 Harrington Drive, Exeter EX4 8PD* T: (01392) 460457 E: cdrkharley@gmail.com

HARLEY, The Ven Michael. b 50. AKC 73 Ch Ch Coll Cant CertEd 74 Lambeth STh 92 Kent Univ MPhil 95. St Aug Coll Cant 74. d 75 p 76. C Chatham St Wm *Roch* 75–78; C-in-c Weeke *Win* 78–81; V Southampton St Mary Extra 81–86; V Hurstbourne Tarrant, Faccombe, Vernham Dean etc 86–99; ACORA Link Officer 91–94; Dioc Rural Officer 94–97; RD Andover 95–99; V Chandler's Ford 99–09; Tutor STETS 03–06; Hon Can Win Cathl 06–15; Adn Win 09–15; P-in-c Win St Faith w St Cross 09–11; Master St Cross Hosp 09–11; rtd 15; PtO *Win* from 16. *28 Simmons Field, Thatcham RG18 4ET* E: mharley50@gmail.com

HARLEY, Peter David. b 59. Sheff Univ BSc 82 Warwick Univ MBA 86. d 09 p 10. OLM Horwich and Rivington *Man* from 09; OLM Blackrod 11–15. *6 Barford Grove, Lostock, Bolton BL6 4NQ* T: (01204) 694611

HARLEY, Canon Robert Patterson. b 53. St Andr Univ MA 75 Cam Univ CertEd 76 Glas Univ PhD 89 Edin Univ BD 97. d 97 p 98. C Edin St Thos 97–00; Chapl Lothian Univ Hosps NHS Trust 98–00; P-in-c Kirriemuir *St And* from 00; Can St Ninian's Cathl Perth from 08. *128 Glengate, Kirriemuir DD8 4JG* T: (01575) 575515 E: robert.harley@gmx.co.uk

HARLEY, Roger Newcombe. b 38. Ely Th Coll 61. d 64 p 65. C Plymouth St Pet *Ex* 64–66; C Heston *Lon* 66–69; C Maidstone All SS w St Phil and H Trin *Cant* 69–73; R Temple Ewell w Lydden 73–79; P-in-c Shirley St Geo 79–81; V 81–84; V Croydon H Sav *S'wark* 85–95; V Forest Row *Chich* 95–03; rtd 03; PtO *Cant* 03–16; *Lich* 17–21. *34 Milltown Way, Leek ST13 5SZ* T: (01538) 387369 E: rogerharley@btinternet.com

HARLEY, Ruth Victoria. b 87. Magd Coll Ox BA 10. Qu Foundn Birm MA 21. d 21. C Watling Valley *Ox* from 21. *14 Beckinsale Grove, Crownhill, Milton Keynes MK8 0DU* M: 07983-990617 E: revruthharley@gmail.com

HARLING, Timothy Charles. b 80. Southn Univ BSc 01 Fitzw Coll Cam BA 04 Qu Coll Cam MA 13. Westcott Ho Cam 02. d 05 p 06. C Romsey *Win* 05–09; Chapl HM Pris Peterborough 09–13; Chapl Qu Coll Cam 13–17; Dean

of Chpl from 17. *Queens' College, Silver Street, Cambridge CB3 9ET* T: (01223) 335511 E: tch42@cam.ac.uk

HARLOW, Mark Jonathan. b 80. Man Univ BSc 01 K Coll Lon MA 10. Ridley Hall Cam 11. d 14 p 15. C Leeds St Geo 14–17; P-in-c Ireland Wood 17–19; V from 19. *St Paul's Vicarage, Raynel Drive, Leeds LS16 6BS* M: 07725-625900 E: mark.harlow@stpaulsirelandwood.org

HARLOW, Canon Richard John St Clair. b 63. Cam Univ BA 85 MA 88. Cranmer Hall Dur 87. d 89 p 90. C Basford w Hyson Green *S'well* 89–94; C Mansfield SS Pet and Paul 94–97; TV Newark 97–01; Chapl Brighton and Sussex Univ Hosps NHS Trust 01–10; Lead Chapl Sussex Partnership NHS Foundn Trust 10–13; Chapl St Pet and St Jas Hospice N Chailey 02–05; R Tadley w Pamber Heath and Silchester *Win* from 13; AD Basingstoke from 15; Hon Can Win Cathl from 17. *The Rectory, The Green, Tadley RG26 3PB* T: 0118-981 4860 M: 07875-969128 E: richard73harlow@aol.com *or* minister@st-marys-church-tadley.org.uk

HARLOW, Archdeacon of. *See* HERRICK, The Ven Vanessa Anne

HARMAN, Karin. *See* VOTH HARMAN, Karin Lee

HARMAN, Kathleen Joyce. b 49. d 03 p 04. C Llangynwyd w Maesteg *Llan* 03–08; R Dowlais and Penydarren 08–16; rtd 16. *33 Orchard Way, Stretton on Dunsmore, Rugby CV23 9HP*

HARMAN, Canon Leslie Davies. b 46. Nottm Univ BTh 76. St Jo Coll Nottm LTh 75. d 76 p 77. C Wandsworth All SS *S'wark* 76–78; C Godstone 78–82; V Thorncombe w Winsham and Cricket St Thomas *B & W* 82–87; TV Hitchin *St Alb* 87–95; V Royston 95–11; RD Buntingford 96–01; Hon Can St Alb 09–11; rtd 11. *1 Berry Meadow, Kingsteignton, Newton Abbot TQ12 3BL* T: (01626) 351757 E: leslie.harman@btopenworld.com

HARMAN, Michael John. b 48. Chich Th Coll 71. d 74 p 75. C Blackpool St Steph *Blackb* 74–79; Chapl RN 79–06; PtO *Ex* 06–08; *Truro* 06–13; P-in-c Wembury *Ex* 08–14; rtd 14; PtO *Ex* from 14. *18 Furzeacre Close, Plymouth PL7 5DZ* T: (01752) 338910 M: 07836-377820 E: revmikeharman@blueyonder.co.uk

HARMAN, Theodore Allan. b 27. Linc Coll Ox BA 52 MA 56 Hatf Coll Dur MA 90. Wells Th Coll 52. d 54 p 55. C Hawkshead and Low Wray *Carl* 54–55; C Kirkby Stephen w Mallerstang 55–57; Asst Chapl Sedbergh Sch 57–84; Sen Chapl 84–87; Tutor Hatf Coll Dur from 88; Admissions Tutor 89–90; Lib and Coll Officer 91–02; Acting Chapl 99–00; Fell from 00; PtO *Dur* from 88. *2 Palmers Close, Church Street Head, Durham DH1 3DN* T: 0191-386 7213 F: 334 3101 E: theoharman@gmail.com

HARMER, Timothy James. b 47. Birm Univ CertEd 68. St Jo Coll Nottm BA 95. d 95 p 96. C Studley *Cov* 95–98; V Tanworth *Birm* 98–05; P-in-c Helsington *Carl* 05–12; P-in-c Underbarrow 05–12; RD Kendal 08–12; rtd 12; PtO *Carl* 12–13; P-in-c Church Coniston 13–15; P-in-c Torver 13–15; R Coniston and Torver 13–16; PtO 16–19. *Address temp unknown* E: tharmer246@btinternet.com

HARMON, Michael Edgar. b 54. Birm Univ BEd 76. Wycliffe Hall Ox 10. d 12 p 13. NSM Aston and Nechells *Birm* 12–15; R Chelmsley Wood 15–20; rtd 20. *Address temp unknown* M: 07900-405455 E: harmon.mike2@gmail.com

HARMSWORTH, Canon Roger James. b 46. Univ of W Ontario BA 87. Huron Coll Ontario MDiv 90. d 90 p 90. Canada 90–96; I Maryborough w Dysart Enos and Ballyfin *C, F & O* 96–01; I Killanne w Killegney, Rossdroit and Templeshanbo 01–17; Treas Ferns Cathl 03–04; Chan 04–17; rtd 17. *Ballinastoll, Killanne, Enniscorthy, Co Wexford, Republic of Ireland* T: (00353) (53) 925 6517 E: precentor.1@hotmail.com

HARNDEN, Peter John. b 63. Coll of Resurr Mirfield 96. d 98 p 99. C Staplehurst *Cant* 98–02; V Tokyngton St Mich *Lon* 02–11; P-in-c Benhilton *S'wark* 11–15; V 15–17; R Harbledown *Cant* from 17. *The Rectory, Summer Hill, Harbledown, Canterbury CT2 8NW* T: (01227) 479377 E: rector.harbledown@btconnect.com

HARNEY, Janice. b 56. d 02 p 03. OLM Pennington *Man* 02–06; PtO 06–11 and from 18; NSM Astley, Tyldesley and Mosley Common 11–18; NSM Glazebury w Hollinfare *Liv* from 18. *10 Hesnall Close, Glazebury, Warrington WA3 5PB* T: (01942) 671481 M: 07811-764355 E: allsaints134@gmail.com

HARONSKI, Boleslaw. b 46. Pemb Coll Ox BA 68 MA 72 DPhil 73. St Mich Coll Llan 80 Westcott Ho Cam 82. d 82 p 83. C Maindee Newport *Mon* 82–85; V Llanishen w Trelleth Grange and Llanfihangel etc 85–89; V Blackwood 89–92; rtd 11. *Tir Llandre, Llanarthney, Carmarthen SA32 8JE*

✠**HARPER, The Rt Revd Alan Edwin Thomas.** b 44. OBE 96. Leeds Univ BA 65. CITC 75. d 78 p 79 c 02. C Ballywillan *Conn* 78–80; I Moville w Greencastle, Upper Moville etc *D & R* 80–82; I Londonderry Ch Ch 82–86; I Belfast

Malone St Jo *Conn* 86–02; Preb St Audoen St Patr Cathl Dublin 90–01; Adn Conn 96–02; Prec Belf Cathl 96–02; Bp Conn 02–07; Abp Arm 07–12; rtd 12. *Forth Cottage, 67 Lisnacroppan Road, Rathfriland, Newry BT61 5NZ* T: (028) 4065 1649 M: 07713-954758 E: a.e.t.harper@gmx.com

HARPER, Canon Alan Peter. b 50. Man Univ BA 73 FCA 83. Ripon Coll Cuddesdon 86. **d** 88 **p** 89. C Newport w Longford and Chetwynd *Lich* 88–91; P-in-c Wilncote 91–94; V 94–98; V Codsall 98–07; Preb Lich Cathl 02–07; RD Penkridge 06–07; Bp's Dom Chapl *Derby* 07–11; P-in-c Mackworth All SS 11–17; P-in-c Kirk Langley 11–17; P-in-c Mugginton and Kedleston 11–17; Hon Can Derby Cathl 12–17; rtd 17. *78 Moatbrook Avenue, Codsall, Wolverhampton WV8 1DH* E: revd.alan8@btinternet.com

HARPER, Andrew. b 61. Leic Poly BA 83. St Mellitus Coll BA 16. **d** 16 **p** 17. C Ramsbottom and Edenfield *Man* 16–19; TV Eccles from 19. *11 Abbey Grove, Eccles, Manchester M30 9QN* M: 07825-081861 E: revandyharper@gmail.com

HARPER, Barry. See HARPER, Malcolm Barry

HARPER, The Ven Brian John. b 61. Liv Univ BA 82. CITC. **d** 85 **p** 86. C Portadown St Columba *Arm* 85–88; C Drumglass w Moygashel 88–89; I Errigle Keerogue w Ballygawley and Killeshil 89–93; I Mullavilly 93–12; I Magheracross *Clogh* from 12; Can Clogh Cathl from 14; Adn Clogh from 17. *27 Craghan Road, Ballinamallard, Enniskillen BT94 2BT* T: (028) 6638 8238 M: 07898-743545 E: magheracross@gmail.com

HARPER, Clive Stewart. b 35. FCIS 71. Ridley Hall Cam 80. **d** 82 **p** 83. C Bromyard *Heref* 82–85; P-in-c Bredenbury and Wacton w Grendon Bishop 85–89; P-in-c Edwyn Ralph and Collington w Thornbury 85–89; P-in-c Pencombe w Marston Stannett and Lt Cowarne 85–89; R Bredenbury w Grendon Bishop and Wacton etc 89–92; R Bilton *Cov* 92–02; rtd 02; Hon C Churchover w Willey *Cov* 02–05; PtO 05–19. *6 Arcade Park, North Shields NE30 4HP* T: 0191-296 6800 E: harperclival@btinternet.com

HARPER, Canon Geoffrey Roger. b 57. Jes Coll Cam BA 79 MA 83. St Jo Coll Nottm 81. **d** 84 **p** 85. C Belper *Derby* 84–87; C Birstall and Wanlip *Leic* 87–90; TV Tettenhall Regis *Lich* 90–97; C Aldridge 97–02; PtO 02–07; Chapl Douglas MacMillan Hospice Stoke-on-Trent 04–07; C W Bromwich Gd Shep w St Jo *Lich* 07–09; PtO *Derby* 09–10; P-in-c Burton Joyce w Bulcote and Stoke Bardolph *S'well* 10–11; V 11–15; Chapl HM Pris Whatton 15–17; Chapl HM Pris Thameside from 17; Hon Can W Ankole from 05. *HM Prison Thameside, Griffin Manor Way, London SE28 0FJ* T: (020) 8317 9777 M: 07954-409635 E: harperrog@gmail.com

HARPER, Gordon William Robert. b 48. Wellington Univ (NZ) BA 70 St Chad's Coll Dur BA 74 Nottm Univ PhD 89. Coll of Resurr Mirfield 74. **d** 75 **p** 76. C Battyeford *Wakef* 75–76; NZ 76–80; P-in-c Byers Green *Dur* 80–83; V Evenwood 83–89; R Wolviston 89–00; V Billingham St Mary 97–01; P-in-c Winlaton 01–06; R 06–13; rtd 13; PtO *Dur* from 13. *66 Rochester Road, Durham DH1 5QD* T: 0191-383 1348 E: gordonharper89@gmail.com

HARPER, Canon Ian. b 51. AKC 78. Oak Hill Th Coll 79. **d** 80 **p** 81. C Sidcup St Jo *Roch* 80–83; C Bushey *St Alb* 83–87; TV Thamesmead *S'wark* 87–92; TR N Lambeth 92–00; V Homerton St Luke *Lon* 00–10; AD Hackney 04–09; V Ladywood St Jo and St Pet *Birm* from 10; AD Cen Birm 12–19; Jt AD Handsworth and Central 19–20; Hon Can Birm Cathl from 16. *St John's Vicarage, Darnley Road, Birmingham B16 8TF* T: 0121-454 0973 *or* 218 5530 M: 07961-537487 E: harper-i1@sky.com

HARPER, James. b 35. St Luke's Coll Ex TDip 57. SWMTC. **d** 90 **p** 91. NSM Pendeen w Morvah *Truro* 90–97; PtO *Win* 09–20. *1 Millstream Mews, 50 Beaconsfield Road, Christchurch BH23 1QT* T: (01202) 477138

HARPER, John Anthony. b 46. AKC 69. **d** 70 **p** 71. C Pet St Mary Boongate 70–73; C Abington 73–75; V Grendon w Castle Ashby 75–82; Asst Dioc Youth Chapl 75–82; R Castor w Sutton and Upton *Pet* 82–94; TV Riverside *Ox* 94–04; V Meppershall and Shefford *St Alb* 04–11; RD Shefford 08–10; RD Ampthill and Shefford 11; rtd 11; PtO *St Alb* 11–18; *Ely* from 12; *Pet* from 12. *54 Chapel Street, Yaxley, Peterborough PE7 3LN* T: (01733) 688923 E: revjohnharper@talktalk.net

HARPER, Joseph Frank. b 38. Hull Univ BA 60 MA 86 MPhil 98 Dur Univ PhD 10. Linc Th Coll 80. **d** 81 **p** 82. C Preston St Cuth *Blackb* 81–83; C Lancaster St Mary 83–87; V Bamber Bridge St Aid 87–92; V Kinsley w Wragby *Wakef* 92–99; R Newhaven *Chich* 99–04; rtd 04; PtO *Dur* 04–20; *Blackb* from 21. *34 Fosbrooke House, 8 Clifton Drive, Lytham St Annes FY8 5RQ* E: j925harper@btinternet.com

HARPER, Ms Lisa Rae. b 67. Cranmer Hall Dur 13. **d** 15 **p** 16. C Cen Telford *Lich* 15–18; C Oakengates, Priors Lee and Wrockwardine Wood from 18. *16 Highgrove*

Meadows, Priorslee, Telford TF2 9RJ M: 07808-924223 E: lisataraharper@yahoo.co.uk

HARPER, Canon Malcolm Barry. b 37. Dur Univ BSc 59. Wycliffe Hall Ox 59. **d** 61 **p** 62. C Harold Wood *Chelmsf* 61–65; C Madeley *Heref* 65–68; V Slaithwaite w E Scammonden *Wakef* 68–75; V Walmley *Birm* 75–03; Hon Can Birm Cathl 96–03; rtd 03; PtO *Birm* from 03. *1 Welcombe Drive, Sutton Coldfield B76 1ND* T: 0121-351 3990 M: 07866-216154 E: canonbarryharper@gmail.com

HARPER, Mrs Margaret. b 51. Nottm Coll of Educn TCert 73 Nottm Univ BEd 74. SAOMC 98. **d** 01 **p** 02. C Slough *Ox* 01–05; P-in-c Leeds St Cypr Harehills *Ripon* 05–09; P-in-c Burmantofts St Steph and St Agnes 05–09; TV Ely 09–14; rtd 14; Hon C Bishop's Cleeve and Woolstone w Gotherington etc *Glouc* 16–17; PtO *Leic* from 19. *14 Peter Laslett Close, Loughborough LE11 2PT* E: margaretharper@waitrose.com

HARPER, Martin Nigel. b 48. Cant Ch Ch Univ Coll PGCE 95 FRICS 88. S Dios Minl Tr Scheme 82. **d** 85 **p** 86. NSM St Leonards Ch Ch and St Mary *Chich* 85–93; NSM Rye 94–95; R Brede w Udimore 08–14; R Brede w Udimore and Beckley and Peasmarsh 14–19; rtd 19. *31 Manor Road, Bexhill-on-Sea TN40 1SP* M: 07760-197954 E: martin.harper48@icloud.com

HARPER, Michael Sydney. b 36. Portsm Dioc Tr Course 86. **d** 87. NSM Leigh Park St Clare CD *Portsm* 87–88; NSM Warren Park 88–05; NSM Leigh Park 96–05; rtd 05; PtO *Portsm* from 07. *17 Hampage Green, Warren Park, Havant PO9 4HJ* T: (023) 9245 4275 E: michael_harper06@tiscali.co.uk *or* michael.har1936@gmail.com

HARPER, Robert James. b 75. St Hild Coll 17. **d** 20 **p** 21. C Wakef St Jo Leeds from 20. *39 Redbarn Close, Leeds LS10 4SZ* M: 07702-875014 E: robertjharper1@aol.com

HARPER, Roger. b 43. Man Univ BSc 64 FCA 80. Local Minl Tr Course 84. **d** 87 **p** 88. NSM Onchan *S & M* 87–97; NSM Douglas St Geo 97–06; PtO from 11. *The Barns, Strawberry Fields, Croit-e-Caley, Colby, Isle of Man IM9 4BZ* T: (01624) 842466 E: roger.harper@mcb.net

HARPER, Roger. See HARPER, Geoffrey Roger

HARPER, Mrs Rosalind Elizabeth. b 82. Keble Coll Ox BA 05. Qu Foundn Birm 18. **d** 20 **p** 21. C Burbage w Aston Flamville *Leic* from 20. *147 Coventry Road, Burbage, Hinckley LE10 2HW* T: (01455) 634055 E: rosalindharper@hotmail.co.uk

HARPER, Canon Rosemary Elizabeth. b 55. Birm Univ BA 76 Lon Univ MA 03 ARCM 75 LRAM 78. NTMTC 96. **d** 99 **p** 00. C Amersham *Ox* 99–03; P-in-c Gt Missenden w Ballinger and Lt Hampden 03–07; V 07–21; rtd 21; Chapl to Bp Buckingham *Ox* from 06; Hon Can Ch Ch from 11. *2 Old Chapel Close, Little Kimble, Aylesbury HP17 0RA* E: rosieswiss@yahoo.com

HARPER, Sally Elizabeth. b 62. Birm Univ BA 82 MA 83 Magd Coll Ox DPhil 89. St Padarn's Inst 18. **d** 19 **p** 20. C St As from 19. *9 Llys y Tywysog, Tremeirchion, St Asaph LL17 0UL* T: (01745) 710488 E: chaplain@stasaphcathedral.wales

HARPER, Canon Timothy James Lincoln. b 54. Lon Univ BMus 76 MA 96 CertEd LRAM. Wycliffe Hall Ox 84. **d** 86 **p** 87. C Morden *S'wark* 86–90; V Deptford St Pet 90–97; R Amersham *Ox* 97–21; Jt AD 17–21; Hon Can Ch Ch from 18; rtd 21. *2 Old Chapel Close, Little Kimble, Aylesbury HP17 0RA* E: harpervic@yahoo.co.uk

HARPHAM, Mrs Diana Joan. b 44. MCSP 66. St Alb Minl Tr Scheme 94. **d** 98 **p** 99. NSM Harrold and Carlton w Chellington *St Alb* 98–01; NSM Bromham w Oakley and Stagsden 01–15; PtO from 15. *129 Stagsden Road, Bromham, Bedford MK43 8QJ* T: (01234) 918691 E: diharpham@gmail.com

HARRATT, James Michael. b 87. Univ of Wales (Ban) BSc 08 St Aug Coll of Th MA 20. Ripon Coll Cuddesdon BA 14. **d** 15 **p** 16. C Rainham *Roch* 15–18; V Bromley SS Pet and Paul from 18. *The Vicarage, 9 St Paul's Square, Bromley BR2 0XH* T: (020) 8464 9462 M: 07969-293648 E: jharratt@outlook.com *or* vicar@bromleyparishchurch.org

HARRATT, Philip David. b 56. Magd Coll Ox BA 79 MA 83. Ripon Coll Cuddesdon 82. **d** 85 **p** 86. C Ewyas Harold w Dulas, Kenderchurch etc *Heref* 85–88; V Chirbury 88–09; V Marton 88–09; V Trelystan w Leighton 88–09; P-in-c Middleton 02–09; RD Pontesbury 01–08; Preb Heref Cathl 03–09; V Embleton w Rennington and Rock *Newc* 09–16; rtd 16; PtO *Newc* As from 17; *Heref* 18–21. *55 Preston Street, Shrewsbury SY2 5PN*

HARRE-YOUNG, Steven Nicholas. b 86. Trin Coll Bris 14. **d** 17 **p** 18. NSM Patchway *Bris* 17–20. *48 Rock Lane, Stoke Gifford, Bristol BS34 8PF*

HARREX, David Brian. b 54. Trin Coll Bris 87. **d** 89 **p** 90. C Bedminster St Mich *Bris* 89–93; V Pilning w Compton

Greenfield 93–00; RD Westbury and Severnside 97–99; AD Bris W 99–00; TR Yate New Town 00–12; C Frampton Cotterell and Iron Acton 07–12; Hon Can Bris Cathl 10–12; TV Yatton Moor *B & W* 12–17; rtd 17; PtO *Bris* from 19. *Rose Cottage, Bath Road, Leonard Stanley, Stonehouse GL10 3LU* T: (01453) 825660 M: 07798-830172 E: davidharrex@gmail.com

HARRIES, John Edward. b 60. Bris Univ BSc 81 PhD 84. Wycliffe Hall Ox 94. **d** 96 **p** 97. C Hyde St Geo *Ches* 96–00; P-in-c Walton 00–15; C Latchford St Jas 00–15; Chapl Sir Thos Boteler High Sch 03–15; V Sutton, Wincle, Wildboarclough and Bosley *Ches* from 15; RD Macclesfield from 19. *St James' Vicarage, Church Lane, Sutton, Macclesfield SK11 0DS* T: (01260) 253945 E: vicar@peakparishes.org.uk

HARRIES, Malcolm David. b 44. BA 99. Oak Hill Th Coll 94. **d** 96 **p** 97. C Rock Ferry *Ches* 96–00; P-in-c Godley cum Newton Green 00–14; rtd 14. *17 Barnes Court, Durham Avenue, Woodford Green IG8 7NJ* E: malcolmharries2@btinternet.com

HARRIES, Sebastian David Tudor. b 86. Man Univ MusB 11 Jes Coll Cam BTh 15. Westcott Ho Cam 13. **d** 16 **p** 17. C Lingfield and Dormansland *S'wark* 16–19; Chapl St Gabr Coll Camberwell from 19; NSM Kennington St Jo w St Jas *S'wark* from 19; PtO *Chelmsf* from 19. *St Gabriel's College, Langton Road, London SW9 6UL* T: (020) 7793 3901 M: 07732-773303 E: sebastian.harries@cantab.net

✠**HARRIES OF PENTREGARTH, The Rt Revd Lord (Richard Douglas).** b 36. Selw Coll Cam BA 61 MA 65 Lon Univ Hon DD 94 FKC 83 FRSL 96. Cuddesdon Coll 61. **d** 63 **p** 64 **c** 87. C Hampstead St Jo *Lon* 63–69; Chapl Westf Coll Lon 67–69; Tutor Wells Th Coll 69–71; Warden Sarum & Wells Th Coll 71–72; V Fulham All SS *Lon* 72–81; Dean K Coll Lon 81–87; Consultant to Abps Cant and York on Inter-Faith Relns 86–06; Bp Ox 87–06; rtd 06; Asst Bp S'wark from 06; Hon Prof Th K Coll Lon from 06; Hon Asst Bp Lon from 14. *House of Lords, London SW1A 0PW* E: harriesr@parliament.uk

HARRIGAN, David Michael. b 84. Ox Min Course 15. **d** 18 **p** 19. C Romford Gd Shep *Chelmsf* from 18. *103 Highfield Road, Romford RM5 3AE* T: (01708) 941789 M: 07598-291807 E: dmharrigan@gmail.com *or* dmharrigan@thegoodshepherd.org.uk

HARRINGTON, Christopher Robert. b 57. Wilson Carlile Coll 99 ERMC 06. **d** 08 **p** 09. C Middle Rasen Gp *Linc* 08–12; P-in-c Heckington Gp 12–13; P-in-c Helpringham w Hale 12–13; R Heckington and Helpringham Gp from 13. *The Rectory, 10 Cameron Street, Heckington, Sleaford NG34 9RW* T: (01529) 460904 E: c.r.harrington@btinternet.com

HARRINGTON, John Christopher Thomas. b 43. Qu Coll Birm 71. **d** 74 **p** 75. C Northampton St Mich *Pet* 74–76; C Paston 76–79; R Doddington *Ely* 79–82; R Benwick St Mary 79–82; R Doddington w Benwick 82–83; CF (TA) 75–86; Chapl Doddington Co Hosp 79–83; V Eastbourne St Mich *Chich* 83–02; R Selsey 02–11; Chapl RNLI 03–11; rtd 11; Custos St Mary's Hosp Chich 11–18; PtO from 11. *43 Kingston Way, Seaford BN25 4NG* T: (01323) 351816 E: jctharrington@tiscali.co.uk

HARRINGTON (formerly CLARK), Melanie Louise. Selw Coll Cam PhD. Ripon Coll Cuddesdon 16. **d** 18 **p** 19. C Lich St Mich w St Mary and Wall 18–21; V Kew St Phil and All SS w St Luke *S'wark* from 21. *St Philip's Vicarage, 70 Marksbury Avenue, Richmond TW9 4JF* T: (020) 8392 1425 *or* 8332 1324 E: melanie.harrington@cantab.net

HARRIS, Mrs Alanna Jane. b 87. Regent's Park Coll Ox BA 08 Anglia Ruskin Univ MA 19. Ridley Hall Cam 16. **d** 19 **p** 20. C St Geo-in-the-East w St Paul *Lon* from 19. *Address temp unknown*

HARRIS, Mrs Alison Ann. b 54. Univ of Wales (Abth) BA 75 Westmr Coll Ox PGCE 76 Ches Univ MTh 07. Qu Coll Birm 07. **d** 08 **p** 09. C Neston *Ches* 08–12; V Witton 12–18; rtd 18; PtO *Ches* from 18. *12 Moorlands Avenue, Cuddington, Northwich CW8 2LU* T: (01606) 882047 M: 07775-449155 E: alisonannharris@hotmail.co.uk

HARRIS, Mrs Arthur Emlyn Dawson. b 27. Ex Univ BSc 47. S'wark Ord Course 83. **d** 86 **p** 87. NSM Frant w Eridge *Chich* 86–87; P-in-c Withyham St Mich 87–95; rtd 95; PtO *Sarum* 96–07; *Chich* from 13. *Pine Lodge, Beacon Gardens, Crowborough TN6 1BD* E: closecelts@btinternet.com

HARRIS, Bernard Malcolm. b 29. Leeds Univ BA 54. Coll of Resurr Mirfield 54. **d** 56 **p** 57. C Shrewsbury St Chad *Lich* 56–60; C Porthill 60–61; V Birches Head 61–66; V W Bromwich St Jas 66–78; V Sedgley All SS 78–93; rtd 93; PtO *Worc* 93–12; *Lich* 09–21. *6 Beacon Lane, Sedgley, Dudley DY3 1NB* T: (01902) 663134 E: bernardharris30@hotmail.com

HARRIS, Brian. b 33. Man Univ BSc. Qu Coll Birm 79. **d** 80 **p** 81. C Lich St Chad 80–81; PtO *Ches* 82–87; NSM Warburton 87–88; P-in-c 88–92; R Gt and Lt Casterton w Pickworth and Tickencote *Pet* 92–98; RD Barnack 94–98; rtd 98; PtO *Pet* 99–07; *St Alb* 06–07; *Ches* 10–14. *16 Westminster Green, Chester CH4 7LE* T: (01244) 675824 E: brookmeadow@btinternet.com

HARRIS, Brian. *See* HARRIS, Reginald Brian

HARRIS, Brian William. b 38. K Coll Lon BD 61 AKC 61. St Boniface Warminster 61. **d** 62 **p** 63. C Liversedge *Wakef* 62–65; C Kirkby *Liv* 65–70; V Dalton 70–79; V Aberford w Saxton *York* 79–91; V Hemingbrough 91–95; rtd 95; PtO *York* from 95; Dom Chapl to Bp Selby 95–03; Rtd Clergy and Widows Officer (York Adnry) 99–19. *2 Furness Drive, Rawcliffe, York YO30 5TD* T: (01904) 638214 E: harrischap@talktalk.net

HARRIS, Mrs Carol. b 68. Dur Univ BSc 87. Lindisfarne Regional Tr Partnership BA 17. **d** 17 **p** 18. C Wheatley Hill, Thornley and Wingate w Hutton Henry *Dur* 17–20; P-in-c Shildon from 20; C Coundon and Eldon from 20. *1A Burnie Gardens, Shildon DL4 1ND* E: carol.harris@durham.anglican.org

HARRIS, Catherine Elizabeth. *See* EDMONDS, Catherine Elizabeth

HARRIS, Christian Edward. b 95. Ex Univ BA 17 Dur Univ BA 21. St Mellitus Coll 18. **d** 21. C Totnes w Bridgetown, Berry Pomeroy etc *Ex* from 21. *The Vicarage, Week, Dartington, Totnes TQ9 6JL* M: 07503-151835 E: christianedwardharris@gmail.com

HARRIS, David Anthony. b 68. **d** 96 **p** 97. Canada 96–11; R Reading St Giles *Ox* from 11. *St Giles's Rectory, Church Street, Reading RG1 2SB* T: 0118-957 2831 E: sgiles.vicar@gmail.com

HARRIS, David Rowland. b 46. Ch Ch Ox BA 69 MA 72. Wycliffe Hall Ox 70. **d** 73 **p** 74. C Virginia Water *Guildf* 73–76; C Clifton Ch Ch w Em *Bris* 76–79; Scripture Union 79–85; V Bedford Ch Ch *St Alb* 85–99; R Ex St Leon w H Trin 99–12; rtd 12; P-in-c Ilsington *Ex* 12–15; V 15–21; PtO from 21. *25 Sett Close, Bovey Tracey, Newton Abbot TQ13 9LR* T: (01626) 836636 E: dandsharris@hotmail.com

HARRIS, Mrs Elaine Sarah. b 43. SWMTC 02. **d** 03 **p** 04. NSM Dyffryn *Llan* 03–06; P-in-c Penyfai 06–12; rtd 12; PtO *Llan* 17–18. *15 Neath Road, Fforest Goch, Pontardawe, Swansea SA8 3JB* T: (01656) 651719 E: revel07@hotmail.com

HARRIS, Elizabeth Anne. b 55. Qu Foundn (Course) 15. **d** 17 **p** 18. OLM Coventry Caludon *Cov* 17–19; OLM Caludon H Cross Cov from 19; OLM Wyken from 21. *48 Coombe Park Road, Coventry CV3 2NX* T: (024) 7672 3364 E: curate@holy-cross.org.uk

HARRIS, Ernest John. b 46. QUB BD 75. **d** 75 **p** 76. C Lisburn Ch Ch *Conn* 75–78; C Coleraine 78–83; I Belfast St Kath 83–90; I Ballinderry 90–11; Preb Conn Cathl 06–11; rtd 11. *10 Little Wenham, Moira, Craigavon BT67 0NN* T: (028) 9210 7385 M: 07842-114854

HARRIS, Geoffrey Daryl. b 39. Open Univ BA 83. St Aid Birkenhead 63. **d** 66 **p** 67. C Eston *York* 66–70; C Iffley *Ox* 70–75; V Bubwith *York* 75–78; V Bubwith w Ellerton and Aughton 78–79; P-in-c Stillingfleet w Naburn 79–80; R Escrick and Stillingfleet w Naburn 80–95; Chapl Qu Marg Sch York 83–94; Hon C Okehampton w Inwardleigh, Bratton Clovelly etc *Ex* 96–99; P-in-c Ashwater, Halwill, Beaworthy, Clawton etc 99–01; R 01–03; rtd 03; C Okehampton w Inwardleigh, Bratton Clovelly etc *Ex* 07–11. *The Old Barnsite, 7 Crossley Moor Road, Kingsteignton, Newton Abbot TQ12 3LE* E: revgdh@btinternet.com

HARRIS, Harriet Anne. b 68. MBE 17. Oriel Coll Ox BA 90 New Coll Ox DPhil 94. St Steph Ho Ox. **d** 00 **p** 01. C Ox St Mary V w St Cross and St Pet 00–06; Chapl Wadham Coll 00–10; Chapl Edin Univ from 10; NSM St Mary's Cathl 10–12. *Chaplaincy Centre, The University of Edinburgh, 1 Bristo Square, Edinburgh EH8 9AL* T: 0131-650 2595 M: 07896-244792 E: h.harris@ed.ac.uk

HARRIS, James David. b 78. Trin Coll Cam MA 01. Ox Min Course 12. **d** 15 **p** 16. NSM Stoke Bishop *Bris* 15–18; Asst Chapl Gtr Athens *Eur* 18–19; PtO *Bris* 19–20; R Long Ashton w Barrow Gurney and Flax Bourton *B & W* from 20; PtO *Eur* from 19. *The Vicarage, 7 Church Lane, Long Ashton, Bristol BS41 9LU*

HARRIS, Canon James Nigel Kingsley. b 37. St D Coll Lamp BA 60. Sarum Th Coll. **d** 62 **p** 63. C Painswick *Glouc* 62–65; C Glouc St Paul 65–67; V Slad 67–77; V Cam 77–78; P-in-c Stinchcombe 77–78; V Cam w Stinchcombe 78–82; V Stonehouse 82–02; Chapl Glos R Hosp NHS Trust 92–02; rtd 02; PtO *Glouc* 03–20; Hon Can Antsiranana Madagascar from 00. *14 Shalford Close, Cirencester GL7 1WG* T: (01285) 885641

HARRIS, James Philip. b 59. Westf Coll Lon BA 82 Cardiff Univ MPhil 12 Univ of Wales PGCE 97. St Mich Coll Llan BD 86. **d** 86 **p** 87. C Newport St Paul *Mon* 86–89; C Bedwellty 89–91; V Newport St Matt 91–96; Chapl Univ of Wales Inst

Cardiff *Llan* 97–99; Chapl Glam Univ 99–03; V Gwernaffield and Llanferres *St As* 03–09; Dioc Dir of Ords 03–09; V Bwlchgwyn and Minera *St As* 09–10; V Minera w Coedpoeth and Bwlchgwyn 10–14; V Minera w Coedpoeth 14–16; TV Alyn Miss Area from 17; AD Alyn 12–16. *The Vicarage, Church Road, Minera, Wrexham LL11 3DA* T: (01978) 753133 M: 07757-595154 E: jamespharris03@aol.com

HARRIS, Canon Jeremy David. b 63. Leeds Metrop Univ MA 00 Univ of Wales (Lamp) BA 04 Cardiff Univ MPhil 07 FCCA 92. St Mich Coll Llan 05. **d** 07 **p** 08. C Monmouth w Overmonnow etc *Mon* 07–09; C Magor 09–10; TV 10–12; TR from 12; AD Netherwent from 14; Can St Woolos Cathl from 17. *The Rectory, Redwick Road, Magor, Caldicot NP26 3GU* M: 07710-410950

HARRIS, Jeremy Michael. b 64. St Steph Ho Ox BTh 93. **d** 93 **p** 94. C Newport St Julian *Mon* 93–95; C Ebbw Vale 95–97; TV 97–98; Dioc Youth Chapl 96–98; TV Bracknell *Ox* 98–05; V Boyne Hill from 05. *The Vicarage, Westmorland Road, Maidenhead SL6 4HB* T: (01628) 626921

HARRIS, Canon John. b 45. St Steph Ho Ox 72. **d** 75 **p** 76. C Wanstead St Mary *Chelmsf* 75–84; V Penponds *Truro* 84–91; V St Gluvias 91–12; RD Carnmarth S 00–12; Hon Can Truro Cathl 01–12; rtd 12; PtO *Truro* 15–21. *The Anchorage, 2 Penlee View Terrace, Penzance TR18 4HY* T: (01736) 351026 E: john.harris2511@btinternet.com

HARRIS, John. b 54. Leeds Univ BSc 75. St Jo Coll Nottm LTh 86. **d** 86 **p** 87. C S Ossett *Wakef* 86–90; V Moldgreen 90–97; P-in-c S Ossett 97–04; V 04–10; P-in-c Luddenden w Luddenden Foot 10–13; rtd 13; PtO *Leeds* 17–18; P-in-c Woolley 18–19; PtO *York* from 19. *51 Aysgarth Rise, Bridlington YO16 7HU* E: nettletonscottage@gmail.com

HARRIS, John Brian. b 53. Hertf Coll Ox BA 76. Ripon Coll Cuddesdon 87. **d** 89 **p** 90. C Witton *Ches* 89–93; R Thurstaston 93–99; V Stockton Heath 99–04; P-in-c Gt Saughall 04–12; P-in-c Lostock Gralam 12–15; V 15–18; rtd 18; PtO *Ches* from 18. *12 Moorlands Avenue, Cuddington, Northwich CW8 2LU* E: revjohnbrianharris@gmail.com

HARRIS, Joshua Lloyd. b 89. Keble Coll Ox BA 10 Trin Coll Cam BA 18. Ridley Hall Cam 16. **d** 19 **p** 20. NSM St Geo-in-the-East w St Paul *Lon* from 19. *Address temp unknown*

HARRIS, Mrs Judith Helen. b 42. Chelsea Coll Lon TCert 64 Westmr Coll Ox MTh 03. St Alb Minl Tr Scheme 83. **dss** 86 **d** 87 **p** 94. Leagrave *St Alb* 86–87; Hon Par Dn 87–91; Team Dn Dunstable 91–94; TV 94–03; rtd 03; PtO *Truro* from 03. *Belmont, Fore Street, Porthleven, Helston TR13 9HN* T: (01326) 563090 E: revdjhharris@btopenworld.com

HARRIS, Julie Christine. b 61. Sarum Coll 15. **d** 17 **p** 18. NSM Wraxall *B & W* 17–20; P-in-c Nailsea Ch Ch w Tickenham 20–21; R from 21. *The Rectory, 1 Christ Church Close, Nailsea, Bristol BS48 1RT* T: (01275) 859210 E: jules.rectorccsqsj@gmail.com

HARRIS, Linda Margaret. b 55. Man Univ BSc 76 UMIST MSc 78 Birkbeck Coll Lon MSc 98. Wycliffe Hall Ox 03. **d** 05 **p** 06. C Cannock *Lich* 05–08; P-in-c Hatch Warren and Beggarwood *Win* 08–13; V Birchwood *Linc* from 13. *St Luke's Vicarage, 78 Jasmin Road, Lincoln LN6 0YR* E: revlinda@btinternet.com

HARRIS, Mrs Mandy June. b 63. Qu Foundn Birm 16. **d** 18 **p** 19. C Sheldon *Birm* 18; C Sheldon and Tile Cross from 18. *St Peter's Church Vicarage, Haywood Road, Birmingham B33 0LH* T: 0121-770 1377 M: 07598-122307 E: mandyjharris@virginmedia.com

HARRIS, Margaret Claire (Sister Margaret Joy). b 53. RGN 85 Homerton Coll Cam BEd 78. Ridley Hall Cam 90. **d** 92. Par Dn Stevenage All SS Pin Green *St Alb* 92–93; C 93–95; CSMV 95–99; OSB from 99. *St Mary's Abbey, 52 Swan Street, West Malling ME19 6JX* T: (01732) 843309

HARRIS, Mark. b 72. Ox Univ MA 94 K Coll Lon MA 12. Oak Hill Th Coll 16. **d** 18 **p** 19. C Kensington Ch Ch *Lon* from 18. *Christians in Parliament APPG, Room 484, Portcullis House, Bridge Street, London SW1A 2LW* E: mark.harris@parliament.uk *or* mark.harris@christchurchkensington.com

HARRIS, Mark Andrew. b 69. Heythrop Coll Lon BD 92 K Coll Lon MA 05 Jes Coll Cam PhD 12. Ridley Hall Cam 06. **d** 10 **p** 11. C Meopham w Nurstead *Roch* 10–13; C Blockhouse Bay NZ 13–14; P-in-c Henderson 14–16; Lect St Jo Coll Auckland from 16. *194 St John's Road, Meadowbank, Auckland 1072, New Zealand* T: (0064) (9) 869 4253 E: m.harris@stjohnscollege.ac.nz

HARRIS, Prof Mark Jonathan. b 66. St Cath Coll Cam BA 88 MA 92 PhD 92. Ripon Coll Cuddesdon BA 01 MA 05. **d** 02 **p** 03. C Cowley St Jas *Ox* 02–04; Chapl Oriel Coll Ox 04–10; Can and Vice Provost St Mary's Cathl Edin 10–12; Prec 12–13; LtO *Edin* from 14; Lect Edin Univ 12–19; Prof Natural Science and Th from 19. *Edinburgh University*

Faculty of Divinity, New College, Mound Place, Edinburgh EH1 2LX M: 07813-676892 E: mark.harris@ed.ac.uk

HARRIS, Canon Martin John. b 54. Trin Coll Cam BA 76 MA. Wycliffe Hall Ox 82. **d** 85 **p** 86. C Lindfield *Chich* 85–88; C Galleywood Common *Chelmsf* 88–91; V Southchurch Ch Ch 91–08; RD Southend 00–05; TR Harlow Town Cen w Lt Parndon from 08; RD Harlow from 09; Hon Can Chelmsf Cathl from 15. *The Rectory, 43 Upper Park, Harlow CM20 1TW* T: (01279) 411100 *or* 434243 M: 07905-672141 E: martinjohnharris@virginmedia.com *or* martinjharris@live.co.uk

HARRIS, Mary Noreen Cecily. *See* SOKANOVIC, Mary Noreen Cecily

HARRIS, Michael. b 34. St Mark & St Jo Coll Lon CertEd 56 ACP 65 MIL 76. Qu Coll Birm. **d** 83 **p** 84. NSM Bournville *Birm* 83–90; NSM Stirchley 90–96; Chapl Univ of Cen England in Birm 92–99; Dean NSMs 96–99; rtd 00; PtO *Birm* 00–12; *Cov* from 00. *33 Bosley Close, Shipston-on-Stour CV36 4QA* T/F: (01608) 661672 M: 07811-489713 E: mike.harris@pikkle.net

HARRIS, Michael Andrew. b 53. Ian Ramsey Coll Brasted 74 Trin Coll Bris 75. **d** 78 **p** 79. C St Paul's Cray St Barn *Roch* 78–82; C Church Stretton *Heref* 82–87; Res Min Penkridge w Stretton *Lich* 87–90; Res Min Penkridge Team 90–92; V Amington *Birm* 92–15; AD Polesworth 07–14; V Highley w Billingsley, Glazeley etc *Heref* from 15. *The Rectory, Church Street, Highley, Bridgnorth WV16 6NA* E: highleyrector@gmail.com

HARRIS, Nicholas Bryan. b 60. Down Coll Cam BA 81 MA 85. Ridley Hall Cam 82. **d** 85 **p** 86. C Walney Is *Carl* 85–88; C S'wark Ch Ch 88–92; PtO *Chich* 92–08. *Wheelwrights, High Street, Fairwarp, Uckfield TN22 3BP* E: box534@yahoo.co.uk

HARRIS, Paul Ian. b 45. MSc. Qu Coll Birm. **d** 82 **p** 83. C The Quinton *Birm* 82–86; V Atherstone *Cov* 86–13; rtd 13; PtO *Cov* from 13; *Leic* 13–21. *31 Woodside, Ashby-de-la-Zouch LE65 2NJ* T: (01530) 589873 E: starpentree@gmail.com

HARRIS, Paul Michael. b 58. Chelsea Coll Lon BSc 79 Oak Hill Th Coll BA 89 Bath Coll of HE CertEd 82 Open Univ BA 04 MA 14. **d** 89. C Finchley Ch Ch *Lon* 89–90; Asst Master St Luke's Sch W Norwood 90–91; Master and Asst Chapl Brent Internat Sch Philippines 91–92; Volunteer Miss Movement Sunningdale 93–94; Past Asst St Joseph's RC Ch Dorking 94–95; Form Master Merton Court Prep Sch Sidcup 95–97; Asst Master Clewborough Ho Prep Sch Camberley 98–01; Teacher St Nic Sch for Girls Church Crookham 01–02; Culford Sch Bury St Edmunds 02–04; Teacher St Marg Prep Sch Calne 05–07. *Maes-yr-Haf, 4 Penllain, Penparc, Cardigan SA43 1RJ* T: (01239) 571082 E: paul.harris.007@hotmail.co.uk

HARRIS, Peter Dudley. b 44. Sir John Cass Coll Lon BSc 72 MA 77. **d** 13 **p** 14. NSM Hanger Hill Ascension and W Twyford St Mary *Lon* from 13. *91 Ashbourne Road, London W5 3DH* T: (020) 8997 7852 M: 07944-576375 E: pete@richard-brise.co.uk

HARRIS, Peter Malcolm. b 52. Em Coll Cam BA 74 MA 79. Trin Coll Bris. **d** 80 **p** 81. C Upton (Overchurch) *Ches* 80–83; Crosslinks from 83; Portugal 93–97; France from 97. *rue de Meunier 4, Ribet, 13990 Fontvieille, France* M: (0033) 8 77 35 61 53 E: harris@crosslinks.org

HARRIS, Peter Samuel. b 68. Dundee Univ BA 98 St Jo Coll Dur BA 04. Cranmer Hall Dur 02. **d** 04 **p** 05. C Walton and Trimley *St E* 04–07; R Dalkeith *Edin* from 07; R Lasswade from 07. *11 Peacock Parkway, Bonnyrigg EH19 3RQ* T: 0131-663 7000 E: revpharris@gmail.com

HARRIS, Raymond. b 36. Nottm Univ BA 58. Lich Th Coll 58. **d** 60 **p** 61. C Clifton St Fran *S'well* 60–63; C Davyhulme St Mary *Man* 63–66; V Bacup Ch Ch 66–82; R Dunsby w Dowsby *Linc* 82–87; R Rippingale 82–87; R Rippingale Gp 87–94; rtd 94. *2 The Bungalow, Swaton Lane, Swaton, Sleaford NG34 0JU* T: (01529) 421343

HARRIS, Rebecca Jane. *See* SWYER, Rebecca Jane

HARRIS (née LEE), Mrs Rebecca Susan. b 62. Man Univ BA 85. Trin Coll Bris 93. **d** 95 **p** 96. C Cirencester *Glouc* 95–99; TV Gt Chesham *Ox* 99–11; V Creech St Michael and Ruishton w Thornfalcon *B & W* 11–20; RD Taunton 18–19; TR White Horse *Sarum* from 20. *The Rectory, Bitham Lane, Westbury BA13 3BU* T: (01373) 822209 E: harrisrs211@gmail.com *or* teamrector@whtministry.org.uk

HARRIS, The Ven Reginald Brian. b 34. Ch Coll Cam BA 58 MA 61. Ridley Hall Cam. **d** 59 **p** 60. C Wednesbury St Bart *Lich* 59–61; C Uttoxeter w Bramshall 61–64; V Bury St Pet *Man* 64–70; V Walmsley 70–80; RD 70–80; Adn Man 80–98; Can Res Man Cathl 80–98; rtd 98; PtO *Derby* 98–18. *9 Cote Lane, Hayfield, High Peak SK22 2HL* T: (01663) 746321 E: aandbharris@btinternet.com

HARRIS, Robert. *See* WYNFORD-HARRIS, Robert William

HARRIS, Preb Robert Douglas. b 57. Ex Univ BEd 80 Bris Univ MEd 96. Chich Th Coll 80. **d** 82 **p** 83. C Portsea St Mary *Portsm* 82–87; V Clevedon St Jo *B & W* 87–92; R Felpham w Middleton *Chich* 92–99; R Felpham 99–04; RD Arundel and Bognor 98–04; P-in-c Southwick 04–06; R 06–10; RD Hove 09–10; P-in-c Ilfracombe, Lee, Woolacombe, Bittadon etc *Ex* 10–16; TR Plympton from 16; Preb Ex Cathl from 17. *St Mary's Vicarage, 209 Ridgeway, Plymouth PL7 2HP* T: (01752) 658762 E: robdharris@btinternet.com

HARRIS, Robert James. b 45. Nottm Univ MA 02 ALCD 73. St Jo Coll Nottm 69. **d** 72 **p** 73. C Sheff St Jo 72–76; C Goole 76–78; V Bramley and Ravenfield 78–91; P-in-c Boulton *Derby* 91–99; RD Melbourne 96–99; P-in-c Hazlewood 99–02; P-in-c Hazlewood and Milford 02–05; V Hazelwood, Holbrook and Milford 05–10; rtd 10. *13 Mill Close, Findern, Derby DE65 6AP* T: (01283) 703024 E: jrjubilate@btinternet.com

HARRIS, Sian Elizabeth. b 54. Kingston Poly BSocSc 75. WEMTC 03. **d** 06 **p** 07. NSM Leominster *Heref* 06–09; Chapl St Mich Hospice Hereford 09–11; TV Tenbury *Heref* 11–16; TR from 16. *The Rectory, Burford, Tenbury Wells WR15 8HG* T: (01584) 819792 M: 07866-492863 E: sianharris@f2s.com

HARRIS, Thomas William. b 54. Univ of Wales (Lamp) MA 04 AKC 76. Linc Th Coll 77. **d** 78 **p** 79. C Norton Woodseats St Chad *Sheff* 78–81; V Barnby Dun 81–91; P-in-c Kirk Bramwith and Fenwick 81–85; Chapl RN 91–94; R Draycot Bris 94–02; P-in-c Cawston w Booton and Brandiston etc *Nor* 02–12; Chapl Norfolk Community Health and Care 02–07; Chapl Cawston Park Hosp 07–09; P-in-c Gt w Lt Massingham, Harpley, Rougham etc *Nor* 12–13; rtd 13; PtO *Nor* from 14. *Blake House, The Common, Hanworth, Norwich NR11 7HP* T: (01263) 761570 E: revtomharris@gmail.com

HARRIS, William Edric Mackenzie. b 46. Sarum & Wells Th Coll 72. **d** 75 **p** 76. C Langney *Chich* 75–79; C Moulsecoomb 80–81; TV 81–85; R W Grinstead 85–16; rtd 16. *10 Alnwick Way, Amble, Morpeth NE65 0GQ* E: williamemharris@gmail.com

HARRIS, William Fergus. b 36. CCC Cam BA 59 MA 63 Edin Univ DipEd 70. Yale Div Sch 59 Westcott Ho Cam 60. **d** 62 **p** 63. C St Andrews St Andr *St And* 62–64; Chapl Edin Univ 64–71; R Edin St Pet 71–83; R Perth St Jo *St And* 83–90; Hon C 90–08; rtd 90; Prov Archivist 91–02; LtO *St And* from 08. *35 St Mary's Drive, Perth PH2 7BY* T: (01738) 621379

HARRIS-EVANS, William Giles. b 46. AKC 68. Bangalore Th Coll. **d** 70 **p** 71. C Clapham H Trin *S'wark* 70–74; Sri Lanka 75–78; V Benhilton *S'wark* 78–86; TR Cov E 86–93; TR Brighouse and Clifton *Wakef* 93–99; V Petersfield *Portsm* 99–10; R Buriton 99–10; rtd 10; PtO *Portsm* from 11. *11 Great Southsea Street, Southsea PO5 3BY* E: wghevans@talktalk.net

HARRIS-FAULKNER, Anthea Brenda Sybil. b 67. St Aug Coll of Th 15. **d** 18 **p** 19. NSM Greenhithe St Mary *Roch* 18–19; NSM Stone from 19. *71 Windsor Road, Gravesend DA12 5BW*

HARRIS-WHITE, John Emlyn. b 34. St Aid Birkenhead 59. **d** 62 **p** 63. C Cricklade w Latton *Bris* 62–63; C Kingswood 63–66; C Ashton-on-Ribble St Andr *Blackb* 66–69; V Heyhouses 69–71; Chapl Roundway Hosp Devizes 71–77; Chapl R Variety Children's Hosp and K Coll Hosp Lon 77–89; Chapl Belgrave Hosp Lon 77–89; Regional Community Relns Co-ord 89–93; rtd 94; Hon C Folkestone St Pet *Cant* 97–01. *40 Tippet Knowes Road, Winchburgh, Broxburn EH52 6UL* E: johnharriswhite@aol.com

HARRISON, Alison Edwina. See HART, Alison Edwina

HARRISON, Mrs Barbara Ann. b 41. Man Univ BA 63 Leic Univ CertEd 64. EMMTC 85. **d** 88 **p** 94. C Immingham *Linc* 88–94; P-in-c Habrough Gp 94–99; V 99–01; rtd 02; PtO *Linc* from 02. *3 Windsor Mews, Louth LN11 9AY* T: (01507) 610015

HARRISON, Canon Barbara Anne. b 34. Westf Coll Lon BA 56 CertEd 57 Hull Univ MA 85. Linc Th Coll 76. **dss** 79 **d** 87 **p** 94. Lakenham St Jo *Nor* 79–80; Chapl York Univ 80–88; Team Dn Sheff Manor 88–93; Par Dn Holts CD *Man* 93–94; C-in-c 94–98; Dioc UPA Officer 93–98; Chapl Rochdale Healthcare NHS Trust 98–02; Chapl Pennine Acute Hosps NHS Trust 02–04; C Bury Ch King *Man* 98–01; C Bury St Paul 98–04; P-in-c Kirkholt 01–04; Hon Can Man Cathl 02–04; rtd 04; PtO *Man* from 04; *Ches* from 17. *36 Homebeck House, Gatley Green, Gatley, Cheadle SK8 4NF* M: 07513-160794 E: barbara.harrison34@hotmail.com

HARRISON, Bruce. b 49. Linc Th Coll 86. **d** 88 **p** 89. C Syston *Leic* 88–90; C Whitby *York* 90–93; V Glaisdale 93–99; R Brotton Parva 99–04; V Coatham and Dormanstown 04–08; Chapl Tees and NE Yorks NHS Trust 04–07; rtd 08; PtO *York* from 08. *65 Guisborough Road, Moorsholm, Saltburn-by-the-Sea TS12 3JA* E: bruce.harrison@live.co.uk

HARRISON, Bruce Mountford. b 49. AKC 71. **d** 72 **p** 73. C Hebburn St Cuth *Dur* 72–75; C Bethnal Green St Jo w

St Simon *Lon* 75–77; P-in-c Bethnal Green St Bart 77–78; TV Bethnal Green St Jo w St Bart 78–80; C-in-c Pennywell St Thos and Grindon St Oswald CD *Dur* 80–85; V Sunderland Pennywell St Thos 85–90; V Gateshead St Helen 90–14; rtd 14. *18 Salkeld Road, Gateshead NE9 5UD*

HARRISON, Sister Cécile. b 29. Bp Lonsdale Coll TCert 51. St Steph Ho Ox 97. **d** 97 **p** 97. CGA from 66; LtO *Eur* 97–12; PtO *Ex* from 13. *4 Coombe Meadows, Chillington, Kingsbridge TQ7 2JL* T: (01548) 532815 E: cgaprasada@gmail.com

HARRISON (née Wilson), Christella Helen. b 62. Leeds Univ MA 11. Yorks Min Course 08. **d** 11 **p** 12. C Pannal w Beckwithshaw *Ripon* 11–14; *Leeds* 14; V Hampsthwaite and Killinghall and Birstwith 14–19. *Home Farm, Whitworth, Spennymoor DL16 7QX* E: revchrissywilson@yahoo.com

HARRISON, Christine Amelia. b 47. STETS 94. **d** 98 **p** 99. NSM Goldsworth Park *Guildf* 98–12; rtd 12; PtO *Guildf* from 12. *2 Abercorn Way, Woking GU21 3NY* T: (01483) 750645 E: revchrissie@btinternet.com

HARRISON, Christopher Dennis. b 57. Clare Coll Cam BA 79 BA 86. Westcott Ho Cam 84. **d** 87 **p** 88. C Camberwell St Geo *S'wark* 87–92; V Forest Hill 92–96; P-in-c Fenny Bentley, Kniveton, Thorpe and Tissington *Derby* 96–98; P-in-c Parwich w Alsop-en-le-Dale 96–98; R Fenny Bentley, Thorpe, Tissington, Parwich etc 98–09; RD Ashbourne 98–09; P-in-c Nottingham All SS, St Mary and St Pet *S'well* 09–11; R 11–17; R Nottingham St Pet and All SS from 18. *24 Pelham Crescent, Nottingham NG7 1AW* T: 0115-941 8927 E: christopher.d.harrison@btinternet.com

HARRISON, Christopher Joseph. b 38. AKC 61 Hull Univ CertEd 68 Bris Univ BEd 75. **d** 62 **p** 63. C Bottesford *Linc* 62–67; C Elloughton *York* 67–68; Asst Master Bishop's Cleeve Primary Sch 68–74; Sen Master 74–78; Dep Hd 78–96; P-in-c Farmington *Glouc* 69–73; C Tredington w Stoke Orchard and Hardwicke 74–86; rtd 96; PtO *Glouc* from 87. *Appledore, 93 Stoke Road, Bishops Cleeve, Cheltenham GL52 8RP* T: (01242) 673452

HARRISON, Crispin. See HARRISON, Michael Burt

HARRISON, David Daniel. b 62. St Paul's Coll Chelt BA 84 Leeds Univ MA 85 Westmr Coll Ox PGCE 88. Westcott Ho Cam 03. **d** 05 **p** 06. C Beckenham St Geo *Roch* 05–09; P-in-c Woodnesborough w Worth and Staple *Cant* 09–12; Chapl Univ Campus Suffolk *St E* 13; PtO 13–16; P-in-c Ringshall w Battisford, Barking w Darmsden etc 16–19; R S Bosmere from 19. *The Rectory, Willisham, Ipswich IP8 4SP* E: ddh25@btinternet.com

HARRISON, David Henry. b 40. Tyndale Hall Bris 65. **d** 68 **p** 69. C Bolton St Paul *Man* 68–72; V Bircle 72–83; V Southport SS Simon and Jude *Liv* 83–91; TR Fazakerley Em 91–99; V Toxteth Park Ch Ch and St Mich w St Andr 99–05; rtd 05; PtO *Blackb* from 06. *55 The Oval, Shevington, Wigan WN6 8EN* T: (01257) 400084 E: revdave@live.co.uk

HARRISON, Miss Doreen. b 32. Leeds Univ BA 53 PGCE 54 Lanc Univ MLitt 78 MA(Ed) 79. **d** 92 **p** 94. C Ambleside w Brathay *Carl* 92–96; Asst P Colton 96–01; P-in-c 01–02; Asst P Rusland 96–01; P-in-c 01–02; Asst P Satterthwaite 96–01; P-in-c 01–02; rtd 02; PtO *Carl* from 02. *Fox How, Ambleside LA22 9LL* T: (015394) 33021

HARRISON, Fred Graham. b 41. Lon Univ BSc 62. Ridley Hall Cam 80. **d** 82 **p** 83. C Lenton *S'well* 82–85; V Ruddington 85–04; rtd 04; PtO *Ches* from 05. *18 Holly Bank, Hollingworth, Hyde SK14 8QL* T: (01457) 765955 E: fg.harrison@talktalk.net

HARRISON, Gloria. b 55. Qu Foundn (Course) 14. **d** 17 **p** 18. OLM Hanley H Ev *Lich* 17–19; NSM Stoke-upon-Trent and Fenton from 19. *18 Ashbourne Grove, Stoke-on-Trent ST1 5QW* T: (01782) 257820

HARRISON, Guy Patrick. b 58. Ox Univ MTh 99 Middx Univ DPsych 16 MBACP 04. Sarum & Wells Th Coll 92. **d** 94 **p** 95. C Wimborne Minster and Holt *Sarum* 94–96; C Wimborne Minster 96–97; Chapl Dorothy House Hospice Winsley 97–01; Chapl Stoke Mandeville Hosp NHS Trust 01–02; Chapl Team Ldr 02–05; Team Ldr and Bereavement Service Manager Bucks Hosps NHS Trust 05–07; Hd Spiritual and Past Care W Lon Mental Health NHS Trust 07–12; Hd Spiritual and Past Care Ox Health NHS Foundn Trust from 12. *Littlemore Mental Health Centre, Sandford Road, Littlemore, Oxford OX4 4XN* T: 08452-191145 M: 07786-843878 E: guy.harrison@oxfordhealth.nhs.uk

HARRISON, Ian David. b 45. Imp Coll Lon BSc 66. Oak Hill Th Coll 93. **d** 96 **p** 97. NSM Tunbridge Wells St Jo *Roch* 96–99; P-in-c Chiddingstone w Chiddingstone Causeway 99–10; rtd 10; PtO *Roch* from 10. *3 Brunswick Terrace, Tunbridge Wells TN1 1TR* T: (01892) 871639 E: ian.harrison.tw@gmail.com

HARRISON, Canon John. b 49. Fitzw Coll Cam BA 71 MA 74. Westcott Ho Cam 74. **d** 77 **p** 78. C Nunthorpe *York* 77–81; C Acomb St Steph and St Aid 81–83; V

Heptonstall *Wakef* 83–91; R Stamford Bridge Gp *York* 91–02; V Easingwold w Raskelf 02–14; RD Easingwold 05–14; Can and Preb York Minster 10–14; rtd 14; PtO *York* from 14. *24 The Manor Beeches, Dunnington, York YO19 5PX* E: john.harrison8@hotmail.co.uk

HARRISON, John. *See* HARRISON, Steven John

HARRISON, John Christopher. b 69. Liv Univ BA 90 MSc 98 Liv Jo Moores Univ PhD 06. SNWTP 07. **d** 10 **p** 11. NSM Hoylake *Ches* from 10. *St Hildeburgh's Vicarage, 1 Stanley Road, Hoylake, Wirral CH47 1HL* T: 0151-632 3897 M: 07834-262166

HARRISON, Mrs Kathryn Maxine. b 70. Ox Min Course 13. **d** 15 **p** 16. C New Windsor *Ox* 15–18; V St Marylebone St Mark Hamilton Terrace *Lon* from 18. *St Mark's Vicarage, 114 Hamilton Terrace, London NW8 9UT* M: 07794-113782 E: mail.kmh22@gmail.com

HARRISON, Keith. *See* HARRISON, Peter Keith

HARRISON, Canon Lyndon. b 47. St Mich Coll Llan 91. **d** 93 **p** 94. C Ebbw Vale *Mon* 93–96; TV 96–01; TV Caldicot 01–05; TR 05–14; Can St Woolos Cathl 12–14; rtd 14; PtO *Mon* from 14. *14 Swallow Drive, Caldicot NP26 5RD* T: (01291) 430041

HARRISON, Mrs Marion Jeanne. b 56. SAOMC 04. **d** 07 **p** 08. C Watercombe *Sarum* 07–11; P-in-c Lt Barningham, Blickling, Edgefield etc *Nor* 11–15; C 15–17; P-in-c Barningham w Matlaske w Baconsthorpe etc 15–17; P-in-c The Lavingtons, Cheverells, and Easterton *Sarum* 17–18; R from 18. *The Vicarage, 25 White Street, West Lavington, Devizes SN10 4LW* T: (01380) 816963 M: 07932-521776 E: marion681@btinternet.com *or* lavingtonrector@gmail.com

HARRISON, Mark. b 60. Global Univ Missouri BA 95 Open Univ BSc 14 St Jo Coll Dur BA 18. Cranmer Hall Dur 16. **d** 18 **p** 19. C Chester le Street *Dur* from 18. *16 Park Road North, Chester le Street DH3 3SD* M: 07975-782891 E: mark.ofelton@gmail.com

HARRISON, Martin. b 58. DCR(R) 78. Trin Coll Bris BA 89. **d** 89 **p** 90. C Heworth H Trin *York* 89–94; Chapl York Distr Hosp 89–94; P-in-c Skelton w Shipton and Newton on Ouse *York* 94–95; R 95–01; V Strensall from 01; RD Easingwold 00–05; C Alne from 17; C Brafferton w Pilmoor, Myton-on-Swale etc from 17; C Coxwold and Husthwaite from 17; C Crayke w Brandsby and Yearsley from 17; C Easingwold w Raskelf from 17; C Skelton w Shipton and Newton on Ouse from 17; C Forest of Galtres from 17. *The Vicarage, 10 York Road, Strensall, York YO32 5UN* T: (01904) 490683 E: revmartinharrison@gmail.com

HARRISON, Maureen Ann. b 39. **d** 08 **p** 09. OLM Sutton *Liv* 08–13; rtd 13. *89 Farndon Avenue, Sutton Manor, St Helens WA9 4DN*

HARRISON, Michael Anthony. b 48. Westhill Coll Birm CertCYW 72 Huddersfield Poly CertEd 88 Leeds Poly BA 91 Leeds Univ MA 98. NOC 94. **d** 97 **p** 98. NSM Thornhill and Whitley Lower *Wakef* 97–99; TV Wrexham *St As* 99–03; V Ruabon 03–11; rtd 11; PtO *St As* from 11; Ban from 12. *15 Vicarage Gardens, Llandudno LL30 1RG* T: (01492) 870701 M: 07910-141410 E: mikeonorme@gmail.com

HARRISON, Michael Burt (Crispin). b 36. Leeds Univ BA 59 Trin Coll Ox BA 62 MA 66. Coll of Resurr Mirfield 59. **d** 63 **p** 64. C W Hartlepool St Aid *Dur* 63–64; C Middlesbrough All SS *York* 64–66; Lic to Offic *Wakef* 67–69 and 78–87 and 97–02 and 06–14; CR from 68; S Africa 69–78 and 87–97 and 03–06; Registrar Coll of Resurr Mirfield 78–84; Vice-Prin 84–87; Superior CR 97–02; LtO *Leeds* from 14. *Community of the Resurrection, Stocks Bank Road, Mirfield WF14 0BN* T: (01924) 483337 E: charrison@mirfield.org.uk

✠**HARRISON, The Rt Revd Michael Robert.** b 63. Selw Coll Cam BA 84 K Coll Lon PhD 97 Bradf Univ MA 99. Ripon Coll Cuddesdon BA 89 Union Th Sem (NY) STM 90. **d** 90 **p** 91 **c** 16. C S Lambeth St Anne and All SS *S'wark* 90–94; Bp's Chapl to Students *Bradf* 94–98; Chapl Bradf Univ 94–98; Chapl Bradf and Ilkley Community Coll 94–98; V Eltham H Trin *S'wark* 98–06; RD Eltham and Mottingham 05–06; Dir Min and Miss *Leic* 06–16; Hon Can Leic Cathl 06–16; Suff Bp Dunwich *St E* from 16; Dioc Warden of Readers and Lic Lay Min from 16. *Robin Hall, Chapel Road, Mendlesham, Stowmarket IP14 5SQ* T: (01473) 252829

HARRISON, Mrs Nona Margaret. b 50. Open Univ BA 80. S Dios Minl Tr Scheme 92. **d** 95 **p** 96. NSM E w W Wellow and Sherfield English *Win* 95–99; NSM Barton Stacey and Bullington etc 99; NSM Hurstbourne Priors, Longparish etc 00–08; PtO 08–15; *Sarum* from 18. *35 Blackthorn Way, Verwood BH31 6TA* T: (01202) 020374 E: nonaharrison@mypostoffice.co.uk

HARRISON, Miss Patricia Mary. b 35. St Kath Coll Lon CertEd 65 Open Univ BA 74. St Mich Ho Ox IDC 59. **dss** 85 **d** 87 **p** 94. NSM Nunthorpe *York* 85–98; rtd 98; PtO

York from 98. *22 Lamonby Close, Nunthorpe, Middlesbrough TS7 0QG* T: (01642) 313524 E: marie.pat@btinternet.com

HARRISON, Paul Graham. b 53. Univ of Wales (Lamp) MA 10. Sarum & Wells Th Coll 76. **d** 79 **p** 80. C Brixham w Churston Ferrers *Ex* 79–82; C Portsea N End St Mark *Portsm* 82–87; V Tiverton St Andr *Ex* 87–94; Chapl Tiverton and Distr Hosp 90–94; P-in-c Astwood Bank *Worc* 94–05; TV Redditch Ch the K 05–08; P-in-c Churchill-in-Halfshire w Blakedown and Broome 08–17; Chapl to Deaf People 94–08; Dioc Adv for Disability Issues 03–08; Hon C Belbroughton w Fairfield and Clent 15–17; RD Stourbridge 13–16; PtO *Cov* 94–17; rtd 17; PtO *Lich* from 17. *8 Truro Close, Lichfield WS13 7SR* T: (01543) 326458 E: connectpharrison@hotmail.com

HARRISON, Mrs Penelope Ann. b 58. St Andr Univ MA 79. Qu Coll Birm MA 09. **d** 09 **p** 10. C Hamstead St Paul *Birm* 09–13; V Marston Green 13–21; rtd 21. *34 Wellesbourne Grove, Stratford-upon-Avon CV37 6PD* M: 07722-446222 E: revdpenny13@gmail.com

HARRISON, Peter Keith. b 44. Open Univ BA 85. St Aid Birkenhead. **d** 68 **p** 69. C Higher Bebington *Ches* 68–71; C Walmsley *Man* 71–74; V Lumb in Rossendale 74–79; V Heywood St Marg 79–87; V Hey 87–95; AD Saddleworth 93–95; Chapl Athens w Kifissia *Eur* 95–98; V Aston Cantlow and Wilmcote w Billesley *Cov* 98–02; V W Burnley All SS *Blackb* 02–09; rtd 09; PtO *Blackb* from 09. *57 West Cliffe, Lytham St Annes FY8 5DR* T: (01253) 735128 E: keithharrison207@gmail.com

HARRISON, The Ven Peter Reginald Wallace. b 39. Selw Coll Cam BA 62. Ridley Hall Cam 62. **d** 64 **p** 65. C Barton Hill St Luke w Ch Ch *Bris* 64–69; Chapl Greenhouse Trust 69–77; Dir Northorpe Hall Trust 77–84; TR Drypool *York* 84–98; AD E Hull 88–98; Adn E Riding 98–06; Can and Preb York Minster 94–06; rtd 06; PtO *York* from 06. *10 Priestgate, Sutton-on-Hull, Hull HU7 4QR* T: (01482) 797110 E: peter@harrisons.karoo.co.uk

HARRISON, Phillip Roger Neil. b 74. Trin Coll Bris 12. **d** 15 **p** 16. C Gtr Corsham and Lacock *Bris* 15–18; V Wroughton and Wichelstowe from 18. *The Vicarage, Church Hill, Wroughton, Swindon SN4 9JS* T: (01793) 812050 E: vicar@wroughton.com

HARRISON, Canon Rachel Elizabeth. b 53. NEOC 98. **d** 01 **p** 02. C Skelton w Upleatham *York* 01–04; P-in-c New Marske 04–06; V 06–12; P-in-c Wilton 04–06; V 06–12; V Redcar 12–20; Ind Chapl 04–20; RD Guisborough 13–19; Can and Preb York Minster 16–20; rtd 20; PtO *York* from 20. *65 Guisborough Road, Moorsholm, Saltburn-by-the-Sea TS12 3JA* E: rachelhere@hotmail.com

HARRISON, Richard Kingswood. b 61. Linc Coll Ox BA 83 MA 88 Leeds Univ BA 90. Coll of Resurr Mirfield 88. **d** 91 **p** 92. C Reading St Giles *Ox* 91–93; Asst Chapl Merchant Taylors' Sch Northwood 93–96; Chapl Ardingly Coll 96–02; R Shill Valley and Broadshire *Ox* 02–04; Chapl Uppingham Sch 04–09; Chapl Lancing Coll from 09; PtO *Ox* 11–19. *Ladywell House, Lancing College, Lancing BN15 0RW* T: (01273) 465961 E: rkh@lancing.org.uk

HARRISON, Robert William. b 62. Mansf Coll Ox BA 84. Qu Coll Birm 87. **d** 89 **p** 90. C Sholing *Win* 89–93; Communications Adv to Bp Willesden *Lon* 93–97; C Cricklewood St Gabr and St Mich 93–97; V Hillingdon St Jo 97–15; V Neasden St Cath w St Paul from 15. *9 Midstrath Road, London NW10 1TD* T: (020) 8452 7322 M: 07961-011040 E: rob.harrison@london.anglican.org *or* st.catherines@gmx.com

HARRISON, Miss Rosemary Elizabeth. b 57. Lindisfarne Regional Tr Partnership 16. **d** 19 **p** 21. NSM Humshaugh w Simonburn and Wark *Newc* 19–20; NSM Ponteland from 20. *20A North Side, Stamfordham, Newcastle upon Tyne NE18 0LA* T: (01661) 855128 M: 07888-834961 E: rosemaryharrison@ymail.com

HARRISON, Stephen George. b 66. Rhodes Univ BA 96. **d** 95 **p** 96. C Newlands S Africa 95–97; R Northlands 97–11; R Westville 11–17; Adn Pinetown 15–16; TR Stroudwater *Glouc* from 17. *The Rectory, Church Road, Leonard Stanley, Stonehouse GL10 3NP* M: 07466-858975 E: rectorstroudwater@gmail.com

HARRISON, Steven John. b 47. Univ of Wales (Abth) BSc 68 PhD 74 FRMetS 74. St And Dioc Tr Course 87. **d** 90 **p** 91. NSM Alloa *St And* 90–94; NSM Bridge of Allan 94–02; NSM Spittal *Newc* 02–10; NSM Scremerston 02–10; P-in-c 06–10; rtd 10; PtO *Newc* from 10. *East Cottage, Plunderheath, Haydon Bridge, Hexham NE47 6JU* T: (01434) 684994 E: johnandaveril@aol.com

HARRISON, Trevor Kenneth. b 54. Leeds Univ LLB 77 Barrister-at-Law 78. St Aug Coll of Th 14. **d** 20 **p** 21. NSM New Groombridge *Chich* from 20. *The Old Bakery, Station*

Road, Groombridge, Tunbridge Wells TN3 9NB T: (01892) 882536 M: 07979-886735 E: revtrev@groombridge.com

HARRISON-MILES, Damian Stewart. b 76. Fitzw Coll Cam BTh 02. Westcott Ho Cam 99. **d** 02 **p** 03. C Willingdon Chich 02–06; P-in-c Nork Guildf 06–11; P-in-c Thorpe 11–15; V from 15. The Vicarage, Church Approach, Egham TW20 8TQ   T: (01932)   565986   M: 07815-848735 E: damomiles@btinternet.com

HARRISON-SMITH, Ms Fiona Jane. b 74. Huddersfield Univ BMus 96 Ox Brookes Univ BA 03 Leeds Univ MA 07. Coll of Resurr Mirfield 05. **d** 07 **p** 08. C Redcar York 07–11; TV Seacroft Leeds 11–16; V Weoley Castle Birm from 16. 83 Marston Road, Birmingham B29 5LS   M: 07709-914786 E: revdfiona@gmail.com

HARRISON-WATSON, Carole. See FORD, Carole

HARRISSON, John Anthony Lomax. b 47. Ex Univ BA 72. Qu Coll Birm 72. **d** 74 **p** 75. C Loughton St Jo Chelmsf 74–81; V Chingford St Anne 81–98; TV Aldrington Chich 98–04; TV Golden Cap Team Sarum 04–09; rtd 09; PtO Ex from 10. 82 Chestnut Way, Honiton EX14 2XF T: (01404) 47905 E: john.harrisson@yahoo.co.uk

HARROLD, Canon Jeremy Robin. b 31. Hertf Coll Ox BA 54 BSc 56 MA 58. Wycliffe Hall Ox. 59 **p** 60. C Rushden Pet 59–61; Bp's Chapl Lon 61–64; Australia 64–67; V Harlesden St Mark Lon 67–72; V Hendon St Paul Mill Hill 72–84; V Stowmarket St E 84–96; RD 90–96; Hon Can St E Cathl 94–96; rtd 96; PtO St E 96–19. 18 Wilkinson Way, Woodbridge IP12 1SS   T: (01394) 380127 E: jeremy@harrold1931.plus.com

HARRON, Canon Gareth Andrew. b 71. QUB BA 92. CITC BTh 95. **d** 95 **p** 96. C Willowfield D & D 95–98; C Dromore Cathl 98–02; I Magheralin w Dollingstown 02–15; I Holywood from 15; Can Dromore Cathl from 12; Can Belf Cathl from 16. The Vicarage, 156 High Street, Holywood BT18 9HT T: (028) 9042 2069 M: 07711-885317 E: garethharron@btinternet.com

HARRON, James Alexander. b 37. GIMechE 61. St Aid Birkenhead 63. **d** 65 **p** 66. C Willowfield D & D 65–69; I Desertmartin D & R 69–80; Dep Sec BCMS (Ireland) 80–84; I Aghalee D & D 84–03; Preb Dromore Cathl 02–03; Chapl HM Pris Maghaberry 86–03; rtd 03. 8 Churchill Avenue, Lurgan, Craigavon BT66 7BW T/F: (028) 3834 6543

HARROP, Mrs Eileen Khean Geok. b 59. Keele Univ BA 83 MA 89 PGCE 83 Wolfs Coll Cam BTh 11. Ridley Hall Cam 08. **d** 12 **p** 13. C Tenterden and Smallhythe Cant 12–16; C Rother and Oxney 13–16; P-in-c Gainford Dur from 16; P-in-c Winston from 16; Pioneer Min from 16. The Vicarage, Low Green, Gainford, Darlington DL2 3DS   T: (01325) 733154 M: 07976-676098 E: ekgharrop@gmail.com

HARROP, Stephen Douglas. b 48. St Jo Coll York CertEd 74 Man Univ DipAdEd 90. Edin Th Coll 77. **d** 79 **p** 82. C Middlesbrough St Martin York 79–80; C Cayton w Eastfield 80–81; C Oldham Man 82–84; V Oldham St Barn 84–89; P-in-c Em Ch Hong Kong 89–93; Ind Chapl and TV Kidderminster St Mary and All SS w Trimpley etc Worc 93–95; Chapl Kidderminster Coll 93–95; Sandwell Chs Link Officer Birm 95–96; Dep Chapl HM Pris Brixton 96–97; Chapl Taichung St Jas Taiwan 97–98; R Lower Merion St Jo USA 98–99; R Essington Lich 99–03; PtO Man 03–04 and 09–13; C Elton St Steph 04–05; P-in-c 05–08; Chapl HM Pris Forest Bank 08–13; P-in-c Petton w Cockshutt, Welshampton and Lyneal etc Lich 13–17; Hon C Adbaston, High Offley, Knightley, Norbury etc 17–18; R Harlaxton Gp Linc 18–20. Address temp unknown M: 07871-987455 E: steph60en@aol.com

HARRY, Bruce David. b 40. JP 77. Culham Coll Ox CertEd 60. NOC 83. **d** 86 **p** 87. NSM Liscard St Thos Ches 86–91; NSM Eastham 91–94; C New Brighton St Jas 94–96; C New Brighton Em 94–96; C New Brighton St Jas w Em 96–98; NSM 98–02; NSM New Brighton All SS 98–02; P-in-c 02–03; PtO 03–19. 21 Sandymount Drive, Wallasey CH45 0LJ T: 0151-639 7232 E: rev_bdh@tiscali.co.uk

HARRY, Usha Praful. b 26. **d** 98 **p** 02. PtO Lon 98–14; NSM Wembley St Jo 14–18; PtO from 18. 157 Ealing Road, Wembley HA0 4BY T: (020) 8903 8873 E: ushaharry157@yahoo.com

HART (formerly **HARRISON**), **Mrs Alison Edwina.** b 53. Newc Univ BEd 75. Linc Th Coll 84. **dss** 86 **d** 87 **p** 94. Loughborough Em Leic 86–89; Par Dn 87–89; C Stockton Dur 89–92; P-in-c Lynesack and Cockfield 92–95; P-in-c Ebchester 95–96; R 96–97; V Medomsley 96–97; V Newc H Cross 97–01; P-in-c Ulgham and Widdrington 01–06; P-in-c Beckermet St Jo and St Bridget w Ponsonby Carl 06–10; rtd 10; PtO Newc 10–20; Mor from 10. 1 Braeval, Carrbridge PH23 3AA E: coolingstreams@yahoo.co.uk

HART, Allen Sydney George. b 38. Chich Th Coll 64. **d** 67 **p** 68. C N Wembley St Cuth Lon 67–71; C W Bromwich All SS Lich 71–74; TV Hucknall Torkard S'well 74–80; V Annesley

Our Lady and All SS 80–86; V Bilborough St Jo 86–99; RD Nottingham W 94–99; P-in-c Clarborough w Hayton 99–03; Asst Chapl HM Pris Ranby 99–03; rtd 03; PtO S'well 03–15. 3 Castleton Close, Hucknall, Nottingham NG15 6TD T: 0115-955 2067 E: a.hart557@ntlworld.com

HART, André Hendrik. b 62. Cape Town Univ BA 86. St Steph Ho Ox 89. **d** 91 **p** 92. C Newbold w Dunston Derby 91–95; P-in-c Clifton and Norbury w Snelston 95–02; Chapl S Derbyshire Community Health Services NHS Trust 95–01; Chapl Derbyshire Mental Health Services NHS Trust 01–02; V Westbury-on-Trym H Trin Bris from 02. Holy Trinity Vicarage, 44 Eastfield Road, Westbury-on-Trym, Bristol BS9 4AG T: 0117-962 1536 or 950 8644

HART, Colin Edwin. b 45. Leeds Univ BA 66 PGCE 67 MPhil 89 Fitzw Coll Cam BA 73 MA 77 K Coll Lon MTh 76 Man Univ PhD 98. Trin Coll Bris 74. **d** 74 **p** 75. C Ware Ch Ch St Alb 74–78; TV Sheff Manor 78–80; V Wombridge Lich 80–87; Lect St Jo Coll Nottm 87–01; Public Preacher S'well 87–01; Hon C Chilwell 87–91; Hon C Trowell 91–01; PtO Ches from 09. 47 Deveraux Drive, Wallasey CH44 4DG T: 0151-630 0749 E: ceh2397@gmail.com

HART, Dagogo. b 50. Birm Bible Inst 77. **d** 82 **p** 83. Nigeria 82–00; C St Cypr Niger Delta 82–88; V 93–96; Chapl to Bp 83–88; Res Min Niger Delta Ch Ch 89–92; Can Res St Steph Cathl Niger Delta 97–00; C W Bromwich St Jas w St Paul Lich 01–06; V 06–15; rtd 15. 43 Ravenscar Road, Surbiton KT6 7PJ M: 07946-761906

HART, David John. b 58. K Coll Lon BD 80. St Mich Coll Llan 83. **d** 85 **p** 86. C Denbigh and Nantglyn St As 85–88; Chapl RAF 88–89; C Llanrhos St As 89–91; V Rhosllannerchrugog 91–01; PtO Lich 11–14 and from 17. Coach House, Brynkinallt, Chirk, Wrexham LL14 5NS E: davidjhart@lineone.net

HART, David Maurice. b 35. Univ Coll Dur BSc 57. Clifton Th Coll 59. **d** 61 **p** 62. C Bolton St Paul Man 61–64; C Hamworthy Sarum 64–70; R W Dean w E Grimstead 70–81; R Farley w Pitton and W Dean w E Grimstead 81–90; V Steeple Ashton w Semington and Keevil 90–03; rtd 03; PtO Sarum from 04. 9 Field Close, Westbury BA13 3AG T: (01373) 827912 E: rotherham1935@gmail.com

HART, Debbie. See HORE, Debbie

HART, Geoffrey Robert. b 49. TISEC 93. **d** 95 **p** 96. P-in-c Edin St Salvador 95–98; C Edin St Cuth 96–98; LtO 98–00; TV Edin St Marg 00–04; NSM Edin St Dav 04–09; P-in-c Edin St Marg 09–12; rtd 12; LtO Edin from 16. 27 Links View, Port Seton, Prestonpans EH32 0EZ T: (01875) 814520 M: 07963-463551

HART, Canon Gillian Mary. b 57. Sheff City Poly BA 79. Carl Dioc Tr Inst 92. **d** 95 **p** 96. C Burgh-by-Sands and Kirkbampton w Kirkandrews etc Carl 95–99; C Aikton 95–99; C Orton St Giles 95–99; Dioc Youth Officer 99–03; Chapl St Martin's Coll Carl 99–03; R Barony of Burgh Carl 03–10; TR Maryport, Netherton and Flimby 10–15; P-in-c Brigham, Gt Broughton and Broughton Moor 14–15; P-in-c Eskdale, Irton, Muncaster and Waberthwaite 15–17; R Black Combe, Drigg, Eskdale etc 17–21; Adv for Women in Min 08–21; Hon Can Carl Cathl 10–21; rtd 21. 21 High Street, Gatehouse of Fleet, Castle Douglas DG7 2HR E: hart.gill@btopenworld.com

HART, Jane Elizabeth. See WARHURST, Jane Elizabeth

HART, Mark. b 61. Chu Coll Cam BA 82 Cam Univ MA 86 PhD 86. Trin Coll Bris BA 98. **d** 98 **p** 99. C Bromborough Ches 98–02; V Plemstall w Guilden Sutton 02–18; RD Ches 09–13; R Nantwich from 18. The Rectory, Church Lane, Nantwich CW5 5RQ T: (01270) 620668 E: markhart61@gmail.com

HART, Canon Michael Anthony. b 50. AKC 71. St Aug Coll Cant 72. **d** 73 **p** 74. C Southwick St Columba Dur 73–76; C Hendon St Alphage Lon 76–78; P-in-c Eltham Park St Luke S'wark 78–83; V 83–85; R Newington St Mary 85–96; P-in-c Camberwell St Mich w All So w Em 85–96; RD S'wark and Newington 93–96; P-in-c Chaldon 96–97; P-in-c Caterham 96–97; TR 98–05; RD 98–05; Hon Can S'wark Cathl 01–05 and 10–15; Can Missr 05–10; TR Catford (Southend) and Downham 10–15; rtd 15; PtO S'wark from 15; Chich from 15. 1 High Beeches, Worthing BN11 4TJ E: m.a.hart@hotmail.co.uk

HART, Preb Michael Stuart. b 39. Univ of Wales (Lamp) BA 61 Lanc Univ MA 72. Wycliffe Hall Ox 61. **d** 63 **p** 64. C W Bromwich St Jas Lich 63–66; C Tarrington w Stoke Edith Heref 66–67; C Putney St Mary S'wark 67–70; V Accrington St Mary Blackb 70–82; RD Accrington 76–82; Hon Can Blackb Cathl 81–91; V Walton-le-Dale 82–91; TR Heavitree w Ex St Paul 91–02; P-in-c Ex St Mary Steps 01–02; TR Heavitree and St Mary Steps 02–07; P-in-c Exwick 05–07; Preb Ex Cathl 02–07; rtd 07; P-in-c Bath H Trin B & W 09–11; PtO 11–13. 23 Conway Crescent, Burnham-on-Sea TA8 2SL T: (01278) 788520 M: 07786-516076 E: m.hart254@btinternet.com

HART, Mrs Mildred Elizabeth. b 49. d 10 p 11. OLM Len Valley *Cant* 10–14; NSM 14–19; rtd 19; PtO *Cant* from 20. *15 Mercer Drive, Harrietsham ME17 1AY* T: (01622) 859753 E: millie.hart@uwclub.net

HART, Mrs Pauline Jayne. b 58. St Mellitus Coll 13. d 15 p 16. NSM Alresford and Frating w Thorrington *Chelmsf* 15–17; NSM Elmstead 16–17; NSM Tenpenny Villages from 17. *8A Manor Road, Wivenhoe, Colchester CO7 9LN* T: (01206) 826318 E: assocpriest@tenpennyvillages.uk

HART, Preb Peter Osborne. b 57. St Jo Coll Nottm. d 92 p 93. C Shipley St Pet *Bradf* 92–97; TV Walsall *Lich* 97–03; TV Cannock 03–09; TV Cannock and Huntington 09–10; V 10–17; V Hatherton 10–17; TV Brereton and Rugeley w Armitage from 17; Preb Lich Cathl from 13. *3 Church Lane, Armitage, Rugeley WS15 4BA*

HART, Peter William. b 60. Liv Univ BA 82 Université de Haute Normandie MèsL 84 Univ of Wales (Swansea) MPhil 92. Sarum & Wells Th Coll 86. d 88 p 89. C Llansamlet *S & B* 88–89; C Sketty 89–92; P-in-c Warndon St Nic *Worc* 92–97; R Berkhamsted St Mary *St Alb* 97–04; V Kew St Phil and All SS w St Luke *S'wark* 04–20; Ecum Adv Kingston Area 05–20; AD Richmond and Barnes 18–20; TR Worc SE from 20. *The Rectory, 6 St Catherine's Hill, Worcester WR5 2EA* T: (01905) 358083 E: pwhart1@aol.com

HART, Robert William. b 76. R Holloway & Bedf New Coll Lon BSc 97 Leeds Univ BA 01 MA 04. Coll of Resurr Mirfield 99. d 02 p 03. C Haydock St Jas *Liv* 02–06; R Hemsworth *Wakef* 06–14; *Leeds* from 14. *The Rectory, 3 Church Close, Hemsworth, Pontefract WF9 4SJ* T: (01977) 610507 E: frrobert@parishofhemsworth.org.uk

HART, Ronald George. b 46. BSc Univ of Wales MA 03 CQSW 77. Sarum & Wells Th Coll. d 85 p 86. C Sittingbourne St Mich *Cant* 85–88; C Walton H Trin *Ox* 88–89; TV 89–96; R Broughton Gifford, Gt Chalfield and Holt *Sarum* 96–05; Chapl UWE *Bris* 05–07; C Mangotsfield 06–07; R Vale of White Hart *Sarum* 07–11; rtd 11; PtO *Sarum* from 11. *Lavenders, 6 Squarey Close, Downton, Salisbury SP5 3LQ* T: (01725) 514772 E: ronhart1@yahoo.co.uk

HART, Mrs Sheila Elizabeth. b 49. ERMC. d 08 p 09. NSM Whinlands *St E* 08–17; NSM Alde Sandlings from 17; RD Saxmundham from 18. *3 Keats Close, Saxmundham IP17 1WJ* T: (01728) 602456 E: sheila.hart49@gmail.com

HART, Mrs Susan Clare. b 67. Ripon Coll Cuddesdon 15. d 17 p 18. C River Were *Sarum* from 17. *8 Rock Lane, Warminster BA12 9JZ*

HART, Prof Trevor Andrew. b 61. St Jo Coll Dur BA 82 Aber Univ PhD 89. d 88 p 88. NSM Bieldside *Ab* 88–95; NSM St Andrews St Andr *St And* 95–13; R from 13; Prof Div St Mary's Coll St Andr Univ from 95; Prin St Mary's Coll 01–06. *The Rectory, Queens Terrace, St Andrews KY16 9QF* M: 07545-322259 E: tah@st-andrews.ac.uk *or* rector.stasstas@gmail.com

HARTE, Matthew Scott. b 46. TCD BA 70 MA 74. CITC 71. d 71 p 72. C Bangor Abbey *D & D* 71–74; C Ballynafeigh St Jude 74–76; I Ardara w Glencolumbkille, Inniskeel etc *D & R* 76–98; I Dunfanaghy, Raymunterdoney and Tullaghbegley 98–13; adn Raphoe 83–13; Preb Howth St Patr Cathl Dublin 07–13; rtd 13. *Largymore, Kilcar, Co Donegal, Republic of Ireland* T: (00353) (74) 973 8434 M: 87-756 5081 E: msharte1@eircom.net

HARTER, Andrew Michael Hatfeild. b 44. K Coll Cam BA 66 MA 69. Ripon Coll Cuddesdon 12. d 13 p 14. NSM Grosmont and Skenfrith and Llangattock etc *Mon* 13–16; PtO from 16; *Heref* from 17. *Ferry Bank, Breinton, Hereford HR4 7PR* T: (01432) 356320 E: andrew@harter.co.uk

HARTERINK, Mrs Joy Frances. b 49. Essex Univ BA 71 Hughes Hall Cam CertEd 72 Lon Univ MSc 87. Oak Hill NSM Course 89. d 92 p 94. NSM Richmond H Trin and Ch Ch *S'wark* 92–05; Chapl Richmond Coll 97–01; PtO *Guildf* 05–15; *Chich* from 16. *8 Portland Close, Littlehampton BN17 6SJ* E: joyharterink@yahoo.com

HARTIGAN, Eileen. b 53. SNWTP 15. d 17 p 18. OLM Walkden and Lt Hulton *Man* from 17. *8 Silverdale Avenue, Little Hulton, Manchester M38 9QJ*

HARTLAND, Ian Charles. b 49. K Coll Lon BD 72 MTh 76 AKC 72 Lon Inst of Educn PGCE 73. Sarum & Wells Th Coll 83. d 84 p 85. C Orpington All SS *Roch* 84–87; Sen Lect Ch Ch Coll Cant 87–95; Adv RE Kent Coun 96–03; HMI of Schs 03–07; PtO *Heref* from 17. *Dormington House, Dormington, Hereford HR1 4ES* T: (01432) 851465 E: ian.c.hartland@hotmail.co.uk

HARTLAND (née CLARKE), Mrs Rachel Frances. b 69. Univ of Wales (Abth) BSc 90. Ox Min Course 12. d 14 p 15. NSM Old Basing and Lychpit *Win* 14–18; NSM Darby Green and Eversley from 18. *Ramtops, 26 Cornfields, Yateley GU46 6YT* E: ramtopsrac@yahoo.co.uk

HARTLESS, Berengaria Isabella de la Tour. b 52. Univ of Wales (Cardiff) BSc 74 Goldsmiths' Coll Lon PGCE 76 Liv Univ MA 03 K Coll Lon DThMin 15. Ox Min Course 90. d 93 p 94. Par Dn High Wycombe *Ox* 93–94; C 94–97; P-in-c Seer Green and Jordans 97–00; OLM Tr Officer (Bucks) 97–00; Dioc Prin of OLM 00–18; Dir of IME (2) from 11; PtO *Cov* 10–18; Hon C Edgehill Churches from 18. *Lloyd's House, Banbury Street, Kineton, Warwick CV35 0JS* T: (01926) 642975 E: beren.hartless@btinternet.com

HARTLEY, Mrs Anne Theresa. b 52. St Cuth Soc Dur BSc 74 Worc Coll of Educn PGCE 75. d 03 p 04. OLM Wychwood *Ox* 03–17; PtO from 17. *The Old House, Upper Milton, Milton-under-Wychwood, Chipping Norton OX7 6EX* T: (01993) 830160 M: 07976-025101 E: anne@thartley.net *or* anne@wychwoodbenefice.org.uk

HARTLEY, Brian. b 41. NOC 82. d 85 p 86. NSM Royton St Paul *Man* 85–91; NSM Oldham St Steph and All Martyrs 91–94; TV E Farnworth and Kearsley 94–97; TR New Bury 97–06; P-in-c Gt Lever 03–06; AD Farnworth 98–05; rtd 06; PtO *Man* from 06. *21 Penryn Avenue, Royton, Oldham OL2 6JR* T: (01706) 849132 E: brian_hartley@tiscali.co.uk

HARTLEY, Christopher Neville. b 56. Hull Univ BA 82 SS Paul & Mary Coll Cheltenham PGCE 84. SNWTP 08. d 10 p 11. OLM Man Victoria Park from 10. *8 Bronte Street, Manchester M15 6QL* T: 0161-232 0644 M: 07783-932386 E: christopherhartley@ymail.com

HARTLEY, Daniel George. b 73. Leeds Univ BA 95. Coll of Resurr Mirfield 96. d 99 p 00. C Richmond w Hudswell *Ripon* 99–03; Chapl HM YOI Deerbolt 03–10; V Ecclesfield *Sheff* 11–15; P-in-c Thurlestone, S Milton, W Alvington etc *Ex* 15; R Thurlestone, S Milton, Churchstow etc from 15. *The Rectory, Thurlestone, Kingsbridge TQ7 3LF*

HARTLEY, Denis. b 54. NTMTC BA 07. d 07 p 15. NSM Wood Green St Mich w Bounds Green St Gabr etc *Lon* 07–12; Chapl HM Pris Thameside 12–16; NSM Thamesmead *S'wark* 15–16; PtO *Cant* 16–17; C Margate All SS 17–20; PtO from 20. *23A Palm Bay Avenue, Margate CT9 3DQ* M: 07957-227764 E: fr-denis@outlook.com

HARTLEY, Dianna Lynn. *See* GWILLIAMS, Dianna Lynn

✠HARTLEY, The Rt Revd Helen-Ann Macleod. b 73. St Andr Univ MTheol 95 Princeton Th Sem ThM 96 Worc Coll Ox MPhil 00 DPhil 05. SAOMC 03. d 05 p 06 c 14. C Wheatley *Ox* 05–07; C Littlemore 07–12; Lect Ripon Coll Cuddesdon 05–12; Tutor 09–12; Tutor St Jo Coll Auckland NZ 12–14; Bp Waikato 14–17; Suff Bp Ripon *Leeds* from 18. *Redwood, New Road, Sharow, Ripon HG4 5BS* M: 07568-536408 E: bishop.helenann@leeds.anglican.org

HARTLEY, John Peter. b 56. Cam Univ BA 78 Leeds Univ PhD 82 Dur Univ BA 84. Cranmer Hall Dur 82. d 85 p 86. C Spring Grove St Mary *Lon* 85–88; C Bexleyheath St Pet *Roch* 88–91; P-in-c Hanford *Lich* 91–00; Faith in the City Officer (Potteries) 91–00; V Eccleshill *Bradf* 00–14; *Leeds* from 14. *The Vicarage, 2 Fagley Lane, Bradford BD2 3NS* T: (01274) 636403 M: 07811-915320 E: john.hartley@leeds.anglican.org

HARTLEY, Canon John William. b 47. St Jo Coll Dur BA 69. Linc Th Coll 70. d 72 p 73. C Poulton-le-Fylde *Blackb* 72–76; C Lancaster St Mary 76–79; V Barrowford 79–87; V Salesbury 87–11; AD Whalley 01–11; Hon Can Blackb Cathl 09–11; rtd 11; PtO *Blackb* from 11. *14 Beech Mount, Ramsgreave, Blackburn BB1 9BP* T: (01254) 243700 E: john.hartley828@btinternet.com

HARTLEY, Julian John. b 57. Oak Hill Th Coll BA 85. d 85 p 86. C Eccleston Ch Ch *Liv* 85–89; V Goose Green 89–00; P-in-c Mosley Common *Man* 00–06; TV Astley, Tyldesley and Mosley Common 06–19; AD Leigh 15–19; V Astley Bridge from 19; AD Walmsley 19–21. *St Paul's Vicarage, Sweetloves Lane, Bolton BL1 7ET* T: (01204) 308410 M: 07378-936969 E: rev.hartley@hartley.me.uk

HARTLEY, Kate. d 20. Chapl HM Pris Bronzefield from 20. *HM Prison Bronzefield, Woodthorpe Road, Ashford TW15 3JL* T: (01784) 425690 E: kate.hartley@sodexogov.co.uk

HARTLEY, Martin John Edward. b 67. Ridley Hall Cam 11. d 13 p 14. C Newton Flotman, Swainsthorpe, Tasburgh, etc *Nor* 13–17; V Mile Cross from 17. *St Catherine's Vicarage, Aylsham Road, Norwich NR3 2RJ* M: 07876-643560 E: mjehartley@gmail.com

HARTLEY, Melanie Zoe. b 79. Sheff Univ BA 01 Open Univ PGCE 06 Dur Univ MA 21. Cliff Th Coll MA 08 St Hild Coll 19. d 21. NSM Baslow and Eyam *Derby* from 21. *Lindum, Cliff Lane, Calver, Hope Valley S32 3WD* M: 07428-017084 E: rev.mel.hartley@gmail.com

HARTLEY, Canon Michael Leslie. b 56. Leeds Univ BSc 77. Ripon Coll Cuddesdon 87. d 89 p 90. C Standish *Blackb* 89–93; V Bamber Bridge St Aid 93–98; TR Colne and Villages

98–08; P-in-c Warton St Paul 08–16; P-in-c Freckleton 16; V Freckleton and Warton St Paul 17; Dioc Ecum Officer 08–17; Hon Can Blackb Cathl 15–17; rtd 17; PtO *Blackb* from 17. *31 Southdown Drive, Thornton-Cleveleys FY5 5BL* T: (01253) 975435 E: canonmichaelhartley@gmail.com

HARTLEY, Canon Nigel John. b 48. Portsm Poly BA. St Jo Coll Nottm. **d** 83 **p** 84. C Ipswich St Marg *St E* 83–86; P-in-c Hintlesham w Chattisham 86–95; Dioc Radio Officer 86–95; P-in-c Gt Finborough w Onehouse, Harleston, Buxhall etc 95–04; RD Stowmarket 96–99; V Aldeburgh w Hazlewood 04–14; RD Saxmundham 05–12; Hon Can St E Cathl 10–14; rtd 14; PtO *St E* 14–18; *Chich* from 14. *Sheppens, Newham Lane, Steyning BN44 3LR* E: nigel.hartley2@btinternet.com

HARTLEY, Paul. b 51. Nottm Univ BTh 88. Linc Th Coll 85. **d** 88 **p** 89. C Clitheroe St Mary *Blackb* 88–91; TV Guiseley w Esholt *Bradf* 91–97; R Ackworth *Wakef* 97–14; *Leeds* 14–17; rtd 17. *27 Upper Carr Lane, Calverley, Pudsey LS28 5PL* E: rev.paulhartley@yahoo.co.uk

HARTLEY, Canon Peter. b 44. St Cath Coll Cam BA 66 MA 69 Avery Hill Coll PGCE 67. Sarum & Wells Th Coll 77. **d** 78 **p** 79. Hon C Freemantle *Win* 78–79; Chr Educn Officer *Pet* 79–81; Dir of Educn 81–90; Dir Coun of Educn and Tr *Chelmsf* 90–09; Hon Can Chelmsf Cathl 92–09; rtd 09; PtO *Nor* from 04. *3 St Mary's Lane, Langham, Holt NR25 7AF* T: (01328) 830624 E: peter.hartley49@btinternet.com

HARTLEY, Peter Mellodew. b 41. Qu Coll Cam BA 63 MA 66 Lon Univ MSc 71 FICE. S'wark Ord Course 80. **d** 83 **p** 84. NSM Salfords *S'wark* 83–97; Chapl Surrey and Sussex Healthcare NHS Trust 97–02; rtd 02; PtO *Chich* from 00; *S'wark* from 02; *Eur* from 05; *Lon* from 14. *Old Timbers, North Lane, West Hoathly, East Grinstead RH19 4QF* T: (01342) 811238 E: petermhartley@btinternet.com

HARTLEY, Sarah Elizabeth. *See* ARCHER, Sarah Elizabeth

HARTLEY, Stephen William Mark. b 50. St Chad's Coll Dur BA 71. Westcott Ho Cam 72. **d** 74 **p** 75. C Holbrooks *Cov* 74–76; C Styvechale 76–79; P-in-c Snitterfield w Bearley 79–81; V 81–83; V Exhall 83–88; V Tilehurst St Cath *Ox* 88–95; TR Cowley St Jas 95–06; TR Hermitage 06–08; TR Cov E 08–15; rtd 15. *25 Manor Park, Longlevens, Gloucester GL2 0HG* M: 07794-484195 E: stephen.hartley@btinternet.com

HARTLEY, Stewart John Ridley. b 47. St Jo Coll Nottm 78. **d** 80 **p** 81. C Altham w Clayton le Moors *Blackb* 80–84; P-in-c Nelson St Phil 84–91; V 91–98; V Gt Marsden w Nelson St Phil 99–03; Hon Can Blackb Cathl 99–03; V Bermondsey St Anne and St Aug *S'wark* 03–12; V Bermondsey St Jas w Ch Ch and St Crispin 03–12; rtd 12; PtO *Leeds* from 17. *8 Weston Park Lane, Otley LS21 2DU* T: (01943) 464106 E: sr.hartley47@gmail.com

HARTLEY, Susan Mary. b 49. Newc Univ MB, BS 73 MRCGP 77. SEITE 99. **d** 02 **p** 03. NSM Spitalfields Ch Ch w All SS *Lon* 02–07; NSM Hainault *Chelmsf* 07–16; Asst Chapl St Joseph's Hospice Hackney 06; PtO *Chelmsf* 16–20; Chapl Barking, Havering and Redbridge Hosps NHS Trust from 17. *272 New North Road, Ilford IG6 3BT* T: (020) 8500 4592 M: 07741-468576 E: suemhartley@btinternet.com

HARTMAN, Mrs Jill Norma. b 57. Cen Sch of Art Lon BA 80. SEITE 08. **d** 11 **p** 16. NSM Upper St Leonards St Jo *Chich* from 11. *21 Nelson Road, Hastings TN34 3RX* T: (01424) 716126 M: 07952-950316 E: jillhartman39@gmail.com

HARTNELL, Canon Bruce John. b 42. Ex Univ BA 64 Linacre Coll Ox BA 66 MA. Ripon Hall Ox 64. **d** 66 **p** 67. C S Stoneham *Win* 66–69; Chapl and Tutor Ripon Hall Ox 69–74; V Knowl Hill w Littlewick *Ox* 74–78; Chapl Southn Univ *Win* 78–83; V Sholing 83–07; add Southampton 93–01; Hon Can Win Cathl 93–07; rtd 07; PtO *Win* from 07. *9 Ash Close, Southampton SO19 5SD* T: (023) 8090 5420 E: bruce.j.hartnell@gmail.com

HARTNELL, Graham Philip. b 50. **d** 08 **p** 08. NSM Flackwell Heath *Ox* 08–15; PtO *Lich* from 15. *93 Planks Lane, Wombourne, Wolverhampton WV5 8DX* T: (01902) 593086 E: g.hartnell@icloud.com

HARTOPP, Mrs Penelope Faye. b 55. Ripon Coll Cuddesdon. **d** 03 **p** 04. C Studley *Cov* 03–04; C Cov E 04–07; TV Godalming *Guildf* 07–11; V Over St Chad *Ches* 11–15; C Budleigh Salterton, E Budleigh w Bicton etc *Ex* 15–19; Chapl HM Pris Channings Wood from 19. *HM Prison Channings Wood, Denbury, Newton Abbot TQ12 6DW* T: (01803) 814647 M: 07884-314752 E: penniehartopp@googlemail.com

HARTREE, Steven John. b 45. FFA 78. WEMTC 96. **d** 99 **p** 00. NSM Highbridge *B & W* 99–03; P-in-c Tintinhull w Chilthorne Domer, Yeovil Marsh etc 03–09; rtd 09; PtO *B & W* from 10. *Chestnuts, Chestnut Lane, Bleadon, Weston-super-Mare BS24 0QD* T: (01934) 811849 M: 07899-660422 E: stevenhartree194@btinternet.com

HARTROPP, Andrew James. b 59. Southn Univ BSc 80 PhD 85 K Coll Lon PhD 03. Oak Hill Th Coll BA 95. **d** 98 **p** 99. C Watford *St Alb* 98–01; C Watford Ch Ch 01–08; Teacher Henrietta Barnett Sch 01–06; NSM White Waltham w Shottesbrooke and Waltham St Lawrence *Ox* 08–12; Research Tutor Ox Cen for Miss Studies 12–16; PtO *Ox* 12–20; R Ibstock w Heather *Leic* from 20. *The Rectory, 2 Hinckley Road, Ibstock LE67 6PB* E: a.hartropp@btinternet.com

HARTSHORNE, Kim. *See* BROWN, Kim

HARTWELL, Mrs Jeanette May. b 65. Aston Univ BSc 88. Qu Coll Birm BA 07. **d** 07 **p** 08. C Brereton and Rugeley *Lich* 07–10; TV Smestow Vale 10–16; Dir Reader Tr from 16; Tutor Qu Coll Birm from 16. *The Vicarage, School Road, Trysull, Wolverhampton WV5 7HR* T: (01902) 896650

HARVEY, Anne. *See* HARVEY, Ruth Anne

HARVEY, Brian. b 51. Hatf Poly BA 74. St As Minl Tr Course 02. **d** 05 **p** 06. NSM Cilcain and Nannerch and Rhydymwyn *St As* 05–09; P-in-c 06–09; R Flint 09–16; P-in-c Bagillt 13–16; TV Estuary and Mountain Miss Area from 17. *The Rectory, Allt Goch, Flint CH6 5NF* T: (01352) 733274 E: brianharvey@mac.com

HARVEY, The Ven Cyril John. b 30. Univ of Wales (Lamp) BA 51. Coll of Resurr Mirfield 51. **d** 53 **p** 54. C Caerau w Ely *Llan* 53–57; C Milford Haven *St D* 57–61; V Castlemartin and Warren 61–65; R Begelly w Ludchurch and Crunwere 65–73; V Haverfordwest St Martin w Lambston 73–88; Can St D Cathl from 85; R Tenby 88–96; Adn St D 91–96; rtd 96; PtO *St D* from 05. *5 Paxton Court, White Lion Street, Tenby SA70 7ET* T: (01834) 845747 E: johnofwales@hotmail.co.uk

HARVEY, Desmond Victor Ross. b 37. QUB BA 59. Princeton Th Sem ThM 63 Fuller Th Sem California DMin 93 St Mich Coll Llan 95. **d** 95 **p** 96. Presbyterian Min 65–95; C Cwmbran *Mon* 95–97; TV 97; PtO from 97; OCM from 98. *Mallory, Llanmaes, Llantwit Major CF61 2XR* T/F: (01446) 792753 E: mallory06@talktalk.net

HARVEY, James. *See* HARVEY, Thomas James

HARVEY, John Christopher. b 65. Univ of Wales (Lamp) BA 86 Nottm Univ BTh 89. Linc Th Coll 86. **d** 89 **p** 90. C Dwygyfylchi *Ban* 89–93; V Llangrannog w Llandysiliogogo w Penbryn *St D* 93–02; RD Glyn Aeron 99–02; P-in-c Llangystennin *St As* 02–04; R 04–09; V Meliden and Gwaenysgor 09–17; P-in-c Bryn a Mor Miss Area from 18; Dioc Voc Adv from 08. *The Vicarage, Ffordd Penrhwylfa, Prestatyn LL19 8HN* T: (01745) 856220

HARVEY, Lt Col John William Arthur. b 43. Guildf Dioc Min Course 98. **d** 01 **p** 02. OLM Aldershot St Aug *Guildf* 01–13; PtO from 13. *59 Knoll Road, Fleet GU51 4PT* T: (01252) 622793 E: father.john@talktalk.net

HARVEY, Jonathan Bromley. b 72. BSc BA PGCE. St Mellitus Coll. **d** 14 **p** 15. C Eastleigh *Win* 14–18; C N Stoneham and Bassett from 18. *45 Stevens Road, Eastleigh SO50 9RH* M: 07515-287108

HARVEY, Lincoln. Univ of Wales (Swansea) BA 92 K Coll Lon MA 01 PhD 08. **d** 09 **p** 10. NSM St John-at-Hackney *Lon* 09–12; NSM Fulham St Andr 12–16; LtO 16–21; Tutor SEITE 06–10; Tutor St Mellitus Coll *Lon* 10–14; Asst Dean 14–20; Tutor 20–21; V St Marylebone Annunciation Bryanston Street from 21. *Church of the Annunciation, Bryanston Street, London W1H 7AH* T: (020) 7723 6434 E: lincoln.harvey@gmail.com

HARVEY, Margaret Claire. b 41. Univ of Wales (Abth) BA 62 DipEd 63 Lon Univ BD 68 Univ of Wales (Trin St Dav) MA 13. Dalton Ho Bris 66. **dss** 68 **d** 80 **p** 97. Flint *St As* 68–74; Lect Trin Coll Bris 74–80; Connah's Quay *St As* 79–80; C 80–86; Bp's Adv for Continuing Clerical Educn 86–98; Hon C Corwen and Llangar 86–87; Dn-in-c Bryneglwys 87–97; P-in-c 97–02; rtd 02; PtO *St As* from 09. *7 Llys Trewithan, St Asaph LL17 0DJ* T: (01745) 583535 E: rev.maggie@outlook.com

✠**HARVEY, The Rt Revd Murray Alexander.** b 63. Univ of Qld BA 85 Deakin Univ Australia DHSc 03 MAPsS 87. St Fran Coll Brisbane BTh 91. **d** 91 **p** 92 **c** 18. C Milton Australia 92–93; C Stafford 94–95; P-in-c Tamborine Mt St Geo 95–02; V Glen Gp *Linc* 02–11; R Clayfield Australia 11–18; Can Res Brisbane 14–18; Bp Grafton from 18. *Bishopsholme, 35 Victoria Street, Grafton NSW 2460, Australia* T: (0061) (2) 6642 4122 E: bishop@graftondiocese.org.au

HARVEY, Nicola Joan. b 70. Liv Jo Moores Univ BEd 93. St Aug Coll of Th 14. **d** 17 **p** 18. C Hadlow *Roch* 17–20; V Marden *Cant* from 20. *The Vicarage, High Street, Marden, Tonbridge TN12 9DR* T: (01622) 831379 M: 07919-075470 E: rev.nickyharvey@gmail.com

HARVEY, Canon Norman Roy. b 43. Nottm Univ DipAE 86. Wycliffe Hall Ox 66. **d** 69 **p** 70. C Clay Cross *Derby* 69–72; C Dronfield 72–76; TV 76–79; P-in-c Rowsley 79–89; Dioc Youth Officer 79–83; Dioc Adv in Adult and Youth Educn 83–89; TR Eckington w Handley and Ridgeway 89–01; R

Eckington and Ridgeway 01–08; RD Bolsover and Staveley 00–05; Hon Can Derby Cathl 00–08; rtd 08; PtO *Derby* 08–13; *Sheff* 09–11. *62 Parklands View, Aston, Sheffield S26 2GW* T: 0114-287 2243 E: norman.harvey3@gmail.com

HARVEY, Oliver Paul. b 33. Magd Coll Ox BA 55 MA 59. Cuddesdon Coll 57. d 59 p 60. C S Norwood St Mark *Cant* 59–61; C Hythe 61–64; Zambia 64–71; Chapl Cant Coll of Tech 71–77; Hon C Cant St Martin and St Paul 73–77; Chapl K Sch Roch 77–88; C Roch St Pet w St Marg 88–90; V Gillingham St Mary 90–00; RD Gillingham 98–00; rtd 00; PtO *Roch* 00–03; *B & W* 05–20. *11 Henley Road, Taunton TA1 5BN* T: (01823) 272825

HARVEY, Miss Pamela Betty. b 33. Dalton Ho Bris IDC 59. dss 68 d 87 p 95. Nottingham St Ann *S'well* 68–72; Bestwood St Matt 72–76; CPAS Staff 76–93; Dir Consultants Division CPAS 93–99; rtd 99; Hon C Glenfield *Leic* 95–04; PtO 04–21. *72 Chestnut Road, Glenfield, Leicester LE3 8DB* T: 0116-232 2959 E: pamela.harvey@mypostoffice.co.uk

HARVEY, Canon Patrick Arnold. b 58. TCD MA. CITC 82. d 85 p 86. C Bandon Union *C, C & R* 85–88; Dean's V Limerick St Mich *L & K* 88–91; Dioc Info Officer 88–91; I Abbeyleix w Ballyroan etc *C, F & O* from 91; Can Ossory Cathl from 97; Chan from 11; Chan Leighlin Cathl *C, F & O* from 10; Can St Patr Cathl Dublin from 13; Can Ferns Cathl *C, F & O* from 14. *The Rectory, Abbeyleix, Portlaoise, Co Laois, R32 C6N1, Republic of Ireland* T/F: (00353) (57) 873 1243 E: patrickharveyone@gmail.com

HARVEY, Paul. *See* HARVEY, Oliver Paul

HARVEY, Peter Eric. b 76. Oak Hill Th Coll 16. d 19 p 19. NSM Wellfield Propr Chpl *Blackb* from 19.

HARVEY, Philip Ian. b 61. Macquarie Univ (NSW) BA 85 DipEd 85 New England Univ NSW MA 94. Cam Th Federation 14. d 17 p 18. C Sprowston w Beeston *Nor* 17–21; C New Catton Ch Ch 19–21; V Weobley w Sarnesfield and Norton Canon *Heref* from 21; R Letton w Staunton, Byford, Mansel Gamage etc from 21. *The Vicarage, Church Road, Weobley, Hereford HR4 8SD* T: (01544) 318147 E: rector@weobleyandstaunton.co.uk

HARVEY, Robert Martin. b 30. S'wark Ord Course 69. d 70 p 71. C Sutton New Town St Barn *S'wark* 70–75; C Leatherhead *Guildf* 76–78; V Wadworth w Loversall *Sheff* 78–96; RD W Doncaster 94–97; rtd 96; PtO *Sheff* 96–13. *58 Thomson Avenue, Doncaster DN4 0NU* T: (01302) 857599

HARVEY, Robin Grant. b 43. Clare Coll Cam BA 64 MA 68 Univ of NSW PhD 74. Linc Th Coll 85. d 87 p 88. C Keynsham *B & W* 87–91; R E w W Harptree and Hinton Blewett 91–97; Chapl Surrey Univ *Guildf* 98–02; P-in-c Cuddington 02–07; V 07–08; rtd 08; PtO *B & W* 09–19. *21 St Cadoc House, Temple Street, Keynsham, Bristol BS31 1HD* T: 0117-986 2295 E: rgharvey.194@btinternet.com

HARVEY, Canon Roland. b 68. St Jo Coll Nottm 99. d 01 p 02. C Skelmersdale St Paul *Liv* 01–05; P-in-c Pemberton St Fran Kitt Green 05–12; P-in-c Garston 12–14; V 14–19; AD Liv South-Childwall 14–19; TR S Widnes 19–21; R from 21; AD Widnes from 19; Hon Can Liv Cathl from 14. *St Mary's Vicarage, Vicarage Close, Hale Village, Liverpool L24 4BH* T: 0151-352 2049 M: 07884-972199 E: rolandharvey68@gmail.com

HARVEY, Ruth Anne. b 59. Leic Univ MB, ChB 83 Open Univ BA 02. St Mellitus Coll BA 12. d 13 p 14. NSM Broomfield *Chelmsf* 13–20; PtO from 20. *1 Beveridge Links, Dunbar EH42 1ZU* E: rev.anneharvey@gmail.com

HARVEY, Simon John. b 63. Trin Coll Bris BA 00. d 00 p 01. C Walsall St Paul *Lich* 00–03; TV Oadby *Leic* 03–10; Warden of Readers 05–10; V Islington St Mary *Lon* 10–19; V Bury St Edmunds St Mary *St E* from 19. *11 Sicklesmere Road, Bury St Edmunds IP33 2BN* M: 07376-060101 E: simon.harvey@sjharvey.org.uk

HARVEY, Canon Steven Charles. b 58. Reading Univ BA 79 Cam Univ PGCE 80 Ox Univ BA 83 MA 88. Ripon Coll Cuddesdon 81. d 84 p 85. C Oldham *Man* 84–87; Chapl and Hd RS St Pet Sch York 87–96; Sen Dep Hd Kingswood Sch Bath 96–03; Educn Officer and Sen Provost Woodard Corp 03–06; PtO *B & W* 96–03; *Lich* 03–06; Hd Master Bury Gr Sch 06–13; PtO *Blackb* 06–13; *Man* 06–13; Can Res Newc Cathl 13–19; rtd 19; PtO *Newc* from 19; *York* from 19. *32 Ascot Close, Northallerton DL7 8BF* T: (01609) 761017 E: harveysteven@btinternet.com

HARVEY, Mrs Susan Esther. b 44. d 11 p 12. OLM Sherston Magna, Easton Grey, Luckington etc *Bris* 11–16; OLM Hullavington, Norton and Stanton St Quintin 15–16; OLM Gauzebrook from 16. *55 The Tarters, Sherston, Malmesbury SN16 0NT* T: (01666) 840696

HARVEY, Thomas James. b 71. Nottm Univ BA 92 Leic Univ MA 96 DipSW 96. Cranmer Hall Dur 09. d 11 p 12. C Cramlington *Newc* 11–14; P-in-c Felton 14–21; P-in-c Longframlington w Brinkburn 14–21;

P-in-c Darlington St Cuth *Dur* from 21; P-in-c Darlington H Trin from 21. *26 Upsall Drive, Darlington DL3 8RB* M: 07722-405253 E: james.harvey@live.com

HARVEY, Tracey Louise. *See* CASWELL, Tracey Louise

HARVEY, Mrs Verity Margaret. b 48. Bris Univ BA 69 Saltley Tr Coll Birm DipEd 70. SAOMC 99. d 02 p 03. NSM Radlett *St Alb* 02–05; NSM Bushey 05–11; Chapl Herts Partnership Univ NHS Foundn Trust from 10; PtO *St Alb* from 12. *28 Field Road, Watford WD19 4DR* T: (01923) 492863 E: verity.harvey@yahoo.co.uk

HARVEY, Wendy Marion. b 46. SEITE 06. d 09 p 10. NSM Hurst Green *S'wark* 09–14; NSM Limpsfield and Tatsfield 14–16 and 18–19; Chapl HM Pris Downview 11–17; Chapl HM Pris High Down from 17; PtO *Lon* 14–20; *Guildf* from 16; *S'wark* 16–18. *HM Prison High Down, Highdown Lane, Sutton SM2 5PJ* T: (020) 7147 6300 M: 07973-428683 E: wendyharvey@talktalk.net

HARVIE, Robert. b 53. d 04 p 05. OLM Godalming *Guildf* 04–19; rtd 19. *4 Bargate Court, Godalming GU7 2NA* T: (01483) 414378 E: robert.harvie@btinternet.com

HARWOOD, Ann Jane. *See* CLARKE, Ann Jane

HARWOOD (formerly SOUTH), Mrs Gillian. b 51. NEOC 87. d 90 p 94. C Rothbury *Newc* 90–93; C Morpeth 93–97; V Amble 97–06; Chapl Northumbria Healthcare NHS Foundn Trust 06–15; rtd 15; PtO *Newc* from 15. *7 Hedgerow Mews, Fallowfield, Ashington NE63 8LH* T: (01670) 810478 E: gillian.harwood@sky.com

HARWOOD, Canon John Rossiter. b 26. Selw Coll Cam BA 51 MA 55. Wycliffe Hall Ox 51. d 53 p 54. C Handsworth St Mary *Birm* 53–55; Tutor Trin Coll Umuahia Nigeria 57–64; Warden Minl Tr Cen Freetown Sierra Leone and Bp's Dom Chapl 64–67; Home Educn Sec CMS 67–75; V Cheltenham Ch Ch *Glouc* 75–91; RD Cheltenham 84–89; Hon Can Glouc Cathl 85–91; rtd 91; PtO *Ex* 91–99; *Chich* 00–18; *Portsm* from 00. *14 Nile Street, Emsworth PO10 7EE* T: (01243) 372215

HARWOOD, Mary Ann. b 46. Cam Inst of Educn CertEd 68. Ox Min Course 04. d 07 p 08. NSM Burghfield *Ox* 07–10; NSM W Downland 10–18; rtd 18; PtO *Ox* from 18. *10 Brook View, South Street, Letcombe Regis, Wantage OX12 9RG* M: 07721-437316 E: maryharwood695@btinternet.com

HARWOOD, Peter James. b 64. Birm Univ MB 88 ChB 88 K Coll Lon MA 02. Wycliffe Hall Ox BA 93 MA 98. d 94 p 95. C Cov H Trin 94–97; C Kensington St Barn *Lon* 97–02; V Woking Ch Ch *Guildf* 02–19; Chapl Woking Hospice 02–19; AD Woking *Guildf* 16–19; Dioc Dir of Miss from 19. *Church House, 20 Alan Turing Road, Surrey Research Park, Guildford GU2 7YF* T: (01483) 790300 E: peter.harwood@cofeguildford.org.uk

HARWOOD, William Francis. b 78. Pemb Coll Ox MA 00 Keble Coll Ox MSt 19 New Coll Ox PGCE 05. Wycliffe Hall Ox BA 18. d 19 p 20. C Kea *Truro* from 19. *169 Treffry Road, Truro TR1 1UF* M: 07823-886788 E: will_harwood@me.com

HASELHURST (née STERLING), Mrs Anne. b 51. Macalester Coll (USA) BA 73. EAMTC 89. d 92 p 94. Par Dn Bury St Edmunds St Jo *St E* 92–94; C 94–95; V Fordham St Pet *Ely* 95–06; P-in-c Kennett 95–06; P-in-c Isleham 05–06; R Cupar *St And* 06–15; R Ladybank 06–15; rtd 15; PtO *St And* from 17. *7 Newmill Gardens, St Andrews KY16 8RY* T: (01334) 209068 E: annehaselhurst@talktalk.net

HASELOCK, Canon Jeremy Matthew. b 51. York Univ BA 73 BPhil 74. St Steph Ho Ox BA 82 MA 86. d 83 p 84. C Pimlico St Gabr *Lon* 83–86; C Paddington St Jas 86–88; Bp's Dom Chapl *Chich* 88–91; P-in-c Boxgrove 91–94; V 94–98; Dioc Adv on Liturgy 91–98; Can and Preb Chich Cathl 94–98; Can Res and Prec Nor Cathl 98–17; rtd 17; Chapl to The Queen from 13; PtO *Lon* from 17. *3 The Terrace, Old Ford Road, London E2 9PH* T: (020) 8980 6087

HASKETT, Mrs Fiona Ann. b 55. SEITE 01. d 04 p 05. NSM Leigh *Roch* 04–09; V Whittington w Weeford *Lich* 09–15; V Hints 09–15; V Headcorn and The Suttons *Cant* from 15. *The Vicarage, 64 Oak Lane, Headcorn, Ashford TN27 9TU* E: fiona.haskett@btopenworld.com

HASKETT, Stephen Ian. b 78. Cranmer Hall Dur. d 13 p 14. C Anchorsholme *Blackb* 13–17; V Blackpool St Jo 17–20; PtO from 20. *2 Hesketh Avenue, Bispham, Blackpool FY2 9JX* M: 07890-248917 E: stevehaskett78@gmail.com

HASKINS, Thomas. b 41. TCD BA 72. CITC 71. d 73 p 74. C Larne and Inver *Conn* 73–78; C Antrim All SS 78–83; I Belfast St Mark 83–90; I Dublin Clontarf *D & G* 90–02; I Dublin St Ann and St Steph 02–08; Can Ch Ch Cathl Dublin 99–08; rtd 08. *7 Gorse Haven, Coolboy, Tinahely, Co Wicklow, Republic of Ireland* T: (00353) (402) 34997 E: tomhaskins2@gmail.com

HASLAM, Andrew James. b 57. Univ Coll Dur BSc 78 Coll of Ripon & York St Jo PGCE 79 Lambeth STh 84. Trin Coll Bris 80. d 83 p 84. C Leyland St Andr *Blackb* 83–86; C

Hartford *Ches* 86–88; V Grimsargh *Blackb* 88–98; V St Helens St Mark *Liv* 98–05; V Birkenhead Ch Ch *Ches* 05–13; PtO from 13. *2 Millview Drive, Wirral CH63 8PL* T: 0151-792 6201 E: andrew.haslam@live.co.uk

HASLAM, John Gordon. b 32. Birm Univ LLB 53. Qu Coll Birm 75. d 77 p 77. Hon C Bartley Green *Birm* 77–79; Hon C Moseley St Mary 79–96; Chapl to The Queen 89–02; PtO *Heref* 97–18. *16 Mill Street, Ludlow SY8 1BE* T/F: (01584) 876663

HASLAM, Michael Henry. b 72. Buckingham Univ BA 93. Trin Coll Bris BA 94 MA 94. d 97 p 98. C Minehead *B & W* 97–00; Chapl Newc Univ 00–04; C Purton and Dioc Ecum Officer *Bris* 04–06; P-in-c N Swindon St Andr 06–09; NSM Alfred Jewel *B & W* from 10; Chapl Taunton Academy 11–17; Chapl Richard Huish Coll Taunton 16–17; Chapl Development Adv *B & W* from 17. *The New Rectory, Cliff Road, North Petherton, Bridgwater TA6 6NY* T: (01278) 662429 M: 07530-677493 E: mike.haslam@hotmail.co.uk

HASLER, Catherine Lesley. b 54. St Mellitus Coll 16. d 18 p 19. OLM Grays Thurrock *Chelmsf* from 18. *28 Orchard Drive, Grays RM17 5AF*

HASLER, Canon John Joseph. b 45. Univ of Wales (Cardiff) MPhil 99. Qu Coll Birm 89. d 90 p 91. C Horfield H Trin *Bris* 90–93; V Bris St Andr Hartcliffe 93–01; V Bris Lockleaze St Mary Magd w St Fran 01–15; AD City 03–06; Hon Can Bris Cathl 08–15; rtd 15. *Address withheld by request* E: joehasler@btinternet.com

HASLER, Kevin John. b 56. RGN 80 RMN 80. St Mich Coll Llan BTh 06. d 06 p 07. NSM Raglan w Llandenny and Bryngwyn *Mon* 06–08; P-in-c Llangwm Uchaf and Llangwm Isaf w Gwernesney etc 08–12; PtO 13–15; V Usk Min Area 15–20; Min Area Ldr Raglan Gp from 20; AD Raglan-Usk from 20. *The Steps, Abergavenny Road, Raglan, Usk NP15 2AA* M: 07836-795753 E: rector@raglanma.org.uk

HASSALL, Mrs Elizabeth Claire. b 80. R Holloway Coll Lon BSc 01 Trin Coll Bris MA 11. BA 08. d 09 p 10. C Bempton w Flamborough, Reighton w Speeton *York* 09–13; V Coxwold and Husthwaite 13–20; R Crayke w Brandsby and Yearsley 13–20; RD Easingwold from 14; C Alne 17–20; C Brafferton w Pilmoor, Myton-on-Swale etc 17–20; C Easingwold w Raskelf 17–20; C Skelton w Shipton and Newton on Ouse 17–20; C Strensall 17–20; C Forest of Galtres 17–20; RD Easingwold 14–19; P-in-c York All SS Pavement w St Crux and St Mich from 20; P-in-c York St Denys from 20; P-in-c York St Helen w St Martin from 20; P-in-c York St Olave w St Giles from 20. *All Saints' Rectory, 52 St Andrewgate, York YO1 7BZ* E: revliz@trundlebug.co.uk

HASSALL, William Edwin. b 41. St Jo Coll Nottm 75. d 77 p 78. C Wellington w Eyton *Lich* 77–80; C Farewell 80–82; V 82–93; C Gentleshaw 80–82; V 82–93; P-in-c Cheddleton 93–94; PtO 97–09; Asst Chapl Birm Heartlands and Solihull NHS Trust 98–01; Chapl Team Ldr 01–06; rtd 06; PtO *Birm* 06–13; C Hatherton *Lich* 09–16; PtO 16–21. *The Vicarage, Buds Road, Rugeley WS15 4NB* T: (01543) 670739 E: revbillhassall@outlook.com

HASSAN, Brian Joseph. b 67. CITC 05. d 08 p 09. NSM Clooney w Strathfoyle *D & R* 08–09; NSM Faughanvale 09–19; P-in-c Ballyscullion from 19. *59 Newton Road, Limavady BT49 0UD* T: (028) 7776 6281 M: 07828-668342 E: brian.hassan2@btinternet.com

HASTED, Marcus Arthur David. b 35. Qu Coll Birm 63. d 66 p 67. C Woodchurch *Ches* 66–69; C W Kirby St Bridget 69–72; V Farndon 72–76; V Farndon and Coddington 76–79; PtO 98–00 and 02–14; NSM Liscard St Mary w St Columba 00–02. *62 South Road, West Kirby, Wirral CH48 3HQ* T: 0151-625 0428

HASTIE-SMITH, Timothy Maybury. b 62. Magd Coll Cam MA 84. Wycliffe Hall Ox 85. d 88 p 89. C Ox St Ebbe w H Trin and St Pet 88–91; Chapl Stowe Sch 91–98; Hd Master Dean Close Sch 98–08; TV S Cotswolds *Glouc* from 08. *The Vicarage, Bibury, Cirencester GL7 5NT* T: (01285) 740301 E: tim.hastie-smith@hotmail.com

HASTINGS, David Kerr. b 40. St Luke's Coll Ex CertEd 63. Ox NSM Course 84. d 87 p 88. Hd Master St Edburg's Sch Bicester 82–89; Asst Chapl HM Pris Grendon and Spring Hill 87–89; NSM Bicester w Bucknell, Caversfield and Launton *Ox* 87–89; Chapl HM Pris Reading 90–92; P-in-c Gt Wishford *Sarum* 92; P-in-c S Newton 92; P-in-c Stapleford w Berwick St James 92; P-in-c Winterbourne Stoke 92; R Lower Wylye and Till Valley 92–95; Chapl HM Pris Ex 96–01; rtd 01; PtO *Ex* from 01. *26 Hoopern Street, Exeter EX4 4LY* T: (01392) 498233 E: david.godsquad@sky.com

HASTINGS, Canon Gary Lee. b 56. NUU BA 82 MA 87 TCD BTh 93. CITC 90. d 93 p 94. C Galway w Kilcummin *T, K & A* 93–95; I Aughaval w Achill, Knappagh, Dugort etc 95–09; I Galway w Kilcummin 09–18; Dom Chapl to Bp Tuam

94–12; Can Tuam Cathl 00–18; Adn Tuam 06–18; Can St Patr Cathl Dublin from 10; Can Killala Cathl *T, K & A* 13–18; I Killiney H Trin *D & G* from 18; Treas Ch Ch Cathl Dublin from 18. *Holy Trinity Rectory, Killiney Road, Killiney, Co Dublin, A96 HD62, Republic of Ireland* T: (00353) (01) 285 2695 E: gryh@me.com *or* rector.htkilliney@dublin.anglican.org

HASTWELL, James Sydney. b 37. Roch Th Coll 67. d 69 p 70. C Croydon St Aug *Cant* 69–73; C Hurstpierpoint *Chich* 73–75; P-in-c Twineham 76; P-in-c Sayers Common 76; P-in-c Albourne 76; R Albourne w Sayers Common and Twineham 76–88; V Forest Row 88–94; rtd 97; PtO *Chich* 97–09; *Nor* from 11. *4 East End Close, Caister-on-Sea, Great Yarmouth NR30 5PG* T: (01692) 678574 E: jen-jim@hotmail.co.uk

HASWELL, Jeremy William Drake. b 60. Qu Mary Coll Lon BSc 84. Ridley Hall Cam 06. d 08 p 09. C St Alb St Paul 08–13; PtO 13–15; C Grayshott *Guildf* 15–18; V from 18. *The Vicarage, 10 Vicarage Gardens, Grayshott, Hindhead GU26 6NH* T: (01428) 605254 E: revjeremy.grayshott@gmail.com

HATCHER, Mark. b 54. Ox Univ BA 77 MA 82 Barrister (Middle Temple) 78 FRSA 94 MCIPR 10. SEITE 09. d 12 p 13. NSM Brockley Hill St Sav *S'wark* 12–15; Reader of The Temple from 15; PtO *S'wark* from 17. *Temple Church Offices, 1 Inner Temple Lane, London EC4Y 1AF* T: (020) 7353 8559 *or* 8293 4969 M: 07801-038389 E: reader@templechurch.com

HATCHETT, Michael John. b 49. Enfield Coll BSc 72 K Coll Lon BD 77 AKC 77. Linc Th Coll 77. d 78 p 79. C Halstead St Andr w H Trin and Greenstead Green *Chelmsf* 78–81; C Greenstead 81–85; V Gt Totham 85–01; R Gt Totham and Lt Totham w Goldhanger 01–06; RD Witham 96–01; Chapl MU 04–06; Dioc Melton and Ufford *St E* 06–15; rtd 15; PtO *St E* 15–21; *Chelmsf* from 21. *Rowan Cottage, 12 Surrey Lane, Tiptree, Colchester CO5 0BH* T: (01621) 815964 E: michael.hatchett@yahoo.co.uk

HATCHETT, Mrs Ruth Merrick. b 54. K Coll Lon BD 77 AKC 77 Open Univ BA 92. EAMTC 03. d 05 p 06. NSM Tolleshunt Knights w Tiptree and Gt Braxted *Chelmsf* 05–06; NSM Melton and Ufford *St E* 06–10; TV Wilford Peninsula 10–20; rtd 20; PtO *Chelmsf* from 21. *Rowan Cottage, 12 Surrey Lane, Tiptree, Colchester CO5 0BH* E: ruth.hatchett@yahoo.com

HATFIELD, Rebecca Alison. See LUMLEY, Rebecca Alison

HATHAWAY, Martin Charles. b 48. St Jo Coll Nottm 93. d 95 p 96. C Weddington and Caldecote *Cov* 95–99; V Potters Green 99–04; C The Heyfords w Rousham and Somerton *Ox* 04–05; C Fritwell w Souldern and Ardley w Fewcott 04–05; TV Dunstable *St Alb* 05–13; rtd 13; PtO *Leic* from 15. *61 Symington Way, Market Harborough LE16 7XA* T: (01858) 288701 E: revd.martinhathaway@tiscali.co.uk

HATHAWAY, Vivienne Ann. b 57. Bucks Chilterns Univ Coll BSc 96. Westcott Ho Cam 00. d 02 p 03. C Bp's Hatfield *St Alb* 02–05; C Bishop's Hatfield, Lemsford and N Mymms 05–07; P-in-c Stevenage St Mary Shephall w Aston 07–14; V Stevenage St Mary Shephall from 14. *St Mary's Vicarage, 148 Hydean Way, Shephall, Stevenage SG2 9YA* T: (01438) 351963 E: vh899@btinternet.com

HATHORNE (née MARSH), Mrs Carol Ann. b 44. W Midl Coll of Educn BA 83. WMMTC 88. d 91 p 94. Par Dn Wednesbury St Paul Wood Green *Lich* 91–93; NSM Pensnett *Worc* 93–97; TV Cannock *Lich* 97–01; NSM Willenhall H Trin 05–11; NSM Bentley Em and Willenhall H Trin 11–12; PtO 12–17 and 20–21. *3 Kirton Grove, Wolverhampton WV6 8RX* E: hathorne@btinternet.com

HATHORNE, Mark Stephen. b 51. Boston Univ MDiv 76. d 00 p 00. C Willenhall H Trin *Lich* 00–01; TV 01–06; TR 06–11; P-in-c Bentley 06–09; TR Bentley Em and Willenhall H Trin 11–13; TV Bilston 13–17; rtd 17; PtO *Lich* 18–20; NSM Cen Wolverhampton from 20. *3 Kirton Grove, Wolverhampton WV6 8RX* T: (01902) 422642 E: mchathorne@virginmedia.com

HATTAWAY, Judith Helen Alison. b 53. Kent Univ BA 79 PGCE 80 Liv Univ MA 02 MBACP 00. STETS 07. d 10 p 11. NSM Hurst *Ox* 10–11; Asst Chapl Broadmoor Hosp Crowthorne 10–11; NSM Frimley *Guildf* 11–14; Asst Chapl Frimley Park Hosp NHS Foundn Trust 11–12; Lead Chapl 12–14; NSM Wokingham St Paul *Ox* from 15. *15 Rayner Drive, Arborfield, Reading RG2 9FB* T: 0118-976 1197 M: 07798-723232 E: judihattaway@mac.com

HATTON, Canon Jane Elizabeth. b 53. SAOMC 95. d 98 p 99. NSM Stevenage St Pet Broadwater *St Alb* 98–04; Chapl E and N Herts NHS Trust 03–17; Hon Can St Alb 16–17; rtd 18; PtO *St Alb* from 18. *2 Dancote, Park Lane, Knebworth SG3 6PB* T: (01438) 811039 E: canonjane@outlook.com

HATTON, Janet Ann. b 56. d 18 p 19. NSM Bromsgrove *Worc* from 18. *255 Pennine Road, Bromsgrove B61 0TN* E: janet.hatton1@btinternet.com

HATTON, Jeffrey Charles. b 49. K Coll Lon BD 70 Bris Univ MA 72. Westcott Ho Cam 72 Episc Th Sch Cam Mass 73. **d** 74 **p** 75. C Nor St Pet Mancroft 74–78; C Earlham St Anne 78–79; Relig Broadcasting Asst IBA 79–82; Hon C Kensington St Barn *Lon* 79–84; Hon C Fulham All SS 85–89; R Win All SS w Chilcomb and Chesil 89–94; Dioc Communications Officer 89–94; P-in-c Salisbury St Thos and St Edm *Sarum* 94–99; R 99–05; rtd 05; Hon C Chalke Valley *Sarum* 06–11; Hon C E Coker w Sutton Bingham and Closworth *B & W* 11–13; Hon C W Coker w Hardington Mandeville, E Chinnock etc 11–13; Hon C Coker Ridge 13–15. *35 Harnwood Road, Salisbury SP2 8DD* T: (01722) 505504

HATTON, Michael Samuel. b 44. St Jo Coll Dur BA 72. Cranmer Hall Dur. **d** 74 **p** 75. C Dudley St Jas *Worc* 74–75; C N Lynn w St Marg and St Nic *Nor* 75–77; C Walsall Wood *Lich* 78–79; Min Shelfield St Mark CD 79–89; V Middleton St Cross *Ripon* 89–97; V Ingol *Blackb* 97–11; rtd 11; PtO *Blackb* from 11. *7 Laurel Avenue, Euxton, Chorley PR7 6AY* T: (01257) 274584

HATWELL, Canon Timothy Rex. b 53. Oak Hill Th Coll BA 85. **d** 85 **p** 86. C Tonbridge St Steph *Roch* 85–90; V Cudham and Downe 90–07; V Falconwood 07–15; R Ightham from 15; RD Shoreham from 16; Hon Can Roch Cathl from 21. *The Rectory, Bates Hill, Ightham, Sevenoaks TN15 9BG* T: (01732) 886827 M: 07799-601546 E: revtim.hatwell@gmail.com

HAUGH, Geoffrey Norman. **d** 13 **p** 14. Ballymore *Arm* 13–14; C Holywood *D & D* 14–17; I Knocknamuckley from 17. *The Rectory, 30 Moss Bank Road, Craigavon BT63 5SL* T: (028) 3883 2121 M: 07568-364573 E: geoff_karen@hotmail.co.uk *or* revghaugh@hotmail.com

HAUGHTON, Peter Steele. b 57. K Coll Lon BD 84 MA 90. Westcott Ho Cam 84. **d** 86 **p** 87. C Cheam Common St Phil *S'wark* 86–90; Chapl Lon Univ Medical Schs 90–94; Educn Adv 94–95; P-in-c Kingston Vale St Jo 95–03; Adv in Ethics and Law K Coll Lon 03–13; PtO *Win* 03–13; C Southampton (City Cen) 13–18; PtO from 18. *95 Bullar Road, Southampton SO18 1GT* T: (023) 8033 5187 M: 07477-578800 E: pshaughton@virginmedia.com

HAUGHTY, Miss Rebecca Mary. b 69. Coll of Resurr Mirfield 09. **d** 11 **p** 12. C Pocklington Wold and Londesborough Wold *York* 11–15; V Coatham and Dormanstown from 15. *9 Blenheim Terrace, Redcar TS10 1QP* M: 07518-412149 E: r.haughty@btinternet.com

HAVELL, Edward Michael. b 38. Dur Univ BA 65. Ridley Hall Cam 66. **d** 68 **p** 69. C Ecclesall *Sheff* 68–71; C Roch St Justus 71–74; P-in-c Holbeach Hurn *Linc* 74–75; C Hollington St Jo *Chich* 75–85; TV Rye 85–92; C E Dereham and Scarning *Nor* 92; rtd 93; PtO *Chich* from 99. *4 Gammons Way, Sedlescombe, Battle TN33 0RQ* T: (01424) 870864 E: havell01@btinternet.com

HAVEY, Kenneth Richard. b 61. St Steph Ho Ox 95. **d** 97 **p** 98. C Corringham *Chelmsf* 97–98; C Leigh St Clem 98–02; R 02–13; P-in-c Hockley 13–20. *PO Box 19, Katsouliana, Kritsa, Lassithi 72051, Crete, Greece* E: kenneth.havey@btinternet.com

HAVILAND, Canon Andrew Mark James. b 65. Leeds Univ BEd 87. STETS 02. **d** 05 **p** 06. NSM N Holmwood *Guildf* 05–08; Chapl Bryanston Sch 08–19; Can and Preb Sarum Cathl 15–19; Sen Chapl Epsom Coll from 19; CF(V) from 15. *Epsom College, College Road, Epsom KT18 4JQ* T: (01372) 821288 M: 07756-698565 E: andrew.haviland@epsomcollege.org.uk

HAWES, Canon Andrew Thomas. b 54. Sheff Univ BA 77 Em Coll Cam MA 79. Westcott Ho Cam 77. **d** 80 **p** 81. C Gt Grimsby St Mary and St Jas *Linc* 80–84; P-in-c Gedney Drove End 84–86; P-in-c Sutton St Nicholas 84–86; V Lutton w Gedney Drove End, Dawsmere 86–89; V Edenham w Witham on the Hill 89–00; V Edenham w Witham on the Hill and Swinstead 00–18; RD Beltisloe 97–13; Can and Preb Linc Cathl 09–18; rtd 18. *Pilkingtons Lodge, Little Bytham, Grantham NG33 4RD* T: (01778) 590035 E: frandrewhawes@gmail.com

HAWES, The Ven Arthur John. b 43. UEA BA 86. Chich Th Coll 65. **d** 68 **p** 69. C Kidderminster St Jo *Worc* 68–72; P-in-c Droitwich 72–76; R Alderford w Attlebridge and Swannington *Nor* 76–92; Chapl Hellesdon and David Rice Hosps and Yare Clinic 76–92; RD Sparham *Nor* 81–91; Mental Health Act Commr 86–94; Hon Can Nor Cathl 88–95; TR Gaywood 92–95; Adn Linc and Can and Preb Linc Cathl 95–08; rtd 08; PtO *S'wark* 10–13; *Nor* 12–17; Hon C Barnham Broom and Upper Yare 17–21; PtO from 21. *29 Market Street, Shipdham, Thetford IP25 7LY* T: (01362) 822441 M: 07803-249834 E: arthur.hawes@yahoo.co.uk

HAWES, The Very Revd Joseph Patricius. b 65. St Chad's Coll Dur BA 87 K Coll Lon MA 12. St Steph Ho Ox 88. **d** 91 **p** 92. C Clapham Team *S'wark* 91–96; P-in-c Barnes St Mich 96–97; TV Barnes 97–03; V Fulham All SS *Lon* 03–18; Dean St E from

18; Hon Can Gaborone Botswana from 11. *The Deanery, The Great Churchyard, Bury St Edmunds IP33 1RS* T: (01284) 748720 M: 07951-600923 E: dean@stedscathedral.org

HAWES, Mrs Joy Elizabeth. b 58. STETS 12. **d** 15 **p** 16. NSM Isle of Wedmore *B & W* 15–19; NSM Yeovil St Mich 19–20; SSM Adv Wells Adnry from 19; Min Support P Axbridge Deanery from 21. *Glencoe, Fishers Hill, Glastonbury BA6 8AH* T: (01458) 830659 M: 07968-156910 E: therevjoy@gmail.com

HAWES, Mary Elizabeth. b 56. SEITE 94. **d** 00 **p** 01. Dioc Children's Adv *Lon* 98–06; Nat Children's Adv Abps' Coun 06–12; Nat Going for Growth (Children and Youth) Adv from 12; NSM Streatham St Leon *S'wark* 00–11; NSM Teddington St Mary w St Alb *Lon* from 11. *47 Traherne Lodge, 64 Walpole Road, Teddington TW11 8PW* T: (020) 7898 1504 E: mary.hawes@churchofengland.org

HAWES, Ms Rachel. b 54. St Hugh's Coll Ox BA 76 MA 80. STETS 05. **d** 07 **p** 08. NSM Kensington St Mary Abbots w Ch Ch and St Phil *Lon* 07–10; NSM Notting Hill St Jo 10–16; P-in-c St Martin Ludgate 14–16; PtO *Chich* 17; NSM Chich St Paul and Westhampnett from 17. *Downcote Cottage, Summersdale Road, Chichester PO19 6PN* T: (01243) 539150 M: 07768-875590 E: rachel.hawes@outlook.com

HAWKEN, Andrew Robert. b 58. K Coll Lon BD 81 AKC 81. St Steph Ho Ox 83. **d** 85 **p** 86. C Ex St Dav 85–88; TV Witney Ox 88–93; V Benson 93–10; AD Aston and Cuddesdon 02–07; Hon Can Ch Ch 09–10; Chapl Midi-Pyrénées and Aude *Eur* 10–16; V E Grinstead St Swithun *Chich* from 16; RD E Grinstead from 21. *The Vicarage, Church Lane, East Grinstead RH19 3AZ* T: (01342) 323307 M: 07397-292926 E: vicareg16@gmail.com

HAWKEN, Rosalind Mary. b 56. York Univ BA 77 Univ of Wales (Cardiff) BTh 02. St Mich Coll Llan 99. **d** 02 **p** 03. C Swansea St Thos and Kilvey *S & B* 02–03; C Gorseinon 03–07. *Society of the Sacred Cross, Tymawr Convent, Lydart, Monmouth NP25 4RN* T: (01600) 860244

HAWKER, The Ven Alan Fort. b 44. Hull Univ BA 65. Clifton Th Coll 65. **d** 68 **p** 69. C Bootle St Leon *Liv* 68–71; C Fazakerley Em 71–73; V Goose Green 73–81; TR Southgate *Chich* 81–98; Can and Preb Chich Cathl 91–98; RD E Grinstead 94–98; Hon Can Bris Cathl 98–10; Adn Swindon 98–99; Adn Malmesbury 99–10; rtd 10; PtO *Cov* 11–21. *21 Paddocks Close, Wolston, Coventry CV8 3GW* T: (024) 7654 4021 E: alanandjen68@gmail.com

HAWKER, Alan John. b 53. K Coll Lon BD 76 AKC 76. Sarum & Wells Th Coll 77. **d** 78 **p** 79. C Coleford w Staunton *Glouc* 78–81; C Up Hatherley 81–84; V Plymouth St Jas Ham *Ex* 84–92; TV Worc SE 92–99; TR Leic Presentation 99–03; P-in-c Leic St Chad 02–03; PtO 09–10; NSM Eyres Monsell 10–11; R Narborough and Huncote 11–19; rtd 19; PtO *Leic* from 19. *318 Victoria Park Road, Leicester LE2 1XE* E: a.hawker87@btinternet.com

HAWKER, Canon Peter John. b 37. OBE 96. Ex Univ BA 59. Wycliffe Hall Ox 69. **d** 70 **p** 71. Asst Chapl Berne *Eur* 70–76; Chapl Berne w Neuchâtel 76–89; Switzerland 86–04; Chapl Zürich w St Gallen, Baden and Zug 90–00; Can Brussels Cathl 86–04; rtd 04. *Schulgasse 10, 3280 Murten, Switzerland* T: (0041) (26) 670 6221 F: 670 6219 E: phawker@anglican.ch

HAWKES, Canon Cecilia Mary (Cilla). b 48. Reading Univ BSc 69 Canley Coll of Educn DipEd 71. EAMTC 99. **d** 02 **p** 03. NSM Takeley w Lt Canfield *Chelmsf* 02–10; NSM Stebbing and Lindsell w Gt and Lt Saling 10–20; NSM Broxted w Chickney and Tilty etc 18–20; Voc Officer Colchester Area 08–20; RD Dunmow and Stansted 10–20; Hon Can Chelmsf Cathl 15–20; rtd 20; PtO *Chelmsf* from 20. *Greenfields, Felsted, Dunmow CM6 3LF* T/F: (01371) 856480 E: cilla@hawkesfarming.co.uk

HAWKES, Mrs Elisabeth Anne. b 56. GRNCM 78 PGCE 80 Kent Univ MA 97. Linc Th Coll 86. **d** 88 **p** 97. Hon Par Dn Finham *Cov* 88–90; Hon Par Dn Bexhill St Pet *Chich* 90–97; Asst to RD Oundle Pet 97–98; NSM 98–00; NSM Benefield and Southwick w Glapthorn 99–00; PtO *Cant* 00–04; Hon Min Can Cant Cathl 03–12; NSM Reculver and Herne Bay St Bart 04–12; Dioc Adv in Liturgy 04–12; NSM Wykeham *Ox* 12–20; rtd 20; PtO *York* from 21. *5 Hawthorne Garth, Beverley HU17 9US* E: revlizhawkes@gmail.com

HAWKES, Mrs Helen Vanda. b 50. Surrey Univ BA 01. STETS 98. **d** 01 **p** 02. NSM N Hayling St Pet and Hayling Is St Andr *Portsm* 01–05; NSM Bedhampton 05–11; rtd 11; PtO *Portsm* from 11. *67 East Lodge Park, Farlington, Portsmouth PO16 1BZ* T: (023) 9222 1409 M: 07724-687095 E: vanda.hawkes@btinternet.com

HAWKES, Keith Andrew. b 28. Oak Hill Th Coll 72. **d** 74 **p** 75. C Gt Yarmouth *Nor* 74–77; C-in-c Bowthorpe CD 77; Chapl Düsseldorf *Eur* 77–83; TV Quidenham *Nor* 83–88;

TR 88–90; RD Thetford and Rockland 86–90; R Wickmere w Lt Barningham, Itteringham etc 90–96; Dioc Rural Officer 90–94; P-in-c Saxthorpe w Corpusty, Blickling, Oulton etc 94–96; R Lt Barningham, Blickling, Edgefield etc 96–98; Bp's Chapl 98; rtd 98; PtO *Nor* 98–00 and from 04; P-in-c Guiltcross 00–03; Chapl Norwich Primary Care Trust 00–02; Chapl Riddlesworth Hall Sch Nor from 04. *Peel Cottage, West Church Street, Kenninghall, Norwich NR16 2EN* T/F: (01953) 888533 E: revkahawkes@aol.com

HAWKES, Canon Martyn John. b 71. Nottm Univ BA 94 St Jo Coll Dur BA 01 MA 04. Cranmer Hall Dur 99. **d** 02 **p** 03. C Is of Dogs Ch Ch and St Jo w St Luke *Lon* 02–05; C Brownswood Park and Stoke Newington St Mary 05–11; V Aldersbrook *Chelmsf* from 11; P-in-c Wanstead St Mary w Ch Ch from 21; AD Redbridge from 19; Hon Can Chelmsf Cathl from 20. *St Gabriel's Vicarage, 12 Aldersbrook Road, London E12 5HH* T: (020) 8989 0315 E: mj_hawkes@yahoo.co.uk

HAWKES, Nigel Anthony Robert. b 59. UEA BSc 80 Edin Univ MSc 82. Ripon Coll Cuddesdon 00. **d** 02 **p** 03. C Chase *Ox* 02–04; C Chipping Norton 04–05; TV Dorchester 05–11; P-in-c Wheatley 11–14; V Albury w Tiddington etc from 14. *The Vicarage, 18 London Road, Wheatley, Oxford OX33 1YA* T: (01865) 872224 E: vicar.wheatley@gmail.com

HAWKES, Ronald Linton. b 54. St Jo Coll York CertEd 75 Leeds Univ BEd 76 Kent Univ MA 96. Linc Th Coll 85. **d** 87 **p** 88. C Finham *Cov* 87–90; TV Bexhill St Pet *Chich* 90–97; V Oundle *Pet* 97–00; P-in-c Benefield and Southwick w Glapthorn 99–00; Dir Post-Ord Tr 98–00; Chapl St Edm Sch Cant 00–03; V Reculver and Herne Bay St Bart *Cant* 03–12; P-in-c Hoath H Cross 04–12; AD Reculver *Cant* 06–12; Hon Min Can Cant Cathl 01–12; R Wykeham *Ox* 12–20; rtd 20. *5 Hawthorne Garth, Beverley HU17 9US* E: reverendronald1954@gmail.com

HAWKES, Vanda. *See* HAWKES, Helen Vanda

HAWKETT, Graham Kenneth. b 20. Bps' Coll Cheshunt 61. **d** 63 **p** 64. C Farncombe *Guildf* 63–67; V Wyke 67–85; rtd 85; PtO *Guildf* 85–14. *Bede House, Beech Road, Haslemere GU27 2BX* T: (01428) 656430

HAWKEY, Canon James Douglas Thomas. b 79. Girton Coll Cam BA 01 MA 05 Selw Coll Cam MPhil 02 PhD 08. Westcott Ho Cam 03 St Thos Aquinas Pontifical Univ Rome 06. **d** 07 **p** 08. C Portsea St Mary *Portsm* 07–10; Min Can and Sacr Westmr Abbey 10–13; Prec Westmr Abbey 13–15; Dean Clare Coll Cam 15–19; Asst Dir of Ords *Ely* 16–19; PV Westmr Abbey 15–19; Can Th Westmr Abbey from 19; Visiting Lect K Coll Lon from 19; Chapl to The Queen from 17. *The Chapter Office, 20 Dean's Yard, London SW1P 3PA* T: (020) 7222 5152 M: 07394-561860 E: james.hawkey@westminster-abbey.org

HAWKINGS, Timothy Denison. b 55. Ex Univ BA 78. St Jo Coll Nottm BA 80. **d** 81 **p** 82. C Penn *Lich* 81–85; TV Stafford 85–94; TR Stratton St Margaret w S Marston etc *Bris* 94–05; P-in-c Axbridge w Shipham and Rowberrow *B & W* 05–11; R 11–21; P-in-c Mark w Allerton 08–10; RD Axbridge 08–14; rtd 21. *12 Fieldins, Winsley, Bradford-on-Avon BA15 2JU* T: (01225) 684908 E: revhawkings@gmail.com

HAWKINS, The Very Revd Alun John. b 44. K Coll Lon BA 66 AKC 66 Univ of Wales (Ban) BD 81. St Deiniol's Hawarden 78. **d** 81 **p** 82. C Dwygyfylchi *Ban* 81–84; R Llanberis 84–89; Tutor Ban Dioc NSM Course 85–93; Dir of Ords *Ban* 86–90; V Knighton and Norton *S & B* 89–93; Chapl Knighton Hosp 89–93; TR Bangor *Ban* 93–06; Adult Educn Officer 93–11; Sec Dioc Bd of Miss 93–11; Can Res and Can Missr Ban Cathl 93–00; Adn Ban 00–04; Dean Ban 04–11; rtd 11; PtO *Ban* from 11. *9 Cil y Craig, Llanfairpwllgwyngyll LL61 5NZ* T: (01248) 717403

HAWKINS (née BRAZIER), Mrs Annette Michaela. b 59. Brighton Univ BEd 95 Homerton Coll Cam BTh. Ridley Hall Cam 07. **d** 09 **p** 10. C Ore St Helen and St Barn *Chich* 09–16; V Salehurst, Hurst Green and Robertsbridge from 16. *4 Glenleigh Walk, Robertsbridge TN32 5DQ* T: (01580) 880282 M: 07900-332791 E: annette@jhbd.co.uk

HAWKINS, Canon Bruce Alexander. b 44. Qu Coll Ox BA 66 MA 71. Sarum Th Coll 66. **d** 68 **p** 69. C Epsom St Martin *Guildf* 68–71; Dioc Youth Chapl *Cant* 72–81; Hon Min Can Cant Cathl 75–99; Dep Dir of Educn 81–86; V Walmer 86–05; RD Sandwich 94–00; Hon Can Cant Cathl 99–05; rtd 05; PtO *Cant* from 05. *88 The Gateway, Dover CT16 1LQ* T: (01304) 240820 E: brucehawkins0701@gmail.com

HAWKINS, Cheryl. b 73. Open Univ LLB 06. Sarum Coll 17. **d** 20 **p** 21. C Westbury-on-Trym H Trin *Bris* from 20. *Address withheld by request* M: 07498-877376 E: curate@westbury-parish-church.org.uk

HAWKINS, Mrs Anne Marilon. b 56. SEITE 98. **d** 01 **p** 02. NSM Epping Distr *Chelmsf* 01–02; C Woodford St Mary w St Phil and St Jas 02–05; P-in-c Hatfield Broad Oak and Bush End 05–07; Ind Chapl Harlow 05–07; Chapl Princess Alexandra

Hosp NHS Trust 07–14; TV Louth *Linc* 15–17; P-in-c Fyfield, Moreton w Bobbingworth etc *Chelmsf* from 17; P-in-c High Laver w Magdalen Laver and Lt Laver etc from 18. *The Rectory, 6 Forest Drive, Fyfield, Ongar CM5 0TP* T: (01277) 899866 E: revcah56@gmail.com

HAWKINS, Clive Ladbrook. b 53. St Pet Coll Ox BA 76 MA 79. Trin Coll Bris 80. **d** 82 **p** 83. C Win Ch Ch 82–86; R Eastrop 86–20; AD Basingstoke 00–08; Hon Can Win Cathl 05–20; rtd 20; PtO *Win* 21. *11 Nether Park Drive, Derby DE22 2TR*

✠**HAWKINS, The Rt Revd David John Leader.** b 49. Nottm Univ BTh 73. St Jo Coll Nottm 69 ALCD 73. **d** 73 **p** 74 **c** 02. C Bebington *Ches* 73–76; Nigeria 76–82; C Ox St Aldate w St Matt 83–86; V Leeds St Geo *Ripon* 86–99; TR 99–02; Area Bp Barking *Chelmsf* 02–14; rtd 14; Hon Asst Bp Leeds from 14. *3 Princes Drive, Skipton BD23 1HN* E: davidjlhawkins@outlook.com or david@davidhawkingsartist.com

HAWKINS, David Kenneth Beaumont. b 36. Em Coll Saskatoon LTh 63. **d** 63 **p** 64. C Northminster Canada 63–69; C Belleville Ch Ch 69–71; I Wellington 71–79; I Barriefield w Pittsburgh 80–85; C St Alb St Paul 85–87; C Hednesford *Lich* 87–92; R Buildwas and Leighton w Eaton Constantine etc 92–95; TV Wrockwardine Deanery 95–01; rtd 01. *PO Box 454, 131 Westwind Crescent, Wellington ON K0K 3L0, Canada* T: (001) (613) 399 5666 E: rowenadavid@sympatico.ca

HAWKINS, Mrs Dorothy. b 46. RGN 77 RM 79. All SS Cen for Miss & Min 07. **d** 14 **p** 15. OLM Worsley *Man* 14–19; rtd 20; PtO *Man* from 20. *4 Ryecroft Lane, Worsley, Manchester M28 2PN* T: 0161-794 5072 E: dh89@btinternet.com

HAWKINS, Ivor Geoffrey. **d** 15 **p** 16. NSM Garthbeibio, Llanerfel and Llangadfan *St As* 15–16; NSM Caereinion 17–20. *Ceunant, Pont Robert, Meifod SY22 6JN* T: (01938) 500483 E: hawkinsceunant@aol.com

HAWKINS, James Reginald. b 39. Ex Univ BA 61 Hull Univ MA 00. Westcott Ho Cam 61. **d** 63 **p** 64. C Cannock *Lich* 63–66; C Wem 66–67; C Cheddleton 67–69; R Yoxall 69–77; R The Quinton *Birm* 77–84; V Bosbury w Wellington Heath etc *Heref* 84–96; P-in-c Ancaster Wilsford Gp *Linc* 96–99; R 99–04; RD Loveden 97–03; rtd 04; PtO *Bris* from 05. *14 Pound Pill, Corsham SN13 9JA* T: (01249) 715353 E: jrhawkins74@outlook.com

HAWKINS, John Colin. b 50. SEITE 97. **d** 00 **p** 01. NSM W Wickham St Jo *S'wark* 00–04; P-in-c Burwash Weald *Chich* 04–11; PtO from 11. *Bell Cottage, Vinehall Road, Mountfield, Robertsbridge TN32 5JN* E: john.c.hawkins@btinternet.com

HAWKINS, The Ven John Edward Inskipp. b 63. K Coll Lon BD 85. Qu Coll Birm 86. **d** 88 **p** 89. C Birchfield *Birm* 88–92; C Poplar *Lon* 92–93; TV 93–99; V W Hendon St Jo 99–15; P-in-c Colindale St Matthias 07–15; AD W Barnet 04–09; Adn Hampstead from 15; Preb St Paul's Cathl from 13. *13 Kingscroft Road, London NW2 3QE* E: jeih.stj@tiscali.co.uk or archdeacon.hampstead@london.anglican.org

HAWKINS, Jonathan Desmond. b 53. FRICS 93. Ox Min Course 04. **d** 07 **p** 08. NSM Walton H Trin *Ox* 07–09; NSM Southcourt 09–10; NSM Haddenham w Cuddington, Kingsey etc 10–16; NSM Wychert Vale from 16. *Croft End, 1A White Hart Lane, Haddenham, Aylesbury HP17 8BB* T: (01844) 299429 M: 07976-281699 E: jon@jdhawkins.co.uk

HAWKINS, Nicholas Milner. b 45. Univ of Wales (Swansea) BA 69 MSc 71. **d** 01 **p** 05. Par Dn Dingestow and Llangovan w Penyclawdd etc *Mon* 01–02; PtO *Ban* 02–03; NSM Nefyn w Tudweiliog w Llandudwen w Edern 03–08; P-in-c Botwnnog w Bryncroes w Llangwnnadl w Penllech 08–12; rtd 12; C Dawlish *Ex* 12–15; C Kenton, Mamhead, Powderham, Cofton and Starcross 12–15; C Dawlish, Cofton and Starcross 15–18. *Harlea, The Strand, Starcross, Exeter EX6 8PA* T: (01626) 899166 M: 07870-264385 E: rev.starcross@gmail.com

HAWKINS, Noel. b 46. St Jo Coll Nottm 82. **d** 84 **p** 85. C Worksop St Jo *S'well* 84–86; C Wollaton Park 86–89; TV Billericay and Lt Burstead *Chelmsf* 89–95; TV Keynsham *B & W* 95–00; V Brislington St Chris and St Cuth *Bris* 00–08; V Brislington St Chris 08–12; P-in-c Hengrove 06–12; rtd 12; PtO *B & W* 13–21. *17 White Horse Drive, Frome BA11 2DA* T: (01373) 451305 E: henbriznl@gmail.com

HAWKINS, Preb Patricia Sally. b 59. LMH Ox BA 80 MA 84 Ex Univ BPhil 85 Ox Univ BTh 04 CQSW 85. St Steph Ho Ox 99. **d** 01 **p** 02. C Stafford *Lich* 01–04; V Oxley 04–14; AD Wolverhampton 08–11; RD Wulfrun 11–14; Can Res Lich Cathl 14–20; Preb Lich Cathl 09–20; V Ellesmere from 20; Preb Lich Cathl from 20; Chapl to The Queen from 20. *The Vicarage, Church Hill, Ellesmere SY12 0HB* E: revpat.hawkins@gmail.com

HAWKINS, Paul Henry Whishaw. b 46. Ex Coll Ox BA 68 MA 74 SS Coll Cam MA 84. St Steph Ho Ox 70. **d** 72 **p** 73. C Fawley *Win* 72–75; C Ealing St Steph Castle Hill *Lon* 75–77; P-in-c Dorney *Ox* 77–78; TV Riverside 78–81; Chapl

SS Coll Cam 82–87; V Plymstock *Ex* 87–97; RD Plymouth Sutton 91–96; TR Plymstock and Hooe 97–00; Preb Ex Cathl 98–00; P-in-c St Pancras w St Jas and Ch Ch *Lon* 00–02; V 02–11; rtd 11; PtO *Bris* 11–20. *Ground Floor Flat, 9 Buckingham Place, Clifton, Bristol BS8 1LJ* T: 0117-946 7506 E: jackie.schubert@hotmail.com

HAWKINS, Peter Edward. b 35. Leeds Univ BA 60. Coll of Resurr Mirfield 60. **d** 62 **p** 63. C Forest Gate St Edm *Chelmsf* 62–65; C Sevenoaks St Jo *Roch* 65–68; Chapl Metrop Police Cadet Corps Tr Sch 68–73; P-in-c Knowle H Nativity *Bris* 73; TV Knowle 73–79; V Westbury-on-Trym H Trin 79–87; TR Solihull *Birm* 87–96; Hon Can Birm Cathl 92–96; rtd 00. *Back Street Cottage, 15 St Andrew's Road, Stogursey, Bridgwater TA5 1TE* T/F: (01278) 733635 E: peterhawkins15@googlemail.com *or* peh.stogursey@tiscali.co.uk

HAWKINS, Peter Michael. b 38. Kelham Th Coll 58. **d** 63 **p** 64. Ox Miss to Calcutta India 63–64; C Calcutta Cathl 64–66; C-in-c Kidderpore 66–68; V Asansol w Burnpur 68–69; C Manningham St Paul and St Jude *Bradf* 70–72; C Bradf Cathl 72–75; V Allerton 75–90; V Pet H Spirit Bretton 90–07; P-in-c Marholm 90–95; rtd 07. *Le Pavillon, Mané Gouélo, RD 765, 56690 Landaul, France* T: (0033) 2 97 59 90 83 M: 6 48 42 78 70 E: peterhawkins@sfr.fr

HAWKINS, Mrs Rachel Ann. b 76. Trin Coll Bris 09. **d** 11 **p** 12. C Long Eaton St Jo *Derby* 11–15; V Rushden St Pet *Pet* from 15. *St Peter's Vicarage, 12 Kensington Close, Rushden NN10 6RR* T: (01933) 356398 E: revrach@hotmail.co.uk

✠**HAWKINS, The Rt Revd Richard Stephen.** b 39. Ex Coll Ox BA 61 MA 65 Ex Univ BPhil 76. St Steph Ho Ox 61. **d** 63 **p** 64 **c** 88. C Ex St Thos 63–66; C Clyst St Mary 66–75; TV Clyst St George, Aylesbeare, Clyst Honiton etc 75–78; TV Cen Ex 78–81; Bp's Officer for Min and Jt Dir Ex and Truro NSM Scheme 78–81; Dioc Dir of Ords 79–81; Adn Totnes 81–88; P-in-c Oldridge and Whitestone 81–87; Suff Bp Plymouth 88–96; Suff Bp Crediton 96–04; rtd 04; Hon Asst Bp Ex 05–19. *3 Westbrook Close, Exeter EX4 8BS* T: (01392) 462622 E: valrid@aol.com

HAWKINS, Canon Richard Whishaw. b 51. Coll of Resurr Mirfield 93. **d** 95 **p** 96. C Weymouth H Trin *Sarum* 95–99; P-in-c Hey *Man* 99–06; TR Medlock Head 06–16; AD Saddleworth 03–09; Hon Can Man Cathl 12–16; rtd 16; PtO *Man* from 16. *45 Otmoor Way, Royton, Oldham OL2 6SD* T: (01706) 844391 M: 07801-241428 E: richardhawkins190@gmail.com

HAWKINS, Steven Andrew. b 51. Nottm Univ BEd 75 Open Univ BSc 91 Bris Poly ADEd 90. STETS 95. **d** 98 **p** 99. C Horfield H Trin *Bris* 98–02; V Brislington St Anne 02–08; P-in-c Knowle St Martin 08–13; V 13–15; rtd 15; P-in-c Knowle H Nativity *Bris* 17–21. *130 Charlton Mead Drive, Bristol BS10 6LH* M: 07929-485006 E: sh1951@outlook.com

HAWKINS, Susan. b 47. Doncaster Coll of Educn CertEd 69 Ches Coll of HE BTh 99. NOC 95. **d** 99 **p** 00. NSM Prestbury *Ches* 99–02; P-in-c Marthall and Chapl David Lewis Cen for Epilepsy 02–09; rtd 09; PtO *Ches* from 09; *Eur* from 18. *3 Thorne Close, Prestbury, Macclesfield SK10 4DE* T: (01625) 829833 E: suehawkins03@virginmedia.com

HAWKINS, Timothy St John. b 59. CCC Ox BA 82. Trin Coll Bris BA 87. **d** 87 **p** 88. C Cheltenham St Mary, St Matt, St Paul and H Trin *Glouc* 87–90; C Cowplain *Portsm* 90–94; V Pennycross *Ex* 94–96; P-in-c St Keverne *Truro* 96–05; P-in-c Gulval and Madron 05–16; V 16–21; rtd 21. *6 Old Tavern Lane, Welshpool SY21 7JD* E: revtimhawkins@hotmail.co.uk

HAWKSLEY, Katharine Mary. b 82. **d** 16 **p** 17. C Chard St Mary w Combe St Nicholas, Wambrook etc *B & W* 16–20; R Cam Vale from 20. *The Rectory, Englands Lane, Queen Camel, Yeovil BA22 7NN* T: (01935) 851465 E: revkhawksley@gmail.com

HAWKSWORTH, Maldwyn Harry. b 45. Aston Univ CertEd 74. St Jo Coll Nottm 87. **d** 89 **p** 90. C Penn *Lich* 89–94; TV Bloxwich 94–09; Local Min Adv (Wolverhampton) 09–15; Local Par Development Adv Wolverhampton Area 10–15; P-in-c Yoxall 09–17; rtd 17; PtO *Lich* 17–21. *118 Haymoor, Lichfield WS14 9SX*

HAWKSWORTH, Peter John Dallas. b 54. St Jo Coll Ox BA 75 MA 79 Solicitor 79. Sarum & Wells Th Coll 89. **d** 91 **p** 92. C Warminster St Denys, Upton Scudamore etc *Sarum* 91–95; P-in-c Salisbury St Mark 95–99; V 99–05; RD Salisbury 03–05; PtO 07–21. *6 Newton Rise, Swanage BH19 2QP* E: confluence@btinternet.com

HAWLEY, Canon Anthony Broughton. b 41. St Pet Coll Ox BA 67 MA 71. Westcott Ho Cam 67. **d** 69 **p** 70. C Wolverhampton St Pet *Lich* 69–72; C-in-c Bermondsey St Hugh CD S'wark 73–84; Hon PV S'wark Cathl 83–84; TR Kirkby *Liv* 84–02; AD Walton 93–02; Hon Can Liv Cathl 96–02; Can Res Liv Cathl 02–11; rtd 11; PtO *Sarum*

from 12. *Pimlico Cottage, Black Lane, Lover, Salisbury SP5 2PQ* T: (01794) 390607 E: anthonybhawley@gmail.com

HAWLEY, The Ven John Andrew. b 50. K Coll Lon BD 71 AKC 71. Wycliffe Hall Ox 72. **d** 74 **p** 75. C Kingston upon Hull H Trin *York* 74–77; C Bradf Cathl Par 77–80; V Woodlands *Sheff* 80–91; TR Dewsbury *Wakef* 91–02; Hon Can Wakef Cathl 98–02; Adn Blackb 02–15; Bp's Adv on UPA 02–15; Bp's Adv on Hospice and Hosp Chapl 13–15; Bp's Adv on Pris Chapl 14–15; rtd 15; PtO *Sheff* from 15; *York* from 15; *Leeds* from 17. *35 Woodland Avenue, Goole DN14 6QT* T: (01405) 762678 M: 07544-952645 E: john.hawley627@gmail.com

HAWLEY, Nigel David. b 51. Coll of Resurr Mirfield 77. **d** 80 **p** 81. C Birch w Fallowfield *Man* 80–84; P-in-c Moston St Jo 84–85; R 85–93; R Reddish 93–06; Co-ord Chapl HM Pris Forest Bank 06–07; Managing Chapl HM Pris Risley 08–16; Lic Preacher *Man* 07–16; rtd 16; PtO *Leeds* from 16. *Rosa Mystica, 31 Barnsley Road, Cawthorne, Barnsley S75 4HW* M: 07812-489776 E: nigelhawley@googlemail.com

HAWORTH, Julie Elizabeth. b 59. St Mich Coll Llan. **d** 09. C Wigan All SS and St Geo *Liv* 09–13; C Wigan St Anne 13–15; C Wigan All SS 15; Chapl Whiteley Village Walton-on-Thames 15–18; PtO *Blackb* 18–20. *19 Redcar Road, Lancaster LA1 4NA* T: (01524) 572356 E: je.haworth@yahoo.co.uk

HAWORTH, Canon Mark Newby. b 50. Aber Univ BSc 73 MICFor 81. Westcott Ho Cam 88. **d** 90 **p** 91. C Cherry Hinton St Andr *Ely* 90–93; C Teversham 90–93; P-in-c Swaffham Bulbeck and Swaffham Prior w Reach 93–94; V 94–02; Sub Warden of Readers 95–02; RD Fordham 96–02; Chapl Framlingham Coll and Brandeston Hall Sch 03; Chapl to Bp Pet 03–05; TR Pendleton *Man* 05–09; P-in-c Lower Kersal 06–09; TR Salford All SS 09–12; Borough Dean Salford 10–12; R Rochdale 12–13; Hon Can Man Cathl 12–13; TR Bury St Edmunds All SS w St Jo and St Geo *St E* 13–19; P-in-c Lark Valley 14–19; TR Lark Valley and N Bury 19–20; RD Thingoe 14–20; Hon Can St E Cathl 16–20; rtd 20; Hon C Exning St Martin w Landwade *St E* 20–21; P-in-c Claydon from 21; Dioc Environment Officer from 20. *The Vicarage, 7 Back Lane, Claydon, Ipswich IP6 0EB* T: (01638) 577196 M: 07932-160009 E: mhaworth50@hotmail.com

HAWORTH, Paul. b 47. G&C Coll Cam BA 68 MA 72. Westcott Ho Cam 75. **d** 78 **p** 79. C Hornchurch St Andr *Chelmsf* 78–81; C Loughton St Mary and St Mich 81–88; TV Waltham H Cross 88–92; TR Becontree S 92–00; P-in-c S Woodham Ferrers 00–11; rtd 11; PtO *Chelmsf* 11–19; *Leeds* 20–21. *25 Cambridge Street, Normanton WF6 1ET* T: (01924) 219360 M: 07986-535425 E: onthemat@btconnect.com

HAWORTH, Stanley Robert. b 48. St Jo Coll Dur BA 69. Sarum & Wells Th Coll 71. **d** 73 **p** 74. C Skipton H Trin *Bradf* 73–76; C Bradf Cathl 76–78; C Grantham *Linc* 78; TV 78–82; V Deeping St James 82–96; V Middlewich w Byley *Ches* 96–01; P-in-c Forcett and Aldbrough and Melsonby *Ripon* 01–12; AD Richmond 08–12; rtd 12; PtO *Pet* from 12. *45 Finedon Road, Irthlingborough, Wellingborough NN9 5TY* T: (01933) 653798 E: stantherevman@hotmail.com

HAWORTH, Stuart. b 43. **d** 94 **p** 95. OLM Bradshaw *Man* 94–01; OLM Turton Moorland 01–08; rtd 08; PtO *Man* from 08. *39 Patterdale Road, Bolton BL2 3LX* T: (01204) 384006

HAWRISH, Mary-Beth Louise Ladine. b 51. **d** 09 **p** 10. OLM Oxshott *Guildf* 09–17; NSM N Hants Downs *Win* 17–20; rtd 20; PtO *Guildf* from 20. *Address withheld by request* E: mhawrish@yahoo.co.uk

HAWTHORN, The Ven Christopher John. b 36. Qu Coll Cam BA 60 MA 64. Ripon Hall Ox 60. **d** 62 **p** 63. C Sutton St Jas *York* 62–66; V Kingston upon Hull St Nic 66–72; V E Coatham 72–79; V Scarborough St Martin 79–91; RD Scarborough 82–91; Can and Preb York Minster 87–01; Adn Cleveland 91–01; rtd 01; PtO *York* from 01. *Wetherlam, 11 Holly Tree Lane, Haxby, York YO32 3YJ* T: (01904) 591008

HAWTHORN, David. b 63. Chich Th Coll 87. **d** 90 **p** 91. C Hartlepool H Trin *Dur* 90–94; C Middlesbrough All SS *York* 94–95; P-in-c Thornaby on Tees 95–96; V S Thornaby 96–02; P-in-c Brighton Annunciation *Chich* 02–04; V Hollinwood and Limeside *Man* 04–18; rtd 18. T: 0161-241 9424 *or* (00351) 262 608 230

HAWTHORN, Philip Alan. b 58. Essex Univ BSc 79. Ripon Coll Cuddesdon 05. **d** 07 **p** 08. C Hardington Vale *B & W* 07–10; P-in-c Charlcombe w Bath St Steph 10–16; R from 16. *The Rectory, Richmond Place, Bath BA1 5PZ* T: (01225) 466114 M: 07973-350560 E: philiphawthorn@btinternet.com *or* philip@ststephensbath.org.uk

HAWTHORNE, John William. b 32. St Aug Coll Cant 74. **d** 77 **p** 78. C Boxley *Cant* 77–80; P-in-c Otham 80–82; P-in-c Langley 80–82; R Otham w Langley 82–83; TR Preston w Sutton Poyntz, Littlemoor etc *Sarum* 83–97; R Tetbury w Beverston *Glouc* 87–01; rtd 01; PtO *Ex* 02–16; *Sarum* from

06; *Bris* 12–19. *19 Long Street, Devizes SN10 1NN* T: (01380) 728056 E: j.hawthorne146@btinternet.com

HAWTHORNE, Juanita Marie. b 63. ERMC 19. d 21. NSM Grimshoe *Ely* from 21. *The Hermitage, 39 High Street, Methwold, Thetford IP26 4NX* E: revjuanita58@gmail.co.uk

HAWTHORNE-STEELE, Isobel. d 14 p 16. Ahoghill w Portglenone *Conn* 14–16; C Belfast St Paul w St Barn from 16. *210 York Street, Belfast BT15 1JJ* T: (028) 9086 9410 M: 07788-553376 E: i.hawthorne@ulster.ac.uk

⊠**HAWTIN, The Rt Revd David Christopher.** b 43. Keble Coll Ox BA 65 MA 70. Wm Temple Coll Rugby 65 Cuddesdon Coll 66. d 67 p 68 c 99. C Pennywell St Thos and Grindon St Oswald CD *Dur* 67–71; C Stockton St Pet 71–74; C-in-c Leam Lane CD 74–79; R Washington 79–88; Dioc Ecum Officer 88–91; Adn Newark *S'well* 92–99; Suff Bp Repton *Derby* 99–06; rtd 06; Hon Asst Bp Sheff 07–20; PtO *Leeds* 19–21. *29 Arran Way, Rothwell, Leeds LS26 0WB*

HAY, David Frederick. b 38. Pemb Coll Ox BA 62 MA 67. Qu Coll Birm 82. d 84 p 85. C Prenton *Ches* 84–88; V Stockport St Sav 88–96; P-in-c Gt Saughall 96–03; rtd 03; PtO *Ches* 04–19; Hon Min Can Ches Cathl from 04; PtO *St As* from 09. *2 Moel View Road, Buckley CH7 2BT* T: (01244) 541342 E: davidfhay@yahoo.com

HAY, Jack Barr. b 31. Bps' Coll Cheshunt 57. d 60 p 61. C Byker St Ant *Newc* 60–63; C Killingworth 63–68; V Cowgate 68–77; V Woodhorn w Newbiggin 77–96; rtd 96; PtO *Newc* from 96. *7 Glebelands, Corbridge NE45 5DS* T: (01434) 632979

HAY, Joanna Jane Louise. *See* DOBSON, Joanna Jane Louise

HAY, John. b 45. CITC 77. d 79 p 80. C Newtownards *D & D* 79–81; I Galloon w Drummully *Clogh* 81–89; I Donacavey w Barr 89–03; Can Clogh Cathl 91–03; Dean Raphoe *D & R* 03–13; I Raphoe w Raymochy and Clonleigh 03–13; rtd 13. *151 Tonnagh Road, Trillick, Omagh BT78 3PJ* M: 07909-530084 E: johnhayfintona@btinternet.com

HAY, Miss Lesley Jean Hamilton. b 48. St Andr Univ MA 71. Westcott Ho Cam 04 Yale Div Sch 05. d 06 p 07. C Shrivenham and Ashbury *Ox* 06–08; C Bethany USA 08; Asst R Hamden 08–10; R Mentone St Jos from 10. *PO Box 161, Mentone AL 35984-0161, USA* T: (001) (256) 634 4476 E: lesleyhay@yahoo.co.uk

HAY, Margaret Ann. b 47. Brunel Univ BTech 71 W Sussex Inst of HE PGCE 95. STETS 02. d 05 p 06. NSM Elson *Portsm* 05–17; PtO from 17. *Bodinnick, 12 Longwater Drive, Gosport PO12 2UP* T: (023) 9234 3303

HAY, Mark Alastair. b 71. St Martin's Coll Lanc BA 94. Trin Coll Bris 11. d 14 p 15. C Longfleet *Sarum* from 14. *32 Linthorpe Road, Poole BH15 2JS* T: (01202) 677573 M: 07792-405803 E: mark.hay@smlpoole.org.uk

HAY, Nicholas John. b 56. Sheff Poly BSc 85. St Jo Coll Nottm 85. d 88 p 89. C Blackb Redeemer 88–91; C Hellesdon *Nor* 91–95; R Widford *Chelmsf* 95–01; Sen Chapl HM Pris Ashfield 01–09; C Bedminster *Bris* 09–15; P-in-c 15–20; V Bedminster and Southville 20–21; C Whitchurch 09–15; V Whitchurch St Aug 15–18; AD Bris S 16–19; Hon Can Bris Cathl 09–21; rtd 21. *Address temp unknown* M: 07905-834869 E: nickhaybristol@gmail.com

HAY, Richard. b 42. CMG 92. Ball Coll Ox BA 63. Cranmer Hall Dur 94. d 96 p 97. C Hastings St Clem and All SS *Chich* 96–99; V Addlestone *Guildf* 99–07; RD Runnymede 02–07; rtd 07; PtO *Guildf* from 07. *15 Fox Close, Woking GU22 8LP* T: (01932) 343585 E: richard.hay3@btinternet.com

HAY, Robin Andrew. b 72. WEMTC 16. d 17 p 18. NSM Evington *Leic* 17–19; NSM Avon-Swift from 19; Hd Learning and Min Development from 17. *St Martin's House, 7 Peacock Lane, Leicester LE1 5PZ* T: 0116-261 5317 E: rob.hay@leccofe.org

HAYCRAFT, Brian Roger Norman. b 43. Oak Hill Th Coll 69. d 73 p 74. C Belsize Park *Lon* 73–76; C Yardley St Edburgha *Birm* 76–79; V Hornchurch H Cross *Chelmsf* 79–03; rtd 03; PtO *Chelmsf* from 04. *12 Hannards Way, Hainault IG6 3TB* T: (020) 8501 1718

HAYDAY, Canon Alan Geoffrey David. b 46. Kelham Th Coll 65. d 69 p 70. C N Evington *Leic* 69–72; C Spalding St Mary and St Nic *Linc* 72–78; V Cherry Willingham w Greetwell 78–86; RD Lawres 84–86; TR Brumby 86–02; RD Manlake 93–99; Can and Preb Linc Cathl 00–02; Dean St Chris Cathl Bahrain 02–09; Adn Gulf 06–09; Hon Can Bahrain from 09; rtd 09. *22 Kestral Drive, Louth LN11 0GE* T: (01507) 600877 M: 07709-873224 E: windhover22@live.co.uk

HAYDEN, Carol Toni. b 64. Leeds Univ BA 05. NOC 02. d 05 p 06. NSM Ainsworth *Man* 05–09; NSM Bury SE 09–11; TV Radcliffe 11–17; TR 17; TV Turton Moorland from 17; Assoc Dir of Ords from 16. *2 Higher Dunscar, Egerton,*

Bolton BL7 9TE T: (01204) 587150 M: 07434-365971 E: c_hayden1@sky.com

HAYDEN, The Ven David Frank. b 47. Lon Univ BD 71. Tyndale Hall Bris 67. d 71 p 72. C Silverhill St Matt *Chich* 71–75; C Galleywood Common *Chelmsf* 75–79; R Redgrave cum Botesdale w Rickinghall *St E* 79–84; RD Hartismere 81–84; V Cromer *Nor* 84–02; P-in-c Gresham 84–98; Chapl Cromer and Distr Hosp Norfolk 84–94; Chapl Norfolk and Nor Health Care NHS Trust 94–00; Chapl Fletcher Hosp Norfolk 85–00; RD Repps *Nor* 95–02; Hon Can Nor Cathl 96–12; Adn Norfolk 02–12; rtd 12; PtO *Nor* 12–17 and from 19; P-in-c Oulton Broad 17–19; P-in-c Oulton St Mich 18–19. *Church Farm House, Church Lane, Lowestoft NR32 3JN* T: (01502) 450022 E: davidf.hayden@gmail.com

⊠**HAYDEN, The Rt Revd John Donald.** b 40. Lon Univ BD 62. Tyndale Hall Bris 63. d 65 p 66 c 03. C Macclesfield Ch Ch *Ches* 65–68; C H Spirit Cathl Dodoma Tanzania 68–69; V Moshi 70–77; Home Sec USCL 77–83; TV Ipswich St Mary at Stoke w St Pet *St E* 83–94; P-in-c Bury St Edmunds St Mary 94–99; V 99–04; Asst Bp Mt Kilimanjaro 03–08; Hon Asst Bp Ches from 08; PtO *Liv* from 16. *45 Birkenhead Road, Hoylake, Wirral CH47 5AF* T: 0151-632 0448 E: johndhayden@gmail.com

HAYDEN, Canon Mark Joseph James. b 68. St Thos Aquinas Pontifical Univ Rome BD 93. H Cross Coll Clonliffe 86. d 92 p 93. In RC Ch 92–99; C Monkstown *D & G* 99–01; I Gorey w Kilnahue, Leskinfere and Ballycanew *C, F & O* from 01; Can Treas Ferns Cathl from 07. *The Rectory, The Avenue, Gorey, Co Wexford, Republic of Ireland* T/F: (00353) (53) 942 1383 E: gorey@ferns.anglican.org

HAYDEN, Michael. b 95. St Jo Coll Nottm BA 16 Oak Hill Th Coll 18. d 20 p 21. C Nor St Andr from 20. *1 Drays Yard, Norwich NR1 1RL* M: 07599-662622 E: michael@standrewsnorwich.org

HAYDOCK, Canon Alan. b 41. Kelham Th Coll 60. d 65 p 66. C Rainworth *S'well* 65–68; C Hucknall Torkard 68–71; TV 71–74; V Bilborough St Jo 74–80; R E Bridgford 80–82; R E Bridgford and Kneeton 82–06; RD Bingham 84–94; Hon Can S'well Minster 86–06; rtd 06; PtO *Leic* 07–20; S'well from 06. *29 The Teasels, Bingham, Nottingham NG13 8TY* T: (01949) 875805 M: 07944-569661

HAYDON, Keith Frank Michael. b 46. Cuddesdon Coll 73. d 75 p 76. C De Beauvoir Town St Pet *Lon* 75–77; C Wells St Thos w Horrington *B & W* 77–80; TV Weston-super-Mare Cen Par 80–84; TV Cowley St Jas *Ox* 84–87; TR 87–95; V Walsingham, Houghton and Barsham *Nor* 95–96; P-in-c 96–99; rtd 01; C Sutton on Plym *Ex* 09–11; C Plymouth St Simon and St Mary 09–11; P-in-c Sutton-on-Plym, Plymouth St Simon and St Mary 11–16; P-in-c Plymouth St Gabr 11–16; PtO from 17. *Address withheld by request*

HAYES, Bruce John. b 75. UCD BA 97 TCD BTh 01. CITC 98. d 01 p 02. C Cregagh *D & D* 01–04; I Abbeystrewry Union *C, C & R* 04–13; Warden of Readers 08–13; I Dalkey St Patr *D & G* from 13. *The Rectory, Barnacoille Park, Church Road, Dalkey, Co Dublin, Republic of Ireland* T: (00353) (1) 280 3369 M: 86-232 7349 E: brucejohnhayes@gmail.com

HAYES, Carmen Miranda. b 61. TCD BTh 08. d 08 p 09. C Portadown St Mark *Arm* 08–11; I Kilcronaghan w Draperstown and Sixtowns *D & R* 11–19; I Errigal w Garvagh from 19; Bp's Dom Chapl from 12. *St Paul's Rectory, 58 Station Road, Garvagh, Coleraine BT51 5LA* M: 07907-579913 E: carmenmirandahayes@hotmail.com

HAYES, David Malcolm Hollingworth. b 42. K Coll Lon BD 68 AKC 68 MPhil 97. d 69 p 70. C Upper Teddington SS Pet and Paul *Lon* 69–70; C Ruislip St Martin 70–75; P-in-c Ludford *Heref* 75–80; P-in-c Ashford Carbonell w Ashford Bowdler 75–80; V Eastcote St Lawr *Lon* 80–90; R Cant St Pet w St Alphege and St Marg etc 90–07; P-in-c Blean 03–07; Master Eastbridge Hosp 90–07; Guardian of the Greyfriars 97–07; rtd 07; PtO *Sarum* 07–21. *Forge Cottage, 3 North Row, Warminster BA12 9AD* T: (01985) 212929 E: dmhforge@btinternet.com

HAYES, David Thomas. b 70. Leeds Univ BA 09. NOC. d 09 p 10. NSM Leeds Belle Is St Jo and St Barn *Ripon* 09–12; NSM Aberford w Micklefield *York* 12–18; NSM Sherburn in Elmet w Saxton 12–18; Chapl Mid Yorks Hosps NHS Trust 17–20; Chapl HM Pris Wealstun from 20; PtO *Leeds* 20–21. *HM Prison Wealstun, Walton Road, Wetherby LS23 7AZ* T: (01937) 444400 M: 07739-364755

HAYES, Denise Angela. b 62. NOC 02. d 05 p 06. C Ashton-in-Makerfield St Thos *Liv* 05–10; P-in-c Litherland St Phil 10–14; P-in-c Pemberton St Fran Kitt Green 14–15; V from 14; P-in-c Marsh Green 14–15; V 15–16; V Kitt Green and Marsh Green 16–19; P-in-c Hattersley *Ches* 19–20; V from 20. *St Barnabas' Vicarage, Hattersley Road East, Hyde SK14 3EQ* M: 07736-523168 E: denisehayes4@aol.com

HAYES, Helen. b 63. d 10 p 11. NSM Bradgate Team *Leic* 10–13; Pioneer P among homeless in W Leic 13–19; PtO 19–20. *179 Starkholmes Road, Starkholmes, Matlock DE4 5JA*

HAYES, Jane. d 16. NSM Parkham, Alwington, Buckland Brewer etc *Ex* from 16. *16 Pengilly Way, Hartland, Bideford EX39 6HR*

HAYES, Canon John Henry Andrew. b 52. BSc. Wycliffe Hall Ox 82. d 84 p 85. C Moreton *Ches* 84–87; R Barrow 87–94; Bp's Chapl 87–94; P-in-c Runcorn St Mich 94–04; P-in-c Runcorn All SS 94–05; P-in-c Runcorn H Trin 04–05; V Runcorn All SS w H Trin 05–15; Hon Can Ches Cathl 08–15; rtd 15; PtO *Ches* from 15. *Crosbies Cottage, Buxworth, High Peak SK23 7NE* E: johnh552@outlook.com

HAYES, Mrs Marion Anne. b 51. Leeds Univ BA 05 Liv Inst of Educn CertEd 72. NOC 02. d 05 p 06. NSM Runcorn All SS w H Trin *Ches* 05–15; rtd 15; PtO *Ches* from 15. *Crosbies Cottage, Buxworth, High Peak SK23 7NE* E: mrsmahayes@gmail.com

HAYES, Michael Gordon William. b 48. St Cath Coll Cam BA 69 MA 73 PhD 73. Ridley Hall Cam 73. d 75 p 76. C Combe Down w Monkton Combe *B & W* 75–78; C Cambridge H Trin *Ely* 78–81; V Bathampton *B & W* 81–88; V Clevedon St Andr and Ch Ch 88–95; C Belper *Derby* 95–00; P-in-c Drayton in Hales *Lich* 00–07; RD Hodnet 01–06; P-in-c Chilton Cantelo, Ashington, Mudford, Rimpton etc *B & W* 07–13; rtd 13; PtO *B & W* from 13. *10 Paddock Close, Creech St Michael, Taunton TA3 5DZ* T: (01823) 444766 E: mhhayes@outlook.com

HAYES, Michael John. b 52. Lanc Univ BA 73. Coll of Resurr Mirfield 75. d 78 p 79. C Notting Hill *Lon* 78–81; C-in-c Hammersmith SS Mich and Geo White City Estate CD 81–88; PtO 98–00; NSM Norwood St Mary 00–03; Chapl Heart of Kent Hospice 12–05; P-in-c Burham and Wouldham *Roch* 12–16; R from 16. *22 Ridley Road, Rochester ME1 1UL* M: 07964-697556 E: mikejhayes@hotmail.co.uk

HAYES, Canon Miranda Jane. b 57. STETS BA 06. d 06 p 07. C Dorking w Ranmore *Guildf* 06–10; P-in-c Earls Barton *Pet* 10–16; RD Wellingborough 15–18; P-in-c Welford w Sibbertoft and Marston Trussell 19; P-in-c Clipston w Naseby and Haselbech w Kelmarsh 19; R Clipston, Haselbech, Kelmarsh, Marston Trussell etc from 19; RD Brixworth from 20; Can Pet Cathl from 17. *The Rectory, 18 Church Lane, Clipston, Market Harborough LE16 9RW* T: (01858) 525342 E: mirandahayes@outlook.com *or* vicar.welfordclipston@outlook.com

HAYES, Peter Rowland. b 53. Melbourne Coll of Div BD 82 MMin 05. d 82 p 83. C Hamilton Australia 82–83; R Wongan Hills w Dalwallinu 84–87; R Kwinana 87–91; CF 91–09; P-in-c Lurgashall *Chich* 14–19; P-in-c w Ebernoe 14–19; rtd 19. *c/o Ms C Hayes, Unit 17, 36 Jerdanefield Road, St Lucia QLD 4067, Australia* E: rowls3613@gmail.com

HAYES, Richard. b 39. K Coll Lon BD 68 AKC 68. d 69 p 70. C Dartford H Trin *Roch* 69–72; C S Kensington St Steph *Lon* 72–76; V Ruislip Manor St Paul 76–82; V Ealing St Pet Mt Park 82–91; R St Edm the King and St Mary Woolnoth etc 91–99; rtd 99; PtO *Lich* 99–04; *Heref* from 00; Hon C Shrewsbury St Alkmund *Lich* 04–07; Hon C Shrewsbury St Chad, St Mary and St Alkmund 07–15; PtO 15–21; OCM from 09. *53 Stiperstones Court, Abbey Foregate, Shrewsbury SY2 6AL* T: (01743) 244668 E: l.r.hayes@btinternet.com

HAYES, Richard Henry. b 65. St Jo Coll Nottm 89. d 92 p 93. C Southborough St Pet w Ch Ch and St Matt *Roch* 92–95; C Downend *Bris* 95–97; V Gravesend St Mary *Roch* 97–02; R Clymping and Yapton w Ford *Chich* from 02. *The Rectory, St Mary's Meadow, Yapton, Arundel BN18 0EE* T: (01243) 552962 M: 07944-804933 E: revrichhayes@me.com

HAYES, Canon Rosemarie Eveline. b 51. Brighton Coll of Educn CertEd 72. NOC 88. d 91 p 94. Par Dn Manston *Ripon* 91–94; C 94–95; C Beeston 95–00; V Horsforth 00–11; P-in-c Kirkstall 06–11; TR Allerton Bywater, Kippax and Swillington 16–20; All Whitkirk 17; Hon Can Ripon Cathl 10–20; rtd 20; PtO *Leeds* 21. *282 Selby Road, Leeds LS15 0PU* E: rosemariehayes@live.co.uk

HAYES, Sarah Caroline. b 61. Man Univ BA 84 Solicitor 90. St Jo Coll Nottm 05 Qu Coll Birm 07. d 09 p 10. NSM Hall Green St Pet *Birm* 09–13; NSM Edgbaston St Germain 13–19; V from 19. *180 Portland Road, Birmingham B16 9TD* T: 0121-429 3431 M: 07891-136654 E: sarahhayes2@me.com *or* sarah@stgermains.org.uk

HAYES, Sarah Elizabeth. b 63. Ch Coll Cam BA 85 MA 89. Wycliffe Hall Ox 08. d 10 p 11. C Chipping Campden w Ebrington *Glouc* 10–13; V Horsell *Guildf* 13–20; Public Preacher *St Alb* from 20; PtO *Glouc* from 20. *3 Old Grammar School, High Street, Chipping Campden GL55 6HB* M: 07878-455644

HAYES, Stephen Anthony. b 57. St Jo Coll Dur BA 80 S Bank Univ PGCE 96. SAOMC 97. d 99 p 00. NSM Kingham w Churchill, Daylesford and Sarsden *Ox* 99–01; NSM Chipping Norton 01–06; Chapl Kingham Hill Sch *Oxon* 99–06; Teacher Arnold Lodge Sch Leamington Spa 06–12; Teacher St Mary's Sch Ascot 15–16; PtO *Ox* 06–16; R Ray Valley from 16. *The Vicarage, Church Walk, Ambrosden, Bicester OX25 2UJ* T: (01869) 247813 E: hayesfamily@freeuk.com

HAYES, Timothy James. b 62. d 89 p 90. C Lache cum Saltney *Ches* 89–94; P-in-c Dukinfield St Jo 94–99; V from 99; P-in-c Millbrook from 17. *37 Harold Avenue, Dukinfield SK16 5NH* T: 0161-308 4708 E: revtimhayes@hotmail.com

HAYHOE, Geoffrey John Stephen. b 57. Portsm Univ BSc 00. Qu Coll Birm 01. d 03 p 04. C Felixstowe St Jo *St E* 03–06; V Geraldine NZ 06–17; R Broadhembury, Dunkeswell, Luppitt, Plymtree, Sheldon, and Upottery *Ex* from 17. *Manor Cottage, Upottery, Honiton EX14 9PN* M: 07864-048575 E: john@hayhoe.net *or* rector.dunkeswell@gmail.com

HAYLER, Mrs Lynn Christina. b 64. d 14 p 15. C S Cotswolds *Glouc* 14–18; TV N Wingfield, Clay Cross and Pilsley *Derby* from 18. *The New Vicarage, Morton Road, Pilsley, Chesterfield S45 8EF* T: (01773) 872293 E: vicar@stmaryspilsley.org

HAYLER, Peter John. b 65. R Holloway Coll Lon BSc 87 Univ of Wales (Cardiff) MPhil 01 Anglia Ruskin Univ DProf 16. Wilson Carlile Coll 89 St Mich Coll Llan 99. d 00 p 04. Ind Chapl *Mon* 95–03; C Pontnewydd 00–03; C Magor 03–06; TV 06–09; C Cambridge Gt St Mary w St Mich *Ely* 09–17; Chapl Univ Staff Cam 09–17; R Shipbourne w Plaxtol *Roch* from 17. *The Rectory, The Street, Plaxtol, Sevenoaks TN15 0QG* T: (01732) 811081 E: rectorswp@gmail.com

HAYLETT, David William. b 44. d 05 p 06. OLM Dorchester *Ox* 05–16; PtO from 16. *8 Westfield Road, Long Wittenham, Abingdon OX14 4RF* T: (01865) 407382 E: familyhaylett@yahoo.com

HAYLOCK, Mrs Jill Caroline. b 54. ERMC 12. d 15 p 16. OLM Loddon, Sisland, Chedgrave, Hardley and Langley *Nor* from 15. *Lodge Farm, Sisland, Norwich NR14 6EE* T: (01508) 520248 E: jillhaylock@aol.com

HAYMAN, Mrs Audrey Doris. b 41. St Mary's Coll Chelt 61 Bris Univ CertEd 61 Cov Coll of Educn 65. Glouc Sch of Min 88. d 91 p 94. NSM Matson *Glouc* 91–98; P-in-c Falfield w Rockhampton 98–02; P-in-c Oldbury-on-Severn 98–02; PtO 02–04; NSM Barnwood from 04. *32 Corncroft Lane, Matson, Gloucester GL4 6XU* T: (01452) 411786 E: audrey.hayman@gmail.com

HAYNES, Miss Catherine Mary. b 68. Man Univ BA 90 Win Univ MA 11. St Mich Coll Llan BD 95. d 96 p 97. C Llantwit Major *Llan* 96–99; C Coity w Nolton 99–01; Dioc Children's Officer 99–01; P-in-c Llangammarch w Llanganten and Llanllеonfel etc *S & B* 01–03; P-in-c Irfon Valley 03–06; R 06–10; V Blaenau Irfon 06–10; Dioc Dir of Educn 02–08; Chapl Haberdashers' Monmouth Sch for Girls from 12; C Rockfield w Monmouth w Overmonnow etc *Mon* from 14; Dioc Children's Adv from 14. *St Thomas's Vicarage, St Thomas Square, Monmouth NP25 5ES* T: (01600) 715159 E: revcmhaynes@btinternet.com

HAYNES, Jonathan Kenneth William. b 84. R Cen Sch Speech & Drama BA 07. Ripon Coll Cuddesdon BA 19. d 19 p 20. C Putney St Mary S'wark from 19. *8 Deodar Road, London SW15 2NN* M: 07841-908382 E: jonathanhaynes838@gmail.com *or* jonathan.haynes@parishofputney.co.uk

HAYNES, Canon Stuart Edward. b 69. Edge Hill Coll of HE 90. SNWTP 07. d 10 p 11. NSM Ormskirk *Liv* from 10; Hon Can Liv Cathl from 19. *11 Fairfield Close, Ormskirk L39 1RN* M: 07534-218122 E: stuart.haynes@liverpool.anglican.org

HAYNES, Valerie Elizabeth Mary-Benedict. b 53. Cant Ch Ch Univ BA 09. St Steph Ho Ox 03. d 05 p 06. C Sheerness H Trin w St Paul *Cant* 05–09; PtO 09–10; P-in-c Skelton w Upleatham *York* 10–14; R from 14; P-in-c Boosbeck and Lingdale 10–14; V from 14. *2 Nidderdale, Skelton-in-Cleveland, Saltburn-by-the-Sea TS12 2FY* T: (01287) 654040 M: 07803-798475 E: revhaynes@btinternet.com

HAYNS, Mrs Clare Julia Yates. b 69. Warwick Univ BA 91 R Holloway Coll Lon MSc 95 DipSW 95. Ripon Coll Cuddesdon 08. d 11 p 12. C Blenheim *Ox* 11–15; Chapl Ch Ch Ox from 15; LtO *Ox* from 17. Christ Church, St Aldates, Oxford OX1 1DP T: (01865) 276236 M: 07801-930702 E: clare.hayns@chch.ox.ac.uk

HAYSMORE, Geoffrey Frederick. b 39. Bps' Coll Cheshunt 63. d 66 p 67. C St Marylebone St Mark w St Luke *Lon* 66–69; C Stockton St Chad *Dur* 69–72; C-in-c Town End Farm CD 72–77; PtO from 95; rtd 01. *139 Lambton Road, Middlesbrough TS4 2ST* T: (01642) 275259 E: g.haysmore@ntlworld.com

HAYTER, Mark Harrison George. b 49. Newc Univ BA 72. WEMTC 10. **d** 12 **p** 13. NSM St Weonards *Heref* 12–14; C Nadder Valley *Sarum* from 14. *High Spinney, Sutton Road, Fovant, Salisbury SP3 5LF* E: revmarkh@icloud.com

HAYTER, Mary Elizabeth. *See* BARR, Mary Elizabeth

HAYTER, Canon Raymond William. b 48. Oak Hill Th Coll 74. **d** 77 **p** 78. C Bermondsey St Jas w Ch Ch *S'wark* 77–80; C Sydenham H Trin 81–83; Asst Chapl HM Pris Brixton 83–84; Chapl HM Youth Cust Cen Stoke Heath 84–88; Chapl HM Pris Maidstone 88–91; CF 91–08; Chapl HM Pris Standford Hill 08–11; Min Can St Woolos Cathl *Mon* 11–14; Can Pastor from 14; rtd 16; PtO *Lon* from 19. *Address withheld by request* E: raymondhayter@hotmail.com

HAYTER, Sandra. *See* RAILTON, Sandra

HAYTON, John Anthony. b 45. TD 81. Heythrop Coll Lon MA 00 ACII 70. Oak Hill Th Coll 93. **d** 96 **p** 97. NSM St Alb St Mich 96–15; PtO from 15; OCM 02–08. *89 Harpenden Road, St Albans AL3 6BY* T: (01727) 761719 *or* 835037 E: john.hayton@ntlworld.com

HAYTON, Mark William. b 59. St Steph Ho Ox 85. **d** 88 **p** 89. C Sittingbourne St Mich *Cant* 88–91; C Kennington 91–94; R Broadstairs 94–07; RD Thanet 96–01; P-in-c Folkestone Trin 07–11; V 11–14; AD Elham 11–14; V Fleet *Guildf* from 14; AD Aldershot from 19. *The Vicarage, Branksomewood Road, Fleet GU51 4JU* T: (01252) 219281 E: vicar@parishoffleet.org.uk

HAYWARD, Canon Christopher Joseph. b 38. TCD BA 63 MA 67. Ridley Hall Cam 63. **d** 65 **p** 66. C Hatcham St Jas *S'wark* 65–69; Warden Lee Abbey Internat Students' Club Kensington 69–74; Chapl Chelmsf Cathl 74–77; P-in-c Darlaston All SS *Lich* 77–83; Ind Chapl 77–83; Can Res Bradf Cathl 83–92; Sec Bd Miss 83–92; R Linton in Craven *Bradf* 92–03; P-in-c Burnsall w Rylstone 97–03; RD Skipton 93–98; Hon Can Bradf Cathl 92–03; rtd 03; PtO *Bradf* 04–14; *Leeds* from 14. *33 Priestley Court, Railway Road, Ilkley LS29 8UU* T: (01943) 818679 M: 07944-617890 E: chrisannh@talktalk.net

HAYWARD, Jeffrey Kenneth. b 47. St Jo Coll Nottm BTh 74. **d** 74 **p** 75. C Stambermill *Worc* 74–77; C Woking St Jo *Guildf* 77–83; V Springfield H Trin *Chelmsf* 83–98; Chapl HM Pris Chelmsf 86–00; Area RD Chelmsf 86–88; RD Chelmsf 88–93; RD Chelmsf N 93–95; Hon Can Chelmsf Cathl 93–98; Chapl HM Pris Wakef 00–05; Chapl HM Pris Long Lartin 05–12; rtd 12; PtO *Chelmsf* from 14. *4 Durham Close, Great Bardfield, Braintree CM7 4UA* T: (01371) 810837

HAYWARD, Mrs Jennifer Dawn. b 38. WMMTC 85. **d** 88 **p** 94. NSM Gt Malvern St Mary *Worc* 88–90; NSM Gt Malvern Ch Ch 88–90; Par Dn 90–94; C 94–96; TV Wirksworth *Derby* 96–04; rtd 04; PtO *Worc* from 04. *26 Barley Crescent, Long Meadow, Worcester WR4 0HW* T: (01905) 29545 M: 07963-089437 E: revjenniehayward@gmail.com

HAYWARD, John Andrew. b 63. Nottm Univ BTh 89 MHCIMA 83. Linc Th Coll 86. **d** 89 **p** 90. C Seaford w Sutton *Chich* 89–92; C St Pancras H Cross w St Jude and St Pet *Lon* 92–95; V Kentish Town St Martin w St Andr 95–08; AD S Camden 05–08; V Merton St Mary *S'wark* from 08. *The Vicarage, 3 Church Path, London SW19 3HJ* T: (020) 8543 6192 E: vicar@stmarysmerton.org.uk

HAYWARD, Preb John Talbot. b 28. Selw Coll Cam BA 52 MA 56. Wells Th Coll 52. **d** 54 **p** 55. C S Lyncombe *B & W* 54–58; R Lamyatt 58–71; V Bruton w Wyke Champflower and Redlynch 58–71; RD Bruton 62–71; R Weston-super-Mare St Jo 71–75; Preb Wells Cathl 73–03; TR Weston-super-Mare Cen Par 75–92; rtd 92; PtO *B & W* from 92. *5 Chelswood Avenue, Weston-super-Mare BS22 8QP* T: (01934) 628431

HAYWARD, Marianne Ruth. b 73. Girton Coll Cam BA 94 MA 98 MB, BCh 97 MRCPsych 03. Coll of Resurr Mirfield BA 20. **d** 20 **p** 21. NSM Elm Park St Nic Hornchurch *Chelmsf* 20–21; NSM Hornchurch St Andr from 21. *Address withheld by request* M: 07904-292993 E: marianne.hayward@talktalk.net

HAYWARD, Martin. b 45. WMMTC 07. **d** 07 **p** 08. Dir Internat Min *Cov* 07–08; NSM Cov St Fran N Radford 07–12; Dean's V Cov Cathl 10–12; rtd 12; PtO *S'wark* from 12; *Cov* 12–15. *31 Waterside Court, Millpond Place, Carshalton SM5 2JT* T: (020) 3652 0551 M: 07917-182579 E: martin.hayward12@sky.com

HAYWARD, Mrs Sarah Lynn. b 77. St Mary's Coll Strawberry Hill BA 99. St Jo Coll Nottm MTh 06. **d** 08 **p** 09. C Dibden *Win* 08–13; P-in-c Braintree St Paul *Chelmsf* 13–19; C Colchester St Luke from 19; C Colchester St Mich Myland from 19; C Langham w Boxted from 19; C W Bergholt and Gt Horkesley from 19; C Wormingford, Mt Bures and Lt Horkesley from 19. *2 Jenner Chase, Colchester CO4 6BJ* M: 07828-046193 E: sarah.hayward@talktalk.net

HAYWARD, Timothy David Mark. b 78. St Andr Univ MTheol 00. Westcott Ho Cam 07. **d** 09 **p** 10. C Buckden w

the Offords *Ely* 09–12; V Bunbury and Tilstone Fearnall *Ches* from 12; RD Malpas from 21. *The New Vicarage, Vicarage Lane, Bunbury, Tarporley CW6 9PE* T: (01829) 261511 M: 07988-994481 E: revtimhayward@gmail.com

HAYWOOD, Christopher John. b 69. Poly Cen Lon BSc 92 Brighton Univ BSc 95 St Jo Coll Lon BA 17. Cranmer Hall Dur 15. **d** 17 **p** 18. C Hugglescote w Donington, Ellistown and Snibston *Leic* 17–21; R Hawridge w Cholesbury and St Leonard *Ox* from 21; V The Lee from 21. *The Vicarage, The Lee, Great Missenden HP16 9LZ* E: rev.chrishaywood@btinternet.com

HAYWOOD, Miss Joanna Margaret. b 59. Open Univ BSc 01 Surrey Univ PGCE 02. ERMC 19. **d** 21. C Trunch Group *Nor* from 21. *3 Swallow Barns, Pond Road, Bradfield, North Walsham NR28 0AB* T: (01692) 406091 M: 07941-096311 E: jo.m.haywood@gmail.com

HAYWOOD, Preb Keith Roderick. b 48. Oak Hill Th Coll 84. **d** 86 **p** 87. C Fazeley *Lich* 86–90; TV Leek and Meerbrook 90–01; Acting TR Hanley H Ev 01–03; TR 03–13; Preb Lich Cathl 07–13; rtd 13; PtO *Lich* from 14. *135 Chase Road, Burntwood WS7 0EB* E: keithrhaywood@gmail.com

HAZEL, Sister. *See* SMITH, Hazel Ferguson Waide

HAZELL, David Peter. b 88. Wycliffe Hall Ox 12. **d** 17. C Herne Bay Ch Ch *Cant* 17–21; C Battle *Chich* from 21. *6 Lily Close, Sedlescombe, Battle TN33 0FS* T: (01424) 870341 E: rev.davidhazell@gmail.com

HAZELTON, Michael John. b 53. UEA BA 76 Bedf Coll Lon PhD 81. Heythrop Coll Lon BD 89. **d** 90 **p** 91. Asst Chapl Helsinki *Eur* 94–95; Asst Chapl Zürich w Winterthur 95–98; R Mablethorpe w Trusthorpe *Linc* 98–02; R Saxonwell 02–05; V Danby w Castleton and Commondale *York* 05–17; V Westerdale 05–17; V Moorsholm 09–17; RD Whitby 16–17; rtd 17; PtO *S'wark* from 17. *19 St Elmos Road, London SE16 6SA* E: mjh_uk@hotmail.com

HAZELWOOD, Ms Jillian. b 32. Bp Otter Coll CertEd 52 St Alb Minl Tr Scheme 82. **d** 87 **p** 94. NSM Wheathampstead *St Alb* 87–02; rtd 02; PtO *St Alb* 02–19. *14 Butterfield Road, Wheathampstead, St Albans AL4 8PU* T/F: (01582) 833146 E: woodhazel@waitrose.com

HAZLEHURST, Anthony Robin. b 43. Man Univ BSc 64. Tyndale Hall Bris 65. **d** 68 **p** 69. C Macclesfield Ch Ch *Ches* 68–71; C Bushbury *Lich* 71–75; P-in-c New Clee *Linc* 75–85; TV Deane *Man* 85–96; V Harwood 96–07; rtd 07; PtO *Man* from 07; *B & W* from 21. *6 Vale End, Nailsea, Bristol BS48 2JS* T: (01275) 819024 E: robinhaz@btinternet.com

HAZLETT, Stephen David. b 56. TCD BTh 88. CITC. **d** 88 **p** 89. C Ballywillan *Conn* 88–90; I Rathcoole 90–95; I Dunluce 95–00; Ind Chapl *Dur* 00–12; TV Sunderland 00–07; Chapl Sunderland Minster 07–12; Chapl Rotterdam w Schiedam Miss to Seafarers *Eur* 12–16; Hon C Rotterdam 12–16; R Kirkcudbright *Glas* from 16; R Gatehouse of Fleet from 16. *The Rectory, 18 Castledykes Road, Kirkcudbright DG6 4AN* T: (01557) 620132 M: 07900-231360 E: stephen.hazlett@greyfriarsstmarys.org.uk

HAZLEWOOD, Canon Andrew Lord. b 54. Essex Univ BSc 76. Wycliffe Hall Ox. **d** 82 **p** 83. C Leckhampton SS Phil and Jas w Cheltenham St Jas *Glouc* 82–85; C Waltham H Cross *Chelmsf* 85–89; R Pedmore *Worc* 89–15; P-in-c Wollaston 09–13; RD Stourbridge 07–13; Hon Can Worc Cathl 10–15; rtd 15; PtO *B & W* from 15. *Wychbury, 3 Cuzco Gardens, Periton Road, Minehead TA24 8DU* T: (01643) 818916 E: andrewhazlewood@gmail.com

HAZLEWOOD, David Paul. b 47. Sheff Univ MB, ChB 70 Campion Hall Ox BA 72 MA 77. Wycliffe Hall Ox 70. **d** 73 **p** 74. C Chapeltown *Sheff* 73–75; Singapore 76; Indonesia 76–88; R Ipswich St Helen *St E* 88–97; V Shirley *Win* 97–11; rtd 11; PtO *Llan* 11–14; *Truro* from 14. *2 Hazelmead, Liskeard PL14 4PY* T: (01579) 324848 E: dphazlewood@gmail.com

✠**HAZLEWOOD, The Rt Revd William Peter Guy.** b 71. De Montfort Univ BA 97. St Steph Ho Ox BTh 01. **d** 01 **p** 02 **c** 20. C Knowle H Nativity and Easton All Hallows *Bris* 01–04; P-in-c Iver Heath *Ox* 04–08; R 08–11; P-in-c Dartmouth and Dittisham *Ex* 11–15; V 15–20; Preb Ex Cathl 17–20; Area Bp Lewes *Chich* from 20. *Knoll Cottage, Knowle Lane, Halland, Lewes BN8 6PR* T: (01273) 425009 M: 07436-293168 E: bishop.lewes@chichester.anglican.org

HEAD, David Nicholas. b 55. Pemb Coll Cam BA 77 MA 81 Westmr Coll of Educn MTh 01. Westcott Ho Cam 78. **d** 81 **p** 82. C Surbiton St Andr and St Mark *S'wark* 81–84; C St Marylebone w H Trin *Lon* 84–89; TV Clapham Team *S'wark* 89–96; Chapl Trin Hospice Lon 89–96; Chapl Princess Alice Hospice Esher 96–03; R Lyng, Sparham, Elsing, Bylaugh, Bawdeswell etc *Nor* 03–14; RD Sparham 13–14; R Aylmerton, Runton, Beeston Regis and Gresham 14–19; rtd 19. *Dane House, The Street, Kettlestone, Fakenham NR21 0AU* T: (01328) 878455 E: david@davidhead.plus.com

HEAD, Peter Ernest. b 38. Lon Univ BSc 59. Ridley Hall Cam 61. d 63 p 64. C Fulwood *Sheff* 63–66; C Belper *Derby* 66–68; Hd RE Shoeburyness Sch Southend-on-Sea 69–74; Hd RE Bilborough Coll 74–79; Public Preacher *S'well* 74–79; NSM Bramcote 74–79; Vice-Prin Totton Coll Southn 79–93; Hon C Hordle *Win* 94–02; rtd 03; PtO *Win* from 02. *44 Lentune Way, Lymington SO41 3PF* T/F: (01590) 678097 E: peter_head@bigfoot.com

HEADING, Margaret Anne. b 66. Leeds Univ BSc 88 Man Univ PhD 91 Aston Univ PGCE 99. Wycliffe Hall Ox BA 01. d 02 p 03. C Fletchamstead *Cov* 02–05; V Ingleby Greenhow, Bilsdale Priory etc *York* from 05. *3 Holmemead, Great Broughton, Middlesbrough TS9 7HQ* T: (01642) 710045

HEADING, Canon Richard Vaughan. b 43. Lon Univ BSc 65 ARCS 65. Coll of Resurr Mirfield 66. d 68 p 69. C Heref St Martin 68–75; P-in-c Birches Head and Northwood *Lich* 75–77; TV Hanley H Ev 77–82; V Heref H Trin 82–92; TR Bedminster *Bris* 92–08; AD Bris S 01–06; Hon Can Bris Cathl 01–08; rtd 08; PtO *Worc* from 09. *18 Timberdine Avenue, Worcester WR5 2BD* T: (01905) 360998 E: ric.heading@gmail.com

HEADLEY, Miss Carolyn Jane. b 50. K Coll Lon MA 74 MCSP 71. Oak Hill Th Coll BA 83. dss 83 d 87 p 94. Kensal Rise St Mark and St Martin Lon 83–87; Par Dn Uxbridge 87–90; Team Dn 90–92; Warden of Readers (Willesden Area) 88–92; Tutor Wycliffe Hall Ox 94–05; P-in-c W Meon and Warnford *Portsm* 05–07; Chapl Portsm Hosps NHS Trust 07–11; Chapl Team Ldr 11–13; PtO *Portsm* 13–14; Chapl Epsom and St Helier Univ Hosps NHS Trust 14–18; rtd 18; PtO *S'wark* from 15; *Guildf* from 18. *17 Hawkwood Rise, Bookham, Leatherhead KT23 4JS* T: (01372) 456330 M: 07777-617516 E: carolynheadley@btinternet.com

HEAGERTY, Alistair John. b 42. MBE 86. Oriel Coll Ox BA 63 MA 67. Lon Coll of Div BD 68. d 68 p 69. C Margate H Trin *Cant* 68–72; CF 72–97; Chapl R Memorial Chpl Sandhurst 92–97; TV Kingswood *Bris* 97–08; rtd 08; PtO *St Alb* from 08. *44 Ferney Road, East Barnet, Barnet EN4 8LF* T: (020) 3234 1003 E: ajheagerty@gmail.com

HEAK, Philip George. b 70. QUB BA 92. CITC BTh 95. d 95 p 96. C Ballymacash *Conn* 95–98; C Galway w Kilcummin *T, K & A* 98–00; Dioc Youth Officer (Cashel) *C, F & O* 00–06; I Naas w Kill and Rathmore *M & K* from 06. *15 Spring Gardens, Naas, Co Kildare, Republic of Ireland* T: (00353) (45) 897206 M: 86-817 2356 E: pheak@eircom.net

HEAL, Miss Felicity Joan. b 42. Portsm Dioc Tr Course 89. d 92. NSM Bramshott and Liphook *Portsm* 92–95; NSM Blendworth w Chalton w Idsworth 95–97; PtO from 97. *25 College Street, Petersfield GU31 4AG* T: (01730) 260410 M: 07712-249608 E: felicity.heal@gmail.com

HEALE, Nicholas James. b 67. St Cath Coll Ox BA 89 DPhil 95 Leeds Univ BA 94. Coll of Resurr Mirfield 95. d 95 p 96. C Syston *Leic* 95–99; V Blackpool St Mich *Blackb* 99–10; P-in-c Skerton St Chad 10–15; V 15–19; P-in-c N and E Blackb from 19. *St Jude's Vicarage, Didsbury Street, Blackburn BB1 3JL*

HEALE, Walter James Grenville. b 40. Wycliffe Hall Ox 77. d 79 p 80. C Walsall *Lich* 79–82; TV Marfleet *York* 82–89; TR 89–94; R Easington w Skeffling, Kilnsea and Holmpton 94–05; P-in-c Owthorne and Rimswell w Withernsea 00–05; rtd 05; P-in-c Easington w Skeffling, Kilnsea and Holmpton *York* 05–06; PtO 06–21. *18 Sloe Lane, Beverley HU17 8ND* T: (01482) 865915

HEALEY, Mrs Hilary Louise. b 51. RSCN 73 SRN 73. STETS 10. d 13 p 14. NSM Ampfield, Chilworth and N Baddesley *Win* 13–16; NSM Win St Faith w St Cross from 16. *178 Oliver's Battery Road South, Winchester SO22 4LF* T: (01962) 865923 M: 07443-437472 E: hilaryhealey24@gmail.com

HEALEY (née Barr), Joanna Margaret Alice. b 93. St Jo Coll Dur BSc 14 Murray Edwards Coll Cam BTh 18. Ridley Hall Cam 16. d 19 p 20. C Berrow and Breane *B & W* from 19. *17 Links Close, Burnham-on-Sea TA8 2JD* M: 07926-905110 E: joanna.barr123@gmail.com

HEALEY, Michael Harry Edmund. b 74. Mansf Coll Ox MA 01 Leeds Univ BA 03. Coll of Resurr Mirfield 01. d 04 p 05. C Norton *Sheff* 04–07; P-in-c Beighton from 07. *The Vicarage, 27 Tynker Avenue, Beighton, Sheffield S20 1DX* T: 0114-248 7635 E: mhehealey@hotmail.com

HEALY (née THOROLD), Mrs Alison Susan Joy. b 59. St Jo Coll Dur BA 80. Ripon Coll Cuddesdon 97 SEITE 03. d 06 p 07. NSM Shooters Hill Ch Ch *S'wark* 06–11; PtO 12–13; R Brant Broughton and Beckingham *Linc* 13–17; R Leadenham 13–17; R Welbourn 13–17; P-in-c Caythorpe 13–17; Chapl Trin Sch Belvedere from 17; NSM Footscray w N Cray *Roch* 17–18; NSM Sidcup St Jo 17–18; NSM Sidcup St Jo w Footscray from 18. *3 Holt Close, Sidcup DA14 5EQ* M: 07962-318728 E: vicardancer@supanet.com *or* ahealy@trinity.bexley.sch.uk

HEANEY, Eileen. b 59. SNWTP 08. d 11 p 12. NSM Burscough Bridge *Liv* 11–13; NSM Scarisbrick 13–15; P-in-c 15–18; V from 19; AD Ormskirk from 20. *473 Southport Road, Scarisbrick, Ormskirk L40 9RF* T: (01704) 880463 E: reveileenheaney@hotmail.co.uk

HEANEY, Canon James Roland. b 59. d 85 p 86. C Ballynafeigh St Jude *D & D* 85–88; C Lisburn Ch Ch Cathl *Conn* 88–90; I Dunganstown w Redcross and Conary *D & G* from 90; Can Ch Ch Cathl Dublin from 05. *The Rectory, Redcross, Co Wicklow, Republic of Ireland* T/F: (00353) (404) 41637 E: rolyheaney@gmail.com

HEANEY, Michael Roger. b 43. TCD BA 66 HDipEd 67 MA 69. CITC 74. d 76 p 77. Chapl St Columba's Coll Dub 76–09; rtd 09. *Montana, Scholarstown Road, Dublin 16, Republic of Ireland* T: (00353) (1) 493 1167 M: 86-265 1791 E: revmheaney@gmail.com

HEANEY, Robert Stewart. b 40. d 01 p 02. C Dunboyne Union *M & K* 01–04; PtO *Ox* 05–08; Sen Lect St Jo Univ Tanzania 10–12; Asst Prof Virginia Th Sem USA from 13; Dir Cen for Angl Communion Studies from 13. *Virginia Theological Seminary, 3737 Seminary Road, Alexandria, VA 22304, USA* T: (001) (703) 370 6600 E: robert.s.heaney@gmail.com

HEANEY, Samuel Stewart. b 44. Open Univ BA 79 Ulster Univ BEd 83 Lon Univ BD 93 QUB MPhil 99. St Deiniol's Hawarden 92. d 92 p 93. In Presbyterian Ch 85–92; C Knockbreda *D & D* 92–96; I Belfast H Trin and St Silas *Conn* 96–02; I Ballyrashane w Kildollagh 02–09; rtd 09. *3 Edgewood Court, Antrim BT41 4PG* T: (028) 9446 1076 E: stewartheaney@yahoo.co.uk

HEANEY, Timothy Daniel. b 59. Trin Coll Bris BA 04. d 04 p 05. C Dursley *Glouc* 04–08; P-in-c Paul *Truro* 08–12; Assoc Chapl Dubai H Trin 12–14; Chapl Jebel Ali Ch Ch 15–19; R Shere, Albury and Chilworth *Guildf* from 19. *The Rectory, The Spinning Walk, Shere, Guildford GU5 9HN* T: (01483) 202394 E: rector@parishofshere.com

HEANEY, Wendy Anne. b 42. St Alb Minl Tr Scheme 90. d 95 p 96. NSM Clifton and Southill *St Alb* 95–99; Asst Chapl HM Pris Bedf 95–99; Chapl 99–02; LtO *St Alb* 99–02; rtd 02; PtO *St Alb* from 03. *34 Meadow Way, Letchworth Garden City SG6 3JB* T: (01462) 641303

HEAP, David Leonard. b 58. Man Univ BA 79. Cranmer Hall Dur 82. d 85 p 86. C Clitheroe St Jas *Blackb* 85–88; C Blackb St Gabr 88–92; V Bare from 92. *St Christopher's Vicarage, 12 Elm Grove, Morecambe LA4 6AT* T: (01524) 411363 E: davidleonardheap@gmail.com

HEARD, James Barrie. b 66. Brunel Univ BA 98 K Coll Lon MA 01 PhD 07. Ridley Hall Cam 03. d 06 p 07. C Fulham All SS *Lon* 06–09; C Chelsea St Luke and Ch Ch 09–13; P-in-c Holland Park 13–18; V from 18; AD Kensington from 20. *2 Aubrey Walk, London W8 7JG* T: (020) 3602 9873 M: 07867-508919 E: vicar@hollandparkbenefice.org

HEARD, Richard Adrian. b 72. Univ of Wales (Swansea) BSc 94 Hull Univ PGCE 96. St Jo Coll Nottm 06. d 08 p 09. C Hackenthorpe *Sheff* 08–11; V W Bessacarr from 11; Jt AD Doncaster from 18. *The Vicarage, 39 Sturton Close, Doncaster DN4 7JG* T: (01302) 953342 M: 07818-850347 E: rev.richardheard@yahoo.co.uk *or* richard.heard@sheffield.anglican.org

HEARD, Stephen Edward. b 53. NTMTC 02. d 04 p 08. NSM Bush Hill Park St Mark *Lon* 04–19; NSM Bush Hill Park St Steph 13–19; Parliamentary Chapl to Bp Lon 07–13; rtd 19. *43 Speed House, Barbican, London EC2Y 8AT* M: 07939-253657 E: seh3@me.com

HEARL, Maria Christina. b 47. New Hall Cam BA 69 MA 70 Ex Univ MA 98 PhD 07 PGCE 70. SWMTC 03. d 07 p 08. NSM Ex St Dav 07–11; NSM Sampford Peverell, Uplowman, Holcombe Rogus etc 11–13; PtO *B & W* 13–15; NSM Wellington and Distr 15–21; rtd 21. *16 Twyford Place, Tiverton EX16 6AP* T: (01884) 256380

HEARN, John Henry. b 49. Trin Coll Bris. d 82 p 83. C Epsom Common Ch Ch *Guildf* 82–85; C Ringwood *Win* 85–88; Chapl Basingstoke Distr Hosp 88–91; Chapl Luton and Dunstable Hosp 91–96; C Ampthill w Millbrook and Steppingley *St Alb* 96–99; P-in-c Wymington w Podington 99–03; V W Acklam *York* 03–14; rtd 14; PtO *Dur* from 14. *18 Thurso Close, Stockton-on-Tees TS19 7JD* E: jhhearn4@gmail.com

HEARN, Jonathan. b 58. Leeds Univ BA 81 GradIPM 85. Westcott Ho Cam 89. d 91 p 92. C Tuffley *Glouc* 91–94; C Milton *Win* 94–02; P-in-c Warwick St Paul *Cov* 02–03; TV Warwick from 03. *St Paul's Vicarage, 33 Stratford Road, Warwick CV34 6AS* T: (01926) 419814 E: revjonathanhearn@btinternet.com

HEARN, Canon Peter Brian. b 31. St Jo Coll Dur 52. d 55 p 56. C Frodingham *Linc* 55–59; R Belton SS Pet and Paul 59–64; PC Manthorpe w Londonthorpe 59–64; V Billingborough 64–73; V Sempringham w Pointon and Birthorpe 64–73;

V Flixborough w Burton upon Stather 73–96; RD Manlake 87–93; Can and Preb Linc Cathl 92–01; rtd 96; PtO *Linc* from 01. *7 St Andrews Drive, Burton-upon-Stather, Scunthorpe DN15 9BY* T: (01724) 720510

HEARN, Trevor. b 36. Sarum Th Coll 61. **d** 64 **p** 65. C Hounslow St Steph *Lon* 64–67; Miss to Seafarers 67–01; UAE 92–01; rtd 01; PtO *Bris* from 01. *37 Elberton Road, Bristol BS9 2PZ* T: 0117-983 6526 E: tvhearn37@btinternet.com

HEATH, Mrs Cynthia Grace. b 46. St Mark & St Jo Coll Lon TCert 68 Open Univ BA 85 ARCM 66 GRSM 68. WMMTC 94. **d** 97 **p** 98. NSM Penkridge *Lich* 97–00; TV 00–07. *2 Hall Farm Road, Brewood, Stafford ST19 9EZ* T: (01902) 850175 E: cynthgren@btinternet.com

HEATH, Henry. b 40. FCII 77. Oak Hill Th Coll 77. **d** 80 **p** 81. NSM Lexden *Chelmsf* 80–86; C Colne Engaine 86; NSM Halstead St Andr w H Trin and Greenstead Green 86–90; NSM W w E Mersea 90–95; R Stanway 95–02; rtd 02; PtO *Chelmsf* 02–05; P-in-c Wormingford, Mt Bures and Lt Horkesley 05–12; PtO *St E* 13–21; *Chelmsf* from 20. *The Mews, Hill House, Long Melford, Sudbury CO10 9BD* M: 07885-306699 E: hillhousemews@aol.com or revhenryheath@gmail.com

HEATH, John Henry. b 41. Chich Th Coll 69. **d** 71 **p** 72. C Crediton *Ex* 71–74; C Tavistock and Gulworthy 74–76; C Brixham 76–77; C Brixham w Churston Ferrers 77–79; R Bere Ferrers 79–85; P-in-c Moretonhampstead, N Bovey and Manaton 85–88; R 88–93; P-in-c Lifton 93–99; P-in-c Kelly w Bradstone 93–99; P-in-c Broadwoodwidger 93–99; R Lifton, Broadwoodwidger, Coryton, Stowford etc 99–01; V Lifton, Broadwoodwidger, Stowford etc 01–03; rtd 03; PtO *Heref* 04–10. *30 Wye Way, Hereford HR1 2NP*

HEATH, Julie Ann. b 62. Nottm Univ BA 09. EMMTC. **d** 06 **p** 07. NSM Kegworth, Hathern, Long Whatton, Diseworth etc *Leic* 06–08; Workplace Chapl 08–14; Chapl Leic Univ 09–13; Chapl Leic Cathl 12–14; PtO from 14. *Fairmount House, 87 Leicester Road, Ashby-de-la-Zouch LE65 1DD* T: (01530) 414549 M: 07801-467348 E: julieannheath@pottersmaze.co.uk

HEATH, Martin Jonathan. b 68. St Jo Coll Nottm 07. **d** 09 **p** 10. C Gt Wyrley *Lich* 09–12; C Harlescott from 12. *Emmanuel Vicarage, Mount Pleasant Road, Shrewsbury SY1 3HY* T: (01743) 350907 M: 07847-370572 E: martinjheath@talktalk.net

HEATH-WHYTE, David Robert. b 68. Fitzw Coll Cam BA 89. Wycliffe Hall Ox BTh 98. **d** 98 **p** 99. C Gt Chesham *Ox* 98–02; V Frogmore *St Alb* 02–14; TR Morden *S'wark* from 14. *The Rectory, London Road, Morden SM4 5QT* T: (020) 8648 3920 or 8685 0012 E: david.hw@morden.church

HEATHER, Mark Duncan Grainger. b 62. Leic Poly LLB 83 Leeds Univ BA 99. Coll of Resurr Mirfield 97. **d** 99 **p** 00. C Leeds St Aid *Ripon* 99–03; V Leeds Halton St Wilfrid 03–10; Bp's Chapl *Guildf* 10–17; R Ashurst *Chich* from 17; V Steyning from 17. *The Vicarage, Station Road, Steyning BN44 3YL* T: (01903) 879877 E: vicarofsteyning@gmail.com or rectorofashurst@gmail.com

HEATHER, Mrs Sally Patricia. b 51. Avery Hill Coll BEd 73. STETS 99. **d** 02 **p** 03. NSM Michelmersh and Awbridge and Braishfield etc *Win* 02–06; TV Basingstoke 06–11; PtO from 11. *8 Sparkford Road, Winchester SO22 4NL* T: (01962) 622550 E: spheather@gmail.com

HEATHFIELD, Rachel Jane. b 70. Surrey Univ BA 91 MA 93. St Mellitus Coll BA 16. **d** 16 **p** 17. C The Quinton *Birm* 16–19; P-in-c from 20. *The Rectory, 773 Hagley Road West, Quinton, Birmingham B32 1AJ* M: 07968-077453 E: rachel@quintonchurch.co.uk

HEATHFIELD, The Ven Simon David. b 67. Birm Univ BMus 88 Fitzw Coll Cam BTh 99. Ridley Hall Cam 96. **d** 99 **p** 00. C Heswall *Ches* 99–02; Voc and Min Adv CPAS 02–05; TR Walthamstow *Chelmsf* 06–14; AD Waltham Forest 12–14; Adn Aston *Birm* from 14. *The Rectory, 773 Hagley Road West, Quinton, Birmingham B32 1AJ* M: 07769-187435 E: simonh@cofebirmingham.com

HEATLEY, Cecil. *See* HEATLEY, William Cecil

HEATLEY, David Henry. b 50. Kent Univ BA 72. Qu Coll Birm 86. **d** 88 **p** 89. C Liss *Portsm* 88–91; V Newchurch and Arreton 91–99; R Greatham w Empshott and Hawkley w Prior's Dean 99–13; Dioc Rural Officer 07–13; rtd 13; PtO *Portsm* from 14. *1 Osborne Chase, Cowes PO31 7FA* T: (01983) 290567 E: dhheatley@btinternet.com

HEATLEY, Canon William Cecil. b 39. QUB BA 61. Ridley Hall Cam 62. **d** 64 **p** 65. C Ballymacarrett St Patr *D & D* 64–69; C Herne Hill St Paul *S'wark* 69–74; TV Sanderstead All SS 75–82; P-in-c Peckham St Sav 82–87; V 87–07; RD Dulwich 97–02; Hon Can S'wark Cathl 01–07; rtd 07; PtO *S'wark* from 07; *Roch* from 07. *37 Bromley College, London Road, Bromley BR1 1PE* T: (020) 8460 9505 E: cecilheatley@yahoo.com

HEATON, Alan. b 36. K Coll Lon BD 64 AKC 64 Nottm Univ MTh 76. **d** 65 **p** 66. C Stockton St Chad *Dur* 65–68; C Englefield Green *Guildf* 68–70; C Winlaton *Dur* 70–74; Chapl Derby Lonsdale Coll 74–79; V Alfreton 79–87; RD 81–86; TR Clifton *S'well* 87–93; P-in-c Rolleston w Fiskerton, Morton and Upton 93–96; rtd 97; PtO *Liv* from 97. *29 The Parchments, Newton-le-Willows WA12 0DX* T: (01925) 292209 E: a.ms-heaton@tiscali.co.uk

HEATON, Sister Elizabeth Ann. b 65. Bath Coll of HE BSc 87. Ripon Coll Cuddesdon 98. **d** 00 **p** 01. C Lostwithiel, St Winnow w St Nectan's Chpl etc *Truro* 00–03; CSF from 03; PtO *B & W* 03–10; *Linc* 10–12; C Branston w Nocton and Potterhanworth 12–15; C Metheringham w Blankney and Dunston 12–15; PtO *Leic* 17–20; R Upper Soar from 20. *The Vicarage, Main Road, Claybrooke Parva, Lutterworth LE17 5AE* T: (01455) 202935 M: 07592-690222 E: uppersoar2019@gmail.com

HEATON, Canon Joseph Anthony Turnley. b 70. Univ of Wales (Abth) BSc 91 PhD 95 St Jo Coll Dur BA 08. Cranmer Hall Dur 06. **d** 08 **p** 09. C Ribbesford w Bewdley and Dowles *Worc* 08–11; P-in-c Rushen *S & M* 11–13; V from 13; Can St German's Cathl from 16. *Rushen Vicarage, Barracks Road, Port St Mary, Isle of Man IM9 5LP* T: (01624) 832275 E: rev.joeheaton@gmail.com

HEATON, Julian Roger. b 62. LSE BSc(Econ) 83. St Steph Ho Ox BA 86 MA 92. **d** 87 **p** 88. C Stockport St Thos w St Pet *Ches* 87–90; Chapl Asst Qu Medical Cen and Univ Hosp Nottm 90–92; V Knutsford St Cross *Ches* 92–01; P-in-c Altrincham St Jo 01–05; Voc Officer (Macclesfield Adnry) 01–05; V Sale St Anne 05–17; RD Bowdon 12–17; R Bury St Mary *Man* from 17; V Bury St Paul from 17. *Bury Rectory, Tithebarn Street, Bury BL9 0JR* T: 0161-764 2452 M: 07564-721331 E: julian.heaton_1@outlook.com

HEATON, Robert Anthony. b 56. **d** 16 **p** 17. NSM Sprotbrough *Sheff* from 16. *24 Field House Road, Sprotbrough, Doncaster DN5 7RP* T: (01302) 570209 M: 07762-929763 E: r.heaton1956@virgin.net or robert.heaton@sheffield.anglican.org

HEATON, Timothy. b 59. STETS 08. **d** 08 **p** 10. NSM Upper Stour *Sarum* 08–11; NSM Gillingham and Milton-on-Stour 11–19; NSM Gillingham, Milton-on-Stour and Silton from 19. *Grange Cottage, Chaffeymoor, Bourton, Gillingham SP8 5BY* T: (01747) 840936 E: tim4heaton@yahoo.co.uk

HEAVISIDES, Canon Neil Cameron. b 50. Selw Coll Cam BA 72 MA 76 Ox Univ BA 74 MA 85. Ripon Hall Ox 72. **d** 75 **p** 76. C Stockton St Pet *Dur* 75–78; Succ S'wark Cathl 78–81; V Seaham w Seaham Harbour *Dur* 81–88; P-in-c Edington and Imber, Erlestoke and E Coulston *Sarum* 88–89; R 89–93; Can Res Glouc Cathl 93–15; rtd 15; Asst Chapl St Jo Coll 15–16. *218 Myreside Street, Glasgow G32 6DX* E: neil.heavisides@gmail.com

HEAZELL, Pamela Fletcher. b 50. NTMTC 96. **d** 99 **p** 00. NSM Hayes St Nic CD *Lon* 99–01; NSM N Greenford All Hallows 01–04; P-in-c 04–08; V 08–17; rtd 17; PtO *B & W* from 18. *3 Wells Road, Glastonbury BA6 9DN* T: (01458) 833752 E: pfheazell@aol.com

HEBBERN, Geoffrey Alan. b 43. MBE 98. **d** 05 **p** 06. NSM Radipole and Melcombe Regis *Sarum* from 05; Asst Chapl HM Pris The Verne from 05. *11 Hawthorn Close, Weymouth DT4 9UG* T/F: (01305) 772205 E: ghebbern@hotmail.com

HEBBLETHWAITE, Brian Leslie. b 39. Magd Coll Ox BA 61 MA 67 Magd Coll Cam BA 63 MA 68 BD 84 DD 06. Westcott Ho Cam 62. **d** 65 **p** 66. C Elton All SS *Man* 65–68; Chapl Qu Coll Cam 68; Dean of Chpl and Fell 69–94; Asst Lect Div Cam Univ 73–77; Lect 77–99; Can Th Leic Cathl 82–00; rtd 99; PtO *Ely* 02–17. *The Old Barn, 32 High Street, Stretham, Ely CB6 3JQ* T: (01353) 648279 M: 07740-307568 E: blh1000@cam.ac.uk

HEBBLEWHITE, David Ernest. b 52. Hull Univ BA 81 Nottm Univ MA 82 CQSW 82. St Jo Coll Nottm MA 95. **d** 97 **p** 98. C Melton Mowbray *Leic* 97–00; TV Cannock *Lich* 00–07; P-in-c Countesthorpe w Foston *Leic* 07–16; R Four Saints 16–19; Warden of Ev 10–14; RD Guthlaxton 10–18; rtd 19; PtO *Leic* from 20. *24 Waverley Road, Blaby, Leicester LE8 4HH* T: 0116-479 0945

HEBDEN, Cynthia Margaret. *See* THOMSON, Cynthia Margaret

HEBDEN, Keith Oliver. b 76. Univ of Wales (Ban) BD 98 MTh 00 Warwick Univ PGCE 01 Birm Univ PhD 08. Qu Coll Birm 07. **d** 09 **p** 10. C Matson *Glouc* 09–12; C Mansfield SS Pet and Paul *S'well* 12–16; C Mansfield St Mark 12–16; Dir Urban Th Unit Sheff from 16; PtO *Leic* 16–20; NSM Didcot St Pet *Ox* from 20. *16 Sherwood Road, Didcot OX11 0BU* E: keithhebden@gmail.com

HEBDEN, Shirley Elizabeth. b 46. d 19. NSM Beeford w Frodingham and Foston *York* from 19; RD N Holderness from 21. *88 Main Street, North Frodingham, Driffield YO25 8LJ*

HEBER, Andrew John. b 63. Nottm Univ BA 86 MA 89 CQSW 89. Trin Coll Bris BA 99. d 99 p 00. C Parr *Liv* 99–03; TV Kirkby 03–12; R Clogherny w Seskinore and Drumnakilly *Arm* 12–18; I Carnmoney *Conn* from 18. *20 Glebe Road, Newtownabbey BT36 6UW* T: (028) 9083 6637 M: 07804-340912 E: andy.heber@googlemail.com

HEBER PERCY, Canon Christopher John. b 41. St Jo Coll Cam BA 64 MA 68. Wells Th Coll 66. d 68 p 69. C Leigh St Mary *Man* 68–71; Asst Ind Chapl 71–80; P-in-c Oldham St Andr 75–78; TV Oldham 78–80; Ind Chapl *Win* 80–90; N Humberside Ind Chapl *York* 90–06; AD E Hull 98–06; Can and Preb York Minster 05–06; rtd 06. *59 Swarcliffe Road, Harrogate HG1 4QZ* T: (01423) 884076

HEBER-PERCY, Colin Michael. b 68. Birkbeck Coll Lon BA 99 K Coll Lon MA 00 PhD 06. Ripon Coll Cuddesdon MTh 16. d 16 p 17. C Vale of Pewsey *Sarum* 16–20; TV Savernake from 20. *Tidcombe Manor Cottage, Tidcombe, Marlborough SN8 3SL* T: (01264) 731386 M: 07823-772043 E: colinheberpercy@gmail.com

HECTOR, Preb Noel Antony. b 61. Sheff Univ LLB 83 Barrister-at-Law 84. Oak Hill Th Coll BA 91. d 91 p 92. C Rodbourne Cheney *Bris* 91–92; C Bris St Mary Redcliffe w Temple etc 92–95; R Wrington w Butcombe *B & W* 95–03; R E Clevedon w Clapton in Gordano etc from 03; Chapl N Bris NHS Trust from 03; RD Portishead *B & W* 10–17; Preb Wells Cathl from 17. *The Rectory, All Saints' Lane, Clevedon BS21 6AU* T/F: (01275) 873257 E: eastcleveub@blueyonder.co.uk

HEDDERLY, Katherine. b 63. St Hugh's Coll Ox BA 85 MA 94. NTMTC BA 06. d 06 p 07. C Bedford Park *Lon* 06–09; C St Martin-in-the-Fields 09–19; V All Hallows by the Tower etc from 19; AD The City from 19. *All Hallows, 43 Trinity Square, London EC3N 4DJ* M: 07855-161415 E: vicar@ahbtt.org.uk

HEDDLE, Duncan. b 34. Wadh Coll Ox BA 57 MA 61 DPhil 64. d 86 p 86. Chapl Aber Univ *Ab* from 86; P-in-c Bucksburn from 90. *2 Douglas Place, High Street, Aberdeen AB24 3EA* T: (01224) 485975 *or* 272137

HEDGECOCK, Jonathan James. b 64. Imp Coll Lon BScEng 86 Ban Univ BTh 09 CEng MIET 89. d 07 p 08. OLM Guildf H Trin w St Mary from 07. *8 Foxglove Gardens, Guildford GU4 7ES* T: (01483) 502199 M: 07785-766631 E: jonathanjhedgecock@hotmail.com

HEDGER, Canon Graham. b 57. Lon Bible Coll BA 79. Ridley Hall Cam 81. d 83 p 84. C Walton *St E* 83–86; TV Mildenhall 86–91; R Swainsthorpe w Newton Flotman *Nor* 91–94; Dioc Evang Officer 91–94; PtO *St E* 95–99; Bp's Chapl and Liaison Officer 99–07; Bp's Policy and Liaison Officer 07–11; P-in-c Clopton w Otley, Swilland and Ashbocking 09–12; Asst Dioc Sec 10–18; Hd of Stewardship 17–18; P-in-c Orebeck *St E* from 18; Hon Can St E Cathl 04–15; RD Loes 20–21. *14 St Peter's Close, Charsfield, Woodbridge IP13 7RG* T: (01473) 737280 M: 07388-117656 E: revgrahamhedger@outlook.com

HEDGES, Mrs Anne Violet. b 53. Ripon Coll Cuddesdon 87. d 89 p 94. C Thetford *Nor* 89–94; P-in-c Garboldisham w Blo' Norton, Riddlesworth etc 94–97; R Guiltcross 97–00; Chapl Riddlesworth Hall Sch Nor 93–00; Dep Chapl HM Pris Leeds 00–01; Chapl HM Pris Leic 01–05; Chapl HM Pris Highpoint 05–09; Chapl HM Pris Bure 09–16; rtd 16; PtO *Nor* from 16. *Address withheld by request*

HEDGES, Ian Charles. b 55. Sarum & Wells Th Coll 79. d 82 p 83. C Chessington *Guildf* 82–85; C Fleet 85–90; Dioc Adv on Homelessness 87–09; Tr Officer for Past Assts 91–00; rtd 20. *Address withheld by request*

HEDGES, The Very Revd Jane Barbara. b 55. St Jo Coll Dur BA 78. Cranmer Hall Dur 78. dss 80 d 87 p 94. Fareham H Trin *Portsm* 80–83; Southampton (City Cen) *Win* 83–87; Par Dn 87–88; Dioc Stewardship Adv *Portsm* 88–93; Can Res Portsm Cathl 93–01; P-in-c Honiton, Gittisham, Combe Raleigh, Monkton etc *Ex* 01–03; TR 03–06; RD Honiton 03–06; Can Steward Westmr Abbey 06–14; Dean Nor from 14. *The Deanery, The Close, Norwich NR1 4EG* T: (01603) 218300 E: dean@cathedral.org.uk

HEDGES, Mrs Jane Rosemary. b 44. RGN 65. S Dios Minl Tr Scheme 86. d 89 p 94. NSM Gillingham *Sarum* 89–04; NSM Gillingham and Milton-on-Stour 04–08; Lic to RD Blackmore Vale 08–12; PtO *Ox* from 16. *89 Derwent Avenue, Headington, Oxford OX3 0AS* T: (01865) 429494 M: 07966-548127 E: denehollow@msn.com

HEDGES, John Michael Peter. b 34. Leeds Univ BA 60. Ripon Hall Ox 60. d 61 p 62. C Weaste *Man* 61–65; V Ashton St Pet 65–74; C Easthampstead *Ox* 74–85; V Tilehurst St Geo

85–91; C Thatcham 91–94; TV 94–99; rtd 99; PtO *Ox* 99–19. *39 Mallard Way, Grove, Wantage OX12 0QG*

HEDLEY, Charles John Wykeham. b 47. R Holloway Coll Lon BSc 69 PhD 73 Fitzw Coll Cam BA 75 MA 79. Westcott Ho Cam 73. d 76 p 77. C Chingford St Anne *Chelmsf* 76–79; C St Martin-in-the-Fields *Lon* 79–84 and 85–86; P-in-c 84–85; Chapl Ch Coll Cam 86–90; TR Gleadless *Sheff* 90–99; R Westmr St Jas *Lon* 99–09; rtd 09. *95 Brighton Belle, 2 Stroudley Road, Brighton BN1 4ZD* E: chequal@googlemail.com

HEDLEY, Mrs Julia Margaret. b 56. Goldsmiths' Coll Lon BA 78 Bedf Coll Lon MSc 85 Liv Univ MTh 03 SRN 80. NOC 97. d 00 p 01. C Altrincham St Geo *Ches* 00–04; PV Ches Cathl 04–07; Bps' Chapl *B & W* 07–13; NSM Kensington St Mary Abbots w Ch Ch and St Phil *Lon* 13–16; PtO *St Alb* from 13; *Cant* 16–19; *Carl* from 20. *Bassenthwaite, Keswick CA12 4QG* T: (01768) 776844

HEDWORTH, Paul Simon James. b 56. Worc Coll of Educn BEd 78. Qu Coll Birm BA(Theol) 84. d 04 p 05. NSM Bacup and Stacksteads *Man* 04–06; Chapl Qu Eliz Gr Sch Blackb 98–06; Chapl Bromsgrove Sch from 06. *Bromsgrove School, Worcester Road, Bromsgrove B61 7DU* T: (01527) 579679 M: 07966-503194 E: hedworthfamily@yahoo.co.uk *or* phedworth@bromsgrove-school.co.uk

HEELEY, Mrs Janet. b 45. d 00 p 01. OLM Lich St Chad 00–10; rtd 10; PtO *Lich* 10–21. *43 High Grange, Lichfield WS13 7DU* T: (01543) 251600

HEELEY, Robert Francis. b 54. NOC 06. d 08 p 09. NSM Hadfield *Derby* 08–12; NSM Charlesworth and Dinting Vale 12–14; NSM Dinting Vale 14–19; rtd 19; PtO *Derby* from 20. *3 Chesham Close, Hadfield, Glossop SK13 1QX* T: (01457) 855541 E: rob.heeley@uwclub.net

HEELEY, Mrs Ruth Mary. b 41. Qu Coll Birm 04. d 06 p 07. NSM Halas *Worc* 06–11; rtd 11; PtO *Worc* 11–17. *24 Willow View Park, Whimple, Exeter EX5 2QT* T: (01404) 758708 E: ruthmh@hotmail.co.uk

HEENAN, Vivienne Mary. b 48. Univ of Wales (Abth) BA 70 SS Paul & Mary Coll Cheltenham PGCE 90. STETS 03. d 06 p 07. NSM Whitwell and Niton *Portsm* 06–11; NSM Ventnor St Cath 11–13; NSM Ventnor H Trin 11–13; NSM Bonchurch 11–13; PtO 13–18; *Worc* from 18. *The Risings, Kington, Worcester WR7 4DH* M: 07740-780767 E: vivienneheenan@outlook.com

HEFFERNAN-ROBINSON, Michael Thomas Edward. *See* ROBINSON, Michael Thomas Edward

HEFFRON, Peter Heinrich. b 69. Ripon Coll Cuddesdon 18. d 21. NSM Northampton St Alb *Pet* from 21. *51 Green Street, Milton Malsor, Northampton NN7 3AT* M: 07976-431691 E: revpeterheffron@heinrichderek.com

HEGARTY, Ms Bernadette Grace. b 58. Man Poly BA 81 Leeds Univ BA 11 CQSW 90. Coll of Resurr Mirfield 09. d 11 p 12. C High Harrogate St Pet *Ripon* 11–14; *Leeds* 14; V Bow Common *Lon* from 14. *St Paul's Vicarage, Leopold Street, London E3 4LA* E: bhgrace@hotmail.co.uk

HEGEDUS, Frank Michael. b 48. St Louis Univ BA 71 Michigan State Univ MA 76 Univ of St Thos St Paul MBA 84. Colgate-Rochester Div Sch DMin 80. d 74 p 74. P-in-c St Paul St Paul's-on-the-Hill USA 87–89; P-in-c Northfields All SS & Dundas H Cross 88–90; R Farmington Advent 89–96; Asst P Orange Trin Ch 97–98; P-in-c Norwalk St Fran 98–99; NSM Budapest *Eur* 99–01; Asst P Huntington Beach St Wilfrid USA 01–02; P-in-c Redlands Trin Ch 02–03; P-in-c Plymouth St Jo 04–05; P-in-c El Cajon St Alb 05–08; P-in-c Del Mar St Pet 08–09; P-in-c El Centro St Pet and St Paul 09; P-in-c Episc Ch in Almaden San Jose 09–10; P-in-c Budapest *Eur* from 11. *1117 Budapest, Szerémi út 7/A - 603, Hungary* T: (0036) (20) 269 5161 E: anglicanbudapest@gmail.com

HEIGHT (formerly WATKINS), Susan Jane. b 58. Qu Coll Birm. d 01 p 02. C Edgbaston St Germain *Birm* 01–05; TV Salter Street and Shirley 05–11; P-in-c N Dulwich St Faith *S'wark* 11–18; V from 18; AD Dulwich from 16. *St Faith's Vicarage, 62 Red Post Hill, London SE24 9JQ* T: (020) 7274 3924 E: office@stfaithschurch.org

HEIGHTON, George. b 55. Qu Coll Birm 08. d 11 p 12. NSM Bilton *Cov* 11–14; C Willenhall 14–17; C Whitley 14–17; V Brailes from 17; R Sutton under Brailes from 17; P-in-c Tysoe w Oxhill and Whatcote from 17. *The Vicarage, Peacock Lane, Tysoe, Warwick CV35 0SG* M: 07730-009098 E: revgeorgeh@outlook.com

HEIGHTON, Miss Janet Elizabeth. b 67. Leeds Poly BSc 92. Ripon Coll Cuddesdon. d 00 p 01. C Leeds Gipton Epiphany *Ripon* 00–04; P-in-c 04–07; TV Upholland *Liv* 07–14; V Rainford from 14. *1 Tudor Close, Rainford, St Helens WA11 8SD* T: (01744) 882200

HEIL, Janet. b 53. Liv Univ BEd 75 St Jo Coll Dur BA 84. Cranmer Hall Dur. dss 85 d 87 p 94. Ashton Ch Ch *Man* 85–91; Par Dn 87–91; Par Dn Scotforth *Blackb* 91–94; C

358

94–95; V Gt Harwood St Bart 95–06; P-in-c Gt Harwood St Jo 02–06; Hon Can Blackb Cathl 04–06; Chapl Oslo w Bergen, Trondheim and Stavanger *Eur* 06–13; rtd 13; PtO *Blackb* 14–17. *4 Hornby Court, Beaumont Park, Lancaster LA1 2LB* E: janetheil@btinternet.com

HEINE, John Karl. b 62. Simpson Univ (USA) BA 84 California State Univ BA 87 Univ of the Pacific MA 89. Wycliffe Hall Ox 16. **d** 18. C Ashtead *Guildf* 18–19; C Gt Bookham from 19. *17 Loraine Gardens, Ashtead KT21 1PD* M: 07930-126622 E: skyehiker@gmail.com

HEININK, Mrs Jennifer Ann. b 54. K Coll Lon BD 75 Sarum Coll MA 10. St Mellitus Coll 13. **d** 14 **p** 15. OLM Cranham Park *Chelmsf* 14–17; NSM from 17. *14 Grosvenor Gardens, Upminster RM14 1DJ* T: (01708) 227374 E: jennyheinink@hotmail.com

HEITZMANN, Pamela. See BARRIE, Pamela

HELD, Ms Catherine Jane. b 54. Edin Univ BA 77. **d** 18 **p** 19. NSM Blyth Valley *St E* from 18. *Oak Cottage, The Street, Rumburgh, Halesworth IP19 0JX* T: (01986) 781760 M: 07771-556391

HELEN, Sister. See LODER, Helen

HELEN JULIAN, Sister. See ENGLISH, Helen Margaret

HELEY, John. b 28. Lon Univ BA 72. Bps' Coll Cheshunt 54. **d** 56 **p** 57. C Claremont St Sav S Africa 57–61; C Wimborne Minster *Sarum* 61–62; V Narborough w Narford *Nor* 62–67; R Pentney St Mary Magd w W Bilney 62–67; V Catton 67–69; LtO *Ox* 69–72; R E w W Rudham *Nor* 72–75; P-in-c Houghton 72–74; V 74–75; V Hunstanton St Edm 75–82; V Hunstanton St Edm w Ringstead 82–83; rtd 88. *24 Kestrel Close, Burnham Market, King's Lynn PE31 8EF* T: (01328) 730036

HELKVIST, Samuel James. **d** 16 **p** 17. NSM Newport St Julian and St Teilo *Mon* from 16. *104 Worcester Court, Tonyrefail, Porth CF39 8JT* M: 07827-932821 E: frsamuel@stteilonewport.org.uk

HELLARD, Dawn Yvonne Lorraine. b 47. St Mich Coll Llan 89. **d** 91 **p** 97. C Llantwit Major *Llan* 91–95; TV Cowbridge 95–05; rtd 05; PtO *Llan* from 05. *10 Maes Lloi, Aberthin, Cowbridge CF71 7HA* T: (01446) 772460 E: dawnhellard05@gmail.com

HELLEWELL, John. b 63. Bris Univ BSc 86 BTh 93. St Jo Coll Nottm MA 94. **d** 94 **p** 95. C Greasbrough *Sheff* 94–98; P-in-c High Hoyland, Scissett and Clayton W *Wakef* 98–04; V Mount Pellon 04–09; Warden of Readers 04–12; V Halifax St Aug and Mount Pellon 09–14; *Leeds* 14–21; V Thornton-le-Moors w Ince and Elton *Ches* from 21. *The Vicarage, Ince Lane, Elton, Chester CH2 4QB* E: revjhell@gmail.com

HELLICAR, Hugh Christopher. b 37. Qu Coll Birm 69. **d** 70 **p** 71. C Bromyard *Heref* 70–73; C Bishop's Castle w Mainstone 73–75; PtO *S'wark* 77–85; *Chich* 83–93; NSM Hove 93–98; rtd 02. *74 Marina, St Leonards-on-Sea TN38 0BJ* T: (01424) 444072 E: rainbow.poetry@hotmail.com

HELLIER, Jeremy Peter. b 53. K Coll Lon BD 75 AKC 75. St Aug Coll Cant 75. **d** 76 **p** 77. C Walton *St E* 76–79; C Ipswich St Fran 79–80; C Wolborough w Newton Abbot *Ex* 80–82; CF 82–84; R Pendine w Llanmiloe and Eglwys Gymyn w Marros *St D* 84–89; TR Widecombe-in-the-Moor, Leusdon, Princetown etc *Ex* 89–94; CF (TAVR) 90–03; RD Moreton *Ex* 91–94; Chapl and Hd RE Wellington Sch Somerset 94–15; rtd 16; Hon Chapl Miss to Seafarers from 02; PtO *B & W* from 15; Dioc Secondary Relig Educn Adv from 18; PtO *Eur* from 17. *15 Stoney Stile Way, Wells BA5 2NS* M: 07493-559210 E: jeremyhellier@hotmail.com

HELLINGS, Mrs Tara Charmian Lashmar. b 68. Ch Ch Ox MA 90. STETS 06. **d** 09 **p** 10. NSM Alton *Win* 09–12; Chapl Alton Coll 11–12; V Crondall and Ewshot *Guildf* from 12. *The Vicarage, Farm Lane, Crondall, Farnham GU10 5QE* M: 07932-184873 E: tartzhellings@yahoo.co.uk

HELLMUTH, Miss Lynn Margaret. b 60. Lon Bible Coll BA 82 Birm Univ PGCE 83. Wycliffe Hall Ox 00. **d** 02 **p** 03. C Twickenham Common H Trin *Lon* 02–05; TV Crawley *Chich* 05–08; V Stoneleigh *Guildf* 08–18; V Hackness w Harwood Dale *York* 18–20; V Ravenscar and Staintondale 18–20; V Scalby 18–20; V Scarborough St Luke 18–20; rtd 20; PtO *York* from 20. *46 Station Court, Railway Street, Hornsea HU18 1QD* E: lynnhellmuth@yahoo.co.uk

HELLYER, Stephen John. b 56. St Cath Coll Cam BA 77 MA 81. Wycliffe Hall Ox 82. **d** 84 **p** 85. C Plymouth St Andr w St Paul and St Geo *Ex* 84–88; Chapl Lee Abbey 88–89; Lon and SE Consultant CPAS 90–94; C Nottingham St Nic *S'well* 94–98; P-in-c Ox St Matt 98–10; R 10–18; rtd 18; PtO *Ox* from 21. *6 Millers Cottages, 17A Mill Street, Eynsham, Witney OX29 4JX* T: (01865) 881246 M: 07811-001712 E: stevejohnhellyer@yahoo.co.uk

HELM, Canon Alistair Thomas. b 53. Aston Univ BSc 75. EAMTC 88. **d** 91 **p** 92. NSM Leic St Jas 91–95; NSM Humberstone 95–04; NSM Emmaus Par Team 04–12; NSM

Giggleswick and Rathmell w Wigglesworth *Bradf* 09–12; NSM Settle 09–12; P-in-c Manningham 12–13; V *Leeds* 13–18; Acting Adn Bradf 15–16; AD Inner Bradf 17–18; rtd 18; Hon C Market Harborough and The Transfiguration etc *Leic* from 19. *61 Tungstone Way, Market Harborough LE16 9GA* M: 07557-375844 E: alistair.helm@btinternet.com

HELM, Catherine Mary. b 64. St Martin's Coll Lanc BEd 86. St Jo Coll Nottm 03. **d** 05 **p** 06. C Heswall *Ches* 05–09; V Burton and Shotwick from 09. *The Vicarage, Vicarage Lane, Burton, Neston CH64 5TJ* T: 0151-353 0453 E: revc.helm@burtonchurch.org.uk

HELM, Preb Nicholas. b 57. Surrey Univ BSc 81 Heythrop Coll Lon MA 10. St Jo Coll Nottm 85. **d** 88 **p** 89. C Old Ford St Paul w St Steph and St Mark *Lon* 88–92; TV Netherthorpe *Sheff* 92–93; V Sheff St Bart 93–98; Bp's Chapl 99–03; Bp's Adv in Spirituality 99–09; Chapl Whirlow Grange Conf Cen Sheff 99–09; CMD Officer *Heref* 10–19; Hon C The Ashfords from 19; Dioc Adv in Spirituality from 20; Preb Heref Cathl from 16. *Jesmond, St Julian's Avenue, Ludlow SY8 1ET* M: 07411-243413 E: n.helm@hereford.anglican.org

HELMS, David Clarke. b 50. Boston Univ BA 72. Yale Div Sch MDiv 77. **d** 77 **p** 77. USA 77–88; Ind Chapl *Worc* 88–97; Ind Chapl Teesside *York* 97–02; Dir Workplace Min for Ch in Soc *Roch* 05–12; P-in-c Dartford St Alb 12–16; rtd 16. *3 Royal Oak Terrace, Gravesend DA12 1JU* T: (01474) 321593 M: 07957-193816

HELVADJIAN, Miss Hannah. b 91. St Mellitus Coll BA 20. **d** 20 **p** 21. C Lache cum Saltney *Ches* from 20. *12 Lindfields, Saltney, Chester CH4 8QD* M: 07932-054887 E: hana@stmarkssaltney.org.uk

HEMINGRAY, Raymond. b 47. Leeds Univ LLB 68 Solicitor 71. ERMC 04. **d** 07 **p** 08. Dioc Registrar *Pet* 74–14; NSM Castor w Sutton and Upton w Marholm 07–14; PtO from 14; *Ely* 11–21. *4 Holywell Way, Peterborough PE3 6SS* T: (01733) 262523 E: rh@raymondhemingray.co.uk

HEMMING, Andrew Martyn. b 56. Bath Univ BSc 78. STETS 08. **d** 11 **p** 12. NSM Axbridge w Shipham and Rowberrow *B & W* 11–14; NSM Wrington w Butcombe and Burrington from 14; SSM Adv Bath Adnry from 19. *Eleuthera, Garston Lane, Blagdon, Bristol BS40 7TF* T: (01761) 462582 M: 07584-124198 E: andrewmhemming@btinternet.com

HEMMING, Terry Edward. b 47. Calvin Coll Michigan MA 84. S Dios Minl Tr Scheme 88. **d** 90 **p** 91. NSM E Win 90–09; Chapl St Swithun's Sch Win 95–07; NSM Hurstbourne Priors, Longparish etc *Win* 09–18; rtd 18; PtO *Win* 18–20; Master St Cross Hosp from 20; PtO *Eur* from 19. *The Chaplain's Lodge, St Cross Road, Winchester SO23 9SD* M: 07714-334570 E: revhemm@yahoo.com

HEMMING-CLARK, Stanley Charles. b 29. Peterho Cam BA 52 MA 56. Ridley Hall Cam 52. **d** 54 **p** 55. C Redhill H Trin *S'wark* 54–56; C Woking St Jo *Guildf* 56–59; V Crockenhill All So *Roch* 59–97; rtd 97; PtO *Guildf* from 97. *St Anthony's, 22 Ashcroft, Shalford, Guildford GU4 8JT* T: (01483) 568197

HEMMINGS, Mrs Caroline Faith Roberts. b 60. Loughb Univ BSc 84 Derby Univ MEd 04. All SS Cen for Miss & Min MTh 18. **d** 18 **p** 19. C Kirk Hallam *Derby* 18–21; C Ilkeston St Jo 18–21; Chapl Swan Valley Angl Community Sch Australia from 21. *Swan Valley Anglican Community School, Locked Bag 2, Ellenbrook WA 6069, Australia*

HEMMINGS, Ms Jane Marie. b 68. Lon Univ BD 91 AKC 91 Heythrop Coll Lon MTh 95 Southn Univ PGCE 08. NTMTC 01. **d** 03 **p** 04. C Bishop's Waltham *Portsm* 03–08; NSM 07–08; C Upham 03–08; NSM 07–08; NSM Akeman *Ox* 08–12; R 12–16; Dir of Ords (Dorchester Area) from 16. *1 The Rookery, Kidlington OX5 1AW* T: (01869) 350224 E: Jane.Hemmings@oxford.anglican.org

HEMMINGS, Roy Anthony. b 48. Univ of Wales (Cardiff) BD 85 MTh 00. St Mich Coll Llan 82. **d** 86 **p** 87. C Rhyl w St Ann *St As* 86–90; CF 90–08; V Maybush and Southampton St Jude *Win* 08–18; rtd 18. *81 Hebron Road, Clydach, Swansea SA6 5EH* M: 07710-774431 E: padreroy48@aol.com

HEMP, Mrs Julia. b 61. Reading Univ BA 82. ERMC 10. **d** 13 **p** 14. C Earlham *Nor* 13–16; C Gressenhall w Longham w Wendling etc 16–18; C Wellingham 17–18; TV Launditch and the Upper Nar *Nor* 18–21; NSM from 21. *Novus House, Hoe, Dereham NR20 4HD* M: 07702-665000 E: reverendjulia@gmail.com

HEMPHILL, John James. b 44. TCD BA 68 MA 72. Oak Hill Th Coll 71. **d** 73 **p** 74. C Dundonald *D & D* 73–78; I Balteagh w Carrick *D & R* 78–02; I Ballyhalbert w Ardkeen *D & D* 02–19; rtd 19. *Address temp unknown* M: 07890-012843

HEMSLEY HALLS, Susan Mary. b 59. Cranmer Hall Dur 93. **d** 95 **p** 96. C Wilnecote *Lich* 95–00; P-in-c Attenborough *S'well* 00–11; V 11–13; Dioc Chapl amongst Deaf People 00–12; Dioc Dir of Ords 12–18; P-in-c S Trin Broads *Nor*

from 18. *The Rectory, Main Road, Fleggburgh, Great Yarmouth NR29 3AG*

HEMSTOCK, Canon Julian. b 51. Trent Poly BSc 74 CEng MIProdE. Sarum & Wells Th Coll 89. **d** 91 **p** 92. C Carrington *S'well* 91–94; C Basford St Aid 94–97; Asst Chapl Qu Medical Cen Nottm Univ Hosp NHS Trust 97–03; Chapl from 03; Hon Can S'well Minster from 13. *Queen's Medical Centre University Hospital, Derby Road, Nottingham NG7 2UH* T: 0115-924 9924 ext 43799 E: julian.hemstock@qmc.nhs.uk

HEMSTOCK, Mrs Pat. b 51. Sarum & Wells Th Coll 89. **d** 91 **p** 95. Par Dn Carrington *S'well* 91–94; Par Dn Basford St Aid 94–95; C 95–97; P-in-c 97–05; V Calverton 05–16; rtd 16; PtO *S'well* from 17. *8 Peacock Drive, Eastwood, Nottingham NG16 3HW*

HEMSWORTH, John Alan. b 45. FGA 67. **d** 02 **p** 03. OLM Droylsden St Andr *Man* 02–10; P-in-c 10–16; C Droylsden St Martin 13–16; rtd 16; PtO *Man* from 16. *13 Keston Avenue, Droylsden, Manchester M43 6BL* M: 07544-306713 E: john.hemsworth@ntlworld.com

HENDERSON, Andrew Douglas. b 36. Trin Coll Cam BA 60 MA 64 Liv Univ DASS 65 MBASW. Cuddesdon Coll 60. **d** 62 **p** 63. C Newington St Paul *S'wark* 62–64; Hon C Camberwell St Luke 65–80; PtO *Lon* 85–06; *Chich* from 06. *4 Western Terrace, Brighton BN1 2LD* T: (01273) 327829

HENDERSON, Ashley. *See* HENDERSON, Peter Ashley

HENDERSON, Daniel Thomas. b 81. Nottm Univ BSc 03. Oak Hill Th Coll BTh 10. **d** 10 **p** 11. C Hailsham *Chich* 10–14; C Hove St Andr 14–18; P-in-c 18–21; V from 21; RD Hove from 18. *St Andrew's Vicarage, 17 Vallance Gardens, Hove BN3 2DB* M: 07734-928877 E: dan-henderson@hotmail.co.uk

HENDERSON, David. *See* HENDERSON, Robert David Druitt

HENDERSON, Mrs Elizabeth. b 42. CITC 96. **d** 99 **p** 00. C Ballymacash *Conn* 99–00; C Finaghy 00–15; Asst Chapl Belfast City Hosp Health and Soc Services Trust 99–05; Asst Chapl Down Lisburn Health and Soc Services Trust 05–15; rtd 15. *39 Garvey Court, Lisburn BT27 4DG* T: (028) 9260 7146

HENDERSON, Mrs Janet Elizabeth. b 53. N Lon Poly BSc 75. Ripon Coll Cuddesdon 05. **d** 06 **p** 07. NSM Ellesborough, The Kimbles and Stoke Mandeville *Ox* 06–09; R 09–18; rtd 18; PtO *Ox* from 18. *Winterfold, The Butts, Church Street, Princes Risborough HP27 9AN* E: jeh@brook-farm.supanet.com

HENDERSON, Mrs Joanne Sarah. b 63. Ripon Coll Cuddesdon 10. **d** 12 **p** 13. C Abu Dhabi St Andr *UAE* 12–16; TV Knaresborough *Leeds* 16–19. *3/17 Western Harbour Breakwater, Edinburgh EH6 6PA* M: 07577-150543 E: revjohenderson@gmail.com

⊕**HENDERSON, The Rt Revd Julian Tudor.** b 54. Keble Coll Ox BA 76 MA 81. Ridley Hall Cam 77. **d** 79 **p** 80 **c** 13. C Islington St Mary *Lon* 79–83; V Hastings Em and St Mary in the Castle *Chich* 83–92; V Claygate *Guildf* 92–05; RD Emly 96–01; Adn Dorking 05–13; Hon Can Guildf Cathl 02–13; Bp Blackb from 13. *Bishop's House, Ribchester Road, Clayton le Dale, Blackburn BB1 9EF* T: (01254) 248234 E: bishop@bishopofblackburn.org.uk

HENDERSON, Lucy. *See* FYFE-JAMIESON, Lucy

HENDERSON, Nicholas Paul. b 48. Selw Coll Cam BA 73 MA 77 Univ of Wales (Lamp) PhD 09. Ripon Hall Ox 73. **d** 75 **p** 76. C St Alb St Steph 75–78; Warden J F Kennedy Ho Cov Cathl 78–79; C Bow w Bromley St Leon *Lon* 79–85; P-in-c W Acton St Martin 85–96; V 96–18; P-in-c Ealing All SS 89–95; V 96–14; rtd 18; PtO *Lon* from 20. *38 Caledonian Wharf, London E14 3EW* E: nicholashenderson@mac.com

HENDERSON, Olive Elizabeth. b 48. St Jo Coll Nottm. **d** 97 **p** 98. Aux Min Tallaght *D & G* 97–99; P-in-c Moviddy Union *C, C & R* 99–01; P-in-c Rathdrum w Glenealy, Derralossary and Laragh *D & G* 01–04; C 04–07; I 07–08; I Killeshin w Cloydagh and Killabban *C, F & O* 08–10; Chapl Kingston Coll Mitchelstown 10–12; I Donoughmore and Donard w Dunlavin *D & G* 12–14; rtd 14. *Strathmore, Grangemellon, Athy, Co Kildare, Republic of Ireland* M: (00353) 87-218 1891 E: oliveernest@hotmail.com

HENDERSON, Patrick James. b 57. R Holloway Coll Lon BA 78 St Mary's Univ Coll Twickenham MA 12 Surrey Univ PGCE 01. St Steph Ho Ox 83. **d** 86 **p** 87. C Hornsey St Mary w St Geo *Lon* 86–90; V Whetstone St Jo 90–95; In RC Ch 95–01; PtO *Lon* 01–02; C Hornsey H Innocents from 02; C Stroud Green H Trin 02–04; P-in-c 04–07; V from 07; C Harringay St Paul from 10; Chapl Greig City Academy from 02. *Holy Trinity Vicarage, Granville Road, London N4 4EL* T: (020) 8340 2051 E: pjhenderson2001@yahoo.co.uk

HENDERSON, Peter Ashley. b 59. St Martin's Coll Lanc PGCE 00. CBDTI 02. **d** 05 **p** 06. NSM Arnside *Carl* 05–08;

NSM Kendal H Trin from 08. *2 Lowther Park, Kendal LA9 6RS* T: (01539) 736079 E: ashleykpc@gmail.com

HENDERSON, Canon Richard. b 69. St Jo Coll Nottm 04. **d** 06 **p** 07. C Beccles St Mich and St Luke *St E* 06–09; TV Sole Bay 09–16; P-in-c Beccles St Mich and St Luke 16–18; R 18–21; P-in-c Worlingham w Barnby and N Cove 19–21; R Beccles w Worlingham, N Cove and Barnby from 21; RD Waveney and Blyth from 20; Hon Can St E Cathl from 20. *The Rectory, 44 Ringsfield Road, Beccles NR34 9PF* T: (01502) 349143 E: richhenderson@btinternet.com

⊕**HENDERSON, The Rt Revd Richard Crosbie Aitken.** b 57. Magd Coll Ox MA 84 DPhil 84. St Jo Coll Nottm 83. **d** 86 **p** 87 **c** 98. C Chinnor w Emmington and Sydenham etc *Ox* 86–89; I Abbeystrewry Union *C, C & R* 89–95; I Ross Union 95–98; Dean Ross 95–98; Chan Cork Cathl 95–98; Bp T, K & A 98–11; TV Heart of Eden *Carl* 11–12; Hon Asst Bp Carl 11–13; rtd 12. *2 Rue Vivienne, 47360 Prayssas, France* E: rcah57@gmail.com

HENDERSON, Robert. b 43. Lambeth STh 94 Union Th Coll Belf BD 06. TCD Div Sch 66. **d** 69 **p** 70. C Drumglass *Arm* 69–72; Chapl Miss to Seamen 72–77; Sen Chapl Mombasa Kenya 77–78; I Mostrim w Granard, Clonbroney, Killoe etc *K, E & A* 78–82; I Belfast St Matt *Conn* 82–92; I Kilroot and Templecorran 92–98; rtd 98. *39 Garvey Court, Lisburn BT27 4DG* T: (028) 9260 7146 E: hclerics1@gmail.com

HENDERSON, Robert David Druitt. b 41. St Edm Hall Ox MA 64 Brunel Univ MA 77 K Alfred's Coll Win PGCE 88. **d** 03 **p** 04. OLM Wylye and Till Valley *Sarum* 03–10; rtd 10; PtO *Sarum* from 11. *Orchard House, Salisbury Road, Steeple Langford, Salisbury SP3 4NQ* T: (01722) 790388 E: henderson.family@virgin.net

HENDERSON, Terry James. b 45. St Deiniol's Hawarden 76. **d** 77 **p** 77. C Wrexham *St As* 77–79; Wilson Carlile Coll of Evang 79–81; TV Langtree *Ox* 81–87; P-in-c Aston Cantlow and Wilmcote w Billesley *Cov* 87–90; V 90–97; V St Peter-in-Thanet *Cant* 97–02; R Elmley Castle w Bricklehampton and Combertons *Worc* 02–12; C Overbury w Teddington, Alstone etc 09–12; rtd 12; PtO *Cov* from 13. *8 Birdhaven Close, Banbury Road, Lighthorne, Warwick CV35 0BE* T: (01926) 640350 E: terryhenderson15@gmail.com

HENDERSON, William Ernest. b 53. CEng 81 MICE 81 Southn Univ BSc 75. St Jo Coll Nottm 87. **d** 89 **p** 90. C Win Ch Ch 89–93; V Stanley *Wakef* 93–14; Leeds 14–17; V Outwood, Stanley and Wrenthorpe 17–18; rtd 18. *1 Drake Hill Cottage, Cumberworth, Huddersfield HD8 8YD*

HENDERSON SMITH, Mrs Judith Hazel. b 55. De Montfort Univ BSc 00 Nottm Univ MA 11. EMMTC 08. **d** 11 **p** 12. NSM Alvaston *Derby* 11–15; NSM Sawley 15–16; V Ault Hucknall and Scarcliffe from 16; Jt Dioc Ecum Officer 12–16. *11 Devonshire Cottages, Churchside, Scarcliffe, Chesterfield S44 6TE* T: (01246) 241835 M: 07920-036867 E: revjudyhs@gmail.com

HENDRA, David Christopher. b 81. Trin Coll Bris 13. **d** 16 **p** 17. C Leic H Trin w St Jo 16–20; C The Mitre Benefice *Nor* from 20. *St Alban's Vicarage, Eleanor Road, Norwich NR1 2RE* E: davehendra@gmail.com *or* dave.hendra@stn.org.uk

HENDRICKSE, Canon Clarence David. b 41. Nottm Univ PGCE 73 MPhil 95 CEng MIMechE 71. St Jo Coll Nottm 71. **d** 74 **p** 75. C St Helens St Helen *Liv* 74–76; C Netherley Ch Ch CD 76–77; TV 78–87; V Liv Ch Ch Norris Green 87–93; V Eccleston Ch Ch 93–06; Hon Can Liv Cathl 96–06; rtd 06; PtO *Carl* from 07; PtO Saldanha Bay from 11. T: (015394) 43058 E: canon.clarence.hendrickse@talktalk.net

HENDRY, Mrs Helen Clare. b 58. Lanc Univ BA 79 Cam Univ PGCE 80. Reformed Th Sem Mississippi MA 85 Oak Hill Th Coll 94. **d** 95. Lect Oak Hill Th Coll 86–08; NSM Muswell Hill St Jas w St Matt *Lon* from 95; NSM Friern Barnet St Pet le Poer from 21. *44 The Grove, London N13 5JR* T: (020) 8882 2186 *or* 8442 0276 E: clare.hendry@gracech.org.uk

HENDRY, Malcolm Graham. b 54. **d** 13 **p** 14. NSM Wrose *Bradf* 13–14; Leeds 14; C Shipley St Paul 15–17; V Cottingley from 17. *81 Littlelands, Bingley BD16 1AL* T: (01274) 560761 M: 07545-073075 E: malg6031@gmail.com

HENDRY, Rosemary. b 52. Lindisfarne Regional Tr Partnership 17. **d** 20 **p** 21. NSM Greenside *Dur* from 20. *Delfin, Lead Road, Greenside, Ryton NE40 4RD* T: 0191-413 6111 M: 07975-744622 E: rosemaryhendry123@gmail.com

HENDY, Canon Graham Alfred. b 45. St Jo Coll Dur BA 67 MA 75 Univ of Wales (Lamp) MTh 03 MPhil 07 Fitzw Coll Cam CertEd 70. Sarum Th Coll 67. **d** 70 **p** 71. C High Wycombe *Ox* 70–75; TV 75–78; V Upton cum Chalvey 78–83; TR 83–90; R S Walsham and Upton *Nor* 90–97; Dioc Lay Tr Officer 90–97; Can Res S'well Minster 97–02; R Upper Itchen *Win* 02–08; rtd 08; PtO *B & W* from 09. *74 Bath Road, Wells BA5 3LJ* T: (01749) 677003 E: grahamhendy@dunelm.org.uk

HENGIST, Barry. b 59. N Lon Poly BA 88. Ripon Coll Cuddesdon 07. **d** 09 **p** 10. C Weybridge *Guildf* 09–13; P-in-c Shirley St Geo *S'wark* 13–17; V from 17. *The Vicarage, 2 The Grove, West Wickham BR4 9JS* M: 07947-068209 E: barryhengist@gmail.com

HENIG, Martin Edward. b 42. St Cath Coll Cam BA 63 MA 66 Worc Coll Ox DPhil 72 DLitt 98 FSA 75. St Steph Ho Ox 08. **d** 10 **p** 11. NSM Osney Ox 10–18; PtO from 18. *16 Alexandra Road, Oxford OX2 0DB* T: (01865) 241118 *or* 278265 E: martin.henig@arch.ox.ac.uk

HENLEY, Christopher Charles. b 57. St Mellitus Coll BA 16. **d** 16 **p** 17. NSM Staines *Lon* 16–18; NSM Staines St Mary and St Pet 18–20; C Hounslow St Steph from 20. *11 Hartington Court, Hartington Road, London W4 3TT* T: (020) 8582 5898 M: 07920-104009 E: christopherhenley57@gmail.com

HENLEY, Dean. b 64. St Chad's Coll Dur BA 93. Westcott Ho Cam 93. **d** 95 **p** 96. C Farncombe *Guildf* 95–99; TV Hale w Badshot Lea 99–06; R Campton, Clophill and Haynes *St Alb* 06–19; rtd 19. *4 Clematis Close, Driffield YO25 6XQ*

HENLEY, James Andrew. **d** 15 **p** 16. C Newport St Paul *Mon* 15–17; TR Cyncoed from 17. *The Rectory, 256 Cyncoed Road, Cardiff CF23 6RU* T: (029) 2075 2138 E: james.henley@gmail.com

HENLEY, John Francis Hugh. b 48. SS Mark & Jo Coll Chelsea CertEd 69. St Mich Coll Llan. **d** 82 **p** 83. C Griffithstown *Mon* 82–85; V St Hilary Greenway 85–90; P-in-c Fulham St Etheldreda w St Clem *Lon* 90–11; V 11–18; C 18; rtd 18; PtO *Lon* from 18; *Nor* from 19. *11 Beatty Road, Great Yarmouth NR30 4BT* T: (01493) 298867

HENNESSY, Carol Joyce. Univ of Wales (Lamp) CertHE 10. **d** 19 **p** 20. Geashill w Killeigh and Ballycommon *M & K* 00–20; OLM Naas w Kill and Rathmore from 20. *Mansfield Lodge, 5 The Way, Prusselstown Green, Athy, Co Kildare, R14 TX94, Republic of Ireland* T: (00353) (59) 864 1188 M: 87-295 9688 E: hennessycarol1@gmail.com

HENNING, Mrs Judy. b 49. Portsm Univ MSc 99. S Dios Minl Tr Scheme 85. **d** 88 **p** 97. C Catherington and Clanfield *Portsm* 88–91; C Leigh Park 91–92; PtO 94–96; Min in Whiteley and Asst to RD Fareham 96–99; C-in-c Whiteley CD 99–04; P-in-c Old Cleeve, Leighland and Treborough *B & W* 04–06; R 06–11; P-in-c Rainham *Roch* 11–13; V 13–17; rtd 17; PtO *Portsm* from 18. *17 Orpine Close, Fareham PO15 5TE* T: (01329) 845946 E: judy.henning@btinternet.com

HENNINGS, John Richard. b 58. Sheff Univ BA 80. Spurgeon's Coll BA 87. **d** 07 **p** 08. SSF from 05; PtO *Ripon* 09–10; *Sheff* 10–11; *Newc* 11–17; *Birm* from 17. *113 Gillott Road, Birmingham B16 0ET* T: 0121-454 8302 E: johnssf@franciscans.org.uk

HENRY, Cornelius Vincent. b 70. K Coll NY BA 92 Heythrop Coll Lon MA 06. NTMTC 07. **d** 09 **p** 10. C Hornchurch St Andr *Chelmsf* 09–13; V Forest Gate St Sav and St Jas from 13. *St Saviour's Rectory, Sidney Road, London E7 0EF* T: (020) 8534 6109 E: revcahenry@gmail.com

HENRY, Miss Jacqueline Margaret. b 40. Open Univ BA 82. Trin Coll Bris 77. **dss** 83 **d** 87 **p** 94. Deptford St Jo *S'wark* 79–82; Catshill and Dodford *Worc* 83–86; The Lye and Stambermill 86–87; Par Dn 87–89; Educn Chapl 89–93; C Tolleshunt Knights w Tiptree and Gt Braxted *Chelmsf* 94–97; Chapl amongst Deaf People 94–97; TV Stantonbury and Willen *Ox* 97–02; rtd 02; PtO *Cant* 02–09; *Roch* from 09. *Address temp unknown*

HENRY, Peter. b 49. BTh. St Jo Coll Nottm. **d** 84 **p** 85. C Sinfin Moor and Blagreaves St Andr CD *Derby* 84–89; V Guernsey St Jo *Win* 89–97; P-in-c Sawley *Derby* N 01–06; rtd 06. *23 Mulberry Close, Stotfold, Hitchin SG5 4NL* T: (01462) 834902 E: henmusic@cwgsy.net

HENRY, Canon Stephen Kenelm Malim. b 37. Brasted Th Coll 58 Bps' Coll Cheshunt 60. **d** 62 **p** 63. C Leic St Phil 62–67; CF 67–70; V Woodhouse *Wakef* 70–01; Hon Can Wakef Cathl 00–01; rtd 01; PtO *Wakef* 01–14; *Leeds* from 14. *1 Yorkstone, Crosland Moor, Huddersfield HD4 5NQ* T: (01484) 644807 E: mandsmalim64@btinternet.com

HENRYHOLLAND, Miss Anne. b 56. **d** 12 **p** 13. NSM Ludgvan, Marazion, St Hilary and Perranuthnoe *Truro* 12–17; Public Preacher from 17. *Tremorran, Truthwall, St Just, Penzance TR19 7QJ* M: 07768-166309 E: missanniehenry@hotmail.com

HENSHALL, Keith. *See* HENSHALL, Ronald Keith

HENSHALL, The Very Revd Nicholas James. b 62. Wadh Coll Ox BA84 MA 88. Ripon Coll Cuddesdon 85. **d** 88 **p** 89. C Blyth St Mary *Newc* 88–92; V Scotswood 92–02; Can Res Derby Cathl 02–08; V High Harrogate Ch Ch *Ripon* 08–14; Dean Chelmsf from 14. *3 Harlings Grove, Chelmsford CM1 1YQ* T: (01245) 294492 E: nicholas.henshall@chelmsfordcathedral.org.uk

HENSHALL, Ronald Keith. b 54. Loughb Coll of Educn CertEd 76. Chich Th Coll 87. **d** 89 **p** 90. C Ribbleton *Blackb* 89–92; TV 95–98; P-in-c Charlestown and Lowland St Kitts-Nevis 92–95; V Ellel w Shireshead *Blackb* 98–02; Cyprus 02–05; Chapl R Alexandra and Albert Sch Reigate 05–06; P-in-c Lerwick and Burravoe *Ab* 06–10; V Holme-in-Cliviger w Worsthorne *Blackb* 10–16; rtd 16; PtO *Man* from 17. *Flat 203, 3 Munday Street, Manchester M4 7AY* M: 07540-133357 E: r.k.henshall@gmail.com

HENSON, Carolyn. b 44. Bedf Coll Lon BA 65 Nottm Univ MTh 88 PhD 97 Solicitor 75. EMMTC 82. **dss** 85 **d** 87 **p** 94. Braunstone *Leic* 85–89; Par Dn 87–89; Adult Educn and Tr Officer *Ely* 89–91; NSM Sutton and Witcham w Mepal 89–95; Chapl Gt Ormond Street Hosp for Children NHS Trust 95–96; NSM Cainscross w Selsley *Glouc* 96–97; Vice Prin EMMTC *S'well* 97–01; R Morley w Smalley and Horsley Woodhouse *Derby* 02–05; rtd 05; Chapl St Mich Hospice Harrogate 09–10; PtO *York* from 09. *45 Harvest Drive, Malton YO17 7BF* E: carolyn.henson2@gmail.com

HENSON, Christopher Lawrence. b 92. Leeds Univ BA 14. Ripon Coll Cuddesdon MA 20. **d** 20 **p** 21. C Kidderminster St Jo and H Innocents *Worc* from 20. *186 Birmingham Road, Kidderminster DY10 2SJ* T: (01562) 632092 M: 07407-403270 E: frchenson@outlook.com

HENSON, Jacqueline Ruth. b 77. Univ of Wales (Ban) BA 98. Ripon Coll Cuddesdon 17. **d** 20 **p** 21. C S Cheltenham *Glouc* from 20. *32 Gratton Road, Cheltenham GL50 2BU* T: (01242) 220053 E: revjacquelinehenson@gmail.com

HENSON, Joanna. b 62. **d** 06 **p** 07. NSM Egton-cum-Newland and Lowick and Colton *Carl* 06–12; rtd 12; PtO *Carl* from 13. *Woodside Cottage, Colton, Ulverston LA12 8HE* T: (01229) 861800 E: joannahenson@aol.com

HENSON, John David. b 49. EMMTC. **d** 00 **p** 01. NSM Beckingham w Walkeringham *S'well* 00–02; NSM Gringley-on-the-Hill 00–02; NSM Misterton and W Stockwith 02–05; C 06–07; C Beckingham w Walkeringham and Gringley 06–07; P-in-c Beckingham and Walkeringham and Misterton etc 07–11; V 11–15; Asst Chapl HM Pris Whatton 00–05; V Beckingham, Walkeringham, Misterton, etc *S'well* 15–19; Sen Police Chapl 03–19; rtd 19. *37 North Crescent, Clipstone Village, Mansfield NG21 9EB* E: jd.henson@btinternet.com

HENSON, Canon John Richard. b 40. Selw Coll Cam BA 62 MA 66. Ridley Hall Cam 62. **d** 65 **p** 66. C Ollerton *S'well* 65–68; Univs Sec CMS 68–73; Chapl Scargill Ho 73–78; V Shipley St Paul *Bradf* 78–83; TR Shipley St Paul and Frizinghall 83–91; V Ilkeston St Mary *Derby* 91–99; V Mickleover St Jo 99–05; Dioc Ecum Officer 96–05; Hon Can Derby Cathl 00–05; rtd 05; PtO *Derby* 05–16; *S'well* from 06; Asst P St Geo Cathl Jerusalem 13–15. *6 Ganton Close, Nottingham NG3 3ET* E: john.henson3@ntlworld.com

HENSON, Shaun Christopher. E Nazarene Coll (USA) BA 94 Duke Univ (USA) MDiv 98 Regent's Park Coll Ox DPhil 07. Duke Div Sch. **d** 04 **p** 05. C Blenheim *Ox* 04–17; C Woodstock and Bladon from 17; Chapl St Hugh's Coll Ox from 07. *St Hugh's College, St Margarets Road, Oxford OX2 6LE* T: (01865) 274955 M: 07795-547555 E: shaun.henson@theology.ox.ac.uk

HENSTRIDGE, Edward John. b 31. Ex Coll Ox BA 55 MA 59 FCIPD 77. Wells Th Coll 55. **d** 57 **p** 58. C Milton *Portsm* 57–62; V Soberton w Newtown 62–69; LtO *Derby* 69–71; PtO *Guildf* 72–84 and from 02; LtO 84–02; Bp's Officer for NSMs 97–01. *Hunters Moon, Lower Ham Lane, Elstead, Godalming GU8 6HQ* T: (01252) 702272 E: johnhn@globalnet.co.uk

HENTHORNE, Thomas Roger. b 30. EAMTC. **d** 79 **p** 80. Hd Master St Mary's Sch St Neots 67–93; NSM St Neots *Ely* 79–04; PtO from 04. *Stapeley, 45 Berkley Street, Eynesbury, St Neots PE19 2ND* T: (01480) 472548 E: roger.henthorne@uwclub.net

HENTON, John Martin. b 48. AKC 71 St Luke's Coll Ex DipEd 72. St Aug Coll Cant 74. **d** 74 **p** 75. C Woolwich St Mary w H Trin *S'wark* 74–77; C Cotham St Mary *Bris* 77–78; C Cotham St Sav w St Mary 78–80; R Filton 80–87; Chapl Ex Sch and St Marg Sch 87–91; V Ex St Dav 91–09; rtd 09; PtO *Ex* from 10. *Upexe Cottage, Upexe, Exeter EX5 5ND* T: (01392) 860038 E: sue@upexe.eclipse.co.uk

HENWOOD (née RENNIE), Gillian Kathleen. b 56. Lanc Univ MA 79 Ches Univ DProf 19 ABIPP 81. CBDTI 94. **d** 97 **p** 98. NSM Whitechapel w Admarsh-in-Bleasdale *Blackb* 97–00; NSM Fellside Team 00–01; Rural Chapl 00–03; Chapl Myerscough Coll 00–03; Bp's Adv for Leisure and Tourism 01–03; C Westmr St Jas *Lon* 03–04; V Nunthorpe *York* 04–09; P-in-c Riding Mill *Newc* 09–10; Chapl Shepherd's Dene Retreat Ho 09–10; Adv for Spirituality and Spiritual Direction 09–10; P-in-c Ribchester w Stydd *Blackb* 10–11; R 11–16; PtO 16–17; P-in-c Grasmere *Carl* 17–19; P-in-c Rydal 17–19; rtd 19; PtO *Carl* from 19. *Keen Ground,*

Hawkshead, Ambleside LA22 0NW M: 07712-526719
E: gillkhenwood@hotmail.com
HENWOOD, Canon Peter Richard. b 32. St Edm Hall Ox BA 55
MA 69. Cuddesdon Coll 56. **d** 57 **p** 58. C Rugby St Andr *Cov*
57–62; C-in-c Gleadless Valley CD *Sheff* 62–71; V Plaistow
St Mary *Roch* 71–97; RD Bromley 79–96; Hon Can Roch
Cathl 88–97; rtd 97; PtO *Cant* 99–14. *Wayside, 1 Highfield
Close, Sandling Road, Saltwood, Hythe CT21 4QP* T: (01303)
230039
HENWOOD (née OAKLEY), Mrs Susan Mary. b 55. Salford
Univ BSc 76. St Jo Coll Nottm 84. **d** 87 **p** 94. Par Dn
Armthorpe *Sheff* 87–91; C Howell Hill *Guildf* 91–96; PtO
Sheff 97–00; *S'well* 97–00; *Cov* 02–04; NSM Bidford-on-Avon
04–15; NSM Heart of England 15–16; NSM Alcester Minster
16–21; rtd 21. *Address temp unknown*
HEPBURN, Ian Malcolm George. b 76. Napier Univ Edin
BSc 00. St Mellitus Coll 16. **d** 19 **p** 20. C Bolton St Pet w
St Phil *Man* 19–20; Lect from 20. *The Vicarage, 91 Chorley
Road, Westhoughton, Bolton BL5 3PG* T: (01942) 814045
E: lecturer@boltonparishchurch.co.uk
HEPBURN, Julia Mary. b 61. St Andr Univ BSc 82 Man
Univ MB, ChB 85. Linc Sch of Th and Min 04. **d** 12 **p** 13.
OLM Springline *Linc* 12–16; OLM Owmby Gp 12–16;
NSM Linc St Mary Magd w St Paul and St Mich from
16. *27 Lee Road, Lincoln LN2 4BQ* M: 07707-027804
E: julia.hepburn@lincoln.anglican.org
HEPPER, Canon Christopher Michael Alan. b 55. Wolv Univ
BSc 78. St Jo Coll Nottm 90. **d** 92 **p** 93. C High Harrogate Ch Ch
Ripon 92–95; Bp's Dom Chapl 95–99; Dioc Communications
Officer 95–97; NSM Ripon H Trin 98–99; P-in-c Poitou-
Charentes *Eur* 99–11; P-in-c Leyburn w Bellerby *Leeds*
11–15; V 15–18; AD Wensley 13–18; Hon Can Ripon Cathl
17–18; NSM Felton *Newc* from 18; NSM Longframlington
w Brinkburn from 18. *West Moor Farm, Longhorsley, Morpeth
NE65 8QX* E: revmichael@btinternet.com
HEPPER, William Raymond. b 62. Kingston Poly BA 83.
Trin Coll Bris BA 98. **d** 98 **p** 99. C Spring Grove St Mary
Lon 98–01; CMS Egypt 01–04; NSM Greenford H
Cross *Lon* 05–08; PtO from 08. *92 Beechmount Avenue,
London W7 3AQ* T: (020) 8578 3437 M: 07917-336657
E: williamhepper@hotmail.com
HEPTINSTALL, Canon Lillian. b 49. EMMTC 99. **d** 02
p 03. NSM Chilwell *S'well* 02–15; Hon Can S'well
Minster 12–15; rtd 15; PtO *S'well* from 16. *8 Cranston
Road, Bramcote, Nottingham NG9 3GU* T: 0115-916 4588
E: heptinstall@ntlworld.com
HEPTINSTALL, Mrs Susan Margaret. b 56. Yorks Min
Course 08. **d** 10 **p** 11. NSM Halifax St Aug and Mount Pellon
Wakef 10–14; *Leeds* 14–17; NSM Bradshaw and Holmfield
from 17. *26 Sandbeds Road, Pellon, Halifax HX2 0JF* T: (01422)
341436 M: 07510-510359 E: vicarsue@gmail.com
HEPWORTH, Canon Ernest John Peter. b 42. K Coll Lon
BD 65 AKC 65 Hull Univ MA 87. **d** 66 **p** 67. C Headingley
Ripon 66–69; Asst Chapl St Geo Hosp Lon 69–71; C Gt
Grimsby St Mary and St Jas *Linc* 71–72; TV 72–74; V Crosby
74–80; V Barton upon Humber 80–04; RD Yarborough
86–92; Can and Preb Linc Cathl 94–04; rtd 04. *63 Ferriby
Road, Barton-upon-Humber DN18 5LQ* T: (01652) 661363
E: ehep01@aol.com
HEPWORTH, Michael David Albert. b 37. Em Coll Cam
BA 59 MA 63 Lon Inst of Educn PGCE 60. Ridley Hall
Cam 65. **d** 67 **p** 68. C Eastbourne All SS *Chich* 67–69;
Teacher Eastbourne Coll 67–69; Asst Chapl Bedford Sch
69–72; Chapl 72–83; Hd Master Birkdale Sch 83–98;
PtO *Sheff* 83–09; *Derby* 83–09; *Guildf* from 10. *6 Elm
Gardens, Claygate, Esher KT10 0JS* T: (01372) 466651
E: michaelhepworth@talktalk.net
HERAPATH, Jonathan James. b 67. Westmr Coll Ox BTh 96
Ox Brookes Univ PGCE 02. St Steph Ho Ox MTh 06. **d** 05
p 06. C Cowley St Jo *Ox* 05–07; Chapl SS Helen and Kath Sch
Abingdon 07–10; Chapl Wadh Coll Ox 10–12; PtO *Portsm* from
12; *Lon* 16–17; NSM St Vedast w St Mich-le-Querne etc 17–19.
11 Dial Place, Warkworth, Morpeth NE65 0UR M: 07745-
405150 E: jonathanherapath@gmail.com
HERBERT, Alison Elizabeth. b 72. St D Coll Lamp BA 93 K Coll
Lon MA 94. St Mellitus Coll BA 19. **d** 19 **p** 20. C Birm St Luke
from 19. *9 Moorland Road, Birmingham B16 9JP* M: 07850-
453024 E: aliherbert@trumail.com
HERBERT, Christopher. b 63. Yorks Min Course 14. **d** 17 **p** 18.
NSM Burghwallis and Campsall *Sheff* from 17. *4 Highfield
Villas, High Street, Norton, Doncaster DN6 9EJ* T: (01302)
702615 E: chris.herbert@sheffield.anglican.org
HERBERT, Christopher John. b 37. Dur Univ BA 60. Cranmer
Hall Dur 60. **d** 62 **p** 63. C Huyton Quarry *Liv* 62–65; C
Rainford 65–68; V Impington *Ely* 68–78; RD N Stowe 76–78;
V Gt Shelford 78–97; RD Shelford 80–85; rtd 97. *North Place,*

Crown Street, Great Bardfield, Braintree CM7 4ST T: (01371)
810516
✠**HERBERT, The Rt Revd Christopher William.** b 44. Univ of
Wales (Lamp) BA 65 Bris Univ PGCE 65 Leic Univ MPhil 02
PhD 08 Herts Univ Hon DLitt 03. Wells Th Coll 65. **d** 67
p 68 **c** 95. C Tupsley *Heref* 67–71; Dioc RE Adv 71–76; Dioc
Dir RE 76–81; Preb Heref Cathl 76–81; V Bourne *Guildf*
81–90; Hon Can Guildf Cathl 85–95; Adn Dorking 90–95;
Bp St Alb 95–09; rtd 09; Hon Asst Bp Guildf from 09; Hon
Asst Bp Win 09–21; Hon Asst Bp Chich 10–14. *1 Beacon
Close, Wrecclesham, Farnham GU10 4PA* T: (01252) 795600
E: cherbert@threeabbeys.org.uk
HERBERT, Clare Marguerite. b 54. St Hild Coll Dur BA 76
New Coll Edin MTh 78 Anglia Ruskin Univ DProf 17. Linc
Th Coll 79. **dss** 81 **d** 87 **p** 94. Clifton St Paul and Asst
Chapl Bris Univ 81–84; Hon Par Dn Bris St Mary Redcliffe
w Temple etc 87–90; Dioc Past Care Adv *Lon* 92–95; Hon C
Clapham Team *S'wark* 94–96; C St Martin-in-the-Fields *Lon*
96–98; R Soho St Anne w St Thos and St Pet 98–07; Dean of
Women's Min Two Cities Area 01–07; Nat Co-ord Inclusive
Ch 07–10; Lect St Martin-in-the-Fields *Lon* 10–14; Tutor
St Aug Coll of Th 14–18; rtd 18; Assoc Tutor (Lead) St Aug
Coll of Th from 18; PtO *S'wark* from 14. *Fiere, 15 Queen Street,
Emsworth PO10 7BJ* T: (01243) 430765 M: 07841-032751
E: herbert.clare@googlemail.com
HERBERT, Canon David Alexander Sellars. b 39. Bris Univ
BA 60. St Steph Ho Ox 65. **d** 67 **p** 68. C St Leonards Ch Ch
Chich 67–81; V Bickley *Roch* 81–09; Hon Can Roch Cathl
92–09; rtd 09; PtO Roch from 09; *S'wark* from 18. *54 High
Street, Chislehurst BR7 5AQ* T: (020) 8467 5230 M: 07545-
645316 E: fatherdavidherbert@btinternet.com
HERBERT, Canon David Roy. b 51. K Coll Lon BD 73
AKC 73 Ches Univ MTh 12. **d** 74 **p** 75. C Sheff St Aid
w St Luke 74–75; C Sheff Manor 75–78; TV Gleadless
Valley 78–83; TV Ellesmere Port *Ches* 83–93; V Tarvin
93–09; Continuing Minl Tr Officer 03–09; CMD Officer
and IME (4-7) Officer 09–21; rtd 21; Hon Can Ches
Cathl from 08. *Address temp unknown* M: 07594-952551
E: davidherbert8510@gmail.com
HERBERT, Mrs Denise Bridget Helen. b 42. Win Univ MA 11
SRN 72 SCM 74. Ripon Coll Cuddesdon. **d** 95 **p** 96. C Ocean
View S Africa 95–97; C Grahamstown Cathl 97–99; Sub-
Dean 99–00; R Jedburgh *Edin* 00–08; rtd 08; R Newport-on-
Tay *St And* 09–15; PtO *Bre* 15–18; LtO from 18; Protection of
Vulnerable Gps Officer from 17; PtO *St And* from 15; *Edin*
from 16. *43 Bridieswell Gardens, Gauldry, Newport-on-Tay
DD6 8RY* T: (01382) 330411 E: dbh.herbert@btinternet.com
HERBERT, Geoffrey William. b 38. Ox Univ MA 62 Birm Univ
PhD 72. Qu Coll Birm 80. **d** 82 **p** 83. C Hall Green Ascension
Birm 82–85; R Sheldon 85–95; rtd 95; PtO *Birm* from 95;
Co-ord for Spiritual Direction 00–05. *28 Lulworth Road,
Birmingham B28 8NS* T: 0121-777 2684
HERBERT, Graham Victor. b 61. St Jo Coll Nottm BA 02. **d** 02
p 03. C Strood St Nic w St Mary *Roch* 02–06; P-in-c Grain w
Stoke 06–09; R Milton next Gravesend w Denton from 09.
The Rectory, Church Walk, Gravesend DA12 2QU T: (01474)
533434 E: grahamherbert@hotmail.co.uk
HERBERT, Ian Charles. b 65. Trin Coll Bris 10. **d** 12 **p** 13.
C Haddenham w Cuddington, Kingsey etc *Ox* 12–16; TV
Grays Thurrock *Chelmsf* 16–17; R Woughton *Ox* from
17. *7 Stonebridge Grove, Monkston Park, Milton Keynes
MK10 9PB* M: 07740-081457 E: ian.herbert@yahoo.co.uk
HERBERT, Canon Jonathan Patrick. b 62. Bris Univ BA 86.
Linc Th Coll 86. **d** 88 **p** 89. C Kirkby *Liv* 88–91; TV Blakenall
Heath *Lich* 91–96; Pilsdon Community 96–10; Chapl to
Travelling People *Sarum* from 15; Can and Preb Sarum Cathl
from 19. *The Friary, Hilfield, Dorchester DT2 7BE* T: (01300)
341345 E: jonathanherbert1@hotmail.co.uk
HERBERT, Peter David. b 83. Pemb Coll Cam BA 05 MSci 05
MA 08 Herts Univ PhD 12. Oak Hill Th Coll BA 13. **d** 13
p 14. C Cromer *Nor* 13–18; TR Thetford from 18. *The Rectory,
6 Redcastle Road, Thetford IP24 3NF* T: (01842) 763579
E: revpeterherbert@gmail.com
HERBERT, Canon Ronald. b 53. Worc Coll Ox BA 75 MA 80 Lon
Univ BD 78 W Kentucky Univ MA 79. Oak Hill Th Coll 75.
d 79 **p** 80. C Welling *Roch* 79–89; V Falconwood 89–90; V
Becontree St Mary *Chelmsf* 90–07; Hon Can Chelmsf Cathl
02–07; V Stonebridge St Mich *Lon* 07–18; rtd 18; PtO *Cant*
18–21. *111 Somerset Road, Folkestone CT19 4NW* T: (01303)
279859 E: ronald.herbert53@gmail.com
HERBERT, Stephen Edward. b 54. Hastings Coll Nebraska
BA 76 Bemidji State Univ MA 81. Seabury-Western Th Sem
MDiv 87. **d** 87 **p** 87. V Lake City Grace Ch USA 87–90; Asst
P Vancouver St Jas Canada 90–00; TV Wythenshawe *Man*
00–06; TR 06–09; P-in-c Byker St Martin *Newc* 09–16; V
16–20; P-in-c Byker St Mich w St Lawr 09–12; P-in-c Byker

St Ant 12–16; V 16–20; Hon Can Newc Cathl 17–20; rtd 20; PtO *Dur* from 21; *Newc* from 21. *10 Blair Close, Sherburn Village, Durham DH6 1RQ*

HERBERT, Canon Timothy David. b 57. Man Univ BA 78 MPhil 88 PhD 04. Ridley Hall Cam 79. **d** 81 **p** 82. C Macclesfield St Mich *Ches* 81–85; V Wharton 85–93; Asst CME Officer 90–93; P-in-c Thanington *Cant* 93–98; Dir of Ords 93–98; Dir Dioc Tr Inst *Carl* 99–14; C Cotehill and Cumwhinton 99–00; C Scotby and Cotehill w Cumwhinton 00–14; P-in-c Aspatria w Hayton and Gilcrux from 14; RD Solway from 16; Hon Can Carl Cathl from 99. *The Vicarage, King Street, Aspatria, Wigton CA7 3AL* T: (016973) 22712 E: therbert@globalnet.co.uk

HERBERT, William. b 52. **d** 18 **p** 19. NSM Woodbridge St Jo and Bredfield *St E* from 18. *Rustic Cottage, Half Moon Lane, Grundisburgh, Woodbridge IP13 6UE* T: (01473) 735381

HEREFORD, Archdeacon of. See CHEDZEY, The Ven Derek Christopher

HEREFORD, Bishop of. See JACKSON, The Rt Revd Richard Charles

HEREFORD, Dean of. See BROWN, The Very Revd Sarah Romilly Denner

HERKES, Richard Andrew. b 54. Kent Univ BA 75. STETS 99. **d** 02 **p** 03. NSM Polegate *Chich* from 02. *31 Wannock Lane, Eastbourne BN20 9SB* T: (01323) 488328

HERKLOTS, Canon John Radu. b 31. Trin Hall Cam BA 53 MA 61. Westcott Ho Cam 54. **d** 55 **p** 56. C Attercliffe w Carbrook *Sheff* 55–60; C Stoke Damerel *Ex* 60–65; V Devonport St Bart 65–72; V Denmead *Portsm* 72–97; RD Havant 82–87; Hon Can Portsm Cathl 86–97; rtd 97; PtO *Heref* 97–02; *Portsm* from 03. *14 Derwent Road, Lee-on-the-Solent PO13 8JG* T: (023) 9255 2652 E: dencliff1@hotmail.com

HERMO, Ole Bertin. b 66. Spurgeon's Coll BA 14. St Mellitus Coll 14. **d** 16 **p** 17. C Hounslow H Trin *Lon* 16–19; V Leic Martyrs from 19. *The Vicarage, 17 Westcotes Drive, Leicester LE3 0QT* M: 07950-644390 E: bertin.hermo@yahoo.com

HERON, David George. b 49. AKC 72. **d** 73 **p** 74. C Stockton St Chad *Dur* 73–77; C Beamish 77–81; R Willington and Sunnybrow 81–95; V Dipton and Leadgate 95–11; rtd 11; PtO *Dur* from 15. *13 Mount Park Drive, Lanchester, Durham DH7 0PQ* E: fatherheron@talktalk.net

HERON, George Dobson. b 34. TD . Cranmer Hall Dur 58. **d** 61 **p** 62. C Benfieldside *Dur* 61–65; C Winlaton 65–68; V Dunston St Nic 68–77; P-in-c Dunston Ch Ch 74–77; V Dunston 77–82; V Gateshead St Helen 82–89; rtd 94; PtO *Dur* 94–17; *Newc* 94–20. *9 Beech House, Snows Green Road, Consett DH8 0HS*

HERON, Nicholas Peter. b 60. Man Univ BA 83 Southn Univ BTh 86. Sarum & Wells Th Coll. **d** 84 **p** 85. C Brinnington w Portwood *Ches* 84–87; Chapl RAF 87–14; P-in-c Wem *Lich* 14–15; P-in-c Lee Brockhurst 14–15; R Wem, Lee Brockhurst etc from 16. *The Rectory, Ellesmere Road, Wem, Shrewsbury SY4 5TU*

HERON, Simon Alexander. b 68. Ridley Hall Cam 05. **d** 07 **p** 08. C Frindsbury w Upnor and Chattenden *Roch* 07–11; P-in-c Lawford *Chelmsf* 11–17; C Ardleigh and The Bromleys 16–17; C Tendring and Lt Bentley w Beaumont cum Moze 16–17; V Lawford, Lt Bentley and The Bromleys 17–20; AD Harwich 16–20; Hon Can Chelmsf Cathl 16–20; V Cheltenham Ch Ch *Glouc* from 20. *The Vicarage, Malvern Road, Cheltenham GL50 2NU* T: (01242) 515983 E: simon.heron@mac.com

HERRICK, The Ven Andrew Frederick. b 58. Univ of Wales (Lamp) BA 80. Wycliffe Hall Ox 80. **d** 82 **p** 83. C Aberystwyth *St D* 82–85; P-in-c Llangeitho and Blaenpennal w Betws Leucu etc 85–86; R 86–88; Youth Chapl 86–88; R Aberporth w Tremain and Blaenporth 88–91; Succ St D Cathl 91–94; V Betws w Ammanford 94–00; TV Aberystwyth 00–15; P-in-c Lampeter w Maestir and Silian and Llangybi and Betws Bledrws 15–18; Hon Can St D Cathl 14–18; V Bro Cybi *Ban* from 18; Adn Anglesey from 18. *Bryn Llewellyn, Penrallt Road, Trearddur Bay, Holyhead LL65 2UG* T: (01407) 861084 E: andyherrick101@gmail.com *or* archdeacon.anglesey@churchinwales.org.uk

HERRICK, Canon David William. b 52. Middx Poly BSc 73. St Jo Coll Nottm 79. **d** 82 **p** 83. C Ipswich St Matt *St E* 82–85; C Nor St Pet Mancroft w St Jo Maddermarket 85–88; V Bury St Edmunds St Geo *St E* 88–96; P-in-c Gt Barton 96–99; Dir Studies Dioc Min Course 99–12; Vice Prin 04–12; Lay Min Tr Officer 12–16; Dioc Warden of Readers and Lic Lay Min 14–16; Hon Can St E Cathl 13–16; rtd 16; PtO *Sarum* 13–17; *Chelmsf* 17–18; P-in-c Gt Hallingbury and Lt Hallingbury from 18; C Hatfield Heath and Sheering from 20; C Hatfield Broad Oak and Bush End from 20. *Glebe House, Church Lane, Sheering, Bishop's Stortford CM22 7NR* T: (01279) 734524 E: davidherrick103@gmail.com

HERRICK (formerly COWLEY), Mrs Jean Louie Cameron. b 39. Sarum Dioc Tr Coll CertEd 59. SAOMC 94. **d** 96 **p** 97. NSM Chorleywood Ch Ch *St Alb* 96–02; NSM Hermitage *Ox* 02–05; PtO *Glouc* from 05. *1 The Maltings, Station Street, Tewkesbury GL20 5NN* T: (01684) 295598 E: jean.herrick@talktalk.net

HERRICK (née RENAUT), The Ven Vanessa Anne. b 58. York Univ BA 80 Anglia Poly Univ MA 96 LTCL 75. St Jo Coll Nottm 80 Ridley Hall Cam 94. **d** 96 **p** 97. C St E Cathl Distr 96–99; Chapl Fitzw Coll Cam 96–02; Fell 01–02; Tutor Ridley Hall Cam 99–02; Dir Min and Vocation *Ely* 03–12; Hon Can Ely Cathl 03–12; R Wimborne Minster *Sarum* 12–15; P-in-c Witchampton, Stanbridge and Long Crichel etc 15; P-in-c Horton, Chalbury, Hinton Martel and Holt St Jas 15; R Wimborne Minster and the N Villages 15–17; Can and Preb Sarum Cathl 14–17; Adn Harlow *Chelmsf* from 17. *Glebe House, Church Lane, Sheering, Bishops Stortford CM22 7NR* T: (01279) 734524 F: 734426 E: a.harlow@chelmsford.anglican.org

HERROD, Kathryn. b 59. Warwick Univ BSc 80 Matlock Coll of Educn PGCE 81. St Jo Coll Nottm MA 97. **d** 97 **p** 98. C Wollaton *S'well* 97–01; R Warsop 01–10; TR Hucknall Torkard 10–17; Dean of Women's Min 15–17; Hon Can S'well Minster 11–17; P-in-c Barnburgh w Melton on the Hill etc *Sheff* from 17; P-in-c Bilham from 17; Asst Dioc Dir of Ords from 17. *1 Fitzwilliam Drive, Harlington, Doncaster DN5 7HY* T: (01709) 898538 E: kathryn.herrod@sheffield.anglican.org *or* revkathryn@btinternet.com

HERRON, Robert Gordon John. b 36. MCIPD 75. Wycliffe Hall Ox 65. **d** 77 **p** 78. C Ditton St Mich *Liv* 77–80; C W Kirby St Bridget *Ches* 80–82; R Gorton Our Lady and St Thos *Man* 82–00; rtd 00; PtO *Ches* from 10. *The Gables, 13 West Road, Bowdon, Altrincham WA14 2LD* E: revgordon@bowdonchurch.org *or* rgjherron@gmail.com

HERRON, Steven Joseph. b 85. All SS Cen for Miss & Min 17. **d** 20. NSM Marown, Foxdale and Baldwin *S & M* from 20. *13 Sunningdale Drive, Onchan, Isle of Man IM3 1EX* M: 07624-308815 E: steven.herron@sodorandman.im

HERTFORD, Archdeacon of. See MACKENZIE, The Ven Janet

HERTFORD, Suffragan Bishop of. See BEASLEY, The Rt Revd Noel Michael Roy

HERTH, Daniel Edwin. b 36. Xavier Univ Cincinnati BS 58. Ch Div Sch of Pacific MDiv 83. **d** 83 **p** 84. C Oakland St Paul USA 83–86; R Alameda Ch Ch 86–97; NSM Gt and Lt Ouseburn w Marton cum Grafton etc *Ripon* 98–01; Chapl HM YOI Wetherby from 99. *The Garden House, 32 Mallorie Park Drive, Ripon HG4 2QF* T/F: (01765) 602558 M: 07779-379420 E: danielherthsr@btinternet.com

HERVÉ, Mrs Beverley Joan. b 62. UWE BSc 99 Greenwich Univ MA 08 Dur Univ BA 19. St Aug Coll of Th 16. **d** 19 **p** 20. NSM Guernsey Ste Marie du Castel *Win* from 19; NSM Guernsey St Matt from 19. *Footprints, 3 St Patrick's Court, Water Lanes, St Peter Port, Guernsey GY1 2EF* T: (01481) 730575 M: 07911-724284 E: footprints@cwgry.net

HERVÉ, Canon John Anthony. b 49. TD 94. Open Univ BA 81 Wolv Univ PGCE 95. Lich Th Coll 70. **d** 73 **p** 74. C Middlesbrough All SS *York* 73–76; CF 76–81; CF (TAVR) 81–08; P-in-c Handsworth St Andr *Birm* 81–86; Hon C Cowley St Jo *Ox* 86–90; Tutor St Steph Ho Ox 86–90; V Sparkbrook St Agatha w Balsall Heath St Barn *Birm* 90–14; P-in-c Highgate 05–10; Hon Can Birm Cathl 05–14; rtd 14. *29 Lytton House, St Luke's Road South, Torquay TQ2 5PA* T: (01803) 295887

HERVEY, Mrs Mary Diana. b 41. St Hugh's Coll Ox BA 63. St And Dioc Tr Course 83 TISEC 96. **d** 92 **p** 94. Par Dn Cupar *St And* 92–94; Asst Chapl St Andr Univ 94–97; Asst P Cen Fife Team 94–97; C Ulverston St Mary w H Trin *Carl* 97–00; P-in-c Barrow St Jo 00–06; rtd 06; PtO *Carl* 08–14; *Bradf* 11–14; *Leeds* 14–16; *Ab* from 18. *Nor Hamar, Baltasound, Unst, Shetland ZE2 9DS* T: (01957) 711331

HESELTINE, Barbara Joan. See FEATHER, Barbara Joan

HESELWOOD, Eric Harold. b 43. Oak Hill Th Coll 84. **d** 86 **p** 87. C Farnborough *Roch* 86–88; V Biggin Hill 88–96; V Orpington All SS 96–98; V Bromley Common St Aug 98–05; rtd 05; PtO *Roch* 06–08; P-in-c Cudham and Downe 08–10; PtO from 10. *34 Victoria Gardens, Biggin Hill, Westerham TN16 3DJ* T/F: (01959) 509131 E: eric.heselwood@ntlworld.com

HESFORD-LOCKE, Richard Nigel. b 61. Coll of Resurr Mirfield 92. **d** 94 **p** 95. C Middlesbrough Ascension *York* 94–97; C Paignton St Jo, St Andr and St Boniface *Ex* 97–98; rtd 98. *2 Windyhill Drive, Bolton BL3 4TH*

HESKETH, Derrick. **d** 12 **p** 13. OLM Blackwell w Tibshelf *Derby* from 12. *61 Peveril Road, Tibshelf, Alfreton DE55 5LR* T: (01773) 872146 E: derrickhesketh61@btinternet.com

HESKETH, The Very Revd Philip John. b 64. K Coll Lon BD 86 AKC 86 PhD 94. Ripon Coll Cuddesdon 92. **d** 94

p 95. C Bearsted w Thurnham *Cant* 94–98; V Chatham St Steph *Roch* 98–05; Can Res Roch Cathl 05–16; Dean Roch from 16. *Chapter Office, Garth House, The Precinct, Rochester ME1 1SX* T: (01634) 843366 F: 401410 E: dean@rochestercathedral.org

HESKETH, The Ven Ronald David. b 47. CB 04. Bede Coll Dur BA 68 FRGS 02. Ridley Hall Cam 69 St Mich Coll Llan 71. **d** 71 **p** 72. C Southport H Trin *Liv* 71–74; Asst Chapl Miss to Seamen 74–75; Chapl RAF 75–98; Command Chapl RAF 98–01; Chapl-in-Chief RAF 01–06; QHC 01–06; Can and Preb Linc Cathl 01–06; Voc Officer *Worc* 06–11; Co-ord Chapl W Mercia Police 09–16; PtO from 16; *Glouc* 15–19; Hon C Tewkesbury w Walton Cardiff and Twyning from 19. *Whistledown, Twyning Green, Twyning, Tewkesbury GL20 6DQ* T: (01684) 299773 E: ron@hesketh.org.uk

HESKINS, Georgiana Mary. *See* BELL, Georgiana Mary

HESKINS, Canon Jeffrey George. b 55. Heythrop Coll Lon MA 94 Princeton Th Sem DMin 00 AKC 78. Chich Th Coll 80. **d** 81 **p** 82. C Primrose Hill St Mary w Avenue Road St Paul *Lon* 81–85; Chapl R Cen Sch of Speech and Drama 81–85; Enfield Deanery Youth Officer 85–88; C Enfield Chase St Mary *Lon* 85–88; TV Kidbrooke St Jas *S'wark* 88–95; R Charlton St Luke w H Trin 95–02; P-in-c Old Charlton St Thos 02; R Charlton 02–07; Dioc Dir of Ords *Linc* 07–19; Min Can and PV Linc Cathl 08–10; Dir IME 4-7 10–18; Chapl Bp Grosseteste Univ from 19; Chapl Lincs Partnership NHS Foundn Trust 20–21; Can and Preb Linc Cathl from 10. *The Chaplaincy Office, Bishop Grosseteste University, Longdales Road, Lincoln LN1 3DY* M: 07387-833757 E: jeffrey.heskins@bishopg.ac.uk

HESKINS, Rachel. b 70. Trevelyan Coll Dur BA 92 Sheff Univ MA 19 Ox Univ PGCE 97. Westcott Ho Cam 15. **d** 16 **p** 17. C Welton and Dunholme w Scothern *Linc* 16–19; V Linc St Jo from 19. *St John's Vicarage, Sudbrooke Drive, Lincoln LN2 2EF* M: 07813-617977 E: rachel@heskins.plus.com

HESLAM, Peter Somers. b 63. Hull Univ BA 89 Keble Coll Ox DPhil 94 Trin Coll Cam BA 96 MA 01. Ridley Hall Cam 93. **d** 96 **p** 97. C Huntingdon *Ely* 96–99; Min Stukeley Meadows LEP 99; Dir Studies EAMTC 99–00; Tutor Ridley Hall Cam 99–05; Dir Capitalism Project Lon Inst of Contemporary Chr 00–04; Fell Faculty of Div Cam Univ from 05; Hon C Cherry Hinton St Jo *Ely* from 00. *Glebe House, 64A Glebe Road, Cambridge CB1 7SZ* T: (01223) 722822 E: psh20@cam.ac.uk

HESLOP, Alan. *See* HESLOP, James Alan

HESLOP, Andrew James. b 66. Man Univ BA 87 PGCE 88. **d** 03 **p** 04. OLM Turton Moorland *Man* 03–18; Chapl Wrightington, Wigan and Leigh NHS Foundn Trust 07–10; Chapl Springhill Hospice 10–14; Chapl Salford R NHS Foundn Trust 14–21; Chapl Leeds Teaching Hosps NHS Trust from 21; PtO *Blackb* 07–10; *Man* from 18. *The Leeds Teaching Hospitals NHS Trust, St James's University Hospital, Beckett Street, Leeds LS9 7TF* T: 0113-206 4658

HESLOP, Caroline Susan. *See* WILSON, Caroline Susan

HESLOP, James Alan. b 37. Codrington Coll Barbados 61. **d** 64 **p** 65. C Bartica Guyana 64–68; P-in-c Long Is Nassau Bahamas 68–71; C Ch Ch Cathl 71–72; C Haxby w Wigginton *York* 72–74; TV 74–76; V York St Olave w St Giles 76–87; V Northampton All SS w St Kath *Pet* 87–88; R Felpham w Middleton *Chich* 88–92; TR Howden *York* 92–94; Warden Coll of St Barn Lingfield 94–95; Warden Morley Retreat and Conf Ho Derby 95–98; R Kirkbride and V Lezayre St Olave Ramsey *S & M* 98–99; P-in-c Woburn w Eversholt, Milton Bryan, Battlesden etc *St Alb* 99–03; rtd 03; Chapl Soc of St Marg 04–05; P-in-c Pau *Eur* 05–06. *1 Coniston Close, Bognor Regis PO22 8ND* T: (01243) 869499

HESLOP, Neil. b 73. Sunderland Univ BSc 95 MSc 03 Sheff Univ BA 15. Coll of Resurr Mirfield 13. **d** 15 **p** 16. C Fenham St Jas and St Basil *Newc* 15–18; C Sugley 18; P-in-c from 18; P-in-c Denton from 20. *Sugley Vicarage, Sugley Drive, Lemington, Newcastle upon Tyne NE15 8RD* T: 0191-267 4633 E: frneil.heslop@gmail.com

HETHERINGTON, Andrew. b 50. Sheff Univ BSc 71. Wycliffe Hall Ox 71. **d** 74 **p** 75. C Leic H Trin w St Jo 74–78; C Leic H Apostles 78–82; V Bootle St Mary w St Paul *Liv* 82–93; TR W Swindon and the Lydiards *Bris* 93–01; P-in-c Chebsey, Ellenhall and Seighford-with-Creswell *Lich* 01–06; V Chebsey, Creswell, Ellenhall, Ranton etc 06–15; rtd 15; PtO *Liv* from 15. *67 Maliston Road, Great Sankey, Warrington WA5 1JS* E: andrewhetherington@btinternet.com

HETHERINGTON, Mrs Charlotte Elizabeth. b 52. Girton Coll Cam BA 74 Maria Grey Coll Lon PGCE 75 Heythrop Coll Lon MA 02. SAOMC 95. **d** 98 **p** 99. NSM Stratfield Mortimer and Mortimer W End etc *Ox* 98–04; C Portsea St Mary *Portsm* 04–17; rtd 17; PtO *Portsm* from 17. *Pitts Farm House, Langrish, Petersfield GU32 1RQ* E: charlottehetherington@hotmail.com

HETHERINGTON, John Carl. b 52. Hull Univ BTh 93. Linc Th Coll 82. **d** 84 **p** 85. C Crosby *Linc* 84–88; TV Cleethorpes 88–93; Chapl RAF 93–07; R Monk Fryston and S Milford York 07–17; rtd 17; PtO *York* from 17. *12 Longbridge Drive, Easingwold, York YO61 3FH* T: (01347) 469087 M: 07709-827122 E: easingwoldrev@gmail.com

HETHERINGTON, Mrs Rachel Marie. b 65. ERMC 05. **d** 08 **p** 12. NSM Northampton Ch Ch *Pet* 08–11; NSM Northampton H Sepulchre w St Andr and St Lawr 08–11; NSM Northampton St Mich w St Edm 08–11; NSM Northampton H Trin and St Paul 08–11; Asst Chapl St Andr Healthcare 11–21; C Kingsthorpe *Pet* 12–16; TV 16–21; C Abington from 21. *Address temp unknown* E: rhetherington10@gmail.com

HEWERDINE, Mark Richard. b 77. Man Univ BA 99. Qu Coll Birm MA 13. **d** 13 **p** 14. C W Didsbury and Withington St Chris *Man* 13–16; P-in-c Ladybarn 16–19; R from 19; C Burnage St Nic from 17. *1 St Chad's Road, Manchester M20 4WH* T: 0161-445 1185 M: 07772-538491 E: markhewerdine@gmail.com

HEWES, John. b 29. Nottm Univ BA 50. Chich Th Coll 79. **d** 81 **p** 82. C Buckland in Dover w Buckland Valley *Cant* 81–84; P-in-c Elmsted w Hastingleigh 84–89; P-in-c Crundale w Godmersham 84–89; RD W Bridge 88–89; R Lydd 89–95; RD S Lympne 89–95; rtd 95; PtO *Cant* from 95. *24 Orchard Drive, Wye, Ashford, TN25 5AT* T: (01233) 750214 E: john.hewes@btinternet.com

HEWES, Timothy William. b 50. Sheff Univ BDS 74. SAOMC 98. **d** 01. NSM Abingdon *Ox* 01–14; NSM Sutton Courtenay w Appleford 14–17; PtO from 17. *25 New Road, Charney Bassett, Wantage OX12 0ER* M: 07771-880117 E: tim.hewes50@icloud.com

HEWETSON, The Ven Christopher. b 37. Trin Coll Ox BA 60 MA 64. Chich Th Coll 67. **d** 69 **p** 70. C Leckhampton St Pet *Glouc* 69–71; C Wokingham All SS *Ox* 71–73; V Didcot St Pet 73–82; R Ascot Heath 82–90; RD Bracknell 86–90; P-in-c Headington Quarry 90–94; Hon Can Ch Ch 92–94; RD Cowley 94; Adn Ches 94–02; rtd 02; Bp's Adv for Spirituality *Ex* 03–07; PtO *Ches* 05–10; *B & W* 09–13. *70 East Street, South Molton EX36 3DQ* E: christopher.hewetson@sky.com

HEWETSON, Canon Robin Jervis. b 39. AKC 63 K Coll Lon MA 93. **d** 64 **p** 65. C Thorpe St Andr *Nor* 64–67; C E Dereham w Hoe 67–69; TV Mattishall w Mattishall Burgh 69–72; R Ingham w Sutton 72–78; R Catfield 75–78; R Taverham w Ringland 78–89; P-in-c Marsham 89–92; P-in-c Burgh 89–92; Dioc Ecum Officer 89–04; Exec Officer Norfolk Ecum Coun 89–04; R Marsham w Burgh-next-Aylsham *Nor* 92–04; Hon Can Nor Cathl 01–04; rtd 04; PtO *Nor* from 04. *83 Soame Close, Aylsham, Norwich NR11 6JF* T: (01263) 734325 E: robin.hewetson@gmail.com

HEWETSON, Canon Valerie Patricia. b 44. St Mary's Coll Dur BSc 66 MSc 70 Leeds Univ MA 75. Linc Th Coll 89. **d** 91 **p** 94. C Kingston upon Hull St Nic *York* 91–94; V Barmby Moor w Allerthorpe, Fangfoss and Yapham 94–98; V Barmby Moor Gp 98–10; RD S Wold 01–06; Can and Preb York Minster 01–10; rtd 10; PtO *York* from 11. *27 Briarsfield, Barmby Moor, York YO24 4HN* T: (01759) 303816 E: valerie.hewetson@btinternet.com

HEWETT, Kristian Sydney. b 92. Jes Coll Cam BA 14 Homerton Coll Cam PGCE 16 Cam Univ BA 20. Westcott Ho Cam 18. **d** 21. C Shrewsbury H Cross *Lich* from 21. *14 Langholm Drive, Shrewsbury SY2 5UN* E: kristian.hewett92@gmail.com

HEWETT, Ruth Ellen. b 60. **d** 16 **p** 17. NSM Ch the King *Newc* from 16. *62 Featherstone Grove, Newcastle upon Tyne NE3 5RJ* T: 0191-217 0367 E: ruthhewett@icloud.com

HEWISH, Mrs Lesley Gillian. b 60. Trin Coll Bris 08. **d** 10 **p** 11. C Tetbury, Beverston, Long Newnton etc *Glouc* 10–13; Chapl HM Pris Eastwood Park 13–18; Chapl HM Pris Leyhill from 18. *HM Prison Leyhill, Wotton-under-Edge GL12 8BT* T: (01454) 264041 M: 07876-775290 E: lesley.hewish@justice.gov.uk

HEWISON, Miss Catherine Ann. b 75. Univ of Wales (Ban) BSc 98. Trin Coll Bris 17. **d** 19 **p** 20. C Gorton and Abbey Hey *Man* from 19. *St Philip's Rectory, Lavington Grove, Manchester M18 7EQ* M: 07732-082537 E: cathhewison@hotmail.com

HEWITT, Caroline Doris. b 62. Man Univ BSc 83 PhD 87. All SS Cen for Miss & Min 12. **d** 15 **p** 16. C Salford All SS *Man* 15–19; TV Wythenshawe from 19; P-in-c Lawton Moor 19–20; V from 20. *St Michael and All Angels Vicarage, Orton Road, Manchester M23 0LH* T: 0161-998 2715 E: revd.caroline.hewitt@gmail.com

HEWITT, Christopher James Chichele (Chich). b 45. Witwatersrand Univ BSc 68 UNISA BA 78 MTh 92 LTCL 69. St Paul's Coll Grahamstown. **d** 78 **p** 79. S Africa 78–99; Chapl St Paul's Coll Grahamstown 84–86; Warden 86–92; Can Grahamstown Cathl 88–93; Chan 92; Sub-Dean 93; Dean and Adn Grahamstown 93–98; USA 99; TR Radcliffe *Man* 00–09; AD Radcliffe and Prestwich 02–09; P-in-c Swinton H

Rood 09–13; V 13–14; C Worsley 13–14; rtd 14; PtO *Man* from 14. *79 Long Lane, Bolton BL2 6EU* T: (01204) 436374 E: chich@rink-hewitt.co.uk

HEWITT, Christopher William. b 63. Nottm Trent Univ BEng 98 PGCE 05 Linc Univ BA 14 Bp Grosseteste Univ MA 19 CEng 01 MIET 01. Linc Sch of Th and Min 10. **d** 15 **p** 16. C Barlings *Linc* 15–18; C S Lawres Gp 15–18; V Walesby Gp from 18; P-in-c Barkwith Gp from 20; RD W Wold from 19. *The Rectory, Otby Lane, Walesby, Market Rasen LN8 3UT* M: 07853-277065 E: cwhewitt@btinternet.com *or* chris.hewitt@lincoln.anglican.org

HEWITT, Colin Edward. b 52. Man Poly BA 80 Em Coll Cam BA 82 MA 86 Maryvale Inst PGCE 08. Westcott Ho Cam 81. **d** 83 **p** 84. C Radcliffe St Thos and St Jo *Man* 83–84; C Langley and Parkfield 84–86; R Byfield w Boddington *Pet* 86–89; R Byfield w Boddington and Aston le Walls 89–91; Chapl RAF 91–09; V Brentwood St Thos *Chelmsf* 09–17; rtd 17; PtO *St E* from 19. *Address withheld by request* T: (01394) 548389 M: 07704-495001 E: colinhewitt@hotmail.com

HEWITT, David Warner. b 33. Selw Coll Cam BA 56 MA 60. Wells Th Coll 57. **d** 59 **p** 60. C Longbridge *Birm* 59–61; C Sheldon 61–64; V Smethwick Old Ch 64–70; V Smethwick 70–78; P-in-c Littlehampton St Jas *Chich* 78–85; V Wick 78–85; V Littlehampton St Mary 78–85; TR Littlehampton and Wick 86–89; PtO *Eur* from 95; rtd 98; Hon Asst Chapl Gtr Athens *Eur* 00–03; PtO *Chelmsf* from 07. *18 Orchard Close, Weaverhead Lane, Thaxted, Dunmow CM6 2JX* T: (01371) 830591 E: tangulls1@mac.com

HEWITT, Canon Francis John Adam. b 42. St Chad's Coll Dur BA 64. **d** 66 **p** 67. C Dewsbury Moor *Wakef* 66–69; C Huddersfield St Jo 69–73; V King Cross 73–81; V Lastingham w Appleton-le-Moors, Rosedale etc *York* 81–94; RD Helmsley 85–94; V Pickering 94–95; V Pickering w Lockton and Levisham 95–07; RD Pickering 94–06; rtd 07; PtO *York* from 07; Can and Preb York Minster from 97. *Michaelmas Cottage, 3 Lime Chase, Kirkbymoorside, York YO62 6BX* T: (01751) 430322 E: francis.hewitt@hotmail

HEWITT, Canon Garth Bruce. b 46. St Jo Coll Dur BA 68. Lon Coll of Div LTh 70. **d** 70 **p** 71. C Maidstone St Luke *Cant* 70–73; Staff Evang CPAS 73–79; Hon C W Ealing St Jo w St Jas *Lon* 73–81; Amos Trust from 85; Dir 88–11; World Affairs Adv *Guildf* 94–96; Regional Co-ord (Lon and SE) Chr Aid 96–12; PtO *S'wark* from 04; P-in-c All Hallows Lon Wall 97–99; V 99–13; Hon C St Clem Eastcheap w St Martin Orgar 13–18; Hon Can Jerusalem from 06. *Amos Trust, St Clement's Church, 1 St Clement's Court, London EC4N 7HB* T: (020) 7588 2638 E: garth@amostrust.org

HEWITT, Guy Arlington Kenneth. b 67. Univ of W Indies BSc 92 MSc 94. SEITE 00. **d** 04 **p** 05. C Ch Ch Barbados 04–06; P-in-c Ruby H Trin 06–07; C Ch Ch 07–08; PtO *S'wark* 15–19. *9 Roehampton Gate, London SW15 5JR* T: (020) 8878 0260 *or* 7299 7150 E: guyhewitt@gmail.com

HEWITT, Jason Lawrence. b 87. St Steph Ho Ox 16. **d** 19 **p** 20. C Cen Barnsley *Leeds* from 19. *St George's Vicarage, 100 Dodworth Road, Barnsley S70 6HL* M: 07395-522289 E: jaylhewitt@hotmail.co.uk

HEWITT, Kenneth Victor. b 30. Lon Univ BSc 49 CertEd 51 MSc 53. Cuddesdon Coll 60. **d** 62 **p** 63. C Maidstone St Martin *Cant* 62–64; C Croydon St Mich 64–67; P-in-c S Kensington St Aug Lon 67–73; V 73–95; Asst Chapl Lon Univ 67–73; rtd 95; PtO *Roch* 95–16. *41 Bromley College, London Road, Bromley BR1 1PE* T: (020) 8464 0014

HEWITT, Laura Jane. b 67. Cranmer Hall Dur 01. **d** 03 **p** 04. C Kingston upon Hull St Aid Southcoates *York* 03–07; V Seamer w East Ayton 07–14; TR Billingham *Dur* 14–17; V New Barnet St Jas *St Alb* from 17; AD Barnet from 21. *St James' Vicarage, 11 Park Road, New Barnet, Barnet EN4 9QA* T: (020) 3654 0649 M: 07500-345058 E: revlaurajane@yahoo.co.uk

HEWITT, Michael David. b 49. K Coll Lon BD 79 AKC 79 CertEd. Qu Coll Birm 79. **d** 80 **p** 81. C Bexleyheath Ch Ch *Roch* 80–84; C Buckland in Dover w Buckland Valley *Cant* 84–89; R Ridgewell w Ashen, Birdbrook and Sturmer *Chelmsf* 89–13; rtd 13. *22 Bromley College, London Road, Bromley BR1 1PE*

HEWITT, Paul Stephen Patrick. b 59. TCD BA 82 MA 87. CITC 83. **d** 86 **p** 87. C Ballymacash *Conn* 86–89; C Ballymena w Ballyclug 89–91; I Glencraig *D & D* 91–12; rtd 12. *18A Old Cultra Road, Holywood BT18 0AE* T: (028) 9042 1847 E: paulsphewitt@btconnect.com

HEWITT, Stephen Wilkes. b 49. Fitzw Coll Cam MA 71. St Jo Coll Nottm 88. **d** 90 **p** 91. C Eaton *Nor* 90–93; V Warwick St Paul *Cov* 93–01; V Newc 90–93; V High Spen and Rowlands Gill *Dur* 02–05; V 05–09; TR Cramlington *Newc* 09–14; rtd 15; PtO *Newc* from 15. *54 Prior Road, Tweedmouth, Berwick-upon-Tweed TD15 2EH*

HEWITT, Canon Timothy James. b 67. St D Coll Lamp BD 88 Win Univ MA 19 MCMI 14 CMgr 14. Ripon Coll Cuddesdon 89. **d** 91 **p** 92. C Milford Haven *St D* 91–94; C Llanelli 94–96; P-in-c Llan-non 96–97; V Clydach *S & B* 98–07; V Ystalyfera from 07; Dioc Voc Adv 07–17; Bp's Officer for Tr and Minl Development from 18; Can Res Brecon Cathl from 15. *The Vicarage, Glan yr Afon Road, Ystalyfera, Swansea SA9 2EP* T: (01639) 842257 E: timothyhewitt@outlook.com

HEWLETT, Mrs Caroline Joan. b 68. Coll of Ripon & York St Jo BEd 92 St Jo Coll Dur BA 01. Cranmer Hall Dur 99. **d** 01 **p** 02. C Leeds St Geo *Ripon* 01–04; C Aldborough w Boroughbridge and Roecliffe 04–06; Chapl Leeds Combined Court Cen 03–06; V Swaledale 06–14; *Leeds* from 14. *The Vicarage, Langhorne Lodge, Langhorne Drive, Reeth, Richmond DL11 6ST* T: (01748) 884706 M: 07866-750211 E: carolinejhewlett@btinternet.com

HEWLETT, David Bryan. b 49. Bris Univ BEd 72. Qu Coll Birm 77. **d** 79 **p** 80. C Ludlow *Heref* 79–81; TV 81–84; V Marden w Amberley and Wisteston 84–92; Lect Glouc Sch for Min 84–92; Field Officer for Lay Min *Heref* 84–91; CME Officer 86–92; Dir Post-Ord Tr 91–92; Hd Master St Fran Sch Pewsey 92–94; Co-ord Chapl Frenchay Healthcare NHS Trust Bris 94–99; Chapl N Bris NHS Trust 99–00; Dir Past Studies OLM Scheme and CME Adv *Linc* 00–04; Par Development Adv (South) 00–04; R Pontesbury I and II *Heref* 04–08; V Corbridge w Halton and Newton Hall *Newc* 08–17; AD Corbridge 09–17; rtd 17; PtO *Heref* from 17. *Broxmere, Bodenham, Hereford HR1 3JB* T: (01568) 797568 E: david.hewlett3@btopenworld.com

HEWLETT, Canon David Jonathon Peter. b 57. Dur Univ BA 79 PhD 83. Ridley Hall Cam 82. **d** 83 **p** 84. C New Barnet St Jas *St Alb* 83–86; Lect CITC 86–90; P-in-c Feock *Truro* 91–95; Jt Dir SWMTC 91–95; Prin 95–03; Adv Local Ord Min 91–95; Hon Can Truro Cathl 01–03; Prin Qu Coll Birm 03–20; Hon Can Birm Cathl 14–20; rtd 20. *The Byre, Stocks Lane, Leigh Sinton, Malvern WR13 5DY* T: (01886) 288217 E: djph0802@gmail.com

HEWLETT, Guy Edward. b 59. Thames Poly CertEd 89 Open Univ BA 90. Oak Hill Th Coll 96. **d** 96 **p** 97. NSM Sudbury St Andr *Lon* 96–99; C Harrow Trin St Mich 99–05; V Harrow Weald St Mich 05–13; Chapl Worcs Acute Hosps NHS Trust 13–17; TR Gornal and Sedgley *Worc* from 17. *The Vicarage, Vicar Street, Sedgley, Dudley DY3 3SD* E: guyhewlett18@gmail.com

HEWLETT-SMITH, Peter Brian. b 40. OBE 87. Ripon Coll Cuddesdon 06. **d** 06. NSM Heckfield w Mattingley and Rotherwick *Win* 06–07; NSM Whitewater 07–10; PtO from 10. *10 Winchfield Court, Pale Lane, Winchfield, Hook RG27 8SP* T: (01252) 842163 M: 07799-404206 E: peter.hewlettsmith@gmail.com

HEWLINS, Pauline Elizabeth. See SEAMAN, Pauline Elizabeth

HEWSON, Douglas Peter. b 43. **d** 12 **p** 13. OLM Milford *Guildf* 12–16; PtO from 16. *Meijendel, Sandy Lane, Milford, Godalming GU8 5BL* T: (01483) 425131 E: peter_hewson@sky.com

HEWSON, Mrs Mandy Carol. b 61. Anglia Ruskin Univ BSc 05. St Mellitus Coll BA 11. **d** 11 **p** 13. NSM E Springfield *Chelmsf* 11–16 and from 20; PtO 16–20. *33 Meon Close, Chelmsford CM1 7QG* T: (01245) 287710 E: mandyhewson@gmail.com

HEYCOCKS, Canon Christian John. b 71. Univ of Wales (Ban) BA 93 MA 96. Westcott Ho Cam 94 CITC 97. **d** 97 **p** 98. C Rhyl w St Ann *St As* 97–00; Chapl RN 00–06; Chapl Univ Staff Cam and C Cambridge Gt St Mary w St Mich *Ely* 06–09; V Sheringham *Nor* from 09; RD Repps 14–20; Hon Can Nor Cathl from 20. *The Vicarage, 10 North Street, Sheringham NR26 8LW* T: (01263) 822089 E: rev.heycocks15@btinternet.com

HEYES, Robert John. b 46. STETS 00. **d** 03 **p** 04. NSM Bramley and Grafham *Guildf* 03–08; NSM Shamley Green 08–11; rtd 11. *Juniper Cottage, 22 Eastwood Road, Bramley, Guildford GU5 0DS* T: (01483) 893706 F: 894001 E: bobheyes@onetel.com

HEYGATE, Stephen Beaumont. b 48. Loughb Univ BSc 71 CQSW 73 PhD 89. St Jo Coll Nottm 86. **d** 88 **p** 89. C Aylestone St Andr w St Jas *Leic* 88–90; V Cosby 90–00; V Evington 00–11; P-in-c Leic St Phil 00–04; rtd 12; PtO *Leic* from 12; *Pet* from 12; Bp's Adv for Healing and Deliverance *Leic* from 04. *4 Gapstile Close, Desborough, Kettering NN14 2TZ* T: (01536) 764106 E: stephenheygate@btinternet.com

HEYHOE, Jonathan Peter. b 53. Man Univ BA 75. Trin Coll Bris 77. **d** 80 **p** 81. C Woking St Pet *Guildf* 80–83; C Heatherlands St D *Sarum* 83–91; Chr Renewal Cen Rostrevor 91–95; PtO *D & D* 91–97; I Ballybay w Mucknoe and Clontibret *Clogh* 98–11; Preb Clogh Cathl 06–11; rtd 11. *11 Rowallon, Warrenpoint, Newry BT34 3TR* T: (028) 4175 4659 M: 07503-920902

HEYN, Lucinda Jane. See MORRISS, Lucinda Jane

HEYWARD, Daniel James. b 74. Ex Univ BA 97 MCIPD. Wycliffe Hall Ox 09. **d** 11 **p** 12. C Reading Greyfriars *Ox* 11–15; C Bris St Phil and St Jacob w Em 15–16; V Ox St Andr from 16. *46 Charlbury Road, Oxford OX2 6UX* M: 07508-346550 E: daniel_heyward@hotmail.com *or* dan.heyward@standrewsoxford.org

HEYWOOD, Mrs Anne Christine. b 44. Sarum Th Coll. **d** 97 **p** 98. C Talbot Village *Sarum* 97–01; TV Shaston 01–09; rtd 10; PtO *Sarum* from 10; *Ox* from 18. *26 Casterbridge Way, Gillingham SP8 4FG* T: (01747) 825259

HEYWOOD, Anthony. *See* HEYWOOD, Richard Anthony

HEYWOOD, David Stephen. b 55. Selw Coll Cam BA 76 MA 80 SS Hild & Bede Coll Dur PhD 89. Cranmer Hall Dur 80. **d** 86 **p** 87. C Cheltenham St Luke and St Jo *Glouc* 86–90; TV Sanderstead All SS *S'wark* 90–98; V Edensor *Lich* 98–03; Deanery and Min Development Officer 03–06; Dir Past Studies Ripon Coll Cuddesdon 06–15; Dep Dioc Dir of Miss *Ox* 17–20; rtd 20; PtO *Ox* from 20. *8 Gravel Lane, Drayton, Abingdon OX14 4HY* M: 07804-680513 E: davidheywood43@gmail.com

HEYWOOD, Deiniol John Owen. *See* KEARLEY-HEYWOOD, Deiniol John Owen

HEYWOOD, Mrs Margaret Anne (Meg). b 52. Luton Coll of HE BSc 81. EMMTC 04. **d** 07 **p** 07. Chapl Ox Min Course 06–12; NSM Ox St Clem 07–08; NSM Thame 09–10; PtO 10–17; NSM DAMASCUS from 17. *The Vicarage, 8 Gravel Lane, Drayton, Abingdon OX14 4HY* T: (01235) 537100 E: revmeg@damascusparish.org.uk

HEYWOOD, Peter. b 46. Cranmer Hall Dur 72. **d** 75 **p** 76. C Blackley St Andr *Man* 75–78; C Denton Ch Ch 78–80; V Constable Lee 80–01; rtd 01; PtO *Man* from 01. *1 Millgate Road, Rossendale BB4 7AS* T: (01706) 212297 M: 07881-543973 E: peterheywood1@sky.com

HEYWOOD, Richard Anthony. b 77. St Jo Coll Dur BA 99. Oak Hill Th Coll 04. **d** 07 **p** 08. C Lt Shelford *Ely* 07–11; TV Thetford *Nor* from 11. *44 Nunsgate, Thetford IP24 3EL* M: 07804-671405 E: tony.heyward@talk21.com

HEZEL, Adrian. b 43. Chelsea Coll Lon BSc 64 PhD 67. NOC 78. **d** 81 **p** 82. NSM Mirfield *Wakef* 81–89; C 89–90; V Shelley and Shepley 90–99; V Hoylake *Ches* 99–08; rtd 08; PtO *Ches* from 09; *St As* from 18. *32 Ffordd Byrnwr Gwair, Mold CH7 1FQ* T: (01352) 756922 E: ahezel@btinternet.com

HIBBERD, Brian Jeffery. b 35. Fitzw Coll Cam MA 62 Southn Univ MA 84. Ridley Hall Cam 58. **d** 60 **p** 61. C Cambridge H Trin *Ely* 60–63; C Doncaster St Mary *Sheff* 63–66; Asst Master Price's Sch Fareham 66–69; Warblington Sch Havant 69–71; Hd Soc and RS Carisbrooke High Sch 71–84; Distr Health Promotion Officer Is of Wight 84–88; SW Herts 88–90; Hd RS Goffs Sch Cheshunt 90–95; rtd 95; Teacher Qu Sch Bushey 95–97; Teacher R Masonic Sch for Girls Rickmansworth 97–00; Hon C Abbots Langley *St Alb* 00–01; PtO from 01. *50 Rosehill Gardens, Abbots Langley WD5 0HF* T: (01923) 267391

HIBBERD, John. b 60. Wadh Coll Ox MA 82. Trin Coll Bris BA 89. **d** 89 **p** 90. C Northolt St Mary *Lon* 89–92; C-in-c Southall Em CD 92–94; Min of Miss Through Faith Miss *Ely* 95–14; Miss Development Adv Sheff and Rotherham Adnry from 14. *14 Hollingswood Way, Sunnyside, Rotherham S66 3ZN* T: (01709) 700351 E: jhibberd14@btinternet.com

HIBBERD, John Charles. b 38. Bernard Gilpin Soc Dur 62 Chich Th Coll 63. **d** 66 **p** 67. C W Drayton *Lon* 66–70; C Noel Park St Mark 70–72; C Ealing St Steph Castle Hill 72–75; V Gunnersbury St Jas 75–84; V Whitton SS Phil and Jas 84–86; Finance and Trust Sec Lon Dioc Fund 87–98; PtO *Lon* 87–98; rtd 98. *18 Pursley Close, Sandown PO36 9QP* T: (01983) 401036 E: johnhibberd0138@talktalk.net

HIBBERT, Gillian Mary. b 40. **d** 09 **p** 10. Chapl Countess of Chester Hosp NHS Foundn Trust from 09. *Whitehaven, Church Walks, Christleton, Chester CH3 7AF* T: (01244) 336544

HIBBERT, Canon Peter John. b 43. Hull Univ BA 71 Lon Univ CertEd 72 MA 79. Sarum & Wells Th Coll 85. **d** 88 **p** 89. C Newsome and Armitage Bridge *Wakef* 88–92; P-in-c Newton Flowery Field *Ches* 92–00; P-in-c Hyde St Thos 97–00; V Handsworth St Jas *Birm* 00–08; P-in-c Altarnon w Bolventor, Laneast and St Clether *Truro* 08–09; P-in-c Micklehurst *Ches* 09–13; P-in-c Hyde St Thos w Godley cum Newton Green 10–17; PtO *Man* 16–18; NSM Hulme Ascension from 18; NSM Chorlton-cum-Hardy St Werburgh 18–20; PtO *Ches* 17–18; Hon Can Ches Cathl 11–18. *203 Petersburg Road, Stockport SK3 9RA* T: 0161-474 1601 E: hibbert631@btinternet.com

HIBBERT, Prof Peter Rodney. b 53. Man Univ LLB 74 Nottm Univ MA 99 Solicitor 77. EMMTC 96. **d** 99 **p** 00. C Knighton St Mary Magd *Leic* 99–01; PtO 01–12; *Birm* from 03; *Leic* from 15; Superior OGS 11–19. *Grange Cottage, 37 Rushes*

Lane, Lubenham, Market Harborough LE16 9TN T: (01858) 433174 E: for.peter@hotmail.com

HIBBERT, Canon Richard Charles. b 62. Trin Coll Bris BA 93. **d** 96 **p** 97. C Luton St Mary *St Alb* 96–00; V Bedford Ch Ch from 00; RD Bedford 10–20; Hon Can St Alb from 13. *Christ Church Vicarage, 115 Denmark Street, Bedford MK40 3TJ* T/F: (01234) 359342 E: vicar@ccbedford.org

HIBBINS, Neil Lance. b 60. St Anne's Coll Ox BA 82 MA 87. St Mich Coll Llan 83. **d** 85 **p** 86. C Griffithstown *Mon* 85–87; C Pontypool 87–88; TV 88–92; Walsall Hosps NHS Trust 92–96; Asst Chapl Manor Hosp Walsall 92–96; R Norton Canes *Lich* from 96. *The Rectory, 81 Church Road, Norton Canes, Cannock WS11 9PQ* T: (01543) 278969 E: neil_hibbins@msn.com

HIBBS, Peter Wilfred. b 56. NOC 05. **d** 08 **p** 09. NSM Gt Snaith *Sheff* from 08. *Peveril, High Street, Snaith, Goole DN14 9HJ* T: (01405) 862517 M: 07885-348498 E: peter.hibbs@sheffield.anglican.org

HICKEN, Kathryn Elizabeth. b 69. Moorlands Coll BA 10. St Mellitus Coll 11. **d** 13 **p** 14. C Holdenhurst and Iford *Win* 13–16; P-in-c Southampton St Mark 16–20; V from 20. *The Vicarage, 54 Archers Road, Southampton SO15 2LU* M: 07590-211015 E: kathy.stmarks@icloud.com

HICKLING, John. b 34. Handsworth Coll Birm 56. Launde Abbey 69. **d** 69 **p** 70. In Methodist Ch 59–69; C Melton Mowbray w Thorpe Arnold *Leic* 69–71; TV 71–75; R Waltham on the Wolds w Stonesby and Saltby 75–84; R Aylestone St Andr w St Jas 84–93; R Husbands Bosworth w Mowsley and Knaptoft etc 93–96; rtd 96; PtO *Leic* 99–19. *28 Oxford Drive, Melton Mowbray LE13 0AL* T: (01664) 560770 E: revd.johnhickling@btinternet.com

HICKMAN, John William. b 38. Barrister-at-Law (Middle Temple) 69 Qu Coll Cam LLM 81. Oak Hill Th Coll 92. **d** 95 **p** 96. NSM Sevenoaks St Nic *Roch* 95–98; P-in-c Stedham w Iping *Chich* 98–04; rtd 04; PtO *Chich* from 05. *Bywood, Selham Road, West Lavington, Midhurst GU29 0EG* T: (01730) 810821

HICKS, Miss Barbara. b 42. Cranmer Hall Dur BA 71. dss 85 **d** 87 **p** 94. Norton Woodseats St Paul *Sheff* 85–87; Par Dn Sheff St Jo 87–94; C 94–02; Chapl Shrewsbury Hosp 96–02; rtd 02; PtO *Sheff* 06–20. *87 Underwood Road, Sheffield S8 8TG* T: 0114-255 8087

HICKS, Clive Anthony. b 58. Man Univ BA 79 Bris Univ PhD 88 Sheff Univ MA 11. Coll of Resurr Mirfield 09. **d** 11 **p** 12. C Budbrooke *Cov* 11–14; V Ossett and Gawthorpe *Leeds* 14–19; R Heart of Eden *Carl* from 19. *Long Marton Rectory, Long Marton, Appleby-in-Westmorland CA16 6BN* T: (017683) 62436 M: 07585-266757 E: cliveahicks@gmail.com

HICKS, Ms Eunice. b 41. Trin Coll Bris BA 00. WEMTC 01. **d** 01 **p** 02. NSM Chew Magna w Dundry and Norton Malreward *B & W* 01–06; NSM Rowledge and Frensham *Guildf* 06–10; rtd 10; PtO *B & W* 11–14; *Eur* from 16. *7 Galbraith Close, Congleton CW12 4WG* T: (01260) 409085 M: 07799-178833 E: revehicks@gmail.com

HICKS, Canon Hazel Rebecca. b 54. Open Univ BA 92. CITC 05. **d** 08 **p** 09. NSM Annagh w Drumaloor, Cloverhill and Drumlane *K, E & A* 08–11; P-in-c Arvagh w Carrigallen, Gowna and Columbkille from 11; Dioc Sec (Elphin and Ardagh) from 16; Can Kilmore Cathl from 16. *Garvary Lodge, 49 Teemore Road, Garvary, Derrylin, Enniskillen BT92 9QB* T: (028) 6774 8422 *or* (00353) (89) 459 3219 M: 07770-852362 E: diocsechazel@gmail.com *or* revhazel08@yahoo.com

HICKS, Miss Joan Rosemary. b 60. Homerton Coll Cam BEd 83. Westcott Ho Cam 87. **d** 90 **p** 94. C Wendover *Ox* 90–95; C Earley St Pet 95–98; P-in-c Beech Hill, Grazeley and Spencers Wood 98–05; P-in-c Cox Green 05–17; V from 17. *The Vicarage, 9 Warwick Close, Maidenhead SL6 3AL* T: (01628) 622139 E: revjrhicks@gmail.com

HICKS, John Michael. *See* PEARSON-HICKS, John Michael

HICKS (née HODGSON), Julia Ruth. b 66. Somerville Coll Ox BA 88 UEA PGCE 89. Westcott Ho Cam 06. **d** 08 **p** 09. C Bridgwater St Mary and Chilton Trinity *B & W* 08–11; R Merriott w Hinton, Dinnington and Lopen from 11; Adv in Women's Min Taunton Adnry from 18. *The Rectory, Church Street, Merriott TA16 5PS* T: (01460) 76406 E: juliahicks1@gmail.com

HICKS, Richard Barry. b 32. Dur Univ BA 55. Sarum Th Coll 59. **d** 61 **p** 62. C Wallsend St Luke *Newc* 61–64; C Tynemouth Ch Ch 64–69; V Tynemouth St Jo 69–75; V Prudhoe 75–82; TV Swanborough *Sarum* 82–86; R Hilperton w Whaddon and Staverton etc 86–97; rtd 97; PtO *Newc* 97–18; *Carl* 98–19. *Lane House, Sawmill Lane, Brampton CA8 1DA* T: (016977) 2156 E: hicks323@btinternet.com

HICKS, Robert Buxton. b 66. Ex Univ BSc 90. Westcott Ho Cam 06. **d** 08 **p** 09. C Bridgwater St Fran *B & W* 08–11; C

Merriott w Hinton, Dinnington and Lopen from 11. *The Rectory, Church Street, Merriott TA16 5PS* T: (01460) 76406 E: bobhicks66@googlemail.com

HICKS, Mrs Valerie Joy. b 47. SRN 69. Cant Sch of Min 82. dss 85 d 87 p 94. Roch St Pet w St Marg 85–89; Hon Par Dn 87–89; Par Dn Thatcham *Ox* 89–93; Team Dn Aylesbury 93–94; TV 94–00; P-in-c Dordon *Birm* 00–09; V 09–10; Dioc Chapl MU 01–06; rtd 10; PtO *Birm* from 10; *Lich* from 11. *12 Rocklands Crescent, Lichfield WS13 6DH* E: val.hicks@virginmedia.com

HICKS, Canon William Trevor. b 47. Hull Univ BA 68 Fitzw Coll Cam BA 70 MA 74. Westcott Ho Cam 68. d 70 p 71. C Cottingham *York* 70–73; C Elland *Wakef* 73–76; V Walsden 76–81; V Knottingley 81–92; R Castleford All SS 92–96; P-in-c Womersley and Kirk Smeaton 96–00; RD Pontefract 94–99; V Bolsover *Derby* 00–11; RD Bolsover and Staveley 05–11; Hon Can Derby Cathl 07–11; rtd 11. *18 Spittal Green, Bolsover, Chesterfield S44 6TP* T: (01246) 827856 E: wtrevorhicks@gmail.com *or* trevorhicks1@aol.com

HICKSON, Gordon Crawford Fitzgerald. b 51. CCC Cam MA 76. d 06 p 07. NSM Ox St Aldate 06–10; PtO 10–11; NSM Cowley St Jas 11–13; PtO 13–21. *31 Orchard Road, Oxford OX2 9BL* T: (01865) 862981 M: 07713-688079 E: gordon.hickson@gmail.com

HIDDEN, Jonathan Martin. b 79. Portsm Univ BSc 00. Wycliffe Hall Ox BTh 13. d 13 p 14. C Guildf Ch Ch 13–17; V Anston *Sheff* from 17. *The Vicarage, 17 Rackford Road, North Anston, Sheffield S25 4DE* M: 07790-018645 E: jonhidden@gmail.com

HIDER, David Arthur. b 46. Lon Univ BSc 67. Sarum & Wells Th Coll 86. d 89 p 90. NSM Southbourne w W Thorney *Chich* 89–91; C Goring-by-Sea 91–94; P-in-c Peacehaven and Telscombe Cliffs 94–99; V 99–09; P-in-c Telscombe w Piddinghoe and Southease 94–99; V Telscombe Village 99–09; V Piddinghoe 99–09; V Southease 99–09; rtd 09; PtO *Chich* from 09. *74 Park Road, Emsworth PO10 8NY* T: (01243) 377636 E: revd_d_hider@msn.com

HIDER, Mrs Melanie Anne. b 53. UEA BA 91 Homerton Coll Cam PGCE 92. d 06 p 07. OLM Nor Lakenham St Alb and St Mark 06–15; NSM Sprowston w Beeston from 15. *10 Brian Avenue, Norwich NR1 2PH* T: (01603) 622373 E: melanie@sprowston.org.uk

HIGGINBOTTOM, Richard. b 48. Lon Univ BD 74. Oak Hill Th Coll. d 74 p 75. C Kenilworth St Jo *Cov* 74–77; C Finham 77–79; P-in-c Attleborough 79–81; V 81–84; Asst Chapl HM Pris Brixton 84–85; Chapl HM Pris Roch 85–92; Camp Hill 92–00; HM YOI Dover 00–03; rtd 03; Port Cath 03–07; Cov 09–19. *c/o Crockford, Church House, 27 Great Smith Street, London SW1P 3AZ* M: 07779-775081

HIGGINBOTTOM, Richard William. b 51. Man Univ BA 73 MA 75. Edin Th Coll 83. d 85 p 86. C Knighton St Mary Magd *Leic* 85–87; C Northleach w Hampnett and Farmington *Glouc* 87–89; V Hayfield *Derby* 89–93; CPAS Min Adv for Scotland 93–08; Community Development Officer Tulloch NET 08–14; rtd 14; PtO *Newc* 16–20; *Eur* 16–20. *36 Meadow Riggs, Alnwick NE66 1AP* M: 07548-209922 E: richwhigg@gmail.com

HIGGINS, Anthony Charles. b 46. d 97 p 98. OLM Swanage and Studland *Sarum* 97–09; PtO 09–19. *The Old School House, School Lane, Studland, Swanage BH19 3AJ* T: (01929) 450691 E: revtonyhiggins@btinternet.com

HIGGINS, Bernard. b 42. Leic Poly BPharm 66 MRPharmS 68. St Jo Coll Nottm 89. d 91 p 92. C Stockport St Geo *Ches* 91–94; C Stockport SW 94–95; P-in-c Dunham Massey St Marg and St Mark 95–98; V 98–00; rtd 00; PtO *Blackb* 01–11; *Carl* 01–13; *Leic* 13–21. *20 Kingfisher Road, Great Glen, Leicester LE8 9DG* T: 0116-259 2624

HIGGINS (née JAMIESON), **Mrs Emma Victoria.** b 89. Edin Univ MA 12 Fitzw Coll Cam MPhil 15. Ridley Hall Cam 13. d 15 p 16. C Rugby W *Cov* 15–18; Chapl HM Pris Gartree from 19; PtO *Cov* from 19. *HM Prison Gartree, Market Harborough LE16 7RP* T: (01858) 426600 M: 07843-878636 E: revemmahiggins@gmail.com *or* emma.higgins@justice.gov.uk

HIGGINS, Canon Godfrey. b 39. St Chad's Coll Dur BA 61 DipEd 63. d 63 p 64. C Brighouse *Wakef* 63–66; C Huddersfield St Jo 66–68; R High Hoyland w Clayton W 68–75; V Marsden 75–83; V Pontefract St Giles 83–04; Hon Can Wakef Cathl 93–04; rtd 04; PtO *Bradf* 05–14; *Leeds* from 14. *2 Holme View, Ilkley LS29 9EL* T: (01943) 603861 E: godfrey.higgins@talktalk.net

HIGGINS, Canon John Leslie. b 43. Open Univ BA 79 Birm Univ MEd 89 PhD 07 CQSW 75. Lich Th Coll 64. d 66 p 67. C Sale St Anne *Ches* 66–69; C Bredbury St Mark 69–72; V Wharton 72–74; Hon C Annan and Lockerbie *Glas* 75–79; V Coseley Ch Ch *Lich* 79–89; R Arthuret *Carl* 89–96; Soc Resp

Officer and Child Protection Co-ord 96–00; C Brampton and Farlam and Castle Carrock w Cumrew 96–00; Hon Can Carl Cathl 96–00; Hon C Annan *Glas* 00–12; Child Protection Adv and Researcher Abps' Coun 00–03; PtO *Carl* from 01; *Eur* 09–12; P-in-c Ankara 12–15; PtO *Glas* from 15. *Green Croft Cottage, The Haggs, Ecclefechan, Lockerbie DG11 3ED* T: (01576) 300796 F: 300790 M: 07867-505644 E: canon-higgins@hotmail.co.uk

HIGGINS, The Ven Kenneth. b 56. TCD BTh 93. CITC 90. d 93 p 94. C Cregagh *D & D* 93–96; Bp's C Movilla 96–00; I 01–09; I Belfast St Donard from 09; Can Down Cathl from 06; Treas Down Cathl from 12; Adn Down from 20. *St Donard's Rectory, 421 Beersbridge Road, Belfast BT5 5DU* T: (028) 9065 2321 M: 07986-866690 E: revkenhiggins@hotmail.com

HIGGINS, The Very Revd Michael John. b 35. OBE 03. Birm Univ LLB 57 G&C Coll Cam LLB 59 PhD 62. Ridley Hall Cam 63. d 65 p 65. C Ormskirk *Liv* 65–67; Selection Sec ACCM 67–74; Hon C St Marylebone St Mark w St Luke *Lon* 69–74; P-in-c Woodlands *B & W* 74–80; V Frome St Jo 74–80; TR Preston St Jo *Blackb* 80–91; Dean Ely 91–03; rtd 03; PtO *Ely* 05–19; *Nor* from 13; *Eur* from 16. *Twin Cottage, North Street, Great Dunham, King's Lynn PE32 2LR* T: (01328) 701058 E: michaelj.higgins@btinternet.com

HIGGINS, Natasha Caroline. See WOODWARD, Natasha Caroline

HIGGINS, Richard Ellis. b 63. Univ of Wales (Lamp) BA 84. St Mich Coll Llan 86. d 89 p 90. C Bargoed and Deri w Brithdir *Llan* 89–92; Zimbabwe 92–94; V Penmaen and Crumlin *Mon* 94–99; Chapl Glan Hafren NHS Trust 94–99; V Rhymney *Mon* 99–02; Chapl Peterborough and Stamford Hosps NHS Foundn Trust 03–12; PtO *Pet* 12–20; R Old Cleeve, Leighland and Treborough *B & W* from 20. *The Rectory, Roadwater, Watchet TA23 0QZ* M: 07910-384332 E: rrhiggins1963@gmail.com

HIGGINS, Rupert Anthony. b 59. Man Univ BA 80. Wycliffe Hall Ox 82. d 85 p 86. C Plymouth St Andr w St Paul and St Geo *Ex* 85–90; C-in-c St Paul 88–90; Assoc V Clifton Ch Ch w Em *Bris* 90–95; V S Croydon Em *S'wark* 95–02; C Langham Place All So *Lon* 02–05; P-in-c Clifton Ch Ch w Em *Bris* 05–09; Asst Vacancy Development Adv Strategy Support 09–10; V Talbot Village *Sarum* from 10. *The Vicarage, 20 Alton Road, Bournemouth BH10 4AE* T: (01202) 939799 E: rupert.higgins@gmail.com

HIGGINS, Mrs Sheila Margaret. b 46. STETS 09. d 10 p 11. NSM Aldingbourne, Barnham and Eastergate *Chich* from 10. *2 Orchard Terrace, The Street, Walberton, Arundel BN18 0PH* T: (01243) 553901 M: 07884-495916 E: smhandaway@tiscali.co.uk *or* smhandaway@hotmail.co.uk

HIGGINS, Canon Timothy John. b 45. Bris Univ BEd 70 Lanc Univ MA 74. Cranmer Hall Dur. d 79 p 80. C Northampton All SS w St Kath *Pet* 79–82; V Whitton St Aug *Lon* 82–90; AD Hampton 86–90; TR Aylesbury *Ox* 90–06; RD 94–04; Hon Can Ch Ch 00–06; Can Res Bris Cathl 06–14; P-in-c City of Bris 06–08; P-in-c Bris St Steph w St Jas and St Jo w St Mich etc 08–14; rtd 14; PtO *Ban* from 15. *Cae Helyg, Tudweiliog, Pwllheli LL53 8PB* T: (01758) 770303 E: tim.tssf@gmail.com

HIGGINSON, Andrew John. b 62. Bradf Univ BTech 85. Trin Coll Bris 02. d 04 p 05. C Quarrington w Old Sleaford *Linc* 04–08; C Silk Willoughby 04–08; P-in-c Freiston, Butterwick w Bennington, and Leverton from 08; RD Holland from 19. *The Rectory, Butterwick Road, Freiston, Boston PE22 0LF* T: (01205) 760480 E: revonline@btopenworld.com

HIGGINSON (née BROOKS), **Hannah Victoria.** b 90. d 14 p 15. C Finchampstead and California *Ox* 14–18; C Wokingham All SS from 18. *3 Drew Crescent, Wokingham RG40 1GD* M: 07976-309668

HIGGINSON, Richard Andrew. b 53. St Jo Coll Cam BA 74 Man Univ PhD 82. EAMTC 02. d 04 p 05. Lect Ridley Hall Cam 89–18; rtd 18; NSM Cambridge St Phil *Ely* 04–11; PtO from 12. *66 Winstanley Court, Cromwell Road, Cambridge CB1 3UR* T: (01223) 246616 M: 07551-249351 E: rah41@cam.ac.uk *or* richard.higginspn@cantab.net

HIGGINSON, Stanley. b 53. d 08 p 09. NSM Wigan St Mich *Liv* 08–15; TV Wigan All SS 15–19; TV Wigan from 20. *12 Clifton Crescent, Wigan WN1 2LB* T: (01942) 235900 E: stanley.higginson33@yahoo.co.uk

HIGGON, David. b 51. Univ of Wales (Swansea) BA 75 Birm Univ MBA 96 Nottm Univ MA 99. EMMTC 96. d 00 p 01. NSM Crich and S Wingfield *Derby* 00–04; Chapl HM Pris Dovegate 04–05; PtO *Derby* 05–07; Chapl HM Pris Ranby 07–11; NSM Crich and S Wingfield *Derby* 11–21; LtO *Mor* 17–21; rtd 21; PtO *Mor* from 21. *Brackloch Cottage, Dundonnell, Garve IV23 2QW* T: (01854) 633226 E: dhiggon@btopenworld.com

HIGGOTT, Bryn Graham. b 54. Birm Poly BA 76 Solicitor 79. NEOC 03. **d** 06 **p** 07. NSM Thirsk *York* 06–08. *15 Spencelayh Close, Wellingborough NN8 4UU* E: bghiggott@gmail.com

HIGGS, Andrew Richard Bowen. b 53. Man Univ BSc 75. St Jo Coll Nottm 81. **d** 85 **p** 86. C Droylsden St Mary *Man* 85–88; C Harlow Town Cen w Lt Parndon *Chelmsf* 88–95; TV 95–02; Chapl Princess Alexandra Hosp NHS Trust 96–02; R Stifford *Chelmsf* from 02. *The Rectory, High Road, North Stifford, Grays RM16 5UE* T: (01375) 372733 E: rector@parishofstifford.co.uk

HIGGS, Garry Richard. b 79. Qu Coll Birm 17. **d** 20 **p** 21. C Rocester, Denstone and Croxden w Hollington *Lich* from 20. *10 Bennion Grove, Denstone, Uttoxeter ST14 5EZ* M: 07757-386845 E: garry.higgs79@gmail.com

HIGGS, Mrs Karen Elizabeth. b 66. SEITE 12. **d** 16 **p** 17. NSM Hartfield w Coleman's Hatch *Chich* 16–18; NSM E Grinstead St Swithun from 18; Chapl Brambletye Sch from 21. *34 Mallard Place, East Grinstead RH19 4TF*

HIGGS, Owen Christopher Goodwin. b 63. St Anne's Coll Ox BA 84 MA 88. St Steph Ho Ox 90. **d** 93 **p** 94. C Teddington St Mark and Hampton Wick *Lon* 93–96; C Lon Docks St Pet w Wapping St Jo 96–00; V Petts Wood *Roch* 00–09; V Bickley 09–14; V Pimlico St Gabr *Lon* from 14. *St Gabriel's Vicarage, 30 Warwick Square, London SW1V 2AD* T: (020) 7834 7520 E: frowen@stgabrielspimlico.com

HIGHAM, Gerald Norman. b 40. St Aid Birkenhead 64. **d** 68 **p** 69. C Garston *Liv* 68–71; C Blundellsands St Nic 71–73; V Bolton All So w St Jas *Man* 73–78; V Tonge w Alkrington 78–84; P-in-c Edenfield 84–86; P-in-c Stubbins 84–86; V Edenfield and Stubbins 86–03; rtd 03; PtO *Blackb* from 03; *Man* from 08. *71 Cherry Tree Way, Rossendale BB4 4JZ* T: (01706) 210143 E: g_higham@sky.com

HIGHAM, John Leonard. b 39. Wycliffe Hall Ox 62. **d** 65 **p** 66. C Prescot *Liv* 65–71; V Hollinfare 71–74; Adult and Youth Service Adv Knowsley 74–76; TV Padgate *Liv* 76–84; V Farnworth 84–89; TR Sutton 89–02; rtd 02; PtO *Liv* from 03. *86 Ormskirk Road, Rainford, St Helens WA11 8DB*

HIGHAM (née ANNS), Canon Pauline Mary. b 49. Bris Univ BEd 71. EMMTC 87. **d** 90 **p** 94. Par Dn Wirksworth w Alderwasley, Carsington etc *Derby* 90–92; Par Dn Lt Berkhamsted and Bayford, Essendon etc *St Alb* 92–94; C 94–96; P-in-c 96–05; R 05–18; Jt RD Hertford and Ware 05–15; Hon Can St Alb 06–18; Hon C Combs and Finborough *St E* from 18. *The Rectory, Woodland Close, Onehouse, Stowmarket IP14 3HL*

HIGHTON, Philip William. b 70. Liv Univ BSc 91 Nottm Univ MSc 92. Oak Hill Th Coll BA 05. **d** 05 **p** 06. C Knutsford St Jo and Toft *Ches* 05–09; V Cheadle All Hallows 09–14; NSM Hartford 14–21; Chapl Hartford C of E High Sch from 14. *2 Trafalgar Close, Northwich CW8 9WQ* T: (01606) 810685

HIGHTON, William James. b 31. St Deiniol's Hawarden. **d** 82 **p** 83. NSM Thornton Hough *Ches* 82–84; C Cheadle 84–88; V Walton 88–99; rtd 99; PtO *Carl* from 01. *15 Mowbray Drive, Burton-in-Kendal, Carnforth LA6 1NF* T: (01524) 782073

HIGHWAY, Andrew David Carnell. b 67. St Mich Coll Llan 09. **d** 12 **p** 13. NSM Llanishen *Llan* 12–15; NSM Eglwysilan and Caerphilly 16–20; NSM Whitchurch from 20. *18 Y Groes, Cardiff CF14 6DX* M: 07969-757742 E: a.highway30@btinternet.com

HIGSON, Lee Matthew. b 76. Univ of Wales (Ban) BTh 97 Cliff Coll MA 17 Middx Univ MA 21 MM 07. St Mellitus Coll 19. **d** 21. C Astley Bridge *Man* from 21. *3 Ivy Bank Road, Bolton BL1 7EQ* M: 07712-003290 E: revleehigson@gmail.com

HIGSON, Peter James. b 55. Glas Univ BD 13. TISEC 06. **d** 19. NSM Middle Esk Moor *York* 19–21. *57 Ptak Way, Bridge of Earn, Perth PH2 9FT* T: (01738) 718688 M: 07724-434494 E: peterjhigson@hotmail.com

HIGTON, Anthony Raymond. b 42. Lon Sch of Th BD 65. Oak Hill Th Coll 65. **d** 67 **p** 68. C Newark Ch Ch *S'well* 67–69; C Cheltenham St Mark *Glouc* 70–75; R Hawkwell *Chelmsf* 75–99; Gen Dir CMJ 99–05; R Jerusalem Ch Ch Israel 03–06; R N w S Wootton *Nor* 06–09; rtd 09; PtO *Ely* 09–15; *Nor* 09–15; Hon C Brough w Stainmore *Carl* 15–17; PtO 17–19. *Kiln Scar, Great Asby, Appleby-in-Westmorland CA16 6HD* T: (017683) 53139 M: 07815-891582 E: tony@higton.info *or* higton01@btinternet.com

HILARY, Sister. *See* JORDINSON, Vera

HILBORN, David Henry Kyte. b 64. Nottm Univ BA 85 PhD 94 Mansf Coll Ox MA 88 SFHEA 18. **d** 02 **p** 02. C Acton St Mary *Lon* 02–06; Dir Studies NTMTC 06–07; Prin 07–12; Asst Dean St Mellitus Coll *Lon* 07–12; Lic Preacher from 06; Prin St Jo Coll Nottm 12–19; Prin Moorlands Coll Christchurch from 19; PtO *Win* from 19. *Moorlands College, Sopley, Christchurch BH23 7AT* T: (01425) 674500 M: 07792-350701 E: david.hilborn@moorlands.ac.uk

HILBORN, Canon Mia Alison Kyte. b 63. City Univ BSc 84 Mansf Coll Ox MA 87. **d** 02 **p** 02. Chapl Team Ldr Guy's and St Thos' NHS Foundn Trust from 01; NSM N Lambeth *S'wark* from 02; NSM S Lambeth St Anne and All SS 17–20; Hon Can S'wark Cathl from 20. *Guy's & St Thomas' NHS Foundation Trust, St Thomas Street, London SE1 9RT* T: (020) 7188 5588 M: 07740-779585 E: mia.hilborn@gstt.nhs.uk

HILDING OHLSSON, Nicolas. b 82. Buenos Aires Bible Inst BA 08. **d** 09 **p** 13. Argentina 09–15; PtO *Guildf* 16–17; C Ashtead from 17. *1 Oakfield Road, Ashtead KT21 2RE* M: 07928-987835 E: ho.nico@gmail.com

HILDITCH, Janet. b 59. St Andr Univ MTheol 81 PhD 87. NOC 92. **d** 94 **p** 95. C Kirkholt *Man* 94–98; Chapl Rochdale Healthcare NHS Trust 97–98; Chapl N Man Health Care NHS Trust 98–00; Chapl Tameside Hosp NHS Foundn Trust 00–15; Hon Can Man Cathl 04–15; LtO *Ab* from 15. *6 Sunnyside, Mid Yell, Shetland ZE2 9BS* T: (01957) 702258 E: janetofhoulland@hotmail.co.uk

HILDITCH, Mrs Rachel Helen. b 87. SS Coll Cam BA 07 MA 11 Clare Coll Cam BTh 15. Ridley Hall Cam 13. **d** 16 **p** 17. C Hampton *Ely* from 16. *8 Tabor Court, Hampton Centre, Peterborough PE7 8GF* M: 07817-737401 E: rhh31@cantab.net

HILDRED, David. b 61. Bath Univ BSc 83 CertEd 83. Wycliffe Hall Ox 86. **d** 89 **p** 90. C Westcliff St Mich *Chelmsf* 89–92; C Rayleigh 92–96; V Sidcup St Andr *Roch* 96–10; AD Sidcup 03–08; R Darfield *Sheff* 10–20; TR Kidderminster E *Worc* from 20. *The Rectory, 30 Leswell Street, Kidderminster DY10 1RP* M: 07906-156239 E: dhildred316@gmail.com

HILDRETH, Steven Marcus. b 47. Leeds Univ LLB 69 Solicitor 78. SNWTP 08. **d** 11 **p** 12. NSM Ches St Paul 11–14; rtd 15; PtO *Ches* from 15. *3 Field Close, Tarvin, Chester CH3 8DL* T: (01829) 749303 E: shildr1027@aol.com

HILES, John Michael. b 32. Qu Coll Cam BA 57 MA 61. Sarum Th Coll 57. **d** 59 **p** 60. C Clifton St Jas *Sheff* 59–62; V Bramley St Fran 62–69; Hon C Holmfirth *Wakef* 69–89; Hon C Upper Holme Valley 89–91; Lic to Offic 91–97; PtO 97–03; *Sarum* 03–15. *22 Oldfield Road, Bishopdown, Salisbury SP1 3GQ* T: (01722) 349951 E: mike.hiles@btinternet.com

HILL, Mrs Alison Elizabeth. b 67. Glos Univ BEd 89. St Mellitus Coll BA 18. **d** 18 **p** 19. C Southampton (St Mary) *Win* 18–21; R Totton from 21. *The Rectory, 92 Salisbury Road, Totton, Southampton SO40 3JA* M: 07810-544710 E: ali@stwins.org

HILL, Andrew Nicholas Luke. b 70. Glam Univ BA 95. Ripon Coll Cuddesdon 15. **d** 19 **p** 20. NSM Cam w Stinchcombe *Glouc* from 19. *15 Marment Road, Dursley GL11 6LA* T: (01453) 519754 M: 07413-278171 E: andrewnlhill@hotmail.com

HILL, Mrs Anne Doreen. b 40. **d** 88 **p** 94. Par Dn Bexleyheath St Pet *Roch* 88–90; Sub Chapl HM Pris Belmarsh 91–96; Dep Chapl 96–99; Hon C Lee St Mildred *S'wark* 93–04; rtd 04; PtO *Sarum* 05–08 and from 14. *64 St Mary's Road, Poole BH15 2LL* T: (01202) 666076 E: adhill40@hotmail.com

HILL, Barry Leon. b 79. Wycliffe Hall Ox BTh 05. **d** 05 **p** 06. C Loughborough Em and St Mary in Charnwood *Leic* 05–09; Dioc Miss Enabler 09–17; TR Market Harborough and The Transfiguration etc from 17; Dioc Resource Ch Enabler from 17. *The Rectory, Rectory Lane, Market Harborough LE16 8AS* E: barry@hill-home.co.uk *or* barry@harborough-anglican.org.uk

HILL, Mrs Carol. b 52. SCRTP 13. **d** 15 **p** 16. OLM Bicester w Bucknell, Caversfield and Launton *Ox* 15–19; NSM from 19. *25 Shaw Close, Bicester OX26 2FN* T: (01869) 600680 E: carolghill@hotmail.co.uk

HILL, Charles Bernard. b 50. Sheff Univ BA 71 Qu Coll Ox DPhil 76. Cant Sch of Min 91. **d** 94 **p** 95. NSM Sandgate St Paul w Folkestone St Geo *Cant* 94–98; NSM Folkestone H Trin w Ch Ch 98–04; Eur Sec Coun for Chr Unity 99–08; PtO *Eur* from 03; Can Gib Cathl 03–08; P-in-c Benenden *Cant* 08–10; P-in-c Sandhurst w Newenden 08–10; P-in-c Benenden and Sandhurst 10–13; rtd 13; PtO *Cant* from 14. *39 Cinque Ports Avenue, Hythe CT21 6HP* T: (01303) 269886 M: 07746-621448 E: cbhill18@hotmail.com

HILL, Christopher David. b 84. Moorlands Coll BA 07. St Mellitus Coll BA 12. **d** 12 **p** 13. C Cricklewood St Gabr and St Mich *Lon* 12–15; R Northolt St Mary 15–21; Miss Tr *Win* from 21. *Diocesan Office, Wolvesey Palace, Winchester SO23 9ND* T: (01962) 710976 E: chris.hill@winchester.anglican.org

HILL, Christopher Glynn. b 43. Tyndale Hall Bris 66. **d** 70 **p** 71. C Longfleet *Sarum* 70–74; LtO *Chelmsf* 74–82; rtd 05. *7 Paddock Close, Benson, Wallingford OX10 6RS* E: clministries@btinternet.com

✠**HILL, The Rt Revd Christopher John.** b 45. KCVO 14. K Coll Lon BD 67 AKC 67 MTh 68. **d** 69 **p** 70 **c** 96. C Tividale *Lich* 69–73; C Codsall 73–74; Abp's Asst Chapl on Foreign Relns *Cant* 74–81; ARCIC from 74; Sec 74–90; Abp's Sec for Ecum Affairs *Cant* 82–89; Hon Can Cant Cathl 82–89; Chapl to The Queen 87–96; Can Res and Prec St Paul's Cathl *Lon* 89–96; Select Preacher Ox Univ 90; Area Bp Stafford *Lich* 96–04; Bp Guildf 04–13; rtd 13; Hon Asst Bp Glouc from 14; Clerk of the Closet 05–14. *Hillview, West End, Ruardean GL17 9TP* T: (01594) 541831 E: christopher.j.hill@outlook.com

HILL, Christopher Murray. b 57. Lanchester Poly Cov BA 78. Ox Min Course 05. **d** 07 **p** 08. NSM Warfield *Ox* 07–11; C 11–13; P-in-c Ely 13–17; TR from 17. *The Vicarage, St Mary's Street, Ely CB7 4HF* T: (01353) 662308 M: 07788-206361 E: chris.hill@stmarysely.org

HILL, The Ven Colin. b 42. Leic Univ BSc 64 Open Univ PhD 88. Ripon Hall Ox 64. **d** 66 **p** 67. C Leic Martyrs 66–69; C Braunstone 69–71; Lect Ecum Inst Thornaby Teesside 71–72; V Worsbrough St Thos and St Jas *Sheff* 72–78; Telford Planning Officer *Lich* 78–96; RD Telford and Telford Severn Gorge *Heref* 80–96; Preb Heref Cathl 83–96; Can Res Carl Cathl 96–04; Dioc Sec 96–04; Adn W Cumberland 04–08; rtd 08; PtO *Carl* from 09. *1A Briery Bank, Arnside, Carnforth LA5 0HW* T: (01524) 762629 E: hill69@tiscali.co.uk

HILL, Canon Colin Arnold Clifford. b 29. OBE 96. Bris Univ 52 Univ of Wales (Ban) MPhil 03. Ripon Hall Ox 55. **d** 57 **p** 58. C Rotherham *Sheff* 57–61; V Brightside St Thos 61–64; R Easthampstead *Ox* 64–73; Chapl RAF Coll Bracknell 68–73; V Croydon St Jo *Cant* 73–84; V Croydon St Jo *S'wark* 85–94; Chapl Abp Whitgift Foundn 73–94; Hon Can Cant Cathl 75–84; Hon Can S'wark Cathl 85–94; Chapl to The Queen 90–99; rtd 94; PtO *Ox* from 11. *4 Farthing House, 11 St Martin's Street, Wallingford OX10 0AL* M: 07837-249949 E: colinatsb@clara.co.uk

HILL, David Rowland. b 34. Lon Univ BSc 55. Qu Coll Birm. **d** 59 **p** 60. C Upper Tooting H Trin *S'wark* 59–61; C Cheam 61–63; C Richmond St Mary w St Matthias 63–68; V Sutton St Nicholas *Linc* 68–82; V Pinchbeck 82–99; rtd 99; PtO *Linc* 99–02 and from 05; *Pet* 04–11. *24 London Road, Spalding PE11 2TA* T: (01775) 768912 E: revdavidhill1934@gmail.com

HILL, David Royston. b 68. Westmr Coll Ox BTh 96 PGCE 97. ERMC 04. **d** 06 **p** 07. C Dereham and Distr *Nor* 06–09; R Quidenham Gp 09–14; R Upper St Leonards St Jo *Chich* from 14; RD Hastings from 20; CF(V) 09–17. *St John's Rectory, 53 Brittany Road, St Leonards-on-Sea TN38 0RD* T: (01424) 423367 M: 07827-815247 E: fatherdavid68@icloud.com *or* rectorstjohns30@gmail.com

HILL, Derek Stanley. b 28. AKC 53. **d** 53 **p** 54. C Rushmere *St E* 53–55; S Africa 55–57; C Boreham Wood All SS *St Alb* 57–59; V Crowfield *St E* 59–67; P-in-c Stonham Aspal 59–61; R 61–67; V Bury St Edmunds St Geo 67–73; P-in-c Ampton w Lt Livermere and Ingham 68–73; V Gazeley w Dalham 73–75; P-in-c Lidgate w Ousden 73–74; P-in-c Gt Bradley 74–78; V Gazeley w Dalham and Moulton 75–78; V Gt Barton 78–86; V Bury St Edmunds All SS 86–93; rtd 93; PtO *St E* from 93. *Whimwillow, 38 Maltings Garth, Thurston, Bury St Edmunds IP31 3PP* T: (01359) 230770

HILL, Eugene Mark. b 48. Univ of Wales (Lamp) BA 71. Sarum Th Coll 71. **d** 73 **p** 74. C Sutton St Nic *S'wark* 73–77; Hon C 77–80; Asst Chapl Emanuel Sch Wandsworth 77–87; Chapl 87–04; Hon C St Helier *S'wark* 83–84; Hon C Caterham 84–98; Dir Chr Studies Course 85–04; PtO 98–07 and from 10; Hon C Croydon St Jo 07–10. *129A Honor Oak Park, London SE23 3LD* M: 07771-708893 E: eugenemarkhill@btinternet.com

HILL, Fiona Elizabeth. b 90. **d** 20 **p** 21. C Scarborough St Columba and St Jas w H Trin *York* from 20. *The New Vicarage, Wains Lane, Staxton, Scarborough YO12 4SF*

HILL, Giles. *See* HILL, Michael John Giles

HILL, Canon Gillian Beryl. b 53. Open Univ BA 86 Portsm Univ PhD 06. S Dios Minl Tr Scheme 87. **d** 90 **p** 94. NSM Southsea St Jude *Portsm* 90–95; C Southsea St Pet 95–01; V Catherington and Clanfield 01–18; Hon Can Portsm Cathl 03–18; rtd 18; PtO *Ex* from 20. *6 Treston Close, Dawlish EX7 0DH* E: gill.vicar@gmail.com

HILL, Ian Maxwell. b 60. Loughb Univ BSc 81 MCIT 85. EMMTC 92. **d** 95 **p** 96. NSM Thurnby Lodge *Leic* 95–00; NSM Thurmaston 00–08; NSM Fosse Team from 08. *Shady Ash, 4 Sturrock Close, Thurnby, Leicester LE7 9QP* T: 0116-243 1609

HILL, Ian Richard. b 69. Wycliffe Hall Ox 04. **d** 06 **p** 07. C Fareham St Jo *Portsm* 06–09; P-in-c Aspenden, Buntingford and Westmill *St Alb* 09–13; R 13–21; V Hinckley St Mary *Leic* from 21. *2 The Rills, Hinckley LE10 1NA* E: vicar.stmaryshinckley@gmail.com

HILL, James. *See* HILL, Kenneth James

HILL, James Aidan Stuart. b 75. Ridley Hall Cam 06. **d** 09 **p** 10. C Cov H Trin 09–13; Asst Chapl Amsterdam w Den Helder and Heiloo *Eur* 13–19; P-in-c Mildmay Grove St Jude and St Paul *Lon* from 19. *71 Marquess Road, London N1 2PT* M: (0031) 62-774 4590 E: jamesincitycentre@gmail.com

HILL, James Alexander Hart. b 82. K Coll Lon BA 05. St Steph Ho Ox 05. **d** 07 **p** 08. C Tottenham St Paul *Lon* 07–11; C Tottenham St Benet Fink 10–11; P-in-c 11–16; V from 16; P-in-c Tottenham St Phil 14–18. *St Benet Fink Vicarage, Walpole Road, London N17 6BH* T: (020) 8888 4541 E: frjameshill@hotmail.co.uk

HILL, Mrs Janice. Sheff Univ BEd 79 Nottm Univ MA 10. St Jo Coll Nottm 05. **d** 07 **p** 08. C Formby H Trin *Liv* 07–10; TV N Meols 10–14; PtO 14–16; Dioc Missr 15–16; P-in-c Blundellsands St Mich 16–17; TR Maghull and Melling 17–21; rtd 21. *15 Rothwell Drive, Southport PR8 2SB* M: 07849-765400 E: janicehill.htc@gmail.com

HILL, Mrs Jennifer Clare. b 50. City Univ BSc 71 FBCO 72. EMMTC 94. **d** 97 **p** 98. NSM Bottesford and Muston *Leic* 97–98; C Glen Parva and S Wigston 98–01; C Walsall Wood *Lich* 01–08; V Shelfield and High Heath 08–10; RD Walsall 05–10; TV Hemel Hempstead *St Alb* 10–13; TR 13–16; Dioc Adv for Women's Min 11–16; rtd 16; PtO *St Alb* from 16; *Ely* 16–18; P-in-c Long Stanton w St Mich 18–19; P-in-c Over 18–19; P-in-c Swavesey 18–19; P-in-c Willingham 18–19; PtO from 19. *57 Water Lane, Oakington, Cambridge CB24 3AL* T: (01223) 635076 M: 07970-949331 E: jennyhill@pawstime.co.uk

HILL, Jonathan Carey. b 68. St Jo Coll Nottm 12. **d** 14 **p** 15. C Cheylesmore *Cov* 14–16; C Fletchamstead 16–18; V Hull St Martin w Transfiguration *York* from 18. *942 Anlaby Road, Hull HU4 6AH* M: 07810-652011 E: jonathan.carey.hill@gmail.com

HILL, Kenneth James. b 43. Leic Univ BA 64 Lon Univ BD 68. Oak Hill Th Coll 65. **d** 69 **p** 70. C Southall Green St Jo *Lon* 69–72; C Blackheath Park St Mich *S'wark* 72–75; C Bath Abbey w St Jas *B & W* 75–83; P-in-c Bath St Mich w St Paul 75–82; R 82–83; R Huntspill 83–91; Omega Order 91–98; PtO *B & W* 91–98; *Bris* 91–98; C Somerton w Compton Dundon, the Charltons etc *B & W* 98–07; rtd 07; PtO *B & W* 08–18; *Sarum* from 14. *14 White Horse Road, Winsey, Bradford-on-Avon BA15 2JZ* T: (01225) 864119 E: kjhill23@btinternet.com

HILL, Laurence Bruce. b 43. Open Univ BA 97. AKC 67. **d** 69 **p** 70. C Feltham *Lon* 69–72; C-in-c Hampstead St Steph 72–77; V Finchley H Trin 77–10; rtd 10. *49 Abbots Gardens, London N2 0JG* T: (020) 8444 0510 E: lorenzohill@yahoo.co.uk

HILL, Mrs Leonora Anne. b 59. Bath Univ BSc 81 Westmr Coll Ox PGCE 93. Ox Min Course 05. **d** 08 **p** 09. C Charlton Kings St Mary *Glouc* 08–12; R Ridgeway *Ox* from 12. *Ridgeway Rectory, Warborough Road, Letcombe Regis, Wantage OX12 9LD* T: (01235) 760112 M: 07867-420234 E: revd.lahill@btinternet.com

HILL, Malcolm Crawford. b 43. Oak Hill Th Coll 68. **d** 71 **p** 72. C Maidstone St Luke *Cant* 71–74; C Longfleet *Sarum* 74–79; V Bexleyheath St Pet *Roch* 79–90; V Lee St Mildred *S'wark* 90–04; rtd 04; PtO *Sarum* from 05. *64 St Mary's Road, Poole BH15 2LL* T: (01202) 666076 E: mchill43@hotmail.com

HILL, Mrs Marjorie Ann. b 38. MCSP 60. St Jo Coll Nottm 92. **d** 94 **p** 95. C Hull St Martin w Transfiguration *York* 94–99; P-in-c Willerby w Ganton and Folkton 99–03; rtd 03; PtO *York* 03–06 and from 10; P-in-c Sigglesthorne w Nunkeeling and Bewholme 06–09; RD N Holderness 07–08. *31 White Gap Road, Little Weighton, Cottingham HU20 3XE* T: (01482) 840544 E: marjoriehill28@gmail.com

HILL, Mark. *See* HILL, Eugene Mark

HILL, Canon Matthew Anthony Robert. b 71. Leeds Univ BA 93 Univ of Wales (Cardiff) BD 96 MPhil 00 Univ of Wales (Trin St Dav) PhD 16. St Mich Coll Llan 94. **d** 97 **p** 98. C Cardiff St Jo *Llan* 97–00; PV Llan Cathl 00–04; P-in-c Dowlais and Penydarren 04–05; R 05–07; Tutor Cardiff Univ and St Mich Coll Llan 04–07; Chapl Univ of Wales Trin St Dav *St D* 07–13; Voc Adv Cardigan Adnry 09–13; Co-ord Voc Adv *St D* 10–13; P-in-c Llanfihangel Ystrad and Cilcennin w Trefilan etc 13–19; P-in-c Carmarthen St Pet and Abergwili etc 19; P-in-c Bro Caerfyrddin from 19; AD from 19; Can St D Cathl from 19. *6 Ael y Bryn, Tanerdy, Carmarthen SA31 2HB* T: (01267) 468432 M: 07964-631997 E: ystrad.matthew@outlook.com

✠**HILL, The Rt Revd Michael Arthur.** b 49. Ridley Hall Cam 74. **d** 77 **p** 78 **c** 98. C Addiscombe St Mary *Cant* 77–81; C Slough *Ox* 81–83; P-in-c Chesham Bois 83–90; R 90–92; RD Amersham 89–92; Adn Berks 92–98; Area Bp Buckingham 98–03; Bp Bris 03–17; rtd 17; Hon Asst Bp B & W from 18. *13 Lime Kiln Lane, Clevedon BS21 6BX* M: 07808-290908 E: mhill1949@gmail.com

HILL, The Rt Revd Michael John Giles. b 43. S Dios Minl Tr Scheme 82. **d** 84 **p** 86. Community of Our Lady and St John from 67; Abbot from 90; PtO Win 84–92 and from 13; Public Preacher 92–13; PtO Portsm from 04; Hon Can Win Cathl from 15. Abbey of Our Lady and St John, Abbey Road, Beech, Alton GU34 4AP T: (01420) 562145 or 563575 F: 561691 E: giles@altonabbey.com

HILL, Miss Naomi Jean. b 75. Coll of Ripon & York St Jo BA 96. Wycliffe Hall Ox BTh 06. **d** 06 **p** 07. C Northampton St Giles Pet 06–10; C Nottingham St Nic S'well 10–14; C Sneinton St Chris w St Phil 10–14; P-in-c from 14; C Nottingham St Ann w Em from 14. St Christopher's Vicarage, 180 Sneinton Boulevard, Nottingham NG2 4GL T: 0115-924 0046 M: 07855-060410 E: naomihillster@gmail.com

HILL, Nicholas John. b 66. St Mellitus Coll BA 15. **d** 17 **p** 18. C Stoke-next-Guildf Guildf 17–20; C Reading Greyfriars Ox from 20. 290 Northumberland Avenue, Reading RG2 8DD M: 07974-228961 E: nick66hill@gmail.com

HILL, Peppie. See HILL, Stephanie Jane

HILL, Canon Peter. b 36. AKC 60. St Boniface Warminster 60. **d** 61 **p** 62. C Gt Berkhamsted St Alb 61–67; R Bedford St Mary 67–69; P-in-c 69–70; V Goldington 69–79; V Biggleswade 79–90; RD 80–85; Hon Can St Alb 85–90; V Holbeach Linc 90–01; RD Elloe E 94–99; P-in-c The Suttons w Tydd 99–01; rtd 01; PtO Nor 01–12; Ely 06–19. 40 Walnut Tree Crescent, Fenstanton, Huntingdon PE28 9LE T: (01480) 461005

✠**HILL, The Rt Revd Peter.** b 50. Man Univ BSc 71 Nottm Univ MTh 90. Wycliffe Hall Ox 81. **d** 83 **p** 84 **c** 14. C Porchester S'well 83–86; V Huthwaite 86–95; P-in-c Calverton 95–04; RD S'well 97–01; Dioc Chief Exec 04–07; Adn Nottingham 07–14; Hon Can S'well Minster 01–07; Area Bp Barking Chelmsf 14–21; rtd 21. 1 The Paddocks, Newark NG24 1SS E: peterhill92@talktalk.net

HILL, Rebecca. b 83. Dur Univ BA 21. St Mellitus Coll 18. **d** 21. C Southport Ch Ch Liv from 21. 10 Ploughmans Close, Southport PR9 8QZ E: rhill23@me.com

HILL, Canon Richard Brian. b 47. Dur Univ BA 68. Cranmer Hall Dur 68 Westcott Ho Cam 70. **d** 71 **p** 72. C Cockermouth All SS w Ch Ch Carl 71–74; C Barrow St Geo w St Luke 74–76; V Walney Is 76–83; Dir of Clergy Tr 83–90; P-in-c Westward, Rosley-w-Woodside and Welton 83–90; V Gosforth All SS Newc 90–05; rtd 05; Hon Can Newc Cathl from 05; Chapl St Mary Magd and H Jes Trust 06–19; Asst Dioc Ecum Officer Newc 08–19; PtO from 19. 56 St Mary Magdalene Hospital, Claremont Road, Newcastle upon Tyne NE2 4NN T: 0191-261 2648 E: r.b.hill@lineone.net

HILL, Richard Hugh Oldham. b 52. CCC Ox BA 74 BA 77 MA 78. Wycliffe Hall Ox 75. **d** 78 **p** 79. C Harold Wood Chelmsf 78–81; C Hampreston Sarum 81–86; TV N Ferriby York 86–97; V Swanland 97–08; R Church Stretton Heref 08–18; RD Condover 11–18; rtd 18; PtO Heref from 19; Rtd Clergy Officer from 20. 5 Whitbatch Close, Ludlow SY8 2PA T: (01584) 318093

HILL, Robert Joseph. b 45. Oak Hill Th Coll BA 81. **d** 81 **p** 82. C W Derby St Luke Liv 81–84; P-in-c Devonport St Mich Ex 84–97; Chapl Morden Coll Blackheath 97–99; TV Manningham Bradf 99–04; P-in-c Davyhulme Ch Ch Man 04–13; rtd 13; PtO Ches from 17; Man from 19. 52 Wellfield Road, Stockport SK2 6AT T: 0161-456 2450 E: rjandh@gmail.com or bobhillmsc@mailas.com

HILL, Rodney Maurice. b 44. Leeds Univ BA 67 FCIPD. Ripon Coll Cuddesdon 04. **d** 05 **p** 06. NSM N Hinksey and Wytham Ox 05–10; NSM Osney 10–12; PtO from 12. 13 Hobson Road, Oxford OX2 7JX T: (01865) 426804 E: rodneymauricehill@hotmail.com

HILL, Canon Roger Anthony John. b 45. Liv Univ BA 67 Linacre Coll Ox BA 69 MA. Ripon Hall Ox 67. **d** 70 **p** 71. C St Helier S'wark 71–74; C Dawley Parva Lich 74–75; C Cen Telford 76–77; TV 77–81; TR 81–88; TR Newark S'well 88–02; RD 90–95; Hon Can S'well Minster 98–02; R Man St Ann 02–07; AD Hulme 05–07; Bp's Missr 07–11; Hon Can Man Cathl 02–11; rtd 11; PtO Man from 11; Chapl to The Queen 01–15. 4 Four Stalls End, Littleborough OL15 8SB T: (01706) 374719 E: hillraj@gmail.com

HILL, Rosemary. **d** 17 **p** 18. C Penarth and Llandough Llan 17–20; TV Llantrisant from 20. Address temp unknown M: 07486-635575 E: vicarptl@llan.org.uk

HILL, Simon George. b 53. Reading Univ BSc 75 MSc 78 K Coll Lon MA 02 Lon Univ DMin 10. S'wark Ord Course 80. **d** 83 **p** 84. NSM Croydon St Aug Cant 83–84; Swaziland 84–86; Fiji 86–88; NSM Croydon St Aug S'wark 88–90; Tanzania 90–94; Uganda 94–96; Swaziland 96–98; PtO S'wark 99–02; Chich 99–02; P-in-c Cockfield w Bradfield St Clare, Felsham etc St E 02–04; R Bradfield St Clare, Bradfield St George etc 04–11; RD Lavenham 09–11; V Copthorne Chich 11–17; R Chevington w Hargrave, Chedburgh w Depden etc

St E 17–21; RD Clare 20–21; rtd 21. 89 Tollgate Lane, Bury St Edmunds IP32 6DF T: (01284) 754110 M: 07840-038384 E: mlima001@btinternet.com

HILL, The Ven Simon James. b 64. Sheff Univ BA 85 Ex Univ PGCE 88 Bris Univ MA 09. Ripon Coll Cuddesdon BA 94. **d** 95 **p** 96. C Manston Ripon 95–98; TV Dorchester Ox 98–03; Dir Berinsfield Progr Ripon Coll Cuddesdon 98–03; R Backwell w Chelvey and Brockley B & W 03–10; Dioc Dir of Clergy Development 10–16; Preb Wells Cathl 14–16; Adn Taunton from 16. 2 Monkton Heights, West Monkton, Taunton TA2 8LU T: (01823) 413315 E: adtaunton@bathwells.anglican.org

HILL, Stephanie Jane (Peppie). b 67. K Coll Lon LLB 88. Wycliffe Hall Ox BTh 05. **d** 05 **p** 15. C Loughborough Em and St Mary in Charnwood Leic 05–06; NSM Leic H Trin w St Jo 14–17; Assoc P Evang Development Market Harborough and The Transfiguration etc from 17. The Rectory, Rectory Lane, Market Harborough LE16 8AS E: pep@hill-home.co.uk or pep@harborough-anglican.org.uk

HILL, Stuart Graeme. b 64. Ripon Coll Cuddesdon BTh 97. **d** 97 **p** 98. C Usworth Dur 97–99; C Monkwearmouth 99–01; TV 01–06; V Upper Derwent York 06–19; C Jarrow and Simonside Dur from 19. St Simon's Vicarage, 134 Wenlock Road, South Shields NE34 9AL T: 0191-660 7927 E: revd.stuarthill@icloud.com

HILL (formerly SAYERS), Susan. b 46. Bp Otter Coll Chich BEd 69 Middx Univ BA 02 Win Univ MA 18. NTMTC 99. **d** 02 **p** 03. NSM Southend Chelmsf 02–12; TV 05–12; Asst Chapl HM Pris Bullwood Hall 02–06; PtO Chelmsf 13–16 and from 18; Hon C Chingford SS Pet and Paul 16–18. 17 Claremont Close, Westcliff-on-Sea SS0 7UA T: (01702) 431843 M: 07557-101314 E: susansayers@yahoo.com

HILL, Walter Henry. **d** 06 **p** 07. Aux Min Cloyne Union C, C & R 06–14; NSM Fermoy Union from 14. Quetta, Glenatore, Conna, Co Cork, Republic of Ireland M: (00353) 87-629 6545 E: whill911@gmail.com

HILL, William. b 44. Man Univ BSc 66 CEng 73 MICE 73. SEITE 95. **d** 98 **p** 99. NSM Farnham Guildf 98–01; P-in-c Smallburgh w Dilham w Honing and Crostwight Nor 01–05; rtd 05; PtO Nor from 05; RD St Benet 07–12; PtO Cant from 20. 2 Kennington Place, Kennington, Ashford TN24 9HZ T: (01233) 612884 E: revd.william.hill@btinternet.com

HILL-BROWN, Rachel Judith. b 65. Westmr Coll Ox BEd 88. St Jo Coll Nottm MTh 07. **d** 07 **p** 09. C Knowle Birm 07–10; C Tanworth 10–11; Hon C Dorridge from 11; Hon Chapl Birm Children's Hosp NHS Foundn Trust 11–19; Chapl Univ Hosp Birm NHS Foundn Trust from 19. 54 Glendon Way, Dorridge, Solihull B93 8SY T: (01564) 772472 E: rhillbrown@googlemail.com

HILL-BROWN, Canon Timothy Duncan. b 65. Westmr Coll Ox BA 87. Wycliffe Hall Ox 91. **d** 93 **p** 94. C Sparkhill w Greet and Sparkbrook Birm 93–97; C Sutton Coldfield H Trin 97–99; P-in-c Short Heath 99–00; V 00–06; V Dorridge from 06; AD Shirley 12–20; Co-AD Kings Norton, Moseley and Shirley 20–21; Hon Can Birm Cathl from 18. 54 Glendon Way, Dorridge, Solihull B93 8SY T: (01564) 772472 E: duncan@stphilipsandstjames.org

HILL-TOUT, Mark Laurence. b 50. AKC 73. **d** 74 **p** 75. C Brighton Resurr Chich 74–77; C Old Shoreham and New Shoreham 77–79; Dioc Stewardship Adv Lewes and Hastings 79–84; P-in-c Stonegate 79–83; R Horsted Keynes 84–89; V St Helens and Sea View Portsm 89–95; P-in-c Wymering 95–99; V 99–06; rtd 06. c/o Crockford, Church House, 27 Great Smith Street, London SW1P 3AZ M: 07758-260936 E: m-m.h-t@hotmail.co.uk

HILLEL, Laurence Christopher Francis. b 54. Bris Univ BA 76 Sheff Univ PGCE 78 SOAS Lon MA 84. Cuddesdon Coll 98. **d** 98 **p** 99. C Pinner Lon 98–00; Chapl Bp Ramsey Sch 01–14; Inter Faith Adv Willesden Area Lon 14–19; NSM Eastcote St Lawr 01–04; NSM Brondesbury St Anne w Kilburn H Trin 04–19; rtd 19; PtO Ex from 20. 10 Cross Street, Lynton EX35 6HG M: 07801-286819 E: lcfhillel@gmail.com

HILLER, Ms Frances. b 53. Greenwich Univ BA 93. NTMTC 07. **d** 09. Chapl to Suff Bp Eur from 09; PtO S'wark from 09. 14 Tufton Street, London SW1P 3QZ T: (020) 7898 1161 E: frances.hiller@churchofengland.org

HILLER, Ms Jane Alison Summer. b 69. UWE BA 96. Trin Coll Bris 17. **d** 19. C Penhill Bris 19–20; C Upper Stratton 19–20; C Fishponds All SS and St Mary from 20. 10 Millfield Drive, Bristol BS30 5NR T: 0117-239 0625 E: revjaneyhiller@gmail.com

HILLIAM, Mrs Cheryl. b 49. EMMTC. **d** 94 **p** 95. C Linc St Faith and St Martin w St Pet 94–98; P-in-c S Ormsby Gp 98–16; rtd 16; PtO Linc 17–20. 17 Queen Street, Horncastle LN9 6BD T: (01507) 523936

HILLIARD, Canon David. b 57. TCD BTh 91. CITC 88. **d** 91 **p** 92. C Holywood *D & D* 91–94; C Seagoe 94–96; I Tartaraghan w Diamond *Arm* from 96; Can Arm Cathl from 16. *The Rectory, 5 Tarthlogue Road, Portadown BT62 1RB* T/F: (028) 3885 1289 E: tartaraghan@armagh.anglican.com

HILLIARD, Ms Lorelli Alison. b 60. St Mary's Coll Dur BSc 82 Dur Univ MA 07. Cranmer Hall Dur 04. **d** 06 **p** 07. C Drypool *York* 06–10; P-in-c Gt Marsden w Nelson St Phil *Blackb* 10–13; V from 13. *St Philip's Vicarage, 1 Victory Close, Nelson BB9 9ED* T: (01282) 697011 E: lorelli.hilliard@googlemail.com

HILLIARD, Martin. b 45. TCD BA 69 BTh 08. CITC 05. **d** 08 **p** 09. C Larne and Inver and Glynn w Raloo *Conn* 08–11; I Kells Gp *C, F & O* 11–17; rtd 17. *21 Crannagh Road, Dublin 14, D14 AY10, Republic of Ireland* T: (00353) (1) 490 8676 M: (00353) 86-108 7432 E: hilliarm@gmail.com

HILLIARD, Robert Godfrey. b 52. Portsm Univ BA(Ed) 97 MA 03. St Mich Coll Llan 72. **d** 75 **p** 76. C Whitchurch *Llan* 75–80; Chapl RNR 77–80; Chapl RN 80–06; Hon Chapl Portsm Cathl 03–06; Chapl Bradfield Coll Berks 06–12; C Cobham and Stoke D'Abernon *Guildf* 13–19; R Stoke D'Abernon 19–21; rtd 21. *18 Nettlecombe Avenue, Southsea PO4 0QN* M: 07786-257395 E: godfreyhilliard@hotmail.co.uk

HILLIER, The Ven Andrew. b 68. Cardiff Univ MTh RGN 92. SWMTC 99. **d** 02 **p** 03. C Castle Cary w Ansford *B & W* 02–05; Chapl RN from 05–21; Chapl of the Fleet and Adn for the RN from 21; QHC from 21; *Royal Naval Chaplaincy Service Headquarters, Tanner Building, HMS Excellent, Whale Island, Portsmouth PO2 8ER* T: 0300-157 7544 E: revandrewhillier@gmail.com

HILLIER, Derek John. b 30. Sarum Th Coll 61. **d** 63 **p** 64. C Salisbury St Mark *Sarum* 63–65; C Weymouth H Trin 65–66; R Caundle Bishop w Caundle Marsh and Holwell 66–75; R The Caundles and Holwell 75–81; R The Caundles w Folke and Holwell 81–02; P-in-c Pulham 70–78; rtd 02; PtO *Sarum* 02–18; *B & W* 02–18. *Saunt House, Bishop's Caundle, Sherborne DT9 5ND* T/F: (01963) 23243 E: hillier899@btinternet.com *or* hilliers899@brimvernd.com

HILLIER, John Frederick. b 43. ARIBA 67. **d** 01 **p** 02. OLM Merton St Mary *S'wark* 01–06; PtO *St Alb* 07; NSM Sandridge 07–13; rtd 13; PtO *St Alb* 13; *Ely* from 14. *70 Royal Way, Trumpington, Cambridge CB2 9AX* T: (01223) 844282 M: 07802-646374 E: johnfhillier@gmail.com

HILLIER (née CHAPMAN), Mrs Linda Rosa. b 54. Middx Univ BA 04. NTMTC 01. **d** 04 **p** 05. C W Drayton *Lon* 04–07; Faith and Work Development Officer Slough *Ox* 07–13; NSM Upton cum Chalvey from 12. *79 Torbay Road, Harrow HA2 9QG* T: (020) 8864 5728 E: lindarosahillier@msn.com

HILLIER, Ms Marilyn Jean. b 51. Ches Coll of HE CertEd 73. NTMTC BA 08. **d** 08 **p** 09. NSM Gt Parndon *Chelmsf* 08–12; PtO from 13. *23 Chapel Hill, Stansted CM24 8AD* T: (01279) 819176 E: lynhillier@btinternet.com

HILLIER, Canon Timothy John. b 55. Westmr Coll Ox CertEd 77. Oak Hill Th Coll 94. **d** 96 **p** 97. C Chertsey *Guildf* 96–00; V 00–04; V Chertsey, Lyne and Longcross from 04; RD Runnymede 07–13; Hon Can Guildf Cathl from 18. *The Vicarage, London Street, Chertsey KT16 8AA* T/F: (01932) 563141 E: timjhillier@gmail.com

HILLMAN, Clive Ralph. b 71. York Univ BSc 92. St Steph Ho Ox BA 93. **d** 96 **p** 97. C Kingston upon Hull St Alb *York* 96–00; Chapl St Jo Coll Cam 02–06; V Betws-y-Coed and Capel Curig w Penmachno etc *Ban* 06–13; P-in-c Leigh St Clem *Chelmsf* from 14. *The Rectory, 80 Leigh Hill, Leigh-on-Sea SS9 1AR* T: (01702) 475967 E: clivehillman@btinternet.com

HILLMAN, Jonathan. b 68. Man Univ BEng 90. Ridley Hall Cam. **d** 00 **p** 01. C N Wingfield, Clay Cross and Pilsley *Derby* 00–03; TV Cove St Jo *Guildf* 03–10; R Windlesham from 10; AD Surrey Heath from 17. *The Rectory, Kennel Lane, Windlesham GU20 6AA* T: (01276) 472363 E: rector@windleshamchurch.org.uk

HILLMAN, Peter. b 69. Spurgeon's Coll Lon BD. NTMTC. **d** 07 **p** 08. C Rayleigh *Chelmsf* 07–11; Public Preacher 12–19; C New Thundersley from 19. *20 Lambeth Road, Benfleet SS7 4BN* T: (01268) 461753 E: pete@legacyweb.org *or* pete.hillman@stmarkscollege.com

HILLMAN, Sarah Catherine. b 68. Selw Coll Cam BA 90 MA 94. St Jo Coll Nottm MA 05. **d** 03 **p** 04. C Sandy *St Alb* 03–06; P-in-c Barkway, Reed and Buckland w Barley 06–11; P-in-c Puddletown, Tolpuddle and Milborne w Dewlish *Sarum* 11–15; R from 15; RD Dorchester from 20. *The Vicarage, The Square, Puddletown, Dorchester DT2 8SL* T: (01305) 848784

HILLS, Elaine. b 45. RN 67. Mon Dioc Tr Scheme 02. **d** 04 **p** 08. NSM Caerleon w Llanhennock *Mon* 04–09; NSM Caerleon and Llanfrechfa 09–18. *15 Church Street, Caerleon, Newport NP18 1AW* M: 07967-349096 E: rev.elaine@btinternet.com

HILLS, Michael John. b 58. MBE 09. Open Univ BA 10. Westcott Ho Cam 87. **d** 88 **p** 89. C Workington St Jo *Carl*

88–91; C Gosforth All SS *Newc* 91–93; TV Seaton Hirst 93–98; Chapl RN 98–19; PtO *Glas* 00–03; *Bre* 03–06; *Newc* 06–19; *Sarum* 10–15; *Portsm* from 16; V Newc St Andr from 19; City Cen Chapl from 19; Chapl RNR from 19. *21 Treherne Road, Newcastle upon Tyne NE2 3NP* T: 0191-285 4464 M: 07900-583922 E: revmikehills@hotmail.com

HILLS, Michael William John. b 54. Univ of Wales (Lamp) BA 84. Westcott Ho Cam 85. **d** 87 **p** 88. C Reddish *Man* 87–91; V Bolton St Phil 91–00; V Northampton St Mich w St Edm *Pet* from 00; P-in-c Northampton H Sepulchre w St Andr and St Lawr 04–07; V from 07. *The Vicarage, 94 St Georges Avenue, Northampton NN2 6JF* T: (01604) 230316 *or* 717855 F: 635673 M: 07932-141428 E: mickhills54@gmail.com

HILLS, Roger Malcolm. b 42. Oak Hill Th Coll 83. **d** 86 **p** 87. NSM Mill Hill Jo Keble Ch *Lon* 86–98; NSM Mill Hill St Mich 86–98; PtO 98–00; V Queensbury All SS 00–07; rtd 07; PtO *Lon* from 08. *22 Sefton Avenue, London NW7 3QD* T: (020) 8959 1931 E: roger.hills2@btinternet.com

HILLS, Canon Sarah Ann St Leger. b 65. Sheff Univ MB, ChB 89 Leeds Univ MA 07. NOC 04. **d** 07 **p** 08. C Millhouses H Trin *Sheff* 07–10; PtO 10–11; Hon C Sheff St Pet and St Oswald 11–14; Bp's Adv in Past Care and Reconciliation 13–14; Can for Reconciliation Min Cov Cathl 14–19; V Holy Is *Newc* from 19. *The Vicarage, Holy Island, Berwick-upon-Tweed TD15 2RX* M: 07557-054641 E: incumbentholyisland@gmail.com

HILLS, Stephen Alan. b 59. Sheff Univ BA 81. Ridley Hall Cam 97. **d** 99 **p** 00. C Southborough St Pet w Ch Ch and St Matt etc *Roch* 99–02; TV 02–19; R Bidborough St Lawr and Southborough St Pet from 19. *The Rectory, Rectory Drive, Bidborough, Tunbridge Wells TN3 0UL* T: (01892) 528081 E: stephen.bidborough@yahoo.co.uk

HILTON, Mrs Barbara Anne. b 59. Lindisfarne Regional Tr Partnership BA 14. **d** 14 **p** 15. C Heighington and Darlington St Matt and St Luke *Dur* 14–17; P-in-c Croxdale and Tudhoe from 17; P-in-c Merrington from 17; P-in-c Byers Green from 20. *St David's Vicarage, 21 York Villas, Spennymoor DL16 6LP* M: 07456-082231 E: barbara17hilton@yahoo.co.uk

HILTON, Clive. b 30. K Coll Lon 54. **d** 58 **p** 59. C Wythenshawe Wm Temple Ch CD *Man* 58–61; C Newton Heath All SS 61–62; C-in-c Oldham St Chad Limeside CD 62–65; V Oldham St Chad Limeside 65–70; P-in-c Gravesend H Family *Roch* 70–71; R Killamarsh *Derby* 71–88; R Broughton w Loddington and Cransley etc *Pet* 88–91; rtd 92; PtO *Man* 92–95; *Pet* from 98; *Ches* 95–99; *Linc* from 98; *Ely* 05–08. *73A Tattershall Drive, Market Deeping, Peterborough PE6 8BZ* T: (01778) 346217

HILTON, Canon Ian Anthony. b 57. St Jo Coll Nottm 83. **d** 86 **p** 87. C Nottingham St Sav *S'well* 86–90; C Aspley 90–97; P-in-c Colchester, New Town and The Hythe *Chelmsf* 97–02; R 02–18; RD Colchester 06–14; CME Adv from 18; Public Preacher from 18; Hon Can Chelmsf Cathl from 12. *Chelmsford Diocesan Board of Finance, 53 New Street, Chelmsford CM1 1AT* M: 07813-538926 E: ihilton@chelmsford.anglican.org

HILTON, John. b 49. Ex Univ BA 70. Cuddesdon Coll 71. **d** 73 **p** 74. C W Derby St Jo *Liv* 73–79; V Orford St Andr 79–96; V Leeds St Wilfrid *Ripon* 96–14; rtd 14; PtO *Man* from 15. *42 College Avenue, Oldham OL8 4DS* T: 0161-624 9172 M: 07970-476406 E: fr.john@btinternet.com

HILTON, Peter. QUB BTh 05 TCD MTh 19. **d** 18 **p** 19. Hillsborough *D & D* 18–19; C Newtownards from 19. *16 Forthill Parade, Bangor BT19 1NW* T: (028) 9127 0635 M: 07746-709240 E: peterhilton36@outlook.com

HILTON, Steven Craig. b 79. JP 11. Southn Univ BA 01 Ox Univ MTh 20 FRSA 16. Westcott Ho Cam 02 Ripon Coll Cuddesdon 17. **d** 19 **p** 20. C Man Cathl from 19. *237 Great Clowes Street, Salford M7 2DZ* M: 07779-604781 E: curate@manchestercathedral.com

HILTON-TURVEY, Keith Geoffrey Michael. b 59. Oak Hill Th Coll BA 03. **d** 03 **p** 04. C S Mimms Ch Ch *Lon* 03–09; P-in-c Cricklewood St Pet 09–15; P-in-c Ledbury w Eastnor *Heref* 15–17; V from 17. *The Rectory, Worcester Road, Ledbury HR8 1PL* E: kwrbht@zoho.com *or* rector@ledburyparishchurch.org.uk

HINCHCLIFFE, Garry Anthony Frank. b 68. New Coll Edin BD 94. Edin Th Coll 90. **d** 94 **p** 95. C Dumfries *Glas* 94–97; P-in-c Motherwell 97–00; P-in-c Wishaw 97–00; V Hampsthwaite and Killinghall *Ripon* 00–04; V Hampsthwaite and Killinghall and Birstwith 04–13; TR Knaresborough 13–14; *Leeds* 14–18; P-in-c Nidd 14–18; TR Knaresborough, Goldsborough, Nidd and Brearton from 19. *The Rectory, High Bond End, Knaresborough HG5 9BT* T: (01423) 202092 E: garry.hinchcliffe@btinternet.com

HINCHCLIFFE, Lesley. b 56. Huddersfield Univ CertEd 02. LCTP 13. **d** 16 **p** 17. NSM Salesbury *Blackb* 16–19; V Fence-in-Pendle and Higham from 19. *10 Lynwood Avenue, Clayton le Moors, Accrington BB5 5RR* T: (01254) 396485 M: 07711-585645 E: lesleyhinchcliffe@hotmail.com

HINCKLEY, Paul Frederick. b 61. Cranfield Inst of Tech MSc 85. Ridley Hall Cam 92. **d** 94 **p** 95. C Ovenden *Wakef* 94–99; TV Billericay and Lt Burstead *Chelmsf* 99–06; R Yateley *Win* 06–10; TV Gt Marlow w Marlow Bottom, Lt Marlow and Bisham *Ox* 10–13; TV Stoke Gifford *Bris* 13–15; V Bradley Stoke 15–20; V Ivybridge, Cornwood, Harford and Sparkwell *Ex* from 20. *The Vicarage, Blachford Road, Ivybridge PL21 0AD* T: (01752) 895227 E: vicar.sdmc@gmail.com

✠**HIND, The Rt Revd John William.** b 45. Leeds Univ BA 66 Lambeth DD 09. Cuddesdon Coll 70. **d** 72 **p** 73 **c** 91. C Catford (Southend) and Downham *S'wark* 72–76; V Forest Hill Ch Ch 76–82; P-in-c Forest Hill St Paul 81–82; Prin Chich Th Coll 82–91; Wiccamical Preb Chich Cathl 82–91; Area Bp Horsham 91–93; Bp Eur 93–01; Asst Bp Chich 93–01; Bp Chich 01–12; rtd 12; Hon Asst Bp Portsm from 12; PtO from 16. *1 Stanley Road, Emsworth PO10 7BD* M: 07768-081106 E: johnwhind@gmail.com

HIND, Ruth Elizabeth. *See* NEWTON, Ruth Elizabeth

HINDER, Richard Alan. b 46. Birm Univ BSc 67 CCC Cam PhD 71 FRAS 70 CEng 82 FIEE 80. S'wark Ord Course 04. **d** 07 **p** 08. NSM Croydon St Matt *S'wark* 07–16; PtO from 16. *18 Mapledale Avenue, Croydon CR0 5TB* E: rahinder@gmail.com

HINDLE, Anne Margaret. *See* BARKER, Anne Margaret

HINDLE, Miss Penelope Jane Bowyn. b 45. Trin Coll Bris 76. **dss** 84 **d** 87 **p** 94. Stoneycroft All SS *Liv* 84–89; Par Dn 87–89; Asst Chapl Broadgreen Hosp *Liv* 87–89; Asst Chapl R Free Hosp Lon 89–93; Chapl N Herts NHS Trust 93–00; Chapl E and N Herts NHS Trust 00–02; rtd 02; PtO *B & W* from 07. *Cleeve House, Level Lane, Charlton Horethorne, Sherborne DT9 4NN* T: (01963) 220055 E: jane.hindle@btinternet.com

HINDLEY, Andrew David. b 59. Univ of Wales (Lamp) BA. Sarum & Wells Th Coll. **d** 82 **p** 83. C Huddersfield St Pet *Wakef* 82–84; C Huddersfield St Pet and All SS 84–86; P-in-c Holmfield 86–91; R Ribchester w Stydd *Blackb* 91–96; Bp's Adv for Leisure and Tourism 91–96; Chapl Ribchester Hosp 91–96; Can Res Blackb Cathl 96–21; rtd 21. *3 Cathedral Close, Blackburn BB1 5AA* T: (01254) 680080 E: ahin259177@aol.com

HINDLEY, Canon Anthony Talbot. b 41. Bernard Gilpin Soc Dur 61 Oak Hill Th Coll 62. **d** 66 **p** 67. C Stoke next Guildf St Jo 66–69; C Eldoret Kenya 70–72; V Menengai 72–78; C Redhill H Trin *S'wark* 78–79; P-in-c Eastbourne All So *Chich* 79–83; V 83–86; V S Malling 86–98; R Wainford *St E* 98–06; RD Beccles and S Elmham 00–03; Hon Can St E Cathl 05–06; rtd 06; PtO *St E* 07–13; *Nor* 07–13; *Ex* from 15. *19 Thorne Park Road, Torquay TQ2 6RU* T: (01803) 445885 M: 07766-546601 E: anthonyhindley1@gmail.com

HINDLEY, Michael Alexander. b 72. Man Metrop Univ BA 94. Wycliffe Hall Ox BTh 05. **d** 05 **p** 06. C Clubmoor *Liv* 05–09; TV Fazakerley Em from 09. *Emmanuel Rectory, Higher Lane, Liverpool L9 9DJ* T: 0151-525 5229 M: 07980-912768 E: revd.mike@btinternet.com

HINDLEY, Roger Dennis. b 48. Birm Univ BA 70 Ox Univ BA 77 MA 83. Ripon Coll Cuddesdon 75 Qu Coll Birm 77. **d** 78 **p** 79. C Rubery *Birm* 78–81; C Henbury *Bris* 81–83; V Erdington St Chad *Birm* 83–89; V Hill 89–05; AD Sutton Coldfield 96–02; Hon Can Birm Cathl 00–05; TR Willington *Newc* 05–12; rtd 11; PtO *Lich* 11–21. *29 Thacker Drive, Lichfield WS13 6NS* T: (01543) 253686

HINDMARSH, Valerie Gail. b 54. Edin Univ BA 75 Jordanhill Coll Glas CertEd 76 Man Metrop Univ CertEd 98 Lon Inst of Educn MA 06 EdD 12. All SS Cen for Miss & Min 15. **d** 17 **p** 18. NSM Norbury *Ches* from 17. *1 Clumber Close, Poynton, Stockport SK12 1PG* T: (01625) 873820 E: val_hindmarsh@hotmail.com

HINE, John Victor. b 36. Open Univ BA 82. Carl Dioc Tr Course 85. **d** 88 **p** 89. NSM Dean *Carl* 88–92; NSM Clifton 88–92; C Millom 92–94; P-in-c Gt Broughton and Broughton Moor 94–02; P-in-c Brigham 99–02; rtd 02; PtO *Carl* from 02. *4 The Paddocks, Thursby, Carlisle CA5 6PB* T: (01228) 712704 E: john.vine@btinternet.com

HINE, Keith Ernest. b 50. Bradf Univ BA Leeds Univ CertEd. NOC 89. **d** 89 **p** 90. C Wilmslow *Ches* 89–94; V Bowdon 94–08; R Tarporley 08–14; C Acton and Worleston, Church Minshull etc 10–14; RD Malpas 10–14; rtd 14; PtO *Ches* from 14. *18 Statham Drive, Lymm WA13 9NW* T: (01925) 752213 E: keithehine@gmail.com

HINE, Patrick Lewis. b 45. **d** 06 **p** 07. OLM Horfield H Trin *Bris* 06–15; PtO 15–19. *16 Red House Lane, Bristol BS9 3RZ* T: 0117-962 3861 E: revpatrickhine@gmail.com

HINES, Mrs Ashley Jane. b 64. Qu Coll Birm 11. **d** 14 **p** 15. OLM Horninglow *Lich* 14–17; Chapl Burton Hosps NHS Foundn Trust 17–20; PtO *Lich* 18–20; C Alrewas from 20; C Wychnor from 20. *24 Church View, Burton-on-Trent DE13 0NQ* T: (01283) 563115 E: revdashleyhines@gmail.com

HINES, Richard Arthur. b 49. Imp Coll Lon MSc 73 PhD 76 K Coll Lon MTh 89. Oak Hill Th Coll 82. **d** 84 **p** 85. C Mile Cross *Nor* 84–87; Lect Oak Hill Th Coll 87–97; Vice-Prin NTMTC 94–97; R Happisburgh, Walcott, Hempstead w Eccles etc *Nor* 97–07; C Bacton w Edingthorpe w Witton and Ridlington 04–07; R Bacton, Happisburgh, Hempstead w Eccles etc 07; R Ch Ch Cathl and the Falkland Is 07–14; rtd 14; P-in-c Aberdeen St Jas *Ab* 15–18; PtO *Ely* from 19; RD Wisbech Lynn Marshland 19–20. *47B Ramnoth Road, Wisbech PE13 2JA* T: (01945) 587742 M: 07933-198943 E: richard.hines@outlook.com

HINEY, Thomas Bernard Felix. b 35. MC 61. Open Univ BA 07. Ridley Hall Cam 67. **d** 69 **p** 70. C Edgbaston St Aug *Birm* 69–71; CF 71–91; Chapl R Hosp Chelsea 91–01; Chapl Mercers' Coll Holborn 99–01; rtd 01. *7B Dagmar Road, Exmouth EX8 2AN* T: (01395) 270688 E: sevenbdagmar@gmail.com

HINGE, Derek Colin. b 36. Imp Coll Lon BSc 58 CChem 60 MRSC 60. St Alb Minl Tr Scheme 84. **d** 88 **p** 89. NSM Bishop's Stortford St Mich *St Alb* 88–08; PtO from 08. *5 Westfield Close, Bishop's Stortford CM23 2RD* T: (01279) 652173 E: derekhinge@gmail.com

HINGLEY, Christopher James Howard. b 48. Trin Coll Ox BA 69 MA 71. Wycliffe Hall Ox 81. **d** 80 **p** 81. C St Jo Cathl Bulawayo Zimbabwe 80–81; C Hillside Ascension 82–84; Tutor Wycliffe Hall Ox 84–88; Chapl Whitestone Sch Bulawayo Zimbabwe 89–04; Headmaster Petra High Sch 04–06; R Petra Schs Bulawayo from 06. *Whitestone School, Private Bag 4, Bulawayo, Zimbabwe* E: hingley@yoafrica.com

HINGLEY (née EDWARDS), Canon Helen. b 55. Natal Univ BSW 75. St Steph Ho Ox 94. **d** 96 **p** 97. C Gravelly Hill *Birm* 96–01; TV Cen Wolverhampton *Lich* 01–05; P-in-c Hamstead St Bernard *Birm* 05–08; V 08–14; AD Handsworth 08–11; Hon Can Birm Cathl 11–14; rtd 14; PtO *Birm* from 14. *4 Adrian Croft, Birmingham B13 9YF* T: 0121-777 2171 E: h.hingley@btinternet.com

HINGLEY, Robert Charles. b 46. Ball Coll Ox BA 69 MA 74 Birm Univ CertEd 73. Qu Coll Birm 70. **d** 73 **p** 74. C Charlton St Luke w H Trin *S'wark* 73–76; Asst Warden Iona Abbey 76–77; TV Langley Marish *Ox* 77–83; V Balsall Heath St Paul *Birm* 83–90; PtO 90–91; V Birm St Luke 91–96; LtO 96–05; Hon C Hamstead St Bernard 05–14; rtd 14; PtO *Birm* from 14; *Lich* 01–16. *4 Adrian Croft, Birmingham B13 9YF* T: 0121-777 2171 E: rob.hingley@btinternet.com

HINGLEY, Roderick Stanley Plant. b 51. St Chad's Coll Dur BA 72. St Steph Ho Ox 74. **d** 75 **p** 76. C Lower Gornal *Lich* 75–79; C Tividale 79–82; C Broseley w Benthall *Heref* 82–84; C Wanstead St Mary *Chelmsf* 84–92; V Romford St Alb from 92. *St Alban's Vicarage, 3 Francombe Gardens, Romford RM1 2TH* T: (01708) 473580

HINGSTON, Barry David. b 63. LSE BSc(Econ) 84. NTMTC BA 08. **d** 08 **p** 09. C Ealing St Paul *Lon* 08–12; P-in-c Greenhill St Jo 12–14; V from 14. *11 Flambard Road, Harrow HA1 2NB* T: (020) 8907 7956 M: 07710-359483 E: barryhingston@btinternet.com or barry@stjohnsharrow.org

HINKLEY, Mrs Maureen. b 41. **d** 04. NSM Hollington St Jo *Chich* from 04. *8 Wadhurst Close, St Leonards-on-Sea TN37 7AZ* T: (01424) 754872 E: hinkley872@btinternet.com

HINKS, Margaret Anne. b 47. Birm Univ MB, ChB 65. Qu Coll Birm 08. **d** 10 **p** 11. NSM Birm St Geo 10–14; NSM Hampton-in-Arden w Bickenhill 14–17; PtO from 17; P-in-c Leam Valley *Cov* 18–20; rtd 21. *29 Birchy Close, Shirley, Solihull B90 1QL* M: 07854-329892 E: anne.hinks@outlook.com

HINKS (née CHAMBERS), Mrs Marion Patricia. b 48. Univ of Wales BDS 72. SWMTC 97. **d** 97 **p** 98. NSM Plymstock and Hooe *Ex* 97–02; NSM Ivybridge w Harford 02–15; rtd 15; PtO *Ex* from 16. *52 Southland Park Road, Wembury, Plymouth PL9 0HQ* T: (01752) 862439

HINKSMAN, Barrie Lawrence James. b 41. K Coll Lon BD 64 AKC 64 Birm Univ PhD 02. St Boniface Warminster 64. **d** 65 **p** 66. C Crosby *Linc* 65–67; Ecum Development Officer Scunthorpe Coun of Chs 67–69; C Chelmsley Wood *Birm* 69–72; TV 72–75; P-in-c Offchurch *Cov* 75–79; Dioc Lay Tr Adv 75–79; PtO 89–90; Hon Chapl Cov Cathl 90–01; PtO *Birm* 01–12; Hon Sen Fell Warw Univ *Cov* 02–09; PtO *Heref* 12–18; *Worc* 16–17. *c/o Crockford, Church House, 27 Great Smith Street, London SW1P 3AZ*

HINSLEY, Robert Charles. b 77. Univ of Wales (Abth) BTh 98 St Jo Coll Dur MATM 06. Cranmer Hall Dur 03.

d 05 **p** 06. C Carlton-in-Lindrick and Langold w Oldcotes *S'well* 05–08; P-in-c Felixstowe St Jo *St E* 08–14; RD Colneys 11–14; TR Ipswich St Mary at Stoke w St Pet and St Fran 14–21; V Stocking Farm and Beaumont Leys *Leic* from 21. *St Luke's Vicarage, 97 Halifax Drive, Leicester LE4 2DR* E: rev.roberthinsley@gmail.com

HINTON, Mrs Frances Mary. b 43. EN(G) 85. EMMTC 89. **d** 92 **p** 94. Par Dn Hornsey Rise Whitehall Park Team *Lon* 92–94; C 94–97; C Upper Holloway 97; TV Barking St Marg w St Patr *Chelmsf* 97–04; rtd 04; PtO *Linc* 17–20. *5 Little Thorpe Lane, Thorpe-on-the-Hill, Lincoln LN6 9BL* T: (01522) 688886

HINTON, Canon James William. b 63. Cov Poly BSc 84 Leeds Univ PGCE 86. St Jo Coll Nottm 00. **d** 02 **p** 03. C Thornbury *Bradf* 02–05; P-in-c Bowling St Steph 05–15; P-in-c Bankfoot 09–15; V Bankfoot and Bowling St Steph *Leeds* from 15; C Lt Horton from 05; Hon Can Bradf Cathl from 17. *St Stephen's Vicarage, 48 Newton Street, Bradford BD5 7BH* T: (01274) 720784 *or* 391537 E: jimmy4hinton@gmail.com *or* jimmy.hinton@leeds.anglican.org

HINTON, Michael Ernest. b 33. K Coll Lon 53 St Boniface Warminster 56. **d** 57 **p** 58. C Babbacombe *Ex* 57–60; S Africa 60–66; P-in-c Limehouse St Pet *Lon* 66–68; R Felmingham *Nor* 68–72; R Suffield 68–72; P-in-c Colby w Banningham and Tuttington 68–72; Bahamas 72–76; P-in-c Mylor w Flushing *Truro* 76–77; V 77–80; R The Deverills *Sarum* 82–87; Bermuda 87–89; Virgin Is 89–91; Chapl Sequoian Retreat and Conf Progr from 91; rtd 98; PtO *St E* 00–01; *Ex* 02–18. *Le Petit Pain, St Ann's Chapel, Kingsbridge TQ7 4HQ* T: (01548) 810124

HINTON, Michael George. b 27. Mert Coll Ox BA 48 MA 51 Reading Univ PhD 59. S Dios Minl Tr Scheme 81. **d** 83 **p** 84. NSM Weston-super-Mare St Paul *B & W* 83–85; NSM Sibertswold w Coldred *Cant* 85–87; NSM Eythorne and Elvington w Waldershare etc 87–95; PtO 95–19. *The College of St Barnabas, Blackberry Lane, Lingfield RH7 6NJ* E: michael@hintonm.co.uk

HINTON, Nigel Keith. b 49. Univ Coll Lon BSc 70 Lon Inst of Educn MA 87 Worc Coll of Educn PGCE 73. Oak Hill NSM Course 89. **d** 92 **p** 93. NSM Cudham and Downe *Roch* 92–07; Asst Chapl St Paul's Sch Barnes 92–07; PtO *Lon* 03–13; NSM Ootacamund St Steph India 08–12; PtO *Roch* 13–15; NSM Dormansland *S'wark* from 15. *St John's Vicarage, The Platt, Dormansland, Lingfield RH7 6QU* T: (01342) 832391 E: nigelk.hinton@gmail.com

HINTON, Paul Robin George. b 64. St Jo Coll Dur BA 86. Qu Coll Birm BA 05. **d** 05 **p** 06. C Rowley Regis *Birm* 05–09; V Warley Woods 09–19; Asst Dioc Dir of Ords 18–19; Hd of Min Formation from 19; PtO from 19. *Diocesan Office, 1 Colmore Road, Birmingham B3 2BJ* T: 0121-426 0400 E: paulh@cofebirmingham.com

HINTON, Robert Matthew. b 69. Lanc Univ BA 91. Cranmer Hall Dur BA 97. **d** 97 **p** 98. C Lache cum Saltney *Ches* 97–99; C Cheadle Hulme St Andr 99–02; V Hale Barns w Ringway 02–09; Ind Chapl *Ripon* 09–13; V Beckenham Ch Ch *Roch* from 13; AD Beckenham 15–19. *Christ Church Vicarage, 18 Court Downs Road, Beckenham BR3 6LR* T: (020) 8650 3487 E: revrobhinton@hotmail.com

HIORNS, Timothy John. b 88. Oak Hill Th Coll 15. **d** 18 **p** 19. C Crowborough *Chich* 18–21. *6 Hunters Mews, Alma Road, Windsor SL4 3SL*

HIPPISLEY-COX, Canon Stephen David. b 63. Sheff Univ BSc 85 PhD 92 Peterho Cam BA 98 MA 02. Westcott Ho Cam 96. **d** 99 **p** 00. C Ollerton w Boughton *S'well* 99–02; NSM Wilford Hill 02–07; P-in-c Willoughby-on-the-Wolds w Wysall and Widmerpool 07–11; R from 11; AD E Bingham from 18; Hon Can S'well Minster from 21. *The Rectory, Keyworth Road, Wysall, Nottingham NG12 5QQ* T: (01509) 889706 E: s.d.hippisley.cox@gmail.com

HIRD, Matthew. b 83. Jes Coll Ox BA 04. St Jo Coll Nottm MA 09. **d** 09 **p** 10. C Penn *Lich* 09–13; V Wolverhampton St Matt from 13. *St Matthew's Vicarage, 14 Sydenham Road, Wolverhampton WV1 2NY* E: matthew_hird@hotmail.com *or* matt@stmatthewswolves.com

HIRONS, Malcolm Percy. b 36. Oriel Coll Ox BA 59 MA 62. Wycliffe Hall Ox 59. **d** 61 **p** 62. C Edgbaston St Aug *Birm* 61–64; Chapl Warw Sch 64–65; C Beverley Minster *York* 65–69; V Barnby upon Don *Sheff* 69–80; P-in-c Kirk Bramwith 75–80; P-in-c Fenwick 75–80; V Norton Woodseats St Paul 80–98; rtd 98; PtO *Nor* 98–16. *Broome Lodge, 8 Lincoln Square, Hunstanton PE36 6DL* T: (01485) 532385

HIRST, David William. b 37. Man Univ BA 78. Brasted Th Coll 59 St Aid Birkenhead 61. **d** 63 **p** 64. C Clayton *Man* 63–64; C Bury St Jo 64–66; C Wynhshawe Wm Temple Ch 67–70; V Oldham St Chad Limeside 70–79; V Friezland 79–91; R Ashton St Mich 91–95; Chapl HM Pris Buckley Hall 95–00; Chapl HM Pris Wolds 00–02;

rtd 02; PtO *Blackb* from 09. *8 Priory Mews, Lytham St Annes FY8 4FT* T: (01253) 730945 M: 07833-353837 E: davidwilliamhirst@btinternet.com

HIRST, Canon Godfrey Ian. b 41. Univ of Wales (Lamp) BA 63 MBIM. Chich Th Coll 63. **d** 65 **p** 66. C Brierfield *Blackb* 65–68; Ind Chapl *Liv* 68–71; TV Kirkby 71–75; Ind Chapl *Blackb* 75–94; P-in-c Treales 75–87; Hon Can Blackb Cathl 83–87 and 94–06; Can Res Blackb Cathl 87–94; V Lytham St Cuth 94–06; AD Kirkham 98–06; rtd 06; PtO *Blackb* from 06. *11 Arundel Road, Lytham St Annes FY8 1AF* T: (01253) 732474 M: 07885-118331 E: godfreyhirst@btinternet.com

HIRST, John Adrian. b 49. St Jo Coll Nottm BTh 78. **d** 78 **p** 79. C Cheltenham St Mark *Glouc* 78–84; TV 84–85; TV Swan *Ox* 85–89; R Denham 89–15; rtd 15; PtO *Ox* from 15. *15 Riverview, Flackwell Heath, High Wycombe HP10 9AT*

HIRST, Canon Judith. b 54. St Mary's Coll Dur BA 76 LMH Ox PGCE 77 Hull Univ MA 86 St Jo Coll Dur BA 94. Cranmer Hall Dur 91. **d** 94 **p** 95. Bp's Adv in Past Care and Counselling *Dur* 94–00; C Dur St Oswald 94–00; Dir Min Formation Cranmer Hall Dur 00–07; Local Min Development Officer Dur and *Newc* 07–11; Local Ch Growth and Development Adv (Missr) *Dur* 11–19; NSM Dur St Marg and Neville's Cross St Jo 12–19; Hon Can Dur Cathl 11–19; rtd 19; PtO *Dur* from 21. *5 Beechways, Durham DH1 4LG* T: 0191-370 9505 E: judy.hirst@durham.anglican.org

HIRST, Margaret. *See* FOSSEY, Margaret

HIRST, Mrs Rachel Ann. b 58. Portsm Poly BA 79 York St Jo Univ MA 11 Hull Univ PGCE 81 ACII 85. NEOC 99. **d** 02 **p** 03. NSM Clifton *York* 02–04; C 04–06; Par Development and Tr Officer (York Adnry) 06–11; V Norton juxta Malton 11–20; RD S Ryedale 13–18; rtd 20; PtO *York* from 20. *13 Florence Grove, York YO30 5UR* T: (01904) 631592 M: 07896-204121 E: rachel.hirst40@gmail.com

HISCOCK, Gary Edward. b 43. Oak Hill Th Coll BA 90. **d** 90 **p** 91. C Cheltenham St Luke and St Jo *Glouc* 90–94; C Hardwicke, Quedgeley and Elmore w Longney 95–96; rtd 96. *25 Bournside Road, Cheltenham GL51 3AL* T: (01242) 513002

HISCOCK, Phillip George. b 47. Southn Univ CertEd 68 MPhil 90 MCIPD 83. STETS 95. **d** 98 **p** 99. NSM Portchester and Chapl Portsm Docks 98–02; Chapl Dunkirk Miss to Seafarers *Eur* 02–08; C Alverstoke *Portsm* 08–15; rtd 15; PtO *Portsm* from 15. *15 Winnham Drive, Fareham PO16 8QE* T: (01329) 314345 M: 07830-362149 E: phillip.hiscock@ntlworld.com *or* philhiscock@gmail.com

HISCOCKS, Nicholas Robin Thomas. b 75. Keble Coll Ox BA 96 MA 01 Anglia Poly Univ MA 01. Ridley Hall Cam 99. **d** 01 **p** 02. C Bromley Ch Ch *Roch* 01–11; V Westbourne Ch Ch Chpl *Win* from 11. *134 Alumhurst Road, Bournemouth BH4 8HU* T: (01202) 767881 E: nick@christchurchwestbourne.com

HISCOX, Miss Denise. b 47. Lon Univ TCert 68 Lanchester Poly Cov BSc 78. WMMTC 98. **d** 01 **p** 02. NSM Cov St Mary 01–05; NSM Leamington Priors All SS 05–07; NSM Leamington Spa H Trin and Old Milverton 05–07; PtO 07–08; NSM Willenhall 08–10; PtO *Newc* from 11. *1 Rogerson Road, Belford NE70 7DB* E: denise@dhiscox.co.uk

HISCOX, Jonathan Ronald James. b 64. Qu Coll Birm 87. **d** 89 **p** 90. C Wiveliscombe *B & W* 89–93; P-in-c Donyatt w Horton, Broadway and Ashill 93–94; TV Ilminster and Distr 94–02; R Rowde and Bromham *Sarum* 02–10; C Upper Wylye Valley from 21. *Address temp unknown*

HISLOP, Martin Gregory. b 55. DL 18. Jas Cook Univ Townsville BA 78 Univ of S Aus MEd 88. **d** 92 **p** 93. C N Mackay St Ambrose Australia 92–93; Dir Studies St Barn Coll of Min 93–94; Chapl Ballarat Univ 95–98; Asst Chapl St Mich Gr Sch 98; Assoc P E St Kilda 98; C Kingston St Luke *S'wark* 00–01; P-in-c 01–05; V from 05. *St Luke's Vicarage, 4 Burton Road, Kingston upon Thames KT2 5TE* T: (020) 8974 8079 E: vicar@kingstonstlukes.uk

HISLOP, Mrs Patricia Elizabeth. b 42. Heythrop Coll Lon MA 03. **d** 08 **p** 09. OLM Ewhurst *Guildf* 08–12; PtO from 12; Birtley Ho Bramley 12–16. *2 Napper Place, Cranleigh GU6 8DZ* T: (01483) 274724 E: patricia.hislop@phrh.co.uk

HITCH, Canon Kim William. b 54. Leic Univ BSc 75 K Coll Lon MA 94 Birm Univ MPhil 08. Trin Coll Bris 76. **d** 78 **p** 79. C Becontree St Mary *Chelmsf* 78–80; C Huyton Quarry *Liv* 80–83; V Hatcham St Jas *S'wark* 83–91; TR Kidbrooke 91–02; R Kidbrooke St Jas from 02; Lewisham Adnry Ecum Officer 03–06; Dir Ords Woolwich Area from 05; Dioc Voc Adv 12–17; AD Charlton 06–19; Hon Can S'wark Cathl from 08. *St James's Rectory, 62 Kidbrooke Park Road, London SE3 0DU* T: (020) 8856 3438 E: k.w.hitch@btinternet.com

HITCHEN, Carol Ann. *See* CLOSE, Carol Ann

HITCHEN, Gillian Françoise-Hélène. b 71. Wycliffe Hall Ox 16. **d** 18 **p** 19. C Parr *Liv* 18–21; P-in-c Orford St Andr from 21. *St Andrew's Vicarage, Poplars Avenue, Warrington WA2 9UE* E: revgillhitchen@gmail.com

HITCHEN, Lisa Jan. *See* MacINNES, Lisa Jan

HITCHENS (*née* GREEN), Mrs Catherine Isabel. b 48. Cant Sch of Min 89. d 92 p 94. C Willesborough *Cant* 92–96; Sen Asst P E Dereham and Scarning *Nor* 96–97; Asst Chapl HM Pris Wayland 96–97; Chapl HM Pris Leic 97–00; Chapl HM YOI Castington 00–02; Chapl HM Pris Cant 02–12; rtd 12. *Dan y Coed, 6 Gybbons Road, Rolvenden, Cranbrook TN17 4LL* E: cathandfred@hotmail.co.uk

HITCHINER, Mrs Elizabeth Ann. b 59. Birm Univ BSc 80. WEMTC 03. d 06 p 07. NSM Cagebrook *Heref* from 06. *Dunan House, Clehonger, Hereford HR2 9SF* T: (01432) 355980

HITCHING, His Honour Judge Alan Norman. b 41. Ch Ch Ox BA 62 MA 66 BCL 63 Barrister-at-Law (Middle Temple) 64. d 01 p 02. NSM High Ongar w Norton Mandeville *Chelmsf* 01–06; PtO from 06. *9 Monkhams Drive, Woodford Green IG8 0LG* T: (020) 8504 4260 E: anhitching@btinternet.com

HITCHINS, Graham Edward David. b 54. S Dios Minl Tr Scheme 91. d 94 p 95. C Bishop's Waltham *Portsm* 94–97; C Upham 94–97; C Honiton, Gittisham, Combe Raleigh, Monkton etc *Ex* 97–98; TV 98–03; Chapl RN 03–10; R Burnham Gp of Par *Nor* 09–18; Corps Chapl Sea Cadet Corps 10–21; Chapl RNR 16–20; rtd 20; PtO *Ex* 18–19; *Sarum* from 21. *Stapleford House, Gold Street, Stalbridge, Sturminster Newton DT10 2LX* T: (01963) 363916 E: revdgrahamhitchins@hotmail.com

HITCHMAN, Keith John. b 62. Middx Univ BSc 90. Trin Coll Bris BA 95. d 95 p 96. C Bestwood *S'well* 95–99; Chapl Glos Univ 99–04; C Cheltenham St Mary, St Matt, St Paul and H Trin *Glouc* 04–07; TV Cheltenham H Trin and St Paul 07–10; Pioneer Min River in the City *Liv* 10–16; V Toxteth Park Ch Ch and St Mich w St Andr from 16. *St Michael's Vicarage, 1B St Michael's Church Road, Liverpool L17 7BD*

HIZA, Douglas William. b 38. Richmond Univ Virginia BA 60 MDiv 63 Mankato State Univ MS 70. Virginia Th Sem 60. d 63 p 64. C Calvary Cathl Sioux Falls USA 63–65; V Sioux Falls Gd Shep 65–66; V Vermillion St Paul 66–69; V New Ulm St Pet 71–80; Chapl Mankato State Univ 74–80; Chapl Hackney Hosp Gp Lon 80–95; Chapl Homerton Hosp Lon 80–95; PtO Lon 96–04; Hon C Smithfield St Bart Gt 04–06; PtO from 06; *S'wark* 06–15. *10 Meynell Crescent, London E9 7AS* T: (020) 8985 7832 *or* 7253 3107 E: hiza@btinternet.com

HOAD, Anne Elizabeth. b 42. Bris Univ BA 63. dss 69 d 94 p 95. Asst Chapl Imp Coll Lon 69–74; S'wark Lay Tr Scheme 74–77; Brixton St Matt *S'wark* 77–80; Charlton St Luke w H Trin 80–94; Project Worker Community of Women and Men 88–91; Voc Adv Lewisham from 91; Asst Chapl Lewisham Hosp *S'wark* 92–93; Hon C Lee Gd Shep w St Pet 94–03; C 03–10; rtd 10; PtO *S'wark* from 11. *14 Silk Close, London SE12 8DL* T: (020) 8297 8761 E: hoadanne@yahoo.co.uk

HOAD, Miss Rosemary Claire. b 60. Cranmer Hall Dur 92. d 94 p 95. C Epsom St Martin *Guildf* 94–97; TV Brentford *Lon* 97–05; V Spring Grove St Mary 05–18; V Egham Hythe *Guildf* from 18. *17 Old School Mews, Staines-upon-Thames TW18 3HX* E: vicar@speh.org.uk

HOAD, Mrs Shona Mary. b 66. Newc Univ BA 88. STETS 07. d 10 p 11. C Dorking St Paul *Guildf* 10–14; V Atworth w Shaw and Whitley *Sarum* 14–18; NSM Whitewater *Win* from 18. *Mattingley Rectory, Vicarage Lane, Hound Green, Hook RG27 8LF* T: 0118-932 6075 M: 07871-740158 E: shonahoad@whitewaterchurches.co.uk

HOARE, Carol. b 46. Lon Univ BA 68 Birm Univ CertEd 69. Qu Coll Birm 86 WMMTC 86. d 91 p 94. NSM Curdworth *Birm* 91–00; PtO from 00. *14 Elms Road, Sutton Coldfield B72 1JF* T: 0121-354 1117 E: c.hoare@btinternet.com

HOARE, Canon David Marlyn. b 33. Bps' Coll Cheshunt 60. d 63 p 64. C Ampthill w Millbrook and Steppingley *St Alb* 63–67; C Bushey 67–70; V Harlington 70–76; V Oxhey All SS 76–81; V Hellesdon *Nor* 81–98; Hon Can Nor Cathl 95–98; rtd 98; PtO *Nor* from 98. *14 Cottinghams Drive, Norwich NR6 6PS* T: (01603) 423418 E: dmhoare@icloud.com

HOARE, Diana Charlotte. b 48. Keele Univ BA 78. WEMTC 02. d 05 p 06. C Bishop's Castle w Mainstone, Lydbury N etc *Heref* 05–09; P-in-c Bucknell w Chapel Lawn, Llanfair Waterdine etc 09–14; V Middle Marches 14–15; P-in-c Walton W w Talbenny and Haroldston W *St D* 15–18; P-in-c Gtr Dewisland from 18. *The Rectory, Calbern, Simpson Cross, Haverfordwest SA62 6EP* T: (01437) 721205 E: diana.hoare540@btinternet.com *or* starstonewell@gmail.com

HOARE (*née* CULLING), Elizabeth Ann. b 58. St Mary's Coll Dur BA 76 St Jo Coll Dur PhD 87 Rob Coll Cam BA 88 PGCE 80. Ridley Hall Cam 86. d 89 p 94. Par Dn S Cave and Ellerker w Broomfleet *York* 89–92; Tutor Cranmer Hall Dur

93–95; P-in-c Cherry Burton *York* 95–00; Abp's Sen Adv on Rural Affairs 95–98; Spiritual Dir York Angl Cursillo 98–00; Chapl Bp Burton Coll York 95–00; PtO *York* 01–02; NSM Cowesby 02–07; NSM Felixkirk w Boltby 02–07; NSM Kirkby Knowle 02–07; NSM Leake w Over and Nether Silton and Kepwick 02–07; Tutor and Lect Cranmer Hall Dur 02–07; Tutor Wycliffe Hall Ox from 07. *Wycliffe Hall, 54 Banbury Road, Oxford OX2 6PW* T: (01865) 274200 *or* 873412 E: eahoare@googlemail.com

HOARE, Janet Francis Mary. *See* MILES, Janet Francis Mary

HOARE, Patrick Gerard. *See* GERARD, Patrick Hoare

HOARE, Patrick Reginald Andrew Reid (Toddy). b 47. TD 80 and Bar 88. Hull Univ MA 90. Wycliffe Hall Ox 77. d 80 p 81. Rotterdam w Schiedam *Eur* 76–77; C Guisborough *York* 80–83; P-in-c Felixkirk w Boltby 83–07; P-in-c Kirkby Knowle 83–07; P-in-c Leake w Over and Nether Silton and Kepwick 83–07; P-in-c Cowesby 83–07; Chapl Yorks Agric Soc 92–09; CF (TA) 82–99; rtd 07; PtO *Ox* from 07. *Pond Farm House, Holton, Oxford OX33 1PY* T: (01865) 873412 E: toddy100@btinternet.com

HOARE, Roger John. b 38. Tyndale Hall Bris 63. d 66 p 67. C Stoughton *Guildf* 66–70; C Chesham St Mary *Ox* 70–73; V Bath St Bart *B & W* 73–83; V Gt Faringdon w Lt Coxwell *Ox* 83–89; Deputation Appeals Org (NE Lon) Children's Soc 89–93; P-in-c Lambourne w Abridge and Stapleford Abbotts *Chelmsf* 93–03; Ind Chapl 93–03; rtd 03; PtO *Chelmsf* from 04. *44 Anchor Road, Tiptree, Colchester CO5 0AP* T: (01621) 817236 E: randd@hoare44.plus.com

✠**HOARE, The Rt Revd Rupert William Noel.** b 40. Trin Coll Ox BA 61 MA 66 Fitzw Ho Cam BA 64 MA 84 Birm Univ PhD 73. Kirchliche Hochschule Berlin 61 Westcott Ho Cam 62. d 64 p 65 c 93. C Oldham St Mary w St Pet *Man* 64–67; Lect Qu Coll Birm 68–72; Can Th Cov Cathl 70–76; R Man Resurr 72–78; Can Res Birm Cathl 78–81; Prin Westcott Ho Cam 81–93; Area Bp Dudley and Hon Can Worc Cathl 93–00; Dean Liv 00–07; rtd 07; Hon Asst Bp Man from 08; PtO *Eur* from 16. *14 Shaw Hall Bank Road, Greenfield, Oldham OL3 7LD* T: (01457) 820375 E: rupert.gesinehoare@gmail.com

HOARE, Canon Simon Gerard. b 37. AKC 61. d 62 p 63. C Headingley *Ripon* 62–65; C Adel 65–68; R Spofforth 68–71; R Spofforth w Kirk Deighton 71–77; V Rawdon *Bradf* 77–85; Hon Can Bradf Cathl 85–02; R Carleton and Lotherscale 85–02; Dioc Ecum Officer 85–94; rtd 02; PtO *Ripon* 02–14; *Leeds* from 14. *Skell Villa, 20 Wellington Street, Ripon HG4 1PH* T: (01765) 692187 E: sghoare@talktalk.net

HOARE, Toddy. *See* HOARE, Patrick Reginald Andrew Reid

HOARE, Mrs Valerie Mary. b 54. Ex Univ BTh 07. SWMTC 04. d 07 p 08. NSM Chard St Mary *B & W* 07–10; C Chard St Mary w Combe St Nicholas, Wambrook etc 10–14; NSM Ilminster and Whitelackington 15–18; rtd 18; PtO *B & W* from 18. *Nyleve, Church Lane, Horton, Ilminster TA19 9RN* T: (01460) 54542 E: cherrybrook@hotmail.co.uk

HOBBINS, Mrs Susan. b 47. Birm Univ CertEd 68. STETS 04. d 07 p 08. NSM Hatherden w Tangley, Weyhill and Penton Mewsey *Win* 07–09; C Pastrow 09–13; PtO *Win* from 13. *Rose Cottage, Upton, Andover SP11 0JP* T: (01264) 736166 E: susanhobbins@icloud.com

HOBBS, Alexander. b 85. Ex Univ BA 07 Leeds Univ MMus 08 Sheff Univ BA 16 AKC 15. Coll of Resurr Mirfield 14. d 17 p 18. C Heavitree and St Mary Steps *Ex* from 17. *10 Sherwood Close, Exeter EX2 5DX* T: (01392) 677153 E: fralexanderhobbs@gmail.com

HOBBS, Mrs Alison Clare. b 58. Imp Coll Lon BSc 80. Lindisfarne Regional Tr Partnership 09. d 12 p 13. NSM Brancepeth *Dur* from 12. *Brancepeth Castle, Brancepeth, Durham DH7 8DF* T: 0191-378 9670 M: 07504-489089 E: alison@brancepethcastle.org.uk *or* alisonhobbs@stbrandon.org.uk

HOBBS (*formerly* DUFFUS), Mrs Barbara Rose. b 51. EMMTC 95. d 98 p 99. C Linc St Faith and St Martin w St Pet 98–00; C Grantham St Wulfram 00–02; P-in-c Brothertoft Gp 02–04; Mental Health Chapl SE Lincs 02–04; P-in-c Hastings St Clem and All SS *Chich* 04–08; rtd 08; PtO *Chich* from 08. *Courtyard Cottage, Main Road, Westfield, Hastings TN35 4QE* T: (01424) 756479 M: 07724-410292 E: barbara.r.hobbs@googlemail.com

HOBBS, Christopher Bedo. b 61. Jes Coll Cam BA 83 BTh 90. Ridley Hall Cam 88. d 91 p 92. C Langham Place All So *Lon* 91–95; C Hull St Jo Newland *York* 95–00; V Selly Park St Steph and St Wulstan *Birm* from 00. *18 Selly Wick Road, Selly Park, Birmingham B29 7JA* T: 0121-472 0050 *or* 472 8253 E: chris.hobbs@sssw.org.uk

HOBBS, Christopher John Pearson. b 60. Sydney Univ BA 82 K Coll Lon BD 89 AKC 89. Wycliffe Hall Ox 89. d 91 p 92. C S Mimms Ch Ch *Lon* 91–94; C Jesmond Clayton Memorial

Newc 94–97; V Oakwood St Thos *Lon* 97–17; V Cheadle Hulme St Andr *Ches* from 17. *2 Orrishmere Road, Cheadle Hulme, Cheadle SK8 5HP* E: christopher.hobbs@blueyonder.co.uk

HOBBS, Edward Quincey. b 74. Bris Univ BSc 95. Wycliffe Hall Ox BA 99. **d** 00 **p** 01. C Stapenhill w Cauldwell *Derby* 00–03; C Newbury *Ox* 03–08; C Brompton H Trin w Onslow Square St Paul *Lon* 08–09; P-in-c Cullompton, Willand, Uffculme, Kentisbeare etc *Ex* 09–15; R Cullompton from 15. *Windyridge, 10 Willand Road, Cullompton EX15 1AP* E: eqhobbs@gmail.com

HOBBS, Ian. *See* HOBBS, Kenneth Ian

HOBBS, James. b 42. K Alfred's Coll Win CertEd 64 Open Univ BA 89 Hull Univ MA 94 Win Univ BUniv 15. Linc Th Coll 66. **d** 68 **p** 69. C Moseley St Mary *Birm* 68–73; V Kingstanding St Mark 73–77; R Rushbrooke *St E* 77–78; R Bradfield St Geo w Rushbrooke 77–78; R Bradfield St Geo 78–80; P-in-c Bradfield St Clare 77–80; P-in-c Felsham w Gedding 77–80; R Bradfield St George w Bradfield St Clare etc 80–84; P-in-c Gt and Lt Whelnetham 84–85; R Gt and Lt Whelnetham w Bradfield St George 85–90; Ecum Chapl for F&HE Grimsby *Linc* 90–97; Chapl Lincs and Humberside Univ (Grimsby Campus) 90–97; Gen Preacher 92–97; V Ingham w Cammeringham w Fillingham 97–01; R Aisthorpe w Scampton w Thorpe le Fallows etc 97–01; P-in-c N w S Carlton 97–01; P-in-c Burton by Linc 97–01; rtd 01; PtO *Linc* 01–04; *Chich* from 04. *Courtyard Cottage, Main Road, Westfield, Hastings TN35 4QE* T: (01424) 756479 M: 07726-302341 E: hobbs.jim1@gmail.com

HOBBS, Jason Michael. b 74. Northumbria Univ BSc 97 Sunderland Univ BA 00. TISEC 07. **d** 10 **p** 11. C Aberdeen St Mary *Ab* from 10. *98 Burnieboozle Crescent, Aberdeen AB15 8NQ* M: 07446-113014 E: jhobbs10@gmail.com

HOBBS, Kenneth Brian. b 47. Sussex Univ BA 68 Lon Inst of Educn PGCE 70. NTMTC 98. **d** 98 **p** 99. NSM Howell Hill *Guildf* 98–01; NSM Shere, Albury and Chilworth 01–11; rtd 11; PtO *Guildf* 11–19; C-in-c Stoneleigh 19–20; Rtd Clergy Officer 18–20. *5 Burdon Park, Cheam SM2 7PS* T: (020) 8643 7878 E: revken.hobbs@gmail.com

HOBBS, Kenneth Ian. b 50. Oak Hill Th Coll 74. **d** 77 **p** 78. C Southborough St Pet w Ch Ch and St Matt *Roch* 77–80; C Hoole *Ches* 80–84; V Barnston 84–95; P-in-c Bedworth *Cov* 95; TR 95–01; RD Nuneaton 00–01; TR Radipole and Melcombe Regis *Sarum* 01–15; RD Weymouth and Portland 08–12; rtd 15; PtO *Ches* from 16. *4 Daryl Road, Wirral CH60 5RD* T: 0151-342 8353 E: kijahobbs@gmail.com

HOBBS, Leslie Robert. b 42. Sussex Univ BA 64 Lon Bible Coll BD 67. EAMTC 02. **d** 02 **p** 03. NSM Somerleyton, Ashby, Fritton, Herringfleet etc *Nor* 02–09; R 09–12; rtd 12; PtO *Nor* from 13. *Nether End Cottage, Blacksmiths Loke, Lound, Lowestoft NR32 5LS* T: (01502) 732536 E: hobbsnec@btinternet.com

HOBBS, Preb Maureen Patricia. b 54. Surrey Univ BSc 76. Westcott Ho Cam 95. **d** 97 **p** 98. C Shrewsbury St Chad w St Mary *Lich* 97–01; R Baschurch and Weston Lullingfield w Hordley 01–09; P-in-c Pattingham w Patshull 09–14; V 14–21; RD Trysull 09–19; Dioc Adv for Women in Min 04–11; Min Development Enabler 19–21; Preb Lich Cathl 12–21; rtd 21. *c/o 13 Furrocks Lane, Ness, Neston CH64 4EH*

HOBBS, Mrs Nicola. b 77. **d** 14 **p** 15. C Broughton w Loddington and Cransley etc *Pet* 14–18; R Broughton w Cransley and Mawsley from 18. *15 Loddington Way, Mawsley, Kettering NN14 1GE* T: (01536) 799522 E: revnicki@familyhobbs.org.uk

HOBBS, Sarah Kathleen. *See* PATTEN, Sarah Kathleen

HOBBS, Sarah Louise. b 47. WEMTC 01. **d** 04 **p** 05. NSM Westbury-on-Severn w Flaxley, Blaisdon etc *Glouc* 05–14; NSM Abenhall w Mitcheldean 11–14; NSM Huntley and Longhope, Churcham and Bulley 12–14; rtd 14; PtO *Glouc* from 15. *Wedgewood House, High Street, Newnham GL14 1AD* T: (01594) 517157 E: shobbs001@btinternet.com

HOBBS, Simon John. b 59. St Steph Ho Ox BA 82 MA. **d** 83 **p** 84. C Middlesbrough Ascension *York* 83–85; C Stainton-in-Cleveland 85–88; C St Marylebone All SS *Lon* 88–90; P-in-c Paddington St Pet 90–94; C-in-c Grosvenor Chpl 94–08; C Hanover Square St Geo 94–08; Chapl Bonn w Cologne *Eur* 08–11; Chapl Sussex Partnership NHS Foundn Trust from 13. *Sussex Partnership NHS Foundation Trust, Swandean, 85 Arundel Road, Worthing BN13 3EP*

HOBDAY, Hannah Elizabeth. b 80. Jes Coll Ox BA 04 MA 15 Selw Coll Cam BA 06 MA 15 Anglia Ruskin Univ MA 16. Ridley Hall Cam 04. **d** 07 **p** 08. C Margate H Trin *Cant* 07–09; C Cliftonville 07–09; C Chesterton St Geo *Ely* 09–15; C Earley St Pet *Ox* from 15; Tutor IME2 from 21. *69 Eastcourt Avenue, Earley, Reading RG6 1HN* T: 0118-966 6701 E: hannah@earleystpeters.org.uk

HOBDAY, Philip Peter. b 81. Ex Coll Ox BA 02 MA 09 Fitzw Coll Cam BA 05 MA 09 Nottm Univ MA 14 Dur Univ

PhD 21. Ridley Hall Cam 03. **d** 06 **p** 07. C St Peter-in-Thanet *Cant* 06–09; Chapl Cant Ch Ch Univ 06–09; Fell Magd Coll Cam 09–15; Chapl 09–14; Dean of Chpl 15; V Earley St Pet *Ox* from 15. *69 Eastcourt Avenue, Earley, Reading RG6 1HH* T: 0118-966 6701 M: 07537-922652 E: philip@earleystpeters.org.uk

HOBDEN, Christopher Martin. b 49. Lon Univ BSc 71. Oak Hill Th Coll 80. **d** 87 **p** 88. NSM St Marylebone All So w SS Pet and Jo *Lon* 87–88; NSM Langham Place All So 88–95. *10 Kent Terrace, London NW1 4RP*

HOBDEN, David Nicholas. b 54. K Coll Lon BD 76 AKC 76 Cam Univ PGCE. Ripon Coll Cuddesdon 77. **d** 78 **p** 79. C Marlborough *Sarum* 78–80; C Salisbury St Thos and St Edm 81–85; V Shalford *Guildf* 85–99; Asst Chapl R Surrey Co Hosp NHS Trust 99–00; Sen Chapl R Surrey Co Hosp NHS Foundn Trust 00–15; rtd 15; PtO *Guildf* from 15. *Greenwood, Oakdene Road, Godalming GU7 1QF* T: (01483) 410177 E: dnhobden@gmail.com

HOBDEN, Geoffrey William. b 46. Trin Coll Bris 80. **d** 82 **p** 83. C Ex St Leon w H Trin 82–86; V Weston-super-Mare Ch Ch *B & W* 86–06; V Weston super Mare Ch Ch and Em 06–11; RD Locking 93–99; rtd 11; PtO *B & W* from 11. *21 Burrington Avenue, Weston-super-Mare BS24 9LP* T: (01934) 707981 M: 07531-648609 E: hobdenshouse@gmail.com

HOBLEY, Ms Susan Elizabeth. b 51. Newc Univ BA 74 Dur Univ PGCE 75. NEOC 98. **d** 01 **p** 02. NSM Millfield St Mark and Pallion St Luke *Dur* 01–05; C Sheff St Mark Broomhill 05–09; V Wath-upon-Dearne 09–16; rtd 16; PtO *Leeds* from 17; *Sheff* from 18. *6 Greenway, Honley, Holmfirth HD9 6NQ*

HOBMAN, David John. b 52. **d** 17. NSM York All SS Pavement w St Crux and St Mich from 17; NSM York H Trin Micklegate from 17; NSM York St Denys from 17; NSM York St Helen w St Martin from 17; NSM York St Lawr w St Nic from 17; NSM York St Olave w St Giles from 17. *41 Manor Park Road, York YO30 5UB*

HOBSON, Alexander. *See* HOBSON, John Alexander

HOBSON, Anthony Peter. b 53. St Jo Coll Cam BA 74. St Jo Coll Nottm 75. **d** 77 **p** 78. C Brunswick *Man* 77–82; R Stretford St Bride 82–92; TR Hackney Marsh *Lon* 92–00; V Leic Martyrs 00–08; Dir St Martin's Ho 09–16; PtO 15–16; C Leic Cathl and Project Dir Leic Cathl Revealed 16–19; rtd 19; PtO *Leic* from 20. *4 Church Road, Aylestone, Leicester LE2 8LB* T: 0116-283 3251 M: 07810-023659 E: petehobson@me.com

HOBSON, Barry Rodney. b 57. Open Univ BA 98. Wilson Carlile Coll 82 EAMTC 97. **d** 98 **p** 99. CA from 85; C Warboys w Broughton and Bury w Wistow *Ely* 98–01; P-in-c Roxwell *Chelmsf* 01–07; RD Chelmsf N 06–07; V Hornchurch St Andr 07–19; rtd 19; Hon C Downham w S Hanningfield and Ramsden Bellhouse *Chelmsf* from 21. *April Cottage, Highwood Road, Edney Common, Chelmsford CM1 3QE* T: (01245) 249099 E: b.hobson@btinternet.com

HOBSON, John Alexander (Alex). b 70. LMH Ox BA 91 MA 02 York Univ MA 94. Wycliffe Hall Ox BA 01. **d** 02 **p** 03. C Aynho and Croughton w Evenley etc *Pet* 02–05; Chapl RAF from 05. *Chaplaincy Services (RAF), HQ Air Command, RAF High Wycombe HP14 4UE* T: (01494) 496800 E: alexhobson17@gmail.com

HOBSON, Canon Patrick John Bogan. b 33. MC 53. Magd Coll Cam BA 56 MA 60 Ox Brookes Univ BA 08. S'wark Ord Course 75 Qu Coll Birm 77. **d** 79 **p** 80. C St Jo in Bedwardine *Worc* 79–81; R Clifton-on-Teme, Lower Sapey and the Shelsleys 81–88; TR Waltham H Cross *Chelmsf* 88–98; Hon Can Chelmsf Cathl 95–98; rtd 98; PtO *Ox* from 09. *24 Cunliffe Close, Oxford OX2 7BL* T/F: (01865) 556206 E: patrick.hobson@btinternet.com

HOBSON, Peter. *See* HOBSON, Anthony Peter

HOBSON, Miss Trudy. b 82. Open Univ BA 09. Coll of Resurr Mirfield BA 15. **d** 16 **p** 17. C Brigg, Wrawby and Cadney cum Howsham *Linc* 16–19; P-in-c Upper Wylye Valley *Sarum* 19–20; TR from 20. *1 Bests Lane, Sutton Veny, Warminster BA12 7AU* M: 07508-066222 E: cowpy27@hotmail.co.uk

HOBSON, Mrs Yvonne Mary. b 45. Ex Univ BTh 03. SWMTC 00. **d** 03 **p** 04. C St Illogan *Truro* 03–06; C Paul 06–10; rtd 10; PtO *Truro* from 16. *8 Donnington Road, Penzance TR18 4PQ* T: (01736) 364354 E: yvonnehobson@btinternet.com

HOCKEN, Glen Rundle. b 59. Kent Univ BA 80 Southlands Coll Lon PGCE 90 ACA 84. Wycliffe Hall Ox 90. **d** 92 **p** 93. C Cogges *Ox* 92–94; C Cogges and S Leigh 94–96; C Boldmere *Birm* 96–99; TV Southgate *Chich* 99–06; Chapl HM Pris Lewes 06–13; Chapl St Pet and St Jas Hospice N Chailey 05–13; Chapl HM Pris Onley 13–16; Chapl HM Pris Moorland 16–19; Chapl HM Pris Wealstun 19; Chapl HM Pris Full Sutton from 19. *HM Prison, Full Sutton, York YO41 1PS* T: (01759) 475100 E: glen.hocken@justice.gov.uk

HOCKEY (née LOOMES), Gaenor Mary. b 65. Hull Univ BA 92 RGN 86. St Jo Coll Nottm MPhil 93. **d** 96 **p** 97. C Charles w Plymouth St Matthias *Ex* 96–00; C Devonport St Aubyn 00–05; PtO 05–06; P-in-c Seer Green and Jordans *Ox* 06–13; R Yeovil H Trin w Barwick *B & W* 13–19; C Marnhull *Sarum* from 19. *The Rectory, New Street, Marnhull, Sturminster Newton DT10 1PY* E: gaenor@protonmail.com

HOCKLEY, Paul William. b 47. Chu Coll Cam BA 68 MA 72 Nottm Univ BA 73. St Jo Coll Nottm 71. **d** 74 **p** 75. C Chatham St Phil and St Jas *Roch* 74–78; C Tunbridge Wells St Jo 78–81; V Penketh *Liv* 81–14; TV Warrington W 14–15; rtd 15; PtO *Sarum* 16–21. *76 Vale Road, Poole BH14 9AU* T: (01202) 730626

HOCKLEY-STILL, Tanya. b 89. Cardiff Univ BA 10 Anglia Ruskin Univ MA 14. Westcott Ho Cam 12. **d** 14 **p** 15. C Stone Cross St Luke w N Langney *Chich* 14–17; P-in-c St Mark, St Sidwell and St Matt 17–18; R Ex St Mark from 18. *St Mark's Rectory, 8 Lamacraft Drive, Exeter EX4 8QS* T: (01392) 423311 M: 07971-442264 E: tanya@stmarksexeter.uk

HOCKNULL, Canon Mark Dennis. b 63. Surrey Univ BSc 85 Univ Coll Lon PhD 89 St Jo Coll Dur BA 93. Cranmer Hall Dur 91. **d** 94 **p** 95. C Prenton *Ches* 94–96; C Runcorn All SS and Runcorn St Mich 96–99; V Gt Meols 99–05; CME Officer *Linc* 05–09; Lic Preacher 05–09; Can Res and Chan *Linc* Cathl 09–17; Hd of Min Tr (Dioc Min Course) 09–17; Tutor Linc Univ from 17. *University of Lincoln, Campus Way, Lincoln LN6 7TS* T: (01522) 886076 E: mhocknull@lincoln.ac.uk

HODDER, Anthony Mark. b 56. Univ of Wales (Newport) CertEd 00 FCCA 90. Ridley Hall Cam 08. **d** 11 **p** 13. C Heref S Wye 11–12; C Ledbury 12–17; PtO from 17. *21 Biddulph Way, Ledbury HR8 2HP* M: 07977-063294 E: tony.hodder@gmail.com

HODDER, Christopher John. b 75. Huddersfield Univ BA 96. St Jo Coll Nottm BTh 00. **d** 01 **p** 02. C Loughborough Em and St Mary in Charnwood *Leic* 01–05; Chapl Derby Univ and Derby Cathl 05–10; P-in-c Wilford Hill *S'well* 10–11; V 11–18; Chapl RAF from 18; PtO *Nor* from 18. *Chaplaincy Service (RAF), HQ Air Command, RAF High Wycombe HP14 4UE* T: (01494) 496800 M: 07833-592800

HODDER, John Kenneth. b 45. Edin Univ MA 68. Cuddesdon Coll 71. **d** 73 **p** 74. C Kibworth Beauchamp *Leic* 73–76; C Whittlesey *Ely* 76–80; R Downham 80–87; P-in-c Coveney 80–81; R 81–87; R Nunney and Witham Friary, Marston Bigot etc *B & W* 87–10; rtd 10; PtO *B & W* from 10. *95 Nunney Road, Frome BA11 4LF* T: (01373) 466063 E: hodderhodder@btinternet.com

HODDER, Matthew John. b 90. **d** 20. C Bexley *Roch* from 20. *29 Hill Crescent , Bexley DA5 2DA* E: matthodder10@gmail.com

HODGE, Anthony Charles. b 43. AKC 66. **d** 67 **p** 68. C Carrington *S'well* 67–69; C Bawtry w Austerfield 69–72; C Misson 69–72; Grenada 72–74; Trinidad and Tobago 74–76; V Tuckingmill *Truro* 76–78; V Worksop St Paul *S'well* 78–81; P-in-c Patrington w Hollym, Welwick and Winestead *York* 81–86; R 86–88; V York St Olave w St Giles 88–08; V York St Helen w St Martin 97–08; Chapl York Coll for Girls 88–96; rtd 08; P-in-c Duloe, Herodsfoot, Morval and St Pinnock *Truro* 08–14; PtO from 14. *3 Tower Hill Gardens, Rhind Street, Bodmin PL31 2FD* T: (01208) 892929 M: 07717-877430 E: achodge@live.co.uk

HODGE, Mrs Joanne Lesley. b 64. Bris Univ BA 87 Open Univ BSc 06 Univ of Wales (Cardiff) PGCE 88. Trin Coll Bris 17. **d** 19 **p** 20. OLM Fromeside *Bris* from 19; OLM Yate from 19. *3 Chatterton Road, Yate, Bristol BS37 4BJ* T: (01454) 880152 M: 07758-648264 E: nijo.hodge@blueyonder.co.uk

HODGE, Canon Michael Robert. b 34. Pemb Coll Cam BA 57 MA 61. Ridley Hall Cam 57. **d** 59 **p** 60. C Harpurhey Ch Ch *Man* 59; C Blackpool St Mark *Blackb* 59–62; V Stalybridge Old St Geo *Man* 62–67; R Cobham w Luddesdowne and Dode *Roch* 67–81; Hon Can Roch Cathl 81–99; R Bidborough 81–99; rtd 99; Hon C Chale *Portsm* 99–06; Hon C Gatcombe 99–06; Hon C Shorwell w Kingston 99–06; Asst to RD W Wight 99–06; PtO from 06. *Braxton Cottage, Halletts Shute, Norton, Yarmouth PO41 0RH* T/F: (01983) 761121 M: 07941-232983 E: michael.hodge.1954@pem.cam.ac.uk

HODGES, Christina Caroline. *See* FFRENCH-HODGES, Christina Caroline

HODGES, Ian Morgan. b 72. Glam Univ BSc 95 Cam Univ BTh(Min) 05. Ridley Hall Cam. **d** 05 **p** 06. C Llantrisant *Llan* 05–11; R Llanilid w Pencoed from 11; AD Bridgend from 18. *The Rectory, 60 Coychurch Road, Pencoed, Bridgend CF35 5NA* T: (01656) 860337 E: revian@lphparish.org.uk

HODGES, Preb Jane Anne Christine. b 62. Leeds Univ BA 84. SEITE 06. **d** 09 **p** 10. C Poplar *Lon* 09–11; TV 11–15; TR from 15; AD Tower Hamlets from 20; Preb St Paul's Cathl from 20. *164 St Leonard's Road, London E14 6PW* T: (020) 7538 9198 E: revjanehodges@hotmail.com

HODGES, Jasper Tor. b 62. Leeds Univ BSc 84 Sheff Univ MEng 85 Lon Univ PGCE 87. Trin Coll Bris BA 94. **d** 94 **p** 95. C Holbeck *Ripon* 94–97; C Ealing St Steph Castle Hill *Lon* 97–04; V Arbourthorne and Norfolk Park *Sheff* 04–18. *All Hallows, Church Lane, High Hoyland, Barnsley S75 4BJ* M: 07850-660513 E: jasplive@gmail.com

HODGES, Keith Michael. b 53. Southn Univ BTh 82 Heythrop Coll Lon MA 04. Chich Th Coll 77. **d** 80 **p** 81. C Sydenham St Phil *S'wark* 80–84; PtO 85; C Leatherhead *Guildf* 86–89; V Aldershot St Aug 89–20; rtd 20; PtO *Guildf* from 20; *Chich* from 20. *4A Normanton Avenue, Bognor Regis PO21 2TX* T: (01243) 862120 E: fatherkeith20@outlook.com

HODGES, Wayne Anthony. **d** 90 **p** 91. PtO *Ban* 17–18; C Bro Ardudwy 18–19; V from 19. *The Vicarage, Porthmadog LL49 9PA* T: (01766) 513187 E: awdhodges63@gmail.com

HODGETT, Ms Tina Elizabeth. b 64. St Mary's Coll Dur BA 88 Leic Univ MBA 05 Cam Univ BTh 08 Sheff Univ PGCE 90. Ridley Hall Cam 06. **d** 08 **p** 09. C Bestwood Em w St Mark *S'well* 08–11; TV Portishead *B & W* 11–17; Evang and Pioneer Team Ldr from 17. *Flourish House, 2 Cathedral Avenue, Wells BA5 1FD* T: (01749) 685105 M: 07759-909106 E: tina.hodgett@bathwells.anglican.org

HODGETTS, Canon Alan Paul. b 54. Birm Poly BSc 78 Heythrop Coll Lon MA 96. St Steph Ho Ox 79. **d** 82 **p** 83. C Perry Barr *Birm* 82–85; C Broseley w Benthall *Heref* 85–87; V Effingham w Lt Bookham *Guildf* 87–96; R Merrow 96–06; Managing Chapl HM Pris Woodhill 06–19; Hon Can Ch Ch *Ox* 16–19; rtd 19; PtO *Ox* from 19. *Address withheld by request*

HODGETTS, Colin William John. b 40. MBE 18. St D Coll Lamp BA 61. Ripon Hall Ox 61. **d** 63 **p** 64. C Hackney St Jo *Lon* 63–68; Hon C St Martin-in-the-Fields 70–76; C Creeksea w Althorne *Chelmsf* 76–79; PtO *Ex* 84–03; C Parkham, Alwington, Buckland Brewer etc 03–07; AD Gambella Ethiopia 11–12; rtd 12; PtO *Ex* 12–17; P-in-c Abbotsham 17–18; PtO *Edin* from 18. *5 Brunton Terrace, Edinburgh EH7 5EH* E: colin@colinhodgetts.co.uk

HODGETTS, Harry Samuel. b 30. Chich Th Coll 63. **d** 65 **p** 66. C Harton Colliery *Dur* 65–68; C Penzance St Mary Truro 68–70; V Penwerris 70–79; V Kettering St Mary *Pet* 79–94; rtd 95; PtO *Win* 03–09. *The Flat, Etal Manor, Etal, Cornhill-on-Tweed TD12 4TL* T: (01890) 820378

HODGINS, Miss Kylie Anne. b 68. SEITE 98 Ridley Hall Cam 00. **d** 02 **p** 03. C Histon and Impington *Ely* 02–07; Chapl Sherborne Sch for Girls 07–08; P-in-c Cottenham *Ely* 08–16; P-in-c Rampton 09–16; V Bricket Wood *St Alb* from 16. *20 West Riding, Bricket Wood, St Albans AL2 3QP* E: kh2@gumnut.me.uk

HODGINS, Philip Arthur. b 57. Lanc Univ BA 78 Bradf Univ MBA 90 MCIPD 94. Linc Th Coll 82. **d** 85 **p** 86. C Norton *Ches* 85–88; C Whitkirk *Ripon* 88–89; PtO *Bradf* 89–90; *Chich* 91–02; Hon C Chiddingly w E Hoathly 02–04; P-in-c 04–09; R from 09; RD Uckfield 06–11. *The Rectory, Rectory Close, East Hoathly, Lewes BN8 6EG* T: (01825) 840270 E: philhodgins@btinternet.com

HODGKINS, Christopher Thomas Alan. b 73. Westcott Ho Cam. **d** 13 **p** 14. C G7 Benefice *Cant* 13–16; C Tenterden, Rother and Oxney 16–21; Rural Business Chapl 16–21; TR Romney Marsh from 21; AD Romney and Tenterden from 21. *The Vicarage, North Street, New Romney TN28 8DR*

HODGKINSON, Mrs Jennifer Mary. b 57. **d** 12 **p** 13. OLM Cromer *Nor* from 12. *29 Fulcher Avenue, Cromer NR27 9SG* T: (01263) 510153 E: jenniehodgkinson1997@gmail.com

HODGKINSON, John David. b 57. Birm Univ BA 78 Edin Univ BD 89. Edin Th Coll 86. **d** 89 **p** 90. C Briercliffe *Blackb* 89–92; C Darwen St Cuth w Tockholes St Steph 92–94; R Harrington *Carl* 94–00; V Walney Is 00–12; TV N Barrow 12–17; P-in-c Barrow St Jo 15–17; rtd 17; PtO *Carl* from 17. *St Francis House, 158 Schneider Road, Barrow-in-Furness LA14 5ER*

HODGSON, Ms Amanda Jane. b 66. Westmr Coll Ox BA 88 Heythrop Coll Lon MA 99. Westcott Ho Cam 94. **d** 96 **p** 97. C Epping Distr *Chelmsf* 96–01; TV Wythenshawe *Man* 01–07; R Streatham St Leon *S'wark* 07–16; TR Wimbledon from 16; Adv for Women's Min Kingston Area from 12. *14 Arthur Road, London SW19 7DZ* T: (020) 8946 2830 *or* 8946 2605 E: rector@stmaryswimbledon.org

HODGSON, Antony. b 66. Dundee Univ MA 88 Jes Coll Cam BA 92 MA 96 Lanc Univ MA 04 K Coll Lon MPhil 10 AKC 10 Lambeth PhD 15 FSAScot 15 Cen Lancs Univ PGCE 21. Westcott Ho Cam 90 Ven English Coll Rome 92. **d** 93 **p** 94. C Chorley St Geo *Blackb* 93–96; C Lytham St Cuth 96–99; V St Annes St Marg from 99. *St Margaret's Vicarage, 24 Chatsworth Road, Lytham St Annes FY8 2JN* T: (01253) 728711 E: antonyantioch76@gmail.com

HODGSON, Barbara Elizabeth. b 46. N Riding Coll of Educn BEd 85. NEOC 06. **d** 08 **p** 09. NSM Bridlington Em

York 08–11; NSM Burton Fleming w Fordon, Grindale etc 11–15; NSM Rudston, Boynton, Carnaby etc from 15. *79 St James Road, Bridlington YO15 3PQ* M: 07734-467174 E: vidara1972@talktalk.net

HODGSON, Canon David Peter. b 56. Fitzw Coll Cam BA 77 MA 81 Nottm Univ BA 82 MTh 85. St Jo Coll Nottm 80. **d** 83 **p** 84. C Guiseley w Esholt *Bradf* 83–86; Asst Chapl Loughb Univ *Leic* 86–89; P-in-c Hatfield Broad Oak *Chelmsf* 89–90; P-in-c Bush End 89–90; P-in-c Hatfield Broad Oak and Bush End 90–97; Ind Chapl Harlow 89–97; R Wokingham All SS *Ox* from 97; AD Sonning 04–13; Hon Can Ch Ch from 09. *The Rectory, 2A Norreys Avenue, Wokingham RG40 1TU* T: 0118-979 2999 E: david@allsaintswokingham.org.uk

HODGSON, Canon Gary Stuart. b 65. Ridley Hall Cam 95. **d** 98 **p** 99. C S Ossett *Wakef* 98–01; V Kirkburton 01–07; Chapl Huddersfield Univ and Hon C Fixby and Cowcliffe 07–09; P-in-c Cottingley *Bradf* 09–14; V 14; *Leeds* 14–16; RD Airedale *Bradf* 10–14; AD *Leeds* 14–16; R Tong and Laisterdyke from 16; Hon Can Bradf Cathl from 13. *The Vicarage, 74 Holme Wood Road, Bradford BD4 9EJ* E: gshodgson@sky.com

HODGSON, John. b 35. St Jo Coll Cam MA 62 Lon Univ BD 61. St Deiniol's Hawarden 80. **d** 81 **p** 82. Hon C Padiham *Blackb* 81–84; C W Burnley All SS 85–87; V 87–95; rtd 95; PtO *Worc* 95–02; *Glouc* 98–02; *Win* from 12. *33 Ticonderoga Gardens, Southampton SO19 9HB* T: (023) 8043 2895

HODGSON, Julia Ruth. *See* HICKS, Julia Ruth

HODKINSON, George Leslie. b 48. Qu Coll Birm 86. **d** 88 **p** 89. C Hall Green St Pet *Birm* 88–91; TV Solihull 91–96; P-in-c Billesley Common 96–00; V 00–05; AD Moseley 01–02; rtd 05; Chapl Countess of Chester Hosp NHS Foundn Trust 05–11; Chapl Cheshire and Wirral Partnership NHS Foundn Trust 05–11; PtO *Lich* 09–21. *2 Birch Close, Four Crosses, Llanymynech SY22 6NH* T: (01691) 839946

HODKINSON, Thomas Martyn. b 92. St Mellitus Coll BA 17 Trin Coll Bris MA 20. **d** 20 **p** 21. C Bournemouth St Clem *Win* from 20. *St Clement's Vicarage, St Clement's Road, Bournemouth BH1 4DZ* M: 07817-141779 E: tom.hodkinson@lovechurch.org.uk or tomhodkinson@hotmail.com

HODSON, Gordon George. b 35. St Chad's Coll Dur BA 59. **d** 60 **p** 61. C Tettenhall Regis *Lich* 60–64; C Rugeley 64–68; V Shrewsbury St Mich 68–74; V Kinnerley w Melverley 74–87; P-in-c Knockin w Maesbrook 75–87; P-in-c Chesbey 87–91; P-in-c Seighford, Derrington and Cresswell 87–91; V Chebsey, Ellenhall and Seighford-with-Creswell 91–00; rtd 00; PtO *Lich* 01–21. *27 Oak Drive, Oswestry SY11 2RU* T: (01691) 662849

HODSON, Keith. b 53. Hatf Coll Dur BA 74. Wycliffe Hall Ox 77. **d** 80 **p** 81. C Ashton-upon-Mersey St Mary Magd *Ches* 80–84; C Polegate *Chich* 84–92; V Baddesley Ensor w Grendon *Birm* 92–08; R Beckbury, Badger, Kemberton, Ryton, Stockton etc *Lich* from 08; RD Edgmond and Shifnal 10–19. *The Rectory, Beckbury, Shifnal TF11 9DG* T: (01952) 750474 E: keithhodson@talk21.com

HODSON, Mrs Margot Rosemary. b 60. Bris Univ BSc 82 PGCE 83 Ox Brookes Univ BA 06. All Nations Chr Coll 87 SAOMC 99. **d** 01 **p** 02. C Grove *Ox* 01–04; Chapl Jes Coll Ox 04–09; P-in-c Haddenham w Cuddington, Kingsey etc *Ox* 09–16; R Wychert Vale 16–19; C Shill Valley and Broadshire from 19; Dir Th and Educn The John Ray Initiative from 19. *The Vicarage, Filkins, Lechlade GL7 3JQ* E: margot.hodson@jri.org.uk

HODSON, Canon Raymond Leslie. b 42. St Chad's Coll Dur BSc 64. **d** 66 **p** 67. C Adlington *Blackb* 66–68; C Cleveleys 68–72; V Ewood 72–77; V Nazeing *Chelmsf* 77–84; R Ampthill w Millbrook and Steppingley *St Alb* 84–95; Chapl Madrid *Eur* 95–04; Can Gib Cathl 02–04; rtd 04. *Los Alcazares 3, 03726 Benitachell (Alicante), Spain* M: (0034) 607 706 904 E: m2813341g@yahoo.co.uk

HODSON, Trevor. b 57. Sheff Univ BA 78 Padgate Coll of Educn PGCE 79 Leeds Univ MA 06. NOC 04. **d** 06 **p** 07. NSM Broadheath *Ches* 06–13; NSM Latchford Ch Ch 13–18; PtO *Liv* 18; TV Lowton and Golborne from 18. *40 Riversdale, Woolston, Warrington WA1 4PZ* T: (01925) 811952 M: 07935-198009 E: th57dearden@outlook.com

HOEY, David Paul. b 57. MBE 20. QUB BD 79. CITC 79. **d** 81 **p** 82. C Belfast Whiterock *Conn* 81–83; C Portadown St Mark *Arm* 83–84; I Cleenish w Mullaghdun *Clogh* 84–90; I Magheracross 90–03; Dir of Ords 91–03; Can Clogh Cathl 95–03; Min Consultant for Ireland CPAS 03–11; I Faughanvale *D & R* from 15; Can Derry Cathl from 18. *St Canice's Rectory, 21 Main Street, Eglinton, Londonderry BT47 3AB* T: (028) 7181 2462 E: dphoey@btinternet.com

HOEY, William Thomas. b 32. CITC 64. **d** 66 **p** 67. C Belfast St Mary *Conn* 66–68; C Lisburn Ch Ch 69–72; I Ballinderry

72–78; I Belfast St Simon w St Phil 78–02; rtd 02. *11 Cairnshill Court, Belfast BT8 6TX* T: (028) 9079 0595

HOFBAUER, Canon Andrea Martina. b 71. Johannes Gutenberg Univ Mainz Ox Univ MTh 04. St Steph Ho Ox 00. **d** 02 **p** 03. C Teignmouth, Ideford w Luton, Ashcombe etc *Ex* 02–05; Chapl Ex Univ 05–09; Tutor SWMTC 05–09; PV Ex Cathl 06–09; Prec Wakef Cathl 09–15; P-in-c Leeds All So and St Aid 15–16; V Leeds St Aid from 16; Hon Can Bradf Cathl from 17. *9 Parkside Green, Leeds LS6 4NY* E: andihofb@gmail.com

HOFFMANN, Miss Rosalind Mary. b 49. **d** 10 **p** 11. OLM Loddon, Sisland, Chedgrave, Hardley and Langley *Nor* 10–19; rtd 19; PtO *Nor* from 19. *Oakhurst, Briar Lane, Hales, Norwich NR14 6SY* T: (01508) 548200 E: ros@hoffman2011.plus.com

HOFREITER, Christian. b 75. Innsbruck Univ MPhil 99 MPhil 01 Wycliffe Hall Ox BA 08 MA 12 Keble Coll Ox MSt 09 DPhil 14. Ox Min Course 09. **d** 10 **p** 10. NSM Ox St Aldate 10–13; PtO *Eur* from 13. *Ebendorferstrasse 8/1, A-1220 Vienna, Austria* E: ch@citykirche.wien

HOGAN, Edward James Martin. b 46. Trin Coll Bris. **d** 85 **p** 86. C St Austell *Truro* 85–88; V Gt Broughton and Broughton Moor *Carl* 88–94; V St Stythians w Perranarworthal and Gwennap *Truro* 94–10; RD Carnmarth N 03–08; rtd 10; PtO *Heref* 15–18. *444 Buckfield Road, Leominster HR6 8SD* T: (01568) 620064 E: martin@houseofhogan.org or martinhogan@gmail.com

HOGAN, Miss Jennie. b 75. Goldsmiths' Coll Lon BA 99 Fitzw Coll Cam BA 03. Westcott Ho Cam 01. **d** 04 **p** 05. C Westmr St Steph w St Jo *Lon* 04–07; C All Hallows by the Tower etc 07–09; Chapl Univ of the Arts 07–20; Chapl Lon Goodenough Trust 09–20; C St Giles Cripplegate w St Bart Moor Lane etc from 11; C Bloomsbury St Geo w Woburn Square Ch Ch from 18; PtO *S'wark* 08–10. *24 Coopers Lane, London NW1 1HA* M: 07515-486806

HOGARTH, Alan Francis. b 58. Oak Hill Th Coll BA 89. **d** 89 **p** 90. C Felixstowe SS Pet and Paul *St E* 89–93; R Beckington w Standerwick, Berkley, Rodden etc *B & W* 93–04; P-in-c Basildon w Aldworth and Ashampstead *Ox* 04–08; P-in-c Heapey and Withnell *Blackb* 08–12; V from 12. *34 Kittiwake Road, Heapey, Chorley PR6 9BA* T: (01257) 231868 E: alan.hogarth@gmail.com

HOGG, Matthew. b 79. **d** 08 **p** 09. C Brompton H Trin w Onslow Square St Paul *Lon* 08–10; C Hammersmith St Paul 10–11; P-in-c Fulham St Alb w St Aug 11–13; V 13–21; Leadership Enabler CPAS from 21. *CPAS, Unit 3, Sovereign Court 1, Sir William Lyons Road, University of Warwick Science Park, Coventry CV4 7EZ* T: 0300-123 0780

HOGG, Neil Richard. b 46. BSc 69. Ridley Hall Cam 82. **d** 84 **p** 85. C Bingham *S'well* 84–87; TV Bushbury *Lich* 87–00; V Worksop St Jo *S'well* 00–11; rtd 11; PtO *York* from 18. *4 Lowick, York YO24 2RF* M: 07585-816697 E: hogg350@btinternet.com

HOGG, William John. b 49. New Coll Ox MA 71 Lon Univ CertEd 72 Crewe & Alsager Coll MSc 88. Edin Th Coll 86. **d** 88 **p** 89. C Oxton *Ches* 88–93; R Bromborough 93–04; P-in-c Radlett *St Alb* 04–05; TR Aldenham, Radlett and Shenley 05–12; rtd 12; PtO *St And* from 12. *Craigwood, Brae Street, Dunkeld PH8 0BA* T: (01350) 727053 E: wijoho@btinternet.com

HOGG, William Ritson. b 47. Leeds Univ BSc 69. Qu Coll Birm. **d** 72 **p** 73. C Bordesley St Oswald *Birm* 72–76; TV Seacroft *Ripon* 76–82; V Hunslet St Mary 82–88; V Catterick 88–97; rtd 07. *c/o Crockford, Church House, 27 Great Smith Street, London SW1P 3AZ* E: bill.denise@yahoo.co.uk

HOGGARD, Mrs Jean Margaret. b 36. NW Ord Course 76. **dss** 79 **d** 87 **p** 94. Northowram *Wakef* 79–94; Par Dn 87–94; C Ovenden 94–00; rtd 00; PtO *Wakef* 01–14; *Leeds* from 14. *13 Joseph Avenue, Northowram, Halifax HX3 7HJ* T: (01422) 201475

HOGGER, Clive Duncan. b 70. Sheff Univ BA 92. Ridley Hall Cam 06. **d** 08 **p** 09. C Fletchamstead *Cov* 08–11; TV Cov E 11–16; R Cov All SS 16–21; AD Cov E 14–18; Acting Adn Cov 17–18; Assoc Adn Doncaster *Sheff* from 21. *18 Central Boulevard, Doncaster DN2 5PE* E: clive.hogger@gmail.com

HOGGER-GADSBY, Alison. b 71. **d** 14 **p** 15. C Coventry Caludon *Cov* 14–18; V Foleshill St Paul from 18; Chapl K Henry VIII Sch Cov from 15; Tutor St Mellitus Coll from 21. *St Margaret's Vicarage, 18 South Avenue, Coventry CV2 4DR* M: 07788-593805 E: alison.hogger@gmail.com

HOLBEN, Bruce Frederick. b 45. STETS 99. **d** 02 **p** 03. NSM W Wittering and Birdham w Itchenor *Chich* from 02. *3 Elmstead Gardens, West Wittering, Chichester PO20 8NG* T: (01243) 514129 M: 07940-759060

HOLBIRD, Derek John. b 50. **d** 17 **p** 18. C Churt and Hindhead *Guildf* from 17. *The Old School House, Fieldway, Haslemere GU27 2AX* T: (01428) 642988

HOLBIRD, Thomas James. b 79. Leeds Univ BSc 00 Cam Univ BTh 11. Ridley Hall Cam 08. **d** 11 **p** 12. C Gerrards Cross and Fulmer *Ox* 11–15; C Brighton St Pet *Chich* from 15; P-in-c Brighton St Matthias from 17. *45 Hollingbury Park Avenue, Brighton BN1 7JQ* T: (01273) 553246 M: 07870-682853 E: tomh@stpetersbrighton.org

HOLBROOK, Canon Barbara Mary. b 58. Nottm Trent Univ BA 94 Nottm Univ MA 04. EMMTC 02. **d** 04 **p** 05. C Chesterfield H Trin and Ch Ch *Derby* 04–08; P-in-c Kimberley *S'well* 08–15; P-in-c Nuthall 08–15; R Kimberley and Nuthall from 15; Hon Can S'well Minster from 13. *The Rectory, 1 Eastwood Road, Kimberley, Nottingham NG16 2HX* T: 0115-938 3565 M: 07766-732514

✠**HOLBROOK, The Rt Revd John Edward.** b 62. St Pet Coll Ox BA 83 MA 87. Ridley Hall Cam 82. **d** 86 **p** 87 **c** 11. C Barnes St Mary *S'wark* 86–89; C Bletchley *Ox* 89–93; C N Bletchley CD 89–93; V Adderbury w Milton 93–02; RD Deddington 00–02; R Wimborne Minster *Sarum* 02–11; P-in-c Witchampton, Stanbridge and Long Crichel etc 02–11; P-in-c Horton, Chalbury, Hinton Martel and Holt St Jas 06–11; RD Wimborne 04–11; Chapl S and E Dorset Primary Care Trust 02–11; Can and Preb Sarum Cathl 06–11; Suff Bp Brixworth *Pet* from 11; Can Pet Cathl from 11. *Orchard Acre, 11 North Street, Mears Ashby, Northampton NN6 0DW* T: (01733) 562492 E: bishop.brixworth@peterborough-diocese.org.uk

HOLCOMBE, Canon Graham William Arthur. b 50. Open Univ BA 99. St Mich Coll Llan. **d** 80 **p** 81. C Neath w Llantwit *Llan* 80–84; Asst Youth Chapl 81–84; PV Llan Cathl 84–86; V Pentyrch 86–00; V Pentyrch w Capel Llanilltterne 00–02; Can Llan Cathl 02–14; Can Res from 14. *1 White House, Cathedral Green, Llandaff, Cardiff CF5 2EB* T: (029) 2056 9521 E: grahamw.holcombe@gmail.com

HOLDAWAY, Graham Michael. b 51. Southn Univ BSc 73. Sarum & Wells Th Coll 74. **d** 77 **p** 78. C Walton-on-Thames *Guildf* 77–81; TV Westborough 81–86; PtO 86–01; NSM Walton-on-Thames 01–02; rtd 06. *7 Mampitts Lane, Shaftesbury SP7 8FN* E: grahamholdaway@mac.com

HOLDAWAY, Mark Daniel James. b 78. Selw Coll Cam BA 99 MA 02. Oak Hill Th Coll BA 07. **d** 07 **p** 08. C Bury St Edmunds St Mary *St E* 07–11; R Kirby-le-Soken w Gt Holland *Chelmsf* from 11. *The Rectory, 10 Thorpe Road, Kirby Cross, Frinton-on-Sea CO13 0LT* T: (01255) 675997 E: mdjholdaway@gmail.com

HOLDAWAY, Canon Stephen Douglas. b 45. Hull Univ BA 67. Ridley Hall Cam 67. **d** 70 **p** 71. C Southampton Thornhill St Chris *Win* 70–73; C Tardebigge *Worc* 73–78; Ind Chapl 73–78; Ind Chapl *Linc* 78–93; Co-ord City Cen Group Min 81–93; TR Louth *Linc* 93–11; RD Louthesk 95–11; rtd 11; Can and Preb Linc Cathl from 00. *36 Wesley Way, Horncastle LN9 6RY* E: stephen.holdaway@btinternet.com

HOLDEN, Christopher Charles. b 54. **d** 11 **p** 12. OLM Codnor *Derby* 11–19; OLM Horsley and Denby 11–19; OLM Denby Gp from 19. *62 Waingroves Road, Waingroves, Ripley DE5 9TD* T: (01773) 746411 E: cholden123@aol.com

HOLDEN, James. b 87. Keble Coll Ox BA 09. Ripon Coll Cuddesdon 15. **d** 17 **p** 18. C Ludgershall and Faberstown *Sarum* 17–18; C Ludgershall and Tidworth 18–21; TV Dorchester and the Winterbournes from 21. *17A Edward Road, Dorchester DT1 2HL*

HOLDEN, James Bryan. b 60. Sheff Univ BA 81. St Steph Ho Ox 14. **d** 16 **p** 20. NSM Claverdon w Preston Bagot *Cov* from 16; NSM Wootton Wawen from 16; C Aston Cantlow and Wilmcote w Billesley 18–19; NSM from 21; Bp's Officer Business Ldr from 21. *49 Cocksparrow Street, Warwick CV34 4ED* M: 07767-321086 E: james.holden@leader.co.uk

HOLDEN, Jennifer. b 80. SOAS BA 03 K Coll Lon PhD 10 New Coll Edin MDiv 19. Scottish Episc Inst 16. **d** 19 **p** 20. C Aberdeen St Jo *Ab* from 19. *8 Hammersmith Road, Aberdeen AB10 6NB* M: 07984-891894 E: jenniferaholden@gmail.com *or* revjennyholden@gmail.com

HOLDEN, Canon John. b 33. MBE 76. Sheff Univ MA 02 ACMA 62. Ridley Hall Cam 65 Selly Oak Coll 71. **d** 67 **p** 68. C Flixton St Jo CD *Man* 67–71; Uganda 71–75; V Aston SS Pet and Paul *Birm* 75–87; RD Aston 86–87; Hon Can Birm Cathl 86–87; R Ulverston St Mary w H Trin *Carl* 87–98; RD Furness 90–94; Hon Can Carl Cathl 91–94; rtd 98; PtO *Carl* 98–16; *Heref* from 99. *3 Alison Road, Church Stretton SY6 7AT* T: (01694) 724167

HOLDEN, Mark Noel. b 61. Collingwood Coll Dur BA 82 Birm Univ MA 95 Edin Univ CQSW 85 Warwick Univ TCert 93. Qu Coll Birm 93. **d** 95 **p** 96. C Brumby *Linc* 95–99; P-in-c Wragby 99–00; R Wragby Gp from 00; RD Horncastle from 12. *The Vicarage, Church Street, Wragby, Lincoln LN8 5RA* T: (01673) 857825

HOLDEN, Paul Edward. b 53. BSc 75 CEng 79 MIM MIBF. Trin Coll Bris 83. **d** 86 **p** 87. C Harpurhey Ch Ch *Man* 86–88; C Harpurhey St Steph 88–93; Sen Min Harpurhey LEP 88–93. *2 Baywood Street, Harpurhey, Manchester M9 5XJ* T: 0161-205 2938

HOLDEN, Richard Gary. **d** 04 **p** 05. C Louth *Linc* 04–07; P-in-c Clee 07–16; P-in-c Cleethorpes St Aid 07–16; R Skegness Gp from 16; RD Calcewaithe and Candleshoe from 20. *The Parsonage, 18 Danial Close, Skegness PE25 1RQ* E: richard.holden70@ntlworld.com

HOLDEN, Mrs Rita. b 45. SAOMC 98. **d** 01 **p** 03. OLM Burghfield *Ox* 01–02; NSM Droitwich Spa *Worc* 02–15; PtO from 15. *40 Nightingale Close, Droitwich WR9 7HB* T: (01905) 772787 M: 07814-621389 E: rita.openv@btinternet.com

HOLDEN, Tony. b 55. Lindisfarne Regional Tr Partnership 07. **d** 16 **p** 17. NSM Esh and Hamsteels *Dur* 16–19; NSM Langley Park 16–19; NSM Waterhouses 16–19; NSM Lumley from 19; NSM E Rainton from 19; NSM W Rainton from 19; NSM Chilton Moor from 20. *The Rectory, South Street, West Rainton, Houghton le Spring DH4 6PA* M: 07425-150040 E: tonyholden709@gmail.com

HOLDER, Adèle Claire. See REES, Adèle Claire

HOLDER, John William. b 41. Chester Coll CertEd 61 Open Univ BA 73 Bath Univ MEd 85. Trin Coll Bris MA 94. **d** 87 **p** 88. C Brockworth *Glouc* 87–91; P-in-c Avening w Cherington 91–95; V Cinderford St Jo 95–05; P-in-c Lydbrook 99–03; P-in-c Coberley, Cowley, Colesbourne and Elkstone 05–13; Hon Can Glouc Cathl 03–13; rtd 13; PtO *Ex* from 13. *8 Elmfield Road, Seaton EX12 2EG* T: (01297) 24351 E: canon.john@holder-net.co.uk

HOLDER, Jonathan Mark. b 83. Ox Brookes Univ BA 08. Trin Coll Bris 16. **d** 19 **p** 20. C Turnham Green Ch Ch *Lon* from 19. *64A Grove Park Road, London W4 3SB* M: 07590-013277 E: jon@christchurchw4.com

HOLDER, Mrs Lydia Jayne. b 89. Univ Coll Falmouth BA 11. Trin Coll Bris BA 19. **d** 19 **p** 20. C Turnham Green Ch Ch *Lon* from 19. *64A Grove Park Road, London W4 3SB* M: 07443-564286 E: lydia@christchurchw4.com

HOLDER, Rodney Dennis. b 50. Trin Coll Cam BA 71 MA 75 MMath 11 Ch Ch Ox MA 75 DPhil 78 FRAS 75 CPhys 91 MInstP 91 CMath 95 FIMA 95. Wycliffe Hall Ox BA 96. **d** 97 **p** 98. C Long Compton, Whichford and Barton-on-the-Heath *Cov* 97–01; C Wolford w Burmington 97–01; C Cherington w Stourton 97–01; C Barcheston 97–01; PtO 01–02; P-in-c The Claydons *Ox* 02–05; Course Dir Faraday Inst for Science and Relig 06–13; rtd 13; PtO *Eur* from 02; *Ely* from 06. *44 St Margaret's Road, Girton, Cambridge CB3 0LT* T: (01223) 364577 E: drandmrsr.holder@virginmedia.com

HOLDER, Shirley Susan. b 50. Lon Univ CertEd 72 BEd 73. ERMC 19. **d** 20 **p** 20. NSM Cambridge Gt St Mary w St Mich *Ely* from 20. *44 St Margaret's Road, Girton, Cambridge CB3 0LT* T: (01223) 364577 M: 07876-752165 E: ssh49@gsm.cam.ac.uk

HOLDING (formerly SMITH), Georgina Leah. b 83. Nottm Univ BA 05 Ox Univ MTh 10. Ripon Coll Cuddesdon 07. **d** 10 **p** 11. C Gt and Lt Coates w Bradley *Linc* 10–14; TV Brereton and Rugeley w Armitage *Lich* 14–20; R Market Deeping *Linc* from 20. *The New Rectory, 13 Church Street, Market Deeping, Peterborough PE6 8DA* E: rev.georgeholding@hotmail.com

HOLDING, Kenneth George Frank. b 27. Sarum & Wells Th Coll 75. **d** 77 **p** 78. C Bexley St Mary *Roch* 77–80; Min Joydens Wood St Barn CD 80–85; R Mereworth w W Peckham 85–92; rtd 92; PtO *York* 92–04; P-in-c Willerby w Ganton and Folkton 04–18. *Address temp unknown*

HOLDRIDGE, The Ven Bernard Lee. b 35. Lich Th Coll 64. **d** 67 **p** 68. C Swinton *Sheff* 67–71; V Doncaster St Jude 71–81; R Rawmarsh w Parkgate 81–88; RD Rotherham 86–88; V Worksop Priory *S'well* 88–94; adn Doncaster *Sheff* 94–01; rtd 01; PtO *Sheff* 01–06; *Guildf* 06–15. *35 Denehyrst Court, York Road, Guildford GU1 4EA* T: (01483) 570791

HOLDSTOCK, Canon Adrian Charles. b 51. Peterho Cam BA MA 75 Nottm Univ MA 03 CMgr FCMI. EMMTC 00. **d** 03 **p** 04. NSM Bosworth and Sheepy Gp *Leic* 03–12; NSM Nailstone and Carlton w Shackerstone 07–12; P-in-c Pet St Mark 12–16; V from 16; Asst Dir Ords from 14; Can Pet Cathl from 20. *The Vicarage, 82 Lincoln Road, Peterborough PE1 2SN* M: 07792-452669 E: adrian.holdstock@peterborough-diocese.org

HOLDSWORTH, Canon Ian Scott. b 52. Sheff Poly BA 75. Oak Hill Th Coll BA 81. **d** 81 **p** 82. C Denham *Ox* 81–84; P-in-c S Leigh 84–89; P-in-c Cogges 84–88; V 88–89; PtO *Pet* 95; NSM Brackley St Pet w St Jas 96–99; P-in-c Northampton St Mary 99–04; V 04–19; Can Pet Cathl 17–19; rtd 19; PtO *York* from 20. *62 Cardigan Road, Bridlington YO15 3JT* T: (01262) 308078 M: 07912-639980 E: canonianh@gmail.com

HOLDSWORTH, Canon John Ivor. b 49. Univ of Wales (Abth) BA 70 Univ of Wales (Cardiff) BD 73 MTh 75 Univ of Wales (Lamp) PhD 96. St Mich Coll Llan 70. **d** 73 **p** 74. C Newport St Paul *Mon* 73–77; CF (TAVR) 75–90; V Abercraf and Callwen

S & B 77–86; Bp's Chapl for Th Educn 80–97; V Gorseinon 86–97; Hon Lect Th Univ of Wales (Swansea) 88–96; Prin and Warden St Mich Coll Llan 97–03; Lect Th Cardiff Univ *Llan* 97–10; Adn St D and V Steynton *St D* 03–10; Adn Cyprus, Chapl Larnaca and Exec Adn Cyprus and the Gulf 10–19; rtd 19; Dir Min Cyprus and the Gulf from 19; Can Th Nicosia from 19. *Ty Newydd, Llansaint, Kidwelly SA17 5HZ* T: (01267) 267350 *or* (00357) (22) 671220 M: (00357) 99-658147 E: archdeaconjohn32@gmail.com

HOLDSWORTH, The Very Revd Kelvin. b 66. Man Poly BSc 89 St Andr Univ BD 92 Edin Univ MTh 96. TISEC 95. d 97 p 98. Prec St Ninian's Cathl Perth *St And* 97–00; R Bridge of Allan 00–06; Chapl Stirling Univ 00–06; Provost St Mary's Cathl *Glas* from 06; R Glas St Mary from 06. *300 Great Western Road, Glasgow G4 9JB* T: 0141-530 8643 E: provost@thecathedral.org.uk

HOLE, Amy Margaret Sinclair. b 73. Edin Univ MA 95 K Coll Lon MA 96. St Hild Coll 17. d 21. C Crookes St Tim *Sheff* from 21; C Sheffield Vine from 21. *St Chad's Vicarage, 9 Linden Avenue, Sheffield S8 0GA* T: 0114-221 6867 M: 07906-312997 E: amy@sttims.org.uk *or* amy@thevinesheffield.org.uk

HOLE, The Very Revd Derek Norman. b 33. De Montfort Univ Hon DLitt 99 Leic Univ Hon LLD 05. Linc Th Coll 57. d 60 p 61. C Knighton St Mary Magd *Leic* 60–62; Dom Chapl to Abp Cape Town 62–64; C Kenilworth St Nic *Cov* 64–67; R Burton Latimer *Pet* 67–73; V Leic St Jas 73–92; Hon Can Leic Cathl 83–92; RD Christianity S 83–92; Provost Leic 92–99; Chapl to The Queen 85–93; rtd 99; PtO *Leic* 00–20. *25 Southernhay Close, Leicester LE2 3TW* T: 0116-270 9988 M: 07799-892615 E: dnhole@btinternet.com

HOLE, Samuel Richard. b 84. Trin Hall Cam BA 06 MA 10 PGCE 07 K Coll Lon MA 11 Selw Coll Cam PhD 16. Westcott Ho Cam 12. d 16 p 17. C S'wark St Geo w St Alphege and St Jude 16–19; C Chelsea St Luke and Ch Ch *Lon* from 19. *29 Burnsall Street, London SW3 3SR* M: 07792-786442 E: samhole@gmail.com *or* samhole@chelseaparish.org

HOLE, Toby Kenton. b 72. Dur Univ BA 94 MA 95 Cam Univ BTh 06. Ridley Hall Cam 03. d 06 p 07. C Islington St Mary *Lon* 06–10; V Woodseats St Chad *Sheff* from 10; C Norton 17–20; P-in-c from 20; C Greenhill from 17; C Norton Lees St Paul from 17; AD Ecclesall 14–20. *St Chad's Vicarage, 9 Linden Avenue, Sheffield S8 0GA* T: 0114-274 9302 *or* 274 5086 M: 07906-312998 E: toby.hole@gmail.com *or* toby.hole@sheffield.anglican.org

HOLFORD, Canon Andrew Peter. b 62. Nottm Univ BSc 84. Cranmer Hall Dur 87. d 90 p 91. C Waltham Cross *St Alb* 90–93; C Northampton St Benedict *Pet* 93–95; V Pet Ch Carpenter 95–04; TR Baldock w Bygrave and Weston *St Alb* 04–13; R Baldock w Bygrave from 13; Hon Can St Alb from 18. *The Rectory, 9 Pond Lane, Baldock SG7 5AS* T: (01462) 896273 E: 2008luddite@googlemail.com

HOLFORD, Canon John Alexander. b 40. Chich Th Coll 65. d 67 p 68. C Cottingley *Bradf* 67–71; C Baildon 71–73; P-in-c Bingley H Trin 73–74; V 74–86; V Woodhall 86–93; C Shelf 93–94; TV Shelf w Buttershaw St Aid 94–99; rtd 99; P-in-c Embsay w Eastby *Bradf* 99–04; Hon Can Bradf Cathl 03–04; PtO 04–14; *Leeds* from 14. *3 Wheelwrights Court, Hellifield, Skipton BD23 4LX* T: (01729) 851740 E: john.holford720@gmail.com

HOLFORD, Margaret Sophia. b 39. SAOMC 95. d 98 p 99. NSM Stevenage St Andr and St Geo *St Alb* 98–03; NSM Ickleford w Holwell 03–05; NSM Holwell, Ickleford and Pirton from 05. *Icknield House, Westmill Lane, Ickleford, Hitchin SG5 3RN* T: (01462) 432794 F: 436618

HOLGATE, Audrey Elizabeth. b 60. NOC 04. d 07 p 08. NSM Ramsbottom and Edenfield *Man* 07–10; V Cadishead 10–21; Chapl Salford City Academy 10–21; rtd 21. *Address temp unknown* M: 07752-526140 E: kaynacg@aol.com

HOLGATE, Canon David Andrew. b 54. Cape Town Univ BA 77 Port Eliz Univ BA 89 Rhodes Univ MTh 90 PhD 94. All Nations Chr Coll 80. d 82 p 84. C Uitenhage St Kath S Africa 82–84; Asst P Port Elizabeth St Hugh 84–87; P-in-c Somerset E All SS 88–89; St Paul's Coll Grahamstown 90–93; CME Officer *Chelmsf* 93–96; P-in-c Felsted 93–96; V Felsted and Lt Dunmow 96–97; Dean of Studies STETS 97–14; Vice-Prin 01–11; Prin 11–14; Can Res Man Cathl from 14. *3 Booth Clibborn Court, Salford M7 4PJ* E: daholgate@googlemail.com

✠**HOLLAND, The Rt Revd Alfred Charles.** b 27. St Chad's Coll Dur BA 50. d 52 p 53 c 70. C W Hackney St Barn *Lon* 52–54; R Scarborough Australia 55–70; Asst Bp Perth 70–77; Bp Newcastle 78–92; rtd 92; Bp Jerusalem 93–94; Australia from 94. *21 Sullivan Crescent, Wanniassa ACT 2903, Australia* T: (0061) (2) 6231 8368 E: acjmholland@bigpond.com

✠**HOLLAND, The Rt Revd Edward.** b 36. AKC 64. d 65 p 66 c 86. C Dartford H Trin *Roch* 65–69; C Mill Hill Jo Keble Ch *Lon* 69–72; Prec Gib Cathl *Eur* 72–74; Chapl Naples Ch Ch 74–79; Chapl Bromley Hosp 79–86; V Bromley St Mark *Roch* 79–86; Suff Bp Eur 86–95; Dean Brussels 86–95; Area Bp Colchester *Chelmsf* 95–01; rtd 01; Hon Asst Bp Lon from 02; Hon Asst Bp Eur from 02. *37 Parfrey Street, London W6 9EW* T: (020) 8746 3636 E: ed.holland@uwclub.net

HOLLAND, Mrs Elizabeth Ann. b 91. Dur Univ BA 12. St Mellitus Coll 15. d 17 p 18. C Berkswell *Cov* 17–20; R Allesley from 20. *The Rectory, Rectory Lane, Allesley, Coventry CV5 9EQ* T: (024) 7640 2006 M: 07377-449873

HOLLAND, Mrs Gillaine. b 67. Kent Inst of Art & Design BA 89. STETS 05. d 08 p 09. C Epsom St Martin *Guildf* 08–09; C Woking St Mary 09–12; Asst Chapl HM Pris Send 11–12; Chapl St Columba's Retreat and Conf Cen 12–16; Pioneer Min *Guildf* from 16. *St Michael's Shared Church, Dartmouth Avenue, Woking GU21 5PJ* T: (01932) 341694 M: 07969-067116 E: rev.gillaine.holland@stmichaelssheerwater.org.uk

HOLLAND, Canon Glyn. b 59. Hull Univ BA Bris Univ CertEd. Coll of Resurr Mirfield 83. d 85 p 86. C Brighouse St Martin *Wakef* 85–89; V Ferrybridge 89–96; Chapl Pontefract Gen Infirmary 89–96; V Middlesbrough All SS *York* from 96; RD Middlesbrough from 21; Can and Preb York Minster from 21. *All Saints' Vicarage, 14 The Crescent, Middlesbrough TS5 6SQ* T: (01642) 820304 E: vicar@allsaintsmbro.co.uk

HOLLAND, Jesse Marvin Sean. b 66. Westmr Coll Ox MTh 03. Oak Hill Th Coll BA 97. d 98 p 99. C Thundersley *Chelmsf* 98–02; P-in-c Tedburn St Mary, Whitestone, Oldridge etc *Ex* 02–06; V Buller NZ 06–08; P-in-c Lyneham w Bradenstoke *Sarum* 08–10; Chapl RAF from 10. *Chaplaincy Services (RAF), HQ Air Command, RAF High Wycombe HP14 4UE* T: (01494) 496800 E: revdjmsholland@aol.com

HOLLAND, John Stuart. b 52. Sarum & Wells Th Coll 77. d 80 p 81. C Wylde Green *Birm* 80–83; C Swanage and Studland *Sarum* 83–85; P-in-c Handley w Pentridge 85–88; TV Preston w Sutton Poyntz, Littlemoor etc 88–95; P-in-c Failsworth St Jo *Man* 95–01; V Ashton Ch Ch 01–07; P-in-c Carbis Bay w Lelant *Truro* 07–10; P-in-c Towednack and Zennor 08–10; P-in-c Oswaldtwistle Immanuel and All SS *Blackb* 10–12; P-in-c Oswaldtwistle St Paul 10–12; V Oswaldtwistle 12–16; AD Accrington 14–16; rtd 16; PtO *Newc* from 16. *33 Tyelaw Meadows, Shilbottle, Alnwick NE66 2JJ* M: 07718-483817 E: johnholland703@yahoo.co.uk

HOLLAND, Lesley Anne. *See* LEON, Lesley Anne

HOLLAND, Mrs Lisa Jayne. b 67. RGN 94. Ridley Hall Cam 16. d 18 p 19. C Duston and Upton *Pet* from 18. *St Francis House, Eastfield Road, Duston, Northampton NN5 6TQ* T: (01604) 590052

HOLLAND, Matthew Francis. b 52. Lon Univ BA 73. Qu Coll Birm. d 79 p 80. C Ecclesall *Sheff* 79–83; TV Gleadless Valley 83–86; V Sheff Gillcar St Silas 88–92; V Sheff St Silas Broomhall 92–98; V Southsea St Simon *Portsm* 98–15; rtd 15; PtO *York* from 15. *6 Rifts Avenue, Saltburn-by-Sea TS12 1QE* T: (01287) 624915 E: matthew758@btinternet.com

HOLLAND, Simon Geoffrey. b 63. MHCIMA 83. Trin Coll Bris BA. d 91 p 92. C Reigate St Mary *S'wark* 91–95; Chapl Lee Abbey 95–99; C Guildf St Sav 99–07; P-in-c Bath Walcot B & W 07–15; R 15–16; Warden Lee Abbey 16–19; Dep Dir Garden Tomb Assn Jerusalem from 19. *The Garden Tomb, PO Box 19462, Jerusalem 9119302, Israel* E: simongh10@gmail.com

HOLLAND, Canon Simon Paul. b 56. Westcott Ho Cam 79. d 81 p 82. C Uckfield *Chich* 81–84; TV Lewes All SS, St Anne, St Mich and St Thos 84–88; TR 88–91; R Glas St Matt 91–95; P-in-c Glas St Kentigern 95–96; R Aldingbourne, Barnham and Eastergate *Chich* 96–12; R Chich St Paul and Westhampnett from 12; P-in-c Chich St Wilfrid 17–21; PtO *Portsm* from 15; Can and Preb Chich Cathl from 10. *The Rectory, Tower Close, Chichester PO19 1QN* T: (01243) 779089 E: simonholland578@btinternet.com

HOLLAND, Mrs Tessa Christine. b 59. Hull Univ BA 81 Heythrop Coll Lon MA 12. STETS 00. d 03 p 04. NSM Storrington *Chich* 03–05; NSM Pulborough 05–07; LtO 07–21. *Hirfron, Pant-y-Dwr, Rhayader LD6 5LR* E: tessaandmark123@gmail.com

HOLLETT, Catherine Elaine. *See* DAKIN, Catherine Elaine

HOLLEY, Paul Robert. b 65. Cranmer Hall Dur 91. d 94 p 95. C Tonge w Alkrington *Man* 94–98; P-in-c Salford St Phil w St Steph 98–00; P-in-c Salford Sacred Trin 99–00; R Salford Sacred Trin and St Phil 00–03; P-in-c La Côte *Eur* 03–10; PtO 10–15; Hon C S Dulwich St Steph *S'wark* 12–14; P-in-c Colbury *Win* 14–16; P-in-c Bodmin w Lanhydrock and Lanivet *Truro* 16–17; TR Bodmin from 17; RD Trigg Minor and Bodmin from 18. *The Rectory, Barons Meadow, Bodmin PL31 2DD* M: 07470-192378 E: paul.holley@mac.com

HOLLIDAY, Canon Andrew. b 62. St Steph Ho Ox 89. **d** 92 **p** 93. C Marton *Blackb* 92–95; C Poulton-le-Fylde 95–97; V Leyland St Jas 97–04; AD Leyland 02–04; P-in-c Darwen St Pet w Hoddlesden 04–10; V Darwen St Pet 10–11; R Standish from 11; Chapl MU from 12; Warden of Readers *Blackb* from 16; Hon Can Blackb Cathl from 12. *The Rectory, 13 Rectory Lane, Standish, Wigan WN6 0XA* T: (01257) 421396 E: holliday321@btinternet.com

HOLLIDAY, Canon Peter Leslie. b 48. Birm Univ BCom 70 MA 92 FCA 79. Qu Coll Birm 81. **d** 83 **p** 84. C Burton *Lich* 83–87; P-in-c Longdon 87–93; PV and Subchanter Lich Cath 87–93; R Stratford-on-Avon w Bishopton *Cov* 93–00; Chief Exec Officer St Giles Hospice Lich 00–17; Chan's V Lich Cathl 02–13; Can Custos Lich Cathl 13–18; Chapl to The Queen 15–18; rtd 18; PtO *Cov* from 18; Bp's Officer for Rtd Clergy and Spouses from 19; PtO *Lich* from 18; Chapter Can Lich Cathl from 19. *60 Needlers End Lane, Balsall Common, Coventry CV7 7AB* T: (01676) 533305 E: plh@europe.com

HOLLIDAY, William John. b 49. Middleton St Geo Coll of Educn TCert 72. CBDTI 05. **d** 07 **p** 08. NSM Kendal St Thos Carl 07–12; TV Loughrigg 12–13; rtd 13; PtO *Carl* from 13. *2 Michaelson Road, Kendal LA9 5JQ* T: (01539) 730701 E: billholliday@googlemail.com

✠**HOLLINGHURST, The Rt Revd Anne Elizabeth.** b 64. Trin Coll Bris BA 96 Hughes Hall Cam MSt 10. **d** 96 **p** 97 **c** 15. C Nottingham St Sav *S'well* 96–99; Chapl Derby Univ and Derby Cathl 99–05; Bp's Dom Chapl and Can Res Man Cathl 05–10; V St Alb St Pet 10–15; Suff Bp Aston *Birm* from 15. *16 Coleshill Street, Sutton Coldfield B72 1SH* T: 0121-426 0400 E: bishopofaston@cofebirmingham.com

HOLLINGHURST, Preb Stephen. b 59. St Jo Coll Nottm 81. **d** 83 **p** 84. C Hyde St Geo *Ches* 83–86; C Cropwell Bishop w Colston Bassett, Granby etc *S'well* 86–90; R Pembridge w Moor Court, Shobdon, Staunton etc *Heref* 90–02; R Presteigne w Discoed, Kinsham, Lingen and Knill from 02; RD Kington and Weobley 95–02, 07–12 and 14–19; Preb Heref Cathl from 08. *The Rectory, St David's Street, Presteigne LD8 2BP* T: (01544) 267777 E: revsteve.hollinghurst@gmail.com

HOLLINGHURST, Stephen Patrick. b 63. Hull Univ BA 84. Trin Coll Bris BA 95 MA 96. **d** 96 **p** 97. C Nottingham St Sav *S'well* 96–99; Chapl Nottm Trent Univ 99–03; Researcher CA 03–13; Tutor 13–19; PtO *Derby* 00–04; Chapl Derby Cathl 04–05; PtO *Birm* from 16; Evang Enabler *Lich* from 20. *Diocese of Lichfield, 1 Three Spires House, Station Road, Lichfield WS13 6HX* M: 07834-070246 E: stevehollinghurst@hotmail.com *or* steve.hollinghurst@lichfield.anglican.org

HOLLINGS, Ms Daphne. b 46. WMMTC 02. **d** 05 **p** 06. NSM Adbaston, High Offley, Knightley, Norbury etc *Lich* 05–09; C Edstaston, Fauls, Prees, Tilstock and Whixall 09–15; C Whitchurch 13–15; rtd 15; PtO *Ban* 15–16; Hon C Uwch Gwyrfai Beuno Sant 16–21. *Nythfa, County Road, Penygroes, Caernarfon LL54 6EY* T: (01286) 880853 E: daphne.hollings785@btinternet.com

HOLLINGS, Robert George. b 48. St Jo Coll Nottm. **d** 94 **p** 95. C Cotmanhay *Derby* 94–97; TV Godrevy *Truro* 97–02; V Newhall *Derby* 02–12; rtd 12; P-in-c Six Pilgrims *B & W* 12–13; PtO *Lich* 15–20. *2 Meadow View, Rolleston-on-Dove, Burton-on-Trent DE13 9AN* E: bobandjacqui@btinternet.com

HOLLINGSBEE, Thomas Richard. b 86. Sheff Univ BSc 07. Oak Hill Th Coll 13. **d** 16 **p** 17. C Higher Openshaw *Man* 16–20; C Knutsford St Jo and Toft *Ches* from 20. *20 George Street, Knutsford WA16 6HP* T: (01565) 755160 E: tom.hollingsbee@stjohnsknutsford.org.uk

HOLLINGSHURST, Canon Christopher Paul. b 63. St Chad's Coll Dur BA 85 Anglia Poly Univ MA 04 Westmr Coll Ox PGCE 86. Ridley Hall Cam 96. **d** 99 **p** 00. C Bourn and Kingston w Caxton and Longstowe *Ely* 99–00; C Papworth 00–03; V Hook *S'wark* 03–14; Voc Adv Wandsworth Adnry 09–12; Dioc Voc Adv 12–13; Dir Ords Kingston Area 13–14; P-in-c W Byfleet *Guildf* 14–16; V 16–21; Can Res Guildf Cathl from 21; Asst Dioc Dir of Ords 18–20. *The Cathedral Office, Stag Hill, Guildford GU2 7UP* T: (01483) 547862

HOLLINGSWORTH, Geoffrey. b 53. MCIPD 85. NOC 86. **d** 86 **p** 87. C Thorne *Sheff* 86–89; V Rawcliffe 89–96; V Airmyn, Hook and Rawcliffe 96–09; P-in-c Pocklington and Owsthorpe and Kilnwick Percy etc *York* 09–10; P-in-c Burnby 09–10; P-in-c Londesborough 09–10; P-in-c Nunburnholme and Warter and Huggate 09–10; P-in-c Shiptonthorpe and Hayton 09–10; R Pocklington Wold 10–18; R Londesborough Wold 10–18; rtd 18; PtO *York* from 18; *Sheff* from 18; *Eur* from 18. *Address withheld by request* T: (01430) 434670 E: geoff.holly145@btinternet.com

HOLLINGSWORTH, James William. b 69. Southn Univ BA 91 SS Coll Cam BA 96 Nottm Univ MA 17. Aston Tr Scheme 92 Ridley Hall Cam 94. **d** 97 **p** 98. C Mildenhall *St E* 97–01; R Barcombe *Chich* 01–20; P-in-c Newick 16–20; V Seaford w Sutton from 20; RD Lewes and Seaford from 21. *The Vicarage, 46 Sutton Road, Seaford BN25 1SH* T: (01323) 893508

HOLLINGSWORTH, Mrs Lucy Jane. b 70. SEITE. **d** 16 **p** 17. NSM Ringmer *Chich* 16–17; NSM Scaynes Hill 17–20; LtO from 21. *The Vicarage, 46 Sutton Road, Seaford BN25 1SH* T: (01323) 893508 E: lucyjhollingsworth@gmail.com

HOLLINGSWORTH, Paula Marion. b 62. Van Mildert Coll Dur BSc 83 Univ of Wales (Lamp) MA 08. Trin Coll Bris BA 91. **d** 91 **p** 94. C Keynsham *B & W* 91–95; C Balsall Heath St Paul *Birm* 95–98; Tutor Crowther Hall CMS Tr Coll Selly Oak 95–01; P-in-c Houghton-on-the-Hill, Keyham and Hungarton *Leic* 01–10; Bp's Adv for CME 01–04; P-in-c Westbury sub Mendip w Easton *B & W* 10–12; V 12–20; V Priddy 12–20; Sub-Dean and Preb Wells Cathl 14–20; Dean of Women's Min 15–20; PtO from 20; Chapl St Paul's Cathl *Lon* from 20. *8B Amen Court, London EC4M 7BU* M: 07909-631977 E: pmhollingsworth@btinternet.com

HOLLINS, Canon Beverley Jayne. b 68. Univ of Wales (Abth) BLib 90. SAOMC 00. **d** 03 **p** 04. C Milton Keynes *Ox* 03–06; LtO 06–07; Newport Deanery Development Facilitator 07–12; P-in-c Hardingstone and Piddington w Horton *Pet* 12–15; V Hardingstone, Piddington w Horton and Quinton and Preston Deanery 15–21; R Weston Favell from 21; RD Gtr Northn from 16; Can Pet Cathl from 18. *The Rectory, Church Way, Weston Favell, Northampton NN3 3BX* T: (01604) 413218 E: beverley.hollins@gmail.com

HOLLINS, John Edgar. b 35. St Jo Coll Cam BA 58 MA 62. Oak Hill Th Coll 58. **d** 60 **p** 61. C Whalley Range St Edm *Man* 60–63; C Highbury Ch Ch *Lon* 63–66; C St Alb St Paul 66–71; Hon C Halliwell St Paul *Man* 71–72; C Ravenhill St Jo 72–73; PtO *Birm* 79–81; V Millbrook *Ches* 81–89; rtd 89; PtO *Truro* from 89. *3 Victoria Close, Liskeard PL14 3HU* T: (01579) 349963 E: johnhollins@live.co.uk

HOLLINS (formerly SHIPP), Patricia Susan. b 54. Univ of Wales BA 76. St Paul's Coll Grahamstown 77 Linc Th Coll 81. **d** 83 **p** 94. C Cyncoed *Mon* 83–87; Par Dn Lawrence Weston *Bris* 89–91; Par Dn Henbury 91–94; V Longwell Green 94–99; Hon Can Bris Cathl 97–99; Chapl Mt Vernon and Watford Hosps NHS Trust 99–00; Sen Co-ord Chapl W Herts Hosps NHS Trust 00–04; Lead Chapl (E) Caring for the Spirit NHS Project 04–09; P-in-c Boxley w Detling *Cant* 09–14; AD N Downs 09–14; Chapl Cam St Edw *Ely* 14–15; Lead Chapl Qu Eliz Hosp King's Lynn NHS Foundn Trust 15–17; PtO *Nor* 17–18. *63 Dorset Avenue, Exeter EX4 1ND* M: 07918-671476

HOLLIS, The Ven Arnold Thaddeus. b 33. JP 87. Stockton State Coll New Jersey BA 74 NY Th Sem MDiv 74 STM 76 DMin 78. Codrington Coll Barbados 56. **d** 59 **p** 60. C Wakef St Jo 60–62; Br Guiana 62–64; P-in-c Horbury Bridge *Wakef* 64–66; C Loughton St Jo *Chelmsf* 66–69; USA 69–77; Hon Chapl RN Bermuda from 77; Chapl HM Pris from 77; Chapl Miss to Seafarers from 90; Hon Can Bermuda Cathl from 87; Adn Bermuda 96–03; rtd 03. *3 Middle Road, Sandys SB 02, Bermuda* T: (001) (441) 234 2025 *or* (441) 234 0834 F: 234 2723 E: athol@logic.bm

HOLLIS, Derek. b 60. Loughb Univ BA 82. Cranmer Hall Dur 83. **d** 86 **p** 87. C Evington *Leic* 86–89; C Arnold *S'well* 89–93; V Beckingham w Walkeringham 93–03; P-in-c Gringley-on-the-Hill 95–03; V Beckingham w Walkeringham and Gringley 03–05; P-in-c Elston w Elston Chapelry 05–11; P-in-c E Stoke w Syerston 05–11; P-in-c Shelton 05–11; P-in-c Sibthorpe 05–11; P-in-c Staunton w Flawborough 05–11; P-in-c Kilvington 05–11; Hon Chapl Miss to Seafarers 03–04; Bp's Adv on Rural Affairs *S'well* 04–11; R Stourhead *St E* 11–18; rtd 18; PtO *Nor* from 20. *13 Queen's Gardens, Hunstanton PE36 6HD* T: (01485) 535283 E: rev.derek.hollis@gmail.com

HOLLIS, Miss Elizabeth Jane. b 92. Ex Univ BA 14 St Jo Coll Dur MA 15. Cranmer Hall Dur 16. **d** 19 **p** 20. C Belmont and Pittington *Dur* from 19. *83 Birkdale Gardens, Durham DH1 2UJ* M: 07985-984827 E: liz_hollis@live.co.uk

HOLLIS, Mrs Lorna Mary. b 40. Cranmer Hall Dur 05. **d** 06 **p** 07. NSM Scarborough St Jas w H Trin *York* 06–19; Asst Chapl Scarborough and NE Yorks Healthcare NHS Trust 06–12; Asst Chapl York Teaching Hosp NHS Foundn Trust 12–20; rtd 20; PtO *York* from 19. *30 Hartford Court, Filey Road, Scarborough YO11 2TP* T: (01723) 351395 E: mary.hollis3@btinternet.com

HOLLIS, Rebecca Catherine. *See* MATHEW, Rebecca Catherine

HOLLIS, Timothy Knowles. b 28. RN Coll Dartmouth 45. St Steph Ho Ox 54. **d** 58 **p** 59. C Oatlands *Guildf* 58–60; C Crawley *Chich* 60–63; C Sotterley w Willingham *St E* 63–69; C Sotterley, Willingham, Shadingfield, Ellough etc 69; R

69–76; Gen Sec L'Arche UK 77–93; rtd 93; PtO *Chich* 93–02; *Glouc* 03–20. *9 Abbots Court Drive, Twyning, Tewkesbury GL20 6JJ* T: (01684) 274903

HOLLIS, Mrs Valerie Elizabeth. b 40. Maria Grey Coll Lon CertEd 61. St Alb Minl Tr Scheme 89. **d** 92 **p** 94. NSM Kempston Transfiguration *St Alb* 92–06; NSM Officer Bedford Adnry 06–10; PtO 06–18; *Ches* from 20. *Address temp unknown*

HOLLOWAY, Canon David Dennis. b 43. Lich Th Coll 65. **d** 68 **p** 69. C Cricklade w Latton *Bris* 68–71; C Bris St Agnes and St Simon w St Werburgh 71–74; V Bitton 74–78; TV E Bris 78–80; P-in-c Tormarton w W Littleton 80–83; Dioc Ecum and Global Partnership Officer 83–93; Hon C Bris St Mich 89–93; V Horfield St Greg 93–00; RD Horfield 97–99; Chapl St Monica Home Westbury-on-Trym 00–07; Hon Can Bris Cathl 92–07; rtd 07; PtO *Ox* from 09; *St Alb* from 16. *76 Marsworth Road, Pitstone, Leighton Buzzard LU7 9AS* T: (01296) 662765 M: 07974-648556

HOLLOWAY, David Ronald James. b 39. Univ Coll Ox BA 62 MA 66. Ridley Hall Cam 65. **d** 67 **p** 68. C Leeds St Geo *Ripon* 67–71; Tutor Wycliffe Hall Ox 71–72; V Jesmond Clayton Memorial *Newc* from 73. *7 Otterburn Terrace, Newcastle upon Tyne NE2 3AP* T: 0191-281 2001 *or* 212 7400 M: 07702-175399 E: david.holloway@church.org.uk

HOLLOWAY, Graham Edward. b 45. Chich Th Coll 69. **d** 72 **p** 73. C W Drayton *Lon* 72–75; P-in-c Hawton *S'well* 75–80; V Ladybrook 80–85; P-in-c Babworth 85–87; R Babworth w Sutton-cum-Lound 87–97; RD Retford 88–93; C Mansfield Woodhouse 97–04; P-in-c Mansfield St Aug 04–12; P-in-c Pleasley Hill 04–12; rtd 12; PtO *S'well* from 13. *6 Aylesbury Way, Forest Town, Mansfield NG19 0GJ* T: (01623) 414616 E: padreg@btinternet.com

HOLLOWAY, Keith Graham. b 45. Linc Coll Ox BA 67. Cranmer Hall Dur. **d** 73 **p** 74. C Gt Ilford St Andr *Chelmsf* 73–78; Hon C Squirrels Heath 78–80; Min Chelmer Village CD 80–87; V E Springfield 87–89; P-in-c Gt Dunmow 89–96; R Gt Dunmow and Barnston 96–02; R Upper Colne 02–10; rtd 10; PtO *Chelmsf* from 10. *5 Martens Meadow, Braintree CM7 3LB* T: (01376) 334976 E: kanddway@aol.com

HOLLOWAY, Michael Sinclair. b 50. UEA BSc 74 Southn Univ PGCE 75. STETS 99. **d** 02 **p** 03. NSM Catherington and Clanfield *Portsm* 02–07; C Bishop's Cleeve *Glouc* 07–08; TV Bishop's Cleeve and Woolstone w Gotherington etc 08–13; V Painswick, Sheepscombe, Cranham, The Edge etc 13–18; rtd 18. *10 Orchard Road, Winchcombe, Cheltenham GL54 5QB* T: (01242) 603421 E: revmike.holloway@gmail.com

✠**HOLLOWAY, The Rt Revd Prof Richard Frederick.** b 33. Lon Univ BD 63 NY Th Sem STM 68 Strathclyde Univ DUniv 94 Aber Univ Hon DD 95 Napier Univ Edin DLitt 00 Glas Univ DD 01 FRSE 95. Edin Th Coll 58. **d** 59 **p** 60 **c** 86. C Glas St Ninian 59–63; P-in-c Glas St Marg 63–68; R Edin Old St Paul 68–80; R Boston The Advent MA USA 80–84; V Ox St Mary Magd 84–86; Bp Edin 86–00; Primus 92–00; rtd 00; Gresham Prof of Div 97–01. *6 Blantyre Terrace, Edinburgh EH10 5AE* T: 0131-446 0696 M: 07710-254500 E: richard@docholloway.org.uk

HOLLOWAY, Simon Anthony. b 50. Sussex Univ BSc 72 Univ of Wales MA 03. Trin Coll Bris 76. **d** 79 **p** 81. C Bushbury *Lich* 79–81; C Castle Church 81–84; P-in-c Sparkbrook Ch Ch *Birm* 84–91; V 91–02; AD Bordesley 92–99; TV Horley *S'wark* 02–11; Chapl SE Cyprus 11–14; P-in-c Kilmington, Stockland, Dalwood, Yarcombe etc *Ex* 14–19; rtd 19; PtO *B & W* from 20; *Eur* from 20. *15 Yarbury Way, Weston-super-Mare BS24 7EP* T: (01934) 253313 E: simonholloway55@yahoo.co.uk

HOLLOWOOD, Graham. b 56. Anglia Ruskin Univ MA 07. St Steph Ho Ox 97. **d** 99 **p** 00. C Newport St Julian *Mon* 99–02; V Newport All SS 02–08; V Glodwick *Man* 08–18; AD Oldham E 14–18; V Royton from 18. *St Mark's Vicarage, 1 Skipton Street, Oldham OL8 2JF* T: 0161-624 4964 M: 07748-106718 E: 1frgraham@gmail.com

HOLLYWELL, Mrs Catherine Ann Mary. b 62. Qu Coll Birm 12. **d** 15 **p** 16. C Derby St Jo 15–16; C Pride Park, Wilmorton, Allenton and Shelton Lock from 16. *St Werburgh's Vicarage, Gascoigne Drive, Spondon, Derby DE21 7GL* M: 07745-735060 E: chollywell@btinternet.com

HOLLYWELL, Julian Francis. b 70. Liv Univ BSc 91 Leeds Univ MA 05. NOC 03. **d** 05 **p** 06. C W Didsbury and Withington St Chris *Man* 05–08; V Spondon *Derby* from 08; RD Derby N 10–17; P-in-c Chaddesden St Phil w Derby St Mark from 20; C Pride Park, Wilmorton, Allenton and Shelton Lock from 20. *St Werburgh's Vicarage, Gascoigne Drive, Spondon, Derby DE21 7GL* T: (01332) 673573 M: 07963-420564 E: fatherjulian@btinternet.com

HOLMAN, Francis Noel. b 37. Sarum Th Coll 62. **d** 65 **p** 66. C Weston Favell *Pet* 65–68; C Eckington *Derby* 68–71; Asst Chapl St Thos Hosp Lon 72–77; Chapl Hope Hosp Salford 77–02; Chapl Salford R Hosp 77–93; Chapl Ladywell Hosp 77–99; Chapl Man and Salford Skin Hosp 88–94; rtd 02; PtO *Man* 03–18. *90 Rocky Lane, Eccles, Manchester M30 9LY* T: 0161-707 1180 E: fnholman@talktalk.net

HOLMAN, Mrs Lesley Anita. b 50. SWMTC 11. **d** 14 **p** 15. NSM Littleham-cum-Exmouth w Lympstone *Ex* 14–20; PtO from 20. *24 Hilltop Avenue, Buckingham MK18 1YJ* T: (01280) 823433 E: lesleyholman3@gmail.com

HOLMDEN, Miss Maria Irene. b 50. Trent Poly TCert 72 BEd 73. Oak Hill Th Coll 90. **d** 92 **p** 94. Par Dn Stratford St Jo and Ch Ch w Forest Gate St Jas *Chelmsf* 92–94; C 94–96; P-in-c Leyton All SS 96–01; V 01–20; rtd 20. *3 Essex Road, London E10 6HP* E: mholmden@live.co.uk

HOLME, Thomas Edmund. b 49. Selw Coll Cam BA 71 MA 75. Coll of Resurr Mirfield 71. **d** 73 **p** 74. C Wyther *Ripon* 73–76; C Wimbledon *S'wark* 76–78; TV 78–79; V Bermondsey St Anne 79–81; V Stamford Baron *Pet* 83–89; P-in-c Tinwell 83–89; Hon Min Can Pet Cathl 84–89; Prec Worc Cathl 89–95; P-in-c Penshurst and Fordcombe *Roch* 95–05; R 05–20; P-in-c Chiddingstone w Chiddingstone Causeway 19–20; rtd 20. *Address temp unknown*

HOLMES, Miss Alexandra Jane. b 74. Ox Brookes Univ BA 96 Portsm Univ MSc 11. Ripon Coll Cuddesdon 13. **d** 16 **p** 17. C Blagdon w Compton Martin and Ubley *B & W* 16–20; NSM Hardington Vale 20–21; V Priddy from 21; V Westbury sub Mendip w Easton from 21. *The Vicarage, Crow Lane, Westbury sub Mendip, Wells BA5 1HB* M: 07979-667324 E: holmesaj@yahoo.com

HOLMES, Andrew David. b 64. All SS Cen for Miss & Min 18. **d** 20 **p** 21. C Haslingden w Grane and Stonefold *Blackb* from 20; C Musbury from 20. *41 Crofters Fold, Heysham, Morecambe LA3 2AH* M: 07460-899451 E: revandrewdholmes@gmail.com

HOLMES, Andrew Keith. b 69. Univ of Wales BEng 93. St Mich Coll Llan BTh 96. **d** 96 **p** 97. C Clydach *S & B* 96–98; C Swansea St Thos and Kilvey 98–00; P-in-c New Radnor and Llanfihangel Nantmelan etc 00–03; V Penrhiwceiber, Matthewstown and Ynysboeth *Llan* 03–16; Tv Aber Valley *Mon* from 16; Chapl St Cadoc's Hosp NHS Trust from 16. *Vicar Ab [V Manselton and Cwmbwrla S & B 16–18; R Fish Hoek S Africa from 18. 4 Fourth Avenue, Fish Hoek 7975, South Africa* E: andrewkeithholmes@gmail.com

HOLMES (née PLATT), Anne Cecilia. b 46. Birm Univ BA 67 Anglia Ruskin Univ MA 09 DProf 18 Ox Univ DipEd 68 MInstGA 96. SAOMC 99. **d** 02 **p** 03. Chapl Headington Sch 02–04; Asst Chapl Oxon & Bucks Mental Health Partnership NHS Trust 04–09; NSM Marston w Elsfield *Ox* 02–12; PtO 12–19; NSM Ox St Giles and SS Phil and Jas w St Marg from 19. *Trinity Cottage, 27 Mill Street, Eynsham, Witney OX29 4JX* T: (01865) 881397 M: 07831-254727 E: anne@ac-holmes.co.uk *or* annececiliaholmes@gmail.com

HOLMES, Brian. b 41. NEOC 92. **d** 95 **p** 96. NSM Darlington St Matt and St Luke *Dur* 95–98; V 98–08; rtd 08; PtO *Dur* from 08. *2 Christchurch Close, Darlington DL1 2YL* T: (01325) 482255 E: revbholmes@hotmail.com

HOLMES (née KENYON), Caroline Elizabeth. b 40. SRN 62. NOC 04. **d** 05 **p** 06. NSM Hale and Ashley *Ches* 05–10; PtO from 10. *1 Broomfield House, 134 Hale Road, Hale, Altrincham WA15 9HJ* T: 0161-233 0761 E: caroline.holmes@rgsit.com

HOLMES, Craig Walter. b 72. Southn Univ BSc 95 R Holloway & Bedf New Coll Lon PhD 01 Fitzw Coll Cam BA 03 MA 07 CCC Cam MPhil 04. Ridley Hall Cam 01. **d** 07 **p** 08. C Egham *Guildf* 07–10; V Hanworth St Rich *Lon* 10–19; Dioc Dir of Ords *Guildf* from 19. *Church House, 20 Alan Turing Road, Surrey Research Park, Guildford GU2 7YF* T: (01483) 790300 E: craig.holmes@cofeguildford.org.uk

HOLMES (formerly WARD), Mrs Elizabeth Joyce. b 42. Open Univ BA. WEMTC 04. **d** 06 **p** 07. OLM Painswick, Sheepscombe, Cranham, The Edge etc *Glouc* 06–11; rtd 11; PtO Truro from 16. *Arbour Cottage, Mount Hawke, Truro TR4 8EE* T: (01209) 890388 E: e.holmes154@btinternet.com

HOLMES, Geoffrey Robert. b 67. Nottm Univ BSc 89 Sheff Univ PhD 13. Ridley Hall Cam BA 92. **d** 93 **p** 94. C Clifton St Jas *Sheff* 93–98; V Worsbrough St Thos and St Jas 98–05. *Address withheld by request* E: geoff.r.holmes@sheffield.ac.uk

HOLMES, Grant Wenlock. b 54. St Steph Ho Ox BA 78 MA 83. **d** 79 **p** 80. C Benhilton *S'wark* 79–82; C-in-c S Kenton Annunciation CD *Lon* 82–86; Tutor Chich Th Coll 86–87; Bp's Dom Chapl *Chich* 86–88; V Mayfield 88–99; P-in-c Mark Cross 97–99; Asst Chapl Lewisham Hosp NHS Trust 99–01; Lead Chapl Kingston Hosp NHS Foundn Trust Surrey 01–14; Hon C Barnes *S'wark* 01–06; V St Alb St Mary Marshalswick from 14. *The Old Rectory, Sumpter Yard, Holywell Hill, St Albans AL1 1BY* T: (01727) 890260 E: wenlockholmes@gmail.com

HOLMES, Mrs Janet Ellen. b 61. Wolv Univ BSc 95 RCN MSc 99 RGN 83. Qu Coll Birm MA 09. **d** 09 **p** 10. C Hadley and Wellington Ch Ch *Lich* 09–12; C Cen Telford 11–12; TV 12–21; Chapl Severn Hospice from 15; PtO *Lich* from 21. *Sutton Bank Farm, Sutton, Newport TF10 8DD* T: (01952) 813658 M: 07980-521064 E: janeteholmes@btinternet.com *or* janet@telfordchurch.co.uk

HOLMES, Canon John Robin. b 42. Leeds Univ BA 64. Linc Th Coll 64. **d** 66 **p** 67. C Wyther *Ripon* 66–69; C Adel 69–73; V Beeston Hill St Luke 73–76; V Holbeck 76–86; RD Armley 82–86; V Manston 86–93; Hon Can Ripon Cathl 89–98; Dioc Missr 93–98; Can Missr *Wakef* 98–07; rtd 07; PtO *Leeds* from 17; *York* from 17. *54 West Crayke, Bridlington YO16 6XW* T: (01262) 424101 M: 07712-044364 E: canon.john@sky.com

HOLMES, Jonathan Michael. b 49. Qu Coll Cam BA 70 MA 74 VetMB 73 PhD 78 MRCVS 73. Ridley Hall Cam 87. **d** 88 **p** 89. Chapl Qu Coll Cam 88–13; Dean of Chpl 94–14; rtd 14; PtO *Ely* from 15. *Queens' College, Cambridge CB3 9ET* T: (01223) 335545 F: 335522 E: jmh38@cam.ac.uk

HOLMES, Nigel Peter. b 48. Nottm Univ BTh 72 Lanc Univ CertEd 72 Lon Univ BD 76 Sheff Univ MEd 84. Kelham Th Coll. **d** 72 **p** 73. C Barrow St Matt *Carl* 72–75; C Derby St Bart 75–78; P-in-c Gt Barlow 78–84; V Carl St Herbert w St Steph 84–91; V Keswick St Jo 91–94; V Mexborough *Sheff* 94–97; P-in-c Nether Hoyland St Pet 97–98; P-in-c Nether Hoyland St Andr 97–98; V Hoyland 98–07; AD Tankersley 04–07; V Monk Bretton *Wakef* 07–09; rtd 09. *6 The Signals, Widdrington, Morpeth NE61 5QU*

HOLMES, Prof Peter Geoffrey. b 32. Bris Univ BSc 59 MSc 69 Leic Univ PhD 74 CEng FIEE. St Deiniol's Hawarden 74. **d** 76 **p** 77. NSM Glen Parva and S Wigston *Leic* 76–02; Prof Nottm Poly 85-92; Prof Nottm Trent Univ 92–96; rtd 02; PtO *Leic* 02–16. *19 Windsor Avenue, Glen Parva, Leicester LE2 9TQ* T: 0116-277 4534 E: peterholmes@iee.org

HOLMES, Peter John. b 41. Reading Univ TCert 63 Open Univ BA 76 K Coll Lon BA 96 AKC 96 MA 97 Glas Univ PhD 02. St Steph Ho Ox 03. **d** 04 **p** 05. NSM Beaconsfield *Ox* 04–08; PtO 08–10; *Pet* 11–13 and from 16. *14 Bayley Close, Uppingham, Oakham LE15 9TG* T: (01572) 821834 E: p.holmes4@icloud.com

HOLMES, Roger Cockburn. b 46. Jes Coll Ox BA 70 MA 84 Edin Univ BD 76. Edin Th Coll 73. **d** 84 **p** 85. Canada 84–88; R Ditchingham w Pirnough *Nor* 88–90; R Hedenham 88–90; R Broome 88–90; R Ditchingham, Hedenham and Broome 90–93; V Helmsley *York* 93–97; PtO *Wakef* 07. *7 Bishopgate, Howden, Goole DN14 7AD* T: (01430) 430880 E: fatherholmes@hotmail.com

HOLMES, Roy Grant. b 37. Ox NSM Course 83. **d** 86 **p** 87. NSM Wokingham St Paul *Ox* 86–07; PtO 07–20. *58 Copse Drive, Wokingham RG41 1LX* T: 0118-978 4141

HOLMES, Stephen. b 54. St Andr Univ MTheol 84. Chich Th Coll 84. **d** 86 **p** 87. C Croydon St Jo *S'wark* 86–89; C Tewkesbury w Walton Cardiff *Glouc* 89–92; P-in-c Bournemouth St Luke *Win* 92–94; V 94–10; P-in-c N Stoneham and Bassett 10–15; rtd 15; PtO *Win* from 16; *Sarum* 16–21. *Palmyra House, 7 St Luke's Road, Bournemouth BH3 7LR* T: (01202) 252201 E: liberanos7@gmail.com

HOLMES, Canon Stephen John. b 50. CertEd 72. Trin Coll Bris 81 Sarum & Wells Th Coll 88. **d** 89 **p** 90. C Skegness and Winthorpe *Linc* 89–93; P-in-c Mablethorpe w Trusthorpe 93–97; V Hadleigh St Barn *Chelmsf* 97–07; R Gt and Lt Leighs and Lt Waltham 07–14; rtd 14; PtO *Chelmsf* from 16; Can Roray Tanzania from 18. *105 Grand Parade, Leigh-on-Sea SS9 1DW* T: (01702) 875381 E: familyholmes@hotmail.co.uk

HOLMES, Stephen Mark. b 65. St Andr Univ MA 87 Pontifical Univ Maynooth BD 04 Edin Univ PhD 13 CCC Cam PGCE 88 FSAScot 98 FRHistS 15. TISEC 11. **d** 04 **p** 04. In RC Ch 04–08; NSM Edin Old St Paul 12–14; P-in-c Edin St Marg 13–14; C Edin St Jo 14–18; R Padstow, St Merryn and St Issey w St Petroc Minor *Truro* 18–20; R Edin H Cross from 20; Tutor Scottish Episc Inst from 16. *18 Barnton Gardens, Edinburgh EH4 6AF* M: 07584-091870 E: rector.hce@gmail.com

HOLMES, Susan. b 46. Leeds Univ LLB 68 Univ of Wales LLM 00. **d** 06 **p** 07. NSM Scotby and Cotehill w Cumwhinton *Carl* 06–11; rtd 11; PtO *Carl* from 11. *Woodside, Great Corby, Carlisle CA4 8LL* T: (01228) 560617 E: susan@gtcorby.plus.com

HOLMES, Trevor Norman. b 61. TCD BSc 82 NUI MBA 94. CITC MTh 15. **d** 13 **p** 15. NSM Julianstown and Colpe w Drogheda and Duleek *M & K* 13–15; NSM Mullingar, Portnashangan, Moyliscar, Kilbixy etc from 15; Vice Pres External and Strategic Affairs Dublin City Univ *D & G* from 14; PtO from 15. *45 Parsons Hall, Rathcoffey Road, Maynooth, Co Kildare,*

Republic of Ireland T: (00353) (1) 629 0182 M: (00353) 87-242 5560 E: trevor.n.holmes@gmail.com

HOLMES, William John. b 49. **d** 97 **p** 98. Aux Min Billy w Derrykeighan *Conn* 97–02; Aux Min Ballymoney w Finvoy and Rasharkin 02–14; NSM Killowen *D & R* from 14. *20 Mountfield Drive, Coleraine BT52 1TW* T: (028) 7035 5993 M: 07780-916795 E: william149@btinternet.com *or* billyh851@gmail.com

HOLROYD, John Richard. b 54. Liv Univ BA 75 PGCE 77. Wycliffe Hall Ox 78. **d** 81 **p** 82. C Gt Stanmore *Lon* 81–84; Min Can, V Choral and Prec St E Cathl 84–89; TV Wolverton *Ox* 89–96; P-in-c Maidenhead St Luke 96–10; P-in-c Cotham St Sav w St Mary and Clifton St Paul *Bris* 10–14; V 14–17; rtd 17. *Bredon, Church Lane, Whittington, Worcester WR5 2RQ* E: richardholroyd@mac.com

HOLROYD, Canon Stephen Charles. b 56. UEA BA 79. St Jo Coll Nottm 84. **d** 87 **p** 88. C Barton Seagrave w Warkton *Pet* 87–91; V Eye 91–97; V Silsoe, Pulloxhill and Flitton *St Alb* 97–14; P-in-c The Stodden Churches 14–19; R from 19; Hon Can St Alb from 20. *Stodden Rectory, High Street, Upper Dean, Huntingdon PE28 0ND* E: stephenholroyd@btinternet.com

HOLROYD-THOMAS, Dominic John. b 94. Dur Univ BA 18. Westcott Ho Cam 14. **d** 17 **p** 18. C Welwyn *St Alb* 17–20; P-in-c Ampthill w Millbrook and Steppingley from 20. *The Rectory, 10 Church Avenue, Ampthill, Bedford MK45 2PN* T: (01525) 795417 E: rector@ampthillbenefice.co.uk

HOLT, Andrew Michael. b 82. K Coll Lon LLB 05. Oak Hill Th Coll BA 18. **d** 18 **p** 19. C Kensington St Helen w H Trin *Lon* 18–21; PtO from 21. *Address temp unknown* M: 07747-843018 E: andrewmholt@outlook.com

HOLT, Mrs Claire Frances. b 66. Bris Univ BSc 88 Kingston Poly PGCE 89. STETS 02. **d** 05 **p** 06. C N Farnborough *Guildf* 05–12; P-in-c Tongham 12–14; V from 14. *The Vicarage, Poyle Road, Tongham, Farnham GU10 1DU* T: (01252) 782790 E: clairefholt@hotmail.com *or* claire@stpaulstongham.org.uk

HOLT, Canon David. b 44. St Jo Coll Dur BSc 67. **d** 70 **p** 71. C Blackley St Pet *Man* 70–73; C Radcliffe St Thos 73–74; C Radcliffe St Thos and St Jo 74–75; V Ashton St Pet 75–79; Dioc Youth Officer *Guildf* 80–85; V Bagshot 85–97; RD Surrey Heath 92–97; V Fleet 97–03; RD Aldershot 98–03; Hon Can Guildf Cathl 99–03; rtd 03; Ox 06–19. *62 Lynwood Drive, Mytchett, Camberley GU16 6BY* T: (01276) 507538 M: 07974-354411 E: david.holt10@ntlworld.com

HOLT, Canon Douglas Robert. b 49. MA. Ridley Hall Cam. **d** 82 **p** 83. C Cambridge St Barn *Ely* 82–84; P-in-c Barn 84–86; V 86–91; V Ealing St Mary *Lon* 91–98; Dioc Dir Strategy Support *Bris* 98–09; Can Res Bris Cathl 98–10; Hon Can and Dioc Dir Strategy Support 10–14; rtd 14; PtO *Bris* 14–16; P-in-c Hove St Jo *Chich* 14–18; PtO *Bris* from 19. *71 High Street, Malmesbury SN16 9AG* E: douglas.holt49@gmail.com

HOLT, Francis Thomas. b 38. Edin Th Coll 79. **d** 81 **p** 82. C Cullercoats St Geo *Newc* 81–83; C Ponteland 83–86; Chapl Worc Coll of HE 86–89; R Worc St Clem 86–93; V Finstall 93–96; Chapl Menorca *Eur* 96–97; rtd 98; PtO *Worc* 97–13; *Newc* from 13. *34 Meadow Grange, Berwick-upon-Tweed TD15 1NW*

HOLT, Jack Derek. b 38. Trin Coll Bris 71. **d** 73 **p** 74. C Daubhill *Man* 73–76; P-in-c Thornham w Gravel Hole 76–79; V 79–83; R Talke *Lich* 83–93; V Cotmanhay *Derby* 93–03; Chapl Derbyshire Mental Health Services NHS Trust 93–03; rtd 03; PtO *Lich* 03–19. *31 Hatherton Close, Newcastle ST5 7SN* T: (01782) 560845

HOLT, James Edward. b 49. St Martin's Coll Lanc BA 94 PGCE 95. NOC 99. **d** 02 **p** 04. NSM Holme-in-Cliviger w Worsthorne *Blackb* 02–03; NSM Whalley 03–12; NSM W Pendleside 12–19; PtO 19–20. *15 Wheatley Close, Fence, Burnley BB12 9QH* T: (01282) 778319 E: jimeholt@btinternet.com

HOLT, Canon Lucinda Jane. b 65. Open Univ BSc 00. Wycliffe Hall Ox 01. **d** 03 **p** 04. C Newton Longville and Mursley w Swanbourne etc *Ox* 03–06; TV Riverside 06–08; V Eton w Eton Wick, Boveney and Dorney 08–13; R Poole *Sarum* from 13; RD Poole and N Bournemouth from 16; Can and Preb Sarum Cathl from 19. *The Rectory, 10 Poplar Close, Poole BH15 1LP* T: (01202) 672694 E: revlucy@tiscali.co.uk *or* lucy.stjamespoole@hotmail.co.uk

HOLT, Michael. b 38. Univ of Wales (Lamp) BA 61. St D Coll Lamp. **d** 63 **p** 64. C Stand *Man* 63–69; V Bacup St Jo 69–03; AD Rossendale 98–00; rtd 03; PtO *Man* from 03. *Address temp unknown* M: 07884-241575 E: hoplite@talktalk.net

HOLT, Shirley Ann. b 98 **p** 99. OLM High Oak, Hingham and Scoulton w Wood Rising *Nor* 98–14; PtO from 14. *Westfield, 59 Church Lane, Wicklewood, Wymondham NR18 9QH* T: (01953) 603668 E: saholt@talk21.com

HOLT, Stephen Richard. b 64. Leeds Univ BA 11. Coll of Resurr Mirfield 09. **d** 11 **p** 12. C Gt Grimsby St Mary and St Jas *Linc* 11–14; C Boston 14–18; V Carr Dyke Gp from 18. *The Vicarage, 6 Walcott Road, Billinghay, Lincoln LN4 4EH* T: (01526) 580654 M: 07722-117519 E: steve.carrdyke@gmail.com

⊕HOLTAM, The Rt Revd Nicholas Roderick. b 54. Collingwood Coll Dur BA 75 K Coll Lon BD 78 AKC 78 FKC 05 Dur Univ MA 89 Hon DCL 05. Westcott Ho Cam 78. d 79 p 80 c 11. C Stepney St Dunstan and All SS *Lon* 79–83; Tutor Linc Th Coll 83–88; V Is of Dogs Ch Ch and St Jo w St Luke *Lon* 88–95; V St Martin-in-the-Fields 95–11; Bp Sarum 11–21; rtd 21. *Flat 2, 5-6 Clarendon Terrace, Brighton BN2 1FD*

HOLTH, Øystein Johan (Stein). b 31. Open Univ BA 75. AKC 54. d 54 p 55. C Greenford H Cross *Lon* 54–56; Br N Borneo and Sarawak 56–63; E Malaysia 63–67; Chapl OHP and St Hilda's Sch Whitby 67–75; P-in-c Pimlico St Barn *Lon* 75–97; Ind Chapl 75–97; rtd 97; PtO *Lon* from 97. *13 Dollis Park, London N3 1HJ* T: (020) 8346 8131 E: steinandclare@holth.de

HOLZAPFEL, Mrs Christine Anne. b 53. Ex Univ BA 74 PGCE 75. WMMTC 04. d 07 p 08. C Worc SE 07–10; P-in-c Finstall 10–12; C Catshill and Dodford 10–12; TV Bromsgrove 12–14; TR 14–17; V Dodford 14–17; Harnhill Cen of Chr Healing 17–20; rtd 20; PtO *Glouc* 19–21. *2 Henbrook Cottage, Worcester Road, Wychbold, Droitwich WR9 0DG* M: 07749-898698 E: c.holzapfel15@gmail.com

HOMDEN, Peter David. b 56. Moorlands Coll BA 06. STETS 07. d 09 p 10. C Heatherlands St Jo *Sarum* from 09. *72 Alexandra Road, Poole BH14 9EW* T: (01202) 241437 M: 07841-699094 E: homdenhome@virginmedia.com

HOMER, Rosemary Louise. b 86. Ripon Coll Cuddesdon 15. d 18 p 19. C Coplow *Leic* 18–21; Chapl Univ Hosps Cov and Warks NHS Trust from 21. *University Hospital Coventry & Warwickshire NHS Trust, Clifford Bridge Road, Coventry CV2 2DX* E: rosiehomer1@gmail.com

HOMFRAY, Kenyon Lee James. b 55. TCD BTh 99 MA 03 Univ of Wales (Cardiff) LLM 02. CITC 96. d 99 p 00. C Convoy w Monellan and Donaghmore *D & R* 99–02; I 02–05; I Bunclody w Kildavin, Clonegal and Kilrush *C, F & O* 05–11; rtd 12. *Garrankyle, Cloneen, Fethard, Co Tipperary, Republic of Ireland*

HONES, Simon Anthony. b 54. Sussex Univ BSc 75. Qu Coll Birm. d 79 p 80. C Win Ch Ch 79–82; C Basing 82–88; Min Chineham CD 88–90; V Surbiton St Matt *S'wark* 90–08; TR 08–11; P-in-c Marchwood *Win* from 11. *St John's Vicarage, Vicarage Road, Marchwood, Southampton SO40 4SX* T: (023) 8086 1496 E: simon.hones@btinternet.com

HONESS, Claire Elizabeth. b 67. Reading Univ BA 89 PhD 97. St Hild Coll 19. d 21. C Barnoldswick w Bracewell *Leeds* from 21. *33 Chapman Court, Barnoldswick BB18 5EE* T: (01282) 853310 M: 07869-471101 E: claire.e.honess@gmail.com

HONEY, Mrs Elizabeth Katherine. b 81. Keble Coll Ox MA 07. Wycliffe Hall Ox 06. d 09 p 10. C Furze Platt *Ox* 09–13; Pioneer Min *Derby* from 13; Dioc Pioneer and Fresh Expressions Enabler from 20. *119 Francis Street, Derby DE21 6DE* T: (01332) 299110 M: 07883-470158 E: revhoney@live.co.uk or benandbethderby@gmail.com

HONEY, Canon Frederick Bernard. b 22. Selw Coll Cam BA 48 MA 72. Wells Th Coll 48. d 50 p 51. C S'wark St Geo 50–52; C Claines St Jo *Worc* 52–55; V Wollaston 55–87; RD Stourbridge 72–83; Hon Can Worc Cathl 75–87; rtd 87. *38 Park Farm, Bourton-on-the-Water, Cheltenham GL54 2HF* T: (01451) 822218

HONEY, Canon Thomas David. b 56. Lon Univ BA 78. Ripon Coll Cuddesdon 80. d 83 p 84. C Mill End and Heronsgate w W Hyde *St Alb* 83–86; C Stepney St Dunstan and All SS *Lon* 86–89; TV High Wycombe *Ox* 89–95; P-in-c Headington Quarry 95–07; Can Res and Treas Ex Cathl 07–10; V Ex St Dav 10–17; Chapl St Mich Hosp Basingstoke 17–19; rtd 20; PtO *Ox* 20–21; *Ex* from 21. *12 Linhay Park, Sandford, Crediton EX17 4LL* E: tomhoney14@icloud.com

HONEYMAN, Jennifer Mary. *See* LANE, Jennifer Mary

HONOUR, Colin Reginald. b 44. Lanc Univ CertEd 69 Man Univ AdDipEd 75 Newc Univ MEd 80. NOC 88. d 91 p 92. NSM Walmsley *Man* 91; C Middleton 92–94; R Holcombe 94–01; P-in-c Hawkshaw Lane 99–01; P-in-c Aldingham, Dendron, Rampside and Urswick *Carl* 01–03; R 03–09; rtd 09; PtO *Carl* from 10. *1 Crow Wood, Heversham, Milnthorpe LA7 7ER* T: (015395) 64357 E: cnchonour@btinternet.com

HONOUR, Derek Gordon. b 59. Bath Univ BSc 84. St Jo Coll Nottm. d 89 p 90. C High Wycombe *Ox* 89–91; C Brightside w Wincobank *Sheff* 91–94; P-in-c Dawley St Jerome *Lon* 94–01; C Derby St Alkmund and St Werburgh 01–05; V Stoke Hill *Guildf* 05–09; P-in-c Derby St Barn 09–13; V from 13. *St Barnabas' Vicarage, 122 Radbourne Street, Derby DE22 3BU* T: (01332) 342553 E: dghonour@ad.co.uk

HONOUR, Mrs Joanna Clare. b 61. Westmr Coll Ox BEd 83. St Jo Coll Nottm 86. d 89 p 94. Par Dn High Wycombe *Ox* 89–91; Par Dn Brightside w Wincobank *Sheff* 91–94; C 94; Dep Chapl HM Pris Wandsworth 95–97; Chapl HM Pris The Mount 97; NSM Dawley St Jerome *Lon* 96–01; Chapl HM Pris Foston Hall 01–05; Chapl HM Pris Coldingley 06–09; Chapl HM Pris Whatton 09–16; Hon Can S'well Minster 15–16; Chapl HM Pris Stafford 16–20; Chapl HM Pris Sudbury from 20. *HM Prison Sudbury, Sudbury, Ashbourne DE6 5HW* T: (01283) 584000 E: jo.honour@justice.gov.uk

HONOUR, Jonathan Paul. b 68. Ox Brookes Univ BSc 90 Greenwich Univ PGCE 91. St Jo Coll Nottm MA 98. d 99 p 00. C Tonbridge St Steph *Roch* 99–03; TV Woodley *Ox* 03–08; V Guernsey H Trin *Win* from 08. *Holy Trinity Vicarage, Brock Road, St Peter Port, Guernsey GY1 1RS* T: (01481) 724382 M: 07752-241255 E: jonhonour@gmail.com

HOOD, Mrs Doreen. b 38. Open Univ BA 90 SRN 59 RFN 61. NEOC 90. d 93 p 94. NSM Cullercoats St Geo *Newc* 93–99; NSM Monkseaton St Pet 99–00; P-in-c Newc St Hilda 00–03; rtd 03; PtO *Newc* from 03. *24 Keswick Drive, North Shields NE30 3EW* T: 0191-253 1762

HOOD, Mrs Elizabeth Mary. b 57. Ex Univ BA 79. ERMC 05. d 08 p 09. C Boxmoor St Jo *St Alb* 08–12; TV Langelei 12–18; TR from 18; AD Hemel Hempstead 15–19. *The Vicarage, 14 Pancake Lane, Hemel Hempstead HP2 4NB* T: (01442) 264860 E: lizziehood@aol.com

HOOD, Jennifer Louise. *See* JOYCE-HOOD, Jennifer Louise

HOOD, Mrs Linda. b 47. Leeds Univ BA 68. St Jo Coll Nottm 07. d 09 p 10. NSM Chase Terrace *Lich* 09–15; NSM Chase Terrace etc 15–17; rtd 17; PtO *Lich* from 18. *13 Mossbank Avenue, Burntwood WS7 4UN* T: (01543) 301728 M: 07786-987114 E: linda_hoodburntwood@hotmail.co.uk

HOOD, Peter Michael. b 47. Sheff Univ BSc 68. Wycliffe Hall Ox 70. d 73 p 74. C Soundwell *Bris* 73–76; P-in-c Walcot St Andr CD 76–77; TV Swindon St Jo and St Andr 77–80; V Esh and Hamsteels *Dur* 80–88; V Stockton St Paul 88–00; P-in-c Herrington 00–05; P-in-c Penshaw 00–05; P-in-c Shiney Row 00–05; R Herrington, Penshaw and Shiney Row 05–07; Lic to Adn Sunderland and Houghton Deanery 07–12; rtd 12; PtO *Dur* from 12. *1 Victory Street East, Hetton le Hole, Houghton le Spring DH5 9DN* T: 0191-526 9187 E: revphood@talktalk.net

HOOD, Stephen William. b 61. d 13 p 14. NSM New Milverton *Cov* 13–16; NSM Wellesbourne from 16; NSM Walton d'Eiville from 16. *Millbrook House, Wasperton, Warwick CV35 8EB* T: (01926) 624579 E: steve.hood@accel.org.uk

HOOK, Canon Ian Kevin. b 57. Trin Coll Bris 93. d 95 p 96. C Dalton-in-Furness *Carl* 95–98; C Newbarns w Hawcoat 98–01; V Barrow St Mark 01–17; RD Barrow 06–11; Hon Can Carl Cathl 10–17; rtd 17. *Craiglea, Brodick, Isle of Arran KA27 8AJ* E: ianhook@dsl.pipex.com

HOOK (*née* KAMINSKI), Mrs Julia Ann. b 55. WEMTC 07. d 10 p 11. NSM Winchcombe *Glouc* from 10; TV from 14. *The Vicarage, Church Road, Alderton, Tewkesbury GL20 8NR* T: (01242) 620636 M: 07715-953076 E: julia.hook@btinternet.com

HOOK, Neil. b 73. Univ of Wales (Swansea) BA 94 Univ of Wales (Cardiff) BD 96. St Mich Coll Llan 94. d 97 p 98. C Brecon St Mary and Battle w Llanddew *S & B* 97–99; Min Can Brecon Cathl 97–99; P-in-c Llanllyr-yn-Rhos w Llanfihangel Helygen 99–00; V Upper Wye 00–05; P-in-c Trallwng w Bettws Penpont w Aberyskir etc 05–09; P-in-c Cynog Honddu 08–09; V Dan yr Eppynt 10–12; V Builth and Llanddewi'r Cwm w Llangynog etc 12–15; V Buallt 15–19; P-in-c Daugleddau LMA *St D* from 19; AD Daugleddau from 19. *St Martin's Vicarage, Barn Street, Haverfordwest SA61 1TD* T: (01437) 769284 E: frhooky@gmail.com

HOOKER, Valerie Jean. b 58. ERMC 19. d 21. C Taverham w Ringland *Nor* from 21. *194 West End, Costessey, Norwich NR8 5AW* T: (01603) 746936 E: valhooker@hotmail.co.uk

HOOPER, Preb Derek Royston. b 33. St Edm Hall Ox BA 57 MA 65. Cuddesdon Coll 57. d 59 p 60. C Gt Walsingham *Nor* 59–62; C Townstall w Dartmouth *Ex* 62–65; V Lynton and Brendon 65–69; C Littleham w Exmouth 70–72; TV 72–79; R Wrington w Butcombe *B & W* 79–94; Preb Wells Cathl 93–94; rtd 94; PtO *Ex* 95–19; *B & W* 95–00 and 16–19. *23 Dagmar Road, Exmouth EX8 2AN* T: (01395) 272831

HOOPER, Geoffrey Michael. b 39. MBE 00. Univ of Wales (Ban) MA 07. K Coll Lon 61. d 66 p 67. C Chesterfield St Mary and All SS *Derby* 66–69; Chapl RAF 69–74; P-in-c Hook Norton w Swerford and Wigginton *Ox* 74–80; P-in-c Gt Rollright 75–80; R Hook Norton w Gt Rollright, Swerford etc 80–82; Warden Mansf Ho Univ Settlement Plaistow 82–00; Dir 86–00; rtd 03; PtO *Ban* from 09. *2 Mount Pleasant, Corris, Machynlleth SY20 9RL* T: (01654) 761392 M: 07740-467426 E: geoffrey.hooper678@btinternet.com

HOOPER, Ian. b 44. St Jo Coll York CertEd 67. Trin Coll Bris. **d** 88 **p** 89. C Martlesham w Brightwell *St E* 88–92; R Pakenham w Norton and Tostock 92–09; RD Ixworth 03–09; rtd 09; PtO *St E* from 09; Dioc Retirement Officer 10–15. *26 Drake Close, Stowmarket IP14 1UP* T: (01449) 770179 E: ianavrilhooper126@btinternet.com

✠**HOOPER, The Rt Revd Michael Wrenford.** b 41. Univ of Wales (Lamp) BA 63. St Steph Ho Ox 63. **d** 65 **p** 66 **c** 02. C Bridgnorth St Mary *Heref* 65–70; P-in-c Habberley 70–78; R 78–81; V Minsterley 70–81; RD Pontesbury 75–80; Preb Heref Cathl 81–02; V Leominster 81–85; TR 85–97; P-in-c Eyton 81–85; RD Leominster 81–97; P-in-c Eye, Croft w Yarpole and Lucton 91–97; Adn Heref 97–02; Suff Bp Ludlow 02–09; Adn Ludlow 02–09; rtd 09; Hon Asst Bp Worc from 10. *6 Avon Drive, Eckington, Pershore WR10 3BU* T: (01386) 751589 E: bishopmichael@btinternet.com

HOOPER, The Ven Paul Denis Gregory. b 52. Man Univ BA 75 Ox Univ BA 80 MA 87. Wycliffe Hall Ox 78. **d** 81 **p** 82. C Leeds St Geo *Ripon* 81–84; Dioc Youth Officer 84–87; Bp's Dom Chapl 87–95; Dioc Communications Officer 87–97; V Harrogate St Mark 95–09; AD Harrogate 05–09; Dir Clergy Development 09–12; Adn Leeds 12–16; Hon Can Ripon Cathl 08–16; rtd 16; PtO *Leeds* from 16. *9 Fulwith Gate, Harrogate HG2 8HS* E: ven.paul.hooper@outlook.com

HOOPER, The Ven Peter George. b 62. Newc Univ BSc 83 PhD 87. Catholic Inst of Toulouse 04 EMMTC 04. **d** 06 **p** 07. C Melton Mowbray *Leic* 06–10; TR Bradgate Team 10–15; R Groby and Ratby 15–16; R Peckleton 15–16; AD Sparkenhoe E 11–16; P-in-c Ab Kettleby and Holwell w Asfordby 16–21; C Old Dalby, Nether Broughton, Saxelbye etc 18–21; AD Framland 16–21; Dioc Rural Officer 11–21; Hon Can Leic Cathl 16–21; Adn France *Eur* from 21. *Address temp unknown* E: peter.hooper@live.com

HOPE, Charles Henry. b 64. Regent's Park Coll Ox BA 87 MA 90 St Jo Coll Dur BA 90 FRGS 82. Cranmer Hall Dur. **d** 90 **p** 91. C Tynemouth St Jo *Newc* 90–94; V 94–03; P-in-c Prudhoe 03–07; V 07–16; P-in-c Keswick St Jo *Carl* 16–18; C Upper Derwent 16–18; V Keswick St Jo w Borrowdale from 18; P-in-c St John's-in-the-Vale, Threlkeld and Wythburn from 18; RD Derwent from 17; CF(V) from 94. *St John's Vicarage, Ambleside Road, Keswick CA12 4DD* T: (01768) 775855 E: charleshope@btopenworld.com

HOPE, Colin Frederick. b 49. St Mich Coll Llan 73. **d** 76 **p** 77. C Warrington St Elphin *Liv* 76–80; V Newton-le-Willows 80–84; CSWG from 84; LtO *Chich* from 88. *The Monastery, Crawley Down, Crawley RH10 4LH* T: (01342) 712074 E: father.colin@cswg.org.uk

HOPE, Henry James. b 86. Ox Univ MSt 09 Hochschule für Musik Franz Liszt, Weimar MA 10 Ox Univ DPhil 14 Sheff Univ BA 20. Coll of Resurr Mirfield 18 Ripon Coll Cuddesdon 20. **d** 21. C Hexham *Newc* from 21. *29 Robson Drive, Hexham NE46 2HZ* M: 07421-462595 E: curate@hexhamabbey.org.uk

HOPE, Robert. b 36. Dur Univ BSc 61. Clifton Th Coll 61. **d** 63 **p** 64. C Woking St Mary *Guildf* 63–66; C Surbiton Hill Ch Ch *S'wark* 66–68; Th Students' Sec IVF 68–71; Hon C Wallington *S'wark* 69–71; C Ox St Ebbe w St Pet 71–74; V Walshaw Ch Ch *Man* 74–87; TR Radipole and Melcombe Regis *Sarum* 87–93; rtd 93; PtO *St D* from 93. *1A Swiss Valley, Felinfael, Llanelli SA14 8BS* T: (01554) 759199

HOPE, Canon Susan. b 49. St Jo Coll Dur BA 83 Sheff Univ MA 04. Cranmer Hall Dur 80. **dss** 83 **d** 87 **p** 94. Boston Spa *York* 83–86; Brightside w Wincobank *Sheff* 86–97; Par Dn 87–89; Dn-in-c 89–94; V 94–97; V Chapeltown 97–02; Dioc Missr 02–07; RD Tankersley 00–02; Dir Tr Wilson Carlile Coll of Evang 07–08; Six Preacher Cant Cathl 99–09; Hon Can Sheff Cathl 00–09; P-in-c Shipley St Paul *Bradf* 09–14; V 14; Leeds 14–16; Dioc Adv in Evang *Bradf* 09–14; *Leeds* 14–16; Hon Can Bradf Cathl 12–16; rtd 16; Chapl Wycliffe Hall Ox 16–18; PtO *Dur* from 18. *14 Sunderland Bridge, Durham DH6 5HD* T: 0191-908 5400 M: 07736-774937 E: shope12443@aol.com

✠**HOPE OF THORNES, The Rt Revd and Rt Hon Lord (David Michael).** b 40. PC 91 KCVO 95. Nottm Univ BA 62 Linacre Ho Ox DPhil 65 Hon FGCM 94. St Steph Ho Ox 62. **d** 65 **p** 66 **c** 85. C W Derby St Jo *Liv* 65–67 and 68–70; Chapl Bucharest *Eur* 67–68; V Orford St Andr *Liv* 70–74; Prin St Steph Ho Ox 74–82; V St Marylebone All SS *Lon* 82–85; Master of Guardians Shrine of Our Lady of Walsingham 82–93; Bp Wakef 85–91; Bp Lon 91–95; Dean of HM Chpls Royal 91–95; Abp York 95–05; rtd 05; P-in-c Ilkley St Marg *Bradf* 05–06; Hon Asst Bp Bradf 05–14; Hon Asst Bp Eur 07–12; Hon Asst Bp Blackb 08–17; PtO *Leeds* from 17; Hon Asst Bp Leeds from 19. *35 Hammerton Drive, Hellifield, Skipton BD23 4LZ* E: dmhhellifield@gmail.com

HOPE-BELL, Mrs Vanessa Anne. b 45. TCD BA 67 Univ of Wales (Swansea) MEd 98. **d** 14 **p** 15. NSM Catheiniog *St D* 14–19; NSM Bro Dinefwr from 19. *The Mill House, Llansadwrn, Llanwrda SA19 8LW* T: (01550) 777239 E: v.hopebell@btinternet.com

HOPEGOOD JONES, Mrs Emma Kate. b 88. K Coll Lon BMus 09 Dur Univ BA. Ripon Coll Cuddesdon 14. **d** 17 **p** 18. C Hanborough and Freeland *Ox* 17–21; P-in-c Hatfield Hyde *St Alb* from 21. *Address temp unknown* M: 07896-558932 E: emma.hopegood.jones@gmail.com

HOPEWELL, Canon Jeffery Stewart. b 52. Leic Univ BA 75 ACA 79. EMMTC 82. **d** 85 **p** 86. NSM Houghton on the Hill w Keyham *Leic* 85–88; NSM Houghton-on-the-Hill, Keyham and Hungarton 88–91; C Syston 91–93; TV 93–97; Bp's Ecum Adv 91–97; P-in-c Wymeswold and Prestwold w Hoton 97–04; V Old Dalby, Nether Broughton, Saxelbye etc 04–15; Dioc Ecum Officer 03–06; Hon Can Leic Cathl 14–15; rtd 15; PtO *Leic* from 15. *23 Weare Close, Billesdon, Leicester LE7 9DY* T: 0116-259 9760 E: jshopewell@btinternet.com

HOPKIN, David James. b 67. Birm Univ BTh 94 Univ of Wales MA 14. Ripon Coll Cuddesdon 98. **d** 99 **p** 00. C Wickford and Runwell *Chelmsf* 99–02; TV Penistone and Thurlstone *Wakef* 02–06; TR 06–14; TR Penistone and Thurlstone *Sheff* from 14; AD Tankersley from 19. *The Vicarage, Shrewsbury Road, Penistone, Sheffield S36 6DY* T: (01226) 370954 or 370006 E: david.hopkin@sheffield.org or fatherdavid.pen@outlook.com

HOPKIN WILLIAMS, Jeffrey. *See* WILLIAMS, Robert Jeffrey Hopkin

HOPKINS, Mrs Angela Joan. b 42. Bp Otter Coll Chich CertEd 64. S Dios Minl Tr Scheme 92. **d** 95 **p** 96. NSM Kingsbury H Innocents *Lon* 95–13; PtO from 13. *3 Regal Way, Harrow HA3 0RZ* T: (020) 8907 1045 E: ahopkins762@btinternet.com

HOPKINS, Brenda Alison. b 63. St Martin's Coll Lanc BA 95 Anglia Poly Univ MA 97. Westcott Ho Cam 95. **d** 97 **p** 98. C Camberwell St Geo *S'wark* 97–00; Chapl Nor City Coll of F&HE 00–03. *Rose Tree Cottage, The Green, Stokesby, Great Yarmouth NR29 3EX*

HOPKINS, Christopher John. b 61. Trin Coll Bris 11. **d** 13 **p** 14. C Somerton w Compton Dundon, the Charltons etc *B & W* 13–16; P-in-c Baltonsborough w Butleigh, W Bradley etc from 16. *The Vicarage, Ham Street, Baltonsborough, Glastonbury BA6 8PX* T: (01458) 851681 E: bruebeneficevicar@btinternet.com

HOPKINS, Gillian Frances. b 55. Bedf Coll Lon BA 76 SS Mark & Jo Univ Coll Plymouth PGCE 77 Cam Inst of Educn MA 91. NTMTC BA 07. **d** 07 **p** 08. C Wickford and Runwell *Chelmsf* 07–10; TV Waltham H Cross 10–16; rtd 16; PtO *Chelmsf* from 16. *15 Ferndown, Woodford Road, London E18 2ED* M: 07973-289801 E: gill_hopkins@yahoo.co.uk

HOPKINS, Henry Charles. b 46. RD 87. Edin Th Coll 65. **d** 71 **p** 72. C Dundee St Salvador *Bre* 71–74; C Dundee St Martin 71–74; Chapl RNVR 72–81; R Monifieth *Bre* 74–78; Chapl Miss to Seamen Kenya 78–85; Singapore 85–92; Offg Chapl NZ Defence Force 89–92; Chapl Miss to Seamen Teesside 92–94; V Middlesbrough St Thos *York* 94–97; V N Thornaby 97–18; rtd 18; PtO *York* 18–21. *28 Windsor Oval, Thornaby, Stockton-on-Tees TS17 8PP* T: (01642) 691798 E: hopkins.harry@yahoo.co.uk

HOPKINS, Ian Richard. b 70. Collingwood Coll Dur BA 92. Wycliffe Hall Ox BTh 00. **d** 00 **p** 01. C Edin St Thos 00–04; I 04–13; C Haydock St Mark *Liv* 13–17; C Liv Cathl from 17. *11 Wagon Lane, Haydock, St Helens WA11 0HZ* T: (01744) 302265

HOPKINS, Kenneth Victor John. b 45. Univ Coll Lon BA 66 Lon Univ BD 69 Hull Univ PhD 84. Tyndale Hall Bris 66. **d** 69 **p** 70. C S Mimms Ch Ch *Lon* 69–72; C Branksome St Clem *Sarum* 72–75; P-in-c Trowbridge St Thos 75–76; V 76–81; R Wingfield w Rowley 76–81; Chapl and Lect NE Surrey Coll of Tech 81–84; Hd Student Services Essex Inst of HE 84–88; Kingston Poly 88–92; Kingston Univ 92–98; Dean of Students 98–03; Pro Vice-Chan 04–06; rtd 06. *Quarry Cottage, Duke Street, Withington, Hereford HR1 3QD* T: (01432) 850933

HOPKINS, Lionel. b 48. MBE 14. Open Univ BA 82. St D Coll Lamp. **d** 71 **p** 72. C Llandeilo Tal-y-bont *S & B* 71–74; C Morriston 74–78; P-in-c Waunarllwydd 78–80; V 80–86; Youth Chapl 84–86; V Llangyfelach 86–96; P-in-c Swansea Ch Ch 96–00; Chapl HM Pris Swansea 96–13; rtd 13. *1051 Llangyfelach Road, Tirdeunaw, Swansea SA5 7HY* E: lionelhopkins22@gmail.com

HOPKINS, Mark James. b 86. Fitzw Coll Cam MA 10. Trin Coll Bris MA 14. **d** 13 **p** 14. C Warley Woods *Birm* 13–17; R Castle Bromwich SS Mary and Marg from 17. *67 Chester Road, Castle Bromwich, Birmingham B36 9DP* M: 07745-805478 E: revmarkhopkins@gmail.com

HOPKINS, Neil James. b 72. Brunel Univ BTh 97 MTh 01. Trin Coll Bris 10. **d** 12 **p** 13. C Portswood Ch Ch *Win* 12–16; V Knaphill w Brookwood *Guildf* from 16. *Trinity House, 2 Trinity Road, Knaphill, Woking GU21 2SY* M: 07557-908383 E: neiljuleshopkins@me.com

HOPKINS, Miss Patricia Mary. b 46. Kingston Poly BEd 78. Trin Coll Bris 83. **dss** 85 **d** 87 **p** 94. Gorleston St Andr *Nor* 85–88; C 87–88; C Woking St Jo *Guildf* 88–90; Team Dn Barnham Broom *Nor* 90–94; TV 94–97; V Otford *Roch* 97–07; rtd 07; PtO *Nor* from 08. *Hill Cottage, Broomhill, East Runton, Cromer NR27 9PF* T: (01263) 512338 E: popkins@greenbee.net

HOPKINS, Peter. b 54. Nottm Univ BSc 75 Imp Coll Lon MSc 79. Oak Hill Th Coll BA 86. **d** 86 **p** 87. C Gee Cross *Ches* 86–90; R Gt Gonerby *Linc* 90–95; R Barrowby and Gt Gonerby 95–19; RD Grantham 01–09; rtd 19. *1 Gregory Close, Harlaxton, Grantham NG32 1JG* E: peterhoppy@gmail.com

HOPKINS, Robert James Gardner. b 42. Bris Univ BSc 64 ACA 76 FCA 81. St Alb Minl Tr Scheme. **d** 79 **p** 80. NSM Chorleywood Ch Ch *St Alb* 79–83; NSM Parr Mt *Liv* 83–97; NSM Crookes St Thos *Sheff* 97–09; NSM Philadelphia St Thos 09–15; PtO 15–21; Dir Angl Ch Planting Initiatives from 92; Missr Fresh Expressions from 05. *70 St Thomas Road, Sheffield S10 1UX* T: 0114-267 8266 *or* 278 9378 E: hopkins.the@gmail.com

HOPKINS, Victor John. b 44. UEA LLB 82. CBDTI 06. **d** 07 **p** 08. NSM Sedbergh, Cautley and Garsdale *Bradf* 07–12; NSM Sedbergh, Cautley and Garsdale *Carl* 12–14; PtO *St E* from 15; *Pet* from 15. *94 Chediston Street, Halesworth IP19 8BJ* T: (01986) 875934 E: csninefour@btinternet.com

HOPKINSON, The Ven Barnabas John. b 39. Trin Coll Cam BA 63 MA 67. Linc Th Coll 63. **d** 65 **p** 66. C Langley All SS and Martyrs *Man* 65–67; C Cambridge Gt St Mary w St Mich *Ely* 67–71; Asst Chapl Charterhouse Sch Godalming 71–75; P-in-c Preshute *Sarum* 75–76; TV Marlborough 76–81; RD 77–81; TR Wimborne Minster and Holt 81–86; Can and Preb Sarum Cathl 83–04; RD Wimborne 85–86; Adn Sarum 86–98; P-in-c Stratford sub Castle 87–98; Adn Wilts 98–04; rtd 04; PtO *B & W* 09–15. *Tanners Cottage, 22 Frog Street, Bampton, Tiverton EX16 9NT* T: (01398) 331611 E: barneyesme@onetel.net

HOPKINSON, Benjamin Alaric. b 36. Trin Coll Ox BA 59. Chich Th Coll 59. **d** 61 **p** 62. C Pallion *Dur* 61–66; Rhodesia 66–67; Botswana 67–74; Hon C Sherwood *S'well* 74–77; Hon C Carrington 74–77; V Lowdham 77–85; R Whitby *York* 85–95; Miss to Seafarers from 85; V Stainton w Hilton *York* 95–01; Chapl Cleveland Constabulary 95–01; rtd 01; PtO *Newc* from 01. *3 Watershaugh Road, Warkworth, Morpeth NE65 0TT* T/F: (01665) 714213 E: benjamin.hopkinson@gmail.com

HOPKINSON, Colin Edward. b 57. BA LLB. Ridley Hall Cam. **d** 84 **p** 85. C Chadwell *Chelmsf* 84–87; C Canvey Is 87–90; P-in-c E Springfield 90–98; RD Chelmsf N 95–99; R Langdon Hills 98–21; rtd 21. *49 Harecroft Road, Otley LS21 2BG* E: cchopkinson@aol.com

HOPKINSON, David John. b 47. Ox NSM Course. **d** 79 **p** 80. NSM Wardington *Ox* 79; Hon C Didcot St Pet 80–83; C Headingley *Ripon* 83–87; P-in-c Leeds All So 87–91; R Middleton Tyas w Croft and Eryholme 91–95; V Leeds Belle Is St Jo and St Barn 95–98; rtd 98; PtO *Ripon* 98–06; *Wakef* 07–12. *11 Old Well Head, Halifax HX1 2BN* T: (01422) 361226

HOPKINSON, William Humphrey. b 48. Lon Univ BSc 69 Dur Univ MA 78 Nottm Univ MPhil 84 Man Poly MSc 90 California State Univ MEd 00 ARIC 73. Cranmer Hall Dur. **d** 77 **p** 78. C Normanton *Derby* 77–80; C Sawley 80–82; V Birtles *Ches* 82–87; Dir Past Studies NOC 82–94; Dir Course Development 90–94; CME Officer *Ches* 87–94; P-in-c Tenterden St Mich *Cant* 94–96; Dir Min and Tr 94–02; Hon Can Cant Cathl 01–02; PtO 03–06; World Faith Manager Harmondsworth Immigration Removal Cen 03–05; Registrar Lon Academy of HE 05–06; Manager Independent Newham Users Forum 07; Asst Prof California State Univ USA from 07; rtd 13. *91 Chobham Road, London E15 1LX* M: 07057-111933 E: bill@bhopkinson.co.uk

HOPLEY, David. b 37. Wells Th Coll 62. **d** 65 **p** 66. C Frome St Jo *B & W* 65–68; R Staunton-on-Arrow w Byton and Kinsham *Heref* 68–81; P-in-c Lingen 68–81; P-in-c Aymestrey and Leinthall Earles w Wigmore etc 72–81; R Buckland Newton, Long Burton etc Sarum 81–02; rtd 02; PtO *B & W* 07–19. *Sunnyside, Clatworthy, Taunton TA4 2EH* T: (01984) 623842

HOPPER, Philip John. b 61. Kent Univ BA 84 Ox Poly PGCE 89. Sarum Coll 18. **d** 20. NSM Pilton w Croscombe, N Wootton and Dinder *B & W* 20–21; NSM Midsomer Norton w Clandown from 21. *13 Waterloo Road, Shepton Mallet BA4 5HG* M: 07596-759584

HOPPER, Canon Robert Keith. b 45. Cranmer Hall Dur 74. **d** 77 **p** 78. C Oxclose *Dur* 77–80; C Hebburn St Jo 80–82; V Lobley Hill 82–04; P-in-c Marley Hill 02–04; V Hillside 04–16; Hon Can Dur Cathl 09–16; rtd 16; PtO *Dur* 16–21. *3 Hallgarth View, High Pittington, Durham DH6 1AS* M: 07960-754744 E: canonbob@durham.uk.net

HOPTHROW, Mrs Elizabeth Rosemary Gladys. b 45. **d** 01 **p** 02. NSM Aylesham w Adisham *Cant* 01–04; NSM Nonington w Wymynswold and Goodnestone etc 01–04; NSM Barham w Bishopsbourne and Kingston 04–11; Chapl Pilgrims Hospice Cant 01–11; Warden The Quiet View from 11; PtO *Cant* from 11. *146 The Street, Kingston, Canterbury CT4 6JQ* T: (01227) 830070 M: 07977-754920 E: lizziehopthrow@gmail.com

HOPWOOD, Adrian Patrick. b 37. N Lon Poly BSc 61 CBiol MRSB. Ox Min Course 87. **d** 90 **p** 91. NSM Chesham Bois *Ox* 90–93; NSM Amersham 93–95; NSM Ridgeway 95–05; rtd 05; PtO *B & W* from 06. *15 Waverley, Somerton TA11 6SH* T: (01458) 274527 E: adrian@proceff.f9.co.uk

HOPWOOD OWEN, Mrs Karen. b 58. Padgate Coll of Educn CertEd 79 St Martin's Coll Lanc DASE 90. **d** 95 **p** 96. OLM Peel *Man* 95–99; OLM Walkden and Lt Hulton 99–13; TV Worsley from 13; AD Eccles 16–20. *8 Landrace Drive, Worsley, Manchester M28 1UY* M: 07964-663225 E: karen.h.owen@ntlworld.com

HORAN, Helene. b 57. Qu Foundn (Course) 14. **d** 17 **p** 18. NSM Chelmsley Wood *Birm* from 17. *7 Rotherby Grove, Marston Green, Birmingham B37 7XL* E: revhelene@virginmedia.com

HORAN, Joan Anne. b 53. BA 74 DipEd 75. **d** 05 **p** 06. Australia 05–09; R Grimshoe *Ely* from 09. *The Rectory, 7 Oak Street, Feltwell, Thetford IP26 4DD* T: (01842) 828034 E: joanhoran123@btinternet.com

HORAN, John Champain. b 52. WMMTC 95. **d** 98 **p** 99. NSM Leckhampton SS Phil and Jas w Cheltenham St Jas *Glouc* 98–08; Dioc Communications Officer 01–02; Chapl 2gether NHS Foundn Trust 05–17; PtO *Glouc* from 17. *34 Pickering Road, Cheltenham GL53 0LB*

HORBURY, Prof William. b 42. Oriel Coll Ox BA 64 MA 67 Clare Coll Cam BA 66 PhD 71 DD 00 FBA 97. Westcott Ho Cam 64. **d** 69 **p** 70. Fell Clare Coll Cam 68–72; CCC Cam from 78; R Gt w Lt Gransden *Ely* 72–78; Lect Div Cam Univ 84–98; Prof Jewish and Early Chr Studies from 98; P-in-c Cambridge St Botolph *Ely* 90–14; PtO 15–20. *5 Grange Road, Cambridge CB3 9AS* T: (01223) 363529 F: 462751 E: wh10000@cam.ac.uk

HORDER, Mrs Catharine Joy. b 51. Battersea Coll of Educn CertEd 72 UWE BA 98. S Dios Minl Tr Scheme 92. **d** 95 **p** 96. C Burrington and Churchill *B & W* 95–00; TV Yatton Moor 00–11; rtd 11. *The Sanctuary, Bridford, Exeter EX6 7HS* T: (01647) 252750

HORE (formerly HART), Debbie. b 56. **d** 11 **p** 16. NSM St Marylebone St Paul *Lon* 11–17; NSM Sawbridgeworth *St Alb* from 17. *St Mary's Lodge, Knight Street, Sawbridgeworth CM21 9AX* M: 07985-649120 E: deacondebs@gmail.com

HORE, Leslie Nicholas Peter. b 40. SWMTC 99. **d** 02 **p** 03. OLM Treverbyn *Truro* 02–10; rtd 10; PtO *Truro* from 16. *Tremore Noweth, Hallaze Road, Penwithick, St Austell PL26 8YW* T: (01726) 851750 E: peterhore@hotmail.co.uk

HORLESTON, Kenneth William. b 50. Oak Hill Th Coll BA 86. **d** 86 **p** 87. C Wednesfield Heath *Lich* 86–89; V Blagreaves *Derby* 89–00; P-in-c Horsley 00–02; P-in-c Denby 00–02; V Horsley and Denby 02–10; C Morley w Smalley and Horsley Woodhouse 06–07; rtd 10. *11 Pegasus Way, Hilton, Derby DE65 5HW* T: (01283) 735600 E: kwhorleston@gmail.com

HORLOCK, Andrew John. b 51. Bath Univ BSc 74 Open Univ MPhil 89 Nottm Univ PhD 99. Ridley Hall Cam 03. **d** 05 **p** 06. C Crich and S Wingfield *Derby* 05–08; P-in-c Lugano *Eur* 08–15; rtd 15; PtO *Eur* from 15. *32 Meadow Close, Lavant, Chichester PO18 0FJ* T: (01243) 950203 M: 07952-180370 E: andyhorlock@hotmail.com

HORLOCK, The Very Revd Brian William. b 31. OBE 78. Univ of Wales (Lamp) BA 55. Chich Th Coll 55. **d** 57 **p** 58. C Chiswick St Nic w St Mary *Lon* 57–61; C Witney *Ox* 61–62; V N Acton St Gabr *Lon* 62–68; Chapl Oslo w Bergen, Trondheim and Stavanger *Eur* 68–89; RD Scandinavia 75–79; Adn 80–89; Hon Can Brussels Cathl 80–89; Dean Gib 89–98; Chapl Gib 89–98; rtd 98; PtO *Eur* from 98; *Sarum* 98–16. *1 Richard's Close, Royal Wootton Bassett, Swindon SN4 7LE* T: (01793) 848344 F: 848378 E: brian@horlocks.com

HORLOCK, Peter Richard. b 76. UWE BA 97. Oak Hill Th Coll BA 04. **d** 04 **p** 05. C Rusholme H Trin *Man* 04–12; Missr to Business Community from 12; C Man St Ann from 12. *63 Burnside Drive, Burnage, Manchester M19 2NA* M: 07890-860022 E: pete@ministry2business.co.uk *or* petehorlock@gmail.com

HORLOCK, Timothy Edward. b 72. Anglia Poly Univ BSc 94 Bath Univ PGCE 96. Ridley Hall Cam 05. d 07 p 08. C Bedford Ch Ch St Alb 07–10; P-in-c Stevenage St Pet Broadwater 10–14; V 14–16; RD Stevenage 13–16; V Chorleywood St Andr from 16. The Vicarage, 37 Quickley Lane, Chorleywood, Rickmansworth WD3 5AE M: 07787-968843 E: tim.horlock@st-andrews.org.uk

HORN, Colin Clive. b 39. CEng MIMechE FEI. Cant Sch of Min. d 83 p 84. NSM Yalding w Collier Street Roch 83–91; V Kemsing w Woodlands 91–98; RD Shoreham 94–98; rtd 99; PtO B & W from 00. Saw Mill Cottage, High Street, Leigh upon Mendip, Radstock BA3 5QQ T/F: (01373) 812736 M: 07885-523190 E: colinhorn@hotmail.com

HORN, David Henry. See RANDOLPH-HORN, David Henry

HORNBUCKLE, Eric Wayne. b 67. d 07. USA 07–08; C Tonbridge St Steph Roch 16–17. 2277 Longview Drive, Woodbridge VA 22191, USA T: (001) (703) 492 9279 E: eric.hornbuckle@gmail.com

HORNBY (née CHRISTIAN), Mrs Helen. b 47. K Coll Lon BA 68 AKC 68 Lon Inst of Educn PGCE 69. Cranmer Hall Dur 00. d 02 p 03. C Briercliffe Blackb 02–07; C Blackpool St Jo 07–11; C Layton and Staining 11–12; rtd 12; PtO Blackb from 12. 2 Arnside Avenue, Lytham St Annes FY8 3SA T: (01253) 711215 E: revhelenhornby@yahoo.co.uk

HORNBY, Matthew. b 75. d 13 p 14. C S Barrow Carl 13–17; R Coppull Blackb from 17. The Vicarage, 209 Chapel Lane, Coppull, Chorley PR7 4NA T: (01257) 791218 M: 07903-136128 E: hornbymatt@gmail.com

HORNE, Mona Lyn Denison. b 38. Gipsy Hill Coll of Educn TCert 58. WEMTC 98. d 99 p 00. OLM Cheltenham St Mark Glouc 99–12; rtd 12; PtO Glouc from 16. 37 Oakdene, Lansdown Road, Cheltenham GL51 6PX T: (01242) 236786 E: lynbrihorne@btinternet.com

HORNE, Simon Timothy. b 62. Ball Coll Ox BA 86 MA 90 Birm Univ PhD 99 RN(MH) 89. Qu Coll Birm BD 94. d 95 p 96. C Basingstoke Win 95–99; C Fordingbridge 99–01; TV Fordingbridge and Breamore and Hale etc 01–11; Chapl RN 11–19; Chapl RNR from 19. 9B West Abercromby Street, Helensburgh G84 9LH M: 07733-960056

HORNER, Graham. b 57. Grey Coll Dur BSc 78 ACA 81. St Jo Coll Nottm 93. d 93 p 94. C Longdon-upon-Tern, Rodington, Uppington etc Lich 93–95; C Wrockwardine Deanery 95–96; TV 96–02; TR 02–07; RD Wrockwardine 02–07; V Gt Wyrley 07–18; V Riccall, Barlby and Hemingbrough York from 18. The Vicarage, 10 Grove Park, Barlby, Selby YO8 5LP E: gandjhorner123@btinternet.com

HORNER, James. d 13 p 14. C Bailieborough w Knockbride, Shercock and Mullagh K, E & A 14–16; I from 16. The Rectory, Bailieborough, Co Cavan, Republic of Ireland T: (00353) (42) 967 5822 M: 87-622 3609 E: ianewhorner@gmail.com

HORNER, Richard Murray. b 61. Dur Univ BSc 83. NTMTC 93. d 96 p 97. C Sherborne w Castleton and Lillington Sarum 96–99; Chapl Rugby Sch from 99. Tudor House, 4 Horton Crescent, Rugby CV22 5DL T: (01788) 544939

HORNER, Sally Jane. b 68. City Univ BSc 94 Cam Univ BTh 08 Cant Ch Ch Univ MA 13. Westcott Ho Cam 06. d 08 p 09. C Peckham St Jo w St Andr S'wark 08–12; Chapl Notts Healthcare NHS Foundn Trust 12–15; Chapl W Lon Mental Health NHS Foundn Trust 15–18; PtO S'wark 14–18; Chapl Ox Health NHS Foundn Trust from 18. Oxford Health NHS Foundation Trust, Corporate Services Building, Littlemore Mental Health Centre, Sandford Road, Littlemore, Oxford OX4 4XN T: (01865) 902760 E: sally.horner@oxfordhealth.nhs.uk

HOROBIN, Canon Timothy John. b 60. St Jo Coll Nottm 92. d 94 p 95. C Nelson St Phil Blackb 94–98; P-in-c Blackpool St Paul 98–00; PtO 05–06; LtO 06–10; P-in-c Lower Darwen St Jas 10–11; V from 11; P-in-c Over Darwen St Jas and Hoddlesden from 17; Hon Can Blackb Cathl from 18. The Vicarage, Johnson New Road, Hoddlesden, Darwen BB3 3NN T: (01254) 53898 M: 07811-074063 E: stjameschurch.lowerdarwen@aol.co.uk

HORREX, Mrs Gay Lesley. b 42. d 96 p 97. OLM Walton-on-Thames Guildf 96–07; rtd 07; PtO Guildf 07–17; Portsm from 08. 25 Pine Walk, Liss GU33 7AT T: (01730) 893827 E: glhorrex@gmail.com

HORROCKS, Judith Anne. b 53. Univ of Calgary BSc 76 Keele Univ MA 99. St Jo Coll Nottm. dss 82 d 87 p 94. Denton Ch Ch Man 82–85; Whalley Range St Edm 85–97; Par Dn 87–97; C 94–97; Chapl Man R Infirmary 88–90; Chapl Christie Hosp NHS Trust Man 95–03; Chapl S Man Univ Hosps NHS Trust 98–03; Lic Preacher Man 97–03; Hon Can Man Cathl 02–03; Multifaith Chapl Co-ord Sheff Hallam Univ 03–05; Chapl St Ann's Hospice Manchester 05–09; Lect Bolton St Pet Man 09–11; Lect Bolton St Pet w St Phil 11–14; Ch in Sch Development Worker 14–17; Lic Preacher 14–17; rtd 17; PtO Eur from 17. Calle Cardon 76, Tamaragua, 35660 Corralejo,

Fuerteventura, Spain T: (0035) 928 345 360 M: 660 068 782 E: judie.horrocks@ymail.com

HORROCKS, Oliver John. b 30. Clare Coll Cam BA 53 MA 57. Westcott Ho Cam 53. d 55 p 56. C Moss Side Ch Ch Man 55–58; C Arnold S'well 58–60; R Ancoats Man 60–67; R Barthomley Ches 67–96; rtd 96; PtO Ches 98–14. 36 Station Road, Alsager, Stoke-on-Trent ST7 2PD T: (01270) 877284

HORROCKS, Robert James. b 56. Grey Coll Dur BSc 78. St Jo Coll Nottm. d 82 p 83. C Denton Ch Ch Man 82–85; R Whalley Range St Edm 85–97; P-in-c Bolton St Paul w Em 97–06; P-in-c Daubhill 05–06; TR New Bury w Gt Lever 06–16; P-in-c Fuerteventura Eur from 17. Calle Cardon 76, Tamaragua, 35660 Corralejo, Fuerteventura, Spain T: (0034) 928 345 360 E: revbobhorrocks@yahoo.co.uk

HORSFALL, Canon Andrew Stuart. b 64. Qu Coll Birm 93. d 06 p 06. Methodist Min 95–06; Chapl E Lancs Hosps NHS Trust 05–09; Chapl Co-ord from 09; NSM Feniscowles Blackb 06–07; Hon C Accrington Ch the King 11–12; Can Res Blackb Cathl 16–20. Royal Blackburn Hospital, Haslingden Road, Blackburn BB2 3HH T: (01254) 263555 or 736849 E: andrew.horsfall@blackburncathedral.co.uk

HORSFALL, David John. b 55. Bris Poly BA 77. St Jo Coll Nottm 87. d 89 p 90. C Chaddesden St Mary Derby 89–92; V Swadlincote 92–11; RD Repton 99–09; R Chesterfield H Trin and Ch Ch 11–20; rtd 20. 73 Spindletree Drive, Oakwood, Derby DE21 2DG T: (01332) 834064 E: djhorsfall@hotmail.com

HORSFALL, Deborah. See NASH, Deborah

HORSHAM, Archdeacon of. See MARTIN, The Ven Angela Frances

HORSHAM, Area Bishop of. See BUSHYAGER, The Rt Revd Ruth Kathleen Frances

HORSINGTON, Timothy Frederick. b 44. Dur Univ BA 66. Wycliffe Hall Ox 67. d 69 p 70. C Halewood Liv 69–72; C Farnworth 72–75; C-in-c Widnes St Jo 72–75; P-in-c Llangarron w Llangrove Heref 75–82; P-in-c Whitchurch w Ganarew 77–82; R Llangarron w Llangrove, Whitchurch and Ganarew 83–84; R Highclere and Ashmansworth w Crux Easton Win 84–09; rtd 09; PtO B & W from 12; Win 12–17. 27 Arlington Close, Yeovil BA21 3TB T: (01935) 410731

HORSLEY, Canon Alan Avery. b 36. St Chad's Coll Dur BA 58 Pacific States Univ MA 84 PhD 85. Qu Coll Birm 58. d 60 p 61. C Daventry Pet 60–63; C Reading St Giles Ox 63–64; C Wokingham St Paul 64–66; V Yeadon St Andr Bradf 66–71; R Heyford w Stowe Nine Churches Pet 71–78; RD Daventry 76–78; V Oakham w Hambleton and Egleton 78–81; V Oakham, Hambleton, Egleton, Braunston and Brooke 81–86; Can Pet Cathl 79–86; V Lanteglos by Fowey Truro 86–88; Provost St Andr Cathl Inverness Mor 88–91; R Inverness St Andr 88–91; P-in-c Culloden St Mary-in-the-Fields 88–91; P-in-c Strathnairn St Paul 88–91; V Mill End and Heronsgate w W Hyde St Alb 91–01; RD Rickmansworth 00–01; rtd 01; PtO Pet 03–14. 22 Vyner Close, Thorpe Astley, Braunstone, Leicester LE3 3EJ T: 0116-289 2695 M: 07503-321553 E: canonalanahorsley@gmail.com

HORSLEY, Peter Alec. b 56. Leeds Metrop Univ CertEd 98. Cranmer Hall Dur 99. d 01 p 02. C Acomb St Steph and St Aid York 01–05; P-in-c Wheldrake w Thorganby 05–08; R Derwent Ings 08–11; V Acomb St Steph and St Aid 11–15; rtd 15; PtO York from 15. 38 Campbell Avenue, Holgate, York YO24 4LA T: (01904) 799095 E: peterhorsley1@icloud.com

HORSMAN, Andrew Alan. b 49. Otago Univ BA 70 Man Univ MA 72 PhD 75. St Steph Ho Ox BA 80 MA 87. d 81 p 82. C Hillingdon All SS Lon 81–84; C Lt Stanmore St Lawr 84–87; TV Haxby w Wigginton York 87–98; V Acomb Moor 98–15; P-in-c York All SS N Street 03–15; rtd 15; PtO York from 19. 24 Mayfair House, Piccadilly, York YO1 9QJ E: andrew@horsmanz.plus.com

HORSWELL, Kevin George. b 55. Jes Coll Cam BA 77 MA 81 Nottm Univ BA 81. St Jo Coll Nottm 79. d 82 p 83. C Bootle Ch Ch Liv 82–86; Chapl LMH Ox 86–91; C Ox St Giles and SS Phil and Jas w St Marg 86–91; R Dodleston Ches 91–00; R Llanaber w Caerdeon Ban 00–15; AD Ardudwy 12–15; V Mold St As 15–16; TV Mold Miss Area from 17. The Vicarage, 8 Church Lane, Mold CH7 1BW T: (01352) 752960

HORTON, Anne. See HORTON, Roberta Anne

HORTON, David Harold. b 49. St Jo Coll Dur BA 72. NEOC 82. d 86 p 87. C Enfield St Jas Lon 86–90; Min Joydens Wood St Barn CD Roch 90–93; V Joydens Wood St Barn 93–99; P-in-c Rosherville 99–04; rtd 04; PtO Roch 09–18. 6 Blaisdon Way, Cheltenham GL51 0WR T: (01242) 241350 E: davidhhorton@gmail.com

HORTON, Jane. See HORTON, Margaret Jane

HORTON, John. b 49. STETS 05. d 07 p 08. NSM Exhall Cov 07–11; NSM Stourdene Gp 11–19; rtd 19; PtO Cov from

386

20. *16 Huntington Court, Lowes Lane, Wellesbourne, Warwick CV35 9RF* E: john.horton123@btinternet.com

HORTON, Mrs Joy. b 52. CertEd 73 Kent Univ MA 98. SEITE 94. **d** 97 **p** 98. C Dartford St Edm *Roch* 97–01; Chapl Bromley Hosps NHS Trust 01–02; C Erith St Jo *Roch* 02–03; PtO 03–04; Chapl Burrswood Chr Cen 04–08; PtO *St E* from 09. *3 Furze Close, Thurston, Bury St Edmunds IP31 3PR* T: (01359) 230649

HORTON, Mrs Margaret Jane. b 60. ARCM 83. Ripon Coll Cuddesdon 13. **d** 15 **p** 16. C Truro St Mary 15–18; Prayer and Discipleship Co-ordinator from 18; Public Preacher from 18. *22 Stret Myghtern Arthur, Nansledan, Newquay TR8 4GJ* T: (01872) 360028 E: jane.horton@truro.anglican.org

HORTON, Ralph Edward. b 41. S'wark Ord Course 75. **d** 78 **p** 79. C Streatham St Leon *S'wark* 78–81; TV Catford (Southend) and Downham 81–88; V Ashford St Matt *Lon* 88–12; rtd 12. *12 Convent Fields, Sidmouth EX10 8QR*

HORTON, Canon Roberta Anne. b 44. Leic Univ BSc 66 CertEd 67 Nottm Univ BCombStuds 82. Linc Th Coll 79. **dss** 82 **d** 87 **p** 94. Cambridge St Jas *Ely* 82–86; Beaumont Leys *Leic* 86–91; Par Dn 87–91; Dioc Dir of Tr 91–00; P-in-c Swithland 94–99; R Woodhouse, Woodhouse Eaves and Swithland 00–14; Hon Can Leic Cathl 94–14; rtd 14; PtO *Leic* from 14. *8B Copeland Road, Birstall, Leicester LE4 3AA* E: rahorton@outlook.com

HORTON, Simon James. b 65. **d** 12 **p** 13. C Goring-by-Sea *Chich* 12–16; P-in-c Saltdean 16–21; V from 21. *The Vicarage, 51 Saltdean Vale, Saltdean, Brighton BN2 8HE* T: (01273) 271683

HORWELL, Elizabeth. b 54. Southn Univ BSc 76 Essex Univ MA 77 Birm Univ PhD 84 Wolv Univ PGCE 94. ERMC 04. **d** 07 **p** 08. C Wanstead St Mary w Ch Ch *Chelmsf* 07–11; R 11–16; rtd 16; PtO *Chelmsf* from 16. *32 Tumulus Way, Colchester CO2 9SD* T: (01206) 521995 M: 07835-450837 E: ehorwell@hotmail.com

HORWOOD, Mrs Juliet Joy. b 51. Ex Univ BSc 73. SWMTC 09. **d** 11. NSM Topsham and Wear *Ex* from 11; Chapl R Devon and Ex NHS Foundn Trust from 11. *20 Higher Shapter Street, Topsham, Exeter EX3 0AW* T: (01392) 875558 E: juliet_horwood@yahoo.co.uk

HOSKIN, Canon David William. b 49. Hatf Coll Dur BSc 71. Wycliffe Hall Ox 72. **d** 75 **p** 76. C Bridlington Priory *York* 75–78; C Rodbourne Cheney *Bris* 78–79; C Bebington *Ches* 79–82; R Lockington and Lund and Scorborough w Leconfield *York* 82–88; V Beverley St Mary 88–10; RD Beverley 97–07; Can and Preb York Minster 05–10; rtd 10. *24 Chestnut Avenue, Driffield YO25 6SH* T: (01377) 538172 E: david@hoskin.eu

HOSKINS, Hugh George. b 46. S Dios Minl Tr Scheme. **d** 84 **p** 85. NSM Hilperton w Whaddon and Staverton etc *Sarum* 84–87; C Calne and Blackland 87–90; R W Lavington and the Cheverells 90–97; Asst Chapl HM Pris Erlestoke 94–97; TR Upper Wylye Valley *Sarum* 97–04; RD Heytesbury 00–03; TR Pewsey and Swanborough 04–10; P-in-c Upavon w Rushall and Charlton 07–10; TR Vale of Pewsey 10–11; rtd 11; PtO *Sarum* from 11. *42 St Mary's Close, Hilperton Marsh, Trowbridge BA14 7PW* T: (01225) 781579 E: hughhoskins9@gmail.com

HOSKINS, John Paul. b 74. Univ Coll Dur BA 95 MA 96 MLitt 07 Trin Coll Cam BA 99 MA 04 Ox Univ MTh 10. Westcott Ho Cam 97 Ripon Coll Cuddesdon 05. **d** 07 **p** 08. C Bakewell *Derby* 07–11; Bp's Chapl *Glouc* 11–16; Min Can Glouc Cathl 13–16; P-in-c Winchcombe from 16. *The Rectory, Langley Road, Winchcombe, Cheltenham GL54 5QP* T: (01242) 603640 E: johnpaul@winchcombeparish.org.uk

HOSKINS, Preb Rosemary Anne. b 56. Surrey Univ BA 03. Wesley Coll Bris 99 STETS 01. **d** 02 **p** 03. NSM Camelot Par *B & W* 02–06; NSM Cam Vale 06–20; Warden of Readers Wells Adnry 05–09; RD Bruton and Cary 10–16; Preb Wells Cathl 09–20; PtO from 21. *Springfields, Weston Bampfylde, Yeovil BA22 7HZ* T: (01963) 440026 E: revroseanne@gmail.com

HOSKINS, Mrs Susan. b 59. Sarum Coll 17. **d** 20 **p** 21. NSM Wrington w Butcombe and Burrington *B & W* from 20. *23 Stowey Road, Yatton, Bristol BS49 4HX* T: (01934) 87143 M: 07972-225850 E: sue-hoskins@outlook.com

HOST, Mrs Charmaine Anne. b 54. Birm Univ BA 00. WMMTC 87. **d** 90 **p** 94. C Westwood *Cov* 90–94; C Whitnash 94–96; V Kineton 96–08; V Combroke w Compton Verney 96–08; P-in-c Warmington w Shotteswell and Radway w Ratley 07–08; Asst Chapl Paris St Mich *Eur* 08–09; P-in-c Bishopswood *Lich* 09–11; V 11–15; P-in-c Brewood 09–11; V 11–15; TV Smestow Vale 15–20; rtd 21. *10 Birch Grove, Wellesbourne, Warwick CV35 9SJ* E: charmainehost@yahoo.co.uk *or* charmainehost@btinternet.com

HOTCHEN, Stephen Jeffrie. b 50. Bradf Coll of Educn. Linc Th Coll 85. **d** 87 **p** 88. C Morpeth *Newc* 87–90; TV High Wycombe *Ox* 90–91; R Dingwall and Strathpeffer *Mor* 91–94; V Rickerscote *Lich* 94–04; R Aylmerton, Runton, Beeston Regis and Gresham *Nor* 04–07; P-in-c Altofts *Wakef* 07–13; P-in-c Badsworth 13–14; *Leeds* 14–19; Dioc Adv on Disability Issues *Wakef* 13–14; *Leeds* 14–19; Chapl Princess of Wales Hospice 13–19; rtd 19; PtO *Lich* 19–21. *36 Devereux Gardens, Great Haywood, Stafford ST18 0WY* M: 07976-387199 E: stephenhotchen@btinternet.com

HOTCHIN, Mrs Hilary Moya. b 52. Birm Univ CertEd 73. WMMTC 85. **d** 88 **p** 94. NSM Redditch St Steph *Worc* 88–91; Par Dn Handsworth *Sheff* 91–94; C 94–96; TV Maltby 96–98; NSM Marfleet *York* 06–08; NSM Sutton St Mich 08–15; PtO 16–17 and 18–20. *8 Whisperwood Way, Bransholme, Hull HU7 4JT* T: (01482) 828015

HOTCHKISS, Mrs Mary. b 79. Cape Town Univ BSocSc 01. Trin Coll Bris 17. **d** 19 **p** 20. C Bris St Aid w St Geo, Fishponds St Jo, and Two Mile Hill from 19. *2 Jockey Lane, Bristol BS5 8NZ* M: 07570-100775 E: revmhotchkiss@gmail.com

HOUGH, Adrian Michael. b 59. Hertf Coll Ox BA 80 MA 84 DPhil 84 MRSC LRPS. Ripon Coll Cuddesdon BA 91. **d** 92 **p** 93. C Martley and Wichenford, Knightwick etc *Worc* 92–96; Asst P Evesham Deanery 96–97; V Badsey w Aldington and Offenham and Bretforton 97–04; C Lerwick and Burravoe *Ab* 04–05; PtO *Worc* 05–06; Bp's Chapl and Asst *Ex* 06–11; Episc V and Chapl 11–16; Dioc Miss and Past Sec 16–20; Dir IME 4-7 08–15; NSM Broadclyst, Clyst Honiton, Pinhoe, Rockbeare etc 19–21; NSM Pinhoe w Poltimore from 21. *76 Causey Lane, Exeter EX1 3SH* T: (01392) 468004 E: adrianmhough@btinternet.com

HOUGH, Miss Carole Elizabeth. b 59. Lon Hosp SRN 81. St Jo Coll Nottm 87. **d** 91 **p** 94. C Beoley *Worc* 91–95; Asst Chapl Addenbrooke's NHS Trust 95–98; Chapl Milton Keynes Hosp NHS Foundn Trust 98–09; Chapl Milton Keynes Primary Care Trust 98–09; Chapl St Jo Hospice Moggerhanger 10–12; Chapl Bucks Healthcare NHS Trust from 13; Chapl Florence Nightingale Hospice 13–19; Chapl MHA Westbury Grange Care Home and Dementia Care from 19. *28 Pettigrew Close, Walnut Tree, Milton Keynes MK7 7LL* M: 07947-257425 E: carolehough59@gmail.com

HOUGH, Michael Jeremy. b 61. Wilson Carlile Coll. Oak Hill Th Coll 00. **d** 02 **p** 03. C Redhill H Trin *S'wark* 02–06; P-in-c Woodmansterne 06–11; R 11–13; V Redhill H Trin from 13. *4 Carlton Road, Redhill RH1 2BX* T: (01737) 773816 M: 07872-525144 E: mick@htredhill.com

HOUGH, Sharron Lesley. b 54. **d** 01 **p** 02. OLM Willenhall H Trin *Lich* 01–05; C Bentley 05–09; P-in-c 09–11; TV Bentley Em and Willenhall H Trin 11–19; rtd 20. *10 Pineneedle Croft, Willenhall WV12 4BY* T: (01902) 410458

HOUGHTON, Barbara Jayne. b 72. St Mellitus Coll 19. **d** 21. C Preston St Steph *Blackb* from 21. *29 Bow Lane, Preston PR1 8ND* M: 07508-706937 E: barbarahoughton1@gmail.com

HOUGHTON, Christopher Guy. b 64. W Surrey Coll of Art & Design BA 86. Oak Hill Th Coll BA 89. **d** 89 **p** 90. C Mossley Hill St Matt and St Jas *Liv* 89–92; C Ashton-in-Makerfield St Thos 92–95; C Southport St Phil and St Paul 95–96; Chapl Chorley and S Ribble NHS Trust 96–01; rtd 01; PtO *Blackb* from 03. *35 Deerfold, Chorley PR7 1UD* E: rev.chris.htn@hotmail.co.uk

HOUGHTON, David John. b 47. Edin Univ BSc(Econ) 68. Cuddesdon Coll 69. **d** 71 **p** 72. C Prestbury *Glouc* 71–74; Prec Gib Cathl *Eur* 74–76; Chapl Madrid 76–78; C Croydon St Jo *Cant* 78–80; Chapl Warw Sch 80–85; P-in-c Isleworth St Fran *Lon* 85–90; USA 90–91; TV Clapham Team *S'wark* 91–01; RD Clapham 93–01; V Clapham H Spirit 02; Chapl Paris St Geo *Eur* 02–07; P-in-c Surbiton St Andr and St Mark *S'wark* 07–10; V 10–12; AD Kingston 09–12; rtd 12; PtO *Chich* from 13; *Roch* from 13; *S'wark* from 14; *Eur* from 18. *2 Milton Drive, Tunbridge Wells TN2 3DE* T: (01892) 541988 M: 07984-854036 E: houghton308@btinternet.com

HOUGHTON, Canon Geoffrey John. b 59. Ridley Hall Cam 87. **d** 90 **p** 91. C Sholing *Win* 90–94; P-in-c Jersey All SS 94–99; V 99–09; P-in-c Jersey St Simon 94–99; V 99–09; P-in-c Jersey H Trin 05–06; R from 06; Vice-Dean Jersey from 99; Hon Chapl Jersey Hospice from 96; Hon Can Win Cathl from 11. *Holy Trinity Rectory, La Rue du Presbytere, Trinity, Jersey JE3 5JB* T/F: (01534) 861110 E: geoffhoughton51@gmail.com

HOUGHTON, Graham. See HOUGHTON, Peter Graham

HOUGHTON, Hugh Alexander Gervase. b 76. St Jo Coll Cam BA 97 MPhil 98 MA 01 Leeds Univ BA 02 Birm Univ PhD 06. Coll of Resurr Mirfield 00. **d** 03 **p** 04. NSM Weoley Castle *Birm* 03–06; NSM Headington Quarry *Ox* 06–09; PtO *Birm* from 09; Research Fell Birm Univ 06–15; Reader NT Textual

Scholarship 15–18; Prof NT Textual Scholarship from 18. *ITSEE, Department of Theology and Religion, University of Birmingham, Edgbaston, Birmingham B15 2TT* T: 0121-415 8341 E: h.a.g.houghton@bham.ac.uk

HOUGHTON, Ian David. b 50. Lanc Univ BA 71 Newc Univ CertEd 74. Sarum & Wells Th Coll 80. **d** 82 **p** 83. C Newc St Geo 82–85; Chapl Newc Poly 85–92; Chapl Northumbria Univ 92–95; Master Newc St Thos Prop Chpl 90–95; Ind Chapl Black Country Urban Ind Miss *Lich* 95–04; Res Min Bilston 95–04; Chapl Pet City Cen 04–08; C Pet St Jo 04–08; P-in-c Osmotherley w Harlsey and Ingleby Arncliffe *York* 08–09; V 09–18; P-in-c Leake w Over and Nether Silton and Kepwick 08–09; V 09–18; P-in-c Felixkirk w Boltby 08–09; V 09–18; P-in-c Kirkby Knowle 08–09; V 09–18; P-in-c Cowesby 08–09; R 09–18; RD Mowbray 14–17; rtd 18. *19 Weavers Green, Northallerton DL7 8FJ* M: 07742-563519

HOUGHTON, Canon Josephine Elizabeth Mayer. b 80. Birm Univ BA 01 PhD 07. St Steph Ho Ox BA 09 MA 14. **d** 09 **p** 10. C Handsworth St Andr *Birm* 09–13; P-in-c Stirchley 13–15; V 15–16; Bp's Dom Chapl 16–19; Asst Dioc Learning Adv *Cov* 16–17; Can Res Birm Cathl from 19. *Birmingham Cathedral, Colmore Row, Birmingham B3 2QB* T: 0121-262 1840 E: canonprecentor@birminghamcathedral.com

HOUGHTON, Matthew Walker. b 71. Ridley Hall Cam 14. **d** 16 **p** 17. C Gt Baddow *Chelmsf* 16–19; C Margaretting w Mountnessing and Buttsbury 19–20; C Ingatestone w Fryerning 19–20; TV Thetford *Nor* from 20. *Cloverfield Vicarage, 24 Foxglove Road, Thetford IP24 2XF* M: 07758-228443 E: matthoughton1@hotmail.co.uk

HOUGHTON, Peter Graham. b 51. St Jo Coll Nottm 85. **d** 87 **p** 88. C Toxteth Park St Clem *Liv* 87–91; Chapl Winwick Hosp Warrington 91–92; Chapl Warrington Community Health Care NHS Trust 93–98; Chapl HM Pris Styal 98–01; Asst Chapl St Helens and Knowsley Hosps NHS Trust 03–04; rtd 04; PtO *Liv* from 04. *10 Burlington Drive, Great Sankey, Warrington WA5 8AB* T: (01925) 711451

HOUGHTON, Prof Peter John. b 47. Chelsea Coll Lon BPharm 68 PhD 73 Cant Ch Ch Univ MA 13 FRPharmS 94 FRSC 95 CChem 95. Dioc OLM tr scheme 05. **d** 08 **p** 09. NSM Balham Hill Ascension *S'wark* 08–12; PtO 12–13; NSM Heref S Wye 13–18; V S Wye Rural Par 18; rtd 18; PtO *Heref* from 19. *The Lodge, Ballingham, Hereford HR2 6NN* T: (01432) 840443 F: 352412 M: 07734-747688 E: peter.houghton@kcl.ac.uk

HOUGHTON, Mrs Rosemary Margaret Anne. b 46. **d** 00 **p** 01. OLM Earlham *Nor* 00–16; PtO from 16. *74 St Mildred's Road, West Earlham, Norwich NR5 8RS* T: (01603) 502752 M: 07808-774811

HOULDERSHAW, Michelle Louse. b 67. **d** 12 **p** 13. OLM Brothertoft Gp *Linc* 12–17; OLM Sibsey w Frithville 12–17; C Skegness Gp 17–20. *6 Bayes Road, Skegness PE25 3AN* M: 07986-433358 E: michelle@sheafhf.com

HOULDING, Preb David Nigel Christopher. b 53. AKC 76. **d** 77 **p** 78. C Hillingdon All SS *Lon* 77–81; C Holborn St Alb w Saffron Hill St Pet 81–85; V Hampstead St Steph w All Hallows from 85; AD N Camden 01–02; Preb St Paul's Cathl from 04. *All Hallows' House, 52 Courthope Road, London NW3 2LD* T: (020) 7267 7833 *or* 7267 6317 F: 7267 6317 M: 07710-403294 E: fr.davidhoulding@gmail.com

HOULTON, David Andrew. b 58. Bradf Univ BEng 80 MPhil 86 Wycliffe Hall Ox BTh 11 CEng 90 EurIng 90 FIChemE 98 SOSc 13. Wycliffe Hall Ox 07. **d** 09 **p** 10. C Old Trafford St Bride *Man* 09–12; NSM Stoke Bishop *Bris* 12–13; V Gargrave w Coniston Cold *Leeds* 13–18; Rural Adv 13–17; I Conwal Union w Gartan *D & R* from 18. *Conwal Rectory, New Line Road, Letterkenny, Co Donegal, F92 PCC2, Republic of Ireland* T: (00353) (74) 912 2573 E: david.houlton@wycliffe.oxon.org

HOULTON, Heather Joy. Bradf Univ BA 83 Open Univ MA 03. Trin Coll Bris MA 14. **d** 13 **p** 14. C Linton in Craven *Leeds* 13–15; C Burnsall w Rylstone 13–15; C Skipton H Trin 15–17; C Keighley 16–17; PtO 17–18; *D & R* from 18. *Address withheld by request*

HOULTON, Neil James. b 54. STETS 04. **d** 07 **p** 08. NSM Pokesdown St Jas *Win* 07–10; NSM Boscombe St Andr from 10; P-in-c from 12. *3 Wilfred Road, Bournemouth BH5 1NB* T: (01202) 462476 E: neil.houlton@ntlworld.com

HOUNSELL, Mrs Susan Mary. b 49. STETS BA 10. **d** 07 **p** 08. NSM W Monkton *B & W* 07–11; NSM W Monkton w Kingston St Mary, Broomfield etc 11–13; rtd 13; PtO *B & W* from 14. *33 Home Orchard, Hatch Beauchamp, Taunton TA3 6TG* T: (01823) 480545 E: susan@sackbuts.co.uk

HOUSE, Graham Ivor. b 44. Oak Hill Th Coll BA 80. **d** 80 **p** 81. C Ipswich St Jo *St E* 80–84; V Ipswich St Andr 84–00; R Monks Eleigh w Chelsworth and Brent Eleigh etc 00–03; rtd 03; PtO *St E* from 03. *6 Through Duncans,*

Woodbridge IP12 4EA T: (01394) 386066 M: 07966-169372 E: graham.house44@gmail.com

HOUSE, Jack Francis. b 35. Bris Univ BEd 70 Lon Univ MA 80 Univ of Wales MTh 94. Bris & Glouc Tr Course 79. **d** 80 **p** 81. NSM Bedminster *Bris* 80–92; PtO 92–94; NSM Knowle H Nativity 94–03; NSM Easton All Hallows 98–03; NSM Brislington St Anne 03–05; rtd 05; PtO *Bris* 05–19. *48 Hendre Road, Bristol BS3 2LR* T: 0117-966 1144 E: rhouse3766@virginmedia.com

HOUSE, Mrs Janet. b 45. UEA BA 67 Keswick Hall Coll PGCE 68 Sussex Univ MA 80. Ripon Coll Cuddesdon 93. **d** 95 **p** 96. C Swindon Ch Ch *Bris* 95–99; TV Worc SE 99–06; rtd 06; PtO *Nor* from 06. *11 Caernarvon Road, Norwich NR2 3HZ* T: (01603) 762259 E: jhouse@waitrose.com

HOUSE, Simon Hutchinson. b 30. Peterho Cam BA 65 MA 67. Cuddesdon Coll 61. **d** 64 **p** 65. C Sutton St Jas *York* 64–67; C Acomb St Steph and St Aid 67–69; V Allestree St Nic *Derby* 69–81; RD Duffield 74–81; V Bitterne Park *Win* 81–91; rtd 91; PtO *Win* 91–12. *22 Stanley Street, Southsea PO5 2DS* T: (023) 9283 8592

HOUSEMAN, Patricia Adele. *See* CAMPION, Patricia Adele

HOUSLEY, Andrew Arthur. b 67. Wilson Carlile Coll 91 Ridley Hall Cam 00. **d** 02 **p** 03. C Ormskirk *Liv* 02–06; V Litherland St Phil 06–09; R Aughton St Mich and Bickerstaffe from 09. *The Rectory, 10 Church Lane, Aughton, Ormskirk L39 6SB* T: (01695) 423204 E: andrew.housley67@gmail.com

HOUSMAN, Arthur Martin Rowand. b 53. MA CertEd. Trin Coll Bris 81. **d** 83 **p** 84. C Croydon Ch Ch Broad Green *Cant* 83–84; C Croydon Ch Ch *S'wark* 85–87; TV Stratton St Margaret w S Marston etc *Bris* 87–93; Chapl Peterhouse Sch Zimbabwe 93–98; Chapl Nor Sch 98–07; Hon PV Nor Cathl 98–07; Hon C Raveningham Gp 08–21; Hon C Waveney Marshlands from 21. *Orchards, Beccles Road, Raveningham, Norwich NR14 6NW* T: (01508) 548322 M: 07790-944860 E: housemartin54@yahoo.com

HOUSSEMAYNE du BOULAY, Miss Sarah Elizabeth. b 82. Kent Univ BA 03 Staffs Univ BA 12. Ripon Coll Cuddesdon 17. **d** 19 **p** 20. C Needham Market w Badley *St E* from 19. *20 Flint Drive, Needham Market, Ipswich IP6 8FL*

HOUSTON, Canon Arthur James. b 54. Trin Coll Bris BA 87. **d** 87 **p** 88. C Chatham St Phil and St Jas *Roch* 87–91; I Carrigaline Union *C, C & R* 91–99; Can Cork Cathl 95–99; Can Ross Cathl 95–99; Dir of Ords 96–99; V Margate H Trin *Cant* 99–08; P-in-c Maidstone St Paul 08–10; AD Thanet 02–08; AD Maidstone 08–10; P-in-c Minster-in-Sheppey 10–12; C Eastchurch w Leysdown and Harty 10–12; C Sheerness H Trin w St Paul 10–12; Min Parkwood CD 12–20; C Maidstone St Luke 12–15; P-in-c Maidstone St Faith from 15; Hon Can Cant Cathl from 03. *11 Maidstone Road, Lenham, Maidstone ME17 2QH* T: (01622) 858020 E: arthurjhouston@googlemail.com

HOUSTON, David William James. b 52. Th Ext Educn Coll. **d** 93 **p** 95. C Lyttelton S Africa 93–96; R Sabie w Lydenburg 96–00; P-in-c Elmsted w Hastingleigh *Cant* 00–06; P-in-c Petham and Waltham w Lower Hardres etc 00–06; V Stone Street Gp 06; R Southfleet *Roch* 06–17; rtd 17. *Landway House, Northfleet Green, Gravesend DA13 9PN* M: 07719-378993 E: david@houstonclan.net

HOUSTON, Helen Sarah. b 70. Bris Univ BA 91. St Jo Coll Nottm MA 95. **d** 95 **p** 96. C Bourne *Guildf* 95–98; PtO *Bris* 98–99; Hon C Chippenham St Pet 99–00; C Ballyholme *D & D* 02–04; C Stretton and Appleton Thorn *Ches* 04–05; Asst to RD Gt Budworth 05; Chapl St Rocco's Hospice 05–11; Hon C Stockton Heath *Ches* 08–11; Chapl Rossall Sch Fleetwood 11–12; Chapl St Geo Sch Blackpool 12–19; Chapl Blackpool Teaching Hosps NHS Foundn Trust from 19. *Blackpool Wyre & Fylde Health Authority, Victoria Hospital, Whinney Heys Road, Blackpool FY3 8NR* E: helen.davehouston@btinternet.com

HOUSTON, Kenneth. *See* HOUSTON, Samuel Kenneth

HOUSTON, Mark Russell. b 68. Bretton Hall Coll BEd 92. St Mellitus Coll 15. **d** 18 **p** 19. C Cross Fell Gp *Carl* 18–21; P-in-c Inglewood Gp from 21; C Penrith w Newton Reigny and Plumpton Wall from 21. *The New Vicarage, Plumpton, Penrith CA11 9PA* E: houstonmark15@gmail.com

HOUSTON, Prof Samuel Kenneth. b 43. QUB BSc 64 PhD 67 FIMA 73 MILT. CITC 81. **d** 85 **p** 86. NSM Belfast St Jas w St Silas *Conn* 85–91; NSM Belfast St Andr 91–18; Prof Mathematical Studies Ulster Univ 96–06; PtO *Conn* from 18. *29 North Circular Road, Belfast BT15 5HB* T: (028) 9077 1830 M: 07929-725319 E: skhouston43@gmail.com

HOUSTON, Thomas Michael. b 99. Trin Coll Bris 14. **d** 17 **p** 18. C Burton Latimer *Pet* 17–21; V Kettering St Andr from 21. *St Andrew's Vicarage, Lindsay Street, Kettering NN16 8RG* E: revtomhouston@gmail.com

HOUSTON, Canon William Paul. b 54. QUB BSSc 76 TCD BTh 78. CITC 78. **d** 81 **p** 82. C Carrickfergus *Conn* 81–83; C Bangor St Comgall *D & D* 83–86; I Gilford 86–90; I Carnalea 90–99; I Clondalkin w Rathcoole *D & G* 99–09; I Castleknock and Mulhuddart w Clonsilla from 09; Min Can St Patr Cathl Dublin 00–14; Can St Patr Cathl Dublin from 14. *The Rectory, 12 Hawthorn Lawn, Castleknock, Dublin 15, Republic of Ireland* T: (00353) (1) 821 3083

HOVER, David James. b 83. Birm Univ LLB 04 Called to the Bar (Lincoln's Inn) 05. Qu Foundn Birm 13. **d** 16 **p** 17. C Four Saints *Leic* 16–19; C Avon-Swift 19; P-in-c Braunstone Town w Thorpe Astley from 19; P-in-c Leicester Forest East from 19. *The Rectory, 36 Woodcote Road, Leicester LE3 2WD* E: revddavehover@gmail.com

HOVER (formerly BENNER), Joanna Susan. b 76. Leic Univ BA 99. Ripon Coll Cuddesdon 15. **d** 17 **p** 18. C Broughton Astley and Croft w Stoney Stanton *Leic* 17–20; C Four Saints from 20. *The Rectory, Nock Verges, Stoney Stanton, Leicester LE9 4LR* E: rev.jo.hover@gmail.com

HOVEY, Richard Michael. b 58. Man Univ BA 95 Imp Coll Lon BScEng 79 Cranfield Inst of Tech MBA 84 CEng 83 MIET 83 EurIng 92. Cranmer Hall Dur 93. **d** 95 **p** 96. C Cheddar *B & W* 95–99; TV Gtr Corsham *Bris* 99–01; TV Gtr Corsham and Lacock 01–05; S Team Ldr CMS 05–14; rtd 14; PtO *Bris* from 05. *80 High Street, Corsham SN13 0HF* T: (01249) 715407 E: richard@richardhovey.co.uk

HOVIL, Jeremy Richard Guy. b 65. K Coll Lon BSc 86 Spurgeon's Coll Lon MTh 99 Stellenbosch Univ ThD 05. Wycliffe Hall Ox BTh 95. **d** 95 **p** 96. C Kensington St Barn *Lon* 95–99; Crosslinks Uganda and S Africa 00–13; Crosslinks UK from 13; PtO *B & W* 14–16; NSM Bath St Bart from 16. *10 The Firs, Bath BA2 5ED* T: (01225) 833850 M: 07860-337113 E: hovil@crosslinks.org

HOW, Gillian Carol. *See* BUNCE, Gillian Carol

HOWARD, Canon Andrew. b 63. Man Univ BA 95 Leeds Univ MA 97. Coll of Resurr Mirfield 95. **d** 97 **p** 98. C Worksop Priory *S'well* 97–01; V Hemlington *York* 01–05; Chapl Teesside Univ 05–13; C Middlesbrough St Jo the Ev and Middlesbrough St Columba w St Paul 05–13; V Cantley *Sheff* from 13; Jt AD Doncaster from 18; Hon Can Sheff Cathl from 21. *St Wilfrid's Vicarage, 200 Cantley Lane, Doncaster DN4 6PA* T: (01302) 285316 E: fatherahoward@gmail.com *or* andrew.howard@sheffield.anglican.org

HOWARD, Arthur Calvin. b 60. Leeds Univ LLB 82 Barrister 83. Wycliffe Hall Ox 00. **d** 03 **p** 04. C Heswall *Ches* 03–04; C Weston 04–07; Chapl E Lancs Hospice 09–11; C Bispham *Blackb* 11–13; V Copp w Inskip 13–17; rtd 17; PtO *Blackb* from 18. *14 St Michael's Close, Blackburn BB2 5DG* M: 07534-254318 E: calvina.howard@gmail.com

HOWARD, Charles William Wykeham. b 52. Southn Univ BTh 81. Sarum & Wells Th Coll 76. **d** 79 **p** 80. C St Mary-at-Latton *Chelmsf* 79–82; Chapl RN 82–06; Chapl Midi-Pyrénées and Aude *Eur* 06–09; V Funtington and Sennicotts *Chich* 10–15; R W Stoke 10–15; R Funtington and W Stoke w Sennicotts 15–17; rtd 17; PtO *Portsm* from 19. *10 Heather Close, Waterlooville PO7 8EE* T: (023) 9225 4123 E: ch@scwwh.com

HOWARD, Clive Eric. b 65. Oak Hill Th Coll BA 99. **d** 99 **p** 00. C Chipping Sodbury and Old Sodbury *Glouc* 99–03; V Tipton St Matt *Lich* 03–13; RD Wednesbury 12–13; V Woodbridge St Jo and Bredfield *St E* 13–21; Chapl James Paget Univ Hosps NHS Foundn Trust from 21. *James Paget Hospital, Lowestoft Road, Gorleston, Great Yarmouth NR31 6LA* E: clive.howard65@gmail.com

HOWARD, Daniel James. b 71. Nottm Univ BA 94. Oak Hill Th Coll 04. **d** 06 **p** 07. C Deane *Man* 06–09; V Thornton Hough *Ches* 09–18. *54 Neston Road, Thornton Hough, Wirral CH63 1JF* T: 0151-336 3429 *or* 336 1654 E: daniel@howardemail.com

HOWARD, Daniel Thomas. b 90. Liv Hope Univ BA 11. St Steph Ho Ox MSt 13. **d** 14 **p** 15. C Anfield St Columba *Liv* 14–17; V Orford St Marg 17–20; V Anfield St Columba from 20. *St Columba's Vicarage, Pinehurst Avenue, Anfield, Liverpool L4 7UQ* E: fr.danielhoward@gmail.com

HOWARD, David John. b 51. Lon Univ BSc 73. Oak Hill Th Coll 74. **d** 77 **p** 78. C Radipole and Melcombe Regis *Sarum* 77–83; R Tredington and Darlingscott w Newbold on Stour *Cov* 83–90; P-in-c Binley 90–94; V 94–04; RD Cov E 95–99; V Potterne w Worton and Marston *Sarum* 04–16; rtd 16; PtO *Cov* from 17. *53 Ivybridge Road, Coventry CV3 5PF* E: dahoward@waitrose.com

HOWARD, David John. b 47. Brasted Th Coll 68 Ripon Hall Ox 70. **d** 72 **p** 73. C Benchill *Man* 72–74; C Sedgley All SS *Lich* 75–77; C-in-c Lostock CD *Man* 77–85; V Lt Hulton 85–88; PtO 90–91; C E and W Leake, Stanford-on-Soar, Rempstone etc *S'well* 91–94; P-in-c Bilborough w Strelley

94–98; Chapl HM YOI Werrington 98–03; Chapl HM Pris Drake Hall 03–14; rtd 14; PtO *Lich* 14–21. *c/o Crockford, Church House, 27 Great Smith Street, London SW1P 3AZ* E: davidjohnhoward@virginmedia.com

HOWARD, Mrs Erika Kathryn. b 49. SRN 70 SCM 72 FRSA. S Dios Minl Tr Scheme 88. **d** 91 **p** 94. NSM New Shoreham and Old Shoreham *Chich* 91–94; C Kingston Buci 94–03; V Sompting 03–17; rtd 17. *207 Upper Shoreham Road, Shoreham-by-Sea BN43 6BE* E: rev.erikahoward@ntlworld.com

HOWARD, Frank Thomas. b 36. Lon Univ BSc 57. Bps' Coll Cheshunt 59. **d** 61 **p** 62. C Macclesfield St Mich *Ches* 61–64; C Claughton cum Grange 64–66; V Lache cum Saltney 66–76; R Stanton *St E* 76–97; RD Ixworth 79–85; P-in-c Hempnall *Nor* 97–01; rtd 01; PtO *Nor* from 01; *St E* 19–21. *55 Heywood Avenue, Diss IP22 4DN* T: (01379) 640819 E: fandrhoward@hotmail.com

HOWARD, Geoffrey. b 30. Barrister-at-Law 83 Lon Univ LLB 77. EMMTC. **d** 85 **p** 86. NSM Barton *Ely* 85–87; NSM Coton 85–87; C W Walton 87–92; TV Daventry, Ashby St Ledgers, Braunston etc *Pet* 92–97; rtd 97; PtO *Ely* 97–00 and 07–17. *11 Porson Court, Porson Road, Cambridge CB2 8ER* T: (01223) 300738 E: geoffreyhoward@mail.com

HOWARD, Geoffrey. b 45. St Jo Coll Dur BA 68. Cranmer Hall Dur 67. **d** 71 **p** 72. C Cheetham Hill *Man* 71–74; C Denton Ch Ch 74–77; V Pendleton St Ambrose 77–91; TR Pendleton St Thos w Charlestown 91–94; AD Salford 86–94; PtO from 04. *20 May Road, Swinton, Manchester M27 5FR* T: 0161-950 7778 E: geoffrey.howard@ntlworld.com

HOWARD, Ian Barry. b 57. Trin Coll Cam BA 81 MA 87. Homerton Coll Cam PGCE 82. SEITE 13. **d** 16 **p** 17. NSM Brize Norton and Carterton *Ox* 16–20; TV from 20; Chapl Cokethorpe Sch Witney from 16. *39 Bluebell Way, Carterton OX18 1JY* T: (01993) 837677 M: 07867-784693 E: ibhoward@btinternet.com *or* ian.barry.howard@gmail.com

HOWARD, John. *See* HOWARD, Nicolas John

HOWARD, Canon John Robert. b 60. NUI BA HDipEd. **d** 84 **p** 85. C Donaghcloney w Waringstown *D & D* 84–88; I Belfast St Ninian *Conn* 88–94; Bp's Dom Chapl 88–94; Chapl Ulster Univ 88–94; I Annahilt w Magherahamlet *D & D* from 94; Chapl HM Pris Maghaberry from 96; Can Dromore Cathl *D & D* from 06; Chan Dromore Cathl from 12. *Annahilt Rectory, 15 Ballykeel Road, Hillsborough BT26 6NW* T: (028) 9263 8218 E: jrobert.howard@btinternet.com

HOWARD, Jon Christopher. b 51. **d** 20 **p** 21. NSM Ystradgynlais *S & B* from 20. *Cartref, 46 Heol Eglwys, Coelbren, Neath SA10 9PF* T: (01639) 700435 M: 07810-820593 E: jon.cartref@gmail.com

HOWARD, Keith. b 55. St Jo Coll Nottm 81. **d** 84 **p** 85. C Llanidloes w Llangurig *Ban* 84–87; R Llansantffraid Glan Conwy and Eglwysbach *St As* 87–00; V Heapey and Withnell *Blackb* 00–07; V Hooton *Ches* from 07. *Hooton Vicarage, Chester Road, Childer Thornton, Ellesmere Port CH66 1QF* T: 0151-339 2020

HOWARD, Canon Michael Charles. b 35. Selw Coll Cam BA 58 MA 63 CQSW 72. Wycliffe Hall Ox 58. **d** 60 **p** 61. C Stowmarket *St E* 60–64; CMS Nigeria 64–71; Hon Can Ondo 70–71; Hon C Southborough St Pet w Ch Ch and St Matt *Roch* 72–73; PtO *Ox* 73–18; rtd 00. *17 Milton Road, Bloxham, Banbury OX15 4HD* T: (01295) 720470

HOWARD, Michael John. b 51. Open Univ BA 78 Dur Univ MA 20 Redland Coll of Educn CertEd 74. **d** 09 **p** 10. OLM Ness Gp *Linc* from 09; RD Elloe W from 19. *East Dean House, East End, Langtoft, Peterborough PE6 9LP* T: (01778) 349576 E: revmichaelj.howard@gmail.com

HOWARD, Nicolas John. b 61. Nottm Univ BTh 90. Aston Tr Scheme 85 Linc Th Coll 87. **d** 90 **p** 91. C Bracknell *Ox* 90–94; P-in-c Oldham St Chad Limeside *Man* 94–96; PtO *Birm* 96–99. *11 Chesterfield Court, Middleton Hall Road, Birmingham B30 1AF* T: 0121-459 4975

HOWARD, Paul David. b 47. Lanchester Poly Cov BA 69. St Jo Coll Nottm 74. **d** 77 **p** 78. C Bedworth *Cov* 77–83; V Newchapel *Lich* 83–93; V Stretton w Claymills 93–04; P-in-c Talke 04–07; R 10–13; Chapl Newcastle-under-Lyme Primary Care Trust 07–13; rtd 13; PtO *Lich* 13–21. *19 Pen y Garreg Close, Bryn-y-Baal, Mold CH7 6TW* M: 07824-099577 E: paulhoward510@gmail.com

HOWARD, Canon Peter Leslie. b 48. Nottm Univ BTh 77 Birm Univ MA 80 Leeds Univ MEd 91. St Jo Coll Nottm LTh 77. **d** 77 **p** 78. C Gospel Lane St Mich *Birm* 77–81; P-in-c Nechells 81–85; V Stanley *Wakef* 85–92; P-in-c Nor Heartsease St Fran 92–16; Hon Can Nor Cathl 10–16; RD Nor E 06–14; rtd 16; PtO *Nor* from 16; Dioc CUF/CUF Link Officer from 02; PtO *Eur* from 16. *Chapel Cottage, 17 Chapel Lane, Coltishall, Norwich NR12 7DR* T: (01603) 738835 E: plhoward@btinternet.com

HOWARD, Robert. *See* HOWARD, John Robert

HOWARD, Canon Robert Weston (Robin). b 28. Pemb Coll Cam BA 49 MA 53. Westcott Ho Cam 51. **d** 53 **p** 54. C Bishopwearmouth St Mich *Dur* 53–56; C Cambridge Gt St Mary w St Mich *Ely* 56–60; Hong Kong 60–66; V Prenton *Ches* 66–75; RD Frodsham 74–82; P-in-c Dunham-on-the-Hill 75–77; V Helsby and Ince 75–77; V Helsby and Dunham-on-the-Hill 77–82; Hon Can Ches Cathl 78–82; V Moseley St Mary *Birm* 82–88; V Chalke Valley W *Sarum* 88–93; rtd 93; PtO *St D* 93–08; *Heref* 93–08; *Ox* 08–18. *4 Hitchmans Drive, Chipping Norton OX7 5BG* T: (01608) 641248 E: roberthoward5@sky.com

HOWARD, Ronald. b 40. AMIBF 65 AMICME 01. Cranmer Hall Dur 86. **d** 88 **p** 89. C Baildon *Bradf* 88–92; P-in-c Sutton 92–96; P-in-c St Tudy w St Mabyn and Michaelstow *Truro* 96–00; P-in-c Keyingham w Ottringham, Halsham and Sunk Is *York* 00–03; R 03–08; RD S Holderness 04–06; rtd 08; PtO *York* 08–18. *Silver Gates, Withernsea Road, Hollym, Withernsea HU19 2QH* T: (01964) 611270 E: ronaldhoward146@btinternet.com

HOWARD, Simon Charles. b 60. Birm Univ BA 81. Ridley Hall Cam 90. **d** 92 **p** 93. C Cambridge St Martin *Ely* 92–96; Chapl St Bede's Sch Cam 92–96; P-in-c Earley Trin *Ox* 96–05; P-in-c Ruscombe and Twyford 05–12; V Ruscombe and Twyford w Hurst 12–16; Sen Chapl Lee Abbey 16–19; Hon C Crosthwaite Kendal *Carl* from 21; Hon C Cartmel Fell from 21; Hon C Winster from 21; Hon C Witherslack from 21. *1 Mountain View, Kendal LA9 4QT* T: (01539) 729638 E: revdsimonhoward92@outlook.com

HOWARD, Thomas Norman. b 40. St Aid Birkenhead 64. **d** 67 **p** 68. C Farnworth and Kearsley *Man* 67–70; C Prestwich St Marg 70–73; V Heyside 73–85; Warden Lamplugh Ho Angl Conf Cen 85–90; Hon C Langtoft w Foxholes, Butterwick, Cottam etc *York* 85–87; C 87–90; V Fence and Newchurch-in-Pendle *Blackb* 90–00; Dioc Ecum Officer 90–95; rtd 00; Hon C Stalybridge H Trin and Ch Ch *Ches* 01–03; PtO 03–04; *Blackb* from 00. *5 Mount Gardens, Morecambe LA4 6AS* T: (01524) 923040 M: 07791-184544 E: jenniferhoward1944@gmail.com

HOWARD, William Alfred. b 47. St Jo Coll Dur BA 69. Wycliffe Hall Ox 74. **d** 77 **p** 79. C Norbiton *S'wark* 77–80; C Mile Cross *Nor* 80–84; R Grimston, Congham and Roydon 84–13; Chapl Norfolk Constabulary 00–13; rtd 13; PtO *Cov* from 14; *Eur* from 16. *21 Daniell Road, Wellesbourne, Warwick CV35 9UD* T: (01789) 508831 E: william.howard@dunelm.org.uk

HOWARD-JONES, Sarah Rachel. b 70. Down Coll Cam BA 93 MA 97 Dur Univ BA 21. Ripon Coll Cuddesdon 19. **d** 21. C Kensal Rise St Martin *Lon* from 21. *63 Linden Avenue, London NW10 5RG* M: 07818-208648 E: sarah.howard-jones@london.anglican.org

HOWARTH, Christopher Robin. b 41. **d** 10 **p** 12. NSM Canley *Cov* 10–18; NSM Westwood 14–18; PtO from 18. *The Vicarage, 47 Glebe Close, Coventry CV4 8DJ* T: (024) 7642 1721 M: 07730-409778 E: christopherrobin41@gmail.com

HOWARTH, David Alexander. b 81. Wycliffe Hall Ox BTh 14. **d** 14 **p** 15. C Bromley Ch Ch *Roch* 14–18; C Hove Bp Hannington Memorial Ch *Chich* from 18. *43 Hogarth Road, Hove BN3 5RH* M: 07740-361097 E: dahowarth1@gmail.com or daveholycross@gmail.com

HOWARTH, Delphine. *See* HOWARTH, Victoria Elizabeth Delphine

HOWARTH, Mrs Henriette. b 66. Utrecht Univ MTh 94. Wycliffe Hall Ox 91. **d** 04 **p** 05. C Sparkbrook Ch Ch *Birm* 04–05; C Springfield 05–09; PtO 09–11; Chapl St Mich C of E Academy 11–14; NSM Peckham All SS *S'wark* 12–14; V Shipley St Paul *Leeds* 17–21. *47 Kirkgate, Shipley BD18 3EH* M: 07701-097881 E: henhowarth@gmail.com

HOWARTH, Lucy Hope. *See* SABLAN, Lucy Hope

HOWARTH, Maxine. b 71. Westcott Ho Cam 17. **d** 19. C Langelei *St Alb* 19–20; C Abbots Langley from 20. *1 Linden Glade, Hemel Hempstead HP1 1XB* E: curateht@gmail.com

HOWARTH, Michael Scott. b 42. SNWTP. **d** 13 **p** 14. NSM Dearnley *Man* 13–14; NSM Dearnley, Wardle and Smallbridge 14–18; PtO from 18. *5 Starfield Avenue, Littleborough OL15 0NG* T: (01706) 371544 M: 07977-164848 E: michael.howarth@zen.co.uk

HOWARTH, Miles. b 58. **d** 08 **p** 09. OLM Failsworth St Jo *Man* 08–12; Spiritual Care Co-ord Dr Kershaw's Hospice Oldham 11–16; NSM Kirkholt *Man* 12–14; P-in-c Denton Ch Ch from 14; C Audenshaw St Steph from 14; C Denton St Lawr from 14; C Haughton St Anne from 14. *15 Grimshaw Street, Failsworth, Manchester M35 0DF* T: 0161-688 7710 M: 07718-326321 E: mhowarth175@gmail.com

HOWARTH, Peter Benjamin. b 73. St Mellitus Coll 13. **d** 17 **p** 18. NSM Holborn St Geo w H Trin and St Bart *Lon* from 17. *7 Babington Court, Orde Hall Street, London WC1N 3JT* M: 07845-283262 E: p.howarth@qmul.ac.uk

HOWARTH, Robert Francis Harvey. b 31. S'wark Ord Course 71. **d** 72 **p** 73. C St Marylebone All So w SS Pet and Jo *Lon* 72–73; C St Helen Bishopsgate w St Martin Outwich 73–78; V Harlow St Mary and St Hugh w St Jo the Bapt *Chelmsf* 78–88; P-in-c Victoria Docks Ascension 88–96; rtd 96; PtO *Chelmsf* 12–16. *14 Quinlan Court, 78 Mill Lane, Danbury, Chelmsford CM3 4HX* T: (01245) 698142

✠**HOWARTH, The Rt Revd Toby Matthew.** b 62. Yale Univ BA 86 Birm Univ MA 91 Free Univ of Amsterdam PhD 01. Wycliffe Hall Ox 89. **d** 92 **p** 93 **c** 14. C Derby St Aug 92–95; Crosslinks India 95–00; The Netherlands 00–02; Vice Prin and Tutor Crowther Hall CMS Tr Coll Selly Oak 02–04; P-in-c Springfield *Birm* 04–11; Bp's Adv on Inter-Faith Relns 05–11; Abp's Sec for Inter-Relig Affairs *Cant* 11–14; Suff Bp Bradf *Leeds* from 14. *47 Kirkgate, Shipley BD18 3EH* T: 0113-353 0290 M: 07811-467999 E: bishop.toby@leeds.anglican.org

HOWARTH, Victoria Elizabeth Delphine. b 50. Keele Univ MSc 06. **d** 11 **p** 12. OLM Penkridge *Lich* 11–15; C 15–20; rtd 20; PtO *Lich* from 20. *Lower Farm House, Bednall, Stafford ST17 0SA* T: (01785) 714527 M: 07412-617211 E: delphine.howarth@ifdev.net

HOWAT, Jeremy Noel Thomas. b 35. Em Coll Cam BA 59 MA 62. Ridley Hall Cam 59. **d** 63 **p** 64. C Sutton *Liv* 63–65; C Kirk Ella *York* 65–66; C Bridlington Quay Ch Ch 66–69; R Wheldrake 69–78; Dioc Youth Officer 69–74; SAMS Argentina 78–81; 90–97; P-in-c Newton upon Ouse *York* 81–82; V Shipton w Overton 81–82; P-in-c Skelton by York 81–82; R Skelton w Shipton and Newton on Ouse 82–89; C Elloughton and Brough w Brantingham 97–99; rtd 99; PtO *York* 00–19. *18 Petersway, York YO30 6AR* T: (01904) 628946 E: nowell@ntlworld.com

HOWDEN, Canon John Travis. b 40. RIBA 62. Sarum Th Coll 66. **d** 69 **p** 70. C S Gillingham *Roch* 69–72; C Banbury *Ox* 72–73; LtO *York* 73–74; Hon C Hull St Jo Newland 74–81; Hon C Stock Harvard *Chelmsf* 82–86; R Doddinghurst and Mountnessing 86–91; P-in-c Pleshey 91–00; Warden Pleshey Retreat Ho 91–00; R Wickham Bishops w Lt Braxted *Chelmsf* 00–05; Hon Can Chelmsf Cathl 97–05; rtd 05; PtO *Chelmsf* from 05. *12A Back Road, Writtle, Chelmsford CM1 3PD* T: (01245) 422023 E: johnhowden7@gmail.com

HOWDLE, Glyn. b 50. Bp Lonsdale Coll BEd 72. St Alb Minl Tr Scheme 90. **d** 01 **p** 02. NSM Aspenden, Buntingford and Westmill *St Alb* 01–11; PtO 11–19. *33 Cappell Lane, Stanstead Abbotts SG12 8BU* T: (01920) 739162 M: 07507-541884 E: glynhowdle@gmail.com

HOWE, Canon Alan Raymond. b 52. Nottm Univ BTh 79. St Jo Coll Nottm 76. **d** 80 **p** 81. C Southsea St Simon *Portsm* 80–83; C Bexleyheath St Pet *Roch* 83–86; TV Camberley St Paul *Guildf* 86–93; P-in-c Mansfield St Jo *S'well* 93–96; P-in-c Wollaton Park 96–02; V 02–05; AD Nottingham W 99–05; V Chilwell 05–16; P-in-c Lenton Abbey 09–16; rtd 16; P-in-c Tollerton *S'well* 16–21; Hon Can S'well Minster 11–21; PtO *Eur* from 18. *158 Prittlewell Chase, Westcliff-on-Sea SS0 0RT* E: revahowe@gmail.com

HOWE, Canon Anthony Graham. b 72. Qu Coll Ox BA 93 MA 99. St Steph Ho Ox BA 00. **d** 01 **p** 02. C Newbury *Ox* 01–04; Dioc Communications Officer *Wakef* 04–05; C Athersley and Monk Bretton 05–06; V Staincliffe and Carlinghow 06–14; *Leeds* 14–15; Chapl Chpl Royal Hampton Court Palace from 15; Dep P in O from 15; Can Chpls R from 17. *Chapel Royal, Hampton Court Palace, East Molesey KT8 9AU* T: (020) 3166 6515 M: 07795-095157 E: chapelroyal@hrp.org.uk or anthony.howe@hrp.org.uk

HOWE, The Ven George Alexander. b 52. St Jo Coll Dur BA 73. Westcott Ho Cam 73. **d** 75 **p** 76. C Peterlee *Dur* 75–79; C Norton St Mary 79–81; V Hart w Elwick Hall 81–85; R Sedgefield 85–91; RD 89–91; V Kendal H Trin *Carl* 91–00; RD Kendal 94–00; Hon Can Carl Cathl 94–15; adn Westmorland and Furness 00–11; Bp's Adv for Ecum Affairs 01–11; Bp's Chapl and Chief of Staff and Dioc Dir of Ords 11–15; rtd 15; PtO *Heref* from 16. *The Old House, Bosbury Road, Cradley, Malvern WR13 5LT* T: (01886) 880220 M: 07879-452763 E: gahowe@hotmail.co.uk

HOWE, Canon Rex Alan. b 29. Ch Coll Cam BA 53 MA 57. Coll of Resurr Mirfield 53. **d** 55 **p** 56. C Barnsley St Pet *Wakef* 55–57; C Helmsley *York* 57–60; V Middlesbrough St Martin 60–67; V Redcar 67–73; V Kirkleatham 67–73; RD Guisborough 67–73; Dean Hong Kong 73–76; Adn Hong Kong 75–76; TR Grantham *Linc* 77–85; RD 78–85; Can and Preb Linc Cathl 81–85; V Canford Cliffs and Sandbanks *Sarum* 85–94; RD Poole 92–94; rtd 94; PtO *Sarum* 94–17. *2 St Nicholas Hospital, St Nicholas Road, Salisbury SP1 2SW* T: (01722) 326677

HOWE, Roy William. b 38. ALCD 67. **d** 66 **p** 67. C Bradf Cathl 66–70; C Barnoldswick w Bracewell 70–72; V Yeadon St Jo 72–79; P-in-c Bainton *York* 79–86; P-in-c Middleton-on-the-Wolds 79–86; P-in-c N Dalton 79–86; RD Harthill 81–87; C Watton w Beswick and Kilnwick 82–86; R Bainton w N Dalton, Middleton-on-the-Wolds etc 86–87; TV Penrith w Newton Reigny and Plumpton Wall *Carl* 87–92; Dioc Chapl to Agric and Rural Life 87–92; V Cornhill w Carham *Newc* 92–98; V Branxton 92–98; P-in-c Coddenham w Gosbeck and Hemingstone w Henley *St E* 98–03; rtd 03; PtO *Truro* 04–21. *Ballaclague, 2 Halvasso Vean, Longdowns, Penryn TR10 9DN* T: (01209) 860552

HOWELL, Andrew John. b 44. Clifton Th Coll 68. **d** 71 **p** 72. C Halliwell St Pet *Man* 71–77; V Facit 77–95; P-in-c Wardle and Smallbridge 95–13; rtd 13; PtO *Man* from 13. *21 Bateman Avenue, Rochdale OL12 9ST* T: (01706) 375082 E: a.howell554@btinternet.com

HOWELL, Brian. b 43. MBE 99. Newc Univ MA 95. Cranmer Hall Dur 11. **d** 11 **p** 12. NSM Blaydon and Swalwell *Dur* 11–13; rtd 13; PtO *Dur* from 14. *Hillcroft House, Sourmilk Hill Lane, Gateshead NE9 5RU* T: 0191-482 3158 M: 07710-000654 E: b_howell2004@yahoo.co.uk

HOWELL (*formerly* WILLIAMS), **David Paul.** b 61. Coll of Resurr Mirfield 91. **d** 93 **p** 94. C Leic St Aid 93–97; P-in-c Edvin Loach w Tedstone Delamere etc *Heref* 97–16; R Ariconium from 16. *The Rectory, Weston under Penyard, Ross-on-Wye HR9 7QA* T: (01886) 821285

HOWELL, Geoffrey Peter. b 52. Selw Coll Cam BA 75 MA 78 Leeds Univ MA 01 K Alfred's Coll Win PGCE 77 LTCL 82. Cranmer Hall Dur 85. **d** 87 **p** 88. C Hartlepool St Luke *Dur* 87–90; TV Burford I, Nash and Boraston *Heref* 90–94; TV Whitton w Greete and Hope Bagot 90–94; TV Burford III w Lt Heref 90–94; TV Tenbury Wells 90–94; P-in-c Cradley w Mathon and Storridge 94–97; Succ Heref Cathl 97–99; Chapl Heref Cathl Jun Sch 97–99; PtO *Heref* 99–16; Min Can St Woolos Cathl *Mon* 02–10; TV Monkton *St D* 10–16; Chapl Dyfed-Powys Police 11–16; rtd 16; PtO *Ox* from 17; Chapl Thames Valley Police 18–19. *33 Brook End, Weston Turville, Aylesbury HP22 5RQ* T: (01296) 614826 M: 07716-328202 E: gphowell@btinternet.com

HOWELL, Mrs Heather Ellen. b 40. Bp Otter Coll Chich TCert 60 Sussex Univ BA 83. Ripon Coll Cuddesdon 00. **d** 01 **p** 02. NSM Newhaven *Chich* 01–06; P-in-c Fletching 06–11; rtd 11; PtO *Chich* from 17. *1 Rookery Way, Seaford BN25 2SA* T: (01323) 873643 E: heather.howell@tiscali.co.uk

HOWELL, Miss Julie Anne. b 65. Ox Univ BA 98 Ox Brookes Univ MA 04. Ripon Coll Cuddesdon 17. **d** 19 **p** 20. C W Downland *Ox* 19–20; C Newbury St Geo and St Jo from 20. *The Vicarage, 1 Chesterfield Road, Newbury RG14 7QB* M: 07919-207137 E: j.howell826@btinternet.com

HOWELL, Mrs Pamela Isobel Anne. b 62. Sheff Univ LLB 84 Solicitor 87. Qu Coll Birm 09. **d** 12 **p** 13. C Whitnash *Cov* 12–15; V Willenhall from 15; AD Cov E 18–19. *St John's Vicarage, Robin Hood Road, Coventry CV3 3AY* T: (024) 7630 3266 E: revpamhowell@gmail.com

HOWELL, Roger Brian. b 43. ALCD 67. **d** 67 **p** 68. C Battersea Park St Sav *S'wark* 67–71; C Southgate *Chich* 71–76; V Pendeen and P-in-c Sancreed *Truro* 76–81; V Bedgrove *Ox* 81–91; R Purley 91–08; RD Bradfield 94–04; rtd 08; PtO *Ox* from 08. *246 Burwell Meadow, Witney OX28 5JJ* T: (01993) 706893

HOWELL, Simon Gordon. b 63. Sheff Univ BMus 84 Bath Coll of HE PGCE 85 Anglia Ruskin Univ MA 07 ACII 90. Ridley Hall Cam 00. **d** 03 **p** 04. C Northwood Em *Lon* 03–06; TV Keynsham *B & W* 06–14; Bp's Inter Faith Officer 10–14; TV Stroud Team *Glouc* from 14; Interfaith Adv from 15. *Holy Trinity Vicarage, 10 Bowbridge Lane, Stroud GL5 2JW* T: (01453) 350387 M: 07971-582332 E: revsimonhowell@blueyonder.co.uk

HOWELL, Thomas William. b 75. New Coll Ox MBiochem 99 Ox Univ Inst of Educn PGCE 00. St Mellitus Coll 16. **d** 19 **p** 20. NSM Ox St Andr from 19. *33 Wentworth Road, Oxford OX2 7TH* T: (01865) 552496 M: 07986-044254 E: tcabmhowell@gmail.com

HOWELL-JONES, The Very Revd Peter. b 62. Huddersfield Poly BMus 84 Bretton Hall Coll PGCE 85. St Jo Coll Nottm 90 MA 96. **d** 93 **p** 94. C Walsall *Lich* 93–98; V Boldmere *Birm* 98–05; Can Res Birm Cathl 05–11; Bp's Adv for Miss 05–11; Asst Dean 07–11; Acting Dean 08–10; Vice-Dean and Can Res Ches Cathl 11–17; Dean Blackb from 17. *The Deanery, Cathedral Close, Blackburn BB1 5AA* M: 07435-969256 E: dean@blackburncathedral.co.uk

HOWELLS, Chan Arthur Glyn. b 32. Univ of Wales (Lamp) BA 54 MA 03. St Mich Coll Llan 54. **d** 56 **p** 57. C Oystermouth *S & B* 56–58; C Llangyfelach 58–64; R Llandefalle and Llyswen w Boughrood etc 64–69; Youth Chapl 67–71; V Landore 70–80; Dioc Missr 80–89; Can Brecon Cathl 80–89; Can Tres Brecon Cathl 89–94; Dir St Mary's Coll Swansea 82–89; V Swansea St Jas *S & B* 89–98; Chan Brecon Cathl 94–98; RD Swansea 96–98; rtd 98. *2 Lilliput Lane, West Cross, Swansea SA3 5AQ* T: (01792) 402123 E: aghow@hotmail.com

HOWELLS (*formerly* SMITHAM), **Canon Elizabeth Ann.** b 62. St D Coll Lamp BA 90 Univ of Wales (Lamp) MA 04. St Mich Coll Llan. **d** 92 **p** 97. C Llangiwg *S & B* 92–94; C Morriston 94–98; P-in-c Llanfair-is-gaer and Llanddeiniolen *Ban* 98–00; V 00–03; V Llanddeiniolen w Llanfair-is-gaer etc 03–04; V Clydau w Egremont and Llanglydwen etc *St D* 04–06; P-in-c Llanpumsaint w Llanllawddog 06–08; V Llanilar w Rhostie and Llangwyryfon etc 09–10; V Llandybie 10–17; P-in-c Llan-llwch w Llangain and Llangynog and Llansteffan etc 17–18; P-in-c Bro Sancler from 18; AD from 18; Hon Can St D Cathl from 18. *The New Vicarage, Millbank Lane, Johnstown, Carmarthen SA31 3HW* T: (01267) 468136

HOWELLS, Euryl. b 60. Univ of Wales (Cardiff) BD 93. St Mich Coll Llan 90. **d** 93 **p** 94. C Deanery of Emlyn *St D* 93–97; V Llangeler w Pen-Boyr 97–03; P-in-c Tre-lech a'r Betws w Abernant and Llanwinio 03–06; Chapl Carmarthenshire NHS Trust 06–08; Chapl R Devon and Ex NHS Foundn Trust 08–09; V Grwp Bro Ystwyth a Mynach *St D* 09–10; PtO from 10; Sen Chapl Hywel Dda Health Bd from 11. *Chaplaincy Office, Glangwili Hospital, Dolgwili Road, Carmarthen SA31 2AF* T: (01267) 227563 E: euryl.howells@virgin.net

HOWELLS, Gordon. b 39. Univ of Wales (Cardiff) BSc 61 DipEd 62. Ripon Coll Cuddesdon 86. **d** 88 **p** 89. C Atherstone *Cov* 88–89; C Lillington 89–92; R Clymping and Yapton w Ford *Chich* 92–97; P-in-c Rackheath and Salhouse *Nor* 97–04; Chapl among Deaf People 97–04; rtd 04; PtO *St As* from 09; *Ban* 14–17. *53 Abbey Road, Rhos on Sea, Colwyn Bay LL28 4NR* T: (01492) 525899 E: ghowells@idnet.com

HOWELLS, Richard Grant. b 62. Univ of Wales (Lamp) BA 83 Anglia Ruskin Univ MA 05. Westcott Ho Cam 83 and 92. **d** 93 **p** 94. NSM Harston w Hauxton and Newton *Ely* 93–15; NSM Nar Valley *Nor* from 15. *Church Farm House, South Acre, King's Lynn PE32 2AD* T: (01760) 755129 M: 07802-432594 E: rhowells@harvardup.co.uk

HOWELLS, Mrs Sandra June. b 52. FBDO 77 FADO 77. Mon Dioc Tr Scheme 90. **d** 93 **p** 97. NSM Caerwent w Dinham and Llanfair Discoed etc *Mon* 93–97; C Griffithstown 97–00; V Penallt and Trellech 00–07; V Trellech and Penallt 07–18; rtd 18; PtO *York* from 19. *4 Dale View, Gravel Hole Lane, Sowerby, Thirsk YO7 1NN*

HOWES, Alan. b 49. Chich Th Coll 76. **d** 79 **p** 80. C Bilborough St Jo *S'well* 79–82; TV Newark w Hawton, Cotham and Shelton 82–89; TV Newark 89–94; V Coseley St Chad *Worc* 94–19; rtd 19; PtO *Lich* from 19. *46 Himley Close, Bilston WV14 0LL* M: 07941-284048 E: alan.howes.49@gmail.com

HOWES, David. b 30. Open Univ BA 75. Roch Th Coll 62. **d** 64 **p** 65. C Highweek *Ex* 64–67; C Clyst St George 67–71; P-in-c Woolfardisworthy w Kennerleigh 71–72; P-in-c Washford Pyne w Puddington 71–72; TR N Creedy 72–73; PtO 74–77; C Walworth *S'wark* 77–78; P-in-c Roundshaw LEP 78–83; R S'wark St Geo 83–90; P-in-c S'wark St Jude 84–90; P-in-c Risley *Derby* 90–93; Bp's Ind Adv 90–93; rtd 93; PtO *Derby* 93–00; *S'well* 95–00; *Win* 01–13; *Lich* 13–14; *Birm* 16–17. *8C Cliff Road, Bridgnorth WV16 4EY* M: 07415-506476

HOWES, Miss Judith Elizabeth. b 44. SRN RSCN. Ripon Coll Cuddesdon 83. **d** 89 **p** 94. Par Dn Ex St Sidwell and St Matt 89–92; Par Dn Brixham w Churston Ferrers and Kingswear 92–94; C 94–95; TV E Darlington *Dur* 95–97; TR 97–02; P-in-c Washington 02–04; P-in-c S Shields St Simon 04–08; C Hedworth 04–08; rtd 08; PtO *Dur* from 08. *25 Firtree Avenue, Harraton, Washington NE38 9BA* E: judithehowes@gmail.com

HOWES, Canon Norman Vincent. b 36. AKC 61. **d** 62 **p** 63. C Radford *Cov* 62–66; V Napton on the Hill 66–72; V Exhall 72–83; R Walton d'Eiville and V Wellesbourne 83–03; RD Fosse 87–93; Hon Can Cov Cathl 89–03; rtd 03; PtO *Cov* 03–21. *6 Brookside Avenue, Wellesbourne, Warwick CV35 9RZ* T: (01789) 470902 E: howes.howes@btinternet.com

HOWES, Stuart James. b 78. Wolv Univ BA 03 Worc Univ PGCE 04. Qu Foundn Birm 15. **d** 17 **p** 18. C Shrewsbury St Giles w Sutton and Atcham *Lich* 17–20; V Hadley and Wellington Ch Ch from 20. *The Vicarage, Church Walk, Wellington, Telford TF1 1RW* T: (01952) 273515 M: 07800-894416 E: rev_stu@outlook.com

HOWETT, Amanda Jane. See FEATHERSTONE, Amanda Jane

HOWITT, Ivan Richard. b 56. Kent Univ BA 81. Sarum & Wells Th Coll 83. **d** 85 **p** 86. C Herne Bay Ch Ch *Cant* 85–87; C St Laur in Thanet 87–90; R Owmby and Normanby w Glentham *Linc* 90–91; P-in-c Spridlington w Saxby and Firsby 90–91; R Owmby Gp 91–99; RD Lawres 96–99; Chapl Hull Miss to Seafarers 99–03; V Hedon w Paull *York* 03–09; P-in-c Sand Hutton 09–12; P-in-c Whitwell w Crambe and Foston 09–12; R Harton 12–13; rtd 13; PtO *York* from 14; *Linc* 16–19. *40 Clipson Crest, Barton-upon-Humber DN18 5GW* M: 07739-316019 E: ivan.howitt@me.com

HOWITZ *(formerly* **TEDD),** Christopher Jonathan Richard. b 74. MBE 20. Ch Ch Ox MEng 96. Oak Hill Th Coll BA 00. d 00 p 01. C Harpurhey Ch Ch *Man* 00–04; P-in-c Higher Openshaw 05–12; Co-Chapl Oman from 12; PtO *Eur* from 16. *PO Box 1982, Ruwi 112, Sultanate of Oman* E: cjhowitz@hotmail.com

HOWLAND, David John. b 55. SEITE 12. d 15. NSM Horsted Keynes *Chich* 15–18; NSM W Green 18–19; NSM Colgate and Roffey from 19; PtO *S'wark* from 15. *13 Holtye Avenue, East Grinstead RH19 3EG* T: (01342) 313094 E: david@davidhowland.co.uk

HOWLES, Gareth Harry. b 80. Ridley Hall Cam 15. d 17 p 19. C Burley in Wharfedale *Leeds* 17–19; C Morton and Riddlesden 19–20; P-in-c Farsley from 20. *Address temp unknown* M: 07795-268997 E: gnhowles@hotmail.co.uk

HOWLES, Kenneth. b 56. Oak Hill Th Coll 91. d 93 p 94. C Leyland St Andr *Blackb* 93–96; C Livesey 96–97; C Ewood 96–97; P-in-c 97–99; V 99–03; P-in-c Blackb Sav 01–03; V Chorley St Jas 03–10; rtd 10. *20 Waverley Drive, Tarleton, Preston PR4 6XX* T: (01772) 815752

HOWLES, Timothy David. b 80. Qu Coll Cam BA 02 LSE MSc 04 Keble Coll Ox MSt 13 DPhil 19. Wycliffe Hall Ox BA 12. d 17 p 18. C Headington Ox 17–20; PtO 20–21. *84 Oxford Road, Old Marston, Oxford OX3 0RD* M: 07775-733846 E: timhowles@outlook.com

HOWLETT, Mrs Elizabeth Mary. b 58. Southn Univ BA 80. WMMTC 99. d 01 p 02. C Salter Street and Shirley *Birm* 01–04; Bp's Adv for Lay Adult Educn and Tr 04–18; PtO from 19; C Bride Valley *Sarum* from 20. *The Lodge, The Othona Communty, Burton Bradstock, Bridport DT6 4RN* E: lizhowlett@outlook.com

HOWLETT, Philip John. b 60. St Mellitus Coll 14. d 17 p 18. NSM Black Notley, Gt Notley and Rayne *Chelmsf* 17–21; NSM Greenstead w Colchester St Anne from 21. *1 Blackwater Avenue, Colchester CO4 3UY* E: howlettphilip@hotmail.com

HOWLETT, Richard Laurence. b 56. Kent Univ BA 79. Trin Coll Bris. d 94 p 95. C Louth *Linc* 94–98; R Marston Morteyne w Lidlington *St Alb* 98–05; V Goldington 05–17; TV Langelei from 17. *St Benedict's Vicarage, Peascroft Road, Hemel Hempstead HP3 8EP* T: (01442) 243934 E: revrhowlett@gmail.com

HOWLETT, Mrs Susannah Elizabeth. b 62. RGN 84. St Mellitus Coll BA 14. d 14 p 15. C Boreham *Chelmsf* 14–18; TV Greenstead w Colchester St Anne from 18. *1 Blackwater Avenue, Colchester CO4 3UY* E: sue_howlett@hotmail.co.uk *or* sue@greensteadwithstanne.org.uk

HOWLETT, Victor John. b 43. S Dios Minl Tr Scheme 90. d 93 p 94. NSM Bris St Andr w St Bart 93–95; NSM Bishopston and Bris St Matt and St Nath 95–96; C Gtr Corsham 96–99; V Wick w Doynton and Dyrham 99–05; AD Kingswood and S Glos 02–05; P-in-c Stratton St Margaret w S Marston etc 05–10; rtd 10; PtO *Bris* 10–19; *B & W* from 15; Hon C Gtr Corsham and Lacock *Bris* from 19. *11 Moor Park, Neston, Corsham SN13 9YJ* T: (01225) 819954 E: victorhowlett@hotmail.co.uk

HOWLETT-SHIPLEY, Ruth Mary. b 65. Univ Coll Lon BSc 86 MB, BS 89 Birm Univ MPH 03. Portsm Dioc Tr Course 17. d 19 p 20. C Shedfield and Wickham *Portsm* from 19. *12 Greenwood Close, Fareham PO16 7UF* M: 07970-407176 E: ruthshipley@hotmail.com

HOWMAN, Anne Louise. b 43. Ex Univ BA 97. SWMTC 97. d 99 p 00. NSM Ex St Dav 99–02; C Salcombe and Malborough w S Huish 02–07; rtd 08. *28 Sentrys Orchard, Exminster, Exeter EX6 8UD*

HOWORTH, Andrew John. b 59. d 15 p 16. NSM Addingham *Leeds* 15–18; NSM Menston w Woodhead from 18; Chapl Bradf Univ from 17. *3 Albany Row, Main Street, Menston, Ilkley LS29 6HA* T: (01943) 879267 E: revahoworth@icloud.com

HOWSE, Martin David. b 58. St Steph Ho Ox 97. d 99 p 00. C Colchester St Jas and St Paul w All SS etc *Chelmsf* 99–03; V Rush Green from 03. *St Augustine's Vicarage, 78 Birkbeck Road, Romford RM7 0QP* T: (01708) 741460 F: 732093 M: 07770-928167 E: martin.howse@virgin.net

HOWSON, Mrs Anne Margaret. b 56. Qu Mary Coll Lon BA 95 Anglia Ruskin Univ BA 09 Lon Inst of Educn PGCE 96. Westcott Ho Cam 07. d 09 p 10. C Saffron Walden w Wendens Ambo, Littlebury etc *Chelmsf* 09–11; C Saffron Walden and Villages 12; P-in-c Brightlingsea 12–17; rtd

17; PtO *Sarum* from 19. *Marshwood House, Whitchurch Canonicorum, Bridport DT6 6RQ* E: revhowson@gmail.com

HOWSON, Edwin John. b 51. ERMC. d 13 p 14. NSM St Osyth *Chelmsf* 13–15; NSM St Osyth and Great Bentley 15–16; PtO *Sarum* from 21. *Marshwood House, Whitchurch Canonicorum, Bridport DT6 6RQ* T: (01297) 489238 E: eddiehowson@gmail.com

HOWSON, James Edward. b 62. Ridley Hall Cam 97 EAMTC 98. d 00 p 01. C Cogges and S Leigh *Ox* 00–05; PtO 05–06; *Eur* 05–06; P-in-c Kiev 06–08; R Alfriston w Lullington, Litlington and W Dean *Chich* 09–14; PtO *Pet* from 14; *Ox* from 17. *1 The Mansions, Pevers Lane, Western Underwood, Olney MK46 5JU* E: jameshowson@rocketmail.com

HOWSON, Philip Michael. b 68. St Jo Coll Nottm 14. d 16 p 17. C Ollerton w Boughton *S'well* 16–19; C Bilsthorpe 18–19; C Eakring 18–19; C Egmanton 18–19; C Kirton 18–19; C Kneesall w Laxton and Wellow 18–19; C Walesby 18–19; V S Leightonstone *Ely* from 19. *The Rectory, Church Lane, Tilbrook, Huntingdon PE28 0JS* M: 07545-325789 E: revphiliphowson@icloud.com

HOY, Michael John. b 30. Reading Univ BSc 52. Oak Hill Th Coll 57. d 59 p 60. C Worthing St Geo *Chich* 59–62; C Tulse Hill H Trin *S'wark* 62–66; R Danby Wiske w Yafforth and Hutton Bonville *Ripon* 66–76; V Camelsdale *Chich* 76–87; V Gt Marsden *Blackb* 87–96; rtd 96. *35 Hardwick Park, Banbury OX16 1YF* T: (01295) 268744

HOY, Stephen Anthony. b 55. Leeds Poly BA 76. Linc Th Coll 92. d 94 p 95. C Glen Parva and S Wigston *Leic* 94–98; V Linc St Jo 98–18; Can and Preb Linc Cathl 15–18; rtd 18; PtO *Chich* from 19. *4 Gordon Avenue, Chichester PO19 8QY* T: (01243) 786374

HOYAL, Richard Dunstan. b 47. Ch Ch Ox BA 67 MA 71 BA 78. Ripon Coll Cuddesdon 76. d 79 p 80. C Stevenage St Geo *St Alb* 79–83; V Monk Bretton *Wakef* 83–89; V Ilkley St Marg *Bradf* 89–04; Dir of Ords 96–04; Hon Can Bradf Cathl 03–04; P-in-c Clifton All SS w St Jo *Bris* 04–12; P-in-c Easton All Hallows 04–12; P-in-c Bris Ch Ch w St Ewen, All SS and St Geo 09–12; rtd 12; PtO *Chich* from 13. *15 Garland Close, Petworth GU22 0QZ* E: richardhoyal@btinternet.com

HOYLAND, John Gregory. b 50. Sussex Univ BEd 73 Westmr Coll Ox MTh 96 Ches Univ DProf 17. Wycliffe Hall Ox 75. d 78 p 79. C Pudsey St Lawr *Bradf* 78–81; P-in-c Long Preston 81–84; V Long Preston w Tosside 84; CPAS Staff 85–87; Chapl York St Jo Coll 87–01; Lect York St Jo Univ 01–16; PtO *York* from 01; rtd 16. *18 Caxton Avenue, York YO26 5SN* T: (01904) 784140 *or* 876533 E: greg@hoyland.me.uk

HOYLE, David Fredric. b 46. Lon Bible Coll. d 02 p 03. NSM Northwood Em *Lon* 02–05; PtO *Win* from 11. *23 Cranleigh Gardens, Bournemouth BH6 5LE* T: (01202) 386305

HOYLE, The Very Revd David Michael. b 57. MBE 20. CCC Cam BA 80 MA 83 Magd Coll Cam PhD 91 UWE Hon DLitt 19. Ripon Coll Cuddesdon 84. d 86 p 87. C Chesterton Gd Shep *Ely* 86–88; Chapl Magd Coll Cam 88–91; Dean and Fell 91–95; V Southgate Ch Ch *Lon* 95–02; Dir Post-Ord Tr Edmonton Area 00–02; Dioc Officer for Min *Glouc* 02–10; Dioc Can Res Glouc Cathl 02–10; Dean Bris 10–19; Dean Westmr from 19. *The Chapter Office, 20 Dean's Yard, London SW1P 3PA* T: (020) 7654 4801 E: david.hoyle@westminster-abbey.org

HOYLE, Pamela Margaret. *See* CLOCKSIN, Pamela Margaret

HOYLE, Philip James. b 77. St Mellitus Coll. d 13 p 14. C Shepherd's Bush St Steph w St Thos *Lon* from 13. *60 Sundew Avenue, London W12 0RR* M: 07989-969257 E: hoylus@hotmail.com

HOYLE, Stephen Jonathan. b 64. Leeds Univ BA 87. Ripon Coll Cuddesdon 88. d 90 p 91. C Lt Stanmore St Lawr *Lon* 90–93; C Lon Docks St Pet w Wapping St Jo 93–96; PtO 01–02; TV Withycombe Raleigh *Ex* from 02. *St John's Vicarage, 3 Diane Close, Exmouth EX8 5QG* T: (01395) 270094

HOYTE, David Anthony. St Mellitus Coll BA 15. d 15 p 16. OLM Forest Gate All SS *Chelmsf* 15–16; C 16–19; V Plaistow SS Phil and Jas and St Mary from 19. *The Rectory, 19 Abbey Street, London E13 8DT* T: (020) 7473 5734

HRYZIUK, Petro. b 57. Lanc Univ BEd 80 Open Univ MA 95. St Jo Coll Nottm 89. d 90 p 91. C Huyton St Geo *Liv* 90–93; C Goose Green 93–96; C Wavertree H Trin 96–98; TV Maghull 98–05; Chapl Shrewsbury and Telford NHS Trust 05–13; Lead Chapl Shrewsbury and Telford Hosp NHS Trust from 13. *Chaplaincy Department, Royal Shrewsbury Hospital, Mytton Oak Road, Shrewsbury SY3 8XQ* T: (01743) 261000 E: petroh@hotmail.com *or* petro.hryziuk@sath.nhs.uk

HUBAND, Richard William. b 39. Trin Coll Cam BA 62 MA 66. Qu Coll Birm 76. d 78 p 79. C Norton *St Alb* 78–81; R Aspley Guise w Husborne Crawley and Ridgmont 81–91; V Elstow 91–03; rtd 03; PtO *Sarum* 04–19. *10 Beveridge Links, Dunbar EH42 1ZU* T: (01368) 868338

HUBBARD, Mrs Gillian Carol. b 63. RGN 84. WEMTC 05. **d** 08 **p** 09. NSM Glouc St Paul and St Steph 08–12; P-in-c Mow Cop *Lich* 12–16; V 16–21; TV Caldicot *Mon* from 21. *The Rectory, 19 Main Road, Portskewett, Caldicot NP26 5SG* T: (01291) 424348 M: 07525-039323 E: gillyhubbard@hotmail.co.uk

HUBBARD, Ian Maxwell. b 43. Surrey Univ BEd 84 Goldsmiths' Coll Lon MA 86 FCollP 83 ACP 83. Sarum & Wells Th Coll 69. **d** 73 **p** 74. Hon C S'wark H Trin w St Matt 73–78; Hon C Camberwell St Mich w All So w Em 78–87; Hon C Dulwich St Barn 87–90; C Battersea St Mary 90–92; V Winscombe *B & W* 92–98; TR Yatton Moor 98–13; RD Portishead 02–10; rtd 13; PtO *B & W* 13–18 and from 19. *38 Wemberham Lane, Yatton, Bristol BS49 4BP* T: (01934) 835859 E: ian.hubbardi@gmail.com

HUBBARD, Ms Judith Frances. b 49. St Alb Minl Tr Scheme 79. **dss** 82 **d** 87 **p** 94. Hemel Hempstead *St Alb* 82–86; Longden and Annscroft w Pulverbatch *Heref* 86–87; Hon C 87–91; Vice Prin WEMTC 91–97; Acting Prin 94–95; Hon C Leominster *Heref* 94–97; Cathl Chapl and Visitors' Officer *Glouc* 97–02; I Kinneigh Union *C, C & R* 02–09; Warden of Readers 05–08; P-in-c Frampton on Severn, Arlingham, Saul etc *Glouc* 09–10; rtd 10. *63 The Meadows, Leominster HR6 8QY* T: (01568) 612779 M: 07958-505881 E: judithfrances@gmail.com

HUBBARD, Julian Richard Hawes. b 55. Em Coll Cam BA 76 MA 81. Wycliffe Hall Ox BA 80 MA 85. **d** 81 **p** 82. C Fulham St Dionis *Lon* 81–84; Chapl Jes Coll and Tutor Wycliffe Hall Ox 84–89; Selection Sec ACCM 89–91; Sen Selection Sec ABM 91–93; V Bourne *Guildf* 93–99; P-in-c Tilford 97–99; RD Farnham 96–99; Can Res Guildf Cathl and Dir Minl Tr 99–05; Adn Ox and Can Res Ch Ch 05–11; Dir Min Division Abps' Coun 11–18; R Compton *Guildf* from 20; Rtd Clergy Officer from 20. *48 Manor Way, Guildford GU2 7RP* E: julianrhhubbard@gmail.com

HUBBARD, Laurence Arthur. b 36. Qu Coll Cam BA 60 MA 64. Wycliffe Hall Ox 60 CMS Tr Coll Chislehurst 65 CMS Tr Coll Selly Oak 93. **d** 62 **p** 63. C Widcombe *B & W* 62–65; CMS Kenya 66–73; V Pype Hayes *Birm* 73–79; P-in-c Norwich-over-the-Water Colegate St Geo *Nor* 79–85; P-in-c Nor St Aug w St Mary 79–85; CMS 85–97; Area Sec Cant and Roch 85–93; Chapl Damascus, Syria 93–97; Miss to Seamen Aqaba, Jordan 97–00; rtd 00; PtO *Glouc* 01–19. *24 Light Close, Corsham SN13 0DF* E: laurencehubbard@supanet.com

HUBBARD, Peter James. b 72. York Univ BA 93 Nottm Univ PGCE 97. Trin Coll Bris BA 03. **d** 04 **p** 05. C Hinckley H Trin *Leic* 04–08; R Karrinyup Australia 08–12; C Meole Brace *Lich* 12–16; V Bayston Hill from 16; Chapl Prestfelde Sch Shrewsbury 12–16. *42 Eric Lock Road West, Bayston Hill, Shrewsbury SY3 0QA* M: 07951-444269 E: peterhubbard1972@hotmail.com

HUBBARD, Roy Oswald. b 32. Lich Th Coll 62. **d** 64 **p** 65. C Baswich *Lich* 64–68; P-in-c Ash 68–70; V Stevenage St Pet Broadwater *St Alb* 71–78; V Flitwick 78–90; RD Ampthill 87–90; R Sharnbrook and Knotting w Souldrop 90–96; rtd 96; PtO *St Alb* 96–16; *Pet* from 96. *27 Cottington Court, Sidmouth EX10 8HD* T: (01395) 708599 E: roynpam11@gmail.com

HUBBLE, Canon Raymond Carr. b 30. Wm Temple Coll Rugby 60. **d** 61 **p** 62. C Newbold w Dunston *Derby* 61–64; Chapl RAF 64–80; Asst Chapl-in-Chief RAF 80–85; QHC 84–85; P-in-c Odiham w S Warnborough and Long Sutton *Win* 85; P-in-c Odiham 85–86; V 86–95; RD 88–95; Hon Can Win Cathl 94–95; rtd 95; PtO *Win* from 95. *Dormers, Centre Lane, Everton, Lymington SO41 0JP*

HUBBUCK, Dominic George. b 75. Univ of Wales (Newport) BA 07. Trin Coll Bris 14. **d** 16 **p** 17. C Yare Valley *Nor* 16–18; C Thorpe St Andr 18–19; Chapl Koinonia Federation from 19. *29 Ormiston Road, London SE10 0LJ* M: 07984-022700 E: dghubbuck@gmail.com

HUCKETT, Andrew William. b 50. AKC 72. St Aug Coll Cant 72. **d** 73 **p** 74. C Chipping Sodbury and Old Sodbury *Glouc* 73–76; Miss to Seafarers 76–14; Chapl Flushing 76–79; Chapl Teesside 79–82; Chapl Lagos Nigeria 82–85; Chapl Mombasa Kenya 85–86; Chapl Milford Haven 86–92; Chapl Medway Ports 92–03; Staff Chapl and Chapl Thames/Medway 03–05; Chapl Southampton 05–14; rtd 14; PtO *Cant* from 14. *24 Chegworth Gardens, Tunstall, Sittingbourne ME10 1RH* M: 07836-261324 E: andrewhuckett@outlook.com

HUCKLE, Stephen Leslie. b 48. Ch Ch Ox BA 70 BA 72 MA 74. Coll of Resurr Mirfield 73. **d** 75 **p** 76. C Wednesbury St Paul Wood Green *Lich* 75–78; C Aylesbury *Ox* 78–85; C Farnham Royal w Hedgerley 85–88; V Fenny Stratford 88–98; V Stirchley *Birm* 98–05; P-in-c Kempston All SS *St Alb* 05–13; V 15–16; P-in-c Biddenham 05–15; V 15–16; rtd 16; PtO *Linc* from 16. *15 Hall Road, Great Hale, Sleaford NG34 9LJ* T: (01529) 461704 E: stephenhuckle48@gmail.com

HUDD, Philip Simon Gorman. b 68. Westmr Coll Ox BA 90 Lanc Univ MA 06. Westcott Ho Cam 91. **d** 93 **p** 94. C Kirkby *Liv* 93–97; TV 97–99; V Lancaster Ch Ch *Blackb* 99–19; AD Lancaster 04–10. *7 Dumbarton Road, Lancaster LA1 3BX*

HUDDERSFIELD, Suffragan Bishop of. *See* GIBBS, The Rt Revd Jonathan Robert

HUDDLESON, Robert Roulston. b 32. QUB BA 55 TCD Div Test 57. **d** 57 **p** 58. C Ballymena w Ballyclug *Conn* 57–59; C Belfast St Pet and St Jas 59–63; Ethiopia 63–69; Exec Asst WCC Geneva 69–75; Dep Sec Gen Syn Bd for Miss and Unity 75–81; Admin Sec *Dur* 81–86; Dioc Sec *Ex* 86–97; rtd 97; PtO *Ex* 97–19. *6 Newton Court, Bampton, Tiverton EX16 9LG* T: (01398) 331412

HUDDLESTON, Geoffrey Roger. b 36. TCD BA 63 MA 67. Ridley Hall Cam 63. **d** 65 **p** 66. C Tonbridge SS Pet and Paul *Roch* 65–69; Chapl RAF 69–85; V Lyonsdown H Trin *St Alb* 85–00; RD Barnet 94–99; rtd 00; PtO *Lich* 01–17 and 19–21. *12 Island Green, Stafford ST17 0QB* T: (01785) 501728 E: grhuddleston@gmail.com

HUDSON, Deborah Elizabeth. *See* MOYO, Deborah Elizabeth

HUDGHTON, Emily Victoria. b 89. Cranmer Hall Dur 14. **d** 17 **p** 18. C Stockton Par Ch *Dur* 17–20; Pioneer Min from 20. *Address withheld by request* E: emily@wynyard.church

HUDGHTON, John Francis. b 56. BA. Cranmer Hall Dur 81. **d** 83 **p** 84. C Stockport St Geo *Ches* 83–85; C Witton 85–87; C Stockport St Alb Hall Street 87–90; V Thornton-le-Moors w Ince and Elton 90–95; Chapl RAF 95–01; P-in-c Burnby *York* 01–03; P-in-c Londesborough 01–03; P-in-c Nunburnholme and Warter and Huggate 01–03; P-in-c Shiptonthorpe and Hayton 01–03; TR Buxton w Burbage and King Sterndale *Derby* 03–17; RD Buxton 11–14; V Hayfield and Chinley w Buxworth from 17. *The Vicarage, 8 Bluebell Close, Hayfield, High Peak SK22 2PG* E: vicarhcb@outlook.com

HUDGHTON, Mark James David. b 88. York Univ MEng 11. Cranmer Hall Dur 14. **d** 17 **p** 18. C Shildon *Dur* 17–20; Pioneer Min from 20. *Address withheld by request* E: mark@wynyard.church

HUDSON, Mrs Alison Margaret. b 64. St Jo Coll Nottm 14 Qu Foundn Birm BA 20. **d** 17 **p** 18. NSM Bradwell and Porthill *Lich* 17–18; NSM Stone St Mich and St Wulfad w Aston St Sav 18–20; C from 20. *Meadow View, Shallowford House, Shallowford, Stone ST15 0NZ* M: 07725-467246 E: alison.hudson4@gmail.com

HUDSON, Andrew Julian. b 57. Cranmer Hall Dur 93. **d** 93 **p** 94. C Moldgreen *Wakef* 93–97; P-in-c Lundwood 97–01; V Dodworth 01–04; Ind Chapl *Chelmsf* from 04; C Aveley and Purfleet 04–13; TV Mardyke 13–17; P-in-c Thundersley from 17. *St Peter's Rectory, Church Road, Benfleet SS7 3HG* M: 07946-115396 E: andyhudson483@btinternet.com

HUDSON, Anthony George. b 39. NOC. **d** 84 **p** 85. C Harrogate St Mark *Ripon* 84–87; P-in-c Hampsthwaite 87–94; P-in-c Killinghall 87–94; P-in-c Hampsthwaite and Killinghall 94–96; V 96–99; rtd 99; PtO *Ripon* 00–14; *Leeds* from 14. *26 Beckwith Crescent, Harrogate HG2 0BQ* T: (01423) 858740

HUDSON, Brainerd Peter de Wirtz Goodwin. *See* GOODWIN HUDSON, Brainerd Peter de Wirtz

HUDSON, Canon Charles Edward Cameron. b 73. Univ Coll Ox BA 94 MA 08. Wycliffe Hall Ox BA 07. **d** 08 **p** 09. C St Margaret's-on-Thames *Lon* 08–11; R Broxbourne w Wormley *St Alb* from 11; RD Cheshunt from 17; Hon Can St Alb from 20. *The Vicarage, Churchfields, Broxbourne EN10 7AU* T: (01992) 444117 E: bwparishoffice@btinternet.com

HUDSON, Christopher John. b 45. Bedf Coll Lon BSc 68 MCIH 73. Cranmer Hall Dur. **d** 77 **p** 78. C Bath Weston St Jo *B & W* 77–80; Youth Chapl 77–80; P-in-c Baltonsborough w Butleigh and W Bradley 80–84; V 84–87; P-in-c Shirwell w Loxhore *Ex* 87–89; P-in-c Kentisbury, Trentishoe, E Down and Arlington 88–89; TR Shirwell, Loxhore, Kentisbury, Arlington, etc 90–91; P-in-c Trentishoe 90–91; RD Shirwell 88–91; R Huntspill *B & W* 91–94; rtd 01; PtO *B & W* 98–09; *Ex* from 06; *B & W* from 17. *Achray, 5 Conigar Close, Hemyock, Cullompton EX15 3RE* T: (01823) 680170 E: revchris@mhbruton.eclipse.co.uk

HUDSON, Daniel James. b 76. Sussex Univ BSc 97. Wycliffe Hall Ox 17. **d** 19. C Gt Aycliffe *Dur* from 19. *St Francis's Vicarage, Burnhope, Newton Aycliffe DL5 7ER* E: revdanielhudson@gmail.com

HUDSON, Mrs Elizabeth Rachel Ann. b 60. Newc Univ BA 81 Avery Hill Coll PGCE 83 Derby Univ MSc 03. Cranmer Hall Dur 15. **d** 17 **p** 18. C Morpeth *Newc* 17–18; C Cramlington 18–20; V Scremerston, Spittal and Tweedmouth from 20; Adv for Counselling and Wellbeing from 19. *The Vicarage, Main Street, Tweedmouth,*

Berwick-upon-Tweed TD15 2AW M: 07974-410409
E: revrachelhudson@gmail.com

HUDSON, John. b 51. Oak Hill Th Coll 84. **d** 86 **p** 87.
C Leyland St Andr *Blackb* 86–89; V Coppull 89–16;
P-in-c Coppull St Jo 10–11; R 11–16; rtd 16. *12 Mallow Way,
Euxton, Chorley PR7 6PU*

HUDSON, John. *See* HUDSON, Reginald John

HUDSON, John Stephen Anthony. b 49. S Dios Minl Tr
Scheme 85 Chich Th Coll 86. **d** 88 **p** 89. C Horsham *Chich*
88–91; TV Littlehampton and Wick 91–15; rtd 15. *166
Little Breach, Chichester PO19 5UA* T: (01243) 931557
E: stephen.hudson@outlook.com

HUDSON, Peter John. b 66. **d** 03 **p** 04. OLM Deptford St Paul
S'wark 03–07; NSM Lewisham St Steph and St Mark from
07. *7A Blackheath Rise, London SE13 7PN* T: (020) 8318
0483 M: 07908-640369 E: frpeter@sky.com

HUDSON, Rachel. *See* HUDSON, Elizabeth Rachel Ann

HUDSON, Reginald John. b 47. FRSA CertSS. Linc Th Coll. **d** 83
p 84. C Merton St Mary *S'wark* 83–86; C Kirk Ella *York* 86–88;
P-in-c Lenborough *Ox* 88–93; V 93–03; P-in-c Tingewick w
Water Stratford, Radclive etc 89–93; P-in-c Water Stratford
93–00; P-in-c Reading St Matt 03–10; rtd 11. *La Columbine,
198 Route de Vimoutiers, 61120 Canapville, France* T: (0033)
(2) 33 67 03 21

HUDSON, Robert Antony. b 82. York Univ BA 04. Wycliffe
Hall Ox BA 09. **d** 10 **p** 11. C Elburton *Ex* 10–14; C Harold
Wood *Chelmsf* 14–18; V from 18. *The Vicarage, 15 Athelstan
Road, Romford RM3 0QB* T: (01708) 376400 M: 07799-
600147 E: roberthudson79@btinternet.com *or*
robhudson@stpetersharoldwood.org

HUDSON, Stephen. *See* HUDSON, John Stephen Anthony

HUDSON, Walter Gerald. b 29. **d** 95 **p** 96. Hon C Eccleston
Park *Liv* 95–99; PtO from 99. *31 Springfield Lane, Eccleston,
St Helens WA10 5EW* T: (01744) 24919

✠**HUDSON-WILKIN, The Rt Revd Rose Josephine.** b 61.
MBE 20. Birm Univ BPhil 00. WMMTC 89. **d** 91 **p** 94 **c** 19.
Par Dn Wolverhampton St Matt *Lich* 91–94; C 94–95; C W
Bromwich Gd Shep w St Jo 95–98; Black Anglican Concern
95–98; V Dalston H Trin w St Phil and Haggerston All SS
Lon 98–14; P-in-c St Mary at Hill w St Andr Hubbard etc
14–19; Chapl to The Queen 07–19; Chapl to Speaker of Ho
of Commons 10–19; PV Westmr Abbey 10–19; Preb St Paul's
Cathl *Lon* 13–19; Suff Bp Dover *Cant* from 19. *The Bishop's
Office, Old Palace, Canterbury CT1 2EE* T: (01227) 459382
E: revdrose@aol.com *or* rhudson-wilkin@diocant.org

HUDSPETH, Ralph. b 46. **d** 06 **p** 07. NSM Ripley w Burnt
Yates *Ripon* 06–12; NSM Lower Wharfedale 12–14; *Leeds*
from 14. *10 Winksley Grove, Harrogate HG3 2SZ* T: (01423)
561918 M: 07810-631826 E: ralphhudspeth@hotmail.com

HUDSPITH, Colin John. b 46. Nottm Univ BA 67. SWMTC 93.
d 96 **p** 97. C Pilton w Ashford *Ex* 96–97; C Barnstaple 97–99;
C Shirwell, Loxhore, Kentisbury, Arlington, etc 99–00;
TV 00–11; rtd 11; PtO *Ex* from 13. *Brackendale, Heanton,
Barnstaple EX31 4DG* T: (01271) 813547

HUDSPITH, Mrs Susan Mary. b 49. St Alb Minl Tr Scheme 79.
dss 82 **d** 87 **p** 94. Luton St Chris Round Green *St Alb* 82–92;
Par Dn 87–88; NSM 88–92; PtO 92–94 and 00–05; NSM Luton
St Mary 94–00; NSM Stevenage St Pet Broadwater 05–08; PtO
08–18. *15 Waverley Close, Stevenage SG2 8RU* T: (01438)
725030

HUFFMAN, John Phillip. b 81. Pittsburgh Univ BA 04 MS 07.
St Aug Coll of Th 16. **d** 19 **p** 20. C Margate H Trin *Cant* from
19. *61 Addiscombe Road, Margate CT9 2SY* M: 07999-479202
E: johnhuffman7@gmail.com

HUGGETT, John Victor James. b 39. Dur Univ BA 64.
Tyndale Hall Bris 64. **d** 66 **p** 67. C Hailsham *Chich* 66–69;
C Worthing St Geo 69–71; C Woking St Pet *Guildf* 71–73;
C Buckhurst Hill *Chelmsf* 73–76; V Meltham Mills *Wakef*
76–78; V Wilshaw 76–78; Jt Ldr Breath Min 79–14; rtd 14;
PtO *Wakef* 79–84; *Roch* from 84; *Chich* from 15. *3 Cannon
House, St John's Close, Tunbridge Wells TN4 9GE* T: (01892)
512520 E: cjphuggett@yahoo.co.uk

HUGGETT, Kevin John. b 62. St Jo Coll Dur BA 83. Trin
Coll Bris 88. **d** 91 **p** 92. C Gt Ilford St Andr *Chelmsf* 91–94;
Regional Manager for Uganda and Sudan CMS 94–01; Hon C
Tonbridge SS Pet and Paul *Roch* 98–01; Chapl Lanc Univ *Blackb*
from 01. *11 Alderman Road, Lancaster LA1 5FW* T: (01524)
843091, 594082 *or* 594071 E: k.huggett@lancaster.ac.uk

HUGGETT, Michael George. b 38. Bris Univ BA 60 Birm Univ
CertEd 61. EMMTC 85. **d** 88 **p** 89. C Sawley *Derby* 88–92;
C Chaddesden St Phil 92–93; P-in-c Alkmonton, Cubley,
Marston Montgomery etc 93–99; R 99–04; rtd 04; PtO *Derby*
from 04. *12 Murray Road, Mickleover, Derby DE3 9LE* T: (01332)
511259 E: m.huggett152@btinternet.com

HUGGINS, Jonathan Paul (John). b 59. Leeds Univ
BSc 80 Bris Univ PhD 83 Dur Univ BA 18. SEITE 12.

d 14 **p** 15. C Kingsdown and Creekside *Cant* 14–17;
P-in-c Len Valley from 17. *Lenham Vicarage, Old Ashford
Road, Lenham, Maidstone ME17 2PX* T: (01622) 850280
E: john.p.huggins1@gmail.com *or* vicar@lvb.org.uk

HUGGINS, Stephen David. b 53. Sussex Univ BEd 75 K
Coll Lon MA 80 Leic Univ DipEd 79. STETS 98. **d** 01 **p** 02.
NSM Bexhill St Aug *Chich* 01–02; NSM Sedlescombe w
Whatlington 02–07; P-in-c Turners Hill 07–09; Angl Chapl
Worth Sch 07–09; TV Bexhill St Pet *Chich* 09–15; rtd 15; PtO
Chich 16–17; Hon C Bexhill St Barn 17–20; P-in-c 20–21. *10
Constable Way, Bexhill-on-Sea TN40 2UH* M: 07926-569152
E: frshuggins@gmail.com

HUGHES, Canon Adrian John. b 57. Newc Univ BA 78 St Jo
Coll Dur BA 82. Cranmer Hall Dur 80. **d** 83 **p** 84. C Shard
End *Birm* 83–86; TV Solihull 86–90; TV Glendale Gp *Newc*
90–94; P-in-c Belford 94–95; V Belford and Lucker 95–06; V
Ellingham 95–02; AD Bamburgh and Glendale 97–06; Asst
Dioc Dir of Ords 98–06; V Cullercoats St Geo from 06; AD
Tynemouth 09–14; Hon Can Newc Cathl from 05; QHC
from 19. *St George's Vicarage, 1 Beverley Gardens, North Shields
NE30 4NS* T: 0191-252 1817 E: revajh@btinternet.com *or*
revajh@virginmedia.com

HUGHES, Canon Alan. b 46. TD MBE 14. Edin Th Coll 71.
d 74 **p** 75. C Edin St Cuth 74–76; P-in-c Wester Hailes
St Luke 76–78; C Marske in Cleveland *York* 78–81; V New
Marske 81–84; V Kirkbymoorside w Gillamoor, Farndale etc
84–94; CF 84–94; V Berwick H Trin and St Mary *Newc* 94–13;
Hon Can Newc Cathl 08–13; rtd 13; PtO *Newc* from 13. *12
Governors Gardens, Berwick-upon-Tweed TD15 1JF* T: (01289)
307640 E: skypilot60@btinternet.com

HUGHES, The Ven Alexander James. b 75. Greyfriars Ox
BA 97 MA 04 St Edm Coll Cam MPhil 99 PhD 11. Westcott
Ho Cam 98. **d** 00 **p** 01. C Headington Quarry *Ox* 00–03;
Bp's Dom Chapl *Portsm* 03–08; P-in-c Portsea St Luke 08–13;
P-in-c Southsea St Pet 08–13; V Southsea St Luke and St Pet
13–14; Adn Cam *Ely* from 14; Hon Can Ely Cathl from 14.
1A Summerfield, Cambridge CB3 9HE T: (01223) 355013
E: archdeacon.cambridge@elydiocese.org

HUGHES, Allan Paul. b 45. Open Univ BA 91 Glam Coll of
Educn CertEd 69. Abp's Sch of Min 01. **d** 02 **p** 03. Chapl
St Olave's Sch York 02–05; NSM Skelton w Shipton and
Newton on Ouse *York* 02–03; Asst to RD Easingwold 03–04;
NSM York All SS Pavement w St Crux and St Mich 04–12;
NSM York St Denys 04–12; rtd 12; PtO York from 12; Asst
Dioc Dir of Ords from 10; Voc Adv *Eur* from 14; PtO *Win*
from 17; *Eur* from 18. *11 Farmers Way, Copmanthorpe,
York YO23 3XU* T: (01904) 269557 M: 07443-518645
E: revd_al@hotmail.co.uk

HUGHES, Andrew Karl William. b 58. St Steph Ho Ox 07
WEMTC 08. **d** 08 **p** 09. NSM Cheltenham *Glouc* 08–09;
C W Bromwich St Fran *Lich* 09–11; P-in-c Weston super
Mare All SS and St Sav *B & W* from 11. *The Vicarage, 46
Manor Road, Weston-super-Mare BS23 2SU* T: (01934) 204217
E: fatherandrew@sky.com

HUGHES, Miss Angela Mary. b 52. Avery Hill Coll CertEd 75.
St Steph Ho Ox 90. **d** 92 **p** 94. Par Dn Kidderminster
St Mary and All SS w Trimpley etc *Worc* 92–94; C 94–96;
P-in-c Gilmorton w Peatling Parva and Kimcote etc *Leic*
96–01; RD Guthlaxton II 99–01; R Wyberton *Linc* 01–09;
V Frampton 01–09; RD Holland W 04–09; R Carnoustie *Bre*
09–13; R Monifieth 09–13; P-in-c Clipston w Naseby and
Haselbech w Kelmarsh *Pet* 13–18; rtd 18; P-in-c Lanercost,
Walton, Gilsand and Nether Denton *Carl* from 18. *The
Vicarage, Lanercost, Brampton CA8 2HQ* T: (016977) 2478
E: ahughes@webleicester.co.uk

HUGHES, Arthur John. b 41. MCIOB 71 MRICS 78.
WEMTC 03. **d** 05 **p** 06. NSM Church Stretton *Heref* 05–11; rtd
11. *Jacey, 4 Lawley Close, Church Stretton SY6 6EL* T: (01694)
722582 E: jonhughes@uwclub.net

HUGHES, Arthur Lewis. b 36. St Deiniol's Hawarden 65.
d 68 **p** 69. C Holywell *St As* 68–71; Lect Watford St Mary
St Alb 71–73; C Watford 73–75; V Thornton in Lonsdale
w Burton in Lonsdale *Bradf* 75–84; V Daubhill *Man* 84–89;
V Castle Town *Lich* 89–00; Chapl Staffs Univ 91–00; rtd
00; PtO *Ches* 00–04; *Pet* from 05. *31 Hunt Close, Towcester
NN12 7AD* T: (01327) 358257

HUGHES, Bernard Patrick. b 35. Oak Hill Th Coll. **d** 65
p 66. C Fulham St Matt *Lon* 65–69; Chapl St Steph Hosp
Lon 69–89; Chapl St Mary Abbots Hosp Lon 69–97; Chapl
Chelsea and Westmr Hosp Lon 89–94; Chapl Westmr
Children's Hosp Lon 89–94; Sen Chapl Chelsea and Westmr
Hosp NHS Foundn Trust 94–97; rtd 97; PtO *Sarum* from 97.
Charis, 6 Priory Park, Bradford-on-Avon BA15 1QU T: (01225)
868679

HUGHES, Miss Carol Lindsay. b 51. Cam Inst of Educn
CertEd 72 Nottm Univ BEd 86. Trin Coll Bris 91. **d** 93 **p** 94.

C Ilkeston St Mary *Derby* 93–97; P-in-c Langley Mill 97–02; V 02–06; P-in-c Oakwood 06–11; RD Heanor 99–06; rtd 11; PtO *Cov* 12–21. *13 Harris Drive, Rugby CV22 6DX*

HUGHES, Clive. b 54. Univ of Wales BA 77 MA 82. St Mich Coll Llan BD 95. **d** 95 **p** 96. C Carmarthen St Dav *St D* 95–97; TV Aberystwyth 97–04; P-in-c Hanmer, Bronington, Bettisfield, Tallarn Green *St As* 04–09; P-in-c Hanmer and Bronington and Bettisfield 09–12; V Hanmer, Bronington, Bettisfield and Penley 12–16; TV Maelor Miss Area from 17. *The Vicarage, Hanmer, Whitchurch SY13 3DE* T: (01948) 830468 E: clivehughes54@gmail.com

HUGHES, Cynthia May. b 45. **d** 10 **p** 11. NSM Middlewich w Byley *Ches* from 10. *Ash Bank Farm, Weaverham Road, Gorstage, Northwich CW8 2SQ* E: thiahughes@hotmail.com

HUGHES, David Howard. b 55. Univ of Wales (Ban). St Mich Coll Llan. **d** 79 **p** 80. C Llanrhos *St As* 79–82; C Eckington w Handley and Ridgeway *Derby* 82–83; C Staveley and Barrow Hill 83–85; TV 85–89; V Whitworth St Bart *Man* 89–00. *2 Cromwell Road, Chesterfield S40 4TH* T: (01246) 277361

HUGHES, Canon David Michael. b 41. Oak Hill Th Coll BD 67. **d** 68 **p** 69. C Tunbridge Wells St Jo *Roch* 68–73; C Crookes St Thos *Sheff* 73–81; V Normanton *Wakef* 81–90; TR Didsbury St Jas and Em *Man* 90–09; AD Withington 00–04; Hon Can Man Cathl 06–09; rtd 09; PtO *Ches* 09–19; *Man* 09–19; *S'well* from 20. *48 Tranby Gardens, Nottingham NG8 2AB* T: 0115-916 8717 M: 07929-114143 E: davidmhughes11@gmail.com

HUGHES, Canon Elizabeth Jane. b 58. K Coll Lon BD 81 AKC 81. Ripon Coll Cuddesdon 81. **dss** 83 **d** 87 **p** 94. Chipping Barnet w Arkley *St Alb* 83–86; Dunstable 86–93; Hon Par Dn 87–93; NSM Boxmoor St Jo 93–03; Chapl Hospice of St Fran Berkhamsted 99–13; Sen Chapl Luton Airport *St Alb* from 13; Hon Can St Alb from 13. *London Luton Airport Operations Ltd, Navigation House, Airport Way, London Luton Airport, Luton LU2 9LY* T: (01582) 405100 E: liz.hughes@stfrancis.org.uk

HUGHES, Canon Evelyn. b 31. Gilmore Ho 73. **dss** 79 **d** 87 **p** 94. Fetcham *Guildf* 79–82; Dioc Adv Lay Min 82–86; Farnborough 83–87; C 87–92; Bp's Adv for Women's Min 87–94; Dn-in-c Badshot Lea CD 92–94; C-in-c 94–96; Hon Can Guildf Cathl 94–96; rtd 96; PtO *Guildf* 96–20. *4 Oaklands, Haslemere GU27 3RD* T: (01428) 651576

HUGHES, Gareth Francis. b 73. St Jo Coll Dur MSc 94 Wolfs Coll Ox MSt 07 GInstP 94. St Mich Coll Llan BD 98. **d** 98 **p** 99. C Haughton le Skerne *Dur* 98–02; TV White Horse *Sarum* 02–06; PtO *Lon* 09–11; Chapl Hertf Coll Ox 11–16; Prec Perth Cathl Australia from 16. *St George's Cathedral, 38 St George's Terrace, Perth WA 6000, Australia* T: (0061) (8) 9325 5766 E: gareth.hughes@perthcathedral.org

HUGHES, The Very Revd Geraint Morgan Hugh. b 34. Keble Coll Ox 58 MA 63. St Mich Coll Llan 58. **d** 59 **p** 60. C Gorseinon *S & B* 59–63; C Oystermouth 63–68; R Llanbadarn Fawr, Llandegley and Llanfihangel etc 68–76; R Llandrindod w Cefnllys 76–86; R Llandrindod w Cefnllys and Disserth 87–98; Can Brecon Cathl 89–98; Prec Brecon Cathl 95–98; RD Maelienydd 95–98; Dean Brecon 98–00; V Brecon St Mary and Battle w Llanddew 98–00; rtd 00. *Hafod, Cefnllys Lane, Penybont, Llandrindod Wells LD1 5SW* T: (01597) 851830

HUGHES, Canon Gwilym Berw. b 42. St Mich Coll Llan. **d** 68 **p** 69. C Conwy w Gyffin *Ban* 68–71; V Llandinorwig 71–75; TV Llandudno 75–80; V Dwygyfylchi 80–96; RD Arllechwedd 88–96; V Bodelwyddan *St As* 96–09; Can Cursal St As Cathl 08–09; rtd 09; PtO *Ban* from 09; *St As* from 10. *Glanfa, Glanyrafon Road, Dwygyfylchi, Penmaenmawr LL34 6UD* T: (01492) 623365

HUGHES, Gwilym Lloyd. b 48. Univ of Wales (Cardiff) BD 76 MA 79 Univ of Wales (Ban) CertEd 84. St Mich Coll Llan 71. **d** 99 **p** 00. NSM Caerwys and Bodfari *St As* 99–14; Warden of Readers 99–02; PtO from 14. *Grove Hall, Bodfari, Denbigh LL16 4DE* E: lloyd.hughes@btconnect.com

HUGHES, Howard. See HUGHES, David Howard

HUGHES, Ian Peter. b 55. Fitzw Coll Cam BA 76 MA 93. Ridley Hall Cam 05. **d** 07 **p** 08. C Wadhurst *Chich* 07–11; C Howell Hill w Burgh Heath *Guildf* 11–17; PtO from 18. *2 Meadow Close, Westcott, Dorking RH4 3GG* E: ian@hughes.name

HUGHES, Preb Ivor Gordon. b 45. Westmr Coll Ox MTh 94 Culham Coll of Educn CertEd 68. Ripon Coll Cuddesdon 75. **d** 77 **p** 78. C Newport w Longford *Lich* 77–79; Children's Work Officer CMS 79–82; V Gt and Lt Bedwyn and Savernake Forest *Sarum* 82–86; P-in-c Urchfont w Stert 86–90; TR Redhorn 90–92; Nat Children's Officer Gen Syn Bd of Educn 92–95; R Yeovil w Kingston Pitney *B & W* 95–06; Preb Wells Cathl 02–06; RD Yeovil 04–06; Chapl St Marg Hospice Yeovil 04–06; P-in-c Klamath Falls and Bonanza USA 06–08; rtd 08; PtO *B & W* from 08; *Sarum* 13–21. *15 Leventon*

Place, Hilperton, Trowbridge BA14 7US T: (01225) 760275 E: hughes6cm@btinternet.com

HUGHES, Canon Jacqueline Louise. b 50. Birm Poly BEd 86 ACP 81. WMMTC 89. **d** 92. NSM Edgbaston St Geo *Birm* 92–95; Tutor Qu Coll Birm 96–00; Educn Chapl Birm City Coun 00–10; Dir of Educn *Birm* 10–15; Hon Can Birm Cathl 14–15; rtd 15; PtO *Birm* 05–16. *267 Stoney Lane, Yardley, Birmingham B25 8YG* T: 0121-628 4184 E: jackielhughes1950@gmail.com

HUGHES, James Thomas. b 74. St Anne's Coll Ox BA 95 Aber Univ PhD 15 Liv Hope PGCE 97. Oak Hill Th Coll BA 02. **d** 03 **p** 04. C Virginia Water *Guildf* 03–07; C Hartford *Ches* 07–16; V Duffield and Lt Eaton *Derby* from 16. *The Vicarage, 2 Vicarage Lane, Duffield, Belper DE56 4EB* E: james.t.hughes@btopenworld.com

HUGHES, John. See HUGHES, Arthur John

HUGHES, John David. b 58. Leeds Univ BA 79 Man Univ PGCE 82. Ripon Coll Cuddesdon 97. **d** 99 **p** 00. C Wythenshawe *Man* 99–06; P-in-c Old Trafford St Jo 06–18; R from 18; AD Stretford 10–15; Dioc Environment Officer from 15. *St John's Rectory, 1 Lindum Avenue, Manchester M16 9NQ* T: 0161-872 0500 E: john_dhughes@yahoo.co.uk

HUGHES, John Lloyd. b 48. **d** 08 **p** 09. NSM Abergavenny St Mary w Llanwenarth Citra *Mon* 08–09 and 11–13; NSM Abergavenny H Trin 11–13; NSM Govilon w Llanfoist w Llanellen 09–11; PtO 13–15; S Africa 14–15; NSM Llantilio Pertholey w Bettws Chpl etc *Mon* from 15; PtO *S & B* from 18. *Emmanuel, 7 Orchard Close, Gilwern, Abergavenny NP7 0EN* T: (01873) 832368 E: john997hughes@btinternet.com

HUGHES, John Malcolm. b 47. Man Univ BSc 68. Coll of Resurr Mirfield 68. **d** 71 **p** 72. C Newton Nottage *Llan* 71–78; V Llanwynno 78–92; R Cadoxton-juxta-Barry 92–11; AD Penarth and Barry 08–11; rtd 11; PtO *Llan* from 14; *Mon* from 14. *3 The Terrace, Rhymney, Tredegar NP22 5LY* T: (01685) 555374 E: fr.johnhughessc@hotmail.com

HUGHES, Canon John Patrick. b 41. Oak Hill Th Coll. **d** 67 **p** 68. C Chorleywood St Andr *St Alb* 67–71; C E Twickenham St Steph *Lon* 71–76; TV High Wycombe *Ox* 77–92; Chapl Wycombe Gen Hosp 77–83; V Harborne Heath *Birm* 92–09; Hon Can Birm Cathl 99–09; rtd 09; PtO *Ox* from 10. *59 Witney Road, Ducklington, Witney OX29 7TS* T: (01993) 358781 M: 07817-465996 E: johnandanniehughes@gmail.com

HUGHES, Canon John Tudor. b 59. Nottm Univ BSc 81 Univ of Wales (Cardiff) BD 84. St Mich Coll Llan 81. **d** 84 **p** 85. C Mold *St As* 84–88; Asst Dioc Youth Chapl 86–90; Dioc Youth Chapl 90–97; Min Can St As Cathl 88–90; Min St As and Tremeirchion 88–90; V Holt 90–96; V Buckley 96–04; RD Mold 00–03; V Gresford 04–09; V Holt and Gresford 09–16; TV Alyn Miss Area from 17; Can Cursal St As Cathl 05–13; Can Res, Preb and Sacr from 13. *The Vicarage, Church Green, Gresford, Wrexham LL12 8RG* T: (01978) 852236 E: tudorhughes53@gmail.com

HUGHES, Jonathan William Llewelyn. b 83. Fitzw Coll Cam BA 05 MA 09. St Mellitus Coll 14. **d** 16 **p** 17. C Nottm Trin BMO *S'well* from 16. *7 Kingston Road, West Bridgford, Nottingham NG2 7AQ* M: 07720-540302

HUGHES, Katherine. See HACKER HUGHES, Katherine Lucy

HUGHES, Lindsay. See HUGHES, Carol Lindsay

HUGHES, Lloyd. See HUGHES, Gwilym Lloyd

HUGHES, Matthew James. b 66. K Coll Lon BD 88. Westcott Ho Cam 89. **d** 91 **p** 92. C Heston *Lon* 91–94; C Fulham All SS 94–96; TV St Laur in Thanet *Cant* 96–01; R Farnborough *Roch* from 01. *The Rectory, Farnborough Hill, Orpington BR6 7EQ* T: (01689) 856931 E: jmath@btinternet.com

HUGHES, Michael John Minto. b 50. Liv Univ MB, ChB 74 Westmr Coll Ox MTh 94. Wycliffe Hall Ox 76. **d** 79 **p** 80. C Stranton *Dur* 79–82; Chapl Intercon Ch Soc Peru 82–86; PtO *Dur* 86–87; *Carl* 87–89; TV Thetford *Nor* 89–97; P-in-c Downham *Ely* 97–05; Hon C Ely 05–13; CMS Uganda 13–18; rtd 18. *44 Merchant Gate, Riverside Square, Bedford MK40 1AS* M: 07542-840685 E: mikeandsue.hughes@gmail.com

HUGHES, Neville Joseph. b 52. NUU BA 79 MBIM 93 CITC 97. **d** 91 **p** 92. NSM Mullabrack w Markethill and Kilcluney *Arm* 91–98; I 00–18; C Portadown St Mark 98–00; Can Arm Cathl 14–18; rtd 18. *24 Derryhale Road, Portadown, Craigavon BT62 4HE* T: (028) 3833 3647 M: 07395-814315

HUGHES, The Ven Paul Vernon. b 53. Ripon Coll Cuddesdon 78. **d** 82 **p** 83. C Chipping Barnet w Arkley *St Alb* 82–86; TV Dunstable 86–93; P-in-c Boxmoor St Jo 93–98; V 98–03; RD Hemel Hempstead 96–03; Adn Bedford 03–19; rtd 19. *156 Buckingham Drive, Luton LU2 9RE*

HUGHES, Mrs Penelope Patricia. b 47. Sheff Univ LLB. WMMTC 95. **d** 98 **p** 99. NSM Whitley *Cov* 98–01; NSM

Leamington Spa H Trin and Old Milverton 01–03; P-in-c Berkswell 03–08; rtd 08; PtO *Cov* from 08. *8 Albany Terrace, Leamington Spa CV32 5LP* T: (01926) 330204 E: penhughes@aol.com

HUGHES, Peter. b 79. Nottm Univ BSc 02. Westmr Th Cen 06. **d** 08 **p** 09. C Bryanston Square St Mary w St Marylebone St Mark *Lon* 08–09; Pioneer Min King's Cross from 10; V Hanley Road from 19. *16 Bewdley Street, London N1 1HB* T: (020) 3432 5396 E: pete.hughes@stsaviours.church

HUGHES, Peter John. b 59. Wolv Poly BA 83 Lon Univ PGCE 85. Wycliffe Hall Ox 90. **d** 92 **p** 93. C Ecclesall *Sheff* 92–96; V Kimberworth 96–05; R Wickersley from 05; P-in-c Ravenfield, Hooton Roberts and Braithwell from 17; AD Rotherham 17–19. *The Rectory, 5 Church Lane, Wickersley, Rotherham S66 1ES* T: (01709) 543111 E: peter.j.hughes59@btinternet.com

HUGHES, Canon Philip. b 47. St Jo Coll Nottm 79. **d** 81 **p** 82. C Dolgellau w Llanfachreth and Brithdir etc *Ban* 81–83; Asst Youth Chapl 82–83; R Llaneugrad w Llanallgo and Penrhosllugwy etc 83–95; R Llanberis w Llanrug 95–03; R Llanberis, Llanrug and Llandinorwig 03; Dioc Youth Chapl 93–98; RD Arfon 00–02; R Llanfair-pwll and Llanddaniel-fab etc 03–12; AD Tindaethwy and Menai 07–10; Can Ban Cathl 10–12; rtd 12; PtO *Ban* from 12. *Afallon, 27 Pengarth, Conwy LL32 8RW* T: (01492) 562866 E: revphiliphughes@yahoo.co.uk

HUGHES, Philip Geoffrey John. b 60. Nottm Univ BCombStuds 82. Qu Coll Birm 86. **d** 89 **p** 90. C Sedgley All SS *Lich* 89–94; V Boscoppa *Truro* 94–96; Chapl Gatwick Airport and Chapl Sussex Police 96–02; P-in-c Harmondsworth *Lon* 02–07; Chapl Heathrow Airport 02–07; Chapl Metrop Police 02–07; V Seghill *Newc* 07–21; AD Bedlington 13–20; Chapl Northumbria Police 07–13; rtd 21. *Address withheld by request* E: phil.hughes@pobroadband.co.uk

HUGHES, Philip Stephen. b 34. Dur Univ BA 59. Coll of Resurr Mirfield 59. **d** 62 **p** 63. C Horfield St Greg *Bris* 62–66; C Bedminster St Mich 66–69; P-in-c Chippenham St Pet 69–71; V 71–83; TR Bedminster 83–91; V Ashton Keynes, Leigh and Minety 91–00; rtd 00; PtO *Worc* from 00. *19 Fairways, Pershore WR10 1HA* T: (01386) 552375 E: p-jhughes@outlook.com

HUGHES, Poppy. See HUGHES, Veronica Jane

HUGHES, Richard Millree. b 33. Univ of Wales BA 56 MA 79. St Mich Coll Llan 56. **d** 58 **p** 59. C Mold *St As* 58–61; V Choral St As Cathl 61–64; V Towyn 64–67; Asst Master Marlborough Sch Woodstock 77–79; R Whitchurch St Mary *Ox* 79–00; rtd 00; PtO *St As* 13–14; P-in-c Llansilin w Llangadwaladr and Llangedwyn 14–16; TV Tanat Valley Miss Area 17–18; PtO from 18. *The Vicarage, Llansilin, Oswestry SY10 7PX* T: (01691) 791876 M: 07798-790369 E: rmillree@aol.com

HUGHES, Canon Sally Lorraine. b 59. Open Univ BA 98. EAMTC 99. **d** 02 **p** 03. NSM Gretton w Rockingham and Cottingham w E Carlton *Pet* 02–05; Asst Chapl Kettering Gen Hosp NHS Trust 02–04; P-in-c Stoke Albany w Wilbarston and Ashley etc *Pet* 05–16; R 16–18; Rural Adv Oakham Adnry 05–06; Can Pet Cathl 17–18; rtd 19. *28 Rushton Road, Wilbarston, Market Harborough LE16 8QL* T/F: (01536) 770998 E: sally@hughes.uk.com

HUGHES, Mrs Sheila. b 52. NOC 92. **d** 95 **p** 96. NSM Birkenhead Priory *Ches* 95–97; C 97–99; P-in-c Northwich St Luke and H Trin 99–01; V 01–07; Bp's Adv for Women in Min 00–07; Chapl Mid Cheshire Hosps Trust 99–07; P-in-c Barrow St Jo *Carl* 07–14; rtd 14; P-in-c Lorton and Loweswater w Buttermere *Carl* 14–17. *7 Pine Tree Avenue, Prenton CH43 9RX* T: 0151-678 4233 E: revsheilahughes@hotmail.co.uk

HUGHES, Sheila Norah. b 40. **d** 06 **p** 07. NSM Ellesmere Port *Ches* 06–10; rtd 10; PtO *Ches* from 10. *13 Bridle Way, Great Sutton, Ellesmere Port CH66 2NJ* T: 0151-339 9777 E: sheila.hughes67@ntlworld.com

HUGHES, Timothy David Llewelyn. b 77. St Mellitus Coll. **d** 13 **p** 14. C Onslow Square and S Kensington St Aug *Lon* 13–15; P-in-c Birm St Luke from 15. *38 Carpenter Road, Birmingham B15 2JJ* M: 07590-692535 E: tim.hughes@gasstreet.church

HUGHES, Trystan Owain. b 72. Univ of Wales (Ban) BD 94 PhD 98. Wycliffe Hall Ox MTh. **d** 05 **p** 07. C Llantwit Major *Llan* 05–09; C Whitchurch 09; Chapl Cardiff Univ 09–13; P-in-c Cardiff Ch Ch Roath Park from 13; Dioc Dir of Ords 13–15; Dir of Voc from 15. *Christ Church Vicarage, 154 Lake Road East, Cardiff CF23 5NQ* T: (029) 2075 8588 *or* 2075 7190 E: trystanhughes@churchinwales.org.uk

HUGHES, Tudor. See HUGHES, John Tudor

HUGHES, Ms Valerie Elizabeth. b 53. Birm Univ BA 75 CertEd 76. Wycliffe Hall Ox 85. **d** 87 **p** 94. C Hallwood *Ches* 87–90; Par Dn Garston *Liv* 90–93; Asst Chapl Liv Univ 93;

Team Dn Gateacre 93–94; TV 94–00; C St Helens St Helen 00–09; TV Newton 09–19; rtd 19. *21 Coronation Drive, Chirk, Wrexham LL14 5LF* E: val.hughes@live.co.uk

HUGHES, Canon Veronica Jane (Poppy). b 60. Ex Univ BA 82 Birkbeck Coll Lon MSc 04. SEITE 07. **d** 10 **p** 11. C Dulwich St Clem w St Pet *S'wark* 10–13; P-in-c Tetbury, Beverston, Long Newnton etc *Glouc* 13–14; R from 14; R Avening w Cherington 14–16; AD Cirencester from 18; Hon Can Glouc Cathl from 21. *The Vicarage, 6 The Green, Tetbury GL8 8DN* T: (01666) 502333 E: poppy_hughes@hotmail.co.uk

HUGHES, Canon William Piers Maximillian. b 76. Ex Univ BA 99. Ripon Coll Cuddesdon 99. **d** 01 **p** 02. C Cley Hill Warminster *Sarum* 01–05; V Blackmoor and Whitehill *Portsm* 05–11; V Petersfield from 11; R Buriton from 11; AD Petersfield 11–16; Acting Adn The Meon 21; Hon Can Portsm Cathl from 15. *12 Dragon Street, Petersfield GU31 4AB* T: (01730) 260464 E: revwillhughes@btinternet.com

HUGHES CAREW, Sion Awen Mihangel. b 85. Edin Univ MA 08 Cardiff Univ LLM 18 St Jo Coll Cam BA 21. Westcott Ho Cam 18 Ven English Coll Rome 20. **d** 21. C Newsham and Horton *Newc* from 21. *59 Albatross Way, Blyth NE24 3QH* M: 07951-565243 E: frsionhc@gmail.com

HUGHESDON, James Carlyle. b 82. Ex Univ BA 05 Anglia Ruskin Univ MA 12. Westcott Ho Cam 10. **d** 12 **p** 13. C Old Ford St Paul and St Mark *Lon* 12–15; V 15–21; V Islington St Mary from 21. *St Mary's Vicarage, Upper Street, London N1 2TU* M: 07841-123869

HUGHMAN, June Alison. b 58. Kingston Poly BSc 81 Southn Univ PhD 84. Trin Coll Bris 86. **d** 89 **p** 94. Par Dn Penge St Jo *Roch* 89–93; C Woking Ch Ch *Guildf* 93–98; V Croydon Ch Ch *S'wark* 98–00; C Uxbridge *Lon* 00–21; Town Cen Min 00–21; P-in-c Cowley *Lon* from 21. *26 Church Road, Hayes UB3 2LH*

HUGO, Canon Keith Alan. b 41. Nottm Univ BA 62. Chich Th Coll 62. **d** 64 **p** 65. C Pontefract St Giles *Wakef* 64–68; C Chesterfield St Mary and All SS *Derby* 68–71; V Allenton and Shelton Lock 71–77; Dioc Communications Officer *Sarum* 77–89; V Potterne 77–84; V Worton 77–84; V Potterne w Worton and Marston 84–89; R Wyke Regis 89–06; Can and Preb Sarum Cathl 84–06; RD Weymouth 94–04; rtd 06; PtO *Sarum* 06–19; *Eur* from 18. *15 Steepdene, Poole BH14 8TE* T: (01202) 734971 E: keith.hugo@ntlworld.com

HUISH, Barnaby Thomas. b 71. St Chad's Coll Dur BA 94 MA 95. Ripon Coll Cuddesdon BA 98. **d** 99 **p** 00. C Darlington H Trin *Dur* 99–02; Prec and Min Can St Alb Abbey 02–06; R Dur St Marg, Neville's Cross St Jo and Bearpark from 06. *St Margaret's Rectory, 10 Westhouse Avenue, Durham DH1 4FH*

HUITSON, Christopher Philip. b 45. Keble Coll Ox BA 66 MA 70. Cuddesdon Coll 67. **d** 69 **p** 70. C Croydon St Sav *Cant* 69–71; Soc Service Unit St Martin-in-the-Fields *Lon* 71–73; C St Alb St Pet 73–77; V Cople 77–78; P-in-c Willington 77–78; V Cople w Willington 78–89; V Leavesden 89–96; V Totteridge 96–11; RD Barnet 99–05; rtd 11; PtO *Sarum* 12–22; *St Alb* 11–16. *Abbotsleigh, 1A Gainsborough Drive, Sherborne DT9 6DS* T: (01935) 815187 E: c.huitson33@btinternet.com

HULBERT, John Anthony Lovett. b 40. Trin Coll Cam BA 63 MA 67. Wells Th Coll 64. **d** 66 **p** 67. C Fareham H Trin *Portsm* 66–70; R Wickham 70–79; RD Bishop's Waltham 74–79; V Bedford St Andr *St Alb* 79–92; RD Bedford 87–92; V Leighton Buzzard w Eggington, Hockliffe etc 92–03; Hon Can St Alb 91–03; C Stansted *Chich* 03–04; P-in-c Lynch w Iping Marsh and Milland 04–10; rtd 10; PtO *Chich* from 10; *Portsm* from 11. *Cherry Trees, Buckshead Hill, Meonstoke, Southampton SO32 3NA* T: (01489) 878289 E: anthonic@btinternet.com

HULBERT, Canon Martin Francis Harrington. b 37. Dur Univ BSc 58 MA 62. Ripon Hall Ox 58. **d** 60 **p** 61. C Buxton *Derby* 60–63; C Eglingham *Newc* 63–67; C-in-c Loundsley Green Ascension CD *Derby* 67–71; P-in-c Frecheville 71–72; R Frecheville and Hackenthorpe *Sheff* 73–77; P-in-c Hathersage *Derby* 77–83; V 83–90; RD Bakewell and Eyam 81–90; R Brailsford w Shirley and Osmaston w Edlaston 90–93; V Tideswell 93–02; RD Buxton 96–99; Hon Can Derby Cathl 89–02; rtd 02; PtO *Derby* from 02. *18 Yokecliffe Crescent, Wirksworth, Matlock DE4 4ER* T: (01629) 825148 E: martin.hulbert1@btinternet.com

HULKS, Mrs Nicola Ann. b 84. Ripon Coll Cuddesdon 12. **d** 15 **p** 16. C Maidenhead St Luke *Ox* 15–19; TV Thatcham from 19. *1 Cowslip Crescent, Thatcham RG18 4DE* T: (01635) 864916 E: nicola.hulks@hotmail.co.uk

HULL, Mrs Bernadette Mary. b 46. E Lon Univ BA 92 PGCE 93. NTMTC 99. **d** 02 **p** 03. NSM Becontree S *Chelmsf* 02–04; NSM Marks Gate 04–09; P-in-c Romford Ascension Collier Row 09–17; rtd 17; PtO *Chelmsf* 18–19. *1 Colin Pond Court, 21 Longhayes Avenue, Romford RM6 5HB* T: (020) 8598 8027 M: 07506-377414 E: revbernadettehull@gmail.com

HULL, The Very Revd Thomas Henry. b 55. QUB BD 79. NTMTC 94. **d** 97 **p** 98. C Kidbrooke *S'wark* 97–99; TV 99–01; I Lecale Gp *D & D* from 01; Min Can Down Cathl 03–06; Dean Down from 06. *Lecale Rectory, 9 Quoile Road, Downpatrick BT30 6SE* T: (028) 4461 3101 *or* 4461 4922 F: 4461 4456 E: henryhull@downcathedral.org

HULL, Timothy David. b 60. Lon Bible Coll 87 K Coll Lon PhD 97. St Jo Coll Nottm BTh 90. **d** 90 **p** 91. C Leyton St Mary w St Edw *Chelmsf* 90–95; Chapl Havering Coll of F&HE 94–98; C Harold Hill St Geo *Chelmsf* 95–98; TV Becontree W 98–05; Co-ord NTMTC 98–01; Registrar 01–05; Tutor St Jo Coll Nottm from 05. *St John's College, Chilwell Lane, Bramcote, Nottingham NG9 3DS* T: 0115-925 1114 E: t.hull@stjohns-nottm.ac.uk

HULL, Suffragan Bishop of. *See* WHITE, The Rt Revd Alison Mary

HULLYER, Paul Charles. b 68. Anglia Poly Univ MA 98 Lambeth MA 04 FRSA 04. Aston Tr Scheme 92 Westcott Ho Cam 94. **d** 97 **p** 98. C Stoke Newington St Mary *Lon* 97–00; C Addlestone *Guildf* 00–03; V Hillingdon All SS *Lon* 03–08; V Pinner from 08; Dir Post-Ord Tr 10–15; CF from 12. *The Vicarage, 2 Church Lane, Pinner HA5 3AA* T: (020) 8866 3869

HULME, Alan John. b 60. Birm Univ BSc 81. Wycliffe Hall Ox BA 90. **d** 91 **p** 92. C Chilwell *S'well* 91–96; TV Roxeth *Lon* 96–02; V S Harrow St Paul 02–08; TR Ely 08–13; Dioc Dir Par Development and Evang *Guildf* 13–18; V Rugby W *Cov* from 19. *St Matthew's Vicarage, 7 Vicarage Road, Rugby CV22 7AJ* T: (01788) 330442 M: 07543-500483 E: alanhulme@m2o.org.uk

HULME (*née* ASHLEY), Mrs Jane Isobel. b 59. Birm Univ BSc 81. **d** 05 **p** 06. NSM S Harrow St Paul *Lon* 05–08; NSM Ely 08–13; PtO *Guildf* 13–18; NSM Rugby W *Cov* from 19. *St Matthew's Vicarage, 7 Vicarage Road, Rugby CV22 7AJ* T: (01788) 330442 E: janehulme59@gmail.com

HULME, Ms Juliette Mary. b 57. Whitelands Coll Lon BEd 81. Cranmer Hall Dur 94. **d** 94 **p** 95. C Crayford *Roch* 94–98; C Leatherhead *Guildf* 98–01; CF 02–05; PtO *Sarum* 05–08; Chapl Wells Cathl Sch 06–18; TV Nadder Valley *Sarum* from 18. *The Rectory, Park Road, Tisbury, Salisbury SP3 6LF* T: (01747) 871957 E: revjmhulme@gmail.com

HULME, Susan. b 52. **d** 08 **p** 09. NSM Kinsley w Wragby *Wakef* 08–12; NSM Brotherton 12–14; *Leeds* from 14; NSM Ferrybridge *Wakef* 12–14; *Leeds* from 14; Chapl Mid Yorks Hosps NHS Trust from 13. *4 Balmoral Drive, Knottingley WF11 8RQ* T: (01977) 676808 E: bedeuk@talk21.com

HULME, Suffragan Bishop of. *Vacant*

HULSE (*formerly* WHITTINGHAM), Mrs Janet Irene. b 49. **d** 03 **p** 04. OLM Pendleton *Man* 03–09; OLM Salford All SS 09–16; Chapl Salford R NHS Foundn Trust 14–20; rtd 20; PtO *Man* from 16. *24 Aylesbury Close, Salford M5 4FQ* T: 0161-736 5878 M: 07905-667308 E: revjhulse@gmail.com

HULSE, Mrs Ruth Carole. b 80. Ripon Coll Cuddesdon 11. **d** 13 **p** 14. C W Heref 13–16; TV 16–21; TR from 21; RD Heref City from 20. *The Vicarage, Vowles Close, Hereford HR4 0DF* T: (01432) 273086 M: 07733-329290 E: ruthhulse@hotmail.co.uk

HULSE, William John. b 42. Dur Univ BA 65. Linc Th Coll 65. **d** 67 **p** 68. C S Westoe *Dur* 67–70; LtO *Newc* 70–72; C Far Headingley St Chad *Ripon* 72–76; R Swillington 76–88; V Shadwell 88–95; V Oulton w Woodlesford 95–02; P-in-c Spennithorne w Finghall and Hauxwell 02–12; Chapl MU 03–09; rtd 12; PtO *Ripon* 13–14; *Leeds* from 14. *5 Hargill Close, Harmby, Leyburn DL8 5QE* T: (01969) 623396 E: wjhulse@btinternet.com

HUMBLE, Reid Thomas. b 87. Oklahoma Chr Univ BA 09 Sheff Univ MA 11. Westcott Ho Cam 12. **d** 16 **p** 17. C Rotherham *Sheff* 16–18; C Walkley 18–19; Asst Chapl Sheff Univ 18–19; P-in-c Southchurch H Trin *Chelmsf* from 19. *The Rectory, 8 Pilgrims Close, Southend-on-Sea SS2 4XF* M: 07588-074156 E: reverend.reidhumble@gmail.com

HUME, Mrs Barbara Christine. b 56. St Mellitus Coll BA 14. NTMTC 94. **d** 97 **p** 98. NSM Romford St Edw *Chelmsf* 97–01; C 01–11; P-in-c Upper Colne 11–17; P-in-c Sible Hedingham w Castle Hedingham 16–17; R The Hedinghams and Upper Colne 17; rtd 18; Ind (Retail) Chapl *Lon* from 18; PtO *Chelmsf* 18–21. *Robins Rest, Moat Street, Gestingthorpe, Halstead CO9 3AT* M: 07707-680562 E: revbarbara8@gmail.com

HUME, Miss Clephane Arrol. b 46. Open Univ BA 87 Edin Univ MTh 98 DipOT 68. Edin Dioc NSM Course 88. **d** 92 **p** 94. NSM Edin St Jo from 92. *26 Findhorn Place, Edinburgh EH9 2JP* T: 0131-667 2996 E: cah@clephane.plus.com

HUME, Ernest. b 45. Linc Th Coll 77. **d** 79 **p** 80. C Ilkeston St Mary *Derby* 79–81; C Sheff Manor 81–82; TV 82–88; V Norton Woodseats St Chad 88–99; V Woodhouse St Jas 99–02; rtd 02. *Shadwell, 6 Canal Bridge, Killamarsh, Sheffield S21 1DJ* T: 0114-248 1769

HUME, Martin. b 54. Coll of Resurr Mirfield 89. **d** 91 **p** 92. C Brentwood St Thos *Chelmsf* 91–94; P-in-c Corringham 94–04; V E Wickham *S'wark* 04–10; rtd 10; PtO *Chich* from 11. *55 Farm Road, Hove BN3 1FD* T: (01273) 206478 M: 07901-553522 E: martinhume@aol.com

HUME, Richard Fletcher. b 68. Qu Foundn (Course) 14. **d** 17 **p** 18. OLM Longton St Mary and St Chad *Lich* 17–18; C Walsall St Gabr Fulbrook from 19. *1A Orchard Road, Walsall WS5 4UT* M: 07887-761147

HUME, Robert Roy. b 47. **d** 09 **p** 10. OLM Ashmanhaugh, Barton Turf etc *Nor* 09–16; PtO from 16. *Owls Dene, Ferry Cott Lane, Horning, Norwich NR12 8PP* T: (01692) 630029 E: robhume1@btinternet.com

HUMM, Andrew James. b 72. St Jo Coll Nottm 10. **d** 12 **p** 13. C Loughborough Em and St Mary in Charnwood *Leic* 12–14; C Loughborough Em 15–16; P-in-c Tiverton St Geo and St Paul *Ex* from 16. *St Paul's Vicarage, Bakers Hill, Tiverton EX16 5NE* E: as_humm@yahoo.com

HUMPHREY, Alan. b 48. Open Univ BA 74. Qu Coll Birm 07. **d** 10 **p** 11. C Kirby Muxloe *Leic* 10–15; R Leicester Forest East 15–18; Warden Community of the Tree of Life 18–21; Chapl Launde Abbey *Leic* from 21; PtO from 18. *Launde Abbey, Launde Road, Launde, Leicester LE7 9XB* T: (01572) 717254 M: 07768-374200 E: alan.humphrey@icloud.com

HUMPHREY, David Lane. b 57. Maine Univ BA 79. St Jo Coll Nottm 84. **d** 88 **p** 89. C Springfield All SS *Chelmsf* 88–91; C Thundersley 91–96; V Standon St Alb 96–04; RD Bishop's Stortford 01–04; R Portland St Matt USA from 04. *11229 NE Prescott Street, Portland OR 97220-2457, USA* T: (001) (503) 252 5720 E: humphrey@iinet.com

HUMPHREY, Timothy Martin. b 62. Ex Univ BA 83. St Jo Coll Nottm 86. **d** 89 **p** 90. C Wallington *S'wark* 89–92; P-in-c 92–97; C Oakley w Wootton St Lawrence *Win* 97–02; Faith Development Field Officer 97–02; V Kensington St Barn *Lon* 02–15; V Tunbridge Wells Ch Ch *Roch* from 17. *The Vicarage, 63 Claremont Road, Tunbridge Wells TN1 1TE* T: (01892) 526644

HUMPHREYS, Mrs Anne-Marie (Anna). b 44. SRN 67 K Coll Lon BD 92 AKC 92 Man Univ MA 96. NOC 92. **d** 95 **p** 96. NSM Manchester Gd Shep and St Barn *Man* 95–98; NSM Burnage St Nic 98–03; Chapl Cen Man Healthcare NHS Trust 96–01; Chapl Cen Man/Man Children's Univ Hosp NHS Trust 01–06; rtd 06; PtO *Ban* 10–17; *St As* from 17. *Eryl Mor, 60 Deganwy Road, Deganwy, Conwy LL31 9DN* T: (01492) 573396

HUMPHREYS, Asa James. b 79. Kent Univ BA 00 St Chad's Coll Dur MA 01 Ches Univ MTh 19. St Jo Coll Nottm 13. **d** 15 **p** 16. C Talbot Village *Sarum* 15–18; P-in-c Heybridge w Langford *Chelmsf* from 18; P-in-c Maldon All SS w St Pet from 21. *The Vicarage, 32 Scraley Road, Heybridge, Maldon CM9 4BL* E: asa_humphreys@hotmail.com

HUMPHREYS, Brian Leonard. b 29. MChS 51 SRCh. Bp Attwell Tr Inst. **d** 87 **p** 88. NSM Maughold *S & M* 87–91; NSM S Ramsey St Paul 91–92; NSM Andreas 92–94; PtO 94–10. *1 Seafield, Ballure Road, Ramsey, Isle of Man IM8 1NL* T: (01624) 813694

HUMPHREYS, John Louis. b 51. Jes Coll Cam BA 72 MA 76 Nottm Univ BA 75. St Jo Coll Nottm 73. **d** 76 **p** 77. C W Bromwich Gd Shep w St Jo *Lich* 76–79; C Woodford Wells *Chelmsf* 79–83; V Werrington *Lich* 83–08; Chapl HM YOI Werrington 83–98; PtO *Lich* 09–18; *S'wark* from 21. *61 Josephine Avenue, Lower Kingswood, Tadworth KT20 7AB* T: (01737) 832922

HUMPHREYS, Lydia Ann. b 60. Sarum & Wells Th Coll 91. **d** 93 **p** 94. C Gaywood *Nor* 93–97; TV Cov E 97–10; P-in-c Kempston Transfiguration *St Alb* 10–14; V 14–17; V Shepshed and Oaks in Charnwood *Leic* from 17. *1 Charles Hall Close, Shepshed, Loughborough LE12 9UP* T: (01509) 506385 E: lydia.humphreys@sky.com

HUMPHREYS, Canon Roger John. b 45. CertEd 66 Open Univ BA 76. Wycliffe Hall Ox 81. **d** 83 **p** 84. Chapl Dragon Sch Ox 83–87; C Ox St Andr 83–87; V Carterton 87–94; R Bladon w Woodstock 94–05; TR Blenheim 05–09; AD Woodstock 01–06; Chapl Cokethorpe Sch Witney 09–13; Hon Can Ch Ch *Ox* 05–14; PtO 09–20; *Eur* 15–19. *12 The Pieces, Bampton, Oxford OX18 2JZ* T: (01993) 850199 M: 07788-717214 E: rev.roger@zen.co.uk

HUMPHREYS, Stephen Robert Beresford. b 52. K Coll Lon BA 98. 74. **d** 76 **p** 77. C Northwood Hills St Edm *Lon* 76–79; C Manningham St Mary and Bradf St Mich 79–81; Chapl Bradf R Infirmary 82–86; C Leeds St Pet *Ripon* 87–90; PtO *B & W* 94–99; C Selworthy, Timberscombe, Wootton Courtenay etc 02–07; C Porlock and Porlock Weir w Stoke Pero etc from 07. *Stowey Farm, Timberscombe, Minehead TA24 7BW* T: (01643) 841265 M: 07973-409536 E: srbh@mac.com

HUMPHRIES, Anthony Roy. b 49. Lon Univ BSc 73. Wycliffe Hall Ox. d 94 p 95. C Worksop St Jo *S'well* 94–96; C Retford St Sav 96–98; TV Grantham *Linc* 98–00; TV Bestwood *S'well* 00–03; V Branston w Tatenhill *Lich* 03–07; P-in-c Gisburn *Bradf* 12–14; P-in-c Gisburn *Blackb* 14–16; PtO *Dur* from 20. *Fell Cottage, 9 High Town, Westgate, Bishop Auckland DL13 1JR* T: (01388) 517283 M: 07809-177343 E: revtonyhumphries@hotmail.com

HUMPHRIES, Benjamin Paul. b 56. Man Univ BA 77 FRGS 85. Qu Coll Birm 82. d 85 p 86. C Hall Green Ascension *Birm* 85–88; P-in-c Belmont *Man* 88–96; Fieldworker USPG Blackb, Bradf, Carl and Wakef 96–98; Area Co-ord Chr Aid (Cumbria, Lancs and Isle of Man) 98–07; C Shepherd's Bush St Steph w St Thos *Lon* 07–12; Chapl Mombasa Miss to Seafarers Kenya 12–15; Chapl Dunkirk Miss to Seafarers *Eur* 15–17; C Shepherd's Bush St Steph w St Thos *Lon* 17–19; V White City from 19. *Church of St Michael and St George, 1 Commonwealth Avenue, London W12 7QR* M: 07712-460680 E: ben.humphries@london.anglican.org

HUMPHRIES, Catherine Elizabeth. *See* NICHOLLS, Catherine Elizabeth

HUMPHRIES, Canon Christopher William. b 52. St Jo Coll Cam BA 73 MA 77 Lon Inst of Educn CertEd 74. St Jo Coll Nottm 77. d 79 p 80. C Eccleshill *Bradf* 79–82; Chapl Scargill Ho 82–86; TV Guiseley w Esholt *Bradf* 86–91; V Filey *York* 91–05; RD Scarborough 98–04; Can Res Ches Cathl 05–14; V Whitegate w Lt Budworth 14–18; Hon Can Ches Cathl 14–18; rtd 18; PtO *York* from 19. *The Meadows, Bempton Lane, Flamborough, Bridlington YO15 1PS* T: (01262) 422150

HUMPHRIES, David. *See* HUMPHRIES, William David

HUMPHRIES, David Graham. b 48. St Mich Coll Llan 67. d 71 p 72. C Neath w Llantwit *Llan* 71–72; C Bishop's Cleeve *Glouc* 81–83; C Cirencester 83–87; V Glouc St Steph 87–96; P-in-c Mickleton 96–03; Assoc P Up Hatherley 03–06; rtd 06; Chapl Glouc Charities Trust 06–20. *19 Gurney Avenue, Tuffley, Gloucester GL4 0YJ* T: (01452) 529582 E: fr.didds@virginmedia.com

HUMPHRIES, David John. b 51. BSc CertEd BD. Edin Th Coll. d 84 p 85. C Styvechale *Cov* 84–88; V Greetland and W Vale *Wakef* 88–96; V Shawbury *Lich* 96–15; R Moreton Corbet 96–15; V Stanton on Hine Heath 96–15; rtd 15; PtO *Lich* from 16. *The New Vicarage, Church Street, Shawbury, Shrewsbury SY4 4NH* T: (01939) 250419

HUMPHRIES, Mrs Janet Susan. b 46. SAOMC 02. d 04 p 05. NSM Potton w Sutton and Cockayne Hatley St Alb 04–07; NSM Caldecote, Northill and Old Warden 07–16; PtO 16–21; *Ely* from 20. *173 Herne Road, Ramsey St Marys, Ramsey, Huntingdon PE26 2SY* T: (01733) 219961 E: janet.humphries73@gmail.com

HUMPHRIES, Mrs Julie Ann. b 64. Birm Univ BA 02 MA 08. Qu Coll Birm 06. d 08 p 09. C Redditch H Trin *Worc* 08–12; TV Salter Street and Shirley *Birm* 12–17; V Salter Street 17–19; PtO *Worc* from 20. *Minfford, Waresley Road, Hartlebury, Kidderminster DY11 7XT* E: juliehumphries27@yahoo.co.uk

HUMPHRIES, Richard James Robert. b 44. Anglia Ruskin Univ MA 12 FRAM 95. EAMTC 99. d 01 p 02. NSM Heybridge w Langford *Chelmsf* 01–02; NSM Maldon All SS w St Pet 02–09; Asst Chapl Mid-Essex Hosp Services NHS Trust 01–04; Chapl Colchester Hosp Univ NHS Foundn Trust 04–09; rtd 09; PtO *Chelmsf* from 09. *20 Rosewood Park, Mistley, Manningtree CO11 1UH* T: (01206) 393240 M: 07803-281036 E: richard.humphries1@btopenworld.com

HUMPHRIES, Robert William. b 36. Open Univ BA 87. SWMTC 96. d 99 p 00. OLM Kenwyn w St Allen Truro from 99. *27 Penhalls Way, Playing Place, Truro TR3 6EX* T: (01872) 862827 E: rev.bobh@btinternet.com

HUMPHRIES, Sara Ann. b 59. Qu Foundn (Course) 15. d 18 p 19. OLM Ashley and Mucklestone and Broughton and Croxton *Lich* from 18. *12 Martin Dale, Loggerheads, Market Drayton TF9 4DH* T: (01630) 673740 M: 07989-731978 E: sarahumphries2@gmail.com

HUMPHRIES, Sidney Mark. b 53. d 13 p 14. NSM Littleham-cum-Exmouth w Lympstone *Ex* 13–17; C 17–18; V Aylesbeare, Clyst St George, Clyst St Mary etc 18–19. *36 Trafalgar Road, Lympstone, Exeter EX8 5HX* M: 07922-117556 E: revsidh@gmail.com

HUMPHRIES, Mrs Susan Joy. b 45. Open Univ BSc 98. Cranmer Hall Dur 05. d 06 p 07. NSM Beverley Minster *York* 06–09; NSM N Cave w Cliffe and Hotham 09–12; P-in-c 12; PtO *Worc* from 12. *119 Old Station Road, Bromsgrove B60 2AS* T: (01527) 577808 M: 07930-803601 E: rev.s.humphries@btinternet.com

HUMPHRIES, Canon William David. b 57. QUB BEd LTCL. CITC. d 86 p 87. C Ballyholme *D & D* 86–90; Min Can Belf Cathl 89–12; V Choral Belf Cathl 90–93; Can Belf Cathl from 12; C Belfast St Anne *Conn* 90–93; I Stormont *D & D*

93–16; I Kilbride *Conn* from 16. *Kilbride Rectory, 7 Rectory Road, Doagh, Ballyclare BT39 0PT* T: (028) 9334 0225 E: wdhumphries@hotmail.com

HUMPHRIS, Richard. b 44. Sarum & Wells Th Coll 69. d 72 p 73. C Cheltenham St Luke and St Jo *Glouc* 72–77; C Lydney w Aylburton 77–82; Chapl RAF 82–85; TV Kippax w Allerton Bywater *Ripon* 85–92; RSPCA 92–95; rtd 95; PtO *York* 98–14. *4 Belle Vue Terrace, Bellerby, Leyburn DL8 5QL* T: (01969) 622004

HUMPHRISS, Canon Reginald George. b 36. Kelham Th Coll 56. d 61 p 62. C Londonderry *Birm* 61–63; Asst Dir RE *Cant* 63–66; Dioc Youth Chapl 63–66; V Preston next Faversham 66–72; P-in-c Goodnestone St Bart and Graveney 71–72; V Spring Park 72–76; R Cant St Martin and St Paul 76–90; R Saltwood 90–01; RD Cant 82–88; Hon Can Cant Cathl 85–01; RD Elham 93–00; rtd 01; PtO *Cant* from 01. *11 Mulberry Court, Stour Street, Canterbury CT1 2NT* T: (01227) 765264 E: reg@humphriss1.plus.com

HUMPHRY, Frances Marian. b 64. Ches Univ MA 20. All SS Cen for Miss & Min 18. d 20 p 21. NSM Wigan *Liv* 20–21; C from 21. *6 Netherwood Grove, Wigan WN3 6NF* M: 07592-024058 E: curate.west@churchwigan.org

HUMPHRYS, Kevin Luke. b 73. Surrey Univ BA 97. St Steph Ho Ox. d 99 p 00. C Moulsecoomb *Chich* 99–03; NSM Colgate and Roffey 16–19; NSM Brighton St Mich and St Paul from 19. *2 Adur Court, 463 Brighton Road, Lancing BN15 8LF* T: (01903) 609260 E: kevin_humphrys@hotmail.com

HUNDLEBY, Alan. b 41. d 86 p 87. OLM Fotherby *Linc* 86–02; NSM Barnoldby le Beck 02–14; NSM Waltham Gp from 14. *35 Cheapside, Waltham, Grimsby DN37 0HE* T: (01472) 827159

HUNG, Frank Yu-Chi. b 45. Birm Univ BSc 68 BA 75 Liv Univ MSc 71. Wycliffe Hall Ox 76. d 78 p 79. C Walton H Trin *Ox* 78–82; C Spring Grove St Mary *Lon* 82–85; TV Wexcombe *Sarum* 85–92; V Hatcham St Jas *S'wark* 92–98; Chapl Goldsmiths' Coll Lon 95–98; Chapl Lon S Bank Univ 98–10; rtd 10; Hon C S'wark St Geo w St Alphege and St Jude from 10. *151 Graham Road, London SW19 3SL* T: (020) 8542 1612

HUNGERFORD, Robin Nicholas. b 47. Redland Coll of Educn CertEd 74. Trin Coll Bris 86. d 88 p 89. C Swindon Dorcan *Bris* 88–92; TV Melbury *Sarum* 92–01; P-in-c Winterbourne Stickland and Turnworth etc 01–05; V Winterborne Valley and Milton Abbas 05–12; rtd 12; PtO *Sarum* from 12; B & W from 19. *Church House, 53A High Street, Heytesbury, Warminster BA12 0EA* T: (01985) 840522

HUNNISETT, John Bernard. b 47. AKC 73. d 73 p 74. C Charlton Kings St Mary *Glouc* 73–77; C Portsea St Mary *Portsm* 77–80; V Badgeworth w Shurdington *Glouc* 80–87; R Dursley 87–99; TR Ross *Heref* 99–07; RD Ross and Archenfield 02–07; Chapl Huggens Coll Northfleet 07–12; rtd 12; PtO *Glouc* from 12. *1 Fernleigh Villas, Old Bristol Road, Nailsworth, Stroud GL6 0LQ* T: (01453) 833491 M: 07970-280274 E: john.hunnisett@me.com

HUNNYBUN, Martin Wilfrid. b 44. Oak Hill Th Coll 67. d 70 p 71. C Ware Ch St Alb 70–74; C Washfield, Stoodleigh, Withleigh etc *Ex* 74–75; TV 75–80; R Braunston *Pet* 80–85; Asst Chapl HM Pris Onley 80–85; R Berry and Kangaroo Valley Sydney Australia 85–94; Sen Chapl Angl Retirement Village 94–98; TV Parkham, Alwington, Buckland Brewer etc *Ex* 98–00; Dioc Ecum Adv 98–00; R Glebe Australia 00–03; rtd 03. *204 Beacon Road, North Tambrine QLD 4272, Australia* T: (0061) (7) 5545 4310 E: m.hunnybun@bigpond.com

HUNT, Andrew Collins. b 54. Reading Univ BA 77 Hull Univ PGCE 79. St Alb Minl Tr Scheme 82 Sarum & Wells Th Coll 89 WEMTC 99. d 00 p 01. NSM Cainscross w Selsley *Glouc* 00–02; NSM Wells St Thos w Horrington *B & W* 07–10; PtO 10–12 and from 16; NSM Polden Wheel 12–16. *58A Cowl Street, Shepton Mallet BA4 5EP* E: andrewhunt151@gmail.com

HUNT, Ashley Stephen. b 50. St Jo Coll Nottm 81. d 83 p 84. C Southchurch H Trin *Chelmsf* 83–86; TV Droitwich *Worc* 86–87; USA 88–91; TV Melton Gt Framland *Leic* 92–93; TV Melton Mowbray 93–98; TV Grantham *Linc* 98–00; Chapl Mental Health 98–01; C Stamford All SS w St Jo *Linc* 00–01; TV Mynyddislwyn *Mon* 02–15; rtd 15. *2 Laurel Drive, The Bryn, Pontllanfraith, Blackwood NP12 2PR*

HUNT, Mrs Beverley Cecilia. b 49. d 08 p 09. NSM E Molesey *Guildf* 08–11; TV Godalming 11–15; PtO 15; P-in-c E Molesey 15–17; C Woking St Pet 17–18; rtd 19; PtO *Guildf* 19–20; V Pirbright 20–21. *1 St John's Rise, Woking GU21 7PN* M: 07495-395225 E: revbev.stmaa@gmail.com

HUNT, Mrs Christina. b 24. Qu Mary Coll Lon BSc 45. S Dios Minl Tr Scheme 78. dss 81 d 87 p 94. Alderbury and W Grimstead *Sarum* 81–87; Hon Par Dn 87–91; Hon Par Dn Alderbury Team 91–94; rtd 94; PtO *Sarum* 94–08 and from 11. *37 Elizabeth Court, Crane Bridge Road, Salisbury SP2 7UX* T: (01722) 336002 E: chrishunt37@btinternet.com

HUNT, Christopher Paul Colin. b 38. Ch Coll Cam BA 62 MA 62. Clifton Th Coll 63. **d** 65 **p** 66. C Widnes St Paul *Liv* 65–68; Singapore 68–70; Malaysia 70–71; Hon C Folkestone St Jo *Cant* 72–73; Iran 74–80; Overseas Service Adv CMS 81–91; P-in-c Claverdon w Preston Bagot *Cov* 91–02; rtd 02; PtO *Worc* from 04. *Birchfield House, 18 Oaklands, Malvern WR14 4JE* T: (01684) 578803 E: pauldianamalvern@gmail.com

HUNT, Christopher Stephen. b 83. Middx Univ BA 16. St Mellitus Coll 19. **d** 21. C Bicester w Bucknell, Caversfield and Launton *Ox* from 21. *2 Tayberry Close, Bicester OX27 8AU* M: 07889-555748 E: chrishunt1@outlook.com

HUNT, Craig Adam. b 86. St Jo Coll Dur BSc 07. St Mellitus Coll BA 12. **d** 12 **p** 13. C Cant St Mary Bredin 12–19; Dioc Dir of Ords *S'well* from 19. *Diocese of Southwell and Nottingham, Jubilee House, 8 Westgate, Southwell NG25 0JH* T: (01636) 814331 M: 07837-830231 E: craig.hunt@dunelm.org.uk

HUNT, David John. b 35. Kelham Th Coll 60. **d** 65 **p** 66. C Bethnal Green St Jo w St Simon *Lon* 65–69; C Mill Hill St Mich 69–73; R Staple Fitzpaine, Orchard Portman, Thurlbear etc *B & W* 73–79; P-in-c E Coker w Sutton Bingham 79–88; V E Coker w Sutton Bingham and Closworth 88–00; RD Merston 85–94; rtd 00; PtO *B & W* 01–11. *Meadowside, Head Street, Tintinhull, Yeovil BA22 8QH* T: (01935) 824554

HUNT, Ernest Gary. b 36. Univ Coll Dur BA 57. Carl Dioc Tr Inst 90. **d** 93 **p** 94. NSM Salesbury *Blackb* 93–95; NSM Blackb St Mich w St Jo and H Trin 95–98; NSM Balderstone 98–01; rtd 01; PtO *Blackb* from 01. *Dunelm, 10 Pleckgate Road, Blackburn BB1 8NN* T: (01254) 52531 E: eg.andk.hunt@talktalk.net

HUNT, Miss Gabrielle Ann. b 59. STETS BA 10. **d** 08 **p** 09. C Salisbury St Fran and Stratford sub Castle *Sarum* 08–12; C Bourne Valley 09–12; TV Avon River from 12. *The Vicarage, High Street, Netheravon, Salisbury SP4 9QP* T: (01980) 670326 E: galehunt@btinternet.com

HUNT, Giles Butler. b 28. Trin Hall Cam BA 51 MA 55. Cuddesdon Coll 51. **d** 53 **p** 54. C N Evington *Leic* 53–56; C Northolt St Mary *Lon* 56–58; Bp's Dom Chapl *Portsm* 58–59; Bp's Chapl *Nor* 59–62; R Holt 62–67; R Kelling w Salthouse 63–67; C Pimlico St Pet w Westmr Ch Ch *Lon* 67–72; V Barkway w Reed and Buckland *St Alb* 72–79; V Preston next Faversham, Goodnestone and Graveney *Cant* 79–92; rtd 92; PtO *Nor* from 93. *The Cottage, The Fairstead, Cley-next-the-Sea, Holt NR25 7RJ* T: (01263) 740471 E: gileshunt@btinternet.com

HUNT, James Castle. b 66. Univ of Ulster BSc 90 MRICS 92. Wycliffe Hall Ox 02. **d** 04 **p** 05. C N Farnborough *Guildf* 04–08; R Bishop's Waltham *Portsm* from 08; R Upham from 08. *The Rectory, Maypole Green, Bishops Waltham, Southampton SO32 1PW* T: (01489) 892618 E: jameshunt1966@gmail.com

HUNT, John Barry. b 46. Lich Th Coll 70 Qu Coll Birm 72. **d** 73 **p** 74. C Auckland St Andr and St Anne *Dur* 73–77; C Consett 77–79; R Lyons 79–89; P-in-c Hebburn St Cuth 89–05; P-in-c Hebburn St Oswald 01–05; V Hebburn St Cuth and St Oswald 05–11; rtd 11; PtO *Dur* from 11. *11 Parklands, Gateshead NE10 8YP* T: 0191-438 3022 E: tyneheaven2@outlook.com

HUNT, John Edwin. b 38. ARCO Dur Univ BA 60 DipEd. EMMTC 78. **d** 81 **p** 82. NSM Newbold w Dunston *Derby* 81–92; NSM Chesterfield St Mary and All SS 92–02. *4 Ardsley Road, Ashgate, Chesterfield S40 4DG* T: (01246) 275141

HUNT, Canon Judith Mary. b 57. Bris Univ BVSc 80 Lon Univ PhD 85 Fitzw Coll Cam BA 90 MRCVS 80. Ridley Hall Cam 88. **d** 91 **p** 94. Par Dn Heswall *Ches* 91–94; C 94–95; P-in-c Tilston and Shocklach 95–03; Bp's Adv for Women in Min 95–00; Can Res Ches Cathl and Dioc Dir of Min 03–09; Adn Suffolk *St E* 09–12; R Whitchurch *Lich* 12–20; P-in-c Edstaston, Fauls, Prees, Tilstock and Whixall 13–18; C 18–20; R Fauls, Tilstock and Whitchurch from 20. *The Rectory, Church Street, Whitchurch SY13 1LB* T: (01948) 667253 E: revjudyhunt@gmail.com

HUNT, The Ven Kevin. b 59. St Jo Coll Dur BA 80 Ox Univ BA 84 MA 88. St Steph Ho Ox 81. **d** 84 **p** 85. C Mansfield St Mark *S'well* 84–85; C Hendon and Sunderland *Dur* 85–88; V Sunderland St Mary and St Pet 88–95; TR Jarrow 95–02; V Walker *Newc* 02–12; AD Newc E 04–12; Hon Can Newc Cathl 10–12; Can Res Newc Cathl 12–15; Asst Dioc Dir of Ords 03–15; PtO 15–19 and from 22; P-in-c Vancouver St Jas Canada 15–17; R from 17; Adn Burrard from 18. *602-1025 Gilford Street, Vancouver BC V6G 2P2, Canada* E: fr.kevin@stjames.bc.ca *or* kevinht10@icloud.com

HUNT, Michael David. b 64. Southn Univ BSc 86. Ox Min Course 09. **d** 12 **p** 13. NSM Wendover and Halton *Ox* 12–16; NSM Risborough from 16. *Autumn Winds, Aylesbury Road,*

Princes Risborough HP27 0JP　T: (01844) 344150　M: 07712-851381 E: midahunt@yahoo.co.uk

HUNT, Paul. *See* HUNT, Christopher Paul Colin

HUNT, Paul Edwin. b 47. Ripon Coll Cuddesdon 93. **d** 95 **p** 96. C Cleobury Mortimer w Hopton Wafers etc *Heref* 95–98; P-in-c Fritwell w Souldern and Ardley w Fewcott *Ox* 98–05; TR Cherwell Valley 05–12; AD Bicester and Islip 05–08; rtd 12; PtO *Pet* from 13. *32 Dalestones, Northampton NN4 9UU* T: (01604) 460539 E: paul.jehu@mac.com *or* paul.e.hunt@me.com

HUNT, Paul Michael. b 57. St Chad's Coll Dur BA 79 K Coll Lon PGCE 80 MA 96 Univ of Wales (Lamp) MTh 04. Chich Th Coll 91. **d** 92 **p** 93. Chapl Brighton Coll 92–93; NSM St Leonards SS Pet and Paul *Chich* 92–93; Chapl Mill Hill Sch Lon 93–98; Hon C Hendon St Paul Mill Hill *Lon* 95–98; P in O 96–98; V Southgate St Andr *Lon* 98–05; Warden of Readers Edmonton Area 01–05; Chapl Emanuel Sch Wandsworth 05–17; rtd 17; PtO *Chich* 18–20; P-in-c Hastings St Clem and All SS from 20. *Flat 3, 87 Pevensey Road, St Leonards-on-Sea TN38 0LR* T: (01424) 441197 E: paul.m.hunt@btinternet.com

HUNT, Canon Peter John. b 35. AKC 58. St Boniface Warminster. **d** 59 **p** 60. C Chesterfield St Mary and All SS *Derby* 59–61; C Matlock and Tansley 61–63; Chapl Matlock Hosp 61–63; Lect Matlock Teacher Tr Coll 61–63; V Tottington *Man* 63–69; CF (TA) 65–67; CF (VR) from 75; V Bollington St Jo *Ches* 69–76; R Wilmslow 76–98; Hon Can Ches Cathl 94–02; P-in-c Brereton w Swettenham 98–02; rtd 02; PtO *Ches* from 02. *1 Varden Town Cottages, Birtles Lane, Over Alderley, Macclesfield SK10 4RZ* T: (01625) 829593 E: canonhari@gmail.com

HUNT, Canon Richard William. b 46. G&C Coll Cam BA 67 MA 71. Westcott Ho Cam 68. **d** 72 **p** 73. C Bris St Agnes and St Simon w St Werburgh 72–77; Chapl Selw Coll Cam 77–84; V Birchfield *Birm* 84–01; R Chich St Paul and Westhampnett 01–11; RD Chich 06–11; Can and Preb Chich Cathl 10–11; rtd 11; PtO *Sarum* from 12; *B & W* from 15. *76 Warminster Road, Bath BA2 6RU* T: (01225) 938529　M: 07504-089009 E: richardhunt040246@gmail.com

HUNT, Ms Rosalind Edna Mary. b 55. Man Univ BA 76. St Steph Ho Ox 86. **d** 88 **p** 94. Chapl Jes Coll Cam 88–92; Hon Chapl to the Deaf *Ely* 92–04; C Cambridge St Jas 00; PtO *Man* from 05; *Ely* from 15. *4 Silverwood Close, Cambridge CB1 3HA* M: 07775-508900 E: ros.hunt@virgin.net

HUNT, Canon Russell Barrett. b 35. NY Univ Virginia Univ Fitzw Ho Cam. Westcott Ho Cam 73. **d** 75 **p** 76. C Leic St Mary 75–78; V Leic St Gabr 78–82; Chapl Leic Gen Hosp 82–95; Hon Can Leic Cathl 88–95; rtd 95; PtO *Leic* 15–20. *33 Braunstone Avenue, Leicester LE3 0JH* T: 0116-254 9101 E: c.p.k@btinternet.com

HUNT, Simon John. b 60. Pemb Coll Ox BA 81 MA 85. St Jo Coll Nottm 87. **d** 90 **p** 91. C Stalybridge St Paul *Ches* 90–93; C Heysham *Blackb* 93–99; V Higher Walton 99–18; rtd 18; PtO *York* from 19. *The Ancient Shepherd, Wrights Lane, Cridling Stubbs, Knottingley WF11 0AS* T: (01977) 674479 E: simon.hunt15@btinternet.com

HUNT, Stephen. b 38. Man Univ BSc 61 MSc 62 PhD 64 DSc 80. Carl Dioc Tr Inst 88. **d** 91 **p** 92. C Broughton *Blackb* 91–95; Chapl Preston Acute Hosps NHS Trust 94–95; V Preston Em *Blackb* 95–03; rtd 03; PtO *Blackb* from 05. *8 Wallace Lane, Forton, Preston PR3 0BA* T: (01524) 792563

HUNT, Timothy Collinson. b 65. Univ of Wales (Cardiff) BD 95 Ox Univ MTh 98. Ripon Coll Cuddesdon 95. **d** 97 **p** 98. C Ex St Dav 97–01; Chapl Blundell's Sch Tiverton from 01. *1B Hillands, 39 Tidcombe Lane, Tiverton EX16 4EA* T: (01884) 242343 E: tch@blundells.org *or* timothy.collinson.hunt@gmail.com

HUNT, Vera Susan Henrietta. b 33. MBE 06. S Dios Minl Tr Scheme 88. **d** 91 **p** 94. Hon Chapl RAD from 91; PtO *Lon* from 03; *Ox* from 08. *54 Highway Avenue, Maidenhead SL6 5AQ* T: (01628) 623909

HUNTE, Roxanne Fay. *See* EVERSLEY, Roxanne Fay

HUNTER, Edwin Wallace. b 43. NUI BA 83 FCIM. CITC 91. **d** 94 **p** 95. NSM Cork St Fin Barre's Union *C, C & R* 94–18; Min Can Cork Cathl 95–18; Bp's Dom Chapl 03–18; rtd 18. *Cedar Lodge, Church Road, Carrigaline, Co Cork, Republic of Ireland* T: (00353) (21) 437 2338

HUNTER, Graham. b 78. K Coll Lon BA 02 Anglia Ruskin Univ MA 10. Ridley Hall Cam 05. **d** 07 **p** 08. C Holloway St Mary Magd *Lon* 07–10; C Hoxton St Jo w Ch Ch 10–11; V from 11. *St John's Vicarage, Crondall Street, London N1 6PT* T: (020) 7739 9823 E: graham@stjohnshoxton.org.uk

HUNTER, Ian Roy. *See* WILLIAMS-HUNTER, Ian Roy

HUNTER, James. b 38. Union Th Coll Belf BD 90. **d** 92 **p** 92. In Presbyterian Ch of Ireland 82–92; V Werneth *Man* 92–98; V Woking St Paul *Guildf* 98–05; Asst Chapl HM

Pris Coldingley 01–05; rtd 06; PtO *Pet* from 06. *31 The Ridings, Desborough, Kettering NN14 2LP* T: (01536) 660328 E: jimo.hunter2@gmail.com

HUNTER, John Crichton. b 38. Univ of Wales (Cardiff) BA 59 DipEd 60 LTCL. St Steph Ho Ox 98. **d** 99 **p** 00. NSM Walham Green St Jo w St Jas *Lon* 99–05; NSM S Kensington St Steph 05–08; PtO from 08. *57 Manor Court, 23 Bagleys Lane, London SW6 2BN* T: (020) 7736 7544 E: frjohnhunter@hotmail.com

HUNTER, Matthew Gawain. b 83. LMH Ox BA 04 Man Univ MA 08 Northumbria Univ MA 11. Ripon Coll Cuddesdon 10. **d** 12 **p** 13. C Halifax *Wakef* 12–15; C Hexham *Newc* 15–18; P-in-c Whorlton from 18. *St John's Vicarage, Whorlton, Newcastle upon Tyne NE5 1NN* E: mwg_hunter@yahoo.co.uk

HUNTER, Michael John. b 45. CCC Cam BA 67 MA 71 PhD 71 Ox Univ BA 75. Wycliffe Hall Ox 73. **d** 76 **p** 77. C Partington and Carrington *Ches* 76–79; CMS 80–90; Uganda 80–89; C Penn Fields *Lich* 90–02; RD Trysull 97–02; V Dore *Sheff* 02–12; rtd 12; PtO *Sheff* 12–14; *Carl* from 12. *18 Linnet Grove, Kendal LA9 7RP* T: (01539) 725093 E: mutagwok@aol.com

HUNTER, Canon Michael Oram. b 40. MBE 10. K Coll Lon BD 64 AKC 64. **d** 65 **p** 66. C Tividale *Lich* 65–68; C Harrogate St Wilfrid *Ripon* 68–70; V Hawksworth Wood 70–78; V Whitkirk 78–86; TR Gt Grimsby St Mary and St Jas *Linc* 86–10; Can and Preb Linc Cathl 89–10; rtd 10; PtO *Leeds* from 17. *12 Osborne Road, Harrogate HG1 2EA* T: (01423) 313825 E: mo.hunter@talktalk.net

HUNTER, Paul Andrew. b 55. Trin Coll Bris 09. **d** 11 **p** 12. OLM Brislington St Chris *Bris* 11–18; NSM Whitchurch St Aug 18–21; NSM Withywood from 21. *17 Friendship Road, Bristol BS4 2RW* T: 0117-971 9390 E: paulzhunter@blueyonder.co.uk

HUNTER, Paul Graham. b 64. Sheff Univ LLB 85 Solicitor 86. St Jo Coll Nottm MA 96. **d** 04 **p** 05. Prin Morogoro Bible Coll Tanzania 04–06; PtO *Blackb* 08–19; C Copp w Inskip 19–20; V from 20. *St Peter's Vicarage, Preston Road, Inskip, Preston PR4 0TT* M: 07731-924289 E: pp.hunter@sky.com

HUNTER, Peter Wells. b 52. Bris Univ BSc 73. Trin Coll Bris BA 91. **d** 91 **p** 92. C New Borough and Leigh *Sarum* 91–97; P-in-c Warminster Ch Ch 97–18; rtd 18; PtO *Sarum* from 19; *Glouc* from 20. *15 Tilting Road, Thornbury, Bristol BS35 1EP* E: peter.wh@btopenworld.com

HUNTER, Stephanie Louise. b 89. Aber Univ MA 13. Ripon Coll Cuddesdon 15. **d** 17 **p** 18. C Cumberworth, Denby, Denby Dale etc *Leeds* 17–21; P-in-c from 21; C Kirkburton and Shelley 17–21; P-in-c from 21. *The Rectory, 43 Hollybank Avenue, Upper Cumberworth, Huddersfield HD8 8NY*

HUNTER, Stephen Albert Paul. b 52. JP 96. NOC 01. **d** 04 **p** 05. NSM Ecclesall *Sheff* 04–13; Bp's Adv for SSM 10–14; Dioc Dir of Ords from 13. *Overhill, Townhead Road, Dore, Sheffield S17 3GE* T: 0114-236 9978 F: 275 9769 M: 07739-949473 E: stephenaphunter@btinternet.com

HUNTER DUNN, Jonathan. b 69. Sussex Univ BSc 91 Uppsala Univ PhD 98. Oak Hill Th Coll BA 09. **d** 10 **p** 11. C Burford w Fulbrook, Taynton, Asthall etc *Ox* 10–15; R Shepton Mallet w Doulting *B & W* from 15. *11 Naisholt Road, Shepton Mallet BA4 5GD* T: (01749) 342420 E: jonathanhunterdunn@gmail.com

HUNTER JONES, Karen Elizabeth. *See* JONES, Karen Elizabeth

HUNTER SMART, Ian Douglas. b 60. St Jo Coll Dur BA 83 MA 99. Edin Th Coll 83. **d** 85 **p** 86. C Cockerton *Dur* 85–89; TV Jarrow 89–92; TV Sunderland 92–98; Chapl Sunderland Univ 92–98; Ecum Chapl Newcastle Coll 98–00; PtO *Dur* from 98; *Ripon* 12–14; *Leeds* from 14. *Gardeners Cottage, Carlton, Richmond DL11 7AG* T: (01325) 710481 E: ihs@dunelm.org.uk

HUNTER SMART, William David. b 75. Bris Univ BSc 97. Wycliffe Hall Ox BA 01. **d** 02 **p** 03. C Watford *St Alb* 02–05; C Muswell Hill St Jas w St Matt *Lon* 05–11; TR Newbury *Ox* 11–15; R Newbury St Nic and Speen from 15. *The Rectory, 64 Northcroft Lane, Newbury RG14 1BN* T: (01635) 47018 E: rector@st-nicolas-newbury.org

HUNTINGDON AND WISBECH, Archdeacon of. *See* MACCURDY, The Ven Hugh Kyle

HUNTINGDON, Suffragan Bishop of. *See* WINTER, The Rt Revd Dagmar

HUNTLEY, David Anthony. b 32. AMInstT 56 MRTvS 78 MILT 98. Lon Bible Coll BA 60 Fuller Sch of World Miss MTh 81 Trin Coll Singapore 65. **d** 64 **p** 65. OMF Internat from 61; Singapore 61–71; Indonesia 72–73; Philippines 74–75; Hong Kong 77–81; Seychelles 82–87; Thailand 88–97; NSM S Croydon Em *Cant* 76–77 and 81–82; NSM S Croydon Em *S'wark* 87–88 and 91–92 and 98–04; PtO from 05. *42 Farnborough Avenue, South Croydon CR2 8HD* T: (020) 8657 5673

HUNTLEY, Denis Anthony. b 56. Saltley Tr Coll Birm CertEd 77. Qu Coll Birm 77. **d** 80 **p** 81. C Llanblethian w

Cowbridge and Llandough etc *Llan* 80–83; TV Glyncorrwg w Afan Vale and Cymmer Afan 83–86; R 86–89; Chapl Asst Walsgrave Hosp Cov 89–92; Chapl Halifax Gen Hosp 92–94; Chapl Calderdale Healthcare NHS Trust 94–97; C Leeds City *Ripon* 97–02; Chapl to the Deaf 97–02; Chapl amongst Deaf People and Adv for Deaf Min 02–06; Chapl amongst Deaf and Deaf-blind People *Chelmsf* 06–14; Lead Min Deaf Community 15–19; Adv on Disability Issues *Chelmsf* 06–19; rtd 19. *21 Bedford Gardens, Leeds LS16 6DH* T: 0113-267 8063 E: denis.huntley@icloud.com

HUNTLEY, Heidi Anne. b 71. Ripon Coll Cuddesdon 07. **d** 09 **p** 10. C Sydenham St Bart *S'wark* 09–12; V Royston St Alb from 12. *The Vicarage, 20 Palace Gardens, Royston SG8 5AD* T: (01763) 243145 E: hahlive@gmail.com

HUNTLEY, Stuart Michael. b 73. BEng BA. Trin Coll Bris. **d** 08 **p** 09. C Jersey St Lawr *Win* 08–09; C Jersey St Helier 09–11; R Port Washington St Steph USA 11–15; R Wulfric Benefice *B & W* 15–20. *Address temp unknown* M: 07479-532355 E: revstuarthuntley@gmail.com

HUNTON, Thomas Mark. b 80. Trin Coll Bris 16. **d** 18 **p** 19. C Chippenham St Paul w Hardenhuish etc *Bris* from 18. *33 Fallow Field Close, Chippenham SN14 6YA* M: 07570-477540 or 07464-505800 E: tomhunton@hotmail.co.uk

HUPFIELD, Mrs Hannah Elizabeth. b 84. New Hall Cam BA 06 MA 10 Anglia Ruskin Univ BA 14 Selw Coll Cam MPhil 17. Westcott Ho Cam 08. **d** 11 **p** 12. C Woodbridge St Mary *St E* 11; C Saxilby Gp *Linc* 12–15; C Stow Gp 12–15; PtO *Ely* 15–20; Asst Chapl Selw Coll Cam 16–18; PtO *Worc* 19–21; V High Lane *Ches* from 21. *The Vicarage, 2 Vicarage Close, High Lane, Stockport SK6 8DL* T: (01663) 766448 E: hannahhupfield@cantab.net

HUPFIELD, Timothy. b 83. K Coll Cam MSci 06 BA 06 MA 09 PGCE 09 Jes Coll Cam BTh 17. Westcott Ho Cam 15. **d** 18 **p** 19. C E Vale and Avon Villages *Worc* 18–21; V Low Marple *Ches* from 21; Dioc Healing Adv from 21. *The Vicarage, 2 Vicarage Close, High Lane, Stockport SK6 8DL* M: 07812-982196 E: timothyhupfield@cantab.net

HURCOMBE, Thomas William. b 45. BD 74 AKC 76. **d** 76 **p** 77. C Hampstead All So *Lon* 76–79; C Is of Dogs Ch Ch and St Jo w St Luke 79–83; C Bromley All Hallows 83–89; C E Greenwich Ch Ch w St Andr and St Mich *S'wark* 89–96; from 16. *39A Warminster Road, London SE25 4DL* M: 07939-289196 E: hurcomt@aol.com

Waterfront Chapl 96–98; C Charlton St Luke w H Trin 97–98; P-in-c S Norwood St Mark 98–14; rtd 14; PtO *S'wark*

HURD, Alun John. b 52. Trin Coll Bris BA 86 New Coll Edin MTh 97. **d** 86 **p** 87. C Chertsey *Guildf* 86–90; Chapl St Pet Hosp Chertsey 86–90; V W Ewell *Guildf* 90–04; Chapl NE Surrey Coll Ewell 01–05; CF (TA) 99–05; Distr P Lower Yorke Peninsula Australia 05–07; P-in-c Gt Wakering w Foulness *Chelmsf* 08–17; P-in-c Barling w Lt Wakering 08–17; P-in-c Rochford and Sutton w Shopland 14–17; P-in-c High Westmorland *Carl* 17–21; rtd 21; PtO *Carl* from 21. *3 Crown Inn Fields, Morland, Penrith CA10 3EB* M: 07941-417135 E: alunjhurd@gmail.com

HURD, Brenda Edith. b 44. Sittingbourne Coll DipEd 75. Cant Sch of Min 87. **d** 92 **p** 94. NSM Birling, Addington, Ryarsh and Trottiscliffe *Roch* 92–02; P-in-c Wrotham 02–12; R 12–14; RD Shoreham 06–15; Hon Can Roch Cathl 09–14; rtd 14; PtO *Roch* from 15. *South View, London Road, Ryarsh, West Malling ME19 5AW* T: (01732) 842255 E: b.hurd@virgin.net

HURFORD, Colin Osborne. b 33. Qu Coll Ox BA 55 MA 59. Wells Th Coll 55. **d** 57 **p** 58. C Barnoldswick w Bracewell *Bradf* 57–61; C Warrington St Elphin *Liv* 61–63; Malaysia 63–70; P-in-c Annscroft *Heref* 71–79; P-in-c Longden 71–79; P-in-c Pontesbury III 71–79; R Longden and Annscroft 79–85; P-in-c Church Pulverbatch 81–85; R Longden and Annscroft w Pulverbatch 85–86; Tanzania 86–87; TR Billingham St Aid *Dur* 87–96; rtd 96; PtO *Heref* from 96; *Lich* 01–10. *14 Station Road, Pontesbury, Shrewsbury SY5 0QY* T: (01743) 792605

HURLE, Canon Anthony Rowland. b 54. Lon Univ BSc Em Coll Cam PGCE. Wycliffe Hall Ox 80. **d** 83 **p** 84. C Ipswich St Mary at Stoke w St Pet *St E* 83–87; TV Barking St Marg w St Patr *Chelmsf* 87–92; V St Alb St Paul 92–20; RD St Alb 95–05; Hon Can St Alb 05–20; rtd 20; PtO *Lon* from 21. *102 Cumberland Road, London W7 2EB* T: (020) 3643 7412 M: 07983-996349 E: tonyhurle99@gmail.com

HURLE (née POWNALL), Mrs Lydia Margaret. b 53. SRN SCM. Wycliffe Hall Ox 78. **dss** 81 **d** 94 **p** 95. Ipswich St Mary at Stoke w St Pet etc *St E* 81–83; NSM St Alb St Paul 93–20; PtO *Chelmsf* from 19; *Lon* from 21. *102 Cumberland Road, London W7 2EB* T: (020) 3643 7412 E: lydiahurle@gmail.com

HURLEY, Mark Tristan. b 57. Trin Coll Bris BA 89. Sarum & Wells Th Coll 89. **d** 91 **p** 92. C Gainsborough All SS *Linc* 91–94; TV Grantham 94–00; V Donington 00–02; V Bicker 00–02;

PtO *Ox* 08–09; Hon C Wolverton 09–12; P-in-c Swanscombe *Roch* 12–20; P-in-c Bishop's Lydeard w Lydeard St Lawrence etc *B & W* from 20. *The Rectory, Church Street, Bishops Lydeard, Taunton TA4 3AT* T: (01823) 432222 E: markcsb@gmail.com *or* rector@bishopslydeardbenefice.org

HURLEY, Robert. b 64. Univ of Wales (Cardiff) BD 86. Ridley Hall Cam 88. **d** 90 **p** 91. C Dagenham *Chelmsf* 90–93; C Egg Buckland *Ex* 93–96; C Devonport St Budeaux 96; P-in-c Camberwell All SS *S'wark* 96–99; V 99–02; R Oldbury *Sarum* 02–04; Chapl Grenoble *Eur* 13–18; C W Cheltenham *Glouc* 18–20; rtd 20. *Address temp unknown* E: janeandbobhurley@aol.com

HURLEY, Susan Elizabeth. b 65. Leeds Univ BA 87 Leic Univ PGCE 88. St Mellitus Coll 14. **d** 16 **p** 17. C Stebbing and Lindsell w Gt and Lt Saling *Chelmsf* 16–21; P-in-c from 21; C Broxted w Chickney and Tilty etc 17–21; P-in-c from 21. *The Rectory, Park Road, Little Easton, Dunmow CM6 2JJ* T: (01371) 859158 E: sue@hurleyathome.com

HURLSTON, Canon Jean Margaret. b 54. Crewe Coll of Educn CertEd 75 Keele Univ BEd 76. **d** 06 **p** 07. OLM High Crompton *Man* 06–10; OLM Oldham 10–11; NSM Oldham St Mary w St Pet from 11; Borough Dean Oldham from 18; Chapl Man Airport from 18; Chapl Tameside and Glossop Integrated Care NHS Foundn Trust from 18; Hon Can Man Cathl from 18. *24 Taunton Lawns, Ashton-under-Lyne OL7 9EL* T/F: 0161-344 2854 M: 07885-406808 E: jeanhurlston@btinternet.com

HURN, Mrs June Barbara. b 32. Birm Univ CertEd 53. Cant Sch of Min 87. **d** 90 **p** 94. NSM Chislehurst St Nic *Roch* from 90. *Hawkswing, Hawkwood Lane, Chislehurst BR7 5PW* T: (020) 8467 2320 E: junehurn@yahoo.co.uk

HURREN, Timothy John. b 46. BEM 19. York Univ BA 74 ACIB 70. NEOC 99. **d** 02 **p** 03. C High Harrogate St Pet *Ripon* 02–14; *Leeds* from 14. *1 South Park Road, Harrogate HG1 5QU* T: (01423) 541696 E: tim.hurren@ntlworld.com

HURRY, Lynn Susan. b 59. Middx Univ BA 05. NTMTC 02. **d** 05 **p** 06. C Southchurch H Trin *Chelmsf* 05–08; V St Mary-at-Latton from 08. *St Mary-at-Latton Vicarage, The Gowers, Harlow CM20 2JP* T: (01279) 424005 E: revlynn@btinternet.com

HURST, Andrew Robert. b 65. Mansf Coll Ox BA 87. ERMC 17. **d** 20 **p** 21. NSM Cambridge St Mark *Ely* from 20; NSM Grantchester from 20. *28 Sedley Taylor Road, Cambridge CB2 8PN* T: (01223) 211418 M: 07966-424967 E: andrewhurst65@outlook.com

HURST, Canon Brian Charles. b 58. Nottm Univ BA Sheff Univ MA 07. Ripon Coll Cuddesdon 82. **d** 84 **p** 85. C Cullercoats St Geo *Newc* 84–87; C Prudhoe 87–88; TV Willington 88–95; V Denton 95–03; RD Newc W 97–98; TV Glendale Gp 03–09; V Bamburgh 09–17; V Ellingham 09–17; AD Bamburgh and Glendale 06–16; V Newc St Geo and St Hilda from 17; Hon Can Newc Cathl from 10. *St George's Vicarage, St George's Close, Newcastle upon Tyne NE2 2TF* T: 0191-281 1628 E: brian.hurst1@btopenworld.com

HURST, Colin. b 49. Linc Th Coll 88. **d** 90 **p** 91. C Wavertree H Trin *Liv* 90–93; C Croft and Stoney Stanton *Leic* 93–95; V Wigan St Andr *Liv* 97–14; AD Wigan W 03–05; AD Wigan 05–08; Hon Can Liv Cathl 03–08; rtd 14; PtO *Liv* 15–21; *Blackb* 16–17. *19 Foxfield Grove, Shevington, Wigan WN6 8AJ* T: (01257) 402261 E: churst6000@gmail.com

HURST, Colin. b 58. Westmr Coll Ox BA 90. St Jo Coll Nottm MA 95. **d** 95 **p** 96. C Warboys w Broughton and Bury w Wistow *Ely* 95–98; P-in-c Wisbech St Mary 98–04; P-in-c Guyhirn w Ring's End 98–04; V Wisbech St Mary and Guyhirn w Ring's End etc 05–07; P-in-c Eye *Pet* 07–14; P-in-c Newborough 07–14; P-in-c Thorney Abbey *Ely* 07–14; V Eye, Newborough and Thorney *Pet* from 14. *The Vicarage, Thorney Road, Eye, Peterborough PE6 7UN* T: (01733) 222334 E: revcolinhurst@gmail.com

HURST, Edward. b 57. SEITE 09. **d** 11 **p** 12. NSM S Gillingham *Roch* 11–17; V Shorne from 17; P-in-c Gravesend H Family w Ifield from 21; PtO *Cant* 14–17; Chapl Kent and Medway NHS and Soc Care Partnership Trust from 13. *The Vicarage, Butchers Hill, Shorne, Gravesend DA12 3EB* T: (01474) 822239 M: 07791-994933 E: notfathered@gmail.com

HURST, Canon Jeremy Richard. b 40. Trin Coll Cam BA 61 MA MPhil FCP. Linc Th Coll 62. **d** 64 **p** 65. C Woolwich St Mary w H Trin *S'wark* 64–69; PtO *Ex* 69–76; *Ox* 76–84; TV Langley Marish 84–85; TR 85–05; Hon Can Ch Ch 05; Chapl Thames Valley Univ Lon 92–98; rtd 05; PtO *Ox* from 05. *Hortus Lodge, 22A Bolton Avenue, Windsor SL4 3JF* T: (01753) 863693

HURST, Ms Joanna. b 74. Cranmer Hall Dur 13. **d** 15 **p** 16. C Kendal H Trin *Carl* 15–18; Chapl Eden Valley Hospice Carl 18–20; PtO *Carl* 18–20; R Lower Windrush *Ox* from

20. *The Rectory, Main Road, Stanton Harcourt, Witney OX29 5RP* T: (01865) 655692

HUSBAND, Mrs Caroline Elizabeth. b 72. STETS BA 14. **d** 14 **p** 15. NSM Paulton w Farrington Gurney and High Littleton *B & W* 14–17; Lic to RD Midsomer Norton 17–18; TV White Horse *Sarum* from 18. *The Vicarage, The Hollow, Dilton Marsh, Westbury BA13 4BU* T: (01373) 596104 M: 07887-621580 E: husbandcc@gmail.com *or* teamvicar@whtministry.org.uk

HUSS, The Ven David Ian. b 75. Jes Coll Ox MPhys 97. Wycliffe Hall Ox BA 07. **d** 07 **p** 08. C Banbury St Paul *Ox* 07–11; I Donegal w Killymard, Lough Eske and Laghey *D & R* from 11; Adn Raphoe from 13. *The Rectory, The Glebe, Donegal, Republic of Ireland* T: (00353) (74) 972 1075 E: donegal@raphoe.anglican.org

HUSTWAYTE, Samantha Jane. b 73. Lon Univ BD 96 Ches Univ MTh 13. St Jo Coll Nottm LTh 13. **d** 13 **p** 14. C Arnold *S'well* 13–17; V Calverton from 17. *The Vicarage, 18 Crookdole Lane, Calverton, Nottingham NG14 6GF* T: 0115-841 0727 M: 07801-364984 E: revsam@hustwayte.co.uk

HUSTWICK, Mrs Joanne Patricia. b 59. Trin Coll Bris 11. **d** 13 **p** 14. C Tong *Bradf* 13–14; *Leeds* 14–15; C Tong and Laisterdyke 15–17; V Birkby and Birchencliffe from 17. *The Vicarage, 4 Brendon Drive, Huddersfield HD2 2DF* T: (01484) 546966 E: jhustwick13@gmail.com

HUTCHEON, Mrs Elsie. b 39. RGN 63 CertEd UEA MEd 98. EAMTC 89. **d** 92 **p** 94. NSM Heigham St Thos *Nor* 92–02; P-in-c Heigham St Barn w St Bart 02–15; RD Nor S 06–09; rtd 15; PtO *Nor* from 16. *6 St Julian's Alley, Norwich NR1 1QD* T: (01603) 629912 E: elsie.hutcheon@tiscali.co.uk *or* elsie.hutcheon@me.com

HUTCHERSON, Justin Francis. b 87. Jes Coll Cam BA 08 MA 11 Univ of E Lon PGCE 11 Open Univ MEd 12 Heythrop Coll Lon MA 12. St Steph Ho Ox BA 12 MA 12. **d** 14 **p** 15. C Corringham and Fobbing *Chelmsf* 14–18; V Clacton St Jas from 18. *St James's Vicarage, 44 Wash Lane, Clacton-on-Sea CO15 1DA* T: (01255) 426602 M: 07515-946575 E: frjustin@cantab.net

HUTCHIN, David William. b 37. Man Univ MusB 58 CertEd 59 DipEd 59 LRAM ARCM LTCL. Glouc Sch of Min 85. **d** 88 **p** 89. NSM Northleach w Hampnett and Farmington *Glouc* 88–94; NSM Cold Aston w Notgrove and Turkdean 88–94; P-in-c Chedworth, Yanworth and Stowell, Coln Rogers etc 94–01; RD Northleach 96–99; PtO *Leic* 01–06; *Derby* 02–06; *Ripon* 06–14; *Leeds* from 14. *6 St Kevin's Court, 34 Queen's Road, Harrogate HG2 0HB* T: (01423) 712733

HUTCHINGS, Ian James. b 49. Ches Coll of HE MA 03. Clifton Th Coll 69 Trin Coll Bris 72. **d** 73 **p** 74. C Parr *Liv* 73–77; C Timperley *Ches* 77–81; V Partington and Carrington 81–96; V Huntington 96–12; Chapl Bp's Blue Coat C of E High Sch 96–08; rtd 12; PtO *Ches* from 12; *Lich* 12–19 and from 21; *Liv* from 16. *52 Hillcrest, Ellesmere SY12 0LJ* T: (01691) 622304 E: ihutchings@aol.com

HUTCHINGS, James Benjamin Balfour. b 62. Ex Univ BA 84. STETS 03. **d** 06 **p** 07. C Ex St Jas 06–09; C Cen Ex 09–11; P-in-c Littleham w Exmouth 11–13; TR Littleham-cum-Exmouth w Lympstone 13–19; RD Aylesbeare 15–19; TR Barnes *S'wark* from 19. *25 Glebe Road, London SW13 0DZ* T: (020) 8741 5422 E: revdjames@stmarybarnes.org

HUTCHINGS, Thomas George. b 84. Qu Coll Cam BA MPhil 07 BA 13. Ridley Hall Cam 11. **d** 14 **p** 15. C Sileby, Cossington and Seagrave *Leic* 14–17; C Cambridge H Sepulchre *Ely* 17–21; Chapl Kingham Hill Sch from 21. *Kingham Hill School, Kingham, Chipping Norton OX7 6TH* T: (01608) 658999 M: 07484-663325 E: tghutchings@gmail.com

HUTCHINS, Miss Katrina Mary. b 62. Dur Univ MA 20. Ripon Coll Cuddesdon 13. **d** 15 **p** 16. C Kingsthorpe *Pet* 15–18; R Mears Ashby and Hardwick and Sywell etc from 18. *The Vicarage, 46 Wellingborough Road, Mears Ashby, Northampton NN6 0DZ* T: (01604) 812907 M: 07710-464675 E: katrinahutchins94@yahoo.co.uk

HUTCHINS, Canon Paul. b 79. Coll of Resurr Mirfield 99 NOC 04. **d** 05 **p** 06. C Royton St Paul *Man* 05–10; TV Swinton and Pendlebury 10–13; P-in-c Southport St Luke *Liv* 13–18; R Failsworth H Family *Man* from 18; R Blackley H Trin from 21; R Lightbowne from 21; Can Wiawso Ghana from 15. *Holy Family Rectory, 190 Lord Lane, Failsworth, Manchester M35 0QS* T: 0161-681 3644 M: 07572-075990 E: fr.hutchins@btinternet.com

HUTCHINS, Richard Frank. b 70. Ox Min Course 14. **d** 17 **p** 18. C Liss *Portsm* 17–20; P-in-c Catherington and Clanfield from 20. *Catherington Vicarage, 330 Catherington Lane, Waterlooville PO8 0TD* E: revrichardhutchins@gmail.com

HUTCHINSON, Alison Joyce. b 62. Leeds Univ BA 84 RMN 90. Aston Tr Scheme 92 Ripon Coll Cuddesdon 94. **d** 97 **p** 98. C Benfieldside *Dur* 97–00; C Bishopwearmouth St Nic 00–02; PtO *Carl* 02–07; C Penrith w Newton Reigny and Plumpton Wall 07–08; PtO 09; Hon C Crathorne *York* 09–16 and 18–19; Hon C Kirklevington w Picton, and High and Low Worsall 09–16 and 18–19; Hon C Rudby in Cleveland w Middleton 09–16 and 18–19; Hon C Whorlton w Carlton and Faceby 16–19; Hon C Whorlton Gp 19–20; Asst Chapl HM Pris Kirklevington Grange 16–20; Chapl HM Pris Littlehey from 20; PtO *Ely* from 20. *HM Prison Littlehey, Perry, Huntingdon PE28 0SR* T: (01480) 335000 E: alison.hutchinson@justice.gov.uk

HUTCHINSON, Canon Andrew Charles. b 63. Univ of Wales (Ban) BA 84 MEd 96. Aston Tr Scheme 85 Chich Th Coll 87. d 89 p 90. C Burnley St Cath w St Alb and St Paul *Blackb* 89–92; C Shrewsbury St Chad w St Mary *Lich* 92–94; Chapl Heref Cathl Sch 94–97; Succ Heref Cathl 94–97; Chapl Solihull Sch from 97; Can St Jo Pro-Cathl Katakwa from 00. *36 Avenbury Drive, Solihull B91 2QZ* T: 0121-704 0171 E: andrewcapecoast@gmail.com *or* hutcha@solsch.org.uk

HUTCHINSON, Andrew George Pearce. b 78. Glos Univ BA 01 PGCE 02. Oak Hill Th Coll BA 08. d 08 p 09. C Normanton *Derby* 08–15; Chapl Monkton Combe Sch Bath from 15. *Monkton Combe School, Church Lane, Monkton Combe, Bath BA2 7HG* T: (01225) 721208 M: 07877-831506 E: andy_hutchinson@hotmail.com

HUTCHINSON, Andrew Paul. b 65. Trin Hall Cam BA 87 MA 91. Solicitor 90. Aston Tr Scheme 92 Ripon Coll Cuddesdon BTh 97. d 97 p 98. C Stanley *Dur* 97–99; C Sunderland 99–01; TV 01–02; Chapl Sunderland Univ 99–02; TV Penrith w Newton Reigny and Plumpton Wall *Carl* 02–09; Chapl Cumbria Campus Cen Lancs Univ 02–07; Chapl Cumbria Univ *Carl* 07–09; R Stokesley w Seamer *York* 09–20; TR St Neots *Ely* from 20. *The Rectory, Church Street, St Neots PE19 2BU* T: (01480) 471297 E: paul.hutchinson5@btinternet.com

HUTCHINSON, Anthony Hugh. b 47. Open Univ BSc 00 Liv Univ MA 09. d 10 p 11. OLM Stafford St Chad *Lich* 10–15; NSM Rough Hills 15; NSM Wolverhampton St Martin and St Steph 15–20; PtO *Cov* from 18; *Lich* from 21. *Kilsall Hall, Kilsall, Shifnal TF11 8PL* T: (01902) 373145 E: fr.tony@softersolutions.co.uk

HUTCHINSON, Canon Cyril Peter. b 37. Dur Univ BA 61. Wm Temple Coll Rugby 61. d 63 p 64. C Birm St Paul 63–67; Prin Community Relns Officer 66–69; Dir Bradf SHARE 69–76; Hon C Manningham *Bradf* 75–76; V Clayton 76–83; RD Bowling and Horton 80–83; TR Keighley St Andr 83–94; Hon Can Bradf Cathl 84–03; rtd 94; Hon C Keighley All SS *Bradf* 94–03; PtO 04–14; *Leeds* from 14. *Wellcroft, Laycock Lane, Laycock, Keighley BD22 0PN* T: (01535) 606145 E: peter_hutchinson@hotmail.co.uk

HUTCHINSON, David. *See* HUTCHINSON, William David

HUTCHINSON, Mrs Esther. b 96. York St Jo Univ BA 17 St Jo Coll Dur BA 19. Cranmer Hall Dur 17. d 20 p 21. C Clifton *S'well* from 20. *1 Osprey Close, Nottingham NG11 8SX* M: 07722-243070 E: e.allin@outlook.com

HUTCHINSON, Mrs Janice Vivien. b 50. All SS Cen for Miss & Min 17. d 18 p 19. OLM W Hallam and Mapperley w Stanley *Derby* from 18. *1 Spencer Street, Stanley Common, Ilkeston DE7 6GA* T: 0115-752 6116

HUTCHINSON, Jeremy Olpherts. b 32. Oriel Coll Ox BA 55 MA 60. Cranmer Hall Dur. d 57 p 58. C Shoreditch St Leon *Lon* 57–60; V Hoxton St Jo w Ch Ch 60–78; Hon C Hackney 78–85; C Highbury Ch Ch w St Jo and St Sav 85–91; P-in-c Hanley Road St Sav w St Paul 91–92; TV Tollington 92–96; rtd 96; PtO *Lon* 96–19. *8 Casimir Road, London E5 9NU* T: (020) 8806 6492 E: jeremy.hutch@virgin.net *or* janddhutchinson@gmail.com

HUTCHINSON, John Charles. b 44. K Coll Lon 64. d 69 p 70. C Portsea All SS *Portsm* 69–71; C Portsea All SS w St Jo Rudmore 71–73; TV Fareham H Trin 73–78; P-in-c Pangbourne *Ox* 78–86; P-in-c Tidmarsh w Sulham 84–86; R Pangbourne w Tidmarsh and Sulham 86–96; PtO from 07. *90 Fir Tree Avenue, Wallingford OX10 0PL* T: (01491) 832445 E: cavea100@outlook.com

HUTCHINSON, Prof John Maxwell. b 48. PPRIBA Robert Gordon Univ Aber Hon DDes 07 Linc Univ DA 15. d 14. NSM St Jo on Bethnal Green *Lon* 14–16; NSM Chingford SS Pet and Paul *Chelmsf* 16–20; PtO 20–21. *95 Falmouth Avenue, London E4 9QR* E: m.hutchinson@blueyonder.co.uk

HUTCHINSON, Jonathan Graham. b 62. Bris Univ BA 01. Trin Coll Bris 98. d 01 p 02. C Church Stretton *Heref* 01–04; P-in-c Aspley *S'well* 04–11; V 11–17; V Sunningdale *Ox* from 17. *The Vicarage, Sidbury Close, Ascot SL5 0PD* T: (01344) 620061 E: htsvicar@gmail.com

HUTCHINSON, Jonathan Mark. b 45. Open Univ BA 73 E Lon Univ MSc 94. Cant Sch of Min 85. d 89 p 90. NSM Wickham Market w Pettistree and Easton *St E* 89–93; V Thorington w Wenhaston, Bramfield etc 94–97; TV Ipswich St Mary at Stoke w St Pet and St Fran 97–02; PtO *B & W* from 02. *35A Milton Lane, Wells BA5 2QS* T: (01749) 938779 E: drmark.hutchinson@hotmail.co.uk

HUTCHINSON, Canon Julie Lorraine. b 55. WMMTC 90. d 93 p 94. C Northampton St Mary *Pet* 93–95; P-in-c Morcott w Glaston and Bisbrooke 95–97; P-in-c Lyddington w Stoke Dry and Seaton etc 97–02; V 03; Dir of Ords and Voc 03–10; Bp's Chapl 11–15; TV Oakham, Ashwell, Braunston, Brooke, Egleton etc 15–18; Can Pet Cathl 04–18; Hon C High Framland Par *Leic* 18–21; Hon C S Framland 18–21. *5 Croxton Lane, Harston, Grantham NG32 1PP* T: (01476) 870083 M: 07949-199135 E: revdjulie@icloud.com

HUTCHINSON, The Ven Karen Elizabeth. b 64. LMH Ox BA 85 MA 89 Kent Univ MA 06 Solicitor 89. Wycliffe Hall Ox. d 01 p 02. C Alton St Lawr *Win* 01–06; V Crondall and Ewshot *Guildf* 06–12; V The Bourne and Tilford 12–16; Hon Can Guildf Cathl 13–16; Adn Nor from 16. *31 Bracondale, Norwich NR1 2AT* T: (01603) 620007 E: archdeacon.norwich@dioceseofnorwich.org

HUTCHINSON, Mark. *See* HUTCHINSON, Jonathan Mark

HUTCHINSON, Maxwell. *See* HUTCHINSON, John Maxwell

HUTCHINSON, Michael Thomas. b 87. St Cath Coll Cam BA 08 MA 12. St Mellitus Coll BA 19. d 19 p 20. C Preston St Cuth *Blackb* from 19. *58 Garstone Croft, Fulwood, Preston PR2 3WY* M: 07933-533205 E: hutchi44@hotmail.com

HUTCHINSON, Paul. *See* HUTCHINSON, Andrew Paul

HUTCHINSON, Peter. *See* HUTCHINSON, Cyril Peter

HUTCHINSON, Peter Francis. b 52. Sarum & Wells Th Coll 87. d 89 p 90. C Honiton, Gittisham, Combe Raleigh, Monkton etc *Ex* 89–93; V Valley Park *Win* 93–17; rtd 17; PtO *Portsm* from 18. *9 Albert Way, East Cowes PO32 6GA* T: (01983) 294615

HUTCHINSON, Canon Raymond John. b 51. Liv Univ BSc 73. Westcott Ho Cam 73. d 76 p 77. C Peckham St Jo *S'wark* 76–78; C Peckham St Jo w St Andr 78–79; C Prescot *Liv* 79–81; V Edgehill St Dunstan 81–87; P-in-c Litherland Ch Ch 87–89; P-in-c Waterloo Park 87–89; V Waterloo Ch Ch and St Mary 90–97; Chapl Wigan and Leigh Health Services NHS Trust 97–01; Chapl Wrightington, Wigan and Leigh NHS Foundn Trust 01–15; P-in-c Wigan All SS *Liv* 04–08; P-in-c Wigan St Geo 05–08; R Wigan All SS and St Geo 08–15; TR Wigan All SS 15; Hon Can Liv Cathl 13–15; rtd 15; PtO *Liv* from 16. *9 Chequers Gardens, Liverpool L19 3PD* T: 0151-291 5803 E: rayh365@gmail.com

HUTCHINSON, Roy William. b 69. Oak Hill Th Coll BA 94. d 17 p 18. C W Hendon St Jo and Cricklewood St Pet *Lon* 17–20; V from 20. *St John's Vicarage, Vicarage Road, London NW4 3PX* T: (020) 8202 3667 M: 07790-317721 E: roy.hutchinson@gmail.com

HUTCHINSON, Canon Stephen. b 38. St Chad's Coll Dur BA 60. d 62 p 63. C Tividale *Lich* 62–68; V Walsall St Andr 68–73; R Headless Cross *Worc* 73–81; TR Redditch, The Ridge 81–91; RD Bromsgrove 85–91; V Stourbridge St Thos 91–03; Hon Can Worc Cathl 88–03; rtd 03; PtO *Worc* from 03. *251 Stourbridge Road, Kidderminster DY10 2XJ* T: (01562) 631658 E: stephen.hutchinson71@virginmedia.com

HUTCHINSON, Canon William David. b 27. Wycliffe Hall Ox 55. d 57 p 58. C Ipswich St Jo *St E* 57–60; R Combs 60–65; V Ipswich St Aug 65–76; R Ewhurst *Guildf* 76–81; V Aldeburgh w Hazlewood *St E* 81–92; RD Saxmundham 83–88; Hon Can St E Cathl 87–92; rtd 92. *Hazlewood, 1 Birch Close, Woodbridge IP12 4UA* T: (01394) 383760 E: wdhutchinson@tiscali.co.uk

HUTCHINSON CERVANTES, Canon Ian Charles. b 62. Cant Univ (NZ) BSc 84 Reading Univ MSc 86 Jes Coll Cam BA 89 MA 92. Westcott Ho Cam 86. d 89 p 90. C Iffley *Ox* 89–92; USPG 92–04; Locum P Caracas Cathl Venezuela 93; P-in-c El Cayo St Andr Belize 93–97; USPG Staff 97–04; Chapl Madrid *Eur* 04–12; World Miss Officer and P-in-c Nuthurst and Mannings Heath *Chich* 12–15; R 15–18; Regional Dir Miss to Seafarers from 18; Hon Can Madrid Cathl from 01; Hon Can Buenos Aires from 02; Hon Can Pelotas from 06; Can Gib Cathl *Eur* from 10. *Mission to Seafarers, St Michael Paternoster Royal, College Hill, London EC4R 2RL* T: (020) 7248 5202 M: 07733-023880

HUTCHISON, Geoffrey John. b 52. Trin Hall Cam MA 76 Lon Univ CertEd 76. Ridley Hall Cam 77. d 79 p 80. C Harold Wood *Chelmsf* 79–83; CF 83–89; Warden Viney Hill Chr Adventure Cen 89–96; P-in-c Viney Hill *Glouc* 89–96; V Wadsley *Sheff* 96–11; Chapl Sheff Children's NHS Foundn Trust 11–14; PtO *Sheff* from 16; *Leeds* 20–21. *14 Canterbury Crescent, Sheffield S10 3RX* T: 0114-230 9286 E: rev.hutch@gmail.com

HUTCHISON, Ross. b 61. Wadh Coll Ox BA 83 MA 86 DPhil 88. SEITE 03. d 06 p 07. NSM Newington St Mary *S'wark* 06–10; NSM Kilburn St Mary w All So and W Hampstead St Jas *Lon*

from 10. *12A Cumberland Mansions, West End Lane, London NW6 1LL* T: (020) 7794 6087 E: rossnw6@gmail.com

HUTSON, Mark Arthur. b 69. Linc Sch of Th and Min 10. d 13 p 16. OLM Barrow and Goxhill *Linc* 13–15; NSM Gt Grimsby St Mary and St Jas 15–18; C Wolds Gateway Group from 18. *The Vicarage, 24 Victoria Road, Keelby, Grimsby DN41 8EH* M: 07745-369630 E: prayerhut1@gmail.com *or* mark.hutson@lincoln.anglican.org

HUTT, Canon David Handley. b 38. Lambeth MA 05 AKC 68. d 69 p 70. C Bedford Park *Lon* 69–70; C Westmr St Matt 70–73; PV and Succ S'wark Cathl 73–78; Chapl K Coll Taunton 78–82; V Bordesley SS Alb and Patr *Birm* 82–86; V St Marylebone All SS *Lon* 86–95; Can Steward Westmr Abbey 95–05; Sub-Dean and Adn Westmr 99–05; rtd 05; PtO *Lon* 06–13; *Eur* from 06. *14A The Quadrangle, Morden College, 19 St Germans Place, London SE3 0PW*

HUTTON, Christopher. b 81. Sussex Univ BSc 04. Wycliffe Hall Ox BTh 10. d 10 p 11. C Southgate *Chich* 10–14; R Ditchingham, Hedenham, Broome, Earsham etc *Nor* from 14. *The Rectory, School Road, Earsham, Bungay NR35 2TF* T: (01986) 895423 E: chrishutton@hotmail.com

HUTTON, Elizabeth. *See* HUTTON, Susan Elizabeth

HUTTON, Griffith Arthur Jeremy. b 31. Trin Hall Cam BA 56 MA 59. Linc Th Coll 56. d 58 p 59. C Hexham *Newc* 58–60; C Gosforth All SS 60–65; V Whitegate *Ches* 65–71; V Whitegate w Lt Budworth 71–78; R Dowdeswell and Andoversford w the Shiptons etc *Glouc* 78–91; V Newnham w Awre and Blakeney 91–96; rtd 96; PtO *Heref* from 99; *Glouc* from 15. *12 Kent Close, Churchdown, Gloucester GL3 2HQ* T: (01452) 712626 E: behindthemower@gmail.com

HUTTON, Matthew Charles Arthur. b 53. DL 20. Ch Ch Ox BA 75 MA 79. St Stephen's Ho SEITE 11. d 14 p 15. OLM Nor St Steph 14–18; PtO 18–19; NSM The Mitre Benefice from 19. *Broom Farm, Chedgrave, Norwich NR14 6BQ* T: (01508) 520775 *or* 528388 E: mcahutton@gmail.com

HUTTON, Sarah Fielding. b 63. d 11 p 12. NSM Shere, Albury and Chilworth *Guildf* from 11; Spiritual Growth Facilitator from 14. *Netley House, Shere Road, Gomshall, Guildford GU5 9QA* T: (01483) 203800 E: sarah@handr.co.uk *or* sarah.hutton@cofeguildford.org.uk

HUTTON, Mrs Serena Quartermaine. b 35. Nottm Univ BA 57 Lon Univ BA 73 Stranmillis Coll PGCE 68 FRSA 87. SAOMC 95. d 98 p 99. OLM Chinnor, Sydenham, Aston Rowant and Crowell *Ox* 98–06; PtO from 06. *Robin Cottage, The Green, Kingston Blount, Chinnor OX9 4SE* T: (01844) 354173 E: serenaqh@btinternet.com

HUTTON, Susan Elizabeth. b 70. Univ of Wales (Cardiff) BD 91. Ripon Coll Cuddesdon 93. d 95 p 96. C W Parley *Sarum* 95–99; C Trowbridge H Trin 99–05; P-in-c 05–09; PtO 09–14; Lic to RD Devizes 14–16; TV Clarendon 16–20; TR Whitton from 20. *The Rectory, Back Lane, Ramsbury, Marlborough SN8 2QH* T: (01672) 520235 E: rector@whittonteam.org.uk

HUXHAM, Canon Peter Richard. b 38. Worc Coll Ox BA 61 MA 74. St Steph Ho Ox 61. d 63 p 64. C Gillingham *Sarum* 63–67; C Osmondthorpe St Phil *Ripon* 67–70; V Parkstone St Osmund *Sarum* 70–75; TR Parkstone St Pet w Branksea and St Osmund 75–92; RD Poole 85–92; Can and Preb Sarum Cathl 85–92; Chapl Taunton and Somerset NHS Trust 92–03; rtd 03; PtO *Sarum* 04–19. *Salterns House, 34 Brownsea View Avenue, Poole BH14 8LQ* T: (01202) 707431

HUXLEY, Canon Stephen Scott. b 30. Linc Th Coll 53. d 56 p 57. C Cullercoats St Geo *Newc* 56–59; C Eglingham 59–60; C N Gosforth 60–63; V Nether Witton and Hartburn and Meldon 63–65; V Tynemouth Priory 65–74; V Warkworth and Acklington 74–78; P-in-c Tynemouth St Jo 78–81; V 81–87; Hon Can Newc Cathl 82–92; V Wylam 87–92; rtd 92; PtO *Newc* 92–10. *7 Langside Drive, Comrie, Crieff PH6 2HR* T: (01764) 679877

HUXLEY-JONES, Craig John. b 85. Cant Ch Ch Univ BA 06 MCollT 09. SEITE 11. d 14 p 15. NSM Hackington *Cant* 14–15; NSM Goudhurst w Kilndown 15–19; Chapl Benenden Sch 14–19; Sen Chapl Ch Hosp Horsham from 19. *2 West Gun Copse, The Avenue, Christ's Hospital, Horsham RH13 0JE* M: 07872-554044

HUXTABLE, Canon Peter Alexander. b 68. Southn Univ BEng 90. St Jo Coll Nottm MTh 01. d 01 p 02. C Kidderminster St Geo *Worc* 01–05; V Bestwood Em w St Mark S'well 05–10; P-in-c Stapleford 10–11; V 11–21; AD Nottm N 16–21; C Broxtowe from 21; Hon Can S'well Minster from 17. *St Martha's Vicarage, 135 Frinton Road, Nottingham NG8 6GR*

HUYTON, Canon Susan Mary. b 57. Birm Univ BA 79. Qu Coll Birm 83. d 86 p 97. C Connah's Quay *St As* 86–89; C Wrexham 89–90; Dn-in-c 90–91; TV 91–99; V Gwersyllt 99–14; AD Gresford 05–12; R Bangor Monachorum,

Worthenbury and Marchwiel 14–16; Miss Area Ldr Maelor Miss Area from 17; AD Dee Valley 14–17; Can Cursal St As Cathl from 08. *The Rectory, 8 Ludlow Road, Bangor-on-Dee, Wrexham LL13 0JG* T: (01978) 780608 E: suehuyton@aol.com

HUZZEY, Canon Peter George. b 48. Trin Coll Bris 74. d 76 p 77. C Bishopsworth *Bris* 76–79; V 86–96; C Downend 79–80; TV Kings Norton *Birm* 80–86; TR Bishopsworth and Bedminster Down *Bris* 97–00; RD Bedminster 98–99; TR Kingswood 00–15; P-in-c Hanham 12–15; Hon Can Bris Cathl 12–15; rtd 15; PtO *Bris* 16–20; Hon C Mangotsfield from 21. *134 Guest Avenue, Emersons Green, Bristol BS16 7DA* T: 0117-983 0725 M: 07397-208088 E: peterhuzzey67@gmail.com

HYATT, Robert Keith. b 34. Em Coll Cam BA 59 MA 63. Ridley Hall Cam 58. d 60 p 61. C Cheltenham St Mary *Glouc* 60–63; Asst Chapl K Edw Sch Witley 63–65; C Godalming *Guildf* 65–69; Hong Kong 69–78; V Claygate *Guildf* 78–91; TV Whitton *Sarum* 91–96 and 99–00; TR 96–99; rtd 00; PtO *B & W* 00–04; *Bris* from 02; May Moore Chapl Malmesbury w Westport and Brokenborough 02–05; Chapl Kennet and N Wilts Primary Care Trust 02–05. *19 Dark Lane, Malmesbury SN16 0BB* T: (01666) 829026 E: bobnhelen@dsl.pipex.com

HYDE, Ann. b 42. d 09 p 10. NSM Bramhall *Ches* 09–12; NSM Low Marple 12–17; PtO from 17. *Mellor View, 25 St Martin's Road, Marple, Stockport SK6 7BY* T: 0161-427 5767 E: ann.hyde@btinternet.com

HYDE, Canon Denise. b 54. WEMTC 05. d 08 p 09. OLM Fairford Deanery *Glouc* 08–12; NSM S Cotswolds from 12; Hon Can Glouc Cathl from 18. *14 Park Street, Fairford GL7 4JJ* T: (01285) 713285 *or* 850283 M: 07816-500269 E: denisehyde15@gmail.com

HYDE, Canon Jacqueline Diane. b 66. Glos Univ BA 12. WEMTC 06. d 09 p 10. NSM S Cheltenham *Glouc* 09–15; V Churchdown St Jo and Innsworth from 15; Dioc Ecum Officer from 13; Hon Can Glouc Cathl from 19. *The Vicarage, 2 St John's Avenue, Churchdown, Gloucester GL3 2DB* T: (01452) 713421 E: revdjacqui@talktalk.net

HYDE, Jane. b 56. All SS Cen for Miss & Min 17. d 18 p 19. NSM Clarksfield and Waterhead *Man* from 18. *2 Old Rectory Gardens, Mellalieu Street, Middleton, Manchester M24 5DN* E: janehyde10@hotmail.com

HYDE, Canon Jeremy Richard Granville. b 52. Sch of Pharmacy Lon BPharm 75 PhD 80. SAOMC 01. d 04 p 05. NSM Furze Platt *Ox* 04–11; AD Maidenhead and Windsor 08–11; V Finham *Cov* 11–17; rtd 17; PtO *Lon* 17–18; NSM Hanwell St Mellitus w St Mark from 18; Can Kigeme Rwanda from 14. *4A Castlebar Park, London W5 1BX* T: (020) 8997 9380 E: jeremy.hyde@btinternet.com

HYDE, Karen. b 68. Univ of Wales (Cardiff) BSc 89 St Hugh's Coll Ox DPhil 94. Ox Min Course 14. d 17 p 18. NSM DAMASCUS *Ox* 17–21; PtO from 21. *Address withheld by request* M: 07526-985395 E: revdkaren.hyde@gmail.com

HYDER-SMITH, Brian John. b 45. FInstAM MCMI MBIM. EAMTC 84. d 87 p 88. NSM Huntingdon *Ely* 87–90; P-in-c Abbots Ripton w Wood Walton 90–98; P-in-c Kings Ripton 90–98; C Whittlesey, Pondersbridge and Coates 98–99; TV 99–04; rtd 04; Hon C Ironstone *Ox* 10–12; PtO *Ely* from 13; *Ox* from 19. *4 Monks Walk, Marcham, Abingdon OX13 6GG* T: (01865) 391697 E: hydersmith@icloud.com

HYDON, Canon Veronica Weldon. b 52. N Lon Poly BA 73 Maria Grey Coll Lon CertEd 74. Aston Tr Scheme 87 Westcott Ho Cam 89. d 91 p 94. Par Dn Poplar *Lon* 91–94; C 94–95; P-in-c Roxwell *Chelmsf* 95–00; Lay Development Officer 95–00; V Forest Gate Em w Upton Cross 00–03; Assoc V Timperley *Ches* 03–07; V Bollington 07–20; RD Macclesfield 14–19; Hon Can Ches Cathl 14–20; rtd 21; PtO *Ches* from 21. *6 Merlin Close, Macclesfield SK10 2AS* T: (01625) 422849 E: vhydon@hotmail.com

HYGATE, Paul. b 72. Bolton Inst of HE BA 95. EMMTC 07. d 10 p 11. NSM Aston on Trent, Elvaston, Weston on Trent etc *Derby* from 10. *38 Oaklands Avenue, Littleover, Derby DE23 2QH* T: (01332) 772779 E: frpaulhygate@gmail.com

HYLAND, Cecil George. b 38. TCD BA 62 MA 78. CITC Div Test. d 63 p 64. C Belfast St Nic *Conn* 63–66; C Monkstown *D & G* 66–68; Ch of Ireland Youth Officer 68–73; Chapl TCD 73–79; I Tullow *D & G* 79–90; I Howth 90–05; Dir of Ords (Dub) 91–98; Can Ch Ch Cathl Dublin 91–05; Cen Dir of Ords 98–05; rtd 05. *34 The Vale, Skerries Rock, Skerries, Co Dublin, Republic of Ireland* T: (00353) (1) 810 6884 M: 86-838 5317 E: cecilhyland@hotmail.com

HYLTON, Jane Lois. *See* NURSEY, Jane Lois

HYSLOP, Mrs Catherine Graham Young. b 53. Carl Dioc Tr Inst 90. d 92 p 94. NSM St Bees *Carl* 92–95; NSM Upperby St Jo 95–98; C Upperby 98–19; Adv for Post-Ord Tr 00–03; Chapl Cumbria Partnership NHS Foundn Trust 05–19; rtd 19; PtO *Carl* from 19. *1 Hillcrest*

Court, High Road, Carlisle CA1 2PU T: (01228) 930572 E: katie.hyslop2010@gmail.com

HYSLOP, Canon Thomas James. b 54. St Andr Univ BD 76. Edin Th Coll 76. **d** 78 **p** 79. C Whitehaven *Carl* 78–81; C Walney Is 81–83; P-in-c Gt Broughton and Broughton Moor 83–85; V 85–88; V Kells 88–95; P-in-c Upperby St Jo 95–97; V 97–03; TR S Carl 03–12; R Upperby 12–19; Dioc Chapl MU 02–19; Hon Can Carl Cathl 06–19; rtd 19; PtO *Carl* from

19. *1 Hillcrest Court, High Road, Carlisle CA1 2PU* T: (01228) 930572 E: jim.hyslop@talk21.com

HYSON, Peter Raymond. b 51. Open Univ BA 80 Bris Univ MSc 05. Oak Hill Th Coll BA 86. **d** 87 **p** 88. C Billericay and Lt Burstead *Chelmsf* 87–92; TV Whitton *Sarum* 92–99; PtO *Lon* 07–14; *Glouc* from 14. *68 Hampton Street, Tetbury GL8 8LE* T: (01666) 311100 M: 07951-767113 E: peter@change-perspectives.com

I

I'ANSON, Frederick Mark. b 43. MRAC 68. Carl Dioc Tr Inst 89. **d** 92 **p** 93. NSM Sedbergh, Cautley and Garsdale *Bradf* 92–98; P-in-c Kirkby-in-Malhamdale w Coniston Cold 98–08; rtd 08; PtO *Bradf* 09–12; *Carl* from 12. *The Bowers, Firbank, Sedbergh LA10 5EG* T: (015396) 21757 M: 07815-552778 E: mark.mmia43@gmail.com

IBBOTSON, David Paul. b 64. Man Univ BSc 85 PGCE 86. STETS 09. **d** 12 **p** 13. C Tewkesbury w Walton Cardiff and Twyning *Glouc* 12–14; Chapl Monmouth Schs 14–16; Chapl Eastbourne Coll 16–18; PtO *Glouc* 16–17; *Chich* from 17; Chapl Malvern Coll from 19. *24 College Road, Malvern WR14 3DD* M: 07876-333390

IBBOTSON, Miss Tracy Alexandra. b 63. Cranmer Hall Dur 01. **d** 03 **p** 04. C Todmorden *Wakef* 03–08; V Airedale w Fryston 08–14; *Leeds* from 14; Adv on Urban Issues *Wakef* 12–14; *Leeds* from 14. *Holy Cross Vicarage, The Mount, Castleford WF10 3JN* T: (01977) 553157 E: ibbotson457@btinternet.com

IBIAYO, David Akindayo Oluwarotimi. b 71. Lagos Univ BSc. Ridley Hall Cam. **d** 06 **p** 07. C Barking St Marg w St Patr *Chelmsf* 06–10; R Vange from 11; P-in-c Bowers Gifford w N Benfleet from 11. *Vange Rectory, 782 Clay Hill Road, Basildon SS16 4NG* T: (01268) 581404 M: 07904-846028 E: david_ibiayo@hotmail.com

ICKE, Robert John. b 69. Regents Th Coll BA 98. All SS Cen for Miss & Min 17. **d** 19 **p** 20. C Stockton Heath *Ches* from 19; C Latchford St Jas from 19; C Latchford Ch Ch from 20. *St James's Vicarage, 14 Manx Road, Warrington WA4 6AJ* M: 07791-611128 E: r.icke@btinternet.com

IDDON, Fiona Margaret Hastings. b 74. Regent's Park Coll Ox BA 95 MA 99 Westmr Coll Ox PGCE 97. St Mellitus Coll 14. **d** 17 **p** 18. C Shrewsbury St Geo w Greenfields *Lich* 17–20; C Meole Brace from 20. *18A Meole Walk, Shrewsbury SY3 9EU* T: (01743) 357262 E: fionamhiddon@gmail.com

IDDON, Jonathan Richard. b 82. **d** 11 **p** 12. C Glascote and Stonydelph *Lich* 11–13; V Fazeley 13–17; V Canwell 13–17; R Drayton Bassett 13–17; R Peel Parishes from 17. *Address withheld by request* E: vicar@stpaulsfazeley.org

IDDON, Roy Edward. b 40. TCert 61 Lanc Univ MA 88. NOC 83. **d** 83 **p** 84. Hd Teacher St Andr Primary Sch Blackb from 83; NSM Bolton St Matt w St Barn *Man* 83–88; Lic to AD Walmsley 88–93; NSM 93–01; NSM Turton Moorland 01–04; NSM Bolton St Phil 04–10; PtO from 11. *28 New Briggs Fold, Egerton, Bolton BL7 9UL* T: (01204) 306589 M: 07792-654445 E: raiddon@aol.com

IDLE, Christopher Martin. b 38. St Pet Coll Ox BA 62. Clifton Th Coll 62. **d** 65 **p** 66. C Barrow St Mark *Carl* 65–68; C Camberwell Ch Ch *S'wark* 68–71; P-in-c Poplar St Matthias *Lon* 71–76; R Limehouse 76–89; R N Hartismere St E 89–95; PtO *S'wark* 95–03; *St E* 01–03; rtd 03; PtO *Roch* 04–16; *S'wark* from 13. *50 Park View House, Hurst Street, London SE24 0EH* T: (020) 3490 7828 E: christophermidle@gmail.com

†IDOWU-FEARON, The Rt Revd Josiah Atkins. b 49. Birm Univ MA. Immanuel Coll Ibadan 67. **d** 71 **p** 71 **c** 90. Abp Kaduna from 01; Warden St Fran Th Coll Wusasa Nigeria 81–84; Provost St Mich Cathl 84–90; Bp Sokoto 90–98; Bp Kaduna 98–15; Abp 02–09; Sec Gen Angl Communion Office from 15; Hon Asst Bp *Lon* from 15; Hon Asst Bp *S'wark* from 18; PV Westmr Abbey from 16; Six Preacher Cant Cathl from 07. *Anglican Consultative Council, St Andrew's House, Tavistock Crescent, London W11 1AP* T: (020) 7313 3900

IEVINS, Mrs Catherine Ruth. b 54. LMH Ox BA 77 MA 80

Solicitor 81. EAMTC 98. **d** 01 **p** 02. C Pet Ch Carpenter 01–05; PtO 05–06; P-in-c Polebrook and Lutton w Hemington and Luddington 06–07; C Barnwell w Tichmarsh, Thurning and Clopton 06–07; R Barnwell, Hemington, Luddington in the Brook etc 07–16; Warden of Readers 12–14; rtd 16; PtO *Ely* 17–18; Hon C Cambridge St Phil from 18. *18 Hemingford Road, Cambridge CB1 3BZ* T: (01223) 242945 E: ci.life9@gmail.com

IEVINS, Paul Janis. b 58. Linc Sch of Th and Min 12. **d** 15 **p** 16. NSM Welton and Dunholme w Scothern *Linc* from 15. *5 Oak Avenue, Dunholme, Lincoln LN2 3QX*

IEVINS, Peter Valdis. b 54. St Jo Coll Ox BA 75 MA 81 Solicitor 79. Westcott Ho Cam 86. **d** 88 **p** 89. C Sawston and Babraham *Ely* 88–91; NSM Pet Ch Carpenter 01–06; LtO 06–16; PtO *Ely* 16–17; NSM Cherry Hinton St Andr from 17. *18 Hemingford Road, Cambridge CB1 3BZ* T: (01223) 242945 M: 07708-216974 E: peterievins54@gmail.com

IFODE-BLEASE, Mariama Oluseun. b 82. St Andr Univ MA 04 Peterho Cam MPhil 05 PhD 13. Ripon Coll Cuddesdon 18. **d** 20 **p** 21. C Westminster St Jas the Less *Lon* from 20. *The Vicarage, Church Field, Watling Street, Radlett WD7 8EE* E: curate@sjp.org.uk

IGWE, Oliver Chimezie. b 72. St Paul's Univ Coll Awka Nigeria BA 96 St Jo Coll Dur MA 01 Birm Univ PhD 07. **d** 96 **p** 97. Nigeria 96–02; PtO *Birm* 03–05; LtO 05–07; Nigeria 07–20; P-in-c Crewe St Andr w St Jo *Ches* from 20; P-in-c Crewe All SS and St Paul w St Pet from 20. *The Vicarage, 14 Danebank Avenue, Crewe CW2 8AA* T: (01270) 569000 M: 07570-940966 E: oliverigwe36@gmail.com

IJAZ, Luke Anthony. b 76. Univ Coll Lon MSci 99 Lon Inst of Educn PGCE 01. Wycliffe Hall Ox BA 06. **d** 07 **p** 08. C Wallington *S'wark* 07–11; C Redhill H Trin 11–13; C Langham Place All So *Lon* from 14. *25 Fitzroy Street, London W1T 6DR* M: 07803-244543 E: luke_ijaz@hotmail.com *or* luke.ijaz@allsouls.org

IKE, Solomon Uche. b 74. ERMC 17. **d** 21. C Madrid *Eur* from 21. *calle Oliva de plasencia 11:3A, 28044 Madrid, Spain* T: (0034) 915 765 109 M: (0034) 631 867 132 E: solomonchidi2000@yahoo.com

IKECHUKWU, Eliakim Chinonyerem. b 62. Calabar Univ Nigeria BA 01 Wolv Univ MA 16 MRes 17. Trin Coll Umuahia 08. **d** 07 **p** 08. Chapl Calabar Univ Nigeria 07–10; Chapl Calabar Pris 10–15; C Calabar Cathl 11–13; Chapl 13–15; PtO *Birm* 15–18; NSM Kings Norton from 18. *53 Wychall Park Grove, Birmingham B38 8AG* T: 0121-458 3289 M: 07958-600772 E: eliakimike@yahoo.com

IKIN, Gordon Mitchell. b 30. AKC 57. **d** 58 **p** 59. C Leigh St Mary *Man* 58–61; V Westleigh St Paul 61–72; V Thornham St Jas 72–95; rtd 95; PtO *Man* 95–08; *Worc* from 14. *3 Lygon Lodge, Newland, Malvern WR13 5AX* T: (01684) 564948

ILIFFE, Mrs Alison Jane. b 63. Birm Poly BA 86. Qu Coll Birm 13. **d** 15 **p** 16. NSM Avon-Swift *Leic* 15–18; TV Market Harborough and The Transfiguration etc from 18. *44 Northampton Road, Market Harborough LE16 9HE* T: (01858) 440225 E: ajiliffe@gmail.com *or* alison@harborough-anglican.org.uk

ILIFFE, Mrs Felicity Mary. b 57. Glam Univ BA 79 Normal Coll Ban PGCE 82. SEITE 06 WEMTC 07. **d** 09 **p** 10. C Ledbury *Heref* 09–13; V Highley w Billingsley, Glazeley etc 13–14; PtO *Pet* 16–21; NSM Weldon w Deene from 21. *70 Chapel Road, Weldon, Corby NN17 3HP* T: (01536) 266842 E: revfliss@gmail.com

ILLINGWORTH, Ms Elizabeth Rose. b 92. Ex Univ BA 14 St Jo Coll Dur MA 20. Cranmer Hall Dur 17. **d** 20. C Tavistock, Gulworthy and Brent Tor *Ex* from 20. *1 St Andrew's Road, Tavistock PL19 9BY* **M:** 07745-988722 **E:** rosie.illingworth8@gmail.com

ILSLEY (*née* ROGERS), **Mrs Anne Frances.** b 50. Heythrop Coll Lon BA 00 RGN 72. Wycliffe Hall Ox 00. **d** 02 **p** 03. NSM Harefield Lon 02–06; NSM Dorchester *Ox* 06–15; rtd 15; PtO *Sarum* 16–21. *1-2 Charlton Hill, Edington, Westbury BA13 4PL* **T:** (01380) 830651 **M:** 07956-374624 **E:** annefi36@aol.com

ILSLEY (*formerly* PHILLIPS), **Mary Alice.** b 53. Ripon Coll Cuddesdon 97. **d** 99 **p** 00. C Addiscombe St Mildred *S'wark* 99–02; TV Basingstoke *Win* 02–12; rtd 13; PtO *Win* 15–20. *42 Topaz Drive, Andover SP10 3EE*

ILTON, Mrs Jennifer Jane. b 38. S Dios Minl Tr Scheme 92. **d** 95 **p** 96. NSM Jersey St Sav *Win* 95–08; PtO from 08. *38 Maison St Louis, St Saviour, Jersey JE2 7LX* **T:** (01534) 722327

ILYAS, Marilyn. b 51. Oak Hill Th Coll 92. **d** 95 **p** 96. C Roch St Pet w St Marg 95–98; TV S Chatham H Trin 98–01; TR 01–12; rtd 12; PtO *Roch* from 12. *5 Pepperidge Way, Hoo, Rochester ME3 9FY* **T:** (01634) 255897

IMPEY, Miss Joan Mary. b 35. Dalton Ho Bris 65. **dss** 74 **d** 87 **p** 94. Kennington St Mark *S'wark* 67–75; Barking St Marg w St Patr *Chelmsf* 75–81; Harwell w Chilton *Ox* 81–87; Par Dn 87–92; Par Dn Didcot All SS 92–94; C 94–97; rtd 98; PtO *Ox* from 99. *15 Loder Road, Harwell, Didcot OX11 0HR* **T:** (01235) 820346

IMPEY, Canon Patricia Irene. b 45. Birm Univ BA 67 Lanc Univ MPhil 01 K Coll Lon PhD 19. Carl Dioc Tr Course 88. **d** 90 **p** 94. Par Dn Blackpool St Paul *Blackb* 90–94; C 94–95; Chapl Asst Victoria Hosp Blackpool 94–95; Asst Chapl Norfolk and Nor Health Care NHS Trust 95–96; Hon C Sprowston w Beeston *Nor* 96; R King's Beck 96–02; V Ecclesfield *Sheff* 02–10; Dean of Women's Min 03–08; Hon Can Sheff Cathl 04–10; rtd 10; PtO *Blackb* from 11. *22 Hala Grove, Lancaster LA1 4PS* **T:** (01524) 36617 **E:** patriciaimpey@btinternet.com

IMPEY, Richard. b 41. Em Coll Cam BA 63 MA 67 Harvard Univ ThM 67 Ches Univ DProf 13. Ridley Hall Cam 67. **d** 68 **p** 69. C Birm St Martin 68–72; Dir of Tr *B & W* 72–79; Dir of Ords 76–79; V Blackpool St Jo *Blackb* 79–95; RD Blackpool 84–90; Hon Can Blackb Cathl 89–95; Dioc Dir of Tr *Nor* 95–00; P-in-c Heigham St Barn w St Bart 00–02; V Wentworth *Sheff* 02–06; Bp's Adv in Par Development 04–10; rtd 06; PtO *Blackb* from 10. *22 Hala Grove, Lancaster LA1 4PS* **T:** (01524) 36617 **E:** richardimpey@btinternet.com

INALL, Mrs Elizabeth Freda. b 47. Univ of Wales (Lamp) MA 06. St Alb Minl Tr Scheme 88. **d** 92 **p** 94. NSM Tring *St Alb* 92–01; C Harpenden St Nic 01–09; P-in-c Milton Ernest, Pavenham and Thurleigh 09–13; rtd 13; PtO *Ches* from 14. *Grange House, Village Road, Christleton, Chester CH3 7AS* **T:** (01244) 336500 **E:** elizabeth@inall.co.uk

INBADAS, Hamilton. b 77. Nesamony Memorial Chr Coll Marthandam BA 97 Leuven Univ Belgium MSc 10 Nottm Univ PhD 15. United Th Coll Bangalore BD 02. **p** 09. Chapl Chr Medical Coll Vellore India 09–10; PtO *S'well* 11–14; LtO *Glas* 15–17; P-in-c Forres *Mor* from 18. *St John's Rectory, Victoria Road, Forres IV36 3BN* **T:** (01309) 672856 **E:** clergystjohnsforres@gmail.com *or* clergy@stjohnsforres.org.uk

INCH, Vivian Ann. b 57. **d** 13 **p** 14. OLM High Wycombe *Ox* 13–16. *Address temp unknown* **E:** vainch73@gmail.com

IND, Dominic Mark. b 63. Lanc Univ BA 87. Ridley Hall Cam 87. **d** 90 **p** 91. C Birch w Fallowfield *Man* 90–93; SSF 93–95; PtO *Glas* 95–96; C Byker St Martin *Newc* 96–98; C Walker 96–98; P-in-c Cambuslang and Uddingston *Glas* 98–07; R Bridge of Allan *St And* 07–18; Chapl Stirling Univ 07–18; Bp's Chapl 07–18; Can St Ninian's Cathl Perth 10–18; Dioc Dir of Ords 11–18; R Helensburgh *Glas* from 18. *The Rectory, 16 William Street, Helensburgh G84 8BD* **T:** (01436) 670297 **E:** ind.dominic@gmail.com

✠IND, The Rt Revd William. b 42. Leeds Univ BA 64. Coll of Resurr Mirfield 64. **d** 66 **p** 67 **c** 87. C Feltham *Lon* 66–71; C Northolt St Mary 71–73; TV Basingstoke *Win* 73–79; Vice-Prin Aston Tr Scheme 79–82; Dioc Dir of Ords *Win* 82–87; Hon Can Win Cathl 84–87; Suff Bp Grantham *Linc* 87–97; Dean Stamford 87–97; Can and Preb Linc Cathl 87–97; Bp Truro 97–08; rtd 08; PtO *Sarum* 16–20. *15 Dean Close, Melksham SN12 7EZ* **T:** (01225) 340979 **E:** frances.bill@blueyonder.co.uk

INESON, David Antony. b 36. ALCD 62. **d** 62 **p** 63. C Sandal St Helen *Wakef* 62–65; C Birm St Geo 66–71; V Horton *Bradf* 71–80; RD Bowling and Horton 78–80; V Sedbergh, Cautley and Garsdale 80–86; C Firbank, Howgill and Killington 81–86; TV Langley and Parkfield *Man* 86–88; TR Banbury *Ox*

92–98; R 98–01; rtd 01; PtO *Ripon* 01–14; *Leeds* 14–21. *11 Church Close, Redmire, Leyburn DL8 4HF* **T:** (01969) 624631 **E:** d.ine70@btinternet.com

✠INESON, The Rt Revd Emma Gwynneth. b 69. Birm Univ BA 92 MPhil 93 PhD 98. Trin Coll Bris BA 99. **d** 00 **p** 01 **c** 19. C Dore *Sheff* 00–03; Chapl Lee Abbey 03–06; Tutor Trin Coll Bris 07–13; Prin 14–19; NSM Bris St Matt and St Nath 06–14; Bp's Chapl 13–14; NSM Stoke Bishop 15–19; Chapl to The Queen 16–19; Suff Bp Penrith *Carl* 19–21; Bp to Abps Cant and York from 21; Cen Chapl MU from 19. *Lambeth Palace, Lambeth Palace Road, London SE1 7JU* **T:** (020) 7898 1200 **E:** emma.ineson@lambethpalace.org.uk

INESON, John Michael. b 57. Leeds Univ BA 12 MA 14 MIGEM 12 FRSA 16. Yorks Min Course 09. **d** 12 **p** 13. NSM Utley *Bradf* 12–14; *Leeds* 14–16; NSM Keighley from 16; NSM Ingrow w Hainworth from 19. *7 Badger Gate, Wilsden, Bradford BD15 0NP* **T:** (01535) 273670 **M:** 07850-204114 **E:** ineson50@btinternet.com

INESON, Mathew David. b 69. Birm Univ BEng 91. Trin Coll Bris BA 99 MA 00. **d** 00 **p** 01. NSM Dore *Sheff* 00–03; Chapl Lee Abbey 03–06; P-in-c Bris St Matt and St Nath 06–14; V 14; Min Inner Ring Partnership 06–14; AD City 10–14; P-in-c Stoke Bishop 14–15; V 15–19; AD Bris W 16–19; P-in-c Crosscrake *Carl* 19–21; P-in-c Kendal H Trin 20–21. *Address temp unknown* **M:** 07398-252715

INGALL, David Lenox. b 81. Jes Coll Cam BA 04 MA 08. Wycliffe Hall Ox BA 08 MA 13. **d** 09 **p** 10. C Holborn St Geo w H Trin and St Bart *Lon* 09–12; C Onslow Square and S Kensington St Aug 12–13; P-in-c St Sepulchre w Ch Ch Greyfriars etc 13–17; R 17–20. *Needs Farm House, Steyning Lane, Partridge Green, Horsham RH13 8ED* **M:** 07824-999726

INGAMELLS, Ronald Sidney. b 32. FCIPD 92. K Coll Lon AKC 56 St Boniface Warminster 56. **d** 57 **p** 58. C Leeds Gipton Epiphany *Ripon* 57–59; P-in-c Gt Yarmouth *Nor* 59–64; Dioc Youth Officer 64–79; NSM Nor St Pet Mancroft 64–79; Sec Tr Development and Chr Educn Nat Coun YMCAs 79–92; Consultant to Romania Euro Alliance YMCAs 93–97; P-in-c Lemsford *St Alb* 79–02; rtd 02; PtO *Ely* 03–16; *Nor* from 16. *5 Riverview Drive, Upton, Norwich NR13 6BH* **E:** rjingamells@btinternet.com

✠INGE, The Rt Revd John Geoffrey. b 55. St Chad's Coll Dur BSc 77 MA 94 PhD 02 Keble Coll Ox PGCE 79. Coll of Resurr Mirfield. **d** 84 **p** 85 **c** 03. Asst Chapl Lancing Coll 84–86; Jun Chapl Harrow Sch 86–89; Sen Chapl 89–90; V Wallsend St Luke *Newc* 90–96; Can Res Ely Cathl 96–03; Vice-Dean 99–03; Suff Bp Huntingdon *Ely* 03–07; Bp Worc from 07; Ld High Almoner from 13. *The Bishop's Office, The Old Palace, Deansway, Worcester WR1 2JE* **T:** (01905) 731599 **F:** 739382 **E:** bishop.worcester@cofe-worcester.org.uk

INGHAM, Anthony William. b 55. Ven English Coll Rome PhB 75 STB 78 NOC 98. **d** 78 **p** 79. In RC Ch 78–98; NSM Tottington *Man* 99–01; CF 01–15; P-in-c Beaulieu-sur-Mer *Eur* from 15. *Presbytère Anglican, 9 rue Paul-Doumer, 06310 Beaulieu-sur-Mer, France* **T:** (0033) 4 93 01 45 61 **E:** chaplain@stmichaelsbeaulieusurmer.org

INGHAM, Carol Helen. *See* PHARAOH, Carol Helen

INGHAM, Gareth. b 71. Qu Foundn Birm 18. **d** 20 **p** 21. C Oakengates, Priors Lee and Wrockwardine Wood *Lich* from 20. *The Vicarage, Ashley Road, St Georges, Telford TF2 9LF* **T:** (01743) 235084 **M:** 07753-336995 **E:** gareth.ingham3@btinternet.com

INGHAM, Malcolm John. b 68. Wycliffe Hall Ox BTh 99. **d** 99 **p** 00. C Moreton-in-Marsh w Batsford, Todenham etc *Glouc* 99–03; C Leckhampton SS Phil and Jas w Cheltenham St Jas 03–04; TV The Ortons, Alwalton and Chesterton *Ely* 04–10; P-in-c Elton w Stibbington and Water Newton 06–10; V Alwalton and Chesterton 10–20; R Badby w Newham and Charwelton w Fawsley etc *Pet* from 20. *The Vicarage, Vicarage Hill, Badby, Daventry NN11 3AP* **T:** (01327) 314428 **E:** vicarofknightley@gmail.com

INGHAM, Mrs Pamela. b 47. MBE 96. NEOC 93. **d** 96 **p** 97. C Newc Epiphany 96–99; C Fawdon 99–00; P-in-c 00–06; Dioc Development Officer for Partners in Community Action 06–10; rtd 10; Hon C Tynemouth St Jo *Newc* 12–15; PtO from 15. *15 St George's Road, Cullercoats NE30 3JZ*

INGLE-GILLIS, Mrs Sally. b 66. **d** 18 **p** 19. C Wentwood *Mon* 18–21; V Usk Min Area from 21. *The Vicarage, 25 St John's Road, Newport NP19 8GR* **M:** 07813-264429 **E:** sallyinglegillis@wentwood.church

INGLE-GILLIS, William Clarke. b 68. Baylor Univ (USA) BA 90 MA 95 K Coll Lon PhD 04. Westcott Ho Cam 02. **d** 04 **p** 05. C Caldicot *Mon* 04–08; Dioc Soc Resp Officer 06–08; P-in-c Caerwent w Dinham and Llanvair Discoed etc 08–14; P-in-c Wentwood 14–17; Tutor St Mich Coll Llan 07–16; V Newport Maindee and Lliswerry *Mon* from 17. *St John's*

Vicarage, St John's Road, Newport NP19 8GR T: (01633) 674155 M: 07722-500805 E: w.c.ingle-gillis@cantab.net

INGLEBY, Canon Anthony Richard. b 48. Keele Univ BA 72. Trin Coll Bris. **d** 83 **p** 84. C Plymouth St Jude *Ex* 83–88; R Lanreath *Truro* 88–97; V Pelynt 88–97; RD W Wivelshire 96–97; P-in-c Stoke Climsland 97–05; P-in-c Linkinhorne 03–05; P-in-c Liskeard and St Keyne 05–16; Chapl Cornwall and Is of Scilly Primary Care Trust 05–09; Hon Can Truro Cathl 04–16; RD W Wivelshire 08–13; C Duloe, Herodsfoot, Morval and St Pinnock 10–16; rtd 16. *91 Compton Avenue, Plymouth PL3 5DD* E: revtonyingleby@gmail.com

INGLEDEW, Peter David Gordon. b 48. AKC 77 Jo Dalton Coll Man CertEd 73 Croydon Coll DASS 92 CQSW 92 Univ Coll Chich BA 03. St Steph Ho Ox 77. **d** 78 **p** 79. C Whorlton *Newc* 78–81; C Poplar *Lon* 81–83; TV 83–85; V Tottenham H Trin 85–90; PtO *Chich* from 90. *11 St Luke's Terrace, Brighton BN2 2ZE* T: (01273) 689765 F: 389115 E: david.ingledew2@ntlworld.com

INGLES, Daniel Edward. b 78. Plymouth Univ BA 00. Ridley Hall Cam 12. **d** 14 **p** 15. C Beaminster Area *Sarum* 14–17; TV Melbury from 17. *The Vicarage, Corscombe, Dorchester DT2 0NU* T: (01935) 891858 E: revdanielingles@hotmail.com

INGLESBY, Richard Eric. b 47. Birm Univ BSc 69 Bris Univ CertEd 74. Wycliffe Hall Ox 85. **d** 87 **p** 88. C Cheltenham Ch Ch *Glouc* 87–92; P-in-c Paulton *B & W* 92–94; V 94–01; P-in-c Farrington Gurney 92–94; V 94–01; P-in-c Moxley *Lich* 01–09; V 09–13; C Darlaston All SS 01–13; C Darlaston St Lawr 01–13; Ecum Adv (Wolverhampton Area) 04–08; RD Wednesbury *Lich* 05–12; Preb Lich Cathl 09–13; rtd 13; PtO *Glouc* from 14. *32 Sandycroft Road, Churchdown, Gloucester GL3 1JH* T: (01452) 541509 E: r_inglesby@hotmail.com

INGLIS, Canon Kelvin John. b 62. Ripon Coll Cuddesdon MTh 00. **d** 00 **p** 01. C Southampton Maybush St Pet *Win* 00–04; V Whitchurch w Tufton and Litchfield 04–17; AD Whitchurch 14–17; R Salisbury St Thos and St Edm *Sarum* from 17; RD Salisbury from 18; Can and Preb Sarum Cathl from 20. *Little Bower, Campbell Road, Salisbury SP1 3BG* T: (01722) 239463 E: kelvin.inglis@tiscali.co.uk

INGRAM, Canon Bernard Richard. b 40. Lon Coll of Div 66. **d** 66 **p** 67. C Bromley Common St Aug *Roch* 66–70; C Gravesend St Geo 70–74; Chapl Joyce Green Hosp Dartford 75–83; V Dartford St Edm *Roch* 75–83; V Strood St Fran 83–04; RD Strood 91–97; Hon Can Roch Cathl 00–04; rtd 04; PtO *Heref* from 05. *1 Hillview Cottage, Upper Colwall, Malvern WR13 6DH* T/F: (01684) 540475

INGRAM, Mrs Clodagh Mary. b 65. Man Poly BA 87. WEMTC 07. **d** 10 **p** 11. C Tuffley *Glouc* 10–13; NSM Churchdown 13–17; P-in-c Upton St Leonards 17–20. *2 Coxmore Close, Hucclecote, Gloucester GL3 3SA* M: 07583-754960 E: rev.clodaghingram@gmail.com

INGRAM, Gary Simon. b 58. K Coll Lon BD AKC. Ripon Coll Cuddesdon. **d** 83 **p** 84. Chapl Nelson and Colne Coll 92–98; C Spalding St Mary and St Nic *Linc* 83–87; C Heaton Ch Ch *Man* 87–89; V Colne H Trin *Blackb* 89–98; RD Pendle 96–98; R Poulton-le-Sands w Morecambe St Laur 98–09; AD Lancaster 98–04; P-in-c Ferring *Chich* 09–11; V from 11. *The Vicarage, 19 Grange Park, Ferring, Worthing BN12 5LS* T: (01903) 241645 E: revgaryingram@googlemail.com

INGRAM, Miss Jennifer Rebecca. b 90. Nottm Univ BA 12 St Jo Coll Nottm MA 13. Cranmer Hall Dur 14. **d** 16 **p** 17. C Wootton *Pet* 16–19; V Earls Barton from 19. *The Vicarage, 7 High Street, Earls Barton, Northampton NN6 0JG* M: 07743-593700 E: revjennyingram@outlook.com

INGRAM, Peter Anthony. b 53. NOC 83. **d** 86 **p** 87. C Maltby *Sheff* 86–89; TV Gt Snaith 89–92; R Adwick-le-Street w Skelbrooke 92–05; AD Adwick 01–05; V Millhouses H Trin 05–15; P-in-c Abbeydale St Jo 11–15; V Abbeydale and Millhouses 15–21; AD Ecclesall 07–11; Hon Can Sheff Cathl 05–21; rtd 21. *38 Boshaw View, Hade Edge, Holmfirth HD9 2TZ*

INGRAMS, Canon Peter Douglas. b 56. Wheaton Coll Illinois BA 77 Ox Univ BA 80. Wycliffe Hall Ox 78. **d** 83 **p** 84. C Rowner *Portsm* 83–86; C Petersfield w Sheet 86–90; V Sheet 90–96; V Locks Heath 96–07; Local Min Officer *Cant* 07–15; Local Min and Growth Adv 15–21; Hon Can Cant Cathl 19–21; rtd 21. *12 Guildford Road, Canterbury CT1 3QD* M: 07876-642788 E: pdingrams56@gmail.com

INKPIN, David Leonard. b 32. Liv Univ BSc 54 CChem MRSC 55. EMMTC 83. **d** 86 **p** 87. NSM Legsby, Linwood and Market Rasen *Linc* 86–04; PtO from 04. *Weelsby House, Legsby Road, Market Rasen LN8 3DY* T: (01673) 843360 E: inkypens@yahoo.co.uk

INMAN, Canon Daniel David. b 84. Wycliffe Hall Ox BA 05 MA 09 Qu Coll Ox MSt 06 DPhil 09. Ripon Coll Cuddesdon 07. **d** 10 **p** 11. C Deddington w Barford, Clifton and Hempton *Ox* 10–13; Sen Chapl Win Coll 13; Chapl and Sen Research

Fell Qu Coll Ox 13–16; Dioc Dir of Ords *Chich* 16–19; C Hove All SS 19; Can Res and Chan Chich Cathl from 19. *2 Vicars Close, Chichester PO19 1PT* T: (01243) 788347 M: 07747-016370 E: chancellor@chichestercathedral.org.uk

INMAN, Malcolm Gordon. b 33. Edin Th Coll 58. **d** 60 **p** 61. C Lundwood *Wakef* 60–63; C Heckmondwike 63–70; V Wrenthorpe 70–75; Chapl Cardigan Hosp 70–73; Asst Chapl Pinderfields Gen Hosp Wakef 72–73; V Cleckheaton St Jo *Wakef* 75–98; rtd 98; PtO *Wakef* 00–07; Hon C Staincliffe and Carlinghow 07–14; *Leeds* from 14. *14 Briestfield Road, Thornhill Edge, Dewsbury WF12 0PW* T: (01924) 437171

INMAN, Canon Thomas Jeremy. b 45. Rhodes Univ BA 67. St Steph Ho Ox 67. **d** 69 **p** 70. C Deptford St Paul *S'wark* 69–72; C Bellville S Africa 72–73; R Malmesbury 73–76; P-in-c Donnington *Chich* 76–80; V Hangleton 80–86; V Bosham 86–10; RD Westbourne 91–99; Can and Preb Chich Cathl 00–10; rtd 10; PtO *Bris* from 10; *Chich* from 13. *35 Hunters Road, Bristol BS15 3EZ* T: 0117-960 5045 M: 07941-834914 E: tjinman45@gmail.com

INNES, Donald John. b 32. St Jo Coll Ox BA 54 MA. Westcott Ho Cam 56. **d** 56 **p** 57. C St Marylebone St Mark Hamilton Terrace *Lon* 56–58; C Walton-on-Thames *Guildf* 58–67; Chapl Moor Park Coll Farnham 67–76; P-in-c Tilford *Guildf* 76–97; rtd 97; PtO *Guildf* 97–20. *19 Whitecroft, Dilton Marsh, Westbury BA13 4DJ* T: (01373) 824724 E: innescribable@gmail.com

✠**INNES, The Rt Revd Robert Neil.** b 59. K Coll Cam BA 82 MA 85 St Jo Coll Dur BA 91 Dur Univ PhD 95. Cranmer Hall Dur 89. **d** 95 **p** 96 **c** 14. C Dur St Cuth 95–97; C Shadforth and Sherburn w Pittington 97–99; Lect St Jo Coll Dur 95–99; P-in-c Belmont *Dur* 99–00; V 00–05; Sen Chapl and Chan Brussels Cathl *Eur* 05–14; Chapl to The Queen 12–14; Bp Eur from 14. *avenue Princesse Paola 15, 1410 Waterloo, Belgium* T: (0032) (2) 213 7480 E: bishop.europe@churchofengland.org

INNES, Canon Ruth. b 56. New Coll Edin BD 00. TISEC 97. **d** 00 **p** 01. Prec St Ninian's Cathl Perth *St And* 00–02; P-in-c Linlithgow and Bathgate *Edin* 02–06; P-in-c Edin St Mark 06–10; R Falkirk 10–16; R Edin St Fillan from 16; Synod Clerk from 17. *St Fillan's Rectory, 8 Buckstone Drive, Edinburgh EH10 6PD* M: 07765-908829 E: ruth@ruthinnes.me.uk

INSLEY, Canon Michael George Pitron. b 47. Trin Coll Ox BA 69 MA 70 Nottm Univ MPhil 85. Wycliffe Hall Ox 69. **d** 72 **p** 73. C Beckenham Ch Ch *Roch* 72–76; P-in-c Cowden 76–79; Lect St Jo Coll Nottm 79–85; V Tidebrook and Wadhurst *Chich* 85–98; P-in-c Stonegate 95–98; Can and Preb Chich Cathl 94–98; P-in-c Horsmonden and Dioc Rural Officer *Roch* 98–03; V Bromley Common St Luke 03–12; Hon Can Th Roch Cathl 06–12; rtd 12; PtO *Sarum* 12–22; *Roch* 13–15. *22 Bridport Road, Dorchester DT1 1RS* T: (01305) 262412 E: michaelinsley@uwclub.net

INSTON, Brian John. b 47. SAOMC 95. **d** 98 **p** 99. C Bentley *Sheff* 98–01; V Balby 01–12; AD W Doncaster 07–11; rtd 12; PtO *Sheff* from 12. *62 Hindburn Close, Doncaster DN4 7RP* T: (01302) 534976 M: 07990-513120 E: bjinston@yahoo.co.uk

INVERNESS, Provost of. *See* STRANGE, The Most Revd Mark Jeremy

✠**IPGRAVE, The Rt Revd Michael Geoffrey.** b 58. OBE 11. Oriel Coll Ox BA 78 MA 94 St Chad's Coll Dur PhD 00 SOAS Lon MA 04. Ripon Coll Cuddesdon BA 81. **d** 82 **p** 83 **c** 12. C Oakham, Hambleton, Egleton, Braunston and Brooke *Pet* 82–85; Asst P Chiba Resurr Japan 85–87; TV Leic Ascension 87–90; TV Leic H Spirit 91–95; TR 95–99; P-in-c Leic St Mary 93–94; Bp's Adv on Relns w People of Other Faiths 91–99; Bp's Dom Chapl 92–99; Hon Can Leic Cathl 94–04; Adv Inter-Faith Relns Abp's Coun 99–04; Sec Ch's Commission Inter Faith Relns 99–04; Hon C Leic Presentation 02–04; Adn S'wark 04–12; P-in-c S'wark St Geo w St Alphege and St Jude 06–07; P-in-c Peckham St Jo w St Andr 09–10; Can Missr 10–12; Area Bp Woolwich 12–16; Dioc Warden of Readers 14–16; Bp Lich from 16. *Bishop's House, 22 The Close, Lichfield WS13 7LG* T: (01543) 306001 E: bishop.michael@lichfield.anglican.org

IPSWICH, Archdeacon of. *See* KING, The Ven Rhiannon Elizabeth

IQBAL, The Ven Javaid. b 71. Birm Univ MA 09. St Jo Coll Nottm BA 97. **d** 97 **p** 99. C Lahore St Thos Pakistan 97–99; P-in-c Lashore Ch Ch 99–00; Dir Miss and Evang Raiwind 98–99; PtO *Leic* 00–05; C Evington 05–07; P-in-c Thurmaston 07–08; TV Fosse Team 08–13; Hon Can Leic Cathl 11–13; TR Aldenham, Radlett and Shenley *St Alb* 13–20; Adn Doncaster *Sheff* from 20. *The New Vicarage, Stainforth Road, Barnby Dun, Doncaster DN3 1AA* M: 07469-580723 E: canoniqbal@gmail.com *or* javaid.iqbal@sheffield.anglican.org

IREDALE, Hilary Grace. b 59. Guy's Hosp Medical Sch MB, BS 82 FRCA 90. Qu Coll Birm 06. **d** 09 **p** 10. NSM Rugby *Cov* 09–13; V Rugby St Geo 13–19; rtd 19. *241 Hillmorton Road, Rugby CV22 5BD* T: (01788) 540355 E: mike.iredale@btinternet.com

IRELAND, David Arthur. b 45. Mert Coll Ox BA 67 MA 71 MICFM 87. Cuddesdon Coll 67. **d** 69 **p** 70. C Chapel Allerton *Ripon* 69–72; C Harpenden St Nic *St Alb* 72–76; R Clifton 76–84; PtO *Guildf* 91–00; NSM Tattenham Corner and Burgh Heath 01–02; NSM Leatherhead and Mickleham 02–12; Chapl Box Hill Sch 05–12; rtd 12; PtO *Guildf* from 12. *St Michael's Lodge, Old London Road, Mickleham, Dorking RG5 6DU* E: rev.ireland43@btinternet.com

IRELAND, Leslie Sydney. b 55. York Univ BA 76. St Jo Coll Nottm 83. **d** 86 **p** 87. C Harwood *Man* 86–89; C Davyhulme St Mary 89–90; V Bardsley 90–99; R Levenshulme St Andr and St Pet 99–06; P-in-c Levenshulme St Mark 05–06; R Levenshulme 06–12; AD Heaton 04–12; R Lenzie *Glas* from 12. *58 Waverley Park, Kirkintilloch, Glasgow G66 2BP* T: 0141-776 3866 M: 07757-946184 E: rector@stcyprianslenzie.com *or* les949@btinternet.com

IRELAND, Mrs Lucy Annabel. b 53. Univ of Zimbabwe BSc 74. St Jo Coll Nottm. **dss** 85 **d** 87 **p** 95. Mansfield St Jo *S'well* 85–87; Hon Par Dn Harwood *Man* 87–89; NSM Bardsley 90–99; C Levenshulme St Andr and St Pet 99–06; C Levenshulme 06–12; NSM Glas E End from 13. *58 Waverley Park, Kirkintilloch, Glasgow G66 2BP* T: 0141-776 3866 M: 07583-884358 E: irelandla@hotmail.com

IRELAND, The Ven Mark Campbell. b 60. St Andr Univ MTheol 81 Sheff Univ MA 01. Wycliffe Hall Ox 82. **d** 84 **p** 85. C Blackb St Gabr 84–87; C Lancaster St Mary 87–89; Sub-Chapl HM Pris Lanc 87–89; V Baxenden *Blackb* 89–97; Dioc Missr *Lich* 98–07; TV Walsall 98–07; V Wellington All SS w Eyton 07–16; Adn Blackb from 16. *19 Clarence Park, Blackburn BB2 7FA* T: (01254) 958836 M: 07866-778791 E: mark.ireland@blackburn.anglican.org

IRELAND, Mrs Mary Janet. b 52. EMMTC 96. **d** 99 **p** 00. NSM Kibworth and Smeeton Westerby and Saddington *Leic* 99–02; C Lutterworth w Cotesbach and Bitteswell 02–05; P-in-c Glen Magna cum Stretton Magna etc 05–13; R Gt w Lt Harrowden and Orlingbury and Isham etc *Pet* 13–17; rtd 17; PtO *Leic* from 18. *19 Links Road, Kibworth Beauchamp, Leicester LE8 0LD* T: 0116-279 6892 E: mary_ireland@btinternet.com

IRELAND, Mrs Sharran. b 49. SEITE 95. **d** 98 **p** 99. C Appledore w Brookland, Fairfield, Brenzett etc *Cant* 98–01; TV St Laur in Thanet 01–03; TR 03–13; rtd 13; PtO *Cant* from 13. *Jamark, 13 Norman Road, Faversham ME13 8PX*

IRESON, David Christopher. b 45. Man Univ TCert 67 Birm Univ BEd 80. St Steph Ho Ox. **d** 93 **p** 94. C Minehead *B & W* 93–97; V St Decumans 97–08; rtd 08; PtO *B & W* 11–14. *50 Camperdown Terrace, Exmouth EX8 1EQ* T: (01395) 263307 M: 07786-943967 E: decuman@hotmail.co.uk

IRESON, Philip. b 52. Newc Univ BSc 73. St Jo Coll Nottm. **d** 84 **p** 85. C Owlerton *Sheff* 84–87; V The Marshland 87–94; PtO *Linc* 90–93; Chapl HM YOI Hatfield 91–92; Bp's Rural Adv *Sheff* 91–00; R Firbeck w Letwell 94–01; V Woodsetts 94–01; Chapl HM Pris and YOI Doncaster 01–11; V Pitsmoor Ch Ch *Sheff* 11–16; P-in-c Ellesmere St Pet 13–16; rtd 16; PtO *Sheff* from 17. *19 Stradbroke Road, Sheffield S13 8LR* M: 07882-027473 E: ireson61@gmail.com

IRETON, Elliott John. b 83. Cranmer Hall Dur 15. **d** 17 **p** 18. C Burscough Bridge *Liv* from 17. *20 Warpers Moss Lane, Burscough, Ormskirk L40 4AQ* M: 07872-952961 E: elliottireton@gmail.com

IRETON, Robert John. b 56. Bris Univ BEd. Oak Hill Th Coll BA. **d** 84 **p** 85. C Bromley Ch Ch *Roch* 84–87; TV Greystoke, Matterdale, Mungrisdale etc *Carl* 87–90; V Falconwood *Roch* 90–97; V Stanwix *Carl* 97–04; P-in-c Erith St Jo *Roch* 04–10; Chapl Trin Sch Belvedere 04–10; P-in-c Brinklow *Cov* 10–11; P-in-c Harborough Magna 10–11; P-in-c Monks Kirby w Pailton and Stretton-under-Fosse 10–11; P-in-c Churchover w Willey 10–11; R Revel Gp 11–13; rtd 13. *7 The Meadows, Bempton, Bridlington YO15 1LU*

IRONS, Nigel Richard. b 59. Aston Univ BSc 77. St Jo Coll Nottm MA 95. **d** 97 **p** 98. C Newchapel *Lich* 97–00; V Burton All SS w Ch Ch 00–14; TR Leek and Meerbrook from 14; RD Leek from 21. *St Edward's Vicarage, 24 Ashenhurst Way, Leek ST13 5SB*

IRONSIDE, John Edmund. b 31. Peterho Cam BA 55 MA 59. Qu Coll Birm 55. **d** 57 **p** 58. C Spring Park *Cant* 57–60; C Guernsey St Sampson *Win* 60–63; Thailand 63–66; R Guernsey St Jo *Win* 66–72; V Sholing 72–82; R Guernsey St Sampson 82–98; Miss to Seamen 82–98; rtd 98; PtO *Win* 98–07; P-in-c Guernsey St Andr 07–11; PtO *Chich* from 11. *1 Johnson Way, Ford, Arundel BN18 0TD* T: (01903) 722884 E: sarniaford@hotmail.co.uk

IRVINE, Alison Elizabeth Gillian. Man Univ BSc. CITI. **d** 17 **p** 18. Tullamore w Durrow, Newtownfertullagh, Rahan etc *M & K* 17–18; C Dunboyne and Rathmolyon from 18. *5 Newcastle Woods Crescent, Enfield, Co Meath, A83 AV24, Republic of Ireland* M: (00353) 87-985 1035 E: revalisonirvine@gmail.com

IRVINE, Mrs Andrea Mary. b 49. Sussex Univ BA 70 Ox Univ PGCE 71. NTMTC 99. **d** 02. NSM Cov H Trin 02–05; PtO 05–06; NSM Cov Cathl 06–12; PtO *Ely* 13–16. *42 Pretoria Road, Cambridge CB4 1HE* T: (01223) 364128 E: andreairvine12@gmail.com

IRVINE (formerly SADLER), Ann Penrith. b 50. STETS 98. **d** 01 **p** 02. C Len Valley *Cant* 01–04; P-in-c Aylesham w Adisham 04–08; C Nonington w Wymynswold and Goodnestone etc 04–08; PtO 08–10. *Pilgrim Cottage, 16 Kilmahamogue Road, Moyarget, Ballycastle BT54 6JH* T: (028) 2076 3748 E: revann@uwclub.net

IRVINE, Mrs Catherine Frances. b 70. K Coll Lon BA 97. Ripon Coll Cuddesdon 99. **d** 01 **p** 02. C Romsey *Win* 01–05; TV Richmond St Mary w St Matthias and St Jo *S'wark* 05–11; Chapl R Holloway and Bedf New Coll *Guildf* 11–19; TR Ouzel Valley *St Alb* from 19. *The Vicarage, Pulford Road, Leighton Buzzard LU7 1AB* T: (01525) 373217 E: rectorcate@gmail.com

IRVINE, Canon Christopher Paul. b 51. Nottm Univ BTh 75 Lanc Univ MA 76 St Martin's Coll Lanc PGCE 77. Kelham Th Coll 73. **d** 76 **p** 76. Chapl Lanc Univ *Blackb* 76–77; C Stoke Newington St Mary *Lon* 77–80; Chapl Sheff Univ 80–85; Chapl St Edm Hall Ox 85–90; Tutor St Steph Ho Ox 85–90; Vice-Prin 91–94; V Cowley St Jo Ox 94–98; Prin Coll of Resurr Mirfield 98–07; Can Res and Lib Cant Cathl 07–17; rtd 17; P-in-c Ewhurst *Chich* from 17; P-in-c Bodiam from 17; RD Rye from 18. *The Rectory, Ewhurst Green, Robertsbridge TN32 5TB* T: (01580) 830268 *or* 830925 E: canonchristopher@outlook.com

IRVINE, Clyde. *See* IRVINE, James Clyde

IRVINE, David John. b 50. Trin Coll Cam BA 72 MA 75. NOC 91. **d** 94 **p** 95. C Hexham *Newc* 94–99; P-in-c Blanchland w Hunstanworth and Edmundbyers etc 99–13; P-in-c Slaley 99–13; P-in-c Healey 03–13; P-in-c Whittonstall 03–13; rtd 13; PtO *St And* from 14. *25 Charles Street, Pittenweem, Anstruther KY10 2QH* T: (01333) 311868 E: davidirvine190@btinternet.com

IRVINE, Donald Andrew. b 45. Trin Coll Bris 94. **d** 96 **p** 97. C Allington and Maidstone St Pet *Cant* 96–99; P-in-c Harrietsham w Ulcombe 99–02; P-in-c Lenham w Boughton Malherbe 00–02; R Len Valley 02–07; TV Whitstable 07–10. *Pilgrim Cottage, 16 Kilmahamogue Road, Moyarget, Ballycastle BT54 6JH* T: (028) 2076 3748 M: 07932-149495 E: don.irvine35@gmail.com

IRVINE, Gareth Iain. b 80. Warwick Univ BSc 03. St Mellitus Coll BA 12. **d** 12 **p** 13. C Westwood *Cov* 12–16; NSM 16–17; V Foleshill St Laur from 17; AD Cov N from 20. *The Vicarage, 142 Old Church Road, Coventry CV6 7ED* M: 07743-932759 E: gareth@stlaurences.org

IRVINE, James Clyde. b 35. QUB BA 57 NUU BPhil(Ed) 83. CITC 59. **d** 59 **p** 60. C Belfast St Luke *Conn* 59–62; C Lisburn Ch Ch Cathl 62–65; R Duneane w Ballyscullion 65–69; I Kilbride 69–74; Hd of RE Ballyclare High Sch 73–98; Bp's C Killead w Gartree 98–05; rtd 05. *1A Rathmena Avenue, Ballyclare BT39 9HX* T: (028) 9332 2933 E: irvineclyde@live.co.uk

IRVINE, Mrs Jennifer Anne. b 81. Warwick Univ BSc 03. St Mellitus Coll BA 12. **d** 12 **p** 13. C Westwood *Cov* 12–16; PtO 17–18; NSM Foleshill St Laur from 18; PtO *Lon* from 21. *The Vicarage, 142 Old Church Road, Coventry CV6 7ED* T: (024) 7668 8271

IRVINE, The Very Revd John Dudley. b 49. Sussex Univ BA 70. Wycliffe Hall Ox BA 80. **d** 81 **p** 82. C Brompton H Trin w Onslow Square St Paul *Lon* 81–85; P-in-c Kensington St Barn 85–94; V 94–01; Dean Cov 01–12; P-in-c Cov St Fran N Radford 06–12; C Cambridge H Trin *Ely* 12–16; rtd 16. *42 Pretoria Road, Cambridge CB4 1HE* T: (01223) 364128 E: jdirvine@lineone.net

IRVINE-CAPEL, The Ven Luke Thomas. b 75. Greyfriars Ox BA 97 MA 01 Leeds Univ MA 99. Coll of Resurr Mirfield 97. **d** 99 **p** 00. C Abertillery w Cwmtillery w Six Bells *Mon* 99–01; Chapl Coleg Gwent 99–01; Min Can St Woolos Cathl 01–03; Sub-Chapl HM Pris Cardiff 02–03; R Cranford *Lon* 03–08; V Pimlico St Gabr 08–13; Dir St Leonards Ch Ch and St Mary etc *Chich* 13–14; R 14–19; P-in-c Hastings St Clem and All SS 17–19; Adn Chich from 19. *The Palace, Canon Lane, Chichester PO19 1PY* T: (01273) 425799 M: 07775-526858 E: ltic75@hotmail.com *or* archchichester@chichester.anglican.org

IRVING, Alexander John Dolman. b 87. UEA BA 08 Lon Sch of Th BTh 13 MTh 14. Wycliffe Hall Ox 14. **d** 17 **p** 18. C Nor St Steph 17–20. *1 Aurania Avenue, Norwich NR1 2RD* M: 07788-413238 E: alex.irving3@gmail.com *or* curate@ststephensnorwich.org

IRVING, Canon Michael John Derek. b 43. LVO 07 DL 09. BEd 80. Qu Coll Birm 80. **d** 81 **p** 82. C Coleford w Staunton *Glouc* 81–84; V Dean Forest H Trin 84–91; RD Forest S 88–91; P-in-c Hempsted and Dir of Ords 91–96; R Minchinhampton 96–08; Hon Can Glouc Cathl 94–08; rtd 08; PtO *Glouc* from 17. *9 Canton Acre, Painswick, Stroud GL6 6QX* T: (01452) 814242 E: mi@vale-view.co.uk

IRVING, Paul John. b 74. Univ of Wales (Ban) BA 96 Bris Univ PGCE 97. Trin Coll Bris BA 10. **d** 10 **p** 11. C Galmington *B & W* 10–14; TV Redditch H Trin *Worc* 14–21; R Staplegrove w Norton Fitzwarren *B & W* from 21. *The Rectory, Staplegrove, Taunton TA2 6AP* E: revpaulirving@outlook.com

IRWIN, Canon Alan David. b 65. TCD BTh 09. CITC 07. **d** 09 **p** 10. C Ballymena w Ballyclug *Conn* 09–12; I Lack *Clogh* from 12; Can Clogh Cathl from 19. *The Rectory, Main Street, Lack, Enniskillen BT93 0DN* T: (028) 6863 1689 E: alan.irwin7@gmail.com

IRWIN, Andrew Trevor Ronald. QUB BEng TCD MTh. CITI. **d** 17 **p** 18. C Donaghcloney w Waringstown *D & D* 17–18; C Seapatrick from 18. *61 Burn Brae Court, Banbridge BT32 4GD* T: (028) 3884 1323 M: 07543-702570 E: irwinan@tcd.ie andrew@bchurch.co.uk *or* andrewtrirwin@gmail.com

IRWIN, John Henry. b 60. ACA 92 FCA 02. St Aug Coll of Th 17. **d** 19 **p** 20. NSM S Hackney St Mich w Haggerston St Paul *Lon* 19–21; PtO from 21; NSM Ipswich St Thos *St E* from 21. *8 Luther Road, Ipswich IP2 8BL* M: 07957-579680

IRWIN, Mrs Patricia Jane. b 49. CBDTI 02. **d** 05 **p** 06. NSM S Carl 05–10; rtd 10; PtO *Carl* from 11. *31 Blackwell Road, Carlisle CA2 4AB* T: (01228) 526885

IRWIN, Patrick Alexander. b 55. BNC Ox BA 77 MA 81 Edin Univ BD 81. Edin Th Coll 77 Liturgisches Inst Trier 79. **d** 81 **p** 82. Hon C Cambridge St Botolph *Ely* 81–84; Chapl BNC Ox 84–92; Lect Th 86–92; CF 92–99; Sen CF 99–10; Chapl Guards Chpl Lon 05–07; Dir of Ords 05–07; Chapl Udruga Hrvata Sv Dominik Gorazde 94–95; PtO *D & G* from 87; *Arm* from 96; *Guildf* 99–02; *Ripon* 00–14; *Leeds* 14–16; Hon V Choral Arm Cathl 02–07; PtO *Eur* 08–10 and 13–20; Chapl Bucharest w Sofia 10–13; Lect St Trivelius Inst Sofia Bulgaria 13–14; Chapl Ankara *Eur* 20–21. *Hedgebank, 8 Paganel Road, Minehead TA24 5ET* T: (01643) 703509 E: patalexirwin@yahoo.co.uk

IRWIN, Stewart. b 53. Sarum & Wells Th Coll 80. **d** 83 **p** 84. C Brighouse *Wakef* 83–87; V Stockton St Jo *Dur* 87–95; V Howden-le-Wear and Hunwick 95–13; rtd 13; PtO *Dur* from 13. *22 South View, Hunwick, Crook DL15 0JW* E: stewart_irwin@talktalk.net

IRWIN, Miss Susan Elizabeth. b 47. Cranmer Hall Dur 77. dss 79 **d** 87 **p** 94. Harborne St Faith and St Laur *Birm* 79–82; Caterham *S'wark* 82–88; Par Dn 87–88; Par Dn Kidlington w Hampton Poyle *Ox* 88–94; C 94–95; TV St Marlow w Marlow Bottom, Lt Marlow and Bisham 95–06; R Powick and Guarlford and Madresfield w Newland *Worc* 06–17; Chapl St Oswald's Hosp from 17; PtO *Eur* from 13. *The Chaplain's House, St Oswald's Hospital, Upper Tything, Worcester WR1 1HR* T: (01905) 29438 M: 07703-350301 E: revsueirwin@gmail.com

IRWIN, Canon William George. b 53. QUB BSc 77. CITC 80. **d** 80 **p** 81. C Lisburn St Paul *Conn* 80–83; C Seagoe *D & D* 83–85; C Newtownards w Movilla Abbey 85–88; I Ballymacash *Conn* 88–16; Preb Conn Cathl 04–16; Treas 12-16; Chan 16; rtd 16. *11 The Willows, Sion Mills, Strabane BT82 9FQ* E: wgirwin@btopenworld.com

IRWIN-CLARK, Peter Elliot. b 49. Univ Coll Lon LLB 71 Barrister 72. Cranmer Hall Dur BA 80. **d** 81 **p** 82. C Kirkheaton *Wakef* 81–86; V Shirley *Win* 86–96; PtO *Chich* 96–97; *S'wark* 97; V Prestonville St Luke *Chich* 97–03; Missr Warham Trust and Faith Development Officer (Basingstoke Adnry) *Win* 03–08; TR Broadwater *Chich* 08–15; rtd 15; PtO *Chich* from 15. *Desmond's Castle, London Road, Handcross, Haywards Heath RH17 6HA* T: (01444) 400307 E: picvic@btinternet.com

ISAAC, Canon David Thomas. b 43. Univ of Wales BA 65. Cuddesdon Coll 65. **d** 67 **p** 68. C Llandaff w Capel Llanilltern *Llan* 67–71; P-in-c Swansea St Jas *S & B* 71–73; Chapl Ch in Wales Youth Coun 73–77; V Llangiwg *S & B* 77–79; Dioc Youth Officer *Ripon* 79–83; Nat Officer for Youth Work Gen Syn Bd of Educn 83–90; Can Res Portsm Cathl 90–14; Dioc Dir of Educn 90–06; Hd Miss and Discipleship 06–14; Warden of Readers 11–14; rtd 14; PtO *Portsm* from 15; AD Is of Wight 16–17; AD Bishop's Waltham from 19. *The Rectory,*

Southwick Road, Wickham, Fareham PO17 6HR M: 07768-997220 E: dtisaac@btinternet.com

ISAAC, Mrs Patricia Jane. b 59. Leeds Univ BA 80 Univ Coll Lon MA 82. STETS 11. **d** 14 **p** 15. C Ryde All SS *Portsm* 14–17; C Swanmore St Mich 14–17; R Shedfield and Wickham from 17. *The Rectory, Southwick Road, Wickham, Fareham PO17 6HR* E: pjisaac@btinternet.com

ISAAC, Sydwell Nzaliseko. b 58. Man Univ BA 16. All SS Cen for Miss & Min 17. **d** 18. C Man Victoria Park 18–19; C Man St Ann from 19. *197 Old Hall Lane, Manchester M14 6HJ* T: 0161-498 0977 M: 07404-265463 E: sydwellisaac@yahoo.co.uk

ISAACS, James Alexander. b 84. Ex Univ BA 06. Oak Hill Th Coll BA 15. **d** 15 **p** 16. C Hailsham *Chich* 15–18; V Riseley w Bletsoe *St Alb* from 18. *The Vicarage, 16 Church Lane, Riseley, Bedford MK44 1ER* M: 07872-111354 E: jisaacs11@gmail.com

ISAACSON, Alan Timothy. b 55. York Univ BA 77 Sheff Univ PGCE 84 Leeds Univ MA 97. NOC 94. **d** 96 **p** 97. C Kimberworth *Sheff* 96–99; TV Brinsworth w Catcliffe and Treeton 99–03; TV Rivers Team 03–07; R Bradfield from 07; Dioc Discipleship Development Officer from 07; AD Ecclesfield 14–19. *The Rectory, High Bradfield, Bradfield, Sheffield S6 6LG* T: 0114-285 1225 E: alan.isaacson@sheffield.anglican.org

ISAACSON, Hilda Ruth. b 57. Leeds Univ BA 10. NOC 07. **d** 09 **p** 10. C Deepcar *Sheff* 09–13; P-in-c 13–18; P-in-c Bolsterstone 14–18; V Cornerstone from 18; Dioc Chapl MU from 21. *The Rectory, High Bradfield, Bradfield, Sheffield S6 6LG* T: 0114-285 1225 M: 07762-075687 E: hilda.isaacson@sheffield.anglican.org

ISABEL, Sister. *See* KEEGAN, Frances Ann

ISHERWOOD, Mrs Claire Virginia. b 54. Liv Univ BDS 76 K Alfred's Coll Win PGCE 92. **d** 10 **p** 11. OLM Camberley St Paul *Guildf* 10–21; Asst Adn Surrey from 20. *37 Watchetts Drive, Camberley GU15 2PQ* M: 07854-549154 E: claire.isherwood@stpaulscamb.co.uk

ISHERWOOD, Canon David Owen. b 46. BA 68 Lon Univ MA 95 MPhil 87. Ridley Hall Cam 76. **d** 78 **p** 79. C Sanderstead All SS *S'wark* 78–82; C Horley 82–84; TV 84–88; P-in-c Streatham Immanuel and St Andr 88–89; V 89–95; TR Clapham Team 95–01; V Clapham H Trin and St Pet 02–15; Hon Can S'wark Cathl 06–15; rtd 15; PtO *Portsm* from 16. *15 Streamleaze, Fareham PO14 4NP* E: davidowenisherwood@gmail.com

ISHERWOOD, Robin James. b 56. Hull Univ BA 78 Uppsala Univ MDiv 92. Ripon Coll Cuddesdon 92. **d** 94 **p** 95. C Bramhall *Ches* 94–98; V Alsager St Mary 98–14; Preacher Charterhouse and Dep Master 14–20; Hon Chapl ATC 99–10; PtO *B & W* from 20. *26 Keyford Gardens, Frome BA11 1JY* T: (01373) 474430 E: revslob@gmail.com

ISIORHO, David John Phillip. b 58. Liv Poly BA 80 Warwick Univ MA 93 Bradf Univ PhD 98. Westcott Ho Cam 87. **d** 90 **p** 91. C Nuneaton St Mary *Cov* 90–93; P-in-c Bradf St Oswald Chapel Green 93–96; P-in-c Brereton *Lich* 96–00; P-in-c Arthingworth, Harrington w Oxendon and E Farndon *Pet* 00–05; P-in-c Maidwell w Draughton, Lamport w Faxton 01–05; V Kempston Transfiguration *St Alb* 05–09; V Handsworth St Jas *Birm* 09–17; P-in-c Charlestown *Truro* from 17; P-in-c Par 17–21; P-in-c Tywardreath w Tregaminion 17–21; R Ashley and Mucklestone and Broughton and Croxton *Lich* from 21. *The Rectory, Charnes Road, Ashley, Market Drayton TF9 4LQ* T: (01630) 672939 E: david.isiorho@outlook.com

ISIORHO (née NORTHALL), Mrs Linda Barbara. b 50. Birm Univ BA 72 Birm City Univ MA 15 Worc Coll of Educn PGCE 75. Qu Coll Birm 88. **d** 90 **p** 94. C Wood End *Cov* 90–91; PtO 91–93; *Bradf* 93–94; NSM Low Moor St Mark 94–96; PtO *Lich* 96–97; NSM Alrewas 97–00; PtO *Pet* 01–05; *Birm* 10–17; *Truro* 17–21. *The Rectory, Charnes Road, Ashley, Market Drayton TF9 4LQ* T: (01630) 672939

ISKANDER, Mrs Susan Mary Mackay. b 64. Ox Univ BA 85 MBA 93. NTMTC 05. **d** 08 **p** 09. NSM Writtle w Highwood *Chelmsf* 08–12; PtO 12–13; P-in-c E Hanningfield 13–15; P-in-c Springfield All SS from 15. *The Rectory, 4 Old School Field, Springfield, Chelmsford CM1 7HU* M: 07710-646297 E: revsusaniskander@gmail.com

ISLE OF WIGHT, Archdeacon of. *See* LEONARD, The Ven Peter Philip

ISLINGTON, Suffragan Bishop of. *See* THORPE, The Rt Revd Richard Charles

ISON, Canon Andrew Phillip. b 60. Imp Coll Lon BEng 82 Penn Univ MSE 83 Univ Coll Lon PhD 87 CEng 92 MIChemE 92. Trin Coll Bris BA 01. **d** 01 **p** 02. C Cleethorpes *Linc* 01–05; V Bestwood Park w Rise Park *S'well* 05–07; Chapl Voorschoten *Eur* 07–12; V Gt and Lt Driffield *York* 12–16;

V Langtoft w Foxholes, Butterwick, Cottam etc 12–16; I Ballisodare w Collooney and Emlaghfad *T, K & A* from 16; Can Tuam Cathl from 18; Can Killala Cathl from 18. *The Rectory, Ballisodare, Co Sligo, Republic of Ireland* M: (00353) 71-913 3217 E: rev.andrew.ison@gmail.com

ISON, The Very Revd David John. b 54. Leic Univ BA 76 Nottm Univ BA 78 K Coll Lon PhD 85. St Jo Coll Nottm 76. d 79 p 80. C Deptford St Nic and St Luke *S'wark* 79–85; Lect CA Tr Coll Blackheath 85–88; V Potters Green *Cov* 88–93; Jt Dir SWMTC *Ex* 93–95; Dioc Officer for CME 93–05; Bp's Officer for NSMs 97–05; Can Res Ex Cathl 95–05; Chan 97–05; Dean Bradf 05–12; Dean St Paul's *Lon* from 12. *The Chapter House, St Paul's Churchyard, London EC4M 8AD* T: (020) 7246 8367 E: dean@stpaulscathedral.org.uk

ISON, Mrs Hilary Margaret. b 55. Leic Univ BA 76 E Lon Univ MA 02 Man Univ MA 09. Gilmore Course 77. d 87 p 94. NSM Deptford St Nic and St Luke *S'wark* 87–88; NSM Potters Green *Cov* 88–90; C Rugby 90–93; Chapl Ex Hospiscare 93–00; C Ex St Mark, St Sidwell and St Matt 99–05; Bp's Adv for Women in Min 02–05; Area Tutor SWMTC 03–05; PV Ex Cathl 04–05; Tutor Coll of Resurr Mirfield 05–08; Selection Sec Min Division 08–17; Hon C Calverley Deanery Bradf 06–12; PtO *Lon* from 14. *The Deanery, 9 Amen Court, London EC4M 7BU* E: hilary@isons.org.uk

ISON-STIERER, Susan Jane. *See* OSMOND, Susan Jane

ISSBERNER, Norman Gunther Erich. b 34. Fitzw Ho Cam BA 58 MA 61. Clifton Th Coll 57. d 59 p 60. C Croydon Ch Ch Broad Green *Cant* 59–61; C Surbiton Hill Ch Ch *S'wark* 61–66; V Egham *Guildf* 66–75; V Wallington *S'wark* 75–86; UK Chmn Africa Inland Miss from 77; Adv on Miss and Evang *Chelmsf* 86–91; P-in-c Castle Hedingham 91–93; V Clacton St Paul 93–99; RD St Osyth 94–99; rtd 99; PtO *Chelmsf* from 99. *14 Darcy Close, Frinton-on-Sea CO13 0RR* T: (01255) 673548 E: nissb@talktalk.net

ISTED, Elisabeth. b 66. Bris Univ BA 87 PhD 94. Ripon Coll Cuddesdon 16. d 18 p 19. C Yeovil St Mich *B & W* 18–21; P-in-c Castle Cary and Ansford from 21. *The Vicarage, Church Street, Castle Cary BA7 7EJ* M: 07890-464201 E: revd.elisabeth.isted@gmail.com

ITALY AND MALTA, Archdeacon of. *See* WALLER, The Ven David James

ITUMU, John Murithi. b 65. Lon Sch of Th BA 04 Heythrop Coll Lon MA 10. Lon Bible Coll 01. d 02 p 03. C Cricklewood St Gabr and St Mich *Lon* 02–07; C Herne Hill *S'wark* 07–10; P-in-c Glouc St Cath 10–12; V 12–18; V St Helier *S'wark* 18–20; R Woodmansterne from 20. *The Rectory, Woodmansterne Street, Banstead SM7 3NL* T: (01737) 423892 M: 07946-000364 E: rector@saintpeterschurch.org.uk

IVE, Jeremy George Augustus. b 57. Rhodes Univ BA 81 Ch Coll Cam PhD 86 K Coll Lon MPhil 95 PhD 12. Wycliffe Hall Ox 89. d 91 p 92. NSM Ivybridge w Harford *Ex* 91–95; P-in-c Abbotskerswell 95–99; P-in-c Tudeley cum Capel w Five Oak Green *Roch* 99–13; V 12–19; V Capel United Ben from 19; Dioc Lay Min Adv 99–01. *The Vicarage, Sychem Lane, Five Oak Green, Tonbridge TN12 6TL* T/F: (01892) 836653 E: jeremy@tudeley.org

IVE (née KNOTT), Canon Pamela Frances. b 58. Bedf Coll of Educn BEd 79. Wycliffe Hall Ox 88. d 90. Par Dn Ivybridge w Harford *Ex* 90–95; Par Dn Abbotskerswell 95–99; Par Dn Capel United Ben *Roch* from 99; Dioc Dir of Ords from 17; Hon Can Roch Cathl from 18. *The Vicarage, Sychem Lane, Five Oak Green, Tonbridge TN12 6TL* T: (01892) 836653 E: pamela.ive@rochester.anglican.org

IVES-SMITH, Mrs Susan Margaret. d 15 p 16. C Tideswell *Derby* 15–18; P-in-c Newbold de Verdun, Barlestone and Kirkby Mallory *Leic* 18–21; P-in-c Peckleton 18–21. *Address temp unknown* E: sueivessmith@live.co.uk

IVESON, Robert George. b 70. Oak Hill Th Coll BA 01. d 01 p 02. C Cheadle All Hallows *Ches* 01–04; C-in-c Cheadle Hulme Em CD 04–14; R Davenham from 14. *4 Waystead Close, Northwich CW9 8NN* T: (01606) 42450 E: rob.iveson@btinternet.com

IVESON, Canon Ronald Edward. b 68. Ches Coll of HE RMN 92. Aston Tr Scheme 95 Oak Hill Th Coll BA 00. d 00 p 01. C Lache cum Saltney *Ches* 00–03; V Bidston 03–21; RD Birkenhead 16–20; V Norley, Crowton and Kingsley from 21; P-in-c Alvanley from 21; Hon Can Ches Cathl from 18. *St John's House, Pike Lane, Kingsley, Frodsham WA6 8EH* E: roniveson@hotmail.com

IVISON, Norman William. b 54. Hull Univ BA 75 DipEd 76 Dur Univ MA(Theol) 12. Trin Coll Bris. d 82 p 83. C Barrow St Mark *Carl* 82–85; Ecum Liaison Officer BBC Radio Furness 82–85; Chapl Barrow Sixth Form Coll 83–85; Dioc Broadcasting Officer *Lich* 85–91; Relig Progr Producer BBC Radio Stoke 85–91; Hon C Bucknall and Bagnall *Lich* 85–91; Asst Producer Relig Progr BBC TV Man 91–93; Producer Relig and Ethics BBC TV Man 93–05; Dir Tr and Events Fresh Expressions 05–08; Dir Communications and Resources 08–15; Dir BowlandMedia 15–18; PtO *Blackb* from 98. *3 Claremont Drive, Clitheroe BB7 1JW* M: 07885-866317 E: norman.ivison@btinternet.com

IVORSON, David. b 51. Mansf Coll Ox MA 73 York Univ BPhil 75 ACA 80. SEITE 05. d 08 p 09. NSM E Grinstead St Swithun *Chich* 08–11; Chapl Whittington Coll Felbridge from 11; PtO *Chich* from 15. *Woodhurst, Portland Road, East Grinstead RH19 4DZ* T: (01342) 316451 M: 07741-491252 E: davidivorson@gmail.com

IVORY, Canon Christopher James. b 54. Reading Univ BSc 76. Qu Coll Birm. d 81 p 82. C Waltham Cross *St Alb* 81–84; C Is of Dogs Ch Ch and St Jo w St Luke *Lon* 84–88; V Streatham Ch Ch *S'wark* 88–03; Lambeth Adnry Ecum Officer 90–95; RD Streatham 00–03; R King's Lynn St Marg w St Nic *Nor* 03–17; TR 17–20; RD Lynn 08–13; Hon Can Nor Cathl 08–20; rtd 20; PtO *Ely* from 21. *Dilland House, 8A Cross Lane Close, Orwell, Royston SG8 5QW* T: (01223) 208602 E: c.j.i@btinternet.com

IZOD, Mrs Wendy Janet. b 47. Sheff Univ BA(Econ) 68. SEITE 98. d 01 p 02. NSM Hever, Four Elms and Mark Beech *Roch* 01–16; P-in-c 16–19; Chapl ATC 01–19; rtd 19. *West Lodge, Stick Hill, Edenbridge TN8 5NJ* T: (01342) 850738 M: 07703-107496 E: izodiham@gmail.com

IZZARD, David Antony. b 55. Trin Coll Bris 92. d 94 p 95. C E Bris 94–98; V Sea Mills 98–16; R Radstock w Writhlington *B & W* 16–21; R Kilmersdon w Babington 16–21. *Address temp unknown* E: david.izzard@btinternet.com

IZZARD (formerly WOODGATE), Elizabeth Mary. b 66. W Sussex Inst of HE BEd 87. St Jo Coll Nottm MTh 02. d 02 p 04. C Crofton *Portsm* 02–03; C Lee-on-the-Solent 03–05; C Rowner and Bridgemary 05–07; NSM Kuwait 07–10; PtO *Portsm* 11–15; V Ringmer *Chich* 15–20; rtd 21. *6 Chestnut Close, Hailsham BN27 3AF*

IZZARD, Canon Susannah Amanda. b 59. Hatf Poly BA 82 Birm Univ MEd 93 Wolv Univ PGCE 92. Trin Coll Bris BA 86. dss 86 d 87 p 01. Birm St Martin w Bordesley St Andr 86–89; Par Dn 87–89; C Handsworth St Jas 89–91; Asst Chapl Qu Eliz Hosp Birm 90–91; Lect Birm Univ 93–02; NSM Selly Oak St Mary 01–12; PtO 12–17; Bp's Adv for Pastoral Care 07–16; Hon Can Birm Cathl 16; PtO *St E* from 17; Bp's Adv for Past Care of Clergy 17–19. *Corner House, Mill Lane, Barnby, Beccles NR34 7PX* M: 07702-571760 E: susannah.izzard@cofesuffolk.org

J

JABLONSKI, Andrew Philip. b 54. St Jo Coll Cam MA 76 Nottm Univ MBA 90 Anglia Ruskin Univ MA 10 CEng 90 FIMechE 02. Ridley Hall Cam 07. d 09 p 10. NSM Grantham, Harrowby w Londonthorpe *Linc* 09–12; C Bromley SS Pet and Paul *Roch* 12–18; P-in-c Mudeford *Win* 18–21; rtd 21. *7 Chewton Way, Walkford, Christchurch BH23 5LS* M: 07736-649401 E: andrewjab@gmail.com

JABLONSKI, Mrs Anne Judith. b 54. Girton Coll Cam BA 76 MA 79. Ridley Hall Cam 07. d 09 p 10. C Grantham St Wulfram *Linc* 09–12; V Bromley SS Pet and Paul *Roch* 12–18; NSM Mudeford *Win* 18–21; rtd 21. *7 Chewton Way, Walkford, Christchurch BH23 5LS* M: 07759-661836 E: annejab1@virginmedia.com

JACK, Fiona Mary. b 57. Ox Univ MA 77. Sarum Coll 17. d 20 p 21. C Ealing St Barn *Lon* from 20. *10 Harrow View Road, London W5 1LZ* T: (020) 8998 8985 M: 07780-704720 E: fjack@greenlightresearch.com

JACK, Judith Ann. *See* JEFFERY, Judith Ann

JACK, Philip Andrew. b 76. Nottm Univ BA 98. Oak Hill Th Coll BA 08. **d** 08 **p** 09. C Ox St Ebbe w H Trin and St Pet 08–12; NSM 12–13; Chapl Canford Sch from 13. *Canford School, Canford Magna, Wimborne BH21 3AD* T: (01202) 841254   M: 07972-078148   E: phil.a.jack@gmail.com   *or* paj@canford.com

JACKLIN, John Frederick. b 30. Oak Hill Th Coll 72. **d** 72 **p** 72. Chile 72–75; C Roxeth Ch Ch *Lon* 75–78; V Selston *S'well* 78–95; rtd 95; PtO *Derby* 97–18. *5 Rose Avenue, Borrowash, Derby DE72 3GA* T: (01332) 669670

JACKMAN, Aaron Anthony. b 83. Leeds Univ BA 04 MMus 06. Westcott Ho Cam 14. **d** 17 **p** 18. C Saddleworth *Man* from 17. *The Vicarage, Woods Lane, Dobcross, Oldham OL3 5AN* M: 07717-893466 E: aaronjackman@cofeinsaddleworth.org.uk

JACKS, David. Nottm Univ BTh 87 Birm Univ MA 95 PhD 08. Linc Th Coll 84. **d** 87 **p** 88. C Oakham, Hambleton, Egleton, Braunston and Brooke *Pet* 87–90; V Weedon Bec w Everdon 90–96; V Weedon Bec w Everdon and Dodford 96–01; V Llandrillo-yn-Rhos *St As* 01–16; AD Llanrwst and Rhos 14–15; V Ashton Ch Ch *Man* from 16. *Christ Church Vicarage, Vicarage Road, Ashton-under-Lyne OL7 9QY* T: 0161-330 1601   M: 07974-937517 E: david.jacks@live.co.uk

JACKSON, Alan. b 44. Newc Univ BA 67 DipEd 68 MEd 79. NEOC 79. **d** 81 **p** 82. NSM Jesmond H Trin *Newc* 81–82; Chapl Bp Wand Sch Sunbury-on-Thames 82–89; V Hanworth St Rich *Lon* 89–10; rtd 10; PtO *Lon* from 11. *7 Uxbridge Road, Feltham TW13 5EG* T: (020) 8898 3093 E: alan44nov@gmail.com

JACKSON, Alison. b 58. St Mellitus Coll. **d** 14 **p** 15. NSM Rye Park St Cuth *St Alb* 14–17; Fresh Expressions Development Officer from 18. *95 New Road, Ware SG12 7BY* T: (01727) 818113 E: ajackson@stalbans.anglican.org

JACKSON, Barry James. b 65. Sheff Univ BEng 87. St Jo Coll Nottm MTh 09. **d** 07 **p** 08. C Leamington Priors St Mary *Cov* 07–10; P-in-c Kineton 10–14; P-in-c Combroke w Compton Verney 10–14; P-in-c Warmington w Shotteswell and Radway w Ratley 10–14; R Edgehill Churches from 14. *The Vicarage, Warwick Road, Kineton, Warwick CV35 0HW* T: (01926) 640248 E: revbarryjackson@btinternet.com

JACKSON, The Very Revd Brandon Donald. b 34. Liv Univ LLB 56 Bradf Univ Hon DLitt 90. Wycliffe Hall Ox. **d** 58 **p** 59. C New Malden and Coombe *S'wark* 58–61; C Leeds St Geo *Ripon* 61–65; V Shipley St Pet *Bradf* 65–77; Relig Adv Yorkshire TV 69–79; Provost Bradf 77–89; Dean Linc 89–97; rtd 97; PtO *Ripon* 98–14; *Leeds* 14–16. *1 Kingston Way, Market Harborough LE16 7XB* T: (01858) 462425 E: brandon.j1@btinternet.com

JACKSON, Mrs Brenda Joan. b 51. All SS Cen for Miss & Min 18. **d** 19 **p** 20. NSM Bakewell, Ashford w Sheldon and Rowsley *Derby* from 19. *27 Castle Mount Crescent, Bakewell DE45 1AT* T: (01332) 554820 *or* (01629) 813143   M: 07805-949918 E: rev.brendajackson@gmail.com

JACKSON, Catherine Louise. b 79. Dur Univ BA 02 Bris Univ MSW 07. Sarum Coll 18. **d** 20 **p** 21. C Broughton Gifford, Gt Chalfield and Holt *Sarum* from 20. *Address withheld by request* E: katiejacks139@gmail.com

JACKSON, Charlotte Lucy. b 88. St Andr Univ MA 10 Middx Univ MA 14 Cam Univ BTh 18. Ridley Hall Cam 16. **d** 19 **p** 20. C Willenhall *Cov* from 19. *St James's Church Vicarage, Abbey Road, Coventry CV3 4BG* T: (024) 7630 3266   M: 07591-474231 E: revcharlottejackson@gmail.com

JACKSON, Christopher John Wilson. b 45. St Pet Coll Ox BA 67 MA 85. Ridley Hall Cam 69. **d** 72 **p** 73. C Putney St Marg *S'wark* 72–76; C Battersea St Pet and St Paul 76–79; TV Preston St Jo *Blackb* 79–87; P-in-c Sandal St Cath *Wakef* 87–90; V Shenley Green *Birm* 90–01; AD Kings Norton 95–99; P-in-c Chesterfield H Trin and Ch Ch *Derby* 01–10; R 10; rtd 10; PtO *Blackb* from 10. *5 Beech Grove, Ashton-on-Ribble, Preston PR2 1DX* T: (01772) 721772 E: chrisaliz76@virginmedia.com

JACKSON, Miss Cynthia. b 42. Open Univ BA 07. S'wark Ord Course 93. **d** 96 **p** 97. NSM Wimbledon *S'wark* 96–12; PtO from 12. *39 Panmuir Road, London SW20 0PZ* T: (020) 8947 5940 E: cyn@cynthiaja.plus.com

JACKSON, David. b 48. Open Univ BA 85. St Deiniol's Hawarden 91. **d** 91 **p** 92. C Scotforth *Blackb* 91–95; Chapl Ox Radcliffe Hosps NHS Trust 95–00; C Banbury *Ox* 95–96; TV 96–98; V Banbury St Hugh 98–07; V Banbury St Fran 07–12; rtd 12; PtO *Eur* from 12. *16 rue Soeur Marie Antoinette, 50720 Barenton, France* E: davyjax.dj@gmail.com

JACKSON, David Reginald Estcourt. b 25. OBE. Qu Coll Cam BA 45 MA 49. Cranmer Hall Dur 80. **d** 81 **p** 82. Hon C Douglas *Blackb* 81–82; C 82–87; rtd 90. *64 The Common, Parbold, Wigan WN8 7EA* T: (01257) 462671

JACKSON, David Robert. b 51. Lon Univ BDS. Linc Th Coll 81. **d** 83 **p** 84. C Hatcham St Cath *S'wark* 83–87; V Sydenham St Bart 87–93; PtO *Lon* 03–05 and 11–16; C St Martin-in-the-Fields 05–11; PtO *Ox* from 16. *Hunter's Rest, 1 Field Court, Duns Tew, Bicester OX25 6LD* M: 07973-657260 E: djsaab@aol.com

JACKSON, Canon Derek Reginald. b 49. K Coll Lon BD 72 AKC 72. **d** 73 **p** 74. C Westhoughton *Man* 73–75; C Kendal H Trin *Carl* 75–78; V Pennington w Lindal and Marton 78–83; Warden of Readers 82–92; V Kendal St Geo 83–94; Hon Can Carl Cathl 89–00; V Applethwaite 94–96; P-in-c Troutbeck 94–96; V Windermere St Mary and Troutbeck 96–00; RD Windermere 98–00; Can Res Bradf Cathl 00–03; P-in-c Bingley All SS 03–10; RD Airedale 05–10; rtd 10; PtO *Carl* from 11. *3 Ellas Orchard, Green Lane, Flookburgh, Grange-over-Sands LA11 7JT* T: (015395) 59086 E: derekjackson2901@hotmail.com

JACKSON, Duncan. b 57. Sussex Univ BSc 78 Essex Univ PhD 84 Glos Univ BA 02. **d** 20 **p** 20. NSM Egremont and Haile *Carl* from 20. *Horse & Groom House, Market Place, Egremont CA22 2AE* T: (01946) 823643   M: 07872-160350 E: duncanjackson62@outlook.com

JACKSON, Mrs Elizabeth Mary. b 41. Man Univ BA 67 Leeds Univ MA 01 York St Jo Univ BEd. Ox Min Course 90. **d** 92 **p** 94. Chapl Reading Hosps 86–95; NSM Reading St Mary the Virgin *Ox* 92–94; Chapl R Berks and Battle Hosps NHS Trust 95–02; NSM Reading Deanery *Ox* 02–07; PtO *Carl* 08–20. *10 Deer Orchard Close, Cockermouth CA13 9JH* E: mjack2bl@aol.com

JACKSON, The Ven Frances Anne (Peggy). b 51. Somerville Coll Ox BA 72 MA 76 ACA 76 FCA 81. Ripon Coll Cuddesdon 85. **d** 87 **p** 94. C Ilkeston St Mary *Derby* 87–90; TM Hemel Hempstead *St Alb* 90–94; TV 94–98; TR Mortlake w E Sheen *S'wark* 98–09; RD Richmond and Barnes 00–05; Hon Can S'wark Cathl 03–09; Dean of Women's Min 04–09; Adn Llan from 09; P-in-c Penmark w Llancarfan w Llantrithyd 09–14; P-in-c St Fagans and Michaelston-super-Ely 14–20. *59 Station Road, Llandaff North, Cardiff CF14 2FB* T: (029) 2056 9179   M: 07770-375480 E: archdeacon.llandaff@churchinwales.org.uk

JACKSON, Miss Freda. b 41. BEM 17. Bp Otter Coll TCert 61. **d** 92 **p** 94. OLM Middleton *Man* 92–94; OLM Middleton and Thornham 94–12; rtd 12; PtO *Man* from 12. *17 Craiglands, Rochdale OL16 4RA* T: (01706) 523520   M: 07974-971683

JACKSON, Ms Gillian Rosemary. b 52. Newc Univ BA 75 PGCE 76 Aber Univ MLitt 80 Nottm Univ MA 04 AFBPsS. EMMTC 01. **d** 04 **p** 05. NSM Bosworth and Sheepy Gp *Leic* 04–08; Dioc Dir Soc Resp 04–08; Bp's Exec Asst 08–10; PtO *S & B* from 17. *3 Oxford Villas, Oxford Road, Hay-on-Wye, Hereford HR3 5BW*

JACKSON, Hannah Louise. *See* HALL, Hannah Louise

JACKSON, Ian. b 53. Jes Coll Ox BA 75. Linc Th Coll 76. **d** 78 **p** 79. C Holbeach *Linc* 78–82; V Newsome *Wakef* 82–85; V Newsome and Armitage Bridge 85–03; TR Em TM 03–04; P-in-c Corfe Castle, Church Knowle, Kimmeridge etc *Sarum* 04–11; R 14–18; R St Aldhelm from 18. *The Rectory, East Street, Corfe Castle, Wareham BH20 5EE* T: (01929) 480257 E: rectorsabpurbeck@gmail.com

JACKSON, Mrs Isobel Margaret. b 69. Uganda Chr Univ BD 04. **d** 04. CMS Uganda 04–05; C Lismore w Cappoquin, Kilwatermoy, Dungarvan etc *C, F & O* 05–10; I Templebreedy w Tracton and Nohoval *C, C & R* from 10. *Templebreedy Rectory, Church Road, Crosshaven, Co Cork, Republic of Ireland* T: (00353) (21) 483 1236   M: 87-743 5424 E: isobel@nijackson.com

JACKSON, Mrs Janet Lesley. b 45. BEM 19. CQSW 78. NEOC 93. **d** 96 **p** 97. NSM Whorlton *Newc* 96–98; Chapl St Oswald's Hospice Newc 98–07; Bereavement Services Co-ord Tynedale Hospice 10–12; Chapl from 12; PtO *Newc* from 10. *1 St Andrews Road, Hexham NE46 2EY* T: (01434) 602929 E: revjan307@btinternet.com

JACKSON, Mrs Joan. b 44. Bolton Coll of Educn CertEd 71 Lanc Univ MA 98. CBDTI 95. **d** 98 **p** 99. NSM Staveley, Ings and Kentmere *Carl* 98–00; Chapl Furness Hosps NHS Trust 98–00; Asst Chapl Bradf Hosps NHS Trust 00–04; NSM Bingley H Trin *Bradf* 03–07; PtO 07–10; *Carl* from 11. *3 Ellas Orchard, Green Lane, Flookburgh, Grange-over-Sands LA11 7JT* T: (015395) 59086 E: jjacksonddp@yahoo.co.uk

JACKSON (née MINTER), Mrs Julie Louise. b 82. Ripon Coll Cuddesdon 15. **d** 18 **p** 19. C Cowplain *Portsm* from 18. *24 Wincanton Way, Waterlooville PO7 8NW* M: 07732-699448   E: julie@stwilfridscowplain.co.uk   *or* juliejackson3732@gmail.com

JACKSON, Miss Kathryn Dianne. b 64. Leeds Univ BA 87 MA 01. St Steph Ho Ox 87. **d** 90 **p** 94. Par Dn Headingley *Ripon* 90–94; C Hawksworth Wood 94–00; P-in-c Scarborough

St Columba *York* 00–14; Chapl St Cath Hospice Scarborough 00–14; R Haxby and Wigginton *York* from 14. *The Rectory, 5 Back Lane, Wigginton, York YO32 2ZH* T: (01904) 765155 E: rectorkathryn@btinternet.com

JACKSON, Laura Marina. b 66. Qu Foundn Birm 17. **d** 19 **p** 20. C Broughton Astley and Croft w Stoney Stanton *Leic* from 19.

JACKSON, Lisa Helen. *See* BARNETT, Lisa Helen

JACKSON, Miss Lynne Margaret. b 74. St Mellitus Coll 16. **d** 19 **p** 20. C Rainhill *Liv* 19–21; TV Sutton from 21. *26 Calder Drive, Rainhill, Prescot L35 0NW* M: 07444-793958 E: lynn-ej@hotmail.com

JACKSON, Malcolm. b 58. NEOC 01. **d** 04 **p** 05. C Guisborough *York* 04–08; V Kirkleatham 08–14; C Whitby w Ruswarp 14–18; P-in-c Hinderwell, Roxby and Staithes etc 18; R from 18. *27 Runswick Lane, Hinderwell, Saltburn-by-the-Sea TS13 5HP* E: maljackoagain@gmail.com

JACKSON, Mrs Margaret Elizabeth. b 47. Lon Univ BSc 68 MSc 95 Univ of Wales (Lamp) MTh 05 FCIPD 91. S'wark Ord Course 80. **dss** 83 **d** 92 **p** 94. Surbiton Hill Ch Ch *S'wark* 83–84; Saffron Walden w Wendens Ambo and Littlebury *Chelmsf* 84–85; Dulwich St Barn *S'wark* 86–97; Hon C 92–97; Personal Asst to Bp *S'wark* 92–94; Selection Sec Min Division 96–00 and from 03; NSM Churt *Guildf* 98–00; NSM The Bourne and Tilford 00–10; NSM Churt and Hindhead 10–14; Convenor STETS 00–02; Dioc Dir of Ords *S'wark* 05–06; Dir of Ords Kingston Area 10–11; PtO *Guildf* from 14. *62 Wheelwrights Lane, Grayshott, Hindhead GU26 6EB* T: (01428) 606074 E: revjackson@btinternet.com

JACKSON, Margaret Jane. b 50. RGN 72 RHV 74. S'wark Ord Course 89. **d** 92 **p** 94. Par Dn Hatcham St Cath *S'wark* 92–94; C 94–98; V Mottingham St Edw 98–17; rtd 17; Hon C Dunster, Carhampton, Withycombe w Rodhuish etc *B & W* from 17. *5 Winsors Lane, Carhampton, Minehead TA24 6NJ* T: (01643) 822501 E: rev.mjackson@gmail.com

JACKSON, Mark Benjamin. b 77. Dur Univ BSc 00. Wycliffe Hall Ox BTh 13. **d** 13 **p** 14. C Langham Place All So *Lon* from 13; C Clerkenwell St Jas and St Jo w St Pet from 18. *4 Owen's Row, London EC1V 4NP* T: (020) 7251 1190 E: mark@inspirelondon.org

JACKSON, Mark Harding. b 51. Open Univ BA 87. Sarum & Wells Th Coll 76. **d** 79 **p** 80. C Hobs Moat *Birm* 79–83; Chapl RN 83–15; PtO *Eur* from 17. *Bush House, 12 Palmer Street, South Petherton TA13 5DB* T: (01460) 242171 M: 07960-733472 E: maundycottage@talktalk.net

JACKSON, Martin. b 56. Clare Coll Cam BA 77 MA 81 St Jo Coll Dur BA 80 MA 97. Cranmer Hall Dur. **d** 81 **p** 82. C Houghton le Spring *Dur* 81–84; C Bishopwearmouth St Mich w St Hilda 84–86; TV Winlaton 86; V High Spen and Rowlands Gill 86–94; P-in-c Benfieldside 94–97; V from 97; P-in-c Castleside from 11; AD Lanchester 00–06. *St Cuthbert's Vicarage, Church Bank, Consett DH8 0NW* T: (01207) 503019 E: martin.jackson@durham.anglican.org

JACKSON, Matthew Christopher. b 75. Univ of Wales (Abth) BD 96 MTh 98. Ripon Coll Cuddesdon. **d** 01 **p** 02. C King's Lynn St Marg w St Nic *Nor* 01–05; V Pembury *Roch* 05–10; R Attleborough w Besthorpe *Nor* from 10; RD Thetford and Rockland 11–21. *The Rectory, Surrogate Street, Attleborough NR17 2AW* T: (01953) 453185 E: therectory@me.com

JACKSON, Mrs Melanie Jane Susann. b 60. UWE BA 83 Leic Univ MA 94. SWMTC 97. **d** 00 **p** 01. C Ottery St Mary, Alfington, W Hill, Tipton etc *Ex* 00–04; PtO 04–08; NSM Linc St Jo 08–14; Chapl Bp Grosseteste Univ from 15; PtO *Linc* 15–18. *Chaplaincy Office, Bishop Grosseteste University, Longdales Road, Lincoln LN1 3DY* E: melanie.jackson@bishopg.ac.uk

✠**JACKSON, The Most Revd Michael Geoffrey St Aubyn.** b 56. TCD BA 79 MA 82 St Jo Coll Cam BA 81 MA 85 PhD 86 Ch Ch Ox MA 89 DPhil 89. CITC 86. **d** 86 **p** 87 **c** 02. C Dublin Zion Ch *D & G* 86–89; Chapl Ch Ch Ox 89–97; Student 93–97; Dean Cork *C, C & R* 97–02; I Cork St Fin Barre's Union 97–02; Chapl and Asst Lect Univ Coll Cork 98–02; Chapl Cork Inst of Tech 98–02; Bp Clogh 02–11; Abp Dublin *D & G* from 11. *The See House, 17 Temple Road, Dartry, Dublin 6, Republic of Ireland* T: (00353) (1) 497 7849 F: 497 6355 E: archbishop@dublin.anglican.org

JACKSON, Michael Ian. b 51. Southn Univ BA 73. STETS 00. **d** 03 **p** 04. Dir St Jo Win Charity 87–13; NSM Twyford and Owslebury and Morestead etc *Win* 03–13; V Kirkby-in-Malhamdale *Leeds* 13–16; rtd 16; PtO *Win* from 17; *Chich* from 21. *Yew Tree Cottage, Kirdford, Billingshurst RH14 0LT* T: (01403) 820963 E: michaelianjackson222@gmail.com

JACKSON, Canon Michael James. b 44. Liv Univ BEng 65 Newc Univ PhD 84 CEng 69 MICE 69. NEOC 82. **d** 84 **p** 85. C Houghton le Spring *Dur* 84–87; V Millfield St Mark 87–95;

V Ponteland *Newc* 95–07; AD Newc W 03–07; Hon Can Newc Cathl 06–07; rtd 07; PtO *Newc* from 07. *1 St Andrews Road, Hexham NE46 2EY* T: (01434) 602929

JACKSON, Nicholas David. b 54. Wadh Coll Ox MA 75 Bris Univ PhD 96. Wycliffe Hall Ox 06. **d** 08 **p** 09. C Branksome Park All SS *Sarum* 08–12; V Southlake *Ox* 12–17; rtd 17; PtO *Win* from 17. *77 Carbery Avenue, Bournemouth BH6 3LW* T: (01202) 388140 E: rev.nickj@gmail.com

JACKSON, Patricia Ann. b 56. **d** 16 **p** 17. NSM Mow Cop *Lich* from 16. *65 Hollington Drive, Stoke-on-Trent ST6 6TZ* T: (01782) 790376 E: patjackson@mypostoffice.co.uk

JACKSON, Paul Andrew. b 65. NEOC 05. **d** 08 **p** 09. NSM Haxby and Wigginton *York* 08–16; V Middle Esk Moor 16–21. *Address temporarily unknown* E: pjacko99@aol.com

JACKSON, Peggy. *See* JACKSON, Frances Anne

JACKSON, Peter. b 88. Dur Univ BSc 09 Sheff Univ BA 20. Coll of Resurr Mirfield 18. **d** 21. C Torre and Torquay St Jo *Ex* from 21; C Torquay St Luke from 21. *28 Barewell Road, Torquay TQ1 4PA* M: 07419-166180 E: pedro88j@aol.com

JACKSON, Peter Jonathan Edward. b 53. St Pet Coll Ox BA 74 MA 78 PGCE 78. St Steph Ho Ox 79. **d** 79 **p** 80. Lect Westmr Coll Ox 79–80; Hon C Ox St Mich w St Martin and All SS 79–80; C Malvern Link w Cowleigh *Worc* 79–82; Chapl Aldenham Sch Herts 82–89; Chapl and Hd RE Harrow Sch 89–01; Lect K Coll Lon 92–99; Dir Chr Educn and Assoc R Washington St Patr USA 01–03; V Southgate Ch Ch *Lon* 03–14; Chapl Nice w Vence *Eur* from 14. *Holy Trinity, 11 rue de la Buffa, 06000 Nice, France* T: (0033) 4 93 87 19 83 M: 7 83 28 39 53 E: peterjejackson@aol.com

JACKSON, Philip Michael. b 74. Chelt & Glouc Coll of HE BA 95 Brunel Univ PGCE 97. Trin Coll Bris BA 05. **d** 06 **p** 07. C W Kilburn St Luke w St Simon and St Jude *Lon* 06–09; C Reigate St Mary *S'wark* 09–13; P-in-c Chipstead 13–14; R 14–17; Chapl Reigate Gr Sch from 17; PtO *S'wark* from 17. *Reigate Grammar School, Reigate Road, Reigate RH2 0QS* T: (01737) 222231 M: 07545-054022 E: phil.jackson74@gmail.com

JACKSON (née PRICE), Mrs Rachel Anne. b 57. **d** 03 **p** 04. OLM Barnham Broom and Upper Yare *Nor* 03–18; PtO from 18. *Red Hall, Red Hall Lane, Southburgh, Thetford IP25 7TG* T: (01362) 821032 E: revrachel@edwardjacksonltd.com

✠**JACKSON, The Rt Revd Richard Charles.** b 61. Ch Ch Ox BA 83 Cranfield Inst of Tech MSc 85. Trin Coll Bris 92. **d** 94 **p** 95 **c** 14. C Lindfield *Chich* 94–98; V Rudgwick 98–09; RD Horsham 05–09; Dioc Adv for Miss and Renewal 09–14; Area Bp Lewes 14–20; Bp Heref from 20. *The Bishop's House, The Palace, Hereford HR4 9BN* E: bishop.hereford@hereford.anglican.org

JACKSON, Richard Hugh. b 44. St Jo Coll York CertEd 66 UEA MA 84. **d** 98 **p** 99. OLM Stalham and E Ruston w Brunstead *Nor* 98–00; OLM Stalham, E Ruston, Brunstead, Sutton and Ingham 00–14; PtO from 14. *The Croft, Camping Field Lane, Stalham, Norwich NR12 9DT* T: (01692) 581389 E: richard.jackson@intamail.com

JACKSON, Robert. b 69. Nottm Univ BA 01. St Jo Coll Nottm 98. **d** 01 **p** 02. C Altham w Clayton le Moors *Blackb* 01–03; C Blackb St Gabr 03–05; TV Westhoughton and Wingates *Man* 05–10; TV Cartmel Peninsula *Carl* 10–15; P-in-c Whitehaven from 15; Lay Development Co-ord from 10. *Autumn Garth, Harras Road, Harras Moor, Whitehaven CA28 6SG* M: 07863-377777 E: revrobjackson@live.co.uk

JACKSON, Robert Brandon. b 61. Lancaster Poly Cov BA 86 Ox Univ BA 88 MA 95. Wycliffe Hall Ox 86. **d** 89 **p** 90. C Bromley Common St Aug *Roch* 89–92; P-in-c Stowe *Ox* 92–97; Asst Chapl Stowe Sch 92–97; Chapl 02–11; Chapl Lord Wandsworth Coll Hook 97–02; PtO *Ox* 11–18; Chapl RNR 16–21; PtO *Glas* from 21. *Woodside, Feorlin Way, Garelochhead, Helensburgh G84 0DF* E: hittiterev@msn.com

JACKSON, Robert Fielden. b 35. St D Coll Lamp BA 57. Sarum Th Coll 57. **d** 59 **p** 60. C Altham w Clayton le Moors *Blackb* 59–62; C Lytham St Cuth 62–64; V Skerton St Chad 64–69; V Preesall 69–90; RD Garstang 85–89; V Wray w Tatham and Tatham Fells 90–00; rtd 00; PtO *Blackb* 00–14. *8 Squirrel's Chase, Lostock Hall, Preston PR5 5NE* T: (01772) 338756

JACKSON, The Ven Robert William. b 49. K Coll Cam MA 73 Man Univ MA. St Jo Coll Nottm 78. **d** 81 **p** 82. C Fulwood *Sheff* 81–84; V Grenoside and Chapl Grenoside Hosp 84–92; V Scarborough St Mary w Ch Ch and H Apostles *York* 92–01; Springboard Missr 01–04; Adn Walsall and Hon Can Lich Cathl 05–09; rtd 09. *4 Glebe Park, Eyam, Hope Valley S32 5RH* T: (01433) 631212 E: archbob@gmail.com or venerablebob@gmail.com

JACKSON, Roger. b 57. Chich Th Coll 85. **d** 88 **p** 89. C Hale *Guildf* 88–92; V Barton w Peel Green *Man* 92–95; P-in-c Long Crendon w Chearsley and Nether Winchendon *Ox* 95–00; V 00–08; V Clevedon St Jo *B & W* 08–14;

P-in-c Fareham SS Pet and Paul *Portsm* from 14. *The Vicarage, 22 Harrison Road, Fareham PO16 7EJ* T: (01329) 281521 E: frrjackson@gmail.com

JACKSON, Canon Ronald William. b 37. **d** 69 **p** 70. C Crofton *Portsm* 69–74; V Wolverhampton St Matt *Lich* 74–85; V Bloxwich 85–89; C Tamworth 89–92; Bp's Officer for Par Miss and Development *Bradf* 92–98; Hon Can Bradf Cathl 94–98; rtd 98; PtO *Bradf* 99–14; *Leeds* 14–16; *Blackb* from 14. *24 Fosbrooke House, Clifton Drive, Lytham St Annes FY8 5RQ* T: (01253) 667024 E: rw.jackson@icloud.com

JACKSON, Ruth Ellen. b 69. Dub City Univ BBS 91. CITC BTh 02. **d** 02 **p** 03. C Portadown St Mark *Arm* 02–05; C Carrigrohane Union *C, C & R* 05–10; I Mountmellick w Coolbanagher, Rosenallis etc *M & K* 10–15; I Dublin Crumlin w Chapelizod *D & G* from 15. *St Mary's Rectory, 118 Kimmage Road West, Dublin 12, Republic of Ireland* M: (00353) 87-052 3450 E: ruthjnoble@gmail.com

JACKSON, Ruth Victoria. *See* HAKE, Ruth Victoria

JACKSON, Sarah Colleen Mitford. b 72. Edin Univ MA 95. St Mellitus Coll 18. **d** 20 **p** 21. NSM Onslow Square and S Kensington St Aug *Lon* from 20. *59 Burlington Road, London SW6 4NH* M: 07740-482810 E: sarah.jackson@crtrust.org

JACKSON, Sarah Diana. b 53. Birkbeck Coll Lon MSc 01 Dorset Ho Sch of Occupational Therapy DipCOT 74. St Aug Coll of Th 09. **d** 12 **p** 13. NSM Wandsworth Common St Mary *S'wark* 12–15; NSM Upper Tooting H Trin w St Aug 15–20; PtO *Sarum* 20–21; NSM Bradford on Avon H Trin, Westwood and Wingfield from 21; PtO *S'wark* from 21. *2 High Street, Norton St Philip, Bath BA2 7LG* T: (01373) 834481 M: 07719-876610 E: mail@sarahjackson.me

JACKSON (*née* STAFF), Mrs Susan. b 59. Leeds Univ BA 82. Ridley Hall Cam 88. **d** 90 **p** 94. Par Dn Mickleover All SS *Derby* 90–93; Par Dn Chatham St Wm *Roch* 93–94; C 94–97; TV Walton Milton Keynes *Ox* 97–13; PtO from 13. *11 Herdwyck Close, Oakridge Park, Milton Keynes MK14 6GR* T: (01908) 317515 E: s.jackson201@btinternet.com

JACKSON, Mrs Tiffany Marie. b 85. Simpson Univ (USA) BA 06 Fuller Th Sem California MA 11. Trin Coll Bris MA 20. **d** 20 **p** 21. C Ross w Walford and Brampton Abbotts *Heref* from 20. *3 Redwood Close, Ross-on-Wye HR9 5UD* M: 07881-420823 E: tiffmjackson2015@gmail.com

JACKSON, Wendy Pamela. *See* JACKSON-HILL, Wendy Pamela

JACKSON, William Stafford. b 48. Sunderland Poly DCYW 83 Sunderland Univ CertEd 96. Linc Th Coll 86. **d** 89 **p** 90. C Heworth St Mary *Dur* 89–91; C Tudhoe Grange 91–92; Churches' Regional Commn in the NE 97–01; NSM Dipton and Leadgate 03–08; V Burnham *Ox* 08–19; rtd 19; PtO *Dur* from 19. *10 Woodland Terrace, Nettlesworth, Chester le Street DH2 3PW* M: 07793-750652

JACKSON, Canon William Stanley Peter. b 39. St Mich Coll Llan 63. **d** 66 **p** 67. C Llandrindod w Cefnllys *S & B* 66–69; C Gowerton w Waunarlwydd 69–73; V Crickadarn w Gwenddwr and Alltmawr 73–79; R Llanfeugan w Llanthetty etc 79–04; Dioc GFS Chapl 84–92; Can Res Brecon Cathl *S & B* 90–04; Prec Brecon Cathl 98–99; Treas Brecon Cathl 99–00; Chan Brecon Cathl 00–04; Dioc Communications Officer 92–94; RD Crickhowell 98–02; rtd 04. *9 St Peter's Avenue, Fforestfach, Swansea SA5 5BX* T: (01792) 541229

JACKSON-HILL, Mrs Wendy Pamela. b 45. Th Ext Educn Coll 99. **d** 00 **p** 02. Community P Woodlands S Africa 02–03; C Crediton, Shobrooke and Sandford etc *Ex* 03–05; P-in-c Southway 05–15; C Tamerton Foliot 06–15; rtd 15; PtO *Cant* from 16. *33 Colmanton Grove, Sholden, Deal CT14 0FF* E: wendyjacksonhill@gmx.com

JACKSON NOBLE, Ruth Ellen. *See* JACKSON, Ruth Ellen

JACKSON-STEVENS, Preb Nigel. b 42. St Steph Ho Ox. **d** 68 **p** 69. C Babbacombe *Ex* 68–73; V Swimbridge 73–75; P-in-c W Buckland 73–75; V Swimbridge and W Buckland 75–84; P-in-c Mortehoe 84–85; P-in-c Ilfracombe, Lee, W Down, Woolacombe and Bittadon 84–85; TR Ilfracombe, Lee, Woolacombe, Bittadon etc 85–08; RD Barnstaple 93–97; Preb Ex Cathl 95–08; rtd 08. *Rose Cottage, Eastacombe, Barnstaple EX31 3NT* T: (01271) 325283 E: jacksonstevens@btinternet.com

JACOB, Mrs Amelia Stanley. b 52. Punjab Univ BA 73. Oak Hill Th Coll. **d** 90 **p** 94. NSM Asian Chr Congregation All SS Tufnell Park *Lon* 90–92; NSM Alperton 92–12; C from 13. *39 Chester Drive, Harrow HA2 7PX* T: (020) 8902 4592 E: ameliastanley39@yahoo.com

JACOB, John Lionel Andrew. b 26. Selw Coll Cam BA 50 MA 54. Westcott Ho Cam 50. **d** 52 **p** 53. C Brightside St Thos *Sheff* 52–55; C Maltby 55–58; V Doncaster Intake 58–67; V Sheff St Aid w St Luke 67–75; TR Sheff Manor 75–82; R Waddington *Linc* 82–91; rtd 91; PtO *Linc* 91–00. *Flat 21,*

Manormead, Tilford Road, Hindhead GU26 6RA T: (01428) 601521

JACOB, Neville Peter. b 60. Kent Univ BA 82 Leeds Metrop Univ PGCE 86. Ripon Coll Cuddesdon 94. **d** 96 **p** 97. C Market Harborough *Leic* 96–97; C Market Harborough Transfiguration 96–97; C Market Harborough and The Transfiguration etc 97–99; Chapl Miss to Seafarers 99–03; P-in-c Copythorne *Win* 03–11; Chapl Ibex 03–09; PtO *Win* 11–16. *3 Elmsleigh Court, Glen Eyre Road, Southampton SO16 3NT* E: raveknave@tinyworld.co.uk

JACOB, The Ven William Mungo. b 44. Hull Univ LLB 66 Linacre Coll Ox BA 69 MA 73 Ex Univ PhD. St Steph Ho Ox 70. **d** 70 **p** 71. C Wymondham *Nor* 70–73; Asst Chapl Ex Univ 73–75; Dir Past Studies Sarum & Wells Th Coll 75–80; Vice-Prin 77–80; Selection Sec and Sec Cttee for Th Educn ACCM 80–86; Warden Linc Th Coll 85–96; Can and Preb Linc Cathl 86–96; Hon C Linc Minster Gp 88–96; Adn Charing Cross *Lon* 96–14; Bp's Sen Chapl 96–00; R St Giles-in-the-Fields 00–15; P-in-c Soho St Anne w St Thos and St Pet 11–13; rtd 15; P-in-c E Dulwich St Jo *S'wark* 15–16; PtO *Lon* from 17; *Nor* from 18. *4 St Mary's Walk, London SE11 4UA* T: (020) 7735 8201 E: wmjacob15@gmail.com

JACOBS, Mrs Brenda Mary. b 61. Birm Univ BA 85 Glos Univ PGCE 04. WEMTC 06. **d** 09 **p** 10. C Holmer w Huntington *Heref* 09–10; C W Heref 10–12; R Pembridge w Moor Court, Shobdon, Staunton etc 12–16; TR Parkham, Alwington, Buckland Brewer etc *Ex* 16–18; PtO from 18. *18 Higher Road, Fremington, Barnstaple EX31 3BG* T: (01271) 345743 E: jacobs200@btinternet.com

JACOBS, Kevin David. b 55. Dur Univ BA 18. SEITE 11. **d** 14 **p** 15. NSM Tunstall and Bredgar *Cant* 14–19; PtO from 19. *10 Beatrice Road, Capel-le-Ferne, Folkestone CT18 7LL* M: 07572-690460 E: frkevin.0614@gmail.com

JACOBS, Prof Michael David. b 41. Ex Coll Ox BA 63 MA 67. Chich Th Coll 63. **d** 65 **p** 66. C Walthamstow St Pet *Chelmsf* 65–68; Chapl Sussex Univ *Chich* 68–72; Student Cllr Leic Univ 72–84; Lect 84–97; Sen Lect 97–00; Dir Past Care Derby, Linc and S'well 84–94; Visiting Prof Bournemouth Univ *Sarum* from 03. *12 Atlantic Road, Swanage BH19 2EG* T/F: (01929) 423068

JACOBS, Peter John. b 33. JP. MICFM. SEITE 96. **d** 96 **p** 97. NSM Boughton under Blean w Dunkirk and Hernhill *Cant* 96–99; NSM Murston w Bapchild and Tonge 99–02; rtd 02; PtO *Cant* from 02. *16 Temple Road, Canterbury CT2 8JD* M: 07780-353108 E: pjacobs631@gmail.com

JACOBSON, Ian Andrew. b 61. FRGS 94. STETS 02. **d** 05 **p** 06. NSM Ewell St Fran *Guildf* 05–08; NSM Headley w Box Hill 08–11; Asst Chapl Gibraltar Cathl *Eur* 11–14; P-in-c St Laur in Thanet *Cant* 14–20; TR from 20; P-in-c Ramsgate St Mark 16–17; AD Thanet 15–17; CF (TA) 07–10; OCM 11–14; PtO *Eur* from 15; Chapl RNR from 21. *The Rectory, 2 Newington Road, Ramsgate CT11 0QT* T: (01843) 582672 M: 07711-716254 E: i.andrew.jacobson@gmail.com

JACQUES, Barry John. b 52. Open Univ BSc 95. Wycliffe Hall Ox 00. **d** 02 **p** 03. NSM Attleborough *Cov* 02–03; C Weddington and Caldecote 03–07; PtO from 07. *23 Ferndale Close, Nuneaton CV11 6AQ* T: (024) 7767 7044 E: bazjac1702@gmail.com

JACQUES, Mrs Margaret Irene. b 53. St Jo Coll Nottm BA 03 Birm Univ MPhil 10. **d** 03 **p** 04. C W Hallam and Mapperley w Stanley *Derby* 03–07; P-in-c Morton and Stonebroom w Shirland 07–12; R 12–16; rtd 16; PtO *Derby* from 16; *Leic* from 21. *63 Jubilee Close, Melbourne, Derby DE73 8GR* T: (01332) 865842 E: margaret@ajacques.plus.com

JACQUES, Martin. b 62. Ch Ch Coll Cant BA 05. Coll of Resurr Mirfield 00. **d** 02 **p** 03. C Margate St Jo *Cant* 02–06; P-in-c Bucharest w Sofia *Eur* 06–09; P-in-c Gainford *Dur* 09–15; P-in-c Winston 09–15; V Tynemouth Priory *Newc* 15–18; V Budleigh Salterton, E Budleigh w Bicton etc *Ex* from 18. *The New Vicarage, Vicarage Road, East Budleigh, Budleigh Salterton EX9 7EF* M: 07706-875741 E: revmartinjacques@gmail.com

JACQUET, Linda. b 44. Hatf Poly BA 84. ERMC 06. **d** 08 **p** 09. NSM Bungay *St E* 08–14; rtd 15; PtO *St E* from 15. *Roseheath, 10 Sun Road, Broome, Bungay NR35 2RW* T: (01986) 896623 M: 07889-684693 E: l.jacquet@talktalk.net

JACQUET, Trevor Graham. b 56. Man Univ BSc 77. Oak Hill Th Coll BA 88. **d** 88 **p** 89. C Deptford St Nic and St Luke *S'wark* 88–92; Chapl HM Pris Brixton 92–95; Chapl HM Pris Elmley 95–08; Chapl HM Pris Belmarsh from 08. *HM Prison Belmarsh, Western Way, London SE28 0EB* T: (020) 8331 4400 F: 8331 4401 E: trevor.jacquet@justice.gov.uk

JAGANNATH, Julia Rosemary. b 67. St Mellitus Coll 16. **d** 19 **p** 20. C Oak Tree Angl Fellowship *Lon* from 19. *3 Roman Close, London W3 8HE* M: 07954-572682 E: juliajag@hotmail.co.uk

JAGE-BOWLER, Canon Christopher William. b 61. Nottm Univ BA 83 Ch Ch Ox PGCE 84 Dur Coll Cam BA 89 MA 95. Ridley Hall Cam 87. **d** 90 **p** 91. C Downend *Bris* 90–94; Chapl Bris Univ 94–96; C Bris St Mich and St Paul 94–96; Asst Chapl Berlin *Eur* 96–97; Chapl from 97; Can Malta Cathl from 10. *Goethestrasse 31, 13158 Berlin, Germany* T/F: (0049) (30) 917 2248 E: office@stgeorges.de

JAGGER, The Ven Ian. b 55. K Coll Cam BA 77 MA 81 St Jo Coll Dur BA 80 MA 87. Cranmer Hall Dur 78. **d** 82 **p** 83. C Twickenham St Mary *Lon* 82–85; P-in-c Willen *Ox* 85–87; TV Stantonbury and Willen 87–94; TR Fareham H Trin *Portsm* 94–98; Dioc Ecum Officer 94–96; RD Fareham 96–98; Can Missr 98–01; Adn Auckland *Dur* 01–06; Dioc Rural Development Officer 01–06; Adn Dur and Can Res Dur Cathl 06–19; rtd 19. *20 The Timbers, Fareham PO15 5NB* E: ruth.ian@jagfam.co.uk

JAGGER (née GREEN), Mrs Ruth Valerie. b 56. Ex Univ CertEd 77. Ox NSM Course 87. **d** 92 **p** 94. NSM Stantonbury and Willen *Ox* 90–98; NSM Fareham H Trin *Portsm* 94–98; NSM Portsm Deanery 98–01; PtO *Dur* 01–19; *Portsm* from 19. *20 The Timbers, Fareham PO15 5NB* E: ruth.jagger@durham.anglican.org *or* ruth.ian@jagfam.co.uk

JAGGS-FOWLER, Robert Mark. b 60. Charing Cross Hosp Medical Sch MB, BS 85 De Montfort Univ LLM 11 St Jo Coll Dur MA 16 FRCGP 09 FRSA 13. Linc Sch of Th and Min 15. **d** 19 **p** 20. NSM Barton upon Humber *Linc* from 19; Chapl Baysgarth Sch from 20. *The Retreat, 6 Park View, Barton-upon-Humber DN18 6AX* T: (01652) 633727 M: 07538-988944 E: bartoncurate@theretreat-barton.com

JAGO, Christine May. b 52. Ex Univ BA 01 SRN 73. SWMTC 92. **d** 94 **p** 95. OLM St Buryan, St Levan and Sennen *Truro* 94–11; rtd 11; PtO *Truro* from 14. *Boscarne House, St Buryan, Penzance TR19 6HR* T: (01736) 810374 E: christinejago337@btinternet.com

JAGO, David. b 48. Shoreditch Coll Lon CertEd 69 Birm Univ BPhil 77. St Steph Ho Ox 95. **d** 97 **p** 98. C S Bank *York* 97–00; V Middlesbrough St Martin w St Cuth 00–05; V Kingston upon Hull St Alb 05–17; rtd 17; PtO *Carl* from 18. *10 Albert Court, Brook Street, Penrith CA11 7XH* T: (01768) 862674

JAKEMAN, Francis David. b 47. Leeds Univ BSc 69. Cuddesdon Coll 71. **d** 74 **p** 75. C Gt Grimsby St Mary and St Jas *Linc* 74–77; Ind Chapl *Lon* 77–88; V Harrow Weald All SS 88–03; V Bexleyheath Ch Ch *Roch* 03–13; AD Erith 04–09; rtd 13; PtO *Ox* from 14. *50 Eastern Avenue, Reading RG1 5SE* T: 0118-327 3326 M: 07899-922883 E: francis.jakeman@gmail.com

JALLAND, Hilary Gervase Alexander. b 50. Ex Univ BA 72. Coll of Resurr Mirfield 74. **d** 76 **p** 77. C St Thos 76–80; C Portsea St Mary *Portsm* 80–86; V Hempton and Pudding Norton *Nor* 86–90; TV Hawarden *St As* 90–93; R Llandysilio and Penrhos and Llandrinio etc 93–03; V Towyn and St George 03–06; rtd 06; PtO *B & W* from 15; *Sarum* from 15. *Flat 7, Sexeys Hospital, Bruton BA10 0AS* T: (01749) 813700 M: 07814-132259 E: hgaj@jalland1504.plus.com

JAMES, Andrew Nicholas. b 54. BSc 76. Trin Coll Bris 77. **d** 80 **p** 81. C Prescot *Liv* 80–83; C Upholland 83–85; V Hindley Green 85–91; V Dean Forest H Trin *Glouc* 91–06; RD Forest S 97–03; P-in-c Hardwicke and Elmore w Longney 06–09; V 09–19; rtd 19; PtO *Glouc* from 20. *6 Dovedale Close, Hardwicke, Gloucester GL2 4JH*

JAMES, Andrew Peter. b 60. Glam Univ BSc 96 Univ of Wales (Cardiff) BTh 99. St Mich Coll Llan 96. **d** 99 **p** 00. C Roath *Llan* 99–01; C Radyr 01–06; TV Whitchurch 06–14; P-in-c St Andrews Major w Michaelston-le-Pit from 14; AD Penarth and Barry from 16. *The Rectory, Lettons Way, Dinas Powys CF64 4BY* T: (029) 2051 2555 E: andrewjames@churchinwales.org.uk

JAMES, Anne Loraine. b 45. St Jo Coll Nottm. **d** 90 **p** 94. NSM Ellon and Cruden Bay *Ab* 90–99; NSM Alford 99–02; P-in-c 02–17; rtd 17. *9 Stewart Place, Alford AB33 8UH* T: (01975) 564151 E: revanne.alford@outlook.com

JAMES, Barry Paul. b 49. BSc. Sarum & Wells Th Coll. **d** 82 **p** 83. C Bitterne Park *Win* 82–86; V Southampton St Mary Extra 86–00; R Fawley 00–14; rtd 14; PtO *Win* from 14. *7 Cleveland Drive, Dibden Purlieu, Southampton SO45 5QR* T: (023) 8087 9872

JAMES, Brunel Hugh Grayburn. b 70. Selw Coll Cam BA 93 MA 97 Leeds Univ MA 02. Wycliffe Hall Ox BA 97. **d** 98 **p** 99. C Thornbury *Bradf* 98–02; R Barwick in Elmet *Ripon* 02–08; Abp's Dom Chapl *York* 08–10; P-in-c Cleckheaton St Luke and Whitechapel *Wakef* 10–13; P-in-c Cleckheaton St Jo 10–13; V Cleckheaton *Leeds* from 13; PtO *York* from 15. *Wayside, Eldon Place, Cleckheaton BD19 5DH* T: (01274) 873471 M: 07811-195280

JAMES, Miss Carolyn Anne. b 65. Coll of Ripon & York St Jo BA 87 Nottm Univ BTh 91 Leeds Univ MA 03. Linc Th Coll 88. **d** 91 **p** 94. Par Dn Middleton St Mary *Ripon* 91–94; C Wetherby 94–97; V Kirkstall 97–05; Chapl and Sen Warden Bp Grosseteste Coll Linc 05–12; P-in-c Manston *Leeds* 12–16; V from 16. *Manston Vicarage, Church Lane, Leeds LS15 8JB* T: 0113-264 2685 E: carolyn.james117@btinternet.com

JAMES, Christyan Elliot. b 68. Westcott Ho Cam. **d** 09 **p** 10. C Maidstone St Martin *Cant* 09–11; rtd 11; Hon C Brighton Gd Shep Preston *Chich* 11–14; PtO 16–20; Hon C Alfriston w Lullington, Litlington, W Dean and Folkington from 20. *Wickham Cottage, 20 Deneside, East Dean, Eastbourne BN20 0JG* T: (01323) 423070 E: christyanj@yahoo.co.uk

JAMES, Colin Robert. b 39. Magd Coll Ox BA 61 MA 65 DipEd 62. SAOMC 93. **d** 96 **p** 97. NSM Wokingham All SS *Ox* 96–13; PtO from 13. *7 Sewell Avenue, Wokingham RG41 1NT* T: 0118-978 1515 E: colinjames@waitrose.com

JAMES, David. See JAMES, Richard David

✠**JAMES, The Rt Revd David Charles.** b 45. Ex Univ BSc 66 PhD 71. St Jo Coll Nottm BA 73. **d** 73 **p** 74 **c** 98. C Portswood Ch Ch *Win* 73–76; C Goring-by-Sea *Chich* 76–78; Chapl UEA *Nor* 78–82; V Ecclesfield *Sheff* 82–90; RD 87–90; V Portswood Ch Ch *Win* 90–98; Hon Can Win Cathl 98; Suff Bp Pontefract *Wakef* 98–02; Bp Bradf 02–10; rtd 10; Hon Asst Bp York from 10. *7 Long Lane, Beverley HU17 0NH* T: (01482) 871240 E: david@davidjames43.karoo.co.uk

JAMES, David Clive. b 40. Bris Univ BA 61 K Coll Lon DipEd 87. Lich Th Coll 62 St Steph Ho Ox 64. **d** 65 **p** 66. C Portslade St Nic *Chich* 65–68; C Haywards Heath St Wilfrid 68–71; Chapl Brighton Poly 71–75; PtO from 75. *The Old Stables, 5 De Warrenne Road, Lewes BN7 1BP* T: (01273) 471851 E: davidcjames@talktalk.net

JAMES, David Henry. b 45. Univ of Wales MB, BCh 68 Univ of Wales (Swansea) MA 92 MRCPsych 75. SWMTC 95. **d** 98. NSM Truro Cathl 98–00; rtd 00; PtO *Truro* 00–03; *Sarum* 03–05; LtO *Arg* from 06. *Glencruitten House, Glencruitten, Oban PA34 4QB* T: (01631) 562431 E: david.james.855@btinternet.com

JAMES, Preb David Howard. b 47. Ex Univ BA 70 MA 73 Pemb Coll Cam CertEd 72. Linc Th Coll 81. **d** 83 **p** 84. C Tavistock and Gulworthy *Ex* 83–86; C E Teignmouth 86–88; C W Teignmouth 86–88; P-in-c Bishopsteignton 88–89; P-in-c Ideford, Luton and Ashcombe 88–89; TV Teignmouth, Ideford w Luton, Ashcombe etc 90–95; P-in-c Sidmouth, Woolbrook, Salcombe Regis, Sidbury etc 95–97; TR 97–13; Preb Ex Cathl 99–13; RD Ottery 03–13; rtd 13; PtO *Ex* from 13. *1 Farm Close, Exeter EX2 5PJ* T: (01392) 424690 E: djexon211@gmail.com

JAMES, David William. b 55. Birm Univ BA 99. Coll of Resurr Mirfield 86. **d** 88 **p** 88. C New Rossington *Sheff* 88–90; V Yardley Wood *Birm* 90–95; P-in-c Allens Cross 95–96; V 96–06; P-in-c Rubery 05–12; V Sutton in Ashfield St Mary *S'well* 12–16; rtd 16; PtO *S'well* from 16. *Address temp unknown* M: 07511-918806 E: david.james5@btinternet.com

JAMES, Glyn. See JAMES, Henry Glyn

JAMES, Canon Godfrey Walter. b 36. Univ of Wales (Lamp) BA 58 Univ of Wales (Cardiff) MA 60 St Pet Coll Ox DipEd 61 BA 63 MA 67. St Mich Coll Llan 63. **d** 64 **p** 65. C Canton St Jo *Llan* 64–71; V Dinas and Penygraig w Williamstown 71–85; V Kenfig Hill 85–01; Hon Can Llan Cathl 96–01; rtd 01; PtO *Llan* from 04. *Albert Edward Prince of Wales Court, Penylan Avenue, Porthcawl CF36 3LY*

✠**JAMES, The Rt Revd Graham Richard.** b 51. Lanc Univ BA 72 Hon FGCM 92. Cuddesdon Coll 72. **d** 75 **p** 76 **c** 93. C Pet Ch Carpenter 75–79; C Digswell *St Alb* 79–82; TV Digswell and Panshanger 82–83; Sen Selection Sec and Sec Cand Cttee ACCM 83–87; Abp's Chapl *Cant* 87–93; Hon Can Dallas from 89; Suff Bp St Germans *Truro* 93–99; Bp Nor 99–19; rtd 19; PtO *Truro* from 19; Hon Asst Bp Truro from 20. *31 Knoll Park, Truro TR1 1FF* M: 07825-134633 E: grj51@icloud.com

JAMES, Helen Alison. See JONES, Helen Alison

JAMES, Henry Glyn. b 26. Keble Coll Ox BA 50 MA 58 Toronto Univ MEd 74. Wycliffe Hall Ox 50. **d** 52 **p** 53. C Edgbaston St Aug *Birm* 52–54; C Surbiton St Matt *S'wark* 54–57; Housemaster Kingham Hill Sch Oxon 57–62; Chapl St Lawr Coll Ramsgate 62–68; Canada 68–73; Hon C Kidmore End *Ox* 74–77; K Jas Coll of Henley 74–87; Hon C Remenham *Ox* 77–88; Chapl The Henley Coll 87–88; Chapl Toulouse *Eur* 88–91; rtd 91; PtO *Win* 93–19. *13 Harbour Road, Bournemouth BH6 4DD* T: (01202) 427697 E: glyn.james55@gmail.com

JAMES, Prof Ian Nigel. b 48. Leeds Univ BSc 69 Man Univ PhD 74. SAOMC 99. **d** 02 **p** 03. NSM Bracknell *Ox* 02–04; NSM Winkfield and Cranbourne 04–10; P-in-c Bootle,

Corney, Whicham and Whitbeck *Carl* 10–15; rtd 15; PtO *Carl* from 15. *19. High Pasture, Crook Road, Kendal LA8 8LY* M: 07808-207422 E: dr.i.n.james@btinternet.com

JAMES, Jane Eva. b 55. Birm Univ BSc 76 W Midl Coll of Educn PGCE 77. St Mich Coll Llan 08. d 11 p 12. NSM Llansantffraid-ym-Mechain and Llanfechain *St As* 11–13; P-in-c Meifod w Llangynyw w Pont Robert w Pont Dolanog 13–16; I Caereinion from 17. *The Vicarage, Meifod SY22 6DH* T: (01938) 500231 M: 07577-166201 E: janevicaragemeifod@btinternet.com

JAMES, Jeffrey Aneurin. b 53. Univ of Wales (Cardiff) BScEcon 80 Bris Univ MSc 85 MHSM 83. WEMTC 98. d 01 p 02. NSM Minchinhampton *Glouc* 01–07; NSM Painswick, Sheepscombe, Cranham, The Edge etc 07–13; NSM Mylor w Flushing *Truro* 13–20; rtd 20; PtO *Truro* from 20. *4 Union Place, Truro TR1 1EP* M: 07917-597056 E: jeff4up@gmail.com

JAMES, Canon Jeremy Richard. b 52. Jes Coll Cam BA 73 MA 77 York Univ CertEd 77. Cranmer Hall Dur 86. d 88 p 89. C Broxbourne w Wormley *St Alb* 88–91; C Hailsham *Chich* 91–99; V Wadhurst 99–18; V Tidebrook 99–18; P-in-c Stonegate 99–18; RD Rotherfield 03–14; Can and Preb Chich Cathl 12–18; rtd 18; PtO *Ely* from 18. *6 Downham Road, Ely CB6 1AH* E: jeremy@jrjames.me

JAMES, Mrs Joanna Elizabeth. b 72. SAOMC. d 06 p 07. C Northwood Em *Lon* 06–10; C S Mimms Ch Ch 10–18; V Hendon St Paul Mill Hill from 18. *St Paul's Vicarage, Hammers Lane, London NW7 4EA* T: (020) 8201 0231 E: revjoannajames@btinternet.com

JAMES, John Charles. b 35. Keble Coll Ox BA 59. Linc Th Coll 68. d 70 p 71. C S Shields St Hilda w St Thos *Dur* 70–77; P-in-c Jarrow Docks 77–78; Adn Seychelles 78–92; V Mylor w Flushing *Truro* 92–05; rtd 06; PtO *Dur* from 11. *172 Westoe Road, South Shields NE33 3PH*

JAMES, Mrs Julie Margaret. b 55. Shenstone Coll of Educn TCert 76 BEd 77. Qu Coll Birm 01. d 04 p 05. NSM Salwarpe and Hindlip w Martin Hussingtree *Worc* 04–06; NSM St Jo in Bedwardine 06–09; NSM Abberton, The Flyfords, Naunton Beauchamp etc 09–14; R Berrow w Pendock, Eldersfield, Hollybush etc from 14. *Thistledown, Pendock, Gloucester GL19 3PW* T: (01531) 650563 M: 07751-465241 E: julie.m.james@btinternet.com

JAMES, Keith Edwin Arthur. b 38. Sarum & Wells Th Coll 85. d 87 p 88. C Hempnall *Nor* 87–91; R Roughton and Felbrigg, Metton, Sustead etc 91–98; V Ascension Is 98–01; rtd 02; Chapl Laslett's *Worc* 02–04; PtO *Nor* from 05. *30 Woodland Rise, Tasburgh, Norwich NR15 1NF* T: (01508) 470032 E: keith.james2011@btinternet.com

JAMES, Canon Keith Nicholas. b 69. Leeds Univ BA 91 Univ of Wales (Lamp) MA 06. St Jo Coll Nottm MA 93. d 93 p 94. C Crosby *Linc* 93–96; P-in-c Cherry Willingham w Greetwell 96–00; R S Lawres Gp 00–03; RD Lawres 01–03; R Ribbesford w Bewdley and Dowles *Worc* 03–11; R Ribbesford w Bewdley and Dowles and Wribbenhall 11–15; RD Kidderminster 07–13; Can Res Nor Cathl from 15; CMD Officer from 15; Dir Min from 20. *25 The Close, Norwich NR1 4DZ* T: (01603) 882339 E: keith.james@dioceseofnorwich.org

JAMES, Malcolm. b 37. CEng MICE MIStructE. NOC 80. d 83 p 84. NSM Ripponden *Wakef* 83–10; PtO 10–14; *Leeds* from 14. *Lower Stones, Bar Lane, Rishworth, Sowerby Bridge HX6 4EY* T: (01274) 677439 E: malcolm@mjconsultancy.demon.co.uk

JAMES, Manon Ceridwen. b 69. Poly of Wales BA 90 Selw Coll Cam BA 93 MA 97 Birm Univ PhD 15. Ridley Hall Cam. d 94 p 97. C Llandudno *Ban* 94–98; P-in-c Glanogwen w St Ann's w Llanllechid 98–99; V 99–05; V Pentir 04–05; Dir of Ords 02–05; C Llanrhos *St As* 05–07; Dioc Dir Lifelong Learning 05–08; R Llanddulas and Llysfaen 08–16; Bp's Adv for Min 12–13; Dir Min 14–18; LtO 15–18; Hon Can St As Cathl 17–18; Dir Formation for Lic Min St Padarn's Inst from 18. *St Padarn's Institute, 54 Cardiff Road, Llandaff, Cardiff CF5 2YJ* T: (029) 2056 3379 M: 07776-591799 E: manoncjames@churchinwales.org.uk

JAMES, Mark. b 70. Sarum Coll 13. d 16 p 17. NSM Portsdown *Portsm* 16–18. *17 Plover Close, Fareham PO14 3PX* M: 07443-577577 E: mark.james@hotmail.co.uk

JAMES, Mark Nicholas. b 55. Jes Coll Ox BA 77 MA 80 PGCE 79. Ridley Hall Cam 03. d 05 p 06. C Gt Dunmow and Barnston *Chelmsf* 05–09; R Bentley Common, Kelvedon Hatch and Navestock 09–19; P-in-c Doddinghurst from 14; rtd 19; PtO *Chelmsf* from 20. *11 Keith Way, Southend-on-Sea SS2 6SG* E: revmarkjames@icloud.com

JAMES, Martin. b 40. ACII. d 94 p 95. OLM N Farnborough *Guildf* 94–08; OLM Camberley St Martin Old Dean 08–09; NSM 09–10; rtd 10; PtO *Guildf* from 10. *43 Ashley Road, Farnborough GU14 7HB* T: (01252) 544698 E: martinjean.james@ntlworld.com

JAMES, Michael Howard. b 55. Bris Univ LLB 73 Solicitor 92. WEMTC 04. d 06 p 07. NSM Clifton H Trin, St Andr and St Pet *Bris* 06–08; NSM Westbury Park LEP 08–15; Chapl Partis Coll Bath 15–19; rtd 19; PtO *Bris* 15–20; Hon C Westbury-on-Trym St Alb from 20; PtO *B & W* from 19. *10 Hill Drive, Failand, Bristol BS8 3UX* T: (01275) 393729 E: mike.james@bathwells.anglican.org

JAMES, Paul Maynard. b 31. Univ of Wales (Ban) BA 52 Fitzw Ho Cam BA 54 MA 58. Ridley Hall Cam 56. d 57 p 58. C Newhaven *Chich* 57–60; Kenya 60–65; SW Area Sec CCCS 65–68; V Shrewsbury St Julian *Lich* 68–76; V Shrewsbury H Trin w St Julian 76–90; P-in-c Woore and Norton in Hales 90–98; Adn Salop's Adv on Evang 90–98; RD Hodnet *Lich* 93–97; rtd 98; PtO *Heref* 00–20; *Lich* 00–13. *Nettledene, Elms Lane, Little Stretton, Church Stretton SY6 6RD* T: (01694) 722559

JAMES, Canon Peter David. b 42. Keble Coll Ox BA 63 Lon Univ BD 67. Tyndale Hall Bris 64. d 67 p 68. C Haydock St Mark *Liv* 67–69; C Ashton-in-Makerfield St Thos 69–74; V Whiston 74–80; V Harlech and Llanfair-juxta-Harlech etc *Ban* 80–94; R Botwnnog w Bryncroes 94–99; V Botwnnog w Bryncroes w Llangwnnadl w Penllech 99–07; Hon Can Ban Cathl 02–07; rtd 07. *Tabor, Llithfaen, Pwllheli LL53 6NL* T: (01758) 750202 E: peter@llithfaen.org.uk

JAMES, Richard Andrew. b 44. Mert Coll Ox BA 67 MA 70. Tyndale Hall Bris. d 70 p 71. C Bebington *Ches* 70–73; C Histon *Ely* 73–77; Chapl Guildf Coll of Tech 77–80; C Guildf St Sav w Stoke-next-Guildford 77–80; Ecum Chapl Bedf Coll of HE *St Alb* 81–83; TV Ipslay *Worc* 84–89; R Mulbarton w Kenningham *Nor* 89–92; rtd 93. *5 Links Way, Harrogate HG2 7EW* T: (01423) 889410 E: e4jameses@icloud.com

JAMES, Richard David. b 45. Cheltenham & Glouc Coll of HE MA 97. Lon Coll of Div 66. d 70 p 71. C Boultham *Linc* 70–74; C New Waltham 74–77; TV Cleethorpes 77–87; TR E Bris 87–99; Partnership P E Bris 99–15; V E Bris St Ambrose and St Leon 99–15; rtd 15; PtO *Bris* from 16. *87 Victoria Park, Kingswood, Bristol BS15 1RZ* T: 0117-329 3528 M: 07824-888427 E: rd.james@live.co.uk

JAMES, Richard David. b 65. Clare Coll Cam MA 88 Lon Hosp MB, BChir 90. Ridley Hall Cam 92. d 95 p 96. C Clifton Ch Ch w Em *Bris* 95–98; C Enfield Ch Ch Trent Park *Lon* 98–00; V 00–17; AD Enfield 09–16; R Heigham H Trin *Nor* from 17. *The Rectory, 17 Essex Street, Norwich NR2 2BL* T: (01603) 622225

JAMES, Richard Lindsay. b 39. Kelham Th Coll 61. d 66 p 67. C Seacroft *Ripon* 66–74; rtd 04. *3 Cavendish Mews, Hove BN3 1AZ* T: (01273) 324672 E: rljames@supanet.com

JAMES, Canon Robert William. b 79. Kent Univ BA 01 SOAS Lon MA 02 NM 10 CCC Cam MPhil 03 St Andr Univ MLitt 13 Nottm Univ MA 17. Westcott Ho Cam 02. d 05 p 06. C St Edm Way and Bradfield St Clare, Bradfield St George etc *St E* 05–07; PtO *Glouc* 12–13; NSM Coleford, Staunton, Newland, Redbrook etc 13–14; V Newnham w Awre and Blakeney 14–19; Can and Chan Wells Cathl *B & W* from 19. *8 The Liberty, Wells BA5 2SU* T: (01749) 674483 E: robdogcollar@yahoo.co.uk

JAMES, Roger Michael. b 44. K Coll Lon BD 66 AKC 66. d 69 p 70. C Frindsbury w Upnor *Roch* 69–72; LtO St Alb 73–78; C Digswell 78–81; R Knebworth 81–92; P-in-c Upper Tean and Local Min Adv (Stafford) *Lich* 92–99; Dir Cottesloe Chr Tr Progr *Ox* 99–03; R Cusop w Blakemere, Bredwardine w Brobury etc *Heref* 03–09; RD Abbeydore 06–09; rtd 09. *Ty Siloh, Llandeilo'r Fan, Brecon LD3 8UD* T: (01874) 636126 E: tysiloh@googlemail.com

JAMES, Sandra Kay. See GARDNER, Sandra Kay

JAMES, Ms Sheridan Angharad. b 71. Univ of Wales (Abth) BA 93 PGCE 94 MPhil 00. SEITE 04. d 07 p 08. C Catford (Southend) and Downham S'wark 07–11; V Hatcham St Cath from 11; Dean of Women's Min Woolwich Area from 12. *St Catherine's Vicarage, 102A Pepys Road, London SE14 5SG* T: (020) 7639 1050 M: 07703-291594 E: revsheridanjames@gmail.com

JAMES, Canon Stephen Lynn. b 53. Oak Hill Th Coll BA 86. d 86 p 87. C Heigham H Trin *Nor* 86–89; C Vancouver St Jo Canada 89–93; R Bebington *Ches* 93–06; R Rusholme H Trin *Man* 06–19; Hon Can Man Cathl 18–19; rtd 19; PtO *Man* from 19. *81 Piper's Lane, Heswall, Wirral CH60 9HR*

JAMES, Canon Stephen Nicholas. b 51. Reading Univ MA 87 Bris Univ EdD 95 ARCM 72 LTCL 72 FTCL 73. SAOMC 01. d 04 p 05. NSM Hanney, Denchworth and E Challow *Ox* 04–07; P-in-c Goetre w Llanover *Mon* 07–13; Dioc Dir Educn 11–15; Bp's Chapl 15–20; Hon Can St Woolos Cathl 14–20; rtd 20; PtO *Mon* from 20. *Pear Tree Cottage, Llanfair Kilgeddin, Abergavenny NP7 9DY* T: (01873) 840229 E: sueandstephen1973@gmail.com

JAMES, Thomas Martin St John. b 85. St Jo Coll Cam MA 12. Westcott Ho Cam 09. **d** 12 **p** 13. C Petersfield *Portsm* 12–15; Chapl RN from 15. *72 Redmill Drive, Lee-on-the-Solent PO13 9JE* T: 0300-157 7544

JAMES, Ms Tracey Louise. b 77. Ripon Coll Cuddesdon 18. **d** 20 **p** 21. C Debenham and Helmingham *St E* from 20. *Address temp unknown* E: traceyjamescurate@gmail.com

JAMES, Canon Veronica Norma. b 59. STETS 99. **d** 02 **p** 03. NSM Ashton Keynes, Leigh and Minety *Bris* 02–05; R Merriott w Hinton, Dinnington and Lopen *B & W* 05–10; R The Guitings, Cutsdean, Farmcote etc *Glouc* 10–14; AD N Cotswold 10–14; Hon Can Glouc Cathl 12–14; R Skipton H Trin *Leeds* 14–19; Hon Can Ripon Cathl 19; rtd 19; PtO *Leeds* 19–21; *York* from 20. *42 Back Lane, Settrington, Malton YO17 8NP* E: veronica.james690@gmail.com

JAMESON, Miss Beverley Joyce. b 60. St Jo Coll Nottm 09. **d** 11 **p** 12. C Cen Telford *Lich* 11–15; TV Droitwich Spa *Worc* 15–17; C Salwarpe and Hindlip w Martin Hussingtree 15–17; Dean of Women's Min 16–17; R Lymm *Ches* from 17. *46 Rectory Lane, Lymm WA13 0AL* T: (01925) 757081 M: 07495-670048 E: bevjameson@live.co.uk

JAMESON, Howard Kingsley. b 63. Warwick Univ BSc 84. Trin Coll Bris 99. **d** 02 **p** 03. C Wareham *Sarum* 02–05; P-in-c Monkton Farleigh, S Wraxall and Winsley 05–11; P-in-c Bradford-on-Avon Ch Ch 10–11; R N Bradford on Avon and Villages 11–12; P-in-c Patchway *Bris* from 12. *86 Oakleaze, Patchway, Bristol BS34 5AW* T: 0117-370 8279 E: revh.jameson@gmail.com

JAMIE, Mrs Katherine Elizabeth. b 81. Cranmer Hall Dur 12. **d** 15 **p** 16. C Easington and Easington Colliery *Dur* 15–18; V Heworth St Mary 18–21; Chapl HM YOI Deerbolt from 21; Chapl HM Pris Kirklevington Grange from 21. *HM Young Offender Institution, Bowes Road, Barnard Castle DL12 9BG* T: (01833) 633200

JAMIESON, Christopher Donald. b 50. Man Univ MEd 89 Westmr Coll Ox BEd 72. All SS Cen for Miss & Min. **d** 13 **p** 14. OLM Turton Moorland *Man* from 13. *25 Timberbottom, Bolton LB2 3DG* T: (01204) 302346 M: 07726-349195 E: roscanvel2@gmail.com

JAMIESON, Douglas. *See* JAMIESON, William Douglas

JAMIESON, Emma Victoria. *See* HIGGINS, Emma Victoria

JAMIESON, Guy Stuart. b 66. Leeds Univ BA 98. Ripon Coll Cuddesdon. **d** 00 **p** 01. C Woodhall *Bradf* 00–03; V Southowram and Claremount *Wakef* 03–14; Leeds 14–16; V Lt Marsden w Nelson St Mary and Nelson St Bede *Blackb* from 16; AD Pendle 18–20. *St Paul's Vicarage, Bentley Street, Nelson BB9 0BS* T: (01282) 615888 M: 07983-678356 E: guyjamieson@btinternet.com

JAMIESON, Ian David. b 73. Leeds Univ BA 99 PGCE 00. St Jo Coll Nottm 11. **d** 13 **p** 14. C Em TM *Leeds* 13–17; P-in-c Bradley from 17; P-in-c Fixby and Cowcliffe from 17. *The Vicarage, 3 St Thomas Gardens, Bradley, Huddersfield HD2 1SL* T: (01484) 427838 M: 07594-552519 E: revianjamieson@gmail.com

JAMIESON, Kenneth Euan Oram. b 24. Roch Th Coll 60. **d** 62 **p** 63. C Bromley SS Pet and Paul *Roch* 62–66; R Colchester St Mary Magd *Chelmsf* 66–71; V Bexleyheath St Pet *Roch* 71–78; P-in-c Maidstone St Faith *Cant* 78–83; P-in-c Maidstone St Paul 78–83; Ind Chapl *St Alb* 83–89; rtd 89; PtO *B & W* 89–19. *Manormead Supported Housing, Tilford Road, Hindhead GU26 6RA* E: kenjy@uwclub.net

JAMIESON, Canon Marilyn. b 52. Cranmer Hall Dur IDC 80. **d** 91 **p** 94. Par Dn Bensham *Dur* 91–93; Par Dn Ryton w Hedgefield 93–94; Chapl Metro Cen Gateshead 94–02 and 06–20; Bp's Sen Chapl 02–05; Hon C Ryton 05–06; Hon Can Dur Cathl 97–20; rtd 20; PtO *Newc* 06–20. *2 Westburn Cottages, Ryton NE40 4EY* T: 0191-413 2164

JAMIESON, Mrs Moira Elizabeth. b 50. **d** 08 **p** 09. C Lenzie *Glas* 08–13; P-in-c Cumbernauld 13–19; rtd 19. *3 Cawder Place, Cumbernauld, Glasgow G68 0BG* T: (01236) 597633 M: 07977-096446 E: jamiemoi60@sky.com

JAMIESON, Peter Grant. b 64. Liv Univ BA 87. Coll of Resurr Mirfield 90. **d** 93 **p** 94. C Charlton Kings St Mary *Glouc* 93–96. *56 East Street, Thame OX9 3JS* M: 07779-148898 E: peterjamieson4@gmail.com

JAMIESON, Miss Rosalind Heather. b 49. CertEd 71. Cranmer Hall Dur 79. **dss** 81 **d** 87 **p** 94. Queensbury All SS *Lon* 81–85; Richmond H Trin and Ch Ch *S'wark* 85–87; Par Dn 87–91; Par Dn Burmantofts St Steph and St Agnes *Ripon* 91–94; C 94–99; TV Seacroft 99–14; *Leeds* 14; rtd 14; PtO *Leeds* from 17; *Man* from 18. *7 Alford Close, Bolton BL2 6NR* E: heather.jamieson2@gmail.com

JAMIESON, Mrs Susan Jennifer. b 49. Liv Univ SRN 71. Dioc OLM tr scheme 97. **d** 00 **p** 01. OLM Clubmoor *Liv* 00–19; rtd 19; PtO *Liv* from 19. *Address withheld by request* E: sue@standrewslive.org.uk

JAMIESON, Thomas Lindsay. b 53. N Lon Poly BSc 74. Cranmer Hall Dur. **d** 77 **p** 78. C Gateshead Fell *Dur* 77–80; C Gateshead 80–84; TV 84–90; P-in-c Gateshead St Cuth w St Paul 90–91; TV Bensham 91–93; P-in-c Ryton w Hedgefield 93–95; R 95–05; R Ryton 05–17; AD Gateshead W 94–98; rtd 17; P-in-c Ryton *Dur* 17–19; PtO from 20. *2 Westburn Cottages, Ryton NE40 4EY* E: tomjbees@outlook.com

JAMIESON, William Douglas. b 38. Oak Hill Th Coll 63. **d** 66 **p** 67. C Shrewsbury St Julian *Lich* 66–68; C Bucknall and Bagnall 68–70; C Otley *Bradf* 70–74; TV Keighley 74–81; V Utley 81–00; rtd 00; PtO *Ches* from 00. *11 The Quay, Frodsham, Warrington WA6 7JG* T: (01928) 731085 M: 07974-947838 E: douglasjamieson@tiscali.co.uk *or* wdouglasjamieson@gmail.com

JAMISON, William Mervyn Noel. b 66. CITC 03. **d** 07 **p** 08. NSM Ballybeen *D & D* 07–10; NSM Comber 10–15; P-in-c Belvoir 15–17; P-in-c Drumbo 17–19; I from 19. *Holy Trinity Church, Ballylesson Road, Belfast BT8 8JT* T: (028) 9082 6048 M: 07808-481669 E: rev.merv@me.com

JANES, Austin Steven. b 75. York Univ BA 97. Ripon Coll Cuddesdon 06. **d** 08 **p** 09. C Crewe St Andr w St Jo *Ches* 08–11; Min Can St Alb Abbey 11–14; TV Hemel Hempstead from 14. *33 Craigavon Road, Hemel Hempstead HP2 6BA* E: revaustin@sky.com

JANES, David Edward. b 40. Lon Univ BSc 67. Glouc Sch of Min 86. **d** 89 **p** 90. NSM Church Stretton *Heref* 89–00; rtd 00; PtO *Heref* 00–20. *Bourton Westwood Farm, 3 Bourton Westwood, Much Wenlock TF13 6QB* T: (01952) 727393

JANICKER, Laurence Norman. b 47. SS Mark & Jo Coll Chelsea DipEd 69. St Jo Coll Nottm 83. **d** 85 **p** 86. C Beverley Minster *York* 85–89; R Lockington and Lund and Scorborough w Leconfield 89–94; V Cov St Geo 94–08; rtd 08; PtO *Nor* from 09. *136 Manor Road, Newton St Faith, Norwich NR10 3LG* T: (01603) 898614 E: winnieaurens@gmail.com

JANSSON, The Very Revd Maria Patricia. b 55. Milltown Inst Dub MRelSc 92. CITC 00. **d** 01 **p** 02. C Galway w Kilcummin *T, K & A* 01–02; C Wexford w Ardcolm and Killurin *C, F & O* 02–04; I 04–09; C Kilscoran w Killinick and Mulrankin 02–04; P-in-c 04–09; I Wexford and Kilscoran Union 10–11; Dean Waterford from 11; I Waterford w Killea, Drumcannon and Dunhill from 11; Preb Ossory Cathl from 12. *Address temp unknown* M: (00353) 87-225 5793 E: miajansson@eircom.net

JANVIER, Philip Harold. b 57. Trin Coll Bris BA 87. **d** 87 **p** 88. C Much Woolton *Liv* 87–90; TV Toxteth St Philemon w St Gabr and St Cleopas 90–97; TR Gateacre from 97. *St Stephen's Rectory, Belle Vale Road, Liverpool L25 2PQ* T/F: 0151-487 9338 E: philjanvier@btinternet.com

JAQUET, Didier Francis. b 76. K Coll Lon LLB 97. ERMC 06. **d** 11 **p** 12. NSM Tring *St Alb* 11–19; NSM Winslow w Gt Horwood and Addington *Ox* from 19. *Address withheld by request* T: (01525) 240465 M: 07420-656955

JAQUISS, Mrs Gabrielle Clair. b 56. Clare Coll Cam BA 79 MA 85 LRAM 76. NOC 06. **d** 08 **p** 09. NSM Bowdon *Ches* 08–11; NSM Hale Barns w Ringway 11–16; V from 16; RD Bowdon from 17. *Ingersley, Belgrave Road, Bowdon, Altrincham WA14 2NZ* T: 0161-928 0717 M: 07843-375494 E: clairjq@aol.com

JARAM, Peter Ellis. b 45. Lon Univ BSc 70 CEng 77 MIET 77 MBIM 88. Linc Th Coll 94. **d** 94 **p** 95. C Bridlington Priory *York* 94–96; C Rufforth w Moor Monkton and Hessay 96–97; C Healaugh w Wighill, Bilbrough and Askham Richard 96–97; P-in-c 97–01; Chapl Askham Bryan Coll 97–01; V Brompton by Sawdon w Hutton Buscel, Snainton etc *York* 01–05; rtd 05; PtO *York* from 05. *74 Eastgate, Pickering YO18 7DY* T: (01751) 477831 E: pwj74@btinternet.com

JARDINE, Canon Anthony. b 38. Qu Coll Birm 64. **d** 67 **p** 68. C Baldock w Bygrave and Clothall *St Alb* 67–71; C N Stoneham *Win* 71–73; P-in-c Ecchinswell cum Sydmonton 73–79; P-in-c Burghclere w Newtown 73–79; R Burghclere w Newtown and Ecchinswell w Sydmonton 79–87; R Wonston and Stoke Charity w Hunton 87–97; P-in-c Chawton and Farringdon 97–04; Dioc Rural Officer 97–04; Hon Can Win Cathl 99–04; rtd 04; Hon C Knight's Enham and Smannell w Enham Alamein *Win* 04–08; PtO *Heref* from 09. *9 Park Green, Kington HR5 3AP*

JARDINE, Canon David John (Brother David). b 42. QUB BA 65 TCD Div Test 67. CITC 67. **d** 67 **p** 68. C Ballymacarrett St Patr *D & D* 67–70; Asst Chapl QUB 70–73; SSF from 73; Asst Chapl HM Pris Belfast 75–79; Chapl 79–85; USA 85–88; Sen Asst Warden Ch of Ireland Min of Healing 88–92; Dir Divine Healing Min 92–17; Dir Equipping for Life 18–20; Can Belf Cathl from 07. *350 Merville Garden Village, Newtownabbey BT37 9TU* T: (028) 9086 1495 M: 07889-572801 E: davidjjardine@gmail.com

JARDINE, Canon Norman. b 47. QUB BSc 72. Trin Coll Bris 74. d 76 p 77. C Magheralin *D & D* 76–78; C Dundonald 78–80; Bp's C Ballybeen 80–88; I Willowfield 88–00; Dir Think Again 00–04; I Ballynafeigh St Jude 04–16; Can Belf Cathl 03–16; rtd 16. *273 Orby Drive, Belfast BT5 6BG* T: (028) 9050 0012 E: norman.jardine2@ntlworld.com

JARDINE, Thomas Parker. b 44. Oak Hill Th Coll BA 87. d 87 p 88. C Crowborough *Chich* 87–91; R Dersingham w Anmer and Shernborne *Nor* 91–00; P-in-c Southport SS Simon and Jude *Liv* 00–03; V Southport SS Simon and Jude w All So 03–09; C Southport All SS 03–09; rtd 09; PtO *Win* 10–19. *16 Donnelly Road, Bournemouth BH6 5NW* E: tomandannjardine@googlemail.com

JARMAN, Christopher (Kit). b 38. QUB BA 63. Wells Th Coll 69. d 71 p 72. C Leckhampton SS Phil and Jas *Glouc* 71–73; Chapl RN 73–93; Chapl Rossall Sch Fleetwood 94; R Stirling *St And* 94–03; Chapl ATC 97–03; rtd 03; LtO *Arg* 04–17; PtO *Pet* from 19. *22 Daventry Road, Kilsby, Rugby CV23 8XF*

JARMAN, Michael Robert. b 48. Trin Coll Bris 07. d 09 p 10. NSM Caerleon and Llanfrechfa *Mon* 09–12; P-in-c Newport Ch Ch 12–18; rtd 18; Chapl Madeira *Eur* from 19. *rua do Quebra Costas 18, 9000-034 Funchal, Portugal* T: (00351) (291) 220674 E: jarmanmichael48@gmail.com *or* htcchaplain@gmail.com

JARRATT, David. b 70. Herts Univ BSc 92 Univ of N Lon PhD 97 UEA PGCE 97. Ox Min Course 10. d 12 p 13. C Felpham *Chich* 12–16; R Lavant 16–21; RD Chich 19–21; C W Bromwich All SS w St Mary and St Phil *Lich* from 21. *33 Reform Street, West Bromwich B70 7PF* M: 07911-132417 E: david.jarratt@btinternet.com

JARRATT, Canon Robert Michael. b 39. K Coll Lon BD 62 AKC 62 NY Th Sem DMin 85. d 63 p 64. C Corby St Columba *Pet* 63–67; Lay Tr Officer *Sheff* 67–71; Ind Chapl *S'wark* 72–80; P-in-c Betchworth 76–80; V Ranmoor *Sheff* 80–01; P-in-c Worsbrough and Dir Post-Ord Tr 01–05; RD Hallam 87–94; Hon Can Sheff Cathl 95–05; rtd 05; PtO *Sheff* 05–20. *69 Barley House, 211 Ecclesall Road, Sheffield S11 8HR* T: 0114-273 7545 M: 07805-017426

JARRATT, Stephen. b 51. Edin Univ BD 76 St Kath Coll Liv CertEd 77. d 78 p 79. C Horsforth *Ripon* 78–81; C Stanningley Th Sem 81–84; P-in-c Fishponds St Jo *Bris* 84–85; V 85–92; V Chapel Allerton *Ripon* 92–04; AD Allerton 97–04; TR Clifton *S'well* 04–08; AD W Bingham 07–08; P-in-c Haxby and Wigginton *York* 08–09; R 09–13; rtd 13; PtO *York* 14–19. *14 Boundary Lane, Chichester PO19 6EP* E: jarratt312@btinternet.com

⛪**JARRETT, The Rt Revd Martyn William.** b 44. K Coll Lon BD 67 AKC 67 Hull Univ MPhil 91. d 68 p 69 c 94. C Bris St Geo 68–70; C Swindon New Town 70–74; C Northolt St Jos *Lon* 74–76; V 76–81; V Hillingdon St Andr 81–83; P-in-c Uxbridge Moor 82–83; V Uxbridge St Andr w St Jo 83–85; Selection Sec ACCM 85–88; Sen Selection Sec 89–91; V Chesterfield St Mary and All SS *Derby* 91–94; Suff Bp Burnley *Blackb* 94–00; Hon Can Blackb Cathl 94–00; Suff Bp Beverley (PEV) *York* 00–12; Hon Asst Bp S'well and Nottm from 01; Dur, Ripon and Sheff 00–12; Man and Wakef 01–12; Bradf 02–12; Liv 03–12; Newc 10–12; Hon Can Wakef Cathl 01–10; rtd 12. *91 Beaumont Rise, Worksop S80 1YG* T: (01909) 477847 E: martyn.jarrett@yahoo.co.uk

JARRETT, René Isaac Taiwo. b 49. Milton Margai Teachers' Coll Sierra Leone TCert 79 Lon Inst of Educn BEd 94. Sierra Leone Th Hall 80. d 83 p 85. Dn Freetown St Luke Sierra Leone 83–85; C Freetown Bp Elwin Memorial Ch 85–89; Hon C St Pancras w St Jas and Ch Ch *Lon* 89–95; C Bloomsbury St Geo w Woburn Square Ch Ch 95–11; rtd 11; PtO *Lon* from 11; *S'wark* from 13. *2 Woburn Mansions, Torrington Place, London WC1E 7HL* T: (020) 7580 5165 M: 07853-348143 E: jarrorene@yahoo.co.uk

JARROW, Suffragan Bishop of. *See* CLARK, The Rt Revd Sarah Elizabeth

JARVIS, Benjamin Joseph Francis. b 86. Coll of Resurr Mirfield BA 19. d 19 p 20. C Monkseaton St Mary *Newc* from 19. *2 Seacombe Avenue, North Shields NE30 3DR* M: 07972-717783 E: revd.bjarvis@gmail.com

JARVIS, Ian Frederick Rodger. b 38. Bris Univ BA 60. Tyndale Hall Bris 61. d 63 p 64. C Penge Ch Ch w H Trin *Roch* 63–67; C Bilston St Leon *Lich* 67–71; V Lozells St Silas *Birm* 71–76; V Chaddesden St Mary *Derby* 76–95; V Newhall 95–02; rtd 02; PtO *Derby* from 02. *29 Springfield Road, Midway, Swadlincote DE11 0BZ* T: (01283) 551589 E: ianandirenejarvis@btinternet.com

JARVIS, Canon Nathan John. b 73. Ox Brookes Univ BA 97 Leeds Univ MA 04. St Steph Ho Ox BTh 06. d 06 p 07. C Hartlepool H Trin *Dur* 06–09; V Kingstanding St Luke *Birm* 09–12; TV Blenheim *Ox* 12–17; Chapl Lic Victuallers'

Sch Ascot from 16; Chapl Ban Univ 18–21; Hon Can Ban Cathl from 18. *Bangor Cathedral, Cathedral Close, Bangor LL57 1LH* T: (01248) 354999 E: fr.nathan@yahoo.com

JARVIS, Mrs Pamela Ann. b 51. Sussex Univ BEd 74. SWMTC 97. d 00 p 01. C Braunton *Ex* 00–03; C Combe Martin, Berrynarbor, Lynton, Brendon etc 03–04; TV 04–10; rtd 10. *Crocnamac, Tomouth Road, Appledore, Bideford EX39 1QD* T: (01237) 420454 M: 07773-900523 E: revpajarvis@btinternet.com

JARVIS, Stephen John. b 55. WEMTC 04. d 07 p 08. NSM Bisley, Chalford, France Lynch, and Oakridge etc *Glouc* 07–18; NSM Nailsworth w Shortwood, Horsley etc 18–21; rtd 21. *8 Ollney Road, Minchinhampton, Stroud GL6 9BX* T: (01453) 884545 M: 07975-565156 E: stephenjarvis88@talktalk.net

JARVIS, Steven Roy. b 73. NE Wales Inst of HE BA 05. WEMTC 04. d 07 p 08. NSM Ludlow *Heref* 07–10; Dioc Youth Officer *Glouc* 10–13; TV White Horse *Sarum* 13–17; C Stratford-upon-Avon, Luddington etc *Cov* from 17. *3 Coopers Close, Stratford-upon-Avon CV37 0RS* M: 07879-442751 E: steve.the.vicar@btinternet.com

JARY, Ms Helen Lesley. b 69. Lanc Univ BA 91. St Jo Coll Nottm 05. d 07 p 08. C Oulton Broad *Nor* 07–11; TV Thetford 11–19; TR Oulton Broad from 19. *212 Bridge Road, Lowestoft NR33 9JX* M: 07990-501683 E: revhelenjary@gmail.com

JASPER, Canon David. b 51. Jes Coll Cam BA 72 MA 76 Keble Coll Ox BD 80 Dur Univ PhD 83 Ox Univ DD 02 Uppsala Univ Hon ThD 07 FRSE 06 FRSA 07. St Steph Ho Ox BA 75 MA 79. d 76 p 77. C Buckingham *Ox* 76–79; C Dur St Oswald 80; Chapl Hatf Coll Dur 81–88; Dir Cen Study of Lit and Th Dur 88–91; Prin St Chad's Coll Dur 88–91; Reader and Dir Cen Study of Lit and Th Glas Univ from 91; Vice-Dean of Div 95–98; Dean of Div 98–02; LtO *Glas* 91–08; NSM Hamilton from 08; P-in-c Cambuslang 14–16; P-in-c Uddingston 14–16; Can Th St Mary's Cathl from 17. *32 Crompton Avenue, Glasgow G44 5TH* E: davidjasper124@gmail.com

JASPER, David Julian McLean. b 44. Dur Univ BA 66. Linc Th Coll 66. d 68 p 69. C Redruth *Truro* 68–72; TV 72–75; V St Just in Penwith 75–86; P-in-c Sancreed 82–86; C Reading St Matt *Ox* 96–00; P-in-c 00–02; R S Petherton w The Seavingtons *B & W* 02–11; rtd 11; RD Trigg Major *Truro* 12–16; PtO from 14. *39 Fore Street, Plympton, Plymouth PL7 1LZ* T: (01752) 331536 M: 07767-814533 E: davidjasper5dy@btinternet.com

JAVELLE, Stéphane Jean Michel. b 71. Provence Univ BA 98. Ripon Coll Cuddesdon 15. d 17 p 18. C Salisbury Plain *Sarum* from 17. *11 The Limes, High Street, Shrewton, Salisbury SP3 4BW* T: (01980) 621318 M: 07740-775070 E: rev.stephane.javelle@eclipso.eu

JAY, Canon Colin. b 62. Keble Coll Ox BA 85 St Jo Coll Dur BA 89. Cranmer Hall Dur 87. d 90 p 91. C Bishopwearmouth St Gabr *Dur* 90–94; C Newton Aycliffe 94; TV 94–96; TV Gt Aycliffe 96–03; AD Sedgefield 99–03; Chapl Co Dur & Darlington Priority Services NHS Trust 03–06; Chapl Tees, Esk and Wear Valleys NHS Foundn Trust from 06; Can Dur Cathl from 18. *The Chaplaincy, West Park Hospital, Edward Pease Way, Darlington DL2 2TS* T: (01325) 552045 E: colin.jay@tewv.nhs.uk *or* colin.jay@nhs.net

JAY, Mrs Sarah Clare. b 65. d 12 p 13. NSM Stranton *Dur* 12–15; NSM Blackwell All SS and Salutation from 15. *All Saints Church, Ravensdale Road, Darlington DL3 8DT* E: colsarjay@yahoo.co.uk

JAYNE, Martin Philip. b 49. Man Univ BA 71 MRTPI 73. Carl Dioc Tr Course 87. d 90 p 91. NSM Natland *Carl* 90–19; Dioc Officer for NSM 04–08; rtd 19; PtO *Carl* from 19. *12 Longmeadow Lane, Natland, Kendal LA9 7QZ* T: (01539) 560942 E: martjay@mac.com

JEAL, David James. b 66. d 15 p 16. NSM Bris Lockleaze St Mary Magd w St Fran 15–16; C 16–19; Chapl RN from 19. *Royal Naval Chaplaincy Service Headquarters, Tanner Building, HMS Excellent, Whale Island, Portsmouth PO2 8ER* T: 0300-157 7544 M: 07814-024321 E: davejeal@blueyonder.co.uk

JEANES, Gordon Paul. b 55. Ox Univ BA 79 MA 82 BD 90 Univ of Wales (Lamp) PhD 99. St Steph Ho Ox 80. d 82 p 83. C S Wimbledon H Trin and St Pet *S'wark* 82–85; C Surbiton St Andr and St Mark 85–90; Chapl St Chad's Coll Dur 90–93; Sub-Warden St Mich Coll Llan 94–98; Lect Th Univ of Wales (Cardiff) 94–98; V Wandsworth St Anne *S'wark* 98–08; P-in-c Wandsworth St Faith 05–08; V Wandsworth St Anne w St Faith 08–21; Dioc Voc Adv 99–21; rtd 21. *Address temp unknown* E: gordon.jeanes@virgin.net

JEANS, The Ven Alan Paul. b 58. MIAAS 84 MIBCO 84 Southn Univ BTh 89 Univ of Wales (Lamp) MA 03. Sarum & Wells Th Coll 86. d 89 p 90. C Parkstone St Pet w Branksea and St Osmund *Sarum* 89–93; P-in-c Bishop's Cannings, All Cannings etc 93–98; Par Development Adv from 98; Can and Preb Sarum Cathl from 02; Adn Sarum from 03;

RD Alderbury 05–07; Dioc Dir of Ords 07–13. *Herbert House, 118 Lower Road, Salisbury SP2 9NW* T: (01722) 336290 F: 411990 E: adsarum@salisbury.anglican.org

JEANS, David Bockley. b 48. Mert Coll Ox BA 71 MA 80 PGCE 73 Man Univ MPhil 98. Trin Coll Bris 83. **d** 85 **p** 86. C Clevedon St Andr and Ch Ch *B & W* 85–88; V Wadsley *Sheff* 88–96; Dir Studies Wilson Carlile Coll of Evang 96; Prin 97–06; Dean Coll of S Cross NZ 06–08; P-in-c Deepcar *Sheff* 08–13; rtd 13; PtO *Sheff* from 13. *112 Airedale Road, Sheffield S6 4AW* T: 0114-221 7829 E: d.jeans1948@gmail.com

JEANS, Miss Eleanor Ruth. b 75. Man Univ BMus 97 GRNCM 97. Ridley Hall Cam 09. **d** 11 **p** 12. C Thurnby w Stoughton *Leic* 11–14; C Kettering Ch the King *Pet* from 14. *11 Churchill Way, Kettering NN15 5DP* M: 07432-602677 E: eleanor@thisman.co.uk

JEAPES (née PORTER), Mrs Barbara Judith. b 47. Cam Inst of Educn TCert 68 Man Univ MA 17. Carl Dioc Tr Inst 91. **d** 94 **p** 95. NSM Egremont and Haile *Carl* 94–09; TV 09–14; rtd 14; PtO *Carl* 14–19; *Ches* from 19. *7 Stretton Walk, Northwich CW9 8GH* T: (01606) 334874 E: barbara.jeapes@btinternet.com

JEAVONS, Mrs Margaret Anne. b 51. Liv Poly BA 72 Bris Univ BA 01 St Kath Coll Liv PGCE 74. Trin Coll Bris 99. **d** 01 **p** 02. C Totnes w Bridgetown, Berry Pomeroy etc *Ex* 01–05; V Sutton St Mich *York* 05–19; P-in-c Bilton St Pet 15–19; AD E Hull 13–19; rtd 19. *4 Collison House, Trinity Lane, Beverley HU17 0AR* E: maggieannejeavons@gmail.com

JEE, Jonathan Noel. b 63. BNC Ox BA 84 MA 88. Wycliffe Hall Ox 85. **d** 88 **p** 89. C Brampton St Thos *Derby* 88–92; TV Hinckley H Trin *Leic* 92–00; V Leamington Priors St Paul *Cov* from 00. *The Vicarage, 15 Lillington Road, Leamington Spa CV32 5YS* T: (01926) 772132 *or* 427149 E: jonathan@stpl.org.uk

JEE, Thomas Peter. b 91. St Jo Coll Ox BA 13 Trin Coll Cam BA 17 MPhil 18 Birm City Univ PGCE 14. Ridley Hall Cam 15. **d** 18 **p** 19. C Woodford Wells *Chelmsf* from 18. *55B Montalt Road, Woodford Green IB8 9RS* M: 07403-463755 E: thomas_jee@hotmail.co.uk

JEEWAN, Alexander. b 71. Univ of E Lon BA 95 PGCE 97. Westcott Ho Cam 13. **d** 15 **p** 16. C Witham and Villages *Chelmsf* 15–18; TV Saffron Walden and Villages from 18. *The Vicarage, Church Street, Great Chesterford, Saffron Walden CB10 1NP* M: 07801-946217 E: alex_jeewan@hotmail.com *or* vicar.camvillages@gmail.com

JEFF, Canon Gordon Henry. b 32. St Edm Hall Ox BA 56 MA 60. Wells Th Coll 59. **d** 61 **p** 62. C Sydenham St Bart *S'wark* 61–64; C Kidbrooke St Jas 64–66; V Clapham St Paul 66–72; V Raynes Park St Sav 73–79; RD Merton 77–79; V Carshalton Beeches 79–86; P-in-c Petersham 86–90; Chapl St Mich Convent 90–96; Hon Can S'wark Cathl 93–96; rtd 96; PtO *B & W* 07–12. *9 Barnetts Well, Draycott, Cheddar BS27 3TF* T: (01934) 744943 E: rumpus9bw@hotmail.com

JEFFCOAT, Rupert Edward Elessing. b 70. St Cath Coll Cam BA 92 MA 96 Salford Univ PhD 16 FRCO 91. WMMTC 02. **d** 05 **p** 06. NSM Brisbane Cathl Australia 05–10. *Arden House, 25 Saunders Avenue, Bedworth CV12 8RJ* T: (024) 7673 4799 E: ruperteejeffcoat@gmail.com

JEFFERIES, Preb Phillip John. b 42. St Chad's Coll Dur BA 65 MA 91. **d** 67 **p** 68. C Tunstall Ch Ch *Lich* 67–71; C Wolverhampton St Pet 71–74; P-in-c Oakengates 74–80; V 80–82; P-in-c Ketley 78–82; V Horninglow 82–00; RD Tutbury 97–00; TR Stafford 00–07; Bp's Adv on Hosp Chapl 82–06; Preb Lich Cathl 99–07; rtd 07; PtO *Lich* 07–21; *Truro* from 16. *16 Morley's Hill, Burton-on-Trent DE13 0TA* T: (01283) 544013 E: pjjefferies@talktalk.net

JEFFERS, Cliff Peter. b 69. York St Jo Univ MA 19. CITC BTh 98. **d** 98 **p** 99. C Limerick City *L & K* 98–01; I Clonenagh w Offerlane, Borris-in-Ossory etc *C, F & O* 01–04; I Athy w Kilberry, Fontstown and Kilkea *D & G* 04–13; Chapl Dub Inst of Tech 13–14; I Fanlobbus Union *C, C & R* from 14. *The Rectory, Sackville Street, Dunmanway, Co Cork, Republic of Ireland* T: (00353) (23) 884 5151 E: cliff4b@gmail.com *or* rector@fanlobbus.ie

JEFFERS, Neil Gareth Thompson. b 78. St Jo Coll Ox BA 99 MA 05. Oak Hill Th Coll MTh 07. **d** 07 **p** 08. C Lowestoft Ch Ch *Nor* 07–11; Chapl Pangbourne Coll from 11. *Sunbeam, Bere Court Road, Pangbourne, Reading RG8 8JY* T: 0118-976 7449 M: 07769-586260 E: neiljeffers2003@yahoo.co.uk

JEFFERSON, Charles Dudley. b 55. St Pet Coll Ox BA 78 MA 81. Ridley Hall Cam 79. **d** 81 **p** 82. C Chadkirk *Ches* 81–84; C Macclesfield St Pet 84–85; C Macclesfield Team 85–89; R Elworth and Warmingham 89–99; Chapl Framlingham Coll 99–01; Chapl Rendcomb Coll Cirencester 01–09; P-in-c Rendcomb *Glouc* 01–09; R Thrapston, Denford and Islip *Pet* 09–15; R Chenderit 15–17; V Balderstone, Mellor and Samlesbury *Blackb* 17–19; P-in-c Walton-on-

Trent w Croxall, Rosliston etc *Derby* 19–21; P-in-c Seale and Lullington w Coton in the Elms 19–21; P-in-c Stapenhill Immanuel 19–21; rtd 21. *12 Ardmillan Lane, Oswestry SY11 2JY* E: revcjefferson@uwclub.net

JEFFERSON, David Charles. b 33. Leeds Univ BA 57. Coll of Resurr Mirfield 57. **d** 59 **p** 60. C Kennington Cross St Anselm *S'wark* 59–62; C Richmond St Mary w St Matthias 62–64; Chapl Wilson's Gr Sch Camberwell 64–93; Chapl Wilson's Sch Wallington 75–99; Public Preacher *S'wark* 64–74; Hon C Carshalton Beeches 74–04; rtd 93; PtO *S'wark* 04–13. *15 Sandown Drive, Carshalton SM5 4LN* T: (020) 8669 0640 *or* 8773 2931

JEFFERY, Graham. b 35. Qu Coll Cam BA 58. Wells Th Coll 58. **d** 60 **p** 61. C Southampton Maybush St Pet *Win* 60–63; Australia 63–66; C E Grinstead St Swithun *Chich* 66–68; C-in-c The Hydneye CD 68–74; V Wick 74–76; C Hove 76–78; P-in-c Newtimber w Pyecombe 78–82; R Poynings w Edburton, Newtimber and Pyecombe 82–92; P-in-c Sullington and Thakeham w Warminghurst 92–95; rtd 96; NSM Edburton *Chich* 97–99; PtO 00–17; NSM Poynings w Edburton, Newtimber and Pyecombe 17–18. *6 Orchard Close, Small Dole, Henfield BN5 9YA*

JEFFERY (née CAW), Canon Hannah Mary. b 69. Birm Univ BMus 90. St Jo Coll Nottm MA 95. **d** 95 **p** 96. C Northampton St Giles *Pet* 95–99; Hon C Hanger Hill Ascension and W Twyford St Mary *Lon* 99–04; TV Northampton Em *Pet* 04–11; CMD Officer 11–16; Chapl Bp Stopford Sch 11–16; R Desborough, Brampton Ash, Dingley and Braybrooke *Pet* from 16; RD Kettering from 17; Can Pet Cathl from 19. *The Vicarage, Lower Street, Desborough, Kettering NN14 2NP* T: (01536) 660415 M: 07761-288326 E: revhj@outlook.com

JEFFERY, Harry Ernest. b 59. **d** 11. NSM Bardney *Linc* from 11. *28 Station Road, Bardney, Lincoln LN3 5UD*

JEFFERY, Mrs Jennifer Ann. b 45. Philippa Fawcett Coll CertEd 66. STETS. **d** 02 **p** 03. NSM Wilton *B & W* 02–05; Chapl Bp Henderson Sch from 07; rtd 15; PtO *B & W* from 15. *4 Southwell, Trull, Taunton TA3 7HU* T: (01823) 286589 M: 07979-285607 E: revjen@sky.com

JEFFERY, Jonathan George Piers. b 63. Man Univ LLB 84. Ripon Coll Cuddesdon 95. **d** 97 **p** 98. C Lee-on-the-Solent *Portsm* 97–01; V Leigh Park from 01; V Warren Park from 01; AD Havant 09–14. *The Vicarage, Riders Lane, Havant PO9 4QT* T: (023) 9247 5276 E: jonathanjeffery7@btinternet.com

JEFFERY (née JACK), Mrs Judith Ann. b 54. Wycliffe Hall Ox 03. **d** 05 **p** 06. C Tetbury, Beverston and Long Newnton *Glouc* 05–10; C Shipton Moyne 05–10; P-in-c Baltonsborough w Butleigh, W Bradley etc *B & W* 10–15; R Crook Peak 15–21; rtd 21. *Old Hall House, Ham Street, Baltonsborough, Glastonbury BA6 8PX* E: judithjack@talktalk.net

JEFFERY, Kenneth Charles. b 40. Univ of Wales BA 64 Linacre Coll Ox BA 67 MA 70. St Steph Ho Ox 64. **d** 67 **p** 68. C Swindon New Town *Bris* 67–68; C Summertown *Ox* 68–71; C Brighton St Pet *Chich* 71–77; V Ditchling 77–00; rtd 01; PtO *Ox* from 19. *Carrick House, 2 South Street, Caulcott, Bicester OX25 4NE* T: (01869) 343114 E: fruitlands@live.co.uk

JEFFERY, Michael Frank. b 48. Linc Th Coll 74. **d** 76 **p** 77. C Caterham Valley *S'wark* 76–79; C Tupsley *Heref* 79–82; P-in-c Stretton Sugwas 82–84; P-in-c Bishopstone 83–84; P-in-c Kenchester and Bridge Sollers 83–84; V Whiteshill *Glouc* 84–92; P-in-c Randwick 92; V Whiteshill and Randwick 93–02; TV Bedminster *Bris* 02–09; P-in-c 09–13; rtd 13; PtO *B & W* 13–21. *1 The Almshouses, High Street, Northleach, Cheltenham GL54 3EU* E: michael@not2arty.com

JEFFERY, Peter James. b 41. Leeds Univ BSc 63. Oak Hill Th Coll 64. **d** 66 **p** 67. C Streatham Park St Alb *S'wark* 66–70; C Northampton St Giles *Pet* 70–73; C Rushden St Pet 73–76; C Rushden w Newton Bromswold 77–78; V Siddal *Wakef* 78–85; V Sowerby Bridge w Norland 85–98; P-in-c Cornholme 98–00; P-in-c Walsden 98–00; V Cornholme and Walsden 00–05; rtd 05; PtO *Wakef* 07–14; *Leeds* from 14. *12 Highcroft Road, Todmorden OL14 5LZ* T: (01706) 839781 E: pandm.jeffery@tiscali.co.uk

JEFFERY, Richard William Christopher. b 43. Ex Univ BA 65. Coll of Resurr Mirfield 66. **d** 68 **p** 69. C Wymering w Widley *Portsm* 68–71; C Salisbury St Mich *Sarum* 71–74; TV Ridgeway 74–80; V Stanford in the Vale w Goosey and Hatford *Ox* 80–89; V Topsham *Ex* 89–09; RD Aylesbeare 01–07; rtd 09; P-in-c Topsham and Wear *Ex* 09–13; PtO from 13. *5 Brownlees, Exminster, Exeter EX6 8SW* T: (01392) 823526 E: richardwcj@gmail.com

JEFFREY, Katrina. See METZNER, Katrina

JEFFREY, William Kenneth. CITI. **d** 17 **p** 18. Killaney w Carryduff *D & D* 17–18; C Ballymacash *Conn* from 18. *79 Kings*

Road, Belfast BT6 7BU T: (028) 9070 3949 M: 07443-462265 E: jeffreyw@tcd.ie *or* williamjeffrey01@btinternet.com

JEFFREYS, David John. b 45. S Dios Minl Tr Scheme 89. **d** 92 **p** 93. NSM Bexhill St Barn *Chich* 92–95; Chapl Hastings and Rother NHS Trust 95–02; Chapl E Sussex Hosps NHS Trust 02–05; Chapl Team Ldr 05–09; rtd 09; PtO *Chich* from 10. *4 Osbern Close, Bexhill-on-Sea TN39 4TJ* T: (01424) 843672 E: frdavid@onetel.com

JEFFREYS (née DESHPANDE), Lakshmi Anant. b 64. Liv Univ BSc 86 St Luke's Coll Ex PGCE 87. Wycliffe Hall Ox BTh 94. **d** 94 **p** 95. C Long Eaton St Jo *Derby* 94–97; Chapl Nottm Trent Univ *S'well* 98–03; PtO *Derby* 03–04; Dioc Miss Adv 04–13; P-in-c Wootton w Quinton and Preston Deanery *Pet* 13–15; V Wootton from 15; Asst Dir Ords from 14. *The Rectory, Water Lane, Wootton, Northampton NN4 6HH* T: (01604) 962061 E: woottonvicar@talktalk.net

JELLEY, Ian. b 54. Newc Univ MA 94 Dur Univ MA 03. NEOC 89. **d** 91 **p** 92. C Jarrow *Dur* 91–95; P-in-c Leam Lane 95–96; Chapl HM Pris Holme Ho 96–01; R Grindon, Stillington and Wolviston *Dur* 01–03; rtd 03; PtO *Dur* from 03. *1 Rievaulx Avenue, Billingham TS23 2BP* E: lun1204@hotmail.co.uk

JELLEY, James Dudley. b 46. Linc Th Coll 78. **d** 80 **p** 81. C Stockwell Green St Andr *S'wark* 80–85; V Camberwell St Phil and St Mark 85–93; PtO 93–96; V Camberwell St Luke 96–13; RD Camberwell 00–06; rtd 13; PtO *S'wark* 13–18; Hon C Brede w Udimore and Beckley and Peasmarsh *Chich* from 18. *Vine Cottage, Main Street, Peasmarsh, Rye TN31 6UL*

✠**JELLEY (née CAPITANCHIK), The Rt Revd Sophie Rebecca.** b 72. Leeds Univ BA 93. Wycliffe Hall Ox MPhil 97. **d** 97 **p** 98 **c** 20. C Shipley St Pet *Bradf* 97–00; CMS Uganda 00–03; C Churt and Hindhead *Guildf* 03–10; V Burgess Hill St Andr *Chich* 10–15; Dir Miss, Min and Discipleship *Dur* 15–20; Can Res Dur Cathl 15–20; Suff Bp Doncaster *Sheff* from 20. *Oak Tree House, 22A Hatchell Drive, Doncaster DN4 6SH* T: (01302) 846610 M: 07884-186689 E: bishopsophie@bishopofdoncaster.org.uk

JELLEYMAN, Susan. b 53. WEMTC 14. **d** 18 **p** 19. NSM Apedale Gp *Heref* from 18. *35 Stretton Farm Road, Church Stretton SY6 6DX* T: (01694) 724031 E: suejellsincs@btinternet.com *or* apedalecurate@gmail.com

JEMMETT, Melanie Jane. b 72. Surrey Univ BA 93 Cam Univ BTh 14 Middx Univ PGCE 96. Westcott Ho Cam 12. **d** 14 **p** 15. C Fawkham and Hartley *Roch* 14–17; V Lamorbey H Redeemer from 17; AD Sidcup from 19. *Holy Redeemer Vicarage, 64 Day's Lane, Sidcup DA15 8JR* T: (020) 8300 1508 E: melaniejemmett@btinternet.com

JENKIN, Canon Charles Alexander Graham. b 54. BScEng. Westcott Ho Cam 81. **d** 84 **p** 85. C Binley *Cov* 84–88; TV Canvey Is *Chelmsf* 88–94; TR Melton Mowbray *Leic* 94–08; RD Framland 98–02; Hon Can Leic Cathl 06–08; V Ipswich St Mary-le-Tower *St E* 08–21; RD Ipswich 12–17; rtd 21; Bp's Interfaith Adv *St E* from 09; Hon Can St E Cathl from 17. *7 Briarwood Avnue, Bury St Edmunds IP33 3QF* E: charles@jenkin.uk.net

JENKIN, Christopher Cameron. b 36. BNC Ox BA 61 MA 64. Clifton Th Coll 61. **d** 63 **p** 64. C Walthamstow St Mary *Chelmsf* 63–68; C Surbiton Hill Ch Ch *S'wark* 68–78; V Newport St Jo *Portsm* 78–88; TR Newbarns w Hawcoat *Carl* 88–01; rtd 01; PtO *Carl* from 01. *Beckside, Orton, Penrith CA10 3RX* T: (01539) 624410 E: chriscjenkin@aol.com

JENKINS, Alan David. b 60. Bris Poly BA 83 Spurgeon's Coll MTh 02. Wycliffe Hall Ox 89. **d** 95 **p** 96. C Tunbridge Wells St Jas w St Phil *Roch* 95–01; TV S Gillingham 01–07; R Gt Bookham *Guildf* from 07; AD Leatherhead from 15. *The Rectory, 2A Fife Way, Bookham, Leatherhead KT23 3PH* T: (01372) 452405 E: alan.jenkins@stnicolasbookham.org.uk

JENKINS, Miss Anne Christina. b 47. Birm Univ BA 70 Hull Univ CertEd 71 St Jo Coll Dur BA 77 Leeds Univ MA 92. Cranmer Hall Dur 75. **dss** 78 **d** 87 **p** 94. E Coatham *York* 78–81; OHP 81–87; PtO *York* 81–87; Ghana 87–88; Par Dn Beeston *Ripon* 88–93; Par Dn Leeds Gipton Epiphany 93–94; V Leeds St Marg and All Hallows 94–99; rtd 99; PtO *York* 00–14; P-in-c Costa Brava *Eur* 12–17; PtO *York* from 19; *Eur* from 18. *28 Hill Cottages, Rosedale East, Pickering YO18 8RG* T: (01751) 417130

JENKINS, Audrey Joan. b 36. TCert 61. St D Coll Lamp. **d** 01 **p** 06. Par Dn Marshfield and Peterstone Wentloog etc *Mon* 01–06; NSM Llanrumney from 06. *10 Cwrt Pencraig, 8 Caerau Crescent, Newport NP20 4HG* T: (01633) 263470

JENKINS, Clifford Thomas. b 38. Westmr Coll Ox MTh 02 IEng MIElecIE. Sarum & Wells Th Coll 74. **d** 77 **p** 78. Chapl Yeovil Coll 77–86; Hon C Yeovil w Kingston Pitney *B & W* 77–80; P-in-c 80–86; Chs FE Liaison Officer B & W, Bris and Glouc 87–90; PtO *B & W* 87–19; FE Adv Gen Syn Bd of Educn and Meth Ch 90–98; rtd 98. *Bethany, 10 Grove Avenue, Yeovil BA20 2BB* T: (01935) 475043

JENKINS, Clive Ronald. b 57. Chich Univ BA 08. Ripon Coll Cuddesdon 81. **d** 84 **p** 85. C E Grinstead St Swithun *Chich* 84–87; C Horsham 87–88; TV 88–90; Dioc Youth Chapl 90–96; P-in-c Amberley w N Stoke and Parham, Wiggonholt etc 93–96; V Southbourne w W Thorney 96–15; RD Westbourne 11–15; P-in-c Wisborough Green 15–20; V from 20; P-in-c Kirdford from 21. *The Vicarage, Billingshurst Road, Wisborough Green, Billingshurst RH14 0DZ* T: (01403) 700339 M: 07812-740720 E: candmjenkins@hotmail.com

JENKINS, David. *See* JENKINS, Richard David

JENKINS, David. *See* JENKINS, William David

JENKINS, David Alan. b 62. Linc Sch of Th and Min 15. **d** 18 **p** 19. C Quarrington w Old Sleaford *Linc* 18–21; P-in-c N Lafford Gp from 21. *The Rectory, 2 All Saints' Close, Ruskington, Sleaford NG34 9FP* M: 07908-738039 E: ajenkins016@gmail.com

JENKINS, The Ven David Harold. b 61. SS Coll Cam BA 84 MA 87 Ox Univ BA 88 MA 94 Univ of Wales (Lamp) PhD 08. Ripon Coll Cuddesdon 86. **d** 89 **p** 90. C Chesterton Gd Shep *Ely* 89–91; C Earley St Pet *Ox* 91–94; V Blackpool St Mich *Blackb* 94–99; V Broughton 99–04; AD Preston 04; Can Res Carl Cathl 04–10; Dir of Educn 04–10; Adn Sudbury *St E* from 10; NSM St Edm Way 16–18. *Sudbury Lodge, Stanningfield Road, Great Whelnetham, Bury St Edmunds IP30 0TL* T: (01284) 386942 M: 07900-990073 E: archdeacon.david@cofesuffolk.org

JENKINS, Prof David Harrison. b 52. **d** 15 **p** 16. NSM St Ishmael's w Llan-saint and Ferryside *St D* 15–18. *17 Parc Y Ffynnon, Ferryside SA17 5TQ* T: (01267) 268230

JENKINS, David Thomas. b 43. Ox Univ MA 94 RIBA 70. S'wark Ord Course 76. **d** 79 **p** 80. NSM Merthyr Tydfil and Cyfarthfa *Llan* 79–86; NSM Brecon St David w Llanspyddid and Llanilltyd *S & B* 86–91; P-in-c Llangiwg 91–92; V 92–01; Chapl Puerto de la Cruz Tenerife *Eur* 02–09; rtd 09. *15 Highmoor, Maritime Quarter, Swansea SA1 1YE* M: 07974-748476 E: jenkins@tinyonline.co.uk

JENKINS, David William. b 43. **d** 12 **p** 13. OLM Busbridge and Hambledon *Guildf* from 12. *Medlar House, 6 Quartermile Road, Godalming GU7 1TG* T: (01483) 416084 E: david.jenkins@djturfcare.co.uk

JENKINS, Canon Eric Robert. b 52. Poly Cen Lon BSc 74. STETS 97. **d** 00 **p** 01. C Weybridge *Guildf* 00–04; R Cobham and Stoke D'Abernon 04–17; RD Leatherhead 08–15; Hon Can Guildf Cathl 15–17; rtd 17. *69 The Glade, Fetcham, Leatherhead KT22 9TF* M: 07747-844689 E: er.jenkins@btinternet.com

JENKINS, Mrs Fiona. b 59. Dur Univ BSc 80 York St Jo Coll MA 04. St Jo Coll Nottm 04. **d** 06 **p** 07. C Settle *Bradf* 06–08; C Linton in Craven 08–14; Leeds 14–15; C Kettlewell w Conistone, Hubberholme etc *Bradf* 08–14; Leeds 14–15; V Burnsall w Rylstone *Bradf* 08–14; Leeds 14–15; V Chipping and Whitewell *Blackb* 15–18; V Chipping 18–21; rtd 21. *7 Lazonby Hall, Lazonby, Penrith CA10 1AZ*

JENKINS, Garry Frederick. b 48. Southn Univ BTh 79. Chich Th Coll 75. **d** 79 **p** 80. C Kingsbury St Andr *Lon* 79–84; C Leigh St Clem *Chelmsf* 84–88; P-in-c Brentwood St Geo 88–94; V 94–18; Chapl NE Lon Foundn Trust 02–18; rtd 18; P-in-c New Brompton St Luke *Roch* from 19. *51 Trinity Road, Gillingham ME7 1JA* E: g.jenkins197@btinternet.com

JENKINS, Canon Gary John. b 59. York Univ BA 80 CertEd 81. Oak Hill Th Coll BA 89. **d** 89 **p** 90. C Norwood St Luke *S'wark* 89–94; P-in-c St Helier 94–95; V 95–01; V Redhill H Trin 01–12; AD Reigate 12; V Bermondsey St Jas and St Anne from 13; AD Bermondsey from 18; Hon Can S'wark Cathl from 06. *St James's Vicarage, 4 Thurland Road, London SE16 4AA* T: (020) 7394 1482 E: garyjjenkins@outlook.com

JENKINS, Glyn Frank. b 34. Keble Coll Ox BA 55 MA 59 DipEd 58. **d** 14 **p** 14. NSM Bassaleg *Mon* from 14. *10 Cwrt Pencraig, 9 Caerau Crescent, Newport NP20 4HG*

JENKINS, Canon Jeanette. b 42. St Jo Coll Nottm 83. **dss** 84 **d** 86 **p** 94. NSM Kilmarnock *Glas* 84–94; NSM Irvine St Andr LEP 84–94; NSM Ardrossan 84–94; Asst Chapl Crosshouse Hosp 86–94; Chapl Ayrshire Hospice 90–02; Can St Mary's Cathl *Glas* from 99; LtO from 12. *4 Gleneagles Avenue, Kilwinning KA13 6RD* T: (01294) 553383 M: 07775-595109 E: revj.jenkins@btinternet.com

JENKINS, John. b 49. **d** 14 **p** 15. NSM Uxbridge *Lon* from 14. *39 Church Road, Uxbridge UB8 3ND* T: (01895) 812670 E: john.jenkins@uxbridgeparish.com

JENKINS, John Francis. b 46. Ripon Hall Ox 77 Ripon Coll Cuddesdon 75. **d** 77 **p** 78. C Filton *Bris* 77–79; C Bris St Andr Hartcliffe 79–84; P-in-c Bris H Cross Inns Court 84–85; V 85–95; R Odcombe, Brympton, Lufton and Montacute *B & W* 95–14; rtd 14. *10 Cursley Path, Wells BA5 1FF* E: johnjenkins382@btinternet.com

JENKINS, John Rhys. b 64. Southn Univ BM 89 MRCGP 94 DRCOG 93. St Mich Coll Llan 09. d 13 p 14. NSM Roath *Llan* 13–19; NSM Canton Cardiff from 19. *1 Thompson Avenue, Cardiff CF5 1EX* E: jrhysj@ntlworld.com

JENKINS, Julian James. b 56. St Mich Coll Llan 97. d 99 p 00. C Whitchurch *Llan* 99–01; TV Aberavon 01–05; TV Cowbridge 05–11; P-in-c Llandyfodwg and Cwm Ogwr from 11. *The Vicarage, Coronation Street, Ogmore Vale, Bridgend CF32 7HE* T: (01656) 840248

JENKINS, Katrina Tracey. b 66. St Aug Coll Cant 19. d 21. C Hersham *Guildf* from 21. *The Parish Office, St Peter's Church Hall, 1 Burwood Road, Hersham, Walton-on-Thames KT12 4AA* M: 07787-308033 E: curate@stpetershersham.com

JENKINS, Canon Lawrence Clifford. b 45. Open Univ BA 77 AKC 70. St Aug Coll Cant. d 71 p 72. C Osmondthorpe St Phil *Ripon* 71–74; C Monkseaton St Mary *Newc* 74–78; V Shiremoor 78–84; V Wheatley Hills *Sheff* 84–95; RD Doncaster 92–95; V Greenhill 95–10; Hon Can Sheff Cathl 08–10; rtd 10; PtO *Sheff* from 11. *10 Chiltern Crescent, Sprotbrough, Doncaster DN5 7PE* T: (01302) 856587 E: lawriejenkins@virginmedia.com

JENKINS, Canon Paul Morgan. b 44. Sussex Univ BEd 68 Fitzw Coll Cam BA 73 MA 76. Westcott Ho Cam 71. d 74 p 75. C Forest Gate St Edm *Chelmsf* 74–77; P-in-c Stourpaine, Durweston and Bryanston *Sarum* 77–83; Chapl Bryanston Sch 77–85; Chapl Repton Sch Derby 84–89; Dean of Chpl 89–91; V W Dean *Chich* 91–97; V E Dean 91–97; R Singleton 91–97; Dir St Columba's Retreat and Conf Cen 97–07; Chapl Community of St Pet Woking 03–07; P-in-c Dunsfold and Hascombe *Guildf* 07–12; Hon Can Guildf Cathl 05–12; Master Hugh Sexey's Hosp Bruton 12–17; PtO *B & W* 17–19. *5 Wren Quad, Bromley College, London Road, Bromley BR1 1PE* T: (01342) 872864 E: pjenkins44@aol.com

JENKINS (née RICHARDSON), Pauline Kate. b 41. RGN 62 Nottm Univ CertEd 80 RNT 83. St Jo Coll Nottm 91. d 94 p 98. Uganda 94–96; PtO *S'well* 96–98; NSM Selston 98–01; NSM Annesley w Newstead 01–03; rtd 03; PtO *S'well* 03–15; *Leic* 07–17; *S'wark* from 17. *45 March Court, Warwick Drive, London SW15 6LE* T: (020) 8789 3396 E: revd.p.k.jenkins@gmail.com

JENKINS, Rhys. See JENKINS, John Rhys

JENKINS, Preb Richard David. b 33. Magd Coll Cam BA 58 MA. Westcott Ho Cam 59. d 61 p 62. C Staveley *Derby* 61–64; C Billingham St Aid *Dur* 64–68; V Walsall Pleck and Bescot *Lich* 68–73; R Whitchurch 73–97; RD Wem and Whitchurch 85–95; P-in-c Tilstock and Whixall 92–95; Preb Lich Cathl 93–97; rtd 97; PtO *Lich* 99–17. *The Council House, Council House Court, Castle Street, Shrewsbury SY1 2AU* T: (01743) 270051

JENKINS, Richard Morvan. b 44. St Mich Coll Llan 65. d 69 p 70. C Tenby *St D* 69–73; V Llanrhian w Llanhywel and Carnhedryn etc 73–80; R Johnston w Steynton 80–93; V St Ishmael's w Llan-saint and Ferryside 93–09; rtd 09; PtO *St D* from 11. *Geirionydd, 7 Dwynant, Furnace Road, Burry Port SA16 0YQ* T: (01554) 834761

JENKINS, Robert. See JENKINS, Eric Robert

JENKINS, Rosemary Edith. b 47. Nottm Univ MA 04 RGN 68 RHV 71. EMMTC 01. d 04 p 05. NSM Bassingham Gp *Linc* 04–08; P-in-c Sibsey w Frithville 08–13; V 13–17; P-in-c Brothertoft Gp 10–13; V 13–17; rtd 17; PtO *Linc* 18–21. *11 Deepdale Drive, Leasingham, Sleaford NG34 8LR* T: (01529) 306816

JENKINS, Mrs Sarah Jean. b 65. Westcott Ho Cam 16. d 18 p 19. C Nacton and Levington w Bucklesham etc *St E* 18–20; C Waldringfield w Hemley and Newbourne 18–20; C Orwell and Deben from 20. *25 Weir Place, Kirton, Ipswich IP10 0QA* T: (01394) 448936 M: 07900-667089 E: revdsarahjenkins@gmail.com

JENKINS, Timothy David. b 52. Pemb Coll Ox BA 73 MLitt 77 MA 82 St Edm Ho Cam BA 84 PhD 01. Ridley Hall Cam 82. d 85 p 86. C Kingswood *Bris* 85–87; Sen Chapl Nottm Univ *S'well* 88–92; Dean of Chpl Jes Coll Cam 92–10; Fell 92–19; Can Th Leic Cathl 04–09; rtd 19. *50 Stanley Road, Cambridge CB5 8LB* T: (01223) 363185 E: tdj22@jesus.cam.ac.uk

JENKINS, Canon William David. b 42. Birm Univ BA 63. St D Coll Lamp LTh 65. d 65 p 66. C Gorseinon *S & B* 65–67; C Llanelli *St D* 67–72; V Clydach *S & B* 72–82; Chapl Gwynedd Hosp NHS Trust 82–97; V Llanrhos *St As* 82–97; RD Llanrwst 84–96; Can Cursal St As Cathl 93–97; TR Tenby *St D* 97–07; rtd 07; PtO *St As* from 09; *St D* from 11. *Kildare, 96 Conway Road, Llandudno LL30 1PP* T: (01492) 860176 M: 07791-738018

JENKINSON, Margaret. b 40. MCSP 62. Carl Dioc Tr Inst 89. d 92 p 94. NSM Preesall *Blackb* 92–96; NSM Lanercost, Walton, Gilsland and Nether Denton *Carl*

96–04; P-in-c Lorton and Loweswater w Buttermere 04–13; rtd 13; PtO *Blackb* from 14. *10 The Conifers, Hambleton, Poulton-le-Fylde FY6 9EP* T: (01253) 702237 E: margaretjenkinson@btinternet.com

JENKYNS, John Thomas William Basil. b 30. Univ of Wales (Lamp) BA 54 St Cath Coll Ox BA 57 MA 62. Wycliffe Hall Ox 54. d 57 p 58. C Neasden cum Kingsbury St Cath *Lon* 57–60; C S Lyncombe *B & W* 60–64; V Gt Harwood St Bart *Blackb* 64–66; R Colne St Bart 66–69; V Chard St Mary *B & W* 69–87; Preb Wells Cathl 87; V Swaffham *Nor* 87–89; V Overbury w Teddington, Alstone etc *Worc* 89–95; rtd 95; PtO *St E* 10–14. *9 Aldeburgh Road, Leiston IP16 4JY*

JENNER, Peter David. b 67. d 95 p 96. C Staines *Lon* 15–18; V Hinchley Wood *Guildf* from 18. *The Vicarage, 98 Manor Road North, Esher KT10 0AD* T: (020) 8398 9095 M: 07824-323815 E: vicar@stchristopherschurch.org.uk

JENNER, Canon Peter John. b 56. Chu Coll Cam BA 77 PhD 80 MA 81. St Jo Coll Nottm 82. d 85 p 86. C Upperby St Jo *Carl* 85–88; Chapl Reading Univ *Ox* 88–96; P-in-c Mellor *Derby* 96–99; V 99–06; V Mellor *Ches* 06–12; RD Chadkirk 08–11; Can Res Ches Cathl 12–15; Chapl Ches Univ from 12. *22 Balmoral Park, Chester CH1 4BQ* E: jennerfamily@btinternet.com *or* p.jenner@chester.ac.uk

JENNER, William George. b 37. Nottm Univ BSc 59 K Coll Lon PGCE 60. d 97 p 98. OLM Gillingham w Geldeston, Stockton, Ellingham etc *Nor* 97–05; PtO from 05. *3 Woodland Drive, Kirby Cane, Bungay NR35 2PT* T: (01508) 518229 E: williamgjenner@gmail.com

JENNETT, The Ven Maurice Arthur. b 34. St Jo Coll Dur BA 60. Cranmer Hall Dur 60. d 62 p 63. C Marple All SS *Ches* 62–67; V Withnell *Blackb* 67–75; V Stranton *Dur* 75–91; Crosslinks Zimbabwe 92–99; Asst P Nyanga Mary Magd 92–93; R 93–99; Can and Adn Manicaland N 97; rtd 99; PtO *Ripon* 01–14; *Leeds* 14–16; *York* from 17. *1 Dulverton Hall, Esplanade, Scarborough YO11 2AR* T: (01723) 372954

JENNINGS, Clive John. b 57. Trin Coll Bris. d 00 p 01. C Milton *B & W* 00–02; C Clevedon St Andr and Ch Ch 02–18; V Clevedon Ch Ch from 18. *12 Princes Road, Clevedon BS21 7SZ* T: (01275) 872134 E: vicar@christchurch-clevedon.org.uk

✠**JENNINGS, The Rt Revd David Willfred Michael.** b 44. AKC 66. d 67 p 68 c 00. C Walton St Mary *Liv* 67–69; C Christchurch *Win* 69–73; V Hythe 73–80; V Romford St Edw *Chelmsf* 80–92; RD Havering 85–92; Hon Can Chelmsf Cathl 87–92; Adn Southend 92–00; Suff Bp Warrington *Liv* 00–09; rtd 09; PtO *Ox* 10–13; Hon Asst Bp Ox from 13; Hon Asst Bp Glouc from 10. *The Laurels, High Street, Northleach, Cheltenham GL54 3ET* T: (01451) 860743 E: bishopdavidjennings@gmail.com

JENNINGS, Duncan William. b 54. UWE MA. STETS 05. d 08 p 09. C Southampton Thornhill St Chris *Win* 08–11; P-in-c 11–21; V from 21. *St Christopher's Vicarage, 402 Hinkler Road, Southampton SO19 6DF* T: (023) 8122 5911

JENNINGS, Canon Frederick David. b 48. K Coll Lon BD 73 AKC 73 Loughb Univ MPhil 98. St Aug Coll Cant 73. d 74 p 75. C Halesowen *Worc* 74–77; PtO *Birm* 78–80; *Leic* 78–80 and 85–87; P-in-c Snibston 80–85; Community Relns Officer 81–84; P-in-c Burbage w Aston Flamville 85–87; R 91–14; Hon Can Leic Cathl 03–10; Project officer for Ch and Soc 11–14; rtd 14; Can Th Leic Cathl from 10; PtO from 14. *59 Pipistrelle Drive, Market Bosworth, Nuneaton CV13 0NW* T: (01455) 698805 M: 07710-205582 E: revdavidjennings@talktalk.net

JENNINGS, Ian Matheson. b 47. Leeds Univ MA 98. NOC 95. d 97 p 97. NSM Hackenthorpe *Sheff* 97–01; Asst Chapl HM Pris and YOI Doncaster 97–98; Chapl 98–01; V Sheff St Cuth 01–06; TR Aston cum Aughton w Swallownest and Ulley 06–15; rtd 15; PtO *Sheff* from 16; Hon C Denham *Ox* from 19. *The Annexe, Kayalami, The Pyghtle, Denham, Uxbridge UB9 5BD* E: ianjennings@denhamparish.church

JENNINGS, Ian Richard. b 65. Liv Univ BA 88 Wolv Poly PGCE 91. Trin Coll Bris 07. d 09 p 10. C Pedmore *Worc* 09–13; C The Lye and Stambermill 13–14; V Low Moor and Oakenshaw *Leeds* from 14. *The Vicarage, Park House Road, Low Moor, Bradford BD12 0HR* M: 07722-019096 E: ianrichardjennings@gmail.com

JENNINGS, Janet. b 38. SCM 71 SRN 74. Oak Hill Th Coll BA 87. d 88 p 97. Par Dn Stevenage St Pet Broadwater *St Alb* 88–90; PtO *St As* 92–14. *5 Elsted Road, Bexhill-on-Sea TN39 3BG* T: (01424) 843669 E: wandjjennings@hotmail.com

JENNINGS, Jonathan Peter. b 61. K Coll Lon BD 83. Westcott Ho Cam 84. d 86 p 87. C Peterlee *Dur* 86–89; C Darlington St Cuth 89–92; Dioc Communications Officer *Man* 92–95; Broadcasting Officer Gen Syn 95–01; PtO *S'wark* 95–98; Hon C Banstead *Guildf* 98–04; Abp Cant's Press Sec 01–08; PtO *Cant* 05–08; *Roch* 05–08; P-in-c Gillingham St Aug 08–16;

RD Gillingham 10–11; C Rainham from 16. *7 Elmstone Road, Gillingham ME8 9BD* E: revjpj@aol.com

JENNINGS, Mrs Natalie Amy. b 95. Ex Univ BA 17. Cranmer Hall Dur 19. **d** 21. C Maund Gp *Heref* from 21. *79 Bridle Road, Hereford HR4 0PW* M: 07422-655321 E: revd.njennings@gmail.com

JENNINGS, Robert Henry. b 46. St Jo Coll Dur BA 69 MA 79. Qu Coll Birm. **d** 72 **p** 73. C Dursley *Glouc* 72–74; C Coleford w Staunton 75–78; TV Bottesford w Ashby *Linc* 78–83; TV Witney *Ox* 83–89; V Lane End w Cadmore End 89–16; rtd 16; PtO *Ox* from 16. *3 Fall Close, Aylesbury HP19 9XR* M: 07866-027542 E: revrobjennings@gmail.com

JENNINGS, Mrs Susan Mary. b 61. MCSP 82. St Jo Coll Nottm BA 15. **d** 15 **p** 16. C Manningham *Leeds* 15–18; C Girlington, Heaton and Manningham 18–21. *Address temp unknown* M: 07963-279153 E: suemaryjennings@gmail.com

JENNINGS, Walter James. b 37. Birm Univ BMus 60 MA 90. Qu Coll Birm 77. **d** 80 **p** 81. Hon C Hampton in Arden *Birm* 80–84; Chapl St Alb Aided Sch Highgate Birm 84–86; C Wotton-under-Edge w Ozleworth and N Nibley *Glouc* 86–89; V Pittville All SS 89–98; rtd 98; Chapl Beauchamp Community 98–00; PtO *Worc* 98–14. *1 Elgar Court, 27 Hampton Park Road, Hereford HR1 1TH* T: (01432) 271841 E: walterlinda.jennings@gmail.com

JENSEN, Alexander Sönderup. b 68. Tübingen Univ 94 St Jo Coll Dur PhD 97 Ox Univ MTh 01. St Steph Ho Ox 97. **d** 99 **p** 00. C Norton St Mich *Dur* 99–02; Lect CITC 02–05; Hon C Ch Ch Cathl Dublin *D & G* 02–05; Lect Murdoch Univ w Perth Th Hall Australia 05–07; Sen Lect 08–15; Prin Perth Th Hall 06–12; Hon C Perth Cathl 05–15; Prin ERMC from 16. *Eastern Region Ministry Course, 1A The Bounds, Lady Margaret Road, Cambridge CB3 0BJ* T: (01223) 760444 E: asj43@cam.ac.uk

JENSEN, Juliet Helen. b 68. Man Univ MB, ChB 92 Univ Coll Lon MSc 97. STETS 11. **d** 13 **p** 14. C Forest Gate Em w Upton Cross *Chelmsf* 13–16; V Glouc St Jas and All SS and Ch Ch from 16. *The Vicarage, 1 The Conifers, Gloucester GL1 4LP* T: (01452) 422349 M: 07946-869324 E: juliet.jensen@protonmail.com

JENSON, Philip Peter. b 56. Ex Coll Ox BA 78 MA 82 Down Coll Cam BA 80 MA 86 PhD 88. Ridley Hall Cam 80. **d** 87 **p** 88. C Gt Warley Ch Ch *Chelmsf* 87–89; Lect Trin Coll Bris 89–05; Lect Ridley Hall Cam 05–21; rtd 21. *Old Church House, Wisbech Road, Littleport, Ely CB6 1RG* T: (01353) 863956 E: ppj22@cam.ac.uk

JEPP, Malcolm Leonard. b 44. SWMTC 06. **d** 09 **p** 10. NSM Meneage *Truro* 09–14; rtd 14; PtO *Truro* from 14. *Polpidnick Cottage, Porthallow, St Keverne, Helston TR12 6PL* T/F: (01326) 281031 M: 07797-505539 E: lenjepp@jeppassociates.co.uk

JEPP (née NUGENT), Mrs Mary Patricia. b 55. Mt St Vincent Univ Canada BA 79 Univ of New Brunswick BEd 80 Open Univ MA 03 Anglia Ruskin Univ MA 14. ERMC 05. **d** 08 **p** 09. C Godmanchester *Ely* 08–11; P-in-c Alconbury cum Weston 11–14; P-in-c Winwick 11–14; P-in-c Hamerton 11–14; P-in-c Gt w Lt Gidding and Steeple Gidding 11–14; P-in-c Upton and Copmanford 11–14; P-in-c Buckworth 11–14; R N Leightonstone 14–17; R Kilmarnock *Glas* 17–20; Hon C W Meon and Warnford *Portsm* from 20; Hon C E Meon from 20; Hon C Langrish from 20. *The Rectory, Doctor's Lane, West Meon, Petersfield GU32 1LR* E: m.jepp@btinternet.com

JEPSON, Mrs Ann Brenda. b 46. Open Univ BA 81 Hockerill Coll Cam CertEd 68. LCTP 10. **d** 11 **p** 12. NSM Hurst Green and Mitton *Bradf* 11–13; NSM Ribchester w Stydd *Blackb* 13–15; rtd 15; PtO *Blackb* from 15; *Man* from 18. *Ribblesdale View, Greenside, Ribchester, Preston PR3 3ZJ* T: (01254) 878177 E: annjepson@btinternet.com

JEPSON, Joanna Elizabeth. b 76. Trin Coll Bris BA 99 UEA MA 03. Ridley Hall Cam 01. **d** 03 **p** 04. C Plas Newton *Ches* 03–06; Chapl Lon Coll of Fashion 06–11; P-in-c Fulham St Pet 06–09; PtO *Portsm* 12–13; CF (VR) from 13; Chapl Wells Cathl Sch 19. *4 The Liberty, Wells BA5 2SU* T: (01749) 673489 E: joeyjep@yahoo.com

JEPSON-BIDDLE, Canon Nicholas Lawrence. b 71. K Coll Lon BA 94 Leeds Univ MA 98. Coll of Resurr Mirfield 96. **d** 98 **p** 99. C Bedford St Andr *St Alb* 98–01; Bp's Dom Chapl and Research Asst *Chich* 01–04; P-in-c Brighton Gd Shep Preston 04–05; TV Putney St Mary *S'wark* 07–10; PV Westmr Abbey 08–10; Can Res Portsm Cathl 10–13; Can Res and Prec Wells Cathl *B & W* from 13. *4 The Liberty, Wells BA5 2SU* T: (01749) 673489 M: 07825-322326 E: nicklb@hotmail.co.uk

JEREMIAH, Anderson Harris Mithra. b 75. Madras Univ BA 95 MA 97 MPhil 98 Edin Univ PhD 09. United Th Coll Bangalore BD 02. **d** 03 **p** 04. C Ranipet St Mary India 03; Chapl Chr Medical Coll and Hosp Vellore 03–05; LtO *Edin* 06–08; C Edin Ch Ch 08–11; PtO *Blackb* 12–14; P-in-c Gisburn 14–16;

NSM Lancaster St Mary w St John and St Anne 16–17; PtO from 17; Bp's Adv for Black, Asian and Minority Ethnic Affairs from 18. *St Paul's Church, 24 Scotforth Road, Lancaster LA1 4ST* T: (01524) 298442 E: a.jeremiah@lancaster.ac.uk

JERMAIN, Jessica-Jil Stapleton. *See* AIDLEY, Jessica-Jil Stapleton

JERSEY, Dean of. *See* KEIRLE, The Very Revd Michael Robert

JERUSALEM AND THE MIDDLE EAST, President Bishop of the Episcopal Church in. *See* LEWIS, Michael Augustine Owen

JERVIS, Christopher. b 53. Loughb Univ BEd 75. Wycliffe Hall *Ox* 80. **d** 82 **p** 83. C Woodford Wells *Chelmsf* 82–85; Chapl Felsted Sch 85–87; Chapl Canford Sch 87–13; C Jersey St Helier *Win* 13–17; Provost Milton Abbey Community 17–19; PtO *Sarum* from 17; *Eur* from 19. *7 Woodlands, Hazelbury Bryan, Sturminster Newton DT10 2DD* T: (01258) 817969 E: cjervis7@gmail.com

JERVIS, William Edward. b 47. MRICS 74. Linc Th Coll 74. **d** 77 **p** 78. C W Bromwich All SS *Lich* 77–80; C Horsham *Chich* 80–86; R W Tarring 86–14; rtd 14; PtO Cyprus and the Gulf from 15; PtO *Chich* from 21. *5 Broadmark Beach, Broadmark Lane, Rustington, Littlehampton BN16 2JF* T: (01903) 367214 M: 07443-034094 E: edward.jervis@tiscali.co.uk

JERWOOD, Eleanor Alice Jerwood. *See* CLACK, Eleanor Alice Jerwood

JESSETT, David Charles. b 55. K Coll Lon BD 77 AKC 77 MTh. Westcott Ho Cam 78. **d** 79 **p** 80. C Aveley *Chelmsf* 79–82; C Walthamstow St Pet 82–85; P-in-c Hunningham *Cov* 85–91; P-in-c Wappenbury w Weston under Wetherley 85–91; Progr Dir Exploring Chr Min Scheme 85–91; Dir CME 87–90; PtO *Cov* 90–97; P-in-c Barford w Wasperton and Sherbourne 97–19; P-in-c Hampton Lucy w Charlecote and Loxley 07–19; rtd 19; PtO *Cov* from 19. *Address temp unknown*

JESSIMAN, Timothy Edward. b 58. Portsm Univ MA 06. Oak Hill Th Coll 88. **d** 91 **p** 92. C Baldock w Bygrave *St Alb* 91–95; C Bideford *Ex* 95–96; TV Bideford, Northam, Westward Ho!, Appledore etc 96–00; Chapl Grenville Coll Bideford 95–00; Chapl N Devon Healthcare NHS Trust 98–00; P-in-c Hartpland *Portsm* 00–06; V 06–13; P-in-c Stokesay *Heref* 13–17; P-in-c Halford w Sibdon Carwood 13–17; P-in-c Wistanstow 13–17; P-in-c Acton Scott 13–17; P-in-c Churchill and Langford *B & W* 17–20; rtd 20. *Address temp unknown*

JESSON, Alan Francis. b 47. TD 89. Loughb Univ MLS 77 Selw Coll Cam MA 87 ALA 70 FLA 91. EAMTC 88. **d** 91 **p** 92. NSM Swavesey *Ely* 91–95; NSM Fen Drayton w Conington and Lolworth etc 95–00; CF (ACF) 92–96; Sen Chapl ACF 96–14; R Outwell *Ely* 00–12; R Upwell St Pet 00–12; rtd 12; PtO *Ely* from 12; *Nor* from 01. *9 Lawn Lane, Sutton, Ely CB6 2RE* T: (01353) 776172

JESSON, Julia Margaret. b 54. St Matthias Coll Bris CertEd 75 Nottm Univ MA 04. EMMTC 01. **d** 04 **p** 05. NSM Stapleford *S'well* 04–07; C Kimberley 07–08; P-in-c E Markham w Askham, Headon w Upton and Grove 08–11; P-in-c Dunham w Darlton, Ragnall, Fledborough etc 08–11; TV Retford Area 11–17; AD Bassetlaw and Bawtry 16–17; V Knotty Ash St Jo Liv from 17. *The Vicarage, Thomas Lane, Liverpool L14 5NR* E: julia.jesson@btinternet.com

JESSOP, Canon Gillian Mary. b 48. Hatf Poly BSc 71 Nottm Univ MEd 85 Homerton Coll Cam PGCE 80. EAMTC 91. **d** 94 **p** 95. C Gt Yarmouth *Nor* 94–97; R Gt w Lt Addington and Woodford *Pet* 97–02; R Paston 02–15; Asst Dir Tr for Readers 00–02; Dir 02–10; RD Pet 10–15; Can Pet Cathl 11–15; rtd 15; PtO *Pet* from 15; *Ely* from 15. *35 Gidding Road, Sawtry, Huntingdon PE28 5TS* T: (01487) 832237 E: rev.gill69@gmail.com

JESSOP, Ms Tracy Jane. b 65. ERMC 16. **d** 19 **p** 20. C Wroxham w Hoveton, Belaugh and Tunstead etc *Nor* 19–20; C Aylsham and Distr from 20. *95 Holman Road, Aylsham, Norwich NR11 6BT* M: 07402-165485 E: tracy_jessop@btinternet.com

JESTY, Mrs Helen Margaret. b 51. York Univ BA 72. Cranmer Hall Dur BA 81. **dss** 82 **d** 87. S Lambeth St Steph *S'wark* 82–86; Norbiton 86–93; Par Dn 87–90; Hon Par Dn 91–93; Chapl Naomi Ho Hospice 05–13; rtd 13. *Fairfield, 1 Downside Road, Winchester SO22 5LT* T: (01962) 849190 E: helen.jesty@btinternet.com

JESUDASON, Leslie Peter Prakash. b 58. Wycliffe Hall Ox 05. **d** 07 **p** 08. C Throop *Win* 07–11; TV Bracknell *Ox* 11–19; V Croydon Ch Ch *S'wark* from 19. *The Vicarage, 34 Longley Road, Croydon CR0 3LH* T: (020) 8703 9205 E: ljesudason@outlook.com

JEVONS, The Ven Alan Neil. b 56. Ex Univ BA 77 Selw Coll Cam BA 80 MA 84. Ridley Hall Cam. **d** 81 **p** 82. C Halesowen *Worc* 81–84; C Heywood St Luke w All So *Man* 84–87; TV Heref St Martin w St Fran 87–93; P-in-c Much Birch w Lt

Birch, Much Dewchurch etc 93–02; RD Ross and Archenfield 98–02; TR Tenbury Wells 02–07; Preb Heref Cathl 02–07; RD Ludlow 05–07; V Llyn Safaddan *S & B* 07–15; C from 15; C The Beacons from 15; Dioc Tourism Officer 07–13; Asst Dioc Soc Resp Officer 09–13; Adn Brecon from 13. *The Vicarage, Llangorse, Brecon LD3 7UG* T: (01874) 658298 E: archdeacon.brecon@churchinwales.org.uk

JEVONS, Harry Clifford. b 46. Bp Otter Coll 01. **d** 04 **p** 05. C Ifield *Chich* 04–07; C Milton *Win* 07–11; C Ermington and Ugborough *Ex* 11–14; C Diptford, N Huish, Harberton, Harbertonford etc 11–14; P-in-c Torquay St Luke 14–16; C Paignton St Jo, St Andr and St Boniface 16–19; PtO from 19. *48 Knapp Park Road, Paignton TQ4 7LA* T: (01803) 525198 M: 07752-219505 E: fr.harry@hotmail.co.uk

JEWELL, Alan David John. b 59. St Cath Coll Ox MA 86. Wycliffe Hall Ox 83. **d** 86 **p** 87. C Walton H Trin *Ox* 86–91; TV Sutton *Liv* 91–97; TV Halewood 97–01; TR 01–12; TR Halewood and Hunts Cross 12–14; V Stretton and Appleton Thorn *Ches* from 14. *The Vicarage, Stretton Road, Stretton, Warrington WA4 4NT* T: (01925) 730276 E: alandjjewell@btopenworld.com

JEWISS, Anthony Harrison. b 39. Virginia Th Sem MDiv 92. **d** 92 **p** 93. Chapl to Bp Los Angeles USA 92–99; Can Prec Los Angeles 99; Dep Exec Officer Episc Ch Cen New York 99–07; rtd 07; Asst Chapl Midi-Pyrénées and Aude *Eur* 09–20. *1775 Ridgeview Circle West, Palm Springs CA 92264, USA* T: (001) (646) 644 6989 E: tonyjewiss@gmail.com

JEWITT, Martin Paul Noel. b 44. AKC 69. St Aug Coll Cant. **d** 70 **p** 71. C Usworth *Dur* 70–74; TV 77–78; Tutor Newton Coll Papua New Guinea 74–77; V Balham Hill Ascension *S'wark* 78–93; R N Reddish *Man* 93–99; V Thornton Heath St Paul *S'wark* 99–10; rtd 10; PtO *Cant* from 10. *12 Abbott Road, Folkestone CT20 1NG* T: (01303) 211491 M: 07981-754738 E: martin.jewitt@virginmedia.com

JEWSON, Dawn. b 56. St Mellitus Coll BA 13. **d** 13 **p** 14. C Southall St Geo *Lon* 13–16; P-in-c Hatfield Heath and Sheering *Chelmsf* from 16; P-in-c Hatfield Broad Oak and Bush End from 20; C Gt Hallingbury and Lt Hallingbury from 20. *The Vicarage, Broomfields, Hatfield Heath, Bishop's Stortford CM22 7EH* T: (01279) 730288 M: 07930-902507 E: rev.dawn.jewson@gmail.com

JEYES, Caroline Helen. *See* WALKER, Caroline Helen

JEYNES, Anthony James. b 44. AKC 68. St Boniface Warminster 68. **d** 69 **p** 70. C Ellesmere Port *Ches* 69–73; C Birkenhead St Pet w St Matt 73–74; R Oughtrington 75–80; C Timperley 80–85; C Eastham 85–89; V New Brighton St Jas 89–96; P-in-c New Brighton Em 94–96; R Tarleton *Blackb* 96–04; P-in-c Kyrenia St Andr and Chapl N Cyprus 04–07; Chapl Paphos 07–09; rtd 09; PtO Cyprus and the Gulf from 09; PtO *Ches* from 19. *6 Maidwell Close, Winsford CW7 3UG* T: (01608) 594572 M: 07485-000839 E: tonyirenejeynes@gmail.com

JINKS, Mrs Elizabeth. b 60. St Aug Coll of Th 16. **d** 19 **p** 20. NSM Holbrook *Chich* from 19. *St Mark's Church, St Mark's Lane, Horsham RH12 5PU* T: (01403) 275403 E: curate@stmarksholbrook.org.uk

JOACHIM, Margaret Jane. b 49. St Hugh's Coll Ox BA 70 MA 74 Birm Univ PhD 77 W Midl Coll of Educn PGCE 71 FGS 91. S Dios Minl Tr Scheme 91. **d** 94 **p** 95. NSM Ealing St Barn *Lon* 94–97; NSM Ealing St Pet Mt Park 97–19; PtO from 19. *8 Newburgh Road, London W3 6DQ* T: (020) 8723 4514 E: margaret.joachim@london.anglican.org

JOBBER, Barry William. b 38. N Staffs Poly BA 84. Cuddesdon Coll 73. **d** 75 **p** 76. C Fenton *Lich* 76–79; V Goldenhill 79–80; PtO *Ches* 90–02 and from 12; NSM Middlewich w Byley 02–08; NSM Witton 08–12; rtd 12. *16 Angus Grove, Middlewich CW10 9GR* T: (01606) 737386 M: 07974-380234 E: barry.jobber@uwclub.net

JOBBINS, John Clive. b 46. Bournemouth Univ BSc 06 Win Univ MA 11. Sarum Coll 08. **d** 15 **p** 16. NSM Winkleigh *Ex* 15–17; NSM Ashreigney 15–17; NSM Broadwoodkelly 15–17; NSM Brushford 15–17; NSM Burrington, Chawleigh, Cheldon, Chulmleigh etc 17–19; PtO from 19. *Vine Croft, Vine Street, Winkleigh EX19 8HN* M: 07745-684505 E: jclivejobbins@gmail.com

JOBLING, Mary. *See* ROLLS, Mary

✠**JOHN, The Rt Revd Andrew Thomas Griffith.** b 64. Univ of Wales LLB. St Jo Coll Nottm BA. **d** 89 **p** 90 **c** 08. C Cardigan w Mwnt and Y Ferwig *St D* 89–91; C Aberystwyth 91–92; TV 92–99; V Henfynyw w Aberaeron and Llanddewi Aberarth etc 99–06; V Pencarreg and Llancrwys 06–08; Adn Cardigan 06–08; Bp Ban from 08. *Ty'r Esgob, Upper Garth Road, Bangor LL57 2SS* T: (01248) 362895 E: bishop.bangor@churchinwales.org.uk

JOHN, Canon Arun Andrew. b 54. **d** 77 **p** 78. India 77–96; S Africa 97–04; TV Manningham *Bradf* 04–11; P-in-c Blackb

St Steph 11–12; P-in-c Blackb St Jas 11–12; V Blackb St Steph and St Jas 12–18; AD Blackb and Darwen 16–18; TR Rothwell, Lofthouse, Methley etc *Leeds* from 18. *Holy Trinity Vicarage, 1 Beech Grove, Rothwell, Leeds LS26 0EF*

JOHN, Barbara. b 34. Gilmore Ho. **dss** 67 **d** 80 **p** 97. Merthyr Tydfil *Llan* 67–71; Loughton St Jo *Chelmsf* 71–73; Newport St Woolos *Mon* 73–78; Asst Chapl Univ Hosp of Wales Cardiff 78–85; C Radyr *Llan* 85–00; rtd 00; PtO *Llan* from 04. *14 Pace Close, Cardiff CF5 2QZ* T: (029) 2055 2989

JOHN, Canon Beverley Hayes. b 49. Qu Coll Birm 83. **d** 85 **p** 86. C Oystermouth *S & B* 85–87; C Morriston 87–88; V Cefn Coed w Vaynor 88–14; P-in-c Penderyn Mellte 12–14; AD Brecon 99–14; Can Res Brecon Cathl 04–14; rtd 14; PtO *S & B* from 14. *63 Kingrosia Park, Clydach, Swansea SA6 5PL* T: (01792) 842911

JOHN, Brother. *See* HENNINGS, John Richard

JOHN, David Wyndham. b 61. Lon Bible Coll. NTMTC. **d** 01 **p** 02. NSM Hampstead Em W End *Lon* 01–04; NSM W Hampstead St Cuth 04–15; P-in-c 06–15; V Iwerne Valley *Sarum* from 15. *The Vicarage, Iwerne Minster, Blandford Forum DT11 8NF* M: 07719-333389 E: david.john@btopenworld.com

JOHN, Jeffrey Philip Hywel. b 53. Hertf Coll Ox BA 75 Magd Coll Ox DPhil 84 Herts Univ Hon DLitt 15. St Steph Ho Ox BA 77 MA 78. **d** 78 **p** 79. C Penarth w Lavernock *Llan* 78–80; Asst Chapl Magd Coll Ox 80–82; Fell and Dean of Div 84–91; Chapl and Lect BNC Ox 82–84; V Eltham H Trin *S'wark* 91–97; Chan and Can Th S'wark Cathl 97–04; Bp's Adv for Min 97–04; Dean St Alb 04–21; Chapl Paris St Geo *Eur* from 21; Hon Fell Hertf Coll Ox from 19. *St George's Anglican Church, 7 rue Auguste Vacquerie, 75116 Paris, France* T: (0033) 1 47 20 22 51 E: drjphjohn@gmail.com

JOHN, Michael Ioannou. b 86. City Univ BA 09. Wycliffe Hall Ox BTh 15. **d** 15 **p** 16. C Muswell Hill St Jas w St Matt *Lon* 15–18; C Clapham H Trin *S'wark* 18–20; C N Lambeth from 20. *St Peter's Vicarage, 308 Kennington Lane, London SE11 5HY* M: 07540-469052 E: michael.john@stpetersvauxhall.org

JOHN, Napoleon. b 55. Punjab Univ BA 76. Lahetysteologisen Inst Ryttyla Finland 84 Oak Hill Th Coll BA 93. **d** 93 **p** 94. C Leyton St Mary w St Edw *Chelmsf* 93–96; C Leyton St Mary w St Edw and St Luke 96–97; P-in-c Becontree St Elisabeth 97–04; V 04–07; TR Walton and Trimley *St E* 07–13; R Hayes *Roch* 13–21; rtd 21. *229 Meadgate Avenue, Chelmsford CM2 7NJ* E: napojohn@gmail.com

JOHN, Robert Michael. b 46. Edin Univ BSc 67 Man Univ MSc 68 PhD 70 Otago Univ BD 78. St Jo Coll Auckland 76. **d** 78 **p** 79. C Tauranga NZ 78–80; C Hastings 80–83; V Waipaoa 83–87; C Swansea St Jas *S & B* 87–88; V Otumoetai NZ 88–94; Chapl Auckland Hosps 94–09; Chapl Univ Hosps of Morecambe Bay NHS Trust 09–11; C N Barrow *Carl* 11–13; rtd 13; PtO *Carl* 13–15; NZ 15–16; P-in-c Onehunga 16. *11 Palmerston Road, Birkenhead, Auckland 0626, New Zealand* E: robertmichaeljohn@btinternet.com

JOHN, Stephen Michael. b 63. Univ of Wales (Lamp) BA 85. Coll of Resurr Mirfield 87. **d** 89 **p** 90. C Coity w Nolton *Llan* 89–91; C Merthyr Dyfan 91–94; V Tredegar St Geo *Mon* 94–99; Chapl HM Pris Gartree 99–04; TV Tenby *St D* 04–12; V Pentyrch and Capel Llanillterne *Llan* from 12; AD Llan from 15. *The Vicarage, Church Road, Pentyrch, Cardiff CF15 9QF* T: (029) 2140 3854 E: vicar@parishofpentyrch.org.uk

JOHN-FRANCIS, Brother. *See* FRIENDSHIP, Roger Geoffrey

JOHNES, Philip Sydney. b 45. St Mich Coll Llan 90. **d** 92 **p** 93. C Cardigan w Mwnt and Y Ferwig *St D* 92–95; V Llanegwad w Llanfynydd 95–10; rtd 10; PtO *St D* from 10. *Keeper's Cottage, Ferryside SA17 5TY* T: (01267) 267081 E: pjohnes@phonecoop.coop

JOHNS, Adam Aubrey. b 34. TCD BA 57 MA 76 NUU BA 75. CITC Div Test 58. **d** 58 **p** 59. C Aghalee *D & D* 58–61; C Derriaghy *Conn* 61–63; I Billy 63–77; I Billy w Derrykeighan 77–03; Can Conn Cathl 98–03; rtd 03. *26 Chatham Road, Armoy, Ballymoney BT53 8TT* T: (028) 2075 1978 E: chathambrae@btinternet.com

JOHNS, Canon Bernard Thomas. b 36. Birm Univ BSc 58. St Mich Coll Llan 61. **d** 63 **p** 64. C Aberavon *Llan* 63–65; C St Andrews Major w Michaelston-le-Pit 65–70; V Cardiff St Andr and St Teilo 70–76; Asst Dioc Dir of Educn 72–91; V Roath 76–88; R Wenvoe and St Lythans 88–02; Dioc Dir Community Educn 91–02; Can Llan Cathl 96–02; rtd 02. *Bay Tree Cottage, 13 Badgers Meadow, Pwllmeyric, Chepstow NP16 6UE* T: (01291) 623254

JOHNS, Mrs Patricia Holly. b 33. Girton Coll Cam BA 56 MA 60 Hughes Hall Cam PGCE 57. Ox NSM Course 87. **d** 90 **p** 94. NSM Wantage *Ox* 90–94; NSM Marlborough *Sarum* 94–95; rtd 95; PtO *Sarum* 95–21. *1 Priory Lodge,*

93 Brown Street, Salisbury SP1 2BX T: (01722) 328007
E: payjohns70@hotmail.com

JOHNS, Thomas Morton. b 43. Oak Hill Th Coll 67. **d** 70
p 71. C N Meols *Liv* 70–73; C Farnborough *Guildf* 73–76;
P-in-c Badshot Lea CD 76–83; Dep Chapl HM Pris Man
83; Chapl HM Youth Cust Cen Wellingborough 83–88;
Chapl HM YOI Swinfen Hall 88–90; Chapl Tr Officer 88–95;
Chapl HM Pris Service Coll 90–95; Asst Chapl Gen of Pris
(HQ) 95–01; Acting Chapl Gen 00–01; P-in-c Colbury
Win 02–08; Chapl Hants Constabulary 02–08; rtd 08;
PtO *Portsm* from 02. *1 Southbrook Mews, Bishops Waltham,
Southampton SO32 1RZ* T: (01489) 891585 M: 07988-
314928 E: tomjohns585@gmail.com

JOHNS-PERRING, Michael James. b 85. York Univ BA 07 Edin
Univ MSc 09 Selw Coll Cam BTh 18. Westcott Ho Cam 16.
d 19 **p** 20. C Surbiton St Andr and St Mark *S'wark* from 19. *1
The Mall, Surbiton KT6 4EH*

JOHNSEN, Edward Andrew. b 67. Birm Univ BTheol 89.
Qu Coll Birm 95. **d** 97 **p** 98. C Birm St Luke 97–01; C
Handsworth St Mary 01–04; PtO 05–06; TV Eden, Gelt
and Irthing *Carl* from 06; RD Brampton from 18. *The
Vicarage, Hayton, Brampton CA8 9HR* T: (01228) 670248
E: edwardajohnsen@gmail.com

JOHNSON, Dom Andrew Edmond. b 59. **d** 08 **p** 09. OSB from
85; PtO *Win* from 09. *Abbey of Our Lady and St John, Abbey
Road, Beech, Alton GU34 4AP* T: (01420) 562145 F: 561691

JOHNSON, Andrew Paul. b 56. W Surrey Coll of Art &
Design BA 79 Kent Coll for Careers CertEd 82 TCD BTh 96.
CITC 93. **d** 96 **p** 97. C Penarth w Lavernock *Llan* 96–99;
R Walton W w Talbenny and Haroldston W *St D* 99–15;
P-in-c Dale and St Brides w Marloes etc from 14; P-in-c Roose
from 19. *The Vicarage, Castle Way, Dale, Haverfordwest
SA62 3RN* T: (01646) 636966 E: frandrew@btinternet.com

JOHNSON, Andrew Paul. b 69. **d** 14 **p** 15. C W Ealing St Jo
w St Jas *Lon* 14–17; P-in-c Perivale from 17. *4 Bethlehem
Close, Perivale, Greenford UB6 7FQ* M: 07958-604708
E: revandyjohnson@me.com

JOHNSON, Andrew Peter. b 67. Westf Coll Lon BA 89 St Jo
Coll Nottm MA 98 LTh 99. Aston Tr Scheme 94. **d** 99
p 00. C Hitchin *St Alb* 99–03; V Batley All SS and Purlwell
Wakef 03–13; R Barton-le-Cley w Higham Gobion and
Hexton *St Alb* from 13. *The Rectory, 2 Manor Farm Close,
Barton-le-Cley, Bedford MK45 4TB* T: (01582) 881873
E: johnsons@care4free.net

JOHNSON, Andrew Peter. **d** 12 **p** 15. NSM Ex Cathl 12–17;
NSM Heavitree and St Mary Steps from 17. *Elm Brook House,
348 Topsham Road, Exeter EX2 6HF* T: (01392) 271059
E: andrewjohnson1@btinternet.com

JOHNSON, Mrs Angela Carolyn Louise. b 52. RGN 76.
STETS 00. **d** 03 **p** 04. NSM Catherington and Clanfield
Portsm 03–07; NSM Denmead from 07. *90 Downhouse Road,
Waterlooville PO8 0TY* T: (023) 9264 4595

JOHNSON, Anthony Peter. b 45. K Coll Lon BD 76 AKC 76
MTh 79. Wells Th Coll 67. **d** 70 **p** 71. C Goldington *St Alb*
70–73; C Hainault *Chelmsf* 73–76; TV Loughton St Mary
76–81; V Scunthorpe All SS *Linc* 81–85; V Alkborough
85–87; Chapl Man Univ and TV Man Whitworth 87–96;
P-in-c Chorlton-cum-Hardy St Werburgh 96–00; R 00–05;
P-in-c Yardley St Cypr Hay Mill *Birm* 05–08; V 08–10; rtd
10; PtO *Birm* 10–16. *St Barnabas' Vicarage, 51 Over Green
Drive, Kingshurst, Birmingham B37 6EY* M: 07842-151492
E: ajohnson940@btinternet.com

JOHNSON, Anthony Warrington. b 40. Goldsmiths' Coll Lon
CertEd 60. St Jo Coll Nottm 86. **d** 88 **p** 89. C Lutterworth
w Cotesbach *Leic* 88–92; V Countesthorpe w Foston
92–06; P-in-c Arnesby w Shearsby and Bruntingthorpe
94–01; rtd 06; Hon C Lutterworth w Cotesbach and
Bitteswell *Leic* 06–09; PtO 13–17. *15 Constable Drive,
Barton Seagrave, Kettering NN15 5UA* T: (01536) 515033
E: tonywjohnson@btinternet.com

JOHNSON, Miss Barbara. b 45. St Jo Coll Nottm 04. **d** 07
p 08. NSM Royston *St Alb* 07–08; NSM Goldington 08–10;
Chapl Beds and Luton Fire and Rescue Service from 07;
PtO *Ely* 10–15 and 16–21; *Ox* from 11. *4 Hicks Lane, Girton,
Cambridge CB3 0JS* T: (01223) 276282 M: 07768-560646

JOHNSON, Barry Charles Richard. b 48. EAMTC 96. **d** 99
p 00. C Gt Burstead *Chelmsf* 99–02; C Bowers Gifford w N
Benfleet 02–04; P-in-c Woodham Mortimer w Hazeleigh
04–06; R Vange 06–10; P-in-c Bowers Gifford w N Benfleet
07–10; V Folkestone St Mary, St Eanswythe and St Sav *Cant*
10–12; rtd 12; P-in-c Gt Parndon *Chelmsf* 13–14; V Staple Tye
14–15; P-in-c Mayland 15–16; C Althorne and Latchingdon
w N Fambridge 15–16; V Mayland and Latchingdon 16;
PtO 16–18. *Lyndon, London Road, Bowers Gifford, Basildon
SS13 2HE* T: (01268) 726318 E: revbj@btinternet.com

JOHNSON, Mrs Brenda Margaret. b 47. TISEC 93. **d** 00.
NSM Edin St Salvador 00–03; NSM Wester Hailes St Luke
00–03; NSM Edin Gd Shep 03–17. *58 Ratho Park Road, Ratho,
Newbridge EH28 8PQ* T: 0131-333 1742 M: 07713-154744
E: brenmj@btinternet.com

JOHNSON, Brian. b 42. S'wark Ord Course 84. **d** 87 **p** 88.
NSM Dulwich St Barn *S'wark* 87–92; NSM Herne Hill 92–94;
PtO 94–96; Chapl HM Pris Man 96–01; P-in-c Rotterdam
Eur 01–02; Operations Manager ICS 03; PtO *Cov* 03; *Ches*
04–19; *Man* 11–17; *Newc* from 18. *42 Sunningdale, Whitley
Bay NE25 9YF* T: 0191-340 0659 E: revbfg13@gmail.com

JOHNSON, Bruce Graham. b 67. All SS Cen for Miss &
Min 15. **d** 18 **p** 19. NSM Heanor *Derby* 18–19; NSM Langley
Mill and Aldercar 18–19; NSM Marlpool 18–19; NSM
Belper Ch Ch w Turnditch 19–20; NSM Ockbrook from
20. *31 Porterhouse Road, Ripley DE5 3FL* T: (01773) 449001
E: revbruce18@gmail.com

JOHNSON, Mrs Catherine Jane. b 78. Collingwood Coll Dur
BA 99 Lanc Univ MA 00. All SS Cen for Miss & Min 18. **d** 20
p 21. C Cheadle All Hallows *Ches* from 20. *74 Boundary
Road, Cheadle SK8 2EP* T: 0161-374 2284 M: 07759-647109
E: catherine.the-johnsons.org.uk

JOHNSON, Christopher Frederick. b 43. MRICS 67.
Ripon Hall Ox 71. **d** 74 **p** 75. C Chatham St Steph *Roch*
74–78; V Slade Green 78–85; V Wilmington 85–95; R
Chevening 95–09; rtd 09; PtO *Roch* from 09. *7 Kennedy
Gardens, Sevenoaks TN13 3UG* T: (01732) 456626
E: c.f.johnson@btinternet.com

JOHNSON, Christopher James. b 88. Cant Ch Ch Univ
BA 11. Ripon Coll Cuddesdon MTh 13. **d** 13 **p** 14.
C Weobley w Sarnesfield and Norton Canon *Heref*
13–16; C Wigston *Leic* from 16. *St Thomas's Vicarage, 9
Hindoostan Avenue, Wigston LE18 4UD* T: 0116-278 2830
E: revchrisjohnson.wbs@gmail.com

JOHNSON, Christopher Neil. b 87. St Benet's Hall Ox BA 10
MA 14. St Steph Ho Ox MSt 10 MLitt 14. **d** 13 **p** 14. C Pickering
w Lockton and Levisham *York* 13–17; V Horbury w Horbury
Bridge *Leeds* from 17; Hon PV Wakef Cathl from 20. *St Peter's
Vicarage, Northgate, Horbury, Wakefield WF4 6AS* T: (01924)
576745 E: fr.christopher.johnson@gmail.com

JOHNSON, Christopher Paul. b 47. Leeds Univ MA 01. St Jo
Coll Nottm BTh 74. **d** 74 **p** 75. C Normanton *Wakef* 74–78;
P-in-c Dewsbury St Mark 78–82; V Harden and Wilsden
Bradf 82–88; P-in-c Holbeck *Ripon* 88–94; V 94–97; Asst
Chapl Leeds Teaching Hosps NHS Trust 97–00; Chapl Bradf
Hosps NHS Trust 00–13; PtO *Leeds* from 13. *6 Suffield
Road, Gildersome, Morley, Leeds LS27 7WA* T: 0113-285 4953
E: christopherjohnson1947@live.co.uk

JOHNSON, Christopher Robert. b 43. Lon Coll of Div 66.
d 70 **p** 71. C Everton St Geo *Liv* 70–71; C Childwall All
SS 71–75; TV Gateacre 75–76; TV Bushbury *Lich* 76–87;
R Burslem 87–10; rtd 10; PtO *Lich* 11–21. *102 Chell
Green Avenue, Stoke-on-Trent ST6 7LA* T: (01782) 850169
E: rob.johnson60@talk21.com

JOHNSON, Colin Leslie. b 41. Trin Coll Cam MA 65. Cheshunt
Coll Cam 62. **d** 93 **p** 94. Publications Dir Chr Educn
Movement 89–01; NSM Brailsford w Shirley and Osmaston
w Edlaston *Derby* 93–04; rtd 04; PtO *Derby* 04–20. *1 Ashmead
Way, Kidlington OX5 2FT* T: (01865) 374254 M: 07915-
531108 E: clj864@outlook.com

JOHNSON, Colin Stewart. b 46. SEITE 99. **d** 02 **p** 03.
NSM Borden *Cant* 02–05; C Charlton-in-Dover 05–06;
P-in-c 06–13; rtd 13; PtO *Cant* from 14. *423 Minster
Road, Minster on Sea, Sheerness ME12 3NS* T: (01795)
857175 M: 07740-775277 E: frcj@dsl.pipex.com

JOHNSON, David. b 68. Cranmer Hall Dur 13. **d** 15 **p** 16. C
Monk Fryston and S Milford *York* 15–19; 20s-40s Multiply
Ldr from 19; C Northallerton w Kirby Sigston from 19. *6
Mayfair Court, Northallerton DL7 8WG* M: 07515-288105
E: davidjohnsonihs@gmail.com

JOHNSON, David. See JOHNSON, John David

JOHNSON, David Alan. b 43. Lon Univ BSc 63 PhD 67. Trin
Coll Bris 78. **d** 80 **p** 81. C Watford *St Alb* 80–85; V Idle *Bradf*
85–08; P-in-c Greengates 08; rtd 08; PtO *Dur* from 09. *15
Blackburn Close, Bearpark, Durham DH7 7TQ* T: 0191-373
7953 E: david@festsoft.co.uk

JOHNSON, David Bryan Alfred. b 36. Kelham Th Coll 56.
d 61 **p** 62. C Streatham St Paul *S'wark* 61–63; C St Thos
Cathl Kuching Malaysia 63–66; V Sibu 66–71; V Worc
St Mich 71–74; Warden Lee Abbey Internat Students' Club
Kensington 74–77; V Plumstead St Mark and St Marg
S'wark 77–86; Chapl W Park Hosp Epsom 86–96; Chapl
Laslett's *Worc* 96–01; rtd 96; PtO *Ox* from 18. *3 St Birinus
Cottages, Wessex Way, Bicester OX26 6DX* T: (01869) 320839
E: dbajohnson1@gmail.com

JOHNSON, David Francis. b 32. Univ Coll Ox BA 55 MA 59. Westcott Ho Cam 55. **d** 57 **p** 58. C Earlsdon *Cov* 57–59; C Willenhall 59–61; C Attenborough w Bramcote *S'well* 61–62; V Ravenstone w Weston Underwood *Ox* 62–66; V Crewe Ch Ch *Ches* 66–70; P-in-c Crewe St Pet 67–70; V Thornton w Allerthorpe *York* 70–79; V N Hull St Mich 79–81; V Leyburn w Bellerby *Ripon* 81–88; V Coxwold and Husthwaite *York* 88–97; rtd 97; PtO *York* 98–03; *Heref* 05–13; *Glouc* 17–20. *26 Capel Court, The Burgage, Prestbury, Cheltenham GL52 3EL* T: (01242) 220506 E: dfjjaj@btinternet.com

JOHNSON, David John. b 49. Lanc Univ BA 72. Linc Th Coll 78. **d** 81 **p** 82. C Stockport St Thos *Ches* 81–84; OGS from 83; C Stockton Heath *Ches* 84–88; V Tranmere St Paul w St Luke 88–99; P-in-c Antrobus 99–02; P-in-c Aston by Sutton 99–02; P-in-c Lt Leigh and Lower Whitley 99–02; V Antrobus, Aston by Sutton, Lt Leigh etc 02–07; C Coppenhall 07–10; rtd 11; PtO *Ches* from 11. *14 Manor Way, Crewe CW2 6JX* T: (01270) 250256

JOHNSON, David William. b 40. Oak Hill Th Coll BD 64. **d** 65 **p** 66. C Tunbridge Wells St Jas *Roch* 65–68; C Kirby Muxloe *Leic* 68–72; V Burton Joyce w Bulcote *S'well* 72–83; V Mitford and Chapl Northgate Mental Handicap Unit Morpeth 83–87; Asst Chapl R Victoria Infirmary Newc 87–89; Chapl R Shrewsbury Hosps NHS Trust 89–04; rtd 04. *42 Hartlands, Bedlington NE22 6JG* T: (01670) 828693

JOHNSON, Preb Derek John. b 36. St Aid Birkenhead 65. **d** 68 **p** 69. C Eccleshall *Lich* 68–73; C Stafford St Mary 73–74; C Stafford St Mary and St Chad 74–75; Chapl New Cross Hosp Wolv 75–96; Preb Lich Cathl 83–96; rtd 96; PtO *St E* 96–21. *6 St Paul's Close, Aldeburgh IP15 5BQ* T: (01728) 452474

JOHNSON, Diana. b 54. RMCS BSc 79 Qu Coll Cam MPhil 92 Anglia Ruskin Univ MA 06. Ridley Hall Cam 95 ERMC 16. **d** 17 **p** 18. NSM Girton *Ely* 17–19; NSM Trumpington 19–21; P-in-c Riding Mill *Newc* from 21. *The Vicarage, Riding Mill NE44 6AT* T: (01434) 682120 E: diana.johnson@cantab.net

JOHNSON, Canon Diana Margaret. b 46. MCSP 68 SRP 68. Cranmer Hall Dur 92. **d** 94 **p** 95. C Birtley *Dur* 94–99; TV Gateshead 99–06; AD 03–06; P-in-c Belmont 06–07; V Belmont and Pittington 07–12; Hon Can Dur Cathl 06–12; rtd 12; PtO *Dur* from 12. *3 Avenue Street, High Shincliffe, Durham DH1 2PT* T: 0191-386 1660 E: dmjohnson462@gmail.com

JOHNSON, Mrs Diane Pearl. b 47. Leeds Univ BA 68 Cam Univ PGCE 69. EAMTC 95. **d** 98 **p** 99. NSM Gt Bowden w Welham, Glooston and Cranoe *Leic* 98–01; C Evington and Leic St Phil 01–04; P-in-c 04–07; rtd 07; PtO *Pet* from 10; *Leic* from 15. *16 Oaklands Park, Market Harborough LE16 8EU* T: (01858) 434118 E: gandi2007@btinternet.com

JOHNSON, Mrs Dorothy. Leic Univ BSc 89 Ox Univ MTh 95 Ox Brookes Univ MA 14 RGN FRSH 91. Qu Coll Birm 77. **dss** 80 **d** 87 **p** 94. Coventry Caludon *Cov* 80–81; Wolston and Church Lawford 81–86; NSM Stoneleigh w Ashow 87–08; Bp's Asst Officer for Soc Resp 87–96; PtO 11–15; *Win* from 16. *119 Hillside Drive, Christchurch BH23 2SZ* M: 07975-893114 E: e.djohnson@btinternet.com

JOHNSON, Douglas Leonard. b 45. St Paul's Coll Chelt CertEd 67 Lon Bible Coll MA 95 Roehampton Univ PhD 13. Tyndale Hall Bris 70. **d** 73 **p** 74. C New Malden and Coombe *S'wark* 73–76; P-in-c Upper Tulse Hill St Matthias 76–82; CPAS Staff 82–88; Lect and Tutor CA Coll 88–91; Dir Crossways Chr Educn Trust 92–08; Hon C Wimbledon Em Ridgway Prop Chpl *S'wark* 91–94; Lect Cornhill Tr Course 94–06; Crosslinks Kenya 08–10; rtd 11; PtO *B & W* from 12. *The Stables, Mudford, Yeovil BA21 5TD* T: (01935) 432304 E: douglasjohnson@btinternet.com

JOHNSON, Elizabeth Anne. b 68. Coll of Ripon & York St Jo BEd 90. Linc Sch of Th and Min 18. **d** 20 **p** 21. C Messingham w E Butterwick, Scotter w E Ferry and Scotton w Northorpe *Linc* 20–21; C Gainsborough and Morton from 21. *32 Morton Terrace, Gainsborough DN21 2RQ* T: (01427) 614397 M: 07798-914596 E: lizjohnson.1968@outlook.com

JOHNSON, Emma Louise. See PARKER, Emma Louise

JOHNSON, Emma Louise. See COLEY, Emma Louise

JOHNSON, Eric. b 38. Nottm Univ BSc 60 Man Univ CertEd 65 Open Univ BA 92 SS Paul & Mary Coll Cheltenham MA 94 Birm Univ BA 06. Qu Coll Birm 74. **d** 77 **p** 78. Sen Lect Cov Tech Coll 66–91; NSM Earlsdon *Cov* 77–81; NSM Wolston and Church Lawford 81–86; NSM Stoneleigh w Ashow and Baginton 90–98; FE Liaison Officer B & W, Bris and Glouc 91–93; Dioc Dir of Educn *Worc* 93–98; rtd 98; PtO *Cov* 11–15; *Win* from 16. *119 Hillside Drive, Christchurch BH23 2SZ* M: 07773-748967 E: e.djohnson@btinternet.com

JOHNSON, Frances Josephine. b 53. Leeds Univ CertEd 74 Open Univ BA 90. NOC 02. **d** 05 **p** 06. C Hall Green St Pet *Birm* 05–08; V Kingshurst from 08; PtO *Lich* from 21. *St Barnabas' Vicarage, 51 Over Green Drive, Birmingham B37 6EY* T: 0121-770 3972 E: revjohnson@btinternet.com

JOHNSON, Geoffrey Stuart. b 39. ALCD 65 Wolv Poly DipEd Sussex Univ DPhil 01. **d** 65 **p** 66. C Worksop St Jo *S'well* 65–68; Taiwan 68–71; C St Andr Cathl Singapore 71–76; Aber Univ *Ab* 76–78; PtO *Heref* 78–82; P-in-c Hoarwithy, Sellack and Hentland 82–84; Chapl Horton Hosp Epsom 84–90; Distr Chapl Brighton HA 90–94; Managing Chapl Brighton Healthcare NHS Trust 94–99; Managing Chapl S Downs Health NHS Trust 94–99; rtd 99; Chapl S Downs Health NHS Trust 00–06; Chapl Sussex Partnership NHS Foundn Trust 06–13; PtO *Chich* 01–14. *Kingfisher, Rope Walk, Ross-on-Wye HR9 7BU* T: (01989) 562002 E: g.johnson479@btinternet.com

JOHNSON, Gillian Margaret. b 55. Bretton Hall Coll CertEd 76 Coll of Ripon & York St Jo MA 03. NOC 00. **d** 03 **p** 04. C Thornhill and Whitley Lower *Wakef* 05–07; C Mirfield 07–10; Curriculum Development Officer Dioc Bd Educn 07–10; Dioc Educn Development Officer 10–14; Dioc Schs' Adv *Leeds* 14–18; Sec Coll of Resurr Mirfield 18–21; rtd 21. *5 Wood Mount, Overton, Wakefield WF4 4SB* M: 07804-477867 E: gilljohnson99@gmail.com

JOHNSON, Harriet. b 69. St Aug Coll of Th 15. **d** 17 **p** 18. NSM Kingsdown *Roch* 17–20; Chapl St Aug Coll of Th from 20. *St Augustine's College of Theology, 52 Swan Street, West Malling ME19 6JX* T: (01732) 252656 E: revharrietjohnson@gmail.com

JOHNSON, Canon Hilary Ann. b 51. RGN 72 RHV 74. S'wark Ord Course 82. **dss** 85 **d** 87 **p** 94. Hon Par Dn Salfords *S'wark* 85–90; Chapl St Geo Hosp Lon 90–94; Chapl St Geo Healthcare NHS Trust Lon 94–15; NSM Wimbledon *S'wark* 95–10; Bp's Adv for Healthcare Chapl 11–15; Hon Can S'wark Cathl 07–15; rtd 15; NSM Chessington *Guildf* 10–21; PtO from 21. *203 Moor Lane, Chessington KT9 2AB* T: (020) 8397 0952 M: 07764-221116 E: hilary1j@gmail.com

JOHNSON, Ian Lawrence. b 44. Wells Th Coll 68. **d** 71 **p** 72. C Benhilton *S'wark* 71–73; C Weymouth H Trin *Sarum* 73–76; R Pewsey 76–81; R Maiden Newton and Valleys 81–83; Youth Officer (Sherborne Area) 81–83; Dioc Youth Officer *Sarum* 83–88; TR Langley and Parkfield *Man* 88–95; P-in-c Haughton St Anne 95–99; Dioc Adv on Evang 95–99; TR Southampton (City Cen) *Win* 99–08; rtd 08. *Farthing Cottage, 71 St Andrew Street, Tiverton EX16 6PL* T: (01884) 251974

JOHNSON, Ian Leslie. b 51. Bede Coll Dur TCert 73. Wycliffe Hall Ox 91. **d** 93 **p** 94. C Evington *Leic* 93–96; C Foxton w Gumley 96–00; P-in-c Foxton w Gumley and Laughton 00–12; Sub Chapl HM Pris Gartree 96–04; Chapl 04–15; Co-ord Chapl 12; rtd 15; PtO *Nor* from 15. *59 Lower Street, Horning, Norwich NR12 8AA* T: (01692) 631287 E: ijoh270951@aol.com

JOHNSON (née SILINS), Ms Jacqueline. b 62. Coll of Ripon & York St Jo BA 85 York St Jo Univ MA 15. Ripon Coll Cuddesdon 01. **d** 03 **p** 04. C Torpoint *Truro* 03–08; P-in-c Harworth *S'well* 08–12; Dioc Min Development Adv 12–19; CMD Officer *Linc* from 19. *Edward King House, Minster Yard, Lincoln LN2 1PU* T: (01522) 504034 M: 07827-291724 E: jackie.johnson@lincoln.anglican.org

JOHNSON, John David. b 38. Claremont Sch of Th 65 St Deiniol's Hawarden 71. **d** 71 **p** 72. C Heref St Martin 71–73; P-in-c Ewyas Harold w Dulas 73–79; P-in-c Kilpeck 73–79; C St Devereux w Wormbridge 73–79; P-in-c Kenderchurch 73–79; P-in-c Bacton 78–79; TR Ewyas Harold w Dulas, Kenderchurch etc 79–81; R Kentchurch w Llangua, Rowlestone, Llancillo etc 79–81; Chapl Napsbury Hosp St Alb 81–96; Chapl Horizon NHS Trust Herts 96–00; Chapl Barnet Healthcare NHS Trust 96–00; Chapl Barnet and Chase Farm Hosps NHS Trust 00–05; Chapl Herts Partnerships NHS Trust 02–03; rtd 03. *10 Highcroft Road, Sharpthorne, East Grinstead RH19 4NX* T: (01342) 810314

JOHNSON, Josephine. See JOHNSON, Frances Josephine

JOHNSON, Mrs Julie Margaret. b 47. **d** 98 **p** 99. OLM Welton and Dunholme w Scothern *Linc* 98–07; NSM Edgeley and Cheadle Heath *Ches* 07–19; rtd 20. *10 Delaford Close, Stockport SK3 8XA* T: 0161-456 6463 E: johnson-julie@sky.com

JOHNSON, Kathryn Ann. **d** 03 **p** 04. C Wrexham *St As* 03–04; C Prestatyn 04–11; V Abergele and St George 11–16; TV Aled Miss Area from 17. *Iscoed, 21 Woodland Road West, Colwyn Bay LL29 7DH* T: (01492) 209311 M: 07801-541380 E: pastorkate123@yahoo.com

JOHNSON, Keith Henry. b 64. Keele Univ BA 91 Leeds Univ BA 97 MA 09 CQSW 91. Coll of Resurr Mirfield 95. **d** 97 **p** 98. C W Bromwich St Fran *Lich* 97–00; P-in-c Willenhall St Giles 00–05; V 05–06; PtO *Lon* 06–08; *Lich* 07–08; *Sheff* 08; P-in-c Handsworth 08–10; R from 10. *St Mary's Rectory, Handsworth Road, Handsworth, Sheffield S13 9BZ* T: 0114-269 3983 E: keithhjohnson@hotmail.com

JOHNSON, Keith Martyn. b 68. St Jo Coll Nottm 04. **d** 06 **p** 07. C Ipsley *Worc* 06–10; V Chatham St Paul w All SS *Roch* 10–16; V Hughenden *Ox* from 16. *The Vicarage, Valley Road, Hughenden Valley, High Wycombe HP14 4PF* T: (01634) 811536 M: 07772-642393 E: keiththevicar@gmail.com

JOHNSON, The Very Revd Keith Winton Thomas William. b 37. K Coll Lon BD 63 Open Univ MA 06 AKC 63. **d** 64 **p** 65. C Dartford H Trin *Roch* 64–69; Chapl Kuwait 69–73; V Erith St Jo *Roch* 73–80; V Bexley St Jo 80–91; V Royston *St Alb* 91–94; R Sandon, Wallington and Rushden w Clothall 94–97; Dean St Chris Cathl Bahrain 97–02; rtd 02; Hon C Balsham, Weston Colville, W Wickham etc *Ely* 04–10; RD Linton 07–09; PtO 10–20. *4 Shetland Avenue, Wilnecote, Tamworth B77 5AT* T: (01827) 251396 E: jkeith1412@gmail.com

JOHNSON, Kenneth William George. b 53. Hull Univ BA 76 PGCE 77. EMMTC 92. **d** 95 **p** 96. NSM Ilkeston H Trin *Derby* 95–99; NSM Sandiacre 99–21; NSM Somercotes from 21; NSM Alfreton from 21; NSM Riddings and Ironville from 21; Chapl Bluecoat Sch Nottm 02–11; PtO *S'well* from 96. *18 Park Avenue, Awsworth, Nottingham NG16 2RA* T: 0115-930 7830 E: kwjohnson@ntlworld.com

JOHNSON, Miss Lesley Denise. b 47. WMMTC 95. **d** 98 **p** 99. NSM Stockingford *Cov* 98–01; TV Cov E 01–10; rtd 10; PtO *Cov* from 12. *212 Sedgemoor Road, Coventry CV3 4DZ* T: (024) 7630 1241

JOHNSON, Louis James. b 80. Chu Coll Cam BA 02 MA 11 Liv Univ MMus 05 PhD 12. St Mellitus Coll BA 20. **d** 20 **p** 21. C St Luke in the City *Liv* from 20. *17 Eton Court, Liverpool L18 3HG* T: 0151-722 8921 M: 07432-894664 E: louis.johnson@cantab.net *or* curate@stlukeinthecity.org.uk

JOHNSON, Malcolm Arthur. b 36. Univ Coll Dur BA 60 MA 64 Lon Metrop Univ Hon MA 02 Lambeth MA 06 K Coll Lon PhD 10 FSA 04. Cuddesdon Coll 60. **d** 62 **p** 63. C Portsea N End St Mark *Portsm* 62–67; Chapl Qu Mary Coll *Lon* 67–74; V St Botolph Aldgate w H Trin Minories 74–92; P-in-c St Ethelburga Bishopgate 85–89; AD The City 85–90; Master R Foundn of St Kath in Ratcliffe 93–97; Bp's Adv for Past Care and Counselling *Lon* 97–01; rtd 02; PtO *Lon* 07–18; *Guildf* 09–17. *1 Foxgrove Drive, Woking GU21 4DZ* T: (01483) 720684 E: malcolm.johnson4@btinternet.com

JOHNSON, Canon Malcolm Stuart. b 35. AKC 60. **d** 61 **p** 62. C Catford St Laur *S'wark* 61–64; Hon C Hatcham St Cath 66–76; P-in-c Kingstanding St Luke *Birm* 76–77; V 77–82; P-in-c Peckham St Jo w St Andr *S'wark* 82–92; V 92–03; Hon Can Sabongidda-Ora from 98; rtd 04. *34 Sheppard's College, London Road, Bromley BR1 1PF* T: (020) 8466 5276

JOHNSON, Canon Margaret Anne Hope. b 52. Fitzw Coll Cam BA 95 MA 99. Ridley Hall Cam 93. **d** 95 **p** 96. C Northampton Em *Pet* 95–97; P-in-c 97–98; TR 98–16; Adv in Women's Min 03–06; Can Pet Cathl 04–16; rtd 16; PtO *Pet* 17–20; Hon C Wellingborough All SS from 20; Hon C Wellingborough All Hallows from 20; Hon C Wellingborough St Andr and St Barn from 20. *3 The Drive, Wellingborough NN8 2DB* T: (01933) 384628 M: 07752-183574 E: revmahj@gmail.com

JOHNSON, Margaret Joan (Meg). b 41. S'wark Ord Course 92. **d** 95 **p** 96. NSM Sanderstead St Mary *S'wark* 95–04; PtO 13–17. *Rose Cottage, 89 Durrington Lane, Worthing BN13 2TQ* E: megjohnson@uwclub.net

JOHNSON, Preb Mark. b 62. Leic Poly BSc 84 Loughb Univ PhD 88. Ripon Coll Cuddesdon 92. **d** 94 **p** 95. C Bishop's Cleeve *Glouc* 94–98; TV Heref S Wye 98–09; R Wormelow Hundred from 09; RD Ross and Archenfield 13–21; Preb Heref Cathl from 16. *Becket House, Much Birch, Hereford HR2 8HT* T: (01981) 540390 E: revmark100@yahoo.co.uk

JOHNSON, Michael. b 42. Birm Univ BSc 63. S'wark Ord Course 68. **d** 71 **p** 72. C Kidbrooke St Jas *S'wark* 71–74; NSM Eynsford w Farningham and Lullingstone *Roch* 74–89; NSM Selling w Throwley, Sheldwich w Badlesmere etc *Cant* 89–12; rtd 12; PtO *Cant* from 12. *1 Halke Cottages, North Street, Sheldwich, Faversham ME13 0LR* T: (01795) 536583 M: 07860-635728 E: onehalke@aol.com

JOHNSON, Canon Michael Anthony. b 51. Ex Univ BA 76. Ripon Coll Cuddesdon 76 Ch Div Sch of the Pacific (USA) 77. **d** 78 **p** 79. C Primrose Hill St Mary w Avenue Road St Paul *Lon* 78–81; C Hampstead St Jo 81–85; TV Mortlake w E Sheen *S'wark* 85–93; V Wroughton *Bris* 93–17; RD 97–99; AD Swindon 99–06; Hon Can Bris Cathl 99–17; PtO 17–19; Acting Adn Bris 18–19; Acting Dean Bris 19–20; Assoc Adn Bris from 21; Assoc Adn Malmesbury from 21. *20 Brettingham Gate, Swindon SN3 1NH* T: 0117-926 4879 M: 07985-963031 E: michaeljohnson@bristoldiocese.org

JOHNSON, Michael Colin. b 37. S'wark Ord Course 77. **d** 80 **p** 81. NSM New Eltham All SS *S'wark* 80–84; NSM Woldingham 84–98; rtd 98; PtO *Chich* 99–07. *The College of*

St Barnabas, Blackberry Lane, Lingfield RH7 6NJ T: (01342) 872832 E: tandem@collegeofstbarnabas.com

JOHNSON, Michael Douglas. b 64. St Jo Coll Nottm 11. **d** 13 **p** 14. C Woodthorpe *S'well* 13–17; R Gedling from 17; P-in-c Lambley from 17. *The Rectory, Rectory Drive, Gedling, Nottingham NG4 4BG* E: michael.johnsons@hotmail.com

JOHNSON, Michael Gordon. b 45. Kelham Th Coll 64. **d** 68 **p** 69. C Holbrooks *Cov* 68–72; C Cannock Lich 72–75; V Coseley Ch Ch 75–79; P-in-c Sneyd 79–82; R Longton 82–88; Chapl Pilgrim Hosp Boston 88–96; TV Jarrow *Dur* 96–98; Chapl Monkton and Primrose Hill Hosp 96–98; R Burghwallis and Campsall *Sheff* 98–10; rtd 10; PtO *Sheff* 10–18; *Leeds* from 17. *8 Harmby Close, Skellow, Doncaster DN6 8PA* T: (01302) 330700 E: junejohnson01@btinternet.com

JOHNSON, Michael Robert. b 68. Aston Business Sch BSc 90. Ridley Hall Cam 94. **d** 97 **p** 98. C E Greenwich *S'wark* 97–00; C Perry Hill St Geo 00–03; Chapl W Lon YMCA 03–05; C Wokingham All SS *Ox* 05–14; Pioneer Min Sonning Deanery 11–18; TV Beaconsfield from 18. *St Thomas's House, Mayflower Way, Beaconsfield HP9 1UF* M: 07737-477193

JOHNSON, Mrs Nancy May. b 46. TCert 67 Sheff Poly MA 86. NOC 00. **d** 02 **p** 03. NSM Sheff Cathl 02–04; Asst Chapl Sheff Teaching Hosps NHS Foundn Trust 04–10; rtd 10; PtO *Sheff* 10–21. *121 Rustlings Road, Sheffield S11 7AB* T: 0114-266 6456 E: nancyjohnson@hotmail.co.uk

JOHNSON, Nicholas Ronald. b 84. Man Univ LLB 05 Cardiff Univ LLM 11 Called to the Bar (Lincoln's Inn) 06. St Steph Ho Ox BA 16. **d** 17 **p** 18. C Glodwick *Man* 17–18; C Royton 18–21; V W Derby St Jo *Liv* from 21. *The Vicarage, 1A Snaefell Avenue, Liverpool L13 7HA* M: 07817-912245 E: father.nicholas@icloud.com

JOHNSON, Canon Nigel Victor. b 48. ARCM 68 LTCL 75 Cam Univ DipEd 69. Linc Th Coll 80. **d** 82 **p** 83. C Lindley *Wakef* 82–85; P-in-c Upperthong 85–87; PtO *Derby* 88–89; NSM Calow and Sutton cum Duckmanton 89–90; R 90–00; RD Bolsover and Staveley 98–00; V Newbold w Dunston 00–15; RD Chesterfield 02–11; Hon Can Derby Cathl 05–15; rtd 15; PtO *Derby* from 15; Spiritual Dir Adv 16–18. *Yew Tree Cottage, Wheatley Road, Two Dales, Matlock DE4 2FF* E: nvjohnson@tiscali.co.uk

JOHNSON, Paul James. b 56. Teesside Coll of Educn BEd 80 Dur Sch of Educn MA 95. NEOC 06. **d** 09 **p** 10. NSM Whorlton w Carlton and Faceby *York* 09–12; PtO from 12; Chapl Ian Ramsey Sch Stockton 12–14; NSM Norton St Mary *Dur* 13–19; NSM Norton St Mich 13–19; NSM Billingham from 19. *18 Priorwood Gardens, Ingleby Barwick, Stockton-on-Tees TS17 0XH* T: (01642) 761941 E: pauljohnson452@btinternet.com

JOHNSON, Canon Peter Frederick. b 41. Melbourne Univ BA 63 Ch Ch Ox BA 68 MA 72. St Steph Ho Ox 68. **d** 69 **p** 70. C Banbury *Ox* 69–71; Tutor St Steph Ho Ox 71–74; Chapl St Chad's Coll Dur 74–80; Vice-Prin 78–80; Chapl K Sch Cant 80–90; PtO *Cant* 80–81; Hon Min Can Cant Cathl 81–90; Can Res Bris Cathl 90–08; rtd 08; PtO *Ox* from 08. *4 St John's Road, Windsor SL4 3QN* T: (01753) 865914 E: pf.johnson@btinternet.com

JOHNSON, Prof Peter Stewart. b 44. Nottm Univ BA 65 PhD 70. Cranmer Hall Dur 01. **d** 03 **p** 04. NSM Dur St Nic 03–14; PtO from 14. *126 Devonshire Road, Durham DH1 2BH* T: 0191-386 6334 M: 07949-680467 E: psjohnson969@gmail.com

JOHNSON, Philip Anthony. b 69. All Nations Chr Coll BA 97 MA 98 FIBMS 94. Ridley Hall Cam 00. **d** 02 **p** 03. C Witham *Chelmsf* 02–06; P-in-c Holland-on-Sea 06–13; V Sleaford *Linc* from 13; RD Lafford from 19. *1A Northfield Road, Quarrington, Sleaford NG34 8RT* E: revdphilip@aol.com

JOHNSON, Phillip Thomas. b 75. City Univ BA 03 Ox Univ BTh 12 Open Univ BA 14 Roehampton Univ MA 14 FRSA. Ripon Coll Cuddesdon 06. **d** 08 **p** 09. C Cheam *S'wark* 08–11; V Weston *Guildf* 11–18; AD Emly 17–18; V Malvern Link w Cowleigh *Worc* from 18. *12 Lambourne Avenue, Malvern WR14 1NL* T: (01684) 566054 E: vicar@mlwc.church

JOHNSON (née DAVIES), Canon Rhiannon Mary Morgan. b 69. St Anne's Coll Ox BA 90 MA 96 Univ of Wales (Cardiff) PhD 94 BD 96. St Mich Coll Llan 94. **d** 97 **p** 98. C Whitchurch *Llan* 97–99; NSM Walton W w Talbenny and Haroldston W *St D* 99–00; Chapl Trin Coll Carmarthen 00; NSM Walton W w Talbenny and Haroldston W *St D* 00–08; P-in-c Walwyn's Castle 08–14; P-in-c Walwyn's Castle and Robeston W 15–19; P-in-c Roose from 19; Dioc Course Dir for Exploring Faith from 11; Can St D Cathl from 15. *The Vicarage, Castle Way, Dale, Haverfordwest SA62 3RN* T: (01646) 636966 E: rhiannonjohnson@churchinwales.org.uk

JOHNSON, Richard Miles. b 59. Bris Univ BSc 82. St Jo Coll Nottm 87. **d** 90 **p** 91. C Bromley SS Pet and Paul *Roch* 90–94; USPG/CMS Philippines 94–97; Ind Chapl *Roch* 97–06; C

Bexleyheath Ch Ch 97–06; Ind Chapl *Worc* from 06; TV Redditch H Trin 06–17. *124 Lyttleton Avenue, Bromsgrove B60 3LB* E: dickim@globalnet.co.uk

JOHNSON, Richard William. b 76. St Cath Coll Cam BA 98 MA Glos Univ PhD 05. Westmr Th Cen. **d** 05 **p** 06. C Symonds Street St Paul NZ 05–09; C Worc City 09–14; V Worc St Nic and All SS w St Helen from 14. *St Helen's Church House, Fish Street, Worcester WR1 2HN* T: (01905) 734625 E: rich@allsaintsworcester.org.uk

JOHNSON, Robert. *See* JOHNSON, Christopher Robert

JOHNSON, Robert Anthony. b 59. Yorks Min Course 14. **d** 16 **p** 17. NSM Thornbury *Leeds* 16–17; NSM Woodhall 16–17; NSM Thornbury, Woodhall and Waterloo from 17. *13 Plumpton Drive, Bradford BD2 1PJ* T: (01274) 618330 E: revdjohnson13@gmail.com

JOHNSON, Ronald George. b 33. Chich Th Coll 75. **d** 76 **p** 77. NSM Shipley *Chich* 76–79; C Brighton St Matthias 79–82; R Barlavington, Burton w Coates, Sutton and Bignor 82–93; rtd 93; PtO *Chich* from 93. *1 Highdown Drive, Littlehampton BN17 6HJ* T: (01903) 732210

JOHNSON, Ruth Alice Edna. *See* LAMBERT, Ruth Alice Edna

JOHNSON (née ROWE), Mrs Shiela. b 43. CITC 93. **d** 96 **p** 97. Aux Min Urney w Denn and Derryheen *K, E & A* 96–97; Aux Min Boyle and Elphin w Aghanagh, Kilbryan etc 97–01; Aux Min Roscommon Gp 97–01; P-in-c Clondevaddock w Portsalon and Leatbeg *D & R* 02–08; rtd 08. *Rainbow's End, Carrickmacafferty, Derrybeg, Co Donegal, Republic of Ireland* T: (00353) (74) 953 2843 M: 087-635 0776 E: revshjohnson@gmail.com

JOHNSON, Simon Benjamin. b 73. Univ Coll Lon BEng 94. Trin Coll Bris 16. **d** 18 **p** 19. C S Harrow St Paul *Lon* from 18. *39 Eastcote Lane, Harrow HA2 8DF* M: 07810-180102 E: simonbjohnson1973@gmail.com

JOHNSON, Stanley. b 42. QUB BSc 63 TCD BTh 89. CITC 86. **d** 89 **p** 90. C Kilmore w Ballintemple, Kildallan etc *K, E & A* 89–96; Adn Elphin and Ardagh 97–01; Can Elphin Cathl 97–01; I Templemichael w Clongish, Clooncumber etc 97–01; I Clondehorkey w Cashel *D & R* 01–09; Can Raphoe Cathl 08–09; rtd 09. *Rainbow's End, Carrickmacafferty, Derrybeg, Co Donegal, Republic of Ireland* T: (00353) (74) 953 2843 M: 87-973 5775 E: revshjohnson@gmail.com or sjohnsons@eircom.net

JOHNSON, Stephen Ashley. b 79. York Univ BA 01 MA 02. Wycliffe Hall Ox BTh 06. **d** 06 **p** 07. C Sunningdale *Ox* 06–09; V Sunninghill and S Ascot 09–21; C Knowle *Birm* from 21. *49 Newton Road, Knowle, Solihull B93 9HN* M: 07799-834250 E: steve79a@gmail.com

JOHNSON, Stephen George. b 75. Ch Ch Coll Cant BA 97. Ridley Hall Cam 14. **d** 16 **p** 17. C Goring and Streatley w S Stoke *Ox* 16–19; R Church Stretton *Heref* from 19. *The Rectory, 4 Ashbrook Meadow, Carding Mill Valley, Church Stretton SY6 6JF* M: 07855-850667 E: stevejohn18@hotmail.com

JOHNSON, Stephen William. b 63. Trent Poly BEd 86 Keele Univ MA 94 Univ Coll Ches BA 05 ALCM 85. NOC 02. **d** 05 **p** 06. NSM Silverdale *Lich* 05–08; PtO *Linc* 09–10; *Lich* 10–12; Community Chapl *Linc* 13–14; P-in-c Market Rasen 14–19; P-in-c Legsby 14–19; P-in-c Linwood 14–19; P-in-c Lissington 14–19; RD W Wold 17–19; TR Gainsborough and Morton from 19. *The Vicarage, 32 Morton Terrace, Gainsborough DN21 2RQ* M: 07766-411090 E: stephenjohnson1963@icloud.com or steve.johnson@lincoln.anglican.org

JOHNSON, Stuart. *See* JOHNSON, Geoffrey Stuart

JOHNSON, Mrs Susan Constance. b 46. EAMTC 01. **d** 03 **p** 04. NSM Heald Green St Cath *Ches* 03–07; PtO 10–19; *Newc* from 18. *42 Sunningdale, Whitley Bay NE25 9YF* T: 0191-340 0659 E: revsusan@talktalk.net

JOHNSON, Miss Susan Elaine. b 44. R Holloway Coll Lon BA 66. EAMTC 99. **d** 02 **p** 03. C Münich Ascension and V Ingolstadt H Trin Germany 03–06; NSM Cwmbran *Mon* 06–09; TV Papworth *Ely* 09–11; rtd 11. *96 The Green, Weasenham, King's Lynn PE32 2TD* T: (01328) 838124 M: 07919-232211 E: revsusan44@btinternet.com

JOHNSON, Mrs Suzanne Joan. b 61. Ripon Coll Cuddesdon 16. **d** 19 **p** 20. NSM Taplow and Dropmore *Ox* from 19. *32 Ferrers Avenue, West Drayton UB7 7AA* M: 07971-240645 E: rev.suzanne@btinternet.com

JOHNSON, Terence John. b 44. Cov Poly BA 89. ALCD 70. **d** 69 **p** 70. C Woodside *Ripon* 69–72; C Leeds St Geo 72–76; C Heworth H Trin *York* 76–81; V Budbrooke *Cov* 81–97; Chapl Wroxall Abbey Sch 83–93; V Stone Ch Ch and Oulton *Lich* 97–02; P-in-c Collingtree w Courteenhall and Milton Malsor *Pet* 02–08; rtd 08; PtO *Pet* from 09. *32 Brick Field, Bletchley, Milton Keynes MK2 2FR* T: (01908) 378051 E: terencejohnson194@btinternet.com

JOHNSON, Thomas Bernard. b 44. BA CertEd. Oak Hill Th Coll. **d** 84 **p** 85. C Birkenhead St Jas w St Bede *Ches* 84–88; R Ashover and Brackenfield *Derby* 88–01; P-in-c Wessington 99–01; R Ashover and Brackenfield w Wessington *Derby* 01–03; RD Chesterfield 97–02; V Swanwick and Pentrich 03–10; Hon Chapl Derbyshire St Jo Ambulance 91–09; rtd 10; PtO *Derby* from 10. *11 The Spinney, Ripley DE5 3HW* T: (01773) 570375 E: t.b.johnson2000@gmail.com

JOHNSON, Canon Victoria Louise. b 75. Leic Univ BSc 96 PhD 00 SS Coll Cam BA 06. Westcott Ho Cam 04 Yale Div Sch 06. **d** 07 **p** 08. C Baguley *Man* 07–10; P-in-c Flixton St Mich 10–15; Can Res Ely Cathl 15–20; Can Res York Minster from 20. *2 Minster Court, York YO1 7JJ* T: (01904) 557200 M: 07713-478609 E: vickyjohnson@cantab.net or precentor@yorkminster.org

JOHNSTON, Alexander Irvine. b 47. Keele Univ BA 70 LRAM. St Alb Minl Tr Scheme 77. **d** 80 **p** 81. NSM Hockerill *St Alb* 80–95; NSM High Wych and Gilston w Eastwick 95–96; TV Bottesford w Ashby *Linc* 96–01; P-in-c St Germans *Truro* 01–12; rtd 12; PtO *Truro* 12–16. *31 Longmeadow Road, Saltash PL12 6DP* T: (01752) 842328 E: alecjohnston@btinternet.com

JOHNSTON, Allen Niall. b 61. Southn Univ BTh 92 Kent Univ MA 97 AMBIM 87 MISM 87 MInstD 00. Sarum & Wells Th Coll 89. **d** 92 **p** 93. C Roehampton H Trin *S'wark* 92–95; Dir Past Services Richmond, Twickenham and Roehampton NHS Trust 95–98; Tutor SEITE 95–97; PtO *Eur* 01–02; Sierra Leone 02–03; Asst P St Jo Cathl Freetown 03; PtO *Ely* 03–08; *D & R* 04–12; Project Dir FoRB Leadership Network 19–20; Dep Dir of Operations Miss and Public Affairs Abps' Coun from 20; PtO *Ely* 21. *Church House, 27 Great Smith Street, London SW1P 3AZ* T: (020) 7898 1116 E: niall.johnston@churchofengland.org

JOHNSTON, Austin. b 50. Huddersfield Poly CertEd 76 BEd 90. Chich Th Coll 92. **d** 94 **p** 95. C Peterlee *Dur* 94–97; C Stockton St Pet 97–00; TR Stanley and Tanfield 00–01; TR Ch the K 01–15; V Stanley and S Moor 15–16; rtd 16. *12 Selwyn House, 29 Selwyn Road, Eastbourne BN21 2LF*

JOHNSTON, Brian. *See* JOHNSTON, Wilfred Brian

JOHNSTON, Mrs Carole Ann. b 58. Worc Coll of Educn BA 84. St Jo Coll Nottm 04. **d** 06 **p** 07. C Ilkley All SS *Bradf* 06–09; TV Turton Moorland *Man* 09–11; PtO *St Alb* 15–21. *21A Orchard Road, Beeston, Sandy SG19 1PJ* T: (01767) 699934 E: carole.johnston@virgin.net

JOHNSTON, Charles James Andrew. b 60. **d** 16 **p** 17. NSM St Mary le Strand w St Clem Danes *Lon* 16–19; PtO *Eur* 19; Chapl Marseille w Aix-en-Provence and the Luberon from 19. *4 rue de Belloi, 13006 Marseille, France* T: (0033) 7 66 01 71 50 E: anglican.marseille@gmail.com

JOHNSTON, David George Scott. b 60. Avery Hill Coll BA 88. SEITE 00. **d** 03 **p** 04. C Frindsbury w Upnor and Chattenden *Roch* 03–06; R Longfield 06–11; C Chislehurst Ch Ch 11–15; V from 15. *The Vicarage, 62 Lubbock Road, Chislehurst BR7 5JK* T: (020) 8467 3185 E: rev.dj@btinternet.com

JOHNSTON, Edith Violet Nicholl. b 28. **d** 87. Par Dn Bentley *Sheff* 87–88; rtd 88; PtO *Sheff* 88–08. *30 Sharman Road, Belfast BT9 5FW* T: (028) 9066 6776

JOHNSTON, Frank. *See* JOHNSTON, William Francis

JOHNSTON, Canon Geoffrey Stanley. b 44. Aston Univ MBA 81 Birm Univ CertEd 78. Kelham Th Coll 64. **d** 68 **p** 69. C Blakenall Heath *Lich* 68–72 and 73–75; C St Buryan, St Levan and Sennen *Truro* 72–73; P-in-c Willenhall St Steph *Lich* 75–76; C W Bromwich All SS 76–77; Lect W Bromwich Coll of Commerce and Tech 78–82; Ind Chapl *Worc* 82–94; TV Halesowen 82–94; NSM Dudley St Fran 94–99; P-in-c 99–08; P-in-c Dudley St Edm 04–08; rtd 08; P-in-c Nerja and Almuñécar *Eur* 08–14; Interim Adn Gib 13–19; Acting Adn Italy and Malta 19. *29 Little Fallows, Milford, Belper DE56 0RY* T: (01773) 270972 M: 07507-391297 E: vengeoffrey@gmail.com or geoff.johnston@europe.anglican.org

JOHNSTON, Mrs Helen Kay. b 48. SRN 70. SAOMC 95. **d** 98 **p** 99. OLM Banbury St Paul *Ox* 98–01; P-in-c Flimby *Carl* 01–03; C Netherton 01–03; PtO *Derby* 04–11; *Lich* from 11. *Merryfields, Whitehorn Avenue, Barleston, Stoke-on-Trent ST12 9EF* T: (01782) 372618

JOHNSTON, Miss Henrietta Elizabeth Ann. b 59. St Jo Coll Dur BA 03. Cranmer Hall Dur 01. **d** 03 **p** 04. C Cov H Trin 03–07; C Dorridge *Birm* 07–11; V Lache cum Saltney *Ches* from 11; P-in-c Chester St Pet 16–17; RD Ches from 19. *St Mark's Vicarage, 5 Cliveden Road, Chester CH4 8DR* T: (01244) 671702 or 675372 M: 07796-948904 E: hennie.johnston@gmail.com

JOHNSTON, Ian. b 61. Hull Univ CertEd 82 BEd 84. LCTP 08. **d** 13 **p** 14. NSM Carl H Trin and St Barn 13–21; P-in-c Rockcliffe and Blackford from 21; Asst Dir of Ords from

16. *Watch Hill, Burgh-by-Sands, Carlisle CA5 6AQ* T: (01228) 576097

JOHNSTON, Ian Harold. b 50. Ex Univ BA 72 McMaster Univ Ontario MA 74 Sheff Univ BA 13. Yorks Min Course 10. d 13 p 14. NSM Adel *Leeds* 13–16; NSM Ireland Wood 13–16; NSM Hampsthwaite and Killinghall and Birstwith 16–18; Min to Business Leeds from 14; rtd 18. *4 Buttercup Close, Killinghall, Harrogate HG3 2WU* M: 07775-602475 E: revianjohnston@gmail.com

JOHNSTON, James. *See* JOHNSTON, Charles James Andrew

JOHNSTON, Kay. *See* JOHNSTON, Helen Kay

JOHNSTON, Lee. b 91. Glas Univ BD 15 MTh 16. d 18 p 19. C Lanark w Douglas *Glas* from 18. *21B High Street, Lanark ML11 7LU* T: (1555) 450095 E: l.johnston.gla@gmail.com

JOHNSTON, Michael David Haigh. b 44. S Dios Minl Tr Scheme 88. d 91 p 92. NSM Wootton *Portsm* 91–95; NSM Ryde H Trin 95–99; NSM Swanmore St Mich 95–99; P-in-c Cowes St Faith 99–03; Asst Chapl Isle of Wight NHS Primary Care Trust 03–11; Chapl HM Pris Kingston (Portsm) 03–05; P-in-c St Lawrence *Portsm* 11–14; rtd 14; PtO *Portsm* from 14. *8 Coniston Drive, Ryde PO33 3AE* T: (01983) 611291 E: rvdmikej@fastmail.fm

JOHNSTON, Niall. *See* JOHNSTON, Allen Niall

JOHNSTON, Canon Robert John. b 31. Oak Hill Th Coll 64. d 64 p 65. C Bebington *Ches* 64–68; I Lack *Clogh* 68–99; Can Clogh Cathl 89–99; rtd 99. *Flat 16, 8 Eastermede Park, Ballymoney BT53 6HP* T: (028) 2766 9317

JOHNSTON, Trevor Samuel. b 72. Ulster Univ BMus 96 TCD BTh 01. CITC 98. d 01 p 02. C Carrickfergus *Conn* 01–04; C Jordanstown and Chapl Jordanstown and Belf Campuses Ulster Univ 04–09; Crosslinks Ireland Team Ldr 09–14; I Belfast All SS *Conn* from 14; P-in-c Belfast St Nic from 20. *All Saints' Rectory, 171 Malone Road, Belfast BT9 6TA* M: 07776-178248 E: trev@tjohnston.net *or* rector@ascbelfast.com

JOHNSTON, Violet. *See* JOHNSTON, Edith Violet Nicholl

JOHNSTON, Wilfred Brian. b 44. TCD BA 67 MA 70. Div Test 68. d 68 p 70. C Seagoe *D & D* 68–73; I Inniskeel *D & R* 73–82; I Castlerock w Dunboe and Fermoyle 82–02; Bp's C Gweedore, Carrickfin and Templecrone 02–08; Dioc Registrar 89–06; Can Derry Cathl 92–02; Preb 99–02; Can Raphoe Cathl *D & R* 05–08; rtd 08. *2 The Apple Yard, Coleraine BT51 3PP* T: (028) 7032 6406 E: b.johnston@talk21.com *or* johnston.brian1944@gmail.com

JOHNSTON, William Francis (Frank). b 30. CB 83. TCD BA 55 MA 69. d 55 p 56. C Orangefield *D & D* 55–59; CF 59–77; Asst Chapl Gen 77–80; Chapl-Gen 80–87; P-in-c Winslow *Ox* 87–91; RD Claydon 89–94; R Winslow w Gt Horwood and Addington 91–95; rtd 95; PtO *Ex* 95–11. *Lower Axehill, Chard Road, Axminster EX13 5ED* T: (01297) 33259

JOHNSTON, Canon William John. b 35. Lon Univ BA 85 MA 90 PhD. CITC 67. d 70 p 71. C Belfast St Donard *D & D* 70–72; C Derg *D & R* 72–78; I Drumclamph w Lower and Upper Langfield 78–91; I Kilskeery w Trillick *Clogh* 91–10; Preb Clogh Cathl 04–10; Prec 09–10; rtd 10. *Ernedene, 61 Dublin Road, Enniskillen BT74 6HN* T: (028) 6632 2268

JOHNSTON, William McConnell. b 33. TCD BA 57. d 58 p 59. C Ballymena w Ballyclug *Conn* 58–61; C Belfast St Thos 61–63; C Finaghy 63–66; R Kambula S Africa 66–74; Dean Eshowe 74–86; R Mtubatuba 86–99; rtd 00; PtO *Chich* from 04. *70 Royal Close, Chichester PO19 7PS* T: (01243) 681280 E: mfundisi.johnston@gmail.com

JOHNSTON, Debra Jayne. b 62. All SS Cen for Miss & Min 15. d 17 p 18. OLM Ainsworth *Man* from 17. *51 Green Bank, Bolton BL2 3NQ*

JOINT, Canon Michael John. b 39. Sarum & Wells Th Coll 79. d 79 p 79. CA from 61; Hon C Chandler's Ford *Win* 79–83; Youth Chapl 79–83; V Lymington 83–95; Co-ord Chapl R Bournemouth and Christchurch Hosps NHS Trust 96–03; Hon Can Win Cathl 00–03; rtd 03; PtO *Win* 03–04 and from 12. *20 Wavendon Avenue, Barton on Sea, New Milton BH25 7LS* T: (01425) 628952 E: michjoin@aol.com

JOLLEY, Mrs Alice Elizabeth. b 95. Grey Coll Dur BA 17 Dur Univ MA 19. Westcott Ho Cam 17. d 19 p 20. C Linc St Nic w St Jo Newport from 19. *14 Nettleham Close, Lincoln LN2 1SJ* T: (01522) 402315 M: 07891-695963 E: mthr.alicejolley@outlook.com

JOLLEY, The Ven Andrew John. b 61. Nottm Univ BSc 83 PhD 06 Warwick Univ MBA 88 CEng 88 MIMechE 88. St Jo Coll Nottm BTh 97. d 98 p 99. C Sparkhill w Greet and Sparkbrook *Birm* 98–02; V Aston SS Pet and Paul 02–08; P-in-c Aston St Jas 05–08; P-in-c Nechells 05–08; V Aston and Nechells 08–16; AD Aston 05–12; Hon Can Birm Cathl 15–16; Adn Bradf *Leeds* from 16. *1 Selborne Grove, Bradford BD9 4NL* T: 0113-353 0292 M: 07973-458403 E: andy.jolley@leeds.anglican.org

JONAS, Alan Charles. b 56. Leeds Univ BA 79 Univ of Wales (Abth) PGCE 80. Wycliffe Hall Ox 92. d 94 p 95. C Hersham *Guildf* 94–98; P-in-c Westcott 98–08; V 08–21; Chapl Priory Sch 01–07; AD Dorking *Guildf* 14–19; rtd 21. *27 Odlehill Grove, Abbotskerswell, Newton Abbot TQ12 5NJ* E: alchasjonas@aol.com

JONAS, Ian Robert. b 54. St Jo Coll Nottm BTh 80. d 80 p 81. C Portadown St Mark *Arm* 80–82; C Cregagh *D & D* 82–85; BCMS Sec *D & G* 85–90; V Langley Mill *Derby* 90–97; I Kilgariffe Union *C, C & R* 97–09; I Carrigrohane Union 09–20; Can Cork Cathl 11–20; Can Cloyne Cathl 11–20; rtd 20. *Address temp unknown* E: revianjonas@yahoo.co.uk

JONES, Adrian. *See* JONES, Michael Adrian Roche

JONES, Alan Pierce. *See* PIERCE-JONES, Alan

JONES, Alison. b 61. NE Surrey Coll of Tech BSc 86 Cardiff Univ BTh 12. d 10 p 11. NSM Swansea St Pet *S & B* 10–11; NSM Cen Swansea 11; C Sketty 11–15; V Swansea St Nic and St Jude 15–20; Can Res Brecon Cathl 18–20; Bp's Officer for Lay Min 18–20; Warden of Readers 18–20. *Address temp unknown* M: 07890-707117 E: alison.rhossili@hotmail.co.uk

JONES, Alison. *See* WAGSTAFF, Alison

JONES, Alison. *See* JONES, Helen Alison

JONES, Alison Fiona Kay. b 67. St Mellitus Coll 11. d 13 p 14. C Burghfield *Ox* 13–17; LtO *S'well* from 17. *Willow Cottage, Norwell Woodhouse, Newark NG23 6NG* M: 07818-806403 E: alison.jones@thepottingshedchurch.org

JONES, Alun. b 52. Leeds Univ BA 96. Cuddesdon Coll 94. d 96 p 97. C Newc St Geo 96–98; C Cowgate 98–99; C Fenham St Jas and St Basil 99–04; P-in-c Carl St Herbert w St Steph 04–07; V from 07. *St Herbert's Vicarage, Blackwell Road, Carlisle CA2 4RA* T: (01228) 523375 E: alun52@sky.com

JONES, Alyson Elizabeth. *See* DAVIE, Alyson Elizabeth

JONES, Ms Amanda Louise. b 69. Cranmer Hall Dur 14. d 16 p 17. C Penrith w Newton Reigny and Plumpton Wall *Carl* from 16. *18 Skirsgill Close, Penrith CA11 8QF* T: (01768) 744687 E: mandyjoness@aol.co.uk

JONES, Mrs Andrea Margaret. b 46. Qu Coll Birm 88. d 90 p 94. Par Dn Kidderminster St Geo *Worc* 90–94; TV 94–95; C Penn Fields *Lich* 95–00; C Gt Wyrley 00–06; rtd 06; PtO *Worc* from 07. *57 Woodward Road, Kidderminster DY11 6NY* T: (01562) 823555 E: aam57@blueyonder.co.uk

JONES, Ms Andrea Susan. b 55. SNWTP 08. d 10 p 11. OLM Davyhulme St Mary *Man* 10–11; C Newton Heath 11–13; C Moston St Jo 11–13; C Moston St Chad 11–13; R Manchester Gd Shep and St Barn 13–17; Borough Dean Man 12–17; Hon Can Man Cathl 16–17; TV Borderlands Miss Area *St As* from 17. *The Rectory, 2 Birch Rise, Hawarden, Deeside CH5 3DD* T: (01244) 520992 E: andysjones@hotmail.co.uk

JONES, The Ven Andrew. b 61. Univ of Wales (Ban) BD 82 PGCE 82 TCD BTh 85 MA 91 Univ of Wales MPhil 93. CITC 82 St Geo Coll Jerusalem 84. d 85 p 86. Min Can Ban Cathl 85–88; R Dolgellau w Llanfachreth and Brithdir etc 88–92; Warden of Readers 91–92; Dir Past Studies St Mich Coll Llan 92–96; Lect Th Univ of Wales (Cardiff) 92–96; Visiting Prof St Geo Coll Jerusalem from 94; Research Fell from 96; R Llanberis w Llannor w Llanfihangel etc *Ban* 96–01; R Llanbedrog w Llannor and Llangian 01–12; Dioc CME and NSM Officer 96–00; AD Llyn and Eifionydd 99–10; Hon Can Ban Cathl 04–05; Can Ban Cathl from 05; Dioc Dir of Ords from 06; Adn Meirionnydd from 10; C Bro Enlli 12–16; V from 16. *Ty'n Llan Rectory, Llanbedrog, Pwllheli LL53 7TU* T/F: (01758) 740919 E: archdeacon.meirionnydd@churchinwales.org.uk

JONES, Andrew. b 64. York Univ BA 85. Westmr Th Sem (USA) MDiv 91 St Jo Coll Nottm 92. d 94 p 95. C Win Ch Ch 94–98; C St Helen Bishopsgate w St Andr Undershaft etc *Lon* 98–04; Min-in-c Grace Ch Hackney from 04. *89 Forest Road, London E8 3BL* T: (020) 7254 5942 M: 07534-669528 E: rev.aj64@btinternet.com *or* info@gracechurchhackney.org.uk

JONES, Andrew. *See* JONES, Ian Andrew

JONES, Preb Andrew Christopher. b 47. Southn Univ BA 69 PhD 75. Ridley Hall Cam 78. d 80 p 81. C Wareham *Sarum* 80–83; P-in-c Symondsbury 83; P-in-c Chideock 83; R Symondsbury and Chideock 84–91; V Shottermill *Guildf* 91–99; P-in-c Bishopsnympton, Rose Ash, Mariansleigh etc *Ex* 99–14; rtd 14; Preb Ex Cathl from 14; PtO from 15. *13 Kingdon Avenue, South Molton EX36 4GJ* E: acjtherectory@btinternet.com

JONES, Andrew Edward. b 71. Ridley Hall Cam 10. d 12 p 13. C Sprowston w Beeston *Nor* 12–15; R Trunch Group from 15. *The Rectory, Knapton Road, Trunch, North Walsham NR28 0QE* T: (01263) 722218 E: revandrewjones@gmail.com

426

JONES, Mrs Anna Holt. b 75. Mert Coll Ox BA 96 Univ Coll Lon MA 98 Peterho Cam MPhil 99 Jes Coll Cam BTh 19. Westcott Ho Cam 17. **d** 19 **p** 20. C Three Rivers Gp *Ely* from 19. *13 Mayfield Close, Ely CB6 3AB* T: (01353) 645944 M: 07751-032166 E: revdannajones@gmail.com

JONES, Anne. *See* FURNESS, Christine Anne

JONES, Anthony. b 43. WEMTC 99. **d** 01 **p** 02. OLM Lydney *Glouc* 01–07; NSM Woolaston w Alvington and Aylburton 07–17; rtd 17; PtO *Glouc* from 19. *2 The Lodge, High Street, St Briavels, Lydney GL15 6TB* T: (01594) 531134 M: 07860-331755 E: jones_rev@yahoo.co.uk

JONES, April Elizabeth. b 46. WEMTC. **d** 12 **p** 13. NSM Badgeworth, Shurdington and Witcombe w Bentham *Glouc* 12–17; rtd 17. *Charnwood, Bryerland Road, Witcombe, Gloucester GL3 4TA* T: (01452) 864469 E: alanjones1944@hotmail.com

JONES, Barbara Christine. b 48. St Hugh's Coll Ox BA 71 MA 74 Lady Spencer Chu Coll of Educn PGCE 74. CBDTI 97. **d** 00 **p** 01. NSM Bolton-le-Sands *Blackb* 00–13; Bp's Adv on Healing 09–16; PtO from 13. *11 Sandown Road, Lancaster LA1 4LN* T: (01524) 65598

JONES, Barry Mervyn. b 46. St Chad's Coll Dur BA 68. **d** 70 **p** 71. C Bloxwich *Lich* 70–72; C Norwood All SS *Cant* 72–76; C New Addington 76–78; Chapl Mayday Univ Hosp Thornton Heath 78–86; Chapl Qu Hosp Croydon 78–86; Chapl St Mary's Hosp Croydon 78–86; Chapl Bromsgrove and Redditch DHA 86–94; Chapl Alexandra Healthcare NHS Trust Redditch 94–00; Chapl Worcs Acute Hosps NHS Trust 00–03; Chapl Team Ldr 03–05; PtO *Worc* from 05. *46 Barlich Way, Redditch B98 7JP* T: (01527) 520659

JONES, Benjamin Jenkin Hywel. b 39. Univ of Wales BA 61. St Mich Coll Llan 61. **d** 64 **p** 65. C Carmarthen St Pet *St D* 64–70; V Cynwyl Gaeo w Llansawel and Talley 70–79; R Llanbadarn Fawr 79–82; V Llanbadarn Fawr w Capel Bangor and Goginan 82–92; V Llanychaearn w Llanddeiniol 92–05; Warden of Readers from 82; Can St D Cathl 86–90; RD Llanbadarn Fawr 89–90; Adn Cardigan 90–06; rtd 06; PtO *St D* from 06. *Dowerdd, Waun Fawr, Aberystwyth SY23 3QF* T: (01970) 617100 E: hywelandanne@btinternet.com

JONES, Benjamin Mark Oscar. b 79. Kent Univ BA 00 Cant Ch Ch Univ PGCE 01. Trin Coll Bris BA 11 MPhil 12. **d** 12 **p** 13. C Folkestone St Jo *Cant* 12–15; C S Croydon Em *S'wark* 15–21; V Hedge End St Luke *Win* from 21. *16 Elliot Rise, Hedge End, Southampton SO30 2RU* M: 07779-494372 E: benmarkjones@hotmail.com

JONES, Bernard Lewis. b 48. Llan Dioc Tr Scheme 89. **d** 93 **p** 94. NSM Aberaman and Abercwmboi w Cwmaman *Llan* 93–99; V Hirwaun 99–13; AD Cynon Valley 08–12; rtd 13; PtO *Llan* from 13; Chapl to Rtd Clergy from 20. *21 Parc Aberaman, Aberaman, Aberdare CF44 6EY* T: (01685) 870607

JONES, Brenda. b 50. Cranmer Hall Dur 02. **d** 04 **p** 05. C Jarrow *Dur* 04–07; C-in-c Bishop Auckland Woodhouse Close CD 07–14; rtd 14; PtO *Dur* from 17. *33 Walden Close, Ouston, Chester le Street DH2 1TF*

JONES, Brenda. *See* CAMPBELL, Brenda

JONES, Canon Brian Howell. b 35. Univ of Wales MPhil 96. St Mich Coll Llan. **d** 61 **p** 62. C Llangiwg *S & B* 61–63; C Swansea St Mary and H Trin 63–70; R New Radnor w Llanfihangel Nantmelan etc 70–75; V Llansamlet 75–89; Dioc Dir of Stewardship 82–89; P-in-c Capel Coelbren 89–94; Dioc Missr 89–95; Can Res Brecon Cathl 89–00; Can Treas Brecon Cathl 90–00; Chan Brecon Cathl 99–00; RD Cwmtawe 89–93; V Killay 95–00; rtd 00. *125 Homegower House, St Helen's Road, Swansea SA1 4DW* T: (01792) 652466 E: b.h.jones@outlook.com

JONES, Canon Brian Michael. b 34. Trin Coll Bris 79 Oak Hill Th Coll BA 82. **d** 84 **p** 84. CMS 82–85; Sierra Leone 84–93; Can Bo from 91; C Frimley *Guildf* 93–99; rtd 99; PtO *Newc* 00–01; Hon C N Tyne and Redesdale 01–08; PtO *Carl* 09–20. *20 Campfield Road, Ulverston LA12 9PB* T: (01229) 480380 E: bmj.retired@btopenworld.com

JONES, Brian Robert. b 53. Surrey Univ BSc 76. SAOMC 02. **d** 05 **p** 06. NSM Greenham Ox from 05. *27 Three Acre Road, Newbury RG14 7AW* T: (01635) 34875

JONES, Canon Bryan Maldwyn. b 32. St Mich Coll Llan. **d** 62 **p** 63. C Swansea St Barn *S & B* 62–69; V Trallwng and Betws Penpont 69–75; V Trallwng, Bettws Penpont w Aberyskir etc 75–00; RD Brecon 80–91; AD 91–99; Hon Can Brecon Cathl 92–00; rtd 00. *Plas Newydd, 8 Camden Crescent, Brecon LD3 7BY* T: (01874) 625063 E: bryanandmary8@gmail.com

JONES, Bryn Parry. b 49. Univ of Wales BSc 98 MCIH 98 FCIH 03. St As Minl Tr Course 04. **d** 06 **p** 10. NSM Connah's Quay *St As* 06–15; P-in-c Pontrobin 15–16; P-in-c Borderlands Miss Area 17–19; rtd 19. *7 Fron Las, Holywell CH8 7HX* T: (01352) 714781

JONES, Bryon. b 34. Open Univ BA 84. St D Coll Lamp 61. **d** 64 **p** 65. C Port Talbot St Theodore *Llan* 64–67; C Aberdare 68–69; C Up Hatherley *Glouc* 69–71; C Oystermouth *S & B* 71–74; V Camrose *St D* 74–77; V Camrose and St Lawrence w Ford and Haycastle 77–04; rtd 04. *31 New Road, Haverfordwest SA61 1TU* T: (01437) 760596

JONES, Cameron Charles Wallace. **d** 14 **p** 15. Carrickfergus *Conn* 14–15; C 15–19; ICM from 19. *28 Bachelors Walk, Dublin 1, D01 P4V6, Republic of Ireland* M: 07742-617224 E: cameron.cw.jones@gmail.com

JONES, Caroline Elizabeth. b 53. W Glam Inst of HE BA 91 Cape Town Univ MA 94 Univ of Wales (Lamp) PhD 01. **d** 16 **p** 17. NSM Llanegwad w Llanfihangel Uwch Gwili *St D* 16–18; NSM St Clears w Llangynin and Llanddowror etc 18; C Cwmaman 18–19; P-in-c Bro Aman from 19. *Y Ficerdy, Vicarage Road, Twyn, Ammanford SA18 1JQ* T: (01269) 822104 M: 07530-959547 E: caroline.jones08@btinternet.com

JONES, Miss Celia Lynn. b 54. Univ of Wales (Lamp) MTh 09. Trin Coll Bris. **d** 01 **p** 08. C Bris St Paul's 01–08; C Barton Hill St Luke w Ch Ch and Moorfields 08–09; TV Magor *Mon* from 09. *The Vicarage, Station Road, Llanwern, Newport NP18 2DW* T: (01633) 413647 E: clynnjones@talktalk.net

JONES, Charles Derek. b 37. K Coll Lon BD 60 AKC 60. **d** 61 **p** 62. C Stockton St Chad *Dur* 61–64; C Becontree St Elisabeth *Chelmsf* 64–66; C S Beddington St Mich *S'wark* 66–73; LtO *Ex* 73–77; PtO *Liv* 77–99; rtd 02. *4 Bryn Glas, Graigfechan, Ruthin LL15 2EX* T: (01824) 705015 E: derek620jones@btinternet.com

JONES, Christopher Howell. b 50. BA FCCA. Oak Hill Th Coll 80. **d** 83 **p** 84. C Leyton St Mary w St Edw *Chelmsf* 83–86; C Becontree St Mary 86–90; P-in-c Bootle St Matt *Liv* 90–93; V 93–99; AD Bootle 97–99; V Ormskirk 99–15; Chapl W Lancashire NHS Trust 99–11; C Liv Cathl 15–18; rtd 18. *9 Mersey Court, Liverpool L23 3AQ* T: 0151-932 1674 E: chrisjonesvic50@gmail.com

JONES, Christopher Mark. b 56. St Jo Coll Cam BA 78 MA 82 Wycliffe Hall Ox BA 81 MA 85. **d** 82 **p** 83. C Walsall *Lich* 82–84; Chapl St Jo Coll Cam 84–89; Chapl Eton Coll from 89; Ho Master 97–10; Ho Masters' Rep 10–17; Dir Boarding from 17. *2 Hodgson House, Eton College, Windsor SL4 6DE* T: (01753) 671330 M: 07794-136258 E: c.m.jones@etoncollege.org.uk

JONES, Christopher Yeates. b 51. STETS 97. **d** 00 **p** 01. NSM Yeovil St Mich *B & W* 00–12; rtd 12; PtO *B & W* from 15. *26 Glenthorne Avenue, Yeovil BA21 4PG* T: (01935) 420886 M: 07944-461154

JONES, Mrs Claire Rachel. b 90. Worc Coll Ox BA 13 St Jo Coll Dur MA 19. Cranmer Hall Dur 17. **d** 19 **p** 20. C Bodmin *Truro* from 19. *Address withheld by request* E: revclairejones@gmail.com

JONES, Clive. b 51. BA 82. Oak Hill Th Coll 79. **d** 82 **p** 83. C Brunswick *Man* 82–85; V Pendlebury St Jo 85–96; V Attleborough *Cov* 96–16; rtd 16; PtO *Derby* 17–19; *S'wark* from 19. *25 Bedford Road, Burton-on-Trent DE15 9JG*

JONES, Clive Morlais Peter. b 40. Univ of Wales (Cardiff) BA 63 CertEd 64 LTCL 71. Chich Th Coll 64. **d** 66 **p** 67. C Llanfabon *Llan* 66–70; PV Llan Cathl 70–75; R Gelligaer 75–85; Prec and Can Llan Cathl 84–85; R Tilehurst St Mich *Ox* 85–94; Chapl Costa Blanca *Eur* 94–97; V Newton St Pet *S & B* 97–06; P-in-c Haarlem *Eur* 07–10; PtO *Ox* from 10; *Eur* from 16. *31 Lowbury Gardens, Compton, Newbury RG20 6NN* T: (01635) 579409 E: clive.jones857@btinternet.com

JONES, Clive Wesley. b 68. St Steph Ho Ox 95. **d** 98 **p** 99. C Swanley St Mary *Roch* 98–02; P-in-c Belvedere St Aug 02–07; V from 07; Chapl Trin Sch Belvedere 02–04; PtO *Chelmsf* 14–18; *S'wark* from 19. *The Vicarage, St Augustine's Road, Belvedere DA17 5HH* T: (020) 8311 6307 E: frclive@tiscali.co.uk

JONES, Colin Stuart. b 56. Southn Univ LLB 77. Coll of Resurr Mirfield 81. **d** 84 **p** 85. C Mountain Ash *Llan* 84–86; C Castle Bromwich SS Mary and Marg *Birm* 86–89; V Kingshurst 89–94; V Perry Barr 94–05; P-in-c Wordsley *Worc* 05–07; TR from 07; RD Kingswinford 10–16. *The Rectory, 13 Dunsley Drive, Stourbridge DY8 5RA* T: (01384) 400709

JONES, Collette Moyra Yvonne. b 50. Liv Univ BSc 71 PhD 75 ALCM 91. SNWTP 08. **d** 11 **p** 12. NSM Gt Sutton *Ches* 11–14; V Aston by Sutton, Lt Leigh and Lower Whitley from 14. *The Vicarage, Street Lane, Lower Whitley, Warrington WA4 4EN* T: (01925) 730158 E: collettejones868@gmail.com

JONES, Daniel. b 78. St Andr Univ MTheol 01 PGCE 02. Qu Coll Birm 06. **d** 08 **p** 09. NSM Barbourne *Worc* 08–11; Chapl St Pet Sch York from 11. *St Peter's School, Clifton, York YO30 6AB* T: (01904) 527412 E: daniel_a_jones@btopenworld.com

JONES, David. b 55. CA Tr Coll 74 St Steph Ho Ox 83. **d** 85 **p** 86. C Fleur-de-Lis *Mon* 85–87; V Ynysddu 87–93; V

Blackwood 93–08; AD Bedwellty 06–08; V Landore and Treboeth S & B from 08. *St Alban's Vicarage, Heol Fach, Treboeth, Swansea SA5 9DE* T: (01792) 310586

JONES, David. *See* JONES, Wilfred David

JONES, David Arthur. b 44. Liv Univ BA 66 Sussex Univ MA 68. St D Coll Lamp LTh 74. **d** 74 **p** 75. C Tenby *St D* 74–76; C Chepstow *Mon* 76–78; P-in-c Teversal *S'well* 78–81; R 81–91; Chapl Sutton Cen 78–89; V Radford All So w Ch Ch and St Mich 91–04; Adv to Urban Priority Par 96–01; Officer for Urban Life and Miss 04–09; rtd 09; PtO *S'well* from 11. *37 Devonshire Road, Nottingham NG5 2EW* T: 0115-962 2115 E: urbanrover@gmail.com

JONES, David Eric. b 72. St Mellitus Coll BA 16. **d** 16 **p** 17. C Croxley Green All SS *St Alb* 16–19; V Beckenham St Jo *Roch* from 19. *The Vicarage, 249 Eden Park Avenue, Beckenham BR3 3JN* M: 07540-120077 E: djones007@me.com

JONES, David Gordon. b 78. Trin Coll Bris 17. **d** 19 **p** 20. C Fromeside *Bris* from 19. *The Vicarage, Mautravers Close, Bradley Stoke, Bristol BS32 8ED* M: 07737-529687 E: davidjones75@msn.com

JONES, David Ian Stewart. b 34. Selw Coll Cam BA 57 MA 61. Westcott Ho Cam 57. **d** 59 **p** 60. C Oldham *Man* 59–63; V Elton All SS 63–66; Chapl Eton Coll 66–70; Sen Chapl 70–74; Hd Master Bryanston Sch 74–82; P-in-c Bris Ch Ch w St Ewen and All SS 82–84; P-in-c Bris St Steph w St Nic and St Leon 82–84; Soc Resp Adv 84–85; Dir Lambeth Endowed Charities 85–94; Hon PV S'wark Cathl 85–94; rtd 94; PtO *Ox* 08–12. *33 St Lucian's Lane, Wallingford OX10 9ER* T: (01491) 836052 E: davidandsuejones@aol.com

JONES, David Mark. b 73. St Mich Coll Llan 03. **d** 06 **p** 07. C Llansamlet S & B 06–08; Min Can Brecon Cathl 08–13; P-in-c Rhondda Fach Uchaf *Llan* from 13. *Ty Nant, Margaret Street, Pontygwaith, Ferndale CF43 3EH* T: (01443) 732321 E: revdmj@yahoo.co.uk

JONES, David Michael. b 48. Oral Roberts Univ BA 09. Chich Th Coll 75. **d** 78 **p** 79. C Yeovil *B & W* 78–84; C Barwick 81–84; V Cleeve w Chelvey and Brockley 84–92; V Heigham St Barn w St Bart *Nor* 92–00; V Writtle w Highwood *Chelmsf* 00–14; rtd 14; PtO *Sarum* from 15. *5 Rope Yard Court, Rope Yard, Royal Wootton Bassett, Swindon SN4 7FD* E: revmjoneswrittle@aol.com

JONES, David Raymond. b 34. Univ of Wales (Lamp) BA 54 St Cath Coll Ox BA 57 MA 61. Wycliffe Hall Ox 58. **d** 58 **p** 59. C Ex St Dav 58–60; C Bideford 60–63; Chapl Grenville Coll Bideford 63–66; Chapl RN 66–89; QHC 84–89; Dir and Warden Divine Healing Miss Crowhurst 89–97; rtd 97; PtO *Chich* from 97. *9 Perrots Lane, Steyning BN44 3NB* T: (01903) 815236 E: maureenroy9@gmail.com

JONES, David Sebastian. b 43. St Cath Coll Cam BA 67 MA 73. Linc Th Coll 66. **d** 68 **p** 69. C Baguley *Man* 68–71; C Bray and Braywood *Ox* 71–73; V S Ascot 73–07; AD Bracknell 96–04; Chapl Heatherwood Hosp E Berks 81–94; Chapl Heatherwood and Wexham Park Hosps NHS Trust 94–07; rtd 07. *Fairhaven, 1 St Clement's Terrace, Mousehole, Penzance TR19 6SJ* T: (01736) 732938

JONES, David Victor. b 37. St Jo Coll Dur BA 59. Cranmer Hall Dur Bossey Ecum Inst Geneva 61. **d** 62 **p** 63. C Farnworth *Liv* 62–65; CF 65–68; Asst Master Hutton Gr Sch Preston 68–97; rtd 02. *10 Houghton Close, Penwortham, Preston PR1 9HT* T: (01772) 745306

JONES, Denise Gloria. b 56. Cov Univ BA 93 Leeds Univ MA 06. WMMTC 95. **d** 98 **p** 99. C Hobs Moat *Birm* 98–02; C Olton and Chapl Birm and Solihull Mental Health Trust 02–06; Chapl Manager Birm Women's NHS Foundn Trust 06–08; TV Bridgnorth, Tasley, Astley Abbotts, etc *Heref* 08–10; PtO *Birm* 10–11; Chapl Co-ord Birm Women's NHS Foundn Trust 11–21; Hon C Yardley Wood *Birm* 14–15; P-in-c Hamstead St Bernard 15–21; V Salter Street from 21. *62 Balmoral Way, Birmingham B14 4NT* M: 07747-385006 E: revddee@aol.com

JONES, Derek Alan. b 81. Reading Univ BA 03. Cranmer Hall Dur 15. **d** 17 **p** 18. C Lt Horton *Leeds* 17–21; P-in-c from 21. *St Oswald's Vicarage, Christopher Street, Bradford BD5 9DH* M: 07880-508174 E: derekalanjones@me.com

JONES, Miss Diana. b 46. Qu Coll Birm 89. **d** 91 **p** 94. Par Dn Harnham *Sarum* 91–94; C 94–95; C Tidworth, Ludgershall and Faberstown 95–00; P-in-c Hazelbury Bryan and the Hillside Par 00–06; rtd 06. *47 Gloucester Road, Trowbridge BA14 0AB* T: (01225) 755826

JONES, Canon Dick Heath Remi. b 32. Jes Coll Cam BA 56. Linc Th Coll 56. **d** 58 **p** 59. C Ipswich St Thos *St E* 58–61; C Putney St Mary *S'wark* 61–65; P-in-c Dawley Parva *Lich* 65–75; P-in-c Lawley 65–75; RD Wrockwardine 70–72; P-in-c Malins Lee 72–75; RD Telford 72–80; P-in-c Stirchley 74–75; TR Cen Telford 75–80; Preb Lich Cathl 76–80; TR Bournemouth St Pet w St Swithun, H Trin etc *Win* 80–96; RD Bournemouth

90–95; Hon Can Win Cathl 91–96; rtd 96; PtO *Sarum* 96–17. *Maltings, Church Street, Fontmell Magna, Shaftesbury SP7 0NY* T: (01747) 812071 E: dick.jones@uwclub.net

JONES, Dominic Jago Francis. St Jo Coll Nottm 09. **d** 11 **p** 12. C Ludgvan, Marazion, St Hilary and Perranuthnoe *Truro* 11–15; C Feock 15–17; C Devoran 15–17; C St Stythians w Perranarworthal and Gwennap 15–17; C Chacewater w St Day and Carharrack 15–17; Chapl Hants Constabulary from 17. *19 Gatcombe, Netley Abbey, Southampton SO31 5PX* M: 07904-500882

JONES, Donald. b 50. BA BSc. St Jo Coll Nottm 79. **d** 82 **p** 83. C Hutton *Chelmsf* 82–86; C E Ham w Upton Park and Forest Gate 86–88; TV 88–96; V Beckton St Mark 89–96; V Nuneaton St Nic *Cov* 96–14; P-in-c Weddington and Caldecote 09–14; RD Nuneaton 01–06; rtd 14; C Atherstone *Cov* 14–15; PtO *S'well* from 19. *28 Holkham Avenue, Beeston, Nottingham NG9 5EQ* T: 0115-837 8852 E: don.jones4718@gmail.com

JONES, Edward. b 36. Dur Univ BA 60. Ely Th Coll 60. **d** 62 **p** 63. C S Shields St Hilda w St Thos *Dur* 62–65; C Cleadon Park 65–68; V Hebburn St Cuth 68–79; R Winlaton 79–00; rtd 00; PtO *Newc* from 01. *10 Melkridge Gardens, Benton, Newcastle upon Tyne NE7 7GQ* T: 0191-266 4388

JONES, Elaine. b 62. SNWTP. **d** 10 **p** 11. C Wavertree St Mary *Liv* 10–14; V Toxteth St Bede w St Clem from 14; C Wavertree St Bridget and St Thos from 19; AD Toxteth and Wavertree from 17. *29 Moel Famau View, Liverpool L17 7ET* M: 07787-550622 E: st.bridgetswavertree@outlook.com

JONES, Miss Elaine Edith. b 58. St Jo Coll Nottm BA 99. **d** 99 **p** 00. C Gainsborough and Morton *Linc* 99–02; C Netherton *Carl* 02–04; TV Maryport, Netherton and Flimby 04–05; Lay Tr Officer 02–05; V Binley *Cov* 05–14; V Peterlee *Dur* from 14. *St Cuthbert's Vicarage, Manor Way, Peterlee SR8 5QW* T: 0191-586 2630 E: reveej@hotmail.co.uk

JONES, Canon Elaine Joan. b 50. Oak Hill Th Coll. **d** 87 **p** 94. Par Dn Tottenham H Trin *Lon* 87–92; Par Dn Clay Hill St Jo and St Luke 92–94; C St Botolph Aldgate w H Trin Minories 94–96; V Hackney Wick St Mary of Eton w St Aug 96–04; AD Hackney 99–04; Can Res Derby Cathl 04–13; rtd 13; Hon Can Derby Cathl from 13; C Derby St Jo from 13. *The Vicarage, 2 Glebe Crescent, Stanley, Ilkeston DE7 6FL* T: 0115-930 2080 M: 07749-867347 E: canonelaine.stjohns@gmail.com

JONES, Mrs Elizabeth. b 52. St Mich Coll Llan 09. **d** 12 **p** 13. NSM Tredegar *Mon* from 12. *Allesley, Ashville, Tredegar NP22 4LN* T: (01495) 726251 E: ejones8@talktalk.net

JONES, Elizabeth Anne. b 66. **d** 14 **p** 16. Chapl Univ Hosps Cov and Warks NHS Trust 14–17; C Bulkington *Cov* 14–18; C Burton Hastings 17–18; Chapl Univ Hosps Cov and Warks NHS Trust from 18. *Morahill, Tamworth Road, Corley, Coventry CV7 8BX*

JONES, Mrs Elizabeth Jane. b 57. Derby Univ BSc 00. St Jo Coll Nottm MTh 02. **d** 02 **p** 03. C Leek and Meerbrook *Lich* 02–05; C Harlescott and Chapl Shropshire Co Primary Care Trust 05–11; R Darlaston St Lawr *Lich* 11–14; TR Darlaston and Moxley 14–18; P-in-c Rocester and Croxden w Hollington 18–19; C Alton w Bradley-le-Moors and Denstone etc 18–19; V Rocester, Denstone and Croxden w Hollington from 19; Chapl JCB Academy from 18. *The Vicarage, Church Lane, Rocester, Uttoxeter ST14 5JZ* T: (01889) 591748 M: 07923-403395 E: revdlizjones@gmail.com

JONES, Mrs Elizabeth Somerset. b 49. St Jo Coll Nottm. **d** 88 **p** 94. NSM Duns *Edin* 88–99; NSM Selkirk 89–90; Dioc Dir of Ords 95–05; NSM Dalkeith from 02; NSM Lasswade from 02. *255 Carnethie Street, Rosewell EH24 9DR* T: 0131-440 2602 E: esomersetjones@btinternet.com

JONES, Lt Col Ellis Glyn. b 42. Victoria Univ Man BDS 67. St Mich Coll Llan. **d** 15 **p** 16. NSM Garthbeibio, Llanerfel and Llangadfan *St As* 15–16; NSM Caereinion from 17. *1 High Street, Llanfair Caereinion, Welshpool SY21 0QS* T: (01938) 811031 E: eglyn@eglynjones.plus.com

JONES, Ernest Edward Stephen. b 39. Lon Univ BD 76. St D Coll Lamp. **d** 66 **p** 67. C N Meols *Liv* 66–69; C Kirkby 69–71; V Farnworth All SS *Man* 71–75; P-in-c Bempton *York* 75–78; R Rufford *Blackb* 78–84; V Cropredy w Gt Bourton and Wardington *Ox* 84–90; R York St Clem w St Mary Bishophill Senior 90–98; P-in-c York All SS N Street 90–98; V Northampton St Benedict *Pet* 98–05; rtd 05; P-in-c Wootton w Glympton and Kiddington *Ox* 05–15; R from 15; AD Woodstock 09–12. *The Rectory, 22 Castle Road, Wootton, Woodstock OX20 1EG* T: (01993) 812543

JONES, Mrs Eva Frances. **d** 16 **p** 17. NSM Newport All SS *Mon* from 16. *16 The Maltings, Llantarnam, Cwmbran NP44 7BB* E: garethandfrancesjones@btinternet.com

JONES, Evan Hopkins. b 38. St Mich Coll Llan 65. **d** 67 **p** 68. C Churston Ferrers w Goodrington *Ex* 67–70; C Tavistock and Gulworthy 70–73; R Ashprington 73–78; V Cornworthy 73–78; R S Hackney St Jo w Ch Ch *Lon* 78–92; AD Hackney

84–89; V Islington St Jas w St Pet 92–08; rtd 08; PtO *Lon* from 08. *5 St James's Close, Bishop Street, London N1 8PH* T: (020) 7226 0104 E: fatherevanjones@btinternet.com

JONES, Frances. *See* JONES, Eva Frances

JONES, Canon Gareth Edward John Paul. b 79. Leeds Univ BA 06 FRSA 15. Coll of Resurr Mirfield 03. **d** 06 **p** 07. C Brighton St Mich *Chich* 06–10; P-in-c Gt Ilford St Mary *Chelmsf* 10–14; V from 14; Dioc Refugee Coord from 18; Chapl Snaresbrook Crown Court from 18; Hon Can Cape Coast Ghana from 21. *St Mary's Vicarage, 26 South Park Road, Ilford IG1 1SS* T: (020) 8478 0546 E: vicar@stmarysilford.org.uk

JONES, Gareth Lewis. b 42. K Coll Lon BD 64 AKC 64. **d** 65 **p** 66. C Risca *Mon* 65–70; PtO *Win* 70–74; *Newc* 74–75; *Sarum* 75; C Pontesbury I and II *Heref* 75–77; P-in-c Presteigne w Discoed 77–79; TV Hemel Hempstead *St Alb* 79–86; R Longden and Annscroft w Pulverbatch *Heref* 86–93; TV Leominster 93–07; rtd 07; PtO *Heref* from 08. *33 Danesfield Drive, Leominster HR6 8HP* T: (01568) 620453

JONES, Prof Gareth Lloyd. b 38. Univ of Wales BA 61 Selw Coll Cam BA 63 MA 67 Yale Univ STM 69 TCD BD 70 Lon Univ PhD 75. Episc Sem Austin Texas Hon DD 90 Westcott Ho Cam 62. **d** 65 **p** 66. C Holywell w Rhoscolyn *Ban* 65–68; USA 68–70; P-in-c Merton *Ox* 70–72; Tutor Ripon Hall Ox 72; Sen Tutor 73–75; Lect Ex Coll Ox 73–77; Tutor and Lib Ripon Coll Cuddesdon 75–77; Lect Th Univ of Wales (Ban) 77–89; Sen Lect 89–95; Reader and Hd of Sch from 95; Prof from 98; Sub-Dean Faculty of Th 80–89; Dean 89–92; Chan Ban Cathl 90–09; Select Preacher Ox Univ 89. *22 Bron-y-Felin, Llandegfan, Menai Bridge LL59 5UY* T: (01248) 712786

JONES, Gary. b 60. **d** 18 **p** 19. NSM Kesgrave *St E* 18–20; NSM Kesgrave w Lt Bealings and Playford from 21. *30 Maycroft Close, Ipswich IP1 6RG* T: (01473) 412329 M: 07714-614095 E: gary.jones590@ntlworld.com

JONES, Glyn. b 71. **d** 12 **p** 13. NSM Ches Ch Ch from 12. *15 Lincoln Drive, Chester CH2 2PQ*

JONES, Glynn. b 56. Ches Univ MA 14 DMin 20. NEOC 91. **d** 94 **p** 95. NSM Glendale Gp *Newc* 97–98; Chapl HM Pris Leeds 97–99; Chapl HM Pris Dur 99–00; Co-ord Chapl HM YOI Wetherby 00–05; Co-ord Chapl HM Pris Wymott 06–07; Co-ord Chapl HM Pris Haverigg 07–16; Chapl from 16; Carl Dioc Chapl to Chapl from 16; Regional Dir (N) Daylight Chr Pris Trust from 16. *10 Blencathra View, Threlkeld Quarry, Keswick CA12 4TY* T: (017687) 79082 E: glynnandlizjones@aol.com *or* glynn@daylightcpt.org

JONES, Godfrey Caine. b 36. Dur Univ BA 59 Lon Univ CertEd 60 Birm Univ MEd 71. St Deiniol's Hawarden 76. **d** 78 **p** 79. Hd Humanities Denbigh High Sch 75–81; NSM Ruthin w Llanrhydd *St As* 78–81; C 83–84; Sen Lect Matlock Coll 81–83; P-in-c Llanfwrog and Clocaenog and Gyffylliog *St As* 84–85; R 85–93; V Ruabon 93–02; RD Llangollen 93–02; rtd 02; Min Pradoe *Lich* 02–08; PtO 08–16; *St As* from 09. *14 Adlington House, Abbey Road, Rhos on Sea, Colwyn Bay LL28 4PU* T: (01492) 471312 E: dodie2822@gmail.com

JONES, Griffith Trevor. b 56. BSc MPS Univ of Wales BD. **d** 87 **p** 88. C Llanfairpwll w Bodwrog and Heneglwys etc *Ban* 87–89; R Llangefni w Tregaean and Llangristiolus etc 89–91; TV Bangor 91–94; Chapl Ysbyty Gwynedd 91–94; LtO *Ban* 94–00; Hon C Bro Tysilio 14–21. *8 Carreg-y-Gad Estate, Ffordd Penmynydd, Llanfairpwllgwyngyll LL61 5QF* T: (01248) 713094 E: gjones2747@aol.com

JONES, Gwynn Rees. b 32. St D Coll Lamp BA 55. **d** 57 **p** 58. C Llangystennin *St As* 57–59; C Llanrhos 59–64; R Cefn 64–68; R Llanfyllin 68–80; V Bistre 80–89; R Flint 89–97; rtd 97; PtO *St As* 09–13. *3 Lon Derw, Abergele LL22 7EA* T: (01745) 825188

JONES, Harold Philip. b 49. Leeds Univ BA 72 St Jo Coll Dur BA 84. Cranmer Hall Dur 82. **d** 85 **p** 86. C Scartho *Linc* 85–88; V Dodworth *Wakef* 88–91; C Penistone and Thurlstone 91–95; C Scunthorpe All SS *Linc* 95–96; TV Brumby 96–02; Chapl Derby Hosps NHS Foundn Trust 02–14; rtd 14. *53 Beech Avenue, Alvaston, Derby DE24 0EA* E: haroldofderby@yahoo.co.uk

JONES, Haydn Llewellyn. b 42. Edin Th Coll 63. **d** 65 **p** 66. C Towcester w Easton Neston *Pet* 65–68; C Northampton St Matt 68–72; CF 72–97; PtO *Roch* 97–98; *Ex* from 98; rtd 99. *11 Lady Park Road, Livermead, Torquay TQ2 6UA* T: (01803) 690483

JONES (née JAMES), Ms Helen Alison. b 59. St Andr Univ BSc 81. EMMTC 93. **d** 96 **p** 97. C Brocklesby Park *Linc* 96–98; PtO 06–08; C Bassingham Gp 08–10; R Dundee St Jo *Bre* 10–14; R Dundee St Marg 10–14; R Dundee St Martin 10–14; NSM Alexandria and Dumbarton *Glas* 14–15. *Shillinghill, 16 School Road, Rhonehouse, Castle Douglas DG7 1UA* M: 07814-789817 E: halisonjones@gmail.com

JONES, Hester. *See* JONES, Susannah Hester Everett

JONES, Hilary Christine. b 55. Ch Ch Coll Cant CertEd 76 Lon Univ BEd 77 Ch Ch Coll Cant MA 06. SEITE. **d** 99 **p** 00. C Kennington *Cant* 99–02; R Cheriton St Martin 02–11; P-in-c Cheriton All So w Newington 06–11; Bp's Adv for Women's Min 04–11; AD Elham 08–11; Asst Chapl Basle *Eur* 11–15; Chapl 15–20; rtd 20; PtO *Ox* from 21. *97 Deeds Grove, High Wycombe HP12 3NY* E: revhilaryjones@gmail.com

JONES, Hugh Vaughan. b 44. **d** 07 **p** 08. C Holyhead *Ban* 07–09; P-in-c Bodedern w Llanfaethlu 09–11; P-in-c Amlwch 11–15; rtd 15; PtO *Ban* from 15. *116 Foryd Road, Kinmel Bay, Rhyl LL18 5LR* M: 07795-578932 E: hughvaughan.santelbod@btinternet.com

JONES, Hugh William Fawcett. b 68. Ripon Coll Cuddesdon. **d** 10 **p** 11. C Boston *Linc* 10–14; V Linc St Nic w St Jo Newport from 14; P-in-c Linc St Mary Magd w St Paul and St Mich from 21; RD Christianity from 17. *The Vicarage, 95 Yarborough Crescent, Lincoln LN1 3NE* E: hugh.wf.jones@talk21.com

JONES, Ian Andrew. b 65. Lanc Univ BA 87. St Mich Coll Llan. **d** 90 **p** 91. C Caerphilly *Llan* 90–96; Chapl RAF from 96. *Chaplaincy Services (RAF), HQ Air Command, RAF High Wycombe HP14 4UE* T: (01494) 496800

JONES, Ian Robert. b 69. Sheff Univ BA 92. Trin Coll Bris 11. **d** 13 **p** 14. C Burscough Bridge *Liv* 13–17; P-in-c Kirkheaton *Leeds* 17–18; R from 18. *The New Rectory, Church Lane, Kirkheaton, Huddersfield HD5 0BH* T: (01484) 532410 M: 07957-502260 E: rector@kirkheatonchurch.org.uk

✠**JONES, The Rt Revd Idris.** b 43. St D Coll Lamp BA 64 NY Th Sem DMin 86. Edin Th Coll 64. **d** 67 **p** 68 **c** 98. C Stafford St Mary *Lich* 67–70; Prec St Paul's Cathl Dundee *Bre* 70–73; P-in-c Gosforth All SS *Newc* 73–80; R Montrose and Inverbervie *Bre* 80–89; Can St Paul's Cathl Dundee 84–92; Chapl Angl Students Dundee Univ 89–92; P-in-c Invergowrie 89–92; TR S Ayrshire TM 92–98; Bp Glas 98–09; Primus 06–09; rtd 09; Hon Fell Univ of Wales (Trin St Dav) from 07; LtO *Glas* from 10. *10 Swan Mews, Eglinton, Kilwinning KA13 7QE* T: (01294) 556873 M: 07702-589481 E: idrisjones43@hotmail.co.uk

JONES, Jacqueline Dorian. b 58. K Coll Lon BD 80 AKC 80 MTh 81. Westcott Ho Cam 84. **dss** 86 **d** 87 **p** 94. Epsom St Martin *Guildf* 86–91; C 87–91; Chapl Chelmsf Cathl 91–97; V Bridgemary *Portsm* 97–03; Can Res S'well Minster 03–18; P-in-c Danbury *Chelmsf* from 18; P-in-c Lt Baddow from 18. *The Rectory, 55 Main Road, Danbury, Chelmsford CM3 4NG*

JONES, Mrs Jacqueline Mary Shore. b 65. York St Jo Univ BA 14 Sheff Univ MA 17. Yorks Min Course 15. **d** 17 **p** 18. C Warmsworth *Sheff* 17–21; P-in-c Stainforth from 21; P-in-c Fishlake w Sykehouse and Kirk Bramwith etc from 21. *St Mary's Vicarage, Field Road, Stainforth, Doncaster DN7 5AQ* M: 07894-262706 E: threadsjj@gmail.com

JONES, Jacqueline Primrose. b 47. **d** 09 **p** 10. NSM Chipping Norton *Ox* 09–12; Chapl Ox Univ Hosps NHS Trust 12–13; Chapl Kath Ho Hospice from 13; NSM Chipping Norton *Ox* 13–19; PtO from 19. *Old Appleyard, 18 Kingham Road, Churchill, Chipping Norton OX7 6NE* T: (01608) 658616 E: jackiejones.churchill@gmail.com

JONES, James Richard. b 65. SS Hild & Bede Coll Dur BA 87 Open Univ MBA 95. Wycliffe Hall Ox 02. **d** 04 **p** 05. C Ashtead *Guildf* 04–08; P-in-c Burscough Bridge *Liv* 08–15; V 15; R Ashtead *Guildf* from 15. *Ashdene, Dene Road, Ashtead KT21 1EE* T: (01372) 805182 E: jrj37@aol.com *or* richard.jones@ashteadparish.org

✠**JONES, The Rt Revd James Stuart.** b 48. KBE 17. Ex Univ BA 70 PGCE 71 Hull Univ Hon DD 99 Lincs & Humberside Univ Hon DLitt 01. Wycliffe Hall Ox 81. **d** 82 **p** 83 **c** 94. C Clifton Ch Ch w Em *Bris* 82–90; V S Croydon Em *S'wark* 90–94; Suff Bp Hull *York* 94–98; Bp Liv 98–13; Bp HM Pris 07–13; rtd 13; Asst Bp York from 14. *The Diocese of York, Amy Johnson House, Amy Johnson Way, York YO30 4XT* T: (01904) 699500

JONES, Jennifer Margaret. b 49. Lon Univ CertEd. Cranmer Hall Dur 87. **d** 89 **p** 94. C Musselburgh *Edin* 89–93; Dn-in-c 93–94; P-in-c 94–95; R 95–02; C Prestonpans 89–93; Dn-in-c 93–94; P-in-c 94–95; R 95–02; NSM Rothiemurchus *Mor* from 07. *Meadowbank, Main Street, Newtonmore PH20 1DD* T: (01540) 673532 E: jennifer.jones32@btinternet.com

JONES, Mrs Joanne. b 64. Warwick Univ BA 88. St Mellitus Coll BA 10. **d** 10 **p** 11. C Maldon All SS w St Pet *Chelmsf* 10–14; P-in-c Writtle w Highwood 14–17; P-in-c Roxwell 15–17; PtO 18–20; Chapl HM Pris Chelmsf from 20. *HM Prison Chelmsford, 200 Springfield Road, Chelmsford CM2 6LQ* T: (01245) 552077 E: joanne.jones3@justice.gov.uk

JONES, John Bernard. b 49. Qu Coll Birm 86. **d** 88 **p** 89. C Mold *St As* 88–91; P-in-c Treuddyn and Nercwys and Eryrys 91–92; V Treuddyn w Nercwys 92–14; RD Mold 95–00;

rtd 14; PtO *St As* from 15. *18 Willow Walk, Leeswood, Mold CH7 4UJ* T: (01352) 770919   M: 07952-071657 E: revjbj@hotmail.com

JONES, John David Emrys. b 36. Trin Coll Carmarthen. **d** 96 **p** 97. NSM Llanfihangel Ystrad and Cilcennin w Trefilan etc *St D* 96–97; P-in-c Llangeitho and Blaenpennal w Betws Leucu etc 97–06; PtO from 06. *Dolfor, Ciliau Aeron, Lampeter SA48 8DE* T: (01570) 470569

JONES, Canon Joyce Rosemary. b 54. Newnham Coll Cam BA 76 MA 82 Coll of Ripon & York St Jo MA 97 Solicitor 79. NOC 94. **d** 97 **p** 98. C Pontefract All SS *Wakef* 97–00; NSM Cumberworth, Denby and Denby Dale 00–01; Dioc Voc Adv 00–01; Asst Chapl Kirkwood Hospice Huddersfield 00–01; P-in-c Shelley and Shepley *Wakef* 01–14; *Leeds* 14–16; R Cumberworth, Denby, Denby Dale etc 16–21; AD Kirkburton 11–18; NSM High Hoyland, Scissett and Clayton W from 21; NSM Skelmanthorpe from 21; Hon Can Wakef Cathl from 10. *15 Busker Lane, Scissett, Huddersfield HD8 9JU* T/F: (01484) 862350 E: joyce.jones@leeds.anglican.org

JONES, Julie Ann. b 59. STETS. **d** 10 **p** 11. NSM W Meon and Warnford *Portsm* 10–11; NSM Portchester 11–14; NSM Purbrook 14–19; Chapl Portsm Hosps Univ NHS Trust 19–21; Chapl S Health NHS Foundn Trust from 21. *Orchard View, Hill Pound, Swanmore, Southampton SO32 2UN* T: (01489) 891402 M: 07800-553920 E: jones59ja@btinternet.com

JONES, Mrs Julie Denise. b 63. CBDTI 03. **d** 06 **p** 07. C Darwen St Pet w Hoddlesden *Blackb* 06–09; P-in-c Wesham and Treales 09–11; V 11–16; rtd 16. *191 Reads Avenue, Blackpool FY1 4HZ* M: 07814-500855 E: juliejones449@btinternet.com

JONES, Karen Elizabeth. b 64. Univ of Ulster BA 87. Wycliffe Hall Ox 04. **d** 06 **p** 07. C Northolt Park St Barn *Lon* 06–07; NSM Longwell Green *Bris* 08–10; Chapl UWE 10–11; C Stoke Gifford 10–16; NSM Woodchester and Brimscombe *Glouc* 16–18; C Chacewater w St Day and Carharrack *Truro* 18–19; C Devoran 18–19; C Feock 18–19; C St Stythians w Perranarworthal and Gwennap 18–19. *Address temp unknown* M: 07799-028802 E: kehunterjones@outlook.com

JONES, Karen Sheila Frances. *See* ROOMS, Karen Sheila Frances

JONES, Karl Rupert Barker. b 63. Salford Univ BSc 87 Lon Univ BD 93 York St Jo Coll MA 01. NOC 05. **d** 07 **p** 08. NSM Utley *Bradf* 07–08; NSM Thwaites Brow 08–10; PtO *Dur* 11–18; NSM Waverton w Aldford and Bruera *Ches* from 18. *The Rectory, Green Lake Lane, Aldford, Chester CH3 6HW*

JONES, Kathryn Mary. *See* BUCK, Kathryn Mary

JONES (née SANDELLS-REES), The Very Revd Kathy Louise. b 68. Univ of Wales (Ban) BTh 96 Leeds Univ MA 13 Northumbria Univ PGCE 11. Qu Coll Birm 90. **d** 92 **p** 97. C Holyhead w Rhoscolyn w Llanfair-yn-Neubwll *Ban* 92–94; C Bangor 94–95; Chapl Gwynedd Hosp Ban 94–99; P-in-c Bangor *Ban* 95–99; V Betws-y-Coed and Capel Curig w Penmachno etc 99–06; Chapl Newcastle upon Tyne Hosps NHS Foundn Trust 06–12; Chapl Team Ldr Northumbria Healthcare NHS Foundn Trust 12–16; Dean Ban from 16; TR Bro Deiniol from 16. *Erw Fach, Hwfa Road, Bangor LL57 2BN* T: (01248) 352515 E: kathyjones@esgobaethbangor.net

JONES, Mrs Kay Sandra. b 61. Linc Univ BA 01. **d** 12 **p** 13. OLM New Clee *Linc* 12–17; P-in-c from 17. *The Rectory, 41 Dunbar Avenue, New Waltham, Grimsby DN36 4PY* T: (01472) 884434 M: 07811-747569 E: revsok@virginmedia.com

JONES, The Very Revd Keith Brynmor. b 44. Selw Coll Cam BA 65 MA 69. Cuddesdon Coll 67. **d** 69 **p** 70. C Limpsfield and Titsey *S'wark* 69–72; Dean's V St Alb Abbey 72–76; P-in-c Boreham Wood St Mich 76–79; TV Borehamwood 79–82; V Ipswich St Mary-le-Tower *St E* 82–96; RD Ipswich 92–96; Hon Can St E Cathl 93–96; Dean Ex 96–04; Dean York 04–12; rtd 12; PtO *St E* from 13. *7 Broughton Road, Ipswich IP1 3QR* T: (01473) 413436 E: keithbjones@gmail.com *or* keithbjones2012@gmail.com

JONES, Keith Ellison. b 47. Wycliffe Hall Ox 72. **d** 75 **p** 76. C Everton St Chrys *Liv* 75–79; C Buckhurst Hill *Chelmsf* 79–81; TV 81–88; TR Leek and Meerbrook *Lich* 88–99; V Formby H Trin *Liv* 99–11; AD Sefton 05–08; Hon Can Liv Cathl 05–08; rtd 11; PtO *Lich* 13–15 and 17–21. *77 Woodhouse Lane, Biddulph, Stoke-on-Trent ST8 7EN*

JONES, Lesley Anne. b 46. Luton Coll of HE CertEd 77. SAOMC 01. **d** 04 **p** 06. NSM Gravenhurst, Shillington and Stondon *St Alb* 04–06; NSM Leagrave 06–16; NSM Officer Bedford Adnry 14–16; rtd 16; PtO *St Alb* from 16. *91 Manton Drive, Luton LU2 7DL* T: (01582) 616888 E: lesleyjones31647@aol.com

JONES, Mrs Lesley Marie. b 66. **d** 12 **p** 13. NSM N Wearside *Dur* 12–13; C Milton Regis w Murston, Bapchild and Tonge *Cant* 13–17; TV Sittingbourne w Bobbing 17–20; R Jarrow and Simonside *Dur* from 20. *St Peter's House, York Avenue, Jarrow NE32 5LP* M: 07881-555580 E: revlesleyjones@gmail.com

JONES, Lloyd. *See* JONES, Gareth Lloyd

JONES, Miss Mair. b 41. Cartrefle Coll of Educn TCert 61. St Mich Coll Llan 91. **d** 93 **p** 97. C Llangollen w Trevor and Llantysilio *St As* 93–97; V Llandrillo and Llandderfel 97–00; R Llanelian w Betws-yn-Rhos w Trofarth 00–03; R Llanelian 03–08; P-in-c Brynymaen 04–08; rtd 08; PtO *St As* from 09. *5 Ffordd Bugail, Colwyn Bay LL29 8TN* T: (01492) 517866 E: jonesmair41@gmail.com

JONES, Malcolm. *See* JONES, Philip Malcolm

JONES, Canon Malcolm Francis. b 44. Open Univ BA 88 Hull Univ MA 96 Univ of Wales (Cardiff) LLM 05 FInstLM 10. Chich Th Coll 67. **d** 70 **p** 71. C Prestbury *Ches* 70–73; Chapl RAF 73–81; R Heaton Reddish *Man* 81–84; CF (ACF) 82–84 and 98–14; CF (TA) 83–84; CF 84–93; CF (R of O) 93–99; TV Cleethorpes *Linc* 93–97; V Ryde H Trin *Portsm* 97–10; V Swanmore St Mich 97–10; rtd 10; P-in-c Win H Trin 10–11; R 11–16; P-in-c 16–17; Hon Can Win Cathl 14–17; PtO *Eur* from 15; *Win* from 17. *Rue des Aubépines, 56580 Bréhan, France* T: (0033) 2 56 34 74 30 M: 07710-543155 E: frmalcolmjones@hotmail.com

JONES, Malcolm Stuart. b 41. Sheff Univ BA 62. Linc Th Coll 64. **d** 66 **p** 67. C Monkseaton St Mary *Newc* 66–69; C Ponteland 69–72; Chapl Lake Maracaibo Venezuela 73–75; C Hexham *Newc* 75–77; P-in-c Killingworth 77–92; V Delaval 92–01; TV Ch the King 01–07; rtd 07; PtO *Newc* from 07. *13 Valeside, Newcastle upon Tyne NE15 9LA* T: 0191-267 7829 E: malcolmjonespcdc@hotmail.com

JONES, Mrs Margaret Angela. b 53. Wolv Univ CertEd 91 Univ of Wales (Lamp) MA 04. Qu Coll Birm BA 99. **d** 99 **p** 00. C Pershore w Pinvin, Wick and Birlingham *Worc* 99–03; TV Solihull *Birm* 03–11; P-in-c Pontesbury I and II *Heref* 11–18; RD Pontesbury 13–17; rtd 18; PtO *Blackb* from 19. *9 Fairview Close, Walmer Bridge, Preston PR4 5RF* E: magz.stgeorges@talktalk.net

JONES, Mrs Margaret Anne. b 47. Lon Univ TCert 68 Ches Coll of HE BTh 04. NOC 01. **d** 04 **p** 05. NSM Altrincham St Geo *Ches* 04–07; C 07–12; C Altrincham St Jo 07–12; P-in-c Whaley Bridge 12–19; Chapl Trin C of E High Sch Man 05–07; PtO *Man* from 06. *12 Moorland Avenue, Sale M33 3FH* M: 07748-645596 E: margaret_jones@talk21.com

JONES, Margaret Mary. b 47. Oak Hill Th Coll 92. **d** 95 **p** 96. C Sydenham H Trin *S'wark* 95–98; V Anerley St Paul Roch 98–09; TV Anerley 09–11; rtd 11; PtO *S'wark* from 12. *10 Lower Road, Redhill RH1 6NN* T: (01737) 247998 E: maggi.jones99@gmail.com

JONES, Mark. *See* JONES, Christopher Mark

JONES, Canon Mark Andrew. b 60. Southn Univ BSc 82 Sussex Univ PGCE 83. Oak Hill Th Coll 88. **d** 91 **p** 92. C Wolverhampton St Luke *Lich* 91–96; I Inishmacsaint *Clogh* 96–01; V Padiham w Hapton and Padiham Green *Blackb* from 01; AD Burnley 10–19; Hon Can Blackb Cathl from 17. *The Vicarage, 1 Arbory Drive, Padiham, Burnley BB12 8JS* T: (01282) 772442 E: jones.padiham@btinternet.com

JONES, Mark Vincent. *See* HALDON-JONES, Mark Vincent

JONES, Martin. b 58. Leeds Univ BA 07. NOC 04. **d** 07 **p** 08. NSM Winwick *Liv* 07–13; Chapl St Helens and Knowsley Hosps NHS Trust 09–13; NSM Aisholt, Enmore, Goathurst, Nether Stowey etc *B & W* 13–17; Chapl Somerset Partnership NHS Foundn Trust 13–17; PtO *Truro* 17–18 and from 19; P-in-c Duloe and Herodsfoot 18–19. *April Cottage, Tredinnick, Liskeard PL14 4PJ* T: (01503) 265862 M: 07943-706693 E: revmartinjones@icloud.com

JONES, Martin David. b 50. Liv Univ MB, ChB 73. **d** 13 **p** 14. OLM Codnor *Derby* 13–19; OLM Horsley and Denby 13–19; OLM Horsley Woodhouse 13–19; OLM Loscoe 13–19; OLM Denby Gp 19–20; rtd 20; PtO *Derby* from 20. *Meadow Rise, Smalley Mill Road, Horsley, Derby DE21 5BL* T: (01332) 882929 M: 07788-641946 E: martinjones2812@gmail.com

JONES, Martin Patrick. b 62. K Coll Lon BDS 85. Dioc OLM tr scheme 02. **d** 05 **p** 06. NSM Kingsnorth and Shadoxhurst *Cant* 05–09; PtO 09–11; NSM Aldington w Bonnington and Bilsington etc 11–13; C Saxon Shoreline 13–18; P-in-c Haywards Heath Ascension *Chich* 18–20; V from 20. *Ascension Vicarage, 1 Redwood Drive, Haywards Heath RH16 4ER* T: (01444) 410729 E: martin.jones62@icloud.com

JONES, Mary Catherine Theresa Bridget. b 41. Westhill Coll Birm CertEd 77 Birm Univ BA 80 MA 09 Leic Univ PhD 17. Qu Coll Birm 04. **d** 05 **p** 06. NSM Bromsgrove St Jo *Worc* 05–08; PtO from 08; *Birm* from 11. *262 Dickens Heath Road, Shirley, Solihull B90 1QJ* T: (01564) 822687 E: theresaj1@btinternet.com

JONES, Canon Mary Nerissa Anna. b 41. MBE 02. Qu Mary Coll Lon BA 86 FRSA 91. Ripon Coll Cuddesdon 86. **d** 88 **p** 94. Par Dn St Botolph Aldgate w H Trin Minories *Lon* 88–93;

P-in-c Wood End *Cov* 93–95; V 95–01; Hon Can Cov Cathl 01; rtd 01; P-in-c Askerswell, Loders and Powerstock *Sarum* 01–10; P-in-c Symondsbury 07–10; PtO from 11. *Church Farm Cottage, West Milton, Bridport DT6 3SL* T: (01308) 485304 E: revnerissa@gmail.com

JONES, Canon Mary Valerie. b 37. Univ of Wales (Ban) BD 84. St Deiniol's Hawarden 84. d 85 p 97. C Holyhead w Rhoscolyn w Llanfair-yn-Neubwll *Ban* 85–87; C Ynyscynhaearn w Penmorfa and Porthmadog 87–90; Dn-in-c Llansantffraid Glyn Ceirog and Llanarmon etc *St As* 90–97; V 97–98; R Overton and Erbistock and Penley 98–04; RD Bangor Isycoed 98–04; Can Cursal St As Cathl 01–04; rtd 04; PtO *St As* 09–18. *Cysgod y Coed, 12 Church View, Ruabon, Wrexham LL14 6TD* T: (01978) 822206

JONES, Maurice Maxwell Hughes. b 32. Clifton Th Coll 56. d 60 p 61. C Islington St Andr w St Thos and St Matthias *Lon* 60–63; Argentina 63–71; C Whitchurch *Llan* 72–73; Area Sec (NW England) SAMS 73–77; V Haydock St Mark *Liv* 78–87; V Paddington Em Harrow Road *Lon* 87–97; rtd 98. *Glyn Orig, Cemmaes, Machynlleth SY20 9PR* T/F: (01650) 511632

JONES, Canon Melville Kenneth. b 40. Open Univ BA 82. St D Coll Lamp. d 66 p 67. C Aberdare *Llan* 66–71; C Caerau w Ely 71–72; Chapl Pontypridd Hosps 72–89; V Graig *Llan* 72–89; P-in-c Cilfynydd 86–89; V Llantwit Fardre 89–07; Chapl E Glam NHS Trust 89–99; RD Pontypridd *Llan* 99–05; Hon Can Llan Cathl 04–07; Chapl Pontypridd and Rhondda NHS Trust 99–01; rtd 07; PtO *Llan* from 10. *Nanteos, 7 Meadow Hill, Church Village, Pontypridd CF38 1RX* T: (01443) 217213 E: melville.k.jones@gmail.com

JONES, Michael. b 49. Leeds Univ BA 71 Man Univ MA 73 Padgate Coll of Educn PGCE 73. Qu Coll Birm 83. d 85 p 86. C Leigh St Mary *Man* 85–88; C-in-c Holts CD 88–93; V Hamer 93–05; rtd 09; PtO *Man* 06–12; *St As* 09–16. *Ty Coch Cottage, Llangynhafal, Ruthin LL15 1RT* T: (01824) 703037 E: mike@ashborn.force9.co.uk

JONES, Michael. *See* JONES, David Michael

JONES, Michael Adrian Roche. b 62. Reading Univ BSc 83 PGCE 84. Trin Coll Bris 07. d 09 p 10. C Bath Weston All SS w N Stoke and Langridge *B & W* 09–13; Bp's Chapl *Leic* 13–17; V Knighton from 17. *Knighton Vicarage, 5 Church Lane, Leicester LE2 3WG* T: 0116-270 4268 E: adrian.jones@zoho.com

JONES, Michael Barry. b 48. MCIEH 88 MIOSH 88. ERMC 04. d 07 p 08. NSM Whittlesey, Pondersbridge and Coates *Ely* 07–12; PtO from 12; Chapl Peterborough and Stamford Hosps NHS Foundn Trust 13–20; rtd 20; PtO *Ely* from 20. *Chaplaincy Department, Peterborough City Hospital, Bretton Gate, Peterborough PE3 9GZ* T: (01733) 203588 E: michael.jones123@sky.com

JONES, Michael Christopher. b 67. Southn Univ BSc 88. St Jo Coll Nottm MTh 03 MA 04. d 04 p 05. C Aldridge *Lich* 04–07; V Lilleshall and Muxton 07–13; V Luton St Mary *St Alb* 13–21; P-in-c Luton St Matt High Town 17–21; V Luton St Mary and St Matt from 21; P-in-c Luton St Paul 18–19. *32 Whitehill Avenue, Luton LU1 3SP* M: 07928-821995 E: vicar@stmarysluton.org

JONES, Michael Denis Dyson. b 39. CCC Cam BA 62 MA 66 Lon Univ MSc 73. Wycliffe Hall Ox. d 76 p 77. C Plymouth St Andr w St Paul and St Geo *Ex* 76–81; V Devonport St Budeaux 81–00; RD Plymouth Devonport 93–95; TV Barnstaple 00–07; RD 03–07; rtd 07. *The Spinney, 40 West Drive, Harrow HA3 6TS* T: (020) 8954 1530

JONES, Michael Kevin. b 57. Llan Ord Course 94. d 98 p 99. NSM Caerau w Ely *Llan* 98–00; NSM Cen Cardiff 01; P-in-c Tremorfa St Phil CD 02–05; Area Fundraising Manager Children's Soc Llan and Mon 98–00; Ch Strategy Manager Wales 01–02; LtO *Llan* 05–09; V Mountain Ash and Miskin from 09; AD Cynon Valley from 13. *5 Lon-y-Felin, Cefn Pennar, Mountain Ash CF45 4ES* T: (01443) 473700 E: jonesm78@sky.com

JONES, Canon Neil Crawford. b 42. Univ of Wales BA 63 K Coll Lon BD 66 AKC 66. d 67 p 68. C Holywell *St As* 67–69; C Rhyl w St Ann 69–73; C Christchurch *Win* 73–77; V Stanmore 77–84; RD Win 82–84; V Romsey 84–07; RD 89–94; Hon Can Win Cathl 93–07; rtd 07; PtO *Nor* from 12. *17 Wroxham Avenue, Swaffham PE37 7SD* T: (01760) 788312 E: neilcj@btinternet.com

JONES, Nerissa. *See* JONES, Mary Nerissa Anna

JONES, Nicholas Godwin. b 58. St Jo Coll Cam BA 81 MA 84 Hughes Hall Cam PGCE 90. Ridley Hall Cam 91. d 93 p 94. C Cambridge H Trin *Ely* 93–97; Chapl St Bede's Sch Cam 97–00; C Fulbourn 97–00; C Gt Wilbraham 97–00; C Lt Wilbraham 97–00; V Harston w Hauxton and Newton 00–03; V Gt Horton *Bradf* 03–10; Chapl HM Pris Man 10–11; Chapl HM Pris Hindley 10–15; Hon C Halifax *Leeds* 13–15; Hon C Siddal 13–15; P-in-c Acton St Mary *Lon* 15–16; R from 16.

The Rectory, 14 Cumberland Park, London W3 6SX T: (020) 8992 8876 *or* 8993 0422 E: nickjones114@gmail.com

JONES, Nicholas Peter. b 55. St Mich Coll Llan. d 82 p 83. C St Andrews Major w Michaelston-le-Pit *Llan* 82–84; C Aberdare 84–88; Youth Chapl 85–89; V Abercynon 88–96; R Llanilid w Pencoed 96–10; AD Bridgend 10; Chapl Miss to Seafarers 12–17; P-in-c Burry Port and Pwll *St D* 17–19; P-in-c Bro Gwendraeth from 19. *The Vicarage, Cae Ffwrnes, Burry Port SA16 0FW* T: (01554) 832936 E: revnickjones@gmail.com

JONES, Nigel David. b 69. Qu Coll Cam MA 95. Westcott Ho Cam 97. d 00 p 01. C Abbots Langley *St Alb* 00–03; TV Dunstable 03–08; V Caversham St Andr *Ox* from 08. *St Andrew's Vicarage, Harrogate Road, Reading RG4 7PW* T: 0118-947 2788

JONES, Nigel Ivor. b 54. Sheff Univ MMin 04. WMMTC 91. d 94 p 95. C Shirley *Birm* 94–99; TV Salter Street and Shirley 99–01; Bp's Voc Adv 95–01; Ind Chapl 96–01; V Olton 01–08; Chapl HM Pris Rye Hill 10–17; PtO *Birm* from 13. *62 Balmoral Way, Birmingham B14 4NT* E: revnigel@aol.com

JONES, Norman. b 50. Oak Hill Th Coll BA 83. d 83 p 84. C Ulverston St Mary w H Trin *Carl* 83–87; V Ch Ch Hong Kong 88–92; TR Eccles *Man* 92–01; AD 95–00; R Haslemere and Grayswood *Guildf* 01–10; RD Godalming 02–07; Chapl Wispers Sch Haslemere 01–10; rtd 11; PtO *Ches* from 11; Chapl E Cheshire Hospice 12–13; V Bangkok Ch Ch Thailand 19–20. *51 Freshwater Drive, Weston, Crewe CW2 5GR* T: (01270) 829141 M: 07484-240446 E: normanjones1950@gmail.com

JONES, Norman Burnet. b 52. St Andr Univ BSc 74 Man Univ PhD 78 CChem 81 CBiol 78. SEITE 08. d 11 p 12. NSM Southgate *Chich* 11–15; PtO *St Alb* from 15. *6 Aldridge Way, Buntingford SG9 9FX* M: 07766-367983 E: normanbjones1@virginmedia.com *or* normanbjones1@gmail.com

JONES, Mrs Patricia Ann. b 43. d 97 p 98. OLM Bincombe w Broadwey, Upwey and Buckland Ripers *Sarum* 97–05; NSM 06–10; rtd 11; PtO *Sarum* 11–19. *23 Camedown Close, Weymouth DT3 5RB* T: (01305) 813056

JONES, Mrs Patricia Anne. b 55. CSS 81. Oak Hill Th Coll 92. d 95 p 00. NSM Mill Hill Jo Keble Ch *Lon* 95–01; NSM Queensbury All SS 01–08; PtO 08–12; TV Thatcham *Ox* 12–19; V London Colney *St Alb* from 19. *St Peter's Vicarage, Riverside, London Colney, St Albans AL2 1QA* E: revpatsy55@gmail.com

JONES, Canon Patrick Geoffrey Dickson. b 28. Ch Ch Ox BA 51 MA 55 Aber Univ MLitt 98. St Deiniol's Hawarden 79. d 82 p 83. NSM Sandbach *Ches* 82–84; R Aboyne *Ab* 84–96; R Ballater 84–96; P-in-c Braemar 84–96; rtd 96; P-in-c Cen Buchan *Ab* 96–98; LtO 06–16; P-in-c Cuminestown 09–15; PtO from 16; Hon Can St Andr Cathl from 01. *2 Kingston Cross, Kingston, Sturminster Newton DT10 2AR* T: (01258) 817967 E: patrickj786@btinternet.com

JONES, Patrick George. b 42. Cant Ch Ch Univ Coll MA 99. Lich Th Coll 69. d 72 p 73. C Chesterton St Geo *Ely* 72–75; P-in-c Waterbeach 75–78; P-in-c Landbeach 76–78; R Charlton-in-Dover *Cant* 78–90; Chapl Cautley Ho Chr Cen 90–06; rtd 06. *36 Windmill Grange, Windmill Lane, Histon, Cambridge CB24 9JF* T: (01223) 232505 E: patrickjones303@btinternet.com

JONES, Paul Evan. b 62. York Univ BA 84 Sarum Coll MA 13 CPFA 89. SEITE 02. d 05 p 06. C Kingstanding St Luke *Birm* 05–09; P-in-c Babbacombe *Ex* 09–17; V from 17; RD Torbay 13–16. *Babbacombe Vicarage, 4 Cary Park, Torquay TQ1 3NH* T: (01803) 323002 E: liberty.hall@me.com

JONES, Pauline Edna. b 55. Liv Univ BA 77. d 10 p 11. OLM Langley *Man* 10–17; Chapl Pennine Acute Hosps NHS Trust 13–17; NSM Bro Eleth *Ban* from 17. *The Rectory, 3 Swn-y-Don, Benllech, Tyn-y-Gongl LL74 8PR* E: broeleth@pjones.wales

JONES, Canon Peter Anthony Watson. b 53. AKC 75. Sarum & Wells Th Coll 76. d 77 p 78. C Hessle *York* 77–81; C Stainton-in-Cleveland 81–82; P-in-c Weston Mill *Ex* 82–84; Chapl Plymouth Poly 82–90; V Gt Ayton w Easby and Newton-in-Cleveland *York* 90–92; C Devonport St Aubyn *Ex* 92–98; P-in-c Yealmpton and Brixton 98–01; Team Chapl Portsm Hosps NHS Trust 01–05; Chapl Portsm Univ 05–09; Can Res Portsm Cathl 05–09; R Havant 09–14; Dioc Interfaith Adv 06–11; rtd 14; Hon C York All SS Pavement w St Crux and St Mich 14–16; Hon C York St Olave w St Giles 14–16; Hon C York St Helen w St Martin 14–16; Hon C York St Denys 14–16; P-in-c Farnsfield *S'well* 16–18; P-in-c Kirklington w Hockerton 16–18; P-in-c Winkburn 16–18; P-in-c Maplebeck 16–18. *28 Blakeney Road, Radcliffe-on-Trent, Nottingham NG12 2GX*

JONES, Peter Brian. b 81. Ulster Univ BA 02 PGCE 03. MTh 14. d 13 p 14. Maghera w Killelagh *D & R* 13–14; C Drumglass w Moygashel *Arm* 14–17; I Mossley *Conn*

from 17; Dioc Warden of Readers from 19. *1 Woodford Manor, Newtownabbey BT36 6FF* T: (028) 9083 2726 E: peterjones917@hotmail.com

JONES, Peter Charles. b 60. Univ of Wales BA 81 MA 82 PGCE 97. St Mich Coll Llan 80. **d** 83 **p** 84. C Pontnewynydd *Mon* 83–85; C Bassaleg 85–87; TV Cwmbran 87–94; V Blaenavon w Capel Newydd 94–01; Chapl CME 00–01; Chapl and Fell Trin Coll Carmarthen 01–05; V Llangennech and Hendy *St D* 05–11; AD Cydweli 08–11; V Keele *Lich* from 11; V Silverdale from 11. *The Vicarage, 21 Pepper Street, Silverdale, Newcastle ST5 6QJ* T: (01782) 624455 E: tadjones@btinternet.com

JONES, Peter David. b 48. S'wark Ord Course 89. **d** 92 **p** 93. NSM Coulsdon St Andr *S'wark* 92–04; PtO from 04. *79 Beverley Road, Whyteleafe CR3 0DU* T: (020) 8668 6398 E: revpeter79@gmail.com

JONES, Peter Owen. b 64. Hull Univ BSc 86. Oak Hill Th Coll BA 08. **d** 08 **p** 09. C Hubberston *St D* 08–11; P-in-c Llanfihangel Genau'r Glyn and Llangorwen 11–17; AD Llanbadarn Fawr 14–17; P-in-c Monkton 17–20; P-in-c S W Pembrokeshire from 20; AD from 20. *The Vicarage, Church Terrace, Monkton, Pembroke SA71 4LW* E: rev.peterjones@outlook.com

JONES, Peter Robin. b 42. Open Univ BA 75 Bp Otter Coll Chich CertEd 68. EMMTC 79. **d** 82 **p** 83. NSM Doveridge *Derby* 82–97; NSM Doveridge, Scropton, Sudbury etc 98–10; NSM S Dales from 11; Bp's Inspector of Th Colls and Courses from 98; PtO *Lich* 93–10. *4 Cross Road, Uttoxeter ST14 7BN* T: (01889) 565123 E: rev.jon@talktalk.net

JONES, Canon Peter Russell. b 48. St Jo Coll Cam BA 71 MA 75 Univ of Wales MTh 86. Wycliffe Hall Ox. **d** 75 **p** 76. C Northampton All SS w St Kath *Pet* 75–79; C Ban Cathl 79–81; Min Can Ban Cathl 79–81; R Pentraeth and Llanddyfnan 81–85; V Conwy w Gyffin 85–14; Lect Univ of Wales (Ban) 89–95; AD Arllechwedd *Ban* 96–09; Can and Treas Ban Cathl 99–09; Chan Ban Cathl 09–14; rtd 14; PtO *St As* from 14; *Ban* from 14. *Encilfa, 14 Victoria Park, Colwyn Bay LL29 7AX* T: (01492) 531711

JONES, The Ven Philip Hugh. b 51. Solicitor. Chich Th Coll 92. **d** 94 **p** 95. C Horsham *Chich* 94–97; V Southwater 97–05; RD Horsham 02–04; Adn Hastings 05–16; rtd 16; P-in-c Slindon, Eartham and Madehurst *Chich* 16–19; R 19–20. *Holly Cottage, Easebourne Lane, Easebourne, Midhurst GU29 9AY* E: venp2005@outlook.com

JONES, Philip Malcolm. b 43. Qu Coll Birm. **d** 04 **p** 05. NSM Birm St Paul 04–08; P-in-c Heathfield St Rich *Chich* 08–13; V 13–15; rtd 15; PtO *Cant* 16–19. *2 The Oast, Gate Court Farm, Station Road, Northiam, Rye TN31 6QT* T: (01797) 252563 E: malcolm@peri.co.uk

JONES, Philip Thomas Henry. b 34. Qu Coll Birm 58. **d** 60 **p** 61. C Castle Bromwich SS Mary and Marg *Birm* 60–67; C Reading St Mary V *Ox* 67–72; C-in-c Reading All SS CD 72–75; V Reading All SS 75–95; PtO *Portsm* from 97; Hon Chapl Portsm Cathl from 97. *13 Oyster Street, Portsmouth PO1 2HZ* T: (023) 9275 6676 E: johnmortiboys@gmail.com

JONES, Canon Phillip Bryan. b 34. St Mich Coll Llan. **d** 61 **p** 62. C Hope *St As* 61–64; C Llanrhos 64–67; V Kerry 67–74; R Newtown w Llanllwchaiarn w Aberhafesp 74–97; RD Cedewain 76–97; Sec Ch in Wales Prov Evang Cttee 80–83; Hon Can St As Cathl 86–93; Can St As Cathl 93–97; rtd 97. *7 Dalton Drive, Shrewsbury SY3 8DA* T: (01743) 351426

JONES, Phillip Edmund. b 56. Man Poly BA 78 Fitzw Coll Cam BA 84 MA 88 GradCIPD 79. Westcott Ho Cam 82. **d** 85 **p** 86. C Stafford St Jo and Tixall w Ingestre *Lich* 85–89; TV Redditch, The Ridge *Worc* 89–95; TV Worc SE 95–08; Ind Chapl 89–17; Team Ldr Worcs Ind Miss 01–08; Team Ldr and Chapl Faith at Work in Worcs 08–11; Miss Development Officer 11–17; C Worc St Barn w Ch Ch 08–17; TR Hanley H Ev *Lich* from 17. *35 Harding Road, Stoke-on-Trent ST3 3BQ* T: (01782) 922540 M: 07586-303831 E: phillip.e.jones@talktalk.net

JONES, Phyllis Gwendoline Charlotte. b 44. **d** 05 **p** 06. OLM Talbot Village *Sarum* 05–12; rtd 13; PtO *Sarum* 13–15; Hon C Tralee w Kilmoyley, Ballymacelligott etc *L & K* from 15. *The New Rectory, Kilgobbin, Camp, Co Kerry, Republic of Ireland* T: (00353) (66) 713 0767 M: (00353) 85-855 8594 E: phyllisjones@eircom.net

JONES, Ray. *See* JONES, David Raymond

JONES, Raymond. b 43. NOC 99. **d** 02 **p** 03. NSM Ashton-in-Makerfield St Thos *Liv* 02–03; C Widnes St Mary w St Paul 03–05; V 05–08; rtd 08; Hon C Farnworth *Liv* 10–13; Hon C E Widnes 13; PtO from 16. *4 Norlands Park, Widnes WA8 5BH*

JONES (née WELCH), Mrs Rebecca Anne. b 79. Leic Univ BSc 00. Wycliffe Hall Ox BTh 10. **d** 09 **p** 10. C Cov Cathl 09–12; C Aston and Nechells *Birm* 12–18; V Leamington

Priors St Mary *Cov* from 18. *28 St Mary's Road, Leamington Spa CV31 1JP* M: 07712-632504

JONES, Rhiannon Elizabeth. *See* KING, Rhiannon Elizabeth

JONES, Rhys. b 69. TCD Div Sch MTh 17. **d** 15 **p** 17. Castledawson *D & R* 15–20; C Clooney w Strathfoyle 17–20; I Balteagh w Carrick from 20; I Tamlaghtard w Aghanloo from 20. *The Rectory, 115 Drumsurn Road, Limavady BT49 0PD* M: 07907-386327 E: rhjones@tcd.ie *or* analogkid04@hotmail.com

JONES, Richard. *See* JONES, James Richard

JONES, Richard Christopher Bentley. b 53. Pemb Coll Ox BA 77 MA 79. SEITE 03. **d** 06 **p** 07. NSM Clapham H Trin and St Pet *S'wark* 06–13; PtO *Heref* 13–17; NSM Wye Brooks Benefice from 17. *Langstone Court, Llangarron, Ross-on-Wye HR9 6NR* T: (01989) 770254 E: richard.jones@langstone-court.org.uk

JONES, Robert. b 45. Culham Coll Ox CertEd 67. St Steph Ho Ox. **d** 85 **p** 86. C High Wycombe *Ox* 85–89; V Beckenham St Barn *Roch* 89–90; C Swanley St Mary 90–91; C Edenbridge 91–13; C Crockham Hill H Trin 91–13; rtd 13. *23 Bromley College, London Road, Bromley BR1 1PE* E: r.jones52@btinternet.com

JONES, Robert Cecil. b 32. Univ of Wales (Abth) BA 54 DipEd 55. Qu Coll Birm 84. **d** 86 **p** 87. C Llanbadarn Fawr w Capel Bangor and Goginan *St D* 86–88; R Llanllwchaearn and Llanina 88–91; R Newport w Cilgwyn and Dinas w Llanllawer 91–98; rtd 98; PtO *Derby* 05–18. *Old Craigstead Works, High Street, Stoney Middleton, Hope Valley S32 4TL* T: (01433) 631857 E: revrobbiejones02@gmail.com

JONES, Robert David. b 73. UCD BSc 97 TCD BTh 07. CITC 04. **d** 07 **p** 08. C Dublin St Patr Cathl Gp *D & G* 07–10; V Dublin Rathmines w Harold's Cross 10–17; R from 17. *25 Airfield Road, Rathgar, Dublin 6, Republic of Ireland* M: (00353) 86-285 4098

JONES, The Ven Robert George. b 55. Hatf Coll Dur BA 77. Ripon Coll Cuddesdon BA 79 MA 87. **d** 80 **p** 81. C Foley Park *Worc* 80–84; V Dudley St Fran 84–92; TR Worc St Barn w Ch Ch 92–06; Dir Development 06–14; RD Worc E 99–05; Hon Can Worc Cathl 03–14; Adn Worc from 14; V Gt Malvern Ch Ch 15–20. *The Archdeacon's House, Walkers Lane, Whittington, Worcester WR5 2RE* T: (01905) 773301 E: rjones@cofe-worcester.org.uk *or* archdeacon.worcester@cofe-worcester.org.uk

JONES, Canon Robert George. b 42. St Mich Coll Llan 93. **d** 95 **p** 96. NSM Treboeth *S & B* 95–02; P-in-c 02–07; P-in-c Landore 03–07; Can Res Brecon Cathl 06–07; rtd 07. *106 Plunch Lane, Mumbles, Swansea SA3 4JE* E: robertgeorgejones@yahoo.co.uk

JONES, Robert William. b 55. Open Univ BA 85 MA 88. Ian Ramsey Coll Brasted 75 Chich Th Coll 76 TCD Div Sch 77. **d** 79 **p** 80. C Seapatrick *D & D* 79; C Bangor Abbey 81–83; I Drumgath w Drumgooland and Clonduff 83–89; I Finaghy *Conn* 89–93; I Kilwaughter w Cairncastle and Craigy Hill 94–98; I Athlone w Benown, Kiltoom and Forgney *M & K* 98–02; Dean Clonmacnoise 02–12; I Trim and Athboy Gp 02–12; I Belfast Malone St Jo *Conn* 12–18; Can Belf Cathl 13–18; I Kiltegan w Hacketstown, Clonmore and Moyne *C, F & O* from 18. *The Rectory, Kiltegan, Co Wicklow, W91 D2E6, Republic of Ireland* T: (00353) (59) 647 3368 M: 85-257 3139 E: kilteganrectory@gmail.com

JONES, Robin Dominic Edwin. b 78. St Chad's Coll Dur BA 00 K Coll Lon MA 01. St Steph Ho Ox MTh 07. **d** 04 **p** 05. C Ealing Ch the Sav *Lon* 04–08; V Hammersmith St Luke 08–12; V Sevenoaks St Jo *Roch* from 12. *St John's Clergy House, 62 Quakers Hall Lane, Sevenoaks TN13 3TX* T: (01732) 451710 M: 07779-299924

JONES, Roderick. b 48. Leeds Univ BA 70 PGCE 72. Westmr Th Sem (USA) 73 Oak Hill Th Coll 74. **d** 76 **p** 77. C Beckenham Ch Ch *Roch* 76–80; C Uphill *B & W* 80–84; R Springfield All SS *Chelmsf* 84–90; Selection Sec ABM 91–96; V Horsell *Guildf* 96–13; rtd 13; PtO *Guildf* from 13. *3 Pine Close, New Haw, Addlestone KT15 3BW* E: revrodjones@btinternet.com

JONES, Canon Roger. b 49. St Mich Coll Llan 84. **d** 86 **p** 87. C Llangynwyd w Maesteg *Llan* 86–90; V Wiston w Walton E and Clarbeston *St D* 90–01; V Pembroke Gp 01–04; TV Monkton 04–16; Can St D Cathl 09–16; rtd 16; PtO *St D* from 17. *32 Oakfield Drive, Kilgetty SA68 0UD* T: (01834) 811797 M: 07971-528933 E: canonrog@gmail.com

JONES, Mrs Rose-Mary Harriett. b 90. Westmr Univ BA 11 St Jo Coll Dur BA 18. Cranmer Hall Dur 16. **d** 19 **p** 20. C N Cornwall Cluster *Truro* from 19. *Address withheld by request* E: revrosejones@gmail.com

JONES, Rupert Trevelyan. b 76. St Hugh's Coll Ox BA 97 MA 05. St Aug Coll Cant 17. **d** 21. NSM Primrose Hill St Mary w Avenue Road St Paul *Lon* from 21. *St Mary the Virgin Parish Office, Elsworthy Road, London NW3 3DJ*

JONES, Russell Frederick. b 55. Man Univ BA 77 Edin Univ BD 84. Edin Th Coll 81. **d** 84 **p** 85. C Croxteth *Liv* 84–87; V Edgehill St Dunstan 87–98; R Glas St Bride 98–08; Hon Chapl Glas Univ 00–06; Chapl Marie Curie Hospice Glasgow 08–14; Chapl Gtr Glas and Clyde NHS from 15. *The Chaplaincy, Gartnavel General Hospital, 1053 Great Western Road, Glasgow G12 0YN* T: 0141-211 3026 E: russell.jones@ggc.scot.nhs.uk

JONES, Mrs Sally Ann. b 41. **d** 09 **p** 10. NSM Teme Valley N *Worc* 09–13; PtO from 13. *2 Old School House, Eastham, Tenbury Wells WR15 8PB* T: (01584) 781526 E: revsally@live.com

JONES, Miss Sally Jennifer. b 86. St Mich Coll Llan. **d** 11 **p** 12. C Bro Ardudwy Uchaf *Ban* 11–13; C Bro Ardudwy 13–14; Min Can St Alb 14–18; P-in-c Munster Square Ch Ch and St Mary Magd *Lon* from 18. *24 Redhill Street, London NW1 4DQ* M: 07842-341748 E: vicar.marymags@gmail.com

JONES, Samuel. b 44. CITC. **d** 86 **p** 87. C Agherton *Conn* 86–88; I Connor w Antrim St Patr 88–97; I Whitehead and Islandmagee 97–01; Bp's C Kilbroney *D & D* 01–10; rtd 10. *2 The Brambles, Coleraine BT52 1PN* T: (028) 7031 0076

JONES, Sarah. *See* EDEN-JONES, Sarah Rachel

JONES, Sarah Charlotte. b 57. SRN 79. SAOMC 01. **d** 04 **p** 05. NSM Forest Edge *Ox* 04–18; rtd 18; PtO *Ox* from 18. *4 Tower Hill, Witney OX28 5ER* T: (01993) 200483 E: sarahtandem@hotmail.com

JONES, Ms Sarah Jane. b 61. St Hugh's Coll Ox BA 95 MA 03 Northumbria Univ MSc 02. Westcott Ho Cam 02. **d** 04 **p** 05. C Ross *Heref* 04–07; P-in-c 07–08; R Ross w Walford and Brampton Abbotts 08–18; P-in-c Cardiff City Par *Llan* from 18. *The Vicarage, 16 Queen Anne Square, Cardiff CF10 3ED* T: (029) 2022 4956

JONES, Sebastian. *See* JONES, David Sebastian

JONES, Canon Sharon Ann. b 60. St Kath Coll Liv BA 82. Cranmer Hall Dur 83. **dss** 85 **d** 87 **p** 94. Rubery *Birm* 85–89; Par Dn 87–89; C-in-c Chelmsley Wood St Aug CD 89–92; PtO *Newc* 92–93; Chapl HM Pris Acklington 93–97; Chapl HM YOI Castington 97–00; Chapl HM Pris Forest Bank 00–06; P-in-c Dearnley *Man* 06–14; P-in-c Wardle and Smallbridge 13–14; V Dearnley, Wardle and Smallbridge 14–16; AD Salford 03–06; AD Rochdale 06–15; TR Saddleworth from 16; Hon Can Man Cathl from 13. *Saddleworth Vicarage, Station Road, Uppermill, Oldham OL3 6HQ* T: (01457) 879977 M: 07738-966271 E: sharonjones@cofesaddleworth.org or sharonjones@cofeinsaddleworth.org.uk

JONES, Mrs Shelagh Deirdre. b 46. St Mary's Coll Dur BA 68. NEOC 01. **d** 04 **p** 05. NSM Burnby *York* 04–07; NSM Londesborough 04–07; NSM Nunburnholme and Warter and Huggate 04–07; NSM Shiptonthorpe and Hayton 04–07; PtO from 07; Chapl HM YOI Wetherby 04–10; PtO *Eur* from 13. *Red Gables, Fair View, Town Street, Shiptonthorpe, York YO43 3PE* T/F: (01430) 871612 E: revd-shelagh@red-gables.org.uk

JONES, Canon Simon. b 63. Trin Coll Bris BA 89. **d** 89 **p** 90. C Hildenborough *Roch* 89–93; C Crofton *Portsm* 93–96; C Northwood Em *Lon* 96–01; Min in charge Ignite 01–07; R Stoke Gifford *Bris* from 07; AD Kingswood and S Glos 11–19; Hon Can Bris Cathl from 17. *119 North Road, Stoke Gifford, Bristol BS34 8PE* T: 0117-979 1656 or 969 2486 F: 959 9264 E: simon@stmichaelsbristol.org

JONES, Canon Simon Matthew. b 72. SS Hild & Bede Coll Dur BA 93 MA 94 Selw Coll Cam PhD 00 Ox Univ MA 02 DPhil 03. Westcott Ho Cam 95. **d** 99 **p** 00. C Tewkesbury w Walton Cardiff and Twyning *Glouc* 99–02; Chapl and Fell Mert Coll Ox from 02; Hon Can Ch Ch *Ox* from 15; Can and Preb Chich Cathl from 16. *Merton College, Oxford OX1 4JD* T: (01865) 276365 or 281793 F: 276361 E: simon.jones@merton.ox.ac.uk

JONES, Stephen. *See* JONES, Ernest Edward Stephen

JONES, Stephen Frederick. b 53. Magd Coll Ox BA 75 MA 79 Lon Univ BD 89 Leeds Univ MA 96. Linc Th Coll BCombStuds 84. **d** 84 **p** 85. C Kingswinford St Mary *Lich* 84–87; Min Can, Succ and Dean's V Windsor 87–94; C Howden *York* 94–96; Chapl St Elphin's Sch Matlock 96–01; C Worksop Priory *S'well* 01–03; R Longton *Lich* 03–13; TR Staveley and Barrow Hill *Derby* from 13. *The Rectory, Church Street, Staveley, Chesterfield S43 3TN* T: (01246) 498603 E: sfjones53@googlemail.com

JONES, Stephen John. b 56. **d** 14 **p** 15. NSM Rednal *Birm* from 14; Bp's Adv on Disability from 16. *19 Meadowfield Road, Rubery, Rednal, Birmingham B45 9BY* T: 0121-460 1173 M: 07866-748932 E: stephen.jones@forumpm.com or revdstevejones@gmail.com

JONES, Canon Stephen Leslie. b 59. Hull Univ BA 80 Lanc Univ MA 06. Sarum & Wells Th Coll 82. **d** 85 **p** 86. C Perry Barr *Birm* 85–88; C Blackpool St Steph *Blackb* 88–90; V Greenlands 90–95; V Carnforth from 95; Hon Can Blackb Cathl from

11. *The Vicarage, North Road, Carnforth LA5 9LJ* T: (01524) 732948 E: stephenjones17@hotmail.com

JONES, Stephen Richard. b 49. Heythrop Coll Lon MA 01. Oak Hill Th Coll 72. **d** 75 **p** 76. C Welling *Roch* 75–79; C Cheltenham St Mark *Glouc* 79–82; V Shiregreen St Jas and St Chris *Sheff* 82–86; P-in-c Harold Hill St Geo *Chelmsf* 86–88; V 88–97; P-in-c Harold Hill St Paul 94–95; V Kippington *Roch* 97–08; RD Sevenoaks 00–05; R Ightham 08–14; RD Shoreham 11–14; rtd 14; PtO *B & W* 15–18; Hon C Beercrocombe w Curry Mallet, Hatch Beauchamp etc from 18. *The Rectory, Hatch Beauchamp, Taunton TA3 6AB* T: (01823) 710712

JONES, Steven Charles. b 64. Ex Univ LLB 93 Barrister-at-Law. Trin Coll Bris 16. **d** 16. C Totnes w Bridgetown, Berry Pomeroy etc *Ex* 16–20; TR Littleham-cum-Exmouth w Lympstone from 20. *The Rectory, 1 Maer Road , Exmouth EX8 2DA* M: 07711-833178 E: stevencharlesjones@icloud.com

JONES, Stewart William. b 57. Heriot-Watt Univ BA 79 Bris Univ BA 88. Trin Coll Bris 86. **d** 88 **p** 89. C Stoke Bishop *Bris* 88–92; P-in-c Brislington St Luke 92–97; Abp's Chapl and Dioc Missr *Cant* 97–03; P-in-c Cant All SS 01–05; AD Cant and Hon Prov Can Cant Cathl 02–05; R Birm St Martin w Bordesley St Andr 05–17; Hon Can Birm Cathl 11–17; V Barlaston *Lich* from 17; PtO *Birm* from 17. *The Vicarage, 2 Longton Road, Stoke-on-Trent ST12 9AA* M: 07793-724949 E: canonstewart@icloud.com

JONES, Susan Catherine. *See* ASHTON, Susan Catherine

JONES, The Very Revd Susan Helen. b 60. Trin Coll Carmarthen BEd 92 MPhil 94 Univ of Wales (Ban) PhD. Ripon Coll Cuddesdon 93. **d** 95 **p** 97. Chapl Univ of Wales (Swansea) *S & B* 95–98; Hon C Sketty 95–98; Dir Past Studies St Mich Coll Llan 98–00; Lect Univ of Wales (Cardiff) *Llan* 98–00; TV Bangor *Ban* 00–09; AD Ogwen 07–09; Can Missr Ban Cathl 10–11; Dean Ban 11–15; TR Bro Deiniol 14–15; Dir of Miss and Min *Derby* 15–18; Can Res Derby Cathl 15–18; Acting Dean Derby 16–17; Dean Liv from 18; Research Fell Glyndŵr Univ from 09. *1 Cathedral Close, Liverpool L1 7BR* T: 0151-702 7220 E: dean@liverpoolcathedral.org.uk

JONES, Susan Jean. b 47. Bp Grosseteste Coll CertEd 68 Heythrop Coll Lon MA 01. SAOMC 93. **d** 96 **p** 97. C S Ascot *Ox* 96–07; NSM 01–07; rtd 07. *Fairhaven, 1 St Clement's Terrace, Mousehole, Penzance TR19 6SJ* T: (01736) 732938

JONES, Susannah Hester Everett. b 67. **d** 07 **p** 08. NSM Bris St Mary Redcliffe w Temple etc 07–13; P-in-c Abbots Leigh w Leigh Woods 13–14; V from 14. *The Vicarage, 51 Church Road, Abbots Leigh, Bristol BS8 3QU* E: hester.jones2@googlemail.com

JONES, Theresa. *See* JONES, Mary Catherine Theresa Bridget

JONES, Timothy Llewellyn. b 67. York Univ BA 90. Ripon Coll Cuddesdon BA 94. **d** 94 **p** 95. C Middlesbrough St Martin *York* 94–96; P-in-c Rounton w Welbury 96–02; Chapl HM YOI Northallerton 96–99; Adv for Young Adults and Voc (Cleveland) 99–02; R Corinth St Paul USA 02–07; P-in-c York St Hilda 07–14; P-in-c York St Lawr w St Nic 07–14; Dioc Dir of Ords *St E* 14–21; Hon C Lark Valley 14–19; Hon C Bury St Edmunds All SS w St Jo and St Geo 14–19; Hon C Lark Valley and N Bury 19–21; Hon Can St E Cathl 17–21; Dir Min and Discipleship *Llan* from 21. *The Diocesan Office, The Court, Coychurch, Bridgend CF35 5EH* T: (01656) 868868 M: 07415-851546 E: timjones@churchinwales.org.uk

JONES, Timothy Richard Nigel. b 54. Collingwood Coll Dur BSc 75 Birm Univ MSc 76 FGS. Trin Coll Bris 84. **d** 86 **p** 87. C Hailsham *Chich* 86–91; V Madley w Tyberton, Preston-on-Wye and Blakemere *Heref* 91–00; R Madley w Tyberton, Peterchurch, Vowchurch etc 00–06; V Taunton St Jas *B & W* 06–17; rtd 17. *Clover Cottage, Little Silver, Tiverton EX16 4LW* T: (01884) 595001 E: tim@bankend.net

JONES, Tracey Anne. b 62. Ripon Coll Cuddesdon 18. **d** 19 **p** 20. NSM Hughenden *Ox* from 19. *101 Cedar Avenue, Hazlemere, High Wycombe HP15 7EF* E: rev.funkyfish@gmail.com

JONES, Canon Tracy Jane. **d** 12 **p** 13. C Seintiau Braint a Chefni *Ban* 12–14; R Bro Padrig 14–18; C Bro Deiniol from 18; Can Ban Cathl from 16. *4 Lon Eryri, Penrhosgarnedd, Bangor LL57 2QF* T: (01248) 361876 E: revtracyjones@gmail.com

JONES, Trevor Blandon. b 43. Oak Hill Th Coll 77. **d** 80 **p** 81. NSM Homerton St Barn w St Paul *Lon* 80–83; NSM Harlow New Town w Lt Parndon *Chelmsf* 83–90; C 90–92; V Leyton Em 92–01; rtd 02; PtO *Chelmsf* from 03. *5 Wheatley Close, Sawbridgeworth CM21 0HS* T: (01279) 600248

JONES, Trevor Edwin. b 49. Heythrop Coll Lon MA 05 K Coll Lon DThMin 12. Ripon Coll Cuddesdon 74. **d** 76 **p** 77. C Cannock *Lich* 76–79; C Middlesbrough Ascension *York* 79–81; V Oldham St Steph and All Martyrs *Man* 81–84; V Perry Beeches *Birm* 84–90; P-in-c Saltley 90–93; P-in-c Shaw Hill 90–93; V Saltley and Shaw Hill 93–97; R Lon Docks St Pet w Wapping St Jo 97–17; rtd 17; PtO *Nor* from 17. *30 Cleaves Drive, Walsingham NR22 6EQ* T: (01328) 821415 M: 07977-260559 E: father.jones@btinternet.com *or* frtejones@aol.com

JONES, The Ven Trevor Pryce. b 48. Southn Univ BEd 76 BTh 79 Univ of Wales (Cardiff) LLM 04 St Jo Coll Dur DThM 13 Herts Univ Hon LLM 18. Sarum & Wells Th Coll 73. **d** 76 **p** 77. C Glouc St Geo 76–79; Warden Bp Mascall Cen *Heref* 79–84; Dioc Communications Officer 81–86; TR Heref S Wye 84–97; Preb Heref Cathl 93–97; OCM 85–97; Adn Hertford and Hon Can St Alb 97–16; Hon Can St Alb 97–16; PtO *Ex* 16–17; Chapter Can Ex Cathl from 17. *3 South Terrace, Longmeadow Road, Lympstone, Exmouth EX8 5LN* T: (01395) 268745 E: tprycejones@gmail.com

JONES, Miss Victoria Kay. b 83. St Mich Coll Llan 09. **d** 12 **p** 13. C Llangwm w Freystrop and Johnston *St D* 12–15; P-in-c Llanedi w Tycroes and Saron from 15; P-in-c Gorslas from 15. *The Vicarage, 56 Black Lion Road, Gorslas, Llanelli SA14 6RU* T: (01269) 845505 M: 07976-836209 E: rev.vjones@gmail.com

JONES, Preb Wilfred David. b 22. Keble Coll Ox BA 47 MA 48. St Mich Coll Llan 47. **d** 48 **p** 49. C Aberaman *Llan* 48–50; C Cardiff St Jo 50–55; Chapl Kelly Coll Tavistock 55–62; V St Decumans *B & W* 62–76; V Ilminster w Whitelackington 76–92; RD Ilminster 78–87; Preb Wells Cathl 81–05; rtd 92; PtO *B & W* 92–06. *Dragons, Lambrook Road, Shepton Beauchamp, Ilminster TA19 0NA* T: (01460) 240967

JONES, Wilfred Lovell. b 39. Lon Univ BD 71 Cam Univ CertEd. St D Coll Lamp 60. **d** 63 **p** 64. C Llanllyfni *Ban* 63–65; C Llanbeblig w Caernarfon 65–68; V Llanwnog w Penstrowed 68–72; V Llanwnnog and Caersws w Carno 72–75; Asst Chapl Dover Coll 77–90; Chapl Wrekin Coll Telford 91–94; V Llangollen w Trevor and Llantysilio *St As* 94–04; AD Llangollen 03–04; rtd 04; PtO *St As* 09–16; Guildf from 16. *21 Ashley Drive, Blackwater, Camberley GU17 0PR* T: (01276) 600643 E: wlwaj@btinternet.com

JONES, Mrs Wyn. b 49. **d** 01 **p** 02. OLM Linslade *Ox* 01–08; OLM Ouzel Valley *St Alb* from 08. *2 Woodside Way, Linslade, Leighton Buzzard LU7 7PN* T: (01525) 373638 E: wjones255@aol.com

JONES-BLACKETT, Enid Olive. b 40. Reading Univ BA 61. **d** 97 **p** 98. OLM Hellesdon *Nor* 97–10; rtd 10; PtO *Nor* from 10. *8 Fastolf Close, Hellesdon, Norwich NR6 5RE* T: (01603) 424769 E: enidjonesblackett@btinternet.com

JONG, Jonathan. b 85. **d** 14 **p** 15. NSM Ox St Mary Magd 14–20; PtO *Chich* 20–21; R Cocking w W Lavington, Bepton and Heyshott from 21. *Cocking Rectory, Mill Lane, Cocking, Midhurst GU29 0HJ* M: 07799-271913 E: jonathan.jong@anthro.ox.ac.uk *or* emailjonhere@gmail.com

JONGMAN, Canon Kären Anngel Irene. b 43. EMMTC 97. **d** 01 **p** 02. NSM Northampton St Mary *Pet* 01–03; NSM Guilsborough w Hollowell and Cold Ashby 03–04; P-in-c Walgrave w Hannington and Wold and Scaldwell 04–18; R Pattishall w Cold Higham and Gayton w Tiffield from 18; Chapl Northants Fire and Rescue Service from 03; Can Pet Cathl 12–13. *The Vicarage, 17 Church Street, Pattishall, Towcester NN12 8NB* M: 07980-881252 E: karenajongman@gmail.com

JORDAN, Anne. b 42. RGN 66. **d** 02 **p** 03. OLM Crofton *Wakef* 02–14; Leeds from 14. *95 Ashdene Avenue, Crofton, Wakefield WF4 1LY* T: (01924) 865527 M: 07450-475184

JORDAN, Anthony John. b 50. Birm Univ BEd 73. LNSM course. **d** 83 **p** 84. Asst Chapl Uppingham Sch 83–86; NSM Uppingham w Ayston and Wardley w Belton *Pet* 83–86; Asst Chapl Sherborne Sch 86–87; NSM Bournemouth St Fran *Win* 88–03; PtO *Leic* 04–06; NSM Leic St Aid 06–08; V Eyres Monsell 08–13; rtd 13. *67 Lethbridge Close, Leicester LE1 2EB* T: 0116-278 0940 M: 07798-860106

JORDAN, Canon Elizabeth Ann. b 58. New Hall Cam MA 82 Anglia Ruskin Univ DProf 16. St Jo Coll Nottm 82. **d** 87 **p** 94. Par Dn Blackpool St Jo *Blackb* 87–90; Par Dn Ewood 90–94; C 94–95; Asst Dir of Ords 90–95; Min Shelfield St Mark CD *Lich* 95–00; Local Min Adv (Wolverhampton) 95–05; OLM Course Ldr and Team Ldr Min Division 03–05; Dir Local Min Development 06–10; C Blakenall Heath 10–11; Lay Educn and Tr Adv *Chelmsf* from 11; Hon C Rawreth from 12; Hon C Rettendon and Hullbridge from 21; Hon Can Chelmsf Cathl from 20. *Diocesan Office, 53 New Street, Chelmsford CM1 1AT* T: (01245) 294454 F: 294477 E: ejordan@chelmsford.anglican.org

JORDAN, Lucy Charlotte Tansley. b 87. St Cuth Soc Dur BA 08 St Mary's Coll Dur PGCE 09. Ripon Coll Cuddesdon 17. **d** 19 **p** 20. C Wells St Cuth w Wookey Hole *B & W* from 19. *7 Deckle Edge Close, Wells BA5 2GP* M: 07983-307197 E: rev.lucy.jordan@outlook.com

JORDAN, Miss Pamela Mary. b 43. Univ of Wales (Cardiff) BSc 64 Ox Univ DipEd 65. WEMTC 02. **d** 05 **p** 06. NSM Coalbrookdale, Iron-Bridge and Lt Wenlock *Heref* 05–13; PtO from 13. *2 Madeley Wood View, Madeley, Telford TF7 5TF* T: (01952) 583254

JORDAN, Patrick Glen. b 69. SEITE 01. **d** 04 **p** 05. C Charlton *S'wark* 04–07; C Catford (Southend) and Downham 07–08; TV 08–16; V Thorpe St Matt *Nor* from 16; C Nor Heartsease St Fran from 19. *St Matthew's Vicarage, Albert Place, Norwich NR1 4JL* T: (01603) 494015 *or* 763695 E: revpatrickjordan@gmail.com

JORDAN, Peter Harry. b 42. Leeds Univ BA 64 Leeds Coll of Educn PGCE 65. Cranmer Hall Dur 70. **d** 73 **p** 74. C Nottingham St Ann w Em *S'well* 77–82; C Edgware *Lon* 77–82; V Everton St Chrys *Liv* 82–94; Dioc Ev and V Bootle St Mary w St Paul 94–02; Chapl Barcelona *Eur* 02–08; rtd 08; PtO *Eur* 08–19; *Ches* from 10. *43 Montpellier House, Montpellier Crescent, Wallasey CH45 9NF* T: 0151-639 7860 E: peterybarbara@gmail.com

JORDAN, Canon Richard William. b 56. Lanchester Poly Cov BSc 78 Sheff Univ MA 07. St Jo Coll Nottm 84. **d** 87 **p** 88. C Blackpool St Jo *Blackb* 87–90; V Ewood 90–95; PtO *Lich* 95–97; Co-ord Walsall Town Cen Min 97–00; Ch Links Projects Officer 00–06; Dioc Ch and Soc Officer *Derby* 06–11; P-in-c Rawreth *Chelmsf* from 11; P-in-c Rettendon and Hullbridge from 17; AD Rochford 15–18; Hon Can Chelmsf Cathl from 15. *The Rectory, Church Road, Rawreth, Wickford SS11 8SH* T: (01268) 766565 E: rev.richard.jordan@gmail.com

JORDAN, Steven Paul. b 52. **d** 11 **p** 12. NSM Church Lench w Rous Lench and Abbots Morton etc *Worc* 11–15; PtO NZ 15–16; NSM Nelson Cathl 16–17; Sub Dean from 17. *48 Weka Street, The Wood, Nelson 7010, New Zealand* M: (0064) 21-294 6105 E: bspj@live.co.uk

JORDAN, Tansley. *See* JORDAN, Lucy Charlotte Tansley

JORDAN, Thomas. b 36. NW Ord Course 76. **d** 79 **p** 80. NSM Prenton *Ches* 79–84; NSM Egremont St Jo 84–91; C 91–96; Ind Chapl 91–96; TV Birkenhead Priory 96–01; rtd 01; PtO *Ches* from 02. *13 Corniche Road, Wirral CH62 5HA* E: thomas.t.jordan@btinternet.com

JORDAN, Trevor. b 44. Lon Hosp MB, BS 67 LRCP 68 MRCS 68 Nottm Univ MA 99. EMMTC 96. **d** 03 **p** 04. NSM Seamer *York* 03–07; PtO 07–11; NSM Long Buckby w Watford and W Haddon w Winwick *Pet* 11–16; rtd 16; PtO *Leic* 16–21. *5 Pretoria Road, Ibstock LE67 6LP* T: (01530) 459619 M: 07887-537244 E: trevor@trevorsweb.net

JORDINSON, Vera (Sister Hilary). b 37. Liv Univ BA 60 CertEd 61. Westcott Ho Cam 88. **d** 89 **p** 94. CSF from 74; Prov Sec 90–01; Gen Sec 96–02; Sec for Miss SSF 96–99; Gift Aid Sec 01–11; LtO *Heref* 89–92; PtO *Lich* 90–92; *Birm* 92–94, 97–06 and from 12; *B & W* 06–10; NSM Birchfield *Birm* 94–96. *37 Firs Close, Watery Lane, Smethwick B67 6DQ* E: hilarycsf@franciscans.org.uk

JØRGENSEN (née BURGESS), Mrs Laura Jane. b 74. Imp Coll Lon BSc 95 ARSM 95. Ripon Coll Cuddesdon BTh 00. **d** 00 **p** 01. C St Alb Abbey 00–01; C Boxmoor St Jo 01–04; Min Can and Sacr St Paul's Cathl *Lon* 04–09; V St Botolph Aldgate w H Trin Minories from 09; PV Westmr Abbey from 10; Dean of Women's Min Two Cities Area *Lon* from 20. *St Botolph's Church, Aldgate High Street, London EC3N 1AB* T: (020) 7283 2154 E: rector@stbotolphs.org.uk

JORYSZ, Canon Ian Herbert. b 62. Van Mildert Coll Dur BSc 84 MA 95 Liv Univ PhD 87. Ripon Coll Cuddesdon BA 89 MA 95. **d** 90 **p** 91. C Houghton le Spring *Dur* 90–93; C Ferryhill 93–95; Research Officer to Bp of Bradwell 95–15; P-in-c S Weald *Chelmsf* 95–00; V 00–15; RD Brentwood 08–15; Bp's Sen Chapl *Man* from 15; Hon Can Man Cathl from 15. *Bishopscourt, Bury New Road, Salford M7 4LE* T: 0161-792 2096 E: bishopschaplain@manchester.anglican.org

JOSEPH EMMANUEL, Brother. *See* DICKSON, Colin James

JOSS, Capt Martin James Torquil. b 60. Univ of Wales (Lamp) BA 79. EAMTC 03. **d** 03 **p** 04. C Harlow Town Cen w Lt Parndon *Chelmsf* 03–07; P-in-c Coalville and Bardon Hill *Leic* 07–09; C Ravenstone and Swannington 07–09; V Coalville w Bardon Hill and Ravenstone 09–17; V Oswaldtwistle *Blackb* from 17. *The Vicarage, 29 Maygill Avenue, Oswaldtwistle, Accrington BB5 3AA* T: (01254) 231038 M: 07875-494588 E: vicarofossy@gmail.com

JOSS-POTHEN, Bethany Deborah Keziah. b 92. Westcott Ho Cam 16. **d** 19 **p** 20. C St Mary-at-Latton *Chelmsf* from 19. *21 Huntley Road, Harlow CM20 2PR* E: reverendbethany@gmail.com

JOSS-POTHEN, Nathan James. b 93. Westcott Ho Cam 16. **d** 19 **p** 20. C Harlow Town Cen w Lt Parndon *Chelmsf* from 19. *21 Huntley Road, Harlow CM20 2PR*

JOWETT, Hilary Anne. b 54. Hull Univ BA 75. Cranmer Hall Dur IDC 80. **dss** 82 **d** 87 **p** 94. Sheff St Jo 80–83; Brampton Bierlow 83–87; Par Dn 87–89; Hon Par Dn Sharrow St Andr 89–95; Chapl Nether Edge Hosp Sheff 89–95; C Sheff St Mark Broomhill 95–97; C Mosborough 97–00; TR Gleadless 00–12; R Dinnington w Laughton and Throapham 12–17; R Dinnington 17–20; rtd 20. *303A Hollinsend Road, Sheffield S12 2NL* T: 0114-239 7619 E: hilaryjowett@live.co.uk

JOWETT, Canon Nicholas Peter Alfred. b 44. St Cath Coll Cam BA 66 MA Nottm Trent Univ MA 14 Bris Univ CertEd 67. Qu Coll Birm 72. **d** 75 **p** 76. C Wales *Sheff* 75–78; TV Sheff Manor 78–83; V Brampton Bierlow 83–89; V Sharrow St Andr 89–98; V Psalter Lane St Andr 98–12; Dioc Ecum Adv 01–09; Hon Can Sheff Cathl 06–12; rtd 12; PtO *Sheff* from 12. *303A Hollinsend Road, Sheffield S12 2NL* T: 0114-239 7619 E: mail@njowett.plus.com

JOWITT, Andrew Robert Benson. b 56. Down Coll Cam BA 78 PGCE 79 MA 81. Wycliffe Hall Ox 88. **d** 90 **p** 91. C Northampton Em *Pet* 90–94; C Barking St Marg w St Patr *Chelmsf* 94–98; TV 98–00; TV Stantonbury and Willen *Ox* 00–17; Bp's Officer for Evang 00–17; rtd 17. *12 Fields View, Sudbury CO10 1BJ* E: jowitts@btinternet.com

JOY, Bernard David. b 50. Sarum & Wells Th Coll 90. **d** 92 **p** 93. C Shortlands *Roch* 92–94; C Henbury *Bris* 94–96; V Bris St Aid w St Geo 96–03; P-in-c Bridgwater St Fran *B & W* 03–07; V 07–16; rtd 16; PtO *Sarum* from 17; *B & W* from 18. *40 Wessex Way, Gillingham SP8 4LX* T: (01747) 834427 M: 07745-291113 E: rev.obejoyful@gmail.com

JOY, Canon Matthew Osmund Clifton. b 40. St Edm Hall Ox BA 62 MA 66. St Steph Ho Ox 62. **d** 64 **p** 65. C Brinksway *Ches* 64–66; C Southwick St Columba *Dur* 66–69; V Hartlepool H Trin 69–85; V Rotherham St Paul, St Mich and St Jo Ferham Park *Sheff* 85–88; V Masbrough 88–95; RD Rotherham 88–93; P-in-c Bordesley St Benedict *Birm* 95–01; V 01–05; Bp's Adv on Chr/Muslim Relns 95–05; rtd 05; PtO *Wakef* 05–14; *Leeds* from 14; *Sheff* 06–18; *Leic* from 19. *22 Stuart Court, High Street, Kibworth Beauchamp, Leicester LE8 0LR* T: 0116-367 0332 E: joy313.matthew@gmail.com

JOYCE, Canon Alison Jane. b 59. Univ of Wales (Swansea) BA 81 Bris Univ MLitt 87 Birm Univ PhD 00 SS Coll Cam PGCE 84. Ripon Coll Cuddesdon BA 87 MA 94. **d** 88 **p** 94. Par Dn Chalgrove w Berrick Salome *Ox* 88–90; Tutor WMMTC 90–95; Tutor Qu Coll Birm 95–96; NSM Moseley St Anne *Birm* 96–04; Dean NSMs 00–03; NSM Birm Cathl 04–05; P-in-c Edgbaston St Bart 05–11; V 11–14; Chapl Birm Univ 05–14; Chapl Elmhurst Sch for Dance 05–14; Hon Can Birm Cathl 06–14; R St Bride Fleet Street w Bridewell etc *Lon* from 14. *St Bride's Rectory, St Bride's Avenue, London EC4Y 8AU* T: (020) 7427 0133 E: alison.joyce@stbrides.com

JOYCE, Anthony Owen. b 35. Selw Coll Cam BA 60 MA 64. Wycliffe Hall Ox 60. **d** 62 **p** 63. C Birm St Martin 62–67; Rhodesia 67–70; V Birm St Luke 70–79; V Downend *Bris* 79–01; RD Stapleton 83–89; rtd 01; PtO *Bris* from 01. *116 Jellicoe Avenue, Stapleton, Bristol BS16 1WJ* T: 0117-956 2510 E: anthonyjoyce@gmail.com

JOYCE, Graham Leslie. b 49. Lon Univ CertEd 71. Trin Coll Bris 87. **d** 89 **p** 90. C Heald Green St Cath *Ches* 89–93; R Church Lawton 93–14; rtd 14; PtO *Ches* from 14. *11 Fields Close, Alsager, Stoke-on-Trent ST7 2ND* T: (01270) 883621 E: revglj@gmail.com

JOYCE, Jennifer Claire. See BRIDGMAN, Jennifer Claire

JOYCE, Miss Joanna Lucy. b 76. Ridley Hall Cam 16. **d** 18 **p** 19. C Stockingford *Cov* from 18. *10 Rossendale Way, Nuneaton CV10 7NS* M: 07730-474129 E: revjoannajoyce@outlook.com

JOYCE, John Barnabas Altham. b 47. St Chad's Coll Dur BA 69 Lon Univ DipEd 86. St Steph Ho Ox 72. **d** 74 **p** 75. C Reading St Giles *Ox* 74–77; C Cowley St Jo 77–80; Dioc Youth and Community Officer 80–87; V Hangleton *Chich* 87–94; Dioc Adv for Schs and Dir Educn 94–99; R Hurstpierpoint 99–13; rtd 13; PtO *Chich* 13–17. *3 Wolstonbury Road, Hove BN3 6EJ* T: (01273) 773150 E: fr.john.joyce@live.co.uk

JOYCE, Margaret. b 47. Oak Hill NSM Course 86. **d** 89 **p** 94. NSM Chadwell Heath *Chelmsf* 89–92; NSM Bath Odd Down w Combe Hay *B & W* from 92; Chapl Bath and West Community NHS Trust from 95. *69 Bloomfield Rise, Bath BA2 2BN* T: (01225) 840864 M: 07841-053454 E: margaretjoyce@stphilipstjames.org

JOYCE, Miss Penelope Anne. b 53. St Mary's Coll Chelt CertEd 74. Wycliffe Hall Ox. **d** 00 **p** 01. C Ox St Clem *Sarum* 11–16; Hon C Salisbury St Fran and Stratford sub Castle 11–16; PtO 17–21; rtd 18. *60 Endless Street, Salisbury SP1 3UH* T: (01722) 416054 M: 07808-181885 E: pennyre.joyce@gmail.com

JOYCE, Philip Rupert. b 38. Selw Coll Cam BA 68 MA 72. Cranmer Hall Dur 68. **d** 70 **p** 71. C Newland St Jo *York* 70–73; C Woolwich St Mary w H Trin *S'wark* 73–77; Chapl Thames Poly 73–77; Chapl S Bank Poly 77–79; rtd 03. *37 Fulcher Avenue, Cromer NR27 9SG* T: (01263) 519405

JOYCE, Canon Terence Alan. b 57. York St Jo Univ MA 10. St Jo Coll Nottm BTh 84. **d** 84 **p** 85. C Mansfield SS Pet and Paul *S'well* 84–88; V Greasley 88–00; Dioc Dir of Ords 99–11; Dir Post-Ord Support and Tr 01–11; Hon Can S'well Minster 02–11; York Adnry Tr Adv and Dioc Adv for Clergy CMD 12–21; NSM Rural E York 12–21; rtd 21. *Address temp unknown*

JOYCE-HOOD, Jennifer Louise. St Mich Coll Llan. **d** 10 **p** 11. C Glanogwen and Llanllechid w St Ann's and Pentir *Ban* 10–13; Chapl Salford R NHS Foundn Trust from 14. *Salford Royal NHS Foundation Trust, Hope Hospital, Stott Lane, Salford M6 8HD* T: 0161-789 7373 E: jennifer.joyce-hood@srft.nhs.uk

JOYNER, Mrs Susan Diane. b 58. Nene Coll Northn BA 79 Open Univ MA 99 Leic Univ PGCE 84. NEOC 05. **d** 08 **p** 09. NSM Upper Coquetdale *Newc* from 08. *The Old Church, Harbottle, Morpeth NE65 7DQ* T: (01669) 650385 E: suejoyner2@aol.com

JOYNES, David. b 51. Leeds Univ BSc 74. Ripon Coll Cuddesdon 12. **d** 13 **p** 14. OLM The Cookhams *Ox* 13–16; NSM from 16. *1 Keeleys Cottages, High Street, Cookham, Maidenhead SL6 9SF* T: (01628) 528622 M: 07753-749228 E: revdavidjoynes@gmail.com

JOYNSON, Gillian Marion. b 57. **d** 16 **p** 17. OLM Cannock and Huntington *Lich* from 16; OLM Hatherton from 16. *2 Deer Close, Huntington, Cannock WS12 4UL* M: 07803-931828 E: gill.joynson@deerbahn.co.uk

JUCKES, Jonathan Sydney. b 61. St Andr Univ MA 83. Ridley Hall Cam BA 87. **d** 88 **p** 89. C Sevenoaks St Nic *Roch* 88–92; Proclamation Trust 92–95; C St Helen Bishopsgate w St Andr Undershaft etc *Lon* 95–98; TR Kirk Ella and Willerby *York* 98–14; R 14–17; President Oak Hill Coll from 18; Public Preacher *Lon* from 18. *Oak Hill College, Chase Side, London N14 4PS* T: (020) 8449 0467 E: johnnyj@oakhill.ac.uk

JUCKES, Canon Nigel Patrick. b 49. St Jo Coll Nottm 74. **d** 77 **p** 78. C Westville S Africa 78–80; R Addington 80–86; R Stanger All So 86–92; R Kloof 93–15; Adn Pinetown 01–06; Hon Can Pietermaritzburg from 06; P-in-c Llandogo w Whitebrook Chpl and Tintern Parva *Mon* from 15. *The Rectory, Llandogo, Monmouth NP25 4TW* T: (01594) 530041 E: nigelpj49@icloud.com

JUDD, Adrian Timothy. b 67. Lanc Univ BA 88 St Jo Coll Dur BA 92 St Thos Aquinas Pontifical Univ Rome MA 18 Huddersfield Univ MSc 18 PGCE 13 Domuni Univ MTh 18. Cranmer Hall Dur 90 Trin Coll Singapore 92. **d** 93 **p** 94. C Dudley St Aug Holly Hall *Worc* 93–97; V Stockbridge Village *Liv* 97–99; V Went Valley *Wakef* 00–14; *Leeds* from 14. *The Vicarage, Marlpit Lane, Darrington, Pontefract WF8 3AB* T: (01977) 704744 E: revjudd@gmail.com

JUDD, Colin Ivor. b 35. Dur Univ BA 61. Ridley Hall Cam 61. **d** 63 **p** 64. C Stratford St Jo w Ch *Chelmsf* 63–66; C Kimberworth *Sheff* 66–68; Area Sec CMS Bradf and Wakef 68–80; V Bradf St Columba w St Andr 80–00; rtd 00; PtO *Bradf* 00–14; *Leeds* from 14. *57 Grosvenor Road, Shipley BD18 4RB* T: (01274) 584775 E: thejudds@saltsvillage.co.uk

JUDD, Mrs Nicola Jane. b 51. K Alfred's Coll Win CertEd 72. S Dios Minl Tr Scheme 87. **d** 90 **p** 94. NSM Abbotts Ann and Upper Clatford and Goodworth Clatford *Win* 90–11; Chapl 90–92; Adv for NSM *Win* 01–05; PtO 11–17; NSM Abbotts Ann and Upper Clatford and Goodworth Clatford from 17. *13 Belmont Close, Andover SP10 2DE* T: (01264) 729075 E: revdnickyannabenefice@gmail.com

JUDD, The Very Revd Peter Somerset Margesson. b 49. DL 09. Trin Hall Cam BA 71. Cuddesdon Coll 71. **d** 74 **p** 75. C Salford St Phil w St Steph *Man* 74–76; Chapl Clare Coll Cam 76–81; C Burnham *Ox* 81–82; TV Burnham w Dropmore, Hitcham and Taplow 82–88; V Iffley 88–97; RD Cowley 94–97; Provost Chelmsf 97–00; Dean Chelmsf 00–13; rtd 13; PtO *Ely* 13–17; Acting Dean Clare Coll Cam 14–15; P-in-c Cambridge Gt St Mary w St Mich *Ely* 17–18; PtO from 18. *18 Baycliffe Close, Cambridge CB1 8EE* T: (01223) 214205 M: 07740-456844 E: peterjudd19@yahoo.co.uk

JUDD, Susan Elizabeth. b 48. Bris Univ BSc 74 Univ of Wales MA 04 ACA 80. STETS 05. **d** 08 **p** 09. NSM Portsm Cathl 08–12; PtO from 12. *16 Bepton Down, Petersfield GU31 4PR* T: (01730) 266819 E: susan.judd@ntlworld.com

JUDGE, Mrs Alison Gwendolyn. b 60. Ch Ch Coll Cant BA 13. SEITE BA 10. **d** 10 **p** 11. C W Wickham St Fran and St Mary *S'wark* 10–14; PtO 14–16; TV Merton Priory from 16. *Christ Church Vicarage, Christchurch Road, London SW19 2NY* T: (020) 8616 5794 E: revalisonjudge@gmail.com

JUDGE, Andrew Duncan. b 50. Cape Town Univ BCom 72 Keble Coll Ox MA 81. Pietermaritzburg Th Sem 82. **d** 83 **p** 84. C Westville S Africa 84–87; R Prestbury 88–94; R Westville 94–01; TV Keynsham *B & W* 01–18; rtd 18; PtO *Sarum* from 20. *4 Alum Close, Trowbridge BA14 7HD* T: (01225) 777491 E: adjudge27@outlook.com

JUDSON, Miss Christine Alison. b 64. Surrey Univ BSc 86 Birm Univ PGCE 88. Ripon Coll Cuddesdon 05. **d** 07 **p** 08. C Highbridge *B & W* 07–10; TV Portishead 10–21; P-in-c The Huntspills and Mark from 21. *Huntspill Rectory, Church Road, West Huntspill, Highbridge TA9 3RN* E: c.judson@btinternet.com

JUDSON, Mrs Mary Ruth. b 47. Bretton Hall Coll DipEd 68. NEOC 89. **d** 92 **p** 94. Par Dn Chester le Street *Dur* 92–94; C 94–96; V Millfield St Mark and Pallion St Luke 96–04; V Hartlepool St Luke 04–11; rtd 11; PtO *Dur* from 12. *5 Caxton Way, Chester le Street DH3 4BW* T: 0191-388 0512 E: maryjudson7@gmail.com

JUDSON, Paul Wesley. b 46. Leic Poly ATD 71. Cranmer Hall Dur 87. **d** 89 **p** 90. C Lobley Hill *Dur* 89–92; C Chester le Street 92–96; Ed Dioc Publications and Sec Dioc Bd of Soc Resp 96–98; C Millfield St Mark and Pallion St Luke 96–04; C Hartlepool St Luke 04–11; Dioc Publications Officer 98–11; Dioc Dir of Communications 02–11; rtd 11; PtO *Dur* from 12. *5 Caxton Way, Chester le Street DH3 4BW* T: 0191-388 0512 E: pwjudson@gmail.com

JUDSON, Peter. b 39. Lon Univ BSc 61 Plymouth Univ PGCE 87. SWMTC 99. **d** 02 **p** 03. OLM Bude Haven and Marhamchurch *Truro* 02–09; rtd 09; PtO *Truro* from 15; *Portsm* from 19. *25 Limewood, St Mary's Road, Hayling Island PO11 9FE* M: 07970-115538 E: mepmeadowcroft@gmail.com

JUKES, John Christopher. b 61. Ex Univ BTh 13 MA 17. SWMTC 10. **d** 13 **p** 14. C Saltash *Truro* 13–16; TV Cen Telford *Lich* 16–17; TV Uttoxeter Area 17–19; V Todmorden w Cornholme and Walsden *Leeds* from 19. *The Vicarage, 7 Fern Valley Chase, Todmorden OL14 7HB* M: 07443-414436 E: johnjukes101@yahoo.co.uk *or* john.jukes@leeds.anglican.org

JUKES, Mrs Maria Elisabeth. b 82. St Mellitus Coll 17. **d** 20 **p** 21. C Oadby *Leic* from 20. *31 Hill Field, Oadby, Leicester LE2 4RW* M: 07960-990319 E: maria.jukes@icloud.com

JUKES (née WEATHERHOGG), Mrs Susanne. b 56. Leeds Univ BA 77 Coll of Ripon & York St Jo PGCE 78. NEOC 98. **d** 01 **p** 02. C Monk Fryston and S Milford *York* 01–05; P-in-c 05–07; Assoc Min Aldborough w Boroughbridge and Roecliffe *Ripon* 07–09; Asst Dir of Ords 07–09; Chapl HM Pris Full Sutton 09–14; V Topcliffe, Baldersby w Dishforth, Dalton etc *York* 14–20; Chapl HM Pris Kirklevington Grange 14–20; rtd 20; PtO *York* 20; *Dur* from 21. *37 Pinfold Lane, Butterknowle, Bishop Auckland DL13 5NU* T: (01388) 710409 M: 07764-375430 E: susanne.jukes@gmail.com

JULIE, Mother. *See* WISEMAN, Julie

JUMP, Elizabeth Anne. b 63. Liv Inst of Educn BA 95. NOC 97. **d** 00 **p** 01. C Walkden and Lt Hulton *Man* 00–03; P-in-c Elton St Steph 03–05; C Ashton Ch Ch 05–06; PtO 06–07; TV Blackbourne *St E* 07–14; R Wroxham w Hoveton and Belaugh *Nor* 14–18; R Wroxham w Hoveton, Belaugh and Tunstead etc from 18. *The Vicarage, 11 Church Lane, Wroxham, Norwich NR12 8SH* T: (01603) 784150 E: rector@wroxhambenefice.org

JÚNIOR, Josias Pereira de Souza. *See* DE SOUZA, Josias Pereira

JUNIPER, Sandra Elizabeth. b 42. SWMTC. **d** 11 **p** 12. NSM Bideford, Northam, Westward Ho!, Appledore etc *Ex* 11–12; PtO from 12. *16 Link House, Nelson Road, Westward Ho!, Bideford EX39 1HS* T: (01237) 238769 E: san.juniper@outlook.com

JUPP, The Rt Revd Roger Alan. b 56. St Edm Hall Ox BA 78 MA 82 Surrey Univ PGCE 96. Chich Th Coll 79. **d** 80 **p** 81 **c** 03. C Newbold w Dunston *Derby* 80–83; C Cowley St Jo *Ox* 83–85; C Islington St Jas w St Phil *Lon* 85–86; V Lower Beeding *Chich* 86–90; Dom Chapl to Bp Horsham 86–91; V Burgess Hill St Jo 90–93; TR Burgess Hill St Jo w St Edw 93–94; PtO 97–98; C Aldwick 98–00; Prin Newton Th Coll Papua New Guinea 00–03; Bp Popondota 03–05; P-in-c St Leonards Ch Ch and St Mary *Chich* 05–06; R St Leonards Ch Ch and St Mary etc 06–12; Hon Asst Bp Chich 05–12; V Long Eaton St Laur *Derby* 12–18; P-in-c Ilkeston H Trin 12–18; rtd 18; PtO *Chich* 19. *1 Johns Road, Radcliffe-on-Trent, Nottingham NG12 2GW* T: 0115-933 1703 E: rajupp1@hotmail.com

JUPP, Vincent John. b 64. St Jo Coll Nottm BA(ThM) 06. **d** 00 **p** 01. C Evington *Leic* 00–03; TV Ascension TM 03–07; R 07–11; AD City of Leic 09–11; R Birstall and Wanlip 11–19; Dioc Transition Enabler 19–21; rtd 21. *Address temp unknown* E: vincejupp@btinternet.com

JUSTICE, Keith Leonard. b 42. Wolv Univ BSc 68 CEng 83 MIMechE 83. Wycliffe Hall Ox 91. **d** 93 **p** 94. C Penwortham St Mary *Blackb* 93–96; C Dovercourt and Parkeston w Harwich *Chelmsf* 96–98; V Wentworth *Sheff* 98–01; Chapl Rotherham Gen Hosps NHS Trust 98–01; Chapl Rotherham Priority Health Services NHS Trust 98–01; R Melrose *Edin* 01–04; P-in-c Royton St Anne *Man* 04–08; P-in-c Lawton Moor 08–13; rtd 13; PtO *Man* from 13; *Ches* from 16. *228A Wythenshawe Road, Manchester M23 0PH* T: 0161-215 1113 E: keithjustice123@gmail.com

JUSTICE, Simon Charles. b 66. Univ of Wales (Lamp) BD 88 Edin Univ MTh 90 Bexley Seabury Th Sem DMin 19. Cranmer Hall Dur 90. **d** 92 **p** 93. C Tilehurst St Mich *Ox* 92–95; R Troy St Paul USA 95–01; R Tigard St Jas 02–04; Can All SS Cathl Albany 98–04; R Edin Ch Ch 04–06; R Corvallis Gd Samaritan USA from 06. *445 NW Elizabeth Drive, Corvallis OR 97330, USA* T: (001) (541) 757 6647 E: simon.justice@gmail.com

JUTSUM, Linda Mary. *See* ELLIOTT, Linda Mary

K

KABOLEH, David Reardon. b 64. Westmr Coll Ox MTh 00. Trin Coll Nairobi 88. **d** 90 **p** 91. C-in-c Nairobi St Phil Kenya 90–92; TV Nairobi St Luke and Immanuel 93–95; NSM Hoddesdon *St Alb* 95–97; NSM Ox St Matt 97–99; NSM Blackbird Leys 99–02; NSM Ox St Aldate 03–04; NSM Akeman 04–07; P-in-c Worminghall w Ickford, Oakley and Shabbington 07–10; R from 10. *The Rectory, 32A The Avenue, Worminghall, Aylesbury HP18 9LE* T: (01844) 338839 E: kaboleh@btinternet.com

KACHIWANDA, Evans Esau. b 62. Univ of Malawi BA 97. Bp Patteson Th Coll (Solomon Is) 87 Virginia Th Sem MTh 04. **d** 89 **p** 91. Chapl to Bp S Malawi 91–92; Sch and Coll Chapl 92–93; Angl Progr Dir 97–98; Chapl and Teacher Malosa Sch 99–04; Headmaster 01–02; Prov Sec Cen Africa 04–05; Lect+Dean Studies Leonard Kamungu Th Coll 05–06; PtO *Blackb* 07–09; Malawi from 09. *All Saints' Church, PO 309, Ntcheu, Malawi* E: ekachiwanda@hotmail.com

KAGGWA, Nelson Sonny. b 58. E Lon Univ BA 91. Bp Tucker Coll Mukono 77. **d** 80 **p** 80. Kenya 80–83; USA 83; Hon C Ox SS Phil and Jas w St Marg 84–85; C W Ham *Chelmsf* 86–87; TV Walthamstow St Mary w St Steph 87–92; PtO *Sheff* 92–95; V Sheff St Paul 96–97; rtd 98. *Al-Salam, 36 Standish Gardens, Sheffield S5 8YD* T: 0114-273 1428 F: 273 1348 M: 07989-261278 E: kaggwanelsonibrahim@msn.com

KAKURU (née ASHBRIDGE), Mrs Clare Patricia Esther. b 80. QUB BTh 03 MTh 07. **d** 07 **p** 08. C Donaghcloney w Waringstown *D & D* 07–12; V Lurgan Ch the Redeemer 12–17; P-in-c Maghaberry from 17. *48 Birchdale, Lurgan, Craigavon BT66 7TR* T: (028) 3832 9420 E: weedoll@gmail.com *or* revclarekakuru@gmail.com

KALENIUK, Nicholas George. b 69. WEMTC. **d** 09 **p** 10. C Claines St Jo *Worc* 09–13; P-in-c Wollaston 13–17; P-in-c Stourbridge St Mich Norton 13–17; V Norton and Wollaston 17–21. *Address temp unknown*

KALSI, Mrs Gina Louise. b 68. Leeds Univ BA 09. NOC 06. d 09 p 10. C Netherthorpe St Steph *Sheff* 09–13; V Malin Bridge 13–20; P-in-c Wadsley 15–16; PtO from 20; Dioc Ecum Missr from 21. *61 Shirland Lane, Sheffield S9 3SQ* M: 07787-578721 E: ginalkalsi@hotmail.co.uk *or* gina.kalsi@sheffield.anglican.org

KAMBLE HANSELL, Anupama. *See* HANSELL, Anupama

KANAGARATNAM, Anjali Miriam. b 72. Birm Univ BA 94 PGCE 95. Trin Coll Bris 17. d 20 p 21. C By Brook *Bris* from 20. *7 Willis Close, Chippenham SN15 3GJ* T: (01249) 652237 E: anjalikanagaratnam@yahoo.co.uk

KANE, Peter David Colin. b 72. K Coll Lon BMus 92 Fitzw Coll Cam BA 05 MA 09 Chich Univ MA 13 ARCO 91 ARCM 94. Wycliffe Hall Ox BA 08. d 09 p 10. C Chich St Paul and Westhampnett 09–13; V Clacton St Jas *Chelmsf* 13–17; P-in-c Heene *Chich* from 18. *Heene Rectory, 4 Lansdowne Road, Worthing BN11 4LY* T: (01903) 339656 E: p.kane.03@cantabgold.net

KANERIA, Rajni. b 57. Bath Univ BPharm 82. Wycliffe Hall Ox 83. d 86 p 87. C Hyson Green *S'well* 86–87; C Hyson Green St Paul w St Steph 87–89; C Harold Hill St Geo *Chelmsf* 89–91; TV Oadby *Leic* 91–97; PtO from 15. *32 Rendall Road, Leicester LE4 6LE* T: 0116-266 6613 E: kanerias@ntlworld.com

KAOMA, Canon John Kafwanka. b 66. Trin Coll Melbourne BTh 97 Ridley Coll Melbourne MA 00. St Jo Sem Lusaka 90. d 93 p 94. C Chingola St Barn Zambia 93–94; PtO Melbourne Australia 94–00; Lect St Jo Coll Kitwe Zambia 00–03; Prin 01–03; Regional Manager (S Africa) CMS 03–06; PtO Lusaka Zambia 04–06; Research Officer Miss Dept Angl Communion Office 06–09; Dir for Miss 09–20; PtO *Lon* 06–12; Hon C Isleworth St Jo 12–14; PtO 15–17; Hon C Heston 17–21; V Whitton St Aug from 21; Hon Can Lusaka from 15. *St Augustine's Vicarage, Hospital Bridge Road, Twickenham TW2 6DE* T: (020) 8894 3764 E: vicarofstaugustinewhitton@aol.com

KARAMURA, Grace Patrick. b 62. Nat Teachers' Coll Uganda DipEd 89 Rob Coll Cam MPhil 95 Leeds Univ PhD 98. Bp Tucker Coll Mukono BD 92. d 92 p 93. C All SS Cathl Kampala Uganda 92–93; C Ebbw Vale *Mon* 98–01; TV 01–03; V Pontyclun w Talygarn *Llan* 03–14. *17 Muchelney Way, Yeovil BA21 3RB* T: (01935) 700371

KAROON, David. b 69. FRAS. Westcott Ho Cam 16. d 17 p 17. C Trumpington *Ely* 17–19; P-in-c W Norfolk Priory Gp 19–21; R from 21. *The Rectory, Church Road, Wimbotsham, King's Lynn PE34 3QG* M: 07596-707469 E: davidshirley@hotmail.com

KASHOURIS, Peter Zacharias. b 66. Peterho Cam BA 89 MA 93. St Steph Ho Ox 92. d 94 p 95. C Hampstead St Jo *Lon* 94–97; R Hartlepool St Hilda *Dur* 97–03; P-in-c Dur St Oswald 03–06; P-in-c Dur St Oswald and Shincliffe from 06; Dioc Ecum Officer 03–09; Chapl St Mary's Coll Dur from 15. *St Oswald's Vicarage, Church Street, Durham DH1 3DG* T: 0191-374 1681 *or* 383 0830 E: pzkashouris@gmail.com

KASIBANTE, Amos Sebadduka. b 54. Trin Coll Cam BA 83 MA 87 Yale Univ STM 89. Bp Tucker Coll Mukono 76. d 79 p 80. C Lyantonde Uganda 79–80; Tutor Bp Tucker Coll Mukono 83–92; Tutor Coll of Ascension Selly Oak 92–95; Prin Simon of Cyrene Th Inst 95–97; Vice Prin St Mich Coll Llan 97–02; Chapl Leic Univ and Co-ord Reader Tr Leic 02–09; P-in-c Burmantofts St Steph and St Agnes *Ripon* 10–14; *Leeds* 14–16; P-in-c Leeds St Cypr Harehills 10–16; V Burmantofts and Harehills from 16; Racial Justice Officer *Ripon* 12–14; *Leeds* from 14. *St Agnes' Vicarage, 21 Shakespeare Close, Leeds LS9 7UQ* T: 0113-248 2648 M: 07990-938122 E: amos.kasibante@virgin.net

KASIBANTE, Sonia Ann. b 69. Open Univ BSc 08. Yorks Min Course BA 16. d 16 p 17. C Gipton and Oakwood *Leeds* 16–20; Chapl Leeds Teaching Hosps NHS Trust from 20. *St Agnes' Vicarage, 21 Shakespeare Close, Leeds LS9 7UQ* T: 0113-248 2648 M: 07506-778171 E: sonia.kasibante@yahoo.co.uk

KASSELL, Colin George Henry. b 42. Ripon Coll Cuddesdon 76. d 68 p 69. In RC Ch 69–75; PtO *Ox* 76–77; C Denham 77–80; V Brotherton *Wakef* 80–84; Chapl and Past Ldr St Cath Hospice Crawley 84–91; R Rogate w Terwick and Trotton w Chithurst *Chich* 91–94; C Heene 94–06; Chapl Worthing Hosp 94–07; rtd 07; P-in-c Worthing St Andr *Chich* 06–15; RD Worthing 10–16; PtO 16–17. *6 Benedict Close, Worthing BN11 2NZ* M: 07802-259310 E: c.kassell@virginmedia.com

KATE, Sister. *See* BURGESS, Kate Lamorna

KAUNHOVEN, Canon Anthony Peter. b 55. Leeds Univ BA 78 Coll of Ripon & York St Jo PGCE 79. Edin Th Coll 79. d 81 p 82. C Leeds St Aid *Ripon* 81–84; C Hawksworth Wood 84–89; V Upper Nidderdale 89–91; Hon C Rawdon *Bradf* 96–99; P-in-c Old Brampton *Derby* 99–07; P-in-c Gt Barlow 04–07; P-in-c Bakewell 07–11; C Ashford w Sheldon

and Longstone 07–11; P-in-c Rowsley 07–11; V Bakewell, Ashford w Sheldon and Rowsley from 11; RD Bakewell and Eyam 12–15; Dioc Ecum Officer from 01; AD Peak from 21; Hon Can Derby Cathl from 11. *The Vicarage, South Church Street, Bakewell DE45 1FD* T: (01629) 814462 E: jazzyrector@aol.com

KAUTZER, Benjamin Allen. b 85. Pt Loma Nazarene Univ (USA) BA 07 Nottm Univ MA 08 St Jo Coll Dur PhD 15. Ripon Coll Cuddesdon 13. d 15 p 16. C Earley St Nic *Ox* 15–19; R Oakley w Wootton St Lawrence *Win* from 19. *9 The Drive, Oakley, Basingstoke RG23 7DA* T: (01256) 420903 M: 07787-838384 E: ben@oww.church

KAVANAGH, The Ven Michael Lowther. b 58. York Univ BA 80 Newc Univ MSc 82 Leeds Univ BA 86 MBPsS 90. Coll of Resurr Mirfield 84. d 87 p 88. C Boston Spa *York* 87–91; C Clifford 89–91; Chapl Martin House Hospice for Children Boston Spa 87–91; V Beverley St Nic *York* 91–97; RD Beverley 95–97; Abp's Dom Chapl and Dioc Dir of Ords 97–05; Chapl HM Pris Full Sutton 05–08; Angl Adv HM Pris Service 08–12; Hd Chapl and Faith Services 12–18; Chapl Gen of Pris and Adn to HM Pris 13–18; rtd 18; NSM Garrowby Hill *York* from 19; Can Th Liv Cathl from 09. *The Rectory, Worsendale Road, Bishop Wilton, York YO42 1ST* T: (01759) 369974 M: 07828-849823 E: mikekavanagh@hotmail.co.uk

KAY, Alasdair Stewart. b 61. St Jo Coll Nottm MA 15. d 14 p 15. NSM Walbrook Epiphany *Derby* 14–15; C Mackworth St Fran 15–18; P-in-c 18–19; R Wyke Regis *Sarum* from 19. *The Rectory, 1 Portland Road, Weymouth DT4 9ES* T: (01305) 784649 M: 07885-858709 E: revaskay@gmail.com

KAY, Audrey Elizabeth. *See* HOLGATE, Audrey Elizabeth

KAY, Clifford. b 60. Leeds Metrop Univ BA 94 Ban Univ MA 09. Ridley Hall Cam 10. d 12 p 13. C Warley *Wakef* 12–14; *Leeds* 14–15; C Halifax St Hilda *Wakef* 12–14; *Leeds* 14–15; V Belton Gp *Linc* from 15; RD Is of Axholme from 17. *All Saints Rectory, 118 High Street, Belton DN19 1NS* E: cliffkay1@gmail.com *or* cliff.kay@cantab.net

KAY, Dennis. b 57. St As Minl Tr Course 96. d 99 p 00. NSM Llangystennin *St As* 99–01; NSM Colwyn Bay w Brynymaen 01–03; NSM Petryal 03–07. *41 Ffordd Ffynnon, Rhuddlan, Rhyl LL18 2SP* M: 07748-312067

KAY, Marjory Marianne Kate. b 61. d 97. NSM Godshill *Portsm* 97–05; NSM Askerswell, Loders, Powerstock and Symondsbury *Sarum* 06–14; PtO from 18. *Court Lodge, Chardstock, Axminster EX13 7BW*

KAY, Peter Richard. b 72. St Cath Coll Cam BA 93 MA 00 PGCE 95. Trin Coll Bris 09. d 11 p 12. C Letchworth St Paul w Willian *St Alb* 11–14; P-in-c Milton Ernest, Pavenham and Thurleigh from 14. *The Vicarage, Thurleigh Road, Milton Earnest, Bedford MK44 1RF* M: 07718-201449 E: rev.peter.kay@outlook.com

KAYE, Canon Alistair Geoffrey. b 62. Reading Univ BSc 85. St Jo Coll Nottm 87. d 90 p 91. C Gt Horton *Bradf* 90–94; C Rushden w Newton Bromswold *Pet* 94–98; V Upper Armley *Ripon* 98–08; Armley Deanery Missr 08–13; AD Armley 05–08; P-in-c Beeston Hill and Hunslet Moor 13–14; Hon Can Ripon Cathl *Leeds* from 13. *St Luke's Vicarage, Malvern View, Leeds LS11 8SG* M: 07881-804104

KAYE, Canon Gerald Trevor. b 32. Man Univ BSc 54. Oak Hill Th Coll. d 56 p 57. C Widnes St Ambrose *Liv* 56–58; C St Helens St Mark 58–62; V Brixton Hill St Sav *S'wark* 62–65; Canada 65–85; Hon Can Keewatin 70–75; Adn Patricia 75–78; V Slough *Ox* 85–97; rtd 97; LtO *Arg* from 08. *Craiguanach, Torlundy, Fort William PH33 6SW* T: (01397) 705395 E: eleanorado@aol.com

KAYE, Peter Alan. b 47. K Coll Lon BD 71 AKC 71 Leic Univ MA 82 CQSW 82. St Aug Coll Cant 71. d 72 p 73. C Fulham All SS *Lon* 72–74; Chapl Rubery Hill, Jo Conolly and Jos Sheldon Hosps Birm 74–80; Hon C Northfield *Birm* 80–83; PtO 99–06; P-in-c Stirchley 06–12; rtd 12; PtO *Birm* 12–15; *Ban* from 12. *Gwrtheyrn, Morfa Bychan, Porthmadog LL49 9YD* T: (01766) 514666 E: peterakaye@gmail.com

KAYE, Simon Keith. b 66. Ridley Hall Cam 11. d 13 p 14. C Eye and Newborough *Pet* 13–14; C Eye, Newborough and Thorney 14–17; V Pet Ch Carpenter from 17. *The Vicarage, 93A Chestnut Avenue, Peterborough PE1 4PE* E: simonkaye748@gmail.com

KAYE, Stephen Michael. b 72. Trin Coll Bris 06. d 08 p 09. C Calverley *Bradf* 08–12; C Washburn and Mid-Wharfe 12–13; C Abbeylands *Ripon* 13–14; *Leeds* 14–18; TV from 18. *St Mary's Vicarage, 50 Cragside Walk, Leeds LS5 3QE* M: 07375-125348 E: revstephenkaye@gmail.com

KAYE, Timothy Henry. b 52. Linc Th Coll 77. d 80 p 81. C Warsop *S'well* 80–83; C Far Headingley St Chad *Ripon* 83–86; P-in-c Birkby *Wakef* 86; TV N Huddersfield 86–91; R Stone St Mich w Aston St Sav *Lich* 91–95; V S Kirkby *Wakef* 95–14; *Leeds* 14–18; rtd 18; PtO *Blackb* 18–20; Hon C Burnley

St Andr w St Marg and St Jas 20–21. *87 Marsden Hall Road North, Nelson BB9 8JH* E: kayetimothy62@gmail.com

KAYLA, Ms Giyanow Sophia. b 62. St Jo Coll Nottm 13. **d** 15 **p** 16. NSM Aston and Nechells *Birm* from 15. *11 Tansley Road, Birmingham B44 0DN* T: 0121-384 1795 M: 07944-365778 E: giyanow@yahoo.co.uk

KAZICH, Ms Anne. b 69. Cranmer Hall Dur 12. **d** 14 **p** 15. C Tanhouse The Oaks CD *Liv* 14–18; NSM Skelmersdale St Paul from 18. *63 Enstone, Skelmersdale WN8 6AW* M: 07935-320832 E: revannekazich@gmail.com

KAZIRO, Godfrey Sam. b 48. BDSc Lon Univ MSc FDSRCPSGlas FFDRCSI. **d** 02 **p** 03. OLM Waterloo St Jo w St Andr *S'wark* 02–12; NSM from 12; PtO *Lon* from 09. *19 Hampshire Road, Hornchurch RM11 3EU* T: (01708) 441609 M: 07845-281593 E: godfrey_kaziro@yahoo.co.uk

KEAL, Barry Clifford. b 57. Leeds Univ BA 06. NOC 03. **d** 06 **p** 07. NSM Halsall, Lydiate and Downholland *Liv* 06–11. *46 Eastway, Liverpool L31 6BS* T: 0151-526 4508 E: barry@keal.me.uk

KEAN, Robert John. b 64. St Mellitus Coll BA 11. **d** 11 **p** 12. C Black Notley *Chelmsf* 11–14; P-in-c Fairstead w Terling and White Notley etc 14; TV Witham and Villages 14–17; Chapl Algarve *Eur* from 17. *Casa do Jardim, rua José de Conceição Conde, 8600-169 Luz (Lagos), Portugal* T: (00351) (282) 789660 E: revrobkean@gmail.com

KEANE, Christian John. b 74. Rob Coll Cam BA 95 MA 99. Wycliffe Hall Ox BA 06 MA 06. **d** 06 **p** 07. C Eastrop *Win* 06–11; C Ex St Leon w H Trin from 11. *St Leonard's Church, Topsham Road, Exeter EX2 4NG* T: (01392) 286995 E: chris.keane@stleonards.church

KEAR, Mrs Cara Lindsay. b 70. St Mellitus Coll BA 19. **d** 19 **p** 20. C Twickenham Common H Trin *Lon* from 19. *404 Chertsey Road, Twickenham TW2 6LP* M: 07704-889852 E: carakear@gmail.com

KEARLEY-HEYWOOD, Deiniol John Owen. b 73. K Coll Lon BA 95 Peterho Cam MPhil 03. Westcott Ho Cam 02. **d** 04 **p** 05. C Paddington St Jo w St Mich *Lon* 04–08; R Prestwood and Gt Hampden *Ox* from 08; AD Wendover from 16. *The Rectory, 140 Wycombe Road, Prestwood, Great Missenden HP16 0HJ* T: (01494) 866530 E: rector@htprestwood.org.uk

KEARNEY, Mrs Sandra. b 55. Bolton Inst of HE BSc 89 Univ Coll Ches BTh 04. NOC 01. **d** 04 **p** 05. C Blackpool Ch Ch w All SS *Blackb* 04–08; R Ordsall and Salford Quays *Man* 18–21; rtd 21. *59 Dove Lane, Darwen BB3 1EA* E: rev.sandra@sky.com

KEARNS, Andrew Philip. b 76. Wycliffe Hall Ox. **d** 09 **p** 10. C Maidenhead St Andr and St Mary *Ox* 09–15; PtO from 18. *5 Walden Avenue, Arborfield, Reading RG2 9HR* E: andrewpkearns@gmail.com

✠**KEARON, The Rt Revd Kenneth Arthur.** b 53. TCD BA 76 MA 79 MPhil 91. CITC 78. **d** 81 **p** 82 **c** 15. C Raheny w Coolock *D & G* 81–84; Lect TCD 82–90; Dean of Res TCD 84–90; I Tullow *D & G* 91–99; Can Ch Ch Cathl Dublin 95–15; Dir Irish Sch Ecum 99–05; Sec Gen Angl Communion Office 05–15; Hon Prov Can Cant Cathl 06–15; Bp L & K 15–21; rtd 21. *1 Priory Gate, Delgany, Co Wicklow, A63 AX56, Republic of Ireland* E: kkearon@gmail.com

KEARTON, Canon Janet Elizabeth. b 54. Univ Coll Lon BSc 78 Birkbeck Coll Lon MSc 81. NEOC 01. **d** 04 **p** 05. C Richmond w Hudswell and Downholme and Marske *Ripon* 04–08; V Hipswell 08–13; Can Res Carl Cathl 13–20; rtd 20. *Bowes Garth, Carperby, Leyburn DL8 4DJ* M: 07816-278267

KEAST, William. b 43. Univ Coll Ox BA 65 DipEd 66. **d** 88 **p** 89. OLM Scotton w Northorpe *Linc* 88–16; OLM Messingham w E Butterwick, Scotter w E Ferry and Scotton w Northorpe from 16. *4 Crapple Lane, Scotton, Gainsborough DN21 3QT* T: (01724) 763190 E: wkeast@hotmail.com

KEATES, Stephanie Louise. b 87. Univ of Wales (Newport) BA 08. Coll of Resurr Mirfield BA 17 MA 18. **d** 18 **p** 19. C Newc St Geo and St Hilda from 18. *Close House, St George's Close, Newcastle upon Tyne NE2 2TF* T: 0191-281 5018 E: revdskeates@gmail.com

KEATES, Thomas Frederick. b 45. Southn Univ BSc 96. WEMTC 09. **d** 12 **p** 13. NSM Thornbury and Oldbury-on-Severn w Shepperdine *Glouc* 12–17; PtO from 17. *80 Knapp Road, Thornbury, Bristol BS35 2HJ* T: (01454) 885058 M: 07905-834870 E: tomkeates@blueyonder.co.uk

KEATING, Mrs Ann Barbara. b 53. Open Univ BA 85. STETS 06. **d** 09 **p** 10. NSM Fisherton Anger *Sarum* 09–11; NSM Avon River 11–13; Asst Chapl Win Univ 12–13; R N Bradford on Avon and Villages *Sarum* from 13; Chapl Wilts Constabulary *Bris* from 16. *The Rectory, 6 Milbourn Close, Winsley, Bradford-on-Avon BA15 2NN* T: (01225) 722230 M: 07702-020733 E: rev.ann.keating@btinternet.com

KEATING, Christopher Robin. b 39. K Coll Lon BD AKC 84. Sarum Th Coll 62. **d** 65 **p** 66. C Baildon *Bradf* 65–67; CF 67–72; V Thornton Heath St Paul *Cant* 72–79; C Harold

Hill St Geo *Chelmsf* 85–89; V Goodmayes All SS 89–07; rtd 07; PtO *York* 09–20; Newc from 19. *Brigwood, Highford Lane, Hexham NE46 2DD* T: (01434) 605793

KEATING, Geoffrey John. b 52. Open Univ BA 94. St Steph Ho Ox 81. **d** 84 **p** 85. C Lancaster Ch Ch w St Jo and St Anne *Blackb* 84–85; C Rotherham *Sheff* 85–87; V Bentley 87–91; V Penponds *Truro* 91–96; V Pet St Jude 96–19; rtd 19; PtO *Ely* from 20. *47 Borthwick Park, Orton Wistow, Peterborough PE2 6YY* E: geoffrey.keating@btinternet.com

KEATING, Mrs Valerie. b 54. Leeds Metrop Univ BSc 87 Huddersfield Univ MEd 92 CertEd 89 FHEA 06. Yorks Min Course 12. **d** 14 **p** 15. NSM Batley All SS and Purlwell *Leeds* 14–16; NSM Batley 16–17; P-in-c Lepton 17–18; P-in-c Emley 17–18; P-in-c Flockton cum Denby Grange 17–18; R Lepton, Emley and Flockton w Denby Grange from 18. *138 Wakefield Road, Lepton, Huddersfield HD8 0LU* T: (01484) 606126 M: 07505-134105 E: valkeating@sky.com

KEAY, Charles Edward. b 70. Glos Univ BA 94. St Steph Ho Ox 01. **d** 03 **p** 04. C Havant *Portsm* 03–07; P-in-c Alford w Rigsby *Linc* 07–11; TV Portsea N and St Mark *Portsm* 11–15; TV Ex St Thos and Em 15–20. *Address temp unknown* M: 07948-600619 E: fathercharles04@gmail.com

KEAY (née Dudley), Mrs Wendy Elizabeth. b 46. City of Sheff Coll CertEd 68. Cranmer Hall Dur 79. dss 81 **d** 87 **p** 94. Cumnor *Ox* 81–89; Par Dn 87–89; Par Dn Hodge Hill *Birm* 89–94; C 94–95; TV 95–98; TV Bucknall *Lich* 98–06; rtd 06; PtO *Lich* 08–21. *26 Swallow Croft, Lichfield WS13 7HF* T: (01543) 306509

KEDDIE, Canon Tony. b 37. Qu Coll Birm 63. **d** 66 **p** 67. C Barnoldswick w Bracewell *Bradf* 66–69; C New Bentley *Sheff* 69–71; TV Seacroft *Ripon* 71–79; V Kippax 79–84; TR Kippax w Allerton Bywater 84–92; R Fountains Gp 92–02; Hon Can Ripon Cathl 94–02; rtd 02; PtO *Ripon* 02–14; *Bradf* 03–14; Leeds from 14. *4A Stone Acre Heights, Meltham, Holmfirth HD9 4EF* E: tbmk@metronet.co.uk

KEDDILTY, Matthew Paul. b 79. St Jo Coll Nottm 12. **d** 14 **p** 15. C Ulverston St Mary w H Trin *Carl* 14–17; V Bishop Auckland *Dur* from 17. *The Vicarage, 4 Conway Grove, Bishop Auckland DL14 6AF* M: 07872-620605 E: matthew.keddilty@hotmail.com

KEEBLE, Annette Thelma. b 54. St Mellitus Coll 16. **d** 18 **p** 19. OLM Tye Green w Netteswell *Chelmsf* 18–21; NSM Harlow Town Cen w Lt Parndon from 21. *54 Sharpecroft, Harlow CM19 4AB* T: (01279) 428478 M: 07740-701798 E: annekensophie@gmail.com

KEEBLE, Philip Wade. b 47. St Seiriol Cen 09. **d** 13. Min Can Ban Cathl 13–14. *12 Glassfordd, Marianglas, Anglesey LL73 8PB* T/F: (01248) 853802 M: 07944-671444 E: keeblephil@gmail.com

KEECH, April Irene. b 52. Penn State Univ BA 76. Trin Coll Bris BA 89. **d** 89 **p** 92. C Walthamstow St Luke *Chelmsf* 89–92; USA 92–95; V Deptford St Jo w H Trin *S'wark* 95–02; Asst Dioc Dir of Ords 96–00; Hon Can S'wark Cathl 99–02; V Hoxton St Jo w Ch Ch *Lon* 02–10; Chapl St Mary Magd Academy Lon from 10; PtO *Lon* 10–15; NSM Old Ford St Paul and St Mark from 15. *13 Regents Wharf, Wharf Place, London E2 9BD* T: (020) 7739 7621 *or* 7697 0123 E: april.keech@smmacademy.org *or* april.keech@btinternet.com

KEECH, Dominic. b 83. Keble Coll Ox BA 05 MA 14 MSt 06 DPhil 10. St Steph Ho Ox 10. **d** 12 **p** 13. C Wantage *Ox* 12–14; Chapl BNC Ox from 14; C Ox St Mary Magd 14–16; LtO 16–17; V Brighton St Nic *Chich* from 17. *2 Windlesham Road, Brighton BN1 3AG* M: 07920-761546

KEEGAN, Frances Ann (Sister Isabel). b 44. Open Univ BA 11 Sarum Coll MA 16 SEN 74. Franciscan Study Cen 87. **d** 99 **p** 00. NSM Sherborne w Castleton and Lillington *Sarum* 99–01; NSM Golden Cap Team 01–08; NSM Crosslacon *Carl* 08–11; P-in-c Brigham, Gt Broughton and Broughton Moor 11–12; rtd 12; PtO *Truro* 13–14; *Sarum* 14–18; P-in-c Kilcolman w Kiltallagh, Killorglin, Knockane etc *L & K* from 18. *Seaview House, Gurrane West, Sunhill, Killorglin, Co Kerry, V93 T2C1, Republic of Ireland* T: (00353) (66) 979 0359 E: revik@hotmail.co.uk

KEEGAN, Graham Brownell. b 40. Nottm Univ CertEd 68. NOC 81. **d** 84 **p** 85. C Highfield *Liv* 84–87; V Ince St Mary 87–95; V Newton in Makerfield St Pet 95–05; rtd 05; PtO *Liv* from 16. *5 Scott Road, Lowton, Warrington WA3 2HD* T: (01942) 713809

KEELER, Alan. b 58. City Univ BSc 81. St Jo Coll Nottm MA 01. **d** 90 **p** 91. C Paddock Wood *Roch* 90–94; V Blendon 94–06; V Plaistow St Mary from 06; AD Bromley 15–21. *St Mary's Vicarage, 74 London Lane, Bromley BR1 4HE* T: (020) 8460 1827 E: agkeeler@tiscali.co.uk

KEELING, Peter Frank. b 34. Kelham Th Coll. **d** 58 **p** 59. C S Elmsall *Wakef* 58–63; C Barnsley St Mary 63–67; V Ravensthorpe 67–73; V Cudworth 73–83; R Downham

438

Market w Bexwell *Ely* 83–00; RD Fincham 83–94; V Crimplesham w Stradsett 85–00; rtd 00; P-in-c Hempton and Pudding Norton *Nor* 00–04; PtO from 04. *23 Cleaves Drive, Walsingham NR22 6EQ* T: (01328) 820310

KEEN, David Mark. b 69. Oriel Coll Ox BA 91. St Jo Coll Nottm BTh 96 MPhil 98. **d** 98 **p** 99. C Yeovil w Kingston Pitney *B & W* 98–02; C Haughton le Skerne *Dur* 02–06; C Preston Plucknett *B & W* 06–17; V from 17. *3 Poplar Drive, Yeovil BA21 3UL* T: (01935) 422286 E: revdmkeen@btinternet.com

KEEN, Michael Spencer. b 41. St Pet Coll Ox BA 68 MA 72 GRSM 62 ARCM Reading Univ CertEd. Westcott Ho Cam 68. **d** 73 **p** 74. NSM W Derby St Jo *Liv* 73–74; NSM Stanley 74–76; Chs Youth and Community Officer Telford *Lich* 77–82; Dioc Unemployment Officer *Sheff* 82–89; NSM Brixton Road Ch Ch *S'wark* 89–92; Employment Development Officer 89–92; PtO 92–99; NSM Camberwell St Giles w St Matt 99–01. *40 Sheppard's College, London Road, Bromley BR1 1PF* T: (020) 8313 0490 E: keen3045@gmail.com

KEEN, Ms Miriam Frances. b 65. Ex Univ BSc 87 Glos Univ MA 10 Westmr Coll of Educn PGCE 88. Wycliffe Hall Ox 04. **d** 05 **p** 06. C Cogges and S Leigh *Ox* 05–14; C N Leigh 13–14; TV Marlborough *Sarum* 14–18; R W Downland *Ox* from 18. *West Downland Rectory, Main Street, Chaddleworth, Newbury RG20 7EW* M: 07954-117093 E: miri.westdownland@gmail.com

KEENE, Canon David Peter. b 32. Trin Hall Cam BA 56 MA 60. Westcott Ho Cam. **d** 58 **p** 59. C Radcliffe-on-Trent *S'well* 58–61; C Mansfield SS Pet and Paul 61–64; V Nottingham St Cath 64–71; R Bingham 71–81; Chapl RAF 72–76; Dioc Dir of Ords *S'well* 81–90; Can Res *S'well* Minster 81–97; rtd 97; PtO *S'well* from 02. *Averham Cottage, Church Lane, Averham, Newark NG23 5RB* T: (01636) 708601

KEENE, Edward John Gerald. b 86. Nottm Univ BA 08. Wycliffe Hall Ox 17. **d** 20 **p** 21. C Lt Shelford *Ely* from 20. *All Saints' Church, Church Street, Little Shelford, Cambridge CB2 5HG* T: (01223) 847815 M: 07804-506984 E: ekeene1286@hotmail.com

KEENE, Mrs Muriel Ada. b 35. dss 83 **d** 87 **p** 94. Dioc Lay Min Adv *S'well* 87–88; Asst Dir of Ords 88–90; Dn-in-c Oxton 90–93; Dn-in-c Epperstone 90–94; Dn-in-c Gonalston 90–94; NSM Lowdham w Caythorpe, and Gunthorpe 94–00; rtd 95; PtO *S'well* from 05. *Averham Cottage, Church Lane, Averham, Newark NG23 5RB* T: (01636) 708601

KEEP, Andrew James. b 55. Collingwood Coll Dur BA 77 Yale Univ STM 84 K Coll Lon MA 14. Sarum & Wells Th Coll 78. **d** 80 **p** 81. C Banstead *Guildf* 80–83; Chapl Qu Eliz Hosp Banstead 80–83; USA 83–84; Chapl Cranleigh Sch Surrey 84–98; Chapl Wells Cathl Sch 98–06; PV Wells Cathl *B & W* 01–06; Chapl Mill Hill Sch Lon 07–10; PtO *Lon* 10–14; NSM St Marg Pattens from 14. *193 Foundling Court, Brunswick Centre, London WC1N 1QF* T: (020) 7837 5327 M: 07740-647813 E: andrew.keep@me.com *or* vicar@stmargaretpattens.org

KEEP, Hugh Charles John Martin. b 45. Qu Coll Birm 90. **d** 92 **p** 93. C Aston Cantlow and Wilmcote w Billesley *Cov* 92–95; P-in-c Hampton Lucy w Charlecote and Loxley 95–02; Chapl Rainsbrook Secure Tr Cen 02–05; rtd 05; PtO *Cov* from 05. *4 Old Town, Stratford-upon-Avon CV37 6BG* T: (01789) 414142 E: hrkeepnet@aol.com

KEETON, Barry. b 40. Dur Univ BA 61 MA 69 MLitt 78 K Coll Lon BD 63 AKC 63. **d** 64 **p** 65. C S Bank *York* 64–67; C Middlesbrough St Cuth 67–69; C Kingston upon Hull St Alb 70–71; V Appleton-le-Street w Amotherby 71–74; Dioc Ecum Adv 74–81; R Ampleforth w Oswaldkirk 74–78; V Howden 78–79; P-in-c Barmby on the Marsh 78–79; P-in-c Laxton w Blacktoft 78–79; P-in-c Wressell 78–79; TR Howden 80–91; Can and Preb York Minster 85–91; RD Howden 86–91; TR Lewes All SS, St Anne, St Mich and St Thos *Chich* 91–96; R Cov St Jo 96–01; RD Cov N 97–01; rtd 01; PtO *Sheff* 01–19; *York* 05–10. *19 Shardlow Gardens, Bessacarr, Doncaster DN4 6UB* T: (01302) 532045 E: barrykeeton116@outlook.com

KEFFORD, Canon Peter Charles. b 44. Nottm Univ BTh 74. Linc Th Coll 70. **d** 74 **p** 75. C W Wimbledon Ch Ch *S'wark* 74–77; C All Hallows by the Tower etc *Lon* 77–81; C-in-c Pound Hill CD *Chich* 81; TV Worth 82–83; TR 83–92; R Henfield w Shermanbury and Woodmancote 92–01; Can Res and Treas Chich Cathl 01–09; Adv for Ord Min and Dioc Dir of Ords 01–06; Dioc Adv for Min 07–09; rtd 09; PtO *Derby* 10–21. *17 North Close, Mickleover, Derby DE3 9JA* T: (01332) 549534 E: peter_kefford@hotmail.com

KEGG, Mrs Georgina. b 47. Oak Hill Th Coll BA 99. EAMTC 02. **d** 05 **p** 06. NSM Mattishall and the Tudd Valley *Nor* 05–11; NSM Moulton *Ches* 12–16; rtd 16; PtO *Ches* from 16. *Old Post Office, Shutley Lane,*

Little Leigh, Northwich CW8 4RP T: (01606) 892667 E: georgina.kegg@btinternet.com

KEGG, Gordon Rutherford. b 45. Reading Univ BSc 66 Imp Coll Lon PhD 71 Lon Univ CertEd 74. Oak Hill Th Coll 88. **d** 90 **p** 91. C Luton Lewsey St Hugh *St Alb* 90–94; TV Hemel Hempstead 94–01; P-in-c Mattishall w Mattishall Burgh, Welborne etc *Nor* 01–08; P-in-c Hockering, Honingham, E and N Tuddenham 04–08; R Mattishall and the Tudd Valley 08–11; rtd 11; P-in-c Moulton *Ches* 11–16. *Old Post Office, Shutley Lane, Little Leigh, Northwich CW8 4RP* T: (01606) 892667 E: gordon.kegg@btinternet.com

KEIGHLEY, Mrs Amanda Jane. b 56. Garnett Coll Lon CertEd 85 Leeds Univ MA 98. Cranmer Hall Dur 04. **d** 07 **p** 08. NSM Is of Dogs Ch Ch and St Jo w St Luke *Lon* 07–12; P-in-c Elm Park St Nic Hornchurch *Chelmsf* 12–13; V from 13. *The Vicarage, 17 St Nicholas Avenue, Hornchurch RM12 4PT* T: (01708) 474639 M: 07889-486354 E: akeighley@clara.co.uk

KEIGHLEY, Andrew Kenneth. b 62. Nottm Univ LLB 84 Solicitor 85. Wycliffe Hall Ox 94. **d** 97 **p** 98. C Westminster St Jas the Less *Lon* 97–00; NSM 00–04; C Brompton H Trin w Onslow Square St Paul 04–06; P-in-c W Hampstead Trin 06–09; V from 09. *10 Lisburne Road, London NW3 2NR* M: 07747-611577

KEIGHLEY, David John. b 48. Open Univ BA 88 CertEd. Sarum & Wells Th Coll 82. **d** 83 **p** 84. C Sawbridgeworth *St Alb* 83–86; TV Saltash *Truro* 86–89; V Lanlivery w Luxulyan 89–00; P-in-c The Candover Valley *Win* 00–08; P-in-c Wield 03–08; P-in-c Hurstbourne Tarrant, Faccombe, Vernham Dean etc 08–16; rtd 16. *Drokensford, Chapel Road, Meonstoke, Southampton SO32 3NJ* T: (01489) 877983 M: 07736-799262 E: davidkeighley@hotmail.com

KEIGHLEY, Martin Philip. b 61. Edin Univ MA 83. Westcott Ho Cam 86. **d** 88 **p** 89. C Lytham St Cuth *Blackb* 88–91; C Lancaster St Mary 91–93; R Halton w Aughton 93–00; V Poulton-le-Fylde 00–04; V Poulton Carleton and Singleton from 04; AD Poulton from 08. *The Vicarage, 7 Vicarage Road, Poulton-le-Fylde FY6 7BE* T: (01253) 883086 E: martinkeigh@btconnect.com

KEIGHLEY, Thomas Christopher. b 51. Open Univ BA 85 K Coll Lon PhD 15. NEOC 00. **d** 03 **p** 04. NSM Upper Nidderdale *Ripon* 03–06; NSM Dacre w Hartwith and Darley w Thornthwaite 06–07; NSM Is of Dogs Ch Ch and St Jo w St Luke *Lon* 07–12; Chapl St Joseph's Hospice Hackney 09–10; NSM Elm Park St Nic Hornchurch *Chelmsf* from 12; Dean SSM Stepney Area *Lon* 09–12; Dean SSM Barking Area from 15. *The Vicarage, 17 St Nicholas Avenue, Hornchurch RM12 4PT* T: (01708) 474639 M: 07889-486354 E: nurprc@nursing.u-net.com

KEILLER, Canon Jane Elizabeth. b 52. Westmr Coll Ox BEd 74. Cranmer Hall Dur 76. dss 80 **d** 87 **p** 94. Cambridge H Trin w St Andr Gt *Ely* 80–86; NSM Cambridge St Barn 86–88 and 90–94; NSM Cambridge H Cross 95–02; Chapl and Tutor Ridley Hall Cam 96–14; Hon Can Ely Cathl from 05; Bp's Adv for Spirituality from 14; PtO from 16. *68 Pierce Lane, Cambridge CB21 5DL* T: (01223) 575776 E: jane.keiller@gmail.com

KEIR, Mrs Gillian Irene. b 44. Westf Coll Lon BA 66 Somerville Coll Ox BLitt 70 Lon Univ MA 95. SAOMC 95. **d** 98 **p** 99. NSM St Alb St Steph 98–08; PtO from 08; NSM Officer St Alb Adnry 06–14. *17 Battlefield Road, St Albans AL1 4DA* T: (01727) 854885 E: gillikeir@gmail.com

KEIRLE, The Very Revd Michael Robert. b 62. Trin Coll Bris BA 89. **d** 89 **p** 90. C Orpington Ch Ch *Roch* 89–92; Zimbabwe 92–95; R Keston *Roch* 95–03; R Guernsey St Martin *Win* 03–17; Vice-Dean Guernsey 13–17; R Jersey St Helier from 17; Dean Jersey from 17. *The Deanery, David Place, Jersey JE2 4TE* T: (01534) 720001 E: dean@jerseydeanery.je

KEITH, Elisabeth Grace. b 77. Sheff Univ BA 02 York St Jo Univ MA 09. Cranmer Hall Dur 13. **d** 16 **p** 17. C Sheff Cathl 16–19; C Ecclesall 19–21; C Sheff St Mark Broomhill from 21. *9 Betjeman Gardens, Sheffield S10 3FW* M: 07904-979713 E: beth.keith@sheffield.anglican.org

KEITH, John. b 25. LRAM 50 LGSM 50 AGSM 51. Cuddesdon Coll 60. **d** 62 **p** 63. C Lee-on-the-Solent *Portsm* 62–65; C Raynes Park St Sav *S'wark* 65–68; rtd 90. *7 Torr An Eas, Glenfinnan PH37 4LS* T: (01397) 722314

KELHAM, Canon Adèle Mary. b 46. St Andr Univ BSc 69. Cranmer Hall Dur 98. **d** 98 **p** 99. Asst Chapl Zürich *Eur* 98–01; P-in-c Bishop Middleham *Dur* 01–05; AD Sedgefield 03–05; P-in-c Lausanne *Eur* 05–13; P-in-c Lausanne w Neuchâtel 13–16; Dioc Adv for Women's Min 05–08; Hon Can from 16; Acting Adn Switzerland from 16. *Poststrasse 28, 5303 Würenlingen, Switzerland* T: (0041) (56) 281 1025 E: kelham@bluewin.ch *or* adele.kelham@europe.anglican.org

KELK, Michael Anthony. b 48. Sarum & Wells Th Coll. d 83 p 84. C Ross w Brampton Abbotts, Bridstow and Peterstow *Heref* 83–86; P-in-c Burghill 86–97; P-in-c Stretton Sugwas 86–97; P-in-c Walford and St John w Bishopswood, Goodrich etc 97–02; P-in-c Llangarron w Llangrove, Whitchurch and Ganarew 02–08; PtO from 11. *Highland Cottage, Fownhope, Hereford HR1 4NX* T: (01432) 860565

KELLAGHER, Christopher John Bannerman. b 55. Aber Univ MA 79 UMIST MSc 88. STETS MA 09. d 09 p 10. NSM Aldershot H Trin *Guildf* from 09. *Amberley, 19 Hillside Road, Aldershot GU11 3LX* T: (01252) 337841 E: cjbk99@gmail.com

KELLEHER, Patrick James. b 67. Ridley Hall Cam 17. d 19 p 20. C Kettering Ch the King *Pet* from 19. *9 Churchill Way, Kettering NN15 5DP* T: (01536) 510715 M: 07966-155601 E: patrick@ctk.org.uk

KELLEN, David. b 52. St Mich Coll Llan 70. d 75 p 76. C Mynyddislwyn *Mon* 75–77; C Risca 77–78; C Malpas 78–81; V Newport All SS 81–88; V St Mellons from 88; R Michaelston-y-Fedw 89–96. *The Vicarage, Ty'r Winch Road, St Mellons, Cardiff CF3 5UP* T: (029) 2079 6560 E: hyweldda1067@gmail.com

KELLETT, Canon Richard. b 64. Leeds Univ BSc 85 PhD 89. St Jo Coll Nottm BTh 95 MA 96. d 96 p 97. C Nottingham St Jude *S'well* 96–00; P-in-c Skegby 00–02; P-in-c Teversall 00–02; R Skegby w Teversal 02–17; AD Newstead 06–17; P-in-c Lenton Abbey 16–20; Hon Can S'well Minster from 10. *Jubilee House, Westgate, Southwell NG25 0JH* T: (01636) 814331 E: richard.kellett@southwell.anglican.org

KELLEY, Neil George. b 64. ARCM 85. Westcott Ho Cam 88. d 91 p 92. C E Bedfont *Lon* 91–93; C Chiswick St Nic w St Mary 93–97; C Kirkby *Liv* 97–99; V Gt Crosby St Faith and Waterloo Park St Mary 99–12; Dioc Adv on Worship and Liturgy 06–12; R Bushey *St Alb* 12–17; PtO *Lon* 13–18; R Chorley St Laur *Blackb* from 17; AD Chorley from 21. *The Rectory, Rectory Close, Chorley PR7 1QW* M: 07980-872203 E: frneilkelley@gmail.com *or* rector@stlaurencechorley.co.uk

KELLEY, Peter John. b 55. Poly of the S Bank BSc 85 Kingston Univ MBA 97 Cant Ch Ch Univ BA 12. SEITE 06. d 09 p 10. NSM Hook *S'wark* 09–15; NSM Tolworth, Hook and Surbiton 15–17; P-in-c Raynes Park St Sav from 17. *95 Lime Grove, New Malden KT3 3TR* T: (020) 8336 1639 M: 07542-961809

KELLOW, Richard James. b 78. Kent Univ BA 00 Cam Univ PGCE 01. Trin Coll Bris MA 12. d 12 p 13. C Histon *Ely* 12–16; C Impington 12–16; TV Duston and Upton *Pet* from 16. *22 Berrywood Road, Northampton NN5 6GB* T: (01604) 289310 E: revrkellow@gmail.com

KELLS, Ms Jill Elizabeth. b 70. Univ of Wales (Cardiff) BSc 91. Trin Coll Bris 16. d 19 p 20. C Bursledon *Win* from 19. *St Paul's Church, 2 Oak Road, Bursledon, Southampton SO31 8DU* M: 07731-838797 E: revjillkells@gmail.com

KELLS, Mary Eileen. b 65. St Andr Univ MA 87 LSE PhD 00. Ripon Coll Cuddesdon 15. d 17 p 18. C Bridgemary *Portsm* 17–18; C Elson 17–18; C Lee-on-the-Solent 18–21. *Address temp unknown* M: 07846-951285 E: maryeileenkells@gmail.com

KELLY, Canon Brian Horace. b 34. St Jo Coll Dur BA 57 MA 69. d 58 p 59. C Douglas St Geo and St Barn *S & M* 58–61; V Foxdale 61–64; V Bolton All So w St Jas *Man* 64–73; V Maughold *S & M* 73–77; Dir of Ords 76–93; V German 77–06; Can and Prec St German's Cathl 80–06; RD Castletown and Peel 97–04; rtd 06; PtO *S & M* from 09. *16 Slieau Whallian Park, St Johns, Isle of Man IM4 3JH* T: (01624) 801479 E: revkelly@manx.net

KELLY, Desmond Norman. b 42. Oak Hill Th Coll BA 95. d 90 p 91. C Braintree *Chelmsf* 90–94; P-in-c Sible Hedingham 94–95; P-in-c Castle Hedingham 94–95; R Sible Hedingham w Castle Hedingham 95–08; rtd 08; PtO *St E* from 11; *Chelmsf* from 11. *Wykhams, Mill Common, Westhall, Halesworth IP19 8RQ* T: (01502) 575493 E: rev.des@btinternet.com

KELLY, John Adrian. b 49. Qu Coll Birm 70. d 73 p 74. C Formby St Pet *Liv* 73–77; Org Sec CECS *Liv*, Blackb and S & M 77–92; Deputation Appeals Org (Lancs and Is of Man) 88–92; PtO *Liv* 77–05; *Blackb* 77–00; *Man* 88–97. *4 Blandford Close, Southport PR8 2DB* E: karin.kelly@btopenworld.com

KELLY, Canon John Dickinson. b 42. Nottm Univ BA 63. Ripon Hall Ox 63. d 65 p 66. C Egremont *Carl* 65–67; C Upperby St Jo 67–70; V Arlecdon 70–73; V Barrow St Aid 73–79; V Milnthorpe 79–83; V Beetham and Milnthorpe 83–85; V Camerton St Pet 85–88; P-in-c Camerton H Trin W Seaton 86–88; V Camerton, Seaton and W Seaton 88–01; P-in-c Kells 01–05; Hon Can Carl Cathl from 00; Chapl N Cumbria Acute Hosps NHS Trust 03–05; rtd 05; P-in-c Kirkland, Lamplugh w Ennerdale *Carl* 05–07; Hon C Whitehaven 07–12; PtO from 12. *10 Stonyhurst Drive, Whitehaven CA28 7RZ* T: (01946) 692630

KELLY, Katie Joanne. b 72. Ox Univ BA 94. Wycliffe Hall Ox 19. d 21. C Mottingham St Edw *S'wark* from 21. *132 William Barefoot Drive, London SE9 3BP* M: 07986-862347 E: katiejk29@icloud.com

KELLY, Malcolm Bernard. b 46. St Mich Coll Llan 72. d 74 p 75. C Tranmere St Paul w St Luke *Ches* 74–77; C Barnston 77–80; R Thurstaston 80–92; R Grappenhall 92–11; rtd 11; PtO *Ches* from 11. *22 Boswell Avenue, Warrington WA4 6DQ* T: (01925) 423871 E: malcolmkelly25@yahoo.co.uk

KELLY, Martin Herbert. b 55. Selw Coll Cam MA 90. Aston Tr Scheme 78 Ripon Coll Cuddesdon 80. d 83 p 84. C Clapham Old Town *S'wark* 83–87; Chapl and Fell Selw Coll Cam 87–92; Chapl Newnham Coll Cam 87–92; Chapl St Piers Hosp Sch Lingfield *S'wark* 95–01; C Limpsfield and Titsey 95–01; Chapl Basildon and Thurrock Gen Hosps NHS Trust 03–04; Chapl Dartford and Gravesham NHS Trust 04–18; PtO *S'wark* 14–15. *Cygnets, Hosey Hill, Westerham TN16 1TB* E: martinkelly300@gmail.com

KELLY, Nigel James (Ned). b 60. N Staffs Poly BSc 83. Ripon Coll Cuddesdon 83. d 86 p 87. C Len Telford *Lich* 86–90; TV 90–92; Chapl RN 92–16; Chapl HM Pris Dovegate 16–20; rtd 20; PtO *Lich* from 20. *Address temp unknown* E: revnkelly@gmail.com

KELLY, Paul. b 60. Qu Coll Birm 02. d 04 p 05. C Ogley Hay *Lich* 04–07; V Stafford St Paul Forebridge 07–11; V Hednesford from 11. *The Vicarage, Church Hill, Hednesford, Cannock WS12 1BD* T: (01543) 426954 M: 07815-452616

KELLY, Canon Peter Hugh. b 46. Sarum & Wells Th Coll 81. d 84 p 85. C Fareham H Trin *Portsm* 84–87; Chapl and Prec Portsm Cathl 87–90; V Eastney 90–97; P-in-c Swanmore St Barn 97–06; V 07–11; RD Bishop's Waltham 03–09; Hon Can Portsm Cathl 07–11; rtd 11; PtO *Portsm* from 11. *16 Rosedale Close, Fareham PO14 4EL* T: (01329) 849567 E: peterkelly@swanmore.net

KELLY, Canon Stephen Alexander. b 61. Man Univ BSc 84. Ridley Hall Cam 03. d 05 p 06. C Meole Brace *Lich* 05–08; C Cen Telford 08–13; Fresh Expressions Adv 12–13; V Northampton St Giles *Pet* from 13; Can Pet Cathl from 18. *St Giles's Vicarage, 2 Spring Gardens, Northampton NN1 1LX* T: (01604) 627680 E: revstevekelly@gmail.com

KELLY, Canon Stephen Paul. b 55. Keble Coll Ox BA 77 MA 07 Leeds Univ MA 06. Linc Th Coll 77. d 79 p 80. C Illingworth *Wakef* 79–82; C Knottingley 82–84; V Alverthorpe 84–93; Dioc Ecum Officer 88–93; TR Bingley All SS *Bradf* 93–03; P-in-c Woolley *Wakef* 03–14; *Leeds* 14–17; Dioc CME Officer *Wakef* 03–14; *Leeds* 14–17; RD Wakef 11–14; AD Leeds 14–17; Hon Can Wakef Cathl 08–17; rtd 17. *416 Leeds Road, Dewsbury WF12 7QE* E: s.p.kelly1995@gmail.com

KELLY, Timothy Patrick. b 73. Trin Hall Cam MA 94 York Univ DPhil 99. St Hild Coll 16. d 19 p 20. C Beverley Minster *York* 19–20; C Beverley St Jo and St Martin w Routh All SS from 20. *23 Outer Trinities, Beverley HU17 0HN* M: 07818-456834 E: tim.kelly@duvelle.co.uk

KELLY-MOORE, The Very Revd Joanne. b 68. Victoria Univ Wellington BA LLB. Bible Coll of NZ BD 99. d 00 p 01. C Remuera St Aidan NZ 00–04; V Remuera St Aidan 04–10; Dean Auckland 10–17; Adn Cant and Can Res Cant Cathl; Dean St Alb from 21. *The Old Rectory, Sumpter Yard, Holywell Hill, St Albans AL1 1BY* M: 07392-983474 E: dean@stalbanscathedral.org

KELSEY, Canon George Robert Joseph. b 61. Imp Coll Lon BSc 83 Newc Univ MSc 84 PhD 92. Cranmer Hall Dur 95. d 97 p 98. C Denton *Newc* 97–01; TV Glendale Gp 01–10; V Norham and Duddo from 10; P-in-c Cornhill w Carham from 10; P-in-c Branxton from 10; AD Norham from 16; Hon Can Newc Cathl from 16. *The Vicarage, Church Lane, Norham, Berwick-upon-Tweed TD15 2LF* T: (01289) 382325 E: robert.josephkelsey@live.com

KELSEY, Mrs Tina Jane. b 69. Chich Univ BA 10. Ripon Coll Cuddesdon 11. d 13 p 14. C Beckenham St Geo *Roch* 13–17; V Edmonton St Pet w St Martin *Lon* from 17. *The Vicarage, St Peter's Road, London N9 8JP* T: (020) 8807 7431 M: 07512-710085 E: tina.jk42@yahoo.co.uk

KELSO, Andrew John. b 47. Lon Univ BA 70 LRAM 73. St Jo Coll Nottm 83. d 85 p 86. C Gorleston St Mary *Nor* 85–87; C Hellesdon 87–90; TV Ipsley *Worc* 90–09; rtd 09; PtO *Worc* from 11. *2 The Close, Throckmorton, Pershore WR10 2JU* T: (01386) 462087 M: 07795-431382 E: andy.kelso@sky.com

KEMBALL, Sister Heather Susan. b 61. St Mellitus Coll 18. d 19 p 20. NSM Alsager Ch Ch *Ches* from 19. *54 Obelisk Way, Congleton CW12 4FY* T: (01260) 278362 M: 07762-914673 E: heather@kemball.com

KEMBER, Ann Elizabeth. b 58. ERMC 12. d 15 p 16. C Wolverton *Ox* 15–18; R Chard St Mary w Combe St Nicholas, Wambrook etc *B & W* from 18. *The Vicarage, Forton Road,*

Chard TA20 2HJ T: (01460) 351521 M: 07490-236179
E: annkember@hotmail.com

KEMP, Canon Alice Mary Elizabeth. b 59. Kent Univ BA 82 Thames Poly PGCE 91. STETS 07. **d** 10 **p** 11. NSM Box w Hazlebury and Ditteridge *Bris* 10–18; NSM Colerne w N Wraxall 11–18; NSM Marshfield w Cold Ashton and Tormarton etc from 18; Hon Can Bris Cathl from 17. *Barn House, Barn Piece, Box, Corsham SN13 8LF* T: (01225) 742128 E: revalicekemp@btinternet.com

KEMP, Canon Allan. b 43. Bps' Coll Cheshunt 65 Oak Hill Th Coll 67. **d** 68 **p** 69. C Tunbridge Wells St Jas *Roch* 68–76; V Becontree St Mary *Chelmsf* 76–90; RD Barking and Dagenham 81–86; V Gt w Lt Chesterford 90–07; Hon Can Chelmsf Cathl 99–07; rtd 07; PtO *Glouc* 16–20. *6 Freemans Orchard, Newent GL18 1TX* T: (01531) 822041 E: canonkemp@waitrose.com

KEMP, Prof Anthony Eric. b 34. St Mark & St Jo Coll Lon CertEd 57 LTCL 63 FTCL 63 Lon Inst of Educn DipEd 70 Sussex Univ MA 71 DPhil 79 Hon FLCM 83 CPsychol 89 FBPsS 97 Helsinki Univ Hon MusDoc 03. SAOMC 96. **d** 98 **p** 99. NSM Wokingham All SS *Ox* 98–05; NSM Wokingham St Paul 05–09; PtO 09–13; *Portsm* from 14. *40 Sea Grove Avenue, Hayling Island PO11 9EU* T: (023) 9378 6659 E: ae.kemp@yahoo.co.uk

KEMP, Christopher Michael. b 48. K Coll Lon BD 71 AKC 71. St Aug Coll Cant 75. **d** 76 **p** 77. C Weaverham *Ches* 76–79; C Latchford St Jas 79–82; P-in-c Sandbach Heath 82–88; V Macclesfield St Paul 88–89; C Cheadle Hulme All SS 89–93; C Oxton 93–98; P-in-c Seacombe 98–02; P-in-c Brereton w Swettenham 02–05; P-in-c Brereton w Eaton and Hulme Walfield 05–10; rtd 10. *1 Orchard Rise, Droitwich WR9 8NU* T: (01905) 774372

KEMP, Hilary Anne. b 65. ERMC 15. **d** 18 **p** 19. NSM Hemel Hempstead St Alb 18–20; NSM Sunnyside w Bourne End from 20. *6 Granville Dene, Bovingdon, Hemel Hempstead HP3 0JE* E: hilarykemp65@gmail.com

KEMP, John Ingham Edwin. b 29. Bris Univ BA 51 PGCE 52 Lon Univ BD 65. Wells Th Coll 63. **d** 65 **p** 66. C Maidenhead St Luke *Ox* 65–70; R Rotherfield Greys 70–78; V Highmore 70–78; Dep Dir Tr Scheme for NSM 78–84; P-in-c Taplow 78–82; TV Burnham w Dropmore, Hitcham and Taplow 82–84; Prin EAMTC 84–92; rtd 92; Chapl Kyrenia Cyprus 92–95; PtO *St E* from 95. *Lea Cottage, The Street, Middleton, Saxmundham IP17 3NJ* T: (01728) 648324 E: revdjgk@waitrose.com

KEMP, John Robert Deverall. b 42. City Univ BSc 65 BD 69. Oak Hill Th Coll 66. **d** 70 **p** 71. C Fulham Ch Ch *Lon* 70–73; C Widford *Chelmsf* 73–79; P-in-c New Thundersley 79–84; V 84–98; Chapl HM Pris Bullwood Hall 79–98; R S Shoebury *Chelmsf* 98–09; rtd 09; PtO *Chelmsf* from 09. *36 Macmurdo Road, Leigh-on-Sea SS9 5AQ* T: (01702) 525978

KEMP, Mrs Karen Margaret. b 64. Victoria Univ Wellington MA 11 Geo Fox Univ DMin 19 RGN 82. ACT BTh 89. **d** 13 **p** 14. C Glouc City and Hempsted 13; Dean Tikanga Pakeha, St Jo Coll Auckland NZ from 14. *The College of St John the Evangelist, St John's Road, Auckland 1072, New Zealand* T: (0064) (9) 521 2725 M: 21-057 3391 E: k.kemp@stjohnscollege.ac.nz

KEMP, Mrs Pamela Ann. b 52. Coll of St Matthias Bris CertEd 73 RMN 98. Ripon Coll Cuddesdon BTh 07. **d** 02 **p** 03. C Portland All SS w St Pet *Sarum* 02–04; C Verwood 04–06; R Highnam, Lassington, Rudford, Tibberton etc *Glouc* 06–11; P-in-c Stokenham, Slapton, Charleton w Buckland etc *Ex* 11–14; R Stokenham, Slapton, Charleton w Buckland etc 14–19; rtd 19; PtO *Truro* from 20. *Plot 177, 5 Sanderling Close, Bude EX23 8GJ* T: (01288) 350660 M: 07989-604543 E: pamelakemp@btinternet.com

KEMP, Ralph John. b 71. Wye Coll Lon BSc 93 Trin Hall Cam BTh 04. Ridley Hall Cam 01. **d** 04 **p** 05. C Astbury and Smallwood *Ches* 04–07; V Burton and Shotwick 07–08; NSM Plas Newton w Ches Ch Ch 09–11; NSM Ches Ch Ch from 11. *38 Ethos Court, City Road, Chester CH1 3AT* M: 07762-847211 E: ralphjkemp@googlemail.com *or* ralph.kemp@christchurchchester.com

KEMP, William. b 67. St Anne's Coll Ox BA 91 Wolfs Coll Cam BTh 99 St Mellitus Coll MA 18 Brunel Univ PGCE 92. Ridley Hall Cam 96. **d** 99 **p** 00. C Kensington St Barn *Lon* 99–04; C Hurstpierpoint *Chich* 04–11; Pioneer Min from 11. *12 Western Road, Hurstpierpoint BN6 9TA* T: (01273) 835645

KEMPSTER, Miss Helen Edith. b 49. **d** 00 **p** 01. OLM Weybridge *Guildf* 00–06; OLM Esher 06–14; PtO 14–15; NSM Headley All SS 15–19; PtO from 19. *Perrymead, May Close, Headley, Bordon GU35 8LR* T: (01428) 713973 E: helen.kempster@btinternet.com

KEMPTHORNE, Renatus. b 39. Wadh Coll Ox BA 60 MA 64. Wycliffe Hall Ox 60. **d** 62 **p** 63. C Stoke *Cov* 62–65; Lect

St Jo Coll Auckland NZ 65–68; R Wytham *Ox* 68–75; Chapl Bp Grosseteste Coll Linc 75–83; V Waimea NZ 83–90; Th Consultant 90–96; Researcher and Educator from 97; rtd 04. *140 Nile Street, Nelson 7010, New Zealand* T: (0064) (3) 546 7447 E: kempthorne@xtra.co.nz

KENCHINGTON, Canon Jane Elizabeth Ballantyne. b 58. Hull Univ BSc 79 Trin Coll Bris MA 05 Hughes Hall Cam PGCE 83. Westcott Ho Cam 88. **d** 90 **p** 94. C Winchcombe, Gretton, Sudeley Manor etc *Glouc* 90–96; PtO 96–99; NSM Dursley 99–02; Dir Reader Tr and Tutor WEMTC 01–06; Dean of Women Clergy 06–09; R Sodbury Vale 09–15; AD Wotton 13–15; Hon Can Glouc Cathl 06–15; TR Solihull *Birm* 15–21; Hon Can Birm Cathl 19–21; rtd 21. *7 Warren Croft, North Nibley, Dursley GL11 6EN* M: 07779-991760 E: janekenchington@gmail.com

KENCHINGTON, Paul Henry. b 54. Worc Coll Ox MA 76. St Jo Coll Nottm BA 81. **d** 82 **p** 83. C Scarborough St Mary w Ch Ch and H Apostles *York* 82–85; C Caversham St Pet and Mapledurham etc *Ox* 85–89; V Flucclecote *Glouc* 89–00; V Kowloon St Andr Hong Kong 00–05; Chapl Versailles w Chevry *Eur* 05–11; P-in-c Combe Down w Monkton Combe and S Stoke *B & W* 11–16; V 16–17; rtd 17; PtO *Glouc* from 19. *4 Painswick Heights, Yokehouse Lane, Stroud GL6 7QS* M: 07825-482225

KENDAL, Gordon McGregor. b 46. Dundee Univ MA 70 Mansf Coll Ox BA 72 MA 76 Lon Univ BA 73 PhD 79 MA 98 St Andr Univ PhD 08 Jordanhill Coll Glas PGCE 88. Edin Th Coll 72. **d** 74 **p** 75. C Bracknell *Ox* 74–77; C Wokingham All SS 77–79; Chapl and Fell Linc Coll Ox 79–83; R Edin St Pet 83–87; Man Gr Sch 88–92; Gen Sec Fellowship of St Alb and St Sergius 92–96; V S Lambeth St Anne and All SS *S'wark* 96–00; rtd 11. *10 Bamff Road, Alyth, Blairgowrie PH11 8DT* T: (01828) 633400

KENDAL, Henry David. b 59. ASVA 83. Lon Bible Coll 90 Oak Hill NSM Course 92. **d** 94 **p** 95. C Roxeth *Lon* 94–99; C Woodside Park St Barn 99–06; V from 06. *78 Woodside Avenue, London N12 8TB* T: (020) 8343 7776 *or* 8343 5775 F: (020) 8446 7492 *or* 8343 5771 M: 07977-521656 E: henrykendal@stbarnabas.co.uk

KENDALL, Edward Jonathan. b 76. Nottm Univ BA 98 Ox Univ PGCE 99. Oak Hill Th Coll BA 10. **d** 10 **p** 11. C Fulham St Pet *Lon* 10–14; C Teddington SS Pet and Paul and Fulwell 14–19; V Fulwell from 19. *45 St James's Avenue, Hampton Hill, Hampton TW12 1HL* M: 07813-610977 E: ed@stmichaelsfulwell.co.uk

KENDALL, Mrs Emma Jane. b 69. R Holloway Coll Lon BA 97. Trin Coll Bris MA 18. **d** 20 **p** 21. C Milverton w Halse, Fitzhead and Ash Priors *B & W* from 20. *Malthouse Cottage, Halse, Taunton TA4 3AF* T: (01823) 433034 M: 07727-105077 E: revemmakendall@gmail.com

KENDALL, Frank. b 40. CCC Cam BA 62 MA 68 FRSA 90. S'wark Ord Course 74. **d** 74 **p** 75. NSM Lingfield *S'wark* 74–75 and 78–82; NSM Sketty *S & B* 75–78; NSM Limpsfield and Titsey *S'wark* 82–84; LtO *Man* 84–89; LtO *Liv* 89–96; NSM Adnry St Helens 96–00; PtO from 01; NSM Farington Moss and Lostock Hall *Blackb* 03–06; PtO from 06. *52 Kingsway, Penwortham, Preston PR1 0ED* T: (01772) 748021 E: fandbkendall@hotmail.com

KENDALL, Giles. b 57. Lon Univ BA 80 Univ Coll Lon BSc 86 Lon Univ PhD 90. STETS BTh 98. **d** 98 **p** 99. C Wareham *Sarum* 98–01; V Sawston *Ely* 01–08; P-in-c Babraham 01–08; P-in-c Kingswinford St Mary *Worc* 08–17; R 17–20; rtd 20. *4 Deneside, South Shields NE34 7RW*

KENDALL, Gordon Sydney. b 41. **d** 72 **p** 74. NSM Old Ford St Paul w St Steph and St Mark *Lon* 72–82; NSM Homerton St Luke 86–92; Asst Chapl Hackney and Homerton Hosp Lon 87–92; Chapl S Devon Healthcare NHS Trust 92–06; rtd 06. *Shiloh, Beech Trees Lane, Ipplepen, Newton Abbot TQ12 5TW* T: (01803) 814054 E: kendallg@uwclub.net

KENDALL, Miss Jacqueline Ann. b 63. Univ of Wales (Abth) BA 85. Cranmer Hall Dur 88. **d** 91 **p** 94. Par Dn Stockport St Sav *Ches* 91–94; C 94–95; C Acton and Worleston, Church Minshull etc 95–96; C Alvanley and Helsby and Dunham-on-the-Hill 96–97; C Timperley 97–01 and 07–10; P-in-c Dodleston 01–07; rtd 10. *Address withheld by request*

KENDRA, Neil Stuart. b 46. JP 96. Leeds Univ BA 67 Bradf Univ MSc 80 PhD 84. Linc Th Coll 67. **d** 69 **p** 70. C Allerton *Liv* 69–72; Ldr Leeds City Cen Detached Youth Work Project 73–75; Dioc Youth Officer *Ripon* 75–77; Lect Ilkley Coll 77–78; Sen Lect Bradf and Ilkley Community Coll 78–88; Hd Community and Youth Studies St Martin's Coll 88–94; Hd Applied Soc Sciences 94–06; Hd Sch Soc Sciences and Business Studies 01–06; P-in-c Settle *Bradf* 06–11; P-in-c Giggleswick and Rathmell w Wigglesworth 08–11; rtd 11; PtO *Bradf* 11–14; *Leeds* from 14. *Cravendale, Belle Hill, Giggleswick, Settle BD24 0BA* T: (01729) 825307

KENDREW, Geoffrey David. b 42. K Coll Lon BD 66 AKC 66. d 67 p 68. C Bourne *Guildf* 67–70; C Haslemere 70–76; V Derby St Barn 76–95; R Deal St Leon w St Rich and Sholden etc *Cant* 95–07; Chapl E Kent NHS and Soc Care Partnership Trust 00–06; Chapl Kent and Medway NHS and Soc Care Partnership Trust 06–07; rtd 07; PtO *Linc* 15–18. *2 Mill Lane, Butterwick, Boston PE22 0JE* T: (01205) 760977 E: david-kendrew@supanet.com

KENDRICK, Dale Evans. b 62. Ch Ch Coll Cant BA 86 Nottm Univ MA 87 Leeds Univ MA 95 Birm Univ PhD 13. Coll of Resurr Mirfield 94. d 95 p 96. C Tividale *Lich* 95–96; C Blakenall Heath 96–97; C Stafford 97–98; Dep Chapl HM Pris Birm 98–01; Chapl HM Pris Drake Hall 01–03; Chapl RAF 03–04; Chapl HM YOI Werrington 04–08; Chapl HM Pris Lewes 08–17. *Roskhill House, Roskhill, Dunvegan, Isle of Skye IV55 8ZD*

KENDRICK, Mrs Helen Grace. b 66. Bris Univ BA 88. SAOMC 96. d 99 p 00. C Icknield *Ox* 99–03; P-in-c Sutton Courtenay w Appleford 03–17; R DAMASCUS from 17; AD Abingdon from 17. *The Vicarage, 3 Tullis Close, Sutton Courtenay, Abingdon OX14 4BD* T: (01235) 848297 E: rector@damascusparish.org.uk

KENNAR, Canon Thomas Philip. b 66. Surrey Univ BA 08. STETS 02. d 05 p 06. C Warblington w Emsworth *Portsm* 05–08; Chapl Portsm Coll 06–08; TR Portsea N End St Mark *Portsm* 08–15; R Havant from 15; Hon Can Cape Coast Ghana from 13; Hon Can Ho from 13; Hon Can Portsm Cathl from 18. *St Faith's Rectory, 5 Meadowlands, Havant PO9 2RP* M: 07881-025592 E: tomkennar@gmail.com

KENNARD, Mark Philip Donald. b 60. Man Univ BSc 82 Cardiff Univ MTh 08. Cranmer Hall Dur 85. d 88 p 89. C Newark w Hawton, Cotham and Shelton *S'well* 88–89; C Newark 89–91; C Cropwell Bishop w Colston Bassett, Granby etc 91–93; P-in-c Shireoaks 93–99; Chapl Bassetlaw Hosp and Community Services NHS Trust 93–96; Chapl RAF 99–16; PtO *Linc* 17–18; P-in-c Digby Gp from 18. *2 Thomas a Becket Close, Digby, Lincoln LN4 3GA* E: digbyrectory@outlook.com

KENNAUGH, Gary. b 80. Trin Coll Bris 12. d 15 p 16. C Lache cum Saltney *Ches* 15–18; V Stalybridge H Trin and Ch Ch from 18. *The Vicarage, 277 Mottram Road, Stalybridge SK15 2RT* T: 0161-304 9024 M: 07388-104316 E: gary@hts.church

KENNEDY, Alan. b 52. Liv Univ BSc 95. NOC 01. d 03 p 04. C Westbrook St Phil *Liv* 03–07; TV Mossley Hill 07–16; TR 16–20; R from 20. *The Vicarage, Rose Lane, Liverpool L18 8DB* T: 0151-724 1915

KENNEDY, Canon Alison Mary. b 66. K Coll Lon BMus 87 Heythrop Coll Lon MA 95 LTCL 90. NTMTC 96. d 99 p 00. C De Beauvoir Town St Pet *Lon* 99–02; TV Walthamstow *Chelmsf* 02–07; TV N Lambeth *S'wark* 07–18; Can Res Chelmsf Cathl from 18; Tutor St Mellitus Coll from 18. *1A Harlings Grove, Chelmsford CM1 1YQ* T: (01245) 491599 E: alison_m_kennedy@hotmail.com

KENNEDY, Ms Caroline Jane. b 62. St Andr Univ MA 85 York Univ PGCE 86. LCTP 11. d 14 p 15. NSM Harraby *Carl* 14–15; NSM Aspatria w Hayton and Gilcrux from 15; Chapl Trin Sch Carl from 15; Chapl Cumbria Univ *Carl* from 19. *4 The Courtyard, Broadwath, Heads Nook, Brampton CA8 9BL* T: (01228) 561885 M: 07506-563393

KENNEDY, Carolyn Ruth. b 59. Univ of Wales (Ban) BA 81 GradCertEd(FE) 85. Ripon Coll Cuddesdon BA 90. d 91 p 94. C Frodingham *Linc* 91–95; Chapl Cov Univ 95–00; R Uffington Gp *Linc* 00–18; rtd 18. *21 Plantagenet Way, Gillingham SP8 4TD* T: (01747) 835981 E: ccd@crk.me.uk

KENNEDY, Christopher John. b 82. Brunel Univ BSc 10. St Mellitus Coll BA 17. d 17 p 18. C Hanworth St Rich *Lon* 17–21; Pioneer P from 21. *1 Bychurch End, Teddington TW11 8PS* M: 07941-435622 E: kennes777@yahoo.co.uk

KENNEDY, David George. b 46. Hull Univ BEd 71 MA 76. Linc Th Coll 77. d 79 p 80. C Linc St Faith and St Martin w St Pet 79–82; V Bilton St Pet *York* 82–90; V New Seaham *Dur* 90–92; Chapl Lincs and Humberside Univ *York* 92–97; P-in-c Barrow St Matt *Carl* 97–99; TR 99–03; Chapl Furness Coll 97–03; P-in-c Blackb St Aid 03–04; V Blackb St Fran and St Aid 04–06; Chapl Nord Pas de Calais *Eur* 06–08; P-in-c Bierley *Bradf* 08–12; V 12–14; *Leeds* 14–15; PtO *Blackb* from 15. *53 Parklands Way, Blackburn BB2 4QS* T: (01254) 600515

KENNEDY, Canon David John. b 57. St Jo Coll Dur BA 78 Nottm Univ MTh 81 Birm Univ PhD 96. St Jo Coll Nottm 79. d 81 p 82. C Tudhoe Grange *Dur* 81–87; C Merrington 84–87; Tutor Qu Coll Birm 88–96; R Haughton le Skerne *Dur* 96–01; Can Res Dur Cathl 01–18; Chapl Grey Coll Dur 01–09; V Corbridge w Halton and Newton Hall *Newc* from 18; AD Corbridge from 19. *The Vicarage, Greencroft Avenue, Corbridge NE45 5DW*

KENNEDY, Gary. b 63. Qu Coll Birm BA 02. d 03 p 04. C New Bury *Man* 03–06; C New Bury w Gt Lever 06; P-in-c Bolton SS Simon and Jude 06–11; TR Broughton 11–16; Chapl Pennine Acute Hosps NHS Trust 16–21; PtO *Blackb* from 18. *Address temp unknown* E: therev.wolf@gmail.com

KENNEDY, Ian Duncan. b 53. d 04 p 05. OLM Whitnash *Cov* 04–07; NSM Leek Wootton 07–08; P-in-c Fillongley and Corley 08–15; V from 15; rtd 18; PtO *Cov* from 18. *27 Primrose Drive, Bedworth CV12 0GL* E: reviankennedy@aol.com

KENNEDY, Mrs Jane Rowston. b 47. Dudley Coll of Educn CertEd 70 Leic Univ DipEd 93. EMMTC 04. d 07 p 08. NSM Avon-Swift *Leic* 07–17; rtd 17; PtO *Leic* 17–21. *9 Anzac Close, Fareham PO14 2JD* M: 07974-909226 E: jrkneeb@gmail.com

KENNEDY, Jason Grant. b 68. Oak Hill Th Coll BA 95. d 98 p 99. C Beccles St Mich *St E* 98–01; R Hollington St Leon *Chich* 01–05; C Tonbridge St Steph *Roch* 05–10; V Ripley *Derby* 10–14; Ch Growth Officer *Derby* Adnry from 14. *Church House, Full Street, Derby DE1 3DR* T: (01332) 388691 E: jason.kennedy@derby.anglican.org

KENNEDY, John Frederick. b 42. Birm Univ BSc 64 PhD 67 DSc 73 BA 12. Qu Coll Birm 05. d 06 p 07. NSM Edgbaston St Geo *Birm* 06–10; PtO from 11; *Heref* from 11; *Worc* from 15. *Kyrewood House, Kyrewood, Tenbury Wells WR15 8FF* M: 07801-624749

KENNEDY, Joseph. b 69. Edin Univ BSc 91 BD 94 Moray Ho Coll of Educn PGCE 97 St Hugh's Coll Ox MSt 00 Keble Coll Ox DPhil 06. St Steph Ho Ox 98. d 02 p 03. C Stratfield Mortimer and Mortimer W End etc *Ox* 02–03; C Abingdon 03–05; Dean of Chpl, Chapl and Fell Selw Coll Cam 05–08; Chapl Newnham Coll Cam 05–08; Prin Coll of Resurr Mirfield 08–11; Hon Can Wakef Cathl 10–11; V Oxton *Ches* from 11; RD Birkenhead from 21. *The Vicarage, Village Way, Prenton CH43 2GQ* T: 0151-652 2402 E: revd.j.kennedy@gmail.com

KENNEDY, Michael Charles. b 39. TCD BA 63 MA 79 BD 79 Open Univ PhD 87. TCD Div Sch 61. d 63 p 64. C Drumglass *Arm* 63–66; I Lisnadill w Kildarton 66–14; Warden Dioc Guild of Lay Readers from 74; Hon V Choral Arm Cathl 75–14; Tutor for Aux Min (Arm) 82–14; Preb Yagoe St Patr Cathl Dublin 92–14; rtd 14. *8 Vicar's Hill, Armagh BT61 7ED* T: (028) 3752 3630 E: michaelkennedy2@btinternet.com

KENNEDY, Paul Alan. b 67. ACA 92. St Steph Ho Ox BA 95. d 95 p 96. C Romford St Andr *Chelmsf* 95–98; C Cheam *S'wark* 98–01; V Steep and Froxfield w Privett *Portsm* 01–08; Bp's Adv on Healing 04–08; R E Win 08–17; AD Win 13–17; P-in-c Win St Faith w St Cross 15–17; P-in-c St Vedast w St Mich-le-Querne etc *Lon* 17–21; R from 21; P-in-c St Mary Aldermary from 17. *St Vedast's Rectory, 4 Foster Lane, London EC2V 6HH* T: (020) 7606 3998 M: 07877-211307 E: priest@vedast.org.uk or paul@moot.uk.net

KENNEDY, Paul Joseph Alan. b 57. Newc Univ MA 93. Sarum & Wells Th Coll 81. d 84 p 85. C Shildon w Eldon *Dur* 84–86; C Shotton *St As* 86–88; V Waterhouses *Dur* 88–93; V Denton *Newc* 93–95; CF 95–98; P-in-c Leam Lane *Dur* 98–99; V 99–05; P-in-c S Westoe 05–15; V 15–16; V Seaham and Dawdon from 16. *Seaham Harbour Vicarage, Maureen Terrace, Seaham SR7 7SN*

KENNEDY, Miss Penelope Ann Cheney. b 49. STETS 08. d 11 p 12. NSM Buckland Newton, Cerne Abbas, Godmanstone etc *Sarum* 11–13; NSM Charminster and Stinsford 13–17; NSM Charminster, Stinsford and the Chalk Stream villages from 17. *Church House, 4 Meadow Bottom, Stratton, Dorchester DT2 9WH* T: (01305) 251422 E: revpenekennedy@yahoo.com

KENNEDY, Brother Philip Bartholomew. b 47. STETS 95. d 98 p 99. SSF from 77; C Plaistow and N Canning Town *Chelmsf* 08–16; PtO 17–19. *Address temp unknown* E: philipbartholomewssf@gmail.com

KENNEDY, Ross Kenneth. b 40. Edin Th Coll 83. d 85 p 86. C Hexham *Newc* 85–89; TV Glendale Gp 89–93; TR Ch the King 93–05; rtd 05; Hon C Dunfermline *St And* 05–17. *12 Calaisburn Place, Dunfermline KY11 4RD* T: (01383) 625887 E: rk.kennedy@talktalk.net

KENNEDY, Samuel (Uell). b 51. Heriot-Watt Univ BSc 72. CBDTI 06. d 07 p 08. NSM Baildon *Bradf* 07–14; Development Officer Min and Miss 02–18; PtO *Leeds* from 15. *The Moorings, Hunsingore, Wetherby LS22 5HY* T: (01423) 358993 E: uell_kennedy@yahoo.co.uk

KENNEDY, Canon Wendy Patricia. b 58. STETS 00. d 03 p 04. NSM Warren Park and Leigh Park *Portsm* 03–07; Dioc Sec 07–18; rtd 18; PtO *Portsm* 07–11 and from 18; Public Preacher 11–18; Interim Dir Discipleship, Voc and Min and Par Development and Evang *Guildf* 18–19; Hon Can Portsm Cathl from 18. *13 Ashcroft Lane, Waterlooville PO8 0AX* T: (023) 9241 3190 E: wendy.kennedy234@gmail.com

KENNERLEY, Katherine Virginia (Ginnie). Somerville Coll Ox BA 58 MA 65 TCD BA 86 Princeton Th Sem DMin 98.

CITC 86. **d** 88 **p** 90. Lect Applied Th CITC 88–93; NSM Bray *D & G* 88–93; I Narraghmore and Timolin w Castledermot etc 93–05; Can Ch Ch Cathl Dublin 96–05; rtd 05; Ed *Search* from 04. *4 Seafield Terrace, Dalkey, Co Dublin, Republic of Ireland* T: (00353) (1) 275 0737 M: 87-647 5092 E: vkennerley@gmail.com

KENNETT, Mrs Jeanette Tracy. b 71. Kent Univ BA 94. St Aug Coll of Th 15. **d** 18 **p** 19. C Tenterden, Rother and Oxney *Cant* from 18. *14 Abbott Way, Tenterden TN30 7BZ* M: 07888-998874 E: caulkhead7@talktalk.net

KENNEY, Canon Peter. b 50. Edin Univ BD 75 Dur Univ MA 97 Essex Univ MA 05. Edin Th Coll 73. **d** 76 **p** 77. C Cullercoats St Geo *Newc* 76–81; TV Whorlton 81–88; TR Ch the King 88–93; P-in-c Newc St Jo 93–02; P-in-c Gosforth St Hugh 02–09; P-in-c Chapel House 09–12; Dioc Adv in Past Care and Counselling 02–12; Min Development Officer 12–18; Hon Can Newc Cathl 04–18; rtd 18; PtO *Newc* from 18. *17 North Farm Court, Throckley, Newcastle upon Tyne NE15 9DW* T: 0191-267 5989 M: 07890-628251 E: peter.kenney5@btinternet.com

KENNING, Canon Michael Stephen. b 47. St Chad's Coll Dur BA 68. Westcott Ho Cam 69. **d** 71 **p** 72. C Hythe *Cant* 71–75; TV Bow w Bromley St Leon *Lon* 75–77; C-in-c W Leigh CD *Portsm* 77–81; V Lee-on-the-Solent 81–92; R N Waltham and Steventon, Ashe and Deane *Win* 92–03; RD Whitchurch 03–08; Hon Can Win Cathl 09–10; rtd 10; PtO *Win* from 10. *20 Teal Crescent, Basingstoke RG22 5QX* T: (01256) 817989 E: michael.kenning@teltoycoed.co.uk

KENNINGTON, The Very Revd John Paul. b 61. Collingwood Coll Dur BA 85. St Steph Ho Ox BA 87 MA 92. **d** 88 **p** 89. C Headington *Ox* 88–91; C Dulwich St Clem w St Pet *S'wark* 91–94; TV Mortlake w E Sheen 94–01; V Battersea St Mary 01–10; Dean Montreal Canada 11–16; NSM Leytonstone St Andr *Chelmsf* 16–18; P-in-c 18; V from 18. *St Andrew's Vicarage, 7 Forest Glade, London E11 1LU* T: (020) 8989 0942 E: jpaulkennington@gmail.com *or* priest.standrews.leytonstone@gmail.com

KENNY, Charles John. b 39. QUB BA 61 MEd 78 LGSM 74. CITC 69. **d** 69 **p** 70. C Belfast St Paul *Conn* 69–71; Hd of RE Grosvenor High Sch 71–94; V Choral Belf Cathl 94–00; Can Belf Cathl 95–00; Treas Belf Cathl 95–00; rtd 00; LtO *Conn* from 84. *45 Deramore Drive, Belfast BT9 5JS* T: (028) 9066 9632 *or* 9032 8332 F: 9023 8855 E: c.kenny142@btinternet.com

KENNY, James Anthony. b 96. York St Jo Univ BA 17 St Jo Coll Dur MA 21. Cranmer Hall Dur 17. **d** 21. C Goodmanham *York* from 21; C Sancton from 21; C Weighton Wold from 21. *70 Market Place, Market Weighton, York YO43 3AW* E: rev.jakenny@gmail.com

KENNY, Mrs Lynda Ann. b 57. Sheff Univ BA 14 MA 17. Yorks Min Course 11. **d** 14 **p** 16. C N Ormesby *York* 14–15; C S Cave and Ellerker w Broomfleet 15–18; Chapl HM Pris Humber 18–19; TV Howden *York* from 19. *The Vicarage, 3 Thimblehall Lane, Newport, Brough HU15 2PX* T: (01430) 266394 M: 07545-471474 E: revd_lyn@yahoo.co.uk

KENRICK, Kenneth David Norman. b 44. RMN. Ripon Hall Ox 70 NW Ord Course 77. **d** 77 **p** 78. C Stockport St Geo *Ches* 77–83; R Stockport St Thos 83–85; R Stockport St Thos w St Pet 86–12; Chapl St Thos Hosp 88–12; Chapl Cheadle R Hosp 88–12; rtd 12; PtO *Ches* from 12. *88 Woodlands Drive, Stockport SK2 5AP* T: 0161-483 0675 E: truefaith_d@hotmail.com

KENSINGTON, Area Bishop of. See TOMLIN, The Rt Revd Graham Stuart

KENT, Alan Gilbert. b 56. Univ of Wales (Ban) BTh 09 Univ of Wales (Trin St Dav) MTh 15. **d** 14 **p** 15. NSM Cardigan w Mwnt and Y Ferwig w Llangoedmor *St D* 14–18; NSM Bro Teifi from 18. *44 Bro Teifi, Cardigan SA43 1DQ* T: (01239) 613907 E: albewaiting@googlemail.com

KENT, Barry James. b 41. **d** 02 **p** 03. OLM Kinson *Sarum* 02–07; NSM Hordle *Win* 07–12; rtd 12; PtO *Win* from 12. *6 Orchard Leigh, 2 Herbert Road, New Milton BH25 6BX* T: (01202) 611348 M: 07733-048534 E: barrykent@minister.com

KENT, Christopher Alfred. b 48. Birm Univ BSc 69 PhD 72 CEng 77 MIChemE 77. St Jo Coll Nottm 82. **d** 84 **p** 85. C Bucknall and Bagnall *Lich* 84–86; Hon C Halesowen *Worc* 86–96; NSM Reddal Hill St Luke 96–01; NSM The Lye and Stambermill from 01. *40 County Park Avenue, Halesowen B62 8SP* T: 0121-550 3132 E: kentca@btinternet.com

KENT, Miss Cindy. b 45. MBE 16. SEITE 05. **d** 07 **p** 08. NSM Whetstone St Jo *Lon* 07–16; P-in-c 10–16; rtd 16; PtO *Cant* from 16. *170 Southsea Avenue, Minster on Sea, Sheerness ME12 2LU* T: (01795) 876469 M: 07879-642100 E: cindykent58@hotmail.com

KENT, David. b 44. CEng MIMechE. NOC. **d** 83 **p** 84. NSM Huddersfield St Pet and All SS *Wakef* 83–98; NSM

Newsome and Armitage Bridge 98–03; NSM Em TM 03–14; Newsome and Armitage Bridge and S Crosland *Leeds* from 14. *2 Hillside Crescent, Huddersfield HD4 6LY* T: (01484) 324049 M: 07949-762186 E: david.kent3@ntlworld.com

KENT, Frank. b 44. Open Univ BA 82 ARCM 76. Ridley Hall Cam. **d** 86 **p** 87. C Faversham *Cant* 86–89; R Lyminge w Paddlesworth, Stanford w Postling etc 89–99; P-in-c Sittingbourne St Mich 99–00; V Sittingbourne St Mary and St Mich 01–04; R Eastry and Northbourne w Tilmanstone etc 04–07; rtd 07; PtO *Cant* from 14. *3 Balfour Road, Walmer, Deal CT14 7HU* T: (01304) 375080 *or* 619366 E: francikeut@tiscali.co.uk

KENT, Hugh. See KENT, Richard Hugh

KENT, Mrs Mary. b 51. Birm Univ BA 72. St Steph Ho Ox 06. **d** 08 **p** 09. NSM Alveston *Cov* 08–13; PtO 13–14; P-in-c Wexham *Ox* 14–18; rtd 18; PtO *Ox* from 18. *16 Ash Road, Princes Risborough HP27 0BQ* M: 07597-382594

KENT, Richard Hugh. b 38. Worc Coll Ox BA 61 MA 63. Chich Th Coll 61. **d** 63 **p** 64. C Emscote *Cov* 63–66; C Finham 66–70; V Parkend *Glouc* 70–75; V Glouc St Aldate 75–86; Chapl and Warden Harnhill Healing Cen 86–96; R N Buckingham *Ox* 96–04; AD Buckingham 00–04; rtd 04; PtO *Pet* from 05; *Ox* 06–12 and 17–19. *10 Booth Close, Pattishall, Towcester NN12 8JP* T: (01327) 830231 E: hugh.hilary38@btinternet.com

KENT-WINSLEY, Cindy. See KENT, Cindy

KENTIGERN-FOX, Canon William Poyntere Kentigern. b 38. AKC 63. **d** 64 **p** 65. C S Mimms St Mary and Potters Bar *Lon* 64–67; C S Tottenham 67–70; R Barrowden and Wakerley *Pet* 70–76; P-in-c Duddington w Tixover 70–76; P-in-c Morcott w S Luffenham 75–76; R Barrowden and Wakerley w S Luffenham 77–79; R Byfield w Boddington 79–86; V Northampton St Mich w St Edm 86–95; V Raunds 95–03; Can Pet Cathl 94–03; RD Higham 97–02; rtd 03; PtO *Linc* 17–20. *41 Parkfield Road, Ruskington, Sleaford NG34 9HT* T: (01526) 830944

KENWARD, Roger Nelson. b 34. Selw Coll Cam BA 58 MA 62. Ripon Hall Ox 58. **d** 60 **p** 61. C Paddington St Jas *Lon* 60–63; Chapl RAF 64–82; Asst Chapl-in-Chief RAF 82–89; P-in-c Lyneham w Bradenstoke *Sarum* 72–76; QHC 85–89; R Laughton w Ripe and Chalvington *Chich* 90–95; Chapl Laughton Lodge Hosp 90–95; rtd 95; NSM Chiddingly w E Hoathly *Chich* 96; PtO from 96. *The Coach House, School Hill, Old Heathfield, Heathfield TN21 9AE* T: (01435) 862618 E: kenwardroger@gmail.com

KENWAY, Ian Michael. b 52. Leeds Univ BA 74 Bris Univ PhD 86. Coll of Resurr Mirfield 74. **d** 76 **p** 77. C Cov E 76–79; C Southmead *Bris* 79–81; P-in-c Shaw Hill *Birm* 82–88; Asst Sec Gen Syn Bd for Soc Resp 88–93; Chapl Essex Univ *Chelmsf* 93–99; Dir Studies Cen for Study of Th 93–99; PtO *S & B* 01–19. *Katerina's House, Symi, 85600 Dodecanese, Greece* M: 07927-429237 E: iankenway@phidoc.net

KENWAY, Robert Andrew. b 56. Bris Univ BA 78. Westcott Ho Cam 80. **d** 82 **p** 83. C Birchfield *Birm* 82–85; C Queensbury All SS *Lon* 87–89; R Birm St Geo 89–97; V Calne and Blackland *Sarum* 97–10; TR Marden Vale from 10. *The Vicarage, 4 Vicarage Close, Calne SN11 8DD* T: (01249) 812340 E: rakenway@gmail.com

KENYON, Caroline Elizabeth. See HOLMES, Caroline Elizabeth

KENYON, Robert Fletcher. b 52. K Coll Lon BSc 73 PhD 80. SEITE 02. **d** 05 **p** 17. C Ashford *Cant* 05–06; PtO *S'wark* 15–16; NSM Brockham Green 16; NSM Leigh 16; NSM Brockham Green and Leigh 17–19; Faith in the Countryside Officer 19. *156 Croydon Road, Reigate RH2 0NG* M: 07979-707529 E: robfleckenyon@gmail.com

KEOGH, Robert Gordon. b 56. CITC. **d** 84 **p** 85. C Mossley *Conn* 84–87; I Taunagh w Kilmactranny, Ballysumaghan etc *K, E & A* 87–90; I Swanlinbar w Tomregan, Kinawley, Drumlane etc 90–02; Preb Kilmore Cathl 98–02; I Drumclamph w Lower and Upper Langfield *D & R* from 02. *Drumclamph Rectory, 70 Greenville Road, Castlederg BT81 7NU* T: (028) 8167 1433 E: rkeogh10@hotmail.co.uk

KEOWN, Paul Gabriel. b 53. Univ of Wales (Swansea) BA 95 PGCE 97 LGSM 76. Ripon Coll Cuddesdon 00 St Steph Ho Ox BTh 06. **d** 02 **p** 03. C Llansamlet *S & B* 02–04; P-in-c Swansea St Nic 04–07; R Haddington *Edin* 07–08; V Salfords *S'wark* 08–12; P-in-c Beckenham St Mich w St Aug *Roch* 12–15; P-in-c Footscray w N Cray 15–16; Dioc Dir of Ords 15–16; P-in-c Erwood Gp w Painscastle Gp *S & B* from 16. *Trefechan, Aberedw, Builth Wells LD2 3UH* T: (01982) 560653 E: frpaulkeown@mac.com

KER, Robert Andrew. **d** 05 **p** 06. Aux Min Larne and Inver *Conn* 05–13; Dioc C 13–16; I Templepatrick w Donegore 16–18. *24 Ravensdale, Newtownabbey BT36 6FA* T: (028) 9083 6901 E: a.ker@btinternet.com

KERL, Ms Elizabeth. b 72. d 13 p 14. NSM Bassaleg *Mon* 13–18; TV Cwmbran from 18. *18 St Peter's Vicarage, 30 Longhouse Grove, Henllys, Cwmbran NP44 6HQ* T: (01633) 974973

KERLEY, Patrick Thomas Stewart. b 42. Linc Th Coll. d 85 p 86. Hon C Thorpe St Andr *Nor* 85–90; C Wymondham 90–94; C Gt Yarmouth 94–95; TV 95–00; TV Wilford Peninsula *St E* 00–07; rtd 07; PtO *Nor* from 08. *3 St Leonard's Close, Wymondham NR18 0JF* T: (01953) 606618 M: 07940-739769 E: patrick_kerley@sky.com

KERNEY, Barbara. *See* SHERLOCK, Barbara Lee Kerney

KERNOHAN, Jason William. b 79. TCD BTh 10. CITC 07. d 10 p 11. C Drumachose *D & R* 10–15; I Eglantine *Conn* from 15. *All Saints' Rectory, 16 Eglantine Road, Lisburn BT27 5RQ* T: (028) 9266 1406 E: jasonkernohan79@gmail.com

KERR, The Ven Alison. b 76. Ripon Coll Cuddesdon 06. d 09 p 10. C Lytchett Minster *Sarum* 09–10; C The Lytchetts and Upton 10–12; P-in-c Whippingham w E Cowes *Portsm* 12–17; P-in-c Newport St Jo 17–19; AD Is of Wight 17–19; V Portsea St Cuth from 19; Adn The Meon from 21. *St Cuthbert's Vicarage, 2 Lichfield Road, Portsmouth PO3 6DE* T: (023) 9307 1792

KERR, Andrew Harry Mayne. b 41. TCD BA 63. Melbourne Coll of Div MMin 98. d 65 p 66. C Belfast St Luke *Conn* 65–68; SCM Sec (Ireland) 68–72; C Clooney *D & R* 72–74; C Swinburne Australia 74–80; I Dallas 80–88; I Mont Albert 88–94; P-in-c W Geelong from 96. *101 Katrina Street, Blackburn North Vic 3130, Australia* T: (0061) (3) 5221 6694 *or* (3) 9893 4946 F: 9893 4946 E: ahmkerr@hotmail.com

KERR, Bryan Thomas. b 70. QUB BD 91 TCD MPhil 96. CITC 94. d 96 p 97. C Enniskillen *Clogh* 96–99; I Garrison w Slavin and Belleek 99–05; I Lisbellaw 05–14; Dioc Communications Officer 00–13; Can Clogh Cathl 12–14; Dean Dromore *D & D* 14–15; I Dromore Cathl 14–15; P-in-c Heversham and Milnthorpe *Carl* from 19; P-in-c Levens from 19. *The Vicarage, Vicarage Road, Levens, Kendal LA8 8PY* E: brykerr@sky.com

KERR, Charles. *See* KERR, Ewan Charles

KERR, David James. b 36. TCD BA 58 MA 61 BD 61 HDipEd 66. TCD Div Sch Div Test 59. d 60 p 61. C Belfast Trin Coll Miss *Conn* 60–63; Dean's V St Patr Cathl Dublin 63–66; Chapl Beechwood Park Sch St Alb 66–01; Hon C Flamstead *St Alb* 74–00; PtO 00–03; rtd 01. *Trumpton Cottage, 12A Pickford Road, Markyate, St Albans AL3 8RU* T: (01582) 841191 E: kerr_david@hotmail.com *or* kerr-david66@hotmail.com

KERR, Canon Derek Preston. b 64. TCD BTh 90. Oak Hill Th Coll 85. d 90 p 91. C Belfast St Donard *D & D* 90–93; C Carrickfergus *Conn* 93–96; I Devenish w Boho Clogh 96–07; I Drummaul w Duneane and Ballyscullion *Conn* from 07; Preb Conn Cathl from 16. *The Vicarage, 1A Glenkeen, Randalstown, Antrim BT41 3JX* T: (028) 9447 2561 E: derekpkerr@gmail.com

KERR, Miss Dora Elizabeth. b 41. QUB BA 65 Southn Univ DipEd 66. St Jo Coll Nottm 82. dss 84 d 87 p 94. Becontree St Mary *Chelmsf* 84–88; Par Dn 87–88; Par Dn Rushden w Newton Bromswold *Pet* 88–93; C Finham and Chapl Walsgrave Hosps NHS Trust 94–00; C Belper *Derby* 00–07; rtd 07; PtO *Cov* from 08. *23 Worcester Close, Allesley, Coventry CV5 9FZ* T: (024) 7640 2413 E: elizabeth@ekerr1.plus.com

KERR, Ewan Charles. b 74. Fitzw Coll Cam BA 96 MA 00. Ripon Coll Cuddesdon MTh 01. d 01 p 02. C Nor St Pet Mancroft w St Jo Maddermarket 01–04; Chapl Glenalmond Coll *St And* 04–07; Chapl St Edw Sch Ox 07–18; LtO *Ox* from 18. *31 Stone Meadow, Oxford OX2 6TD* E: charlie.kerr@oxford.anglican.org

KERR, Canon Jean. b 46. Man Univ MA 93 SS Hild & Bede Coll Dur CertEd 69. NOC 84. d 87 p 94. NSM Peel *Man* 87–93; Par Dn Dixon Green 88–89; Par Dn New Bury 89–93; Par Dn Gillingham St Mark *Roch* 93–94; C 94–98; Chapl Medway Secure Tr Cen 98–01; Warden of Ev *Roch* 98–05; NSM Roch St Justus 01–05; Hon Can Roch Cathl 03–05; Can Missr 05–16; Tr Officer for Lay Minl Educn *Roch* 03–05; Bp's Officer for Miss and Unity 05–16; rtd 16; PtO *Cant* 17–20; *Roch* from 17. *30 Scholars Close, Deal CT14 9FA* T: (01304) 360546 M: 07791-503123 E: jeankerr146@yahoo.co.uk

KERR, Karlene Theresa Kamella. b 58. d 13 p 14. C Harefield *Lon* 13–14; C Wealdstone H Trin 14–16; PtO 16–18; C Gaywood *Nor* 17–18; TV from 18; Dioc Ecum Officer from 18; Bp's Adv for Black, Asian and Minority Ethnic Affairs from 20. *28 Jermyn Road, King's Lynn PE30 4AE* T: (01553) 768264 M: 07989-467276 E: karlenekerr@aol.com *or* vicar@stfaithsgaywoodlep.org.uk

KERR, Canon Nicholas Ian. b 46. Em Coll Cam BA 68 MA 72. Westcott Ho Cam 74. d 77 p 78. C Merton St Mary *S'wark* 77–80; C Rainham *Roch* 80–84; Chapl Joyce Green Hosp Dartford 84–90; V Dartford St Edm *Roch* 84–90; V Lamorbey H Redeemer 90–11; RD Sidcup 98–03; Hon Can Roch Cathl

02–11; rtd 11; PtO *Roch* from 11. *11 Cobdown Grove, Rainham, Gillingham ME8 7PN* T: (01634) 389960 M: 07885-619595 E: mizeki@mac.com

KERR, Canon Paul Turner. b 47. Man Univ MA 92. Cranmer Hall Dur 68. d 71 p 72. C Kingston upon Hull St Martin *York* 71–72; C Linthorpe 72–76; C Cherry Hinton St Jo *Ely* 76–78; Chapl Addenbrooke's Hosp Cam 76–78; TV Rochdale *Man* 78–84; Chapl Birch Hill Hosp 78–84; V New Bury *Man* 84–87; TR 87–93; C Gillingham St Mark *Roch* 93–98; RD Gillingham 96–98; V Roch St Justus 98–11; RD Roch 02–11; CF (TA) 90–03; CF (ACF) 06–17; Chapl Roch Cathl 11–16; Hon Can Roch Cathl 11–16; rtd 12; PtO *Cant* 17–20; *Roch* from 17. *30 Scholars Close, Deal CT14 9FA* T: (01304) 360546 E: ptkerr@hotmail.co.uk

KERR, Canon Stephen Peter. b 46. TCD BA 68 Edin Univ BD 71 MPhil 80. d 71 p 72. C Belfast H Trin *Conn* 72–76; C Ballywillan 76–78; Lect Linc Th Coll 78–87; Dioc Officer for Adult Educn and Minl Tr *Worc* 87–99; P-in-c Ombersley w Doverdale 87–13; P-in-c Hartlebury 08–13; P-in-c Elmley Lovett w Hampton Lovett and Elmbridge etc 10–13; Bp's Th Adv 99–07; RD Droitwich 07–13; Hon Can Worc Cathl 93–13; rtd 13; PtO *Worc* from 13. *27 Witton Avenue, Droitwich WR9 8NX* T: (01905) 776423 E: stephen.kerr46@yahoo.co.uk

KERR, Terence Philip. b 54. QUB BD 97. CITC 97. d 99 p 00. C Antrim All SS *Conn* 99–01; I Drummaul w Duneane and Ballyscullion 01–07; I Belfast St Aid 07–12; rtd 13; P-in-c Maghera w Killelagh *D & R* 16–17; I from 17. *69 Tobermore Road, Maghera BT46 5DN* T: (028) 7964 2252 M: 07727-877833 E: terryrevkerr@talktalk.net

KERRIDGE, Benjamin. b 82. Clare Coll Cam BA 04. Coll of Resurr Mirfield 11. d 14 p 15. C Hornsey St Mary w St Geo *Lon* 14–17; V Hornsey H Innocents from 17. *99 Hillfield Avenue, London N8 7DG*

KERRY, Martin John. b 55. Ox Univ MA 78. St Jo Coll Nottm BA 81 MTh 83. d 82 p 83. C Everton St Geo *Liv* 82–85; LtO *S'well* 85–04; Chapl Asst Nottm City Hosp 85–89; Chapl 89–94; Hd Chapl Nottm City Hosp NHS Trust 94–04; Lead Chapl (NE) Caring for the Spirit NHS Project 04–07; Chapl Manager Sheff Teaching Hosps NHS Foundn Trust 07–18; rtd 18. *14 Avondale Road, Chesterfield S40 4TF* T: (01246) 202144 E: martinkerry101@gmail.com

KERSHAW, Johanna. b 81. Clare Coll Cam BA 12 St Andr Univ MA 04 Oriel Coll Ox MSt 05 DPhil 10. Westcott Ho Cam 10. d 13 p 14. C Todmorden w Cornholme and Walsden *Leeds* 13–17; C Wrenthorpe 17; C Outwood, Stanley and Wrenthorpe 17–20; C N Wakefield from 20. *St Anne's Vicarage, 121 Wrenthorpe Road, Wrenthorpe Road, Wakefield WF2 0JS* T: (01924) 373758 M: 07979-042694 E: revdjokershaw@gmail.com

KERSHAW, Savile. b 37. Bernard Gilpin Soc Dur 60 Chich Th Coll 61. d 64 p 65. C Staincliffe *Wakef* 64–66; C Saltley *Birm* 66–68; C Birm St Aid Small Heath 68–72; PtO 88–02; rtd 02. *74 Longmore Road, Shirley, Solihull B90 3EE* T: 0121-744 3470

KERSLAKE, Marc Richard. b 67. SWMTC 14. d 17 p 18. C Whimple, Talaton, Clyst St Lawr and Clyst Hydon *Ex* 17–21; P-in-c 21; TR Broadclyst, Clyst Honiton, Clyst Hydon etc from 21. *The Rectory, Grove Road, Whimple, Exeter EX5 2TP* M: 07958-557068 E: marckerslake@hotmail.co.uk

KERSLEY, Stuart Casburn. b 40. CEng MIET. Trin Coll Bris. d 82 p 83. C Lancing w Coombes *Chich* 82–87; TV Littlehampton and Wick 87–90; R Kingston Buci 90–98; V Kirdford 98–06; rtd 06; Hon C Appleshaw, Kimpton, Thruxton, Fyfield etc *Win* 06–12; PtO *Chich* 12–17. *7 Hormare Crescent, Storrington, Pulborough RH20 4PW*

KERSWILL, Canon Anthony John. b 39. Lambeth STh 85. Linc Th Coll 72. d 73 p 73. C Boultham *Linc* 73–76; P-in-c N Kelsey and Cadney 76–83; V Gainsborough St Geo 83–91; V Bracebridge 91–00; P-in-c Linc St Swithin 00–01; V Linc All SS 01–05; RD Christianity 96–02; Can and Preb Linc Cathl 02–05; rtd 05; Chapl Trin Hosp Retford 05–12; PtO *S'well* 12–20. *1 Ridgeway, Nettleham, Lincoln LN2 2TL* E: tonyvic931@gmail.com

KERSWILL, Vanessa Jane. b 78. St Mellitus Coll 15. d 18 p 19. C Abbots Langley *St Alb* 18–20; P-in-c Watford St Pet from 20. *Address withheld by request* T: (01923) 465064 E: vicar@stpeterswatford.org.uk

KERSYS-HULL, Mrs Polly Ruth. b 91. Cant Ch Ch Univ BA 13. St Mellitus Coll MA 17. d 17 p 18. C Leytonstone St Jo *Chelmsf* from 17; C Leytonstone H Trin and St Aug Harrow Green from 21. *34 Leyspring Road, London E11 3BX* M: 07510-053841 E: polly@kersys-hull.co.uk

KERTON-JOHNSON, Peter. b 41. St Paul's Coll Grahamstown. d 81 p 82. S Africa 81–99; PtO *Sarum* 99–00; P-in-c Stoke sub Hamdon *B & W* 00–11; Chapl St Marg Hospice Yeovil

07–08; rtd 11. *50 Brutton Way, Chard TA20 2HB* T: (01460) 419761 M: 07932-753872 E: kertonjohnson@sky.com

KESARI, Godfrey Freeda. b 73. Nesamony Memorial Chr Coll Marthandam BSc 93 United Th Coll Bangalore BD 99. Princeton Th Sem ThM 01. **p** 05. PtO *Birm* 05–07; C Bridlington Priory *York* 07–10; V Southwater *Chich* from 10; Dioc Interfaith Adv from 18. *The Vicarage, Church Lane, Southwater, Horsham RH13 9BT* T: (01403) 730229 M: 07709-947056 E: revdgodfrey@yahoo.co.uk

KESLAKE, Peter Ralegh. b 33. Sarum & Wells Th Coll. **d** 83 **p** 84. C Glouc St Geo w Whaddon 83–86; P-in-c France Lynch 86–91; V Chalford and France Lynch 91–03; rtd 03; PtO *Glouc* 04–18. *4 Farmcote Close, Eastcombe, Stroud GL6 7EG* E: qml@live.co.uk

KESTER, Jonathan George Frederick. b 66. Ex Univ BA 90 FRSA 14. Coll of Resurr Mirfield 91. **d** 93 **p** 94. C Cheshunt *St Alb* 93–96; Chapl to Bp Edmonton *Lon* 96–00; Hon C Munster Square Ch Ch and St Mary Magd 96–00; V Gt Ilford St Mary *Chelmsf* 00–08; P-in-c Hampstead Em W End *Lon* 08–13; V from 13; P-in-c W Hampstead St Cuth from 16; Asst Dir of Ords 09–17; CMP 00–14; AD N Camden *Lon* 16–20; AD S Camden 18–20; AD Camden from 20. *Emmanuel Vicarage, Lyncroft Gardens, London NW6 1JU* T: (020) 7435 1911 E: frjonathan@mac.com

KESTERTON, David William. b 59. Man Univ BSc 80. Cranmer Hall Dur 85. **d** 88 **p** 89. C Cheddleton *Lich* 88–92; TV Dunstable *St Alb* 92–97; Chapl Dunstable Coll 92–97; PtO *St Alb* 12–13; C Luton All SS w St Pet 13–14; P-in-c 14–17; V from 17; AD Luton from 19. *All Saints' Vicarage, Shaftesbury Road, Luton LU4 8AH* T: (01582) 526662 M: 07957-228102 E: dkesterton1@gmail.com

KESTEVEN, Elizabeth Anne. b 79. Newc Univ LLB 01. St Steph Ho Ox 05. **d** 08 **p** 09. C Bris St Steph w St Jas and St Jo w St Mich etc 08–12; C Bedminster 12–13; C Whitchurch 12–13; P-in-c Fishponds All SS 13–19; P-in-c Fishponds St Mary 13–19; V Fishponds All SS and St Mary from 19. *11 Vicar's Close, Bristol BS16 3TH* T: 0117-965 0856 M: 07973-917720 E: lizzie.kesteven@live.co.uk

KESTON, Marion. b 44. Glas Univ MB, ChB 68 Edin Univ MTh 95. St And Dioc Tr Course 87 Edin Th Coll 92. **d** 90 **p** 94. NSM W Fife Team Min *St And* 90–93; C Dunfermline 93–96; Priest Livingston LEP *Edin* 96–04; P-in-c Kinross *St And* 04–11; rtd 11; LtO *St And* 11–18; LtO *Mor* from 18. *60 Manse Road, Nairn IV12 4RS* T: (01667) 456587 E: marionkeston2@gmail.com

KETLEY, Christopher Glen. b 62. Aston Tr Scheme 91 Coll of Resurr Mirfield 93. **d** 95 **p** 96. C Gt Crosby St Faith *Liv* 95–98; C Swinton and Pendlebury *Man* 98–00; V Belfield 00–08; R Elgin w Lossiemouth *Mor* 08–18; R Dufftown 08–12; R Aberlour 08–12; Syn Clerk 14–18; R Castle Douglas *Glas* from 18; R Dalbeattie from 18. *68 St Andrew Street, Castle Douglas DG7 1EN* M: 07932-183069

KETLEY, Michael James. b 39. Oak Hill Th Coll 79. **d** 81 **p** 82. C Bedhampton *Portsm* 81–85; R St Ive w Quethiock *Truro* 85–86; NSM Basildon St Andr w H Cross *Chelmsf* 89–90; C Barkingside St Cedd 90–92; P-in-c 92–95; R Hadleigh St Jas 95–08; rtd 08; PtO *Chelmsf* from 08. *40 Commonhall Lane, Hadleigh, Benfleet SS7 2RN* T: (01702) 428971 E: mikeketley@aol.com

KETTLE, Alan Marshall. b 51. Leeds Univ BA 72. Wycliffe Hall Ox MA 78. **d** 78 **p** 79. C Llantwit Fardre *Llan* 78–81; Prov RE Adv Ch in Wales 81–84; Chapl Llandovery Coll 84–92; P-in-c Cil-y-Cwm and Ystrad-ffin w Rhandir-mwyn etc *St D* 85–92; Chapl W Buckland Sch Barnstaple 92–11; rtd 11; PtO *Llan* 11–12; P-in-c Colwinston, Llandow and Llysworney from 12; PtO *St D* from 15. *Moat Farm, Llysworney, Cowbridge CF71 7NQ* T: (01446) 679186 E: kettlesatmoat@hotmail.co.uk

KETTLE, Martin Drew. b 52. New Coll Ox BA 74 Selw Coll Cam BA 76 Cam Univ MA 85. Ridley Hall Cam 74. **d** 77 **p** 78. C Enfield St Andr *Lon* 77–80; Chapl Ridley Hall Cam 80–84; V Hendon St Paul Mill Hill *Lon* 85–98; AD W Barnet 90–95; PtO *Ely* 03–04; Hon C Huntingdon 04–06; Hon C E Leightonstone 06–10; Hon C Hamerton, Winwick and Gt w Lt Gidding and Steeple Gidding 09–10; PtO *Ox* 11–19. *19 Windrush Quay, Witney OX28 1YL* M: 07554-213344 E: mdkettle@msn.com

KETTLE, Mrs Patricia Mary Carole. b 41. Worc Coll of Educn CertEd 61. Dalton Ho Bris 66. **d** 87 **p** 94. C Wonersh Guildf 87–98; C Wonersh w Blackheath 98–01; rtd 01; PtO *Guildf* from 02; Dioc Widow/Widowers' Officer from 13. *Wakehurst Cottage, Links Road, Bramley GU5 0AL* T: (01483) 898856 E: patsykettle@talktalk.net

KETTLE, Peter. b 51. K Coll Lon BD 74 AKC 74. St Aug Coll Cant 74. **d** 75 **p** 76. C Angell Town St Jo *S'wark* 75–78; C Putney St Mary 78–80; V Raynes Park St Sav 80–85; PtO

85–20; *Lon* 03–13; NSM S Kensington H Trin w All SS 13–19. *46 Allenswood, Albert Drive, London SW19 6JX* T: (020) 8785 3797 E: peter@levelsix.plus.com

KEULEMANS, Andrew Francis Charles. b 68. Univ of Wales (Abth) BSc 90 ACP 71. St Jo Coll Nottm BTh 93. **d** 94 **p** 95. C Mold *St As* 94–97; TV Wrexham 97–02; Chapl Loretto Sch Musselburgh 02–10; R Musselburgh and Prestonpans *Edin* 10–15; PtO 15–17; Chapl Shrewsbury Sch from 17. *Shrewsbury School, Kingsland, Shrewsbury SY3 7BA* T: (01743) 280500 E: andrewkeulemans@btinternet.com *or* ak@shrewsbury.com

KEULEMANS, Michael Desmond. b 42. SS Mark & Jo Univ Coll Plymouth TCert 65 Univ of Wales (Ban) MTh 06 DMin 10. St As Minl Tr Course 02. **d** 92 **p** 93. PtO *St As* 03–11; Hon C Llanfyllin, Bwlchycibau and Llanwddyn 11–13; PtO *Lich* 13–15; *Blackb* from 16. *4 Wakefield Crescent, Standish, Wigan WN6 0AU* T: (01257) 425320 E: mdkeulemans43@gmail.com

KEVILL-DAVIES, Christopher Charles. b 44. AKC 69. St Aug Coll Cant 70. **d** 70 **p** 71. C Folkestone St Sav *Cant* 70–75; V Yaxley *Ely* 75–78; R Chevington w Hargrave and Whepstead w Brockley *St E* 78–86; PtO *St Alb* 86–89; NSM Stansted Mountfitchet *Chelmsf* 87–89; R Barkway, Reed and Buckland w Barley *St Alb* 89–97; R Chelsea St Luke and Ch Ch *Lon* 97–05; rtd 06; PtO *S'wark* from 06; Hon Min Can S'wark Cathl from 06; PtO *Lon* from 19. *York House, 35 Clapham Common South Side, London SW4 9BS* T: (020) 7622 9647 E: christopherkd@hotmail.com

KEVIN, Brother. See GOODMAN, Kevin Charles

KEVIS, Lionel William Graham. b 55. York Univ BA. Wycliffe Hall Ox 83. **d** 86 **p** 87. C Plaistow St Mary *Roch* 86–90; R Ash 90–00; R Ridley 90–00; P-in-c Bidborough 00–02; P-in-c Leigh 00–09; V from 09; RD Tonbridge 03–10. *The Vicarage, The Green, Leigh, Tonbridge TN11 8QJ* T: (01732) 833022

KEW, Canon William Richard. b 45. Lon Univ BD 69. ALCD 68. **d** 69 **p** 70. C Finchley St Paul Long Lane *Lon* 69–72; C Stoke Bishop *Bris* 72–76; C Hamilton and Wenham USA 76–79; R Rochester All SS 79–85; Exec Dir SPCK 85–95; Co-ord Russian Min Network 95–00; Convenor US Angl Congregation 00–02; V Franklin Apostles 02–06; R Franklin Resurr 06–07; Development Dir Ridley Hall Cam 07–15; rtd 15; PtO *Ely* 12–16; Hon Can Missr Owerri from 12. *2272 Lewisburg Pike, Franklin TN 37064, USA* E: richardkew@aol.com

KEY, Christopher Halstead. b 56. St Jo Coll Dur BA 77 K Coll Lon MTh 78. Ridley Hall Cam 79. **d** 81 **p** 82. C Balderstone *Man* 81–84; C Wandsworth All SS *S'wark* 84–88; C-in-c W Dulwich Em CD 88–93; V W Dulwich Em 93–95; R Ore St Helen and St Barn *Chich* 95–13; RD Hastings 03–13; V Maidstone St Luke *Cant* 13–20; rtd 20; PtO *York* from 21. *83 Thoresby Road, York YO24 3EN* E: revchriskey@gmail.com

KEY, Roderick Charles Halstead. b 57. MTh. **d** 84 **p** 85. C Up Hatherley *Glouc* 84–87; V Glouc St Paul 87–04; TR Trunch *Nor* 04–14; V Chippenham St Andr w Tytherton Lucas *Bris* from 14. *St Andrew's Vicarage, 54A St Mary Street, Chippenham SN15 3JW* T: (01249) 652788

KEY, Roger Astley. b 49. Coll of Resurr Mirfield 72. **d** 74 **p** 75. PtO *Wakef* 74–75; P-in-c Khomasdal Grace Ch Namibia 75–77; R Luderitz 77–81; Adn The South 80–86; R Walvis Bay 81–85; Personal Asst to Bp Windhoek 85–86; Dean Windhoek 86–00; V Hopton w Corton *Nor* 00–19; rtd 19; PtO *Nor* from 19. *The Fairstead, 1 Back Street, Horsham St Faith, Norwich NR10 3JP* M: 07733-028048 E: thekeybunch@aol.com

KEYES, Graham George. b 44. St Cath Coll Cam BA 65 MA 68 Lanc Univ MA 74 Nottm Univ MTh 85 MPhil 92. EMMTC 82. **d** 84 **p** 85. C Evington *Leic* 84–86; Vice-Prin NEOC 86–89; C Monkseaton St Mary *Newc* 86–89; P-in-c Newc St Hilda 89–94; TV Ch the King 94–99; rtd 99; PtO *Newc* from 09. *1 East Avenue, Newcastle upon Tyne NE12 9PH* T: 0191-259 9024 E: graham.keyes@btinternet.com

KEYT, Fitzroy John. b 34. Linc Th Coll. **d** 67 **p** 68. C Highters Heath *Birm* 67–70; Hon C Sheldon 70–73; V Miles Australia 73–76; R Rayton 76–86; R Coolangatta 86–98; P-in-c Clayfield 98–01. *58 Thompson Street, Zillmere QLD 4034, Australia* T: (0061) (7) 3314 3011 E: dskeyt@optusnet.com.au

KEYTE, Mrs Christine Evi. b 73. UNISA BA 98 Anglia Ruskin Univ MA 15. Westcott Ho Cam 13. **d** 14 **p** 15. C Rustington *Chich* 14–17; V Crawley Down All SS from 17. *The Vicarage, Vicarage Road, Crawley Down, Crawley RH10 4JJ* T: (01342) 718741 E: vicar@allsaintscrawleydown.org

KHAKHRIA, Rohitkumar Prabhulal (Roy). b 60. Sheff Univ BSc 82 PGCE 83. Oak Hill Th Coll 94. **d** 96 **p** 97. C Muswell Hill St Jas w St Matt *Lon* 96–01; C Stoughton *Guildf* 01–04; V Boscombe St Jo *Win* from 04. *St John's Vicarage, 17*

Browning Avenue, Bournemouth BH5 1NR   T: (01202) 396667 *or* 301916   F: 301916 E: roykhakhria@me.com

KHAMBATTA, Neville Holbery. b 48. St Chad's Coll Dur BA 74. S'wark Ord Course 81. **d** 84 **p** 85. Asst Chapl Emanuel Sch Wandsworth 84–87; Hon C Thornton Heath St Jude w St Aid *S'wark* 84–87; Asst Warden Horstead Cen 87–01; Hon C Coltishall w Gt Hautbois and Horstead *Nor* 87–01; V Ludham, Potter Heigham, Hickling and Catfield 01–11; rtd 11; PtO *Nor* from 11. *The Spinney, Butchers Common, Neatishead, Norwich NR12 8XH*   T: (01692) 630231 E: nevilleandval@gmail.com

KHAN, Rana Youab. b 71. St Thos Th Coll Karachi MDiv 99. **d** 99 **p** 01. C Lahore St Andr Pakistan 99–01; V Lahore St Paul 01–03; V Lahore St Jo 03–09; Pris Chapl and Bp's Interfaith Adv 04–09; Internat Inter-Faith Dialogues Asst ACC 09–13; NSM Belmont *Lon* 13–15; C Mill Hill Jo Keble Ch 16–17; V Crickhowell w Cwmdu and Tretower *S & B* from 17; AD Gtr Brecon from 20. *The Rectory, Rectory Road, Crickhowell NP8 1DW*   T: (01873) 810944   M: 07729-805100 E: revrana@hotmail.com *or* rector@crickhowellparish.org.uk

KHAN, Rayman Anthony. b 63. Ripon Coll Cuddesdon 09. **d** 11 **p** 12. C Tamworth *Lich* 11–15; TV Bromsgrove *Worc* from 15. *12 Kidderminster Road, Bromsgrove B61 7JW*   T: (01527)   577172   M: 07952-170840 E: rev.stjohns.bromsgrove@gmail.com

KHARITONOVA, Natalia. *See* CRITCHLOW, Natalia

KHOVACS, Ivan Patricio. b 68. **d** 14 **p** 15. NSM Willesborough w Sevington *Cant* 14–15; NSM Westmr St Jas *Lon* from 15. *3 St Peter's House, 119 Eaton Square, London SW1W 9AL*   M: 07540-418621 E: ivankhovacs@gmail.com

KHOVACS, Mrs Julie Marie. b 67. Regent Coll Vancouver MA 00 Leeds Univ MA 05. Westcott Ho Cam 09. **d** 11 **p** 12. C Ashford *Cant* 11–15; C Pimlico St Pet w Westmr Ch Ch *Lon* from 15. *3 St Peter's House, 119 Eaton Square, London SW1W 9AL*   M: 07540-418623 E: revjuliekho@gmail.com *or* julie.khovacs@stpetereatonsquare.co.uk

KICHENSIDE, David Alexander. b 78. St Jo Coll Nottm BA 10. **d** 10 **p** 11. C Lilleshall and Muxton *Lich* 10–14; TV S Chatham H Trin *Roch* from 14. *26 Mayford Road, Chatham ME5 8SZ* E: david.kichenside@gmail.com

KICHENSIDE, Mark Gregory. b 53. Nottm Univ BTh 83. St Jo Coll Nottm 80. **d** 83 **p** 84. C Orpington Ch Ch *Roch* 83–86; C Bexley St Jo 86–90; V Blendon 90–93; V Welling 93–00; R Flegg Coastal Benefice *Nor* 00–05; RD Gt Yarmouth 02–05; TV Walton and Trimley *St E* 10–17; V Felixstowe Ch Ch 17–18; rtd 18. *36 Coombe Meadows, Chillington, Kingsbridge TQ7 2JL*   M: 07933-997480 E: mgkichenside@gmail.com

KIDD, Mrs Ruth. b 62. Southn Univ BSc 83 Westmr Coll of Educn PGCE 84. **d** 12 **p** 13. OLM Lightwater *Guildf* from 12. *11 Aplin Way, Lightwater GU18 5TY*   T: (01276) 471193   M: 07738-263057 E: ruth.kidd@btinternet.com *or* ruth@allsaintslightwater.org.uk

KIDDLE, The Ven John. b 58. Qu Coll Cam BA 80 MA 83 Heythrop Coll Lon MTh 02. Ridley Hall Cam 79. **d** 82 **p** 83. C Ormskirk *Liv* 82–86; V Huyton Quarry 86–91; V Watford St Luke *St Alb* 91–08; RD Watford 99–04; Officer for Miss and Development 08–15; Hon Can St Alb 05–10; Can Res St Alb 10–15; Dir Miss 11–15; Adn Wandsworth *S'wark* from 15; P-in-c Earlsfield St Jo from 19. *Kingston Episcopal Area Office, 620 Kingston Road, London SW20 8DN*   T: (020) 8545 2440 E: john.kiddle@southwark.anglican.org

KIDDLE, Mark Brydges. b 34. ACP 61. Wycliffe Hall Ox. **d** 63 **p** 64. C Scarborough St Luke *York* 63–66; C Walthamstow St Sav *Chelmsf* 66–71; V Nelson St Bede *Blackb* 71–76; V Perry Common *Birm* 76–79; R Grayingham *Linc* 79–84; V Kirton in Lindsey 79–84; R Manton 79–84; Hon C St Botolph Aldgate w H Trin Minories *Lon* 85–91; Hon C St Clem Eastcheap w St Martin Orgar 91–08. *12 Tudor Rose Court, 35 Fann Street, London EC2Y 8DY* E: mk@fpsi.org

KIDDLE, Martin John. b 42. Open Univ BA 80. St Jo Coll Nottm 74. **d** 76 **p** 77. C Gt Parndon *Chelmsf* 76–80; Asst Chapl HM Pris Wakef 80–81; Asst Chapl HM Youth Cust Cen Portland 81–88; Chapl HM Pris Cardiff 88–97; Chapl HM Pris Channings Wood 97–02; rtd 02; PtO *Ex* 02–09. *2 Cricketfield Close, Chudleigh, Newton Abbot TQ13 0GA*   T: (01626) 853980 E: mkiddle@talktalk.net

KIDDLE, Miss Susan Elizabeth. b 44. Birm Univ BSc 66 Nottm Univ CertEd 67. **d** 89 **p** 95. OLM Waddington *Linc* 89–97; OLM Bracebridge 98–06; PtO from 06. *Rose Cottage, 30 Finningley Road, Lincoln LN6 0UP*

KIDDY, Claire Elizabeth. b 60. ERMC 15. **d** 18 **p** 19. NSM Beccles St Mich and St Luke *St E* 18–21; NSM Hundred River and Wainford from 21. *Wissett Lodge, Lodge Lane, Wissett, Halesworth IP19 0JQ*   T: (01986) 873173 E: revclairekiddy@gmail.com

KIGGELL, Mrs Anne Kirk. b 36. Liv Univ BA 57. SAOMC 99. **d** 02 **p** 03. OLM Basildon w Aldworth and Ashampstead *Ox* 02–09; PtO from 09. *6 Quarry Hollow, Headington, Oxford OX3 8JR*   T: (01865) 766235 E: anne.kiggell@btinternet.com

KILCOOLEY, Christine Margaret Anne. *See* ROBINSON, Christine Margaret Anne

KILDARE, Archdeacon of. *See* STEVENSON, The Ven Leslie Thomas Clayton

KILDARE, Dean of. *See* WRIGHT, The Very Revd Timothy

KILFORD, William Roy. b 38. Bris Univ BA 60. Sarum & Wells Th Coll 82. **d** 84 **p** 85. C Herne *Cant* 84–87; Chapl Wm Harvey Hosp Ashford 87–93; R Mersham w Hinxhill *Cant* 87–93; P-in-c Sevington 87–93; V Reculver and Herne Bay St Bart 93–95; Chapl Paphos Cyprus 95–98; P-in-c Doddington, Newnham and Wychling *Cant* 98–02; P-in-c Teynham w Lynsted and Kingsdown 98–02; P-in-c Norton 98–02; AD Ospringe 01–02; rtd 02; Chapl Nord Pas de Calais *Eur* 02–04; Hon C Burton Fleming w Fordon, Grindale etc *York* 04–08; Chapl St Jo Hosp Cant 08–09; P-in-c Burpham *Chich* 09–13; P-in-c Poling 09–13; PtO *Leic* 14–17; Hon C Daventry *Pet* 14–17; PtO *Cant* 18–21. *12A St Nicholas' Hospital, Church Hill, Harbledown, Canterbury CT2 9AD* E: revkilford@aol.com

KILGOUR, Christine Mary. *See* CROMPTON, Christine Mary

KILGOUR, Christopher Richard Hargrave. b 74. York Univ BSc 97 MSc 00. Oak Hill Th Coll BA 13. **d** 13 **p** 14. C Chalk *Roch* 13–17; V Northaw and Cuffley *St Alb* from 17. *The Vicarage, 58 Hill Rise, Cuffley, Potters Bar EN6 4RG*   M: 07446-516945 E: chris@kilgour.org.uk

KILGOUR, Richard Eifl. b 57. Edin Univ BD 85. Edin Th Coll 81. **d** 85 **p** 86. C Wrexham *St As* 85–88; V Whitford 88–97; Ind Chapl 89–97; R Newtown w Llanllwchaiarn w Aberhafesp 97–03; RD Cedewain 01–03; Provost St Andr Cathl *Ab* 03–15; R Aberdeen St Andr 03–15; P-in-c Aberdeen St Ninian 03–15; Gen Sec Internat Chr Maritime Assn 15–16; R Motherwell *Glas* from 18; R Wishaw from 18. *The Rectory, 14 Crawford Street, Motherwell ML1 3AD* E: newrect@hotmail.com

KILLALA AND ACHONRY, Archdeacon of. *See* MACWHIRTER, The Ven Stephen Joseph

KILLALA, Dean of. *See* GRIMASON, The Very Revd Alistair John

KILLALOE, KILFENORA AND CLONFERT, Dean of. *See* SMYTHE, The Very Revd Roderick Lindsay.

KILLWICK, Canon Simon David Andrew. b 56. K Coll Lon BD 80 AKC 80. St Steph Ho Ox 80. **d** 81 **p** 82. C Worsley *Man* 81–84; TV 84–97; P-in-c Moss Side Ch Ch 97–06; R from 06; Hon Can Man Cathl from 04; AD Hulme 07–12. *Christ Church Rectory, Monton Street, Manchester M14 4LT*   T/F: 0161-226 2476 E: frskillwick@btinternet.com *or* rector.ccmside@gmail.com

KILMISTER, David John. b 46. Open Univ BA 88. **d** 06 **p** 07. OLM Chippenham St Paul w Hardenhuish etc *Bris* 06–20; OLM Kington St Michael 06–20; PtO from 20. *22 The Common, Langley Burrell, Chippenham SN15 4LQ*   T/F: (01249) 650926   M: 07747-331971 E: djkilmster@sky.com

KILMORE, Archdeacon of. *See* MACCAULEY, The Ven Craig William Leslie

KILMORE, Dean of. *See* CROSSEY, The Very Revd Nigel Nicholas

KILMORE, ELPHIN AND ARDAGH, Bishop of. *See* GLENFIELD, The Rt Revd Samuel Ferran

KILNER, Canon Frederick James. b 43. Qu Coll Cam BA 65 MA 69. Ridley Hall Cam 67. **d** 70 **p** 71. C Harlow New Town w Lt Parndon *Chelmsf* 70–74; C Cambridge St Andr Less *Ely* 74–79; P-in-c Milton 79–88; R 88–94; P-in-c Ely 94–96; P-in-c Chettisham 94–96; P-in-c Prickwillow 94–96; P-in-c Stretham w Thetford 94–96; P-in-c Stuntney 95–96; TR Ely 96–08; Hon Can Ely Cathl 88–08; Hon C Somersham w Pidley and Oldhurst and Woodhurst 08–15; RD St Ives from 10; PtO from 15. *125 High Street, Somersham, Huntingdon PE28 3EN*   T: (01487) 842864 E: kilner@btinternet.com

KILNER, Mrs Valerie June. b 42. Univ of Wales (Abth) BSc 64 Hughes Hall Cam PGCE 65 MICFM 91. EAMTC 98. **d** 98 **p** 99. NSM Ely 98–08; PtO from 08. *125 High Street, Somersham, Huntingdon PE28 3EN*   T: (01487) 842864 E: vjkilner@btinternet.com

KILPATRICK, Alan William. b 64. Oak Hill Th Coll BA 96. **d** 96 **p** 97. C Ealing St Paul *Lon* 96–01; Assoc R Mt Pleasant USA 01–04; P-in-c Prestonville St Luke *Chich* 04–09; R Diep River S Africa 09–13; I Knocknamuckley *D & D* 13–15; Min Hope Community Ch Craigavon 15–17; PtO *B & W* from 18. *139A Bleary Road, Portadown, Craigavon BT63 5NG* E: alanwkilpatrick@gmail.com

KILPATRICK, Edmund Stuart. b 52. d 12 p 13. NSM Southowram *Leeds* from 12. *17 Athol Green, Halifax HX3 5RN* T: (01422) 259196

KIM, Byung Jun. b 82. Yonsei Univ S Korea BTh 10. Angl Th Sem Seoul MDiv 13. d 13 p 16. C Yaksu-dong and Dioc Officer Dept of Tr and Educn Seoul Korea 13–14; C Pet All SS 15–19; R Abington from 19. *15 Honeysuckle Way, Northampton NN3 3QE* M: 07961-469048 E: prayandwork@gmail.com

KIMARU, Benson Mbure. b 54. St Andr Coll Kabare 81. d 83 p 84. V Mitinguu Kenya 85; Dioc Radio Producer 86–88; Asst to Provost Nairobi 88; V Kangaru 89–90; V Kayole 91–94; V Nyari 95–98; V Maringo 99–02; V Githurai 03–05; PtO *Sheff* 06–07; NSM Brightside w Wincobank 07; NSM Penistone and Thurlstone *Wakef* 07–09; Chapl SW Yorks Partnership NHS Foundn Trust from 09; Chapl Leeds and York Partnership NHS Foundn Trust from 13; PtO *S'well* 11–16; *Leeds* from 17. *41 Holgate Mount, Worsbrough, Barnsley S70 6SR* T: (01226) 891185 M: 07919-988131 E: benititu@gmail.com

KIMBER, Geoffrey Francis. b 46. Univ Coll Lon BA 67 Birm Univ MPhil 01. St Jo Coll Nottm 86. d 88 p 89. C Buckhurst Hill *Chelmsf* 88–92; R Arley *Cov* 92–02; P-in-c Ansley 97–02; CMS Romania 02–07; R Birm Bp Latimer w All SS 07–12; rtd 12; PtO *Ex* from 13; *Eur* from 18. *10A Belle Vue Court, Belle Vue Road, Paignton TQ4 6ER* T: (01803) 556773 E: geoff.kimber@gmail.com

KIMBER, Mrs Gillian Margaret. b 48. Bedf Coll Lon BA 70 Nottm Univ MPhil 11. Oak Hill Th Coll 89. d 91. NSM Buckhurst Hill *Chelmsf* 91–92; C Arley *Cov* 92–97; C Ansley 97–02; CMS Romania 02–07; PtO *Birm* 07–12; rtd 12; LtO *Ex* from 13; PtO *Eur* from 18. *10A Belle Vue Court, Belle Vue Road, Paignton TQ4 6ER* T: (01803) 556773 M: 07581-666199 E: deacon_gill@yahoo.co.uk

KIMBER, Mrs Jennifer Carole Mary. b 47. Keele Univ BA 70. d 15 p 16. NSM Lampeter w Maestir and Silian and Llangybi and Betws Bledrws *St D* 15–20. *15 Carnoustie Grove, Bingley BD16 1QF* T: (01274) 231924 M: 07740-463486 E: jcm.kimber@gmail.com

KIMBER, John Keith. b 45. Bris Univ BSc 66. St Mich Coll Llan. d 69 p 70. C Caerphilly *Llan* 69–72; Chapl Birm Univ 72–75; TR Bris St Agnes and St Simon w St Werburgh 75–82; P-in-c Bris St Paul w St Barn 80–82; Hon C Westbury-on-Trym H Trin 82–83; Area Sec (Wales) USPG 83–89; TR Halesowen *Worc* 89–92; Chapl Geneva *Eur* 92–01; Chapl Monte Carlo 01–02; TR Cen Cardiff *Llan* 02–06; V Cardiff City Par 07–10; rtd 10; PtO *Llan* from 10; *Eur* from 15. *13 Meadow Street, Cardiff CF11 9PY* T: (029) 2023 5809 E: johnkeith.k@gmail.com

KIMBER, Canon Jonathan Richard. b 69. K Coll Cam BA 91 MA 95 St Jo Coll Dur MA 02 K Coll Lon PhD 15. Cranmer Hall Dur 99. d 02 p 03. C Weston Favell *Pet* 02–05; P-in-c Northampton St Benedict 05–10; V 10–15; Can Pet Cathl 14–15; Dioc Dir Min and Discipleship *Worc* from 15. *16 Lowesmoor Wharf, Lowesmoor, Worcester WR1 2RS* T: (01905) 732812 E: jkimber@cofe-worcester.org.uk

KIMBER, Stuart Francis. b 53. Qu Eliz Coll Lon BSc 74 Fitzw Coll Cam BA 79 MA 83. Ridley Hall Cam 77. d 80 p 81. C Edgware *Lon* 80–83; C Cheltenham St Mark *Glouc* 83–84; TV 84–92; C Hawkwell *Chelmsf* 92–01; V Westcliff St Andr 01–15; rtd 15; PtO *Birm* from 18. *210 Staple Lodge Road, Birmingham B31 3DL* M: 07758-468052 E: revskimber@blueyonder.co.uk

KIMBERLEY, Canon Carol Lylie Wodehouse, Countess of. b 51. St Hugh's Coll Ox BA 73 MA 77 CertEd 74. Ripon Coll Cuddesdon 87. d 89 p 94. NSM Hambleden Valley *Ox* 89–02; P-in-c Hormead, Wyddial, Anstey, Brent Pelham etc *St Alb* 02–12; P-in-c Sandon, Wallington and Rushden w Clothall 10–11; RD Buntingford 06–11; Hon Can St Alb 10–12; rtd 12; PtO *Ox* from 12; *St Alb* from 12. *29 Institute Road, Marlow SL7 1BJ* T: (01628) 487920 E: carolkimberley6@gmail.com

KIMMIS, Ms Sally Elizabeth. b 59. Westcott Ho Cam 08. d 10 p 11. C King's Lynn St Marg w St Nic *Nor* 10–14; P-in-c Foulsham, Guestwick, Stibbard, Themelthorpe etc 14–17; P-in-c N Elmham, Billingford, Bintree, Guist etc 16–17; P-in-c Bawdeswell w Foxley 16–17; TR Heart of Norfolk from 17. *The Vicarage, 48 Holt Road, North Elmham, Dereham NR20 5JQ* T: (01362) 668850 M: 07548-741159 E: heartofnorfolkrector@gmail.com

KINAHAN, Canon Timothy Charles. b 53. Jes Coll Cam BA 75. CITC 77. d 78 p 79. C Carrickfergus *Conn* 78–81; Papua New Guinea 81–84; I Belfast Whiterock *Conn* 84–90; I Gilnahirk *D & D* 90–06; I Helen's Bay from 06; Can Belf Cathl from 04; Preb Monmohenock St Patr Cathl Dublin from 12. *The Rectory, 2 Woodland Avenue, Helen's Bay, Bangor BT19 1TX* T: (028) 9185 3601 E: timothykinahan@btinternet.com

KINCH, Christopher David. b 81. K Alfred's Coll Win BTh 02. St Steph Ho Ox 03. d 05 p 06. C Long Eaton St Laur *Derby* 05–09; TV Swindon New Town *Bris* 09–11; Partnership P Bris S 11–15; P-in-c Knowle H Nativity 12–16; CF(V) 10–16; CF from 16. *c/o MOD Chaplains (Army)* T: (01264) 383430 F: 381824 E: frchristopherkinch@gmail.com *or* christopher.kinch981@mod.gov.uk

KINCHIN-SMITH, John Michael. b 52. Fitzw Coll Cam MA. Ridley Hall Cam 79. d 82 p 83. C Sanderstead All SS *S'wark* 82–87; TV Halesworth w Linstead, Chediston, Holton etc *St E* 87–92; R Mursley w Swanbourne and Lt Horwood *Ox* 92–02; R Newton Longville and Mursley w Swanbourne etc 03–06; R Chinnor, Sydenham, Aston Rowant and Crowell 06–13; rtd 13; PtO *Nor* from 13; RD Gt Yarmouth 16–21; PtO *Eur* from 16. *The Old Vicarage, Duke Road, Gorleston, Great Yarmouth NR31 6LL* T: (01493) 717739 E: johnks1881@aol.com

KINDER, David James. b 55. EAMTC 01. d 04 p 05. NSM Warboys w Broughton and Bury w Wistow *Ely* 04–08; Chapl HM Pris Littlehey from 08. *Chaplain, HM Prison Littlehey, Perry, Huntingdon PE28 0SR* T: (01480) 335252 E: david.kinder@justice.gov.uk

KINDER, Mark Russell. b 66. Univ of Wales (Swansea) BA(Econ) 88. St Jo Coll Nottm 91. d 94 p 95. C Pheasey *Lich* 94–98; TV Tettenhall Regis 98–07; P-in-c Walsall St Paul 07–11; V 11–20; C Walsall St Matt 07–11; V Walsall St Luke 11–20; C Walsall Pleck and Bescot 11–20; Chapl HM Pris and YOI Stoke Heath from 20. *HM Prison, Stoke Heath, Market Drayton TF9 2JL* T: (01630) 636000

KINDER, Mrs Sylvia Patricia. b 61. Ridley Hall Cam 03. d 05 p 06. C Warboys w Broughton and Bury w Wistow *Ely* 05–09; C Werrington *Pet* 09–12; P-in-c Hampton *Ely* 13–18; V from 18. *105 Eagle Way, Hampton Vale, Peterborough PE7 8EL* T: (01733) 240196 M: 07876-204624 E: vicar@hamptonchurch.co.uk *or* sylvia@5kinders.com

KING, Mrs Angela Margaret. b 45. Bedf Coll Lon BA 67 Lon Inst of Educn PGCE 68. SEITE 00. d 03 p 04. NSM Bromley St Andr *Roch* 03–15; P-in-c 11–15; rtd 15; PtO *Roch* from 16. *4 Avondale Road, Bromley BR1 4EP* T/F: (020) 8402 0847 E: angelaking45@hotmail.com

KING, Annabel Ingrid. b 57. SWMTC 14. d 16 p 17. NSM Callington Cluster *Truro* 16–20; NSM Maker w Rame, Millbrook, St John and Torpoint from 20. *12 Trefloyd Close, Kelly Bray, Callington PL17 8DP* T: (01579) 382765 E: annabelking@gmail.com

KING, Mrs Barbara Anne. b 55. St Mich Coll Sarum BEd 78. SNWTP 07. d 13 p 14. NSM Christleton *Ches* 13–16; NSM Tarvin from 16. *17 Cathcart Green, Guilden Sutton, Chester CH3 7SR* T: (01244) 300756 E: barbara.king65@yahoo.com

KING, Benjamin John. b 74. Down Coll Cam BA 96 MA 00 Harvard Univ MTh 03 Dur Univ PhD 07. Westcott Ho Cam 97. d 00 p 06. C Boston the Advent USA 00–06; Chapl Harvard Univ 06–09; Asst Prof Ch Hist Univ of the South 09–14; Assoc Prof 14–20; Assoc Dean for Academic Affairs and Prof Ch Hist from 20. *University of the South, 335 Tennessee Avenue, Sewanee TN 37383, USA* T: (001) (931) 598 1619 E: bjking@sewanee.edu

KING, Benjamin William. b 76. Dijon Univ BA 97 Man Univ BA 98 Univ Coll Lon MA Cam Univ BA 05. Ridley Hall Cam 03. d 06 p 07. C Stanwix *Carl* 06–10; TV Chigwell and Chigwell Row *Chelmsf* 10–15; TR 15–19; V Forest Gate St Mark from 19. *The Vicarage, 4A Tylney Road, London E7 0LS* T: (020) 8555 2988 M: 07752-708207 E: kingbw2001@yahoo.com *or* ben.king@stmarksforestgate.org.uk

KING, Caroline Naomi. b 62. New Coll Edin BD 94. Ripon Coll Cuddesdon 94. d 97 p 98. C Wheatley *Ox* 97–12; TV Dorchester from 12. *The Vicarage, 49 The Green North, Warborough, Wallingford OX10 7DW* T: (01865) 858525 M: 07540-051798 E: reverend.caroline@gmail.com

KING, Charles Edward Bruce. b 81. St Cath Coll Cam BA 04. St Mellitus Coll MA 18. d 18 p 19. C St Alb St Mich from 18. *1 Blue House Hill, St Albans AL3 6AD*

KING, Clare Maria. b 68. St Andr Univ BD 91 K Coll Lon MPhil 98. Westcott Ho Cam 91. d 94. Hon C Norbury St Phil *S'wark* 94–96; Chapl Croydon Coll 95–96; Asst Chapl Cen Sheff Univ Hosps NHS Trust 96–01; C Leic Presentation 02–08; C Leic St Chad from 08. *The Vicarage, 12 Saddington Road, Fleckney, Leicester LE8 8AW* T: 0116-240 2215 E: cmking@leicester.anglican.org

KING, David Charles. b 52. K Coll Lon 73 Coll of Resurr Mirfield 77. d 78 p 79. C Saltburn-by-the-Sea *York* 78–81; Youth Officer 81–85; P-in-c Crathorne 81–85; Par Educn Adv *Wakef* 85–91; Min Coulby Newham LEP *York* 91–94; P-in-c Egton w Grosmont 94–00; P-in-c Goathland and Glaisdale 99–00; V Middle Esk Moor 00–07; PtO 12–13; V Middlesbrough St Martin w St Cuth 13–19; Chapl Cleveland

Police 13–19; rtd 19. *16 Ellerby Lane, Runswick, Saltburn-by-the-Sea TS13 5HS* M: 07977-729612 E: meaux1@hotmail.co.uk

KING, David John. b 67. W Sussex Inst of HE BEd 91. St Steph Ho Ox 98. **d** 00 **p** 01. C Bexhill St Pet *Chich* 00–03; TV 03–08; V Eastbourne St Andr from 08; RD Eastbourne from 21. *St Andrew's Vicarage, 425 Seaside, Eastbourne BN22 7RT* T: (01323) 723739 E: frdavidking@talktalk.net *or* frdavid@tiscali.co.uk *or* vicar@standrewseastbourne.org.uk

KING, David Michael. b 73. St Jo Coll Dur BA 95 PGCE 96 Cam Univ BA 02. Ridley Hall Cam 00. **d** 03 **p** 04. C Claygate *Guildf* 03–07; C Redhill H Trin *S'wark* 07–10; C Wallington 10–11; V Wallington St Patr from 12. *12 Mallard Way, Wallington SM6 9LZ* M: 07901-700958 E: david.king@stpats.org.uk

KING, Canon David Russell. b 42. Univ of Wales (Lamp) BA 67. St D Coll Lamp. **d** 68 **p** 69. C Barrow St Geo w St Luke *Carl* 68–72; P-in-c Kirkland 72–74; V Edenhall w Langwathby 72–73; P-in-c Culgaith 72–73; V Edenhall w Langwathby and Culgaith 73–74; V Flookburgh 75–79; V Barrow St Jas 79–82; P-in-c Bolton w Ireby and Uldale 82–83; R 83–90; R Burgh-by-Sands and Kirkbampton w Kirkandrews etc 90–00; P-in-c Aikton and Orton St Giles 95–00; R Barony of Burgh 00–02; P-in-c Gt Broughton and Broughton Moor 02–05; V Brigham, Gt Broughton and Broughton Moor 05–07; Hon Can Carl Cathl 01–07; rtd 07; PtO *Carl* 08–10; Hon C Aspatria w Hayton and Gilcrux from 10. *27 King Street, Aspatria, Wigton CA7 3AF* T: (016973) 23580 E: candrking@gmail.com

KING, David William Anthony. b 42. Ch Ch Ox BA 63 MA 68. Westcott Ho Cam 63. **d** 65 **p** 66. C Cayton w Eastfield *York* 65–68; C Southbroom *Sarum* 68–71; V Holt St Jas 71–72; R Hinton Parva 71–72; V Holt St Jas and Hinton Parva 72–75; P-in-c Horton and Chalbury 73–75; R Holt St Jas, Hinton Parva, Horton and Chalbury 75–79; TV Melton Mowbray w Thorpe Arnold *Leic* 79–83; V Foxton w Gumley and Laughton and Lubenham 83–90; P-in-c Boreham *Chelmsf* 90–00; R Tendring and Lt Bentley w Beaumont cum Moze 00–06; rtd 06; PtO *Ely* from 06. *14 The Hythe, Reach, Cambridge CB25 0JQ* T: (01638) 742924 E: dking66@btinternet.com

KING, Mrs Elaine Rosemary. b 55. Qu Coll Birm. **d** 13 **p** 14. NSM Ward End w Bordesley Green *Birm* 13–17; NSM Birm Cathl from 17. *283 George Road, Erdington, Birmingham B23 7SD* M: 07582-407188 E: rev.eking@hotmail.co.uk

KING, Eleanor Olwen. b 61. Leeds Univ BSc 82 Strathclyde Univ MSc 84. STETS 11. **d** 14 **p** 15. C Alfred Jewel *B & W* 14–18; R Aisholt, Enmore, Goathurst, Nether Stowey etc from 18. *The Rectory, 25 St Mary Street, Nether Stowey, Bridgwater TA5 1LJ* M: 07803-243823 E: eleanor.king@hotmail.com

KING, Ellen Francis. See LOUDON, Ellen Francis

KING, Canon Fergus John. b 62. St Andr Univ MA Edin Univ BD 89 UNISA DTh 06. Edin Th Coll 86. **d** 89 **p** 90. Chapl St Jo Cathl Oban *Arg* 89–92; C Oban St Jo 89–92; Tanzania 92–98; Hon Can and Can Th Tanga from 01; PtO *S'wark* 99–03; Hon C Thamesmead 03–05; R Kotara South Gd Shep Australia from 05. *The Rectory, 10 Melissa Avenue, Adamstown Heights NSW 2289, Australia* T: (0061) (2) 4943 0103 M: 40-377 2431 E: revfking@bigpond.net.au

KING, Helen Sarah Elizabeth. See BLAINE, Helen Sarah Elizabeth

KING, Mrs Jacqueline May. b 67. St Mellitus Coll 18. **d** 21. C Southminster and Steeple *Chelmsf* from 21. *The Vicarage, Fambridge Road, Althorne, Chelmsford CM3 6BZ* E: jacqui.king67@gmail.com

KING, James Anthony. b 46. CBE 76. K Coll Lon BA 69 AKC 69 Lon Inst of Educn DipEd 77. SAOMC 99. **d** 01 **p** 02. NSM Gerrards Cross and Fulmer *Ox* 01–03; NSM S Tottenham St Ann *Lon* 03–08; NSM Chalfont St Peter *Ox* 08–15; PtO from 15. *7 Meadowcroft, Chalfont St Peter, Gerrards Cross SL9 9DH* T: (01753) 887386

KING, Canon Jeffrey Douglas Wallace. b 43. AKC 67. **d** 68 **p** 69. C S Harrow St Paul *Lon* 68–71; C Garforth *Ripon* 71–74; V Potternewton 74–83; TR Moor Allerton 83–99; RD Allerton 85–89; P-in-c Thorner and Dioc Ecum Officer 99–08; Hon Can *Ripon* Cathl 90–08; rtd 08; PtO *Ripon* 09–14; *Leeds* from 14. *17 Barleyfields Terrace, Wetherby LS22 6PW* T: (01937) 520646

KING, Jennifer. b 48. **d** 08 **p** 09. OLM Chorlton-cum-Hardy St Clem *Man* 08–20; rtd 20; PtO from *Man* from 20. *8 St Clements Road, Manchester M21 9HU* T: 0161-861 0898 M: 07918-702572

KING, Jeremy Norman. See CLARK-KING, Jeremy Norman

KING, Mrs Joanna Claire. b 72. Chelt & Glouc Coll of HE BEd 96. Ripon Coll Cuddesdon 12. **d** 14 **p** 15. C Pagham *Chich* 14–18; P-in-c N Bersted 18–19; V from 19. *350 Chichester Road, Bognor Regis PO21 5BX* M: 07960-266601 E: joannaclaireking@gmail.com

KING, John Andrew. b 50. Qu Coll Birm 72. **d** 75 **p** 76. C Halesowen *Worc* 75–77; C Belper Ch Ch and Milford *Derby* 78–81; PtO from 87. *3 Holly House Lane, Blackbrook, Belper DE56 2DE* T: (01773) 823467 E: jaking49@hotmail.com

KING, John Charles. b 27. St Pet Hall Ox BA 51 MA 55. Oak Hill Th Coll 51. **d** 53 **p** 54. C Slough *Ox* 53–57; V Ware Ch Ch *St Alb* 57–60; Ed C of E Newspaper 60–68; LtO *St Alb* 60–70; Teacher Fran Bacon Sch St Alb 68–71; Boston Gr Sch 71–88; LtO *Linc* 74–92; rtd 92. *6 Somersby Way, Boston PE21 9PQ* T: (01205) 363061 E: johnc.king@talktalk.net

KING, John Frederick. b 47. **d** 05 **p** 06. NSM Buckingham *Ox* 05–21; NSM Blackthorn Chase from 21. *Wood End Farm, 2 Wood End, Nash, Milton Keynes MK17 0EL* T: (01908) 501860 E: john@kingsfold100.co.uk

KING, Joseph Stephen. b 39. St Chad's Coll Dur BA 62 MPhil 83. **d** 64 **p** 65. C Lewisham St Mary *S'wark* 64–69; Hon C Milton next Gravesend Ch Ch *Roch* 70–85; V 85–07; rtd 07; PtO *Roch* from 07. *13 Bannister Drive, Hutton, Brentwood CM13 1YX* T: (01277) 201900 E: patandjoe48@hotmail.com

KING, Mrs Katharine Mary. b 63. St Hugh's Coll Ox BA 85 MA 89 SS Coll Cam BA 88. Ridley Hall Cam 86. **d** 89 **p** 94. C Ipswich St Aug *St E* 89–91; NSM Bures 92–02; NSM Bures w Assington and Lt Cornard 02–13; PtO *Chelmsf* 14–15; NSM Coggeshall w Markshall 15–20; NSM Cressing w Stisted and Bradwell etc 15–20; NSM Coggeshall, Markshall, Cressing etc from 20. *The House, The Street, Bradwell, Braintree CM77 8EL* T: (01376) 563357 E: kkingchurch@gmail.com

KING, Malcolm Charles. b 37. Chich Th Coll 67. **d** 70 **p** 71. C Mill End *St Alb* 70–72; Chapl RAF 72–76; R W Lynn *Nor* 76–81; V Croxley Green All SS *St Alb* 81–90; V Grimsby St Aug *Linc* 90–99; Asst Local Min Officer 90–95; V Bury w Houghton and Coldwaltham and Hardham *Chich* 99–02; rtd 02; OGS from 90; PtO *Chich* 02–11; Warden Community of St Pet Woking 02–03. *20 The Quadrangle, Morden College, 19 St Germans Place, London SE3 0PW* T: (020) 8858 5313

KING, Malcolm Stewart. b 56. Univ of Wales (Lamp) MA 09. Sarum & Wells Th Coll 77. **d** 80 **p** 81. C Farnham *Guildf* 80–83; C Chertsey and Chapl St Pet Hosp Chertsey 83–86; V Egham Hythe *Guildf* 86–91; TR Cove St Jo 91–98; RD Aldershot 93–98; V Dorking w Ranmore 98–04; Hon Can Guildf Cathl 99–04; RD Dorking 01–04; P-in-c Portsea N End St Mark *Portsm* 04–06; TR 06–07; Warden Iona Community *Arg* 07–10; R Robina w Mermaid Beach Australia 10–12; PtO *Carl* 12–13; TR Stroud Team *Glouc* 13–16; AD Stroud 13–16; rtd 16; PtO *Glouc* from 18. *The Rectory, School Hill, Bourton-on-the-Water, Cheltenham GL54 2AW* T: (01451) 821282 E: malcolmsking@btinternet.com

KING (née COWIE), Mrs Margaret Harriet. b 53. Glas Univ BSc 76 AMA 85 FMA 97. TISEC 95. **d** 98 **p** 99. NSM Montrose and Inverbervie *Bre* 98–05; Dioc Dir of Ord 00–05; TV N Hinckford *Chelmsf* 05–13; TR 13–20; rtd 20; PtO *Chelmsf* from 20; *St E* from 20. *13 Hall Road, Wenhaston, Halesworth IP19 9EP* T: (01502) 478746 M: 07989-659073 E: mandgking39@hotmail.com

KING, Marie. b 40. CertEd 78. **d** 03 **p** 04. OLM Addiscombe St Mildred *S'wark* 03–10; PtO from 10. *8 Annandale Road, Croydon CR0 7HP* T: (020) 8654 2651 E: marie.king@virgin.net

KING, Martin Harry. b 42. St Jo Coll Cam MA 68 MBCS 85. SAOMC 03. **d** 05 **p** 06. NSM Wheathampstead *St Alb* 05–12; Dioc Environment Officer 08–09; rtd 12; PtO *St Alb* from 13. *29 Parkfields, Welwyn Garden City AL8 6EE* T: (01707) 328905 E: revdmartin.king@cantab.net

KING, Martin Peter James. b 73. Bris Univ BEng 95. Oak Hill Th Coll BA 05. **d** 05 **p** 06. C Leamington Priors St Paul *Cov* 05–09; V Rudgwick *Chich* from 10. *The Vicarage, Cox Green, Rudgwick, Horsham RH12 3DD* T: (01403) 822127 E: martinthevicar@googlemail.com *or* vicar@rudgwickchurch.org.uk

KING, Martin Quartermain. b 39. Reading Univ BA 61. Cuddesdon Coll 62. **d** 64 **p** 65. C S Shields St Hilda w St Thos *Dur* 64–66; C Newton Aycliffe 66–71; V Chilton Moor 71–78; R Middleton St George 78–91; R Sedgefield 91–04; RD 91–96; Chapl Co Dur & Darlington Priority Services NHS Trust 91–04; rtd 04; PtO *Dur* from 04; *Eur* from 09. *3 White House Drive, Sedgefield, Stockton on Tees TS21 3BX* T: (01740) 620424 E: martin.king@durham.anglican.org *or* mqking@btinternet.com

KING, Mrs Melanie Jane. b 58. Hull Univ BA 83 SS Hild & Bede Coll Dur PGCE 91. Lindisfarne Regional Tr Partnership 13. **d** 15 **p** 16. NSM Brompton w Deighton *York* 15–18; PtO from 19. *19 Weavers Green, Northallerton DL7 8FJ* M: 07938-054338 E: revmelking@gmail.com

KING, Nicholas Bernard Paul. b 46. Wycliffe Hall Ox 72. **d** 75 **p** 76. C Pitsmoor w Wicker *Sheff* 75–78; C Erdington St Barn *Birm* 78–80; C Sutton Coldfield H Trin 80–84; V Lynesack

Dur 84–92; rtd 93; PtO *Dur* from 17. *16 Chatsworth Avenue, Bishop Auckland DL14 6AX* T: (01388) 605614

KING, Nigel Edward. b 44. St Cath Coll Ox BA 66 MA 69. **d** 16 **p** 17. NSM Three Cliffs *S & B* from 16. *36 East Cliff, Pennard, Swansea SA3 2AS* T: (01792) 233124 M: 07850-583153 E: nigeledward.king@btopenworld.com

KING, Patrick Stewart. b 84. St Chad's Coll Dur BA 06 Jes Coll Cam MPhil 10. Westcott Ho Cam 08. **d** 10 **p** 11. C Dorchester *Sarum* 10–13; C Wokingham St Paul *Ox* 13–16; Voc Advocate Wollaston Th Coll Australia 16–17; R Fremantle and Palmyra from 17. *St John's Anglican Church, 24 Adelaide Street, Fremantle WA 6160, Australia* T: (0061) (8) 9335 2213 F: 9335 2005 E: patrick.s.king@gmail.com

KING, Paul Derwent. b 39. Ball Coll Ox BA 62 MA 65. Cuddesdon Coll 63. **d** 65 **p** 66. C Portsea N End St Mark *Portsm* 65–67; C Iffley *Ox* 67–70; Asst Chapl Nottm Univ *S'well* 70–72; Chapl Southn Univ *Win* 72–78; V Headington *Ox* 78–86; RD Cowley 81–86; V Ox St Mary Magd 86–89; rtd 04. *60 Abingdon Road, Oxford OX1 4PE* T: (01865) 437066

KING, Penelope Ann. *See* WARNER, Penelope Ann

KING, Peter. b 78. St Hild Coll 18. **d** 21. C Kirkleatham *York* from 21. *All Saints House, 47 South Avenue, Redcar TS10 5LL* M: 07912-218452 E: pete1king@hotmail.com

KING, Peter Duncan. b 48. TD. K Coll Lon LLB 70 AKC 70 Fitzw Coll Cam BA 72 MA 77. Westcott Ho Cam 70. **d** 80 **p** 81. NSM Notting Hill *Lon* 80–84; NSM Mortlake w E Sheen *S'wark* 84–18; Dean MSE 99–16; PtO 18–20. *49 Leinster Avenue, London SW14 7JW* T: (020) 8876 8997 F: 8287 9329 E: kingpd@hotmail.com

KING, Canon Philipa Ann. b 65. Westcott Ho Cam 91. **d** 95 **p** 96. C Cambridge Ascension *Ely* 95–00; TV 00–02; TR from 02; Hon Can Ely Cathl from 11. *2 Stretten Avenue, Cambridge CB4 3EP* T: (01223) 366665 *or* 315000 M: 07816-833363 E: pipking@btinternet.com *or* rectoratcastle@btinternet.com

KING (née JONES), The Ven Rhiannon Elizabeth. b 72. Ex Univ BA 93 Brunel Univ MA 95 Anglia Ruskin Univ MA 05. Ridley Hall Cam 98. **d** 00 **p** 01. C Huntingdon *Ely* 00–04; R Fulbourn 04–10; V Gt Wilbraham 04–10; R Lt Wilbraham 04–10; Transforming Ch Co-ord *Birm* 10–14; Dir of Miss 14–19; Adn Ipswich *St E* from 19. *Picton House, 167 Valley Road, Ipswich IP1 4PQ* M: 07595-880584 E: archdeacon.rhiannon@cofesuffolk.org

KING, Canon Robert Dan. b 57. Sarum & Wells Th Coll 92. **d** 94 **p** 95. C Heref H Trin 94–97; TV W Heref 97–00; V Weobley w Sarnesfield and Norton Canon 00–14; P-in-c Letton w Staunton, Byford, Mansel Gamage etc 00–04; R 04–14; Preb Heref Cathl 10–14; R Kelso *Edin* from 14; Hon Can St Mary's Cathl from 20. *St Andrew's Rectory, 6 Forestfield, Kelso TD5 7BX* T: (01573) 224163 E: rectorofkelso@gmail.com

KING, The Ven Robin Lucas Colin. b 59. Dundee Univ MA 81. Ridley Hall Cam 87. **d** 89 **p** 90. C Ipswich St Aug *St E* 89–92; V Bures 92–02; C Assington w Newton Green and Lt Cornard 00–02; V Bures w Assington and Lt Cornard 02–13; RD Sudbury 06–13; Hon Can St E Cathl 08–13; Adn Stansted *Chelmsf* from 13. *The House, The Street, Bradwell, Braintree CM77 8EL* T: (01376) 563357 M: 07813-633096 E: a.stansted@chelmsford.anglican.org

KING, Mrs Rowena Niesje. b 77. Univ of Qld BAppSc 97 Chas Sturt Univ NSW BTh 13 Ox Univ MTh 15. Ripon Coll Cuddesdon WEMTC. **d** 15 **p** 16. C Dursley *Glouc* 15–18; R Bourton-on-the-Water w Clapton etc from 18. *The Rectory, School Hill, Bourton-on-the-Water, Cheltenham GL54 2AW* T: (01451) 821282 E: revrowena@gmail.com

KING, Canon Stuart John. b 77. **d** 10 **p** 11. NSM Winnersh *Ox* 10–14; Chapl Bearwood Coll Wokingham 10–14; P-in-c Ashford St Matt *Lon* from 14; P-in-c Stanwell from 16; Hon Can Sekondi Ghana from 20. *St Matthew's Vicarage, 99 Church Road, Ashford TW15 2NY* T: (01784) 252459 E: fr_stuart@smam.org.uk

KING, Canon Walter Raleigh. b 45. New Coll Ox BA 67 MA 74. Cuddesdon Coll 71. **d** 74 **p** 75. C Wisbech SS Pet and Paul *Ely* 74–77; C Barrow St Geo w St Luke *Carl* 77–79; P-in-c Clifford *Heref* 79–83; P-in-c Cusop 79–83; P-in-c Hardwick 79–83; P-in-c Whitney w Winforton 81–84; R Cusop w Clifford, Hardwicke, Bredwardine etc 83–86; R Heref St Nic 86–92; Dir of Ords 86–92; Preb Heref Cathl 86–92; TR Huntingdon *Ely* 92–01; RD 94–99; Hon Can Ely Cathl 99–01; Vice Dean and Can Res Chelmsf Cathl 01–10; rtd 10; PtO *Lon* 11–21; *S'wark* 13–21. *8 Woodlands, Clapham Common North Side, London SW4 0RJ* E: walterking@btinternet.com

KING, William. b 46. **d** 14 **p** 15. OLM N Beltisloe Gp *Linc* 14–19. *Tanglewood, Grantham Road, Old Somerby, Grantham NG33 4AB* M: 07568-075680 E: bill.king@hotmail.co.uk

KING, Zoë Elisabeth. St Mich Coll Llan. **d** 06 **p** 07. C Neath *Llan* 06–10; P-in-c Llansawel, Briton Ferry 10–15;

AD Neath 12–15; P-in-c Tongwynlais 15–21; C St Fagans and Michaelston-super-Ely 19–21; C Pentyrch and Capel Llanilltterne 19–21; C Radyr 19–21; Min Area Ldr Barry from 21; Dioc Officer for IME from 15. *The Rectory, 3 Park Road, Barry CF62 6NU* T: (029) 2081 0437 E: revdzoeking@gmail.com

KING-BROWN, Ian Barry. b 53. St Cuth Soc Dur BA 80 PGCE 81. Sarum & Wells Th Coll 84. **d** 86 **p** 87. C Winchmore Hill St Paul *Lon* 86–89; Hon Chapl Chase Farm Hosp Enfield 86–88; Hon Chapl Harley Street Area Hosps 88–90; Hon Chapl RAM 89; C St Marylebone w H Trin *Lon* 89–94; rtd 94; Hon Chapl Regent's Coll Lon 96–05; PtO *Lon* from 11. *Flat 4, 9 Welbeck Street, London W1G 9YB* T: (020) 3624 4433 E: ibkb13@gmail.com

KING-SMITH, Preb Giles Anthony Beaumont. b 53. Univ Coll Ox BA 75. Trin Coll Bris 86. **d** 88 **p** 89. C Gtr Corsham *Bris* 88–92; V Two Mile Hill St Mich 92–96; TV Ilfracombe, Lee, Woolacombe, Bittadon etc *Ex* from 96; RD Barnstaple 10–17; Preb Ex Cathl from 14. *The Vicarage, Springfield Road, Woolacombe EX34 7BX* T: (01271) 870467 E: gkingsmith53@gmail.com

KINGDOM, Paul Anthony. b 62. Ex Univ BA 83 Win Univ MA 18 FCA 86 ATII 87. STETS 07. **d** 10 **p** 11. NSM Burnham *B & W* 10–14; NSM Chapel Allerton 15–16; NSM Wedmore w Theale and Blackford 15–16; NSM Dulverton w Brushford, Brompton Regis etc 16–20; R Silverton, Butterleigh, Bickleigh and Cadeleigh *Ex* from 20. *The Rectory, 21A King Street, Silverton, Exeter EX5 4JG* M: 07803-922605 E: revpaulkingdom@gmail.com

KINGMAN, Paul Henry Charles. b 64. Reading Univ BSc 86. Wycliffe Hall Ox BTh 95. **d** 95 **p** 96. C Whitton *Sarum* 95–99; C Harold Wood *Chelmsf* 99–03; V Stone Ch Ch and Oulton *Lich* from 03. *Christ Church Vicarage, Bromfield Court, Stone ST15 8ED* T: (01785) 812669

✠**KINGS, The Rt Revd Graham Ralph.** b 53. Hertf Coll Ox BA 77 MA 80 Utrecht Univ PhD 02. Ridley Hall Cam 78. **d** 80 **p** 81 **c** 09. C Harlesden St Mark *Lon* 80–84; CMS Kenya 85–91; Dir Studies St Andr Inst Kabare 85–88; Vice Prin 89–91; Lect Miss Studies Cam Th Federation 92–00; Overseas Adv Henry Martyn Trust 92–95; Dir Henry Martyn Cen Westmr Coll Cam 95–00; Hon C Cambridge H Trin *Ely* 92–96; Hon C Chesterton St Andr 96–00; V Islington St Mary *Lon* 00–09; Area Bp Sherborne *Sarum* 09–15; Can and Preb Sarum Cathl 09–15; Miss Th Angl Communion 15–17; Hon Asst Bp S'wark 15–20; Hon Asst Bp Dur 16–17; P-in-c S'wark H Trin w St Matt 17–18; Hon C 18–20; Hon Asst Bp Ely from 20. *46 Green End Road, Cambridge CB4 1RY* E: grahamrkings@gmail.com

KINGS, Jean Alison. *See* THORN, Jean Alison

KINGSLEY, Miss Mary Phyllis Lillian. b 48. K Coll Lon BSc 76 Lon Inst of Educn MA 87. ERMC 96. **d** 09 **p** 10. NSM Croxley Green All SS *St Alb* 09–13; NSM Bushey 13–18; C 18–19; rtd 19. *19 The Cloisters, Rickmansworth WD3 1HL* T: (01923) 771172 E: mplk@waitrose.com

KINGSMILL-LUNN, Brooke. *See* LUNN, Brooke Kingsmill

KINGSTON, Desmond. *See* KINGSTON, John Desmond George

KINGSTON, Eric. b 24. **d** 69 **p** 70. C Ballymacarrett St Patr *D & D* 69–72; C Knock 72–76; I Annahilt w Magherahamlet 76–93; Can and Prec Dromore Cathl 93; rtd 93. *38 Kinedale Park, Ballynahinch BT24 8YS* T: (028) 9756 5715

KINGSTON, John Desmond George. b 40. TCD BA 63 MA 66. CITC 64. **d** 64 **p** 65. C Arm St Mark w Aghavilly 64–70; Hon V Choral Arm Cathl 70–95; Chapl Portora R Sch Enniskillen 70–01; LtO *Clogh* 70–01; Can Clogh Cathl 96–01; rtd 01. *Ambleside, 45 Old Rossory Road, Enniskillen BT74 7LF* T: (028) 6632 4493

KINGSTON, Kenneth Robert. b 42. TCD BA 65 MA 69. **d** 66 **p** 67. C Enniscorthy *C, F & O* 66–69; C Ballymena w Ballyclug *Conn* 70–72; C Drumragh w Mountfield *D & R* 72–78; I Badoney Lower w Greenan and Badoney Upper 78–84; I Desertmartin w Termoneeny 84–13; Can Derry Cathl 97–13; rtd 13. *1 Fairlea Heights, Moneymore, Magherafelt BT45 7UQ* T: (028) 8674 7905 E: kennethkingstonfairlea@gmail.com

KINGSTON, Malcolm Trevor. b 75. QUB BSc 97 MSc 98 TCD BTh 04. CITC 01. **d** 04 **p** 05. C Portadown St Mark *Arm* 04–07; I Kilmore St Aid w St Sav 07–14; I Arm St Mark from 14. *St Mark's Rectory, 14 Portadown Road, Armagh BT61 9EE* T: (028) 3752 2970 E: malcolm.kingston@btinternet.com

KINGSTON, Canon Michael Joseph. b 51. K Coll Lon BD 73 AKC 73. St Aug Coll Cant 73. **d** 74 **p** 75. C Reading H Trin *Ox* 74–77; C New Eltham All SS *S'wark* 77–83; V Plumstead Ascension 83–94; Sub-Dean Greenwich N 92–94; V Sydenham St Bart 94–18; RD W Lewisham 04–16; Hon Can S'wark Cathl 15–18; rtd 18; PtO *Ox* from 19. *23*

Windmill Avenue, Bicester OX26 3DX T: (01869) 354990
E: michaelkingston@btinternet.com
KINGSTON, Michael Marshall. b 54. St Jo Coll Nottm MA 94.
d 96 p 97. C Drayton w Felthorpe *Nor* 96–99; R Gt and Lt
Plumstead w Thorpe End and Witton 99–09; RD Blofield
06–08; Chapl Norfolk Primary Care Trust 01–09; TR Hempnall
Nor 09–20; RD Depwade 13–16; rtd 20; PtO *Nor* from 21.
30 Frederick Grove, Hethersett, Norwich NR9 3FW M: 07792-
020652 E: mmkingston@btinternet.com
KINGSTON, Robert George. b 46. TCD BA 68 Div Test 69. d 69
p 72. C Belfast St Thos *Conn* 69–72; C Kilkenny St Canice
Cathl *C, F & O* 72–75; I Ballinasloe w Taughmaconnell *L & K*
77–79; I Maryborough w Dysart Enos and Ballyfin *C, F & O*
79–85; I Lurgan w Billis, Killinkere and Munterconnaught
K, E & A 85–88; Registrar Kilmore 87–92; I Lurgan etc w
Ballymachugh, Kildrumferton etc *K, E & A* 88–92; I Tallaght
D & G 92–98; Warden of Readers 93–98; I Mallow Union
C, C & R 98–07; I Carrickmacross w Magheracloone *Clogh*
07–13; Chapl Mageough Home *D & G* from 13. *Chaplain's
Apartment, The Mageough, Cowper Road, Dublin 6, Republic
of Ireland* T: (00353) (1) 555 2179 M: 89-400 1720
E: rgk@eircom.net
KINGSTON-UPON-THAMES, Area Bishop of. *See* CHEETHAM,
The Rt Revd Richard Ian
KINGTON, Canon David Bruce. b 45. Trin Coll Bris 72. d 72
p 73. C Wellington w Eyton *Lich* 72–77; C Boscombe St Jo
Win 77–81; R Michelmersh, Timsbury, Farley Chamberlayne
etc 81–98; R Michelmersh and Awbridge and Braishfield
etc 98–10; RD Romsey 95–05; Hon Can Win Cathl 02–10;
rtd 11; PtO *Win* from 11. *St Swithun's Cottage, Main
Road, Littleton, Winchester SO22 6QS* T: (01962) 882698
E: dbrucek245@gmail.com
KINKEAD, John Alfred Harold. b 84. TCD BA 06 MA 11. CITC
BTh 10. d 10 p 11. C Cregagh *D & D* 10–13; C Taney *D & G*
13–15; Chan V St Patr Cathl Dublin from 13; P-in-c Wicklow
w Killiskey *D & G* 15–17; I from 17. *The Rectory, Brickfield
Lane, Wicklow, Co Wicklow, A67 Y478, Republic of
Ireland* T: (00353) (404) 32491 M: (00353) 86-172 7654
E: kinkeadj@gmail.com
KINNA, Preb Michael Andrew. b 46. Chich Th Coll 84.
d 86 p 87. C Leominster *Heref* 86–90; TV Wenlock
90–93; R Broseley w Benthall, Jackfield, Linley etc 94–11;
P-in-c Coalbrookdale, Iron-Bridge and Lt Wenlock 07–11;
RD Telford Severn Gorge 03–10; Preb Heref Cathl 07–11;
rtd 11; PtO *Heref* 11–19; *Lich* 18–19; *Linc* from 19. *48
Jaguar Drive, North Hykeham, Lincoln LN6 9SE* T: (01522)
884664 M: 07752-888114
KINNAIRD, Jennifer. b 41. Hull Univ BA 62 Ex Univ
PGCE 63. NEOC 94. d 97 p 98. NSM Corbridge w
Halton and Newton Hall *Newc* 97–11; rtd 11; PtO *Newc*
from 11. *17 Glebelands, Corbridge NE45 5DS* T: (01434)
632695   E: j.kinnaird@btopenworld.com   or
j.kinnaird1356@btinternet.com
KINNAIRD, Keith. b 42. Chich Coll 72. d 75 p 76. C
Didcot St Pet *Ox* 75–78; C Abingdon w Shippon 78–82;
P-in-c Sunningwell 82–90; P-in-c Radley 88–90; R Radley
and Sunningwell 90–95; Chapl Abingdon Hosp 79–92; V
Old Shoreham *Chich* 95–00; V New Shoreham 95–00; V
Caversham St Andr *Ox* 00–07; Voc Adv and Adv for Min
of Healing 00–07; rtd 07; PtO *Ox* 07–18. *2 Weaver Row,
Garston Lane, Wantage OX12 7DZ* T/F: (01235) 760867
E: keithkinnaird@btinternet.com
KINNEY, Robert Scott. b 81. Univ of Chicago BA 04
Univ of Illinois MS 08 Bris Univ PhD 15. d 14 p 16.
PtO *Eur* 16–19; Hon C Vienna from 19. *Schottengasse
7/2/4/11A, Wien 1010, Austria* T/F: (001) (773) 771 0771
E: curate@christchurchvienna.org
KINRADE, Nicol Wendy. b 73. St Chad's Coll Dur BA 97 Newc
Univ MA 98. Westcott Ho Cam 13. d 15 p 16. C Ditchling,
Streat and Westmeston *Chich* 15–18; P-in-c Highbrook
and W Hoathly from 18. *The Vicarage, North Lane, West
Hoathly, East Grinstead RH19 4QF* T: (01342) 810183
E: mother.nicol@gmail.com
KINSELLA, Nigel Paul. b 66. Wolv Univ LLB 95. Westcott
Ho Cam 00. d 02 p 03. C Attleborough w Besthorpe
Nor 02–03; C Quidenham Gp 03–05; R E w W Harling,
Bridgham w Roudham, Larling etc 05–10; CF from 10.
c/o MOD Chaplains (Army) T: (01264) 383430 F: 381824
E: nigelkinsella@btinternet.com
KINSEY, Canon Bruce Richard Lawrence. b 59. K Coll Lon
BD 81 AKC 81 MTh 86 MA 94 Down Coll Cam MA 95 Balliol
Coll Ox MA 15. Wycliffe Hall Ox. d 84 p 85. C Gt Stanmore
Lon 84–88; C Shepherd's Bush St Steph w St Thos 88–91;
Chapl and Fell Down Coll Cam 91–01; Hd Philosophy and
RS Perse Sch Cam 01–10; Sen Tutor 10–14; Fell and Chapl
Ball Coll Ox from 14; PtO *Ely* 07–18; *Ox* from 17; Hon

Can Ely Cathl from 17. *Balliol College, Broad Street, Oxford
OX1 3BJ* T: (01865) 277777 E: bruce@balliol.ox.ac.uk
KINSEY, Russell Frederick David. b 34. Sarum Th Coll 59.
d 62 p 63. C Twerton *B & W* 62–66; C N Cadbury 66–75; C
Yarlington 66–75; P-in-c Compton Pauncefoot w Blackford
66–75; P-in-c Maperton 66–75; P-in-c N Cheriton 66–75; TV
Camelot Par 76–79; V Pill 79–82; P-in-c Easton-in-Gordano
w Portbury and Clapton 80–82; V Pill w Easton in Gordano
and Portbury 82–92; rtd 94. *25 Newbourne Road, Weston-
super-Mare BS22 8NF*
KINYANJUI, Peter Thiongo. b 65. St Paul's Coll Limuru 91.
d 94 p 94. C Jericho St Phil Kenya 94; V Kajiado St Jo 95; Adn
Loitokitok 95–96; V Thogoto 97–00; USA 01–06; PtO *Chelmsf*
from 11. *91 Blake Avenue, Barking IG11 9SB* M: 07557-
223160 E: mabipeter@yahoo.co.uk
KIPLING, Miss Susan Jane. b 49. Girton Coll Cam BA 70
MA 73. Westcott Ho Cam 04. d 06 p 08. C Old Basing
and Lychpit *Win* 06–07; C N Hants Downs 07–10; R
Brington w Whilton and Norton etc *Pet* 10–17; rtd 17;
PtO *Win* from 18. *Westbourne, Goodworth Clatford, Andover
SP11 7QX* T: (01264) 352579 E: suekipling@btinternet.com
KIPPAX, Canon Michael John. b 48. Open Univ BA 82.
SWMTC 89. d 92 p 93. C Camborne *Truro* 92–95; C
Woughton *Ox* 95–96; TV 96–98; R St Illogan *Truro* 98–12;
Hon Can Truro Cathl 08–12; rtd 12; PtO *Glouc* from 16.
33 Berkeley Crescent, Lydney GL15 5SH T: (01594) 840049
E: mikekippax@gmail.com
KIRBY, Antony Philip. b 60. Leeds Univ BA 11. Yorks Min
Course 08. d 11 p 12. C Richmond w Hudswell and
Downholme and Marske *Leeds* 11–15; P-in-c Barningham w
Hutton Magna and Wycliffe 15–18; P-in-c Gilling and Kirkby
Ravensworth 15–18; R Holmedale from 19. *The Vicarage, Gilling
West, Richmond DL10 5JG* T: (01748) 850349 M: 07594-
615190 E: antonykirby01@btinternet.com
KIRBY, David Graham. b 58. Univ of Wales (Cardiff) BA 80.
Wycliffe Hall Ox BA 85 MA 92. d 86 p 87. C Northallerton
w Kirby Sigston *York* 86–89; C Southport Ch Ch *Liv* 89–92;
R Bishop Burton w Walkington *York* 92–07; R Weston Favell
Pet 07–20; Warden Lay Past Min 10–20; rtd 20. *Address temp
unknown* E: kirbydg@gmail.com
KIRBY, Mrs Elizabeth. b 56. City Univ BSc 79. ERMC 06.
d 10 p 11. NSM Bury St Edmunds All SS w St Jo and St Geo
St E 10–12; C Ipswich St Mary at Stoke w St Pet and St Fran
12–14; P-in-c Elmton *Derby* 14–18; P-in-c Whitwell 14–18; R
Elmton w Creswell and Whitwell w Steetley 18–19; rtd 19.
Address temp unknown E: liz.kirby@btinternet.com
KIRBY, Miss Kathryn Margaret. b 52. Girton Coll Cam
BA 74 MA 78 Hughes Hall Cam PGCE 75 Leeds Univ MA 08
MCLIP 82. Coll of Resurr Mirfield 06. d 07 p 08. NSM Sale
St Paul *Ches* 07–09; NSM Gatley 09–10; V Macclesfield
St Paul 10–15; rtd 15; PtO *Truro* from 15; *Ches* 15–18. *Chy
Lowen, 1 Rowan Road, Wadebridge PL27 7SN* T: (01208)
369963 M: 07745-434266 E: k.m.kirby@btinternet.com
KIRBY, Canon Michael Christopher. b 63. BSc BTh MSc
MA PhD CSci FHEA. d 13 p 14. NSM Blackb Cathl 13–16;
PV Ches Cathl 16–18; Chapl Countess of Chester Hosp
NHS Foundn Trust 17; PtO *Ches* from 17; Chapl Liv Cathl
18–20; Can Res Liv Cathl from 20. *3 Homerton Road, Liverpool
L6 8NL* T: 0151-228 6178 E: mkirby1821@aol.com or
mike.kirby@liverpoolcathedral.org.uk
KIRBY, Paul Michael. b 51. Seabury-Western Th Sem
DMin 99. Wycliffe Hall Ox 74. d 76 p 77. C Gateacre *Liv*
76–79; C Barton Seagrave w Warkton *Pet* 79–83; V Bidston
Ches 83–93; V Ormskirk *Liv* 93–99; Team Ldr Chapl E
Kent Hosps NHS Trust 99–00; Sen Team Ldr Chapl E Kent
Hosps Univ NHS Foundn Trust 00–14; Chapl Manager
E and Coastal Kent Primary Care Trust 08–14; Bp's Adv
for Hosp Chapl *Cant* 02–14; rtd 14; Min Burry Green
Chpl from 19. *Orchard Cottage, Burry Green, Reynoldston,
Swansea SA3 1HR* T: (01792) 390303 M: 07552-230672
E: kirby74@btinternet.com
KIRBY, Richard Arthur. b 48. Lon Univ BSc 69. d 05 p 06.
OLM Wellington All SS w Eyton *Lich* 05–07; NSM 11–16;
PtO 07–11; rtd 16; PtO *S'well* from 17. *16 Dover Back Close,
Ravenshead, Nottingham NG15 9ER*
KIRBY, Simon Thomas. b 67. Lon Bible Coll BA 92.
NTMTC 00. d 03 p 04. C Woodside Park St Barn *Lon*
03–06; Lic Preacher 06–11; Chapl Wren Academy 08–12;
C Friern Barnet St Jas *Lon* 11–12; V Cogges and S Leigh
Ox from 13; V N Leigh 13–16. *Cogges Priory, Church Lane,
Witney OX28 3LA* T: (01993) 702155 M: 07862-254540
E: simonkirby@gmail.com
KIRBY, Stennett Roger. b 54. St Pet Coll Ox BA 75 MA 79.
Sarum & Wells Th Coll 75. d 77 p 78. C Belsize Park *Lon*
77–79; NSM Plumstead St Nic *S'wark* 88; C Leic Ch Sav
90–91; TV Hanley H Ev *Lich* 91–95; P-in-c Walsall St Pet

95–01; V 01–07; V W Ham *Chelmsf* 07–18; rtd 18. *11 Aulton Crescent, Hinckley LE10 0XA* T: (01455) 371542 E: srkirby2016@outlook.com

KIRBY, Vanessa Catherine. b 65. Leeds Univ MA 09. Cranmer Hall Dur 19. **d** 20 **p** 21. C Middlesbrough St Oswald and St Chad *York* from 20. *19 Ventnor Road, Middlesbrough TS5 6DX* M: 07804-234388 E: rev.vanessakirby@gmail.com

KIRK, Alastair James. b 71. St Jo Coll Dur BSc 93 PhD 98 Fitzw Coll Cam BA 06. Ridley Hall Cam 04. **d** 07 **p** 08. C Tong *Bradf* 07–10; C Laisterdyke 08–10; Chapl Warw Univ *Cov* 10–14; V Burley in Wharfedale *Leeds* from 14. *The Vicarage, 21 Southfield Road, Burley in Wharfedale, Ilkley LS29 7PB* T: (01943) 863216 M: 07725-991073 E: alastair_kirk@yahoo.co.uk

KIRK, Andrew. See KIRK, John Andrew

KIRK, Clive John Charles. b 37. TD 81. FIBMS 66. Guildf Dioc Min Course 95. **d** 98 **p** 99. OLM E Molesey St Paul *Guildf* 98–04; NSM E Horsley and Ockham w Hatchford and Downside 04–10; rtd 10; PtO *Guildf* from 10. *63 Send Barns Lane, Send, Woking GU23 7BS* T: (01483) 211799 E: candakirk@btinternet.com

KIRK, Miss Erika Cottam. b 55. Nottm Univ LLB 76. St Jo Coll Nottm MA 98. **d** 98 **p** 99. NSM Epperstone *S'well* 98–03; NSM Gonalston 98–03; NSM Oxton 98–03; NSM Calverton 98–03; NSM Woodborough 98–03; NSM Burton Joyce w Bulcote and Stoke Bardolph 03–08; NSM Edingley w Halam 08–10; NSM Gedling 11–16; Warden Sacrista Prebend Retreat Ho 16–18; PV S'well Minster from 18. *24 St Helen's Crescent, Burton Joyce, Nottingham NG14 5DW* T: 0115-931 4125 E: erika.kirk@btinternet.com

KIRK, The Ven Gavin John. b 61. Southn Univ BTh Heythrop Coll Lon MA *Guildf* LLM 20. Chich Th Coll 83. **d** 86 **p** 87. C Seaford w Sutton *Chich* 86–89; Chapl and Succ Roch Cath 89–91; Min Can 89–91; Hon PV 91–98; Asst Chapl K Sch Roch 91–98; Can Res Portsm Cathl 98–03; Can Res and Prec Linc Cathl 03–16; Adn Linc from 16; PtO *S'well* from 06. *Edward King House, The Old Palace, Lincoln LN2 1PU* T: (01522) 504039 E: archdeacon.lincoln@lincoln.anglican.org

KIRK, Miss Geraldine Mercedes. b 49. Hull Univ MA 89. **d** 87 **p** 94. Ind Chapl *Linc* 87–99; P-in-c Bridgwater St Jo *B & W* 99–14; Chapl Somerset Primary Care Trust 99–14; rtd 14; PtO *B & W* from 15. *121 Newton Road, Bath BA2 1RU* T: (01225) 400688 E: revkirk52@gmail.com

KIRK, John Andrew. b 37. Lon Univ BD 61 AKC 61 MPhil 75 Fitzw Ho Cam BA 63 Radboud Univ Nijmegen PhD 11. Ridley Hall Cam 61. **d** 63 **p** 64. C Finchley Ch Ch *Lon* 63–66; Argentina 66–79; SAMS 79–81; CMS 82–90; Dean of Miss Selly Oak Colls 90–99; Dept of Th Birm Univ 99–02; PtO *Glouc* from 99; rtd 02. *The Old Stable, Market Square, Lechlade GL7 3AB* T: (01367) 253254

KIRK, Natalie Roberta. See GARRETT, Natalie Roberta

KIRK, Canon Steven Paul. b 59. Ex Univ LLB 80 Univ of Wales (Cardiff) BD 87 LLM 94. St Mich Coll Llan 84. **d** 87 **p** 88. C Ebbw Vale *Mon* 87–89; PV Llan Cathl 89–91; PV and Succ 91–94; V Port Talbot St Agnes w Oakwood *Llan* 94–01; TR Aberavon 01–07; AD Margam 06–07; V Ystrad Mynach w Llanbradach from 07; Can Llan Cathl from 07; AD Merthyr Tydfil and Caerphilly from 14. *The Vicarage, Cedar Way, Ystrad Mynach, Hengoed CF82 7DR* T: (01443) 813246

KIRK-SPRIGGS, Graham Voysey. b 91. Sheff Hallam Univ BA 12. Ripon Coll Cuddesdon BA 17. **d** 17 **p** 18. C Nor St Pet Mancroft w St Jo Maddermarket 17–21; C Sprowston w Beeston from 21. *63 Recreation Road, Norwich NR2 3PA* T: (01603) 456112 M: 07393-532321 E: graham.kirk-spriggs@outlook.com

KIRKBRIDE, Martin Lea. b 51. Oak Hill Th Coll BA 94. **d** 97 **p** 98. C Lancaster St Thos *Blackb* 97–00; TV Hampreston *Sarum* 00–05; V Lenton *S'well* 05–11; Dioc Learning Adv *Cov* 11–14; Assoc Min Cov Cathl 12–14; P-in-c Wembury *Ex* 14–18; C 19; PtO *B & W* 19–21; P-in-c Wellington and Distr from 21. *17 The Fairways, Sherford, Taunton TA1 3PA* M: 07983-852456 E: martinkirkbride@aol.com

KIRKBY, Canon John Victor Michael. b 39. Lon Univ BScEng 62 BD 73. Ridley Hall Cam 65. **d** 67 **p** 68. C Muswell Hill St Jas *Lon* 67–70; Chapl Hatf Poly *St Alb* 71–75; V Wootton 75–86; RD Elstow 82–86; R Byfleet *Guildf* 86–92; P-in-c Potten End w Nettleden *St Alb* 92–97; V 97–05; TV Gt Berkhamsted, Gt and Lt Gaddesden etc 05–08; Chapl Ashridge Business Sch 92–08; rtd 08; PtO *St Alb* from 08; Can Masindi Uganda from 09. *3 Hillside Gardens, Berkhamsted HP4 2LE* T: (01442) 872725 E: jvmkirkby@aol.com

KIRKER, Richard Ennis. b 51. Sarum & Wells Th Coll 72. **d** 77. C Hitchin *St Alb* 77–78; Chief Exec LGCM 79–08. *10 Coopers Close, London E1 4BB* T: (020) 7791 1802 M: 07798-805428 E: richard@richardkirker.com

KIRKHAM, Mrs Judith Mary. b 52. **d** 13 **p** 14. OLM Stalmine w Pilling *Blackb* 13–19; OLM Waterside Par 13–19; OLM Over Wyre from 20. *4 Stalmine Country Park, Neds Lane, Stalmine, Poulton-le-Fylde FY6 0LW* T: (01253) 702711 M: 07508-884528 E: judithkirkham@hotmail.com

KIRKHAM, June Margaret. b 54. EMMTC 99. **d** 02 **p** 03. C Nottingham St Jude *S'well* 02–06; P-in-c Broxtowe 06–11; V 11–19; rtd 19. *12 Lyndhurst Avenue, Grimsby DN33 2AW*

KIRKLAND, Richard John. b 53. Leic Univ BA 75. Cranmer Hall Dur 76. **d** 79 **p** 80. C Knutsford St Jo and Toft *Ches* 79–82; C Bebington 82–89; V Poulton Lancelyn H Trin 89–95; V Hoole 95–20; rtd 21. *100 Upton Grange, Chester CH2 1BG* E: j.kirkland@hender.org.uk

KIRKMAN, Richard Marsden. b 55. Cranmer Hall Dur. **d** 87 **p** 88. C Bridlington Priory *York* 87–90; TV Thirsk 90–96; R Escrick and Stillingfleet w Naburn 96–21; RD Derwent 01–11; P-in-c Bubwith w Skipwith 11–21; rtd 21. *Appletree House, West Scrafton, Leyburn DL8 4RU* E: richarmk.777@gmail.com

KIRKMAN, Trevor Harwood. b 51. Trin Hall Cam BA 73 MA 77. EMMTC 94. **d** 96 **p** 97. NSM Hickling w Kinoulton and Broughton Sulney *S'well* 96–01; NSM Keyworth and Stanton-on-the-Wolds and Bunny etc 01–10; P-in-c Plumtree 10–11; R from 11; Dioc Registrar and Bp's Legal Adv *Leic* 02–19. *Orchard End, 8 Back Lane, Long Clawson, Melton Mowbray LE14 4NA* T: (01664) 823788 E: trevorkirkman@btinternet.com

KIRKPATRICK, Nigel David Joseph. b 68. CITC BTh 96. **d** 96 **p** 97. C Portadown St Columba *Arm* 96–99; C Lecale Gp *D & D* 99–01; I Killinchy w Kilmood and Tullynakill 01–07; I Gilnahirk 07–19; I Kilroot and Templecorran *Conn* from 19. *Kilroot Rectory, 29 Downshire Gardens, Carrickfergus BT38 7LW* T: (028) 9070 4123

KIRKPATRICK, Reginald. b 48. **d** 07 **p** 08. OLM Ditchingham, Hedenham, Broome, Earsham etc *Nor* from 07. *18 Clark Road, Ditchingham, Bungay NR35 2QQ* T: (01986) 893645 E: revregkirk@uwclub.net

KIRKSTALL, Suffragan Bishop of. See SLATER, The Rt Revd Paul John

KIRKUP, Nigel Norman. b 54. K Coll Lon BD 79 AKC 79. **d** 80 **p** 80. Hon C Catford (Southend) and Downham *S'wark* 80–83; Hon C Surbiton St Andr and St Mark 83–85; Hon C Shirley St Geo 85–93; PtO *Lon* 96–09. *6 Shore Cottages, Silverdale, Carnforth LA5 0TS* M: 07817-458076 E: nigelkirkup@hotmail.com

KIRKWOOD, Canon David Christopher. b 40. Pemb Coll Ox BA 63. Clifton Th Coll 63. **d** 65 **p** 66. C Wilmington *Roch* 65–68; C Green Street Green 68–72; Youth and Area Sec BCMS 72–73; Educn and Youth Sec 73–80; Hon C Sidcup Ch Ch *Roch* 74–80; V Rothley *Leic* 80–92; RD Goscote II 84–88; RD Goscote 88–90; P-in-c Toxteth St Philemon w St Gabr and St Cleopas *Liv* 92–95; TR 95–01; TR Harlow Town Cen w Lt Parndon *Chelmsf* 01–07; AD Toxteth and Wavertree *Liv* 96–01; AD Harlow *Chelmsf* 04–07; Hon Can Chelmsf Cathl 07; rtd 07. *7 Dunoon Close, Sinfin, Derby DE24 9NF* E: davidk@minternet.org

KIRLEW, John Richard Francis. b 52. STETS 92. **d** 05 **p** 06. NSM Castle Cary w Ansford *B & W* 05–08; P-in-c Colwyn *S & B* 08–13; V 13–15; Dioc Rural Life Adv 09–15; TV Three Valleys *Sarum* from 15. *The Rectory, Holwell, Sherborne DT9 5LF* T: (01963) 23570 E: richard.kirlew@btinternet.com

KIRTON, Canon Richard Arthur. b 43. Dur Univ BA 67 MA 73. Wycliffe Hall Ox 68. **d** 69 **p** 70. C Warsop *S'well* 69–72; C Newark St Mary 72–75; Lect Kolej Theolojo Malaysia 76–79; Dean of Studies Th Sem Kuala Lumpur 79–82; P-in-c Kuala Lumpur St Gabr 79–81; Hon Can Kuala Lumpur from 88; P-in-c Bleasby w Halloughton *S'well* 83–89; V Thurgarton w Hoveringham 83–89; V Thurgarton w Hoveringham and Bleasby etc 89–91; Bp's Adv on Overseas Relns 85–91; Tutor Wilson Carlile Coll of Evang 91–98; P-in-c Ollerton w Boughton *S'well* 98–08; rtd 08; PtO *S'well* from 08. *Hill Top, Mosscar Close, Warsop, Mansfield NG20 0BW* T: (01623) 842915 M: 07803-627574 E: richardkirton1@btinternet.com

KISA, Robert. b 82. St Jo Coll Nottm BA 16. **d** 16 **p** 17. C Liv All SS from 17. *19 Lockerby Road, Liverpool L7 0HG* M: 07815-690760 E: kisarobert@gmail.com

KISH, Paul Alexander. b 68. K Coll Lon BD 92 AKC 92 Leeds Univ MA 96. St Steph Ho Ox 96. **d** 98 **p** 99. C Prestbury *Glouc* 98–01; Chapl Sutton Valence Sch Kent 01–13; PtO *Cant* 14–16; V Yalding w Collier Street *Roch* from 16; PtO *Cant* from 20. *The Vicarage, Vicarage Road, Yalding, Maidstone ME18 6DR* T: (01622) 814182 M: 07760-355434 E: pkish@btinternet.com *or* vicar@yaldingchurches.co.uk

KISSEL, Mathias. b 65. d 19. NSM Basle *Eur* from 19. *Uhlandstrasse 4, 4053 Basle, Switzerland* E: mathias.kissel@anglicanbasel.ch

KISSELL, Barrington John. b 38. Lon Coll of Div 64. d 67 p 68. C Camborne *Truro* 67–71; C Chorleywood St Andr *St Alb* 71–00; C Bryanston Square St Mary w St Marylebone St Mark *Lon* from 00; Dir Faith Sharing Min from 74. *Garden Flat, 19 Lena Gardens, London W6 7PY* T: (020) 7258 5040 E: bkissell1@aol.com

KISSELL, Jonathan Mark Barrington. b 66. Glos Univ BA 93. Trin Coll Bris 99. d 01 p 02. C Stevenage St Pet Broadwater *St Alb* 01–05; C Dublin St Patr Cathl Gp *D & G* 05–11; Chapl Arbour Hill Pris 05–11; PtO *S'wark* 12–13; Asst Chapl YMCA from 14; C Surbiton St Matt *S'wark* 13–15; C Tolworth, Hook and Surbiton 15–16; PtO *Lon* 16; C Teddington St Mark and Hampton Wick 16–17; C Hampton Wick 17–21. *Address temp unknown*

KITCHEN, Andrew Jonathan. b 79. Nottm Univ BA 01 Sheff Hallam Univ MSc 08. St Mellitus Coll 18. d 19 p 20. C Onslow Square and S Kensington St Aug *Lon* 19–20; C Wrexham *St As* from 20. *Address temp unknown*

KITCHEN, Ian Brian. b 60. Worc Coll Ox BA 81 Southn Univ PGCE 82. Wycliffe Hall Ox 98. d 00 p 01. C Brandesburton and Leven w Catwick *York* 00–03; P-in-c Coxwold and Husthwaite 03–11; V 11–12; P-in-c Crayke w Brandsby and Yearsley 03–11; R 11–12; R Derwent Ings 12–19; P-in-c Fountains Gp *Leeds* from 19. *The Rectory, Ringbeck Road, Kirkby Malzeard, Ripon HG4 3SL* E: dulloldman@gmail.com

KITCHEN, Martin. b 47. N Lon Poly BA 71 K Coll Lon BD 76 AKC 77 Man Univ PhD 88. S'wark Ord Course 77. d 79 p 80. Lect CA Tr Coll Blackheath 79–83; Hon C Kidbrooke St Jas *S'wark* 79–83; Chapl Man Poly 83–88; TV Man Whitworth 83–86; TR 86–88; Adv In-Service Tr *S'wark* 88–95; Dioc Co-ord of Tr 95–97; Can Res S'wark Cathl 88–97; Can Res Dur Cathl 97–05; Sub-Dean 99–05; Dean Derby 05–07; P-in-c S Rodings *Chelmsf* 08–11; rtd 11; PtO *Newc* from 12. *4 Town Farm Close, Wall, Hexham NE46 4DH* T: (01434) 689696

KITCHEN, Mrs Rachel Jane. b 75. Surrey Univ BA 97. St Mellitus Coll 18. d 19 p 20. C Onslow Square and S Kensington St Aug *Lon* 19–20; C Wrexham *St As* from 20. *Address temp unknown* M: 07773-776742

KITCHENER, Christopher William. b 46. Open Univ BA. Sarum & Wells Th Coll 82. d 84 p 85. C Bexleyheath Ch Ch *Roch* 84–88; V Gravesend St Mary 88–97; V Biggin Hill 97–07; V St Mary Cray and St Paul's Cray 07–11; rtd 11; Bp's Officer for Retired Clergy Widows and Widowers *Roch* from 11; PtO from 11. *22 Renton Drive, Orpington BR5 4HH* T: (01732) 761766 E: chriskitchener4@gmail.com

KITCHENER, Mrs Evarina Carol. b 51. Stockwell Coll of Educn CertEd 70 Heythrop Coll Lon MA 00. Cant Sch of Min 89. d 92 p 94. NSM Gravesend St Mary *Roch* 92–97; NSM Biggin Hill 97–07; Asst Chapl Bromley Hosps NHS Trust 98–99; Distr Evang Miss Enabler S Prov URC 99–01; Par Development Officer *Roch* 01–07; C Chislehurst St Nic 07–11; P-in-c Seal St Lawr 11–12; V 12–16; P-in-c Underriver 11–12; V 12–16; V Seal Chart w Underriver 16; rtd 16. *22 Renton Drive, Orpington BR5 4HH* E: carolkitchener2@gmail.com

KITCHENER, Canon Michael Anthony. b 45. Trin Coll Cam BA 67 MA 70 PhD 71. Cuddesdon Coll 70. d 71 p 72. C Aldwick *Chich* 71–74; C Caversham *Ox* 74–77; Tutor Coll of Resurr Mirfield 77–83; Prin NEOC *Dur* 83–90; Hon Can Newc Cathl 84–90; Can Res and Chan Blackb Cathl 90–95; P-in-c Rydal *Carl* 95–99; Warden Rydal Hall and Ldr Rydal Hall Community 95–99; Can Res Nor Cathl 99–05; Dioc Dir of Ords 99–04; Bp's Officer for Ord and Initial Tr 04–05; rtd 05; LtO *Edin* 06–10; LtO *Arg* from 10. *Croft Cottage, Creag an Tairbh Beag, Ford, Lochgilphead PA31 8RH* T: (01546) 810062 E: kitcheners@yahoo.co.uk

KITCHIN, Kenneth. b 46. Trin Coll Bris. d 89 p 90. C Barrow St Mark *Carl* 89–93; C Dalton-in-Furness 93–95; P-in-c Dearham 95–01; P-in-c Clifton 01–07; P-in-c Dean 01–07; P-in-c Mosser 01–07; R Clifton, Dean and Mosser 07–10; rtd 10; PtO *Carl* from 10. *7 Allerdale, Cockermouth CA13 0BN* E: kenkitchin@yahoo.co.uk

KITCHING, Daphne. b 48. Yorks Min Course. d 09 p 10. NSM Swanland *York* 09–17; PtO 17–21; *Leeds* 20–21. *21 Old Pond Place, North Ferriby HU14 3JE* T: (01482) 635159 E: daphnekitching@hotmail.com

KITCHING, Miss Elizabeth. b 49. Trent Park Coll of Educn CertEd 74. St Jo Coll Nottm. d 01 p 02. C Northallerton w Kirby Sigston *York* 01–05; V Cloughton and Burniston w Ravenscar etc 05–13; V Hackness w Harwood Dale 05–13; rtd 13; PtO *York* from 13. *31 Osgodby Crescent, Scarborough YO11 3JP* M: 07889-425025 E: elizabethkitching@btinternet.com

KITE, Paul Anthony. b 64. SEITE BA 14. d 14 p 15. C W Sheppey *Cant* 14–17; TV N Downs 17–20; P-in-c W Sheppey from 20. *Address temp unknown* E: revkite@btinternet.com

KITELEY, Robert John. b 51. Hull Univ BSc 73 Univ of Wales (Abth) MSc 75 Lon Univ PhD 82. Trin Coll Bris. d 83 p 84. C Bebington *Ches* 83–88; C Hoole 88–91; V Plas Newton 91–99; R Ashtead *Guildf* 99–14; rtd 14. *2 Doreen Close, Farnborough GU14 9HB* T: (01276) 428834 E: johntew51@gmail.com

KITLEY, Canon David Buchan. b 53. St Jo Coll Dur BA. Trin Coll Bris 78. d 81 p 82. C Tonbridge St Steph *Roch* 81–84; C-in-c Southall Em CD *Lon* 84–91; V Dartford Ch Ch *Roch* 91–09; RD Dartford 98–07; V Kippington 09–20; rtd 20; Bp's Adv for Overseas Links *Roch* from 09; Hon Can Roch Cathl from 05; Hon Can Mpwapwa from 05. *93A Yew Tree Road, Tunbridge Wells TN4 0BJ* T: (01892) 523618 E: kitley@clara.net

KITSON, Kevin. b 64. d 14 p 15. NSM Dur N 14–16; PtO 17–20. *Stenhill Cottage, North Petherwin, Launceston PL15 8NN* M: 07950-341110 E: kevinkitson64@gmail.com

KITTO, Ms Michele Claire. b 74. Cam Univ BEd 98 Buckingham Univ MEd 21. Sarum Coll 18. d 20 p 21. Chapl Millfield Jun Sch Somerset from 17; NSM Glastonbury w Meare *B & W* from 20. *Ivernia, Cinnamon Lane, Glastonbury BA6 8BN* M: 07748-966450 E: kitto.m@millfieldprep.com *or* glastonburycurate@yahoo.com

KIVETT, Michael Stephen. b 50. Bethany Coll W Virginia BA 72. Chr Th Sem Indiana MDiv 76 Sarum & Wells Th Coll 76. d 77 p 78. C Harnham *Sarum* 77–80; C E Dereham Nor 80–83; R S Walsham and V Upton 83–88; Chapl Lt Plumstead Hosp 84–88; V Chard St Mary *B & W* 88–99; TR Chard and Distr 99–04; RD Crewkerne and Ilminster 93–98; R Staplegrove w Norton Fitzwarren 04–20; rtd 20; PtO *B & W* from 20. *11 Tellisford Lane, Norton St Philip, Bath BA2 7LL* T: (01373) 834587 E: kivett@btinternet.com

KIYAGA, Innocent Nathan. b 87. Redcliffe Coll Glouc BA 12. Lon Sch of Th MA 13. d 15 p 16. Min for Internat Miss Dio Mbeere Kenya 15–16; NSM Upton *Ex* from 16; Asst Chapl Univ of St Mark and St Jo 16–17; Chapl St Cuthbert Mayne Sch Torquay from 17; RD Torbay *Ex* from 21. *The Haven, St Katherines Road, Torquay TQ1 4DE* M: 07964-532187 E: nathan@kiyaga.com

KLAIR, Sarbjit Singh. b 65. Bath Univ BSc 88 FCA 92. Ridley Hall Cam 15. d 17 p 18. C Thames Ditton *Guildf* 17–21. *4 Quinton Road, Thames Ditton KT7 0AX* M: 07711-752778 E: sarb.klair@gmail.com

KLIMAS, Canon Lynda. b 58. Jes Coll Cam BA 89 MA 93. Cranmer Hall Dur 89. d 90 p 94. Par Dn Sandy *St Alb* 90–93; Par Dn Bishop's Stortford St Mich 93–94; C 94–98; P-in-c Weston and C Baldock w Bygrave 98–03; TV Baldock w Bygrave and Weston 03–04; V Cople, Moggerhanger and Willington 04–13; R Maulden from 13; RD Ampthill and Shefford from 13; Hon Can St Alb from 13. *The Rectory, Clophill Road, Maulden, Bedford MK45 2AA* T: (01525) 403139 E: rev.l.klimas@btinternet.com

KNAPP, Antony Blair. b 48. Imp Coll Lon BSc 68. NOC 86. d 89 p 90. C Bolton St Jas w St Chrys *Bradf* 89–92; V Kettlewell w Conistone, Hubberholme etc 92–00; TR Swindon Dorcan *Bris* 00–13; rtd 13; PtO *Llan* from 14. *5 Mountjoy Place, Penarth CF64 2TB* T: (01793) 525130

KNAPP, Canon Bryan Thomas. b 61. Trin Coll Bris BA 91. d 91 p 92. C S Gillingham *Roch* 91–95; V Chatham St Paul w All SS 95–09; V Paddock Wood from 09; RD 13–19; Hon Can Roch Cathl from 15. *The Vicarage, 169 Maidstone Road, Paddock Wood, Tonbridge TN12 6DZ* T: (01892) 833917 E: bryan@standrewspw.org.uk

KNAPP (née STOCKER), Canon Rachael Ann. b 64. Bris Univ BA 86. Trin Coll Bris BA 91. d 91 p 94. C Ditton *Roch* 91–95; C Chatham St Paul w All SS 95–08; Chapl Bennett Memorial Dioc Sch Tunbridge Wells from 08; Hon Can Roch Cathl from 18. *The Vicarage, 169 Maidstone Road, Paddock Wood, Tonbridge TN12 6DZ* T: (01892) 833917 *or* 521595 E: knapp@bennett.kent.sch.uk

KNEE-ROBINSON, Keith Frederick. b 40. Thames Poly BSc 75 MICE 76. SAOMC 99. d 01 p 02. OLM Caversham St Pet and Mapledurham *Ox* 01–10; OLM Caversham Thameside and Mapledurham 10–12; rtd 12; PtO *Ox* from 12. *8 Hewett Close, Reading RG4 7ER* T: 0118-947 7868 E: kkrmill@globalnet.co.uk

KNEEBONE, Canon Patricia Jane. b 53. Man Univ BA 74 Lon Univ BD 94. SWMTC 08. d 10 p 11. NSM Newquay *Truro* 10; Hon Can Truro Cathl from 15. *34 Henver Road, Newquay TR7 3BN* M: 07966-703924 E: janekneebone@gmail.com

KNEEN, Preb Michael John. b 55. Univ Coll Lon BSc 76 MSc 77 St Jo Coll Dur BA 85. Cranmer Hall Dur 83. d 86 p 87. C Bishop's Castle w Mainstone *Heref* 86–90; TV Bridgnorth, Tasley, Astley Abbotts, etc 90–08; TV Leominster

08–10; TR 10–20; RD 14–19; Preb Heref Cathl 18–20; rtd 20; PtO *Heref* from 21. *The Cwm, Meadow Street, Weobley, Hereford HR4 8SF* T: (01544) 318080 E: mjkneen@btinternet.com

KNIBBS, Peter John. b 55. Birm Univ BDS 78 DDS 93. SWMTC 04. **d** 07 **p** 08. NSM St Illogan *Truro* 07–11; P-in-c Chacewater w St Day and Carharrack 11–14; C 14; P-in-c St Stythians w Perranarworthal and Gwennap 11–14; P-in-c Devoran 11–14; P-in-c Feock 11–14; V Monkseaton St Mary *Newc* 14–16; rtd 16; PtO *Newc* from 16; Hon C N Shields 17–21. *85 Wellesley Drive, Blyth NE24 3UZ* T: (01670) 302546 E: peter.knibbs@lineone.net

KNIGHT, The Very Revd Alexander Francis (Alec). b 39. OBE 06. St Cath Coll Cam BA 61 MA 65. Wells Th Coll. **d** 63 **p** 64. C Hemel Hempstead *St Alb* 63–68; Chapl Taunton Sch 68–75; Dir Bloxham Project 75–81; Dir of Studies Aston Tr Scheme 81–83; P-in-c Easton and Martyr Worthy *Win* 83–91; Adn Basingstoke 90–98; Can Res Win Cathl 91–98; Dean Linc 98–06; rtd 06; PtO *Sarum* from 15. *Shalom, Clay Street, Whiteparish, Salisbury SP5 2ST* T: (01794) 884402 E: sheelagh_knight@hotmail.com

KNIGHT, Canon Andrew James. b 50. Grey Coll Dur BA 72 Ox Univ BA 74 MA 81 Univ of Wales MTh 08. Wycliffe Hall Ox 72. **d** 75 **p** 76. Min Can Brecon Cathl *S & B* 75–78; C Brecon w Battle 75–78; C Morriston 78–82; V 89–00; V Llanwrtyd w Llanddulas in Tir Abad etc 82–89; RD Cwmtawe 97–00; V Sketty 00–15; Can Res Brecon Cathl 98–04; Treas Brecon Cathl 04–15; rtd 15; PtO *S & B* from 15. *105 Frampton Road, Gorseinon, Swansea SA4 4YE* T: (01792) 736159 E: andrewknight@phonecoop.coop

KNIGHT, Andrew Ronald. b 67. **d** 06 **p** 07. C Wolstanton *Lich* 06–09; V 09–14; Chapl Staffs and Stoke on Trent Partnership NHS Trust 09; R Shrewsbury St Giles w Sutton and Atcham *Lich* from 14. *The Rectory, 127 Abbey Foregate, Shrewsbury SY2 6LY* T: (01743) 600691 E: andykn@talktalk.net

KNIGHT, Andrew William. b 71. Hull Univ BSc 92 PhD 96. St Jo Coll Nottm 12. **d** 14 **p** 15. C Mottram in Longdendale *Ches* 14–17; P-in-c Partington and Carrington from 17; PtO *Man* from 19. *St Mary's Vicarage, Manchester Road, Partington, Manchester M31 4FB* M: 07899-724760 E: andrewknight247@gmail.com

KNIGHT, Ann Elaine. b 66. **d** 21. OLM Tyseley *Birm* from 21. *76 Tenby Road, Birmingham B13 9LX* T: 0121-778 6174 M: 07768-451549 E: annknight69@yahoo.co.uk

KNIGHT, Mrs Barbara. b 46. St Alb Minl Tr Scheme 86. **d** 90 **p** 94. NSM Weston and Ardeley *St Alb* 90–95; C Norton 95–97; R Barkway, Reed and Buckland w Barley 97–05; rtd 05; PtO *Glouc* from 14. *332 London Road, Charlton Kings, Cheltenham GL52 6YJ*

KNIGHT, Mrs Barbara Mary. b 43. SRN 64 SCM 70. EMMTC 94. **d** 97 **p** 98. NSM Market Harborough and The Transfiguration etc *Leic* 97–99; C Church Langton cum Tur Langton etc 99–02; P-in-c Billesdon and Skeffington 02; R Church Langton cum Tur Langton etc 02–07; rtd 07; PtO *Blackb* from 07. *1 Whittlewood Drive, Accrington BB5 5DJ* T: (01254) 395549 E: revbarbarak@btopenworld.com

KNIGHT, David Alan. b 59. Lanc Univ BA 81. Ripon Coll Cuddesdon 82. **d** 85 **p** 86. C Stretford All SS *Man* 85–88; C Charlestown 88–89; TV Pendleton St Thos w Charlestown 89–94; V Tysoe w Oxhill and Whatcote *Cov* 94–05; RD Shipston 04–05; Chapl Marie Curie Cen Solihull 06–08; Chapl St Richard's Hospice Worc 06–15; Chapl Mary Stevens Hospice Stourbridge 15–17; Bp's Health Service Adv *Worc* 12–17; Chapl St Wilfrid's Hospice Eastbourne 17–19; Lead Chapl Sussex Community NHS Foundn Trust from 19; V Fletching *Chich* from 21. *Sussex Community NHS Foundation Trust, Brighton General Hospital, Elm Grove, Brighton BN2 3EW* T: (01273) 696011 E: davidalanknight@outlook.com

KNIGHT, Canon David Charles. b 45. Lon Univ BA 66 St Edm Hall Ox BA 68 MA 73 ATCL 63. St Steph Ho Ox 68. **d** 70 **p** 71. C Northwood H Trin *Lon* 70–73; C Stevenage All SS Pin Green *St Alb* 73–77; C Cippenham CD *Ox* 77–78; TV W Slough 78–83; Dep Min Can Windsor 81–08; R Lt Stanmore St Lawr *Lon* 83–91; Ecum Officer to Bp Willesden 83–91; Prec and Can Res Chelmsf Cathl 91–01; V Ranmoor *Sheff* 01–08; rtd 08; PtO *Ox* from 09. *12 Bankside, Headington, Oxford OX3 8LT* T: (01865) 761476 E: davidcknight45@gmail.com

KNIGHT, Canon David Lansley. b 33. Em Coll Cam BA 58 MA 61 PGCE 76. Ridley Hall Cam 57. **d** 59 **p** 60. C Chatham St Steph *Roch* 59–63; C Plymouth St Andr *Ex* 63–65; V Gravesend St Aid *Roch* 65–71; V Bexley St Mary 71–98; RD Sidcup 93–97; Hon Can Roch Cathl 97; rtd 98; PtO *Chich* 98–19. *1 Newlands Avenue, Bexhill-on-Sea TN39 4HA* T: (01424) 212120

KNIGHT, Mrs Dawn Marie. b 68. RGN 90. Qu Foundn (Course) 16. **d** 19 **p** 20. C Allestree St Nic

Derby from 19; C Quarndon from 19. *28 Earlswood Drive, Mickleover, Derby DE3 9LN* M: 07789-070260 E: dawnmarieknight@hotmail.co.uk *or* revdawn68@gmail.com

KNIGHT (née SMITH), Frances Mary. b 48. St Jo Coll York CertEd 69. EMMTC 98. **d** 03 **p** 04. NSM Braunstone *Leic* 03–07; NSM The Abbey Leic 07–12; rtd 12; PtO *Leic* from 15. *32 Aster Way, Burbage, Hinckley LE10 2UQ* T: (01455) 618218 E: frances.knight@mypostonline.co.uk

KNIGHT, Gavin Rees. b 65. St Andr Univ MTheol 94. Ripon Coll Cuddesdon MTh 96. **d** 98 **p** 99. C Solihull *Birm* 98–02; P-in-c Fulham St Andr *Lon* 02–05; P-in-c Fulham St Alb w St Aug 04–05; Chapl Mon Sch 05–11; V Summertown *Ox* from 11. *The Vicarage, 33 Lonsdale Road, Oxford OX2 7ES* M: 07833-251939 E: vicar@stmichaels-summertown.org.uk

KNIGHT, Isaac John. b 91. St Jo Coll Dur BA 13. Wycliffe Hall Ox 16. **d** 19 **p** 20. C Flackwell Heath *Ox* from 19. *12 Green Crescent, Flackwell Heath, High Wycombe HP10 9JQ* M: 07494-409303 E: revisaacknight@gmail.com

KNIGHT, Joel Matthew. b 88. Nottm Univ BA 11. Wycliffe Hall Ox 14. **d** 17 **p** 18. C Ox St Ebbe w H Trin and St Pet from 17. *81 Marlborough Road, Oxford OX1 4LX* M: 07773-780998 E: jknightgy@gmail.com

KNIGHT, Canon John Bernard. b 34. Fuller Th Sem California DMin 91 ACIS 60. Oak Hill Th Coll 61. **d** 65 **p** 66. C Morden *S'wark* 65–69; USA 69–71; V Summerfield *Birm* 71–07; Hon Can Birm Cathl 01–07; rtd 07; PtO *Birm* from 07; *Worc* from 08. *102 High Haden Road, Cradley Heath B64 7PN* T: 0121-559 0108 E: home@jandmknight.go-plus.net

KNIGHT, Canon John Francis Alan Macdonald. b 36. Coll of Resurr Mirfield 59. **d** 61 **p** 62. C Gwelo Rhodesia 61–66; R Melfort 66–68; C Highlands and P-in-c Chikwaka, Mrewa, Hoyuyu, and Mtoko 68–70; LtO Mashonaland 70–75; R Umtali Zimbabwe 76–81; Dean Mutare 81–87; TR Northampton Em *Pet* 87–97; RD Northn 88–92; P-in-c Greens Norton w Bradden and Lichborough 97–05; Bp's Adv for Min of Healing 99–05; Can Pet Cathl 01–05; rtd 05; PtO *Pet* 06–11; P-in-c Weedon Bec w Everdon and Dodford 11–17; PtO from 17. *The Rectory, High Street, Marston St Lawrence, Banbury OX17 2DB* T: (01295) 368682 E: theknights16@tiscali.co.uk

KNIGHT, Jonathan Morshead. b 59. Fitzw Coll Cam BA 81 MA 85 Jes Coll Cam PhD 91 Jes Coll Ox MA 87 Worc Coll Ox DPhil 02 W Lon Inst of HE PGCE 82 Sheff Univ PGCE 00. Wycliffe Hall Ox 86. **d** 88 **p** 89. C Hillingdon St Jo *Lon* 88–91; NSM Baslow *Derby* 91–92; NSM Curbar and Stoney Middleton 91–92; Lect Bibl Studies Sheff Univ 91–92; Research Fell 92–94; NSM Sheff St Paul 92–94; Bp's Research Asst *Ely* 94–98; Min Whittlesford LEP 95–96; Bp's Dom Chapl 96; Sec Doctrine Commn 96–98; P-in-c Holywell w Needingworth *Ely* 98–01; Tutor Westcott Ho Cam 98–99; OCM from 99; CF (TAVR) 00–03; Hon Lect Th Kent Univ 00–03; Chapl Worc Coll Ox 02–03; Visiting Fell York St Jo Univ from 07; Tutor Grey Coll Dur 10–21; PtO *S & M* from 21; NSM St German's Cathl from 21. *St Germans Cathedral, Derby Road, Peel, Isle of Man IM5 1HH* T: (01624) 844830 M: 07549-170031 E: jonathanknight5@hotmail.com

KNIGHT, Joseph Daniel. b 83. Trin Coll Bris MA 18. **d** 18 **p** 19. C Newnham w Awre and Blakeney *Glouc* from 18. *The Old Library, High Street, Newnham GL14 1AD* M: 07950-712282 E: joeknight@outlook.com

KNIGHT, Keith Kenneth. b 36. Southn Univ BSc 58. Wycliffe Hall Ox 59. **d** 62 **p** 63. C Lower Darwen St Jas *Blackb* 62–64; C Leyland St Andr 64–68; P-in-c Blackb All SS 68–71; Dioc Youth Chapl 71–88; Hon C Burnley St Pet 71–74; Warden Scargill Ho 88–01; rtd 01; PtO *Bradf* 01–14; *Leeds* from 14. *4 The Hawthorns, Sutton-in-Craven, Keighley BD20 8BP* T: (01535) 632920

KNIGHT, Mrs Margaret Owen. b 34. Oak Hill Th Coll 78. dss 80 **d** 87 **p** 94. Chorleywood St Andr *St Alb* 80–04; Par Dn 87–94; C 94–04; rtd 94; PtO *St Alb* 04–19. *15A Blacketts Wood Drive, Chorleywood, Rickmansworth WD3 5PY* T: (01923) 283832 E: moknight@waitrose.com

KNIGHT, Michael Andrew. b 87. Warwick Univ BA 09. Trin Coll Bris 17. **d** 20. C Charles w Plymouth St Matthias *Ex* from 20. *261 North Road West, Plymouth PL1 5DH* E: mike@stmplymouth.org.uk

KNIGHT, Canon Michael Richard. b 47. St Jo Coll Dur BA 69 MA 79 Fitzw Coll Cam BA 73 MA 78 St Cross Coll Ox MA 92. Westcott Ho Cam 71. **d** 74 **p** 75. C Bishop's Stortford St Mich *St Alb* 74–75; C Bedford St Andr 75–79; Chapl Angl Students Glas 79–86; V Riddings and Ironville *Derby* 86–91; Lib Pusey Ho 91–94; Fell St Cross Coll Ox 92–94; V Chesterfield St Mary and All SS *Derby* 94–13; P-in-c Chesterfield SS Aug 05–09; Hon Can Derby Cathl 06–13; rtd 13; PtO *S'well* from 14. *1 Leabrook Close, Nottingham NG11 8NW*

KNIGHT, Paul Jeremy. b 53. d 94 p 95. CA 77–04 and from 13; C Adderley *Lich* 94–96; C Drayton in Hales 94–96; C Moreton Say 94–96; C Adderley, Ash, Calverhall, Ightfield etc 96–97; V Birstall *Wakef* 97–14; *Leeds* 14–20; AD 14–18; rtd 20; PtO *Llan* from 21. *35 North Terrace, Maerdy, Ferndale CF43 4DD*

KNIGHT, Peter John. b 51. AKC 73 Ch Ch Coll Cant CertEd 77. Sarum & Wells Th Coll 79. d 80 p 81. C Greenford H Cross *Lon* 80–83; C Langley Marish *Ox* 83; NSM W Acton St Martin *Lon* 88–90; C E Acton St Dunstan w St Thos 90–92; V Malden St Jo *S'wark* 92–02; Co-ord Chapl HM Pris Long Lartin 02–05; TR Malvern Link w Cowleigh *Worc* 05–10; V 10–17; RD Malvern 13–17; rtd 17; PtO *Glouc* from 18. *29 Albert Road, Evesham WR11 4JZ* E: pjknight1951@gmail.com

KNIGHT, Peter Malcolm. b 55. Trin Hall Cam BA 76 MA 80 Lon Hosp MB, BS 76 Leeds Univ MA 12 MRCGP 85. Trin Coll Bris BA 94. d 94 p 95. C Quidenham *Nor* 94–97; R Thurton w Ashby St Mary, Bergh Apton etc 97–14; RD Loddon 99–05; NSM Tunis St Geo Tunisia 14–19; PtO *Nor* 14–19; RD Trigg Major *Truro* from 19; P-in-c Trigg Major CD from 19; P-in-c Launceston from 19; P-in-c Boyton, N Tamerton, Werrington etc from 19. *The Rectory, Dunheved Road, Launceston PL15 9JE* T: (01566) 777607 E: tl.triggmaj@gmail.com

KNIGHT, Philip Stephen. b 46. Ian Ramsey Coll Brasted 74 Oak Hill Th Coll 75. d 77 p 78. C Pennycross *Ex* 77–80; C Epsom St Martin *Guildf* 80–83; V Clay Hill St Jo *Lon* 83–86; TV Washfield, Stoodleigh, Withleigh etc *Ex* 86–90; Chapl ATC from 86; Chapl S Warks Hosps 90–94; Chapl S Warks Health Care NHS Trust 94–05; PtO *Cov* from 05; *Ex* 10–21; rtd 11. *Coombeside, 122 Alexandria Road, Sidmouth EX10 9HG* T: (01395) 514168 E: psk54@hotmail.co.uk

KNIGHT, Rhona Anton. b 60. Lon Univ MB, BS 85 Surrey Univ MA 04 FRCGP 06 Dur Univ MA 16. Ridley Hall Cam 14. d 16 p 17. C Sleaford *Linc* 16–19. *Charis, 5 Griffiths Close, Oakham LE15 6FP* M: 07599-447431 E: revrhona@btinternet.com

KNIGHT, Canon Roger George. b 41. Culham Coll Ox CertEd 63. Linc Th Coll 65. d 67 p 68. C Bris St Andr Hartcliffe 67–69; Hd Master Twywell Sch Kettering 69–74; V Naseby *Pet* 74–79; P-in-c Haselbech 74–79; R Clipston w Naseby and Haselbech 79–82; C Arthingworth w Kelmarsh and Harrington 79–82; TR Corby SS Pet and Andr w Gt and Lt Oakley 82–88; R Irthlingborough 88–99; RD Higham 89–94; R Burton Latimer 99–03; Can Pet Cathl 92–03; rtd 03; PtO *Pet* from 03. *9 Hollow Wood Road, Burton Latimer, Kettering NN15 5RB* T: (01536) 669618 E: rogerknight41@outlook.com

KNIGHT, Roger Ivan. b 54. K Coll Lon BD 79 AKC 79. Ripon Coll Cuddesdon 79. d 80 p 81. C Orpington All SS *Roch* 80–84; C St Laur in Thanet *Cant* 84–87; R Cuxton and Halling *Roch* from 87. *The Rectory, 6 Rochester Road, Cuxton, Rochester ME2 1AF* T: (01634) 717134 E: roger@cuxtonandhalling.org.uk

KNIGHT, Stephen. *See* KNIGHT, Philip Stephen

KNIGHT, Ms Sue Elizabeth. b 47. Southlands Coll Lon CertEd 68. SEITE 01. d 03 p 04. NSM Lee St Mildred *S'wark* 03–09; NSM Cheltenham St Mary w St Matt and St Luke *Glouc* 12–14; rtd 14; PtO *Glouc* from 20. *11 Giffard Way, Leckhampton, Cheltenham GL53 0PW* T: (01242) 234363

KNIGHT, Mrs Susan Jane. b 57. Open Univ BSc 99. NTMTC BA 09. d 09 p 10. C Harlow Town Cen w Lt Parndon *Chelmsf* 09–12; TV 12–16; P-in-c Roydon 15–16; rtd 16. *11 Sweetbriar Lane, Holcombe, Dawlish EX7 0JZ* E: sue@kerryknight.co.uk

KNIGHT, Mrs Susan Margaret. d 02 p 03. C Clydach *S & B* 02–03; C Cen Swansea 04–05; TV 05–16; rtd 16; PtO *S & B* from 16. *21 Parklands Court, Sketty, Swansea SA2 8LZ* T: (01792) 683049

KNIGHT, William Lawrence. b 39. Univ Coll Lon BSc 61 PhD 65. Coll of Resurr Mirfield 75. d 77 p 78. C Bp's Hatfield *St Alb* 77–81; Asst Chapl Brussels Cathl *Eur* 81–84; V Pet H Spirit Bretton 84–89; P-in-c Marholm 84–89; TR Riverside *Ox* 89–04; rtd 04; PtO *Chich* from 15. *90 Norfolk Gardens, Littlehampton BN17 5PF* T: (01903) 716750 E: wlnight@tiscali.co.uk

KNIGHT-SCOTT, Catherine Mary. Selw Coll Cam BA 83 MA 00 Goldsmiths' Coll Lon PGCE 11. Ripon Coll Cuddesdon 12. d 14 p 15. C Orpington All SS *Roch* 14–18; P-in-c Footscray w N Cray 18; P-in-c Sidcup St Jo 18; V Sidcup St Jo w Footscray from 18. *St John's Vicarage, Church Avenue, Sidcup DA14 6BU* E: revcathyks@gmail.com

KNIGHTS, Christopher Hammond. b 61. St Jo Coll Dur BA 83 PhD 88. Linc Th Coll 87. d 89 p 90. C Stockton St Pet *Dur* 89–92; C Chich St Paul and St Pet 92–94; Tutor Chich Th Coll 92–94; V Ashington *Newc* 94–00; V Monkseaton St Mary 00–04; Dioc Moderator Reader Tr 03–10; P-in-c Scotswood 04–11; R Kelso *Edin* 11–13; R Coldstream 11–13;

Development Worker Hawick Acorn Project 13–14; Ch and Community Development Worker Musselburgh 14–16; PtO *Edin* 13–16; *Newc* 14–16; P-in-c Southampton Lord's Hill and Lord's Wood *Win* 16–21; V from 21. *The Vicarage, 1 Tangmere Drive, Southampton SO16 8GY* T: (023) 8073 1091 M: 07486-425069 E: revchrisknights@gmail.com

KNIGHTS, James William. b 34. AKC 66. d 67 p 68. C Kettering St Andr *Pet* 67–71; V Braunston w Brooke 71–81; V Dudley St Jo *Worc* 81–97; rtd 97; PtO *Worc* from 98. *192 Brook Farm Drive, Malvern WR14 3SL* T: (01684) 561358

KNIGHTS JOHNSON, Nigel Anthony. b 52. Ealing Tech Coll BA 74 Westmr Coll Ox MTh 99. Wycliffe Hall Ox 78. d 80 p 81. C Beckenham Ch Ch *Roch* 80–84; CF 84–07; R Ockley, Okewood and Forest Green *Guildf* 07–17; rtd 17; PtO *Ox* from 17; *Eur* from 16. *134 Main Road, Long Hanborough, Witney OX29 8JY* E: nigelknightsjohnson@gmail.com

KNOTT, Barry James Frederick. b 64. Cant Ch Ch Univ BSc 00. St Aug Coll of Th 15. d 17 p 18. C Allington and Maidstone St Pet *Cant* 17–20; C Barming Heath 17–20; C Lympne and Saltwood 20–21; R from 21. *The Rectory, Rectory Lane, Saltwood, Hythe CT21 4QA* M: 07891-199459 E: barryjfknott@msn.com

KNOTT, The Ven Graham Keith. b 53. Oak Hill Th Coll BA 80. d 80 p 81. C Normanton *Derby* 80–83; C Ripley 83–87; TV Newark w Hawton, Cotham and Shelton *S'well* 87–89; TV Newark 89–97; P-in-c Mansfield St Jo 97–06; AD Mansfield 03–06; P-in-c Croajingolong Australia 06–09; P-in-c Watford *St Alb* 09–11; R Maffra Australia 11–15; R Leongatha from 15; Adn Gippsland from 15. *PO Box 271, Leongatha VIC 3953, Australia* T: (0061) (3) 5662 5043 E: grahamjune74@gmail.com

KNOTT, Preb Janet Patricia. b 50. Avery Hill Coll CertEd 71. S Dios Minl Tr Scheme MTS 91. d 92 p 94. NSM Clutton w Cameley *B & W* 92–99; Chapl R Sch Bath 94–98; Chapl R High Sch Bath 98–99; R Farmborough, Marksbury and Stanton Prior *B & W* 99–20; Chapl Bath Spa Univ 99–20; RD Chew Magna 04–14; Preb Wells Cathl 07–20; rtd 20; PtO *B & W* from 21. *3 Sunnyside, Clutton Hill, Clutton, Bristol BS39 5QG* E: jpknott@btinternet.com

KNOTT, John Wensley. b 51. Fitzw Coll Cam MA 75 FIA 84. S Dios Minl Tr Scheme 87. d 90 p 91. NSM Canford Magna *Sarum* 90–94; NSM Northchurch and Wigginton *St Alb* 94–95; NSM Munich Ascension Germany 95–97; PtO *Eur* from 09; NSM Colne and Villages *Blackb* 12–14; R Foulridge, Laneshawbridge and Trawden from 14. *Christ Church Vicarage, Keighley Road, Colne BB8 7HF* E: john.knott51@icloud.com

KNOTT, Pamela Frances. *See* IVE, Pamela Frances

KNOTT, Wendy Gillian. b 47. Adelaide Univ BA 78. Melbourne Coll of Div BD 95. d 94 p 96. NSM Sandy Bay Australia 94–98; NSM New Town St Jas 98–01; NSM Franklin w Esperance 01–05; Hon Chapl Ch Coll Tasmania 97–06; R Wick *Mor* 06–17; P-in-c Thurso 06–17; rtd 17. *39 Ormlie Road, Thurso KW14 7EB* E: rev.wendy@btinternet.com

KNOWERS, Stephen John. b 49. K Coll Lon BD 72 AKC 72. d 73 p 74. C Bp's Hatfield *St Alb* 73–77; C Cheshunt 77–81; P-in-c Barnet Vale St Mark 81–83; V 83–85; Chapl S Bank Poly 85–92; Chapl S Bank Univ 92–94; V Croydon St Pet 94–06; P-in-c Croydon St Aug 04–06; V S Croydon St Pet and St Aug 06–07; V Shirley St Jo 07–15; AD Croydon Addington 11–15; rtd 15; PtO *Eur* from 15. *Narva Mnt 6-19, Tallinn 10117, Estonia* T: (00372) 5802 4920 E: frstiiv@hotmail.com

KNOWLES, Andrew John. b 66. Wimbledon Sch of Art BA 88. St Jo Coll Nottm 05. d 07 p 08. C Long Buckby w Watford and W Haddon w Winwick and Ravensthorpe *Pet* 07–11; V Camberley St Mary *Guildf* from 11; Asst Dioc Dir of Ords from 15. *St Mary's Vicarage, 37 Park Road, Camberley GU15 2SP* T: (01276) 685167 *or* 425310 E: vicar@stmaryscamberley.org.uk

KNOWLES, Canon Andrew William Allen. b 46. St Cath Coll Cam BA 68 MA 72. St Jo Coll Nottm 69. d 71 p 72. C Leic H Trin 71–74; C Cambridge H Trin *Ely* 74–77; C Woking St Jo *Guildf* 77–81; V Goldsworth Park 81–93; V Wyke 93–98; Dioc Officer Educn and Development of Lay People 93–98; Can Res Chelmsf Cathl 98–11; rtd 11; PtO *Carl* from 12. *68 Appleby Road, Kendal LA9 6HE* T: (01539) 723478 E: andrew.knowles@btinternet.com

KNOWLES, Charles Howard. b 43. Sheff Univ BSc 65 Fitzw Coll Cam BA 69 MA 73. Westcott Ho Cam 67. d 69 p 70. C Bilborough St Jo *S'well* 69–72; V Choral S'well Minster 72–82; V Cinderhill 82–94; AD Nottingham W 91–94; V Cov St Mary 94–06; AD Cov S 96–02; C Burnsall w Rylstone *Bradf* 06–08; C Linton in Craven 06–08; C Kettlewell w Conistone, Hubberholme etc 06–08; rtd 08; PtO *Bradf* 08–14; *Leeds* 14–16. *Ivy Cottage, Linton, Skipton BD23 5HH*

KNOWLES, Clay. *See* KNOWLES, Melvin Clay

KNOWLES, Clifford. b 35. Open Univ BA 82. NW Ord Course 74. **d** 77 **p** 78. C Urmston *Man* 77–80; V Chadderton St Luke 80–87; V Heywood St Luke w All So 87–95; AD Heywood and Middleton 92–95; PtO *Linc* 95–98; rtd 00; PtO *Linc* from 02. *12B Far Lane, Coleby, Lincoln LN5 0AH* T: (01522) 810720

KNOWLES, Canon Eric Gordon. b 44. WMMTC 79. **d** 82 **p** 83. NSM Gt Malvern St Mary *Worc* 82–83; NSM Malvern H Trin and St Jas 83–90; NSM Lt Malvern, Malvern Wells and Wyche 90–99; NSM Lt Malvern 99–00; P-in-c 00–13; V 13–20; Hon Can Worc Cathl from 05. *45 Wykewane, Malvern WR14 2XD* T: (01684) 567439 E: skypilot@homecall.co.uk

✠**KNOWLES, The Rt Revd Graeme Paul.** b 51. CVO 12. AKC 73 FKC 11. St Aug Coll Cant 73. **d** 74 **p** 75. c 03. C St Peter-in-Thanet *Cant* 74–79; C Leeds St Pet *Ripon* 79–81; Chapl and Prec Portsm Cathl 81–87; Chapter Clerk 85–87; V Leigh Park *Portsm* 87–93; RD Havant 90–93; Adn Portsm 93–99; Dean Carl 99–03; Bp S & M 03–07; Dean St Paul's *Lon* 07–12; Hon Asst Bp St E from 12; Hon Asst Bp Ely from 12; PtO *Lon* from 12; PV Westmr Abbey from 14; PtO *Linc* 16–19; Can Res St E Cathl 17–18. *102A Barons Road, Bury St Edmunds IP33 2LY* T: (01284) 723823 E: graemeknowles@hotmail.co.uk

KNOWLES, James Russell. b 80. Sydney Univ BA 01. Oak Hill Th Coll BTh 13. **d** 13 **p** 14. C High Ongar w Norton Mandeville *Chelmsf* 13–16; C Enfield Ch Ch Trent Park *Lon* 16–21; V Eastbourne All SS *Chich* from 21. *All Saints' Centre, 21A Grange Road, Eastbourne BN21 4HE* M: 07791-371808 E: vicar@allsaintseastbourne.com

KNOWLES, Mrs Jane Frances. b 44. GGSM 66 Lon Inst of Educn TCert 67. Ox Min Course 90. **d** 93 **p** 94. NSM Sandhurst *Ox* 93–97; C Wargrave 97–99; P-in-c Ramsden, Finstock and Fawler, Leafield etc 99–01; V Forest Edge 01–09; rtd 09; PtO *Sarum* from 10. *41 Martin's Road, Keevil, Trowbridge BA14 6NA* T: (01380) 870325 E: jane.knowles2@btinternet.com

KNOWLES, John Geoffrey. b 48. Man Univ BSc 69 Lon Univ MSc 75 Ox Univ PGCE 70 FRSA. WMMTC 95. **d** 98 **p** 99. NSM The Lickey *Birm* 99; R Hutcheson's Gr Sch 99–04; P-in-c Woodford *Ches* 05–12; V 12; Dioc Warden of Readers 05–16; NSM Norbury 13–14; NSM Handforth 13–18; rtd 18; PtO *Ches* from 18. *15 Clare Avenue, Handforth, Wilmslow SK9 3EQ* T: (01625) 526531 E: john.knowles92@btinternet.com

KNOWLES, Melvin Clay. b 43. Stetson Univ (USA) BA 66 Ex Univ MA 73. Ripon Coll Cuddesdon 75. **d** 77 **p** 78. C Minchinhampton *Glouc* 77–80; St Helena 80–82; TV Haywards Heath St Wilfrid *Chich* 82–88; Adult Educn Adv 88–94; TR Burgess Hill St Jo w St Edw 94–00; V Burgess Hill St Jo 00–09; rtd 09; PtO *Chich* from 14. *20 Fairfield Road, Burgess Hill RH15 8QA* T: (01444) 254429 E: cknowles@waitrose.com *or* mclayknowles@gmail.com

KNOWLES, Philip Andrew. b 63. Leeds Univ BA 07. NOC 04. **d** 07 **p** 08. C Blackb St Mich w St Jo and H Trin 07–10; C Blackb St Thos w St Jude 07–10; P-in-c Lt Marsden w Nelson St Mary and Nelson St Bede 10–11; V 11–15; V Sheff St Cath Richmond Road from 15; Jt AD Attercliffe 18–21; AD from 21. *St Catherine's Vicarage, 300 Hastilar Road South, Sheffield S13 8EJ* T: 0114-239 9598 M: 07813-966257 E: philip.knowles1@btinternet.com *or* philip.knowles@sheffield.anglican.org

KNOWLES, Richard John. b 47. EAMTC 00. **d** 01 **p** 02. C Burlingham St Edmund w Lingwood, Strumpshaw etc *Nor* 01–04; TV Gt Yarmouth 04–10; rtd 11; PtO *Nor* 11–13. *21 rue de Parthenay, 79340 Ménigoute, France* T: (0033) 5 49 70 68 13 E: revrjk@hotmail.co.uk

KNOX, Canon Geoffrey Martin. b 44. Dur Univ BA 66 Sheff City Coll of Educn DipEd 73. St Chad's Coll Dur 63. **d** 67 **p** 68. C Newark St Mary *S'well* 67–72; PtO *Derby* 72–74; V Woodville 74–81; RD Repton 79–81; V Long Eaton St Laur 81–00; V Somercotes 00–09; RD Alfreton 04–09; Hon Can Derby Cathl 08–09; rtd 09; PtO *Truro* from 16. *9 Treveryn Parc, Budock Water, Falmouth TR11 5EH* T: (01326) 373142

KNOX, Canon Ian Stephen. b 44. Leeds Univ LLB 64 Solicitor 66 Brunel Univ MPhil 03. **d** 05 **p** 05. PtO *Cov* 05–06; *Newc* from 06; Exec Dir 40:3 Trust from 05. *16 East Moor, Loughoughton, Alnwick NE66 3JB* T: (01665) 572939 E: office@fortythreetrust.com *or* ian@knox.org.uk

KOBUS van WENGEN (née SHUTE), Rosemary Margaret. b 38. Westf Coll Lon BA 60 Leiden Univ MA 77 PhD 81. SEITE 98. **d** 01 **p** 02. NSM Benenden *Cant* 01–10; NSM Sandhurst w Newenden 04–10; NSM Benenden and Sandhurst 10–11; PtO from 11. *Beach House, Grange Road, St Michaels, Tenterden TN30 6EF* T: (01580) 764857 E: rosemaryvanwengen@gmail.com

KOCH, John Dunbar. b 77. Washington & Lee Univ BA 00 Humboldt Univ Berlin PhD 14. Trin Episc Sch for Min Penn MDiv 07. **d** 07 **p** 08. C Wiesbaden Austria 07–09; C Vienna *Eur* 09–12; R Harrods Creek St Fran USA from 12. *436 Club Lane, Louisville KY 40207, USA* T: (001) (502) 544 5711 E: jadykoch@gmail.com

KOEPPING, Elizabeth Rosalind. b 47. Edin Univ MA 71 Man Univ MA 73 Univ of Qld PhD 81 Westmr Coll Ox MTh 98. **d** 09 **p** 10. NSM Edin Ch Ch 09–14; PtO *Eur* 11–14; P-in-c Heidelberg 14–16; PtO *Ox* 16–21. *Blenheim Cottage, The Slade, Charlbury, Chipping Norton OX7 3SJ* T: (01608) 811400 E: e.koepping@ed.ac.uk

KOH, Mrs Yunghee. b 68. Roehampton Inst MA 00 PGDE 08 Dur Univ BA 11. St Aug Coll of Th 15. **d** 17 **p** 18. C Wimbledon *S'wark* 17–20; C Battersea St Luke from 20. *30 Canford Road, London SW11 6NZ* M: 07533-386918 E: yungheekoh05@yahoo.co.uk *or* yunghee@stlukeschurch.org.uk

KOLLTVEIT, Emily Alice. b 75. Ripon Coll Cuddesdon 18. **d** 20 **p** 21. C Primrose Hill St Mary w Avenue Road St Paul *Lon* from 20. *Flat 2, St John's Hall, St John's Wood High Street, London NW8 7NE* M: 07947-792869 E: rev.emkolltveit@gmail.com

KOMOR, The Ven Michael. b 60. Univ of Wales BSc 83. Chich Th Coll 83. **d** 86 **p** 87. C Mountain Ash *Llan* 86–89; C Llantwit Major 89–91; TV 91–00; V Ewenny w St Brides Major 00–05; R Coity, Nolton and Brackla 05–14; R Coity, Nolton and Brackla w Coychurch from 14; AD Bridgend 04–10 and 15–18; Can Llan Cathl from 14; Adn Margam from 18; C Llansantffraid, Bettws and Aberkenfig 18–20. *The Paddock, Derllwyn Road, Tondu, Bridgend CF32 9HD* T: (01656) 725921 E: archdeacon.margam@churchinwales.org.uk

KOMOROWSKI, Diane Nicole. b 75. Birm Univ BSc 96. St Mellitus Coll 19. **d** 21. C Lupset *Leeds* from 21; C Thornes from 21. *1 St James's Court, Wakefield WF2 8DN* M: 07903-044570 E: revddiane@gmail.com

KONIG, Peter Montgomery. b 44. Univ of Wales (Lamp) MA 10. Westcott Ho Cam 80. **d** 82 **p** 83. C Oundle *Pet* 82–86; Chapl Westwood Ho Sch Pet 86–92; Chapl Pet High Sch 92–95; Chapl Worksop Coll Notts 95–99; Chapl Glenalmond Coll *St And* 99–04; rtd 04; PtO *Pet* from 04. *Crossways, Main Street, Yarwell, Peterborough PE8 6PR* T: (01780) 782873 M: 07764-586619 E: pandakonig@talktalk.net

KOPSCH, Hartmut. b 41. Sheff Univ BA 63 Univ of BC MA 66 Lon Univ PhD 70. Trin Coll Bris 78. **d** 80 **p** 81. C Cranham Park *Chelmsf* 80–85; V Springfield *Birm* 85–92; V Dover St Martin *Cant* 92–96; R Bath Walcot *B & W* 96–06; rtd 06; PtO *Glouc* 07–09; *Bris* from 09. *10 St Edyths Road, Bristol BS9 2ES* T: 0117-968 8683 E: hartmuvandjane@gmail.com

KORMI, Emmanuel Barine. b 58. **d** 16. NSM Hatcham St Cath *S'wark* from 16; Chapl Lewisham and Greenwich NHS Trust from 18. *50 Wild Goose Drive, London SE14 5LL*

KORMOS, Endre. b 86. Coll of Resurr Mirfield BA 16. **d** 16 **p** 17. C Wallsend St Pet and St Luke *Newc* 16–20. *Address temp unknown* E: frkormos@protonmail.com

KORN, Sam Christopher. b 89. Trin Hall Cam MA 14. Westcott Ho Cam 12 Bossey Ecum Inst Geneva 13. **d** 14 **p** 15. C E Barnet *St Alb* 14–17; V Aintree St Giles w St Pet *Liv* 17–19; Chapl St Mary Magd Academy Lon from 19; C Pimlico St Mary Bourne Street *Lon* from 20. *St Mary Magdalene Academy, 475 Liverpool Road, London N7 8PG* T: (020) 7697 0123 M: 07900-827371 E: sam.korn@cantab.net *or* sam.korn@smmacademy.org

KORNAHRENS, Canon Wallace Douglas. b 43. St Andr Univ PhD 08. The Citadel Charleston BA 66 Gen Th Sem (NY) STB 69. **d** 69 **p** 70. USA 69–72; C Potters Green *Cov* 72–75; Chapl Community of Celebration Wargrave Oxon 75–76; P-in-c Cumbrae (or Millport) *Arg* 76–78; R Grantown-on-Spey *Mor* 78–83; R Rothiemurchus 78–83; R Edin H Cross 83–18; Hon Can St Mary's Cathl from 14; rtd 18. *114 Broomfield Crescent, Edinburgh EH12 7NF*

KOSLA, Mrs Ann Louise. b 56. Middx Univ BA 04. NTMTC 01. **d** 04 **p** 05. NSM Thorley *St Alb* 04–07; NSM Chelmsf S Deanery 08–10; NSM Boreham *Chelmsf* 10–12; V Church Langley 12–20; Chapl St Clare Hospice from 20; NSM Vale of Roding *Chelmsf* from 21. *The Rectory, 66 High Road, Chigwell IG7 6QB* T: (01375) 480427 *or* (01279) 773700 M: 07563-548337 E: annkosla@gmail.com

KOSLA, Charles Antoni. b 58. Cam Th Federation MA 12. Ridley Hall Cam 97. **d** 99 **p** 00. C Widford *Chelmsf* 99–03; C Thorley *St Alb* 03–07; Dioc Adv for Miss and Evang *Chelmsf* 07–17; Hon C E Springfield 08–12; Hon C Church Langley 12–18; TV Grays Thurrock 18–21; TR Vale of Roding from 21. *The Rectory, 66 High Road, Chigwell IG7 6QB* T: (01375) 480427 M: 07753-634021 E: charliekosla@gmail.com

KOUBLE (née MACKIE), Fiona Mary. b 66. Anglia Ruskin Univ BA 94 MSc 95 St Jo Coll Dur BA 09 RGN 88. Cranmer

Hall Dur 07. **d** 11 **p** 12. C Hillsborough and Wadsley Bridge *Sheff* 11–13; V Ardsley from 13. *Christ Church Vicarage, Doncaster Road, Barnsley S71 5EF* M: 07817-167386 E: fionakouble@yahoo.co.uk

KOUSSEFF, Mrs Karen Patricia. b 60. Ex Univ BA 83. STETS 06. **d** 09 **p** 10. NSM Lower Dever *Win* 09–17; NSM Win St Bart and St Lawr w St Swithun 18–19; P-in-c 19–21; R from 21; AD Win from 17. *St Bartholomew's House, 1 Abbey Hill Close, Winchester SO23 7AZ* T: (01962) 850956 E: karen.kousseff@outlook.com

KOVOOR, Canon George Iype. b 57. Delhi Univ BA 77 Serampore Univ BD 80. Union Bibl Sem Yavatmal 78. **d** 80 **p** 80. Chapl Leprosy Miss Hosp Kothara India 80–81; Assoc Presbyter Shanti Nivas Ch Faridabad 82; Presbyter Santokh Majra 83; Dean St Paul's Cathl Ambala 84–88; Chapl St Steph Hosp Delhi 88–90; C Derby St Aug 90–94; Min Derby Asian Chr Min Project 90–94; Tutor Crowther Hall CMS Tr Coll Selly Oak 94–97; Prin 97–05; Hon Can Worc Cathl 01–05; Prin Trin Coll Bris 05–13; R New Haven St Jo Connecticut USA 13–16; R Darien St Paul from 16; Chapl to The Queen from 03; Can Th Niger Delta N from 10; Can Missiologist Sabah from 10. *471 Mansfield Avenue, Darien, CT 06820, USA* T: (001) (203) 655 8773

KOZAK, Robert Jozef. b 84. SS Coll Cam BTh 15 K Coll Lon MA 18. Westcott Ho Cam 12. **d** 15 **p** 16. C Leavesden *St Alb* 15–18; P-in-c Letchworth from 18. *The Rectory, 39 South View, Letchworth Garden City SG6 3JJ* T: (01462) 684822 E: father.kozak@gmail.com

KRAFT (née STEVENS), Mrs Jane. b 45. SRN 66 SCM 68. NTMTC 01. **d** 03 **p** 04. NSM Finchley St Mary *Lon* 03–07; TV Chipping Barnet *St Alb* 07–14; rtd 15; PtO *St Alb* 15–17; *Ox* from 15. *66 Yeovil Road, Owlsmoor, Sandhurst GU47 0TE* T: (01276) 36402 M: 07803-868482 E: revd.janekraft@btinternet.com

KRAMER, Beaman Kristopher (Kris). b 67. Mars Hill Coll (USA) BS 88 Duke Univ (USA) MTS 95. Wycliffe Hall Ox MTh 98. **d** 98 **p** 99. C Hersham *Guildf* 98–99; C Paddington St Jo w St Mich *Lon* 99–00; R Radford Grace USA 00–10; PtO *Ox* 10–12; Chapl St Edm Hall Ox 12–13; Fellows' Chapl Magd Coll Ox 12–13; USA from 13; R Morganton St Mary and St Steph from 20. *506 W Sumter Street, Shelby NC 28150, USA* E: frkris@gmail.com

KRAMER, Mrs Caroline Anne. b 70. Wycliffe Hall Ox BTh 98. **d** 98. C Oatlands *Guildf* 98–99; USA 00–10; C Wokingham All SS *Ox* 10–13; C Ponte Vedra Beach USA from 13. *506 W Sumter Street, Shelby NC 28150, USA* E: revcarolinekramer@googlemail.com

KRAMER, Maxwell James. b 85. Ball Coll Ox BA 07 MA 11 St Jo Coll Cam BA 10 MPhil 11 MA 15. Westcott Ho Cam 08. **d** 13 **p** 14. NSM Cambridge St Mary Less *Ely* 13–17; Min Can and Prec Cant Cathl from 17. *5 The Precincts, Canterbury CT1 2EE* M: 07796-673081 E: max_kramer@hotmail.com

KRAUSS, Andrew John. Jes Coll Ox MPhys 05 Leeds Univ BA 10 Sheff Univ MA 11 St Jo Coll Dur PhD 18. Coll of Resurr Mirfield 08. **d** 11 **p** 12. C Cottingham *York* 11–14; Asst Chapl Paris St Geo *Eur* 14–17; Chapl and Dean of Chpl CCC Cam 17–18; PtO *Ox* 19; C Cottesloe 19–20; TV from 20; PtO *Eur* from 19; *Chich* from 19. *Address withheld by request* E: andrewjkrauss@gmail.com

KRAWIEC, Christopher James Michael. b 86. St Jo Coll Dur BA 16. Cranmer Hall Dur 12. **d** 15 **p** 16. C Gt Harwood *Blackb* 15–19; R Poulton-le-Sands w Morecambe St Laur from 19. *The Rectory, Church Walk, Morecambe LA4 5PR* M: 07596-669987 E: c.krawiec@icloud.com

KREJCI, Kvetoslav Tomas. b 68. Chas Univ Prague PhD 01 PhD 17 Blackfriars Ox MPhil 16 Solicitor 07. St Steph Ho Ox 16. **d** 18 **p** 19. C Reading St Giles *Ox* from 18. *10 Jesse Terrace, Reading RG1 7RT* M: 07984-838866 E: pater_tomas@outlook.com

KRINKS, Philip Lewis. b 72. Magd Coll Ox BA 95 MA 99 INSEAD MBA 00 K Coll Lon PhD 11 MA 12. Westcott Ho Cam 12. **d** 14 **p** 15. C Battersea St Mary *S'wark* 14–16; C E Win 16–17; C Win St Faith w St Cross 16–17; P-in-c 17–21; R from 21. *St Anne's, Petersfield Road, Winchester SO23 0JD* M: 07899-813650 E: philip@krinks.com

KRONBERGS, Paul Mark. b 55. NEOC 02. **d** 05 **p** 06. NSM Middlesbrough St Columba w St Paul *York* from 05. *39 Northumberland Grove, Stockton-on-Tees TS20 1PB* T: (01642) 365160 E: fr-paul.kronbergs@hotmail.co.uk

KRONENBERG, John Simon. b 59. Greenwich Univ BSc 85 Open Univ BA 00 MRICS 87 MBEng 94. Ripon Coll Cuddesdon BTh 05. **d** 02 **p** 03. C Chandler's Ford *Win* 02–06; V Hinchley Wood *Guildf* 06–15; V Redhill St Jo *S'wark* from 15. *St John's Vicarage, Church Road, Redhill RH1 6QA* M: 07500-954963 E: vicar@stjohnsredhill.org.uk

KROUKAMP, Nigel John Charles. b 53. Cen Lancs Univ BSc 93 Bolton Inst of HE CertEd 86 RNMH 75 RGN 78. LCTP 05. **d** 08 **p** 09. NSM Colne and Villages *Blackb* 08–14; rtd 14; PtO *Blackb* from 14. *56 Kelswick Drive, Nelson BB9 0SZ* T: (01282) 698261 M: 07725-858433 E: nigelkroukamp@googlemail.com

KTORIDES, Nicholas. b 59. Sheff Univ MA 97. Ridley Hall Cam. **d** 14 **p** 15. C Gorleston St Andr *Nor* 14–16; C Lowestoft St Andr 16–18; C Oulton St Mich 18–19; PtO *Ox* 19–20; Hon C Akeman from 20. *The Rectory, Alchester Road, Chesterton, Bicester OX26 1UW* M: 07812-170911

KUHRT, The Ven Gordon Wilfred. b 41. Lon Univ BD 63 Middx Univ DProf 01. Oak Hill Th Coll 65. **d** 67 **p** 68. C Illogan *Truro* 67–70; C Wallington *S'wark* 70–73; V Shenstone *Lich* 73–79; P-in-c S Croydon Em *Cant* 79–81; V S Croydon Em *S'wark* 81–89; RD Croydon Cen *Cant* 81–84; RD Croydon Cen *S'wark* 85–86; Hon Can S'wark Cathl 87–89; Adn Lewisham 89–96; Dir Chief Sec ABM 96–98; Min Division Abps' Coun 99–06; rtd 06; Hon C Ilmington w Stretton-on-Fosse etc *Cov* 06–12; PtO *Ox* from 12. *87 Churchway, Haddenham, Aylesbury HP17 8DT* T: (01844) 698358 E: omkuhrt@tiscali.co.uk

KUHRT, Martin Gordon. b 66. Nottm Univ LLB 88. Trin Coll Bris 93. **d** 96 **p** 97. C Morden *S'wark* 96–00; Chapl Lee Abbey 00–02; TV Melksham *Sarum* 02–08; C Atworth w Shaw and Whitley 07–08; C Broughton Gifford, Gt Chalfield and Holt 07–08; P-in-c Bedgrove *Ox* 08–09; V from 09. *2 Earlswood Close, Aylesbury HP21 7PG* T: (01296) 435546 E: makuhrt555@btinternet.com *or* martin@holyspiritbedgrove.org

KUHRT, Stephen John. b 69. Man Univ BA 91 Lon Inst of Educn PGCE 93. Wycliffe Hall Ox BA 03. **d** 03 **p** 04. C New Malden and Coombe *S'wark* 03–07; P-in-c 07–17; V from 17. *The Vicarage, 6 Filbert Terrace, Cambridge Avenue, New Malden KT3 4JZ* T: (020) 8942 0915 E: stephenkuhrt@ccnm.org

KUIN LAWTON, Theresa (Tess). b 69. St Aid Coll Dur BA 91 PGCE 92 TCD MPhil 96 Bris Univ PhD 11. Ox Min Course 06. **d** 07 **p** 08. C Bampton w Clanfield *Ox* 07–10 and from 17; Chapl Magd Coll Sch Ox 09–17; Chapl, Fell and Tutor Worc Coll Ox from 17; Voc Adv Ox Univ from 17; AD Witney *Ox* from 19; V Black Bourton from 20. *Worcester College, Walton Street, Oxford OX1 2HB* T: (01865) 278300 E: chaplain@worc.ox.ac.uk

KUIPER, Wim. b 61. Twente Univ MA 86 Maastricht Univ PhD 94. Westcott Ho Cam 18. **d** 20 **p** 21. C Sunderland St Matt and St Wilfrid *Dur* from 20. *2 Whitebark, Sunderland SR3 2NX* M: 07394-555152 E: wimkuiper.br@gmail.com

KUPONIYI, Samson. b 69. Ibadan Univ Nigeria BSc 90. Ripon Coll Cuddesdon 17. **d** 20 **p** 21. C Burnham *Ox* from 20. *12 Hatchgate Gardens, Burnham, Slough SL1 8DD* M: 07771-728826 E: skuponiyi@yahoo.co.uk

KURK, Pamela Ann. b 56. Univ of Wales (Ban) BTh 06 Heythrop Coll Lon MA 10. **d** 04 **p** 05. NSM Wandsworth St Mich w St Steph *S'wark* 04–11; Chapl St Cecilia's Wandsworth C of E Sch 07–19; P-in-c Battersea St Mich *S'wark* 13–17; NSM Clapham Common St Barn 17–19; TV Caterham from 19. *The Rectory, 8 Whyteleafe Hill, Whyteleafe CR3 0AA* T: (020) 8763 8504 M: 07774-437471 E: vicar@stlukeswhyteleafe.co.uk

KURZ, Nathaniel William. b 84. Trin Coll Bris BA 15. **d** 15 **p** 16. C Esher *Guildf* 15–18; C E Molesey St Mary 18–21; V from 21. *The Vicarage, St Mary's Road, East Molesey KT8 0ST* M: 07912-037246

KUSTNER, Ms Jane Lesley. b 54. Lanchester Poly Cov BA 76 FCA 79. St Steph Ho Ox 03. **d** 05 **p** 06. C Waterloo St Jo w St Andr *S'wark* 05–08; P-in-c Lewisham St Swithun 08–17; AD E Lewisham 13–17; P-in-c Mariannridge S Africa 17–19; Chapl Bromley Coll from 19. *Chaplain's House, Bromley College, London Road, Bromley BR1 1PE* T: (020) 8460 4712 E: chaplain@bandscolleges.org

KUTAR, Diane Leslie. b 68. Bradf Univ BSc 89 Brighton Univ MA 09. St Mellitus Coll 18. **d** 21. C Sawtry, Glatton and Holme w Conington *Ely* from 21. *2 Bell Field, Brampton, Huntingdon PE28 4PT* M: 07887-992257 E: diane@dkutar.com

KUTIWULU, Calixte. b 63. Qu Coll Birm 12. **d** 92 **p** 93. In RC Ch Democratic Republic of Congo 92–03; C Pet St Mary Boongate 14–16; C Paston 16–18. *1A Mead Close, Peterborough PE4 6BS* M: 07417-433229 E: ckutiwulu@yahoo.co.uk

KYRIACOU, Brian George. b 42. Lon Univ LLB 64. Oak Hill Th Coll 79. **d** 81 **p** 82. C Becontree St Mary *Chelmsf* 81–83; C Becontree St Cedd 83–85; C Becontree W 85; TV 85–87; V Shiregreen St Jas and St Chris *Sheff* 87–92; TV Schorne *Ox* 92–98; V Edmonton All SS w St Mich *Lon* 98–07; rtd 07; PtO *Chelmsf* from 07. *3 Cranford Close, Frinton-on-Sea CO13 9LF* T: (01255) 763782 M: 07970-719094 E: briankyriacou71@gmail.com

KYRIAKIDES-YELDHAM, Preb Anthony Paul Richard. b 48. Birkbeck Coll Lon BSc 82 Warwick Univ MSc 90 Univ of Wales (Lamp) MMin 10 Ex Univ PhD 17 CQSW 83 CPsychol 91. K Coll Lon BD 73 AKC 73. **d** 74 **p** 75. C Dalston H Trin w St Phil *Lon* 74–78; NSM Lon Docks St Pet w Wapping St Jo 79–81; NSM Hackney Wick St Mary of Eton w St Aug 81–85; NSM Wandsworth Common St Mary *S'wark* 85–87; Chapl Wandsworth HA Mental Health Unit 87–93; Chapl Springfield Univ Hosp Lon 87–93; PtO *Ex* 94–98; LtO 98–08; Sen Chapl Plymouth Hosps NHS Trust 98–08; P-in-c Kingsbridge and Dodbrooke *Ex* 08–11; Preb Ex Cathl 07–11; Chapl Imp Coll Healthcare NHS Trust 11–12; rtd 13;
PV Westmr Abbey from 13; Chapl 13–15; Chapl Marie Curie Hospice 15–20; Bp's Adv for Healthcare Chapl *Lon* 18–21; Chapl Barts Health NHS Trust from 21; PtO *Ex* from 11. *Flat 14, 19 Page Street, London SW1P 4JX* M: 07929-775228 E: aprkyriakides@gmail.com

KYTE, Eric Anthony. b 62. Leeds Univ BSc 84 PGCE 85. Trin Coll Bris BA 98. **d** 98 **p** 99. C Pudsey St Lawr and St Paul *Bradf* 98–01; P-in-c Gisburn and Hellifield 01–11; V Roslyn NZ from 11; V Gen Dunedin 13–15. *373 Highgate, Roslyn, Dunedin, New Zealand* E: eric@calledsouth.org.nz

KYUMU MOTUKO, Norbert. *See* CHUMU MUTUKU, Norbert

L

LA STACEY, Mrs Rosalind Ruth. b 54. New Hall Cam MA 81 Bulmershe Coll of HE PGCE 94. Ripon Coll Cuddesdon 09. **d** 11 **p** 12. C Easthampstead *Ox* 11–14; V Eton w Eton Wick, Boveney and Dorney from 14. *The Vicarage, 69A Eton Wick Road, Eton Wick, Windsor SL4 6NE* T: (01753) 852268 E: revlastacey@gmail.com

LA TOUCHE, Francis William Reginald. b 51. Linc Th Coll 73. **d** 76 **p** 77. C Yate *Bris* 76–77; C Yate New Town 77–79; Chapl Vlissingen (Flushing) Miss to Seamen *Eur* 79–83; Port Chapl Hull Miss to Seamen 83–91; V Burstwick w Thorngumbald *York* 91–02; PtO *Ches* 11–14; *York* from 16. *45 Lee Street, Hull HU8 8NN* E: frank.latouche@gmail.com

LABRAN, Stuart. b 79. Leeds Univ BA 00 PGCE 02 Clare Coll Cam MPhil 09. Westcott Ho Cam 07. **d** 09 **p** 10. C Stratford-upon-Avon, Luddington etc *Cov* 09–12; Asst Chapl Emanuel Sch Wandsworth from 17; NSM Kennington St Jo w St Jas *S'wark* from 19. *Flat 3, 24 Peckham Rye, London SE15 4JR* E: stuartlabran@hotmail.com

LACEY, Canon Allan John. b 48. Sheff Univ MA 02. Wycliffe Hall Ox. **d** 82 **p** 83. C Greasbrough *Sheff* 82–85; R Treeton 85–92; V Thorpe Hesley 92–00; R Rossington 00–07; CMS Uganda 07–13; Can Em Cathl Arua from 12; rtd 13; PtO *Leic* 14–16; *Derby* from 17; *Sheff* 17–21. *45 High Street, Staveley, Chesterfield S43 3UU* T: (01246) 470422 M: 07887-473540 E: allanandanne@btinternet.com

LACEY, Carol Ann. b 62. Qu Coll Birm 07. **d** 09 **p** 10. NSM Leic St Anne, St Paul w St Aug 09–14; V Brampton Bierlow *Sheff* 14–18; Chapl LOROS Hospice from 19. *22A Chapel Street, Blaby, Leicester LE8 4GB* T: 0116-231 3771 M: 07971-519705 E: carolannlacey@gmail.com

LACEY, Colin Brian. **d** 10 **p** 11. C Ballymena w Ballyclug *Conn* 10–13; I Belfast St Pet and St Jas from 13. *St Peter's Rectory, 17 Waterloo Park West, Belfast BT15 5HX* T: (028) 9077 7053 M: 07563-531082 E: brianlacey@hotmail.co.uk

LACEY, Eric. b 33. Cranmer Hall Dur 69. **d** 71 **p** 72. C Blackpool St Jo *Blackb* 71–75; V Whittle-le-Woods 75–88; R Heysham 88–98; rtd 98; PtO *Blackb* from 98. *143 Bredon Avenue, Chorley PR7 6NS* T: (01257) 273040

LACEY, Nigel Jeremy. b 59. St Jo Coll Nottm BTh 94. **d** 94 **p** 95. C Mildenhall *St E* 94–97; C Selly Park St Steph and St Wulstan *Birm* 97–01; Chapl St Mary's Hospice 97–01; P-in-c W Wycombe w Bledlow Ridge, Bradenham and Radnage *Ox* 01–09; R 09–16; P-in-c Burton and Sopley *Win* 16–21; R Hopton, Corton and Gunton *Nor* from 21. *The Rectory, 36 Gunton Church Lane, Lowestoft NR32 4LF* M: 07761-852619 E: nigellacey405@btinternet.com

LACK, Miss Catherine Mary. b 59. Clare Coll Cam BA 81 Ox Univ MTh 00 ARCM 78. Qu Coll Birm 90. **d** 92 **p** 94. C Leiston *St E* 92–95; TV Ipswich St Mary at Stoke w St Pet and St Fran 95–98; Chapl Keele Univ *Lich* 98–07; Cultural and Relig Affairs Manager Yarl's Wood Immigration Removal Cen 07–08; Warden Ferrar Ho Lt Gidding 08–09; Chapl Newc Univ 09–18; Master Newc St Thos Prop Chpl 09–18; PtO *Worc* from 19; Glouc from 19. *Pear Tree Cottage, Church Street, Bredon, Tewkesbury GL20 7LA* T: (01684) 772838 M: 07582-033125 E: catherine.lack50@gmail.com

LACK, Martin Paul. b 57. St Jo Coll Ox MA 79 MSc 80. Linc Th Coll 83. **d** 86 **p** 87. C E Bowbrook and W Bowbrook *Worc* 86–89; C Bowbrook S and Bowbrook N 89–90; R Teme Valley S 90–01; rtd 01. *Colbridge Cottage, Bottom Lane, Whitbourne, Worcester WR6 5RT* T: (01886) 821978

LACKENBY, George Joseph. b 48. **d** 13 **p** 14. NSM Harlow Green and Lamesley *Dur* from 13. *68*
Ashford, Gateshead NE9 6YG T: 0191-421 9173 E: george.lackenby@hotmail.co.uk

LACKEY, Michael Geoffrey Herbert. b 42. Oak Hill Th Coll 73. **d** 75 **p** 76. C Hatcham St Jas *S'wark* 75–81; V New Barnet St Jas *St Alb* 81–91; V Hollington St Jo *Chich* 91–02; Dir Crowhurst Chr Healing Cen 02–05; rtd 05; Hon C Gt Amwell w St Margaret's and Stanstead Abbots *St Alb* 05–09; PtO from 10. *5 Vicarage Close, St Albans AL1 2PU* E: glackey@virginmedia.com

LACON, Susanna Margaret. **d** 18 **p** 19. OLM Thaxted, The Sampfords, Radwinter and Hempstead *Chelmsf* from 18. *c/o Crockford, Church House, 27 Great Smith Street, London SW1P 3AZ* E: susannah.lacon@ttsrh.org

LACY, Melanie June. b 75. TCD BA 98 All Hallows Coll Dublin MA 00. CITC 98. **d** 00. C Bangor St Comgall *D & D* 00–02; N Ireland Regional Co-ord Crosslinks 02–06; C Knutsford St Jo and Toft *Ches* 06–09; Dir Youth and Children's Min Oak Hill Coll from 10; NSM Knutsford St Jo and Toft *Ches* from 19. *125 Severn Way, Holmes Chapel, Crewe CW4 8FS* T: (020) 8449 0467 F: 8441 5996 E: mell@oakhill.ac.uk

LADD, Mrs Anne de Chair. b 56. Nottm Univ BA 78 Birm Univ CQSW 80. St Jo Coll Nottm 83. **dss** 86 **d** 87 **p** 94. Bucknall and Bagnall *Lich* 86–91; Par Dn 87–91; NSM Bricket Wood *St Alb* 91–01; Chapl Garden Ho Hospice Letchworth 98–06; Befriending Co-ord Mencap 07–08; Soc worker 09–11; Chapl Nottm Univ Hosp NHS Trust 11–17; Hon C Chilwell *S'well* 15–17; P-in-c Allens Cross *Birm* from 17. *19 Bodenham Road, Birmingham B31 5DP* M: 07800-980953 E: laddanne@gmail.com *or* anne.stbs@gmail.com

LADD, Nicholas Mark. b 57. Ex Univ BA 78 Selw Coll Cam BA 81 MA 97 Anglia Ruskin Univ MA 03. Ridley Hall Cam 79. **d** 82 **p** 83. C Aston SS Pet and Paul *Birm* 82–86; TV Bucknall and Bagnall *Lich* 86–91; V Bricket Wood *St Alb* 91–01; V Cambridge St Barn *Ely* 01–09; Dean and Lect St Jo Coll Nottm 09–17; Hon C Chilwell *S'well* 15–17; C Allens Cross *Birm* from 17; Bp's Adv for Clergy Formation and IME from 17. *30 Lickey Square, Rednal, Birmingham B45 8HB* T: 0121-445 4400 M: 07540-425381 E: nick.ladd57@gmail.com

LADDS, Alexander John. b 72. Univ of Wales (Abth) BD 94. LCTP 13. **d** 16 **p** 17. NSM Broughton, Marton and Thornton Leeds from 16; Chapl Giggleswick Sch from 16. *Giggleswick School, Giggleswick, Settle BD24 0DE* T: (01729) 893190 E: ajladds@giggleswick.org.uk

✠**LADDS, The Rt Revd Robert Sidney.** b 41. Lon Univ BEd 71 LRSC 72. Cant Sch of Min 79. **d** 80 **p** 81 **c** 99. C Hythe *Cant* 80–83; R Bretherton *Blackb* 83–91; Chapl Bp Rawstorne Sch Preston 83–87; Bp's Chapl for Min and Adv Coun for Min *Blackb* 86–91; P-in-c Preston St Jo 91–96; R Preston St Jo and St Geo 96–97; Hon Can Blackb Cathl 93–97; Adn Lancaster 97–99; Suff Bp Whitby *York* 99–08; rtd 09; Hon Asst Bp Lon from 09; Hon C Hendon St Mary and Ch Ch 09–15; Hon C Lon Docks St Pet w Wapping St Jo from 15; PtO *Nor* from 21. *St Peter's Clergy House, Wapping Lane, London E1W 2RW* T: (020) 7488 3864 E: episcopus70@gmail.com

LADIPO, Canon Adeyemi Olalekan. b 37. Trin Coll Bris 63. **d** 66 **p** 76. C Bilston St Leon *Lich* 66–68; Regional V Canonbury St Steph *Lon* 85–87; Sec for Internat Miss BCMS 87–90; Hon C Bromley SS Pet and Paul *Roch* 89–90; V Herne Hill *S'wark* 90–99; Hon Can Jos from 95; V S Malling *Chich* 99–02; rtd 02; PtO *Chich* from 03; *S'wark* from 07. *63 Elm Grove, London SE15 5DB* T: (020) 7639 8150 E: adeyemiladipo@hotmail.com

LAFFERTY, Miss Kim Elvin. b 62. RGN 85 RM 89. Wycliffe Hall Ox 10. **d** 12 **p** 13. C Horwich and Rivington *Man* 12–15; TV Farnworth, Kearsley and Stoneclough 15–21; R Alyth *St And* from 21; R Blairgowrie from 21; R Coupar Angus from 21. *The Rectory, 10 Rosemount Park, Blairgowrie PH10 6TZ* T: (01250) 875426 *or* (01204) 294831 M: 07703-417640 E: kelafferty@hotmail.co.uk

LAFFORD, Sylvia June. b 46. Middx Univ BA 04. NTMTC 01. **d** 04 **p** 05. NSM Hayes St Edm *Lon* 04–12; Asst Chapl Hillingdon Hosps NHS Foundn Trust 10–13; PtO *Lon* from 13; *Pet* from 13. *18 Blenheim Croft, Brackley NN13 7ET* T: (01280) 700122 E: sylvia.lafford@btinternet.com

LAIDLAW, Juliet. *See* MONTAGUE, Juliet

LAIN-PRIESTLEY, The Ven Rosemary Jane. b 67. Kent Univ BA 89 K Coll Lon MA 02. Carl Dioc Tr Course 92. **d** 96 **p** 97. C Scotforth *Blackb* 96–98; C St Martin-in-the-Fields *Lon* 98–06; Dean of Women's Min Two Cities Area 06–15; Adn Charing Cross 16–19; Bp's Adv on Policy and Strategy from 19. *The Old Deanery, Dean's Court, London EC4V 5AA* T: (020) 3837 5205 E: rosemary.lainpriestley@london.anglican.org

LAIRD, Alisdair Mark. b 60. Auckland Univ BA 84. Trin Coll Bris BA 92. **d** 92 **p** 93. C Linthorpe *York* 92–98; V Hull St Cuth 98–06; P-in-c Alne 06–07; P-in-c Brafferton w Pilmoor, Myton-on-Swale etc 06–07; LtO 07–08; PtO 08–20; Chapl Hull and E Yorks Hosps NHS Trust 09–20; V Easington w Skeffling, Keyingham, Ottringham etc *York* from 20; RD S Holderness from 21. *The Vicarage, Northside, Patrington, Hull HU12 0PA* T: (01964) 630327 E: mail@trackways.net

LAIRD, Canon John Charles. b 32. Sheff Univ BA 53 MA 54 St Cath Coll Ox BA 58 MA 62 Lon Univ DipEd 70. Ripon Hall Ox 56. **d** 58 **p** 59. C Cheshunt *St Alb* 58–62; Chapl Bps' Coll Cheshunt 62–64; Vice-Prin 64–67; Prin 67–69; V Keysoe w Bolnhurst and Lt Staughton *St Alb* 69–01; Hon Can St Alb 87–02; LtO 01–15. *The College of St Barnabas, Blackberry Lane, Lingfield RH7 6NJ* T: (01342) 872838

LAIRD, Stephen Charles Edward. b 66. Oriel Coll Ox BA 88 MA 92 MSt 93 K Coll Lon MTh 91 Kent Univ PhD 06 FSA 14 FHEA 12. Wycliffe Hall Ox MPhil 96. **d** 94 **p** 95. C Ilfracombe, Lee, Woolacombe, Bittadon etc *Ex* 94–98; Chapl Kent Univ *Cant* 98–03; Dean of Chapl from 03; Hon Lect from 98; Chapl Kent Inst of Art and Design 98–02; Hon C Hackington *Cant* from 03; P-in-c Blean 09–21; V from 21. *24 Tyler Hill Road, Blean, Canterbury CT2 9HT* T: (01227) 763373 M: 07970-438840 E: s.c.e.laird@kent.ac.uk

LAJEUNESSE, Michel. *See* ERLEWYN-LAJEUNESSE, Michel David Siva

LAKE, David Michael. b 57. St Mary's Sem Oscott 76. St Jo Coll Nottm BA 01. **d** 01 **p** 02. C Lilleshall, Muxton and Sheriffhales *Lich* 01–05; P-in-c Crick and Yelvertoft w Clay Coton and Lilbourne *Pet* 05–09; R 09–20; rtd 20. *Address temp unknown* E: d.m.lake@btinternet.com

LAKE, Eileen Veronica. *See* CREMIN, Eileen Veronica

LAKE, Jeffrey Ronald. b 70. Univ of N Colorado MA 93 LSHTM MSc 06 Cov Univ PhD 98. SEITE 12. **d** 15 **p** 16. NSM St Bride Fleet Street w Bridewell etc *Lon* from 15. *106 Florin Court, 6-9 Charterhouse Square, London EC1M 6EY* T: (020) 7251 8173 E: jeffrey_r_lake@yahoo.com.sg *or* jeffrey.lake@btinternet.com

LAKE, Kevin William. b 57. St Mich Coll Llan 97. **d** 99 **p** 00. C Penarth w Lavernock *Llan* 99–02; Chapl Marie Curie Cen Holme Tower 02–04; P-in-c Cwm Ogwr *Llan* 04–06; P-in-c Llandyfodwg and Cwm Ogwr 06–08; V Aberdare St Fagan 08–12; V Caerleon and Llanfrechfa *Mon* 12–15; P-in-c Barry All SS *Llan* 15–16; TV Barry 16–20; rtd 20. *18B Park Road, Barry CF62 6NW* E: kevin.lake1957@gmail.com

LAKE, The Very Revd Stephen David. b 63. Southn Univ BTh. Chich Th Coll 85. **d** 88 **p** 89. C Sherborne w Castleton and Lillington *Sarum* 88–92; P-in-c Branksome St Aldhelm 92–96; V 96–01; RD Poole 00–01; Can Res and Sub-Dean St Alb 01–11; Dean Glouc from 11. *The Deanery, 1 Miller's Green, Gloucester GL1 2BP* T: (01452) 524167 E: dean@gloucestercathedral.org.uk

LAKE, Vivienne Elizabeth. b 38. Westcott Ho Cam 84. **dss** 86 **d** 87 **p** 94. Chesterton Gd Shep *Ely* 86–90; C 87–90; Ecum Min K Hedges Ch Cen 87–90; NSM Bourn Deanery *Ely* 90–01; NSM Papworth Everard 94–96; PtO from 01. *15 Storey's House, Mount Pleasant, Cambridge CB3 0BZ* T: (01223) 369523 E: vel.camb@gmail.com

LAKEY, Michael John. b 70. Ches Coll of HE BA 98 MTh 01 St Jo Coll Dur PhD 08. St Steph Ho Ox 13. **d** 14 **p** 15. Lect Ripon Coll Cuddesdon 08–19; NSM Dorchester *Ox* 14–19; V Chalgrove w Berrick Salome from 19. *58 Brinkinfield Road, Chalgrove, Oxford OX44 7QX* T: (01865) 890392 M: 07534-197280 E: revmichaellakey@gmail.com

LALL, Canon Julia Carole. b 56. Ch Ch Coll Cant CertEd 78 BEd 79. ERMC 07. **d** 10 **p** 11. C Bacton w Wyverstone, Cotton and Old Newton etc *St E* 10–13; P-in-c S Hartismere 13–17; R from 17; Hon Can St E Cathl from 17; Spiritual Dir Cursillo from 19. *The Rectory, Stanwell Green, Thorndon, Eye IP23 7JL* T: (01379) 678064 M: 07837-785607 E: julia.lall@hotmail.co.uk

LAMB, Alison. *See* EARL, Alison

LAMB, Alyson Margaret. b 55. LMH Ox BA 77 MA 80. Ridley Hall Cam 03. **d** 05 **p** 06. C York St Mich-le-Belfrey 05–09; V Eastbourne St Jo *Chich* 09–13; Can and Preb Chich Cathl 12–13; Chapl Paris St Mich *Eur* 13–17; P-in-c Mitford and Hebron *Newc* 17–21; rtd 21. *Address withheld by request*

LAMB, Bruce. b 47. Keble Coll Ox BA 69 MA 73. Coll of Resurr Mirfield 70. **d** 73 **p** 74. C Romford St Edw *Chelmsf* 73–76; C Canning Town St Cedd 76–79; V New Brompton St Luke *Roch* 79–83; Chapl RN 83–87; C Rugeley *Lich* 87–88; V Trent Vale 88–92; Bereavement Cllr Cruse 94–99; Hon C Chorlton-cum-Hardy St Clem *Man* 98–99; Asst Chapl N Man Health Care NHS Trust 99–02; P-in-c Barton w Peel Green *Man* 02–14; rtd 14; PtO *Ches* from 14. *11 Kennet Drive, Congleton CW12 3BR* T: (01260) 273707

LAMB, Canon Christopher Avon. b 39. Qu Coll Ox BA 61 MA 65 Birm Univ MA 78 PhD 87. Wycliffe Hall Ox BA 63. **d** 63 **p** 64. C Enfield St Andr *Lon* 63–69; Pakistan 69–75; Tutor Crowther Hall CMS Tr Coll Selly Oak 75–78; Co-ord BCMS/CMS Other Faiths Th Project 78–87; Dioc Community Relns Officer *Cov* 87–92; Can Th *Cov* Cathl from 92; Sec Inter Faith Relns Bd of Miss 92–99; R Warmington w Shotteswell and Radway w Ratley *Cov* 99–06; rtd 06; PtO *Cov* from 06. *8 Brookside Avenue, Wellesbourne, Warwick CV35 9RZ* T: (01789) 842060 E: christopherlamb00@gmail.com

LAMB, David Andrew. b 60. Liv Inst of HE BA 94 Man Univ MA 01 PhD 12. NOC 90. **d** 94 **p** 95. C Formby H Trin *Liv* 94–97; C St Helens St Matt Thatto Heath 97–98; C Halewood 98–01; Lect Liv Hope 99–00; V Birkenhead St Jas w St Bede *Ches* 01–08; NSM Wallasey St Nic w All SS 08–12; V Ashton Hayes 12–18; rtd 18. *Uwch-y-Llanw, Aber Place, Llandudno LL30 3AR* E: david.a.lamb@btinternet.com

LAMB, Mrs Jean Evelyn. b 57. Reading Univ BA 79 Nottm Univ MA 88. St Steph Ho Ox 81. **dss** 84 **d** 88 **p** 01. Leic H Spirit 84–87; Asst Chapl Leic Poly 84–87; Par Dn Beeston S'well 88–91; Hon C and Artist in Res Nottingham St Mary and St Cath 92–95; Hon Par Dn Sneinton St Steph w St Alb 97–01; NSM Rolleston w Fiskerton, Morton and Upton 01–02; PtO 02–04; C Bilborough St Jo 04–11; C Bilborough w Strelley 04–11; C Colwick 11–12; C Gedling from 12. *St Alban's House, 4 Dale Street, Nottingham NG2 4JX* T: 0115-958 5892 M: 07851-792552

LAMB, Mary. b 52. **d** 10 **p** 11. OLM Framlingham w Saxtead *St E* 10–13; NSM 13–18; PtO *St E* from 18. *2 The Coach House, The Square, Dennington, Woodbridge IP13 8AB* T: (01728) 638897 E: marylamb1952@gmail.com

LAMB, Nicholas Henry. b 52. St Jo Coll Dur BA 74. St Jo Coll Nottm 76. **d** 79 **p** 80. C Luton Lewsey St Hugh *St Alb* 79–84; Bethany Fellowship 84–86; In Bapt Min 86–94; PtO *Chich* 97–99; C E Grinstead St Swithun 99–04; V Forest Row 04–13; Asst Chapl Highgate Sch Lon 13–16; rtd 16. *27 Tower House Close, Cuckfield, Haywards Heath RH17 5EQ* E: revnhlamb@hotmail.com

LAMB, Philip Richard James. b 42. Sarum & Wells Th Coll. **d** 83 **p** 84. C Wotton-under-Edge w Ozleworth and N Nibley *Glouc* 83–86; TV Worc SE 86–91; R Billingsley w Sidbury, Middleton Scriven etc *Heref* 91–96; R St Dominic, Landulph and St Mellion w Pillaton *Truro* 96–11; rtd 11; PtO *Truro* from 15. *3 Trelinnoe Gardens, South Petherwin, Launceston PL15 7TH* T: (01566) 776805 E: p.lamb1571@btinternet.com

LAMB, Phillip. b 68. NEOC 00. **d** 03 **p** 04. C Bridlington Priory *York* 03–06; V Hornsea w Atwick 06–16; V Hornsea, Atwick and Skipsea 16–17; P-in-c Hull St Mary Sculcoates 17–18; V from 18; P-in-c Sculcoates 17–18; V from 18. *St Paul's Vicarage, 10 Bridlington Avenue, Hull HU2 0DU* M: 07803-239611 E: imagine.peace9@yahoo.com

LAMB, Scott Innes. b 64. Edin Univ BSc 86 Fitzw Coll Cam BA 92 Heythrop Coll Lon MA 15. Ridley Hall Cam 90. **d** 93 **p** 94. C E Ham w Upton Park and Forest Gate *Chelmsf* 93–97; V W Holloway St Luke *Lon* 97–00; P-in-c Hammersmith H Innocents 00–03; Chapl RN 03–09; V Bexley St Jo *Roch* 09–12; TR Bexley 12–18; R Guernsey Ste Marie du Castel *Win* from 18; V Guernsey St Matt from 18. *The Rectory, La Rue de la Lande, Castel, Guernsey GY5 7EJ* T: (01481) 256793 E: lambscott@sky.com

LAMB, William Robert Stuart. b 70. Ball Coll Ox BA 91 MA 95 Peterho Cam MPhil 94 Sheff Univ PhD 10 FHEA 07. Westcott Ho Cam 92. **d** 95 **p** 96. C Halifax *Wakef* 95–98; TV Penistone and Thurlstone 98–01; Chapl Sheff Univ 01–10; Can Res

Sheff Cathl 05–10; Vice-Prin Westcott Ho Cam 10–17; V Ox St Mary V w St Cross and St Pet from 17. *9A Norham Gardens, Oxford OX2 6PS* T: (01865) 279114 M: 07761-325449 E: william.lamb@oriel.ox.ac.uk

LAMBERT, David Francis. b 40. Oak Hill Th Coll 72. **d** 74 **p** 75. C Paignton St Paul Preston *Ex* 74–77; C Woking Ch Ch *Guildf* 77–84; P-in-c Willesden Green St Gabr *Lon* 84–91; P-in-c Cricklewood St Mich 85–91; V Cricklewood St Gabr and St Mich 92–93; R Chenies and Lt Chalfont, Latimer and Flaunden *Ox* 93–01; Chapl Izmir (Smyrna) w Bornova *Eur* 01–03; TV Brixham w Churston Ferrers and Kingswear *Ex* 03–05; rtd 05; PtO *Ex* from 12. *33 Singer Court, Manor Crescent, Paignton TQ3 2BP*

LAMBERT, David Hardy. b 44. AKC 66. **d** 67 **p** 68. C Marske in Cleveland *York* 67–72; V 85–09; V N Ormesby 73–85; RD Guisborough 86–91; rtd 09; PtO *York* from 10. *13 Fell Briggs Drive, Marske-by-the-Sea, Redcar TS11 6BU* T: (01642) 490235

LAMBERT, David Joseph. b 66. Coll of Resurr Mirfield 99. **d** 01 **p** 02. C Camberwell St Geo *S'wark* 01–04; C Walworth St Jo 04–06; V Stoke Newington St Faith, St Matthias and All SS *Lon* from 06. *St Matthias Vicarage, Wordsworth Road, London N16 8DD* T: (020) 7254 5063 E: frdavidlambert@aol.com

LAMBERT, John Connolly. b 61. Univ of Wales (Ban) BTh 04. EAMTC 01. **d** 04 **p** 05. C Paris St Mich *Eur* 04–08; C Preston-on-Tees and Longnewton *Dur* 08–10; P-in-c 10–20. *25 Danesmoor Crescent, Darlington DL3 8NJ*

LAMBERT, Malcolm Eric. b 58. Leic Univ BSc 80 Fitzw Coll Cam BA 89 Nottm Univ MPhil 02 RMN 84. Ridley Hall Cam 87. **d** 90 **p** 91. C Humberstone *Leic* 90–94; R S Croxton Gp 94–99; R Birstall and Wanlip 99–05; TR Leic Resurr 05–07; RD Christianity N 05–07; Warden of Readers 97–05; Dir Angl Th Inst Belize 08–09; TR Chigwell and Chigwell Row *Chelmsf* 09–15; P-in-c Annesley w Newstead *S'well* 15; V Annesley w Newstead and Kirkby Woodhouse 15–18; P-in-c Crookes St Tim *Sheff* 18–21; rtd 21. *5 Calver Crescent, Sapcote, Leicester LE9 4JD* E: malcolm.lambert@gmail.com

LAMBERT, Miss Olivia Jane. b 48. Matlock Coll of Educn BEd 70. Trin Coll Bris 84. **dss** 86 **d** 87 **p** 94. York St Luke 86–90; Par Dn 87–90; Chapl York Distr Hosp 86–90; Par Dn Huntington *York* 90–94; C 94–95; TV S 95–00; TV Marfleet 00–07; C Harrogate St Mark *Ripon* 07–08; rtd 08; PtO *Leeds* from 11. *7 Almsford Place, Harrogate HG2 8EH* T: (01423) 202243

LAMBERT, Canon Philip Charles. b 54. St Jo Coll Dur BA 75 Fitzw Coll Cam BA 77 MA 81. Ridley Hall Cam 75. **d** 78 **p** 79. C Upper Tooting H Trin *S'wark* 78–81; C Whorlton *Newc* 81–84; P-in-c Alston cum Garrigill w Nenthead and Kirkhaugh 84–87; TV Alston Team 87–89; R Curry Rivel w Fivehead and Swell *B & W* 89–01; RD Crewkerne and Ilminster 98–01; TR Dorchester *Sarum* 01–06; RD 02–06; Can Res Truro Cathl 06–14; Asst Chapl Gtr Athens *Eur* 14–17. *1 Jacksons Close, Kerridge, Macclesfield SK10 5GF* M: 07475-370839 E: pclambert54@gmail.com

LAMBERT (née JOHNSON), Mrs Ruth Alice Edna. Leic Univ BA 80 PGCE 93 Nottm Univ MA 01 Birm Univ MPhil 08 RGN 85. EMMTC 98. **d** 01 **p** 02. C Mountsorrel Ch Ch and St Pet *Leic* 01–04; Chapl Univ Hosps Leic NHS Trust 04–07; P-in-c Belmopan St Ann Belize 08–09; Chapl Barking, Havering and Redbridge Hosps NHS Trust 09–12; Sen Chapl Guy's and St Thos' NHS Foundn Trust 12–15; Lead Chapl Sherwood Forest Hosps NHS Foundn Trust 15–18; Hd of Chapl Sheff Teaching Hosps NHS Foundn Trust 18–21; rtd 21. *5 Calver Crescent, Sapcote, Leicester LE9 4JD* E: ruth.lambert@gmail.com

LAMBERT, Mrs Ruth Eleanor. b 52. ERMC. **d** 14 **p** 15. OLM Mile Cross *Nor* from 14. *22 Blomefield Road, Norwich NR3 2RA* T: (01603) 410565 E: ruthless52@hotmail.com

LAMBERT, William John. Man Univ BMus 81. St Mich Coll Llan. **d** 13 **p** 14. C Upper Ebbw Valleys *Mon* 13–16; P-in-c Kenmore w Brookfield Australia 16–18; P-in-c St Ishmael's w Llan-saint and Ferryside *St D* 18–19; P-in-c Bro Cydweli from 19. *The Vicarage, Water Street, Ferryside SA17 5RT* T: (01267) 267559 E: williamlambert314@hotmail.com

LAMBETH, Archdeacon of. *See* GATES, The Ven Simon Philip

LAMBOURN, David Malcolm. b 37. Lanc Univ BEd 76 Man Univ MEd 78 Warwick Univ PhD 01. Linc Th Coll 63. **d** 65 **p** 66. C Camberwell St Geo *S'wark* 65–67; C Mottingham St Andr w St Alban 67–70; rtd 03. *47 Earsham Street, Bungay NR35 1AF* E: david_lambourn@mac.com

LAMDIN, Canon Keith Hamilton. b 47. Bris Univ BA 69. Ripon Coll Cuddesdon 86. **d** 86 **p** 87. Adult Educn Officer *Ox* 83–98; Team Ldr Par Resources Dept 88–94; Dioc Dir Tr 94–08; Prin Sarum Coll 08–15; NSM Cowley St Jo *Ox* 98–06; P-in-c Upper Kennet *Sarum* 08–10; Hon Can Ch Ch *Ox* 97–08; Hon Can Kimberley S Africa from 08; Can and Preb Sarum Cathl 09–15; PtO from 15. *2 Forge Close,*

West Overton, Marlborough SN8 4PG T: (01672) 861550 E: khlamdin@gmail.com

LAMEY, Canon Richard John. b 77. Keble Coll Ox BA 98 MA 02 Em Coll Cam BA 01 MA 05. Westcott Ho Cam 99. **d** 02 **p** 03. C Stockport SW *Ches* 02–05; P-in-c Newton in Mottram 05–11; P-in-c Newton in Mottram w Flowery Field 11–12; V Newton w Flowery Field 12; RD Mottram 08–12; R Wokingham St Paul *Ox* from 12; AD Sonning from 18; Hon Can Ch Ch from 21. *St Paul's Rectory, Holt Lane, Wokingham RG41 1ED* T: 0118-327 9116 E: rector@spauls.co.uk

LAMMAS, Miss Diane Beverley. b 47. Trin Coll Bris 76. **dss** 79 **d** 87 **p** 94. Lenton Abbey *S'well* 79–84; Wollaton Park 79–84; E Regional Co-ord and Sec for Voc and Min CPAS 84–89; Hon C Cambridge St Paul *Ely* 87–90; Voc and Min Adv CPAS 89–92; Sen Voc and Min Adv CPAS 92–95; R Hethersett w Canteloff w Lt and Gt Melton *Nor* 95–12; RD Humbleyard 98–03; rtd 12; PtO *Nor* from 13. *3 Turnberry Close, Lowestoft NR33 9JN* T: (01502) 218599 E: di.lammas@yahoo.co.uk

LAMMENS, Erwin Bernard Eddy. b 62. Catholic Univ Leuven BA 86 Gregorian Univ Rome MDiv 90. Grootseminarie Gent 84. **d** 87 **p** 88. In RC Ch 87–96; Asst Chapl Antwerp St Boniface *Eur* 98–05; TV Harwich Peninsula *Chelmsf* 05–10; R Wivenhoe from 10. *The Rectory, 44 Belle Vue Road, Wivenhoe, Colchester CO7 9LD* T: (01206) 822511 E: erwinlammens@btinternet.com

LAMMING, Sarah Rebecca. b 77. Middx Univ BA 02. Westcott Ho Cam 03 Yale Div Sch 05. **d** 06 **p** 07. C Handsworth St Jas *Birm* 06–09; USA from 09. *1000 Spa Road, Apt #202, Annapolis MD 21403, USA* E: fr.sarah@gmail.com

LAMOND, Stephen Paul. b 64. Trin Coll Bris BA 99. **d** 99 **p** 00. C Weston-super-Mare Ch Ch *B & W* 99–02; C Congresbury w Puxton and Hewish St Ann 02–03; Chapl RAF from 03. *Chaplaincy Services (RAF), HQ Air Command, RAF High Wycombe HP14 4UE* T: (01494) 496800

LAMONT, Charles John David. b 91. **d** 14 **p** 15. C Wisley w Pyrford *Guildf* 14–18; P-in-c S Wimbledon St Andr *S'wark* from 18. *St Andrew's Vicarage, 105 Hartfield Road, London SW19 3TJ* M: 07786-265939 E: charlie@standrewswimbledon.com

LAMONT, Canon Euphemia Margaret (Fay). b 53. N Coll of Educn BA 98. TISEC 00. **d** 00 **p** 00. C Monifieth and Carnoustie *Bre* 00–07; P-in-c Dundee St Ninian from 07; Can St Paul's Cathl Dundee from 08. *St Ninian's Church House, Kingsway East, Dundee DD4 7RW* T: (01382) 453818 M: 07931-222092 E: flamont53@sky.com

LAMONT, Roger. b 37. Jes Coll Ox BA 60 MA 62 MBACP 00. St Steph Ho Ox 59. **d** 61 **p** 62. C Northampton St Alb *Pet* 61–66; V Mitcham St Olave *S'wark* 66–73; V N Sheen St Phil and All SS 73–85; P-in-c Richmond St Luke 82–85; Chapl St Lawr Hosp Caterham 85–93; Chapl Surrey Oaklands NHS Trust 94–01; rtd 01; PtO *S'wark* from 01. *36 Hillcroft Court, Chaldon Road, Caterham CR3 5XB* T: (01883) 340803 E: rmglamont@gmail.com

LAMONT, Ms Veronica Jane (Ronni). b 56. Bp Grosseteste Coll CertEd 77 Anglia Poly Univ MA 06. St Jo Coll Nottm 90. **d** 92 **p** 94. Par Dn St Alb St Pet 92–94; C 94–96; TV Hemel Hempstead 96–01; V Bexley St Jo *Roch* 01–08; PtO *Cant* from 08; *Roch* from 08; Dioc Faith and Nuture Adv *Cant* from 15. *86 Ufton Lane, Sittingbourne ME10 1EX* T: (01795) 553603 M: 07802-793910 E: ronni@lamonts.org.uk *or* rlamont@diocant.org

LAMPARD, Ms Ruth Margaret. b 65. St Jo Coll Dur BA 87 Jes Coll Cam BA 99 MA 04 Heythrop Coll Lon MA 04. Westcott Ho Cam 97 Berkeley Div Sch 99. **d** 00 **p** 01. C Ealing St Pet Mt Park *Lon* 00–04; C Eastcote St Lawr 01–04; Hon C Norton St Alb 05–06; PtO *S'wark* 06–12; Chapl to Bp Kensington *Lon* 07–08; C W Brompton St Mary w St Peter and St Jude 08–13; Chapl Chapter 1 13–15; Hon C Waterloo St Jo w St Andr *S'wark* from 13; Chapl The ME Trust from 19. *St Barnabas' Vicarage, 146A Lavenham Road, London SW18 5EP* T: (020) 8874 7768 M: 07870-651240 E: ruthlampard3@gmail.com

LANCASTER, Mrs Jennifer. b 48. NEOC 00. **d** 03 **p** 04. C Walker *Newc* 03–07; TV Jarrow *Dur* 07–12; rtd 12; PtO *Newc* from 12. *2 Heathdale Gardens, High Heaton, Newcastle upon Tyne NE7 7QR* E: jenny.lancaster@gmail.com

LANCASTER, John Rawson. b 47. BSc. NOC. **d** 82 **p** 83. C Bolton St Jas w St Chrys *Bradf* 82–86; V Barnoldswick w Bracewell 86–12; rtd 12; PtO *Bradf* 13–14; *Leeds* from 14. *Harold's Laithe, High Bradley Lane, Bradley, Keighley BD20 9ES* T: (01535) 634264

LANCASTER, Ronald. b 31. MBE 93. St Jo Coll Dur BA 53 MA 56 Hon MSc 09 FRSC 83 CChem 83. Cuddesdon Coll 55. **d** 57 **p** 58. C Morley St Pet w Churwell *Wakef* 57–60; C High Harrogate St Pet *Ripon* 60–63; LtO *Ely* 63–88; Chapl Kimbolton Sch 63–88; Asst Chapl 88–91; PtO *Ely* 88–16; rtd 96; PtO *St Alb* 13–18; *Ely* from 18. *7 High*

Street, Kimbolton, Huntingdon PE28 0HB T: (01480) 860498
E: ronlancaster31@outlook.com

LANCASTER, Archdeacon of. *See* PICKEN, The Ven David
Anthony

LANCASTER, Suffragan Bishop of. *See* DUFF, The Rt Revd
Jillian Louise Calland

LANCHANTIN-PIGGOTT, Mrs Eve Line. b 51. Sorbonne
Univ Paris BA 79 MA 80 MPhil 83. Protestant Inst of Th
Paris BDiv 95 MDiv 99. **d** 07 **p** 08. C Ashford *Cant* 07–10;
PtO 15–16; TV Ashford Town 16–21; rtd 21. *Address temp
unknown* M: 07949-349543 E: evelanchantin@gmail.com

LAND, Edward Charles. b 79. Trin Coll Bris 13. **d** 15 **p** 16.
C Heigham St Thos *Nor* 15–17; C The Mitre Benefice
from 17; P-in-c Costessey from 19. *The Vicarage, Folgate
Lane, Costessey, Norwich NR8 5DP* M: 07917-285072
E: edward@costesseyparish.org

LAND, Michael Robert John. b 43. Ripon Hall Ox BA 72 MA.
d 72 **p** 73. C Newbury St Nic *Ox* 72–73; C Newbury 73–75;
TV Chigwell *Chelmsf* 75–80; V Walthamstow St Andr 80–08;
rtd 08; PtO *Heref* 08–17. *20 St Mary's Lane, Burghill, Hereford
HR4 7QL* T: (01432) 760452 E: mrland117@gmail.com

LANDALL, Allan Roy. b 55. Qu Coll Birm BA 98. **d** 98 **p** 99.
C Thurnby w Stoughton *Leic* 98–02; R Walsoken *Ely* from
02. *The Rectory, Church Road, Wisbech PE13 3RA* T: (01945)
583740 E: arlandall@btinternet.com

LANDAU, Christopher David. b 80. Trin Coll Cam BA 01
MA 05 MPhil 02 Oriel Coll Ox DPhil 17. Ripon Coll
Cuddesdon MPhil 12. **d** 13 **p** 14. C W Kilburn St Luke and
Harrow Road St Pet *Lon* 13–17; C Ox St Aldate 17–21; Hon
Chapl Ch Ch 18–21; Chapl Ox Pastorate 18–21; Dir ReSource
from 21. *49 Arundel Close, Telford TF3 2LX* T: (01865)
761852 M: 07703-958086 E: cdlandau@gmail.com or
christopherlandau@resource-arm.net

LANDER, Mrs Elizabeth Anne. b 69. St Andr Univ BSc 93 Ox
Univ PGCE 94. Wycliffe Hall Ox 00. **d** 02 **p** 03. C Glascote
and Stonydelph *Lich* 02–07; C Beckenham St Jo *Roch* 08–13;
V 13–18; Chapl Alleyn's Sch Dulwich from 19; NSM Dulwich
St Barn *S'wark* from 19. *122 Woodwarde Road, London
SE22 8UT* M: 07790-212302 E: landerliz@yahoo.co.uk

LANDRY, Peter George. b 87. Pretoria Univ BTh 11. St Mellitus
Coll MA 20. **d** 20 **p** 21. C Bletchley *Ox* from 20. *14 Hamilton
Lane, Bletchley, Milton Keynes MK3 5LU* M: 07491-499988
E: peter.george.landry@gmail.com

LANE, Alexander John. b 71. Leeds Univ BA 02. Coll of
Resurr Mirfield 99. **d** 02 **p** 03. C Eastbourne St Andr
Chich 02–06; C Littlehampton and Wick 06–08; V
Hunslet w Cross Green *Ripon* 08–12; V Twickenham All
SS *Lon* from 12; CMP from 08. *All Saints' House, Church
View Road, Twickenham TW2 5BX* T: (020) 8894 3580
E: vicar.allsaintstwickenham.org.uk

LANE, Mrs Amanda Mary. b 59. Hull Univ BA 82 Ch Ch
Coll Cant PGCE 97. SEITE 13. **d** 16 **p** 17. NSM The Six *Cant*
from 16. *Meadvale, Maidstone Road, Borden, Sittingbourne
ME9 7QA* T: (01795) 842478 M: 07986-785659
E: amandamarylane@gmail.com

LANE, Andrew Harry John. b 49. MBE 92. Lanc Univ BA 71.
Cuddesdon Coll 71. **d** 73 **p** 74. C Abingdon w Shippon *Ox*
73–78; Chapl Abingdon Sch 75–78; Chapl RAF 78–94; rtd
94; PtO *Nor* 94–01 and from 21; Public Preacher 01–21;
RD Repps 02–05. *Society of St Luke, 32B Beeston Common,
Sheringham NR26 8ES* T: (01263) 825623 F: 820334
E: andrewssl@me.com

LANE, Anthony Richard. b 42. St Jo Coll Nottm 07. **d** 09
p 10. C Gtr Athens *Eur* 09–17; PtO from 17; *Ex* from 19. *6
Kingfisher Close, Newton St Cyres, Exeter EX5 5DH* T: (01392)
851975 M: 07860-530760 E: lane.tony42@gmail.com

LANE, Canon Antony Kenneth. b 58. Ripon Coll
Cuddesdon 84. **d** 87 **p** 88. C Crediton and Shobrooke
Ex 87–90; C Amblecote *Worc* 90–94; C Sedgley All SS
94–95; TV 95–00; R Crayford *Roch* 00–17; AD Erith 09–14;
P-in-c Gillingham St Aug 17–20; Hon Can Roch Cathl 09–20;
rtd 20; PtO *Ex* from 20. *2 Lily Vale Mews, Havelock Road,
Torquay TQ1 4LZ* T: (01803) 322271 M: 07928-769882
E: ak.lane@btinternet.com

LANE, Bernard Charles. b 59. Cam Coll of Art & Tech BA 81
Anglia Poly Univ MA 01. Trin Coll Bris BA 91 Ridley Hall
Cam 99. **d** 01 **p** 02. C Sittingbourne St Mary and St Mich *Cant*
01–05; Chapl N Bris NHS Trust 10–16; TV Broadclyst, Clyst
Honiton, Pinhoe, Rockbeare etc *Ex* 16–21; TV Broadclyst,
Clyst Honiton, Clyst Hydon etc from 21. *Rockbeare Vicarage,
Rockbeare, Exeter EX5 2EG* T: (01404) 758759 M: 07756-
797071 E: tvclystvalley@gmail.com

LANE, Christopher Paul. b 80. Regent's Park Coll Ox MA 01.
St Mellitus Coll 17. **d** 19 **p** 20. C Walsall St Pet *Lich* from
19. *40 Princes Avenue, Walsall WS1 2DG* M: 07919-453413
E: revchrislane@gmail.com

✠LANE, The Rt Revd Elizabeth Jane Holden (Libby). b 66.
St Pet Coll Ox BA 89 MA 93. Cranmer Hall Dur 91. **d** 93
p 94 **c** 15. C Blackb St Jas 93–96; PtO *York* 96–99; Family
Life Educn Officer *Ches* 00–02; TV Stockport SW 02–07;
Asst Dir of Ords 05–07; V Hale and Ashley 07–15; Dean of
Women in Min 10–15; Suff Bp Stockport 15–19; Bp Derby
from 19. *The Bishop's House, 6 King Street, Duffield, Belper
DE56 4EU* T: (01332) 840132 E: bishop@bishopofderby.org

LANE, Gareth Ernest. b 71. Westmr Univ BSc 94
Univ of Wales MA 08. Wycliffe Hall Ox 08. **d** 10
p 11. C Bedgrove *Ox* 10–14; TV Aylesbury from 14.
28 Domino Way, Aylesbury HP18 0FZ T: (01296)
328523 M: 07919-332859 E: garethlane@hotmail.com or
gareth@churchonberryfields.org

LANE, George David Christopher. b 68. St Pet Coll Ox
BA 89 MA 93. Cranmer Hall Dur 91. **d** 93 **p** 94. C Blackb
St Jas 93–96; C Beverley Minster *York* 96–99; V Heald
Green St Cath *Ches* 99–07; PtO 07–18; *Man* 08–12; Chapl
Man Airport from 12; Lic Preacher from 12. *Bishop's Lodge,
Back Lane, Dunham Town, Altrincham WA14 4SG* T: 0161-
489 2838 or 928 5611 E: george.lane@manairport.co.uk or
george_dcl@yahoo.co.uk

LANE, Hannah Kate. b 85. Keele Univ BSc 07 PGCE 08 Man
Metrop Univ MA 13. St Mellitus Coll 19. **d** 21. C Turton
Moorland *Man* from 21. *173 Chapeltown Road, Bromley
Cross, Bolton BL7 9AJ* M: 07840-065268 or 07825-085220
E: lane.hk8@gmail.com

LANE, Iain Robert. b 61. CCC Ox BA 83. Ripon Coll
Cuddesdon BA 86 MA 88. **d** 87 **p** 88. C Rotherhithe St Mary
w All SS *S'wark* 87–91; V Bierley *Bradf* 91–00; Can Res St Alb
00–08; Admin St Alb Cen for Chr Studies from 08; PtO *St Alb*
from 08. *Hill House, Wild Hill, Hatfield AL9 6EB* T: (01707)
660485 E: iain.lane@christianstudies.org.uk or
iain@iainlane.uk

LANE, Jennifer Mary. b 73. Leeds Univ BA 08 MA 12. NOC 05.
d 08 **p** 09. C Crosland Moor and Linthwaite *Wakef* 08–11;
P-in-c Crofton and Warmfield 11–14; Par Educn Adv 11–14;
P-in-c E Richmond *Leeds* 14–16; R E Dere street 16–19; R Lower
Swale from 19. *The Rectory, Manor Lane, Ainderby Steeple,
North Allerton DL7 9PY* E: jennilane2013@btinternet.com or
jenni.lane@leeds.anglican.org

LANE, Jessica. *See* SAVILL, Jessica

LANE, John Ernest. b 39. OBE 94. MBIM 76 Cranfield Info
Tech Inst MSc 80. Handsworth Coll Birm 58. **d** 80 **p** 80.
In Methodist Ch 62–80; Hon C Peckham St Jo w St Andr
S'wark 80–95; Hon C Greenwich St Alfege 98–99; Dir
St Mungo Housing Assn 80–94; Dir Corporate Affairs from
94; PtO *S'wark* 95–98; *Lich* 02–14. *2 Tregony Rise, Lichfield
WS14 9SN* T: (01543) 415078

LANE, Libby. *See* LANE, Elizabeth Jane Holden

LANE, Mrs Lilian June. b 37. Stockwell Coll Lon TCert 59.
d 02 **p** 03. OLM E Knoyle, Semley and Sedgehill *Sarum*
02–08; OLM St Bartholomew 08–09; Chapl St Mary's
Sch Shaftesbury from 09. *Ashmede, Watery Lane,
Donhead St Mary, Shaftesbury SP7 9DP* T: (01747) 828427
E: rev.jlane@icloud.com

LANE, Mrs Linda Mary. b 41. Lon Univ BD 87 ACIB 66.
Gilmore Ho 67. **dss** 82 **d** 87 **p** 94. Hadlow *Roch* 82–94;
Hon Par Dn 87–94; PtO 94–96; C Dartford H Trin 96–97;
V Kensworth, Studham and Whipsnade *St Alb* 97–03; rtd
03; PtO *Wakef* 05–10. *Carey Cottage, The Green, Cleasby,
Darlington DL2 2QZ* T: (01325) 464544

LANE, Malcolm Clifford George. b 48. JP. ACIB. St D
Coll Lamp. **d** 02 **p** 05. Par Dn Abergavenny St Mary w
Llanwenarth Citra *Mon* 02–08; P-in-c Michaelston-y-Fedw
08–14; Asst Chapl Gwent Healthcare NHS Trust 02–14;
rtd 14; PtO *Mon* from 15; *Heref* from 16. *14 Coed y Brenin,
Llantilio Pertholey, Abergavenny NP7 6PY* T: (01873) 858464
E: st8711@msn.com

LANE, Canon Martin John. b 69. Open Univ BSc 03 Cardiff
Univ LLM 08. Coll of Resurr Mirfield 92. **d** 95 **p** 96. C Liss
Portsm 95–98; C Warren Park and Leigh Park 98–00; TV
Littlehampton and Wick *Chich* 00–04; P-in-c Harting w
Elsted and Treyford cum Didling 04–10; RD Midhurst
06–10; V Bosham from 10; RD Westbourne from 15; Can
and Preb Chich Cathl from 18. *The Vicarage, Bosham
Lane, Bosham, Chichester PO18 8HX* T: (01243) 573228
E: vicar@boshamchurch.org.uk

LANE, Robert David. b 66. St Steph Ho Ox 05. **d** 07
p 08. C Corringham *Chelmsf* 07–10; V Petts Wood *Roch*
10–17; P-in-c Borden *Cant* from 17. *The Vicarage, School
Lane, Borden, Sittingbourne ME9 8JS* M: 07807-224748
E: fr.robert.lane@gmail.com

LANE, Ms Rosalind Anne. b 69. Trevelyan Coll Dur BA 91
Heythrop Coll Lon MTh 93 Man Univ MA 01 Ches Univ
DProf 16. Westcott Ho Cam. **d** 95 **p** 96. C Huddersfield

St Pet and All SS *Wakef* 95–99; Sub Chapl HM Pris and YOI New Hall 97–99; Asst Chapl HM Pris and YOI Doncaster 99–01; Chapl 01; Chapl HM Pris Wymott 01–05; Kirkham 05–08; Whitemoor 08–11; Ashwell 11; Chapl N Essex Partnership NHS Foundn Trust 11–12; Chapl Cambs and Pet NHS Foundn Trust 12–15; Chapl Peterborough and Stamford Hosps NHS Foundn Trust 12–15; Chapl K Ely from 15. *King's, Barton Road, Ely CB7 4EW* T: (01353) 660700 E: roslane@kingsely.org

LANE, Roy Albert. b 42. Bris Sch of Min 82. d 85 p 86. NSM Bedminster *Bris* 85–97; PtO 97–02; NSM Bishopsworth and Bedminster Down 02–12; rtd 12; PtO *Bris* from 12. *20 Ashton Drive, Bristol BS3 2PW* T: 0117-983 0747 M: 07701-002485 E: roypeg@blueyonder.co.uk

LANE, Simon. *See* DOUGLAS LANE, Charles Simon Pellew

LANE, Stuart Alexander Rhys. *See* LANE, Alexander John

LANE, Terry. b 50. STETS 94. d 97 p 98. NSM Freemantle *Win* 97–99; Chapl HM Pris Kingston (Portsm) 99–01; Chapl HM Pris Parkhurst 01–06; Co-ord Chapl HM Pris Win 06–10; rtd 10; PtO *Win* 10–16. *24 Claremont Crescent, Southampton SO15 4GS* E: samaritan1949@gmail.com

LANE, William Henry Howard. b 63. Bris Poly BA 85. Trin Coll Bris 00. d 02 p 03. C Frome H Trin *B & W* 02–06; P-in-c Woolavington w Cossington and Bawdrip 06–07; R 07–11; RD Sedgemoor 09–11; V Bridgwater H Trin and Durleigh from 11. *The New Vicarage, Hamp Avenue, Bridgwater TA6 6AN* T: (01278) 455022 E: reverend.lane@gmail.com

LANG, William David. b 51. K Coll Lon BD 74 MA 94 AKC 74. St Aug Coll Cant 74. d 75 p 76. C Fleet *Guildf* 75–79; C Ewell St Fran 79–82; C W Ewell 79–82; V Holmwood 82–92; R Elstead 92–10; V Thursley 92–10; P-in-c Redhorn *Sarum* 10–12; P-in-c Bishop's Cannings, All Cannings etc 11–12; TR Cannings and Redhorn 12–16; rtd 16. *60 St Marys Gardens, Hilperton Marsh, Trowbridge BA14 7PQ* E: william@lang.net

LANGAN, Canon Eleanor Susan. b 56. Homerton Coll Cam BEd 78. Ripon Coll Cuddesdon 84. d 87 p 94. Hon Par Dn Grays Thurrock *Chelmsf* 87–89; LtO 89–94; NSM Creeksea w Althorne, Latchingdon and N Fambridge 94–95; NSM S Woodham Ferrers 95–99; NSM Overstrand, Northrepps, Sidestrand etc *Nor* 99–03; Chapl Norfolk and Nor Univ Hosps NHS Foundn Trust 00–10; Lead Chapl 10–19; V Nor St Helen from 19; Chapl Gt Hosp Nor from 19; Hon Can Nor Cathl from 18. *Calthorpe Lodge, Great Hospital, Bishopgate, Norwich NR1 4EL*

LANGDON, Ms Susan Mary. b 48. RN 69. Ripon Coll Cuddesdon 01. d 03 p 04. C Amesbury *Sarum* 03–06; Jt Ldr Pilgrimage Community of St Wite 06–19; Warden Pilsdon Community from 19; PtO *Sarum* from 16. *Pilsdon Manor, Pilsdon, Bridport DT6 5NZ* T: (01308) 868308 E: suelangdon@btinternet.com

LANGDON-DAVIES, Mrs Stella Mary. b 44. Bris Univ BSc 85 Nottm Univ MBA 97. St Jo Coll Nottm MTh 01. d 01 p 02. C Stamford All SS w St Jo *Linc* 01–04; V Heme Cant 04–06; P-in-c Saxonwell *Linc* 06–08; rtd 08; PtO *Leic* 14–19; *Linc* 15–18. *5 Manor Paddock, Allington, Grantham NG32 2DL* T: (01400) 281395 M: 07976-380659 E: stellalangdondavies@btinternet.com

LANGDON-GRIFFITHS (née Erving), Christel Estelle Ann. b 79. Liv Univ BSc 01 St Jo Coll Dur BA 15. Cranmer Hall Dur 13. d 15 p 16. C Walton St Luke *Liv* 15–17; C Wavertree St Mary 17–18. *Christ Church Vicarage, 30 Wash Lane, Warrington WA4 1HT* M: 07477-594790 E: christel.erving@outlook.com

LANGDON-GRIFFITHS, Daniel Steven. b 82. St Jo Coll Dur BA 14. Cranmer Hall Dur 11. d 14 p 15. C Sutton *Liv* 14–17; Chapl Midi-Pyrénées and Aude *Eur* 18–21; PtO *Ches* from 21. *Christ Church Vicarage, 30 Wash Lane, Warrington WA4 1HT* M: 07411-795237 E: dan.langdon.griffiths@gmail.com

LANGDON-SMITH, Thomas Robert. b 83. Liv Hope Univ BA 05. St Mellitus Coll 16. d 19 p 20. C Liv Ch Ch Norris Green from 19. *9 Kingsland Crescent, Liverpool L11 7AN* M: 07800-652662 E: tomlangdonsmith@gmail.com

LANGDOWN, Jennifer May. b 48. STETS 95. d 98 p 99. C S Petherton w The Seavingtons *B & W* 98–02; R Curry Rivel w Fivehead and Swell 02–12; rtd 12; PtO *B & W* from 15. *61 Vereland Road, Hutton, Weston-super-Mare BS24 9TH* T: (01934) 815499 M: 07850-245948 E: mrsvic7548@gmail.com

LANGERHUIZEN, Sandra Marilyn. b 45. d 11 p 12. NSM Birkenhead St Jas w St Bede *Ches* 11–15; rtd 15; PtO *Ches* from 15. *43 Shamrock Road, Birkenhead CH41 0EG* T: 0151-652 3109 E: w.langerhuizen@btinternet.com

LANGFORD, David Laurence. b 51. d 88 p 89. OLM Scotton w Northorpe *Linc* 88–16; OLM Messingham w E Butterwick, Scotter w E Ferry and Scotton w Northorpe from 16. *1 Westgate, Scotton, Gainsborough DN21 3QX* T: (01724) 763139

LANGFORD, Peter Francis. b 54. Sarum & Wells Th Coll 76. d 79 p 80. C N Ormesby *York* 79–82; Ind Chapl 83–91; V Middlesbrough St Chad 91–96; R Easington w Liverton 96–07; rtd 07; PtO *York* from 07. *32 Furlong Road, Stamford Bridge, York YO41 1PX*

LANGFORD, Peter Julian. b 33. Selw Coll Cam BA 58. Westcott Ho Cam 59. d 60 p 61. C E Ham St Mary *Chelmsf* 60–67; Hon C 67–68; Hon C E Ham w Upton Park 68–71; Hon C Beccles St Mich *St E* 71–76; Warden Ringsfield Hall Suffolk 71–87; P-in-c Ringsfield w Redisham *St E* 76–80; TV Seacroft *Ripon* 87–98; rtd 98; PtO *St E* 99–21. *22 Alexander Road, Beccles NR34 9UD* T: (01502) 710034

LANGHAM, Paul Jonathan. b 60. Ex Univ BA 81 Fitzw Coll Cam BA 86 MA 91. Ridley Hall Cam 84. d 87 p 88. C Bath Weston All SS w N Stoke *B & W* 87–91; Chapl and Fell St Cath Coll Cam 91–96; V Combe Down w Monkton Combe and S Stoke *B & W* 96–10; P-in-c Clifton Ch Ch w Em *Bris* 10–15; V from 15. *Christ Church Clifton Church Office, Linden Gate, Clifton Down Road, Bristol BS8 4AH* T: 0117-973 6524 E: paul.langham@ccweb.org.uk

LANGILLE, Canon Melvin Owen. b 58. St Mary's Univ Halifax NS BA 79. Atlantic Sch of Th MDiv 82. d 82 p 83. Dn-in-c Falkland Canada 82; R Lockeport and Barrington 83–86; R French Village 87–90; R Cole Harbour St Andr 90–96; R Yarmouth H Trin 97–03; P-in-c Brora *Mor* 03–09; P-in-c Dornoch 03–09; R Arpafeelie from 09; R Cromarty from 09; R Fortrose from 09; Syn Clerk 07–12; Dioc Dir of Ords 08–14; Can St Andr Cathl Inverness 07–12 and from 13. *The Rectory, 1 Deans Road, Fortrose IV10 8TJ* T: (01381) 622241 M: 07780-512990 E: mel@sagart.me.uk

LANGLANDS, John Craig. Suffolk Coll BA 07. Qu Coll Birm 14. d 15 p 16. NSM Allesley Park and Whoberley *Cov* 15–18; C 18–21. *52 Brookside Avenue, Coventry CV5 8AF* T: (024) 7667 5236 M: 07588-664962 E: jlanglands@sky.com

LANGLEY, Andrew Paul. b 64. Cardiff Univ BTh 11 Regent's Park Coll Ox MSt 12 DPhil 18. Wycliffe Hall Ox 16. d 18 p 19. C Dartmouth and Dittisham *Ex* 18–21; V from 21. *St Saviour's Church, Church Close, Dartmouth TQ6 9DH* T: (01803) 835540

LANGLEY, Jean. *See* PHILLIPS, Jean

LANGLEY, Mrs Morag Ellen. b 53. Bris Univ BA 74 St Luke's Coll Ex PGCE 76. d 16 p 17. NSM Tyndale *Glouc* from 16. *Charlecote, Orchard Street, Wotton-under-Edge GL12 7EZ* T: (01453) 845147 M: 07411-207720 E: morag914@btinternet.com

LANGLEY, Canon Myrtle Sarah. b 39. TCD BA 61 HDipEd 62 MA 67 Bris Univ PhD 76 Lon Univ BD 66 FRAI. Dalton Ho Bris 64. d 88 p 94. Dir Chr Development for Miss *Liv* 87–89; Dir Dioc Tr Inst *Carl* 90–98; Dioc Dir of Tr 90–98; Hon Can Carl Cathl 91–98; P-in-c Long Marton w Dufton and w Milburn 98–06; rtd 06; PtO *Carl* from 07. *Grania, 5 Farbrow Road, Carlisle CA1 3HW* T: (01228) 539291 E: canonmlangley@hotmail.com

LANGLEY, The Ven Robert. b 37. St Cath Soc Ox BA 61. St Steph Ho Ox. d 63 p 64. C Aston cum Aughton *Sheff* 63–68; Midl Area Sec Chr Educn Movement 68–71; HQ Sec Chr Educn Movement 71–74; Prin Ian Ramsey Coll Brasted 74–77; Can Res St Alb and Dir St Alb Minl Tr Scheme 77–85; Can Res Newc Cathl 85–01; Dioc Missr 85–98; Dioc Dir of Min and Tr 98–01; Adn Lindisfarne 01–07; Local Min Development Officer 01–07; rtd 08; PtO *Newc* from 08; *York* 09–19. *1 Castle Farm Mews, Jesmond, Newcastle upon Tyne NE2 3RG* T: 0191-284 9526 E: r.langley648@btinternet.com

LANGMAN, Barry Edward. b 46. RD . Master Mariner 73. Cant Sch of Min 87. d 90 p 91. NSM St Margarets-at-Cliffe w Westcliffe etc *Cant* 90–92; C Sandgate St Paul w Folkestone St Geo 92–95; P-in-c Headcorn 95–01; V 01–08; rtd 08; PtO *Cant* 08–14; *Ches* from 15. *23 Birkdale Close, Macclesfield SK10 2UA* T: (01625) 662287 E: barrylangman@yahoo.co.uk

LANGNER, Mrs Elizabeth Ann. b 79. d 20 p 21. C Norton Lees St Paul *Sheff* from 20. *70 Lees Hall Avenue, Sheffield S8 9JF* T: 0114-258 1198 M: 07859-065940 E: bethjwinkley@gmail.com *or* beth.stpauls@gmail.com

✠**LANGRISH, The Rt Revd Michael Laurence.** b 46. Birm Univ BSocSc 67 Fitzw Coll Cam BA 73 MA 77 Ex Univ Hon DD 07. Ridley Hall Cam 71. d 73 p 74 c 93. C Stratford-on-Avon w Bishopton *Cov* 73–76; Chapl Rugby Sch 76–81; P-in-c Offchurch *Cov* 81–87; Dioc Dir of Ords 81–87; P-in-c Rugby 87–91; Hon Can Cov Cathl 90–93; TR Rugby 91–93; Suff Bp Birkenhead *Ches* 93–00; Bp Ex 00–13; rtd 13; Hon Asst Bp Chich from 13; Hon Asst Bp Eur from 18; PtO from 18. *39 The Meadows, Walberton, Arundel BN18 0PB* T: (01243) 551704 E: langrishm@btinternet.com

✠**LANGSTAFF, The Rt Revd James Henry.** b 56. St Cath Coll Ox BA 77 MA 81 Nottm Univ BA 80. St Jo Coll Nottm 78. **d** 81 **p** 82 **c** 04. C Farnborough *Guildf* 81–84 and 85–86; P-in-c 84–85; P-in-c Duddeston w Nechells *Birm* 86; V 87–96; RD Birm City 95–96; Bp's Dom Chapl 96–00; P-in-c Short Heath 98–00; R Sutton Coldfield H Trin 00–04; AD Sutton Coldfield 02–04; Suff Bp Lynn *Nor* 04–10; Bp Roch 10–21; Bp HM Pris 13–20; rtd 21. *Address temp unknown*

LANGTON, Robert. b 45. SAOMC 97. **d** 00 **p** 01. C Boyne Hill *Ox* 00–03; Chapl St Mich Hospice St Leonards-on-Sea 03–08; TV Cwmbran *Mon* 08–15; rtd 10; Hon C Cwmbran *Mon* 15–16; rtd 15; PtO *Cov* from 16. *4 Margetts Close, Kenilworth CV8 1EN* T: (01926) 259523 E: robertlangton.langton@gmail.com

LANHAM, Geoffrey Peter. b 62. Cam Univ MA 84 Ox Univ MPhil 86 Win Univ MA 19. Wycliffe Hall Ox 86. **d** 89 **p** 90. C Southborough St Pet w Ch Ch and St Matt *Roch* 89–92; C Harborne Heath *Birm* 92–00; C Birm St Paul 00–07; Deanery Missr 00–09; C Birm Cathl 07–09; V Selly Park Ch Ch 09–19; V Knowle from 19. *The Vicarage, 1811 Warwick Road, Knowle, Solihull B93 0DS* T: (01564) 779123

LANHAM, Richard Paul White. b 42. Dur Univ BA 64. Wycliffe Hall Ox 65. **d** 67 **p** 68. C Gerrards Cross *Ox* 67–69; C Horwich H Trin *Man* 69–72; C Worsley 72–74; V Accrington St Andr *Blackb* 74–80; V Shillington *St Alb* 80–85; V Upper w Lower Gravenhurst 80–85; rtd 85; PtO *St Alb* from 85. *10 Alexander Close, Clifton, Shefford SG17 5RB* T: (01462) 813520

LANKESTER, Mrs Jane Elizabeth. b 53. Qu Mary Coll Lon BScEcon 74 SS Mark & Jo Univ Coll Plymouth MA 04. SWMTC 05. **d** 08 **p** 09. NSM Totnes w Bridgetown, Berry Pomeroy etc *Ex* 08–12; TV Honiton, Gittisham, Combe Raleigh, Monkton etc 12–18; rtd 18. *63 Cleeve Drive, Ivybridge PL21 9BP* E: jane.lankester@gmail.com

LANKSHEAR, Jane Frances. See MAINWARING, Jane Frances

LANNON, Joseph. b 61. QUB BD 83 PhD 02 Cranfield Univ MSc 85. SWMTC 15. **d** 17. C Newton Abbot *Ex* 17–18; C Newton Ferrers w Revelstoke 18–19; C Brixton, Newton Ferrers, Revelstoke etc 19–21; R Callington Cluster *Truro* from 21. *Church Hill House, Church Hill, Holbeton, Plymouth PL8 1LN* T: (01752) 830214 E: revjoelannon@gmail.com

LANSDALE, Canon Charles Roderick. b 38. Leeds Univ BA 59. Coll of Resurr Mirfield 59. **d** 61 **p** 62. C Nunhead St Antony *S'wark* 61–65; Swaziland 65–71; V Benhilton *S'wark* 72–78; TR Catford (Southend) and Downham 78–87; TR Moulsecoomb *Chich* 87–97; V Eastbourne St Mary 97–08; Can and Preb Chich Cathl 98–08; rtd 08; PtO *Chich* from 08. *102 Channel View Road, Eastbourne BN22 7LJ* T: (01323) 646655

LANYON-HOGG, Mrs Anne Chester. b 49. St Anne's Coll Ox BA 71 MA 75 Worc Coll of Educn PGCE 92. WEMTC 01. **d** 04 **p** 05. NSM Colwall w Upper Colwall and Coddington *Heref* 04–19; NSM Malvern H Trin and St Jas *Worc* 07–14; PtO from 14; Bp's Adv for SSM *Heref* 15–19; rtd 19; PtO *Heref* from 19. *Ty'r Gorwel, Betws Ifan, Beulah, Newcastle Emlyn SA38 9QL* M: 07891-868676 E: stillannelh@gmail.com

LANYON JONES, Keith. b 49. Southn Univ BTh 79. Sarum & Wells Th Coll 74. **d** 77 **p** 78. C Charlton Kings St Mary *Glouc* 77–81; Sen Chapl Rugby Sch 81–99; LtO *Truro* 83–00; P-in-c St Cleer 00–15; C St Ive and Pensilva w Quethiock 02–15; Chapl Kelly Coll Tavistock 08–15; rtd 15. *The Old Forge, 17A St John Street, Wells BA5 1SW*

LAOTAN, Anthony Olanrewaju. b 77. Yorks Min Course 12. **d** 16 **p** 17. C Idle *Leeds* 16–20; V Stamford Ch Ch *Linc* from 20. *The Vicarage, 3 Northfields Court, Stamford PE9 1RA* M: 07716-936336 E: olanonline@yahoo.com *or* vicar@christchurchstamford.org

LAPWOOD, Robin Rowland John. b 57. Selw Coll Cam MA. Ridley Hall Cam 80. **d** 82 **p** 83. C Bury St Edmunds St Mary *St E* 82–86; P-in-c Bentley w Tattingstone 86–93; P-in-c Copdock w Washbrook and Belstead 86–93; TV High Wycombe *Ox* 93–96; P-in-c Marcham w Garford 96–02; Chapl Summer Fields Sch *Ox* 02–12; PtO *Ox* from 12. *Rose Cottage, Challow Road, Wantage OX12 9DN* E: robin.lapwood@gmail.com

LARCOMBE, Paul Richard. b 57. Portsm Poly BSc 79 CEng MIET. Trin Coll Bris 94. **d** 96 **p** 97. C Werrington *Pet* 96–98; C Longthorpe 98–00; V Pet St Paul 00–07; TR Worle *B & W* 07–16; PtO from 16. *55 Forest Drive, Weston-super-Mare BS23 2UG* T: (01934) 270470 E: plarcombe@mac.com

LARGE, Stephen James. b 48. All SS Cen for Miss & Min 15. **d** 17 **p** 18. NSM Burnley St Cuth *Blackb* 17–20; NSM Brierfield 17–20; PtO from 20. *11 Sandiway Drive, Briercliffe, Burnley BB10 2JS*

LARGE, William Roy. b 40. Dur Univ BA DipEd Newc Univ MLitt 15. Edin Th Coll 82. **d** 84 **p** 85. C Leamington Priors All SS *Cov* 84–88; V Bishop's Tachbrook 88–99; Warden of Readers and Sen Tutor 88–99; TV N Tyne and Redesdale *Newc* 99–01; TR 01–05; rtd 05; PtO *Newc* from 05. *4 Osborne Court, Osborne Avenue, Newcastle upon Tyne NE2 1LE* T: 0191-281 1894 E: wr.large@btinternet.com

LARK, William Donald Starling. b 35. Keble Coll Ox BA 59 MA 63. Wells Th Coll 59. **d** 61 **p** 62. C Wyken *Cov* 61–64; C Christchurch *Win* 64–66; V Yeovil St Mich *B & W* 66–75; V Earley St Pet *Ox* 75–85; V Prittlewell St Mary *Chelmsf* 85–88; V Dawlish *Ex* 88–00; rtd 00; P-in-c Lanzarote *Eur* 00–05. *Las Alondras, 6 Cummings Court, Cummings Cross, Liverton, Newton Abbot TQ12 6HJ* T: (01626) 824966 E: lanzalarks@btinternet.com

LARKEY, Canon Deborah Frances. b 63. Univ of Wales (Abth) BA 85 Sarum Coll MA 17 Liv Inst of Educn PGCE 90. Dioc OLM tr scheme 95 NOC 03. **d** 98 **p** 99. OLM Toxteth St Cypr w Ch Ch *Liv* 98–01; OLM Edge Hill St Cypr w St Mary 01–04; C Netherton 04–07; TV Vale of Pewsey *Sarum* 07–11; TR from 11; Can and Preb Sarum Cathl from 17. *The Vicarage, Church Road, Woodborough, Pewsey SN9 5PH* T: (01672) 851746 E: deborahlarkey@btinternet.com

LARKIN, Andrew Brian. b 70. Warwick Univ BEng 92 PhD 95. Trin Coll Bris BA 06. **d** 06 **p** 07. C Littleover *Derby* 06–08; C Brailsford w Shirley, Osmaston w Edlaston etc 08–10; R Fenny Bentley, Thorpe, Tissington, Parwich etc 10–16; RD Ashbourne 12–16; P-in-c Claverdon w Preston Bagot *Cov* 16–20; P-in-c Wootton Wawen 16–20; P-in-c Barford w Wasperton and Sherbourne from 19; P-in-c Hampton Lucy w Charlecote and Loxley from 19. *The Rectory, 2 Church Lane, Barford, Warwick CU35 8ES* M: 07758-704452 E: andy@larkin.me.uk

LARKIN, Karen Maria. See GREENIDGE-SILCOTT, Karen Maria

LARKIN, Lucy. b 66. Birm Univ BA 87 MPhil 91 PhD 01 Westmr Coll Ox PGCE 89. **d** 08 **p** 09. C Hawthorn Australia 08–10; C St Pet Cathl Adelaide 10–11; Tutor SWMTC from 13; PtO *Truro* 13–14; Public Preacher from 14. *3 The Cedars, Truro TR1 2FD* T: (01872) 241716 M: 07757-917473 E: lucylarkin@swmtc.org.uk

LARKIN, Canon Peter John. b 39. ALCD 62. **d** 62 **p** 63. C Liskeard w St Keyne *Truro* 62–65; C Rugby St Andr *Cov* 65–67; Sec Bp Cov Call to Miss 67–68; V Kea *Truro* 68–78; P-in-c Bromsgrove St Jo *Worc* 78–81; R Torquay St Matthias, St Mark and H Trin *Ex* 81–97; Can Sokoto Nigeria 91–98; Can Kaduna from 98; TR Plymouth Em, St Paul Efford and St Aug *Ex* 97–00; rtd 00; PtO *Ex* 00–16; *Truro* 08–21. *12 De Luci Park, Truro TR1 2FB* T/F: (01872) 859328 E: mollypeterlarkin@tiscali.co.uk

LARKIN, Canon Susan Jane. b 52. MBE 07. Qu Foundn (Course) 10. **d** 12 **p** 13. NSM Garretts Green and Tile Cross *Birm* 12–18; NSM Garretts Green and Lea Hall from 18; Hon Can Birm Cathl from 21. *48 Horrell Road, Birmingham B26 2PD* T: 0121-574 3152 E: susanjlarkin@hotmail.co.uk

LARKIN, Mrs Treena Maud. b 72. Wolv Univ BSc 93 Keele Univ MSc 07. St Mellitus Coll BA 18. **d** 19 **p** 20. C Penn Fields *Lich* from 19. *131 Church Road, Bradmore, Wolverhampton WV3 7EN* T: (01902) 655485 M: 07971-049571 E: treenalarkin@hotmail.com

LASKEY, Cyril Edward. b 44. RMN 71 RGN 74. Llan Dioc Tr Scheme 85. **d** 88 **p** 89. NSM Troedrhiwgarth *Llan* 88–93; NSM Caerau St Cynfelin 94–01; P-in-c Glyncorrwg and Upper Afan Valley 01–10; rtd 10; PtO *Llan* from 11. *207 Bridgend Road, Maesteg CF34 0NL* T: (01656) 734639

LASLETT, Christopher John. b 42. Leeds Univ BA 64 Lon Univ PGCE 73. Lich Th Coll 64. **d** 66 **p** 67. C Bradf St Clem 66–69; C Upper Armley *Ripon* 69–70; PtO *Dur* 71–72; Hon C Stranton 79–81; PtO *Ripon* 87–88; rtd 07. *135 King Edward Road, Thorne, Doncaster DN8 4BZ*

LAST, Eric Cyril. b 30. Oak Hill Th Coll 77. **d** 79 **p** 80. C Wandsworth All SS *S'wark* 79–83; V Earlsfield St Andr 83–88; V S Merstham 88–96; Asst RD Reigate 92–96; rtd 96; Hon C Upper Tean *Lich* 96–10; PtO 10–16. *16 Whitehaven Castle, Flatt Walks, Whitehaven CA28 7RA* T: (01946) 692716 M: 07594-668598 E: eric.last1@btinternet.com

LAST, Mrs Estella Ruth. b 76. Brunel Univ LLB 98. SEITE 11. **d** 14 **p** 15. C Herne *Cant* 14–18; P-in-c Bridge from 18; Bp's Adv for Women's Min from 19. *The Vicarage, 23 High Street, Bridge, Canterbury CT4 5JZ* T: (01227) 206272 E: estellalast@gmail.com

LAST, Canon Michael Leonard Eric. b 60. St Jo Coll Nottm 92. **d** 94 **p** 95. C Tettenhall Wood *Lich* 94–98; V Pelsall 98–02; V Alton w Bradley-le-Moors and Oakamoor w Cotton 02–09; P-in-c Mayfield and Denstone w Ellastone and Stanton 06–09; I Saskatchewan Gateway Canada 09–11; R Adderley,

Ash, Calverhall, Ightfield etc *Lich* 11–17; P-in-c Keith *Mor* from 17; P-in-c Huntly from 17; P-in-c Aberchirder from 17; P-in-c Fochabers from 17; P-in-c Dufftown from 18; Can St Andr Cathl Inverness from 19. *Holy Trinity Rectory, Seafield Avenue, Keith AB55 5BS* T: (01542) 882782 M: 07591-750575 E: rev.last@lastrose.uk

LATHAM, Christine Elizabeth. b 46. S'wark Ord Course 87. **d** 90 **p** 94. Par Dn Battersea St Pet and St Paul *S'wark* 90–94; Par Dn S'wark Ch 94; C 94–97; C Merstham and Gatton 97–05; Chapl E Surrey Learning Disability NHS Trust 97–05; Chapl R Marsden NHS Foundn Trust 05–10; rtd 10; PtO *S'wark* from 10. *4 Bromley College, London Road, Bromley BR1 1PE* T: (020) 3489 7213 E: christine.latham@talktalk.net

LATHAM, Henry Nicholas Lomax. b 64. Reading Univ BA 86. Wycliffe Hall Ox BTh 93. **d** 93 **p** 94. C Aberystwyth *St D* 93–99; P-in-c Stoke Poges *Ox* 99–08; V 08–17; R Headley and Box Hill w Walton on the Hill *Guildf* from 17. *The Rectory, Breech Lane, Walton on the Hill, Tadworth KT20 7SD* T: (01737) 812105 E: isaiah61@uwclub.net

LATHAM, John Montgomery. b 37. Univ of NZ BA Cam Univ MA Cant Univ (NZ) MEd. Westcott Ho Cam 60. **d** 62 **p** 63. C Camberwell St Geo *S'wark* 62–65; Chapl Trin Coll Cam 65–70; Chapl Wanganui Colleg Sch NZ 71–79; Min Enabler New Brighton 96–01; V Christchurch St Luke 98–02; rtd 02. *43 Rugby Street, Christchurch 8014, New Zealand* T: (0064) (3) 355 6654 F: 355 6658 E: latham@xtra.co.nz

LATHAM, Robert Benedict Neil. b 73. Ripon Coll Cuddesdon 15. **d** 18 **p** 19. C Fromeside *Bris* 18–21; Min Can and Sacr Westmr Abbey from 21. *The Chapter Office, 20 Dean's Yard, London SW1P 3PA* T: (020) 7222 5152

LATHAM, Robert Norman. b 53. Qu Coll Birm 82. **d** 85 **p** 86. C Tamworth *Lich* 85–89; TV Wordsley *Worc* 89–96; P-in-c Hallow 96–97; R Hallow and Grimley w Holt 97–18; rtd 19; PtO *Cov* from 19. *30 Elmdene Road, Kenilworth CV8 2BX* T: (01926) 716142 E: letsstartatthecross@gmail.com

LATHAM, Roger Allonby. b 69. Leic Univ BA 90 Warwick Univ MA 92 Leeds Univ PGCE 93 Nottm Univ PhD 07. St Jo Coll Nottm BTh 98. **d** 99 **p** 00. C Paston *Pet* 99–02; TV Cartmel Peninsula *Carl* 02–09; Officer for IME 4-7 08–18; Vice-Prin LCTP and C Beacon TM 09–16; Dir Cumbria Chr Learning 16–18; Dir Cuddesdon: Glouc and Heref from 18; Public Preacher *Heref* from 18. *12 College Green, Gloucester GL1 2LX* T: (01452) 874969 E: rogerlatham54@aol.com or roger.latham@rcc.ac.uk

LATHAM (*née* WEBSTER), **Mrs Rosamond Mary.** b 54. Coll of Ripon & York St Jo BEd 90 MA 00 Birm Univ MPhil 13. Westcott Ho Cam 00. **d** 02 **p** 03. C Frodingham *Linc* 02–05; TV Dur N 05–07; TV Dorchester *Ox* 07–13; P-in-c Alford w Rigsby *Linc* 13–18; P-in-c Bilsby w Farlesthorpe 13–18; P-in-c Hannah cum Hagnaby w Markby 13–18; P-in-c Saleby w Beesby and Maltby 13–18; P-in-c Well 13–18; P-in-c Willoughby 14–18; R Alford Gp 18–20; RD Calcewaithe and Candleshoe 17–20; rtd 21. *3 Florentine's Court, Allhallowgate, Ripon HG4 1WB* M: 07779-784320 E: rosmlatham@gmail.com

LATHAM, Trevor Martin. b 56. BD 84. Ripon Coll Cuddesdon 84. **d** 86 **p** 87. C Cantril Farm *Liv* 86–89; TV Croxteth Park 89–98; V 98–99; TR Walton-on-the-Hill 99–19; rtd 19. *The Walton Cornerstone, 2 Liston Street, Liverpool L4 5RT*

LATHE, Canon Anthony Charles Hudson. b 36. Jes Coll Ox BA 59 MA 64. Lich Th Coll 59. **d** 61 **p** 62. C Selby Abbey *York* 61–63; V Hempnall *Nor* 63–72; R Woodton w Bedingham 63–72; R Fritton w Morningthorpe w Shelton and Hardwick 63–72; R Topcroft 63–72; R Banham 72–76; TR Quidenham 76–83; P-in-c New Buckenham 78–79; V Heigham St Thos 83–94; Hon Can Nor Cathl 87–99; RD Nor S 90–94; P-in-c Sheringham 94–99; rtd 99; PtO *Nor* 99–06; *St Alb* from 07. *15A Kingsdale Road, Berkhamsted HP4 3BS* T: (01442) 863115

LATIMER, Andrew John. b 78. Qu Coll Cam MA 04 Lon Univ MB, BS 05. Oak Hill Th Coll BTh 10. **d** 10 **p** 11. C Limehouse *Lon* 10–19; LtO *S'wark* from 19. *49 Devonshire Drive, London SE10 8JZ* M: 07740-287545 E: andrew@thelatimers.net or andrew.latimer@greenwich.church

LATIMER, Carol. b 45. Trent Park Coll of Educn CertEd 67 Stirling Univ BA 97 MLitt 04 MITI 14. TISEC 11. **d** 17. NSM Aberdour *St And* from 17; NSM Burntisland from 17; NSM Inverkeithing from 17. *6 Hawkcraig Road, Aberdour, Burntisland KY3 0XB* T: (01383) 860450 E: carollatimer98@gmail.com

LATIMER, Clifford James. b 45. City Univ BSc 68. **d** 99 **p** 00. OLM Burntwood *Lich* 99–10; rtd 10; PtO *Lich* 11–14 and 15–19. *6 Bradwell Lane, Rugeley WS15 4RW*

LATTEY, Susan. See CUMMING-LATTEY, Susan Mary Ruth

LATTIMER, Nicholas William. b 84. Leeds Univ BA 08. Trin Coll Bris 12. **d** 15 **p** 16. C Woodside *Leeds* 15–19; C Burley from 19. *12 Beech Walk, Adel, Leeds LS16 8NY* T: 0113-281 7309 M: 07912-321377 E: nicklattimer@hotmail.com or nick.lattimer@leeds.anglican.org

LATTIMORE, Anthony Leigh. b 35. Dur Univ BA 57. Lich Th Coll 60. **d** 62 **p** 63. C Aylestone *Leic* 62–66; C-in-c Eyres Monsell CD 66–69; V Eyres Monsell 69–73; V Somerby, Burrough on the Hill and Pickwell 73–86; RD Goscote I 80–86; R Glenfield 86–95; rtd 95; PtO *Leic* 95–12; *Pet* 95–11. *28 Elizabeth Way, Uppingham, Oakham LE15 9PQ* T: (01572) 823193

LATTY, Howard James. b 54. SRCh 71. WEMTC 98. **d** 01 **p** 02. NSM Bath St Mich w St Paul *B & W* 01–08; NSM Chewton Mendip w Ston Easton, Litton etc from 08. *The Rectory, Lower Street, Chewton Mendip, Radstock BA3 4GP* T: (01761) 241189

LAU, Fung Ming. b 60. St Mellitus Coll BA 16. **d** 16 **p** 17. NSM Westminster St Jas the Less *Lon* from 16. *3 Strutton Court, 54 Great Peter Street, London SW1P 2HH* T: (020) 7233 4027 M: 07834-611610

LAU, Paul Chow Sing. b 49. Nat Chengchi Univ BA 74 Chinese Univ of Hong Kong MDiv 80. **d** 80 **p** 81. C Hong Kong H Trin Hong Kong 80–82; V Macao St Mark Macao 82–83; P-in-c Hong Kong Ch of Our Sav Hong Kong 83–94; V Angl Chinese Miss Ch Dio Wellington NZ 94–01; Chapl Chinese Congregation *Lon* 01–19; rtd 19. *3 Strutton Court, 54 Great Peter Street, London SW1P 2HH* T: (020) 7233 4027

LAUCKNER, Averil Ann. b 55. Lanc Univ BSc 76. Ripon Coll Cuddesdon 03. **d** 04 **p** 05. C Royston *St Alb* 04–07; C Lich Ch Ch and Lich St Mich w St Mary and Wall 07–09; P-in-c Lich Ch Ch 09–11; P-in-c Hatfield Hyde *St Alb* 11–14; V 14–19; rtd 19; PtO *Birm* from 19. *28 Upper Clifton Road, Sutton Coldfield B73 6BP* E: averil.lauckner@btinternet.com

LAUENER (*née* MULLINER), **Angela Margaret.** b 54. Collingwood Coll Dur BSc 75 Sheff City Poly MSc 91 Sheff Hallam Univ PhD. Yorks Min Course 12. **d** 14 **p** 15. NSM Ranmoor *Sheff* 14–17; NSM Abbeydale and Millhouses from 17; Asst Bp's Adv in Spirituality from 15. *82 Pingle Road, Sheffield S7 2LL* T: 0114-236 2188 M: 07949-403992 E: angielauener@me.com or angela.lauener@sheffield.anglican.org

LAUNDERS-BROWN, Eleanor. b 71. St Mellitus Coll 19. **d** 21. C E Scarsdale *Derby* from 21. *5 Croft House Way, Bolsover, Chesterfield S44 6FF* M: 07720-775796 E: revellielb@gmail.com

LAUNDON, Timothy James. b 83. CCC Cam MA 07 SS Coll Cam BTh 11. Westcott Ho Cam 09. **d** 12 **p** 13. C Wetherby *Leeds* 12–16; Chapl Hants Hosps NHS Foundn Trust 16–17; NSM New Windsor *Ox* 18–19; V Ludgershall and Tidworth *Sarum* from 19. *The Rectory, 10 St James's Street, Ludgershall, Andover SP11 9QF* T: (01264) 393026 E: revtimlaundon@gmail.com

LAURENCE, The Ven John Harvard Christopher. b 29. Trin Hall Cam BA 53 MA 57. Westcott Ho Cam 53. **d** 55 **p** 56. C Linc St Nic w St Jo Newport 55–59; V Crosby 59–74; Can and Preb Linc Cathl 74–79 and 85–94; Dioc Missr 74–79; Bp's Dir of Clergy Tr *Lon* 80–85; Adn Lindsey Linc 85–94; rtd 94; PtO *Linc* 94–97. *5 Haffenden Road, Lincoln LN2 1RP* T: (01522) 531444

LAURENCE, John-Daniel. b 79. Mansf Coll Ox MPhys 02. Trin Coll Bris BA 09 MA 10. **d** 10 **p** 11. C Aberystwyth *St D* 10–15; TV 15–19; Tutor St Padarn's Inst from 19. *St Padarn's Institute, 54 Cardiff Road, Llandaff, Cardiff CF5 2YJ* E: jd.laurence@stpadarns.ac.uk

LAURENCE, Preb Julian Bernard Vere. b 60. Kent Univ BA 82. St Steph Ho Ox 86. **d** 88 **p** 89. C Yeovil St Mich *B & W* 88–91; Chapl Yeovil Coll 90–91; Chapl Yeovil Distr Hosp 91; P-in-c Barwick *B & W* 91–94; V Taunton H Trin from 94; Dioc Adv in Deliverance Min from 14; Preb Wells Cathl from 17. *Holy Trinity Vicarage, 15 The Square, Hillyfields, Taunton TA1 2LU* T: (01823) 354800 E: frjulianssc@gmail.com

LAURIE, Canon Donovan Hugh. b 40. Man Univ MSc. Oak Hill NSM Course. **d** 82 **p** 83. NSM Cudham and Downe *Roch* 82–84; C Tunbridge Wells St Jas 84–88; P-in-c Ventnor St Cath *Portsm* 88–99; V 99–04; P-in-c Ventnor H Trin 88–99; V 99–04; P-in-c Bonchurch 00–03; R 03–04; Hon Chapl St Cath Sch Ventnor 88–04; Hon Can Portsm Cathl 01–04; rtd 04; PtO *Roch* from 05. *39 Cleveland, Tunbridge Wells TN2 3NH* T: (01892) 539951 E: mail@dhl1524.plus.com

LAUT, Graham Peter. b 37. Chich Th Coll 63. **d** 67 **p** 68. C Corringham *Chelmsf* 67–68; C Leytonstone St Marg w St Columba 68–71; P-in-c Leytonstone St Andr 71–75; V 75–80; V Romford Ascension Collier Row 80–06; rtd 06; PtO *Chelmsf* from 07. *11 Archers Close, Billericay CM12 9YF* T: (01277) 630395 E: graham8470@gmail.com

LAUTENBACH, Edward Wayne. b 59. Univ Coll Ches BTh 04. St Paul's Coll Grahamstown 85. **d** 88 **p** 88. C Weltevredenpark St Mich S Africa 88–89; Asst P Florida St Gabr 89–91; Sen Asst P Bryanston St Mich 91–94; R Brakpan St Pet 94–99; P-in-c Grange St Andr Ches 99–04; P-in-c Runcorn H Trin 99–04; V Prenton 04–15; V Branksome St Aldhelm Sarum 15–16; Chapl R Berks NHS Foundn Trust 17; PtO Cov 17–18; P-in-c Hermitage 18–19; TR from 19. The Rectory, Yattendon, Thatcham RG18 0UR M: 07828-534655 E: waynelautenbach@gmail.com

LAUTENBACH, Mrs Glynnis Valerie. b 59. Leeds Univ BA 08. NOC 05. **d** 08 **p** 09. C Oxton Ches 08–15; PtO Sarum 15–16; P-in-c Burghfield Ox 17–18; R from 18. The Rectory, Hollybush Lane, Burghfield Common, Reading RG7 3JL T: 0118-983 2115 E: glynn.laut@gmail.com

LAVARELLO-SMITH, Mrs Lorna Mary. b 64. Qu Coll Birm 10. **d** 13 **p** 14. C Billing Pet 13–16; S Africa from 16. Address temp unknown E: lavarellosmith@gmail.com

LAVELLE, Elizabeth Mary Nicola. b 63. ERMC. **d** 16 **p** 17. NSM Welwyn Garden City St Alb 16–18; C 18–20; NSM from 20. 24 Cheviots, Hatfield AL10 8JT M: 07803-601162 E: lizlavelle01@gmail.com

LAVENDER, Christopher Piers. b 61. Ridley Hall Cam 08. **d** 10 **p** 11. C Headcorn and The Suttons Cant 10–13; P-in-c Allington and Maidstone St Pet from 13; P-in-c Barming Heath from 13; P-in-c Maidstone St Paul from 21; AD Maidstone from 20. The Rectory, Poplar Grove, Maidstone ME16 0DE T: (01622) 267307 M: 07910-442247 E: chris_piers@yahoo.com

LAVENDER, Mark Harley. b 70. Sheff Univ BSc 91 Univ Coll Lon PhD 95 Lon Inst of Educn PGCE 97. Ridley Hall Cam 14. **d** 16 **p** 17. C Crofton St Paul Roch 16–20; V Broadbridge Heath Chich from 20. St John's House, Church Road, Broadbridge Heath, Horsham RH12 3LD M: 07816-668153 E: revdoclav@hotmail.com

LAVERTY, Walter Joseph Robert. b 49. CITC 70 Glouc Th Course 73. **d** 73 **p** 74. C Belfast St Donard D & D 73–77; C Ballymacarrett St Patr 77–82; I Kilwarlin Upper w Kilwarlin Lower 82–86; I Orangefield w Braniel 86–14; Warden of Readers 96–14; Can Down Cathl 97–00; Preb Down Cathl 97–00; Treas Down Cathl 01–14; rtd 14. 6 Hanwood Heights, Dundonald, Belfast BT16 1XU T: (028) 9573 8743 E: barbaralaverty58@hotmail.com

LAVERY, Edward Robinson. Lon Univ BA. St Aid Birkenhead 65. **d** 67 **p** 68. C Belfast Trin Coll Miss Conn 67–69; C Belfast St Mary Magd 69–71; CF (TA) 70–95; OCM from 75; I Belfast St Phil Conn 71–74; I Craigs w Dunaghy and Killagan 74–83; I Ballymoney w Finvoy and Rasharkin 83–05; Dioc Info Officer 83–05; Can Conn Cathl 96–05; Treas Conn Cathl 98–01; Chan Conn Cathl 01–05; rtd 05; P-in-c Ballyscullion D & R 09–15. 11 Drumnamallaght Park, Ballymoney BT53 7QZ T: (028) 2766 9147 E: robin.lavery2@gmail.com

LAVIN, Alexandra Elizabeth. b 67. **d** 12 **p** 13. NSM Sheldon Birm 12–16; P-in-c 16–18; V Sheldon and Tile Cross from 18. St Thomas's Vicarage, Rotherfield Road, Birmingham B26 2SH T: 0121-384 5666 M: 07963-558242 E: alexpost@blueyonder.co.uk

LAW, Andrew Philip. b 61. BNC Ox BA 83 MA 93 G&C Coll Cam PGCE 86 Leic Univ MBA 04. WEMTC 90. **d** 93 **p** 94. C Tupsley w Hampton Bishop Heref 93–95; Chapl Heref Sixth Form Coll 94–95; Chapl City of Lon Freemen's Sch 95–97; LtO Guildf 95–97; Chapl and Hd RS Heref Cathl Sch 97–02; Chapl Malvern Coll 02–18; Ho Master 05–07; Fell Harris Manchester Coll Ox 13; PtO Heref 12; Worc from 18. 1 The Moorlands, Malvern WR14 4PS T: (01684) 563481 E: apl@malcol.org

LAW, David Richard. b 60. Keble Coll Ox BA 82 DD 15 Wolfs Coll Ox MA 89 DPhil 89. NOC 98 Predigerseminar Preetz Germany 99. **d** 01 **p** 02. NSM Ashton-upon-Mersey St Martin Ches 01–09; NSM Timperley 09–14; NSM Altrincham from 14. 2 Winston Close, Sale M33 6UG T: 0161-962 0297 E: david.r.law@manchester.ac.uk

LAW, Mrs Elizabeth Ann. b 49. Doncaster Coll of Educn CertEd 70 Loughb Univ MA 00. EAMTC 97. **d** 01 **p** 02. C Wickham Bishops w Lt Braxted Chelmsf 01–05; P-in-c Rattlesden w Thorpe Morieux, Brettenham etc St E 05–08; R 08–11; rtd 11; PtO St E 11–13; Hon C Gt Finborough w Onehouse, Harleston, Buxhall etc 13–15; Hon C Combs and Lt Finborough 13–15; Hon C Bildeston w Wattisham and Lindsey etc 15–17; Asst Dioc Dir of Ords 08–13; PtO from 18. 15 Manor Road, Bildeston, Ipswich IP7 7BG T: (01449) 740085 M: 07743-785282 E: rev.liz@btinternet.com

LAW, Jeremy Thomson. b 61. Univ of Wales (Abth) BSc 82 Southn Univ BTh 89 Ox Univ DPhil 00. Sarum & Wells Th Coll 84. **d** 87 **p** 88. C Wimborne Minster and Holt Sarum 87–90; C Highfield Ox 90–94; Chapl and Lect Ex Univ 94–03; Dean of Chpl Cant Ch Ch Univ from 03; PtO Roch from 13. Canterbury Christ Church University, North Holmes Road, Canterbury CT1 1QU T: (01227) 782747 E: jeremy.law@canterbury.ac.uk

LAW, John Francis. b 35. Bps' Coll Cheshunt 65. **d** 67 **p** 68. C Styvechale Cov 67–71; P-in-c Cov St Anne and All SS 71–73; TV Cov E 73–77; P-in-c Fillongley 77–82; P-in-c Corley 77–82; V Fillongley and Corley 82–00; RD Nuneaton 90–95; rtd 00; PtO Cov from 00. 10 Brodick Way, Nuneaton CV10 7LH T: (024) 7632 5582 E: johnflaw@sky.com

LAW, Canon John Michael. b 43. Open Univ BA 79. Westcott Ho Cam 65. **d** 68 **p** 69. C Chapel Allerton Ripon 68–72; C Ryhope Dur 72–73; Mental Health Chapl Fulbourn Hosp Cam 74–04; Chapl Ida Darwin Hosp Cam 74–96; Hon Can Ely Cathl 04–05; rtd 04; PV Ely Cathl 06–08; PtO from 08. 2 Suffolk Close, Ely CB6 3EW T: (01353) 659084

LAW, Nicholas Charles. b 58. Trin Coll Bris BA 89. **d** 89 **p** 90. C Goldington St Alb 89–92; C Teignmouth, Ideford w Luton, Ashcombe etc Ex 92–97; R Bere Ferrers from 97; RD Tavistock 11–20. The Rectory, Bere Alston, Yelverton PL20 7HH T: (01822) 840229 E: nick123law@gmail.com

LAW, Peter James. b 46. Ridley Hall Cam 85. **d** 87 **p** 88. C Bournemouth St Jo w St Mich Win 87–91; V Chineham 91–96; V Luton Lewsey St Hugh St Alb 96–11; rtd 11; PtO Portsm from 13; Guildf from 16; Win from 16. 7 Anmore Drive, Waterlooville PO7 6DY T: (023) 9226 8336 E: revpjl@btinternet.com

LAW, Richard Anthony Kelway. b 57. UWIST BEng 79. St Jo Coll Nottm MA(TS) 01 99. **d** 01 **p** 02. C Brundall w Braydeston and Postwick Nor 01–04; V Hollingworth w Tintwistle Ches 04–14; TV N Wingfield, Clay Cross and Pilsley Derby 14–20; rtd 20. Address temp unknown

LAW, Canon Robert Frederick. b 43. St Aid Birkenhead 67. **d** 69 **p** 70. C Bengeo St Alb 69–72; C Sandy 72–76; P-in-c St Ippolyts 76–81; Chapl Jersey Gp of Hosps 81–84; V Crowan w Godolphin Truro 84–92; RD Kerrier 90–91; R St Columb Major w St Wenn 92–02; RD Pydar 95–02; P-in-c St Minver 02–05; Hon Can Truro Cathl 98–05; rtd 05; PtO York from 07; Eur from 06. 24 Parkfield, Stillington, York YO61 1JW T: (01347) 810940 M: 07842-111525 E: robertlaw43@btinternet.com

LAW, Simon Anthony. b 55. Middx Univ BA 93 K Coll Lon MA 10. NTMTC 94. **d** 96 **p** 97. NSM Forest Gate St Mark Chelmsf 96–98; C Becontree W 98–99; TV 99–02; TR 02–07; V Becontree St Cedd 07–10; R Pitsea w Nevendon from 10. The Rectory, Rectory Road, Pitsea, Basildon SS13 2AA T: (01268) 556874 E: simon@revlaw.co.uk

LAW-JONES, Peter Deniston. b 55. Newc Univ BA 77 Nottm Univ BTh 87 Lanc Univ MA 03 Man Univ PGCE 81. Linc Th Coll 84. **d** 88 **p** 88. C Chorley St Laur Blackb 87–91; V Feniscliffe 91–96; V St Annes St Thos 96–13; AD Kirkham 09–13; Chapl Blackpool, Wyre and Fylde Community NHS Trust 97–04; TR Salter Street and Shirley Birm 13–17; V Shirley 17–20; rtd 20. 24 Clive Avenue, Lytham St Annes FY8 2RU M: 07902-580237 E: pljz1000@gmail.com

LAWAL, Miss Basirat Adebanke Amope (Ade). b 67. Lon Bible Coll BTh 02. SAOMC 03. **d** 05 **p** 06. C Blurton Lich 05–09; V Wyther Ripon 09–13; Racial Justice Officer 10–14; Leeds 14–15; Chapl Leeds Teaching Hosps NHS Trust 13–15; P-in-c Gillingham St Mary Roch 15–17; C Roch St Justus 17–21; PV Roch Cathl 17–21; C Roch St Pet w St Marg from 21; C Borstal from 21. 82 Hathaway Court, Esplanade, Rochester ME1 1QY

LAWES, Geoffrey Hyland. b 37. St Jo Coll Dur BA 58 Hertf Coll Ox BA 60 MA 64 Newc Univ PGCE 76 Med 79. Cranmer Hall Dur 61. **d** 63 **p** 64. C Millfield St Mark Dur 63–66; C Jarrow Grange 66–69; Hon C 69–86; Hd of RE Boldon Sch 71–88; Hd of Sixth Year 88–90; LtO Dur 86–90; V Collierley w Annfield Plain 90–05; rtd 05; Hon C Satley, Stanley and Tow Law Dur 05–06; PtO from 06. Netherwood, St Mary's Avenue, Crook DL15 9HY T: (01388) 766585 E: geofflawes@gmail.com

LAWES, Jonathan Mark. b 90. St Jo Coll Cam MEng 12 Middx Univ BA 21. Oak Hill Th Coll 18. **d** 21. C Laleham Lon from 21. 251 Staines Road, Staines-upon-Thames TW18 2RS M: 07850-815780 E: johnny.lawes@allsaintslaleham.org.uk

LAWES, Matthew James. b 86. Trin Coll Ox MMath 08. Oak Hill Th Coll 17. **d** 20 **p** 21. C Fulwood Sheff from 20. 23 Hallamshire Close, Sheffield S10 4FJ M: 07964-096501 E: mjlawes@gmail.com

LAWES, Timothy Stanley. b 57. Nottm Univ BTh 88. Linc Th Coll 85. **d** 88 **p** 89. C Wymondham Nor 88–92; R Felmingham, Skeyton, Colby, Banningham etc 92–96; Sweden 96–12; Asst V Byske 98–09; TR Skelleftea Landsforsamling 11–12; V Swaffham and Sporle Nor 12–16;

Sweden from 16. *Vintergatan 69A, 932 32 Skelleftehamn, Sweden* E: timothylawes@hotmail.com

LAWLESS, Mrs Patricia Elizabeth. b 36. Bris Univ BA 58 PGCE 59. S Dios Minl Tr Scheme 91. **d** 93 **p** 94. NSM Frome Ch Ch *B & W* 93–95; NSM Mells w Buckland Dinham, Elm, Whatley etc 96; NSM Frome St Jo and St Mary 96–00; Chapl Victoria Hosp Frome 96–98; rtd 00; PtO *B & W* from 00. *22 Braithwaite Way, Frome BA11 2XG* T: (01373) 466106

LAWLEY, Peter Gerald Fitch. b 52. Chich Th Coll 77. **d** 80 **p** 81. C Pet St Jo 80–83; C Daventry 83–87; P-in-c Syresham w Whitfield 87–90; TV Cen Telford *Lich* 90–98; V Priors Lee and St Georges' 98–12; rtd 12; PtO *Lich* 13–20. *11 Kingsley Drive, Muxton, Telford TF2 8DH* T: (01952) 606160 E: peterlawley12@gmail.com

LAWLEY, Rosemary Ann. b 47. WMMTC 00. **d** 03 **p** 04. NSM Kinver and Enville *Lich* 03–07; TV Kidderminster St Mary and All SS w Trimpley etc *Worc* 07–15; TR Kidderminster Ismere 15–18; Ind Chapl 07–18; Hon Can Worc Cathl 15–18; rtd 18; PtO *Worc* from 19; *Heref* from 19. *Almain, Bridgnorth Road, Highley, Bridgnorth WV16 6HE* T: (01746) 862301 E: rosemarylawley@gmail.com

LAWLOR, Anne Louise. b 61. UEA BEd 83 Surrey Univ Roehampton BA 02 Lucy Cavendish Coll Cam BTh 12. Westcott Ho Cam 10. **d** 12 **p** 13. C Everton St Pet w St Chrys *Liv* 12–16; Chapl Liv Women's NHS Foundn Trust 16–17; TV Kirkby *Liv* from 17. *9 Redwood Way, Liverpool L33 4DU* T: 0151-548 0962 M: 07904-346101 E: annelawlor92@yahoo.co.uk

LAWLOR, Colin Robert. b 63. Lanc Univ BA 89 MPhil 97 St Martin's Coll Lanc PGCE 90. Chich Th Coll 90. **d** 93 **p** 94. C Moulsecoomb *Chich* 93–97; TV 97–99; Chapl Brighton Univ 99–18; P-in-c Stanmer w Falmer 13–18; V Waterlooville *Portsm* from 18; Asst Dir of Ords from 20. *The Vicarage, 5 Deanswood Drive, Waterlooville PO7 7RR* M: 07733-225263

LAWLOR, Paul. b 60. Nottm Univ BSc 82. St Jo Coll Nottm 06. **d** 08 **p** 09. C Warsop *S'well* 08–11; TV Redditch H Trin *Worc* from 11; RD Bromsgrove 16–21; AD Redditch and Bromsgrove from 21. *The Vicarage, 219 St George's Road, Redditch B98 8EE* T: (01527) 62375 M: 07807-611090 E: paul@pjlawlor.me.uk

LAWRANCE, Robert William. b 63. Jes Coll Ox BA 85 MA 89 Man Univ MA 93. Ripon Coll Cuddesdon BA 87. **d** 88 **p** 89. C Astley *Man* 88–91; Lect Bolton St Pet 91–94; V Bury St Jo w St Mark 94–00; Chapl Bury Healthcare NHS Trust 95–00; Dir of Ords *Dur* 00–08; Chapl Hatf Coll Dur 00–05; Chapl Collingwood Coll Dur 05–08; TR Dur N 08–15; AD Dur 10–15; Hon Can Dur Cathl 10–15; Hon Chapl Dur and Darlington Fire and Rescue Brigade 09–15; V Newc St Fran from 15; AD Newc E from 17. *St Francis Vicarage, 66 Cleveland Gardens, Newcastle upon Tyne NE7 7QH* T: 0191-266 1071 E: robert.lawrance@newcastle.anglican.org

LAWRENCE, Mrs Anastasia Jane. b 63. Cam Coll of Art & Tech GMus 85 Kingston Poly PGCE 86. St Jo Coll Nottm 14. **d** 17 **p** 18. C Albrighton, Boningale and Donington *Lich* 17–20; P-in-c Street w Walton and Compton Dundon *B & W* 20; R from 20. *The Rectory, Vestry Close, Street BA16 0HZ* T: (01458) 841373 M: 07708-050310 E: revanalawrence@gmail.com

LAWRENCE, Anthony Christian. b 71. St Steph Ho Ox 19. **d** 21. C Ventnor St Cath *Portsm* from 21; C Ventnor H Trin from 21; C Bonchurch from 21. *The Vicarage, 55 Clarence Road, Wroxall, Ventnor PO38 3BY* T: (01983) 852532 M: 07753-523797 E: fr.tonylawrence@outlook.com *or* tonyschickens@btinternet.com

LAWRENCE, Charles Anthony Edwin. b 53. AKC 75. St Aug Coll Cant 75. **d** 76 **p** 77. C Mitcham St Mark *S'wark* 76–80; C Haslemere *Guildf* 80–82; P-in-c Ashton H Trin *Man* 82–84; V 84–93; AD Ashton-under-Lyne 91–93; V Saddleworth 93–97; V Effingham w Lt Bookham *Guildf* 97–05; Chapl Manor Ho Sch 97–05; R Shere, Albury and Chilworth *Guildf* 05–09; R Northfield *Birm* 09–15; rtd 15; PtO *Birm* 15–20; *Heref* from 17. *The Heath, Munslow, Craven Arms SY7 9ET* T: (01584) 841862 E: fathercharles@hotmail.co.uk

LAWRENCE, Canon David Ian. b 48. Univ Coll Lon BSc 74 AIMLS 71 MRSB 76. Glouc Sch of Min 84 Sarum & Wells Th Coll 87. **d** 88 **p** 89. C Wotton St Mary *Glouc* 88–91; P-in-c Cheltenham St Mich 91–93; V 93–06; V Coleford, Staunton, Newland, Redbrook etc 06–11; Hon Can Glouc Cathl 06–11; rtd 12; PtO *Sarum* 12–22. *14 Clappentail Park, Lyme Regis DT7 3NB* T: (01297) 442140

LAWRENCE, Isaac Sartaj. b 72. Peshawar Univ BSc 95 Philippine Chr Univ MBA 97. Lich Th Coll 06. **d** 08 **p** 09. C Ripon H Trin 08–12; V Scotby and Cotehill w Cumwhinton *Carl* from 12. *The Vicarage, Lambley Bank, Scotby, Carlisle CA4 8BX* T: (01228) 513205 M: 07588-646918 E: revisaac.lawrence@gmail.com

LAWRENCE, James Andrew. b 87. Leeds Univ BA 05. Yorks Min Course 13. **d** 16 **p** 17. C Otley *Leeds* 16–19. *9 Bransdale Close, London NW6 4QH* M: 07545-211776 E: revjimmylawrence@gmail.com

LAWRENCE, James Conrad. b 62. St Jo Coll Dur BA 85. Ridley Hall Cam 85. **d** 87 **p** 88. Min Bar Hill LEP *Ely* 87–92; Min Bar Hill 92–93; Deanery Adv in Evang 90–93; CPAS Evang 93–98; PtO *Cov* from 93; Springboard Missr from 97; CPAS Dir Evang Projects from 99; LtO *Cov* from 21. *20 Cotton Mill Spinney, Cubbington, Leamington Spa CV32 7XH* T: (01926) 426761 *or* 334242 F: 337613 E: jlawrence@cpas.org.uk

LAWRENCE, John Graham Clive. b 47. ACIB. Trin Coll Bris. **d** 78 **p** 79. C Chatham St Phil and St Jas *Roch* 78–83; V Roch St Justus 83–97; Asst Chapl HM Pris Roch 83–97; UK Dir CMJ 97–00; Internat Co-ord Light to the Nations UK 00–10; Chapl Maidstone and Tunbridge Wells NHS Trust 03–04; Chapl W Kent NHS and Soc Care Trust 05–06; Chapl Kent and Medway NHS and Soc Care Partnership Trust 06–08; Chapl Team Ldr Bucks Healthcare NHS Trust 08–10; rtd 10. *55 Elmshurst Gardens, Tonbridge TN10 3QT* T: (01732) 490549 M: 07984-951534 E: jgcl138@gmail.com

LAWRENCE, Mrs Judith Patricia. b 53. WEMTC 01. **d** 04 **p** 05. C Glastonbury w Meare *B & W* 04–09; PtO 09–11; Chapl Somerset Community Health NHS Trust 10–11; Chapl Somerset Partnership NHS Foundn Trust 10–11; Asst Chapl Taunton and Somerset NHS Foundn Trust 10–11; Chapl 11–18; rtd 18. *12 Glanvill Road, Street BA16 0TN* T: (01458) 445451 E: j.lawrence123@btinternet.com

LAWRENCE, Canon Katherine Anne. b 75. Cranmer Hall Dur 14. **d** 16 **p** 17. C Win Cathl 16–19; Can Wellington NZ from 19. *12 Eccleston Hill, Thorndon, Wellington 6011, New Zealand* E: canon@wellingtoncathedral.org.nz

LAWRENCE, Leslie. b 44. S'wark Ord Course 86. **d** 88 **p** 89. NSM Stanwell *Lon* 88–92; C Hounslow H Trin w St Paul 92–97; P-in-c Norwood St Mary 97–06; R 06–09; rtd 09; PtO *Lon* from 11. *22 Chestnut Road, Ashford TW15 1DG* T: (01784) 241773 E: leslielawrencestd@googlemail.com

LAWRENCE, Lorraine Margaret. b 58. Open Univ BA 08. SEITE 08. **d** 11 **p** 12. NSM Gravesend St Geo *Roch* 11–15; C Wye *Cant* from 15. *The Vicarage, Pilgrims Way, Hastingleigh, Ashford TN25 5HP* T: (01233) 750987 M: 07894-034409 E: lorraine_lawrence@btinternet.com

LAWRENCE, Canon Patrick Henry Andrew. b 51. TCD Div Test 79 BA 81. **d** 81 **p** 82. C Templemore *D & R* 81–84; C Kilkenny St Canice Cathl *C, F & O* 84–85; I Templebreedy w Tracton and Nohoval *C, C & R* 85–92; I Geashill w Killeigh and Ballycommon *M & K* 92–98; Can Kildare Cathl 92–09; Adn Kildare 93–09; Adn Meath 97–09; Warden of Readers 97–09; I Julianstown and Colpe w Drogheda and Duleek 98–09; I Monkstown *D & G* 09–15; Preb Monmohenock St Patr Cathl Dublin 00–12; Chan St Patr Cathl Dublin 12–15; Chapl St Vincent's Univ Hosp Dublin 15–17; rtd 17. *Sidebrook House, Rochfortbridge, Mullingar, Co Westmeath, N91 Y327, Republic of Ireland* T: (00353) (44) 922 2109 M: (00353) 86-056 2944

LAWRENCE, Canon Peter Anthony. b 36. Lich Th Coll 67. **d** 69 **p** 70. C Oadby *Leic* 69–74; P-in-c Northmarston and Granborough *Ox* 74–81; P-in-c Hardwick St Mary 74–81; P-in-c Quainton 76–81; P-in-c Oving w Pitchcott 76–81; TR Schorne 81–91; RD Claydon 84–88; V Ivinghoe w Pitstone and Slapton 91–97; Hon Can Ch Ch 97; rtd 97; PtO *Ox* 99–07; *Worc* from 01. *Hill House, Back Lane, Malvern WR14 2HJ* T: (01684) 564075 E: peter.molly2@waitrose.com

LAWRENCE (née MASON), Sarah Catherine. b 79. K Coll Lon BA 02 PGCE 03 Chu Coll Cam MPhil 06 Birm Univ PhD 17. Ridley Hall Cam 05. **d** 08 **p** 10. NSM Carr Dyke Gp *Linc* 08–10; C Shifnal and Sheriffhales *Lich* 10–13; C Tong 11–13; PtO *Linc* 16–19; Officer for IME from 18. *Address withheld by request* T: (01522) 729190 M: 07766-348170 E: revsarahlawrence@btinternet.com *or* sarah.lawrence@lincoln.anglican.org

LAWRENCE, Canon Simon Peter. b 60. TD. Nottm Univ BTh 88 MA 97 Indiana State Univ DMin 01. St Jo Coll Nottm 85. **d** 88 **p** 89. C Holbeach *Linc* 88–90; C Alford w Rigsby 90–91; R Rattlesden w Thorpe Morieux and Brettenham *St E* 91–93; V Churchdown *Glouc* 93; V Maenclochog w Henry's Moat and Mynachlogddu etc *St D* 93–94; R Overstrand, Northrepps, Sidestrand etc *Nor* 95–98; CF (TA) 89–05; CF (ACF) 90–05; PtO *Nor* 02–06; Public Preacher 06–07; R Stalham, E Ruston, Brunstead, Sutton and Ingham 07–21; P-in-c Smallburgh w Dilham w Honing and Crostwight 16–18; R 18–21; RD St Benet 12–19; Dioc Chapl MU 11–19; Hon Can Nor Cathl 17–21. *Rosalida, Happisburgh, Norwich NR12 0PN* E: simon.stalham@btinternet.com

LAWRENCE (née FOREMAN), Mrs Vanessa Jane. b 73. Ch Ch Coll Cant BA 95. Westcott Ho Cam. **d** 00 **p** 01. C

N Stoneham *Win* 00–04; NSM Swaythling 04–07; NSM Chilworth w N Baddesley 07–10; NSM Ampfield 08–10; NSM Ampfield, Chilworth and N Baddesley from 10; Chapl S Health NHS Foundn Trust from 09. *164 Botley Road, North Baddesley, Southampton SO52 9EE* T: (023) 8073 6671 E: vanessalawrence@btconnect.com

LAWRENCE, Victor John. b 43. ACII. Oak Hill Th Coll. d 83 p 84. C Paddock Wood *Roch* 83–87; R Milton next Gravesend w Denton 87–09; RD Gravesend 05–09; rtd 09. *5 Riplingham, 41 Gaudick Road, Eastbourne BN20 7LW* E: victorjlaw@googlemail.com

LAWRENCE-MARCH, David Lawrence. b 61. Univ of Wales (Lamp) BA 83. Coll of Resurr Mirfield 83. d 85 p 86. C Pet St Jude 85–89; Chapl St Aug Sch Kilburn 89–92; C Kilburn St Aug w St Jo *Lon* 89–90; C Paddington St Mary 90–92; Chapl Bearwood Coll Wokingham 92–96; R Holt w High Kelling *Nor* 96–98; Sen Chapl Bedford Sch 98–09; Chapl Ardingly Coll 09–17; PtO *Lon* 14–17; P-in-c Shanklin St Sav *Portsm* 17–20; P-in-c Lake 17–20; V Long Eaton St Laur *Derby* from 20; P-in-c Ilkeston H Trin from 20. *St Lawrence Vicarage, Regent Street, Long Eaton, Nottingham NG10 1JX* E: fatherdlm@icloud.com

LAWRENSON, Ronald David. b 41. CITC 68. d 71 p 72. C Seapatrick *D & D* 71–78; Min Can Down Cathl 78–79; V Choral Belf Cathl 79–86; Bp's C Tynan w Middletown and Aghavilly *Arm* 86–90 and 91–93; Hon V Choral Arm Cathl 87–02; Bp's C Tynan w Middletown 92–93; I Donaghmore w Donaghmore Upper 93–98; rtd 02. *Riverbrook Apartments, 5 Brooklands Drive, Whitehead, Carrickfergus BT38 9SL* T: (028) 9337 3625

LAWRINSON, Leslie Norman. b 35. IEng MCIPD 90 MCMI 84. d 99 p 00. OLM Onchan *S & M* 99–05; NSM Scarisbrick *Liv* 05–08; rtd 08; PtO *S & M* from 09. *8 Hillary Wharf Apartments, South Quay, Douglas, Isle of Man IM1 5BL* T: (01624) 627664 M: 07749-687469

LAWRY, Richard Henry. b 57. Bris Univ BA 79 Wolfs Coll Cam PGCE 81. St Jo Coll Nottm MA 01. d 99 p 00. C Macclesfield Team *Ches* 99–02; P-in-c Stalybridge St Paul 02–06; V 06–09; V Norbury 09–19; R Blakeney w Cley, Wiveton, Glandford etc *Nor* from 19; RD Holt from 20; RD Repps from 20. *The Rectory, Back Lane, Blakeney, Holt NR25 7NP* T: (01263) 740686 E: revrichardlawry@gmail.com

LAWS, Clive Loudon. b 54. UEA BEd 76 Leeds Univ CertEd 75. Wycliffe Hall Ox 79. d 82 p 83. C Newcastle w Butterton *Lich* 82–85; C Gabalfa *Llan* 85–88; R Pendine w Llanmiloe and Eglwys Gymyn w Marros *St D* 89–94; CF 89–94; PtO *B & W* 95–96; C Portishead 96–02; TV 02–08; P-in-c High Laver w Magdalen Laver and Lt Laver etc *Chelmsf* 08–10; Chapl St Clare Hospice 08–10; rtd 10. *36 Alexandra Close, Illogan, Redruth TR16 4RS* T: (01209) 843117 E: clive_anne@yahoo.co.uk

LAWSON, Canon Alma Felicity. b 51. St Hugh's Coll Ox BA 73 MA 78. St Jo Coll Nottm. d 98 p 99. Dean of Min and Dir of Ords *Wakef* 93–00; Hon C Wakef Cathl 98–00; V Gildersome 00–14; *Leeds* 14–17; RD Birstall 10–14; P-in-c Drighlington 12–17; Hon Can Wakef Cathl 01–17; rtd 17. *23 Banks Bridge Close, Barnoldswick BB18 6YP* E: felicity.lawson@outlook.com

LAWSON, Anne. *See* LAWSON, Sarah Anne

LAWSON, Canon David McKenzie. b 47. Glas Univ MA 69 Edin Univ BD 76. Edin Th Coll 73. d 76 p 77. C Glas St Mary 76–82; V Keighley All SS *Bradf* 82–85; Chapl Asst Univ Coll Hosp Lon 85–91; Hon C St Pancras w St Jas and Ch Ch *Lon* 86–91; R Smithfield St Bart Gt 91–93; Hon C Buckingham St Jas 94–00; TV Chambersbury *St Alb* 00–03; TR 03–09; TR Langelei 09–17; RD Hemel Hempstead 08–15; Hon Can St Alb 12–17; rtd 18; PtO *St Alb* from 18. *8 Nightingale Lodge, Cowper Road, Berkhamsted HP4 3ED* T: (01442) 872158 M: 07939-473717 E: davidmlawson@btinternet.com

LAWSON, Felicity. *See* LAWSON, Alma Felicity

LAWSON, Gary Austin. b 53. Man Univ BA 80. Ripon Coll Cuddesdon 80. d 82 p 83. C Nunhead St Antony *S'wark* 82–86; Hon C Reddish *Man* 86–87; Hon C Longsight St Jo w St Cypr 87–88; V Wythenshawe St Rich 88–98; Chapl Bolton Inst of F&HE 98–03; C Bolton St Pet 98–03; TR Westhoughton and Wingates 03–13; C Daisy Hill 11–13; TR Daisy Hill, Westhoughton and Wingates 13–14; rtd 14. *4 Brookfold Road, Stockport SK4 5EJ* T: 0161-442 7970 E: garyaustinlawson@btinternet.com

LAWSON, James Barry. b 68. Edin Univ MA 91 New Coll Ox DPhil 96. Coll of Resurr Mirfield 98. d 99 p 00. C Poplar *Lon* 99–02; Chapl CCC Cam 02–07; Bp's Sen Chapl *Sarum* 07–08; V Stoke Newington Common St Mich *Lon* 09–17; Vice-Prin St Steph Ho Ox 17–19; PtO *Lon* 20–21; V Enfield Chase St Mary from 21; Dir Ords Edmonton Area from 21. *30 The Ridgeway, Enfield EN2 8QH*

LAWSON, Canon John Alexander. b 62. Sheff Univ BA 84 Nottm Univ MA 97 PhD 06. St Jo Coll Nottm 85. d 87 p 88. C Wellington All SS w Eyton *Lich* 87–92; TV Dewsbury *Wakef* 92–98; P-in-c Birchencliffe 98–05; Dioc Vocations Adv and Asst Dir of Ords 02–05; Can Res Wakef Cathl 05–19; Dioc Dir Tr 05–16; Warden Wakef Min Scheme 06–08; Prin Mirfield Hub Leeds Sch of Min from 16; Hon Can Wakef Cathl *Leeds* from 19. *St Giles's Vicarage, 9 The Mount, Pontefract WF8 1NE* M: 07816-502014 E: john.lawson@leeds.anglican.org

LAWSON, Jonathan Halford. b 68. St Chad's Coll Dur BA 90 Heythrop Coll Lon MA 04. Westcott Ho Cam 91. d 93 p 94. C Sedgefield *Dur* 93–96; C Usworth 96–97; TV 97–00; TV Epping Distr *Chelmsf* 00–04; Chapl St Hild and St Bede Coll *Dur* 04–14; V Newc St Gabr from 14. *St Gabriel's Vicarage, 9 Holderness Road, Newcastle upon Tyne NE6 5RH* T: 0191-908 7835 E: vicarofheaton@gmail.com

LAWSON, Canon June Margaret. b 62. Birm Univ BA 83 Didsbury Coll of Educn PGCE 84 St Jo Coll York MA 02. NOC 00. d 02 p 03. C Huddersfield H Trin *Wakef* 02–05; Dir Adult Chr Educn Mirfield Cen 05–08; Dir Mirfield Cen 08–19; PV Wakef Cathl *Leeds* 05–19; Dean of Women's Min *Wakef* 09–14; *Leeds* 14–19; Clergy Development Officer Wakefield Area 17–19; AD Wakef 17–19; V Pontefract from 19; Hon Can Wakef Cathl from 17. *St Giles's Vicarage, 9 The Mount, Pontefract WF8 1NE* E: june.lawson@leeds.anglican.org

LAWSON, Mrs Katherine Ellen. b 53. SEITE 11. d 14 p 15. NSM Hove All SS *Chich* 14–17; NSM Saltdean from 17. *Moray Cottage, 31 Oaklands Avenue, Saltdean, Brighton BN2 8LQ* T: (01273) 709330 M: 07878-959327 E: rev.kate.lawson@gmail.com

LAWSON, Matthew James. b 67. St Andr Univ MTheol 91 FRSA 02. Ripon Coll Cuddesdon MTh 94. d 94 p 95. C Bedford St Andr *St Alb* 94–97; Chapl and Hd RS St Jo Sch Leatherhead 97–07; Tutor Dioc Min Course *Guildf* 98; Chapl Hurstpierpoint Coll 07–10. *54 Hipwell Court, Olney MK46 5QB* M: 07768-515950 E: frlawson@aol.com

LAWSON, The Ven Michael Charles. b 52. Sussex Univ BA 75. Trin Coll Bris 75. d 78 p 79. C Horsham *Chich* 78–81; C St Marylebone All So w SS Pet and Jo *Lon* 81–87; V Bromley Ch Ch *Roch* 87–99; Adn Hampstead *Lon* 99–10; R Guildf St Sav 10–12; rtd 12; Chapl HM Pris Littlehey from 13; PtO *Ely* from 13. *HM Prison Littlehey, Perry, Huntingdon PE28 0SR* T: (01480) 335252 E: venmlawson@gmail.com *or* michael.lawson@justice.gov.uk

LAWSON, Penelope Ann. b 54. d 16. NSM Bishopsnympton, Charles, E Anstey, High Bray etc *Ex* from 16. *Bottreaux Mill Farm, Bottreaux Mill, South Molton EX36 3PS* T: (01398) 341278 E: plawson@btconnect.com

LAWSON, Miss Sarah Anne. b 66. Ches Coll of HE BA 87 Univ of Wales MA 12. Ridley Hall Cam. d 00 p 01. C Hollingworth w Tintwistle *Ches* 00–05; V Haslington w Crewe Green 05–14; V Acton and Worleston, Church Minshull etc from 14. *St Mary's Vicarage, Chester Road, Acton, Nantwich CW5 8LG* T: (01270) 628864 E: revanne@uwclub.net *or* crosscountryparishes@outlook.com

LAWSON-JONES, Christopher Mark. b 68. Open Univ BA 98 Ripon Coll Cuddesdon MA 17. St Mich Coll Llan 98. d 00 p 01. C Risca *Mon* 00–03; Chapl Cross Keys Campus Coleg Gwent 00–03; TV Cyncoed 03–06; Dioc Soc Resp Officer 04–06; P-in-c Magor 06–09; TR 09–12; TR Cyncoed 12–17; AD Bassaleg 12–17; Chapl Miss to Seafarers S Wales Ports from 17. *55 William Belcher Drive, St Mellons, Cardiff CF3 0NZ* M: 07540-793653 E: marklawsonjones@gmail.com

LAWTON, Christopher. *See* LAWTON, Robin David Christopher

LAWTON, Capt Christopher Michael. b 65. Wilson Carlile Coll 89 St Padarn's Inst BA 21. d 21. C Aber-Morfa Miss Area *St As* from 21. *The Vicarage, 7 Parc Gwellyn, Kinmel Bay, Rhyl LL18 5HN* T: (01745) 331891 M: 07527-311025 E: clawton106@btinternet.com *or* christopherlawton@churchinwales.org.uk

LAWTON, Donald John William. b 48. Huron Coll Ontario BMin 77. d 77 p 78. I Elsa Mayo Canada 77–80; C Ch Ch Cathl Whitehorse 80–13; C Eastling w Ospringe and Stalisfield w Otterden *Cant* 13–14; C Selling w Throwley, Sheldwich w Badlesmere etc 13–14; V High Downs 14–17; Co-Warden of Readers 14–17; rtd 17. *PO Box 612, Garibaldi Highlands, BC V0N 1T0, Canada* E: donaldjlawton@gmail.com

LAWTON, Robin David Christopher. b 73. St Jo Coll Dur BATM 14. Cranmer Hall Dur 12. d 14 p 15. C Leyburn w Bellerby *Leeds* 14–17; P-in-c Crakehall 17–18; P-in-c Hornby 17–18; P-in-c Patrick Brompton and Hunton 17–18; P-in-c Spennithorne w Finghall and Hauxwell 17–18; R Lower Wensleydale from 18. *The Vicarage,*

Patrick Brompton, Bedale DL8 1JN T: (01677) 450920
E: chris.lawton@leeds.anglican.org

LAWTON, Siân Lesley. b 77. St Jo Coll Dur BA 15. St Mellitus
Coll MA 19. **d** 19 **p** 20. C Masham and Healey *Leeds* from
19; C W Tanfield and Well w Snape and N Stainley from 19.
The Vicarage, Patrick Brompton, Bedale DL8 1JN T: (01677)
450920 M: 07583-874203 E: revsianlawton@gmail.com

LAXON, Canon Colin John. b 44. FRSA. Cant Sch of Min 86.
d 89 **p** 90. C Folkestone St Mary and St Eanswythe *Cant*
89–94; P-in-c Barrow St Jas *Carl* 94–01; Soc Resp Officer
01–09; C Brampton and Farlam and Castle Carrock w
Cumrew 01–02; TV Eden, Gelt and Irthing 02–06; C Carl
St Cuth w St Mary 06–09; Hon Can Carl Cathl 06–09;
rtd 09; PtO *Carl* 09–13. *15 Knowefield Avenue, Carlisle
CA3 9BQ* T: (01228) 544215 E: c.laxon@btinternet.com

LAY, Mrs Alison Margaret. b 57. **d** 07 **p** 09. OLM Needham
Market w Badley *St E* 07–08; OLM Combs and Lt
Finborough 08–12; PtO from 12. *Hideaway, Park Road,
Needham Market, Ipswich IP6 8BH* T: (01449) 721115
E: alidivineone@gmail.com

LAY, Geoffrey Arthur. b 54. Leic Poly BA 77 Man Univ MA 83
Lon Univ BD 88. Ridley Hall Cam 90. **d** 92 **p** 93. C St Neots
Ely 92–95; P-in-c Long Stanton w St Mich 95–01; P-in-c Dry
Drayton 95–97; R Chailey *Chich* 01–06; Chapl Chailey
Heritage Hosp Lewes 01–06; rtd 06; PtO *Chich* 12–17. *77 Firle
Road, Peacehaven BN10 7QH* T: (01273) 588048

LAYBOURNE, Teresa Margaret. *See* WALTON, Teresa Margaret

LAYFIELD, Mrs Vanessa Denise. b 63. Salford Univ
BA 10 Staffs Univ DipSW 05. All SS Cen for Miss &
Min 18. **d** 20. NSM Nantwich *Ches* from 20. *Tower
Barn, Lyneal, Ellesmere SY12 0QG* M: 07984-318885
E: vanessadlayfield@gmail.com

LAYNESMITH, Mark David. b 74. York Univ BA 97 MA 99.
Ripon Coll Cuddesdon BA 01. **d** 02 **p** 03. C Tadcaster w
Newton Kyme *York* 02–05; Chapl Reading Univ *Ox* from 05;
PtO from 19. *30 Shinfield Road, Reading RG2 7BW* T: 0118-
987 1495

LAYTON, Miss Norene. b 39. Trin Coll Bris 84. dss 86
d 87 **p** 94. Lindfield *Chich* 86–92; Par Dn 87–92; Par Dn
Loughborough Em *Leic* 92–94; C Loughborough Em and
St Mary in Charnwood 94–96; V Hengrove *Bris* 96–04;
rtd 04; PtO *Leic* 14–18. *104 Outwoods Drive, Loughborough
LE11 3LU* T: (01509) 218127

LAYZELL, Martyn Paul. b 75. Wycliffe Hall Ox 08. **d** 10 **p** 11.
C Onslow Square and S Kensington St Aug *Lon* 10–20; V
Battersea Rise St Mark *S'wark* from 20. *St Mark's Church,
Battersea Rise, London SW11 1EJ* M: 07891-015221 *or* 07702-
968022 E: martyn.layzell@smbr.church

LAZENBY, Caroline. b 49. SCTEI 16. **d** 19 **p** 20. OLM
N Holmwood *Guildf* from 19. *96 Dukes Ride, North
Holmwood, Dorking RH5 4UA* T: (01306) 640208
E: caroline.lazenby254@gmail.com

LE BAS, Canon Jennifer Anne. b 60. Hull Univ BSc 81 Univ
of Wales (Lamp) MA 06. S Dios Minl Tr Scheme 90. **d** 93
p 94. C Alverstoke *Portsm* 93–96; C Elson 97–01; P-in-c
Gosport Ch Ch and Dioc FE Officer 01–04; PtO *Roch* 05–06;
P-in-c Seal SS Pet and Paul 06–12; V from 12; RD Sevenoaks
from 21; Hon Can Roch Cathl from 19. *The Vicarage,
Church Street, Seal, Sevenoaks TN15 0AR* M: 07510-522292
E: sealpandp@gmail.com

LE BILLON, Mrs Janet. b 42. STETS 99. **d** 02 **p** 03. NSM
Guernsey St Jo *Win* 02–06; NSM Guernsey Ste Marie du
Castel 06–09; NSM Guernsey St Matt 06–09; PtO from 09;
Chapl Princess Eliz Hosp Guernsey 02–17. *Tranquillité, Clos
des Quatre Vents, St Martin, Guernsey GY4 6SU* T: (01481)
234283 E: revjanleb@gmail.com

LE BRUN POWELL, Edward Llywelyn. Univ of Wales
(Trin St Dav) BD 12 Cardiff Univ MTh 16. St Mich Coll
Llan 13. **d** 16 **p** 17. C Milford Haven *St D* 16–17; C
Llandaff *Llan* 17–19; C Eglwysilan and Caerphilly 19–20;
TV 20–21; V Cov St Mary from 21. *Address temp unknown*
E: fatheredward.25@gmail.com

LE COUTEUR, Tracy. *See* BROMLEY, Tracy Le Couteur

LE GRYS, Alan Arthur. b 51. K Coll Lon BD 73 AKC 73
MTh 90. St Aug Coll Cant 73. **d** 74 **p** 75. C Harpenden St Jo
St Alb 74–77; C Hampstead St Jo *Lon* 77–81; Chapl Westf
Coll and Bedf Coll 81–83; V Stoneleigh *Guildf* 84–91; Lect
Ripon Coll Cuddesdon 91–96; Prin SEITE 96–05; Hon PV
Roch Cathl from 96; PtO from 06; *Chich* from 15. *2 Blenheim
Avenue, Chatham ME4 6UU* T: (01634) 814298 M: 07958-
547053 E: a.legrys@btinternet.com

LE ROSSIGNOL, Richard Lewis. b 52. Aston Univ BSc 75.
Oak Hill Th Coll BA 79. **d** 79 **p** 80. C E Ham St Paul *Chelmsf*
79–81; C Willesborough w Hinxhill *Cant* 81–85; PtO
85–94; NSM Brabourne w Smeeth 94–01; NSM Mersham
w Hinxhill and Sellindge 01–06; NSM Smeeth w Monks

Horton and Stowting and Brabourne 06–07; P-in-c 07–14;
P-in-c Mersham w Hinxhill and Sellindge 07–14; V A20
Benefice 14–17; rtd 17; PtO *Cant* from 18. *Stanelaw, Station
Road, St Margarets-at-Cliffe, Dover CT15 6AY* T: (01304)
853155 E: rller@btinternet.com

LE SÈVE, Mrs Jane Hilary. b 63. SS Hild & Bede Coll Dur BA 86.
EAMTC 01. **d** 04 **p** 05. NSM Brightlingsea *Chelmsf* 04–08; TV
Greenstead w Colchester St Anne 08–15; P-in-c Wickham
Bishops w Lt Braxted from 15; Asst Dir of Ords from 15. *The
Rectory, 1 Church Road, Wickham Bishops, Witham CM8 3LA*
E: revhilary@btinternet.com

LE SUEUR, Paul John. b 38. Lon Univ BSc 59. Wycliffe
Hall Ox 60. **d** 62 **p** 63. C Mortlake w E Sheen *S'wark*
62–65; C Witney Ox 65–69; R Sarsden w Churchill 69–74;
P-in-c Clifton Hampden 74–77; P-in-c Rotherfield Greys
H Trin 77–82; V 82–90; V Blacklands Hastings Ch Ch and
St Andr *Chich* 90–97; V Ticehurst and Flimwell 97–00;
rtd 00; PtO *Chich* from 01; *Ox* 14–20. *19 Tynemouth Rise,
Monkston, Milton Keynes MK10 9JB* T: (01908) 233521
E: halomanpj@gmail.com

LE VASSEUR, Mrs Linda Susan. b 48. Shenstone Coll of
Educn CertEd 70. S Dios Minl Tr Scheme 92. **d** 95 **p** 96. NSM
Guernsey Ste Marie du Castel and Guernsey St Matt *Win*
95–01; NSM Guernsey St Sav and Guernsey St Marguerite
de la Foret 01–14; P-in-c Guernsey St Jo 14–16; Sen Chapl
Princess Eliz Hosp Guernsey from 00. *Princess Elizabeth
Hospital, Rue Mignot, St Martin, Guernsey GY4 6UU* T: (01481)
725241 ext 4699

LE VAY, Clare Forbes Agard Bramhall Joanna. b 41. St Anne's
Coll Ox BA 64 MA 66 Univ of Wales (Abth) MSc 72 PhD 86.
Westcott Ho Cam 86. **d** 88 **p** 94. C Stamford Hill St Thos *Lon*
88–89; C Hackney 89–92; Asst Chapl Brook Gen Hosp Lon
92–95; Asst Chapl Greenwich Distr Hosp Lon 92–95; Chapl
Greenwich Healthcare NHS Trust 95–01; PtO *S'wark* 02–06;
Lon 04–06; *Glouc* 09–14. *Thalia, Middle Street, Uplands,
Stroud GL5 1TG* T: (01453) 451844 M: 07816-468112
E: clarelevay@yahoo.com

LE-WORTHY, Michael Raymond. b 50. **d** 98 **p** 99. OLM
Glascote and Stonydelph *Lich* 98–12; NSM 12–20; NSM
Tamworth 12–15; rtd 20; PtO *Lich* from 20. *5 Carter Close,
Tamworth B79 8UE* E: michael.leworthy1@btinternet.com

LEA, Carolyn Jane. *See* COOKE, Carolyn Jane

LEA, Canon Montague Brian. b 34. OBE 00. St Jo Coll Cam
BA 55 Lon Univ BD 71. St Jo Coll Nottm 68. **d** 71 **p** 72. C
Northwood Em *Lon* 71–74; Chapl Barcelona *Eur* 74–79;
V Hove Bp Hannington Memorial Ch *Chich* 79–86; Adn
N France *Eur* 86–94; Chapl Paris St Mich 86–94; Hon
Can Gib Cathl from 95; R Chiddingly w E Hoathly *Chich*
94–96; Chapl The Hague *Eur* 96–00; rtd 01; PtO *Chich*
from 01. *35 Summerdown Lane, East Dean, Eastbourne
BN20 0LE* T: (01323) 423226 E: brian.lea@greenbee.net

LEA (née WETHERELL), Philippa Clare. b 80. Univ of Wales
(Cardiff) BSc 02. Trin Coll Bris BA 08. **d** 09 **p** 10. C W Derby
St Mary and St Jas *Liv* 09–13; TV Kirkby from 13. *The Rectory,
Old Hall Lane, Kirkby, Liverpool L32 5TH* M: 07770-892639
E: philippaclea@yahoo.co.uk

LEA-WILSON, Nicholas Hugh. b 61. Man Poly BA 83 Leeds
Univ BA 08 MLI 90. NOC 05. **d** 08 **p** 09. C Gateacre *Liv*
08–12; P-in-c Knowsley 12–14; TV 4Saints Team from 14.
The Vicarage, Tithebarn Road, Prescot L34 0JA T: 0151-546
4266 M: 07968-290553

LEACH, Alan Graham. b 46. Univ Coll Ches BTh 04
Master Mariner 73. NOC 04. **d** 05 **p** 06. NSM Neston
Ches 05–08; NSM Heswall 08–17; rtd 17; PtO *Ches* from
17. *8 Hill Top Lane, Ness, Neston CH64 4EL* T: 0151-336
5046 M: 07802-622143 E: alan.leach5@btinternet.com

LEACH, Andrew John Philip. b 54. Univ of Wales (Lamp)
BA 77 Univ of Wales (Abth) PGCE 78. WEMTC 07. **d** 10
p 11. NSM Painswick, Sheepscombe, Cranham, The Edge
etc *Glouc* from 10. *Melrose Cottage, Cheltenham Road,
Painswick GL6 6SJ* T: (01452) 813609 M: 07564-448692
E: ajpleach@googlemail.com

LEACH, Miss Bethia Morag. b 62. Sheff Univ BA 84 Liv Inst
of Educn PGCE 85. Ripon Coll Cuddesdon 95. **d** 97 **p** 98.
C Stafford *Lich* 97–00; TV Bilston 00–07; V Pennsett *Worc*
07–10; rtd 10. *66 Lichfield Road, Walsall WS4 2DJ* T: (01922)
446956 E: bethialeach@virginmedia.com

LEACH, James Roger. b 66. Ball Coll Ox BA 89 MA 99.
Wycliffe Hall Ox BA 98. **d** 99 **p** 00. C Knowle *Birm* 99–06; C
Gerrards Cross and Fulmer *Ox* 06–20; TV Langtree from 20.
*St Mary's House, High Street, Whitchurch on Thames, Reading
RG8 7DF* E: jamesleach.whitchurch@gmail.com

LEACH, John. b 52. K Coll Lon BD 79 AKC 79 St Jo Coll
Dur MA 83 Lambeth STh 02. **d** 81 **p** 82. C N Walsham w
Antingham *Nor* 81–85; C Crookes St Thos *Sheff* 85–89; V
Styvechale *Cov* 89–97; Dir Angl Renewal Min 97–02; R

Jersey St Lawr *Win* 02–04; Par Development Adv *Mon* 04–09; V Folkestone St Jo *Cant* 09–13; PtO 13–14; Developing Discipleship Adv and Tr *Linc* 14–18; Growing Disciples Officer from 18. *105 Nettleham Road, Lincoln LN2 1RU* E: john.leach@lincoln.anglican.org

LEACH, Mrs Rebecca Mary. b 65. St Aid Coll Dur BA 87 Bris Univ PGCE 90. ERMC 05. **d** 08 **p** 09. C E Barnet *St Alb* 08–11; C Harpenden St Nic 11–16; V St Alb St Steph from 16. *St Stephen's Vicarage, 14 Watling Street, St Albans AL1 2PX* T: (01727) 862598 E: vicar@ststephenandstjulian.org

LEACH, Samuel Mark. b 76. Westmr Coll Ox BEd 99. Ridley Hall Cam 05. **d** 08 **p** 09. C Walsall St Paul *Lich* 08–11; TV Wednesfield 11–18; R Upton *Ex* from 18. *Upton Rectory, Furzehill Road, Torquay TQ1 3JG* M: 07915-668714 E: vicar@stmags.org.uk

LEACH, Stephen Lance. b 42. St Steph Ho Ox 66. **d** 69 **p** 70. C Higham Ferrers w Chelveston *Pet* 69–72; TV Ilfracombe H Trin *Ex* 72; TV Ilfracombe, Lee and W Down 72–74; V Barnstaple St Mary 74–77; R Goodleigh 74–77; P-in-c Barnstaple St Pet w H Trin 76–77; P-in-c Landkey 77–79; TR Barnstaple and Goodleigh 77–79; TR Barnstaple, Goodleigh and Landkey 79–82; V Paignton St Jo, St Andr and St Boniface 82–95; Chapl Paignton and Kings Ash Hosps 82–95; Gen Sec ACS 95–08; rtd 08; Public Preacher *Birm* 95–15; PtO *Ex* from 15. *16 Kings Avenue, Paignton TQ3 2AR* T: (01803) 552335

LEACH, Stephen Winston. b 47. St Chad's Coll Dur BSc 70 Linacre Coll Ox BA 72 MA 76. Ripon Hall Ox 70. **d** 73 **p** 74. C Swinton St Pet *Man* 73–77; C Oldham St Chad Limeside 77–79; V Shaw 79–87; V St Just in Penwith *Truro* 87–14; V Sancreed 87–14; rtd 14. *Porthpean, 4 Bentham Avenue, Fleetwood FY7 8RH* T: (01253) 771624 E: windsorleach@aol.com

LEACH, Timothy Edmund. b 41. Dur Univ BA 63. Ridley Hall Cam 63. **d** 65 **p** 66. C Ecclesfield *Sheff* 65–68; C Stocksbridge 68–71; C-in-c W Bessacarr CD 71–80; V Goole and Hon Chapl Miss to Seamen 80–95; V Wath-upon-Dearne *Sheff* 95–08; rtd 08; PtO *Sheff* from 09. *6 Sawn Moor Avenue, Thurcroft, Rotherham S66 9DQ* T: (01709) 701263

LEADER, Miss Janette Patricia. b 46. EAMTC 94. **d** 97 **p** 98. C Desborough, Brampton Ash, Dingley and Braybrooke *Pet* 97–01; V Wellingborough St Barn 01–12; rtd 12; PtO *Pet* from 14. *15 Salisbury Road, Peterborough PE4 6NL* T: (01733) 685672 E: revjanleader@virginmedia.com

LEAF, Edward David Hugh. b 65. Oak Hill Th Coll BA 97. **d** 98 **p** 99. C Bath St Bart *B & W* 98–01; C Minehead 01–05; V Chadderton Em *Man* from 05. *Emmanuel Vicarage, 15 Chestnut Street, Chadderton, Oldham OL9 8HB* T: 0161-681 1310 E: stgeorgechadderton@icloud.com

LEAH, William Albert. b 34. K Coll Lon BA 56 AKC 57 K Coll Cam MA 63. Ripon Hall Ox 60. **d** 62 **p** 63. C Falmouth K Chas *Truro* 62–63; Chapl K Coll Cam 63–67; Min Can Westmr Abbey 67–74; V Hawkhurst *Cant* 74–83; Hon Min Can Cant Cathl 78–83; V St Ives *Truro* 83–94; rtd 98. *Trerice Cottage, Sancreed Newbridge, Penzance TR20 8QR* T: (01736) 810987 E: w.leah1934@gmail.com

LEAHY, Canon David Adrian. b 56. Open Univ BA 90. Qu Coll Birm. **d** 85 **p** 86. C Tile Cross *Birm* 85–88; C Warley Woods 88–91; V Hobs Moat 91–07; AD Solihull 97–04; V Four Oaks from 07; AD Sutton Coldfield 13–19; Jt AD Aston and Sutton Coldfield 19; Hon Can Birm Cathl from 18. *The Vicarage, 26 All Saints Drive, Sutton Coldfield B74 4AG* T: 0121-308 5315 E: revaleahy@gmail.com

LEAK, Adrian Scudamore. b 38. Ch Ch Ox BA 60 MA 65 BD 89 FSA 17. Cuddesdon Coll 64. **d** 66 **p** 67. C Cov St Mark 66–69; C Dorchester *Ox* 69–73; V Badsey *Worc* 73–80; V Wickhamford 73–78; V Badsey w Aldington and Wickhamford 78–80; P-in-c Monkwearmouth St Pet *Dur* 80–81; V Choral and Architect York Minster 81–86; Can Res and Prec Guildf Cathl 86–90; Hon C Guildf H Trin w St Mary 96–00; Hon C Worplesdon 00–06; P-in-c Withyham St Mich *Chich* 06–13; rtd 13; PtO *Guildf* from 14. *Flat 1, 10 Joseph's Road, Guildford GU1 1DW* T: (01483) 579503 E: adrian.leak@btinternet.com

LEAK, Harry Duncan. b 30. St Cath Coll Cam BA 53 MA 57. Ely Th Coll 53. **d** 54 **p** 55. S Africa 54–57; Portuguese E Africa 57–61; C Eccleshall *Lich* 62–64; V Normacot 64–66; V Stoke upon Trent 66–68; V Hanley All SS 68–71; R Swynnerton 71–80; PtO 80–03; rtd 92. *15 Sutherland Road, Tittensor, Stoke-on-Trent ST12 9JQ* T: (01782) 374341

✠**LEAKE, The Rt Revd David.** b 35. CBE 03. ALCD 59 LTh 74. **d** 59 **p** 60 **c** 69. V Watford *St Alb* 59–61; Lect 61–63; SAMS Argentina 63–69; Asst Bp Paraguay 69–73; Asst Bp N Argentina 69–80; Bp N Argentina 80–90; Bp Argentina 90–02; rtd 02; Hon Asst Bp Nor from 03; PtO from 03. *The Anchorage, Lower Common, East Runton, Cromer NR27 9PG* T: (01263) 513536 E: obispodavid@gmail.com

LEAKE, Duncan Burton. b 49. Leeds Univ BA 71 Leeds and Carnegie Coll PGCE 72 Keele Univ MA 85. Oak Hill Th Coll 90. **d** 92 **p** 93. C Stanwix *Carl* 92–97; C Chasetown *Lich* 97–00; V Chase Terrace 00–14; rtd 14; PtO *Lich* from 15. *12 Outwoods Close, Weston, Stafford ST18 0JR* E: revduncan@outlook.com *or* rev.dbl@googlemail.com

LEAKE, Roger Norman Simon. b 59. Dur Univ BSc 80 Coll of Ripon & York St Jo PGCE 81. Sarum Coll 16. **d** 19 **p** 20. NSM Chalke Valley *Sarum* from 19. *The Killick, Wylye Road, Hanging Langford, Salisbury SP3 4NW* T: (01722) 792862 E: revrleake@gmail.com

LEAL, Mrs Clare Elizabeth. b 61. FCIH 97. Ripon Coll Cuddesdon 16. **d** 19 **p** 20. NSM Summertown *Ox* from 19. *19 Edgeway Road, Marston, Oxford OX3 0HD* E: curate@stmichaels-summertown.org.uk

LEAL, John Xavier. b 64. **d** 14 **p** 14. NSM Rock Ferry *Ches* 14–16; R Rossington *Sheff* 16–19; P-in-c New Rossington 16–19; R Coppenhall *Ches* from 19. *The Rectory, 198 Ford Lane, Crewe CW1 3TN* T: (01270) 215151 E: priestxman@gmail.com

LEAMY, Stuart Nigel. b 46. Pemb Coll Ox BA 68 MA 73 ACA 76 FCA 81. Sarum Th Coll 68. **d** 70 **p** 71. C Upholland *Liv* 70–78; LtO *Lon* 78–83 and 94–97; NSM Pimlico St Mary Bourne Street 97–16; PtO from 16. *92 Gloucester Road, Hampton TW12 2UJ* T: (020) 8979 9068 E: leamy@blueyonder.co.uk

LEAN, The Very Revd David Jonathan Rees. b 52. Coll of Resurr Mirfield 74. **d** 75 **p** 76. C Tenby *St D* 75–79; C Tenby w Gumfreston 80–81; V Llanrhian w Llanhywel and Carnhedryn etc 81–88; V Haverfordwest St Martin w Lambston 88–00; RD Roose 99–00; Can St D Cathl 00–17; TV Dewisland 01–09; TR 09–17; Dean St D 09–17; rtd 17; PtO *St D* from 17. *The Garth, Serpentine Road, Tenby SA70 8DD* T: (01834) 843341 E: jonathanlean1@gmail.com

LEAR, Peter Malcolm. b 45. FCMA. SEITE 95. **d** 98 **p** 99. NSM Ham St Andr *S'wark* 98–03; Chapl to Bp Kingston 98–99; NSM Wandsworth St Anne 03–04; NSM Upper Coquetdale *Newc* 04–11; rtd 11; PtO *York* from 11. *39 Farmanby Close, Thornton Dale, Pickering YO18 7TD* T: (01751) 470190 E: peterlear@learpm.com

LEARMONT, Oliver James. b 62. UEA BA 83 Wolv Univ LLM 96 SS Coll Cam BTh 07. Westcott Ho Cam 05. **d** 07 **p** 08. C Hitchin *St Alb* 07–11; P-in-c E Bridgford and Kneeton *S'well* 11–18; P-in-c Flintham 11–18; P-in-c Car Colston w Screveton 11–18; V N Bradley, Southwick, Heywood and Steeple Ashton *Sarum* from 18. *The Vicarage, 62 Church Lane, North Bradley, Trowbridge BA14 0TA* T: (01225) 774845 E: oliver.learmont@btinternet.com

LEARMOUTH, Michael Walter. b 50. FCA. Oak Hill Th Coll 84. **d** 84 **p** 85. C Harlow St Mary and St Hugh w St Jo the Bapt *Chelmsf* 84–89; V Hainault 89–97; TR Harlow Town Cen w Lt Parndon 97–00; TR Barnsbury *Lon* 00–19; AD Islington 08–14; rtd 19; PtO *York* from 20. *7 Montague Street, York YO23 1JB*

LEARY, Thomas Glasbrook. b 42. AKC 66. **d** 67 **p** 68. C W Bromwich All SS *Lich* 67–70; TV Croydon St Jo *Cant* 70–75; C Limpsfield and Titsey *S'wark* 75–83; V Sutton New Town St Barn 83–92; V Merton St Mary 92–07; RD Merton 98–01; rtd 07; PtO *Heref* from 07; *S & B* 12–14. *Conduit Cottage, Livesey Road, Ludlow SY8 1EZ* T: (01584) 875619 E: glassbrook@msn.com

LEATHARD, Preb Brian. b 56. Sussex Univ BA Cam Univ MA Loughb Univ PhD 91. Westcott Ho Cam 79. **d** 82 **p** 83. C Seaford w Sutton *Chich* 82–85; Chapl Loughb Univ *Leic* 85–89; V Hampton Hill *Lon* 89–06; R Chelsea St Luke and Ch Ch from 06; Dir of Ords 99–09; Preb St Paul's Cathl from 05. *The Rectory, 64A Flood Street, London SW3 5TE* T: (020) 7352 6331 *or* 7351 7365 E: brianleathard@chelseaparish.org

LEATHARD, Prof Helen Louise. b 47. Chelsea Coll Lon BSc 70 K Coll Lon PhD 74 St Martin's Coll Lanc MA 06 FBPhS 06. LCTP 12. **d** 13 **p** 14. NSM Slyne w Hest and Halton w Aughton *Blackb* 13–17; rtd 17; PtO *Blackb* from 17. *29 Coronation Way, Lancaster LA1 2TQ* T: (01524) 849495 E: helenleathard@btinternet.com

LEATHERBARROW, Andrew James Howard. b 68. All SS Cen for Miss & Min 12. **d** 15 **p** 16. C Rainhill *Liv* 15–18; V Stoneycroft All SS from 18. *The Vicarage, 7 Saints Close, Liverpool L13 4AT* T: 0151-228 3581 M: 07769-276734

LEATHERBARROW, Mrs Laura Lee. b 70. **d** 14 **p** 15. C E Widnes *Liv* 14–18; V Croxteth Park from 18. *The Vicarage, 7 Saints Close, Liverpool L13 4AT* M: 07780-448274 E: revlauraleatherbarrow@gmail.com

LEATHERS, Preb Brian Stanley Peter. b 61. Nottm Univ BSc 83. Oak Hill Th Coll BA 89. **d** 89 **p** 90. C Watford *St Alb* 89–92; C Welwyn w Ayot St Peter 92–96; V Heacham *Nor* 96–99; P-in-c Stapenhill Immanuel *Derby* 99–00; V 00–09; P-in-c Denstone w Ellastone and Stanton 09–10;

P-in-c Mayfield 09–10; V Alton w Bradley-le-Moors, Ellastone w Stanton, and Mayfield from 10; RD Uttoxeter from 11; Preb Lich Cathl from 18. *The New Vicarage, Limekiln Lane, Alton, Stoke-on-Trent ST10 4AR* T: (01538) 702469 E: briantopsey@gmail.com

LEATHERS, Daniel Brian. b 88. Derby Univ BA 10 Trin Hall Cam BTh 15. Ridley Hall Cam 12. d 15 p 16. C Whitfield *Derby* 15–18; V Haydock St Mark *Liv* from 18. *2 Stanley Bank Road, St Helens WA11 0UW* M: 07526-660791 E: dan_leathers@hotmail.co.uk

LEATON, Martin John. b 46. Clifton Th Coll 68. d 71 p 72. C Kenilworth St Jo *Cov* 71–74; C Stratford-on-Avon w Bishopton 74–77; P-in-c Meriden 77–81; R Meriden and Packington 82–84; R Heanton Punchardon w Marwood *Ex* 84–87; PtO 95–97; P-in-c Rampton w Laneham, Treswell, Cottam and Stokeham *S'well* 97–06; P-in-c N and S Leverton 03–06; rtd 06; Hon C Tysoe w Oxhill and Whatcote *Cov* 06–17; PtO *Heref* 17–19. *7 Centurian Way, Credenhill, Hereford HR4 7FF* T: (01432) 761374 E: martinjleaton@gmail.com

LEAVER, David Noel. b 63. Hatf Coll Dur BA 85. Wycliffe Hall Ox 89. d 91 p 92. C Blackheath Park St Mich *S'wark* 91–95; C Upton (Overchurch) *Ches* 95–98; C Wilmslow 98–99; PtO from 99. *42 Hill Top Avenue, Cheadle Hulme, Cheadle SK8 7HY* T: 0161-485 4302 E: davidleaver@btconnect.com

LEAVER, Mrs Janice Patricia. b 56. EAMTC 03. d 06 p 07. C Desborough, Brampton Ash, Dingley and Braybrooke *Pet* 06–09; TV Wilford Peninsula *St E* 09–18; rtd 18. *17 Elmhurst Court, Hamblin Road, Woodbridge IP12 1HB* M: 07913-977218 E: janpatleaver@gmail.com

LEAVER (née SMYTH), Mrs Lucinda Elizabeth Jane. b 67. New Hall Cam BA 88 MA 92. Wycliffe Hall Ox BTh 93. d 93 p 94. C Cambridge St Barn *Ely* 93–97; Chapl St Kath Hall Liv Hope 97–98; TV Stockport SW *Ches* 99–01; Chapl Stockport Gr Sch from 99; Chapl Univ Hosp of S Man NHS Foundn Trust 14–17; Chapl Man Univ NHS Foundn Trust 17–19; PtO *Eur* from 16; *Man* from 19. *42 Hill Top Avenue, Cheadle Hulme, Cheadle SK8 7HY* T: 0161-456 9000

LEAWORTHY, John Owen. b 40. Univ of Wales (Swansea) BSc 62. Oak Hill Th Coll 80. d 82 p 83. C Compton Gifford *Ex* 82–85; C Plymouth Em w Efford 85–86; P-in-c Marks Tey w Aldham and Lt Tey *Chelmsf* 86–88; R 88–89; Chapl HM Pris Full Sutton 89–91; NSM Portree *Arg* 96–04; rtd 05; PtO *Chelmsf* from 05. *46 Wilkin Drive, Tiptree, Colchester CO5 0QP* T: (01621) 810905 E: jleaworthy@btinternet.com

LEBEY, Nicholas Kwabena. b 82. Cranmer Hall Dur 19. d 21. C Tolworth, Hook and Surbiton *S'wark* from 21. *127 Hamilton Avenue, Surbiton KT6 7QA* M: 07933-785179 E: kwabnich@gmail.com

LECK, Stuart David. b 62. Cant Ch Ch Univ BA 11 ACIB 84. SEITE 03. d 06 p 07. NSM Brockley Hill St Sav *S'wark* 06–10; NSM Nunhead St Antony w St Silas 10–12; C Catford (Southend) and Downham 12–14; TV from 14. *St Barnabas' Vicarage, 1 Churchdown, Bromley BR1 5PS* T: (020) 8698 4851 M: 07811-384420 E: stuart.leck@btinternet.com

LECKEY, Paul Robert. b 61. QUB. Ripon Coll Cuddesdon Aston Tr Scheme. d 96 p 97. C Leavesleigh Win 96–01; P-in-c Upton St Leonards *Glouc* 01–13; V Hall Green Ascension *Birm* 13–17; V Balsall Heath and Edgbaston SS Mary and Ambrose 17–20; rtd 20. *Address temp unknown* E: rev.leckey@virginmedia.com

LECLÉZIO, Ms Marie Katryn. b 62. Natal Univ BA 83 All Nations Chr Coll MA 00. WEMTC 05. d 08 p 09. C Halas *Worc* 08–12; TV 12–21; Deanery Miss Enabler from 12; C Bredon w Bredon's Norton from 21; P-in-c Elmley Castle w Bricklehampton and Combertons from 21; P-in-c Overbury w Teddington, Alstone etc from 21. *The Rectory, 22 Parkwood Road, Elmley Castle, Pershore WR10 3HT*

LEDGER, Mrs Margaret Phyllis. b 42. d 04 p 05. OLM Newburn *Newc* 04–17; rtd 17; PtO *Newc* from 17. *14 Woodside Avenue, Throckley, Newcastle upon Tyne NE15 9BE* T: 0191-267 2953 E: margaret.p.ledger@btinternet.com

LEDWARD, John Archibald. b 30. Lon Univ BD 58 Man Univ MA 81 FRSA 85. ALCD 57. d 58 p 59. C St Helens St Helen *Liv* 58–62; V Dearham *Carl* 62–66; V Wirehouse 66–71; V Daubhill *Man* 71–77; R Newcastle w Butterton *Lich* 77–88; R Rockland St Mary w Hellington, Bramerton etc *Nor* 88–94; P-in-c Kirby Bedon w Bixley and Whitlingham 92–94; R Rockland St Mary w Hellington, Bramerton etc 94–95; RD Loddon 92–95; rtd 95; PtO *Nor* from 95. *41 Lackford Close, Brundall, Norwich NR13 5NL* T: (01603) 714745

LEE, Agnes Elizabeth. b 31. Open Univ BA 87 Whitelands Coll Lon TCert 51 ACP 76. NOC 97. d 98 p 99. NSM Dewsbury *Wakef* 98–02; rtd 02; PtO *Wakef* 02–14; *Leeds* from 14. *1 Moor Park Court, Dewsbury WF12 7AU* T: (01924) 467319

LEE, Andrew. *See* LEE, Sang Youn

LEE, Anne Louise. *See* WILKINS, Anne Louise

LEE, Anthony Maurice. b 35. Bps' Coll Cheshunt 62. d 65 p 66. C Pinner *Lon* 65–71; Asst Youth Chapl *Glouc* 71–72; V Childswyckham 72–73; R Aston Somerville 72–73; V Childswyckham w Aston Somerville 73–91; P-in-c Buckland 88–91; P-in-c Stanton w Snowshill 88–91; R Childswyckham w Aston Somerville, Buckland etc 91–94; RD Winchcombe 86–94; rtd 94. *Lysander House, 6 Lutyens Court, Upper Rissington, Cheltenham GL54 2RG*

LEE, Canon Brian. b 37. Linc Th Coll 78. d 80 p 81. C Duston *Pet* 80–84; P-in-c Spratton 84–89; V 89–06; Jt P-in-c Maidwell w Draughton, Lamport w Faxton 89–01; Jt P-in-c Cottesbrooke w Gt Creaton and Thornby 89–06; RD Brixworth 94–01; Can Pet Cathl 98–06; rtd 06; PtO *Pet* from 06. *1 Bishops Way, Corby NN18 0TJ* T: (01536) 747195 E: revbrianlee@gmail.com

LEE, Canon Brian Ernest. b 32. ACA 59 FCA 70. Linc Th Coll 60. d 62 p 63. C Birch St Jas *Man* 62–65; C Withington St Paul 65–66; R Abbey Hey 66–70; Hon C Gatley *Ches* 86–88; V Egremont St Jo 88–97; RD Wallasey 91–96; OGS from 92; Hon Can Ches Cathl 96–97; rtd 97; PtO *Nor* from 97. *St Fursey House, Convent of All Hallows, Ditchingham, Bungay NR35 2DZ* T: (01986) 892308 F: 894215 E: blee@ogs.net

LEE, Brian John. b 51. K Coll Lon BD 78 AKC 78. Coll of Resurr Mirfield 78. d 79 p 80. C Ham St Rich *S'wark* 79–82; C Surbiton St Andr and St Mark 82–85; V Shirley St Geo 85–93; C V St Botolph Aldgate w H Trin Minories *Lon* 93–08; rtd 08. *6 Shore Cottages, Silverdale, Carnforth LA5 0TS* T: (01524) 701381 M: 07905-756024 E: brianlee51@icloud.com

LEE, Mrs Carol Joyce. b 59. d 20 p 21. C Finningley w Auckley *Sheff* from 20. *20 Headingley Close, Kirk Sandall, Doncaster DN3 1SS* T: (01302) 881232 M: 07548-251065 E: revcaroljl@gmail.com

LEE, Christopher James. b 52. FIBMS 77. St Mich Coll Llan 10. d 13 p 14. NSM Caerau w Ely *Llan* 13–20; NSM Roath St Sav from 20. *10 Coronation Road, Cardiff CF14 4QY* T: (029) 2061 8054 M: 07831-500738

LEE, Christopher John Bodell. b 82. Kingston Univ BA 01 Cam Univ BTh 11. Ridley Hall Cam 08. d 07 p 11. C Onslow Square and S Kensington St Aug *Lon* 11–14; P-in-c Cobbold Road St Sav w St Mary 15–18; V from 18. *St Saviour's Vicarage, Cobbold Road, London W12 9LN* T: (020) 8743 4769 M: 07966-632161 E: revchris7@gmail.com

LEE, David Alexander. b 83. Imp Coll Lon MSci 05 PhD 10. Oak Hill Th Coll BA 14. d 14 p 15. C Fulham St Pet *Lon* 14–21. *31 Burnthwaite Road, London SW6 5BQ* E: david.a.lee@gmail.com

LEE, The Ven David John. b 46. Bris Univ BSc 67 Fitzw Coll Cam BA 76 MA 79 Birm Univ PhD 96. Ridley Hall Cam 74. d 77 p 78. C Putney St Marg *S'wark* 77–80; Tutor Bp Tucker Th Coll Uganda 80–86; Tutor Crowther Hall CMS Tr Coll Selly Oak 86–91; P-in-c Wishaw and Middleton *Birm* 91–96; Can Res Birm Cathl 96–04; Dir Dioc Bd for Miss 96–04; Adn Bradf 04–15; rtd 15; Adn for Miss Resources 15–16; PtO *Birm* 16–20; P-in-c Aston and Nechells 20–21; PtO *Lich* from 17; *Birm* from 21. *16 Tudor Hill, Sutton Coldfield B73 6BH* T: 0121-681 4347 M: 07711-671351 E: davidjlee@blueyonder.co.uk

LEE, David John. b 58. Open Univ BA 87. ERMC 18. d 20 p 21. C Fowlmere, Foxton, Shepreth and Thriplow *Ely* from 20. *Dove Cottage, 37 Church Street, Harston, Cambridge CB22 7NP* M: 07895-378724 E: davidjohnlee36@gmail.com

LEE, The Ven David Stanley. b 30. Univ of Wales (Cardiff) BSc 51. St Mich Coll Llan 56. d 57 p 58. C Caerau w Ely *Llan* 57–60; C Port Talbot St Agnes 60–70; Ind Chapl 60–70; R Merthyr Tydfil 70–72; Chapl Merthyr Tydfil Hosp 70–91; R Merthyr Tydfil and Cyfarthfa *Llan* 72–91; RD Merthyr Tydfil 82–91; Can Llan Cathl 84–97; Adn Llan 91–97; R Llanfabon 91–97; rtd 97; PtO *Llan* from 97; *Mon* from 98. *2 Old Vicarage Close, Llanishen, Cardiff CF14 5UZ* T: (029) 2075 2431

LEE, David Wight Dunsmore. b 39. Wells Th Coll 61. d 63 p 64. C Middlesbrough St Oswald *York* 63–67; C Northallerton w Kirby Sigston 67–69; R Limbe W Thyolo and Mulanje Malawi 69–71; R S Highlands 71–75; V Newington Transfiguration *York* 76–81; P-in-c Sheriff Hutton 81–85; P-in-c Sheriff Hutton and Farlington 85–97; V Sheriff Hutton, Farlington, Stillington etc 97–04; rtd 04; PtO *York* 04–20. *Kirkstone Cottage, Main Street, Oswaldkirk, York YO62 5XT* T: (01439) 788283 E: dwdlee@talk21.com or dawdle@dwdlee.plus.com

LEE, Edmund Hugh. b 53. Trin Coll Ox BA 75 MA 79 Goldsmiths' Coll Lon BMus 83 K Coll Lon MA 98. Ripon Coll Cuddesdon 93. d 95 p 96. C Malden St Jas *S'wark* 95–99; TV Mortlake w E Sheen 99–08. *67 North Worple Way, London SW14 8PP* T: (020) 8876 5270

LEE, Elizabeth. *See* LEE, Agnes Elizabeth

LEE, Franklin. *See* LEE, On Yip Franklin

LEE, Hugh. *See* LEE, John Charles Hugh Mellanby

LEE, James Alexander. b 85. Warwick Univ BA 07 K Coll Lon MA 13 Middx Univ BA 21. Oak Hill Th Coll 18. d 21. C Stanton-by-Dale w Dale Abbey and Risley *Derby* from 21. *41 St John's Road, Ilkeston DE7 5PA* M: 07729-885604 E: jimmylee42@gmail.com

LEE, Mrs Jane. b 71. Teesside Univ BA 96. St Mellitus Coll BA 19. d 19 p 20. C W Pendleside *Blackb* from 19. *19 Nab View, Whalley, Clitheroe BB7 9YG* M: 07769-951978 E: jane.lee1271@gmail.com

LEE, Mrs Janet. b 58. d 13 p 14. OLM Clifton Ch Ch w Em *Bris* from 13. *45 Alma Road, Clifton, Bristol BS8 2DE* E: janet.lee@ccweb.org.uk

LEE, Mrs Jayne Christine. b 53. Dundee Univ MA 75. d 06 p 07. OLM Roberttown w Hartshead *Wakef* 06–10; OLM Heckmondwike 06–10; OLM Liversedge w Hightown 06–10; OLM Hartshead, Hightown, Robertttown and Scholes 10–14; *Leeds* from 14. *58 Prospect View, Liversedge WF15 8BD* T: (01924) 235868 E: jayneclee@hotmail.com

LEE, Mrs Jennifer. b 42. Westf Coll Lon BA 64 CQSW 78. NOC 01. d 03 p 04. NSM Millhouses H Trin *Sheff* 03–06; PtO 06–13; NSM Compton w Shackleford and Peper Harow *Guildf* 07–12; rtd 12; PtO *Guildf* from 12. *The Old Barn, Peper Harow, Godalming GU8 6BQ* T: (01483) 424468 E: revjennylee@gmail.com

LEE, John Charles Hugh Mellanby. b 44. Trin Hall Cam BA 66 MA 69 Brunel Univ MTech 71. Ox NSM Course 78. d 81 p 82. NSM Amersham on the Hill *Ox* 81–88; NSM Ox St Aldate w St Matt 88–93; NSM Wheatley 93–95; Dioc Development Officer Miss in Work and Economic Life 95–02; P-in-c Ox St Mich w St Martin and All SS 02–09; LtO 09–13; NSM Wheatley 13–14; NSM Beckley, Forest Hill, Horton-cum-Studley and Stanton St John 14–21; PtO from 21. *64 Observatory Street, Oxford OX2 6EP* T: (01865) 316245 M: 07879-426625 E: hugh.lee@btinternet.com

LEE, John Michael Andrew. b 62. Leeds Univ BA 84. Trin Coll Bris 88. d 90 p 91. C Norbiton *S'wark* 90–94; C Leic H Trin w St Jo 94–02; R York St Paul 02–19; RD City of York 18–19; 20s-40s Team Ldr from 19; P-in-c York St Barn from 18. *42 East Mount Road, York YO24 1BD* E: johnmalee@btinternet.com or john.lee@yorkdiocese.org

LEE, John Samuel. b 47. Chich Th Coll 74. d 77 p 78. C Bramley *Ripon* 77–80; C Bideford *Ex* 81–84; TV Littleham w Exmouth 84–90; P-in-c Sidbury 90–91; TV Sidmouth, Woolbrook, Salcombe Regis, Sidbury etc 91–04; rtd 04; Hon C Torquay St Jo *Ex* 17–18; Hon C Torre and Torquay St Jo 18–20. *Westward Ho!, Torpark Road, Torquay TQ2 5BQ* T: (01803) 293086 E: lee352@sky.com

LEE, Jonathan James Wilton. b 66. QC 15. Sheff Univ BEng 88. Trin Coll Bris 19. d 21. NSM Kingsthorpe *Pet* from 21. *42 Fallow Walk, Northampton NN2 8DE* M: 07956-456574 E: jonathan@redcourt.co.uk

LEE, Jonathon Wei Sing. Clare Coll Cam BA 09 MSci 09 MA 12. Oak Hill Th Coll BA 17. d 18 p 19. C Ashton-on-Ribble St Andr *Blackb* 18–21; R Bispham from 21. *Address withheld by request* E: jwslee2@gmail.com

LEE, Joseph Patrick. b 53. St Jos Coll Upholland 72 Ushaw Coll Dur 75. d 78 p 79. In RC Ch 78–99; NSM Charlton *S'wark* 99–09; NSM E Greenwich 09–17; NSM Charlton from 17. *11 Troughton Road, School Square, London SE10 0BT* T: (020) 8465 5212 M: 07872-347058 E: joe@charlton.church

LEE, Mrs Judith Mary. b 44. Doncaster Coll of Educn TCert 65. d 06 p 07. OLM Frenchay and Winterbourne Down *Bris* 06–16; OLM Frenchay and Stapleton 16–20; NSM from 20. *8 Beaufort Road, Frampton Cotterell, Bristol BS36 2AD* T: (01454) 772381 E: jrplee@btinternet.com

LEE, Canon Kenneth Peter. b 45. Em Coll Cam BA 67 MA 71. Cuddesdon Coll 67. d 69 p 70. C Stoke Poges *Ox* 69–72; C Witton *Ches* 72–74; V Frankby w Greasby 74–92; R Christleton 92–10; Hon Can Ches Cathl 05–10; rtd 10; PtO *Ches* from 10. *16 Rookery Drive, Tattenhall, Chester CH3 9QS* T: (01829) 770292 E: leepf@btinternet.com

LEE, Luke Gun-Hong. b 37. Univ of Yon Sei BTh 62. St Jo Coll Morpeth 64. d 67 p 68. Lic to Offic Taejon Korea 67–79; C Bloxwich *Lich* 79–83; TV Dunstable *St Alb* 83–90; V Croxley Green All SS 90–07; rtd 07; PtO *Ox* 07–20; *Lon* from 08. *101 Lark Vale, Aylesbury HP19 0YP* T: (01296) 423133 E: luke.gh.lee@gmail.com

LEE, Mrs Margaret. b 48. Coll of Ripon & York St Jo BEd 71. NEOC 03. d 06 p 07. NSM Houghton le Spring *Dur* 06–19; rtd 19; PtO *Dur* from 19. *2 Rectory View, Shadforth, Durham DH6 1LF* T: 0191-372 0595 E: marglee372@outlook.com

LEE, Martin Paul. b 66. Leeds Univ BA 13 Teesside Univ MEd 15. Aston Tr Scheme 91 Linc Th Coll 93 St Steph Ho Ox 94. d 96 p 97. C Wells St Thos w Horrington *B & W* 96–00; P-in-c Brent Knoll, E Brent and Lympsham 00–01; R 01–08; RD Axbridge 03–08; V Long Benton *Newc*

08–21; AD Newc E 12–17; TR Sherborne w Castleton, Lillington and Longburton *Sarum* from 21. *The Vicarage, Abbey Close, Sherborne DT9 3LQ* M: 07725-593100 E: martinlee903@btinternet.com

LEE, Mary Elizabeth. See DUNN, Mary Elizabeth

LEE, Matthew Thomas. b 87. Trin Coll Cam BA 08. Wycliffe Hall Ox BA 17. d 18 p 19. C New Borough and Leigh *Sarum* from 18. *7 Ethelbert Road, Wimborne BH21 1BH* M: 07743-130268

LEE, Michael. b 45. d 07 p 08. OLM Chickerell w Fleet *Sarum* 07–11; NSM 11–15; PtO 15–22. *45 Lower Way, Chickerell, Weymouth DT3 4AR* T: (01305) 777031 E: michael.lynda@googlemail.com

LEE, Ms Michele Julie. b 57. Open Univ BSc 10. St Mellitus Coll BA 16. d 15 p 16. NSM Paddington St Steph w St Luke *Lon* from 15; NSM Bayswater from 15; Chapl Chelsea and Westmr Hosp NHS Foundn Trust from 15; Chapl Imp Coll Healthcare NHS Trust from 15. *37 Cumberland Mansions, Nutford Place, London W1H 5ZB* T: (020) 7262 7892 M: 07985-743650 E: m_lee157@sky.com or michele.lee@imperial.nhs.uk

LEE, Preb Nicholas Knyvett. b 54. Trin Coll Cam BA 76 MA 77. Cranmer Hall Dur 82. d 85 p 86. C Brompton H Trin w Onslow Square St Paul *Lon* 85–11; C Onslow Square and S Kensington St Aug from 11; Chapl R Brompton and Harefield NHS Trust 86–90; Chapl R Brompton and Harefield NHS Foundn Trust from 94; Preb St Paul's Cathl *Lon* from 16. *St Paul's Church House, Onslow Square, London SW7 3NX* T: 08456-447533 or (020) 7052 0324 E: nicky.lee@htb.org.uk

LEE, On Yip Franklin. b 82. York Univ BA 04 MA 06 Leeds Univ MA 07 Cam Univ BTh 12. Westcott Ho Cam 09. d 12 p 13. C Spalding St Mary and St Nic *Linc* 12–15; Min Can and Succ Windsor 15–18; Chapl St Geo Sch Windsor 15–18; Chapl St Jo Cathl Hong Kong 18–21; Sub-Dean H Trin Cathl from 21; P-in-c St Aug Chapl from 21. *Holy Trinity Cathedral, 135 Ma Tau Chung Road, Kowloon City, Kowloon, Hong Kong* E: franklinleeuk@yahoo.co.uk or flee@hkskh.org

LEE, Peter. See LEE, Kenneth Peter

LEE, Peter Alexander. b 44. Hull Univ BSc(Econ) 65. Ex & Truro NSM Scheme 80. d 83 p 84. NSM Ex St Sidwell and St Matt 83–89; NSM Ex St Dav 90–98; C Paignton St Jo, St Andr and St Boniface 98–01; PtO 01–03; Hon C Ex St Dav from 03. *Windyridge, Beech Avenue, Exeter EX4 6HF* T: (01392) 254118

LEE, Canon Raymond John. b 30. St Edm Hall Ox BA 53 MA 57. Tyndale Hall Bris 54. d 56 p 57. C Tooting Graveney St Nic *S'wark* 56–59; C Muswell Hill St Jas *Lon* 59–62; V Woking St Mary *Guildf* 62–70; V Gt Crosby St Luke *Liv* 70–82; Dioc Adv NSM 79–95; V Allerton 82–94; P-in-c Altcar 94–98; Hon Can Liv Cathl 89–95; rtd 95; PtO *Liv* from 98. *15 Barkfield Lane, Liverpool L37 1LY* T: (01704) 872670 E: rjlee@btinternet.com

LEE, Rebecca Susan. See HARRIS, Rebecca Susan

LEE, Richard. See LEE, Thomas Richard

LEE, Robert David. QUB BD 75. CITC 77. d 77 p 78. C Comber *D & D* 77–83; I Mt Merrion 83–87; CMS 89–92; Egypt 89–97; R Peebles *Edin* 97–11; P-in-c Innerleithen 97–11; rtd 11; LtO *Edin* from 11; PtO *Eur* from 17. *Flat 6, 32 Montgomery Street, Edinburgh EH7 5JS* T: 0131-623 1850 E: robindavidlee@gmail.com

LEE, Roderick James. b 50. Linc Th Coll 88. d 90 p 91. C Rushden w Newton Bromswold *Pet* 90–93; C Kingsthorpe w Northampton St Dav 93–94; TV 94–99; R Mears Ashby and Hardwick and Sywell etc 99–04; P-in-c Corby St Columba 04–12; RD Corby 07–12; Chapl Northants Fire and Rescue Service *Pet* 08–15. *41 Kingswell Road, Northampton NN2 6QB* T: (01604) 716199 M: 07806-262822 E: revrjl@btinternet.com

LEE, Sang Youn (Andrew). b 65. Pontifical Gregorian Univ BPh 95 BTh 98 MTh 00. St Steph Ho Ox 10. d 98 p 99. In RC Ch 98–06; C Goldthorpe w Hickleton *Sheff* 12–14; P-in-c Dalton 14–19; P-in-c Ryecroft St Nic 14–19; P-in-c Eyres Monsell *Leic* from 19; P-in-c Narborough and Huncote from 19. *St Hugh's Vicarage, 51 Pasley Road, Leicester LE2 9BU* M: 07870-885705 E: frandrewlee@yahoo.co.kr

LEE, Sarah Louise. b 65. BEM 21. Sheff Univ BA 88 Hughes Hall Cam PGCE 89. Trin Coll Bris 19. d 21. C Kingsthorpe *Pet* from 21. *42 Fallow Walk, Northampton NN2 8DE*

LEE, Steven Michael. b 56. Van Mildert Coll Dur BA 78. Trin Coll Bris 80. d 83 p 84. C Beckenham St Jo *Roch* 83–86; C Leic Martyrs 86–90; V Coalville and Bardon Hill 90–95; P-in-c Kibworth and Smeeton Westerby and Saddington 95–00; P-in-c Foxton w Gumley and Laughton 96–00; R Kibworth and Smeeton Westerby and Saddington 00–06; Chapl St Lawr Coll Ramsgate 06–08; R Newcastle w Butterton *Lich* 08–14; V Holmer w Huntington *Heref* from

14. *The New Vicarage, Holmer, Hereford HR4 9RG* T: (01432) 273200 E: revslee@btinternet.com

LEE, Stuart Graham. b 73. Roehampton Inst BA 94 Heythrop Coll Lon MA 10. St Steph Ho Ox BTh 00. **d** 00 **p** 01. C Eltham H Trin *S'wark* 00–03; TV Wimbledon 03–10; TV Mortlake w E Sheen 10–16; Chapl Richmond Charities Almshouses from 16. *The Richmond Charities, 8 The Green, Richmond TW9 1PL* T: (020) 8948 4188 E: stuartlee73@blueyonder.co.uk

LEE, Stuart Michael. b 67. SEITE 06. **d** 09 **p** 10. NSM St Jo on Bethnal Green *Lon* 09–14; NSM Bethnal Green St Barn from 14. *29 Brierly Gardens, London E2 0TE* T: (020) 8980 1699 M: 07855-703766 E: stuartm.lee@virgin.net *or* stuartmlee@me.com

LEE, Thomas Richard. b 52. AKC 73 FRSA 03 FRSocMed. St Aug Coll Cant 74. **d** 75 **p** 76. C Leam Lane CD *Dur* 75–80; Chapl RAF 80–09; Fell K Coll Lon 99–00; Prin Armed Forces Chapl Cen Amport Ho 03–06; Hon C St Mary le Strand w St Clem Danes *Lon* 06–09; QHC 06–09; TR Egremont and Haile *Carl* 09–18; Regional Chapl (N) RAF Air Cadets from 16; rtd 18; PtO *Carl* from 18; RD Calder from 20. *20 Abbey Vale, St Bees CA27 0EF* M: 07841-398088 E: lee535877@aol.com

LEE, Veronica. b 47. Redland Coll of Educn TCert 68 Open Univ BA 84 Bris Poly MEd 89. STETS 02. **d** 05 **p** 06. NSM Bishopston and St Andrews *Bris* 05–17; P-in-c Bris Lockleaze St Mary Magd w St Fran 17–19; PtO 19–21; *Ex* from 19. *38 High Street, Ide, Exeter EX2 9RW* T: (01392) 493385 E: vronlee@hotmail.com

LEE, Young. b 75. Korea Univ BA 98. St Mellitus Coll BA 12. **d** 12 **p** 13. C Walthamstow *Chelmsf* 12–15; P-in-c Barking St Erkenwald 15–20; V from 20. *St Erkenwald Vicarage, Levett Road, Barking IG11 9JZ* T: (020) 8507 9017 M: 07800-969706

LEE-BARBER, Evelyn Mary. b 62. **d** 13 **p** 14. NSM Bath Abbey w St Jas *B & W* from 13. *6 Cranhill Road, Bath BA1 2YF* T: (01225) 421170 M: 07920-847322 E: evelyn@evelynleebarber.plus.com

LEE-PHILPOT, Derreck Anthony John. b 56. Ripon Coll Cuddesdon 08. **d** 11 **p** 12. NSM Cholsey and Moulsford *Ox* 11–16; C Seaford w Sutton *Chich* from 16. *St Luke's House, Seaford Road, Seaford BN25 3SP* T: (01323) 893391 E: derreck3147@gmail.com *or* dlp@seafordparish.org.uk

LEECE, Roderick Neil Stephen. b 59. Wadh Coll Ox BA 81 MA 85 Leeds Univ BA 84 ARCM 85. Coll of Resurr Mirfield 82. **d** 85 **p** 86. C Portsea St Mary *Portsm* 85–91; V Stamford Hill St Bart *Lon* 91–05; R Hanover Square St Geo from 05. *21A Down Street, London W1J 7AW* T: (020) 7629 0874 E: rector@stgeorgeshanoversquare.org

LEECH, Pieter-Jan Bosdin. b 73. K Alfred's Coll Win BA 96. St Jo Coll Nottm 08. **d** 10 **p** 11. C Stalham, E Ruston, Brunstead, Sutton and Ingham *Nor* 10–13; R Yare Valley from 13; Jt RD Blofield from 17. *The Rectory, 73 The Street, Brundall, Norwich NR13 5LZ* M: 07504-171311 E: peter.leech@live.co.uk

LEEDS, Archdeacon of. *See* AYERS, The Ven Paul Nicholas

LEEDS, Bishop of. *See* BAINES, The Rt Revd Nicholas

LEEKE, Charles Browne. b 39. Stranmillis Coll CertEd 62. CITC 80. **d** 83 **p** 84. C Ballymoney w Finvoy and Rasharkin *Conn* 83–86; I Faughanvale *D & R* 86–97; Chapl Port Londonderry Miss to Seamen 92–97; Bp's Dom Chapl *D & R* 92–96; Can Derry Cathl 96–00; I Drumragh w Mountfield 97–00; Reconciliation Development Officer *D & D* 00–06; Can Dromore Cathl 05–06; rtd 06; I Dromara w Garvaghy *D & D* 08–13. *41 Beechfield Lodge, Aghalee, Craigavon BT67 0GA* T: (028) 9265 0179 M: 07712-870799 E: charlieleeke@yahoo.co.uk

LEEKE, Canon Stephen Owen. b 50. EAMTC 82 Ridley Hall Cam 83. **d** 84 **p** 85. C Cherry Hinton St Andr *Ely* 84–87; P-in-c Warboys 87–91; P-in-c Bury 87–91; P-in-c Wistow 87–91; R Warboys w Broughton and Bury w Wistow 91–01; RD St Ives 92–01; V Cambridge St Martin 01–15; Hon Can Ely Cathl 05–15; rtd 15; PtO *Ely* from 15. *11 Sycamore Lane, Ely CB7 4TP* E: stephen.leeke9@gmail.com *or* stephen@leeke.me.uk

LEEMAN, Miss Penelope Anne. b 51. SNWTP 10. **d** 12 **p** 13. C Kirkdale St Athanaseus with St Mary *Liv* 12–16; C Maghull and Melling 17–19; rtd 19. *10 Garth Court, Haigh Road, Liverpool L22 3XL* E: pleeman22@gmail.com

LEES (née LESLIE), Amanda Louise Thornton. b 69. Univ Coll Dur BA 90. St Jo Coll Nottm MA 16. **d** 16 **p** 17. NSM Blidworth w Rainworth *S'well* 16–18; Bp's Chapl from 18. *Jubilee House, Westgate, Southwell NG25 0JH* T: (01636) 817996 E: chaplain@southwell.anglican.org

LEES, Brian James. b 52. Lon Univ BA 74 Leeds Univ BA 08 Univ of Wales (Abth) PGCE 75. NOC 05. **d** 08 **p** 09. NSM Hutton Cranswick w Skerne, Watton and Beswick *York* 08–11; P-in-c 11–16; P-in-c Nafferton w Wansford 14–16;

rtd 16; PtO *York* from 16. *The Old Post House, 20 Main Street, Beswick, Driffield YO25 9AS* T: (01377) 270806 E: brianlees2019@gmail.com

LEES, Charles Alan. b 38. RGN TCert. WMMTC 78. **d** 81 **p** 82. NSM Yardley St Cypr Hay Mill *Birm* 81–84 and 86–87; Hon C Dorridge 84–86; Chapl E Birm Hosp 85–87; Hon C Leamington Spa H Trin and Old Milverton *Cov* 89–90; PtO *Birm* 95–01. *8 Fairlawn Close, Leamington Spa CV32 6EN*

LEES, Preb Christopher John. b 58. Fitzw Coll Cam BA 80 Birkbeck Coll Lon MA 86 Liv Univ MTh 04 FCIPD. NOC 01. **d** 04 **p** 05. NSM Wilmslow *Ches* 04–14; Asst Dir of Ords 07–14; C Colyton, Musbury, Southleigh and Branscombe *Ex* 15–20; Bp's Officer for SSM from 16; Nat Officer for SSM Nat Min Team Abps' Coun from 20; Preb Ex Cathl from 19. *3 Vicarage Street, Colyton EX24 6LJ* T: (01297) 551351 E: info@johnleescareers.com

LEES, Jane. b 62. Ripon Coll Cuddesdon 05. **d** 07 **p** 08. NSM Ox St Matt from 07. *36 Canning Crescent, Oxford OX1 4XB* T: (01865) 250672 *or* 251616

LEES, John Raymond. b 57. Selw Coll Cam BA 78 MA 82. St Steph Ho Ox 89. **d** 91 **p** 92. C Eastbourne St Mary *Chich* 91–93; Min Can and Succ St Paul's Cathl *Lon* 93–98; TR Swindon New Town *Bris* 98–01; Asst to AD Swindon and C Highworth w Sevenhampton and Inglesham etc 01–02; PtO *Lon* 02–05; *Pet* 04–06; *Ely* 04–06; Can Res and Prec Wakef Cathl 06–09; rtd 09; PtO *Lich* 09–14; *Nor* from 14; Hon PV Nor Cathl from 15. *The Beeches, 58 Church Lane, Sprowston, Norwich NR7 8AZ*

LEES, Joshua Marcus. b 91. Staffs Univ BA 13 MA 16. Wycliffe Hall Ox MTh 19. **d** 19 **p** 20. C Onslow Square and S Kensington St Aug *Lon* from 19. *Address withheld by request* E: josh.lees@htb.org

LEES, Mrs Kathleen Marion. b 30. Birkbeck Coll Lon BA 60. S'wark Ord Course 77. **dss** 80 **d** 87 **p** 94. Epping St Jo *Chelmsf* 80–86; Hon C Hunstanton St Mary w Ringstead Parva, Holme etc *Nor* 87–88; PtO 88–94; Chapl King's Lynn and Wisbech Hosps NHS Trust 94–00; NSM Gaywood *Nor* 94–00; rtd 00; PtO *Nor* 00–16; *Chich* from 16. *24 Ramsay Hall, 9-13 Byron Road, Worthing BN11 3HN*

LEES, Peter John. b 39. St Jo Coll Nottm 91. **d** 95 **p** 96. NSM Buckie and Turriff *Ab* 95–00; P-in-c Fraserburgh 00–01; R 01–06; rtd 06; P-in-c Turriff *Ab* 08–09; LtO from 15. *7 Whitefield Court, Buckie AB56 1EY* T: (01542) 835011 M: 07929-668027

LEES, Stephen. b 55. St Jo Coll York CertEd 77 BEd 78 Nottm Univ MA 96. St Jo Coll Nottm 88. **d** 90 **p** 91. C Mansfield St Jo *S'well* 90–93; TV Bestwood 93–98; V Baxenden *Blackb* 98–08; P-in-c Halifax All SS *Wakef* 08–14; *Leeds* 14–18; V 18–20; rtd 20. *Address temp unknown* E: theleeslot@blueyonder.co.uk

LEES, Stephen David. b 63. Sheff City Poly BA 84 St Jo Coll Dur BA 09 Bradf Coll of Educn PGCE 92. Cranmer Hall Dur 07. **d** 09 **p** 10. C Frizinghall St Marg *Bradf* 09–13; C Wrose 13–14; C Bolton St Jas w St Chrys 13–14; V *Leeds* 14–21; Chapl Bradf Teaching Hosps NHS Foundn Trust from 21. *Bradford Royal Infirmary, Duckworth Lane, Bradford BD9 6RJ* T: (01274) 542200 E: stelees51@gmail.com *or* steve.lees@leeds.anglican.org

LEES, Stuart Charles Roderick. b 62. Trin Coll Bris BA. **d** 89 **p** 90. C Woodford Wells *Chelmsf* 89–93; C Brompton H Trin w Onslow Square St Paul *Lon* 93–97; Chapl Stewards Trust 93–97; P-in-c Fulham Ch Ch *Lon* 97–03; V from 03. *Christ Church Vicarage, 40 Clancarty Road, London SW6 3AA* T: (020) 7736 4261 E: stuart@ccfulham.com

LEES-SMITH, Anthony James. b 77. Selw Coll Cam BA 99 MA 02 St Jo Coll Dur BA 08 MA 09 Westmr Inst of Educn PGCE 02. Cranmer Hall Dur 06. **d** 09 **p** 10. C Chesterton Gd Shep *Ely* 09–12; V Evington *Leic* from 12; AD City of Leic from 20. *The Vicarage, Rectory Gardens, Leicester LE2 2FU* T: 0116-215 5500 M: 07967-353857 E: singers99.als@gmail.com

LEESE, Mrs Jane Elizabeth. b 50. Man Univ BA(Econ) 72 Avery Hill Coll PGCE 73. Sarum Th Coll 93. **d** 96 **p** 97. NSM Kempshott *Win* 96–01; NSM Herriard w Winslade and Long Sutton etc 01–08; NSM N Hants Downs 08–16; rtd 16; PtO *Win* from 16; Clergy Widows and Widowers Officer (Win Adnry) 16–19. *15 Waverley Avenue, Basingstoke RG21 3JN* T: (01256) 471193 M: 07754-296994 E: reverendjane@hotmail.co.uk

LEESON, Bernard Alan. b 47. Bris Univ CertEd 68 Open Univ BA 75 Southn Univ MA 78 Sheff Univ PhD 97 FCollP 92 FRSA 92. EMMTC 84. **d** 87 **p** 88. Dep Hd Master Ripley Mill Hill Sch 80–91; NSM Breadsall *Derby* 87–91; Hd St Aid C of E Tech Coll Lancs 91–06; NSM Officer *Blackb* 92–96; Clergy Support and Development Officer 06–09; PtO 91–92; LtO 92–17; rtd 17; PtO *Blackb* from 17. *The Lodge, Daggers Lane, Preesall, Poulton-le-Fylde FY6 0QN* T: (01253) 811020 E: leeson@mail.org

LEFFLER, Christopher. b 33. Em Coll Cam BA 57 MA 61. Linc Th Coll. **d** 59 **p** 60. C Bermondsey St Mary w St Olave and St Jo *S'wark* 59–60; C Herne Hill St Paul 60–63; C-in-c Canley CD *Cov* 63–67; R Gt and Lt Glemham *St E* 67–72; R Badwell Ash w Gt Ashfield, Stowlangtoft etc 72–82; R Trimley 82–99; rtd 99; PtO *St E* 99–20; *Ely* from 21. *308 High Street, Felixstowe IP11 9QJ* T: (01394) 672279 M: 07765-785958 E: chrisleffler@uwclub.net

LEFFLER, Jeremy Paul (Jem). b 62. Westmr Coll Ox BEd 88. Wycliffe Hall Ox BTh 94. **d** 94 **p** 95. C Ormskirk *Liv* 94–97; C Much Woolton 97–00; P-in-c Widnes St Ambrose 00–03; V 03–12; P-in-c Birkdale St Jo 12–21; rtd 21. *Address temp unknown*

LEFROY, John Perceval. b 40. Trin Coll Cam BA 62. Cuddesdon Coll 64. **d** 66 **p** 67. C Maidstone St Martin *Cant* 66–69; C St Peter-in-Thanet 69–74; V Barming Heath 74–82; V Upchurch w Lower Halstow 82–05; P-in-c Iwade 95–05; rtd 05; PtO *Sarum* from 06. *23 Heather Avenue, Melksham SN12 6FX* T: (01225) 704012 E: jclefroy@tiscali.co.uk

LEFROY, Matthew William. b 62. Trin Coll Cam BA 84 Keele Univ PGCE 91. St Jo Coll Nottm MTh 02. **d** 02 **p** 03. C Portswood Ch Ch *Win* 02–06; TV Madeley *Heref* 06–13; RD Telford Severn Gorge 11–13; V Lilleshall and Muxton *Lich* from 13; RD Edgmond and Shifnal from 20. *The Vicarage, 25 Church Road, Lilleshall, Newport TF10 9HE* T: (01952) 604281

LEFROY-OWEN, Neal. b 62. Bradf Univ BA 99. NOC 00. **d** 03 **p** 04. C Sandal St Cath *Wakef* 03–06; Asst Chapl HM Pris Hull 06–08; Chapl HM Pris Lindholme 08–12; Chapl HM Pris Wakef 12–14; P-in-c Warley *Leeds* 15–16; P-in-c Halifax St Hilda 15–16; V Warley and Halifax St Hilda 16–17. *2 Kitten Clough, Halifax HX2 0JJ* E: revneal.owen@gmail.com

LEGG, Adrian James. b 52. St Jo Coll Nottm BTh 82. **d** 82 **p** 83. C Haughton le Skerne *Dur* 82–85; C Llanishen and Lisvane *Llan* 85–89; V Llanwddyn and Llanfihangel-yng-Nghwynfa etc *St As* 89–93; V Llansadwrn w Llanwrda and Manordeilo *St D* 93–10; Chapl Wadham Sch Crewkerne 11–15; C Yeovil St Mich *B & W* 12–14; PtO *S & B* from 15; *St D* from 17. *Llys Esgob, Abergwili, Carmarthen SA31 2JG* E: adrianlegg@btinternet.com

LEGG, Alison Grant. See MILBANK, Alison Grant

LEGG, Joanna Susan Penberthy. See PENBERTHY, Joanna Susan

LEGG, Margaret. b 50. SEITE. **d** 07 **p** 08. NSM Paddington St Jo w St Mich *Lon* 07–20; PtO from 20; Chapl Imp Coll Healthcare NHS Trust from 16. *Flat 2, 134 Elgin Avenue, London W9 2NS* T: (020) 3532 5300 E: margaret.rose.legg@gmail.com

LEGG, Richard. b 37. Selw Coll Cam BA 62 MA 66 Brunel Univ MPhil 77 NY Th Sem DMin 85. Coll of Resurr Mirfield 63. **d** 65 **p** 66. C Ealing St Pet Mt Park *Lon* 65–68; Chapl Brunel Univ 68–78; Wychcroft Ho (Dioc Retreat Cen) *S'wark* 78–81; C Chipping Barnet w Arkley *St Alb* 81–83; TV 83–85; R St Buryan, St Levan and Sennen *Truro* 85–93; Subwarden St Deiniol's Lib Hawarden 93; PtO *Ches* 93; TV Beaminster Area *Sarum* 93–97; P-in-c Veryan w Ruan Lanihorne *Truro* 97–00; rtd 01; PtO *Truro* 03–09; *B & W* 10–18. *27A Bath Road, Wells BA5 3HR* T: (01749) 670468

LEGG, Roger Keith. b 35. Lich Th Coll 61. **d** 63 **p** 64. C Petersfield w Sheet *Portsm* 63–66; C Portsea St Mary 66–70; Rhodesia 70–75; V Clayton *Lich* 75–00; rtd 01; PtO *Lich* 01–14. *High Crest, Chapel Lane, Hookgate, Market Drayton TF9 4QP* T: (01630) 672766 E: rogjud@talktalk.net

LEGG, Miss Ruth Helen Margaret. b 52. Hull Univ BA 74 Homerton Coll Cam CertEd 75. Trin Coll Bris 86. **d** 88 **p** 94. C Clevedon St Andr and Ch Ch *B & W* 88–92; C Nailsea Ch Ch 92–96; C Nailsea Ch Ch w Tickenham 96–97; V Pill, Portbury and Easton-in-Gordano 97–16; rtd 16; PtO *Sarum* 17–22. *11 Sunridge Shades, 11-15 Belle Vue Road, Poole BH14 8TW* T: (01202) 002572 E: ruthhmlegg@gmail.com

LEGG, Sandra Christine. See FACCINI, Sandra Christine

LEGGATE, Colin Archibald Gunson. b 44. Bris Sch of Min 86. **d** 88 **p** 89. NSM Brislington St Luke *Bris* 88–97; Asst Chapl Frenchay Healthcare NHS Trust Bris 97–99; Asst Chapl N Bris NHS Trust 99–09; rtd 09; PtO *Heref* from 09. *5 Merrivale Crescent, Ross-on-Wye HR9 5JU* T: (01989) 564536 E: colin.leggate@tiscali.co.uk

LEGGE, Robert James. b 63. BSc 92. Ox Min Course. **d** 09 **p** 10. C Walton H Trin *Ox* 09–13; TV Kidderminster E *Worc* from 13. *38 Comberton Avenue, Kidderminster DY10 3EG* M: 07809-227660 E: rjlegge@live.co.uk

LEGGE, Trevor Raymond. b 42. Liv Univ BEng 63. **d** 11 **p** 12. NSM Oughtrington and Warburton *Ches* 11–16; PtO from 16. *17 Wychwood Avenue, Lymm WA13 0NE* T: (01925) 756872 E: trlegge@talktalk.net

LEGGETT, James Henry Aufrere. b 61. Oak Hill Th Coll 91. **d** 93 **p** 94. C Hensingham *Carl* 93–97; C-in-c Ryde St Jas Prop Chpl *Portsm* from 97. *84 Pellhurst Road, Ryde PO33 3BS* T: (01983) 565621 *or* 566381 E: james.leggett@stjamesryde.com

LEGGETT, Nicholas William Michael. b 62. Glos Univ BA 10 FCMI. St Steph Ho Ox 00. **d** 02 **p** 04. C Clevedon St Jo *B & W* 02–06; P-in-c Bridgwater H Trin and Durleigh 06–07; V 07–10; V Tile Hill *Cov* 10–18; R Chenderit *Pet* from 18; C Culworth w Sulgrave and Thorpe Mandeville etc from 21; Hon Chapl ATC from 04; CF(V) from 12. *Chenderit Rectory, 17 Astrop Road, Middleton Cheney, Banbury OX17 2PG* M: 07925-419068 E: leggett1uwe@yahoo.co.uk

LEGH, Mrs Jane Mary. b 52. BEM 17. Southn Univ BSc 73. Qu Coll Birm 08. **d** 09 **p** 10. NSM S Dales *Derby* from 09; NSM Boylestone, Church Broughton, Dalbury, etc 09–21; P-in-c 17–21. *Cubley Lodge, Cubley, Ashbourne DE6 2FB* T: (01335) 330297 E: jane.legh@cubleylodge.com

LEGOOD, Giles Leslie. b 67. MBE 14. K Coll Lon BD 88 AKC 88 Heythrop Coll Lon MTh 98 Derby Univ DMin 04. Ripon Coll Cuddesdon 90. **d** 92 **p** 93. C N Mymms *St Alb* 92–95; Chapl R Veterinary Coll *Lon* 95–07; Chapl R Free and Univ Coll Medical Sch 95–07; Chapl RAuxAF 04–07; Chapl RAF from 07; QHC from 18. *Chaplaincy Services (RAF), HQ Air Command, RAF High Wycombe HP14 4UE* T: (01494) 496800

LEHANEY, Frank George. b 44. MCIT 75 MILT 99 MIAM 78. **d** 99 **p** 00. OLM Brockham Green *S'wark* 99–07; NSM 07–14; OLM Leigh 99–07; NSM 07–14; Chapl Surrey and Sussex Healthcare NHS Trust 99–09; PtO *S'wark* from 14. *Twelve Trees, Small's Hill Road, Leigh, Reigate RH2 8PE* T: (01306) 611201

LEICESTER, Archdeacon of. See WORSFOLD, The Ven Richard Vernon

LEICESTER, Bishop of. See SNOW, The Rt Revd Martyn James

LEICESTER, Dean of. See MONTEITH, The Very Revd David Robert Malvern

LEIGH, Mrs Alison Margaret. b 40. CertEd 63 Goldsmiths' Coll Lon BEd 75. Sarum & Wells Th Coll 85. **d** 87 **p** 94. C Chessington *Guildf* 87–90; C Green Street Green *Roch* 90–92; Dn-in-c E Peckham and Nettlestead 92–94; P-in-c 94–95; R 95–01; rtd 01; PtO *Heref* from 02. *17 Orchard Green, Marden, Hereford HR1 3ED* T: (01432) 882032

LEIGH, Mary Elizabeth. b 42. K Coll Lon BA 64 Univ of Wales (Lamp) MMin 06. Westcott Ho Cam 89. **d** 91 **p** 94. NSM Chesterfield St Mary and All SS *Derby* 91–92; C Hall Green Ascension *Birm* 92–94; Asst P Yardley St Edburgha 94–97; Chapl and Tutor NOC 97–08; rtd 08; PtO *Lich* 99–11; *Derby* from 14; *Lon* 16–19. *Downing Cottage, Jaggers Lane, Hathersage, Hope Valley S32 1AZ* T: (01433) 650567 M: 07796-980636 E: mel@leigh.me

LEIGH, Michael John. b 69. Leeds Univ BA 02 LWCMD 93. Coll of Resurr Mirfield 00. **d** 02 **p** 03. C N Hull St Mich *York* 02–06; P-in-c Newby 06–14; V 14–20; V Cloughton and Burniston 14–20; RD Scarborough 16–20; Chapl Scargill Ho from 20; V Cloughton and Burniston w Ravenscar etc *York* from 14. *Scargill House, Kettlewell, Skipton BD23 5HU* T: (01756) 760500 E: famleigh77@gmail.com

LEIGH, Nathan Daniel. b 90. Moorlands Coll BA 17. St Mellitus Coll MA 19. **d** 19 **p** 20. NSM Southampton (St Mary) *Win* from 19. *St Matthew's Vicarage, 12-14 Kings Park Road, Southampton SO15 2AT* M: 07434-958003 E: nathan.l2012la@gmail.com

LEIGH, Richenda Mary Celia. See WHEELER, Richenda Mary Celia

LEIGH, Mrs Ruth Margaret. b 56. Warwick Univ BA 02. Ripon Coll Cuddesdon 19. **d** 21. OLM Westbury, Worthen and Yockleton *Heref* from 21. *14 Jubilee Mews, Westbury, Shrewsbury SY5 9EZ* T: (01743) 884658 E: ruthleigh56@gmail.com

LEIGH-HUNT, Nicolas Adrian. b 46. MIEx 70. Qu Coll Birm 85. **d** 87 **p** 88. C Tilehurst St Geo *Ox* 87–91; TV Wexcombe *Sarum* 91–99; TR 99–02; TR Savernake 02–11; RD Pewsey 97–10; rtd 11; PtO *Sarum* 15–20. *Steeles Cottage, Eastcourt, Burbage, Marlborough SN8 3AG* T: (01672) 810953 E: leighhunt@aol.com

LEIGHLIN, Dean of. See GORDON, The Very Revd Thomas William

LEIGHTON, Adrian Barry. b 44. LTh. Lon Coll of Div 65. **d** 69 **p** 70. C Erith St Paul *Roch* 69–72; C Ipswich St Marg *St E* 72–75; P-in-c Ipswich St Helen 75–82; R 82–88; P-in-c Holbrook w Freston and Woolverstone 88–97; P-in-c Wherstead 94–97; R Holbrook, Freston, Woolverstone and Wherstead 97–98; RD Samford 90–93; P-in-c Woore and Norton in Hales *Lich* 98–09; Local Min Adv (Shrewsbury) 99–09; rtd 09; PtO *Ches* 09–18. *2 Tollgate Drive, Audlem, Crewe CW3 0EA* T: (01270) 812209 E: adrianleighton@btinternet.com

LEIGHTON, Alan Granville Clyde. b 37. MInstM AMIDHE. S'wark Ord Course 73. **d** 76 **p** 77. C Silverhill St Matt *Chich*

76–79; C Eston *York* 79–82; V 82–84; TR Eston w Normanby 84–02; rtd 02; PtO *York* 02–15. *Priory Lodge, 86B Church Lane, Eston, Middlesbrough TS6 9QR* T: (01642) 504798 F: 283016

LEIGHTON, Anthony Robert. b 56. Trin Coll Bris BA 88. **d** 88 **p** 89. C Harrow Trin St Mich *Lon* 88–92; TV Ratby cum Groby *Leic* 92–94; TR Bradgate Team 94–00; P-in-c Newtown Linford 95–98; V Thorpe Acre w Dishley 00–08; NSM S Croxton Gp 08–14; Master Wyggeston's Hosp Leic from 14; NSM Leic H Apostles from 14. *The Master's House, Wyggeston's Hospital, 160 Hinckley Road, Leicester LE3 0UX* T: 0116-254 8682 E: tony0leighton@btinternet.com

LEIGHTON, Mrs Catherine Mary Alexandra. b 72. Surrey Univ BMus 93 Man Metrop Univ PGCE 08. Trin Coll Bris 16. **d** 18 **p** 19. C Tettenhall Regis *Lich* from 18. *12 Windmill Lane, Wolverhampton WV3 8HJ* M: 07903-164242 E: cmaleighton@icloud.com

LEIGHTON, Simon Andrew. b 90. Lon Sch of Th BA 13. Trin Coll Bris 16. **d** 18 **p** 19. C Lawrence Weston and Avonmouth *Bris* 18–20; C Shirehampton from 20. *11 Severn Road, Shirehampton, Bristol BS11 9TE* M: 07876-613629 E: revsimonleighton@gmail.com

LEIGHTON, Mrs Susan. b 58. Bretton Hall Coll BEd 80. Trin Coll Bris BA 89. **p** 94. Par Dn Harrow Weald All SS *Lon* 89–92; NSM Ratby cum Groby *Leic* 92–96; C Bradgate Team 96–00; Asst Warden of Readers 96–00; NSM Thorpe Acre w Dishley 00–08; TV S Croxton Gp 08–10; P-in-c 10–14; P-in-c Burrough Hill Pars 10–14; NSM Leic Martyrs 15–17; P-in-c Leic St Theodore from 17; Chapl for Deaf People from 15. *The Master's House, Wyggeston's Hospital, 160 Hinckley Road, Leicester LE3 0UX* T: 0116-254 8682 M: 07766-476490 E: susan.leighton2@btinternet.com

LEIGHTON PLOM, Ashley James. b 85. St Mellitus Coll BA 20. **d** 20. C St Dav from 20. *3 Cowley View, Glenthorne Road, Exeter EX4 4XA* M: 07855-305519 E: aescleal@gmail.com

LEIPER, Nicholas Keith. b 34. SS Coll Cam BA 55 MB 58 BChir 58 MA 65. St Jo Coll Nottm LTh 82. **d** 84 **p** 85. C Bidston *Ches* 84–87; TV Gateacre *Liv* 87–92; P-in-c Bickerstaffe 92–94; P-in-c Melling 92–94; V Bickerstaffe and Melling 94–00; rtd 00; PtO *Liv* from 00. *31 Weldale House, Chase Close, Southport PR8 2DX* T: (01704) 566393

LEITHEAD, Mrs Lynette. b 54. Kent Univ BA 08. SEITE. **d** 08 **p** 09. NSM Kippington *Roch* 08–13 and 17–19; NSM Sundridge w Ide Hill and Toys Hill 13–16; PtO 16–17; NSM W Sevenoaks from 19. *45 Chipstead Park, Sevenoaks TN13 2SL* T: (01732) 742272 M: 07958-145959 E: lynetteleithead@hotmail.co.uk

LEMMEY, William Henry Michael. b 59. Jes Coll Cam BA 81 Jes Coll Ox PGCE 82. Westcott Ho Cam 03. **d** 05 **p** 06. C Milton *Win* 05–09; R Porlock and Porlock Weir w Stoke Pero etc *B & W* 09–20; V Aylesbeare, Clyst St George, Clyst St Mary etc *Ex* from 20. *The Vicarage, Greenway, Woodbury, Exeter EX5 1LU* T: (01395) 232161 E: revbillwhitecross@gmail.com

LENANDER, Laura Sian. b 86. Univ of the Arts Lon BA 09 Goldsmiths' Coll Lon MA 13 Dur Univ BA 21. St Mellitus Coll 18. **d** 21. C Cen Telford *Lich* from 21. *Address temp unknown* M: 07738-590365 E: llenander@gmail.com

LENG, Bruce Edgar. b 38. St Aid Birkenhead 68. **d** 69 **p** 70. C Sheff St Swithun 69–74; TV Yate New Town *Bris* 78–82; R Handsworth *Sheff* 82–95; R Thrybergh 95–05; Warden for Past Workers 96–05; rtd 05; PtO *Sheff* from 06. *41 Hall Close Avenue, Whiston, Rotherham S60 4AH* M: 07908-448337 E: brucelenguk@gmail.com

LENNOX, Joan Baxter. *See* LYON, Joan Baxter

LENNOX, Mark. Ulster Univ BA St Jo Coll Nottm MA. CITC. **d** 09 **p** 10. NSM Maghera w Killelagh *D & R* 09–12; NSM Camus-juxta-Mourne 12–15; Bp's C 15–18; I Killyman Arm from 18. *The Rectory, 85 Dungorman Road, Dungannon BT71 6SE* T: (028) 8772 2324 *or* 8772 2500 M: 07752-152991 E: mark.lennox6@btopenworld.com *or* killyman@armagh.anglican.org

LENOX-CONYNGHAM, Canon Andrew George. b 44. Magd Coll Ox BA 66 MA 73 CCC Cam PhD 73. Westcott Ho Cam 72. **d** 74 **p** 75. C Poplar *Lon* 74–77; TV 77–80; Chapl Heidelberg *Eur* 80–82; 91–95; Chapl R Marsden Hosp 95–96; Chapl Ch Coll Cam 82–86; Chapl and Fell St Cath Coll Cam 86–91; V Birm St Luke 96–14; AD Cen Birm 04–12; Hon Can Birm Cathl 14; rtd 14; PtO *Birm* from 14. *9 Hitches Lane, Birmingham B15 2LS* T: 0121-446 6783 E: lenox@birm.eclipse.co.uk

LENS VAN RIJN, Robert Adriaan. b 47. St Jo Coll Nottm 78. **d** 80 **p** 81. C Gt Baddow *Chelmsf* 80–83; C Edgware *Lon* 83–86; C Derby St Pet and Ch Ch w H Trin 86–90; Chapl Eindhoven *Eur* 91–00; Chapl Burrswood Chr Cen 04–08; rtd 08; PtO *York* 09–18; Chapl Dove Ho Hospice Hull 09–18. *De Jongestraat 3, 4453 BP 's-Heerenhoek, The Netherlands* T: (0031) (113) 268763 E: rlvr@iae.nl

LENTHALL, Mrs Nicola Yvonne. b 73. Southn Univ BA 95 Anglia Ruskin Univ MA 02. Westcott Ho Cam. **d** 99 **p** 00. C Leighton Buzzard w Eggington, Hockliffe etc *St Alb* 99–03; V Kensworth, Studham and Whipsnade from 03; RD Dunstable from 19. *The Vicarage, Clay Hall Road, Kensworth, Dunstable LU6 3RF* T: (01582) 872223 E: revnicolalenthall@btinternet.com

LENTON, John Robert. b 46. Ex Coll Ox BA 69 Harvard Univ MBA 74. Oak Hill Th Coll. **d** 00 **p** 02. NSM Muswell Hill St Jas w St Matt *Lon* 00–09; NSM Hampstead St Jo Downshire Hill Prop Chpl 09–10; NSM Bramley *Win* 10–14; NSM Sherfield-on-Loddon and Stratfield Saye etc 14–21; rtd 21; PtO *Win* from 21. *31A Kings Avenue, London N10 1PA* M: 07714-237235 E: john.lenton@gmail.com

LENTON, Sarah Edwina. b 48. K Coll Lon BD 72. St Mellitus Coll 15. **d** 16 **p** 17. NSM Bedford Park *Lon* 16–18; NSM Covent Garden St Paul 18–20; NSM Westmr St Matt from 20; NSM St Mary le Strand w St Clem Danes from 20; Chapl W End Theatres from 16. *10 Saltcoats Road, London W4 1AR* T: (020) 8994 1380 E: sarah.lenton@virgin.net

LENTON de DICKIN, Mrs Patricia Margarita. b 72. STETS MA 08. **d** 08 **p** 09. C Epsom Common Ch Ch *Guildf* 08–09; C Oxshott 09–12; P-in-c Mereworth w W Peckham *Roch* 12–19; R Mereworth, Wateringbury and W Peckham 19; TV S Gillingham from 19. *The Vicarage, 90 Wigmore Road, Gillingham ME8 0SX*

LEON (*née* HOLLAND), Mrs Lesley Anne. b 52. Univ Coll Chich BA 04. STETS 04. **d** 07 **p** 08. NSM Northanger *Win* from 07; PtO *Portsm* from 11. *11A Tilmore Gardens, Petersfield GU32 2JQ* E: lesley.leon@ntlworld.com

LEONARD, Mrs Andrea Susan. b 60. SEITE 13. **d** 15 **p** 16. C Roch St Justus 15–19; P-in-c Luton Ch Ch from 19. *Christ Church, Luton Road, Chatham ME4 5BT* T: (01634) 845537 M: 07752-626644 E: andumiak@gmail.com *or* andrea@luton.church

LEONARD, Ms Ann Cressey. b 50. Open Univ BA 90 Lon Univ MA. S Dios Minl Tr Scheme 90. **d** 94 **p** 95. C Portsea St Cuth *Portsm* 94–96; C Farlington 96–00; Asst to RD Petersfield 00–03; Deanery Co-ord for Educn and Tr 00–03; V Hayling Is St Andr 03–15; V N Hayling St Pet 03–15; Dioc Ecum Officer 02–03; rtd 15; PtO *Portsm* from 15. *10 Trent Way, Lee-on-the-Solent PO13 8JF* T: (023) 9263 7673 E: anncleonard@gmail.com

LEONARD, John Francis. b 48. Lich Th Coll 69. **d** 72 **p** 73. C Chorley St Geo *Blackb* 72–75; C S Shore H Trin 75–80; V Marton Moss 81–89; V Kingskerswell w Coffinswell *Ex* 89–18; P-in-c Abbotskerswell 06–18; rtd 18. *Windermere, 19 Fisher Road, Newton Abbot TQ12 2NA*

LEONARD, Canon John James. b 41. Southn Univ BSc 62. Sarum Th Coll 63. **d** 65 **p** 66. C Loughborough Em *Leic* 65–70; V New Humberstone 70–78; C-in-c Rushey Mead CD 78–85; V Leic St Theodore 85–05; Hon Can Leic Cathl 96–05; RD Christianity N 97–05; rtd 05; PtO *Leic* from 05. *1339 Melton Road, Syston, Leicester LE7 2EP* T: 0116-269 2691 E: j2.leonard@btinternet.com

LEONARD, Nicola Susan. *See* TERRY, Nicola Susan

LEONARD, The Ven Peter Philip. b 70. Trin Coll Bris BA 94. **d** 97 **p** 98. C Haslemere *Guildf* 97–00; C Haslemere and Grayswood 00–01; C Woodham 01–06; PtO 07–10; *Portsm* 12–14; Can Res Portsm Cathl 14–19; Adn Is of Wight from 19; TR Newport and Carisbrooke from 20. *5 The Boltons, Wootton Bridge, Ryde PO33 4PB* T: (01983) 884432 M: 07817-722219 E: peterleonard200@gmail.com *or* peter.leonard@portsmouth.anglican.org

LEONARD-JOHNSON, Canon Philip Anthony. b 35. Selw Coll Cam BA 58 MA 60. Linc Th Coll 63. **d** 65 **p** 66. C Wymondham *Nor* 65–68; Zimbabwe 69–82; V Drayton in Hales *Lich* 82–92; R Adderley 82–92; P-in-c Moreton Say 88–92; S Africa 92–98; rtd 97; Hon Can Grahamstown from 97; PtO *Lich* 99–14. *Hillside, Mount Lane, Market Drayton TF9 1AG* T: (01630) 655480 E: philipandjohnson@hotmail.com

LEONARDI, Preb Jeffrey. b 49. Warwick Univ BA 71 UEA PhD 09. Carl Dioc Tr Course 85. **d** 88 **p** 89. C Netherton *Carl* 88–91; V Cross Canonby 91–97; V Allonby 91–97; Bp's Adv for Past Care and Counselling *Lich* 97–14; C Colton, Colwich and Gt Haywood 97–10; C Abbots Bromley, Blithfield, Colton, Colwich etc 11–14; Preb Lich Cathl 12–14; rtd 14; PtO *St D* from 14; Hon Research Fell Univ of Wales Trin St Dav from 14. *Llwyncelyn, Cribyn, Lampeter SA48 7NH* T: (01570) 470526 E: jeff.leonardi@btinternet.com

LEPINE, Ayla Rowanna. b 83. Victoria Univ (BC) BA 03 Courtauld Inst of Art MA 05 PhD 11 Jes Coll Cam BA 17 MPhil 18. Westcott Ho Cam 15. **d** 18 **p** 19. C Hampstead St Jo *Lon* 18–20; Chapl K Coll Cam from 20. *King's College, Cambridge CB2 1ST* T: (01223) 331212 M: 07791-683042 E: ayla.lepine@gmail.com

LEPINE, The Very Revd Jeremy John. b 56. BA. St Jo Coll Nottm 82. **d** 84 **p** 85. C Harrow Trin St Mich *Lon* 84–88; TV Horley *S'wark* 88–95; Evang Adv Croydon Area Miss Team 95–02; Dioc Evang Adv and Hon Chapl S'wark Cathl 97–02; R Wollaton *S'well* 02–13; AD Nottm N 08–13; Hon Can S'well Minster 09–13; Dean Bradf 13–14; *Leeds* 14–21; rtd 21. *4 Moorway Lane, Littleover, Derby DE23 2FR*

LEPINE, Michelle Yvonne. b 72. Salford Univ BA 95 Leeds Univ PGCE 03. St Hild Coll 18. **d** 21. C Ripon H Trin *Leeds* from 21. *14 Filey Avenue, Ripon HG4 2DH* M: 07818-828575 E: m.lepine@holytrinityripon.org.uk

LEPLEY, Mrs Kim Angela. b 60. St Mellitus Coll BA 12. **d** 12 **p** 13. C Takeley w Lt Canfield *Chelmsf* 12–15; C Gt Wakering w Foulness 15–17; P-in-c 17–19; C Barling w Lt Wakering 15–17; P-in-c 17–19; C Rochford and Sutton w Shopland 15–17; P-in-c 17–19; TR Roach Par from 19. *The Vicarage, 2 New Road, Great Wakering, Southend-on-Sea SS3 0AH* T: (01702) 216725 M: 07540-065837 E: revd.kim@outlook.com

LEPP, Susan Elizabeth. b 76. Alberta Univ BSc 04 Nottm Univ MSc 09 Dur Univ BA 19. Wycliffe Hall Ox 14. **d** 16 **p** 17. C Langley Marish *Ox* 16–20; P-in-c Hambleden Valley from 20. *St Katharine's Convent, Parmoor, Frieth, Henley-on-Thames RG9 6NN* M: 07930-520562 E: revdsuelepp@gmail.com

LEPPARD, Ms Heather Sian. b 85. Open Univ BA 09 Em Coll Cam BA 14. Westcott Ho Cam 12. **d** 15 **p** 16. C Harnham *Sarum* 15–19; V Old Basing and Lychpit *Win* from 19. *The Vicarage, Church Lane, Old Basing, Basingstoke RG24 7DJ* M: 07745-731729 E: vicar@stmarysoldbasing.org.uk *or* revheatherleppard@gmail.com

LEPPINGTON, Dian Marjorie. b 45. Leeds Univ BA 85. Cranmer Hall Dur 81. **dss** 83 **d** 87 **p** 94. Potternewton *Ripon* 83–85; Ind Chapl 85–97; Chapl Teesside Univ *York* 97–04; Can and Preb York Minster 03–04; Par Resources Adv *Man* 05–14; rtd 13; PtO *Man* 13–17; *York* from 14; *Eur* from 16. *39 Derwent Mews, York YO10 3DN* T: (01904) 500253 E: dleppington.shanks@gmail.com

LERRY, Keith Doyle. b 49. St Mich Coll Llan 69. **d** 72 **p** 73. C Caerau w Ely *Llan* 72–75; C Roath St Martin 75–84; V Glyntaff 84–11; rtd 11. *8 Wenvoe Terrace, Barry CF62 7AS*

LESITER, The Ven Malcolm Leslie. b 37. Selw Coll Cam BA 61 MA 65. Cuddesdon Coll 61. **d** 63 **p** 64. C Eastney *Portsm* 63–66; C Hemel Hempstead *St Alb* 66–71; TV 71–73; V Leavesden 73–88; RD Watford 81–88; V Radlett 88–93; Hon Can St Alb Abbey 90–93; Adn Bedford 93–03; rtd 03; PtO *Ely* 03–08; *Chelmsf* from 04. *349 Ipswich Road, Colchester CO4 0HN* T: (01206) 841479 E: mllesiter@hotmail.com

LESLIE, Christopher James. b 42. Open Univ BA 75. Wycliffe Hall Ox 97. **d** 05 **p** 06. NSM Loddon Reach *Ox* 05–18; PtO from 18. *Church Farm House, Church Lane, Shinfield, Reading RG2 9BY* T: 0118-988 8642 E: cj.leslie@btinternet.com

LESLIE, David Rodney. b 43. Liv Univ MEd 94 Birm Univ PhD 01 AKC 67. **d** 68 **p** 69. C Belmont *Lon* 68–71; C St Giles Cripplegate w St Bart Moor Lane etc 71–75; TV Kirkby *Liv* 76–84; TR Ditton St Mich 84–98; V Ditton St Mich w St Thos 98–03; V Croxteth Park 03–08; rtd 08; PtO *Ches* from 09. *10 Eversley Close, Frodsham WA6 6AZ* T: (01928) 732463 E: david.leslie3@gmail.com

LESLIE, Canon Richard Charles Alan. b 46. ACIB 71. St Alb Minl Tr Scheme 76. **d** 79 **p** 91. NSM Redbourn *St Alb* 79–88; NSM Newport Pagnell w Lathbury and Moulsoe *Ox* 88–94; Stewardship Adv St Alb Adnry 94–97; TV Borehamwood 97–05; TV Elstree and Borehamwood 05–15; Hon Can St Alb 14–15; rtd 15; PtO *St Alb* from 15. *17 George Street, Hemel Hempstead HP2 5HJ* T: (01442) 769834 E: rcaleslie@idreamtime.com

LESTER, David Charles. b 46. BSc. **d** 99 **p** 00. NSM Trowell *S'well* 99–02; NSM Trowell, Awsworth and Cossall 02–06; rtd 06; PtO *York* from 07. *25 Ruby Street, Saltburn-by-the-Sea TS12 1EF* E: d.c.lester@hotmail.co.uk

LESTER, Stephanie Helen. *See* WARRELL, Stephanie Helen

LESTER, Canon Trevor Rashleigh. b 50. CITC 83. **d** 89 **p** 90. NSM Douglas Union w Frankfield *C, C & R* 89–93; Bp's V and Lib Kilkenny Cathl and C Kilkenny w Aghour and Kilmanagh *C, F & O* 93–95; I Abbeystrewry Union *C, C & R* 95–03; Dean Waterford *C, F & O* 03–11; I Waterford w Killea, Drumcannon and Dunhill 03–11; I Kilmoe Union *C, C & R* 11–17; Can Cork and Ross Cathls 14–17; rtd 17. *The Old White Farmhouse, Garrendruig, Kilbrittain, Co Cork, Republic of Ireland* M: (00353) 86-313 4617 E: lester@eircom.net *or* trevorlester3725@eircom.net

L'ESTRANGE, Timothy John Nicholas. b 67. Surrey Univ BA 90 FRSA 18. St Steph Ho Ox BA 92 MA 96. **d** 93 **p** 94. C Halesworth w Linstead, Chediston, Holton etc *St E* 93–96; Dom Chapl to Bp Horsham *Chich* 96–98; R Beeding and Bramber w Botolphs 98–08; R Monken Hadley *Lon* 08–11; V N

Acton St Gabr from 11. *St Gabriel's Vicarage, 15 Balfour Road, London W3 0DG* T: (020) 8259 2138 M: 07845-211617 E: sacerdotal@gmail.com *or* vicar@saintgabrielacton.org

LETALL, Ronald Richard. b 29. ACII 76. Linc Th Coll 82. **d** 84 **p** 85. C Scarborough St Martin *York* 84–86; C Middlesbrough St Thos 86–88; R Kirby Misperton w Normanby, Edston and Salton 88–90; TV Louth *Linc* 90–94; rtd 94; PtO *Sheff* from 95; *Wakef* 95–97; *Chich* 97–20. *6 Windlesham Court, Grand Avenue, Worthing BN11 5AE*

LETCHER, Canon David John. b 34. K Coll Lon 54. Chich Th Coll 56. **d** 58 **p** 59. C St Austell *Truro* 58–62; C Southbroom *Sarum* 62–64; R Odstock w Nunton and Bodenham 64–72; RD Alderbury 68–73 and 77–82; V Downton 72–85; Can and Preb Sarum Cathl 79–99; TV Dorchester 85–97; RD 89–95; rtd 97; PtO *Sarum* 97–15; CF 97–00; PtO *Ex* 12–15; *Truro* 17–21. *15 Tregavethan View, Threemilestone, Truro TR3 6SS* T: (01872) 274615

LETCHFORD, Mrs Angela Maria. b 70. Nottm Univ BSc 91 Lanc Univ PGCE 92. All SS Cen for Miss & Min 18. **d** 20 **p** 21. OLM Lancaster St Thos *Blackb* from 20. *45 Lune Drive, Morecambe LA3 3RZ* T: (01524) 389163 E: a_letchford@yahoo.co.uk

LETHBRIDGE, Christopher David. b 43. NOC 90. **d** 93 **p** 94. NSM S Elmsall *Wakef* 93–95; C Knottingley 95–97; R Badsworth 97–01; P-in-c Bilham *Sheff* 01–13; Chapl HM YOI Hatfield 01–03; Chapl HM Pris Moorland 03–12; rtd 13; PtO *Sheff* 13–19. *25 Mayfield, Scawthorpe, Doncaster DN5 7UA* T: (01302) 483084

LETHEREN, William Neils. b 37. St Aid Birkenhead 61. **d** 64 **p** 65. C Liv St Mich 64–67; V 71–75; C Kirkdale St Athanasius 67–69; C Walsall Wood *Lich* 69–71; V W Derby St Jas *Liv* 75–84; R Newton in Makerfield Em 84–88; V Garston 88–04; rtd 04; PtO *Liv* from 16. *24 Pitville Avenue, Liverpool L18 7JG* T: 0151-724 5543

LETMAN, Mrs Sally Janet. b 60. Univ of Wales (Abth) BA 82. ERMC 18. **d** 20 **p** 21. C Capel St Mary w Lt and Gt Wenham *St E* from 20. *The Rectory, Days Road, Capel St Mary, Ipswich IP9 2LE* T: (01473) 312225 M: 07773-360264 E: sallyjletman@gmail.com

LETSCHKA, Mrs Alison Clare. b 58. Sussex Univ BA 79 Anglia Ruskin Univ BA 08. Westcott Ho Cam 06. **d** 08 **p** 09. C Haywards Heath St Wilfrid *Chich* 08–12; TV Bexley *Roch* 12–18; P-in-c W Grinstead *Chich* from 18. *Hookshile, Church Road, Partridge Green, Horsham RH13 8JS* M: 07950-152229 E: acletschka@yahoo.co.uk

LETSOM-CURD, Clifford John. *See* CURD, Clifford John Letsom

LEUNG, Peter. b 36. Trin Coll Singapore BTh 60 St Andr Univ PhD 73. SE Asia Sch of Th MTh 69. **d** 60 **p** 61. Singapore 60–62 and 65–76; Br N Borneo 62–63; Malaysia 63–65; Lect Congr Coll Man 76–77; USPG 77–83; PtO *Roch* 83–89; CCBI 83–90; CTBI from 90; PtO *S'wark* 88–94; Hon C Shortlands *Roch* 90–01; Regional Sec (S and E Asia) CMS 91–99; rtd 99. *35 Tufton Gardens, West Molesey KT8 1TD* T: (020) 8650 4157

LEVANWAY, William Douglas. b 85. Belmont Univ Nashville BA 07 Vanderbilt Univ (USA) MDiv 12 K Coll Lon PhD 17. St Steph Ho Ox 15. **d** 17 **p** 18. C Fulham All SS *Lon* 17–20; USA from 20. *15 Highland Meadow Drive, Jackson MS 39211, USA* E: willlevanway@gmail.com

LEVASIER, Joanna Mary. b 68. Jes Coll Cam BA 89 MA 90. Wycliffe Hall Ox 07. **d** 09 **p** 10. C Ashtead *Guildf* 09–12; C Burpham from 12. *272 London Road, Guildford GU4 7LF* T: (01483) 853023 E: j.levasier@ntlworld.com *or* jo@burphamchurch.org.uk

LEVELL, Peter John. b 40. Bris Univ BA 62 CertEd 63. STETS 99. **d** 02 **p** 03. NSM Guildf St Sav 02–10; rtd 10; PtO *Guildf* from 11; *Lon* from 15. *23 Mountside, Guildford GU2 4JD* T: (01483) 871656 E: plevell@ntlworld.com

LEVERTON, Mrs Judith. b 55. Eaton Hall Coll of Educn CertEd 76. St Jo Coll Nottm 02. **d** 04 **p** 05. C Doncaster St Jas *Sheff* 04–07; TV Rivers Team 07–15; rtd 15; Chapl to Deaf People *Sheff* 09–15; PtO from 19. *35 Wayford Avenue, Bramley, Rotherham S66 2ST* M: 07960-573529 E: judy.leverton@yahoo.co.uk

LEVERTON, Canon Michael John. b 52. K Coll Lon BD 76 AKC 76 MTh 77. Cant Sch of Min 84. **d** 87 **p** 88. NSM Elham w Denton and Wootton *Cant* 87–92; C Yelverton, Meavy, Sheepstor and Walkhampton *Ex* 92–93; TV 93–98; C Tavistock and Gulworthy 98–00; P-in-c Stevenage All SS Pin Green *St Alb* 00–10; P-in-c Ardeley 10–12; P-in-c Benington w Walkern 10–12; P-in-c Cottered w Broadfield and Throcking 10–12; V Ardeley, Benington, Cottered w Throcking etc 12–19; RD Buntingford 18–19; Hon Can St Alb 14–19; rtd 19; PtO *St Alb* from 19. *15 Lingfield Road, Stevenage SG1 5SG* E: michael.leverton@btinternet.com

LEVETT, Julie. b 60. **d** 10 **p** 11. OLM Knaphill w Brookwood *Guildf* from 10. *7 Larks Way, Knaphill, Woking GU21 2LE* T: (01483) 850623 E: julie-levett@ntlworld.com

LEVINSOHN, Matthew James. b 79. Ex Univ BA 01 Bris Univ PGCE 04. Trin Coll Bris MA 14. **d** 17 **p** 18. C Salisbury St Fran and Stratford sub Castle *Sarum* 17–21; P-in-c Preston-on-Tees and Longnewton *Dur* from 21. *The Vicarage, Quarry Road, Eaglescliffe, Stockton-on-Tees TS16 9BD* M: 07816-386623 E: matt.levinsohn@gmail.com

LEW, Henry. b 39. **d** 96 **p** 97. LtO *D & G* from 99; NSM Delgany from 10. *Lotts Cottage, Drummin West, The Downs, Delgany, Co Wicklow, Republic of Ireland* T: (00353) (1) 287 2957 M: 87-628 8049 E: healew@outlook.com

LEWER ALLEN, Mrs Patricia (Paddy). b 47. UNISA BA 79 HDipEd 85 Cape Town Univ BA 86 SRN 70. Th Ext Educn Coll 94. **d** 97 **p** 98. P-in-c Dunbar *Edin* 98–08; R Crieff *St And* 08–18; R Comrie 08–18; R Lochearnhead 08–18; Dioc Dir of Ords 10–18; rtd 18; PtO *Arg* from 19. *99 Alexandra Palace, Dunoon PA23 8AH* T: (01369) 705458 M: 07810-746121 E: paddyallen27@gmail.com

LEWES AND HASTINGS, Archdeacon of. *See* DOWLER, The Ven Robert Edward Mackenzie

LEWES, Area Bishop of. *See* HAZLEWOOD, The Rt Revd William Peter Guy

LEWIS, Alaric Mark Edward. b 66. **d** 92 **p** 93. USA 92–14; PtO *Eur* 14–15; Chapl Costa del Sol E 15–18; V Nor Colegate and Tombland from 18; Dioc Voc Outreach Officer from 18. *8 Robert Gybson Way, Norwich NR3 3PH* T: (01603) 663757 E: st.george.alaric@gmail.com

LEWIS, Aled Wyn. b 77. St Jo Coll Dur LLB 98. St Mich Coll Llan 14. **d** 16 **p** 18. NSM Tregaron Gp *St D* 16–19; NSM Lampeter from 19. *Afallon, Ystrad Meurig SY25 6AD* T: (01974) 831518 E: aled.lewis40@gmail.com

LEWIS, Prof Andrew Dominic Edwards. b 49. St Jo Coll Cam LLB 71 MA 74. SWMTC 04. **d** 07 **p** 08. NSM St Endellion w Port Isaac and St Kew *Truro* 07–12; NSM St Minver 07–12; NSM N Cornwall Cluster 12–19; Preb St Endellion from 18; PtO from 19. *Moorgate, Advent, Camelford PL32 9QH* T: (01840) 211161 E: a.d.e.lewis@ucl.ac.uk

LEWIS, Angela Jane. *See* HANNAFIN, Angela Jane

LEWIS, Ann Elizabeth. b 56. SWMTC 15. **d** 18 **p** 19. C Ilfracombe, Lee, Woolacombe, Bittadon etc *Ex* from 18. *Osborne House, West Down, Ilfracombe EX34 8NG* T: (01271) 865405 E: annlewis333@aol.com

LEWIS, Benjamin William Donald. b 78. Northumbria Univ BA 00. Ripon Coll Cuddesdon 12. **d** 14 **p** 15. C Goldington *St Alb* 14–17; V Wellingborough St Mark *Pet* from 17; Warden Lay Min Northn Adnry from 19. *St Mark's Vicarage, 142 Queensway, Wellingborough NN8 3SD* T: (01933) 673893 M: 07977-243197 E: ben.lewis33@live.co.uk

LEWIS, Miss Bethany Lynn. b 82. SOAS Lon BSc 03 PGCE 04. SEITE BA 16. **d** 16 **p** 17. C Bromley St Mark *Roch* 16–20; TV Cheam *S'wark* from 20; V Belmont from 21. *The Vicarage, Belmont Rise, Sutton SM2 6EA* M: 07516-951540 E: bethlynnlewis@hotmail.com *or* beth@cheamparish.org.uk

LEWIS, Brian James. b 52. Cant Univ (NZ) BA 75. St Jo Coll Auckland 76. **d** 78 **p** 79. C Ashburton NZ 78–80; C Shrub End *Chelmsf* 80–82; P-in-c Colchester St Barn 82–84; V 84–88; P-in-c Romford St Andr 88–90; R 90–99; RD Havering 93–97; R Lt Ilford St Mich 99–18; rtd 18. *St Matthias' Vicarage, 48 Rushgrove Avenue, London NW9 6QY* E: brianlewis2014@btinternet.com

LEWIS, The Very Revd Christopher Andrew. b 44. Bris Univ BA 69 CCC Cam PhD 74. Episc Th Sch Cam Mass 69 Westcott Ho Cam 70. **d** 73 **p** 74. C Barnard Castle *Dur* 73–76; Dir Ox Inst for Ch and Soc 76–79; Tutor Ripon Coll Cuddesdon 76–79; Sen Tutor 79–81; Vice-Prin 81–82; P-in-c Aston Rowant w Crowell *Ox* 78–81; V Spalding St Mary and St Nic *Linc* 82–87; Can Res Cant Cathl 87–94; Dir of Minl Tr 89–94; Dean St Alb 94–03; Dean Ch Ch *Ox* 03–14; rtd 14; PtO *St E* from 15. *The Old Brewery, 16 Victoria Road, Aldeburgh IP15 5ED* T: (01728) 454263 E: christopher.lewis@chch.ox.ac.uk

LEWIS, David Antony. b 48. Dur Univ BA 69 Nottm Univ MTh 84. St Jo Coll Nottm 81. **d** 83 **p** 84. C Gateacre *Liv* 83–86; V Toxteth St Cypr w Ch 86–01; V Edge Hill St Cypr w St Mary 01–07; AD Liv N 94–03; Urban Development Adv 07–08; rtd 08; PtO *Ex* from 20. *48 Coulsdon Road, Sidmouth EX10 9JP* T: (01395) 516762 E: davenwend@gmail.com

LEWIS, David Hugh. b 45. Oak Hill Th Coll 88. **d** 90 **p** 91. C Oakham, Hambleton, Egleton, Braunston and Brooke *Pet* 90–94; R Ewhurst *Guildf* 94–01; RD Plymouth Moorside 01–03; P-in-c Anglesey Gp *Ely* 03–04; V 04–11; rtd 11. *95 Myrtlebury Way, Exeter EX1 3XB* T: (01392) 467547 E: revdavidhlewis08@btinternet.com

LEWIS, David Tudor Bowes. b 63. Keele Univ BA 85 Univ of Wales (Cardiff) BTh 90. St Mich Coll Llan 87. **d** 90 **p** 91. C Llangollen w Trevor and Llantysilio *St As* 90–93; C Bistre 93–97; V Berse and Southsea 97–02; V Bwlchgwyn w Berse w Southsea 02–04; R Overton and Erbistock and Penley 04–11; AD Bangor Isycoed 09–11; TR Hawarden 11–17; TV Aled Miss Area 17–18; Miss Area Ldr 18–20; Miss Area Ldr Bryn a Mor Miss Area from 20. *The Vicarage, Llanasa Road, Gronant, Prestatyn LL19 9SP* T: (01492) 549515 E: david.lewis962@btinternet.com

LEWIS, Canon David Vaughan. b 36. Trin Coll Cam BA 60 MA 64. Ridley Hall Cam 60. **d** 62 **p** 63. C Rugby St Matt *Cov* 62–65; Asst Chapl K Edw Sch Witley 65–71; Hon C Rainham *Chelmsf* 71–76; V Stoke Hill *Guildf* 76–87; V Wallington *S'wark* 87–03; Hon Can S'wark Cathl 95–03; RD Sutton 97–00; rtd 03; PtO *Ely* 03–21. *11 The Meadows, Haslingfield, Cambridge CB23 1JD* T: (01223) 874029 E: davidmargylewis@gmail.com

LEWIS, Canon David Watkin. b 40. Univ of Wales (Lamp) BA 61. Wycliffe Hall Ox 61. **d** 63 **p** 64. C Skewen *Llan* 63–66; Field Tr Officer Prov Youth Coun Ch in Wales 66–68; C Gabalfa *Llan* 68–71; P-in-c Marcross w Monknash and Wick 71–73; R 73–83; RD Llantwit Major and Cowbridge 81–83; V Baglan 83–10; Can Llan Cathl 00–10; Treas Llan Cathl 04–10; rtd 10; PtO *Llan* from 14. *23 St Illtyd's Close, Baglan, Port Talbot SA12 8BA* T: (01639) 821778 E: davidlewis322@btinternet.com

LEWIS, Edward John. b 58. JP 93. Univ of Wales BEd 80 BA 82 Surrey Univ MA 07 FRSA 97 MInstD 01. Chich Th Coll 82. **d** 83 **p** 84. C Llangiwg *S & B* 83–85; C Morriston 85–87; Asst Chapl Morriston Hosp 85–87; V Tregaron w Ystrad Meurig and Strata Florida *St D* 87–89; Chapl Tregaron Hosp 87–89; Chapl Manor Hosp Walsall 89–92; Distr Co-ord Chapl Walsall Hosps 90–92; Sen Chapl Walsall Hosps NHS Trust 92–00; Chapl Walsall Community Health Trust 92–00; Chief Exec and Dir Tr Gen Syn Hosp Chapl Coun 00–10; PtO *St Alb* 02–10; P-in-c Watford St Jo 10–11; V Kenton *Lon* from 11; Visiting Lect St Mary's Univ Twickenham from 04; PV Westmr Abbey 07–12; Chapl to The Queen from 08; PtO *Lich* 00–16. *St Mary's Vicarage, 3 St Leonard's Avenue, Harrow HA3 8EJ* T: (020) 8907 2914 M: 07500-557953 E: fr@fredward.org.uk

LEWIS, Ella Pauline. b 41. SWMTC 94. **d** 98. NSM Paignton Ch Ch and Preston St Paul *Ex* 98–07; NSM Torquay St Luke 07–15; rtd 15; PtO *Ex* from 07. *Roselands, 5 Great Headland Road, Paignton TQ3 2DY* T: (01803) 555171 E: paulinelewis@eclipse.co.uk *or* eplewis@sky.com

LEWIS, Eric. b 47. NEOC 04. **d** 07 **p** 08. NSM Monkseaton St Mary Newc 07–11; P-in-c Ovingham 11–16; rtd 16; PtO *Newc* from 16. *1 Bideford Gardens, Whitley Bay NE26 1QW* E: e.lewis129@gmail.com

LEWIS, Gary. b 61. Lanc Univ BA 85. Ripon Coll Cuddesdon 86. **d** 89 **p** 90. C Blackb St Mich w St Jo and H Trin 89–92; C Altham w Clayton le Moors 92–95; V Lea 95–01; V Skerton St Luke 01–14; V Cockerham w Winmarleigh and Glasson from 14. *The Vicarage, 5 Lancaster Road, Cockerham, Lancaster LA2 0EB* T: (01524) 791390 E: garylewislewis@btinternet.com

LEWIS, Graham Rhys. b 54. Loughb Univ BTech 76 Cranfield Inst of Tech MBA 89. Ridley Hall SEITE 95. **d** 98 **p** 99. NSM S Gillingham *Roch* 98–16; TV 12–16; NSM Burwash, Burwash Weald and Etchingham *Chich* 16–20; C from 20. *The Vicarage, Burwash Common, Etchingham TN19 7NA* T: (01435) 882172 M: 07508-882407 E: grahamstp@gmail.com

LEWIS, Gwynne. *See* LEWIS, Hywel Gwynne

LEWIS, Ms Hannah Margaret. b 71. CCC Cam BA 93 MA 96 Birm Univ PhD 03. Qu Coll Birm 95. **d** 97 **p** 98. C Cannock *Lich* 97–00; NSM Cen Telford 00–06; Team Ldr Past Services for Deaf Community *Liv* from 06. *9 Hougoumont Avenue, Liverpool L22 0LL* T: 0151-705 2130 E: hannah.lewis@liverpool.anglican.org

LEWIS, Hubert Godfrey. b 33. Univ of Wales (Lamp) BA 59. **d** 60 **p** 61. C Merthyr Tydfil *Llan* 60–64; C Caerphilly 64–66; PtO *S'wark* 66–76; Cant 76–82; Hon C Shirley St Jo *S'wark* 82–93; Hon C Whitchurch *Llan* from 94. *2 Heol Wernlas, Cardiff CF14 1RY* T: (029) 2061 3079

LEWIS, Hywel Gwynne. b 37. FCA 75. St D Dioc Tr Course 94. **d** 97 **p** 98. NSM Henfynyw w Aberaeron and Llanddewi Aberarth etc *St D* 97; PtO *St D* from 07. *Danycoed, Lampeter Road, Aberaeron SA46 0ED* T: (01545) 570577

LEWIS, Preb Ian Richard. b 54. Sheff Univ BA 76 Ox Univ BA 83 MA 87. Wycliffe Hall Ox 81. **d** 84 **p** 85. C Rusholme H Trin *Man* 84–88; C Sandal St Helen *Wakef* 88–91; V Bath St Bart *B & W* from 91; Preb Wells Cathl from 11. *St Bartholomew's Vicarage, 6A*

Oldfield Road, Bath BA2 3ND T/F: (01225) 422070
E: ian.ir.lewis@btinternet.com *or* ianlewis@stbartsbath.org

LEWIS, James Michael. b 51. Trin Coll Carmarthen CertEd 73 Open Univ BA 86 MA 91. St Mich Coll Llan 98. **d** 02 **p** 03. NSM Laleston w Tythegston and Merthyr Mawr *Llan* 02–09; NSM Laleston and Merthyr Mawr 09–13; NSM Laleston and Merthyr Mawr w Penyfai 13–16; PtO from 16. *19 Austin Avenue, Laleston, Bridgend CF32 0LG* T: (01656) 660648 M: 07951-300206 E: mike.laleston@hotmail.co.uk

LEWIS, Jane Rosemary. b 59. **d** 13 **p** 14. OLM Southlake *Ox* 13–17; PtO 17–18; NSM Reading St Mark and All SS from 18. *Address withheld by request* M: 07703-266451 E: revdjanelewis@gmail.com

LEWIS, Mrs Jayne Lisa. b 63. Hull Univ BA 84 Leic Univ PGCE 99. Qu Coll Birm 12. **d** 15 **p** 16. C Market Harborough and The Transfiguration etc *Leic* 15–19; P-in-c Whatborough Gp from 19. *The Vicarage, Halstead Road, Tilton on the Hill, Leicester LE7 9LB* T: 0116-259 7244 M: 07875-011924 E: jaynelewis28@gmail.com

LEWIS, Jemima Catherine. b 83. Bris Univ BA 05. Win Sch of Miss 17. **d** 21. NSM King's Worthy *Win* from 21; NSM Headbourne Worthy from 21. *The Meads, Pudding Lane, Headbourne Worthy, Winchester SO23 7JL* M: 07841-523100 E: jemimalewis@live.co.uk

LEWIS, Mrs Jennifer Jane. b 56. Man Univ BA 78. All SS Cen for Miss & Min 12. **d** 15 **p** 16. OLM Eccles *Man* from 15. *4 Welbeck Road, Eccles, Manchester M30 9EH* T: 0161-707 6230 E: jennylewis@dsl.pipex.com

LEWIS, Jocelyn Vivien. b 49. Trevelyan Coll Dur BSc 70 Sheff Univ PhD 75. EMMTC 91. **d** 94 **p** 95. NSM Brimington *Derby* 94–99; P-in-c Whittington 99–09; Dioc Dir Reader Tr 99–09; P-in-c New Whittington 04–09; rtd 09. *13 Gower Crescent, Chesterfield S40 4LX* T: (01246) 229539 E: jocelyn@gandjlewis.plus.com

LEWIS, The Ven John Arthur. b 34. Jes Coll Ox BA 56 MA 60. Cuddesdon Coll 58. **d** 60 **p** 61. C Prestbury *Glouc* 60–63; C Wimborne Minster *Sarum* 63–66; R Eastington and Frocester *Glouc* 66–70; V Nailsworth 70–78; Chapl Memorial and Querns Hosp Cirencester 78–88; V Cirencester *Glouc* 78–88; RD 84–88; Hon Can Glouc Cathl 85–98; Adn Cheltenham 88–98; rtd 98; PtO *Glouc* from 98. *5 Silverie Mead, Bishop's Cleeve, Cheltenham GL52 7YY* T: (01242) 678425

LEWIS, John Herbert. b 42. Selw Coll Cam BA 64 MA 68. Westcott Ho Cam 64. **d** 66 **p** 67. C Wyken *Cov* 66–70; C Bedford St Andr *St Alb* 70–73; Lib Pusey Ho and Bp's Chapl for Graduates *Ox* 73–77; TV Woughton 78–82; TV Gt Chesham 82–88; P-in-c Newport Pagnell w Lathbury and Moulsoe 88–91; R 91–07; rtd 07; PtO *Ox* from 08. *54 Sparrows Way, Oxford OX4 7GE*

LEWIS, John Horatio George. b 47. Southn Univ BEd 72 MA 85. Ox NSM Course 86. **d** 89 **p** 90. NSM Newbury *Ox* 89–04; PtO *Win* 94–04; P-in-c Borden *Cant* 05–08; V 08–16; AD Sittingbourne 09–15; rtd 16; PtO *Lich* from 16. *Crossing Cottage, Shorthill, Lea Cross, Shrewsbury SY5 8JE* T: (01743) 860714 M: 07973-406622 E: jhgl240415@gmail

LEWIS, John Malcolm. b 41. Reading Univ BEd. Trin Coll Bris. **d** 82 **p** 83. C Kingswood *Bris* 82–85; TV Weston-super-Mare Cen Par *B & W* 85–91; Dioc Children's Adv *Nor* 91–97; TV Bishopsworth and Bedminster Down *Bris* 97–06; Hon Min Can Bris Cathl 04–06; rtd 06; PtO *Sarum* from 14. *35 Lodge Way, Weymouth DT4 9UU* T: (01305) 776560 E: monandjohn@btinternet.com

LEWIS, Canon John Pryce. b 65. Trin Coll Carmarthen BA 87. Wycliffe Hall Ox 92. **d** 94 **p** 95. C Carmarthen St Pet *St D* 94–97; V Nevern and Y Beifil w Eglwyswrw and Meline etc 97–07; V Henfynyw w Aberaeron and Llanddewi Aberarth etc 07–19; P-in-c Glyn Aeron (Coastal) from 19; AD from 19; Can St D Cathl from 14. *The Vicarage, Panteg Road, Aberaeron SA46 0EP* T: (01545) 570433 E: vicar@aberaeronparish.org.uk

LEWIS, Joycelyn Augusta. See LEWIS-GREGORY, Joycelyn Augusta

LEWIS, Kevin James. b 76. Nottm Univ BA 98. St Jo Coll Nottm MTh 04 MA(MM) 05. **d** 05 **p** 06. C Southgate *Chich* 05–09; C St Helier *S'wark* 09–17; V Carshalton Beeches from 17. *38 Beeches Avenue, Carshalton SM5 3LW* M: 07739-139389 E: kevin@goodshepherdcarshalton.org

LEWIS, Leslie. b 28. LRAM 56. St Aid Birkenhead 61. **d** 63 **p** 64. C Eastham *Ches* 63–66; C W Kirby St Bridget 66–72; V Rainow w Saltersford 72–73; V Rainow w Saltersford and Forest 73–02; Dioc Clergy Widows and Retirement Officer 88–93; rtd 02; PtO *Ches* from 02. *25 Appleby Close, Macclesfield SK11 8XB* T: (01625) 616395

LEWIS, Marjorie Ann. See BROOKS, Marjorie Ann

LEWIS, Mark John. b 68. Ripon Coll Cuddesdon. **d** 16 **p** 17. C Whitewater *Win* 16–20; PtO from 20. *10 Canberra Close,*

Yateley GU46 7PZ T: (01252) 650090 M: 07776-397617 E: revd.mark.lewis@gmail.com

LEWIS, Mrs Mary Carola Melton. b 51. LRAM 72 S Glam Inst HE CertEd 76 Lon Univ BD 93. St Mich Coll Llan 97. **d** 98 **p** 99. NSM Aberedw w Llandeilo Graban and Llanbadarn etc *S & B* 98–03; PtO *Arg* 13–18; rtd 18. *2C North Road, Wells BA5 2TJ* M: 07833-767273 E: mcmlewis@aol.com

LEWIS, Michael. See LEWIS, James Michael

✠**LEWIS, The Most Revd Michael Augustine Owen.** b 53. Mert Coll Ox BA 75 MA 79. Cuddesdon Coll 75. **d** 78 **p** 79 **c** 99. C Salfords *S'wark* 78–80; Chapl Thames Poly 80–84; V Welling 84–91; TR Worc SE 91–99; RD Worc E 93–99; Hon Can Worc Cathl 98–99; Suff Bp Middleton *Man* 99–07; Bp Cyprus and the Gulf from 07; Pres Bp Episc Ch Jerusalem and Middle E from 19. *PO Box 22075, CY 1517-Nicosia, Cyprus* T: (00357) (22) 671220 F: 674553 E: bishop@spidernet.com.cy *or* michael.lewis_2000@yahoo.com

LEWIS, Canon Michael David Bennett. b 41. Portsm Univ MA 01. St Mich Coll Llan 65. **d** 68 **p** 69. C Penarth w Lavernock *Llan* 68–72; Chapl RAF 72–74; C Llanishen and Lisvane *Llan* 74–77; V Penyfai w Tondu 77–82; Chapl Ardingly Coll 82–90; R Merrow *Guildf* 90–95; RD Guildf 94–95; V Southsea H Spirit *Portsm* 95–11; RD Portsm 06–11; Hon Can Portsm Cathl 06–11; rtd 11; PtO *St D* from 11. *Stepping Stones, Reynalton, Kilgetty SA68 0PG* T: (01834) 891531 M: 07808-609912 E: jandmleiws@btinternet.com

LEWIS, Michael John. b 37. LLAM 86. St Aid Birkenhead 64. **d** 66 **p** 67. C Whitnash *Cov* 66–69; C Nuneaton St Nic 69–73; TV Basildon St Martin w H Cross and Laindon *Chelmsf* 73–79; V W Bromwich St Jas *Lich* 79–85; TV Buxton w Burbage and King Sterndale *Derby* 85–95; P-in-c Brampton St Mark 95–02; rtd 02; PtO *Lich* 03–19. *15 Langley Street, Basford, Stoke-on-Trent ST4 6DX* T: (01782) 622762 E: michael.lewis@talktalk.net

LEWIS, Patrick Mansel. See MANSEL LEWIS, Patrick Charles Archibald

LEWIS, Pauline. See LEWIS, Ella Pauline

LEWIS, Peter. See LEWIS, Thomas Peter

LEWIS, Peter Andrew. b 67. Pemb Coll Ox MA PhD Univ of Wales (Abth) Bris Univ BA Univ of Wales (Trin St Dav) MPhil 13. Trin Coll Bris 92. **d** 96 **p** 97. C Cardigan w Mwnt and Y Ferwig *St D* 96–98; C Gabalfa *Llan* 98–01; V Aberpergwm and Blaengwrach 01–04; V Vale of Neath 04–12; AD Neath 10–12; V Pontypridd St Cath 12–15; TV Pontypridd 15–20; V Abercynon from 20; Voc Adv from 20. *67 Grovers Field, Abercynon, Mountain Ash CF45 4PQ* T: (01443) 742090 E: revpeterlewis@gmail.com

LEWIS, Peter Richard. b 40. Dur Univ BA 62. Qu Coll Birm 62. **d** 64 **p** 65. C Moseley St Mary *Birm* 64–67; C Sherborne w Castleton and Lillington *Sarum* 67–71; P-in-c Bishopstone w Stratford Tony 72–80; V Amesbury 80–02; rtd 02; PtO *Sarum* 02–20; *B & W* 05–19. *Rose Cottage, Silton Road, Bourton, Gillingham SP8 5DE*

LEWIS, The Very Revd Richard. b 35. Fitzw Ho Cam BA 78 MA 63. Ripon Hall Ox 58. **d** 60 **p** 61. C Hinckley St Mary *Leic* 60–63; C Sanderstead All SS *S'wark* 63–66; V S Merstham 67–72; V S Wimbledon H Trin 72–74; P-in-c S Wimbledon St Pet 72–74; V S Wimbledon H Trin and St Pet 74–79; V Dulwich St Barn 79–90; Chapl Alleyn's Foundn Dulwich 79–90; RD Dulwich *S'wark* 83–90; Hon Can S'wark Cathl 87–90; Dean Wells *B & W* 90–03; Warden of Readers 91–03; rtd 03; PtO *Worc* 03–08; *B & W* 08–19. *1 Monmouth Court, Union Street, Wells BA5 2PX* T: (01749) 672677 M: 07788-413525 E: dean.richard@btinternet.com

LEWIS, Canon Richard Charles. b 44. Univ of Wales (Lamp) MA 94 Sheff Univ MEd 96. ALCD 69. **d** 69 **p** 70. C Kendal H Trin *Carl* 69–72; C Chipping Barnet *St Alb* 72–76; V Watford Ch Ch 76–12; Chapl Abbot's Hill Sch Herts 81–96; Hon Can St Alb Abbey 90–12; Chapl from 12; Chapl Trin Hosp Retford from 12; PtO *S'well* from 12. *Rectory Farm, Rectory Road, Retford DN22 7AY* T: (01777) 710260 E: dick@ccwatford.u-net.com

LEWIS, Robert. b 38. St Pet Coll Ox BA 62 MA 66. Cuddesdon Coll 62. **d** 64 **p** 65. C Kirkby *Liv* 64–67 and 70–71; TV 71–75; Chapl St Boniface Coll Warminster 68–69; Tutor St Aug Coll Cant 69–70; Abp's Dom Chapl and Dir of Ords *York* 76–79; TR Thirsk 79–92; Chapl Oslo w Bergen, Trondheim, Stavanger etc *Eur* 93–96; P-in-c Danby *York* 96–98; V 98–04; RD Whitby 98–04; rtd 04; PtO *York* from 04. *17 Meadowfields, Chapel Street, Thirsk YO7 1TH* T: (01845) 523256 E: maureen240@btinternet.com

LEWIS, Canon Robert George. b 53. Lanc Univ BEd 76. Ripon Coll Cuddesdon. **d** 78 **p** 79. C Liv Our Lady and St Nic w St Anne 78–81; Asst Dir of Educn 81–88; P-in-c Newchurch 88–89; P-in-c Glazebury 88–89; R Newchurch and Glazebury 89–94; R Winwick 94–09; R Glazebury w Hollinfare 04–09; AD Winwick 01–09; Chapl Liv Univ 09–20; Chapl Liv Jo

Moores Univ 09–20; Bp's Adv Sector Min 11–20; Chapl Liv Cathl from 20; P-in-c Toxteth St Marg from 14; Can Liv Cathl from 01. *10 Ladychapel Close, Liverpool L1 7BZ* T: 0151-707 2988   M: 07789-402954   E: thelewises@hotmail.com   *or* bob.lewis@liverpool.anglican.org

LEWIS, Roger Gilbert. b 49. St Jo Coll Dur BA 70. Ripon Hall Ox 70. **d** 72 **p** 73. C Boldmere *Birm* 72–76; C Birm St Pet 76–77; TV Tettenhall Regis *Lich* 77–81; V Ward End *Birm* 81–91; rtd 91; PtO *Birm* 91–06. *8 Tudor Terrace, Ravenhurst Road, Birmingham B17 9SB* M: 07845-558376

LEWIS, Simon Wilford. b 66. Westmr Coll Ox BTh 94 Roehampton Inst PGCE 95. STETS 03. **d** 06 **p** 07. C Ventnor St Cath, Ventnor H Trin and Bonchurch *Portsm* 06–09; P-in-c Brent Knoll, E Brent and Lympsham *B & W* 09–18; R Blagdon w Compton Martin and Ubley from 18. *Easton House, Church Street, Blagdon, Bristol BS40 7SJ* E: rev.simonlewis@gmail.com

LEWIS, Thomas Peter. b 45. Selw Coll Cam BA 67 MA. Ripon Hall Ox 68. **d** 70 **p** 71. C Bp's Hatfield *St Alb* 70–74; C Boreham Wood All SS 74–78; Chapl Haileybury Coll 78–85; Chapl Abingdon Sch 86–03; R Narberth w Mounton w Robeston Wathen etc *St D* 03–14; rtd 10; PtO *St D* from 15. *Nantyfelin, Old St Clears Road, Johnstown, Carmarthen SA31 3HN* T: (01267) 234667 E: revtplewis@btinternet.com

LEWIS, Trevor Arnold. b 55. York St Jo Univ BA 12. NEOC 06. **d** 09 **p** 10. NSM Middlesbrough St Martin w St Cuth *York* 09–10; NSM Osmotherley w Harlsey and Ingleby Arncliffe 10–17; NSM Leake w Over and Nether Silton and Kepwick 10–17; NSM Felixkirk w Boltby 10–17; NSM Kirkby Knowle 10–17; NSM Cowesby 10–17; C Hurstbourne Tarrant, Faccombe, Vernham Dean etc *Win* 17–20; C Pastrow from 20; RD Andover from 18. *The Vicarage, The Dene, Hurstbourne Tarrant, Andover SP11 0AH* T: (01264) 736565 E: revtrev@pastrowfamily.org.uk

LEWIS, Vera Elizabeth. b 45. Lon Univ BA 66 Univ of Wales (Abth) DipEd 67. St As Minl Tr Course 82. **d** 85 **p** 97. NSM Garthbeibio and Llanerfyl and Llangadfan *St As* 85–86; C 87–88; NSM Llanfair Caereinion w Llanllugan 85–86; C 87–88; Dn-in-c Llanrhaeadr-ym-Mochnant etc 88–96; Dn-in-c Llanddulas and Llysfaen 96–97; R 97–03; rtd 03; P-in-c Henllan and Llannefydd and Bylchau *St As* 12–15; NSM Caerwys and Bodfari 15–16; NSM Denbigh Miss Area 17–21. *Heulwen, Bronwylfa Square, St Asaph LL17 0BU* T: (01745) 584261 E: vera.lewis2@btinternet.com

LEWIS, Canon Walter Arnold. b 45. NUI BA 68 TCD MPhil 91. TCD Div Sch Div Test 71. **d** 71 **p** 72. C Belfast Whiterock *Conn* 71–73; C Belfast St Mark 73–80; Bp's C Belfast St Andr 80–84; I Belfast St Thos 84–12; Can Belf Cathl 97–12; rtd 12. *145 Mountsandel Road, Coleraine BT52 1TA* T: (028) 7034 0929 M: 07715-358127 E: waltera.lewis@btinternet.com

LEWIS, William George Rees. b 35. Hertf Coll Ox BA 59 MA 63. Tyndale Hall Bris 61. **d** 63 **p** 64. C Tenby w Gumfreston *St D* 63–66; C Llanelli St Paul 66–69; R Letterston 69–73; R Letterston w Llanfair Nantygof, Jordanston etc 73–84; R Jordanston w Llanstinan 73–78; R Letterston w Llanfair Nant-y-Got etc 78–84; R Hubberston w Herbrandston and Hasguard etc 84–88; R Hubberston 89–90; Prov Officer for Evang and Adult Educn 90–94; V Gabalfa *Llan* 94–00; rtd 00; PtO *St D* from 00. *5 Westaway Drive, Hakin, Milford Haven SA73 3EG* T: (01646) 692280 E: billandchlorislewis@gmail.com

LEWIS, William Rhys. b 20. St Mich Coll Llan 53. **d** 55 **p** 56. C Ystrad Mynach *Llan* 55–58; C Bassaleg *Mon* 58–59; V Cwmtillery 59–62; V Newport St Andr 62–64; TR Ebbw Vale 64–73; R Llangattock and Llangyndir *S & B* 73–78; V Swansea St Luke 78–85; rtd 85; PtO *Llan* from 85. *6 Beech Avenue, Llantwit Major CF61 1RT* T: (01446) 796741

LEWIS-ANTHONY, Justin Griffith. b 64. LSE BA 86 Kent Univ PhD 12. Ripon Coll Cuddesdon BA 91 MA 97. **d** 92 **p** 93. C Cirencester *Glouc* 92–98; Prec Ch Ch Ox 98–03; R Hackington *Cant* 03–13; Assoc Dean of Students Virginia Th Sem USA 13–16; Research Fell Ripon Coll Cuddesdon 16–17; Dep Dir Angl Cen Rome 18–20; R Chingford SS Pet and Paul *Chelmsf* from 20; PtO *Eur* from 18; *St Alb* 20–21. *2 The Green Walk, London E4 7ER* T: (020) 8529 1291 E: rector@parishofchingford.org.uk

LEWIS-GREGORY, Mrs Joycelyn Augusta. b 60. Qu Coll Birm. **d** 08 **p** 09. C Hall Green St Pet *Birm* 08–12; P-in-c Cotteridge 12; V 12–16; Bp's Adv for Minority Ethnic Angl from 12; PtO from 16. *28 Arton Croft, Birmingham B24 8RA* M: 07932-443769 E: revjoycelyn@gmail.com

LEWIS-MORRIS, Catherine Mary. *See* DAWKINS, Catherine Mary

LEWIS-NICHOLSON, Russell John. b 45. Oak Hill Th Coll 79. **d** 81 **p** 82. C Clayton *Bradf* 81–84; Australia from 84; rtd 10.

5 Rawlinson Street, Croydon Vic 3136, Australia T: (0061) (3) 972 3653 M: 42-935 8490 E: dreamrider17@hotmail.com

LEWISHAM AND GREENWICH, Archdeacon of. *See* CUTTING, The Ven Alastair Murray

LEWORTHY, Graham Llewelyn. b 47. Reading Univ BA 69. S Dios Minl Tr Scheme 91. **d** 94 **p** 95. C Sark *Win* 94–11; rtd 11. *Summerland Nursing Home, Mount Durand, St Peter Port, Guernsey GY1 1DX*

LEWRY, Glyn Hugh Brendon. b 63. **d** 14 **p** 15. NSM Sampford Peverell, Uplowman, Holcombe Rogus etc *Ex* 14–18; TR from 18. *The Rectory, Blackdown View, Sampford Peverell, Tiverton EX16 7BE* T: (01884) 243727 E: revglyn01@gmail.com

LEYDEN, Mrs Anna Louise. b 87. St Pet Coll Ox BA 08 MA 17. Qu Foundn Birm 17. **d** 20 **p** 21. C Ches Ch Ch from 20. *36 Chester Road, Huntingdon, Chester CH3 6BW* M: 07879-204514 E: anna.leyden@hotmail.com

LEYLAND, Derek James. b 34. Lon Univ BSc 55. Qu Coll Birm 58. **d** 60 **p** 61. C Ashton-on-Ribble St Andr *Blackb* 60–63; V 80–87; C Salesbury 63–65; V Preston St Oswald 65–67; V Pendleton 67–74; Dioc Youth Chapl 67–69; Ind Youth Chapl 70–74; R Brindle 74–80; V Garstang St Helen Churchtown 87–94; Sec SOSc 90–94; rtd 94; PtO *Blackb* from 94. *Greystocks, Goosnargh Lane, Goosnargh, Preston PR3 2BP* T: (01772) 865682

LEYLAND, Ty John. b 49. Aston Univ BSc 68. St Jo Coll Nottm 89. **d** 91 **p** 92. C Lich St Mary w St Mich 91–94; TV Willenhall H Trin 94–99; P-in-c The Ridwares and Kings Bromley 99–08; R 08–18; rtd 18. *4 Ellsmore Meadow, Lichfield WS13 6NJ* E: ty.leyland@gmail.com

LEYSHON, Simon. b 63. Trin Coll Carmarthen BA 86 Southn Univ BTh 89 Univ of Wales (Abth) MEd 07. Sarum & Wells Th Coll. **d** 89 **p** 90. C Tenby *St D* 89–92; TV 92–96; Chapl and Hd RS Llandovery Coll 96–02; PtO *St D* from 02; Chapl Lord Wandsworth Coll Hook 02–13; Hd Cransley Sch Northwich 13–16; PtO *Ches* 13–16; Hd Moon Hall Sch Reigate 16; Dep Hd ACS Internat Sch Cobham from 17; Interim Hd 18–19; PtO *S'wark* 17–18; *Guildf* from 19. *24 Poplar Close, Epsom KT17 3LH* E: simonleyshon@yahoo.co.uk

LIBBY, Canon John Ralph. b 55. Trin Coll Cam BA 83. Ridley Hall Cam 89. **d** 91 **p** 92. C Enfield St Andr *Lon* 91–93; C Northwood Em 93–96; V Denton Holme *Carl* 96–14; RD Carl 04–10; Nat Dir Langham Partnership from 15; NSM Stanwix *Carl* from 16; Hon Can Carl Cathl from 08. *14 East Block, Shaddon Mill, Shaddongate, Carlisle CA2 5WD* E: john.libby@btinternet.com

LICHFIELD, Archdeacon of. *See* WELLER, The Ven Susan Karen

LICHFIELD, Bishop of. *See* IPGRAVE, The Rt Revd Michael Geoffrey

LICHFIELD, Dean of. *See* DORBER, The Very Revd Adrian John

LICKESS, Canon David Frederick. b 37. St Chad's Coll Dur BA 63. **d** 65 **p** 66. C Howden *York* 65–70; V Rudby in Cleveland w Middleton 70–07; Can and Preb York Minster 90–07; RD Stokesley 93–00; rtd 07; PtO *York* from 07; *Leeds* from 17. *Bridge House, Snape, Bedale DL8 2SZ* T: (01677) 470077 E: davidlickess@gmail.com

LIDDELL, Mark. b 55. Birm Univ BA 00. Coll of Resurr Mirfield 96. **d** 98 **p** 99. C Wednesbury St Jas and St Jo *Lich* 98–00; C Walsall St Andr 00–01; P-in-c 01–05; V 06–08; V Nuneaton St Mary *Cov* 08–18; V Ocker Hill *Lich* from 18. *St Mark's Vicarage, Ocker Hill Road, Tipton DY4 0UT*

LIDDELL, Canon Peter Gregory. b 40. St Andr Univ MA 63 Linacre Ho Ox BA 65 MA 70 Andover Newton Th Sch DMin 75. Ripon Hall Ox 63. **d** 65 **p** 66. C Bp's Hatfield *St Alb* 65–71; USA 71–76; P-in-c Kimpton w Ayot St Lawrence *St Alb* 77–83; Dir of Past Counselling 80–05; Hon Can St Alb 99–05; rtd 05. *12 Old Hall Court, Horn Hill, Whitwell, Hitchin SG4 8AS* T: (01438) 871135 E: petermary.liddell@btinternet.com

LIDDELL, Roxane Harriet. b 68. City of Lon Poly BSc 90 Middx Univ PGCE 09. Westcott Ho Cam 16. **d** 18 **p** 19. C Stoke Newington St Mary *Lon* from 18. *Basement Flat, St Mary's Rectory, Stoke Newington Church Street, London N16 9ES* M: 07957-283238 E: roxaneliddell@hotmail.com

LIDDELOW, Peter William. b 33. Oak Hill NSM Course. **d** 82 **p** 83. NSM Finchley Ch Ch *Lon* 82–84; NSM S Mimms Ch Ch 84–11; PtO *St Alb* 95–18; Chapl Magic Circle 02–16; rtd 16. *23 King's Road, Barnet EN5 4EF* T: (020) 8441 2968 E: pliddelow@hotmail.co.uk

LIDGATE, Mrs Jacqueline Margaret. b 56. **d** 01 **p** 02. Hon C Milton Australia 01–02; C Indooroopilly 02–04; P-in-c Jimboomba 04–07; P-in-c Coolum 07–10; Chapl St Andr Angel Coll 08–10; PtO *S'well* 10–11; NSM Brampton St Thos *Derby* 11; PtO *S'well* 13–16; *Sheff* 15–16; P-in-c Firbeck w Letwell 16–18; PtO from 18. *4 Granary Court, Carlton-*

in-Lindrick, Worksop S81 9JZ T: (01909) 733820
E: pandjlidgate@sky.com

LIDSTONE, Vernon Henry. b 43. SWMTC 89. d 92 p 93. NSM Bovey Tracey SS Pet, Paul and Thos w Hennock *Ex* 92–94; Sub-Chapl HM Pris Channings Wood 92–96; Asst Dioc Chr Stewardship Adv *Ex* 92–93; Dioc Chr Stewardship Adv 93–96; Dioc Officer for Par Development *Glouc* 96–97; Chapl HM Pris Leyhill 97–03; rtd 03; PtO *Glouc* from 17. *The Pike House, Saul, Gloucester GL2 7JD* T: (01452) 741410 E: vernon@lidstone.net

LIEBERT, Ms Sarah Jane. b 66. Pemb Coll Ox BA 88 MA 14 Imp Coll Lon MSc 89 Fitzw Coll Cam BA 13. Westcott Ho Cam 11. d 14 p 15. C Upper Tooting H Trin w St Aug *S'wark* 14–19; V Stonebridge St Mich *Lon* from 19. *St Michael's Vicarage, Hillside, London NW10 8LB* T: 07958-163211 E: liebertsj@gmail.com

LIEVESLEY, Hannah Felicity. b 71. Univ of Cen England in Birm BA 93. St Jo Sch of Miss Nottm 14. d 16 p 17. C Farsley *Leeds* 16–19; TV Headingley 19–21; TR Headingley and All Hallows from 21. *St Chad's Vicarage, Otley Road, Leeds LS16 5JT* T: 0113-210 3497 M: 07582-036290 E: hannah.lievesley@leeds.anglican.org

LIEVESLEY, Mrs Joy Margaret. b 48. Lady Mabel Coll CertEd 69. Guildf Dioc Min Course 98. d 00 p 01. NSM Farnham *Guildf* 00–14; NSM Frimley 15–18; PtO from 18. *3 Kingfisher Close, Church Crookham, Fleet GU52 6JP* T: (01252) 690223 E: joy.lievesley@ntlworld.com

LIGGINS, Andrew David. b 85. St Cath Coll Cam BA 06. Oak Hill Th Coll BA 16. d 17 p 18. C Southport SS Simon and Jude w All So *Liv* 17–20; V from 20. *The Vicarage, 72 Roe Lane, Southport PR9 7HT* M: 07901-787586 E: andy.liggins@stsimonsouthport.org.uk

LIGHT, Canon Madeline Margaret. b 54. Girton Coll Cam BA 77 MA 80 Lon Inst of Educn PGCE 78. EAMTC 96. d 99 p 00. C Eaton *Nor* 99–02; P-in-c Nor St Helen 02–09; Chapl Gt Hosp Nor 02–09; P-in-c Nor St Steph 09–16; V from 16; Hon Can Nor Cathl from 16. *12 The Crescent, Chapel Field Road, Norwich NR2 1SA* T: (01603) 920598 E: madelinelight@gmail.com

LIGHT, Mrs Penelope Ann. b 46. Madeley Coll of Educn TCert 71 N Lon Poly BEd 81. WEMTC 06. d 09 p 10. NSM Cirencester *Glouc* 09–16; rtd 16. *Toad Cottage, 22 Bingham Close, Cirencester GL7 1HJ* T: (01285) 640125 E: jonpen22@tiscali.co.uk

LIGHTBOWN, Richard Andrew. b 66. Buckingham Univ MBA 07. Ripon Coll Cuddesdon MA 13. d 13 p 14. C Schorne *Ox* 13–16; R Winslow w Gt Horwood and Addington from 16. *The Vicarage, Vicarage Road, Winslow, Buckingham MK18 3BJ* T: (01296) 712564 M: 07711-234546 E: alightbown@hotmail.co.uk

LIGHTOWLER, Joseph Trevor. b 33. d 79 p 80. Hon C Leverstock Green *St Alb* 79–80; Hon C Chambersbury 80–84; C Woodmansterne *S'wark* 84–88; R Odell and Pavenham *St Alb* 88–97; rtd 97; PtO *St Alb* 97–18. *25 Yeats House, 2 Wordsworth Close, Kings Park, St Albans AL3 4GG* T: (01727) 866906

LILBURN, Robert Irvine Terence. b 47. CITC 07. d 10 p 11. NSM Kilternan *D & G* 10–11; NSM Powerscourt w Kilbride from 11. *13 Churchfields, Dundrum Road, Milltown, Dublin 14, Republic of Ireland* T: (00353) (1) 260 0003 M: 86-886 5361 E: terrylilburn@gmail.com

LILES, Malcolm David. b 48. Nottm Univ BA 69. St Steph Ho Ox 69. d 71 p 72. C Corby Epiphany w St Jo *Pet* 71–74; C New Cleethorpes *Linc* 74–76; TV Lt Coates 76–77; TV Gt and Lt Coates w Bradley 78–82; Soc Resp Sec 82–93; Hon C Gt Grimsby St Mary and St Jas 82–93; P-in-c Grimsby All SS 88–93; TV Dronfield w Holmesfield *Derby* 93–98; TR Crawley *Chich* 98–14; rtd 14; PtO *Sheff* from 15; Sec Rtd Clergy Assn from 18. *473 City Road, Sheffield S2 1GF* T: 0114-453 7964 M: 07702-203273 E: malcolm.liles48@gmail.com

LILEY, The Ven Christopher Frank. b 47. Nottm Univ BEd 70. Linc Th Coll 72. d 74 p 75. C Kingswinford H Trin *Lich* 74–79; TV Stafford 79–84; V Norton *St Alb* 84–96; RD Hitchin 89–94; V Shrewsbury St Chad w St Mary *Lich* 96–01; P-in-c Shrewsbury St Alkmund 96–01; Adn Lich 01–13; Can Res and Treas Lich Cathl 01–13; rtd 13; PtO *Worc* from 14. *15 Holloway Drive, Pershore WR10 1JL* T: (01386) 561608 E: lileyc@aol.com

LILEY, Peter James. b 60. Liv Univ BA 82 Westmr Coll Ox PGCE 83. Oak Hill Th Coll 91. d 93 p 94. C Exning St Martin w Landwade *St E* 93–96; V Acton w St Waldingfield 96–00; TV Bottesford w Ashby *Linc* 00–05; TR 05–12; Lic Preacher 12–14; R Mablethorpe w Trusthorpe from 14; R Sutton, Huttoft and Anderby from 14. *The Vicarage, 7A Huttoft Road, Sutton-on-Sea, Mablethorpe LN12 2QZ* T: (01507) 443948 E: rev.p.liley@btinternet.com

LILEY, Canon Stephen John. b 65. Liv Univ BA 87 MMus 88 ARCM 93. Wycliffe Hall Ox 97. d 99 p 00. C Throop *Win* 99–03; V Clapham *St Alb* from 03; RD Elstow 08–10; RD Sharnbrook from 15; Hon Can St Alb from 18. *The Vicarage, Green Lane, Clapham, Bedford MK41 6ER* T: (01234) 352814 E: the.lileys@ukgateway.net

LILLEY, Mrs Alexandra Mary. b 80. St Pet Coll Ox BA 01 MA 06. St Mellitus Coll BA 14. d 14 p 15. C Shadwell St Paul w Ratcliffe St Jas *Lon* 14–17; P-in-c Tufnell Park St Geo and All SS from 17; Dean of Women's Min Stepney Area from 20. *St George's Vicarage, 72 Crayford Road, London N7 0ND* M: 07986-433658 E: alexandra_lilley@hotmail.com

LILLEY, Canon Christopher Howard. b 51. FCA 75 FTII 83. LNSM course 83 St Jo Coll Nottm 91. d 85 p 86. OLM Skegness and Winthorpe *Linc* 85–93; C Limber Magna w Brocklesby 93–96; PtO *S'well* 96–97; P-in-c Middle Rasen Gp *Linc* 96–97; R 97–02; V Scawby, Redbourne and Hibaldstow 02–10; P-in-c Bishop Norton, Waddingham and Snitterby 06–10; P-in-c Kirton in Lindsey w Manton 06–10; RD Yarborough 02–09; Hon C Mablethorpe w Trusthorpe from 10; Hon C Sutton, Huttoft and Anderby from 10; Can and Preb Linc Cathl from 05. *The Chrysalis, 12 Hillside Avenue, Sutton-on-Sea, Mablethorpe LN12 2JH* T: (01507) 440039 E: c.lilley@btinternet.com

LILLEY, Ivan Ray. b 32. Bps' Coll Cheshunt 58. d 61 p 62. C Kettering SS Pet and Paul 61–64; C Gt Yarmouth *Nor* 64–75; P-in-c Tottenhill w Wormegay *Ely* 76–83; P-in-c Watlington 76–83; P-in-c Holme Runcton w S Runcton and Wallington 76–83; V Tysoe w Oxhill and Whatcote *Cov* 83–86; C Langold *S'well* 87–91; P-in-c 91–98; rtd 98; PtO *Nor* from 98. *Linden Lea, 41 Cedar Drive, Attleborough NR17 2EY* T: (01953) 452710 E: ivanlinlea@hotmail.co.uk

LILLEY (formerly EDWARDS), Lynda Jane. b 65. Qu Coll Birm. d 11 p 12. NSM Allesley *Cov* 11–15; NSM Meriden 15–20; P-in-c 17–20; P-in-c Chesterton from 20; P-in-c Lighthorne from 20; P-in-c Newbold Pacey w Moreton Morrell from 20. *The Rectory, Lighthorne, Warwick CV35 0AR* T: (01926) 651735 M: 07747-846293 E: vicar.midfosse@gmail.com

LILLEY, Thomas Robert. b 84. UEA BA 05 PGCE 06 Fitzw Coll Cam BTh 11. Westcott Ho Cam 08. d 11 p 12. C Attleborough w Besthorpe *Nor* 11–14; P-in-c Southchurch H Trin *Chelmsf* 14–17; Chapl Canon Slade Sch Bolton from 17. *Canon Slade School, Bradshaw Brow, Bolton BL2 3BP* T: (01204) 333343 M: 07984-181919 E: tom.lilley@gmail.com *or* contact@canon-slade.bolton.sch.uk

LILLICRAP, Peter Andrew. b 65. Hatf Poly BEng 87 CEng 93 MIMechE 93. Trin Coll Bris 00. d 02 p 03. C Kineton *Cov* 02–04; C Napton-on-the-Hill, Lower Shuckburgh etc 04–07; V Acton and Worleston, Church Minshull etc *Ches* 07–13; V Layton and Staining *Blackb* from 13; AD Blackpool from 19. *St Mark's Vicarage, 163 Kingscote Drive, Blackpool FY3 8EH* T: (01253) 392895 E: peterlillicrap@gmail.com

LILLICRAP, Canon Stephen Hunter. b 58. Newc Univ MB, BS 81 MRCGP 85. SEITE 00. d 03 p 04. C Wye w Brook and Hastingleigh etc *Cant* 03–08; C Stone Street Gp 06–08; C Mersham w Hinxhill and Sellindge 08; P-in-c Teynham w Lynsted and Kingsdown 08–14; P-in-c Norton 08–14; V Kingsdown and Creekside 14–20; V High Downs 19–20; V Kingsdown, Creekside and High Downs from 20; AD Ospringe from 11; Hon Can Cant Cathl from 14. *The Vicarage, 76 Station Road, Teynham, Sittingbourne ME9 9SN* T: (01795) 522510 M: 07971-224094 E: steve.lillicrap@btopenworld.com

LILLIE, Judith Virginia. *See* THOMPSON, Judith Virginia

LILLINGTON (née POLLIT), Mrs Ruth Mary. b 65. SS Paul & Mary Coll Cheltenham BA 88. St Jo Coll Nottm 88. d 90 p 94. Par Dn Caverswall *Lich* 90–92; Par Dn Caverswall and Weston Coyney w Dilhorne 92–93; Par Dn Luton St Mary *St Alb* 93–94; C 94–97; Chapl Luton Univ 93–97; NSM Clifton Ch Ch w Em *Bris* from 16. *12 St Edyth's Road, Bristol BS9 2ES* E: ruthy.lillington@ccweb.org.uk

LILLISTONE, Canon Brian David. b 38. SS Coll Cam BA 61 MA 65. St Steph Ho Ox 61. d 63 p 64. C Ipswich All Hallows *St E* 63–66; C Stokesay *Heref* 66–71; P-in-c Lyonshall w Titley 71–76; R Martlesham w Brightwell *St E* 76–03; Hon Can St E Cathl 98–03; rtd 03; PtO *St E* 03–19. *23 Woodland Close, Risby, Bury St Edmunds IP28 6QN* T: (01284) 811330 E: brianlillistone23@gmail.com

LIMA, Luiz Henrique. *See* DE ANDRADE LIMA, Luiz Henrique

LIMBERT, Chrichton. b 57. Reading Univ BSc 79 St Jo Coll Cam PhD 87. St Mellitus Coll BA 12. d 12 p 13. C Ouzel Valley *St Alb* 12–15; V Southgate Ch Ch *Lon* from 15. *Christchurch Vicarage, 1 The Green, London N14 7EG* M: 07711-751501 E: frch138@btinternet.com

LIMBRICK, Gordon. b 36. Open Univ BA 88. St Jo Coll Nottm. d 87 p 91. Hon C Troon *Glas* 87–90; Hon C Yaxley

Ely 90–97; Hon C Yaxley and Holme w Conington 97–04; rtd 04; PtO *Pet* 98–14 and from 15; *Ely* from 04. *271 Broadway, Yaxley, Peterborough PE7 3NR* T: (01733) 243170 E: revgordonlimbrick@gmail.com

LIMERICK AND ARDFERT, Dean of. *Vacant*

LIMERICK, ARDFERT AND AGHADOE, Archdeacon of. *See* LUMBY, The Ven Simon John

LIMERICK, ARDFERT, AGHADOE, KILLALOE, KILFENORA, CLONFERT, KILMACDUAGH AND EMLY, Bishop of. *Vacant*

LINCOLN, Archdeacon of. *See* KIRK, The Ven Gavin John

LINCOLN, Bishop of. *Vacant*

LINCOLN, Dean of. *See* WILSON, The Very Revd Christine Louise

LIND, Jeremy Robert. b 55. ERMC 15. d 18 p 19. NSM Newmarket St Mary w Exning St Agnes *St E* from 18. *Nutbeam, Ducksen Road, Mendlesham, Stowmarket IP14 5SE* T: (01449) 766646 M: 07500-794303 E: lind05@btinternet.com

LIND-JACKSON, Peter Wilfrid. b 35. Leeds Univ BA 67. Linc Th Coll 67. d 68 p 69. C Heref St Martin 68–71; P-in-c Burghill 71–78; V 78–82; V Barnard Castle *Dur* 82–83; P-in-c Whorlton 82–83; V Barnard Castle w Whorlton 83–00; rtd 00; PtO *Ripon* 03–14; *Leeds* from 14. *5 Gill Lane, Barnard Castle DL12 9AS* T: (01833) 630027 E: lindjacksons@googlemail.com

LINDECK, Peter Stephen. b 31. Oak Hill Th Coll 57. d 59 p 60. C Homerton St Luke *Lon* 59–62; C Salterhebble All SS *Wakef* 62–63; C Islington St Andr w St Thos and St Matthias *Lon* 64–67; PtO *Derby* 67–68; *St Alb* 67–68; V Toxteth Park St Bede *Liv* 68–74; V Kano St Geo Nigeria 74–76; C Netherton *Liv* 76–77; C Ollerton and Boughton *S'well* 77–80; V Whitgift w Adlingfleet and Eastoft *Sheff* 80–86; P-in-c Swinefleet 81–86; V Kilnhurst 86–94; Chapl Montagu Hosp Mexborough 86–94; rtd 94; PtO *Sheff* 94–06; *Leic* 14–19. *27 Stuart Court, High Street, Kibworth Beauchamp, Leicester LE8 0LR* T: 0116-279 6347 E: peter32.lindeck@gmail.com

LINDISFARNE, Archdeacon of. *See* SOURBUT GROVES, The Ven Catherine Ann

LINDLEY (née FLYNN), Mrs Anna Therese. b 42. Leeds Univ BSc 63 Surrey Univ MPhil 72 Westmr Coll Ox DipEd 64. Yorks Min Course 08. d 09 p 11. NSM York St Mich-le-Belfrey 09–12; rtd 16; PtO *York* from 17. *35 Manor Garth, Wigginton, York YO32 2WZ*

LINDLEY, Mrs Danie Maria. b 71. N Riding Coll of Educn BA(QTS) 93. Lindisfarne Regional Tr Partnership BA 16. d 15 p 16. NSM Chester le Street *Dur* 15–18; P-in-c Windy Nook St Alb from 18; P-in-c Gateshead Fell from 18. *The Vicarage, Coldwell Park Drive, Gateshead NE10 9BY* M: 07902-477474

LINDLEY, Graham William. b 47. CIPFA 77. d 97 p 98. OLM E Crompton *Man* 97–02; NSM Newhey 02–08; P-in-c 08–13; P-in-c Belfield 09–17; rtd 17; PtO *Man* from 17. *37 Jordan Avenue, Shaw, Oldham OL2 8DQ* T: (01706) 845677 E: g.lindley7@ntlworld.com

LINDLEY, Canon Richard Adrian. b 44. Hull Univ BA 65 Man Univ MA 79 Win Univ PhD 14. Cuddesdon Coll 66. d 68 p 69. C Ingrow w Hainworth *Bradf* 68–70; PtO *Birm* 70–74; TV Ellesmere Port *Ches* 74–79; V Westborough *Guildf* 79–80; TR 80–84; Dir of Educn *Birm* 84–96; Hon Can Birm Cathl 96; Dir of Educn *Win* 96–04; Hon Can Win Cathl 03–04; rtd 04; PtO *Win* 04–13; NSM Win Cathl 13–16; PtO from 16. *28 Denham Close, Winchester SO23 7BL* T: (01962) 621851 M: 07743-758639 E: richardlindley4@gmail.com

LINDNER, Christoph Walter. b 67. St Mellitus Coll BA 12. d 12 p 13. NSM Gerrards Cross and Fulmer *Ox* 12–16; R Denham from 16. *The Rectory, Ashmead Lane, Denham, Uxbridge UB9 5BB* M: 07905-530996 E: rector@denhamparish.church

LINDOE, Jacqualine. b 56. St Mellitus Coll 12. d 16 p 17. OLM Prittlewell St Mary *Chelmsf* from 16. *37 Hill Road, Southend-on-Sea SS2 6JT* M: 07810-825694 E: revjackystmarys@icloud.com

LINDOP, Andrew John. b 57. Cam Univ MA. Cranmer Hall Dur 80. d 82 p 83. C Brinsworth w Catcliffe *Sheff* 82–85; C S Shoebury *Chelmsf* 85–89; V Mosley Common *Man* 89–99; V Astley Bridge 99–11; AD Walmsley 02–10; TR Ramsbottom and Edenfield from 11. *St Andrew's Vicarage, 2 Henwick Hall Avenue, Ramsbottom, Bury BL0 9YH* T/F: (01706) 826482 E: andylindop95@tiscali.co.uk

LINDOP, Canon Kenneth. b 45. Linc Th Coll 71. d 74 p 75. C Leic St Phil 74–77; C Cov H Trin 77–80; P-in-c Cubbington 80–82; V 82–07; RD Warwick and Leamington 91–96; Jt P-in-c Leamington Spa H Trin and Old Milverton 03–07;

Hon Can Cov Cathl 04–07; rtd 07; PtO *B & W* from 09. *2 Grove House, Blue Anchor, Minehead TA24 6JU* T: (01643) 821940 M: 07711-389551 E: rev.lindop@gmail.com

LINDSAY, Anne. *See* LINDSAY, Mary Jane Anne

LINDSAY, Anthony. b 38. Trin Coll Bris 92. d 89 p 90. CMS 76–92; Dioc Admin Bo Sierra Leone 89–92; C Rainham w Wennington *Chelmsf* 93–96; R Quendon w Rickling and Wicken Bonhunt etc 96–03; rtd 03; PtO *York* 03–07 and from 10; P-in-c Langtoft w Foxholes, Butterwick, Cottam etc 07–10; Rtd Clergy and Widows Officer (E Riding) from 12. *5 Bursary Court, Pickering YO18 8BF* T: (01751) 476849 M: 07398-038929 E: ptlindsay1@gmail.com

LINDSAY, Calum Oran. b 73. Edin Univ BEng 97. Ridley Hall Cam 09. d 11 p 12. C St Margaret's-on-Thames *Lon* 11–14; PtO 15–18. *3821 University Boulevard, Dallas TX 75205, USA* E: revcalumlindsay@gmail.com

LINDSAY, Canon David Macintyre. b 46. Trin Hall Cam BA 68 MA 72. Cuddesdon Coll 68. d 71 p 72. C Gosforth All SS *Newc* 71–74; C Keele *Lich* 74–78; PtO *St E* 79–80; Chapl Haberdashers' Aske's Sch Elstree 80–06; rtd 06; PtO *St Alb* 06–07; *Portsm* from 07; Co-ord Reader Tr 10–15; Hon Can Portsm Cathl from 20. *Kentmere, Ashling Close, Waterlooville PO7 6NQ* T: (023) 9225 7662 M: 07769-814165 E: lindsay_d46@hotmail.com

LINDSAY, Canon John Carruthers. b 50. Edin Univ MA 72 BD 82. Edin Th Coll 79. d 82 p 83. C Broughty Ferry *Bre* 82–84; C Edin St Hilda 84–85; TP 85–88; C Edin St Fillan 84–85; TP 85–88; R N Berwick 88–15; R Gullane 88–15; Can St Mary's Cathl 00–15; rtd 15; PtO *Eur* from 18. *2 West Meikle Pinkerton Cottages, Dunbar EH42 1RX* M: 07977-520277 E: canonjohnlindsay@icloud.com

LINDSAY, Mrs Linda. b 53. Lindisfarne Regional Tr Partnership 13. d 15 p 16. NSM Crook *Dur* from 15; P-in-c from 20. *16 Priors Path, Ferryhill DL17 8UA* T: (01740) 655649 M: 07940-985217 E: linda.lindsay16@btinternet.com

LINDSAY (née CLEALL), Mrs Mary Jane Anne. b 54. Keele Univ BA 77 Herts Univ PGCE 92. SAOMC 00. d 03 p 04. C Chipping Barnet *St Alb* 03–07; Chapl Portsm Hosps NHS Trust 07–17; rtd 17; PtO *Portsm* from 17. *Kentmere, Ashling Close, Waterlooville PO7 6NQ* T: (023) 9225 7662 E: annelindsay54@hotmail.com

LINDSAY, Richard John. b 46. Sarum & Wells Th Coll 74. d 78 p 79. C Aldwick *Chich* 78–81; C Almondbury w Farnley Tyas *Wakef* 81–84; V Mossley *Man* 84–15; rtd 15; PtO *Man* 15–20; *Leeds* from 17. *Post Box Cottage, 15 Lindley Road, Elland HX5 0TE* T: (01422) 649250 E: lindsay.patricia@ymail.com

LINDSAY-SCOTT, Jonathan Mark. b 82. Bath Univ MEng 06. Ridley Hall Cam 11. d 14 p 15. C Romiley *Ches* from 17; Min Wallington Springfield Ch *S'wark* from 17. *49 Stanley Park Road, Carshalton SM5 3HT* T: (020) 8404 6064 E: jon@springfieldchurch.org.uk

LINDSAY-SMITH, Kevin Roy. b 55. d 05 p 06. OLM Glascote and Stonydelph *Lich* 05–15; rtd 15. *Address temp unknown* E: lindsay-smith1@sky.com

LINDSEY, John (Sami). b 73. Ch Ch Ox BA 95 Cranfield Univ MSc 97. Trin Coll Bris 11. d 13 p 14. C Leic H Trin w St Jo 13–16; C Emmaus Par Team 14–15; P-in-c from 16; TV Oadby from 21. *254 Kimberley Road, Leicester LE2 1LJ* M: 07850-326991 E: samilindsey@googlemail.com

LINDSEY, Judith Irene. b 50. d 19. NSM Huntington *York* from 19. *5 Lang Road, Huntington, York YO32 9SD* T: (01904) 274372 E: lindsey=j@sky.com

LINDSEY, Archdeacon of. *Vacant*

LINECAR, Rhian Wynn. b 52. Univ of Wales BMus 73 K Alfred's Coll Win CertEd 74. St Mich Coll Llan 13. d 15 p 16. NSM Cardiff City Par *Llan* from 15; NSM Cardiff Dewi Sant from 15. *Ty Llwyd, Drope Road, St George's-super-Ely, Cardiff CF5 6EP* T: (01446) 760007 M: 07545-425221 E: rlinecar@gmail.com

LINES, Graham Martin. b 55. St Jo Coll Nottm 97. d 99 p 00. C Crosby *Linc* 99–02; C Bottesford w Ashby 02–03; TV 03–14; V Crowle Gp from 14. *The Vicarage, Church Street, Crowle, Scunthorpe DN17 4LE* E: grahamlines62@gmail.com

LINES, Nicholas David John. b 64. York St Jo Univ MA 16. St Jo Coll Nottm 94. d 96 p 97. C Burton All SS w Ch Ch *Lich* 96–01; P-in-c Rodbourne Cheney *Bris* 01–02; R from 02. *St Mary's Rectory, 298 Cheney Manor Road, Swindon SN2 2PF* T: (01793) 522379 E: nick.lines1@gmail.com

LINFORD, Susan. b 51. STETS 10. d 13 p 14. OLM Bride Valley *Sarum* 13–16; NSM 16–21; PtO from 21. *North Hill Cottage,*

Shipton Lane, Burton Bradstock, Bridport DT6 4NQ T: (01308) 897363 E: sue.linford@btopenworld.com

LING, Canon Adrian Roger. b 66. Goldsmiths' Coll Lon BA 89 Leeds Univ BA 02. Coll of Resurr Mirfield 00. d 02 p 03. C Mill End and Heronsgate w W Hyde *St Alb* 02–06; P-in-c Flegg Coastal Benefice *Nor* 06–08; R 08–12; R S and W Lynn from 12; PtO *Ely* from 17; Hon Can Nor Cathl from 18; CMP from 13. *All Saints' Rectory, 33 Goodwins Road, King's Lynn PE30 5QX* T: (01553) 771779 E: adrianrling@btinternet.com

LING, Timothy Charles. b 61. Ex Univ BA 85 Selw Coll Cam BA 91. Ridley Hall Cam 89. d 92 p 93. C Gerrards Cross and Fulmer *Ox* 92–96; C Woking St Pet *Guildf* 96–00; V Bathford *B & W* 00–09; PtO 10–18; NSM Bath St Bart from 18. *26 Mendip Gardens, Bath BA2 2UT* T: (01225) 722622 M: 07760-785829 E: tim@stbartsbath.org

LINGARD, Colin. b 36. Kelham Th Coll 58. d 63 p 64. C Middlesbrough St Martin *York* 63–66; C Stainton-in-Cleveland 66–71; V Eskdaleside w Ugglebarnby 71–77; P-in-c Redcar w Kirkleatham 77; V Kirkleatham 78–86; RD Guisborough 83–86; V Linc St Botolph 86–89; Dioc Dir of Readers 86–89; R Washington *Dur* 89–93; P-in-c Middleton St George 93–97; R 97–01; Chapl Teesside Airport 97–01; rtd 01; PtO *Dur* from 01; *Leeds* 20–21. *29 Belgrave Terrace, Hurworth Place, Darlington DL2 2DW* M: 07752-179418 E: jlingard3@gmail.com

LINGARD, Jennifer Mary. See ALIDINA, Jennifer Mary

LINGS, Canon George William. b 49. Nottm Univ BTh 74 Ox Univ PGCE 75 Lambeth MLitt 93 Man Univ PhD 09. St Jo Coll Nottm 70. d 75 p 76. C Harold Wood *Chelmsf* 75–78; C Reigate St Mary *S'wark* 78–85; V Deal St Geo *Cant* 85–97; First Dir CA Sheff Cen for Ch Planting and Evang 97–17; NSM Norfolk Park St Leonard CD *Sheff* 97–03; NSM Arbourthorne and Norfolk Park 03–05; Hon Can Sheff Cathl 11–17; rtd 17; PtO *Sheff* from 17. *28 Norfolk Road, Sheffield S2 2SX* T: 0114-270 1780

LINGWOOD, Preb David Peter. b 51. Lon Univ BEd 73 Southn Univ BTh 80. Sarum & Wells Th Coll 75. d 78 p 79. C Ashford St Hilda *Lon* 78–81; TV Redditch, The Ridge *Worc* 81–86; TR Blakenall Heath *Lich* 86–96; V Rushall 96–04; RD Walsall 98–03; TR Stoke-upon-Trent 04–16; RD Stoke 07–14; Preb Lich Cathl 02–16; rtd 16; PtO *Worc* from 17. *32 Fairoak Drive, Bromsgrove B60 3PN* E: canonlingwood@gmail.com

LINN, Frederick Hugh. b 37. Em Coll Cam BA 61 MA 65. Ripon Hall Ox 61. d 63 p 64. C Bramhall *Ches* 63–68; V Liscard St Mary 68–71; V Liscard St Mary w St Columba 71–74; V Wybunbury 74–82; R Eccleston and Pulford 82–98; rtd 98; PtO *Ches* from 98; *St As* from 09. *4 Stonewalls, Burton, Rossett, Wrexham LL12 0LG* T: (01244) 571942 E: hugh.linn@btinternet.com

LINNEGAR, George Leonard. b 33. CGA. Kelham Th Coll 63. d 62 p 63. C Wellingborough St Mary *Pet* 62–65; LtO *Lich* 65–69; PtO *B & W* 69–80; Hon C Lewes All SS, St Anne, St Mich and St Thos *Chich* 80–86; C 87–99; rtd 99; PtO *Chich* from 99. *20 Morris Road, Lewes BN7 2AT* T: (01273) 478145

LINNEY, Barry James. b 64. Spurgeon's Coll BD 97 Anglia Poly Univ MA 02 Univ of Wales (Trin St Dav) MMin 14. Westcott Ho Cam 99. d 01 p 02. C Chingford SS Pet and Paul *Chelmsf* 01–04; V Cherry Hinton St Andr *Ely* 04–15; P-in-c Chatham St Steph *Roch* 15–17; V from 17. *St Stephen's Vicarage, 55 Pattens Lane, Chatham ME4 6JR* T: (01634) 305786 E: barryjameslinney@gmail.com

LINNEY, The Ven Gordon Charles Scott. b 39. CITC 66. d 69 p 70. C Agherton *Conn* 69–72; Min Can Down Cathl *D & D* 72–75; V Dublin St Cath w St Jas *D & G* 75–80; Preb Tipperkevin St Patr Cathl Dublin 77–80; I Glenageary *D & G* 80–04; Adn Dublin 88–04; Lect CITC 89–93; rtd 04. *208 Upper Glenageary Road, Glenageary, Co Dublin, Republic of Ireland* T: (00353) (1) 284 8503 M: 87-254 1775 E: linney.gordon@gmail.com

LINS, Hannah Melanie. b 78. St Mellitus Coll 14. d 17 p 18. C Bicton, Montford w Shrawardine and Fitz *Lich* 17–21; P-in-c from 21; C Leaton and Albrighton w Battlefield 17–21; P-in-c from 21. *41 Grange Road, Shrewsbury SY3 9DG* T: (01743) 232598 E: revhannahlins@gmail.com

LINTERN, John. b 61. Linc Th Coll BTh 93. d 93 p 94. C Preston on Tees *Dur* 93–96; Asst Dioc Youth Adv 96–99; P-in-c W Pelton 96–07; P-in-c Pelton 99–07; V Pelton and W Pelton from 07; AD Chester le Street and Houghton from 21. *The Vicarage, West Pelton, Stanley DH9 6RT* T: 0191-370 2146 F: 07971-114359 E: john.lintern@durham.anglican.org

LINTERN, Robert George. b 43. d 10 p 11. OLM Codsall *Lich* 10–17; PtO 17–20. *66 Ravenhill Drive, Codsall, Wolverhampton WV8 1BL* M: 07971-403157 E: lintern@gmail.com

LINTON, Mrs Angela Margaret. b 45. SAOMC 97. d 00 p 01. NSM Langtree *Ox* from 00. *10 Yew Tree Court, Goring,*

Reading RG8 9HF T/F: (01491) 874236 M: 07884-346552 E: dormouse62@yahoo.co.uk

LINTON, Barry Ian. b 76. Glas Univ BSc 98 TCD BTh 04 MCIBS 01. CITC 01. d 04 p 05. C Enniskillen *Clogh* 04–08; I Drumcliffe w Lissadell and Munninane *K, E & A* 08–15; Adn Elphin and Ardagh 12–15; I Drumragh w Mountfield *D & R* 15–20; I Drumgath w Drumgooland and Clonduff *D & D* from 20. *29 Cross Road, Hilltown, Newry BT34 5TF* M: 07931-600920

LINZEY, Prof Andrew. b 52. K Coll Lon BD 73 PhD 86 AKC 73 Lambeth DD 01 Win Univ Hon DD 11. St Aug Coll Cant 75. d 75 p 76. C Charlton-in-Dover *Cant* 75–77; Chapl and Lect Th NE Surrey Coll of Tech 77–81; Chapl Essex Univ *Chelmsf* 81–92; Dir of Studies Cen for Study of Th 87–92; Sen Research Fell Mansf Coll Ox 92–00; Tutor Chr Ethics 93–00; Special Prof Th Nottm Univ 92–96; Special Prof St Xavier Univ Chicago from 96; Hon Prof Birm Univ 97–07; Sen Research Fell Blackfriars Hall Ox 00–06; Dir Ox Cen for Animal Ethics from 06; Hon Prof Win Univ from 07; Hon Research Fell St Steph Ho Ox 08–19. *91 Iffley Road, Oxford OX4 1EG* T: (01865) 201565 E: andrewlinzey@aol.com *or* director@oxfordanimalethics.com

LION, Christopher Mark. b 84. St Mellitus Coll 12. d 15 p 16. C Gerrards Cross and Fulmer *Ox* 15–19; PtO from 19. *1 Manor House Mews, Oxford Road, Gerrards Cross SL9 7DW* M: 07796-115951 E: candclion@gmail.com *or* chris.lion@saintjames.org.uk

LIPOVSKY, Attila (Gregory). b 79. Pécs Th Coll Hungary BA 04 St Steph Ho Ox 16. d 03 p 03. PtO *Ox* 16–17; C Cambridge St Mary Less *Ely* 17–19; V Weymouth St Paul *Sarum* from 19. *St Paul's Vicarage, 58 Abbotsbury Road, Weymouth DT4 0BJ* M: 07796-963703 E: gregorio.hu@gmail.com

LIPPIATT, Michael Charles. b 39. Oak Hill Th Coll BD 71. d 71 p 72. C Ardsley *Sheff* 71–74; C Lenton *S'well* 74–78; V Jesmond H Trin *Newc* 78–96; rtd 96. *69 Lansdowne Crescent, Stanwix, Carlisle CA3 9ES* T: (01228) 537080

LIPPIETT, Canon Peter Vernon. b 47. Lon Univ MB, BS 73 MRCGP 80 Univ of Wales (Lamp) MA 08. Ripon Coll Cuddesdon 86. d 88 p 89. C Pinner Lon 88–91; V Twyford and Owslebury and Morestead *Win* 91–99; P-in-c Rydal *Carl* 99–03; Warden Rydal Hall and Ldr Rydal Hall Community 99–03; Dioc Spirituality Adv *Portsm* 03–10; Hon Can Portsm Cathl 10; rtd 11; PtO *Win* from 11. *Pax Lodge, Cox's Hill, Twyford, Winchester SO21 1PQ* T: (01962) 717438 E: peterlippiett@gmail.com

LIPSCOMB, Canon Timothy William. b 52. Chich Th Coll 82. d 85 p 86. C Sevenoaks St Jo *Roch* 85–89; C Stanningley St Thos *Ripon* 89–92; V Armley w New Wortley 92–05; AD Armley 98–05; R Preston St Jo and St Geo *Blackb* 05–17; AD Preston 08–14; Hon Can Blackb Cathl 10–17; rtd 17; P-in-c Bryn a Mor Miss Area *St As* from 20. *Beach Lawn, 123 Peulwys Lane, Old Colwyn, Colwyn Bay LL29 8YF* T: (01492) 512759 M: 07855-396452 E: lavisherminegourmet@gmail.com

LIPSCOMBE, Brian. b 37. Bris Univ BA 62. Tyndale Hall Bris 62. d 64 p 65. C Eccleston Ch Ch *Liv* 64–66; C Halliwell St Pet *Man* 66–69; C Frogmore *St Alb* 69–72; V Richmond Ch Ch *S'wark* 72–75; TV Mortlake w E Sheen 76–80; P-in-c Streatham Vale H Redeemer 80–85; V 85–91; R Norris Bank *Man* 91–96; V Droylsden St Martin 96–02; rtd 02; PtO *Ripon* 02–14; *Bradf* 13–14; *Leeds* from 14. *15 St Anne's Drive, Leeds LS4 2SA* T: 0113-275 1893 M: 07743-168641

LISK, Canon Stewart. b 62. Regent's Park Coll Ox BA 84 MA 88. St Mich Coll Llan 86. d 88 p 89. C Glan Ely *Llan* 88–92; Chapl Cardiff Inst of HE 92–96; Chapl Welsh Coll of Music and Drama 92–96; Asst Chapl Univ of Wales (Cardiff) 92–96; V Glan Ely 96–06; AD Llan 04–06; V Roath from 06; AD Cardiff 17–21; Can Llan Cathl from 14. *Roath Vicarage, Waterloo Road, Cardiff CF23 5AD* T: (029) 2048 4808 *or* 2048 7854 E: stewartlisk@live.co.uk

LISSENDEN, Steven John. b 64. St Mellitus Coll 16. d 19 p 20. OLM Wickford and Runwell *Chelmsf* from 19. *102 Bruce Grove, Wickford SS11 8QH* T: (01268) 763670 M: 07944-959300 E: revsteveliss@gmail.com

LISTER, Mrs Jennifer Grace. b 44. Totley Hall Coll CertEd 65. NOC 87. d 92 p 94. C Cowgate *Newc* 92–95; C Wall and Lich St Mary w St Mich 95–96; P-in-c Yoxall and Asst P The Ridwares and Kings Bromley 96–07; rtd 07; PtO *Cov* from 09. *81 Kingsley Road, Bishops Tachbrook, Leamington Spa CV33 9RZ* T: (01926) 427922 E: jenny.lister@waitrose.com

LISTER (née AISBITT), Mrs Joanne. b 69. St Jo Coll Dur BA 91. St Steph Ho Ox 91. d 93. NSM Mill End and Heronsgate w W Hyde *St Alb* 93–96. *Address temp unknown* E: listerwilliam@hotmail.com

LISTER, Joseph Hugh. b 38. Tyndale Hall Bris 61. **d** 64 **p** 65. C Pemberton St Mark Newtown *Liv* 64–68; Hon C Braintree *Chelmsf* 68–71; C Darfield *Sheff* 71–73; P-in-c Sheff St Swithun 73–75; TV Sheff Manor 76–80; TR Winfarthing w Shelfanger *Nor* 80–81; P-in-c Burston 80–81; P-in-c Gissing 80–81; P-in-c Tivetshall 80–81; R Winfarthing w Shelfanger w Burston w Gissing etc 81–88; P-in-c Sandon, Wallington and Rushden w Clothall *St Alb* 88–89; R 89–93; R Nether and Over Seale *Derby* 93–96; V Lullington 93–96; R Seale and Lullington 96–98; Dean Ndola Repton 96–98; Zambia 99–02; rtd 02; Hon C Hartington, Biggin and Earl Sterndale *Derby* 02–04; C Stoke Canon, Poltimore w Huxham and Rewe etc *Ex* 05–06; PtO *Carl* 10–16; *Derby* 17–20. *Cliff Cottage, Thorpe, Ashbourne DE6 2AW* T: (01335) 350383 E: joeandgillie@gmail.com

LISTER, Miss Mary Phyllis. b 28. St Andr Ho Portsm 52. **dss** 80 **d** 87. Inkberrow w Cookhill and Kington w Dormston *Worc* 80–82; Ancaster *Linc* 82–87; C 87–88; rtd 88; PtO *Worc* 88–00; *Leic* 15–20. *6 Stuart Court, High Street, Kibworth Beauchamp, Leicester LE8 0LR* T: 0116-279 3763

LISTER, Peter. b 42. Leeds Univ BA 64 Newc Univ PGCE 75. Coll of Resurr Mirfield 63. **d** 65 **p** 66. C Monkseaton St Pet *Newc* 65–68; C Cramlington 68–70; Hon C 71–78; C Morpeth 79–83; V Shilbottle 83–88; Asst Dioc Dir of Educn 83–88; Dir of Educn 88–95; Hon Can Newc Cathl 88–95; Dioc Dir of Educn *Lich* 95–06; rtd 07; PtO *Lich* 07–09; *Cov* from 09. *81 Kingsley Road, Bishops Tachbrook, Leamington Spa CV33 9RZ* T: (01926) 427922 E: peterlister@globalnet.co.uk

LISTER, Peter William Ryley. b 56. Linc Sch of Th and Min 08. **d** 10 **p** 11. OLM Bourne *Linc* 10–19; OLM Edenham w Witham on the Hill and Swinstead from 19. *4 Linden Rise, Bourne PE10 9TD* T: (01778) 423730 E: pwr.lister@btinternet.com

LISTER, William Bernard. b 67. Keble Coll Ox BA 88 MA 92. St Steph Ho Ox BA 91. **d** 92 **p** 93. C Mill End and Heronsgate w W Hyde *St Alb* 92–96; CF 96–06; Sen CF 06–12; Chapl Florence w Siena *Eur* 12–21. *Address temp unknown* M: (0039) 328-180 4196

LISVANE, Lady (Constance Jane). b 51. Lanchester Poly Cov BA 73. WEMTC 10. **d** 13 **p** 14. C Cusop w Blakemere, Bredwardine w Brobury etc *Heref* 13–17; NSM from 17. *Blakemere House, Blakemere, Hereford HR2 9JZ* T: (01981) 500478 E: jane@blakemerehouse.myzen.co.uk

LITHERLAND, Terence. b 46. **d** 93 **p** 94. OLM Horwich and Rivington *Man* 93–16; OLM Blackrod 11–15; rtd 16. *61 Tomlinson Street, Horwich, Bolton BL6 5QR* T: (01204) 692201 M: 07436-019274 E: tlitherland36@gmail.com

LITTLE, Andrew. b 27. Open Univ BA 83 UEA BA 03. AKC 51. **d** 52 **p** 53. C Fulham All SS *Lon* 52–54; C Epsom St Barn *Guildf* 54–61; V Northwood *Lich* 61–72; V Stowe 72–85; P-in-c Hixon 72–85; V Hixon w Stowe-by-Chartley 86–89; rtd 89; PtO *Nor* 89–09; Hon PV Nor Cathl 93–09. *4 Capel Court, The Burgage, Prestbury, Cheltenham GL52 3EL* T: (01242) 285800

LITTLE, Bryan Martin. b 80. Edin Univ MA 01. Cranmer Hall Dur 15. **d** 17 **p** 18. C E Clevedon w Clapton in Gordano etc *B & W* 17–21; P-in-c Highbridge from 21. *The Vicarage, 81A Church Street, Highbridge TA9 3HS* M: 07816-955713

LITTLE, Ms Christine. b 60. Lanc Univ BA 83. St Jo Coll Nottm 88. **d** 91 **p** 94. Par Dn Meltham *Wakef* 91–94; C Hatcham St Jas *S'wark* 94–99; P-in-c 99–04; C Nottingham St Pet and All SS *S'well* 04–07; C Nottingham All SS, St Mary and St Pet 07–14; C Bestwood Em and St Mark w Rise Park from 14. *5 Hatton Close, Arnold, Nottingham NG5 9QG* T: 0115-840 7209 E: revchrissielittle@gmail.com

LITTLE, Derek Peter. b 50. St Jo Coll Dur BA 72. Trin Coll Bris. **d** 75 **p** 76. C Bradley *Wakef* 75–78; C Kidderminster St Geo *Worc* 78–82; V Lepton *Wakef* 82–85; E Regional Sec CPAS 85–88; V Canonbury St Steph *Lon* 88–96; R Bedhampton *Portsm* 96–99; rtd 09. *Sunnyside House, 14 Culimore Road, West Wittering, Chichester PO20 8HB* T: (01243) 671114 E: littlederek20@gmail.com

LITTLE, George Nelson. b 39. CITC 70. **d** 72 **p** 73. C Portadown St Mark *Arm* 72–76; I Newtownhamilton w Ballymoyer and Belleek 76–80; I Aghaderg w Donaghmore *D & D* 80–82; I Aghaderg w Donaghmore and Scarva 82–05; Can Dromore Cathl 93–05; Treas Dromore Cathl 93–05; Chan Dromore Cathl 03–05; rtd 05. *41 Carn Valley, Rathfriland, Newry BT34 5GA* T: (028) 4023 9102

LITTLE, Ian Dawtry Torrance. b 49. Keele Univ BEd 72. SWMTC 81. **d** 85 **p** 86. NSM St Stythians w Perranarworthal and Gwennap *Truro* 85–97; NSM Chacewater w St Day and Carharrack 97–06; PtO from 06. *Kernyk, Crellow Fields, Stithians, Truro TR3 7RE*

LITTLE, James Harry. b 57. York Univ BA 79. Qu Coll Birm 84. **d** 87 **p** 88. C Wollaton *S'well* 87–90; C N Wheatley, W

Burton, Bole, Saundby, Sturton etc 90–93; R E Markham w Askham, Headon w Upton and Grove 93–06; P-in-c Dunham w Darlton, Ragnall, Fledborough etc 04–06; TR Howden *York* from 06; RD 10–15. *The Minster Rectory, Market Place, Howden, Goole DN14 7BL* T: (01430) 432056 E: revjlittle@aol.com

LITTLE, Martin. See LITTLE, Bryan Martin

LITTLE, Matthew. b 68. Scotus Coll Bearsden BD 00. **d** 99 **p** 00. Chapl St Andr Hospice Airdrie from 09; NSM Glas St Mary 17–20; R Hamilton from 20; R Uddingston from 20. *6 Rowanden Avenue, Bellshill ML4 3EW* T: (01698) 615059 *or* (01236) 772046 M: 07813-954610 E: matthew.little1968@gmail.com

LITTLE, Nigel James. b 73. Middx Univ BA 93. Oak Hill Th Coll 98. **d** 01 **p** 02. C Highgate St Mich *Lon* 01–07; TV Kirk Ella and Willerby *York* 07–12; Chapl Felsted Sch from 12. *Stavells, Braintree Road, Felsted, Dunmow CM6 3DR* T: (01371) 822600 E: nigel_little@yahoo.com

LITTLE, Canon Stephen Clifford. b 47. Man Univ MEd 81. AKC 72. **d** 72 **p** 73. C Grange St Andr *Ches* 72–73; C E Runcorn w Halton 73–75; P-in-c Newbold *Man* 75–77; P-in-c Broughton and Milton Keynes *Ox* 77–82; Sector Min Milton Keynes Chr Coun 77–84; TR Warwick *Cov* 84–93; R Harvington and Norton and Lenchwick *Worc* 93–96; R Harvington 96–98; Exec Officer Dioc Bd for Ch and Soc *Man* 98–05; Exec Officer Dioc Bd for Min and Soc 01–05; Hon Can Man Cathl 00–05; PtO from 05; *Ex* from 20. *Howden Lodge, Willand Old Village, Willand, Cullompton EX15 2RJ* T: (01884) 32663 M: 07795-821476 E: stephenlittle@essell.org.uk

LITTLEFORD, Peter John. b 40. St Mark & St Jo Coll Lon CertEd 63 ACP 65 Birkbeck Coll Lon BSc 70 Lon Inst of Educn DipEd 73 MA 76. SAOMC 96. **d** 99 **p** 00. Chapl De Montfort Univ *Leic* 99–01; NSM Bedf St Mark *St Alb* 99–01; NSM Bedford St Mich 01–04; NSM Elstow 04–10; rtd 10; PtO *St Alb* from 10. *1 Bindon Abbey, Bedford MK41 0AZ* T: (01234) 356645 E: peterlittleford@btinternet.com

LITTLEJOHN, Keith Douglas. b 59. Ripon Coll Cuddesdon BTh 03. **d** 03 **p** 04. C Horsham *Chich* 03–07; P-in-c Bolney 07–19; P-in-c Cowfold 07–19; V Goring-by-Sea from 19. *12 Compton Avenue, Goring-by-Sea, Worthing BN12 4UJ* T: (01903) 242525 M: 07905-544366 E: keithdlj@aol.com

LITTLER, Alison Susan. **d** 12 **p** 13. NSM Caldicot *Mon* 12–14; NSM Magor 14–18; NSM Panteg and Griffithstown 18–20; NSM Mid Torfaen from 20. *Panteg Rectory, The Highway, New Inn, Pontypool NP4 0PH* T: (01495) 755278 E: alisonlittler1@btinternet.com

LITTLER, Eric Raymond. b 36. AMIC 93. Roch Th Coll 65. **d** 68 **p** 69. C Hatfield Hyde *St Alb* 68–73; Chapl Welwyn Garden City Hosp 70–73; TV Pemberton St Jo *Liv* 73–78; Chapl Billinge Hosp Wigan 76–81; V Pemberton St Fran Kitt Green *Liv* 78–81; V White Notley, Faulkbourne and Cressing *Chelmsf* 81–88; V Westcliff St Andr 88–96; Chapl Westcliff Hosp 88–96; Chapl Southend HA 89–96; R E and W Tilbury and Linford *Chelmsf* 96–98; Chapl Orsett Hosp 96–98; RD Thurrock *Chelmsf* 96–98; R Gt Oakley w Wix and Wrabness 98–02; Chapl Essex Rivers Healthcare NHS Trust 98–02; rtd 02; PtO *Sarum* from 98; *Chelmsf* 02–19; *B & W* from 02; Chapl St Jo Hosp Heytesbury 03–08. *Minster Hall, 1 Pound Row, Warminster BA12 8NQ* T: (01985) 218818 E: ericandsuzette@uwclub.net

LITTLEWOOD, Alan James. b 51. Man Poly BEd 77. **d** 95 **p** 96. OLM Gosberton *Linc* 95–97; OLM Gosberton, Gosberton Clough and Quadring 97–01; C Bourne 01–03; P-in-c Leasingham and Cranwell 03–08; P-in-c Ancaster Wilsford Gp 08–14; P-in-c Barkston and Hough Gp 11–14; rtd 15; PtO *Linc* 16–19. *37 Parklands Drive, Harlaxton, Grantham NG32 1HX* T: (01476) 563085 E: alanjlittlewood@gmail.com

LITTLEWOOD, Alistair David. b 68. St Cath Coll Ox BA 89. Qu Coll Birm 93. **d** 96 **p** 97. C Keyworth and Stanton-on-the-Wolds *S'well* 96–00; Chapl Birm Univ 00–05; P-in-c Edwinstowe *S'well* 05–10; P-in-c Perlethorpe 05–10; Hon C Mansfield Deanery 10–12; PtO *S'well* from 12. *24 The Heathers, Boughton, Newark NG22 9HE* E: 1alistairlittlewood@gmail.com

LITTLEWOOD, Miss Jacqueline Patricia. b 52. Linc Th Coll 77. **dss** 80 **d** 87 **p** 94. Crayford *Roch* 80–84; Gravesend H Family w Ifield 84–87; Par Dn 87–93; rtd 93; NSM Gravesend St Aid *Roch* from 93; NSM Milton next Gravesend Ch Ch from 06. *25 Beltana Drive, Gravesend DA12 4BT* T: (01474) 560106 E: jpl7skypilot@gmail.com

LITTLEWOOD, Mrs Penelope Anne. b 47. WEMTC 05. **d** 08 **p** 09. NSM Burghill *Heref* 08–12; P-in-c 12–17; NSM Pipe-cum-Lyde and Moreton-on-Lugg 08–12; P-in-c 12–17; NSM Stretton Sugwas 08–12; P-in-c 12–17; rtd 17; PtO

Heref from 18; Dioc Chapl MU from 18. *Cobwebs, Burghill, Hereford HR4 7RL* T: (01432) 760835 M: 07734-347327 E: penny.cobwebs@virgin.net

LITTON, Alan. b 42. Ridley Hall Cam 66. **d** 69 **p** 70. C Bolton St Bede *Man* 69–71; C Ashton St Mich 71–73; V Haslingden St Jo Stonefold *Blackb* 73–77; Ind Chapl *York* 77–81; V Crewe All SS and St Paul *Ches* 81–84; Ind Chapl *Liv* 84–89; V Spotland *Man* 89–94; R Newchurch *Liv* 94–02; P-in-c Croft w Southworth 99–02; R Newchurch Culcheth w Croft 02; rtd 02; PtO *Liv* 03–08 and from 11; Hon C Burtonwood 08–11. *3 Rosemary Close, Great Sankey, Warrington WA5 1TL* T: (01925) 222944 E: littonalan@gmail.com

LITZELL, Sven Anders. b 80. Wheaton Coll Illinois BA 03 Stockholm Univ MSc 04. Ridley Hall Cam 10. **d** 12 **p** 13. C Holborn St Geo w H Trin and St Bart *Lon* 12–15; Prior Community of St Anselm *Cant* 15–18; PtO *S'wark* 15–18; R Westville St Eliz S Africa from 18. *St Elizabeth's Church, 45 Salisbury Avenue, Westville, Durban 3629, KwaZulu-Natal, South Africa* T: (0027) (31) 266 4325 E: anders@litzell.se

LIVERPOOL, Archdeacon of. *See* MACGURK, The Ven Michael Joseph Patrick

LIVERPOOL, Bishop of. *See* BAYES, The Rt Revd Paul

LIVERPOOL, Dean of. *See* JONES, The Very Revd Susan Helen

LIVESEY, Rachel Elizabeth. *See* DALE, Rachel Elizabeth

LIVESLEY, John. b 80. Magd Coll Ox BA 02 MSt 03 MA 07 Leeds Univ MA 07. Coll of Resurr Mirfield 04. **d** 07 **p** 08. C Swinton and Pendlebury *Man* 07–10; P-in-c Tudhoe Grange *Dur* 10–19; P-in-c Cassop cum Quarrington 10–19; V Bowburn and Tudhoe Grange from 19. *St Andrew's Vicarage, St Andrew's Road, Spennymoor DL16 6NE* T: (01388) 814817 M: 07796-117568 E: johnlivesley1980@yahoo.co.uk

LIVINGSTONE, Jonathan David. b 84. St Andr Univ MA 06. Scottish Episc Inst 14. **d** 17 **p** 18. C Hamilton *Glas* 17–20; C Uddingston 17–20; C Smithfield Gt St Bart *Lon* 20–21; Chapl Barts Health NHS Trust from 20. *16 Osborne Road, London E7 0PH* M: 07947-863501 E: jonathan.livingstone@nhs.net

LIYANAGE, Sylvester. b 78. Kingston Univ BEng 01 Surrey Univ MSc 03 Cam Univ BTh 08. Ridley Hall Cam 05. **d** 08 **p** 09. C Kingston Hill St Paul *S'wark* 08–12; TV Gt Chesham *Ox* 12–19. *Fabriksgatan 36C, 702 23 Orebro, Sweden* E: s.liyanage@btinternet.com

LLANDAFF, Archdeacon of. *See* GREEN, The Ven Roderick Ernest Alexander

LLANDAFF, Bishop of. *See* OSBORNE, The Rt Revd June

LLANDAFF, Dean of. *See* CAPON, The Very Revd Gerwyn Huw

✠**LLEWELLIN, The Rt Revd John Richard Allan.** b 38. Fitzw Ho Cam BA 64 MA 78. Westcott Ho Cam 61. **d** 64 **p** 65 **c** 85. C Radlett *St Alb* 64–68; C Johannesburg Cathl S Africa 68–71; V Waltham Cross *St Alb* 71–79; R Harpenden St Nic 79–85; Hon Can Truro Cathl 85–92; Suff Bp St Germans 85–92; Suff Bp Dover *Cant* 92–99; Bp at Lambeth (Hd of Staff) 99–03; rtd 03; PtO *Truro* 04–07; Hon Asst Bp Cant from 08. *15A The Precincts, Canterbury CT1 2EL* T: (01227) 764645 M: 07850-185869 E: rllewellin@clara.co.uk

LLEWELLYN, Brian Michael. b 47. Univ of Wales (Cardiff) LLM 99 MRICS 73. Sarum & Wells Th Coll 78. **d** 80 **p** 81. C Farncombe *Guildf* 80–83; Chapl RAF 83–87; R Hethersett w Canteloff w Lt and Gt Melton *Nor* 87–95; RD Humbleyard 94–95; P-in-c Smallburgh w Dilham w Honing and Crostwight 95–98; R 98–00; P-in-c Ypres *Eur* 10–16; P-in-c Chich from 17. *19 James Avenue, Herstmonceux, Hailsham BN27 4PB* T: (01323) 832899 E: bllewy@gmail.com

LLEWELLYN, Canon Christine Ann. b 46. Univ of Wales (Ban) BA 69 DipEd 70. **d** 89 **p** 97. NSM Arthog w Fairbourne w Llangelynnin w Rhoslefain *Ban* 90–93; NSM Holyhead w Rhoscolyn w Llanfair-yn-Neubwll 93–94; C 94–95; C Holyhead 95–97; TV 97–04; TR 04–11; Hon Can Ban Cathl 03–07; Can Cursal Ban Cathl 07–11; rtd 12; PtO *Ban* from 12; AD Llifon and Talybolion 13–15. *The Old School, Rhoscolyn, Holyhead LL65 2RQ* T: (01407) 741593

LLEWELLYN, Neil Alexander. b 55. LWCMD 78. Westcott Ho Cam 79 Sarum & Wells Th Coll 83. **d** 84 **p** 85. C Heref St Martin 84–86; Chapl Rotterdam Miss to Seamen *Eur* 86–89; R Docking w The Birchams and Stanhoe w Barwick *Nor* 89–92; Chapl Ypres *Eur* 92–95; Toc H 92–95; CF 95–06; P-in-c Newport w Cilgwyn and Dinas w Llanllawer *St D* 06–07; V Newport w Cilgwyn and Nevern and Y Beifil etc 07–11; V Newport w Cilgwyn and Dinas w Llanllawer etc 11–18; P-in-c W Cemaes from 18. *The Rectory, Long Street, Newport SA42 0TJ* T: (01239) 820380

LLEWELLYN, Richard Morgan. b 37. MBE 76 OBE 79 CB 91. FCMI 81. Sarum & Wells Th Coll 91. **d** 93 **p** 94. C Brecon St Mary and Battle w Llanddew *S & B* 93–95; Min Can Brecon Cathl 93–95; Chapl Ch Coll Brecon 95–14. *Field*

House, Llangattock, Crickhowell NP8 1HL T: (01873) 810116 E: morgan.llewellyn@btinternet.com

LLEWELLYN-MACDUFF, Ms Lindsay. b 75. Kent Univ BA 97. St Mich Coll Llan 97. **d** 99 **p** 00. C Milton next Sittingbourne *Cant* 99–01; C Barham w Bishopsbourne and Kingston 01–03; C Margate All SS and Westgate St Sav 03–05; P-in-c Gt Finborough w Onehouse, Harleston, Buxhall etc *St E* 05–09; Chapl HM Pris Littlehey 10–14; Bp's Dom Chapl *Roch* from 14. *Bishopscourt, 24 St Margaret's Street, Rochester ME1 1TS* T: (01634) 814439 E: lindsay.llewellyn-macduff@rochester.anglican.org

LLEWELYN, Miss Gabrielle Jane. b 48. Trin Coll Bris 08. **d** 09 **p** 10. NSM Fair Oak *Win* 09–12; Chapl HM Pris Northd 12–15; PtO *Newc* from 12. *149 Gloster Park, Amble, Morpeth NE65 0HQ* M: 07817-731036 E: gllewelyn60@gmail.com

LLOYD, Canon Bernard James. b 29. AKC 56. **d** 57 **p** 58. C Laindon w Basildon *Chelmsf* 57–65; V E Ham St Geo 65–82; RD Newham 76–82; Hon Can Chelmsf Cathl 82–94; R Danbury 82–94; P-in-c Woodham Ferrers 87–90; rtd 94; PtO *Chelmsf* from 94. *Chanterelle, 47 Seaview Avenue, West Mersea, Colchester CO5 8HE* T: (01206) 383892

LLOYD, The Ven Bertram Trevor. b 38. Hertf Coll Ox BA 60 MA 64. Clifton Th Coll 62. **d** 64 **p** 65. C S Mimms Ch Ch *Lon* 64–70; V Wealdstone H Trin 70–84; RD Harrow 77–82; P-in-c Harrow Weald St Mich 80–84; V Harrow Trin St Mich 84–89; Adn Barnstaple *Ex* 89–02; Preb Ex Cathl 91–02; rtd 02; PtO *Ex* from 06. *8 Pebbleridge Road, Westward Ho!, Bideford EX39 1HN* T: (01237) 424701 E: trevorlloyd152@outlook.com

LLOYD, Mrs Carole Barbara. b 53. Sheff Univ BA 74 Coll of Ripon & York St Jo MA 03 Leeds Metrop Univ PGCE 93. NOC 00. **d** 03 **p** 04. C Bolton St Jas w St Chrys *Bradf* 03–06; C Gt Aycliffe and Chilton *Dur* 06–07; TV Gt Aycliffe 07–09; P-in-c Chilton 09–11; P-in-c Kelloe and Coxhoe 08–11; P-in-c Swanwick and Pentrich *Derby* 11–12; V 12–15; rtd 15; PtO *Derby* 15–17 and 18–20; P-in-c Ilkeston St Mary 17–18; PtO *S'well* 19–20; *Leeds* 20–21. *37 Cricketers Green, Yeadon, Leeds LS19 7YS* T: 0113-250 5465 M: 07948-836523 E: carole.lloyd@amnos.co.uk

LLOYD, David Edgar Charles. b 59. St Mich Coll Llan 97. **d** 99 **p** 00. C Newton Nottage *Llan* 99–03; V Newcastle from 03. *The Vicarage, 1 Walters Road, Bridgend CF31 4HE* T: (01656) 655999 E: frdavidlloyd@hotmail.com

LLOYD, David John. b 52. Lon Univ BD 82. Burgess Hall Lamp 73. **d** 76 **p** 77. C Pembroke St Mary w St Mich *St D* 76–77; C Llanelli 77–80; V Cil-y-Cwm and Ystrad-ffin w Rhandir-mwyn etc 80–82; Oman 82–84; R Llanllwchaearn and Llanina *St D* 84–88; V Llangennech and Hendy 88–90; PtO *St Alb* 91–95; V Bampton w Clanfield *Ox* 96–17; AD Witney 02–03; rtd 17; PtO *S & B* from 18. *26 Palace Avenue, Llanelli SA15 1NA* T: (01554) 228836 E: revdjlloyd@hotmail.co.uk

LLOYD, David Zachary. b 80. Wycliffe Hall Ox BA 01 Anglia Ruskin Univ MA 10 Solicitor 05. Ridley Hall Cam 08. **d** 10 **p** 11. C Hampton St Mary *Lon* 10–13; C Heigham St Thos *Nor* 13–17; C Nor Lakenham St Alb and St Mark 15–17; C The Mitre Benefice from 17; P-in-c 20–21; Chapl City Coll Nor 17–20. *Church View Barn, Hawes Green, Shotesham St Mary, Norwich NR15 1UW* M: 07916-295154 E: davidzacharylloyd@gmail.com or david.lloyd@stn.org.uk

LLOYD, Dennis John. b 46. BSc 70 MSc 74 PhD 81. S Dios Minl Tr Scheme. **d** 90 **p** 91. C Hamworthy *Sarum* 90–92; Chapl UEA *Nor* 92–97; P-in-c Malvern St Andr *Worc* 97–99; V 99–01; Chapl Defence Evaluation Research Agency 97–01; RD Malvern *Worc* 98–01; P-in-c Rowlands Castle *Portsm* 01–11; Warden of Readers 01–11; rtd 11; PtO *Portsm* from 11. *24 Forest Hills, Newport PO30 5NQ* E: revdrdjlloyd@aol.com

LLOYD, Derek James. b 78. Birm Univ BA 00 Leeds Univ BA 03. Coll of Resurr Mirfield 02. **d** 04 **p** 05. C Burnley St Andr w St Marg and St Jas *Blackb* 04–07; C W Burnley All SS 07–09; V Cross Heath *Lich* 09–17; V Newcastle St Paul 09–17; V Toxteth Park St Agnes and St Pancras *Liv* 17–20; Catholic Miss Enabler from 17; CMP from 05. *Address temp unknown*

LLOYD, Dyfrig Cennydd. b 80. K Coll Lon BA 01. Ripon Coll Cuddesdon 01. **d** 04 **p** 05. C Llandysul w Bangor Teifi and Llanfairollwyn etc *St D* 04–06; C Bro Teifi Sarn Helen 06–07; TV 07–11; V Cardiff Dewi Sant *Llan* from 11; AD Cardiff from 21. *6 Rachel Close, Cardiff CF5 2SH* T: (029) 2056 6001

LLOYD, Edward Gareth. b 60. K Coll Cam BA 81 MA 85 Dur Univ PhD 98. Ridley Hall Cam 85. **d** 88 **p** 89. C Chester Dur 88–91; C Monkwearmouth St Pet 91–92; P-in-c 92–96; TV Monkwearmouth 97–99; V Birtley from 99. *6 Ruskin Road, Birtley, Chester le Street DH3 1AD* T: 0191-410 2115 E: gareth@dunelm.org.uk

LLOYD, Eileen. *See* TAVERNOR, Eileen

LLOYD, Gareth. *See* LLOYD, Edward Gareth

LLOYD, Miss Jane Elisabeth. b 52. Th Ext Educn Coll BA 08. **d** 99 **p** 05. C Letaba S Africa 99–15; rtd 15; PtO *St E* from 20. *59 Station Road, Sudbury CO10 2SP* T: (01787) 374108 M: 07960-986445 E: janeelloyd@icloud.com

LLOYD, Jonathan Joseph Barrington. b 88. St Cuth Soc Dur BA 09 Clare Coll Cam BA 15 Dur Univ PGCE 10. Westcott Ho Cam 13. **d** 16 **p** 17. C Jarrow *Dur* 16–18; C Jarrow and Simonside 18–19; Prec and Min Can St Alb Abbey from 19. *1 Dean Moore Close, St Albans AL1 1DW* M: 07462-855550 E: jjblloyd@hotmail.co.uk *or* precentor@stalbanscathedral.org

LLOYD, Canon Jonathan Wilford. b 56. Surrey Univ & City of Lon Poly BSc 80 N Lon Poly MA 86 Goldsmiths' Coll Lon CQSW 82 DASS 82. S'wark Ord Course 87. **d** 90 **p** 91. NSM Sydenham St Bart *S'wark* 90–93; P-in-c 93–94; Dir of Soc Resp 91–95; Bp's Officer for Ch in Soc 95–97; Hon PV S'wark Cathl 91–97; Chapl Team Ldr Bath Univ *B & W* 97–04; P-in-c Charlcombe w Bath St Steph 04–09; Chapl Denmark *Eur* 09–14; Adn Germany and N Eur 10–14; Can Brussels Cathl 10–14; PtO from 14; P-in-c Bridge *Cant* 14–16; P-in-c Littlebourne and Ickham w Wickhambreaux etc 14–16; Asst Dir of Ords 15–16; R W Vancouver St Steph Canada 16–21; Co Ecum Officer Chs Together in Somerset from 21; PtO *B & W* from 21. *11 Moss Close, Wells BA5 1FX* T: (01749) 705103 E: canonjonathanlloyd@gmail.com

LLOYD, Marc Andrew. b 78. LMH Ox BA 99 Middx Univ MA 02. Oak Hill Th Coll 04. **d** 07 **p** 08. C Eastbourne H Trin *Chich* 07–11; P-in-c Warbleton and Bodle Street Green 11–12; R Warbleton, Bodle Street Green and Dallington from 12; RD Dallington from 14. *Warbleton Rectory, Rookery Lane, Rushlake Green, Heathfield TN21 9QJ* T: (01435) 830421 M: 07812-054820 E: marc_lloyd@hotmail.com

LLOYD, Michael Francis. b 57. Down Coll Cam BA 79 MA 82 St Jo Coll Dur BA 83 Worc Coll Ox DPhil 97. Cranmer Hall Dur 81. **d** 84 **p** 85. C Locks Heath *Portsm* 84–87; Asst Chapl Worc Coll Ox 89–90; Chapl Ch Coll Cam 90–94; Chapl Fitzw Coll Cam 95–96; Hon C Westminster St Jas the Less *Lon* 96–03; Tutor St Steph Ho Ox 03–05; Tutor St Paul's Th Cen *Lon* 06–13; C St Andr Holborn 06–10; Chapl Qu Coll Ox 10–13; Prin Wycliffe Hall Ox from 13; LtO *Ox* from 19. *Wycliffe Hall, 54 Banbury Road, Oxford OX2 6PW* T: (01865) 274200 F: 274215 E: michael.lloyd@wycliffe.ox.ac.uk

LLOYD, Canon Nigel James Clifford. b 51. Nottm Univ BTh 81 Lambeth STh 90 Win Univ MA 10. Linc Th Coll 77. **d** 81 **p** 82. C Sherborne w Castleton and Lillington *Sarum* 81–84; R Lytchett Matravers 84–92; TR Parkstone St Pet w Branksea and St Osmund 92–02; R Parkstone St Pet and St Osmund w Branksea 02–12; Ecum Officer (Sherborne Area) 92–00; Dioc Ecum Officer 00–01; RD Poole 01–09; V Broadstone 12–17; Can and Preb Sarum Cathl 02–17; rtd 17; PtO *Sarum* from 18. *23 Laurel Close, Corfe Mullen, Wimborne BH21 3TD* T: (01202) 699883 M: 07940-348776 E: canon.nigel@gmail.com

LLOYD (née WALMSLEY), Patricia Jane. b 62. Bris Univ BSc 83 PhD87 Trin Coll Cam BTh 01. Ridley Hall Cam 99. **d** 01 **p** 02. C Bowdon *Ches* 01–05; V Over Peover w Lower Peover 05–19; P-in-c Haslington w Crewe Green and Wheelock from 19. *163 Crewe Road, Haslington, Crewe CW1 5RL* T: (01270) 582088 M: 07785-752023 E: vicarjanelloyd@gmail.com

LLOYD, Rebecca Joanne. b 78. Univ of Wales (Ban) BA 00 K Coll Lon MMus 01 PhD 06 Jes Coll Cam BA 13 MA 18. Westcott Ho Cam 11. **d** 14 **p** 15. C S Dulwich St Steph *S'wark* 14–17; Bp's Dom Chapl *Lich* from 17; PV Lich Cathl from 17. *Bishop's House, 22 The Close, Lichfield WS13 7LG* T: (01543) 306000 E: rebecca.lloyd@lichfield.anglican.org

LLOYD, Richard Gary. b 75. Ex Coll Ox BA 98 St Jo Coll Dur MA 00. Cranmer Hall Dur 98. **d** 00 **p** 01. C Didben *Win* 00–03; Asst Chapl Charterhouse Sch Godalming 04–07; Sen Chapl 07–11; C Claygate *Guildf* 11–13; P-in-c E Molesey St Mary 13–18; V 18–20; P-in-c W Molesey 17–20; PtO *Lon* from 21. *Saxon Stables, West End Lane, Haslemere GU27 2EN* M: 07753-835744 E: richardlloyd.rhema@gmail.com

LLOYD, Richard John. b 32. Univ of Wales (Lamp) BA 52 LTh 54. **d** 54 **p** 56. C Manselton *S & B* 54–56; C Sketty 56–59; C Swansea St Mary and H Trin 59–63; CF (TA) 59–65; V Elmley Castle w Netherton and Bricklehampton *Worc* 63–69; Chapl Dragon Sch Ox 69–82; Chapl St Hugh's Coll Ox 75–80; P-in-c Ox St Marg 75–76; Chapl Magd Coll Ox 75–82; Prec and Chapl Ch Ch *Ox* 82–87; R Alvescot w Black Bourton, Shilton, Holwell etc 87–95; P-in-c Broughton Poggs w Filkins, Broadwell etc 94–95; R Shill Valley and Broadshire 95–01; rtd 01; PtO *Glouc* from 02; *Ox* from 02. *3 The Lanes, Bampton OX18 2JG*

LLOYD, Mrs Sandra Edith. b 48. Sarum & Wells Th Coll 83. **dss** 86 **d** 87 **p** 94. Freshwater *Portsm* 86–87; C 87–89; C Whitwell 89–95; V 95–14; C Niton 89–95; P-in-c 95–96; R 96–14; R St Lawrence 96–04; rtd 14; PtO *Portsm* from 14. *St Kenelm, Guyers Road, Freshwater PO40 9QA* T: (01983) 756865 E: rhadegunde@aol.com

LLOYD, Sarah Jane. MBE 12. Leic Univ BA 88. Ripon Coll Cuddesdon MA 15. **d** 15 **p** 16. C Old Basing and Lychpit *Win* 15–18; C Basingstoke 18–19; V Shalford *Guildf* from 19. *The Vicarage, East Shalford Lane, Guildford GU4 8AE* E: vicar.shalford@icloud.com

LLOYD, Simon Christopher. b 65. Newc Poly BSc 88 Surrey Univ MSc 89. All SS Cen for Miss & Min 17. **d** 20 **p** 21. C Lt Marsden w Nelson St Mary and Nelson St Bede *Blackb* from 20. *The Old Post Office, Stopper Lane, Rimington, Clitheroe BB7 4DU* M: 07977-488586 E: simon.christopher.lloyd@outlook.com

LLOYD, Stephen Russell. b 47. Worc Coll Ox BA 69 MA 77 CertEd. Oak Hill Th Coll 76. **d** 77 **p** 78. C Canonbury St Steph *Lon* 77–80; C Braintree *Chelmsf* 80–92; V Braintree St Paul 92–01; V Ipswich St Andr *St E* 01–14; rtd 14; PtO *St E* from 14; *Chelmsf* from 18. *26 Endsleigh Court, Colchester CO3 3QN* T: (01206) 560172 E: stephenrlloyd@btinternet.com

LLOYD, Canon Stuart George Errington. b 49. TCD BA 72. **d** 75 **p** 76. C Cloughfern *Conn* 75–79; C Cregagh *D & D* 79–82; I Eglantine *Conn* 82–89; I Ballymena w Ballyclug 89–15; Can Conn Cathl 97–15; Preb 97–01; Prec 01–15; rtd 15. *123 Knockan Road, Broughshane, Ballymena BT43 7JA* T: (028) 2586 2705 E: sgelloyd@btinternet.com

LLOYD, Trevor. *See* LLOYD, Bertram Trevor

LLOYD-EVANS, Charlotte Louise. b 70. Bris Univ BEng 92. St Padarn's Inst 14 Qu Th Coll Newfoundland 15. **d** 17 **p** 18. Asst Chapl Abu Dhabi and Al Ain UAE 17–20; P-in-c Greenhithe St Mary *Roch* from 20; P-in-c Swanscombe from 20. *The Rectory, Swanscombe Street, Swanscombe DA10 0JZ* T: (01322) 383160 M: 07808-584122 E: revcharlielloydevans@gmail.com

LLOYD HUGHES, Gwilym. *See* HUGHES, Gwilym Lloyd

LLOYD-JAMES, Duncan Geraint. b 66. St Steph Ho Ox BTh 94. **d** 94 **p** 96. C St Leonards Ch Ch and St Mary *Chich* 94–96; C Rottingdean 96–99; R Brede w Udimore 99–07; rtd 07; PtO *Guildf* 08–10. *18 Sudeley Place, Brighton BN2 1HF* T: (01273) 606550 M: 07511-772256 E: duncanlj@btinternet.com

LLOYD JONES, Ieuan. b 31. St Cath Coll Cam BA 51 MA 54 FBIM. Sarum & Wells Th Coll 80. **d** 83 **p** 84. NSM Claygate *Guildf* 83–89; PtO *Ox* 89–06; *Guildf* 07–17. *2C Aldersey Road, Guildford GU1 2ES* T: (01483) 449605 E: lloyd.jones4@ntlworld.com

LLOYD MORGAN, Richard Edward. b 48. Trin Coll Cam MA 70 Ox Univ DipEd 71. SEITE 95. **d** 98 **p** 99. NSM Clapham St Paul *S'wark* 98–03; Chapl K Coll Cam 03–15; rtd 15; PtO *Eur* from 15; *S'wark* from 17; *Lon* from 17. *111 Narbonne Avenue, London SW4 9LQ* T: (020) 8673 4149 E: richard.lloydmorgan@gmail.com

LLOYD-RICHARDS, David Robert. b 48. Open Univ BA 84 Hull Univ MA 87. St D Coll Lamp. **d** 71 **p** 72. C Skewen *Llan* 71–73; C Neath w Llantwit 73–76; Miss to Seamen 76–77; V Pontlottyn w Fochriw *Llan* 77–84; R Merthyr Dyfan 84–90; Chapl Barry Neale-Kent Hosp 84–90; Tutor Open Univ 85–10; Sen Chapl Univ Hosp of Wales NHS Trust 90–95; Sen Chapl Univ Hosp of Wales and Llandough NHS Trust 95–00; Sen Chapl Manager Cardiff and Vale NHS Trust 00–08; rtd 08. *Jeantique, La Butte, La Trinité des Laitiers, Gace, 61230 Orne, France* T: (0033) (2) 33 36 11 15 E: robertlloydrichards@googlemail.com

LLOYD ROBERTS, Mrs Kathleen Ada May. b 49. Bordesley Coll of Educn CertEd 71. Qu Coll Birm 03. **d** 06 **p** 07. NSM Temple Balsall *Birm* 06–09; V from 09. *The Master's House, Temple Balsall, Knowle, Solihull B93 0AL* T: (01564) 772415 E: klloydroberts@leveson.org.uk

LLOYD WILLIAMS, The Ven Martin Clifford. b 65. Westmr Coll Lon BEd 87. Trin Coll Bris BA 93. **d** 93 **p** 94. C Bath Walcot *B & W* 93–97; R Bath St Mich w St Paul 97–14; R Bath St Mich Without 14–15; RD Bath 10–15; Adn Brighton and Lewes *Chich* from 15; R Ovingdean 19–20. *12 Walsingham Road, Hove BN3 4FF* M: 07305-412784 E: archbandl@chichester.anglican.org

LO, Peter Kwan Ho. b 54. Chinese Univ of Hong Kong BD 84 Stirling Univ MBA 92 K Coll Lon LLB 99. **d** 84 **p** 85. Hong Kong 84–91; PtO *Chich* 02–03; C Uckfield 03–06; R Monterey Park USA 07–19; Hon C N Pt St Pet Hong Kong from 19. *133 East Graves Avenue, Monterey Park CA 91755-3915, USA* T: (001) (626) 571 2714 E: peterkwanholo@hotmail.com

lo POLITO, Nicholas. b 59. Catholic Th Union Chicago MDiv 85 MA(Theol) 87 Birm Univ PhD 10. Comboni Miss. **d** 85 **p** 86. In RC Ch 85–94; Egypt 86–88; Sudan 88–91;

Italy 91–94; Asst Chapl Malta and Gozo *Eur* 94–98; C Castle Bromwich SS Mary and Marg *Birm* 98–01; TV Salter Street and Shirley 01–05; Chapl Birm Univ 05–13; P-in-c Highgate 13–16; Chapl St Alb Academy 13–16; V Potternewton w Lt London *Leeds* from 16. *St Martin's Vicarage, St Martin's View, Leeds LS7 3LB* T: 0113-262 4271 E: nlopolito@hotmail.com

LOACH, Michael Graham. b 72. Bris Univ BA 94 Chelt & Glouc Coll of HE PGCE 95 Heythrop Coll Lon MA 03 St Jo Coll Dur MA 12. Cranmer Hall Dur 10. **d** 12 **p** 13. C W Kirby St Bridget *Ches* 12–15; V Higher Bebington from 15; P-in-c Tranmere St Paul w St Luke from 21. *Christ Church Vicarage, King's Road, Bebington, Wirral CH63 8LX* T: 0151-609 0943 M: 07878-338546 E: mgloach@gmail.com

LOADER, Michael John. b 43. Hull Univ BSc 64 Chelsea Coll Lon MSc 72. **d** 05 **p** 14. Asst Chapl Nicosia Cyprus *Cyprus* 05–12; NSM Tavistock and Gulworthy *Ex* 13–15; NSM Tavistock, Gulworthy and Brent Tor 15–20; PtO from 20. *20 Edgcumbe Drive, Tavistock PL19 0ET* T: (01822) 613231 M: 07799-766755 E: michaelloader@supanet.com

LOAT, Canon Andrew Graham. b 61. Aber Univ BD 83 Univ of Wales (Ban) MTh 00. St Jo Coll Nottm. **d** 87 **p** 88. C Llangynwyd w Maesteg *Llan* 87–90; C Llansamlet *S & B* 90–91; R Whitton and Pilleth and Cascob etc 91–98; R Llandrindod w Cefnllys and Disserth 98–09; R Lower Ithon Valley 09–14; V Upper Ithon Valley 09–14; Warden of Readers 02–08; AD Maelienydd 06–14; Can Res Brecon Cathl 03–14; P-in-c Llanbadarn Fawr and Elerch and Penrhyncoch etc *St D* 14–19; P-in-c Bro Padarn from 19; AD from 19; Hon Can St D Cathl from 16. *The Vicarage, Llanbadarn Fawr, Aberystwyth SY23 3TT* T: (01970) 624638 E: vicarage.llanbadarn@gmail.com

LOBB, Edward Eric. b 51. Magd Coll Ox BA 74 MA 76. Wycliffe Hall Ox 73. **d** 76 **p** 77. C Haughton St Mary *Man* 76–80; C Rusholme H Trin 80–84; P-in-c Whitfield *Derby* 84–90; V 90–92; V Stapenhill w Cauldwell 92–03; rtd 03; PtO *Derby* 03–05. *Middleton House, Beith KA15 1HX* T: (01505) 500232

LOBB, Miss Josephine Mary. b 57. SRN 83. **d** 96 **p** 97. OLM St Germans *Truro* 96–06; NSM Saltash 06–12; TV 12–17; rtd 17. *19 Lowertown Close, Landrake, Saltash PL12 5DG* T: (01752) 851488 E: jolobb@btinternet.com

LOBO, Nived Joseph. b 90. Ox Univ BA 20. Wycliffe Hall Ox 18. **d** 21. C Portswood Ch Ch *Win* from 21. *6 Royston Close, Southampton SO17 1TB* E: revnivlobo@gmail.com

LOBSINGER, Eric John. b 78. Washington Univ AB 00 JD 03 Kyushu Univ Japan LLM 04 LLD 07. **d** 10 **p** 15. USA 10–13; Jun Chapl Mert Coll Ox 13–14; Jun Dean St Steph Ho Ox 13–14; C Hornsey H Innocents *Lon* 15–17; V Ruislip St Mary from 17. *9 The Fairway, Ruislip HA4 0SP* E: fr.eric.lobsinger@gmail.com

LOCHEAD, Samuel George. b 92. SS Coll Cam BA 14 MEd 17 PGCE 15 Cam Univ BA 19. Westcott Ho Cam 19. **d** 20 **p** 21. C Corbridge w Halton and Newton Hall *Newc* from 20. *15 Hallgarth Close, Corbridge NE45 5BS* M: 07557-640339 E: samlochead92@googlemail.com

LOCK, Mrs Beverley. b 59. Loughb Univ BA 81 York St Jo Univ MA 12 Bris Univ PGCE 82. CBDTI 01. **d** 04 **p** 05. C Kendal St Geo *Carl* 04–07; C Beacon TM 07–08; P-in-c Orton and Tebay w Ravenstonedale etc 08–16; P-in-c Shap w Swindale and Bampton w Mardale 08–16; TR Loughrigg from 16. *The Vicarage, Millans Park, Ambleside LA22 9BW* T: (015394) 33205 E: reverend.beverley@gmail.com

LOCK, Mrs Jacqueline. b 43. **d** 08 **p** 09. OLM High Wycombe *Ox* from 08. *15 Kingsley Crescent, High Wycombe HP11 2UN* T: (01494) 532216 M: 07976-719909 E: jackie@thelocks.org.uk

LOCK, Nicholas George. b 62. **d** 06 **p** 07. OLM Melksham *Sarum* 06–10; OLM Atworth w Shaw and Whitley 07–10; OLM Broughton Gifford, Gt Chalfield and Holt 07–10. *4 Murray Walk, Melksham SN12 7AZ* T: (01225) 353906 M: 100966 E: nicklock42@hotmail.com

LOCK, Paul Alan. b 65. St Chad's Coll Dur BA 86. Coll of Resurr Mirfield 87. **d** 89 **p** 90. C Upholland *Liv* 89–92; C Teddington SS Pet and Paul and Fulwell *Lon* 92–95; V 95–99; V Skelmersdale St Anne *Liv* 99–04; Dioc Dir of Educn *Blackb* 13–14; C Dalton *Liv* 16–17; P-in-c 17–20; C Upholland 16–17; P-in-c 17–20; R Up Holland and Dalton from 20. *The Rectory, 1A College Road, Upholland, Skelmersdale WN8 0PY* T: 07813-019863 E: paul.a_lock@btinternet.com

LOCK, The Ven Peter Harcourt D'Arcy. b 44. AKC 67. **d** 68 **p** 69. C Meopham *Roch* 68–72; C Wigmore w Hempstead 72; C S Gillingham 72–77; R Hartley 77–83; R Fawkham and Hartley 83–84; V Dartford H Trin 84–93; Hon Can Roch Cathl 90–01; V Bromley SS Pet and Paul 93–01; RD Bromley 96–01; Adn Roch and Can Res Roch Cathl 01–09; rtd 09; PtO *Cant* from 11; *Roch* from 11. *53*

Preston Park, Faversham ME13 8LH T: (01795) 529161 E: peter.lock123@btinternet.com

LOCK, Thomas. b 38. **d** 05 **p** 06. OLM N Poole Ecum Team *Sarum* 05–11; rtd 11; PtO *Sarum* from 11. *Smithy's Lodge, 75 Tatnam Road, Poole BH15 2DP* M: 07970-021768 E: thomaslock04@gmail.com

LOCKE, Mrs Jennifer Margaret. b 52. Edin Univ BEd 74. Ox Min Course 06. **d** 08 **p** 09. NSM Wexham *Ox* 08–11; TV Risborough 11–17; rtd 17; PtO *Ox* from 18. *7 Lynbury Place, 14 South Park Crescent, Gerrards Cross SL9 8HJ* T: (01753) 880546 E: revjmlocke@gmail.com

LOCKE, Nigel Richard. *See* HESFORD-LOCKE, Richard Nigel

LOCKE, Robert Andrew. b 62. St Steph Ho Ox 89. **d** 92 **p** 93. C Colchester St Jas, All SS, St Nic and St Runwald *Chelmsf* 92–95; CF 95–00; V Burnham *Chelmsf* 00–04. *14 Armstrong Road, Edinburgh EH14 2BF* M: 07545-320484 E: rablocke1603@gmail.com

LOCKE, Stephen John. b 60. St Chad's Coll Dur BA 82. Sarum & Wells Th Coll 84. **d** 86 **p** 87. C Blackb St Mich w St Jo and H Trin 86–89; C Oswaldtwistle Immanuel and All SS 89–92; V Blackb St Mich w St Jo and H Trin 92–98; Chapl to the Deaf 98–04; V Owton Manor *Dur* from 04. *The Vicarage, 18 Rossmere Way, Hartlepool TS25 5EF* T: (01429) 290278 E: frlockessc@ntlworld.com

LOCKETT, Preb Paul. b 48. Sarum & Wells Th Coll 73. **d** 76 **p** 77. C Horninglow *Lich* 76–78; C Tewkesbury w Walton Cardiff *Glouc* 78–81; P-in-c W Bromwich St Pet *Lich* 81–90; R Norton Canes 90–95; V Longton St Mary and St Chad 95–12; Dean's V Lich Cathl 91–12; Preb Lich Cathl 04–12; rtd 12; P-in-c Hempton and Pudding Norton *Nor* 12–16; Chantry P Shrine of Our Lady of Walsingham 12–16; P-in-c Shrewsbury All SS w St Mich *Lich* 16–19; Chapl to The Queen 12–18; PtO *Lich* from 19. *119 Wenlock Road, Shrewsbury SY2 6JX* T: (01743) 272948

LOCKETT, Simon David. b 66. Stirling Univ BA 96. Wycliffe Hall Ox 00. **d** 02 **p** 03. C Ray Valley *Ox* 02–06; R Madley w Tyberton, Peterchurch, Vowchurch etc *Heref* from 06. *The Vicarage, Madley, Hereford HR2 9LP* T: (01981) 250245 E: simonlizlockett@hotmail.com

LOCKEY, Malcolm. b 45. Sunderland Poly BA 67 Newc Univ DipEd 68 FRSA 75. NEOC 87. **d** 90 **p** 91. NSM Yarm *York* 90–97; C 97–98; TV Whitby w Aislaby and Ruswarp 98–03; Hon Chapl Miss to Seafarers 98–03; Chapl RNLI 00–03; P-in-c Coldstream *Edin* 04–09; R Kelso 05–09; Offg Chapl RAF and Chapl ATC 02–03; rtd 09; PtO *Newc* 10–13; NSM Bilbrook and Coven *Lich* 13–14; V Coven 14–17; PtO 17–19. *Ashtree House, Ashbrook Lane, Abbots Bromley, Rugeley WS15 3DW* T: (01283) 841947 M: 07710-467785 E: fr.mac1945@gmail.com

LOCKHART, Canon Clare Patricia Anne (Sister Clare). b 44. Bris Univ BA 74 Newc Univ MLitt 96. Cranmer Hall Dur 84. **d** 87 **p** 94. Sisters of Charity from 63; Chapl Asst Sunderland Distr Gen Hosp 84–89; Chapl 89–94; Chapl City Hosps Sunderland NHS Trust 94–95; NSM N Hylton St Marg Castletown *Dur* 87–95; P-in-c 95–99; NSM Eoropaidh *Arg* from 99; PtO *Dur* 02–14; Dioc Supernumerary *Arg* from 09; P-in-c Stornoway 11–12; Hon Can St Jo Cathl Oban from 17. *The Sisters of Charity, Carmel, 7A Gress, Isle of Lewis HS2 0NB* T: (01851) 820484 *or* 820734 E: srclarecarmel@btinternet.com

LOCKHART, David. b 68. QUB BSc 90 TCD BTh 93. CITC 90. **d** 93 **p** 94. C Belfast St Mary w H Redeemer *Conn* 93–96; I Belfast St Steph w St Luke 96–03; I Cloughfern 03–18; I Glynn w Raloo from 18; I Larne and Inver from 18. *The Rectory, 8 Lower Cairncastle Road, Larne BT40 1PQ* T: (028) 2827 2788 E: dandblockhart@btinternet.com

LOCKHART, Eileen Ann. b 52. Open Univ BA 93 ACII 74. EAMTC 95. **d** 98 **p** 99. NSM Shenfield *Chelmsf* 98–17; rtd 17. *6 Granary Meadow, Wyatts Green, Brentwood CM15 0QD* T/F: (01277) 822537 E: eileenlockhart@gmail.com

LOCKHART, Raymond William. b 37. Qu Coll Cam BA 58 MA 61 LLB 60. St Jo Coll Nottm 72. **d** 74 **p** 75. C Aspley S'well 74–76; V 81–88; R Knebworth *St Alb* 76–81; Warden Stella Carmel Haifa (CMJ) Israel 88–91; R Jerusalem Ch Ch 91–99; Dir CMJ 99–02; rtd 02; PtO *B & W* 03–16; *Chich* from 16. *18 The Vincent, Redland Hill, Redland, Bristol BS6 6BJ* M: 07474-355944 E: raylockhart1@gmail.com

LOCKLEY, Miss Pauline Margaret. b 41. **d** 02. OLM Stoke-upon-Trent *Lich* 02–13; PtO 13–19. *Highfields, 89 Tolkien Way, Stoke-on-Trent ST4 7SJ* T: (01782) 849806

LOCKLEY, Philip Jonathan. b 81. Newc Univ BA 02 St Hugh's Coll Ox MSt 04 New Coll Ox DPhil 10 St Jo Coll Dur MA 17. Cranmer Hall Dur 15. **d** 17 **p** 18. C Ox St Clem 17–21; P-in-c Washington *Dur* from 21. *27 Wroxton, Washington NE38 7NU* M: 07817-549099 E: pjlockley@gmail.com

LOCKYER, David Ralph George. b 41. Wells Th Coll 65. **d** 67 **p** 68. C Bottesford *Linc* 67–69; C Eling *Win* 69–72; C Eling, Testwood and Marchwood 72–73; TV 73–77; TR Speke St Aid *Liv* 77–84; V Halifax St Jude *Wakef* 84–96; Chapl Halifax R Infirmary 84–96; V Banwell *B & W* 96–06; rtd 06. *The Old Quarry, Stour Provost, Gillingham SP8 5SB* T: (01747) 839970

LOCOCK (née MILES), Mrs Jillian Maud. b 33. Lon Univ BSc 55. NOC 81. **dss** 84 **d** 87 **p** 95. Didsbury Ch Ch *Man* 84–86; Chapl Asst Man R Infirmary 85–87; Chapl Asst Withington Hosp Man 86–88; Chapl Asst RN 88–93; NSM Dumbarton *Glas* 93–96; PtO *Ex* 02–18. *Glebe Cottage, Dousland, Yelverton PL20 6LU* T: (01822) 854098 E: rjbirtles@aol.com

LODER, Sister Helen. b 43. S'wark Ord Course 91. **d** 94 **p** 95. Soc of St Marg from 70; Hon C S Hackney St Mich w Haggerston St Paul *Lon* 94–01; Hon C Bethnal Green St Matt w St Jas the Gt 02–10; PtO from 10. *St Saviour's Priory, 18 Queensbridge Road, London E2 8NS* T: (020) 7613 1464 E: helenloder@aol.com

LODGE, Prof Anne Elizabeth. NUI BEd PhD Man Univ MEd. CITI. **d** 16 **p** 18. Raheny w Coolock *D & G* 16–18; NSM Dublin Clontarf from 18. *70 Dunluce Road, Clontarf, Dublin 3, Republic of Ireland* M: (00353) 86-373 6995 E: anne.lodge454@gmail.com *or* lodgea@tcd.ie

LODGE, The Ven Michael John. b 53. Wycliffe Hall Ox 87. **d** 89 **p** 90. C Highworth w Sevenhampton and Inglesham etc *Bris* 89–93; P-in-c Cheltenham St Luke and St Jo *Glouc* 93–05; TR Rayleigh *Chelmsf* 05–17; RD Rochford 08–15; Adn Chelmsf from 17; Hon Can Chelmsf Cathl from 12. *The Archdeacon's Lodge, 459 Rayleigh Road, Benfleet SS7 3TH* T: (01268) 779345 E: a.southend@chelmsford.anglican.org

LODGE, Petrina. **d** 18 **p** 19. C Llyn Safaddan *S & B* from 18. *Yr Hen Ffermdy, Llanywern, Brecon LD3 7UP* T: (01874) 658878

LODGE, Robin Paul. b 60. Bris Univ BA 82 Ch Ch Coll Cant PGCE 83. Chich Th Coll 88. **d** 90 **p** 91. C Calne and Blackland *Sarum* 90–94; Asst Chapl St Mary's Sch Calne 90–94; TV Wellington and Distr *B & W* 94–03; V Highbridge 03–09; V Taunton St Andr from 09; Warden of Readers Taunton Adnry from 17. *The Vicarage, 118 Kingston Road, Taunton TA2 7SR* T: (01823) 352471 M: 07772-567059 E: robin.lodge1@btinternet.com

LODGE, Roy Frederick. b 38. MBE 97. Lon Univ MB BTh DPhil 92. Tyndale Hall Bris 63. **d** 66 **p** 67. C Tardebigge *Worc* 66–67; Chapl and Warden Probation Hostel Redditch 67–69; Chapl RAF 69–75; C Kinson *Sarum* 76; LtO *Pet* 76–77; Asst Chapl HM Pris Stafford 77–78; Chapl HM Pris Ranby 78–84; Chapl HM Pris Long Lartin 84–93; Chapl HM Pris Service Coll 87–93; Chapl HM Pris Hewell Grange 93–98; Chapl HM Pris Brockhill 93–98; rtd 98; PtO *Cov* from 98; *Glouc* from 99; *St Alb* 12–17. *44 Eton Road, Stratford-upon-Avon CV37 7ER* T: (01789) 204850 E: lodgeconstantia1@btinternet.com

LODGE, Sally Nicole. b 61. Keele Univ BA 83 St Jo Coll Dur BA 09. Cranmer Hall Dur 07. **d** 09 **p** 10. C Halstead Area *Chelmsf* 09–12; P-in-c Witham 12–14; TR Witham and Villages 14–19; AD Witham 16–19; Hon Can Chelmsf Cathl 16–19; TR New Windsor *Ox* from 19. *Holy Trinity Vicarage, 73 Alma Road, Windsor SL4 3HD* M: 07747-612817 E: sally.lodge@btinternet.com

LODWICK, Canon Brian Martin. b 40. Leeds Univ BA 61 MPhil 76 Linacre Coll Ox BA 63 MA 67 Univ of Wales PhD 87 FSA 19 FRHistS 20. St Steph Ho Ox 61. **d** 64 **p** 65. C Aberaman *Llan* 64–66; C Newton Nottage 66–73; R Llansannor and Llanfrynach w Penllyn etc 73–94; R Llandough w Leckwith 94–04; RD Llantwit Major and Cowbridge 83–94; Warden of Readers 92–03; Chan Llan Cathl 92–02; Treas Llan Cathl 02–04; Chapl Llandough Hosp 94–99; Chapl Cardiff and Vale NHS Trust 99–00; Chapl Cardiff and Vale NHS Trust 00–01; rtd 01; PtO *Llan* from 04. *26 New Road, Neath Abbey, Neath SA10 7NH*

LODWICK, Stephen Huw. b 64. Plymouth Poly BSc 85. St Mich Coll Llan. **d** 94 **p** 95. C Clydach *S & B* 94–95; Chapl St Woolos Cathl *Mon* 95–98; R Grosmont and Skenfrith and Llangattock etc 98–01; CF from 01. *c/o MOD Chaplains (Army)* T: (01264) 887405

LOEWE, The Very Revd Jost Andreas. b 73. St Pet Coll Ox BA 95 MA 99 MPhil 97 Selw Coll Cam PhD 01 FRHistS 11. Westcott Ho Cam 97. **d** 01 **p** 02. C Upton cum Chalvey *Ox* 01–04; C Cambridge Gt St Mary w St Mich *Ely* 04–09; Chapl Trin Coll Melbourne Australia 09–12; Lect Th Trin Coll Th Sch 10–12; Dean Melbourne from 12. *St Paul's Cathedral, 209 Flinders Lane, Melbourne VIC 3000, Australia* T: (0061) (3) 9653 4333 F: 9653 4307 E: dean@stpaulscathedral.org.au

LOEWENDAHL, David Jacob (Jake). b 50. St Coll Cam BA 74 MA 77. Ripon Coll Cuddesdon 75. **d** 77 **p** 78. C Walworth S'wark 77–80; Chapl St Alb Abbey 80–83; Chapl St Alb Sch 80–83; Team Ldr Community Service Volunteers 84–90; PtO

Lon 83–90; R E and W Tilbury and Linford *Chelmsf* 90–95; V Menheniot *Truro* 95–98; RD W Wivelshire 97–98; rtd 98; PtO *Truro* from 98. *Bank Barn, Woodlands Farm, Sweetshouse, Bodmin PL30 5FE* T: (01208) 871384 M: 07816-430292

LOFT, Edmund Martin Boswell. b 25. St Jo Coll Cam BA 49 MA 55. Ely Th Coll 49. **d** 51 **p** 52. C Carl H Trin 51–54; C Barrow St Geo 54–56; V Allonby w W Newton 56–62; V Fillongley *Cov* 62–77; V Earlsdon 77–90; rtd 90; PtO *Sheff* 90–09. *41 Brook Road, Sheffield S8 9FH* T: 0114-250 9979 E: martinloft@gmail.com

LOFTHOUSE, Canon Brenda. b 33. RGN 60 RM 62 RNT 69. NOC 84. **d** 87 **p** 94. Hon Par Dn Greengates *Bradf* 87–89; Par Dn Farsley 89–94; V Bolton St Jas w St Chrys 94–00; Hon Can Bradf Cathl 98–00; rtd 00; PtO *Bradf* 00–14; Leeds from 14. *33 Myrtle Court, Bingley BD16 2LP* T: (01274) 771476

LOFTHOUSE, Mrs Diane Lesley. b 66. Yorks Min Course 08. **d** 11 **p** 12. NSM Moor Allerton and Shadwell *Ripon* 11–14; *Leeds* 14–16; NSM Roundhay St Edm 16–19; Chapl St Gemma's Hospice 15–19; Chapl Harrogate and Distr NHS Foundn Trust from 19. *33 Jackson Avenue, Leeds LS8 1NP* T: 0113-266 6495 E: dianelofthouse@virginmedia.com

LOFTS, Sally Anne. See BAYLIS, Sally Anne

LOFTUS, Francis. b 52. Newc Univ BA 73 St Andr Univ BPhil 76 York St Jo Coll PGCE 76 FRSA 94. NEOC 93. **d** 96 **p** 97. Hd Master Barlby High Sch 90–10; NSM Barlby and Riccall *York* 96–10; P-in-c 10–13; NSM Hemingbrough 06–10; P-in-c 10–13; V Riccall, Barlby and Hemingbrough 13–17; rtd 17; PtO *York* from 17; *St Alb* from 17. *19 Green Lane, North Duffield, Selby YO8 5RR* M: 07850-839419 E: francisloftus@btinternet.com

LOFTUS, John Michael. b 52. Sheff Univ BSc 74 Solicitor 77. **d** 00 **p** 01. OLM Hundred River *St E* 00–13; NSM Hundred River and Wainford 13–20; P-in-c Wrentham, Covehithe w Benacre etc 20–21; V from 21. *Keld House, Hulver Street, Henstead, Beccles NR34 7UE* T: (01502) 476257 F: 533001 E: jloftus@nortonpeskett.co.uk

LOGAN, Ms Alexandra Jane. b 73. Trin Coll Carmarthen BA 94. Ridley Hall Cam 99. **d** 02 **p** 03. C Penwortham St Mary *Blackb* 02–07; V Bethnal Green St Jas Less *Lon* 07–13; Chapl Co-ord Cumbria Univ *Blackb* from 14. *University of Cumbria, Bowerham Road, Lancaster LA1 3JD* E: alexandra.logan@cumbria.ac.uk

LOGAN, Elizabeth Jane. b 59. **d** 10 **p** 11. NSM Copthorne *Chich* 10–15; NSM Crawley Down All SS 15–19; rtd 19; PtO *Chich* from 20. *Fermandy House, Fermandy Lane, Crawley Down, Crawley RH10 4UB* T: (01342) 713338 E: elogan674@gmail.com

LOGAN, Ms Joanne. b 64. Ch Coll Cam BA 87 St Jo Coll Dur BA 04 MA 05 PhD 19. Cranmer Hall Dur 02. **d** 05 **p** 06. C Harrogate St Mark *Ripon* 05–09; PtO *Leeds* 11–12; *St Alb* 12–17; *Dur* from 17; Tutor Lindisfarne Coll of Th from 18. *11 Beechways, Durham DH1 4LG* T: 0191-386 8346 *or* 270 4144 E: jo_logan@btopenworld.com *or* jo@lindisfarnect.org

LOGAN, Kevin. b 43. Oak Hill Th Coll 73. **d** 75 **p** 76. C Blackb Sav 75–78; C Leyland St Andr 78–82; V Gt Harwood St Jo 82–91; V Accrington Ch Ch 91–08; rtd 08; PtO *Blackb* from 08. *119 Kingsway, Church, Accrington BB5 5EL* T: (01254) 396139 M: 07776-007694 E: kevinlogan1@hotmail.co.uk

LOGUE, Mrs Rosemary Christine. TCD BTh 93 Dub City Univ MA 01. CITC 90. **d** 93 **p** 94. C Clooney w Strathfoyle *D & R* 93–96; I Londonderry St Aug 96–03; I Tullyaughnish w Kilmacrennan and Killygarvan 03–05; I Sixmilecross w Termonmaguirke *Arm* 05–08; P-in-c Cambuslang *Glas* 08; I Kilskeery w Trillick *Clogh* 11–18; rtd 18. *17 Dunhugh Park, Londonderry BT47 2NL* T: (028) 7134 7480 E: r.logue@btinternet.com

LOH, Tom. b 79. UEA BSc 01. Wycliffe Hall Ox BTh 11. **d** 11 **p** 12. C Billericay and Lt Burstead *Chelmsf* 11–14; P-in-c Westcliff St Mich from 14; P-in-c Westcliff St Andr 16–19; P-in-c Southend St Jo from 21. *St Michael's Vicarage, 5 Mount Avenue, Westcliff-on-Sea SS0 8PS* T: (01702) 478462 M: 07905-743419 E: tomloh79@yahoo.co.uk

LOMAS, Anthony David. b 59. Cranfield Inst of Tech BSc 81. WEMTC 04. **d** 07 **p** 08. C Sevenhampton w Charlton Abbots, Hawling etc *Glouc* 07–11; R Redmarley D'Abitot, Bromesberrow, Pauntley etc 11–16; Chapl Aquitaine *Eur* from 16. *lieu-dit Labrande, 47800 Agnac, France* T: (0033) 6 72 31 72 87 E: revtonylomas@gmail.com

LOMAS, Mrs Catherine Mary. b 72. St Jo Coll Cam MA 93. STETS 07. **d** 10 **p** 11. C Wellingborough All SS *Pet* 11–14; C Cogenhoe and Gt and Lt Houghton w Brafield 11–14; LtO 15–16; V Irchester w Stanton Cross from 16. *The Vicarage, 19 Station Road, Irchester, Wellingborough NN29 7EH* T: (01933) 312674 E: revdcatherine@encircled.uk

LOMAX, Canon Barry Walter John. b 39. Lambeth STh Lon Coll of Div 63. **d** 66 **p** 67. C Sevenoaks St Nic *Roch* 66–71;

C Southport Ch Ch *Liv* 71–73; V Bootle St Matt 73–78; P-in-c Litherland St Andr 76–78; V New Borough and Leigh *Sarum* 78–94; Can and Preb Sarum Cathl 91–02; R Blandford Forum and Langton Long 94–02; rtd 02; PtO *Sarum* 03–19. *Shiloh, 2 Colborne Avenue, Wimborne BH21 2PZ* T: (01202) 856104 E: barry.lomax@talktalk.net

LOMAX, Eric John. b 64. St Jo Coll Dur BA 96 Leeds Univ PGCE 04. Cranmer Hall Dur 93. **d** 96 **p** 97. C Goodshaw and Crawshawbooth *Man* 96–00; V Copmanthorpe *York* 00–01; P-in-c Colsterworth Gp *Linc* 10–17; V Kempston All SS *St Alb* from 17; V Biddenham from 17. *The Vicarage, Church End, Kempston, Bedford MK43 8RH* E: ericjohnlomax64@aol.com

LOMAX, Kate Jane. b 73. RGN 96. St Jo Coll Nottm BA 02. **d** 02 **p** 03. C Luton St Mary *St Alb* 02–04; Asst Chapl Cam Univ Hosps NHS Foundn Trust 04–05; Chapl 05–07; NSM Penn Fields *Lich* 08–10; NSM Bayston Hill 10–16; PtO *St Alb* 17–18; NSM Luton St Paul 18–19; P-in-c from 19. *7 Corder Close, St Albans AL3 4NH* T: (01727) 758489 E: kate.lomax@virginmedia.com

LOMAX, Canon Timothy Michael. b 73. Derby Univ BEd 95 Nottm Univ MA 11. Ridley Hall Cam 05. **d** 07 **p** 08. C Penn Fields *Lich* 07–10; V Bayston Hill 10–16; Dir Miss *St Alb* from 16; Can Res St Alb from 16. *7 Corder Close, St Albans AL3 4NH* T: (01727) 758489 E: tim.lomax1@virginmedia.com

LONDON (St Paul's), Dean of. *See* ISON, The Very Revd David John

LONDON, Archdeacon of. *See* MILLER, The Ven Luke Jonathan

LONDON, Bishop of. *See* MULLALLY, The Rt Revd and Rt Hon Dame Sarah Elisabeth

LONEY, Mark William James. b 72. Cen Lancs Univ BSc 94 MA 97 TCD BTh 03. CITC 00. **d** 03 **p** 04. C Larne and Inver *Conn* 03–06; I Aghoghill w Portglenone 06–11; TV Digswell and Panshanger *St Alb* 12–15; I Dungiven w Bovevagh *D & R* from 15. *The Rectory, 14 Main Street, Dungiven, Londonderry BT47 4LB* T: (028) 7774 1394 *or* 7774 1226 E: rev.loney@btopenworld.com

LONG, Canon Anne Christine. b 33. Leic Univ BA 56 Ox Univ DipEd 57 Lon Univ BD 65 ALBC. **dss** 80 **d** 87 **p** 94. Lect St Jo Coll Nottm 73–84; Acorn Chr Healing Trust 85–98; Stanstead Abbots *St Alb* 85–92; Hon Par Dn 87–92; Hon Par Dn Camberley St Paul *Guildf* 92–94; Hon C 94–03; Hon Can Guildf Cathl 96–03; PtO *Sarum* from 06. *3 Chiselbury Grove, Salisbury SP2 8EP* T: (01722) 341488 E: annelong33@talktalk.net *or* anneclong33@gmail.com

LONG, Anthony Auguste. b 45. Linc Th Coll 79. **d** 81 **p** 82. C Kingswinford St Mary *Lich* 81–84; TV Ellesmere Port Ches 84–87; V Witton 87–97; P-in-c Wybunbury w Doddington 97–02; V 02–10; rtd 10; PtO *Ches* from 10. *23 Osborne Grove, Shavington, Crewe CW2 5BY* T: (01270) 561113 E: tojolong@hotmail.co.uk

LONG, Anthony Robert. b 48. SS Mark & Jo Coll Chelsea CertEd 70 Southn Univ BTh 93 UEA MA 96 Lambeth MA 04. Chich Th Coll 74. **d** 77 **p** 78. C Chiswick St Nic w St Mary *Lon* 77–80; C Earley St Pet *Ox* 80–85; P-in-c Worstead w Westwick and Sloley *Nor* 85–92; R Worstead, Westwick, Sloley, Swanton Abbot etc 92–16; P-in-c Tunstead w Sco' Ruston 85–16; Chapl Nor Cathl 85–16; rtd 16; PtO *Nor* from 17. *The Elms, The Street, Hemsby, Great Yarmouth NR29 4EU* T: (01493) 731727

LONG, Christopher William. b 47. MBE 94. Nottm Univ BTh 78 Open Univ BA 80. Linc Th Coll 75. **d** 78 **p** 79. C Shiregreen St Jas and St Chris *Sheff* 78–81; V 81–82; Chapl RAF 82–05; I Enniscorthy w Clone, Clonmore, Monart etc *C, F & O* 05–15; Adn Ferns 08–15; Adn Cashel, Waterford and Lismore 14–15; rtd 15. *20 Grange Mor Park, Grange Road, Rosslare, Co Wexford, Y35 X361, Republic of Ireland* T: (00353) (53) 913 2749 M: (00353) 87-695 0613 E: chriswlong1@eircom.net

LONG, David William. b 47. St Aug Coll Cant 70. **d** 72 **p** 73. C Stanley *Liv* 72–73; C W Derby St Luke 73–76; C Cantril Farm 76–79; V Warrington St Barn 79–81; V Westbrook St Jas 82–96; V Ince St Mary 96–12; AD Wigan E and Hon Can Liv Cathl 03–05; rtd 12; PtO *Blackb* from 14; *Liv* from 16. *25 Almond Brook Road, Standish, Wigan WN6 0TB* T: (01257) 400720

LONG, Mrs Frances Mary. b 58. SEITE 98. **d** 01 **p** 02. NSM Caterham *S'wark* 01–05; Chapl Surrey and Sussex Healthcare NHS Trust 01–03; C Riddlesdown *S'wark* 05–08; P-in-c Purley St Mark 08–12; P-in-c Purley St Swithun 08–12; PtO 12–14; NSM Caterham from 14. *56 Roffes Lane, Chaldon, Caterham CR3 5PT* T: (01883) 340257 M: 07903-019620 E: franyb8@hotmail.com

LONG, Frederick Hugh. b 43. EMMTC 90. **d** 90 **p** 91. NSM Grantham *Linc* 90–00; C 00–01; TV 01–02; V Grantham

St Anne New Somerby and Spitalgate 02–08; rtd 08; Hon C Drybrook, Lydbrook and Ruardean *Glouc* 08–13; PtO from 14. *2 Unlawater House, Unlawater Lane, Newnham GL14 1BJ* T: (01594) 510739

LONG, Geoffrey Lawrence. b 47. La Sainte Union Coll BTh 93 PGCE 94. Portsm Dioc Tr Course 88. **d** 89 **p** 98. NSM Whippingham w E Cowes *Portsm* 89–01; Chapl HM Pris Maidstone 01–12; rtd 12; PtO *Ely* from 13. *2 Fallowfield, Littleport, Ely CB6 1GY* T: (01353) 360702 E: geoffrey.long@outlook.com

LONG, Hermione Jane. *See* MORRIS, Hermione Jane

LONG, John. b 48. ACIB 72. Yorks Min Course 09. **d** 10 **p** 11. NSM Utley *Bradf* 10–14; *Leeds* 14–16; NSM Keighley from 16. *Rosslyn House, Could Street, Haworth, Keighley BD22 8AY* T: (01535) 646592 E: haworthlongs@tiscali.co.uk

LONG, Canon John Sydney. b 25. Lon Univ BSc 49. Wycliffe Hall Ox 50. **d** 51 **p** 52. C Plaistow St Andr *Chelmsf* 51–54; C Keighley *Bradf* 54–57; C-in-c Horton Bank Top CD 57–59; V Buttershaw St Aid 59–64; V Barnoldswick w Bracewell 64–85; Hon Can Bradf Cathl 77–91; RD Skipton 83–90; R Broughton, Marton and Thornton 85–91; rtd 91. *1 Church Villa, Carleton, Skipton BD23 3DQ* T: (01756) 799095

LONG, Katherine Claire. b 74. Univ of Wales (Lamp) BA 00 Aber Univ MSc(Econ) 15. Ripon Coll Cuddesdon 19. **d** 21. C Blackwell All SS and Salutation *Dur* from 21. *Address withheld by request* M: 07927-972461 E: revkatherinelong@gmail.com *or* curate@allsaintsblackwell.org.uk

LONG, Peter Ronald. b 48. Cuddesdon Coll 71. **d** 73 **p** 74. Chapl RAFVR 74–99; C Bodmin *Truro* 73–75; C Newquay 75–76; Asst Youth Chapl 75–76; Dioc Youth Chapl 76–79; PtO *Eur* 76, 78–85 and 87–98; Public Preacher *Truro* 77; P-in-c Mawgan w St Martin-in-Meneage 79–82; Chapl Helston-Meneage Community and Geriatric Hosp 80–95; Miss to Seamen 80–98; P-in-c Cury w Gunwalloe *Truro* 80–82; R Cury and Gunwalloe w Mawgan 83–98; PtO *Ex* 82–93; Ecum Th in UK Rail Ind from 97; rtd 08. *26 Jubilee Street, Newquay TR7 1LA* M: 07780-976113 E: ipsn2009@yahoo.co.uk

LONG, Samuel Allen. b 48. EAMTC 03. **d** 05 **p** 06. NSM Barrow *St E* 05–08; NSM Pakenham w Norton and Tostock 08–10; P-in-c Badwell and Walsham 10–15; C Hepworth, Hinderclay, Wattisfield and Thelnetham 15; rtd 15; PtO *St E* from 15. *16 Drury Close, Rougham, Bury St Edmunds IP30 9JE* T: (01359) 271936 M: 07732-971925 E: samlong167@aol.com

LONGBOTTOM, Canon Frank. b 41. Birm Univ MA 15. Ripon Hall Ox 65. **d** 68 **p** 69. C Epsom St Martin *Guildf* 68–72; Chapl St Ebba's Hosp Epsom 68–72; Chapl Qu Mary's Hosp Carshalton 68–72; Chapl Henderson Hosp Sutton 68–72; Chapl Highcroft Hosp Birm 72–94; Chapl Northcroft Hosp Birm 74–94; Dioc Adv for Past Care of Clergy & Families *Birm* 89–94; Bp's Adv 94–06; Bp's Adv on Health and Soc Care *Birm* 01–06; P-in-c Middleton 99–00; Hon Can Birm Cathl 91–06; rtd 07; PtO *Birm* from 09. *46 Sunnybank Road, Sutton Coldfield B73 5RE* T/F: 0121-350 5823

LONGBOTTOM, Canon Paul Edward. b 44. Kent Univ MA 02 AKC 67. **d** 68 **p** 69. C Rainham *Roch* 68–71; C Horsell 71–75; C Dunton Green 71–75; V Penge Lane H Trin 75–84; V Chatham St Wm 84–94; V Shorne and Dioc Dir of Ords 94–09; Hon Can Roch Cathl 96–09; rtd 09; PtO *Roch* from 09; *Cant* from 10. *30 Doubleday Drive, Bapchild, Sittingbourne ME9 9PJ* T: (01795) 428300 E: paul.longbottom@ymail.com

LONGDEN, Lee Paul. b 70. Peterho Cam BA 91 MA 95 Ches Coll of HE MTh 03 Birm Univ ThD 12 Huddersfield Univ MSc 13 FRCO 91 LLCM 93 ARCM 93 LRSM 96 FHEA 12 SFHEA 17 FInstLM 13. Qu Coll Birm 03. **d** 05 **p** 06. C Langley and Parkfield *Man* 05–08; V Ashton Ch 08–15; Hon Assoc Dir of Ords 09–15; Vice Prin All SS Cen for Miss and Min 15–18; PtO *Man* 15–18; R Kersal Moor from 18; Extraordinary Sen Lect NW Univ S Africa from 13; Hon Research Fell Qu Foundn Birm from 18. *Address withheld by request* T: 0161-792 5362 E: rectorofkersal@gmail.com

LONGDON, Anthony Robert James. b 44. STETS 00. **d** 03 **p** 04. OLM N Bradley, Southwick and Heywood *Sarum* 03–08; OLM N Bradley, Southwick, Heywood and Steeple Ashton 08–14; PtO from 14. *1A Holbrook Lane, Trowbridge BA14 0PP* T/F: (01225) 754771

LONGE, Canon David John Hastings. b 75. New Coll Edin BD 99. Ripon Coll Cuddesdon 07. **d** 09 **p** 10. C N Lambeth *S'wark* 09–15; Chapl to Abp in Jerusalem 15–18; R Matlaske *Nor* from 18. *The Rectory, The Street, Matlaske, Norfolk NR11 7AQ* T: (01263) 577252 M: 07881-950294 E: djhlonge@gmail.com

LONGE, James Robert. b 46. EAMTC 02. **d** 04 **p** 05. NSM Pakenham w Norton and Tostock *St E* 04–07; NSM St Edm Way 07–14; rtd 14; PtO *St E* from 14. *Bush House, Bradfield St Clare, Bury St Edmunds IP30 0EQ*

LONGFELLOW, Erica Denise. b 74. Duke Univ (USA) BA 97 Linc Coll Ox MSt 98 DPhil 01. SEITE 02. **d** 05 **p** 06. NSM Kew St Phil and All SS w St Luke *S'wark* 05–09; NSM Surbiton St Andr and St Mark 09–11; Chapl and Dean of Div New Coll Ox from 11. *New College, Holywell Street, Oxford OX1 3BN* T: (01865) 279555 E: chaplain@new.ox.ac.uk

LONGFOOT, Canon Richard. b 46. Oak Hill Th Coll 76. **d** 78 **p** 79. C Chaddesden St Mary *Derby* 78–81; C Cambridge St Martin *Ely* 81–83; R Folksworth w Morborne 83–89; R Stilton w Denton and Caldecote 83–89; R Stilton w Denton and Caldecote etc 90–11; RD Yaxley 02–07; Hon Can Ely Cathl 04–11; rtd 11; PtO *Ely* 11–16; *Pet* from 12. *5 Westfield Close, Yaxley, Peterborough PE7 3NW* T: (01733) 247700 E: richard.lfoot@lineone.net

LONGMAN, Edward. b 37. Hatf Coll Dur BSc 62 Fitzw Coll Cam BA 66 MA 70. Clifton Th Coll 62. **d** 66 **p** 67. C Lower Homerton St Paul *Lon* 66–72; C Parr *Liv* 72–73; TV 74–85; PtO 87–02; *Ches* from 96. *21 Canadian Avenue, Hoole, Chester CH2 3HG* T: (01244) 317544 F: 400450 M: 07779-650791 E: ted.longman@firsschool.org

LONGMAN, Edward George. b 35. St Pet Hall Ox BA 58 MA 62. Westcott Ho Cam 59. **d** 61 **p** 62. C Sheff St Mark Broomhall 61–65; V Brightside St Thos 65–74; V Yardley St Edburgha *Birm* 74–84; RD Yardley 77–84; Hon Can Birm Cathl 81–96; R Sutton Coldfield H Trin 84–96; RD Sutton Coldfield 94–96; Chapl Gd Hope Distr Gen Hosp Sutton Coldfield 84–90; P-in-c Cerne Abbas w Godmanstone and Minterne Magna *Sarum* 96–02; RD Dorchester 00–02; rtd 02; PtO *B & W* 04–14. *5 Old Wells Road, Shepton Mallet BA4 5XN* T: (01749) 343699 E: ted@roseted.co.uk *or* longmanrose@gmail.com

LONGUET-HIGGINS, John. b 62. Leeds Univ BA 85. St Jo Coll Nottm 88. **d** 91 **p** 92. C Kidlington w Hampton Poyle *Ox* 91–95; TV N Huddersfield *Wakef* 95–01; V Painswick, Sheepscombe, Cranham, The Edge etc *Glouc* 02–12; R Ashleworth, Corse, Hartpury, Hasfield etc from 12. *The Rectory, Over Old Road, Hartpury, Gloucester GL19 3BJ* T: (01452) 700965 E: vicar.westof7@gmail.com

LONSDALE, Mrs Gillian. b 36. Qu Mary Coll Lon BA 57 MA 59 Ex Univ MPhil 81 AIMSW 61. SWMTC 96. **d** 99 **p** 00. NSM Duloe, Herodsfoot, Morval and St Pinnock *Truro* 99–06; NSM Lansallos and Talland 01–03; RD W Wivelshire 03–06; rtd 06; PtO *Newc* from 11. *2 Garden Terrace, Whittingham, Alnwick NE66 4RD* T: (01665) 574907 E: lonsdale828@btinternet.com

LONSDALE, Ms Linda. b 49. SWMTC 08. **d** 10 **p** 11. NSM Alderley Edge *Ches* 10–13; P-in-c Beetham *Carl* 13–17; rtd 17; PtO *Ches* from 18. *The Woodlands, 13 Wood Lane, Goostrey, Crewe CW4 8NE* E: rev@jandll.plus.com

LOOKER, Clare Margaret. *See* FLEMING, Clare Margaret

LOOMES, Gaenor Mary. *See* HOCKEY, Gaenor Mary

LOPES, Marco Gonzaga. *See* FILIPE LOPES, Marco Gonzaga

LORD, Andrew Michael. b 66. Warwick Univ BSc 87 Birm Univ MA 99 PhD 10 Fitzw Coll Cam BA 02. Ridley Hall Cam 00. **d** 03 **p** 04. C Long Buckby w Watford *Pet* 03–06; C W Haddon w Winwick and Ravensthorpe 03–06; R Trowell, Awsworth and Cossall *S'well* 06–19; P-in-c Didcot All SS *Ox* from 19. *140 Lydalls Road, Didcot OX11 7EA* T: (01235) 813244 E: revandylord@gmail.com *or* vicar@didcotallsaints.org.uk

LORD, Clive Gavin. b 69. St Martin's Coll Lanc BA. St Steph Ho Ox BTh. **d** 96 **p** 97. C Penwortham St Leon *Blackb* 96–98; C Blackpool St Mary 98–01; P-in-c 01–04; V 04–06; Chapl Blackpool, Fylde and Wyre Hosps NHS Trust from 06. *Chaplaincy Office, Victoria Hospital, Whinney Heys Road, Blackpool FY3 8NR* T: (01253) 306875

LORD, Mrs Deborah Alice. b 69. Reading Univ BSc 90 Univ of Wales (Swansea) PGCE 93. St Jo Coll Nottm 10. **d** 13 **p** 14. C Toton *S'well* 13–17; PtO *Ox* from 19; *S'well* 17–19. *The Rectory, 140 Lydalls Road, Didcot OX11 7EA* E: debbie.lord@gmail.com *or* debbie.lord99@gmail.com

LORD, Mrs Sharon Ruth. b 68. Staffs Univ BSc 03 RGN 89 RM 92. Cranmer Hall Dur 13. **d** 15 **p** 16. C Burton All SS w Ch Ch *Lich* 15–17; C Branston and Burton All SS w Ch Ch 17–18; R Pakefield *Nor* from 18. *Pakefield Rectory, Causeway, Pakefield Street, Lowestoft NR33 0JZ* M: 07711-030203 E: rev@lord-family.co.uk

LORDING, Miss Claire Ann. b 75. Roehampton Inst BA 96. Ripon Coll Cuddesdon BTh 96. **d** 99 **p** 00. C Ledbury *Heref* 99–02; TV Tenbury Wells 02–08; TR 08–10; P-in-c Clee Hill 09–10; TR Tenbury 10–15; RD Ludlow 10–15; P-in-c Pershore w Pinvin, Wick and Birlingham *Worc* from 15. *58 Three Springs Road, Pershore WR10 1HS* T: (01386) 300053 *or* 552071 E: vicar@pershoreabbey.org.uk

LORT-PHILLIPS, Mrs Elizabeth Priscilla. b 47. STETS 02. **d** 05 **p** 06. NSM Redhorn *Sarum* 05–12; NSM Cannings and Redhorn 12–15; rtd 15; PtO *St D* from 15. *Garron, Lawrenny, Kilgetty SA68 0PU* T: (01834) 891634 E: e.lortphillips@btinternet.com

LOTHIAN, Iain Nigel Cunningham. b 59. Aber Univ MA 84 Leeds Univ MA 05 Bath Univ PGCE 86. NOC 02. **d** 05 **p** 06. C Sheff St Pet Abbeydale 05–09; C Sheff St Pet and St Oswald 09; PtO 09–17; P-in-c Crosspool 17–21; C Lodge Moor St Luke 17–21; R Edin St Jas from 21. *19 Claremont Road, Edinburgh EH6 7NQ* E: if.lothian@blueyonder.co.uk

LOTT, Eric John. b 34. Lanc Univ MLitt 70 PhD 77. Richmond Th Coll BD 59. **d** 60 **p** 61. Miss Dornakal India 60–62; Lect Andhra Union Th Coll 62–64; Lect Andhra United Th Coll 65–75; Prof United Th Coll Bangalore 77–88; Wesley Hall Ch and Community Project Leics 88–94; rtd 94; PtO *Leic* 94–15 and 20–21. *16 Main Road, Old Dalby, Melton Mowbray LE14 3LR* T: (01664) 822405 E: eric.lott@tiscali.co.uk

LOUDEN, Canon Terence Edmund. b 48. Ch Coll Cam BA 70 MA 74. Sarum & Wells Th Coll 72. **d** 75 **p** 76. C Portsea N End St Mark *Portsm* 75–78; C-in-c Leigh Park St Clare CD 78–81; R Chale 81–88; R Niton 81–88; P-in-c Whitwell 82–84; V Cosham 88–96; V E Meon 96–13; V Langrish 96–13; CME Officer 96–03; Hon Can Portsm Cathl 92–13; rtd 13; Hon Can Cape Coast Ghana from 12; PtO *Portsm* from 13. *34 Claire Gardens, Waterlooville PO8 0JH* T: (023) 9259 6525 M: 07715-869531 E: terrylouden@btinternet.com

LOUDON, (née KING), Canon Ellen Francis. b 67. Liv Poly BA 90 Liv Univ MA 96 PhD 11. Trin Coll Bris 06. **d** 08 **p** 09. C Everton St Pet w St Chrys *Liv* 08–12; P-in-c Walton St Jo 14–15; P-in-c Walton St Luke 12–15; V 15–16; AD Walton 13–16; Hon Can Liv Cathl 13–19; Can Res Liv Cathl from 19. *3 Cathedral Close, Liverpool L1 7BR* T: 0151-521 2113 M: 07718-806891 E: ellen@ellenloudon.com *or* ellen.loudon@liverpool.anglican.org

LOUGHBOROUGH, Archdeacon of. *See* WOOD, The Ven Claire

LOUGHBOROUGH, Suffragan Bishop of. *Vacant*

LOUGHRAN, Mrs Deborah Jayne. b 72. Cranmer Hall Dur 12. **d** 14 **p** 15. C Hetton-Lyons w Eppleton *Dur* 14; C Gt Aycliffe 14–17; Chapl Miss for Deaf from 16; R Oakengates, Priors Lee and Wrockwardine Wood *Lich* from 17; RD Telford from 20. *The New Rectory, Church Road, Wrockwardine Wood, Telford TF2 7AH* T: (01952) 617667 M: 07885-762837 E: rev_debbie@hotmail.com

LOUIS, Ms Emma Christine. b 69. Coll of Ripon & York St Jo BA 92 St Jo Coll Dur BA 96. Cranmer Hall Dur 94. **d** 97 **p** 98. C Birm St Martin w Bordesley St Andr 97–00; Arts Development Officer 97–00; Asst Chapl Harrogate Health Care NHS Trust 00–02; Chapl Co-ord St Mich Hospice Harrogate 01–02; Asst Chapl Birm Heartlands and Solihull NHS Trust 02–04; Lead Chapl Black Country Partnership NHS Foundn Trust 04–20; Lead Chapl Black Country Healthcare NHS Foundn Trust from 20; PtO *Birm* from 05; *Worc* from 14. *Black Country Healthcare NHS Foundation Trust, Edward Street, West Bromwich B70 8NL* T: 0121-612 8067 M: 07817-564014 E: elouis@nhs.net

LOVATT, Bernard James. b 31. Lich Th Coll 64. **d** 65 **p** 66. C Burford III w Lt Heref 65–67; C Cleobury Mortimer w Hopton Wafers 67–68; C Bradford-on-Avon H Trin *Sarum* 68–69; C Wootton Bassett 69–72; C Broad Town 69–72; R Bishopstrow and Boreham 72–79; P-in-c Brighton St Geo *Chich* 79–83; V Brighton St Anne 79–83; V Brighton St Geo and St Anne 83–86; P-in-c Kemp Town St Mark and St Matt 85–86; V Brighton St Geo w St Anne and St Mark 86–95; rtd 95; PtO *Ex* 95–19. *7 Cambridge Terrace, Salcombe Road, Sidmouth EX10 8PL* T: (01395) 514154

LOVATT, Deborah Anne. b 68. Ex Univ BA 92 MA 95 Dur Univ MA 21. All SS Cen for Miss & Min 18. **d** 21. C Warrington St Elphin *Liv* from 21. *38 Bretton Avenue, Warrington WA1 2GP* M: 079440-33885 E: debbie.lovatt@gmail.com

LOVATT, Mrs Pamela. b 50. **d** 98 **p** 99. OLM Warrington St Ann *Liv* 98–14; OLM Warrington H Trin and St Ann from 14; Chapl 5 Boroughs Partnership NHS Foundn Trust from 99. *59 Amelia Street, Warrington WA2 7QD* T: (01925) 650849 *or* 655221 E: pam.lovatt@ntlworld.com

LOVATT, William Robert. b 54. SS Coll Cam BA 75 MA 78 K Coll Lon PGCE 77. Oak Hill Th Coll 85. **d** 87 **p** 88. C Devonport St Budeaux *Ex* 87–90; Asst Chapl Paris St Mich *Eur* 90–94; P-in-c Lenton *S'well* 94–00; V 00–04; V Eastbourne All SS *Chich* 04–20; RD Eastbourne 06–09; rtd 20. *7 Hazel Road, Angmering, Littlehampton BN16 4FR* T: (01903) 779250 M: 07772-774580 E: robertlovatt777@hotmail.co.uk

LOVE, Mrs Alison Jane. b 63. Lanc Univ BA 84 Westmr Coll Ox PGCE 85 Win Univ BA 11. STETS 08. **d** 11 **p** 12. NSM Chippenham St Pet *Bris* 11–14; P-in-c Draycot 14–16; R

16–21; AD N Wilts 19–21; C Cirencester *Glouc* from 21. *5 Brewin Close, Cirencester GL7 1GY* E: alisonjlove1@gmail.com

LOVE, Ms Anette. b 53. Matlock Coll of Educn CertEd 74 Nottm Univ BEd 75. Cranmer Hall Dur 88. **d** 90 **p** 94. Par Dn Gresley *Derby* 90–92; C Heanor 92–94; C Loscoe 94–02; V Heath 02–15; rtd 15; PtO *Derby* from 15. *3 Chase View, Crich, Matlock DE4 5DZ* T: (01773) 852180 M: 07713-955249 E: anette.love@btinternet.com

LOVE, Joel Andrew. b 77. Birm Univ BA 99 MPhil 04 PhD 08 Cam Univ BA 11. Westcott Ho Cam 09. **d** 11 **p** 12. C Lancaster St Mary w St John and St Anne *Blackb* 11–15; V Roch St Pet w St Marg from 15; P-in-c Borstal from 21. *The Vicarage, 138 Delce Road, Rochester ME1 2EH* M: 07519-620889 E: joel.loves.trees@gmail.com

LOVE, Richard Angus. b 45. AKC 67. **d** 68 **p** 69. C Balham Hill Ascension *S'wark* 68–71; C Amersham *Ox* 71–73; R Scotter w E Ferry *Linc* 73–79; P-in-c Petham w Waltham and Lower Hardres w Nackington *Cant* 79–85; R Petham and Waltham w Lower Hardres etc 85–90; V Sittingbourne H Trin w Bobbing 90–02; P-in-c Aldington w Bonnington and Bilsington etc 02–10; rtd 10; PtO *Cant* from 10. *45 Greystones Road, Bearsted, Maidstone ME15 8PD* E: revralove@msn.com

LOVE, Robert. b 45. Bradf Univ BSc 68 PhD 74 NE Lon Poly PGCE 89. Trin Coll Bris. **d** 75 **p** 76. C Bowling St Jo *Bradf* 75–79; TV Forest Gate St Sav w W Ham St Matt *Chelmsf* 79–85; P-in-c Becontree St Elisabeth 85–96; V S Hornchurch St Jo and St Matt 96–10; AD Havering 08–10; rtd 10; PtO *Chelmsf* from 11. *7 Chelmer Drive, South Ockendon RM15 6EE* T: (01708) 530915 M: 07767-279598 E: revboblove@tiscali.co.uk

LOVEDAY, Mrs Jean Susan. b 47. Ex Univ BTh 10. SWMTC 09. **d** 11 **p** 16. NSM Braunton *Ex* 11–14; NSM Combe Martin, Berrynarbor, Lynton, Brendon etc 14–18; NSM Lynton, Brendon, Countisbury etc 18–19; PtO from 19. *Castle Garden, Castle Hill, Lynton EX35 6JA* T: (01598) 752699 E: jean.loveday35@gmail.com

LOVEDAY, Joseph Michael. b 54. AKC 75. St Aug Coll Cant 75. **d** 78 **p** 79. C Kettering SS Pet and Paul 78–81; C Upper Teddington SS Pet and Paul *Lon* 81–84; CF 84–09; rtd 09; PtO *Ox* from 13; Pet from 16. *6 Mansell Close, Towcester NN12 7AY*

LOVEDAY, Susan Mary. b 49. Sussex Univ BA 70 Surrey Univ MSc 81. STETS 94. **d** 97 **p** 98. NSM New Haw *Guildf* 97–03; NSM Egham Hythe 03–19; Ecum Co-ord Churches Together in Surrey 00–18; PtO from 19. *10 Abbey Gardens, Chertsey KT16 8RQ* T: (01932) 561576 E: sueloveday97@gmail.com

LOVEGROVE, Anne Maureen. b 44. Oak Hill Th Coll 88. **d** 90 **p** 94. Par Dn Thorley *St Alb* 90–94; C 94–95; V Croxley Green St Oswald 95–02; V Letchworth St Paul w Willian 02–09; rtd 09; PtO *St Alb* from 09; *Ox* 09–20. *24 Chenies Avenue, Amersham HP6 6PP* T: (01494) 763151 E: annelovegrove1@gmail.com

LOVEGROVE, Michael John Bennett. b 42. FCII FCIPD ACIArb. SEITE. **d** 00 **p** 01. NSM Saffron Walden w Wendens Ambo, Littlebury etc *Chelmsf* 00–08; TV 05–08; rtd 08; PtO *Chelmsf* from 09. *Craigside, 8 Beck Road, Saffron Walden CB11 4EH* T: (01799) 528232 M: 07485-411898 E: lovegrove8_@btinternet.com

LOVELESS, Martin Frank. b 46. N Bucks Coll of Educn CertEd 68. Wycliffe Hall Ox 72. **d** 75 **p** 76. C Caversham *Ox* 75–81; V Carterton 81–86; Chapl RAF 86–02; Chapl K Coll Taunton 02–04; PtO *Heref* 04–05 and from 07; P-in-c Glossop *Derby* 05–07. *74 Cheltenham Road East, Gloucester GL3 1AD* T: (01452) 534527 M: 07810-002079 E: martinloveless@hotmail.com

LOVELESS, Mrs Natalie Louise. b 78. Southn Univ BA 01. SEITE 08. **d** 11 **p** 12. NSM Horsham *Chich* 11–14; TV 14–19; V Rustington from 19. *The Vicarage, Claigmar Road, Rustington, Littlehampton BN16 2NL* E: revnloveless@gmail.com

LOVELL, Mrs Cara Frances. b 79. Cant Ch Ch Univ Coll BSc 01 Sheff Hallam Univ MSc 10. St Mellitus Coll MA 18. **d** 18 **p** 19. NSM Hampton St Mary *Lon* from 18. *St Mary's Vicarage, 7 Church Street, Hampton TW12 2EB* M: 07879-404201 E: cara.lovell@hampton-church.org.uk

LOVELL, Charles Nelson. b 34. Oriel Coll Ox BA 57 MA 61. Wycliffe Hall Ox. **d** 59 **p** 60. C Walsall St Matt *Lich* 59–63; C St Giles-in-the-Fields *Lon* 63; Argentina 64–73; C Cambridge H Trin *Ely* 64; V Esh *Dur* 67–75; V Hamsteels 67–75; Chapl Winterton Hosp Sedgefield 75–83; R Stanhope *Dur* 83–86; Chapl Horn Hall Hosp Weardale 83–97; R Stanhope w Frosterley *Dur* 86–97; V Eastgate w Rookhope 86–97; RD Stanhope 87–97; rtd 97; PtO *Dur* 97–15. *10 Riverside, Wolsingham, Bishop Auckland DL13 3BP* T: (01388) 527038 E: charlesn@uklovell.co.uk

LOVELL, Mrs Gillian Jayne. b 58. Univ of Wales (Ban) BA 79 PGCE 80. Qu Coll Birm MA 04. **d** 04 **p** 05. C

Burnham *Ox* 04–08; P-in-c Burghfield 08–10; R 10–16; R Sulhamstead Abbots and Bannister w Ufton Nervet 10–14; Par Development Adv (Bucks) from 16. *28 Peters Close, Prestwood, Great Missenden HP16 9ET*

LOVELL, Helen Sarah. *See* HOUSTON, Helen Sarah

LOVELL, Keith Michael Beard. b 43. K Coll Lon 67. **d** 68 **p** 69. C Romford St Edw *Chelmsf* 68–73; P-in-c Elmstead 73–79; V Tollesbury w Salcot Virley 79–09; rtd 09; PtO *Chelmsf* from 09. *14 Brierley Avenue, West Mersea, Colchester CO5 8HG* T: (01206) 386626

LOVELL, Kevin John. b 62. Salford Univ BSc 83 Leic Univ MSc 03 Dur Univ MA 19. Ripon Coll Cuddesdon 18. **d** 19 **p** 20. C Prestwood and Gt Hampden *Ox* from 19. *28 Peters Close, Prestwood, Great Missenden HP16 9ET* T: (01494) 868845 E: kevin@htprestwood.org.uk

LOVELL (née STANTON), Mrs Kimberley Rebecca. b 88. Trin Coll Bris 14. **d** 17 **p** 18. C Plymouth St Jude *Ex* 17–20; TV Brixton, Newton Ferrers, Revelstoke etc from 20; C Holbeton from 20. *The Rectory, 8 Court Road, Newton Ferrers, Plymouth PL8 1DL* M: 07305-155375 E: rev.k.lovell@gmail.com

LOVELUCK, Canon Graham David. b 34. Univ of Wales (Abth) BSc 55 PhD 58 CChem FRSC. St Deiniol's Hawarden 77. **d** 78 **p** 79. NSM Llanfair Mathafarn Eithaf w Llanbedrgoch *Ban* 78–87; NSM Llaneugrad w Llanallgo and Penrhosllugwy etc 87–96; P-in-c 96–03; R 03–04; Dioc Dir of Educn 92–03; Can Cursal Ban Cathl 00–04; rtd 04; PtO *Ban* from 11. *Gwenallt, Marianglas LL73 8PE* T: (01248) 853741 E: grahamloveluck@outlook.com

LOVEMAN, Mrs Ruth. b 45. STETS 01. **d** 04 **p** 05. NSM Portsea N End St Mark *Portsm* 04–09; NSM Cowplain 09–12; NSM Blendworth w Chalton w Idsworth 12–15; PtO from 15. *3 Cotwell Avenue, Waterlooville PO8 9AP* T: (023) 9259 1933 E: ruthlvm@googlemail.com

LOVERIDGE, Douglas Henry. b 52. Sarum & Wells Th Coll. **d** 84 **p** 85. C Earley St Pet *Ox* 84–88; V Hurst 88–03; Asst Chapl R Berks NHS Foundn Trust 03–07; Chapl Mid-Essex Hosp Services NHS Trust 07–09; Chapl W Herts Hosps NHS Trust 09–16; PtO *St Alb* from 16. *All Saints' Vicarage, Churchfields, Hertford SG13 8AE* T: (01992) 584899 or (01923) 217994 E: dhloveridge@hotmail.com

LOVERIDGE, Emma Warren. b 65. St Jo Coll Cam BA 87 MA 90 PhD 01. **d** 99 **p** 00. NSM Highbury Ch Ch w St Jo and St Sav *Lon* 99–02; NSM Islington St Mary 03–05; Prin Adv to Abp York 06–07; PtO *Lon* from 14; *Ex* from 19. *Address withheld by request* T: (020) 3542 9935 M: 07774-859215 E: eloveridge@rafanhouse.co.uk

LOVERIDGE (née RODEN), Canon Joan Margaretha Holland (Jo). b 57. K Coll Lon BD 78 AKC 78 Regent's Park Coll Ox MTh 98. SAOMC 95. **d** 97 **p** 98. NSM Caversham St Jo *Ox* 97–98; C Earley St Pet 98–03; P-in-c Burghfield 03–07; AD Bradfield 04–07; P-in-c Hertford All SS *St Alb* 07–08; TR Hertford from 08; Hon Can St Alb from 14; RD Hertford and Ware 15–21. *All Saints' Vicarage, Churchfields, Hertford SG13 8AE* T: (01992) 584899 E: jonloveridge@hotmail.com

LOVERING, Mrs Jennifer Mary. b 39. Eastbourne Tr Coll CertEd 59. Wycliffe Hall Ox 81. **dss** 84 **d** 87 **p** 94. Abingdon w Shippon *Ox* 84–87; Par Dn Abingdon 87–94; C 94–97; rtd 98; PtO *Ox* 01–18. *5 Monksmead, Brightwell-cum-Sotwell, Wallingford OX10 0RL* T: (01491) 825329 E: jandmlovering@tiscali.co.uk

LOVERN, Mrs Sandra Elaine. b 48. Trin Coll Bris BA 07. **d** 07 **p** 08. NSM Chew Magna w Dundry, Norton Malreward etc *B & W* 07–21. *Address temp unknown* M: 07515-031564 E: sandra_lovern@yahoo.com

LOVESEY, Katharine Patience Beresford. b 62. Trin Coll Bris 00. **d** 03 **p** 04. C Nor Lakenham St Jo and All SS and Tuckswood 03–08; C Stoke H Cross w Dunston, Arminghall etc 08–10; P-in-c Aldborough Hatch *Chelmsf* from 12; P-in-c Gt Ilford St Jo from 18. *Aldborough Hatch Vicarage, 89 St Peter's Close, Ilford IG2 7QN* T: (020) 8599 5413 E: revklovesey@gmail.com

LOVESMITH (née WELLBELOVE), Mrs Sophie Rebecca. b 86. Chich Univ BA 08. St Mellitus Coll BA 18. **d** 18 **p** 19. C Camberley St Paul *Guildf* from 18. *3 Upper Gordon Road, Camberley GU15 2HJ* T: (01276) 700210 M: 07709-690632 E: sophiewellbelove@gmail.com

LOVETT, Frances Mary Anderson. b 46. Plymouth Univ BA 92. NOC 00. **d** 03 **p** 04. Ind Chapl *Liv* 03–10; NSM Newton in Makerfield St Pet 03–05; Hon Chapl Liv Cathl 05–10; rtd 10; PtO *Liv* from 10. *11 Riverside Close, Bideford EX39 2RX* T: (01237) 471846 M: 07989-099483 E: fran.lovett@googlemail.com or fran.lovett@gmail.com

LOVETT, Francis Roland. b 25. Glouc Th Course. **d** 85 **p** 86. NSM Ludlow *Heref* 85–91; rtd 92; PtO *Heref* 96–05. *7 Poyner Road, Ludlow SY8 1QT* T: (01584) 872470

LOVETT, Ian Arthur. b 43. NE Lon Poly BSc 74. Linc Th Coll 85. **d** 87 **p** 88. C Uppingham w Ayston and Wardley w Belton *Pet* 87–91; R Polebrook and Lutton w Hemington and Luddington 91–04; Asst to RD Corby 05–08; rtd 08; PtO *Pet* 09–17. *38 Northbrook, Corby NN18 9AX* T: (01536) 747644

LOVETT, Canon Ian James. b 49. JP 99. CertEd 72 BTh 89 MA 92. S'wark Ord Course 73. **d** 76 **p** 77. NSM Gravesend St Geo *Roch* 76–77; NSM Willesborough w Hinxhill *Cant* 77–83; NSM Landcross, Littleham, Monkleigh etc *Ex* 83–85; C Compton Gifford 85–86; TV Plymouth Em w Efford 86–92; TV Plymouth Em, St Paul Efford and St Aug 93–97; Chapl Aintree Univ Hosp NHS Foundn Trust Liv 97–10; Bp's Adv for Hosp Chapl *Liv* 03–10; Hon Can Liv Cathl 08–10; TV Bideford, Northam, Westward Ho!, Appledore etc *Ex* 11–16; rtd 16. *11 Riverside Close, Bideford EX39 2RX* T: (01237) 471846 M: 07989-085534

LOW, Prof Adrian Andrew. b 56. UEA BSc 77 Hull Univ MSc 78 Nottm Univ MA 10 CertEd 82 FBCS FIMA CEng CITP. EMMTC 08. **d** 10 **p** 11. NSM Alrewas *Lich* 10–14; NSM Wychnor 10–14; C Abbots Bromley, Blithfield, Colton, Colwich etc 14–15; Chapl Costa del Sol W *Eur* 15–21. *Griffin Lodge, Bellamour Way, Colton, Rugeley WS15 3LL* T: (01889) 577888 E: a.a.low@staffs.ac.uk

LOW, Alastair Graham. b 43. Brunel Univ BSc 68 Reading Univ PhD 74. Ripon Coll Cuddesdon 90. **d** 92 **p** 93. C Brighton Gd Shep Preston *Chich* 92–96; TV Horsham 99–08; Chapl Surrey and Sussex Healthcare NHS Trust 02–08; rtd 08; PtO *Ox* from 08. *3 Sheepway Court, Iffley, Oxford OX4 4JL* T: (01865) 777257 E: glowpigs@gmail.com

LOW, Mrs Christine Mabel. b 48. Southlands Coll Lon CertEd 69 SS Mark & Jo Univ Coll Plymouth BEd 87. SWMTC. **d** 99 **p** 00. NSM Bideford, Northam, Westward Ho!, Appledore etc *Ex* 99–03; P-in-c Thornton in Lonsdale w Burton in Lonsdale *Bradf* 03–08; NSM Bingley All SS and Bingley H Trin 08–12; PtO *Sheff* from 12. *61 Woodburn Drive, Chapeltown, Sheffield S35 1YT* T: 0114-453 5199 M: 07717-096495 E: revchris.low@gmx.com

LOW, Canon David Michael. b 39. Cape Town Univ BA 60. Cuddesdon Coll 61. **d** 63 **p** 64. C Portsea St Cuth *Portsm* 63–65; S Africa 65–69; C Havant *Portsm* 69–72; V St Helens 72–88; V Sea View 81–88; V Sandown Ch Ch 88–95; V Lower Sandown St Jo 88–95; R Brading w Yaverland 95–01; Hon Can Portsm Cathl 00–01; rtd 01. *Copeland, Lane End Close, Bembridge PO35 5UF* T: (01983) 874306

LOW, Mrs Jennifer Anne. b 49. St Anne's Coll Ox MA 70 Nottm Univ PGCE 71. Trin Coll Bris 01. **d** 03 **p** 04. C Bris St Andr Hartcliffe 03–07; P-in-c Lawrence Weston and Avonmouth 07–14; Deanery Growth Officer Bris W 07–14; rtd 14; PtO *Bris* from 14. *4 Sheepwood Close, Henbury BS10 7BT* E: revjennylow@gmail.com

LOW, Robbie. *See* LOW, William Roberson

LOW, Terence John Gordon. b 37. Oak Hill Th Coll 75. **d** 77 **p** 78. C Kensal Rise St Martin *Lon* 77–79; C Longfleet *Sarum* 79–83; P-in-c Maiden Newton and Valleys 83–84; TV Melbury 84–88; TV Buckhurst Hill *Chelmsf* 88–92; R Gt Hallingbury and Lt Hallingbury 92–01; rtd 01; PtO *Sarum* 02–16. *37 Vicarage Lane, Charminster, Dorchester DT2 9QF* T: (01305) 260180 E: terrylow@talktalk.net

LOW, William Roberson (Robbie). b 50. Pemb Coll Cam BA 73 MA 77. Westcott Ho Cam 76. **d** 79 **p** 80. C Poplar *Lon* 79–83; Chapl St Alb Abbey 83–88; V Bushey Heath 88–03; rtd 10. *3 Trewince Lane, Bodmin Hill, Lostwithiel PL22 0AJ* T: (01208) 871517 E: robbielow2@hotmail.com

LOWATER, Canon Jennifer Blanche. b 34. Eastbourne Tr Coll TCert 54. Sarum & Wells Th Coll 82. dss 85 **d** 87 **p** 94. Locks Heath *Portsm* 85–88; Hon C 87–88; NSM Southsea St Pet 88–94; NSM Hook w Warsash 94–01; Asst Dir of Ords 91–99; Hon Can Portsm Cathl 95–97; rtd 97. *27 Beck Lodge, 8 Botley Road, Park Gate, Southampton SO31 1EZ* T: (01489) 885835 E: jlowater@tiscali.co.uk

LOWDE, Glenn Frederick. b 54. Qu Foundn Birm 19. **d** 20 **p** 21. NSM Bilton *Cov* from 20. *18 Linnell Road, Rugby CV21 4AN* T: (01788) 572611 M: 07843-442304 E: gfl1954@icloud.com

LOWDON, Christopher Ian. b 63. Plymouth Univ LLB 93 Barrister 94. Aston Tr Scheme 86 St Mich Coll Llan 04. **d** 06 **p** 07. C Chaddesden St Phil *Derby* 06–09; TV Buxton w Burbage and King Sterndale 09–13; P-in-c Maughold and S Ramsey *S & M* 13; V 13–19; R Dollar *St And* from 19. *St James's Rectory, 12 Harviestoun Road, Dollar FK14 7HF* T: (01259) 742494 E: rector@sjgd.org.uk

LOWE, Anthony Richard. b 45. York Univ BA 66. Qu Coll Birm 66. **d** 69 **p** 70. C Greasbrough *Sheff* 69–71; C Thrybergh 71–75; P-in-c Sheff St Mary w St Simon w St Matthias 75; P-in-c Sheff St Barn and St Mary 75–78; V Shiregreen St Hilda 78–85; V Hoxne w Denham St Jo and Syleham *St E* 85–89;

P-in-c Fressingfield w Weybread and Wingfield 86–89; R Hoxne w Denham, Syleham and Wingfield 90–05; rtd 06; PtO *Cant* 16–19. *9 Alfred Road, Dover CT16 2AB* T: (01304) 214047

LOWE, Mrs Brenda June. b 53. Cranmer Hall Dur 75. **d** 88 **p** 94. Chapl to Families Trin Coll and Mortimer Ho Bris 86–91; NSM Clifton Ch Ch w Em *Bris* 88–91; Asst Chapl Southmead Health Services NHS Trust 86–91; NSM Marple All SS *Ches* 91–96; PtO *Man* 91–97; Asst Chapl Wythenshawe Hosp Man 94–96; Chapl Stockport Acute Services NHS Trust 96–98; Sen Chapl Stockport NHS Foundn Trust 98–16. *55 Woodlands Road, Handforth, Wilmslow SK9 3AU* T: 01625-525718 E: malowe@mail.com *or* brendalowem@gmail.com

LOWE, Christopher Alan. b 75. Imp Coll Lon MEng 97. Oak Hill Th Coll MTh 08. **d** 08 **p** 09. C Cambridge St Andr Less *Ely* 08–13; C Chesterton Gd Shep from 13. *3 Iceni Way, Cambridge CB4 2NZ* T: (01223) 354207 M: 07962-060786

LOWE, Mrs Elaine Mary. b 55. **d** 98 **p** 99. OLM Bardsley *Man* from 98. *5 Danisher Lane, Bardsley, Oldham OL8 3HU* T: 0161-633 4535 E: elaine@thelowes.f2s.com

LOWE, Mrs Heather Jocelyn. b 63. Bradf Univ BA 84. Ridley Hall Cam 12. **d** 14 **p** 15. C Harrington *Carl* 14–17; C Distington 14–17; R Brigstock w Stanion and Lowick and Sudborough *Pet* from 17. *14 Willow Lane, Stanion, Kettering NN14 1DT* M: 07587-172062 E: heatherlowe020@btinternet.com

LOWE, Mrs Janet Eleanor. b 56. Univ Coll Lon BSc 77. NTMTC 98. **d** 01 **p** 02. C Hendon St Paul Mill Hill *Lon* from 01. *12 Frobisher Road, London N8 0QS* T: (020) 8340 8764 E: janlowe@btinternet.com

LOWE, Canon Jonathan David. b 66. ACII 04. Trin Coll Bris 08. **d** 10 **p** 11. C Icknield Way Villages *Chelmsf* 10–13; P-in-c Steeple Bumpstead and Helions Bumpstead 13–15; P-in-c Ridgewell w Ashen, Birdbrook and Sturmer 14–15; R Two Rivers from 15; AD Hinckford 15–21; Hon Can Chelmsf Cathl from 16. *The Vicarage, 3 Church Street, Steeple Bumpstead, Haverhill CB9 7DG* T: (01440) 731687 M: 07771-850705 E: vicar@2rivers.faith

LOWE, Keith Gregory. b 50. Sarum & Wells Th Coll 91. **d** 93 **p** 94. C Wallasey St Hilary *Ches* 93–94; C W Kirby St Bridget 94–98; V Sandbach Heath w Wheelock 98–01; V High Lane 01–04; Chapl Stockport NHS Trust 01–04; Asst Chapl Sheff Teaching Hosps NHS Trust 04–06; Chapl Sheff Teaching Hosps NHS Foundn Trust 06–15; rtd 15. *41 Ramsey Avenue, Bishopthorpe, York YO23 2SQ* T: (01904) 848894 E: brigidnkeith@talktalk.net

LOWE, Canon Michael Arthur. b 46. Lon Univ BD 67 Hull Univ MA 85. Cranmer Hall Dur 75. **d** 76 **p** 77. C Thorpe Edge *Bradf* 76–79; C N Ferriby *York* 79–84; TV 84–86; Dir Past Studies Trin Coll Bris 86–91; V Marple All SS *Ches* 91–00; RD Chadkirk 95–00; Dir of Miss and Unity 00–05; C Delamere 00–02; C Wilmslow 05–08; Hon Can Ches Cathl 00–08; rtd 08; Dioc Ecum Officer *Ches* 09–15; Hon C Cheadle 10–17; PtO from 17. *55 Woodlands Road, Handforth, Wilmslow SK9 3AU* T: (01625) 525718 E: malowe@mail.com

LOWE, Preb Stephen Arthur. b 49. Nottm Univ BSc 71. Cuddesdon Coll 71. **d** 74 **p** 75. C Mansfield St Mark *S'well* 74–77; Chapl Martyrs' Sch Papua New Guinea 77–78; P-in-c Nambaiyufa 79; V Kirkby Woodhouse *S'well* 80–86; V Beeston 86–99; TR Wenlock *Heref* 99–14; RD Condover 06–11; Preb Heref Cathl 10–14; rtd 14; PtO *B & W* from 20. *Faith Cottage, West Lambrook, South Petherton TA13 5HA* T: (01460) 249447 E: stephen@slowe.eclipse.co.uk

✠**LOWE, The Rt Revd Stephen Richard.** b 44. Lon Univ BSc 66. Ripon Hall Ox 68. **d** 68 **p** 69 **c** 99. C Gospel Lane St Mich *Birm* 68–72; C-in-c Woodgate Valley CD 72–75; V E Ham w Upton Park *Chelmsf* 75–76; TR E Ham w Upton Park and Forest Gate 76–88; Hon Can Chelmsf Cathl 85–88; Adn Sheff 88–99; Can Res Sheff Cathl 88–99; Suff Bp Hulme *Man* 99–09; rtd 09; PtO *St As* 09–11 and 12–17; P-in-c Towyn 11–12; I Aled Miss Area 17–18; Hon Asst Bp Liv from 15. *2 Pen y Glyn, Bryn-y-Maen, Colwyn Bay LL28 5EW* T: (01492) 533510 M: 07801-505277 E: lowehulme@btinternet.com

LOWE, Ms Tessa Louise. b 71. SS Hild & Bede Coll Dur BA 92 Sir John Cass Coll Lon MBA 07. SWMTC 15. **d** 18 **p** 19. C Lann Pydar *Truro* from 18. *22 Stret Myghtern Arthur, Nansledan, Newquay TR8 4GJ* M: 07843-439102 E: tesslowe71@gmail.com

LOWE, Theresa Caroline. b 66. BA 88. Sarum Coll 17. **d** 19 **p** 20. NSM Two Rivers *Chelmsf* from 19. *The Vicarage, 3 Church Street, Steeple Bumpstead, Haverhill CB9 7DG* T: (01440) 731687 M: 07919-154185 E: theresa@tclowe.co.uk

LOWELL, Ian Russell. b 53. AKC 75. St Aug Coll Cant 75. **d** 76 **p** 77. C Llwynderw *S & B* 76–79; C Swansea St Mary w H Trin and St Mark 79–81; Chapl Ox Hosps 81–83; TV Gt and Lt Coates w Bradley *Linc* 83–88; V Wellingborough

St Mark *Pet* 88–02; V Northampton St Alb 02–13; Chapl Northants Ambulance Service 92–03; Officer for Major Emergencies 03–13; rtd 13; PtO *Truro* from 14. *24 Gwel Lewern, Eastern Green, Penzance TR18 3AX* T: (01736) 361924 E: ianlowell@btinternet.com

LOWEN, Mrs Anne Lois. b 60. Sarum Coll MA 17 DipCOT 82. ERMC 03. **d** 06 **p** 07. NSM Basle *Eur* from 06; Asst Chapl from 11. *The Anglican Church in Basel, St Johanns-Ring 92, 4056 Basel, Switzerland* T: (0041) (61) 731 1485 E: anne.lowen@anglicanbasel.ch

LOWER, David John. b 77. Huddersfield Univ BA 99. Wycliffe Hall Ox 08. **d** 10 **p** 11. C Sileby, Cossington and Seagrave *Leic* 10–14; P-in-c Clacton St Paul *Chelmsf* 14–19; V from 19; C Holland-on-Sea from 14. *St Paul's Vicarage, 7 St Albans Road, Clacton-on-Sea CO15 6BA* T: (01255) 475900 E: david.lower@btinternet.com

LOWMAN, The Ven David Walter. b 48. K Coll Lon BD 73 AKC 73. St Aug Coll Cant 73. **d** 75 **p** 76. C Notting Hill *Lon* 75–78; C Kilburn St Aug w St Jo 78–81; Selection Sec and Voc Adv ACCM 81–86; TR Wickford and Runwell *Chelmsf* 86–93; Dioc Dir of Ords 93–01; C Chelmsf All SS 93–01; C Chelmsf Ascension 93–01; Hon Can Chelmsf Cathl 93–01; Adn Southend 01–13; Adn Chelmsf 13–16; rtd 16; PtO *Chelmsf* from 16. *16 Kelvin Court, Fourth Avenue, Frinton-on-Sea CO13 9DT* T: (01255) 676793 E: davidlowman@uwclub.net

LOWNDES, Harold John (Nobby). b 31. SAOMC 96. **d** 99 **p** 00. OLM Lamp *Ox* from 99. *98 Wolverton Road, Haversham, Milton Keynes MK19 7AB* T: (01908) 319939

LOWNDES, Canon Richard Owen Lewis. b 63. Univ of Wales (Ban) BD 86. Coll of Resurr Mirfield 87. **d** 89 **p** 90. C Milford Haven *St D* 89–91; C Roath St German *Llan* 91–94; Chapl Cardiff Royal Infirmary 91–94; V Tylorstown w Ynyshir *Llan* 94–96; Asst Chapl St Helier NHS Trust 96–98; Chapl Team Ldr W Middx Univ Hosp NHS Trust 98–03; Chapl Team Ldr Ealing Hosp NHS Trust 01–03; Chapl Team Ldr Univ Hosp Southn NHS Foundn Trust 03–11; Hon Can Win Cathl 11; Coaching and Lay Tr Officer *Llan* from 11; Dir Min and Discipleship 15–21; Can Llan Cathl from 19. *The Diocesan Office, The Court, Coychurch, Bridgend CF35 5EH* T: (01656) 868859 M: 07825-954564

LOWRIE, David Andrew. b 81. **d** 14 **p** 15. C Gt Crosby St Luke *Liv* 14–18; NSM from 18. *26 Thorndale Road, Liverpool L22 9QR* E: lowzie@yahoo.co.uk

LOWRIE, Ronald Malcolm. b 48. Bath Spa Univ MA 07. Ripon Hall Ox 70. **d** 72 **p** 73. C Knowle *Birm* 72–75; C Bourton-on-the-Water w Clapton *Glouc* 75–79; R Broadwell, Evenlode, Oddington and Adlestrop 79–81; TV Trowbridge H Trin *Sarum* 81–88; P-in-c Westwood and Wingfield 88–90; R 90–13; P-in-c Bradford-on-Avon Ch Ch 03–10; Chapl Wilts and Swindon Healthcare NHS Trust 88–05; rtd 13. *89 Thestfield Drive, Staverton, Trowbridge BA14 8TT* T: (01225) 768310 E: rmlowrie@btinternet.com

LOWRY, Canon Stephen Harold. b 58. QUB BSc 79 CertEd 80. CITC 82. **d** 85 **p** 86. C Coleraine *Conn* 85–88; I Greenisland 88–98; I Dromore Cathl *D & D* 98–13; Dean Dromore 02–13; I Killaney w Carryduff from 13; Can Belf Cathl from 13. *The Rectory, 700 Saintfield Road, Carryduff, Belfast BT8 8BU* T: (028) 9081 2342 or 9081 3489 M: 07834-584932 E: stephenlowry@me.com

⊕**LOWSON, The Rt Revd Christopher.** b 53. Heythrop Coll Lon MTh 96 Univ of Wales (Cardiff) LLM 03 AKC 75. St Aug Coll Cant 76 Pacific Sch of Relig Berkeley STM 78. **d** 77 **p** 78 **c** 11. C Richmond St Mary w St Matthias *S'wark* 77–79; C Richmond St Mary w St Matthias and St Jo 79–82; P-in-c Eltham H Trin 82–83; V 83–91; R Buriton *Portsm* 91–99; V Petersfield 91–99; RD 95–99; Adn Portsdown 99–06; Bp's Liaison Officer for Pris 00–03; Bp's Adv to Hosp Chapl 03–06; Dir Min Division Abps' Coun 06–11; PV Westmr Abbey 06–11; Bp Linc 11–21; rtd 21; PtO *Lon* from 21. *58A Ashley Gardens, Ambrosden Avenue, London SW1P 1QG* E: christopher.lowson@yahoo.co.uk

LOWSON, Elizabeth Margaret. York Univ BA 04 MA 06 Surrey Univ PhD 10 St Jo Coll Cam BA 16. Westcott Ho Cam 14. **d** 17 **p** 18. C Gt Missenden w Ballinger and Lt Hampden *Ox* 17–21; R Woodford St Mary w St Phil and St Jas *Chelmsf* from 21. *The Rectory, 8 Chelmsford Road, London E18 2PL* T: (020) 8504 7981 M: 07955-275338 E: rector@stmaryswoodford.org.uk

LOWTH, Miss Emma Patricia. Jes Coll Cam BA 08. Wycliffe Hall Ox BA 19. **d** 19 **p** 20. C Gipsy Hill Ch Ch *S'wark* from 19. *Address withheld by request* M: 07789-693520 E: revemmalowth@gmail.com

LOWTHER, Ms Kareen Anne. b 59. Loughb Univ BSc 81. WMMTC 98. **d** 01 **p** 02. C Lich St Mich w St Mary and Wall 01–04; TV Bloxwich 04–13; TV

Penkridge 13–15; C Lt Aston 16–17; PtO from 18. *17 Leyfields, Lichfield WS13 7NJ* M: 07940-936033 E: kareenlowther@hotmail.com

LOWTHER, Peter Mark. b 56. GTCL 77. NTMTC BA 08. **d** 08 **p** 09. C Pimlico St Pet w Westmr Ch Ch *Lon* 08–15; P-in-c Aldeburgh w Hazlewood *St E* from 15; P-in-c Whinlands 15–17; R Alde Sandlings 17–21; rtd 21. *50 Whitethorn Lane, Letchworth Garden City SG6 2DJ* M: 07801-258503 E: mark@thelowthers.com

LOWTON, Preb Nicholas Gerard. b 53. St Jo Coll Ox BA 76 FRSA 94. Glouc Sch of Min 86. **d** 89 **p** 90. NSM Prestbury *Glouc* 89–94; V Black Mountains Gp *Heref* from 10; RD Abbeydore from 14; Preb Heref Cathl from 20. *Forest Mill, Craswall, Hereford HR2 0PW* T: (01981) 510675 E: lowton.nicholas@virgin.net

LOXHAM, Edward. b 49. Lanc Univ BEd 78 Man Univ MEd 89. **d** 04 **p** 05. OLM Birkdale St Pet *Liv* 19–19; rtd 19; PtO *Liv* 19–21. *34 Alma Road, Southport PR8 4AN* T: (01704) 568141

LOXHAM, Geoffrey Richard. b 40. Hull Univ BA 62. Cranmer Hall Dur. **d** 65 **p** 66. C Darwen St Barn *Blackb* 65–68; C Leyland St Andr 68–72; V Preston St Mark 72–79; V Edgeside *Man* 79–91; P-in-c Heapey and Withnell *Blackb* 91–92; V 92–99; V Grimsargh 99–10; rtd 10; PtO *Blackb* from 10. *63 Preston Road, Preston PR3 3AY* T: (01772) 780511 E: geoffreyloxham@gmail.com

LOXLEY, Harold. b 43. NOC 79. **d** 82 **p** 83. NSM Sheff St Cecilia Parson Cross 82–87; C Gleadless 87–90; V Sheff St Cath Richmond Road 90–14; rtd 14; PtO *Sheff* from 14. *508 Richmond Road, Sheffield S13 8NB* E: father.loxley@sky.com

LOXTON, John Sherwood. b 29. Bris Univ BSc 50 Birm Univ BA 53. Handsworth Coll Birm 50 Chich Th Coll 80. **d** 80 **p** 81. In Meth Ch 50–80; C Haywards Heath St Wilfrid *Chich* 80–82; TV 82–89; V Turners Hill 89–96; rtd 96; PtO *Chich* 96–10; *Win* 13–17. *2 Blackbird Court, Andover SP10 5PA* T: (01264) 358179 E: jsloxton@virgimedia.com

LOXTON, Canon Susan Ann. b 57. EAMTC 02. **d** 05 **p** 06. NSM Colchester, New Town and The Hythe *Chelmsf* 05–08; P-in-c Fressingfield, Mendham, Metfield, Weybread etc *St E* 08–13; C Hoxne w Denham, Syleham and Wingfield 08–13; R Sancroft from 13; RD Hoxne 13–21; RD Hartismere 14–21; RD Hartismere and Hoxne from 21; Hon Can St E Cathl from 17. *The Rectory, Doctors Lane, Stradbroke, Eye IP21 5HU* T: (01379) 388493 E: revloxton@gmail.com

LUBBE, Linda Mary. b 61. Witwatersrand Univ BA 82 UNISA BTh 89 MTh 97 DTh 04. Rosebank Bible Coll 82. **d** 00 **p** 02. C Yeoville S Africa 00–05; C St Andrews 05–09; P-in-c 09–13; Adn Waterberg 14–18; Hon C Oxborough w Foulden and Caldecote *Nor* from 18; Hon C Hilborough w Bodney from 18; Hon C Mundford w Lynford from 18. *The Rectory, Elm Place, Gooderstone, King's Lynn PE33 9BX* T: (01366) 328921 M: 07724-783391 E: lindal@senco.co.za

LUCAS, Anthony Stanley. b 41. Man Univ BA 62 K Coll Lon MA 99. Qu Coll Birm 63. **d** 65 **p** 66. C N Hammersmith St Kath *Lon* 65–69; C W Wimbledon Ch Ch *S'wark* 69–74; C Caterham 74–78; P-in-c Stockwell St Mich 78–86; V 86–91; R S'wark St Geo the Martyr w St Jude 91–94; P-in-c S'wark St Alphege 92–94; R S'wark St Geo w St Alphege and St Jude 95–06; rtd 06; PtO *S'wark* from 10. *23 Comers Road, London SE16 4DW* T: (020) 7064 9088 E: tonyslucas@btinternet.com

LUCAS, The Ven Brian Humphrey. b 40. CB 93. FRSA 93 Univ of Wales (Lamp) BA 62. St Steph Ho Ox 62. **d** 64 **p** 65. C Llandaff w Capel Llanilltern *Llan* 64–67; C Neath w Llantwit 67–70; Chapl RAF 70–87; Asst Chapl-in-Chief RAF 87–91; Chapl-in-Chief RAF 91–95; QHC from 88; PtO *Llan* from 88; Can and Preb Linc Cathl 91–95; P-in-c Caythorpe 96–00; R 00–03. *Pen-y-Coed, 6 Arnhem Drive, Caythorpe, Grantham NG32 3DQ* T: (01400) 272085 E: brian@pen-y-coed.co.uk

LUCAS, Mrs Carolyn. b 61. Surrey Univ MSc 06. SEITE 06. **d** 09 **p** 10. NSM New Malden and Coombe *S'wark* 09–18; NSM Tolworth, Hook and Surbiton from 18. *10 Presburg Road, New Malden KT3 5AH*

LUCAS, Clive. b 52. St Mellitus Coll 15. **d** 16 **p** 17. OLM Westcliff St Andr *Chelmsf* from 16; OLM Westcliff St Mich from 16. *501 Woodgrange Drive, Southend-on-Sea SS1 3EQ* T: (01702) 585000 M: 07951-356143 E: lucasclive@ymail.com or lucasclive@gmail.com

LUCAS, Glyn Andrew. b 63. Oak Hill Th Coll. **d** 09 **p** 10. C Cheadle *Ches* 09–12; R Stanton-by-Dale w Dale Abbey and Risley *Derby* 12–18; V Woking St Jo *Guildf* from 18. *St John's Vicarage, St John's Hill Road, Woking GU21 7RQ* T: (01483) 726039

LUCAS, Mrs Jane Eleanor. b 49. SWMTC 00. **d** 03 **p** 04. NSM N Creedy *Ex* 03–07; NSM Burrington, Chawleigh, Cheldon, Chulmleigh etc 07–08; P-in-c Ashwater, Halwill, Beaworthy, Clawton etc 08–15; R 15–19; RD Holsworthy 17–19; rtd

19; PtO *Ex* from 19. *Galilee, 31 North Street, South Molton EX36 3AW* E: therev.rectory62@gmail.com

LUCAS, Julia Mary. *See* MYLES, Julia Mary

LUCAS, Lorna Yvonne. b 48. Bp Lonsdale Coll TCert 69. EMMTC 95. **d** 98 **p** 99. NSM Haxey and Owston *Linc* 98–00; NSM Scawby, Redbourne and Hibaldstow 00–04; NSM Lea Gp 05–16; PtO from 16. *4 Willingham Road, Lea, Gainsborough DN21 5EH* T: (01427) 811463

LUCAS, Mark Wesley. b 62. Man Univ BSc 83. Oak Hill Th Coll BA 94. **d** 94 **p** 95. C Harold Wood *Chelmsf* 94–98; Dir Oast Ho Retreat Cen *Chich* 98–00; Co-ord for Adult Educn (E Sussex Area) 98–00; V Polegate 00–10; R Barton Seagrave w Warkton *Pet* from 10. *The Rectory, St Botolph's Road, Kettering NN15 6SR* T: (01536) 628501 M: 07788-100757 E: rector@stbots.church

LUCAS, Preb Richard Charles. b 25. Trin Coll Cam BA 49 MA 57. Ridley Hall Cam. **d** 51 **p** 52. C Sevenoaks St Nic *Roch* 51–55; Cand Sec CPAS 55–61; Asst Sec 61–67; R St Helen Bishopsgate w St Martin Outwich *Lon* 61–80; P-in-c St Andr Undershaft w St Mary Axe 77–80; R St Helen Bishopsgate w St Andr Undershaft etc 80–98; Preb St Paul's Cathl 85–98; rtd 98. *16 Merrick Square, London SE1 4JB* T: (020) 7407 4164

LUCAS, Ms Susan Catherine. b 59. City of Lon Poly BSc 90. STETS 97. **d** 00 **p** 01. C Streetly *Lich* 00–02; C Pheasey 02–04; Chapl HM Pris Albany 04–09; Chapl HM Pris Wandsworth 09–11; Chapl HM Pris High Down 11–15; Chapl HM YOI Aylesbury 15–18; PtO *St Alb* from 17; *Ox* from 18. *Address withheld by request*

LUCAS, Susan Joyce. b 61. Bedf Coll Lon BA 83 Univ of Wales (Swansea) PGCE 90 Birkbeck Coll Lon MPhil 95 PhD 07 Leeds Univ MA 08. **d** 08 **p** 09. NSM Anfield St Marg *Liv* 08–12; C Walton-on-the-Hill 12–14; P-in-c Gt Crosby St Faith and Waterloo Park St Mary 14–16; TR E Ham H Trin *Chelmsf* from 16. *The Vicarage, Navarre Road, London E6 3AQ* T: (020) 8586 7520 M: 07976-901389 E: revsue85@icloud.com

LUCKETT, Nicholas Frank. b 43. Ch Ch Ox BA 65 DipEd 66 MA 69. OLM course 95. **d** 98 **p** 99. Hd Master St Edw C of E Middle Sch Leek 94–00; OLM Ipstones w Berkhamsytch and Onecote w Bradnop *Lich* 98–02; NSM Siddington w Preston *Glouc* 02–07; NSM S Cerney w Cerney Wick, Siddington and Preston 07–08; rtd 08; PtO *Nor* from 09. *The Beeches, 10 Pauls Lane, Overstrand, Cromer NR27 0PE* T: (01263) 576895 E: nandeluckett@hotmail.com

LUCKETT, Virginia. b 67. **d** 11 **p** 12. NSM Isleworth All SS *Lon* 11–17; NSM Golden Cap Team *Sarum* 18–20; TV from 20. *Abbott's Wootton Cottage, Wootton Fitzpaine, Bridport DT6 6NL* M: 07812-056564 E: virginia.luckett@gmail.com

LUCKING, Mrs Linda Pauline. b 61. St Jo Coll Nottm BA 10. **d** 10 **p** 11. C Caverswall and Weston Coyney w Dilhorne *Lich* 10–17; P-in-c 17–20; Chapl N Staffs Combined Healthcare NHS Trust 13–17; PtO *Lich* from 20. *5 Welsh Close, Lightwood Grange, Stoke-on-Trent ST3 4TQ* T: (01782) 321246 M: 07778-896584 E: linda.lucking.me@gmail.com

LUCKING, Paul Anthony. b 58. Open Univ BA 94. Qu Foundn (Course) 17. **d** 19 **p** 20. NSM Chell *Lich* from 19. *5 Welsh Close, Stoke-on-Trent ST3 4TQ* M: 07775-898654 E: rev.paul.lucking@gmail.com

LUCKMAN, David Thomas William. b 71. Oak Hill Th Coll BA 95 K Coll Lon PGCE 96. CITC 98. **d** 00 **p** 01. C Portadown St Mark *Arm* 00–02; C Enniskillen *Clogh* 02–03; I Galloon w Drummully and Sallaghy 03–04; N Ireland Field Worker ICM 05–08; C Ardmore w Craigavon *D & D* 10–11; C Donaghcloney w Waringstown 12–13; Crosslinks Ireland Team Ldr from 15. *64 Dromore Road, Lurgan, Craigavon BT66 7JQ* T: (028) 3832 4936 M: 07742-513845

LUCKRAFT, Christopher John. b 50. K Coll Lon BD 80 AKC 80. Ripon Coll Cuddesdon 80. **d** 81 **p** 82. C Sherborne w Castleton and Lillington *Sarum* 81–84; Bermuda 84–87; Chapl RN 87–07; R Merrow *Guildf* 07–16; rtd 16; PtO *Sarum* 17–22. *10 Windy Ridge, Beaminster DT8 3SR* T: (01308) 862547 E: chrisluckraft@sky.com

LUDKIN, Miss Linda Elaine. b 50. NEOC 02. **d** 05 **p** 06. NSM Dunnington *York* 05–10; NSM Ireland Wood *Ripon* 10–14; *Leeds* 14–16; rtd 16; PtO *York* 15–20; *Leeds* from 17. *Address temp unknown* E: l.e.ludkin@btinternet.com

LUDLOW, Brian Peter. b 55. Lon Univ MB, BS 78 Birm Univ MMedSc 90 LRCP 78 MRCS 78 MRAeS 87 AFOM 90 MFOM 92 FFOM 01. WEMTC 01. **d** 04 **p** 05. NSM Winchcombe *Glouc* 04–06; NSM Cainscross w Selsley 06–09; NSM Rodborough 09–15; NSM The Stanleys 12–13; NSM The Stanleys w Selsley 13–15; C Gingin-Chittering Australia 15–21; C Toodyay-Goomalling 15–21; NSM Chenies and Lt Chalfont, Latimer and Flaunden *Ox* from 21. *The Rectory, Church Lane, Latimer, Chesham HP5 1UA* E: revdocbrian@gmail.com

LUDLOW, Miss Joy Elizabeth. b 90. Cardiff Univ BMus 12. Trin Coll Bris MA 17. **d** 17 **p** 18. C Thornbury and Oldbury-on-Severn w Shepperdine *Glouc* 17–20; P-in-c from 20. *The Vicarage, 27 Castle Street, Thornbury, Bristol BS35 1HQ* M: 07875-776089 E: joyeludlow@outlook.com

LUDLOW, Mrs Lesley Elizabeth. b 43. SEITE 97 OLM course 04. **d** 06 **p** 07. NSM Allington and Maidstone St Pet *Cant* 06–10; NSM Bearsted w Thurnham 11–13; rtd 13; PtO *Cant* from 13. *37 Tudor Avenue, Maidstone ME14 5HJ* T: (01622) 673536 M: 07778-027031 E: lesley.ludlow@blueyonder.co.uk

LUDLOW, Prof Morwenna Ann. b 70. Trin Coll Ox BA 92 St Jo Coll Ox DPhil 97. SWMTC 13. **d** 15 **p** 16. C Ex Cathl 15–18; Can Th Ex Cathl from 18. *Address withheld by request* E: m.a.ludlow@exeter.ac.uk

LUDLOW, Archdeacon of. *See* GIBSON, The Ven Fiona Ruth

LUDLOW, Suffragan Bishop of. *Vacant*

LUFF, Mrs Caroline Margaret Synia. b 44. St Hild Coll Dur BA 65 Bris Univ CertEd 66. SWMTC 87. **d** 90 **p** 94. NSM Teignmouth, Ideford w Luton, Ashcombe etc *Ex* 90–07; Chapl Trin Sch Teignmouth 97–11; C Diptford, N Huish, Harberton, Harbertonford etc *Ex* 07–16; C Ermington and Ugborough 11–16; rtd 16. *1 Elm Grove, Teignmouth TQ14 8SA* T: (01626) 778265 E: pgandcmsl@btinternet.com

LUFF, John Edward Deweer. b 46. STETS 04. **d** 07 **p** 08. NSM Guernsey St Peter Port *Win* 07–14; Chapl States of Guernsey Health and Soc Care 07–16; Chapl HM Pris Guernsey 12–16; PtO *Win* 15–16; P-in-c Sparkbrook St Agatha w Balsall Heath St Barn *Birm* 16–20; PtO *Win* from 20. *Le Courtil la Chapelle, Rohais de Haut, St Andrew, Guernsey GY6 8YX* T: (01481) 256774

LUFF, Matthew John. b 70. Brighton Univ BA 95. Wycliffe Hall Ox 07. **d** 09 **p** 10. C Broadwater *Chich* 09–13; P-in-c Worthing H Trin 13–16; V Southbourne w W Thorney *Chich* from 16. *The Vicarage, 271 Main Road, Emsworth PO10 8JE* T: (01243) 375576 M: 07875-190203 E: matthewluff39@gmail.com

LUFF, Preb Philip Garth. b 42. St Chad's Coll Dur BA 63. **d** 65 **p** 66. C Sidmouth St Nic *Ex* 65–69; C Plymstock 69–71; Asst Chapl Worksop Coll Notts 71–74; V Gainsborough St Jo *Linc* 74–80; V E Teignmouth *Ex* 80–89; P-in-c W Teignmouth 85–89; TR Teignmouth, Ideford w Luton, Ashcombe etc 90–07; RD Kenn 01–05; Preb Ex Cathl 02–07; Chapl S Devon Healthcare NHS Trust 85–07; Chapl Trin Sch Teignmouth 88–97; rtd 07; PtO *Ex* 07–19. *1 Elm Grove, Teignmouth TQ14 8SA* T: (01626) 778265 E: pgandcmsl@btinternet.com

LUGG, Donald Arthur. b 31. St Aid Birkenhead 56. **d** 59 **p** 60. C Folkestone H Trin w Ch Ch *Cant* 59–62; V Seasalter 62–66; Iran 67–73; V Cliftonville *Cant* 74–94; rtd 94; PtO *Cant* from 94. *Redcroft, Vulcan Close, Whitstable CT5 4LZ* T: (01227) 770434

LUKE, Anthony. b 58. Down Coll Cam BA 81 MA 85. Ridley Hall Cam 82. **d** 84 **p** 85. C Allestree *Derby* 84–87; C Oakham, Hambleton, Egleton, Braunston and Brooke *Pet* 87–88; V Allenton and Shelton Lock *Derby* 88–02; Dir Reader Tr 95–97; Warden of Readers *Derby* 97–00; R Aston on Trent, Elvaston, Weston on Trent etc from 02; RD Melbourne 07–18. *The Rectory, Rectory Gardens, Aston-on-Trent, Derby DE72 2AZ* T: (01332) 792658 E: theramsrev@gmail.com

LUMB, Anna Louise. b 73. Birm Univ BA 94 Leeds Univ PGCE 95 MA 12. St Hild Coll 19. **d** 21. C Harden and Wilsden, Cullingworth and Denholme *Leeds* from 21. *86 Towngate, Northowram, Halifax HX3 7EG* T: (01422) 201580 M: 07787-155970 E: anna.lumb@leeds.anglican.org *or* annalumb@hotmail.com

LUMBY, Jonathan Bertram. b 39. Em Coll Cam BA 62 MA 66 Lon Univ PGCE 66. Ripon Hall Ox 62. **d** 64 **p** 65. C Moseley St Mary *Birm* 64–65; Asst Master Enfield Gr Sch 66–67; C Hall Green Ascension *Birm* 67–70; V Melling *Liv* 70–81; P-in-c Milverton w Halse and Fitzhead *B & W* 81–82; R 82–86; P-in-c Gisburn and Dioc Rural Adv *Bradf* 90–93; P-in-c Easton w Colton and Marlingford *Nor* 95–98; Dioc Missr 95–98; R Eccleston and Pulford *Ches* 98–05; rtd 05; Hon C Redmarley D'Abitot, Bromesberrow, Pauntley etc *Glouc* 05–08. *Valentines Cottage, Hollybush, Ledbury HR8 1ET* T: (01531) 650641 E: jonathanlumby@gmail.com

LUMBY, The Ven Simon John. b 56. Hull Univ BSc 80 Open Univ MTh 01. St Jo Coll Nottm 99. **d** 01 **p** 04. C Wirksworth *Derby* 01–06; R Clifton Campville w Edingale and Harlaston *Lich* 06–10; P-in-c Thorpe Constantine 06–10; P-in-c Elford 06–10; Chapl OHP 10–13; P-in-c Killarney w Aghadoe and Muckross *L & K* from 14; Adn Limerick, Ardfert and Aghadoe from 16. *The Rectory, Rookery Close, Rookery Road, Killarney, Co Kerry, V93 DPC3 , Republic of Ireland* T: (00353) (64) 663 1832 E: rector@churchthesloes.ie

LUMGAIR, Michael Hugh Crawford. b 43. Lon Univ BD 71. Oak Hill Th Coll 66. **d** 71 **p** 72. C Chorleywood Ch Ch *St Alb*

71–74; C Prestonville St Luke *Chich* 74–75; C Attenborough *S'well* 75–80; R Tollerton 80–91; V Bexleyheath St Pet *Roch* 91–06; rtd 06; PtO *Roch* from 06. *11 Bromley College, London Road, Bromley BR1 1PE* T: (020) 8290 2011 E: michaellumgair@gmail.com

LUMLEY (*née* **HATFIELD**), **Rebecca Alison.** b 76. St Andr Univ MTheol 99 St Jo Coll Dur MA 02. Cranmer Hall Dur 02. **d** 04 **p** 05. C Haughton le Skerne *Dur* 04–09; V Windy Nook St Alb 09–11; V Beverley St Mary *York* from 11; Chapl Bp Burton Coll York 11–13. *St Mary's Vicarage, 15 Molescroft Road, Beverley HU17 7DX* T: (01482) 881437 M: 07584-906812 E: vicar.stmarys.beverley@gmail.com

LUMMIS, Elizabeth Howieson. *See* McNAB, Elizabeth Howieson

LUMSDON, Keith. b 45. Linc Th Coll 68. **d** 71 **p** 72. C S Westoe *Dur* 71–74; C Jarrow St Paul 74–77; TV Jarrow 77–88; V Ferryhill 88–07; P-in-c Cornforth 03–07; V Cornforth and Ferryhill 07–15; AD Sedgefield 05–15; rtd 15; PtO *Dur* from 15. *32 Witton Road, Ferryhill DL17 8QE*

LUND, David Peter. b 46. NOC 88. **d** 91 **p** 92. C Maghull *Liv* 91–94; V Hindley All SS 94–01; V Teddington St Mark and Hampton Wick *Lon* 01–14; rtd 14; PtO *Win* from 15. *7 Stourvale Avenue, Christchurch BH23 2EU* M: 07813-493761

LUND (*née* **BEST**), **The Ven Karen Belinda.** b 62. Qu Coll Birm 92. **d** 94 **p** 95. C Southall Green St Jo *Lon* 94–97; C Northolt Park St Barn 97–00; V Gillingham St Barn *Roch* 00–08; P-in-c Roxwell *Chelmsf* 08–14; Lay Discipleship Adv (Bradwell Area) 08–14; TV Turton Moorland *Man* 14–17; Adn Man from 17. *14 Moorgate Avenue, Manchester M20 1HE* T: 0161-448 1976 M: 07909-231280 E: archmanchester@manchester.anglican.org

LUNN, Preb Brooke Kingsmill. b 32. TCD BA 62 MA 66. Chich Th Coll 62. **d** 64 **p** 65. C Northolt Park St Barn *Lon* 64–66; C N St Pancras All Hallows 66–68; P-in-c Hornsey St Luke 68–79; V Stroud Green H Trin 79–02; AD W Haringey 90–95; Preb St Paul's Cathl 96–02; rtd 02; PtO *Lon* from 02. *The Charterhouse, Charterhouse Square, London EC1M 6AN* T: (020) 7251 5143

LUNN, David. b 47. Bris Univ BSc 69 St Jo Coll Dur BA 73. Cranmer Hall Dur. **d** 74 **p** 75. C Aigburth *Liv* 74–77; C Slough *Ox* 77–81; P-in-c Haversham w Lt Linford 81–84; R Haversham w Lt Linford, Tyringham w Filgrave 84–93; RD Newport 86–92; TR Walton Milton Keynes 93–12; Dioc Ecum Officer 00–10; rtd 12; Hon C Billing *Pet* from 13. *38 Riverwell, Northampton NN3 5EG* T: (01604) 784241

LUNN, Edward James. b 85. St Jo Coll Dur BA 12. Cranmer Hall Dur 09. **d** 12 **p** 13. C Acomb St Steph and St Aid *York* 12–17; V Greenhill *Sheff* from 17; C Norton Lees St Paul from 17; C Norton from 17; C Woodseats St Chad from 17. *St Peter's Vicarage, Reney Avenue, Sheffield S8 7FN* T: 0114-237 5326 M: 07834-532768 E: nedlunn@gmail.com *or* ned@saintpeters.co

LUNN, Graham Edward. b 86. Wycliffe Hall Ox BA 08 MA 12. St Steph Ho Ox MTh 11. **d** 11 **p** 12. C Reading St Mark and All SS *Ox* 11–15; Shrine P Shrine of Our Lady of Walsingham 15–16; C Beckenham St Jas w St Mich and St Aug *Roch* 16–20. *Address temp unknown*

LUNN, Ms Helen Mary. b 61. Leic Univ BA 83 Newc Univ MA 99. Lindisfarne Regional Tr Partnership 14. **d** 17 **p** 18. NSM Byker St Mich w St Lawr *Newc* 17–19; NSM Byker St Martin from 19. *26 Copland Terrace, Newcastle upon Tyne NE2 1YB* T: 0191-670 4442 M: 07806-668580 E: lunnhelen@yahoo.co.uk

LUNN, Leonard Arthur. b 42. Culham Coll of Educn CertEd 64. Trin Coll Bris 69. **d** 72 **p** 73. C Walthamstow St Mary w St Steph *Chelmsf* 72–75; V Collier Row St Jas 75–85; V Collier Row St Jas and Havering-atte-Bower 86–87; Sen Chapl St Chris Hospice Sydenham *S'wark* 87–04; Hon C Redlynch and Morgan's Vale *Sarum* 04–06; Hon C Forest and Avon 06–09; PtO from 09. *Summerhayes, Whiteshoot, Redlynch, Salisbury SP5 2PR* T: (01725) 510322 E: len.lunn@btopenworld.com

LUNN, Mrs Lucy Ann (**Lucie**). b 71. Lanc Univ BA 93. Cranmer Hall Dur 11. **d** 13 **p** 14. C Binsey *Carl* 13–17; P-in-c Aldingham, Dendron, Rampside and Urswick from 18. *The Vicarage, Church Road, Great Urswick, Ulverston LA12 0TA* T: (01229) 587200 M: 07825-241366 E: revlucielunn@btinternet.com

LUNN, Maureen Susan. b 48. Middx Univ BSc 00. NTMTC BA 07. **d** 07 **p** 15. NSM Enfield St Jas *Lon* 07–10; NSM Enfield Chase St Mary 10–18; rtd 18; PtO *Lon* from 18. *62 First Avenue, Enfield EN1 1BN* T: (020) 8366 0592 E: mo@stmarymagdalene.church

LUNN, Mrs Rosemary Christine. b 51. Bris Univ BA 72. Trin Coll Bris 98. **d** 00 **p** 01. NSM Stoke Bishop *Bris* 00–01; C Chippenham St Pet 01–04; Hon Min Can

Bris Cathl 02–04; P-in-c Wraxall *B & W* 04–09; R 09–12; P-in-c Evercreech w Chesterblade and Milton Clevedon 12–17; C Bruton and Distr 12–17; V Alham Vale 17–18; rtd 18; Palace Pastor Wells *B & W* from 19. *357B Nore Road, Portishead, Bristol BS20 8EY* M: 07786-118762 E: rosemarylunn@btinternet.com *or* palace.pastor@bathwells.anglican.org

LUNN, Sarah Anne. b 63. Lanc Univ BMus 84 Man Metrop Univ MA 93. Cranmer Hall Dur 00. **d** 02 **p** 03. C Kirkby Lonsdale *Carl* 02–07; P-in-c Long Marton w Dufton and w Milburn 07–08; TV Heart of Eden 08–10; TR 10–17; R 17–18; P-in-c Kirkby Thore w Temple Sowerby and Newbiggin 11–17; C Brough w Stainmore, Musgrave and Warcop 15–17; Dioc Rural Officer 09–18; P-in-c Chollerton w Birtley and Thockrington *Newc* from 18; P-in-c St Oswald in Lee w Bingfield from 19; AD Bellingham from 20; Jt Bp's Rural Affairs Adv from 19. *The Vicarage, Chollerton, Hexham NE46 4TF* T: (01434) 681721 E: sarahlunn63@gmail.com

LUNNON, Canon Robert Reginald. b 31. K Coll Lon BD 55 AKC 55 Kent Univ MA 99. St Boniface Warminster 55. **d** 56 **p** 57. C Maidstone St Mich *Cant* 56–58; C Deal St Leon 58–62; V Sturry 63–68; V Norbury St Steph 68–77; V Orpington All SS *Roch* 77–96; RD Orpington 79–95; Hon Can Roch Cathl 96; rtd 96; PtO *Cant* from 96. *10 King Edward Road, Deal CT14 6QL* T: (01304) 364898 E: robert.lunnon@btinternet.com

LUNT, Colin Peter. b 54. York Univ BA 75 Bris Univ MA 02. Trin Coll Bris 95. **d** 97 **p** 98. C Westbury-on-Trym H Trin *Bris* 97–00; V Coalpit Heath 00–21; rtd 21. *23 Cleeve Hill, Bristol BS16 6ET* E: colin@lunt.co.uk

LUNT, Margaret Joan. b 44. Leeds Univ MB, ChB 68. Cranmer Hall Dur 91. **d** 94 **p** 95. C Stanford-le-Hope w Mucking *Chelmsf* 94–97; C Rayleigh 97–00; TV 00–03; TV Rivers Team *Sheff* 03–10; rtd 10; Hon C Todwick *Sheff* 10–12; PtO from 14. *1 Rodwell Close, Treeton, Rotherham S60 5UF* T: 0114-269 4479 E: margaretlunt@yahoo.co.uk

LURIE, Miss Gillian Ruth. b 42. LRAM 62 GNSM 63. Gilmore Ho 68. **d** 87 **p** 94. Camberwell St Phil and St Mark *S'wark* 74–76; Haddenham *Ely* 76–79; Dioc Lay Min Adv *Pet* 79–86; Longthorpe 79–81; Pet H Spirit Bretton 81–86; Bramley *Ripon* 86–93; C 87–88; Team Dn 88–93; P-in-c Methley w Mickletown 93–98; R 98–01; rtd 02; PtO *Cant* 02–17. *42A Cuthbert Road, Westgate-on-Sea CT8 8NR* T/F: (01843) 831698 E: gillandjean@hotmail.com

LURY, Anthony Patrick. b 49. K Coll Lon BD 71 AKC 71. St Aug Coll Cant 71. **d** 72 **p** 73. C Richmond St Mary w St Matthias *S'wark* 72–76; P-in-c Streatham Hill St Mary 76–81; V Salfords 81–90; V Emscote *Cov* 90–01; P-in-c Ascot Heath *Ox* 01–06; NSM The Churn 06–10; PtO *St E* from 11. *8 St Anthonys Crescent, Ipswich IP4 4SY* T: (01473) 273395 E: anthonylury@gmail.com

LUSCOMBE, John Nickels. b 45. Birm Univ BA 99. AKC 68. **d** 69 **p** 70. C Stoke Newington St Faith, St Matthias and All SS *Lon* 69–74; V Tottenham St Phil 74–81; Zimbabwe 82–86; V Queensbury All SS *Lon* 86–99; V Estover *Ex* 99–01; Dioc Ecum Officer 99–01; V Norton *St Alb* 01–10; RD Hitchin 02–07; rtd 10. *8 Manor Way, Totnes TQ9 5HP* T: (01803) 864514 E: jnluscombe@btinternet.com

✠**LUSCOMBE, The Rt Revd Lawrence Edward** (**Ted**). b 24. Dundee Univ LLD 87 MPhil 91 PhD 93 ACA 52 FSA 80 FRSA 87. K Coll Lon 63. **d** 63 **p** 64 **c** 75. C Glas St Marg 63–66; R Paisley St Barn 66–71; Provost St Paul's Cathl Dundee *Bre* 71–75; R Dundee St Paul 71–75; Bp Bre 75–90; Primus 85–90; rtd 90; PtO *Bre* 90–08; LtO *St And* from 05; LtO *Bre* from 08; LtO *Glas* from 08. *Woodville, Kirkton of Tealing, Dundee DD4 0RD* T: (01382) 380331

LUSCOMBE, Matthew Thomas. b 80. Southn Univ BSc 01 Ox Brookes Univ BA 10. Trin Coll Bris MA 19. **d** 19 **p** 20. C The Mitre Benefice *Nor* 19–20; C Yare Valley from 20; C Costessey from 20. *19 Ipswich Grove, Norwich NR2 2LU* M: 07774-896341 E: matt.luscombe@dioceseofnorwich.org

LUSTY, Tom Peter. b 71. Glas Univ BD 94 Leeds Univ MA 06. Coll of Resurr Mirfield 97. **d** 99 **p** 00. C Billingshurst *Chich* 99–02; Asst Chapl Leeds Teaching Hosps NHS Trust 02–06; Chapl Wheatfields Hospice 06–11; P-in-c Far Headingley St Chad *Ripon* 11–14; TV Headingley *Leeds* 14–19; V Bramhope 19–21; V Upper Wharfedale and Littondale from 21. *The Vicarage, Westgate, Kettlewell, Skipton BD23 5QU* E: tom.lusty@leeds.anglican.org *or* stgiles.tom@gmail.com

LUTHER, Canon Richard Grenville Litton. b 42. Lon Univ BD 64. Tyndale Hall Bris 66. **d** 68 **p** 69. C Preston St Mary *Blackb* 68–70; C Bishopsworth *Bris* 70–71; C Radipole *Sarum* 72–76; TV Radipole and Melcombe Regis 77–90; TR Hampreston 90–07; Can and Preb Sarum Cathl 00–07; rtd 07; PtO *Sarum* from 07. *49 North Street, Charminster, Dorchester DT2 9RN* T: (01305) 251547 E: rglluther@gmail.com

LUZ (formerly **FAWCETT**), **Mrs Laura Joy.** b 82. Fitzw Coll Cam BA 03 Cen Sch Speech & Drama MA 07 Pemb Coll Cam MPhil 14. Westcott Ho Cam 13. **d** 15 **p** 16. C Putney St Mary *S'wark* 15–18; V Dalston H Trin w St Phil and Haggerston All SS *Lon* from 18. *All Saints' Vicarage, Livermere Road, London E8 4EZ* T: (020) 7254 5062　M: 07815-115826 E: vicar@trinitysaintsunited.co.uk

LYALL, Canon Graham. b 37. Univ of Wales (Lamp) BA 61. Qu Coll Birm 61. **d** 63 **p** 64. C Middlesbrough Ascension *York* 63–67; C Kidderminster St Mary *Worc* 67–72; V Dudley St Aug Holly Hall 72–79; P-in-c Barbourne 79–81; V 81–93; RD Worc E 83–89; TR Malvern Link w Cowleigh 93–04; Hon Can Worc Cathl 85–04; rtd 04; PtO *Worc* from 04. *44 Victoria Street, Worcester WR3 7BD* T: (01905) 20511 E: lambourne43@hotmail.co.uk

LYDDON, David Andrew. b 47. Lon Univ BDS 70 LDS 70. SWMTC 90. **d** 93 **p** 94. NSM Tiverton St Pet *Ex* 93–95; NSM Tiverton St Pet w Chevithorne 95–96; NSM W Exe 96–01; NSM Tiverton St Geo and St Paul 01–19; PtO from 19. *Hightrees, 19 Patches Road, Tiverton EX16 5AH* T: (01884) 257250 E: lyddons@yahoo.co.uk

LYDON, Mrs Barbara. b 34. Gilmore Ho 64. **dss** 72 **d** 87 **p** 94. Rastrick St Matt *Wakef* 72–85; Upper Hopton 85–87; Par Dn 87; Dn-in-c Kellington w Whitley 87–94; P-in-c 94–95; rtd 95; PtO *Leeds* 94–14; *Leeds* from 14. *17 Garlick Street, Brighouse HD6 3PW* T: (01484) 722704

LYES-WILSDON, Canon Patricia Mary. b 45. Open Univ BA 87 ALA 65. Glouc Sch of Min 84 Qu Coll Birm 86. **d** 87 **p** 94. C Thornbury *Glouc* 87–94; P-in-c Cromhall w Tortworth and Tytherington 94–03; Asst Dioc Dir of Ords 90–98; Dioc Voc Officer 94–01; RD Hawkesbury 98–04; R Cromhall, Tortworth, Tytherington, Falfield etc 02–09; Dioc Adv for Women's Min 01–09; Hon Can Glouc Cathl 02–09; rtd 09; PtO *Glouc* from 16. *24 Maple Avenue, Thornbury, Bristol BS35 2JW*

LYNAS, Mrs Angela. b 56. ERMC. **d** 14 **p** 15. NSM Cheshunt *St Alb* 14–18; NSM Beane Valley from 18. *8 Parkwood Close, Broxbourne EN10 7PF* E: clergy.angela@gmail.com

LYNAS, Preb Stephen Brian. b 52. MBE 00. St Jo Coll Nottm BTh 77. **d** 78 **p** 79. C Penn *Lich* 78–80; Relig Progr Org BBC Radio Stoke-on-Trent 81–84; C Hanley H Ev *Lich* 81–82; C Edensor 82–84; Relig Progr Producer BBC Bris 85–88; Relig Progr Sen Producer BBC S & W England 88–91; Hd Relig Progr TV South 91–92; Community (and Relig) Affairs Ed Westcountry TV 92–96; Abps' Officer for Millennium 96–01; Dioc Resources Adv *B & W* 01–07; Sen Chapl and Adv to Bps B & W and Taunton 07–17; rtd 17; Hon C Deanery of Glastonbury *B & W* 17–21; Preb Wells Cathl 07–21. *Old Honeygar Cottage, Honeygar Lane, Westhay, Glastonbury BA6 9TS* T: (01458) 860763 E: stephen@lynas.org.uk

LYNCH, Aimee Elizabeth. b 93. Birm Univ BA 14. Qu Foundn Birm 15. **d** 18 **p** 19. C Walney Is *Carl* 18–19; C Dalton-in-Furness and Ireleth-with-Askam 19–21; TV S Barrow from 21; C N Barrow from 21. *98A Roose Road, Barrow-in-Furness LA13 9RL* E: revdalynch@gmail.com *or* aew155@outlook.com

LYNCH, Eithne Elizabeth Mary. b 45. TCD BTh. CITC 94. **d** 97 **p** 98. C Douglas Union w Frankfield *C, C & R* 97–01; I Kilmoe Union 01–10; I Mallow Union 10–19; Min Can Cork Cathl 98–07; Bp's Dom Chapl 99–19; Can Cork and Ross Cathls 09–19; rtd 19. *49 Willowbank Court, Mideton, Co Cork, P25 TH26, Republic of Ireland* M: (00353) 86-253 5002 E: eithnelynch9@gmail.com

LYNCH, Gerard James. b 77. QUB BA 00. St Steph Ho Ox MSt 20. **d** 20 **p** 21. C Devizes St Jo w St Mary *Sarum* from 20. *52 Queens Road, Devizes SN10 5HW* M: 07521-440622 E: rev@revlynch.co.uk

LYNCH, Michael Paul. b 54. Open Univ BA(Ed) 80 Birm Univ TCert 77. St Mellitus Coll 12. **d** 14 **p** 16. C St Marylebone All SS *Lon* 14–15; C Paddington St Jas 15–17; C St Giles-in-the-Fields 17–19; PtO from 19. *8 Dudley Mansions, 17 Hanson Street, London W1W 6TJ* T: (020) 7637 4062 E: reverend.michael.lynch@gmail.com

LYNCH, Ms Sally Margaret. b 60. St Jo Coll Dur BA 81 UEA MA 94 FRSA 96. Westcott Ho Cam 04. **d** 08 **p** 09. C Romford St Edw *Chelmsf* 08–11; V Maidenhead St Luke *Ox* from 11. *St Luke's Vicarage, 26 Norfolk Road, Maidenhead SL6 7AX* T: (01628) 783033 E: sally514@btinternet.com

LYNCH, Mrs Victoria Murray. b 09 **p** 10. Youth Min and Dioc Resources Development Officer *L & K* 07–12; LtO 09–12; P-in-c Fiddown w Clonegam, Guilcagh and Kilmeaden *C, F & O* from 19. *The Rectory, Banagher, Piltown, Carrick-on-Suir, Co Tipperary, E32 VP08, Republic of Ireland* T: (00353) (51) 602270 E: victorialynch.rev@gmail.com

LYNCH-WATSON, Graham Leslie. b 30. AKC 55. **d** 56 **p** 57. C New Eltham All SS *S'wark* 56–60; C W Brompton St Mary *Lon*

60–62; V Camberwell St Bart *S'wark* 62–66; V Purley St Barn 67–77; C Caversham *Ox* 77–81; C Caversham St Pet and Mapledurham etc 81–85; P-in-c Warwick St Paul *Cov* 85–86; V 86–92; rtd 92; PtO *Ox* 96–00. *72 Park Gardens, Bath Road, Banbury OX16 9HQ*

LYNES, Ann Louise. b 79. Moray Ho Edin BSc 01. Ripon Coll Cuddesdon BA 12. **d** 13 **p** 14. C Barnes *S'wark* 13–17; V Northwood H Trin *Lon* from 17; AD Harrow from 21. *Holy Trinity Vicarage, Gateway Close, Northwood HA6 2RP* T: (01923) 822990 E: vicar@htnorthwood.co.uk

LYNESS, Nicholas Jonathan. b 55. Oak Hill Th Coll BA 97. **d** 97. C Reading Greyfriars *Ox* 97–98; PtO *St Alb* from 13. *2 Flint Cottages, Mill End, Sandon, Buntingford SG9 0RN* T: (01763) 288172　M: 07802-730485

LYNETT, Canon Anthony Martin. b 54. K Coll Lon BD 75 AKC 75 Darw Coll Cam PGCE 76. Sarum & Wells Th Coll 77. **d** 78 **p** 79. C Swindon Ch Ch *Bris* 78–81; C Leckhampton SS Phil and Jas w Cheltenham St Jas *Glouc* 81–83; Asst Chapl HM Pris Glouc 83–88; Chapl 91–98; V Coney Hill *Glouc* 83–88; Chapl HM YOI Deerbolt 88–91; P-in-c Glouc St Mark 91–99; P-in-c Glouc St Mary de Crypt w St Jo, Ch Ch etc 98–99; Chapl HM Pris Wellingborough 99–01; V Wellingborough All SS *Pet* 01–19; P-in-c Wellingborough All Hallows 10–19; RD Wellingborough 07–15; Can Pet Cathl 12–19; rtd 19. *14 Thornbridge Close, Rushden NN10 9NJ* E: tartleknock@btinternet.com

LYNN, Anthony Hilton. b 44. Goldsmiths' Coll Lon TCert 66 Open Univ BA 80. SAOMC 95. **d** 98 **p** 99. NSM Stanford in the Vale w Goosey and Hatford *Ox* 98–00; NSM Cherbury w Gainfield 00–03; TV Hermitage 03–13; rtd 13; PtO *Ox* 13–19; *Nor* 20; TV Aylsham and Distr from 20. *29 Yaxley's Lane, Aylsham, Norwich NR11 6DY* T: (01263) 735524 E: revtonylynn@btinternet.com

LYNN, Mrs Antonia Jane. b 59. Girton Coll Cam BA 80 MA 84. St Steph Ho Ox 82. **dss** 84 **d** 87. Portsm Cathl 84–87; Dn-in-c Camberwell St Mich w All So w Em *S'wark* 87–91; Par Dn Newington St Mary 87–91; PtO 91–94; Chapl Horton Hosp Epsom 91–94; Gen Sec Guild of Health from 94; Hon Par Dn Ewell *Guildf* 94–99. *7 Kingsmead Close, West Ewell, Epsom KT19 9RD* T: (020) 8786 8983 E: antonia.j.lynn@gmail.com

LYNN, Frank Trevor. b 36. Keble Coll Ox BA 61 MA 63. St Steph Ho Ox 61. **d** 63 **p** 64. C W Derby St Mary *Liv* 63–65; C Chorley *Ches* 65–68; V Altrincham St Jo 68–72; Chapl RN 72–88; Hon C Walworth St Jo *S'wark* 88–90; C Cheam 90–96; rtd 99. *7 Kingsmead Close, West Ewell, Epsom KT19 9RD* T: (020) 8786 8983 E: j.t.lynn@btinternet.com

LYNN, Peter Anthony. b 38. Keele Univ BA 62 St Jo Coll Cam BA 64 MA 68 PhD 72. Westcott Ho Cam 67. **d** 68 **p** 69. C Soham *Ely* 68–72; Min Can St Paul's Cathl *Lon* 72–78; PtO *St Alb* 78–86; Min Can and Sacr St Paul's Cathl *Lon* 86–88; C Westmr St Matt 89–91; V Glynde, W Firle and Beddingham *Chich* 91–03; rtd 03; PtO *Chich* from 16. *119 Stanford Avenue, Brighton BN1 6FA* T: (01273) 553361 E: lentteupal@gmail.com

LYNN, Trevor. See LYNN, Frank Trevor

LYNN, Archdeacon of. See BENTLEY, The Ven Ian Robert

LYNN, Suffragan Bishop of. See STEEN, The Rt Revd Jane Elizabeth

LYON, Adrian David. b 55. Coll of Resurr Mirfield 84. **d** 87 **p** 88. C Crewe St Andr *Ches* 87–90; C Altrincham St Geo 90–91; TV Accrington *Blackb* 91–00; TR Accrington Ch the King 00–10; P-in-c St Annes St Anne 10–11; V 11–21; AD Kirkham 17–21; rtd 21. *7 Margate Road, Lytham St Annes FY8 3EG* E: david.lyon1955@gmail.com

LYON, Miss Jane Madeline. b 50. Derby Univ MA 05. Ripon Coll Cuddesdon 07. **d** 09 **p** 10. NSM Derby St Andr w St Osmund 09–12; Asst Chapl Derby Hosps NHS Foundn Trust 12–14; C Marlpool *Derby* 14–16; rtd 16; PtO *Derby* 16–17 and from 20; C Belper 17–20. *19 John O'Gaunts Way, Belper DE56 0DA* T: (01773) 826884　M: 07974-806636 E: janelyon0910@tiscali.co.uk

LYON, Joan Baxter. b 50. Strathclyde Univ BA 70. TISEC 94. **d** 96 **p** 00. NSM Glas E End 96–00; Asst Chapl Luxembourg *Eur* 05–11; TV Sole Bay *St E* 11–15; P-in-c Aberdeen St Ninian *Ab* from 15. *8 Seaton Stables, Don Street, Old Aberdeen, Aberdeen AB24 1XS* T: (01224) 740791　M: 07513-421700 E: joanblyon@gmail.com

LYON, John Forrester. b 39. Edin Th Coll CertEd 95. **d** 95 **p** 96. C Greenock *Glas* 95–98; C Gourock 95–98; Chapl Ardgowan Hospice 95–98; Chapl HM Pris Greenock 97–04; P-in-c Glas Gd Shep and Ascension 98–07; Chapl Rosshall Academy from 02; rtd 07; PtO *Bre* from 09. *28 Demondale Road, Arbroath DD11 1TR* T: (01241) 433601

LYON, John Harry. b 51. S Dios Minl Tr Scheme 86. **d** 89 **p** 90. NSM S Patcham *Chich* 89–91; C Chich St Paul and St Pet 91–94; R Earnley and E Wittering 94–04; V E

Preston w Kingston 04–16; rtd 16; PtO *Chich* from 16. *58 Kendal Close, Littlehampton BN17 6SZ* T: (01903) 368650 E: frjohnlyon@gmail.com

LYON, Mark John. b 82. St Steph Ho Ox 08. **d** 11 **p** 12. C Brighton St Mich and St Paul *Chich* 11–15; C W Tarring 15–16; P-in-c 16–18; R Maybridge and W Tarring from 18. *West Tarring Rectory, Glebe Road, Worthing BN14 7PF* E: frmarklyon@gmail.com

LYON TUPMAN, William James Andrew Henry. b 94. Girton Coll Cam BA 14 K Coll Lon MA 19 Girton Coll Cam MA 21 AKC 19. Westcott Ho Cam 19. **d** 21. C St Neots *Ely* from 21. *56 Stone Hill, St Neots PE19 6AA* M: 07940-795026 E: fr.w.lyontupman@gmail.com

LYONS, Bruce Twyford. b 37. K Alfred's Coll Win CertEd 61. Tyndale Hall Bris. **d** 70 **p** 71. C Virginia Water *Guildf* 70–73; Chapl Ostend w Knokke and Bruges *Eur* 73–78; V E Ham St Paul *Chelmsf* 78–85; V St Alb Ch Ch 85–91; Chapl Wellingborough Sch 92–95; P-in-c Stogumber w Nettlecombe and Monksilver *B & W* 96–98; P-in-c Ostend w Knokke and Bruges *Eur* 98–00; NSM Newbury Deanery Ox 01; Chapl Milton Abbey Sch Dorset 01–02; rtd 02; PtO *Sarum* 01–11; *Win* from 16; *B & W* from 18; *Eur* 01–21. *Linhayes, West Street, Somerton TA11 6NB* E: bruce.lyons1@virgin.net

LYONS, Canon Edward Charles. b 44. Nottm Univ BTh 75 LTh. St Jo Coll Nottm 71. **d** 75 **p** 76. C Cambridge St Martin *Ely* 75–78; P-in-c Bestwood Park *S'well* 78–85; R W Hallam and Mapperley *Derby* 85–98; P-in-c Brownsover CD *Cov* 98–02; V Brownsover 02–06; V Clifton w Newton and Brownsover 07–09; RD Rugby 99–06; Dioc Ecum Officer 03–06; Hon Can Cov Cathl 07–09; rtd 09; PtO *Cov*

10–20. 68 Juliet Drive, Rugby CV22 6LY T: (01788) 333277 E: ted.lyons@virginmedia.com

LYONS, Margaret Rose Marie. b 47. **d** 89. OLM Gainsborough All SS *Linc* 89–91; Hon C Low Moor *Bradf* 04–05; Hon C Oakenshaw, Wyke and Low Moor 06–12; Hon C Wyke 12–14; *Leeds* from 14. *1C Common Road, Low Moor, Bradford BD12 0TN* M: 07940-558062

LYONS, Paul. b 67. Ulster Univ BA 91. TCD Div Sch BTh 98. **d** 98 **p** 99. C Seapatrick *D & D* 98–03; I Greenisland *Conn* 03–18; I Camus-juxta-Bann *D & R* from 18. *39 Belvedere Park, Castlerock, Coleraine BT51 4XW* T: (028) 7084 8774 or 7034 3918 M: 07791-472225 E: revpaul.lyons@btinternet.com *or* macosquin@derry.anglican.org

LYSSEJKO, Janet Lesley. b 64. **d** 10 **p** 11. OLM Walmersley Road, Bury *Man* 10–15; NSM Bury, Roch Valley from 15. *31 Burrs Lea Close, Bury BL9 5HT* T: 0161-764 6882 E: janet.lyssejko@gmail.com

LYTHALL, Andrew Simon. b 86. Keele Univ BSc 07 St Jo Coll Dur BA 09 MA 11. Cranmer Hall Dur 07. **d** 10 **p** 11. C Stockport St Geo *Ches* 10–13; V Offerton St Alb and Stockport St Thos 13–17; Prec Birm Cathl 17–18; PtO *Lich* from 18. *St Martin's House, 17 Daffodil Road, Walsall WS5 3DQ* M: 07706-036425 E: aslythall@gmail.com *or* canonliturgist@birminghamcathedral.com

LYTHALL, Jennifer Elizabeth. See MAYO-LYTHALL, Jennifer Elizabeth

LYTTLE, Norma Irene. b 47. CITC. **d** 01 **p** 02. Aux Min Drumachose *D & R* 01–04; Aux Min Dungiven w Bovevagh 04–07; Bp's C Leckpatrick w Dunnalong 07–09; I 09–17; rtd 17. *Kurin House, 58 Kurin Road, Garvagh, Coleraine BT51 5NT* T: (028) 2955 7782 M: 07912-652714

M

MABBS, Miss Margaret Joyce. b 24. St Hilda's Coll Ox BA 45 MA 47 DipEd 46. S'wark Ord Course 79. **dss** 82 **d** 87 **p** 94. Eltham Park St Luke *S'wark* 82–05; NSM 87–05; PtO from 05. *70 Westmount Road, London SE9 1JE* T: (020) 8850 4621

MABEY, Mrs Johanna Stacey. b 65. ERMC 14. **d** 17 **p** 18. NSM Alde Sandlings *St E* from 17. *Trinity House, The Terrace, Aldeburgh IP15 5HH* T: (01728) 454417 M: 07729-795009 E: mabeyfamily@btinternet.com

MABUZA (*née* Morris), **Catharine Mary.** b 75. Regent's Park Coll Ox BA 96 MA 00. Ridley Hall Cam 99. **d** 01 **p** 02. C Malpas *Mon* 01–06; C Reading Greyfriars *Ox* 06–12; Par Development Adv (Berks) 12–17; V Warfield from 17. *The Vicarage, Church Lane, Warfield, Bracknell RG42 6EE* T: (01344) 884477 M: 07785-990208 E: vicar@warfield.org.uk *or* catharine.mabuza@warfield.org.uk

MAC BRUITHIN, Críostóir (Chris). **d** 15 **p** 16. Londonderry St Aug *D & R* 15–16; C Enniskillen *Clogh* 16–19; I Castlerock w Dunboe and Fermoyle *D & R* from 19. *The Rectory, 52 Main Street, Castlerock, Coleraine BT51 4RA* T: (028) 7055 6883 M: 07514-468730 E: criostoir316@gmail.com

McADAM, Gordon Paul. b 66. QUB BSc 88 TCD BTh 93. CITC 90. **d** 93 **p** 94. C Drumglass w Moygashel *Arm* 93–96; I Dungiven w Bovevagh *D & R* 96–02; I Loughgall w Grange *Arm* 02–17; I Aghalee *D & D* from 17. *The Rectory, 39 Soldierstown Road, Aghalee, Craigavon BT67 0ES* T: (028) 9209 0989 E: gpmcadam@sky.com *or* aghalee@dromore.anglican.org

McADAM, Ms Laura Elizabeth. b 85. Ripon Coll Cuddesdon BA 19. **d** 19 **p** 20. C Buckfastleigh, Dean Prior, Littlehempston etc *Ex* from 19. *Address withheld by request* E: dartcurate@gmail.com *or* laura.e.mcadam@gmail.com

McALISTER, Canon David. b 39. St Jo Coll Nottm 83. **d** 87 **p** 88. NSM Arpafeelie *Mor* 87–93; NSM Cromarty 87–93; NSM Fortrose 87–93; C Broughty Ferry *Bre* 93–95; P-in-c Nairn *Mor* 95–09; P-in-c Kishorn 08–09; P-in-c Lochalsh 08–09; P-in-c Poolewe 08–09; Chapl Inverness Airport 98–09; Can St Andr Cathl Inverness 01–09; OCM 03–09; rtd 09; LtO *Mor* from 10. *36 Feddon Hill, Fortrose IV10 8SP* T: (01381) 622530 E: friedmacon@aol.com

McALISTER, Margaret Elizabeth Anne (Sister Margaret Anne). b 55. St Mary's Coll Dur BA 78 Ex Univ PGCE 79. Wycliffe Hall Ox 83 SAOMC 99. **d** 01 **p** 02. ASSP from

91; NSM Cowley St Jas *Ox* 01–04; NSM Cowley St Jo 04–09; NSM Ox St Mary Magd 09–11; Asst Chapl St Jo Home 11–14; PtO *Ox* from 11; *S'wark* from 15. *25 Orchard Road, Richmond TW9 4AQ* T: (020) 8876 5079 E: margaretanne@socallss.co.uk

McALLEN, James. b 38. Lon Univ BD 71. Oak Hill Th Coll 63. **d** 66 **p** 67. C Blackheath St Jo *S'wark* 66–69; C Edin St Thos 69–73; V Selby St Jas *York* 73–80; V Wistow 75–80; V Houghton *Carl* 80–91; Gen Sec Lon City Miss 92–03; Hon C Blackheath St Jo *S'wark* 94–04; rtd 04; PtO *Carl* from 04. *205 Brampton Road, Carlisle CA3 9AX* T: (01228) 540505 E: jmcallen@btinternet.com

McALLEN, Julian William. b 71. Lon Guildhall Univ BA 94 Avery Hill Coll PGCE 95. Wycliffe Hall Ox 11. **d** 13 **p** 14. C Epsom Common Ch Ch *Guildf* 15–17; C Finchampstead and California *Ox* from 17. *The Vicarage, Vicarage Close, Finchampstead, Wokingham RG40 4JW* M: 07817-745378 E: julianmcallen@hotmail.com

McALLEN, Robert Roy. b 41. Bps' Coll Cheshunt 62. **d** 65 **p** 66. C Seagoe *D & D* 65–67; C Knockbreda 67–70; CF 70–96; Chapl R Memorial Chpl Sandhurst 87–92; Chapl Guards Chpl Lon 92–96; PtO *Guildf* 96–98; R Ockley, Okewood and Forest Green 98–06; rtd 06; PtO *Chich* 12–17. *Maranatha, Church Street, Rudgwick, Horsham RH12 3EG* T: (01403) 823172

McALLISTER, Crystal. b 72. Ripon Coll Cuddesdon 17 CMS 17. **d** 20 **p** 21. C Upper Wreake *Leic* from 20. *1 Palmerston Road, Melton Mowbray LE13 0SS* M: 07890-020012 E: pioneercrystal136@gmail.com

MACAN, Peter John Erdley. b 36. Bp Gray Coll Cape Town 57. **d** 60 **p** 61. C Matroosfontein S Africa 60–64; C Maitland Gd Shep 64–67; C S Lambeth St Ann *S'wark* 68–71; V Nunhead St Silas 72–81; P-in-c Clapham H Spirit 81–87; TV Clapham Team 87–90; V Dulwich St Clem w St Pet 90–02; rtd 02; PtO *S'wark* from 04; Retirement Officer Croydon Area from 08. *19 The Windings, South Croydon CR2 0HW* T: (020) 8657 1398 E: peter.macan@virgin.net

McARTHUR, Mrs Claire-Louise. b 70. Qu Coll Birm 13. **d** 16 **p** 17. C Walsgrave on Sowe *Cov* 16–19; R Stoke St Mich, Coventry from 19. *Stoke Rectory, 365A Walsgrave Road, Coventry CV2 4BG* T: (024) 764 43691 M: 07532-260027 E: revclairestoke@gmail.com

McARTHUR, Duncan Walker. b 50. Strathclyde Univ BSc 73 Moore Th Coll Sydney ThL 80 Melbourne Univ BD 82 Newc Univ MA 94. **d** 82 **p** 82. C Hornsby Australia 82–85; Asst Chapl Barker Coll Hornsby 86–88; Asst Min 88–89; P-in-c Harraby *Carl* 90–93; R Hurstville Australia 93–95; Hon Asst P Wauchope St Matt from 99; Chapl St Columba Sch Port Macquarie from 02. *43 Narran River Road, Wauchope NSW 2446, Australia* T: (0061) (2) 6585 1147 *or* (2) 6583 6999 F: 6583 6982 M: 41-282 8341 E: dmcarthe@bigpond.net.au

MACARTHUR, Helen Anne. b 45. Ulster Univ BEd 90 QUB MSc 96. CITC 05. **d** 08 **p** 09. NSM Derriaghy w Colin *Conn* 08–11; P-in-c Ardclinis and Tickmacrevan w Layde and Cushendun 11–19; rtd 19. *16 Halftown Road, Lisburn BT27 5RD* M: 07818-027040 E: helenmacar@btinternet.com

McARTHUR-EDWARDS, Mrs Judith Sarah. b 71. Westmr Coll Ox BTh 94. Cranmer Hall Dur 97. **d** 99 **p** 00. C Cradley *Worc* 99–02; C Quarry Bank 02–03; Asst Chapl Frimley Park Hosp NHS Trust 04–05; Asst Chapl R Surrey Co Hosp NHS Foundn Trust 05–16; Asst Chapl St Geo Univ Hosps NHS Foundn Trust 16–20; Chapl Brighton and Sussex Univ Hosps NHS Trust from 20. *Chaplain's Office, Royal Sussex County Hospital, Eastern Road, Brighton BN2 5BE* T: (01273) 696955 E: scott_edwards@btopenworld.com

MACARTNEY, Gerald Willam. b 52. TCD BTh 03. CITC. **d** 03 **p** 04. C Drumglass w Moygashel *Arm* 03–05; I Milltown 05–14; Dioc Communications Officer 09–10 and 11–14; I Drumgath w Drumgooland and Clonduff *D & D* 14–19; rtd 19. *7 Brompton Park, Portadown, Craigavon BT62 3SP* T: (028) 3887 0858 M: 07850-040027 E: gwmac@btinternet.com

McATEER (née ROBINSON), Canon Katharine Mary. b 51. NUU BA 73. CITC 03. **d** 06 **p** 07. NSM Conwal Union w Gartan *D & R* 06–08; NSM Londonderry Ch Ch, Culmore, Muff and Belmont from 08; Can Derry Cathl from 20. *27 Northland Road, Londonderry BT48 7NF* T: (028) 7137 4544 F: 7127 1991 M: 07813-885145 E: kmcateer51@gmail.com

MACAULAY, Jide. *See* MACAULAY, Rowland Ayoola Babajide

MACAULAY, John Roland. b 39. Man Univ BSc 61 Liv Inst of Educn PGCE 80. Wells Th Coll 61. **d** 63 **p** 64. C Padgate Ch Ch *Liv* 63–66; C Upholland 66–73; TV 73–75; V Hindley St Pet 75–81; Chapl Liv Coll 81–96; Sub-Chapl HM Pris Risley 85–96; R Lowton St Luke *Liv* 96–05; rtd 05; PtO *Liv* from 16. *83 Severn Road, Culcheth, Warrington WA3 5ED* T: (01925) 502639 E: macaulay.j@sky.com

MACAULAY, Kenneth Lionel. b 55. Edin Univ BD 78. Edin Th Coll 74. **d** 78 **p** 79. C Glas St Ninian 78–80; Dioc Youth Chapl 80–87; P-in-c Glas St Matt 80–87; R Glenrothes *St And* 87–89; Chapl St Mary's Cathl *Glas* 89–92; Min Glas St Mary 89–92; Min Glas St Serf 92–94; PtO 94–96; NSM Glas St Oswald 96–98; P-in-c 98–01; Chapl HM Pris Glas (Barlinnie) 99–00; P-in-c Dumbarton *Glas* 01–06; R 06–19; R Alexandria 14–19; rtd 19. *21 Lochfergus Crescent, Coylton, Ayr LA6 6GA* T: (01292) 571438 M: 07734-187250 E: frkenny@sky.com *or* frkenny@icloud.com

MACAULAY, Kenneth Russell. b 63. Strathclyde Univ BSc 85. TISEC 95. **d** 98 **p** 99. C Edin Old St Paul 98–01; C Edin St Pet 01–06; Dir Coracle Trust 01–09; Warden Epiphany Ho *Truro* 09–12; Public Preacher from 09. *Lismore, Perranuthnoe, Penzance TR20 9NF* E: kandbmacaulay@googlemail.com

McAULAY, Mark John Simon. b 71. Lanc Univ LLB 92 Leeds Univ BA 04 Heythrop Coll Lon MA 11 Barrister-at-Law (Inner Temple) 93. Coll of Resurr Mirfield 02. **d** 04 **p** 05. C Ruislip St Martin *Lon* 04–07; V New Southgate St Paul 07–18; V Eastbourne St Sav and St Pet *Chich* from 18. *St Saviour's Vicarage, Spencer Road, Eastbourne BN21 4PA* E: frmarkmcaulay@hotmail.com

MACAULAY, Philip Richard. b 86. Middx Univ BA 18 St Jo Coll Dur MA 21. Lon Sch of Th 15 Cranmer Hall Dur 19. **d** 21. C Sandy *St Alb* from 21. *14 Pyms Way, Sandy SG19 1BZ* M: 07977-849670 E: p.macaulay@gmail.com

MACAULAY, Rowland Ayoola Babajide. b 65. Thames Valley Univ LLB 96. Westcott Ho Cam 11. **d** 13 **p** 20. C E Ham w Upton Park and Forest Gate *Chelmsf* 13–14; C Leytonstone St Marg w St Columba 18–20. *160 Stewart Road, London E15 2BD* M: 07521-130179 E: ramacaulay@gmail.com

MACAULAY, Simon Mark James. b 73. Liv Univ BA 98 MMus 07 Dur Univ MA 20. Westcott Ho Cam 18. **d** 20. C Formby St Pet *Liv* from 20. *3 Kenton Close, Formby, Liverpool L37 7EA* M: 07736-648702 E: smjmacaulay@mac.com

McAUSLAND, Canon William James. b 36. Edin Th Coll 56. **d** 59 **p** 60. C Dundee St Mary Magd *Bre* 59–64; R 71–79; R Glas H Cross 64–71; Chapl St Marg Old People's Home 79–85; R Dundee St Marg *Bre* 79–01; Chapl St Mary's Sisterhood 82–87; Chapl Ninewells Hosp Dundee 85–01; Can St Paul's Cathl Dundee *Bre* 93–01; rtd 01; Hon Can from 01; NSM Monifieth *Bre* from 03. *18 Broadford Terrace, Broughty Ferry, Dundee DD5 3EF* T: (01382) 737721 E: billmcausland@talktalk.net

McAVOY, George Brian. b 41. MBE 78. TCD BA 61 MA 72. Div Test 63. **d** 63 **p** 65. C Cork St Luke w St Ann *C, C & R* 63–66; I Timoleague w Abbeymahon 66–68; Chapl RAF 68–88; Asst Chapl-in-Chief RAF 88–95; QHC 91–95; Chapl Fosse Health NHS Trust 95–98; Chapl Oakham Sch 98–03; rtd 03; PtO *Pet* 03–11 and from 18; *Leic* from 05; Past Care and Counselling Adv *Pet* 04–10. *1 The Leas, Cottesmore, Oakham LE15 7DG* T: (01572) 812404 M: 07967-967803 E: gbm825@outlook.com *or* brianmcavoy41@gmail.com

McAVOY, Philip George. b 63. Imp Coll Lon BSc 85 SS Coll Cam BA 90. Westcott Ho Cam 88. **d** 91 **p** 92. C W End *Win* 91–95; TV Swanage and Studland *Sarum* 95–00; P-in-c Littleton *Lon* 00–06; V Weston *Guildf* 06–10; PtO 10–13. *Four Acorns, Molesey Road, Walton-on-Thames KT12 3PP* T: (01932) 225098 E: pandk.mac@btinternet.com

MACBAIN, Patrick. b 77. G&C Coll Cam BA 99. Oak Hill Th Coll BTh 06. **d** 09 **p** 10. C Worksop St Anne *S'well* 09–13; V Danehill *Chich* from 13; RD Uckfield from 16. *The Vicarage, Lewes Road, Danehill, Haywards Heath RH17 7ER* T: (01825) 790269 E: pmacbain@hotmail.com

MacBEAN, Gordon Robert. b 70. St Aug Coll of Th 17. **d** 20. C Welling *Roch* from 20. *52 Clifton Road, Welling DA16 1QD* E: revdmacbean@gmail.com

McBETH, David Ronald. BEM 16. TCD BTh 06. **d** 06 **p** 07. C Glendermott *D & R* 06–09; Australia 09–11; I Dungiven w Bovevagh *D & R* 11–15; I Clooney w Strathfoyle from 15. *All Saints' Rectory, 20 Limavady Road, Londonderry BT47 6JD* T: (028) 7134 4306 M: 07817-729374 E: allsaintsclooney@btinternet.com

McBRIDE, Ms Catherine Sarah. b 64. Trent Poly BSc 87. Ridley Hall Cam 06. **d** 08 **p** 09. C Meole Brace *Lich* 08–12; C Busbridge and Hambledon *Guildf* 12–17; V Drayton in Hales *Lich* from 17. *The Vicarage, Mount Lane, Market Drayton TF9 1AQ* T: (01630) 653505 E: vicarofstmarys@gmail.com

McBRIDE, Mrs Katharine Alexandra. b 76. Bath Spa Univ BA 98 PGCE 99. St Hild Coll 17. **d** 19 **p** 20. C Strensall *York* from 19. *The Barn, Sycamore Farm, 72 The Village, Strensall, York YO32 5XA* E: revkmcbride@gmail.com

McBRIDE, The Ven Stephen Richard. b 61. QUB BSc 84 TCD BTh 89 MA 92 QUB PhD 96. CITC 84. **d** 87 **p** 88. C Antrim All SS *Conn* 87–90; I Belfast St Pet 90–95; Bp's Dom Chapl 94–02; I Antrim All SS from 95; Adn Conn from 02; Prec Belf Cathl from 02. *The Vicarage, 10 Vicarage Gardens, Antrim BT41 4JP* T/F: (028) 9446 2186 M: 07718-588191 E: archdeacon@connor.anglican.org

McCABE, Alan. b 37. Lon Univ BScEng 61. Ridley Hall Cam 61. **d** 63 **p** 64. C Bromley SS Pet and Paul *Roch* 63–67; PV Roch Cathl 67–70; V Bromley H Trin 70–77; V Westerham 77–88; V Eastbourne St Jo *Chich* 88–99; rtd 00; PtO *Chich* 00–14. *Dairy Cottage, Dunorlan Farm, Halls Hole Road, Tunbridge Wells TN2 4RE* T: (01892) 458620 E: romymccabe@gmail.com

McCABE, Carol. b 49. **d** 03 **p** 04. OLM Blackrod *Man* 03–14; OLM Horwich and Rivington 11–14; PtO from 14. *1 Newlands Drive, Blackrod, Bolton BL6 5SD* T: (01204) 669775 E: carol.mccabe2@ntlworld.com

McCABE, John Hamilton. b 59. St Edm Hall Ox MA 82 PGCE 84 Ches Univ PhD 15. Trin Coll Bris MA 01. **d** 01 **p** 02. C Burpham *Guildf* 01–05; LtO 05–06; R Byfleet from 06; Dioc Adv for Sports Min from 17. *The Rectory, 81 Rectory Lane, Byfleet, West Byfleet KT14 7LX* T: (01932) 342374 M: 07710-094357 E: john.h.mccabe@btinternet.com

McCABE, The Ven John Trevor. b 33. RD 78. Nottm Univ BA 55. Wycliffe Hall Ox 57. **d** 59 **p** 60. C Compton Gifford *Ex* 59–63; P-in-c Ex St Martin, St Steph, St Laur etc 63–66; Chapl RNR 63–03; Chapl Ex Sch 64–66; V Capel *Guildf* 66–71; V Scilly Is *Truro* 71–74; TR Is of Scilly 74–81; Can Res Bris Cathl 81–83; V Manaccan w St Anthony-in-Meneage and St Martin *Truro* 83–96; RD Kerrier 87–90 and 94–96; Chmn Cornwall NHS Trust for Mental Handicap 91–00; Hon Can Truro Cathl 93–96; Adn Cornwall 96–99; rtd 00; Non Exec Dir Cornwall Healthcare NHS Trust from 99; PtO *Truro* 99–09. *1 Sunhill, School Lane, Budock Water, Falmouth TR11 5DG* T: (01326) 378095

McCAFFERTY, Andrew. *See* McCAFFERTY, William Andrew

McCAFFERTY, Canon Christine Ann. b 43. FCA 76. Gilmore Course 76. **dss** 79 **d** 87 **p** 94. Writtle w Highwood *Chelmsf* 79–94; C 87–94; Chapl to Bp Bradwell 87–92; Dioc NSM Officer 87–94; TR Wickford and Runwell 94–00; Hon C Lt Baddow 00–09; Hon Can Chelmsf Cathl 91–09; rtd 09; PtO *Chelmsf* from 09. *68 Galleywood Road, Great Baddow, Chelmsford CM2 8DN* T: (01245) 690043 E: jcmccafferty@hotmail.co.uk

McCAFFERTY (*née* BACK), **Mrs Esther Elaine.** b 52. Saffron Walden Coll CertEd 74. Trin Coll Bris 79 Oak Hill Th Coll BA 81. **dss** 81 **d** 87 **p** 94. Collyhurst *Man* 81–84; Upton (Overchurch) *Ches* 84–88; Par Dn 87–88; Par Dn Upper Holloway St Pet w St Jo *Lon* 88–90; Min in charge 90–97; P-in-c Pitsea w Nevendon *Chelmsf* 97–02; R Basildon St Martin 02–18; RD Basildon 99–04; rtd 18; PtO *Chelmsf* from 19. *58 Gwynne Park Avenue, Woodford Green IG8 8AB* T: (020) 8502 9790 M: 07947-001172 E: emccafferty@talk21.com

McCAFFERTY, Keith Alexander. *See* DUCKETT, Keith Alexander

McCAFFERTY, William Andrew. b 49. Open Univ BA 93. SWMTC 94. **d** 97 **p** 98. NSM Lapford, Nymet Rowland and Coldridge *Ex* 97–00; CF 00–04; TR Crosslacon *Carl* 04–08; R Forfar *St And* 08–14; R Lunan Head 08–14; CF (TA) 09–14; rtd 14. *29 Willow Drive, Durrington, Salisbury SP4 8DE* T: (01980) 652584 M: 07891-119684 E: normandy08@btinternet.com

McCAGHREY, Mark Allan. b 66. Warwick Univ BSc 87. St Jo Coll Nottm BTh 93. **d** 94 **p** 95. C Byfleet *Guildf* 94–97; V Lowestoft St Andr *Nor* 97–12; R Mattishall and the Tudd Valley from 12; RD Dereham in Mitford from 16. *The Vicarage, Back Lane, Mattishall, Dereham NR20 3PU* T: (01362) 882260 E: mark.mccaghrey@matvchurch.uk

McCALLA, Preb Sandra Sheron. Lucy Cavendish Coll Cam BTh 12 Heythrop Coll Lon MA 16 Barrister-at-Law. Westcott Ho Cam. **d** 12 **p** 13. C Poplar *Lon* 12–15; V Heston 16–21; Bp's Chapl from 21; Preb St Paul's Cathl from 21. *The Old Deanery, Dean's Court, London EC4V 5AA* T: (020) 3837 5200

McCAMLEY, Gregor Alexander. b 42. TCD BA 64 MA 67. CITC 65. **d** 65 **p** 66. C Holywood *D & D* 65–68; C Bangor St Comgall 68–72; I Carnalea 72–80; I Knock 80–07; Stewardship Adv 89–07; Can Down Cathl 90–07; Dioc Registrar 90–95; Adn Down and Chan Belf Cathl 95–07; rtd 07. *1 Rocky Lane, Seaforde, Downpatrick BT30 8PW* T: (028) 4481 1111

McCAMMON, John Taylor. b 42. QUB BSc 65 Lon Univ BD 70. Clifton Th Coll 67. **d** 71 **p** 72. C Lurgan Ch the Redeemer *D & D* 71–75; I Kilkeel 75–82; I Lisburn Ch Ch Cathl *Conn* 82–98; Treas Lisburn Ch Ch Cathl 94–96; Prec Lisburn Ch Ch Cathl 96; Chan Lisburn Ch Ch Cathl 96–98; Can Lisburn Ch Ch Cathl 85–98; CMS Kenya 99–05; CMS Ireland 05–09; rtd 09; PtO *Conn* from 09; *Eur* 15–20. *9 Beechfield Park, Coleraine BT52 2HZ* T: (028) 7032 6046 E: jmmccammon@hotmail.com

McCANN, Alan. *See* McCANN, Thomas Alan George

McCANN, Michael Joseph. b 61. Man Univ BSc 82 TCD BTh 91 FCA. **d** 91 **p** 92. C Derryloran *Arm* 91–94; I Dunmurry *Conn* 94–99; I Kilroot and Templecorran 99–18. *Address temp unknown*

McCANN, Roland Neil. b 39. Serampore Coll BD 73. Bp's Coll Calcutta. **d** 70 **p** 73. C Calcutta St Jas India 70–73; V Calcutta St Thos 73–74; C Earley St Bart *Ox* 74–77; C-in-c Harlington Ch Ch *Lon* 77–99; rtd 99; PtO *Lon* 02–13. *195 Park Road, Uxbridge UB8 1NP* T: (01895) 259265

McCANN, Stephen Thomas. b 60. Benedictine Coll Kansas BA 83 Boston Coll (USA) MA 89 Creighton Univ Nebraska MA 94. Pontifical Gregorian Univ 96. **d** 97 **p** 98. In RC Ch 97–01; Rydal Hall *Carl* 02–05; C Kendal H Trin 05–10; I Ballydehob w Aghadown *C, C & R* from 10; Chapl Lay Min from 14. *The Rectory, Church Road, Ballydehob, Co Cork, Republic of Ireland* T: (00353) (28) 37117 E: ballydehobrector@gmail.com

McCANN, Thomas Alan George. b 66. Ulster Univ BA 90 TCD BTh 93 QUB MPhil 99. CITC 90. **d** 93 **p** 94. C Carrickfergus *Conn* 93–00; I Woodburn H Trin from 00. *20 Meadow Hill Close, Carrickfergus BT38 9RQ* T: (028) 9336 2126 E: rector@holytrinitycarrick.org.uk

McCARTAN, Mrs Audrey Doris. b 50. Keele Univ CertEd 71 BEd 72 Lanc Univ MA 75 Northumbria Univ MSc 99. NEOC 01. **d** 04 **p** 05. NSM Gosforth St Hugh *Newc* 04–07; P-in-c Heddon-on-the-Wall 07–20; P-in-c Longhorsley from 20. *St Helen's Vicarage, Drummonds Close, Longhorsley, Morpeth NE65 8UU* E: audreymccartan@btinternet.com

McCARTER, Mrs Suzanne. b 63. Hull Univ BA 85 PGCE 86. CBDTI 04. **d** 07 **p** 08. C Standish *Blackb* 07–10; C Cullingworth *Bradf* 10–13; TV Harden and Wilsden, Cullingworth and Denholme 13–14; *Leeds* 14–21; V Hampsthwaite and Killinghall and Birstwith from 21; Area Missr S Craven Deanery *Bradf* 10–13. *The Vicarage, Wreaks Road, Birstwith, Harrogate HG3 2NJ* E: suzanne_mccarter@msn.com

McCARTHY, Christopher James. b 61. NEOC 04. **d** 06 **p** 07. C Bessingby *York* 06–08; C Bridlington Quay Ch Ch 06–08; V Bridlington Em 08–15; P-in-c Skipsea and Barmston w Fraisthorpe 08–12; V 12–15; P-in-c Doncaster St Jas *Sheff* from 15. *15 Grange View, Doncaster DN4 0XL* E: chrismbrid@aol.com

MacCARTHY, Denis Francis Anthony. b 60. St Patr Coll Maynooth BD 85 CITC 05. **d** 85 **p** 86. In RC Ch 85–05; C Bandon Union *C, C & R* 06–08; I from 10; I Mallow Union 08–10. *The Rectory, Castle Road, Bandon, Co Cork, Republic of Ireland* T: (00353) (23) 884 1259 E: noden1@eircom.net

MacCARTHY, Lorraine Valmay. *See* REED, Lorraine Valmay

MacCARTHY, Stephen Samuel. b 49. ACII 81 Univ Coll Chich BA 02. **d** 01. NSM Burgess Hill St Edw *Chich* 01–10; NSM Albourne w Sayers Common and Twineham 10–17; NSM Burgess Hill St Jo 17–19; rtd 19. *St Edward's House, 9 Coopers Close, Burgess Hill RH15 8AN* T: (01444) 248520 M: 07802-734903 E: ssmaccarthy@aol.com

McCARTNEY, Adrian Alexander. b 57. Stranmillis Coll BEd 79 TCD BTh 86. CITC 86. **d** 88 **p** 89. C Jordanstown w Monkstown *Conn* 88–91; Bp's C Monkstown 91–94; I 94–96; C Belvoir *D & D* 02–03; Dir Boring Wells (Fresh Expressions) 03–17; I Belvoir *D & D* from 17. *The Rectory, 86B Beechill Road, Belfast BT8 7QN* T: (028) 9064 3777 M: 07970-626384 E: adrian@boringwells.org *or* adrian@belvoirparish.co.uk

McCARTNEY, Ellis. b 47. Univ Coll Lon BSc 73 Lon Inst of Educn MA 82. NTMTC 94. **d** 97 **p** 98. NSM Tollington *Lon* 97–05. *6 Elfort Road, London N5 1AZ* T: (020) 7226 1533 E: macfour@btinternet.com

McCARTNEY, Robert Charles. CITC. **d** 85 **p** 85. C Portadown St Mark *Arm* 85–88; I Errigle Keerogue w Ballygawley and Killeshil 88–89; CF 89–04; I Belfast St Donard *D & D* 04–08; I Aghalee 08–15; rtd 15; P-in-c Clonfert Gp *L & K* 17–19; P-in-c Shinrone w Aghancon etc from 19. *The Rectory, Magheramore, Shinrone, Birr, Co Offaly, R42 XN65, Republic of Ireland* M: 07484-602420 *or* (00353) 87-759 4468 E: dunroamin.mccartney@btopenworld.com

McCARTY, Colin Terence. b 46. Loughb Univ BTech 68 PhD 71 Lon Univ PGCE 73 FRSA 89. EAMTC 91. **d** 94 **p** 95. NSM Exning St Martin w Landwade *St E* 94–16; Bp's Officer for Self-Supporting Min 09–16; rtd 16; PtO *Ely* from 96; *St E* from 16. *1 Seymour Close, Newmarket CB8 8EL* T: (01638) 669400 *or* (01223) 552716 F: 553537 M: 07970-563166 E: test_and_eval@btinternet.com

McCAULAY, Stephen Thomas John. b 61. Leeds Univ BA 98 Cardiff Univ MTh 14. Coll of Resurr Mirfield 96. **d** 98 **p** 99. C Chaddesden St Phil *Derby* 98–02; V Mackworth St Fran 02–04; CF 04–16; R Lympne and Saltwood *Cant* 16–19; R Washburn and Mid-Wharfe *Leeds* from 19. *The Vicarage, Askwith, Otley LS21 2HX* T: (01943) 513340 E: stephen.mccaulay@leeds.anglican.org

McCAULEY, The Ven Craig William Leslie. b 72. Glam Univ BA 95 TCD BTh 99 York St Jo Univ MA 18. CITC 96. **d** 99 **p** 00. C Seapatrick *D & D* 99–02; C Kill *D & G* 02–04; I Lurgan w Billis, Killinkere and Munterconnaught *K, E & A* from 04; Adn Kilmore from 10; Can St Patr Cathl Dublin from 16. *The Rectory, Virginia, Co Cavan, Republic of Ireland* T: (00353) (49) 854 8465 E: virginia@kilmore.anglican.org

McCAUSLAND, Norman. b 58. TCD BTh 89. CITC 89. **d** 89 **p** 90. C Portadown St Columba *Arm* 89–91; P-in-c Clonmel Union *C, C & R* 91–94; Miss to Seamen 91–94; CMS 94–95; Bp's V and Lib Ossory Cathl *C, F & O* 96; Chapl and Tutor CITC 96–00; PV Ch Ch Cathl Dublin *D & G* 96–00; CMS 00–01; LtO *D & G* 01–13; I Raheny w Coolock from 13. *The Rectory, 403 Howth Road, Raheny, Dublin 5, Republic of Ireland* T: (00353) (1) 831 3929 M: 86-837 0450 E: raheny@dublin.anglican.org

M'CAW, Stephen Aragorn. b 61. Magd Coll Cam BA 83 Lon Univ MB, BS 86 FRCS 90 MRCGP 92. Cranmer Hall Dur 97. **d** 99 **p** 00. C Thetford *Nor* 99–02; R Steeple Aston w N Aston and Tackley *Ox* 02–10; Ab Woodstock 06–09; TR Keynsham *B & W* from 10; RD Chew Magna from 17. *68 Park Road, Keynsham, Bristol BS31 1DE* T: 0117-986 4437 E: samcaw@talk21.com

⊕**McCLAY, The Rt Revd David Alexander.** b 59. TCD MA 87. **d** 87 **p** 88 **c** 20. C Magheralin w Dollingstown *D & D* 87–90; I Kilkeel 90–01; I Willowfield 01–20; P-in-c Mt Merrion 07–20; Can Belf Cathl 05–20; Adn Down *D* 13–20; Bp *D & D* from 20. *The See House, 32 Knockdene Park South, Belfast BT5 7AB* T: (028) 9082 8850 M: 07854-395797 E: bishop@downdromorediocese.org

McCLEAN, Derek Alistair. b 69. Poly of Wales BA 92 QUB PGCE 94. Ridley Hall Cam 08. **d** 10 **p** 11. C Drayton *Nor* 10–13; R Hethersett w Canteloff w Lt and Gt Melton from 13. *The Rectory, 27 Norwich Road, Hethersett, Norwich NR9 3AR* M: 07889-284921 E: revdmac@gmail.com

McCLEAN, Dominic Joseph James Albert Francis. b 59. Trin & All SS Coll Leeds BEd 82 De Montfort Univ MSc 07. Allen Hall Qu Coll Birm. **d** 89 **p** 11. NSM Leic St Aid 10–11; NSM Burbage w Aston Flamville 11–13; P-in-c Bosworth and Sheepy Gp 13–15; P-in-c Nailstone and Carlton w Shackerstone 13–15; Dioc Voc Dir *Ban* 15–16; Dioc Dir

Discipleship and Voc from 16; C Bro Cyfeiliog and Mawddwy 15–16. *The Vicarage, Porthmadog LL49 9PA* T: (01766) 513187

McCLEAN, Lydia Margaret Sheelagh. *See* COOK, Lydia Margaret Sheelagh

McCLEAN, Robert Mervyn. b 38. Greenwich Univ BTh 91. Edgehill Th Coll Belf 57. **d** 85 **p** 88. NSM Seapatrick *D & D* 85–99; rtd 99. *2 Kiloanin Crescent, Banbridge BT32 4NU* T: (028) 4062 7419

McCLEAVE, George. b 42. **d** 12 **p** 13. NSM Stokesley w Seamer *York* 12–15; rtd 15; PtO *York* 15–20. *52 The Stripe, Middlesbrough TS9 5PU* T: (01642) 714254 E: gmccleave@btinternet.com

McCLELLAN, Andrew David. b 71. St Jo Coll Cam BA 93 MA 96. Oak Hill Th Coll BA 05. **d** 05 **p** 06. C Sevenoaks St Nic *Roch* 05–09; P-in-c Bromley St Jo 09–12; V from 12; Chapl St Olave's Gr Sch Orpington 09–15. *St John's Vicarage, 9 Orchard Road, Bromley BR1 2PR* T: (020) 8460 1844 M: 07931-731062 E: saintjohnsbromley@gmail.com

McCLELLAN, Susan. b 66. Open Univ BSc 13. Qu Foundn Birm 19. **d** 21. C Cov Cathl from 21. *St Andrew's Vicarage, Church Lane, Shottery, Stratford-upon-Avon CV37 9HQ* M: 07855-479734 E: sumcclellan@googlemail.com *or* su.mcclellan@embraceme.org

McCLELLAND (*née* FARLEY), Mrs Claire Louise. b 69. Man Univ BA 91 Heythrop Coll Lon MTh 99. Westcott Ho Cam 96. **d** 99 **p** 00. C Sherborne w Castleton and Lillington *Sarum* 99–00; C Weymouth H Trin 00–02; Chapl Barts and The Lon NHS Trust 02–03; Chapl Ealing Hosp NHS Trust 03–06; Chapl W Middx Univ Hosp NHS Trust 03–06; NSM S Lambeth St Anne and All SS *S'wark* 06–08; NSM Pimlico St Pet w Westmr Ch Ch *Lon* 08–12; NSM Charminster and Stinsford *Sarum* 12–16; TV Dorchester and the Winterbournes 16–20; P-in-c Upper Weardale *Dur* from 20. *The Vicarage, 14 Burnfoot, St John's Chapel, Bishop Auckland DL13 1QH* T: (01388) 537063 E: clairemcclelland@icloud.com

McCLELLAND, Clifford Stanley. b 60. Trin Coll Bris BA 16. **d** 16 **p** 17. C Headbourne Worthy *Win* 16–18; C King's Worthy 16–18; C Upper Dever 16–18; Chapl HM Pris Win from 18. *HM Prison, Romsey Road, Winchester SO22 5DF* T: (01962) 723000 M: 07753-224078 E: cliff@cliffandsarah.co.uk

McCLELLAND, Sarah Perrée. b 68. St Andr Univ BSc 91 Qu Coll Cam MB, BChir 94 MRCP 96 MRCGP 99. Trin Coll Bris MA 16. **d** 16 **p** 17. C King's Worthy *Win* 16–18; C Headbourne Worthy 16–18; C Upper Dever 16–18; P-in-c Valley Park from 18. *35 Ragland Close, Chandler's Ford, Eastleigh SO53 4NH* M: 07753-224092 E: sarah@cliffandsarah.co.uk

McCLENAGHAN, John Mark. b 61. TCD BTh 05. CITC 02. **d** 05 **p** 06. C Portadown St Columba *Arm* 05–08; I Keady w Armaghbreague and Derrynoose 08–13; Hon V Choral Arm Cathl 07–13; I Aghalurcher w Tattykeeran, Cooneen etc *Clogh* from 13; Dioc Registrar from 17. *Colebrook Rectory, 8 Owenskerry Lane, Fivemiletown BT75 0SP* T: (028) 8953 1822 E: aghalurcher@clogher.anglican.org *or* colebrooke@clogher.anglican.org

MACCLESFIELD, Archdeacon of. *See* BISHOP, The Ven Ian Gregory

McCLINTOCK, Darren John. b 77. Hull Univ BA 98 Open Univ MA(TS) 00. St Jo Coll Nottm 98. **d** 01 **p** 02. C Drypool *York* 01–04; C Bilton *Ripon* 04–05; TV 05–15; Dioc Ecum Adv 08–09; Chapl Wakefield Hospice 15–18; Chapl Leeds Teaching Hosps NHS Trust 18–20; Chapl Harrogate and Distr NHS Foundn Trust from 20. *Harrogate and District NHS Foundation Trust, Harrogate District Hospital, Lancaster Park Road, Harrogate HG2 7SX* T: (01423) 885959 E: darrenjmcclintock1977@gmail.com

McCLURE, Mrs Catherine Abigail. b 63. Birm Univ BA 84 SS Hild & Bede Coll Dur PGCE 85. Ripon Coll Cuddesdon BTh 07. **d** 03 **p** 04. C Cirencester *Glouc* 03–07; Chapl Glos Hosps NHS Foundn Trust 07–13 and from 17; Chapl Cheltenham Ladies' Coll 13–16; Bp's Healthcare Chaplaincy Adv *Glouc* from 18. *Gloucestershire Hospitals NHS Foundation Trust, Cheltenham General Hospital, Sandford Road, Cheltenham GL53 7AN* T: 03004-224286 M: 07824-476505 E: mcclure.staverton@gmail.com *or* katie.mcclure@nhs.net

McCLURE, Jennifer Lynne. *See* MOBERLY, Jennifer Lynne

McCLURE, The Ven Timothy Elston. b 46. St Jo Coll Dur BA 68. Ridley Hall Cam 68. **d** 70 **p** 71. C Kirkheaton *Wakef* 70–73; C Chorlton upon Medlock *Man* 74–79; Chapl Man Poly 74–82; TR Man Whitworth 79–82; Gen Sec SCM 82–92; Bp's Soc and Ind Adv and Dir Chs' Coun for Ind and Soc Resp LEP *Bris* 92–99; Hon Can Bris Cathl 92–12; Hon C Cotham St Sav w St Mary 96; Chapl Lord Mayor's Chpl 96–99; Adn Bris 99–12; rtd 12. *Elephant Cottage, 55 South Street, Bridport DT6 3NZ* E: tim@mcclure.me.uk

McCLUSKEY, Coralie Christine. b 52. Univ of Wales (Cardiff) BEd 74. SAOMC 98. **d** 01 **p** 02. C Welwyn w

Ayot St Peter *St Alb* 01–04; P-in-c Datchworth 04–05; TV Welwyn 05–11; P-in-c Eaton Bray w Edlesborough 11–12; V 12–16; Agric Chapl for Herts 09–13; Agric Chapl for Beds 13–16; rtd 16. *Castle View, Oaklands, Builth Wells LD2 3ER* E: coralie_mccluskey@yahoo.co.uk

McCLUSKEY, James Terence. b 65. Coll of Resurr Mirfield 01. **d** 03 **p** 04. C Swanley St Mary *Roch* 03–06; V Prittlewell St Luke *Chelmsf* 06–18; R Colchester St Jas and St Paul w All SS etc from 18. *50B Priory Street, Colchester CO1 2QB* T: (01206) 860419 M: 07739-404082 E: jamestmccluskey202@btinternet.com

McCOACH, Jennifer Sara. *See* CROFT, Jennifer Sara

McCOLLUM, The Ven Alastair Colston. b 69. Whitelands Coll Lon BA 91 Anglia Poly Univ MA 98. Westcott Ho Cam 95. **d** 96 **p** 97. C Hampton All SS *Lon* 96–98; C S Kensington St Aug 98–00; Chapl Imp Coll 98–00; TV Papworth *Ely* 00–08; V Kilmington, Stockland, Dalwood, Yarcombe etc *Ex* 08–13; R Victoria St Jo Canada from 13; Adn Tolmie from 14. *3896 Cadboro Bay Road, Victoria BC V8N 4G6, Canada* E: amccollum@bc.anglican.ca

McCOLLUM, Charles James. b 41. TCD BTh 89. CITC 85. **d** 89 **p** 90. C Larne and Inver *Conn* 89–91; Bp's C Belfast Whiterock 91–96; I Belfast St Pet and St Jas 96–08; I Dunleckney w Nurney, Lorum and Kiltennel *C, F & O* 08–12; Can Ossory Cathl 12; rtd 12. *Curragho, Cavan, Republic of Ireland* M: (00353) 87-288 5019 E: charlesjmccollum@gmail.com

McCONAGHIE, Colin Andrew. b 75. CITC MTh 12. **d** 11 **p** 12. C Drumglass w Moygashel *Arm* 11–14; C Dunboyne and Rathmolyon *M & K* 14–17; I Carrickmacross w Magheracloone *Clogh* from 17. *The Rectory, Drumconrath Road, Carrickmacross, Co Monaghan, Republic of Ireland* M: (00353) 87-346 6190 E: revcolinmcc@gmail.com *or* carrickmacross@clogher.anglican.org

McCONNAUGHIE, Adrian William. b 66. Jes Coll Ox BA 89 MA 06 Lon Univ PhD 93 Cam Univ PGCE 96. Trin Coll Bris BA 08. **d** 08 **p** 09. C Bath Abbey w St Jas *B & W* 08–11; Chapl Mon Sch 11–13; Chapl Brentwood Sch from 13; C Warley Ch Ch and Gt Warley St Mary *Chelmsf* from 15. *Mitre House, 6 Shenfield Road, Brentwood CM15 8AA* T: (01277) 203280 E: awm@brentwood.essex.sch.uk

McCONNELL, Canon Brian Roy. b 46. St Paul's Coll Grahamstown. **d** 71 **p** 72. C Plumstead S Africa 71–74; C St Geo Cathl Cape Town 74–77; C Prestwich St Marg *Man* 77–79; R Sea Point S Africa 79–85; V Liscard St Mary w St Columba *Ches* 85–90; V Altrincham St Geo 90–06; RD Bowdon 95–03; Hon Can Ches Cathl 97–06; Can Res Carl Cathl 06–13; rtd 13; PtO *B & W* from 15. *30 Gunville Gardens, Milborne Port, Sherborne DT9 5FF* T: (01963) 251511 M: 07759-603583 E: brianles1@btinternet.com

McCORMACK, Alan William. b 68. Jes Coll Ox BA 90 MA 94 DPhil 94. CITC 93. **d** 96 **p** 97. C Knock *D & D* 96–98; Dean of Res and Chapl TCD 98–07; Succ St Patr Cathl Dublin 98–06; Abp's Dom Chapl *D & G* 03–07; P-in-c St Botolph without Bishopgate *Lon* 07–15; P-in-c St Vedast w St Mich-le-Querne etc 07–15; Dean Goodenough Coll from 15; PtO *Lon* 15–17; NSM Hanover Square St Geo from 17; PtO *Eur* from 16. *Goodenough College, London House, Mecklenburgh Square, London WC1N 2AB* T: (020) 7837 8888 E: mccorma@gmail.com

McCORMACK, Colin. b 47. QUB BSc 70 DipEd 71. St Jo Coll Nottm BA 75. **d** 78 **p** 79. C Carl St Jo 78–81; C Ballynafeigh St Jude *D & D* 81–84; V Harraby Carl 84–89; NSM Carl H Trin and St Barn 95–99; Asst Chapl Costa Blanca *Eur* 00–04; Chapl Torrevieja 04–08; I Clonallon and Warrenpoint w Kilbroney *D & D* 11–18. *3C The Pines, Hillsborough BT26 6NT* T: (028) 9268 9518 E: colinmccormack6@btinternet.com

McCORMACK, Canon David Eugene. b 34. Wells Th Coll 66. **d** 68 **p** 69. C Lillington *Cov* 68–71; C The Lickey *Birm* 71–75; V Highters Heath 75–82; V Four Oaks 82–00; Hon Can Birm Cathl 95–00; rtd 00; PtO *Linc* from 00; *Pet* from 00; *Birm* from 05. *27 Rockingham Close, Market Deeping, Peterborough PE6 8BY* T: (01778) 217043 E: jandmccormack@aol.com

McCORMACK, George Brash. b 32. ACIS 65 FCIS 75. S'wark Ord Course 82. **d** 85 **p** 86. Hon C Crofton St Paul *Roch* 85–89; C Crayford 89–91; R Fawkham and Hartley 91–97; rtd 97; PtO *Roch* 98–19. *11 Turnpike Drive, Pratts Bottom, Orpington BR6 7SJ* E: geomacc@uwclub.net

McCORMACK, Ian Douglas. b 80. St Anne's Coll Ox BA 02 MA 06 MSt 03 Leeds Univ MA 10. Coll of Resurr Mirfield 07. **d** 10 **p** 11. C Horbury w Horbury Bridge *Wakef* 10–13; V Grimethorpe w Brierley 13–14; *Leeds* 14–18; P-in-c Nottingham St Geo w St Jo *S'well* 18–21; V from 21. *St George's Vicarage, Strome Close, Nottingham NG2 1HD* E: fatherianmccormack@hotmail.com

McCORMACK, John Heddon. b 58. Chich Th Coll 85. **d** 88 **p** 89. C Cleobury Mortimer w Hopton Wafers *Heref* 88–90;

C Lymington *Win* 90–92; C Portsea N End St Mark *Portsm* 92–95; Chapl St Barn Hospice Worthing 95–06. *10 Columbia Walk, Worthing BN13 2ST* T: (01903) 263700 M: 07974-603518 E: humanrites1@sky.com

McCORMACK, Canon Kevan Sean. b 50. Chich Th Coll 77. **d** 80 **p** 81. C Ross *Heref* 80–81; C Ross w Brampton Abbotts, Bridstow and Peterstow 81–83; C Leominster 83; TV 84–87; Chapl R Hosp Sch Holbrook 87–00; R Woodbridge St Mary *St E* 00–20; Hon Can St E Cathl 09–20; Chapl to The Queen 14–20; rtd 20; PtO *St E* from 20. *Croft Cottage, Church Lane, Bromeswell, Woodbridge IP12 2PJ* T: (01394) 460707 E: bimbling2012@gmail.com

McCORMACK, Canon Lesley Sharman. b 50. EAMTC. **d** 88 **p** 94. Hon Par Dn Chevington w Hargrave and Whepstead w Brockley *St E* 88–95; Asst Chapl W Suffolk Hosp Bury St Edm 88–95; Chapl Kettering Gen Hosp NHS Foundn Trust 95–09; Chapl Cransley Hospice 09–10; NSM Kettering SS Pet and Paul 09–18; Bp's Hosp Chapl Adv 00–12; Can Pet Cathl 03–18; rtd 18; PtO *Pet* from 19. *Barnbrook, Water Lane, Chelveston, Wellingborough NN9 6AP* T: (01933) 626636 E: mccormack26@outlook.com

MacCORMACK, Michael Ian. b 54. Kent Univ BA 77 Ch Ch Coll Cant MA 87 Bris Univ PGCE 78. STETS 02. **d** 05 **p** 06. NSM Martock w Kingsbury Episcopi and Ash *B & W* 05–19; PtO from 19; *Sarum* 19–21; NSM Upper Stour from 21. *11 Manor Gardens, Wincanton BA9 9QR* M: 07470-667118 E: revmikemac@gmail.com *or* revmac@upperstour.org.uk

McCORMACK, Mrs Susan. b 60. NEOC 00. **d** 03 **p** 04. C Newburn *Newc* 03–07; P-in-c Fawdon 07–13; TR Willington from 13. *St Mary's Vicarage, 67 Churchill Street, Wallsend NE28 7TE* T: 0191-209 9995 M: 07452-35974 E: revsue14mack@gmail.com

McCORMICK, Mrs Anne Irene. b 67. Sheff Univ BA 89 Hull Univ PGCE 90 Cardiff Univ MTh 11. Ripon Coll Cuddesdon 90. **d** 92 **p** 94. C Spalding St Mary and St Nic *Linc* 92–96; C Gt Grimsby St Mary and St Jas 96–01; C Gt and Lt Coates w Bradley 98–16; TV from 16; Chapl Rotherham, Doncaster and S Humber NHS Foundn Trust 07–12; Chapl N Lincs and Goole NHS Foundn Trust 12–16. *Glebe House, 11 Church Lane, Limber, Grimsby DN37 8JN* T: (01469) 561082 M: 07903-749266

McCORMICK, David Mark. b 68. Univ of Wales (Ban) BD 89. Ripon Coll Cuddesdon 90. **d** 92 **p** 93. C Holbeach *Linc* 92–96; TV Gt Grimsby St Mary and St Jas 96–01; Prin Linc Min Tr Course 01–09; CME Officer 09–12; TV Gt and Lt Coates w Bradley 12–15; Chapl St Andr Hospice Grimsby 12–15; PtO *Linc* 17–19; TR Gt and Lt Coates w Bradley from 19. *St Nicolas' Vicarage, Great Coates Road, Great Coates, Grimsby DN37 9NS* E: david.mccormick@lincoln.anglican.org *or* rector@glcbchurches.org

McCOSH, Andrew James. b 58. Newman Univ BA 17. **d** 14 **p** 15. NSM Shelfield and High Heath *Lich* 14–18; P-in-c 18–21. *4 Larch Close, Lichfield WS14 9UR* E: revandystmarks@virginmedia.com

McCOUBREY, William Arthur. b 36. CEng MIMechE. Sarum & Wells Th Coll 86. **d** 89 **p** 90. C Bedhampton *Portsm* 89–92; V Stokenham w Sherford *Ex* 92–96; R Stokenham w Sherford and Beesands, and Slapton 96–02; rtd 02; PtO *Portsm* from 02; *Chich* from 02. *19 Warblington Road, Emsworth PO10 7HE* T: (01243) 374011

McCOULOUGH, David. b 61. Man Univ BA 84 St Jo Coll Dur BA 88 Leeds Univ MA 01. Cranmer Hall Dur 86. **d** 89 **p** 90. C Man Apostles w Miles Platting 89–92; C Elton All SS 92–94; V Halliwell St Marg 94–98; Min Can Ripon Cathl 98–01; Chapl Univ Coll of Ripon and York St Jo 98–01; Ind Chapl *S'well* 01–07; Chapl Boots PLC 01–07; C Nottingham St Pet and St Jas 01–02; C Nottingham St Pet and All SS 02–07; Assoc Dir Partnerships 07–09; Dir from 09; P-in-c Edingley w Halam 07–14. *Jubilee House, Westgate, Southwell NG25 0JH* T: (01636) 817246 E: davidmcc@southwell.anglican.org

McCOULOUGH, Thomas Alexander. b 32. AKC 59. **d** 60 **p** 61. C Norton St Mich *Dur* 60–63; USPG India 63–67; P-in-c Derby St Jas 67–72; Ind Chapl *York* 72–82; P-in-c Sutton on the Forest 82–96; Dioc Sec for Local Min 82–89; Lay Tr Officer 89–96; rtd 96; PtO *Newc* from 96. *1 Horsley Gardens, Holywell, Whitley Bay NE25 0TU* T: 0191-298 0332 E: tg.mcc@hotmail.com

McCRACKEN, Victor John. b 61. **d** 19 **p** 20. NSM Athelington, Denham, Horham, Hoxne etc *St E* from 19. *Catlyn House, Wingfield, Diss IP21 5QZ* T: (01379) 388812

McCREA, Christina Elizabeth. b 53. **d** 08 **p** 09. NSM Glanogwen and Llanllechid w St Ann's and Pentir *Ban* 08–14; NSM Bro Ogwen from 14. *2 Bron-y-Waun, Rhiwlas, Bangor LL57 4EX* T: (01248) 372249 E: christinaemcc@aol.com

McCREADIE, Mrs Lesley Anne. b 51. Bp Otter Coll CertEd 73 Open Univ BA 93. STETS BA 10. **d** 10 **p** 11. NSM Sherborne w Castleton, Lillington and Longburton *Sarum* 10–16; TV from 16; Chapl St Antony's Leweston Sch Sherborne from 17. *5 Kings Close, Longburton, Sherborne DT9 5PW* T: (01963) 210548 E: revdlesley@aol.com

McCROSKERY, Canon Andrew. b 74. Glas Univ BD 97 TCD MPhil 99. CITC 98. **d** 99 **p** 00. C Newtownards *D & D* 99–02; Dean's V Cork Cathl *C, C & R* 02–04; I Youghal Union 04–08; Chapl Univ Coll Cork 04–08; Bp's Dom Chapl 03–08; Min Can Cork Cathl 04–08; I Dublin St Bart w Leeson Park *D & G* from 08; Chapl St Mary's Home 08–19; Chapl St Jo Ho from 20; Can Ch Ch Cathl Dublin *D & G* from 19. *The Rectory, 12 Merlyn Road, Ballsbridge, Dublin 4, Republic of Ireland* T: (00353) (1) 269 4813 E: wolfram100@hotmail.com *or* vicar@stbartholomews.ie

McCULLAGH, Danielle Susan. Northumbria Univ BA. **d** 16 **p** 17. Mallusk *Conn* 16–17; C Lisburn Ch Ch Cathl 17–21; TV from 21. *82 Thornleigh Drive, Lisburn BT28 2DS* M: 07964-882269 E: danielle_199@hotmail.co.uk *or* danielle@lisburncathedral.org

McCULLAGH, Elspeth Jane Alexandra. *See* SAVILLE, Elspeth Jane Alexandra

McCULLAGH, Canon John Eric. b 46. TCD BA 68 BTh 88 QUB DipEd 70. **d** 88 **p** 89. C Stillorgan w Blackrock *D & G* 88–91; Chapl and Hd of RE Newpark Sch Dub 90–91; I Clondalkin w Rathcoole *D & G* 91–99; Sec Gen Syn Bd of Educn 99–08; I Rathdrum w Glenealy, Derralossary and Laragh *D & G* 08–14; Can Ch Ch Cathl Dublin 99–14; Treas Ch Ch Cathl Dublin 09–14; rtd 14. *Harcourt Villa, Kimberley Road, Greystones, Co Wicklow, Republic of Ireland* T: (00353) (1) 287 1408 M: 86-837 0384 E: jemccullagh@gmail.com

McCULLOCH, Alistair John. b 59. Univ of Wales (Lamp) BA 81 Leeds Univ BA 86 Lon Univ MA 07. Coll of Resurr Mirfield 84. **d** 87 **p** 88. C Portsm Cathl 87–90; C Portsea St Mary 90–94; V Reading St Matt *Ox* 94–95; PtO *S'wark* 99; Chapl King's Coll Hosp NHS Trust 00–04; Chapl R Marsden NHS Foundn Trust 04–21; Bp's Adv for Hosp Chapl *S'wark* 18–21; Dir Ords Woolwich Area from 21. *St George's Rectory, Maniple Street, London SE1 4LW* M: 07929-765752 E: mccullocha95@gmail.com

McCULLOCH, Andrew Stewart. b 71. St Mellitus Coll 16. **d** 19 **p** 20. C Cogges and S Leigh *Ox* from 19. *1 Cherry Tree Court, Witney OX28 1GQ* E: andy@coggesparish.com

McCULLOCH, Mrs Celia Hume. b 53. Leeds Univ BA 08. NOC 05. **d** 08 **p** 09. C Cheetham *Man* 08–10; rtd 10; PtO *Man* 11–13; *Carl* 12–18. *Stonelea, 1 Heads Drive, Grange-over-Sands LA11 7DY* M: 07943-366331 E: cranfieldcmc@btinternet.com

MacCULLOCH, Prof Diarmaid Ninian John. b 51. Kt 12. Chu Coll Cam BA 72 MA 76 PhD 77 Ox Univ DD 01 FSA 78 FRHistS 81 FBA 01. Ripon Coll Cuddesdon 86. **d** 87. NSM Clifton All SS w St Jo *Bris* 87–88; Tutor Wesley Coll Bris 78–90; Fell St Cross Coll Ox from 95; Sen Tutor 96–00; Lect Th Ox Univ from 95; Prof Hist of Ch 97–19; Fell Campion Hall from 20. *Campion Hall, Brewer Street, Oxford OX1 1QS* T: (01865) 278490 *or* 286100 E: diarmaid.macculloch@theology.ox.ac.uk

✠**McCULLOCH, The Rt Revd Nigel Simeon.** b 42. KCVO 13. Selw Coll Cam BA 64 MA 69. Cuddesdon Coll 64. **d** 66 **p** 67 **c** 86. C Ellesmere Port *Ches* 66–70; Dir Th Studies Ch Coll Cam 70–75; Chapl 70–73; Dioc Missr *Nor* 73–78; P-in-c Salisbury St Thos and St Edm *Sarum* 78–81; R 81–86; Adn Sarum 79–86; Can and Preb Sarum Cathl 79–86; Suff Bp Taunton *B & W* 86–92; Preb Wells Cathl 86–92; Bp Wakef 92–02; Bp Man 02–13; Ld High Almoner 97–13; rtd 13; Hon Asst Bp Carl from 13. *Stonelea, 1 Heads Drive, Grange-over-Sands LA11 7DY* E: n.mcculloch374@btinternet.com

McCULLOCK, Patricia Ann. *See* FULLER, Patricia Ann

McCULLOUGH, Mrs Aphrodite Maria. b 47. Derby Univ MSc 95. EMMTC 97. **d** 00 **p** 01. NSM Kirby Muxloe *Leic* 00–04; TV 04–08; rtd 08; PtO *Leic* from 08. *33 Alton Road, Leicester LE2 8QB* T: 0116-283 7887 E: aphro.mccullough@btinternet.com

McCULLOUGH, Canon Roy. b 46. MBE 13. Brasted Th Coll 69 Linc Th Coll 70. **d** 73 **p** 74. Chapl Highfield Priory Sch Lancs 73–77; C Ashton-on-Ribble St Andr *Blackb* 73–77; V Rishton 77–86; V Burnley St Matt w H Trin 86–97; RD Burnley 91–97; Chapl Victoria Hosp Burnley 86–91; V Walton-le-Dale St Leon w Samlesbury St Leon *Blackb* 97–11; Hon Can Blackb Cathl 97–11; rtd 11; PtO *Blackb* 11–20; Carl from 11. *Wescoe, Kirkby Thore, Penrith CA10 1XE* T: (01768) 361656 E: randjmcc@googlemail.com

McCURDY, The Ven Hugh Kyle. b 58. Portsm Poly BA Univ of Wales (Cardiff) PGCE. Trin Coll Bris. **d** 85 **p** 86. C Egham *Guildf* 85–88; C Woking St Jo 88–91; V Histon *Ely* 91–05;

P-in-c Impington 98–05; RD N Stowe 94–05; Hon Can Ely Cathl 04–05; Adn Huntingdon and Wisbech from 05. *Whitgift House, The College, Ely CB7 4DL* T: (01353) 658404 *or* 652709 F: 652745 E: archdeacon.handw@elydiocese.org

McDERMOTT, Christopher Francis Patrick. b 54. Southeastern Coll USA BA 84 Wheaton Coll Illinois MA 87 Heythrop Coll Lon MA 06. EAMTC. d 95 p 96. C Gt Ilford St Clem and St Marg *Chelmsf* 95–99; PtO from 06; Chapl Sussex Univ *Chich* from 14. *The Chaplaincy, University of Sussex, Southern Ring Road, Falmer, Brighton BN1 9RH* T: (01273) 877123 M: 07952-700391 E: chrismcd54@aol.com *or* c.mcdermott@sussex.ac.uk

McDERMOTT, John Alexander James. b 52. Lon Univ BSc 74 MSc 77 K Coll Cam BA 80 MA 84 CertEd 75. Westcott Ho Cam 78. d 81 p 82. C Bethnal Green St Jo w St Bart *Lon* 81–84; P-in-c Walkern *St Alb* 84–86; R Benington w Walkern 86–87; PtO *Newc* 12–17; P-in-c Amble from 17. *The Vicarage, Straffen Court, Amble, Morpeth NE65 0HA* T: (01665) 713327 M: 07804-181543 E: johnmcdermott35@hotmail.co.uk

McDERMOTT, Jordan Donald. b 95. Ban Univ BMus 16 Sheff Univ BA 20. Coll of Resurr Mirfield 18. d 21. C Accrington St Andr, St Mary and St Pet and Church Kirk *Blackb* from 21. *5 Queen's Road, Accrington BB5 6AR* M: 07843-186247 E: frjordanmcd@gmail.com

MacDERMOTT, Linda Karen. b 65. Ox Brookes Univ BA 12. Ripon Coll Cuddesdon 17. d 19 p 20. C Kington w Huntington, Old Radnor, Kinnerton etc *Heref* from 19. *5 Gravel Hill Drive, Kington HR5 3AE* M: 07546-259039 E: lindamacdermott@yahoo.co.uk

McDERMOTT, Mrs Stroma Gillian. b 65. York St Jo Univ BA 13. Yorks Min Course MA 16. d 16 p 17. C Wetherby *Leeds* 16–19; TV Knaresborough, Goldsborough, Nidd and Brearton from 19. *4 Greengate Drive, Knaresborough HG5 9EN* T: (01423) 860584 M: 07791-499036 E: stroma.mcdermott@ntlworld.com *or* stroma.mcdermott@leeds.anglican.org

MacDONALD, Preb Alan Hendry. b 49. St Steph Ho Ox 86. d 88 p 89. C Heavitree w Ex St Paul 88–91; C Withycombe Raleigh 91–92; TV 92–95; R Silverton, Butterleigh, Bickleigh and Cadeleigh 95–19; RD Tiverton 00–02 and 08–12; RD Cullompton 08–12; Preb Ex Cathl 10–19; rtd 19; PtO *Ex* from 19. *14 Applemede, Silverton, Exeter EX5 4JX* E: almac1@talktalk.net

MacDONALD, Alastair Robert. b 72. Edin Univ MA 94 MTh 03. TISEC. d 02 p 03. C Edin St Thos 02–06; Asst Chapl Amsterdam w Den Helder and Heiloo *Eur* 06–13; P-in-c Insch *Ab* from 13; P-in-c Fyvie from 13. *The Rectory, 17 South Road, Insch AB52 6XG* T: (01464) 820477 M: 07513-400081 E: macinsch@gmail.com

McDONALD, Barbara Joy. b 58. d 12 p 13. OLM Gt Bookham *Guildf* from 12. *3 Fiona Close, Great Bookham KT23 3JU* T: (01372) 454187 E: barbarajoymcdonald@gmail.com

McDONALD, Carollyn Elisabeth. b 54. Edin Univ BSc 76. EMMTC 07. d 09 p 10. C Sawley *Derby* 09–13; C Ashbourne St Oswald w Mapleton from 13; C Ashbourne St Jo from 13; C Clifton from 13; C Norbury w Snelston from 17; P-in-c Fenny Bentley, Thorpe, Tissington, Parwich etc from 17; Asst Dir of Ords from 20. *2A Windmill Lane, Ashbourne DE6 1EY* T: (01335) 664132 E: revcarollyn@peakfive.org

MacDONALD, Colin. b 47. St Jo Coll Nottm 87. d 89 p 90. C Limber Magna w Brocklesby *Linc* 89–92; P-in-c Barrow and Goxhill 92–97; V 97–99; R Hemingby 99–02; V Fulletby 99–02; R Belchford 99–02; TV Wilford Peninsula *St E* 02–09; rtd 09; P-in-c Siddal *Wakef* 09–12; PtO *Leeds* from 19. *5 Southdale Gardens, Ossett WF5 8BB* T: (01924) 276965

MacDONALD, Helen Maria. See BARTON, Helen Maria

McDONALD, Ian Henry. b 40. TD. St Aid Birkenhead 65. d 68 p 69. C Kingston upon Hull H Trin *York* 68–70; C Drumglass *Arm* 70–73; I Eglish w Killylea 73–80; I Maghera w Killelagh *D & R* 80–91; I Killowen 91–98; I Errigal w Garvagh 98–05; Can Derry Cathl 94–00; Preb 00–05; CF (TAVR) 91–05; rtd 05. *77 Saintfield Road, Ballygowan, Newtownards BT23 6HN* T: (028) 9752 8861 M: 07740-708402

McDONALD, James Alexander. b 88. Leeds Univ BSc 10 Ox Brookes Univ MA 16. Ripon Coll Cuddesdon BA 14. d 14 p 15. C Brackley St Pet w St Jas *Pet* 14–17; C York St Lawr w St Nic 17–19; C York All SS Pavement w St Crux and St Mich 17–19; C York St Denys 17–19; C York St Helen w St Martin 17–19; C York St Olave w St Giles 17–19; C York H Trin Micklegate 17–19; TV Langelei *St Alb* from 19; CF (ACF) from 17. *The Vicarage, 1 The Glebe, Kings Langley WD4 9HY* M: 07981-429338 E: james.a.mcdonald@live.co.uk

McDONALD, Prof James Damian (Jack). b 66. Pemb Coll Cam BA 87 MA 91 K Coll Lon MA 96 Strasbourg Univ Dr Théol 07 SS Hild & Bede Coll Dur PGCE 88. Qu Coll Birm 90. d 92 p 93. C Camberwell St Geo *S'wark* 92–95; Chapl G&C Coll Cam 95–99; Fell and Dean 99–06; Sen Proctor Cam Univ 02–03; Headmaster Sancton Wood Sch 06–09; PtO *Eur* 09–11; P-in-c Leuven 11–19; Asst Chapl and Can Th Brussels Cathl from 11. *29 Rue Capitaine Crespel, B1050 Brussels, Belgium* T: (0032) (49) 737 9365 E: president@anglican.be

MACDONALD, Mrs Janice Margaret. b 57. SCRTP 13. d 15 p 16. NSM Aldermaston and Woolhampton *Ox* 15–19; NSM Newbury St Nic and Speen from 19. *3 Heathland, Baughurst, Tadley RG26 5NF* T: 0118-981 3590 M: 07760-481854 E: macdonalds88@hotmail.co.uk *or* jmacdonald.awb@gmail.com

McDONALD, Lawrence Ronald. b 32. St Alb Minl Tr Scheme 84. d 87 p 88. NSM Sharnbrook and Knotting w Souldrop *St Alb* 87–90; C Bromham w Oakley and Stagsden 90–93; P-in-c Renhold 93–98; rtd 99; P-in-c Stevington *St Alb* 99–02; PtO from 02. *16 Townsend Road, Sharnbrook, Bedford MK44 1HY* T: (01234) 782849

MACDONALD, Malcolm Crawford. b 75. St Andr Univ MA 97 MLitt 98. Wycliffe Hall Ox BTh 05. d 05 p 06. C Kensington St Barn *Lon* 05–09; V Loughton St Mary *Chelmsf* from 09. *The Vicarage, 4 St Mary's Close, Loughton IG10 1BA* T: (020) 8508 7892 M: 07821-011435 E: malcolm@stmarysloughton.com

MACDONALD, Martin Stanley Harrison. b 51. Dur Univ BSc 72 ACA 75 FCA 82. SAOMC 98. d 01 p 02. NSM Tring *St Alb* 01–08; PtO *Wakef* 09–10; NSM Luddenden w Luddenden Foot 10–14; *Leeds* 14–21; NSM Erringden *Wakef* 10–15; *Leeds* 14–21; AD Calder Valley 15–17; PtO 21. *Broad Head End, Cragg Vale, Hebden Bridge HX7 5RT* T: (01422) 881543 M: 07777-691347 E: mshmacdonald@gmail.com

McDONALD, Robert William. b 72. Otago Univ BA 94 MA 96 Fitzw Coll Cam BA 06 MA 10 MPhil 07 PhD 12 LTCL 95. Ridley Hall Cam 04. d 10 p 11. C Shrewsbury St Geo w Greenfields *Lich* 10–13; Tutor Ridley Hall Cam from 13; Academic Dean from 18. *Ridley Hall, Ridley Hall Road, Cambridge CB3 9HG* T: (01223) 741068 F: 746581 E: rwm40@cam.ac.uk

MACDONALD, Sarah Jane Futcher. See McDONALD HADEN, Sarah Jane Futcher

McDONALD, Scott James. d 15 p 16. Willowfield *D & D* 15–16; C Down Cathl 16–19; V Lecale Gp 19–20; I Newry from 20. *Address temp unknown* M: 07429-132144 E: s.mcdonald.hammer@gmail.com

MACDONALD (formerly WIFFIN), Susan Elizabeth. b 51. Edin Th Coll 93. d 96 p 97. NSM Jedburgh *Edin* 96–98; C Galashiels 98–01; P-in-c Fochabers and Dioc Miss Co-ord *Mor* 01–04; Can St Andr Cathl Inverness 03–04; Miss and Min Officer *Ab* 05–07; R Edin Ch Ch 07–19; Dean Edin 12–16; Hon Can St Mary's Cathl 17–19; rtd 19. *4 Morningside Road, Edinburgh EH10 4DD* T: 0131-229 6556 *or* 229 0090 E: susan@6a.org.uk

MACDONALD, Warren. b 54. Monash Univ Aus BEng Leeds Univ MPhil Gothenburg Univ PhD 00 CEng CPEng MIEAust. Trin Coll Bris 93. d 95 p 96. NSM Iford *Win* 95–98; PtO 98–12 and from 20; *Sarum* 11–21. *5 St James's Square, Bournemouth BH5 2BX* T: (01202) 422131 F: 422101 M: 07774-497872 E: warren@warrenmacdonald.com *or* w.macdonald@imperial.ac.uk

McDONALD HADEN, Sarah Jane Futcher. b 90. Nottm Univ BA 12. St Mellitus Coll MA 16. d 16 p 17. C Hope Ch Islington *Lon* 16–20; LtO *Glouc* from 20. *17 White Cross Square, Cheltenham GL53 7AY* M: 07957-669157 E: sarah.futchermcdonald@gmail.com *or* sarah@cnc.org.uk

MACDONALD-MILNE, Canon Brian James. b 35. CCC Cam BA 58 MA 62 St Pet Coll Ox MA 81. Cuddesdon Coll 58. d 60 p 61. C Fleetwood St Pet *Blackb* 60–63; Solomon Is 64–78; Vanuatu 78–80; Acting Chapl Trin Coll Ox 81; Acting Chapl St Pet Coll Ox 81–82; Relief Chapl HM Pris Grendon and Spring Hill 81–82; Research Fell Qu Coll Birm 82–83; Hon Asst P Bordesley SS Alb and Patr *Birm* 82–83; R Landbeach *Ely* 83–88; V Waterbeach 83–88; OCM 83–88; R Radwinter w Hempstead *Chelmsf* 88–97; RD Saffron Walden 91–97; P-in-c The Sampfords 95–97; rtd 97; PtO *Ely* from 97; *Chelmsf* from 02; Dioc Rep Melanesian Miss and Papua New Guinea Ch Partnership from 99; Chapl Ely Chapter Guild of Servants of the Sanctuary 00–15; Adv Melanesian Brotherhood 05–13; PtO Melanesia from 05; Can Honiara from 07. *39 Way Lane, Waterbeach, Cambridge CB25 9NQ* T: (01223) 861631 E: bj.macdonaldmilne@homecall.co.uk

MACDONNELL, The Very Revd David. b 80. TCD BEd 02 BTh 09 MA 09. CITC. d 09 p 10. C Dublin Ch Ch Cathl Gp *D & G* 09–14; Treas V St Patr Cathl Dublin 11–14; I Dunfanaghy, Raymunterdoney and Tullaghbegley *D & R* 14–18; Dean Ossory *C, F & O* from 18; I Kilkenny w Aghour and Kilmanagh from 18. *The Deanery, The Close, Coach Road,*

Kilkenny, R95 K2XC, Republic of Ireland T: (00353) (56) 772
1516 E: ossorydean@gmail.com
McDONNELL, Mrs Mavis Marian. b 42. d 98 p 99.
OLM Warrington St Ann *Liv* 98–12; rtd 12. *32 Shaws
Avenue, Warrington   WA2 8AX   T: (01925)   634408*
E: mmavis@aol.com
McDONOUGH, David Sean. b 55. d 89 p 90. C Moseley
St Mary *Birm* 89–92; TV Glascote and Stonydelph
Lich 92–11; R Anstey and Thurcaston w Cropston *Leic*
11–21; rtd 21. *35 Hillcrest Close, Tamworth B79 8PA*
E: davidsmcdonough@outlook.com
McDONOUGH, Terence. b 57. St Jo Coll Nottm LTh 86. d 89
p 90. C Linthorpe *York* 89–94; TV Heworth H Trin 94–98;
V Heworth Ch Ch 98–11; P-in-c York St Thos w St Maurice
06–09; V Fulford 11–21; RD City of York 12–18; rtd 21; PtO
York from 21. *Address temp unknown*
McDOUGALL, David Robin. b 61. Avery Hill Coll CertEd
BEd 84. Ridley Hall Cam 85. d 87 p 88. C Bletchley *Ox*
87–91; C High Wycombe 91–93; C E Twickenham St Steph
Lon 93–02; P-in-c Upper Sunbury St Sav 02–14; AD
Spelthorne 10–14; R Bletchley *Ox* from 14. *The Rectory, 101
Whalley Drive, Bletchley, Milton Keynes MK3 6HX* T: (01908)
630305 *or* 366531
McDOUGALL, Mrs Denise Alma. b 48. Ban Coll TCert 69.
NOC 00. d 03 p 04. NSM Waterloo Ch Ch and St Jo
Liv 03–09; Chapl St Fran of Assisi City Academy
Liv 05–09; NSM Gt Crosby St Faith and Waterloo
Park St Mary *Liv* 09–13; rtd 13; PtO *Liv* from 16. *58
Hartley Crescent, Southport PR8 4SQ*   T: (01704) 550590
E: revdenisemcdougall@gmail.com
McDOUGALL, Sally-Anne. b 64. Glas Univ BMus 86 Edin
Univ BD 04. TISEC 01. d 04 p 11. C Glas St Marg 04–06; C
Studley *Sarum* 10–12; Bp's Dom Chapl *Linc* 12–17; PV *Linc*
Cathl 13–17; Can Res and Prec Linc Cathl 17–20; Dep Dir
RSCM from 20; PtO *Sarum* from 21. *Royal School of Church
Music, 19 The Close, Salisbury SP1 2EB* T: (01722) 424848
E: smcdougall@rscm.com
MacDOUGALL, William Duncan. b 47. Anglia Ruskin Univ
MA 04. St Jo Coll Nottm BTh 74 LTh 74. d 74 p 75. C
Highbury New Park St Aug *Lon* 74–77; C Tunbridge Wells
St Jo *Roch* 77–78; SAMS Argentina 78–82; V Rashcliffe and
Lockwood *Wakef* 83–87; V Tonbridge St Steph *Roch* 87–03; RD
Tonbridge 01–03; Dir Past and Evang Studies Trin Coll Bris
03–12; rtd 12; P-in-c Bradley Stoke N CD *Bris* 12–15; PtO *Roch*
16–19; C Chiddingstone w Chiddingstone Causeway 19–21;
C Penshurst and Fordcombe 19–21; C Penshurst, Fordcombe
and the Chiddingstone Chs 21. *The Rectory, Chiddingstone,
Edenbridge TN8 7AH* T: (01892) 870442 M: 07710-067239
E: williammacdougall0@gmail.com
McDOWALL, Julian Thomas. b 39. CCC Cam BA 62 MA 67
Barrister 61. Linc Th Coll 62. d 64 p 65. C Rugby St Andr
Cov 64–70; C-in-c Stoke Hill CD *Guildf* 70–72; V Stoke Hill
72–76; R Elstead 76–91; V Thursley 82–91; TV Wellington
and Distr *B & W* 91–93; C Lymington *Win* 93–04; rtd 04;
PtO *Win* from 04. *Juniper Cottage, 20 Solent Avenue, Lymington
SO41 3SD* T: (01590) 676750
McDOWALL, Robert Angus (Robin). b 39. AKC 66. d 67
p 68. C Bishopwearmouth St Mich w St Hilda *Dur* 67–69; CF
69–05; Sen CF 80–91; Asst Chapl Gen 91–94; QHC 93–05;
rtd 05; PtO *York* 05–19. *c/o Crockford, Church House, 27 Great
Smith Street, London SW1P 3AZ*
McDOWALL, Roger Ian. b 40. AKC 64. d 65 p 66. C Peterlee
Dur 65–68; C Weaste *Man* 68–70; C Tonge Moor 70–73; V
Whitworth St Bart 73–80; TV Torre *Ex* 80–88; V Torre All
SS 88–00; Chapl S Devon Tech Coll Torbay 80–00; rtd 04;
PtO *Ex* from 14. *Upper Borohaye, 51 Petitor Road, Torquay
TQ1 4QF* T: (01803) 324223 E: roger@sagart.co.uk
✠**McDOWELL, The Most Revd Francis John.** b 56. QUB
BA 78. CITC BTh 93. d 96 p 97 c 11. C Antrim *Conn* 96–99;
I Ballyrashane w Kildollagh 99–02; I Dundela St Mark *D & D*
02–11; Bp Clogh 11–20; Abp Arm from 20. *Church House,
46 Abbey Street, Armagh BT61 7DZ* T: (028) 3752 7144
E: archbishop@armagh.anglican.org
McDOWELL, Canon Peter Kerr. b 69. QUB BA 91. CITC
BTh 94. d 94 p 95. C Lisburn St Paul *Conn* 94–98; C
Arm St Mark 98–99; I Belfast Upper Malone (Epiphany)
Conn 99–05; I Ballywillan from 05; Can St Patr Cathl
Dublin from 11. *The Rectory, 10 Coleraine Road, Portrush
BT56 8EA*   T: (028)   7082   4298   M: 07724-072944
E: revpetermcdowell@hotmail.co.uk
McDOWELL, Sheilah Rosamond Girgis. b 72. d 05. NSM
Hammersmith H Innocents and St Jo *Lon* 05–13; PtO from
13. *36 Avenue Gardens, Teddington TW11 0BH* T: (020) 8943
9259 E: rosamond.mcdowell@btinternet.com

McDOWELL, William. b 61. Ox Min Course 12. d 15 p 16.
NSM E Downland *Ox* from 15. *16 Culver Road, Newbury
RG14 7AS* M: 07877-358161 E: mcdowell@ntlworld.com
McELHINNEY, Robert Stephen. b 70. Aston Univ BSc 91.
CITC BTh 05. d 05 p 06. C Kill *D & G* 05–08; C Drumglass
w Moygashel *Arm* 08–11; P-in-c Derryvolgie *Conn* 11–15;
I 15–18; Miss Dir SAMS (Ireland) from 18. *SAMS Ireland, 1
Irwin Crescent, Lurgan, Craigavon BT66 7EZ* T: (028) 3831
0144 E: smcelh@gmail.com *or* stephen@samsireland.com
McENDOO, Canon Neil Gilbert. b 50. TCD BA 72. CITC 75.
d 75 p 76. C Cregagh *D & D* 75–79; C Dublin St Ann *D & G*
79–82; I Dublin Rathmines w Harold's Cross 82–17; Can
Ch Ch Cathl Dublin 92–02; Preb 02–05; Chan 05–15; Prec
15–17; rtd 17. *21 Derreen Drive, Harbour View, Wicklow Town,
Co Wicklow, A67 NC86, Republic of Ireland* M: (00353) 87-
989 3118 E: neil.mcendoo@gmail.com
McEUNE, Patrick John. b 55. Sarum Coll MA 12. d 04 p 05.
NSM White Horse *Sarum* 04–12; TV 07–12; Bp's Chapl
08–12; R Bradwell on Sea and St Lawrence *Chelmsf* 12–14;
P-in-c Fingringhoe w E Donyland and Abberton etc
14–18; C W w E Mersea, Peldon, Gt and Lt Wigborough
15–18; R Binbrook Gp *Linc* from 18. *The Rectory, Louth
Road, Binbrook, Market Rasen LN8 6BJ* M: 07411-761883
E: mceune@gmail.com *or* frpatrick@btinternet.com
MACEY, Preb Anthony Keith Frank. b 46. St Steph Ho Ox 69.
d 71 p 72. C St Thos 71–76; V Wembury 76–88; RD
Ivybridge 83–91; V Cockington 88–12; RD Torbay 98–03;
Preb Ex Cathl 05–12; rtd 12; PtO *Ex* from 12. *28 All Saints
Road, Torquay TQ1 3RD* T: (01803) 329540
MACEY, Michael David. b 81. Ex Univ BA 03 St Jo Coll Dur
MATM 08. Cranmer Hall Dur 03. d 05 p 06. C Dartmouth
and Dittisham *Ex* 05–08; Min Can and Prec Westmr Abbey
08–14; V Boxmoor St Jo *St Alb* from 14; AD Hemel Hempstead
from 20; PV Westmr Abbey from 14. *Boxmoor Vicarage,
10 Charles Street, Hemel Hempstead HP1 1JH* T: (01442)
243258 M: 07972-266881 E: vicar@stjohnsboxmoor.org.uk
McFADDEN, Canon Ronald Bayle. b 30. TCD BA 53 MA 55.
d 54 p 55. C Drumglass *Arm* 54–58; S Africa 58–62; Bp's Dom
Chapl *D & D* 62–64; C Dundela St Mark 62–64; V Pateley
Bridge and Greenhow Hill *Ripon* 64–73; V Knaresborough
St Jo 73–79; P-in-c Knaresborough H Trin 78–79; Can Res
Ripon Cathl 79–90; rtd 90; Chapl Qu Mary's Sch Baldersby
Park 90–00; PtO *Ripon* 90–14; Leeds 14–16; York 97–13. *12 Ure
Bank Terrace, Ripon HG4 1JG* T: (01765) 604043
McFADYEN, Donald Colin Ross. b 63. Wolfs Coll Cam
BTh 00 Peterho Cam MPhil 02 SS Coll Cam PhD 06. Ridley
Hall Cam 97. d 01 p 02. NSM Haslingfield w Harlton
and Gt and Lt Eversden *Ely* 01–05; P-in-c Bassingbourn
05–12; P-in-c Whaddon 05–12; Course Dir Ridley Hall
Cam 05–08; V Orton Longueville w Bottlebridge *Ely*
12–14; P-in-c Orton Waterville 14; V The Ortons 14–16;
P-in-c Sawtry and Glatton 16–17; RD Yaxley 14–16; V
Warmington, Tansor and Cotterstock etc *Pet* from 20.
*The Vicarage, 4 Stamford Lane, Warmington, Peterborough
PE8 6TW* M: 07595-539507 E: donald.mcfadyen@me.com
or vicar.warmingtonbenefice@gmail.com
McFADYEN (formerly TALBOT), Canon Mair Josephine. b 59.
Univ Coll Lon BA 84. Ridley Hall Cam 85. d 88 p 94. C Gt
Yarmouth *Nor* 88–94; Sen Asst P Raveningham Gp 94–99;
Chapl Norfolk Mental Health Care NHS Trust 94–02;
Bp's Adv for Women's Min *Nor* 01–04; P-in-c Watton w
Carbrooke and Ovington 02–06; Project Manager Magd Gp
06–10; Chapl Norfolk Community Health and Care NHS
Trust 10–16; NSM Nor St Geo Colegate 14–17; Hon Can Nor
Cathl 02–17; rtd 17; PtO *Nor* from 17. *Crow Hall Barn, Crow
Hall Lane, Cawston, Norwich NR10 4TA* T: (01603) 872562
E: mair.mcfadyen@gmail.com
McFADYEN, Canon Phillip. b 44. K Coll Lon BD 69 AKC 69
MTh 70 ATD. St Aug Coll Cant 69. d 71 p 72. C Sheff
St Mark Broomhall 71–74; Chapl Keswick Hall Coll of
Educn 74–79; V Swardeston *Nor* 79–81; P-in-c E Carleton
79–81; P-in-c Intwood w Keswick 79–81; R Swardeston w
E Carleton, Intwood, Keswick etc 81–90; R Ranworth w
Panxworth, Woodbastwick etc 90–05; Dioc Clergy Tr Officer
90–98; P-in-c Nor St Geo Colegate 05–17; Relig Adv Anglia
TV 01–17; Hon Can Nor Cathl 97–17; rtd 17; PtO *Nor* from
17; Bp's Officer for Visual Arts from 01. *Crow Hall Barn, Crow
Hall Lane, Cawston, Norwich NR10 4TA* T: (01603) 872562
E: phillipmcfadyen@hotmail.com
McFARLAND, Darren William. b 71. QUB BA 93. CITC
BTh 96. d 96 p 97. C Greystones *D & G* 96–98; PV Ch Ch
Cathl Dublin 97–99; P-in-c Clydebank *Glas* 99–02; Asst Dioc
Miss 21 Co-ord 99–02; R Paisley H Trin and St Barn 02–11; V
Headington *Ox* from 11. *The Vicarage, 33 St Andrew's Road,
Oxford OX3 9DL*   T: (01865) 761094   M: 07773-772610
E: vicar.headington@gmail.com

McFARLAND, Jonathan Hamilton. CITI. **d** 16 **p** 17. Carnalea *D & D* 16–17; C Urney w Sion Mills *D & R* from 17. *112 Melmount Road, Sion Mills, Strabane BT82 9PY* T: (028) 8165 9309 M: 07866-583991 E: jhmcfarland1969@gmail.com

McFARLANE, Catherine. b 72. Trin Coll Ox MA 93 Heythrop Coll Lon MA 98. ERMC 16. **d** 18 **p** 19. NSM Marston Morteyne w Lidlington *St Alb* 18–19; C 19–21; R St Bartholomew *Sarum* from 21. *The Rectory, Semley, Shaftesbury SP7 9AU* M: 07816-790447

MACFARLANE, Elizabeth Clare. b 71. St Hugh's Coll Ox BA 92 MA 03 St Cross Coll Ox DPhil 12. Ripon Coll Cuddesdon BA 02. **d** 03 **p** 04. C Watford St Mich *St Alb* 03–06; TV Gt Marlow w Marlow Bottom, Lt Marlow and Bisham *Ox* 06–11; Chapl and Fell St Jo Coll Ox from 11. *St John's College, Oxford OX1 3JP* T: (01865) 277660 F: 277435 E: elizabeth.macfarlane@sjc.ox.ac.uk

MACFARLANE, Iain Philip. b 64. Essex Univ BSc 85 W Sussex Inst of HE PGCE 88. Trin Coll Bris BA 99. **d** 99 **p** 00. C Fishponds St Jo *Bris* 99–03; TV Yate from 03. *The Vicarage, 57 Brockworth, Bristol BS37 8SJ* T: (01454) 322921

McFARLANE, Iain Scott. b 70. St Jo Coll Nottm 02. **d** 04 **p** 05. C Malvern St Andr and Malvern Wells and Wyche *Worc* 04–07; V Taunton Lyngford *B & W* 07–14; P-in-c Boyatt Wood *Win* 14–19; Chapl Countess Mountbatten Hospice from 20. *Countess Mountbatten Hospice, Botley Road, West End, Southampton SO30 3JB* M: 07834-191507 E: revmcfarlane@gmail.com

✠**McFARLANE, The Rt Revd Janet Elizabeth.** b 64. Sheff Univ BMedSci 87 St Jo Coll Dur BA 92. Cranmer Hall Dur 93. **d** 93 **p** 94 **c** 16. Par Dn Stafford *Lich* 93–94; C 94–96; Chapl and Min Can Ely Cathl 96–99; Dioc Communications Officer *Nor* 99–16; Hon PV Nor Cathl 00–09; Bp's Chapl 01–09; Adn Nor 09–16; Warden of Readers 15–16; Suff Bp Repton *Derby* 16–20; Can Res Lich Cathl from 20; Hon Asst Bp Lich from 20. *6 Vicars Close, Lichfield WS13 7LE* T: (01543) 251146 E: jan.mcfarlane@lichfield-cathedral.org

MACFARLANE, Nigel Ian. b 56. Qu Foundn (Course) 13. **d** 18 **p** 19. NSM Drayton in Hales *Lich* from 18. *19 Pendrel Close, Buntingsdale, Market Drayton TF9 2ET* T: (01630) 638016 E: curateofstmarys@gmail.com

McGAFFIN, Canon Judith Hilary. CITC. **d** 09 **p** 10. NSM Donagheady *D & R* 09–14; I Fahan Lower and Upper from 14; Can Raphoe Cathl from 21. *The Rectory, Cahir O'Doherty Avenue, Buncrana, Co Donegal, F93 D710, Republic of Ireland* M: 07834-561433 E: judimcgaffin@aol.com

McGARRIGLE, John James Samuel (Don). b 51. QUB BSc 77 CEng 85 MIET 85. ERMC 12. **d** 14 **p** 15. C Ketton, Collyweston, Easton-on-the-Hill and Tinwell *Pet* 14–17; C Ketton and Tinwell 17–18; P-in-c Gt Casterton and Tickencote and Lt Casterton w Pickworth from 18. *48 Main Street, Greetham, Oakham LE15 7NL* T: (01572) 811343 M: 07802-401798 E: escapeenergy@btconnect.com

McGARVEY, Mrs Muriel Dorothy. b 51. Dur Univ BA 18. SEITE 12. **d** 14 **p** 15. NSM Eynsford w Farningham and Lullingstone *Roch* 14–20; R from 20. *17 Tilmans Mead, Farningham, Dartford DA4 0BY* T: (01322) 863050 M: 07969-175768 E: revdmcgarvey@gmail.com

McGEARY, Peter. b 59. K Coll Lon BD AKC. Chich Th Coll 84. **d** 86 **p** 87. C Brighton St Pet and St Nic w Chpl Royal *Chich* 86–90; C St Marylebone All SS *Lon* 90–95; P-in-c Hayes St Anselm 95–97; V 97–98; V St Geo-in-the-East St Mary from 98; PV Westmr Abbey from 00. *The Clergy House, All Saints Court, 68 Johnson Street, London E1 0BQ* T/F: (020) 7790 0973 E: mcgeary@pmcg.demon.co.uk

McGEENEY, Noel. b 59. St Patr Coll Maynooth 80. **d** 83 **p** 84. PtO *St Alb* 11–13; TV Ouzel Valley from 13. *The Vicarage, 2 Reach Lane, Heath and Reach, Leighton Buzzard LU7 0AL* T: (01525) 237633 M: 07401-782427 E: saggart@yahoo.com

MacGEOCH, Preb David John Lamont. b 64. Bath Univ BSc 90 CQSW 90. Westcott Ho Cam 97. **d** 99 **p** 00. C Midsomer Norton w Clandown *B & W* 99–03; V Puriton and Pawlett 03–08; P-in-c Glastonbury w Meare 08–11; V from 11; RD Glastonbury from 11; Preb Wells Cathl from 20. *The Vicarage, 24 Wells Road, Glastonbury BA6 9DJ* T: (01458) 834281 E: vicarabbeyparish@btinternet.com

McGEOCH, Ms Helen Marie. b 68. Redcliffe Coll Glouc BA 12. Ripon Coll Cuddesdon 17. **d** 21. C Glouc St Jas and All SS and Ch Ch from 21. *34 Randwick Road, Tuffley, Gloucester GL4 0NJ* M: 07729-615993 E: helen.mcgeoch@sky.com

McGHIE, Clinton Adolphus. b 41. Univ of W Indies. **d** 78 **p** 79. Jamaica 78–96; PtO *Chelmsf* 96–97; P-in-c Highams Park All SS 97–02; V 02–11; rtd 11. *10 Sussex Way, Billericay CM12 0FA* T: (01277) 634389 E: clint1010@sky.com

MacGILLIVRAY, Jonathan Martin. b 53. Aber Univ MA 75. Coll of Resurr Mirfield. **d** 80 **p** 81. C Hulme Ascension *Man*

80–84; P-in-c Birch St Agnes 84–85; R 85–91; V Hurst 91–96; Chapl Tameside Gen Hosp 92–96; Dir of Ords and OLM Officer *Man* 96–02; V Carrington *S'well* 02–13; P-in-c Darton *Leeds* 13–16; P-in-c Cawthorne 13–16; V Darton w Staincross and Mapplewell 16–18; rtd 18. *Rosa Mystica, 31 Barnsley Road, Cawthorne, Barnsley S75 4HW* E: j.macg@virgin.net

McGINLEY, Canon Jack Francis. b 36. ALCD 65. **d** 65 **p** 66. C Erith St Paul *Roch* 65–70; C Morden *S'wark* 70–74; V New Catton Ch Ch *Nor* 74–94; RD Nor N 84–89; Hon Can Nor Cathl 90–94; R Carlton-in-the-Willows *S'well* 94–02; R Colwick 96–02; rtd 02; PtO *Nor* 03–16; *Bris* 17–19. *82 Railton Jones Close, Stoke Gifford, Bristol BS34 8BF* T: 0117-979 3870 E: jack.mcginley14@btinternet.com

McGINLEY, John Charles. b 69. Birm Univ BSocSc 90. Trin Coll Bris BA 96. **d** 96 **p** 97. C Hounslow H Trin w St Paul *Lon* 96–00; TV Hinckley H Trin *Leic* 00–04; TR 04–09; V Leic H Trin w St Jo 09–20; C 20–21; P-in-c Emmaus Par Team 14–16; P-in-c Leic H Apostles 17–21; Hon Can Leic Cathl 18–21; Public Preacher *Lon* from 21; Exec Dir 10,000 New Ch Project from 21. *St Edmund The King Church, Lombard Street, London EC3V 9EA* E: 19stj69@gmail.com

McGINTY, Canon Nicola Jane. b 61. Bath Univ BSc 83 Warwick Univ MBA 06. Qu Coll Birm MA 09. **d** 09 **p** 10. NSM Barrow upon Soar w Walton le Wolds *Leic* 09–12; NSM Wymeswold and Prestwold w Hoton 09–12; PtO from 12; Hon Can Leic Cathl from 18. *5 Station Road, Rearsby, Leicester LE7 4YX* T: (01664) 424869 E: nicky@njmcginty.co.uk

McGIRR, Canon William Eric. b 43. CITC 68. **d** 71 **p** 72. C Carrickfergus *Conn* 71–74; C Mt Merrion *D & D* 74–77; I Donacavey w Barr *Clogh* 77–88; I Ballybeen *D & D* 88–94; I Magheraculmoney *Clogh* 94–10; Can Clogh Cathl 95–10; Chan Clogh Cathl 06–10; rtd 10. *11 Castle Manor, Kesh, Enniskillen BT93 1RT* T: (028) 6863 2221 E: eric@gallagh.com

McGIVERN, Ann Margaret. *See* SIMPSON, Ann Margaret

McGLADDERY, David John. b 62. Homerton Coll Cam BEd 85 Univ of Wales (Cardiff) MA 93 Ox Brookes Univ MA 17. St Mich Coll Llan 02. **d** 05 **p** 06. NSM Monmouth w Overmonnow etc *Mon* 05–09; V 09–18; AD Monmouth 13–18; Asst Chapl Mon Sch 05–18; Can St Woolos Cathl *Mon* 17–18; R Horfield H Trin *Bris* from 18. *The Rectory, 11 Audrey Walk, Bristol BS9 4SJ* T: 0117-401 3042 E: rector.horfield@gmail.com

McGLINCHEY, Patrick Gerard. b 59. NUU BA 82 Nottm Univ BTh 95 MA 06 QUB PhD 13. St Jo Coll Nottm 93. **d** 95 **p** 96. C Kettering Ch the King *Pet* 95–97; C Gorleston St Andr *Nor* 97–02; Assoc Min Cliff Park Community Ch 99–02; Chapl and Dean of Res QUB 03–09; TCD from 09; Lect Ch of Ireland Th Inst from 09. *26 Riverside, Watery Lane, Clondalkin, Dublin 22, Republic of Ireland* T: (00353) (1) 499 7279 M: (00353) 89-475 3105 *or* 07500-464542 E: patrickmcglinchey@theologicalinstitute.ie

McGLYNN, Mrs Lesley Anne. b 59. St Mellitus Coll BA 16. **d** 15 **p** 16. OLM Canvey Is *Chelmsf* 15–19; NSM from 19. *3 Thorney Bay Road, Canvey Island SS8 0HG* T: (01268) 693218 M: 07795-844105 E: lesleymcglynn@hotmail.co.uk

McGOVERN, Leisa Caroline. *See* POTTER, Leisa Caroline

McGOWAN, Anthony Charles. b 57. Jes Coll Cam BA 79 MA 83. Coll of Resurr Mirfield 80. **d** 82 **p** 83. C Milford Haven *St D* 82–85; C Penistone and Thurlstone *Wakef* 85–88; Asst Chapl Radcliffe Infirmary Ox 91–94; Chapl Radcliffe Infirmary NHS Trust 94–99; Chapl Ox Radcliffe Hosps NHS Trust 99–04; V Northampton H Trin and St Paul *Pet* from 05. *The Vicarage, 24 Edinburgh Road, Northampton NN2 6PH* T: (01604) 711468 E: anthony.mcgowan@tiscali.co.uk

McGOWAN, Daniel Richard Hugh. b 71. Oak Hill Th Coll. **d** 03 **p** 04. C Peterlee *Dur* 03–07; TV Morden *S'wark* 07–16; V Banbury St Paul *Ox* from 16. *St Paul's House, Bretch Hill, Banbury OX16 0LR*

McGOWAN, James. b 83. York St Jo Coll BA 04 St Jo Coll Dur BA 11 Ches Univ MA 17 St Hild Coll Dur PGCE 05. Cranmer Hall Dur 08. **d** 11 **p** 12. C St German's Cathl *S & M* 11–14; C W Coast 12–14; V Malew and Santan 14–19; V Fenham St Jas and St Basil *Newc* from 19; Chapl Dame Allan's Schs Newc from 19. *The Vicarage, Wingrove Road North, Newcastle upon Tyne NE4 9EJ* M: 07485-055178 E: revdjamesmcgowan@outlook.com

McGRATH, Gavin John. b 53. Marietta Coll (USA) BA 76 Trin Episc Sch for Min MDiv 81 Dur Univ PhD 90. **d** 81 **p** 82. USA 81–87 and 99–05; C Fulwood *Sheff* 87–95; Assoc Th Prof Trin Episc Sch for Min Ambridge 99–05; PtO *S'wark* 07–12; C Sevenoaks St Nic *Roch* 12–21; rtd 21. *Forbes Lodge, Edinburgh Road, Gifford, Haddington EH41 4JE* E: mcgrath.gavin@gmail.com

McGRATH, Joanna Ruth. *See* COLLICUTT McGRATH, Joanna Ruth

McGRATH, John. b 49. Salford Univ BSc 78 Univ of Wales (Lamp) MA 10 Man Poly CertEd 79. NOC 82. **d** 85 **p** 86. C Horwich *Man* 85–88; P-in-c Hillock 88–89; V 89–94; V York St Luke 94–97; V Hollinwood *Man* 97–02; P-in-c Oldham St Chad Limeside 97–02; V Hollinwood and Limeside 02–03; TV Turton Moorland 03–07; P-in-c Littleborough, Calderbrook and Shore 07–13; V Littleborough 13–14; rtd 14; PtO *Blackb* 15–17; Hon C Burnley St Pet and St Steph 17–19. *15 Hall Park Avenue, Burnley BB10 4JJ* T: (01282) 760256 E: johnbede@live.co.uk

McGREGOR, Alexander Scott. b 72. Ch Ch Ox BA 95 MA 00 Barrister 96. SAOMC 03. **d** 06 **p** 07. NSM Harrow St Mary *Lon* 06–09; NSM Pimlico St Mary Bourne Street 09–14; NSM Pimlico St Barn 09–15; NSM Clerkenwell H Redeemer from 15; Legal Adv Legal Office Nat Ch Inst 06–08; Dep Legal Adv Gen Syn and Abps' Coun 09–19; Chief Legal Adv from 19; Dep Solicitor Ch Commrs 16–19; Official Solicitor from 19; Dep Chan *Ox* 07–13; Chan from 13. *Church House, 27 Great Smith Street, London SW1P 3AZ* T: (020) 7898 1748 E: alexander.mcgregor@churchofengland.org

MacGREGOR, Donald Alexander Thomson. b 52. Loughb Univ BSc 75 Nottm Univ MA 97 Leic Univ CertEd 78. St Jo Coll Nottm 91. **d** 93 **p** 94. C Walmley *Birm* 93–96; C Braunstone *Leic* 96–97; TV 97–99; Chapl Loughb Univ 99–04; V Fishguard w Llanychar and Pontfaen w Morfil etc *St D* 04–13; P-in-c Llanrhian and Mathry w Grandstone etc 13–17; AD Dewisland and Fishguard 13–14; rtd 17; PtO *St D* from 17. *Amber Cottage, 1 Lower Moor, St Davids, Haverfordwest SA62 6RP* E: donmacg@live.co.uk

McGREGOR, Mrs Eileen. b 50. Ex Univ BA 71. STETS 07. **d** 10 **p** 11. NSM Fulham All SS *Lon* 10–16; NSM Chiswick St Nic w St Mary 16–20; rtd 20; PtO *Lon* from 20. *44 Abinger Road, London W4 1EX* T: (020) 8994 2088 M: 07899-928785 E: mcgeileen@aol.com

McGREGOR, Mrs Lorraine Louise. b 59. Sarum Th Coll 02. **d** 05 **p** 06. OLM Colehill *Sarum* from 05. *Tapiola, Marianne Road, Wimborne BH21 2SQ* T: (01202) 886519 E: lorry886519@gmail.com

McGREGOR, Mrs Lynn. b 61. Ches Coll of HE BTh 00. NOC 97. **d** 00 **p** 01. C Colne and Villages *Blackb* 00–03; C Gt Harwood 03–06; P-in-c Wigan St Mich *Liv* 06–07; V 07–10; P-in-c Platt Bridge 10–17; rtd 17. *29 Moor Lane, Darwen BB3 0EJ*

MacGREGOR, Preb Neil. b 35. Keble Coll Ox BA 60 MA 80. Wells Th Coll. **d** 65 **p** 66. C Bath Bathwick St Mary w Woolley *B & W* 65–70; R Oare w Culbone 70–74; C Lynton, Brendon, Countisbury and Lynmouth *Ex* 70–74; P-in-c Kenn w Kingston Seymour *B & W* 74–76; R 76–80; R Wem and V Lee Brockhurst *Lich* 80–01; P-in-c Loppington w Newtown 95–01; RD Wem and Whitchurch 95–01; Preb Lich Cathl 97–01; rtd 01; PtO *Heref* 01–20. *19 Castle View Terrace, Ludlow SY8 2NG* T: (01584) 872671 E: neil@springhatch.plus.com

McGREGOR, Nigel Selwyn. b 47. FCA 69. Sarum & Wells Th Coll 87. **d** 89 **p** 90. C Charlton Kings St Mary *Glouc* 89–92; P-in-c Seale *Guildf* 92–95; P-in-c Puttenham and Wanborough 92–95; R Seale, Puttenham and Wanborough 95–04; R Barming *Roch* 04–12; rtd 12; PtO *York* from 12. *14 Chestnut Croft, Hemingbrough, Selby YO8 6UD* E: nigelmcgregor@ymail.com

McGREGOR, Stephen Paul. b 55. **d** 03 **p** 04. OLM Tonge Fold *Man* 03–10; OLM Leverhulme 10–20; rtd 20; PtO *Man* from 20. *32 Rawcliffe Avenue, Bolton BL2 6JX* T: (01204) 391205 E: steve.mcgregor@sky.com

McGUFFIE, Duncan Stuart. b 45. Man Univ MA 70 Regent's Park Coll Ox DPhil 80. S Dios Minl Tr Scheme 84. **d** 85 **p** 85. C Sholing *Win* 85–89; V Clavering and Langley w Arkesden etc *Chelmsf* 89–10; rtd 10; PtO *Sheff* 11–21. *Ferry Hill Farm, Barmby-on-the-Marsh, Goole DN14 7HX* T: (01757) 630589 E: virginia.mcguffie5@gmail.com

McGUINNESS, Canon Gordon Baxter. b 57. St Andr Univ BSc 79 BNC Ox MSc 80. Oak Hill NSM Course 86. **d** 89 **p** 90. NSM Loudwater *Ox* 89–92; C Chilwell *S'well* 92–01; TR Ellesmere Port *Ches* 01–09; R from 09; Hon Can Ches Cathl from 14. *The Rectory, Vale Road, Whitby, Ellesmere Port CH65 9AY* T: 0151-356 8351 *or* 355 2516 E: revgordon@supanet.com *or* revgogs@icloud.com

McGURK, The Ven Michael Joseph Patrick. b 68. St Jo Coll Nottm 05. **d** 07 **p** 08. C Haughton St Mary *Man* 07–09; C Harpurhey 09–10; R 10–17; AD N Man 12–17; Adn Liv from 17. *445 Aigburth Road, Liverpool L19 3PA* M: 07811-360432 E: rev.mikemcgurk@hotmail.co.uk

MACHA, David. b 65. Keele Univ BA 88 CertEd 88 St Jo Coll Dur BA 97 Nottm Univ MA 03 SOAS MA 20. Cranmer Hall Dur 94. **d** 97 **p** 98. C Loughborough Em and St Mary in Charnwood *Leic* 97–01; CMS Tanzania 02–09; R Linton in Craven *Bradf* 09–14; *Leeds* 14–19; P-in-c Burnsall w Rylstone *Bradf* 09–14; *Leeds* 14–19; R Linton, Burnsall and Rylstone

from 19. *The Rectory, Hebden Road, Grassington, Skipton BD23 5LA* T: (01756) 752575 E: mchdmacha@gmail.com

McHAFFIE, Canon Alistair. b 57. Oak Hill Th Coll 92. **d** 94 **p** 95. C Braintree *Chelmsf* 94–98; R Falkland Is 98–03; V Leyland St Jo *Blackb* 03–18; AD Leyland 11–16; R Preston Risen Lord from 18; AD Preston 19–21; Hon Can Blackb Cathl from 17. *St Matthew's Vicarage, 20 Fishwick View, Preston PR1 4YA* E: alistair@mchaffie.com *or* alistairmchaffie@rocketmail.com

McHALE, John Michael. b 61. Ch Ch Coll Cant BA 84 Univ of Wales (Cardiff) BTh 08 Kingston Univ PGCE 89. St Mich Coll Llan 03. **d** 08 **p** 09. NSM Llandingat w Myddfai *St D* 08–10; Chapl Llandovery Coll 08–10; Chapl Lich Cathl Sch and Prec's V Lich Cathl 10–12; Chapl Wycliffe Coll Glos 12–19; V Berkeley w Wick, Breadstone, Newport, Stone etc *Glouc* 19–20; PtO 20–21. *44 Courthill Park, Auldgirth, Dumfries DG2 0RR* M: 07912-043374 E: revjohn61@gmail.com

MACHAM, Canon Anna. b 77. Trin Coll Ox BA 98 Cam Univ BA 02 MPhil 04. Ridley Hall Cam 00. **d** 04 **p** 05. C Cheshunt *St Alb* 04–07; Succ S'wark Cathl 07–13; Chapl K Coll Lon 07–13; P-in-c Camberwell St Phil and St Mark *S'wark* 13–19; Can Res Sarum Cathl from 19. *54 The Close, Salisbury SP1 2EL* E: a.macham@btinternet.com

McHARDY, David William. b 61. Edin Univ BD 88 BD 90 PhD 97 Aber Coll of Educn DCE 82. Edin Th Coll 85. **d** 88 **p** 03. C Dumfries *Glas* 88–89; Lect in World Religions Open Univ 97–08; Hon C Oldmeldrum *Ab* 99–08; P-in-c 08; Chapl Blue Coat Sch Reading 08–10; V Meir Heath and Normacot *Lich* from 10. *St Francis's Vicarage, Sandon Road, Stoke-on-Trent ST3 7LH* T: (01782) 398585 M: 07938-956755 E: david.mchardy@hotmail.co.uk

MACHELL, Georgina. b 59. Open Univ MEd 05 Mutare Coll Zimbabwe CertEd 81. Linc Sch of Th and Min 09. **d** 12 **p** 13. OLM Ruskington Gp *Linc* 12–13; OLM N Lafford Gp 13–17; R E Loveden from 17. *The Rectory, 117 Ermine Street, Ancaster, Grantham NG32 3QL* M: 07970-835611 E: rectoreastloveden19@gmail.com

McHENRY, Brian Edward. b 50. CBE 08. New Coll Ox BA 73 MA 77 Cant Ch Ch Univ BA 12 Barrister 76. SEITE 05. **d** 08 **p** 09. C Deptford St Paul *S'wark* 08–11; V Orpington All SS *Roch* 11–17; rtd 17; PtO *Cant* from 18. *14 Richmond Gardens, Canterbury CT2 8ES* T: (01227) 781899 M: 07780-308220 E: brian@mchenry.co.uk

MACHIN, Mrs Jacqueline June. b 62. STETS. **d** 10 **p** 11. C Romsey *Win* 10–14; R The Downs from 14. *c/o Crockford, Church House, 27 Great Smith Street, London SW1P 3AZ* E: revdjax@downsbenefice.org.uk

MACHIN, Roy Anthony. b 38. BA 79. Oak Hill Th Coll 76. **d** 79 **p** 80. C Halliwell St Pet *Man* 79–83; V Eccleston St Luke *Liv* 83–91; V Kendal St Thos and Crook *Carl* 91–99; V Wigan St Barn Marsh Green *Liv* 99–03; rtd 03; PtO *Man* from 03. *56 Ferndown Road, Harwood, Bolton BL2 3NN* T/F: (01204) 362220 E: roy.machin@ntlworld.com

MACHIRIDZA, Canon Douglas Tafara. b 71. Univ of Zimbabwe BSW 99 Birm Univ BPhil 07 St Edm Coll Cam BTh 10. Westcott Ho Cam 08. **d** 10 **p** 11. C Perry Barr *Birm* 10–14; C Perry Beeches 10–14; V Handsworth St Andr 14–20; P-in-c Handsworth St Jas 18–20; AD Handsworth and Central from 20; Hon Can Birm Cathl from 21. *12 Nursery Drive, Handsworth, Birmingham B20 2SW* T: 0121-448 4897 M: 07887-741029 E: dtmachiridza@yahoo.co.uk *or* ad.handsworthandcentral@cofebirmingham.com

McHUGH, Brian Robert. b 50. Keele Univ BA 72 Keele Univ CertEd 73 IEng 92 MIMA 98 CMath 98. S Dios Minl Tr Scheme 79. **d** 82 **p** 83. NSM Sarisbury *Portsm* 82–86; NSM Shedfield 86–06; NSM Shedfield and Wickham 07–18; Perm to Offic Cyprus and the Gulf from 10; PtO *Portsm* from 18. *28 Siskin Close, Bishops Waltham, Southampton SO32 1RQ* T: (01489) 896658 E: brian.mchugh@bcs.org.uk

McHUGH, Michael. b 57. **d** 87 **p** 88. In RC Ch 87–05; NSM Cley Hill Warminster *Sarum* 05–07; C Salisbury St Thos and St Edm 07–10; TV Vale of Pewsey 10–12; TR Savernake from 12. *The Rectory, Church Street, Great Bedwyn, Marlborough SN8 3PF* T: (01672) 870779 E: mtmch@hotmail.com

McILROY (née NEWBY), Mrs Claire. b 77. UWE BSc 00 Ox Brookes Univ MA 09. Trin Coll Bris 12. **d** 14 **p** 15. C Torpoint *Truro* 14–15; C Antony w Sheviock from 14; C Antony w Sheviock and Torpoint 14–18; Asst Chapl Univ of St Mark and St Jo from 18. *16 Compton Park Road, Plymouth PL3 5BU* M: 07766-556321 E: revclairemcilroy@gmail.com

McINDOE, Darren Lee. b 76. Univ of Wales (Lamp) BA 97. Trin Coll Bris BA 05. **d** 06 **p** 07. C Stratford St Jo w Ch Ch and St Jas *Chelmsf* 06–09; C Forest Gate Em w Upton Cross 09–10; R Burslem *Lich* 10–19; TV Hanley H Ev 13–19; P-in-c Tye Green w Netteswell *Chelmsf* from 19; PtO *Eur* from 16. *The Rectory, Tawney Road, Harlow CM18 6QR* M: 07886-502307 E: rev.darren.mcindoe@gmail.com

MACINNES, Canon David Rennie. b 32. Jes Coll Cam BA 55 MA 59. Ridley Hall Cam 55. d 57 p 58. C Gillingham St Mark *Roch* 57–61; C St Helen Bishopsgate w St Martin Outwich *Lon* 61–67; Prec Birm Cathl 67–78; Angl Adv ATV 67–82; Cen TV 82–93; Dioc Missr *Birm* 79–87; Hon Can Birm Cathl 81–87; R Ox St Aldate w St Matt 87–94; R Ox St Aldate 95–02; Hon Can Ch Ch 98–02; rtd 02. *Pear Tree Cottage, Milcombe, Banbury OX15 4RS* T: (01295) 721119 E: david@macinnes.org.uk

MacINNES, Harry Campbell. b 67. Nottm Poly BA 89. Wycliffe Hall Ox BTh 94. d 97 p 98. C E Twickenham St Steph *Lon* 97–00; P-in-c St Margaret's-on-Thames 00–04; R Shill Valley and Broadshire *Ox* from 04. *The Rectory, Church Lane, Shilton, Burford OX18 4AE* T: (01993) 845954 E: harrymacinnes@yahoo.co.uk

MacINNES (née HITCHEN), Mrs Lisa Jan. b 73. Linc Univ NZ BPR&TM 95 Graduate Sch of Educn Dip Teaching 01. Trin Coll Bris BA 09. d 09 p 10. C Brinnington w Portwood *Ches* 09–12; V Hallwood Ecum Par from 12. *The Vicarage, 6 Kirkstone Crescent, Beechwood, Runcorn WA7 3JQ* T: (01928) 713101 *or* 716050 M: 07769-800915

MACINTOSH, Andrew Alexander. b 36. St Jo Coll Cam BA 59 MA 63 BD 80 DD 97. Ridley Hall Cam 60. d 62 p 63. C S Ormsby Gp *Linc* 62–64; Lect St D Coll Lamp 64–67; LtO *Ely* 67–04; Chapl St Jo Coll Cam 67–69; Asst Dean 69–79; Dean 79–02; Lect Th from 70; Pres 95–99; PtO *Ely* from 14. *St John's College, Cambridge CB2 1TP* T: (01223) 338709 E: aam1003@cam.ac.uk

McINTOSH, Ian MacDonald. b 64. Jes Coll Cam BA 86 K Coll Lon PhD 00. Trin Coll Bris BA 90. d 90 p 91. C Belmont *Lon* 90–92; C Pinner 92–95; Chapl Leic Univ 96–02; TV Leic H Spirit 96–02; Co-ord Reader Tr 00–02; Dir Cen for Ecum Studies Westcott Ho Cam 02–04; C Milton Ernest, Pavenham and Thurleigh *St Alb* 02–06; Hon C 06–08; RD Sharnbrook 04–06; Lect and Dir Studies ERMC *Ely* 06–07; Prin 07–15; PtO *St Alb* from 08; Hon Can St E Cathl 12–15; Hd Formation Nat Min Team Abps' Coun 15–21; Dir Miss and Min *York* from 21. *The Diocese of York, Amy Johnson House, Amy Johnson Way, York YO30 4XT* T: (01904) 699500 E: ian.mcintosh@yorkdiocese.org

McINTOSH, Mrs Nicola Ann. b 60. Trin Coll Bris 87. d 90 p 94. Par Dn Queensbury All SS *Lon* 90–93; Par Dn Ruislip Manor St Paul 93–94; C 94–95; NSM Clarendon Park St Jo w Knighton St Mich *Leic* 96–02; Asst Dioc Dir of Ords 00–02; V Milton Ernest, Pavenham and Thurleigh *St Alb* 02–08; PtO 08–12; Lead Chapl Bedford Hosp NHS Trust 12–21; Hon Can St Alb 18–21. *Address temp unknown*

McINTYRE, Preb Robert Mark. b 69. Nottm Univ BA 91. Coll of Resurr Mirfield 92. d 94 p 95. C Wednesbury St Jas and St Jo *Lich* 94–97; TV Wolstanton 97–05; P-in-c Rickerscote 05–10; V 10–11; C Stafford 05–11; V Walsall St Gabr Fulbrook from 11; RD Walsall from 20; Preb Lich Cathl from 15; CMP from 97. *St Gabriel's Vicarage, Walstead Road, Walsall WS5 4LZ* T: (01922) 622583 E: stgabriels.frmark@gmail.com

MACIVER, Donald. b 46. Heriot-Watt Univ BSc 69 Nazarene Th Coll Man ThB 82 Lon Univ BD 82. d 08 p 09. OLM Heatons *Man* 08–14; NSM Cloughton and Burniston *York* 14–17; NSM Newby 14–17; NSM Hackness w Harwood Dale 14–17; NSM Ravenscar and Staintondale 14–17; NSM Scarborough St Luke 14–17; NSM Scalby 14–17; rtd 18; PtO *York* from 18. *38 Newlands Avenue, Scarborough YO12 6PS* E: dmaciver19@yahoo.com

McIVER, Lyn Cavell. b 56. SNWTP. d 10 p 11. C Toxteth Park Ch Ch and St Mich w St Andr *Liv* 10–13; TV E Widnes from 13. *St John's House, 134 Greenway Road, Widnes WA8 6HA* M: 07791-650911

MACK, Mrs Gillian Frances. b 50. SCM 72. Cant Sch of Min 84. d 87 p 94. NSM Deal St Geo Cant 87–88; NSM Deal St Leon and St Rich and Sholden 88–92; Par Dn 93–94; C 94–97; rtd 97; PtO *Cant* 97–06; Hon Chapl Cautley Ho Chr Cen 98–06; Pioneer Min Craven Adnry *Bradf* 08–11; Hon C Hurst Green and Mitton 06–07; P-in-c 07–13; V 13–14; V Hurst Green and Mitton *Blackb* 14–15; Hon C Waddington *Bradf* 06–14; Hon C Waddington *Blackb* 14–15; PtO from 15. *Halfpenny House, 7 Bowland Close, Longridge, Preston PR3 3TU* T: (01772) 783983 E: gfmack@talktalk.net

McKAE, William John. b 42. Liv Univ BSc 63 St Mark & St Jo Coll Lon PGCE 64. Wells Th Coll 68. d 71 p 72. C Tranmere St Paul w St Luke *Ches* 71–74; C Midsomer Norton *B & W* 74–75; TV Birkenhead Priory *Ches* 75–80; R Oughtrington 80–91; Chapl Asst Hope, Salford R and Ladywell Hosps Man 91–92; Lic Preacher *Man* 91–92; R Heaton Reddish 92–06; rtd 06; PtO *Ches* from 06. *3 Grantham Close, Wirral CH61 8SU* T: 0151-648 0858 E: john.g4ila@tiscali.co.uk

MACKARILL, Ian David. b 54. York St Jo Univ BA 09. NEOC 01. d 04 p 05. NSM Waggoners *York* 04–12; NSM Woldsburn

11–12; V Lesbury w Alnmouth *Newc* 12–20; V Longhoughton w Howick 12–20; rtd 20; PtO *Newc* from 20. *27 Kirkwell Cottages, High Hauxley, Morpeth NE65 0JN* T: (01665) 798934 E: ianmackarill@gmail.com

McKAY, Alastair James Mark. b 63. York Univ BA 85 Leeds Univ PGCE 87 E Mennonite Univ (USA) MA 99 Univ of Wales (Trin St Dav) DMin 14. St Mellitus Coll 12. d 15 p 16. C St Martin-in-the-Fields *Lon* from 15; NSM Highgate All SS from 19. *26 Midhurst Avenue, London N10 3EN* T: (020) 8883 1336 M: 07999-492511 E: ajmmckay@gmail.com

MACKAY, Alison. *See* PHILLIPSON, Alison

MACKAY, James Hugh. b 57. Ridley Hall Cam. d 09 p 10. C Walesby *Linc* 09–13; R Stilton w Denton and Caldecote etc *Ely* 13–15; P-in-c Elton 13–15; PtO *Derby* 16–17; P-in-c Old Dalby, Nether Broughton, Long Clawson, Hose, Harby, and Stathern from 17. *The Vicarage, 1 Church Lane, Old Dalby, Melton Mowbray LE14 3LB* T: (01664) 823475 E: revjamiemackay@btinternet.com

McKAY, Jennifer Susan. UCD MVB 91 Cam Univ PhD 98 FRCPath 08 MRCVS 91. All SS Cen for Miss & Min 16. d 19 p 20. NSM Gt Budworth *Ches* from 19. *Address withheld by request* E: mckayjenny56@gmail.com

MACKAY, Miss Margaret. b 59. St Martin's Coll Lanc BEd 82. Lindisfarne Regional Tr Partnership 12. d 14 p 15. NSM High Spen and Rowlands Gill *Dur* 14–18; P-in-c Gateshead from 18. *48 Cedarway, Gateshead NE10 8LD* T: 0191-438 3808 M: 07910-697308 E: margaretmackay1@talktalk.net

McKAY, Margaret McLeish. *See* HALE, Margaret McLeish

MACKAY, Paul Douglas. b 60. Trin Coll Bris. d 00 p 01. C Becontree St Mary *Chelmsf* 00–03; V Mile Cross *Nor* 03–16; RD Nor N 10–16; P-in-c Prittlewell St Mary *Chelmsf* 16–20; V from 20. *Prittlewell Vicarage, 489 Victoria Avenue, Southend-on-Sea SS2 6NL* T: (01702) 343470 E: revpaulstmarys@hotmail.com

MACKAY, Phyllis Marion. *See* BAINBRIDGE, Phyllis Marion

MACKAY, Rupert. b 61. Oak Hill Th Coll BA 00. d 00 p 01. C Knutsford St Jo and Toft *Ches* 00–04; Min Hadley Wood St Paul Prop Chpl *Lon* from 04. *28 Beech Hill, Barnet EN4 0JP* T/F: (020) 8449 2572 E: rupmac@mac.com

McKay, Stephen Andrew. b 75. Univ of Wales (Swansea) BA 98. Trin Coll Bris 19. d 21. C Tadley w Pamber Heath and Silchester *Win* from 21. *The Vicarage St Mary's, Bishopswood Road, Tadley RG26 4HQ* M: 07759-151576 E: revstevemckay@gmail.com

MACKAY, William James. b 61. QUB BTh 98. d 16 p 17. C Andreas, Ballaugh, Jurby and Sulby *S & M* from 16; Pioneer Min from 19. *38 Cronk Cullyn, Colby, Isle of Man IM9 4PS* T: (01624) 815045 E: william.mackay@sodorandman.im

McKEARNEY, Andrew Richard. b 57. Selw Coll Cam MA. Edin Th Coll 81. d 82 p 83. Prec St Ninian's Cathl Perth *St And* 82–84; Chapl St Mary's Cathl *Edin* 84–88; R Hardwick and Toft w Caldecote and Childerley *Ely* 88–94; RD Bourn 92–94; V Chesterton Gd Shep 94–06; V Iffley *Ox* from 06. *The Rectory, Mill Lane, Iffley, Oxford OX4 4EJ* T: (01865) 773516 E: vicar@iffleychurch.org.uk

McKEE, Nicholas John. b 71. Nottm Univ MEng 94. Ridley Hall Cam 05. d 08 p 09. C Didsbury St Jas and Em *Man* 08–11; V Astley Bridge 11–18; AD Walmsley 17–18; PtO from 18; Dir of Voc *Blackb* from 18. *Diocesan Offices, Clayton House, Walker Industrial Estate, Walker Road, Guide, Blackburn BB1 2QE* T: (01254) 503082 E: nick.mckee@blackburn.anglican.org

McKEE, Patrick Joseph. b 49. Ripon Coll Cuddesdon 92. d 94 p 95. C Oakham, Hambleton, Egleton, Braunston and Brooke *Pet* 94–97; V Ryhall w Essendine and Carlby 97–19; rtd 19. *66 Coppice Road, Ryhall, Stamford PE9 4HY* T: (01780) 752145 E: revpaddymckee@gmail.com

McKEE HANNA, Patricia Elizabeth. TCD BA HDipEd PhD 15 QUB BD NUU MA. d 99 p 00. NSM Nenagh *L & K* from 99; NSM Drumcliffe w Kilnasoolagh from 00; Chapl Limerick Univ 01–04. *Seafield Cottage, Baile an tSagart, Tromara West, Quilty, Co Clare, V95 Y0P4, Republic of Ireland* T: (00353) (65) 708 7965 M: (00353) 87-660 6003 E: hannape@tcd.ie

McKEGNEY, Canon John Wade. b 47. TCD BA 70 MA 81. CITC 70. d 72 p 73. C Ballynafeigh St Jude *D & D* 72–75; C Bangor St Comgall 75–80; I Drumgath w Drumgooland and Clonduff 80–83; I Gilnahirk 83–90; I Arm St Mark 90–13; Can Arm Cathl 01–13; rtd 13. *Tan y Bwlch, 2 Magheramenagh Gardens, Portrush BT56 8SU* T: (028) 7082 5019 M: 07801-866555 E: johnwmckegney@gmail.com

MacKEITH (née GODFREY), Mrs Ann Veronica. b 35. Bris Univ BSc 57 CertEd. Gilmore Course 78. dss 79 d 87 p 94. Bishopwearmouth Ch Ch *Dur* 79–83; Bishopwearmouth St Gabr 83–86; Ryhope 86–88; Par Dn 87–88; Par Dn Darlington H Trin 88–94; C 94–95; Family Life Officer 95–97; rtd 98; PtO *Chich* from 15. *26 Withdean Court,*

London Road, Brighton BN1 6RN T: (01273) 552376
E: annmackeith@talktalk.net

McKELLEN, Pamela Joyce. b 47. Homerton Coll Cam TCert 69
BEd 70. Cranmer Hall Dur 01. **d** 02 **p** 03. C Ox St Matt 02–04;
P-in-c Radley and Sunningwell 04–15; P-in-c Kennington
09–15; R Radley, Sunningwell and Kennington 15–16;
AD Abingdon 07–12; rtd 16; PtO Ox from 16. *9 Hazels
Paddock, Cold Ash, Thatcham RG18 9LD* T: (01635) 864274
E: pammckellen13@gmail.com

McKELVEY, Mrs Jane Lilian. b 48. Liv Inst of Educn BA 94. N
Bapt Coll 94. **d** 97 **p** 98. C Aughton St Mich *Liv* 97–01; TV
Gateacre 01–17; rtd 17. *Beth Abba, Wheathill Road, Liverpool
L36 5US* E: revjanemc1@yahoo.co.uk

**McKELVEY, The Very Revd Robert Samuel James
Houston.** b 42. TD QVRM 00 OBE 10. QUB BA 65
MA(Ed) 88 Garrett-Evang Th Sem DMin 93. CITC 67.
d 67 **p** 68. C Dunmurry *Conn* 67–70; CF (TAVR) 70–99;
P-in-c Kilmakee *Conn* 70–77; I 77–81; Sec Gen Syn Bd
of Educn (N Ireland) 81–01; Preb Newcastle St Patr Cathl
Dublin 89–01; Dean Belf 01–11; rtd 11. *9 College Park,
Coleraine BT51 3HE* T: (028) 7035 3621 M: 07802-207825
E: houston.mckelvey@btinternet.com

McKEMEY, Mrs Norma Edith. b 47. St Mary's Coll Chelt
CertEd 71. STETS BA 10. **d** 10 **p** 11. NSM Swindon Ch Ch
Bris 10–17; PtO 17–20. *Bethany, Greens Lane, Wroughton,
Swindon SN4 0RJ* T: (01793) 845917 M: 07760-457739
E: mckemeyn@talktalk.net

McKENDREY, Susan Margaret. b 55. **d** 02 **p** 03. NSM Allonby,
Cross Canonby and Dearham *Carl* 02–08; TV Maryport,
Netherton, Flimby and Broughton Moor 08–21; rtd 21.
Address temp unknown E: s.mckendrey@btinternet.com

MACKENNA, Anne Doreen Crystabelle. b 57. **d** 18. NSM
Leytonstone St Andr *Chelmsf* 18–20; PtO from 21. *Address
withheld by request*

MACKENNA, Christopher. *See* MACKENNA, Robert
Christopher Douglass

McKENNA, Edward Patrick. b 48. Liv Univ BTh 02. NOC 05.
d 06 **p** 07. NSM Stretton and Appleton Thorn *Ches* 06–09;
Asst Chapl HM Pris Risley 05–09; P-in-c Low Marple *Ches*
09–14; V 14–20; rtd 20. *18 Hermitage Avenue, Romiley,
Stockport SK6 4JH* T: 0161-536 1649 M: 07986-896810
E: ed1mckenna@aol.com

McKENNA (née ALLEN), Mrs Jacqueline Lesley. b 54.
EMMTC 99. **d** 02 **p** 03. NSM Huthwaite *S'well* 02–05;
P-in-c Shireoaks 05–12; Asst Chapl Notts Healthcare NHS
Trust 07–12; Chapl Doncaster and Bassetlaw Teaching
Hosps NHS Foundn Trust 12–19; P-in-c Blyth and Scrooby w
Ranskill *S'well* 19–20; rtd 20. *155 Worcester Avenue, Mansfield
Woodhouse, Mansfield NG19 8QY*

McKENNA, Lindsay Taylor Francis. b 62. Glas Univ MA 83
Aber Univ BD 86. Edin Th Coll 87. **d** 87 **p** 88. C Broughty
Ferry *Bre* 87–90; C Wantage *Ox* 90–93; V Illingworth *Wakef*
93–99; Dir CARA 99–02; V Hanworth All SS *Lon* 02–08;
Provost St Paul's Cathl Dundee *Bre* 08–09; R Dundee St Paul
08–09; PtO *Win* 09–10; P-in-c Catford St Andr *S'wark* 10–11;
V from 11; Dir Ords Woolwich Area from 13. *St Andrew's
Parsonage, 119 Torridon Road, London SE6 1RG* T: (020) 8697
2600 E: fatherlindsay@gmail.com

MACKENNA, Richard William. b 49. Pemb Coll Cam BA 71
MA 75. Ripon Coll Cuddesdon BA 77 MA 81. **d** 78 **p** 79. C
Fulham St Dionis *Lon* 78–81; C Paddington St Jas 81–85;
Tutor Westcott Ho Cam 85–89; V Kingston All SS w St Jo
S'wark 90–91; PtO 94–01; *Nor* 99–04. *Flat 5, 11 Grassington
Road, Eastbourne BN20 7BJ* T: (01323) 730477

MACKENNA, Robert Christopher Douglass. b 44. Oriel
Coll Ox BA 72 MA 75 MBAP 85. Cuddesdon Coll 71. **d** 73
p 74. C Farncombe *Guildf* 73–77; C Tattenham Corner
and Burgh Heath 77–80; P-in-c Hascombe 80–90; R 90–00;
RD Godalming 91–96; Hon Can Guildf Cathl 99–00; Dir
St Marylebone Healing and Counselling Cen from 00;
NSM St Marylebone w H Trin *Lon* 00–14; PtO *Chelmsf*
16–21. *17 Victory Road, London E11 1UL* T: (020) 8989 8551
E: chris_anne@aol.co.uk

MACKENZIE, Andrew John Kett. b 46. Southn Univ BA 68.
Guildf Dioc Min Course 98. **d** 91 **p** 92. Fullbrook Sch New
Haw 76–99; OLM Woodham *Guildf* 91–99; C Aldershot
St Mich 99–05; V Effingham w Lt Bookham 05–15; rtd 15; Hon
C Charminster and Stinsford *Sarum* 15–17; Hon C Bradford
Peverell, Stratton, Frampton etc 15–17; PtO from 18. *8
Charlotte Close, Charminster, Dorchester DT2 9PY* T: (01305)
251532 M: 07511-756407 E: revandymac1@btinternet.com

MACKENZIE, Miss Ann. b 54. CertEd 76. Trin Coll Bris 82.
dss 85 **d** 87 **p** 94. Normanton *Wakef* 85–90; Par Dn 87–90;
Par Dn Bletchley *Ox* 90–94; C 94–98; TV W Swindon and the
Lydiards *Bris* 98–04; P-in-c E Springfield *Chelmsf* 04–18; rtd

18; PtO *Cant* 18–21. *3 Jacinth Drive, Sittingbourne ME10 5AP*
E: ann.mackenzie@btinternet.com

MCKENZIE, Mrs Ann Elizabeth. b 45. Leic Univ BA 67
PGCE 68. STETS 95. **d** 98 **p** 99. NSM Appleshaw, Kimpton,
Thruxton, Fyfield etc *Win* 98–15; rtd 15; PtO *Win* from
15. *34 Hilly Orchard, Stroud GL5 4LQ* M: 07733-112975
E: ann.mckenzie@waitrose.com

MACKENZIE, David Stuart. b 45. Open Univ BA 95 FRSA 00.
Linc Th Coll 66. **d** 69 **p** 70. C Bishopwearmouth St Mary V
w St Pet CD *Dur* 69–72; C Pontefract St Giles *Wakef* 72–74;
Chapl RAF 74–02; Chapl St Clem Danes 97–02; Chapl OHP
02–08; RD Whitby *York* 04–08; QHC from 09; PtO *Ely* from
09; *Pet* from 19. *57 London Road, Godmanchester, Huntingdon
PE29 2HZ* T: (01480) 413120 E: dsm3557@gmail.com

MACKENZIE, Ian William. b 46. Trin Coll Bris 93. **d** 95
p 96. C Bideford *Ex* 95–96; C Bideford, Northam,
Westward Ho!, Appledore etc 96–99; TV Littleham w
Exmouth 99–11; rtd 11; PtO *Heref* from 13. *Ballavayre,
New Street, Ledbury HR8 2EL* T: (01531) 579009
E: billandmaggiemackenzie@gmail.com

MACKENZIE, The Ven Janet. b 62. Westmr Coll Ox BEd 86
Anglia Ruskin Univ BA 08. Westcott Ho Cam 04. **d** 06
p 07. C Sandy *St Alb* 06–10; P-in-c Luton St Aug Limbury
10–14; V 14–16; AD Luton 12–16; Adn Hertford and
Hon Can St Alb from 16. *Glebe House, St Mary's Lane,
Hertingfordbury, Hertford SG14 2LE* T: (01727) 818158
E: archdherts@stalbans.anglican.org

MACKENZIE, Jennifer Gaines. b 63. Auburn Univ Alabama
BA 88. Virginia Th Sem MDiv 04. **d** 04 **p** 05. C Washington
St Dav USA 04–07; C Alexandria Ch Ch 07–09; C Burke Gd
Shep 11–12; P-in-c Oak Hill Epiphany 12–13; Adn Wigan
and W Lancashire *Liv* 15–21; Dean's Adv for New Initiatives
Virginia Th Sem USA from 21. *Virginia Theological Seminary,
3737 Seminary Road, Alexandria VA 22304, USA* T: (001)
(703) 370 6600 M: 07464-548015

MCKENZIE (née DOORES), Mrs Jennifer Mary. b 78. Hull
Univ BA 99 St Jo Coll Dur BA 03. Cranmer Hall Dur 01.
d 04 **p** 05. C Old Swinford Stourbridge *Worc* 04–08; V
Cam w Stinchcombe *Glouc* 08–17; V S Cerney w Cerney
Wick, Siddington and Preston from 17. *The Vicarage, Silver
Street, South Cerney, Cirencester GL7 5TP* T: (01285) 860221
E: mckenzie.jennifer@btinternet.com

MacKENZIE, John Christopher Newman. b 67. Trin
Coll Bris 02. **d** 04 **p** 05. C Staplehurst *Cant* 04–07;
P-in-c Willesborough 07–13; P-in-c Sevington 07–13; R
Willesborough w Sevington 13–16; TR Ashford Town 16–20;
Jt AD Ashford 18–20; V W Holloway St Luke *Lon* from 20.
St Luke's Church, Hillmarton Road, London N7 9JE T: (020)
7607 4892 E: mackthevicar@hotmail.com

MACKENZIE, Peter Sterling. b 65. Univ Coll Lon BSc 88. Oak
Hill Th Coll BA 95. **d** 95 **p** 96. C Roxeth *Lon* 95–00; TV 00–08;
V W Ealing St Jo w St Jas 08–18; V Hayes St Edm from 18.
The Vicarage, 1 Edmund's Close, Hayes UB4 0HA M: 07780-
562605

MACKENZIE, Canon Peter Thomas. b 44. Lon Univ
LLB 67 Westmr Coll Ox MTh 97 Univ of E Lon MA 01.
Cuddesdon Coll 68. **d** 70 **p** 71. C Leigh Park *Portsm* 70–75;
P-in-c Sittingbourne St Mary *Cant* 75–82; V Folkestone St Sav
82–90; RD Elham 89–90; R Cant St Martin and St Paul 90–99;
RD Cant 95–99; V Goudhurst w Kilndown 99–07; Hon
Can Cant Cathl 97–07; AD Cranbrook 01–06; rtd 07; PtO
Cant 09–11; P-in-c Turvey St Alb 11–14; P-in-c Stevington
11–14; PtO *Leic* 15–20; *Pet* from 17; *Eur* from 16; Hon C
Market Harborough and The Transfiguration etc *Leic* from
20. *5 Madeline Close, Great Bowden, Market Harborough
LE16 7HX* T: (01858) 440049 E: canonmack@talk21.com

MCKENZIE, Robin Peter. b 61. Sheff Univ BEng 82 Birm
Univ MSc(Eng) 87 Dur Univ BA 02 Warwick Univ EngD 02
CEng MIET. Cranmer Hall Dur 00. **d** 03 **p** 04. C Shrewsbury
St Chad w St Mary *Lich* 03–07; P-in-c Hilton *Ely* 07–11;
P-in-c Fenstanton 07–17; PtO from 18. *324 Trowell Road,
Nottingham NG8 2DT* E: mckenzie_robin@hotmail.com

MACKENZIE, Simon Peter Munro. b 52. Univ Coll Ox BA 74.
Coll of Resurr Mirfield 82. **d** 85 **p** 86. C Tipton St Jo *Lich*
85–91; V Perry Beeches *Birm* 91–13; P-in-c Lochgilphead *Arg*
from 13; P-in-c Inveraray from 13; P-in-c Kilmartin from 13;
P-in-c Is of Arran from 13. *Bishopton House, Bishopton Road,
Lochgilphead PA31 8PY* E: dr.lachlan@zen.co.uk

McKENZIE, Stephen George. b 58. Leeds Univ BSc 80
Imp Coll Lon PhD 85. Oak Hill Th Coll 03. **d** 05 **p** 06. C
Barton Seagrave w Warkton *Pet* 05–08; P-in-c Swynnerton
and Tittensor *Lich* 08–09; C Broughton w Croxton
and Cotes Heath w Standon 08–09; R Cotes Heath and
Standon and Swynnerton etc 09–19; rtd 19. *Address temp
unknown* M: 07986-558861

MACKENZIE, William. *See* MACKENZIE, Ian William

MACKENZIE MILLS, David Graham. b 75. Bris Univ BA 96 St Jo Coll Dur BA 01. Cranmer Hall Dur. **d** 01 **p** 02. C Glas St Marg 01–04; Chapl Trin Coll Cam 04–09; Min Can and Prec Cant Cathl 09–12; R Kinross *St And* from 13. *36 Manse Road, Milnathort, Kinross KY13 9YQ*   T: (01577) 863795 E: frdavidkinross@gmail.com

McKEON, Linda Mary. b 64. **d** 09 **p** 10. OLM Gentleshaw *Lich* 09–16; P-in-c 16–20; P-in-c Farewell 16–20; V Farewell and Gentleshaw from 20. *The Vicarage, Buds Road, Rugeley WS15 4NB*   T: (01543) 670739 E: lynn.mckeon@btinternet.com

McKEOWN, Lucy. b 40. Hatf Poly BSc 78. **d** 20 **p** 21. C Ithon Valley *S & B* from 20. *Forest Lodge, Abbeycwmhir, Llandrindod Wells LD1 6PH*   T: (01597) 851930 E: lucymckeown@btinternet.com

McKEOWN, Trevor James. b 53. Glos Univ BA 12. CITC 01. **d** 04 **p** 05. Aux Min Dromore Cathl *D & D* from 04. *39 Cedar Park, Portadown, Craigavon BT63 5LL*   T: (028) 3832 1217 *or* 9269 3968 E: trevor.mckeown3@hotmail.com

McKERAN, James Orville. b 71. Kent Univ BA 94 K Coll Lon MA 06 Leeds Univ MA 08 Solicitor 98 ACIArb 08 FRGS 11 MCMI 13 FCMI 16 FZS 18. Coll of Resurr Mirfield 06. **d** 08 **p** 09. C Altrincham St Geo and Altrincham St Jo *Ches* 08–11; Chapl Trafford Coll 08–11; Tutor SSM Lesotho 11–12; Asst P Maseru St Jo and Maseru E 11–12; V Gen Botswana 12–15; Dean Gaborone 12–15; R Lobatse St Mark and Chapl Athlone Hosp 15–17; V Witley *Guildf* from 18. *Witley Vicarage, Petworth Road, Witley, Godalming GU8 5LT*   T: (01428) 681867 M: 07493-695875 E: vicar@witleyallsaints.org.uk

MacKICHAN, Gillian Margaret. b 34. Cam Univ CertEd 56 CQSW 80. S Dios Minl Tr Scheme 90. **d** 93 **p** 94. NSM Upper Kennet *Sarum* 93–04; TV 95–04; RD Marlborough *Sarum* 02–04; rtd 04; PtO *Sarum* 04–05 and from 14. *West Bailey, Lockeridge, Marlborough SN8 4ED*   T: (01672) 861629 E: g.mackichan@btinternet.com

MACKIE, Andrew. b 53. Glas Univ BSc 74 CEng MIET. SAOMC 00. **d** 00 **p** 01. OLM Purley *Ox* 00–18. *The Brambles, Stevenson Approach, Great Cornard, Sudbury CO10 0WD*   M: 07900-213350 E: mackie.family@btinternet.com

MACKIE, Fiona Mary. *See* KOUBLE, Fiona Mary

McKILLOP, Mrs Caroline Annis. b 47. Glas Univ MB, ChB 72 PhD 77. TISEC 95. **d** 98 **p** 99. NSM Glas St Matt 98–01; Chapl Stobhill NHS Trust 99–00; NSM Glas St Mary 02–12; LtO from 12. *Flat 1, 6 Kirklee Gate, Glasgow G12 0SZ*   T: 0141-339 7000 E: carolinemckillop@yahoo.co.uk

McKILLOP, Iain Malcolm. b 54. Man Univ BA 75 Man Poly PGCE 76 Kingston Univ MA 95. Guildf Dioc Min Course 07. **d** 10 **p** 11. NSM Effingham w Lt Bookham *Guildf* 10–15; NSM W Byfleet 15–18; PtO *S'wark* from 18. *10 Hopfield Avenue, Byfleet, West Byfleet KT14 7PE*   T: (01932) 341687 E: imckillopi@aol.com

McKINLEY, Canon Arthur Horace Nelson. b 46. TCD BA 69 MA 79. CITC 70. **d** 70 **p** 71. C Taney Ch Ch *D & G* 71–76; I Dublin Whitechurch from 76; Preb Dunlavin St Patr Cathl Dublin from 91. *The Vicarage, Whitechurch Road, Rathfarnham, Dublin 16, Republic of Ireland*   T: (00353) (1) 493 3953 *or* (1) 493 4972 E: whitechurchparish@eircom.net *or* office@whitechurchparish.com

✠**McKINNEL, The Rt Revd Nicholas Howard Paul.** b 54. Qu Coll Cam BA 75 MA 79. Wycliffe Hall Ox BA 79 MA 86. **d** 80 **p** 81 **c** 12. C Fulham St Mary Fnd Lon 80–83; Chapl Liv Univ 83–87; P-in-c Hatherleigh *Ex* 87–88; R Hatherleigh, Meeth, Exbourne and Jacobstowe 88–94; P-in-c Plymouth St Andr w St Paul and St Geo 94–95; TR Plymouth St Andr and Stonehouse 95–12; RD Plymouth Sutton 01–06; Preb Ex Cathl 02–12; Suff Bp Crediton 12–15; Suff Bp Plymouth from 15. *108 Molesworth Road, Stoke, Plymouth PL3 4AQ*   T: (01752) 500059 E: bishop.of.plymouth@exeter.anglican.org

McKINNEY, Canon Mervyn Roy. b 48. St Jo Coll Nottm. **d** 81 **p** 82. C Tile Cross *Birm* 81–84; C Bickenhill w Elmdon 84–89; V Addiscombe St Mary *S'wark* 89–93; V Addiscombe St Mary Magd w St Martin 93–99; P-in-c W Wickham St Fran 99–02; V W Wickham St Fran and St Mary 02–14; AD Croydon Addington 04–11; Hon Can S'wark Cathl 05–14; rtd 14; PtO *Chelmsf* from 15. *12 Dedham Mill, Mill Lane, Dedham, Colchester CO7 6DJ*   T: (01206) 323565 E: mervmckinney@btinternet.com

MacKINNON, Canon Karen Audrey. b 64. Ex Univ BA 85 Cardiff Univ MTh 13. Linc Th Coll 92. **d** 92 **p** 94. Par Dn Filton *Bris* 92–93; Par Dn Bris Lockleaze St Mary Magd w St Fran 93–94; C 94–96; P-in-c 96–98; V 98–00; Asst Chapl Southn Univ Hosps NHS Trust 00–02; Chapl 02–04; Dep Manager 04–11; Spiritual Care Manager Univ Hosp Southn NHS Foundn Trust from 11; Hon Can Win Cathl from 14. *Chaplaincy Department, MP 201, Univ Hospital Southampton*

NHS Trust, Tremona Road, Southampton SO16 6YD   T: (023) 8120 8517 E: karen.mackinnon@uhs.nhs.uk

McKINNON, Neil Alexander. b 46. Wycliffe Hall Ox 71. **d** 74 **p** 75. C Deptford St Nic w Ch Ch *S'wark* 74–76; C St Helier 76–79; Min W Dulwich All SS and Em 79–81; TV Thamesmead 87–95; R S'wark H Trin w St Matt 95–16; rtd 16. *7 The Quadrangle, Morden College, 19 St Germans Place, London SE3 0PW*   M: 07745-287103 E: neilatelephant@yahoo.com

MACKINTOSH, Canon Robin Geoffrey James. b 46. Rhodes Univ BCom 71 Cranfield Inst of Tech MBA 78. Ripon Coll Cuddesdon BA 85 MA 91. **d** 86 **p** 87. C Cuddesdon *Ox* 86; C Cannock *Lich* 86–89; R Girton *Ely* 89–01; Exec Dir The Leadership Inst 01–06; PtO *Cant* 03–21; Dir Min and Tr 06–14; rtd 14; Hon Can Cant Cathl 09–14. *4 Loop Court Mews, Sandwich CT13 9HF* E: robmackintosh@btinternet.com

McKITTRICK, The Ven Douglas Henry. b 53. St Steph Ho Ox 74. **d** 77 **p** 78. C Deptford St Paul *S'wark* 77–80; C W Derby St Jo *Liv* 80–81; TV St Luke in the City 81–89; V Toxteth Park St Agnes and St Pancras 89–97; V Brighton St Pet w Chpl Royal *Chich* 97–02; RD Brighton 98–02; Can and Preb Chich Cathl 98–02; Adn Chich 02–18; rtd 18; PtO *York* from 19. *3 Poplar Avenue, Kirkbymoorside, York YO62 6ES*   T: (01751) 430867

MACKLEY, Robert Michael. b 78. Ch Coll Cam BA 99 MA 03 Em Coll Cam PhD 16. Westcott Ho Cam 00. **d** 03 **p** 04. C Clerkenwell H Redeemer *Lon* 03–06; C Clerkenwell St Mark 03–06; C Liv Our Lady and St Nic 06–09; Asst Chapl Em Coll Cam 09–12; V Cambridge St Mary Less *Ely* from 12; RD Cambridge S 16–21. *The Vicarage, 1B Summerfield, Cambridge CB3 9HE*   T: (01223) 356641 *or* 366202   M: 07866-445877 E: vicar@lsm.org.uk

MACKNESS, The Ven Paul Robert. b 73. Univ of Wales (Lamp) BA 96 Univ of Wales (Cardiff) BA 01. St Mich Coll Llan 98. **d** 01 **p** 02. C Llanelli *St D* 01–04; P-in-c Maenordeifi and Capel Colman w Llanfihangel etc 04–05; R 05–07; R Maenordeifi Gp 07–10; AD Cemais and Sub-Aeron 08–10; V Haverfordwest 10–14; Bp's Chapl 14–18; Can St D Cathl from 14; Asst Dioc Warden Ords from 15; Adn St D from 18; P-in-c Jeffreyston w Reynoldston and Loveston etc 18–20. *The Vicarage, 7 Churchill Park, Jeffreyston, Kilgetty SA68 0SD*   T: (01267) 236597 E: archdeacon.stdavids@churchinwales.org.uk

MACKNIGHT, Glen. b 62. Lindisfarne Regional Tr Partnership 10. **d** 13 **p** 14. C Herrington, Penshaw and Shiney Row *Dur* 13–16; V Hillside from 16. *All Saints' Vicarage, Rowanwood Gardens, Gateshead NE11 0DP*   M: 07983-572472 E: glenmacknight@mac.com *or* admin@hillsidechurch.co.uk

McKNIGHT, Thomas Raymond. b 48. QUB BEd 71. CITC 74. **d** 77 **p** 78. C Lisburn Ch Ch Cathl *Conn* 77–80; C Carrickfergus 80–82; I Kilcronaghan w Draperstown and Sixtowns *D & R* 82–86; I Magheragall *Conn* 86–91; CF 91–07; I Urney w Sion Mills *D & R* 07–11; rtd 11. *5 Pembury Mews, Brompton on Swale, Richmond DL10 7SG*   T: (01748) 810348 E: raymcknight2003@hotmail.com

MACKRIELL, Peter John. b 64. Mansf Coll Ox BA 85 MA 93 Man Univ PGCE 87. St Jo Coll Nottm BTh 93 MA 94. **d** 94 **p** 95. C Hale and Ashley *Ches* 94–96; C Marple All SS 96–98; V Brandwood *Birm* 98–01; V Pontblyddyn *St As* 01–05; Chapl to Deaf People 01–11; Dioc Communications Officer 06–11; V Kelsall *Ches* 11–18; P-in-c Maelor Miss Area *St As* from 18; Dir Studies for Past Workers *Ches* 15–19; Hd of Counselling Services from 19. *The Rectory, 4 Sundorne, Overton, Wrexham LL13 0EB*   T: (01978) 710294   M: 07795-972325 E: revpeter@maelormissionarea.uk

MACKRILL, Mrs Deirdre Anne. b 49. ACIS 95. SAOMC 01. **d** 05 **p** 06. NSM Hemel Hempstead *St Alb* 05–09; NSM St Keverne *Truro* 11–16; NSM St Ruan w St Grade and Landewednack 11–16; NSM St Keverne, St Ruan w St Grade and Landewednack 17–19; rtd 19; PtO *Truro* from 19. *Rosenithon House, Rosenithon, St Keverne, Helston TR12 6QR*   T: (01326) 281178 E: deirdre.mackrill@btinternet.com

MACKRILL, Robert John. b 51. Univ Coll Lon BSc 73 RIBA 79. EMMTC 92. **d** 93 **p** 94. NSM Stamford All SS w St Jo *Linc* 93–97; P-in-c Stamford Ch Ch 97–10; RD Aveland and Ness w Stamford 09–10; C Oakham, Hambleton, Egleton, Braunston and Brooke *Pet* 10; TV Oakham, Ashwell, Braunston, Brooke, Egleton etc 11; rtd 11; PtO *Pet* from 12; *Linc* 15–18; Chapl HM Pris Stocken from 19. *HM Prison, Stocken Hall Road, Stretton, Oakham LE15 7RD*   T: (10780) 795161 E: robert.mackrill@justice.gov.uk

McLACHLAN, Devin Shepard. b 73. Harvard Univ AB 96. Episc Div Sch (USA) MDiv 02. **d** 04 **p** 05. C St Mark's Cathl Seattle USA 04–07; R Newton Messiah 07–11; Asst Chapl Brent Ho Chicago Univ 11–14; Asst Chapl Jes Coll Cam 15–18; PtO *Ely* 14–16; C Cambridge Gt St Mary w St Mich from 16; Bp's Interfaith Adv from 18. *Great St Mary's Church, St Mary's Passage, Cambridge CB2 3PQ*   T: (01223)

747277   M: 07478-646463   E: revmcdev@gmail.com   *or* dm695@cam.ac.uk

MacLACHLAN (*née* **GRIFFITHS**), **Mrs Margaret.** b 44. Birm Poly CertEd 81 Open Univ BA 82 SRN 67. WMMTC 92. **d** 95 **p** 96. NSM Tile Cross *Birm* 95–08; NSM Garretts Green 07–08; NSM Garretts Green and Tile Cross 08–13; PtO from 13; Chapl Heart of England NHS Foundn Trust from 08. *5 Chester Road, Birmingham B36 9DA* T: 0121-747 2340 E: revmac@talktalk.net

MacLACHLAN, Michael Ronald Frederic. b 39. Wycliffe Hall Ox 75. **d** 75 **p** 76. C Mansfield SS Pet and Paul *S'well* 75–78; P-in-c Newark Ch Ch 78–80; TV Newark w Hawton, Cotham and Shelton 80–86; P-in-c Sparkhill St Jo *Birm* 86–90; P-in-c Sparkbrook Em 86–90; V Sparkhill w Greet and Sparkbrook 90–92; RD Bordesley 90–92; P-in-c Kugluktuk Canada 92–97; R Stoke-next-Guildf *Guildf* 97–05; rtd 05; Hon C Drayton Bassett *Lich* 05–12; PtO *Cov* from 13. *36A Grendon Road, Polesworth, Tamworth B78 1NU* T: (01827) 893109 E: michaelmcalachan@gmail.com

MacLACHLAN, Canon Sheila Elizabeth. b 52. SRN 73 Kent Univ MA 89. Wycliffe Hall Ox 80. **dss** 83 **d** 87 **p** 94. Chapl Kent Univ *Cant* 83–94; Dep Master Rutherford Coll 87–94; Dn-in-c Kingsnorth w Shadoxhurst *Cant* 94; P-in-c Kingsnorth and Shadoxhurst 94–15; AD Ashford 03–09; Hon Can Cant Cathl 08–15; rtd 15; PtO *Cant* from 15. *33 Josephs Way, New Romney TN28 8AQ* T: (01797) 690461   M: 07771-691164 E: revsheila25@sky.com

MacLAREN, Canon Clare. b 67. Edin Univ LLB 88 Leeds Univ MA 14. Linc Th Coll BTh 95. **d** 95 **p** 96. C Benchill *Man* 95–98; C Bilton *Ripon* 98–03; TV Seacroft 03–10; P-in-c Heaton St Martin *Bradf* 10–14; *Leeds* 14–15; P-in-c Heaton St Barn *Bradf* 10–14; *Leeds* 14–15; Can Res Newc Cathl from 15. *55 Queens Terrace, Newcastle upon Tyne NE2 2PL* T: 0191-435 0834   M: 07952-760168 E: claremaclaren@gmail.com   *or* clare.maclaren@newcastlecathedral.org.uk

MacLAREN, Duncan Arthur Spencer. b 69. Oriel Coll Ox BA 90 MA 96 K Coll Lon MA 97 PhD 03 Napier Univ Edin MA 12. Oak Hill Th Coll 92. **d** 94 **p** 95. C Ox St Clem 94–97; Chapl St Edm Hall Ox 97–04; Assoc R Edin St Paul and St Geo 04–09; R Edin St Jas 09–13; Dir Top Storey Media 13–15; Chapl NHS Tayside 15–18; Hd Spiritual Care and Bereavement NHS Lothian from 18; LtO *Edin* from 13. *8 Keith Terrace, Edinburgh EH4 3NJ* M: 07902-294878

MacLAREN (*née* **ALEXANDER**), **Mrs Jane Louise.** b 69. LMH Ox BA 90 MA 96. Oak Hill Th Coll BA 95. **d** 95 **p** 96. C Ox St Clem 95–98; Chapl St Aug Sch 98–02; Chapl Ox Brookes Univ 02–04; Assoc R Edin St Paul and St Geo 04–09; NSM Edin St Jas 09–21; P-in-c Edin SS Phil and Jas from 21. *8 Keith Terrace, Edinburgh EH4 3NJ* M: 07709-905528

McLAREN, Jessica Jean. b 83. Bournemouth Univ BA 06 Thames Valley Univ MA 10 St Jo Coll Dur BA 17. Cranmer Hall Dur 14. **d** 17 **p** 18. C Leagrave *St Alb* 17–20; V Wilbury from 20. *103 Bedford Road, Letchworth Garden City SG6 4DU* M: 07743-345314 E: vicar-stw@outlook.com

McLAREN, Richard Francis. b 46. S'wark Ord Course 72. **d** 75 **p** 76. C Charlton St Luke w H Trin S'wark 75–78; C Kensington St Mary Abbots w St Geo *Lon* 78–81; Hon C St Marylebone w H Trin 82–96; P-in-c 96–97; Development Officer CUF 97; Chmn Art and Christianity Enquiry Trust 97–11; Hon C Regent's Park St Mark *Lon* 97–11; rtd 11; PtO *Lon* from 12. *The Chapter House, 2 East Wing, Stoneleigh Abbey, Kenilworth CV8 2LF* M: 07788-416525 E: richardmclaren8@hotmail.co.uk

McLAREN, Canon Robert Ian. b 62. Bris Univ BSc 84 St Jo Coll Dur BA 87. Cranmer Hall Dur 85. **d** 88 **p** 89. C Birkenhead Ch Ch *Ches* 88–90; C Bebington 90–95; V Cheadle All Hallows 95–05; V Poynton 05–19; RD Cheadle 09–16; V Church Hulme from 19; Hon Can Ches Cathl from 14. *The Vicarage, 74A London Road, Holmes Chapel, Crewe CW4 7BD* T: (01477) 668695 E: vicar@stlukesholmeschapel.uk

McLAREN-COOK, Paul Raymond. b 43. Wollaston Th Coll 63. **d** 66 **p** 67. C Mt Lawley Australia 66–67; C Perth Cathl 67–69; R Carnarvon 69–72; V Seremban Malaysia 72–76; Warden Coll of Th 74–76; R Kensington 76–79; R Narrogin 79–84; P-in-c Wellington Australia 84; R Eugowra 84–86; P-in-c Berrigan 86–87; P-in-c Hay 87–88; P-in-c Yass 88; R Moruya 88–90; R Heywood 90–92; R Warracknabeal 92–95; Chapl Ballarat Base and St Jo of God Hosps 95–00; Can Res Ballarat Cathl 95–00; R Kansas City St Mary USA 00–03; R Stanway *Chelmsf* 03–13; rtd 13; Warden Ascot Priory 03–21; PtO *Ox* 14–21. *10 St Peter's Place, Montrose DD10 8PL* E: mclarencook@btinternet.com

McLARNON, Mrs Sylvia Caroline Millicent. b 45. S Dios Minl Tr Scheme 92. **d** 95 **p** 96. C Burgess Hill St Andr *Chich* 95–09; rtd 09; Chapl St Pet and St Jas Hospice N Chailey

from 05; PtO *Chich* from 14. *23 The Warren, Burgess Hill RH15 0DU* T: (01444) 233902

McLAUGHLIN, Adrian Robert. QUB BTh MTh PhD PGCE. **d** 07 **p** 08. C Bangor Abbey *D & D* 07–13; LtO 13–14; I Dunmurry *Conn* from 14. *The Rectory, 27 Church Avenue, Dunmurry, Belfast BT17 9RS* T: (028) 9061 0984 E: revadrian@btinternet.com *or* revdadrian@gmail.com

McLAUGHLIN, Hubert James Kenneth. b 45. CITC 85. **d** 88 **p** 89. NSM Donagheady *D & R* 88–89; NSM Glendermott 89–98; P-in-c Inver w Mountcharles, Killaghtee and Killybegs 98–02; I 02–10; rtd 10. *9 Cadogen Park, Londonderry BT47 5QW* T: (028) 7134 8916 E: kenandmart@yahoo.com

McLAUGHLIN, Capt Michael Anthony. b 48. **d** 97 **p** 98. C Gt Chart *Cant* 97–01; C-in-c Parkwood CD 01–11; rtd 11; PtO *Roch* from 12. *12 Medway Road, Gillingham ME7 1NH* M: 07977-051681 E: macl@blueyonder.co.uk

MACLAURIN, Ms Anne Fiona. b 62. St Andr Univ MA 84. Ridley Hall Cam. **d** 99 **p** 00. C Crookes St Thos *Sheff* 99–04; TV 04–05; Miss P Philadelphia St Thos 05–10; V Cambridge St Barn *Ely* from 10. *The Vicarage, 57 St Barnabas Road, Cambridge CB1 2BX*

MACLAY, Canon Christopher Willis. b 64. Stirling Univ BA 88 Reading Univ MA 92. Trin Coll Bris BA 01. **d** 01 **p** 02. C Bedhampton *Portsm* 01–05; P-in-c Ashington, Washington and Wiston w Buncton *Chich* 05–11; R 11–12; Chapl Versailles w Chevry *Eur* 12–15; V Bream *Glouc* from 15; AD Forest S from 16; Hon Can Glouc Cathl from 19. *St James's Vicarage, Coleford Road, Bream, Lydney GL15 6ES* T: (01594) 368558 E: chris.maclay@gmail.com

McLAY, The Ven Robert James. b 49. Cant Univ (NZ) BA 71. St Jo Coll Auckland. **d** 73 **p** 74. C Fendalton NZ 73–75; Hon C Yardley St Edburgha *Birm* 75–77; V Banks Peninsular NZ 77–80; V Marchwiel 80–83; V Huntly 83–89; Lect St Jo Coll 86–88; V Stokes Valley 89–93; V Pauatahanui 93–04; V Brooklyn 04–14; Can Wellington Cathl 96–00; Adn Wellington 07–13. *189 No 3 Line, Wanganui East, Wanganui 4500, New Zealand* T: (0064) (4) 343 2211 E: el.mclay@clear.net.nz *or* mclayrobert726@gmail.com

MACLEAN, Canon Allan Murray. b 50. Edin Univ MA 72. Cuddesdon Coll 72. **d** 76 **p** 77. Chapl St Mary's Cathl *Edin* 76–81; Tutor Edin Univ 77–80; R Dunoon *Arg* 81–86; R Tighnabruaich 84–86; Provost St Jo Cathl Oban 86–99; R Oban St Jo 86–99; R Ardbrecknish 86–99; R Ardchattan 89–99; Hon Can St Jo Cathl Oban from 99; LtO *Edin* from 00; PtO *Mor* from 00; P-in-c Edin St Vin 15–20. *5 North Charlotte Street, Edinburgh EH2 4HR* T: 0131-225 8609 E: editoredge@aol.com

MacLEAN, Christopher Gavin. b 57. Kent Univ BA 85. SEITE 10. **d** 13 **p** 14. C Walmer *Cant* 13–17; P-in-c Brookland, Fairfield, Brenzett w Snargate etc 17–19; TV Romney Marsh from 20. *All Saints' Rectory, Park Street, Lydd, Romney Marsh TN29 9AY* E: busyonasunday@gmail.com

McLEAN, Donald Stewart. b 48. TCD BA 70. CITC 70. **d** 72 **p** 73. C Glendermott *D & R* 72–75; I Castledawson 75–87 and 03–12; I Londonderry Ch Ch 87–03; Dioc Dir of Ords 79–96; Adn Derry 96–12; Can Derry Cathl 91–12; rtd 12. *99 Oldtown Road, Castledawson, Magherafelt BT45 8BZ* T: (028) 7946 8656   M: 07710-387436 E: donaldmclean@btinternet.com

McLEAN, Mrs Eileen Mary. b 44. City Univ BSc 67. NOC 85. **d** 88 **p** 94. Par Dn Burley in Wharfedale *Bradf* 88–92; Par Dn Nottingham St Pet and St Jas *S'well* 92–94; C 94–02; AD Nottingham Cen 98–02; V Bamburgh *Newc* 02–08; V Ellingham 02–08; rtd 08; PtO *Ripon* 08–13; *Sarum* 15–20. *8 Fordington Dairy, Athelstan Road, Dorchester DT1 1FD* T: (01305) 260126 E: eileen.mclean6@btinternet.com

McLEAN, Mrs Elizabeth Mary. b 79. All SS Cen for Miss & Min 16. **d** 19 **p** 20. C Fulwood Ch Ch *Blackb* from 19. *3 The Turnpike, Fulwood, Preston PR2 3NT* E: emmclean@hotmail.co.uk

MacLEAN, Lawrence Alexander Charles. b 61. K Coll Lon BD 84 AKC 84. Chich Th Coll 86. **d** 88 **p** 89. C Cirencester *Glouc* 88–91; C Prestbury 91–96; PtO 01–02; Chapl Florence w Siena *Eur* 02–11; V Gt and Lt Torrington and Frithelstock *Ex* 11–14; RD Torrington 12–14; V Hove St Barn and St Agnes *Chich* 14–18; P-in-c Hove St Andr 14–18; Dioc Development Officer 14–18; Chapl Monte Carlo *Eur* 18–20; rtd 21. *Address temp unknown* M: 07807-640189 E: lm61@live.co.uk

McLEAN, Canon Margaret Anne. b 62. Birm Univ BA 91 Heythrop Coll Lon MA 99. Qu Coll Birm 88. **d** 91 **p** 94. Par Dn Bedford All SS *St Alb* 91–94; C 94; Chapl St Alb High Sch for Girls 94–98; Asst Soc Resp Officer *Derby* 98–99; Chapl Huddersfield Univ *Wakef* 99–02; P-in-c Scholes 02–09; P-in-c Cleckheaton St Luke and Whitechapel 02–09; P-in-c Battyeford 09–14; Dioc Tr Officer (Reader Formation) 09–14; *Leeds* 14–19; V Battyeford 14–19; Hon Can Wakef Cathl 11–19; Can Res York Minster from

19. *York Minster, Minster Yard, York YO1 7HH* T: (01904) 557200 M: 07777-673172 E: m.a.mclean@btinternet.com *or* missioner@yorkminster.org

McLEAN, Canon Robert Hedley. b 47. St Jo Coll Dur BA 69. Ripon Hall Ox 69. **d** 71 **p** 72. C Redhill St Jo *S'wark* 71–74; C S Beddington St Mich 74–77; C-in-c Raynes Park H Cross CD 77; P-in-c Motspur Park 77–80; V 80–84; V Tadworth 84–00; Asst RD Reigate 92–93; RD Reigate 93–00; R Morpeth *Newc* 00–12; AD 04–08; Chapl Northd Mental Health NHS Trust 00–09; Chapl Northumbria Healthcare NHS Foundn Trust 00–09; rtd 12; P-in-c Wylam *Newc* 12–16; Hon Can Newc Cathl from 11; Hon Can Asante Mampong Ghana from 15; PtO *Newc* from 16. *65 Dene Road, Wylam NE41 8HB* T: (01661) 852065 E: rhm47@hotmail.co.uk

McLEAN, Thomas Paul. b 86. Bath Univ BSc 08 Sarum Coll MA 16 Leeds Univ MA 17. Coll of Resurr Mirfield BA 16. **d** 17 **p** 18. C Higham Ferrers w Chelveston *Pet* 17–19; Chapl K Coll Cam 20. *Residentie Justus Lipsiuscollege, Minderbroedersstraat 15, 3000 Leuven, Belgium* E: frtom.mclean@gmail.com

MacLEAY, Canon Angus Murdo. b 59. Univ Coll Ox BA 81 MA 86 Man Univ MPhil 92 Solicitor 83. Wycliffe Hall Ox 85. **d** 88 **p** 89. C Rusholme H Trin *Man* 88–92; V Houghton *Carl* 92–01; R Sevenoaks St Nic *Roch* from 01; Hon Can Roch Cathl from 15. *The Rectory, Rectory Lane, Sevenoaks TN13 1JA* T: (01732) 740340 F: 742810 E: angus.macleay@stnicholas-sevenoaks.org

MacLEOD, Alan Roderick Hugh (Roddie). b 33. St Edm Hall Ox BA 56 MA 61 Ox Univ DipEd 62. Wycliffe Hall Ox 56. **d** 58 **p** 59. C Bognor St Jo *Chich* 58–61; Chapl Wadh Coll Ox 62; Hd of RE Picardy Boys' Sch Erith 62–68; C Erith St Jo *Roch* 63–69; Dean Lonsdale Coll Lanc Univ 70–72; Hd of RE K Edw VI Sch Totnes 72–73; Dir of Resources St Helier Boys' Sch Jersey 73–84; V Shipton Bellinger *Win* 84–02; rtd 02; PtO *Win* 02–15. *Pippins Toft, Lashmar's Corner, East Preston, Littlehampton BN16 1EZ* T: (01903) 783523

McLEOD, David Leo Roderick. b 71. Westmr Coll Ox BA 92 DipCOT 96. **d** 05 **p** 06. OLM Coddenham w Gosbeck and Hemingstone w Henley *St E* 05–10; OLM Crowfield w Stonham Aspal and Mickfield 05–10; Chapl Team Co-ord Univ Campus Suffolk 07–10; Chapl Team Co-ord Suffolk New Coll 07–10; C Wokingham St Sebastian *Ox* 10–15; V Greenham from 15; AD Newbury from 20. *St Mary's Vicarage, New Road, Greenham, Thatcham RG19 8RZ* T: (01635) 41075 M: 07706-429805 E: davidmcleod01@btinternet.com

McLEOD, Everton William. b 57. Oak Hill Th Coll 89. **d** 91 **p** 92. C New Ferry *Ches* 91–93; C Moreton 93–98; Chapl R Liv Univ Hosp NHS Trust 98–01; R Weston-super-Mare St Nic w St Barn *B & W* 01–11; V Trentham *Lich* 11–16; V Hanford 11–16; TV Hampreston *Sarum* 16–19; rtd 19; Chapl St Jo Hosp Heytesbury 20–21. *8 Tozer Way, Whaddon, Salisbury SP5 3FT* T: (01722) 711275

MACLEOD, Gordon Ian. b 67. Lon Univ LLB 07 Moray Ho Edin DipSW 89. All SS Cen for Miss & Min 17. **d** 20 **p** 21. C Maghull and Melling *Liv* from 20. *8 Welbeck Road, Southport PR8 4AE* T: (01704) 569917 M: 07876-352156 E: gordonimacleod@gmail.com

MACLEOD, John Bain Maclennan. b 50. Aber Univ LLB 86 Solicitor 89. TISEC 03. **d** 06 **p** 08. NSM Hamilton *Glas* 06–12; C Annan 12–18; C Eastriggs 12–18; C Gretna 12–18; C Lockerbie 12–18; C Moffat 12–18; rtd 18; LtO *Glas* from 18. *Greenrig Barn, Greenrig Road, Hawksland, Lesmahagow, Lanark ML11 9QB* T: (01555) 664866 M: 07826-163415 E: macleod.greenrig@btinternet.com

MacLEOD, John Malcolm (Jay). b 61. Harvard Univ AB 84 Pemb Coll Ox BA 87 MA 91. Linc Th Coll MDiv 93. **d** 93 **p** 94. C Chesterfield SS Aug *Derby* 93–96; C Stalybridge St Paul *Ches* 96–98; P-in-c Micklehurst 98–03; P-in-c Bedford All SS *St Alb* 03–13; Dioc Interfaith Adv 03–13; R New London USA from 13. *184 Shindagan Road, Wilmot Flat NH 03287, USA* E: jaymacleod@mac.com

McLEOD, Neil Raymond. b 61. Trin Coll Bris 06. **d** 08 **p** 09. C N w S Wootton *Nor* 08–12; P-in-c Newport and Widdington *Chelmsf* 12–13; V Newport w Widdington, Quendon and Rickling 13–21. *111 Southwick Road, Sunderland SR5 1HQ* E: vicar4nqrwchurches@gmail.com

McLEOD, Paul Douglas. b 66. Cuddesdon Coll BTh 95. **d** 98 **p** 99. C Morpeth *Newc* 98–02; V Newbiggin Hall 02–10; RD Towcester 11–21. *The Vicarage, 24A High Street, Silverstone, Towcester NN12 8US* T: (01327) 858101 M: 07780-834099 E: revpaulmcleod@btinternet.com

MacLEOD, Roderick. See MacLEOD, Alan Roderick Hugh

MacLEOD, Talisker Isobel Alaethea Tuesday. b 81. St Andr Univ MA 03. Ripon Coll Cuddesdon BTh 11. **d** 11 **p** 12. C Hove All SS *Chich* 11–15; R Cherbury w Gainfield *Ox* from

15. *The Vicarage, Buckland, Faringdon SN7 8QN* M: 07887-773579 E: talisker@alathea.org.uk

McLOUGHLIN, Ian Livingstone. b 38. CEng MICE 64. Carl Dioc Tr Course 78. **d** 83 **p** 84. NSM Stanwix *Carl* 83–88; C Barrow St Geo w St Luke 88–90; R Kirkby Thore w Temple Sowerby and Newbiggin 90–01; rtd 01; PtO *Carl* from 01; *Bradf* 01–10. *29 Wordsworth Drive, Kendal LA9 7JW* T: (01539) 728209 E: nohastle@googlemail.com

McLOUGHLIN, John Robert. b 70. QUB BEng 92 Open Univ MSc 02. CITC BTh 09. **d** 09 **p** 10. C Arm St Mark 09–11; I Clonfeacle, Derrygortreavy and Eglish 11–18; I Aghavea Clogh from 18. *256 Belfast Road, Lurgan, Brookeborough, Enniskillen BT94 4DS* T: (028) 8953 1210 M: 07488-371680 E: johnnymcloughlin@gmail.com

McLOUGHLIN, Ms Tracey. b 65. Liv Hope Univ Coll BA 05. SNWTP 09. **d** 12 **p** 13. C Skelmersdale St Paul *Liv* 12–16; TV Warrington E from 16. *The Vicarage, 1 Briers Close, Fearnhead, Warrington WA2 0DN* M: 07990-545489

McLUCKIE, Canon John Mark. b 67. St Andr Univ BD 89. Edin Th Coll MTh 91. **d** 91 **p** 92. C Perth St Ninian *St And* 91–94; Chapl K Coll Cam 94–96; TV Glas E End 96–00; Assoc R Edin St Jo 00–03; PtO 08–09; Chapl R Marsden NHS Foundn Trust 10–12; Vice Provost St Mary's Cathl *Edin* 12–19; R Edin Old St Paul from 19; Hon Can St Mary's Cathl from 19. *Lauder House, 39 Jeffrey Street, Edinburgh EH1 1DH* M: 07967-411884 E: john.mcluckie@hotmail.co.uk *or* rector@osp.org.uk

MACLURE, David Samuel. b 80. York Univ BA 02 MA 06. Oak Hill Th Coll BA 14. **d** 14 **p** 15. C Isleworth St Jo w St Mary *Lon* 14–17; V from 17. *The New Vicarage, St John's Road, Isleworth TW6 6NY* E: davidmaclure@gmail.com

MacLUSKIE, Canon Linda. b 55. Lanc Univ MA 99. CBDTI 95. **d** 98 **p** 99. NSM Halton w Aughton *Blackb* 98–02; NSM Bolton-le-Sands 02–10; P-in-c Sandylands 10–11; V from 11; P-in-c Overton 17–19; AD Lancaster and Morecambe 14–17; Hon Can Blackb Cathl from 18. *St John's Vicarage, 2 St John's Avenue, Morecambe LA3 1EU* T: (01524) 411039 M: 07827-923222 E: lindamacluskie55@gmail.com

McMAHON, Stephen. b 66. Newc Univ BSc 87 MSc 89 Leeds Univ BA 03 Edin Univ MSc 17. Coll of Resurr Mirfield 01. **d** 03 **p** 04. C Lancaster St Mary w St John and St Anne *Blackb* 03–07; P-in-c Lowther and Askham and Clifton and Brougham *Carl* 07–10; P-in-c Kirkby Thore w Temple Sowerby and Newbiggin 07–10; Chapl Rossall Sch Fleetwood 10; NSM Lancaster St Mary w St John and St Anne *Blackb* 10–11; V Blyth St Cuth *Newc* 11–16; P-in-c Ipswich St Paul Australia 16–18; R Ipswich St Paul from 18. *11 Baystone Place, Raceview, Ipswich QLD 4305, Australia* E: steve1345.mcmahon@gmail.com

McMANN, Canon Judith. b 46. Hull Univ BTh 96. EMMTC MA 98. **d** 98 **p** 99. NSM Gt Grimsby St Mary and St Jas *Linc* 98–08; NSM Caistor Gp 08–18; NSM Caistor from 18; Can and Preb Linc Cathl from 05. *23 Grasby Crescent, Grimsby DN37 9HE* T: (01472) 887523 E: mcmann@btopenworld.com

McMANNERS, John Roland. b 46. Liv Univ LLB 68. Cranmer Hall Dur 99. **d** 01 **p** 02. C Monkwearmouth *Dur* 01–05; P-in-c Bishopwearmouth St Gabr 05–15; rtd 15; PtO *Dur* from 16. *40 Bek Road, Durham DH1 5LD* T: 0191-567 5200

McMANUS-THOMPSON, Elizabeth Gray. See THOMPSON, Elizabeth Gray McManus

MacMATH, Terence Handley. See HANDLEY MacMATH, Terence

McMICHAEL, Andrew Hamilton. b 48. Univ of Wales (Ban) BA 77. Chich Th Coll 87. **d** 89 **p** 90. C Chorley St Geo *Blackb* 89–92; C Burnley St Andr w St Marg 92–94; Chapl Burnley Health Care NHS Trust 92–94; R Eccleston *Blackb* 94–99; V Lt Marsden w Nelson St Mary 99–04; P-in-c Tain, Lochinver and Invergordon St Ninian *Mor* 04–07; P-in-c Harrington *Carl* 07–09; R Port Glas 09–13; rtd 13. *11 Howard Court, 77 Albert Road, Southport PR9 9LN*

MacMILLAN, Douglas Middleton. b 41. RCM DMus 13 St Thos Hosp Lon MB, BS 66 FRCS 70 FTCL 82 AMusLCM 80 FLCM 83. Guildf Dioc Min Course 96. **d** 00. NSM Guildf Cathl 00–02; PtO 02–04; NSM E and W Clandon 04–11; rtd 12; PtO *Guildf* from 12; *Lon* from 17. *Rivendell, 50 Speedwell Close, Guildford GU4 7HE* T: (01483) 533019 E: douglas.oriana@btinternet.com

McMULLEN (née **Woodcock**), **Mrs Anne Caroline**. b 63. Man Metrop Univ BA 97 Man Univ MA 07 RGN. SNWTP 08. **d** 10 **p** 11. C Newton in Mottram *Ches* 10–11; C Newton w Flowery Field 11–13; V 13–17; Chapl HM Pris Forest Bank 17–21; Dep Manager of Chapl Man Univ NHS Foundn Trust from 21; PtO *Man* from 16; *Ches* from 17. *Manchester University NHS Foundation Trust, Cobbett House, Manchester Royal Infirmary, Oxford Road, Manchester M13 9WL* T: 03003-309444

McMULLON, Andrew Brian. b 56. Sheff Univ BSc Cardiff Univ MTh 06. St Jo Coll Nottm. **d** 83 **p** 84. C Stainforth *Sheff* 83–86; V Blackb Redeemer 86–90; Chapl RAF 90–13; V Sedbergh, Cautley and Garsdale *Carl* 13–20; P-in-c Firbank, Howgill and Killington 15–20; V Western Dales 20; Chapl Ypres *Eur* from 20. *St George's Memorial Church, 52 Elverdingsestraat, 8900 Ieper, Belgium* E: yprespadre@outlook.com

McMURRAY, Matthew Paul. b 79. Trin Hall Cam BTh 11. Westcott Ho Cam 08. **d** 11 **p** 12. C Hawes Side and Marton Moss *Blackb* 11–14; C Fleetwood St Pet and St Dav 14–16; V Lostock Hall and Farington Moss from 16. *St James's Vicarage, 76A Brownedge Road, Lostock Hall, Preston PR5 5AD* T: (01772) 315404 E: frmatthew@cantab.net

McMURTAREY, Simon Alexander. b 79. Wycliffe Hall Ox BA 00 MA 05. Ripon Coll Cuddesdon MTh 13. **d** 12 **p** 13. C Four Marks *Win* 12–15; Chapl Dur Sch from 15. *5 Monmount Court, Durham DH1 4PD* T: 0191-386 0724 E: revsimontssf@gmail.com

McNAB (née **LUMMIS**), **Mrs Elizabeth Howieson**. b 44. Lon Univ BDS 68 LDS 68. St Jo Coll Nottm 85. **d** 88 **p** 95. NSM Lerwick *Ab* from 88; NSM Burravoe from 88. *Waters Edge, Bridge of Walls, Shetland ZE2 9NP* T: (01595) 809441 E: j.mcnab840@btinternet.com

McNAIR SCOTT, Benjamin Guthrie. b 76. K Coll Lon BA 98 MA 05. Ridley Hall Cam 05. **d** 07 **p** 08. NSM Guildf Ch Ch from 07; Chapl St Cath Sch Bramley from 12. *21 Lancaster Avenue, Guildford GU1 3JR* T: (01483) 455645 M: 07968-617084 E: benjaming@lycos.co.uk *or* benji@christchurchguildford.com

McNALLY, Nicola Mary. b 63. Bath Univ BSc 85 Linacre Coll Ox DPhil 91. Ripon Coll Cuddesdon 17. **d** 20 **p** 21. C Tideswell *Derby* from 20. *Pursglove Lodge, Pursglove Road, Tideswell, Buxton SK17 8LG* M: 07963-428228 E: nicola.curate@outlook.com

McNALLY, Paul. b 83. Wycliffe Hall Ox 15. **d** 17 **p** 18. C Accrington St Jas and St Paul *Blackb* 17–19; C Accrington Ch Ch 19–21; V from 21. *3 Bentcliffe Gardens, Accrington BB5 2NX* M: 07816-491522 E: revd.paul.mcnally@gmail.com

McNAMARA, Barbara. See SMITH, Barbara Mary

McNAUGHTAN-OWEN, James Thomas. b 48. Liv Univ MA 00. Linc Th Coll 77. **d** 80 **p** 81. C Palmers Green St Jo *Lon* 80–84; C Timperley *Ches* 84–87; C Bramhall 87–92; V Latchford St Jas 92–14; RD Gt Budworth 96–03; rtd 14. *9 Melton Road, Runcorn WA7 4AH*

MACNAUGHTON, Mrs Diana. b 54. St Hugh's Coll Ox BA 76 MA 90 Northumbria Univ MA 11 Dur Univ PGCE 78. NEOC 95. **d** 98 **p** 99. NSM Gosforth All SS *Newc* 98–01; C Willington 01–04; Chapl Team Ldr Northumbria Healthcare NHS Foundn Trust 04–11; P-in-c Byker St Silas *Newc* 11–16; rtd 16; PtO *Newc* 16–18; Hon C Tweedmouth 18–19; Hon C Spittal 18–19; Hon C Scremerston 18–19; Hon C Scremerston, Spittal and Tweedmouth 19–20. *St John's Vicarage, 129 Main Street, Spittal, Berwick-upon-Tweed TD15 1RP* M: 07950-627799 E: dmacnaughton@btinternet.com

McNAUGHTON, John. b 29. St Chad's Coll Dur BA 53. **d** 54 **p** 55. C Thorney Close CD *Dur* 54–58; C-in-c E Herrington St Chad CD 58–62; PC E Herrington 62–66; CF 66–94; V Hutton Cranswick w Skerne, Watton and Beswick *York* 94–99; rtd 99; PtO *York* 99–19. *47 Southgate, Cranswick, Driffield YO25 9QX* T: (01377) 270869

MACNAUGHTON, Mrs Pamela Jean. b 63. Ox Min Course. **d** 08 **p** 09. NSM Bishopthorpe *York* 08–20; NSM Acaster Malbis 08–20; NSM Appleton Roebuck w Acaster Selby 08–20; Dioc Adv for Pioneer Min 12–14; CPAS from 13. *Repton House, 39 Hickton Road, Swanwick, Alfreton DE55 1AF* E: workspacepjm@aol.com

⊞**MACNAUGHTON, The Rt Revd William Malcolm**. b 57. Qu Coll Cam BA 80. Ridley Hall Cam 79. **d** 81 **p** 82 **c** 21. C Haughton le Skerne *Dur* 81–85; P-in-c Newton Hall 85–90; TV Shoreditch St Leon and Hoxton St Jo *Lon* 90–00; AD Hackney 94–99; V Hoxton St Jo w Ch Ch 00–02; R Hambleden Valley *Ox* 02–07; AD Wycombe 05–07; Chief of Staff to Abp York 07–20; Can and Preb York Minster 16–20; Suff Bp Repton *Derby* from 21. *Repton House, 39 Hickton Road, Swanwick, Alfreton DE55 1AF* T: (01332) 840132 M: 07933-344746 E: malcolm.macnaughton@derby.anglican.org

MacNEANEY, Jonathan Niall Agnew. b 88. Oriel Coll Ox BA 09. Ripon Coll Cuddesdon MTh 13. **d** 13 **p** 14. C Hadleigh St Jas and Hadleigh St Barn *Chelmsf* 13–14; C Epping Distr 14–17; C Kensington St Mary Abbots *Lon* 17–20; C Fulham All SS from 20. *1 Langton Court, 1 Portinscale Road, London SW15 2HR* E: macneaneyj@gmail.com

McNEE, Canon William Creighton. Ulster Univ MA NUU MA FCIPD. **d** 82 **p** 83. C Larne and Inver *Conn* 82–84; I Donagheady *D & R* 84–91; I Kilwaughter w Cairncastle and Craigy Hill *Conn* 91–93; I Ardstraw w Baronscourt, Badoney Lower etc *D & R* 93–04; P-in-c Londonderry Ch Ch 04–05; I 05–08; I Londonderry Ch Ch, Culmore, Muff and Belmont 08–09; Bp's Dom Chapl 96–07; Can Derry Cathl 00–09; rtd 09. *14 Tartnakilly Road, Limavady BT49 9NA* T: (028) 7727 8873 M: 07770-767737 E: billmcnee@usa.net

McNEICE, Kathleen Mary. b 51. SEITE. **d** 07 **p** 08. NSM Folkestone Trin *Cant* 07–21; rtd 21. *2B Wear Bay Crescent, Folkestone CT19 6AX* T: (01303) 278791 M: 07786-365533 E: katemcneice@gmail.com

McNEIL, Ann. See CAFFYN, Ann

McNEIL, Kyle Gillies. b 86. Univ Coll Dur BA 09. St Steph Ho Ox BA 14. **d** 14 **p** 15. C Cockerton *Dur* 14–17; P-in-c Horden from 17; P-in-c Blackhall, Castle Eden and Monkhesleden from 17. *St Mary's Vicarage, 4 Stapylton Drive, Horden, Peterlee SR8 4HY* E: kyle.g.mcneil@gmail.com

McNELLY, Mrs Nicola. b 62. Cranmer Hall Dur 07. **d** 09 **p** 10. Chapl St Mary's Cathl *Edin* 09–10; C 10–12; Provost St Jo Cathl Oban *Arg* 12–17; R Ardbrecknish 12–17; Can Cumbrae 13–17; R Edin St Cuth from 17. *The Rectory, 6 Westgarth Avenue, Edinburgh EH13 0BD* T: 0131-441 7580 M: 07825-440580 E: stcuthbertsrector@gmail.com

McNICOL, Andrew Keith. b 45. Westmr Coll of Educn CertEd 69 Open Univ BA 79 Westmr Coll Ox MA 90. Westcott Ho Cam 92. **d** 92 **p** 93. C Whitstable *Cant* 92–95; V Ferring *Chich* 95–00; P-in-c Willesborough *Cant* 00–06; P-in-c Tunstall w Rodmersham 06–11; R Tunstall and Bredgar 11–14; rtd 14; PtO *Cant* from 15. *63 Shearwater Avenue, Whitstable CT5 4DY* T: (01227) 264592 E: keiththerector@gmail.com

McPHATE, The Very Revd Gordon Ferguson. b 50. Aber Univ MB, ChB 74 Fitzw Coll Cam BA 77 MA 81 MD 88 Surrey Univ MSc 86 Edin Univ MTh 94 FRCPEd 98. Westcott Ho Cam 75. **d** 78 **p** 79. NSM Sanderstead All SS *S'wark* 78–81; Hon PV S'wark Cathl 81–86; Lect Lon Univ 81–86; Chapl St Andr Univ *St And* 86–02; Lect 86–93; Sen Lect 93–02; Dean *Ches* 02–17; rtd 17; PtO *Ban* from 18. *50 Llys Onnen, Llandudno Junction LL31 9JZ*

McPHEE, Mrs Margaret Theresa Maria. b 65. Nottm Univ BA 88 Anglia Ruskin Univ PGCE 97 FCIPD 04. ERMC 09. **d** 12 **p** 13. C Mile Cross *Nor* 12–13; C Stalham, E Ruston, Brunstead, Sutton and Ingham 13–16; R Horsford, Felthorpe and Hevingham from 16. *1B Gordon Godfrey Way, Horsford, Norwich NR10 3SG* M: 07759-913802 E: revmargaretmcphee@gmail.com

MACPHERSON, Aian Jonathan. b 84. BSc 07 St Jo Coll Dur BA 13. Cranmer Hall Dur 10. **d** 13 **p** 14. C Drypool *York* 13–17; TV Marfleet from 17. *107 Amethyst Road, Hull HU9 4JG* M: 07929-733555 E: aian.macpherson2012@gmail.com

McPHERSON, Canon Andrew Lindsay. b 58. St Jo Coll Dur BA 79 MCIPD 84. **d** 88 **p** 89. C Bitterne *Win* 88–92; V Weston 92–99; V Holdenhurst and Iford from 99; P-in-c Southbourne St Chris from 07; P-in-c Bournemouth H Epiphany 12–14; AD Bournemouth 08–16; Hon Can Win Cathl from 16. *The Vicarage, 53A Holdenhurst Avenue, Bournemouth BH7 6RB* T: (01202) 425978 E: andy@stsaviours.net

MACPHERSON, Canon Anthony Stuart. b 56. Qu Coll Birm 77. **d** 80 **p** 81. C Morley St Pet w Churwell *Wakef* 80–84; C Penistone 84–85; P-in-c Thurlstone 85–86; TV Penistone and Thurlstone 86–88; V Grimethorpe 88–95; P-in-c Westgate Common 95–96; V 96–07; P-in-c Horbury Junction 02–07; RD Wakef 99–07; Hon Can Wakef Cathl 06–07; Can Missr Wakef 07–15; Can Pastor and Sub Dean Wakef *Leeds* 15–19; P-in-c Beadnell *Newc* 19–20; P-in-c Ellingham 19–20; P-in-c N Sunderland 19–20; V Beadnell, Ellingham and N Sunderland from 20. *The Vicarage, 155 Main Street, North Sunderland, Seahouses NE68 7TU* M: 07780-990354 E: canontonymac@gmail.com

MACPHERSON, Ms Catherine Annunciata. b 86. Univ of Wales (Lamp) BA 07 Em Coll Cam MPhil 10. Westcott Ho Cam 08. **d** 10 **p** 11. C Mirfield *Wakef* 10–14; P-in-c Fawdon *Newc* 14–20; V Blyth St Mary from 20. *St Mary's Vicarage, 51 Marine Terrace, Blyth NE24 2JP* M: 07961-699486 E: revcatherinemac@gmail.com

MacPHERSON, David Alan John. b 42. Lon Univ BD 75 Open Univ BA 83 Hatf Poly MSc 89. Clifton Th Coll 69 Trin Coll

Bris 72. **d** 72 **p** 73. C Drypool St Columba w St Andr and St Pet *York* 72–76; Asst Chapl HM Pris Hull 72–76; P-in-c Bessingby and Carnaby *York* 76–78; Chapl RAF 78–83; P-in-c Chedgrave w Hardley and Langley *Nor* 83–87; R 87–97; Chapl Langley Sch Nor 83–97; P-in-c Brington w Whilton and Norton *Pet* 97–98; R Brington w Whilton and Norton etc 98–02; rtd 02; PtO *Pet* 02–14 and from 18; Chapl to Retired Clergy and Clergy Widows' Officer 10–14. *24 Coldstream Close, Daventry NN11 9HL* T: (01327) 704500

MacPHERSON, Ewan Alexander. b 43. Toronto Univ BA 74. Wycliffe Coll Toronto MDiv 78. **d** 78 **p** 79. C Toronto St Cuth Canada 78–81; C Toronto Apostles 81–86; V Priddy and Westbury sub Mendip w Easton *B & W* 86–06; rtd 06. *20 Tuddington Gardens, Wells BA5 2EJ* T: (01749) 675876

MACPHERSON, Peter Sinclair. b 44. Lich Th Coll 68. **d** 71 **p** 72. C Honiton, Gittisham and Combe Raleigh *Ex* 71–72; C Bideford 72–74; C Devonport St Mark Ford 74–75; V Thorncombe *Sarum* 75–79; TV Dorchester 79–85; Chapl Jersey Gp of Hosps 85–90; Chapl Derriford Hosp Plymouth 90–98; rtd 98; PtO *Ex* 04–09. *Pump Cottage, 1 Rosemary Lane, Musbury, Axminster EX13 6AT* T: (01297) 552524

McQUAID, Mrs Jennifer Claire. b 79. Univ of Wales (Abth) BA 01. St Mellitus Coll BA 13 MA 14. **d** 14 **p** 15. NSM Hitchin *St Alb* 14–15; C 15–16; C Hitchin and St Paul's Walden 16–18; V Letchworth St Paul w Willian from 18. *177 Pixmore Way, Letchworth Garden City SG6 1QT* E: jennifercmcquaid@gmail.com

McQUILLEN, Brian Anthony. b 45. Ripon Hall Ox 73. **d** 75 **p** 76. C Northfield *Birm* 75–78; C Sutton Coldfield H Trin 78–80; V Bearwood 80–89; V Glouc St Geo w Whaddon 89–96; R St Martin in Looe *Truro* 96–11; RD W Wivelshire 98–03 and 06–08; rtd 11; PtO *Truro* 14–19; P-in-c St Goran w Caerhays from 19. *The Vicarage, Gorran, St Austell PL26 6HN* T: (01726) 883184 E: revincq75@gmail.com

McREYNOLDS, Canon Kenneth Anthony. b 48. **d** 83 **p** 84. C Ballymena w Ballyclug *Conn* 83–86; I Rathcoole 86–96; I Lambeg 90–16; Can Conn Cathl 08–16; rtd 16. *35 Hazelgrove Avenue, Lurgan, Craigavon BT66 7TF* T: (028) 3815 2145 E: kenmcreynolds@hotmail.com

MacROBERT, Iain. b 49. Wolv Univ BA 80 PGCE 81 Birm Univ MA 85 PhD 89. **d** 00 **p** 00. NSM S Queensferry *Edin* from 00. *21 Long Crook, South Queensferry EH30 9XR* T: 0131-319 1558 *or* (01506) 600292 F: 0131-319 1558 E: iain0macrobert@aol.com

McROBERTS, Ms Tracey. b 68. QUB BTh 99 PGCE 00 Dub City Univ MA 09. CITC 08. **d** 09 **p** 10. C Belfast St Thos *Conn* 09–12; I Belfast St Matt from 12; Bp's Dom Chapl from 11. *Shankill Rectory, 51 Ballygomartin Road, Belfast BT13 3LA* T: (028) 9071 4325 M: 07718-490040 E: tracey.mcroberts@btinternet.com

McROSTIE, Lyn. b 50. Canberra Univ BA 77 Portsm Univ MA 03 MInfSc 81. STETS 95. **d** 98 **p** 99. C Portsea St Cuth *Portsm* 98–02; P-in-c Shadwell St Paul w Ratcliffe St Jas *Lon* 02–04; Course Ldr NTMTC 04–06; P-in-c Northwood *Portsm* 06–07; R 07–11; P-in-c Gurnard 06–07; V 07–11; P-in-c Cowes St Faith 06–07; V 07–11; P-in-c Elizabeth Australia from 11; Ldr Angl Min Playford from 12; Adn The Para 14–19; P-in-c Prospect and Kilburn from 18. *13 Ashley Street, Elizabeth North SA 5113, Australia* T: (0061) (8) 8287 6722 E: lyn.mcrostie@mcrostie.com

MACROW-WOOD, The Ven Antony Charles. b 60. York Univ BA 82 Jes Coll Cam BA 91 ACA 86. Westcott Ho Cam 89. **d** 92 **p** 93. C Swindon St Jo and St Andr *Bris* 92–96; TV Preston w Sutton Poyntz, Littlemoor etc *Sarum* 96–04; P-in-c N Poole Ecum Team 04–06; TR 06–15; Adn Dorset from 15; Can and Preb Sarum Cathl from 12. *28 Merriefield Drive, Broadstone BH18 8PB* E: amacrowwood@mac.com *or* addorset@salisbury.anglican.org

MacSWAIN, Robert Carroll. b 69. Liberty Univ USA BA 92 Princeton Th Sem MDiv 95 Edin Univ MTh 96 St Andr Univ PhD 10. Virginia Th Sem 00. **d** 01 **p** 02. C Kinston St Mary USA 01–04; Chapl and Fell St Chad's Coll Dur 05–08; Instructor Univ of the South USA 09–10; Asst Prof 10–15; Assoc Prof from 15. *The School of Theology, University of the South, Sewanee TN 37383-0001, USA* E: robert.macswain@sewanee.edu

McTEER, Canon Robert Ian. b 56. Chich Th Coll 90. **d** 92 **p** 93. C S Shields All SS *Dur* 92–95; P-in-c Auckland St Helen 95–97; V from 97; Chapl Bishop Auckland Hospitals NHS Trust 95–98; Chapl S Durham Healthcare NHS Trust 98–02; Hon Can Koforidua from 07. *The Vicarage, 8 Manor Road, St Helen Auckland, Bishop Auckland DL14 9EN* T: (01388) 604152 E: fr.r.mcteer@btinternet.com

McTERNAN, Ms Margaret Siobhan. b 70. Edin Univ LLB 92 Dundee Univ MSc 95 DipSW 95. **d** 11 **p** 12. C Glas St Marg

11–21. Flat 0/1, 9 Kennoway Drive, Glasgow G11 7UA T: 0141-337 2604 M: 07738-054461 E: maggsmct@gmail.com

McTIGHE, Ann-Margaret. b 67. Brunel Univ BSc 97 PGCE 98. Trin Coll Bris BA 10. **d** 10 **p** 11. C Woodford St Mary w St Phil and St Jas *Chelmsf* 10–12; C Woodford Wells 12–14; Pioneer Min Olympic Park 14–19; C Stratford St Paul and St Jas *Chelmsf* 14–19; C Stratford St Jo w Ch Ch 15–19; Fresh Expressions Development Officer *St Alb* from 19; PtO *Lon* from 15. *29 Gun Tower Mews, Rochester ME1 3GU* M: 07940-892391 E: revanniemct@gmail.com

MacVANE, Ms Sara Ann Andrew. b 44. Wellesley Coll (USA) BA 66 Univ of Wales (Ban) BA 05. EAMTC 03. **d** 05 **p** 06. C Rome *Eur* 05–09; Asst Dir Angl Cen Rome 05–09; P-in-c Nord Pas de Calais *Eur* 09–11; Asst Chapl Zürich 11–14; PtO 14–21. *60 rue Victor Hugo, 93170 Bagnolet, France* E: macvanesara@gmail.com

McVEAGH, Paul Stuart. b 56. Southn Univ BA 78. Oak Hill Th Coll BA 88. **d** 88 **p** 89. C Bebington *Ches* 88–92; Crosslinks Portugal 92–95; R High Halstow w All Hallows and Hoo St Mary *Roch* 95–02; V Westerham 02–15; P-in-c Ashburnham w Penhurst *Chich* 15–17; rtd 17. *91 Warrington Road, Paddock Wood, Tonbridge TN12 6JS* E: pmcveagh@aol.com

MACVEAN, Mrs Amanda Sharon. b 58. K Alfred's Coll Win BEd 80. STETS 09. **d** 12 **p** 13. C Banstead *Guildf* 12–16; V Effingham w Lt Bookham from 16. *The Rectory, 4 Leewood Way, Effingham, Leatherhead KT24 5JN* T: (01372) 458314 E: rev.mandymacvean@gmail.com

McVEETY, Canon Ian. b 46. NOC 82. **d** 85 **p** 86. C Langley and Parkfield *Man* 85–89; V Castleton Moor 89–99; AD Heywood and Middleton 95–99; V Baguley 99–12; AD Withington 06–12; Hon Can Man Cathl 07–12; rtd 12; PtO *Man* from 12. *873 Walmersley Road, Bury BL9 5LE* T: 0161-797 3575 E: imcveety22@btinternet.com

McVEIGH, Miss Dorothy Sara. b 67. QUB BA 89 TCD BTh 93. CITC 90. **d** 93 **p** 94. C Belfast St Matt *Conn* 93–96; C Carrickfergus 96–99; C Lurgan Ch the Redeemer *D & D* 99–04; I Annaghmore *Arm* from 04. *54 Moss Road, Portadown, Craigavon BT62 1NB* T: (028) 3885 2751 M: 07786-454346 E: mcveigh423@btinternet.com

McVEIGH, Samuel. b 49. MBE TD DL 14. CITC 77. **d** 79 **p** 80. C Drumragh w Mountfield *D & R* 79–82; I Dromore *Clogh* 82–90; I Drumachose *D & R* 90–21; Can Derry Cathl 01–21; Can St Patr Cathl Dublin 18–21; rtd 21. *15 Apollo Gardens, Portrush BT56 8SG* M: 07889-769412 E: mcveigh_family@yahoo.co.uk

McVEIGH, Sandra. See BARTON, Sandra

McWATT, Glenn Ellsworth. b 48. S'wark Ord Course 89. **d** 92 **p** 93. NSM Tulse Hill H Trin and St Matthias *S'wark* 92–99; C New Malden and Coombe 99–03; C Reigate St Mary 03–08; C Gillingham St Mark *Roch* 08–12; P-in-c Grain w Stoke 12–14; rtd 14. *16 Fittleworth Garden, Rustington, Littlehampton BN16 3EW* T: (01903) 774750 E: glennmcwatt@btinternet.com

McWHINNEY, Susan Elizabeth. b 59. Newnham Coll Cam BA 80 MB, BChir 83 MA 84 Sheff Univ BA 16. Yorks Min Course 13. **d** 16 **p** 17. NSM Baildon *Leeds* 16–17; NSM Calverley 17–21; NSM Upper Aire from 21. *The Vicarage, Kirkby Malham, Skipton BD23 4BS* E: sue.mcwhinney@leeds.anglican.org

McWHIRTER, James Angus. b 58. Portsm Poly BA 91 Trin Coll Carmarthen PGCE 93. St Steph Ho Ox 00. **d** 02 **p** 03. C Shifnal *Lich* 02–06; CF 07–18; Chapl RNR from 18. *29 Coniston Road, Edith Weston, Oakham LE15 8HP* E: revdjames.mcwh@btopenworld.com

McWHIRTER (née BELL), Canon Jennifer Kathryn. b 77. Harper Adams Univ Coll BSc 99 QUB MTh 10. CITC BTh 04. **d** 04 **p** 05. Asst Chapl R Gp of Hosps Health and Soc Services Trust 04–06; Asst Chapl Belfast City Hosp Health and Soc Services Trust 04–06; Chapl Belfast Health and Soc Care Trust 06–13; C Belfast St Anne *Conn* 04–06; C Belfast St Nic 06–08; I Templepatrick w Donegore 08–13; Bp's Dom Chapl 08–13; Dir CME Ch of Ireland Th Inst 13–16; Chapl Ch of Ireland Min to Deaf People from 13; P-in-c Killala w Dunfeeny, Crossmolina, Kilmoremoy etc *T, K & A* 16–20; I Aughaval w Achill, Knappagh, Dugort etc from 20; Dioc Dir of Ords from 17; St Patr Cathl Dublin from 18. *The Rectory, Newport Road, Westport, Co Mayo, Republic of Ireland* M: (00353) 85-877 8650 E: revjkmcwhirter@yahoo.co.uk

McWHIRTER, The Ven Stephen Joseph. b 64. Open Univ BA 02. St Jo Coll Nottm MTh 11. **d** 13 **p** 13. C Lisburn St Paul *Conn* 13–15; I Killala w Dunfeeny, Crossmolina, Kilmoremoy etc *T, K & A* from 15; Adn Killala and Achonry from 17; Adn Tuam from 18. *The Rectory, Newport Road, Westport, Co Mayo, Republic of Ireland* M: (00353) 85-877 8650 E: vensj@mcwhirter.ie

McWILLIAMS, Amelia. CITC. **d** 09 **p** 10. NSM Brackaville w Donaghendry and Ballyclog *Arm* 09–12; NSM Portadown St Mark 12–20; NSM Clogherny w Seskinore and Drumnakilly from 20. *47 Alexander Avenue, Armagh BT61 7JD* T: (028) 3752 7456 E: amcwilliams861@btinternet.com

McWILLIAMS, Evan. *See* McWILLIAMS, Patrick Evan

McWILLIAMS, John Alan. b 46. Yorks Min Course 16. **d** 17. NSM S Holderness Deanery from 17. *5 Beechwood Views, Roos, Hull HU12 0HQ*

McWILLIAMS, Laura Jane. *See* HEWITT, Laura Jane

McWILLIAMS, Patrick Evan. b 86. Savannah Coll of Art and Design BFA 08 MA 09 York Univ PhD 16 St Jo Coll Dur BATM 18. Cranmer Hall Dur 15. **d** 18 **p** 19. C Spalding St Mary and St Nic *Linc* 18–21; C Smithfield Gt St Bart *Lon* from 21; Chapl Barts Health NHS Trust from 21. *Flat 49, 28 Bartholomew Close, London EC1A 7ES* M: 07598-910722 E: rev.dr.mcwilliams@gmail.com

MACY, Jonathan Edward Gordon. b 68. Oak Hill Th Coll BA 96 Heythrop Coll Lon MTh 98 K Coll Lon PhD 04. Wycliffe Hall Ox MTh 09. **d** 10 **p** 11. C Plumstead St Jo w St Jas and St Paul *S'wark* 10–14; TV Thamesmead from 14. *62-64 Battery Road, London SE28 0JT* T: (020) 8836 9069 M: 07910-988014 E: jegmacy@googlemail.com

MADANAT, Carolyn. b 72. Wycliffe Hall Ox 19. **d** 21. C Kingston Hill St Paul *S'wark* from 21. *33A Queens Road, Kingston upon Thames KT2 7SF* E: carolyn.madanat@stpaulskingston.org.uk

MADDEN, Kenneth Usher. b 48. St Jo Coll Dur BA 70 Lon Inst of Educn PGCE 73. WEMTC 06. **d** 09 **p** 10. NSM Newent and Gorsley w Cliffords Mesne *Glouc* 09–13; NSM Bath St Mich Without *B & W* from 13; C Bath Abbey w St Jas 18–21; rtd 21; PtO *B & W* from 21. *Odd Down Lodge, Upper Bloomfield Road, Bath BA2 2RU* T: (01225) 353071 M: 07894-208501 E: kenandlibby@virginmedia.com

MADDEN, Michael John. b 60. Lanc Univ BSc 81 Brunel Univ MBA 92 Open Univ MPhil 08 Lon Sch of Th MTh 12. St Mellitus Coll 17. **d** 19 **p** 20. NSM Hanborough and Freeland *Ox* from 19. *2 Hutchcombe Farm Close, Oxford OX2 9HG* T: (01865) 865743 M: 07768-450534 E: curate_mike@hanboroughparish.co.uk

MADDISON, Simon Christopher. b 63. St Steph Ho Ox 10. **d** 12 **p** 13. C Hendon St Alphage *Lon* 12–15; V Edmonton St Aldhelm 15–18; PtO from 19; V Cross Heath *Lich* from 19; V Newcastle St Paul from 19. *St Michael's Presbytery, Linden Grove, Newcastle ST5 9LJ* T: (01782) 614287 M: 07906-156932 E: fr.simon.ssc@outlook.com

MADDOCK, Claire Louise. *See* McCLELLAND, Claire Louise

MADDOCK, David John Newcomb. b 36. Qu Coll Cam BA 60 MA 64. Oak Hill Th Coll 60. **d** 62 **p** 63. C Bispham *Blackb* 62–65; R 82–93; RD Blackpool 90–93; Miss Payne Bay Canada 65-69; R Frobisher Bay 70; R Walsoken *Ely* 70–77; V Ore Ch *Chich* 77–82; V Fowey *Truro* 93–02; Chapl Cornwall Healthcare NHS Trust 94–02; rtd 02; PtO *Chich* 14–19; *Blackb* 19–20. *23 Fosbrooke House, 8 Clifton Drive, Lytham St Annes FY8 5RQ* E: david.maddock764@btinternet.com

MADDOCK, Nicholas Rokeby. b 47. ABSM 72 Birm Coll of Educn CertEd 73. Linc Th Coll 82. **d** 82 **p** 83. C Romford St Edw *Chelmsf* 82–87; V Sway *Win* 87–94; V Taunton St Mary *B & W* 94–04; R Wrington w Butcombe and Burrington 04–17; rtd 17; PtO *B & W* from 18. *3 Friary Close, Clevedon BS21 7QA* T: (01275) 870751 M: 07735-501659 E: nr.maddock@gmail.com

MADDOCK, Philip Arthur Louis. b 47. Open Univ BA 82 Lanc Univ MPhil 02. Oak Hill Th Coll 75. **d** 78 **p** 79. C New Ferry *Ches* 78–81; C Barnston 81–82; V Over St Jo 82–85; V Norley and Chapl to the Deaf 85–88; P-in-c Treales and Chapl to the Deaf *Blackb* 88–96; Chapl to the Deaf *Lich* 96–02; C Yoxall and The Ridwares and Kings Bromley 98–02; Adv for Deaf and Disabled People Min Division 03–12; rtd 12; NSM Alrewas and Wychnor *Lich* 03–13; PtO *Blackb* from 14; *Lich* from 19. *35 Hampshire Crescent, Stoke-on-Trent ST3 4TR* E: pcmaddock@gmail.com

MADDOCK-LYON, John Frederick. b 38. K Coll Lon AKC 62 BD 64. **d** 64 **p** 65. C Woodchurch *Ches* 64–67; C Higher Bebington 67–70; V Sandbach Heath 70–80; V Egremont St Jo 80–88; Chapl Br Emb and Athens St Paul *Eur* 88–91; rtd 99; PtO *Newc* from 05. *29 Robson's Way, Amble, Morpeth NE65 0GA* T: (01665) 711126 E: rivendel66@yahoo.co.uk

MADDOCKS, Alison Julie. b 63. Birm Univ BSc 84 Loughb Univ MBA 92. St Jo Coll Nottm MTh 03. **d** 03 **p** 04; C Wollaton *S'well* 03–06; Retail Chapl Birm City Cen 06–08; Ind Chapl *S'well* 08–11; C Nottingham All SS, St Mary and St Pet 08–11; P-in-c Breadsall *Derby* 11–17; Stewardship and Resources Officer *Worc* from 17. *16 Lowesmoor Wharf, Lowesmoor, Worcester WR1 2RS* T: (01905) 20537 E: amaddocks@cofe-worcester.org.uk

MADDOX, Derek Adrian James. b 64. Kingston Poly BA 88. Trin Coll Bris 02. **d** 04 **p** 05. C Mitcham St Mark *S'wark* 04–07; P-in-c S Yardley St Mich *Birm* 07–08; V 08–13; P-in-c Withywood *Bris* from 13; P-in-c Bris St Andr Hartcliffe from 13. *St Oswald's Vicarage, Cheddar Grove, Bristol BS13 7EN* E: derekmaddox8@gmail.com

MADDOX, Hugh Inglis Monteath. b 37. CCC Cam BA 60. Westcott Ho Cam 61. **d** 63 **p** 64. C Attercliffe *Sheff* 63–66; C Maidstone All SS w St Phil *Cant* 66–67; C Folkestone St Mary and St Eanswythe 67–69; C St Martin-in-the-Fields *Lon* 69–73; R Sandwich *Cant* 73–81; V St Peter-in-Thanet 81–84; V Red Post *Sarum* 84–03; rtd 03; PtO *Sarum* from 03. *36 Corfe Road, Stoborough, Wareham BH20 5AD* T: (01929) 550872

MADDOX, Phillipa Louise. b 71. St Mellitus Coll BA 20. **d** 20 **p** 21. C Leavesden *St Alb* from 20. *49 Ross Crescent, Watford WD25 0DA* M: 07900-618690 E: phillipamaddox@gmail.com or rev.phillipa@allsaintslife.com

MADDY, Kevin. b 58. Selw Coll Cam BA 83 MA 87 GRNCM 79 FRSA 96. Westcott Ho Cam 81. **d** 85 **p** 86. C St Peter-in-Thanet *Cant* 85–88; Chapl RAF 88–02; CF 02–07; Chapl Miss to Seafarers and R Yokohama Ch Ch 07–11; V Monk Bretton *Wakef* 11–14; P-in-c Lundwood 11–14; P-in-c Hackington *Cant* 14–21; R from 21; Chapl Abp's Sch Cant from 14; AD Cant 17–19. *The Rectory, St Stephen's Green, Canterbury CT2 7JU* T: (01227) 477171 M: 07720-499403 E: revkmaddy@gmail.com

MADELEY, Mark Keith. b 68. AVCM 96. Oak Hill Th Coll BA 93. **d** 93 **p** 94. C Mickleover All SS *Derby* 93–96; C Charlesworth and Dinting Vale 96–99; Chapl Chr Tours (UK) Ltd 99–00; NSM Moldgreen and Rawthorpe *Wakef* 99–00; V Coley 00–11; R Weston-super-Mare St Nic w St Barn *B & W* from 12. *Uphill Rectory, 3 Old Church Road, Uphill, Weston-super-Mare BS23 4UH* T/F: (01934) 620156 M: 07947-159795 E: mark@mibtravel.co.uk

MADELEY, Timothy Philip. b 86. Derby Univ LLB 07 BPP Univ LLM 08. Ridley Hall Cam 13. **d** 16 **p** 17. C Bentham, Burton-in-Lonsdale, Chapel-le-Dale etc *Leeds* 16–19; V Bushmead *St Alb* from 19. *73 Hawkfields, Luton LU2 7NW* T: (01582) 454081 M: 07307-191582 E: tim@christchurch-bushmead.org.uk

MADGWICK, Mrs Philippa Jane. b 60. Magd Coll Ox BA 84 MA 88 DPhil 88 Anglia Ruskin Univ BA 09. SAOMC 04 ERMC 05. **d** 07 **p** 08. NSM St Alb St Steph 07–17; SSMs' Officer *St Alb* Adnry 14–17; R Empingham, Edith Weston, Lyndon, Manton etc *Pet* from 17. *19 Digby Drive, North Luffenham, Oakham LE15 8JS* T: (01780) 721286 E: rectorrwb@gmail.com

MADIN, Jacob Lloyd. b 92. Man Univ BA 14. Cranmer Hall Dur 14. **d** 16 **p** 17. C Walsall St Matt *Lich* 16–18; C York St Hilda 18–19; 20s-40s Team Ldr from 19; C Scarborough St Mary w Ch Ch and H Apostles from 19. *160 Dean Road, Scarborough YO12 7JH* M: 07403-271274

MADINDA, John Yohana. b 63. Ox Cen for Miss Studies MA 05. Lon Bible Coll BA 96. **d** 98 **p** 00. Lect St Phil Th Coll Tanzania 97–05; Prin 05–15; C Bunwell, Carleton Rode, Tibenham, Gt Moulton etc *Nor* 15–16; TV Long Stratton and Pilgrim TM from 16. *Old Church House, Chapel Road, Carleton Rode, Norwich NR16 1RN* T: (01953) 789240 M: 07486-352758 E: jymadinda@yahoo.com

MADZORERA, Rainah Huschu. b 59. SCTEI 20. **d** 21. NSM Aylesbury *Ox* from 21; Chapl Ox Health NHS Foundn Trust from 21. *110 Fowler Road, Aylesbury HP19 7QG*

MAFFEI, Andrea Jane. b 68. ERMC 16. **d** 18 **p** 19. C Flitwick *St Alb* 18–21; V Kempston Transfiguration from 21. *The Vicarage, Cleveland Street, Kempston, Bedford MK42 8DW*

MAGEE, Keith Robert. b 60. Trin Coll Bris BA 95 Bris Univ PGCE 96. Westcott Ho Cam 99 Seabury-Western Th Sem 00. **d** 01 **p** 02. C S Woodham Ferrers *Chelmsf* 01–05; V Moulsham St Jo 05–12; V Knighton St Mary Magd *Leic* 12–16; V Braunstone Park 16–20; TR Dorchester and the Winterbournes *Sarum* from 20. *38 Herringston Road, Dorchester DT1 2BS* M: 07766-645135 E: keith.magee@btinternet.com

MAGGS, Sophie Claire. *See* BANNISTER, Sophie Claire

MAGINNIS, Samuel Robert Henry. b 85. St Steph Ho Ox 17. **d** 19 **p** 20. C Loughton St Jo *Chelmsf* from 19. *12 The Greens Close, Loughton IG10 1QE* E: rev.smlt@gmail.com

MAGNESS, Anthony William John. b 37. New Coll Ox BA 62 MA 65 Ch Coll Liv PGCE 76. Coll of Resurr Mirfield 78. **d** 80 **p** 81. C Gt Crosby St Faith *Liv* 80–83; C Newc St Jo 83–85; P-in-c Newc St Luke 85–88; P-in-c Newc St Andr 88; V Newc St Andr and St Luke 89–99; Chapl Hunter's Moor Hosp 89–95; P-in-c Cambois *Newc* 99–00; P-in-c Sleekburn 99–00; V Cambois and Sleekburn 00–03; rtd 03; PtO *Newc* from 03. *59 Firtree Crescent, Newcastle upon Tyne NE12 7JU* T/F: 0191-268 4596

MAGNUSSON, Lisbet Maria. b 50. Mid-Sweden Univ BSc(Econ) 85 Uppsala Univ MDiv 93 ML 98. Past Inst Uppsala 93. **p** 94. In Ch of Sweden 94–98; C Crosby *Linc* 98–99; TV Gainsborough and Morton 99–04; P-in-c Swallow and Chapl Doncaster and S Humber Healthcare NHS Trust 04–06; Sweden from 06. *Haggkullevagen 26, 184 37 Akersberga, Stockholm, Sweden* T: (0046) (8) 5816 1478 *or* (0) 7 0340 3870 M: 70-638 9996 E: lisbet.magnusson@svenskakyrkan.se

MAGORRIAN, Brian Geoffrey. b 64. St Aid Coll Dur BSc 85 York Univ DPhil 89. St Jo Coll Nottm. **d** 01 **p** 02. C Bishopwearmouth St Gabr *Dur* 01–04; P-in-c Brough w Stainmore, Musgrave and Warcop *Carl* 04–10; C Whitfield *Derby* 10–14; V Walton St Jo 14–17. *41 New Hall Street, Macclesfield SK10 3AB* M: 07751-357194 E: brianmagorrian@tiscali.co.uk

✠**MAGOWAN, The Rt Revd Alistair James.** b 55. Leeds Univ BSc 77 Ox Univ MTh 02. Trin Coll Bris 78. **d** 81 **p** 82 **c** 09. C Owlerton *Sheff* 81–84; C Dur St Nic 84–89; Chapl St Aid Coll 85–89; V Egham *Guildf* 89–00; RD Runnymede 93–98; Adn Dorset *Sarum* 00–09; Can and Preb Sarum Cathl 00–09; Suff Bp Ludlow *Heref* 09–20; Adn Ludlow 09–20; rtd 20; Hon Asst Bp Lich from 21. *19 Kenton Drive, Shrewsbury SY2 6TH*

MAGOWAN, Harold Victor. b 34. QUB BA 55 BSc(Econ) 66 DipEd 69 ACII 69 FCII 73. TCD Div Sch Div Test 57. **d** 57 **p** 58. C Antrim All SS w Muckamore *Conn* 57–59. *6 Fold Mews, 22 Ballyholme Road, Bangor BT20 5JS* T: (028) 9146 5091

MAGOWAN, Ian Walter. b 51. St Paul's Coll Chelt CertEd 73 Ulster Poly BEd 82 TCD BTh 07. CITC 04. **d** 07 **p** 08. C Killowen *D & R* 07–10; I Connor w Antrim St Patr *Conn* from 10. *Connor Rectory, 50 Church Road, Kells, Ballymena BT42 3JU* T: (028) 2589 1254 M: 07810-636167 E: iwmagowan@hotmail.co.uk

MAGOWAN, Margaret Louise. b 57. SRN 77 SCM 80. WEMTC 11. **d** 14 **p** 15. NSM Church Stretton *Heref* 14–20. *19 Kenton Drive, Shrewsbury SY2 6TH*

MAGRATH, Richard David. b 84. Homerton Coll Cam BA 06 Jes Coll Cam BA 18. Ridley Hall Cam 16. **d** 19 **p** 20. C Finchley St Mary *Lon* from 19. *28 Hendon Lane, London N3 1TR* E: richard@richardmagrath.com

MAGUIRE, Alan. b 45. CBDTI 03. **d** 06 **p** 07. NSM Croglin and Holme Eden and Wetheral w Warwick *Carl* 06–09; NSM Carl H Trin and St Barn 09–12; P-in-c Lowther and Askham and Clifton and Brougham 12–17; rtd 17. *16 Harker Park Road, Harker Park, Carlisle CA6 4HS* T: (01228) 672891 E: alan.maguire2017@outlook.com

MAGUIRE, Canon Brian William. b 33. Hull Univ BTh 84 MA 88. Coll of Resurr Mirfield 70. **d** 72 **p** 73. C Guisborough *York* 72–76; TV Haxby w Wigginton 76–77; TR 78–89; V Huddersfield St Pet and All SS *Wakef* 89–00; Hon Can Wakef Cathl 94–00; rtd 00; PtO *Wakef* 00–14; *Leeds* 14–16; Bp's Dom Chapl *Wakef* 03–04; PtO *Lich* 12–21. *33 Chapel Lane, Lichfield WS14 9BA* T: (01543) 305936 E: bwmaguire@virginmedia.com

MAGUIRE, Luke Karl. b 87. Warwick Univ BA 09 Leeds Univ BA 11. Coll of Resurr Mirfield 09. **d** 12 **p** 13. C Rochdale *Man* 12–13; C Salford All SS 13–15; P-in-c Stretford All SS 15–18; R from 18. *The Rectory, 233 Barton Road, Stretford, Manchester M32 9RB* T: 0161-865 1350 E: lukekarlmaguire@googlemail.com

MAGUIRE (*formerly* **GRATTON**)**, Canon Patricia Margaret.** b 46. Leeds Univ BTh 94 MA 96 SRN 67 TCert 84 CertEd 88. EMMTC 89 NOC 96. **d** 97 **p** 98. NSM Shipley St Pet *Bradf* 97–99; C Brighouse and Clifton *Wakef* 99–00; Chapl Wakef Cathl Sch 00–05; P-in-c Lupset *Wakef* 05–11; P-in-c Thornes 00–11; RD Wakef 08–11; Hon Can Wakef Cathl 08–11; rtd 11; PtO *Lich* 12–21. *33 Chapel Lane, Lichfield WS14 9BA* T: (01543) 305936 E: revmaguire@virginmedia.com

MAGUIRE, Sarah Alison. *See* EDMONDS, Sarah Alison

MAHAJANGA, Bishop of. *See* SPEERS, Samuel Hall

MAHER, David James. b 70. St Jo Coll Dur BA 01. Cranmer Hall Dur 98. **d** 01 **p** 02. C Hounslow H Trin w St Paul and St Mary *Lon* 01–04; C Staines 04–07; Chapl to Bp Kensington 04–07; V Chesterton Gd Shep *Ely* from 07; RD Cambridge N 14–19. *The Good Shepherd Vicarage, 51 Highworth Avenue, Cambridge CB4 2BQ* T: (01223) 351844 *or* 312933 E: vicar@churchofthegoodshepherd.co.uk

MAHER, Capt Ian. b 58. Open Univ BA 97 MEd 01. CA Tr Coll 88 Yorks Min Course 11. **d** 12 **p** 13. Multifaith Chapl Co-ord Sheff Hallam Univ 06–18; Hon C Sheff Cathl 12–14; Min Can from 14. *3 Parsonage Street, Walkley, Sheffield S6 5BL* T: 0114-232 2330 *or* 225 4577 M: 07791-639820 E: ian.maher@sheffield.anglican.org

MAHILUM, Bello. b 60. **d** 10 **p** 11. NSM Notting Hill St Jo *Lon* 10–14; PtO 16–19; Chapl R Brompton and Harefield NHS Foundn Trust from 19; NSM Notting Hill All SS w St Columb *Lon* from 19; NSM Notting Hill St Mich and Ch Ch from 19. *5 Faith Court, Cooper's Road, London SE1 5HD* T: (020) 3731 7111 M: 07738-330861 E: blmahilum@gmail.com

MAHON, Stephanie Mary. *See* SOKOLOWSKI, Stephanie Mary

MAIDEN, Charles Alistair Kingsley. b 60. Trent Poly BSc 84. St Jo Coll Nottm LTh 88. **d** 89 **p** 90. C Porchester *S'well* 89–93; C Selston 93–96; P-in-c Huthwaite 96–11; V from 11. *The Vicarage, Blackwell Road, Huthwaite, Sutton-in-Ashfield NG17 2QT* T: (01623) 555053 E: charliemaiden@hotmail.com

MAIDMENT, Ross James. b 90. Regent's Park Coll Ox BTh 15 Cardiff Univ MTh 16 MPhil 21. St Padarn's Inst 16. **d** 17 **p** 18. C Rumney *Mon* 17–20; Chapl Win Coll from 20; Chapl RNR from 21. *Winchester College, College Street, Winchester SO23 9NA* M: 07498-210383 E: rjm2@wincoll.ac.uk

MAIDMENT, Thomas John Louis. b 43. Lon Univ BSc 65. St Steph Ho Ox. **d** 67 **p** 68. C Westmr St Steph w St Jo *Lon* 67–73; P-in-c Twickenham Common H Trin 73–77; V 77–80; V Heston 80–98; V Bolton-le-Sands *Blackb* 98–08; P-in-c Tunstall w Melling and Leck 02–03; AD Tunstall 99–05; rtd 08; PtO *Blackb* from 08. *69 Aintree Road, Thornton-Cleveleys FY5 5HW* T: (01253) 829399 E: t.j.l.m@btinternet.com

MAIDSTONE, Archdeacon of. *See* SEWELL, The Ven Andrew William

MAIDSTONE, Suffragan Bishop. *See* THOMAS, The Rt Revd Roderick Charles Howell

MAIN, Clive Timothy. b 53. St Andr Univ MA 75 Cam Univ PGCE 76. Oak Hill Th Coll BA 94. **d** 96 **p** 97. C Alperton *Lon* 96–00; V Highbury New Park St Aug 00–12; TR Hackney Marsh 12–19; R Homerton from 19. *St Barnabas' Rectory, 111 Homerton High Street, London E9 6DL* T: (020) 8533 1156 E: clivemain@outlook.com

MAINE, Michael John. b 57. Leeds Univ BA 11 FGMS 95. Coll of Resurr Mirfield 09. **d** 11 **p** 12. C Willingdon *Chich* 11–15; V Cuckfield 15–20; V Cuckfield and Bolney from 20; RD Cuckfield from 16. *The Vicarage, 5 Barrowfield, Cuckfield, Haywards Heath RH17 5ER* M: 07895-415143 E: michaeljmaine@btinternet.com

MAINES, Canon Trevor. b 40. Leeds Univ BSc 63. Ripon Hall Ox 63. **d** 65 **p** 66. C Speke All SS *Liv* 65–70; C Stevenage St Geo *St Alb* 70–73; V Dorridge *Birm* 73–78; Org Sec CECS Ex 79–80; Hon C Tiverton St Pet *Ex* 79–80; Org Sec (Wales) CECS 80–87; Hon C Newton Nottage *Llan* 81–83; PtO *Mon* 83–87; V Arlesey w Astwick *St Alb* 87–95; RD Shefford 91–95; V Goldington 95–05; rtd 05; Hon Can St Alb 04–05; rtd 05; Hon C Beedon and Peasemore w W Ilsley and Farnborough *Ox* 05–07; Hon C Brightwalton w Catmore, Leckhampstead etc 05–07; PtO from 12. *1 Adlam Villas, Greenham Road, Newbury RG14 7HX* T: (01635) 551352 E: trevor.maines@ntlworld.com

MAINEY, Ian George. b 51. CertEd 73. Oak Hill Th Coll BA 87. **d** 87 **p** 88. C Denton Holme *Carl* 87–91; V Hensingham 91–02; RD Calder 01–02; TR Deane *Man* 02–09; P-in-c Birkdale St Jas *Liv* 09–19; V 19–21; P-in-c Birkdale St Pet 09–21; rtd 21. *Address temp unknown* E: ian.mainey@gmail.com

MAINWARING (*née* **LANKSHEAR**)**, The Ven Jane Frances.** b 70. Leeds Univ BA 92 Trin Coll Carmarthen MPhil 97 PhD 99. EAMTC 98. **d** 00 **p** 01. C Sudbury and Chilton *St E* 00–03; TV Hitchin *St Alb* 03–16; TV Hitchin and St Paul's Walden 16–20; RD Hitchin 15–20; Hon Can St Alb 19–20; Adn St Alb from 20. *41 Wymondley Road, Hitchin SG4 9PR* T: (01727) 818121 E: archd@stalbans.anglican.org

MAIRS, Canon Adrian Samuel. b 43. Oak Hill Th Coll 76. **d** 78 **p** 79. C Rugby St Matt *Cov* 78–82; P-in-c Mancetter 82–84; V 84–08; P-in-c Hartshill 97–01; Hon Can Cov Cathl 03–08; rtd 08; PtO *Blackb* from 14. *15 Salter Fell Road, Lancaster LA1 2PX* T: (01524) 382206

MAITLAND, The Hon Sydney Milivoje Patrick. b 51. Edin Univ BSc MRTPI. St Jo Coll Nottm. **d** 86 **p** 87. Hon C Glas St Geo 86–01; C Glas St Bride 03–11; P-in-c Glas All SS from 11. *14 Kersland Street, Glasgow G12 8BL* T: 0141-339 4573 E: sydneymaitland@btinternet.com

MAJOR, James Edward. b 54. Trin Coll Bris 78. **d** 81 **p** 82. C Parr *Liv* 81–84; V Burton Fleming w Fordon *York* 84–85; V Grindale and Ergham 84–85; P-in-c Wold Newton 84–85; V Burton Fleming w Fordon, Grindale etc 85–91; V Bilton St Pet 91–15; R Woodhall Spa Gp *Linc* 15–19; rtd 19; PtO *York* from 20. *5 Old Chapel Close, Long Riston, Hull HU11 5LA* E: revrichardmajor@gmail.com

MAJOR, Richard John Charles. b 63. Massey Univ (NZ) BA 85 Ex Coll Ox BA 91 MA 93 Magd Coll Ox DPhil 91. St Steph Ho Ox 92. **d** 94 **p** 95. C Truro Cathl 94–97; C Putney St Mary

S'wark 97–98; Chapl Florence w Siena *Eur* 98–01; USA from 01. *Nansough Manor, Ladock, Truro TR2 4PB* T: (01726) 883315 *or* (001) (718) 442 1589 F: (718) 442 4555 E: email@richardmajor.com

MAK, Marcus Andreas. b 81. Ox Brookes Univ BA 10 St Jo Coll Dur BA 15. Cranmer Hall Dur 13. **d** 15 **p** 16. C N Poole Ecum Team *Sarum* 15–16; C Creekmoor 17–19; V Felixstowe Ch Ch *St E* from 19. *1 Parsonage Close, Felixstowe IP11 2QR* M: 07978-588524 E: revmmak@gmail.com

MAKANJUOLA, Mrs Olufolake Oluyomi. b 60. New England Coll BA 84. St Aug Coll of Th 15. **d** 17 **p** 18. C Roch St Pet w St Marg 17–20; P-in-c Croydon St Andr *S'wark* from 20; C Croydon St Jo from 20. *The Vicarage, 20A Haling Park Road, South Croydon CR2 6NE* M: 07714-770769 E: lekkipen@gmail.com

MAKEL, Arthur. b 39. AKC 63. **d** 64 **p** 65. C Beamish *Dur* 64–68; Ind Chapl *York* 68–72; Ind Chapl and P-in-c Scotton w Northorpe *Linc* 72–81; R Epworth 81–89; P-in-c Wroot 81–89; R Epworth and Wroot 89–92; R Sigglesthorne and Rise w Nunkeeling and Bewholme *York* 92–04; P-in-c Aldbrough, Mappleton w Goxhill and Withernwick 98–04; rtd 04; PtO *York* 04–11. *43 Lowfield Road, Beverley HU17 9RF* T: (01482) 865798 E: arthur-makel@makelhouse.karoo.co.uk

MAKEPEACE, David Norman Harry. b 51. Magd Coll Ox BA 74. Trin Coll Bris 83. **d** 85 **p** 86. C Romford Gd Shep *Chelmsf* 85–88; Tanzania 88–89; C York St Paul 89–91; TV Radipole and Melcombe Regis *Sarum* 91–98; V Sandgate St Paul w Folkestone St Geo *Cant* 98–00; PtO from 01. *Flat 1, 33 Augusta Gardens, Folkestone CT20 2RT* T: (01303) 259342

MAKEPEACE, Preb James Dugard. b 40. Keble Coll Ox BA 63 MA 67. Cuddesdon Coll 63. **d** 65 **p** 66. C Cullercoats St Geo *Newc* 65–68; Lib Pusey Ho and Chapl Wadh Coll Ox 68–72; V Romford St Edw *Chelmsf* 72–79; V Tettenhall Regis *Lich* 79–80; TR 80–99; RD Trysull 87–97; Preb Lich Cathl 96–99; rtd 00; PtO *Lich* 00–21; *Worc* from 17. *3 Shaw Lane, Albrighton, Wolverhampton WV7 3DS* T: (01902) 375472 E: jamesdugard@hotmail.com

⌖**MAKHULU, The Most Revd Walter Paul Khotso.** b 35. CMG 00. Kent Univ Hon DD 88 Gen Th Sem NY Hon DD 99. St Pet Rosettenville Selly Oak Coll. **d** 57 **p** 58 **c** 79. S Africa 57–61; Bechuanaland 61–63; C Poplar All SS w St Frideswide *Lon* 64–66; C Pentonville St Silas w Barnsbury St Clem 66–68; V Battersea St Phil *S'wark* 68–72; V Battersea St Phil w St Bart 72–75; Bp Botswana 79–00; Abp Cen Africa 80–00; rtd 00; Hon Asst Bp Lon from 03. *16 Downside, 8-10 St John's Avenue, London SW15 2AE* T: (020) 8704 1220 E: makhulu@btinternet.com

MAKIN, Martin Stephen. b 77. Salford Univ BSc 98 BSc 03. St Mellitus Coll 17. **d** 20 **p** 21. C Bredbury St Mark *Ches* from 20. *12 Eastwood Drive, Marple, Stockport SK6 7PW* T: 0161-427 8473 M: 07879-737800 E: martinandnaomi@outlook.com

MAKIN, Miss Pauline. b 45. Cranmer Hall Dur 75. **dss** 78 **d** 87 **p** 94. Ashton-in-Makerfield St Thos *Liv* 78–89; Par Dn 87–89; Par Dn Rainford 89–94; C 94–95; C Farnworth 95–10; Asst Dioc Chapl to the Deaf 89–10; rtd 10; PtO *Liv* from 16. *50 Farm Meadow Road, Orrell, Wigan WN5 8TE* T: (01695) 624995 E: paulinemakin@aol.com

MAKIN, Susan. b 65. **d** 13 **p** 14. NSM Hoxton St Anne w St Columba *Lon* 13–14; C St John-at-Hackney 14–17; V Hackney Wick St Mary of Eton w St Aug from 17. *The Vicarage, 95 Eastway, London E9 5JA* T: (020) 7018 2904 M: 07949-532978 E: sue.makin@london.anglican.org

MÄKIPÄÄ, Tuomas. b 78. Helsinki Univ 97. **d** 05 **p** 10. C Helsinki *Eur* 05–12; Chapl from 12. *Kalasatamankatu 15 A 35, 00580 Helsinki, Finland* T: (00358) (50) 309 9132 E: tuomas.makipaa@anglican.fi

MAKOWER, Canon Malory. b 38. TCD BA 61 MA 68 St Jo Coll Ox MA 64 DPhil 64. Ridley Hall Cam 64. **d** 66 **p** 67. C Onslow Square St Paul *Lon* 66–69; Tutor Ridley Hall Cam 69–71; Sen Tutor 71–76; P-in-c Lode and Longmeadow *Ely* 76–84; Warden EAMTC 77–79; Prin 79–84; Dir of Post-Ord Tr for NSM *Nor* 84–90; C Gt Yarmouth 84–89; TV 89–95; Dioc NSM Officer 88–95; Hon Can Nor Cathl 94–97; Prin LNSM Tr Scheme 94–97; rtd 97; PtO *Nor* from 98. *114 Yarmouth Road, Lowestoft NR32 4AQ* T: (01502) 574769 E: m.makower@outlook.com

MAKUMBE, Tendai Puwai. b 72. Birm City Univ BSc 14. Bp Gaul Th Coll Harare 98. **d** 00 **p** 01. C Bonda Miss Zimbabwe 00–02; PtO *Birm* from 15. *30 Spring Road, Edgbaston, Birmingham B15 2HA* M: 07737-466697 E: t.papaya@yahoo.com

MALAM, Susan Mary. b 70. St Mellitus Coll BA 14. **d** 14 **p** 15. NSM Witham and Villages *Chelmsf* from 14; Chapl Mid-Essex Hosp Services NHS Trust from 18. *15 Ramsey Road, Halstead CO9 1EL* T: (01245) 515244 E: sue.malam18@gmail.com

MALAN, Victor Christian de Roubaix. b 39. Cape Town Univ BA 60 Linacre Coll Ox BA 63 MA 68. Wycliffe Hall Ox 61. **d** 63 **p** 64. C Springfield *Birm* 63–66; P-in-c 66–67; C New Windsor *Ox* 67–69; Chapl St Jo Coll Cam 69–74; V Northampton All SS w St Kath *Pet* 74–86; V Stockport St Geo *Ches* 86–89; R N Mundham w Hunston and Merston *Chich* 89–06; rtd 06; PtO *Cant* 07–15; *Chich* from 16. *2 The Hermitage, North Mundham, Chichester PO20 1LE* T: (01243) 781054

MALAY, Prof Jessica Lin. b 61. St Martin's Univ Washington (USA) BA 85 Warwick Univ MA 89 Kent Univ PhD 04 Dur Univ MA 18. St Hild Coll 15. **d** 18 **p** 19. NSM Almondbury w Farnley Tyas *Leeds* from 18. *88 Long Lane, Honley, Holmfirth HD9 6EB* T: (01484) 300963 M: 07541-941208 E: jlmalay@gmail.com *or* jessica.malay@leeds.anglican.org

MALBON, Canon John Allin. b 36. Oak Hill Th Coll 62. **d** 65 **p** 66. C Wolverhampton St Jude *Lich* 65–68; C Hoole *Ches* 68–71; P-in-c Crewe Ch Ch 71–75; V 75–79; V Plemstall w Guilden Sutton 79–01; Hon Can Ches Cathl 96–01; rtd 01; PtO *Ches* from 02. *22 Hawksey Drive, Nantwich CW5 7GF* T: (01270) 611584 E: janjon@hotmail.com

MALCOLM, Andrew Alexander. b 55. Open Univ BA 99 Leic Univ MSc 99 Leeds BA 08 Man Metrop Univ MRes 11. NOC 05. **d** 08 **p** 09. NSM Singleton *Blackb* 08–15; V Langho Billington 12–15; PtO from 15; *Ches* from 16. *32 Main Road, Higher Kinnerton, Chester CH4 9AJ* T: (01244) 661549 M: 07957-846428 E: andrew.malcolm34@btinternet.com

MALCOLM, Mercia Alana. *See* FLANAGAN, Mercia Alana

MALE, Canon David Edward. b 62. Southn Univ BA 83 St Jo Coll Dur BA 90. Cranmer Hall Dur 88. **d** 91 **p** 92. C Leic St Chris 91–94; C Kirkheaton *Wakef* 94–98; P Missr Huddersfield 99–06; Dioc Fresh Expressions Adv *Ely* 06–15; Tutor Ridley Hall Cam 06–15; Nat Adv for Pioneer Development Abps' Coun 15–18; Dir Evang and Discipleship from 18; Hon Can Ely Cathl from 14. *Church House, 27 Great Smith Street, London SW1P 3AZ* M: 07825-578679 E: dave.male@churchofengland.org

MALEK, Mark Mayool. b 44. Khartoum Univ BSc 69 Salford Univ BSc 76 Bradf Coll of Educn PGCE 93. **d** 03 **p** 04. NSM Horton *Bradf* 03–04; NSM Bradf St Oswald Chapel Green 03–04; NSM Lt Horton 04–14; *Leeds* 14–19; rtd 19. *26 Martlett Drive, Bradford BD5 8QG* T: (01274) 732712

MALES, Jeanne Margaret. b 49. Reading Univ BA 71 Lon Univ MPhil 73 Surrey Univ PhD 86 AFBPsS 75 CPsychol 88. S'wark Ord Course 93. **d** 96 **p** 97. NSM Caterham *S'wark* 96–00; C Addington 00–03; V 03–15; rtd 15; PtO *S'wark* from 15; *Cant* from 16. *Collingwood House, 53 High Street, Sandwich CT13 9EG* T: (01304) 275027 E: revjeanne2@gmail.com

MALINS, Mrs Judith. b 47. Bris Univ BA 69. STETS 97. **d** 00 **p** 01. NSM Wilton w Netherhampton and Fugglestone *Sarum* 00–04; P-in-c Kingston, Langton Matravers and Worth Matravers 04–10; P-in-c Wrington w Butcombe and Burrington *B & W* 10–12; rtd 12; PtO *B & W* from 12. *87 Knightcott Road, Banwell BS29 6HR* T: (01934) 824162 E: judith.malins@btinternet.com

MALKIN, Thomas Ross. Hertf Coll Ox BA 86. Trin Coll Bris BA 98 MPhil 00. **d** 99 **p** 00. C Old Trafford St Bride *Man* 99–03; P-in-c Firswood and Gorse Hill 03–10; R from 10. *The Rectory, 24 Canute Road, Stretford, Manchester M32 0RJ* T: 0161-865 1802

MALKINSON, Canon Christopher Mark. b 47. Chich Th Coll 84. **d** 86 **p** 87. C Stroud and Uplands w Slad *Glouc* 86–89; V Cam w Stinchcombe 89–00; P-in-c Tywardreath w Tregaminion *Truro* 00–02; P-in-c St Sampson 00–02; V Padstow 02–17; P-in-c St Merryn and St Issey w St Petroc Minor 16–17; R Padstow, St Merryn and St Issey w St Petroc Minor 17; RD Pydar 03–13; Hon Can Truro Cathl 07–17; rtd 17. *101 Summercourt Way, Brixham TQ5 0RB* E: chrismalk@hotmail.com

MALKINSON, Michael Stephen. b 43. St Steph Ho Ox 65. **d** 68 **p** 69. C New Addington *Cant* 68–71; C Blackpool St Steph *Blackb* 71–74; V Wainfleet St Mary *Linc* 74–81; R Wainfleet All SS w St Thos 74–81; P-in-c Croft 80–81; V Lund *Blackb* 81–93; V Heyhouses on Sea 93–00; R Balcombe *Chich* 00–09; P-in-c Staplefield Common 00–03; rtd 09; PtO *Worc* from 10. *8 Haines Avenue, Wyre Piddle, Pershore WR10 2RQ* T: (01386) 556102 E: malkinson@msn.com

MALLAS, Mrs Wendy Norris. b 42. Reading Univ MA 91 Cov Coll of Educn CertEd 63. STETS 00. **d** 03 **p** 04. NSM Liss *Portsm* 03–07; NSM Blackmoor and Whitehill 07–12; PtO 12–15; NSM Bordon *Guildf* 07–19; PtO *Portsm* from 19. *Mayfield, 45 Hogmoor Road, Whitehill, Bordon GU35 9ET* T: (01420) 478883 E: wendy.mallas@gmail.com *or* wendy.mallas@mayfieldjays.co.uk

MALLETT, John Christopher. b 44. EAMTC. **d** 82 **p** 83. NSM Hethersett w Canteloff *Nor* 82–85; NSM Hethersett w Canteloff w Lt and Gt Melton 85–90; Chapl Wayland Hosp Norfolk 88–94; Chapl Norwich Community Health Partnership NHS Trust 94–00; PtO *Nor* 00–03; NSM Hethersett w Canteloff w Lt and Gt Melton 03–10; rtd 10; PtO *Nor* from 10. *2 Bailey Close, Hethersett, Norwich NR9 3EU* T: (01603) 811010 E: christophersheila@tiscali.co.uk

MALLETT, The Ven Marlene Rosemarie. b 59. Sussex Univ BA 81 Warwick Univ PhD 94. SEITE 01. **d** 04 **p** 05. C Brixton Road Ch Ch *S'wark* 04–07; P-in-c Angell Town St Jo 07–13; V 13–20; Dir Ords Kingston Area 13–20; Dioc Public Policy Adv 15–20; Hon Can S'wark Cathl 13–20; Adn Croydon from 20. *Croydon Episcopal Area Office, 6 St Peter's Road, Croydon CR0 1HD* T: (020) 8256 9630 E: rosemarie.mallett@gmail.com

MALLINSON, Peter Albert. b 57. St Jo Coll Nottm 06 BA(ThM) 12. **d** 08 **p** 09. NSM Allestree St Edm and Darley Abbey *Derby* 08–12; TV Canvey Is *Chelmsf* 12–17; V Bury, Coldwaltham, Hardham and Houghton *Chich* from 17. *The Vicarage, Church Lane, Bury, Pulborough RH20 1PB* T: (01798) 839057 E: peter6hq@btinternet.com *or* vicar@arunchurches.com

MALLINSON, Canon Ralph Edward. b 40. Oriel Coll Ox BA 63 MA 66. St Steph Ho Ox 63. **d** 66 **p** 67. C Bolton St Pet *Man* 66–68; C Elton All SS 68–72; V Bury St Thos 72–76; V Bury Ch King 76–81; P-in-c Goodshaw 81–82; V 82–84; V Goodshaw and Crawshawbooth 84–93; AD Rossendale 83–93; V Unsworth 93–06; Hon Can Man Cathl 92–06; Vice Prin Dioc OLM Scheme 98–06; rtd 06; PtO *Man* 06–21. *18 Woodgate Avenue, Bury BL9 7RU* T: 0161-797 2006 E: ralphmallinsonis@gmail.com

MALLON, Allister. b 61. Sheff Univ BA 83 TCD BTh 89 MA. CITC. **d** 87 **p** 88. C Ballymoney w Finvoy and Rasharkin *Conn* 87–90; C Belfast St Mary w H Redeemer 90–92; Bp's C Belfast St Mary Magd 92–00; Bp's C Stoneyford 00–11; Chapl R Gp of Hosps Health and Soc Services Trust 00–11; rtd 11. *64 Magheralave Meadows, Lisburn BT28 3NT* M: 07719-833034 E: bigal@talk21.com *or* allistersanna@gmail.com

MALMESBURY, Archdeacon of. *See* BRYAN, The Ven Christopher Paul

MALONE, Richard Patrick. b 66. Wycliffe Hall Ox BTh 03. **d** 03 **p** 04. C Fulham Ch Ch *Lon* 03–06; C Battersea St Pet and St Paul *S'wark* 06–12; P-in-c from 12. *The Vicarage, 43 Fowler Close, London SW11 2ES* T: (020) 7738 9943 M: 07973-104941

MALONEY, Ms Fiona Elizabeth. b 60. Bradf Univ BSc 82 St Jo Coll Dur BA 91. NOC 91. **d** 92 **p** 94. Par Dn Castleton Moor *Man* 92–94; C 94–96; C Pendlebury St Jo 96–99; C Fatfield *Dur* 99–03; NSM Harrow Trin St Mich *Lon* 03–05; NSM Wealdstone H Trin 05–21; PtO *St Alb* from 21. *The Vicarage, Thornton Road, Potters Bar EN6 1JJ*

MALONEY, Terence Mark. b 63. York Univ BSc 84 Dur Univ MA 09. Cranmer Hall Dur 88. **d** 91 **p** 92. C Blackley St Andr *Man* 91–96; P-in-c Pendlebury St Jo 96–99; P-in-c Fatfield *Dur* 99–03; P-in-c Harrow Trin St Mich *Lon* 03–05; V Wealdstone H Trin 05–21; V Lt Heath *St Alb* from 21. *The Vicarage, Thornton Road, Potters Bar EN6 1JJ* E: mark@cofe.org.uk

MALTBY, Canon Geoffrey. b 38. Leeds Univ BA 62. Wells Th Coll 68. **d** 70 **p** 71. C Mansfield St Mark *S'well* 70–73; V Skegby 73–78; V Carrington 78–87; C Rainworth 87–90; Chapl for People w Learning Disability (Mental Handicap) 90–03; Hon Can S'well Minster 99–03; rtd 03; PtO *S'well* from 03. *18 Beverley Close, Rainworth, Mansfield NG21 0LW* T: (01623) 474452

MALTBY, Canon Judith Diane. b 57. Univ of Illinois BA 79 Newnham Coll Cam PhD 92 FRHistS 99. S Dios Minl Tr Scheme 89. **d** 92 **p** 94. Tutor Sarum & Wells Th Coll 87–93; Hon Par Dn Wilton w Netherhampton and Fugglestone *Sarum* 92–93; Chapl and Fell CCC Ox from 93; Reader Ch Hist Ox Univ from 04; Can Th Leic Cathl from 04; Hon Can Ch Ch *Ox* from 06; Can Th Win Cathl 11–18. *Corpus Christi College, Oxford OX1 4JF* T: (01865) 276722 E: judith.maltby@ccc.ox.ac.uk

MAMBU, Kutukenda Jules. b 64. Man Metrop Univ BA 08. **d** 92 **p** 94. C Prestwich St Mary *Man* 16; C Ashton 16–18; P-in-c Denton St Lawr from 18; P-in-c Haughton St Anne from 18. *131 Town Lane, Denton, Manchester M34 2DJ* T: 0161-320 4895 M: 07897-697503 E: mambujules@hotmail.com

MAN, Archdeacon of the Isle of. *Vacant*

MANCHESTER, Canon John Charles. b 45. Lon Univ BD 69. ALCD 68. **d** 69 **p** 70. C Scarborough St Martin *York* 69–73; C Selby Abbey 73–76; P-in-c Old Malton 76–79; V 79–10; RD Bulmer and Malton 85–91; Can and Preb York Minster 05–10; rtd 10; PtO *York* from 10. *18 Castle Howard Road, Malton YO17 7AY* T: (01653) 690671 E: johncmanchester@gmail.com

MANCHESTER, Archdeacon of. *See* LUND, The Ven Karen Belinda

MANCHESTER, Bishop of. *See* WALKER, The Rt Revd David Stuart

MANCHESTER, Dean of. *See* GOVENDER, The Very Revd Rogers Morgan

MANCO, Gwenda Diane. b 54. NOC 97. **d** 99 **p** 00. NSM Rochdale *Man* 99–02; NSM Dearnley 02–04; Asst Chapl HM Pris Buckley Hall 99–03; Chapl HM Pris Styal 03; NSM Spotland *Man* 04–06; NSM Dearnley 06–13; NSM Littleborough 13–14. *5 Stansfield Hall, Littleborough OL15 9RH* T: (01706) 370264 M: 07966-217252

MANDER, Patricia Margaret. b 51. **d** 13 **p** 14. OLM Haddenham w Cuddington, Kingsey etc *Ox* 13–16; NSM Wychert Vale 16 and from 19; PtO 16–19. *7 Stockwell Furlong, Haddenham, Aylesbury HP17 8HD* T: (01844) 290985

MANDER, Peter John. b 52. Liv Univ BEd 75 Anglia Ruskin Univ MA 09. Sarum & Wells Th Coll 85. **d** 87 **p** 88. C Hale and Ashley *Ches* 87–90; TV Grantham *Linc* 90–00; P-in-c Quarrington w Old Sleaford 00–08; P-in-c Silk Willoughby 00–08; RD Lafford 03–07; Can and Preb Linc Cathl 05–08; R Ellon *Ab* 08–15; R Cruden Bay 08–15; TV N Tyne and Redesdale *Newc* 15–18; rtd 18; PtO *Newc* from 18. *181 Gloster Park, Amble, Morpeth NE65 0HQ* M: 07929-140425 E: peter.mander@gmail.com

MANDER, Canon Thomas Leonard Frederick. b 33. Roch Th Coll 59 Ely Th Coll 60. **d** 62 **p** 63. C Cov St Mary 62–66; V Bishop's Tachbrook 66–70; V Earlsdon 70–76; V Chesterton 76–83; R Lighthorne 76–83; V Newbold Pacey w Moreton Morrell 76–83; Hon Can Cov Cathl 80–92; P-in-c S Leamington St Jo 83–84; V 84–92; rtd 92; PtO *Cov* 92–15. *59 Murcott Road East, Whitnash, Leamington Spa CV31 2JJ* T: (01926) 339950

MANDERSON, Robert Dunlop (Leslie). b 35. LDS 59 FDS 65. Ox Min Course 92. **d** 94 **p** 95. NSM Maidenhead St Andr and St Mary *Ox* 94–00; PtO 00–02; NSM Chipping Norton 02–03; rtd 03; PtO *Ox* 03–04; *Ely* from 04. *14 Nursery Walk, Cambridge CB4 3PR* T: (01954) 782388 E: lesmanderson@gmail.com

MANHOOD, Phyllis. *See* DELVES, Phyllis

MANKEL, Jens Thomas. b 66. Heythrop Coll Lon MA 14. Trin Coll Bris 95. **d** 19 **p** 20. NSM Guildf St Sav from 19; Ch Planting and Fresh Expressions Adv from 16. *8 Selbourne Road, Guildford GU4 7JP* M: 07935-828559 E: jens.mankel@cofeguildford.org.uk

MANLEY, Mrs Gillian. b 59. St Martin's Coll Lanc BEd 80. St Jo Coll Nottm MA 00. **d** 00 **p** 01. C Eckington and Ridgeway *Derby* 00–04; TV Wirksworth 04–09; V Blackwell w Tibshelf from 09; C Pinxton 14–20; RD Alfreton 16–18; AD Hardwick 18–20. *The Vicarage, 67 High Street, Tibshelf, Alfreton DE55 5NU* T: (01773) 873305

MANLEY, Mrs Jane Elizabeth. b 58. Ox Min Course 05. **d** 08 **p** 09. C Bracknell *Ox* 08–11; C Crowthorne 11–12; V Ruislip Manor St Paul *Lon* 12–18; Dean of Women's Min Willesden Area 13–18; R Aldermaston and Woolhampton *Ox* from 18. *The Rectory, Wasing Lane, Aldermaston, Reading RG7 4LX* M: 07711-613057 E: jane.e.manley@btinternet.com

MANLEY, Canon Michael Alan. b 60. SS Hild & Bede Coll Dur BA 82. Trin Coll Bris. **d** 86 **p** 87. C Accrington St Jo w Huncoat *Blackb* 86–90; V Preston St Luke and St Oswald 90–96; V Blackpool St Jo 96–07; Can Res Carl Cathl from 07; RD Carl 10–16. *1 The Abbey, Carlisle CA3 8TZ* T: (01228) 542790 E: canonmissioner@carlislecathedral.org.uk

MANLEY, Pamela Mary. b 54. All SS Cen for Miss & Min 15. **d** 17 **p** 18. OLM Hope St Jas and Pendlebury St Jo *Man* from 17. *7 Hamilton Close, Prestwich, Manchester M25 9JS*

MANLEY-COOPER, Simon James. b 46. S Dios Minl Tr Scheme 91. **d** 94 **p** 95. NSM Soho St Anne w St Thos and St Pet *Lon* 94–96; Ind Chapl 94–96; P-in-c Bedford St Mich *St Alb* 96–01; Ind Chapl 96–01; R Bramfield, Stapleford, Waterford etc 01–02; Chapl E and N Herts NHS Trust 03–11; rtd 11; PtO *St Alb* from 11. *19 Barnfield Road, Harpenden AL5 5TH* T: (01582) 460797 E: manleyc35@gmail.com

MANN, Alexandrina Elizabeth. b 67. Westmr Coll Ox BA 92 PGCE 93 Birm Univ MA 95 FGA 90. Trin Coll Bris 01. **d** 03 **p** 04. C Austrey and Warton *Birm* 03–06; V Hanbury, Newborough, Rangemore and Tutbury *Lich* 06–13; C Branston 13; C Cannock and Huntington 13–20; P-in-c Heath *Derby* from 20. *Address temp unknown* M: 07761-263849 E: alexandra.shalom@virgin.net

MANN, Mrs Angela. b 58. Bath Univ BA 80 Bris Univ PGCE 83. Trin Coll Bris 92. **d** 94 **p** 95. C Marlborough *Sarum* 94–97; PtO 97–98; *Ox* 98–09; TV The Claydons and Swan from 09. *The*

Rectory, Grendon Underwood, Aylesbury HP18 0SY T: (01296) 771100 E: angela.mann858@gmail.com

MANN, Canon Charmion Anne Montgomery. b 36. Liv Univ BA 57 CertEd 62 AdDipEd 79 Univ of Wales (Lamp) MA 06. Trin Coll Bris 80. **dss** 82 **d** 87 **p** 94. Bris St Nath w St Kath 82–84; Bris St Matt and St Nath 84–85; Asst Chapl Bris City Hosp 85–88; Chapl Bris Maternity Hosp 88–94; Chapl Bris R Hosp for Sick Children 88–94; Chapl Bris R Infirmary 88–94; Hon Can Bris Cathl 93–00; P-in-c Lacock w Bowden Hill 94–00; C Gtr Corsham 97–00; rtd 00; PtO *Bris* 00–06; *Sarum* 01–06; *Ex* from 07. *1 Gracey Court, Woodland Road, Broadclyst, Exeter EX5 3GA* T: (01392) 461451 E: charmion.mann@gmail.com

MANN, Christopher John. b 57. Glas Univ BSc 79. Westcott Ho Cam 83. **d** 86 **p** 87. C Worc SE 86–89; Min Can and Sacr St Paul's Cathl *Lon* 89–96; R Upminster *Chelmsf* 96–06; Chapl to Bp Bradwell 06–10; C Corringham 07–10; P-in-c Christchurch *Win* 10–14; Chapl Al Ain UAE 15–16; P-in-c Shenfield *Chelmsf* from 16. *The Rectory, 41 Worrin Road, Shenfield, Brentwood CM15 8DH* T: (01277) 220360 M: 07931-116897 E: fatherchris@domus.org.uk

MANN, David. b 57. St Jo Coll Dur BA 78. Ridley Hall Cam. **d** 82 **p** 83. C Monkwearmouth St Andr *Dur* 82–86; Chapl Sheff Cathl 86–87; C Leeds St Geo *Ripon* 87–94; V Ripon H Trin 94–06; Asst Dir of Ords 02–06; Nat Adv for Pre-Th Educn and Selection Sec Min Division 06–09; Dioc Voc Adv *York* from 09. *64 Strensall Road, Huntington, York YO32 9SH* T: (01904) 768668 E: david.mann@yorkdiocese.org

MANN, Ivan John. b 52. Brunel Univ BTech 74 Southn Univ BTh 80. Sarum & Wells Th Coll 75. **d** 78 **p** 79. C Hadleigh w Layham and Shelley *St E* 78–81; C Whitton and Thurleston w Akenham 81–83; V Leiston 83–86; PtO 86–89; R Aldringham w Thorpe, Knodishall w Buxlow etc 89–93; V Ipswich St Jo 93–96; Chapl St Mary's Convent Wantage 96–00; asst Chapl R Berks and Battle Hosps NHS Trust 00; TV Gt Yarmouth *Nor* 00–03; Team Member Loyola Hall Jesuit Spirituality Cen Prescot 03–04; Prec and Hon Can Cumbrae *Arg* 04–06; Can St Jo Cathl Oban 04–06; rtd 06. *140 Somerleyton Gardens, Norwich NR2 2BS* T: (01603) 929591 E: ivan@ivanmann.f2s.com

MANN, Mrs Joan. b 40. **d** 98. NSM Eastbourne St Mary *Chich* 98–02; NSM The Hydneye 02–10; NSM Hampden Park and The Hydneye from 10. *39 Cherry Garden Road, Eastbourne BN20 8HF* T: (01323) 728259 E: joan.mann@hotmail.co.uk

MANN, John Owen. b 55. QUB BD 77 MTh 86 MPhil 98 Ulster Univ Hon DLitt 18. CITC 79. **d** 79 **p** 81. C Cloughfern *Conn* 79–82; C Knock *D & D* 82–85; I Ballyrashane w Kildollagh *Conn* 85–89; R Bentworth and Shalden and Lasham *Win* 89–93; RD Alton 92–93; I Cloughfern *Conn* 93–02; I Belfast Malone St Jo 02–11; Dean Belf 11–17; I Belfast St Anne *Conn* 11–17; Preb Clonmethan St Patr Cathl Dublin 99–17; TR Swanage and Studland *Sarum* from 17. *The Rectory, 12 Church Hill, Swanage BH19 1HU* T: (01929) 422916

MANN, Julia Corinne. b 52. Open Univ BA 92 Anglia Poly Univ BA 03 RGN 91. **d** 08 **p** 09. OLM Bury St Edmunds All SS w St Jo and St Geo *St E* 08–13; NSM 13–19; NSM Lark Valley from 14; NSM Lark Valley and N Bury from 19. *Orchard House, 13 Orchard Street, Bury St Edmunds IP33 1EH* T: (01284) 753984 E: jc.mann@btinternet.com

MANN, Mrs Patricia Ann. b 62. STETS 08. **d** 11 **p** 12. C Havant *Portsm* 11–15; Chapl RN Coll Greenwich from 15; C Greenwich St Alfege *S'wark* from 15. *39 Burney Street, London SE10 8EX* T: (020) 8269 4750 M: 07890-304670 E: patmann17@yahoo.co.uk *or* pmann@ornc.org

MANN, Paul William. b 63. Leeds Univ BSc 84 CEng MIET. EAMTC 01. **d** 04 **p** 05. NSM Lawford *Chelmsf* 04–17; PtO 17–18; NSM Wormingford, Mt Bures and Lt Horkesley from 18; NSM Colchester St Mich Myland from 18; NSM Colchester St Luke from 18; NSM Langham w Boxted from 18; NSM W Bergholt and Gt Horkesley from 18. *8 Cherrywoods, Great Bentley, Colchester CO7 8QF* T: (01206) 252420 E: paul.mann@riffhams.co.uk

MANN, Peter Eric. b 51. St Jo Coll Dur BA 73. Westcott Ho Cam 73. **d** 75 **p** 76. C Barrow St Jo *Carl* 75–78; C Egremont 78–80; V Carl St Luke Morton 80–86; TR Egremont and Haile 86–93; P-in-c Barrow St Geo w St Luke 93–99; TR S Barrow 99–06; P-in-c Barrow St Jo 95–96; RD Furness 94–01; RD Barrow 01–06; Hon Can Carl Cathl 95–06; TR Harwich Peninsula *Chelmsf* 06–15; RD Harwich 09–14; rtd 15; PtO *Blackb* 16–17 and from 20. *20 Brantwood Avenue, Morecambe LA4 6HB* T: (01524) 4199252 M: 07989-084493 E: cookbird@gmail.com

MANN, Canon Rachel. b 70. Qu Coll Birm 03. **d** 05 **p** 06. C Stretford St Matt *Man* 05–08; P-in-c Burnage St Nic 08–18; R 18–21; C Ladybarn 17–21; AD Withington 19–21; C Bury St Mary from 21; AD Bury and Rossendale from 21; Min Can

Man Cathl 14–17; Hon Can Man Cathl from 17. *The Rectory, 408 Kingsway, Burnage, Manchester M19 1PL* T: 0161-432 7009 M: 07834-403195 E: rachelmann994@gmail.com

MANN, Robin. b 45. Fitzw Coll Cam BA 76 MA 80 MRTPI 73. Ridley Hall Cam 73. **d** 77 **p** 78. C Wetherby *Ripon* 77–80; V Hipswell 80–86; V Mamble w Bayton, Rock w Heightington etc *Worc* 86–96; V Avon Valley *Sarum* 96–02; R Selworthy, Timberscombe, Wootton Courtenay etc *B & W* 02–07; rtd 07; PtO *Glouc* 14–20; *B & W* from 21. *6 Apple Tree Drive, Winscombe BS25 1AY* T: (01934) 842650 E: robin284kjo@gmail.com

MANN, Samuel Andrew. b 93. Univ of S Wales BA 14. Ripon Coll Cuddesdon BA 17. **d** 17 **p** 18. C Coalbrookdale, Iron-Bridge and Lt Wenlock *Heref* 17–20; R Apedale Gp from 20. *The Rectory, Hope Bowdler, Church Stretton SY6 7DD* T: (01694) 722942 E: sam.mann.1993@gmail.com

MANN, Mrs Susan Mary. b 66. Coll of Ripon & York St Jo BA 89 Loughb Univ PGCE 90. St Mellitus Coll BA 12. **d** 12 **p** 13. C Wickford and Runwell *Chelmsf* 12–16; P-in-c Orsett and Bulphan and Horndon on the Hill 16–19; R from 19. *The Rectory, School Lane, Orsett, Grays RM16 3JS* T: (01375) 891254 E: suemann23@hotmail.com

MANN, Mrs Tessa Gillian. b 62. Nottm Univ BA 84. STETS 05. **d** 08 **p** 09. C Bourne Valley *Sarum* 08–17; C Salisbury St Fran and Stratford sub Castle 11–17; C N Bradford on Avon and Villages from 18. *Turleigh Cross, 24 Dane Rise, Winsley, Bradford-on-Avon BA15 2NB* T: (01225) 309374 M: 07588-533283 E: revtgm86@gmail.com

MANN, Wendy Martin. *See* MARTIN, Wendy Helen

MANNERS, Jennifer Helen Edith. b 50. K Coll Lon MB, BS 73 AKC 73. **d** 06 **p** 07. OLM Bearsted w Thurnham *Cant* 06–13; PtO 13–14; *Portsm* from 15. *Address withheld by request* E: jhemanners@hotmail.com

MANNERS, Susan Jane. b 70. Homerton Coll Cam BEd 94. St Aug Coll Cant 19. **d** 21. NSM Stour Downs *Cant* from 21. *The Rectory, Bower Road, Mersham, Ashford TN25 6NN* T: (01233) 500414 M: 07534-278643 E: susan_manners@hotmail.com

MANNING, Adrian Peter. b 63. St Cath Coll Cam BA 84 MA 88 K Coll Lon PGCE 88. Ridley Hall Cam 92. **d** 95 **p** 96. C Oxhey All SS *St Alb* 95–97; Asst Chapl Bedford Sch 97–02; Chapl St Geo Sch Harpenden 02–15; V Ivinghoe w Pitstone and Slapton and Marsworth *Ox* 15–20; PtO from 20. *40 Skidmore Way, Rickmansworth WD3 1TA* E: revadrianmanning@gmail.com

MANNING, Mrs Ann. b 42. Liv Univ CertEd 75. St Jo Coll Nottm 93 NOC 94. **d** 95 **p** 96. NSM Grasmere *Carl* 95–96; NSM Delamere *Ches* 96–99; C Middlewich w Byley 99–02; Chapl Mid Cheshire Hosps Trust 99–02; P-in-c Dunton w Wrestlingworth and Eyeworth *St Alb* 02–05; R 05–08; rtd 08; PtO *Ches* from 10. *27 Barley Croft, Great Boughton, Chester CH3 5SP* T: (01244) 316781 E: revmanning@hotmail.co.uk

MANNING, David Godfrey. b 47. Trin Coll Bris 73. **d** 76 **p** 77. C Richmond H Trin and Ch Ch *S'wark* 76–79; C Anston *Sheff* 79–83; V Blackpool St Mark *Blackb* 83–91; V Creech St Michael *B & W* 91–08; PtO 10–12 and 15–17. *163 Eaton Crescent, Taunton TA2 7UF* T: (01823) 253195 M: 07502-222875

MANNING, Mrs Jean Margaret. b 46. Oak Hill NSM Course 07. **d** 08 **p** 09. NSM Herstmonceux and Wartling *Chich* 08–13; PtO from 13. *Little Bathurst Farm, Cowbeech Road, Rushlake Green, Heathfield TN21 9QA* T/F: (01435) 831105 M: 07711-052131

MANNING, Neville Alexander. b 41. Lon Univ BD 68. ALCD 68. **d** 68 **p** 69. C Belvedere All SS *Roch* 68–71; C Hollington St Leon *Chich* 71–73; C Hersham *Guildf* 73–77; V Dawley St Jerome *Lon* 77–94; R Denton w S Heighton and Tarring Neville *Chich* 94–06; rtd 06; PtO *Chich* from 15. *7 Salvador Close, Eastbourne BN23 5TB* T: (01323) 479359

MANNINGS, Andrew James. b 52. Trent Park Coll of Educn CertEd 73. St Jo Coll Nottm 90. **d** 92 **p** 94. C Over St Chad *Ches* 92–93; C Sale St Anne 93–96; C Timperley 96–98; P-in-c Egremont St Jo 98–04; P-in-c Liscard St Mary w St Columba 03–04; V Liscard Resurr 04–17; RD Wallasey 02–07; rtd 17; PtO *Ches* from 19. *4 Grasmere Drive, Wallasey CH45 4PQ* T: 0151-512 5353 M: 07505-413754 E: frandrew2004@yahoo.co.uk

MANNINGS, Mrs Kimberley. b 89. Man Univ BA 11 Edge Hill Univ PGCE 12. St Mellitus Coll 15. **d** 18 **p** 19. C Prescot *Liv* from 18. *2 Spencer Close, Liverpool L36 0XT* M: 07969-731420 E: manningskimberley@gmail.com

MANOUCH, Miss Sarah Jane. b 65. SEITE 12. **d** 15 **p** 16. NSM W Wittering and Birdham w Itchenor *Chich* 15–20; R E Dean, Singleton, and W Dean from 20. *The Rectory, Singleton, Chichester PO18 0EZ* M: 07468-854864 E: priestvalleyparish@gmail.com

MANSEL LEWIS, Patrick Charles Archibald. b 53. Solicitor 79. St Mich Coll Llan 01. **d** 04 **p** 05. NSM Llandeilo Fawr and Taliaris *St D* 04–12; NSM Llanelli 12–17; NSM Bro Lliedi 17–20; NSM Bro Dyfri from 20. *Capel Isaf, Manordeilo, Llandeilo SA19 7BS* T: (01558) 822942 M: 07792-921327 E: patmanlew@btconnect.com

MANSELL, Carol. b 52. Lon Bible Coll BA 75 Nottm Univ MA 86 CQSW 86 Leic Univ MBA 05 Anglia Ruskin Univ MA 11. ERMC 08. **d** 10 **p** 11. NSM Rattlesden w Thorpe Morieux, Brettenham etc *St E* 10–13; P-in-c Monks Eleigh w Chelsworth and Brent Eleigh etc 13–19; P-in-c Ipswich All Hallows from 19. *All Hallows Vicarage, Reynolds Road, Ipswich IP3 0JH* M: 07788-157147

MANSELL, The Ven Clive Neville Ross. b 53. Leic Univ LLB 74 Solicitor 77. **d** 82 **p** 83. C Gt Malvern St Mary *Worc* 82–85; Min Can Ripon Cathl 85–89; R Kirklington w Burneston and Wath and Pickhill 89–02; AD Wensley 98–02; Adn Tonbridge *Roch* 02–17; rtd 17; PtO *Leeds* from 17; Chapter Can Ripon Cathl from 18. *10 Watermill Lane, North Stainley, Ripon HG4 3LA*

MANSELL, Paul John. b 67. Staffs Univ MSc 05. Ripon Coll Cuddesdon 05. **d** 07 **p** 08. C Schorne *Ox* 07–10; V Forest Edge from 10. *The Vicarage, Mount Skippett, Ramsden, Chipping Norton OX7 3AP* T: (01993) 868687 M: 07983-707560

MANSFIELD, Alastair John Fraser. b 60. Ex Univ BA 82 Ch Coll Cam PGCE 84 City Univ MSc 92. SEITE. **d** 99 **p** 00. C Palmers Green St Jo *Lon* 99–02; P-in-c Enfield St Mich 02–07; Chapl RN from 08. *Royal Naval Chaplaincy Service Headquarters, Tanner Building, HMS Excellent, Whale Island, Portsmouth PO2 8ER* T: 0300-157 7544 E: alastair.mansfield@gmail.com

MANSFIELD, Ms Coralie Patricia. b 58. Nene Coll Northn BA 95. Ripon Coll Cuddesdon. **d** 13 **p** 14. NSM Olney *Ox* 13–17; P-in-c Sherington w Chicheley, N Crawley, Astwood etc from 17. *The Rectory, 21 School Lane, Sherington, Newport Pagnell MK16 9NF*

MANSFIELD, Glen Robert. b 76. St Jo Coll Ox BA 97. Oak Hill Th Coll BA 11. **d** 11 **p** 12. C Aldershot H Trin *Guildf* 11–15; C Rhyl w St Ann *St As* 15–16; C Aber-Morfa Miss Area 17–18; I from 18. *122 Rhuddlan Road, Rhyl LL18 2RD* T: (01745) 798864 E: tellspartans@yahoo.co.uk or glen@parishofrhyl.co.uk

MANSFIELD, Gordon Reginald. b 35. Lon Univ BA CertEd. Clifton Th Coll 58. **d** 64. C Carl St Jo 63–65; C Westcombe Park St Geo *S'wark* 65–68; C Rashcliffe *Wakef* 68–70; V Woodlands *Sheff* 70–80; V Steeple Bumpstead and Helions Bumpstead *Chelmsf* 80–02; PtO *Ely* 03–04 and from 13; *Heref* 04–13; *S & B* 04–13. *25 Rampton End, Willingham, Cambridge CB24 5JB* T: (01954) 261540

MANSFIELD, Julian Nicolas (Nick). b 59. K Coll Lon BD AKC. Edin Th Coll 83. **d** 85 **p** 86. C Kirkby *Liv* 85–89; TV Ditton St Mich 89–96; P-in-c Preston St Oswald *Blackb* 96–01; V Penwortham St Leon from 01. *St Leonard's Vicarage, Marshall's Brow, Penwortham, Preston PR1 9HY* T: (01772) 742367 E: nickthevic1@gmail.com

MANSFIELD, Robert William. b 45. **d** 88 **p** 89. OLM Louth *Linc* from 88. *The Old Railway House, Stewton, Louth LN11 8SD* T: (01507) 327533

MANSFIELD, Simon David. b 55. Brunel Univ BSc 81 Lon Univ MA 94 Univ of Wales (Ban) MPhil 06 Glyndŵr Univ PhD 17. Ripon Coll Cuddesdon 88. **d** 90 **p** 91. C N Harrow St Alb *Lon* 90–93; C Birchington w Acol and Minnis Bay *Cant* 93–97; TV Accrington *Blackb* 97–00; TV Accrington Ch the King 00–05; P-in-c Wednesfield St Greg *Lich* 05–15; V Hockerill *St Alb* from 15. *Hockerill Vicarage, 4A All Saints Close, Bishop's Stortford CM23 2EA* T: (01279) 506542 E: smansfeeld@toucansurf.com

MANSFIELD, Canon Stephen McLaren. b 59. FGA. Cranmer Hall Dur 86. **d** 89 **p** 90. C Poynton *Ches* 89–92; C Bromborough 92–94; V Bidston 94–02; C Heswall 02–09; V Birkenhead St Jas w St Bede 09–18; P-in-c Backford and Capenhurst from 18; P-in-c Gt Saughall from 18; Hon Can Ches Cathl from 16. *Belmont Cottage, Church Road, Saughall, Chester CH1 6EP* E: steve.mansfield@mac.com

MANSHIP, Charmian Margaret. b 45. RCM BMus 68 ARCM 65 GRSM 67 FRCO 68. SAOMC 95. **d** 98 **p** 99. NSM Abingdon *Ox* 98–04; Succ and Min Can Worc Cathl 04–10; PtO from 11. *22 Stanmore Road, Worcester WR2 4PW* T: (01905) 421147 M: 07986-657110 E: charmian@manships.co.uk

MANSHIP, David. b 27. Keble Coll Ox BA 52 MA 58 ARCO. Qu Coll Birm 52. **d** 54 **p** 55. C Hackney St Jo *Lon* 54–58; C Preston Ascension 58–61; C St Andr Holborn 61–65; Members' Tr Officer C of E Youth Coun 65–68; Clergy Tr Officer 68–70; Dir of Educn *Win* 70–79; Hon Can Win Cathl 74–79; R Old Alresford 76–79; V Abingdon w Shippon *Ox* 79–89; TR Abingdon 89–93; V Shippon 89; RD Abingdon 87–90; rtd

93; PtO *Ox* 93–03; *Worc* from 04. *22 Stanmore Road, Worcester WR2 4PW* T: (01905) 421147 E: david@manships.co.uk

MANSLEY, Caroline Anne Bimson. b 58. Bris Univ BA 80 TCD MTh 12. CITI 09. **d** 11 **p** 12. Par Dn Willowfield *D & D* 11–12; C Magheraculmoney *Clogh* 12–16; TV Ashford Town *Cant* 16–21; Jt AD Ashford 18–21; rtd 21. *Address temp unknown* M: 07580-634488 E: caroline@mansley.net

MANSLEY, Colin Edward. b 56. Edin Univ MA 80 Ox Univ BA 85 Leic Univ MA 06. Ripon Coll Cuddesdon 83. **d** 86 **p** 87. C Worle *B & W* 86–89; C Baguley *Man* 89–91; C Radcliffe St Mary 91; TV Radcliffe 91–96; V Bartley Green *Birm* 96–08; R Trefnant w Tremeirchion w Cefn *St As* 08–16; I Denbigh Miss Area 17–19; AD Denbigh 14–19; rtd 19. *Address withheld by request* E: colin@archangel.clara.co.uk

MANSON-BRAILSFORD, Andrew Henry. b 64. NUU BA 86 Liv Univ MPhil 98 Sussex Univ DPhil 09. Ripon Coll Cuddesdon 87. **d** 90 **p** 91. C Warrington St Elphin *Liv* 90–93; C Torrisholme *Blackb* 93–96; V Brighton St Geo w St Anne and St Mark *Chich* from 96; RD Brighton 10–15; Chapl St Mary's Hall Brighton from 97. *St George's House, 6 Sussex Mews, Brighton BN2 1GZ* T: (01273) 625538 or 279448 E: revmanson-brailsford@hotmail.co.uk

MANTERFIELD, Mrs Barbara Ann Danyer. b 58. Newc Univ BA 79 St Luke's Coll Ex PGCE 80. Linc Sch of Th and Min 17. **d** 20 **p** 21. OLM Grantham, Harrowby w Londonthorpe *Linc* from 20. *9 Granta Crescent, Grantham NG31 9PJ* T: (01476) 565782 M: 07825-287883 E: barbaramanterfield@icloud.com

MANTLE, Michael. b 82. **d** 15 **p** 16. C St Helen Bishopsgate w St Andr Undershaft etc *Lon* 16–21; Sydney St Thos Australia from 21. *c/o St Thomas' Church, Corner of Church and McLaren Streets, North Sydney NSW 2060, Australia* E: michaeljmantle@gmail.com

MANTON, Paul Arthur. b 45. Oak Hill Th Coll BD 77. **d** 77 **p** 78. C Wolverhampton *Lich* 77–80; Ind Chapl *Lon* 80–87; Hon C St Marylebone All So w SS Pet and Jo 80–87; PtO 03–18. *75 Homefield Gardens, London N2 0XL* T: (020) 3224 3001 M: 07847-425946 E: paulikann@me.com

MANUEL, Paul. b 55. Univ of Wales (Ban) BA 76 Lon Sch of Th MA 09 ACIS 79 FCIS 88. SAOMC 97. **d** 00 **p** 01. NSM Luton St Paul *St Alb* 00–03; C Chorleywood Ch Ch 03–07; P-in-c New Milverton *Cov* 07–10; V St Alb 40 Warwick and Leamington 10–14; rtd 15; PtO *St Alb* from 19. *50 Roundwood Lane, Harpenden AL5 3EP* E: paul.manuel4@ntlworld.com

MAPES, David. Brunel Univ BSc 71 CEng 72 MIET 74 MIMechE 78 EurIng 89 FInstD 77 MBACP 99. NTMTC 07. **d** 07 **p** 08. NSM Feltham *Lon* 07–10; P-in-c Southampton St Mark *Win* 10–15; Hon C The Downs 15–17; PtO from 17. *5 Pigeonhouse Field, Sutton Scotney, Winchester SO21 3NJ* T: (01962) 761260 M: 07885-635378 E: davemapes@aol.com

MAPLE, David Charles. b 34. Sarum Th Coll 64. **d** 66 **p** 66. C Buckland in Dover *Cant* 66–67; C St Laur in Thanet 67–71; Chapl RAF 71–75; P-in-c Ivychurch w Old Romney and Midley *Cant* 75–76; P-in-c Newchurch 75–78; P-in-c Burmarsh 75–78; P-in-c St Mary in the Marsh 75–76; R Dymchurch 76–78; P-in-c Dymchurch w Burmarsh and Newchurch 78–81; Hon Min Can Cant Cathl 79–18; Abp's Dioc Chapl 81–91; Chapl St Jo Hosp Cant 91–95; rtd 95; PtO *Cant* 98–18. *1 Mount Pleasant, Blean, Canterbury CT2 9EU* T: (01227) 459044

MAPLE, John Philip. b 50. Chich Th Coll 71. **d** 74 **p** 79. C Notting Hill St Mich and Ch Ch *Lon* 74–75; LtO 78–79; C Barnsbury St Dav w St Clem 79–80; C Cotham St Sav w St Mary *Bris* 80–83; TV St Marylebone Ch Ch *Lon* 83–91; R St Marylebone St Paul 91–99; P-in-c Fulham St Alb w St Aug 99–04; P-in-c Fulham St Pet 99–02; Community Min Adv 04–15; rtd 15; PtO *Lon* from 15. *314 South Lambeth Road, London SW8 1UQ* T: (020) 7627 3575 M: 07736-546588 E: maplefoster@hotmail.com

MAPLEY, Mrs Barbara Jean. b 46. Guy's Hosp Medical Sch MCSP 69. Oak Hill NSM Course 86. **d** 89 **p** 94. NSM Kelvedon *Chelmsf* 89–93; C Witham 93–94; TV 94–01; R Belbroughton w Fairfield and Clent *Worc* 01–11; rtd 12; PtO *Ox* from 12. *2 Leamington Gate, Coxwell Road, Faringdon SN7 7FP* T: (01367) 615509

MAPSTONE, Canon Trevor Anthony. b 63. Lanc Univ BSc 84 MA 96 K Coll Lon MA 16. St Jo Coll Nottm 86. **d** 89 **p** 90. C Hoole *Ches* 89–92; C Lancaster St Thos *Blackb* 92–96; V Harrow Trin St Mich *Lon* 96–03; Dir of Ords Willesden Area 98–03; V S Croydon Em *S'wark* 03–19; AD Croydon Cen 09–16; P-in-c Caterham from 19; Hon Can S'wark Cathl from 14. *The Rectory, 5 Whyteleafe Road, Caterham CR3 5EG* T: (01883) 373083

MARBUS, Alida Janny. *See* WHITTOCK, Alida Janny

MARCH, Alan Mervyn. b 48. Open Univ BA 91 CPFA 73. EAMTC 00. **d** 03 **p** 04. NSM Northampton St Alb *Pet* 03–06; NSM Northampton Ch Ch from 06; NSM Northampton H Sepulchre w St Andr and St Lawr from 06; NSM Northampton St Mich w St Edm from 06; NSM Northampton H Trin and St Paul from 06. *236 Beech Avenue, Northampton NN3 2LE* T: (01604) 405722 E: march100@o2.co.uk *or* alanmarch2016@outlook.com

MARCH, Andrew. b 81. UEA BA 03. St Jo Coll Nottm MA 09. **d** 09 **p** 10. C Werrington and Wetley Rocks *Lich* 09–12; V Allesley Park and Whoberley *Cov* from 12. *St Christopher's Vicarage, 99 Buckingham Rise, Coventry CV5 9HF* M: 07816-998642 E: revandymarch@gmail.com

MARCH, Charles Anthony Maclea (Tony). b 32. CCC Cam BA 55 MA 70. Oak Hill Th Coll 55. **d** 57 **p** 58. C S Croydon Em *Cant* 57–60; C Eastbourne H Trin *Chich* 60–63; V Whitehall Park St Andr Hornsey Lane *Lon* 63–67; V Tunbridge Wells H Trin w Ch Ch *Roch* 67–82; V Prestonville St Luke *Chich* 82–97; rtd 97; PtO *Roch* 99–14. *17 Buckingham Road, Oakham LE15 6RX* T: (01572) 756113

MARCH, Gerald. b 44. Nottm Univ BA 75. Oak Hill Th Coll 92. **d** 95 **p** 96. C Sandgate St Paul w Folkestone St Geo *Cant* 95–99; P-in-c Southampton St Mark *Win* 99–03; V 03–09; rtd 09; PtO *Ox* from 10; *Cov* 13–15. *Dovetrees, 2B Curbridge Road, Witney OX28 5JR* E: rev.gerald@gmail.com

MARCH, Jonathan. b 79. Wycliffe Hall Ox. **d** 05 **p** 06. C Brompton H Trin w Onslow Square St Paul *Lon* 05–11; V Oseney Crescent St Luke from 11. *1 Bartholomew Road, London NW5 2AH* T: (020) 7916 0050 E: jon@slkt.org.uk

MARCH, Peter John. b 75. Cov Univ BA 97 Univ Coll Worc PGCE 98. SWMTC 10. **d** 13 **p** 14. C Heavitree and St Mary Steps *Ex* 13–16; P-in-c Torquay St Luke 16–18; V from 18; P-in-c Torre All SS 16–18; V Torre and Torquay St Jo from 18. *All Saints' Vicarage, 45 Barton Road, Torquay TQ1 4DT*

MARCHAND, Canon Rex Anthony Victor (Toby). b 47. K Coll Lon BD 69 AKC 69. St Aug Coll Cant 69. **d** 70 **p** 71. C Leigh Park *Portsm* 70–73; C Bp's Hatfield *St Alb* 73–80; R Deal St Leon and St Rich and Sholden *Cant* 80–95; RD Sandwich 91–94; Hon Can Cant Cathl 94–95; V Bishop's Stortford St Mich *St Alb* 95–12; RD Bishop's Stortford 03–06; Hon Can St Alb 08–12; rtd 12; PtO *Cant* from 13. *12 Langton Close, Deal CT14 6UL* T: (01304) 371419 E: ravmarchand@gmail.com

MARCHANT, John Bennet. b 46. St Jo Coll Nottm. **d** 06 **p** 07. Aux Min Powerscourt w Kilbride *D & G* 06–12; P-in-c Dublin Clontarf 12–13; P-in-c Dublin Irishtown w Donnybrook 13–14; Bp's C 14–21; Chapl Dublin City Univ 07–21; rtd 21. *Address temp unknown* M: (00353) 87-239 3682 E: revjmarchant@gmail.com

MARCHANT (formerly ROWLAND), Sally Margaret. b 58. SEITE. **d** 10 **p** 11. C Melton Mowbray *Leic* 10–13; TV Totton *Win* 13–20; rtd 20; PtO *Ex* from 20. *The Heights, Renney Road, Heybrook Bay, Plymouth PL9 0BD* E: sallymmarchant@gmail.com

MARCHMENT, Mrs Ethel Diane. b 53. Ridley Hall Cam. **d** 11 **p** 12. NSM Douglas St Ninian *S & M* 11–14; NSM W Coast 14–18; PtO *Chich* from 18. *181 Bowmans Close, Steyning BN44 3SR* E: revdimarchment@gmail.com

MARCUS, Mrs Candice Ann. b 52. FInstLEx 80. Trin Coll Bris 05. **d** 07 **p** 08. C Timsbury and Priston *B & W* 07–10; C Timsbury w Priston, Camerton and Dunkerton 10–11; TV Whitton *Sarum* 11–18; rtd 18; PtO *B & W* from 19. *Willow Tree Cottage, Throop Road, Templecombe BA8 0HR* M: 07788-437063 E: revcandicemarcus@gmail.com

MARCUSSEN, Mrs Yolande Roberta. b 47. SEITE 98. **d** 01 **p** 02. NSM Bromley Common St Aug *Roch* 01–03; NSM Orpington All SS 03; Asst Chapl HM Pris *Roch* 01–03; Chapl 03–06; rtd 06; PtO *Roch* from 09. *24 Lucerne Road, Orpington BR6 0EP* T: (01689) 833599 E: yolande.marcussen@ntlworld.com

MARGAM, Archdeacon of. *See* KOMOR, The Ven Michael

MARGARET ANNE, Sister. *See* McALISTER, Margaret Elizabeth Anne

MARGARET JOY, Sister. *See* HARRIS, Margaret Claire

MARIES, Phillip John. **d** 15 **p** 16. C Normanton *Leeds* 15–18; C Cen Barnsley from 18. *186 Racecommon Road, Barnsley S70 6JY* E: philmaries@gmail.com

MARK, Catherine. *See* OKORONKWO, Catherine Chinyere Mark

MARKBY, Ms Jane Elizabeth. b 67. Em Coll Cam BA 88 Homerton Coll Cam PGCE 89. Ridley Hall Cam 00. **d** 02 **p** 03. NSM Edmonton All SS w St Mich *Lon* 02–06; Chapl Haberdashers' Aske's Sch Elstree 06–10; Chapl Berkhamsted Sch Herts from 10. *Adelbert House, Mill Street, Berkhamsted HP4 2BA* T: (01442) 358095 E: jmarkby@berkhamstedschool.org

MARKBY, Peter John Jenner. b 38. Em Coll Cam BA 60. Clifton Th Coll 62. **d** 64 **p** 65. C Tufnell Park St Geo *Lon* 64–68; C Crowborough *Chich* 68–73; C Polegate 73–77; R Southover 77–02; rtd 02; PtO *Chich* from 02. *44 Warren Drive, Lewes BN7 1HD* T: (01273) 875724 M: 07944-618340 E: petermarkby@gmail.com

MARKS, Canon Allan Willi. b 56. Cranmer Hall Dur 92. **d** 94 **p** 95. C Barnoldswick w Bracewell *Bradf* 94–96; C Willington *Newc* 96–98; TV 98–02; V Newc H Cross 02–09; P-in-c Newc Ch Ch w St Ann 09–17; V Newc Ch Ch w St Anne from 17; AD Newc Cen 13–17; Hon Can Newc Cathl from 16. *St Ann's Vicarage, 11 Gibson Street, Newcastle upon Tyne NE1 6PY* T: 0191-232 0516 E: fatherallan@sky.com

MARKS, Dennis Ray. b 37. Lon Univ BSc 58 PhD 67 PGCE 59 Univ of Wales (Ban) BTh 04 CChem 85 MRSC 85. **d** 06 **p** 07. OLM Woking St Mary *Guildf* 06–12; PtO from 12. *Green Tiles, Shaftesbury Road, Woking GU22 7DU* T: (01483) 762030 E: ray.marks@mypostoffice.co.uk

MARKS, Timothy John. b 45. Man Univ BA 76 Anglia Poly Univ MA 96. **d** 88 **p** 89. NSM Burton and Sopley *Win* 88–91; R Croxton and Eltisley *Ely* 91–96; R Graveley w Papworth St Agnes w Yelling etc 91–96; Dir Network Counselling and Tr 96–05; Nat Adv for Personal/Spiritual Development YMCA 05–07. *102 Woodfarm Road, Malvern WR14 4PP* T: (01684) 564925 M: 07817-465213 E: tim@timmarksconsulting.com

MARL, David John. b 42. ARCA 67. **d** 01 **p** 02. OLM Okeford *Sarum* 01–12; rtd 12; PtO *Sarum* 12–20. *St Probus, Marston Road, Sherborne DT9 4BL* T: (01935) 398673 E: burgoyne.marl@gmail.com

MARLEY, Alan Gordon. b 59. Birm Univ BA 89. Qu Coll Birm 87. **d** 89 **p** 90. C Blandford Forum and Langton Long *Sarum* 89–93; Chapl HM YOI Aylesbury 93–97; I Fermoy Union *C, C & R* 97–03; Bp's Dom Chapl 99–03; Dean Cloyne 03–18; I Cloyne Union 03–18; Dioc Dir of Ords 05–18; Chapl Univ Coll Cork from 18. *The Chaplaincy, Iona, University College Cork, College Road, Cork, T12 PY24, Republic of Ireland* T: (00353) (21) 490 2459 E: alan.marley@ucc.ie

MARLOW, Jonathan James. b 76. SS Hild & Bede Coll Dur MEng 99 St Jo Coll Dur MA 21. Wycliffe Hall Ox BTh 06. **d** 06 **p** 07. C Elburton *Ex* 06–10; P-in-c Pennycross 10–15; V 15–18; Assoc Tutor Univ of St Mark and St Jo 10–15; Asst Dioc Dir of Ords 12–17; Miss and Min Development Team Ldr 18–20; Dioc Dir of Ords *Cant* from 20. *Diocesan House, Lady Wootton's Green, Canterbury CT1 1NQ* T: (01227) 459401 M: 07753-454585 E: jmarlow@diocant.org

MARLOW (née SIBBALD), Mrs Olwyn Eileen. b 57. Aston Tr Scheme 85 Linc Th Coll 87. **d** 89 **p** 94. Par Dn Wythenshawe St Martin *Man* 89–93; Par Dn Baguley 93–94; C 94–95; Asst Chapl Cen Man Healthcare NHS Trust 95–00; NSM Newall Green St Fran *Man* 97–98; rtd 01; NSM Wythenshawe *Man* 01–05; PtO from 05; *Ches* from 05. *28 Arcadia Avenue, Sale M33 3SA* T: 0161-962 9292 E: olwynem@sky.com

MARLOW, Ms Tracy Margaret. b 64. St Mellitus Coll 12. **d** 15 **p** 16. C Rayleigh *Chelmsf* 15–19; TV 19–21; V St Helier *S'wark* from 21. *The Vicarage, 193 Bishopsford Road, Morden SM4 6BH* M: 07886-442264 E: t-marlow@hotmail.co.uk

MARNHAM, Preb Charles Christopher. b 51. Jes Coll Cam BA 73 MA 77. Cranmer Hall Dur. **d** 77 **p** 78. C Brompton H Trin *Lon* 77–78; C Brompton H Trin w Onslow Square St Paul 78–80; C Linthorpe *York* 80–84; R Haughton le Skerne *Dur* 84–95; V Ches Square St Mich w St Phil *Lon* 95–19; Preb St Paul's Cathl 10–19; rtd 19; PtO *Lon* from 19. *68 Home Close, Wolvercote, Oxford OX2 8PT* E: charles@stmichaelschurch.org.uk

MARNS, Canon Nigel Geoffrey. b 63. Univ of Wales (Abth) BSc(Econ) 85 Birm Univ BD 92 MA 10. Qu Coll Birm 90. **d** 93 **p** 94. C Addington *S'wark* 93–96; P-in-c W Bromwich Gd Shep w St Jo *Lich* 96–01; V Bromsgrove St Jo *Worc* 01–09; R Ludgvan, Marazion, St Hilary and Perranuthnoe *Truro* from 09; Hon Can Truro Cathl from 16. *The Rectory, Ludgvan, Penzance TR20 8EZ* T: (01736) 740784 E: canon@nigelmarns.plus.com

MÁRQUEZ-PICÓN, Edilberto. b 57. Bible Sem Alliance Peru BA 80 Westmr Coll Ox MTh 93. St Steph Ho Ox 92. **d** 94 **p** 95. C Reading St Jo *Ox* 94–98; C New Malden and Coombe *S'wark* 98–01; P-in-c Bucklebury w Marlston *Ox* 01–08; P-in-c Bradfield and Stanford Dingley 04–08; P-in-c Woodley 08–09; V from 09. *6 Denmark Avenue, Woodley, Reading RG5 4RS* T: 0118-969 6540 M: 07777-665820 E: vicar1992@hotmail.com

MARR (née PARKER), Mrs Anne Elizabeth. b 46. Hull Univ BSc 67 CertEd 68. NEOC 91. **d** 96 **p** 12. NSM Whorlton *Newc* 96–97; NSM Chapel House 97–14; Chapl Newc City Health NHS Trust 96–01; Chapl Newc Mental Health Unit 01–14; rtd 14; PtO *Newc* from 14. *26 The Chesters, Newcastle upon Tyne NE5 1AF* T: 0191-267 4808 E: marr1af@btinternet.com

MARR, Derek Paul. b 33. Dur Univ TCert 69. **d** 00 **p** 01. OLM Chapel House *Newc* 00–03; PtO from 03. *26 The Chesters, Newcastle upon Tyne NE5 1AF* T: 0191-267 4808

MARR, Canon Donald Radley. b 37. K Coll Lon 57. St Aid Birkenhead 61. **d** 64 **p** 65. C Macclesfield St Mich *Ches* 64–66; C Sale St Anne 66–67; V Marthall 67–72; C W Kirby St Bridget 72–76; R Waverton 76–83; R Nantwich 83–87; RD 86–87; RD Malpas 87–91; V Bunbury 87–91; rtd 91; Dioc Rural Officer *Ches* 91–07; Hon Can Ches Cathl 91–92; PtO from 07. *St Boniface, 5 Hockenhull Crescent, Tarvin, Chester CH3 8LJ* T: (01829) 741302 E: revsdonaldandmargaret@btinternet.com

MARRIAGE, Sophia Briony. b 71. Rob Coll Cam BA 93 Edin Univ PhD 98 Glas Univ MTh 05. TISEC 03. **d** 05 **p** 06. C Edin St Martin 05–11; R Edin St Mark from 11. *15 Viewforth Terrace, Edinburgh EH10 4LJ* T: 0131-229 8939 *or* 629 1219 E: sophia.marriage@stmarksportobello.org

MARRIOTT (née REID), Mrs Amanda Joy. b 63. Nottm Univ BTh 92. Linc Th Coll 89. **d** 92 **p** 96. Par Dn Rothwell *Ripon* 92–94; C 94–95; C Manston 95–97; C Wetherby 97–01; P-in-c Water Eaton *Ox* 01–06; AD Milton Keynes 05–06; P-in-c Sherington w Chicheley, N Crawley, Astwood etc 06–09; R 09–15; TR Duston and Upton *Pet* from 15. *The Rectory, 3 Main Road, Duston, Northampton NN5 6JB* T: (01604) 752591 E: aj.marriott123@gmail.com

MARRIOTT, Stanley Richard. b 36. AKC 60 Warwick Univ MA 92. **d** 61 **p** 62. C Coleshill *Birm* 61–64; C Maxstoke 61–64; V Ansley *Cov* 64–78; Org Sec (E Midl) CECS 79–83; P-in-c Baxterley w Hurley and Wood End and Merevale etc *Birm* 83–84; R 84–87; R Newton Regis w Seckington and Shuttington 87–97; rtd 97; PtO B & W 97–19. *Dunkery Pleck, Wootton Courtenay, Minehead TA24 8RH* T: (01643) 841058

MARROW, David Edward Armfield. b 42. Nottm Univ BA 65 MA. Tyndale Hall Bris 65. **d** 67 **p** 68. C Clifton Ch Ch w Em *Bris* 67–70; BCMS Ethiopia 70–75; N Area Sec BCMS 75–77; C-in-c Ryde St Jas Prop Chpl *Portsm* 77–84; V Worthing St Geo *Chich* 84–07; rtd 07. *West View, 65 St Michael's Road, St Helens, Ryde PO33 1YJ* T: (01983) 872729 E: davidmarrow@btinternet.com

MARROW, John Willam. b 70. Wilson Carlile Coll 92 St Mellitus Coll BA 18. **d** 18 **p** 19. C Farnham *Guildf* 18–21; V W Ewell from 21. *All Saints' Vicarage, 7 Church Road, West Ewell, Epsom KT19 9QY* M: 07766-220884 E: johnwmarrow@hotmail.com

MARRY, Sarah Louise. **d** 11 **p** 12. C Douglas Union w Frankfield *C, C & R* 11–15; P-in-c Cork St Ann's Union 15–19; I Clonsast w Rathangan, Thomastown etc *M & K* from 19. *The Rectory, Monasterois, Edenderry, Co Offaly, Republic of Ireland* T: (00353) (46) 973 1585 M: (00353) 86-171 3936

MARSDEN, Canon Andrew Philip. b 63. Keble Coll Ox BA 85 MA 90 Birm Univ MA 86. Wycliffe Hall Ox BA 90. **d** 91 **p** 92. C Newport St Jo *Portsm* 91–94; C Cowplain 94–97; V Wokingham St Sebastian *Ox* from 97; Hon Can Ch Ch from 15. *St Sebastian's Vicarage, Nine Mile Ride, Wokingham RG40 3AT* T: (01344) 761050 E: revamarsden@tiscali.co.uk

MARSDEN, Canon Carole. b 44. Avery Hill Coll TCert 65 Sheff Poly DipEd 81. NOC 88. **d** 91 **p** 94. NSM Saddleworth *Man* 91–92; Par Dn 92–94; C 94–95; P-in-c Oldham St Paul 95–02; C Werneth 98–02; P-in-c Shap w Swindale and Bampton w Mardale *Carl* 02–08; P-in-c Orton and Tebay w Ravenstonedale etc 07–08; rtd 08; PtO *Carl* 09–16; RD Appleby 09–13; P-in-c Kirkby Stephen w Mallerstang etc 16–18; Hon Can Carl Cathl 11–18; PtO *Blackb* from 13. *Fairfield, Faraday Road, Kirby Stephen CA17 4QL* T: (017683) 71279 M: 07866-006849 E: carole.sam@hotmail.co.uk

MARSDEN, Faith Edith Mary. b 54. **d** 18 **p** 19. NSM Acton w Gt Waldingfield *St E* 18–21; V from 21. *4 Chapel Close, Great Waldingfield, Sudbury CO10 0UB* T: (01787) 312002 M: 07525-450444 E: femarsden@hotmail.co.uk

MARSDEN, The Very Revd John Joseph. b 53. York Univ BA 74 Nottm Univ MTh 81 Kent Univ PhD 88. St Jo Coll Nottm 77. **d** 80 **p** 81. C Leigh St Mary *Man* 80–83; Hon C Chatham St Steph *Roch* 83–91; Ind Chapl 83–91; Lect Systematic Th CITC and TCD from 91; I Newbridge w Carnalway and Kilcullen *M & K* 97–16; I Kildare w Kilmeague and Curragh 06–16; Dean Kildare 06–16; rtd 16. *Firgrove House, Military Road, Killiney, Co Dublin, Republic of Ireland* T: (00353) (1) 211 5684 M: 87-949 9177 E: johnmarsden@eircom.net

MARSDEN, Robert. b 59. Ch Ch Ox BA 81 PGCE 82. Oak Hill Th Coll BA 92. **d** 92 **p** 93. C Sevenoaks St Nic *Roch* 92–95; Chapl Fettes Coll Edin 95–99; C-in-c Buxton Trin Prop Chpl *Derby* from 99. *37 Temple Road, Buxton SK17 9BA* T: (01298) 73656 E: bobinbuxton@sky.com

MARSDEN, Robert James. b 56. Ch Ch Coll Cant BEd 79. Oak Hill Th Coll 90. **d** 94 **p** 95. C Margate H Trin *Cant* 94–98; P-in-c Brinton, Briningham, Hunworth, Stody etc *Nor* 98–08;

P-in-c Gressenhall w Longham w Wendling etc 08–16; RD Dereham in Mitford 13–15; P-in-c The Lulworths, Winfrith Newburgh and Chaldon *Sarum* 16–20; PtO from 21. *Address temp unknown* E: revrobert.lulworth@camelhome.co.uk

MARSDEN, Samuel Edward. b 44. Keble Coll Ox BA 66 MA 85. Linc Th Coll 66. **d** 68 **p** 69. C Liskeard w St Keyne *Truro* 68–72; R Gerrans w St Anthony in Roseland 72–77; V Kowloon Ch Ch Hong Kong 77–81; P-in-c Ingrave *Chelmsf* 81–82; P-in-c Gt Warley w Childerditch 81–82; R Gt Warley w Childerditch and Ingrave 82–89; R Gilgandra Australia 89–93; R Kelso 94–00; Adn Wylde 00–01; R Parkes 01–07; Adn Bathurst 05–07; R Coffs Harbour 07–10; rtd 10; PtO *Ely* 10–12; *Truro* from 16. *7 Penmare Court, Hayle TR27 4RD* T: (01736) 756669 E: samuelmarsden@hotmail.com

MARSH, Anderson Jason. b 74. STETS 06. **d** 09. NSM Sheet *Portsm* from 09. *12 Rother Close, Petersfield GU31 4DN* T: (01730) 268156 E: amarsh@rotherbank.co.uk

MARSH, Carol Ann. *See* HATHORNE, Carol Ann

MARSH, Colin Arthur. b 54. Edin Univ PhD 02. St Jo Coll Nottm 79. **d** 82 **p** 83. C Kirkby *Liv* 82–86; TV St Luke in the City 86–91; P-in-c Chingola St Barn Zambia 91–95; PtO *Edin* 95–03; Tutor United Coll of Ascension Selly Oak 03–06; Ecum Development Officer Chs Together *Birm* 06–20; PtO from 04; rtd 20. *19 St Denis Road, Birmingham B29 4LN*

MARSH, David. b 32. St Jo Coll Dur BA 54. Cranmer Hall Dur. **d** 57 **p** 58. C Bilston St Leon *Lich* 57–62; Lic to Offic Dio Maseno Kenya 63–66; Chapl Scargill Ho 67–69; Adn S Maseno 70–72; V Meole Brace *Lich* 72–77; V Westlands St Andr 77–86; V Trentham 86–96; P-in-c Alstonfield, Butterton, Warslow w Elkstone etc 96–99; rtd 99; PtO *Ches* from 99; Chapl Mid Cheshire Hosps NHS Foundn Trust 02–16. *31 Spring Gardens, Nantwich CW5 5SH* T: (01270) 610079 E: dlmarsh@talktalk.net

MARSH, Mrs Deborah Lindsay. b 59. Westcott Ho Cam 13. **d** 15 **p** 16. C Hardingstone, Piddington w Horton and Quinton and Preston Deanery *Pet* 15–18; TV Oakham, Ashwell, Braunston, Brooke, Egleton etc from 18. *The Rectory, 3 Paddock Close, Whissendine, Oakham LE15 7HW* M: 07919-385314 E: debmarsh37@yahoo.com

MARSH, Mrs Elizabeth Alexandra (Sandra). b 60. QUB BA 94. St Aug Coll Cant 17. **d** 18 **p** 19. C Eastry and Woodnesborough *Cant* 18–21; R Calehill w Westwell from 21. *The Vicarage, Pett Lane, Charing, Ashford TN27 0DL* T: (01233) 713996 M: 07788-715443 E: revsandramarsh@btinternet.com

MARSH, Francis John. b 47. York Univ BA 69 DPhil 76 ATCL 65 ARCM 66 ARCO 71. Oak Hill Th Coll 72 Selw Coll Cam 73. **d** 75 **p** 76. C Cambridge St Matt *Ely* 75–78; C Pitsmoor w Wicker *Sheff* 79; C Pitsmoor w Ellesmere 79–81; C Crookes St Thos 81–85; V S Ossett *Wakef* 85–96; RD Dewsbury 93–96; Adn Blackb 96–01; Bp's Adv on Hosp Chapls 96–01; P-in-c Emley *Wakef* 11–14; *Leeds* 14–17; P-in-c Flockton cum Denby Grange *Wakef* 11–14; *Leeds* 14–17. *Bark House Mews, Bark Close, Shelley, Huddersfield HD8 8JR* T: (01484) 981530 E: john.marsh774@gmail.com

MARSH, John. b 53. Open Univ BSc 95 MSc 04. Guildf Dioc Min Course 07. **d** 10 **p** 11. OLM Ockley, Okewood and Forest Green *Guildf* 10–18; NSM Ewhurst w Okewood and Forest Green from 16. *Address temp unknown* E: home@john-marsh.co.uk

MARSH, Leonard Stuart Alexander. b 55. Hull Univ BA 77 SOAS Lon MA 00. Linc Th Coll 77. **d** 79 **p** 80. C Eltham St Barn *S'wark* 79–81; C Camberwell St Giles 81–83; Hon C Clifton St Paul *Bris* 83–86; Asst Chapl Bris Univ 83–86; Area Sec (Dio S'wark) USPG 86–91; Chapl Guildhall Sch of Music and Drama *Lon* 91–97; Chapl City Univ 91–98; NSM Clerkenwell H Redeemer and St Mark 94–95; P-in-c Finsbury St Clem w St Barn and St Matt 95–01; P-in-c Upper Norwood All SS *S'wark* 01–08; V 08–21; AD Croydon N 12–17; rtd 21. *93 Campbell Road, London N17 0BF*

MARSH, Canon Margaret Evaline. b 47. Univ of Wales (Lamp) MA 08. STETS 96. **d** 99 **p** 00. NSM Tattenham Corner and Burgh Heath *Guildf* 99–03; NSM Epsom St Martin 03–04; P-in-c Walton-on-the-Hill 04–15; Hon Can Guildf Cathl 10–15; PtO from 15. *9 Westways, Epsom KT19 0PH* T: (020) 8224 0607 M: 07894-302749 E: maggiemarsh17@gmail.com

MARSH, Max Joseph. b 94. S Bank Univ BA 16 Sheff Univ BA 18. Coll of Resurr Mirfield 18. **d** 21. C Lewisham St Mary *S'wark* from 21. *36D Clarendon Rise, London SE13 5EY* E: frmaxmarsh@gmail.com

MARSH, Michael John. b 47. Reading Univ BA 69 DipEd 70 York Univ MA 91 Leeds Univ BA 07. Coll of Resurr Mirfield 05. **d** 07 **p** 08. NSM Castleford *Wakef* 07–11; Knottingley and Kellington w Whitley *Leeds* 11–20; PtO

21. *9 Highland Close, Pontefract WF8 2JZ* M: 07884-952282
E: frmike.marsh@hotmail.com

MARSH, Peter Charles Ernest. b 57. Southn Univ CertEd 03
IEng 87. WEMTC 04. **d** 06 **p** 07. NSM Wotton-under-
Edge w Ozleworth *Glouc* 06–09; PtO 14–15; NSM Tyndale
from 15. *1 Pitt Court Villas, Pitt Court, North Nibley, Dursley
GL11 6EB* T: (01453) 547521 E: pcemarsh@tiscali.co.uk

MARSH, Phillip Edward. b 73. Univ of Wales (Abth) BSc 94
Ch Ch Coll Cant PGCE 96. Wycliffe Hall Ox BTh 02. **d** 02
p 03. C Hubberston *St D* 02–05; C Werrington *Pet* 05–09;
P-in-c Wilford *S'well* 09–11; R 11–19; PtO *Ely* 19–21; TV Ely
from 21. *47 Elderberry Close, Ely CB6 2FQ* M: 07766-314957

MARSH, Robert Charles. b 58. Linc Univ BA 13. Linc Sch of
Th and Min 09. **d** 13 **p** 14. NSM Whitwick, Thringstone and
Swannington *Leic* 13–15; NSM Desford and Kirby Muxloe
from 15. *43 Chevin Avenue, Leicester LE3 6PX* M: 07557-
536926 E: ministry@family-marsh.uk

MARSH, Roger Philip. b 44. K Coll Lon BD 72 AKC 72 Sussex
Univ MA 95 K Alfred's Coll Win CertEd 66 FRSA 21. St Aug
Coll Cant 73. **d** 73 **p** 74. C Leagrave *St Alb* 73–76; Asst Youth
Officer 76–77; Resources Officer 77–80; Chapl Marlborough
Coll 80–86; Hd Master St Geo Sch Windsor 95–99; Chapl Lancing
Coll 99–09; rtd 09; PtO *Cant* from 09; Chapl St Edm Sch
Cant 10–11; Chapl Heathfield Sch Ascot 11–12; Acting
Hd Master Lancing Coll Prep Sch Worthing 14; PtO *Chich*
14–19. *107 College Road, Deal CT14 6BU* T: (01304) 362851
E: rogermarsh573@gmail.com

MARSH, Sandra. *See* MARSH, Elizabeth Alexandra

MARSH, Canon Shelley Ann. b 54. SRN 75 SCM 76.
St Jo Coll Nottm 84. **d** 89 **p** 94. Hon C Glas Gd Shep
and Ascension 89–96; P-in-c Johnstone and Renfrew
96–06; R Bishopbriggs 06–16; Chapl Paisley Univ
98–00; rtd 16; Hon Can St Mary's Cathl *Glas* from 17.
9 Moredun Square, Perth PH2 0DE T: (01738) 575040
E: revshelleymarsh@ntlworld.com

MARSH, Steven Philip. b 73. Lon Inst BA 96 Cov Univ
MA 98 Lon Sch of Th BA 05. Ripon Coll Cuddesdon
MA 13. **d** 13 **p** 14. C Crofton *Portsm* 13–17; TV Ouzel
Valley *St Alb* from 17. *4 Warneford Way, Leighton Buzzard
LU7 4PX* M: 07817-872163 E: s.p.marsh@hotmail.com *or*
rev.steve.marsh@hotmail.com

MARSH, Susan Edith. b 42. Southn Univ BA 63 CertEd 64.
SAOMC 01. **d** 01 **p** 02. NSM Bp's Hatfield *St Alb* 01–05;
NSM Bishop's Hatfield, Lemsford and N Mymms
05–15; rtd 15; PtO *St Alb* from 15. *141 Handside Lane,
Welwyn Garden City AL8 6TA* T: (01707) 329744
E: susanianmarsh@ntlworld.com

MARSH, William Jack. b 92. Man Univ BA 13 Middx Univ
BA 21. Oak Hill Th Coll 18. **d** 21. C Rusholme *Man* from
21. *3A Eileen Grove West, Manchester M14 5NW* M: 07892-
854651 E: willjackmarsh@hotmail.com

MARSHALL, Alexander Robert. b 43. Glouc Sch of Min 84.
d 87 **p** 88. NSM Newtown w Llanllwchaiarn w Aberhafesp
St As 87–00; P-in-c Mochdre 00–06. *8 Bromley College,
London Road, Bromley BR1 1PE* T: (020) 8464 9727
E: revalexandermarshall17@gmail.com

MARSHALL, Mrs Alison Mary. b 54. Middx Hosp MB, BS 79
MRCGP 84. SAOMC 98. **d** 01 **p** 02. NSM Reading St Jo *Ox*
01–14; PtO 14–19; Progr Co-ordinator Iona Community *Arg*
14–15; NSM Macclesfield Team *Ches* from 20. *79 Byrons Lane,
Macclesfield SK11 7JS* T: (01625) 477171 M: 07740-944102
E: ali.m@rshall.org.uk

MARSHALL, Amanda Jane. b 64. Nottm Univ BA 86
Glam Univ MSc 04. Wycliffe Hall Ox 15. **d** 18 **p** 19. C
Ashbourne St Oswald w Mapleton *Derby* from 18; C
Ashbourne St Jo from 18; C Clifton from 18; C Norbury
w Snelston from 18. *The New Vicarage, Clifton, Ashbourne
DE6 2GL* T: (01335)   343009 M: 07557-567751
E: revamandamarshall@gmail.com

MARSHALL, Andrew Stephen. b 74. UNISA BTh 00. **d** 99
p 00. C Port Elizabeth St Hugh S Africa 00–02; C Port
Elizabeth St Jo 02; C Easthampstead *Ox* 03–06; Sen Chapl
Southn Solent Univ *Win* 06–09; Chapl Portsm Univ 09–17;
Dioc Interfaith Adv 11–17; Chapl R Veterinary Coll *Lon* from
17. *Royal Veterinary College, 4 Royal College Street, London
NW1 0TU* T: (020) 7468 5000 E: asmarshall@rvc.ac.uk

MARSHALL, Mrs Angela. b 48. Trin Coll Bris 74. **d** 88 **p** 96.
Hon Par Dn Newcastle St Geo *Lich* 88–92; LtO *Eur* 92–94; Dn
Versailles 94–96; Asst Chapl 96–04; PtO *St E* 04–07; Hon C
Collier Row St Jas and Havering-atte-Bower *Chelmsf* 07–15;
rtd 15; PtO *Eur* 15–20. *Sous le Figuier, Hameau de Manieu,
32100 Condom, France* E: rev.ange@hotmail.co.uk

MARSHALL, Canon Bryan John. b 40. Chich Th Coll 63.
d 65 **p** 66. C Poulton-le-Fylde *Blackb* 65–68; C S Shore
H Trin 68–70; V Wesham 70–74; PV Chich Cathl 74–82;

V Boxgrove 82–91; P-in-c Tangmere 82–84; R 84–91;
R Westbourne 91–95; V E Preston w Kingston 95–03;
Can and Preb Chich Cathl 94–10; rtd 03. *11 Priory
Close, Boxgrove, Chichester PO18 0EA* T: (01243) 536337
E: boxgrovebryan@gmail.com

MARSHALL, Mrs Christine Anne. b 40. Leeds Univ BSc 64.
d 95 **p** 96. OLM Holbrook, Stutton, Preston, Woolverstone
etc *St E* 95–05; PtO 05–06 and 09–13; *Truro* from 15. *8 Castle
View Park, Mawnan Smith, Falmouth TR11 5HB* T: (01326)
250656 E: marshall616@btinternet.com

MARSHALL, Preb Christopher John Bickford. b 32. TD 78.
AKC 56. **d** 57 **p** 58. C Leatherhead *Guildf* 57–60; C Crewkerne
B & W 60–63; V Long Sutton 63–72; V Long Sutton w Long
Load 72–76; V Wiveliscombe 76–93; RD Tone 78–87; Preb
Wells Cathl 88–96; P-in-c Chipstable w Huish Champflower
and Clatworthy 93; R Wiveliscombe w Chipstable, Huish
Champflower etc 93–96; rtd 96; PtO *B & W* from 96. *Tap
Cottage, High Street, Milverton, Taunton TA4 1LL* T: (01823)
400419

MARSHALL, Craig Laurence. b 64. Southn Univ BEd 87
Open Univ MA 93. St Jo Coll Nottm MTh 01. **d** 01 **p** 02.
C Staplegrove w Norton Fitzwarren *B & W* 01–04; Chapl
K Coll Taunton 04–06; R Aisholt, Enmore, Goathurst,
Nether Stowey etc *B & W* 06–14; RD Quantock 12–14; V
Hurstbourne Priors, Longparish etc *Win* 14–20; Dioc Rural
Officer 14–20; AD Whitchurch 17–20; R Lower Wharfedale
Leeds from 20. *Hayfield House, Strait Lane, Huby, Leeds
LS17 0EA* T: (01423) 733341 E: craig785@btinternet.com *or*
craig.marshall@leeds.anglican.org

MARSHALL, David Charles. b 52. St Chad's Coll Dur BA 73.
Trin Coll Bris 74. **d** 76 **p** 77. C Meole Brace *Lich* 76–78; C
W Teignmouth *Ex* 78–80; C Broadwater St Mary *Chich*
80–84; V Newcastle St Geo *Lich* 84–92; Chapl Versailles
w Chevry *Eur* 92–04; Min Southgate LEP *St E* 04–07;
P-in-c Collier Row St Jas and Havering-atte-Bower *Chelmsf*
07–15; V 15; AD Havering 10–14; rtd 15; PtO *Eur* from 15.
Sous le Figuier, Hameau de Manieu, 32100 Condom, France
E: dmrevdave6@gmail.com

MARSHALL, Canon David Evelyn. b 63. New Coll Ox BA 85
Birm Univ MA 88 PhD 96. Ridley Hall Cam 88. **d** 90 **p** 91.
C Roundhay St Edm *Ripon* 90–92; Chapl Ex Coll Ox 95–98;
Lect St Paul's United Th Coll Limuru Kenya 98–99; P-in-c
Buckden and Hail Weston *Ely* 99–00; Abp's Dom Chapl
Cant 00–05; Hon Can All SS Cathl Cairo from 02; PtO
S'wark 05–09; *Carl* from 09; Assoc Prof Duke Div Sch USA
13–16; WCC from 18. *St Ursula, Jubiläumsplatz 2, 3005 Berne,
Switzerland* E: revdem63@yahoo.com

MARSHALL, Derek Stanley. b 53. All SS Cen for Miss &
Min 11. **d** 14 **p** 15. NSM Tranmere St Cath *Ches* 14–18;
Chapl YMCA Birkenhead 14–18; P-in-c Leasowe from 18.
70 Castleway North, Wirral CH46 1RW M: 07746-943178
E: derekmarshall@yahoo.co.uk

MARSHALL, The Very Revd Geoffrey Osborne. b 48.
St Jo Coll Dur BA 71. Coll of Resurr Mirfield 71. **d** 73
p 74. C Waltham Cross *St Alb* 73–76; C Digswell 76–78;
P-in-c Belper Ch Ch and Milford *Derby* 78–86; V Spondon
86–93; Chapl Derby High Sch 87–01; RD Derby N 90–95;
Can Res Derby Cathl 93–02; Dioc Dir of Ords 95–00; TR
Wrexham *St As* 02–08; AD 02–08; Dean Brecon *S & B* 08–14;
Warden of Readers 08–14; V Brecon St Mary w Llanddew
08–11; P-in-c Llanddew 11–14; rtd 14; PtO *Derby* 14–16 and
from 18; Hon C Morley and Smalley 16–18; Dioc Clergy
Widows' and Widowers' Officer from 21. *36 Saundersfoot
Way, Oakwood, Derby DE21 2RH* T: (01332)   280452
E: brecondeanery@btinternet.com

MARSHALL, Mrs Gillian Kathryn. b 54. Glouc Sch of
Min 84. **d** 87 **p** 97. NSM Newtown w Llanllwchaiarn
w Aberhafesp *St As* 87–98; P-in-c Betws Cedewain and
Tregynon and Llanwyddelan 98–02; V 02–06. *8 Bromley
College, London Road, Bromley BR1 1PE* T: (020) 8464 9727
E: revalexandermarshall17@gmail.com

MARSHALL, Graham George. b 38. Dur Univ BA 60
St Chad's Coll Dur. **d** 65 **p** 66. C Ashton-on-Ribble St Mich
Blackb 65–67; C Lancaster St Mary 67–71; R Church Eaton
Lich 71–75; Prec Man Cathl 75–78; R Reddish 78–85; V
Chadderton St Luke 87–02; rtd 02; PtO *Man* from 02.
7 The Woods, Rochdale OL11 3NT T: (01706)   642139
E: pizzicatoman@sky.com

MARSHALL (née CHADWICK), Mrs Helen Jane. b 63. UEA
BA 84. St Jo Coll Nottm MTh 91. **d** 91 **p** 94. Par Dn Easton H
Trin w St Gabr and St Lawr and St Jude *Bris* 91–94; C 94–95;
PtO *Ox* 95–98; Lect St Paul's Th Coll Limuru Kenya 98–99;
PtO *Ely* 99–00; Chapl K Coll Lon 01–05; P-in-c Addiscombe
St Mildred *S'wark* 05–06; V 06–09; PtO *Carl* 09–13; NSM
Keswick St Jo w Borrowdale 13–19; Chapl Berne *Eur* from 19.
St Ursula, Jubiläumsplatz 2, 3005 Berne, Switzerland T: (0041)

(31) 351 0343 E: helenmarshall2592@yahoo.co.uk or chaplain@stursula.ch

MARSHALL, James Hudson. b 48. Sheff Univ CertEd 70 Open Univ BA 74 Cumbria Univ BA 08. LCTP 05. **d** 08 **p** 09. NSM Lamplugh w Ennerdale *Carl* 08–13; P-in-c 11–13; rtd 14; PtO *Carl* from 14. *28 Arlecdon Road, Arlecdon, Frizington CA26 3UX* E: revjimmarshall@gmail.com

MARSHALL, Mrs Jean. b 36. SWMTC 84. **d** 87 **p** 94. NSM Stratton *Truro* 87–89; NSM Bodmin w Lanhydrock and Lanivet 89–94; P-in-c Lezant w Lawhitton and S Petherwin w Trewen 94–98; rtd 98; Hon C Bodmin w Lanhydrock and Lanivet *Truro* 00–06; PtO from 06. *10 Springwell View, Love Lane, Bodmin PL31 2QP* T: (01208) 79891

MARSHALL, John. b 37. Kelham Th Coll 53. **d** 62 **p** 63. C Winshill *Derby* 62–64; C Chaddesden St Phil 64–65; Chapl HM YOI Morton Hall 65–75; V Swinderby *Linc* 66–77; R Church Aston *Lich* 77–84; V Auckland St Andr and St Anne *Dur* 84–02; P-in-c Hunwick 88–90; Chapl Bishop Auckland Gen Hosp 84–94; Chapl Bishop Auckland Hospitals NHS Trust 94–98; Chapl S Durham Healthcare NHS Trust 98–00; rtd 02; PtO *Derby* 02–06 and 08–19; Hon C S Darley, Elton and Winster 06–08; Hon C Darley, S Darley and Winster 08; PtO *Dur* from 19. *11 Village Close, Newton Aycliffe DL5 4UD*

MARSHALL, John. b 50. St Luke's Coll Ex CertEd 74 W Lon Inst of HE DEHC 79. S'wark Ord Course 88. **d** 91 **p** 92. Hon C Brixton Hill St Sav *S'wark* 91–95; Hon C Clapham St Jas from 95. *57A Kingscourt Road, London SW16 1JA* T: (020) 8769 3665 M: 07873-712091 E: ajohn20002000@yahoo.co.uk

MARSHALL, John Linton. b 42. Worc Coll Ox BA 64 MA 68 Bris Univ MLitt 75. Wells Th Coll 66. **d** 68 **p** 69. C Bris St Mary Redcliffe w Temple etc 68–71; Tutor Sarum & Wells Th Coll 71–73; PtO *Pet* 74–77; LtO *S'well* 77–81; V Choral S'well Minster 79–81; R Ordsall 81–88; P-in-c Grove 84–88; RD Retford 84–88; V Northowram *Wakef* 88–99; P-in-c Glouc St Mark and St Mary de Crypt w St Jo etc 99–00; R Glouc St Mary de Lode and St Mary de Crypt etc 00–09; rtd 09; PtO *Glouc* from 15. *166 Calton Road, Gloucester GL1 5ER*

MARSHALL, Mrs Judith Elizabeth. b 53. St Hild Coll Dur BEd 75. SCTEI 17. **d** 19 **p** 20. OLM Chipping Norton *Ox* from 19. *8 Church Street, Chipping Norton OX7 5NT* T: (01608) 643303 M: 07753-492654 E: joulesmarshall53@gmail.com

MARSHALL, Mrs Julie. b 62. **d** 08 **p** 09. OLM Bucknall *Lich* from 08. *27 Meadow Avenue, Wetley Rocks, Stoke-on-Trent ST9 0BD* T: (01782) 550993 E: julie.marshall@stokecoll.ac.uk

MARSHALL, Ms Karen Lesley. b 59. Coll of Ripon & York St Jo BA 82 Leeds Metrop Univ BSc 96 Huddersfield Univ MA 05. NEOC 04. **d** 07 **p** 08. C Horsforth *Ripon* 07–11; P-in-c Leeds All SS w Osmondthorpe 11–14; P-in-c Urmston *Man* 14–15; P-in-c Davyhulme Ch Ch 14–15; V Davyhulme Ch Ch and Urmston 15–19; P-in-c Hebden Bridge and Heptonstall *Leeds* from 19. *12 Becketts Close, Heptonstall, Hebden Bridge HX7 7LJ* E: karenlmarshall21@gmail.com

MARSHALL, Keith William. **d** 11 **p** 12. C Portadown St Mark *Arm* from 11. *4 Killycomain Drive, Portadown, Craigavon BT63 5JJ* E: keithmarshall777@yahoo.com

MARSHALL, Mrs Margaret Elizabeth. b 60. New Hall Cam BA 81 MA 84. EAMTC 01. **d** 04 **p** 05. C St Neots *Ely* 04–09; P-in-c Riversmeet *St Alb* 09–13; R 13–17; rtd 17; PtO *Ely* from 17; *St Alb* from 17. *80 Hardwick Road, Eynesbury, St Neots PE19 2SD*

MARSHALL, Melanie Kirsten. b 80. Ch Ch Ox BA 02 MSt 06 Toronto Univ MA 07 BNC Ox DPhil 11 Em Coll Cam MA 12. Westcott Ho Cam 10. **d** 13 **p** 14. C Bedford Park *Lon* 13–15; Chapl Linc Coll Ox 15–20; Chapl Mert Coll Ox from 20. *Merton College, Merton Street, Oxford OX1 4JD* M: 07967-762558 E: mthrmelanie@gmail.com

MARSHALL, Michael David. b 51. BSc. Trin Coll Bris. **d** 84 **p** 85. C Kennington St Mark *S'wark* 84–88; V Streatham Park St Alb 88–96; RD Tooting 93–96; V Blackheath St Jo 96–06; RD Charlton 01–06; Chapl Bishop's Stortford Coll 06–11; V St Austell *Truro* 11–15; rtd 15; PtO *Nor* from 16. *12 Aspen Way, Cringleford, Norwich NR4 6UA* E: mikemarshall51@hotmail.com

✠**MARSHALL, The Rt Revd Michael Eric.** b 36. Ch Coll Cam BA 58 MA 60. Cuddesdon Coll 58. **d** 60 **p** 61 **c** 75. C Birm St Pet 60–62; Tutor Ely Th Coll 62–64; Min Can Ely Cathl 62–64; Chapl Lon Univ 64–69; V St Marylebone All SS 69–75; Suff Bp Woolwich *S'wark* 75–84; Episc Dir Angl Inst Missouri 84–92; Abps' Adv Springboard for Decade of Evang 92–97; Hon Asst Bp Lon 84–07; Hon Asst Bp Chich from 92; Can and Preb Chich Cathl 90–99; Bp in Res Upper Chelsea H Trin *Lon* 97–02; R 02–07; rtd 07; PtO *Eur* from 18. *18 Grosvenor Court, 99 Sloane Street, London SW1X 9PF* M: 07710-215131 E: augustinest12345@gmail.com

MARSHALL, Mrs Michèle Jane. b 60. SEN 82. NTMTC 05. **d** 08 **p** 09. C Orsett and Bulphan and Horndon on the Hill *Chelmsf* 08–11; C Pitsea w Nevendon 11–13; C Woodham Ferrers and Bicknacre 13–19; C S Woodham Ferrers 13–19; P-in-c E and W Tilbury and Linford from 19; Lead Chapl (Essex) St Andr Healthcare from 13. *The Rectory, 24 Somerset Road, Linford, Stanford-le-Hope SS17 0QA* E: mjmarshall@fastmail.co.uk

MARSHALL, Peter John Charles. b 35. Bris Univ BA 60. Ridley Hall Cam 60. **d** 62 **p** 63. C Lindfield *Chich* 62–65; Schools Staff Scripture Union 65–83; Hon C Nottingham St Nic *S'well* 65–67; Hon C Cheadle Hulme St Andr *Ches* 67–83; V Ilkley All SS *Bradf* 83–98; RD Otley 92–97; rtd 98; PtO *Ches* 00–03; *St As* from 03; *Ban* 11–17. *55 Chesterton Court, Railway Road, Ilkley LS29 8UW* T: (01943) 725116 M: 07740-081305 E: revmarsh35@gmail.com

MARSHALL, Richard Arthur Howard. Regent's Park Coll Ox BA 88 MA 92 SS Coll Cam PGCE 89. Wycliffe Hall Ox BTh 99. **d** 98 **p** 99. C Broughton *Man* 98–02; Asst Chapl Sedbergh Sch 02–03; Sessional Chapl HM Pris Man 02–04; V Blackb Redeemer 04–20; PtO *Ches* from 20. *Address withheld by request*

MARSHALL, Robert David. b 52. TCD BA 75 MA 00 Solicitor 77. CITC 99. **d** 02 **p** 03. NSM Stillorgan w Blackrock *D & G* from 02. *The Tontine, 84 The Rise, Mount Merrion, Co Dublin, Republic of Ireland* T: (00353) (1) 288 6170 or (1) 649 2137 F: 649 2649 M: 86-815 3089 E: curate@stillorgan.dublin.anglican.org

MARSHALL, Robert Paul. b 60. Sheff Univ BA 81 PhD 14 St Jo Coll Dur MA 85. Cranmer Hall Dur 81. **d** 83 **p** 84. C Kirkstall *Ripon* 83–85; C Otley *Bradf* 85–87; Dioc Communications Officer 87–91; P-in-c Embsay w Eastby 87–91; Dioc Communications Officer *Lon* 91–95; P-in-c S Kensington St Aug 95–00; Media Adv to Abp York 95–05; Communications Adv *Sheff* 04–13; Public Relns Adv Fresh Expressions from 05; Hd of Marketing St Mary's Univ Coll Twickenham *Lon* 05–07; Hon C Kensington St Mary Abbots w Ch Ch and St Phil 07–13; PtO *Ely* 08–13; *Derby* 08–13; *Sarum* 08–13; P-in-c E Ham w Upton Park and Forest Gate *Chelmsf* 13; TR 13–15; TV St Alb 14–18; Min Digswell St Jo CD *St Alb* 15–16; P-in-c Digswell and Panshanger 16–18; R Digswell from 18. *The Rectory, 354 Knightsfield, Welwyn Garden City AL8 7NG* T: (01707) 592088 M: 07917-272833 E: robmarshalluk@gmail.com

MARSHALL, Sarah. b 75. E Lon Univ BA 97 Herts Univ MA 15 MCIPD 15. ERMC 16. **d** 19 **p** 20. C Tring *St Alb* from 19. *Address withheld by request*

MARSHALL, Simon. b 54. Kingston Poly BSc 77 Leeds Univ PGCE 78 MA(Ed) 79. Qu Coll Birm 91. **d** 93 **p** 94. C Gt Clacton *Chelmsf* 93–97; TV Chigwell and Chigwell Row 97–02; C Woodford Wells 02–19; rtd 19; PtO *Glouc* from 20. *25 Brecon Close, Quedgeley, Gloucester GL2 4TS* M: 07752-599672 E: simonmarshall6@icloud.com

MARSHALL, Simon Hardy. b 69. Bp Grosseteste Coll BA 92. St Jo Coll Nottm 00. **d** 02 **p** 03. C Bartley Green *Birm* 02–05; TV Solihull from 05. *Oak Cottage, Bryanston Road, Solihull B91 1BS* T: 0121-704 4730

MARSHALL, Mrs Sonia Margaret Cecilia. b 49. Westf Coll Lon BA 71 Nottm Univ MA 03. EMMTC 01. **d** 03 **p** 04. NSM Deeping St James *Linc* from 03; PtO *Pet* from 12. *135C Eastgate, Deeping St James, Peterborough PE6 8RB* T: (01778) 346420 E: curate@dsj.org.uk or sonia.marshall@btinternet.com

MARSHALL, Mrs Tracy Ann. b 70. Man Metrop Univ BEd 05. All SS Cen for Miss & Min 13. **d** 16 **p** 17. C Didsbury St Jas and Em *Man* 16–19; TV Atherton and Hindsford w Howe Bridge from 19. *Howe Bridge Rectory, Leigh Road, Atherton, Manchester M46 0PH* M: 07837-624872 E: revtracymarshall@outlook.com

MARSHALL, Trevor. b 60. SEITE 08. **d** 11 **p** 12. C Bognor *Chich* 11–15; PtO 16–18; P-in-c Tangmere and Oving from 18. *St Andrew's Rectory, 21 Gibson Road, Tangmere, Chichester PO20 2JA* T: (01243) 785089 M: 07900-158982 E: trevor.marshall9@icloud.com

MARSHALL, William John. b 35. TCD BA 57 BD 61 PhD 75. TCD Div Sch 59. **d** 59 **p** 60. C Ballyholme *D & D* 59–61; India 62–72; Asst Dean of Residence TCD 73–76; I Rathmichael *D & G* 76–92; Can Ch Ch Cathl Dublin 90–02; Chan Ch Ch Cathl Dublin 91–02; Vice-Prin CITC 92–02; rtd 02. *115 The Elms, Abberley, Killiney, Co Dublin, Republic of Ireland* T: (00353) (1) 239 0832 E: rail1948@eircom.net

MARSHMAN, Mrs Elizabeth Maryan. b 53. York St Jo Coll CertEd 74 Leeds Univ BEd 75. NEOC 03. **d** 06 **p** 07. C Clifton *York* 06–10; P-in-c Lockington and Lund and Scorborough w Leconfield 10–14; R 14–18; rtd 18; PtO *York* from 19. *36 Main Street, Kilnwick, Driffield YO25 9JD* E: emmarshman@yahoo.co.uk

MARSTON, Benjamin Charles. b 85. St Cuth Soc Dur BA 06. Wycliffe Hall Ox BA 19. **d** 19 **p** 20. C Retford St Sav *S'well* from 19. *25 Laurel Grove, Retford DN22 7WD* E: benjamincmarston@gmail.com

MARSTON, David Howarth. b 48. St Jo Coll Dur BA 69. Edin Th Coll 69. **d** 71 **p** 72. C Kendal H Trin *Carl* 71–75; PtO *Glas* 75–78; NSM Barrow St Matt *Carl* 79–86; PtO *York* 86–91; Liv 91–93 and 99–00; NSM Southport All SS and All So 93–99; NSM Southport St Luke 00–09; PtO from 11. *33 Sandringham Road, Ainsdale, Southport PR8 2NY* T: (01704) 578303

MARSTON, James Duncan. b 75. Surrey Univ BSc 96 Dur Univ MA 19. Westcott Ho Cam 17. **d** 19 **p** 20. C Alde Sandlings *St E* from 19. *The Rectory, Aldeburgh Road, Friston, Saxmundham IP17 1NP* E: marstonjames@hotmail.com

MARSTON, William Thornton. b 59. Worc Coll Ox BA 81 MA 85 Cam Univ CertEd 83. St Steph Ho Ox BA 87. **d** 88 **p** 89. C Beckenham St Geo *Roch* 88–92; C-in-c Middleton-on-Sea CD *Chich* 97–99; V Middleton 99–21; rtd 21. *Address temp unknown* E: w.marston@btinternet.com

MARSZALEK, Mrs Rachel Emma. b 74. St Jo Coll Nottm 08. **d** 11 **p** 12. C Belper *Derby* 11–14; V Ealing All SS *Lon* from 14. *All Saints' Vicarage, Elm Grove Road, London W5 3JH* T: (020) 8823 9160 M: 07906-632972 E: revrachelemma@gmail.com

MART, Terence Eugene. b 47. CertEd 76 BA 82 Ban Univ MA 19. St Jo Coll Nottm LTh 87. **d** 87 **p** 88. C Prestatyn *St As* 87–91; Chapl Theatr Clwyd Mold 87–91; R Llangystennin *St As* 91–01; RD Llanrwst 96–00; V Llanfair DC, Derwen, Llanelidan and Efenechtyd 01–07. *31 Pengarth, Conwy LL32 8RW*

MARTELL, Samantha Tara. b 70. Girton Coll Cam BA 92. Ripon Coll Cuddesdon 14. **d** 17 **p** 18. C Meon Bridge *Portsm* 17–20; P-in-c Ryde All SS 20–21; P-in-c Swanmore St Mich 20–21; TV Bridgemary, Elson and Rowner from 21. *Address temp unknown* E: revsamantha@alpha-omega.me

MARTIN, Mrs Adele Joan. b 51. BSc 74. Cranmer Hall Dur 05. **d** 07 **p** 08. C Seacroft *Ripon* 07–11; P-in-c Dinsdale w Sockburn *Dur* 11–16; P-in-c Hurworth 11–16; Chapl HM YOI Deerbolt 11–15; PtO *Leeds* from 17. *30 Darnborough Gate, Ripon HG4 2TF* E: adele.martin@leeds.anglican.org

MARTIN, Andrew Philip. b 78. **d** 14 **p** 15. C Selly Park St Steph and St Wulstan *Birm* from 14. *103 Bournbrook Road, Selly Park, Birmingham B29 7BY* T: 0121-247 6763 M: 07799-990179 E: andy.martin@sssw.org.uk

MARTIN, The Ven Angela Frances. b 66. SEITE 05. **d** 08 **p** 09. C Henfield w Shermanbury and Woodmancote *Chich* 08–12; C Worth, Pound Hill and Maidenbower 12–14; V Forest Row from 14; RD E Grinstead 19–21; Adn Horsham from 21. *The Vicarage, Ashdown Road, Forest Row RH18 5BW* T: (01342) 458263 E: revd.angelamartin@gmail.com *or* archhorsham@chichester.anglican.org

MARTIN, Angela Lee. b 61. EMMTC 00. **d** 03 **p** 04. NSM Derby St Barn 03–08; P-in-c Hatton 08–19; rtd 19; PtO *Derby* from 19. *9 Scarsdale Avenue, Allestree, Derby DE22 2LA* T: (01332) 552937 M: 07967-180531 E: hattonlee1968@yahoo.co.uk

MARTIN, Anne Elizabeth. b 61. Qu Foundn (Course) 15. **d** 18 **p** 19. OLM Oxley and Wednesfield St Greg *Lich* 18–20; C from 20. *30 Lodge Road, Wolverhampton WV10 6TH* T: (01902) 784917 M: 07709-616052 E: annieinwolves@blueyonder.co.uk

MARTIN, Benjamin Graham. b 85. Ex Univ BSc 07. Oak Hill Th Coll BA 20. **d** 20 **p** 21. C Hove Bp Hannington Memorial Ch *Chich* from 20. *47 Nevill Avenue, Hove BN3 7NB* T: (01273) 700234 E: revbenmartin@gmail.com

MARTIN, Brendan James. b 84. Oak Hill Th Coll. **d** 16 **p** 17. C Angmering *Chich* 16–19; R Frant w Eridge from 19. *The Rectory, Church Lane, Frant, Tunbridge Wells TN3 9DX* M: 07783-880257 E: revbjmartin@gmail.com

MARTIN, Bryan Robert. b 71. TCD BTh 01. CITC 98. **d** 01 **p** 02. C Magheralin w Dollingstown *D & D* 01–04; C Knockbreda 04–07; I Dromore *Clogh* 07–10; I Donaghcloney w Waringstown *D & D* 10–21; Can Dromore Cathl 16–21; I Drumglass w Moygashel *Arm* from 21. *26 Circular Road, Dungannon BT71 6BE* T: (028) 8775 2281 E: bryan.martin@btinternet.com

MARTIN, Canon Cameron Anthony Brian. b 56. Cape Town Univ BA 93 Cant Univ (NZ) MBA 02 MA 05. St Bede's Coll Umtata 82. **d** 84 **p** 85. C Nigel Ch the K S Africa 84–86; R Ennerdale St Nic 87–89; R Eldorado Park Transfiguration 89–90; P-in-c Kenwyn 90–95; R Woodlands 95–02; Adn Mitchell's Plain 98–02; Dioc Admin Kimberley and Kuruman 02–05; Can from 03; P-in-c Brumby *Linc* 05–07; TR from 07; RD Manlake 14–20. *St Hugh's Rectory, 114 Ashby Road, Scunthorpe DN16 2AG* T: (01724) 487412 M: 07887-802784 E: cameron.martin@ntlworld.com *or* cameron.martin@lincoln.anglican.org

MARTIN, Caroline Evelyn. *See* BECKETT, Caroline Evelyn

MARTIN, Christopher Edward. b 70. Bris Poly BA 92 ACA 97. Trin Coll Bris 07. **d** 09 **p** 10. C Newton Flotman, Swainsthorpe, Tasburgh, etc *Nor* 09–12; C Whimple, Talaton and Clyst St Lawr *Ex* 12–13; P-in-c 13–16; R Whimple, Talaton, Clyst St Lawr and Clyst Hydon 16–20; C Bradninch 13–17; TR Golden Cap Team *Sarum* from 20. *The Old Dairy, Whitchurch Canonicorum, Bridport DT6 6RF* T: (01297) 561065 E: chris@goldencapchurches.org

MARTIN, Christopher John. b 45. Ball Coll Ox BA 67 MA 87 Aber Univ MTh 09. Wycliffe Hall Ox 86. **d** 88 **p** 89. C Edin St Thos 88–90; R Duns 90–00; Chapl Lyon *Eur* 00–13; rtd 13; PtO *Eur* from 16; *Edin* from 16. *10 Kirkhill Terrace, Edinburgh EH16 5DQ* E: revchris.martin45@gmail.com

MARTIN, David Howard. b 47. Worc Coll Ox BEd 79. AKC 70 St Aug Coll Cant 70. **d** 71 **p** 72. C Sedgley All SS *Lich* 71–75; Dioc Youth Chapl *Worc* 75–81; P-in-c Worc St Andr and All SS w St Helen 75–81; R Newland, Guarlford and Madresfield 81–91; R Alvechurch 91–13; rtd 13; PtO *Worc* from 13. *4 Denison Close, Malvern WR14 2EU* T: (01684) 577425 E: davidandlizmartin@gmail.com

MARTIN, David Raymond. **d** 14 **p** 15. Howth *D & G* 14–15; C Hillsborough *D & D* 15–18; Dir ICM from 18. *28 Bachelors Walk, Dublin 1, Republic of Ireland* M: (00353) 85-806 9659 E: drmartin79@gmail.com *or* david@irishchurchmissions.ie

MARTIN, David Thomas. **d** 16 **p** 17. C Clydach *S & B* 16–18; C-in-c from 18; C Llangiwg from 16. *The Vicarage, Woodland Park, Ynystawe, Swansea SA6 5AR* T: (01792) 842787 E: davidtmartin@icloud.com

MARTIN, Dennis James. b 50. St Mellitus Coll. **d** 13 **p** 14. OLM Woodford Wells *Chelmsf* 13–17; NSM 17–20; rtd 20; PtO *Chelmsf* from 20; *Nor* from 21. *7 Knighton Drive, Woodford Green IG8 0NY* T: (020) 8504 6279 M: 07753-191072 E: dennis.martin9@btinternet.com

MARTIN, Edward James Russell. b 76. Hull Univ BA 98 Leeds Univ BA 02 MA 06. Coll of Resurr Mirfield 00. **d** 03 **p** 04. C Carrington *S'well* 03–06; P-in-c Chapel St Leonards w Hogsthorpe *Linc* 06–09; R Scartho 09–14; V Grimsby St Aug 14–19; V Gt Grimsby St Andr w St Luke and All SS 14–19; V Edenham w Witham on the Hill and Swinstead from 19. *The Vicarage, Church Lane, Edenham, Bourne PE10 0LS* M: 07736-711360 E: edward.martin@lincoln.anglican.org

MARTIN, Mrs Eileen. b 43. City of Portsm Coll of Educn TCert 65. **d** 03 **p** 15. OLM Queen Thorne *Sarum* 03–08; C Is of Scilly *Truro* 15–18; rtd 18. *Mellyns, Church Road, St Mary's, Isles of Scilly TR21 0NA* T: (01720) 423660 E: rev_eileenm@yahoo.co.uk

MARTIN, Miss Eileen Susan Kirkland. b 45. LCST 66. Cranmer Hall Dur 77. **dss** 83 **d** 86. Kilmarnock *Glas* 84–86; Par Dn Heanor *Derby* 87–92; PtO 92–95. *1 Malin Court, Hardings Close, Hemel Hempstead HP3 9AQ* T: (01442) 216768 E: eileen_martin8@yahoo.co.uk

MARTIN, Elizabeth Anne. *See* DADY, Elizabeth Anne

MARTIN, Glenn. b 52. Qu Coll Birm 84. **d** 86 **p** 87. C Chatham St Wm *Roch* 86–89; Chapl Pastures Hosp Derby 89–94; Chapl Kingsway Hosp Derby 89–94; Sen Chapl S Derbys Mental Health NHS Trust 94–97; Sen Chapl Community Health Sheff NHS Trust 97–01; Professional Development Officer for Chapl and Spiritual Healthcare 01–07; NSM Gilmorton, Peatling Parva, Kimcote etc *Leic* 04–07; NSM Guilsborough w Hollowell and Cold Ashby *Pet* 07–08; NSM Cottesbrooke w Gt Creaton and Thornby 07–08; NSM Spratton 07–08; NSM W Haddon w Winwick and Ravensthorpe 07–08; R Sutton Bonington w Normanton-on-Soar *S'well* 08–11; P-in-c Derby St Andr w St Osmund 11–13; P-in-c Allenton and Shelton Lock 11–13; rtd 13; PtO *Derby* 13–19; *Leic* from 14; *S'well* from 14. *27 Shields Crescent, Castle Donington, Derby DE74 2JS* T: (01332) 818858 E: glenn.martinrev@btinternet.com

MARTIN, Graham Rowland. b 39. Liv Univ CertEd 58 Lon Univ BD 70 Bris Univ BEd 73 FRSA LCP. Wells Th Coll 71. **d** 71 **p** 72. Hon C Glouc St Cath 71–76; P-in-c Brookthorpe w Whaddon 76–78; PtO 78–80; Hon C Hucclecote 80–82; Hon C Tuffley 82–88; NSM Hardwicke, Quedgeley and Elmore w Longney 88–89; V Kemble, Poole Keynes, Somerford Keynes etc 89–96; P-in-c Bibury w Winson and Barnsley 96–04; Dioc Ecum Officer 96–04; rtd 04; PtO *Glouc* from 04; Ox 16–20. *Wharf Cottage, Wharf Lane, Lechlade GL7 3AU* T: (01367) 252825 E: graham.martin@appleinter.net

MARTIN, James Alwyn. b 47. St Paul's Coll Grahamstown 76. **d** 78 **p** 79. C Highlands St Mary Rhodesia 78–80; P-in-c Lowveld Zimbabwe 80–84; Adn Victoria 82–87; R Masvingo St Mich 84–87; R Borrowdale Ch 87–98; adn Harare S 96–98; Dean Bulawayo 98–04; V Aldershot St Mich *Guildf* 05–16; rtd 16; PtO *Cov* 16–21. *11 Margetts Close, Kenilworth CV8 1EN* T: (01926) 853120 M: 07749-770035

MARTIN, Canon Jessica Heloise. b 63. Trin Hall Cam BA 86 PhD 93. EAMTC 00. **d** 03 **p** 04. NSM Trin Coll Cam 03–09; NSM Fen Ditton *Ely* 08–09; NSM Horningsea 08–09; NSM Teversham 08–09; P-in-c Duxford 10–16; P-in-c Hinxton 10–16; P-in-c Ickleton 10–16; P-in-c Whittlesford 15–16; Bp's Adv for Women's Min 14–16; Hon Can Ely Cathl 14–16; Can Res Ely Cathl from 16. *Powchers Hall, The College, Ely CB7 4DL* M: 07780-704006 E: j.martin@elycathedral.org

MARTIN, John Eric Terence. b 75. SS Coll Cam MA 99 MEng 99. Wycliffe Hall Ox BTh 10. **d** 10 **p** 11. C Wolverhampton St Luke *Lich* 10–13. *18 Galileo Gardens, Cheltenham GL51 0GA* M: 07941-978856 E: john@gracechurchcheltenham.org

MARTIN, John Henry. b 42. St Jo Coll Cam BA 63 MA 67. St Jo Coll Nottm BA 73. **d** 73 **p** 74. C Ecclesall *Sheff* 73–77; C Hednesford *Lich* 77–82; V Walsall Pleck and Bescot 82–92; V Whittington w Weeford 92–08; V Hints 05–08; rtd 08; PtO *Glouc* 15–20; *Bris* from 19. *64 Cricklade Road, Highworth, Swindon SN6 7BL* E: john.h.martin642@gmail.com

MARTIN, John Hunter. b 42. St Andr Univ MLitt 12 AKC 64. **d** 65 **p** 66. C Mortlake w E Sheen *S'wark* 65–69; C-in-c Bermondsey St Hugh CD 69–72; V Bermondsey St Anne 72–78; P-in-c Lt Ouse *Ely* 78; V Littleport 78–89; V Attercliffe *Sheff* 89–90; P-in-c Darnall 89–90; TR Darnall-cum-Attercliffe 90–96; TR Attercliffe, Darnall and Tinsley 96; R Kirk Sandall and Edenthorpe 96–07; rtd 07; PtO *Glas* from 09. *Salara Haven, Sandgreen, Gatehouse of Fleet, Castle Douglas DG7 2DU* T: (01557) 815068 E: vanessaandjohnmartin@gmail.com

MARTIN, Kathleen Linda Bernardette. b 51. **d** 18 **p** 19. C Mid Loes *St E* from 18. *Firs Farm, Monewden, Woodbridge IP13 7DE* T: (01473) 737285 E: b.a.martin@btconnect.com

MARTIN, Kevin. b 73. Surrey Univ BA 01 Heythrop Coll Lon MTh 03 Roehampton Univ MSc 10. Sarum Coll MA 18. **d** 17 **p** 18. C Shaftesbury *Sarum* 17–18; C St Bartholomew 18–20; TR Bemerton from 20. *Bemerton Rectory, 96 St Michael's Road, Salisbury SP2 9LE* T: (01722) 679655 M: 07968-622585 E: rector.bemerton@protonmail.com

MARTIN, Mrs Laura Mary. b 77. Leeds Univ BHSc 01 MHSc 05. **d** 20 **p** 21. C Bilton *Leeds* from 20. *7 Blenheim Court, Harrogate HG2 9DT* M: 07973-890766 E: laura.martin@leeds.anglican.org

MARTIN, Lee. *See* MARTIN, Angela Lee

MARTIN (née BULLEN), Mrs Marilyn Patricia. b 46. Liv Hope Univ Coll BA(Theol) 00 MA 05. NOC 06. **d** 06 **p** 07. NSM Stretton and Appleton Thorn *Ches* 06–09; Asst Chapl HM YOI Thorn Cross 06–17; rtd 17; PtO *Ches* from 13; *Liv* from 17. *Address withheld by request* E: malmartin@btinternet.com

MARTIN, Michelle Karen. *See* BUTCHER, Michelle Karen

MARTIN, Preb Nicholas Roger. b 53. St Jo Coll Dur BA 74. Ripon Coll Cuddesdon 75. **d** 77 **p** 78. C Wolvercote w Summertown *Ox* 77–80; C Kidlington 80–82; TV 82–84; V Happisburgh w Walcot *Nor* 84–85; P-in-c Hempstead w Lessingham and Eccles 84–85; R Happisburgh w Walcot, Hempstead, Lessingham etc 85–89; R Blakeney w Cley, Wiveton, Glandford etc 89–97; TR Totnes w Bridgetown, Berry Pomeroy etc *Ex* 97–05; RD Totnes 99–03; Co-ord Chapl HM Pris Channings Wood 05–15; Bp's Adv for Prisons *Ex* 15–17; Preb Ex Cathl 14–17; PtO from 17. *1 Indio Road, Bovey Tracey, Newton Abbot TQ13 9BT* E: nmartin497@aol.com

MARTIN, Nicholas Worsley. b 52. Sarum & Wells Th Coll 71. **d** 75 **p** 76. C Llandaff w Capel Llanilltern *Llan* 75–79; C Cardiff St Jo 79; C Caerphilly 79–83; TV Hemel Hempstead *St Alb* 83–93; Chapl Hemel Hempstead Gen Hosp 83–93; PtO *Chich* 94–98; *Truro* 98–99; NSM Penzance St Mary w St Paul 99–02; rtd 02; NSM Penzance St Mary w St Paul and St Jo *Truro* 02–07; PtO from 16. *1 Redinnick Gardens, Penzance TR18 4JF* T: (01736) 350506

MARTIN, Canon Penelope Elizabeth. b 44. Cranmer Hall Dur 83. **dss** 86 **d** 87 **p** 94. Seaham w Seaham Harbour *Dur* 86–89; Par Dn 87–89; Par Dn Cassop cum Quarrington 89–93; Par Dn Sherburn w Pittington 93–94; C 94–95; V 95–02; R Shadforth 95–02; R Pittington, Shadforth and Sherburn 02–03; Hon Can Dur Cathl 01–03; rtd 03; PtO *Dur* from 03. *34A Rosemount, Durham DH1 5GA* T: 0191-386 1742 E: penelizmartin@gmail.com

MARTIN, Preb Peter. b 50. MCIH 75. Linc Th Coll 82. **d** 84 **p** 85. C Taunton H Trin *B & W* 84–86; C Bath Bathwick 86–88; R Cannington, Otterhampton, Combwich and Stockland 88–15; RD Sedgemoor 00–06; Warden of Readers Taunton Adnry 06–14; Chapl Cannington Coll 89–15; Preb Wells Cathl *B & W* 09–15; rtd 15; PtO *B & W* from 15. *55 Irnham Road, Minehead TA24 5DW* T: (01643) 706552 E: revd.petermartin@gmail.com

MARTIN, Philip James. b 58. Cam Univ BA. Coll of Resurr Mirfield. **d** 84 **p** 85. C Pontefract St Giles *Wakef* 84–88; C

Wantage *Ox* 88–90; C Didcot All SS 90; V Alderholt *Sarum* 90–17; V Branksome St Aldhelm from 17. *The Vicarage, St Aldhelm's Road, Poole BH13 6BT* T: (01202) 032193 E: frphilipmartin@gmail.com

MARTIN, Richard. b 34. Rhodes Univ BA 54 Em Coll Cam BA 57 MA 58. Wells Th Coll 57. **d** 59 **p** 60. C Portsea St Mary *Portsm* 59–60; C Bloemfontein Cathl S Africa 60–62; R Wepener 62–64; R Odendaalsrus 64–67; R Newton Park St Hugh 67–76; Chapl St Bede's Coll Umtata 77–79; R Hillcrest 79–87; C Aldershot St Mich *Guildf* 87–94; R Wick *Mor* 94–99; P-in-c Thurso 94–99; rtd 99; Hon C Diptford, N Huish, Harberton, Harbertonford etc *Ex* 99–01; PtO 01–03; LtO *Mor* 03–19; PtO *Blackb* from 19. *16 Fosbrooke House, 8 Clifton Drive, Lytham St Annes FY8 5RQ* E: martin@chilledthames.co.uk

MARTIN, Richard Arthur. b 59. Leeds Univ BA 91 MA 97 Cant Ch Ch Univ Coll PGCE 03. SEITE 07. **d** 09 **p** 10. C Gravesend St Aid *Roch* 09–12; P-in-c Gravesend H Family w Ifield 12–19; R 19–20; Bp's Adv for Inter-Faith Concerns 15–20; P-in-c Hardwicke and Elmore w Longney *Glouc* from 20. *Church House, Cornfield Drive, Hardwicke, Gloucester GL2 4QJ* M: 07593-092758 E: revramartin@btinternet.com *or* vicar@hardwicke-elmore-longney.church

MARTIN, Richard Charles de Villeval. b 41. St Jo Coll Ox BA 63 MA 67. Ox Ord Course. **d** 84 **p** 85. NSM Ox St Thos w St Frideswide and Binsey 84–04; Asst Chapl Highgate Sch Lon 86–92; Asst Master Magd Coll Sch Ox 92–02; Chapl 94–02; rtd 04; LtO *Ox* 05–12; PtO 12–16. *1 Ritchie Court, 380 Banbury Road, Oxford OX2 7PW* T: (01865) 510694 E: rickycmartin@icloud.com

✠**MARTIN, The Rt Revd Robert Markland.** b 49. Trin Coll Cam BA 71 MA 74 FCA 80. Trin Coll Bris BA 91. **d** 91 **p** 92 **c** 08. C Kingswood *Bris* 91–95; V Frome H Trin *B & W* 95–08; RD Frome 03–08; Suff Bp Marsabit Kenya 08–11; Bp 11–16; rtd 16; Hon Asst Bp *B & W* from 16; PtO *Eur* from 17. *Willowgate, 1 Egford Hill, Egford, Frome BA11 3JH* E: robandsuemartin@gmail.com

MARTIN, Robin. *See* MARTIN, Thomas Robin

MARTIN, Robin Hugh. b 35. Rhodes Univ BA 56. **d** 58 **p** 59. C Darnall *Sheff* 58–62; C-in-c Kimberworth Park 62–65; LtO 65–66; LtO *Newc* 67–71; PtO *Sheff* 65–66; *Newc* 67–71; *Man* 79–93; *Heref* 97–07; *Lich* 97–99 and 11–21; P-in-c Maesbury 99–11. *Offa House, Treflach, Oswestry SY10 9HQ* T: (01691) 657090

MARTIN, Roger Allen. b 38. Westmr Coll Lon CertEd 59 Birkbeck Coll Lon BA 64 FRMetS 79. SAOMC 97. **d** 99 **p** 00. NSM Bramfield, Stapleford, Waterford etc *St Alb* 99–06; NSM Broxbourne w Wormley 06–10; rtd 10; PtO *St Alb* from 10. *41 The Avenue, Bengeo, Hertford SG14 3DS* T: (01992) 422441 E: roger.martin@ntlworld.com

MARTIN, Canon Roger Ivor. b 42. MCMI. Cant Sch of Min. **d** 85 **p** 86. NSM Saltwood *Cant* 85–90; P-in-c Crundale w Godmersham 90–01; Dioc Exec Officer for Adult Educn and Lay Tr 90–96; CME Officer 94–96; Chapl to Bp Maidstone *Cant* 96–01; R Saltwood 01–09; Hon Can Cant Cathl 09; rtd 09; PtO *Cant* from 09; Hon C Aldington w Bonnington and Bilsington etc 11–12; AD Elham 18–19. *Kwetu, 23 Tanners Hill Gardens, Hythe CT21 5HY* T: (01303) 237204 M: 07791-939713 E: rogmartin@btinternet.com

MARTIN, Ronald Charles John Richard. b 61. Bris Univ BA 92. Wesley Coll Bris 88. **d** 15 **p** 15. Lead Chapl Dorset Co Hosp NHS Foundn Trust from 15; C Sherborne w Castleton, Lillington and Longborton *Sarum* from 15. *The Old Coach House, South Street, Sherborne DT9 3LZ* M: 07701-091627

MARTIN, Rosanna Mary. *See* STUART-MARTIN, Rosanna

MARTIN, Rupert Gresley. b 57. Worc Coll Ox BA 78 Ox Univ MA 95. Trin Coll Bris 89. **d** 91 **p** 92. C Yateley *Win* 91–95; V Sandal St Helen *Wakef* 95–14; *Leeds* 14–21; rtd 21. *17 Oldfield Road, Bristol BS8 4QQ*

MARTIN, Stephen Maurice. b 80. Dur Univ BA 21. Lindisfarne Coll of Th 19. **d** 21. C Lanchester and Burnhope *Dur* from 21; C Harelaw and Annfield Plain from 21. *The Vicarage, St Ives Road, Consett DH8 7SN* T: (01207) 509730 M: 07917-532032 E: stephen.martinfd@outlook.com

MARTIN, Steven. b 50. Qu Coll Birm BA 08. **d** 08 **p** 09. C Malvern St Andr and Malvern Wells and Wyche *Worc* 08–12; TV Brierley Hill 12–15; rtd 15; PtO *Ex* from 16. *Hope Cottage, Chittlehampton, Umberleigh EX37 9QN* E: revstevenmartin@btinternet.com

MARTIN, Steven Edward. b 81. Ex Univ BA 03 MA 04 Bris Univ PhD 10 LRSM 03. St Steph Ho Ox BTh 17. **d** 15 **p** 16. C Tavistock, Gulworthy and Brent Tor *Ex* 15–19; R Colyton, Musbury, Southleigh and Branscombe 19–20; R Colyton, Musbury, Northleigh and Southleigh from 21. *The Vicarage, Vicarage Street, Colyton EX24 6LJ* M: 07866-582519 E: stevenemartin@gmail.com

MARTIN, Mrs Susan Jane. b 69. SEITE BA 10. d 10 p 11. C Minster-in-Sheppey *Cant* 10–12; C W Sheppey 12–14; P-in-c Reculver and Herne Bay St Bart and Hoath from 14. *The Vicarage, 25 Dence Park, Herne Bay CT6 6BQ* T: (01227) 360948 E: revsuemartin@btinternet.com

MARTIN, Mrs Susan Mary. b 49. UEA BEd 94. ERMC 04. d 09 p 10. NSM Gayton, Gayton Thorpe, E Walton, E Winch etc *Nor* 09–13; Chapl Norfolk Hospice 13–21; NSM Ashwicken w Leziate, Bawsey etc *Nor* from 21; PtO *Ely* from 19. *The Gables, Lynn Road, Gayton, King's Lynn PE32 1QJ* T: (01553) 636303 M: 07801-701677 E: revdsuemartin@gmail.com

MARTIN, Sylvia. b 43. Sarum Th Coll 94. d 97 p 98. NSM Locks Heath *Portsm* 97–02; PtO 02–04; NSM Fareham H Trin 04–07; Chapl Fareham Coll of F&HE 04–07; rtd 07; PtO *Portsm* from 07. *9 Harvester Drive, Fareham PO15 5NR* T: (01329) 312269

MARTIN, Thomas Robin. b 40. Bernard Gilpin Soc Dur 63 Bps' Coll Cheshunt 64. d 67 p 68. C Ripley *Derby* 67–70; C Ilkeston St Mary 70–74; V Chinley w Buxworth 74–83; V Knighton St Mich *Leic* 83–85; V Thurmaston 85–05; rtd 05; C Leic Resurr 08; C Braunstone Park 09; C Birstall and Wanlip 10–11; PtO from 14. *22 Sycamore Road, Birstall, Leicester LE4 4LT* T: 0116-267 1651 E: tr.martin@btinternet.com

MARTIN, Ms Wendy Helen. b 59. Portsm Univ BSc 96 Surrey Univ PGCE 92 SRN 80 SCM 81. Qu Foundn (Course) 17. d 19 p 20. NSM Garretts Green and Lea Hall *Birm* from 19. *9 Emerald Court, 960A Alum Rock Road, Birmingham B8 2LS* T: 0121-679 9582 M: 07543-829571 E: wendy164@btinternet.com

MARTIN, William Harrison. b 38. Sarum & Wells Th Coll 91. d 87 p 88. NSM Rushen *S & M* 92–97; C German 92–97; V Lonan and Laxey 97–08; rtd 08; PtO *S & M* from 09. *Crossag Villa, Crossag Road, Ballasalla, Isle of Man IM9 3EF* T: (01624) 825982 E: billmartin@manx.net

MARTIN-DOYLE, Mrs Audrey Brenda. b 35. Cranmer Hall Dur 80. dss 82 d 87 p 95. The Lye and Stambermill *Worc* 82–86; Chapl Lee Abbey 86–88; Ldr Aston Cottage Community 88–93; C Cheltenham St Mary, St Matt, St Paul and H Trin *Glouc* 94–97; rtd 97; PtO *Glouc* 97–20. *39 Moorend Street, Cheltenham GL53 0EH* T: (01242) 510352 E: amartindoyle@gmail.com

MARTIN-SCOTT, Guy Edmund. b 88. Trin Coll Bris 16. d 18 p 19. C Coxley w Godney, Henton and Wookey *B & W* from 18. *1 Cartwright Close, Coxley, Wells BA22 1DB* E: revdguy@gmail.com *or* curate@chwchurches.co.uk

MARTINEAU, Canon David Richards Durani. b 36. AKC 59. d 60 p 61. C Ches St Jo 60–64; C St Mark's Cathl George S Africa 64; C Riversdale 64–66; R Beaufort W and Victoria W 66–69; C Jarrow St Paul *Dur* 69–72; TV 72–75; TR Jarrow 76–85; V Gildersome *Wakef* 85–00; Hon Can Wakef Cathl 94–00; rtd 00; PtO *Linc* from 00; Hon Asst Chapl Voorschoten *Eur* 02–03. *Harlough, St Chad, Barrow-upon-Humber DN19 7AU* T: (01469) 531475 E: davidmartineau@gmail.com

MARTINEAU, Canon Jeremy Fletcher. b 40. OBE 03. K Coll Lon BD 65 AKC 65. d 66 p 67. C Jarrow St Paul *Dur* 66–73; Bp's Ind Adv 69–73; P-in-c Raughton Head w Gatesgill *Carl* 73–80; Chapl to Agric 73–80; Ind Chapl *Bris* 80–90; Nat Rural Officer Gen Syn Bd of Miss 88–03; Hon Can Cov Cathl 01–03; rtd 04; LtO *St D* from 05. *11 New Hill Villas, Goodwick SA64 0DT* T: (01348) 874886 E: jeremy.m@talktalk.net

MARTINSON, Matthew Allan. b 74. Mattersey Hall BA 03. St Jo Coll Nottm. d 09 p 10. C Beverley St Nic *York* 09–12; V Bramsholme 12–19; P-in-c Carl H Trin and St Barn from 19; P-in-c Carl St Luke Morton from 19. *The Vicarage, 104 Housesteads Road, Carlisle CA2 7XG* T: (01228) 538983 E: matt@tp4c.co.uk

MARTLEW, Andrew Charles. b 50. Nottm Univ BTh 76 Lanc Univ MA 80. Linc Th Coll 72. d 76 p 77. C Poulton-le-Fylde *Blackb* 76–79; Hon C Lancaster Ch Ch 79–80; Malaysia 81–83; V Golcar *Wakef* 83–89; Dioc Schs Officer 89–95; V Warmfield 89–95; Dioc Dir of Educn *York* 95–02; CF (TA) 87–02; CF 02–10; Chapl HM Pris Ranby 10–11; rtd 11; PtO *Wakef* 10–13; V Womersley 13–14; *Leeds* 14–20; PtO *York* from 11; *Leeds* 20–21. *Balne Moor Farm, Balne Moor Road, Balne, Goole DN14 0EN* T: (01405) 862484 E: andrew.martlew42@gmail.com

MARTLEW, Catherine Linda. *See* GABRIEL, Catherine Linda

MARVIN, David Arthur. b 51. St Jo Coll Nottm 96. d 97 p 98. C Mansfield St Jo *S'well* 97–01; P-in-c Greasley *S'well* 01–11; V 11–19; rtd 19.

MARWOOD, Timothy John Edmonds. b 51. Open Univ BA 89 Lon Inst of Educn MA 91 Whitelands Coll Lon CertEd 72. S'wark Ord Course 92. d 95 p 96. NSM Putney St Mary *S'wark* 95–00; PtO *Ex* 00–07; P-in-c Petersham *S'wark* 07–11; V 11–21; P-in-c Earlsfield St Jo 15–17; Chapl K Coll Sch Wimbledon 08–10; AD Richmond and Barnes *S'wark* 10–15;

Hon Can S'wark Cathl 08–21; rtd 21; PtO *Lon* from 21. *6A School Road, Hampton Hill, Hampton TW12 1QL* M: 07973-518742 E: timmarwood@yahoo.co.uk

MASCALL, Mrs Margaret Ann. b 43. LRAM 64 Bris Univ CertEd 65 St Jo Coll Dur BA 71 MA 79. Cranmer Hall Dur 69. dss 76 d 87 p 94. Hertford St Andr *St Alb* 75–79; Herne Bay Ch Ch *Cant* 79–82; Seasalter 82–84; Whitstable 84–90; Par Dn 87–90; PtO 91–94; Hon C Hackington 94–95; V Newington w Hartlip and Stockbury 95–03; rtd 03; PtO *Cant* from 03. *48 Holmside Avenue, Minster on Sea, Sheerness ME12 3EY* T: (01795) 663095

MASCARENHAS, Felix Pedro Antonio. b 55. Bombay Univ BA 80 Pontifical Univ Rome JCD 88. Pilar Major Th Sem Goa BTh 81. d 82 p 82. In RC Ch 82–02; C Chich St Paul and Westhampnett 02–06; V Brighton Gd Shep Preston from 06. *The Vicarage, 272 Dyke Road, Brighton BN1 5AE* T: (01273) 882987 M: 07814-739312 E: felixmas@hotmail.com *or* vicar@goodshepherdbrighton.org.uk

MASEKO, Miss Lindiwe. b 72. Univ of Wales BTh 03 Roehampton Univ MA 07. Wycliffe Hall Ox MTh 17. d 17 p 18. C Deptford St Jo w H Trin and Ascension *S'wark* from 17. *3 Orchard Hill, London SE13 7QZ* M: 07817-283818 E: lindi98@hotmail.com

MASH, William Edward John. b 54. Imp Coll Lon BSc 75 Open Univ MA 00 ARCS. St Jo Coll Nottm 87. d 89 p 90. C Beverley Minster *York* 89–93; V Elloughton and Brough w Brantingham 93–01; P-in-c Newcastle St Geo *Lich* 01–08; V 08–10; P-in-c Knutton 06–08; V 08–10; Chapl Town Cen and Newcastle Coll 01–10; Team Ldr Black Country Urban Ind Miss *Lich* 10–19; Dioc Officer for Miss in the Economy 10–19; PtO *Worc* 12–19; rtd 20; PtO *Lich* from 20. *20 Mahogany Drive, Stafford ST16 2TS* T: (01785) 509231 M: 07714-103007 E: william.e.j.mash@gmail.com

MASHEDER, Canon Peter Timothy Charles. b 49. AKC 71. St Aug Coll Cant 71. d 72 p 73. C Barkingside St Fran *Chelmsf* 72–75; C Chingford SS Pet and Paul 75–91; P-in-c High Laver w Magdalen Laver and Lt Laver etc 91–98; R 98–07; RD Ongar 98–04; R Ray Valley *Ox* 07–14; AD Bicester and Islip 08–13; Hon Can Ch Ch 13–14; rtd 14; Hon C Honiton, Gittisham, Combe Raleigh, Monkton etc *Ex* 14–15; P-in-c Bere Regis and Affpuddle w Turnerspuddle *Sarum* 15–19; PtO *Ex* from 19; Hon C Abingdon *Ox* from 19. *2 Musson Close, Abingdon OX14 5RE* E: chasmash@ic24.net

MASHITER, Mrs Marion. b 48. CBDTI 01. d 04 p 05. NSM Burneside *Carl* 04–07; NSM Beacon TM 07–10; NSM Natland from 10; NSM Old Hutton and New Hutton from 10. *The Maples, 5 Esthwaite Avenue, Kendal LA9 7NN* T: (01539) 731957 M: 07748-771836 E: revquackers5@gmail.com

MASIH, Emmanuel Nazir. *See* NAZIR MASIH, Emmanuel

MASIH, Haroon Barkat. b 60. d 09 p 11. PtO *Lon* from 19. *12 Garden Court, Stanmore HA7 4TE* T: (020) 3665 4158 M: 07830-365259 E: rev.haroon.masih@gmail.com

MASIH, Wilson. b 61. St Mellitus Coll BA 11. d 11 p 12. NSM Hanwell St Mellitus w St Mark *Lon* 11–15; NSM Southall Ch Redeemer 15–21; V from 21. *The Vicarage, 299 Allenby Road, Southall UB1 2HE* M: 07950-255515 E: masih37@aol.com

MASKELL, Amanda Jane. b 66. St Mellitus Coll 15. d 17 p 18. C Gillingham St Mark *Roch* 17–21; P-in-c Gillingham St Aug from 21. *1 St Barnabas Close, Gillingham ME7 4BU* M: 07496-023554 E: revamanda2017@gmail.com

MASKELL, John Michael. *See* MILLER-MASKELL, John Michael

MASKELL, Roland Wyndham (Wyn). d 17 p 18. NSM Carmarthen St Dav *St D* 17–20; P-in-c Bro Aeron Mydr from 20. *The Vicarage, Felinfach, Lampeter SA48 8AE* E: wynmaskell@btconnect.com

MASKELL, Miss Rosemary Helen. b 58. Ripon Coll Cuddesdon. d 00 p 01. C Goodrington *Ex* 00–04; V Littleport *Ely* 04–13; R Huntingdon St Barn and the Riptons 13–18; P-in-c Horsham St Faith, Spixworth and Crostwick *Nor* from 18; Chapl Norwich Internat Airport from 18. *The Rectory, Buxton Road, Spixworth, Norwich NR10 3PR* T: (01603) 898258 M: 07794-938501 E: rhmaskell@gmail.com

MASKREY, Mrs Susan Elizabeth. b 43. Cranmer Hall Dur IDC 70. dss 76 d 92 p 94. Littleover *Derby* 76–77; Sec to Publicity Manager CMS Lon 77–78; Stantonbury and Willen *Ox* 78–88; Billingham St Aid *Dur* 88–95; C 92–95; Asst Chapl HM Pris Holme Ho 94–95; Asst Chapl HM Pris Preston 95–01; Chapl HM Pris Kirkham 01–05; rtd 05; PtO *Blackb* from 05. *c/o the Bishop of Blackburn, Bishop's House, Ribchester Road, Blackburn BB1 9EF*

MASLEN, Mrs Linda Jane. b 62. Leeds Univ BA 83 Leic Univ MBA 95. Yorks Min Course 12. d 15 p 16. C Halifax St Aug and Mount Pellon *Leeds* 15–19; C Halifax w Siddal 17–19; Ldr Bradf City Cen Resource Ch from 19. *The Rectory, 8 Redwing Drive, Bradford*

BD6 3YD M: 07595-949153 E: linda_maslen@hotmail.com *or* linda.maslen@leeds.anglican.org

MASLEN (*formerly* CHILD), Mrs Margaret Mary. b 44. ALA 76 Open Univ BA 79. S Dios Minl Tr Scheme 89. **d** 92 **p** 94. C Portishead *B & W* 92–93; C Ilminster w Whitelackington 93–94; C Ilminster and Distr 94–96; C Tatworth 96–99; C Chaffcombe, Cricket Malherbie etc 99–00; TV Chard and Distr 00–05; Chapl Taunton and Somerset NHS Trust 97–05; rtd 05; Hon C Sherston Magna, Easton Grey, Luckington etc *Bris* 06–07; Hon C Hullavington, Norton and Stanton St Quintin 06–07; PtO from 07; *Glouc* from 14. *2 Woods Close, Sherston, Malmesbury SN16 0LF* T: (01666) 840387 E: maslens@tiscali.co.uk

MASLEN, Richard Ernest. b 34. S Dios Minl Tr Scheme 89. **d** 92 **p** 93. NSM Sherston Magna, Easton Grey, Luckington etc *Bris* 92–93; NSM Ilminster w Whitelackington *B & W* 93–94; NSM Ilminster and Distr 94–96; P-in-c Tatworth 96–99; TV Chard and Distr 99–00; rtd 00; PtO *B & W* 00–05; *Bris* from 05; *Glouc* from 16. *2 Woods Close, Sherston, Malmesbury SN16 0LF* T: (01666) 840387 E: maslens@tiscali.co.uk

MASLIN, Ian. b 65. Cranmer Hall Dur 14. **d** 16 **p** 17. C Cranleigh *Guildf* 16–20; P-in-c Dunsfold and Hascombe from 20. *The Rectory, Church Green, Dunsfold, Godalming GU8 4LT* M: 07825-815170 E: ianmaslin831.im@gmail.com

MASON, Adrian Stanley. b 54. Hatf Poly BSc 77. Ripon Coll Cuddesdon 77. **d** 80 **p** 81. C Mill End and Heronsgate w W Hyde *St Alb* 80–83; TV Axminster, Chardstock, Combe Pyne and Rousdon *Ex* 83–87; TV Halesworth w Linstead, Chediston, Holton etc *St E* 87–88; R Brandon and Santon Downham 88–91; R Glemsford, Hartest w Boxted, Somerton etc 91–95; Min Can St E Cathl 95–97; R S Hartismere 06–11; P-in-c Stoke by Nayland w Leavenheath and Polstead 11–15; R Mid Elloe Gp *Linc* 15–19; rtd 19; PtO *S'well* from 19. *48 Queensway, Worksop S81 0AD* E: fr.adrian.mason@gmail.com

MASON, Ambrose. *See* MASON, Thomas Henry Ambrose

MASON, Andrew. b 73. **d** 10 **p** 11. NSM Chelsea St Jo w St Andr *Lon* from 10. *Flat 2, 465 Kings Road, London SW10 0LU* T: (020) 7351 1447 E: andymason73@yahoo.com *or* andy@stjohnchelsea.org

MASON, Miss Anna Louise. b 86. Glos Univ BEd 07. St Mellitus Coll MA 18. **d** 18 **p** 19. C Pentonville St Silas w All SS and St Jas *Lon* from 18. *260 Caledonian Road, London N1 0NG* M: 07793-277012 E: anna.mason@kxc.org.uk

MASON, Anne La'thangue. b 56. St Mellitus Coll 17. **d** 19 **p** 20. OLM Colchester St Luke *Chelmsf* from 19; OLM Langham w Boxted from 19; OLM W Bergholt and Gt Horkesley from 19. *11 Hillridge, Highwoods, Colchester CO4 9UJ* T: (01206) 851792 M: 07895-970834 E: revdannemason@gmail.com

⋈**MASON, The Rt Revd Beverley Anne.** Trin Coll Bris BA 00. **d** 01 **p** 03 **c** 18. C Rusthall *Roch* 01–02; C Rainham 02–05; V Upper Norwood St Jo *S'wark* 05–12; AD Croydon N 10–12; P-in-c Bingley All SS *Bradf* 12–13; V 13–16; Adn Richmond and Craven *Leeds* 16–18; Suff Bp Warrington *Liv* from 18. *Bishop's House, 34 Central Avenue, Eccleston Park, Prescot L34 2QP* T: 0151-705 2140 E: revdbeverley@yahoo.co.uk *or* bishopofwarrington@liverpool.anglican.org

MASON, Ms Chantal Marie. b 73. Ex Univ BA 96 St Luke's Coll Ex PGCE 98. Trin Coll Bris MA 08. **d** 08 **p** 09. C Alphington, Shillingford St George and Ide *Ex* 08–12; Bp's Chapl *Chelmsf* 12–15; Chapl Ex Univ 15–18; Priest, Publicity and Media Co-ord Lee Abbey 18–20; PtO *Ex* 18–20; C Bath Abbey w St Jas *B & W* from 20. *48 Devonshire Buildings, Bath BA2 4SU* M: 07896-101245

MASON, Charles Oliver. b 51. Jes Coll Cam BA 73 MA 99 St Jo Coll Dur BA 79. **d** 80 **p** 81. C Cheltenham St Mary, St Matt, St Paul and H Trin *Glouc* 80–84; C Enfield Ch Ch Trent Park *Lon* 84–88; P-in-c W Hampstead St Cuth 88–93; V 93–01; AD N Camden 98–01; V Braintree *Chelmsf* 01–16; rtd 16; P-in-c Waltham St Lawrence *Ox* 16–20; V Waltham St Lawrence and Shottesbrooke from 20. *The Parsonage, School Road, Waltham St Lawrence, Reading RG10 0NU* T: 0118-934 1054 E: revdcom@btinternet.com

MASON, Christina Mary. b 42. Univ of Wales BMus 63 MA 67 BSc(Econ) 70 Dundee Univ PhD 84 Middx Univ MSc 02. St Jo Coll Nottm 81. **d** 83 **p** 10. LtO *Bre* 83–92; PtO *Nor* 09–10; NSM Gt and Lt Ellingham, Rockland and Shropham etc 10–18; P-in-c from 18. *9 Charles Avenue, Watton, Thetford IP25 6BY* T: (01953) 797622 E: ctrewartha@tiscali.co.uk

MASON, Christopher David. b 51. Lanc Univ BA 72 Leic Univ MEd 82. EAMTC 91. **d** 94 **p** 95. NSM Pet St Mary Boongate 94–00 and 03–05; P-in-c Newborough 00–02; Chapl Pet High Sch 05–10; PtO *Pet* 10–12; Hon C Charfield and Kingswood w Wickwar etc *Glouc* 12–16; PtO from 18. *47 Hartley Close, Chipping Sodbury, Bristol BS37 6NW* M: 07749-903658 E: revd.chris.mason@gmail.com

MASON, Damien David Robert. b 85. Edin Univ BD 11. St Steph Ho Ox MTh 15. **d** 15 **p** 16. C Hendon St Mary and Ch Ch *Lon* 15–18; V Brookfield St Mary from 18. *The Vicarage, 85 Darmouth Park Road, London NW5 1SL* T: (020) 7267 5941 M: 07505-723596 E: frdamienmason@gmail.com

MASON, David Gray. b 37. Birm Univ LDS 61 K Coll Lon MPhil 94. St Alb Minl Tr Scheme 83. **d** 95 **p** 95. NSM Biddenham *St Alb* 95–98; P-in-c Felmersham 98–05; NSM Sharnbrook, Felmersham and Knotting w Souldrop 05–12; RD Sharnbrook 06–12; PtO 12–20. *2A Devon Road, Bedford MK40 3DF* T/F: (01234) 309737 E: david.mason93@ntlworld.com

MASON, Dawn Lavinia. b 53. Ripon Coll Cuddesdon 95. **d** 97 **p** 98. C Wisbech St Aug *Ely* 97–00; V Emneth and Marshland St James 00–09; P-in-c Elm and Friday Bridge w Coldham 04–09; V Fen Orchards 09–20; rtd 20. *1 Sturgeon Way, Barham, Ipswich IP6 0ST* M: 07840-491584 E: dmason889@btinternet.com

MASON, Mrs Elizabeth Ann. b 42. Homerton Coll Cam TCert 64 Open Univ BA 90. Ox Min Course 91. **d** 94 **p** 95. NSM Worminghall w Ickford, Oakley and Shabbington *Ox* 94–95; NSM Swan 95–98; TV 98–05; rtd 05; PtO *Ox* from 06. *35 Common Road, North Leigh, Witney OX29 6RD* T: (01993) 883966

MASON, Francis Robert Anthony. b 56. Trin Coll Bris BA 90. **d** 90 **p** 91. C Denham *Ox* 90–94; P-in-c Jersey Grouville *Win* 94–98; R 98–04; R Tendring and Lt Bentley w Beaumont cum Moze *Chelmsf* 07–15; C Gt Oakley w Wix and Wrabness 13–15; R Fakenham w Alethorpe *Nor* from 15; P-in-c Fulmodeston w Croxton 15–21; rtd 21. *Address temp unknown* E: revmason@btinternet.com

MASON, Jonathan Patrick. b 55. Univ of Wales (Trin St Dav) MA 12. Edin Th Coll 90. **d** 92 **p** 93. C Edin Ch Ch 92–94; C Edin Old St Paul 94–96; R St Andrews All SS *St And* 96–14; Chapl St Andr Univ 97–14; Dioc Dir of Ords 02–11; Can St Ninian's Cathl Perth 07–14; PtO *Newc* 15–16; P-in-c Kirkwhelpington, Kirkharle, Kirkheaton and Cambo 16–20; P-in-c Bolam w Whalton and Hartburn w Meldon 17–20; P-in-c Nether Witton 17–20; Bp's Rural Affairs Adv 16–20; rtd 20. *36 High Street, Belford NE70 7NJ* M: 07922-559854

MASON, Ms Josephine Margaret. b 41. Edin Univ BMus 64. WMMTC 88. **d** 93 **p** 94. Chapl Asst S Birm Mental Health NHS Trust 91–06; C Birm St Jo Ladywood 93–01; C Ladywood St Jo and St Pet 01–06; rtd 06; PtO *Birm* from 06. *340 Selly Oak Road, Birmingham B30 1HP* T: 0121-451 1412 E: jo.mason@freeuk.com *or* josephinemargaretmason@yahoo.co.uk

MASON, Julia Ann. b 43. St Jo Coll Nottm 89. **d** 91 **p** 95. NSM Troon *Glas* 91–93; NSM Ayr, Maybole and Girvan 93–05; LtO *Edin* from 08; PtO *Glas* from 08. *13/2 Rocheid Park, Edinburgh EH4 1RU* T: 0131-343 1165 E: revdjuliamason@btinternet.com

MASON, Canon Kenneth Staveley. b 31. ARCS 53 Lon Univ BSc 53 BD 64. Wells Th Coll 56. **d** 58 **p** 59. C Kingston upon Hull St Martin *York* 58–61; C Pocklington w Yapham-cum-Meltonby, Owsthorpe etc 61–63; C Millington w Gt Givendale 61–63; V Thornton w Allerthorpe 63–69; Sub-Warden St Aug Coll Cant 69–76; Abp's Adv in Past Min 76–77; Dir Cant Sch of Min 77–81; Prin 81–89; Sec to Dioc Bd of Min *Cant* 77–87; Six Preacher Cant Cathl 79–84; Hon Can Cant Cathl 84–89; Prin Edin Th Coll 89–94; Prin TISEC 95; Can St Mary's Cathl *Edin* 89–96; rtd 95; PtO *Ripon* 96–14; *Leeds* from 14. *2 Williamson Close, Ripon HG4 1AZ* T: (01765) 607041

MASON, Mrs Kimberley Sarah. b 82. Sheff Univ BA 04 Dur Univ MA 18. **d** 18 **p** 19. C Harrogate St Mark *Leeds* from 18. *156 Pannal Ash Road, Harrogate HG2 9AJ* M: 07761-356464 E: kim.mason@leeds.anglican.org

MASON, Lesley Jane. b 55. MBE 21. Newnham Coll Cam BA 76 FInstD. St Jo Coll Nottm 04. **d** 07 **p** 08. NSM Busbridge and Hambledon *Guildf* 07–10; Chapl HM Pris Send from 10. *HM Prison Send, Ripley Road, Woking GU23 7LJ* T: (01483) 471000 E: ljmason@btinternet.com

MASON, Canon Nigel Frederick. b 60. Wycliffe Hall Ox 93. **d** 95 **p** 96. C Highbury Ch Ch w St Jo and St Sav *Lon* 95–98; C Seaford w Sutton *Chich* 98–01; R Rotherfield w Mark Cross from 01; Can and Preb Chich Cathl from 19. *The Rectory, Mayfield Road, Rotherfield, Crowborough TN6 3LU* T: (01892) 852536

MASON, Nigel James. b 56. Culham Coll of Educn BEd 78. St Steph Ho Ox 95. **d** 97 **p** 98. C Hove *Chich* 97–00; V Kemp Town St Mary 00–07; Chapl St Mary's Hall Brighton 03–07; V Smethwick *Birm* 07–13; P-in-c Smethwick St Matt w St Chad 10–13; Chapl Ex Hospiscare 13–18; C Aylesbeare, Clyst

St George, Clyst St Mary etc *Ex* 18–20; Bp's Chapl from 20. *4 Velwell Road, Exeter EX4 4LE* T: (01392) 345902

MASON, Paul. b 51. Cranmer Hall Dur 93. d 93 p 94. C Handforth *Ches* 93–97; V Partington and Carrington 97–04; V Church Hulme 04–18; rtd 19; PtO *Ches* from 19. *10 Church Street, Sandbach CW11 1FX* E: paulandsuemason@tiscali.co.uk

MASON, Mrs Pauline. b 49. LCTP. d 08 p 09. NSM Chorley St Geo *Blackb* 08–12; V Wrightington 12–17; rtd 17; PtO *Cant* from 18. *3 Vicarage Lane, St Margarets-at-Cliffe, Dover CT15 6AB* E: revvypolly@btinternet.com

MASON, Peter Charles. b 45. K Coll Lon BD 72 AKC 72 Birm Univ PGCE 89. St Aug Coll Cant 72. d 73 p 74. C Ilkeston St Mary *Derby* 73–76; C Bridgnorth St Mary *Heref* 76–78; TV Bridgnorth, Tasley, Astley Abbotts, etc 78–88; RE Teacher from 89; rtd 10; PtO *Heref* 89–04; St D from 04; St E from 19. *24 The Glade, Thetford IP24 1JR* M: 07974-128958 E: masonpeterc@gmail.com

MASON, Canon Peter Joseph. b 34. Lon Univ BA 58. Coll of Resurr Mirfield 58. d 60 p 61. C Belhus Park CD *Chelmsf* 60–63; LtO *Eur* 63–64; Asst Chapl Lon Univ 64–70; Chapl City Univ 66–70; R Stoke Newington St Mary 70–78; V Writtle *Chelmsf* 78–81; P-in-c Highwood 78–81; V Writtle w Highwood 81–86; R Shenfield 86–93; Hon Can Chelmsf Cathl 89–00; P-in-c Maldon All SS w St Pet 93–95; V 95–00; RD Maldon and Dengie 95–00; rtd 00; PtO *Chelmsf* from 00. *8 Canuden Road, Chelmsford CM1 2SX* T: (01245) 351465 E: petermason32@waitrose.com

MASON, Phillip Richard (Rolf). b 79. St Pet Coll Ox BA 00. Ripon Coll Cuddesdon 15. d 17 p 18. C Holbeck *Leeds* from 17. *St Peter's Vicarage, St Peter's Court, Leeds LS11 5NR* M: 07894-429214 E: revrolfmason@yahoo.com

MASON, Robert Herbert George. b 48. ACII. Oak Hill Th Coll 82. d 84 p 85. C Ware Ch Ch *St Alb* 84–88; V Eastbourne All So *Chich* 88–98; P-in-c Poole *Sarum* 98–01; R 01–11; rtd 11; PtO *Portsm* from 11; Chapl Miss to Seafarers 98–11. *63 Tredegar Road, Southsea PO4 9BJ* T: (023) 928 24712 E: revbobmelmason@hotmail.com

MASON, Mrs Sally Lynne. b 52. EMMTC 05. d 08 p 09. NSM Alfreton *Derby* 08–12; NSM Blackwell w Tibshelf from 12; Spiritual Dir Derby Angl Cursillo 13–18. *27 Stretton Road, Morton, Alfreton DE55 6GW* T: (01773) 873508 E: spiritualdirector@derbycursillo.co.uk

MASON, Mrs Sally-Anne. b 55. Open Univ BA 86 C F Mott Coll of Educn CertEd 77. SNWTP 07. d 10 p 11. NSM Childwall St Dav *Liv* 10–19; NSM Stoneycroft All SS 10–19; NSM Mossley Hill from 19. *2 Reedale Road, Liverpool L18 5HL* T: 0151-724 1142 M: 07889-584885 E: revsallymason@hotmail.com

MASON, Sarah Catherine. *See* LAWRENCE, Sarah Catherine

MASON, Simon Ion Vincent. b 60. Birm Univ BA 82. Trin Coll Bris BA 00. d 00 p 01. C Nottingham St Nic *S'well* 00–05; P-in-c Newent and Gorsley w Cliffords Mesne *Glouc* 05–15; R from 15; AD Severn Vale from 16. *The Rectory, 43 Court Road, Newent GL18 1SY* T: (01531) 820248

MASON, Stephen David. b 65. Univ of Wales (Lamp) BA 87. Ripon Coll Cuddesdon 89. d 92 p 93. C Gt Grimsby St Mary and St Jas *Linc* 92–97; V Southborough St Thos *Roch* 97–02; V Paddington St Jo w St Mich *Lon* from 02. *18 Somers Crescent, London W2 2PN* T: (020) 7262 1732 F: 7706 4475 E: parishadmin@stjohns-hydepark.com

MASON, Terry Mathew. b 56. Trin Coll Bris 94. d 96 p 97. C Bexleyheath Ch Ch *Roch* 96–99; P-in-c Stone 99–03; V Broadway w Wickhamford *Worc* 03–11; RD Evesham 05–10; P-in-c Wootton Wawen *Cov* 11–14; P-in-c Claverdon w Preston Bagot 11–14; AD Alcester 11–14; Deanery Missr 11–14; R Ditton Priors w Neenton, Burwarton etc *Heref* 14–21; rtd 21. *10 Falcon Road, Walton Cardiff, Tewkesbury GL20 7TJ* E: terrymason56@gmail.com

MASON, The Ven Thomas Henry Ambrose. b 51. Solicitor 75. Oak Hill Th Coll BA 86. d 86 p 87. C W Drayton *Lon* 86–89; Field Officer Oak Hill Ext Coll 89–94; Eur Sec ICS 94–95; Dir of Tr *Eur* 95–03; Dir Min and Dir of Ords 01–03; Can Brussels Cathl 00–03; Hon Can Brussels Cathl 03–07; R Grosmont and Skenfrith and Llangattock etc *Mon* 03–08; Dir Min 06–21; Adn Mon 13–21; rtd 21. *County House, 100 The Struet, Brecon LD3 7LS* E: ambrosemason@gmail.com

MASSEY, Alison June. b 63. d 13 p 14. C Stourdene Gp *Cov* 13–16; R Draycote Gp 16–19; PtO 19–20; V Fillongley and Corley from 20. *The Vicarage, 16 Holbeche Crescent, Fillongley, Coventry CV7 8ES* M: 07837-124509 E: reverendalimassey@gmail.com

MASSEY, Mrs Elizabeth Ann. b 53. N Staffs Poly BSc 75. STETS 04. d 07 p 08. C Whitton *Sarum* 07–10; TV Marden Vale 10–17; rtd 17; PtO *Sarum* 18–20. *Fairacre,*

Upavon Road, North Newnton, Pewsey SN9 6JT T: (01980) 630256 M: 07777-800084 E: ea.massey@btinternet.com

MASSEY, George Douglas. b 44. St Jo Coll Nottm 91. d 93 p 94. C Higher Bebington *Ches* 93–98; V Messingham *Linc* 98–14; rtd 14. *12 Holme Lane, Messingham, Scunthorpe DN17 3SG* T: (01724) 762823

MASSEY, Mrs Kate Ishbel. b 77. Aber Univ MB, ChB 99. Qu Coll Birm 08. d 11 p 12. C Kenilworth St Nic *Cov* 11–13; C Meriden 13–15; V Stockingford from 15; Dean Women's Min from 15. *Stockingford Vicarage, 90 Church Road, Nuneaton CV10 8LG* T: (024) 7632 5359 E: revkatemassey@gmail.com

MASSEY, Keith John. b 46. Oak Hill Th Coll 69. d 72 p 73. C Bermondsey St Jas w Ch Ch *S'wark* 72–76; C Benchill *Man* 76–82; V Clifton Green 82–97; V Flixton St Jo 97–11; rtd 11; PtO *Man* from 11. *42 Curzon Road, Stockport SK2 5DH* T: 0161-285 3298 E: keithjmassey@yahoo.co.uk

MASSEY, Michelle Elaine. *See* WARD, Michelle Elaine

MASSEY, Peter. *See* MASSEY, William Peter

MASSEY, Peter William. b 45. St Mark & St Jo Coll Lon TCert 66 Open Univ BA 75. WMMTC 96. d 99 p 00. Lay Tr Officer *Heref* 97–09; NSM Holmer w Huntington 99–03; NSM Heref St Pet w St Owen and St Jas 03–15; rtd 15; PtO *Heref* 15–17; *Blackb* from 17. *51 Copeland Drive, Standish, Wigan WN6 0XR* T: (01257) 427153 M: 07803-826728 E: pwmassey@btinternet.com

MASSEY, Shellie. *See* WARD, Michelle Elaine

MASSEY, Wayne Philip. b 74. Brunel Univ BSc 97. Wycliffe Hall Ox BA 05. d 06 p 07. C Clifton Ch Ch w Em *Bris* 06–12; TV Bishopston and St Andrews from 12. *8 Windsor Road, Bristol BS6 5BP*

MASSEY, William Peter. b 50. CITC 96. d 99 p 00. C Fermoy Union *C, C & R* 99–00; C Carrigrohane Union and Kinsale Union 00–03; PtO *Eur* 04–13; P-in-c Lorgues w Fayence 13–16 and 17–20; PtO 16–17. *1801 chemin des Pailles, 83510 Lorgues, France* T: (0033) 4 94 99 40 74 E: peter@themasseys.fr

MASSHEDAR, Richard Eric. b 57. Nottm Univ BTh 86. Linc Th Coll 83. d 86 p 87. C Cassop cum Quarrington *Dur* 86–89; C Ferryhill 89–91; V Leam Lane 91–94; P-in-c Hartlepool St Paul 94–96; V from 96. *St Paul's Vicarage, 6 Hutton Avenue, Hartlepool TS26 9PN* T: (01429) 272934 E: masshedar@gmail.com

MASSIAH, Amrela Celeste. b 60. Westcott Ho Cam. d 07 p 08. C Lee St Marg *S'wark* 07–09; C Thamesmead 09–11; Asst Chapl RN Coll Greenwich 11–12; Hong Kong 12–16; P-in-c St Phil St Martin Barbados from 16. *Address temp unknown* T: (001) (246) 435 0634 E: acmassiah@yahoo.co.uk

MASSINGBERD-MUNDY, Roger William Burrell. b 36. TD. Univ of Wales (Lamp) BA 59. Ridley Hall Cam 59. d 61 p 62. C Benwell St Jas *Newc* 61–64; C Whorlton 64–72; TV 73; P-in-c Healey 73–85; Dioc Stewardship Adv 73–85; Hon Can Newc Cathl 82–85; CF (TA) 63–68; CF (TAVR) 71–83; R S Ormsby w Ketsby, Calceby and Driby *Linc* 85–86; P-in-c Harrington w Brinkhill 85–86; P-in-c Haugh 85–86; P-in-c Oxcombe 85–86; P-in-c Ruckland w Farforth and Maidenwell 85–86; P-in-c Somersby w Bag Enderby 85–86; P-in-c Tetford and Salmonby 85–86; R S Ormsby Gp 86–96; RD Bolingbroke 88–96; rtd 96; Chapl Taverham Hall Sch 03–08; PtO *Nor* from 02. *The Old Post Office, West Raynham, Fakenham NR21 7AD* T: (01328) 838611 F: 838698 E: revmassingberd@gmail.com

MASSON, Canon Philip Roy. b 52. Hertf Coll Ox BA 75 Leeds Univ BA 77. Coll of Resurr Mirfield 75. d 78 p 79. C Port Talbot St Theodore *Llan* 78–82; V Penyfai w Tondu 82–92; Dioc Dir Post-Ord Tr 85–88; Warden of Ords 88–01; R Newton Nottage from 92; AD Margam 01–06 and 12–18; Can Llan Cathl from 02. *The Rectory, 64 Victoria Avenue, Porthcawl CF36 3HE* T: (01656) 782042 or 786899 E: philipmasson@hotmail.com or office@parishofporthcawl.org.uk

MASTERMAN, Malcolm. b 49. City Univ MSc 00. K Coll Lon 73 Chich Th Coll 76. d 77 p 78. C Peterlee *Dur* 77–80; Chapl Basingstoke Distr Hosp 80–85; Chapl Freeman Hosp Newc 85–95; Tr and Development Officer Hosp Chapl Coun 96–00; Sen Chapl N Dur Healthcare NHS Trust 00–02; Sen Chapl Co Durham and Darlington Acute Hosps NHS Trust 02–06; Lead Chapl S Tees Hosps NHS Foundn Trust 06–14; rtd 14; Bp's Adv on Hosp Chapl (Whitby Area) *York* from 06; PtO from 14; *Dur* from 14. *8 Fulthorpe Grove, Wynyard, Billingham TS22 5QZ* T: (01740) 644787 E: malhel49@btinternet.com

MASTERMAN, Miss Patricia Hope. b 28. St Mich Ho Ox 59. dss 79 d 87. Asst CF 79–90; rtd 90; PtO *Chich* from 90. *33 Sea Lane Gardens, Ferring, Worthing BN12 5EQ* T: (01903) 245231

MASTERS, Mrs Carol. b 61. SNWTP 11. d 13 p 14. OLM Denton Ch Ch *Man* 13–19; TV Gorton and Abbey Hey from 19. *46*

Ashbrook Avenue, Denton, Manchester M34 2GH T: 0161-320 5485 M: 07759-130000 E: carol1masters@aol.com

MASTERS, Kenneth Leslie. b 44. Leeds Univ BA 68. Cuddesdon Coll 68. **d** 70 **p** 71. C Wednesbury St Paul Wood Green *Lich* 70–71; C Tettenhall Regis 71–75; TV Chelmsley Wood *Birm* 75–79; R Harting *Chich* 79–87; V Rustington 87–00; TR Beaminster Area *Sarum* 00–09; rtd 09; PtO *B & W* from 10; *Sarum* 15–20. *9 Carrington Way, Wincanton BA9 9NX* T: (01963) 824209 E: k2masters4@btinternet.com

MASTERS, Rupert Paul Falla. b 52. Hull Univ BA 74 Ex Univ PGCE 75 Lon Inst of Educn MA 88. **d** 10 **p** 11. OLM Stoughton *Guildf* from 10. *32 Sheepfold Road, Guildford GU2 9TT* T: (01483) 573785 E: rupert.masters@talk21.com

MASTERS, Ms Vivien Claire. b 63. Yorks Min Course. **d** 14 **p** 15. C Kippax w Allerton Bywater *Leeds* 14–16 C Allerton Bywater, Kippax and Swillington 16–18; TV Leverhulme *Man* from 18. *7 Alford Close, Bolton BL2 6NR* T: (01204) 285981 E: masters.vivien77@gmail.com

MASTIN, Brian Arthur. b 38. Peterho Cam BA 60 MA 63 BD 80 Mert Coll Ox MA 63 MSNTS 64 MSOTS 64 FHA 14. Ripon Hall Ox 62. **d** 63 **p** 64. Asst Lect Hebrew Univ Coll of N Wales (Ban) 63–65; Lect Hebrew 65–82; Sen Lect 82–98; Chapl Ban Cathl 63–65; LtO 65–98; rtd 98; PtO *Ely* 98–17. *2A Gurney Way, Cambridge CB4 2ED* T: (01223) 355078 E: brianarthurmastin@gmail.com

MATCHETT, Canon Christopher Jonathan. b 65. QUB BSSc TCD BTh 98. **d** 98 **p** 99. C Ballynafeigh St Jude *D & D* 98–01; C Holywood 01–04; I Magheracross *Clogh* 04–11; I Newtownards *D & D* from 11; Can Down Cathl from 17. *The Rectory, 36 Belfast Road, Newtownards BT23 4TT* T: (028) 9181 2527 *or* 9181 3193 M: 07875-179060 E: chris.matchett@btinternet.com

MATHER, David Jonathan. b 65. New Coll Ox BA 88 MA 95. St Steph Ho Ox BTh 95. **d** 95 **p** 96. C Pickering w Lockton and Levisham *York* 95–98; P-in-c Bridlington H Trin and Sewerby w Marton 98–99; V from 99. *Sewerby Vicarage, Cloverley Road, Bridlington YO16 5TX* T: (01262) 675725

MATHER, Mrs Elizabeth Ann. b 45. CertEd 66. Dalton Ho Bris IDC 70 St Jo Coll Nottm 92. **d** 94 **p** 95. NSM Littleover *Derby* 94–02; LtO St Alb 02–05; rtd 05; PtO *York* 05–10. *Angel Court, 2 Rose Street, Fortrose IV10 8TN* T: (01381) 621745 E: revlibby@gmail.com

MATHER, James William. b 63. Sheff Univ BA 86. St Steph Ho Ox 88. **d** 91 **p** 92. C Doncaster St Leon and St Jude *Sheff* 91–94; C Cantley 94–95; V Lakenheath *St E* 95–01; P-in-c Downham Market w Bexwell *Ely* 01–02; P-in-c Crimplesham w Stradsett 01–02; R Downham Market and Crimplesham w Stradsett 02–19; R Downham Market and Stradsett from 19; RD Fincham and Feltwell 06–09. *The Rectory, King's Walk, Downham Market PE38 9LF* T: (01366) 382187

MATHER, Leila Isabella Nadezhda. b 90. Bris Univ BA 13 Cam Univ BA 19. Westcott Ho Cam 17. **d** 20 **p** 21. C Charminster, Stinsford and the Chalk Stream villages *Sarum* from 20. *Church House, 1 Church Lane, Charminster, Dorchester DT2 9QR* E: revdleilamather@gmail.com

MATHER, William Bernard George. b 45. St Jo Coll Nottm 77. **d** 79 **p** 80. C St Leonards St Leon *Chich* 79–82; TR Netherthorpe *Sheff* 82–90; V Littleover *Derby* 90–02; Assoc Dir SOMA UK 02–05; TR Drypool *York* 05–10; rtd 10. *Angel Court, 2 Rose Street, Fortrose IV10 8TN* T: (01381) 621745 E: williammather@gmail.com

MATHERS, Alan Edward. b 36. Lon Univ BA FPhS. Oak Hill Th Coll 61. **d** 64 **p** 65. C Ox St Matt 64–66; C Bootle St Leon *Liv* 66–68; C Hampreston *Sarum* 68–70; P-in-c Damerham 70–71; V Queniborough *Leic* 71–76; USA 76–77; V Tipton St Matt *Lich* 77–86; P-in-c Tipton St Paul 77–84; V 85–86; V Sutton Ch Ch *S'wark* 86–95; Chapl Cannes *Eur* 95–98; rtd 98; PtO *Chich* from 98; *S'wark* from 98. *52 The Meadow, Copthorne, Crawley RH10 3RQ* T: (01342) 713325 E: alanandmuriel2@gmail.com

MATHERS, David Michael Brownlow. b 43. Em Coll Cam BA 65 MA 69. Clifton Th Coll 65. **d** 67 **p** 68. C Branksome St Clem *Sarum* 67–70; C Bromley Ch Ch *Roch* 70–73; V Bures *St E* 73–80; Brazil 80–82; P-in-c Old Newton w Stowupland *St E* 82–86; V 87–90; V Thurston 90–11; RD Ixworth 94–03; rtd 11; P-in-c Laughton w Ripe and Chalvington *Chich* 11–17; PtO *St E* from 17. *3 Bracken Row, Thurston, Bury St Edmunds IP31 3PT* T: (01359) 231734 E: lyndavidmathers@gmail.com

MATHERS, Derek. b 48. NOC 82. **d** 85 **p** 86. C Huddersfield St Jo *Wakef* 85–86; C N Huddersfield 86–88; TV Almondbury w Farnley Tyas 88–92; V Marsden 92–02; R Badsworth 02–12; rtd 12; PtO *Leeds* from 19. *17 Union Street, Slaithwaite, Huddersfield HD7 5ED* T: (01484) 846018 E: father.derek49@yahoo.com

MATHERS, Kenneth Ernest William. b 56. Trin Coll Bris 93. **d** 95 **p** 96. C Bournemouth St Jo w St Mich *Win* 95–99; NSM Darenth *Roch* 99–04; Chapl Dartford and Gravesham NHS Trust 01–04; Chapl N Devon Healthcare NHS Trust 05–16. *42 Brynsworthy Park, Roundswell, Barnstaple EX31 3RB* T: (01271) 346293 E: revkmathers@btinternet.com

MATHERS (*née* **STEWART**)**, Mrs Kim Deborah.** b 61. Southn Univ LLB 82. Trin Coll Bris 86. **d** 89 **p** 94. Par Dn Bitterne *Win* 89–93; NSM Stoke Bishop *Bris* 93–95; NSM Bournemouth St Jo w St Mich *Win* 95–99; P-in-c Darenth *Roch* 99–04; TR Newton Tracey, Horwood, Alverdiscott etc *Ex* 04–15; RD Torrington 09–12; Tutor SWMTC from 15; TV Sidmouth, Woolbrook, Salcombe Regis, Sidbury etc *Ex* from 20. *The Vicarage, Harcombe Lane, Sidford, Sidmouth EX10 9QN* E: kim.mathers@sidvalley.org.uk *or* kim@swmtc.org.uk

MATHEW, Mrs Alison Kate. b 65. Glas Coll of Tech BA 86 Glas Univ MPH 95 Kingston Univ BA 08. Ripon Coll Cuddesdon 10. **d** 12 **p** 13. C Spring Grove St Mary *Lon* 12–15; C Radley, Sunningwell and Kennington *Ox* from 15. *Kennington Vicarage, Ross Court, The Avenue, Kennington, Oxford OX1 5AD* M: 07980-262912 E: alisonmathew@gmail.com

MATHEW, Laurence Allen Stanfield. b 47. Sarum Th Coll 99. **d** 02 **p** 03. OLM Warminster Ch Ch *Sarum* 02–12; NSM Ross w Walford and Brampton Abbotts *Heref* 12–17; rtd 17; PtO *Sarum* from 17; *Glouc* from 21. *Yew Tree House, 2 The Walled Garden, Newent GL18 1EW* M: 07747-108342

MATHEW (*née* **HOLLIS**)**, Rebecca Catherine.** b 78. St Martin's Coll Lanc BA 99. Ripon Coll Cuddesdon BTh 03. **d** 03 **p** 04. C Broughton *Blackb* 03–07; C Mirihana Ch Ch Sri Lanka 07–08; Chapl St Thos Coll Mt Lavina 08–11; TV Bicester w Bucknell, Caversfield and Launton *Ox* 11–17; V Allestree St Nic *Derby* 17–21; P-in-c Quarndon 17–21; V Sale St Paul *Ches* from 21. *28 Kilvert Drive, Sale M33 6PN* E: revdrebh@hotmail.com

MATHEW, Shemil. b 82. Mahatma Gandhi Univ Kerala BA 04 Madurai Univ MA 07 Glos Univ BA 07 MA 14 Ox Univ MTh 14. **d** 14 **p** 15. C Aynho and Croughton w Evenley etc *Pet* 14–17; Chapl Ox Brookes Univ from 17. *Brookes Chaplaincy, Oxford Brookes University, Gipsy Lane, Headington, Oxford OX3 0BP* M: 07388-872951 E: revshemil@gmail.com

MATHIAS, Steffan Idris Mano. b 87. K Coll Lon BA 08 MA 10 PhD 15 AKC 15. Coll of Resurr Mirfield 15. **d** 17 **p** 18. C Lewisham St Mary *S'wark* 17–20; P-in-c Streatham St Pet 20–21; V from 21; Dir Ords Kingston Area from 21. *St Peter's Vicarage, 113 Leigham Court Road, London SW16 2NS* M: 07811-981703 E: steffanmathias@gmail.com

MATHIAS-JONES, Edward Lloyd. b 71. Univ of Wales (Lamp) BA 93. St Mich Coll Llan BD 96. **d** 97 **p** 98. C Llanelli *St D* 97–00; C Milford Haven 00–04; V Newport St Steph and H Trin *Mon* 04–16; V Grangetown *York* from 16. *St Hilda's Vicarage, Clynes Road, Middlesbrough TS6 7LY* E: frmathias-jones@aol.com *or* frmathiasjones@aol.com

MATHOLE, Paul Mark. b 76. St Anne's Coll Ox BA 98 R Holloway Coll Lon MA 00 PhD 04. Oak Hill Th Coll 07. **d** 10 **p** 11. C Rusholme H Trin *Man* 10–20; R from 20. *Holy Trinity Rectory, Platt Lane, Manchester M14 5NF* M: 07733-185670 E: paulmathole@gmail.com

MATLOCK, Miss Catherine Elizabeth. b 66. York Univ BSc 87 Ex Univ MA 15. Qu Foundn Birm 16. **d** 18 **p** 19. C Kings Norton *Birm* from 18. *53 Lanchester Road, Kings Norton B38 9AQ* M: 07443-475554 E: curate@kingsnorton.org.uk

MATLOOB, Canon Nazir Ahmad Barnabas. b 48. Punjab Univ BA 79. Gujranwala Th Sem BTh 77 BD 81 MDiv 83. **d** 78 **p** 78. Pakistan 78–93; PtO *Chelmsf* 94–97; C Forest Gate All SS 98–06; C Lt Ilford St Barn 06; Inter-Faith Worker Newham Deanery 07–20; Hon Can Chelmsf Cathl 12–20; rtd 20. *64 Henderson Road, London E7 8EF* T: (020) 8552 4280

MATSON de LAURIER, Mrs Sarah Kennerley. b 46. EMMTC 00. **d** 02 **p** 03. NSM Hilton w Marston-on-Dove *Derby* 02–14; PtO from 14. *1 Park Way, Etwall, Derby DE65 6HU* T: (01283) 732859 E: pskmdl@aol.com *or* peteandrev@gmail.com

MATTACKS, Mrs Lesley Anne. b 58. Birm Univ BA 79 K Coll Lon MA 86 Leeds Univ BA 07 W Lon Inst of HE PGCE 80. NOC 04. **d** 07 **p** 08. C Birkenshaw w Hunsworth *Wakef* 07–10; P-in-c Middlestown 10–14; *Leeds* 14–15; Dioc Tr Officer (Reader Formation) *Wakef* 10–14; *Leeds* 14–15; V Brownhill from 15. *St Saviour's Vicarage, 24 Intake Lane, Batley WF17 0BT* T: (01924) 471999 M: 07952-375176 E: revles.mattacks@hotmail.co.uk

MATTAPALLY, Sebastian Thomas. b 57. N Bengal Univ BA 77 Pontifical Salesian Univ BTh 84 Pontifical Gregorian Univ LTh 98 DTh 05. **d** 83 **p** 83. In RC Ch 83–00; PtO *Eur* 01–04; C Patcham *Chich* 05–07; P-in-c Kirdford 07–10; V Eastbourne St Mich 10–17; R Springline *Linc* from 17. *The New Vicarage, Church Hill, Ingham, Lincoln LN1 2YE* T: (01522) 731793 E: smattapally@btinternet.com

MATTHEW, Dawn Rachel. b 69. St Mellitus Coll BA 20. **d** 20 **p** 21. C Hinckley St Jo *Leic* from 20. *2 Brascote Road, Hinckley LE10 9YE* M: 07543-247180 E: revddawnmatthew@gmail.com

MATTHEWS, Canon Anna Ruth. b 78. Rob Coll Cam BA 99 MA 03 MPhil 03. Westcott Ho Cam 01. **d** 03 **p** 04. C Abbots Langley *St Alb* 03–06; Min Can St Alb Abbey 06–12; V Cambridge St Benedict *Ely* from 12; Dioc Dir of Ords 12–19; Hon Can Ely Cathl from 15. *61 St Bartholomew's Court, Riverside, Cambridge CB5 8HG* T: (01223) 321312 E: vicar@stbenetschurch.org

MATTHEWS, Canon Campbell Thurlow. b 33. Lon Univ BA 56 Dur Univ DipEd 57. St Jo Coll Nottm 70. **d** 71 **p** 72. C Ryton *Dur* 71–74; Chapl R Victoria Infirmary Newc 74–82; V Greenside *Dur* 74–82; R Wetheral w Warwick *Carl* 82–93; RD Brampton 83–91; P-in-c Farlam and Nether Denton 87–93; P-in-c Gilsland 87–93; Hon Can Carl Cathl 87–00; P-in-c Thornthwaite cum Braithwaite and Newlands 93–00; P-in-c Borrowdale 97–00; rtd 00; PtO *Carl* from 00; *Newc* from 01. *Barn Croft, Applethwaite, Keswick CA12 4PN* T: (017687) 74899 E: ctm18@gmail.com

MATTHEWS, Celia Inger. b 30. St Chris Coll Blackheath 50. **d** 86 **p** 94. Dioc Missr *St And* from 86; rtd 95. *24 Barossa Place, Perth PH1 5HH* T: (01738) 623578 E: celia.matthews@icloud.com

MATTHEWS, Canon Colin John. b 44. Jes Coll Ox BA 67 MA 71 Fitzw Coll Cam BA 70 MA 74. Ridley Hall Cam 68. **d** 71 **p** 72. C Onslow Square St Paul *Lon* 71–74; C Leic H Apostles 74–78; Bible Use Sec Scripture Union 78–89; Dir Ch Cen Guildf St Sav 89–95; V Burpham 95–12; RD Guildf 01–06; Hon Can Guildf Cathl 02–12; rtd 12; PtO *Guildf* from 12. *Bargate, Little Tangley, Wonersh Common, Wonersh, Guildford GU5 0PW* T: (01483) 575334 M: 07787-575923 E: colinjmatthews@gmail.com

MATTHEWS, David John. b 90. Kent Univ BA 11. St Mellitus Coll 14. **d** 17 **p** 18. C Onslow Square and S Kensington St Aug *Lon* 17–21; C S Kensington St Luke from 21. *12 Wharfedale Street, London SW10 9AL* M: 07545-972620

MATTHEWS, David William. b 49. St Paul's Coll Grahamstown 88. **d** 90 **p** 91. C Port Eliz St Sav S Africa 90–91; C Port Eliz St Paul 91–94; R Zwartkops River Valley Par 94–00; Chapl Miss to Seafarers 00–03; R Boxford, Edwardstone, Groton etc *St E* 03–09; P-in-c Southampton St Anne Bermuda 09–16; PtO *Win* from 17. *148 Sullivan Road, Sholing, Southampton SO19 0HX* T: (023) 8032 4938 E: deltawhiskey5@gmail.com

MATTHEWS, David William Grover. b 73. Acadia Univ (NS) BA 93 Toronto Univ MDiv 98. Trin Coll Toronto 95. **d** 98 **p** 99. C Newport St Teilo *Mon* 98–00; NSM Cobbold Road St Sav w St Mary *Lon* 00–03; P-in-c Hammersmith H Innocents 03–05; P-in-c Hammersmith H Innocents and St Jo from 05. *35 Paddenswick Road, London W6 0UA* T: (020) 8741 6480 *or* 8748 2286 E: holyinnocentsw6@yahoo.com

MATTHEWS, Mrs Deborah Lynne. b 57. Southn Univ BTh 98 MCIPD 92. Ripon Coll Cuddesdon MTh 01. **d** 00 **p** 01. C Southampton (City Cen) *Win* 00–04; V Clapham St Paul *S'wark* 04–17; P-in-c Clapham H Spirit 12–13; Dir IME Kingston Area 13–17; AD Lambeth N 13–17; V Verwood *Sarum* from 17. *The Vicarage, 34 Dewlands Way, Verwood BH31 6JN* T: (01202) 823707

MATTHEWS, Mrs Diana Elizabeth Charlotte. b 43. MCSP 65. **d** 93 **p** 96. OLM Merrow *Guildf* 93–11; rtd 11; PtO *Guildf* from 11. *Avila, 13 Wells Road, Guildford GU4 7XQ* T: (01483) 839738 E: diana.matthews@ntlworld.com

MATTHEWS, Elis Alun. b 82. York Univ BA 04 Cam Univ BTh 15. Ridley Hall Cam 12. **d** 15 **p** 16. C E Ham St Paul *Chelmsf* 15–18; V Spring Grove St Mary *Lon* from 18. *St Mary's Vicarage, Osterley Road, Isleworth TW7 4PW* T: (020) 8569 7312 M: 07739-020288 E: rev.elis.matthews@gmail.com

MATTHEWS, Frederick Peter. b 45. Grey Coll Dur BA 66 MA 68 K Coll Lon PGCE 68 Lon Univ BSc(Econ) 75. Sarum & Wells Th Coll 70. **d** 72 **p** 73. C W Wickham St Jo *Cant* 72–74; C Sholing *Win* 74–77; LtO 78–79; V Woolston 79–03; P-in-c Over Wallop w Nether Wallop 03–07; Dioc Ecum Officer 03–07; rtd 07; PtO *Sarum* from 07; *Win* 07–14. *19 Berkshire Road, Salisbury SP2 8NY* T: (01722) 340508 E: fpetermatthews@hotmail.co.uk

MATTHEWS, George Charles Wallace. b 27. Sarum Th Coll 58. **d** 60 **p** 61. C Coppenhall St Paul *Ches* 60–63; C Lewes St Anne *Chich* 63–67; V Wheelock *Ches* 67–76; V Mossley 76–93; rtd 93; PtO *Ches* 93–14. *145 Primrose Avenue, Haslington, Crewe CW1 5QB* T: (01270) 587463

MATTHEWS, Gerald Lancelot. b 31. Bris Univ LLB 50. Ripon Hall Ox 55. **d** 57 **p** 58. C The Quinton *Birm* 57–60; C Olton 60–63; V Brent Tor *Ex* 63–72; P-in-c Lydford w Bridestowe and Sourton 70–72; TR Lydford, Brent Tor, Bridestowe and Sourton 72–78; P-in-c Black Torrington, Bradford w Cookbury etc 78–90; PtO 90–19; rtd 94. *The Larches, Black Torrington, Beaworthy EX21 5PU* T: (01409) 231228

MATTHEWS, Harold James. b 46. Leeds Univ BSc 68 Fitzw Coll Cam BA 70 MA 74 Goldsmiths' Coll Lon PGCE 71. Westcott Ho Cam 68. **d** 71 **p** 72. C Mossley Hill St Matt and St Jas *Liv* 71–74; C Stanley 74–76; TV Hackney *Lon* 76–78; Chapl Forest Sch Snaresbrook 78–83; Hd Master Vernon Holme Sch *Cant* 83–88; Hd Master Heath Mt Sch Hertf 88–06; Chapl Roedean Sch Brighton 06–08; Chapl Kent Coll Pembury 10–16; PtO *Roch* 11–16; *Glouc* from 17; *Eur* from 10. *Flat 1, 12 Ashford Road, Cheltenham GL50 2EN* T: (01242) 231153 M: 07515-857110 E: hjmatth46@hotmail.co.uk

MATTHEWS, Hayley Deborah Yeshua. b 68. Ridley Hall Cam 05. **d** 07 **p** 08. C Lancaster St Mary w St John and St Anne *Blackb* 07–10; Chapl MediaCityUK *Man* 10–13; R Birch w Fallowfield 13–17; Dir Lay Tr *Leeds* from 17. *Diocese of Leeds, 17-19 York Place, Leeds LS1 2EX* T: 0113-353 0283 E: hayley.matthews@leeds.anglican.org

MATTHEWS, Canon Joan Muriel. b 53. NOC 89. **d** 92 **p** 94. C Aughton St Mich *Liv* 92–97; R Wavertree St Mary 97–06; AD Toxteth and Wavertree 04–06; Hon Can Liv Cathl 04–06 and 07–16; P-in-c Newton in Makerfield St Pet 06–07; P-in-c Earlestown 06–07; TR Newton 08–16; AD Winwick 09–16; rtd 16; PtO *Liv* from 17. *130 Belvedere Road, Newton-le-Willows WA12 0LG* T: (01925) 299668 E: revjoan@hotmail.com

MATTHEWS, John Goodman. b 77. Univ of Wales BTh 99. St Mich Coll Llan 99. **d** 02 **p** 03. C Lampeter and Llanddewibrefi Gp *St D* 02–05; P-in-c Aberporth w Tremain w Blaenporth and Betws Ifan 05–07; V 07–09; V Aberporth w Blaenporth w Betws Ifan 09; P-in-c Tregarth and Llandygai and Maes y Groes *Ban* 09–14; V Bro Ogwen from 14. *Pentir Vicarage, Pentir, Bangor LL57 4YB* T: (01248) 364991 E: fatherjohnmatthews@btinternet.com

MATTHEWS, Lewis William (Bill). b 29. St Jo Coll Dur BA 53 MSc 76. **d** 55 **p** 56. C Eston *York* 55–57; Ind Chapl *Sheff* 57–61; V Copt Oak *Leic* 61–64; R Braunstone 64–70; V Thornaby on Tees St Paul *York* 70–72; TR Thornaby on Tees 72–78; Dir Dioc Bd for Soc Resp *Lon* 79–84; PtO 84–94; Warden Durning Hall Chr Community Cen Forest Gate 84–94; rtd 94; Hon C Jersey Gouray St Martin *Win* 94–06; PtO from 06. *2 Malvern, La Ruelle es Ruaux, St Brelade, Jersey JE3 8BB* T: (01534) 498368 M: 07797-731143 E: revmatthews163@gmail.com

MATTHEWS, Canon Melvyn William. b 40. St Edm Hall Ox BA 63 MA 68. K Coll Lon BD 66 AKC 67. **d** 67 **p** 68. C Enfield St Andr *Lon* 67–70; Asst Chapl Southn Univ *Win* 70–72; Lect Univ of Nairobi Kenya 72–76; V Highgate All SS *Lon* 76–79; P-in-c Clifton St Paul *Bris* 79–87; Sen Chapl Bris Univ 79–87; Dir Ammerdown Cen for Study and Renewal 87–93; V Chew Magna w Dundry *B & W* 93–97; Can and Chan Wells Cathl 97–05; rtd 05; PtO *B & W* from 05. *36 Mondyes Court, Milton Lane, Wells BA5 2QX* T: (01749) 672068 M: 07791-875319 E: mwmatthews@onetel.com or melvyn.matthews@icloud.com

MATTHEWS, Michael Raymond. b 55. JP 96. Huddersfield Univ MBA 96 Leeds Univ BA 04 CQSW 82. Coll of Resurr Mirfield 02. **d** 04 **p** 05. C Featherstone and Purston cum S Featherstone *Wakef* 04–07; P-in-c Haslingfield w Harlton and Gt and Lt Eversden *Ely* 07–10; TV Lordsbridge 10–13; RD Bourn 10–13; P-in-c Nassington w Yarwell and Woodnewton w Apethorpe *Pet* 13–15; V Nassington, Apethorpe, Thornhaugh etc 15; PtO 15–18; Chapl All SS C of E Primary Sch from 18. *8A Woodgate, Helpston, Peterborough PE6 7ED* T: (01733) 253768 E: frmichaelmatthews@btinternet.com

MATTHEWS, Paul. b 47. Brunel Univ BTech 70. S Dios Minl Tr Scheme 89. **d** 92 **p** 93. NSM Goring-by-Sea *Chich* 92–12; P-in-c Chidham 12–14; V 14–18; rtd 18. *7 Denton Close, Goring-by-Sea, Worthing BN12 4TZ* E: frpaulmatthews@btinternet.com

MATTHEWS, Peter. *See* MATTHEWS, Frederick Peter

MATTHEWS, Peter John. b 69. Leic Poly BEng 92. Wycliffe Hall Ox 07. **d** 09 **p** 10. C Catterick *Ripon* 09–13; Chapl St Fran Xavier Sch Richmond 09–13; P-in-c Old Trafford St Bride *Man* 13–18; R from 18; Young Adults Missr Man Adnry from 13. *St Bride's Rectory, 33 Shrewsbury Street, Manchester M16 9BB* T: 0161-226 1251 M: 07590-698333 E: peter@stbrides.uk

MATTHEWS, Canon Rodney Charles. b 36. Sarum Th Coll 62. **d** 64 **p** 65. C Gt Clacton *Chelmsf* 64–68; C Loughton St Mary 68–74; TV 74–76; V Goodmayes All SS 76–87; V Woodford Bridge 87–02; Hon Chapl Sail Tr Assn from 89; P-in-c Barkingside St Cedd *Chelmsf* 90–92; Hon Can Chelmsf Cathl 99–02; rtd 02; PtO *Chelmsf* from 03. *93 King's Head Hill, London E4 7JG* T: (020) 8529 4372 E: canonrodney@ntlworld.com

MATTHEWS, Canon Roger Charles. b 54. Man Univ BSc 75 Nottm Univ MA 02 Fuller Th Sem California DMin 10 MBCS 82 CEng 90. Trin Coll Bris 87. **d** 89 **p** 90. C Gt Baddow *Chelmsf* 89–93; P-in-c Chigwell Row 93–94; TV Chigwell and Chigwell Row 94–96; Dioc Miss Officer 96–00; Millenium Ecum Officer 98–00; Bp's Adv for Miss and Min 01–12; Dean of Miss and Min 12–20; Chief Exec and Dioc Sec from 20; Hon C Gt Baddow *Chelmsf* from 01; Hon Can Chelmsf Cathl from 00. *42 Riffhams Drive, Great Baddow, Chelmsford CM2 7DD* T: (01245) 478959 *or* 294409 E: rmatthews@chelmsford.anglican.org

MATTHEWS, Canon Roy Ian John. b 27. TD 71. St Cath Soc Ox BA 52 MA 56. St Steph Ho Ox 52. **d** 54 **p** 55. C Barnsley St Mary *Wakef* 54–58; V Staincliffe 58–65; CF (TA) 58–92; V Penistone w Midhope *Wakef* 65–72; V Brighouse 72–84; Hon Can Wakef Cathl 76–92; V Darrington 84–92; Dioc Schs Officer 84–89; Dep Dir of Educn 85–89; rtd 92; PtO *Wakef* 92–14; *Leeds* 14–16; *York* 92–96 and 17–20; P-in-c Selby Abbey 96–97. *14 Spring Walk, Brayton, Selby YO8 9DS* T: (01757) 707259

MATTHEWS, Canon Royston Peter. b 39. Univ of Wales (Lamp) BA 61. St Mich Coll Llan 61. **d** 64 **p** 65. C Fairwater CD *Llan* 64–67; C Cadoxton-juxta-Barry 67–71; V Bettws *Mon* 71–84; V Abergavenny H Trin 84–05; Hon Can St Woolos Cathl 05; rtd 05; PtO *Win* 08–20; Clergy Widows and Widowers Officer (Bournemouth Adnry) from 18. *1 Hoburne Gardens, Christchurch BH23 4PP* T: (01425) 271216 E: roymatt1@aol.com

MATTHEWS, Sandra Dawn. b 62. Sheff Univ BA 85 Univ of Wales (Cardiff) PGCE 94 Nottm Univ NPQH 01. Win Sch of Miss 19. **d** 21. NSM Ringwood w Ellingham and Harbridge etc *Win* from 21. *1 Hoburne Gardens, Christchurch BH23 4PP* T: (01425) 271216 M: 07598-988875 E: sandradm@aol.com

MATTHEWS, Simon David. b 64. Nottm Univ BA 91 Univ Coll Lon MPhil 93 Univ of Wales (Lamp) CertHE 10. Qu Foundn Birm MA 16. **d** 15 **p** 16. C Wistow *Leic* from 15. *4 Ensbury Gardens, Leicester LE5 6FB* T: 0116-243 2255 M: 07763-974419 E: simondmatthews@btinternet.com

MATTHEWS, Canon Stuart James. b 37. St Jo Coll Dur BA 60. Bps' Coll Cheshunt 60. **d** 62 **p** 63. C Horsham *Chich* 62–65; C Rednal *Birm* 65–67; Min Brandwood St Bede CD 67–68; C Northfield 68–73; V Thurcroft *Sheff* 73–82; RD Laughton 79–82; R Sprotbrough 82–00; RD Adwick 84–89; Hon Can Sheff Cathl 92–00; rtd 00; PtO *Sheff* from 00. *43 Dinnington Road, Woodsetts, Worksop S81 8RL* T: (01909) 560160

MATTHEWS, Timothy John. b 73. Univ of Wales (Cardiff) BScEcon 97 PhD 00 ACA 03. Wycliffe Hall Ox 06. **d** 08 **p** 09. C Brompton H Trin w Onslow Square St Paul *Lon* 08–11; C Onslow Square and S Kensington St Aug 11–14; C Bournemouth Town Cen *Win* 14–17; P-in-c Bournemouth St Clem from 17. *St Swithuns, 1 Gervis Road, Bournemouth BH1 3ED* T: (01202) 241077

MATTHEWS, William. *See* MATTHEWS, Lewis William

MATTHEWS, William John Joseph. b 48. **d** 08 **p** 08. NSM Lee-on-the-Solent *Portsm* 08–10; TV St Helens Town Cen *Liv* 11–15; TV Wigan All SS 15–16; TR 16–18; rtd 18; PtO *Liv* from 18. *Belmont, 20 Kingsway, Waterloo, Liverpool L22 4RQ* T: 0151-281 4879 E: revbillmatthews@outlook.com

MATTHEWS-LOYDALL, Mrs Elaine. b 63. Bp Otter Coll BA 85. St Jo Coll Nottm LTh 89. **d** 90 **p** 94. Par Dn Nottingham All SS *S'well* 90–94; C 94–95; Asst Chapl to the Deaf 91–93; Chapl to the Deaf 93–99; Chapl for Deaf People *Leic* 99–10; TV Leic H Spirit 99–10. *Lower Waterhead Farm, Lesmahagow, Lanark ML11 0HP*

MATTHIAE, Canon David. b 40. Fitzw Ho Cam BA 63 MA 69. Linc Th Coll 63. **d** 65 **p** 66. C New Addington *Cant* 65–70; C Charlton-by-Dover SS Pet and Paul 70–72; C Charlton-in-Dover 72–75; V Cant All SS 75–84; P-in-c Tunstall 84–87; R Tunstall w Rodmersham 87–05; RD Sittingbourne 88–94; Hon Can Cant Cathl 99–05; rtd 05; PtO *Ely* 06–16 and from 17. *7 Bustlers Rise, Duxford, Cambridge CB22 4QU* T: (01223) 835471 M: 07719-716240 E: david@matthiae.demon.co.uk

MATTHIAS, Canon John Rex. b 61. St Mich Coll Llan. **d** 94 **p** 95. C Llandrillo-yn-Rhos *St As* 94–98; R Llanfair Talhaearn and Llansannan etc 98–03; V Petryal 03–10; P-in-c Betws-yn-Rhos 03–10; Warden of Readers 09–10; P-in-c Newport St Julian *Mon* 10–12; V Mold *St As* 12–15; Can Prec St As Cathl from 15. *Cefn Coed, Upper Denbigh Road, St Asaph LL17 0RR* E: rexmatthias61@gmail.com

MATTHIAS, Paul. b 47. Philippa Fawcett Coll CertEd 75 Kent Univ DipEd 84. Cant Sch of Min 92. **d** 94 **p** 95. Head RE Hever Sch Maidstone 80–94; Chapl Ch Ch High Sch Ashford 94–07; NSM Gillingham St Aug *Roch* 94–10; P-in-c New Brompton St Luke 10–17; rtd 17; PtO *Roch* from

18; *Cant* from 18. *9 Pembroke Gardens, Rainham, Gillingham ME8 8TD* T: (01634) 267134 E: p.matthias@sky.com

MATTOCK, Colin Graham. b 38. Chich Th Coll. **d** 84 **p** 85. C Hove All SS *Chich* 84–87; C Bexhill St Pet 87–90; V Henlow St Alb 90–96; V Linslade *Ox* 96–00; P-in-c Pebworth w Dorsington and Honeybourne *Glouc* 00–02; R Pebworth, Dorsington, Honeybourne etc 02–10; AD Campden 06–10; rtd 10; PtO *Glouc* from 17. *14 Mullings Court, Cirencester GL7 2AW* T: (01285) 653828 E: colin.mattock@btinternet.com

MATTOCKS, Mrs Margaret Muriel. b 61. **d** 06 **p** 07. C Tettenhall Regis *Lich* 06–09; V Burntwood 09–15; P-in-c Hammerwich 13–15; TR Burntwood, Chase Terrace etc 15–18; RD Lich 14–18; V Codsall from 18. *The Vicarage, 48 Church Road, Codsall, Wolverhampton WV8 1EH*

MATUMONA, Guy Diakiese. *See* DIAKIESE, Guy Matumona

MAUCHAN, Andrew. b 44. Hertf Coll Ox BA 65 MA 69 Man Univ CertEd 66 Huddersfield Univ MA 10. Oak Hill Th Coll 88. **d** 90 **p** 91. C Bridlington Priory *York* 90–94; V Alverthorpe *Wakef* 94–01; R Wombwell *Sheff* 01–07; rtd 07; PtO *Leeds* from 17. *Hollins Barn, Top o' the Hill, Slaithwaite, Huddersfield HD7 5UA* T: (01484) 846371 E: andrew.mauchan@yahoo.co.uk

MAUDE, Gillian Hamer. b 53. St Anne's Coll Ox BA 75 MA 79 Edin Univ MSc 77. St Steph Ho Ox 99. **d** 01 **p** 02. C Hackney Wick St Mary of Eton w St Aug *Lon* 01–05; P-in-c Goodrington *Ex* 05–06; V 06–14; V Goodrington and Collaton St Mary 14–15; RD Torbay 09–13; P-in-c Jarrow *Dur* 15–18; R Jarrow and Simonside 18–19; rtd 19; PtO *Newc* from 20. *44 Swansfield Park Road, Alnwick NE66 1AR* M: 07527-169016 E: revgilly.pilgrim@gmail.com

MAUDLIN, David. b 39. EAMTC 92. **d** 95 **p** 96. NSM Bury St Edmunds St Jo *St E* 95–97; NSM Haverhill w Withersfield 97–98; P-in-c The Sampfords and Radwinter w Hempstead *Chelmsf* 98–04; RD Saffron Walden 00–04; rtd 04; PtO *Leic* 04–13; P-in-c Leic St Mary 13–20; PtO *Pet* from 04; *Eur* 04–20. *3 Goldfinch Road, Uppingham LE15 9UJ* T: (01572) 820181 E: dmaudlin@btinternet.com

MAUDSLEY, Canon George Lambert. b 27. St Jo Coll Nottm 74. **d** 75 **p** 76. C Binley *Cov* 75–77; Chapl Barn Fellowship Winterborne Whitechurch 77–83; V Salford Priors *Cov* 83–94; RD Alcester 87–92; Hon Can Cov Cathl 91–94; rtd 94; PtO *Cov* from 94. *12 Moorlands Lodge, Moorlands Avenue, Kenilworth CV8 1RT* T: (01926) 512206 E: lambert.maudsley@yahoo.co.uk

MAUDSLEY, Keith. b 51. York Univ BA 72. Ripon Hall Ox 72. **d** 75 **p** 76. C Rugby St Andr *Cov* 75–79; C Cambridge Gt St Mary w St Mich *Ely* 79–82; Chapl Girton Coll 79–82; P-in-c Binley *Cov* 82–89; RD Cov E 87–89; P-in-c Leek Wootton 89–91; Dioc Policy Development Adv 89–91; Dioc Adv on UPA *Liv* 91–97; Soc Resp Officer 91–97; R Lymm *Ches* 97–17; rtd 17; PtO *Ches* from 17. *21 Sandy Lane, Lymm WA13 9HJ* T: (01925) 759178 E: keith.maudsley@gmail.com

MAUDSLEY, Canon Michael Peter. b 38. St Andr Univ BSc 61. Oak Hill Th Coll 65. **d** 67 **p** 68. C Blackpool St Mark *Blackb* 67–70; C Hartford *Ches* 70–72; R Balerno *Edin* 72–82; V Stapenhill w Cauldwell *Derby* 82–91; Assoc R Edin St Paul and St Geo 91–95; C 00–03; R 95–00; rtd 03. *44 Buckstone Loan, Edinburgh EH10 6UG*

MAUDSLEY, Philip. b 73. St Martin's Coll Lanc BA(QTS) 96. St Jo Coll Nottm 13. **d** 15 **p** 16. C Fulwood Ch Ch *Blackb* 15–19; P-in-c Moston St Chad *Man* 19–21; P-in-c Moston St Mary 19–21; V Banstead *Guildf* from 21. *Address temp unknown* E: philmaudsley7@gmail.com

MAUDSLEY, Richard Leonard. b 55. Trent Park Coll of Educn BEd 76. NTMTC 04. **d** 07 **p** 08. NSM Clay Hill St Jo and St Luke *Lon* 07–09; NSM Silverton, Butterleigh, Bickleigh and Cadeleigh *Ex* 09–17; C Tiverton St Andr from 17. *The Parish Rooms, Bickleigh, Tiverton EX16 8RF* T: (01884) 855705 E: rlmaudsley@icloud.com

MAUGHAN, Angela. b 54. Newc Univ BA 93. NEOC 94. **d** 97 **p** 98. C Willington *Newc* 97–01; V Weetslade from 01. *Weetslade Vicarage, 59 Kirklands, Burradon, Cramlington NE23 7LE* T: 0191-268 9366 E: angmaughan@aol.com

MAUGHAN, Canon Geoffrey Nigel. b 48. CCC Cam BA 69 MA 73 Wycliffe Hall Ox MA 98. Oak Hill Th Coll 75. **d** 77 **p** 78. C New Malden and Coombe *S'wark* 77–81; C Abingdon w Shippon *Ox* 81–89; TV Abingdon 89–98; Dir of Min and Chapl Wycliffe Hall Ox 98–07; V Cumnor *Ox* 07–16; Hon Can Ch Ch 15–16; rtd 16; PtO *Ox* from 16. *1 The Old Workshop, North Green, West Hanney, Wantage OX12 0LU* T: (01235) 869160 E: geoff.maughan@btinternet.com

MAUND, Mrs Margaret Jennifer. b 42. RGN 64 RM 65. Llan Dioc Tr Scheme 89. **d** 94 **p** 97. NSM Cymmer and Porth *Llan* 94–97; NSM Pwllgwaun w Llanddewi Rhondda 97–04. *27 Mill Street, Tonyrefail, Porth CF39 8AB* T: (01443) 670085

MAUNDER, Alan John. b 52. UWIST BSc 74. Oak Hill Th Coll 88. d 90 p 91. C Birkenhead Ch Ch *Ches* 90–95; P-in-c Poulton 95–05; V Cwmaman *St D* 05–16; rtd 16; PtO *St D* 16–17; *Mon* from 17. *2 Newgale Row, Cwmbran NP44 3QJ* T: (01269) 822426 E: aljomau@tiscali.co.uk

MAUNDER, Miss Vicky Alexandra. b 73. Leeds Univ BA 95. Ripon Coll Cuddesdon BA 01. d 02 p 03. C Swaythling *Win* 02–05; C Pimlico St Pet w Westmr Ch Ch *Lon* 05–07; TV Kingston All SS w St Jo *S'wark* 07–12; TV Kingston 12–19; V W End *Win* from 19. *The Vicarage, Elizabeth Close, West End, Southampton SO30 3LT* M: 07762-673350 E: stjameswe.vicar@gmail.com

MAURICE, David Pierce. b 50. Pemb Coll Cam BA 72 MA 76 BChir 76. Dioc OLM tr scheme. d 01 p 02. OLM Marlborough *Sarum* 01–20; rtd 20. *Isbury House, Kingsbury Street, Marlborough SN8 1JA* T: (01672) 514119 E: david_maurice2000@yahoo.com

✠**MAURICE, The Rt Revd Peter David.** b 51. St Chad's Coll Dur BA 72. Coll of Resurr Mirfield. d 75 p 76 c 06. C Wandsworth St Paul *S'wark* 75–79; TV Mortlake w E Sheen 79–85; V Rotherhithe H Trin 85–96; RD Bermondsey 91–96; V Tooting All SS 96–03; Adn Wells, Can Res and Preb Wells Cathl *B & W* 03–06; Suff Bp Taunton 06–15; rtd 15; PtO *Cant* 16–19. *14 Saltwood Road, Maidstone ME15 6UY* E: pmaurice51@hotmail.co.uk

MAURITZ, Willem Jacobus. b 72. Fontys Univ Netherlands BA 98 Stoas Univ BSc 00 Surrey Univ MSc 04. St Mellitus Coll BA 14. d 14 p 15. C Tunbridge Wells St Jas *Roch* 14–18; V Copthorne *Chich* from 18. *Copthorne Vicarage, Church Road, Copthorne, Crawley RH10 3RD* M: 07799-076690 E: wim.mauritz@gmail.com or vicar.copthorne@gmail.com

MAW, Mrs Jacqueline. b 59. Wycliffe Hall Ox 04. d 06 p 07. C Iwerne Valley *Sarum* 06–10; TV Wareham 10–16; C Aldershot H Trin *Guildf* 16–21; TR W Wight *Portsm* from 21. *Shalfleet Vicarage, 4 Manor Green, Shalfleet, Newport PO30 4QT* M: 07747-561375 E: mawdiva@gmail.com

MAWBEY, Diane. *See* COUTURE, Diane

MAWDESLEY, Mrs Joy Maria. b 67. Keele Univ BA 90 CQSW 90. Ripon Coll Cuddesdon 14. d 16 p 17. C Newbury St Nic and Speen *Ox* from 16. *14 Strawberry Hill, Newbury RG14 1XJ* M: 07786-106636 E: joymawdesley@macace.net or joy@st-nics.org

MAWDITT, Stephen Donald Harvey. b 56. d 96 p 97. OLM Ashill w Saham Toney *Nor* 96–05; OLM Watton w Carbrooke and Ovington 00–05; Min Ashill Fountain of Life 05–17; Sen Min 17–19; rtd 19; PtO *Nor* from 20. *43 Cressingham Road, Ashill, Thetford IP25 7DG* T: (01760) 440363 E: themawditts@tiscali.co.uk *or* s.mawditt@folchurch.co.uk

MAWHINNEY, Alan Mark. b 67. Dur Univ BA 90 MA 00. St Steph Ho Ox 15. d 17 p 18. C Seaham and Dawdon *Dur* 17–20; P-in-c S Shields St Hilda w St Thos from 20; P-in-c S Westoe from 20. *40 Lawe Road, South Shields NE33 2EU* E: fathermarkmawhinney@gmail.com

MAWHINNEY, Mrs Stephanie. b 69. Magd Coll Ox BA 90. St Mellitus Coll 19. d 21. C Hillock and Unsworth *Man* from 21. *146A Markland Hill Lane, Bolton BL1 5NZ* T: (01204) 840823 M: 07722-799872 E: stephmawhinney@gmail.com

MAWSON, Canon Arthur Cyril. b 35. St Pet Coll Ox BA 56 MA 61. Wycliffe Hall Ox 61. d 62 p 63. C Walsall *Lich* 62–66; V Millhouses H Trin *Sheff* 66–73; Selection Sec ACCM 73–79; Can Res and Treas Ex Cathl 79–98; Dioc Dir of Ords 81–87; rtd 99; PtO *Ox* from 08. *4 Woodlands Close, Headington, Oxford OX3 7RY* T: (01865) 764099 E: pandamaw@outlook.com

MAWSON, David Frank. b 44. Selw Coll Cam BA 65 MA 69. Linc Th Coll 79. d 80 p 81. C Tunstall *Lich* 80–83; C Blakenall Heath 83–84; TV 84–90; Chapl Goscote Hosp Walsall 87–90; V Pelsall *Lich* 90–94; V Tividale 94–99; V Shrewsbury All SS w St Mich 99–07; rtd 07; PtO *Lich* 07–11.

MAXFIELD-COOTE, Ms Olivia Constance. b 86. Kent Univ BA 09 Univ Coll Lon MA 10 Jes Coll Cam BTh 14. Westcott Ho Cam 12. d 15 p 16. C Black Notley *Chelmsf* from 15; C Black Notley, Gt Notley and Rayne 15–18; TV Epping Distr from 18. *9 Seymour Chase, Epping CM16 6FE* M: 07939-297048 E: o.maxfieldcoote@gmail.com

MAXIM, Claire Margaret Astrid. b 68. Birm Univ BEng 90 Reading Univ MBA 03 Warwick Univ EdD 21 MIET 95. Qu Coll Birm 07. d 10 p 11. C Ampfield, Chilworth and N Baddesley *Win* 10–14; V Ludgershall and Faberstown *Sarum* 14–18; Chief Exec Officer Arthur Rank Cen from 18. *Arthur Rank Centre, Rural Innovation Centre, Avenue H, Stoneleigh Park, Kenilworth CV8 2LG* T: (024) 7685 3060 *or* (01926) 817044 E: clairemaxim@btinternet.com

MAXTED, Neil Andrew. b 58. Aston Tr Scheme 88 Sarum & Wells Th Coll 90. d 92 p 93. C Folkestone St Sav *Cant* 92–96; CF 96–05; P-in-c Frome Ch Ch *B & W* 05–15; V Frome St Mary 11–15; V Frome Ch Ch w St Mary 15–18; rtd 19. *30 Mendip Vale, Coleford, Radstock BA3 5PP*

MAXWELL, Christopher John Moore (Bill). b 31. Qu Coll Cam MA 75 MRCS 59 LRCP 59. Trin Coll Bris 74. d 75 p 76. SAMS Chile 75–81; Hon C Homerton St Luke *Lon* 81–94; Chapl Ibiza *Eur* 94–99; rtd 99; PtO *Chich* 99–08; *Win* from 08. *Willowbank, Sycamore Close, Milford on Sea, Lymington SO41 0RY* T: (01590) 643110 E: abmaxwell@btinternet.com

MAXWELL, Marcus Howard. b 54. Liv Univ BSc 76 Man Univ MPhil 89. St Jo Coll Nottm BA 79. d 80 p 81. C Chadderton St Matt *Man* 80–84; V Bircle 84–93; P-in-c Heaton Mersey 93–02; TR Heatons 02–19; AD Heaton 98–04 and 13–18; rtd 20; PtO *Ches* from 20. *45 Radnor Drive, Wallasey CH45 7PS* T: 0151-936 9863 E: mhmaxwell18@gmail.com

MAY, Adrian. b 70. LSE BSc 94. Wycliffe Hall Ox 09. d 12 p 13. NSM Notting Hill St Pet *Lon* from 12. *15 Highlever Road, London W10 6PP* E: adrian@stpetersnottinghill.org.uk

MAY, Charles Henry. b 29. LTh 58. d 58 p 59. C Bethnal Green St Jas Less *Lon* 58–61; C Woking St Pet *Guildf* 61–64; Area Sec (W Midl) CPAS 64–67; V Homerton St Luke *Lon* 67–80; Home Sec SAMS 80–84; V Fulham Ch Ch *Lon* 84–94; rtd 94; PtO *Ely* 94–19; *Pet* from 94; *Linc* 95–15. *16 Kilverstone, Werrington, Peterborough PE4 5DX* T: (01733) 328108 E: clergy.c.may@gmail.com

MAY, Mrs Deborah Kim. b 60. Trin Coll Bris. d 01 p 02. C Haughley w Wetherden and Stowupland *St E* 01–04; R Ashwater, Halwill, Beaworthy, Clawton etc *Ex* 04–08; R Melville Australia from 08. *56 McLean Street, Melville WA 6156, Australia* T: (0061) (8) 9330 1550 F: 9317 4378 M: 41-817 8688 E: revd.debbie@gmail.com

MAY, Janet Isabel. b 51. Lon Univ CertEd 72. d 00 p 01. OLM Gt and Lt Ellingham, Rockland and Shropham etc *Nor* 00–05; PtO from 05. *The Mill House, 4 Church Street, Great Ellingham, Attleborough NR17 1LE* T: (01953) 452198 E: rev.may@btopenworld.com

MAY, Mrs Janet Margaret. b 69. SWMTC 15. d 18 p 19. C Burrington, Chawleigh, Cheldon, Chulmleigh etc *Ex* from 18. *The Rectory, Chawleigh, Chulmleigh EX18 7HJ* T: (01769) 580791 M: 07792-821143 E: janetmay69@gmail.com

MAY, Preb John Alexander Cyril. b 52. K Coll Lon BD 77 PhD 98 Ch Ch Ox PGCE 78. Linc Th Coll 79. d 80 p 81. C Tynemouth Ch Ch *Newc* 80–82; C Tynemouth Ch Ch w H Trin 82–85; C Tynemouth St Aug 82–85; TV Glendale Gp 85–90; V Wotton-under-Edge w Ozleworth, N Nibley etc *Glouc* 90–07; P-in-c St Endellion w Port Isaac and St Kew *Truro* 07–12; P-in-c St Minver 07–12; R N Cornwall Cluster 12–14; Preb St Endellion 07–14; rtd 14. *The Lawns, 31 St Peter Street, Tiverton EX16 6NW* T: (01208) 881041 E: johnmay187@hotmail.com

MAY, Peter Richard. b 43. St Jo Coll Cam BA 64 MA 68 MICE 70. Trin Coll Bris 77. d 79 p 80. C Lancaster St Thos *Blackb* 79–85; V Darwen St Barn 85–91; Chapl Lyon w Grenoble *Eur* 91–92; Chapl Lyon 92–94; PtO *S'wark* 94–95; TR Horley 95–02; rtd 03; PtO *Chich* 04–11. *North Lodge, Exminster, Exeter EX6 8AT* T: (01392) 823047 E: openhearts.2@btinternet.com

MAY, Roger Austin. b 45. SWMTC 07. d 10 p 11. NSM Bodmin w Lanhydrock and Lanivet *Truro* 10–15; rtd 15; PtO *Truro* from 15. *12 Hanson Road, Liskeard PL14 3NT* T: (01579) 342924 M: 07779-349257 E: rev_bluejeans@me.com

MAY, Preb Simon George. b 47. Ex Univ BA 69 Univ of Wales (Ban) CertEd 72 FCA 77. Sarum & Wells Th Coll 86. d 88 p 89. C Tamworth *Lich* 88–92; V Whitchurch *Ex* 92–07; Warden of Readers (Plymouth Adnry) 00–07; RD Tavistock 02–07; C Barnstaple 07–17; Preb Ex Cathl 09–17; rtd 17; P-in-c Upton *Ex* 17–18; PtO from 20. *10 Rogers Close, Tiverton EX16 6UW* T: (01884) 259470 E: simon@sgmay.me.uk

MAY, Toby Sebastian. b 67. Bris Univ BEng 89. St Jo Coll Nottm MTh 02. d 02 p 03. C Kendal St Thos *Carl* 02–06; V Alsager Ch Ch *Ches* 06–18; V Whitfield *Derby* from 18. *16 Scotty Brook Crescent, Glossop SK13 8UG* E: toby@mays-in-grace.co.uk

MAYBEE, Christine. *See* DALE, Christine

MAYBURY, Canon John Montague. b 30. G&C Coll Cam BA 53 MA 57. Ridley Hall Cam 53. d 55 p 56. C Allerton *Liv* 55–59; C Rowner *Portsm* 59–62; V Wroxall 62–67; V Southsea St Simon 67–78; V Crofton 78–91; Hon Can Portsm Cathl 81–95; C Locks Heath 91–95; rtd 95; PtO *Portsm* from 95. *19 Netley Road, Titchfield Common, Fareham PO14 4PE* T: (01489) 584168 E: jandbmaybury@talktalk.net

MAYBURY, Canon Paul Dorian. b 58. Trin Coll Bris 93. d 95 p 96. C Spondon *Derby* 95–99; V Gawthorpe and Chickenley Heath *Wakef* 99–02; P-in-c Ossett cum Gawthorpe 01–02; V Ossett and Gawthorpe 02–13; RD Dewsbury 08–13; Hon Can Wakef Cathl 13; Spirituality Co-ord and Bp's Missr SE Cyprus 13–16; Can Res Bradf Cathl *Leeds* from 16. *3*

Cathedral Close, Bradford BD1 4EG T: (01274) 777720 E: pauldmaybury@gmail.com

MAYCOCK, Ms Jane Ellen. b 66. Somerville Coll Ox BA 90 MA 95 Glas Univ MPhil 98. Cranmer Hall Dur 90. **d** 92 **p** 94. Par Dn Harrow Trin St Mich *Lon* 92–94; C 94–95; C Kendal H Trin *Carl* 95–99; Dir of Ords 01–07. *The Rectory, Longlands Road, Bowness-on-Windermere, Windermere LA23 3AS* T: (015394) 43063 E: j.e.maycock@btinternet.com

MAYELL, Howard John. b 50. Bris Sch of Min 81. **d** 84 **p** 88. NSM Patchway *Bris* 84–86; NSM Weston-super-Mare Cen Par *B & W* 87–88; C N Stoneham *Win* 88–91; P-in-c Black Torrington, Bradford w Cookbury etc *Ex* 91–97; C Ledbury w Eastnor *Heref* 97–98; TV Ledbury 98–17; V Cider Churches 17–18; rtd 18. *2 Shepherds Close, Ledbury HR8 2XF* T: (01531) 631530

MAYER, Alan John. b 46. AKC 70. St Aug Coll Cant 70. **d** 71 **p** 72. C Stanningley St Thos *Ripon* 71–74; C St Helier *S'wark* 74–79; TV Wimbledon 79–85; V Reigate St Luke S Park 85–00; R Oxted and Tandridge 00–11; rtd 11; PtO *S'wark* 11–14. *17 Saxon Crescent, Horsham RH12 2HX* E: aandkmayer@gmail.com

MAYER, Graham Keith. b 46. St Cath Coll Ox BA 68 Nottm Univ PGCE 69 Ex Univ MA 93. Linc Th Coll 78. **d** 80 **p** 81. C Paignton St Jo, St Andr and St Boniface *Ex* 80–93; PtO 93–96; P-in-c Christow, Ashton and Bridford 96–10; P-in-c Dunchideock 97–10; V Christow, Ashton, Bridford, Dunchideock etc 10–18; RD Kenn 05–10; P-in-c Colbury *Win* from 18. *The Vicarage, Deerleap Lane, Totton, Southampton SO40 7EH* E: teignway@gmail.com *or* grahammayer46@yahoo.com

MAYER-JONES, Miss Fiona Ruth. b 70. Westcott Ho Cam 08. **d** 10 **p** 11. C Beverley Minster *York* 10–14; V Northallerton w Kirby Sigston from 14; RD Mowbray from 17. *27 Mowbray Road, Northallerton DL6 1QT* E: revdfmj@gmail.com

MAYES, Miss Alexier Olwen. St Mich Coll Llan 08. **d** 11 **p** 12. C Bistre *St As* 11–14; V Kerry, Llanmerewig, Dolfor and Mochdre 14–16; TV Cedewain Miss Area 17–18; P-in-c Borderlands Miss Area from 18. *The New Vicarage, Mold Road, Connah's Quay, Deeside CH5 4QL* E: rev.alex@btinternet.com

MAYES, Canon Andrew Dennis. b 56. K Coll Lon BD 79 AKC 79 Man Univ MA 97 Univ of Wales DMin 07. Armenian Orthodox Sem Jerusalem 79 St Steph Ho Ox 80. **d** 81 **p** 82. C Hendon St Alphage *Lon* 81–84; C Hockley *Chelmsf* 84–87; V Kingstanding St Mark *Birm* 87–92; V Saltdean *Chich* 92–01; P-in-c Ovingdean 01–09; CME Officer 01–09; Course Dir St Geo Coll and C St Geo Cathl Jerusalem 09–11; R E Blatchington and Bishopstone *Chich* 11–16; Chapl Limassol St Barn Cyprus 18–20; PtO *Heref* from 20; Hon Can Niger Delta from 96. *Vine Cottage, 20A Etnam Street, Leominster HR6 8AQ* E: andrew.mayes@gmail.com

MAYES, Aonghus William Alun. **d** 05 **p** 06. C Cregagh *D & D* 05–10; I Moy w Charlemont *Arm* from 10; Dioc Communications Officer 10–11. *The Rectory, 37 The Square, Moy, Dungannon BT71 7SG* T: (028) 8778 4312 M: 07748-710148 E: aonghusmayes@yahoo.ie

✠**MAYES, The Rt Revd Michael Hugh Gunton.** b 41. TCD BA 62 Lon Univ BD 85. TCD Div Sch Div Test 64. **d** 64 **p** 65 **c** 93. C Portadown St Columba *Arm* 64–68; USPG Kobe Japan 68–69; Tokyo 69–70; Yokkaichi 70–74; Area Sec USPG C & O, C, C & R, L & K and T, K & A 75–93; I Cork St Mich Union *C, C & R* 75–86; Adn Cork, Cloyne and Ross 86–93; I Moviddy Union 86–88; I Rathcooney Union 88–93; Bp K, E & A 93–00; Can Elphin Cathl 93–00; Bp L & K 00–08; rtd 08. *5 Rockfield Crescent, Church Road, Blackrock, Cork, T12 R9X3, Republic of Ireland* T: (00353) (21) 496 7688 E: mhg.mayes@gmail.com

MAYES, Canon Stephen Thomas. b 47. St Jo Coll Nottm 67. **d** 71 **p** 72. C Cullompton *Ex* 71–75; C Cheltenham St Mark *Glouc* 76–84; P-in-c Water Orton *Birm* 84–91; V 91–12; AD Coleshill 99–05; Hon Can Birm Cathl 05–12; rtd 12; P-in-c Barston *Birm* 12–14; PtO from 14; Cov from 18; *Lich* from 19. *47 Yew Tree Lane, Solihull B91 2NX* T: 0121-704 1356 E: stmayes@yahoo.co.uk

✠**MAYFIELD, The Rt Revd Christopher John.** b 35. G&C Coll Cam BA 57 MA 61 Cranfield Inst of Tech MSc 83. Wycliffe Hall Ox 61. **d** 63 **p** 64 **c** 85. C Birm St Martin 63–67; Lect 67–71; V Luton St Mary *St Alb* 71–80; RD Luton 74–80; Adn Bedford 80–85; Suff Bp Wolverhampton *Lich* 85–92; Area Bp Wolverhampton 92–93; Bp Man 93–02; rtd 02; Hon Asst Bp Worc from 02. *23 Petunia Close, Worcester WR5 3RT* T: (01905) 764822 E: christophermayfield54@gmail.com

MAYFIELD, Timothy James Edward. b 60. LMH Ox BA 82. Trin Coll Bris BA 88. **d** 88 **p** 89. C Ovenden *Wakef* 88–92; V Mount Pellon 92–03; V Cheltenham Ch Ch *Glouc* 03–19; V Earsdon and Backworth *Newc* from 19; AD Tynemouth

from 19. *The Vicarage, 5 Front Street, Earsdon, Whitley Bay NE25 9JU* T: 0191-252 9393

MAYHEW, The Hon David Francis. b 51. Ch Ch Ox BA 72 MA 76 Wycliffe Hall Ox BA 75. NEOC 89. **d** 91 **p** 92. NSM High Elswick St Paul *Newc* 91–94; Toc H 91–94; V Mitford *Newc* 94–09; C Longhorsley and Hebron 07–09; Chapl Northgate and Prudhoe NHS Trust 94–09; V Cov H Trin 09–16; rtd 16; PtO *Cov* 18–21. *119 Cannon Hill Road, Coventry CV4 7DF* M: 07720-964586 E: davidfmayhew@gmail.com

MAYHEW (née GURNEY), Jean Elizabeth. b 39. OBE 97. New Hall Cam BA 61 MA 85 K Coll Lon BD 84 AKC 84 PGCE 85 Ulster Univ Hon DUniv 98 FKC 00. SEITE 02. **d** 05 **p** 06. NSM Maidstone St Paul *Cant* 05–10; PtO from 11. *Pump Hill, Kilndown, Cranbrook TN17 2SG* T: (01580) 211820 F: 212232 M: 07773-404554 E: jean@jmayhew.free-online.co.uk *or* mayhew.jean@gmail.com

MAYLAND, Mrs Jean Mary. b 36. JP 77. LMH Ox BA 58 MA 61 TCert 60. St Deiniol's Hawarden 91. **d** 91 **p** 94. NSM York Minster 91–93; Lect and Tutor NOC 91–93; Lect NEOC 93–96; Dioc Ecum Officer *Dur* 93–96; Local Unity Officer Dur Ecum Relns Gp 93–96; Assoc Sec CCBI 96–99; Co-ord Sec for Ch Life CTBI 99–03; Asst Gen Sec 99–03; PtO *Lon* 97–03; *S'wark* 97–00; *Chelmsf* 00–03; rtd 03; PtO *York* 03–09; *Newc* from 04. *Carntyne Residential Home, Battle Hill, Hexham NE46 2EB* T: (01434) 600195 E: jeanmayland@btinternet.com

MAYLES, Helena Rosemary Laura. *See* ROULSTON, Helena Rosemary Laura

MAYLOR, David Charles. b 59. Lanc Univ BSc 80 Edge Hill Coll of HE PGCE 81. St Jo Coll Nottm 89. **d** 91 **p** 92. C Hindley All SS *Liv* 91–94; P-in-c Spalding St Paul *Linc* 94–07; Chapl United Lincs Hosps NHS Trust 99–07; Lic Gen Preacher *Linc* 07–12; Music Dir Stamford St Geo w St Paul 07–12; P-in-c Barnack w Ufford and Bainton *Pet* 12–16; V Barnack w Ufford, Bainton, Helpston and Wittering 16–20; rtd 20. *Address temp unknown* E: dmaylor@btinternet.com

MAYNARD, Adam Richard. b 86. Cranmer Hall Dur 12. **d** 15 **p** 16. C Liv Ch Ch Norris Green 15–18; V Everton St Geo from 18. *St George's Vicarage, 40 Northumberland Terrace, Liverpool L5 3QG* T: 0151-263 6005 E: rev.adam.maynard@gmail.com *or* vicar@stgeorgeseverton.com

MAYNARD, Benjamin Luke. b 82. Moorlands Bible Coll BA 15 Trin Coll Bris MA 20. **d** 20. C Newton Abbot *Ex* from 20. *St Bartholomew's House, 1 St Bartholomew Way, Ogwell, Newton Abbot TQ12 6YW* M: 07908-309091 E: benlukemaynard@gmail.com *or* ben@newtonabbotparishes.co.uk

MAYNARD, Gay Caroline. b 50. Sarum Coll 13. **d** 16 **p** 17. C Warminster St Denys and Upton Scudamore *Sarum* 16–17; C River Were 17–19; C Cley Hill Villages from 19. *Stone Cottage, 32 Huntenhull Green, Corsley, Warminster BA12 7QB* T: (01373) 832490 M: 07809-245516 E: revgmaynard@gmail.com

MAYNARD, John William. b 37. Lon Univ BSc 58. Ripon Hall Ox 60. **d** 62 **p** 63. C St Laur in Thanet *Cant* 62–67; C S Ashford Ch Ch 67–70; V Pagham *Chich* 70–00; rtd 00. *2 West Checkstone, 2 Douglas Avenue, Exmouth EX8 2AU* T: (01395) 222675

MAYNARD, Jonathan Mark (Josh). b 80. Ex Univ BA 02. Trin Coll Bris BA 09. **d** 10 **p** 11. C Woodchester and Brimscombe *Glouc* 10–15; V Styvechale *Cov* from 15. *Styvechale Vicarage, 16 Armorial Road, Coventry CV3 6GJ* T: (024) 7641 6074 M: 07825-795257 E: jmaynard1044@googlemail.com

MAYNARD, Joshua Phillip. b 88. St Mich Coll Llan BTh 14. **d** 14 **p** 15. C Hubberston and Herbrandston *St D* 14–17; TV Monkton 17–20; P-in-c S W Pembrokeshire from 20. *The Vicarage, 13 Reginald Close, Hundleton, Pembroke SA71 5RZ* M: 07849-991706 E: revjoshmaynard@gmail.com

MAYNARD, Canon Richard Edward Buller. b 42. AKC 66. **d** 67 **p** 68. C St Ives *Truro* 67–71; C Falmouth K Chas 71–74; V St Germans 74–85; RD E Wivelshire 81–85; TR Saltash 85–08; Hon Can Truro Cathl 82–08; Chapl St Barn Hosp Saltash 90–93; Chapl Cornwall Healthcare NHS Trust 93–02; Chapl N and E Cornwall Primary Care Trust 02–06; Chapl Cornwall and Is of Scilly Primary Care Trust 06–08; rtd 08; C Altarnon w Bolventor, Laneast and St Clether *Truro* 11–12; PtO from 15. *Harewood, Dunheved Road, Launceston PL15 9JJ* T: (01566) 779135 E: canonrichardmaynard@btinternet.com *or* rebmaynard@btinternet.com

MAYNE, Canon Brian John. b 52. Univ of Wales (Cardiff) BA 73 LTCL 75 MRICS 81. NEOC 82 Coll of Resurr Mirfield 84. **d** 85 **p** 86. C Stainton-in-Cleveland *York* 85–89; P-in-c Rounton w Welbury 89–96; Chapl HM YOI Northallerton 89–96; Chapl HM YOI Lanc Farms 96–10; Chapl HM Pris Kirkham 10–17;

Hon Can Blackb Cathl 09–17; rtd 17; PtO *Blackb* from 17. *Address withheld by request* E: b_mayne@btinternet.com

MAYNE, Fiona Elizabeth. b 72. Ripon Coll Cuddesdon 18. **d** 21. C Hutton and Locking *B & W* from 21. *13 Wayfarer Close, Weston-super-Mare BS24 8BL* M: 07788-419347 E: fionamayne@yahoo.co.uk

MAYO, Christopher Paul. b 68. Heythrop Coll Lon BD 91 Birm Univ PGCE 96. Qu Coll Birm 91. **d** 93 **p** 94. C Wednesfield *Lich* 93–94; C Bilston 94–95; Miss P E Sutherland *Mor* 10–17; P-in-c Tain 12–17; P-in-c Thurso 17–19; P-in-c Wick 17–19; P-in-c Brora 17–19; Dioc Miss Officer 17–19. *9 Academy Street, Brora KW9 6QP* T: (01408) 600818 M: 07860-333892 E: frchrismayo@gmail.com *or* chris.mayo@theauldkirk.org

MAYO, Deborah Ann. *See* MURPHY, Deborah Ann

MAYO, Inglis John. b 46. FCA. Ripon Hall Ox 74. **d** 77 **p** 78. C Bitterne Park *Win* 77–81; C Christchurch 81–86; P-in-c Sturminster Marshall *Sarum* 86–89; P-in-c Kingston Lacy and Shapwick 86–89; V Sturminster Marshall, Kingston Lacy and Shapwick 89–00; P-in-c Lilliput 00–06; V 06–08; rtd 08; PtO *Sarum* 08–18; *Win* from 08. *49B St Catherine's Road, Bournemouth BH6 4AQ* T: (01202) 424971 E: inglis.mayo@btinternet.com

MAYO, Robert William. b 61. Keble Coll Ox BA 83 Trin Coll Carmarthen PhD 00. Cranmer Hall Dur 85. **d** 87 **p** 88. C Luton Lewsey St Hugh *St Alb* 87–90; Hd Cam Univ Miss and NSM Bermondsey St Jas w Ch Ch *S'wark* 90–95; Chapl S Bank Univ 95–98; Dir Youth Work Tr Ridley Hall Cam 98–05; V Shepherd's Bush St Steph w St Thos *Lon* 05–19; Chapl HM YOI Roch 19–21; Chapl HM Pris Wormwood Scrubs from 21. *HM Prison Wormwood Scrubs, Du Cane Road, London W12 0TU* T: (020) 8588 3200 M: 07377-515558 E: bobmayo43@gmail.com

MAYO, Mrs Susan. b 53. Didsbury Coll Man BEd 78. St Jo Coll Nottm 08. **d** 10 **p** 11. NSM Edgeley and Cheadle Heath *Ches* 10–15; NSM Cheadle All Hallows 15–17; Chapl Stockport Academy 11–15; TV Penkridge *Lich* from 17. *3 Bitham Close, Penkridge, Stafford ST19 5HT* T: (01785) 715605 E: mayos32@btinternet.com

MAYO-LYTHALL, Ms Jennifer Elizabeth. b 83. St Jo Coll Dur BA 10. Cranmer Hall Dur 07. **d** 10 **p** 11. C Norbury *Ches* 10–14; Transforming Lives Together Development Officer 14–16; NSM Offerton St Alb and Stockport St Thos 14–17; V Walsall St Martin *Lich* from 17. *St Martin's House, 17 Daffodil Road, Walsall WS5 3DQ* T: (01922) 277695 *or* 635217 M: 07749-949830 E: jenny_m86@hotmail.com

MAYO-SMITH, Peter. b 49. Open Univ BA 80. Ridley Hall Cam 05. **d** 06 **p** 07. C Greengates *Bradf* 06–09; C Idle 06–09; C Cottingley 08–09; P-in-c Haworth 09–14; *Leeds* 14–15; R Haworth and Cross Roads cum Lees 15–17; P-in-c Cross Roads cum Lees *Bradf* 09–14; *Leeds* 14–15; P-in-c Oxenhope *Bradf* 10–13; C Bingley All SS *Leeds* 17–20; rtd 20. *11 Ffordd Porthdy, Rhuddlan, Rhyl LL18 6HZ* M: 07880-866222 E: peter@mayo-smith.net

MAYOR, Henry William. b 39. Oriel Coll Ox BA 62. Westcott Ho Cam 62. **d** 64 **p** 65. C The Quinton *Birm* 64–66; C Dudley St Thos and St Luke *Worc* 67–71; R Birch St Agnes *Man* 71–83; Community Chapl Aylesbury *Ox* 83–89; Community Chapl Aylesbury w Bierton and Hulcott 89; R Cheetham St Luke and Lower Crumpsall St Thos *Man* 89–96; R Cheetham and Lower Crumpsall 97–01; rtd 01; PtO *Man* from 01. *18 Sycamore Close, Heaton Road, Manchester M20 4PH* M: 07958-639967 E: henrywmayor@hotmail.com

MAYOR, Janet Hilary. *See* TAYLOR, Janet Hilary

MAYOSS, Anthony (Aidan). b 31. Leeds Univ BA 55. Coll of Resurr Mirfield 55. **d** 57 **p** 58. C Meir *Lich* 57–62; Lic to Offic *Wakef* 62–72 and 78–84; CR from 64; S Africa 73–75; Asst Chapl Lon Univ 76–78; Bursar CR 84–90; rtd 98; PtO *Lon* 98–07; LtO *Leeds* from 14. *House of the Resurrection, Stocks Bank Road, Mirfield WF14 0BN* T: (01924) 483330 E: amayoss@mirfield.org.uk

MAYOSS-HURD, Susan Patricia. b 59. Lanc Univ BA 81. Cranmer Hall Dur 82. **dss** 84 **d** 87 **p** 94. Ribbesford w Bewdley and Dowles *Worc* 84–88; Par Dn 87–88; Chapl W Heath Hosp 88–96; C W Heath *Birm* 88–96; V 96–03; V Peachland St Marg Canada 03–11. *108-5970 Princess Street, Peachland BC V0H 1X7, Canada* T: (001) (250) 767 9682 E: revsuemh@shaw.ca

MAZUR, Mrs Ann Carol. b 47. St Mich Coll Sarum CertEd 69. TISEC 01. **d** 04 **p** 05. NSM St Ninian's Cathl Perth *St And* 04–07; Prec 07–12; Chapl Craigclowan Sch Perth 04–07; rtd 12; PtO *Linc* 16–19. *Fairmead, Langton-by-Wragby, Market Rasen LN8 5PX* T: (01673) 857720 E: ann@mazur.org.uk

MBANUDE, Chidiebere. p 16. NSM Croydon St Andr *S'wark* from 16. *61A Church Street, Croydon CR0 1RH* M: 07448-478236 E: chychyltd@gmail.com

MDUMULLA, Jonas Habel. b 50. Nairobi Univ Hull Univ BTh 87 MA 89. St Phil Coll Kongwa. **d** 74 **p** 75. Tanzania 74–82; C Sutton St Jas and Wawne *York* 82–96; P-in-c Carlton and Drax 96–15; Ind Chapl 96–15; rtd 15; PtO *York* 16–20. *26 Riverside Court, Rawcliffe, Goole DN14 8TD* T: (01405) 839327 E: mdumulla@btinternet.com

MEAD, Arthur Hugh. b 39. K Coll Cam BA 60 MA 64 New Coll Ox BLitt 66. St Steph Ho Ox 61. **d** 80 **p** 80. NSM Hammersmith St Jo *Lon* 80–05; NSM Hammersmith H Innocents and St Jo 05–09; Chapl St Paul's Sch Barnes 82–97; Dep P in O 85–90 and 95–09; P in O 90–95; Reader of The Temple 95–15; PtO *Lon* from 18. *11 Dungarvan Avenue, London SW15 5QU* T: (020) 8876 5833

MEAD, Elveen. b 67. Trin Coll Bris 15. **d** 17 **p** 18. C Gauzebrook *Bris* 17–20; P-in-c Stratton St Margaret w S Marston etc from 20. *The Rectory, Kenwin Close, Swindon SN3 4NY* E: rev.elveen@gmail.com

MEAD, Mrs Lynda Roberta. b 44. Open Univ BA 91. STETS. **d** 99 **p** 00. NSM Hythe *Win* 99–04; PtO 04–09; NSM Boldre w S Baddesley 09–16; rtd 17; PtO *Win* from 17. *22 Furzedale Park, Hythe, Southampton SO45 3HW* T: (023) 8084 8901

MEAD, Nicholas Charles. b 50. Newc Univ BEd 73 Reading Univ MA 76 Middx Univ PhD 16 FRSA 10. Ridley Hall Cam 83. **d** 85 **p** 86. C Bilton *Cov* 85–88; C Whittlesey *Ely* 88–89; Hd RS Neale-Wade Community Coll March 89–97; Fell Farmington Inst for Chr Studies Ox from 95; Sen Lect RE Westmr Coll 97–00; Sen Lect RE Ox Brookes Univ 00–13; Assoc Lect from 12. *9 Yarnells Road, Oxford OX2 0JY* T: (01865) 240865 E: nmead@brookes.ac.uk

MEAD, Peter Tony. b 63. St Jo Coll Dur BA 08. Cranmer Hall Dur 06. **d** 08 **p** 09. C Yeovil H Trin w Barwick *B & W* 08–12; Chapl Yeovil Distr Hosp NHS Foundn Trust 08–10; R St Leonards St Ethelburga and St Leon *Chich* 12–16; R Arbroath *Bre* from 16; R Auchmithie from 16; Chapl NHS Tayside from 16. *St Mary's Rectory, 2 Springfield Terrace, Arbroath DD11 1EL* T: (01241) 873392 M: 07791-642598 E: pete.mead@sky.com

MEADER, Jennifer Lindsay. b 68. UEA BA 89. Westcott Ho Cam. **d** 01 **p** 02. C Teversham and Cherry Hinton St Andr *Ely* 01–05; C Westmr St Jas *Lon* 05–19; NSM Covent Garden St Paul from 19; Chapl W End Theatres from 19. *St Paul's Church, Bedford Street, London WC2E 9ED* M: 07501-829491 E: revlindsaym@gmail.com

MEADER, Philip John. b 44. Oak Hill Th Coll 73. **d** 75 **p** 76. C E Ham St Paul *Chelmsf* 75–77; CMJ 77–90; TV Lowestoft and Kirkley *Nor* 90–94; V Lowestoft St Andr 94–96; R Panfield and Rayne *Chelmsf* 96–09; RD Braintree 06–09; rtd 09; PtO *Chich* from 09. *39 Langdale Avenue, Chichester PO19 8JQ* T: (01243) 528783

MEADOWS, Mrs Freda Angela. b 46. CertEd 68. Oak Hill Th Coll 93. **d** 96 **p** 97. NSM N Wembley St Cuth *Lon* 96–01; NSM Roxeth 01–07; rtd 07; PtO *Lon* 07–12; *B & W* from 12. *38 Maple Rise, Radstock BA3 3LH* T: (01761) 435320 M: 07887-484497 E: fred@famead.net

MEADWAY, Prof Jeanette Valerie. b 47. Edin Univ MB, ChB 69 FRCP 87 FRCPEd 87. Oak Hill NSM Course 89. **d** 93 **p** 94. NSM Stratford St Jo w Ch Ch and St Jas *Chelmsf* 93–14; NSM Stratford St Paul and St Jas 14–19; V Plaistow St Martin from 19; PtO *Lon* 99–03; Hon Prof Gulu Univ Uganda from 09; Can Mbale Cathl from 09; Hon Prof Busitema Univ from 15. *4 Glebe Avenue, Woodford Green IG8 9HB* T: (020) 8504 1958 E: revjeanettem16@gmail.com

MEAKIN, David John. b 61. Hull Univ BA 82 Dur Univ MA 96 Hughes Hall Cam PGCE 83 Lambeth STh 88. Westcott Ho Cam 86. **d** 88 **p** 89. C Upminster *Chelmsf* 88–92; Prec and Sacr Dur Cathl 92–97; V Ryhope 97–04; P-in-c Schorne *Ox* 04–11; TR from 11; AD Claydon from 11. *The Rectory, 1 Green Acres Close, Whitchurch, Aylesbury HP22 4JP* T: (01296) 641606 E: d.meakin@btinternet.com

MEARA, The Ven David Gwynne. b 47. Oriel Coll Ox BA 70 MA 73. Lambeth STh 76 Cuddesdon Coll 71. **d** 73 **p** 74. C Whitley Ch Ch *Ox* 73–77; Chapl Reading Univ 77–82; V Basildon 82–87; P-in-c Aldworth and Ashampstead 85–87; V Basildon w Aldworth and Ashampstead 87–94; RD Bradfield 90–94; V Buckingham w Radclive cum Chackmore 94–97; P-in-c Nash w Thornton, Beachampton and Thornborough 96–97; R Buckingham 97–00; RD 95–00; Hon Can Ch Ch 98–00; R St Bride Fleet Street w Bridewell etc *Lon* 00–14; Adn Lon 09–14; P-in-c St Mary Aldermary 10–12; rtd 14; PtO *Ox* from 14. *Stonewalls Barn, 10 The Closes, Kidlington OX5 2DP* T: (01865) 803729 E: david.meara14@gmail.com

MEARDON, Canon Brian Henry. b 44. Reading Univ BSc 66 PhD 71. Oak Hill Th Coll MPhil 84. **d** 79 **p** 80. C Reading St Jo *Ox* 79–82; V Warfield 82–09; Hon Can Ch 03–09; rtd 09; Hon C Bemerton *Sarum* 10–12; PtO from 12.

382 Devizes Road, Salisbury SP2 9LY T: (01722) 501300 E: brian.meardon@googlemail.com

MEARDON, Mark James. b 73. Southn Univ BSc 94. Trin Th Coll Singapore MTS 07 St Jo Coll Nottm MA 09. d 09 p 10. C Hazlemere *Ox* 09–17; V from 17; Chapl Pipers Corner Sch from 18. *17 Southcote Way, Penn, High Wycombe HP10 8JG* T: (01494) 812748 M: 07905-887125 E: mark.meardon@gmail.com or mark.hazlemere@gmail.com

MEARDON, Trevor John. b 78. d 16 p 17. C Southmead *Bris* 16–18; C Patchway 18–20; V Pype Hayes *Birm* from 20. *St Mary's Vicarage, 1162 Tyburn Road, Birmingham B24 0TB* M: 07947-610169 E: trev.meardon@gmail.com

MEARS, Mrs Hannah Marie. b 80. St Cuth Soc Dur BA 02 St Mary's Ho Dur MA 03. Trin Coll Bris 06. d 08 p 09. NSM Henbury *Bris* 08–09; C St Austell *Truro* 09–13; V Rugby W *Cov* 13–17; Dioc Voc Adv *Ex* from 19. *The Rectory, 27 West End Road, Bradninch, Exeter EX5 4QS* T: (01392) 881733 E: hannah.mears@exeter.anglican.org

MEARS, Oliver Harry John. b 80. Ball Coll Ox BA 02. Trin Coll Bris BA 08. d 09 p 10. C St Austell *Truro* 09–13; NSM Rugby W *Cov* 13–14; V 14–17; P-in-c Bradninch *Ex* from 17; C Cullompton from 17. *The Rectory, 27 West End Road, Bradninch, Exeter EX5 4QS* T: (01392) 881733 M: 07806-420473

MEARS, Phillip David. b 40. Dur Univ BA 62. d 65 p 66. C Sandylands *Blackb* 65–68; C Chorley St Geo 68–71; V Leyland St Ambrose 71–81; Chapl Warrington Distr Gen Hosp 81–00; PtO *Ches* 81–06; Hon C Schorne *Ox* 06–15. *4 Newell Close, Bedgrove, Aylesbury HP21 7FE* T: (01296) 655237

MEATH AND KILDARE, Bishop of. *See* STOREY, The Most Revd Patricia Louise

MEATH, Archdeacon of. *See* STEVENSON, The Ven Leslie Thomas Clayton

MEATHREL, Timothy James. b 78. Ox Brookes Univ BSc 99. Wycliffe Hall Ox BTh 07. d 08 p 09. C Harborne Heath *Birm* 08–13; C Clifton Ch Ch w Em *Bris* 13–17; V Northwood Em *Lon* from 17. *Emmanuel Vicarage, 3 Gatehill Road, Northwood HA6 3QB* M: 07818-401372 E: tim.meathrel@ecn.org.uk

MEATS, Canon Alan John. b 41. Univ of Wales (Cardiff) BA 62 DipEd 63 Lon Univ BD 70 Trin Coll Carmarthen MTh 00. St Mich Coll Llan 68. d 70 p 71. C Pontypridd St Cath *Llan* 70–73; TV Ystradyfodwg 73–75; Dioc Inspector of Schs 73–75 and 83–89; V Llandeilo Tal-y-bont *S & B* 75–83; RD Llwchwr 81–83; V Aberdare St Fagan *Llan* 83–89; V Felin-foel *St D* 89–01; Asst Dioc Dir of Educn 89–92; Dioc Dir of Educn 92–97; V Pen-bre 01–07; Can St D Cathl 94–07; rtd 07; PtO *S & B* from 12. *45A Capel Road, Llanelli SA14 8SL* T: (01554) 229427

MECHANIC, Mrs Bridget Elisheva. b 54. Cape Town Univ TDip 74 Nazarene Th Coll Man BA 08 Anglia Ruskin Univ MA 10. Ridley Hall Cam 08. d 10 p 11. C Ipswich St Jo *St E* 10–13; rtd 13; Academic Supervisor Africa Sch of Miss S Africa 13–14; P-in-c Escomb *Dur* 14–19; P-in-c Etherley 14–19; P-in-c Witton Park 14–19; P-in-c Hamsterley and Witton-le-Wear 14–19. *123 Coed Celynen Drive, Abercarn, Newport NP11 5AT* E: elishevamechanic@gmail.com

MECHANIC, Rodney Ian (Roni). b 48. Man Univ MA(Theol) 00. d 78 p 78. S Africa 78–98; P-in-c Shebbear, Buckland Filleigh, Sheepwash etc *Ex* 98–01; Australia 01–02; TV Heatons *Man* 02–08; TV Mildenhall *St E* 08–13; rtd 13; Tr Dir Africa Sch of Miss S Africa 13–14; Hon C Escomb *Dur* 14–19; Hon C Etherley 14–19; Hon C Witton Park 14–19; Hon C Hamsterley and Witton-le-Wear 14–19; PtO 19. *123 Coed Celynen Drive, Abercarn, Newport NP11 5AT* T: (01388) 768898 E: ronimechanic@gmail.com

MECREDY, Ruth. b 60. STETS 09. d 12 p 13. NSM Broughton Gifford, Gt Chalfield and Holt *Sarum* from 12. *9 Little Parks, Holt, Trowbridge BA14 6QR* T: (01225) 783197 E: rmecredy@gmail.com

MEDFORTH, Allan Hargreaves. b 27. Qu Coll Cam BA 48 MA 52. Westcott Ho Cam 50. d 51 p 52. C Hexham *Newc* 51–55; PV S'well Minster 55–59; V Farnsfield 59–72; RD S'well 66–72; V St Alb St Pet 72–95; RD St Alb 74–84; rtd 95; PtO St Alb from 95. *62 Cuckmans Drive, St Albans AL2 3AF* T: (01727) 836437 E: allan.medforth@talktalk.net

MEDHURST, Mrs June. b 44. St Hild Coll Dur TCert 66. NOC 99. d 02 p 03. C Silsden *Bradf* 02–06; P-in-c Oxenhope 06–10; Chapl Manorlands Hospice Keighley 04–09; PtO *Bradf* 10–14; *Leeds* from 14. *100 Langley Lane, Baildon, Shipley BD17 6TD* T: (01274) 599177 E: medjune@tiscali.co.uk

MEDHURST, Prof Kenneth Noel. b 38. Edin Univ MA 61 Man Univ PhD 69. d 91 p 93. NSM Baildon *Bradf* 91–06; NSM Oxenhope 06–09; Can Th Bradf Cathl *Leeds* from 00; PtO *Bradf* 10–14; *Leeds* from 14. *100 Langley Lane, Baildon, Shipley BD17 6TD* T: (01274) 599177

MEDLEY, Steven Thomas. b 70. Moorlands Coll BA 02. Qu Foundn Birm 14. d 15 p 16. C Chivers Coton w Astley *Cov* 15–19; Pioneer Min from 19. *6 St Christian's Croft, Coventry CV3 5GY* T: (024) 7667 2268 M: 07751-384297 E: steve.medley42@gmail.com

MEDLICOTT, Rebecca. b 75. Witwatersrand Univ BA 96 BA 98. Ripon Coll Cuddesdon 19. d 21. C Wokingham All SS *Ox* from 21. *25 Fairfax, Bracknell RG42 1YT* T: (01344) 442792 M: 07843-567234 E: becky@warfield.org.uk

MEDWAY, Daron. b 72. Univ of N Lon BA 98. Wycliffe Hall Ox BTh 04. d 04 p 05. C Crofton *Portsm* 04–08; V Penge St Jo *Roch* 08–13; P-in-c Weston *Win* from 13. *Weston Vicarage, Weston Lane, Southampton SO19 9HG* T: (023) 8044 8421 M: 07900-574691 E: d.medway@mac.com

MEE, Colin Henry. b 36. Reading Univ BSc 58. Bris Sch of Min 83. d 85 p 86. NSM Stanton St Quintin, Hullavington, Grittleton etc *Bris* 85–87; C Swindon Ch Ch 88–90; TV Washfield, Stoodleigh, Withleigh etc *Ex* 90–95; TR 95–99; Chapl Marie Curie Foundn (Tidcombe Hall) 95–99; rtd 99; PtO *B & W* from 02. *31 Paganel Road, Minehead TA24 5EU* T: (01643) 706048 E: mee.mavcol@talktalk.net

MEE, Gerard Henry. b 72. St Mary's Coll Twickenham BA 13. Sarum Coll 13. d 16 p 17. NSM Thorpe *Guildf* from 16. *229 Albert Drive, Woking GU21 5RD* M: 07746-915418 E: gerardmee@yahoo.com

MEEK, Anthony William. b 45. ACIB. Ox NSM Course 80. d 83 p 84. NSM Gt Chesham *Ox* 83–01; PtO *Ex* from 01; Clergy Widow(er)s Officer 02–12. *The Willows, Orley Road, Ipplepen, Newton Abbot TQ12 5SA* T: (01803) 814370 E: frtonymeek@aol.com

MEERING, Laurence Piers Ralph. b 48. Man Univ BSc 70. Trin Coll Bris 79. d 81 p 82. C Downend *Bris* 81–84; C Crofton *Portsm* 84–87; V Witheridge, Thelbridge, Creacombe, Meshaw etc *Ex* 87–94; TV Southgate *Chich* 94–02; TV Walton H Trin *Ox* 02–07; P-in-c Bedgrove 02–07; P-in-c Newton Longville and Mursley w Swanbourne etc 07–08; R 08–09; V Newton Longville, Mursley, Swanbourne etc 09–14; AD Mursley 11–14; rtd 14; PtO *B & W* from 15. *21 St Michael's Gardens, South Petherton TA13 5BD* T: (01460) 242653 E: laurencemeering@yahoo.co.uk

MEESAM, Melanie Louise. b 77. St Andr Univ MTheol 01 Hull Univ MA 05 DipSW 04. St Hild Coll 17. d 19 p 20. NSM Hull St Cuth *York* from 19. *31 Sutton Road, Hull HU6 7DR*

MEESON, Andrew Scott. b 86. Man Univ MB, ChB 09. Oak Hill Th Coll MTheol 15. d 15 p 16. C Whittle-le-Woods *Blackb* 15–18; V Leyland St Jo from 18. *St John's Vicarage, Leyland Lane, Leyland PR25 1XB* M: 07532-271740 E: andyandamymeeson@aol.co.uk

MEGARRELL, Miss Joanne Myrtle. b 70. QUB BA 93 PGCE 94. CITC BTh 03. d 03 p 04. C Moira *D & D* 03–12; I from 12. *1 Main Street, Moira, Craigavon BT67 0LE* T: (028) 9261 3359 E: joanne@moiraparish.org.uk

MEHEN, Donald Wilfrid. b 44. Birkbeck Coll Lon BSc 72 CertEd 66. d 00 p 01. OLM Sproughton w Burstall, Copdock w Washbrook etc *St E* 00–13; NSM 13–14; rtd 14; PtO *St E* from 14; RD Samford 13–15. *19 The Link, Bentley, Ipswich IP9 2DJ* T: (01473) 310383 E: donmehen@gmail.com

MEIGHEN, Alan Hugh. b 54. d 15 p 16. NSM Killingworth *Newc* from 15. *4 Hazelwood, Killingworth, Newcastle upon Tyne NE12 6FF* T: 0191-268 1953 M: 07709-647892 E: alanmeighen@btinternet.com

MEIKLE, Ross Alexander. b 90. St Jo Coll Dur BA 17. Cranmer Hall Dur 14. d 17 p 18. C Witney *Ox* 17–21; V Reading St Luke w St Bart from 21. *St Luke's Church, Erleigh Road, Reading RG1 5LH* T: 0118-966 6389 E: rev.ross.redlands@gmail.com

MEIN, The Very Revd James Adlington. b 38. Nottm Univ BA 60. Westcott Ho Cam 61. d 63 p 64. C Edin St Columba 63–67; Bp's Dom Chapl 65–67; Malawi 67–72; R Grangemouth *Edin* 72–82; P-in-c Bo'ness 76–82; TV Livingston LEP 82–90; R Edin Ch Ch 90–04; Can St Mary's Cathl 90–01; Syn Clerk 00–01; Dean Edin 01–04; rtd 04. *Cardhu, Bridgend, Linlithgow EH49 6NH* T: (01506) 834317 E: jim@meins.plus.com

MEIRIONNYDD, Archdeacon of. *See* JONES, The Ven Andrew

MELANIPHY, Miss Angela Ellen. b 55. SRN 79. Cranmer Hall Dur 87. d 90 p 94. Par Dn Leytonstone St Jo *Chelmsf* 90–94; C 94–95; TV Harlow Town Cen w Lt Parndon 95–06; R Fowlmere, Foxton, Shepreth and Thriplow *Ely* from 15. *The Rectory, High Street, Fowlmere, Royston SG8 7SU* E: rector@thefourchurchbenefice.org

MELCHOR, Stuart Floyd. b 64. St Mellitus Coll 14. d 17 p 18. C Northolt St Jos *Lon* 17–21; P-in-c Tokyngton St Mich from 21. *Tokyngton Vicarage, St Michael's Avenue, Wembley HA9 6SL*

MELDRUM, Andrew John Bruce. b 66. Univ of Wales (Abth) LLB 89 Lon Univ MA 98. Westcott Ho Cam 91. d 94 p 95. C Paddington St Jas *Lon* 94–99; P-in-c Brookfield St Anne,

Highgate Rise 99–02; V from 02; Communications Adv to Bp Edmonton from 00; AD S Camden 08–16. *St Anne's Vicarage, 106 Highgate West Hill, London N6 6AP* T/F: (020) 8340 5190 E: javintner@aol.com

MELLARS, Paul David. b 72. York St Jo Univ BA 15. Yorks Min Course 12. **d** 15 **p** 16. C Clifton St Jas *Sheff* 15–17; C Hoyland 17–18; C Stainforth 18–19; C Fishlake w Sykehouse and Kirk Bramwith etc 18–19; TV Dronfield w Holmesfield *Derby* from 19. *11 Rothay Close, Dronfield Woodhouse, Dronfield S18 8PR*

MELLERUP, Miss Eiler Mary. b 37. Saffron Walden Coll CertEd 58. **d** 96 **p** 97. OLM Happisburgh, Walcott, Hempstead w Eccles etc *Nor* 96–08; PtO from 08. *Channings, The Crescent, Walcott, Norwich NR12 0NH* T: (01692) 651393

MELLESS, Miss Claire Louise. b 75. Nottm Trent Univ BA 10. Cranmer Hall Dur 17. **d** 19 **p** 20. C Ravenshead *S'well* from 19. *1 Cromford Court, Ravenshead, Nottingham NG15 9GG* M: 07709-315065 E: claire.melless@yahoo.com

MELLOR, Canon Kenneth Paul. b 49. Southn Univ BA 71 Leeds Univ MA 72. Cuddesdon Coll 72. **d** 73 **p** 74. C Cottingham *York* 73–76; C Ascot Heath *Ox* 76–80; V Tilehurst St Mary 80–85; V Menheniot *Truro* 85–94; Hon Can Truro Cathl 90–94; Can Res and Treas Truro Cathl 94–03; RD W Wivelshire 88–94; R Guernsey St Peter Port *Win* 03–14; P-in-c Sark 03–14; Dean Guernsey 03–14; Hon Can Win Cathl 03–14; rtd 14; PtO *Win* 14–20; Master St Nic Hosp Salisbury 16–21; PtO *Sarum* from 16. *Address temp unknown* M: 07720-506863 E: kpaulmellor@cwgsy.net

MELLOR, Roy. b 52. Lanc Univ BA 92. Cuddesdon Coll 94. **d** 96 **p** 97. C Oakdale *Sarum* 96–00; TV Kingsthorpe w Northampton St Dav *Pet* 00–03; R Blisworth and Stoke Bruerne w Grafton Regis etc 03–10; P-in-c Collingtree w Courteenhall and Milton Malsor 09–10; rtd 10; PtO *Dur* 11–15; *Ox* from 15; *Eur* from 16. *7 Honeysuckle Way, Ambrosden, Bicester OX25 2AN* M: 07914-767191 E: roy_mellor2002@yahoo.co.uk

MELLORS, Derek George. b 38. Bris Univ CertEd 60 Lon Univ BSc 71 Nottm Univ DipEd 74 Liv Univ MEd 83. NOC 81. **d** 84 **p** 85. NSM Eccleston Ch Ch *Liv* 84–92; C Lowton St Mary 92–93; V Ashton-in-Makerfield St Thos 93–99; rtd 99; PtO *Liv* from 00. *20 Millbrook Lane, Eccleston, St Helens WA10 4QU* T: (01744) 28424

MELLOWSHIP, Robert John. b 52. St Mich Coll Llan BD 92. **d** 92 **p** 93. C Brecon St Mary and Battle w Llanddew *S & B* 92–94; Min Can Brecon Cathl 92–94; C Pontypool *Mon* 94–95; TV 95–97; P-in-c Bressingham w N and S Lopham and Fersfield *Nor* 97–07; P-in-c Roydon St Remigius 04–07; R Upper Waveney 07–12; rtd 12. *51 Sharman Avenue, Watton, Thetford IP25 6EG* T: (01953) 889917 E: robmellowship@msn.com

MELLUISH, Preb Mark Peter. b 59. Oak Hill Th Coll. **d** 89 **p** 90. C Ashtead *Guildf* 89–93; V Ealing St Paul *Lon* from 93; P-in-c Hanwell St Mellitus w St Mark from 14; P-in-c W Ealing St Jo w St Jas from 19; Preb St Paul's Cathl from 13. *St Paul's Vicarage, 102 Elers Road, London W13 9QE* T: (020) 8567 4628 *or* 8799 3779 F: 8567 4628 E: mark@stpaulsealing.com

MELOT, Mrs Sheila Mary. b 48. Bris Univ BA 69 MLitt 76. Trin Coll Bris 15. **d** 17 **p** 18. OLM Bishopston and St Andrews *Bris* 17–19. *11 Elm Tree Park, Yealmpton, Plymouth PL8 2ED* M: 07818-001119 E: sheilamelot@gmail.com

MELTON, Anne. b 44. N Riding Coll of Educn CertEd 65. Cranmer Hall Dur 80. **dss** 83 **d** 87 **p** 94. Newton Aycliffe *Dur* 83–88; Par Dn 87–88; Par Dn Shildon w Eldon 88–94; Asst Dir of Ords 88–94; P-in-c Usworth 94–96; TR 96–06; rtd 06; PtO *Dur* 07–20. *4 Lindisfarne, High Shincliffe, Durham DH1 2PH* T: 0191-374 0823

MELVIN, Gordon Thomas. b 55. BA 86. Sarum & Wells Th Coll 86. **d** 88 **p** 89. C Linc St Faith and St Martin w St Pet 88–91; TV Horsham *Chich* 91–94; Chapl Horsham Gen Hosp 91–94; Chapl Ipswich Hosp NHS Trust 94–00; Sen Chapl 00–04; Chapl Local Health Partnerships NHS Trust 94–00; Sen Chapl 00–04; Retreat Ldr from 04; PtO *St E* 04–20. *50 Constable Road, Ipswich IP4 2UZ* T: (01473) 233517 E: gordon.melvin@keme.co.uk

MENDEL, Canon Thomas Oliver. b 57. Down Coll Cam BA 79 MA 82. Cranmer Hall Dur 79. **d** 81 **p** 82. Chapl Down Coll Cam 81–86; Fell 84–86; Hon C Cambridge St Mary Less *Ely* 81–86; V Minsterley *Heref* 86–92; R Habberley 86–92; Chapl Shrewsbury Sch 93–95; Chapl Milan w Genoa and Varese *Eur* 95–96; Chapl Copenhagen w Aarhus 96–04; Sen Chapl Malta and Gozo 04–08; Can and Chan Malta Cathl 04–08; V Eastbourne St Mary *Chich* from 08. *St Mary's Vicarage, 2 Glebe Close, Eastbourne BN20 8AW* T: (01323) 720420 E: tomendel@talktalk.net

MENDHAM, Vivien Evelyn. **d** 18 **p** 19. OLM Lexden *Chelmsf* from 18. *Address withheld by request* E: viv@stleonardslexden.org.uk

MENIN, The Rt Revd Malcolm James. b 32. Univ Coll Ox BA 55 MA 59. Cuddesdon Coll 55. **d** 57 **p** 58 **c** 86. C Southsea H Spirit *Portsm* 57–59; C Fareham SS Pet and Paul 59–62; V Nor St Jas w Pockthorpe 62–72; P-in-c Nor St Martin 62–74; P-in-c Nor St Mary Magd 68–72; V Nor St Mary Magd w St Jas 72–86; RD Nor E 81–86; Hon Can Nor Cathl 82–86; Suff Bp Knaresborough *Ripon* 86–97; rtd 97; PtO *Nor* 97–04; Hon Asst Bp Nor from 00; PtO from 16. *32C Bracondale, Norwich NR1 2AN* T: (01603) 627987

MENNIE, Joel John. b 83. Ox Brookes Univ BA 06. Trin Coll Bris BA 16. **d** 16 **p** 17. C Bath Twerton-on-Avon *B & W* 16–20; V Bognor *Chich* from 20. *The Vicarage, 17 Victoria Drive, Bognor Regis PO21 2RH* M: 07527-545692 E: joel.mennie@mac.com

MENNISS, Canon Andrew Philip. b 49. Univ of Wales (Swansea) BSc 73. Sarum & Wells Th Coll 83. **d** 85 **p** 86. C Horsell *Guildf* 85–89; V Bembridge *Portsm* 89–14; RD E Wight 95–00; Hon Can Portsm Cathl 09–14; rtd 14; PtO *Birm* from 14. *102 Sunnybank Road, Sutton Coldfield B73 5RL* M: 07762-228629 E: andrewpm49@gmail.com

MENON, Nicholas Anthony Thotekat. b 39. Mert Coll Ox BA 61 MA 65. St Steph Ho Ox 61. **d** 63 **p** 64. C Paddington Ch Ch *Lon* 63–66; Hon C 66–70; V Thorpe *Guildf* 70–76; V Ox SS Phil and Jas w St Marg 76–79; Chapl Surrey Univ *Guildf* 79–82; Chapl and Ho Master Cranleigh Sch Surrey 82–00; Asst Chapl Malvern Coll 00–06; rtd 04; PtO *Worc* from 05; *Heref* from 06. *Pilgrim Cottage, 187 West Malvern Road, Malvern WR14 4BB* T: (01684) 577189 E: nicholasmenon159@btinternet.com

MENON, Suresh Vijayan. b 64. Man Poly BA 88. Oak Hill Th Coll 96. **d** 98 **p** 99. C Braintree *Chelmsf* 98–02; C Leic H Trin w St Jo 02–05; C Ox St Ebbe w H Trin and St Pet 10–14; PtO *Guildf* 18–20; P-in-c Frimley Green and Mytchett 20–21; V from 21. *The Vicarage, 37 Sturt Road, Frimley Green, Camberley GU16 6HY* E: mail2suresh.menon@gmail.com *or* suresh@st-andrewschurch.org.uk

MENSINGH, Gregg Richard. b 69. Portsm Univ BSc 94. Westcott Ho Cam 95. **d** 97 **p** 98. C Birchfield *Birm* 97–01; V Gravelly Hill 01–12; R Botley *Portsm* from 12; V Curdridge from 12; R Durley from 12; AD Bishop's Waltham 14–19. *The Rectory, 46 High Street, Botley, Southampton SO30 2EA* T: (01489) 780994 E: gregg.mensingh@gmail.com

MENTZEL, Kevin David. b 60. Reading Univ BSc 82 Down Coll Cam BA 87 MA 91 QUB MTh 04 Heythrop Coll Lon MA 09. Ridley Hall Cam 85. **d** 88 **p** 89. C Ditton *Roch* 88–91; Asst Chapl Eton Coll 91–93; Asst Chapl R Hosp Sch Holbrook 93–94; Sen C Fulham St Dionis *Lon* 94–97; CF 97–15; CF (Army Reserve) from 15. *Ragstone Barn, Faringdon Road, Shippon, Abingdon OX13 6LL* T: (01235) 534488 E: kdmentzel@gmail.com

MENZIES, James Kingsley. b 86. St Jo Coll Dur BA 08. Cranmer Hall Dur 08. **d** 10 **p** 11. C Hetton-Lyons w Eppleton *Dur* 10–14; TV Portland *Sarum* 14–21; TV Weymouth Ridgeway 21; TR from 21. *The Vicarage, 2 Primula Close, Weymouth DT3 6SL* E: jameskmenzies@yahoo.com

MENZIES, Stanley Hay. b 33. Edin Univ MA 55 BD 58. New Coll Edin 55. **d** 02 **p** 03. NSM Boston Spa *York* 02–10; rtd 10; PtO *York* 10–20. *Cairn Croft, 2 Crag Gardens, Bramham, Wetherby LS23 6RP* T/F: (01937) 541047

MEON, Archdeacon of the. *See* KERR, The Ven Alison

MEPHAM, Ali Henry. b 75. Trin Coll Bris BA 07. **d** 07 **p** 08. C Warminster Ch Ch *Sarum* 07–10; TV The Lytchetts and Upton 10–16; V Fair Oak *Win* 16–20; Sen Interim Min *Glouc* from 21. *The Rectory, Redmarley, Gloucester GL19 3HS* M: 07546-170008 E: amepham@glosdioc.org.uk

MEPHAM, Alistair Gregory Simon. *See* MEPHAM, Ali Henry

MEPHAM, Mrs Kathryn Mary. b 75. Sarum Coll 15. **d** 17 **p** 18. C Bishopstoke *Win* 17–20; C Fair Oak 17–20; P-in-c Redmarley D'Abitot, Bromesberrow, Pauntley etc *Glouc* from 20. *The Rectory, Redmarley, Gloucester GL19 3HS* T: (01531) 650344 M: 07512-222635

MEPHAM, Kevin Aubrey. b 55. Sarum & Wells Th Coll 85. **d** 88 **p** 89. NSM Sidley *Chich* 88–90; C Hollington St Leon 90–94; V Horam 94–99; P-in-c Hastings All So 99–03; V Alkham w Capel le Ferne and Hougham *Cant* 03–05; P-in-c Sedlescombe w Whatlington *Chich* from 12. *The Rectory, Church Hill, Sedlescombe, Battle TN33 0QP* E: mephamka@aol.com

MEPHAM, Stephen Richard. b 64. K Coll Lon BD 85 AKC 85 Heythrop Coll Lon MA 18. Linc Th Coll 87. **d** 89 **p** 90. C Newark *S'well* 89–92; C Cheshunt *St Alb* 92–95; C-in-c Turnford St Clem CD 95–98; V Rickmansworth 98–06; PtO 20. *48 Durban Road West, Watford WD18 7DR* E: srmepham@virginmedia.com

MERCER, Jacob Laurence Charles. b 88. Peterho Cam BA 11. Wycliffe Hall Ox BA 18. **d** 18 **p** 19. C Bermondsey St Jas and St Anne *S'wark* from 18. *161 Lynton Road, London SE1 5QX* M: 07833-462066

MERCER, James John. b 56. Bp Otter Coll Chich BEd 79 Lon Inst of Educn MA 85. Ridley Hall Cam 00. **d** 02 **p** 03. C Heref St Pet w St Owen and St Jas 02–07; V Harrow Weald All SS *Lon* 07–18; Lic Lay Min Tr Officer Willesden Area 08–14; Warden Lay Min 16–18; C St Aldhelm *Sarum* from 18. *The Rectory, St George's Close, Langton Matravers, Swanage BH19 3HZ* T: (01929) 422454 M: 07713-236709 E: james_staldhelm@icloud.com

MERCER, Jarred Austin. b 86. SE Coll (USA) BA 09 St Andr Univ MLitt 10 Qu Coll Ox DPhil 15. St Steph Ho Ox 13. **d** 15 **p** 16. C Ox St Mary Magd 15–18; Jun Chapl Mert Coll Ox 15–17; Asst Chapl 17–20; R Newburyport USA from 20. *52B Washington Street, Newburyport MA 01950-2426, USA* E: jarred.mercer@gmail.com

MERCER, Lt Col Nicholas Justin. b 62. St Andr Univ BD 85 Cardiff Univ LLM 99 Ox Univ MTh 14 Solicitor 91. Ripon Coll Cuddesdon 08. **d** 11 **p** 12. C Gillingham and Milton-on-Stour *Sarum* 11–14; Asst Chapl Sherborne Sch 14–17; R Ch Ch Cathl and the Falkland Is 18–19; R Bolton Abbey *Leeds* from 19. *The Old Rectory, Bolton Abbey, Skipton BD23 6AL* M: 07912-619533 E: mercer-family@hotmail.com

MERCER, The Ven Nicholas Stanley. b 49. Selw Coll Cam BA 72 MA 76 PGCE 73 Spurgeon's Coll BA 78 Lon Bible Coll MPhil 86. Cranmer Hall Dur 95. **d** 95 **p** 95. C Northwood Hills St Edm *Lon* 95–98; C Pimlico St Mary Bourne Street 98–03; Dir of Min 03–07; V Gen Lon Coll of Bps 07–17; Dir of Ords 03–17; Lic Preacher 03–17; Hon C Wilton Place St Paul from 04; Adn Lon 15–16; P-in-c St Botolph without Bishopgate 15–16; Preb St Paul's Cathl 08–17; rtd 17; PtO *Lon* from 17; *Eur* 18–19. *42 Broomhouse Road, London SW6 3QX* M: 07782-250377 E: frnick@gmail.com

MERCER, Canon Timothy James. b 54. Fitzw Coll Cam BA 76 MA 80. Westcott Ho Cam 78. **d** 81 **p** 82. C Bromley SS Pet and Paul *Roch* 81–85; R Swanscombe 85–96; Chapl Bromley Hosps NHS Trust 96–09; Chapl S Lon Healthcare NHS Trust 09–14; Hon Can Roch Cathl from 10; Dep Hd of Chapl King's Coll Hosp NHS Foundn Trust 14–18. *75 Tintagel Road, Orpington BR5 4LH* E: mercer180@btinternet.com

MERCER-TURNER, Christine Margaret. *See* TURNER, Christine Margaret

MERCERON, Daniel John. b 58. Lon Univ BA 81. Westcott Ho Cam 88. **d** 90 **p** 91. C Clevedon St Jo *B & W* 90–94; CF 94–14; P-in-c Alfriston w Lullington, Litlington and W Dean *Chich* 14–15; R Alfriston w Lullington, Litlington, W Dean and Folkington 15–17; Chapl Wellington Coll Berks 17–18; Chapl Eastbourne Coll from 19. *The Chaplaincy, Eastbourne College, Old Wish Road, Eastbourne BN21 4JY* E: djmerceron@eastbourne-college.co.uk

MERCHANT, Robert Ian. b 73. Keele Univ BA 98. Wycliffe Hall Ox BA 00 MA 05. **d** 01 **p** 02. C Harborne Heath *Birm* 01–04; Prin Lect Spirituality and Health Staffs Univ *Lich* 05–09; Dep Dir Cen for Ageing and Mental Health 05–09; NSM Cheltenham St Mark *Glouc* 05–06; C Cheltenham St Mich and Cheltenham St Luke and St Jo 06–10; R Ashleworth, Corse, Hartpury, Hasfield etc 10–12; Dir Dispersed Learning St Mellitus Coll 12–16; Dir St Mellitus Coll Chelmsf 16–21; Dean of Miss, Min and Educn *Chelmsf* from 21; PtO *Lon* 12–13; NSM Hornsey Rise from 13; Public Preacher *Chelmsf* from 17. *3 Highcroft Road, London N19 3AQ* T: (020) 7281 1459

MERCHANT, Mrs Tamsin Laetitia Rachel. b 70. Wycliffe Hall Ox BTh 01. **d** 01 **p** 02. C Harborne Heath *Birm* 01–04; Sen Chapl Glos Univ 04–12; V Hornsey Rise *Lon* from 12. *3 Highcroft Road, London N19 3AQ* T: (020) 7281 1459 E: revtamsinmerchant@gmail.com

MERCURIO, Canon Frank James Charles. b 46. Webster Univ (USA) BA 73 MA 75. St Alb Minl Tr Scheme 87. **d** 89 **p** 90. C Cheshunt *St Alb* 89–93; TV Hitchin 93–00; RD 94–00; TR Tring 00–07; P-in-c Alfreton *Derby* 07–16; P-in-c Riddings and Ironville 08–16; Hon Can Derby Cathl 15–16; rtd 16. *81 Queen Street, Eckington, Sheffield S21 4FD* E: frankmercurio@dialstart.net

MEREDITH, Ian. b 53. Univ of Wales BA 85 K Coll Lon MTh 89 Edin Univ MTh 96 Dur Univ PhD 07. K Coll Lon 86. **d** 02 **p** 03. Assoc Min Dumfries *Glas* 02–06; NSM Annan 06–07; NSM Eastriggs 06–07; NSM Gretna 06–07; NSM Lockerbie 06–07; NSM Moffat 06–07; R Ayr 07–13; R Girvan 07–13; R Maybole 07–13; P-in-c Portchester *Portsm* 13–17; V from 17; AD Fareham from 17. *The Vicarage, 164 Castle Street, Portchester, Fareham PO16 9QH* T: (023) 9237 5422 E: irev@ymail.com

MEREDITH, Canon Roland Evan. b 32. Trin Coll Cam BA 55 MA 59. Cuddesdon Coll 55. **d** 57 **p** 58. C Bishopwearmouth St Mich *Dur* 57–59; Dioc Chapl *Birm* 59–60; C Kirkby *Liv* 60–63; V Hitchin St Mary *St Alb* 63–72; TR Preston St Jo *Blackb* 72–76 and 76–79; RD Preston 72–79; Hon Can Blackb Cathl 77–79; TR Witney *Ox* 79–94; P-in-c Hailey w Crawley 79–82; RD Witney 89–97; Hon Can Ch Ch 92–97; rtd 94; PtO *Ox* 97–21; *Eur* from 98. *37 Otters Court, Priory Mill Lane, Witney OX28 1GJ* T: (01993) 703698 M: 07971-370647 E: roland@canonmeredith.free-online.co.uk

MERIVALE, Charles Christian Robert. b 44. Cranmer Hall Dur 76. **d** 78 **p** 79. C Highbury Ch Ch w St Jo *Lon* 78–81; P-in-c Hawes *Ripon* 81–82; P-in-c Hardrow and St Jo w Lunds 81–82; V Hawes and Hardraw 82–84; Chapl R Cornwall Hosps Trust 85–92; PtO *B & W* 92–00; *Ex* 00–02; TV Shebbear, Buckland Filleigh, Sheepwash etc 02–08; rtd 08; PtO *B & W* 10–19. *The Cider House, Coxs Close, North Cadbury, Yeovil BA22 7DY* T: (01963) 440917 M: 07934-780766 E: christianandjane@hotmail.co.uk

MERRICK, Caroline Jane. b 65. SCRTP 14. **d** 17 **p** 18. C Walton-on-Thames *Guildf* from 17. *Parish Office, St Mary's Church Hall, Church Street, Walton-on-Thames KT12 2QS* E: caroline@waltonparish.org.uk

MERRICK, Richard Christopher. b 57. Qu Coll Birm 08. **d** 11 **p** 12. C Bushbury *Lich* 11–14; V Heath Town from 14. *Holy Trinity Vicarage, Bushbury Road, Wolverhampton WV10 0LY* T: (01902) 772840 E: revrichht@gmail.com

MERRIMAN, Stephen Richard. b 74. Leeds Univ BA 02. Coll of Resurr Mirfield 99. **d** 02 **p** 03. C Littlehampton and Wick *Chich* 02–06; TV 08–16; C Brighton St Matthias 06–08; V Chich St Wilfrid 16–17; C Arundel w Tortington and S Stoke 17–20; R W Chiltington from 20. *The Rectory, East Street, West Chiltington, Pulborough RH20 2JY* T: (01798) 669207 E: fr-smerriman@sky.com *or* rector@westchiltington@outlook.com

MERRINGTON, Bill. b 55. Sheff Hallam Univ BSc 78 Birm Univ MPhil 95 Warwick Univ PhD 03. Cranmer Hall Dur 80. **d** 83 **p** 84. C Harborne Heath *Birm* 83–88; V Leamington Priors St Paul *Cov* 88–99; RD Warwick and Leamington 97–99; R Ilmington w Stretton-on-Fosse etc 99–07; R Tredington and Darlingscott 05–07; RD Shipston 99–03; Hon Can Cov Cathl 01–07; Sen Chapl Bournemouth Univ *Sarum* 07–18; PtO *Win* 09–17; Chapl HM Pris Full Sutton 18–20; Chapl Pocklington Sch from 20. *Pocklington School, West Green, Pocklington, York YO42 2NJ* T: (01759) 321200

MERRINGTON, Mrs Hilary. b 47. **d** 14 **p** 15. NSM Norley, Crowton and Kingsley *Ches* from 14. *Cartref, Ball Lane, Kingsley, Frodsham WA6 8HP* T: (01928) 788087 E: hilary.merrington@btinternet.com

MERRIOTT, Pamela Ann. b 51. SNTS. **d** 12 **p** 13. OLM Abbots Bromley, Blithfield, Colton, Colwich etc *Lich* 12–20; rtd 20; PtO *Lich* from 20. *The Oaklands, 1 Billington Avenue, Little Haywood, Stafford ST18 0UZ* T: (01889) 881030 M: 07967-717181 E: davidmerriott@btinternet.com

MERRY, David Thomas. b 48. St Chad's Coll Dur BA 70. AKC 73. **d** 74 **p** 75. C Cirencester *Glouc* 74–78; TV Bridgnorth, Tasley, Astley Abbotts and Oldbury *Heref* 78–83; P-in-c Quatford 81–83; P-in-c Stroud H Trin *Glouc* 83–87; V 87–01; Chapl Stroud Gen Hosp 83–93; Chapl Severn NHS Trust 93–01; Chapl Cheltenham Ladies' Coll 01–13; Hon Min Can Glouc Cathl 04–13; rtd 13; PtO *Glouc* from 19. *3 Rose Hill, Far Wells Road, Bisley, Stroud GL6 7AQ* T: (01452) 770517

MERRY, Philip John. b 58. ERMC 11. **d** 14 **p** 15. NSM Gt and Lt Bealings w Playford and Culpho *St E* 14–17; P-in-c Badwell and Walsham 17–18; V from 18. *The Rectory, The Causeway, Walsham-le Willows, Bury St Edmunds IP31 3AB* T: (01359) 258806 M: 07900-058418 E: philipmerry@hotmail.co.uk

MERRY, Rex Edwin. b 38. AKC 67. **d** 68 **p** 69. C Spalding St Jo *Linc* 68–73; C Boxmoor St Jo *St Alb* 73–83; TV Hemel Hempstead 83–95; V Farley Hill St Jo 95–06; rtd 06; PtO *St Alb* 06–18. *4 Wellcroft, Hemel Hempstead HP1 3EG* T: (01442) 401122 E: rex.merry@yahoo.co.uk

MERRY, Thomas. *See* MERRY, David Thomas

MERRY, Tommy Philip. b 85. UEA BA 08 Sheff Univ BA 13. Coll of Resurr Mirfield 10. **d** 13 **p** 14. C Hanley H Ev *Lich* 13–16; TV Stoke-upon-Trent and Fenton from 16; P-in-c Fenton 16. *10 Fenton Hall Close, Stoke-on-Trent ST4 4PU* T: (01782) 846087 M: 07585-954122 E: frtommymerry@gmail.com

MERRYWEATHER, Mrs Rosalynd. b 50. Hull Coll of Educn CertEd 72. NEOC. **d** 00 **p** 01. NSM Beverley St Nic *York* 00–12; PtO from 12. *10 West Close, Beverley HU17 7JJ* T: (01482) 867958 E: rmerryweather@rmerryweather.karoo.co.uk

MESLEY-SPONG, Terence John. b 32. Roch Th Coll 63. **d** 66 **p** 67. C Forton *Portsm* 66–68; Rhodesia 68–80; Zimbabwe 80–84; R Christow, Ashton, Trusham and Bridford *Ex* 84–86; Chapl Puerto de la Cruz Tenerife *Eur* 86–93; Miss to Seamen 86–93; rtd 93; PtO *Win* 93–13; Chapl R Bournemouth and Christchurch Hosps NHS Trust 97–98. *14B Stuart Road, Highcliffe, Christchurch BH23 5JS* T: (01425) 277833

MESSAM, Paul James. b 65. Lon Coll of Printing BA 87. Cranmer Hall Dur 01. **d** 03 **p** 04. C Market Harborough and The Transfiguration etc *Leic* 03–07; P-in-c Bulkington *Cov* 07–16; Lead Chapl Cov Blue Coat C of E Sch 07–15; P-in-c Elstow *St Alb* from 16. *Abbey Vicarage, Church End, Elstow, Bedford MK42 9XT* T: (01234) 261477 M: 07711-098209 E: vicar@elstow-abbey.org.uk

MESSENGER, Paul. b 38. Univ of Wales (Lamp) BA 63. Coll of Resurr Mirfield 63. **d** 65 **p** 66. C Battersea St Luke *S'wark* 65–69; C Ainsdale *Liv* 69–71; V Wigan St Steph 71–74; Asst Chapl St Marg Convent E Grinstead 74–76; Chapl Kingsley St Mich Sch W Sussex 74–76; P-in-c Southwater *Chich* 76–81; V 81–97; R Sullington and Thakeham w Warminghurst 97–07; rtd 07; PtO *Chich* 12–17. *122 Ninfield Road, Bexhill-on-Sea TN39 5BB* T: (01424) 220044 E: paulmessenger@uwclub.net

MESSER, David Harry. b 61. MCIH 93. EAMTC 01. **d** 04 **p** 05. C Stanton, Hopton, Market Weston, Barningham etc *St E* 04–07; R 07–17; C Hepworth, Hinderclay, Wattisfield and Thelnetham 15–17; RD Ixworth 14–17; R Walkington, Bishop Burton, Rowley etc *York* from 17. *The Rectory, 2 Little Weighton Road, Walkington, Beverley HU17 8SP* E: davidharrymesser93@gmail.com

MESSERVY, Mrs Cassandra Margaret. b 75. Ox Brookes Univ BA 99 PGCE 02 Cardiff Univ LLM 21. Ripon Coll Cuddesdon 09 BTh 15. **d** 11 **p** 12. C Beaconsfield *Ox* 11–14; NSM Seer Green and Jordans 14–15; NSM Chalfont St Giles, Seer Green and Jordans 15–17; C 18–21; R Wychert Vale from 21. *Wychert Vale Benefice Office, St Mary's Centre, Station Road, Haddenham, Aylesbury HP17 8AJ* T: (01844) 291108 E: cassamesservy@gmail.com

MESSHAM, Canon Barbara Lynn. b 52. Bretton Hall Coll CertEd 75. STETS 96. **d** 99 **p** 00. C The Bourne and Tilford *Guildf* 99–03; V Guildf All SS 03–13; RD Guildf 06–11; Hon Can Guildf Cathl 10–13; P-in-c Deerhurst and Apperley w Forthampton etc *Glouc* 13–18; C Tewkesbury w Walton Cardiff and Twyning 13–18; rtd 18; PtO *Glouc* from 19. *Waysmeet, Innerstone Lane, Redmarley, Gloucester GL19 3JH* M: 07932-615132 E: barbara@messhams.co.uk *or* barbaramessham@gmail.com

MESSINGER, Jacqueline Violet. b 51. St Mellitus Coll 16. **d** 19 **p** 20. OLM Lexden *Chelmsf* from 19. *3 Baines Close, Colchester CO3 4AL* T: (01206) 760742 M: 07886-468596 E: jacquie@stleonardslexden.org.uk

METCALF, Preb Michael Ralph. b 37. Clare Coll Cam BA 61 MA 65 Birm Univ MA 80. Ridley Hall Cam 63. **d** 64 **p** 65. C Downend *Bris* 64–67; PtO *Birm* 68–78; *Lich* 72–81; Lect W Midl Coll of Educn 72–77; Sen Lect 77–81; Dioc Dir of Educn *Lich* 83–94; V Stafford St Paul Forebridge 94–05; Preb Lich Cathl 91–05; RD Stafford 00–05; rtd 05; PtO *Heref* 87–08; *Lich* 05–21. *196 Stone Road, Stafford ST16 1NT* T/F: (01785) 600260 E: prebmetcalf@hotmail.com *or* berylm@ntlworld.com

METCALFE, Alistair Andrew. b 77. Warwick Univ BA 99 St Jo Coll Dur BA 18. Cranmer Hall Dur 16. **d** 18 **p** 19. C Bebington *Ches* 18–20; V Ipswich St Aug *St E* from 20. *The Vicarage, 2 Bucklesham Road, Ipswich IP3 8TJ* E: alistairmetcalfe@gmail.com

METCALFE, Bernard. *See* METCALFE, William Bernard

METCALFE, Jacqueline Carol. b 52. Nottm Univ BA 73 Lon Inst of Educn PGCE 74 Anglia Ruskin Univ MA 14. ERMC 15. **d** 20 **p** 21. NSM Milton Ely from 20. *36 The Rowans, Milton, Cambridge CB24 6YU* M: 07765-424642 E: jacques0701@gmail.com *or* jackie.metcalfe@allsaintsmilton.org.uk

METCALFE, Canon Ronald. b 41. BA. Edin Th Coll 67. **d** 69 **p** 70. C Saltburn-by-the-Sea *York* 69–72; P-in-c Crathorne 73–77; Youth Officer 73–77; Dioc Adult Tr Officer 78–88; Can Res York Minster 88–00; Sec for Miss and Min 88–00; V Kendal H Trin *Carl* 00–07; rtd 07; PtO *Dur* 08–21. *50 Carlton Moor Crescent, Darlington DL1 4RF* T: (01325) 367219 E: ronaldmetcalfe90@outlook.com

METCALFE, Canon William Bernard. b 47. St Jo Coll Cam BA 69 MA 73 Ball Coll Ox BA 71. Ripon Hall Ox 70. **d** 72 **p** 73. C Caversham *Ox* 72–75; C Aylesbury 75–79; Ind Chapl 75–79; TV Thamesmead *S'wark* 79–84; TR Totton *Win* 84–94; R Gt Bentley and Frating w Thorrington *Chelmsf* 94–10; V Gt Bentley 12–13; RD St Osyth 99–17; Hon Can Chelmsf Cathl 06–12; rtd 12; PtO *Ox* from 13. *60 Elmhurst Road, Reading RG1 5HY* T: 0118-975 6586 E: bernard.metcalfe@btinternet.com

METHUEN, Canon Charlotte Mary. b 64. Girton Coll Cam BA 85 MA 89 New Coll Edin BD 91 PhD 95. Edin Th Coll 87. **d** 98 **p** 99. C E Netherlands *Eur* 98–01; C Bonn w Cologne 01–03; Hon Asst Chapl 03–05; Dioc Dir of Tr 03–05; Hon C Offenbach (Old Catholic Ch) 05–07; Hon C Bottrop (Old Catholic Ch) from 08; Lect Ecclesiastical Hist Ox

Univ 05–11; Dioc Can Th *Glouc* 07–13; Lect Ripon Coll Cuddesdon 09–11; Lect Ch History Glas Univ from 11. *2/1, 34 Keir Street, Glasgow G41 2NW* T: 0141-429 4716 E: charlotte.methuen@glasgow.ac.uk

METIVIER, Canon Robert John. b 31. Lon Univ BA 68. Lambeth STh 61 Ch Div Sch of the Pacific (USA) BD 66 MDiv 69 Codrington Coll Barbados 56. **d** 60 **p** 61. Trinidad and Tobago 61–64 and 68–78; USPG 66–67; C Gt Berkhamsted *St Alb* 78–82; V Goff's Oak St Jas 82–90; V Tokyngton St Mich *Lon* 90–01; Hon Can Trinidad from 98; rtd 01; PtO *Lon* from 02. *17 Willowcourt Avenue, Kenton, Harrow HA3 8ET* T: (020) 8909 1371 E: ej.metivier@googlemail.com

METZ, Susanna Elizabeth. b 50. Immaculata Univ (USA) BA 72 W Chester State Coll (USA) MA 82 Univ of the S (USA) MDiv 96 DMin 03. **d** 96 **p** 97. C Battle Creek St Jo USA 96–07; R 07–11; TV Shebbear, Buckland Filleigh, Sheepwash etc *Ex* from 11; RD Torrington 15–20. *The Rectory, Petrockstow, Okehampton EX20 3HQ* T: (01837) 810621 E: petrockstowevicaris@gmail.com

METZNER (née JEFFREY), Mrs Katrina. b 73. St Jo Coll Ox BA 96 MA 01. St Steph Ho Ox 97. **d** 99 **p** 00. C Glouc St Geo w Whaddon 99–00; C Parkstone St Pet and St Osmund w Branksea *Sarum* 00–04; PtO *S'wark* 05–16; *Edin* from 18. *The Rectory, 2 May Terrace, North Berwick EH39 4BA* T: (01620) 892154 E: katemetzner@sky.com

METZNER, Simon David. b 64. Magd Coll Ox BA 85 K Coll Lon MA 95 St Luke's Coll Ex PGCE 93. St Steph Ho Ox 98. **d** 00 **p** 01. C Branksome St Aldhelm *Sarum* 00–04; V Tooting All SS *S'wark* 04–16; R N Berwick *Edin* from 16; R Gullane from 16. *The Rectory, 2 May Terrace, North Berwick EH39 4BA* T: (01620) 892154 E: simonmetzner@sky.com

MEWIS, Canon David William. b 47. Leeds Inst of Educn CertEd 68 Leeds Poly BEd 83. NOC 87. **d** 90 **p** 91. C Skipton Ch Ch *Bradf* 90–92; R Bolton by Bowland w Grindleton 92–12; C Waddington, Hurst Green and Mitton 05–12; RD Bowland 99–08; Hon Can Bradf Cathl 00–12; rtd 12; PtO *Bradf* 13–14; *Leeds* from 14; *Blackb* from 14. *23 Darkwood Crescent, Chatburn, Clitheroe BB7 4AL* T: (01200) 440335 E: dwm.dmewis@gmail.com

MEYER, Jonathan Peter. b 55. Keble Coll Ox BA 76 MA 95. SAOMC 03. **d** 05 **p** 06. NSM Kintbury w Avington *Ox* 05–08; NSM W Woodhay w Enborne, Hampstead Marshall etc 05–09; P-in-c Ewelme, Brightwell Baldwin, Cuxham w Easington 09–17; Hon C Benson w Ewelme 17–18; R Winchelsea and Icklesham *Chich* from 18. *The Rectory, St Thomas Street, Winchelsea TN36 4EB* T: (01797) 226254 E: revdjonathan@btinternet.com

MEYER, William John. b 46. ACIB. Cranmer Hall Dur 83. **d** 85 **p** 86. C Merrow *Guildf* 85–89; V Grayshott 89–98; R Binfield *Ox* 98–11; rtd 11. *27A Oxford Drive, Bognor Regis PO21 5QU* E: bill.meyer@hotmail.com

MEYNELL, Canon Andrew Francis. b 43. Westcott Ho Cam 70. **d** 73 **p** 74. C Cowley St Jas *Ox* 73–79; TV 79–81; P-in-c Halton 81–95; V Wendover 81–95; P-in-c Monks Risborough 95–98; TV Risborough 98–08; Dir Ords Bucks Adnry 95–08; Hon Can Ch Ch 01–08; rtd 08; PtO *Ox* from 09. *Pettits House, The Green, Great Milton, Oxford OX44 7NT* T: (01844) 277912 E: andrew.meynell@oxford.anglican.org

MEYNELL, Mrs Honor Mary. b 37. EMMTC 84. **d** 87 **p** 94. NSM Kirk Langley *Derby* 87–03; NSM Mackworth All SS 87–03; NSM Mugginton and Kedleston 87–03; rtd 04; PtO *Derby* 04–18. *The Coachman's Cottage, Meynell Langley, Kirk Langley, Ashbourne DE6 4NT* T: (01332) 824207

MEYNELL, Mark John Henrik. b 70. New Coll Ox MA 93. Ridley Hall Cam MA 97. **d** 97 **p** 98. C Fulwood *Sheff* 97–01; Dean Kampala Evang Sch of Th Uganda 01–05; C Langham Place All So *Lon* 05–14; Hon C from 14; PtO *Ox* from 18. *29 Raymond Road, Maidenhead SL6 6DF* T: (01628) 780776 M: 07725-048617 E: mark.meynell@langham.org

MEYRICK, Christopher George Cyril. b 85. Newc Univ BA 08. Ripon Coll Cuddesdon 18. **d** 20 **p** 21. C Fulham All SS *Lon* from 20. *70A Fulham High Street, London SW6 3LG* M: 07766-934594 E: curate@allsaints-fulham.org.uk

✠**MEYRICK, The Rt Revd Cyril Jonathan.** b 52. St Jo Coll Ox BA 73 MA 77. Sarum & Wells Th Coll 74. **d** 76 **p** 77 **c** 11. C Bicester *Ox* 76–78; Bp's Dom Chapl 78–81; Tutor Codrington Coll Barbados 81–84; TV Burnham w Dropmore, Hitcham and Taplow *Ox* 84–90; TR Tisbury *Sarum* 90–98; Link Officer Black Angl Concerns 90–98; RD Chalke 97–98; Can Res Roch Cathl 98–05; Dean Ex 05–11; P-in-c Cen Ex 06–11; Suff Bp Lynn *Nor* 11–21; rtd 21; Provost Woodard Corp (S Division) from 17; PtO *Ox* from 21. *Claydon House, Mollington Road, Claydon, Banbury OX17 1EN* T: (01295) 690752 E: cjmeyrick45@icloud.com

MEYRICK, Thomas Henry Corfe. b 67. Magd Coll Ox BA 88 MA 92 Leeds Univ PhD 05. St Steph Ho Ox BA 94. **d** 95 **p** 96.

C Bierley *Bradf* 95–99; Chapl Oriel Coll Ox 99–04; P-in-c Ox St Thos w St Frideswide and Binsey 04–05; P-in-c Newbold de Verdun and Kirkby Mallory *Leic* 05–10; P-in-c Barlestone 09–10; R Newbold de Verdun, Barlestone and Kirkby Mallory 10–17; AD Sparkenhoe W 08–15; P-in-c Peckleton 16–17; R Keyworth and Stanton-on-the-Wolds and Bunny etc *S'well* from 17. *The Rectory, Nottingham Road, Keyworth, Nottingham NG12 5FD* E: rector@ksbb.org.uk

MIALL, Mrs Hazel Henrietta. b 49. Open Univ BSc 97 DipCOT 70. St Mellitus Coll BA 12. **d** 12. NSM Southgate Ch Chs *Lon* 12–19; PtO from 19. *85 Conway Road, London N14 7BD* T: (020) 8882 6738 M: 07980-740587 E: hazelhmiall@btinternet.com

MICHAEL, Canon Ian MacRae. b 40. Aber Univ MA 62 Hertf Coll Ox DPhil 66. Westcott Ho Cam 77. **d** 79 **p** 80. C Kings Heath *Birm* 79–82; Vice-Provost St Paul's Cathl Dundee *Bre* 82–88; V Harborne St Faith and St Laur *Birm* 88–03; RD Edgbaston 91–98; Hon Can Birm Cathl 00–03; rtd 03; PtO *Birm* 03–13; LtO *St And* from 04; NSM St Andrews All SS from 05. *46 Argyle Court, St Andrews KY16 9BW* T: (01334) 473901

MICHAEL, Stephen David. b 71. Ripon Coll Cuddesdon 01. **d** 03 **p** 04. C St Blazey *Truro* 02–05; C Tywardreath w Tregaminion 03–07; C Lanlivery w Luxulyan 03–07; P-in-c Treverbyn 07–13; P-in-c Boscoppa 07–13. *1 Treverby Road, Stenalees, St Austell PL26 8TL* M: 07886-734492 E: sdm554@gmail.com

MICHAELS, David Albert Emmanuel. b 49. Bede Coll Dur BA 72 Barrister-at-Law (Inner Temple) 73. Westcott Ho Cam 86. **d** 88 **p** 89. C Hampstead St Jo *Lon* 88–91; TV Wolvercote w Summertown *Ox* 91–04; P-in-c Launceston *Truro* 04–13; rtd 13; PtO *Ox* from 15. *5 Northmoor Place, Northmoor Road, Oxford OX2 6XB* T: (01865) 558035 E: david.michaels@dunelm.org.uk

MICHAUX, Mrs Teresa Mary. b 56. STETS 09. **d** 12 **p** 13. NSM Swindon St Jo and St Andr *Bris* 12–18; TV Marden Vale *Sarum* from 18. *7 Richmond Road, Calne SN11 9UW* M: 07963-399645 E: tmx256@hotmail.co.uk

MICHELL, Philip Leonard. b 69. Trin Coll Bris 08. **d** 10 **p** 11. C Brailsford w Shirley, Osmaston w Edlaston etc *Derby* 10–13; R Hulland, Atlow, Kniveton, Bradley and Hognaston from 13. *The Rectory, 16 Eaton Close, Hulland Ward, Ashbourne DE6 3EX* T: (01335) 371947 M: 07815-940409 E: phil.michell@live.co.uk

MICKLEFIELD, Andrew Mark. b 71. K Alfred's Coll Win BEd 93. Ridley Hall Cam 04. **d** 06 **p** 07. C Alton *Win* 06–10; R Itchen Valley 10–14; V Alton from 14. *St Lawrence Vicarage, Church Street, Alton GU34 2BW* T: (01420) 88794 M: 07749-483407 E: andrewmicklefield@gmail.com

MICKLETHWAITE, Andrew Quentin. b 67. Univ Coll Dur BA 89. Trin Coll Bris BA 94. **d** 94 **p** 95. C Abington *Pet* 94–97; TV Duston 97–04; V Castle Donington and Lockington cum Hemington *Leic* 04–18; PtO from 18. *The Rectory, Wigston Road, Blaby, Leicester LE8 4FU* E: revandrew67@yahoo.co.uk

MICKLETHWAITE, Jane Catherine. b 56. Lanc Univ BSc 78. Trin Coll Bris 92. **d** 95 **p** 96. C Kings Heath *Pet* 96–98; Chapl Nene Coll of HE Northn 97–98; PtO *Pet* 98–01; NSM Kings Heath 01–04; PtO *Leic* 04–06; Chapl E Midl Airport 06–15; NSM Loughborough All SS w H Trin 13–15; Chapl to Internat Students Leic Univ 15–18; P-in-c Blaby from 18. *The Rectory, Wigston Road, Blaby, Leicester LE8 4FU* E: j.micklethwaite@yahoo.co.uk

MIDDLEBROOK, The Ven David John. b 61. Newc Univ BSc 83 Cranfield Inst of Tech MSc 85. Trin Coll Bris BA 98. **d** 98 **p** 99. C Chorleywood Ch Ch *St Alb* 98–02; TV Hemel Hempstead 02–08; P-in-c Watford St Luke 08–12; V 12–19; RD Watford 09–19; Hon Can St Alb 13–19; Adn Bedford from 19. *17 Lansdowne Road, Luton LU3 1EE*

MIDDLEDITCH, Terry Gordon. b 30. Univ of Wales (Lamp) BA 62 St Martin's Coll Lanc PGCE 68. St D Coll Lamp 59. **d** 63 **p** 64. C Poulton-le-Fylde *Blackb* 63–65; C-in-c Heysham 65–67; Sch Master 68–88; Hon C Cheltenham St Pet *Glouc* 75–87; Hon C Badgeworth w Shurdington 75–87; Hon C Up Hatherley 75–87; C Poulton-le-Sands w Morecambe St Laur *Blackb* 88–91; V Stalmine 91–00; rtd 00; PtO *Blackb* from 00. *100 Charles Street, Newark NG24 1RL* M: 07879-426173 E: terry.middleditch@gmail.com

MIDDLEMISS, Fritha Leonora. b 47. Man Univ BA 68 CertEd 69. Glouc Sch of Min 86. **d** 89 **p** 94. NSM Bengeworth *Worc* 89–94; NSM Stoulton w Drake's Broughton and Pirton etc 94–96; Chapl Malvern Girls' Coll 96–03; Asst Chapl HM Pris Long Lartin 03–08; PtO *Cov* from 18. *3 Arden Close, Wilmcote, Stratford-upon-Avon CV37 9WB* M: 07962-046195 E: frithamidlemiss@hotmail.com

MIDDLEMISS, Mrs Justine. b 68. Aston Univ BSc 90 Ripon Coll Cuddesdon BTh 05 K Coll Lon MA 12. Ripon

Coll Cuddesdon 00. **d** 02 **p** 03. C Lee St Marg *S'wark* 02–06; P-in-c Beddington 06; R 06–13; TR Sutton 13–18; P-in-c Kenley from 18; P-in-c Purley St Barn from 18. *The Vicarage, Valley Road, Kenley CR8 5DJ* M: 07956-452021 E: revdjustine@gmail.com

MIDDLESEX, Archdeacon of. *See* FRANK, The Ven Richard Stephen

MIDDLETON, Alan Derek. b 46. St Jo Coll Dur BA 68 MA 85 Sheff Univ MMin 00 Bris Univ PGCE 70. Qu Coll Birm. **d** 72 **p** 73. C Cannock *Lich* 72–76; Warden St Helen's Youth and Community Cen Bp Auckd 76–79; V Darlington St Jo *Dur* 79–89; TR E Darlington 89–90; V Upper Norwood All SS *S'wark* 90–99; TR Warlingham w Chelsham and Farleigh 99–11; Bp's Ecum Adv 96–11; AD Caterham 05–11; rtd 11; PtO *Dur* from 11. *21 Boste Crescent, Durham DH1 5US* T: 0191-386 4467 E: alan.middleton21@btinternet.com

MIDDLETON, Mrs Alison Jayne. b 71. Leic Univ BA 92. Ripon Coll Cuddesdon 13. **d** 16 **p** 17. C Gleneagles *Pet* 16–20; C Rotherham *Sheff* from 20; C Masbrough from 20. *7 Oxley Court, Rotherham S60 2RE* M: 07891-608612 E: rev.ali.j.middleton@gmail.com

MIDDLETON, Arthur. *See* MIDDLETON, Thomas Arthur

MIDDLETON, Barry Glen. b 41. Lich Th Coll 68. **d** 70 **p** 71. C Westhoughton *Man* 70–73; C Prestwich St Marg 73–74; TV Buxton w Burbage and King Sterndale *Derby* 74–77; Chapl Worc R Infirmary 77–83; Chapl Fairfield Hosp Hitchin 83–85; P-in-c Erpingham w Calthorpe *Nor* 85–86; R Erpingham w Calthorpe, Ingworth, Aldborough etc 86–92; R Badingham w Bruisyard, Cransford and Dennington *St E* 92–96; V Sidcup St Jo *Roch* 96–98; V Gt and Lt Bardfield w Gt and Lt Saling *Chelmsf* 98–00; rtd 00; PtO *St E* 00–18. *20 Lynwood Avenue, Felixstowe IP11 9HS* T: (01394) 286506 E: bgm.jfm@btinternet.com

MIDDLETON, David Jeremy. b 68. Ex Univ BSc 90. Wycliffe Hall Ox 01. **d** 03 **p** 04. C Ipswich St Jo *St E* 03–06; Hon C Wimbledon Park St Luke *S'wark* 06–09; C Fulwood *Sheff* 09–11; C Heeley and Gleadless Valley 11–12; V Gleadless Valley from 12. *The Vicarage, 5 Blackstock Close, Sheffield S14 1AE* T: 0114-239 3808 E: djm.middleton@googlemail.com

MIDDLETON, Hugh Charles. b 50. Nottm Univ BTh 77. Linc Th Coll 73. **d** 77 **p** 78. C New Sleaford *Linc* 77–81; C Grantham 81; TV 81–83; R Caythorpe 83–95; P-in-c Bracebridge Heath 97–00; V 00–15; P-in-c Bracebridge 07–15; rtd 15. *3 Roman Close, Navenby, Lincoln LN5 0GW* T: (01522) 415494

MIDDLETON, Miss Jennifer Ann. b 82. St Jo Coll Dur BA 03. St Jo Coll Nottm 06. **d** 08 **p** 09. C Fatfield *Dur* 08–12; NE Regional Dir Urban Saints 12–15; PtO *Dur* 14–15; C Aldridge *Lich* from 16. *6 Linley Close, Aldridge, Walsall WS9 0ES* M: 07775-330935 E: jenpuddleduck@hotmail.com

MIDDLETON, Canon Michael John. b 40. Dur Univ BSc 62 Fitzw Ho Cam BA 66 MA 70. Westcott Ho Cam 63. **d** 66 **p** 67. C Newc St Geo 66–69; V 77–85; Chapl St Geo Gr Sch Cape Town S Africa 69–72; Chapl K Sch Tynemouth 72–77; R Hexham *Newc* 85–92; Hon Can Newc Cathl 90–92; Adn Swindon *Bris* 92–97; Can and Treas Westmr Abbey 97–04; rtd 04; PtO *Carl* 05–19. *2 Cleveland Mews, Cleveland Road, Chichester PO19 7AD* T: (01243) 530580

MIDDLETON, Canon Rodney. b 54. St Andr Univ BD 80. St Steph Ho Ox 80. **d** 82 **p** 83. C Walton St Mary *Liv* 82–87; C-in-c Kew St Fran CD 87–94; V Kew 94–95; Chapl Southport and Formby Distr Gen Hosp 87–95; V Haydock St Jas *Liv* 95–17; Asst Chapl Costa Blanca *Eur* from 17; Hon Can Wiawso Ghana from 13. *Urb El Aspre, Carrer Les Fonts 19, 03792 Orba, Alicante, Spain* T: (0034) 678 318 688 E: rodmid169@yahoo.co.uk

MIDDLETON, Canon Thomas Arthur. b 36. Dur Univ MLitt 95 FRHistS 04. K Coll Lon AKC 61 St Boniface Warminster 61. **d** 62 **p** 63. C Sunderland *Dur* 62–63; C Auckland St Helen 63–67; C Winlaton 67–70; C-in-c Pennywell St Thos and Grindon St Oswald CD 70–79; Chapl Grindon Hall Hosp 73–79; R Boldon *Dur* 79–03; Adv in Stewardship Dur Adnry 87–92; Tutor St Chad's Coll Dur 93–07; Acting Prin 96–97; Hon Fell from 07; Hon Can Dur Cathl 98–03; rtd 03; PtO *Dur* 03–15. *24 Peregrine Drive, Chelmsford CM2 8XY* T: (01245) 901634 E: tamiddleton@talktalk.net

MIDDLETON, Wendy Josephine. b 59. LMH Ox BA 80 MA 85 Birm Univ MSc 81. Ox Min Course 14. **d** 17 **p** 18. NSM Goring and Streatley w S Stoke *Ox* from 17. *1 Milldown Avenue, Goring, Reading RG8 0AG* T: (01491) 875435 E: wendy.middleton@tiscali.co.uk

MIDDLETON, Suffragan Bishop of. *See* DAVIES, The Rt Revd Mark

MIDDLETON-DANSKY, Serge Wladimir. b 45. Cuddesdon Coll 74. **d** 77 **p** 78. C Wisbech SS Pet and Paul *Ely* 77–79; LtO

Adnry Riviera *Eur* from 80; C Ox St Giles and SS Phil and Jas w St Marg 83–86; PtO 86–88; *Truro* 88–90; P-in-c Zennor and Towednack 90–96; PtO 97–99; LtO from 99. *The Old Vicarage, Zennor, St Ives TR26 3BY* T: (01736) 796955

MIDDLEWICK, Robert James. b 44. Lon Univ BD 76 K Alfred's Coll Win CertEd 67. Ripon Coll Cuddesdon 75. **d** 77 **p** 78. C Bromley SS Pet and Paul *Roch* 77–81; C Belvedere All SS 81–84; P-in-c Lamberhurst 85–88; P-in-c Matfield 85–88; V Lamberhurst and Matfield 88–99; rtd 09. *4 St James Court, Wood Street, Tunbridge Wells TN1 2QS* E: middlewick@btinternet.com

MIDGLEY, Stephen Nicholas. b 60. Jes Coll Cam BA 83 MA 86 Lon Hosp MB, BS 86. Wycliffe Hall Ox. **d** 97 **p** 98. C Hove Bp Hannington Memorial Ch *Chich* 97–01; C Cambridge H Sepulchre *Ely* 01–04; P-in-c Cambridge St Andr Less 04–09; V from 09. *St Andrew the Less Vicarage, 21 Parsonage Street, Cambridge CB5 8DN* T: (01223) 353794 *or* 750450 E: steve.midgley@christchurchcambridge.org.uk

MIDLANE, Colin John. b 50. Qu Mary Coll Lon BA 72. Westcott Ho Cam 73 Sarum & Wells Th Coll 77. **d** 78 **p** 79. C Bethnal Green St Pet w St Thos *Lon* 78–82; P-in-c Haggerston All SS 82–88; Chapl Hengrave Hall Ecum Cen 88–89; P Cllr St Botolph Aldgate *Lon* 89–94; C St Botolph Aldgate w H Trin Minories 93–94; TV Haywards Heath St Wilfrid *Chich* 94–97; C Brighton St Geo w St Anne and St Mark 97–01; Chapl Brighton and Sussex Univ Hosps NHS Trust 01–03; rtd 03; PtO *Lon* from 04. *30 Damien Court, Damien Street, London E1 2HL* T: (020) 7791 0001

MIDWINTER, Sister Josie Isabel. b 46. Open Univ BA 84 Univ of Wales (Lamp) MA 98. CA Tr Coll IDC 71. **d** 87 **p** 99. CA from 71; CMS 84–93; Uganda 85–91; Kenya 92–96; C Didcot All SS *Ox* 98–05; P-in-c Drayton St Pet (Abingdon) 05–10; rtd 06; PtO *Ox* from 10. *32 Barnes Close, Didcot OX11 8JN* T: (01235) 759398 E: josie.midwinter@lineone.net

MIDWOOD, Canon Peter Stanley. b 47. CertEd 69 York St Jo Univ Hon BEd 19. Linc Th Coll 80. **d** 82 **p** 83. C Garforth *Ripon* 82–85; C-in-c Grinton w Arkengarthdale, Downholme and Marske 85–86; C-in-c Melbecks and Muker 85–86; V Swaledale 86–97; R Romaldkirk w Laithkirk 97–08; AD Richmond 97–08; R Walkingham Hill 08–13; Hon Can Ripon Cathl 05–13; rtd 13; PtO *Nor* from 14. *4 Larch Crescent, Holt NR25 6TU* E: ps.midwood@gmail.com

MIELL (née OOSTRA), Catharina Henriët. b 60. Uppsala Univ MDiv 92. **p** 92. C Linköping Cathl Sweden 92–93; V Simrishamn 93–96; V Lund Cathl 96–99; V Stora Köpinge 99–01; V Brösarp - Tranås 01–04; C Upton cum Chalvey *Ox* 04–05; PtO *Win* 11–16; V Sotenäs Pastorat Sweden from 16. *Mastgatan 7, 45650 Smögen, Sweden* E: henrietmiell@gmail.com

MIELL, David Keith. b 57. Lanc Univ BSc 78 PhD 81 Trin Coll Cam BA 85. Westcott Ho Cam 83. **d** 86 **p** 87. C Blackbird Leys CD *Ox* 86–88; C Blackbird Leys 88–89; C Walton Milton Keynes 89–90; TV 90–96; RD Milton Keynes 93–95; TR Upton cum Chalvey 96–05; AD Burnham and Slough 02–05; PtO 05–08; *Sarum* 10–11; P-in-c Ringwood *Win* 11–16; rtd 16; PtO *Win* from 16. *Mastgatan 7, 45650 Smögen, Sweden* M: (0046) 76-794 9110 E: dkmiell@gmail.com

MIER, Miss Catherine Elizabeth. b 60. Bris Univ BSc 81 Chelsea Coll Lon MSc 84 Dur Univ BA 95. Cranmer Hall Dur 93. **d** 96 **p** 97. C Royston *St Alb* 96–00; C Bilton *Cov* 00–04; P-in-c Wellesbourne 04–14; V 14–17; P-in-c Walton d'Eiville 04–14; R 14–17; AD Fosse 11–17; R Arden Marches from 18; AD Alcester from 19. *The Vicarage, 3 Manor Mews, Studley B80 7PR* T: (01527) 852830 E: kate.mier1@gmail.com

MIGHALL, Robert. b 33. St Pet Coll Ox BA 57 MA 61. Wycliffe Hall Ox 57. **d** 58 **p** 59. C Stoke *Cov* 58–62; C Rugby St Andr 62–64; V Newbold on Avon 64–76; V Combroke w Compton Verney 76–96; V Kineton 76–96; rtd 96. *40 Rempstone Road, Wimborne BH21 1RP* T: (01202) 883522

MIHILL, Dennis George. b 31. St Alb Minl Tr Scheme 78. **d** 81 **p** 82. NSM Harpenden St Nic *St Alb* 81–86; C Sawbridgeworth 86–89; V Motspur Park *S'wark* 89–96; rtd 96; PtO *St Alb* 96–98 and 01–08; Hon C Biddenham 98–01; PtO *Roch* from 06. *7 Bourchier Close, Sevenoaks TN13 1PD* T: (01732) 459760 E: d.mihill@sky.com

MILBANK (née LEGG), Canon Alison Grant. b 54. Girton Coll Cam BA 78 MA 81 PGCE 79 Lanc Univ PhD 88. EMMTC 05. **d** 06 **p** 07. NSM Lambley *S'well* 06–09; PV S'well Minster 09–17; Can Res S'well Minster from 17. *Burgage Hill Cottage, Burgage, Southwell NG25 0EP* T: (01636) 819224 M: 07738-873279 E: alison.milbank@nottingham.ac.uk *or* alison.milbank@southwellminster.org.uk

MILBANK, Arabella Mary. *See* ROBINSON, Arabella Mary Milbank

MILES, Mrs Beverley Anne. b 54. **d** 09 **p** 15. NSM Findon Valley *Chich* 09–15; P-in-c 15–21; Chapl Care for Veterans Worthing 14–21; V Scaynes Hill *Chich* from 21. *The Vicarage, Vicarage Lane, Scaynes Hill, Haywards Heath RH17 7PB* M: 07786-924942 E: beverley_miles@hotmail.com

MILES, Damian Stewart. *See* HARRISON-MILES, Damian Stewart

MILES, Daniel James. b 85. York St Jo Coll BA 06 York St Jo Univ MA 12 PGCE 08 Dur Univ BA 19. Ridley Hall Cam 16. **d** 19 **p** 20. C Erringden *Leeds* from 19. *12 Phoenix Court, Todmorden OL14 5SJ* M: 07538-916546 E: daniel.miles@leeds.anglican.org

MILES, Gerald Christopher Morgan. b 36. Peterho Cam BA 57 MA 72 Cranfield Inst of Tech MSc 72 CEng MIET. Wycliffe Hall Ox 74. **d** 76 **p** 77. C Tunbridge Wells St Jas *Roch* 76–80; V Leigh 80–90; R Addington w Trottiscliffe 90–91; P-in-c Ryarsh w Birling 90–91; R Birling, Addington, Ryarsh and Trottiscliffe 91–00; Chapl ATC 80–11; rtd 00; PtO *Roch* from 00. *2 Spa Close, Hadlow, Tonbridge TN11 0JX* T/F: (01732) 852323 E: gcmmiles@btinternet.com

MILES (née HOARE), Ms Janet Francis Mary. b 48. St Aid Coll Dur BA 70 Bris Univ MEd 84. Sarum & Wells Th Coll 91. **d** 93 **p** 94. C Bruton and Distr *B & W* 93–98; P-in-c Llangarron w Llangrove, Whitchurch and Ganarew *Heref* 98–04; P-in-c Dixton 02–04; P-in-c Chewton Mendip w Ston Easton, Litton etc *B & W* 04–07; Dir Studies WEMTC 04–07; rtd 11; PtO *B & W* 11–15; *Ex* from 12. *The Sanctuary, Bridford, Exeter EX6 7HS* T: (01647) 252750 E: jfm2@btinternet.com

MILES, Jillian Maud. *See* LOCOCK, Jillian Maud

MILES, Julie. b 64. Open Univ BA 03 York St Jo Coll PGCE 05. Linc Sch of Th and Min 16. **d** 20 **p** 21. C Frodingham and New Brumby *Linc* from 20. *Address withheld by request* E: julie.miles@lincoln.anglican.org

MILES, Miss Sharon Elizabeth Ann. b 66. Westcott Ho Cam 00. **d** 02 **p** 03. C Shrub End *Chelmsf* 02–05; P-in-c Rivenhall 05–10; P-in-c St Osyth 10–15; V St Osyth and Great Bentley from 15. *The Vicarage, The Bury, St Osyth, Clacton-on-Sea CO16 8NX* T: (01255) 822055 E: revdsmiles@hotmail.com

MILES, Stephen John. b 44. Monash Univ Aus BA 66 Worc Coll Ox DipEd 68 Univ Coll Lon MA 75 California Univ PhD 80. Melbourne Coll of Div BTheol 86. **d** 87 **p** 88. C E Malvern St Jo Australia 87; C Clifton Hill St Andr 87–89; Chapl Co-ord and Angl Chapl Monash Med Cen 89–97; Asst Chapl Bonn w Cologne *Eur* 97–00; Chapl 00–03; Perm to Offic Melbourne Australia from 03. *67 Caroline Street, South Yarra VIC, Australia* T: (0061) (3) 9866 1463 E: stephenmiles@iprimus.com.au

MILES, Mrs Susan. b 63. LTCL 85. STETS 10. **d** 13 **p** 14. C White Horse *Sarum* 13–16; Chapl S Warks Gen Hosps NHS Trust from 16. T: (01926) 495321 M: 07545-497254 E: reverendsusanmiles@btinternet.com

MILFORD, Canon Catherine Helena. b 39. LMH Ox BA 61 MA 65 FRSA 92. Gilmore Course 81. **dss** 82 **d** 87 **p** 94. Heaton St Barn *Bradf* 82–88; Par Dn 87–88; Adult Educn Adv *Win* 88–96; TR Barnham Broom *Nor* 96–00; P-in-c Reymerston w Cranworth, Letton, Southburgh etc 96–00; TR Barnham Broom and Upper Yare 00–04; Hon Can Nor Cathl 00–04; rtd 04; PtO *Bradf* 05–14; *Leeds* from 14. *6 Leylands Grove, Bradford BD9 5QP* E: cthmilford6@gmail.com

MILFORD, Graham Alan. b 57. Trin Coll Bris 00. **d** 02 **p** 03. C Wolborough and Ogwell *Ex* 02–08; P-in-c Newburgh w Westhead *Liv* 08–10; V 10–16; C Maghull and Melling 17–18; TV Sutton 18–20. *Allerton Vicarage, Harthill Road, Liverpool L18 3HU* T: 0151-724 1561 M: 07508-818634 E: grahammilford@btinternet.com

MILFORD, Mrs Nicola Claire. b 75. Liv Univ BTh 03. Trin Coll Bris 00 NOC 02. **d** 04 **p** 05. C Alphington, Shillingford St George and Ide *Ex* 04–08; Dioc Adv NSM *Liv* from 11; P-in-c Sefton 13–16; TV Mossley Hill 16–20; R Allerton All Hallows from 20; AD Liv South-Childwall from 19. *Allerton Vicarage, Harthill Road, Liverpool L18 3HU* T: 0151-724 1561 M: 07816-567598 E: nicola@allhallowsallerton.org.uk

MILLAR, Alexander. *See* MILLAR, John Alexander Kirkpatrick

MILLAR, Andrew Charles. b 48. Hull Univ BSc 69. Cuddesdon Coll 71. **d** 73 **p** 74. C Rushmere *St E* 73–76; C Ipswich All Hallows 76–79; Dioc Youth Chapl *Sheff* 79–83; Youth Chapl *Win* 83–92; V Colden 92–08; V Twyford and Owslebury and Morestead etc 08–10; rtd 10; PtO *St As* from 13. *22 Fford Bryn Estyn, Mold CH7 1TJ* T: (01352) 754745 E: acmillar@btinternet.com

MILLAR, Christine. *See* WHEELER, Christine

MILLAR, David Glassell. b 43. Dur Univ BSc 64 St Cath Coll Cam MA 66 MA 71 Birkbeck Coll Lon BSc 78 Leeds Univ MSc 80. Cuddesdon Coll 66. **d** 68 **p** 69. C Pershore w Wick *Worc* 68–72; C Malden St Jas *S'wark* 72–73; V W Dean *Chich*

73–75; rtd 08. *5 Beacon Hill, London N7 9LY* T/F: (020) 7607 3809 E: davidgmillar@hotmail.com

MILLAR, Gary. b 67. St Mich Coll Llan 88. **d** 91 **p** 92. C Tonyrefail w Gilfach Goch *Llan* 91–93; C Barry All SS 93–95; TV Cowbridge 95–97; I Dromara w Garvaghy *D & D* 97–01; I Kilkeel 01–08; I Belfast St Paul w St Barn *Conn* 08–12; I Ahoghill w Portglenone 12–18; I Kilrea, Tamlaght O'Crilly Upper and Lower *D & R* from 18. *2 Moneygran Road, Kilrea, Coleraine BT51 5SJ* T: (028) 2954 0257 M: 07817-968357 E: revgarymillar@btinternet.com

✠**MILLAR, The Rt Revd John Alexander Kirkpatrick (Sandy).** b 39. Trin Coll Cam BA 62 MA 66. Cranmer Hall Dur 74. **d** 76 **p** 77 **c** 05. C Brompton H Trin w Onslow Square St Paul *Lon* 76–85; V 85–05; Hon C 05–11; Hon C Onslow Square and S Kensington St Aug from 11; P-in-c Tollington 03–10; AD Chelsea 89–94; Preb St Paul's Cathl from 97; Asst Bp Uganda from 05; Hon Asst Bp Lon from 06; Hon Asst Bp St E from 12. *37 Alde Lane, Aldeburgh IP15 5DZ* E: sandy.millar@techademic.net

MILLAR, Canon Sandra Doreen. b 57. Univ of Wales (Cardiff) BA 79 Warwick Univ MA 94 PhD 99. Ripon Coll Cuddesdon 98. **d** 00 **p** 01. C Chipping Barnet w Arkley *St Alb* 00–03; TV Dorchester *Ox* 03–07; Dioc Children's Officer *Glouc* 07–13; Hd of Projects and Development Abps' Coun from 13; Public Preacher *Glouc* from 13; Hon Can Glouc Cathl from 14. *Church House, 27 Great Smith Street, London SW1P 3AZ* T: (020) 7898 1458 M: 07976-823986 E: sandra.millar@churchofengland.org or revdocsand@gmail.com

MILLARD, Malcolm Edoric. b 38. Lon Univ BA 60 AKC 60 Lon Inst of Educn PGCE 61. St Jo Coll Nottm 80. **d** 77 **p** 81. Dn Banjul Cathl The Gambia 77–79; Dn Lamin St Andr 79–81; P-in-c 81–82; P-in-c Fajara St Paul 82–88; V Gen 86–88; CMS Miss Partner 89–95; C S Shoebury *Chelmsf* 95–97; C Rainham w Wennington 97–02; P-in-c N Ockendon 02–08; PtO *Sarum* from 08. *29 Moorcombe Drive, Preston, Weymouth DT3 6NP* T: (01305) 834060 E: weeksmary@gmail.com

MILLARD, Paul Richard. b 77. York St Jo Coll BSc 99 Dur Univ BA 19 CIMA 08. Cranmer Hall Dur 14. **d** 16 **p** 17. C Clifton *York* 16–20; R York St Paul from 20; P-in-c York St Barn from 20. *St Paul's Rectory, 100 Acomb Road, York YO24 4ER* E: revpaulmillard@gmail.com

MILLER, Adrian David. b 74. Open Univ BSc 02. St Jo Coll Nottm MTh 06. **d** 06 **p** 07. C Newton Flotman, Swainsthorpe, Tasburgh, etc *Nor* 06–09; TV 09–14; R Mulbarton w Bracon Ash, Hethel and Flordon from 14. *The Rectory, The Common, Mulbarton, Norwich NR14 8JS* T: (01508) 571167 M: 07539-636365 E: adrian@mulbchurch.org.uk

MILLER, Mrs Alison. b 75. Liv Univ BSc 97 St Jo Coll Dur BATM 15. Cranmer Hall Dur 13. **d** 15 **p** 16. C Lanchester and Burnhope *Dur* 15–18; NSM Tanfield w Burnopfield and Dipton 19–21; TV Lark Valley and N Bury *St E* from 21. *The Rectory, West Stow, Bury St Edmunds IP28 6ET* T: (01284) 728714 E: teamvicarlvnb@btinternet.com

MILLER, Andrew. See MILLER, Ronald Andrew John

MILLER, Andrew Philip. b 72. Liv Univ BSc 94 PhD 98. Cranmer Hall Dur 09. **d** 11 **p** 12. C Barnard Castle w Whorlton *Dur* 11–15; V Tanfield w Burnopfield and Dipton 15–21; TR Lark Valley and N Bury *St E* from 21. *The Rectory, West Stow, Bury St Edmunds IP28 6ET* T: (01284) 728714 E: teamrectorlvnb@btinternet.com

MILLER, Mrs Annette. b 53. W Midl Coll of Educn BEd 83. LCTP 07 Cranmer Hall Dur 12. **d** 13 **p** 14. NSM Levens *Carl* 13–17; PtO 17–18; NSM Arnside from 18. *Airton, Eden Park Road, Grange-over-Sands LA11 6BW* T: (015395) 33840 E: miller3637@btinternet.com

MILLER, Anthony. See MILLER, Ronald Anthony

MILLER, Charles. See MILLER, Ernest Charles

MILLER, Charles Irvine. b 35. Nottm Univ BEd 76. Bps' Coll Cheshunt 61. **d** 63 **p** 64. C Anlaby Common St Mark *York* 63–66; C Whitby 66–68; R Ingoldmells w Addlethorpe *Linc* 68–72; P-in-c Bishop Norton 72–76; V Scunthorpe St Jo 76–83; Chapl Manor Hosp Walsall 83–89; rtd 89; PtO *Ely* 89–98 and 99–18; Hon C Isleham 98–99. *The Old Studio, 6 Chapel Street, Duxford, Cambridge CB22 4RJ*

MILLER, The Ven Darren Noel. b 67. Birm Univ BSocSc 89. Chich Th Coll BTh 95 Coll of Resurr Mirfield 94. **d** 95 **p** 96. C Weoley Castle *Birm* 95–98; C Shard End 98–00; V Castle Vale St Cuth 00–06; AD Sutton Coldfield 04–06; TR Cheam *S'wark* 06–18; AD Sutton 13–18; Hon Can S'wark Cathl 16–18; Adn Ashford *Cant* from 18. *The Archdeaconry, Pett Lane, Charing, Ashford TN27 0DL* T: (01233) 712649 M: 07548-232377 E: darren.miller@archdeacashford.org

MILLER, Canon David George. b 54. Oriel Coll Ox BA 76 MA 80 BD 06 Ex Univ PhD 13. Ripon Coll Cuddesdon 78. **d** 81 **p** 82. C Henfield w Shermanbury and Woodmancote

Chich 81–84; C Monk Bretton *Wakef* 84–87; V Rastrick St Jo 87–93; TR Helston and Wendron *Truro* from 93; P-in-c W Kerrier from 19; RD Kerrier from 17; Chapl R Cornwall Hosps Trust 95–01; Chapl W of Cornwall Primary Care Trust 01–06; Hon Can Truro Cathl from 06. *St Michael's Rectory, Church Lane, Helston TR13 8PF* T: (01326) 572516 E: millerourrectory@googlemail.com

MILLER, David James Tringham. b 45. AKC 70. Sarum & Wells Th Coll 76. **d** 77 **p** 78. C Abington *Pet* 77–80; TV Corby SS Pet and Andr w Gt and Lt Oakley 80–83; V Kettering All SS 83–94; RD Kettering 87–94; V Pet All SS 94–09; rtd 09; C Penrith w Newton Reigny and Plumpton Wall *Carl* 10–11; PtO 11–16. *27 Drovers Terrace, Penrith CA11 9EN* T: (01768) 840406

MILLER, David Robert. b 47. Middx Univ BA 98. ERMC 94. **d** 08 **p** 09. C Eaton Socon *St Alb* 08–12; rtd 12; PtO *St Alb* from 12. *32 Cornwall Court, Eaton Socon, St Neots PE19 8PR* T: (01480) 471132 E: davidmiller.rev@gmail.com

MILLER, Ernest Charles. b 56. Franklin & Marshall Coll (USA) BA 78 Univ of Michigan MA 79 Keble Coll Ox DPhil 90. Nashotah Ho MDiv 82. **d** 82 **p** 83. C Dallas St Andr USA 82–84; Warden Ho of SS Greg and Macrina 84–90; Asst Chapl Keble Coll Ox 84–88; P-in-c New Marston *Ox* 91–96; Ramsey Prof Th Nashotah Ho Wisconsin USA 96–00; R New York Transfiguration USA 00–04; Adjunct Prof Ch Hist Gen Th Sem 02–04; TR Abingdon *Ox* from 06. *The Rectory, St Helen's Court, Abingdon OX14 5BS* T: (01235) 532722 M: 07726-743924 E: rector@sthelens-abingdon.org.uk

MILLER, Gareth. See MILLER, John Gareth

MILLER, The Very Revd Geoffrey Vincent. b 56. Dur Univ BEd 78 Newc Univ MA 94. St Jo Coll Nottm 81. **d** 83 **p** 84. C Jarrow *Dur* 83–86; TV Billingham St Aid 86–92; Dioc Urban Development Officer 91–97; Community Chapl Stockton-on-Tees 92–94; P-in-c Darlington St Cuth 94–96; V 96–99; Soc Resp Officer 97–99; Can Res Newc Cathl 99–05; Dioc Urban Officer 99–05; Adn Northd and Can Res Newc Cathl 05–18; Dean Newc from 18. *26 Mitchell Avenue, Newcastle upon Tyne NE2 3LA* T: 0191-232 1939 E: g.miller@newcastle.anglican.org or dean@newcastlecathedral.org.uk

MILLER, Graham William. b 71. St Andr Univ BD 94 Dur Univ MA 98. Westcott Ho Cam 99. **d** 01 **p** 02. C Ex St Dav 01–03; C Sunderland St Mary and St Pet and Sunderland Pennywell St Thos *Dur* 03–07; C Paddington St Jas *Lon* 07–14; R Greenford H Cross from 14. *The Rectory, 75 Oldfield Lane South, Greenford UB6 9JT* T: (020) 8575 5402 M: 07851-013457 E: graham.miller@london.anglican.org

✠**MILLER, The Rt Revd Harold Creeth.** b 50. TCD BA 73 MA 78. St Jo Coll Nottm BA 75. **d** 76 **p** 77 **c** 97. C Carrickfergus *Conn* 76–79; Dir Ext Studies St Jo Coll Nottm 79–84; Chapl QUB 84–89; I Carrigrohane Union *C, C & R* 89–97; Bp's Dom Chapl 91–97; Can Cork and Cloyne Cathls 94–96; Treas Cork Cathl 96–97; Can Cork Cathl 96–97; Preb Tymothan St Patr Cathl Dublin 96–97; Bp D & D 97–19; rtd 19. *29 Dromore Road, Lurgan, Craigavon BT66 7LD* E: haroldcreethmiller@gmail.com

MILLER, Ian Daukes Douglas. St Hugh's Coll Ox BA 96 Warwick Univ MA 97 Called to the Bar (Gray's Inn) 99. Oak Hill Th Coll 17. **d** 19 **p** 20. C Maidenhead St Andr and St Mary *Ox* from 19. *Address withheld by request*

MILLER (née BLUNDEN), Mrs Jacqueline Ann. b 63. Leic Univ BA 86 SS Coll Cam BA 90. Ridley Hall Cam 88. **d** 91 **p** 19. Par Dn Bedford St Paul *St Alb* 91–94; C 94–95; PtO *Lon* 05–18; Hon C St Andr-by-the-Wardrobe w St Ann, Blackfriars and St Martin Ludgate 16–19; NSM Pimlico St Pet w Westmr Ch Ch from 19. *The Rectory, St Andrew's House, 35 St Andrew's Hill, London EC4V 5DE* M: 07742-104065 E: jacquimiller77@gmail.com

MILLER, John David. b 76. Ch Ch Ox BA 98 MA 07. Oak Hill Th Coll BA 10. **d** 10 **p** 11. C Bath St Bart *B & W* 10–13; NSM Box w H Trin and St Pet 16–18. *33A Bushmead Avenue, Bedford MK40 3QH* M: 07821-180901 E: johnmiller.jdm@gmail.com

MILLER, Canon John David. b 50. Nottm Univ BTh 73 Lanc Univ CertEd 74 Newc Univ MA 93. Kelham Th Coll 68. **d** 74 **p** 75. C Horden *Dur* 74–79; C Billingham St Aid 79–80; TV 80–84; TR S Shields All SS 84–10; Hon Can Dur Cathl 04–10; rtd 10; PtO *Dur* from 10. *6 Tynedale Road, South Shields NE34 6EX* T: 0191-455 6911

MILLER, John Gareth. b 57. St Jo Coll Dur BA 78 Hull Univ MA 11. Ridley Hall Cam 79 Ven English Coll Rome 80. **d** 81 **p** 82. C Addiscombe St Mary *Cant* 81–84; TV Melbury *Sarum* 84–88; TR 88–91; V Leamington Priors All SS *Cov* 91–94; PtO *Ox* 15–17; R Akeman from 17; AD Bicester and Islip from 18. *The Rectory, Troy Lane, Kirtlington, Kidlington OX5 3HA* T: (01869) 350224 E: jgarethmiller@gmail.com

MILLER (*née* **BAILEY**), **Judith Elizabeth Anne.** b 61. UEA MSc 14 RSCN 84 RGN. **d** 99 **p** 00. OLM Blyth Valley *St E* 99–07; OLM Bungay H Trin w St Mary 11–13; OLM Wainford 11–13; NSM Bungay 13–18; NSM Sole Bay from 18. *Moonrakers, Back Road, Wenhaston, Halesworth IP19 9DY* T: (01502) 478882 E: judym61@btinternet.com

MILLER (*née* **Donaldson**), **Mrs Katherine.** b 90. St Jo Coll Dur BA 12 St Cath Coll Ox PGCE 14. St Mellitus Coll MA 18. **d** 19. C Fulham St Matt *Lon* from 19. *2A Clancarty Road, London SW6 3AB* M: 07403-674406 E: katherine@stmf.org.uk

MILLER, Kathryn Rebecca. b 63. Ex Univ BSc 84 Abth Univ MSc 86 UEA PhD 10 Wolfs Coll Cam BTh 15. Ridley Hall Cam 13. **d** 15 **p** 16. C Speke St Aid w All SS *Liv* 15–18; V Becontree St Mary *Chelmsf* from 18. *The Vicarage, 191 Valance Wood Road, Dagenham RM8 3AH* T: (020) 8592 2822 M: 07914-529310 E: katie.miller.063@gmail.com

MILLER, The Ven Luke Jonathan. b 66. SS Coll Cam BA 87 MA 91. St Steph Ho Ox BA 90. **d** 91 **p** 92. C Oxhey St Matt *St Alb* 91–94; C Tottenham St Mary *Lon* 94–95; V 95–10; AD E Haringey 05–10; Adn Hampstead 10–15; P-in-c Winchmore Hill H Trin 11–12; P-in-c St Andr-by-the-Wardrobe w St Ann, Blackfriars 15–17; R St Andr-by-the-Wardrobe w St Ann, Blackfriars and St Martin Ludgate from 17; Adn Lon from 16; P-in-c St Botolph without Bishopgate 16–18; Chapl to The Queen from 20. *The Rectory, St Andrew's House, 35 St Andrew's Hill, London EC4V 5DE* T: (020) 3837 5204 E: archdeacon.london@london.anglican.org

MILLER, Mark George. b 69. Cranmer Hall Dur 10. **d** 12 **p** 13. C Stockton *Dur* 12–16; P-in-c Stockton Par Ch from 16. *Stockton Parish Church, High Street, Stockton-on-Tees   TS18 1SP   T: (01642)   611734* E: mark@stocktonparishchurch.org.uk

MILLER, Martin Michael. b 55. St Jo Coll Dur BSc 78. Trin Coll Bris 94. **d** 96 **p** 97. C Leamington Priors St Paul *Cov* 96–99; C Bermondsey St Anne and St Aug *S'wark* 99–05; R Newhaven *Chich* from 05. *The Rectory, 36 Second Avenue, Newhaven BN9 9HN* T: (01273) 515251 E: southcoastmillers@gmail.com

MILLER, Michael Andrew. b 58. Ripon Coll Cuddesdon 03. **d** 05 **p** 06. C Hockerill *St Alb* 05–08; P-in-c Kensal Town St Thos w St Andr and St Phil *Lon* 08–12; V 12–16; V Northwood Hills St Edm from 16. *St Edmund's Vicarage, 2 Pinner Road, Northwood HA6 1QS* T: (020) 8866 9230 M: 07778-617482 E: mmiller832@btinternet.com

MILLER, Michael Daukes. b 46. Qu Coll Cam MA 71 Lon Univ BCh 70 MB 71 MRCGP 74. Glouc Th Course 82. **d** 85 **p** 94. NSM Lydney w Aylburton *Glouc* 85–95; NSM Lydney 95–06; Asst Chapl HM Pris Ex 07–19; PtO Ex from 07. *99 East Street, South Molton EX36 3DF* E: mmiller@btinternet.com

MILLER, Canon Paul. b 49. Oak Hill Th Coll 71. **d** 74 **p** 75. C Upton *Ex* 74–77; C Farnborough *Guildf* 77–78; P-in-c Torquay St Luke *Ex* 78–81; V 81–86; V Green Street Green *Roch* 86–94; V Green Street Green and Pratts Bottom 94–01; RD Orpington 96–01; V Shortlands 01–12; Hon Can Roch Cathl 00–12; AD Beckenham 09–12; Chapl Is of Scilly *Truro* 12–15; rtd 15; Chapl to The Queen 05–19; PtO *Cant* from 16; *Roch* 16–20. *11 Bishopswood, Kingsnorth, Ashford TN23 3RD* T: (01233) 365176 M: 07940-582040 E: paulmiller@roundisland.net

MILLER, Canon Philip Harry. b 58. Leeds Univ BA 79. Chich Th Coll 80. **d** 82 **p** 83. C Reddish *Man* 82–86; R Lower Broughton Ascension 86–94; P-in-c Cheetwood St Alb 91–94; P-in-c Langley and Parkfield 95–00; TR 00–10; V Langley from 10; AD Heywood and Middleton 10–15; Hon Can Man Cathl from 07. *The Rectory, Wood Street, Middleton, Manchester M24 5GL* T: 0161-643 5013 E: canonphil@hotmail.co.uk

MILLER, Philip Howard. b 40. Tyndale Hall Bris 67. **d** 72 **p** 73. Argentina 72–73; C Rusholme H Trin *Man* 73–74; SAMS Paraguay 74–77; C Toxteth St Cypr w Ch Ch *Liv* 78–80; V Burscough Bridge 80–85; V Woodbridge St Jo *St E* 85–91; P-in-c Combs 91–92 and 93–96; Chapl Burrswood Chr Cen 92–93; V Yoxford and Peasenhall w Sibton *St E* 96–01; rtd 01; PtO *St E* 07–17. *Salta, 54 Orchard Close, Melton, Woodbridge IP12 1LD* T: (01394) 388615 E: phm914@lineone.net

MILLER, Philip Hugh Owen. b 62. **d** 13 **p** 14. NSM Beccles St Mich and St Luke *St E* 13–17; P-in-c Hundred River and Wainford 17–20; R from 20. *The Rectory, 27 School Road, Ringsfield, Beccles NR34 8NZ* T: (01502) 714786 E: revphilm@btinternet.com

MILLER, Richard Bracebridge. b 45. Lon Coll of Div 66 Wycliffe Hall Ox 68. **d** 70 **p** 71. C Lee Gd Shep w St Pet *S'wark* 70–74; C Roehampton H Trin 74–77; C Earley St Pet *Ox* 77–80; V Aldermaston w Wasing and Brimpton 80–96; C Newbury 96–01; PtO 03–18; *Lon* from 20. *18 Telford Court, Old College Road, Newbury RG14 1TF* T: (01635) 550418 M: 07870-555474 E: richard.b.miller@btinternet.com

MILLER, The Ven Robert Stephen. b 71. QUB BSc 92. CITC BTh 95. **d** 95 **p** 96. C Lurgan Ch the Redeemer *D & D* 95–99; I Tullylish 99–03; I Maghera w Killelagh *D & R* 03–10; I Londonderry Ch Ch, Culmore, Muff and Belmont from 10; Adn Derry from 12. *The Rectory, 1B Heathfield, Londonderry BT48 8JD* T: (028) 7135 2396 *or* 7135 8925 M: 07711-748406 E: rector@cccmsp.org *or* archdeacon@derry.anglican.org

MILLER, Ronald Andrew John. b 46. **d** 96 **p** 97. OLM Heywood *Man* 96–09; PtO *St As* from 12; *Ban* 16–18. *16 Bryn Morfa, Bodelwyddan, Rhyl LL18 5TP* T: (01745) 530055 E: rajlinmiller@btinternet.com

MILLER, Ronald Anthony. b 41. City Univ BSc 63 CEng CPA MRAeS. S'wark Ord Course 69. **d** 72 **p** 80. NSM Crookham *Guildf* 72–73 and 80–85; NSM New Haw 85–95; NSM Effingham w Lt Bookham 95–04; PtO 05–09; NSM Nork 09–11; rtd 11. *76 Bramley Avenue, Melbourn, Royston SG8 6HG* M: 07710-294786 E: ramiller@sky.com

MILLER, Rosamund Joy. *See* SEAL, Rosamund Joy

MILLER, Miss Sarah Lydia. b 65. St Andr Univ BD 90 Hughes Hall Cam PGCE 91. EAMTC 98. **d** 01 **p** 02. NSM Nor St Pet Mancroft w St Jo Maddermarket 01–03; C Wythenshawe *Man* 03–07; C Tewkesbury w Walton Cardiff and Twyning *Glouc* 07–11; V Newbiggin Hall *Newc* 11–18. *c/o 16 Hungerford Road, Bath BA1 3BU* E: sarahmiller1413@gmail.com

MILLER, Stuart William. b 71. Univ of Wales (Cardiff) BA 92. Trin Coll Bris BA 97. **d** 97 **p** 98. C Fordingbridge *Win* 97–98; C Bursledon 98–02; V W Moors *Sarum* 02–05; Chapl Bournemouth and Poole Coll of FE *Win* 05–10; C Bournemouth Town Cen 05–10; V Moordown 10–16; V Winton, Moordown and Charminster 16–17. *53 Victoria Road, Bournemouth BH1 4RT*

MILLER, Canon Thomas Paul. b 49. **d** 90 **p** 90. Asst R NY St Mich USA 90–94; P-in-c Woodstock St Greg 94–03; Can Lit and the Arts NY 03–13; P-in-c Stromness *Ab* from 15. *Quarrybrae, Hillside Road, Stromness KW16 3HR* T: (01856) 850691 E: tmiller.stromness@btinternet.com

MILLER, Timothy Ian. b 85. Ustinov Coll Dur MA 09 St Jo Coll Dur MATM 14. Cranmer Hall Dur 12. **d** 14 **p** 15. C Primrose Hill St Mary w Avenue Road St Paul *Lon* 14–17; P-in-c Highgate All SS from 17; P-in-c Highgate St Aug from 21. *All Saints' Vicarage, 1B Church Road, London N6 4QH* M: 07588-644217 E: revtimiller@gmail.com

MILLER, William David. b 45. Man Univ BA 66. Linc Th Coll 69. **d** 71 **p** 72. C Newc St Geo 71–74; C Corbridge w Halton 74–77; C N Gosforth 77–81; TV Whorlton 81–90; Chapl K Sch Tynemouth 90–09; rtd 09; PtO *Newc* from 09; *Dur* 15–19. *7 Strawberry Terrace, Hazlerigg, Newcastle upon Tyne NE13 7AR* T: 0191-236 5024 E: millers@talktalk.net

MILLER-MASKELL, John Michael. b 45. Sarum & Wells Th Coll 86. **d** 88 **p** 89. C Swanborough *Sarum* 88–91; Chapl RAF 91–95; P-in-c Ollerton w Boughton *S'well* 95–97; P-in-c Capel *Guildf* 97–02; TV Walton H Trin *Ox* 02–03; Healing Co-ord Acorn Chr Foundn 03–04; rtd 04; PtO *Chich* 04–10; P-in-c Chailey 10–18. *Garden Cottage, Thornhill, Ashurst Wood, East Grinstead RH19 3SL* M: 07852-741515 E: revjohn8099@gmail.com

MILLEST, Daniel John. b 86. St Mellitus Coll. **d** 13 **p** 14. C Onslow Square and S Kensington St Aug *Lon* 13–14; Malaysia from 14. *C-20-6, The Capers, Jalan Enam, 51000, Kuala Lumpur, Malaysia* E: dan.millest@htbb.org

MILLGATE, Victor Frederick. b 44. St Mich Coll Llan 81. **d** 83 **p** 84. C Pembroke St Mary w St Mich *St D* 83–85; V Manorbier and St Florence w Redberth 85–04; TR Carew 04–09; AD Castlemartin 03–09; rtd 09. *3 Grove Drive, Pembroke SA71 5QB* T: (01646) 621683

MILLIER, Gordon. b 28. St Aid Birkenhead 63. **d** 65 **p** 66. C Congresbury *B & W* 65–69; P-in-c Badgworth w Biddisham 69–76; R Weare w Badgworth and Biddisham 76–84; R Pilton w Croscombe, N Wootton and Dinder 84–93; rtd 93; PtO *Ex* 93–19. *28 Withy Close, Canal Hill, Tiverton EX16 4HZ* T: (01884) 253128

MILLINCHIP (*née* **DAVENPORT**), **Susan Jane.** b 56. Somerville Coll Ox MA 79. All SS Cen for Miss & Min 10. **d** 14 **p** 15. NSM Witton *Ches* 14–20; NSM Whitegate w Lt Budworth from 20. *2 Manor Grove, Northwich CW8 1JE* T: (01606) 784042 M: 07591-942297 E: revjanemillinchip@outlook.com

MILLINGTON, Stuart. b 45. Lich Th Coll 67. **d** 70 **p** 71. C Boulton *Derby* 70–73; C Moseley St Mary *Birm* 73–76; TV Staveley and Barrow Hill *Derby* 76–82; R Wingerworth 82–99; RD Chesterfield 91–97; P-in-c Elton All SS *Man* 99–09; P-in-c Woolfold 07–09; V Kirklees Valley 09–10; AD Bury 05–10; rtd 10; PtO *Man* 10–12; *Wakef* 10–14; *Leeds* from 14. *33 Westways, Wrenthorpe, Wakefield WF2 0TE* T: (01924) 375996 E: stumillington@btinternet.com

MILLS, Alexandra. b 56. Univ of Wales (Abth) BMus 78 CertEd 79. Ripon Coll Cuddesdon 88. **d** 90 **p** 94. Par Dn Earlsfield St Andr *S'wark* 90–94; C Kingston All SS w St Jo 94–99; C Brixton Road Ch Ch 99–00; PtO from 05. *121A Tranmere Road, London SW18 3QP* T: (020) 8944 1641 M: 07900-543806 E: perfidafalerina@yahoo.co.uk

MILLS, Anne. *See* MILLS, Leslie Anne

MILLS, Anthony James. b 55. Nottm Univ BA. Linc Th Coll. **d** 84 **p** 85. C Mexborough *Sheff* 84–86; C Howden *York* 86–89; V Fylingdales and Hawsker cum Stainsacre 89–95; V Scarborough St Sav w All SS 95–09; P-in-c Scarborough St Martin 02–05; V 05–09; R Failsworth H Family *Man* 09–17; rtd 17; PtO *Leeds* from 17. *2 Kaye Hill, Cullingworth, Bradford BD13 5HT* T: (01535) 270553 E: aj.mills@hotmail.com

MILLS, David Francis. b 51. Oak Hill Th Coll 76. **d** 79 **p** 80. C Rodbourne Cheney *Bris* 79–82; C Wolverhampton St Matt *Lich* 82–85; CF 85–88; TV Braunstone *Leic* 88–95; Past Asst to Adn Leic 95–97; C Barkestone w Plungar, Redmile and Stathern 97–99; C Bottesford and Muston 97–99; C Harby, Long Clawson and Hose 97–99; C Vale of Belvoir 00–02; R Winfarthing w Shelfanger w Burston w Gissing etc *Nor* 02–20; rtd 20. *Station House, North Road, Hemsby, Great Yarmouth NR29 4EZ* E: revdfmills1812@gmail.com

MILLS, David Graham Mackenzie. *See* MACKENZIE MILLS, David Graham

MILLS, Mrs Elizabeth Frances Margaret. b 56. Westhill Coll Birm BEd 78. Qu Foundn (Course) 15. **d** 17 **p** 18. NSM Wigginton *Lich* 17–20; rtd 20. *21 Robinsons Croft, Chester CH3 5YB* T: (01244) 733936 E: firstclassliz999@gmail.com

MILLS, Canon Geoffrey Charles Malcolm. b 33. Wycliffe Hall Ox 59. **d** 61 **p** 62. C Buckhurst Hill *Chelmsf* 61–65; C Ecclesall *Sheff* 65–69; V Endcliffe 69–78; R Whiston 78–99; Hon Can Sheff Cathl 96–99; rtd 99; PtO *Sheff* from 99. *8 Hall Road, Rotherham S60 2BP* T: (01709) 373863 E: gcmills@blueyonder.co.uk

MILLS, Gordon Derek. b 35. Lich Th Coll 60. **d** 63 **p** 64. C W Derby St Mary *Liv* 63–65; C Clifton w Glapton *S'well* 65–67; V N Wilford St Faith 67–72; V Farnsfield 72–82; P-in-c Kirklington w Hockerton 77–82; P-in-c Brindle and Asst Dir of Educn *Blackb* 82–86; V Gt Budworth *Ches* 86–88; P-in-c Antrobus 87–88; V Gt Budworth and Antrobus 88–92; V Gt Budworth 92–00; rtd 00; PtO *Blackb* 01–04; *York* 04–07; *Bradf* 04–07; *Dur* 04–15; *Leeds* from 17. *Holmelands House, Raby Lane, East Cowton, Northallerton DL7 0BW* T: (01325) 378798 E: derek.mills77@gmail.com

MILLS, Canon Hubert Cecil. b 44. TCD BA 66 MA 71 HDipEd 73. CITC 67. **d** 67 **p** 68. C Dublin Rathfarnham *D & G* 67–72; C Dublin St Steph and St Ann 72–77; I Holmpatrick w Balbriggan and Kenure 77–86; I Killiney H Trin 86–11; Min Can St Patr Cathl Dublin 69–92; Succ St Patr Cathl Dublin 77–92; Preb Rathmichael St Patr Cathl Dublin 92–01; Treas St Patr Cathl Dublin 01–11; rtd 11. *2 Verona, Queens Park, Monkstown, Co Dublin, Republic of Ireland* T: (00353) (1) 214 3689 M: 87-286 8743 E: cecil.mills@alterum.com

MILLS, Ian Kenneth. b 83. QUB BMus 04 MA 06 PhD 16 TCD MTh 18. CITI 15. **d** 17 **p** 18. Agherton *Conn* 17–18; C Larne and Inver 18–21; P-in-c Chew Stoke w Nempnett Thrubwell *B & W* from 21; P-in-c Winford w Felton Common Hill from 21. *The Rectory, 4 Parsonage Lane, Winford, Bristol BS40 8DG* T: 07751-859945 E: imills@tcd.ie

MILLS, Jennifer Clare. *See* TOMLINSON, Jennifer Clare

MILLS, Mrs Leslie Anne. b 44. K Alfred's Coll Win CertEd 65. SWMTC 99. **d** 02 **p** 03. NSM Kilmington, Stockland, Dalwood, Yarcombe etc *Ex* 02–16; rtd 16; PtO *Ex* from 16. *2 Church Lane, Feniton, Honiton EX14 3BY* T: (01404) 850923

MILLS, Martin. b 58. **d** 14 **p** 15. NSM Bolney *Chich* 14–20; NSM Cuckfield and Bolney from 20; NSM Cowfold 14–20; NSM Lower Beeding and Cowfold from 20. *19 Honeywood Road, Horsham RH13 6AE* T: (01403) 267284

MILLS, Michael Henry. b 51. AKC 73. St Aug Coll Cant. **d** 74 **p** 75. C Newton Aycliffe *Dur* 74–78; C Padgate *Liv* 78–79; TV 79–95; V Frodsham *Ches* 95–19; rtd 19; PtO *Ches* from 19. *4 Grove Terrace, Helsby, Frodsham WA6 0QG* T: (01928) 727230 E: mikehmills@mac.com

MILLS, Michael John. b 52. St Andr Univ BSc 75 Cam Univ PGCE 76. Cranmer Hall Dur 97. **d** 99 **p** 00. C Brockmoor *Worc* 99–03; P-in-c St Leonards St Ethelburga *Chich* 04–09; P-in-c St Leonards St Leon 04–09; R St Leonards St Ethelburga and St Leon 09–11; TV Glascote and Stonydelph *Lich* 11–18; Resource Min Tamworth Deanery 18–20; rtd 20. *21 Robinsons Croft, Chester CH3 5YB* T: (01244) 733936 M: 07789-913013 E: michael.mills1912@gmail.com

MILLS, Peter James. b 32. Univ Coll Lon LLB 58. **d** 99 **p** 00. NSM Woodchurch *Ches* 99–03; rtd 03; PtO *Ches* from 03. *6 West Heath Court, Gerard Road, West Kirby,*

Wirral CH48 4ES T: 0151-625 3314 M: 07989-374499 E: pjmills@uwclub.net *or* rev.peter@holycrosswoodchurch.uk

MILLS, Roger Conrad. b 58. Selw Coll Cam BA 79 MA 83. St Jo Coll Nottm 83. **d** 85 **p** 86. C Jesmond H Trin *Newc* 85–88; C Alnwick 88–91; Chapl Newc Univ 91–00; P-in-c Newc St Barn and St Jude 95–97; V Kingston Park 00–18; rtd 18; PtO *Newc* from 19. *4 The Grove, Morpeth NE61 1HY* E: rogermills123@yahoo.co.uk

MILLS, Stephen Paul. b 70. Sheff Univ BA 00 Brighton Univ PGCE 09. St Steph Ho Ox MTh 18. **d** 17 **p** 18. C Preston St Jo w Brighton St Aug and St Sav *Chich* 17–18; C Steyning 18–21; C Ashurst 18–21; P-in-c Chich St Wilfrid from 21; Chapl Bp Luffa Sch Chich 21. *7 Durnford Close, Chichester PO19 3AG* E: stephenmills@hotmail.com

MILLSON, Mrs Margaret Lily. b 41. CertEd 61. EMMTC 83. **dss** 86 **d** 87 **p** 94. NSM Bottesford w Ashby *Linc* 86–01; P-in-c St Tudy w St Mabyn and Michaelstow *Truro* 01–10; rtd 10; PtO *Truro* from 16. *Winterbourne, 2 Gwelmeneth Park, St Cleer, Liskeard PL14 5HU* T: (01579) 346338 E: mlmillson@aol.com

MILLWOOD, Stephen Grant. b 44. Sheff City Coll of Educn CertEd 77 Open Univ BA 92. St Jo Coll Nottm 92. **d** 94 **p** 95. C Anston *Sheff* 94–98; V Kimberworth Park 98–09; Bp's Urban Adv 05–09; rtd 09; PtO *Sheff* from 09. *6 Quarryfield Drive, Sheffield S9 5AG* T: 0114-243 4948 E: steveandjanetm@mac.com

MILMINE, Canon Neil Edward Douglas. b 46. Kent Univ BSc 70. Wycliffe Hall Ox 80. **d** 82 **p** 83. C Hailsham *Chich* 82–86; C Horsham 86; TV 86–93; V Patcham 93–11; Can and Preb Chich Cathl 00–11; RD Brighton 02–09; rtd 11; PtO *Chich* from 12; *S'wark* 12–14. *8 The Willows, Barcombe, Lewes BN8 5FJ* T: (01273) 401521 E: n.milmine@yahoo.co.uk

MILNE, Alan. b 54. RMN SRN TCert. Cranmer Hall Dur 89. **d** 91 **p** 92. C Hartlepool St Luke *Dur* 91–94; P-in-c Dalton le Dale 94–00; V 00–05; P-in-c Hawthorn 94–00; R 00–05; R Hawthorn and Murton 05–17; AD Easington 03–15; rtd 17; PtO *Dur* from 18. *5 Park Lane, Murton, Seaham SR7 9QS*

MILNE, Miss Christine Helen. b 48. LTCL 71. S'wark Ord Course 83. **dss** 86 **d** 87 **p** 90. S Lambeth St Steph *S'wark* 86–89; Par Dn 87–89; C Wainuiomata NZ 89–92; C Eastbourne 93; Chapl Nga Tawa Sch Marton 94–02; Chapl Palmerston North Hosp 04–13; Chapl Auckland City Hosp 13–17; PtO from 17. *7 Hobson Street, Levin 5510, New Zealand* T: (0064) (6) 367 3233 *or* 21-2617045 M: (0064) 21-261 7045 E: hmilne@xtra.co.nz

MILNE, Canon James Harley. b 73. Univ of Wales (Lamp) BD 94 New Coll Edin MTh 96. TISEC 95. **d** 98 **p** 99. C Dundee St Mary Magd *Bre* 98–01; Chapl St Marg Res Home Dundee 98–01; R Dundee St Marg *Bre* 01–09; Chapl Ninewells Hosp Dundee 01–09; R Glas St Bride 09–15; Can St Paul's Cathl Dundee *Bre* 08–09; Hon Can St Paul's Cathl Dundee 09–15; Min Can and Sacr St Paul's Cathl *Lon* 15–19; Can Res and Prec St Paul's Cathl from 19. *6 Amen Court, London EC4M 7BU* T: (020) 7246 8331

MILNE SMITH, Christopher. *See* SMITH, Christopher Milne

MILNER, David. b 38. St Aid Birkenhead 63. **d** 66 **p** 67. C Ulverston H Trin *Carl* 66; C Ulverston St Mary w H Trin 66–68; C Mickleover All SS *Derby* 68–71; C Mickleover St Jo 68–71; V 71–82; P-in-c Sandiacre 82–86; P-in-c Doveridge 86–97; P-in-c Sudbury and Somersal Herbert 92–97; R Doveridge, Scropton, Sudbury etc 98–03; RD Longford 86–96 and 01–03; rtd 03; PtO *Lich* 04–08 and 17–21. *21 Greenwood Park, Hednesford WS12 4DQ* T: (01543) 428972

✠**MILNER, The Rt Revd Ronald James.** b 27. Pemb Coll Cam BA 49 MA 52. Wycliffe Hall Ox 51. **d** 53 **p** 54 **c** 88. Succ Sheff Cathl 53–58; V Westwood *Cov* 58–64; V Fletchamstead 64–70; R Southampton St Mary w H Trin *Win* 70–72; P-in-c Southampton St Matt 70–72; LtO 72–73; TR Southampton (City Cen) 73–83; Hon Can Win Cathl 75–83; Adn Linc 83–88; Can and Preb Linc Cathl 83–88; Suff Bp Burnley *Blackb* 88–93; rtd 93; Hon Asst Bp S'well and Nottm from 94. *7 Crafts Way, Southwell NG25 0BL* T: (01636) 816256

MILNER, William David. b 52. St Jo Coll Nottm. **d** 93 **p** 94. C Wollaton *S'well* 93–97; P-in-c Daybrook 97; C W Bridgford 98–99; TV Clifton 99–04; P-in-c Collingham w S Scarle and Besthorpe and Girton 04–10; P-in-c E Trent 10–11; P-in-c Farndon w Thorpe, Hawton and Cotham 11–17; AD Newark and S'well 12–17; rtd 17; PtO *Leic* from 19; *S'well* from 17. *Mill Pond, Old Forge Lane, Granby, Nottingham NG13 9PS* T: (01949) 850504

MILNES, David Ian. b 45. Chich Th Coll 74. **d** 76 **p** 77. C Walthamstow St Sav *Chelmsf* 76–80; C Chingford SS Pet and Paul 80–83; P-in-c Gt Ilford St Alb 83–87; V 87–09; rtd 09; PtO *Chich* from 15. *Walsingham House, Main Road, Hadlow Down, Uckfield TN22 4ES* T: (01825) 830076 E: frmilnes@aol.com

MILSON, Julian James. b 70. De Montfort Univ BEd 96. Oak Hill Th Coll BA 04. **d** 04 **p** 05. C Bramcote *S'well* 04–07; C Hove Bp Hannington Memorial Ch *Chich* 07–18; Crosslinks from 18. *Calle de los Centelles 54, 8-27, 46006 Valencia, Spain* E: joolsm@mac.com

MILTON, Miss Angela Daphne. b 50. FInstLEx 79. Oak Hill Th Coll 84. **d** 87 **p** 94. NSM Watford *St Alb* 87–95; NSM St Alb St Mary Marshalswick 95–97; C Stevenage St Mary Shephall w Aston 97–02; P-in-c E Molesey St Paul *Guildf* 02–05; V E Molesey 05–10; rtd 10; PtO *St Alb* from 10. *75 Furtherfield, Abbots Langley WD5 0PN* T: (01923) 519453 E: angelamilton@msn.com

MILTON-THOMPSON, Jonathan Patrick. b 51. Nottm Univ BA 76. Oak Hill Th Coll 86. **d** 88 **p** 89. C Bispham *Blackb* 88–92; C Darfield *Sheff* 92; C-in-c Gt Houghton CD 92–03; P-in-c Livesey *Blackb* 03–11; V 11–19; P-in-c Blackb St Barn 10–14; V 14–19; rtd 20. *Address temp unknown* E: jarpmt51@hotmail.co.uk

MILVERTON, The Revd and Rt Hon Lord (Fraser Arthur Richard Richards). b 30. Bps' Coll Cheshunt. **d** 57 **p** 58. C Beckenham St Geo *Roch* 57–59; C Sevenoaks St Jo 59–60; C Gt Bookham *Guildf* 60–63; V Okewood 63–67; R Christian Malford w Sutton Benger etc *Bris* 67–93; Public Preacher 93–95; rtd 95; PtO *Sarum* from 96. *7 Betjeman Road, Marlborough SN8 1TL* T: (01672) 514068

MILVERTON, Mrs Ruth Erica. b 32. Open Univ BA 78 Southn Univ MA 82. Sarum Th Coll 83. **dss** 86 **d** 87 **p** 95. Weymouth H Trin *Sarum* 86–87; Hon Par Dn 87–95; NSM 95–02; Dioc NSM Officer 89–97; rtd 02; PtO *Sarum* 02–20. *4 Compass South, Rodwell Road, Weymouth DT4 8QT* T: (01305) 788930 E: rev.milv.compass@care4free.net

MILWAIN, James Callum. b 90. UCL BSc 11. Ripon Coll Cuddesdon BA 19. **d** 19 **p** 20. C Chesterfield St Mary and All SS *Derby* from 19. *8 Birkdale Drive, Chesterfield S40 3JL* T: 07735-303185 E: milwain@gmail.com *or* curate@crookedspire.org

MINAY, Francis Arthur Rodney. b 44. Westcott Ho Cam 66. **d** 68 **p** 69. C Edenbridge *Roch* 68–73; C Bromley St Mark 73–75; V Tudeley w Capel 75–79; TV Littleham w Exmouth *Ex* 79–82; P-in-c Bolton Percy and Asst Chapl to Arts and Recreation in the NE *York* 82–06; rtd 06; LtO *Mor* 07–14; PtO from 14. *Rosedyke, Achintee, Strathcarron IV54 8YX* T: (01520) 722144 E: francisandjaney@btinternet.com

MINCHIN, Anthony John. b 35. St Cath Coll Cam BA 59 MA. Wells Th Coll 59. **d** 61 **p** 62. C Cheltenham St Pet *Glouc* 61–64; C Bushey *St Alb* 64–67; V Cheltenham St Mich *Glouc* 67–74; V Lower Cam 74–82; V Tuffley 82–92; R Huntley and Longhope 92–00; rtd 00; PtO *Glouc* 00–17. *2 Melbourne Drive, Stonehouse GL10 2PJ* T: (01453) 828899

MINCHIN, Charles Scott. b 51. Trin Coll Cam BA 72 MA 75. Linc Th Coll 73. **d** 75 **p** 76. C Gt Wyrley *Lich* 75–78; TV Wilnecote 78–82; C Tamworth 82–84; C-in-c Glascote CD 84–88; R Brierley Hill *Worc* 88–03; P-in-c Stonehouse *Glouc* 03–16; TV Stroudwater 16–18; rtd 18; PtO *Glouc* from 19. *278 Linden Road, Gloucester GL1 5DU* T: (01452) 901262 E: cminchin@talktalk.net

MINCHIN, Christopher David. b 88. Newc Univ BA 11 RCA(Lon) MA 14. Coll of Resurr Mirfield 16. **d** 18 **p** 19. C Benwell and Scotswood *Newc* from 18. *14 Bentinck Road, Newcastle upon Tyne NE4 6UU* E: revd@chrisminchin.com

MINETT STEVENS, Mrs Christina Noelle. b 68. Hull Univ BSc 92 Sheff Univ BA 14. Coll of Resurr Mirfield 12. **d** 14 **p** 15. C Scarborough St Mary w Ch Ch and H Apostles *York* 14–17; V Hornsea, Atwick and Skipsea from 17. *The Vicarage, 9 Newbegin, Hornsea HU18 1AB* E: vicar@hornseabenefice.org

MINION, Canon Arthur. b 65. TCD BTh 92. CITC 89. **d** 92 **p** 93. C Bandon Union *C, C & R* 92–95; I Taunagh w Kilmactranny, Ballysumaghan etc *K, E & A* 95–99; I Shinrone w Aghancon etc *L & K* 99–08; I Crosspatrick Gp *C, F & O* 08–12; I Wexford and Kilscoran Union from 12; Can Ferns Cathl from 14. *The Rectory, Park, Co Wexford, Y35 X2T4, Republic of Ireland* T: (00353) (53) 914 0652 M: 86-825 1065 E: minionarthur@gmail.com

MINION, Hazel Elizabeth Alice. b 47. TCD BA 68 HDipEd 69. CITC 00. **d** 03 **p** 04. Aux Min Templebreedy w Tracton and Nohoval *C, C & R* 03–04; Aux Min Carrigaline Union from 04; Chapl Ashton Sch Cork 03–07. *22 Inchvale Drive, Shamrock Lawn, Douglas, Cork, Republic of Ireland* T: (00353) (21) 436 1924 E: hminion22@hotmail.com

MINKKINEN, Mrs Janet Mary. b 63. Ox Brookes Univ BA 12. **d** 10 **p** 12. NSM Cippenham *Ox* 10–14; V 14–19; V Burnham from 19. *The Rectory, The Precincts, Burnham, Slough SL1 7HU* M: 07856-047960 E: janetminkkinen@hotmail.co.uk

MINNS, David Andrew. b 59. St Jo Coll Nottm 95. **d** 97 **p** 98. C Burpham *Guildf* 97–00; C Knaphill w Brookwood 00–04; R

Ewhurst 04–17; R Churn Valley *Glouc* from 17. *The Rectory, Gloucester Road, Stratton, Cirencester GL7 2LJ* T: (01285) 655199 E: dlkminns@gmail.com

MINTER, Julie Louise. *See* JACKSON, Julie Louise

MINTERN, Mrs Juliette Melinda. b 55. Homerton Coll Cam CertEd 76 UEA BEd 77. Ripon Coll Cuddesdon 13. **d** 16 **p** 17. C Wokingham St Paul *Ox* 16–19; V Lambourn Valley from 19. *The Vicarage, 4 Newbury Street, Lambourn, Hungerford RG17 8PD* M: 07749-844600 E: julieuk98@aol.com *or* revjulie.mintern@lambournvalley.org

MINTON, Bernard John. b 68. St Chad's Coll Dur BA 89 Sheff Univ PhD 14 MRICS 00. Coll of Resurr Mirfield 00. **d** 04 **p** 05. C Lancing w Coombes *Chich* 04–08; TV Ouzel Valley *St Alb* from 08; R Dunstable 14–19. *St Barnabas' Vicarage, Vicarage Road, Leighton Buzzard LU7 2LP* T: (01525) 372149 E: linsladevicar@gmail.com

MIR, Amene Rahman. b 58. Man Univ BA 81 PhD 93. Coll of Resurr Mirfield 81. **d** 83 **p** 84. C Walton St Mary *Liv* 83–87; Chapl Walton Hosp Liv 83–87; PtO *Man* 87–90; Asst Chapl Salford Mental Health Unit 90–94; Chapl Salford Mental Health Services NHS Trust 94–96; Chapl R Marsden NHS Trust 96–04; LtO *Lon* 96–04; PtO *S'wark* 96–04. *9 Mylne Close, Upper Mall, London W6 9TE* T: (020) 8741 7961 E: amenemir@ymail.com

MIRZANIA, Ms Bassirat Bibi. b 43. Tehran Univ MS 74 Thames Valley Coll of HE BSc 83. **d** 04 **p** 05. Chapl Persian Community UK and NSM Guildf Ch Ch w St Martha-on-the-Hill 04–13; rtd 13; PtO *Guildf* from 13. *Shiraz, 11 Nelson Gardens, Guildford GU1 2NZ* T: (01483) 569316 E: bassi.mirzania@btinternet.com

MITCHELL, Alec Silas. b 52. Man Univ BA 75 MPhil 95. N Bapt Coll 77 Coll of Resurr Mirfield 98. **d** 99 **p** 99. C Ashton *Man* 99–05; TV 05–07; P-in-c Haughton St Anne 07–18; Dioc Officer for Racial Justice 02–18; Borough Dean Tameside 10–18; C Denton Ch Ch 13–18; C Denton St Lawr 13–18; C Audenshaw St Steph 13–18; rtd 18. *Cybi's Well, 4 Stanley Crescent, Holyhead LL65 1DD* M: 07436-589604

MITCHELL, Alison Jane. b 68. All SS Cen for Miss & Min. **d** 16 **p** 17. NSM Reddish *Man* from 16. *19 Finchway Road, Stockport SK5 6EZ* T: 0161-442 3226 M: 07540-792409 E: alison@alisonmitchell.org.uk

MITCHELL, Andrew Patrick (Paddy). b 37. English Coll Valladolid 59 Ripon Coll Cuddesdon 84. **d** 64 **p** 65. In RC Ch 64–85; C Woolwich St Mary w St Mich *S'wark* 85–87; V E Wickham 87–94; P-in-c Walsall St Andr *Lich* 94–00; TV Sedgley All SS *Worc* 00–03; rtd 03; PtO *Birm* 03–07. *714 Pershore Road, Selly Oak, Birmingham B29 7NR* T: 0121-415 5828 E: paddy3739@hotmail.co.uk

MITCHELL, Anne-Marie. b 57. **d** 13 **p** 14. NSM Camberley St Mich Yorktown *Guildf* from 13. *13 Verran Road, Camberley GU15 2ND* T: (01276) 682802

MITCHELL, Anthony. b 54. St Jo Coll Nottm 05. **d** 07 **p** 08. C Plas Newton w Ches Ch Ch 07–10; P-in-c Halton 10–20; V from 20. *27 Halton Brow, Halton, Runcorn WA7 2EH* T: (01928) 563636 E: vicar@haltonparish.org.uk

MITCHELL, Ashley. *See* MITCHELL, Christopher Ashley

MITCHELL, Mrs Brenda Margaret. b 53. Leeds Univ BA 06. NOC 03. **d** 06 **p** 07. C Golcar *Wakef* 06–10; P-in-c Oldham Moorside *Man* 10–16; rtd 16. *20 Oakfield Drive, Baildon, Shipley BD17 6AW* T: (01274) 596202 E: brenda_m_mitchell@hotmail.com

MITCHELL, Miss Catherine Amy. b 62. Cov Poly BEng St Jo Coll Dur BA 13 MA 17. Cranmer Hall Dur 11. **d** 13 **p** 14. C Croxdale and Tudhoe *Dur* 13–17; C Merrington 13–17; TV Gornal and Sedgley *Worc* from 17. *22 The Straits, Dudley DY3 3AB* T: (01902) 677897 E: revcatherinemitchell13@gmail.com

MITCHELL, Christian Strang. b 72. Ripon Coll Cuddesdon 12. **d** 14 **p** 15. C Uckfield *Chich* 14–17; V Heathfield from 17. *Heathfield Vicarage, Hailsham Road, Heathfield TN21 8AF* T: (01435) 862744 M: 07796-008426 E: revchristianmitchell@gmail.com

MITCHELL, Christopher Allan. b 51. Newc Univ BA 72. Oak Hill Th Coll 82. **d** 84 **p** 85. C Guisborough *York* 84–87; C Thornaby on Tees 87–88; TV 88–92; V Dent w Cowgill *Bradf* 92–98; R Barney, Fulmodeston w Croxton, Hindringham etc *Nor* 98–03; R Hulland, Atlow, Kniveton, Bradley and Hognaston *Derby* 03–11; RD Ashbourne 09–11; rtd 11; PtO *York* from 12. *42 Melton Avenue, York YO30 5QG* T: (01904) 623872 E: pennychris51@btinternet.com

MITCHELL, Christopher Ashley. b 69. Leeds Univ BA(Econ) 91. Ridley Hall Cam 92. **d** 95 **p** 96. Min Can St As Cathl 95–98; CF 98–02; Chapl RAF from 02. *Chaplaincy Services (RAF), HQ Air Command, RAF High Wycombe HP14 4UE* T: (01494) 496800 E: ashley.mitchell258@mod.gov.uk

MITCHELL, Canon David George. b 35. QUB BA 56. Sarum Th Coll 59. **d** 61 **p** 62. C Westbury-on-Trym H Trin *Bris* 61–64; C Cricklade w Latton 64–68; V Fishponds St Jo 68–77; RD Stapleton 76–77; TR E *Bris* 77–87; R Syston 87–94; V Warmley 87–94; P-in-c Bitton 87–94; R Warmley, Syston and Bitton 94–01; RD Bitton 87–93; Hon Can *Bris* Cathl 87–01; rtd 01; P-in-c Chedworth, Yanworth and Stowell, Coln Rogers etc *Glouc* 01–09; AD Northleach 04–09; PtO *Bris* from 01; *Glouc* 15–21. *32 Flower Way, Longlevens, Gloucester GL2 9JD* T: (01452) 500119 E: canongeorgemitchell@btinternet.com

MITCHELL, Preb David Norman. b 35. Tyndale Hall Bris 64. **d** 67 **p** 68. C Marple All SS *Ches* 67–70; C St Helens St Helen *Liv* 70–72; V S Lambeth St Steph *S'wark* 72–78; P-in-c Brixton Road Ch Ch 73–75; SE Area Sec CPAS 78–81; R Uphill *B & W* 81–92; TR 92–01; Chapl Weston Area Health NHS Trust 86–01; Preb Wells Cathl *B & W* 90–10; rtd 01; PtO *B & W* from 02. *3 Pizey Close, Clevedon BS21 7TP* T: (01275) 349176 E: davidnmitchell@talktalk.net

MITCHELL, Canon Edwin. b 44. St Jo Coll Nottm BTh 74. **d** 74 **p** 75. C Worksop St Jo *S'well* 74–77; C Waltham Abbey *Chelmsf* 77–80; V Whiston *Liv* 80–91; R Wombwell *Sheff* 91–99; V Mortomley St Sav High Green 99–11; P-in-c Stocksbridge 06–07; AD Ecclesfield 01–07; Hon Can Sheff Cathl 07–11; rtd 11; PtO *Bradf* 12–14; *Leeds* from 14. *3 North View, Lothersdale, Keighley BD20 8EX* T: (01535) 631837 E: theedmitchell@gmail.com

MITCHELL, Elizabeth Edgar. b 43. **d** 14. NSM S Cheltenham *Glouc* 14–18; rtd 18; PtO *Glouc* from 19. *1 Coach House Mews, Commercial Street, Cheltenham GL50 2AU* T: (01242) 241311

MITCHELL, Elizabeth Jane. **d** 16 **p** 17. C Bath Abbey w St Jas *B & W* 16–19; V Sway *Win* from 19. *The Vicarage, Station Road, Sway, Lymington SO41 6BA*

MITCHELL, Geoffrey. b 36. SS Coll Cam BA 60 MA 64 Nottm Univ MA 97 CEng 66 FIMechE 76 FCIT 92. EMMTC 88. **d** 91 **p** 92. NSM Oaks in Charnwood and Copt Oak *Leic* 91–94; NSM Loughborough All SS w H Trin 94–00; P-in-c Oaks in Charnwood and Copt Oak 00–03; NSM Shepshed and Oaks in Charnwood 03–04; Dioc NSM Officer 98–02; rtd 04; PtO *Leic* 04–20. *36 Brick Kiln Lane, Shepshed, Loughborough LE12 9EL* T: (01509) 502280 E: mitchell.household@talk21.com

MITCHELL, Geoffrey Peter. b 30. Liv Univ BEng 57 Man Univ MSc 68. Wells Th Coll 57. **d** 59 **p** 60. C Bradford cum Beswick *Man* 59–61; R Man St Pet Oldham Road w St Jas 61–64; LtO 64–68; Hon C Unsworth 68–86; V Woolfold 86–95; rtd 95; PtO *Man* from 95. *14 Redfearn Wood, Rochdale OL12 7GA* T: (01706) 638180 E: geoffrey@geoffreymitchell.plus.com

MITCHELL, George. *See* MITCHELL, David George

MITCHELL, Geraint Owain. b 71. Lincs & Humberside Univ BA 96 Leeds Univ BA 02 Linc Univ MA 14. Coll of Resurr Mirfield 99. **d** 02 **p** 03. C Bridlington Em *York* 02–05; V Brigg, Wrawby and Cadney cum Howsham *Linc* 05–20; V Bonby 10–20; V Worlaby 10–20; V New Mills *Derby* from 20. *The Vicarage, Church Lane, New Mills, High Peak SK22 4NP* T: (01663) 743225 E: vicar@newmillschurch.co.uk

MITCHELL, Gordon Frank Henry. b 26. QFSM . FIFireE. Sarum & Wells Th Coll 74. **d** 77 **p** 78. NSM Alderbury and W Grimstead *Sarum* 77–91; NSM Alderbury Team 91–96; PtO 96–07 and from 14. *Seefeld, Southampton Road, Whaddon, Salisbury SP5 3EB* T: (01722) 710516 E: rev.mitchell@btinternet.com

MITCHELL, Mrs Helen Miranda. b 55. **d** 10 **p** 11. NSM Sudbury and Chilton *St E* 10–17; NSM Petersfield *Portsm* from 18. *9 Monks Orchard, Petersfield GU32 2JJ* T: (01730) 710682 E: helenoldvic@hotmail.com

MITCHELL, Helen Rosemary. b 64. SCRTP 15. **d** 18 **p** 19. NSM Shottermill *Guildf* from 18; PtO *Portsm* from 18. *Address withheld by request* E: revhelenmitchell@shottermillparish.org.uk

MITCHELL, Ian. *See* MITCHELL, Stuart Ian

MITCHELL, Jane. *See* MITCHELL, Elizabeth Jane

MITCHELL, Karen Irene. b 68. Westcott Ho Cam 07. **d** 09 **p** 10. C Cheshunt *St Alb* 09–13; P-in-c Bridgemary *Portsm* 13–17; V 17–20; P-in-c Elson 13–17; V 17–20; AD Gosport 16–20; R Stevenage St Andr and St Geo *St Alb* from 20. *The Rectory, Cuttys Lane, Stevenage SG1 1UP* M: 07834-322943 E: revd.karenmitchell@btinternet.com

MITCHELL, Kevin. b 49. Newc Univ BSc 71 Ox Univ BA 83. Ripon Coll Cuddesdon 81. **d** 83 **p** 84. C Cantril Farm *Liv* 83–86; Chapl N Middx Hosp 86–90; C Gt Cambridge Road St Jo and St Jas *Lon* 86–90; P-in-c Cricklewood St Pet 90–96; V Whetstone St Jo 96–10; rtd 10. *32 Guildford Street, Brighton BN1 3LS* T: (01273) 203429 E: kevin.mitchell.49@googlemail.com

MITCHELL, Mrs Lisa Jane. b 71. Qu Foundn Birm 17. **d** 19 **p** 20. C W Bromwich All SS *Lich* 19–20; C W Bromwich All SS w St Mary and St Phil from 20. *3 Tiverton Drive, West Bromwich B71 1DA* E: lisajmitchell26@outlook.com

MITCHELL, Owain. *See* MITCHELL, Geraint Owain

MITCHELL, Paddy. *See* MITCHELL, Andrew Patrick

MITCHELL, Rachel Elizabeth. b 60. St Jo Sch of Miss Nottm 14. **d** 17 **p** 18. C Radcliffe-on-Trent and Shelford *S'well* 17–19; R Wiverton in the Vale from 19. *The Vicarage, 2 Dobbin Close, Cropwell Bishop, Nottingham NG12 3GR* M: 07944-992178 E: revdremitchell@gmail.com

MITCHELL, Canon Richard John Anthony. b 64. St Martin's Coll Lanc BA 85 PGCE 86. Sarum & Wells Th Coll 88. **d** 91 **p** 92. C Kendal H Trin *Carl* 91–95; TV Kirkby Lonsdale 95–04; P-in-c Badgeworth, Shurdington and Witcombe w Bentham *Glouc* 04–09; R 09–16; AD Glouc N 04–09; AD Severn Vale 09–16; Hon Can Glouc Cathl 10–16; Can Res Glouc Cathl from 16. *4A Millers Green, Gloucester GL1 2BN* E: richard.mitchell@talk21.com

MITCHELL, Robert Hugh. b 53. Ripon Coll Cuddesdon. **d** 82 **p** 83. C E Dulwich St Jo *S'wark* 82–86; C Cambridge Gt St Mary w St Mich *Ely* 86–90; Chapl Girton Coll Cam 86–90; Asst Chapl Win Coll 90–91; Asst Chapl Addenbrooke's NHS Trust 91–93; Chapl Portsm Hosps NHS Trust 93–95; Chapl Mental Health Chapl Portsm Health Care NHS Trust 93–95; Chapl R Free London NHS Foundn Trust 95–14; PtO *Lon* from 14. *The Undercroft, Stoneleigh Abbey, Kenilworth CV8 2LF* E: roberthughmitchell@mac.com

MITCHELL, Robert McFarlane. b 50. Man Univ BA 72 Lambeth STh 92. Wycliffe Hall Ox 73. **d** 75 **p** 76. C Tonbridge SS Pet and Paul *Roch* 75–80; CF 80–08; P-in-c Tillington *Chich* 08–17; P-in-c Duncton 08–17; P-in-c Upwaltham 08–17; rtd 17. *11 Cross Bank, Skipton BD23 6AH* M: 07530-852896 E: revbobm@btinternet.com

MITCHELL, Mrs Sally. b 58. St Aug Coll of Th. **d** 19 **p** 20. NSM W Grinstead *Chich* from 19. *26 Little Bridges Close, Southwater, Horsham RH13 9HH*

MITCHELL, Sarah Rachel. *See* TAN, Sarah Rachel

MITCHELL, Stephen Andrew John. b 56. Ch Ch Coll Cant CertEd 78 K Coll Lon AKC 77 BD 80 MA 02 Lambeth STh 90 Heythrop Coll Lon MTh 05 PhD 10. Coll of Resurr Mirfield 80. **d** 82 **p** 83. C Chatham St Steph *Roch* 82–87; C Edenbridge 87–91; V from 91; P-in-c Crockham Hill H Trin 91–14; Chapl Invicta Community Care NHS Trust 91–06; Chapl Kent and Medway NHS and Soc Care Partnership Trust from 06. *The Vicarage, Mill Hill, Edenbridge TN8 5DA* T: (01732) 862258 F: 864335 E: ssppvicarage@hotmail.com

MITCHELL, Canon Stephen John. b 51. Ex Univ BA 73 Fitzw Coll Cam BA 78 MA. Ridley Hall Cam 76. **d** 79 **p** 80. C Gt Malvern St Mary *Worc* 79–81; Prec Leic Cathl 82–85; R Barrow upon Soar w Walton le Wolds 85–02; P-in-c Gazeley w Dalham, Moulton and Kentford *St E* 02–04; V Dalham, Gazeley, Higham, Kentford and Moulton 05–16; P-in-c Mildenhall 14–16; RD 08–15; Min Can St E Cathl 05–10; Hon Can St E Cathl 10–16; rtd 16. *93 Bantocks Road, Great Waldingfield, Sudbury CO10 0XT* T: (01787) 370416 E: smitch4517@aol.com

MITCHELL, Canon Stuart. b 53. Cranmer Hall Dur 01. **d** 03 **p** 04. C Pocklington and Owsthorpe and Kilnwick Percy etc *York* 03–06; P-in-c Edith Weston w N Luffenham and Lyndon w Manton *Pet* 06–10; P-in-c Preston and Ridlington w Wing and Pilton 06–10; C Empingham and Exton w Horn w Whitwell 06–10; R Empingham, Edith Weston, Lyndon, Manton etc 11; R Stour Valley *St E* 11–20; RD Clare 16–20; Hon Can St E Cathl 17–20; rtd 20; PtO *Ely* from 21. *47 Ward Way, Witchford, Ely CB6 2JR* E: stuart.mitchell@btinternet.com

MITCHELL, Stuart Ian. b 50. Wadh Coll Ox BA 71 DPhil 74. S'wark Ord Course 81. **d** 85 **p** 87. NSM Charlton St Luke w H Trin *S'wark* 85–86; NSM Kidbrooke St Jas 86–88; NSM Newbold w Dunston *Derby* 88–94; C 94–96; C Newbold and Gt Barlow 96–97; P-in-c Matlock Bank 97–03; RD Wirksworth 98–03; P-in-c Mackworth All SS 03–10; P-in-c Mugginton and Kedleston 03–10; P-in-c Kirk Langley 03–10; rtd 10; PtO *Derby* 10–18; *Chelmsf* from 19. *Old Stores, 138 Church Street, Braintree CM7 5LA* M: 07989-147158 E: sianmitchell050787@yahoo.com

MITCHELL, Wendy Mary. b 47. Glas Univ MA 70 Callendar Park Coll of Educn Falkirk PGCE 71. Trin Coll Bris 99. **d** 01 **p** 02. C Yatton Moor *B & W* 01–07; TV Parkham, Alwington, Buckland Brewer etc *Ex* 07–17; rtd 17; PtO *B & W* from 18; Dioc Chapl MU from 19. *25 St Michael's Gardens, South Petherton TA13 5BD* T: (01460) 249027 E: wendymarym@aol.com

MITCHELL-INNES, Canon Charles William. b 47. Pemb Coll Cam BA 69 MA 73. Sarum Th Coll 83. **d** 86 **p** 87. Asst Chapl Sherborne Sch 86–89; Chapl Milton Abbey Sch Dorset 90–96;

Conduct Eton Coll 96–07; rtd 07; V of the Close Sarum Cathl 07–14; PtO 14–19; Can and Preb Sarum Cathl from 13. *South Bank, South Street, Sherborne DT9 3LZ* T: (01935) 812656 E: charlesm-i@hotmail.com

MITCHELL-INNES, James Alexander. b 39. Ch Ch Ox BA 64 MA 66. Lon Coll of Div 65. **d** 67 **p** 68. C Cullompton *Ex* 67–71; Nigeria 71–75; P-in-c Puddletown w Athelhampton and Burleston *Sarum* 75–78; R Puddletown and Tolpuddle 78–82; V Win Ch Ch 82–92; V Titchfield *Portsm* 92–98; rtd 98; PtO *Win* from 99. *115 Battery Hill, Winchester SO22 4BH* T: (01962) 859039 E: jmitchellinnes@gmail.com

MITCHINSON, Canon Ronald. b 35. Westmr Coll Ox MA 91. Linc Th Coll 66. **d** 68 **p** 69. C Heworth St Mary *Dur* 68–72; C Banbury *Ox* 72–73; TV 73–76; NZ 76–82; TR Banbury *Ox* 82–86; RD Deddington 84–86; Ind Chapl 86–92; Hon Can Ch Ch 90–92; TV Brayton *York* 92–96; Sen Chapl Selby Coalfield Ind Chapl 92–96; rtd 96; PtO *York* 04–11. *2 The Cottages, The Green, Stillington, York YO61 1JY* T: (01347) 810064 E: ronmitchinson@mac.com

MITRA, Avijit (Munna). b 53. Keble Coll Ox BA 76. Ox NSM Course 84. **d** 88 **p** 89. NSM Abingdon *Ox* 88–96; Asst Chapl Abingdon Sch 88–96; Sen Chapl Ch Hosp Horsham 96–09; Asst Chapl and Hd Classics K Sch Roch 09–14; C S Gillingham *Roch* 14–21; rtd 21. *40 Draycott Avenue, Taunton TA2 7QF* M: 07713-727708 E: avijit@mitra1953.plus.com

MITRA, Mrs Nicola Jane. b 54. St Hugh's Coll Ox BA 76 MA 81 PGCE 77. Ox Min Course 92. **d** 94 **p** 95. NSM Abingdon *Ox* 94–96; Asst Chapl Ch Hosp Horsham 96–08; Chapl Maidstone and Tunbridge Wells NHS Trust 08–21; PtO *Roch* 10–21; rtd 21. *40 Draycott Avenue, Taunton TA2 7QF*

MITSON, Mrs Carol Mae. b 46. SRN SCM. Oak Hill NSM Course 89. **d** 93 **p** 94. NSM Lawford *Chelmsf* 93–96; NSM Elmstead 96–98; NSM Harwich 96–98; NSM Dedham 98–00; PtO from 01. *Drift Cottage, The Drift, Dedham, Colchester CO7 6AH* T/F: (01206) 323116 E: johnandcarolmitson@talktalk.net

MITSON, Miss Joyce. b 37. Man Univ CertEd 64. Trin Coll Bris 77. **dss** 79 **d** 87 **p** 94. Wellington w Eyton *Lich* 79–85; Farnworth *Lich* 85–91; Par Dn 87–91; Team Dn Bilston *Lich* 91–94; TV 94; Lich Local Min Adv 91–94; C W Bromwich St Jas 94–97; C W Bromwich St Jas w St Paul 97–98; rtd 98; PtO *Man* 00–12. *13 Birkenhills Drive, Bolton BL3 4TX* T: (01204) 655081

MITTON, Christopher Michael James. b 84. Leeds Univ BA 08. Trin Coll Bris MA 13. **d** 13 **p** 14. C Holbeck *Leeds* 13–17; C Birm St Luke 17–19; LtO from 19. *Address withheld by request* E: chris@anchorchurch.uk

MITTON, Canon Michael Simon. b 53. Ex Univ BA 75. St Jo Coll Nottm 76. **d** 78 **p** 79. C High Wycombe *Ox* 78–82; TV Kidderminster St Geo *Worc* 82–89; Dir Angl Renewal Min 89–97; Dep Dir Acorn Chr Foundn 97–03; Renewing Min Project Officer *Derby* 03–06; Miss and Min Development Adv 06–09; Dioc Fresh Expressions Adv 09–13; Fresh Expressions Officer 13–17; P-in-c Derby St Paul 09–19; Hon Can Derby Cathl 11–19; rtd 19; PtO *Derby* from 20. *264 Broadway, Derby DE22 1BN* T: (01332) 552448 E: michaelmitton@btinternet.com

MOAT, Nigel Paul. b 66. Linc Sch of Th and Min 16 ERMC 19. **d** 20 **p** 21. C W Norfolk Priory Gp *Ely* from 20. *The Rectory, 6 Rectory Lane, Watlington, King's Lynn PE33 0HU* M: 07421-117112 E: nigelmoat@gmail.com

MOAT, Terry. b 61. Nottm Univ BTh 92. Aston Tr Scheme 86 Linc Th Coll 88. **d** 92 **p** 93. C Caterham *S'wark* 92–96; Hon C Tynemouth Priory *Newc* 04–06; C Morpeth 06–09; V Choppington from 09. *The Vicarage, Scotland Gate, Choppington NE62 5SX* T: (01670) 822216 E: cofeparish.choppington@outlook.com

MOATE, Gerard Grigglestone. b 54. BA 82 Essex Univ PhD 14 FRSA 01. Oak Hill Th Coll 79. **d** 82 **p** 83. C Mildmay Grove St Jude and St Paul *Lon* 82–85; C Hampstead St Jo 85–88; P-in-c Pinxton *Derby* 88; V Charlesworth and Dinting Vale 88–95; V Dedham *Chelmsf* 95–15; RD Dedham and Tey 98–03; Chapl Bloxham Sch 15–17; PtO *Ox* from 15; *Lon* from 17; *Glouc* 19–20; P-in-c Sherborne, Windrush, the Barringtons etc from 20. *The Vicarage, Windrush, Burford OX18 4TS* T: (01451) 844613 M: 07906-357707 E: gerard@moate.org

MOATE, Phillip. b 47. RGN 70 RNT 75. NOC 87. **d** 90 **p** 91. NSM Upper Holme Valley *Wakef* 90–92; NSM Almondbury Deanery 92–94; NSM Honley *Wakef* 94–95; P-in-c Roos and Garton w Tunstall, Grimston and Hilston *York* 95–02; R Lockington and Lund and Scorborough w Leconfield 02–09; rtd 09; PtO *York* 09–21. *58 Pilmar Lane, Roos, Hull HU12 0HN* T: (01964) 671321 E: phillipmoate@btinternet.com

MOATE, Miss Rachel Patricia. b 76. Southn Univ BSc 97 MSc 98. ERMC 18. **d** 20 **p** 21. NSM Bishop's Stortford *St Alb* from 20. *Address withheld by request* M: 07917-660739 E: r.moate@btinternet.com

MOATT, Richard Albert. b 54. K Coll Lon BD 76 AKC 76. Linc Th Coll 80. **d** 81 **p** 82. C Egremont and Haile *Carl* 81–85; V Addingham, Edenhall, Langwathby and Culgaith 85–04; P-in-c Skirwith, Ousby and Melmerby w Kirkland 98–04; R Cross Fell Gp 04–13; RD Penrith 09–13; Hon Can Carl Cathl 10–13; R Lewes St Anne and St Mich and St Thos etc *Chich* 13–20; rtd 20. *Address temp unknown* E: moatt@btinternet.com

MOBBERLEY, Keith John. b 56. BA. Westcott Ho Cam. **d** 84 **p** 85. C Coventry Caludon *Cov* 84–87; C Kenilworth St Nic 87–92; V Keresley and Coundon 92–98; P-in-c Hatton w Haseley, Rowington w Lowsonford etc 98–00; R 00–21; rtd 22. *Address temp unknown*

MOBBERLEY, Mrs Susan. b 57. Kent Univ BA 79. Westcott Ho Cam 81. **dss** 84 **d** 90 **p** 94. Coventry Caludon *Cov* 84–87; LtO 87–92; NSM Keresley and Coundon 92–98; NSM Hatton w Haseley, Rowington w Lowsonford etc 98–21. *Address temp unknown* E: sumob@tiscali.co.uk

MOBERLY (née McCLURE), Mrs Jennifer Lynne. b 62. Ball State Univ (USA) BSc 84 Dur Univ PhD 10. Cranmer Hall Dur 98. **d** 01 **p** 02. C Belmont *Dur* 01–07; C Belmont and Pittington 07–08; Chapl St Mary's Coll Dur 09–12; Tutor Cranmer Hall Dur from 10. *St John's College, 3 South Bailey, Durham DH1 3RJ* E: j.l.moberly@durham.ac.uk

MOBERLY, Richard Hamilton. b 30. Trin Hall Cam BA 53 MA 57. Cuddesdon Coll 53. **d** 55 **p** 56. C Walton St Mary *Liv* 55–59; C Kensington St Mary Abbots w St Geo *Lon* 59–63; R Chingola Zambia 63–66; V Kennington Cross St Anselm *S'wark* 67–73; TV N Lambeth 74–80; Ind Chapl 80–95; rtd 95; PtO *S'wark* 95–18. *Flat 2, 1 Chester Way, London SE11 4UT* T: (020) 7735 2233 E: richard@richardmoberly.org.uk

MOBERLY, Robert Walter Lambert. b 52. New Coll Ox MA 77 Selw Coll Cam MA 80 Trin Coll Cam PhD 81. Ridley Hall Cam 74. **d** 81 **p** 82. C Knowle *Birm* 81–85; Lect Dur Univ from 85; PtO *Dur* from 85. *Department of Theology, Abbey House, Palace Green, Durham DH1 3RS* T: 0191-334 3953 E: r.w.l.moberly@durham.ac.uk

MOBEY, Jonathan Lee. b 73. Pemb Coll Cam MA 95 St Edm Hall Ox BM, BCh 98 MRCGP 02. Wycliffe Hall Ox BA 07. **d** 08 **p** 09. NSM Ox St Andr 08–11; R Harwell w Chilton from 11. *The Rectory, Church Lane, Harwell, Didcot OX11 0EZ* T: (01235) 799376 E: rectora@harwellandchiltonchurches.org.uk

MOBSBY, Canon Ian Jonathan. b 68. Leeds Univ BHSc 93 Anglia Ruskin Univ MA 06 SROT 93. EAMTC 00. **d** 04 **p** 05. C Westmr St Matt *Lon* 04–11; C St Mary Aldermary 11–12; P-in-c 12–15; P-in-c Camberwell St Luke *S'wark* 15–19; Par Miss Enabler Woolwich Area 15–19; R *S'wark* Ch Ch from 19; Asst Dean for Fresh Expressions from 19; Can for Miss Th Dio Niagara Canada from 20. *The Rectory, 49 Colombo Street, London SE1 8DP* E: ian.mobsby@southwark.anglican.org *or* ian.christchurch.southwark@gmail.com

MOCK, David Lawrence. b 64. Whitman Coll Washington BA 86 Heythrop Coll Lon MTh 01. Trin Coll Bris BA 98. **d** 98 **p** 99. C Tadworth *S'wark* 98–01; P-in-c Sutton St Geo *Ches* 01–02; C Macclesfield Team 01–02; TV 02–17; P-in-c Barnton 17–21; P-in-c Northwich St Luke 18–21; Chapl Man Univ NHS Foundn Trust from 21. *50 Norley Road, Sandiway, Northwich CW8 2JU* T: (01606) 642052 M: 07591-757126 E: revdavem@gmail.com

MOCK, Mrs Ruth Elizabeth. b 66. York Univ BA 87 Lon Inst of Educn MA 98. All SS Cen for Miss & Min 14. **d** 17 **p** 18. C Stretton and Appleton Thorn *Ches* 17–19; V Sandiway from 19. *50 Norley Road, Sandiway, Northwich CW8 2JU* T: (01606) 883286 E: mockvicar@gmail.com

MOCKFORD (née WATKINS), Mrs Betty Anne. b 45. Leeds Univ BA 66 Nottm Univ CertEd 67. EAMTC 94. **d** 97 **p** 98. C Ipswich St Aug *St E* 97–00; P-in-c Charsfield w Debach, Monewden, Hoo etc 01–06; rtd 06; PtO *St E* from 06. *Mirembe, 10 Castle Brooks, Framlingham, Woodbridge IP13 9SF* T: (01728) 724193 M: 07890-110741

MOCKFORD, Preb Peter John. b 57. Nottm Univ BSc 79 St Jo Coll Dur BA 88. Cranmer Hall Dur 86. **d** 89 **p** 90. C Tamworth *Lich* 89–94; V Blurton 94–11; P-in-c Dresden 04–11; V Blurton and Dresden 11–19; P-in-c Longton Hall 08–13; Preb Lich Cathl from 15; rtd 19; PtO *B & W* from 19. *Homeleigh, Barton Lane, Ruishton, Taunton TA3 5LW* E: mockford.peter@gmail.com

MODY, Rohintan Keki. b 63. New Coll Ox BA 85 MA 88 Fitzw Coll Cam MPhil 05 Aber Univ PhD 08. Oak Hill Th Coll BA 00. **d** 00 **p** 01. C Wolverhampton St Luke *Lich* 00–03; C Virginia Water *Guildf* 08–11; P-in-c Throop *Win*

11–16; Lect Evang Th Coll of Asia from 17. *57 Hume Avenue, Parc Palais #03-04, Singapore 598753, Republic of Singapore* E: romody@hotmail.com

MOFFAT, Canon George. b 46. Edin Univ BD 77 Open Univ BA 87 Bradf Univ MA 04. Edin Th Coll 67. **d** 72 **p** 73. C Falkirk *Edin* 73–76; C Edin St Pet 76–81; Chapl Edin Univ 77–81; C Heston *Lon* 81–84; V S Elmsall *Wakef* 84–93; TR Manningham *Bradf* 93–97; R Bolton Abbey 07–12; Hon Can Bradf Cathl 02–12; rtd 12; Chapl to The Queen 00–16; PtO *Glouc* from 16. *Fir Cottage, The Stenders, Mitcheldean GL17 0JE* T: (01594) 543668 E: rev.g.moffat@gmail.com

MOFFAT, Richard Bruce. b 65. All SS Cen for Miss & Min 15. **d** 18 **p** 19. OLM Tottington *Man* from 18. *110 Summerseat Lane, Ramsbottom, Bury BL0 9TP*

MOFFATT, Joseph Barnaby. b 72. Fitzw Coll Cam BA 96 MA 99. Ripon Coll Cuddesdon MTh 99. **d** 99 **p** 00. C Cen Wolverhampton *Lich* 99–03; C Chelsea St Luke and Ch Ch *Lon* 03–09; V Teddington St Mary w St Alb from 09; P-in-c Teddington SS Pet and Paul from 16; AD Hampton 14–19. *The Vicarage, 11 Twickenham Road, Teddington TW11 8AQ* T: (020) 8977 2767

MOFFATT, Ms Lorraine Susan. b 56. LCTP 12. **d** 15 **p** 16. NSM Sandylands *Blackb* 15–16; C 16–19; C Overton 17–19; V from 19. *St Helen's Vicarage, Chapel Lane, Overton, Morecambe LA3 3HU* T: (01524) 858234 E: lozmof55@gmail.com

MOFFATT, Canon Neil Thomas. b 46. Fitzw Coll Cam BA 68 MA 72. Qu Coll Birm 69. **d** 71 **p** 72. C Charlton St Luke w St Paul *S'wark* 71–74; C Walworth St Pet 74–75; C Walworth 75–77; V Dormansland 77–86; TR Padgate *Liv* 86–96; V 96–98; TR Thatcham 98–10; AD Newbury 02–10; S Africa 10–11; Hon Can Ch Ch *Ox* 10–11; rtd 11; PtO *Ox* 11–18 and from 21; *Cov* 11–20. *28 Battle Road, Newbury RG14 6QU* T: (01635) 841369 E: revd.tom.moffatt@gmail.com

MOFFETT-LEVY, Joanna. b 45. **d** 11 **p** 12. NSM Ox St Mich w St Martin and All SS 11–15; NSM Osney 15–20; rtd 20. *15 Third Acre Rise, Oxford OX2 9DA* T: (01865) 862715 M: 07765-175164 E: jo.moffett-levy@virginmedia.com

MOGER, Canon Peter John. b 64. Mert Coll Ox BA 85 BMus 86 MA 89 St Jo Coll Dur BA 93 ARSCM 08 Hon FGCM 10. Cranmer Hall Dur 89. **d** 93 **p** 94. C Whitby *York* 93–95; Prec, Sacr and Min Can Ely Cathl 95–01; V Godmanchester 01–05; Nat Worship Development Officer Abps' Coun 05–10; PtO *Ely* 05–10; Sec Liturg Commn 09–10; Can Res and Prec York Minster 10–19; P-in-c Eoropaidh *Arg* from 19; P-in-c Stornoway from 19. *St Peter's House, 19 Churchill Drive, Stornoway HS1 2NP* T: (01851) 704435 M: 07970-694021 E: petermoger.stpetersstornoway@gmail.com

MOGHAL, Dominic Jacob. *See* MUGHAL, Dominic Jacob

MOGRIDGE, Christopher James. b 31. Culham Coll of Educn CertEd 62 LCP 70 FCollP 86. St Steph Ho Ox 93. **d** 94 **p** 95. NSM Wellingborough St Andr *Pet* 94–98; NSM Ecton 98–02; rtd 02; PtO *Pet* 02–19. *April Cottage, Little Harrowden, Wellingborough NN9 5BB* T: (01933) 678412

MOIR, Canon Nicholas Ian. b 61. G&C Coll Cam BA 82 MA 86 Ox Univ BA 86 MA 91 Lon Univ MTh 92. Wycliffe Hall Ox 84. **d** 87 **p** 88. C Enfield St Andr *Lon* 87–91; Bp's Dom Chapl *St Alb* 91–94; Chapl St Jo Coll Cam 94–98; V Waterbeach and R Landbeach *Ely* 98–07; RD N Stowe 05–07; V Chesterton St Andr from 07; P-in-c Cambridge St Clem from 14; RD Cambridge N 11–14 and 19–20; Hon Can Ely Cathl from 12. *The Vicarage, 10 Lynfield Lane, Cambridge CB4 1DR* T: (01223) 303469 E: nicholas.moir@standrews-chesterton.org

MOLE, David Eric Harton. b 33. Em Coll Cam BA 54 MA 58 PhD 62. Ridley Hall Cam 55. **d** 59 **p** 59. C Selly Hill St Steph *Birm* 59–62; Tutor St Aid Birkenhead 62–63; Chapl Peterho Cam 63–69; Ghana 69–72; Lect Qu Coll Birm 72–76; Tutor USPG Coll of the Ascension Selly Oak 76–87; C Burton *Lich* 87–93; Chapl Burton Gen Hosp 90–93; Chapl Ostend w Knokke and Bruges *Eur* 93–98; rtd 98; PtO *Birm* from 99. *48 Green Meadow Road, Selly Oak, Birmingham B29 4DE* T: 0121-475 1589 E: susananddavidmole@yahoo.co.uk

MOLE, Jonathan Roger. b 67. Jes Coll Cam BA 91 MA 94 Lon Univ MB, BS 94 MRCP 98 FRCA 00. St Mellitus Coll 16. **d** 19 **p** 20. C Gamston and Bridgford *S'well* from 19. *21 Melton Road, West Bridgford, Nottingham NG2 7NW*

MOLESWORTH, Mrs Helen Joan. b 66. Ex Univ LLB 86 Solicitor 89. St Mellitus Coll 16. **d** 18 **p** 19. C Malpas and Threapwood and Bickerton *Ches* 18–21. *The Cooperage, Coopers Lane, St Martins, Oswestry SY11 3QB* T: (01691) 773827 M: 07712-381977 E: revdhelenmolesworth@gmail.com

MOLL, Christopher David Edward. b 67. St Cath Coll Cam BA 89 MA 93 Covenant Th Sem St Louis DMin 17. Ridley Hall Cam 94. **d** 98 **p** 99. C Byker St Mark and Walkergate St Oswald *Newc* 98–02; C Eastrop *Win* 02–06; V Wembdon

B & W from 07. *The Vicarage, 12 Greenacre, Wembdon, Bridgwater TA6 7RD* T: (01278) 423647 E: ed@sgw.org.uk

MOLL, Nicola. b 47. Bedf Coll Lon BA 69. TISEC 99. **d** 03 **p** 04. C Edin Gd Shep 03–17; C Edin St Salvador 03–06; TV 06–08; P-in-c 08–17; rtd 17; PtO *Edin* from 18. *9/3 Forth Street, Edinburgh EH1 3JX* T: 0131-558 3729 E: nicolamjmoll3@gmail.com

MOLL, Randell Tabrum. b 41. Lon Univ BD 65. Wycliffe Hall Ox 62. **d** 66 **p** 67. C Drypool St Columba w St Andr and St Pet *York* 66–70; Asst Chapl HM Pris Hull 66–70; Asst Master Hull Gr Sch 66–70; C Netherton *Liv* 70–74; C Sefton 70–72; Ind Chapl 70–74 and 92–99; Belgium 75–76; P-in-c Brockmoor *Lich* 76–81; Team Ldr Black Country Urban Ind Miss 76–81; Dir Chilworth Home Services 81–84; Asst Master Bp Reindorp Sch Guildf 84–90; France and Iraq 91; Chapl Sedbergh Sch 92; Sen Chapl Miss in the Economy (Merseyside) 92–99; Hon Can Liv Cathl 97–99; Chapl Campsfield Ho Immigration and Detention Cen 00–02; Sen Chapl Immigration Detention Services 01–02; Team Ldr Workplace Min *St Alb* 03–07; rtd 08; PtO *St Alb* from 08; *Ox* from 17. *Penn Cottage, Green End, Granborough, Buckingham MK18 3NT* T/F: (01296) 670970 E: randellmoll@yahoo.co.uk

MOLLAN, Patricia Ann Fairbanks. b 44. QUB BSc 67 PhD 70 BD 97. **d** 97 **p** 98. Aux Min *D & D* from 97; Aux Min Lecale Gp 02–04; Dep Dir Ch's Min of Healing from 04. *Echo Sound, 69 Killyleagh Road, Downpatrick BT30 9BN* T: (028) 4482 1620 F: 9073 8665 E: pat@mollan.net

MOLLAN, Prof Raymond Alexander Boyce. b 43. QUB MB, BCh 69 BAO 69 MD 84 MTh 98 FRCS FRCSE FRCSI. CITC 97. **d** 97 **p** 98. NSM Saintfield *D & D* 97–01; NSM Carryduff 01–02; NSM Comber 02–10; NSM Orangefield w Braniel 10–15; NSM Ch's Min of Healing - The Mount Belfast from 15. *Echo Sound, 69 Killyleagh Road, Downpatrick BT30 9BN* T: (028) 4482 1620 E: rab@mollan.net

MOLLOY, Mrs Heather. b 54. Bradf Univ BTech 76. **d** 95 **p** 96. OLM Harwood *Man* from 95; AD Walmsley 15–17. *7 Fellside, Bolton BL2 4HB* T: (01204) 520395 E: randhmolloy@hotmail.com

MOLLOY, Peter Liam. b 73. Regent Coll Vancouver MA 00. **d** 00 **p** 01. C Christopher Lake St Chris Canada 00–06; P Westport St Paul 06–17; P Port Perry 17–19; R Buxted and Hadlow Down *Chich* from 20. *The Rectory, Church Road, Buxted, Uckfield TN22 4LP* T: (01825) 733103 E: bhdrector@gmail.com

MOLONEY, Francis Deogratias. b 94. Staffs Univ BA 16. St Mellitus Coll 16. **d** 19 **p** 20. C Redditch H Trin *Worc* from 19. *120 Carthorse Lane, Redditch B97 6SZ* M: 07916-637923 E: francisdeogratiasmoloney@gmail.com

MOLONY, Canon Nicholas John. b 43. St Jo Coll Dur BA 67 Birm Univ MA 78 Fuller Th Sem California DMin 06. Qu Coll Birm 67. **d** 70 **p** 71. C Beaconsfield *Ox* 70–75; P-in-c Chesham Ch Ch 75–80; TV Gt Chesham 80–81; P-in-c Weston Turville 81–90; P-in-c Stoke Mandeville 87–89; P-in-c Gt Marlow 90–93; P-in-c Bisham 90–93; TR Gt Marlow w Marlow Bottom, Lt Marlow and Bisham 93–10; rtd 10; Hon Can Kimberley and Kuruman from 08; PtO *Ox* from 11. *9 Culverton Hill, Princes Risborough HP27 0DZ* T: (01844) 273895 E: nick.molony@btopenworld.com

MOLTON, Robert. b 62. Coll of SS Mark and Jo Plymouth BA 84 Leeds Univ PGCE 85. Birm Bible Inst 92 Trin Coll Bris 18. **d** 20 **p** 21. C Forest Heath *St E* from 20. *2 Elmcroft Close, Beck Row, Bury St Edmunds IP28 8RP* M: 07787-746090 E: bobmolton100notout@gmail.com

MOLUDY, Omid. b 81. All SS Cen for Miss & Min. **d** 14 **p** 14. NSM Heatons *Man* from 14; Miss Support P for Cultural Diversity from 15. *12 Neston Way, Handforth, Wilmslow SK9 3BX* M: 07590-363521 E: omidmoludy@gmail.com *or* omid.moludy@manchester.anglican.org

MOLYNEUX, Ms Tina Mercedes. b 68. Ox Min Course 07. **d** 10 **p** 11. NSM Burchetts Green *Ox* from 10; Voc Adv Berks Area from 17; LtO from 19. *1 Littlewick Place, Coronation Road, Littlewick Green, Maidenhead SL6 3RA* T: (01628) 822813 E: tina.molyneux@btconnect.com *or* tina.molyneux@oxford.anglican.org

MONAGHAN, Mrs Hilary Alice. b 78. Edin Univ MA 01 Cam Univ BA 04. Ridley Hall Cam 02. **d** 06 **p** 07. C Gerrards Cross and Fulmer *Ox* 06–10; NSM Clifton Ch Ch w Em *Bris* 12–13; NSM Malmesbury w Westport and Brokenborough 13–16; NSM Gt Somerford, Lt Somerford, Seagry, Corston etc 13–16; NSM Malmesbury and Upper Avon 16–17; Chapl Westonbirt Sch from 13; Asst Dioc Dir of Ords *Bris* from 12; PtO from 17. *St Edyth's Vicarage, Avonleaze, Bristol BS9 2HU* T: (01666) 881382 E: alicemon7@gmail.com

MONAGHAN, John Emanuel. b 80. Carlow Coll BSc 02 UEA MSc 06. Trin Coll Bris 10. **d** 13 **p** 14. C Malmesbury w

Westport and Brokenborough *Bris* 13–16; C Gt Somerford, Lt Somerford, Seagry, Corston etc 13–16; C Malmesbury and Upper Avon 16–17; V Sea Mills from 17. *St Edyth's Vicarage, Avonleaze, Bristol BS9 2HU* T: 0117-968 6965 E: vicar@stedyths.org.uk

MONBERG, Canon Ulla Stefan. b 52. Copenhagen Univ BA 79. Westcott Ho Cam 88. d 90 p 94. C Westmr St Jas *Lon* 90–94; Dean Women's Min and Area Dir of Ords Cen Lon 94–99; Dean Women's Min Kensington 94–99; C Paddington St Jo w St Mich *Lon* 96–98; P-in-c S Kensington H Trin w All SS 98–02; Dir of Ords Two Cities Area 99–02; Denmark from 02; Dioc Adv for Women's Min *Eur* 04–05; Dioc Dir of Tr 05–16; Dioc Dir Minl Development from 16; Can Brussels Cathl *Eur* from 10. *Borgmester Jensens Alle 9, 2th, DK-2100 Copenhagen 0, Denmark* T: (0045) 3526 0660 E: ulla.monberg@churchofengland.org

MONDON, Simon Charles. b 57. WEMTC. d 02 p 03. OLM Worfield *Heref* 02–09; V Goodrich, Marstow, Welsh Bicknor, Llangarron etc 09–15; V Clun Valley 15–20; rtd 20; PtO *Heref* from 21. *Bether Chapel House, Llanwrtyd Wells LD5 4TE* T: (01591) 610891 E: revsimon@btinternet.com

MONDS, Canon Anthony John Beatty. b 53. d 97 p 00. OLM Queen Thorne *Sarum* 97–04; C Sherborne w Castleton, Lillington and Longburton 04–06; V Piddle Valley, Hilton, Cheselbourne etc 06–15; Bp's Dom Chapl from 15; Can and Preb Sarum Cathl from 18. *Kirkhams, Flamstone Street, Bishopstone, Salisbury SP5 4BZ* M: 07808-614597 E: bishops.chaplain@salisbury.anglican.org *or* tony.monds@btinternet.com

MONEME, Dozie Chukwubulkem. b 79. W Africa Th Sem Lagos BA 10. d 08 p 10. Nigeria 08–11; PtO *S'wark* 11–13; C Orpington Ch Ch *Roch* 14–16; TV Eccleston *Liv* 16–20; P-in-c Barton *Portsm* from 20. *St Paul's Vicarage, Staplers Road, Newport PO30 2HZ* M: 07915-530670 E: chuu200@yahoo.com

MONEY, John Charles. b 69. Wycliffe Hall Ox 01. d 03 p 04. C Porchester *S'well* 03–06; TV Plymouth St Andr and Stonehouse *Ex* 06–13; Chapl RN from 13. *Royal Naval Chaplaincy Service Headquarters, Tanner Building, HMS Excellent, Whale Island, Portsmouth PO2 8ER* T: 0300-157 7544 M: 07766-836529 E: johncharlesmoney@aol.com

MONEY, Mrs Lynn Astrid. b 59. St Martin's Coll Lanc BEd 80. WEMTC 03. d 06 p 07. C Letton w Staunton, Byford, Mansel Gamage etc *Heref* 06–09; R Bredenbury 09–14; TV Dunstable *St Alb* 14–18; R The Ashfords *Heref* from 18. *St Mary's House, Donkey Lane, Ashford Carbonel, Ludlow SY8 4DA* M: 07791-349406 E: revlynnmoney@gmail.com

MONGER, Paul James. b 54. Reading Univ BEd 77 Greenwich Univ MSc 99. NTMTC 07. d 10 p 11. NSM Chingford St Edm *Chelmsf* 10–15; PtO from 15. *64 Trinity Road, Shrewsbury SY3 7PD* M: 07739-905363 E: hampshireboy@ymail.com

MONIE, Rachel Jane. b 70. Sheff Univ BA 92 Chu Coll Cam BTh 17. Ridley Hall Cam 15. d 17 p 18. C Perranzabuloe and Crantock w Cubert *Truro* 17–21; NSM from 21; C St Agnes and Mount Hawke w Mithian 17–21; NSM from 21. *The Vicarage, 6 Penwinnick Parc, St Agnes TR5 0UQ* M: 07507-673575 E: rachel.monie@gmail.com

MONK, Carol Lorna. b 57. STETS 08. d 11 p 12. NSM Ash *Guildf* 11–15 and from 17; PtO 15–17. *The Hawthorns, 2 Rowhill Avenue, Aldershot GU11 3LU* T: (01252) 313239 E: carol.monk159@btinternet.com

MONK, Mrs Mary. b 38. CertEd 58. S'wark Ord Course 85. d 88 p 94. NSM Lee Gd Shep w St Pet *S'wark* 88–99; NSM Harpenden St Jo *St Alb* 99–07; rtd 07; PtO *St Alb* 07–19. *3 Hawthorn Close, Harpenden AL5 1HN* T: (01582) 462057

MONK, Paul Malcolm Spenser. b 65. Ex Univ BSc 86 PhD 90 Leeds Univ MA 07 CChem MRSC. NOC 05. d 07 p 08. C Oldham *Man* 07–09; TV Medlock Head 09–17; V Clarksfield and Waterhead from 17. *St Barnabas Vicarage, 1 Arundel Street, Oldham OL4 1NL* T: 0161-624 7708 M: 07854-776410 E: paul_and_jo_monk@yahoo.co.uk

MONK, Simon William Andrew. b 80. d 16 p 17. C Churchdown St Jo and Innsworth *Glouc* 16–19. *47 Elmbridge Road, Gloucester GL2 0NX* T: (01452) 526364 E: simonmonk47@gmail.com

MONK, Stephen David. b 74. Leuven Univ Belgium STB 03. Qu Coll Birm 05. d 00 p 01. C Knighton St Mary Magd *Leic* 06–08; C Wigston Magna 08–11; P-in-c Darley *Derby* 11–12; C S Darley, Elton and Winster 11–12; R Darley, S Darley and Winster from 12. *10 Normanhurst Park, Darley Dale, Matlock DE4 3BQ* T: (01629) 734257 E: rev.stephenmonk@btinternet.com

MONKHOUSE, William Stanley. b 50. Qu Coll Cam BA 72 MA 76 MB, BChir 75 Nottm Univ PhD 85 MA 06. EMMTC 04. d 06 p 07. C Wirksworth *Derby* 06–08; P-in-c Old Brampton 08–09; P-in-c Gt Barlow 08–09; P-in-c Old Brampton and

Gt Barlow 09–11; R 11; P-in-c Loundsley Green 09–11; Asst Dir of Ords 09–11; I Maryborough w Dysart Enos and Ballyfin *C, F & O* 11–14; Chapl Midlands and Portlaoise Pris 11–14; Chapl Midland Regional Hosp Portlaoise 11–14; V Burton St Aid and St Paul *Lich* 14–19; V Burton St Modwen 14–19; rtd 19. *28 Rangemore Street, Burton-on-Trent DE14 2ED* T: (01283) 892241 E: wsmonkhouse@gmail.com

MONKS, Ian Kay. b 36. K Coll Lon BA 60 Lon Inst of Educn PGCE 61. Oak Hill NSM Course 90. d 93 p 94. NSM Woodford Bridge *Chelmsf* 93–06; PtO from 06. *46 Summit Drive, Woodford Green IG8 8QP* T: (020) 8550 2390 E: irquemonachi@hotmail.co.uk

MONMOUTH, Archdeacon of. *See* REES, The Ven Ian Kendall
MONMOUTH, Bishop of. *See* VANN, The Rt Revd Cherry Elizabeth
MONMOUTH, Dean of. *See* BLACK, The Very Revd Ian Christopher

MONRO, Alexander James. b 55. Oriel Coll Ox BA 77 Lon Hosp MB, BS 80 MRCP 86 MRCGP 88. STETS 09. d 12 p 13. NSM Hunstanton St Mary w Ringstead Parva etc *Nor* 12–16 and 19–20; NSM Hunstanton St Edm w Ringstead 16–20; NSM Hunstanton and Saxon Shore from 20. *Manor Cottage, Church Place, Docking, King's Lynn PE31 8LW* T: (01485) 518342 E: alexander.monro@btinternet.com

MONTAGUE (*née* **LAIDLAW), Mrs Juliet.** b 52. Nottm Univ BTh 82. Linc Th Coll 78. dss 82 d 87 p 94. Gainsborough All SS *Linc* 82–86; Chapl Linc Cathl and Linc Colls of FE 86–92; Dn-in-c Gedney Hill and Whaplode Drove *Linc* 92–94; P-in-c 94–99; P-in-c Crawley and Littleton and Sparsholt w Lainston *Win* 99–03; R 03–08; R The Downs 08–13; Hon C Shedfield and Wickham *Portsm* from 13. *The Vicarage, 52 Brooklynn Close, Waltham Chase, Southampton SO32 2RZ* T: (01489) 895012 E: revdjuliet@gmail.com

MONTAGUE-YOUENS, Canon Hubert Edward. b 30. Ripon Hall Ox 55. d 58 p 59. C Redditch St Steph *Worc* 58–59; C Halesowen 59–62; V Kempsey 62–69; V Kidderminster St Geo 69–72; R Ribbesford w Bewdley and Dowles 72–81; RD Kidderminster 74–81; Hon Can Worc Cathl 78–81; TR Bridport *Sarum* 81–86; RD Lyme Bay 82–86; V Easebourne *Chich* 86–89; Chapl K Edw VII Hosp Midhurst 86–89; rtd 89; PtO *Glouc* 89–95 and 98–12; P-in-c Twyning 96–98. *The Manor House, High Street, Bewdley DY12 2DJ* T: (01299) 402075

MONTEITH, The Very Revd David Robert Malvern. b 68. St Jo Coll Dur BSc 89 Nottm Univ BTh 92 MA 93 Leic Univ Hon LLD 16. St Jo Coll Nottm 90. d 93 p 94. C Kings Heath *Birm* 93–97; C St Martin-in-the-Fields *Lon* 97–02; P-in-c S Wimbledon H Trin and St Pet *S'wark* 02–09; TR Merton Priory 09; AD Merton 04–09; Can Res and Chan Leic Cathl 09–13; Dean Leic from 13. *The Deanery, 23 St Martins, Leicester LE1 5DE* T: 0116-261 5356 M: 07952-238291 E: david.monteith@leccofe.org

MONTGOMERIE, Canon Alexander (Sandy). b 47. Open Univ BA 19. St Jo Coll Nottm 89. d 94 p 96. NSM Irvine St Andr LEP *Glas* 94–21; NSM Ardrossan 94–21; Dioc Ecum Relns Co-ord 05–21; Can St Mary's Cathl 16–20; rtd 20. *105 Sharphill Road, Saltcoats KA21 5QU* T/F: (01294) 465193 E: sandy.montgomerie@btinternet.com

MONTGOMERIE, Andrew Simon. b 60. Keble Coll Ox BA 82. Ridley Hall Cam 83. d 85 p 86. C Childwall All SS *Liv* 85–87; C Yardley St Edburgha *Birm* 87–90; TV Solihull 90–96; V Balsall Common 96–05; P-in-c Eyam *Derby* 05–11; C Baslow w Curbar and Stoney Middleton 06–11; R Baslow and Eyam 11–12; RD Bakewell and Eyam 07–12; R Iver Heath *Ox* from 12. *The Rectory, 2 Pinewood Close, Iver SL0 0QS* T: (01753) 654470 M: 07545-385629 E: asmontgomerie@hotmail.co.uk

MONTGOMERY, Canon Ian David. b 44. St Andr Univ LLB 66 Univ of the South (USA) DMin 02 FCA 69. Wycliffe Hall Ox 71. d 75 p 76. C Fulham St Dionis *Lon* 75–78; Chapl Amherst Coll USA 78–83; R New Orleans St Phil 83–93; R Nashville St Bart 92–97; R Menasha St Thos 97–09; rtd 09; SAMS Peru 09–13; Can from 10. *189 North Street, Chester VT 05143, USA* T: (001) (802) 875 5446 E: frianm@aol.com

MONTGOMERY (*née* **YOUATT), Canon Jennifer Alison.** b 49. St Aid Coll Dur BSc 70 Homerton Coll Cam PGCE 71. NOC 89. d 92 p 94. NSM Ripon H Trin 92–14; *Leeds* 14–19; Warden of Readers from 99; Dioc Adv on Women's Min from 10; Hon Can Ripon Cathl 10–16; PtO 19–21. *12 Clotherholme Road, Ripon HG4 2DA* E: littlethorpe@btinternet.com

MONTGOMERY, Jennifer Susan. b 54. QUB MB, BCh 77 Leeds Univ MA 05. NOC 02. d 05 p 06. NSM Ackworth *Wakef* 05–10; P-in-c Goodshaw and Crawshawbooth *Man* 10–18; rtd 18; PtO *D & D* from 18. *15 Ballygelagh Road, Ardkeen, Newtownards BT22 1JQ* T: (028) 4273 8079 M: 07780-764233 E: jsm1954@hotmail.com

MONTGOMERY, Kevin Francis Martin. b 73. St Mellitus Coll MA 20. d 20 p 21. C Corby St Columba *Pet* from 20. *5 Hood Court, Corby NN17 2RH* T: (01536) 647727 M: 07512-822422 E: kevin@thedigitalchristian.com

MONTGOMERY, Rachel. *See* TREWEEK, Rachel

MONTGOMERY, Richard Anthony. b 59. All SS Cen for Miss & Min 19. d 21. NSM Gt Sutton *Ches* from 21. *17 Rugby Road, Ellesmere Port CH65 5DP* M: 07941-424215 E: revricky@outlook.com

MONTGOMERY, Timothy Robert. b 59. Hull Univ BA 82 Cam Univ PGCE 83. EAMTC 90. d 93 p 94. Dir Romsey Mill Community Cen *Ely* 93–94; NSM Cambridge St Phil 93–96; Chief Exec Kepplewray Cen Broughton-in-Furness 96–00; NSM Kendal St Thos *Carl* 96–00; V 00–13; Bp's Leadership and Strategy Adv 11–15; Hon Can Carl Cathl 06–15; Dir Miss Wigan *Liv* from 15. *Transforming Wigan, Wigan Investment Centre, Waterside Drive, Wigan WN3 5BA* T: (01942) 705260 M: 07985-290493 E: tim.montgomery@liverpool.anglican.org

MONTGOMERY, Archdeacon of. *See* WILSON, The Ven Barry Frank

MOODEY, Jeremy Michael. b 62. Leeds Univ BA 83. St Mellitus Coll 18. d 21. NSM Gt Chesham *Ox* from 21. *14 Chartridge Lane, Chesham HP5 2JJ* T: (01494) 775471 M: 07712-777371 E: jeremy@stmaryschesham.org *or* jeremy.moodey@gmail.com

MOODY, Canon Christopher John Everard. b 51. New Coll Ox BA 72 Lon Univ MSc 90. Cuddesdon Coll BA 74. d 75 p 76. C Fulham All SS *Lon* 75–79; C Surbiton St Andr and St Mark *S'wark* 79–82; Chapl K Coll Lon 82–87; V S Lambeth St Anne and All SS *S'wark* 87–95; RD Lambeth 90–95; P-in-c Market Harborough *Leic* 95–97; P-in-c Market Harborough Transfiguration 95–97; TR Market Harborough and The Transfiguration etc 97–05; Hon Can Leic Cathl 04–05; V Greenwich St Alfege *S'wark* 05–19; Hon Can S'wark Cathl 18–21; rtd 19. *99 Bostall Lane, London SE2 0JX* E: chrisjemoody@btinternet.com

MOODY, George Richard. b 65. Clare Coll Cam BA 88 MA 91 Ox Brookes Univ MA 14. Ripon Coll Cuddesdon 11. d 14 p 15. NSM Vale *Ox* 14–18; TV Three Valleys *Sarum* from 18. *The Rectory, Church Street, Yetminster, Sherborne DT9 6LG* T: (01935) 873214 E: revgeorgemoody@gmail.com

MOODY, Canon Ivor Robert. b 57. K Coll Lon BD 80 AKC Anglia Ruskin Univ MA 03. Coll of Resurr Mirfield. d 82 p 83. C Leytonstone St Marg w St Columba *Chelmsf* 82–85; C Leigh-on-Sea St Marg 85–88; V Tilbury Docks 88–96; Chapl Anglia Ruskin Univ 96–10; Hon Can Chelmsf Cathl 09–10; Vice-Dean and Can Res Chelmsf Cathl from 10. *83 Ridgewell Avenue, Chelmsford CM1 2GF* T: (01245) 267773 *or* 294493 E: vicedean@chelmsfordcathedral.org.uk *or* ivor.moody@chelmsfordcathedral.org.uk

MOODY, John Kelvin. b 30. St Fran Coll Brisbane ThL 55. d 56 p 57. C Warwick Australia 56–57; C Southport 57–58; C Dalby 58–61; C Earl's Court St Cuth w St Matthias *Lon* 61–64; Chapl Ankara *Eur* 64–69; Chapl Istanbul 64–66; Chapl Palma 69–75; Chapl Tangier 75–79; Can Gib Cathl 74–79; Hon Can Gib Cathl from 79; Australia from 79; rtd 01. *1 Short Street, Watsons Bay NSW 2030, Australia* T: (0061) (2) 9337 2871 E: jm986672@bigpond.net.au

MOOKERJI, Michael Manoje. b 45. Baring Union Coll Punjab BSc 69. Ridley Hall Cam 83. d 85 p 86. C Heanor *Derby* 85–92; V Codnor and Loscoe 92–93; V Codnor 93–02; V Winshill 02–15; C Hartshorne and Bretby 13–15; rtd 15; PtO *Derby* from 15; Retirement Chapl 15–20. *1 Plymouth Walk, Church Gresley, Swadlincote DE11 9GU* T: (01283) 335582 M: 07481-765018 E: michael.mookerji@live.co.uk

MOON, John Charles. b 23. Sarum Th Coll 49. d 51 p 52. C Bottesford *Linc* 51–54; C Habrough 54–55; V Immingham 55–61; V Weaste Man 61–67; V Spalding St Jo *Linc* 67–82; V Spalding St Jo w Deeping St Nicholas 82–86; rtd 86; PtO *Linc* 87–02. *14 Harrox Road, Moulton, Spalding PE12 6PR* T: (01406) 370111

MOON, Nicola Jane. b 71. Bradf Univ BSc 94 Sheff Univ PhD 99. Ox Min Course 13. d 15 p 16. C Harbury and Ladbroke *Cov* 15–18; C Stoneleigh w Ashow 18–19; P-in-c 19–20; PtO from 20. *Forge Cottage, Hockley Lane, Ettington, Stratford-upon-Avon CV37 7SS* T: (024) 7641 5506 M: 07891-012660 E: njmoon@outlook.com

MOON, Preb Philip. b 59. CCC Ox BA 80 Warwick Univ PhD 92. Wycliffe Hall Ox BTh 01. d 01 p 02. C Otley *Bradf* 01–05; V Lt Aston *Lich* 05–16; V Bishopswood from 16; V Brewood from 16; Preb Lich Cathl from 18. *Brewood Vicarage, 15 Sandy Lane, Brewood, Stafford ST19 9ET* E: familyofmoon@aol.com

MOON, Canon Philip Russell. b 56. Em Coll Cam BA 78 MA 81 Reading Univ PGCE 79. Wycliffe Hall Ox BA 82.

d 85 p 86. C Crowborough *Chich* 85–87; Hd of CYFA (CPAS) 87–94; V Lowestoft Ch Ch *Nor* 94–04; P-in-c Hove Bp Hannington Memorial Ch *Chich* 04–06; V from 06; RD Hove 05–08; Can and Preb Chich Cathl from 15. *82 Holmes Avenue, Hove BN3 7LD* T: (01273) 985219 E: phil@moons.org.uk

MOON, Sarah Ann. b 70. Huddersfield Univ BSc 93 Newc Univ PhD 97 PGCE 98. Lindisfarne Regional Tr Partnership 13. d 16 p 17. C Killingworth *Newc* 16–20; P-in-c 20–21. *27 Mount Close, Killingworth, Newcastle upon Tyne NE12 6GE* M: 07762-111862 E: sarah@lleuad.co.uk

MOONEY, Mrs Julie. b 66. Cranmer Hall Dur 11. d 13 p 14. C Newc H Cross 13–16; TV Willington from 16. *Battle Hill Vicarage, Berwick Drive, Wallsend NE28 9ED* M: 07443-410781 E: m-jmooney@hotmail.com

MOONEY, The Very Revd Paul Gerard. b 58. St Patr Coll Maynooth BD 84 Asian Cen for Th Studies and Miss Seoul ThM 92 Protestant Th Faculty Brussels DrTheol 02. d 84 p 85. In RC Ch 84–90; Chapl Miss to Seamen Korea 90–94; Hon Can Pusan from 94; Chapl Antwerp Miss to Seamen 94–97; Asst Chapl Antwerp St Boniface *Eur* 94–97; C Galway w Kilcummin *T, K & A* 97–98; I New w Old Ross, Whitechurch, Fethard etc *C, F & O* 98–07; Hon Chapl New Ross and Waterford Miss to Seamen 98–07; Prec Ferns Cathl *C, F & O* 01–07; Adn Ferns 02–07; Chapl Seoul Cathl Korea 07–11; Dean Ferns *C, F & O* from 11; I Ferns w Kilbride, Toombe, Kilcormack etc from 11; Prec Ossory Cathl from 14; Prec Leighlin Cathl from 14. *The Deanery, Ferns, Enniscorthy, Co Wexford, Republic of Ireland* T: (00353) (53) 936 6124 M: 85-707 2964 E: pgmoon@hotmail.com *or* dean@ferns.anglican.org

MOOR, Canon Simon Alan. b 65. Nottm Univ BTh 93. Linc Th Coll 90. d 93 p 94. C Skegness and Winthorpe *Linc* 93–96; C Airedale w Fryston *Wakef* 96–98; V Hoylandswaine and Silkstone w Stainborough 98–11; Bp's Adv for Ecum Affairs 08–11; V Huddersfield St Pet *Leeds* 11–19; Hon Can Wakef Cathl from 11; AD Huddersfield 17–19; Jt AD Kirkburton 18–19; R Bedale and Leeming and Thornton Watlass from 19. *The Rectory, North End, Bedale DL8 1AF* T: (01677) 988175 E: simon.moor@leeds.anglican.org *or* samoor@bedale.church

MOORE, Albert William. b 47. WMMTC 91. d 94 p 95. C Hobs Moat *Birm* 94–98; V Dosthill 98–06; V Hill 06–13; rtd 13; PtO *Birm* from 13; *Derby* from 14; *Lich* from 19. *40 Main Street, Walton-on-Trent, Swadlincote DE12 8LZ* E: billmoore313@gmail.com

MOORE, Anna. b 73. SEITE 14. d 16 p 17. C Reigate St Mark *S'wark* 16–19; R Betchworth and Buckland from 19. *The Rectory, Old Reigate Road, Betchworth RH3 7DE* M: 07939-388607 E: rectorbetchworthandbuckland@gmail.com

MOORE, Anthony Michael. b 71. Ex Univ BA 94 Leeds Univ BA 98 MA 99 PhD 10 Cam Univ MA 10. Coll of Resurr Mirfield 96. d 99 p 00. C Carnforth *Blackb* 99–03; Fell and Past Tutor Coll of Resurr Mirfield 03–04; C Wilton Place St Paul *Lon* 04–07; Chapl and Fell St Cath Coll Cam 07–12; Dean of Chpl 12; Can Res Lich Cathl 13–17; Vice-Dean 14–17; V Rottingdean *Chich* from 17. *The Vicarage, Steyning Road, Rottingdean, Brighton BN2 7GA* T: (01273) 281302 E: fr.anthony@stmargaret.org.uk

MOORE, Anthony Richmond. b 36. Clare Coll Cam BA 59 MA 63. Linc Th Coll 59. d 61 p 62. C Roehampton H Trin *S'wark* 61–66; C New Eltham All SS 66–70; P Missr Blackbird Leys CD *Ox* 70–81; Dioc Ecum Officer 80–98; TV Dorchester 81–93; R Enstone and Heythrop 93–01; rtd 01; PtO *Ox* 01–14. *13 Cobden Crescent, Oxford OX1 4LJ* T: (01865) 244673

MOORE, Arlene. b 64. Dundee Univ BSc 87 N Coll of Educn PGCE 90 TCD BTh 95. CITC 92. d 95 p 96. C Portadown St Mark *Arm* 95–99; PtO *Sheff* 99–02 and 03–09; C Crookes St Thos 02–03; Chapl Belfast Health and Soc Care Trust 09–10; P-in-c Monkstown *Conn* 09–16; P-in-c Rathcoole from 16. *25 Lindara Park, Larne BT40 2GD* T: (028) 2827 2082 M: 07450-284484 E: sendmyemails2me@yahoo.com

MOORE, Canon Bernard Geoffrey. b 27. New Coll Ox BA 47 MA 52. Ely Th Coll 49. d 51 p 52. C Chorley St Pet *Blackb* 51–54; Bp's Dom Chapl 54–55; C-in-c Blackpool St Mich CD 55–67; Chapl Victoria Hosp Blackpool 58–67; V Morecambe St Barn *Blackb* 67–81; R Standish 81–88; Hon Can Blackb Cathl 86–92; RD Chorley 86–92; V Charnock Richard 88–92; rtd 92; PtO *Ex* 92–00; *Carl* 01–10; *Win* 00–12. *16 Calgarth Park, Ambleside Road, Troutbeck Bridge, Windermere LA23 1LF* E: anammoore@hotmail.com

MOORE, Bernard George. b 32. Qu Coll Birm 57. d 60 p 62. C Middlesbrough St Columba *York* 60–62; C Kimberley Cathl S Africa 62–64; R Kimberley St Matt 64–69; Chapl RN 70–74; C Milton *Portsm* 74–76; V Glenfield NZ 76–80; V Kaitala 80–84; V Gisborne 84–86; rtd 97. *45 Feasegate*

Street, Manurewa 2102, New Zealand T: (0064) (9) 267 6924
E: freesaxon2000@yahoo.com

✠**MOORE, The Rt Revd Bruce Macgregor.** b 31. Univ of NZ BA 55. Coll of Resurr Mirfield. d 57 p 58 c 92. C Blackpool St Steph *Blackb* 57–61; NZ from 61; Hon Can Auckland 78–96; Adn Manukau 81–90; Asst Bp Auckland 92–97. *5 Pokaka Crescent, Taupo 3330, New Zealand* T: (0064) (7) 378 4849 E: brucemoore@xtra.co.nz

MOORE, Caroline Judith. *See* FALKINGHAM, Caroline Judith

MOORE, Miss Catherine Joy. b 63. Bretton Hall Coll BEd 85 Anglia Poly Univ MEd 94. St Mellitus Coll BA 10. d 10 p 11. NSM Springfield All SS *Chelmsf* 10–13; NSM Chelmsf Cathl from 13. *33 Church Street, Witham CM8 2JP* T: (01376) 501128 M: 07860-459465 E: katejmoore@aol.com

MOORE, Charles David. b 59. Dundee Univ BSc 82 BArch 85 Open Univ MA 96 RIBA 86. St Jo Coll Nottm 91. d 93 p 94. C Deane *Man* 93–97; Crosslinks 98–02; R and Sub Dean Mutare Zimbabwe 98–02; R Bermondsey St Mary w St Olave, St Jude etc *S'wark* from 02. *The Rectory, 193 Bermondsey Street, London SE1 3UW* T: (020) 7357 0984

MOORE, Christopher Baden. b 58. d 12 p 13. NSM Stretton and Appleton Thorn *Ches* 12–14; C Stockport St Geo 14–15; V Over St Chad 15–20; rtd 21; Chapl St Luke's Cheshire Hospice from 21. *35 Hillside Road, Appleton, Warrington WA4 5PX* E: chrismoore58@aol.com

MOORE, Christopher John. b 73. Stirling Univ BA 95 K Coll Lon MA 98 PGCE 99 Anglia Ruskin Univ MA 13. Westcott Ho Cam 11. d 13 p 14. C Croydon St Jo *S'wark* 13–17; R Man Clayton St Cross w St Paul from 17. *The Rectory, 54 Clayton Hall Road, Manchester M11 4WH* M: 07793-144841 E: christophermoore100@hotmail.com

MOORE, Canon Colin Frederick. b 49. CITC 69. d 72 p 73. C Drumglass w Moygashel *Arm* 72–80; I Newtownhamilton w Ballymoyer and Belleek 80–15; Hon V Choral Arm Cathl 85–96; Can and Preb Arm Cathl 97–15; rtd 15; Asst Dioc and Prov Registrar *Arm* 96–09; Dioc and Prov Registrar from 09. *8 Willow Dean, Markethill, Armagh BT60 1QG* T: (028) 3755 1992 E: cf.moore@btinternet.com

MOORE, Darren Lee. b 73. Kingston Univ BEng 95. Oak Hill Th Coll BA 01. d 01 p 02. C Camberwell All SS *S'wark* 01–04; P-in-c Tranmere St Cath *Ches* 04–07; V 07–12. *104 St Fabian's Drive, Chelmsford CM1 2PR*

MOORE, Darren Richard. b 70. Univ of Wales (Abth) BD 91 St Jo Coll York MA(Ed) 03 Leeds Univ MA 04 Hull Univ PGCE 97. Coll of Resurr Mirfield 02. d 04 p 05. C Scarborough St Martin *York* 04–07; R Brayton 07–09; Chapl Ranby Ho Sch Retford 09–11; Asst Dir of Ords *Ripon* 12–14; *Leeds* 14–15; P-in-c Leeds Halton St Wilfrid 11–15; Chapl Barnard Castle Sch 15–21; R Yarm w Kirklevington, Picton and Worsall *York* from 21. *The Rectory, Westgate, Yarm TS15 9QT* T: (01642) 964664 M: 07545-657154 E: frdmoore@icloud.com

MOORE, David James Paton. b 60. Sheff Univ BSc 82. Cranmer Hall Dur 88. d 91 p 92. C Pemberton St Mark Newtown *Liv* 91–94; C St Helens St Helen 94–97; V Canonbury St Steph *Lon* 97–07; NSM Easton H Trin w St Gabr and St Lawr and St Jude *Bris* 08–17; P-in-c from 17. *65 Chelsea Park, Bristol BS5 6AH* M: 07557-932304

MOORE, David Metcalfe. b 41. Hull Univ BA 64 PhD 69. Trin Coll *Bris* 76. d 78 p 79. C Marple All SS *Ches* 78–82; V Loudwater *Ox* 82–90; V Chilwell *S'well* 90–93; rtd 93; PtO *Ely* 05–16. *12 Rhugarve Gardens, Linton, Cambridge CB21 4LX* T: (01223) 894315 E: davidmmoore@mypostoffice.co.uk

MOORE, Douglas Gregory. b 49. Bris Univ BA 71 CertEd 72. Coll of Resurr Mirfield 87. d 89 p 90. C Hessle *York* 89–93; P-in-c Micklefield w Aberford 93–95; V Aberford w Micklefield 95–04; P-in-c Darwen St Cuth w Tockholes St Steph *Blackb* 04–14; rtd 14; PtO *York* from 15. *53 Saxon Road, Whitby YO21 3NU* T: (01947) 602329 E: douglasgmoore@yahoo.co.uk

MOORE, Geoffrey David. b 51. Poly Cen Lon BA 73. ERMC 04. d 07 p 08. NSM Brackley St Pet w St Jas *Pet* 07–11; NSM Aston-le-Walls, Byfield, Boddington, Eydon etc 11–20; rtd 20; PtO *Pet* from 21. *Address temp unknown* E: geoff@ccvp.co.uk

MOORE, Geoffrey Robert. b 46. WEMTC 03. d 06 p 07. NSM Upton-on-Severn, Ripple, Earls Croome etc *Worc* from 06. *12 Hillview Gardens, Ryall, Upton-upon-Severn, Worcester WR8 0QJ* M: 07961-505871 E: revgrmoore@gmail.com

MOORE, Gillian Mary. *See* MORGAN, Gillian Mary

MOORE, Mrs Hannah Térèse. b 74. UNISA BA 95 Rand Afrikaans Univ TDip 98. St Mellitus Coll BA 16. d 16 p 17. C Badshot Lea and Hale *Guildf* 16–20; R Elstead from 20; V Thursley from 20; C Compton w Shackleford and Peper Harow 20; R Shackleford and Peper Harow from 20. *The Rectory, Thursley Road, Elstead, Godalming GU8 6DG* T: (01252) 705941 M: 07748-983525 E: revd.hannah@gmail.com

MOORE, Henry James William. b 33. TCD BA 55 MA 70. d 56 p 57. C Mullabrack *Arm* 56–61; C Drumglass 61–63; I Clogherny 63–81; I Ballinderry, Tamlaght and Arboe 81–08; Can Arm Cathl 90–08; Chan 98–01; Prec 01–08; rtd 08. *20 Laragh Road, Beragh, Omagh BT79 0TH* T: (028) 8075 7384

✠**MOORE, The Rt Revd Henry Wylie.** b 23. Liv Univ BCom 50 Leeds Univ MA 72. Wycliffe Hall Ox 50. d 52 p 53 c 83. C Farnworth *Liv* 52–54; C Middleton *Man* 54–56; CMS 56–60; Iran 57–60; R Burnage St Marg *Man* 60–63; R Middleton 60–74; Home Sec CMS 74–80; Exec Sec CMS 80–83; Bp Cyprus and the Gulf 83–86; Gen Sec CMS 86–90; rtd 90; Asst Bp Dur 90–94; PtO *Heref* 94–16. *20 Fosbrooke House, 8 Clifton Drive, Lytham St Annes FY8 5RQ*

MOORE, Miss Hilary Jane. b 62. St Jo Coll Nottm 12. d 15 p 16. NSM Chesterfield SS Aug *Derby* from 15; NSM Brampton St Mark from 15; NSM Brampton St Thos from 19; NSM Chesterfield St Mary and All SS from 19; NSM Walton St Jo from 19. *9 Mellor Way, Chesterfield S40 2UA* M: 07399-159655 E: hilary90@hotmail.co.uk

MOORE, Preb Hugh Desmond. b 37. St Cath Soc Ox BA 58 MA 64. St Steph Ho Ox 58. d 61 p 62. C Kingston St Luke *S'wark* 61–68; Asst Chapl Lon Univ 68–70; Chapl Edgware Community Hosp 70–92; Chapl Barnet and Chase Farm Hosps NHS Trust 92–99; V Hendon St Alphage *Lon* from 70; AD W Barnet 85–90; Preb St Paul's Cathl from 95. *The Vicarage, Montrose Avenue, Edgware HA8 0DN* T: (020) 8952 4611

MOORE, Canon James Kenneth. b 37. AKC 62. St Boniface Warminster 62. d 63 p 64. C W Hartlepool St Oswald *Dur* 63–66; C-in-c Manor Park CD *Sheff* 66–76; TV Sheff Manor 76–78; R Frecheville and Hackenthorpe 78–87; V Bilham 87–91; V Sheff St Oswald 91–02; Hon Can Sheff Cathl 93–02; rtd 02; PtO *Sheff* 02–20. *115 Greenhill Main Road, Sheffield S8 7RG* T: 0114-283 9634

MOORE (*formerly* BEVAN), **Ms Janet Mary.** b 46. Bris Poly CertEd 86. WMMTC. d 98 p 99. C Bishop's Cleeve *Glouc* 98–02; V Overbury w Teddington, Alstone etc *Worc* 02–08; Faith Co-ord Surrey Police *Guildf* 08–11; rtd 11; PtO *Glouc* from 15. *8 St John's Close, Cirencester GL7 2JA* T: (01285) 640077 E: therevjan@gmail.com

MOORE, Janis. b 47. d 05 p 06. OLM Bridport *Sarum* 05–17; PtO from 17. *61 North Allington, Bridport DT6 5DZ* T: (01305) 425644 E: janis@bridport-team-ministry.org

MOORE, John Arthur. b 33. Cuddesdon Coll 70. d 71 p 72. Hon C Gt Burstead *Chelmsf* 71–74; Chapl Barnard Castle Sch 74–97; rtd 97; PtO *Dur* from 96; *Ripon* 02–14; *Leeds* 14–16. *39 Woodside, Barnard Castle DL12 8DY* T: (01833) 690947 E: j.d.mooremoore@btinternet.com

MOORE, John Bishop. b 53. Haverford Coll (USA) BA 75 Columbia Univ MBA 78 Sheff Univ MA 18. ERMC. d 08 p 09. C Paris St Mich *Eur* 08–12; Asst Chapl 12–15; V Guernsey St Steph *Win* 15–21; Bp Dover's Adv for Deliverance Min 16–21; Vice-Dean Guernsey *Win* 17–21; Asst Dioc Dir of Ords *Cant* 17–20; rtd 21. *7 place du Tisart, 60300 Borest, France* T: (0033) 3 44 69 29 45 E: frjohnbishopmoore@gmail.com

MOORE, John Cecil. b 37. TCD BA 61 MA 67 BD 69. CITC 62. d 62 p 63. C Belfast St Matt *Conn* 62–65; C Holywood *D & D* 65–70; I Ballyphilip w Ardquin 70–77; I Mt Merrion 77–79; I Donaghcloney w Waringstown 79–02; Treas Dromore Cathl 90–93; Chan Dromore Cathl 93–02; rtd 02. *22 Kensington Court, Dollingstown, Craigavon BT66 7HU* T: (028) 3832 1606 E: canonjohnmoore@gmail.com

MOORE, John Henry. b 35. Nottm Univ BMus 56 CertEd 57 MA 61. EMMTC 87. d 90 p 91. NSM Gotham *S'well* 90–95; NSM Kingston and Ratcliffe-on-Soar 90–95; NSM Bunny w Bradmore 95–00; P-in-c 97–00; rtd 00. *19 Hall Drive, Gotham, Nottingham NG11 0JT* T: 0115-983 0670 E: revjhm@btinternet.com

MOORE, Canon John Richard. b 35. Lambeth MA 01. St Jo Coll Nottm 56. d 59 p 60. C Northwood Em *Lon* 59–63; V Burton Dassett *Cov* 63–66; Dioc Youth Chapl 63–71; Dir Lindley Lodge Educn Trust Nuneaton 71–82; TR Kinson *Sarum* 82–88; Gen Dir CPAS 88–96; Hon Can Cov Cathl 95–01; Internat Dir ICS 96–01; rtd 01; PtO *Cov* 01–18. *2 Milligan Court, Merlin Way, Warwick CV34 6UG* T: (01926) 835612 M: 07821-009738 E: johnrmoore150@gmail.com

MOORE, Canon John Richard. b 45. Linc Th Coll 80. d 82 p 83. C Gt Grimsby St Mary and St Jas *Linc* 82–86; V Skirbeck Quarter 86–95; P-in-c Coningsby w Tattershall 95–99; R 99–06; R Bain Valley Gp 06–10; Can and Preb Linc Cathl 09–10; rtd 11; PtO *Linc* 15–18. *23 Church Lane, Hutton, Alford LN13 9RD* T: (01507) 490246 E: moorejr1605@btinternet.com

MOORE, Joseph Andrew. b 92. K Coll Lon BA 15 St Jo Coll Dur BA 19. Cranmer Hall Dur 16. d 19 p 20. C

Croydon St Jo *S'wark* 19–20; C Walworth St Chris from 20. *115A Wells Way, London SE5 7SZ* M: 07984-277979 E: joe.moore@hotmail.com

MOORE, Canon Joyce. b 48. TCD BA 70 HDipEd 71 ARIAM 68. CITC 98. **d** 01 **p** 02. NSM Camlough w Mullaglass *Arm* 01–07; NSM Drogheda w Ardee, Collon and Termonfeckin from 07; Hon V Choral Arm Cathl 07–16; Can Arm Cathl from 16. *Dundalk Road, Dunleer, Co Louth, Republic of Ireland* T: (00353) (41) 685 1327 E: am.drogheda@armagh.anglican.org

MOORE, Margaret Louise. b 62. DipOT 85. SAOMC 04. **d** 06 **p** 07. C Bishop's Hatfield, Lemsford and N Mymms *St Alb* 06–10; C Letchworth St Paul w Willian 10–17; Chapl Garden Ho Hospice Letchworth 09–17; TR Sutton *Liv* from 17. *Sutton Rectory, 225 Gartons Lane, Clock Face, St Helens WA9 4RB* T: (01744) 602871 M: 07729-385830 E: louisemoore85@btinternet.com or suttonparish@btconnect.com

MOORE, Matthew Edward George. b 38. Oak Hill Th Coll 77. **d** 77 **p** 78. C Larne and Inver *Conn* 77–80; I Desertmartin w Termoneeny *D & R* 80–84; I Milltown *Arm* 84–96; I Culmore w Muff and Belmont *D & R* 96–06; Dioc Warden for Min of Healing 97–06; Can Derry Cathl 04–06; rtd 06. *90 Baronscourt Road, Newtownstewart, Omagh BT78 4EZ* M: 07598-840976 E: matt-audreymoore@hotmail.co.uk

MOORE, Canon Michael Mervlyn Hamond. b 35. LVO 99. Pemb Coll Ox BA 60 MA 63. Wells Th Coll 60. **d** 62 **p** 63. C Bethnal Green St Matt *Lon* 62–66; Chapl Bucharest w Sofia and Belgrade *Eur* 66–67; Asst Gen Sec C of E Coun on Foreign Relns 67–70; Gen Sec 70–72; Abp's Chapl on Foreign Relns *Cant* 72–82; Hon C Walworth St Pet *S'wark* 67–75; Hon C Walworth 75–80; Hon Can Cant Cathl 74–90; Chapl Chpl Royal Hampton Court Palace 82–99; Dep P in O 92–99; rtd 99. *The College of St Barnabas, Blackberry Lane, Lingfield RH7 6NJ* T: (01342) 872859 E: mmhm@collegeofstbarnabas.com

MOORE, Michael Peter John. b 60. Qu Coll Birm 05. **d** 08 **p** 09. C Pet St Mary Boongate 08–11; V from 11; RD Pet from 20. *St Mary's Vicarage, 214 Eastfield Road, Peterborough PE1 4BD* T: (01733) 554815 E: revmikemoore@gmail.com

MOORE, Nicholas James. b 84. Magd Coll Ox BA 07 MSt 08 Keble Coll Ox DPhil 15. Wycliffe Hall Ox 09. **d** 14 **p** 15. C Stranton *Dur* 14–17; Tutor Cranmer Hall Dur from 17. *St John's College, 3 South Bailey, Durham DH1 3RJ* T: 0191-334 3894 M: 07969-393031 E: njmoore121@gmail.com or nicholas.j.moore@durham.ac.uk

MOORE, The Ven Paul Henry. b 59. Ball Coll Ox BA 82 DPhil 86. Wycliffe Hall Ox 87. **d** 89 **p** 90. C Ox St Andr 89–93; V Kildwick *Bradf* 93–01; V Cowplain *Portsm* 01–14; RD Havant 04–09; Hon Can Portsm Cathl 13–14; Adn for Miss Development *Win* 14–20; PtO 20; P-in-c Hathersage w Bamford and Derwent and Grindleford *Derby* from 20; Hon Can Win Cathl 14–20. *The Vicarage, Church Bank, Hathersage, Hope Valley S32 1AJ* T: (01433) 410036 E: vicarpaul1@gmail.com

MOORE, Philip. b 49. York Univ MA 71 Leeds Univ MA 05 PGCE 72. NOC 02. **d** 05 **p** 06. NSM Heworth Ch Ch *York* 05–09; P-in-c York St Thos w St Maurice 09–14; PtO from 14. *14 Whitby Avenue, York YO31 1ET* T: (01904) 425250 E: phil.moore@stthomaswithstmaurice.org.uk

MOORE, Raymond. b 47. QUB BSc 70. **d** 87 **p** 88. Aux Min Belfast All SS *Conn* 87–95; NSM 95–96; Aux Min Kilmakee 96–04; P-in-c Drung w Castleterra, Larah and Lavey etc *K, E & A* 04–09; NSM Albert Park Australia 09–12; P-in-c Belfast St Simon w St Phil *Conn* from 13. *21 Kilwarlin Avenue, Hillsborough BT26 6LQ* T/F: (028) 9268 2789 M: 07746-583471 E: rev.raymond.moore@gmail.com

MOORE, Richard Bernard Roger. b 60. Qu Foundn (Course) 16. **d** 19 **p** 20. C Kenilworth St Nic *Cov* from 19. *4 Chase Cottages, Chase Lane, Kenilworth CV8 1PR* M: 07753-431186 E: eglise@sky.com

MOORE, Canon Richard Norman Theobald. b 39. St Andr Univ BSc 62 Lon Univ BD 66. Clifton Th Coll. **d** 66 **p** 67. C Stowmarket *St E* 66–69; C New Humberstone *Leic* 69–72; P-in-c Leic Martyrs 73; V 73–84; Chapl Manor Hosp Epsom 84–94; Chapl Surrey Oaklands NHS Trust 94–00; rtd 00; PtO *Guildf* 02–07; *St E* 07–21; *Eur* 06–16; Can Dornakal India from 04. *9 Cramner Cliff Gardens, Felixstowe IP11 7NH* T: (01394) 273889

MOORE, Richard William Robert. b 39. UCD BA 70 TCD HDipEd 71. CITC 98. **d** 01 **p** 02. Aux Min Drogheda w Ardee, Collon and Termonfeckin *Arm* 01–05; Aux Min Dundalk w Heynestown from 05; Aux Min Ballymascanlan w Creggan and Rathcor from 05. *Dundalk Road, Dunleer, Co Louth, Republic of Ireland* T: (00353) (41) 685 1327 E: richwmoore@yahoo.ie

MOORE, Robert Allen. b 32. Univ of the Pacific BA 54 Boston Univ STB 58 STM 59. **d** 63 **p** 63. USA 63–80; V Farington *Blackb* 80–83; TV Preston St Jo 83–85; P-in-c Fleetwood St Pet 85–87; V Leyland St Jas 87–97; rtd 97; PtO *Blackb* from 97. *19 Lea Road, Whittle-le-Woods, Chorley PR6 7PF* T: (01257) 265701

MOORE, Mrs Roberta. b 46. CITC 03. **d** 06 **p** 07. Aux Min Drung w Castleterra, Larah and Lavey etc *K, E & A* 06–09; NSM Albert Park Australia 09–12; P-in-c Belfast St Aid *Conn* 13–20; rtd 20. *21 Kilwarlin Avenue, Hillsborough BT26 6LQ* T/F: (028) 9268 2789 M: 07746-583470 E: bobbiemoore1@gmail.com

MOORE, Robin Alan. b 42. Lon Univ BA 71 Garnett Coll Lon CertEd 75. S Dios Minl Tr Scheme 91. **d** 94 **p** 95. NSM Barcombe *Chich* 94–06; PtO from 07; Portsm from 18. *The Moorings, 6 Foxes Close, Sandown PO36 9AF* E: robin@starfish5.plus.com

MOORE, Robin Hugh. b 52. CertEd BEd QUB BD. **d** 84 **p** 85. C Derryloran *Arm* 84–86; C Knock *D & B* 86–89; Bp's C Belfast St Steph w St Luke *Conn* 89–94; I 94–96; I Whitehouse 96–03; Bp's C Belfast St Mary Magd 03–07; I Belfast St Mark from 07; P-in-c Belfast St Mary w H Redeemer from 12. *9 Sycamore Park, Newtownabbey BT37 0NR* T: (028) 9086 9569 E: moorerobin@sky.com

MOORE (née THOMASON), Mrs Sara Elizabeth. b 82. Liv Univ BA 03. Qu Foundn Birm 18. **d** 20 **p** 21. C Moseley St Mary and St Anne *Birm* from 20. *4 Woodrough Drive, Birmingham B13 9EP* T: 0121-748 2162 M: 07855-766152 E: curate@moseleychurch.org.uk

MOORE, Shaun Christopher. b 52. Open Univ BA 92 K Coll Lon MA 10 NE Lon Poly CertEd 75. NTMTC BA 08. **d** 08 **p** 09. NSM Leyton St Mary w St Edw and St Luke *Chelmsf* 08–11; TV Walthamstow 11–12; PtO 12–14; V Harold Hill St Geo 14–21; rtd 21; PtO *Chelmsf* from 21. *90 Elmbridge, Harlow CM17 0JU* M: 07720-771481 E: shaunmoore@freeola.com

MOORE, Simon Quentin. b 61. Sheff Univ BA 83 PGCE 84. St Jo Coll Nottm MA 99. **d** 00 **p** 01. C St Alb St Paul 00–03; TV Digswell and Panshanger 03–10; P-in-c Letchworth St Paul w Willian 10–13; V 13–17; C Sutton *Liv* from 20. *Sutton Rectory, 225 Gartons Lane, Clock Face, St Helens WA9 4RB* E: sqmoore@btinternet.com

MOORE, Thomas Sydney. b 50. St Paul's Coll Grahamstown 77. **d** 79 **p** 80. C Rondebosch St Thos S Africa 79–82 and 83–84; C Bredasdorp 82–83; R Green Pt 84–88; C Bushey *St Alb* 97–08; C Aldershot St Mich *Guildf* 08–19; rtd 19. *3 College Court, Old Sticklepath Hill, Sticklepath, Barnstaple EX31 2BG* E: ts.moore@virgin.net

MOORE, William. See MOORE, Albert William

MOORE-BICK, Miss Elizabeth Mary. b 77. Qu Coll Cam BA 99 MA 03 Anglia Poly Univ BA 04 Brighton Univ PGCE. Westcott Ho Cam 02. **d** 05 **p** 06. C Hillingdon St Jo *Lon* 05–09; TV Clarendon *Sarum* 09–15; Chapl Salisbury Cathl Sch 15. *The Gore, West End, Herstmonceux, Hailsham BN27 4NZ* M: 07803-044217 E: lizmoore_bick@yahoo.co.uk

MOORE BROOKS, Dorothy Anne. b 66. York Univ BA 87 Hughes Hall Cam PGCE 88. Ridley Hall Cam 96. **d** 98 **p** 99. C S Kensington St Jude *Lon* 98–01; PtO 02–08; Chapl Gt Ormond Street Hosp for Children NHS Trust 02–08; NSM Hoddesdon *St Alb* 01–10; Chapl Isabel Hospice 08–10; Chapl Gt Ormond Street Hosp NHS Foundn Trust from 10; LtO Amersham Deanery 10–17; PtO *Lon* 14–18; *Ox* from 17. *Great Ormond Street Hospital, Great Ormond Street, London WC1N 3JH* T: (020) 7813 8232 or (01494) 730876 E: moorebrooks@sky.com or dorothy.moorebrooks@gosh.nhs.uk

MOORES, Jonathan Ian. b 75. Glos Univ BA 10. Trin Coll Bris MA 12. **d** 12 **p** 13. C Denton Holme *Carl* 12–16; TV Atherton and Hindsford w Howe Bridge *Man* 16–19; TV New Bury w Gt Lever 19–20; P-in-c Leverhulme from 20. *St Stephen and All Martyrs Vicarage, Radcliffe Road, Bolton BL2 1NZ* M: 07753-427329 E: revjonathanmoores@outlook.com

MOORES, Samantha Jane. See DUDDLES, Samantha Jane

MOORHEAD, Michael David. b 52. BSc BA MSc. St Steph Ho Ox. **d** 83 **p** 84. C Kilburn St Aug w St Jo *Lon* 83–87; C Kenton 87–89; Chapl Cen Middx Hosp NHS Trust 89–19; V Harlesden All So *Lon* 89–21; P-in-c Willesden St Matt 92–02; Preb St Paul's Cathl 13–21; rtd 21. *Flat 20, 2 Hillside, London NW10 8GE* E: frmichaelmoorhead@gmail.com

MOORHOUSE, Peter. b 42. Liv Univ BSc 64 Hull Univ CertEd. Linc Th Coll 79. **d** 81 **p** 82. C Horsforth *Ripon* 81–85; R Ackworth *Wakef* 85–96; Dep Chapl HM Pris Leeds 96–97; Chapl HM Pris Stocken 97–98; Chapl HM Pris Everthorpe 98–07; rtd 07; PtO *York* from 07. *65 Eastfield Lane, Dunnington, York YO19 5ND* T: (01904) 481055

MOORSOM, Christopher Arthur Robert. b 55. Ox Univ BA. Sarum & Wells Th Coll 79. **d** 82 **p** 83. C Bradford-on-Avon H Trin *Sarum* 82–85; R Broad Town, Clyffe Pypard and Tockenham 85–89; V Banwell *B & W* 89–96; R Upper Stour *Sarum* 96–14; Prec and Can Res Derby Cathl 14–18; PtO *B & W* from 19. *31 Castle Street, Stogursey, Bridgwater TA5 1TG* E: chris@moorsom.co.uk

MORAN, Patricia Margaret. b 54. Dur Univ BA 77 PGCE 81 Loyola Univ MA 99 Newc Univ PhD 10. Lindisfarne Regional Tr Partnership 12. **d** 14 **p** 15. NSM Monkseaton St Mary *Newc* 14–18; P-in-c Bywell and Mickley from 18. *Bywell Vicarage, 9 Meadowfield Road, Stocksfield NE43 7PY* T: (01661) 842272 E: patmoran54@gmail.com

MORAY, Shena Alison. b 61. St Hild Coll 17. **d** 18 **p** 19. C Newby *York* from 18. *9 Green Lane, Scarborough YO12 6HL* M: 07576-443765 E: revmoray@gmail.com

MORAY, ROSS AND CAITHNESS, Bishop of. *See* STRANGE, The Most Revd Mark Jeremy

MORAY, ROSS AND CAITHNESS, Dean of. *See* SIMPSON, The Very Revd Alison Jane

MORBY, Preb Helen Mary. b 62. Wolv Univ BA 99. Ripon Coll Cuddesdon 99. **d** 01 **p** 02. C Lich St Chad 01–04; V Farnworth *Liv* 04–12; AD Widnes 05–07; Hon Can Liv Cathl 05–12; P-in-c Kinnerley w Melverley and Knockin w Maesbrook *Lich* 12–16; P-in-c Maesbury 12–16; R Kinnerley w Melverley, Knockin w Maesbrook and Maesbury 16–18; R Edgmond w Kynnersley and Preston Wealdmoors from 18; V Tibberton w Bolas Magna and Waters Upton from 18; Preb Lich Cathl from 18. *The Rectory, High Street, Edgmond, Newport TF10 8JR* E: helen.morby@btinternet.com

MORE, Ajay Yohan. b 68. **d** 14 **p** 15. C Alperton *Lon* 14–17; C Ealing St Steph Castle Hill 17–18; C Greenhill St Jo from 18. *56 Devon Close, Perivale, Greenford UB6 7DR* T: (020) 7912 9173 M: 07868-662703 E: ajay_kavita@hotmail.com

MORE, Canon Richard David Antrobus. b 48. St Jo Coll Dur BA 70. Cranmer Hall Dur 70. **d** 72 **p** 73. C Macclesfield St Mich *Ches* 72–77; Chapl Lee Abbey 77–82; V Porchester S'well 82–96; RD Gedling 90–96; Bp's Dom Chapl *Chelmsf* 96–01; Dioc Dir of Ords 01–13; Dioc NSM Officer 01–13; Hon Can Chelmsf Cathl 96–13; rtd 13; PtO *Chich* from 14. *16 Russell Street, Chichester PO19 7EL* T: (01243) 839943 E: richardmore16@gmail.com

MORELAND, Andrew John. b 64. St Jo Coll Nottm 09. **d** 11 **p** 12. C Bridlington Priory *York* 11–14; V Seamer w East Ayton 14–17; V Seamer, E Ayton and Cayton from 17. *The Vicarage, 3 Stockshill, Seamer, Scarborough YO12 4QG* T: (01723) 866284 M: 07784-020848 E: andrew.moreland@btinternet.com

MORETON, Harley. *See* MORETON, Philip Norman Harley

MORETON, Preb Mark. b 39. Jes Coll Cam BA 64 MA 68. Westcott Ho Cam 63. **d** 65 **p** 66. C Portsea All SS *Portsm* 65–70; C St Martin-in-the-Fields *Lon* 70–72; Chapl Jes Coll Cam 72–77; R Stafford St Mary and St Chad *Lich* 77–79; P-in-c Stafford Ch Ch 77–79; TR Stafford 79–91; P-in-c Marston w Whitgreave 77–79; V W Bromwich All SS 91–04; Preb Lich Cathl 99–04; rtd 04; PtO *Worc* from 05. *Rosemont, Dry Mill Lane, Bewdley DY12 2BL* T: (01299) 401965

MORETON, Philip Norman Harley. b 28. Linc Th Coll. **d** 57 **p** 58. C Howden *York* 57–60; C Bottesford *Linc* 60–65; V Linc St Giles 65–70; V Bracebridge Heath 71–77; V Seasalter *Cant* 77–84; TV Whitstable 84–88; rtd 88; PtO *York* 96–06; *Linc* 15–18. *112 Grantham Road, Bracebridge Heath, Lincoln LN4 2QF* T: (01522) 534672 M: 07851-717891 E: moretonjosie@googlemail.com

MOREY, Miss Lydia Mary. b 66. Down Coll Cam BA 89 MA 92 Dur Univ BA 17 MA 20 Nottm Univ MA 19 Lon Inst of Educn PGCE 90. Ridley Hall Cam 15 Trin Th Coll Singapore 16 Ox Min Course 17. **d** 18 **p** 19. NSM Swindon St Jo and St Andr *Bris* from 18. *10 Lion Mews, Newbury Street, Lambourn, Hungerford RG17 8YY* T: (01488) 724790 M: 07967-135403 E: moreylydiam@gmail.com

MORFILL, Mrs Mary Joanna. b 46. Seaford Coll of Educn TCert 67. STETS 01. **d** 04 **p** 08. NSM Swanmore St Barn *Portsm* 04–14; PtO from 14; Chapl MU from 12. *Whistlers, New Road, Swanmore, Southampton SO32 2PF* T: (01489) 878227 M: 07906-755145 E: mary@swanmore.net

MORGAN, Adrian. b 85. Univ of Wales (Abth) BA 06 MPhil 08 PhD 12 Peterho Cam BA 13 MA 18. Ridley Hall Cam 11. **d** 14 **p** 15. C Gorseinon *S & B* 14–17; P-in-c 17–20; V Casllwchwr and Gorseinon from 20; Chapl Gower Coll Swansea from 14; Dioc Ecum Officer *S & B* from 15. *The Vicarage, 40 Princess Street, Gorseinon, Swansea SA4 4US* T: (01792) 892849 E: adrian@stcath.org.uk

MORGAN, Mrs Adrienne Elizabeth. b 58. Liv Univ BA 80 PGCE 81. All SS Cen for Miss & Min 16. **d** 18

p 19. OLM Harwood *Man* from 18. *13 Fossgill Avenue, Bolton BL2 3FR* T: (01204) 598337 M: 07917-652955 E: aem13@btinternet.com

MORGAN, Alison Jean. b 59. Girton Coll Cam BA 82 MA 85 Darw Coll Cam PhD 86. EMMTC 93. **d** 96 **p** 97. NSM Oadby *Leic* 96–97; NSM Leic H Trin w St Jo 97–08; Dir Rooted in Jesus from 02; Thinker and Writer ReSource 04–16; Assoc Mathetes Trust from 17; PtO *B & W* from 08. *10 Dairy Close, Wells BA5 2ND* T: (01749) 679865 E: ajm@alisonmorgan.co.uk

MORGAN, Andrew Paul. b 80. **d** 14 **p** 15. C Trentham *Lich* 14–17; V Heref St Pet w St Owen and St Jas from 17. *The Vicarage, 102 Green Street, Hereford HR1 2QW* M: 07880-730295 E: vicar@spsj.org.uk

✠**MORGAN, The Rt Revd Barry Cennydd.** b 47. Lon Univ BA 69 Selw Coll Cam BA 72 MA 74 Univ of Wales PhD 86. Westcott Ho Cam 70. **d** 72 **p** 73 **c** 93. Chapl Bryn-y-Don Community Sch 72–75; C St Andrews Major w Michaelston-le-Pit *Llan* 72–75; Ed *Welsh Churchman* 75–82; Lect Th Univ of Wales (Cardiff) 75–77; Chapl and Lect St Mich Coll Llan 75–77; Warden Ch Hostel Ban 77–84; Chapl and Lect Th Univ of Wales (Ban) 77–84; In-Service Tr Adv *Ban* 78–84; Dir of Ords 82–84; Can Ban Cathl 83–84; TR Wrexham *St As* 84–86; Adn Meirionnydd *Ban* 86–93; R Criccieth w Treflys 86–93; Bp Ban 93–99; Bp Llan 99–17; Abp Wales 03–17; rtd 17. *Crud yr Allt, Westbourne Crescent, Cardiff CF14 2BL* T: (029) 2061 8458

MORGAN, Charles Nicholas Brendan. b 55. MBE 91. Open Univ BSc 94 Leeds Univ BA 08. NOC 05. **d** 08 **p** 09. C Derwent Ings *York* 08–12; R Howardian Gp 12–18; rtd 18; PtO *York* from 19. *Ivy Cottage, Main Street, Linton on Ouse, York YO30 2AS* M: 07902-033174 E: dadintheditch@hotmail.com

✠**MORGAN, The Rt Revd Christopher Heudebourck.** b 47. Lanc Univ BA 73 Heythrop Coll Lon MTh 91. Kelham Th Coll 66. **d** 73 **p** 74 **c** 01. C Birstall *Leic* 73–76; Asst Chapl Brussels *Eur* 76–80; P-in-c Redditch St Geo *Worc* 80–81; TV Redditch, The Ridge 81–85; V Sonning *Ox* 85–96; Prin Berks Chr Tr Scheme 85–89; Dir Past Studies Ox Min Course 92–96; Dioc Can Res Glouc Cathl and Officer for Min 96–01; Area Bp Colchester *Chelmsf* 01–13; rtd 13; Hon Asst Bp Chich from 14. *6 Wellington Court, Grand Avenue, Worthing BN11 5AB* T: (01903) 246184 E: chrishmorgan47@gmail.com

MORGAN, Christopher Laurence John. b 66. **d** 12 **p** 13. NSM Stepney St Dunstan and All SS *Lon* 12–16; PtO 16–17; NSM Stoke Newington St Andr 17–19; Chapl to Bp Stepney from 19; PtO *S'wark* from 16. *13 Ursula Court, 146 Brownfield Street, London E14 6NF* M: 07894-099039

MORGAN, David Bramwell. b 82. Open Univ BA 08. Ripon Coll Cuddesdon BA 15. **d** 17 **p** 18. C Havant *Portsm* 17–19; C Soberton, Newtown and Hambledon from 19; C Meon Bridge from 19. *The Vicarage, Church Lane, Hambledon, Waterlooville PO7 4RT* M: 07590-008964 E: david.morgan@oxon.org

MORGAN, David Farnon Charles. b 43. Leeds Univ BA 68. Coll of Resurr Mirfield 68. **d** 70 **p** 71. C Swinton St Pet *Man* 70–73; C Langley All SS and Martyrs 73–75; R Salford St Clem w St Cypr Ordsall 75–76; R Salford Ordsall St Clem 76–86; V Adlington *Blackb* 86–11; AD Chorley 98–04; rtd 11. *1 Holly Close, Farishes Lane, South Ferriby, Barton-upon-Humber DN18 6HG* T: (01652) 408500 E: morgyvic@talktalk.net

MORGAN, David Joseph. b 47. Bp Burgess Hall Lamp 66 St Deiniol's Hawarden 74. **d** 74 **p** 75. C Pembroke Dock *St D* 74–77; C Burry Port and Pwll 77–80; Miss to Seafarers 80–12; Sen Chapl and Sec Welsh Coun 85–12; rtd 12. *19 Clos Bevan, Gowerton, Swansea SA4 3GY* T: (01792) 923368

MORGAN, Canon Enid Morris Roberts. b 40. St Anne's Coll Ox BA 61 Univ of Wales (Ban) MA 73. United Th Coll Abth BD 81. **d** 84 **p** 97. C Llanfihangel w Llanafan and Llanwnnws etc *St D* 84–86; Dn-in-c 86–93; Dir Bd of Miss Ch in Wales 93–00; V Llangynwyd w Maesteg *Llan* 00–05; Hon Can Llan Cathl 02–05; rtd 05; PtO *St D* from 11. *Rhiwlas, Cliff Terrace, Aberystwyth SY23 2DN* T: (01970) 624648

MORGAN, Gareth James Lloyd. b 86. Ches Univ BA 08. St Mellitus Coll BA 20. **d** 20 **p** 21. C Speke St Aid w All SS *Liv* from 20. *108 Bray Road, Liverpool L24 3TW* M: 07989-698833 E: speke.curate@gmail.com

MORGAN, Gareth Morison Kilby. b 33. Bris Univ BA 56. Cuddesdon Coll 57 Bangalore Th Coll. **d** 61 **p** 62. C St Helier *S'wark* 61–65; Chapl Scargill Ho 65–70; Dir RE *Linc* 71–74; Dioc Dir of Educn *St E* 74–81; TR Hanley H Ev *Lich* 81–89; TR Cen Telford 89–92; Warden Glenfall Ho *Glouc* 92–98; rtd 98; Chapl Hants Partnership NHS Trust 08–11; PtO *Win* 00–11; *Ely* from 12. *102 Lambs Lane, Cottenham, Cambridge CB24 8TA* T: (01954) 201696 E: morgan3341@virginmedia.com

MORGAN, Geoffrey. *See* MORGAN, James Geoffrey Selwyn

MORGAN, Gerwyn. *See* MORGAN, William Charles Gerwyn

MORGAN *(formerly* **MOORE), Mrs Gillian Mary.** b 70. NTMTC. **d** 09 **p** 10. NSM Harwich Peninsula *Chelmsf* 09–13; Chapl St Helena Hospice Colchester 13–19; NSM Lawford *Chelmsf* 15–17; NSM Lawford, Lt Bentley and The Bromleys 17–19; TV N Hinckford 19–20; TR from 20. *The Vicarage, Gages Road, Belchamp St Paul, Sudbury CO10 7BT* T: (01787) 584993 M: 07875-982456 E: revgillmorgan@outlook.com

MORGAN, Glyn. b 33. Univ of Wales (Ban) BA 55 MA 69. Coll of Resurr Mirfield 55. **d** 57 **p** 58. C Dolgellau *Ban* 57–60; C Conway 60–63; V Corris 63–68; Hd of RE Friars' Sch Ban 69–70; LtO *Ban* 70–71; Hd of RE Oswestry Boys' Modern Sch 70–74; Hd of RE Oswestry High Sch for Girls 74–79; Hon C Oswestry H Trin *Lich* 71–79; Hd of RE Fitzalan Sch Oswestry 79–88; V Meifod and Llangynyw *St As* 88–01; RD Caereinion 89–01; rtd 01; PtO *St As* from 08. *Crib y Gwynt Annexe, Trefnanney, Meifod SY22 6XX* T: (01691) 828797

MORGAN, Graham. b 47. Kt 00. S'wark Ord Course. **d** 83 **p** 84. NSM S Kensington St Steph *Lon* 83–90; NSM Hammersmith H Innocents 90–02; NSM Bedford Park from 02. *24 Charleville Court, Charleville Road, London W14 9JG* T: (020) 7381 3211 E: grahammorgan1@btinternet.com

MORGAN, Henry. b 45. Hertf Coll Ox BA 68. Westcott Ho Cam 68. **d** 70 **p** 71. C Lee St Marg *S'wark* 70–73; C Newington St Paul 73–76; V Camberwell St Mich w All So w Em 76–84; V Kingswood 84–93; PtO 93–03; *Sheff* 03–11; *Worc* from 11. *2 Brook Cottage, Eckington Road, Birlingham, Pershore WR10 3DA* M: 07714-569375 E: henry.morgan10@btinternet.com

MORGAN, Ian Stephen. b 50. Open Univ BA 88. Sarum & Wells Th Coll 86. **d** 88 **p** 89. C Baldock w Bygrave *St Alb* 88–91; C S Elmham and Ilketshall *St E* 91–95; V Bungay H Trin w St Mary 95–05; R Lt Barningham, Blickling, Edgefield etc *Nor* 05–10; rtd 10. *88 Beech Road, Saxmundham IP17 1FP* T: (01728) 604154 M: 07808-451350 E: smorganciho@yahoo.co.uk

MORGAN, James Geoffrey Selwyn. b 59. Ex Univ BA 81 PGCE 82 Open Univ MPhil 97 K Coll Lon PhD 14. Cranmer Hall Dur 88. **d** 91 **p** 92. C Reading St Agnes w St Paul *Ox* 91–93; C Bromham w Oakley and Stagsden *St Alb* 94–95; PtO *Pet* 95–98; C Epsom St Martin *Guildf* 98–01; Tutor Ox Cen for Miss Studies 01–05; Lic Preacher *Ox* 01–05; PtO *Guildf* 01–17; Chapl Imp Coll Healthcare NHS Trust 11–13; Lead Chapl 13–16; Lead Chapl N Middx Univ Hosp NHS Trust from 16; Chapl Ox Univ Hosps NHS Foundn Trust from 16; PtO *Lon* from 11; *Ox* from 16. *North Middlesex University Hospital NHS Trust, North Middlesex Hospital, Sterling Way, London N18 1QX* T: (020) 8887 2000 M: 07483-360721 E: jgs_morgan@icloud.com

MORGAN, Mrs Jane Elizabeth. b 60. MBE 13. Keele Univ MA 96. SNWTP 11. **d** 14 **p** 15. NSM Southport H Trin *Liv* 14–17; NSM Halsall, Lydiate and Downholland 17–18; P-in-c Newburgh w Westhead 18–20; V Ainsdale from 20. *St John's Vicarage, 708 Liverpool Road, Southport PR8 3QE* E: revjanemorgan@hotmail.com

MORGAN, John Laurence. b 41. Melbourne Univ BA 62 Oriel Coll Ox BA 69 MA 73 DPhil 76. **d** 68 **p** 69. Acting Chapl Oriel Coll Ox 69; and Chapl 70–76; USA 77–78; Australia 78–13; PtO *Ely* from 13; *Eur* from 14. *PO Box 918, Moe, VIC 3825, Australia* T: (0061) (3) 5127 3091 E: john.morgan@uq.edu.au

MORGAN, John William. b 51. **d** 15 **p** 16. NSM Tenby *St D* 15–20; NSM Narberth and Tenby LMA from 20. *Avalon, 80 Upper Hill Park, Tenby SA70 8JG* T: (01834) 843625 E: jmorg410@aol.com

MORGAN, John William Miller. b 34. Lon Univ BSc 56. Wycliffe Hall Ox 61. **d** 63 **p** 64. C St Alb Ch Ch 63–68; V Luton St Matt High Town 68–79; V Mangotsfield *Bris* 79–90; P-in-c Stanton St Quintin, Hullavington, Grittleton etc 90–95; R Hullavington, Norton and Stanton St Quintin 95–99; rtd 99; PtO *Bris* from 00. *3 Bouverie Park, Stanton St Quintin, Chippenham SN14 6EE* T: (01666) 837670 E: morganssq@tiscali.co.uk

MORGAN, Joseph. *See* MORGAN, David Joseph

MORGAN, Kathleen Irene. b 52. St Martin's Coll Lanc CertEd 74. WEMTC 93. **d** 96 **p** 97. NSM Barnwood *Glouc* 96–99; C Coney Hill 99–02; V Churchdown St Jo and Innsworth 02–14; rtd 14; PtO *Worc* from 15; *Glouc* from 14. *12 Pyke Road, Tewkesbury GL20 8DX* T: (01684) 298988 E: revkaty@aol.com

MORGAN, Prof Linda Marianne. b 48. Bris Univ BSc 69 Surrey Univ MSc 72 Lon Univ PhD 77 FRCPath 01. STETS 99. **d** 02 **p** 03. NSM Claygate *Guildf* 02–18; PtO from 18; Dioc Spiritual Direction Co-ord from 20. *8 Melbury Close, Claygate KT10 0EX* T: (01372) 462911 E: lindamorgan@htclaygate.org

MORGAN, Mrs Marian Kathleen Eleanor. b 38. Birm Univ MA 94 FCMI 82. WEMTC. **d** 00 **p** 01. NSM Cusop w Blakemere, Bredwardine w Brobury etc *Heref* 00–03; P-in-c New Radnor and Llanfihangel Nantmelan etc *S & B* 03–07; rtd 08; Hon C Aberedw w Llandeilo Graban and Llanbadarn etc *S & B* 10–13; Hon C Bryngwyn and Newchurch and Llanbedr etc 10–13; PtO 13–16. *Carob Tree House, 4 Koukkoulas Street, Nata, 8525 Paphos, Cyprus* E: mkemorgan@btinternet.com

MORGAN, Mark Anthony. b 58. LLB. Chich Th Coll. **d** 84 **p** 85. C Thorpe St Andr *Nor* 84–87; C Eaton 87–90; V Southtown 90–92; PtO from 92. *Nethergate End, The Street, Saxlingham Nethergate, Norwich NR15 1AJ* T: (01508) 498003

MORGAN, Mark Steven Glyn. b 60. Essex Univ BSc 83 RGN 86. Ridley Hall Cam 95. **d** 97 **p** 99. C Herne Bay Ch Ch *Cant* 97–02; TV Ipswich St Mary at Stoke w St Pet and St Fran *St E* 02–18; rtd 18. *72 Cemetery Road, Ipswich IP4 2HZ*

MORGAN, Martin Paul. b 46. St Steph Ho Ox 71. **d** 73 **p** 74. C Kettering St Mary *Pet* 73–76; C Fareham SS Pet and Paul *Portsm* 76–80; V Portsea Ascension 80–94; V Rottingdean *Chich* 94–15; rtd 15; PtO *Chich* from 16. *116 The Welkin, Lindfield, Haywards Heath RH16 2PL*

MORGAN, Nicholas John. b 69. Surrey Univ MBus 91 Sheff Univ BA 15 MA 18. Yorks Min Course 13. **d** 15 **p** 16. C Masham and Healey *Leeds* 15–18; C W Tanfield and Well w Snape and N Stainley 15–18; P-in-c Bramham *York* from 18. *The Vicarage, Church Causeway, Thorp Arch, Wetherby LS23 7AE* T: (01937) 849471 *or* 844402 M: 07387-728009 E: revnjmorgan@gmail.com

MORGAN, Canon Nicholas John. b 50. K Coll Lon BD 71 AKC 71 CertEd. St Aug Coll Cant 72. **d** 73 **p** 74. C Wythenshawe Wm Temple Ch *Man* 73–76; C Southam w Stockton *Cov* 76–79; V Braiiles 79–16; R Sutton under Brailes 79–16; P-in-c Tysoe w Oxhill and Whatcote 06–16; RD Shipston 90–98; Hon Can Cov Cathl 03–16; rtd 16; PtO *Cov* from 16; *Glouc* from 19. *21 Marshall Avenue, Shipston-on-Stour CV36 4HN* T: (01608) 664151

MORGAN, Nicola. b 64. Nottm Univ BA 86. Linc Th Coll BTh 95. **d** 95 **p** 96. C Lillington *Cov* 95–98; C Gospel Lane St Mich *Birm* 98–01; P-in-c Gt Paxton *Ely* 01–05; P-in-c Lt Paxton 01–05; P-in-c Diddington 01–05; V The Paxtons w Diddington 05; PtO *Pet* 06–08; P-in-c Hallaton and Allexton, w Horninghold, Tugby etc *Leic* 08–12; R Quantock Coast *B & W* from 12. *The Rectory, High Street, Stogursey, Bridgwater TA5 1PL* T: (01278) 732873 E: nickymorgan25@btinternet.com

MORGAN, Philip. b 51. Lon Univ BSc 75 Univ of Wales (Cardiff) BD 78. St Mich Coll Llan 75. **d** 78 **p** 79. C Swansea St Nic *S & B* 78–81; C Morriston 81–83; C Swansea St Mary w H Trin 83–84; USA from 84. *17476 Hawthorne Avenue, Culpeper VA 22701-8003, USA* E: padre4u@hotmail.com

MORGAN, Canon Philip Brendan. b 35. G&C Coll Cam BA 59 MA 63. Wells Th Coll 59. **d** 61 **p** 62. C Paddington Ch Ch *Lon* 61–66; C Trunch w Swafield *Nor* 66–68; P-in-c Nor St Steph 68–72; Sacr Nor Cathl 72–74; Can Res and Sub-Dean St Alb 74–81; Hon Can St Alb 81–94; R Bushey 81–94; RD Aldenham 91–94; Can Res and Treas Win Cathl 94–01; rtd 01; PtO *Win* from 01. *9 Clifton Hill, Winchester SO22 5BL* T: (01962) 867549

MORGAN, Canon Reginald Graham. b 25. St D Coll Lamp BA 46 LTh 48. **d** 48 **p** 49. C Chirk *St As* 48–50; C Llangollen and Trevor 50–55; R Llanwyddelan w Manafon 55–66; V Rhuddlan 66–94; RD St As 78–94; Hon Can St As Cathl 83–89; Can St As Cathl from 89; rtd 94; PtO *St As* 10–13. *Manafon, 49 Ffordd Ffynnon, Rhuddlan, Rhyl LL18 2SP* T: (01745) 591036

MORGAN, Rhys Bryn. b 65. E Lon Univ BA 94. St Mich Coll Llan 00. **d** 02 **p** 03. C Carmarthen St Pet *St D* 02–05; P-in-c Cil-y-Cwm and Ystrad-ffin w Rhandir-mwyn etc 05–09; PtO *Birm* from 18. *9 Homecroft Road, Birmingham B25 8XN* M: 07393-327094 E: rhysbmorgan@gmail.com

MORGAN, Canon Richard Mervyn. b 50. Wadh Coll Ox BA 73 MA 75 K Alfred's Coll Win PGCE 74. **d** 92 **p** 93. CMS 85–94; Kenya 88–94; PtO *S'wark* 95–96; R Therfield w Kelshall *St Alb* 96–18; RD Buntingford 11–16; Tutor ERMC 99–11; Hon Can St Alb 14–18; rtd 18; PtO *Glouc* from 19. *9 Five Acres, Dursley GL11 4JP* T: (01453) 549062 E: therfieldrectory1@btinternet.com

MORGAN, Richard Thomas. b 70. Peterho Cam BA 91 MA 95. Wycliffe Hall Ox 94. **d** 96 **p** 97. C Bath Twerton-on-Avon *B & W* 96–99; Chapl Lee Abbey 99–01; R Marks Tey and Aldham *Chelmsf* 01–08; C Fisherton Anger *Sarum* 08–12; R Paoli USA from 12. *212 West Lancaster Avenue, Paoli PA 19301, USA* T: (001) (610) 644 4040 E: revrichardmorgan@googlemail.com

MORGAN, Robert Chowen. b 40. St Cath Coll Cam BA 63 MA 67. St Chad's Coll Dur 64. **d** 66 **p** 67. C Lancaster St Mary *Blackb* 66–76; Lect Th Lanc Univ 67–76; Fell Linacre Coll Ox from 76; Lect Th Ox Univ 76–97; Reader from 97; P-in-c Sandford-on-Thames *Ox* 87–20; NSM Littlemore w Sandford-on-Thames from 20. *Lower Farm, Sandford-on-Thames, Oxford OX4 4YR* T: (01865) 748848 E: robert.morgan@theology.ox.ac.uk

MORGAN, Roger William. b 40. Mert Coll Ox BA 62 Cam Univ MA 67. Ridley Hall Cam 80. **d** 81 **p** 82. NSM Cambridge St Paul *Ely* 81–84; V Corby St Columba *Pet* 84–90; V Leic H Trin w St Jo 90–08; C-in-c Leic St Leon CD 01–08; Hon Can Leic Cathl 06–08; Missr ReSource 08–16; Dir Mathetes Trust from 16; PtO *B & W* from 15. *10 Dairy Close, Wells BA5 2ND* T: (01749) 679865 E: rogerwmorgan@outlook.com

MORGAN, Russell Dean. b 80. R Agric Coll MSc 08. Ridley Hall Cam 15. **d** 17 **p** 18. C Cullompton *Ex* 17–19. *Postfach 11 29, 35001 Marburg, Germany* M: 07710-538111 E: russell.d.morgan@gmail.com

MORGAN, Stephen. See MORGAN, Ian Stephen

MORGAN, Stephen John. b 67. UEA BA 89 SS Coll Cam BA 02 MA 05. Westcott Ho Cam 99. **d** 02 **p** 03. C Pitlochry and Kilmaveonaig *St And* 02–04; P-in-c E Knoyle, Semley and Sedgehill *Sarum* 05–08; P-in-c St Bartholomew 08–09; R 09–15; RD Chalke 12–15; Chapl RN 15–18; P-in-c Liskeard and St Keyne *Truro* 17; V from 17; RD W Wivelshire from 18. *The Rectory, Church Street, Liskeard PL14 3AQ* T: (01579) 347411 E: stevethevicar@gmail.com

MORGAN, Stephen Roy David. b 62. Qu Foundn (Course) 17. **d** 19 **p** 20. NSM Burntwood, Chase Terrace etc *Lich* from 19. *54 Lichfield Road, Walsall WS4 2DJ* M: 07305-852152 E: s.morgan12@virginmedia.com

MORGAN, Canon Steve Shelley. b 48. St Mich Coll Llan 67. **d** 71 **p** 72. C Llanharan w Peterston-super-Montem *Llan* 71; C Llandaff w Capel Llanilltern 71–74; C Neath w Llantwit 74–77; TV Merthyr Tydfil and Cyfarthfa 77–91; V Merthyr Tydfil Ch Ch 91–13; RD Merthyr Tydfil 93–04; Can Llan Cathl 98–13; rtd 13; PtO *Llan* from 14. *33 Parc Cwm Pant Bach, Merthyr Tydfil CF48 1TQ* T: (01685) 268571 M: 07870-241681 E: smorgan842@yahoo.com

MORGAN, Mrs Susan Dianne. b 53. Univ of Wales (Lamp) BA 74 Westmr Coll Ox PGCE 75. NOC 03. **d** 05 **p** 06. C Droylsden St Martin *Man* 05–07; P-in-c Kirkholt 08–13; rtd 13; PtO *Man* 13–14; Hon C Langley 14–15; NSM Rochdale 15–17; NSM Langley from 17. *Address withheld by request* M: 07837-706037 E: sue_morgan14@hotmail.com

MORGAN, Taff. See MORGAN, Charles Nicholas Brendan

MORGAN, Teresa Jean. b 68. Clare Coll Cam BA 90 MA 94 PhD 95 Oriel Coll Ox MA 98 BA 01 LRAM 91. SAOMC 00. **d** 02 **p** 03. NSM Littlemore *Ox* 02–20; NSM Littlemore w Sandford-on-Thames from 20. *Oriel College, Oxford OX1 4EW* T: (01865) 728807 E: teresa.morgan@oriel.ox.ac.uk

MORGAN, Thomas Robert. b 81. Lanc Univ BA 03 UEA PGCE 06. Trin Coll Bris 18. **d** 20 **p** 21. C Swindon St Aug *Bris* from 20. *26 Upper Pavenhill, Purton, Swindon SN5 4DQ* E: tom@patternchurch.org

MORGAN, Mrs Victoria Louise. b 78. Ripon Coll Cuddesdon BA 16. **d** 17 **p** 18. C Havant *Portsm* 17–19; P-in-c Blendworth w Chalton w Idsworth from 19; P-in-c Rowlands Castle from 19. *The Vicarage, Church Lane, Hambledon, Waterlooville PO7 4RT* M: 07429-187233 E: revvickiemorgan@gmail.com

MORGAN, William Charles Gerwyn. b 30. Univ of Wales (Lamp) BA 52. St Mich Coll Llan 52. **d** 56 **p** 57. C Hubberston *St D* 56–62; V Ambleston w St Dogwells 62–68; Miss to Seamen 68–93; V Fishguard w Llanychar *St D* 68–84; V Fishguard w Llanychar and Pontfaen w Morfil etc 85–93; Can St D Cathl 85–93; Chan St D Cathl 91–93; rtd 93; PtO *St D* from 12. *Wrth y Llan, Pontycleifion, Cardigan SA43 1DW* T: (01239) 613943

MORGAN-GUY, John Richard. b 44. St D Coll Lamp BA 65 Univ of Wales PhD 85 Univ of Wales (Trin St Dav) DD 09 ARHistS 80 FRHistS 05 FRSM 81 FSA 18. St Steph Ho Ox 65. **d** 67 **p** 68. C Canton St Cath *Llan* 67–68; C Roath St Sav 68–70; Chapl Llandough Hosp 70–71; C Machen and Rudry *Mon* 71–74; R Wolvesnewton w Kilgwrrwg and Devauden 74–80; PtO *B & W* 80–93; V Betws Cedewain and Tregynon and Llanwyddelan *St As* 93–97; RD Cedewain 97; Lect Univ of Wales (Lamp) 98–03 and 07–08; Research Fell 04–07; Research Fell Cen for Adv Welsh & Celtic Studies 99–04; Tutor Welsh Nat Cen for Ecum Studies Carmarthen 00–09; Hon Research Fell Univ of Wales (Trin St Dav) from 03; Chapl 13–15; PtO *St D* 10–16; Visiting Fell Ox Brookes Univ 10. *Tyngors, Silian, Lampeter SA48 8AS* T: (01570) 422710 E: j.morgan-guy@uwstd.ac.uk

MORGAN-JONES, Canon Christopher John. b 43. Bris Univ BA 66 Chicago Univ MBA 68 McMaster Univ Ontario MA 69. Cuddesdon Coll 70. **d** 73 **p** 74. C Folkestone St Sav *Cant* 73–76; P-in-c Swalecliffe 76–82; V Addington 82–84; V Addington *S'wark* 85–92; RD Croydon Addington 85–90; V Maidstone All SS and St Phil w Tovil *Cant* 92–14; Hon Can Cant Cathl 99–14; rtd 14; PtO *Cant* from 14. *35 Shearwater Avenue, Whitstable CT5 4DX* T: (01227) 271172 E: cmorganjones1@gmail.com

MORGAN LUNDIE, Ben Robert. b 71. Univ Coll Lon BSc 93. Wycliffe Hall Ox 16. **d** 18 **p** 19. C Budock *Truro* from 18. *The Rectory, Old Church Road, Mawnan Smith, Falmouth TR11 5HY*

MORGANS, Ms Jenny Louise. b 84. Birm Univ BA 05 Edin Univ MSc 09. Qu Coll Birm 12. **d** 16 **p** 17. C N Lambeth *S'wark* 16–20; Chapl K Coll Lon from 20. *26 Canning Street, Brighton BN2 0EF* M: 07817-493336 E: jenny.morgans@kcl.ac.uk

MORIARTY, Patrick John. b 66. St Jo Coll Ox MA 88 K Coll Lon MA 95 PGCE 89 FRSA 16. ERMC 14. **d** 17 **p** 18. NSM E Barnet *St Alb* 17–18; NSM St Alb St Steph from 18. *73 Oxhey Avenue, Watford WD19 4HB* T: (01923) 816885 M: 07990-836956 E: father.patrick@myphone.coop

MORIARTY, Mrs Susan Margaret. b 43. Cartrefle Coll of Educn TCert 65. St As Minl Tr Course. **d** 02 **p** 09. Par Dn Gorsedd w Brynford, Ysgeifiog and Whitford *St As* 02–15; rtd 16; PtO *St As* from 16. *7 St Michael's Drive, Caerwys, Mold CH7 5BS* T: (01352) 720874 E: reverendsuecaerwys@hotmail.co.uk

MORING, Sally Margaret. b 61. St Martin's Coll Lanc BEd 84 Middx Univ BA 06. NTMTC 03. **d** 06 **p** 07. NSM Northolt St Mary *Lon* 06–09; V Hayes St Edm 09–17; R Wendover and Halton *Ox* from 17. *The Vicarage, 34A Dobbins Lane, Wendover, Aylesbury HP22 6DH* T: (01296) 696136 E: vicar@stmarywendover.org

MORISON, John Donald. b 34. ALCD 60. **d** 61 **p** 62. C Rayleigh *Chelmsf* 61–64; C St Austell *Truro* 64–67; V Meltham Mills *Wakef* 67–71; Youth Chapl *Cov* 71–76; S Africa 76–82; Can Port Elizabeth 80–82; Bardsley Missr 82–86; LtO *S'wark* 82–86; Dioc Missr *Derby* 86–99; V Quarndon 86–99; rtd 99; PtO *Sarum* 01–13. *Flat 1, Canford Place, 59 Cliff Drive, Canford Cliffs, Poole BH13 7JX* T: (01202) 709377 E: kayandjohn@waitrose.com

MORITZ, Michael Andreas Peter. b 82. Portsm Univ BSc 03 K Coll Lon PGCE 05. St Mellitus Coll BA 19. **d** 19 **p** 20. C Locks Heath *Portsm* from 19. *11 Laurel Road, Locks Heath, Southampton SO31 6QG* M: 07865-091517 E: mikemoritz82@gmail.com

MORLEY, Alison Ruth. b 67. Sarum Coll MA 13. STETS 05 Ripon Coll Cuddesdon 13. **d** 13 **p** 14. C Devizes St Jo w St Mary *Sarum* 13–15; P-in-c Upper Wylye Valley 15–18; R Seaview, St Helens, Brading and Yaverland *Portsm* from 18. *The Vicarage, Eddington Road, Seaview PO34 5EF* M: 07500-007437

MORLEY, Andrew John. b 69. Liv Jo Moores Univ BA 92. St Mellitus Coll BA 17. **d** 17 **p** 18. NSM Onslow Square and S Kensington St Aug *Lon* from 17; Pres World Vision Internat from 19. *The Dormer Cottage, Bridle Lane, Loudwater, Rickmansworth WD3 4JG* M: 07738-808999 E: andrewmorley0@gmail.com

MORLEY, Gareth Lee. b 82. St Mellitus Coll BA 20. **d** 20 **p** 21. C High Wycombe *Ox* from 20. *St James' Vicarage, Plomer Hill, High Wycombe HP13 5NB* T: (01494) 708403 M: 07809-460695

MORLEY, Georgina Laura (George). b 63. Dur Univ BA 84 Nottm Univ MTh 95 PhD 99. Cranmer Hall Dur. **d** 03 **p** 03. Dir Studies NEOC 99–04; NSM Osmotherley w Harlsey and Ingleby Arncliffe *York* 03–08; Lect Cranmer Hall Dur 07–10; rtd 10. *Beacon Hill, High Street, Low Pittington, Durham DH6 1BE* T: 0191-372 0385

MORLEY, John. b 43. AKC 67. St Deiniol's Hawarden 67. **d** 68 **p** 69. C Newbold on Avon *Cov* 69–73; C Solihull *Birm* 73–77; C-in-c Elmdon Heath CD 76–77; Chapl RAF 77–93; TR Wallingford *Ox* 93–99; RD 95–99; Dean St Paul's Cathl and Chapl Nicosia 99–02; V Henlow and Langford *St Alb* 02–08; RD Shefford 06–08; PtO *Leic* 08–11 and 13–21; *Pet* from 08; *Lich* 09–11; *Win* from 21; P-in-c Gaulby *Leic* 11–12; Spiritual Dir Leic Angl Cursillo 12–17. *4 Rockbourne Road, Sherfield-on-Loddon, Hook RG27 0SR* T: (01256) 242609 M: 07900-892566 E: revjmorley@talktalk.net

MORLEY, Jonathan Edward. b 93. Dur Univ BA 21. St Mellitus Coll 18. **d** 21. C Aldridge *Lich* from 21. *5 Whetstone Lane, Walsall WS9 8PB* M: 07938-533411 E: jonathan.morley@hotmail.com

MORLEY, Keith. b 44. St Chad's Coll Dur BA 66 Open Univ BSc 93. **d** 67 **p** 68. C S Yardley St Mich *Birm* 67–70; C Solihull 70–73; V Shaw Hill 73–77; P-in-c Burton Coggles *Linc* 77–79;

P-in-c Boothby Pagnell 77–79; V Lenton w Ingoldsby 77–79; P-in-c Bassingthorpe w Bitchfield 77–79; R Ingoldsby 79–87; RD Beltisloe 84–87; P-in-c Old Dalby and Nether Broughton *Leic* 87–94; RD Framland 88–90; rtd 04; PtO *Linc* 03–13. *10 Gracey Court, Woodland Road, Broadclyst, Exeter EX5 3GA*

MORLEY, Canon Leslie James. b 45. K Coll Lon BD 67 AKC 67 MTh 68. St Boniface Warminster 68. **d** 69 **p** 70. C Birm St Pet 69–72; C W Brompton St Mary *Lon* 72; C W Brompton St Mary w St Pet 73–74; Chapl Nottm Univ *S'well* 74–80; Dir Post-Ord Tr 80–85; Can Res and Vice-Provost S'well Minster 80–85; Hon Can S'well Minster 85–99; Chapl Bluecoat Sch Nottm 85–99; R Nottingham St Pet and St Jas *S'well* 85–99; AD Nottingham Cen 90–93; Dioc Rural Officer *Ripon* 99–10; Hon Chapl Yorks Agric Soc *York* from 09; rtd 10; PtO *Dur* from 13. *Beacon Hill, High Street, Low Pittington, Durham DH6 1BE* T: 0191-372 0385 M: 07879-470752 E: leslie@lesliemorley.plus.com

MORLEY, Robert Rushforth. b 58. Kent Univ BA 80 MA 85 Bath Spa Univ MA 02. ERMC 18. **d** 20 **p** 21. NSM Milan w Lake Como *Eur* from 20. *via Rotta 6, Travaco Siccomario (PV) 27020, Italy* M: (0039) 347-370 6240 E: robert@rushforthmorley.com

MORLEY, Stephen Raymond. b 55. Birm Univ LLB 76. STETS 07. **d** 10 **p** 11. C Aisholt, Enmore, Goathurst, Nether Stowey etc *B & W* 10–14; V Bures w Assington and Lt Cornard *St E* 14–21; RD Sudbury 19–21; rtd 21. *Beeches, Crowcombe, Taunton TA4 4AE* M: 07723-786688 E: steve.morley@btinternet.com

MORLEY, Terence Martin Simon. b 49. SS Hild & Bede Coll Dur CertEd 78. St Steph Ho Ox 71. **d** 74 **p** 75. C Kingston upon Hull St Alb *York* 74–76; C Middlesbrough All SS 76–77; PtO *Dur* 77–78; Hon C Worthing St Andr *Chich* 78–80; C Brighton Ch Ch *Chich* 80–82; C Hove St Patr 80–82; C Ayr *Glas* 83–86; C Maybole 83–84; P-in-c Coatbridge 86–88; R 88–92; P-in-c 92; V Plymouth St Jas Ham *Ex* 93–09; Chapl Plymouth Community Services NHS Trust 96–98; rtd 09. *37 Great College Street, Brighton BN2 1HJ*

MORLEY, Trevor. b 39. Man Univ BSc 62 MPS 62 MRSPH 84. Ripon Hall Ox 65. **d** 67 **p** 68. C Compton Gifford *Ex* 67–70; Chapl Hammersmith Hosp Lon 70–83; Hon C N Hammersmith St Kath *Lon* 70–83; Chapl Univ Coll Hosp Lon 83–94; Chapl Univ Coll Lon Hosps NHS Trust 94–99; Chapl St Luke's Hosp for the Clergy 89–99; V Linthwaite *Wakef* 99–06; rtd 06; PtO *Sheff* from 06. *19 Queenswood Road, Sheffield S6 1RR* T: 0114-232 5232 E: tmqwr@tiscali.co.uk

MORLEY-BUNKER, John Arthur. b 27. Wells Th Coll 67. **d** 68 **p** 69. C Horfield H Trin *Bris* 68–71; P-in-c Easton All Hallows 71–75; V 75–82; RD Bris City 74–79; V Horfield St Greg 82–93; rtd 93; PtO *Bris* 93–11. *1 Knoll Court, Knoll Hill, Bristol BS9 1QX* T: 0117-968 5837

MORLEY-JONES, Anthony Roger. St Mich Coll Llan. **d** 04 **p** 05. NSM Cydweli and Llandyfaelog *St D* 04–12; P-in-c 12–15; rtd 15; PtO *St D* from 15. *11 Westhill Crescent, Cydweli SA17 4US* T: (01554) 890458

MORPHY, George David. b 49. Birm Univ BEd 71 Lon Univ BA 75 Warwick Univ MA 90. WMMTC. **d** 89 **p** 90. NSM Ribbesford w Bewdley and Dowles *Worc* 89–06; NSM Barbourne from 06; Dioc Dir of Educn 99–11. *41 Hallow Road, Worcester WR2 6BX* T: (01905) 422007 M: 07867-525779 E: morphy611@btinternet.com

MORRALL, Heather Lynne. *See* COOKE, Heather Lynne

MORRELL, Mrs Jennifer Mary. b 49. NOC 84. **d** 87 **p** 94. Par Dn Crewe All SS and St Paul *Ches* 87–90; Par Dn Padgate *Liv* 90–94; C 94–95; TV Kirkby 95–00; V Croxteth Park 00–02; PtO *Arg* from 13; Welcome Cen Co-ord Iona Community 13–15. *5 Mellendean Farm Cottage, Kelso TD5 8HF* M: 07880-757607 E: shazandjen@gmail.com

MORRELL, Paul Rodney. b 49. SRN 70. SWMTC 91. **d** 93 **p** 94. C Heavitree w Ex St Paul 93–02; C Heavitree and St Mary Steps 02–05; TV 05–16; rtd 16; PtO *Ex* from 17. *9 Coburg Place, Cullompton EX15 1XN*

MORRELL, His Honour Peter Richard. b 44. Univ Coll Ox MA 71 Solicitor 70 Barrister-at-Law (Gray's Inn) 74. ERMC 06. **d** 08 **p** 09. NSM Uppingham w Ayston and Wardley w Belton *Pet* 08–10; NSM Nassington w Yarwell and Woodnewton w Apethorpe 10–12; PtO from 12; *Eur* from 09. *Swallow Cottage, Apethorpe Road, Nassington, Peterborough PE8 6QT* T/F: (01780) 782281 M: 07860-573597 E: petermorrell@sulehay.co.uk

MORRELL, Mrs Susan Marjorie. b 46. Open Univ BA 94. SEITE 93. **d** 96 **p** 97. NSM E Peckham and Nettlestead *Roch* from 96; Chapl Kent Coll Pembury 99–00. *7 Pippin Road, East Peckham, Tonbridge TN12 5BT* T: (01622) 871150

MORRIS, Miss Alison Mary. b 58. W Midl Coll of Educn BEd 81 Wolv Univ PGCE 00 MA 02. Qu Coll Birm 06. **d** 09

p 10. NSM Pelsall *Lich* from 09. *32 Chestnut Road, Leamore, Walsall WS3 1BD* T: (01922) 477734 M: 07837-649756

MORRIS, Mrs Ann. b 52. N Co Coll Newc CertEd 73. WEMTC 00. **d** 03 **p** 04. C Churchdown St Jo and Innsworth *Glouc* 03–07; P-in-c Barnwood 07–17; rtd 17. *5 Chaceley Close, Quedgeley, Gloucester GL2 4WW*

MORRIS (née SHAW), Mrs Anne. b 47. LMH Ox BA 69 MA 72 Lon Univ BD 82. NOC 01. **d** 03 **p** 04. NSM Leamington Priors All SS *Cov* 03–18; NSM Leamington Spa H Trin 03–18; rtd 18; PtO *Cov* from 18. *20 Hayle Avenue, Warwick CV34 5TW* T: (01926) 403512 E: am.gm@hotmail.co.uk

MORRIS, Anne. *See* MORRIS, Margaret Anne

MORRIS, Anthony David. b 61. Aston Univ BSc 83. Qu Coll Birm 06. **d** 09 **p** 10. NSM Droitwich Spa *Worc* 09–13; NSM Stoke Prior, Wychbold and Upton Warren 13–14; P-in-c Bowbrook N 14–20; P-in-c Bowbrook S 14–20; C Stoke Prior, Wychbold and Upton Warren 14–20; V Bowbrook from 20. *The Parsonage, Church Lane, Tibberton, Droitwich WR9 7NW* T: (01905) 345169 M: 07891-837194 E: revdm777@gmail.com

MORRIS, Beti Elin. b 36. CertEd 57. Sarum & Wells Th Coll 87. **d** 89 **p** 97. C Llangeitho and Blaenpennal w Betws Leucu etc *St D* 89–92; C-in-c Pencarreg and Llanycrwys 92–97; V 97–05; rtd 05. *Bro Mihangel, Maes y Tren, Felinfach, Lampeter SA48 8AH* E: betimorris345@btinternet.com

MORRIS, Catharine Mary. *See* MABUZA, Catharine Mary

MORRIS, Canon Christopher John. b 45. K Coll Lon AKC 67 BD 68. **d** 68 **p** 69. C W Bromwich All SS *Lich* 68–72; C Porthill 72–74; Min Can Carl Cathl 74–77; Ecum Liaison Officer BBC Radio Carl 74–77; Dioc Communications Officer *Carl* 77–83; V Thursby 77–83; Angl Adv Border TV 82–91; V Upperby St Jo *Carl* 83–91; P-in-c Lancecost w Kirkcambeck and Walton 91–99; P-in-c Gilsland w Nether Denton 96–99; R Lancercost, Walton, Gilsland and Nether Denton 99–10; RD Brampton 98–05; Hon Can Carl Cathl 98–10; rtd 10; PtO *Carl* from 10. *15 Nook Lane Close, Dalston, Carlisle CA5 7JA* T: (01228) 711872 E: chrisandmarjorie.morris@btinternet.com

MORRIS, David. *See* MORRIS, Anthony David

MORRIS, Preb David Meeson. b 35. Trin Coll Ox BA 56 MA 60. Chich Th Coll 57. **d** 60 **p** 61. C Westmr St Steph w St Jo *Lon* 60–65; Lib Pusey Ho 65–68; Chapl Wadh Coll Ox 67–68; C Sheff St Leon Norwood 68–69; Ind Chapl 68–72; C Brightside St Marg 69–72; R Adderley *Lich* 72–82; V Drayton in Hales 72–82; RD Tutbury 82–95; Chapl Burton Gen Hosp 82–90; P-in-c Burton St Modwen *Lich* 82; V Burton 82–99; Preb Lich Cathl 93–99; P-in-c Shobnall 94–99; rtd 99; PtO *Lich* 99–16; *Heref* 99–20. *Watling House, All Stretton, Church Stretton SY6 6HH* T: (01694) 722243

MORRIS, David Michael. b 59. Ox Univ MA 84 Cam Univ PGCE 91. Sarum & Wells Th Coll 82. **d** 84 **p** 85. C Angell Town St Jo *S'wark* 84–87; C Mitcham SS Pet and Paul 87–90; V Llandygwydd and Cenarth w Cilrhedyn etc *St D* 90–98; Lect Th St D Coll Lamp 90–19; Hd RE Lampeter Comp Sch 98–19. *11 Eaton Road, Cressington, Liverpool L19 0PN* M: 07527-648421 E: michaelmorris712@hotmail.com

MORRIS, Canon David Pryce. b 39. St Mich Coll Llan 62. **d** 63 **p** 64. C Colwyn Bay *St As* 63–70; R St George 70–76; Dioc Children's Adv 75–87; V Bodelwyddan and St George 76–79; V Connah's Quay 79–95; St As Dioc Adult Lay Tr Team 88–06; Ed *St Asaph Diocesan News* from 89; Dioc Communications Officer *St As* 90–06; V Shotton 95–06; Hon Can St As Cathl 96–00; Can Cursal St As Cathl 00–06; rtd 07; PtO *St As* from 09. *7 Rhuddlan Road, Buckley CH7 3QA* T: (01244) 540779 M: 07711-519752 E: daviddandpmorris@talktalk.net

MORRIS, David Thomas. Ban Univ BTh 07 Cardiff Univ MTh 10. St Mich Coll Llan. **d** 09 **p** 10. C Merthyr Tydfil St Dav and Abercanaid *Llan* 09–12; C Cardiff St Mary w St Dyfrig and St Samson 12–16; P-in-c Grangetown w Cardiff St Dyfrig and St Samson 16–19; TV E Vale from 19; Voc Adv 13–19; Dioc Dir of Ords from 19. *The Vicarage, 9 Heol St Cattwg, Pendoylan, Cowbridge CF71 7UG* T: (01446) 760512 E: dtmorris@sky.com *or* davidmorris@churchinwales.org.uk

MORRIS, Dennis Gordon. b 41. ALCM 58. St D Coll Lamp. **d** 67 **p** 68. C Neath w Llantwit *Llan* 67–92; V Troedrhiwgarth 92–10; rtd 10. *12 Cwrt yr Hen Ysgol, Tondu, Bridgend CF32 9GE*

MORRIS, Mrs Elizabeth Anne. b 59. BA 05. **d** 00 **p** 01. OLM Darsham and Westleton w Dunwich *St E* 00–04; C Hadleigh, Layham and Shelley 04–06; C Yoxmere 06–09; Asst Chapl Aquitaine *Eur* from 10. *Maison Neuve, Plaisance, 24560 Issigeac, France* T: (0033) 5 53 23 40 51 E: cookingcurate@gmail.com

MORRIS, Geoffrey. *See* MORRIS, Martin Geoffrey Roger

MORRIS, Geoffrey David. b 43. Fitzw Coll Cam BA 65 MA 69 Westmr Coll Ox DipEd 67. NOC. **d** 82 **p** 83. C Man Clayton St Cross w St Paul 82–85; V Lower Kersal 85–03; P-in-c Priors

Hardwick, Priors Marston and Wormleighton *Cov* 03–08; Asst Chapl HM Pris Rye Hill 03–07; rtd 08; PtO *Cov* from 08. *20 Hayle Avenue, Warwick CV34 5TW* T: (01926) 403512 E: am.gm@hotmail.co.uk

MORRIS, Graham Edwin. b 60. Sarum & Wells Th Coll 83. **d** 86 **p** 87. C Coalbrookdale, Iron-Bridge and Lt Wenlock *Heref* 86–90; TV Bilston *Lich* 90–99; R Northwood *Portsm* 99–05; V Gurnard 99–05; P-in-c Ventnor H Trin 05–06; V 06–12; P-in-c Ventnor St Cath 05–06; V 06–12; P-in-c Bonchurch 05–06; R 06–12; RD E Wight 05–12; P-in-c Ryde All SS 12–18; P-in-c Swanmore St Mich 12–18; Hon Can Portsm Cathl 11–18; V Cirencester *Glouc* from 18. *41 Rendcomb Drive, Cirencester GL7 1YN* E: revcanongraham@gmail.com

MORRIS, Hayley Jayne. b 64. **d** 16 **p** 17. OLM Gt Ilford St Andr *Chelmsf* from 16. *15 Mistley Thorn, 5 Cranbrook Rise, Ilford IG1 3QP* E: hayleyjaym@yahoo.co.uk

MORRIS, Preb Henry James. b 47. Lon Univ BSc 69. Wycliffe Hall Ox MA. **d** 79 **p** 80. C Woodford Wells *Chelmsf* 79–82; C Gt Baddow 82–87; R Siddington w Preston *Glouc* 87–01; RD Cirencester 97–01; TR Madeley *Heref* 01–12; Preb Heref Cathl 09–12; rtd 12; PtO *Lich* 12–21. *2 Waveney Avenue, Perton, Wolverhampton WV6 7RA* T: (01902) 757797 E: henrym@dircon.co.uk

MORRIS (née LONG), Hermione Jane. b 66. Univ of Wales (Swansea) BSc 97 RGN 88. St Mich Coll Llan 05. **d** 07 **p** 08. C Bassaleg *Mon* 07–11; R Llanfyllin, Bwlchycibau and Llanwddyn *St As* 11–14; R Llanfyllin w Llanwddyn and Bwlchycibau 14–16; I Vyrnwy Miss Area 17–20; P-in-c Tanat-Vyrnwy from 20. *The Rectory, Coed Llan Lane, Llanfyllin SY22 5BW* T: (01691) 648306

MORRIS, Miss Jane Elizabeth. b 50. York Univ BA 71 CertEd 72 MSc 80. NEOC 92. **d** 92 **p** 94. NSM York St Mich-le-Belfrey 92–95; C Leeds St Geo *Ripon* 95–05; V Cricklewood St Gabr and St Mich *Lon* 05–19; rtd 19; PtO *Lon* 19–20; Hon C W Ealing St Jo w St Jas from 20. *50A Mattock Lane, London W13 9NS* M: 07702-301328 E: jane.morris100@gmail.com

MORRIS, Canon Jeremy Nigel. b 60. Ball Coll Ox MA 81 DPhil 86 Clare Coll Cam BA 92. Westcott Ho Cam 90. **d** 93 **p** 94. C Battersea St Mary *S'wark* 93–96; Dir Studies Westcott Ho Cam 96–01; Vice-Prin 97–01; Dean and Chapl Trin Hall Cam 01–10; Dean K Coll Cam 10–14; Trin Hall Cam from 14; Hon Can Ely Cathl from 19. *Trinity Hall, Cambridge CB2 1TJ* T: (01223) 332500 E: jnm20@cam.ac.uk *or* jnm20@trinhall.cam.ac.uk

MORRIS, Mrs Joanna. b 69. UWE BSc 99 RGN 90. Trin Coll Bris 18. **d** 20 **p** 21. C Stoke Bishop *Bris* from 20. *30 Queens Gate, Stoke Bishop, Bristol BS9 1TZ* T: 0117-968 2486 M: 07773-793352 E: iamthisjoanna@gmail.com

MORRIS, Mrs Joanna Elizabeth. b 60. N Riding Coll of Educn CertEd 81. Qu Coll Birm 07. **d** 09 **p** 10. C Riddings and Ironville *Derby* 09–13; R Whittington from 13. *The Rectory, 84 Church Street North, Old Whittington, Chesterfield S41 9QP* E: jomorris17@gmail.com

MORRIS, John Douglas. b 37. Cam Univ BA 58 Lon Inst of Educn PGCE 60 Univ of E Africa MEd 67 Ex Univ PhD 87. S Dios Minl Tr Scheme 94. **d** 95 **p** 96. NSM Twyford and Owslebury and Morestead *Win* 95–01; PtO from 01; Chapl Twyford Sch *Win* 95–05. *9 Parkside Gardens, Winchester SO22 5NA* T: (01962) 852033 E: johnmarymorris@btopenworld.com

MORRIS, John Dudley. b 33. Ball Coll Ox BA 57 MA 61. Wycliffe Hall Ox 58. **d** 60 **p** 61. C Tonbridge SS Pet and Paul *Roch* 60–65; C Enfield Ch Ch Trent Park *Lon* 65–69; Chapl Elstree Sch Woolhampton 70–74; Hd Master Handcross Park Sch W Sussex 74–89; V Rudgwick *Chich* 89–98; RD Horsham 93–98; rtd 98; PtO *Chich* from 98. *Address temp unknown*

MORRIS, John Owen. b 56. Nottm Univ BA 82 Ex Univ MA 06. Linc Th Coll 79. **d** 82 **p** 83. C Morriston *S & B* 82–84; C Kingstone w Clehonger and Eaton Bishop *Heref* 84–87; P-in-c Lugwardine w Bartestree and Weston Beggard 87–92; Chapl RN 92–13; Chapl Lord Wandsworth Coll Hook 13–15; PtO *Ex* 15–17; V The Bourne and Tilford *Guildf* from 17. *The Vicarage, 2 Middle Avenue, Farnham GU9 8JL* T: (01252) 713929 M: 07970-667219 E: vicar@thebourne.org.uk

MORRIS, Jonathan Richard. b 57. Lanc Univ BA 78 Trin Coll Ox MSc 84. WEMTC 99. **d** 02 **p** 03. C Taunton St Andr *B & W* 02–06; C Wulfric Benefice from 06; RD Crewkerne 12–20; Dioc Inter Faith Adv from 18. *The Rectory, New Street, North Perrott, Crewkerne TA18 7ST* T: (01460) 72356 E: jonbea@cooptel.net

MORRIS, Kevin John. b 63. Univ of Wales (Ban) BMus 84 Lon Univ MA 12. Westcott Ho Cam 85. **d** 88 **p** 89. C Roath *Llan* 88–91; C Holborn St Alb w Saffron Hill St Pet *Lon* 91–96; V Bedford Park from 96; P-in-c Acton Green 15–16; V from 16; Dir Post-Ord Tr 99–10. *The Vicarage, Priory Gardens, London W4 1TT* T: (020) 8994

0139 *or* 8994 1380 E: stpetersactongreen@gmail.com *or* parishoffice@smaaa.org.uk

MORRIS, Kirsteen Helen Grace. b 44. STETS 99. **d** 02 **p** 03. NSM Cowes H Trin and St Mary *Portsm* 02–12; rtd 12; PtO *Portsm* from 12. *Meda, Medham Farm Lane, Cowes PO31 8PH* T: (01983) 289585 F: 292919

MORRIS, Mrs Lynne. b 48. STETS 07. **d** 10 **p** 11. NSM Horton, Chalbury, Hinton Martel and Holt St Jas *Sarum* 10–14; NSM Witchampton, Stanbridge and Long Crichel etc 11–14; PtO 14–15; NSM W Moors from 15. *2 Garth Close, St Leonards, Ringwood BH24 2RG* E: lynnemorrislp@btinternet.com

MORRIS, Mrs Lynne Margaret. b 53. SEN. WMMTC 95. **d** 98 **p** 99. NSM Wrockwardine Wood *Lich* 98–01; Chapl Birm Community Healthcare NHS Foundn Trust 01–17; rtd 17; PtO *Lich* from 17. *5 Kingston Road, Trench, Telford TF2 7HT* T: (01952) 618158 E: revlynne.morris@yahoo.co.uk

MORRIS, Margaret Anne. b 61. Man Univ BA 82 MA 91 Ches Univ DProf 16. NOC 94. **d** 96 **p** 97. C Bury St Pet *Man* 96–98; C Accrington St Jo w Huncoat *Blackb* 98–01; V Knuzden from 01. *St Oswald's Vicarage, 68 Bank Lane, Blackburn BB1 2AP* T: (01254) 698321 E: revannemorris@gmail.com

MORRIS, Canon Margaret Jane. Ox Univ MTh 96 Leic Univ Hon LLM 96. EMMTC 86. **d** 89 **p** 94. NSM Quorndon *Leic* 89–96; Chapl for People affected by HIV 94–05; NSM Loughborough All SS w H Trin 96–98; Chapl Asst Leic R Infirmary NHS Trust 98–00; Chapl Asst Univ Hosps Leic NHS Trust 00–10; Hon Can Leic Cathl 97–10; rtd 10; PtO *Leic* 10–13; *Derby* from 18. *2 Chatsworth Close, Sandiacre, Nottingham NG10 5PF* T: 0115-949 7997 E: margaretmorris.147@gmail.com

MORRIS, Martin Geoffrey Roger. b 41. Trin Coll Cam BA 63 MA 67. St D Coll Lamp 63. **d** 66 **p** 67. C Newport St Paul *Mon* 66–72; R Lampeter Velfrey *St D* 72–74; R Lampeter Velfrey and Llanddewi Velfrey 74–08; RD St Clears 83–98; Can St D Cathl 92–08; Chan St D Cathl 03–08; rtd 08; PtO *St D* from 08. *Greenfield Cottage, Gilfach Hill, Lampeter Velfrey, Narberth SA67 8UL* T: (01834) 831241

MORRIS, Ms Mary. b 27. Birm Univ BA 49 CertEd 50 MA 56. dss 68 **d** 87 **p** 94. Kinver *Lich* 83–87; Kinver and Enville 87; Hon Par Dn 87–94; Hon C 94–11; PtO 11–12. *12 Pavilion End, Prestwood, Stourbridge DY7 5PF* T: (01384) 877245

MORRIS, Michael. *See* MORRIS, David Michael

MORRIS, Michael Alan. b 46. Jes Coll Cam BA 70 MA 74. Coll of Resurr Mirfield 79. **d** 81 **p** 82. C Leamington Priors All SS *Cov* 81–83; C Milton *Portsm* 83–88; R Petworth *Chich* 88–90; R Egdean 88–90; Chapl St Pet Hosp Chertsey 90–95; Hon C Thorpe *Guildf* 90–95; P-in-c Harbledown *Cant* 95–97; R 97–16; rtd 16; Chapl St Nic Hosp Cant 95–00; Asst Dir of Ords *Cant* from 18. *Hopbine, 4 The Oast Paddock, Durlock Road, Staple, Canterbury CT3 1JX* T: (01304) 814096 E: michael@themorrises.co.uk

MORRIS, Michael James. b 70. Univ of Wales (Abth) BScEcon 92. Qu Coll Birm BA. **d** 00 **p** 01. C Tupsley w Hampton Bishop *Heref* 00–04; TV Watling Valley *Ox* 04–12; TR from 12. *21 Edzell Crescent, Westcroft, Milton Keynes MK4 4EU* T: (01908) 507123 E: mike.morris@wvep.org

MORRIS (née ROBERTS), Canon Nia Wyn. b 64. Univ of Wales (Ban) BA 86 PGCE 87 CQSW 90 Anglia Poly Univ MA 00. Westcott Ho Cam 98. **d** 00 **p** 01. C Rhyl w St Ann *St As* 00–03; R Bala 03–14; AD Penllyn and Edeirnion 12–13; R Llanllwchaiarn and Newtown w Aberhafesp 14–16; I Cedewain Miss Area from 17; AD Cedewain from 14; Can Cursal St As Cathl from 15. *The Rectory, 3 Old Barn Lane, Newtown SY16 2PT* T: (01686) 951395 M: 07833-302312 E: niawyn1000@yahoo.com

MORRIS, Preb Norman Foster Maxwell. b 46. Ex Univ BA 68 MA 71 K Coll Lon MTh 85 Univ of Wales (Cardiff) MA 91 Cheltenham & Glouc Coll of HE MA 98 Leic Univ PGCE 69. S'wark Ord Course 75. **d** 78 **p** 79. C Hackbridge and N Beddington *S'wark* 78–81; Chapl Tonbridge Sch 81–85; Chapl Mon Sch 85–00; Asst Warden Jones Almshouses Mon 89–00; R Wentnor w Ratlinghope, Myndtown, Norbury etc *Heref* 00–16; P-in-c Churchstoke w Hyssington 04–16; RD Clun Forest 11–16; Preb Heref Cathl 12–16; CF (ACF) 02–12; rtd 16; TV Cedewain Miss Area *St As* 16–20; TV Tanat-Vyrnwy from 20. *The Vicarage, Llanrhaeadr ym Mochnant, Oswestry SY10 0JZ* T: (01691) 780827 M: 07974-771069 E: revnormmorris@gmail.com

MORRIS, Canon Paul David. b 56. St Jo Coll Nottm BTh 79. **d** 80 **p** 81. C Billericay and Lt Burstead *Chelmsf* 80–84; C Luton Lewsey St Hugh *St Alb* 84–89; Dioc Adv on Evang *S'well* 89–00; Dioc Millennium Officer 97–01; Min Tommy's (ch for the unchurched) 96–01; C Barton in Fabis 01–02; C Gotham 01–02; C Thrumpton 01–02; C Kingston and Ratcliffe-on-Soar 01–02; C Sutton Bonington w Normanton-on-Soar 01–02; Dir Evang Chr Associates Internat 02–04; Assoc Eur Dir 04–06; Eur Dir 06–08; Brussels Team 08–09; P-in-c Derby St Pet and Ch Ch w H Trin 09–16; V 16–20; Prin Chapl Derby City Cen Chapl 12–20; Prin Chapl Workplace Chapl in Derbyshire 12–20; Bp's Appts Officer 15–17; Hon Can Derby Cathl 12–20; rtd 20; PtO *Guildf* from 21. *71 Portsmouth Road, Guildford GU2 4BS* **M:** 07877-883390 **E:** pdmorris5@gmail.com

MORRIS, Peter. b 45. Leeds Univ CertEd 66. Tyndale Hall Bris 68. **d** 71 **p** 72. C Southport SS Simon and Jude *Liv* 71–74; Min-in-c Ch Ch Netherley LEP 74–76; V Bryn *Liv* 76–91; R Redenhall, Harleston, Wortwell and Needham *Nor* 91–05; rtd 05; PtO *Roch* from 15. *9 Bromley College, London Road, Bromley BR1 1PE* **T:** (020) 8460 3455 **E:** petermorris203@btinternet.com

MORRIS, The Ven Philip Gregory. b 50. Leeds Univ BA 71 MPhil 74. Coll of Resurr Mirfield 71. **d** 73 **p** 74. C Aberdare *Llan* 74–77; C Neath w Llantwit 77–80; V Cymmer and Porth 80–88; TV Llantwit Major 88–01; Dioc Missr 88–99; Can Res Llan Cathl 00–01; Adn Margam 02–15; TV Aberavon 02; P-in-c Kenfig Hill 02–05; P-in-c Ewenny w St Brides Major 05–15; rtd 15; PtO *Llan* from 15. *12 Groeswen, Llantwit Major CF61 2UA* **T:** (01446) 796459

MORRIS, Philip John. b 50. FCIPD 96. St Mich Coll Llan 97. **d** 99 **p** 00. NSM Builth and Llanddewi'r Cwm w Llangynog etc *S & B* 99–04; NSM Aberedw w Llandeilo Graban and Llanbadarn etc 04–13; LtO from 14. *Lochaber, 22 North Road, Builth Wells LD2 3BU* **T:** (01982) 552390 **E:** pip@pipmorris.plus.com

MORRIS, Canon Raymond. b 48. Open Univ BA 88. NOC 80. **d** 83 **p** 84. C Tonge w Alkrington *Man* 83–86; R Blackley St Paul 86–91; V Heyside 91–14; AD Tandle 02–09; C Royton St Anne 12–14; Hon Can Man Cathl 07–14; rtd 14; PtO *Man* from 14. *46 Penthorpe Drive, Royton, Oldham OL2 6JL* **T:** (01706) 842192

MORRIS, Raymond Arthur. b 42. Trin Coll Ox BA 64 MA 66 Lon Univ LLB 71 CQSW 72. Clifton Th Coll 66. **d** 67 **p** 91. C Greenstead *Chelmsf* 67–68; PtO *York* 69–91; NSM Linthorpe 91–12; PtO from 12. *3 Medina Gardens, Middlesbrough TS5 8BN* **T:** (01642) 593726 **E:** morris101@btinternet.com

MORRIS, Canon Robert John. b 45. Leeds Univ BA 67. Coll of Resurr Mirfield 74. **d** 76 **p** 77. C Beeston Hill St Luke *Ripon* 76; C Holbeck 76–78; C Moseley St Mary *Birm* 78–83; P-in-c Handsworth St Jas 83–88; V 88–99; P-in-c Handsworth St Mich 86–87; AD Handsworth 92–99; TR Kings Norton 99–15; Hon Can Birm Cathl 97–15; rtd 15; PtO *Birm* from 15; Dioc Retirement Officer from 17. *61 Oxford Street, Stirchley, Birmingham B30 2LH* **T:** 0121-247 0355 **M:** 07973-389427 **E:** morrisrob4@aol.com

✠**MORRIS, The Rt Revd Roger Anthony Brett.** b 68. Imp Coll Lon BSc 89 Trin Coll Cam BA 92 MA 08 ARCS 89. Ridley Hall Cam 90. **d** 93 **p** 94 **c** 14. C Northleach w Hampnett and Farmington etc *Glouc* 93–96; P-in-c Sevenhampton w Charlton Abbotts and Hawling etc 96–00; P-in-c Dowdeswell and Andoversford w the Shiptons etc 96–00; R Sevenhampton w Charlton Abbots, Hawling etc 00–03; Dioc Dir Par Development and Evang *Cov* 03–08; Adn Worc 08–14; Area Bp Colchester *Chelmsf* from 14. *1 Fitzwalter Road, Colchester CO3 3SS* **T:** (01206) 576648 **M:** 07590-696212 **E:** b.colchester@chelmsford.anglican.org

MORRIS, Mrs Sally Jane. b 69. Imp Coll Lon BSc 91. Qu Coll Birm 07. **d** 10 **p** 11. NSM Bowbrook S *Worc* 10–13; NSM Chipping Campden w Ebrington *Glouc* 13–14; NSM Vale and Cotswold Edge 14–15; NSM Lawford *Chelmsf* 15–17; NSM Lawford, Lt Bentley and The Bromleys from 17. *1 Fitzwalter Road, Colchester CO3 3SS* **T:** (01206) 576648 **M:** 07920-588994 **E:** sjmorris@mypostoffice.co.uk

MORRIS (née GILES), Preb Sarah Jayne. b 76. Aston Univ BSc 98. St Jo Coll Nottm MTh 07. **d** 06 **p** 07. C Cen Telford *Lich* 06–10; Chapl HM YOI Stoke Heath 10–17; Chapl HM Pris Drake Hall from 17; PtO *Lich* 10–16; Dioc Co-ord Chapl for Pris from 16; Preb Lich Cathl from 18. *HM Prison and Young Offender Institution, Drake Hall, Eccleshall, Stafford ST21 6LQ* **T:** (01785) 774100 **E:** sarah.morris@justice.gov.uk

MORRIS, Shaun Anthony. b 64. Keele Univ BSocSc 85. Oak Hill Th Coll 04. **d** 06 **p** 07. C Westlands St Andr *Lich* 06–10; C Hanford 10–17; P-in-c 17–20; V from 20; C Trentham 10–17; RD Stoke-on-Trent from 18. *Hanford Vicarage, 76 Church Lane, Stoke-on-Trent ST4 4QD* **T:** (01782) 657848 **E:** morris.shaun@btinternet.com

MORRIS, Simon John. b 83. St Jo Coll Dur BA 05. St Steph Ho Ox BA 07. **d** 08 **p** 09. C Tottenham St Mary *Lon* 08–11; V from 11. *St Mary's Vicarage, Lansdowne Road, London N17 9XE* **E:** fr.morris@hotmail.com

MORRIS, Stanley James. b 35. Keble Coll Ox BA 58 MA 63. Chich Th Coll 59. **d** 61 **p** 62. C Tunstall Ch Ch *Lich* 61–64;

C W Bromwich All SS 64–67; V Wilnecote 67–88; V Alrewas and Wychnor 88–00; rtd 01; PtO *Derby* 01–18. *44 Pinfold Close, Repton, Derby DE65 6FR* **T:** (01283) 703453

MORRIS, Stephanie Ruth. b 72. All SS Cen for Miss & Min 16. **d** 19 **p** 20. NSM Sutton, Wincle, Wildboarclough and Bosley *Ches* from 19. *St James' Vicarage, Church Lane, Sutton, Macclesfield SK11 0DS* **M:** 07703-578003 **E:** stephmorris1106@btinternet.com

MORRIS, Stephen Bryan. b 54. Linc Th Coll 88. **d** 90 **p** 91. C Glouc St Geo w Whaddon 90–94; C Glouc St Mark and St Mary de Crypt w St Jo etc 94–02; C Barnwood 02–03; Chapl for the Deaf 94–13; Dioc Chapl among Deaf and Adv on Disability 13–15; Chapl among Deaf 15–20; rtd 20. *5 Chaceley Close, Quedgeley, Gloucester GL2 4WW* **T:** (01452) 610450

MORRIS, Stephen Francis. b 52. St Jo Coll Nottm BTh 79. **d** 79 **p** 80. C N Hinksey *Ox* 79–82; C Leic H Apostles 82–85; TV Shenley and Loughton *Ox* 85–88; TV Watling Valley 88–95; V Chatham St Wm *Roch* 95–98; TR S Chatham H Trin 98–00; Lect Nottingham St Mary and St Cath *S'well* 00–07; Lect Nottingham All SS, St Mary and St Pet 07–14; AD Nottingham Cen 02–08; Dioc Ecum Officer 10–14; P-in-c Newark w Coddington 14–17; rtd 17; C Newark w Coddington *S'well* 17; C Nottingham St Mary Lace Market 17–18; PtO from 19. *21 Private Road, Sherwood, Nottingham NG5 4DD*

MORRIS, Steven Ralph. b 62. UEA BA 84 MA 85. Wycliffe Hall Ox 08. **d** 10 **p** 11. C Ealing St Steph Castle Hill *Lon* 10–13; C Neasden St Cath w St Paul 13–15; V N Wembley St Cuth 15–21; C S Kenton 20–21; C Cowley 20–21. *26 King's Avenue, London W5 2SH* **E:** steve_stcuthberts@hotmail.com

MORRIS, Canon Stuart Collard. b 43. AKC 66. St Boniface Warminster 66. **d** 67 **p** 68. C Hanham *Bris* 67–71; C Whitchurch 71–74; P-in-c Westerleigh and Wapley w Codrington and Dodington 74–77; P-in-c Holdgate w Tugford *Heref* 77–82; P-in-c Abdon w Clee St Margaret 77–82; R Diddlebury w Bouldon and Munslow 77–82; P-in-c Sotterley, Willingham, Shadingfield, Ellough etc *St E* 82–87; RD Beccles and S Elmham 83–94; P-in-c Westhall w Brampton and Stoven 86–88; P-in-c Flixton w Homersfield and S Elmham 86–92; V Bungay H Trin w St Mary 87–94; P-in-c Hadleigh w Layham and Shelley 94–96; R Hadleigh 96–99; Dean Bocking 94–99; RD Hadleigh 94–98; Hon Can St E Cathl 87–99; rtd 99; PtO *Ely* 07–14; Hon C Tottenhill w Wormegay 14–16; Hon C Watlington 14–16; Hon C Holme Runcton w S Runcton and Wallington 14–16; PtO *Derby* 16–18; *Man* from 18; *Nor* from 20. *18 Malthouse Cottages, Norwich Road, Dereham NR20 3AW* **M:** 07467-122709 **E:** stuartmorris20@gmail.com

MORRIS, Canon Timothy David. b 48. Lon Univ BSc 69. Trin Coll Bris. **d** 75 **p** 76. C Edin St Thos 75–77; R Edin St Jas 77–83; R Troon *Glas* 83–85; R Galashiels *Edin* 85–02; R Edin Gd Shep 02–08; Dean Edin 92–01; Hon Can St Mary's Cathl from 01; rtd 08; Canada 08–10; LtO *Edin* from 10. *2 The Firs, Foulden Newton, Berwick-upon-Tweed TD15 1UL* **T:** (01289) 386615 **M:** 07979-196824 **E:** tim@foulden.org.uk

MORRIS, Mrs Tracey. b 78. Bradf Univ BSc 00 Sheff Univ BA 16. St Hild Coll 16. **d** 19 **p** 20. NSM Lodge Moor St Luke *Sheff* from 19. *20 Blackbrook Road, Sheffield S10 4LP* **M:** 07882-589685 **E:** tracey.mozza@hotmail.com

MORRIS, Trudie Elizabeth. b 53. UEA BA 91 PGCE 92 Leic Univ MBA 04 Cam Univ BTh 12 Anglia Ruskin Univ PhD 19. Westcott Ho Cam 10. **d** 12 **p** 13. C Fowlmere, Foxton, Shepreth and Thriplow *Ely* 12–15; P-in-c Derby St Andr w St Osmund 15–16; P-in-c Allenton and Shelton Lock 15–16; V Pride Park, Wilmorton, Allenton and Shelton Lock 16–18; R Stand *Man* 18–20; rtd 20; PtO *Nor* from 20. *18 Malthouse Cottages, Norwich Road, Dereham NR20 3AW* **M:** 07710-494871 **E:** revtrudie@gmail.com

MORRIS, Mrs Valerie Ruth. b 46. St Hugh's Coll Ox BA 68 MA 72. Gilmore Course 76. **dss** 78 **d** 87 **p** 05. Drayton in Hales *Lich* 78–82; Burton 82–90; Par Dn 87–91; PtO *Heref* 04–05; Hon C Church Stretton 05–11; PtO from 11. *Watling House, All Stretton, Church Stretton SY6 6HH* **T:** (01694) 722243 **E:** vrmorris46@gmail.com

MORRIS, Victor Bernard. b 50. **d** 14 **p** 15. OLM Wigginton *Lich* 14–20; PtO from 20. *14 Wentworth Drive, Lichfield WS14 9HN* **E:** vicbmorris@yahoo.co.uk

MORRIS, Vincent Sidney. **d** 18 **p** 19. C Bro Tysilio *Ban* 18–21; Miss Area Ldr Bro Cwyfan from 21. *The Vicarage, Tan y Ffordd, Llansadwrn, Menai Bridge LL59 5SH* **T:** (01248) 811342 **E:** vincesmorris@outlook.com

MORRIS, William Hazlitt. b 62. Trin Coll Cam BA 84 MA 88 Virginia Univ LLM 89 Solicitor 88. NTMTC BA 09. **d** 09 **p** 10. NSM St Martin-in-the-Fields *Lon* 09–19. *Address temp unknown*

MORRISON, Ailsa. *See* SPACKMAN, Ailsa

MORRISON, Barry John. b 44. Pemb Coll Cam BA 66 MA 70. ALCD 69. **d** 69 **p** 70. C Stoke Bishop *Bris* 69–72; C Edgware *Lon* 72–76; Chapl Poly Cen Lon 76–83; Hon C Langham Place All So 76–83; P-in-c W Hampstead St Luke 83–88; V 88–98; Chapl Westf Coll 84–92; R Rushden St Mary w Newton Bromswold *Pet* 98–08; rtd 08; PtO *Pet* 09–21. *11 Lytham Park, Oundle, Peterborough PE8 4FB* T: (01832) 274242 E: gandbmorrison@btinternet.com

MORRISON, Bryony Clare. b 47. Lon Univ CertEd 77 Brentwood Coll of Educn BEd 86. NTMTC 96. **d** 99 **p** 00. C Epping Distr *Chelmsf* 99–05; TV 05–17; Chapl Epping Forest Primary Care Trust 02–05; rtd 17; PtO *Sarum* from 18. *Dibley House, 562 Ringwood Road, Poole BH12 4LY* T: (01202) 461360 M: 07850-876304 E: revmorry@gmail.com

MORRISON, Diana Mary (Sister Diana). b 43. St Kath Coll Liv CertEd 64. EAMTC 02. **d** 05 **p** 06. NSM Breadsall *Derby* 05–13; PtO from 13; *Man* 14–18. *Convent of the Holy Name, Morley Road, Oakwood, Derby DE21 4TB* E: dianachn@tiscali.co.uk

MORRISON, Edward John Scott. b 89. York Univ BA 10. St Steph Ho Ox BA 14. **d** 15 **p** 16. C Cantley *Sheff* 15–18; P-in-c Mexborough from 18. *The Vicarage, Church Street, Mexborough S64 0ER* E: esmorrison@hotmail.com

MORRISON, Iain Edward. b 36. St Steph Ho Ox 76. **d** 78 **p** 79. C Brighton St Aug and St Sav *Chich* 78–81; C Felpham w Middleton 81–83; P-in-c Barnham and Eastergate 83–85; R Aldingbourne, Barnham and Eastergate 85–91; V Jarvis Brook 91–98; R Hastings St Clem and All SS 98–03; rtd 03; P-in-c Arlington, Folkington and Wilmington *Chich* 03–10; PtO from 15; *Win* from 19. *46 Homeforde House, Grigg Lane, Brockenhurst SO42 7QX* T: (01590) 623719 E: iain.iona@gmail.com

MORRISON, Preb James Wilson Rennie. b 42. Aber Univ MA 65. Linc Th Coll 76. **d** 78 **p** 79. C Whitley Ch Ch *Ox* 78–81; R Burghfield 81–87; CF 87–97; P-in-c Burghill *Heref* 97–03; V 03–11; P-in-c Stretton Sugwas 97–03; R 03–11; P-in-c Pipe-cum-Lyde 97–03; P-in-c Pipe-cum-Lyde and Moreton-on-Lugg *Heref* 03–11; Preb Heref Cathl 08–11; rtd 11; PtO *Heref* 13–21. *Brambles, 8 Dernside Close, Wellington, Hereford HR4 8BP* T: (01432) 830911 E: jimmym67@btinternet.com

MORRISON, The Ven John Anthony. b 38. Jes Coll Cam BA 60 MA 64 Linc Coll Ox MA 68. Chich Th Coll 61. **d** 64 **p** 65. C Birm St Pet 64–68; C Ox St Mich 68–71; Chapl Linc Coll Ox 68–74; C Ox St Mich w St Martin and All SS 71–74; V Basildon 74–82; RD Bradfield 78–82; V Aylesbury 82–89; RD 85–89; TR 89–90; Adn Buckingham 90–98; P-in-c Princes Risborough w Ilmer 96–97; Adn Ox and Can Res Ch Ch 98–05; rtd 05; PtO *Ox* from 05. *39 Crown Road, Wheatley, Oxford OX33 1UJ* T: (01865) 876625 E: morrison039@btinternet.com

MORRISON, Keith Charles. b 63. Anglia Ruskin Univ MA 17. Wycliffe Hall Ox 99. **d** 01 **p** 02. C Ipswich St Aug *St E* 01–04; Asst Chapl Cam Univ Hosps NHS Foundn Trust 04–13; Chapl Arthur Rank Ho Brookfields Hosp Cam 13–16; Chapl Arthur Rank Hospice Cam from 16; LtO *Ely* from 05. *Arthur Rank Hospice, Cherry Hinton Road, Shelford Bottom, Cambridge CB22 3FB* T: (01223) 675771 M: 07798-865651 E: keith.morrison@arhc.org.uk

MORRISON, Myrtle. b 64. Wilson Carlile Coll 84 CITI 16. **d** 17 **p** 18. Ardmore w Craigavon *D & D* from 17. *23 Mandeville Manor, Portadown, Craigavon BT62 3UP* T: (028) 3833 4307 M: 07774-565914 E: myrtlechurcharmy@btinternet.com

MORRISON, Richard James. b 55. Sarum & Wells Th Coll 87. **d** 89 **p** 90. C Boston *Linc* 89–93; P-in-c Digby 93–99; V Whaplode Drove 99–16; V Gedney Hill 99–16; P-in-c Whaplode 10–14; P-in-c Holbeach Fen 10–14; V Elloe Fen Gp 17; rtd 17; PtO *Win* from 19. *35 Danestream Court, Sea Road, Milford on Sea, Lymington SO41 0DA* T: (01590) 645295

MORRISON, Canon Robin Victor Adair. b 45. Nottm Univ BA 67. Bucharest Th Inst 67 Ripon Hall Ox 68. **d** 70 **p** 71. C Hackney St Jo *Lon* 70–73; Chapl Newc Univ 73–76; P-in-c Teversal *S'well* 76–78; Chapl Sutton Cen 76–78; Asst Hd Deans Community Sch Livingston *Edin* 78–80; R Edin St Columba 80–81; Chapl Birm Univ 81–88; Prin Soc Resp Officer *Derby* 88–96; TV Southampton (City Cen) *Win* 96–01; Ind Chapl 96–01; Non Exec Dir Southampton and SW Hants HA 00–01; Officer for Ch and Soc Ch in Wales Prov Coun 01–11; Hon Can Llan Cathl 09–11; rtd 11; PtO *Lon* from 18. *Headley, The Broadway, Laleham, Staines-upon-Thames TW18 1RZ* E: revrobinmorrison@gmail.com

MORRISS (formerly HEYN), Lucinda Jane. b 68. Ripon Coll Cuddesdon 07. **d** 10 **p** 11. C Goring and Streatley w S Stoke *Ox* 10–14; TV Hermitage 14–18; Bp's Adv for Women in Ord Min

14–18; P-in-c Cusop w Blakemere, Bredwardine w Brobury etc *Heref* 18–21; R from 21; DEAN of Women's Min from 20. *The Rectory, Cusop, Hay-on-Wye, Hereford HR3 5RF* T: (01497) 821877 E: luci.borderlinkbenefice@outlook.com

MORROW, David. b 63. NUU BSc 86 TCD BTh 89. CITC 86. **d** 89 **p** 90. C Portadown St Mark *Arm* 89–91; C Ballymena w Ballyclug *Conn* 91–94; I Tempo and Clabby *Clogh* 94–01; I Kilcronaghan w Draperstown and Sixtowns *D & R* 01–11; Bp's Dom Chapl 07–11; rtd 11. *Address temp unknown* M: 07540-134601 E: davidmorrow763@btinternet.com

MORROW, Canon Joseph John. b 54. JP 87. Edin Univ BD 79 Dundee Univ LLB 92 NY Th Sem DMin 87. Edin Th Coll 76. **d** 79 **p** 80. Chapl St Paul's Cathl Dundee *Bre* 79–82; P-in-c Dundee St Martin 82–85; R 85–90; P-in-c Dundee St Jo 85–08; P-in-c Dundee St Ninian 02–07; Can St Paul's Cathl Dundee 00–08; Hon Can St Paul's Cathl Dundee from 08; Dioc Chan 08–14; PtO from 09. *Miltonhaugh, Tealing, Dundee DD4 0QZ* T: (01382) 380501 E: j.jmorrow@btinternet.com

MORROW, Keri Anne. b 72. R Cen Sch Speech & Drama BSC 95. ERMC 16. **d** 19 **p** 20. C Pet St Mary Boongate from 19. *21 College Park, Peterborough PE1 4AW* T: (01733) 601092 M: 07949-708303 E: revkerimorrow@gmail.com

MORROW, Nigel Patrick. b 68. Dur Univ BA 94 TCD MPhil 02 Anglia Ruskin Univ MA 05. Westcott Ho Cam 03. **d** 05 **p** 06. C Linc St Botolph and Linc St Pet-at-Gowts and St Andr 05–08; C Camberwell St Giles w St Matt *S'wark* 08–10; Chapl K Coll Lon 08–10; Chapl and Inter Faith Adv Brunel Univ 11–12; PtO 12–13; S'wark 13–14; C Lt Ilford St Mich *Chelmsf* 14–21; Chapl Camden and Islington NHS Foundn Trust 14–19; Sen Chapl HM Pris Chelmsf 19; Chapl HM Pris Wayland from 21; PtO *St E* from 21. *HM Prison Wayland, Griston, Thetford IP25 6RL* T: (01953) 804100 E: patrick.morrow2@justice.gov.uk

MORSE, Mrs Elisabeth Ann. b 51. New Hall Cam MA 73 Qu Eliz Coll Lon MSc 74 Heythrop Coll Lon MA 97. S'wark Ord Course 91. **d** 94 **p** 95. C Wimbledon *S'wark* 94–99; C Fulham All SS *Lon* 99–08; V Battersea St Luke *S'wark* 08–16; rtd 16; PtO *S'wark* from 16; *Lon* from 21. *31 Elm Bank Gardens, London SW13 0NU* E: morseelisabeth@yahoo.co.uk

MORSE, Ms Gita. b 55. Wolv Univ CertEd 10. Qu Coll Birm 10. **d** 13 **p** 14. NSM Sparkhill St Jo *Birm* 13–16; NSM Harborne St Faith and St Laur 16–17. *54 Park Hill Road, Harborne, Birmingham B17 9HJ* M: 07716-496154 E: gmorse@mypostoffice.co.uk

MORSON, Mrs Eleanor. b 42. CA Tr Coll 63 TISEC 95. **d** 96 **p** 96. NSM Kirkwall *Ab* 96–01; R Edin St Mark 01–05. *4 Broadshaw Mews, Leazes Parkway, Newcastle upon Tyne NE15 9QL* T: 0191-264 6885

MORSON, John. b 41. CA Tr Coll 62. **d** 88 **p** 92. NSM Duns *Edin* 88–89; CF 89–92; R Kirkwall *Ab* 92–01; R Stromness 92–01; NSM Edin St Mark 01–05; rtd 06. *4 Broadshaw Mews, Leazes Parkway, Newcastle upon Tyne NE15 9QL* T: 0191-264 6885

MORT, Alister. b 52. BSc BA. Oak Hill Th Coll. **d** 82 **p** 83. C Cheadle Hulme St Andr *Ches* 82–85; C Rodbourne Cheney *Bris* 86–87; TV 87–90; V New Milverton *Cov* 90–05; PtO 05–09; TR Bishton *Ripon* 09–14; rtd 14; Tutor Johannesburg Bible Coll S Africa from 14. *c/o J Mort Esq, 168 Tachbrook Road, Leamington Spa CV31 3EF* E: alister9mort@gmail.com

MORTER, Canon Ian Charles. b 54. AKC 77. Coll of Resurr Mirfield 77. **d** 78 **p** 79. C Colchester St Jas, All SS, St Nic and St Runwald *Chelmsf* 78–82; C Brixham w Churston Ferrers *Ex* 82–83; TV 84–86; TV Sidmouth, Woolbrook, Salcombe Regis, Sidbury etc 86–95; P-in-c Exminster and Kenn 95–00; TR Littleham w Exmouth 00–10; RD Aylesbeare 07–10; Preb Ex Cathl 06–18; Can Res Ex Cathl 10–17; rtd 17; Hon PV Ex Cathl from 18. *17 Bapton Lane, Exmouth EX8 3JS* E: ian.morter@talktalk.net

MORTIBOYS, John William. b 45. K Coll Lon BD 69 AKC 69. Sarum Th Coll 71. **d** 71 **p** 72. C Reading All SS *Ox* 71–95; PtO *Portsm* from 97. *13 Oyster Street, Portsmouth PO1 2HZ* T: (023) 9275 6676 F: 9266 2626 E: johnmortibos@gmail.com

MORTIMER, Aileen Jane. b 46. Edin Univ MA 67 CQSW 70. ERMC 05. **d** 08 **p** 09. NSM E Bergholt and Brantham *St E* 08–13; rtd 13; PtO *St E* from 13. *20 Leggatt Drive, Bramford, Ipswich IP8 4ET* T: (01473) 747419 E: ajmortimer@hotmail.co.uk

MORTIMER, Anthony John. b 42. Sarum & Wells Th Coll 68. **d** 71 **p** 72. C Heref St Martin 71–79; V Kingstone 79–85; P-in-c Clehonger and Eaton Bishop 80–85; TR Pinhoe and Broadclyst *Ex* 85–05; rtd 05; PtO *Ex* from 06. *97 Egremont Road, Exmouth EX8 1SA* T: (01395) 271390 E: themortimers@totalise.co.uk

MORTIMER, Elizabeth Anne. *See* DUDLEY, Elizabeth Anne
MORTIMER, Helen Teän. *See* GREENHAM, Helen Teän

MORTIMER, Jonathan Michael. b 60. Bris Univ BA 83. Oak Hill Th Coll BA 92. **d** 92 **p** 93. C Rugby St Matt *Cov* 92–96; C Southgate *Chich* 96–98; TR 98–07; Through Faith Miss Ev 07–11; V Peckham All SS *S'wark* from 11. *78 Talford Road, London SE15 5NZ* T: (020) 7252 7549 E: mortimerj@btinternet.com

MORTIMER, Canon Lawrence George. b 45. St Edm Hall Ox BA 67 MA 71. St Chad's Coll Dur. **d** 70 **p** 71. C Rugby St Andr *Cov* 70–75; V Styvechale 75–89; Dioc Broadcasting Officer 80–89; Dioc Communications Officer 89–03; P-in-c Wootton Wawen 95–10; P-in-c Claverdon w Preston Bagot 03–10; Hon Can Cov Cathl 98–10; rtd 10; PtO *Lich* 11–21. *3 Top Street, Whittington, Oswestry SY11 4DR* T: (01691) 657986 E: l.mortimer@btinternet.com

MORTIMER, Canon Peter Jackson. b 41. TD 73 MBE 95. St Jo Coll York CertEd 63 Essex Univ MA 71 DUniv 09 UEA DUniv 09 FRSA 97 Hon GCM 07. EAMTC 97. **d** 98 **p** 99. NSM Needham Market w Badley *St E* 98–02; NSM Ringshall w Battisford, Barking w Darmsden etc 98–02; Bp's Ecum Adv 02–16; Chapl to Suffolk Fire Service from 03; Hon Can St E Cathl 06–11; Hon Fell UEA *Nor* from 07; PtO *St E* 11–19. *20 Leggatt Drive, Bramford, Ipswich IP8 4ET* T: (01473) 747419 E: petermortimer@hotmail.co.uk

MORTIMER (née LAY), Mrs Sarah Elizabeth. b 66. Qu Coll Ox MA 88. Sarum Coll 18. **d** 20 **p** 21. C Sunninghill and S Ascot *Ox* from 20. *57 Lily Hill Road, Bracknell RG12 2RX* T: (01344) 421520 M: 07876-188519 E: sarah.e.mortimer@ntlworld.com

MORTIMORE, David Jack. b 42. Master Mariner 69. St Mich Coll Llan 90. **d** 91 **p** 92. C Pembroke St Mary w St Mich *St D* 91–92; C Bargoed and Deri w Brithdir *Llan* 92–97; PtO 98–02; P-in-c Llangeinor 02–04; P-in-c Llangeinor and the Garw Valley 04–12; rtd 12; PtO *St D* from 13. *10 Lawrenny Street, Neyland, Milford Haven SA73 1TB* T: (01646) 602555 E: cleddau39@gmail.com

MORTIMORE, Robert Edward. b 39. Kelham Th Coll 61 Wells Th Coll 66. **d** 69 **p** 70. C Byfleet *Guildf* 69–72; C Fitzroy NZ 72–75; C Remuera 76–78; Min Bell Block 77–79; V Te Kuiti 79–85; Offic Min Auckland 86–89; Sen Asst P Whangarei 89–92; V Avondale 92–98; V Milford 98–04; Offic Min from 04. *69 Crawford Crescent, Kamo, Whangarei 0112, New Zealand* T/F: (0064) (9) 435 1285 E: b.jmortimore@xtra.co.nz

MORTIMORE, Robin Malcolm. b 46. **d** 11 **p** 12. NSM Yardley St Edburgha *Birm* 11–15; PtO from 15. *33 Stonebow Avenue, Solihull B91 3UP* T: 0121-705 9116 M: 07812-728526 E: robinmortimore@hotmail.com

MORTIS, Lorna Anne. b 54. Moray Ho Coll of Educn DipEd 76 Open Univ BA 88. TISEC 95. **d** 98 **p** 99. NSM Gullane and N Berwick *Edin* 98–02; P-in-c Edin St Marg 02–08; NSM Prestonpans and Musselburgh 08–10; R Airdrie *Glas* 10–14; Bp's Dom Chapl 11–14; rtd 14; LtO *Edin* from 15. *Rosebank, 2 School Cottages, Athelstaneford, North Berwick EH39 5BE* T: (01620) 880505 M: 07779-553807 E: lorna.mortis@btinternet.com

MORTON, Adrian Ian. b 65. Brighton Poly BSc 87 Brunel Univ MSc 93. Ridley Hall Cam 98. **d** 00 **p** 01. C Kettering Ch the King *Pet* 00–04; P-in-c Bozeat w Easton Maudit 04–06; P-in-c Wollaston and Strixton 04–06; V Wollaston w Strixton and Bozeat etc from 06. *The Vicarage, 81 Irchester Road, Wollaston, Wellingborough NN29 7RW* T: (01933) 664256 E: adrianmorton762@btinternet.com

MORTON, Albert George. b 34. Saskatchewan Univ BA 61 McGill Univ Montreal MA 73. Em Coll Saskatoon 56. **d** 61 **p** 61. Canada 61–65; C Stanford-le-Hope *Chelmsf* 66–69; V Linc St Geo Swallowbeck 69–82; R Lt Munden w Sacombe *St Alb* 82–89; R The Mundens w Sacombe 89–96; rtd 96; PtO *Sarum* 00–22. *10 Church Green, Bishop's Caundle, Sherborne DT9 5NN* T: (01963) 23383 E: amorton1@waitrose.com

MORTON, Christine Marjorie. b 60. **d** 13 **p** 14. NSM Marton *Blackb* 13–18; NSM Treales from 18. *7 Trinity Gardens, Thornton-Cleveleys FY5 2UA* T: (01253) 824657

MORTON, Mrs Christine Mary. b 39. Linc Th Coll 78. **dss** 80 **d** 87 **p** 94. Ore St Helen and St Barn *Chich* 80–84; Southwick St Mich 84–85; Winchmore Hill St Paul *Lon* 85–87; Par Dn 87–94; C 94–99; Hon C 00–02; rtd 00; PtO *Lon* from 02. *122 Bourne Hill, London N13 4BD* T: (020) 8886 3157

MORTON, Clive Frederick. b 47. Lon Univ BA 70 Birm Univ MA 98. Cranmer Hall Dur 78. **d** 80 **p** 81. C Countesthorpe w Foston *Leic* 80–83; C Glen Parva and S Wigston 83–86; Asst Chapl HM Youth Cust Cen Glen Parva 83–86; V Birm St Pet 86–98; Miss Partner CMS 99–02; Chapl St Petersburg *Eur* 99–02; Lect St Petersburg Th Academy and Sem 99–02; V Kingsbury H Innocents *Lon* 02–12; rtd 13; PtO *Truro* from 16. *14 Penmare Court, Hayle TR27 4RD* M: 07947-883559 E: cfmpam@gmail.com

MORTON, Howard Knyvett. b 30. St Jo Coll Cam BA 51 MA 67. Linc Th Coll 55. **d** 57 **p** 58. C Hatfield Hyde *St Alb* 57–60; Hd RE Heaton Gr Sch Newc 60–66; 72–75; CMS 66–72; Regional Org Oxfam 88–91; Grainger Gr Sch Newc 91–94; LtO *Newc* 73–93; Dioc World Development Officer 94–95; rtd 95; PtO *Dur* 95–98; *Newc* from 96. *17 Cragside View, Rothbury, Morpeth NE65 7YU*

MORTON, Mrs Jacqueline Mavis. b 46. UEA BSc 67 York Univ BSc 82. EMMTC 97. **d** 00 **p** 01. NSM Sibsey w Frithville *Linc* 00–14; NSM Alford w Rigsby 14–18; NSM Well 14–18; NSM Saleby w Beesby and Maltby 14–18; NSM Bilsby w Farlesthorpe 14–18; NSM Hannah cum Hagnaby w Markby 14–18; NSM Willoughby 14–18; NSM Alford Gp from 18. *37 Tothby Lane, Alford LN13 0AQ* T: (01507) 622639 E: jacqui.morton@talktalk.net

MORTON, Jennifer. b 50. Bedf Coll Lon BA 72 Leic Univ PGCE 73. EMMTC 87. **d** 90 **p** 94. C New Mills *Derby* 90–94; Chapl Asst Nottm City Hosp NHS Trust 94–98; Chapl Basford Hosp Nottm 94–98; Chapl S Derbyshire Acute Hosps NHS Trust 98–02; Vice Prin EMMTC *S'well* 02–10; rtd 10; PtO *S'well* from 10. *5 Fellbarrow Close, West Bridgford, Nottingham NG2 6QQ* T: 0115-981 2616

MORTON, Jennifer Pam. b 49. **d** 15 **p** 16. NSM Dorchester *Ox* from 15. *8 Toot Baldon, Oxford OX44 9NG* T: (01865) 343302

MORTON, Philip John. b 79. Birm Univ BA 05 St Jo Coll Dur BATM 11 Dur Univ MA 12. Cranmer Hall Dur 09. **d** 12 **p** 13. C Maney *Birm* 12–16; P-in-c Badsey w Aldington and Offenham and Bretforton *Worc* 16–18; P-in-c Cleeve Prior and The Littletons 16–18; V E Vale and Avon Villages from 18. *The Vicarage, 33 High Street, Badsey, Evesham WR11 7EJ* T: (01386) 832599 E: revphilipmorton@gmail.com

MORTON, Rex Gerald. b 61. St Jo Coll Nottm 96. **d** 98 **p** 99. C Bury St Edmunds All SS *St E* 98–01; C Woodside Park St Barn *Lon* 01–07; V Golders Green 07–20; rtd 20. *5 Weston Mews, Sandwich Road, Snowdown, Dover CT15 4FA* M: 07590-216311 E: rexgmorton@gmail.com

MORTON, Sister Rita. b 34. Wilson Carlile Coll. **dss** 85 **d** 87 **p** 94. CA from 76; Par Dn Harlow New Town w Lt Parndon *Chelmsf* 87–89; C Harold Hill St Geo 89–94; rtd 94; NSM Elm Park St Nic Hornchurch *Chelmsf* 94–05; PtO from 05. *38 Havering Court Care Home, Havering Road, Romford RM1 4YW* T: (01708) 874820

MORTON, Rosemary Jane. b 79. LRAM 02 Lon Univ BMus 03. Westcott Ho Cam 07. **d** 10 **p** 11. C Coggeshall w Markshall *Chelmsf* 10–14; Min Can and Succ St Paul's Cathl *Lon* from 14. *The Chapter House, St Paul's Churchyard, London EC4M 8AD* T: (020) 7246 8338 E: rjmorton@cantab.net

MORTON, Mrs Sheila. b 44. Leeds Univ. Sarum & Wells Th Coll 79. **dss** 84 **d** 87 **p** 94. HM Forces Düsseldorf 84–86; Cov St Mary 86–89; Par Dn 87–89; Par Dn Boston Spa *York* 89–92; C Flitwick *St Alb* 93–00; R Wilden w Colmworth and Ravensden 00–14; rtd 14; PtO *St Alb* 14–19; *Ely* from 15. *11 Roundhouse Drive, Perry, Huntingdon PE28 0DJ* T: (01480) 810363 E: revsheila827@gmail.com

MORTON, Mrs Susan Ann. b 58. Ex Univ BA 80 Warwick Univ PGCE 84. Ripon Coll Cuddesdon 10. **d** 12 **p** 13. NSM Hambleden Valley *Ox* from 12. *The Vicarage, Turville, Henley-on-Thames RG9 6QU* M: 07808-517347 E: suemorton131@gmail.com

MORTON, Mrs Theresa Claire. b 72. Birm Univ BN 94 MHSc 98 RNMH 94. Qu Foundn Birm 17. **d** 20 **p** 21. C Northfield *Birm* from 20. *Address withheld by request*

MOSEDALE, Jonathan Ralph. b 69. Imp Coll Lon BSc 90 York Univ MSc 91 Trin Coll Ox DPhil 95. Protestant Th Inst Montpellier Lic 99 Ripon Coll Cuddesdon 07. **d** 09 **p** 10. C St Endellion w Port Isaac and St Kew *Truro* 09–12; C St Minver 09–12; C N Cornwall Cluster 12–13; PtO from 16. *The Flat, 43-45 Molesworth Street, Wadebridge PL27 7DR* M: 07760-275087 E: mosedale@metanoa.com

MOSELEY, Canon Hugh Martin. b 47. St Jo Coll Dur BA 70. Westcott Ho Cam 71. **d** 73 **p** 74. C Hythe *Cant* 73–77; P-in-c Eythorne w Waldershare 77–83; V Ringmer *Chich* 83–99; RD Lewes and Seaford 93–97; P-in-c E Dean w Friston and Jevington 99–00; R 00–03; TR Rye 03–09; Can and Preb Chich Cathl 07–09; rtd 09; PtO *Cant* from 11; *Chich* from 15; Hon C Winchelsea and Icklesham 11–15. *Rushey Green Mill, Rushey Green, Ringmer, Lewes BN8 5JB* T: (01273) 813260 E: annabelle.moseley@btinternet.com

MOSELEY, Michael. b 45. Oak Hill Th Coll 02. **d** 04 **p** 05. NSM Forty Hill Jes Ch *Lon* 04–07; P-in-c Murston w Bapchild and Tonge *Cant* 07–12; rtd 12; PtO *Cant* from 12. *56 Park Drive, Sittingbourne ME10 1RD* T: (01795) 556258 E: michaelmoseley07@googlemail.com

MOSELEY, Roger Henry. b 38. Edin Th Coll 60. **d** 63 **p** 64. C Friern Barnet All SS *Lon* 63–66; C Grantham St Wulfram *Linc* 66–69; P-in-c Swaton w Spanby 69–73; P-in-c Horbling 69–73; V Soberton w Newtown *Portsm* 73–80; V Sarisbury 80–03; rtd 03; PtO *Portsm* from 03. *1 Birchdale Close, Warsash, Southampton SO31 9PT* T: (01489) 572052 E: rhmoseley29@gmail.com

MOSES, The Very Revd John Henry. b 38. KCVO 06. Nottm Univ BA 59 PhD 65. Linc Th Coll 62. **d** 64 **p** 65. C Bedford St Andr *St Alb* 64–70; P-in-c Cov St Pet 70; P-in-c Cov St Mark 71–73; TR Cov E 73–77; RD 73–77; Adn Southend *Chelmsf* 77–82; Provost Chelmsf 82–96; Chmn Coun of Cen for Th Study Essex Univ 87–96; Dean St Paul's *Lon* 96–06; rtd 06; PtO *S'well* from 17. *Chestnut House, Burgage, Southwell NG25 0EP* T: (01636) 814880 E: johnmoses.southwell@gmail.com

MOSES, Preb Leslie Alan. b 49. Hull Univ BA 71 Edin Univ BD 76. Edin Th Coll 73. **d** 76 **p** 77. C Edin Old St Paul 76–79; R Leven *St And* 79–85; R Edin Old St Paul 85–95; P-in-c Edin St Marg 86–92; V St Marylebone All SS *Lon* 95–19; AD Westmr St Marylebone 01–19; Preb St Paul's Cathl 10–19; rtd 19; Warden of Spirituality *Linc* from 20. *17 Geralds Close, Lincoln LN2 4AL* M: 07973-878040 E: alan.moses@lincoln.anglican.org

MOSFORD, Canon Denzil Huw Erasmus. b 56. Florida State Univ MTh 04 AKC 78. St D Coll Lamp 74 Sarum & Wells Th Coll 77. **d** 79 **p** 80. C Clydach *S & B* 79–82; V 87–97; Jamaica 82–85; V Ystalyfera *S & B* 85–87; Dioc World Miss Officer 91–10; RD Cwmtawe 93–97; V Gorseinon 97–10; AD Llwchwr 00–10; Hon Can Brecon Cathl 01–04; Can Res Brecon Cathl 04–10; Dir of Min Miss to Seafarers 10–14; P-in-c Dafen *St D* from 14; P-in-c Llanelli 16–17; P-in-c Bro Lliedi from 17; AD from 17; Dioc Ecum Officer from 14; Can St D Cathl from 18. *The Vicarage, 1 Cysgod Y Llan, Llanelli SA15 3HD* T: (01554) 746034 E: huw.mosford@gmail.com

MOSLEY, Robin Howarth. b 46. Birm Univ LLB 67 Leeds Univ BA 09 Solicitor 71. NOC 06. **d** 09 **p** 10. NSM Ches St Mary 09–11; V Brereton 11–17; rtd 17; PtO *Ches* from 17. *Brookside, Sandy Lane, Higher Kinnerton, Chester CH4 9BJ* T: (01244) 660341 M: 07818-568017 E: rev.robinmosley@gmail.com

MOSS, Alan Charles. b 81. St Mellitus Coll 16. **d** 18 **p** 19. C Collier Row St Jas and Havering-atte-Bower *Chelmsf* 18–21; C Walthamstow from 21. *9 Irons Way, Romford RM5 3RJ* M: 07928-770220 E: alanmoss1981@gmail.com

MOSS, Canon Barbara Penelope. b 46. St Anne's Coll Ox BA 66 MA 70 Lon Univ BD 97 Middx Univ MA 00. EAMTC 95. **d** 97 **p** 98. NSM Leytonstone H Trin and St Aug Harrow Green *Chelmsf* 97–00; C Cambridge Gt St Mary w St Mich *Ely* 00–05; P-in-c Gothenburg w Halmstad, Jönköping etc *Eur* 05–16; Chapl Gothenburg Univ and Chalmers Univ of Tech 05–16; Hon Can *Eur* 12–16; rtd 16; PtO *S'wark* from 17; *Eur* from 16; *Chelmsf* from 20. *327 Holly Court, Greenroof Way, London SE10 0BP* M: 07492-232453 E: barmoss.bm@gmail.com

MOSS, Catherine. b 53. ERMC. **d** 09 **p** 10. NSM Guilsborough and Hollowell and Cold Ashby etc *Pet* from 09. *Saxon Spires Practice, West Haddon Road, Guilsborough, Northampton NN6 8QE* T: (01604) 740210 F: 740869 M: 07779-000897 E: cattimoss@aol.com

MOSS, Christopher Ashley. b 52. Ex Univ BA 73 Southn Univ DASS 78 CQSW 78. Wycliffe Hall Ox 89. **d** 91 **p** 92. C Malvern H Trin and St Jas *Worc* 91–96; V Longdon, Castlemorton, Bushley, Queenhill etc from 96; RD Upton 11–21. *The Vicarage, Longdon, Tewkesbury GL20 6AT* T/F: (01684) 833256 E: cmoss.lcbq@gmail.com

MOSS, David. b 60. WEMTC 12. **d** 15 **p** 16. NSM Gt Hanwood and Longden and Annscroft etc *Heref* 15–19; R Westbury, Worthen and Yockleton from 19. *The Rectory, Westbury, Shrewsbury SY5 9QX* T: (01743) 884165 E: davidmosswwy@gmail.com

MOSS, David Sefton. b 59. Sunderland Poly BSc 80 Anglia Poly Univ MA 05 MRPharmS 81. Ridley Hall Cam 91. **d** 93 **p** 94. C Highworth w Sevenhampton and Inglesham etc *Bris* 93–97; V Bedminster St Mich 97–17; P-in-c Alveston and Littleton-on-Severn w Elberton 17–19; C Almondsbury and Olveston 17–19; V N Severnside from 19. *St Helen's Vicarage, Gloucester Road, Alveston, Bristol BS35 3QT* T: (01454) 415190 M: 07890-262334 E: mossds@gmail.com

MOSS, Canon Denis. b 32. St Jo Coll Auckland LTh 83. **d** 74 **p** 75. NZ 74–92; Chapl Budapest *Eur* 92–10; Hon Can Malta Cathl 01–10; PtO from 16. *8353 Zalaszántó, Zrínyi M utca 39, Hungary* T: (0036) (83) 572003 F: 572004 E: denismoss@t-online.hu

MOSS, The Ven Leonard Godfrey. b 32. K Coll Lon BD 59 AKC 59. **d** 60 **p** 61. C Putney St Marg *S'wark* 60–63; C Cheam 63–67; R Much Dewchurch w Llanwarne and

Llandinabo *Heref* 67–72; Dioc Ecum Officer 69–83; V Marden w Amberley 72–78; V Marden w Amberley and Wisteston 78–84; P-in-c 92–94; Preb Heref Cathl 79–97; Can Heref Cathl 84–91; Dioc Soc Resp Officer 84–91; Adn Heref 91–97; rtd 97; PtO *Heref* 97–20. *10 Saxon Way, Ledbury HR8 2QY* T: (01531) 631195

MOSS, Miss Lucy Margaret. b 85. Cant Ch Ch Univ BA 07. St Jo Coll Nottm MTh 15. **d** 15 **p** 16. C Spennymoor and Whitworth *Dur* 15–18; C Easington and Easington Colliery 18–21; R from 21; V Hawthorn from 21. *The Rectory, 5 Tudor Grange, Easington Village, Peterlee SR8 3DF* M: 07891-491386 E: lucymoss1@hotmail.com

MOSS, Mrs Nelva Elizabeth. b 44. Bp Grosseteste Coll TCert 66 Sussex Univ BEd 73. S Dios Minl Tr Scheme 90. **d** 93 **p** 94. NSM Bincombe w Broadwey, Upwey and Buckland Ripers *Sarum* 93–96; NSM Langtree *Ox* 96–98; TV 98–09; rtd 09; PtO *Sarum* 11–20. *5 Wynnes Rise, Sherborne DT9 6DH* T: (01935) 814329 E: nelvamoss@hotmail.com

MOSS, Peter Hextall. b 34. Clare Coll Cam BA 59 MA 62. Linc Th Coll 59. **d** 61 **p** 62. C Easington Colliery *Dur* 61–63; C Whickham 63–65; C-in-c Town End Farm CD 65–72; TV Mattishall *Nor* 72–75; P-in-c Welborne 75–84; P-in-c Mattishall w Mattishall Burgh 75–84; P-in-c Yaxham 80–84; TR Hempnall 84–89. *High House Cottage, Gunn Street, Foulsham, Dereham NR20 5RN* T: (01362) 683823 E: pandgmoss@gmail.com

MOSS, Mrs Rosemary Ellis Jane. b 60. SS Paul & Mary Coll Cheltenham BEd 82. Qu Foundn Birm 18. **d** 20 **p** 21. NSM Warndon St Nic *Worc* from 20. *76 Hanbury Road, Stoke Prior, Bromsgrove B60 4DN* T: (01527) 836307 M: 07762-916615 E: revdrosiemoss@gmail.com

MOSSE, Mrs Barbara Ann. b 51. CertEd 73 Open Univ BA 77 Univ of Wales (Lamp) MA 99 Lambeth STh 83. CA Tr Coll IDC 81. **d** 90 **p** 95. CA 81–91; NSM Southbourne w W Thorney *Chich* 90–93; Community Mental Health Chapl Fareham/Gosport 94–97; NSM Purbrook *Portsm* 95–03; Team Chapl Portsm Hosps NHS Trust 01–09; Asst Dioc Spirituality Adv *Portsm* 05–09; PtO 03–15. *Drogo, 1 Grenfield Court, Emsworth PO10 7SA* T: (01243) 376155 E: barbaramosse@btinternet.com

MOSSMAN, Margaret. b 46. NOC 97. **d** 00 **p** 01. NSM Beighton *Sheff* 00–02; C 02–04; V Owston 04–12; rtd 12; PtO *Pet* from 12. *32 Tennyson Road, Rothwell, Kettering NN14 6JH* T: (01536) 660928 E: mmossman@hotmail.co.uk

MOSSOP, Patrick John. b 48. St Jo Coll Cam MA 70 LLB Solicitor. Linc Th Coll BTh 93. **d** 93 **p** 94. C Halstead St Andr w H Trin and Greenstead Green *Chelmsf* 93–97; Assoc Chapl Essex Univ 97–99; Chapl 99–04; V Forest Gate Em w Upton Cross 04–09; TR Plaistow and N Canning Town 09–14; rtd 14; PtO *Chelmsf* 15–18; Hon C Wanstead H Trin Hermon Hill from 18. *18 Aileen Walk, London E15 4BB* M: 07908-688078 E: patmossop2@gmail.com

MOSTON, William Howard. b 47. **d** 10 **p** 11. OLM E Crompton *Man* from 10. *36 Clough Road, Shaw, Oldham OL2 8QD* T: (01706) 847940 M: 07440-947328 E: whmoston@hotmail.com

MOTE, Gregory Justin. b 60. Oak Hill Th Coll BA 83. **d** 86 **p** 87. C W Ealing St Jo w St Jas *Lon* 86–90; C St Helen Bishopsgate w St Andr Undershaft etc 90–95; V Poulton Lancelyn H Trin *Ches* 96–04; PtO *Blackb* from 04. *22 Evergreen Avenue, Leyland PR25 3AW* E: gjmote@aol.com

MOTHERSALE, Hugh Robert. b 43. Essex Univ BA 70 MSc 73. **d** 11 **p** 12. OLM Halstead Area *Chelmsf* 11–15; NSM 15–18; rtd 18; PtO *Chelmsf* 18–21. *10 Park Lane, Earls Colne, Colchester CO6 2RJ* T: (01787) 222211 M: 07803-699268 E: hrmsteam@btinternet.com

MOTHERSOLE, John Robert. b 25. Lon Univ MA 99. Chich Th Coll. **d** 84 **p** 85. NSM Hayes St Anselm *Lon* 84–93; NSM Hayes St Edm 93–98; P-in-c St Mary Aldermary 98–10; rtd 10; PtO *Lon* 10–18. *116 Nestles Avenue, Hayes UB3 4QD* T: (020) 8848 0626 E: jm014t1045@blueyonder.co.uk

MOTION, Ruth Caroline. b 67. Surrey Univ BA 88 PGCE 89. Sarum Coll 18. **d** 21. NSM Cheddar, Draycott and Rodney Stoke *B & W* from 21. *21 Oak Apple Drive, Bridgwater TA6 3UW* T: (01278) 322056 M: 07729-264213 E: motionruth@gmail.com

MOTT, Mrs Marjorie. b 51. Westf Coll Lon BSc 72 Univ Coll Lon PhD 78. **d** 15 **p** 16. NSM Greenhill St Jo *Lon* 15–18; PtO 18–20; NSM Roxeth from 20. *Address withheld by request* M: 07595-616227 E: marj@ccrharrow.org

MOTT, Peter John. b 49. Ch Coll Cam BA 70 MA 75 Dundee Univ PhD 73. St Jo Coll Nottm BA 79. **d** 80 **p** 81. C Hull St Jo Newland *York* 80–83; C Selly Park St Steph and St Wulstan *Birm* 83–87; C Mosborough *Sheff* 87–92; R Colne St Bart *Blackb* 92–98; TV Colne and Villages 98–01; P-in-c Keighley St Andr *Bradf* 01–14; *Leeds* 14; Dioc Ecum Officer *Bradf*

04–14; *Leeds* 14; rtd 14; PtO *York* from 14. *Cornerways, 13 Hall Park, Heslington, York YO10 5DT* T: (01904) 206958 E: petermott57@gmail.com

MOTT, Wendy Sandra. b 59. St Mellitus Coll 16. **d** 18 **p** 19. OLM Corringham and Fobbing *Chelmsf* from 18. *Ambleside, 35 Conrad Road, Stanford-le-Hope SS17 0AT* T: (01375) 642017 E: revwendy@ubocaf.org.uk

✠**MOTTAHEDEH, The Rt Revd Iraj Kalimi.** b 32. United Th Coll Bangalore 56. **d** 59 **p** 60 **c** 86. C Isfahan St Luke Iran 59–62; V Shiraz St Simon 62–66; V Tehran St Paul 67–75; V Isfahan St Luke 75–83; Adn Iran 83–86; Asst Bp Iran 86–90; Bp Iran 90–02; Pres Bp Episc Ch Jerusalem and Middle E 00–02; rtd 02; Interim Bp Iran 02–04; Hon Asst Bp Birm and Lich from 05. *2 Highland Road, Newport TF10 7QE* T: (01952) 813615 E: bishraj@btinternet.com

MOTTERSHEAD, Derek. b 39. Open Univ BA 74 BEd. Chich Th Coll 65. **d** 69 **p** 70. C Walthamstow St Barn and St Jas Gt *Chelmsf* 69–72; C Chelmsf All SS 72–77; P-in-c Cold Norton w Stow Maries 77–80; V Leytonstone St Andr 80–92; V Eastbourne St Sav and St Pet *Chich* 92–04; Miss to Seafarers 92–04; rtd 04; PtO *Cant* 05–06 and from 11; Hon C Preston next Faversham, Goodnestone and Graveney 06–10. *Sherwood, 25B The Paddock, Spring Lane, Canterbury CT1 1SX* T: (01227) 453118 E: dmottershead11@btinternet.com

MOTTERSHEAD, Nicholas John Leigh. b 66. Reading Univ BSc 88 Cant Ch Ch Univ BA 15 FCA 91. SEITE 12. **d** 15 **p** 16. NSM St Olave Hart Street w All Hallows Staining etc *Lon* from 15; NSM St Kath Cree from 15; NSM St Sepulchre w Ch Ch Greyfriars etc 21; P-in-c from 21; PtO *Roch* from 16. *47 Barnmead Road, Beckenham BR3 1JF* T: (020) 8289 3858 M: 07950-010640 E: nickmottershead@hotmail.com

MOTTRAM, Andrew Peter. b 53. AKC 77. Ripon Coll Cuddesdon 77. **d** 78 **p** 79. C E Bedfont *Lon* 78–81; C Bp's Hatfield *St Alb* 81–84; V Milton Ernest 84–91; V Thurleigh 84–91; P-in-c Heref All SS 91–06; RD Heref City 02–03; Ch Buildings Officer *Worc* 09–18; rtd 18; PtO *Heref* from 06. *Mulberry Dock, Pencombe, Bromyard HR7 4SH* M: 07960-726717 E: andrew.mottram@btinternet.com

MOTTRAM, Joseph Christopher. b 83. Leeds Univ MPhys 05 PhD 09. Cranmer Hall Dur 18. **d** 20 **p** 21. C Cirencester *Glouc* from 20. *54 Alexander Drive, Cirencester GL7 1UH* T: (01285) 885618 M: 07746-211093 E: joemottram@cirenparish.co.uk *or* josephmottram@hotmail.com

MOTYER, Stephen. b 50. Pemb Coll Cam BA 73 MA 77 Bris Univ MLitt 79 K Coll Lon PhD 93. Trin Coll Bris 73. **d** 76 **p** 77. Lect Oak Hill Th Coll 76–83; C Braughing, Lt Hadham, Albury, Furneux Pelham etc *St Alb* 83–87; Lect Lon Sch of Th from 87; PtO *Lon* 87–13; *St Alb* from 87. *7 Hangar Ruding, Watford WD19 5BH* T: (020) 8386 6829 *or* (01923) 826061 E: s.motyer@ntlworld.com

MOUGHTIN, Ross. b 48. St Cath Coll Cam BA 70 St Jo Coll Dur BA 75. **d** 76 **p** 77. C Litherland St Paul Hatton Hill *Liv* 76–79; C Heswall *Ches* 79–84; Chapl Edw Unit Rochdale Infirmary 83–92; V Thornham w Gravel Hole *Man* 84–92; V Aughton Ch Ch *Liv* 92–18; Chapl W Lancashire NHS Trust 94–11; rtd 18; PtO *Liv* 19–21; *Ches* from 20. *11 Orchard View, Aughton, Ormskirk L39 5AD* T: (01695) 227027 E: ross.moughtin@gmail.com

MOUGHTIN, Sharon. b 76. St Jo Coll Dur BA 97 MA 98 Worc Coll Ox DPhil 04. Westcott Ho Cam 05. **d** 06 **p** 07. C Walworth St Pet *S'wark* 06–10; Dioc Miss Th Angl Communion 10–11; Hon C S'wark St Geo w St Alphege and St Jude 10–15; Hon C Walworth St Pet 15–21; Hon C N Lambeth from 21. *6 Blenheim Gardens, London SW2 5ET* M: 07980-611347 E: sharonmoughtin@gmail.com

MOUGHTIN-MUMBY, Andrew Denis Paul. b 78. Birm Univ BA 00 SS Coll Cam BA 05 MA 09. Westcott Ho Cam 03. **d** 06 **p** 07. C Walworth St Chris *S'wark* 06–10; R Walworth St Pet from 10; AD S'wark and Newington 14–20; PV Westmr Abbey from 14. *St Peter's Rectory, 12 Villa Street, London SE17 2EJ* T: (020) 7703 3139 E: rector@stpeterswalworth.org

MOUK, Mae Elizabeth. *See* CHRISTIE, Mae Elizabeth

MOUL, Russell Derek. b 56. Reading Univ BA 83. Oak Hill Th Coll 97. **d** 99 **p** 00. C Harold Wood *Chelmsf* 99–02; C Harold Hill St Paul 02–03; V 03–21; rtd 21. *Address temp unknown*

MOULAND, Norman Francis. b 38. OLM course 98. **d** 99 **p** 00. OLM Verwood *Sarum* 99–18; PtO from 18. *13 Park Drive, Verwood BH31 7PE* T: (01202) 825320

MOULD, Mrs Jacqueline. b 66. QUB BD 88. CITC BTh 91. **d** 91 **p** 92. C Belfast St Aid *Conn* 91–94; C Drumragh w Mountfield *D & R* 94–96; NSM Kinson *Sarum* 97–00; C Belvoir *D & D* 03–19; P-in-c Greenisland *Conn* from 20. *10A Ballyclough Road, Lisburn BT28 3UY* T: (028) 9264 7912 E: jacmould@gmail.com

MOULD, Jeremy James. b 63. Nottm Univ BA 85 TCD BTh 91. CITC 88. **d** 91 **p** 92. C Mossley *Conn* 91–94; C Drumragh w Mountfield *D & R* 94–96; C Kinson *Sarum* 97–00; I Templepatrick w Donegore *Conn* from 19. *10A Ballyclough Road, Lisburn BT28 3UY* T: (028) 9264 7912 E: jermould@gmail.com

MOULDEN, David Ivor. b 52. Cant Ch Ch Univ BA 02. SEITE 05. **d** 08 **p** 09. C Madeley *Heref* 08–12; V Canonry *Cant* from 12; P-in-c Aylesham 18–19. *The Vicarage, Queen's Road, Ash, Canterbury CT3 2BG* E: davidmoulden@hotmail.com

MOULDER, Kenneth. b 53. Lon Univ BEd 75. Ridley Hall Cam 78. **d** 81 **p** 82. C Harold Wood *Chelmsf* 81–84; C Darfield *Sheff* 84–88; V Walkergate *Newc* 88–92; P-in-c Byker St Mark 90–92; V Byker St Mark and Walkergate St Oswald 92–21; rtd 21. *Address temp unknown*

MOULES-JONES, Roy Llewellyn. **d** 17 **p** 18. C Bro Deiniol *Ban* 17–18; C Bro Cwyfan 18–21; Min Area Ldr Bro Dwynwen from 21. *Bridin, Gaerwen LL60 6AS* T: (01248) 715349 E: llewmoules-jones@esgobaethbangor.net

MOULT, Jane Elizabeth Kate. b 61. Trin Coll Bris 91. **d** 94 **p** 95. C St Jo in Bedwardine *Worc* 94–97; NSM Bilton *Cov* 97–99; Chapl Staunton Harold Hosp 00–01; Sen Chapl Leics Partnership NHS Trust 01–07; PtO *Leic* 07–14. *17 The Leascroft, Ravenstone, Coalville LE67 2BL* T: (01530) 833160

MOULT, Simon Paul. b 66. Trin Coll Bris BA 94. **d** 94 **p** 95. C St Jo in Bedwardine *Worc* 94–97; C Bilton *Cov* 97–99; P-in-c Thringstone St Andr *Leic* 99–05; RD Akeley S 03–05; Chapl Cov and Warks Partnership NHS Trust from 05; Chapl Geo Eliot Hosp NHS Trust Nuneaton from 05. *The Chaplaincy, George Eliot Hospital, College Street, Nuneaton CV10 7DJ* T: (024) 7686 5046 *or* 7635 1351 E: simon.moult@covwarkpt.nhs.uk

MOUNCER, David Peter. b 65. Univ of Wales (Abth) BA 86. Oak Hill Th Coll BA 94. **d** 94 **p** 95. C Folkestone St Jo *Cant* 94–98; Min Grove Green LEP 98–03; R Brampton St Thos *Derby* 03–07; C Chesterfield Deanery 07–16; C Old Brampton and Gt Barlow *Derby* 16–21; C Loundsley Green 16–21; rtd 21. *Address temp unknown* E: therevdp@tiscali.co.uk

MOUNSEY, William Lawrence Fraser. b 51. St Andr Univ BD 75. Edin Th Coll 76. **d** 78 **p** 79. C Edin St Mark 78–81; Chapl RAF 81–90 and 96–06; R Dalmahoy and Chapl Heriot-Watt Univ *Edin* 90–96; PtO *Eur* from 06; C Roslin (Rosslyn Chpl) *Edin* 06–11; C Edin St Vin from 11. *9 Upper Coltbridge Terrace, Edinburgh EH12 6AD* M: 07967-322651 E: wlfm@hotmail.co.uk

✠**MOUNSTEPHEN, The Rt Revd Philip Ian.** b 59. Southn Univ BA 80 Magd Coll Ox MA 87 PGCE. Wycliffe Hall Ox 85. **d** 88 **p** 89 **c** 18. C Gerrards Cross and Fulmer *Ox* 88–92; V W Streatham St Jas *S'wark* 92–98; Hd Pathfinders CPAS 98–02; Dir CY Network 01–02; Hd Min 02–07; Dep Gen Dir 04–07; Chapl Paris St Mich *Eur* 07–12; Exec Ldr CMS 12–18; Hon Can *Eur* from 12; Bp Truro from 18. *Lis Escop, Feock, Truro TR3 6QQ* T: (01872) 862657 M: 07775-528556 E: bishop@truro.anglican.org

MOUNT, Canon Judith Mary. b 35. Bedf Coll Lon BA 56 Lon Univ CertEd 57. Ripon Coll Cuddesdon 81. **dss** 83 **d** 87 **p** 94. Carterton *Ox* 83–85; Charlton on Otmoor and Oddington 85–87; Dioc Lay Min Adv and Asst Dir of Ords 86–89; Par Dn Islip w Charlton on Otmoor, Oddington, Noke etc 87–94; C 94–95; Assoc Dioc Dir Ords and Adv for Women in Ord Min 89–95; Hon Can Ch Ch 92–95; rtd 95; PtO *Ox* 95–10; *Glouc* 99–20. *Lathams, Bell Lane, Poulton, Cirencester GL7 5JF* T: (01285) 850242 E: jmount315@gmail.com

MOUNTAIN, John Raymond. b 46. LCTP 11. **d** 12 **p** 13. NSM Appley Bridge and Parbold *Blackb* 12–16; PtO from 16. *50 The Common, Parbold, Wigan WN8 7EA* T: (01257) 463919 M: 07542-000996 E: john_mountain@talktalk.net

MOUNTFORD, Canon Brian Wakling. b 45. MBE 16. Newc Univ BA 66 Cam Univ MA 73 Ox Univ MA 90. Westcott Ho Cam 66. **d** 68 **p** 69. C Westmr St Steph w St Jo *Lon* 68–69; C Paddington Ch Ch 69–73; Chapl SS Coll Cam 73–78; V Southgate Ch Ch *Lon* 78–86; V Ox St Mary V w St Cross and St Pet 86–16; Chapl St Hilda's Coll Ox 89–20; Acting Chapl CCC Ox 18; Hon Can Ch Ch Ox 98–16; rtd 16; PtO *Ox* from 16. *The Old Barn, Mill Street, Islip, Kidlington OX5 2SY* T: (01865) 682237 M: 07789-222760 E: brian.mountford@oriel.ox.ac.uk

MOURANT, Julia Caroline. b 58. Sheff Univ BA 79. St Jo Coll Nottm 82. **dss** 84 **d** 92 **p** 94. Cropwell Bishop w Colston Bassett, Granby etc *S'well* 84–86; Marple All SS *Ches* 86–89; Harlow St Mary and St Hugh w St Jo the Bapt *Chelmsf* 89–92; NSM 92–04; Asst Dir of Min 98–04; CME Officer 00–02; PtO *Win* 04–05; Lay Tr Officer 05–07; Voc, Recruitment and Selection Officer 07–15; PtO from 15; *Sarum* 18–20. *The Rectory, Church Lane, Ellisfield, Basingstoke RG25 2QR* T: (01256) 381217 E: julia.caroline@btinternet.com

MOURANT, Sidney Eric. b 39. Lon Univ BD 73. Oak Hill Th Coll. **d** 89 **p** 90. C Oxton *Ches* 89–92; V Douglas All SS and St Thos *S & M* 92–96; I Rathkeale w Askeaton, Kilcornan and Kilnaughtin *L & K* 96–00; I Nenagh 00–04; rtd 04. *12 Breezemount, Hamiltonsbawn, Armagh BT61 9SB* T: (028) 3887 2203 M: (00353) 87-239 9785

MOURANT, Stephen Philip Edward. b 54. St Jo Coll Nottm BTh 83. **d** 83 **p** 84. C Cropwell Bishop w Colston Bassett, Granby etc *S'well* 83–86; C Marple All SS *Ches* 86–89; P-in-c Harlow St Mary and St Hugh w St Jo the Bapt *Chelmsf* 89–90; V 90–04; P-in-c Bitterne *Win* 04–08; C Fair Oak 08–11; C Farleigh, Candover and Wield from 11. *The Rectory, Church Lane, Ellisfield, Basingstoke RG25 2QR* T: (01256) 381217   E: stephen.mourant@btinternet.com   or stevemourant@btinternet.com

MOUSIR-HARRISON, Stuart Nicholas. b 68. SW Poly Plymouth BSc 89 Nottm Univ MSc 92 St Martin's Coll Lanc PhD 99 St Jo Coll Dur BA 99. Cranmer Hall Dur. **d** 00 **p** 01. C Oadby *Leic* 00–03; C W Malling w Offham *Roch* 03–07; C Mereworth w W Peckham 03–07; P-in-c Dallington *Pet* 07–12; Chapl Northn Univ from 07. *125 Kingsley Road, Northampton NN2 7BT* T: (01604) 892468

MOWBRAY, David. b 38. Fitzw Ho Cam BA 60 MA 64 Lon Univ BD 62. Clifton Th Coll. **d** 63 **p** 64. C Northampton St Giles *Pet* 63–66; Lect Watford St Mary *St Alb* 66–70; V Broxbourne 70–77; R Broxbourne w Wormley 77–84; V Hertford All SS 84–91; V Darley Abbey *Derby* 91–03; Asst Chapl Derby R Infirmary 91–94; Chapl Derbyshire Mental Health Services NHS Trust 99–03; rtd 03; PtO *Linc* 17–20. *4 Marigold Close, Lincoln LN2 4SZ* T: (01522) 546753 E: davidanddiana@hotmail.co.uk

MOWBRAY, James Edward. b 78. Univ of Wales (Abth) BTh 00 Leeds Univ BA 03. Coll of Resurr Mirfield 01. **d** 03 **p** 04. C Perry Street *Roch* 03–07; V Swanley St Mary 07–14; P-in-c Kettering St Mary *Pet* from 14. *St Mary's Vicarage, 175 Avondale Road, Kettering NN16 8PN* E: frjames78@gmail.com

MOWBRAY, Ms Jill Valerie. b 54. Sussex Univ BEd 76 Lon Inst of Educn MA 86 Anglia Poly Univ MA 01. Ridley Hall Cam 99. **d** 01 **p** 02. C Tufnell Park St Geo and All SS *Lon* 01–04; V Whitton SS Phil and Jas 04–09; CME Adv *Chelmsf* from 09; C Walthamstow from 10. *41 Fraser Road, London E17 9DD* T: (020) 8520 9740 E: revjillmowbray@googlemail.com

MOWFORTH, Mark. b 64. Reading Univ BSc 86. Trin Coll Bris 93. **d** 96 **p** 97. C Buckingham *Ox* 96–98; C High Wycombe 98–03; P-in-c Prestwood and Gt Hampden 03–07. *Flat 2, 118 Totteridge Road, High Wycombe HP13 6EX* T: (01494) 521097

MOWLL, John William Rutley. b 42. Sarum Th Coll 63. **d** 66 **p** 67. C Oughtibridge *Sheff* 66–69; C Hill *Birm* 69–73; Ind Chapl and V Upper Arley *Worc* 73–78; P-in-c Upton Snodsbury and Broughton Hackett etc 78–81; R 81–83; V Boughton under Blean w Dunkirk *Cant* 83–89; V Boughton under Blean w Dunkirk and Hernhill 89–07; RD Ospringe 95–01; Hon Min Can Cant Cathl 96–07; rtd 07; Chapl to The Queen 00–12; PtO *Cant* 07–16 and from 21. *Holly Cottage, Water Lane, Ospringe, Faversham ME13 8TS* T: (01795) 597597

MOXLEY, Mrs Elizabeth Jane. b 52. St Jo Coll Nottm. **d** 05 **p** 06. C Aston Clinton w Buckland and Drayton Beauchamp *Ox* 05–08; R 08–17; rtd 17; PtO *Portsm* from 18. *34 Granville Road, Cowes PO31 7JF* E: elizabethmoxley@hotmail.com

MOY, Miss Elizabeth. b 55. Leeds and Carnegie Coll CertEd 76. LCTP 07. **d** 10 **p** 13. NSM Harden and Wilsden, Cullingworth and Denholme *Bradf* 10–14; *Leeds* from 14. *3 Parkside Court, Cross Roads, Keighley BD22 9DS* T: (01535) 645991

MOY (née PLUMB), Mrs Nicola Louise. b 80. Birm Univ BA 01 Bris Univ MA 03 PGCE 04. St Jo Coll Nottm 06. **d** 08 **p** 09. C Wolverhampton St Jude *Lich* 08–12; C Turnham Green Ch Ch *Lon* 13–19; V from 19. *The Vicarage, 2 Wellesley Road, London W4 4BL* T: (020) 8996 0366 M: 07595-082918 E: nicolalouisemoy@gmail.com or nicola.moy@christchurchw4.com

MOY, Richard John. b 78. St Cath Coll Cam BA 99. Trin Coll Bris MA 03. **d** 04 **p** 05. C Wolverhampton St Jude *Lich* 04–07; Pioneer Min Wolv City Cen 07–10; Fresh Expressions Adv 10–12; V Turnham Green Ch Ch *Lon* 12–19; C 19–21; NSM from 21. *The Vicarage, 2 Wellesley Road, London W4 4BL* T: (020) 8996 0366 E: notintheratrace@yahoo.co.uk or richard.moy@christchurchw4.com

MOYES, Stephanie Abigail. See WATSON, Stephanie Abigail

MOYNAGH, David Kenneth. b 46. LRCP 70 MRCS 70 MRCGP 76 Lon Univ MB, BS 70. S Dios Minl Tr Scheme 88. **d** 91 **p** 92. NSM Ore St Helen and St Barn *Chich* 91–99; PtO *Win* from 01. *Barncroft, Southampton Road, Boldre, Lymington SO41 8PT* T: (01590) 622268

MOYNAGH, Michael Digby. b 50. Southn Univ BA 73 Lon Univ MA 74 Aus Nat Univ PhD 78 Bris Univ MA 85. Trin Coll Bris. **d** 85 **p** 86. C Northwood Em *Lon* 85–89; P-in-c Wilton *B & W* 89–90; TR 90–96; Dir Cen for Futures Studies St Jo Coll Nottm 96–04; Co-Dir Tomorrow Project 04–14; Fresh Expressions Team *Ox* from 05; PtO from 19. *14 Dale Close, Oxford OX1 1TU* T: (01865) 722551 E: michael.moynagh@wycliffe.ox.ac.uk

MOYNAN, David George. b 53. **d** 86 **p** 87. C Seagoe *D & D* 86–88; C Taney *D & G* 88–89; I Arklow w Inch and Kilbride 89–94; Dioc Stewardship Adv 92–15; Dioc Ch of Ireland Bps' Appeal Rep 92–15; I Kilternan 94–15; Dioc Dir Decade of Evang 96–15; Can Ch Cath Cathl Dublin 97–15; NZ from 15. *250 Annesbrooke Drive, Wakatu, Nelson 7011, New Zealand* M: (0064) 21-0826 6278 E: moynandg.nz@gmail.com

MOYO (née Hudghton), Deborah Elizabeth. b 92. Nottm Univ BA 13. St Mellitus Coll 16. **d** 18 **p** 19. C Carlton *S'well* from 18; C Colwick from 18. *5 Langton Close, Colwick, Nottingham NG4 2BW*

MOYSE, Mrs Pauline Patricia. b 42. Ex Univ CertEd 62. S Dios Minl Tr Scheme 88. **d** 91 **p** 94. NSM Fleet *Guildf* 91–92; C 93–97; Chapl Farnborough Coll of Tech 96–97; P-in-c Stoneleigh *Guildf* 97–02; Warden of Readers 97–07; Dioc Adv Lay Min 01–07; rtd 07; Tr Officer for Past Assts *Guildf* 07–09; PtO 09–18; *Win* from 17. *Beechend, 2 Hillcrest, Fleet GU51 4PZ* T: (01252) 671382 E: pauline.moyse42@gmail.com

MUBARAK, Riaz. b 70. **d** 01 **p** 03. Pakistan 01–14; P-in-c W Winch w Setchey, N Runcton and Middleton *Nor* 14–15; R Middlewinch from 15; Chapl Norfolk Constabulary from 18. *The New Rectory, Rectory Lane, West Winch, King's Lynn PE33 0NR* T: (01553) 841519 E: rev.riaz.mubarak@gmail.com

MUCKLE, Andrew Philip. b 69. Bris Univ BVSc 93 Middx Univ MSc 04. Coll of Resurr Mirfield BA 16. **d** 16 **p** 17. C Gillingham and Milton-on-Stour *Sarum* 16–19; V W Moors from 19. *The Vicarage, 57 Glenwood Road, West Moors, Ferndown BH22 0EN* M: 07505-007498 E: andymuckle@outlook.com

MUDD, Mrs Linda Anne. b 59. WMMTC 00. **d** 03 **p** 04. C Exhall *Cov* 03–07; Chapl Geo Eliot Hosp NHS Trust Nuneaton 07–11; TV Coventry Caludon *Cov* 11–19; V Mancetter from 19. *The Vicarage, Quarry Lane, Atherstone CV9 1NL* E: linda.mudd@btinternet.com

MUDGE, Frederick Alfred George. b 31. Leeds Univ BSc 58 Univ of Wales BD 67. St Mich Coll Llan 58. **d** 61 **p** 62. C Cwmavon *Llan* 61–64; PV Llan Cathl 64–70; R Llandough w Leckwith 70–88; V Penarth All SS 88–96; rtd 96; PtO *Llan* from 07. *Pathways, 6 Fairwater Road, Llandaff, Cardiff CF5 2LD*

MUDIE, Martin Bruce. b 54. Goldsmiths' Coll Lon BA 76. Sarum & Wells Th Coll 92. **d** 92 **p** 93. C Bromley St Mark *Roch* 92–95; rtd 95; PtO *B & W* 02–03; Hon C Glastonbury w Meare 03–10; PtO from 10. *20 Oriel Road, Street BA16 0JL* T: (01458) 448034 E: mmudie5@gmail.com

MUFFETT, Mrs Sarah Susan. b 53. STETS 02. **d** 05 **p** 06. NSM Okeford *Sarum* 05–13; rtd 13; PtO *Sarum* 13–22. *Highlands, High Street, Child Okeford, Blandford Forum DT11 8EH* T: (01258) 860010 E: sarahmuffett@btopenworld.com

MUGAN, Canon Miriam Ruth. b 56. RNMH 77. Oak Hill Th Coll 93. **d** 96 **p** 97. NSM St Alb St Sav 96–07; P-in-c Croxley Green All SS 07–12; V from 12; Hon Can St Alb from 19. *All Saints' Vicarage, The Green, Croxley Green, Rickmansworth WD3 3HJ* T: (01923) 772109 E: miriam.mugan@btopenworld.com

MUGGE, Martijn. b 69. Oak Hill Th Coll BA 12. **d** 12 **p** 13. C Wombwell *Sheff* 12–15; P-in-c Conisbrough from 15. *The Vicarage, 8 Castle Avenue, Conisbrough, Doncaster DN12 3BT* M: 07732-492998 E: mugge@onetel.com or martijn.mugge@sheffield.anglican.org

MUGGERIDGE, Ms Sara Ann (Sally). b 49. Westf Coll Lon BA 73 Brunel Univ MBA 92 Cant Ch Ch Univ BTh 13. **d** 15 **p** 16. C St Steph Walbrook and St Swithun etc *Lon* 15–17; PtO *Cant* 18–21. *The Old Farm House, Pike Road, Eythorne, Dover CT15 4DJ* M: 07770-381911 E: revdsallymuggeridge@gmail.com

MUGGLETON, James. b 55. Bris Univ BA 80. Chich Th Coll 81 EAMTC 99. **d** 01 **p** 02. NSM E Leightonstone *Ely* 01–03; C 03–04; C Buckworth and Alconbury cum Weston 04; R Barney, Fulmodeston w Croxton, Hindringham etc *Nor* 04–15; R Barney, Hindringham, Thursford, Great Snoring, Little Snoring and Kettlestone and Pensthorpe from 15. *The Rectory, The Street, Hindringham, Fakenham NR21 0AA* T: (01328) 878159 E: jamie@muggs.myzen.co.uk

MUGHAL, Dominic Jacob. b 59. Asian Soc Inst Manila MSc 88 Edin Univ MTh 93 Leeds Univ MPhil 04. St Jo Coll

Nottm 05. **d** 07 **p** 08. C Fairweather Green *Bradf* 07–09; Community Outreach P 09–13; C Thornbury 09–13; C Woodhall 09–13; C Bradf St Aug Uncliffe 09–13; C Bradf St Clem 09–13; Pakistan Miss Partner CMS 13–15; C Tong and Laisterdyke *Leeds* 15–16; TV Seacroft from 16. *St James's Vicarage, 47 St James Approach, Leeds LS14 6JJ* M: 07821-246891 E: dominic_moghal@hotmail.com

MUGRIDGE, Mrs Gloria **Janet**. b 45. R Holloway Coll Lon BA 66. S Dios Minl Tr Scheme 92. **d** 95 **p** 96. NSM Dorchester *Sarum* 95–97; Asst Chapl Weymouth Coll 95–97; Chapl 97–04; NSM Melbury *Sarum* 97–02; NSM Stour Vale 04–06; PtO from 12. *27 St John's Priory, 1 Shaftesbury Road, Wilton, Salisbury SP2 0JN* T: (01722) 742386 E: janetmug@aol.com

MUIR, Charmaine Fiona. b 74. Wycliffe Hall Ox 18. **d** 20 **p** 21. C Cant St Mary Bredin from 20. *38 Nunnery Road, Canterbury CT1 3LS* E: charmaine.muir@smb.org.uk

MUIR, David Murray. b 49. Glas Univ MA 70. St Jo Coll Nottm BA 72. **d** 76 **p** 77. C Fulham St Mary N End *Lon* 76–80; C Aspley *S'well* 80; India 81–85; Dir Ext Studies St Jo Coll Nottm 85–02; C Upton (Overchurch) *Ches* 02–04; Adult Educn and Par Development Adv *Ex* 04–08; Pioneer Min Okehampton Deanery 08–14; rtd 14. *14 Llewellyn Way, Weston-super-Mare BS22 7QF* M: 07971-917930 E: davidmurraymuir@gmail.com

MUIR, David Trevor. b 49. TCD BA MLitt 93. CITC 75. **d** 78 **p** 79. C Dublin Clontarf *D & G* 78–80; C Monkstown St Mary 80–83; I Kilternan 83–94; I Delgany 94–97; Can Ch Ch Cathl Dublin 95–97; Chapl to Ch of Ireland Assn of Deaf People 97–15; rtd 15. *Luogh North, Doolin, Co Clare, Republic of Ireland* T: (00353) (65) 707 4778 F: 707 4871 M: 87-921 1501 E: muirdt@gmail.com

MUIR, Peter Robert James. b 49. Ex Univ BScEng 71. **d** 09 **p** 10. OLM Thursley *Guildf* 09–13; NSM 13–19; OLM Elstead 09–13; NSM 13–19; PtO 19–20. *Dervenakion 8, 8560 Pegeia, Paphos, Cyprus* T: (00357) 2662 3051 M: (00357) 99-951776 E: petermuir@cellarworld.co.uk

MUKHERJEE, Supriyo. b 42. Calcutta Univ BA 70 Serampore Th Coll BD 76 Derby Univ MA 97. Bp's Coll Calcutta 70. **d** 75 **p** 76. India 75–91; C Crook *Dur* 91–92; V Nelson in Lt Marsden *Blackb* 92–95; Dioc Community Relns Officer *Cov* 95–02; TV Cov E 95–02; rtd 02; PtO *Cov* 02–04. *30 Ulverscroft Road, Coventry CV3 5EZ* T: (024) 7650 1559

MUKHOLI, Patrick John Eshuchi. b 60. Nairobi Univ BSc 86 Aber Univ MTh 09. Nairobi Evang Graduate Sch of Th MDiv 98. **d** 98 **p** 99. Dioc Youth Adv and C Ukunda St Steph Kenya 98–02; Dioc Miss and Communications Officer 99–02; Chapl St Aug Prep Sch 99–02; NSM Blackbird Leys *Ox* 02–08; Youth Worker 03–09; Prin Bp Hannington Th Coll Mombasa Kenya 10–12; NSM Penhill *Bris* 13–17; NSM Upper Stratton 13–17; C Wokingham St Paul *Ox* 17–20; C Winkfield and Cranbourne 20–21. *54 Vulcan Drive, Bracknell RG12 9GN* M: 07448-794154 E: pmukholi@yahoo.com

MUKUNGA, James. b 74. Univ of Zimbabwe BA 00. Bp Gaul Th Coll Harare 95. **d** 97 **p** 99. Zimbabwe 97–04; R Kadoma All SS 01–02; R Mabelreign St Pet and Lect Bp Gaul Coll 02–04; PtO *Ox* 04–06; C High Wycombe 06–07; C Peckham St Sav *S'wark* 07–10; PtO 11–12. *7 Neville Close, London SE15 5UE* M: 07886-235698 E: james_mukunga@yahoo.com

MULCAHY, Richard Patrick. b 67. SW Poly Plymouth BSc 90. St Mich Coll Llan 02. **d** 05 **p** 06. NSM Bassaleg *Mon* 05–16; NSM Bedwas w Machen w Michaelston-y-Fedw w Rudry from 16. *9 High Cross Drive, Rogerstone, Newport NP10 9AB* M: 07940-997741 E: richard-mulcahy@ntlworld.com

MULCOCK, Nathan Peter. b 91. Trin Coll Ox BA 12 MA 16. St Steph Ho Ox 15. **d** 17 **p** 18. C Stevenage St Andr and St Geo St Alb 17–21. *Community of the Resurrection, Stocks Bank Road, Mirfield WF14 0BN* T: (01924) 483310 E: nmulcock@mirfield.org.uk

MULFORD, Robert. b 57. Middx Poly CertEd 79 Open Univ BA 87 MA 93 Oak Hill Th Coll BA 03. ERMC 05. **d** 07 **p** 08. C Billing *Pet* 07–11; PtO 11–12; V Westfield and Guestling *Chich* 12–19; rtd 19; PtO *Ex* from 20. *9 Moor View Close, Sidmouth EX10 9UP* M: 07748-960896 E: revmulford@gmail.com

MULHALL, Canon James Gerard. b 60. NUI DipSW 92 CQSW 92. Carlow Coll BA 95. **d** 86 **p** 87. C Clonmel w Innislounagh, Tullaghmelan etc *C, F & O* 09–10; C Lismore w Cappoquin, Kilwatermoy, Dungarvan etc 10–17; P-in-c Kells Gp from 17; Can Kilkenny Cathl from 18. *The Priory, Kells, Co Kilkenny, Republic of Ireland* T: (00353) (56) 772 8367 M: (00353) 87-240 1913 E: jamesgmulhall@gmail.com

MULHOLLAND, Canon Nicholas **Christopher** John. b 44. Chich Th Coll 77. **d** 79 **p** 80. C Thornbury *Glouc* 79–83; R Boxwell, Leighterton, Didmarton, Oldbury etc 83–11; RD Tetbury 00–03; Hon Can Glouc Cathl 06–11; rtd 11; PtO *Bris* from 11; *Glouc* from 15. *Little Badminton Farmhouse,*

Little Badminton, Badminton GL9 1AB T: (01454) 218427 E: revmulholland@btinternet.com

✠MULLALLY, The Rt Revd and Rt Hon Dame Sarah Elisabeth. b 62. DBE 05. S Bank Univ BSc 84 MSc 92 Bournemouth Univ Hon DSc 01 Wolv Univ Hon DSc 04 Herts Univ Hon DSc 05 RGN 84. SEITE 98. **d** 01 **p** 02 **c** 15. C Battersea Fields *S'wark* 01–06; TR Sutton 06–12; Can Res and Treas Sarum Cathl 12–15; Suff Bp Crediton *Ex* 15–18; Bp Lon from 18. *The Old Deanery, Dean's Court, London EC4V 5AA* T: (020) 3837 5200 E: bishop.london@london.anglican.org

MULLANEY, Daniel Robert John. b 83. Warwick Univ BSc 04 Keble Coll Ox MPhil 17. Wycliffe Hall Ox BA 15. **d** 19 **p** 20. C Higher Openshaw *Man* from 19. *10 Redacre Road, Manchester M18 8RU* T: (01612) 308363 E: daniel@stclementschurchmanchester.org

MULLANEY, Mrs Jane Megan. b 48. Kingston Poly BA 72. **d** 04 **p** 05. OLM Kenilworth St Jo *Cov* 04–15; rtd 15; PtO *Cov* from 15. *5 Knightlow Close, Kenilworth CV8 2PX* T: (01926) 850723 E: jane_m_mullaney536@btinternet.com

MULLEN, Canon Charles William. b 64. CITC BTh 92. **d** 92 **p** 93. C Lecale Gp *D & D* 92–95; I Gorey w Kilnahue, Leskinfere and Ballycanew *C, F & O* 95–00; Dean's V St Patr Cathl Dublin from 00; Preb Rathmichael St Patr Cathl Dublin from 08. *35A Kevin Street Upper, Dublin 8, Republic of Ireland* T: (00353) (1) 453 9472 M: 87-261 8878 E: deans.vicar@stpatrickscathedral.ie

MULLEN, Lee Ross. b 73. Cranmer Hall Dur 05. **d** 07 **p** 08. C Chelmsf St Andr 07–11; V Southend St Sav Westcliff 11–21; V Creech St Michael and Ruishton w Thornfalcon *B & W* from 21. *The Rectory, Creech St Michael, Taunton TA3 5PP* E: revdlee@me.com

MULLEN, Peter John. b 42. Liv Univ BA 70 Middx Univ PhD 00. St Aid Birkenhead 66. **d** 70 **p** 71. C Manston *Ripon* 70–72; C Stretford All SS *Man* 72–73; C Oldham St Mary w St Pet 73–74; LtO 74–77; V Tockwith and Bilton w Bickerton *York* 77–89; PtO 97–98; P-in-c St Mich Cornhill w St Pet le Poer etc *Lon* 98–03; R 03–12; P-in-c St Sepulchre w Ch Ch Greyfriars etc 98–12; Chapl City Inst Stock Exchange 98–12; rtd 12; PtO *Chich* from 14. *3 Naomi Close, Eastbourne BN20 7UU* E: rpetermullen@gmail.com

MULLER, Ms Ank. b 75. Radboud Univ Nijmegen MA 04. ERMC 07. **d** 09. C E Netherlands *Eur* 09–10; C Rotterdam 10–14; Chapl Vlissingen (Flushing) Miss to Seafarers 10–16; PtO 17–21. *Schuitvaartgracht 37, 4382 GH Vlissingen, The Netherlands* M: (0031) 68-174 4385 E: aagmuller@gmail.com

MÜLLER, Anton Michael. b 61. Grey Coll Dur BA 83 MA 91 PGCE 84. Trin Coll Bris 97. **d** 99 **p** 00. C Sandgate St Paul w Folkestone St Geo *Cant* 99–03; TV Penrith w Newton Reigny and Plumpton Wall *Carl* 03–04; P-in-c Dacre 03–04; Chapl N Cumbria Mental Health NHS Trust 03–04; Chapl Eden Valley Hospice Carl 05–08; PtO *Carl* from 08; Tutor Cumbria Chr Learning from 09; PtO *Blackb* 13–15; V Scorton and Barnacre and Calder Vale from 15; Ecum Officer for Churches Together in Lancs from 15; Tutor All SS Cen for Miss and Min 18–21. *St Peter's Vicarage, Snowhill Lane, Scorton, Preston PR3 1AY* T: (01524) 791229 M: 07525-395923 E: antonandsue@gmail.com or unitedparishoffice@gmail.com

MULLETT, Janette Constance. b 58. SWMTC 17. **d** 19 **p** 20. NSM Highertown and Baldhu *Truro* from 19. *Epiphany House, Kenwyn Church Road, Truro TR1 3DR* E: manager@epiphanyhouse.co.uk

MULLEY, Mrs Margery **Ann** Oclanis. b 38. **d** 07 **p** 08. OLM Iwerne Valley *Sarum* 07–12; NSM 12; PtO *Cov* from 13. *17 South Parade, Harbury, Leamington Spa CV33 9HZ*

MULLIGAN, Ronald Leslie. b 53. LCTP. **d** 08 **p** 09. NSM Haslingden w Grane and Stonefold *Blackb* 08–11; NSM Blackb St Thos w St Jude 11–13; NSM Blackb St Mich w St Jo and H Trin 11–13; NSM N and E Blackb 13–14; Chapl Airedale NHS Foundn Trust from 14. *3 Chatburn Close, Rossendale BB4 8UT* T: (01706) 220749 E: ronmulligan@talktalk.net

MULLIN, Horace Boies (**Dan**). b 44. **d** 00 **p** 01. OLM Mildenhall *St E* 00–13; rtd 13; PtO *St E* from 13. *47 Oak Drive, Beck Row, Bury St Edmunds IP28 8UA* T: (01638) 718200 E: dan.marthan@btinternet.com

MULLINER, Angela Margaret. *See* LAUENER, Angela Margaret

MULLINER, Canon Denis Ratliffe. b 40. LVO 15. BNC Ox BA 62 MA 66. Linc Th Coll 70. **d** 72 **p** 73. C Sandhurst *Ox* 72–76; Chapl Bradfield Coll Berks 76–00; Chapl Chpl Royal Hampton Court Palace 00–15; Can 10–15; Dep P in O 00–15; rtd 15; PtO *Nor* from 15. *The Patch, Hillington, King's Lynn PE31 6DN*

MULLINER, Eliska Fiona **Jo**. b 71. Bp Otter Coll BA 94 W Sussex Inst of HE PGCE 98. Ridley Hall Cam 12. **d** 14 **p** 15. C Lymington *Win* 14–17; TV Redruth w Lanner and Treleigh *Truro* 17–19; R Bridge of Allan *St And* from 19; Chapl Stirling

Univ from 19. *The Rectory, 21 Fountain Road, Bridge of Allan, Stirling FK9 4AT* T: (01786) 357603 M: 07493-657187 E: jomulliner@cantab.net

MULLINGS, Paulette Patricia Yvonne. b 53. d 07 p 08. NSM Cobbold Road St Sav w St Mary *Lon* 07–17; NSM Hammersmith H Innocents and St Jo from 17. *53A Melina Road, London W12 9HY* T: (020) 7386 1262 M: 07751-374857 E: pmullings@aol.com *or* paulette.mullings@london.anglican.org

MULLINS, Caroline Anne. b 56. Ex Univ BA 78 St Anne's Coll Ox CertEd 79. SEITE 04. d 07 p 08. NSM Wandsworth St Paul *S'wark* 07–11; NSM Hinchley Wood *Guildf* from 11. *1 Chesterfield Drive, Esher KT10 0AH* T: (020) 8224 3334 E: rev.carolinemullins@gmail.com

MULLINS, Mrs Margaret. b 49. Southn Univ CertEd 70. Sarum & Wells Th Coll 94. d 94 p 95. C Bishopstoke *Win* 94–98; TV Bicester w Bucknell, Caversfield and Launton *Ox* 98–10; rtd 10. *5 Hardings Lane, Fair Oak, Eastleigh SO50 8GL* E: m.mullins@ntlworld.com

MULLINS, Peter Matthew. b 60. Ch Ch Ox BA 82 MA 86 Irish Sch of Ecum MPhil 90. Qu Coll Birm 82. d 84 p 85. C Caversham St Pet and Mapledurham etc *Ox* 84–88; PtO *D & G* 88–89; TV Old Brumby *Linc* 89–94; Clergy Tr Adv 94–99; TR Gt and Lt Coates w Bradley 99–17; Can and Preb Linc Cathl 02–17; RD Grimsby and Cleethorpes 05–10; R Haworth and Cross Roads cum Lees *Leeds* from 17. *78 Prince Street, Haworth, Keighley BD22 8JD* E: p.m.mullins@virgin.net

MULLINS, Timothy Dougal. b 59. St Jo Coll Dur BA 81. Wycliffe Hall Ox 83. d 85 p 86. C Reading Greyfriars *Ox* 85–89; C Haughton le Skerne *Dur* 89–95; Chapl Eton Coll 95–05; Chapl Radley Coll 05–12; C Ches Square St Mich w St Phil *Lon* 12–17; Chapl Stowe Sch from 17. *Stowe School, Buckingham MK18 5EH* T: (01280) 818000 E: timmullins1010@gmail.com

MULLINS, Mrs Yvonne Beryl. b 69. Witwatersrand Univ BPrimEd 90 BEd 93. Ripon Coll Cuddesdon 16. d 19 p 20. C Shelswell *Ox* from 19. *10C St Michael's Close, Fringford, Bicester OX27 8DW* M: 07545-299517 E: y.mullins@outlook.com

MULLIS, Robert Owen. b 49. Open Univ BA 77 Glam Univ MSc 00 St Paul's Coll Chelt CertEd 71. St Mich Coll Llan 90. d 93 p 94. NSM Llangenni and Llanbedr Ystrad Yw w Patricio *S & B* 93–03; NSM Llantilio Pertholey w Bettws Chpl etc *Mon* 03–06; PtO *Heref* 06–19; NSM Eardisley w Bollingham, Willersley, Brilley etc 19–20; rtd 20; PtO *Heref* from 20. *Church Gate, Almeley, Hereford HR3 6LB* T: (01544) 327801 E: bob.mullis@hotmail.co.uk

MULRENAN, David John. b 57. d 18 p 19. NSM Four Rivers *St E* from 18. *4 Sunnyside Cottages, The Thorofare, Brundish, Woodbridge IP13 8BB* T: (01728) 628063 M: 07881-481745 E: djmulrenan@gmail.com

MULRYNE, Thomas Mark. b 70. St Cath Coll Cam BA 91 MA 95 Lon Inst of Educn PGCE 93. Oak Hill Th Coll BA 02. d 02 p 03. C W Streatham St Jas *S'wark* 02–06; C Gt Clacton *Chelmsf* 06–19; V from 19. *112 Woodlands Close, Clacton-on-Sea CO15 4RU* T: (01255) 425159 E: mark_and_caroline_mulryne@hotmail.com

MULVANEY, James Eric John. b 89. Melbourne Univ BA 10 K Coll Lon MA 13. St Mellitus Coll BA 16. d 16 p 17. C Onslow Square and S Kensington St Aug *Lon* 16–17; C Clapham H Trin *S'wark* from 17. Flat B, 6 Old Town, London SW4 0JY M: 07867-499599 E: jamie.mulvaney@holytrinityclapham.org

MUMBY, Andrew. *See* MOUGHTIN-MUMBY, Andrew Denis Paul

MUMFORD, Prof David Bardwell. b 49. St Cath Coll Cam BA 71 MA 75 Bris Univ MB, ChB 81 MD 92 Edin Univ MPhil 89 MRCPsych 86. Bp's Coll Calcutta 71 Cuddesdon Coll 73. d 75. C Bris St Mary Redcliffe w Temple etc 75–76; NSM 76–82; NSM Edin St Columba 82–86; NSM Calverley *Bradf* 86–92; PtO *B & W* 92–06 and from 11. *14 Clifton Vale, Clifton, Bristol BS8 4PT* T: 0117-927 2221 M: 07501-134525 E: david.mumford@bristol.ac.uk

MUMFORD, David Christopher. b 47. Mert Coll Ox BA 68 MA 74 York Univ MSW CQSW 81. Linc Th Coll 84. d 86 p 87. C Shiremoor *Newc* 86–89; C N Shields 89–91; V Byker St Ant 91–97; RD Newc E 96–97; V Cowgate 97–02; Internat Co-ord Internat Fellowship of Reconciliation 02–07; R Brechin *Bre* 07–15; R Tarfside 07–15; Dean Bre 08–12; rtd 15; PtO *Eur* from 15; LtO *Edin* from 16. *10 Temple Mains Steading, Innerwick, Dunbar EH42 1EF* T: (01368) 840361 E: dmumford@phonecoop.coop

MUMFORD, Geoffrey Robert. b 70. York Univ BSc 92 St Jo Coll Nottm MA 00. d 00 p 01. C Rowley Regis *Birm* 00–03; TV Darwen St Pet w Hoddlesden *Blackb* 03–08; P-in-c Copmanthorpe *York* 08–09; V from 09; P-in-c Askham Bryan 08–09; V from 09; P-in-c Bolton Percy 08–09; R from 09; RD New Ainsty from 16. *The Vicarage, 17 Sutor Close,*

Copmanthorpe, York YO23 3TX T: (01904) 707716 M: 07980-569450 E: vicar@stgileschurchcopmanthorpe.org

MUMFORD, Grenville Alan. b 34. Richmond Th Coll. d 78 p 78. C Witham *Chelmsf* 78–81; C-in-c Gt Ilford St Marg CD 81–85; V Gt Ilford St Marg 85–87; P-in-c Everton and Mattersey w Clayworth *S'well* 87–89; R 89–96; RD Bawtry 93–96; rtd 96; PtO *Ches* 96–18. *146 Audlem Road, Nantwich CW5 7EB* T: (01270) 610221 E: mumford7eb@btinternet.com

MUMFORD, Lesley Anne. *See* CHEETHAM, Lesley Anne

MUMFORD, Thomas James. b 90. York Univ BA 15 Peterho Cam BA 18. Westcott Ho Cam 16. d 19 p 20. C Sudbury and Chilton *St E* 19–21; P-in-c Ipswich St Mary-le-Tower from 21. *St Mary-le-Tower Vicarage, 18 Kingsfield Avenue, Ipswich IP1 3TA* E: rev.tommumford@outlook.com

MUNBY, Canon David Philip James. b 52. Pemb Coll Ox BA 75 MA 80. St Jo Coll Nottm 76. d 78 p 79. C Gipsy Hill Ch Ch *S'wark* 78–82; C-in-c W Dulwich Em CD 82–88; V Barnsley St Geo *Wakef* 88–14; Leeds 14–18; Asst Dioc Ecum Officer *Wakef* 99–01; Can Bungoma from 04; rtd 18; PtO *Leeds* 18–21; *Dur* from 20. *8 Greenfield Drive, Eaglescliffe, Stockton-on-Tees TS16 0HE* E: david.7munby@gmail.com

MUNCEY, William. b 49. Oak Hill Th Coll BA 80. d 80 p 81. C Wandsworth St Mich *S'wark* 80–84; C Morden 84–88; TV 88–01; RD Merton 00–01; P-in-c Croydon Ch Ch 01–04; V 04–12; NSM Shelswell *Ox* 12–18; PtO *Ely* from 19. *12 Church Street, Histon, Cambridge CB24 9EP* E: munceybill@gmail.com

MUNCH, Philip Douglas. b 55. Witwatersrand Univ BMus. Cranmer Hall Dur. d 88 p 89. C Wlvis Bay Namibia 88–89; P-in-c 89–92; Warden Ho of Prayer Luderitz 92–99; Prec Port Elizabeth S Africa 99–02; Warden Emmaus Ho of Prayer Northampton from 02; NSM Northampton St Mich w St Edm *Pet* from 02. *Emmaus House of Prayer, St Michael's Church, Perry Street, Northampton NN1 4HL* T: (01604) 627669 F: 230316 E: pdmunch@gmail.com

MUNCHIN, David Leighfield. b 67. Imp Coll Lon BSc 88 K Coll Lon MA 00 Heythrop Coll Lon PhD 09. Ripon Coll Cuddesdon 89. d 92 p 93. C Golders Green *Lon* 92–96; Prec and Min Can St Alb Abbey 96–02; P-in-c Hatfield Hyde 02–10; TR Welwyn from 10. *The Rectory, 2 Ottway Walk, Welwyn AL6 9AS* T: (01438) 714150 M: 07787-567747 E: rector@welwyn.org.uk *or* davidmunchin@outlook.com

MUNCHIN, Ysmena Rachael. *See* PENTELOW, Ysmena Rachael

MUNDAY, Clive Ian. b 57. BNC Ox BA 78 MA 85. St Mellitus Coll BA 17. d 17 p 18. C Bridgnorth and Morville Par *Heref* 17–21; PtO from 21. *41 Innage Lane, Bridgnorth WV16 4HS* T: (01746) 766197 M: 07763-177152 E: clive_munday@btinternet.com

MUNDAY, Elaine Jeanette. b 56. SWMTC. d 10 p 11. NSM Bodmin w Lanhydrock and Lanivet *Truro* 10–17; TV Bodmin from 17. *70 St Mary's Crescent, Bodmin PL31 1NP* T: (01208) 77945 E: elaine.munday@bodminway.org

MUNDAY, Nicholas John. b 54. Jes Coll Cam BA 76 PGCE 77 MA 97. Ripon Coll Cuddesdon BTh 13. d 11 p 12. C Monmouth w Overmonnow etc *Mon* 11–14; R S Lafford *Linc* 14–19; Discipleship Development Adv 14–19; rtd 19; PtO *St Alb* from 19. *1 Tithebarn, Felmersham, Bedford MK43 7JF* T: (01234) 782800 E: n.j.munday@btinternet.com

MUNDAY, Mrs Sandra Anne. b 61. St Jo Sem Wonersh BTh 89 Ripon Coll Cuddesdon 97. d 99 p 00. C Esher *Guildf* 99–02; Team Chapl R United Hosp Bath NHS Trust 02–03; PtO *B & W* 03–17; Hon C Chew Stoke w Nempnett Thrubwell 17–20. *3 Eriskay Gardens, Westbury BA13 3GH*

MUNDEN, Alan Frederick. b 43. Nottm Univ BTh 74 Birm Univ MLitt 80 Dur Univ PhD 87. St Jo Coll Nottm. d 74 p 75. C Cheltenham St Mary *Glouc* 74–76; C Cheltenham St Mary, St Matt, St Paul and H Trin 76; Hon C Jesmond Clayton Memorial *Newc* 76–80; C 80–83; V Cheylesmore *Cov* 83–01; R Weddington and Caldecote 01–03; rtd 03; Hon C Jesmond Clayton Memorial *Newc* from 03; PtO *Dur* 11–19. *11 The Crescent, Benton, Newcastle upon Tyne NE7 7ST* T: 0191-266 1227 E: alan.munden@church.org.uk

MUNDY, David Hugh. b 58. Lon Univ BSc 80 Newc Univ PhD 88 Sheff Univ MA 16. Yorks Min Course 12. d 15 p 16. NSM Chapel-en-le-Frith *Derby* 15–16; NSM Bakewell, Ashford w Sheldon and Rowsley 16–17; NSM Dinting Vale 17–18; NSM Glossop from 17; P-in-c from 18; Asst Dir of Ords *Derby* from 18. *103 Station Road, Hadfield, Glossop SK13 1AR* T: (01457) 856554 E: dhmundy@btinternet.com

MUNDY, Kay. b 67. d 14 p 15. C Deerhurst and Apperley w Forthampton etc *Glouc* from 14; Chapl to Bp Tewksbury from 18. *2 College Green, Gloucester GL1 2LY* T: (01452) 835563 E: kmundy@glosdioc.org.uk

MUNDY, Paul Kevin. b 68. Westcott Ho Cam 11. d 13 p 14. C Barcombe *Chich* 13–17; C Newick 17–20; R from 20;

P-in-c Chailey from 21. *The Rectory, 36A Allington Road, Newick, Lewes BN8 4NB* T: (01825) 723186 M: 07717-000281 E: paul@barcombe.net *or* church.newick@gmail.com

MUNEZA, Steve. b 80. Redcliffe Coll Glouc MA 10. **d** 14 **p** 16. Youth Min Bujumbura Burundi 14–15; NSM Dur N 15–19; Dir Minl Formation and Mixed Mode Tr Cranmer Hall Dur from 19. *25 Barnard Close, Durham DH1 5XN* T: 0191-384 5954 *or* 334 3863 E: stevemuneza@gmail.com

MUNGAVIN, Ross Andrew. b 89. Open Univ BA 15. Oak Hill Th Coll BA 20. **d** 20 **p** 21. C Gerrards Cross and Fulmer *Ox* from 20. *54 The Uplands, Gerrards Cross SL9 7JG* T: (01753) 883311 M: 07979-571955 E: ross-mungavin@hotmail.com

MUNNS, Ms Alice Wiliemhina (Mina). b 78. York Univ BA 99 St Jo Coll Dur BA 15 Derby Univ PGCE 00. Cranmer Hall Dur 13. **d** 15 **p** 16. C Selston *S'well* 15–18; P-in-c Cresswell and Lynemouth *Newc* from 18. *33 Till Grove, Ellington, Morpeth NE61 5ER* M: 07960-250497 E: minamunns90@gmail.com

MUNNS, Stuart Millington. b 36. OBE 77. St Cath Coll Cam BA 58 MA 62 MCIPD 91. Cuddesdon Coll 58. **d** 60 **p** 61. C Allenton and Shelton Lock *Derby* 60–63; C Brampton St Thos 63–65; C-in-c Loundsley Green Ascension CD 65–66; Bp's Youth Chapl 66–72; Nat Dir of Community Industry 72–77; Hon C Hornsey Ch Ch *Lon* 72–77; Dioc Missr *Liv* 77–82; V Knowsley 77–82; P-in-c Stramshall *Lich* 82–88; V Uttoxeter w Bramshall 82–88; RD Uttoxeter 82–87; P-in-c Kingstone w Gratwich 84–88; P-in-c Marchington w Marchington Woodlands 84–88; P-in-c Checkley 86–88; PtO *B & W* 88–90; NSM Wells St Thos w Horrington 90–94; P-in-c Fosse Trinity 94–02; rtd 02; Dioc Pre-Th Educn Co-ord *B & W* 02–06; PtO from 03; *Eur* from 07. *Applewood House, Ham Street, Baltonsborough, Glastonbury BA6 8PX* T: (01458) 851443 M: 07791-111904 E: munns@cantab.net

MUÑOZ-TRIVIÑO, Daniel. b 75. Hatf Coll Dur BA 99 Madrid Univ PhD 16. Wycliffe Hall Ox MTh 01. **d** 01 **p** 02. C Hazlemere *Ox* 01–04; TV Gt Marlow w Marlow Bottom, Lt Marlow and Bisham 04–09; Chapl Los Olivos Retreat Cen Spain from 09; PtO *Ox* 13–16; LtO from 16. *Calle Sierra Nevada, 22 29630 Málaga, Spain* T: (0034) 958 068 001 E: daniel.munoz@facultadseut.org

MUNRO, Alexander Ian. b 78. Leic Univ LLB. St Mellitus Coll BA 17. **d** 17 **p** 18. C W Molesey *Guildf* 17–21; V from 21. *The Vicarage, 518 Walton Road, West Molesey KT8 2QF* M: 07889-456266 E: alex.munro@spwm.org.uk

MUNRO, Duncan John Studd. b 50. Magd Coll Ox BA 72 MA 76 Warwick Univ MBA 96. Wycliffe Hall Ox 73. **d** 76 **p** 77. C Ecclesall *Sheff* 76–77; C Sheff St Barn and St Mary 78–80; LtO 80–86; PtO 97–05; LtO *Edin* 06–17; PtO Glouc 13–15 and from 20; Public Preacher 15–20. *Hosanna House, 43 Cudnall Street, Charlton Kings, Cheltenham GL53 8HL* T: (01242) 321712 M: 07802-871156 E: duncan.munro@munrostrategic.co.uk *or* dmunro@glosdioc.org.uk

MUNRO, Ingrid Phyllis. b 51. Herts Univ BEd 80. St Jo Coll Nottm MA 96 St Alb Minl Tr Scheme 83. **d** 98 **p** 99. NSM Walbrook Epiphany *Derby* 98–01 and 05–09; NSM Alvaston from 09. *40 Brisbane Road, Mickleover, Derby DE3 9JZ*

MUNRO, Robert. b 40. Leeds Univ BA 62 Bris Univ PGCE 63. SWMTC 95. **d** 98 **p** 99. NSM Saltash *Truro* 98–03; NSM Calstock 03–11; PtO 14–21. *15 Valley Road, Saltash PL12 4BT* T: (01752) 844731 M: 07729-907889 E: munrobob88@gmail.com

MUNRO, Robert Speight. b 63. Bris Univ BSc 84 Reformed Th Sem (USA) DMin 08 Man Univ PGCE 92. Oak Hill Th Coll BA 93. **d** 93 **p** 94. C Hartford *Ches* 93–97; R Davenham 97–03; R Cheadle from 03; RD from 16. *The Rectory, 1 Depleach Road, Cheadle SK8 1DZ* T: 0161-428 3440 *or* 428 8050 E: rob@munro.org.uk

MUNRO-SMITH, Alison Jean. *See* WATERS, Alison Jean

MUNT, Mrs Linda Christine. b 55. NEOC 92. **d** 95 **p** 96. C Beverley St Nic *York* 95–98; Chapl E Yorkshire Hosps NHS Trust 97–99; V Bridlington Em *York* 99–03; P-in-c Skipsea w Ulrome and Barmston w Fraisthorpe 02–03; Chapl Martin House Hospice for Children Boston Spa 03–05; Hon C Boston Spa, Thorp Arch w Walton etc 03–05; V Market Weighton *York* 05–10; V Sancton 05–10; R Goodmanham 05–10; PtO 10–12; V Attercliffe and Darnall *Sheff* 12–15; PtO *York* 16–18; P-in-c Garrowby Hill 18–19; R from 19. *Foxfields, Worsendale Road, Bishop Wilton, York YO42 1ST* M: 07888-668663 E: garrowbyvicar@gmail.com

MURCH, Canon Robin Norman. b 37. Wells Th Coll. **d** 67 **p** 68. C Wisbech St Aug *Ely* 67–70; C Basingstoke *Win* 70–73; C Whitstable All SS *Cant* 73–75; C Whitstable All SS w St Pet 75–76; V Queenborough 76–99; Hon Can Cant Cathl 96–99; rtd 99; PtO *Ex* 00–19. *3 Narenta, 2 Barton Crescent, Dawlish EX7 9QL* T: (01626) 863532 M: 07836-514528

MURDOCH, Alexander Edward Duncan. b 37. Oak Hill Th Coll 68. **d** 71 **p** 72. C Kensington St Helen w H Trin *Lon* 71–72; C Kensington St Barn 73–74; CF 74–78; C W Kirby St Bridget *Ches* 78–84; V N Shoebury *Chelmsf* 84–87; V W Poldens *B & W* 87–96; R Gayhurst w Ravenstone, Stoke Goldington etc *Ox* 96–07; rtd 07. *Hopp House, Back Lane, Old Bolingbroke, Spilsby PE23 4EU* T: (01790) 763603

MURDOCH, David John. b 58. Birm Univ BSocSc 81 Leeds Univ MA 03. Ripon Coll Cuddesdon 81. **d** 84 **p** 85. C Penwortham St Leon *Blackb* 84–87; C Wirksworth w Alderwasley, Carsington etc *Derby* 87–89; R Shirland 89–97; Dioc World Development Officer 96–00; P-in-c New Mills 97–01; V 01–05; RD Glossop 04–05; TR Wilford Peninsula *St E* 05–19; rtd 19; P-in-c Horsted Keynes *Chich* from 19. *The Rectory, Station Road, Horsted Keynes, Haywards Heath RH17 7ED* T: (01825) 790317 E: revdave@timicomail.co.uk

MURDOCH, Canon Lucy Eleanor. b 41. STETS BTh 99. **d** 99 **p** 00. NSM Warbleton and Bodle Street Green *Chich* 99–02; NSM Rye 02–12; TV 03–12; RD 10–11; P-in-c Fletching 12–16; Can and Preb Chich Cathl 10–16; rtd 16. *Cottenham, Tubwell Lane, Maynards Green, Heathfield TN21 0BY* M: 07508-931198 E: dog.home@uwclub.net

MURFET, Edward David. b 36. Qu Coll Cam BA 59 MA 63. Chich Th Coll 59. **d** 61 **p** 62. C Croydon St Mich *Cant* 61–64; C Hunslet St Mary and Stourton *Ripon* 64–65; C Hackney Wick St Mary of Eton w St Aug *Lon* 65–69; Chapl Berne *Eur* 69–71; Chapl Naples 71–74; Chapl Rome 74–77; LtO *Bris* 78–81; Gen Sec CEMS 81–86; C Leeds St Pet *Ripon* 87–89; P-in-c 89–90; C Leeds City 91–93; Min Can Ripon Cathl 93–03; rtd 03; PtO *Ripon* 03–14; *Leeds* from 14. *3 Old Deanery Close, St Marygate, Ripon HG4 1LZ* T: (01765) 608422

MURFET, Gwyn. b 44. Linc Th Coll 71. **d** 74 **p** 75. C Scalby w Ravenscar and Staintondale *York* 74–77; P-in-c S Milford 77–83; R 83–84; V Kirkby Ireleth *Carl* 84–05; rtd 05; PtO *Carl* 11–14. *75 Portsmouth Street, Walney, Barrow-in-Furness LA14 3AJ* T: (01229) 471157

MURGATROYD-SHIPP, Elizabeth Ann. b 81. Leic Univ BA 02 Ox Brookes Univ MA 09. Ripon Coll Cuddesdon BA 06. **d** 07 **p** 08. C Wymondham *Nor* 07–11; Bp's Chapl *Worc* 11–16; Min Can Worc Cathl 12–16; P-in-c Melbourn *Ely* from 16; P-in-c Meldreth from 16. *The Vicarage, Vicarage Close, Melbourn, Royston SG8 6DY* T: (01763) 220626 E: vicar.melbournmeldreth@gmail.com

MURLEY, Anthony James Raymond. b 82. Univ Coll Lon BA 04. St Steph Ho Ox 12. **d** 14 **p** 15. C Small Heath *Birm* 14–18; P-in-c Brighton Annunciation *Chich* 18–21; V from 21. *Annunciation Vicarage, 89 Washington Street, Brighton BN2 9SR* M: 07462-555487 E: anthony.murley@ssho.ox.ac.uk *or* anthony.murley@me.com

MURPHIE, Andrew Graham. b 65. Reading Univ BA 86. St Jo Coll Nottm BTh 91 MA 92. **d** 92 **p** 93. C Boulton *Derby* 92–96; C Marston on Dove w Scropton 96–97; V Hilton w Marston-on-Dove 98–18; RD Longford 04–15; P-in-c Crosthwaite Keswick *Carl* from 18; P-in-c Upper Derwent from 21. *Crosthwaite Vicarage, Vicarage Hill, Keswick CA12 5QB* E: andymurphie@btinternet.com

MURPHY, Andrew John. b 46. Edin Univ LLB 67 MA 68. Ox Min Course 14. **d** 95 **p** 16. NSM Aberdeen St Marg *Ab* 95–98; NSM Fraserburgh 98–01; Hon Asst C Bridge of Don St Luke's Miss 01–06; NSM Finchley St Mary *Lon* 16–17. *Flat 2, 50B Birdhurst Road, South Croydon CR2 7EB* M: 07920-596990 E: andrew.murphy@advocates.org.uk

MURPHY, Anthony Michael. **d** 11 **p** 12. NSM Moviddy Union *C, C & R* 11–12; NSM Carrigaline Union from 12. *9 Riverside, Church Road, Carrigaline, Co Cork, Republic of Ireland* M: (00353) 87-832 7347 E: tmurphy@tmahr.com

MURPHY, Christopher Campbell. b 84. Hatf Coll Dur BA 06. Wycliffe Hall Ox 09. **d** 12 **p** 13. C Bovey Tracey SS Pet, Paul and Thos w Hennock *Ex* 12–16; C Barnston *Ches* from 16. *8 Antons Road, Wirral CH61 9PT* T: 0151-648 9440 M: 07595-742970 E: christopher.c.murphy@gmail.com

MURPHY, Mrs Deborah Ann. b 67. Newc Univ BA 89. Qu Coll Birm BD 92. **d** 93 **p** 94. C Bloxwich *Lich* 93–97; TV Gt Grimsby St Mary and St Jas *Linc* 97–00; Chapl N Lincs and Goole Hosps NHS Trust 99–00; PtO *St Alb* 01–05; Asst Chapl Walsall Healthcare NHS Trust 05–08; TV Blakenall Heath *Lich* 08–10; Chapl Heart of England NHS Foundn Trust 10–12; Chapl Walsall Healthcare NHS Trust 12–14; C Pheasey *Lich* 12–15; P-in-c 14–18; *Linc* from 19. *c/o Crockford, Church House, 27 Great Smith Street, London SW1P 3AZ* E: deborahamurphy8@gmail.com

MURPHY, Jack. b 72. NOC 83. **d** 86 **p** 87. C Armley w New Wortley *Ripon* 86–90; C Hawksworth Wood 90–94; rtd 94; PtO *York* 96–20. *24 Dulverton Hall, Esplanade, Scarborough YO11 2AR*

MURPHY, Ms Julia Mary. b 58. Essex Univ BA 81 Lon Bible Coll BTh 00. Wycliffe Hall Ox MTh 07. **d** 07 **p** 08. C Thetford *Nor* 07–11; TV Forest Gate St Sav w W Ham St Matt *Chelmsf* 11–12; Chapl Essex Univ 12–19. *The Vicarage, Burwash Common, Etchingham TN19 7NA* T: (01435) 882172 M: 07779-266034 E: revjuliamurphy@gmail.com

MURPHY, Keith Anthony. b 72. St Jo Coll Nottm 10. **d** 12 **p** 13. C Ware Ch Ch *St Alb* 12–16; C Cheshunt 16–17; C Eggbuckland w Estover *Ex* from 17. *The Vicarage, 70 Inchkeith Road, Plymouth PL6 6EJ* M: 07980-745437 E: keithmurphymusic@gmail.com

MURPHY, Rosalyn Frances Thomas. b 55. Marquette Univ (USA) BA 85 Ustinov Coll Dur MTh 00 Union Th Sem Virginia MDiv 99 St Jo Coll Dur PhD 05. Cranmer Hall Dur 04. **d** 05 **p** 06. C Dur St Nic 05–08; P-in-c Blackpool St Thos *Blackb* 08–12; V 12–18; Prior Community of St Anselm *Cant* 18–20; P-in-c Longford *Cov* from 20. *Address temp unknown*

MURPHY, Shirley. **d** 18 **p** 19. C Narberth w Mounton w Robeston Wathen etc *St D* 18–20; C Narberth and Tenby LMA from 20. *16 Redstone Court, Narberth SA67 7EU* E: revshirleymurphy@gmail.com

MURPHY, Stephen Charles James. b 55. All SS Cen for Miss & Min 17. **d** 19 **p** 20. NSM Prestbury *Ches* from 19. *12-14 Silver Street, Bollington, Macclesfield SK10 5QL* M: 07976-728721

MURPHY, Wendy Susan. b 54. St Jo Coll Nottm 12. **d** 13 **p** 14. NSM Carlton-in-the-Willows *S'well* from 13. *The Rectory, Church Street, Carlton, Nottingham NG4 1BJ* M: 07905-868230 E: rev.wm2254@gmail.com

MURPHY, William Albert. b 43. MBE 98. Lon Univ BD 73 QUB MTh 78. **d** 73 **p** 74. C Lisburn Ch Ch *Conn* 73–79; Supt and Chapl Ulster Inst for the Deaf 79–98; Chapl HM Pris The Maze 82–00; Dioc Dir Ords *Conn* 92–13; Chapl Ch of Ireland Min to Deaf People 98–13; Can Belf Cathl 04–13; rtd 13. *2 Maghaberry Manor, Moira, Craigavon BT67 0JZ* T: (028) 9261 9140 E: murphy43@btinternet.com

MURPHY, Mrs Yvonne Letita. b 52. Brunel Univ BA 90 PGCE 91. SEITE 95. **d** 98 **p** 99. NSM Hampton St Mary *Lon* 98–01; NSM Staines St Mary and St Pet 01–04; Chapl Bp Wand Sch Sunbury-on-Thames 98–04; P-in-c Kennington *Cant* 04–09; TV High Wycombe *Ox* 09–12; rtd 12; PtO *Guildf* from 12. *41 Jersey Close, Chertsey KT16 9PA* T: (01932) 429288 E: ylm.bum@virgin.net

MURRAY, Alan. b 61. St Jo Coll Nottm BTh 92. **d** 92 **p** 93. C Wombwell *Sheff* 92–95; C Mortomley St Sav High Green 95–99; P-in-c Doncaster St Jas 99–01; V 01–13; V Normanton *Wakef* 13–14; *Leeds* from 14. *All Saints' Vicarage, 140 High Street, Normanton WF6 1NR* T: (01924) 893100 E: vicarofallsaints@gmail.com

MURRAY, Andrew James. b 72. Loughb Univ BEng 95 PhD 01. Trin Coll Bris 10. **d** 12 **p** 13. C Clifton Ch Ch w Em *Bris* 12–15; P-in-c Lawrence Weston and Avonmouth from 15. *The Vicarage, 335 Long Cross, Lawrence Weston, Bristol BS11 0NN* T: 0117-325 8722

MURRAY, Mrs Anne. b 53. MCSP 75. NOC 03. **d** 06 **p** 07. NSM Fairfield *Liv* 06–10; NSM Liv All SS 11–20; rtd 20. *11 Elstree Road, Liverpool L6 8NU* M: 07981-432475

MURRAY, Christopher James. b 49. Open Univ BA 78. St Jo Coll Nottm 79. **d** 81 **p** 82. C Heatherlands St Jo *Sarum* 81–84; C Hamworthy 84–90; R Passenham *Pet* 90–17; rtd 17; PtO *Ox* from 18. *7 The Holt, Buckingham MK18 7EF* T: (01280) 812430 E: chris.murray66@outlook.com

MURRAY, David. b 54. All SS Cen for Miss & Min 18. **d** 20 **p** 21. NSM Sale St Anne *Ches* from 20. *7 Denbury Drive, Altrincham WA14 4LX* M: 07985-032180 E: d3.murray@hotmail.co.uk

MURRAY, David McIlveen. b 36. ALCD 61. **d** 61 **p** 62. C Mortlake w E Sheen *S'wark* 61–64; C Lyncombe *B & W* 64–67; C Horsham *Chich* 67–73; V Devonport St Bart *Ex* 73–79; R Chalfont St Peter *Ox* 79–95; RD Amersham 86–89; R Lower Windrush 95–03; rtd 03; PtO *Glouc* from 03. *Collum End Farm, 88 Church Road, Leckhampton, Cheltenham GL53 0PD* T: (01242) 528008

MURRAY, Canon Elaine Mary Edel. b 58. TCD BTh 05 MICS 97. CITC 02. **d** 05 **p** 06. Bp's V and Lib Kilkenny Cathl *C, F & O* 05–11; C Kilkenny w Aghour and Kilmanagh 05–08; V 08–11; I Carrigaline Union *C, C & R* from 11; Can Cork Cathl from 19; Can Ross Cathl from 19. *The Rectory, Church Road, Carrigaline, Co Cork, Republic of Ireland* T: (00353) (21) 437 2224 M: 87-236 3100 E: emit@eircom.net

MURRAY, Elizabeth. b 57. **d** 10 **p** 11. NSM Eastwood and Brinsley w Underwood *S'well* 10–13; P-in-c Elston w Elston Chapelry from 13; P-in-c E Stoke w Syerston from 13; P-in-c Kilvington from 13; P-in-c Shelton from 13; P-in-c Sibthorpe from 13; P-in-c Staunton w Flawborough from 13; P-in-c Farndon w Thorpe, Hawton

and Cotham from 18. *The Rectory, Top Street, Elston, Newark NG23 5NP* T: (01636) 525417 E: reveimurray24@gmail.com

MURRAY, Elizabeth Ruth. **d** 03 **p** 04. C Antrim All SS *Conn* 03–06; I Woodschapel w Gracefield *Arm* from 06. *The Rectory, 140 Ballyronan Road, Magherafelt BT45 6HU* T: (028) 7941 8311 E: eruthmurray@gmail.com

MURRAY, Gordon John. b 33. St Cath Coll Cam BA 57 MA 61. Clifton Th Coll 57. **d** 59 **p** 60. C Heref St Jas 59–61; C Uphill *B & W* 62–65; C-in-c Reading St Mary Castle Street Prop Chpl *Ox* 65–68; Ed *English Churchman* 65–71; Prin Kensit Coll Finchley 68–75; Hd of RE Sandown High Sch 76–78; rtd 98. *18 Longcroft, Felixstowe IP11 9QH* T: (01394) 273372

MURRAY, Canon Heather. b 62. RGN 82. NEOC 04. **d** 07 **p** 08. NSM Burnopfield *Dur* 07–12; P-in-c Harelaw and Annfield Plain 12–18; AD Lanchester 14–18; P-in-c Belmont and Pittington 18–21; V from 21; AD Dur from 18; Hon Can Dur Cathl from 16. *Belmont Vicarage, Broomside Lane, Durham DH1 2QW* T: 0191-386 1545 E: heather.murray@durham.anglican.org

MURRAY, Preb Ian Hargraves. b 45. Man Univ BSc 71. St Jo Coll Nottm 79. **d** 81 **p** 82. C Erith St Paul *Roch* 81–84; C Willenhall H Trin *Lich* 84–87; TV 87–92; P-in-c Moxley 92–00; C Darlaston St Lawr 99–00; TR Glascote and Stonydelph 00–14; RD Tamworth 04–09; Preb Lich Cathl 11–14; rtd 14; PtO *S'well* from 15. *9 Wenlock Drive, Hucknall, Nottingham NG15 8HX* E: rockin.rev@ntlworld.com

MURRAY, John Grainger. b 45. CITC 67. **d** 70 **p** 71. C Carlow Union *C, F & O* 70–72; C Limerick City *L & K* 72–77; I Rathdowney w Castlefleming, Donaghmore etc *C, F & O* 77–14; Can Leighlin Cathl 83–88; Preb Ossory Cathl 83–88; Treas Ossory and Leighlin Cathls 88–89; Chan Ossory and Leighlin Cathls 89–90; Prec Ossory and Leighlin Cathls 90–92; Adn Ossory and Leighlin 92–14; Adn Cashel, Waterford and Lismore 94–14; rtd 14. *Vicarstown, Stradbally, Co Laois, Republic of Ireland* T: (00353) (57) 864 1686 M: 87-248 8241 E: venjgm@gmail.com

MURRAY, John Louis. b 47. Keble Coll Ox BA 67 MA 69. **d** 82 **p** 83. Asst Chapl Strasbourg *Eur* 82–05; P-in-c 05–09; PtO from 09. *Aumônerie Anglicane, 12 avenue de la Forêt Noire, 67000 Strasbourg, France* T: (0033) 3 88 36 12 25

MURRAY, Mrs Kim Margaret. b 58. **d** 07 **p** 09. OLM Camberley St Mich Yorktown *Guildf* 07–18; OLM Camberley St Martin Old Dean from 18. *9 Dorchester Court, 283 London Road, Camberley GU15 3JJ* T: (01276) 23354 E: k.murray208@btinternet.com

MURRAY, Mrs Margaret Janice. b 46. Carl Dioc Tr Course. **dss** 86 **d** 87 **p** 94. Walney Is *Carl* 86–87; Hon Par Dn 87–89; Par Dn Carl H Trin and St Barn 89–94; Chapl Cumberland Infirmary 90–94; C Harraby *Carl* 94–97; P-in-c 97–00; V 00–02; Chapl to the Deaf and Hard of Hearing 94–02; rtd 02; PtO *Carl* from 02. *6 Follyskye Cottages, Tindale Fell, Brampton CA8 2QB* T: (016977) 46400

MURRAY, Paul Ridsdale. b 55. BEd. St Steph Ho Ox 80. **d** 83 **p** 84. C Hartlepool St Oswald *Dur* 83–86; C S Shields All SS 86–88; V Sacriston and Kimblesworth 88–94; P-in-c Waterhouses 94–98; P-in-c Chopwell 98–20; rtd 20; PtO *Newc* from 99. *2 Finchale View, West Rainton, Houghton le Spring DH4 6SD* T: 0191-670 6094 M: 07803-906727 E: prmurray@msn.com

MURRAY, Philip. b 88. CCC Cam BA 10 MA 14 PhD 13. Westcott Ho Cam 15. **d** 18 **p** 19. C Stockton St Pet *Dur* from 18; C Elton from 18. *12 Kendal Road, Stockton-on-Tees TS18 4PU* M: 07825-331119 E: frphilipmurray@gmail.com

MURRAY, Rachel Eleanor. b 70. Univ of Wales (Swansea) BA 92. Westcott Ho Cam 16. **d** 18 **p** 19. C Winchcombe *Glouc* from 18. *22 Delavale Road, Winchcombe, Cheltenham GL54 5HN* E: revrachel@winchcombeparish.org.uk

MURRAY, Roy John. b 47. Open Univ BA 92 Wolv Poly CertEd 89 RGN 75 RMN 77. WMMTC 01. **d** 04 **p** 05. NSM Solihull *Birm* 04–08; C Torquay St Jo and Ellacombe *Ex* 08–11; P-in-c Torquay St Jo 11–13; rtd 13; NSM Solihull *Birm* 13–18; NSM Upminster *Chelmsf* from 18. *6 Gaynes Park Road, Upminster RM14 2HH* T: (01708) 225374 M: 07768-436363 E: roy.murray@upminsterparish.co.uk

MURRAY, Ruth. *See* MURRAY, Elizabeth Ruth

MURRAY, The Very Revd Sarah Elisabeth. b 70. Aber Univ BTh 12. TISEC 10. **d** 13 **p** 14. Dioc C *Mor* 13–16; Vice-Provost St Andr Cathl Inverness 16–17; Provost from 17. *15 Ardross Street, Inverness IV3 5NS* T: (01463) 233535 M: 07794-532052 E: revsarahmurray@gmail.com or provost@invernesscathedral.org

MURRAY, Mrs Sheila Elizabeth. b 53. Ripon Coll Cuddesdon 10. **d** 11 **p** 12. NSM Taunton St Mary *B & W* 11–14; NSM Taunton St Mary and St Jo 14–17; NSM Ripon Cathl Benefice *Leeds* 17–19; rtd 19; PtO *St E*

from 21. *24 Hornbeam Road, Saxmundham IP17 1FZ*
E: revsmurray@btinternet.com

MURRAY, Canon Stephen Michael. b 74. Windsor Univ Ontario BA 97. Trin Coll Toronto MDiv 03. **d** 03 **p** 04. C Dundas St Jas Canada 03–06; R Hamilton Resurr 06–11; Chapl Ghent *Eur* from 11; P-in-c Knokke 11–16; Can Brussels Cathl from 20. *Ekkergemstraat 16, 9000 Ghent, Belgium* T: (0032) (9) 336 4722 M: (0032) 49-745 1809 E: saintjohnsghent@gmail.com

MURRAY (née GOULD), Mrs Susan Judith. b 61. Poly of Wales BSc 83 Open Univ MA 95. St Jo Coll Nottm 90. **d** 91 **p** 94. Par Dn Stokesley *York* 91–94; CMS 94–95; Argentina 95–03; P-in-c Haddlesey w Hambleton and Birkin *York* 03–09; TV Crawley *Chich* 09–17; V Three Bridges 17–18; V Bisley, Chalford, France Lynch, and Oakridge etc *Glouc* from 18; AD Stroud from 19. *The Vicarage, Manor Street, Bisley, Stroud GL6 7BJ* T: (01452) 770897 E: vicar@bisleybenefice.org.uk

MURRAY, Thomas Christopher. b 87. St Luke's Coll Ex BSc 09. Trin Coll Bris BA 19. **d** 19 **p** 20. C Ox St Andr from 19. *St Andrew's Church, Linton Road, Oxford OX2 6UG* M: 07851-600778 E: tcm202@gmail.com

MURRAY, Canon William Robert Craufurd. b 44. St Chad's Coll Dur BA 66. **d** 68 **p** 69. C Workington St Mich *Carl* 68–71; C Harrogate St Wilfrid *Ripon* 71–74; P-in-c Sawley 74; V Winksley cum Grantley and Aldfield w Studley 74; R Fountains 75–81; V Hutt NZ 81–87; V Fendalton and Chapl Medbury Sch 87–00; V Merivale 00–09; Can Christchurch Cathl 91–09; rtd 09. *92 Tauhina Avenue, Lincoln 7608, New Zealand* T: (0064) (3) 325 2196 E: craufurd@xtra.co.nz

MURRAY-LESLIE, Adrian John Gervase. b 46. Lich Th Coll 67. **d** 69 **p** 70. C Sheff St Cuth 69–73; C Mosborough 73–75; C-in-c Mosborough CD 75–80; P-in-c Edale and Warden The Peak Cen 80–11; rtd 11. *Woodside House, New Road, Barlborough, Chesterfield S43 4HY* T: (01246) 819021 E: adrian@murray-leslie.org.uk

MURRAY-PETERS, Mrs Nancy Susan. b 48. WEMTC 09. **d** 11 **p** 12. NSM Worc St Barn w Ch Ch 11–14; NSM Peopleton and White Ladies Aston w Churchill etc 14–18; rtd 18. *Wee Wee Cottage, Worcester Road, Wyre Piddle, Pershore WR10 2HR* T: (01386) 553286 E: nmp.murraypeters@btinternet.com

MURRELL, Canon John Edmund. b 28. Westcott Ho Cam. **d** 66 **p** 67. C Ivychurch w Old Romney and Midley *Cant* 66–70; R Bardwell *St E* 70–75; PtO *Ely* 75–77; V Wenhaston w Thorington and Bramfield w Walpole *St E* 77–86; V Thorington w Wenhaston and Bramfield 86–92; P-in-c Walberswick w Blythburgh 86–92; V Thorington w Wenhaston, Bramfield etc 92–93; RD Halesworth 85–90; Hon Can St E Cathl 89–93; rtd 93; PtO *St E* 93–16. *Strickland Cottage, 12 Lorne Road, Southwold IP18 6EP* T: (01502) 722074

MURRILLS, Mrs Rosemary Jill. b 62. Cam Coll of Art & Tech BSc 84 Brunel Univ MSc 93. ERMC 09. **d** 12 **p** 13. NSM Hartford and Houghton w Wyton *Ely* 12–15; NSM Upper St Leonards St Jo *Chich* 15–17; rtd 17. *4 Hobart Court, 5 Ellenslea Road, St Leonards-on-Sea TN37 6HX* M: 07525-186205 E: rev.murrills@btinternet.com

MURRIN, Robert Staddon. b 42. Reading Univ BA 68 Open Univ MA 96. WMMTC 90. **d** 93 **p** 95. NSM Peterchurch w Vowchurch, Turnastone and Dorstone *Heref* 93–95; NSM Tupsley w Hampton Bishop 95–97; Chapl Kemp Hospice Kidderminster 97–05; PtO *Heref* 06–18. *Albion Cottage, Peterchurch, Hereford HR2 0RP* T: (01981) 550656 *or* 550467 F: 550432

✠**MURSELL, The Rt Revd Alfred Gordon.** b 49. BNC Ox BA 70 MA 73 BD 87 Birm Univ Hon DD 05 ARCM 74. Cuddesdon Coll 71. **d** 73 **p** 74 **c** 05. C Walton St Mary *Liv* 73–77; V E Dulwich St Jo *S'wark* 77–86; Tutor Sarum & Wells Th Coll 87–91; TR Stafford *Lich* 91–99; Prov Birm 99–02; Dean 02–05; Area Bp Stafford *Lich* 05–10; rtd 10; Can Th Leic Cathl from 10; LtO *Glas* from 10. *The Old Manse, Borgue, Kirkcudbright DG6 4SH* T: (01557) 870307 E: gordon.mursell@btinternet.com

MURTHEN, Mark Anthony. b 77. UEA BA 99 MA 00. Oak Hill Th Coll BA 14. **d** 14 **p** 15. C Deane *Man* 14–17; C Muswell Hill St Jas w St Matt *Lon* from 17. *St James Church, St James Lane, London N10 3DB* T: (020) 8883 6277 E: markmurthen@gmail.com

MUSINDI, Mrs Beatrice Nambuya Balibali. b 64. Birm Univ MA 94. Bp Tucker Coll Mukono BD 90. **d** 03 **p** 04. C Caerleon w Llanhennock *Mon* 03–07; C Malpas 07–08; PtO *Cant* 09–14; Chapl Dover Immigration Removal Cen 14; Chapl HM YOI Roch from 14. *HM Young Offender Institution, 1 Fort Road, Rochester ME1 3QS* T: (01634) 803100 M: 07989-469938 E: beatrice.musindi@hotmail.co.uk

MUSINDI, Philip. b 63. Bp Tucker Coll Mukono BD 91 Univ of Wales (Cardiff) MA 94. **d** 87 **p** 90. C and Sch Chapl Naigana Uganda 87–89; C Builth and Llanddewi'r Cwm w Llangynog etc *S & B* 92–94; C Newport St Teilo *Mon* 94–97; P-in-c Newport St Matt 97–04; V Newport St Andr 04–09; Min Thanet St Andr CD *Cant* 09–11; V Reading Street from 11; Visitors' Chapl Cant Cathl from 18; Jt AD Thanet from 21. *St Andrew's House, 29 Reading Street, Broadstairs CT10 3AZ* T: (01843) 579945 E: philip.musindi@hotmail.co.uk

MUSIWACHO, Taurayi Theresa. b 69. Seke Teachers' Coll Zimbabwe TDip 95. ERMC 13. **d** 16 **p** 17. C Royston *St Alb* 16–19; R Lt Berkhamsted and Bayford, Essendon etc from 19. *1 Little Berkhamsted Lane, Little Berkhamsted, Hertford SG13 8LU* E: revtmusi@gmail.com

✠**MUSK, The Rt Revd Bill Andrew.** b 49. Ox Univ BA 70 MA 75 Fuller Th Sem California ThM 80 UNISA D Litt et Phil 84. Trin Coll Bris. **d** 81 **p** 82 **c** 08. C All SS Cathl Cairo Egypt 81–86; CMS 88–89; NSM Belmont *S'wark* 88–89; NSM Sutton Ch 88–89; TV Maghull *Liv* 89–97; V Tulse Hill H Trin and St Matthias *S'wark* 97–08; Hon Can S'wark Cathl 07–08; Area Bp N Africa and R Tunis St Geo 08–15; rtd 15; PtO *Chich* from 15. *45 Bolney Avenue, Peacehaven BN10 8HG* T: (01273) 969171 E: billamusk@gmail.com

MUSKER, Mrs Hilary. b 56. St Mellitus Coll 15. **d** 15 **p** 16. NSM Barkingside St Laur *Chelmsf* 15–18; NSM Chingford SS Pet and Paul from 18. *13 Deacon Way, Woodford Bridge IG8 8DF* E: hilary.musker@parishofchingford.org.uk

MUSKETT, David John. b 63. Southn Univ BA 85. Ripon Coll Cuddesdon 87. **d** 90 **p** 91. C Kempston Transfiguration *St Alb* 90–93; C Ampthill w Millbrook and Steppingley 93–96; V Milford *Guildf* 96–06; C Stoughton 06–10.

MUSSER, Ms Christine. b 55. Ex Univ 96. **d** 00 **p** 01. C Torpoint *Truro* 00–03; P-in-c Boscastle w Davidstow 03–07; P-in-c Pirbright *Guildf* 07–17; V 17–19; rtd 19. *Address temp unknown* E: revdchrismusser@aol.com

MUSSON, David John. b 46. Open Univ BA 86 Univ of Wales (Lamp) MPhil 96 Univ of Wales (Ban) PhD 00. Linc Th Coll 70. **d** 73 **p** 74. C New Sleaford *Linc* 73–76; C Morton 76–80; P-in-c Thurlby 80–86; R Quarrington w Old Sleaford 86–99; P-in-c Silk Willoughby 86–87; R 87–99; PtO *Chich* from 01. *Flat 9, Regency Court 4-5, South Cliff, Eastbourne BN20 7AE* T: (01323) 723345

MUSSON, Helen Elizabeth. b 59. UMIST BSc 80 Man Metrop Univ PGCE 94. St Aug Coll Cant 19. **d** 21. C Orpington Ch Ch *Roch* from 21. *Cudham and Downe Vicarage, The Boundary, Hangrove Hill, Downe, Orpington BR6 7LQ* T: (01959) 540012 E: helen.e.musson@gmail.com

MUSSON, Mrs Joanne Chatterley. b 60. Qu Coll Birm 07. **d** 09 **p** 10. C Redditch Ch the K *Worc* 09–13; P-in-c Claines St Jo from 13; C Worc City 13–14; P-in-c Worc St Geo w St Mary Magd from 14. *The Vicarage, Claines Lane, Worcester WR3 7RN* M: 07590-514115

MUSSON, John Keith. b 39. Nottm Univ BSc 61 PhD 66 CEng MIMechE. St As Minl Tr Course 85. **d** 88 **p** 89. Assoc Prin NE Wales Inst of HE 80–93; NSM Holywell *St As* 88–93; C 93–95; R Caerwys and Bodfari 95–02; PtO *Lich* 02–21; *St As* from 09. *4 Hayes View, Oswestry SY11 1TP* T: (01691) 656212 E: musson908@btinternet.com

MUSSON, William John. b 58. UMIST BSc 80 Open Univ MA 02. St Jo Coll Nottm 88. **d** 91 **p** 92. C Nantwich *Ches* 91–94; C Finchley Ch Ch *Lon* 94–97; V Lynchmere and Camelsdale *Chich* 97–10; V Cudham and Downe *Roch* from 10; AD Orpington from 18. *Cudham and Downe Vicarage, The Boundary, Hangrove Hill, Downe, Orpington BR6 7LQ* T: (01959) 540012 E: stpandp@googlemail.com

MUST, Mrs Shirley Ann. b 35. St Mich Ho Ox 61. dss 82 **d** 87 **p** 94. Highbury New Park St Aug *Lon* 82–84; Walthamstow St Jo *Chelmsf* 84–93; Hon Par Dn 87–93; PtO *Cant* 93–94; Hon C Herne Bay Ch Ch 94–05; PtO 05–12. *24 Nightingale Avenue, Whitstable CT5 4TR* T/F: (01227) 772160

MUSTARD, Canon James Edmond Alexander. b 74. Ex Univ BA 95 Clare Coll Cam BA 04 MA 08 K Coll Lon MA 13. Westcott Ho Cam 02 Berkeley Div Sch 04. **d** 05 **p** 06. C Nor St Pet Mancroft w St Jo Maddermarket 05–08; C Pimlico St Pet w Westmr Ch Ch *Lon* 08–12; R E Barnet *St Alb* 12–18; AD Barnet 16–18; Can Res and Prec Ex Cathl from 18. *6 Cathedral Close, Exeter EX1 1EZ* M: 07763-973647 E: james.mustard@exeter-cathedral.org.uk

MUSTOE, Canon Alan Andrew. b 52. Man Univ BA 74. Qu Coll Birm. **d** 78 **p** 79. C Chatham St Wm *Roch* 78–82; R Burham and Wouldham 82–88; Dioc Info Officer 83–88; V Strood St Nic w St Mary 88–99; V Orpington All SS 99–10; AD Orpington 05–10; R Chislehurst St Nic 10–20; Hon Can Roch Cathl 16–20; rtd 20; PtO *Ox* from 20. *Ghillies Retreat, 12*

Walnut Close, Great Missenden HP16 9AL M: 07725-909733
E: andrewalan7@icloud.com

MUTCH, Canon Sylvia Edna. b 36. St Mich Ho Ox 57. **dss 79**
d 87 **p** 94. Clifton *York* 79–95; Par Dn 87–94; C 94–95; Chapl
Clifton Hosp York 81–94; R Elvington w Sutton on Derwent
and E Cottingwith *York* 95–01; Can and Preb York Minster
98–01; rtd 01; PtO *York* 01–18. *18 Waite Close, Pocklington,*
York YO42 2YU T: (01759) 307894

MUTEMWAKWENDA, Jones Chibuye. b 63. Trin Coll Bris
BA 05. Mindolo Th Coll Zambia 89. **d** 92 **p** 93. C Lusaka
Cathl Zambia 93–95; Chapl Univ Teaching Hosp Lusaka
93–94; P-in-c Choma 95–98; Adn Lusaka 96–98; V Gen
99–02; PtO *B & W* 03–06; *Bris* 08–14; P-in-c Easton All
Hallows 15–19; V from 19. *All Hallows Church, All Hallows*
Road, Easton, Bristol BS5 0HH T: 0117-909 9545 *or* 955 1804
E: jonesgladys99@hotmail.com

MUTETE, Lameck. b 61. Bp Gaul Th Coll Harare 94. **d** 96
p 97. C Harare St Luke Zimbabwe 96–97; Asst P Harare
Cathl 97–01; P-in-c 01; Adn Harare E 01; Can Harare 01–04;
PtO *Bradf* 04; P-in-c Tattenhall and Handley *Ches* 04–10; R
10–11; R Tattenhall w Burwardsley and Handley from 11;
PtO *Birm* from 14. *The Rectory, Chester Road, Gatesheath,*
Tattenhall, Chester CH3 9AH T: (01829) 770245 M: 07940-
512748 E: lameckmutete@yahoo.co.uk

MUTHALALY, Varghese Malayil Lukose (Saju). b 79. S Asia
Bible Coll Bangalore BTh 01. Wycliffe Hall Ox BTh 08. **d** 08
p 09. C Lancaster St Thos *Blackb* 08–11; C Kendal St Thos and
Crook *Carl* 11–15; P-in-c Gillingham St Mark *Roch* 15–19; V
from 19. *St Mark's Vicarage, 173 Canterbury Street, Gillingham*
ME7 5TU T: 01634 570489 E: sajudoj@yahoo.com

MUTHUVELOE, Samuel Rajakumar. b 50. Colombo Univ MB,
BS 76 MRCGP 91 DRCOG 84. Ripon Coll Cuddesdon 13.
d 16 **p** 17. OLM Bletchley Ox 16–19; OLM Stantonbury and
Willen from 19; PtO *St Alb* from 17. *21 Lower Stonehayes,*
Great Linford, Milton Keynes MK14 5ES T: (01908)
668829 M: 07854-745669 E: sam.muthuveloe@gmail.com

MUTIKANI, Mrs Martha Tsungai Zivito. b 66. SEITE 12.
d 15 **p** 16. NSM Reigate St Luke S'wark 15–17; NSM S
Beddington and Roundshaw 17–19; NSM Horley 19–21;
NSM Isfield *Chich* from 21; NSM Uckfield from 21; NSM
Lt Horsted from 21; PtO *Win* from 19. *The Parsonage,*
Station Road, Isfield, Uckfield TN22 5EY M: 07901-568549
E: mtzmutikani20@hotmail.com

MUTTER, Richard Douglas. b 73. **d** 14 **p** 15. C Cleobury
Mortimer w Hopton Wafers etc *Heref* 14–17; R Arden Valley
Cov from 17. *The Vicarage, Church Road, Snitterfield, Stratford-*
upon-Avon CV37 0LN E: richard_mutter@hotmail.com

MUTUKU, Norbert. *See* CHUMU MUTUKU, Norbert

MUXLOW, Judy Ann. b 47. Univ of Wales (Cardiff) BSc 69
St Luke's Coll Ex CertEd 73. SEITE. **d** 00 **p** 01. Chapl Ch
Ch High Sch Ashford 00–03; Bp's Officer for NSM
Cant 03–07; NSM Biddenden and Smarden 00–06; NSM
Appledore w Brookland, Fairfield, Brenzett etc 06–08;
NSM Wittersham w Stone and Ebony 06–08; NSM
Woodchurch 06–08; PtO *Roch* 00–12; *Cant* 09–19. *29 The*
Meadows, Biddenden, Ashford TN27 8AW T: (01580) 291016
E: judy@mucat.eclipse.co.uk

✠**MWAMBA, The Rt Revd Musonda Trevor Selwyn.** b 58.
LLB 81 Ox Univ BA 83 MA 88 MPhil 98. St Steph Ho
Ox 81. **d** 84 **p** 85 **c** 05. C Notting Hill All SS w St Columb
Lon 84; R Luanshya and Voc Dir Cen Zambia 85–86; Prov
Sec Cen Africa and Dioc Sec Botswana 87–96; Asst Chapl
Keble Coll Ox 96–98; NSM Wolvercote w Summertown *Ox*
97–99; NSM Botswana 99–02; V Gen 02–05; Bp Botswana
05–13; TR Barking *Chelmsf* 13–16; TR Barking St Marg
17–19; Hon Asst Bp Chelmsf from 13. *Address temp unknown*
E: musondamwamba@gmail.com

MWANDIA, Nicholas Kyalo. b 64. Anglia Ruskin Univ
BA 09 K Coll Lon MA 10 MPhil 18. ERMC 16. **d** 14 **p** 16.
PtO *St Alb* 17; C Luton St Mary 17–21; C Luton St Matt
High Town 17–21; C Luton St Mary and St Matt from
21; P-in-c Woodside from 21. *St Matthew's Vicarage,*
85 Wenlock Street, Luton LU2 0NN T: (01582) 253537
E: nickmwandia@stmarysluton.org

MYATT, Francis Eric. b 60. St Jo Coll Nottm 89. **d** 92 **p** 93. C
W Derby St Luke *Liv* 92–95; TV Sutton 95–98; V Liv St Chris
Norris Green 98–01; CF 01–13; C Walton St Jo *Liv* 13–15; V
from 15. *66 Roseworth Avenue, Liverpool L9 8HF*

MYCOCK, Malcolm George Robert. b 71. Wycliffe
Hall Ox 15. **d** 17 **p** 18. C Bucknall *Lich* from 17.
St John's Parsonage, 28 Greasley Road, Stoke-on-Trent
ST2 8JE   T: (01782)   915813   M: 07908-200782
E: malcolm1cor13.13@gmail.com

MYERS, Alison Margaret. b 66. Bris Univ BSc 88. SEITE 04.
d 07 **p** 08. NSM Cambourne *Ely* 07–10; TV Lordsbridge
10–17; TR 17–21; Hon Can Ely Cathl 19–21; Warden Launde
Abbey *Leic* from 21; P-in-c Loddington from 21. *The Warden's*
House, Launde Road, Launde, Leicester LE7 9XB T: (01572)
717254 M: 07884-370933 E: warden@launde.org.uk

MYERS, Duncan Frank. b 57. Warwick Univ BSc. St Jo Coll
Nottm 81. **d** 84 **p** 85. C Upton cum Chalvey *Ox* 84–86; C
Farnborough *Guildf* 86–90; Chapl Nottm Poly S'well 90–92;
Chapl Nottm Trent Univ 92–95; Sen Past Adv 95–02; Hon
Min Can Dur Cathl 04–08; Chapl Hatf Coll Dur 06–08;
Chapl Salford Univ *Man* 08–12; Chapl Lon S Bank Univ
S'wark 12–14; Nat Adv for HE Abps' Coun 14–15; Hon Min
Can S'wark Cathl from 13; Chapl Surrey Univ *Guildf* from
20; PV Guildf Cathl from 20. *6 Cathedral Close, Guildford*
GU2 7TL

MYERS, Canon Gillian Mary. b 57. Warwick Univ BSc 78
Nottm Univ MA 96. St Jo Coll Nottm 83. **d** 95 **p** 97. NSM
Nottingham St Jude S'well 95–97; NSM Gedling 97–00;
P-in-c Nottingham All SS 00–02; Succ, Sacr and Min Can
Dur Cathl 02–08; Can Res Man Cathl 08–12; Can Res
and Prec S'wark Cathl 12–20; rtd 20; PtO S'wark from
20; *Guildf* from 20. *6 Cathedral Close, Guildford GU2 7TL*
E: gilly@myers.uk.net

MYERS, Paul Henry. b 49. ALA 72. Qu Coll Birm 74. **d** 77 **p** 78.
C Baildon *Bradf* 77–80; C W Bromwich All SS *Lich* 80–83;
Chapl RAF 83–86; V Milton *Lich* 87–92; C Baswich 96–99;
C Hixon w Stowe-by-Chartley 99–02; TV Mid Trent 02–05;
TR Blakenall Heath 05–14; rtd 14. *110 Buxton Road, Leek*
ST13 6EJ E: rev.paulmyers@btinternet.com

MYERS, Peter Daniel. b 83. Man Univ BA 04 Glos Univ
MA 14 Cam Univ PhD 20. Oak Hill Th Coll MTh 13.
d 13 **p** 14. NSM Cambridge St Andr Less *Ely* 13–20;
Lect Ethiopian Grad Sch of Th Addis Ababa Ethiopia
from 20. *Address temp unknown* M: 07930-222217
E: peterdanielmyers@gmail.com

MYERS, Robert William John. b 57. Aus Nat Univ BSc 80
Newc Univ Aus DipEd 82. Trin Coll Bris 93. **d** 95 **p** 96. C
Addiscombe St Mary Magd w St Martin S'wark 95–98; C
Surbiton St Matt 98–03; P-in-c Blayney Australia 04–10;
I Bellarine from 10. *PO Box 365, Drysdale VIC 3222,*
Australia   T: (0061)   (3)   5251   2571   M: 48-857   4855
E: rwj127@hotmail.com

MYERS, Sally Ann. b 65. Leic Univ BA 86 Nottm Univ MA 06
Cam Univ PhD 14 De Montfort Univ PGCE 07. EMMTC 02.
d 06 **p** 07. C Grantham St Wulfram *Linc* 06–08; Vice-Prin Dioc
Min Tr Course 08–09; Dir of Studies EMMTC 09–14; Prin Linc
Sch of Th 14–21; PtO *Ely* 20–21; Dir Focal Min *Sheff* from 21.
The Vicarage, Christchurch Road, Wath-upon-Dearne, Rotherham
S63 6NW   M: 07708-343241 E: sally.myers@cantab.net *or*
sally.myers@sheffield.anglican.org

MYLES (née LUCAS), Mrs Julia Mary. b 63. Westhill Coll
Birm BEd 85 Birm Univ MA 92. Lindisfarne Regional
Tr Partnership 10. **d** 13 **p** 14. C Alnwick *Newc* 13–17;
P-in-c Arle Valley *Win* 17–20; Chapl Earl Mountbatten
Hospice from 20. *Earl Mountbatten Hospice, Halberry Lane,*
Newport PO30 2ER   T: (01983) 533331 M: 07716-771164
E: juliamyles@btinternet.com

MYLNE, Mrs Christine. b 44. Open Univ BA 76 Univ of Wales
(Lamp) MA 03. St Alb Minl Tr Scheme 89 NEOC 04. **d** 04
p 05. NSM Norham and Duddo *Newc* 04–06; NSM Cornhill
w Carham 04–06; NSM Branxton 04–06; P-in-c Challoch
Glas 06–11; rtd 11; P-in-c Glenurquhart *Mor* 11–17; LtO
from 18. *2 Wester Moniack Cottages, Kirkhill, Inverness*
IV5 7PQ   T: (01463) 831668 E: christinemylne@gmail.com
or christine.mylne@btinternet.com

MYNORS, Canon James Baskerville. b 49. Peterho Cam BA 70
MA 74. Ridley Hall Cam 70 St Jo Coll Nottm 77. **d** 78 **p** 80.
Hon C Leic H Apostles 78–79; C Virginia Water *Guildf* 79–83;
C Patcham *Chich* 83–88; P-in-c Fowlmere and Thriplow *Ely*
88–01; Sen Tutor EAMTC 88–90; Vice-Prin 90–97; P-in-c Gt
w Lt Abington 01–07; P-in-c Hildersham 01–07; Dioc Rural
Miss Officer 04–07; R Aldwincle, Clopton, Pilton, Stoke
Doyle etc *Pet* 07–17; Can Pet Cathl 13–17; rtd 17; PtO *Ox*
17–19; Hon C Cherbury w Gainfield from 19. *4 Malthouse*
Paddock, Buckland, Faringdon SN7 8RH M: 07546-279939
E: jim@mynors.me.uk

MYRES, Peter John Lukis. b 67. Trin Coll Bris 16. **d** 18
p 19. C Malvern Chase *Worc* from 18. *17 Whitborn Close,*
Malvern WR14 2SP E: peter.myres1@btinternet.com *or*
curate@chaseteam.org

N

NADARAJAH (née GOODDEN), Mrs Stephanie Anne. b 81. Fitzw Coll Cam MA 04. Ripon Coll Cuddesdon MTh 10. **d** 10 **p** 11. C Caterham *S'wark* 10–15; V Worcester Park Ch Ch w St Phil 15–21; C Cheam from 21. *9 Avon Close, Worcester Park KT4 7AQ* E: stephnadarajah@gmail.com

NADEN, Anthony Joshua. b 38. Jes Coll Ox BA 62 MA 64 SOAS Lon PhD 73. Wycliffe Hall Ox 60. **d** 62 **p** 63. C Rowner *Portsm* 62–66; C Fisherton Anger *Sarum* 69–72; Ghana 72–10; PtO *Ox* from 10. *Lost Marbles, 31 Reading Road, Pangbourne, Reading RG8 7HY* T: 0118-984 2368 E: lostmarbles31@gmail.com

NADIN, Dennis Lloyd. b 37. St D Coll Lamp BA 60 Man Univ MEd 81. Ridley Hall Cam 60. **d** 64 **p** 65. C Childwall All SS *Liv* 64–67; P-in-c Seacroft *Ripon* 67–69; Project Officer Grubb Inst 69–70; Lect CA Tr Coll Blackheath 70–72; Community Educn Essex Co Coun 73–80; Public Preacher *Chelmsf* from 73; PtO *St Alb* 01–03. *The Hermitage, 201 Willowfield, Harlow CM18 6RZ* T: (01279) 325904 E: nadennadinsociety@yahoo.co.uk

NAGEL, Canon Lawson Chase Joseph. b 49. Univ of Michigan BA 71 K Coll Lon PhD 82 ARHistS 75. Sarum & Wells Th Coll 81. **d** 83 **p** 84. C Chiswick St Nic w St Mary *Lon* 83–86; C Horsham *Chich* 86; TV 86–91; V Aldwick 91–19; rtd 19; Sec Gen Confraternity of the Blessed Sacrament 85–10; Hon Can Popondota from 05; PtO *Eur* from 07; *Chich* from 19. *22 Bishopsgate Walk, Chichester PO19 6FG* T: (01243) 537831 E: fatherlawson@gmail.com

NAGEL, Lucy Mary. *See* WEBB, Lucy Mary

NAHABEDIAN, Canon Harold George. b 39. Toronto Univ BA 63 MA 66. Trin Coll Toronto STB 70 Armenian Orthodox Sem Jerusalem 70. **d** 73 **p** 74. C Vancouver St Jas Canada 73–76; Chapl Trin Coll Toronto 76–81; V Toronto St Thos 81–83; P-in-c Toronto St Mary Magd 83–88; R 88–09; Hon Can Toronto from 93; rtd 09; P-in-c Strasbourg *Eur* 10–13; Hon C Toronto St Martin-in-the-Fields Canada from 14. *33 Amroth Avenue, Toronto ON M4C 4H3, Canada* E: hj.nahabedian@gmail.com

NAIRN, Canon Stuart Robert. b 51. K Coll Lon BD 75 AKC 75 Univ of Wales (Lamp) MTh 04 FRSA 01. St Aug Coll Cant 75. **d** 76 **p** 77. C E Dereham *Nor* 76–80; TV Hempnall 80–88; V Narborough w Narford 88–99; R Pentney St Mary Magd w W Bilney 88–99; R Narborough w Narford and Pentney 99–10; P-in-c Castleacre, Newton, Westacre and Southacre 97–10; R Nar Valley from 11; RD Lynn 91–99; RD Breckland 06–17; Hon Can Nor Cathl from 03. *The Rectory, Main Road, Narborough, King's Lynn PE32 1TE* T: (01760) 338552 or 338562 E: nairn.nvgrectory@btinternet.com

NAIRN-BRIGGS, The Very Revd George Peter. b 45. AKC 69. St Aug Coll Cant 69. **d** 70 **p** 71. C Catford St Laur *S'wark* 70–73; C Raynes Park St Sav 73–75; V Salfords 75–81; V St Helier 81–87; Dioc Soc Resp Adv *Wakef* 87–97; Can Res Wakef Cathl 92–97; Provost Wakef 97–00; Dean Wakef 00–07; rtd 07; PtO *Wakef* 09–14; *Leeds* from 14. *Abbey House, 2 St James Court, Park Avenue, Wakefield WF2 8DN* T: (01924) 291029 M: 07770-636840 E: nairnbriggs@btinternet.com

NAISH, Miss Annie Claire. b 65. St Jo Coll Dur BA 04 MA 08. Cranmer Hall Dur. **d** 05 **p** 06. C Gorleston St Andr *Nor* 05–09; Dioc Ecum Miss Enabler *B & W* 09–11; Missr Lee Abbey Movement 11–16; Bp's Enabler of Miss *Edin* from 16. *21A Grosvenor Crescent, Edinburgh EH12 5EL* T: 0131-538 7033 E: mission@dioceseofedinburgh.org

NAISH, Mrs Joanna Mary. b 60. Bris Univ BA 81 Southn Univ MA 92 Sheff Univ PGCE 82. STETS 06. **d** 09 **p** 10. NSM Woodford Valley w Archers Gate *Sarum* 09–17; NSM Amesbury 13–17; NSM Nadder Valley from 17. *Coombe Warren, Hindon Lane, Tisbury, Salisbury SP3 6QQ* T: (01747) 871820 E: revdjoannanaish@gmail.com

NAISH, Canon Timothy James Neville. b 57. St Jo Coll Ox BA 80 MA 88 Bris Univ PhD 05. WMMTC 86. **d** 87 **p** 88. CMS 81–00; C Cov H Trin 87; Dir Th Formation Dio Shaba Zaïre 88–91; Research Fell, Tutor, and Lect Qu Coll Birm 92–93; Tutor and Lect Bp Tucker Th Coll Uganda 93–00; R Hanborough and Freeland *Ox* 00–06; Dir Studies Ox Min Course 06–09; Dean 09–18; Lect Ripon Coll Cuddesdon 06–18; Asst Chapl Campsfield Ho Immigration Removal Cen 07–15; Can Res and Lib Cant Cathl from 18. *19 The Precincts, Canterbury CT1 2EP* T: (01227) 762862 E: tim.naish@canterbury-cathedral.org

NALL, Sheila Ann. b 48. Univ of Wales (Ban) BA 69. WMMTC 00. **d** 03 **p** 04. NSM Worc St Wulstan 03–07; Chapl

HM Pris Hewell 07–09; PtO *Worc* from 15. *Rose Cottage, Greenhill Lane, Hallow, Worcester WR2 6LG* T: (01905) 864117 E: rev.sheila.nall@gmail.com

NAM, Mark Yan Ying Sum. b 81. Glam Univ LLB 05. Trin Coll Bris MA 20. **d** 20 **p** 21. C Longwell Green *Bris* from 20; C Oldland from 20. *85 Bath Road, Longwell Green, Bristol BS30 9DF* M: 07925-174476 E: rev.marknam@icloud.com

NANCARROW, Mrs Rachel Mary. b 38. Cam Inst of Educn TCert 59. EAMTC 87. **d** 90 **p** 94. NSM Girton *Ely* 90–95; P-in-c Foxton 95–01; P-in-c Shepreth 98–01; C Fulbourn and Gt and Lt Wilbraham 01–03; rtd 03; PtO *Pet* from 04. *Thimble Cottage, 11 Geeston, Ketton, Stamford PE9 3RH* T: (01780) 729382

NANKIVELL, Christopher Robert Trevelyan. b 33. Jes Coll Ox BA 55 MA 63 Birm Univ MSocSc 79. Linc Th Coll 56. **d** 58 **p** 59. C Bloxwich *Lich* 58–60; C Stafford St Mary 60–64; P-in-c Malins Lee 64–72; Soc Welfare Sector Min to Milton Keynes Chr Coun 73–76; Tutor Qu Coll Birm 76–81; rtd 96. *77 Pereira Road, Birmingham B17 9JA* T: 0121-427 1197

NAPIER, Graeme Stewart Patrick Columbanus. b 66. Magd Coll Ox BA MA MPhil LRSM. St Steph Ho Ox. **d** 95 **p** 96. C Inverness St Andr *Mor* 95–98; Asst P St Laurence Ch Ch Australia 98–02; Min Can and Succ Westmr Abbey 02–10; Prec St Geo Cathl Perth Australia 10–16; PtO *Ox* 16–18; R New York St Jo in the Village USA from 18. *St John's in the Village, 224 Waverly Place, New York, NY 10014-2405, USA* T: (001) (212) 243 6192 M: (001) (972) 822 0099 E: rector@stjvny.org

NAPIER, Jennifer Beryl. *See* BLACK, Jennifer Beryl

NASCIMENTO DE JESUS COOK, Mrs Anesia. b 62. Mogidas Cruces Univ BA 86 York St Jo Univ MA 12. Porto Allegre Th Sem BTh 91. **d** 91 **p** 93. Brazil 91–94; LtO *St Alb* 96–97; C Dinnington *Sheff* 97–99; P-in-c Shiregreen St Jas and St Chris 99–07; P-in-c Shiregreen St Hilda 05–07; V Shiregreen 07–08; C Rotherham 08–15; V Sheff St Pet and St Oswald from 15. *St Peter's Vicarage, 17 Ashland Road, Sheffield S7 1RH* T: 0114-250 9716 M: 07952-833858 E: anjesus@postmaster.co.uk *or* anesia.cook@sheffield.anglican.org

NASH, David. b 25. K Coll Lon BD 51 AKC 51. **d** 52 **p** 53. C Buckhurst Hill *Chelmsf* 52–58; Min St Cedd CD Westcliff 58–66; R Rivenhall *Chelmsf* 66–83; P-in-c Boscastle w Davidstow *Truro* 83–85; TR 85–90; rtd 90; PtO *Truro* 90–14. *9 Boscundle Avenue, Falmouth TR11 5BU* E: revdavid@btinternet.com

NASH, Preb David John. b 41. Pemb Coll Ox BA 64 MA 70. Wells Th Coll 65. **d** 67 **p** 68. C Preston Ascension *Lon* 67–70; TV Hackney 70–75; TV Clifton *S'well* 76–82; V Winchmore Hill St Paul *Lon* 82–98; AD Enfield 87–91; R Monken Hadley 98–08; AD Cen Barnet 00–04; Preb St Paul's Cathl 96–08; rtd 08; PtO *Lon* from 08; *St Alb* from 10. *36 Birkbeck Road, Enfield EN2 0DX* T: (020) 8367 6873 E: prebdjnash@yahoo.co.uk

NASH (formerly HORSFALL), Mrs Deborah. b 66. Sheff Univ BA 14. Yorks Min Course 11. **d** 14 **p** 15. C S Ossett *Leeds* 14–18; R Thornhill and Whitley Lower from 18. *51 Frank Lane, Dewsbury WF12 0JW* M: 07834-788618 E: revdhorsfall@gmail.com

NASH, Mrs Ingrid. b 36. SRN 57 RNT 80 BEd 78. S'wark Ord Course 91. **d** 94 **p** 95. NSM Eltham Park St Luke *S'wark* 94–06; PtO *Roch* 97–17; *S'wark* from 06. *13 Crookston Road, London SE9 1YH* T: (020) 8850 0750

NASH, Canon James Alexander. b 56. St Jo Coll Nottm BA 94. **d** 97 **p** 98. C Trunch *Nor* 97–01; R Stratton St Mary w Stratton St Michael etc 01–10; R The Ch in the Woottons from 10; RD Lynn from 13; Hon Can Nor Cathl from 15. *The Rectory, 47 Castle Rising Road, South Wootton, King's Lynn PE30 3JA* T: (01553) 671381 E: jamesnash8@talktalk.net

NASH, James David Gifford. b 76. New Coll Ox MEng 98. Wycliffe Hall Ox BTh 03. **d** 03 **p** 04. C Plymouth St Andr and Stonehouse *Ex* 03–07; Hon C Preston All SS *Blackb* 07–11; C W Preston 11–16; V Ashton-on-Ribble St Andr from 17. *The Vicarage, 240 Tulketh Road, Ashton-on-Ribble, Preston PR2 1ES* T: (01772) 726848 M: 07889-424907 E: jdgnash@gmail.com

NASH, Mrs Jane. b 58. ERMC 05. **d** 08 **p** 09. C Kempston All SS and Biddenham *St Alb* 08–11; V Chadsmoor *Lich* 11–17; rtd 17; PtO *Ox* from 18. *8 Weston Court, Weston Road, Aston Clinton, Aylesbury HP22 5YT*

NASH, Paul. b 59. Liv Univ MA 03 Glos Univ MA 14. WMMTC 94. **d** 97 **p** 98. C Aston SS Pet and Paul *Birm* 97–02; Asst Chapl Birm Children's Hosp NHS Trust 02–04;

Sen Chapl Birm Children's Hosp NHS Foundn Trust 05–18; Chapl and Spiritual Care Team Ldr Birm Women's NHS Foundn Trust from 18; Tutor St Jo Coll Nottm from 02. *13 Jaffray Road, Birmingham B24 8AZ* T: 0121-384 6034 *or* 333 8526 F: 333 8527 E: paulandsal@msn.com

NASH, Paul. *See* NASH, William Paul

NASH, Penelope Jane. b 71. Trin Coll Bris 04. **d** 06 **p** 07. C Downend *Bris* 06–09; TV Gt Berkhamsted, Gt and Lt Gaddesden etc *St Alb* 09–18; Chapl Wycombe Abbey Sch from 18. *Wycombe Abbey School, Abbey Way, High Wycombe HP11 1PE* T: (01494) 520381 E: nashp@wycombeabbey.com

NASH, Robin Louis. b 51. Open Univ BA 87. Aston Tr Scheme 80 Chich Th Coll 82. **d** 84 **p** 85. C Lymington *Win* 84–86; C Andover w Foxcott 86–90; R Kegworth *Leic* 90–01; P-in-c Bournemouth St Alb *Win* 01–10; V 10–14; V Bournemouth St Luke 10–14; rtd 14; PtO *Win* from 14. *6 Shreen Way, Gillingham SP8 4EL* T: (01747) 823183 E: my_quarters@yahoo.co.uk

NASH, Sally Ann. b 57. Sussex Univ BA 78 Sheff Univ DMinTh 03 Ox Brookes Univ MA 10 Birmingham Univ PhD 16 PGCE 79. Qu Coll Birm 10. **d** 12 **p** 13. Dir Midl Inst for Children, Youth and Miss St Jo Coll Nottm from 99; Team Ldr from 18; NSM Hodge Hill *Birm* from 12. *Wellman, 13 Jaffray Road, Erdington, Birmingham B24 8AZ* T: 0121-384 6034 *or* 0115-968 3222 M: 07824-542104 E: revsally12@gmail.com

NASH, Thomas James. b 82. SS Hild & Bede Coll Dur BA 03 MA 04. Wycliffe Hall Ox 07. **d** 09 **p** 10. C St Helen Bishopsgate w St Andr Undershaft etc *Lon* 09–14; C Sevenoaks St Nic *Roch* 14–20; V Tunbridge Wells St Jo from 20. *St John's Vicarage, 1 Amherst Road, Tunbridge Wells TN4 9LG* E: t.nash@stjohnstw.org

NASH, William Paul. b 48. St Mich Coll Llan 86. **d** 87 **p** 88. C Pembroke Dock *St D* 87–89; P-in-c Llawhaden w Bletherston and Llanycefn 89–90; V 90–92; P-in-c E Brixton St Jude *S'wark* 92–96; V 96–99; V Cwmaman *St D* 99–04; R Pendine w Llanmiloe and Eglwys Gymyn w Marros 04–11; TR Monkton 11–17; rtd 17. *29 Bush Street, Pembroke Dock SA72 6XD* E: rev.paulnash@gmail.com

NASH-WILLIAMS, Mark Christian Victor. b 64. Trin Hall Cam BA 86 MA 90 PGCE 87. Qu Coll Birm BD 01. **d** 02 **p** 03. C Edgmond w Kynnersley and Preston Wealdmoors *Lich* 02–06; P-in-c Stamfordham w Matfen *Newc* 06–14; R Alston Moor from 14; Bp's Adv for Environment from 19. *Parsonage House, Brampton Road, Alston CA9 3AA* T: (01434) 382558 E: vicar@alstonmoorcofe.org.uk

NASH-WILLIAMS, Canon Piers le Sor Victor. b 35. Trin Hall Cam BA 57 MA 61. Cuddesdon Coll 59. **d** 61 **p** 62. C Milton Win 61–64; Asst Chapl Eton Coll 64–66; PtO *Chich* 66–68; C Furze Platt *Ox* 69–72; V Newbury St Geo Wash Common 72–73; TV Newbury 73–91; R Ascot Heath 91–01; Hon Can Ch Ch 01; rtd 01; PtO *Ox* from 02. *18 Chiltern Close, Newbury RG14 6SZ* T: (01635) 31762

NASHASHIBI, Pauline. b 48. **d** 11 **p** 12. NSM Finsbury Park St Thos *Lon* 11–15; NSM Hornsey St Mary w St Geo 15–16; PtO from 16. *36A Woodstock Road, London N4 3EX* T: (020) 7263 8268 E: prnashashibi89@gmail.com

NASON, Canon Thomas David. b 44. Open Univ BA 92 ACA 68 FCA 78. Ripon Coll Cuddesdon 84. **d** 86 **p** 87. C Banstead *Guildf* 86–89; Chapl Prebendal Sch Chich 89–14; PV Chich Cathl 89–14; Can and Preb Chich Cathl 06–14; PtO from 14. *The Gables, Hambrook Hill South, Hambrook, Chichester PO18 8UJ* T: (01243) 573716 M: 07732-114279

NASSAR, Nadim. b 64. Near E Sch of Th BTh 88. **d** 03 **p** 04. Prin Trin Foundn for Christianity and Culture 03–05; Dir Awareness Foundn from 05; Hon C Upper Chelsea H Trin *Lon* 03–11; Hon C Upper Chelsea H Trin and St Sav from 11; PtO *S'wark* from 13. *Awareness Foundation, Lodge House, 69 Beaufort Street, London SW3 5AH* T: (020) 7730 8830 M: 07961-968193 E: director@awareness-foundation.com

NATHANAEL, Martin Moses. b 43. Lon Univ BEd 73 K Coll Lon MTh 77. Ripon Coll Cuddesdon 77. **d** 79 **p** 80. C Hampton All SS *Lon* 79–82; P-in-c Kensal Town St Thos w St Andr and St Phil 82–83; Hd Div Bp Stopford Sch Lon 83–91; TV Tring *St Alb* 91–00; rtd 00. *43 Morehall Close, York YO30 4WA* T: (01904) 691201 E: martin.nathanael@btinternet.com

NATHANIAL. b 82. BA 04 MA 15. BD 09. **d** 10 **p** 12. P Kasauli Ch Ch India 12–15; PtO *Eur* 17–18; Chapl Prague from 18. *Pat'anka 2614/11A, 16000 Praha 6 - Dejvice, Czech Republic* T: (00420) 233 310 266 M: 737 039 082 E: nathanialbm@gmail.com

NATHANIEL, Canon Garth Edwin Peter. b 61. Brunel Univ BTh 99. Lon Bible Coll 96. **d** 98 **p** 99. NSM Hanwell St Mary w St Chris *Lon* 98–99; C Lt Stanmore St Lawr

99–01; P-in-c Brockmoor *Worc* 02–07; TV Brierley Hill 07–10; RD Kingswinford 08–10; TR Ipsley from 10; RD Bromsgrove 15–16; Hon Can Worc Cathl from 15. *The Rectory, Icknield Street, Ipsley, Redditch B98 0AN* T: (01527) 522847 M: 07949-490265 E: g.nathaniel@btinternet.com

NATNAEL, Daniel. b 66. Wycliffe Hall Ox 10. **d** 12 **p** 13. C Goldsworth Park *Guildf* 12–15; Chapl Twyford C of E Academies Trust 15–17; C Camberley St Paul *Guildf* 17–20; Min-in-c Deepcut from 20. *The Vicarage, 3 Spartali Place, Deepcut, Camberley GU16 6FR* T: (01276) 504023 M: 07815-137714 E: rev.dnatnael@gmail.com *or* dnatnael@yahoo.co.uk

NATTRASS, Elizabeth Jane. b 59. CBDTI 97. **d** 00 **p** 01. C Dalston w Cumdivock, Raughton Head and Wreay *Carl* 00–03; TV S Barrow 03–08; P-in-c 08; TR 08–10; P-in-c York St Olave w St Giles 10–19; P-in-c York St Helen w St Martin 10–19; P-in-c York All SS Pavement w St Crux and St Mich 10–19; P-in-c York St Denys 10–19; P-in-c York H Trin Micklegate 13–19; P-in-c York St Lawr w St Nic 15–19; V Gosforth St Nic *Newc* from 19; AD Newc Cen from 19. *St Nicholas' Vicarage, 17 Rectory Road, Newcastle upon Tyne NE3 1XR* E: nattrassjane@aol.com

NATTRASS, Michael Stuart. b 41. CBE 98. Man Univ BA 62. Cuddesdon Coll 62. **d** 64 **p** 65. C Easington Colliery *Dur* 64–65; C Silksworth 65–68; PtO *S'well* 68–72; LtO *Dur* 72–76; PtO *Lon* 76–78 and from 05; Hon C Pinner 78–05; rtd 05; PtO *Eur* from 18. *36 Waxwell Lane, Pinner HA5 3EN* T: (020) 8866 0217 F: 8930 0622

NAUDÉ, John Donald. b 62. Ridley Hall Cam 95. **d** 97 **p** 98. C Kettering Ch the King *Pet* 97–00; C-in-c Gleneagles CD 00–06; Dioc Disability Adv 05–06; V Crookhorn *Portsm* 06–12; Dean Liwonde Bible Coll Malawi 12–16; C Hurstpierpoint *Chich* from 16; Dioc Disability Adv from 16. *The Presentation Vicarage, 1 Marylands, New England Road, Haywards Heath RH16 3JZ* T: (01444) 616291 M: 07534-554587 E: john@naudeuk.com

NAUMANN, Canon David Sydney. b 26. Ripon Hall Ox 54. **d** 55 **p** 56. C Herne Bay Ch Ch *Cant* 55–58; Asst Chapl United Sheff Hosps 58–60; V Reculver *Cant* 60–64; Dioc Youth Chapl 63–70; R Eastwell w Boughton Aluph 65–67; V Westwell 65–67; Warden St Gabr Retreat Ho Westgate 68–70; V Littlebourne *Cant* 70–82; RD E Bridge 78–82; Hon Can Cant Cathl 81–00; R Sandwich 82–91; RD 85–90; rtd 91; PtO *Cant* from 91. *2 The Forrens, The Precincts, Canterbury CT1 2ER* T: (01227) 458939

NAUNTON, Hugh Raymond. b 38. Whitelands Coll Lon CertEd 69 Open Univ BA 75 Roehampton Univ Hon BEd 17. Bernard Gilpin Soc Dur 59 Chich Th Coll 60. **d** 63 **p** 64. C Stanground *Ely* 63–66; NSM Woolwich St Mary w H Trin *S'wark* 66–67; NSM Wandsworth St Anne 67–69 and 71–73; NSM Paddington St Sav *Lon* 69–71; NSM Cuddington *Guildf* 73–78; Hd RE Raynes Park High Sch 69–76; Hd RE Paddington Sch 76–78; Sen Teacher and Hd RE Ch Sch Richmond 79–93; Hon C Cheam Common St Phil *S'wark* 79–95; C Cheam 95–02; TV Selsdon St Jo w St Fran 02–03; rtd 03; PtO *Guildf* 73–18; *S'wark* from 66. *35 Farm Way, Worcester Park KT4 8RZ* T: (020) 8337 6685 M: 07581-412607 E: h.naunton@hotmail.com

NAWROCKYI, Nicholas Daniel. b 85. Dur Univ BA 06 MA 07 Leeds Univ BA 10. Coll of Resurr Mirfield 09. **d** 12 **p** 13. C Gt Grimsby St Mary and St Jas *Linc* 12–16; Min Cleethorpes St Fran CD from 16; V Cleethorpes St Aid from 19; V Clee from 19; RD Grimsby and Cleethorpes from 20. *St Nicolas' Vicarage, Great Coates Road, Great Coates, Grimsby DN37 9NS* T: (01472) 459218 M: 07912-681092 E: nick.nawrockyi@lincoln.anglican.org

NAYLOR, Alison Louise. *See* CHESWORTH, Alison Louise

NAYLOR, Anne-Marie. b 66. St Andr Univ BSc 88 Nazarene Th Coll Man MA 16. Cranmer Hall Dur 16. **d** 18 **p** 19. C Marton, Siddington w Capesthorne etc *Ches* 18–20; R Astbury and Smallwood from 20. *23 Dalebrook Road, Somerford, Congleton CW12 4YD* T: (01260) 228294 E: revd.naylor@gmail.com

NAYLOR, Barry. *See* NAYLOR, James Barry

NAYLOR, Fiona. b 68. CQSW 93. St Jo Coll Nottm 02. **d** 05 **p** 08. C Len Valley *Cant* 05–06; Hon C Lower Darwen St Jas *Blackb* 07–10; P-in-c Lea 10–12; PtO 12–14 and from 18. *82 Pear Tree Avenue, Coppull, Chorley PR7 4NL* T: (01257) 793283 E: revfionanaylor@sky.com

NAYLOR, Canon Frank. b 36. Lon Univ BA 58 Liv Univ MA 63. NW Ord Course 75. **d** 75 **p** 76. NSM Eccleston Ch Ch *Liv* 75–92; Asst Dioc Chapl to the Deaf 92–94; Sen Chapl from 94; Hon Can Liv Cathl from 01. *27 Daresbury Road, Eccleston, St Helens WA10 5DR* T: (01744) 757034

NAYLOR, Graham David. b 65. Open Univ LLB 14. Ridley Hall Cam 18. **d** 20 **p** 21. C Lavenham w Preston *St E* from 20. *41 Spire Chase, Sudbury CO10 1PZ* E: grahamdnaylor@gmail.com

NAYLOR, Grant Lambert. b 87. Univ of Wales (Lamp) BA 09. St Steph Ho Ox MTh 11. **d** 11 **p** 12. C Auckland St Helen *Dur* 11–15; P-in-c Sheff St Matt 15–17; V from 17; Miss Development Adv from 15. *St Matthew's Vicarage, 9 Ashdell Road, Sheffield S10 3DA* T: 0114-266 5681 E: father.naylor@gmail.com

NAYLOR, Ian Stuart. b 63. Wycliffe Hall Ox. **d** 01 **p** 02. C Ipswich St Marg *St E* 01–04; P-in-c Martlesham w Brightwell 04–11; P-in-c Coalbrookdale, Iron-Bridge and Lt Wenlock *Heref* 11–20; R 20–21; RD Telford Severn Gorge 13–21; TV Wrockwardine Deanery *Lich* from 21. *Address temp unknown* M: 07712-309848 E: iandjnaylor@hotmail.co.uk

NAYLOR, Canon James Barry. b 50. Lon Univ BSc 71 St Benet's Hall Ox BA 75. Wycliffe Hall Ox 72. **d** 76 **p** 76. C Catford (Southend) and Downham *S'wark* 76–79; TV 79–82; P-in-c Lewisham St Swithun 82–87; V E Dulwich St Jo 87–97; RD Dulwich 90–97; P-in-c Blythburgh w Reydon *St E* 97–99; P-in-c Wrentham w Benacre, Covehithe, Frostenden etc 97–99; P-in-c Southwold 97–99; P-in-c Uggeshall w Sotherton, Wangford and Henham 97–99; TR Sole Bay 99–02; Chapl Supervisor St Felix Sch Southwold 99–02; Can Res Leic Cathl 02–15; C The Abbey Leic 02–08; P-in-c 08–15; C Leic H Spirit 02–08; P-in-c 08–15; rtd 15; PtO *Leic* from 15; Chapl Trin Hosp Leic from 09. *7 Gavin Close, Thorpe Astley, Braunstone, Leicester LE3 3UG*

NAYLOR, Miss Jean. b 29. Linc Th Coll 77. **dss** 79 **d** 87. Charlton St Luke w H Trin *S'wark* 79–84; Crofton Park St Hilda w St Cypr 84–89; Par Dn 87–89; rtd 89; PtO *Wakef* 89–14; *Leeds* from 14. *12 Winter Terrace, Barnsley S75 2ES* T: (01226) 204767

NAYLOR, Martin. b 72. Leeds Univ BA 10 Darw Coll Cam PhD 98 Hertf Coll Ox BA 94 ALCM 90. Coll of Resurr Mirfield 08. **d** 10 **p** 11. C Bedford All SS *St Alb* 10–14; P-in-c Batley All SS and Purlwell *Leeds* 14–16; P-in-c Hanging Heaton 14–16; V Batley from 16. *The Vicarage, Churchfield Street, Batley WF17 5DL* T: (01924) 473049 E: martin.mna@gmail.com

NAYLOR, Canon Peter Aubrey. b 33. Kelham Th Coll 54 Ely Th Coll 57. **d** 58 **p** 59. C Shepherd's Bush St Steph *Lon* 58–62; C Portsea N End St Mark *Portsm* 62–66; Chapl HM Borstal Portsm 64–66; V Foley Park *Worc* 66–74; V Maidstone All SS w St Phil and H Trin *Cant* 74–81; P-in-c Tovil 79–81; V Maidstone All SS and St Phil w Tovil 81–91; Hon Can Cant Cathl 79–93; RD Sutton 80–86; R Biddenden and Smarden 91–93; P-in-c Leic St Marg and All SS 93–96; P-in-c Leic St Aug 93–96; TR The Abbey Leic 96; rtd 98; PtO *Chich* 98–02; P-in-c Crowborough St Jo 02–09; PtO from 15. *1 Hobart Quay, Eastbourne BN23 5PB*

NAYLOR, Peter Henry. b 41. MIMechE. Chich Th Coll 64. **d** 67 **p** 68. C Filton *Bris* 67–70; C Brixham *Ex* 70–72; C Leckhampton St Pet *Glouc* 72–76; V Brockworth 76–94; P-in-c Gt Witcombe 91–94; RD Glouc N 91–94; P-in-c The Ampneys w Driffield and Poulton 94–95; R 95–99; P-in-c Cheltenham Em w St Steph 99–07; rtd 07; PtO *Glouc* from 16. *20 Glebe Farm Court, Up Hatherley, Cheltenham GL51 3EB*

NAYLOR, Russell Stephen. b 45. Leeds Univ BA 70. St Chad's Coll Dur 70. **d** 72 **p** 73. C Chapel Allerton *Ripon* 72–75; Ind Chapl *Liv* 75–81; P-in-c Burtonwood 81–83; V 83–05; rtd 05; PtO *Ches* from 05; *St As* from 16. *6 Hillside Avenue, Runcorn WA7 4BW* M: 07730-137917 E: russnaylor@ntlworld.com

✠**NAZIR-ALI, The Rt Revd Michael James.** b 49. Karachi Univ BA 70 St Edm Hall Ox BLitt 74 MLitt 81 Fitzw Coll Cam MLitt 77 ACT ThD 85 Lambeth DD 05 Bath Univ Hon DLitt 03 Greenwich Univ Hon DLitt 03 Kent Univ Hon DD 04 Westmr Coll Penn (USA) DHumLit 04 Nashotah Ho Wisconsin Hon DD 10. Ridley Hall Cam 70. **d** 74 **p** 76 **c** 84. C Cambridge H Sepulchre w All SS *Ely* 74–76; Tutorial Supervisor Th Cam Univ 74–76; Sen Tutor Karachi Th Coll Pakistan 76–81; Provost Lahore 81–84; Bp Raiwind 84–86; Asst to Abp Cant 86–89; Co-ord of Studies and Ed Lambeth Conf 86–89; Hon C Ox St Giles and SS Phil and Jas w St Marg 86–89; Gen Sec CMS 89–94; Asst Bp S'wark 89–94; Hon C Limpsfield and Titsey 89–94; Can Th Leic Cathl 92–94; Bp Roch 94–09; President Ox Cen for Tr Research Advocacy and Dialogue from 09; Visiting Prof Th and RS Univ of Greenwich from 96; Hon Fell St Edm Hall Ox from 99; Hon Fell Fitzw Coll Cam from 06; Hon Asst Bp Roch from 11.

NAZIR MASIH, Emmanuel. b 72. Westcott Ho Cam 14. **d** 00 **p** 01. PtO *Ely* 14–17; C Milton *Portsm* 16–19; P-in-c Middlesbrough Ascension *York* from 19. *Ascension Vicarage, Penrith Road, Middlesbrough TS3 7JR* M: 07949-817487 E: naziremmanuel@yahoo.com

NDEGWA, Timothy. b 81. **d** 04 **p** 05. Kenya 04–11; PtO *S'wark* 11–14 and 16; NSM Lee Gd Shep w St Pet from 16.

St Alban's Parsonage, 132 William Barefoot Drive, London SE9 3BP M: 07504-829190 E: timobet@gmail.com

NDUKU, Chika Felix. b 71. Ridley Hall Cam 15. **d** 17 **p** 18. C Chadwell Heath *Chelmsf* from 17. *St Peter's Vicarage, 29 Warrington Road, Dagenham RM8 3JH* M: 07799-565754

NEAL, Alan. b 27. Trin Coll Bris 82. **d** 84 **p** 85. Hon C Broughty Ferry *Bre* 84–85; P-in-c Dundee St Ninian 85–86; R Lockerbie and Annan *Glas* 86–94; rtd 94. *c/o Mr and Mrs Graham Rew, 3 Vallance Drive, Lockerbie DG11 2DU*

NEAL, Canon Anthony Terrence. b 42. Open Univ BA 84 Leeds Univ CertEd 73 Univ of Wales MPhil 12. Chich Th Coll 65. **d** 68 **p** 69. C Cross Green St Sav and St Hilda *Ripon* 68–73; NSM Hawksworth Wood 73–78; Asst Chapl and Hd RE Abbey Grange High Sch 73–81; NSM Farnley *Ripon* 78–81; Dioc Adv in RE *Truro* 81–85; Children's Officer 85–87; Stewardship Adv *Truro* 87–88; P-in-c St Erth 81–84; V 84–96; P-in-c Phillack w Gwithian and Gwinear 94–96; P-in-c Hayle 94–96; TR Godrevy 96–06; Hon Can Truro Cathl 94–06; C Chacewater w St Day and Carharrack 10–13; C St Stythians w Perranarworthal and Gwennap 10–13; C Devoran 10–13; C Feock 10–13; PtO from 13. *11 Adelaide Street, Camborne TR14 8HH* T: (01209) 712733 E: steamerneal@talktalk.net

NEAL, James Frederick Charles. b 87. Nottm Univ BA 08. Trin Coll Bris 12. **d** 14 **p** 15. C Ashton-upon-Mersey St Mary Magd *Ches* 14–16; C Cambridge St Barn *Ely* 16–20; C Chorlton-cum-Hardy St Werburgh *Man* 20–21; R from 21. *St Werburgh's Rectory, 388 Wilbraham Road, Manchester M21 0UH* M: 07734-360421 E: james.neal@stwchorlton.org

NEAL, John Edward. b 44. Nottm Univ BTh 74 Heythrop Coll Lon MA 04. Linc Th Coll 70. **d** 74 **p** 75. C Lee St Marg *S'wark* 74–77; C Clapham St Jo 77; C Clapham Ch Ch and St Jo 77–81; P-in-c Eltham St Barn 81–83; V 83–98; Sub-Dean Eltham 89–90; Sub-Dean Greenwich S 91–96; RD Greenwich S 97–01; V Eltham St Jo 98–09; rtd 09; PtO *Eur* 10–16; P-in-c Touraine 16–19; Chapl from 19. *4 Square Mantegna, 37000 Tours, France* T: (0033) 2 47 64 07 92 E: johnlesneal@orange.fr

NEAL, Stephen Charles. b 44. K Coll Lon BSc 66 MCMI 76. NOC 90. **d** 93 **p** 94. C Walmsley *Man* 93–96; P-in-c Bolton St Matt w St Barn 96–98; TV Halliwell 98–02; Chapl Bolton Hospice 02–05; PtO *Man* 05–08; *Derby* from 08; *Eur* from 08; rtd 09; Asst Chapl Univ Hosps of Derby and Burton NHS Foundn Trust from 09. *21 Utah Close, Hilton, Derby DE65 5JA* T: (01283) 480450 M: 07775-794890 E: stephencneal@yahoo.co.uk

NEALE, Andrew Jackson. b 58. Oak Hill Th Coll 97. **d** 99 **p** 00. C Harold Hill St Geo *Chelmsf* 99–02; C Bentley Common, Kelvedon Hatch and Navestock 02–03; TV Chigwell and Chigwell Row 03–10; PtO 10–17; C High Ongar w Norton Mandeville 17–19. *12 Barker Way, Acres Avenue, Ongar CM5 0FJ* M: 07787-802085 E: andy.neale2pray@btopenworld.com

NEALE, Canon David. b 50. Lanchester Poly Cov BSc 72. St Mich Coll Llan BD 83. **d** 83 **p** 84. Min Can St Woolos Cathl *Mon* 83–87; Chapl St Woolos Hosp Newport 85–87; R Blaina and Nantyglo *Mon* 87–91; Video and Tech Officer Bd of Miss 91–01; TV Cyncoed *Mon* 99–01; Creative Resources Officer 01–03; V Maindee Newport *Mon* 03–16; AD Newport 09–16; Can St Woolos Cathl 12–16; rtd 16. *4 Legion Row, Navigation Street, Trethomas, Caerphilly CF83 8JA* T: (029) 2140 6670 E: revdneale@googlemail.com

NEALE, Edward. *See* NEALE, James Edward McKenzie

NEALE, Geoffrey Arthur. b 41. Brasted Th Coll 61 St Aid Birkenhead 63. **d** 65 **p** 66. C Stoke *Cov* 65–68; C Fareham H Trin *Portsm* 68–71; TV 71–72; R Binstead 72–77; TR Bottesford w Ashby *Linc* 77–80; V Horncastle w Low Toynton 80–90; V Brigg 90–95; V Blockley w Aston Magna and Bourton on the Hill *Glouc* 95–01; Local Min Officer 95–01; V Heath and Reach *St Alb* 01–05; TV Billington, Egginton, Hockliffe etc 06; RD Dunstable 02–04; rtd 06; PtO *Cant* from 06. *46 Cavendish Road, Herne Bay CT6 5BB* T: (01227) 360717 M: 07703-174761 E: revd.geoffn@gmail.com

NEALE, Hannah. b 40. BEM 21. SEITE. **d** 99 **p** 00. NSM Mitcham St Mark *S'wark* 99–00; NSM Merton St Jo 00–09; NSM Merton Priory 09; PtO from 09. *55 Boyd Road, London SW19 2DF* T: (020) 8648 5405

NEALE, Canon James Edward McKenzie (Eddie). b 38. MBE 04. Selw Coll Cam BA 61 Nottm Trent Univ Hon DLitt 00 Nottm Univ Hon DD 03. Clifton Th Coll 61. **d** 63 **p** 64. C Everton St Ambrose w St Tim *Liv* 63–72; Relig Adv BBC Radio Merseyside 72–76; V Bestwood St Matt *S'well* 76–86; Dioc Urban Officer 86–91; V Nottingham St Mary and St Cath 91–03; Hon Can S'well Minster 91–03; rtd 03; PtO *S'well* from 03. *Church Cottage, Church Lane, Maplebeck, Nottingham NG22 0BS* T: (01636) 636559

NEALE, Mrs Jan Celia. b 42. EMMTC 92. **d** 92 **p** 94. C Gt and Lt Coates w Bradley *Linc* 92–96; TV 96–01; TV Chambersbury *St Alb* 01–07; rtd 07; PtO *St Alb* 08–19. *1 Dickens Close, St Albans AL3 5PP* T: (01727) 853936

NEALE, Paul Edward. b 46. Portsm Coll of Tech BSc 68. **d** 07 **p** 08. OLM Cromer *Nor* 07–16; rtd 16; PtO *Nor* from 16. *30 Fulcher Avenue, Cromer NR27 9SG* T: (01263) 513563 E: paulneale127@btinternet.com

NEALE, Mrs Sandra Anne. b 50. Yorks Min Course 12. **d** 13 **p** 14. NSM Lt Horton *Bradf* 13–14; *Leeds* 14–17; NSM Queensbury 17–20; PtO 20–21. *4 Foxcroft Close, Queensbury, Bradford BD13 2DG* T: (01274) 816168 M: 07729-338618 E: sandineale@hotmail.co.uk

NEALE-STEVENS, Mrs Harriet Anna. b 82. R Holloway Coll Lon BMus 03 Goldsmiths' Coll Lon MA 04 Cam Univ BTh 17. Westcott Ho Cam 15. **d** 17 **p** 18. C Henfield w Shermanbury and Woodmancote *Chich* 17–20; R Harting w Elsted and Treyford cum Didling from 20. *The Rectory, South Harting, Petersfield GU31 5QB* E: revdharriet@yahoo.com

NEARY (née TAYLOR), Mrs Joanna Beatrice. b 74. Warwick Univ BA 96 Homerton Coll Cam PGCE 97. St Jo Coll Nottm 04. **d** 06 **p** 07. C Northolt St Jos *Lon* 06–09; NSM Charminster and Stinsford *Sarum* 10–12; TV Beaminster Area from 12. *The Vicarage, Orchard Mead, Broadwindsor, Beaminster DT8 3RA* T: (01308) 867816 M: 07939-062409 E: revneary@gmail.com

NEAUM, Canon Andrew David Irwin. b 45. Lon Univ BA 67 PGCE 68. St Paul's Coll Grahamstown 72. **d** 74 **p** 75. C Salisbury Rhodesia 74–77; R Gatooma Zimbabwe 77–82; V St Helena 82–85; Adn 84–85; R Skipton Australia 85–89; R Ararat 89–95; Can Ballarat 93–95; R Wodonga 95–03; R Shepparton 03–13; Can Wangaratta 02–13; Hon C Boldre w S Baddesley *Win* from 13. *Address temp unknown* E: andrew.neaum@gmail.com

NEAUM, David Andrew. b 79. Trin Coll Melbourne BA 01 SS Coll Cam BA 06 Em Coll Cam MPhil 08 PhD 16. Westcott Ho Cam 04 Yale Div Sch 06. **d** 07 **p** 08. NSM Cambridge St Mary Less *Ely* 07–08; C Marnhull *Sarum* 08–11; C Ox St Mary V w St Cross and St Pet 11–13; Asst Chapl Keble Coll Ox 11–12; Chapl and Fell St Cath Coll Cam 13–19; Dean 16–19; PtO *Guildf* from 19; Tutor Local Min Progr from 19. *The Rectory, Coxcombe Lane, Chiddingfold, Godalming GU8 4QA* M: 07411-675157 E: david.neaum@gmail.com

NEAVE, Garry Reginald. b 52. Leic Univ BA 72 MA 73 PGCE 74 MCMI. S'wark Ord Course. **d** 82 **p** 83. NSM Harlow St Mary Magd *Chelmsf* 82–87 and from 92; NSM St Mary-at-Latton 87–92; Chapl and Asst Prin Harlow Tertiary Coll 84–99; Dir Student Services and Admin W Herts Coll 99–04; Educn Dir Girls' Day Sch Trust 04–10; Nat FE 16-19 Adv Abps' Coun 11–17; Nat FE and HE Policy Adv from 17. *35 Perry Spring, Harlow CM17 9DQ* T: (01279) 411775 E: garry.neave@churchofengland.org

NEED, Canon Philip Alan. b 54. AKC 75. Chich Th Coll 76. **d** 77 **p** 78. C Clapham Ch Ch and St Jo *S'wark* 77–79; C Luton All SS w St Pet *St Alb* 80–83; V Harlow St Mary Magd *Chelmsf* 83–89; P-in-c Chaddesden St Phil *Derby* 89–91; Bp's Dom Chapl *Chelmsf* 91–96; R Bocking St Mary 96–13; Dean Bocking 96–13; RD Braintree 00–06 and 09–13; Dioc Dir of Ords 13–20; Hon Can Chelmsf Cathl 07–20; rtd 20; PtO *Chelmsf* from 20. *1 County Place, Chelmsford CM2 0RF* T: (01245) 698354 E: philiplambley@uwclub.net

NEED, Stephen William. b 57. K Coll Lon BD 79 MTh 83 PhD 93 AKC 79 FRSA 95. **d** 08 **p** 08. Dean St Geo Coll Jerusalem 05–11; C St Geo Cathl 08–11; P-in-c Stock Harvard *Chelmsf* 11–20; R from 20; P-in-c W Hanningfield from 11. *The Rectory, 61 High Street, Stock, Ingatestone CM4 9BN* T: (01277) 840442

NEEDHAM, Mrs Marian Ruth. b 52. Birm Univ BMus 74 City Univ MA 96. NOC 06. **d** 08 **p** 09. NSM Ches H Trin 08–12; NSM Dodleston 12–15; NSM Chase *Ox* 15–17; rtd 18; PtO *Ox* from 18. *September House, 58B Mill Street, Kidlington OX5 2EF* T: 07804-032938

NEEDHAM, Peter Douglas. b 56. Chich Th Coll 86. **d** 88 **p** 88. SSF 76–00; C S Moor *Dur* 88–90; Chapl RN 91–93; LtO *Newc* 91–96; LtO *Lon* 97–99; C Ealing Ch the Sav 99–02; P-in-c Grimethorpe *Wakef* 02–05; V Grimethorpe w Brierley 05–12; Chapl Barnsley Hosp NHS Foundn Trust 12–19; V Athersley and Carlton *Leeds* from 19. *The Vicarage, 27 Laithes Lane, Barnsley S71 3AF* T: (01226) 245361 E: needham278@aol.com

NEEDLE, Paul Robert. b 45. Oak Hill Th Coll 67. **d** 70 **p** 71. C Gt Horton *Bradf* 70–74; C Pudsey St Lawr 74–77; Hon C Horton and Chapl St Luke's Hosp Bradf 78–80; NSM Irthlingborough *Pet* 87–90; NSM Gt w Lt Addington 90–94; NSM Gt w Lt Addington and Woodford 94–98; Bp's Media Adv 94–02; NSM Higham Ferrers w Chelveston 02–06;

Bp's Communications Officer *Eur* 05–17; P-in-c Costa Azahar 07–12; PtO 05–07 and from 12; *Pet* 07–13 and from 15; Hon C Higham Ferrers w Chelveston 13–15. *2 Swallow Drive, Rushden NN10 6EG* M: 07712-463806 E: paulneedle@aol.com

NEEDS, Michael John. b 42. Open Univ BA 82 Univ of Wales (Swansea) MSc 84 PhD 87. Wycliffe Hall Ox 91. **d** 93 **p** 94. C Aberystwyth *St D* 93–96; R Llanllwchaearn and Llanina 96–06; rtd 06; P-in-c Martletwy w Lawrenny and Minwear etc *St D* 07–09. *Flat 10, Chartley, 22 The Avenue, Sneyd Park, Bristol BS9 1PE* E: mneeds@talktalk.net

NEIL, Prof Peter Sydney. b 62. Edin Univ MA 83 MEd 86 QUB PhD 95 MDiv 03 Cardiff Univ MPhil 10 Univ of Wales DMin 16 FHEA FRSA. **d** 08 **p** 09. NSM Elerch w Penrhyncoch w Capel Bangor and Goginan *St D* 08–09; NSM Ayr *Glas* 09–13; Vice Chan Bp Grosseteste Univ from 13; Gen Preacher *Linc* from 13; Can and Preb Linc Cathl from 14. *Vice Chancellor's House, Bishop Grosseteste University, Longdales Road, Lincoln LN1 3DY* T: (01522) 523166 M: 07816-953859 E: vicechancellor@bishopg.ac.uk

NEILL, Barbara June. b 39. St Jo Coll Nottm. **d** 00 **p** 01. NSM Bestwood Park w Rise Park *S'well* 00–09; rtd 09; PtO *S'well* from 10. *17 Harvest Close, Nottingham NG5 9BW* T: 0115-975 3378 E: barbjn@live.co.uk

✠**NEILL, The Rt Revd John Robert Winder.** b 45. TCD BA 66 MA 69 Jes Coll Cam BA 68 MA 72 NUI Hon LLD 03. Ridley Hall Cam 67. **d** 69 **p** 70 c 86. C Glenageary *D & G* 69–71; Lect CITC 70–71 and 82–84; Dioc Registrar (Ossory, Ferns and Leighlin) *C, F & O* 71–74; Bp's V, Lib and Registrar Kilkenny Cathl 71–74; I Abbeystrewry *C, C & R* 74–78; I Dublin St Bart w Leeson Park *D & G* 78–84; Chapl Community of St Jo the Ev 78–84; Dean Waterford *C, F & O* 84–86; Prec Lismore Cathl 84–86; Adn Waterford 84–86; I Waterford w Killea, Drumcannon and Dunhill 84–86; Bp T, K & A 86–97; Bp C & O *C, F & O* 97–02; Abp Dublin *D & G* 02–11; Preb Cualaun St Patr Cathl Dublin 02–11; rtd 11. *3 Whitegate Lawn, Freshford Road, Kilkenny, Co Kilkenny, R95 P92N, Republic of Ireland* T: (00353) (56) 771 5449 E: jrwneill55@gmail.com

NEILL, Richard Walter. b 67. Wadh Coll Ox BA 89 Em Coll Cam BA 92. Westcott Ho Cam 90. **d** 93 **p** 94. C Abbots Langley *St Alb* 93–97; C Wisley w Pyrford *Guildf* 97–00; V Winkfield and Cranbourne *Ox* 00–08; V Isle of Wedmore *B & W* from 08; RD Axbridge 19–20. *The Vicarage, Manor Lane, Wedmore BS28 4EL* T: (01934) 713566 E: richardneill1967@sky.com or wedmorevic@gmail.com

NEILL, Canon Robert Chapman. b 51. Lon Univ BD 82. CITC 77. **d** 77 **p** 78. C Lurgan Ch the Redeemer *D & D* 77–82; I Tullylish 82–88; I Mt Merrion 88–98; I Drumbo 98–16; Can Down Cathl 07–16; rtd 16. *149 Coopers Mill Avenue, Dundonald, Belfast BT16 1WR* T: (028) 9041 0832 E: r4cneill@btinternet.com

NEILL, William Barnett. b 30. TCD BA 61. **d** 63 **p** 64. C Belfast St Clem *D & D* 63–66; C Dunndonald 66–72; I Drumgath 72–80; I Drumgooland 76–80; I Mt Merrion 80–83; I Dromore Cathl 83–97; Adn Dromore 85–97; rtd 97. *10 Cairnshill Court, Saintfield Road, Belfast BT8 4TX* T: (028) 9079 2969

NEILL, William Benjamin Alan. b 46. Open Univ BA 76. CITC 68. **d** 71 **p** 72. C Dunmurry *Conn* 71–74; C Coleraine 75–77; C Dublin St Ann w St Steph *D & G* 77–78; I Convoy w Monellan and Donaghmore *D & R* 78–81; I Faughanvale 81–86; I Waterford w Killea, Drumcannon and Dunhill *C, F & O* 86–97; Dean Waterford 86–97; Prec Lismore Cathl 86–97; Prec Cashel Cathl 87–97; Can Ossory and Leighlin Cathls 96–97; I Dalkey St Patr *D & G* 97–12; Can Ch Ch Cathl Dublin 04–12; rtd 12. *Cleevaun, 77 Ballinclea Heights, Killiney, Co Dublin, Republic of Ireland* T: (00353) (1) 202 4849 E: neillben77@gmail.com

NEILSON, Christopher James. b 75. St Mellitus Coll BA 20. **d** 20 **p** 21. C Burscough Bridge *Liv* from 20. *The Vicarage, 12 New Acres, Newburgh, Wigan WN8 7TU* M: 07876-402947 E: chrisneilson4@gmail.com

NELLIST, Canon Valerie Ann. b 48. SRN 69 SCM 71. St And Dioc Tr Course 87. **d** 90 **p** 94. NSM All Souls Fife *St And* 90–99; R Aberdour 99–13; R Burntisland 99–13; R Inverkeithing 99–13; Hon Can St Ninian's Cathl Perth 97–13; rtd 13; PtO *St And* from 13. *28 Glamis Gardens, Dalgety Bay, Dunfermline KY11 9TD* T: (01383) 824066 E: valnellist@btinternet.com

NELMES, Mrs Christine. b 41. St Mary's Coll Chelt Dip Teaching 63 UWE BA 97. S Dios Minl Tr Scheme 92. **d** 95 **p** 96. NSM Winscombe *B & W* 95–99; PtO 00–03; P-in-c Mark w Allerton 03–08; rtd 08; PtO *B & W* from 09. *Yarrow Farm, Yarrow Road, Mark, Highbridge TA9 4LW* T: (01278) 641650 E: revcnelmes@googlemail.com

NELSON, Christopher James. b 57. Lanc Univ MA 91. Aston Tr Scheme 83 St Jo Coll Nottm BTh 88. **d** 88 **p** 89.

C Blackpool St Thos *Blackb* 88–90; C Altham w Clayton le Moors 90–92; V Knuzden 92–01; V Penwortham St Mary from 01; AD Leyland 04–11. *St Mary's Vicarage, 14 Cop Lane, Penwortham, Preston PR1 0SR* T: (01772) 743143 M: 07858-772421 E: kitnel@btinternet.com

✠**NELSON, The Rt Revd Hugh Edmund.** b 72. Worc Coll Ox BA 94. Ripon Coll Cuddesdon 07. **d** 09 **p** 10 **c** 20. C Newington w Hartlip and Stockbury *Cant* 09–12; C Iwade 09–12; C Upchurch w Lower Halstow 09–12; V Goudhurst w Kilndown 12–20; Suff Bp St Germans *Truro* from 20. *Lis Escop, Feock, Truro TR3 6QQ* T: (01872) 862657 E: hugh.nelson@truro.anglican.org

NELSON, Jane. b 42. **d** 94 **p** 99. Par Dn Muchalls *Bre* 94–99; C 99–04; Asst Chapl Grampian Healthcare NHS Trust 93–97; NSM Brechin *Bre* 04–14; NSM Tarfside from 05; P-in-c from 15. *4 St Michael's Road, Newtonhill, Stonehaven AB39 3RW* T: (01569) 730967 E: nelson.jane1@btinternet.com

NELSON, Julie. b 52. St Aid Coll Dur BA 73 Ex Univ MA 95 PhD 05. SWMTC 92. **d** 95 **p** 96. NSM Tavistock and Gulworthy *Ex* 95–01; Germany 01–04; P-in-c Kirklington w Burneston and Wath and Pickhill *Ripon* 04–10; AD Wensley 08–10; Dioc Adv on Women's Min 08–10; R Panfield and Rayne *Chelmsf* 10–15; Dioc Rural Officer 10–15; rtd 15; PtO *Carl* from 19. *Whitehaven, Whiteway, Stroud GL6 7EP* E: rev.julienelson@gmail.com

NELSON (née SEGGIE), Karen Angela. b 75. Roehampton Univ BA 13. Ripon Coll Cuddesdon MTh 15. **d** 15 **p** 16. C Milton next Gravesend Ch Ch *Roch* 15–20; C Gravesend St Aid 15–20; C Gravesend H Family w Ifield 15–20; C Dartford St Alb from 20; C Dartford St Edm from 20; Chapl Kent and Medway NHS and Soc Care Partnership Trust from 20. *Holy Trinity Vicarage, 2 Waltham Road, Gillingham ME8 6XQ* E: revkarenanelson@gmail.com

NELSON, Marcus John Reginald. b 81. QUB LLB 03. Wycliffe Hall Ox BA 11. **d** 11 **p** 12. C Plymouth St Andr and Stonehouse *Ex* 11–15; V Bris St Matt and St Nath 15–18; V Gabalfa *Llan* 18–20; P-in-c Tremorfa St Phil CD 18–20; V Gabalfa and Tremorfa from 21. *St Mark's Vicarage, North Road, Cardiff CF14 3BL* M: 07731-424874 E: marcusjrnelson@gmail.com

NELSON, Mark. b 72. Ripon Coll Cuddesdon 16. **d** 19 **p** 20. C Winslow w Gt Horwood and Addington *Ox* from 19. *16 Station Road, Winslow, Buckingham MK18 3ES* T: (01296) 291493 M: 07414-633450 E: revmarknelson@outlook.com

NELSON, Michael Andrew Kahrs. b 82. Univ of Wales (Ban) BSc 06. Ripon Coll Cuddesdon BA 16. **d** 16 **p** 17. C Horsham *Chich* 16; C Holbrook 16–19; C Gravesend St Geo *Roch* 19–20; V Gillingham H Trin from 20. *Holy Trinity Vicarage, 2 Waltham Road, Gillingham ME8 6XQ* M: 07572-782519 E: mike@htt.org.uk

NELSON, Sister Norma Margaret. b 34. Liv Univ DASS 77 CQSW 77. CA Tr Coll IDC 60. **d** 93 **p** 94. Team Dn Kirkby *Liv* 93–94; TV 94–95; rtd 95; PtO *Liv* from 95. *15 Pateley Close, Kirkby, Liverpool L32 4UT* T: 0151-292 0255

NELSON, Canon Paul John. b 52. Nottm Univ BCombStuds 84. Linc Th Coll 81. **d** 84 **p** 85. C Waltham Cross *St Alb* 84–87; C Sandridge 87–90; V 90–98; R Hundred River *St E* 98–13; C Wainford 06–13; R Hundred River and Wainford 13–15; RD Beccles and S Elmham 03–11; Hon Can St E Cathl 08–15; rtd 15; PtO *St E* from 16. *7 Queens Road, Beccles NR34 9DU* T: (01502) 713392 E: hedgeparson@btinternet.com

NELSON, Peter Joseph. b 46. Nottm Poly BSc 73. N Bapt Coll 82 NEOC 99. **d** 99 **p** 99. In Bapt Min 85–99; Chapl R Hull Hosps NHS Trust 94–99; Sen Chapl 02–11; NSM Sutton St Mich *York* 99–06; rtd 11; PtO *York* from 11. *Cobblestones, 1 Low Street, Sancton, York YO43 4QZ* T: (01430) 828779 E: peternelson46@live.co.uk

NELSON, Ralph Archbold. b 27. St Cuth Soc Dur BA 50. Bps' Coll Cheshunt 50. **d** 52 **p** 53. C Penwortham St Mary *Blackb* 52–57; C Eglingham *Newc* 57–58; V Featherstone *Wakef* 58–80; V Kirkham *Blackb* 80–92; RD 88–91; rtd 92; PtO *Blackb* 92–11. *6 Blundell Lane, Penwortham, Preston PR1 0EA* T: (01772) 742573

NELSON, Robert Towers. b 43. MBE 17. Liv Coll of Tech BSc 65 MSOSc. NW Ord Course 76. **d** 79 **p** 80. NSM Liv Our Lady and St Nic w St Anne 79–83; NSM Liscard St Thos *Ches* 83–87; P-in-c 87–12; V 12–20; Hon C from 20; Ind Missr from 87; Asst Sec SOSc from 89; PtO *Liv* 89–98; Chapl Wirral and W Cheshire Community NHS Trust 98–03. *5 Sedbergh Road, Wallasey CH44 2BR* T: 0151-630 2830 E: rtnelson43@gmail.com

NELSON, Warren David. b 38. TCD BA 67. **d** 68 **p** 69. C Belfast St Mich *Conn* 68–70; I Kilcooley w Littleton,

Crohane, Killenaule etc *C, F & O* 70–76; Chapl Coalbrook Fellowship Hosp Ho Thurles 76–94; PtO (Cashel, Waterford and Lismore) *C, F & O* 93–94; I Lurgan w Billis, Killinkere and Munterconnaught *K, E & A* 94–98; rtd 98. *6 Mucklagh, Tullamore, Co Offaly, Republic of Ireland* T: (00353) (57) 932 4218

NELSON, William. b 38. Oak Hill Th Coll 74. **d** 76 **p** 77. C Hensingham *Carl* 76–81; V Widnes St Paul *Liv* 81–89; R Higher Openshaw *Man* 89–03; AD Ardwick 96–00; rtd 03; PtO *S'well* from 03. *215 Stapleford Road, Trowell, Nottingham NG9 3QE* T: 0115-932 2910 E: revwilliamnelson@gmail.com

NENER, Canon Thomas Paul Edgar. b 42. Liv Univ MB, ChB FRCSEd 71 FRCS 71. Coll of Resurr Mirfield 78. **d** 80 **p** 81. C Warrington St Elphin *Liv* 80–83; V Haydock St Jas 83–95; V W Derby St Jo 95–10; Hon Can Liv Cathl 95–10; rtd 10; PtO *Lich* 16–17; *Liv* from 16; *Ches* from 21. *64 Bromborough Road, Wirral CH63 7RH* T: 0151-352 9362 M: 07484-131166

NENO, David Edward. b 62. SS Mark & Jo Univ Coll Plymouth BA 85. Ripon Coll Cuddesdon 85. **d** 88 **p** 89. C Chapel Allerton *Ripon* 91; C Acton St Mary *Lon* 91–94; V Kingsbury H Innocents 94–02; R Brondesbury Ch Ch and St Laur 02–12; V Ealing St Pet Mt Park from 12; AD Ealing from 21. *St Peter's Vicarage, 56 Mount Park Road, London W5 2RU* T: (020) 8997 1620 M: 07976-905294 E: david.neno@virginmedia.com *or* david.neno@london.anglican.org

NESBITT, Heather Hastings. b 48. S'wark Ord Course 88. **d** 90 **p** 94. Par Dn Camberwell St Luke *S'wark* 90–94; C Addiscombe St Mary Magd w St Martin 94–01; TV Sutton St Jas and Wawne *York* 01–10; rtd 10; PtO *Linc* 17–20. *21 Glengarry Way, Greylees, Sleaford NG34 8XU* T: (01529) 419298 E: h.nesbitt@yahoo.co.uk

NESBITT, Patrick Joseph. b 72. St Martin's Coll Lanc BA 96. St Jo Coll Nottm 00. **d** 03 **p** 04. C Blackpool St Thos *Blackb* 03–07; TV Kinson and W Howe *Sarum* 07–13; C Canford Magna from 16. *16 Croft Road, Ringwood BH24 1TA* M: 07879-660100 E: patricknesbitt72@hotmail.com

NESBITT, Canon Ronald. b 58. Sheff Univ LLB. CITC 82. **d** 85 **p** 86. C Ballymena w Ballyclug *Conn* 85–88; C Holywood *D & D* 88–90; I Helen's Bay 90–96; I Bangor Abbey from 96; Can Belf Cathl from 04. *The Abbey Rectory, 5 Downshire Road, Bangor BT20 3TW* T: (028) 9146 0173 *or* 9145 1087 E: ronnienesbitt@aol.com *or* bangorabbeyparish@gmail.com

NESBITT, Mrs Sarah Joy. b 62. Bath Univ BSc 84. Ox Min Course 15. **d** 18 **p** 19. C Shiplake w Dunsden and Harpsden *Ox* from 18. *The Ashes, 112 The Street, Crowmarsh Gifford, Wallingford OX10 8EJ* M: 07770-930756 E: revsarahjoy@icloud.com

NESBITT, Miss Wilhelmina. b 65. Qu Coll Birm 98. **d** 00 **p** 01. C Bridgnorth, Tasley, Astley Abbotts, etc *Heref* 00–04; TV Saddleworth *Man* 04–08; I Fanlobbus Union *C, C & R* 08–13; R Greenock *Glas* from 17. *St John's Rectory, 96 Finnart Street, Greenock PA16 8HL* T: (01475) 732441

NETHERWAY, Diana Margaret. b 47. Bp Otter Coll 94. **d** 96. NSM Northwood *Portsm* from 96; NSM Gurnard 96–14; Asst Chapl Isle of Wight NHS Trust from 09; NSM Gurnard w Cowes St Faith *Portsm* from 14. *138 Bellevue Road, Cowes PO31 7LD* T: (01983) 298505 E: dnetherway1@gmail.com

NETHERWOOD, Mrs Anne Christine. b 43. Liv Univ BArch 66 Lon Univ BD 92 ARIBA 68. St Deiniol's Hawarden 88. **d** 91 **p** 94. NSM Ellesmere and Welsh Frankton *Lich* 91–94; C Dudleston 94–97; C Criftins 94–97; C Criftins w Dudleston and Welsh Frankton 97; P-in-c 97–10; rtd 10; PtO *Lich* 10–12 and 17–21; Hon C Pradoe 12–16. *11 Cottage Fields, St Martins, Oswestry SY11 3EJ* T: (01691) 778495 E: anne@annenetherwood.co.uk

NEVELL, Simeon Zvi Benjamin. b 84. York Univ BSc 06 Cant Ch Ch Univ PGCE 07. Cranmer Hall Dur 17. **d** 19 **p** 20. C The Six *Cant* from 19. *15 Oak Lane, Upchurch, Sittingbourne ME9 7AT* M: 07552-231908 E: simeonnevell@gmail.com

NEVILL, Mrs Jacqueline Irene. b 40. Anglia Ruskin Univ BA 11. ERMC 05. **d** 07 **p** 08. C Algarve *Eur* 07–14; Rwanda 14–18; PtO *Heref* from 20. *11 Stoneleigh Drive, Belmont, Hereford HR2 7YZ* M: 07552-384702 E: jackienevill1940@gmail.com

NEVILL, James Michael. b 50. Cranmer Hall Dur 84. **d** 86 **p** 87. C Sowerby Bridge w Norland *Wakef* 86–91; CF 91–94; TV Broadwater *Chich* 94–99; Chapl St Mich Hospice Hereford 99–05; Spiritual Care Co-ord St Cath Hospice Crawley 05–15; rtd 15; PtO *Chich* from 15. *Teviotdale, Ivy Close, Ashington, Pulborough RH20 3LW* E: mikenevill1509@sky.com

NEVILLE, Michael Robert John. b 56. Hatf Coll Dur BA 80 Hughes Hall Cam PGCE 81. Wycliffe Hall Ox 82. **d** 85 **p** 86. C E Twickenham St Steph *Lon* 85–88; Asst Dir Proclamation Trust 88–93; R Fordham *Chelmsf* 93–11; P-in-c Upper Chelsea St Sav and St Simon *Lon* 11; V Upper Chelsea St Simon from 11; PtO *Eur* from 16. *St Simon Zelotes Vicarage,*

34 Milner Street, London SW3 2QF T: (020) 7589 8999
E: mike.neville@btinternet.com *or* sszoffice@aol.co.uk

NEVILLE, Paul Stewart David. b 61. Wycliffe Hall Ox 98.
d 00 **p** 01. C Chester le Street *Dur* 00–03; R Middleton
St George and Sadberge 03–13; P-in-c Stockton H Trin w
St Mark from 13; AD Stockton from 17. *The Vicarage, 76
Fairfield Road, Stockton-on-Tees TS19 7BP* T: (01642) 640863
E: prevnev@gmail.com

NEW, David John. b 37. Lon Univ BScEng 58. Chich Th
Coll 65. **d** 67 **p** 68. C Folkestone St Mary and St Eanswythe
Cant 67–72; C Kings Heath *Birm* 72–74; V S Yardley St Mich
74–83; V Moseley St Agnes 83–00; rtd 00; PtO *Worc* from
00. *6 Falmouth, Worcester WR4 0TE* T: (01905) 458084
E: davidnew@talktalk.net

NEW, Canon Thomas Stephen. b 30. K Coll Cam BA 52
MA 56. Cuddesdon Coll 52. **d** 54 **p** 55. C Greenford H Cross
Lon 54–55; C Old St Pancras w Bedford New Town St Matt
55–58; C Woodham *Guildf* 58–64; V Guildf All SS 64–72; V
Banstead 72–93; RD Epsom 76–80; Hon Can Guildf Cathl
79–93; Sub-Chapl HM Pris Downview 88–93; rtd 93; PtO *Ex*
from 94. *St Katharine's, North Street, Denbury, Newton Abbot
TQ12 6DJ* T: (01803) 813775

NEWARK, Archdeacon of. See RAMSEY, The Ven Victoria
Claire

NEWBOLD, Mrs Caroline Sarah. b 62. K Alfred's Coll
Win BA 83 Homerton Coll Cam PGCE 85. St Mellitus
Coll BA 10. **d** 10 **p** 11. C Yiewsley *Lon* 10–13; Chapl Lady
Margaret Sch 13–19; NSM Ealing St Steph Castle Hill
Lon from 13. *St Stephen's Vicarage, Sherborne Gardens,
London W13 8AQ* T: (020) 8810 4929 M: 07958-073583
E: caroline@ststephens-ealing.org

NEWBOLD, Stephen Mark. b 60. Trin Coll Bris 01. **d** 03 **p** 04.
C Roxeth *Lon* 03–09; V Ealing St Steph Castle Hill from 09;
AD Ealing 15–21. *St Stephen's Vicarage, Sherborne Gardens,
London W13 8AQ* T: (020) 8810 4929

NEWBON, Michael Charles. b 59. Oak Hill Th Coll 92.
d 94 **p** 95. C Bedford St Jo and St Leon *St Alb* 94–99;
V Luton St Fran 99–11; P-in-c Georgeham *Ex* 11–15; R
from 15. *The Rectory, Newberry Road, Georgeham, Braunton
EX33 1JS* T: (01271) 890616 E: mikenewbon@aol.com

NEWBORN, Carol Margaret. b 45. **d** 05 **p** 06. OLM
Styvechale *Cov* 05–17; NSM Napton-on-the-Hill, Lower
Shuckburgh etc 17–19; NSM Priors Hardwick, Priors
Marston and Wormleighton 17–19; PtO 19–21. *76
The Park Paling, Coventry CV3 5LL* T: (024) 7650 3707
E: carol_newborn@hotmail.co.uk

NEWBY, Canon Ailsa Ballantyne. b 56. Collingwood
Coll Dur BA 78 Heythrop Coll Lon MA 09. St Steph Ho
Ox 98. **d** 98 **p** 99. C Streatham Ch Ch *S'wark* 98–01; V
S Lambeth St Anne and All SS 01–10; Dir IME Kingston
Area 04–10; TR Putney St Mary 10–17; Hon Can S'wark
Cathl 15–17; Can Res Ripon Cathl *Leeds* from 17. *St Peter's
House, Minster Close, Ripon HG4 1QP* T: (01765) 604108
E: canonailsa@riponcathedral.org.uk

NEWBY, Claire. See McILROY, Claire

NEWBY, Mrs Susan. b 48. Lady Spencer Chu Coll of Educn
CertEd 70 BEd 71. **d** 04 **p** 05. OLM Adderbury w Milton *Ox*
04–10; NSM Banbury 10–16; rtd 16; PtO *Arg* from 18. *Tigh na
Baigh, Bayhead, Isle of North Uist HS6 5DS* M: 07824-470877
E: revnewby@hotmail.co.uk

NEWCASTLE, Bishop of. See HARDMAN, The Rt Revd
Christine Elizabeth

NEWCASTLE, Dean of. See MILLER, The Very Revd Geoffrey
Vincent

NEWCOMBE, Andrew Charles. b 70. Melbourne Univ
BA 92 BMus 93 Ox Univ BTh 09 Monash Univ Aus
DipEd 96 LTCL 93. St Steph Ho Ox 03. **d** 05 **p** 06. C
Tottenham St Mary *Lon* 05–08; C Edmonton St Alpheage
and Ponders End St Matt 08–11; V Hoxton H Trin w
St Mary 11–21. *Address temp unknown* M: 07931-700675
E: andrewnewcombe@yahoo.co.uk

NEWCOMBE, John Adrian. b 61. Univ of Wales (Lamp) BA 83
SS Paul & Mary Coll Cheltenham PGCE 85. Ripon Coll
Cuddesdon 90. **d** 92 **p** 93. C Stroud and Uplands w Slad *Glouc*
92–96; C Nailsworth 96–01; P-in-c Childswyckham w Aston
Somerville, Buckland etc 01–05; TV Winchcombe from 05. *5
Bramley Close, Toddington, Cheltenham GL54 5ED* T: (01242)
621592 E: jridlernewcom@btinternet.com

NEWCOMBE, Jonathan Charles Dymoke. b 75. St Anne's
Coll Ox BA 97 MA 09 Fitzw Coll Cam BA 04 MA 09. Ridley
Hall Cam 02. **d** 07 **p** 08. NSM Wimbledon Em Ridgway
Prop Chpl *S'wark* 07–10; Asst Chapl Tervuren *Eur* 10–14; C
Cambridge H Sepulchre *Ely* 14–18; C Huntingdon from 18.
36 Claytons Way, Huntingdon PE29 1UT M: 07535-501110
E: revcharlienewc@gmail.com

NEWCOMBE, Canon Timothy James Grahame. b 47. AKC 75.
St Aug Coll Cant 75. **d** 76 **p** 77. C Heref St Martin 76–79;
C Hitchin *St Alb* 79–85; R Croft and Stoney Stanton *Leic*
85–91; P-in-c Launceston *Truro* 91–92; V 92–97; TR 97–03;
Hon Can Truro Cathl 01–03; Chapl Cornwall Healthcare
NHS Trust 96–03; V Wotton St Mary *Glouc* 03–12; rtd 12.
18 Kempley Road, Okehampton EX20 1DS T: (01837) 52901
E: tnewco@btinternet.com

✠**NEWCOME, The Rt Revd James William Scobie.** b 53. Trin
Coll Ox BA 74 MA 78 Selw Coll Cam BA 77 MA 81. Ridley
Hall Cam 75. **d** 78 **p** 79 **c** 02. C Leavesden *St Alb* 78–82;
P-in-c Bar Hill LEP *Ely* 82–92; V Bar Hill 92–94; Tutor Ridley
Hall Cam 83–88; P-in-c Dry Drayton *Ely* 89–94; RD N Stowe
93–94; Can Res Ches Cathl and Dioc Dir of Ords 94–02;
Dir of Educn and Tr 96–02; Suff Bp Penrith *Carl* 02–09; Bp
Carl from 09; Clerk of the Closet from 15. *Bishop's House,
Ambleside Road, Keswick CA12 4DD* T: (01768) 773430
E: bishop.carlisle@carlislediocese.org.uk

NEWELL, Christopher David. b 53. Ex Univ MA 03 Win
Univ PhD 15. S'wark Ord Course 84. **d** 87 **p** 88. C Stockwell
St Mich *S'wark* 87–90; Asst Chapl R Lon Hosp (Whitechapel)
90–92; Asst Chapl R Lon Hosp (Mile End) 90–92; R Birch
St Agnes *Man* 92–96; P-in-c Longsight St Jo w St Cypr 94–96;
R Birch St Agnes w Longsight St Jo w St Cypr 97; R Lansallos
and V Talland *Truro* 97–98; Asst P Liskeard and St Keyne
00–02; C Duloe, Herodsfoot, Morval and St Pinnock 02–03;
P-in-c 03–05; C Lansallos and Talland 02–03; Chapl Cornwall
Partnership NHS Foundn Trust 02–16; P-in-c St Goran w
Caerhays *Truro* 14–17; rtd 17. *5 The Old School Mews, Bices
Court, Kenwyn Street, Truro TR1 3DU* T: (01872) 496086
E: christophernewell@talk21.com

NEWELL, David Walter. b 37. Nottm Univ BSc 57.
WEMTC 01. **d** 03 **p** 04. OLM Painswick, Sheepscombe,
Cranham, The Edge etc *Glouc* from 03. *Firle Cottage,
Blakewell Mead, Painswick GL6 6UR* T: (01452) 812083
E: d.newell083@btinternet.com

NEWELL, Canon Edmund John. b 61. Univ Coll Lon BSc 83
Nuff Coll Ox DPhil 88 MA 89 FRHistS 98 FRSA 08. Ox
Min Course 89 Ripon Coll Cuddesdon 92. **d** 94 **p** 95. C
Deddington w Barford, Clifton and Hempton *Ox* 94–98;
Bp's Dom Chapl 98–01; Chapl Headington Sch 98–01;
Can Res St Paul's Cathl *Lon* 01–08; Chan St Paul's Cathl
03–08; Can Res and Sub-Dean Ch Ch *Ox* 08–13; Prin
Cumberland Lodge Windsor from 13; PtO *Ox* from 13;
Hon Can Ch Ch from 14. *Cumberland Lodge, The Great
Park, Windsor SL4 2HP* T: (01784) 497786 F: 497799
E: enewell@cumberlandlodge.ac.uk

NEWELL, Peter James. b 56. SEITE 12. **d** 15 **p** 16. NSM
Kennington *Cant* 15–16; NSM Ashford Town 16–19;
P-in-c Shepherds Lees from 19. *The Vicarage, Vicarage
Lane, Selling, Faversham ME13 9RD* T: (01227) 938374
E: peternewell06@gmail.com *or* peter.newell06@outlook.com

NEWELL, Rachel Leanne. See AKERS, Rachel Leanne

NEWEY, Edmund James. b 71. Linc Coll Ox BA 95 MA 97 Em
Coll Cam BA 99 Man Univ PhD 08. Westcott Ho Cam 97.
d 00 **p** 01. C Birch w Fallowfield *Man* 00–03; R Newmarket
St Mary w Exning St Agnes *St E* 03–07; V Handsworth
St Andr *Birm* 07–13; AD Handsworth 11–13; Can Res and
Sub-Dean Ch Ch *Ox* 13–20; R Rugby St Andr *Cov* from
20. *The Rectory, Church Street, Rugby CV21 3PH* M: 07986-
530511 E: ejnewey@phonecoop.coop

NEWHAM, Simon Frank Eric. b 65. Sheff Univ BSc 87 MSc 89.
Trin Coll Bris BA 00. **d** 00 **p** 01. C Horsham *Chich* 00–04;
P-in-c Wisborough Green 04–09; V 09–10; RD Petworth
06–09; TR Ifield 10–17; R 17–19; V Brockenhurst *Win* from
19; V Boldre w S Baddesley from 19. *The Vicarage, Meerut
Road, Brockenhurst SO42 7TD* T: (01590) 624163

NEWING, Peter. b 33. Birm Univ CertEd 55 Dur Univ BA 63
Bris Univ BEd 76 State Univ NY BSc 85 EdD 88 Worc Univ
BA 12 FRSA 60 FSAScot 59 ACP 67 MCollP 86 FCollT 95
APhS 63 FVCM 01. Cranmer Hall Dur 63. **d** 65 **p** 66. C
Blockley w Aston Magna *Glouc* 65–69; P-in-c Taynton 69–75;
P-in-c Tibberton 69–75; R Brimpsfield w Elkstone and Syde
75–83; R Brimpsfield, Cranham, Elkstone and Syde 83–97;
P-in-c Daglingworth w the Duntisbournes and Winstone
95–97; R Brimpsfield w Birdlip, Syde, Daglingworth etc
97–01; C Redmarley D'Abitot, Bromesberrow, Pauntley etc
01–02; NSM 02–10; rtd 02; PtO *Heref* 02–17 and 20; *Worc*
from 04; *Glouc* from 10. *36 Born Court, New Street, Ledbury
HR8 2DX* T: (01453) 790766 E: profnewing@btinternet.com

NEWITT, Mark Julian. b 76. Bradf Univ BSc 97 St Jo Coll
Dur BA 02. Cranmer Hall Dur 00. **d** 03 **p** 04. C Billing *Pet*
03–06; Asst Chapl Sheff Teaching Hosps NHS Foundn
Trust from 06. *Chaplaincy Services, Royal Hallamshire
Hospital, Glossop Road, Sheffield S10 2JF* T: 0114-271 1900
E: mark.newitt@sth.nhs.uk

NEWLAND, Mrs Patricia Frances. b 35. Edin Univ MA 56. EAMTC 96. **d** 97 **p** 98. NSM Duxford *Ely* 97–02; NSM Hinxton 97–02; NSM Ickleton 97–02; rtd 02; PtO *Ely* 02–07. *Ickelton Lodge, 14 Frogge Street, Ickleton, Saffron Walden CB10 1SH* T: (01799) 530268 F: 531146 E: patricia.newland@googlemail.com

NEWLANDS, Canon Christopher William. b 57. Bris Univ BA 79. Westcott Ho Cam 81. **d** 84 **p** 85. C Bishop's Waltham *Portsm* 84–87; Hon C Upham 85–87; Prec, Sacr and Min Can Dur *Cathl* 87–92; Chapl Bucharest w Sofia *Eur* 92–95; V Shrub End *Chelmsf* 96–04; Bp's Chapl 04–10; P-in-c Lancaster St Mary w St John and St Anne *Blackb* 10–11; V 11–21; Hon Can Blackb *Cathl* 18–21; rtd 21. *14 Swaylands Road, Belvedere DA17 6LS* T: (01322) 412533 E: cnewlands@gmail.com

NEWLANDS, Prof George McLeod. b 41. Edin Univ MA 63 BD 66 DLitt 05 Heidelberg Univ PhD 70 Wolfs Coll Cam MA 73 FRSE 08. **d** 82 **p** 82. Lect Cam Univ 73–86; Fell and Dean Trin Hall Cam 82–86; Prof Div Glas Univ 86–08; PtO *Glas* from 86; Hon Fell New Coll Edin Univ from 10. *49 Highsett, Cambridge CB2 1NZ* T: (01223) 569984 M: 07786-930941 E: newlands71@hotmail.com

NEWLYN, Canon Edwin. b 39. AKC 64. **d** 65 **p** 66. C Belgrave St Mich *Leic* 65–68; Miss to Seamen 68–81; Chapl Santos Brazil 68–69; Asst Chapl Glas and C Glas St Gabr 69–73; Chapl E Lon S Africa 73–76; R W Bank St Pet 75–76; V Fylingdales *York* 81; P-in-c Fylingdales and Hawsker cum Stainsacre 81; V 81–88; RD Whitby 85–92; Sec Dioc Adv Cttee for Care of Chs 87–01; P-in-c Goathland 88–99; Can and Preb York Minster 90–08; rtd 01; PtO *York* 01–18. *The Garden Flat, 12 Royal Crescent, Whitby YO21 3EJ* T: (01947) 604533 *or* 606578 F: 602798 E: edwin.newlyn@talktalk.net

✠**NEWMAN, The Rt Revd Adrian.** b 58. Bris Univ BSc 80 MPhil 89. Trin Coll Bris 82. **d** 85 **p** 86 **c** 11. C Forest Gate St Mark *Chelmsf* 85–89; V Hillsborough and Wadsley Bridge *Sheff* 89–96; RD Hallam 94–96; R Birm St Martin w Bordesley St Andr 96–05; Hon Can Birm *Cathl* 01–05; Dean Roch 05–11; Area Bp Stepney *Lon* 11–18; rtd 19; PtO *Lon* from 19; *Chelmsf* from 20. *Priory Mews, The Street, Little Dunmow, Dunmow CM6 3HT* E: adriannewman145@gmail.com

NEWMAN, Alastair James Morley. b 82. Rob Coll Cam BA 06 MA 08 MSci 06. Westcott Ho Cam 17. **d** 20 **p** 21. C Wimbledon *S'wark* from 20. *Address withheld by request* E: revalastair@gmail.com

NEWMAN, Alison Myra. b 55. K Coll Lon BD 77. SEITE 99. **d** 02 **p** 03. C Bromley SS Pet and Paul *Roch* 02–06; C Shortlands 06–08; C Farnborough 08–15; V Biggin Hill from 15. *The Vicarage, 10 Church Road, Biggin Hill, Westerham TN16 3LB* T: (01959) 540482 E: vicar@movingchurch.org

NEWMAN, Christopher David. *See* NEWMAN-DAY, Christopher David

NEWMAN, Daniel Robert. b 85. BNC Ox BA 06 MA 12 BM, BCh 09 Fitzw Coll Cam BA 12 Anglia Ruskin Univ MA 14. Ridley Hall Cam 10. **d** 13 **p** 14. C Radipole and Melcombe Regis *Sarum* 13–16; C Woking St Jo *Guildf* 16–20; R The Sherbornes w Pamber *Win* from 20. *The Rectory, Vyne Road, Sherborne St John, Basingstoke RG24 9HX* T: (01256) 541607 E: daniel.r.newman@gmail.com *or* rector.sherbornewithpamber@gmail.com

NEWMAN, David. *See* NEWMAN, Richard David

NEWMAN, David Maurice Frederick. b 54. Hertf Coll Ox BA 75 MA 79. St Jo Coll Nottm. **d** 79 **p** 80. C Orpington Ch Ch *Roch* 79–83; C Bushbury *Lich* 83–86; V Ockbrook *Derby* 86–97; TR Loughborough Em and St Mary in Charnwood *Leic* 97–09; RD Akeley E 99–06; Hon Can Leic *Cathl* 06–09; Adn Loughborough 09–17; Warden Launde Abbey 17–21; rtd 21; PtO *Pet* from 17. *The Long House, 33 High Street, Barrow upon Soar, Loughborough LE12 8PY* M: 07817-664189

NEWMAN, Mrs Diana Joan. b 43. Sarum Th Coll 81. **dss** 84 **d** 87 **p** 94. Parkstone St Pet and St Osmund w Branksea *Sarum* 84–13; NSM 87–13; TV 96–02; PtO *Sarum* from 14. *62 Vale Road, Poole BH14 9AU* T/F: (01202) 745136 E: diana.n@sky.com

NEWMAN, Ms Elizabeth Ann. b 57. K Coll Lon BD 79 Hull Univ CQSW 81. **d** 05 **p** 06. OLM Charlton *S'wark* 05–14; NSM 14–17; R from 17; Chapl Blackheath Bluecoat C of E Sch 11–14; Chapl Lewisham and Greenwich NHS Trust 14–17; Bp's Visitor for Clergy Spouses *S'wark* from 15; Women's Min Adv Woolwich Area from 20. *66 Annandale Road, London SE10 0DB* T: (020) 8305 0642 *or* 8858 8175 M: 07922-587263 E: rector@charlton.church

NEWMAN, Elizabeth Margot. b 50. Reading Univ BA 92. Ox Min Course 09. **d** 12 **p** 13. NSM Earley St Nic *Ox* 12–21; PtO from 21. *37 Sevenoaks Road, Earley, Reading RG6 7NT* T: 0118-926 5557 E: revlibby.newman@yahoo.co.uk

NEWMAN, Gillian Ann. b 60. St Mellitus Coll 15. **d** 17. NSM S Hackney St Jo w Ch Ch *Lon* 17–20; Chapl Guy's

and St Thos' NHS Foundn Trust from 18; Chapl Princess Alexandra Hosp NHS Trust from 18. *Priory Mews, The Street, Little Dunmow, Dunmow CM6 3HT* M: 07815-172424 E: gillie09ann@live.co.uk

NEWMAN, Canon Helen Margaret. b 58. York Univ BA 80 Nottm Univ MA 02. EMMTC 99. **d** 02 **p** 03. NSM Thorpe Acre w Dishley *Leic* 02–05; NSM Loughborough Em and St Mary in Charnwood 05–09; Chapl LOROS Hospice 09–17; Chapl Launde Abbey *Leic* 17–21; PtO *Pet* from 17; Hon Can Leic Cathl from 16. *The Long House, 33 High Street, Barrow upon Soar, Loughborough LE12 8PY* M: 07814-444538

NEWMAN, James Edwin Michael. b 59. Nottm Univ BA 80 Ox Univ BA 90 MA 05. Wycliffe Hall Ox 88. **d** 91 **p** 92. C Bidston *Ches* 91–95; C Cheadle from 95. *4 Cuthbert Road, Cheadle SK8 2DT* M: 07590-525217 E: mike@thenewmanfamily.org

NEWMAN, Ms Jennifer Margaret. b 73. K Alfred's Coll Win BEd 95. St Mellitus Coll 16. **d** 19 **p** 20. C Derby St Alkmund and St Werburgh from 19. *27 Wheeldon Avenue, Derby DE22 1HP* M: 07717-807237 E: jenny.newman@stwderby.org *or* jenmnewman73@hotmail.com

NEWMAN, Kevin Richard. b 74. Warwick Univ BSc 95 PGCE 96. Oak Hill Th Coll BA 06. **d** 06 **p** 07. C Crowborough *Chich* 06–10; C Bromley Ch Ch *Roch* 10–14. *Christ Church, 150 High Street, Banstead SM7 2NZ* M: 07920-843385 E: kev@kevandfran.co.uk

NEWMAN, Mrs Lynda Elizabeth. b 61. Univ of Wales (Swansea) DipEd 81 BEd 83 MEd 93. St Mich Coll Llan 07. **d** 10 **p** 11. NSM Neath *Llan* 10–13; TV 13–19; C Llansawel, Briton Ferry 16–19; TR Neath from 19; Asst Dioc Children's Officer from 12. *The Rectory, London Road, Neath SA11 1LE* T: (01639) 633354 E: lenewman@hotmail.co.uk

NEWMAN, Michael Alan. b 40. Chich Th Coll 67. **d** 70 **p** 71. C Kilburn St Aug *Lon* 70–73; C St Geo-in-the-East St Mary 75–78; rtd 78. *April Cottage, Georges Lane, Storrington, Pulborough RH20 3JH* T: (01903) 744354 E: tcepriest@tiscali.co.uk *or* michael.newman@talktalk.net

NEWMAN, Preb Michael John. b 50. Leic Univ BA 72 MA 75. Cuddesdon Coll 73. **d** 75 **p** 76. C Tettenhall Regis *Lich* 75–79; C Uttoxeter w Bramshall 79–82; R Norton Canes 82–89; TR Rugeley 89–06; TR Brereton and Rugeley 06–15; RD Rugeley 07–15; Preb Lich Cathl 02–15; rtd 15; PtO *Lich* from 16. *2 Firs Close, Weeping Cross, Stafford ST17 0DW* T: (01785) 660158 E: eileenandmichael@outlook.com

NEWMAN, Paul Anthony. b 48. Lon Univ BSc 70 Sarum Coll MA 18 Win Univ MA 18. Coll of Resurr Mirfield 73. **d** 76 **p** 77. C Catford St Laur *S'wark* 76–81; TV Grays All SS and Lt Thurrock St Mary *Chelmsf* 81–83; Youth Chapl W Ham Adnry 83–87; P-in-c Forest Gate All SS 83–89; V 89–91; Dep Chapl HM Pris Wormwood Scrubs 91–92; Chapl HM Pris Downview and Asst Chapl HM Pris High Down 92–02; Chapl HM Pris Win 02–07; Chapl HM Pris Kingston (Portsm) 07–13; rtd 13; PtO *Win* 07–13. *5 Cranworth House, Cranworth Road, Winchester SO22 6EJ* T: (01962) 863138 E: paulnewman603@yahoo.com

NEWMAN, Richard David. b 38. BNC Ox BA 60 MA 63. Lich Th Coll 60. **d** 62 **p** 63. C E Grinstead St Swithun *Chich* 62–66; C Gt Grimsby St Jas *Linc* 66–69; C Gt Grimsby St Mary and St Jas 69–73; TV 73–74; V St Nicholas at Wade w Sarre *Cant* 74–75; P-in-c Chislet w Hoath 74–75; V St Nicholas at Wade w Sarre and Chislet w Hoath 75–81; V S Norwood H Innocents 81–84; V S Norwood H Innocents *S'wark* 85–04; rtd 04; PtO *B & W* from 04. *10 Hardy Court, Lang Road, Crewkerne TA18 8JE* T: (01460) 271496 E: david.newman123@btinternet.com

NEWMAN-DAY, Christopher David. b 81. Bath Univ BSc 02 Anglia Ruskin Univ BA 10. Ridley Hall Cam 07. **d** 11 **p** 12. C Canonbury St Steph *Lon* 11–14; V Bethnal Green St Jas Less from 14. *St James the Less Vicarage, St James's Avenue, London E2 9JD* T: (020) 8980 1612 M: 07921-505744 E: rev.newmanday@gmail.com

NEWMARCH, Christine Anne. b 54. St Mellitus Coll 15. **d** 17 **p** 18. C Witham and Villages *Chelmsf* from 17. *Hobbits, 159 High Street, Kelvedon, Colchester CO5 9JA* T: (01376) 571623 E: christinenewmarch@hotmail.co.uk

NEWNES, Steven William. b 61. **d** 14 **p** 15. C Brockworth *Glouc* 14–18; NSM 18; Chapl HM Pris Long Lartin from 18; PtO *Glouc* from 18. *HM Prison, South Littleton, Evesham WR11 8TZ* T: (01386) 295100 E: bullincs17@sky.com

NEWNHAM, Carol Ann. St Mellitus Coll. **d** 15 **p** 16. OLM Becontree St Thos *Chelmsf* 15–18; NSM Theydon Par from 18. *Theydon Garnon Vicarage, Fiddlers Hamlet, Epping CM16 7PQ*

NEWNHAM, Eric Robert. b 43. FCA. Sarum & Wells Th Coll 70. **d** 75 **p** 76. C Blackheath Ascension *S'wark* 75–06; NSM Deptford St Jo w H Trin and Ascension 06–13; PtO

13–17. *27 Morden Hill, London SE13 7NN* T: (020) 8692 6507 or 8691 6559 E: e.n@btopenworld.com

NEWNHAM, Osmond James. b 31. TD 84. Leeds Univ BA 55. Coll of Resurr Mirfield 55. **d** 57 **p** 58. C Salisbury St Mark *Sarum* 57–60; CF (R of O) 59–71; C Pewsey *Sarum* 60–62; R Chickerell w Fleet 62–94; CF (TA) 71–86; rtd 96. *32 Woodpecker Drive, Poole, Dorset BH17 7SY* T: (01202) 658386

NEWPORT, Prof Kenneth George Charles. b 57. Columbia Union Coll (USA) BA 83 Andrews Univ (USA) MA 84 Linacre Coll Ox MSt 85 St Hugh's Coll Ox DPhil 88. NOC 98. **d** 00 **p** 01. Reader Chr Thought Liv Hope 99–01; Prof Th and RS Liv Hope Univ from 01; Asst Vice Chan from 05; Hon Research Fell Man Univ from 98; NSM Bolton St Pet 00–11; NSM Bolton St Pet w St Phil from 11; PtO *Liv* from 00; Hon Can Man Cathl from 16. *Theology and Religious Studies, Liverpool Hope, Hope Park, Taggart Avenue, Liverpool L16 9JD* T: 0151-291 3510 F: 291 3772 E: knewport@hope.ac.uk

NEWPORT, Archdeacon of. *See* WILLIAMS, The Ven Jonathan Simon

NEWSOME, Preb David Ellis. b 55. St Jo Coll Dur BA 77. Westcott Ho Cam 80. **d** 82 **p** 83. C Finchley St Mary *Lon* 82–85; C Fulham All SS 85–87; Bp's Dom Chapl *Birm* 87–91; V Gravelly Hill 91–00; P-in-c Stockland Green 93–96; AD Aston 95–00; TR Tettenhall Regis *Lich* 00–08; Dioc Dir of Ords 08–15; Preb Lich Cathl 15; rtd 16; PtO *Lich* from 16; *Heref* 16–19; *Birm* from 19. *36 Highbridge Road, Sutton Coldfield B73 5QB* T: 0121-354 9203 E: davidenewsome@gmail.com

NEWSOME, Monica Jane. b 55. MBE 16. WMMTC 96. **d** 99 **p** 00. NSM Kingshurst *Birm* 99–00; Asst Chapl HM YOI Stoke Heath 00–10; Chapl HM Pris Swinfen Hall 10–15; rtd 15; PtO *Heref* 17–19; *Lich* from 17; *Birm* from 19. *36 Highbridge Road, Sutton Coldfield B73 5QB* T: 0121-354 9203 E: m.j.newsome2@gmail.com

NEWSON, Julie. b 60. Southn Univ BA 97. Bp Otter Coll 00. **d** 03. NSM Brighton St Pet w Chpl Royal *Chich* 03–09; NSM Brighton Chpl Royal 09–10; Dn-in-c Brighton St Luke Queen's Park from 10. *St Luke's Vicarage, Queen's Park Terrace, Brighton BN2 9YA* T: (01273) 570978 M: 07803-750147 E: julie.newson@btinternet.com

NEWSTEAD, Dominic Gerald Bruno. b 65. Wycliffe Hall Ox BTh 95. **d** 95 **p** 96. C Windlesham *Guildf* 95–00; Asst Chapl Fontainebleau *Eur* 00–05; V Southwater *Chich* 05–09; C Bebington *Ches* 09–16; V Lt Heath *St Alb* 16–20; Chapl Tervuren *Eur* from 20. *Hoornzeelstraat 24, 3080 Tervuren, Belgium* T: (0032) (2) 767 3435 E: dominicnewstead@icloud.com *or* dominic@stpaulstervuren.org

NEWTON, Angela Margaret. b 48. RGN 70. Ripon Coll Cuddesdon 06. **d** 07 **p** 08. NSM Luton St Aug Limbury *St Alb* 07–12; PtO 12–18; NSM Christchurch *Win* 12–20; Chapl R Bournemouth and Christchurch Hosps NHS Foundn Trust 14–20; rtd 20; PtO *Win* from 21. *23 Regency Crescent, Christchurch BH23 2UF* T: (01202) 950010 M: 07940-824206 E: angelanewton48@gmail.com

NEWTON, Barrie Arthur. b 38. Dur Univ BA 61. Wells Th Coll 61. **d** 63 **p** 64. C Walton St Mary *Liv* 63–67; C N Lynn w St Marg and St Nic *Nor* 67–69; Chapl Asst The Lon Hosp (Whitechapel) 69–71; Chapl K Coll Hosp Lon 72–77; P-in-c Bishops Sutton w Stowey *B & W* 77–81; P-in-c Compton Martin w Ubley 79–81; P-in-c Bridgwater St Jo w Chedzoy 81–83; Chapl St Mary's Hosp Praed Street Lon 83–94; Chapl St Mary's NHS Trust Paddington 94–99; rtd 00; PtO *Lon* from 04. *10 Brondesbury Park Mansions, 132 Salusbury Road, London NW6 6PD* T/F: (020) 7328 0397 E: newrie@btinternet.com

NEWTON, Brian Karl. b 30. Keble Coll Ox BA 55 MA 59. Wells Th Coll 56. **d** 58 **p** 59. C Barrow St Geo *Carl* 58–61; Trinidad and Tobago 61–69 and 71–77; Gen Ed USPG 69–71; P-in-c Gt Coates *Linc* 77; TV Gt and Lt Coates w Bradley 78–88; V Burgh le Marsh 88–94; R Bratoft w Irby-in-the-Marsh 88–94; V Orby 88–94; R Welton-le-Marsh w Gunby 88–94; rtd 94; PtO *Linc* 94–97 and 18–21. *17 Stuart Court, High Street, Kibworth Beauchamp, Leicester LE8 0LR* T: 0116-279 6242

NEWTON, David. *See* NEWTON, Michael David

NEWTON, David. *See* NEWTON, Raymond David

NEWTON, David Ernest. b 42. Sarum & Wells Th Coll 72. **d** 74 **p** 75. C Wigan All SS *Liv* 74–80; V Choral York Minster 80–85; R Ampleforth w Oswaldkirk 85–86; P-in-c E Gilling 85–86; R Ampleforth and Oswaldkirk and Gilling E 86–97; V Ampleforth w Oswaldkirk, Gilling E etc 98–01; RD Helmsley 94–99; P-in-c Overton *Blackb* 01–10; PtO from 20. *4 Lunesdale Court, Derwent Road, Lancaster LA1 3ET* T: (01524) 599101 E: davidnoot@aol.com

NEWTON, Derek. b 50. NEOC 89. **d** 92 **p** 93. NSM Houghton le Spring *Dur* 92–96; C 06–09; NSM Deanery of Houghton 97–06; P-in-c Chilton Moor 09–20; rtd 20. *1 Fields View, East Rainton, Houghton le Spring DH5 9GA*

NEWTON, Canon Fiona Olive. b 46. GTCL 67. WMMTC 96. **d** 99 **p** 00. C Southam and Ufton *Cov* 99–03; P-in-c Laxfield, Cratfield, Wilby and Brundish *St E* 03–04; R 04–13; C Hoxne w Denham, Syleham and Wingfield 06–13; R Worlingworth, Southolt, Tannington, Bedfield etc 12–13; R Bedfield, Brundish, Cratfield, Laxfield etc 13; RD Hoxne 07–13; RD Hartismere 08–10; Hon Can St E Cathl 11–13; rtd 13; PtO *Nor* from 14; LtO *Mor* from 15. *Manor Farm Cottage, 67 Langham Road, Field Dalling, Holt NR25 7LG* T: (01328) 830947 *or* (01599) 544345 E: fionanewton46@gmail.com

NEWTON, Canon George Peter Howgill. b 62. Pemb Coll Cam BA 84 MA 88. Oak Hill Th Coll BA 83. **d** 93 **p** 94. C Blackpool St Thos *Blackb* 93–99; P-in-c Aldershot H Trin *Guildf* 99–03; V from 03; AD Aldershot 11–19; Chapl Farnborough Coll of Tech 00–08; Hon Can Guildf Cathl from 18. *2 Cranmore Lane, Aldershot GU11 3AS* T: (01252) 320618 E: g@gjsk.prestel.co.uk

NEWTON, Canon Graham Hayden. b 47. AKC 69. St Aug Coll Cant 70. **d** 70 **p** 71. C St Mary-at-Lambeth *S'wark* 70–73; TV Catford (Southend) and Downham 73–78; P-in-c Porthill *Lich* 78–79; TV Wolstanton 79–86; V Stevenage H Trin *St Alb* 86–96; TR Dunstable 96–04; RD 96–02; R Barton-le-Cley w Higham Gobion and Hexton 04–12; Hon Can St Alb 04–12; rtd 12; PtO *St Alb* 12–15; *Win* from 12. *23 Regency Crescent, Christchurch BH23 2UF* T: (01202) 950010 E: revdghnewton@gmail.com

NEWTON, Holly Jane. b 86. Bath Spa Univ BA 10. Sarum Coll 19. **d** 21. C White Horse *Sarum* from 21. *37 Timor Road, Westbury BA13 2GA* E: hnewton86@gmail.com

NEWTON, John. b 39. AKC 65. **d** 66 **p** 67. C Whipton *Ex* 66–68; C Plympton St Mary 68–74; V Broadwoodwidger 74–81; R Kelly w Bradstone 74–81; R Lifton 74–81; Chapl All Hallows Sch Rousdon 81–94; LtO *Ex* 81–94; rtd 99. *Flat 2, 5 Eyewell Green, Seaton EX12 2BN* T: (01297) 625887 E: lyinclight@live.co.uk

NEWTON, Louis Kalbfield. b 44. N Texas State Univ BA 73. Westcott Ho Cam 90. **d** 93 **p** 94. C Walthamstow St Pet *Chelmsf* 93–97; USA from 97; rtd 09. *265 Fell Street, Apt 207, San Francisco CA 94102-5151, USA* M: (415) 621 3409 E: louisknewton@yahoo.com

NEWTON, Michael David. b 89. Trin Hall Cam BA 11 MA 15 PGCE 12. Cranmer Hall Dur 13. **d** 15 **p** 16. C Ely 15–17; TV Lordsbridge from 17. *The Vicarage, 92 Swaynes Lane, Comberton, Cambridge CB23 7EF* E: mdavidn16@gmail.com

NEWTON, Canon Nigel Ernest Hartley. b 38. St Jo Coll Nottm 87. **d** 89 **p** 90. C Largs *Glas* 89–92; Angl Chapl Ashbourne Home Largs 89–92; P-in-c Eyemouth *Edin* 92–95; Chapl Miss to Seamen 92–95; P-in-c Challoch *Glas* 95–92; R 04–06; Can St Mary's Cathl 04–06; Hon Can St Mary's Cathl from 06; rtd 06; P-in-c Stranraer *Glas* 10–13. *Glenairlie, 7 Wigtown Road, Newton Stewart DG8 6JZ* T: (01671) 401228 M: 07885-436892 E: glenairlie@btinternet.com

NEWTON, Peter. b 39. St Jo Coll Nottm 73. **d** 75 **p** 76. C Porchester *S'well* 75–79; R Wilford 79–99; rtd 99; Warden Advent Ho Healing Min Birmingham USA 99–12; PtO *Leic* 00–21. *20 Main Street, Eaton, Grantham NG32 1SE* T: (01476) 870024 E: newtonji@hotmail.com

NEWTON, Raymond David. b 43. K Coll Lon BSc 65. Linc Th Coll 65. **d** 67 **p** 68. C Ipswich St Matt *St E* 67–71; C E w W Bharash *Linc* 71–74; R Chelmondiston w Harkstead *St E* 74–78; R Chelmondiston w Harkstead and Shotley w Erwarton 78–91; R Chelmondiston and Erwarton w Harkstead 91–04; rtd 04; PtO *St E* from 16. *Langley Cottage, 4 Church Road, Chelmondiston, Ipswich IP9 1HS* T: (01473) 780117 M: 07718-808970

NEWTON, Richard. b 47. Trin Coll Bris 72. **d** 73 **p** 74. C Fareham St Jo *Portsm* 73–76; C Cheltenham St Mark *Glouc* 76–83; P-in-c Malvern St Andr *Worc* 83–95; TR Kingswood *Bris* 95–99; Master St Jo Hosp Bath 00–07; rtd 07; PtO *Worc* from 08. *61 Columbia Drive, Worcester WR2 4DB* T: (01905) 426702 E: 2antiques41@talktalk.net

NEWTON, Richard John Christopher. b 60. Bris Univ BSc 81. Qu Coll Birm 85. **d** 88 **p** 89. C Bris Ch the Servant Stockwood 88–92; C Dorking w Ranmore *Guildf* 92–96; P-in-c Hagley *Worc* 96–00; R from 00; Hon C Belbroughton w Fairfield and Clent from 15. *The Rectory, 6 Middlefield Lane, Hagley, Stourbridge DY9 0PX* T: (01562) 882442 E: richardn.kathy@gmail.com

NEWTON, Ruth Elizabeth. b 71. Cen Lancs Univ BA 93 Huddersfield Univ PGCE 13. St Jo Coll Nottm MTh 01. **d** 02 **p** 03. C Caldbeck, Castle Sowerby and Sebergham *Carl* 02–06; V Hutton Cranswick w Skerne, Watton and Beswick *York* 06–11; RD Harthill 10–11; P-in-c Kirklington w Burneston and Wath and Pickhill *Ripon* 11–14; *Leeds*

14–15; Can Res Ripon Cathl from 15; C Ripon Cathl Benefice *Leeds* from 17; Lay Tr Officer Ripon Area 17–18. *16 Orchard Close, Sharow, Ripon HG4 5BE* M: 07805-265171 E: revdruthnewton@gmail.com

NEWTON, Ruth Katherine. b 58. **d** 10 **p** 11. NSM Rowley w Skidby *York* 10–15; NSM Walkington, Bishop Burton, Rowley etc 15–18; rtd 18; PtO *York* from 18. *6 Manor Barns, Little Weighton, Cottingham HU20 3UA* T: (01482) 841875   E: newtonrk@newtonrk.karoo.co.uk   *or* ruth.newton@yorkdiocese.org

NEWTON, Mrs Sonya Teresa. b 74. Trin Coll Bris 17. **d** 19 **p** 20. C Coney Hill *Glouc* from 19. *8 Bittern Avenue, Abbeydale, Gloucester GL4 4WA* E: howdoyoulikeyours@hotmail.com

NGOY, Lusa. *See* NSENGA-NGOY, Lusa

NIBLETT, James Raemond John. b 86. Bris Bapt Coll BA 09. Trin Coll Bris MA 20. **d** 20 **p** 21. C Vale and Cotswold Edge *Glouc* from 20. *12 Fereby Close, Chipping Camden   GL55 6ET   E: rev.j.niblett@gmail.com   or* jay@stjameschurchcampden.co.uk

NICE, Canon John Edmund. b 51. Univ of Wales (Ban) BA 73. Coll of Resurr Mirfield 74. **d** 76 **p** 77. C Oxton *Ches* 76–79; C Liscard St Mary w St Columba 79–82; V Latchford St Jas 82–92; TR Holyhead w Rhoscolyn w Llanfair-yn-Neubwll *Ban* 92–95; TR Holyhead 95–04; RD Llifon and Talybolion 97–01; AD 01–04; R Llandudno 04–17; Can Cursal Ban Cathl 02–04; Can and Preb Ban Cathl 04–17; AD Arllechwedd 10–15; rtd 17; PtO *St As* from 14; *Ban* from 17. *61 The Dale, Abergele LL22 7DT* E: john.nice2@btopenworld.com

NICHOL, Canon William David. b 58. Hull Univ BA 84. Ridley Hall Cam 84. **d** 87 **p** 88. C Hull St Jo Newland *York* 87–90; C Kirk Ella 90–92; TV 92–98; P-in-c Powick *Worc* 98–99; R Powick and Guarlford and Madresfield w Newland 99–05; V Malvern H Trin and St Jas 05–19; RD Malvern 07–13 and 17–19; P-in-c Pedmore 19–21; P-in-c Wollescote 19–21; R Pedmore and Wollescote from 21; Hon Can Worc Cathl from 17. *The Rectory, Pedmore Lane, Stourbridge DY9 0SW* E: davidnichol1958@gmail.com

NICHOLAS, Jonathan. b 78. Cranmer Hall Dur 08. **d** 10 **p** 11. C Lt Horton *Bradf* 10–14; C Oldbury, Langley and Londonderry *Birm* 14–15; V Sutton Coldfield St Chad from 15. *The Vicarage, 41 Hollyfield Road, Sutton Coldfield B75 7SN* T: 0121-329 2995 E: vicar@stchadsc.org.uk

NICHOLAS, Malcolm Keith. b 46. Open Univ BA 79 FIBMS 71. S Dios Minl Tr Scheme 81. **d** 84 **p** 85. NSM Gatcombe *Portsm* 84–92; NSM Shorwell w Kingston 88–92; C Hartley Wintney, Elvetham, Winchfield etc *Win* 92–96; TV Grantham *Linc* 96–02; V Grantham, Harrowby w Londonthorpe 02–03; V Carr Dyke Gp 03–11; rtd 11; PtO *Nor* from 12. *6 Ashey Place, Ryde PO33 2WA* T: (01983) 810086 E: malnic46@gmail.com

NICHOLAS, Paul James. b 51. Univ of Wales (Lamp) BA. Coll of Resurr Mirfield 73. **d** 74 **p** 75. C Llanelli *St D* 74–78; C Roath *Llan* 78–84; P-in-c Leic St Pet 84–87; V Shard End *Birm* 87–96; rtd 96; PtO *Birm* from 96. *50 Delrene Road, Shirley, Solihull B90 2HJ* T: 0121-745 7339

NICHOLAS, Peter John. b 78. BNC Ox MA 00 MSc 02. Wycliffe Hall Ox 10. **d** 12 **p** 13. C Langham Place All So *Lon* from 12; P-in-c Clerkenwell St Jas and St Jo w St Pet from 18. *14 Steadman Court, 165 Old Street, London EC1V 9ND* T: (020) 7251 1190 E: pete@inspirelondon.org

NICHOLAS ALAN, Brother. *See* WORSSAM, Nicholas Alan

NICHOLAS-LETCH, Carol Ann. b 46. **d** 19 **p** 19. NSM Wissey Valley *Ely* 19–20; C from 20. *Honey Trees, Furlong Drove, Stoke Ferry, King's Lynn PE33 9SX* T: (01366) 500704 E: caroln153@hotmail.com

NICHOLL, Mrs Karen. b 65. Bradf Univ BA 99 Leeds Univ BA 07. Coll of Resurr Mirfield 05. **d** 07 **p** 08. C Lindley *Wakef* 07–10; P-in-c Gomersal 10–14; *Leeds* 14–19; V from 19; P-in-c Birkenshaw w Hunsworth from 19. *St Paul's Vicarage, 6 Vicarage Gardens, Birkenshaw, Bradford BD11 2EF* T: (01274) 683776 E: nicholl.karen@googlemail.com

NICHOLLS (née HUMPHRIES), Mrs Catherine Elizabeth. b 53. Anglia Poly Univ MA 97. Trin Coll Bris BA 87. **d** 87 **p** 94. C Bath Twerton-on-Avon *B & W* 87–90; Personnel Manager and Tr Officer TEAR Fund 90–95; Hon C Norbiton *S'wark* 91–95; PtO *Ely* 95–97; Dir Past Studies EAMTC 97–03; Vice Prin 01–03; Hon Min Can Pet Cathl 97–03; PtO *Nor* 03–05 and from 10; Dioc Dir CME 05–10. *North Cottage, King John's Thorn, Hethel, Norwich NR14 8HE* T: (01508) 570557 E: cathynicholls@allbelievers.org

NICHOLLS (née TOVAR), Mrs Gillian Elaine. b 48. Sussex Univ CertEd 69. Trin Coll Bris BA 86. **dss** 86 **d** 87 **p** 94. Tonbridge SS Pet and Paul *Roch* 86–00; Dar Pn 87–94; C 94–00; V Gillingham H Trin 00–10; rtd 10; PtO *Ox* from 11. *29 The Gables, Haddenham, Aylesbury HP17 8AD* T: (01844) 291993 E: gilltovar2008@gmail.com

NICHOLLS, Helen. **d** 18 **p** 19. NSM Bro Lliedi *St D* from 18. *The Ridge, 6 Trosserch Road, Llangennech, Llandeilo SA14 8AQ* E: hnicholls28@googlemail.com

NICHOLLS, Irene Elizabeth. b 41. **d** 09 **p** 10. OLM Penkridge *Lich* 09–14; PtO 14–21. *79 Croydon Drive, Penkridge, Stafford ST19 5DW* T: (01785) 714686 E: irenenicholl2@gmail.com

NICHOLLS, Canon Janet Elizabeth. b 64. Southlands Coll Lon BEd 86. ERMC 09. **d** 12 **p** 13. NSM Panfield and Rayne *Chelmsf* 12–15; NSM Finchingfield and Cornish Hall End etc 12–15; Dioc Rural Officer from 15; Public Preacher from 15; Hon Can Chelmsf Cathl from 20. *Park House, Braintree Road, Shalford, Braintree CM7 5HQ* T: (01371) 851317 E: jnicholls@chelmsford.anglican.org

✠**NICHOLLS, The Rt Revd John.** b 43. AKC 66. **d** 67 **p** 68 **c** 90. C Salford St Clem Ordsall *Man* 67–69; C Langley All SS and Martyrs 69–72; V 72–78; Dir Past Th Coll of Resurr Mirfield 78–83; Can Res Man Cathl 83–90; Suff Bp Lancaster *Blackb* 90–97; Bp Sheff 97–08; rtd 08; Hon Asst Bp Derby from 09; Hon Asst Bp Man from 12. *75 Rowton Grange Road, Chapel-en-le-Frith, High Peak SK23 0LD* T: (01298) 938249 M: 07773-244946 E: jnseraphim@gmx.com

NICHOLLS, Keith Barclay. b 57. Nottm Univ BA 78. Wycliffe Hall Ox 03. **d** 05 **p** 06. C Bisley and W End *Guildf* 05–09; V Burchetts Green *Ox* 09–20; rtd 20. *4 Fullers Close, Chesham HP5 1LU* E: kbnicholls@hotmail.com

NICHOLLS, Canon Mark Richard. b 60. LSE BSc(Econ) 82 Leeds Univ BA 88. Coll of Resurr Mirfield 86. **d** 89 **p** 90. C Warrington St Elphin *Liv* 89–92; V Wigan St Andr 92–96; R North End St Marg Zimbabwe 96–00; Shrine P Shrine of Our Lady of Walsingham 00–02; V Mill End and Heronsgate w W Hyde *St Alb* 02–07; P-in-c Rotherhithe St Mary w All SS *S'wark* 07–10; R from 10; P-in-c Bermondsey St Kath w St Bart 14–20; AD Bermondsey 13–18; Hon Can Manicaland Zimbabwe from 14. *St Mary's Rectory, 72A St Marychurch Street, London SE16 2JE* M: 07909-546659 E: mmarini2001@aol.com

NICHOLLS, Robert Graham. b 56. Sheff Univ BEng 77 CEng MIET 07. STETS 05. **d** 08 **p** 09. NSM Fair Oak *Win* from 08. *20 The Spinney, Eastleigh SO50 8PF* T: (023) 8069 3716 M: 07837-804366 E: bob.nicholls27@gmail.com

NICHOLLS, Roger Frank. b 43. Ox Univ MA Cam Univ DipEd. **d** 01 **p** 02. OLM Kenwyn w St Allen *Truro* 01–04; NSM Truro St Paul and St Clem 04–08; NSM Truro St Geo and St Jo 04–08; P-in-c Mylor w Flushing 08–13; rtd 13; PtO *Truro* from 16. *8 Truro Vean Terrace, Truro TR1 1HA* T: (01872) 275753

NICHOLLS, Simon James. b 53. Anglia Ruskin Univ MA 08 Trent Park Coll of Educn CertEd 76. Ridley Hall Cam. **d** 00 **p** 01. C Nuneaton St Nic *Cov* 00–04; R Markfield, Thornton, Bagworth and Stanton etc *Leic* 04–19; rtd 19. *29 Coppice Drive, Heanor DE75 7BW* T: (01773) 772853 E: simonnichols24@gmail.com

NICHOLLS, Barry Edward. b 40. ACA 63 FCA 73. S'wark Ord Course 66. **d** 69 **p** 70. NSM Surbiton St Andr and St Mark *S'wark* 69–92; Dean for MSE Kingston Area 90–92; Hon Can S'wark Cathl 90–92; PtO 99–01; NSM Upper Tooting H Trin 01–04; NSM Upper Tooting H Trin w St Aug 04–12; rtd 12; PtO *S'wark* from 12; *Chich* from 21. *Wind Demons, West Bracklesham Drive, Bracklesham Bay, Chichester PO20 8PF* T: (01243) 671479 M: 07740-152309 E: barrynichols@btinternet.com

NICHOLLS, Mrs Elizabeth Margaret. b 45. WEMTC 00. **d** 02 **p** 03. NSM Ledbury *Heref* 02–05; NSM Boxwell, Leighterton, Didmarton, Oldbury etc *Glouc* 05–10; rtd 10; PtO *Glouc* from 16. *27 Noverton Lane, Prestbury, Cheltenham GL52 5DD* T: (01242) 572249

NICHOLS, Frank Bernard. b 43. Kelham Th Coll 64. **d** 68 **p** 69. C Luton St Andr *St Alb* 68–72; C Cheshunt 72–76; C-in-c Marsh Farm CD 76–81; PtO Brisbane Australia 08–10; PtO *Nor* from 10. *15A Wells Road, Walsingham NR22 6DL* T: (01328) 821459 M: 07503-932804 E: lyngateman@hotmail.co.uk

NICHOLS, Howard Keith. b 41. CCC Ox BA 64 MA 68 CEng 86 FIEE 92 EurIng 94. WEMTC 98. **d** 01 **p** 02. NSM Ledbury *Heref* 01–04; NSM Boxwell, Leighterton, Didmarton, Oldbury etc *Glouc* 04–10; PtO from 16. *27 Noverton Lane, Prestbury, Cheltenham GL52 5DD* T: (01242) 572249

NICHOLS, Mark Steven. b 68. Lon Bible Coll BA 94 Ridley Hall Cam 95. **d** 97 **p** 98. C Balham Hill Ascension *S'wark* 97–99. *29 New Road, Norton, Doncaster DN6 9HW* M: 07875-636737 E: mark@mark-nichols.co.uk

NICHOLS, Robert Warren. b 54. Biola Univ (USA) BA 77 Fuller Th Sem California MA 81. SAOMC 93. **d** 96 **p** 97. C Headington Quarry *Ox* 96–00; Sen Asst P Wymondham *Nor* 00–05; Lect 01–05; R Caston, Griston, Merton, Thompson etc *Nor* 05–16; rtd 16; PtO *Nor* from 17. *The Old Rectory,*

Station Road, Hillington, King's Lynn PE31 6DE T: (01485) 609294 E: revbobnichols@gmail.com

NICHOLS, Stephen Robert Chamberlain. b 73. Ch Coll Cam BA 96 MA 00 SOAS Lon MA 98 Bris Univ PhD 11. Wycliffe Hall Ox BA 06. **d** 09 **p** 10. C Plymouth St Andr and Stonehouse *Ex* 09–14; C Langham Place All So *Lon* 14–21; V Lindfield *Chich* from 21. *The Vicarage, 137 High Street, Lindfield, Haywards Heath RH16 2HR* M: 07960-063174 E: stephen.nichols@lindfield.info

NICHOLSON, Andrew John. b 69. Leeds Univ BA 93 MA 00. St Jo Coll Nottm MTh 04. **d** 05 **p** 06. C E Richmond *Ripon* 05–09; P-in-c Barwick in Elmet 09–14; *Leeds* 14–15; P-in-c Thorner *Ripon* 09–14; *Leeds* 14–15; R Elmete Trin 16–21. *2 Fellows Gardens, College Road, Ardingly, Haywards Heath RH17 6SQ.* M: 07512-314312 E: reverandy1@gmail.com

NICHOLSON, Mrs Barbara Ruth. b 39. Nor City Coll TCert 59. **d** 02 **p** 03. OLM Reculver and Herne Bay St Bart *Cant* 02–11; PtO from 11. *34 Cliff Avenue, Herne Bay CT6 6LZ* T: (01227) 364606 F: 365384 E: barbaranicholson@me.com

NICHOLSON, Brian Warburton. b 44. ALCD 73 LTh 74. St Jo Coll Nottm 70. **d** 73 **p** 74. C Canford Magna *Sarum* 73–77; C E Twickenham St Steph *Lon* 77–80; V Colchester St Jo *Chelmsf* 80–96; R Oakley w Wootton St Lawrence *Win* 96–09; rtd 09; PtO *Win* 09–20. *Nuthatches, 16 St Vigor Way, Colden Common, Winchester SO21 1UU* T: (01962) 713433 E: brian.nic@talktalk.net

NICHOLSON, Christina Olive. b 59. **d** 08 **p** 09. OLM Mossley Hill *Liv* 08–12; C Ince Ch Ch w Wigan St Cath 12–15; C Hindley Green 15–16; TV Wigan All SS 16–19; TV Wigan from 20. *St Andrew's Vicarage, 3A Mort Street, Wigan WN6 7AU* E: tina2nic@sky.com

NICHOLSON, David. b 57. Sarum & Wells Th Coll 80. **d** 83 **p** 84. C Trevethin *Mon* 83–85; C Ebbw Vale 85–87; V Newport St Steph and H Trin 87–95; V Abertillery w Cwmtillery w Six Bells 95–97; Hon Chapl Miss to Seamen 87–97; P-in-c Cudworth *Wakef* 97–98; P-in-c Lundwood 01–04; V Cudworth 98–14; *Leeds* from 14; Dioc Urban Officer *Wakef* 08–14; *Leeds* from 14; Chapl to The Queen from 14. *The Vicarage, St John's Road, Cudworth, Barnsley S72 8DE* T: (01226) 710279 E: frnicholson@aol.com

NICHOLSON, Dorothy Ann. b 40. Surrey Univ Roehampton MSc 04. S'wark Ord Course 81. **dss** 84 **d** 87 **p** 94. Carshalton Beeches S'wark 84–88; Par Dn 87–88; Par Dn Brixton Road Ch Ch 88–89; C Malden St Jo 89–95; V Balham St Mary and St Jo 95–05; rtd 05. *17 Bromley College, London Road, Bromley BR1 1PE* T: (020) 3754 9987 E: nichoda@uwclub.net

NICHOLSON, Gary. b 62. Open Univ BA 89. Cranmer Hall Dur 91 NEOC 92. **d** 95 **p** 96. NSM Whitworth w Spennymoor *Dur* 95–97; NSM Spennymoor, Whitworth and Merrington 97–00; C Coundon and Eldon 00–02; P-in-c from 02. *St James's Vicarage, 2A Collingwood Street, Coundon, Bishop Auckland DL14 8LG* E: frgary@hotmail.com

NICHOLSON, Mary. See NICHOLSON, Yuet-Yee Mary

NICHOLSON, Michael James Wesley. b 89. Ch Coll Cam BA 11. Oak Hill Th Coll BA 20. **d** 20 **p** 21. C Cambridge St Andr Less *Ely* from 20. *48 Beacon Rise, 160 Newmarket Road, Cambridge CB5 8AX* M: 07895-761585 E: michael@cccam.org.uk

NICHOLSON, Canon Nigel Patrick. b 46. DL 07. Sarum & Wells Th Coll 72. **d** 75 **p** 76. C Farnham *Guildf* 75–78; C Worplesdon 78–81; CF (ACF) from 80; P-in-c Compton *Guildf* 81–85; R Compton w Shackleford and Peper Harow 85–89; R Cranleigh 89–12; RD 95–00; Hon Can Guildf Cathl 01–12; rtd 12; PtO *Chich* from 12; *Guildf* from 12; *Portsm* from 12. *Banford House, 25 Portsmouth Road, Liphook GU30 7DJ* T: (01428) 724979 E: nicholson.banford@outlook.com

NICHOLSON, Paul Shannon. b 52. York Univ BA 74 Middx Univ BA 02 Heythrop Coll Lon MA 07 ARCO 74 ARCM 75. NTMTC 99. **d** 02 **p** 03. C Primrose Hill St Mary w Avenue Road St Paul *Lon* 02–06; P-in-c Chalk Farm from 06; P-in-c Belsize Park from 06. *St Saviour's Vicarage, 30 Eton Villas, London NW3 4SQ* T: (020) 7586 6522 M: 07971-223764 E: paul.nicholson@london.anglican.org

NICHOLSON, Canon Peter Charles. b 25. OBE 92. Lambeth MA 89. Chich Th Coll 57. **d** 59 **p** 60. C Sawbridgeworth *St Alb* 59–62; Min Can, Prec and Sacr Pet Cathl 62–67; V Wroxham w Hoveton *Nor* 67–74; V Lyme Regis *Sarum* 74–80; Gen Sec St Luke's Hosp for the Clergy 80–93; NSM Harlington *Lon* 80–87; Min Can Ch Ch *Ox* from 87; Can and Preb Chich Cathl 89–93; rtd 93. *St Luke's Cottage, 13 Brearley Close, Uxbridge UB8 1JJ* T: (01895) 233522

NICHOLSON, Peter Charles. b 44. Oak Hill Th Coll 74. **d** 76 **p** 77. C Croydon Ch Ch Broad Green *Cant* 76–80; C Gt Baddow *Chelmsf* 80–88; TV 88–96; V Westcliff St Mich 96–13; rtd 13; PtO *Chelmsf* from 14. *Kiononia, 25 Eastwood*

Park Drive, Leigh-on-Sea SS9 5RP T: (01702) 527444 E: pedinic@yahoo.co.uk

NICHOLSON, Canon Rodney. b 45. Mert Coll Ox BA 68 MA 71. Ridley Hall Cam 69. **d** 72 **p** 73. C Colne St Bart *Blackb* 72–75; C Blackpool St Jo 75–78; V Ewood 78–90; V Clitheroe St Paul Low Moor 90–14; P-in-c Chatburn and Downham 03–14; Hon Can Blackb Cathl 06–14; rtd 14; PtO *York* from 15; RD S Wold 17–19. *96 Shipman Road, Market Weighton, York YO43 3RB* T: (01430) 650271 E: rodnic03@gmail.com

NICHOLSON, Roland. b 40. Sarum & Wells Th Coll 72. **d** 74 **p** 75. C Morecambe St Barn *Blackb* 74–78; V Feniscliffe 78–90; V Sabden and Pendleton 90–02; C Poulton-le-Fylde 02–04; C Poulton Carleton and Singleton 04–07; rtd 08; PtO *Blackb* from 08. *25 St Mary's Court, Church Lane, Mellor, Blackburn BB2 7JE*

NICHOLSON, Miss Velda Christine. b 44. Charlotte Mason Coll of Educn TCert 65. Cranmer Hall Dur 81. **dss** 82 **d** 87 **p** 94. Gt and Lt Driffield *York* 82–86; Newby 86–88; Par Dn 87–88; Team Dn Cramlington *Newc* 88–94; TV 94–96; PtO from 96; rtd 04. *24 Glendale, Amble, Morpeth NE65 0RG* T: (01665) 713796

NICHOLSON, Yuet-Yee Mary. b 60. Man Univ MB, ChB 91 MRCGP 96 Win Univ PGCE 11. Sarum Coll 13. **d** 16 **p** 17. C Brockenhurst *Win* 16–19; C Southampton St Mark 19–20; PtO from 21. *Pikes Post, Chapel Lane, Burley, Ringwood BH24 4DJ* T: (01425) 404155 M: 07799-811888 E: pikespost@tiscali.co.uk

NICKLAS-CARTER, Derath May. See DURKIN, Derath May

NICKOLS, James Alexander. b 75. Regent's Park Coll Ox BA 96. Ridley Hall Cam 98. **d** 00 **p** 01. C Plymouth St Jude *Ex* 00–04; C Camberwell All SS S'wark 04–08; Hon C Camberwell Ch Ch 09–18; PtO *Ox* 13–16; Min Chich Immanuel BMO from 18. *Flint Lodge, Lavant, Chichester PO18 0BH* M: 07875-010350 E: james@immanuelchichester.com

NICKOLS-RAWLE, Peter John. b 44. St Luke's Coll Ex CertEd 73. Sarum & Wells Th Coll 76. **d** 78 **p** 79. C Ex St Thos 78–80; Old and New Shoreham *Chich* 80–86; P-in-c Donnington 86–90; Chapl RAF 90–92; TV Ottery St Mary, Alfington, W Hill, Tipton etc *Ex* 92–97; V Breage w Germoe and Godolphin *Truro* 98–01; rtd 01; PtO *Truro* 01–05. *14 The Copse, Exmouth EX8 4EY* T: (01395) 270068

NICKSON, Canon Ann Louise. b 58. New Hall Cam BA 80 Fitzw Coll Cam BA 95 Solicitor 81. Ridley Hall Cam PhD 98. **d** 98 **p** 99. C Sanderstead All SS S'wark 98–01; P-in-c Norbury St Steph and Thornton Heath 01–05; V 05–10; AD Croydon N 06–10; TR Mortlake w E Sheen from 10; Hon Can S'wark Cathl from 10. *The Rectory, 170 Sheen Lane, London SW14 8LZ* T: (020) 8876 4816 E: annnickson@aol.com

NICOL, David Christopher. b 56. Westmr Coll Ox BEd 84 Ox Univ Inst of Educn 91. SAOMC 95. **d** 98 **p** 99. NSM Deddington w Barford, Clifton and Hempton *Ox* 98–01; V Longnor, Quarnford and Sheen *Lich* 01–08; P-in-c Woore and Norton in Hales 09–12; Local Par Development Adv Shrewsbury Area 10–12; TV Leek and Meerbrook *Lich* 15–20; rtd 20. *6 Hill View, Leek ST13 5TA* E: fr.david@tinyworld.co.uk

NICOL, Harvie Thomas. b 61. Aston Tr Scheme 95 St Jo Coll Nottm 97. **d** 99 **p** 00. C Balderstone *Man* 99; C S Rochdale 00–03; TV Ashton 03–08; P-in-c Ashton St Pet 03–08; V Formby St Luke *Liv* 08–19; V Bury, Roch Valley *Man* from 19; V Bircle from 19. *St Thomas's Vicarage, Pimhole Road, Bury BL9 7EY* T: 0161-764 1157

NICOLE, Bruce. b 54. K Coll Lon MA 96 ACIB. Wycliffe Hall Ox 89. **d** 91 **p** 92. C Headley All SS *Guildf* 91–95; V Camberley St Mich Yorktown 95–20; RD Surrey Heath 02–06; rtd 20; PtO *Guildf* from 21; *Win* from 21. *20 Greenfields Avenue, Alton GU34 2ED* E: revbrucenicole@gmail.com

NICOLL, Miss Angela Olive Woods. b 50. Linc Th Coll 77. **dss** 79 **d** 87 **p** 94. Catford St Laur S'wark 79–83; Peckham St Jo w St Andr 83–88; Par Dn 87–88; Par Dn New Addington 88–94; C 94–02; S Africa 02–06; PtO *Ely* 06–10; Nor from 14. *15 Manor Park, Watton, Thetford IP25 6HH* T: (01953) 889074

NIECHCIAL, Stephen Alexander. b 53. St Chad's Coll Dur BA 74 MA 19 CQSW 85. St Steph Ho Ox 12. **d** 14 **p** 15. C Sidcup St Jo *Roch* 14–18; C Beckenham St Jas w St Mich and St Aug 16–17; V Petts Wood from 18. *St Francis's Vicarage, 60 Willett Way, Petts Wood, Orpington BR5 1QE* T: (01689) 829971 M: 07976-011494 E: revdstephenn@outlook.com

NIEMIEC, Paul Kevin. b 56. EAMTC 03. **d** 05 **p** 06. Youth Officer *Pet* 97–08; NSM Thrapston, Denford and Islip 05–08; TV Barnstaple *Ex* 08–11; TV Ouzel Valley *St Alb* 11–17; TV Heacham and Snettisham *Nor* 17–18; RD Heacham and Rising 17–18; rtd 18. *52 Culloden Drive, Kettering NN15 5DF* E: pkniemiec@gmail.com

NIGHTINGALE, Canon John Brodie. b 42. Pemb Coll Ox BA 64 Qu Coll Cam BA 67. Westcott Ho Cam 65. **d** 67 **p** 68. C Wythenshawe St Martin *Man* 67–70; Nigeria 70–76; P-in-c Amberley w N Stoke *Chich* 76–79; Adult Educn Adv 76–79; Asst Home Sec Gen Syn Bd for Miss and Unity 80–84; Miss Sec 84–87; P-in-c Wolverton w Norton Lindsey and Langley *Cov* 87–95; Dioc Miss Adv 87–95; V Rowley Regis *Birm* 95–07; Hon Can Birm Cathl 01–07; Warden of Readers 03–07; rtd 07; PtO *Birm* from 07; *Lich* 15–21. *19 Berberry Close, Birmingham B30 1TB* T: 0121-458 6182 M: 07811-128831

NIGHTINGALE, Philip James. b 82. Birm Univ BA 05. Wycliffe Hall Ox BA 17. **d** 18 **p** 19. C Rushden St Mary w Newton Bromswold *Pet* from 18. *36 Meadow Sweet Road, Rushden NN10 0GA* M: 07815-095964 E: philnightingale@hotmail.com

NIGHTINGALE, Susan Kay. b 44. Keele Univ BA 66 Seabury-Western Th Sem DMin 99. S'wark Ord Course 90. **d** 93 **p** 94. NSM St Giles Cripplegate w St Bart Moor Lane etc *Lon* 93–99; PtO *York* 93–99; Asst Chapl H Trin Geneva *Eur* 99–02; P-in-c Sutton on the Forest *York* 03–06; NSM Forest of Galtres 06–12; rtd 12; PtO *York* from 12. *27 East Mount Road, York YO24 1BD* T: (01904) 689742 E: suenightingale3@gmail.com

NIMMO, The Very Revd Alexander Emsley. b 53. Aber Univ BD 76 PhD 97 Edin Univ MPhil 83 FSAScot 93. Edin Th Coll 76. **d** 78 **p** 79. Prec St Andr Cathl Inverness *Mor* 78–81; P-in-c Stornoway *Arg* 81–83; R 84; R Edin St Mich and All SS 84–90; Chapl HM Pris Saughton 87–90; R Aberdeen St Marg *Ab* from 90; Can St Andr Cathl from 96; Syn Clerk 01–08; Episc Visiting Chapl HM Pris Peterhead 04–07; Dean Ab 08–17; Hon Can Connecticut USA 16–19. *St Margaret's Clergy House, Gallowgate, Aberdeen AB25 1EA* T: (01224) 644969 F: 630767 E: alexander306@btinternet.com

NIND, Robert William Hampden. b 31. Ball Coll Ox BA 54 MA 60. Cuddesdon Coll 54. **d** 56 **p** 57. C Spalding St Mary and St Nic *Linc* 56–60; Jamaica 60–67; P-in-c Battersea St Bart *S'wark* 67–70; V Brixton St Matt 70–82; LtO 82–84; Ind Chapl 84–89; Ind Chapl *Ox* 89–95; rtd 95; PtO *Ox* 15–18. *19 Binswood Avenue, Headington, Oxford OX3 8NY* T: (01865) 766604 E: b467@btinternet.com

NISBECK, Peter. b 51. SOAS Lon BA 73 Aston Univ MSc 94. NOC 03. **d** 06 **p** 07. NSM Newcastle w Butterton *Lich* from 06. *The Village Farmhouse, Clayton Road, Newcastle ST5 4AB* T: (01782) 662379 E: peternisbeck@hotmail.com

NISBET, Tessa Jane. b 66. **d** 14 **p** 15. C Heatherlands St Jo *Sarum* 14–18; R Hamworthy from 18. *St Michael's Rectory, 1 St Michael's Close, Poole BH15 4QT* T: (01202) 674878 M: 07789-602682 E: tessafuhri@gmail.com

NISSEN, Peter Edlef. b 76. Copenhagen Univ BA 99 MA 05 and 11. St Steph Ho Ox 14. **d** 16 **p** 17. C Alyn Miss Area *St As* 16–18. *19 Acacia Court, Llay, Wrexham LL12 0TX* T: (01978) 448902 M: 07805-921053 E: revd.peter.nissen@gmail.com

NIXON, David John. b 59. St Chad's Coll Dur BA 81 Ex Univ PhD 02. St Steph Ho Ox 88. **d** 91 **p** 92. C Plymouth St Pet *Ex* 91–94; Chapl Ex Univ 94–03; P-in-c Stoke Damerel 03–09; P-in-c Devonport St Aubyn 03–09; R Stoke Damerel and Devonport St Aubyn 09–13; RD Plymouth Devonport 11–13; Dean of Studies SWMTC 13–18; PtO *Ex* 13–18; TR Ex St Thos and Em from 18; RD Christianity from 18; Public Preacher *Truro* from 14. *Emmanuel Vicarage, 49 Okehampton Road, Exeter EX4 1EL* T: (01392) 667192 E: rev.dave@virgin.net

NIXON, Frances (Isobel). b 34. TCD BA 62. **d** 94 **p** 95. NSM Rossorry *Clogh* from 94. *59 Granshagh Road, Enniskillen BT92 2BL* T: (028) 6634 8723 M: 07710-307263 E: agfin@btinternet.com

NIXON, Ms Naomi Jane. b 75. Keele Univ BA 97. St Jo Coll Nottm MA 00. **d** 01 **p** 02. C Ludlow, Ludford, Ashford Carbonell etc *Heref* 01–04; Chapl N Warks and Hinckley Coll of FE 04–12; Dioc Learning Adv for Minl Development *Cov* from 12; NSM Lillington and Old Milverton 10–17; C St Clare in Cov Cathl 17–21; Gen LtO from 18. *Cathedral and Diocesan Offices, 1 Hill Top, Coventry CV1 5AB* T: (024) 7652 1304 E: naomi.nixon@covcofe.org

NIXON, Pauline Margaret. b 49. **d** 05 **p** 06. NSM Perranzabuloe *Truro* 05–10; NSM Crantock w Cubert 09–10; NSM Perranzabuloe and Crantock w Cubert 10–12; Chapl Mt Edgcumbe Hospice 12; PtO *Blackb* from 13; *B & W* from 21. *5 The Green, Winscombe BS25 1AL*

NIXON, Canon Phillip Edward. b 48. Ch Ch Ox MA 73 DPhil 73 Trin Coll Cam BA 80 K Coll Lon MA 00. Westcott Ho Cam 78. **d** 81 **p** 82. C Leeds Halton St Wilfrid *Ripon* 81–84; V Goring *Ox* 84; V Goring w S Stoke 84–03; RD Henley 94–02; Hon Can Ch Ch 00–03; P-in-c Northampton St Jas *Pet* 03–13; Warden of Readers 05–12; rtd 13; PtO *Ox*

from 13. *32 Cedar Road, Oxford OX2 9EB* T: (01865) 241385 E: phillipn@btinternet.com

NIXON, Mrs Tonya. b 69. Plymouth Univ BSc 93 St Mark & St Jo Coll Lon PGCE 94. Qu Coll Birm 06. **d** 09 **p** 10. C Farmborough, Marksbury and Stanton Prior *B & W* 09–13; P-in-c Huntspill 13–18; P-in-c Mark w Allerton 13–18; R The Huntspills and Mark 18–19; C Highbridge 13–19; R Braydon Brook *Bris* from 19. *The Rectory, 1 Days Court, Crudwell, Malmesbury SN16 9HG* T: (01666) 575216 E: vicarbraydon@gmail.com

NIXON, William Samuel. Reading Univ BSc 94 TCD BTh 00. **d** 00 **p** 01. C Lisburn St Paul *Conn* 00–02; C Hillsborough *D & D* 02–06; P-in-c Edin Clermiston Em 06–08; I Killaney w Carryduff *D & D* 08–12; I Drumbeg from 12; Warden of Readers from 08; Chapl HM Pris Hydebank Wood 08–17. *The Rectory, 64 Drumbeg Road, Dunmurry, Belfast BT17 9LE* T: (028) 9543 6592 M: 07764-277771 E: cazza_willie@hotmail.com

NIXSON, Rosemary Clare. *See* WARD, Rosemary Clare

NJENGA, Lukas. b 68. Natal Univ BTh 97 MTh 98 Birm Univ PhD. Trin Coll Nairobi. **d** 92 **p** 93. V Kitengela Kenya 92–96; R Sobantu S Africa 96–01; Lect Carlile Coll Nairobi 01–02; R Glas St Geo 02–05; Chapl Glas Caledonian Univ 05–11; Chapl York St Jo Univ 11–14; Chief Exec Officer Heart for the City from 14. *Heart for the City, Purpose Centre, 582 London Road, Glasgow G40 1DZ* T: 0141-258 1060 M: 07534-719450 E: admin@heartforthecity.co.uk

NJOKA, Stanley. b 80. Middx Univ BA 09. St Andr Coll Kabare 01. **d** 04 **p** 05. Kenya 04–06; PtO *Lon* 06–07; *S'wark* 08–10; NSM Peckham St Jo w St Andr 10–11; NSM Camberwell St Giles w St Matt 11–17; Min Camberwell St Matt CD from 17; Chapl King's Coll Hosp NHS Foundn Trust 10–19; Lead Chapl Surrey and Sussex Healthcare NHS Trust from 19. *Surrey and Sussex Healthcare NHS Trust, East Surrey Hospital, Canada Avenue, Redhill RH1 5RH* T: (01737) 768511 M: 07846-759133 E: stanley.njoka@nhs.net

NJOKU, Chinenye Ngozi. b 63. Trin Coll Bris. **d** 09 **p** 10. C Goldington *St Alb* 09–13; I Garrison w Slavin and Belleek *Clogh* 13–20; Preb Clogh Cathl 19–20; P-in-c Wembley St Jo *Lon* from 20. *The Vicarage, 3 Crawford Avenue, Wembley HA0 2HX* M: 07515-171579 E: gozy78@hotmail.com

NJOROGE, John Kibe Mwangi. b 47. **d** 79 **p** 79. C Llantwit Major *Llan* 07–10; Chapl HM Pris Elmley from 11. *HM Prison Elmley, Church Road, Eastchurch, Sheerness ME12 4DZ* T: (01795) 882130 E: john.njoroge@justice.gov.uk

NJUE, James Mbugua. b 86. CA Tr Coll Nairobi 06. **d** 10 **p** 11. C Mbeere Cathl Kenya 09–12; Bp's Chapl 11–12; V St Phil Rwika 12–13; Dioc Communications Dir 09–17; Dioc Sec 13–17; PtO *S'wark* 17–18; C Addington 18–20; P-in-c Thornton Heath St Jude w St Aid from 20. *56 Viney Bank, Court Wood Lane, Croydon CR0 9JT* M: 07508-182583 E: mbugua.james@hotmail.com

NJUGUNA, Daniel Cahira. b 73. St Jo Coll Nottm BA 04. **d** 00 **p** 01. Kenya 00–03; C Balderton and Barnby-in-the-Willows *S'well* 04–06; TV Hucknall Torkard 06–11; V Wednesbury St Paul Wood Green *Lich* from 11. *St Paul's Vicarage, 68 Wood Green Road, Wednesbury WS10 9QT* M: 07817-577436 E: daniel.njuguna@btinternet.com *or* vicar@paulandluke.co.uk

NOAKES, Mrs Dorothy. b 35. Derby Coll of Educn CertEd 55 Ex Univ BEd 85 BPhil(Ed) 92. **d** 96 **p** 97. OLM Helston and Wendron *Truro* 96–05; rtd 05. *6 Tenderah Road, Helston TR13 8NT* T: (01326) 573239 E: dorothynoakes@gmail.com

NOBBS, Canon Charles Henry ffrench. b 67. Hatf Coll Dur BSc 89 St Jo Coll Dur BA 99 CEng 96. Cranmer Hall Dur 97. **d** 99 **p** 00. C Northampton St Giles *Pet* 99–02; C Collingtree w Courteenhall and Milton Malsor 02–11; Min Grange Park LEP 11–16; Police Chapl Co-ord from 03; Pioneer and Ch Planting Enabler 13–16; Pioneer and New Initiatives Tr Officer 16–19; Dir Miss *Pet* from 19; Can Pet Cathl from 15. *Bouverie Court, 6 The Lakes, Bedford Road, Northampton NN4 7YD* T: (01604) 887000 M: 07742-013599 E: charlie@dunelm.org.uk *or* charlie.nobbs@peterborough-diocese.org.uk

NOBEL, Johannes. b 81. Evang Th Faculty Leuven BA 03 Utrecht Univ MA 05 St Jo Coll Dur MA 08. Cranmer Hall Dur 06. **d** 08 **p** 09. C Norton St Mary *Dur* 08–12; C Stockton St Chad 08–12; V Heslington *York* 12–20; P-in-c Osbaldwick w Murton from 20; Dioc Environmental Officer from 20. *The Vicarage, 80 Osbaldwick Lane, York YO10 3AX* T: (01904) 870814 *or* 412300 E: johannes.nobel@gmail.com *or* jan.nobel@gmail.com

NOBES, Mrs Gillian Mary. b 65. Lon Univ BA 90. Ripon Coll Cuddesdon MA 12. **d** 12 **p** 13. C Broughton, Bossington, Houghton and Mottisfont *Win* 12–16; P-in-c Highcliffe 16–19; R Guernsey St Sampson 19–21; PtO from 21. *Zedkar, Clos du Filage, Le Frie Baton Road, St Saviour, Guernsey GY7 9PL* M: 07781-140985 E: nobes@guernsey.net

NOBLE, Ann Carol. *See* PHILP, Ann Carol

NOBLE, Anne Valerie. b 60. Univ Coll Ox BA 82 Toronto Univ MSc 84 PhD 91. St Jo Coll Nottm 04. **d** 07 **p** 08. C Wollaton S'well 07–11; TV Clifton 11–17; NSM Abbots Bromley, Blithfield, Colton, Colwich etc *Lich* from 17. *The New Rectory, Bellamour Way, Colton, Rugeley WS15 3JW* T: (01889) 576449 E: anoblerev@gmail.com

NOBLE, Brenda Gaye. b 68. All SS Cen for Miss & Min 16. **d** 19 **p** 20. C S Widnes *Liv* 19–21; C Widnes St Jo and St Paul from 21. *47 Leighton Drive, St Helens WA9 3GS* M: 07591-457221 E: brennoble@themountsthelens.co.uk

NOBLE, Christopher John Lancelot. b 58. Oak Hill Th Coll 88. **d** 90 **p** 91. C Tonbridge SS Pet and Paul *Roch* 90–95; P-in-c Stansted w Fairseat and Vigo 95–98; R from 98. *The Rectory, 9 The Coach Drive, Meopham, Gravesend DA13 0SZ* T: (01732) 822494

NOBLE, Canon Eileen Joan. b 45. NEOC 90. **d** 93 **p** 94. C Gosforth All SS *Newc* 93–96; C Cramlington 96–97; TV 97–01; V Ashington 01–06; rtd 06; Hon C Monkseaton St Mary *Newc* 07–15; Hon Can Newc Cathl from 12; PtO from 14. *34 Gorsedene Road, Whitley Bay NE26 4AH* E: revnoble2000@yahoo.com

NOBLE, Jack Michael. b 89. Bris Univ BA 12 Sheff Univ BA 14 MA 15. Coll of Resurr Mirfield 12. **d** 15 **p** 16. C Ruislip St Martin *Lon* 15–18; C St Marylebone w H Trin from 18; Chapl St Marylebone C of E Sch from 18; Chapl Univ of Westmr from 18. *The Chaplain's House, 12 Linhope Street, London NW1 6HN* M: 07765-771547 E: frjacknoble@gmail.com *or* chaplain@stmarylebone.org

NOBLE, Canon Paul Vincent. b 54. Leeds Univ BA 75 PGCE 76 Ox Univ BA 81 MA 85. St Steph Ho Ox 79. **d** 82 **p** 83. C Prestbury *Glouc* 82–85; P-in-c Avening w Cherington 85–90; R The Suttons w Tydd *Linc* 90–98; R Skirbeck St Nic 98–19; RD Holland 15–19; V Linc All SS from 19; Can and Preb Linc Cathl from 18. *The Vicarage, 33A Croft Street, Lincoln LN2 5AX* E: frpnoble@gmail.com

NOBLE, Canon Philip David. b 46. Glas Univ BSc 67 Edin Univ BD 70. Edin Th Coll 67. **d** 70 **p** 71. C Edin Ch Ch 70–72; C Port Moresby Papua New Guinea 72–73; P-in-c Sakarina 73–75; R Cambuslang *Glas* 76–83; R Uddingston 76–83; Ev Prestwick 83–85; R 85–11; Can St Mary's Cathl 99–11; rtd 11; LtO *Mor* from 12. *28 Duncraig Street, Inverness IV3 5DJ* T: (01463) 233612 E: philipdnoble@btopenworld.com

NOBLE, Robert. b 43. TCD BA 66 BD 73. **d** 68 **p** 69. C Holywood *D & D* 68–71; Chapl RAF 71–98; Chapl Holmewood Ho Sch Tunbridge Wells 98–04; PtO *Chich* 01–08; *Heref* from 08. *Temperance Cottage, Weston under Penyard, Ross-on-Wye HR9 7NX* T: (01989) 566748 E: rjnobles@tiscali.co.uk

NOBLET, David. b 62. Cranmer Hall Dur 97. **d** 99 **p** 00. C Standish *Blackb* 99–03; P-in-c Langho Billington 03–11; LtO from 11; Chapl HM Pris Kirkham 08–12; Chapl HM Pris Lanc Farms from 12. *HM Prison Lancaster Farms, Stone Row Head, Lancaster LA1 3QZ* T: (01524) 563584 E: davidnoblet@aol.com

NOBLETT, The Ven William Alexander. b 53. CBE 12. Southn Univ BTh 78 Westmr Coll Ox MTh 99. Sarum & Wells Th Coll 74. **d** 78 **p** 79. C Sholing *Win* 78–80; I Ardamine w Kiltennel, Glascarrig etc *C, F & O* 80–82; Chapl RAF 82–84; V Middlesbrough St Thos *York* 84–87; Dep Chapl HM Pris Wakef 87–89; Chapl 89–92; Chapl HM Pris Nor 92–97; Chapl HM Pris Full Sutton 97–01; Chapl Gen of Pris and Adn to HM Pris 01–12; Can and Preb York Minster 01–12; Hon Can Liv Cathl 09–12; rtd 12; PtO *York* 12–17; *Eur* from 12; *Pet* 15–20; *Ely* from 16; Chapl to The Queen from 05. *Address withheld by request* E: williamnoblett@hotmail.com

NOCK, Roland George William. b 62. St Andr Univ BSc 84 BD 89. Edin Th Coll 91. **d** 91 **p** 92. C Dunfermline *St And* 91–93; C W Fife Team Min 91–93; R Cupar 93–96; CF 96–99. *46 Heol y Parc, Cefneithin, Llanelli SA14 7DL* T: (01269) 845847

NODDER, Marcus Charles Colmore. b 67. Pemb Coll Cam BA 89 PGCE 90. Oak Hill Th Coll BA 01. **d** 01 **p** 02. C Denton Holme *Carl* 01–04; C Limehouse *Lon* from 04; P-in-c St Pet Barge from 12. *St Peter's Barge, Hertsmere Road, London E14 4AL* T: (020) 7515 7947 M: 07727-713744 E: mnodder@googlemail.com *or* m.nodder@stpetersbarge.org

NODDINGS, John Henry. b 39. Chich Th Coll 80. **d** 81 **p** 82. C Southborough St Pet w Ch Ch and St Matt *Roch* 81–83; C Prittlewell St Mary *Chelmsf* 83–86; V Clay Hill St Jo *Lon* 86–88; V Clay Hill St Jo and St Luke 88–02; Chapl Chase Farm Hosp Enfield 88–94; Chapl Chase Farm Hosps NHS Trust 94–95; P-in-c Gt Coxwell w Buscot, Coleshill etc *Ox* 03–10; rtd 03; PtO *Sarum* 10–11. *9 Fisherton Island, Salisbury SP2 7TG* T: (01722) 320177 E: johnnoddings@btinternet.com

NODDINGS, John Michael. b 69. Oak Hill Th Coll BA 97 Catholic Univ Leuven STB 02 Heythrop Coll Lon MTh 04. Allen Hall Westcott Ho Cam 16. **d** 02 **p** 19. In RC Ch 02–14; C

Corringham and Fobbing *Chelmsf* from 18. *The Glebe House, High Road, Fobbing, Stanford-le-Hope SS17 9JH* T: (01375) 466811 E: jmnoddings@icloud.com

NOEL, Rachel Naomi. b 75. BSc MBA MA. STETS. **d** 14 **p** 15. C Fordingbridge and Hyde and Breamore etc *Win* 14–18; P-in-c Pennington from 18. *The Vicarage, 29 Ramley Road, Lymington SO41 8HF* T: (01590) 462022 E: vicar@penningtonchurch.uk

NOGHIU, Bernard. b 74. Pontifical Lateran Univ BA 00. St Jos Th Inst Romania 90. **d** 99 **p** 00. In RC Ch 99–08; NSM Leyton Em *Chelmsf* 18–19; C Prittlewell St Mary 19–21; C Prittlewell St Pet w Westcliff St Cedd from 21; C Prittlewell St Steph from 21. *2 Redstock Road, Southend-on-Sea SS2 5DJ* M: 07417-407910 E: bernardnoghiu@gmail.com

NOKE, Christopher. b 48. Ex Coll Ox BA 69 MA 79 LSE MSc 78 ACA 72 FCA 79. SEITE 03. **d** 06 **p** 07. NSM Raynes Park St Sav and S Wimbledon All SS *S'wark* 06–16; P-in-c S Wimbedon All SS from 17. *Cedar Lodge, Church Road, Ham, Richmond TW10 5HG* T: (020) 8948 7986 E: christophernoke@gmail.com

NOKES, Michael David Patrick. b 44. York St Jo Coll MA 05. **d** 02 **p** 03. CA from 88; NSM Heworth Ch Ch *York* 02–08; PtO *Bradf* 02–11; *Ripon* 03–14; *Leeds* 14–16; *York* 08–20; rtd 10. *5 Fox Covert, York YO31 9EN* T: (01904) 674879 M: 07776-252440 E: mdpnokes@gmail.com

NOKES, Canon Peter Warwick. b 48. Leic Univ BA 71. Westcott Ho Cam 79. **d** 81 **p** 82. C Northfield *Birm* 81–84; C Ludlow *Heref* 84–87; P-in-c Writtle w Highwood *Chelmsf* 87–91; V 91–92; P-in-c Epping St Jo 92–95; P-in-c Coopersale 93–95; TR Epping Distr 95–99; R Nor St Pet Mancroft w St Jo Maddermarket 99–15; Hon Can Nor Cathl 10–15; rtd 15; Chapl Beauchamp Community 15–18. *23 Cockshot Road, Malvern WR14 2TT* M: 07711-384009 E: pwnokes@gmail.com

NOKES, Robert Harvey. b 39. Keble Coll Ox BA 61 MA 65. Qu Coll Birm 61. **d** 63 **p** 64. C Totteridge *St Alb* 63–67; C Dunstable 67–73; V Langford 73–90; R Braughing w Furneux Pelham and Stocking Pelham 90–04; PtO *Ox* from 04. *92 Western Drive, Hanslope, Milton Keynes MK19 7LE* T: (01908) 337939 E: r.nokes@easykey.com

NOLAN, James Charles William. b 44. Chich Th Coll 75. **d** 77 **p** 78. C Crewe St Andr *Ches* 77–79; C Sale St Anne 79–83; R Holme Runcton w S Runcton and Wallington *Ely* 83–14; V Tottenhill w Wormegay 83–14; R Watlington 83–14; rtd 14; PtO *Nor* from 14. *26 Holt Road, Langham, Holt NR25 7BX*

NOLAN, Marcus. b 54. Bris Univ BEd. Ridley Hall Cam. **d** 83 **p** 84. C Dagenham *Chelmsf* 83–86; C Finchley St Paul and St Luke *Lon* 86–90; V W Hampstead Trin 90–98; rtd 99; PtO *Derby* 00–06 and 14–19. *16 Cartwright Close, Melbourne, Derby DE73 8LA*

NOLES, Jeremy Andrew. b 67. St Jo Coll Nottm 02. **d** 04 **p** 05. C Southchurch Ch Ch *Chelmsf* 04–07; C Colchester St Jo 07–12; V Colchester St Luke 12–16; Chapl HM Pris Highpoint 16–18; Chapl HM Pris Chelmsf 18–19; Grants Officer Allchurches Trust Ltd 16–19; Hd of Grants and Relationships from 19. *Allchurches Trust Ltd, Beaufort House, Brunswick Road, Gloucester GL1 1JZ* M: 07748-761191 E: jeremy.noles@allchurches.co.uk

NOLLAND, John Leslie. b 47. New England Univ (NSW) BSc 67 Clare Coll Cam PhD 78. Moore Th Coll Sydney ThL 70 BD 71. **d** 71 **p** 72. Res Min Cabramatta Australia 71–74; Asst Prof NT Studies Regent Coll Vancouver Canada 78–86; Tutor Trin Coll Bris from 86; Vice Prin 91–97 and 06–07. *6 Phoenix Grove, Bristol BS6 7XY* T: 0117-924 4896 E: john.nolland@ntlworld.com

NOPPEN, Ms Chantal Mary. b 83. Newc Univ BMus 06 Clare Coll Cam BTh 12. Westcott Ho Cam 10. **d** 13 **p** 14. C Byker St Martin *Newc* 13–17; C Byker St Mich w St Lawr 13–17; TV N Wearside *Dur* from 17. *The Team Rectory, 28 Rotherham Road, Sunderland SR5 5QS* E: c.noppen+revd@gmail.com

NORBURN, Christopher Richard. b 62. Cov Poly BSc 85. Aston Tr Scheme 92 Ridley Hall Cam 94. **d** 96 **p** 97. C Exning St Martin w Landwade *St E* 96–99; P-in-c Redgrave cum Botesdale w Rickinghall 99–01; R from 01. *The Rectory, Bury Road, Rickinghall, Diss IP22 1HA* T: (01379) 898685 E: chris.norburn@breathemail.net

NORBURN, Mrs Lesley Jane. b 62. **d** 19 **p** 20. NSM Blackbourne *St E* from 19. *9 Orchard Close, Great Livermere, Bury St Edmunds IP31 1JN* T: (01359) 269570 E: lesley.norburn@btinternet.com

NORBURY, Robert John. b 60. Southn Univ BA 83 Univ of Wales (Ban) BTh 07. S'wark Ord Course 01. **d** 04 **p** 05. NSM Eltham Park St Luke *S'wark* 04–07; PtO *Chich* 07–08; NSM Crowborough St Jo 08–12; P-in-c 09–13; V 13–15; V Brighton St Mich and St Paul 15–20; V Durrington from 20; Chapl Wandsworth Primary Care Trust 09–10; Dir of Ords

Croydon Area *S'wark* 10–12. *The Vicarage, Bramble Lane, Worthing BN13 3JE* T: (01903) 268109 M: 07715-595828 E: frrobnorbury@aol.com

NORBY, Dean Luverne. d 11 **p** 12. C Edin St Paul and St Geo 11–14; P-in-c Aberdour *St And* from 14; P-in-c Burntisland from 14; P-in-c Inverkeithing from 14. *The Rectory, Inverkeithing Road, Aberdour, Burntisland KY3 0RS* T: (01383) 861000 M: 07821-712500 E: dean@allsoulsfife.org.uk

NORFIELD, David Jonathan. b 67. Humberside Univ BA 89 Anglia Poly Univ MA 97. Linc Th Coll 94 Westcott Ho Cam 95. **d** 97 **p** 98. C Halstead St Andr w H Trin and Greenstead Green *Chelmsf* 97–01; V Moulsham St Jo 01–04; Chapl RAF from 04. *Chaplaincy Services (RAF), HQ Air Command, RAF High Wycombe HP14 4UE* T: (01494) 496800 E: davidnorfield@hotmail.com

NORFOLK, Kirsten. *See* RICHARDS, Kirsten

NORFOLK, Archdeacon of. *See* BETTS, The Ven Steven James

NORKETT, Alan. b 45. Sarum & Wells Th Coll 85. **d** 87 **p** 88. C Shrewsbury St Giles w Sutton and Atcham *Lich* 87–90; V Mow Cop 90–94; NSM Astbury and Smallwood *Ches* 96–97; NSM Sandbach Heath w Wheelock 97–98; C Castleford All SS and Whitwood *Wakef* 98–01; C Glass Houghton 98–01; R Shrawley, Witley, Astley and Abberley *Worc* 01–10; rtd 10; PtO *Worc* from 11. *15 New Road, Far Forest, Kidderminster DY14 9TQ* T: (01299) 269355 E: alan.norkett@uwclub.net

NORMAN, Andrew Bryan. b 90. Selwyn Coll Cam BA 11 MA 15. Ripon Coll Cuddesdon BA 14. **d** 15 **p** 16. C Cartmel Peninsula *Carl* 15–19; P-in-c Arnside from 19; P-in-c Beetham from 19. *The Parsonage, Stanley Street, Beetham, Milnthorpe LA7 7AS* E: revdabn@gmail.com

NORMAN, Andrew Herbert. b 54. K Coll Lon BD 77 AKC 77 Lon Univ PhD 88. St Steph Ho Ox 77. **d** 78 **p** 79. C Deal St Leon w Sholden *Cant* 78–81; C Maidstone All SS and St Phil w Tovil 81–84; V Tenterden St Mich 84–93; Chapl Benenden Hosp 86–91; Dir Post-Ord Tr *Cant* 91–93; R Guildf St Nic 93–20; Hon Can Guildf Cathl 05–20; rtd 20; PtO *Ex* from 21. *35 Primley Road, Sidmouth EX10 9LD* E: ahnorman14@gmail.com

NORMAN, Canon Andrew Robert. b 63. Univ Coll Ox BA 84 MA 99 Selw Coll Cam BA 94 MA 99 Birm Univ MPhil 08 AIL 89. Ridley Hall Cam 92. **d** 95 **p** 96. Asst Chapl Paris St Mich *Eur* 95–00; C Clifton Ch Ch w Em *Bris* 00–02; Abp's Asst Sec for Ecum and Angl Affairs *Cant* 02–05; Abp's Prin Sec for Internat, Ecum and Angl Communion Affairs 05–08; Prin Ridley Hall Cam 08–17; Dir Min and Miss *Leeds* from 17; Hon Prov Can Cant Cathl from 06; Hon Can Ely Cathl 12–17; Hon Can Wakef Cathl *Leeds* from 17. *Church House, 17-19 York Place, Leeds LS1 2EX* T: 0113-353 0280 F: 249 1129 E: andrew.norman@leeds.anglican.org

NORMAN, Ann. *See* NORMAN, Margaret Ann

NORMAN, Catherine. b 51. Nottm Univ BSc 73 N Counties Coll Newc CertEd 74. Linc Th Coll 95. **d** 95 **p** 96. C Scartho *Linc* 95–99; V Ulceby Gp 99–02; TV Guiseley w Esholt *Bradf* 02–08; P-in-c Rawdon 08–13; V 13–14; *Leeds* 14; RD Otley *Bradf* 09–14; AD Ilkley *Leeds* 14; rtd 14; PtO *Leeds* from 17. *3 Borrowdale Croft, Yeadon, Leeds LS19 7FN* E: caytenorman@aol.com

NORMAN, Mrs Elizabeth Ann. b 43. SAOMC 95. **d** 98 **p** 99. OLM Amersham *Ox* 98–04; PtO *Ex* from 04. *26 Dunlin Drive, Yelland, Barnstaple EX31 3TX* T: (01271) 624181 E: liznorman1971@gmail.com

NORMAN, The Ven Garth. b 38. St Chad's Coll Dur BA 62 MA 68 UEA MEd 84 Cam Inst of Educn PGCE 68. **d** 63 **p** 64. C Wandsworth St Anne *S'wark* 63–66; C Trunch w Swafield *Nor* 66–71; R Gimingham 71–77; TR Trunch 77–83; RD Repps 75–83; Prin Chiltern Chr Tr Course *Ox* 83–87; C W Wycombe w Bledlow Ridge, Bradenham and Radnage 83–87; Dir of Tr *Roch* 88–94; Adn Bromley and Bexley 94–03; Hon Can Roch Cathl 91–03; rtd 03; PtO *S'well* 03–09; Chapl to Rtd Clergy 04–09; PtO *Ely* 10–16. *12 Scotsdowne Road, Trumpington, Cambridge CB2 9HU* T: (01223) 844303

NORMAN, Gary. b 64. Newc Univ BA 87. Ripon Coll Cuddesdon 02. **d** 04 **p** 05. C Spennymoor and Whitworth *Dur* 04–09; P-in-c Croxdale and Tudhoe 08–16; P-in-c Merrington 09–16; V Cornforth and Ferryhill from 16. *St Luke's Vicarage, Church Lane, Ferryhill DL17 8LT* T: (01740) 655232

NORMAN, Jillianne Elizabeth. b 59. Ridley Hall Cam 85. **d** 88 **p** 94. Par Dn Fishponds St Jo *Bris* 88–92; PtO 92–94; Hon C Warmley, Syston and Bitton 94–21; Chapl Univ Hosps Bris NHS Foundn Trust 02–20; Chapl Univ Hosps Bris and Weston NHS Foundn Trust from 20; PtO *B & W* from 20; *Bris* from 21. *74 Blackhorse Road, Mangotsfield, Bristol BS16 9AY* T: 0117-956 1551 *or* 342 6799 F: 904 6894 E: jilliannenorman@blueyonder.co.uk

NORMAN, Linda Mary. b 48. Man Univ BSc 69 CertEd 70 St Jo Coll Dur BA 82. **dss** 83 **d** 87. York St Mich-le-Belfrey 83–88;

Par Dn 87–88; rtd 88. *23 Ainsty Avenue, Dringhouses, York YO24 1HH* T: (01904) 706152

NORMAN, Luke. b 78. St Steph Ho Ox 14 Ripon Coll Cuddesdon 17. **d** 21. C Headington *Ox* from 21. *19 Westlands Drive, Headington, Oxford OX3 9QR* M: 07707-866062 E: lavietranquille@icloud.com

NORMAN, Lynette Dianne. b 52. Sussex Univ CertEd 73 Univ of Wales (Ban) BEd 89. Ripon Coll Cuddesdon 00. **d** 02 **p** 03. C Welshpool w Castle Caereinion *St As* 02–04; R Llanrwst 04–11; C Llanrhaeadr ym Mochnant etc 11–15; V 15–16; I Tanat Valley Miss Area 17–19. *Address temp unknown* M: 07889-184517

NORMAN, Margaret Ann. b 48. N Lon Poly CertEd 76 ALA 73. SEITE 09. **d** 11. NSM Erith St Paul *Roch* 11–13; NSM Erith Ch Ch 13–18; rtd 18. *27 Kempton Close, Erith DA8 3SR* T: (01322) 340902 E: ann.norman@hotmail.com

NORMAN, Michael John. b 61. St Jo Coll Ox BSc 83 Univ Coll Lon MSc 84. Aston Tr Scheme 89 St Jo Coll Nottm 91. **d** 93 **p** 94. C Haughton le Skerne *Dur* 93–97; R Sapcote and Sharnford w Wigston Parva *Leic* 97–21; RD Sparkenhoe W 02–07; rtd 21. *Address temp unknown* M: 07895-320985 E: micknorman@msn.com

NORMAN, Michael John. b 59. Southn Univ LLB 82. Wycliffe Hall Ox 82. **d** 85 **p** 86. C Woodley St Jo the Ev *Ox* 85–89; C Uphill *B & W* 89–92; TV 92–98; R Bath St Sav w Swainswick and Woolley 98–19; V Watford St Luke *St Alb* from 19. *St Luke's Vicarage, Devereux Drive, Watford WD17 3DD* T: (01923) 242208 E: michael.stlukes@gmail.com

NORMAN, Peter John. b 42. Culham Coll of Educn TCert 66 Lon Inst of Educn DipEd 83 MA 86. STETS 95. **d** 98 **p** 99. NSM Bath Weston All SS w N Stoke and Langridge *B & W* 98–13; PtO 14–18 and from 20. *5 Rockliffe Avenue, Bathwick, Bath BA2 6QP* T: (01225) 463348 E: peterjnorman@sky.com

NORMAN, Timothy. b 68. Jes Coll Cam BA 91 Univ Coll Lon PhD 95. Spurgeon's Coll 95 Wycliffe Hall Ox BA 00. **d** 01 **p** 02. C Chipping Norton *Ox* 01–04; Asst Chapl Paris St Mich *Eur* 04–06; PtO 06–08; C Rugby W *Cov* 09–14; PtO from 15; *Ox* from 15; *Lich* 18. *Fir Lodge, Forest Road, Hayley Green, Warfield, Bracknell RG42 6DB* M: 07545-564918 E: tim@theminster.org

NORMAN, Canon William Beadon. b 26. Trin Coll Cam BA 49 MA 55. Ridley Hall Cam 52. **d** 52 **p** 53. C Beckenham St Jo *Roch* 52–54; CMS Miss and Tutor Buwalasi Th Coll Uganda 55–65; Hon Can Mbale 63–65; V Alne *York* 65–74; RD Warley *Birm* 74–79; V Blackheath 74–79; Hon Can Birm Cathl 78–91; TR Kings Norton 79–91; RD 82–87; Warden Dioc Readers Bd 84–91; rtd 91; PtO *S'wark* 92–19; Preacher Lincoln's Inn 94–06. *37 Cloudesdale Road, London SW17 8ET* T: (020) 8673 9134 F: 8675 6890 E: bbnorman@hotmail.com

NORMAN-WALKER, Anna Elizabeth. b 67. RGN 89. St Jo Coll Nottm BA 03. **d** 03 **p** 04. C Cullompton, Willand, Uffculme, Kentisbeare etc *Ex* 03–06; TV 06–10; Chapl Stover Sch Newton Abbot 06–08; RD Cullompton *Ex* 09–10; Can Res Ex Cathl 10–17; Dioc Missr 10–14; Chan 14–17; R Streatham St Leon *S'wark* from 17. *1 Becmead Avenue, London SW16 1UH* T: (020) 8769 4366 M: 07557-053567 E: rectorstleonards@btinternet.com

NORMAND, Stephen Joseph William. b 48. N Texas State Univ BSEd 80. Sarum & Wells Th Coll 90. **d** 92 **p** 93. C Norton *St Alb* 92–94; C St Alb St Pet 95–97; Chapl Oaklands Coll 95–97; TV Horsham *Chich* 97–01; R Wimbotsham w Stow Bardolph and Stow Bridge etc *Ely* 01–04; rtd 04; PtO *Ely* 05–09; *S'wark* 13–16; *Chich* from 19. *The Alms Houses, 14 St Mary's House, Normandy, Horsham RH12 1JL* T: (01403) 210824 M: 07854-493883 E: snormand4@gmail.com

NORRINGTON, Canon Paul Richard. b 57. Brighton Poly BSc 80. Trin Coll Bris 96. **d** 98 **p** 99. C Prittlewell St Pet w Westcliff St Cedd *Chelmsf* 98–02; R Colchester Ch Ch w St Mary V from 02; AD Colchester from 14; Hon Can Chelmsf Cathl from 15. *The Rectory, 21 Cambridge Road, Colchester CO3 3NS* T: (01206) 563478 E: paul.nozzer@btinternet.com

NORRIS, Alexander Frederick. b 74. Westmr Coll Ox BTh 96. St Aug Coll of Th MA 19. **d** 19 **p** 20. NSM St Giles Cripplegate w St Bart Moor Lane etc *Lon* from 19. *501 Howard House, Dolphin Square, London SW1V 3PG* M: 07786-257047 E: curate@stgileschurch.com

NORRIS, Preb Alison. b 55. St Andr Univ MTheol 77 Dur Univ PGCE 78. Cant Sch of Min 80. **dss** 82 **d** 87 **p** 94. Warlingham w Chelsham and Farleigh *S'wark* 82–85; Willingham *Ely* 85–90; Hon Par Dn 87–90; Hon Par Dn Worle *B & W* 90–94; NSM Milverton w Halse and Fitzhead 94–02; P-in-c Deane Vale 02–10; R 10–19; Preb Wells Cathl 14–19; rtd 19; PtO *B & W* from 20. *26 Palmers Mead, Wellington TA21 8FG* T: (01823) 663181 E: revalison@revsnorris.co.uk

NORRIS, Allan Edward. b 43. St Jo Coll Dur BA 72. Cranmer Hall Dur 69. **d** 73 **p** 74. C Plumstead St Jo w St Jas and St Paul

S'wark 73–78; C Battersea Park St Sav 78–82; C Battersea St Geo w St Andr 78–82; V Grain w Stoke *Roch* 82–92; R Sissinghurst w Frittenden *Cant* 92–12; rtd 12; PtO *Cant* from 13. *17 Abbots Road, Faversham ME13 8DD* T: (01795) 227927 E: allannorris@talktalk.net

NORRIS, Andrew David. b 54. St Andr Univ BSc 78 Lon Univ MPhil 80 CPsychol. EAMTC 87. **d** 90 **p** 91. C Worle *B & W* 90–94; R Milverton w Halse and Fitzhead 94–08; RD Tone 01–07; Nat Chapl Adv Methodist Homes for the Aged 08–14; Past Care Manager St Monica Trust Bris 14–19; PtO *B & W* from 14; Bris 14–19; rtd 19. *26 Palmers Mead, Wellington TA21 8FG* T: (01823) 663181 M: 07498-490299 E: revandrew@revsnorris.co.uk

NORRIS, Frances Wendy. ERMC 18. **d** 21. C Haverhill w Withersfield *St E* from 21. *St Mary's Church, High Street, Haverhill CB9 8AX* M: 07497-349345 E: revwendy@gmx.com

NORRIS, Julie Mary. b 63. Westmr Coll Ox BA 84 Fitzw Coll Cam MPhil 88 Birm Univ PhD 03. Wesley Ho Cam 86. **d** 06 **p** 06. C Orwell Gp *Ely* 06–09; P-in-c Gt w Lt Abington 09–16; P-in-c Hildersham 09–16; P-in-c Balsham, Weston Colville, W Wickham etc 10–16; RD Granta 11–16; PtO 16–19; C Orwell Gp from 19. *67 High Street, Barrington, Cambridge CB22 7QX* T: (01223) 870120 E: revjulienorris@gmail.com

NORRIS, Mark. b 68. Brunel Univ BEng 90. Oak Hill Th Coll BA 93. **d** 93 **p** 94. C Roby *Liv* 93–97; C St Helens St Helen 97–00; TV Gateacre 00–09; Asst Dioc Dir of Ords 05–09; Leadership Development Adv (Voc) CPAS 09–12; V Keresley and Coundon *Cov* from 12. *Keresley Vicarage, 34 Tamworth Road, Coventry CV6 2EL* T: (024) 7633 2717 E: vicar@keresley.church

NORRIS, Paul. b 48. **d** 10 **p** 11. OLM Woughton *Ox* from 10. *20 Thirsk Gardens, Bletchley, Milton Keynes MK3 5LH* T: (01908) 371824 M: 07840-296676 E: paul88547@gmail.com

NORTH, Andrew James. b 80. Open Univ BA 10 Nottm Trent Univ PGCE 11. St Jo Coll Nottm MA 16. **d** 16 **p** 17. C Mulbarton w Bracon Ash, Hethel and Flordon *Nor* 16–19; CF from 19. *c/o MOD Chaplains (Army)* T: (01264) 383430 E: rev.north@btinternet.com

NORTH, Christopher David. b 69. Trin Coll Bris BA 01. **d** 01 **p** 02. C Bathampton w Claverton *B & W* 01–05; P-in-c Chilcompton w Downside and Stratton on the Fosse 05–17; RD Midsomer Norton 12–17; Dioc Dir of Ords *Bris* 17–20; Nat Discernment Adv Abps' Coun from 20; PtO *B & W* from 19. *National Ministry Team, Church House, 27 Great Smith Street, London SW1P 3AZ* T: (020) 7898 1826 E: chris.north@churchofengland.org

NORTH, Preb David Roland. b 45. Lich Th Coll 70 Qu Coll Birm 72. **d** 73 **p** 74. C Salesbury *Blackb* 73–76; C Marton 76–79; V Penwortham St Leon 79–87; R Whittington St Jo *Lich* 87–10; P-in-c W Felton 96–10; RD Oswestry 02–09; Chapl Robert Jones/Agnes Hunt Orthopaedic NHS Trust 00–01; Preb Lich Cathl 07–10; rtd 11; PtO *Lich* 11–21; St As 11–16. *Honeycroft, Daisy Lane, Whittington, Oswestry SY11 4EA* T: (01691) 676130

NORTH, Lyndon Percival. b 55. Lon Bible Coll BA 77. NTMTC. **d** 00 **p** 01. NSM Sudbury St Andr *Lon* 00–04 and 05–12; C Roxbourne St Andr 04–05; V from 12; PtO *Eur* from 17. *St Andrew's Vicarage, Malvern Avenue, Harrow HA2 9ER* T: (020) 8422 3633 M: 07716-302101 E: revlnorth@aol.com

NORTH, Canon Mark Richard. b 71. St Steph Ho Ox 03. **d** 05 **p** 06. C Sevenoaks St Jo *Roch* 05–09; V Burnham *Chelmsf* 09–18; RD Maldon and Dengie 17–18; P-in-c Brentwood St Thos 18–20; V from 20; Hon Can Chelmsf Cathl from 17. *The Vicarage, 91 Queens Road, Brentwood CM14 4EY* T: (01277) 231629 M: 07776-231681 E: frmarknorth@btinternet.com

NORTH, Michael Henry. b 50. SWMTC 11. **d** 13 **p** 14. NSM Stokenham, Slapton, Charleton w Buckland etc *Ex* 13–17; NSM Willand, Uffculme, Kentisbeare etc 17–18; P-in-c Meneage *Truro* 18–21; PtO from 21. *Staplehurst, Bowling Green, Constantine, Falmouth TR11 5AP* M: 07590-648121 E: northrnm@btinternet.com

NORTH, Paul. b 73. All SS Cen for Miss & Min 17. **d** 19 **p** 20. C Wistaston *Ches* from 19. *St Mary the Virgin, Church Lane, Wistaston, Crewe CW2 8HA* E: revd.paul@stmaryswistaston.org.uk

✠**NORTH, The Rt Revd Philip John.** b 66. York Univ BA 88. St Steph Ho Ox BA 91 MA 01. **d** 92 **p** 93 **c** 15. C Sunderland St Mary and St Pet *Dur* 92–96; V Hartlepool H Trin 96–02; AD Hartlepool 00–02; P Admin Shrine of Our Lady of Walsingham 02–08; P-in-c Hempton and Pudding Norton *Nor* 04–07; TR Old St Pancras *Lon* 08–15; Suff Bp Burnley *Blackb* from 15; Can Res Blackb Cathl from 16; P-in-c Burnley St Mark 19–20; CMP from 97. *Diocesan Offices, Clayton House, Walker Industrial Estate, Walker Road,*

Guide, Blackburn BB1 2QE T: (01254) 503087 M: 07919-180788 E: bishop.burnley@blackburn.anglican.org

NORTH, Preb Robert. b 54. Lon Univ BSc 77. Ripon Coll Cuddesdon 78. **d** 81 **p** 82. C Leominster *Heref* 81–86; TV Heref St Martin w St Fran, Dewsall etc 86–92; P-in-c Heref St Nic 92–97; TR W Heref 97–20; Dir of Ords 92–00; Dioc Chapl MU 05–08; Preb Heref Cathl 94–20; rtd 20; PtO *Heref* from 21. *Oakleigh, 210 Ledbury Road, Hereford HR1 1RJ* T: (01432) 359147 M: 07813-359956 E: robnorth28@gmail.com

NORTH, William Walter. b 77. Ox Brookes Univ BA 03. St Jo Coll Nottm 07. **d** 09 **p** 10. C N Farnborough *Guildf* 09–13; R Barming *Roch* from 13; RD Malling from 19. *The Rectory, Church Lane, Barming, Maidstone ME16 9HA* T: (01622) 726263 M: 07887-680474 E: revwilnorth@hotmail.co.uk

NORTH WEST EUROPE, Archdeacon of. See VAN LEER, The Ven Samuel Wall

NORTHALL, Linda Barbara. See ISIORHO, Linda Barbara

NORTHALL, Ms Sarah Elizabeth. b 69. Ex Univ BA 91 PGCE 92. Ox Min Course 09. **d** 12 **p** 13. C Iffley *Ox* 12–16; P-in-c Wollescote *Worc* 16–18; P-in-c Pedmore 16–18; V Worc St Wulstan from 19. *St Wulstan's Vicarage, Cranham Drive, Worcester WR4 9PA* E: revsarahnorthall@gmail.com

NORTHAM, Mrs Susan Jillian. b 36. Oak Hill Th Coll 87. **d** 89. NSM Enfield Ch Ch Trent Park *Lon* 89–91; Par Dn 91–94; C 94–97; rtd 97; PtO *Lon* from 02. *5 Beech Hill Avenue, Barnet EN4 0LW* T/F: (020) 8440 2723

NORTHAMPTON, Archdeacon of. See ORMSTON, The Ven Richard Jeremy

NORTHCOTT, Susan. b 62. St Padarn's Inst 18. **d** 20 **p** 21. NSM Llangiwg *S & B* from 20. *6 Ynysderw Road, Pontardawe, Swansea SA8 4EG* T: (01792) 863814 E: sue.northcott@outlook.com

NORTHERN, Elaine Joy. See TIPP, Elaine Joy

NORTHEY, Edward Alexander Anson. b 81. Trin Coll Bris BA 08. Wycliffe Hall Ox 09. **d** 11 **p** 12. C Barrow St Mark *Carl* 11–14; Chapl Univ Hosps of Morecambe Bay NHS Foundn Trust 14–17; Chapl RN from 17. *Royal Naval Chaplaincy Service Headquarters, Tanner Building, HMS Excellent, Whale Island, Portsmouth PO2 8ER* T: 0300-157 7544 M: 07952-938797 E: edwardnorthey@gmail.com

NORTHEY (née GANT), Canon Joanna Elizabeth. b 75. Dur Univ BSc 96 Ox Univ PGCE 97. Trin Coll Bris BA 09. **d** 09 **p** 10. C Swindon Ch Ch *Bris* 09–11; C Barrow St Mark *Carl* 11–14; TV S Barrow 14–17; PtO *Portsm* 18; C Warblington w Emsworth from 18; Hon Can Mampong Ghana from 15. *1 Godwin Close, Emsworth PO10 7XT* M: 07807-188912 E: revjonorthey@gmail.com

NORTHFIELD, Stephen Richmond. b 55. Lon Univ BSc 77. Southn Univ BTh 84. Sarum & Wells Th Coll 79. **d** 82 **p** 83. C Colchester St Jas, All SS, St Nic and St Runwald *Chelmsf* 82–85; C Chelmsf All SS 85–89; V Ramsey w Lt Oakley and Wrabness 89–95; V Hatfield Peverel w Ulting from 95. *The Vicarage, Church Road, Hatfield Peverel, Chelmsford CM3 2LE* T: (01245) 380958 E: srnorthfield@aol.com

NORTHING, Ross. b 58. St Steph Ho Ox 92. **d** 94 **p** 95. CA from 87; C Up Hatherley *Glouc* 94–98; C Cheltenham St Steph 94–95; C Cheltenham Em w St Steph 95–98; V Stony Stratford *Ox* 98–11; R Calverton 98–11; R Stony Stratford w Calverton from 12. *St Mary and St Giles Vicarage, 14 Willow Lane, Stony Stratford, Milton Keynes MK11 1FG* T: (01908) 562148 F: 565132 E: r.northing@btinternet.com

NORTHOLT, Archdeacon of. See PICKFORD, The Ven Catherine Ruth

NORTHOVER, Kevin Charles. b 57. Coll of Resurr Mirfield 89. **d** 91 **p** 92. C Kingston upon Hull St Alb *York* 91–94; V Moorends *Sheff* 94–00; R Guernsey St Michel du Valle *Win* 00–16; Vice-Dean Guernsey 07–13; Sen Vice-Dean 13–16; Chapl HM Pris Guernsey 00–16; rtd 16; CMP 99–09. *Ker Maria, 73 River Holme View, Brockholes, Holmfirth HD9 7BP* E: revkevnorthover@gmail.com

NORTHUMBERLAND, Archdeacon of. See WOOD, The Ven Rachel Astrid

NORTON, Anthony Bernard. b 40. Man Univ BA 62. Linc Th Coll 63. **d** 65 **p** 66. C Westbury-on-Trym H Trin *Bris* 65–68; C Bris St Agnes w St Simon 68–70; P-in-c Bris St Werburgh 70–72; TV Bris St Agnes and St Simon w St Werburgh 72–77; V Lakenham St Alb *Nor* 77–85; TV Trunch 85–93; TV Halesworth w Linstead, Chediston, Holton etc *St E* 93–99; TV Blyth Valley 99–05; RD Halesworth 98–01; rtd 05; PtO *St E* 06–08; P-in-c Heveningham 12–16; PtO 20–21. *6 Bramblewood Way, Halesworth IP19 8JT* T: (01986) 875374 E: anthonynorton@btinternet.com

NORTON, Benjamin James. b 80. Hull Univ BTh 05 Nottm Univ MTh 13. St Jo Coll Nottm 06. **d** 07 **p** 08. C Bridlington Em *York* 07–12; C Marton-in-Cleveland 12–15; C Wawne 15–18; C Sutton Park and Wawne 18–20; C-in-c Kingswood CD from 20. *1 Richmond*

Lane, Kingswood, Hull HU7 3AE   M: 07780-606314
E: thepartycanstart@yahoo.co.uk

NORTON, Howard John. b 41. Fitzw Coll Cam BA 64 MA 68. S'wark Ord Course 78 St Jo Coll Nottm 79. **d** 80 **p** 81. C Sutton Ch Ch *S'wark* 80–82; C Morden 82–84; V Motspur Park 84–88; PtO *Chich* from 03. *Rye View, The Strand, Winchelsea TN36 4JY*   T: (01797) 226524 E: howard@ryeview.net

NORTON, Michael Clive Harcourt. b 34. Selw Coll Cam BA 58 MA 60 Union Th Sem (NY) STM 69 Univ of NSW MCom 81 MACE 84. Wells Th Coll 56 Bossey Ecum Inst Geneva 57. **d** 58 **p** 59. C Gt Ilford St Jo *Chelmsf* 58–62; NSW Sec Aus Coun Chs Australia 62–68; C Manhattan St Steph USA 68–69; C-in-c Mortdale Australia 69–77; R Mortdale 77–79; Assoc Chapl and Hd RS Cranbrook Sch Sydney 79–85; R Hunter's Hill 85–00; rtd 00. *7 Dulwich Road, Chatswood NSW 2067, Australia*   T: (0061) (2) 9411 8606   F: 9410 2069   M: 41-704 1779 E: chnorton@bigpond.com

NORTON, Michael James Murfin. b 42. Lich Th Coll 66. **d** 67 **p** 68. C W Bromwich St Fran *Lich* 67–70; C Wellington Ch Ch 70–72; C Norwood All SS *Cant* 72–76; V Elstow *St Alb* 76–82; Asst Chapl HM Pris Wakef 82–83; Chapl HM Pris Camp Hill 83–86; Parkhurst 86-88; Win 88–93; V Somborne w Ashley *Win* 93–03; rtd 03; PtO *Win* from 17. *20 Cloverbank, Kings Worthy, Winchester SO23 7TP*   T: (01962) 621621 E: mandjnorton@gmail.com

NORTON, Paul James. b 55. Oak Hill Th Coll BA 86. **d** 86 **p** 87. C Luton St Fran *St Alb* 86–89; C Bedworth *Cov* 89–95; TV Hitchin *St Alb* 95–02; V Portsdown *Portsm* 03–07; rtd 07; PtO *Portsm* from 11. *23 Oxford Road, Southsea PO5 1NP*

NORTON, Canon Peter Eric Pepler. b 38. TCD BA 61 G&C Coll Cam PhD 64. Cranmer Hall Dur 78. **d** 80 **p** 81. C Ulverston St Mary w H Trin *Carl* 80–83; P-in-c Warcop, Musgrave, Soulby and Crosby Garrett 83–84; R 84–90; OCM 83–90; V Appleby and R Ormside *Carl* 90–04; P-in-c Kirkby Thore w Temple Sowerby and Newbiggin 01–04; RD Appleby and Hon Can Carl Cathl 00–04; rtd 04; PtO *Nor* 05–08. *Ard na Cree, Church Hill, Wicklow, Co Wicklow, Republic of Ireland*   T: (00353) (404) 62648   M: 07802-334575 E: pepnorton@gmail.com

NORTON, Sam Charles. b 70. Trin Coll Ox BA 92 MA 99 Heythrop Coll Lon MA 00. Westcott Ho Cam 97. **d** 99 **p** 00. C Stepney St Dunstan and All SS *Lon* 99–02; R W w E Mersea *Chelmsf* 03–10; P-in-c Peldon w Gt and Lt Wigborough 03–10; R W w E Mersea, Peldon, Gt and Lt Wigborough 10–18; C Fingringhoe w E Donyland and Abberton etc 15–18; V Parkend and Viney Hill *Glouc* from 18; Assoc Dioc Dir of Ords and Voc Adv from 18. *The Vicarage, Lower Road, Yorkley, Lydney GL15 4TN*   M: 07771-349319 E: revsamnorton@gmail.com

NORTON, (née FISHER), Mrs Susan Alexandra. b 54. Man Univ BA 75 Hughes Hall Cam PGCE 76. NEOC 01. **d** 04 **p** 05. NSM York St Olave w St Giles and York St Helen w St Martin 04–09. *21 Wentworth Road, York YO24 1DG*   T: (01904) 634911 E: e.norton@tinyworld.co.uk

NORWICH, Archdeacon of. See HUTCHINSON, The Ven Karen Elizabeth

NORWICH, Bishop of. See USHER, The Rt Revd Graham Barham

NORWICH, Dean of. See HEDGES, The Very Revd Jane Barbara

NORWOOD, Andrew David. b 65. Lon Bible Coll BA 91. Cranmer Hall Dur 92. **d** 94 **p** 95. C Headingley *Ripon* 94–97; C Handsworth St Mary *Birm* 97–00; PtO *Leic* 01–02; Chapl Univ of the Arts 02–12; PtO *S'wark* 06–13; *Lon* 12–17; NSM Pimlico St Mary Bourne Street 17–19; Chapl Univ Coll 18; C Lt Venice from 20. *14 Philip Court, Hall Place, London W2 1LS*   T: (020) 7723 7266   M: 07411-737224 E: adn272@yahoo.co.uk

NORWOOD, David John. b 40. SS Paul & Mary Coll Cheltenham BEd 82. Linc Th Coll 65. **d** 68 **p** 69. C Hitchin St Mary *St Alb* 68–71; P-in-c Luanshya Zambia 72–76; C Littlehampton St Jas *Chich* 76–77; P-in-c Chacewater *Truro* 77–79; Chapl R Cornwall Hosp Treliske 77–79; Hd RE Red Maids Sch Bris 82–85; Appeals Organiser Children's Soc 86–94; P-in-c Clarkston *Glas* 94–96; R 96–99; R Dalbeattie 99–05; rtd 05; PtO *St D* from 13. *Dove Cottage, Wellfield Terrace, Ferryside SA17 5SD*   T: (01267) 267125 E: norwood794@btinternet.com

NORWOOD, Paul James. b 71. **d** 08 **p** 09. OLM S Lynn *Nor* 08–19; OLM Hempton and Pudding Norton 19–21; V Bedford St Martin *St Alb* from 21. *St Andrew's Vicarage, 1 St Edmond Road, Bedford MK40 2NQ*   M: 07886-276467 E: frpaul@stmartinsbedford.com

NORWOOD, Canon Philip Geoffrey Frank. b 39. Em Coll Cam BA 62 MA 66. Cuddesdon Coll 63. **d** 65 **p** 66. C New Addington *Cant* 65–69; Abp's Dom Chapl 69–72; V Hollingbourne 72–78; P-in-c Wormshill and Huckinge

74–78; V St Laur in Thanet *Cant* 78–88; RD Thanet 86–88; V Spalding St Mary and St Nic *Linc* 88–98; RD Elloe W 96–98; R Blakeney w Cley, Wiveton, Glandford etc *Nor* 98–05; RD Holt 02–05; Hon Can Nor Cathl 03–05; rtd 05; PtO *Leic* from 14. *30 Home Close Road, Houghton-on-the-Hill, Leicester LE7 9GT*   T: 0116-241 0255 E: pandanorwood@hotmail.com

NOTHHELFER-BATTEN, Sibylle Eva. See BATTEN, Sibylle

NOTT, Canon George Thomas Michael. b 34. Ex Coll Ox BA 58 MA 62 Birm Univ MEd 88 Cov Univ PhD 95. Coll of Resurr Mirfield. **d** 60 **p** 61. C Solihull *Birm* 60–69; Chapl K Sch Worc and Min Can Worc Cathl 69–77; P-in-c Worc St Nic and Children's Officer 77–87; P-in-c Worc St Andr and All SS w St Helen 82–84; Droitwich Spa 87–89; V Broadheath, Crown East and Rushwick 89–04; Chapl Worc Coll of HE 89–96; RD Martley and Worc W 95–03; Hon Can Worc Cathl 99–04; P-in-c Worc St Mich 00–01; rtd 04; PtO *Worc* from 06. *17 Wirlpiece Avenue, Worcester WR4 0NF*   T: (01905) 729494 E: mnott17@btinternet.com

NOTT, Philip James. b 69. Nottm Trent Univ BA 92. Ridley Hall Cam 95. **d** 98 **p** 99. C Kersal Moor *Man* 99–01; C Ealing St Mary *Lon* 01–04; Chapl Thames Valley Univ 01–04; P-in-c Broxtowe *S'well* 04–06; P-in-c Easton H Trin w St Gabr and St Lawr and St Jude *Bris* 06–16; Min Inner City Partnership 06–16; V Aston and Nechells *Birm* 16–19; PtO *Bris* from 20. *Lee Abbey House, 2 Filwood Broadway, Bristol BS4 1JN*   T: 0117-239 0147   M: 07863-086143 E: revphilipjnott@gmail.com

NOTTINGHAM, Archdeacon of. See WILLIAMS, The Ven Philip Andrew

NOVIS, Timothy Wellington George. b 70. Trin Coll Toronto BA 93 MDiv 96. **d** 96 **p** 96. C Guelph St Geo Canada 96–98; R Hornby St Steph 98–05; Chapl Ridley Coll 05–08; Chapl Wellington Coll Berks 08–17; Chapl Marlborough Coll from 17. *Marlborough College, Marlborough SN8 1PA*   T: (01672) 892200 E: twgn@marlboroughcollege.org

NOWELL, Canon John David. b 44. AKC 67. **d** 68 **p** 69. C Lindley *Wakef* 68–70; C Lightcliffe 70–72; V Wyke *Bradf* 72–80; V Silsden 80–92; V Baildon 92–14; *Leeds* 14; rtd 14; Hon Can Bradf Cathl 00–14; PtO *Leeds* from 17. *Fairview, Carlisle Road, Pudsey LS28 8LW* E: john@johnnowell.com

NOWÉN, Lars Fredrik. b 71. Summit Pacific Coll BC BTh 93 Regent Coll Vancouver MCS 98. **d** 98 **p** 99. Dn Halifax St Geo Canada 98–99; P-in-c Meadow Lake and Loon Lake 99–04; C Pelton and W Pelton *Dur* 04–07; P-in-c St Bees *Carl* 07–10; Chapl St Bees Sch Cumbria 07–10; Chapl Chelsea Academy 11–12; Sen Chapl Algarve *Eur* 13–15; P-in-c Edmonton Ch the K Canada from 15. *8804 160 St NW, Edmonton AB T5R 2H7, Canada*   T: (001) (780) 807 3136 E: revlfnowen@gmail.com

NOY, Rufus William. b 63. St Mich Coll Llan 11. **d** 13 **p** 14. C Blaenavon w Capel Newydd *Mon* 13–16; P-in-c 16–17; P-in-c Upper Torfaen 17–20; TV Leominster *Heref* from 20. *The New Vicarage, Kimbolton, Leominster HR6 0EJ* E: reverend.noy@gmail.com

NOYCE, Colin Martley. b 45. Brasted Th Coll 73 Ridley Hall Cam 74. **d** 76 **p** 77. C Cambridge St Jas *Ely* 76–78; Chapl RN 78–82; R Mistley w Manningtree *Chelmsf* 82–86; Miss to Seamen Kenya 86–89; Trinidad and Tobago 89–90; V Four Marks *Win* 90–99; Chapl Pilgrims Hospices E Kent 99–01; Chapl and Dir Ch Ch and Ras Morbat Clinics Yemen 01–03; Chapl Limassol St Barn and Miss to Seafarers 03–05; rtd 05; PtO *Chelmsf* 06–09; *Portsm* from 08. *64 Whitwell Road, Southsea PO4 0QS*   T: (023) 9275 3517 E: candinoyce@sky.com

NOYCE, Preb Graham Peter. b 62. Bedf Coll Lon BSc 84. Trin Coll Bris BA 92. **d** 92 **p** 93. C Sketty *S & B* 92–94; C Swansea St Jas 94–96; C Kensal Rise St Mark and St Martin *Lon* 96–04; TV 04–11; V Kensal Rise St Martin from 11; AD Brent 13–18; Preb St Paul's Cathl from 17. *26 Ashburnham Road, London NW10 5SD*   T: (020) 8960 6211   M: 07515-702862 E: graham@noycefamily.co.uk

NOYES, Gary Robert. b 50. Ripon Coll Cuddesdon. **d** 14 **p** 14. C Ipsley *Worc* 14–15; P-in-c Abberton, The Flyfords, Naunton Beauchamp etc 15–20; C from 20; P-in-c Peopleton and White Ladies Aston w Churchill etc 15–20; R from 20; C Fladbury, Hill and Moor, Wyre Piddle etc from 15; C Stoulton w Drake's Broughton and Pirton etc from 17. *The Rectory, Peopleton, Pershore WR10 2EE*   T: (01905) 841563 E: granoyes@gmail.com

NSENGA-NGOY, Canon Lusa. b 77. Cranmer Hall Dur. **d** 08 **p** 09. C Staplehurst *Cant* 08–12; V Gravesend St Aid *Roch* 12–17; Black, Asian and Minority Ethnic Miss and Min Enabler *Leic* from 17; Hon Can Leic Cathl from 17. *St Martin's House, 7 Peacock Lane, Leicester LE1 5PZ*   T: 0116-261 5200 E: lusansenga@gmail.com

✠NTAHOTURI, The Most Revd Bernard. b 48. St Jo Coll Cam MA. Bp Tucker Coll Mukono 68. d 73 c 97. Burundi 73–17; Bp Matana 97–17; Abp Burundi 05–16; Dir Angl Cen Rome 17–18; rtd 18. *Address temp unknown*

NTOYIMONDO, Samuel. b 54. All Nations Chr Coll BA 02 Wolv Univ BA 05 Qu Foundn for Ecum Th Educn MA 11. Butare Th Sch Rwanda 80. d 84 p 87. Pastor Mutunda Rwanda 84–87; Pastor Butare 87–92; Dioc Sec Kigeme 92–94; Germany 96–99; PtO *Birm* 08–11; Chapl HM Pris Wellingborough 11–12; Chapl HM Pris Nottm 13–15; Chapl HM Pris Stocken 13–15; Chapl HM YOI Glen Parva 15–17; Chapl HM Pris Swinfen Hall from 17. *HM Prison Swinfen Hall, Swinfen, Lichfield WS14 9QS* T: (01543) 484000 E: samuel.ntoyimondo@justice.gov.uk

NUGENT, Canon Alan Hubert. b 42. Dur Univ BA 65 MA 78. Wycliffe Hall Ox 65 United Th Coll Bangalore 66. d 67 p 68. C Mossley Hill St Matt and St Jas *Liv* 67–71; C Bridgnorth St Mary *Heref* 71–72; Chapl Dur Univ 72–78; P-in-c Bishopwearmouth Ch Ch 78–85; P-in-c Brancepeth 85–94; Dioc Dir of Educn 85–97; Hon Can Dur Cathl 86–97; Dir of Miss and Tr Development Forum *Linc* 97–03; Can and Preb Linc Cathl 98–03; Can Res and Subdean Linc Cathl 03–11; rtd 11; PtO *Linc* 17–20. *2 The Link, Wellingore, Lincoln LN5 0BJ*

NUGENT, David Richard. b 54. MInstPS 84 Liv Poly BA 87. Oak Hill Th Coll BA 95. d 95 p 96. C Birkenhead St Jas w St Bede *Ches* 95–99; V Blundellsands St Mich *Liv* 99–02; Asst Chapl Wirral and W Cheshire Community NHS Trust 02–03; Asst Chapl Cheshire and Wirral Partnership NHS Foundn Trust 03–16; P-in-c Gt Saughall *Ches* 13–16; rtd 16; PtO *Ches* from 18. *92 Easton Road, Wirral CH62 1DS* E: david.jan.nugent@gmail.com

NUGENT, Mary Patricia. *See* JEPP, Mary Patricia

NUNN, Ms Alice Candida. b 52. Ripon Coll Cuddesdon 95. d 97 p 98. C Margate St Jo *Cant* 97–01; V Winterton Gp *Linc* from 01. *The Vicarage, High Street, Winterton, Scunthorpe DN15 9PU* T: (01724) 732262

NUNN, The Very Revd Andrew Peter. b 57. Leic Poly BA 79 Leeds Univ BA 82. Coll of Resurr Mirfield 80. d 83 p 84. C Manston *Ripon* 83–87; C Leeds Richmond Hill 87–91; Chapl Agnes Stewart C of E High Sch Leeds 87–95; V Leeds Richmond Hill *Ripon* 91–95; Personal Asst to Bp S'wark 95–99; Hon PV S'wark Cathl 95–99; Sub-Dean, Prec and Can Res S'wark Cathl 99–12; Dean S'wark from 12; Dioc Warden of Readers 01–14. *51 Bankside, London SE1 9JE* T: (020) 7928 3336 M: 07961-332051 E: andrew.nunn@southwark.anglican.org

NUNN, Mrs Christine Jane. b 47. d 05 p 06. OLM Kesgrave *St E* 05–13; NSM 13–17; rtd 17; PtO *St E* from 17. *37 Bracken Avenue, Kesgrave, Ipswich IP5 2PP* T: (01473) 622363

NUNN, Peter Rawling. b 51. St Cath Coll Ox BA 73 Sheff Univ MSc 74. Oak Hill Th Coll BA 85. d 85 p 86. C Bispham *Blackb* 85–87; C-in-c Anchorsholme 87–89; V 89–08; P-in-c Preston Risen Lord 08–17; rtd 17; PtO *Blackb* from 17. *13 Meadows Avenue, Thornton-Cleveleys FY5 2TN* E: peter.r.nunn@zohomail.eu

NUNNERLEY, William John Arthur. b 27. Univ of Wales (Lamp) BA 54. St Chad's Coll Dur. d 56 p 57. C Tredegar St Geo *Mon* 56–60; Chapl RN 60–81; QHC from 79; R Barnoldby le Beck *Linc* 81–92; R Waltham 81–92; rtd 92; PtO *B & W* 00–14. *Juniper Cottage, 82B Lower Street, Merriott TA16 5NW* T: (01460) 76049

NUNNEY, Sheila Frances. b 49. SRN 74 RSCN 74 SCM 75. Oak Hill Th Coll BA 92. d 92 p 94. C Swaffham *Nor* 92–96; Chapl Asst Norfolk and Nor Health Care NHS Trust 96–00; Chapl 00–01; Chapl Norfolk Primary Care Trust 01–09; Chapl Norfolk & Waveney Mental Health NHS Foundn Trust 03–09; rtd 09; PtO *Nor* from 09. *9 Coralie Court, Westfield View, Norwich NR4 7FJ* T: (01603) 924655 E: sfn60@btinternet.com

NURMAHI, Shakeel Emmanuel Benjamin. b 96. Dur Univ BA 17 MA 21. Trin Coll Bris 14 Cranmer Hall Dur 19. d 21. C Oakham, Ashwell, Braunston, Brooke, Egleton etc *Pet* from 21. *The Vicarage, 67 Church Street, Langham, Oakham LE15 7JE* M: 07717-282597 E: shakeelnurmahi@virginmedia.com *or* shakeel@oakhamteam.org.uk

NURSEY (née HYLTON), Mrs Jane Lois. b 56. Leeds Univ BA 78. d 07 p 08. OLM Dereham and Distr *Nor* from 07; Chapl Norfolk and Nor Univ Hosps NHS Foundn Trust from 11. *Chaplaincy Department, Norfolk and Norwich University Hospital, Colney Lane, Norwich NR4 7UY* T: (01603) 287470 E: nursey1@btinternet.com

NUTH, Stephen William. b 55. St Jo Coll Nottm 93. d 95 p 96. C Wadhurst and Stonegate *Chich* 95–99; R Marks Tey and Aldham *Chelmsf* 99–01; PtO *St E* 01–04;

P-in-c Woburn w Eversholt, Milton Bryan, Battlesden etc *St Alb* 04–08; V from 08. *The Vicarage, Park Street, Woburn, Milton Keynes MK17 9PG* T: (01525) 290225 E: stephen.nuth@googlemail.com

NUTT, Angela Karen. b 66. Homerton Coll Cam BEd 89. STETS 08. d 11 p 12. C Totton *Win* 11–15; C Copythorne 11–15; P-in-c Freemantle 15–18; Asst Dioc Dir of Ords and IME Adv 18–20; Voc Adv and Dioc Dir of Ords *Win* from 20; PtO from 19. *The Diocesan Office, Old Alresford Place, Old Alresford, Alresford SO24 9DH* T: (01962) 737300 M: 07825-167198 E: revdangi@gmail.com

NUTT, Susan Mary. b 45. BEM 15. d 99 p 00. OLM Blackbourne *St E* 99–13; NSM 13–15; rtd 15; PtO *St E* from 15; Hon Chapl St Nic Hospice Care Bury St Edmunds from 08. *Portelet, Blacksmith Lane, Barnham, Thetford IP24 2NE* T: (01842) 890409 E: suenutt@hotmail.co.uk

NUTTALL, Michael John Berkeley. b 36. K Coll Lon AKC 60. St Boniface Warminster 61. d 61 p 62. C Chapel Allerton *Ripon* 61–64; C Stanningley St Thos 64–68; V Leeds Gipton Epiphany 68–76; P-in-c Stainby w Gunby *Linc* 76–83; R N Witham 76–83; R S Witham 76–83; TV Bottesford w Ashby 83–88; I Adare w Kilpeacon and Croom *L & K* 88–94; I Adare and Kilmallock w Kilpeacon, Croom etc 94–01; Chapl Limerick Univ 88–95; Adn Limerick 92–01; rtd 01; PtO *York* 12–17. *29 Dulverton Hall, Esplanade, Scarborough YO11 2AR* T: (01723) 340129 E: adnmichaelnuttall@yahoo.com

NUTTER, Ms Tracy Jane. b 58. NTMTC. d 10 p 11. NSM Prittlewell St Steph *Chelmsf* 10–14; NSM Rayleigh from 14. *8 Ailsa Road, Westcliff-on-Sea SS0 8BL* T: (01702) 342470 E: t.nutter@virgin.net *or* tracy.nutter@parishofrayleigh.org.uk

NUTU HALL, Ela. *See* HALL, Liliana Miheala Nutu

NUZUM, Daniel Robert. b 73. TCD BTh 99 UCC PhD 16 RGN 94. d 99 p 00. C Bandon Union *C, C & R* 99–01; I Templebreedy w Tracton and Nohoval 02–09; Chapl Cork Univ Hosp from 09; Can Cork Cathl *C, C & R* from 14; Can Cloyne Cathl from 14. *Cork University Hospital, Wilton, Cork, Republic of Ireland* T: (00353) (21) 454 6400

NWAEKWE, Augustine Ugochukwu. b 75. Leuven Univ Belgium MA 07. St Paul's Univ Coll Awka Nigeria 95. d 98 p 00. LtO Dio Mbaise Nigeria 98–04; Asst Chapl Brussels *Eur* 06–13; Chapl Ostend from 13; Chapl Bruges from 13; Chapl Knokke from 16. *Torhoutsesteenweg 132, 8200 Sint Andries, Belgium* T: (0032) (47) 320 9763 M: (0032) 48-499 5790 E: stpetersbrugge@skynet.be

NWOGBE, David Nwabueze. *See* PETERSON, David Nwabueze Nwogbe

NWOGU, Okwunna Nketa. b 66. Uyo Univ Nigeria LLB 02 BL 02 Sunderland Univ LLM 12. Trin Coll Umuahia Nigeria 91. d 94 p 95. Can Aba Cathl Nigeria 02–08; Adn from 08; Chapl Law Sch Enugu 05–06; PtO *Dur* 12–13; NSM The Boldons 13–17; USA from 17. *125 Elm Street, West Orange NJ 07052, USA* E: revdokwunnanwogu@yahoo.com

NYAONGO, Jairo Omondi. b 73. d 14 p 15. C Mill End and Heronsgate w W Hyde *St Alb* 14–17; V Luton St Aug Limbury from 17. *St Augustine's Vicarage, 215 Icknield Way, Luton LU3 2JR* M: 07763-104640 E: jnyaongo@hotmail.com

NYATSANZA, Petros Hamutendi. b 69. Redcliffe Coll Glouc BA 04 Fuller Th Sem California MA 18. Bp Gaul Th Coll Harare 95. d 95 p 96. R Greendale St Luke Zimbabwe 95–96; C Highfields St Paul 96–97; R Mufakose St Luke 97–01; PtO *Glouc* 02–04; P-in-c Rounds Green *Birm* 04–08; V Goodmayes All SS *Chelmsf* 08–18; NSM All SS Cathl Nairobi Kenya 18–21; Chapl Luton and Dunstable Univ Hosp NHS Foundn Trust from 21. *Address temp unknown* E: petrosnyatsanza@yahoo.co.uk

NYE, Canon David Charles. b 39. K Coll Lon BD 65 Glos Univ MA 01. d 63 p 64. C Charlton Kings St Mary *Glouc* 63–67; C Yeovil St Jo w Preston Plucknett *B & W* 67–70; V Lower Cam *Glouc* 70–74; Min Can Glouc Cathl 74–79; Dir of Ords 74–79; Prin Glouc Th Course 74–79; V Glouc St Mary de Lode and St Nic 74–76; V Maisemore 76–79; Chapl Grenville Coll Bideford 79–81; V Leckhampton SS Phil and Jas w Cheltenham St Jas *Glouc* 81–95; Hon Can Glouc Cathl 88–04; RD Cheltenham 89–95; P-in-c Northleach w Hampnett and Farmington 95–00; P-in-c Cold Aston w Notgrove and Turkdean 95–00; R Northleach w Hampnett and Farmington etc 00–04; RD Northleach 99–04; rtd 04. *3 Blackberry Field, Prestbury, Cheltenham GL52 5LT* T: (01242) 268964 E: dcnye@btinternet.com

NYIRONGO, David. b 79. Wycliffe Hall Ox. d 11 p 12. C Penketh *Liv* 11–14; C Warrington W 14–15; TV Pontypridd *Llan* 15–18; TV Tolworth, Hook and Surbiton *S'wark* 18–21; C Upper Tooting H Trin w St Aug from 21. *14 Upper Tooting Park, London SW17 7SW* E: nyirongodavy@gmail.com

O

OADES, Michael Anthony John. b 45. Brasted Th Coll 69 Sarum & Wells Th Coll 71. **d** 73 **p** 74. C Eltham Park St Luke *S'wark* 73–78; C Coulsdon St Andr 78–81; P-in-c Merton St Jas 81–86; V 86–87; V Benhilton 87–10; rtd 10; PtO *Truro* from 14. *Cranleigh, Penbothidno, Constantine, Falmouth TR11 5AU* T: (01326) 341304 E: michaelandsylvia@btinternet.com

OAKDEN, David Ian. b 60. **d** 10 **p** 11. OLM Shere, Albury and Chilworth *Guildf* from 10. *102 New Road, Chilworth, Guildford GU4 8LU* T: (01483) 578230 E: david.oakden@yahoo.co.uk

OAKE, Canon Barry Richard. b 47. MRICS 71. Ripon Coll Cuddesdon 83. **d** 85 **p** 86. C Wantage *Ox* 85–88; C Warlingham w Chelsham and Farleigh *S'wark* 88–91; R N w S Wootton *Nor* 91–05; R Thorpe St Andr 05–15; rtd 15; V Nor St Helen 15–18; Chapl Gt Hosp Nor 15–18; Chapl among Deaf and Hearing-Impaired People *Nor* 01–18; Hon Can Nor Cathl 07–18; PtO from 19. *2A Cliff Road, Cromer NR27 0BU* T: (01263) 514192 E: barryoake@gmail.com

OAKES, Miss Jennifer May. b 43. Trin Coll Bris 78. **dss** 82 **d** 87 **p** 94. Wilncote *Lich* 82–85; Stoneydelph St Martin CD 82–85; Bentley 85–89; Par Dn 87–89; Par Dn Hixon w Stowe-by-Chartley 89–94; C 94–98; Par Dn Fradswell, Gayton, Milwich and Weston 93–94; C 94–98; P-in-c Standon and Cotes Heath 98–00; rtd 03; Hon C Alfrick, Lulsley, Suckley, Leigh and Bransford *Worc* 03–04; PtO *Lich* 05–17. *Willow Rise, Ashbourne Road, Whiston, Stoke-on-Trent ST10 2JE* T: (01538) 260013

OAKES, Canon Jeremy Charles. b 51. ACA 75 FCA 81. Westcott Ho Cam 75. **d** 78 **p** 79. C Evington *Leic* 78–81; C Ringwood *Win* 81–84; P-in-c Thurnby Lodge *Leic* 84–89; TV Oakdale *Sarum* 89–95; P-in-c Canford Cliffs and Sandbanks 95–03; V 03–14; rtd 14; Can and Preb Sarum Cathl from 03; PtO 16–20. *5 Townsend Road, Corfe Castle, Wareham BH20 5ET* T: (01929) 480181 E: oakesjeremyc@gmail.com

OAKES, John Cyril. b 49. AKC 71. St Aug Coll Cant 71. **d** 72 **p** 73. C Broseley w Benthall *Heref* 72–76; C Cannock *Lich* 76–79; TV 79–83; V Rough Hills 83–09; P-in-c Wolverhampton St Steph 94–09; rtd 09; PtO *Lich* from 09; *Worc* from 10. *Glendower, Bull Street, Gornal Wood, Dudley DY3 2NQ* T: (01384) 232097 M: 07821-199122 E: classfortyseven@hotmail.co.uk

OAKES, Canon Leslie John. b 28. AKC 53. **d** 54 **p** 55. C Bedford Leigh *Man* 54–58; C Walsall St Matt *Lich* 58–60; Chapl Selly Oak Hosp Birm 60–64; V Longbridge *Birm* 64–93; Hon Can Birm Cathl 84–93; rtd 93; PtO *Birm* 93–18. *108 Hole Lane, Birmingham B31 2DF* T: 0121-476 8514 E: joakes123@talktalk.net

OAKES, Robert. b 47. Chan Sch Truro 79. **d** 82 **p** 83. NSM Probus, Ladock and Grampound w Creed and St Erme *Truro* 82–84; TV Bodmin w Lanhydrock and Lanivet 85–88; R S Hill w Callington 88–03; RD E Wivelshire 95–00; Bp's Adv on Healing Min 98–03; Hon Can Truro Cathl 01–03; C Calstock 06–14; C St Dominic, Landulph and St Mellion w Pillaton 12–14; Chapl Cornwall and Is of Scilly Primary Care Trust 09–13; rtd 14; PtO *Truro* from 14. *Kernick House, 11 Trelawney Rise, Callington PL17 7PT* T: (01579) 389109 M: 07890-099248 E: oakesrobert@hotmail.co.uk

OAKES, Simon Paul. b 77. SS Coll Cam BA 00 MA 03 PhD 06. Coll of Resurr Mirfield 11. **d** 13 **p** 14. C Walsall St Gabr Fulbrook *Lich* 13–16; V Holbrooks *Cov* from 16. *St Luke's Vicarage, Rotherham Road, Coventry CV6 4FE* T: (024) 7668 8604 E: frsimonoakes@outlook.com

OAKEY-JONES, Ms Angela Jean. b 71. Keele Univ BA 93. NTMTC BA 08. **d** 08 **p** 09. C Rushmere *St E* 08–11; P-in-c Ipswich All Hallows 11–16; R Cheriton w Newington *Cant* 16–19; Spiritual Care Worker St Eliz Hospice Ipswich 19. *18 Chatsworth Drive, Rushmere St Andrew, Ipswich IP4 5XA* T: (01473) 325828 M: 07930-141091 E: revangelaoj@gmail.com

OAKHAM, Archdeacon of. *Vacant*

OAKLAND, Mrs Sarah Marie. b 54. UEA BEd 85. EAMTC 99. **d** 02 **p** 03. C Diss *Nor* 02–06; V Chessington *Guildf* 06–11; R E w W Harling, Bridgham w Roudham, Larling etc *Nor*

11–15; rtd 15. *Sea Holly, Fearns Close, Cromer NR27 0DZ* E: sarahoakland@hotmail.com

OAKLEY, Hilary Robert Mark. b 53. Univ of Wales (Ban) BSc 75 Ox Univ BA 78 MA 81 MCIPD 91. Ripon Coll Cuddesdon 76. **d** 79 **p** 80. C Birm St Pet 79–82; C Cambridge Gt St Mary w St Mich *Ely* 82–86; Chapl Girton Coll Cam 82–86; Chapl Zürich w St Gallen and Winterthur *Eur* 86–88; NSM Lon 88–92; PtO *St Alb* 92–13; NSM Hitchin and St Paul's Walden 13–19; rtd 19. *Casa Campestre Buzón 16C, Calle Fuente del Conde 170, 14978 Iznájar (Córdoba), Spain* M: 07769-648174 E: hilaryoakley@hotmail.com

OAKLEY, Jeremy Steven. b 52. Birm Univ BA 99. Trin Coll Bris 95. **d** 97 **p** 98. C Walsall *Lich* 97–02; V Penn Fields 02–16; P-in-c W Bromwich St Jas w St Paul 16–18; rtd 18; PtO *Lich* from 20. *Guildwood, Old Weston Road, Bishops Wood, Stafford ST19 9AG*

OAKLEY, Canon Mark David. b 68. K Coll Lon BD 90 AKC 90. St Steph Ho Ox 90. **d** 93 **p** 94. C St John's Wood *Lon* 93–96; Bp's Chapl 96–00; P-in-c Covent Garden St Paul 00–03; R 03–05; AD Westmr St Marg 04–05; Chapl RADA 03–05; Adn Germany and N Eur 05–08; Chapl Copenhagen 05–08; P-in-c Grosvenor Chpl *Lon* 08–10; Can Res St Paul's Cathl 10–18; Fell and Dean St Jo Coll Cam from 18; Dep P in O from 96; PtO *Eur* from 18; Can Th Wakef Cathl *Leeds* from 20. *St John's College, Cambridge CB2 1TP* T: (01223) 338600 E: mdo26@cam.ac.uk

OAKLEY, Robert Paul. b 51. Sheff Univ BScTech 72 PGCE 74 Open Univ MA(Theol) 97. St Jo Coll Nottm 87. **d** 89 **p** 90. C Heatherlands St Jo *Sarum* 89–92; V Burton All SS w Ch Ch *Lich* 92–99; V Gt Wyrley 99–07; Tutor Wilson Carlile Coll of Evang 07–12; V Totley *Sheff* 12–16; rtd 16; PtO *Derby* from 18. *34 James Clarke Road, Willington, Derby DE65 6RD* M: 07971-325222

OAKLEY, Stephen Alfred. b 66. **d** 13 **p** 14. NSM Lundwood *Wakef* 13–14; *Leeds* 14–19; NSM Cen Barnsley from 19. *9 Parkland View, Barnsley S71 5LG* T: (01226) 781797 E: stephenoakley66@googlemail.com

OAKLEY, Susan Mary. *See* HENWOOD, Susan Mary

OAKLEY, Timothy Crispin. b 45. Qu Coll Cam BA 66 MA 70 Bris Univ PGCE 69. St Jo Coll Nottm 73. **d** 76 **p** 77. C Bromley Common St Aug *Roch* 76–79; C Fairfield *Liv* 79–81; CMS Kenya 82–90; P-in-c Beaford, Roborough and St Giles in the Wood *Ex* 91–96; Chapl St Andr Sch Turi Kenya 96–98; V Woodford Halse w Eydon *Pet* 99–10; RD Brackley 03–05; rtd 10; PtO *Heref* 12–21. *Sunny Bank, Clive Avenue, Church Stretton SY6 7BL* T: (01694) 724225 E: tim@taitaoakleys.co.uk

OATES, Alan. b 32. S'wark Ord Course 79. **d** 80 **p** 81. NSM Rayleigh *Chelmsf* 80–87; TV Jarrow *Dur* 87–92; P-in-c Stella 92–95; R 95–97; rtd 97; PtO *Dur* 98–14; *Newc* from 00. *1 The Haven, North Shields NE29 6YH* T: 0191-258 6984

OATES, Douglas. b 39. Bolton Coll of Educn CertEd 74 Ches Coll of HE BTh 97. NOC 94. **d** 97 **p** 98. NSM Balderstone *Man* 97–01; NSM Oldham St Barn 01–06; P-in-c 03–06; P-in-c Waterhead 05–06; TV Medlock Head 06–09; rtd 09; PtO *Man* from 09. *43 Devonport Crescent, Royton, Oldham OL2 6JX* T: (01706) 849929 M: 07743-993381

OATES, Canon John. b 30. Kelham Th Coll 53. **d** 57 **p** 58. C Hackney Wick St Mary of Eton w St Aug *Lon* 57–60; Development Officer C of E Youth Coun 60–64; Sec C of E Coun Commonwealth Settlement 64–65; Gen Sec 65–72; Sec C of E Cttee on Migration & Internat Affairs 68–72; Hon Can Bunbury from 69; V Richmond St Mary w St Matthias *S'wark* 70–79; P-in-c Richmond St Jo 76–79; V Richmond St Mary w St Matthias and St Jo 79–84; RD Richmond and Barnes 79–84; R St Bride Fleet Street w Bridewell etc *Lon* 84–00; AD The City 97–00; Preb St Paul's Cathl 97–00; rtd 00; PtO *S'wark* 03–18; *Lon* from 01. *27 York Court, Albany Park Road, Kingston upon Thames KT2 5ST* E: john@oates.co.uk

OATES, Michael Graham. b 62. Leic Poly BSc 84. Aston Tr Scheme 87 Cranmer Hall Dur 89. **d** 92 **p** 93. C Enfield St Andr *Lon* 92–96; TV N Poole Ecum Team *Sarum* 96–07; PtO 07–08; Chapl Dorset HealthCare University NHS Foundn Trust from 14. *51 Ringwood Road, Poole BH14 0RE* T: (01202) 731389 E: oates@madasafish.com *or* michael.oates@dhuft.nhs.uk

OATES (*née* **ADAMS**), **Canon Ruth.** b 47. Bris Univ BSc 69. SEITE 97. **d** 00 **p** 01. C Rainham *Roch* 00–03; V Gravesend St Mary 03–13; RD Gravesend 09–13; P-in-c Ash 13–17; P-in-c Ridley 13–17; Hon Can Roch Cathl 11–17; rtd 17; PtO Ex from 18. *19 Fluder Crescent, Kingskerswell, Newton Abbot TQ12 5JE*

OATRIDGE, Andrew Philip. b 77. Sheff Univ MMath 00. Oak Hill Th Coll MTh 10. **d** 10 **p** 11. C Chapeltown *Sheff* 10–13; Crosslinks Hungary from 13. *Zsigmond király utca 17, 2051 Biatorbágy, Hungary* E: andyzsofi@gmail.com

OBAN, Provost of. *See* CAMPBELL, The Very Revd Margaret Ruth

OBEDOZA, William. b 58. NTMTC 05. **d** 08 **p** 09. C Walthamstow St Sav *Chelmsf* 08–12; V Woodford St Barn from 12. *St Barnabas' Vicarage, 127 Snakes Lane East, Woodford Green IG8 7HX* T: (020) 3659 4023 M: 07916-281227 E: fatherobedoza@gmail.com

O'BENEY, Robin Mervyn. b 35. Ely Th Coll 61. **d** 64 **p** 65. C Liss *Portsm* 64–65; C Portsea St Cuth 65–68; Hon C Wymondham *Nor* 74–76; R Swainsthorpe w Newton Flotman 76–80; NSM Sparkenhoe Deanery *Leic* 87–90; V Billesdon and Skeffington 90–91; rtd 95; PtO *Heref* 10–15. *19 Bridge Street, Kington HR5 3DL* T: (01544) 230416 E: roobeney@gmail.com

OBIDIEGWU, Dennis Chiedu. Cape Coast Univ Ghana BA 13. St Nic Th Coll Ghana 08. Ghana 14–18; Chapl Tangier Eur from 18. *St Andrew, rue d'Angleterre 50, Tangier, Morocco* M: (00212) 622-295203 E: rvndden@gmail.com

OBIN, Raymond Clive. b 63. Girton Coll Cam BA 85 MA 89. Wycliffe Hall Ox BTh 07. **d** 04 **p** 05. NSM Bucklebury w Marlston *Ox* 04–12; NSM Bradfield and Stanford Dingley 04–12; Asst Dir of Ords (Berks) from 12; PtO *Win* from 13; LtO *Ox* from 15. *Solfonn, Enborne Row, Wash Water, Newbury RG20 0LY* T: (01635) 38212 E: raymond@obin.org.uk

OBIORA, Arthur Cuenyem. b 42. JP 91. **d** 95 **p** 95. NSM Hatcham St Cath *S'wark* 95–12; PtO from 12. *126 Perry Hill, London SE6 4EY* T: (020) 8699 3845

OBORNE, Mrs Martine Amelia. b 57. St Hilda's Coll Ox MA 80. SEITE BA 09. **d** 09 **p** 10. C Islington St Mary *Lon* 09–12; P-in-c Chiswick St Mich 12–15; V from 15. *St Michael's Vicarage, 60 Elmwood Road, London W4 3DZ* T: (020) 8994 3173 M: 07842-199556 E: maoborne@hotmail.com *or* vicar@stmichael-suttoncourt.org.uk

O'BOYLE, Liam Patrick Butler. b 66. Nottm Univ BA 90 MA 98. EMMTC 98. **d** 01 **p** 02. C Cinderhill *S'well* 01–06; TV Clifton 06–10; Dioc Partnerships Officer from 10; C Chilwell from 11; C Lenton Abbey from 11. *23 Fellows Road, Beeston, Nottingham NG9 1AQ* T: 0115-943 1032 E: liam.oboyle@ntlworld.com *or* liam.o'boyle@southwell.anglican.org

O'BRIEN, Andrew Peter. b 81. Jes Coll Cam BA 03. Wycliffe Hall Ox BTh 14. **d** 14 **p** 15. C Wimbledon Park St Luke *S'wark* 14–19; PtO from 19. *37 Lucien Road, London SW19 8EL*

O'BRIEN, David. b 62. Moorlands Th Coll BA 99. CBDTI 01. **d** 04 **p** 05. C Bispham *Blackb* 04–08; C S Shore H Trin 08–10; P-in-c Shelton and Oxon *Lich* 10–18; V 18–19; Uplands Nursing Home 15–17; V Blackpool St Thos *Blackb* from 19. *St Thomas's Vicarage, 80 Devonshire Road, Blackpool FY3 8AE*

O'BRIEN, Capt David. b 48. Wilson Carlile Coll 87. **d** 16 **p** 17. NSM Upton Ascension *Ches* from 16. *1 Caldy Close, Chester CH2 2BZ* T: (01244) 375782 M: 07828-206090 E: daveobrienca@hotmail.com

O'BRIEN, Mrs Elaine. b 55. CITC 94. **d** 97 **p** 98. Aux Min Killynan *Arm* 97–00; Aux Min Gilnahirk *D & D* 00–06; Bp's C Clogherny w Seskinore and Drumnakilly *Arm* 06–08; R 08–11; I Whitehouse *Conn* from 11. *The Rectory, 283 Shore Road, Newtownabbey BT37 9SR* T: (028) 9036 9955 M: 07703-618119 E: elaineobrien1@btinternet.com

O'BRIEN, George Edward. b 32. Clifton Th Coll 61. **d** 64 **p** 65. C Denton Holme *Carl* 64–68; V Castle Town *Lich* 68–88; Chapl St Geo Hosp Stafford 88–94; Chapl Kingsmead Hosp Stafford 88–94; Chapl Foundation NHS Trust Stafford 94–99; rtd 99; PtO *Lich* 99–17. *Abily, 185 Tixall Road, Stafford ST16 3XJ* T: (01785) 244261 E: georgemary18@tiscali.co.uk

O'BRIEN, Kevin Michael. b 60. Herts Univ BA 82. St Steph Ho Ox BTh 04. **d** 01 **p** 02. C Uppingham w Ayston and Wardley w Belton *Pet* 01–04; Asst Chapl Wellington Coll Berks 04–06; Bp's Chapl and Office Manager *Eur* 06–10; V Burgess Hill St Jo *Chich* 10–19; RD Hurst 11–18; I Drumcliffe w Kilnasoolagh *L & K* from 19. *Lisheen, Ballynacally, Ennis, Co Clare, V95 XWR0, Republic of Ireland*

O'BRIEN, Mary Veronica. *See* GUBBINS, Mary Veronica

O'BRIEN, Shelagh Ann. *See* STACEY, Shelagh Ann

O'BRIEN, Thomas Anthony. b 72. Open Univ BSc 09 TCD MSc 10 MTh 18. TCD Div Sch 12. **d** 16 **p** 18. Howth *D & D* 16–18; NSM Holmpatrick w Balbriggan and Kenure from 18. *75 Trimleston, Hamlet Lane, Balbriggan, Co Dublin, Republic of Ireland* M: (00353) 87-650 2504 E: revtobrien@gmail.com

O'CALLAGHAN, Regan Robert Rehe. b 67. Brunel Univ BA 97 K Coll Lon MA 98 Anglia Poly Univ MA 01. Westcott Ho Cam 99. **d** 01 **p** 02. C Whitton St Aug *Lon* 01–03; C St Jo on Bethnal Green 03–04; NSM 04–14; PtO from 14. *Emmanuel Vicarage, Lyncroft Gardens, London NW6 1JU* T: (020) 7419 8384 E: reganocallaghan@googlemail.com

OCHOLA, George Otieno. b 58. Lon Sch of Th BTh 02. St Jo Sch of Miss Kokise. **d** 88 **p** 89. Kenya 88–99; PtO *Lon* 00–08; NSM Watford St Mich *St Alb* 08–10; Chapl W Herts Hosps NHS Trust 10–19; Chapl King's Coll Hosp NHS Foundn Trust from 19; PtO *St Alb* from 19. *King's College Hospital NHS Foundation Trust, Denmark Hill, London SE5 9RS* T: (020) 3299 9000 M: 07866-359120 E: georgeochola@hotmail.com

OCKFORD, Paul Philip. b 46. St Chad's Coll Dur BA 67. St Steph Ho Ox 68. **d** 70 **p** 71. C Streatham St Pet *S'wark* 70–74; C Cheam 74–77; P-in-c Eastrington *York* 77–79; TV Howden 80–83; R Sherburn and W and E Heslerton w Yedingham 83–92; V Bampton, Morebath, Clayhanger and Petton *Ex* 92–98; R Goodmanham *York* 98–04; V Market Weighton 98–04; V Sancton 98–04; rtd 04. *78 Wold Road, Pocklington, York YO42 2QG* E: rocktord@msn.com

O'CONNELL, Peter David. b 69. St Edm Hall Ox BA 91 MA 97 Cant Ch Ch Univ BA 12. SEITE 09. **d** 12 **p** 13. C Henfield w Shermanbury and Woodmancote *Chich* 12–16; R Godstone and Blindley Heath *S'wark* from 16. *The Rectory, 17 Ivy Mill Lane, Godstone RH9 8NH* T: (01883) 741945 E: peter.oconnell@cheerful.com

O'CONNELL, William Anthony. b 61. STETS. **d** 10 **p** 11. C Milton *Win* 10–13; P-in-c Lyddington and Wanborough and Bishopstone etc *Bris* 13–20. *Address temp unknown* E: villagevicar@hotmail.co.uk

O'CONNOR, Canon Brian Michael McDougal. b 42. St Cath Coll Cam BA 67 MA 69. Cuddesdon Coll 67. **d** 69 **p** 70. C Headington *Ox* 69–71; Sec Dioc Past and Redundant Chs Uses Cttees 72–79; P-in-c Merton 72–76; V Rainbow Hill 79–97; RD Gillingham 81–88; Hon Can Roch Cathl 89–97; Dean Auckland NZ 97–00; Hon Can from 00; PtO *Ox* 00–02 and 04–16; P-in-c Lt Missenden 02–04; rtd 04. *The Lawn, 64 Fore Street, Otterton, Budleigh Salterton EX9 7HB* T: (01395) 488898 M: 07740-702161 E: canonmichaeloc@aol.com

O'CONNOR, Canon Daniel. b 33. Univ Coll Dur BA 54 MA 67 St Andr Univ PhD 81. Cuddesdon Coll 56. **d** 58 **p** 59. C Stockton St Pet *Dur* 58–62; C W Hartlepool St Aid 62–63; Cam Miss to Delhi 63–70; USPG India 70–72; Chapl St Andr Univ *St And* 72–77; R Edin Gd Shep 77–82; Prin Coll of Ascension Selly Oak 82–90; Dir Scottish Chs Ho (Chs Together in Scotland) 90–93; Can Res Wakef Cathl 93–96; Bp's Adv on Inter-Faith Issues 93–96; rtd 96; Hon C Cupar *St And* 12–13; PtO from 13. *15 School Road, Balmullo, St Andrews KY16 0BA* T: (01334) 871326 E: danoconnor@btinternet.com

O'CONNOR, Martin John. b 48. UCD BComm 73. **d** 11 **p** 12. NSM Dublin St Ann and St Steph *D & G* from 11. *137 Braemor Road, Churchtown, Dublin, D14 YE92, Republic of Ireland* T: (00353) (1) 298 8900 M: 87-207 0907 E: m.oconnor91@upcmail.ie

O'CONNOR, Michael. *See* O'CONNOR, Brian Michael McDougal

O'CONNOR, Stephen James. b 62. K Coll Lon BSc 93 MSc 01 Lanc Univ PhD 08. Ripon Coll Cuddesdon BA 19. **d** 19 **p** 20. C Walmer and Cornilo *Cant* from 19. *35 Church Path, Deal CT14 9TH* M: 07921-313869 E: sjoconnor@hotmail.co.uk

ODDY, Joan Winifred. b 34. **d** 97 **p** 98. OLM Kessingland w Gisleham *Nor* 97–99; OLM Kessingland, Gisleham and Rushmere 99–04; rtd 04; PtO *Nor* from 04. *3 The Paddocks, Kessingland, Lowestoft NR33 7SE* T: (01502) 742001

ODDY-BATES, Mrs Julie Louise. b 61. SRN 82 SCM 85. Ridley Hall Cam 04. **d** 06 **p** 07. C Watton w Carbrooke and Ovington *Nor* 06–07; C Ashill, Carbrooke, Ovington and Saham Toney 07–09; P-in-c Gillingham w Geldeston, Stockton, Ellingham etc 09–18; C Loddon, Sisland, Chedgrave, Hardley and Langley 09–16; rtd 18. *Old Chapel House, Priory Lane, Grimoldby, Louth LN11 8SP* E: jlo32@tiscali.co.uk

O'DELL, Colin John. b 61. WEMTC 03. **d** 06 **p** 07. C Bishop's Cleeve *Glouc* 06–09; Chapl RAF from 09. *Chaplaincy Services (RAF), HQ Air Command, RAF High Wycombe HP14 4UE* T: (01494) 496800 E: revdcolin@hotmail.co.uk

ODLING-SMEE, George William. b 35. K Coll Dur MB, BS 59 FRCS 68 FRCSI 86. **d** 77 **p** 78. Hon Can Down *Conn* 77–90; NSM Belfast St Geo 90–02. *The Boathouse, 24 Rossglass Road South, Killough, Downpatrick BT30 7RA* T: (028) 4484 1868 F: 4484 1143 E: wodlingsmee@gmail.com

ODOEMENA, Prince Doms. b 88. Oak Hill Th Coll BA 17. **d** 11 **p** 12. C Walthamstow St Barn and St Jas Gt *Chelmsf* 17–19; C Forest Gate Em w Upton

Cross 19–20. *The Vicarage, 2 Regent Gardens, Ilford IG3 8UL* M: 07529-989241 E: princedoms@me.com *or* podoemena@chelmsford.anglican.org

O'DONNELL, Mrs Mollie. b 39. Portsm Poly BA 91. STETS 97. **d** 00 **p** 03. NSM Calbourne w Newtown and Shalfleet *Portsm* 00–09; rtd 09; PtO *Portsm* 09–15. *36 Medina Court, Old Westminster Lane, Newport PO30 5PW*

O'DONNELL, Paula Ella. See CHALLEN, Paula Ella

O'DONOGHUE, Mark Ronald. b 69. St Aid Coll Dur BA 91 Solicitor 93. Oak Hill Th Coll BA 04. **d** 04 **p** 05. C St Helen Bishopsgate w St Andr Undershaft etc *Lon* 04–11; C Kensington St Mary Abbots w Ch Ch and St Phil 11–16; V Kensington Ch Ch 17–21; AD Kensington 16–20. *9 Eldon Road, London W8 5PU*

O'DONOGHUE, Mrs Sarah Helen. b 75. Ches Coll of HE BA 96 Liv Hope PGCE 97. St Mellitus Coll 13. **d** 15 **p** 16. C Aughton Ch Ch *Liv* 15–19; V from 19. *22 Long Lane, Aughton, Ormskirk L39 5AT* M: 07847-931323 E: revsarahodonoghue@gmail.com

O'DONOVAN, Canon Oliver Michael Timothy. b 45. Ball Coll Ox BA 68 MA 71 DPhil 75. Wycliffe Hall Ox 68. **d** 72 **p** 73. Tutor Wycliffe Hall Ox 72–77; Prof Systematic Th Wycliffe Coll Toronto 77–82; Regius Prof Moral and Past Th Ox Univ 82–06; Can Res Ch Ch *Ox* 82–06; Prof Chr Ethics Edin Univ 06–12; Hon Prof St Andr Univ *St And* from 13; Can Prov and Can Th York Minster from 15; PtO 15–20. *6A Comely Park, Dunfermline KY12 7HU* E: oliver.odonovan@ed.ac.uk

O'DOWD-SMYTH, Christine. CITC. **d** 09 **p** 10. NSM Lismore w Cappoquin, Kilwatermoy, Dungarvan etc *C, F & O* 09–14; P-in-c Fiddown w Clonegam, Guilcagh and Kilmeaden 14; Dioc Spokesperson for Healing Min from 14. *Eldon, 16 John's Hill, Waterford, Republic of Ireland* T: (00353) (51) 304423 M: 87-293 3461 E: odowdsmythchristine@gmail.com

OEHRING, Alexander James. b 81. Hull Univ BA 02. Cranmer Hall Dur 16. **d** 18 **p** 19. C Walton-on-Thames *Guildf* 18–21; R Colne *Blackb* from 21. *30 Grenfell Gardens, Colne BB8 9PL* M: 07920-098867 E: alexanderoehring@hotmail.com

OEHRING, Anthony Charles. b 56. Sheff City Poly BA 79 CQSW 79 Kent Univ MA 02. Ridley Hall Cam 86. **d** 88 **p** 89. C Gillingham *Sarum* 88–91; TV S Gillingham *Roch* 91–00; P-in-c Faversham *Cant* 00–12; C Preston next Faversham, Goodnestone and Graveney 02–12; P-in-c The Brents and Davington w Oare and Luddenham 03–06; AD Ospringe 02–11; Co-ord Chapl HM Pris E Sutton Park 12–13; Co-ord Chapl HM Pris Blantyre Ho 12–13; Hon Can Cant Cathl 06–13; Managing Chapl HM Pris Ford 13–20; rtd 20; PtO *Sarum* 13–20; Hon C Poole from 20. *The Church Office, St James's Church, Church Street, Poole BH15 1JP* M: 07847-307475 E: acoehring@virginmedia.com

OEPPEN, Canon John Gerard David. b 44. St D Coll Lamp. **d** 67 **p** 68. C-in-c Cwmmer w Abercregan CD *Llan* 67–70; TV Glyncorrwg w Afan Vale and Cymmer Afan 70–71; C Whitchurch 71–74; V Aberavon H Trin 74–78; V Bargoed and Deri w Brithdir 78–86; R Barry All SS 86–08; Can Llan Cathl 04–08; rtd 08; PtO *Llan* from 08. *6 Heol Fioled, Barry CF63 1HB*

OESTREICHER, Canon Paul. b 31. OM(Ger) 95. Univ of NZ BA 53 MA 56 Cov Poly Hon DLitt 91 Sussex Univ Hon LLD 05 Lambeth DD 08 Otago Univ Hon DD 09. Linc Th Coll 56. **d** 59 **p** 60. C Dalston H Trin w St Phil *Lon* 59–61; C S Mymms K Chas 61–68; Asst in Relig Broadcasting BBC 61–64; Assoc Sec Internat Affairs Dept BCC 64–69; V Blackheath Ascension *S'wark* 68–81; Dir of Tr 69–72; Hon Can S'wark Cathl 78–81; Asst Gen Sec BCC 81–86; Can Res Cov Cathl 86–97; Dir of Internat Min 86–97; Humboldt Fell Inst of Th Free Univ of Berlin 92–93; rtd 98; PtO *Cov* 98–10; *Chich* 03–17; Hon Chapl Sussex Univ 04–09. *Apartment 42, 8 Leeds Street, Te Aro, Wellington 6011, New Zealand* M: (0064) 27-264 1580 E: paul.oestreicher.nz@gmail.com

O'FARRELL, James Mark. b 08. NSM Dublin Sandford w Milltown *D & G* from 08. *138 Meadow Grove, Dundrum, Dublin 14, Republic of Ireland* T: (00353) (1) 296 6222 E: amofharp@gmail.com

O'FERRALL, Patrick Charles Kenneth. b 34. OBE 89. New Coll Ox BA 58 MA 60. **d** 00 **p** 01. OLM Godalming *Guildf* 00–04; PtO from 04. *Pear Tree House, 66 Firgrove Hill, Farnham GU9 8LW* T: (01252) 724498 E: patrickoferrall@gmail.com

OFFER, The Ven Clifford Jocelyn. b 43. Ex Univ BA 67 FRSA 97. Westcott Ho Cam 67. **d** 69 **p** 70. C Bromley SS Pet and Paul *Roch* 69–74; TV Southampton (City Cen) *Win* 74–83; TR Hitchin *St Alb* 83–94; Adn Nor and Can Res Nor Cathl 94–08; rtd 08; PtO *Heref* from 09. *Chase House, Peterstow, Ross-on-Wye HR9 6JX* T: (01989) 567874

OFFORD, Mrs Judith Anne. b 50. **d** 19 **p** 20. NSM Sudbury w Ballingdon and Brundon *St E* 19–20; NSM Sudbury and Chilton 19–20; NSM Chadbrook from 20. *98 Melford Road, Sudbury CO10 1JY* T: (01787) 315689 E: judithofford@btinternet.com

O'FLAHERTY, Mrs Sheila Mary. b 53. Huddersfield Univ MA 08 Man Univ CertEd 00. SNWTP 11. **d** 13 **p** 14. NSM Heatons *Man* 13–15; NSM Coldhurst and Oldham St Steph 15–18; P-in-c Newton w Flowery Field *Ches* from 18; PtO *Man* from 18. *St Mary's Vicarage, 39 Bradley Green Road, Hyde SK14 4NA* T: 0161-368 1489 M: 07803-084422 E: revsheila@oflaherty.co.uk

OGBEDE, Mrs Olufunke Oladunni. b 48. Lon Inst of Educn MA 81. **d** 05 **p** 06. OLM S Lambeth St Anne and All SS *S'wark* 05–13; NSM Stockwell St Andr and St Mich 13–18; PtO from 18. *Flat 11, 2 Allingham Road, London SW4 8EG* M: 07944-424931 E: fundunni@aol.com

OGILVIE, Ian Douglas. b 37. Em Coll Cam BA 59 MA 63. Linc Th Coll 59. **d** 61 **p** 62. C Clapham H Trin *S'wark* 61–63; C Cambridge Gt St Mary w St Mich *Ely* 63–66; Chapl Sevenoaks Sch 66–77; Hon C Sevenoaks St Nic *Roch* 67–77; Chapl Malvern Coll 77–84; Hd Master St Geo Sch Harpenden 84–87; LtO *St Alb* 84–87; Bp's Dom Chapl 87–89; P-in-c Aldenham 87–91; Appeals Dir Mind 89–91; Fund Raising Dir Br Deaf Assn 91–94; NSM Tring *St Alb* 92–94; PtO from 94; Fund Raising Dir R Nat Miss to Deep Sea Fishermen from 94; PtO *Ox* from 11; *Eur* from 17. *The White House, 19 Lower Icknield Way, Marsworth, Tring HP23 4LN* T: (01296) 661479 E: ia.ogilve@gmail.com

OGILVIE, Pamela. b 56. Brunel Univ MA 89 CQSW 82. Qu Coll Birm 01. **d** 03 **p** 04. C Hill *Birm* 03–07; V Billesley Common 07–15; rtd 15; PtO *Birm* from 15; *Lich* from 16. *Address withheld by request* E: pamelaogilvie@outlook.com

OGILVIE-BERRY, Amanda Jayne. b 75. Leeds Univ BA 05. St Hild Coll 19. **d** 21. C Huddersfield St Pet *Leeds* from 21. *The Rectory, 10 The Dell, Huddersfield HD2 2FD* M: 07921-140450 E: amanda.ogilvie-berry@leeds.anglican.org *or* manda_berry@yahoo.co.uk

OGILVIE THOMPSON, Christopher William. b 58. Witwatersrand Univ BSc 83. Ox Min Course 14. **d** 16 **p** 17. NSM Bentley, Binsted and Froyle *Win* from 16. *Mill Court House, Mill Court, Upper Froyle, Alton GU34 4JF* T: (01420) 23125 M: 07776-178690 E: christopherot@me.com

OGLE, The Very Revd Catherine. b 61. Leeds Univ BA 82 MPhil 85 MA 91 Fitzw Coll Cam BA 87. Westcott Ho Cam 85. **d** 88 **p** 94. C Middleton St Mary *Ripon* 88–91; Relig Progr Ed BBC Radio Leeds 91–95; NSM Leeds St Marg and All Hallows 91–95; P-in-c Woolley *Wakef* 95–01; P-in-c Huddersfield St Pet and All SS 01–03; V Huddersfield St Pet 03–10; RD Huddersfield 09–10; Chapl Huddersfield Univ 03–06; Hon Can Wakef Cathl 08–10; Dean Birm 10–17; Dean Win from 17. *The Deanery, The Close, Winchester SO23 9LS* E: dean@winchester-cathedral.org.uk

OGLESBY, Canon Leslie Ellis. b 46. Univ Coll Ox BA 69 MA 73 City Univ MPhil 73 Fitzw Coll Cam BA 73 MA 77 Lambeth PhD 12. Ripon Coll Cuddesdon 77. **d** 78 **p** 79. C Stevenage St Mary Shephall *St Alb* 78–80; Dir St Alb Minl Tr Scheme 80–87; V Markyate Street *St Alb* 80–87; Dir CME 87–94; Hon Can St Alb 93–01; TR Hitchin 94–01; Adult Educn and Tr Officer *Ely* 01–04; Dioc Dir Minl and Adult Learning 04–12; Dir Min 12; Hon Can Ely Cathl 04–12; rtd 12; PtO *Ely* from 12; *St Alb* from 12. *55 Swansholme Gardens, Sandy SG19 1HN* E: oglesbyes75@yahoo.co.uk

OGLESBY-ELONG, Mrs Elizabeth Jane. b 73. Roehampton Inst BA 95 Man Univ BPhil 98. Westcott Ho Cam 00. **d** 03 **p** 04. C S Dulwich St Steph *S'wark* 03–06; P-in-c Camberwell St Mich w All So w Em 06–07; V 07–14; AD S'wark and Newington 13–14; V Eltham Park St Luke 14–21; V Biggleswade *St Alb* from 21. *The Vicarage, Shortmead Street, Biggleswade SG18 0AT* T: (01767) 312243

O'GRADY, Anthony Donald. b 87. RNMH 11 Sheff Univ BA 15. Coll of Resurr Mirfield 12. **d** 15 **p** 16. C Newc Ch Ch w St Anne 15–18; V Woodhorn w Newbiggin from 18. *34A Front Street, Newbiggin-by-the-Sea NE64 6PS* M: 07519-683355 E: fr.aogrady@hotmail.com

O'GRADY, Jack. b 86. **d** 21. C Wandsworth All SS *S'wark* from 21. *Address withheld by request*

OGRAM, Mrs Ann. b 44. WEMTC 04. **d** 06 **p** 07. NSM Clun w Bettws-y-Crwyn and Newcastle *Heref* 06–14; NSM Clun Valley 14–15; PtO *B & W* from 15. *21 Orchard Drive, Sandford, Winscombe BS25 5RD* M: 07970-072836 E: ann@ogram.com

OGUGUO, Barnabas Ahuna. b 47. Rome Univ BA 70 BD 74 Glas Univ MTh 84 PhD 90 Strathclyde Univ PGCE 93. **d** 73 **p** 74. Nigeria 73–93; RE Teacher Lenzie Academy *Glas* 93–96; Bearsden Academy from 96; Hon C Lenzie 95–05; P-in-c Glas St Matt 05–07; P-in-c Cumbernauld 07–09; R

09–13; rtd 13; LtO *Glas* from 14. *32 Carron Crescent, Lenzie, Glasgow G66 5PJ* T: 0141-578 9802 M: 07757-502054 E: bahunog01@yahoo.co.uk

OGUNYEMI, Dele Johnson. b 56. Obafemi Awolowo Univ BA 90. SEITE 04. **d** 07 **p** 08. NSM Plumstead All SS *S'wark* 07–11; C Nunhead St Antony w St Silas 11–14; P-in-c 14–15; V from 15. *St Antony with St Silas Vicarage, Athenlay Road, London SE15 3EP* T: (020) 7639 4261 M: 07958-396118 E: djogunyemi@tiscali.co.uk

OGUNYINKA, Olasupo. b 59. ACMA 96. Yorks Min Course 13. **d** 15 **p** 16. NSM Beeston *Leeds* 15–18; NSM Morley 18–20; TV from 21. *36 Holmwood Avenue, Leeds LS6 4NJ* T: 0113-275 7574 M: 07780-806010 E: olasupo.ogunyinka@ntlworld.com

OH, Abraham (Taemin). b 75. St Steph Ho Ox 08. **d** 11 **p** 12. C Colchester St Jas and St Paul w All SS etc *Chelmsf* 11–14; P-in-c Enfield St Geo *Lon* 14–18; V from 18. *St George's Vicarage, 706 Hertford Road, Enfield EN3 6NR* M: 07737-161317 E: taemin.oh@gmail.com

O'HARE, Phelim Sean. b 71. QUB BA 94 Gregorian Univ Rome STB 97 St Thos Aquinas Pontifical Univ Rome MA 98 St Mary's Coll Twickenham PGCE 02. **d** 97 **p** 98. In RC Ch 97–12; Chapl Cathl Sch Llan 12–14; NSM Canton Cardiff *Llan* 12–14; TV 14–17; P-in-c Cardiff St German w St Sav 17–21; AD Kings Norton, Moseley and Shirley *Birm* from 21. *5 Pickenham Road, Birmingham B14 4TG* E: phelimohare@gmail.com

OHEN, John Chuks. b 42. **d** 06 **p** 07. NSM Clapham St Jas *S'wark* 06–12; PtO from 12. *47 Kirkstall Gardens, London SW2 4HR* T: (020) 8671 0028 M: 07758-935906 E: revjohn.ohen@gmail.com

OHLSSON, Nicolas Hilding. *See* HILDING OHLSSON, Nicolas

OKEKE, Christian Chukwudi. b 71. Strathclyde Univ MSc 09. United Th Coll Harare BTheol 04. **d** 05 **p** 06. C Avondale Zimbabwe 05; C Glas St Silas 05–08; P-in-c Glas Gd Shep and Ascension 08–15; Chapl Strathclyde Univ 08–15; Chapl Princess Alexandra Hosp NHS Trust from 15; Hon C Tye Green w Netteswell *Chelmsf* from 16; P-in-c Staple Tye from 19. *The Rectory, Perry Road, Harlow CM18 7NP* T: (01279) 424064 M: 07748-590407 E: bishopc7@yahoo.com

OKEKE, Ifeanyichukwu Ernest. b 68. Pontifical Univ Rome LTh 17. ERMC 13. **d** 17 **p** 18. C Elmswell *St E* from 17. *14 Loch Rannoch Close, Elmswell, Bury St Edmunds IP30 9FA* T: (01359) 241624 M: 07717-158500 E: elmswellcurate1@gmail.com

✠**OKEKE, The Rt Revd Ken Sandy Edozie.** b 41. Nigeria Univ BSc 67 Man Univ MA 94. Igbaja Sem Nigeria. **d** 76 **p** 76 **c** 00. Nigeria 76–80 and 87–89; Chapl to Nigerians in UK and Irish Republic 80–87; Hon Can Kwara from 85; Hon Adn from 98; C Man Whitworth 89–95; Chapl Inst of Higher Learning Man 89–95; CMS 95–01; PtO *S'wark* 96–02; Bp on the Niger 00–11; Hon Asst Bp Roch from 16. *50 Essex Road, Longfield DA3 7QL* T: (01474) 709627 E: kengozi8@yahoo.com

OKELLO, Modicum. b 53. Trin Coll Bris BA 90. St Paul's Coll Limuru 76 Wycliffe Hall Ox 86. **d** 78 **p** 79. Kenya 78–80; Uganda 80–86; NSM Goodmayes All SS *Chelmsf* 91–92; C Barking St Marg w St Patr 92–96; C Stratford St Jo and Ch Ch w Forest Gate St Jas 96–99; TV Forest Gate St Sav w W Ham St Matt 99–10; P-in-c Hall Green St Mich *Birm* 10–14; PtO *Chelmsf* from 18. *217 Abbeville Apartments, 37 London Road, Barking IG11 8FW* E: modicum@btinternet.com

O'KELLY, Martin. **d** 11 **p** 16. C Bray *D & G* 16–19; I Kingscourt w Syddan *M & K* from 19. *St Ernan's Rectory, Church Lane, Lisasturrin, Kingscourt, Co Cavan, A82 P7D5, Republic of Ireland* T: (00353) (42) 966 7255 M: (00353) 85-740 6063 E: revmartinokelly@gmail.com

O'KELLY, Ruth Julia. **d** 14 **p** 15. Mullingar, Portnashangan, Moyliscar, Kilbixy etc *M & K* 14–15; C Dublin Rathfarnham *D & G* 15–19; C Clane w Donadea and Coolcarrigan *M & K* from 19. *Hewetson School, Millicent North, Clane, Naas, Co Kildare, W91 CA34 , Republic of Ireland* M: 86-081 3126 E: revruthokelly@gmail.com

OKORONKWO, Catherine Chinyere Mark. b 71. **d** 16 **p** 17. C Streetly *Lich* 16–19; V Swindon All SS w St Barn *Bris* from 19. *St Barnabas' Vicarage, 2 Ferndale Road, Swindon SN2 1EX* M: 07879-989577 E: cathymarko@yahoo.co.uk

OKPALA, Chibuzor Kenechukwu. b 86. Greenwich Univ BSc 07. **d** 16. NSM Harmondsworth *Lon* from 17. *13 Gunmaker Court, Neath Hill, Milton Keynes MK14 6JL* M: 07916-347570 E: chiokpala08@gmail.com

OLADIPO, Jesutosin (Tosin). b 79. Reading Univ BA 00. St Mellitus Coll BA 18. **d** 18 **p** 19. C St John-at-Hackney *Lon* 18–19; C Hackney 19–21; C Leyton St Mary w St Edw and St Luke *Chelmsf* 19–21; Abp's Chapl *Cant* from 21. *Lambeth Palace, Lambeth Palace Road, London SE1 7JU* T: (020) 7898 1200 E: tosin.oladipo@gmail.com *or* tosin.oladipo@lambethpalace.org.uk

OLADUJI, Christopher Temitayo. b 57. Awosika Th Coll Nigeria 84. **d** 87 **p** 88. C Ilutitun Ebenezer Nigeria 87; Asst P Ondo Cathl 88; NSM W Ham *Chelmsf* 89–93; NSM Peckham St Jo w St Andr *S'wark* 97–98; NSM E Ham St Geo *Chelmsf* 99–01; NSM Hackney Wick St Mary of Eton w St Aug *Lon* 02–04; NSM Smithfield St Bart Gt 04–13; NSM Plaistow and N Canning Town *Chelmsf* 13–17; NSM Plaistow SS Phil and Jas and St Mary from 17; NSM Plaistow St Martin from 17; Chapl Barts Health NHS Trust from 15. *103 Browning Road, London E12 6RB* T: (020) 8472 6506 M: 07985-465401 E: coladuji@yahoo.com

OLADUNJOYE, Oluwayemi Abiodun. b 82. Fed Univ of Tech Akure BTech 10 UWE MSc 14. Immanuel Coll Ibadan 10. **d** 11 **p** 12. C Lafiaji Nigeria 11–15; C Lagos Cathl 15–17; PtO *Birm* 17–18; LtO 18–19; PtO 19–21; NSM Edgbaston St Germain from 21. *23 Westley Court, West Bromwich B71 1HH* M: 07958-530375 E: yemmyola2@yahoo.com

OLANCZUK, Jonathan Paul Tadeusz. b 49. EAMTC 94. **d** 96 **p** 97. C Haverhill w Withersfield *St E* 96–00; P-in-c Badingham w Bruisyard, Cransford and Dennington 00–04; P-in-c Rendham w Sweffling 00–04; R Upper Alde 04–17; rtd 17; PtO *St E* from 17; *Nor* from 17. *82 Park Drive, Worlingham, Beccles NR34 7DL* T: (01502) 470079 M: 07766-953558 *or* 07944-186526 E: olanczuk@me.com

OLD, Arthur Anthony George (Tony). b 36. Clifton Th Coll 69. **d** 71 **p** 72. C Clitheroe St Jas *Blackb* 71–73; C Bispham 73–77; V Haslingden St Jo Stonefold 77–81; TV Lowestoft and Kirkley *Nor* 81–83; Chapl to the Deaf *Cant* 83–01; P-in-c Hernhill 83–85; C Preston next Faversham, Goodnestone and Graveney 85–01; rtd 01; PtO *Cant* 01–15. *62 Knaves Acre, Headcorn, Ashford TN27 9TJ* T: (01622) 891498

OLDFIELD, Jonathan Thomas. b 54. Bede Coll Dur TCert 76. NEOC 04. **d** 07 **p** 08. NSM Crakehall *Leeds* 07–16; NSM Hornby 07–16; NSM Patrick Brompton and Hunton 07–16; NSM Spennithorne w Finghall and Hauxwell 12–16; R Slaidburn w Tosside 16–20; rtd 20; PtO *Leeds* 20–21. *6 Lakeber Close, Bentham, Lancaster LA2 7JL* E: joldfield12@btinternet.com

OLDFIELD, Canon Roger Fielden. b 45. Qu Coll Cam BA 67 MA 71 Lon Univ BD 75. Trin Coll Bris 75. **d** 75 **p** 76. C Halliwell St Pet *Man* 75–80 and 03–10; V 80–03; AD Bolton 93–02; Hon Can Man Cathl 00–10; rtd 10; PtO *Man* from 11. *70 Eastgrove Avenue, Bolton BL1 7HA* T: (01204) 305228 E: rogerandruth@googlemail.com

OLDHAM, Susan Yvonne. b 60. SWMTC BTh 14. **d** 10 **p** 11. NSM Georgeham *Ex* 10–14; P-in-c Dolton from 14; P-in-c Iddesleigh w Dowland 14–15; P-in-c Monkokehampton 14–15; R Dolton, Dowland, Iddesleigh etc from 15. *The Rectory, Cleave Hill, Dolton, Winkleigh EX19 8QT* T: (01805) 804264 E: susan.oldham7@btinternet.com

OLDROYD, David Christopher Leslie. b 42. FRICS. S Dios Minl Tr Scheme. **d** 85 **p** 86. NSM Four Marks *Win* 85–90; PtO *Portsm* from 06; *Guildf* from 08; *Chich* from 12. *18 Rozeldene, Grayshott, Hindhead GU26 6TW* T: (01428) 606620 E: chrisoldroyd@live.co.uk

OLDROYD, Mrs Sheila Margaret. b 40. Liv Univ BSc 63. St Steph Ho Ox 98. **d** 99 **p** 00. NSM Cotgrave *S'well* 99–03; NSM Keyworth and Stanton-on-the-Wolds and Bunny etc 03–08; rtd 08; PtO *S'well* from 08. *27 Lowlands Drive, Keyworth, Nottingham NG12 5HG* T: 0115-937 6344 E: revdmargaret@gmail.com

OLEY, Mrs Carolyn Joan Macdonald. b 44. Ox Min Course 05. **d** 08 **p** 09. NSM Lambfold *Pet* 08–12; R 12–16; Hon C Chenderit from 18; RD Brackley from 20. *10 The Green, Evenley, Brackley NN13 5SQ* T: (01280) 701311 M: 07483-851425 E: carolyn.oley@btinternet.com

OLHAUSEN, William Paul. b 67. Wycliffe Hall Ox BA 97. **d** 98 **p** 99. C Reading Greyfriars *Ox* 98–01; Sub Chapl HM YOI Reading 98–01; C Cambridge H Trin *Ely* 01–04; I Carrigrohane Union *C, C & R* 04–08; Chapl Monkton Combe Sch Bath 08–11; I Killiney Ballybrack *D & G* from 11. *The Rectory, Killiney Avenue, Killiney, Co Dublin, Republic of Ireland* T: (00353) (1) 285 2228 M: 87-166 0356 E: wolhausen@googlemail.com *or* stmatthiaskilliney@gmail.com

OLISA, Tagbo Brown Ikechukwu. b 63. St Mellitus Coll 11. **d** 12 **p** 13. NSM Harmondsworth *Lon* from 17. *140 Burlington Road, Thornton Heath CR7 8PH* T: (020) 8771 5743 M: 07740-101419 E: brown.olisa@btinternet.com

OLIVER, David Leath. b 41. **d** 96. Old Catholic Ch Germany 96–01; PtO *Eur* 10–11; Asst Chapl Helsinki 11–19; rtd 19. *Ajurinkatu 5 A 1, 65100 Vaasa, Finland* M: (00358) 407-325250 E: tuulandavid@yahoo.com

OLIVER, Canon David Ryland. b 34. Univ of Wales (Lamp) BA 56 St Cath Coll Ox BA 58 MA 62. Wycliffe Hall Ox 56. **d** 58 **p** 59. C Carmarthen St Pet *St D* 58–61; C Llangyfelach

S & B 61–63; R Aberedw w Llandeilo Graban etc 63–66; R Llanbadarn Fawr, Llandegley and Llanfihangel etc 66–67; LtO Llan 68–70; LtO Ban 70–73; V Nefyn w Pistyll w Tudweiliog w Llandudwen etc 73–74; V Abercraf and Callwen S & B 74–77; V Llangyfelach 77–79; R Llanllwchaearn and Llanina St D 79–83; V Cwmaman 83–94; Can St D Cathl from 90; RD Dyffryn Aman 93–94; V Cynwyl Gaeo w Llansawel and Talley 94–99; rtd 99; PtO St D 05–17. Maes y Gelynen, 40 Heol Bryngwili, Cross Hands, Llanelli SA14 6LR T: (01269) 840146 or 843157 E: drylandoliver@yahoo.co.uk

OLIVER, Diane Margaret. b 49. d 14 p 15. OLM Cheddleton, Horton, Longsdon and Rushton Spencer Lich 14–19; PtO 19–21. 17 Cauldon Close, Leek ST13 5SH T: (01538) 373800 E: dmoliver@btinternet.com

OLIVER, Mrs Dorothea Louise. b 59. UWE BSc 03 Bournemouth Univ BSc 07 SRN 81. Sarum Coll 18. d 20 p 21. NSM Cheddar, Draycott and Rodney Stoke B & W from 20. Barn Close, Wet Lane, Draycott, Cheddar BS27 3TG T: (01934) 744739 M: 07767-892313 E: theaoliver@hotmail.com

OLIVER, Gordon. See OLIVER, Thomas Gordon

✠**OLIVER, The Rt Revd John Keith.** b 35. G&C Coll Cam BA 59 MA 63 MLitt 65. Westcott Ho Cam 59. d 64 p 65 c 90. C Hilborough w Bodney Nor 64–68; Chapl Eton Coll 68–72; R S Molton w Nymet St George Ex 73–75; P-in-c Filleigh w E Buckland 73–75; P-in-c Warkleigh w Satterleigh and Chittlehamholt 73–75; P-in-c High Bray w Charles 73–75; TR S Molton, Nymet St George, High Bray etc 75–82; P-in-c N Molton w Twitchen 77–79; RD S Molton 74–80; TR Cen Ex 82–85; Adn Sherborne Sarum 85–90; P-in-c W Stafford w Frome Billet 85–90; Can Res Sarum Cathl 85–90; Bp Heref 90–03; rtd 03; Hon Asst Bp S & B from 04; PtO Heref from 05. The Old Vicarage, Glascwm, Llandrindod Wells LD1 5SE T/F: (01982) 570771

OLIVER, John Kenneth. b 47. Brunel Univ MA 92 ALBC 70. EAMTC 98. d 00 p 01. C E Ham St Paul Chelmsf 00–03; V Stratford New Town St Paul 03–05; TV Totton Win 05–12; rtd 12; PtO Win from 12. 91B Wentworth Avenue, Bournemouth BH5 2EH T: (01202) 417666 E: revjohnoliver@btinternet.com

OLIVER, Jonathan Andrew. b 79. Cam Univ MPhil 11. Ridley Hall Cam 08. d 11 p 12. C Sholing Win 11–15; Pioneer Min 15–18; Lead Pioneer Min Southn 18–21; Pioneer Min Monty's Community Hub from 21. Peartree Vicarage, 65 Peartree Avenue, Southampton SO19 7JN M: 07946-048585

OLIVER (née TROMANS), Judith Anne. b 54. Liv Univ BSc 76 Lanc Univ PGCE 77 Birm Univ MA 07. WMMTC. d 96 p 97. C Old Swinford Stourbridge Worc 96–99; C Pensnett 99–01; Asst to Suff Bp Dudley 99–01; P-in-c Dudley Wood 01–08; V 08–10; TV Dudley 10–15; Hon Can Worc Cathl 11–15; rtd 15; PtO Worc from 15; Sub-dean rtd clergy from 16. 37 Haden Park Road, Cradley Heath B64 7HF T: (01384) 832095 M: 07903-104862 E: juditholiver@blueyonder.co.uk

OLIVER, Louise Elizabeth. b 69. Bedf Coll of Educn BA 92 Southn Univ PGCE 95 Kingston Univ MA 04. Sarum Coll 17. d 20 p 21. C Clacton St Jas Chelmsf from 20. 99 Park Square East, Jaywick, Clacton-on-Sea CO15 2NR T: (01255) 476677 M: 07816-756771 E: louise@stjamesclacton.org.uk

OLIVER, Mark Leonard. b 61. d 14 p 15. OLM New Haw Guildf 14–20; PtO Chelmsf 20–21; NSM Clacton St Jas from 21. 99 Park Square East, Jaywick, Clacton-on-Sea CO15 2NR T: (01255) 476677 E: markthechurch@gmail.com

OLIVER, Canon Philip Maule. b 38. Birm Univ LLB 59. Wells Th Coll 62. d 64 p 65. C Chesterton Lich 64–67; C Tettenhall Wood 67–71; V Milton 71–78; V Ixworth and Bardwell St E 78–92; P-in-c Honington w Sapiston and Troston 81–92; TR Blackbourne 92–08; RD Ixworth 85–94; Hon Can St E Cathl 00–08; rtd 08; PtO St E from 08. 25 Millfield Road, Barningham, Bury St Edmunds IP31 1DX

OLIVER, Ryland. See OLIVER, David Ryland

OLIVER, Prof Simon Andrew. b 71. Mansf Coll Ox BA 93 MA 98 Peterho Cam BA 97 MA 00 PhD 03. Westcott Ho Cam 95. d 98 p 99. NSM Teversham Ely 99–01; NSM Cherry Hinton St Andr 98–01; Chapl Hertf Coll Ox 01–05; Lect Univ of Wales (Lamp) St D 05; Sen Lect 06–09; Assoc Prof Nottm Univ S'well 09–15; Can Th S'well Minster 11–15; Van Mildert Prof Div Dur Univ from 15; Can Res Dur Cathl from 15. University of Durham, Department of Theology, Abbey House, Palace Green, Durham DH1 3RS T: 0191-334 3293 E: simon.oliver@durham.ac.uk

✠**OLIVER, The Rt Revd Stephen John.** b 48. AKC 69. St Aug Coll Cant 70. d 71 p 72 c 03. C Clifton S'well 71–75; P-in-c Newark Ch Ch 75–79; R Plumtree 79–85; Sen Producer BBC Relig Broadcasting Dept Lon 85–87; Chief Producer 87–91; TR Leeds City Ripon 91–97; Can Res and Prec St Paul's Cathl Lon 97–03; Area Bp Stepney 03–10; rtd 10; Hon

Asst Bp S'wark from 20. 6 Riverside, Southwell NG25 0HA E: stepoliver7@gmail.com

OLIVER, Canon Susan Jacqueline. b 54. Univ Coll Lon LLB 78 CQSW 86. Qu Coll Birm 03. d 05 p 06. C Fladbury w Wyre Piddle and Moor etc Worc 05–09; TV Louth Linc 09–12; P-in-c Pensnett Worc 12–17; V 17–18; P-in-c Churchill-in-Halfshire w Blakedown and Broome 18–21; C Belbroughton w Fairfield and Clent 18–21; Dioc Warden of Readers 17–21; Hon Can Worc Cathl 17–21; rtd 21. 16 Allesborough Drive, Pershore WR10 1JH M: 07843-750451 E: sueoliver778@gmail.com

OLIVER, Suzanne Marie. See PATTLE, Suzanne Marie

OLIVER, Canon Thomas Gordon. b 48. Nottm Univ BTh 72 DipAdEd 80 Lon Univ MA 15 ALCD 72. St Jo Coll Nottm 68. d 72 p 73. C Thorpe Edge Bradf 72–76; C Woodthorpe S'well 76–80; V Huthwaite 80–85; Dir Past Studies St Jo Coll Nottm 85–94; Dir of Min and Tr Roch 94–09; R Meopham w Nurstead 09–13; Hon Can Roch Cathl 95–13; rtd 13; PtO Roch from 13. 112 Bush Road, Cuxton, Rochester ME2 1HA T: (01634) 735137 E: canongordon.oliver@gmail.com

OLIVER, Mrs Trudi. b 65. Brighton Univ BA 09. Trin Coll Bris BA 11. d 11 p 12. C Southampton Lord's Hill and Lord's Wood Win 11–14; P-in-c Gravesend St Mary Roch 14–18; V from 18; Chapl St Geo Sch Gravesend from 14. The Vicarage, 57 New House Lane, Gravesend DA11 7HJ T: (01474) 353612 M: 07432-131079 E: revtrudi@gmail.com

OLIVER, Canon Wendy Louise. b 54. Aston Tr Scheme 93 Oak Hill Th Coll 94. d 96 p 97. C Walmsley Man 96–99; P-in-c Goodshaw and Crawshawbooth 99–08; AD Rossendale 04–08; V Harwood from 08; AD Walmsley 10–14; Hon Can Man Cathl from 11. The Vicarage, Stitch Mi Lane, Bolton BL2 4HU T: (01204) 525196 E: wendyloliver@gmail.com

OLIVIER, The Very Revd Bertrand Maurice Daniel. b 62. Ecole des Cadres Paris BA 84. S'wark Ord Course 93. d 96 p 97. C Walworth St Jo S'wark 96–00; V Southfields St Barn 00–05; RD Wandsworth 03–05; V All Hallows by the Tower etc Lon 05–18; Dean Montreal Canada from 18; Hon Can St Paul's Cathl Nicosia from 18; PtO Eur from 16. The Cathedral Office, 1444 Union Avenue, Montreal QC H3A 2B8, Canada T: (001) (514) 843 6577 E: bertrand.olivier@montrealcathedral.ca

OLLIER, Mrs Jane Sarah. b 60. Leeds Univ BA 81 Ex Univ MA 05. SWMTC 02. d 05 p 06. NSM Seaton and Beer Ex 05–07; C Ottery St Mary, Alfington, W Hill, Tipton etc 07–10; P-in-c Ex St Mark, St Sidwell and St Matt 10–16; Membership Services Officer Angl Cen Rome 16–18; PtO Ex from 18. Belbury View, Lower Broad Oak Road, West Hill, Ottery St Mary EX11 1UF

OLLIER, Canon Timothy John Douglas. b 44. Trin Hall Cam BA 66 MA 69. Cuddesdon Coll 66. d 68 p 69. C Silksworth Dur 68–71; C St Marylebone w H Trin Lon 71–74; C Winlaton Dur 74–77; R Redmarshall and V Bishopton w Gt Stainton 77–88; P-in-c Grindon and Stillington 83–88; V Gainford and R Winston 88–00; AD Barnard Castle 88–00; P-in-c Egglescliffe 00–03; R 03–13; AD Stockton 01–07; Hon Can Dur Cathl 94–13; rtd 13; PtO Dur from 14. 14 Low Coniscliffe, Darlington DL2 2JY T: (01325) 495458 E: timdollie3@gmail.com

OLLIFF, Roland. b 61. Leeds Univ BTh 95 Ex Coll Ox MA 00. Coll of Resurr Mirfield 93. d 95 p 96. C Bickleigh and Shaugh Prior Ex 95–98; CF 98–07; Sen CF 07–10; Dep Asst Chapl Gen 10–15; Dir of Ords 09–15; V Crookham Guildf 15–17; Bp's Chapl from 17. 59 Brookside, Jacob's Well, Guildford GU4 7NS T: (01483) 590500 M: 07956-028128 E: roland.olliff@gmail.com or roland.olliff@cofeguildford.org.uk

OLLIVE, Preb Patricia Ann. b 55. St Luke's Coll Ex BA 91. Ripon Coll Cuddesdon BTh 05. d 05 p 06. C Backwell w Chelvey and Brockley B & W 05–09; P-in-c Shapwick w Ashcott and Burtle 09–11; P-in-c W Poldens 09–11; V Polden Wheel 11–15; V Bridgwater St Mary and Chilton Trinity 15–20; Preb Wells Cathl 18–20; rtd 20. 10 Brookside Close, Trull, Taunton TA3 7LH M: 07840-387121 E: ollivetrish@hotmail.co.uk

OLLMAN, Mrs Elaine Margaret. b 45. SNWTP 07. d 10 p 11. NSM Frankby w Greasby Ches 10–12; P-in-c Delamere 12–14; R 14–19; rtd 19; PtO Ches from 19. 5 Leslie Avenue, Wirral CH49 1RS T: 0151-677 4930 M: 07599-511887 E: revemollman@btinternet.com

OLNEY, Dorian Frederick. b 50. Kingston Poly BA 71 Anglia Poly Univ MA 03 MIL 88 MCIPD 88. Ridley Hall Cam 96. d 98 p 99. C Glenfield Leic 98–02; Chapl ATC 99–01; TV Newark S'well 02–07; P-in-c Shenstone Lich 07–09; P-in-c Stonnall 07–09; V Shenstone and Stonnall 09–13; R Sissinghurst w Frittenden Cant 13–19; rtd 19. 61 Tiverton Road, Loughborough LE11 2RU E: fred.olney01@gmail.com

OLOKOSE, Folorunso Oladosu. b 70. Lyon Univ MA 08. Trin Coll Bris 11. d 13 p 14. C Cobham and Stoke D'Abernon

Guildf 13–17; V Oatlands from 17. *5 Beechwood Avenue, Weybridge KT13 9TE* E: folo.olokose@gmail.com

O'LOUGHLIN, Mrs Kathryn. b 60. Man Univ BSc 81 Win Univ MA 08. STETS 96. **d** 99 **p** 00. NSM Basing *Win* 99–03; PtO 03–08; C N Hants Downs 08–16; Tutor STETS 08–11; PtO *Win* from 17; *Portsm* from 18. *4 South Downs Close, Swanmore, Southampton SO32 2FR* T: (01489) 890515 E: kathy.oloughlin@gmail.com

OLSEN, Arthur <u>Barry</u>. b 37. Univ of NZ BA 61 Melbourne Coll of Div BD 73. ACT ThL 64. **d** 64 **p** 64. C Nelson All SS NZ 64–67; V Ahaura 67–69; V Motupiko 69–70; V Amuri 70–73; Maori Miss and C Dunedin St Matt 73–76; V Brooklyn 77–81; C Hersham *Guildf* 81–84; P-in-c Botleys and Lyne 84–95; V 95–03; P-in-c Long Cross 84–95; V 95–03; Chapl NW Surrey Mental Health Partnership NHS Trust 85–03; rtd 03; Hon C Rotherfield Peppard and Kidmore End etc *Ox* 03–12; PtO from 13; *St Alb* 13–18. *29 Sandhill Way, Aylesbury HP19 8GU* E: barry.o22@virgin.net

OLSSON-GISLESKOG, Catharina. *See* GISLESKOG, Catharina Irene Gunilla Margaretha Elizabeth Olsson

OLSWORTH-PETER, Edward James. b 77. UWE BA 99. Wycliffe Hall Ox BTh 04. **d** 04 **p** 05. C Guildf Ch Ch w St Martha-on-the-Hill 04–07; C Upper Chelsea St Sav and St Simon *Lon* 07–10; V Sydenham H Trin and St Aug *S'wark* 10–15; Dioc Fresh Expressions Adv *Ely* 15–18; Nat Adv for Pioneer Development Abps' Coun from 18; PtO *Guildf* from 19. *Ministry Division, Church House, Great Smith Street, London SW1P 3AZ* T: (020) 7898 1000 E: revedop@gmail.com *or* ed.olsworth-peter@churchofengland.org

OLUKANMI, Miss Stella Grace Oluwafunmilayo Olanrewaju. b 57. St Jo Coll Nottm BTh 95 LTh 92. **d** 96 **p** 97. C Gt Ilford St Jo *Chelmsf* 96–01; V Barkingside St Cedd 01–15; P-in-c Walthamstow St Andr from 15. *St Andrew's Vicarage, 37 Sutton Road, London E17 5QA* T: (020) 8527 3969 E: stella.sta@btinternet.com

OLUMUYIWA, Canon Olubunmi <u>Taiwo</u>. b 67. Ibadan Univ Nigeria BA 93 Birm Univ MPhil 07 PhD 11. Immanuel Coll Ibadan 88. **d** 93 **p** 94. C Owo St Patr Nigeria 93–94; C Somolu St Paul 94–95; C Ch Ch Cathl Lagos 95–97; Chapl Owo Dioc Angl Gr Sch 97–99; V Orisunmibare-Bodija Ch Ch 99–05; Can Ibadan N from 99; Adn Ibadan N 05–08; PtO *Birm* 03–18; Asst Chapl Univ Hosp Birm NHS Foundn Trust 16–18; Chapl HM Pris Oakwood from 18. *HM Prison Oakwood, Oaks Drive, Featherstone, Wolverhampton WV10 7QD* T: (01902) 799700 M: 07534-270120 E: olumuyiwataiwo37@gmail.com *or* taiwo.olumuyiwa@uk.g4s.com

O'MALLEY, Canon Brian Denis <u>Brendan</u>. b 40. Univ of Wales (Lamp) MA 97 MPhil 00 MHCIMA 60. Oscott Coll (RC) LTh 77 Coll of Resurr Mirfield 82. **d** 77 **p** 83. In RC Ch 77–81; Warden St Greg Retreat Rhandirmwyn *St D* 80–83; Chapl and Min Can St D Cathl 83–85; V Wiston w Ambleston, St Dogwells, Walton E etc 85–88; V Wiston w Clarbeston and Walton E 89; R Walton W w Talbenny and Haroldston W 89–98; Chapl Pembrokeshire Coll of FE 93–98; Officer for Past Care and Counselling *St D* 95–98; Officer for Par Development and Renewal 98–00; Chapl St D Coll Lamp 98–07; Dioc Officer for Lay Tr *St D* 00–07; Can St D Cathl 01–07; rtd 07; PtO *St D* from 07. *Millbank, North Road, Lampeter SA48 7HZ* T: (01570) 422148

O'MAOIL MHEANA, Patrick John. b 66. Coll of Resurr Mirfield 12. **d** 14 **p** 15. C Paulsgrove *Portsm* 14–17; R Airdrie *Glas* 17–20. *Address temp unknown* E: paji65@hotmail.com

OMOBUDE, Boyle <u>Osaro</u>. b 69. Ushaw Coll Dur 07. **d** 11 **p** 15. In RC Ch 11–14; Chapl Tees, Esk and Wear Valleys NHS Foundn Trust from 12; NSM Fenham St Jas and St Basil *Newc* 15–20; PtO from 20; *York* 17–21. *St Margaret's Vicarage, 14 Heighley Street, Newcastle upon Tyne NE15 6AR* E: omobude@btinternet.com

OMOLE, Canon Oluremi Richard. b 63. **d** 05 **p** 07. NSM Dur N 05–14; Chapl City Hosps Sunderland NHS Foundn Trust from 14; Hon Can Dur Cathl from 21. *7 Frensham Way, Meadowfield, Durham DH7 8UR* T: 0191-378 9756 E: romole@sky.com

⊞**OMUKU, The Rt Revd Precious Sotonye.** b 47. Ibadan Univ Nigeria BSc 73. Lagos Angl Dioc Sem 00. **d** 02 **p** 03 c 16. V Ikoyi Nativity Nigeria 02–06; LtO *Lon* 07–08; PtO *S'wark* 07–08; Hon C Morden from 08; Hon Asst Bp S'wark from 16. *4 Litchfield Avenue, Morden SM4 5QS* T: (020) 8640 7311 M: 07790-593392 E: precious.omuku@yahoo.com

O'NEILL, Canon Gary. b 57. K Coll Lon BD 79 AKC 79 Liv Univ MA 06 Ches Univ MProf 16. Westcott Ho Cam 80. **d** 81 **p** 82. C Oldham Man 81–84; C Birch w Fallowfield 84–87; R Moston St Chad 87–97; Can Res Birm Cathl 97–07; Dir Studies for Ords *Ches* 07–20; Bp's Adv for Minl Development Review 15–20; Can Res Blackb Cathl from 20. *Blackburn*

Cathedral, Cathedral Close, Blackburn BB1 5AA T: (01254) 277430 M: 07976-729449

O'NEILL, Mrs Gillian. b 73. Westmr Coll Ox BTh 95. Ripon Coll Cuddesdon MTh 12. **d** 12 **p** 13. C W Dulwich All SS *S'wark* 12–16; V E Dulwich St Jo from 16. *St John's Parish Office, Goose Green Community Centre, 62A East Dulwich Road, London SE22 9AT* T: (020) 8693 3897 E: gill_oneilluk@hotmail.com

O'NEILL, Robert Patrick. b 66. Herts Univ BA 96. Ridley Hall Cam 06. **d** 08 **p** 09. NSM Lt Berkhamsted and Bayford, Essendon etc *St Alb* 08–09; C Luton St Mary 09–12; P-in-c Caddington 12–16; V from 16; P-in-c Farley Hill St Jo 12–16; V from 16. *The Vicarage, Collings Wells Close, Caddington, Luton LU1 4BG* T: (01582) 731692 E: rob@vicar.org.uk

O'NEILL, Victoria Elaine. *See* BRYSON, Victoria Elaine

ONGYERTH, Michael George. b 50. **d** 13 **p** 14. OLM Crowland *Linc* 13–19; V Elloe Fen Gp from 19. *22 North Street, Crowland, Peterborough PE6 0EF*

ONIONS, Mrs Angela Ann. b 33. STETS 01. **d** 02. NSM Bradford-on-Avon H Trin *Sarum* 02–08; PtO from 08; *B & W* from 14. *27 Berryfield Road, Bradford-on-Avon BA15 1SX* T: (01225) 309001 M: 07719-726461 E: r.a.onions@btinternet.com

ONUIGBO, Maria Helena. b 73. Westcott Ho Cam. **d** 10 **p** 15. NSM Brockley Hill St Sav *S'wark* 11–14; C S Beddington and Roundshaw 14–18; R Manchester Gd Shep and St Barn *Man* 18–21. *Address temp unknown* M: 07898-311943 E: mariaobafemi@hotmail.com

ONUNWA, The Ven Udobata Rufus. b 47. Univ of Nigeria BA 78 MA 82 PhD 85. Trin Coll Umuahia 72. **d** 74 **p** 75. Chapl Owerri Cathl Nigeria 74–75; Chapl Univ of Nigeria 75–78 and 82; Chapl to Abp Nigeria 78–79; P-in-c Osebuala St Paul 78–79; Lect Trin Th Coll Umuahia 79–81; Hon Can Okigwe-Orlu 84–89; Can Res Calabar 90–91; V St Jude 92–96; Adn 94–96; Tutor Crowther Hall CMS Tr Coll Selly Oak 97–02; NW Regional Dir Crosslinks 03–05; P-in-c Grange St Andr *Ches* 05–09; rtd 09. *76 Firedrake Croft, Coventry CV1 2DR* M: 07766-724510 E: uonunwa@yahoo.co.uk

ONWUKA, Mrs Kechinyere Chimuemelulau. **d** 17 **p** 18. NSM Enfield St Jas *Lon* from 17. *48 Clydesdale, Enfield EN3 4RJ*

ONYEKWELU, Mrs Ada. b 54. Ibadan Univ Nigeria BSc 83 SEN 98. **d** 07 **p** 08. NSM Selsdon St Fran CD *S'wark* 07–16; NSM S Croydon St Pet and St Aug from 16. *80 Tedder Road, South Croydon CR2 8AQ* T: (020) 8657 4018 E: a_onye@yahoo.co.uk

OOSTERHOF, Canon Liesbeth. b 61. Ripon Coll Cuddesdon 02. **d** 04 **p** 05. C E Bergholt and Brantham *St E* 04–07; R Shoreline from 07; Dioc Adv for Women's Min 11–16; Dean of Women's Min 16–18; RD Samford from 15; Hon Can St E Cathl from 16. *The Rectory, Rectory Field, Chelmondiston, Ipswich IP9 1HY* T: (01473) 781902 E: l.oosterhof@btinternet.com

OOSTRA, Catharina Henriët. *See* MIELL, Catharina Henriët

OPALA, Lisa Maria. b 73. Cranmer Hall Dur 19. **d** 21. NSM Nunthorpe *York* from 21; Chapl S Tees Hosps NHS Foundn Trust from 17. *The Vicarage, 2 Lanbaurgh Road, Hutton Rudby, Yarm TS15 0HL* T: (01642) 701245 M: 07538-153748 E: lisaopala@gmail.com *or* lisa.opala@nhs.net

OPALA, Robert. b 62. Catholic Univ of Lublin BTh 87 MTh 88 Chr Th Academy Warsaw PhD 99. Milltown Inst Dub MA 06 STL 08. **d** 10 **p** 11. In RC Ch 10–16; PtO *York* 16–17; C Crathorne 17–19; C Kirklevington w Picton, and High and Low Worsall 17–19; C Rudby in Cleveland w Middleton 17–19; C Whorlton w Carlton and Faceby 18–19; R Whorlton Gp from 19. *The Vicarage, 2 Langbaurgh Road, Hutton Rudby, Yarm TS15 0HL* M: 07729-661764 E: robertopala62@yahoo.co.uk

OPENSHAW, Steven Paul. b 62. Open Univ BA 91 Birm Univ MSc 01. All SS Cen for Miss & Min 09. **d** 12 **p** 13. C Ramsbottom and Edenfield *Man* 12–16; P-in-c Elton St Steph 16–18; P-in-c Walshaw Ch Ch 16–20; V from 20. *37 Gisburn Drive, Bury BL8 3DH* T: 0161-797 5121 M: 07963-100345 E: revsteveopenshaw@gmail.com

OPIE, Steven Philip. b 86. Ridley Hall Cam 16. **d** 19 **p** 20. C Loughton St Mary *Chelmsf* 19–21; C Leyton St Mary w St Edw and St Luke from 21. *Leyton Vicarage, 4 Vicarage Road, London E10 5EA* E: steve@stmarysloughton.com

OPPERMAN, Graham William. b 40. Th Educh Coll 98. **d** 00 **p** 03. C Linden St Thos S Africa 00–04; NSM Aberdour *St And* 04; NSM Burntisland 04; NSM Inverkeithing 04; TV Jarrow *Dur* 05–10; rtd 10; Hon C Cwmbran *Mon* 10–15; Hon C Usk Min Area from 15. *The Rectory, Parc Road, Llangybi, Usk NP15 1NL* T: (01633) 450811 M: 07792-451622 E: graham@deanery.info

OPPERMAN, Mrs Jennifer Catharine. b 57. ERMC 09. **d** 12 **p** 13. Nsm Pet Cathl 12–16 and 19–21; Lay Voc Officer 16–20; rtd 21. *Littleworth Mission, Main Road, Deeping St Nicholas, Spalding PE11 3EN* T: (01775) 630497 M: 07912-380464 E: jenny@littleworthmission.com

ORAM, Anthony. b 63. York St Jo Univ BA 08 Hull Univ PGCE 09. St Jo Coll Nottm 12. **d** 15 **p** 16. C Kingston upon Hull St Aid Southcoates *York* 15–19; V Cottesmore and Burley, Clipsham, Exton etc *Pet* from 19. *The Rectory, 38 Main Street, Cottesmore, Oakham LE15 7DJ* M: 07740-257173 E: anthony@theorams.com

ORAM, Roland Martin David. b 45. Trin Coll Cam BA 68 ARCM 70. Cranmer Hall Dur. **d** 78 **p** 79. C Aspley *S'well* 78–81; Chapl Alleyn's Sch Dulwich 81–88; Chapl Versailles w Grandchamp and Chevry *Eur* 88–92; Chapl Denstone Coll Uttoxeter 92–01; C Hanford and Trentham *Lich* 02–10; rtd 10; PtO *Lich* 10–18; *Ches* from 10. *12 Ash Grove, Rode Heath, Stoke-on-Trent ST7 3TD* T: (01270) 747271 E: orams45@btinternet.com

ORAM, Stephen John. b 58. **d** 84 **p** 85. C Kidderminster St Jo *Worc* 84–88; Chapl RAF 88–92; P-in-c Brislington St Anne *Bris* 92–97; V Cricklade w Latton 97–04; Co-ord Chapl N Bris NHS Trust 04–16; Chapl Univ Hosps Bris NHS Foundn Trust 16–18; rtd 18; PtO *Bris* 16–19; Hon C N Severnside from 19; PtO *Mon* from 18. *9 Cutter Close, Newport NP19 7LN* E: stephen.oram@blueyonder.co.uk

ORAMS, Ronald Thomas. b 49. ACMA 80. **d** 08 **p** 09. NSM Laxfield, Cratfield, Wilby and Brundish *St E* 08–13; NSM Four Rivers 13–19; PtO from 19. *Crane Lodge, Bickers Hill, Laxfield, Woodbridge IP12 8DP* T: (01986) 798901 M: 07721-682183 E: ron.orams@btinternet.com

ORCHARD, Canon George Richard. b 41. Ex Coll Ox BA 62 BA 64 MA 66. Ripon Hall Ox 62. **d** 65 **p** 66. C Greenhill St Pet *Derby* 65–70; Member Ecum Team Min Sinfin Moor 70–78; V Sinfin Moor *Derby* 76–78; TR Dronfield 78–86; Can Res Derby Cathl 86–92; Hon Can Derby Cathl 92–06; P-in-c Baslow 92–93; P-in-c Curbar and Stoney Middleton 92–93; V Baslow w Curbar and Stoney Middleton 93–06; rtd 06; PtO *Chich* from 07; *Cant* 07–21. *7 Love Lane, Rye TN31 7NE* T: (01797) 225916 E: richardorchard41@yahoo.co.uk

ORCHARD, Helen Claire. b 65. Sheff Univ BA 87 PhD 96 Em Coll Cam MPhil 02 Ox Univ MA 06 Heythrop Coll Lon MA 18. Westcott Ho Cam 01. **d** 03 **p** 04. C Merrow *Guildf* 03–06; Chapl and Fell Ex Coll Ox 06–11; TV Wimbledon *S'wark* from 11. *St Matthew's House, 10 Coombe Gardens, London SW20 0QU* T: (020) 8286 4584 E: orchard.helen@gmail.com

ORCHARD, Richard. *See* ORCHARD, George Richard

O'REILLY, Brian. **d** 07 **p** 08. C Seagoe *D & D* 07–10; I Cobh and Glanmire *C, C & R* 10–14; I Rathcooney Union from 10. *The Rectory, Rathdrum, Co Wicklow, Republic of Ireland* T: (00353) (404) 43814 M: 86-223 0271 E: brianor@eircom.net

O'REILLY, Clare Maria. *See* KING, Clare Maria

O'REILLY, Canon Philip Jonathon. b 66. Portsm Poly BSc 87 Kent Univ MA 97 MRICS. Westcott Ho Cam 93. **d** 93 **p** 94. C Selsdon St Jo w St Fran *S'wark* 93–96; TV Staveley and Barrow Hill *Derby* 96–01; V Wistow *Leic* from 01; Hon Can Leic Cathl from 10. *The Vicarage, 12 Saddington Road, Fleckney, Leicester LE8 8AW* T: 0116-240 2215 E: philipreilly@leicester.anglican.org

O'REILLY, William Anthony. b 62. St Mellitus Coll 12. **d** 15 **p** 16. NSM Bow w Bromley St Leon *Lon* 15–18; NSM Old Ford St Paul and St Mark from 20. *48 Ridgdale Street, London E3 2TW* M: 07798-914298

ORFORD, Barry Antony. b 49. Univ of Wales (Ban) BA 71 MTh 97 PhD 01. St Steph Ho Ox 71. **d** 73 **p** 74. C Monmouth *Mon* 73–77; V Choral St As Cathl 77–81; CR 83–96; PtO *St As* 97–99; Hon Asst Chapl Univ of Wales (Ban) *Ban* 99–01; Lib Pusey Ho 01–14; PtO *Lon* 14–18; P-in-c St Dunstan in the West 16–19; PtO from 19. *8 Hampstead Square, London NW3 1AB* E: barry.orford@stx.ox.ac.uk

ORFORD, Canon Keith John. b 40. FCIT. EMMTC 76. **d** 79 **p** 80. NSM Matlock Bank *Derby* 79–99; NSM Wirksworth 99–20; Hon Can Derby Cathl 00–10; rtd 20; PtO *Derby* from 20. *27 Lums Hill Rise, Matlock DE4 3FX* T/F: (01629) 55349 E: keith.orford@btinternet.com

ORGAN, Mrs Alma. b 45. Bordesley Coll of Educn CertEd 66. WEMTC 08. **d** 09 **p** 10. NSM Worc St Barn w Ch Ch 09–12; NSM Pershore w Pinvin, Wick and Birlingham 12–15; PtO from 15. *14 Ongrils Close, Pershore WR10 1QE* T: (01386) 554248 M: 07531-461810 E: piglet1723@btinternet.com

ORGAN, Peter. b 73. K Coll Lon BA 97 Birm Univ MA 01. Qu Coll Birm 99. **d** 01 **p** 02. C E Wickham *S'wark* 01–05; TV Thamesmead 05–11; V E Wickham from 11; AD Plumstead from 20. *St Michael's Vicarage, Upper Wickham Lane, Welling DA16 3AP* T: (020) 8304 1214 E: revpeterorgan@gmail.com

ORME, Christopher Malcolm. b 60. City Univ BSc 83. Wycliffe Hall Ox 03. **d** 05 **p** 06. C Shrewsbury H Cross *Lich* 05–08; P-in-c Meanwood *Ripon* 08–12; V 12–15; R Thorley *St Alb* 15–18; rtd 19; PtO *B & W* from 19. *9 Abbey View Gardens, Bath BA2 6DQ* E: rev.chris.orme@gmail.com

ORME, Mrs Delia. b 57. STETS 01. **d** 08 **p** 09. NSM Haslemere and Grayswood *Guildf* 08–12; NSM Seale, Puttenham and Wanborough 12–19; NSM Elstead from 19; NSM Thursley from 19; NSM Compton w Shackleford and Peper Harow 20; NSM Shackleford and Peper Harow from 20. *Nightingale Cottage, Peat Common, Elstead, Godalming GU8 6DX* T: (01252) 702217 E: delia.orme@btinternet.com

ORME, Edward John Gilbert. b 42. Man Univ BSc 64. Ox Min Course 04. **d** 07 **p** 08. NSM Reading St Agnes w St Paul and St Barn *Ox* 07–12; rtd 12; PtO *Ox* 12–15. *191 Carr Lane, Dronfield Woodhouse, Dronfield S18 8XF* M: 07901-528971 E: eddie.orme@yahoo.co.uk

ORMROD, Jonathan Robert. b 63. Open Univ BSc 04. Wycliffe Hall Ox 06 Ripon Coll Cuddesdon 09. **d** 11 **p** 12. C Llantrisant *Llan* 11–14; P-in-c Sully from 14; P-in-c Wenvoe and St Lythans from 14; C St Andrews Major w Michaelston-le-Pit from 14. *The Rectory, Port Road, Wenvoe, Cardiff CF5 6DF* T: (029) 2059 5347 E: jonormrod@yahoo.co.uk

ORMROD, Canon Paul William. b 57. Liv Univ BA 80 MTh 08. Westcott Ho Cam 80. **d** 83 **p** 84. C Prescot *Liv* 83–86; TV Padgate 86–95; V Formby St Pet 95–13; Chapl Madrid *Eur* 13–18; Chapl Montreux w Villars from 19; Hon Can from 18. *St John's Church House, avenue de Chillon, 92 CH-1820 Montreux-Territet, Switzerland* T: (0041) (21) 963 4354 E: paul.ormrod1@gmail.com

ORMSTON, Derek. b 43. St D Coll Lamp. **d** 67 **p** 68. C Ogley Hay *Lich* 67–70; C Tettenhall Regis 70–74; P-in-c Leek All SS 74–79; TV Leek and Meerbrook 79–83; Youth Chapl *Bris* 83–87; R Brinkworth w Dauntsey 87–12; Chapl New Coll Swindon 87–12; rtd 12; PtO *Sarum* 13–20. *49 Lime Kiln, Royal Wootton Bassett, Swindon SN4 7HF* T: (01793) 852779

ORMSTON, The Ven Richard Jeremy. b 61. Southlands Coll Lon BA 83 Brunel Univ MTh 98. Oak Hill Th Coll BA 87. **d** 87 **p** 88. C Rodbourne Cheney *Bris* 87–91; R Collingtree w Courteenhall and Milton Malsor *Pet* 91–01; RD Wootton 96–01; R Oundle w Ashton and Benefield w Glapthorn 01–14; RD Oundle 03–13; Can Pet Cathl from 03; Adn Northn from 14; RD Towcester from 21. *Westbrook, 11 The Drive, Northampton NN1 4RZ* T: (01604) 714015 E: archdeacon.northampton@peterborough-diocese.org.uk

O'ROURKE, Canon Brian Joseph Gerard. b 58. TCD BA 82 HDipEd 83. CITC 89. **d** 92 **p** 93. Chapl E Glendalough Sch 90–96; C Newcastle w Newtownmountkennedy and Calary *D & G* 92–96; Bp's C 96–98; I 98–00; I Cork St Ann's Union *C, C & R* 00–15; I Maryborough w Dysart Enos and Ballyfin *C, F & O* 15–17; Bp's C Lismore w Cappoquin, Kilwatermoy, Dungarvan etc 17–19; I Tullow w Shillelagh, Aghold and Mullinacuff from 19; Can Ossory Cathl from 17; Can Kilkenny Cathl from 18; Hon Chapl Miss to Seafarers from 00. *The Rectory, Barrack Street, Tullow, Co Carlow, R93 X722, Republic of Ireland* M: (00353) 86-807 9452 E: bjgorourke@gmail.com or tullow.leighlin@gmail.com

O'ROURKE, Shaun. b 58. NOC 02. **d** 05 **p** 06. C Gorton and Abbey Hey *Man* 05–08; P-in-c Heaton Reddish 08–12; Borough Dean Stockport 10–12; P-in-c Swimbridge, W Buckland, Landkey, and E Buckland *Ex* from 12; RD Shirwell 12–18. *The Rectory, Barnstaple Hill, Swimbridge, Barnstaple EX32 0PH* T: (01271) 830950 M: 07914-361905 E: revd.shaun@gmail.com

ORPIN, Mrs Gillian. b 32. SRN 53. Oak Hill Th Coll 82. **d** 87 **p** 95. Par Dn Passenham *Pet* 87–92; rtd 92; NSM Oban St Jo *Arg* 92–95; Dioc Chapl 95–98; PtO *St Alb* from 98. *11 Berwick Way, Sandy SG19 1TR* T: (01767) 680629 E: gillian.orpin@talktalk.net

ORR, Andrew Dermot Harman. b 66. Sheff Univ BSc 89. CITC BTh 92. **d** 92 **p** 93. C Ballymacash *Conn* 92–95; I Castlecomer w Colliery Ch, Mothel and Bilboa *C, F & O* 95–00; I Castleknock and Mulhuddart w Clonsilla *D & G* 00–09; I Tullow w Shillelagh, Aghold and Mullinacuff *C, F & O* 09–18; Dioc Registrar 95–00 and 12–18; Adn Ossory and Leighlin 14–18; P-in-c Youghal Union *C, C & R* from 18. *13 The Pinnacles, Midleton, Co Cork, Republic of Ireland* T: (00353) (24) 92350 M: 87-419 6051 E: andreworr1234@gmail.com

ORR, David Cecil. b 33. TCD BA 56 MA 68. **d** 57 **p** 58. C Drumragh *D & R* 57–60; I Convoy 60–70; I Maghera w Killelagh 70–80; I Drumragh w Mountfield 80–84; Dean Derry 84–97; I Templemore 84–97; Miss to Seamen 84–97; rtd 97. *Kilrory, 11 Broomhill Court, Londonderry BT47 6WP* T: (028) 7134 8183 E: dcecilorr@btopenworld.com

ORR, Mrs Helen McGowan. b 71. Magd Coll Cam BA 93 MA 98 Anglia Ruskin Univ MA 14. Ridley Hall Cam 12. d 14 p 15. C Chesterton St Andr *Ely* 14–17; C Cambridge Gt St Mary w St Mich from 17. *Great St Mary's Church, St Mary's Passage, Cambridge CB2 3PQ* T: (01223) 747273

ORR, Mark. b 61. St Jo Coll Nottm BA 14. d 14 p 15. C Clifton *S'well* 14–17; R Carlton-in-Lindrick and Langold w Oldcotes from 17. *The Rectory, 21 Grange Close, Carlton-in-Lindrick, Worksop S81 9DX* M: 07568-585638 E: odman001@yahoo.co.uk

ORR, Robert Vernon. b 50. Westmr Univ 80 MIQA 89. Wycliffe Hall Ox 96. d 98 p 99. C Cowley St Jas *Ox* 98–01; P-in-c Reading St Agnes w St Paul 01–02; R Reading St Agnes w St Paul and St Barn 02–18; rtd 18; PtO *Ox* from 19. *17 East Street, Oxford OX2 0AU* T: (01865) 806171 E: vernon.orr@gmail.com

ORR, William James Craig. TCD BTh 01. CITC 98. d 01 p 02. C Lurgan Ch the Redeemer *D & D* 01–07; I Muckamore *Conn* 07–16; I Killead w Gartree 07–16; I Portadown St Mark *Arm* from 16. *The Rectory, 56 Brownstown Road, Portadown, Craigavon BT62 3PY* T: (028) 3815 6771 M: 07850-156942 *or* 07806-882783 E: william-orr@sky.com *or* william@stmarksportadown.org

ORR-EWING, Canon Francis Ian Lance (Frog). b 75. Regent's Park Coll Ox BA 97. Wycliffe Hall Ox MTh 00. d 00 p 01. C Ox St Aldate 00–03; V Camberwell All SS *S'wark* 03–10; PtO *Ox* 10–13; NSM Amersham Deanery 13–19; PtO *Lich* 17–19; Can Th Win Cathl from 18; Research Fell Win Univ from 18. *Applebarn, Bull Lane, Chalfont St Peter, Gerrards Cross SL9 8RH* T: (01753) 886540 M: 07712-175851 E: rector@latimerminster.org

ORRIDGE, Harriet Grace. b 72. St Jo Coll Nottm. d 09 p 10. C Ironstone Villages *Leic* 09–13; P-in-c Saxonwell *Linc* 13–21. *Address temp unknown*

ORTON, Giles Anthony Christopher. b 59. Qu Coll Ox MA 82. St Steph Ho Ox 12. d 16 p 17. NSM Long Eaton St Laur *Derby* 16–20; NSM Ilkeston H Trin 16–20; P-in-c Derby St Anne from 20. *Brun Meadows, Brun Lane, Kirk Langley, Ashbourne DE6 4LU* T: (01332) 824233 M: 07768-827101 E: frgilesorton@fastmail.fm

ORTON, Peter Joseph. b 57. d 03 p 04. OLM Burton St Chad *Lich* 03–10; NSM Burton St Aid and St Paul 10–17; NSM Burton 15–17; P-in-c Stevenage All SS Pin Green *St Alb* 17–19; V from 19. *All Saints' Vicarage, 100 Derby Way, Stevenage SG1 5TJ* M: 07837-387412 E: pete.orton@outlook.com

ORTON, Canon Richard. b 33. Keble Coll Ox BA 56 MA 60 Leeds Univ. Lich Th Coll 60. d 61 p 64. C Penistone w Midhope *Wakef* 61–62; Hon C Meltham 62–69; Hon C Horsforth *Ripon* 69–72; C Far Headingley St Chad 72–75; V Hellifield *Bradf* 75–80; R Bowland 78–80; R Hutton *Chelmsf* 80–87; R Wallasey St Hilary *Ches* 87–00; Dioc Ecum Officer 92–99; RD Wallasey 96–99; Hon Can Ches Cathl 97–00; rtd 00; C Gt Sutton *Ches* 01–05; PtO from 05. *137 Brimstage Road, Barnston, Wirral CH60 1XF* T: 0151-348 4911 E: rokeblox@gmail.com

O'RYAN, Mrs Elizabeth Ann. b 63. Birm Univ BA 84 Glas Univ MTh 11 Roehampton Inst PGCE 85. TISEC 09. d 11 p 12. NSM Greenock *Glas* 11–14; C Dumbarton 14–19; C Alexandria 14–19; R Haddington *Edin* from 19. *6 Church Street, Haddington EH41 3EX* T: (01620) 826667 M: 07949-667135 E: lizoryan@talktalk.net

OSBORN, Andrew Talbot. b 62. d 94 p 95. Australia 94–13; PtO *Blackb* 13–14; R Heysham from 14. *The Rectory, Main Street, Heysham, Morecambe LA3 2RN* T: (01524) 851013 E: andrewinheysham@gmail.com

OSBORN, Charlotte Elizabeth. b 56. Birm Univ BA 77 Cardiff Univ MTh 14 Trin Hall Cam PGCE 78. ERMC 15. d 17 p 18. NSM Oakham, Ashwell, Braunston, Brooke, Egleton etc *Pet* 17–20; PtO *Nor* 20–21; P-in-c Ford and Etal *Newc* from 21; P-in-c Lowick and Kyloe w Ancroft from 21. *Old School House, Branxton, Cornhill-on-Tweed TD12 4SW* M: 07957-367457 E: ceosborn@mail.com

OSBORN, Canon David Ronald. b 42. Bris Univ BA 66 Leeds Univ CertEd 72 Bath Univ MEd 80. Clifton Th Coll 62. d 66 p 67. C Farndon *S'well* 66–69; P-in-c W Bridgford 69–72; Asst Dioc Dir Educn *Carl* 72–77; P-in-c Kirkandrews-on-Eden w Beaumont and Grinsdale 72–77; Hd RE and Chapl Dauntsey's Sch Devizes 77–83; V Southbroom *Sarum* 83–86; Hd RE Bexhill High Sch 86–90; TV Langtree *Ox* 93–95; TR 95–97; TR Bracknell 97–06; rtd 06; P-in-c Llantilio Crossenny w Penrhos, Llanvetherine etc *Mon* 06–14; AD Abergavenny 11–14; Can St Woolos Cathl from 12; PtO 14–19. *51 Cornpoppy Avenue, Monmouth NP25 5SD* M: 07803-618464 E: d.osborn42@btinternet.com

OSBORN, David Thomas. b 58. K Coll Lon BD 79 AKC 79 PGCE 80. Linc Th Coll 82. d 83 p 84. C Bearsted w

Thurnham *Cant* 83–86; Chapl RAF 86–90; R Bassingham *Linc* 90–91; V Aubourn w Haddington 90–91; V Carlton-le-Moorland w Stapleford 90–91; R Thurlby w Norton Disney 90–91; Chapl RAF from 91. *Chaplaincy Services (RAF), HQ Air Command, RAF High Wycombe HP14 4UE* T: (01494) 496800 E: stclementdanes1@btconnect.com

OSBORN, Sally Jane. b 75. d 20 p 21. C Leeds St Aid from 20. *2 Wike Lane, Bardsey, Leeds LS17 9EB* E: sally.osborn@leeds.anglican.org

OSBORNE, Canon Brian Charles. b 38. St Andr Univ MA 61. Clifton Th Coll 61. d 63 p 64. C Skirbeck H Trin *Linc* 63–68; V 80–03; P-in-c New Clee 68–71; V 71–75; V Derby St Aug 75–80; Chapl Pilgrim Hosp Boston 84–88; RD Holland E *Linc* 85–95; Can and Preb Linc Cathl 92–03; rtd 03; Chapl to The Queen 97–08; PtO *Linc* 15–18. *3 Newlands Road, Haconby, Bourne PE10 0UT* T: (01778) 570818

OSBORNE, Preb David Robert. b 50. Birm Univ BSc 71 MEd 86 Bris Univ PGCE 73. Cranmer Hall Dur 78. d 80 p 81. C Penkridge w Stretton *Lich* 80–85; R Longdon-upon-Tern, Rodington, Uppington etc 85–94; R Pilton w Croscombe, N Wootton and Dinder *B & W* 94–13; RD Shepton Mallet 01–07; Sub-Dean Wells Cathl 11–13; rtd 13; PtO *B & W* from 14; Preb Wells Cathl from 11. *10 Millbrook Gardens, Castle Cary BA7 7EF* T: (01963) 351275 M: 07719-391485 E: drosborne@btinternet.com

OSBORNE, David Victor. b 36. Dur Univ BA 59 Univ of Wales MA 99. Cranmer Hall Dur. d 62 p 63. C Kennington Cross St Anselm *S'wark* 62–66; C Sandal St Helen *Wakef* 66–67; R Ancoats *Man* 67–73; V Claremont H Angels 73–80; R Breedon cum Isley Walton and Worthington *Leic* 80–87; V Beaumont Leys 87–92; V Billesdon and Skeffington 92–01; rtd 01; PtO *Leic* 02–17; *Pet* from 02. *Rose Cottage, 12 Barlows Lane, Wilbarston, Market Harborough LE16 8QB* T: (01536) 770400

OSBORNE, Mrs Elizabeth Rachel. b 85. Goldsmiths' Coll Lon MA 10 St Cath Coll Cam MA 11 BTh 17. Ridley Hall Cam 15. d 19 p 20. C Oseney Crescent St Luke *Lon* from 19. *30A Hadley Street, London NW1 8SS* M: 07877-186450 E: osborne.lizzie@gmail.com

OSBORNE, Canon Gerald Edward Richard. b 63. Ch Ch Ox MA 85 Wye Coll Lon MSc 86. d 99 p 00. OLM Pewsey and Swanborough *Sarum* 99–10; OLM Vale of Pewsey from 10; RD Pewsey from 12; Can and Preb Sarum Cathl from 14. *Lower Farm House, Milton Lilbourne, Pewsey SN9 5LQ* T: (01672) 563459 F: 564271 M: 07747-603795 E: gerald.osborne@lawnfarm.co.uk

OSBORNE, Graham Daking. b 51. Univ of Wales MPhil 13 City Univ ACII 74 FCII 77. Ripon Coll Cuddesdon 94. d 96 p 97. C Cirencester *Glouc* 96–00; V Glouc St Cath 00–09; AD Glouc City 03–08; R Leatherhead and Mickleham *Guildf* from 09. *The Rectory, 3 St Mary's Road, Leatherhead KT22 8EZ* T: (01372) 372313 E: revgdo@me.com

OSBORNE, The Ven Hayward John. b 48. New Coll Ox BA 70 MA 73. Westcott Ho Cam 71. d 73 p 74. C Bromley SS Pet and Paul *Roch* 73–77; C Halesowen *Worc* 77–80; TV 80–83; TR Worc St Barn w Ch Ch 83–88; V Moseley St Mary *Birm* 88–01; AD Moseley 94–01; Hon Can Birm Cathl 00–01; Adn Birm 01–18; P-in-c Allens Cross 08–09; rtd 18; PtO *Birm* from 18; *Worc* from 19. *30A Roden Avenue, Kidderminster DY10 2RE* T: (01562) 745638 M: 07752-091371 E: hs.osborne@btinternet.com

OSBORNE, Iain George. b 69. Qu Coll Ox BA 92 Man Univ MA 93 Cam Univ BTh 17. Ridley Hall Cam 15. d 17 p 18. C Oakham, Ashwell, Braunston, Brooke, Egleton etc *Pet* 17–20; R The Ramseys and Upwood *Ely* from 20. *The Rectory, 18 Hollow Lane, Ramsey, Huntingdon PE26 1DE* M: 07935-549947 E: iaingosborne@gmail.com *or* iain@ramseysandupwood.org

OSBORNE, Preb Jonathan Lloyd. b 62. MBE 20. Ripon Coll Cuddesdon 95. d 97 p 98. C Mill End and Heronsgate w W Hyde *St Alb* 97–00; Asst Chapl Ealing Hosp NHS Trust 00–03; Chapl Team Ldr 03–10; Asst Chapl W Middx Univ Hosp NHS Trust 00–03; Chapl Team Ldr 03–10; Chapl Team Ldr Meadow House Hospice 03–10; Chapl W Lon Mental Health NHS Trust 03–10; Sen Chapl Metrop Police *Lon* from 10; PtO *St Alb* from 10; Hon Min Can S'wark Cathl from 03; PtO *Roch* from 10; PV Westmr Abbey from 10; Preb St Paul's Cathl *Lon* from 13; Hon C St Andr-by-the-Wardrobe w St Ann, Blackfriars and St Martin Ludgate from 16; Dep P in O from 17. *Senior Chaplain Metropolitan Police Service, Room 7 New Scotland Yard, Victoria Embankment, London SW1A 2JL* T: (020) 7928 9203

OSBORNE, Julian Marcus. b 60. Loughb Univ BSc 82 Lancs Poly MBA 91. St Mellitus Coll 18. d 19 p 20. NSM Tarporley *Ches* from 19. *3 Dingle Way, Cuddington,*

Northwich CW8 2UW T: (01606) 888392 M: 07421-323699 E: jcrcosborne@gmail.com

✠OSBORNE, The Rt Revd June. b 53. Man Univ BA 74. Wycliffe Hall Ox 78. dss 80 d 87 p 94 c 17. Birm St Martin 80–84; Old Ford St Paul and St Mark *Lon* 84–95; Par Dn Old Ford St Paul w St Steph and St Mark 87–94; P-in-c Old Ford St Paul and St Mark 94–95; Can Res and Treas Sarum Cathl 95–04; Bp's Dom Chapl 95–97; Dean Sarum 04–17; Bp Llan from 17. *Llys Esgob, The Cathedral Green, Llandaff, Cardiff CF5 2YE* T: (029) 2056 2400 F: 2057 7129 E: bishop.llandaff@churchinwales.org.uk

OSBORNE, Canon Malcolm Eric (**Max**). b 64. EN(G) 87 RMN 92. St Jo Coll Nottm 94. d 96 p 97. C Walton *St E* 96–99; C Ipswich St Matt 99–02; Soc Resp Adv 99–02; V Newmarket All SS 02–21; RD Mildenhall 19–21; R Horringer from 21; RD Thingoe from 21; Asst Dioc Dir of Ords from 16; Hon Can St E Cathl from 20. *The Rectory, Manor Lane, Horringer, Bury St Edmunds IP29 5PY* E: max9@btinternet.com

OSBORNE, Canon Marianne Lily-May. St Mich Coll Llan. d 09 p 10. C Tenby *St D* 09–11; P-in-c Burton and Rosemarket 11–14; P-in-c St Issell's and Amroth w Crunwere and Marros 14–17; Children and Youth Development Chapl 11–17; P-in-c Prendergast w Rudbaxton 17–19; P-in-c Daugleddau LMA from 19; Dioc Min Area Development Officer from 17; Can St D Cathl from 19. *54 Glenfields Road, Haverfordwest SA61 1EB* T: (01437) 214612 E: marianneosbor@aol.com

OSBORNE, Mark Alexander. b 68. Univ of Wales (Swansea) BA 95. Ridley Hall Cam 16. d 18 p 19. C Chesterton Gd Shep *Ely* 18–21; Chapl HM Pris Highpoint from 21. *HM Prison Highpoint, Stradishall, Newmarket CB8 9YG* T: (01440) 743100 M: 07900-552377 E: markosborne8@gmail.com

OSBORNE, Mark William. b 67. Univ of Wales BA 89 Lon Univ MTh 06. Coll of Resurr Mirfield 94. d 94 p 95. C Goldthorpe w Hickleton *Sheff* 94–97; C-in-c Southey Green St Bernard CD 97–01; P-in-c Walham Green St Jo w St Jas *Lon* 01–12; V 12–18; Chapl Paris St Geo *Eur* from 18. *St George, 7 rue Auguste-Vacquerie, 75116 Paris, France* T: (0033) 1 47 20 22 51 E: chaplain@stgeorgesparis.org

OSBORNE, Norma Roberta. b 36. d 97 p 03. NSM Upper Tooting H Trin *S'wark* 02–03; NSM Tooting St Aug 02–03; NSM Wandsworth St Mich 03–06; NSM Wandsworth St Mich w St Steph 06–07; PtO 07–14 and from 17. *7 Riverside Drive, Richmond TW10 7QA* T: (020) 8255 0280

OSBORNE, Ralph. b 38. Bernard Gilpin Soc Dur 62 Clifton Th Coll 63. d 66 p 67. C Harpurhey Ch Ch *Man* 66–68; C Chorlton on Medlock St Sav 68–71; C Wilmington *Roch* 71–74; V St Mary Cray and St Paul's Cray 74–85; P-in-c Bath St Steph *B & W* 85–88; P-in-c Charlcombe 86–88; R Charlcombe w Bath St Steph 88–03; rtd 03; PtO *B & W* 09–14. *406 Bath Road, Saltford, Bristol BS31 3DH* T: (01225) 872536

OSBOURNE, Canon David John. b 56. Linc Th Coll 78. d 79 p 80. C Houghton le Spring *Dur* 79–82; C Spalding St Jo *Linc* 82–83; C Spalding St Jo w Deeping St Nicholas 83–84; V Swineshead 84–94; RD Holland W 86–92; P-in-c Boultham 94–01; R from 01; RD Christianity 08–17; Can and Preb Linc Cathl from 12. *The Rectory, 2A St Helen's Avenue, Lincoln LN6 7RA* T/F: (01522) 682026 E: david.osbourne@hotmail.co.uk

OSBOURNE, Steven John. b 59. St Jo Coll Nottm 92. d 94 p 95. C Bushbury *Lich* 94–98; C Tamworth 98–03; V Caverswall and Weston Coyney w Dilhorne 03–17; RD Cheadle 07–14; rtd 17. *8 Vicarage Crescent, Caverswall, Stoke-on-Trent ST11 9EW* T: (01782) 312570 or 388037 E: steve.osbourne@btopenworld.com

OSGOOD (*née* Shipton), Mrs Eileen Kay. b 81. Cardiff Univ BMus 03. St Mellitus Coll MA 15. d 15 p 16. C Chertsey, Lyne and Longcross *Guildf* 15–19; C New Malden and Coombe *S'wark* from 19. *2 California Road, New Malden KT3 3RU* T: 07891-953164 E: eilsosgood@sjnm.org

OSGOOD, Graham Dean. b 39. Lon Univ BSc 62 ALCD 71. St Jo Coll Nottm 71. d 71 p 72. C Bebington *Ches* 71–76; V Gee Cross 76–05; rtd 05; PtO *Ox* 08–21. *4 Lower Close, Bodicote, Banbury OX15 4DZ* T: (01295) 266848 E: grahamosgood55@yahoo.co.uk

O'SHAUGHNESSY, Mrs Janice Florence. b 51. STETS 95. d 98 p 99. NSM Bembridge *Portsm* 98–02; Asst Chapl Isle of Wight Healthcare NHS Trust 99–02; C Catherington and Clanfield *Portsm* 02–07; P-in-c Arreton 07–09; V 09–20; P-in-c Newchurch 07–09; V 09–20; P-in-c Gatcombe 07–09; rtd 20. *Address temp unknown* E: colleenaluinn@aol.com

OSISIOGU, Lawrence Eberendu. b 60. Qu Foundn Birm 16. d 14 p 16. PtO *Birm* from 18. *107 Pitfield Road, Birmingham B33 0NY* T: 0121-572 3855 M: 07507-706332 E: eberelaw@yahoo.com

ÓSKARSDÓTTIR, Miss Nina Kristin. b 89. MF Norwegian Sch of Th BA MTh Wycliffe Hall Ox 15. p 16. PtO *Ox* 17–20; C Northwood Em *Lon* from 21. *54 Rofant Road, Northwood HA6 3BE* M: 07541-397460 E: nina.oskarsdottir@ecn.org.uk

OSLER, Philip. b 55. SEITE 99. d 02 p 03. NSM Staplehurst *Cant* 02–07; C Thurlestone, S Milton, W Alvington etc *Ex* 07–09; P-in-c 09–13; PtO 13–16; NSM Bourne Valley *Sarum* 16–21; PtO *Truro* from 21. *Cobbler's Cottage, Duloe, Liskeard PL14 4QF* E: philip.osler.55@hotmail.co.uk

OSMAN, Canon David Thomas. b 49. Bradf Univ BTech 72 Newc Univ MA 93. Trin Coll Bris 75. d 78 p 79. C Stranton *Dur* 78–81; C Denton Holme *Carl* 81–84; V Preston on Tees *Dur* 84–97; P-in-c Hebburn St Jo 97–18; P-in-c Jarrow Grange 00–18; rtd 18; PtO *Dur* from 18; Hon Can Owo Nigeria from 07. *5 Scotts Court, Gateshead NE10 8JG*

OSMAN, Stephen William. b 53. Matlock Coll of Educn CertEd 74 Teesside Poly CQSW 80. Cranmer Hall Dur 88. d 90 p 91. C Newbarns w Hawcoat *Carl* 90–93; TV Marfleet *York* 93–00; P-in-c Gotham *S'well* 00–10; P-in-c Barton in Fabis 02–10; P-in-c Thrumpton 02–10; P-in-c Kingston and Ratcliffe-on-Soar 02–10; P-in-c Herrington, Penshaw and Shiney Row *Dur* 10–14; R 14–19; rtd 19; PtO *Dur* from 20. *2 The Spinney, Spennymoor DL16 6HZ*

OSMASTON, Canon Amiel Mary Ellinor. b 51. Ex Univ BA 73 St Jo Coll Dur BA 84. Cranmer Hall Dur 82. dss 84 d 87 p 94. Chester le Street *Dur* 84–88; Par Dn 87–88; Dir Miss and Past Studies Ridley Hall Cam 89–96; Min Development Officer *Ches* 96–03; C Lache cum Saltney 00–03; Min Development Officer *Carl* 03–16; C Penrith w Newton Reigny and Plumpton Wall 03–16; Hon Can Carl Cathl 05–16; rtd 16; PtO *Carl* from 18. *The Rock, Charney Well Lane, Grange-over-Sands LA11 6DB*

OSMOND, Andrew Mark. b 62. Leeds Univ LLB 85. Wycliffe Hall Ox 02. d 02 p 09. C Cheltenham St Mary, St Matt, St Paul and H Trin *Glouc* 02–03; NSM Cheltenham St Mark 09–11; Chapl Glouc Docks Mariners' Ch from 12. *11 Sandhurst Road, Gloucester GL1 2SE* T: (01452) 699552 M: 07906-314463 E: andy@marinersgloucester.org.uk

OSMOND, David Methuen. b 38. Qu Coll Birm 75. d 77 p 78. C Yardley St Edburgha *Birm* 77–80; V Withall 80–89; R W Coker w Hardington Mandeville, E Chinnock etc *B & W* 89–95; PtO 96–98; rtd 98; Hon C Castle Town *Lich* 01–03; PtO *Blackb* 05–10; *Heref* 14–16; *Lich* 17–18. *56 Essex Road, Church Stretton SY6 6AY* T: (01694) 328329 E: dandhosmond@hotmail.co.uk

OSMOND, Mrs Heather Christine. b 44. ABSM 64 ARCM 65 Birm Poly CertEd 65. Qu Coll Birm 83. dss 84 d 87 p 97. Brandwood *Birm* 84–85; Withall 85–89; Par Dn 87–89; PtO *B & W* 89–01; P-in-c Castle Town *Lich* 01–03; rtd 04; PtO *Blackb* 05–09; *Heref* 14–16; *Lich* 17–19. *56 Essex Road, Church Stretton SY6 6AY* T: (01694) 328329 E: dandhosmond@hotmail.co.uk

OSMOND (*formerly* ISON-STIERER), Susan Jane. b 79. Ripon Coll Cuddesdon 16. d 18 p 19. C Bridgwater St Mary and Chilton Trinity *B & W* 18–21; V from 21. *St Mary Magdalene Vicarage, Whirligig Lane, Taunton TA1 1SQ* M: 07934-804889 E: revsuse@gmail.com

OSMOND, Tobias Charles. b 74. Plymouth Univ BSc 96. Ripon Coll Cuddesdon BTh 99. d 99 p 00. C Wilton *B & W* 99–02; C Bath Abbey w St Jas 02–05; I Midhurst and Craighurst Canada 05–11; P-in-c Wells St Thos w Horrington *B & W* 11–17; V 17–19; P-in-c Chewton Mendip w Ston Easton, Litton etc 11–19; RD Shepton Mallet 16–19; V Taunton St Mary and St Jo from 19. *St Mary Magdalene Vicarage, Whirligig Lane, Taunton TA1 1SQ* T: (01823) 337305 E: vicar@stmarymagdalenetaunton.org.uk

OSSORY AND LEIGHLIN, Archdeacon of. See ELMES, The Ven Ruth Katherine

OSSORY, Dean of. See MACDONNELL, The Very Revd David

OSTLER, Mrs Christine Anne. b 46. Bp Otter Coll CertEd 68. Westcott Ho Cam 07. d 09 p 10. NSM Gt w Lt Harrowden and Orlingbury and Isham etc *Pet* 09–12; P-in-c Wellingborough St Barn 12–17; rtd 17; Hon C Wellingborough All Hallows *Pet* from 18; Hon C Wellingborough All SS from 18. *19B Castle Street, Wellingborough NN8 1LW* T: (01933) 226730 E: c.ostler@btinternet.com

OSTLI-EAST (*formerly* EAST), Peter Alan. b 61. Southn Univ LLB 82. Cranmer Hall Dur 90. d 93 p 94. C Combe Down w Monkton Combe and S Stoke *B & W* 93–97; PtO *Bris* 06–09; TV Bourne Valley *Sarum* 09–15; P-in-c 15–20; R from 20; C Salisbury St Fran and Stratford sub Castle 09–18. *The Vicarage, Winterbourne Earls, Salisbury SP4 6HA* T: (01980) 611350 M: 07805-581269 E: revpeterbvt@gmail.com

O'SULLIVAN, Mrs Hazel. b 50. Open Univ BA 16. S Dios Minl Tr Scheme 91. d 94 p 95. C Cove St Jo *Guildf* 94–98;

TV Headley All SS 98–02; V Bordon 02–04; Chapl Whiteley Village 04–11; rtd 11; PtO *Win* 12–15; *Portsm* 15–19; C Alverstoke from 19. *3 The Avenue, Gosport PO12 2JS* T: (023) 9252 6664 E: hosull@hotmail.co.uk

O'SULLIVAN, Mrs Hazel May. b 64. Surrey Univ BSc 86 ACA 90. SEITE 09. **d** 12 **p** 13. C Reigate St Mary *S'wark* 12–15; P-in-c W Wickham St Fran and St Mary 15–19; V from 19. *St Mary's Vicarage, The Avenue, West Wickham BR4 0DX* M: 07810-698906 E: osullivan_hazel@yahoo.co.uk

O'SULLIVAN, Miss Helen. b 77. Homerton Coll Cam BEd 00. Trin Coll Bris 16. **d** 18 **p** 19. C N Hants Downs *Win* 18–21; P-in-c Hurstbourne Priors, Longparish etc from 21. *10 Pigeonhouse Field, Sutton Scotney, Winchester SO21 3NJ* M: 07596-749950 E: revhelenosullivan18@gmail.com

O'SULLIVAN, Helen Louise. b 68. Westmr Coll Ox BTh 96. St Steph Ho Ox 06. **d** 08 **p** 09. C Chinnor, Sydenham, Aston Rowant and Crowell *Ox* 08–11; P-in-c Brighstone and Brooke w Mottistone *Portsm* 11–13; R 13–16; P-in-c Shorwell w Kingston 11–13; V 13–16; P-in-c Chale 11–13; R 13–15; Chapl St Paul's Cathl *Lon* 16–19; V Warkworth, Acklington and Shilbottle *Newc* from 19. *The Vicarage, 11 Dial Place, Warkworth, Morpeth NE65 0UR* E: aswvicarage@gmail.com

O'SULLIVAN, Kate. b 67. Coll of Resurr Mirfield 14 Qu Foundn Birm 16. **d** 17 **p** 18. C Reddish *Man* 17–19; C Man Victoria Park 19–21; Min Area Ldr Mid Torfaen *Mon* from 21. *St Hilda's Vicarage, 2 Sunnybank Road, Griffithstown, Pontypool NP4 5LT* M: 07854-598269 E: revdkateosullivan@gmail.com

O'SULLIVAN, Richard Norton. b 59. Glas Coll of Tech BSc 80. Gregorian Univ Rome PhB 85 STB 88 STL 90. **d** 89 **p** 90. In RC Ch 89–96; NSM Clarkston *Glas* 00–02; P-in-c Glas St Oswald 02–06; P-in-c Peterhead *Ab* 06–09; R from 09; R Longside from 09; R Old Deer from 09. *The Rectory, 19 York Street, Peterhead AB42 1SN* T: (01779) 472217 E: richardosullivan01@talktalk.net

OSUNSANMI, Sunkanmi Ebunoluwa. b 71. Univ of Benin MB, BS 97 K Coll Lon MSc 13 MRCPsych 07. Trin Coll Bris 15. **d** 15 **p** 16. PtO *Birm* 15–17; *Glouc* 17–19; NSM Glouc St Jas and All SS and Ch Ch from 19. *Tangley House, Pamington, Tewkesbury GL20 8LX* M: 07785-785647 E: osunsanmi@doctors.org.uk

OSWIN, Frank Anthony (Tony). b 43. Chich Th Coll 69. **d** 71 **p** 72. C Radford *Cov* 71–74; C Shrub End *Chelmsf* 74–76; V Layer de la Haye 76–80; V Eastwood St Dav 80–93; TR Withycombe Raleigh *Ex* 93–10; rtd 10; PtO *Ex* from 13. *39 West Cliff Park Drive, Dawlish EX7 9ER* T: (01626) 888897

OTIENO, Rebecca Ruth. b 85. St Hild Coll 15. **d** 18 **p** 19. NSM Hillsborough and Wadsley Bridge *Sheff* from 18. *19 Birley Spa Lane, Sheffield S12 4EA*

OTTER, Martin John. b 65. Liv Poly BSc 87 Leeds Univ BA 11. Yorks Min Course 08. **d** 11 **p** 12. C Sherburn in Elmet w Saxton *York* 11–18; C Aberford w Micklefield 15–18; V Marston Moor from 18; Chapl Stockton Hall Hosp from 15. *The Vicarage, Wetherby Road, Rufforth, York YO23 3QF* M: 07842-106044 E: martin@theottersholt.plus.com

OTTEY, Canon John Leonard. b 34. AKC 60 Nottm Univ BA 70. **d** 61 **p** 62. C Grantham St Wulfram *Linc* 61–64; R Keyworth *S'well* 70–85; P-in-c Stanton-on-the-Wolds 71–85; P-in-c E Retford 85–87; V 87–99; P-in-c w Retford 85–87; R 87–99; Hon Can *S'well* Minster 93–99; rtd 99; PtO *Linc* from 00; *S'well* 04–11. *1 The Orchards, Grantham NG31 9GW* T: (01476) 578762

OTTLEY, David Ronald. b 57. Lanc Univ BA 78. Sarum & Wells Th Coll 79. **d** 81 **p** 82. C Urmston *Man* 81–85; Lect Bolton St Pet 85–87; P-in-c Halliwell St Thos 87–88; V Bolton St Thos 88–98; TR Halliwell 98–03; P-in-c Goostrey *Ches* 03–05; V Goostrey w Swettenham 05–09; rtd 09; PtO *Ches* from 10; *Man* from 10; Chapl HM Pris Forest Bank 16–20. *77 Ravenscroft, Holmes Chapel, Crewe CW4 7HJ* E: ottley696@btinternet.com

OTTO, Andrew James. b 63. St Pet Coll Ox BA 86 MA 90 Bris Univ BA 01. Trin Coll Bris 99. **d** 01 **p** 02. C Trowbridge H Trin *Sarum* 01–05. *37 Timor Road, Westbury BA13 2GA* T: (01373) 858357

OTTO, Mrs Melanie. b 67. Whitelands Coll Lon BSc 89. Sarum Coll BA 16. **d** 16 **p** 18. C N Bradford on Avon and Villages *Sarum* 16–17; C White Horse 17–21; P-in-c Bris St Paul's from 21; P-in-c Eastville St Anne w St Mark and St Thos from 21. *St Werburgh's Rectory, 15 St Werburgh's Park, Bristol BS2 9YT* M: 07948-598558 E: melanievotto@gmail.com

OTULE, Robert Samuel. b 66. Univ of E Lon BA 01. St Mellitus Coll 10. **d** 18 **p** 19. C Stratford St Jo w Ch Ch *Chelmsf* from 18. *29 Maryland Park, London E15 1HB* M: 07507-211481

OTUO-ACHEAMPONG, Gilbert Duah. b 79. Cape Coast Univ Ghana BSc 05 Roehampton Univ MA 18. St Nic Th Coll Ghana 08. **d** 09 **p** 10. P-in-c Abonkoso St Thos Ghana 11–12; Chapl St Monica Coll 11–18; C Kumawu St Pet 15; C Nsuta St Jos 15–18; Dioc Evang Dir Mampong 15–18; PtO *S'wark* from 18. *St Anselm's Vicarage, 286 Kennington Road, London SE11 5DU* M: 07594-154483

OUGH, John Christopher. b 51. Lon Univ CertEd 74 Open Univ BA 82. SWMTC 91. **d** 94 **p** 95. C Plymouth Em, St Paul Efford and St Aug *Ex* 94–97; P-in-c Diptford, N Huish, Harberton and Harbertonford 97–01; P-in-c Halwell w Moreleigh 97–01; R Diptford, N Huish, Harberton, Harbertonford etc 01–14; C Ermington and Ugborough 10–14; rtd 14; PtO *Truro* from 15. *Carndu, Rosenithon, St Keverne, Helston TR12 6QR* T: (01326) 281079 E: johnoughrev@gmail.com

OULD, Preb Julian Charles. b 57. MHCIMA 77. Coll of Resurr Mirfield 80. **d** 83 **p** 84. C Hebburn St Cuth *Dur* 83–86; C Pet H Spirit Bretton 86–90; R Peakirk w Glinton 90–95; R Peakirk w Glinton and Northborough 95–96; TR Is of Scilly *Truro* 96–98; R 98–06; TR Totnes w Bridgetown, Berry Pomeroy etc *Ex* 06–20; RD Totnes 06–18; Preb Ex Cathl 16–20; rtd 20; PtO *Ex* from 20; PV Ex Cathl from 20. *24 Old Park Avenue, Exeter EX1 3WE* T: (01392) 531415 E: julianould@gmail.com

OULD, Peter. b 74. Man Univ BA 96. Wycliffe Hall Ox BTh 05. **d** 05 **p** 06. C Ware Ch Ch *St Alb* 05–11; PtO *Cant* from 12. *3 Goudhurst Close, Canterbury CT2 7TZ* T: (01227) 456209 E: mail@peter-ould.net

OUTEN (*née* BAILEY), **Mrs Joyce Mary Josephine.** b 33. St Gabr Coll Lon CertEd 69. S'wark Ord Course 80. **dss** 83 **d** 87 **p** 94. Par Dn Woolwich St Mary w St Mich *S'wark* 87–89; Par Dn Rusthall *Roch* 89–94; C 94–97; rtd 97; Asst Chapl Kent and Cant Hosps NHS Trust 97–99; Asst Chapl E Kent Hosps NHS Trust 99–00; TV Whitstable *Cant* 00–07; PtO 07–19. *34 Station Road, Minster, Ramsgate CT12 4BZ* T: (01843) 446569 E: joyceouten03@gmail.com

OVENDEN, Canon John Anthony. b 45. LVO 07. Open Univ BA 80 BA 93 K Coll Lon MA 96 Ox Univ MA 12. Sarum & Wells Th Coll 71. **d** 74 **p** 75. C Handsworth *Sheff* 74–77; C Isfield *Chich* 77–80; C Uckfield 77–80; P-in-c Stuntney *Ely* 80–85; Min Can, Prec and Sacr Ely Cathl 80–85; V Primrose Hill St Mary w Avenue Road St Paul *Lon* 85–98; Can Windsor and Chapl in Windsor Gt Park 98–12; rtd 12; Dean of Chpl and Fell Harris Manchester Coll Ox 12–15; Chapl Mansf Coll Ox 14–20; Dir English Hymnal Co 93–00; Chapl to The Queen 07–15; PtO *Glouc* from 17. *Little Croft, Great Rissington, Cheltenham GL54 2LN* T: (01451) 821533 E: jandcovenden@gmail.com

OVEREND, Alan. b 53. Sheff Univ BA 75. Oak Hill Th Coll 84. **d** 86 **p** 87. C Aughton St Mich *Liv* 86–89; P-in-c Eccleston Park 89–92; V 92–99; V Ainsdale 99–07; V Billinge 07–17; rtd 17; PtO *Ches* from 18. *4 Hazelwood Road, Barnton, Northwich CW8 4SJ*

OVEREND, Barry Malcolm. b 49. K Coll Lon BD 71 AKC 71. St Aug Coll Cant 71. **d** 72 **p** 73. C Nailsworth *Glouc* 72–74; C High Harrogate Ch Ch *Ripon* 75–78; V Collingham w Harewood 78–87; V Far Headingley St Chad 87–10; rtd 10; PtO *Bradf* 10–14; *Leeds* from 14. *46 Langford Lane, Burley in Wharfedale, Ilkley LS29 7EJ* T: (01943) 968248 E: barry.sue.overend@gmail.com

OVEREND, Canon Paul. b 66. Coll of Ripon & York St Jo BA 88 Hull Univ MA 96 Univ of Wales (Cardiff) PhD 04. Coll of Resurr Mirfield 88. **d** 93 **p** 94. C Cayton w Eastfield *York* 93–96; Asst Chapl Univ of Wales (Cardiff) *Llan* 96; Sen Chapl 97–03; Tutor 03–04; Tutor St Mich Coll Llan 03–04; Teaching Fell Liv Hope Univ 04–05; Dir Initial Minl Formation *Sarum* 05–06; Vice Prin Sarum OLM Scheme 05–06; Prin OLM 06–08; Tutor STETS and Co-ord for Locally Deployable Ord Min 08–09; Tutor STETS 11–12; C Wymondham *Nor* 12–13; Lay Development Officer 14–18; Asst Dir of Ords 15–18; Hon PV Nor Cathl 16–18; Can Res and Chan Linc Cathl from 18. *3A Vicars Court, Lincoln LN2 1PT* E: paul.overend@gmail.com *or* chancellor@lincolncathedral.com

OVERINGTON, Canon David Vernon. b 34. ALCD 60. **d** 60 **p** 61. C Penge Ch Ch w H Trin *Roch* 60–62; C Lenton *S'well* 62–65; PC Brackenfield w Wessington *Derby* 65–71; P-in-c Cubley w Marston Montgomery 71–76; R Bridgetown Australia 76–79; Par P Denmark 79–85; Can Bunbury 84–85; R E Fremantle w Palmyra Australia 85–90; Field Officer Angl Dept of Educn 90–93; R Wembley 93–99; Hon Can Perth from 96; rtd 99; P-in-c Longside *Ab* 99–03; P-in-c New Pitsligo 99–03; P-in-c Old Deer 99–03; P-in-c Strichen 99–03; PtO *Roch* from 04; *Guildf* from 17. *7 Kingsmead, 98 Foley Road, Claygate, Esher KT10 0NB* E: overington@talktalk.net

OVERTHROW, Royston John. b 45. Southn Univ BTh 94. Portsm Dioc Tr Course 84. **d** 85. NSM Portsm Cathl 85–91; PtO 91–94; Bp's Dom Chapl *Sarum* 94–02; NSM Marlborough 02–04; rtd 04; PtO *Sarum* from 04. *19*

Bratton Avenue, Devizes SN10 5BA T: (01380) 722404
E: roy.overthrow@btinternet.com

OVERTON, Charles Henry. b 51. CCC Ox BA 74 MA 77 Fitzw Coll Cam PGCE 75 BA 79 MA 85. Ridley Hall Cam 77. **d** 80 **p** 81. C Tonbridge SS Pet and Paul *Roch* 80–84; Asst Chapl St Lawr Coll Ramsgate 84–87; P-in-c Aythorpe w High and Leaden Roding *Chelmsf* 88–95; P-in-c Hughenden *Ox* 95–01; P-in-c Chalfont St Peter 05–08; R 08–16; rtd 16; PtO *Heref* from 17. *The Vallets, Letton, Hereford HR3 6DN* T: (01544) 327912 E: charlesoverton@hotmail.com

OVERTON, John Michael. b 48. CCC Ox BA 71 MA 74 CPA 77 MRSC 01. Ripon Coll Cuddesdon 11. **d** 12 **p** 13. NSM New Mills *Derby* 12–16; NSM Buxton w Burbage and King Sterndale 16–21; rtd 21. *6 Brown Edge Close, Buxton SK17 7AS* T: (01298) 24845 E: jm.overton@btinternet.com

OVERTON-BENGE, Angela Margaret. b 46. UEA BA 99 Anglia Poly Univ MA 04. EAMTC 94. **d** 97 **p** 98. NSM Moulsham St Jo *Chelmsf* 97–01; Ind Chapl 01–04; C Aveley and Purfleet 01–04; Bp's Soc and Ind Adv *Bris* 04–17; C Swindon All SS w St Barn 06–17; C Swindon St Aug 06–17; Hon Can Bris Cathl 12–17; C Black Combe, Drigg, Eskdale etc *Carl* from 17. *The Rectory, Bootle, Millom LA19 5TH*

OWEN, Mrs Carole Janice. b 55. **d** 01 **p** 02. NSM Cley Hill Warminster *Sarum* 01–07; NSM Warminster St Denys and Upton Scudamore 07–17; PtO from 17; Chapl Gt Western Hosps NHS Foundn Trust from 14. *11 Stuart Green, Warminster BA12 9NU* T: (01985) 214849 E: richardowen50@hotmail.com

OWEN, Caroline Ann. b 59. Univ of Wales (Abth) BA 80 PGCE 81. St Mich Coll Llan 03. **d** 05 **p** 06. NSM Bangor *Ban* 05–09; V Cadoxton-juxta-Neath and Tonna *Llan* 09–12; V Dan yr Eppynt *S & B* 12–16; P-in-c Dowlais and Penydarren *Llan* from 16. *The Rectory, Gwernllwyn Uchaf, Dowlais, Merthyr Tydfil CF48 3NA* T: (01685) 558660 E: calowen18@gmail.com

OWEN, Christine Rose. b 62. Univ of Wales (Ban) BA 83 PGCE 84. Qu Coll Birm 86. **d** 88 **p** 94. C Ynyscynhaearn w Penmorfa and Porthmadog *Ban* 88–90; Chapl Lon Univ 90–96; Hon C St Marylebone w H Trin 94–96; Min Can and Prec Worc Cathl 96–00; R Llansantffraid Glan Conwy and Eglwysbach *St As* 00–12; AD Llanrwst 09–12; V Colwyn Bay w Brynymaen 12–16; TV Aled Miss Area from 17. *The Vicarage, 27 Walshaw Avenue, Colwyn Bay LL29 7UY* T: (01492) 539522 E: revdchristine@btinternet.com

OWEN, Christopher David. b 73. Trin Coll Bris 10. **d** 12 **p** 13. C Walton-on-Thames *Guildf* 12–16; TV High Wycombe *Ox* from 16. *70 Marlow Road, High Wycombe HP11 1TH* M: 07890-422357 E: cdowen1973@gmail.com

OWEN, Clifford. See OWEN, Phillip Clifford

OWEN, Daniel James. b 71. Anglia Poly Univ BSc 94 TCD BTh 00. CITC 97. **d** 00 **p** 01. C Belfast St Donard *D & D* 00–03; I Rathcooney Union *C, C & R* 03–09; I Kilgariffe Union 09–15; Chapl St Columba's Coll Dub from 15. *8 Hurley Lane, St Columba's College, Kilmashogue Lane, Rathfarnham, Dublin 16, Republic of Ireland* T: (00353) (1) 493 2219 E: danielsonja@gmail.com

OWEN, David Cadwaladr. b 56. Grey Coll Dur BSc 77 Univ Coll Worc PGCE 99. WEMTC 00. **d** 03 **p** 04. NSM Pershore w Pinvin, Wick and Birlingham *Worc* 03–07; TV Droitwich Spa 07–14; P-in-c Salwarpe and Hindlip w Martin Hussingtree 10–14; V Loddon, Sisland, Chedgrave, Hardley and Langley *Nor* from 14; RD Loddon from 16. *The Vicarage, 4 Market Place, Loddon, Norwich NR14 6EY* M: 07837-800009 E: david.chetvalley@gmail.com

OWEN, Canon David William. b 31. Down Coll Cam BA 55 MA 58. Linc Th Coll 55. **d** 57 **p** 58. C Salford St Phil w St Steph *Man* 57–61; C Grantham St Wulfram *Linc* 61–65; V Messingham 65–70; V Spilsby w Hundleby 70–77; R Aswardby w Sausthorpe 71–77; R Langton w Sutterby 71–77; R Halton Holgate 73–77; P-in-c Firsby w Gt Steeping 75–77; P-in-c Lt Steeping 75–77; TR Louth 77–92; Chapl Louth Co Hosp 77–92; RD Louthesk *Linc* 82–89; Can and Preb Linc Cathl 85–92; TR Swan *Ox* 92–97; RD Claydon 94–96; rtd 97; PtO *Ox* 10–19. *19 Stephen Road, Headington, Oxford OX3 9AY* T: (01865) 766585 E: davidowen9@sky.com

OWEN, Miss Denise. b 65. Warwick Univ BA 87 Westmr Coll of Educn PGCE 92. Coll of Resurr Mirfield 12. **d** 14 **p** 15. C Spotland and Oakenrod *Man* 14–17; P-in-c Oldham Moorside 17–18; V from 18; C Clarksfield and Waterhead from 17. *1 Glebe Lane, Oldham OL1 4SJ* T: 0161-652 0292 E: therevd.dowen@yahoo.co.uk

OWEN, Edgar. b 26. WMMTC. **d** 82 **p** 83. NSM Garretts Green *Birm* 82–88; NSM Stechford 88–94; rtd 94; PtO *Birm* from 94. *36 Colbourne Court, 116 Station Road, Stechford, Birmingham B33 8AE* T: 0121-783 5603 E: edgar.owen78@gmail.com

OWEN (*formerly* **DOWLAND-OWEN**), **Edward Farrington.** b 73. St D Coll Lamp BA 95 Trin Coll Carmarthen PGCE 96 FVCM 99. S Wales Ord Course 00 St Mich Coll Llan 03. **d** 04 **p** 05. C Llandaff *Llan* 04–08; P-in-c Llandyfodwg and Cwm Ogwr 08–10; C Penarth and Llandough 10–13; TV Cowbridge 13–17; P-in-c Margam 17; V 17–21; V Grangetown w Cardiff St Dyfrig and St Sansom from 21; Dioc Spirituality Adv from 12; P Assoc Shrine of Our Lady of Walsingham from 05. *St Paul's Vicarage, Llanmaes Street, Cardiff CF11 7LR* M: 07403-935555 E: vicar.grangetown@outlook.com

OWEN, Gary John. b 72. City Univ BSc 93 Fitzw Coll Cam BA 97 MA 01. Ridley Hall Cam 95. **d** 98 **p** 99. C Welshpool w Castle Caereinion *St As* 98–01; TV Wrexham 01–10; R Eynsford w Farningham and Lullingstone *Roch* 10–19; TR Newton Tracey, Horwood, Alverdiscott etc *Ex* from 19. *The Rectory, High Bickington, Umberleigh EX37 9AY* M: 07947-358050 E: revgaryowen@gmail.com

OWEN, Geoffrey Neill. b 55. Chich Th Coll. **d** 85 **p** 86. C Streatham St Pet *S'wark* 85–89; C Battersea Ch Ch and St Steph 89–91; TV Surbiton St Andr and St Mark 91–97; V Merton St Jas 97–08; V Battersea Ch Ch and St Steph from 08; RD Battersea 10–16. *Christ Church Vicarage, Candahar Road, London SW11 2PU* T: (020) 7228 1225 E: geoffreyowen1956@gmail.com

OWEN, Glyn John. b 56. Open Univ BA 91 Nottm Univ MSc 93 St Jo Coll Dur BA 05. Cranmer Hall Dur 01. **d** 03 **p** 04. C Whiston *Sheff* 03–07; V Rudston w Boynton, Carnaby and Kilham *York* 07–15; P-in-c Burton Fleming w Fordon, Grindale etc 07–15; V Rudston, Boynton, Carnaby etc from 15; RD Bridlington 12–17. *The Vicarage, Rudston, Driffield YO25 4XA* T: (01262) 420313 E: revglynowen@btinternet.com

OWEN, Graham Anthony. b 54. Birm Univ BA 77. Trin Coll Bris 92. **d** 94 **p** 95. C Wiveliscombe w Chipstable, Huish Champflower etc *B & W* 94–98; R 98–09; V Frome H Trin 09–21; RD Frome 17–20; rtd 21. *Address temp unknown* E: graham-owen@hotmail.co.uk

OWEN, Miss Hannah Mair. b 72. **d** 13 **p** 14. NSM Carmarthen St Pet and Abergwili etc *St D* 13–16; C Cwmaman 16; C Catheiniog 16–18; P-in-c Llandybie 18–19. *Address temp unknown* E: revmair@gmail.com

OWEN, Harry Dennis. b 47. Oak Hill Th Coll 73. **d** 76 **p** 77. C Fulham Ch Ch *Lon* 76–81; V Byker St Mark *Newc* 81–89; V Plumstead All SS *S'wark* 89–14; RD Plumstead 03–14; rtd 14. *13 Ratton Road, Eastbourne BN21 2LU* T: (01323) 419425 E: h.d.owen@talk21.com

OWEN, James Thomas. See McNAUGHTAN-OWEN, James Thomas

OWEN, Canon John Edward. b 52. Middx Poly BA 75. Sarum & Wells Th Coll BTh 81. **d** 81 **p** 82. C S Ashford Ch Ch *Cant* 81–85; TV Bemerton *Sarum* 85–91; V St Leonards and St Ives *Win* 91–95; R N Stoneham 95–09; V Steep and Froxfield w Privett *Portsm* from 09; Hon Can Portsm Cathl from 18. *The Vicarage, 77 Church Road, Steep, Petersfield GU32 2DF* T: (01730) 264282 E: revjohnowen@gmail.com

OWEN, Karen. See HOPWOOD OWEN, Karen

OWEN, Keith Robert. b 57. Warwick Univ BA Ox Univ BA MA 85 Hull Univ MA(Ed) 89. St Steph Ho Ox 79. **d** 82 **p** 83. C Headingley *Ripon* 82–85; Chapl Grimsby Colls of H&FE 85–90; Chapl for Educn *Linc* 85–90; P-in-c Linc St Botolph 90–95; Chapl to Caring Agencies Linc City Cen 90–95; V Steeton *Bradf* 95–01; Chapl Airedale NHS Trust 95–01; P-in-c Penzance St Mary w St Paul *Truro* 01–02; P-in-c Penzance St Jo 01–02; TR Penzance St Mary w St Paul and St Jo 02–12; C from 12; P-in-c Newlyn St Pet from 12; C Paul from 12. *24 Chapel Street, Penzance TR18 4AP* T: (01736) 365079 E: stpetersnewlyn@hotmail.co.uk

OWEN, Kenneth Phillip. b 56. Liv Univ BA 77 PGCE 78. NOC 92. **d** 95 **p** 96. C Heswall *Ches* 95–01; V Frankby w Greasby from 01. *The Vicarage, 14 Arrowe Road, Greasby, Wirral CH49 1RA* T: 0151-678 6155 E: kennethpowen@gmail.com

OWEN, Mair. See OWEN, Hannah Mair

OWEN, Mark. b 63. RMN. St Mich Coll Llan 03. **d** 05 **p** 06. C Tredegar *Mon* 05–08; V Rhymney 08–14; P-in-c Mynyddislwyn 14–18; P-in-c Blackwood w Fleur-de-Lis 15–18; TR Upper Islwyn from 18; AD Bedwellty from 15. *The Vicarage, Commercial Street, Pengam, Blackwood NP12 3UA* T: (01443) 836805 E: fathermarkowen12@gmail.com

OWEN, Myles Ronald. b 85. Sheff Univ BA 07. Ripon Coll Cuddesdon 09. **d** 12 **p** 13. C Bowdon *Ches* 12–16; NSM Cranleigh *Guildf* 17–18; Chapl Greycoat Hosp Sch from 19; PtO *S'wark* from 20. *Grey Coat Hospital, Horseferry Road, London SW1P 2DY* T: (020) 7969 1998

OWEN, Paul Jonathan. b 59. S Bank Poly BSc 81 Anglia Poly Univ MA 03. Ridley Hall Cam 00. **d** 02 **p** 03. C

Seaford w Sutton *Chich* 02–06; R Denton w S Heighton and Tarring Neville 06–11; V Seaford w Sutton 11–20; rtd 20; PtO *B & W* from 21. *6 St John's Close, Weston-super-Mare BS23 2LP* T: (01934) 204410 E: revpowen@gmail.com

OWEN, Phillip Clifford. b 42. G&C Coll Cam BA 65 MA 69 Birm Univ PhD 07. Ridley Hall Cam 71. **d** 73 **p** 74. C Stowmarket *St E* 73–76; C Headley All SS *Guildf* 76–81; TV 81–89; P-in-c Clifton-on-Teme, Lower Sapey and the Shelsleys *Worc* 89–97; R 97–02; Dioc Ecum Officer 89–02; P-in-c Corfu *Eur* 03–08; P-in-c Ostend 08–12; rtd 12; PtO *Ely* from 13; *Eur* from 18. *147 Sapley Road, Hartford, Huntingdon PE29 1YH*   T: (01480)   435488   M: 07887-745632 E: cliffordret@gmail.com

OWEN, Mrs Phyllis Elizabeth. b 48. NTMTC. **d** 05 **p** 06. NSM Southend *Chelmsf* 05–20; NSM Southend All SS from 21; NSM Westcliff St Alban and Southend St Mark from 21. *42 Harcourt Avenue, Southend-on-Sea SS2 6HU*   T: (01702) 353049 E: thephiz@blueyonder.co.uk

OWEN, Raymond Philip. b 37. Man Univ BScTech 60 AMCST 60. Chich Th Coll 65. **d** 67 **p** 68. C Elland *Wakef* 67–70; C Lindley 70–73; V Bradshaw 73–80; Ind Chapl *Dur* 80–91; TR Hanley H Ev *Lich* 91–99; Bp Stafford's Past Aux 03–04; rtd 04; PtO *Lich* 04–07; C Alton w Bradley-le-Moors and Denstone etc 07–17; PtO 17–21. *Dove House, Bridge Hill, Mayfield, Ashbourne DE6 2HN* M: 07747-601379 E: revrayowen@hotmail.com

OWEN, Canon Richard Llewelyn. b 27. Univ of Wales (Lamp) BA 51. St Mich Coll Llan 51. **d** 53 **p** 54. C Holyhead w Rhoscolyn w Llanfair-yn-Neubwll *Ban* 53–57; C Porthmadog 57–59; R Llanfechell w Bodewryd, Rhosbeirio etc 59–67; Youth Chapl 66–67; V Penrhyndeudraeth and Llanfrothen 67–77; R Llangefni w Tregaean and Llangristiolus etc 77–89; Can Ban Cathl 82–93; Hon Can Ban Cathl from 93; Treas Ban Cathl 86–93; Can Missr and V Ban Cathl 89–93; RD Arfon 92–93; rtd 93; PtO *Ban* from 93. *Bodowen, Great Orme's Road, Llandudno LL30 2BF* T: (01492) 872765

OWEN, Richard Matthew. b 49. Sheff Univ BA 70 Leeds Univ CertEd 73. NOC 84. **d** 87 **p** 88. NSM Chorlton-cum-Hardy St Werburgh *Man* 87–89; C N Reddish 89–91; PtO *York* 91–96 and 97–03; NSM York St Olave w St Giles 96–97; PtO *Cant* from 12. *17 Mill Lane, St Radigunds, Canterbury CT1 2AW* T: (01227) 784430   M: 07789-923516 E: richardowen100@gmail.com

OWEN, Ronald Alfred. b 44. Wilson Carlile Coll 73 Sarum & Wells Th Coll 80. **d** 81 **p** 82. C Wotton St Mary *Glouc* 81–83; CF 83–97; P-in-c Salcombe *Ex* 97–02; V Salcombe and Malborough w S Huish 02–06; RD Woodleigh 00–03; rtd 07; PtO *B & W* from 07. *9 Reedmoor Gardens, Bridgwater TA6 3SL* T: (01278) 433801   M: 07540-102030 E: owenrarev@gmail.com

OWEN, Sally Ann. See ROBERTSON, Sally Ann

OWEN, Stuart James. b 68. Sunderland Poly BA 91. Ripon Coll Cuddesdon BTh 00. **d** 00 **p** 01. C Hendon St Mary and Ch Ch *Lon* 00–04; P Missr Edmonton St Mary w St Jo 04–08; V Edmonton All SS w St Mich 08–20; AD Enfield 16–20; TV Gt Berkhamsted, Gt and Lt Gaddesden etc *St Alb* from 20. *The Rectory, Rectory Lane, Berkhamsted HP4 2DH* T: (01442) 879739 E: fr.stuart@gmail.com

OWEN, Susan Elizabeth. See WYATT, Susan Elizabeth

OWEN-JONES, Mrs Ingrid. b 41. **d** 11 **p** 12. OLM W Hallam and Mapperley w Stanley *Derby* 11–15; PtO 15–20; *Win* from 19. *Bron Erw, 1 Harfield Crescent, Medstead, Alton GU34 5TE*   T: (01420) 446467   M: 07977-808041 E: ingrid@ipoj.co.uk

OWEN-JONES, Peter Charles. b 57. Ridley Hall Cam 92. **d** 94 **p** 95. C Leverington and Wisbech St Mary *Ely* 94–97; R Haslingfield w Harlton and Gt and Lt Eversden 97–05; P-in-c Glynde, W Firle and Beddingham *Chich* 05–20; V from 20. *The Vicarage, The Street, Firle, Lewes BN8 6NP* T: (01273) 858005   M: 07973-265953 E: peter@halcyon7.co.uk

OWEN-JONES, Peter John. b 47. RMCS BScEng 68 CEng 74 MIMechE 84 MBIM 87 FPWI 89. EMMTC 85. **d** 88 **p** 89. NSM Holbrook and Lt Eaton *Derby* 88–00; NSM W Hallam and Mapperley w Stanley 01–13; RD Erewash 12–13; MSE Officer 11–13; rtd 13; PtO *Derby* 13–19; *Win* from 19. *Bron Erw, 1 Harfield Crescent, Medstead, Alton GU34 5TE*   T: (01420) 446467   M: 07771-828018 E: peter@ipoj.co.uk

OWENS, Christopher Lee. b 42. SS Mark & Jo Coll Chelsea 61 Lon Inst of Educn TCert. Linc Th Coll 66. **d** 69 **p** 70. C Dalston H Trin w St Phil *Lon* 69–72; C Portsea N End St Mark *Portsm* 72–81; TV E Ham w Upton Park and Forest Gate *Chelmsf* 81–92; C Is of Dogs Ch Ch and St Jo w St Luke *Lon* 92–98; P-in-c Chingford St Edm *Chelmsf* 98–02; V 02–07; rtd 07; PtO *Chelmsf* from 08. *67 Disraeli Road, London E7 9JU* T: (020) 8555 6337 E: owenseaster@gmail.com

OWENS, Mrs Janet. b 49. Liv Univ MEd 99. NOC 90. **d** 13 **p** 14. NSM Stockport St Sav *Ches* 13–14; NSM Offerton St Alb and Stockport St Thos 14–18; rtd 18; PtO *Ches* from 18. *6 Chelworth Manor, 37 Manor Road, Bramhall, Stockport SK7 3LX* T: 0161-312 4683   M: 07990-570778 E: revandrog@gmail.com

OWENS, Mrs Margaret Jean. b 49. Man Univ BSc 70 Birm Univ MSc 72. St Jo Coll Nottm BA(ThM) 03. **d** 01 **p** 02. NSM Hurdsfield *Ches* 01–07; V Disley 07–18; rtd 18; PtO *Ches* from 19. *7 Ridge View, Macclesfield SK11 8DB* T: (01625) 501242   M: 07775-801613 E: mowens44@btinternet.com

OWENS, Canon Patricia Margaret. **d** 07 **p** 08. NSM Buckley *St As* 07–10; NSM Ruabon and Rhosymedre 10–16; NSM Offa Miss Area from 17; Hon Can St As Cathl from 14. *The Clappers, Pont-y-Capel Lane, Gresford, Wrexham LL12 8RS* T: (01978) 854855

OWENS, Stephen Graham Frank. b 49. Ch Coll Cam BA 71 MA 75 CertEd 72. Qu Coll Birm 73. **d** 75 **p** 76. C Stourbridge St Mich Norton *Worc* 75–80; Tanzania 80–88; V Dudley Wood *Worc* 88–99; P-in-c Mamble w Bayton, Rock w Heightington etc 99–02; V 02–14; rtd 14; PtO *Worc* from 15. *9 Waterlaide Road, Hartlebury, Kidderminster DY11 7TP* T: (01299) 251176

OWERS, Ian Humphrey. b 46. Em Coll Cam BA 68 MA 72. Westcott Ho Cam 71. **d** 73 **p** 74. C Champion Hill St Sav *S'wark* 73–77; V Peckham St Sav 77–82; P-in-c E Greenwich Ch Ch w St Andr and St Mich 82–83; V 83–94; P-in-c Westcombe Park St Geo 85–94; RD Greenwich 92–94; PtO *St E* 01–07; *Bradf* 03–10; *Sheff* from 10. *The Rectory, Village Street, Adwick-le-Street, Doncaster DN6 7AD* M: 07808-613252

OWERS, Julie. See UPTON, Julie

OXBORROW, Alison Louise. b 68. Nottm Univ BA 90 Lon Sch of Th BA 04 Solicitor 92. St Jo Coll Nottm 08. **d** 11 **p** 12. C Didsbury St Jas and Em *Man* 11–14; PtO 14–15; Chapl Springhill Hospice 15–20; PtO *Lich* from 20. *The Vicarage, School Lane, Stoke-on-Trent ST3 3DU* M: 07870-917710

OXBROW, Canon Mark. b 51. Reading Univ BSc 72 Fitzw Ho Cam BA 75 MA 79. Ridley Hall Cam 73. **d** 76 **p** 77. C Luton Ch Ch *Roch* 76–80; TV Newc Epiphany 80–88; Chapl Newc Mental Health Unit 80–88; Regional Sec Eur CMS 88–01; Communication Resources Sec 94–97; Internat Miss Dir 01–03; Asst Gen Sec 03–08; Internat Co-ord Faith2Share Network 08–18; Dir Guided Study Progr Ox Cen for Miss Studies from 18; LtO *Ox* 07–20; NSM Cowley St Jas from 20; PtO *Eur* from 19; Hon Can Brussels Cathl from 98. *Oxford Centre for Mission Studies, St Philip and St James Church, Woodstock Road, Oxford OX2 6HR* M: 07984-631816 E: moxbrow@ocms.ac.uk

OXENFORTH, Colin Bryan. b 45. St Chad's Coll Dur BA 67. **d** 69 **p** 70. C Bromley St Andr *Roch* 69–72; C Nunhead St Antony *S'wark* 72–76; V Toxteth St Marg *Liv* 76–89; V Brixton St Matt *S'wark* 89–00; V Pemberton St Jo *Liv* 00–10; rtd 10; PtO *Liv* from 10. *Flat 3, 5 Walmer Road, Liverpool L22 5NL* T: 0151-721 2018 E: crosbyboy@sky.com

OXFORD (Christ Church), Dean of. See PERCY, The Very Revd Prof Martyn William

OXFORD, Archdeacon of. See CHAFFEY, The Ven Jonathan Paul Michael

OXFORD, Bishop of. See CROFT, The Rt Revd Steven John Lindsey

OXLEY, Canon Christopher Robert. b 51. Sheff Univ BA 73 PGCE 74. Wycliffe Hall Ox BA 78 MA 83. **d** 79 **p** 80. C Greasbrough *Sheff* 79–82; C Doncaster St Leon and St Jude 82–84; Asst Chapl Brussels *Eur* 84–87; V Humberstone *Leic* 87–93; V Beaumont Leys 93–05; RD Christianity S 98–01; P-in-c Leic St Anne 05–09; P-in-c Leic St Paul and St Aug 05–09; V Leic St Anne, St Paul w St Aug 09–11; P-in-c Avon-Swift 11–17; Dir Post-Ord Tr 04–09; Hon Can Leic Cathl 10–17; Cathedral Chaplain Leic Cathl from 15; rtd 17; PtO *Leic* from 18. *The Vicarage, Vicarage Drive, Foxton, Market Harborough LE16 7RJ* M: 07803-878879

OXLEY, Canon David William. b 63. TCD BA 85 BTh 89. CITC 85. **d** 89 **p** 90. C Dublin Ch Ch Cathl Gp *D & G* 89–92; Clerical V Ch Ch Cathl Dublin 90–92; I Templebreedy w Tracton and Nohoval *C, C & R* 92–96; Min Can Cork Cathl 95–96; I Tullow w Shillelagh, Aghold and Mullinacuff *C, F & O* 96–02; I Dublin Santry w Glasnevin and Finglas *D & G* from 02; Succ St Patr Cathl Dublin from 07; Can St Patr Cathl Dublin from 19. *The Rectory, Church Street, Finglass, Dublin 11, Republic of Ireland* T: (00353) (1) 834 1015   M: 86-881 6486 E: revdwo@hotmail.com

OXLEY, Ms Helen Mary. b 64. TCD BA 88 MA 91 HDipEd 89 Univ of Wales (Trin St Dav) MMin 11. **d** 11 **p** 12. NSM Dunleckney w Nurney, Lorum and Kiltennel *C, F & O* 11–19; PtO from 19. *11 Ashbrook, Tullow Hill, Tullow, Co Carlow, R93 P865, Republic of Ireland* T: (00353) (59) 918 0975 M: 86-378 6980 E: revheleno@gmail.com

OXLEY, Mrs Paula Jane. b 51. Sheff Univ BA 74 Nottm Univ MA 00 PGCE 75. EMMTC 93. **d** 93 **p** 94. NSM Birstall and Wanlip *Leic* 93–95; C Beaumont Leys 95–05; NSM Leic St Anne, St Paul w St Aug 05–14; PtO *Cov* from 13; *Leic* 14–17; P-in-c Foxton w Gumley and Laughton from 17. *The Vicarage, Vicarage Road, Foxton, Market Harborough LE16 7RJ* T: (01858) 540439 E: oxleypj@btinternet.com

OXTOBY, David Antony. b 72. Huddersfield Univ BSc 98. Ridley Hall Cam 08. **d** 10 **p** 11. C Stamford St Geo w St Paul *Linc* 10–13; P-in-c Sutton Bridge 13–14; C The Suttons w Tydd 13–14; V Sutton Bridge and Tydd St Mary 14–18; TR Rayleigh *Chelmsf* 18–21; Nat Discernment Adv Abps' Coun from 21. *National Ministry Team, Church House, 27 Great Smith Street, London SW1P 3AZ* M: 07595-387652 E: david@oxtobyhome.co.uk *or* david.oxtoby@churchofengland.org

OYEBODE, Olukayode Olugboyega. b 57. Lagos Univ BA 81. Lagos Angl Dioc Sem 09. **d** 11 **p** 12. C Lagos Ch on the Peninsular Nigeria 11–15; V Oniru Ch of Living Souls 15–17; rtd 17; PtO *S'wark* 19–20. *Address temp unknown* M: (00234) 803-302 2977 *or* 07375-482670 E: ooyebode57@yahoo.co.uk

P

PACEY, Graham John. b 52. Open Univ BA 81 Leeds Univ CertEd 74 Teesside Poly AdDipEd 85. NEOC 90. **d** 93 **p** 94. C Kirkleatham *York* 93–96; V Middlesbrough St Agnes 96–00; R Skelton w Upleatham 00–09; V Boosbeck and Lingdale 07–09; R Guisborough 09–13; RD 11–13; rtd 13; PtO *York* from 14. *16 Exeter Street, Saltburn-by-the-Sea TS12 1BN* T: (01287) 280883 E: g.pacey@ntlworld.com

PACEY, James Stewart. b 84. Nottm Trent Univ BA 07 Cam Univ BTh 15 Sheff Univ MA 20. Westcott Ho Cam 12. **d** 15 **p** 16. C Hucknall Torkard *S'well* 15–18; V Carrington 18–21; Chapl Nottm Univ Hosp NHS Trust from 21. *31 Lime Grove, Stapleford, Nottingham NG9 7GF* M: 07595-035342 E: revjamespacey@gmail.com

PACK, Barbara Denise. b 62. Lanc Univ BEd 86 Dur Univ PGCE 18. All SS Cen for Miss & Min 15. **d** 18 **p** 19. NSM Blackb St Aid, St Luke, St Mark and St Phil from 18. *41 Pendle Road, Leyland PR25 5TU* T: (01772) 304201 E: barcarr@sky.com

PACKER, Catherine Ruth. *See* PICKFORD, Catherine Ruth

⌖**PACKER, The Rt Revd John Richard.** b 46. Keble Coll Ox BA 67 MA. Ripon Hall Ox 67. **d** 70 **p** 71 **c** 96. C St Helier *S'wark* 70–73; Chapl Abingdon St Nic Ox 73–77; Tutor Ripon Hall Ox 73–75; Tutor Ripon Coll Cuddesdon 75–77; V Wath-upon-Dearne w Adwick-upon-Dearne *Sheff* 77–86; RD Wath 83–86; TR Sheff Manor 86–91; RD Attercliffe 90–91; Adn W Cumberland *Carl* 91–96; P-in-c Bridekirk 95–96; Suff Bp Warrington *Liv* 96–00; Bp Ripon and Leeds 00–14; rtd 14; Hon Asst Bp Newc from 14. *Devonshire House, Alma Place, Whitley Bay NE26 2EQ* T: 0191-253 4321 E: bppacker@googlemail.com

PACKER, Peter Aelred. b 48. St Jo Coll Dur BA 70 St Chad's Coll Dur PhD 79 Strathclyde Univ MBA 00. Ven English Coll Rome 95. **d** 96 **p** 97. SSM 91–98; Hon C S Lambeth St Anne and All SS *S'wark* 96–98; OSB and LtO *Ox* 98–99; Bp's Adv in Miss and Resources *Glas* 99–00; PtO *S'wark* 08–09; Hon C Deptford St Paul 09–10; P-in-c Peckham St Jo w St Andr 10–18; rtd 18; PtO *Eur* from 19. *Address withheld by request* M: 07932-648034 E: packerpunch@gmail.com

PACKMAN, James Morley. b 76. SS Hild & Bede Coll Dur MMath 99. Oak Hill Th Coll BA 04. **d** 04 **p** 05. C Eastbourne All SS *Chich* 04–08; R Frant w Eridge 08–18; RD Rotherfield 15–18; R Nailsea St Thos *B & W* from 18. *10 Ilminster Close, Nailsea, Bristol BS48 4YU* T: (01275) 853227

PADDICK, Graham. b 47. S'wark Ord Course. **d** 89 **p** 90. C St Helier *S'wark* 89–93; P-in-c Thornton Heath St Paul 93–96; V 96–98; V Dormansland 98–14; Chapl MU 03–08; AD Godstone *S'wark* 08–12; Dir Ords Croydon Area 96–14; rtd 14; PtO *S'wark* 14–16. *14 Went Hill Gardens, Eastbourne BN22 0QP* T: (01323) 502970 M: 07866-820547 E: graham.paddick@gmail.com

PADDISON, Mrs Jennifer Sheila. b 70. Cranmer Hall Dur. **d** 07 **p** 08. C Newc H Cross 07–11; Chapl Nottm Trent Univ *S'well* 12–18; PtO *Ely* from 19; *Leic* 11–20; Chapl K Sch Pet from 20. *The King's Cathedral School, Park Road, Peterborough PE1 2UE* T: (01733) 751541 E: paddison.j@kings.peterborough.sch.uk

PADDISON, Canon Michael David William. b 41. Oak Hill Th Coll 75. **d** 77 **p** 78. C Gt Warley Ch Ch *Chelmsf* 77–80; C Rayleigh 80–83; R Scole, Brockdish, Billingford, Thorpe Abbots etc *Nor* 83–95; RD Redenhall 89–94; R Reepham, Hackford w Whitwell, Kerdiston etc 95–06; RD Sparham 00–05; Hon Can Nor Cathl 02–06; rtd 06; PtO *Nor* from 06. *4 North Street, Castle Acre, King's Lynn PE32 3BA* T: (01760) 755648 E: m.s.paddison@gmail.com

PADDISON, Robert Michael. b 70. Cranmer Hall Dur. **d** 07 **p** 08. C Whorlton *Newc* 07–11; P-in-c Barrow upon Soar w Walton le Wolds *Leic* 11–18; P-in-c Wymeswold and Prestwold w Hoton 11–18; Pioneer Min *Ely* from 18. *The Vicarage, 2 Bardolph Way, Alconbury Weald, Huntingdon PE28 4BP* T: (01480) 454114 M: 07905-136836 E: rev.paddison@outlook.com

PADDOCK, The Very Revd John Allan Barnes. b 51. Liv Univ BA 74 MA 91 Ox Univ BA 77 MA 81 Glas Univ PhD 05 Cardiff Univ LLM 08 Man Univ PGCE 75 FRSA 94. St Steph Ho Ox 75. **d** 80 **p** 81. C Matson *Glouc* 80–82; Asst Chapl Madrid *Eur* 82–83; Chapl R Gr Sch Lanc 83–86; Hon C Blackb Ch Ch w St Matt 83–86; Chapl RAF 86–91; OCM 92–94; Chapl St Olave's Gr Sch Orpington 91–94; PtO *Blackb* 94–97; Chapl R Russell Sch Croydon 97–00; Hon C Bickley *Roch* 97–00; V Folkestone St Pet *Cant* 00–03; Hon Min Can Cant Cathl 01–03; V Glouc St Geo w Whaddon 03–08; Dean Gib *Eur* 08–17; rtd 17. *Address withheld by request*

PADFIELD, Joseph Michael. b 70. Dur Univ BA 91 Birm Univ MSocSc 95 DipSW 95. St Aug Coll Cant 18. **d** 21. C E Blatchington and Bishopstone *Chich* from 21. *83 Sherwood Road, Seaford BN25 3ED* T: (01323) 672848 E: fatherjoepadfield@gmail.com

PADFIELD, Jude. b 75. St Mellitus Coll. **d** 12 **p** 13. C St Jas in the City *Liv* 12–16; P-in-c 16–18; V from 18. *6 Lady Chapel Close, Liverpool L1 7BZ* T: 0151-706 0259 M: 07835-824177 E: jude.padfield@stjamesinthecity.org.uk *or* judepadfield@yahoo.co.uk

PADFIELD, Stephen James. b 68. Ex Univ BA 90 Univ Coll Dur PGCE 92. Trin Coll Bris BA 00 MA 01. **d** 01 **p** 02. C Luton Ch Ch *Roch* 01–05; Chapl R Russell Sch Croydon 05–12; Chapl Dulwich Coll 12–15; Hon C Dulwich St Barn *S'wark* 12–15; Chapl K Sch Roch from 15. *Deanery Lodge, Kings Orchard, Rochester ME1 1TG* M: 07747-775385 E: padfieldstephen@gmail.com *or* spadfield@kings-rochester.co.uk

PADLEY, Miss Karen. b 68. RGN 89. St Jo Coll Nottm MA 00. **d** 00 **p** 01. C Broxtowe *S'well* 00–04; V Marlpool *Derby* from 04; P-in-c Heanor from 16; P-in-c Langley Mill and Aldercar from 16; RD Heanor 13–18; AD SE Derbyshire from 18. *All Saints' Vicarage, 85 Ilkeston Road, Heanor DE75 7BP* T: (01773) 712097 E: padleykaren@gmail.com

PADLEY, Kenneth Peter Joseph. b 78. Ex Coll Ox BA 00 MA 04 CCC Ox DPhil 16. Ripon Coll Cuddesdon BA 03 MSt 04. **d** 05 **p** 05. C Cen Swansea *S & B* 04–07; Warden of Ch Hostel and Chapl Ban Univ 07–12; Dir of Ords 11–12; V St Alb St Mich from 12; RD St Alb from 20. *St Michael's Vicarage, St Michael's Street, St Albans AL3 4SL* T: (01727) 835037 E: kennethpadley@gmail.com

PADMORE, Lynn Beverley. b 51. EMMTC. **d** 06 **p** 07. NSM Beaumont Leys *Leic* 06–09; TV Ascension TM 09–14; rtd 14; PtO *Nor* from 14. *Brightmore, 13 Clifton Way, Overstrand, Cromer NR27 0NG* T: (01263) 576720 E: lynn.padmore@hotmail.co.uk

PAGAN, Canon Keith Vivian. b 37. St Jo Coll Dur BA 60 MA 66. Chich Th Coll 60. **d** 62 **p** 63. C Clacton St Jas *Chelmsf* 62–64; C Wymondham *Nor* 64–70; P-in-c Guestwick 70–80; P-in-c Kettlestone 70–79; V Hindolveston 70–80; R Islay *Arg* 80–98; R Campbeltown 80–98; Miss to Seamen 80–98; Can St Jo Cathl Oban *Arg* 85–98; Can Cumbrae 85–98; Hon Can Cumbrae from 99; rtd 98; LtO *Arg* from 04. *Mariefield, Southend, Campbeltown PA28 6RW* T: (01586) 830310

PAGDEN (née TREWARTHA), Mrs Wendy Jane. b 59. Lon Bible Coll BA 91 Bulawayo Teacher Tr Coll CertEd 79. St Mellitus Coll MA 16. **d** 16 **p** 17. NSM Marks Tey and Aldham *Chelmsf* 16–19; NSM Stanway from 19. *6 Komodo Drive, Stanway, Colchester CO3 8DE* T: (01206) 844677 M: 07816-039832 E: revwendypagden@gmail.com *or* pioneer@stalbrights.org

PAGE, David. b 48. Bris Univ BA 70 Leic Univ MA 74 Southn Univ PGCE 74. St Jo Coll Nottm 81. **d** 83 **p** 84. C Morden *S'wark* 83–86; V Wimbledon St Luke 86–91; P-in-c Clapham Common St Barn 91–92; V 92–08; rtd 08; PtO *Chich* from 13. *Rye View, The Strand, Winchelsea TN36 4JY* T: (01797) 226524 E: david@ryeview.net

PAGE, Canon David James. b 62. Liv Univ BSc 83 Qu Coll Ox DPhil 87. Trin Coll Bris BA 93 MA 95. **d** 96 **p** 97. C Knutsford St Jo and Toft *Ches* 96–99; R Elworth and Warmingham 99–11; V Elworth from 11; RD Congleton 13–18; Hon Can Ches Cathl from 19. *The Rectory, 2 Taxmere Close, Sandbach CW11 1WT* T: (01270) 762415 E: vicar@stpeters-elworth.org.uk

PAGE, Gill Lydia. b 53. Bp Grosseteste Coll PGCE 91 Derby Lonsdale Coll BCombStuds 85 Sheff Univ BA 12 MA 18. Yorks Min Course 10. **d** 12 **p** 13. NSM Todmorden w Cornholme and Walsden *Leeds* 12–15; PtO *S'well* 15–16; NSM Clifton 16–19; rtd 19; PtO *S'well* from 19. *2 Pierson Street, Newark NG24 4JG* M: 07974-704374 E: gillpagetod@yahoo.co.uk

PAGE, Gillian Fiona. b 55. Hull Coll of Educn CertEd 76. Cranmer Hall Dur 08. **d** 10 **p** 11. C W Bolton *Man* 10–13; TV Walkden and Lt Hulton 13–21; rtd 21. *42 Keighley Road, Cowling, Keighley BD22 0BH* M: 07866-936323 E: gill91@btopenworld.com

PAGE, Mrs Heather. b 54. **d** 13 **p** 14. NSM Hadley and Wellington Ch Ch *Lich* 13–16; NSM Oakengates, Priors Lee and Wrockwardine Wood 16–17; NSM Cen Telford 17–19; rtd 20; PtO *Lich* from 20. *46 Appledore Gardens, Wellington, Telford TF1 1RR* T: (01952) 249165 E: h.page@blueyonder.co.uk

PAGE, John Jeremy. b 56. Keble Coll Ox BA 79 MA 82 New Coll Edin BD 86. Edin Th Coll 83. **d** 86 **p** 87. C Wetherby *Ripon* 86–89; TV Wrexham *St As* 89–92; Chapl Hymers Coll Hull 92–98; Chapl Charterhouse Sch Godalming 98–03; TR Hale w Badshot Lea *Guildf* 03–10; R Elstead 10–19; V Thursley 10–19; rtd 19; PtO *York* from 21. *Address withheld by request* E: john@padblack.co.uk

PAGE, Jonathan Michael. b 58. Ripon Coll Cuddesdon 97. **d** 99 **p** 00. C Littlemore *Ox* 99–02; V Chaddesden St Phil *Derby* 02–09; P-in-c Derby St Mark 07–09; V Chaddesden St Phil w Derby St Mark 09–10; RD Derby N 06–10; P-in-c Belper Ch Ch w Turnditch 10–13; V 13–21; C Ambergate and Heage 10–12; RD Duffield 10–18; P-in-c Hazelwood, Holbrook and Milford from 21; PtO *Eur* from 17. *Address temp unknown* E: fatherjpage@gmail.com

PAGE, Judy. b 42. Keele Univ DipEd 63 BA 63 Westmr Coll Ox BTh 02. TISEC 03. **d** 05 **p** 06. C Paisley H Trin and St Barn *Glas* 05–13; PtO *Win* from 14. *109B Priory Road, Southampton SO17 2JS* T: (023) 8032 1241 E: revjudypage@live.co.uk

PAGE, Lynda Christina. b 55. STETS 04. **d** 07 **p** 08. NSM Blackmoor and Whitehill *Portsm* 07–14; P-in-c Lyng, Sparham, Elsing, Bylaugh, Bawdeswell etc *Nor* 14–16; PtO from 17. *The Sycamores, 28 King's Lynn Road, Hunstanton PE36 5HT* T: (01485) 534605 M: 07790-494296 E: lyn.page@willow-bank.co.uk

PAGE, Canon Michael John. b 42. K Coll Lon BD 66 AKC 66. **d** 67 **p** 68. C Rawmarsh w Parkgate *Sheff* 67–72; C-in-c Gleadless Valley CD 72–74; TR Gleadless Valley 74–77; V Lechlade *Glouc* 77–86; RD Fairford 81–86; V Winchcombe, Gretton, Sudeley Manor etc 86–02; Hon Can Glouc Cathl 91–02; RD Winchcombe 94–99; Chapl E Glos NHS Trust 94–02; rtd 02; PtO *Sheff* 03–20. *18 Brocco Bank, Sheffield S11 8RR* T: 0114-266 3798 E: michael278@me.com

PAGE, Owen Richard. b 53. FIBMS 83. Linc Th Coll 89. **d** 91 **p** 92. C Gt Bookham *Guildf* 91–94; V Kings Heath *Pet* 94–99; TR Daventry, Ashby St Ledgers, Braunston etc 99–07; RD Daventry 00–07; ACUPA Link Officer 00–07; CUF Project Officer 00–05; Can Pet Cathl 07; V Todmorden *Wakef* 07–13; P-in-c Cornholme and Walsden 12–13; V Todmorden w Cornholme and Walsden *Leeds* 13–15; Asst Dir of Ords 09–15; AD Calder Valley 13–15; TR Clifton *S'well* 15–19; rtd 19; PtO *S'well* from 19. *2 Pierson Street, Newark NG24 4JG* M: 07980-639631 E: owenroage@yahoo.com

PAGE, Sean. b 58. All SS Cen for Miss & Min 17. **p** 18. OLM Collyhurst *Man* from 18; Chapl HM Pris Man from 20. *HM Prison Manchester, 1 Southall Street, Manchester M60 9AH* T: 0161-817 5600

PAGE, Canon Thomas William. b 57. Sarum & Wells Th Coll 84. **d** 87 **p** 88. C Caterham *S'wark* 87–91; C Cheam 91–95; P-in-c Cranham *Chelmsf* 95–04; R Chingford SS Pet and Paul 04–12; V Chelmsf Ascension 12–14; P-in-c Chelmsf All SS 14; V Chelmsf Ascension from 14; AD Chelmsf N 15–18; Dioc NSM Officer from 99; Hon Can Chelmsf Cathl from 15. *Ascension Vicarage, 57 Maltese Road, Chelmsford CM1 2PB* T: (01245) 269906 E: frtom1@priest.com

PAGE, Canon Trevor Melvyn. b 41. Dur Univ BA 63 Fitzw Coll Cam BA 67 MA 72. Westcott Ho Cam 64. **d** 67 **p** 68. C Millhouses H Trin *Sheff* 67–69; Chapl Sheff Univ 69–74; V Doncaster Intake 74–82; Can Res Sheff Cathl 82–00; Dioc Dir of In-Service Tr 82–95; Dioc Dir of Ords and Post-Ord Tr 82–00; R Bradfield 00–06; Hon Can Sheff Cathl 01–06; rtd 06; PtO *Sheff* 06–18. *39 Benty Lane, Sheffield S10 5NF* T: 0114-268 3879

PAGE, William George. b 42. Linc Th Coll 83. **d** 85 **p** 86. C Boston *Linc* 85–89; V Sibsey w Frithville 89–07; RD Holland E 95–97; rtd 07; PtO *York* from 08. *20 Marshall Drive, Pickering YO18 7JT* T: (01751) 476915 E: dunvicaring@btinternet.com

PAGE-CLARK, Howard David. b 53. Fitzw Coll Cam MA 77. **d** 97 **p** 98. OLM Lytchett Minster *Sarum* 97–10; OLM The Lytchetts and Upton from 10. *37 Gorse Lane, Poole BH16 5RR* T: (01202) 620239 E: hdpc@talktalk.net

PAGE DAVIES, David John. b 36. St Cath Soc Ox BA 58 MA 62. St D Coll Lamp 58. **d** 60 **p** 61. C Rhosddu *St As* 60–68; Chr Aid Area Sec (Glos, Herefords and Worcs) 68–85; Midl Regional Co-ord 78–85; Area Co-ord (Devon and Cornwall) 86–01; LtO *Truro* 86–01; PtO 01–09; rtd 01. *3 Chyenhal Cottages, Buryas Bridge, Penzance TR19 6AN* T: (01736) 732466 E: johnp-d@tiscali.co.uk

PAGE-TURNER, Canon Edward Gregory Ambrose Wilford. b 31. Qu Coll Birm 57. **d** 60 **p** 61. C Helmsley *York* 60–64; C Kensington St Phil Earl's Court *Lon* 64–67; C Walton-on-Thames *Guildf* 67–70; V Seend *Sarum* 70–71; V Seend and Bulkington 71–79; R Bladon w Woodstock *Ox* 79–87; P-in-c Begbroke 80–86; P-in-c Shipton-on-Cherwell 80–86; P-in-c Hampton Gay 80–85; RD Woodstock 84–87; P-in-c Wootton by Woodstock 85–87; R Patterdale *Carl* 87–89; R Askerswell, Loders and Powerstock *Sarum* 89–01; RD Lyme Bay 92–98; RD Beaminster 94–97; Can and Preb Sarum Cathl 99–01; rtd 01; PtO *Sarum* 01–18; B & W 02–05; *Eur* 02–06. *The Old School House, 9 School House Close, Beaminster DT8 3AH* T: (01308) 861410 E: canong.pageturner@btinternet.com

PAGET, Richard Campbell. b 54. Collingwood Coll Dur BA 76 Rob Coll Cam BA 87 MA 90. Ridley Hall Cam 85. **d** 88 **p** 89. Chapl Metrop Police *Lon* 89–92; C Gipsy Hill Ch Ch *S'wark* 88–92; R Chatham St Mary w St Jo *Roch* 92–98; P-in-c Brenchley 99–00; V from 00; RD Paddock Wood 06–10. *The Vicarage, 8 Broadoak, Brenchley, Tonbridge TN12 7NN* T: (01892) 722140

PAGET, Robert James Innes. b 35. AKC 59. **d** 60 **p** 61. C Attenborough w Bramcote *S'well* 60–63; C Cheltenham St Mark *Glouc* 63–72; P-in-c Pilsley *Derby* 72–73; TV N Wingfield, Pilsley and Tupton 73–89; R Pinxton 89–97; P-in-c Ambergate and Heage 94–00; PtO *Derby* 06–20. *1A Jeffries Lane, Crich, Matlock DE4 5DT* T: (01773) 852072

PAGET-WILKES, The Ven Michael Jocelyn James. b 41. ALCD 69. **d** 69 **p** 70. C Wandsworth All SS *S'wark* 69–74; V Hatcham St Jas 74–82; V Rugby St Matt *Cov* 82–90; Adn Warwick 90–09; rtd 09; PtO *Glouc* from 16. *64 Tarlton, Cirencester GL7 6PA* T: (01285) 770553 E: michael.pw@btinternet.com

PAILING, Canon Crispin Alexander. b 75. Qu Coll Ox BA 98 MA 01 Birm Univ PhD 08. Ripon Coll Cuddesdon BA 02. **d** 03 **p** 04. C Four Oaks *Birm* 03–06; P-in-c Perry Barr 06–10; V 10–14; AD Handsworth 13–14; R Liv Our Lady and St Nic from 14; Hon Can Liv Cathl from 19. *St Nicholas' House, 71 Woodlands Road, Aigburth, Liverpool L17 0AL* T: 0151-727 4872 *or* 236 5287 E: crispin.pailing@queens.oxon.org *or* rector@livpc.co.uk

PAILING, Canon Rowena Fay. b 77. Qu Coll Ox BA 99 MA 02 Birm Univ PhD 08. Ripon Coll Cuddesdon BA 02. **d** 03 **p** 04. C Four Oaks *Birm* 03–04; C Gravelly Hill 04–07; P-in-c Handsworth St Mich 07–12; Dir Past Studies Coll of Resurr Mirfield 12–18; PtO *Birm* 12–15; *Liv* from 14; Can Res Blackb Cathl from 18; Vice Dean from 19. *1 Cathedral Close, Blackburn BB1 5AA* E: missioner@blackburncathedral.co.uk

PAIN, Isaac Timothy. b 86. Southn Univ BA 09 PGCE 10. Oak Hill Th Coll BA 17. **d** 17 **p** 18. C Burgess Hill St Andr

Chich 17–20; P-in-c Cranfield and Hulcote w Salford St Alb from 20. *The Rectory, Court Road, Cranfield, Bedford MK43 0DR* M: 07738-301996 E: isaacpain@hotmail.com

✠**PAIN, The Rt Revd Richard Edward.** b 56. Bris Univ BA 79 Univ of Wales (Cardiff) BD 84. St Mich Coll Llan 81. d 84 p 85 c 13. C Caldicot Mon 84–86; P-in-c Cwmtillery 86–88; V 88–91; V Six Bells 88–91; V Risca 91–98; V Overmonnow w Wonastow and Michel Troy 98–03; V Monmouth w Overmonnow etc 03–08; Adn Mon 08–13; P-in-c Mamhilad w Monkswood and Glascoed Chapel 08–13; Warden of Ords 01–06; Can St Woolos Cathl 03–13; Bp Mon 13–19; rtd 19. *Address temp unknown*

PAINE, Alasdair David MacConnell. b 60. Trin Coll Cam BA 82 MA 86 Colorado State Univ MSc 84. Wycliffe Hall Ox 94. d 96 p 97. C Ex St Leon w H Trin 96–01; V Westbourne Ch Ch Chpl Win 02–11; V Cambridge H Sepulchre Ely from 11. *The Round Church Vicarage, Manor Street, Cambridge CB1 1LQ* T: (01223) 518218 E: alasdair.paine@stag.org

PAINE, Peter Stanley. b 46. K Coll Lon BD 69 AKC 69. Cuddesdon Coll 69. d 71 p 72. C Leeds St Aid Ripon 71–74; C Harrogate St Wilfrid 74–78; V Beeston Hill H Spirit 78–82; TV Seacroft 82–90; V Martham w Repps w Bastwick Nor 90–94; V Martham and Repps w Bastwick, Thurne etc 94–04; P-in-c Foremark and Repton w Newton Solney Derby 04–08; V 08–11; rtd 11; PtO Liv from 16. *Beachway House, 27 Stratford Close, Southport PR8 2RT* E: peterspaine@gmail.com

PAINE, Canon William Barry. b 58. CITC. d 84 p 85. C Glendermott D & R 84–86; C Lurgan St Jo D & D 86–88; I Kilbarron w Rossnowlagh and Drumholm D & R 88–91; CF 91–00; I Tynan w Middletown and Aghavilly Arm 00–09; I Ballinderry, Tamlaght and Arboe from 09; Can Arm Cathl from 17. *The Rectory, 10 Brookmount Road, Cookstown BT80 0BB* T: (028) 7941 8500 E: bpaine.888@hotmail.co.uk

PAINTER, Christopher Mark. b 65. Cranmer Hall Dur. d 00 p 01. C Melksham Sarum 00–03; Chapl Wilts and Swindon Healthcare NHS Trust 02–03; TV Eccles Man 03–07; PtO Ches 13–14; NSM Hale Barns w Ringway 14–15; P-in-c Calstock Truro 15–17; P-in-c St Dominic, Landulph and St Mellion w Pillaton 15–17; R Tamar Valley from 17; RD E Wivelshire from 17. *Oaklands House, Albaston, Gunnislake PL18 9EZ* E: revchrispainter@gmail.com

PAINTER, The Ven David Scott. b 44. Worc Coll Ox BA 68 MA 72 LTCL 65. Cuddesdon Coll 68. d 70 p 71. C Plymouth St Andr w St Paul and St Geo Ex 70–73; Chapl Plymouth Poly 71–73; C St Marylebone All SS Lon 73–76; Abp's Dom Chapl and Dir of Ords Cant 76–80; V Roehampton H Trin S'wark 80–91; RD Wandsworth 85–90; PV Westmr Abbey 81–91; Can Res and Treas S'wark Cathl 91–00; Dioc Dir of Ords 91–00; Adn Oakham and Can Res Pet Cathl 00–11; rtd 11; Hon C Towcester Deanery 11–17; R Brington w Whilton and Norton etc Pet 17–19; LtO from 19. *3 Meeting Lane, Towcester NN12 6JX* T: (01327) 438392 M: 07976-687059

PAINTING, Stephen Nigel. b 60. Trin Coll Bris 01. d 03 p 04. C Heanton Punchardon w Marwood Ex 03–08; TV Beaconsfield Ox 08–11; Chapl Lee Abbey 11–14; TV Wellington and Distr B & W 14–16; PtO Ex 17–18; P-in-c Heanton Punchardon, Marwood and W Down from 18. *The Rectory, Heanton, Barnstaple EX31 4DG* T: (01271) 812605

PAIRMAN, David Drummond. b 47. GGSM CertEd. Chich Th Coll 82. d 84 p 85. C Cowes St Mary Portsm 84–87; C Hawkchurch Sarum 87–88; C Marshwood Vale 87–95; rtd 95. *Chestnut Cottage, Old Pinn Lane, Exeter EX1 3RF* T: (01392) 464488

PAISEY, Gerald Herbert John. b 31. Wm Booth Memorial Coll 51 Leic Univ CertEd 62 Nottm Univ DipAdEd 70 MPhil 77 Lanc Univ MA 78 K Coll Lon PhD 91. St Alb Minl Tr Scheme 80. d 88 p 90. NSM Montrose Bre 88–90; NSM Inverbervie 88–90; Lect Robert Gordon Univ Ab 89–97; P-in-c Stonehaven and Catterline Bre 90–01; rtd 01; Tutor Open Univ 90–05; PtO Bre 03–07; LtO Edin from 08. *40 South Middleton, Uphall, Broxburn EH52 5GB* T: (01506) 865937

PAISEY, Canon Jeremy Mark. b 58. Aber Univ LLB 81 Solicitor 83. Coates Hall Edin 92. d 94 p 95. C Turriff Ab 94–97; C Buckie 94–97; C Banff 94–97; C Cuminestown 94–97; C Portsoy 94–97; P-in-c Buckie from 97; C Portsoy 97–16; P-in-c Banff from 98; Can St Andr Cathl from 08. *All Saints' Rectory, 14 Cluny Square, Buckie AB56 1HA* T: (01542) 832312 M: 07817-261435 E: jpaisey@aol.com

PAISLEY, Canon Samuel Robinson (Robin). b 51. Man Univ BSc 72. Edin Th Coll BD 91. d 91 p 92. C St Mary's Cathl Glas 91–95; P-in-c Bishopbriggs 95–06; Teaching Consultant Glas Univ 95–99; Chapl Stobhill NHS Trust 95–99; Bp's Adv in Min Glas 99–07; R Dumfries 06–16; Chapl NHS Dumfries and Galloway 06–16; rtd 16; Hon Can St Mary's Cathl Glas from 16; PtO

16–18; LtO from 18. *30 Grampian Way, Bearsden, Glasgow G61 4RW* M: 07464-234308 E: essrpg@gmail.com

PAKENHAM, Kia Louise. b 73. RGN 95. SCRTP 15. d 18 p 19. NSM Wonersh w Blackheath Guildf from 18. *Goblins, Elmbridge Road, Cranleigh GU6 8NW* T: (01483) 277919 M: 07971-077664 E: kiapakenham@icloud.com

PALAIRET, Agnes Ka Yee. b 84. Aber Univ BSc 06 MSc 07. Trin Coll Bris 17. d 19 p 20. C Bris St Mary Redcliffe w Temple etc from 19. *1A Colston Parade, Bristol BS1 6RA* M: 07727-275157 E: aggy.palairet@stmaryredcliffe.co.uk

PALIN, Elizabeth. b 62. Hull Univ BA 85 Birm Univ MA 11. WEMTC 08. d 11 p 12. Dir Glenfall Ho Glouc 08–13; NSM N Cheltenham 11–13; C 13–16; TV 16–18; TV Stroudwater from 18. *St Mary's House, The Street, Frampton on Severn, Gloucester GL2 7ED* T: (01452) 741147 M: 07807-113858 E: tv1stroudwater@gmail.com

PALK, Deirdre Elizabeth Pauline. b 41. Reading Univ BA 63 Lon Univ MA 94 Leic Univ PhD 02 AIL 77 FIOSH 96 FRHistS 06. S'wark Ord Course 81. dss 84 d 87. Wanstead H Trin Hermon Hill Chelmsf 84–88; Hon Par Dn 87–88; Hon Par Dn Walthamstow St Pet 88–93; Hon Chapl UPA Projects 93–97; Tutor NTMTC 97–01; rtd 01. *3 Ashdon Close, Woodford Green IG8 0EF* T: (020) 8498 0649

PALLANT, Canon Roger Frank. b 35. Trin Coll Cam BA 57 MA 61. Wells Th Coll 57. d 59 p 60. C Stafford St Mary Lich 59–62; C Ipswich St Mary le Tower St E 62–65; Dioc Youth Chapl 62–65; Development Officer C of E Youth Coun 65–70; Hon C Putney St Mary S'wark 66–71; Org Sec New Syn Gp 70–71; R Hintlesham w Chattisham St E 71–80; V Ipswich All Hallows 80–88; Hon Can St E Cathl 85–00; P-in-c Sproughton w Burstall 88–00; Dioc Officer for OLM 88–00; RD Samford 93–99; rtd 00; PtO St E from 00. *163 Fircroft Road, Ipswich IP1 6PT* T: (01473) 461148

PALLENT, Ian. b 70. Newc Poly BA 91. Ridley Hall Cam 05. d 07 p 08. C Bayston Hill Lich 07–10; R Jersey St Ouen w St Geo Win from 10. *The Rectory, La Route du Marais, St Ouen, Jersey JE3 2GG* T: (01534) 481800 or 485686 M: 07870-630433 E: ianpallent@hotmail.com

PALLETT, Canon Ian Nigel. b 59. Leeds Univ BA 80. Linc Th Coll 81. d 84 p 85. C Halesowen Worc 84–88; C Mansfield Woodhouse S'well 88–91; R Morton and Stonebroom Derby 91–98; P-in-c Heanor 98–01; V 01–03; P-in-c Dingwall Mor 03–11; P-in-c Strathpeffer 03–11; R Dingwall 11–16; R Strathpeffer 11–16; P-in-c Invergordon St Ninian 15–16; Chapl NHS Grampian from 16; Can St Andr Cathl Inverness Mor from 09. *23 Stuart Street, Ardersier, Inverness IV2 7RS* T: 03454-566000 or (01667) 460030 E: pallett3000@btinternet.com

PALLIS, Mrs Maria. b 60. NOC 96. d 99 p 00. C Chapel Allerton Ripon 99–03; P-in-c Collingham w Harewood 03–11; P-in-c Spofforth w Kirk Deighton 07–11; V Banstead Guildf 11–20; RD Epsom 14; rtd 20. *10A Brewery Lane, Billingborough, Sleaford NG34 0LN* E: mariapallis@hotmail.com

PALMER, Abigail Louise. b 79. Leeds Univ BA 01 PGCE 02. St Hild Coll 15. d 17 p 18. C Pannal w Beckwithshaw Leeds 17–21; V Lindley from 21. *2 Lidget Street, Huddersfield HD3 3JB* E: abbie.palmer@leeds.anglican.org

PALMER, Alister Gordon. b 46. Univ of Tasmania BA 73 DipEd 74. Trin Coll Bris 76 Ridley Hall Cam 78. d 80 p 81. C Patchway Bris 80–83; C Bushbury Lich 83–86; V Wednesfield Heath 86–93; NSM Independent Ch Community Work 93–98; Dioc Officer for Min Tas Australia 98–02; Dir Angl Miss 99–02; C Smestow Vale Lich 02–03; V Knowle St Barn Bris 03–07; P-in-c Inns Court H Cross 05–07; V Filwood Park 07–13; rtd 13; PtO Bris from 18. *4 Rowberrow, Bristol BS14 0AD* T: (01275) 832208 E: agpal46@hotmail.co.uk

PALMER, Andrew Richmond. b 84. St Chad's Coll Dur BA 06. Oak Hill Th Coll MA 14. d 14 p 15. C Hampstead St Jo Downshire Hill Prop Chpl Lon 14–18; PtO S'wark from 18. *Christ Church Balham, 15 Chestnut Grove, London SW12 8JA* T: (020) 3302 6640 M: 07866-584293 E: andy.palmer@live.com

PALMER, Angus Douglas. b 40. St Chad's Coll Dur BA 62. d 63 p 64. C Wallsend St Pet Newc 63–66; C Newc H Cross 66–69; C Bottesford Linc 69–70; R Penicuik Edin 70–84; R W Linton 77–84. *6 Hackworth Gardens, Wylam NE41 8EJ* T: (01661) 853786 E: angusandjanet@gmail.com

PALMER, Antony Paul Steven. b 84. Ox Brookes Univ BA 06. St Mellitus Coll 13. d 16 p 17. C Chandler's Ford Win 16–19; V Bitterne from 19. *Bitterne Vicarage, 2 Bursledon Road, Southampton SO19 7LW* T: (023) 8044 3770 M: 07590-111838 E: tony@bitterneparish.org

PALMER, Canon Christopher John Ingamells. b 71. d 98 p 99. C Emscote Cov 98–02; TV Mortlake w E Sheen S'wark 02–10; AD Richmond and Barnes 05–10; TR Merton Priory

10–18; Can Res and Chan Ex Cathl from 18. *Exeter Cathedral Office, 1 The Cloisters, Exeter EX1 1HS* T: (01392) 255573

PALMER, David Edward. *See* HAGAN-PALMER, David Edward

PALMER, Derek James. b 54. Man Univ BA 77. Qu Coll Birm 77. **d** 79 **p** 80. C Leek *Lich* 79–83; CF 83–92; R Riviera Beach St Geo USA 92–95; C S Ockendon and Belhus Park *Chelmsf* 95–98; V Walthamstow St Mich 98–00; Chapl Salford Univ *Man* 00–06; AD Salford 02–03; P-in-c Droylsden St Andr 06–09; TR Oldham 09–11; V Oldham St Mary w St Pet from 11; Bp's Adv on New Relig Movements from 02. *The Rectory, Prince Charlie Street, Oldham OL1 4HJ* T: 0161-633 1560 M: 07979-121635 E: vicarofoldham@gmail.com

PALMER, Elizabeth. *See* BLATCHLEY, Elizabeth

PALMER, Graham. b 31. Em Coll Cam BA 53 MA 57. Qu Coll Birm 56. **d** 58 **p** 59. C Camberwell St Giles *S'wark* 58–61; C Kilburn St Aug *Lon* 61–67; P-in-c Fulham St Alb 67–73; V 73–92; V Fulham St Alb w St Aug 92–97; rtd 97; PtO *Lon* 97–13. *7 Wellington Court, 116 Knightsbridge, London SW1X 7PL* T: (020) 7584 4036

PALMER, Hugh. b 50. Pemb Coll Cam BA 72 MA 76. Ridley Hall Cam 73. **d** 76 **p** 77. C Heigham H Trin *Nor* 76–80; Bp's Chapl for Tr and Miss 80–84; C St Helen Bishopsgate w St Andr Undershaft etc *Lon* 85–95; C Fulwood *Sheff* 95–97; V 97–05; Hon Can Sheff Cathl 01–05; R Langham Place All So *Lon* 05–20; Chapl to The Queen 12–20; rtd 20; PtO *Lon* from 20; *Glouc* from 20. *63 Brighton Road, Cheltenham GL52 6BA* M: 07576-418081 E: hghp50@gmail.com

✠**PALMER, The Rt Revd Ian Stanley.** b 50. K Coll Lon BD 71. Cranmer Hall Dur 73. **d** 75 **p** 76 **c** 13. C Huyton St Mich *Liv* 75–78; Chapl Dur Univ 78–83; V Collierley w Annfield Plain 83–90; Dir Evang Newc Australia 90–92; R Belmont N and Redhead 93–00; Adn Upper Hunter and R Muswellbrook 00–05; R Queanbeyan 05–13; Adn Chapl 09–13; Adn S Canberra and Queanbeyan 09–13; Bp Bathurst 13–19; rtd 19. *50/123 Boundary Road, Mount Duneed VIC 3217, Australia* M: (0061) 41-124 2596 E: palmeris50@fastmail.fm

PALMER, Mrs Jane Alexandra. b 83. Univ of Wales (Ban) BA 05 Homerton Coll Cam PGCE 06. St Jo Sch of Miss Nottm MA 16. **d** 16 **p** 17. C Trowbridge St Jas and Keevil *Sarum* 16–19; V Atworth w Shaw and Whitley from 19. *The Vicarage, Corsham Road, Shaw, Melksham SN12 8EH* M: 07530-513243 E: revjanepalmer@gmail.com

PALMER, John Richard Henry. b 29. AKC 52. **d** 53 **p** 54. C Englefield Green *Guildf* 53–57; P-in-c Brewarrina Australia 57–62; C Wareham w Arne *Sarum* 62–63; PC Derby St Jo 63–66; Chapl Holloway Sanatorium Virginia Water 66–70; Chapl Brookwood Hosp Woking 70–94; rtd 94; PtO *Truro* from 94. *Lightning Ridge, Pentreath Road, The Lizard, Helston TR12 7NY* T: (01326) 290654

PALMER, Judith Angela. b 47. Bris Univ MB, ChB 71. NOC 02. **d** 05 **p** 06. NSM Strensall *York* 05–14; PtO from 14. *6 Portisham Place, Strensall, York YO32 5AZ* T: (01904) 613356 E: j.palmer@phonecoop.coop

PALMER, Mrs Julia Elizabeth. b 57. Hull Univ BA 80. St Jo Coll Nottm MA 98. **d** 99 **p** 00. C Snodland All SS w Ch Ch *Roch* 99–03; P-in-c Sutton Bonington w Normanton-on-Soar *S'well* 03–08; P-in-c Sutton in Ashfield St Mary 08–11; PtO *Lon* 18–19; V W Acton St Martin from 19. *St Martin's Vicarage, 25 Birch Grove, London W3 9SP* M: 07939-043959 E: juliapalmer12@gmail.com

PALMER, Mrs June Ann. b 42. **d** 11 **p** 12. OLM Elmton and Whitwell *Derby* 11–14; OLM E Scarsdale from 14. *22 Field Drive, Shirebrook, Mansfield NG20 8BN* T: (01623) 744835

PALMER, Mrs Kathleen. b 50. **d** 19 **p** 20. NSM Brandon *St E* from 19. *Address temp unknown* E: palm427@aol.com

PALMER, Kay. b 52. **d** 18 **p** 19. NSM Ipswich St Mary at Stoke w St Pet and St Fran *St E* 18–21; NSM Ipswich St Mary Stoke from 21. *Address temp unknown* E: revkay@switmparish.org.uk

PALMER, Kevin Anthony. b 59. St Steph Ho Ox. **d** 01 **p** 02. C Tunstall *Lich* 01–04; R Wednesbury St Jas and St Jo 04–13; V Longton St Mary and St Chad from 13; CMP 02–20. *St Mary and St Chad's Presbytery, 269 Anchor Road, Stoke-on-Trent ST3 5DN* T: (01782) 313142 E: frkevinpalmer@live.co.uk

PALMER, Marc Richard. b 72. St Jo Coll Dur BA 96. Cranmer Hall Dur 93 Qu Foundn Birm 96. **d** 98 **p** 99. C Chester le Street *Dur* 98–03; TV Bensham 03–08; V Bensham and Teams 08–10; V Nor St Mary Magd w St Jas 10–18; P-in-c Drayton from 18. *The Rectory, 46 School Road, Drayton, Norwich NR8 6EF* E: revmarcpalmer@outlook.com

PALMER, Marion Denise. b 42. Open Univ BA 82 SRN 64 SCM 66. Linc Th Coll 84. **dss** 86 **d** 87 **p** 94. Poplar *Lon* 86–90; Par Dn 87–90; Par Dn Gillingham St Mary *Roch* 90–94; C 94–96; C Farnborough 96–02; Par Dn *St E* from 04. *14 Prestwick Avenue, Felixstowe IP11 9LF* T: (01394) 671588

PALMER, Canon Maureen Florence. b 38. Qu Eliz Coll Lon BSc 60 PhD 64. Ripon Coll Cuddesdon. **dss** 85 **d** 87 **p** 94.

Tupsley *Heref* 85–88; C 87–88; Par Dn Talbot Village *Sarum* 88–91; Chapl Birm Cathl 91–96; Can Pastor and Can Res Guildf Cathl 96–06; Sub-Dean 99–06; rtd 06; PtO *Heref* from 06. *28A Green Street, Hereford HR1 2QG* T: (01432) 353771 E: palmer349@btinternet.com

PALMER, Michael Christopher. b 43. MBE 00. AKC 67 CQSW 76. **d** 68 **p** 69. C Easthampstead *Ox* 68–71; Miss to Seamen 71–73; Hong Kong 73; LtO *Ox* 76–79; LtO *Truro* 79–83; Dioc Soc Resp Adv 83–98; Bp's Dom Chapl 85–87; V Devoran 87–98; rtd 98; PtO *Truro* 98–08; *Ox* 08–10; *Chich* from 10. *5 Little Drove, Little Drove Mews, Singleton, Chichester PO18 0FX* M: 07717-222385 E: nettiepalmer@hotmail.co.uk

PALMER, Nigel Shaun. b 50. Ch Ch Ox BA 71 MA 84. St Steph Ho Ox BA 15. **d** 17 **p** 18. NSM Kentish Town *Lon* 17–20; NSM Croydon St Mich w St Jas *S'wark* 20–21; PtO *Lon* from 20; *Nor* from 21. *The Manor House, 13 Park Vista, London SE10 9LZ* M: 07710-423790 E: nigel1palmer@btinternet.com

PALMER, Mrs Patricia. b 51. STETS. **d** 09 **p** 10. NSM Basingstoke *Win* from 09. *97 Packenham Road, Basingstoke RG21 8YA* T: (01256) 412986 E: revpat@ntlworld.com

PALMER, Paul. b 62. ERMC 17. **d** 21. NSM Croxley Green All SS *St Alb* from 21. *58 Clarkfield, Mill End, Rickmansworth WD3 8FL* M: 07740-871289 E: revpaulpalmer@gmail.com

PALMER, Steven Roy. b 51. Birm Univ BSc 71. WMMTC 91. **d** 94 **p** 95. C Sheldon *Birm* 94–97; P-in-c Duddeston w Nechells 97–99; V Nechells 99–03; R Billing *Pet* 03–16; RD Northn 06–07; rtd 16; PtO *Birm* from 16. *63 Steyning Road, Birmingham B26 1JE* T: 0121-707 4677 E: stevenpalmer951@btinternet.com

PAMMENT, Derek. b 55. Staffs Univ MBA 98. Qu Foundn (Course) 16. **d** 19 **p** 20. NSM Trentham *Lich* from 19. *Stag Villa, Milwich, Stafford ST18 0EG* T: (01889) 505190 M: 07977-022558 E: modernisation@btopenworld.com

PAMPHILON-GREEN, Sister Phaedra Kay. b 64. Anglia Ruskin Univ MA 12. St Mellitus Coll 12. **d** 14 **p** 15. C Gainsborough and Morton *Linc* 14–17; R Bletchingley and Nutfield *S'wark* from 17. *The Rectory, Outwood Lane, Bletchingley, Redhill RH1 4LR* M: 07775-954144 E: pamphilon@gmail.com

PAMPLIN, Canon Richard Lawrence. b 46. Lon Univ BScEng 68 Dur Univ BA 75 NY Th Sem DMin 85. Wycliffe Hall Ox 75. **d** 77 **p** 78. C Greenside *Dur* 77–80; C Sheff St Barn and St Mary 80–84; R Wombwell 84–90; P-in-c Madeley *Heref* 90–91; TR 91–01; Chapl Berne w Neuchâtel *Eur* 01–07; Can Gib Cathl 04–07; Chapl Viña del Mar w Valparaiso Chile 07–12; rtd 12; PtO *Cant* from 12; *Eur* from 18. *126 Downs Road, Folkestone CT19 5PX* T: (01303) 779126 E: richard.l.pamplin@gmail.com

PAMPLIN, Samantha Jane. *See* FERGUSON, Samantha Jane

PANG, Mrs Heather Marian. b 46. St Jo Coll Nottm BA 08. SNWTP 09. **d** 11 **p** 12. NSM Gt Saughall *Ches* 11–20; rtd 20; PtO *Ches* from 20. *20 Oakland Drive, Wirral CH49 6JL* T: 0151-677 2690 E: wingonheather@gmail.com

PANG, Wing-On. b 43. Manitoba Univ BA 67 SOAS Lon MA 70. Oak Hill Th Coll 85. **d** 87 **p** 88. C Pennycross *Ex* 87–91; TV Mildenhall *St E* 91–96; Assoc P Kowloon St Andr Hong Kong 96–08; rtd 08; PtO *Ches* from 09. *20 Oakland Drive, Wirral CH49 6JL* T: 0151-677 2690 E: wingonheather@gmail.com

PANGBOURNE, John Godfrey. b 36. Ridley Hall Cam 82. **d** 84 **p** 85. C Ashtead *Guildf* 84–88; V Ore Ch Ch *Chich* 88–03; rtd 03; PtO *Ex* 04–06; Hon C Ottery St Mary, Alfington, W Hill, Tipton etc from 06. *Meon Croft, Toadpit Lane, West Hill, Ottery St Mary EX11 1TR* T: (01404) 812393

PANKHURST, Ian Charles. b 50. Trin Coll Cam BA 72 Lon Inst of Educn PGCE 88. SAOMC 01. **d** 04 **p** 05. C Watford St Luke *St Alb* 04–10; P-in-c Watford St Andr 10–15; V from 13. *2 Albert Road North, Watford WD17 1QE* T: (01923) 249139 E: ian_pankhurst@btinternet.com

PANTER, The Ven Richard James Graham. b 48. Oak Hill Th Coll 73. **d** 76 **p** 77. C Rusholme H Trin *Man* 76–80; C Toxteth St Cypr w Ch Ch *Liv* 80–85; V Clubmoor 85–96; P-in-c Litherland St Jo and St Jas 96–02; AD Bootle 99–02; V Orrell Hey St Jo and St Jas 02–11; Adn Liv 02–17; rtd 17. *115 Papillon Drive, Liverpool L9 9HL* T: 0151-705 2154

PANTING, Nigel Roger. b 47. St Pet Coll Ox BA 69 PGCE 70. Local Minl Tr Course 06. **d** 11. NSM Ruskington Gp *Linc* 11–13; NSM N Lafford Gp from 13. *The Cottage, Roxholm, Sleaford NG34 8NE* T: (01526) 832020 M: 07866-808737 E: nigelpanting@yahoo.co.uk

PANTLING, Rosemary Caroline. b 60. Ex Coll Ox BA 83 MA 89 Anglia Poly Univ MA 03 Birm Univ PGCE 84. EAMTC 98. **d** 01 **p** 02. NSM Bishop's Tachbrook *Cov* 01–08; P-in-c Cubbington 08–10; PtO 10–16; NSM Lillington and Old Milverton from 16; Chapl S Warks Gen Hosps NHS

Trust from 16. *22 Touchstone Road, Heathcote, Warwick CV34 6EE* T: (01926) 316597 E: revrosyp@gmail.com

PANTON, Alan Edward. b 45. K Coll Lon BD 67 AKC 67. d 68 p 69. C Eltham St Jo *S'wark* 68–73; C Horley 73–78; V Dallington *Pet* 78–07; rtd 07; PtO *Pet* from 09. *12B The Avenue, Dallington, Northampton NN5 7AN*

PANTRY, John Richard. b 46. Oak Hill NSM Course 90. d 93 p 94. NSM Alresford *Chelmsf* 93–04; NSM W w E Mersea 04–10; NSM W w E Mersea, Peldon, Gt and Lt Wigborough 10–18; PtO 18–21. *48 Empress Avenue, West Mersea, Colchester CO5 8EX* T/F: (01206) 386910 E: johnpantry@outlook.com

PAPADOPULOS, The Very Revd Nicholas Charles. b 66. G&C Coll Cam BA 88 MA 92 Barrister-at-Law (Middle Temple) 90. Ripon Coll Cuddesdon. d 99 p 00. C Portsea N End St Mark *Portsm* 99–02; Bp's Dom Chapl *Sarum* 02–07; Hon Chapl 07–10; V Pimlico St Pet w Westmr Ch Ch *Lon* 07–13; Can Res Cant Cathl 13–18; Dir IME 4-7 13–18; Dean Sarum from 18. *The Deanery, 7 The Close, Salisbury SP1 2EF* T: (01722) 555110 M: 07903-620018 E: n.papadopulos@salcath.co.uk

PAPE, David. b 54. d 98 p 99. OLM S'wark St Geo w St Alphege and St Jude from 98; OLM Waterloo St Jo w St Andr from 98. *10 Stopher House, Webber Street, London SE1 0RE* T: (020) 7928 3503 M: 07986-099959 E: revpape@hotmail.co.uk

PAPWORTH, Daniel John. b 69. Plymouth Poly BSc 90. Trin Coll Bris BA 98 MA 00. d 99 p 00. C Galbfa *Llan* 99–02; PtO *B & W* 03–04; Asst Chapl Dudley Gp of Hosps NHS Trust 04–07; Chapl R Devon and Ex NHS Foundn Trust 07–08; TV N Cheltenham *Glouc* 08–13; PtO from 13; *Worc* 14–17; *Bris* 15–19. *7 Campden Road, Cheltenham GL51 6AA* T: (01242) 575649 E: papworth@gmail.com

PAPWORTH, Miss Shirley Marjorie. b 33. CA Tr Coll. d 88 p 94. Par Dn Hornchurch H Cross *Chelmsf* 88–93; rtd 93; Chapl Havering Primary Care Trust 93–08; NSM Hornchurch St Andr *Chelmsf* 93–08; PtO from 08. *14 Paines Brook Court, 14 Paines Brook Way, Romford RM3 9JN* T: (01708) 370177

PARBURY, Mrs Heather Christina Winifred. b 56. d 01 p 02. C Long Compton, Whichford and Barton-on-the-Heath *Cov* 01–05; C Barcheston 01–05; C Cherington w Stourton 01–05; C Wolford w Burmington 01–05; TV Cherwell Valley *Ox* 05–08; P-in-c Pangbourne w Tidmarsh and Sulham 08–10; R 10–20; AD Bradfield 17–20; Chapl MU 10–20; rtd 20; Hon C Brailes *Cov* from 20; Hon C Sutton under Brailes from 20; Hon C Tysoe w Oxhill and Whatcote from 20. *Address temp unknown* E: parbury@btinternet.com

PARE, Stephen Charles. b 53. Sussex Univ BEd 75. St Mich Coll Llan 78. d 80 p 81. C Cardiff St Jo *Llan* 80–83; P-in-c Marcross w Monknash and Wick 83; TV Llantwit Major 83–91; V Penmark w Porthkerry 91–06; P-in-c Llansantffraid, Bettws and Aberkenfig 06–18; Chapl Cardiff Wales Airport 93–06; rtd 18. *24 Davis Avenue, Bryncethin, Bridgend CF32 9JJ* E: scpare@gmail.com

PARES, John. b 57. Bedf Coll Lon BA 79. Westcott Ho Cam 08. d 10 p 11. C Diss *Nor* 10–14; P-in-c Pokesdown St Jas *Win* 14–21; rtd 21. *Swallow Cottage, Offham, Lewes BN7 3QD* M: 07972-075459 E: j.pares@virginmedia.com

PARFFETT, Allan John. b 51. Open Univ BA 97 CQSW 76. Qu Coll Birm MA 00. d 98 p 99. C Hall Green Ascension *Birm* 98–00; Soc Worker 00–09; rtd 09. *20 Kiln Close, Corfe Mullen, Wimborne BH21 3UR* T: (01202) 690164

PARFITT, Anthony Colin. b 44. Ox Univ Inst of Educn CertEd 66 Open Univ BA 71 Plymouth Univ MPhil 84. SWMTC 93. d 96 p 97. NSM Langport Area *B & W* 96–00; NSM Bruton and Distr 01–06; PtO 07–18; *Sarum* 16–21. *Woodside, 13 Ashton Rise, Hilperton, Trowbridge BA14 7QZ* T: (01225) 356193 M: 07930-144522 E: tonyparfitt1@gmail.com

PARFITT, Brian John. b 49. Ex Coll Ox BA 71 MA 76. Wycliffe Hall Ox 71. d 74 p 75. C Newport St Mark *Mon* 74–78; R Blaina 78–83; R Blaina and Nantyglo 83–86; Chapl Blaina and Distr Hosp Gwent 83–86; Regional Consultant (W Midlands and Wales) CPAS 86–95; V Magor w Redwick and Undy *Mon* 95–98; TR Magor 98–06; Local Min Officer *Glouc* 06–14; P-in-c Highnam, Lassington, Rudford, Tibberton etc 14–15; rtd 15; PtO *Win* from 16. *11 Eynham Avenue, Southampton SO19 5LA* T: (023) 8044 7962 M: 07847-359062 E: brianparfitt@btinternet.com

PARFITT, David George. b 65. De Montfort Univ Leic BA 87 Bris Univ MA 12. Wycliffe Hall Ox BTh 95. d 95 p 96. C Malpas *Mon* 95–98; C Bassaleg 98–00; TV 00–01; V Malpas 01–16; rtd 16. *c/o Crockford, Church House, 27 Great Smith Street, London SW1P 3AZ*

PARFITT, George Rudolf William. b 54. WMMTC 96. d 99 p 00. OLM Highnam, Lassington, Rudford, Tibberton etc *Glouc* 99–08; NSM Hardwicke and Elmore w Longney from 08. *66 Holbeach Drive, Kingsway, Quedgeley, Gloucester GL2 2BF* T: (01452) 728180 E: george.parfitt@btinternet.com

PARFITT, Mrs Janet Lesley. b 49. St Hilda's Coll Ox BA 70 MA 73. WEMTC 12. d 16. NSM Bitterne *Win* 16–20; PtO from 20. *11 Eynham Avenue, Southampton SO19 5LA* T: (023) 8044 7962 E: janetparfitt1@btinternet.com

PARFITT, Preb John Hubert. b 29. Southn Univ MA 72 BPhil. Qu Coll Birm 78. d 80 p 81. C Fladbury, Wyre Piddle and Moor *Worc* 80–82; C Malvern Link w Cowleigh 82; V Hanley Castle, Hanley Swan and Welland 82–83; Dir RE *B & W* 84–93; Preb Wells Cathl 85–05; rtd 93; PtO *B & W* 93–14; *Sarum* 06–17; Master Hugh Sexey's Hosp Bruton 95–05; PtO *B & W* 15–18. *3 Willow Farm Cottages, Brister End, Yetminster, Sherborne DT9 6NH* T: (01935) 873260

PARFITT, Susan Mary. b 42. Bris Univ BA 63 CertEd 68. Bris Minl Tr Scheme 82. dss 84 d 87 p 94. Assoc Dir of Ords *Bris* 84–86; CME Officer 87–91; Dir Past Care and Counselling *S'wark* 91–01; rtd 01; PtO *Bris* from 02. *Garden Cottage, Rectory Gardens, Bristol BS10 7AQ*

PARISH, Mrs Mary Eileen. b 48. Nottm Univ BA 70. STETS BTh 98. d 98 p 99. NSM Worthing Ch the King *Chich* 98–08; NSM Worthing St Matt 08–16; rtd 16; PtO *Chich* from 16. *The Heritage, 10 Winchester Road, Worthing BN11 4DJ* T: (01903) 236909 E: frmary@hotmail.co.uk

PARISH, Nicholas Anthony. b 58. Oak Hill Th Coll BA 84 Kingston Univ MA 97. Ridley Hall Cam 84. d 86 p 87. C Eltham H Trin *S'wark* 86–89; C Barnes St Mary 89–91; V Streatham St Paul 91–96; Ind Chapl *Ox* 96–07; P-in-c Bracknell 07–14; AD 04–12; Hon Can Ch Ch 08–14; P-in-c Epsom St Martin *Guildf* 14–16; V from 16. *35 Burgh Heath Road, Epsom KT17 4LP* E: nick.parish@ntlworld.com

PARISH, Canon Stephen Richard. b 49. Liv Univ MTh 05. Oak Hill Th Coll 74. d 77 p 78. C Chadderton Ch Ch *Man* 77–81; C Chell Lich 81–82; TV 82–88; V Warrington St Ann *Liv* 88–14; P-in-c Warrington H Trin 06–14; V Warrington H Trin and St Ann 14–15; Hon Can Liv Cathl 14–15; rtd 15; PtO *Liv* from 16. *26 Leamington Close, Warrington WA5 3PY* T: (01925) 711830 E: bloovee@outlook.com

PARK, Christopher John. b 62. Sheff Poly BA 83. Cranmer Hall Dur 00. d 02 p 03. C Didsbury St Jas and Em *Man* 02–08; P-in-c Alne *York* 08–17; P-in-c Brafferton w Pilmoor, Myton-on-Swale 08–17; C Huntington from 17. *402 Huntington Road, York YO31 9HU* E: pastaparko@parkfamily.me.uk

PARK, Canon John Charles. b 55. St Pet Coll Ox BA 77 St Mary's Coll Newc PGCE 81. Cranmer Hall Dur 00. d 02 p 03. C Morpeth *Newc* 02–06; R Bothal and Pegswood w Longhirst from 06; AD Morpeth from 13; Hon Can Newc Cathl from 17. *Bothal Rectory, Longhirst Road, Pegswood, Morpeth NE61 6XF* T: (01670) 510793 E: johnp2910@gmx.co.uk

PARK, Tarjei Erling Alan. b 64. W Lon Inst of HE BA 88 Lanc Univ MA 89 Pemb Coll Ox DPhil 96. Ripon Coll Cuddesdon 92. d 94 p 95. C Lancaster St Mary w St John and St Anne *Blackb* 94–98; V Enfield St Mich *Lon* 98–01; Asst Dir Post-Ord Tr 98–03; V Golders Green 01–06; C St Pancras w St Jas and Ch Ch 06–08; rtd 09; PtO *Lon* 12–18. *22 Colman Court, Christchurch Avenue, London N12 0DT* T: (020) 8445 7985 M: 07929-465991 E: tarjei.park@pmb.oxon.org

PARK, Trevor. b 38. MBE 05. Lon Univ BA 64 Open Univ PhD 90 Lambeth STh 81. Linc Th Coll 64. d 66 p 67. C Crosthwaite Keswick *Carl* 66–68; Asst Chapl Solihull Sch 69–71; Chapl St Bees Sch and V St Bees *Carl* 71–77; V Dalton-in-Furness 77–84; V Natland 84–97; Hon Can Carl Cathl 86–97; RD Kendal 89–94; Sen Chapl Oslo w Bergen, Trondheim and Stavanger *Eur* 97–05; rtd 05; P-in-c St Petersburg *Eur* 06–07; PtO *Carl* 09–19. *7 Peck Mill, St Bees CA27 0EJ*

PARKER, Angus Michael Macdonald. b 53. Bris Univ BSc 74. St Jo Coll Nottm 80. d 83 p 84. C Northampton St Giles *Pet* 83–86; C Attenborough *S'well* 86–96; V Pennycross *Ex* 96–09; P-in-c Bitterne *Win* 09–18; rtd 18. *6 Cotehele Close, Callington PL17 7TP* E: angusmmparker@gmail.com

PARKER, Miss Anika Lois. b 74. BMus BMin. d 06 p 07. NSM Redland *Bris* 06–10; PtO *Ox* from 15. *5 Belle Avenue, Reading RG6 7BL* M: 07935-225844 E: anikaparker@gmail.com

PARKER, Mrs Ann Jacqueline. b 41. Dur Inst of Educn TCert 63 Sunderland Poly TCert 65 Open Univ BA 82. WEMTC 91. d 95 p 96. NSM Pilning w Compton Greenfield *Bris* 95–98; NSM Almondsbury and Olveston 98–03; Asst Chapl N Bris NHS Trust 98–19; PtO *Bris* 11–21. *49 Green Street, Chepstow NP16 5DP* E: annatdibley@btinternet.com

PARKER, Anne Elizabeth. See MARR, Anne Elizabeth

PARKER, Anne Margaret. See BARKER, Anne Margaret

PARKER, Mrs Brenda. b 36. d 00 p 01. OLM Eccleston Ch Ch *Liv* 00–06; rtd 06; PtO *Liv* from 16. *22 Selkirk Drive, Eccleston, St Helens WA10 5PE* T: (01744) 757495

PARKER, Carole Maureen. See PROUSE, Carole Maureen

PARKER, David Anthony. b 38. St Chad's Coll Dur BA 62. d 64 p 65. C Palmers Green St Jo *Lon* 64–65; C Kenton 65–71; C

W Hyde St Thos *St Alb* 71–75; P-in-c Brinksway *Ches* 76–80; V 80–83; V Weston 83–92; NSM Cheadle Hulme All SS 97–98; C Offerton 98–00; TV Crosslacon *Carl* 00–02; rtd 02; C Cheadle Hulme All SS *Ches* 02–12; PtO 12–18; *Ely* from 18. *36A St Mary's Street, Ely CB7 4ES*

PARKER, Prof David Charles. b 53. OBE 15. St Andr Univ MTheol 75 Leiden Univ DTh 90 FSA 09 FBA 12. Ridley Hall Cam 75. **d** 77 **p** 78. C Hendon St Paul Mill Hill *Lon* 77–80; C Bladon w Woodstock *Ox* 80–85; C-in-c Shipton-on-Cherwell 80–85; C-in-c Begbroke 80–85; C-in-c Hampton Gay 80–85; Lect Qu Coll Birm 85–93; Sen Angl Tutor 89–93; Lect Birm Univ 93–96; Sen Lect 96–98; Reader in NT Textual Criticism and Palaeography from 98; Prof Th 02–17; Prof Digital Philology 17–20; Dir Inst Textual Scholarship and Electronic Editing 05–17; PtO *Heref* 03–17. *Dumbleton Cottage, 24 Church Street, Bromyard HR7 4DP* T: 0121-415 2415 E: d.c.parker@bham.ac.uk

PARKER, Canon David John. b 33. St Chad's Coll Dur BA 55 Hull Univ MA 85. Linc Th Coll 57. **d** 59 **p** 60. C Tynemouth Ch Ch *Newc* 59–60; C Ponteland 60–63; C Byker St Mich 63–64; C-in-c Byker St Martin CD 64–69; V Whorlton 69–72; TR 73–80; Ind Chapl *Linc* 80–84; Master Newc St Thos Prop Chpl 84–89; Lic Preacher *Man* 90–98; Dioc Exec Officer for Soc Resp 90–96; Dioc Exec Officer for Ch and Soc 97–98; Hon Can Man Cathl 97–98; rtd 98; PtO *Newc* from 98. *4 The Kylins, Morpeth NE61 2DJ* T: (01670) 516218 M: 07398-789093 E: dp8876228@gmail.com

PARKER, David John. b 57. Em Coll Cam BA 79 MA 83 Qu Coll Ox DPhil 84. Qu Coll Birm 12. **d** 15 **p** 16. NSM Selly Oak St Mary *Birm* from 15. *1 Spirehouse Lane, Blackwell, Bromsgrove B60 1QE* T: 0121-445 1901 E: davidparker124@btinternet.com

PARKER, Canon David Louis. b 47. Lon Univ LLB 70. Wycliffe Hall Ox BA 79 MA 82. **d** 80 **p** 81. C Broadwater St Mary *Chich* 80–84; TR Ifield 84–97; R Lavant 97–12; RD Chich 01–06; Can and Preb Chich Cathl 03–12; rtd 12; PtO *Chich* 12–17. *6 Queens Gate, 1 Osborne Road, Southsea PO5 3LX*

PARKER (née JOHNSON), Mrs Emma Louise. b 82. St Mary's Coll Dur BA 05 MA 06. Ridley Hall Cam 07. **d** 09 **p** 10. C Cockfield *Dur* 09–12; C Lynesack 09–12; C Evenwood 09–12; C Easington and Easington Colliery 12–14; P-in-c 14–18; Dep Warden Cranmer Hall Dur from 18. *Cranmer Hall, St John's College, 3 South Bailey, Durham DH1 3RJ* T: 0191-334 3851 E: cran.depwarden@durham.ac.uk

PARKER, Canon Janet Elizabeth. b 54. Cranmer Hall Dur 05. **d** 07 **p** 08. C Sale St Anne *Ches* 07–10; V High Lane 10–20; RD Chadkirk 11–18; Hon Can Ches Cathl 16–20; rtd 20; PtO *Newc* from 20. *6 Front Row, Cambo, Morpeth NE61 4AY* E: revjanetparker@btinternet.com

PARKER, Mrs Joanna Caroline. b 63. UEA BA 95 Leeds Univ MA 07 RGN 85 RM 92. NOC 04. **d** 07 **p** 08. C Pocklington Wold *York* 07–11; V Hyde St Geo *Ches* 11–17; V New Milverton *Cov* from 17. *The Vicarage, 2 St Mark's Road, Leamington Spa CV32 6DL* T: (01926) 421004 E: vicar@st-marks.net

PARKER, Joanne Catherine. b 63. Liv Univ BSc 85 Hughes Hall Cam PGCE 87. Qu Foundn Birm 19. **d** 21. C Exhall *Cov* from 21. *42 Lancaster Road, Rugby CV21 2QW* M: 07729-325092 E: parkerjo42@gmail.com

PARKER, Mrs Joanne Clare. b 76. St Hild Coll 17. **d** 19 **p** 20. C Eastfield *York* from 19. *7 Malling Avenue, Eastfield, Scarborough YO11 3FA* M: 07988-973219 E: jopkr76@gmail.com

PARKER, John David. b 61. Ridley Hall Cam 00. **d** 02 **p** 03. C Aston cum Aughton w Swallownest and Ulley *Sheff* 02–06; TV Rugby *Cov* 06–12; V Newbold Pacey w Moreton Morrell 12–18; R Lighthorne 12–18; V Chesterton 12–18; V Wath-upon-Dearne *Sheff* from 18. *The Vicarage, Church Street, Wath-upon-Dearne, Rotherham S63 7RD* E: parkersuk@aol.com

PARKER, Jonathan Edward. **d** 17 **p** 18. C Fishguard w Llanychar and Pontfaen w Morfil etc *St D* 17–18; C Llanwnda, Goodwick w Manorowen and Llanstinan 17–18; C W Cemaes 18–20; P-in-c Dyffryn Teifi from 20. *Terra Cotta, Station Road, Newcastle Emlyn SA38 9BX* T: (01348) 871868 E: jparker.rev@gmail.com

PARKER, Justin Trevelyan. b 71. Reading Univ LLB 92. WEMTC 11. **d** 12 **p** 13. NSM Cleobury Mortimer w Hopton Wafers etc *Heref* 12–19; R Bromfield from 19. *The Vicarage, Bromfield, Ludlow SY8 2JP* M: 07932-606420

PARKER, Canon Lynn. b 54. SS Mark & Jo Univ Coll Plymouth BEd 94. SWMTC 04. **d** 07 **p** 08. NSM S Hill w Callington *Truro* 07–10; P-in-c Antony w Sheviock 10–15; P-in-c Torpoint 10–15; C Maker w Rame and St John w Millbrook 12–15; V Antony w Sheviock and Torpoint 15–19; V St Germans w Antony and Sheviock from 19; Hon Can Truro Cathl from 15. *The New Vicarage, 17 Quay Road, St Germans, Saltash PL12 5LY* E: parker30@hotmail.com

PARKER, Margaret Grace. *See* TORDOFF, Margaret Grace

✠**PARKER, The Rt Revd Matthew John.** b 63. Man Univ BA 85 SS Coll Cam BA 88 MA 92. Ridley Hall Cam 85. **d** 88 **p** 89 **c** 21. C Twickenham St Mary *Lon* 88–91; Chapl Stockport Gr Sch 91–94; C Stockport St Geo *Ches* 91–93; P-in-c Stockport St Mark 93–94; TV Stockport SW 94–00; TR Leek and Meerbrook *Lich* 00–13; RD Leek 07–13; Adn Stoke-upon-Trent 13–21; Area Bp Stafford from 21. *Ash Garth, 6 Broughton Crescent, Barlaston, Stoke-on-Trent ST12 9DD* T: (01782) 373308 E: bishop.stafford@lichfield.anglican.org

PARKER, Michael. b 54. **d** 07 **p** 11. C Ebbw Vale *Mon* 07–09; Hon C Llanhilleth w Six Bells 09–10; Hon C Abertillery w Cwmtillery w Llanhilleth etc 10–17; P-in-c 17–21; rtd 21. *Address temp unknown* E: mikeparker54@gmail.com

PARKER, Canon Michael Alan. b 70. St Jo Coll Dur BA 91. CITC BTh 93. **d** 96 **p** 97. C Dundela St Mark *D & D* 96–00; I Carnalea from 00; Can Belf Cathl from 15. *St Gall's Rectory, 171 Crawfordsburn Road, Bangor BT19 1BT* T: (028) 9185 3366 *or* 9185 3810 E: carnalea@down.anglican.org *or* stgalloffice@btconnect.com

PARKER, Canon Michael John. b 54. Cam Coll of Art and Tech BA 76 Lon Univ BD 85. Trin Coll Bris 82. **d** 85 **p** 86. C Leic H Trin w St Jo 85–88; P-in-c Edin Clermiston Em 88–90; I Edin St Thos 90–03; Can St Mary's Cathl 94–03; NSM Edin St Paul and St Geo 03–06; Gen Sec Evang Alliance Scotland 03–06; Middle E Dir Middle E Chr Outreach 06–09; Internat Dir from 13; Sen Min All SS Cathl Cairo 09–13; Hon Can from 09; PtO *Edin* 06–14. *4 Liberton Place, Edinburgh EH16 6NA* E: canonmikep@gmail.com

PARKER, Canon Michael John. b 57. BSc Nottm Univ MA 04. Wycliffe Hall Ox 80. **d** 83 **p** 84. C Heigham H Trin *Nor* 83–86; C Muswell Hill St Jas w St Matt *Lon* 86–90; R Bedford St Jo and St Leon *St Alb* 90–98; V Knowle *Birm* 98–18; AD Solihull 04–09; Hon Can Birm Cathl 05–18. *82 Wilsdon Way, Kidlington OX5 1TX*

PARKER, Nicolas. *See* PARKER, Robert Nicolas

PARKER, Nigel Howard. b 69. St Jo Coll Dur BSc 90. CITC BTh 97. **d** 97 **p** 98. C Holywood *D & D* 97–00; Outreach Development Officer Think Again 00–04; I Bangor St Comgall from 04. *1A Maxwell Road, Bangor BT20 3RA* T: (028) 9146 0712 E: nigel@parkers123.plus.com *or* nigel@bangorparishchurch.org.uk

PARKER, Philip Vernon. b 60. Birm Univ BSc 82 PGCE 83 Heythrop Coll Lon MA 09. Wycliffe Hall Ox BA 89. **d** 90 **p** 91. C Walkergate *Newc* 90–93; Chapl Shiplake Coll Henley 93–96; C Lindfield *Chich* 97–99; Team Ldr Titus Trust 99–04; Chapl Cranleigh Sch Surrey 04–12; CF (TA) 97–05; P-in-c Frimley Green and Mytchett *Guildf* 13–19; Chapl Loretto Sch Musselburgh 19–20; R Appleton *Ox* from 20; R Besselsleigh from 20; Chapl Cothill Ho Sch from 20. *The Rectory, Oaksmere, Appleton, Abingdon OX13 5JS*

PARKER, Canon Richard Bryan. b 64. Sheff Poly BA 87. Coll of Resurr Mirfield 92. **d** 95 **p** 96. C Norton *Sheff* 95–98; C Hoyland 98–00; V Moorends 00–08; V Hoyland from 08; Dioc Warden of Readers 10–13; Hon Can Sheff Cathl from 10. *The Vicarage, 104 Hawshaw Lane, Hoyland, Barnsley S74 0HH* T: (01226) 749231

PARKER, Richard Frederick. b 36. Oak Hill Th Coll 72. **d** 74 **p** 75. C Wootton *St Alb* 74–76; C Hove Bp Hannington Memorial Ch *Chich* 76–81; R Northwood *Portsm* 81–88; V W Cowes H Trin 81–88; V Aldershot H Trin *Guildf* 88–98; R Spaxton w Charlynch, Goathurst, Enmore etc *B & W* 98–03; rtd 03; PtO *B & W* from 19. *47 Banneson Road, Nether Stowey, Bridgwater TA5 1NS* T: (01278) 733883 E: ricktherec@hotmail.com

PARKER, Robert Nicolas. b 71. Nottm Univ BA 93 PGCE 95. Ridley Hall Cam 95. **d** 98 **p** 99. C Yardley St Edburgha *Birm* 98–02; Asst P Eugene St Mary USA 02–05; P-in-c Coleshill *Birm* 05–08; V 08–21; P-in-c Maxstoke 05–08; V 11–21; AD Yardley and Solihull from 21; Bp's Ecum Adv from 12. *Address temp unknown* E: nickthevicparker@btinternet.com

PARKER, Roger Thomas Donaldson. b 55. Simon Fraser Univ BC BA 80 Univ of Wales (Cardiff) LLB 84 Univ Coll Lon LLM 85. Coll of Resurr Mirfield 95. **d** 95 **p** 96. C Swinton and Pendlebury *Man* 95–02; V Burnley St Cath w St Alb and St Paul *Blackb* from 02. *St Catherine's Parsonage, 156 Todmorden Road, Burnley BB11 3ER* T: (01282) 424587 M: 07977-291166 E: frrogerparker@aol.com

PARKER, Roland John Graham. b 48. AKC 72 Hull Univ BA(Ed) 83. St Aug Coll Cant 71. **d** 74 **p** 75. C Linc St Faith and St Martin w St Pet 74–78; V Appleby 78–84; Ind Chapl 78–84; V N Kelsey 84–92; V Cadney 84–92; P-in-c Waddington 92–97; R 97–11; rtd 11. *29 Castle Street, Kirkcudbright DG6 4JD* T: (01557) 330317 E: rolapark2@btinternet.com

PARKER, Russell Edward. b 48. Man Univ BA 80. St Jo Coll Nottm MTh 82. **d** 81 **p** 82. C Walmsley *Man* 81–85; V Coalville and Bardon Hill *Leic* 85–90; Dir Acorn Chr Foundn

90–14; Internat Ambassador from 14; PtO *Guildf* 20–21; NSM Rowledge from 21. *Pinewood House, Black Pond Lane, Lower Bourne, Farnham GU10 3NW* M: 07919-335291 E: russparker7@icloud.com

PARKER, Stephen. b 88. Ches Univ BA 09 St Jo Coll Dur MA. St Steph Ho Ox BA 12. **d** 13 **p** 14. C Worksop Priory *S'well* 13–16; V S Leamington St Jo *Cov* from 16; AD Warwick and Leamington 18–19. *St John's Vicarage, Tachbrook Street, Leamington Spa CV31 3BN* E: stephen.parker88@gmail.com *or* priest@stjohnsleamingtonspa.org.uk

PARKER, Prof Stephen George. b 65. Birm Univ BEd 89 MA 97 PhD 03 FRHistS. Qu Coll Birm 96. **d** 98. Teaching Asst Westhill Coll of HE Birm 98–01; Sen Lect Th Univ Coll Ches 01–04; Hd RS Cadbury Sixth Form Coll 04–08; Hd Postgraduate Studies in Educn Worc Univ 08–12; Prof Hist of Relig and Educn 13–17. *University of Worcester, Henwick Grove, Worcester WR2 6AJ* T: (01905) 542165 E: s.parker@worc.ac.uk

PARKER, Canon Thomas Richard. b 52. Imp Coll Lon BScEng 73 Keele Univ MEd 83. Cranmer Hall Dur. **d** 94 **p** 95. C Chadkirk *Ches* 94–08; RD 04–08; P-in-c Stalybridge H Trin and Ch Ch 08–11; V 11–17; Hon Can Ches Cathl 13–17; rtd 18. *Naze View, Lesser Lane, Combs, High Peak SK23 9UZ* E: tomparker121@gmail.com

PARKER, Timothy Percy. b 58. Man Univ BA. St Jo Coll Nottm. **d** 85 **p** 86. C Pitsmoor Ch Ch *Sheff* 85–87; C Kimberworth 87–89; C Brightside w Wincobank 89–91; C Upper Armley *Ripon* 91–95; TV Billingham St Aid *Dur* 95–97; V Billingham St Luke 97–12; Chapl Harrogate and Distr NHS Foundn Trust 12–16; P-in-c Hunmanby w Muston *York* 16–18; R Hertford from 18. *The Vicarage, 6 Northgate, Hunmanby, Filey YO14 0NT* T: (01723) 448351 E: timparker17@gmail.com

PARKER-McGEE, Robert Thomas. b 78. Leeds Univ BA 10 Dur Univ MA 17. Coll of Resurr Mirfield 07. **d** 10 **p** 11. C Gornal and Sedgley *Worc* 10–14; P-in-c Geddington w Weekley *Pet* 14–18; Practical Tr Co-Ord for Preaching and Worship 15–18; V Orpington All SS *Roch* 18–19; R Boxford, Edwardstone, Groton etc *St E* from 19. *The Rectory, School Hill, Boxford, Sudbury CO10 5JT* M: 07588-801593 E: rparkermcgee@gmail.com

PARKERSON, Trevor Richard. b 46. Qu Coll Birm 06. **d** 08 **p** 09. NSM Ashby-de-la-Zouch and Breedon on the Hill *Leic* 08–15; PtO *Lich* 14–19; *Leic* from 15. *36 Ashby Road, Woodville, Swadlincote DE11 7BY* T: (01283) 225408

PARKES, Arthur Burnham. b 42. Univ of Wales MSc 72 PhD 76 FIBiol 94 LTCL 82. St Mich Coll Llan 11. **d** 12 **p** 13. NSM Cyncoed *Mon* 12–16; NSM Bedwas w Machen w Michaelston-y-Fedw w Rudry from 16. *17 Bramshill Drive, Pontprennau, Cardiff CF23 8NX* T: (029) 2048 1970 M: 07950-454926 E: arthur.b.parkes@virginmedia.com

PARKES, Mrs Celia Anne. b 50. STETS 06. **d** 09 **p** 10. NSM Bursledon *Win* 09–11; NSM Southampton (City Cen) 11–15; NSM Margaretting w Mountnessing and Buttsbury *Chelmsf* 15–17; NSM Ingatestone w Fryerning 15–17; NSM Napton-on-the-Hill, Lower Shuckburgh etc *Cov* 17–20; NSM Priors Hardwick, Priors Marston and Wormleighton 17–20; rtd 20. *Address temp unknown* M: 07842-151387 E: m.parkes345@btinternet.com

PARKES, Edward Patrick. b 58. Crewe & Alsager Coll BEd 80 Ban Univ MTh 11. SWMTC 10. **d** 11 **p** 12. Dioc Miss Resources Adv *Ex* from 11; NSM Dawlish 11–12; NSM Ex Cathl 12–14; C Yelverton, Meavy, Sheepstor and Walkhampton 14–16; C Sampford Spiney w Horrabridge 14–16; P-in-c Wolborough and Ogwell 16; TR Newton Abbot from 17; RD Newton Abbot from 18; Tutor SWMTC from 14. *The Rectory, 5 Coach Place, Newton Abbot TQ12 1ES* T: (01626) 681498 M: 07960-102001 E: epp@sky.com

PARKES, Jack Christopher. b 53. Leeds Univ BA 81 Hughes Hall Cam PGCE 82. Yorks Min Course 14. **d** 15 **p** 16. NSM Cleckheaton *Leeds* 15–17; Chapl HM Pris Leeds from 16. *HM Prison Leeds, 2 Gloucester Terrace, Armley, Leeds LS12 2TJ* T: 0113-203 2600 M: 07890-724223 E: fr.jack@outlook.com

PARKES, Kevin. b 62. Trent Poly BA 84. Sarum & Wells Th Coll BTh 90. **d** 88 **p** 89. C Wandsworth St Anne *S'wark* 88–92; USPG 92–95; Trinidad and Tobago 93–95; Kingston Area Miss Team *S'wark* 95–01; V Wandsworth Common St Mary 01–09; AD Tooting 07–09; Chapl Univ Coll Lon Hosps NHS Foundn Trust 09–13; Chapl Hillingdon Hosps NHS Foundn Trust 13–14; Chapl King's Coll Hosp NHS Foundn Trust 14–15; Chapl Lewisham and Greenwich NHS Trust from 15. *University Hospital Lewisham, Lewisham High Street, London SE13 6LH* T: (020) 8333 3000 E: bloomsbury1@hotmail.com *or* kevinparkes@nhs.net

PARKES, Patrick. See PARKES, Edward Patrick

PARKHILL, Alan John. b 43. TCD BA 66. CITC 68. **d** 67 **p** 68. C Knockbreda *D & D* 67–70; Asst Warden Elswick Lodge Newc 71–72; C Bangor St Comgall *D & D* 73–78; Bp's C Kilmore 78–81; I Kilmore and Inch 82–86; I Clonfeacle w Derrygortreavy *Arm* 86–09; rtd 09. *1 Rodney Park, Bangor BT19 6FN* T/F: (028) 9147 3916 E: aparkhill1@btinternet.com

PARKIN, Christopher. See PARKIN, Melvyn Christopher

PARKIN, George David. b 37. Cranmer Hall Dur BA 60. **d** 62 **p** 63. C Balderstone *Man* 62–65; C Tunstead 65–67; C Gateshead Fell *Dur* 69–73; CMS Nigeria 74–76; V Walton Breck *Liv* 80–92; V Rawtenstall St Mary *Man* 92–97; P-in-c Constable Lee 02–07; rtd 07; PtO *Man* 08 and from 16. *174 Bury Road, Rawtenstall, Rossendale BB4 6DJ* E: pamandco@googlemail.com

PARKIN, Gillian Elizabeth. b 48. Heref Coll of Educn CertEd 69. Trin Coll Bris. **d** 13 **p** 14. OLM By Brook *Bris* 13–20; NSM from 20; OLM Colerne w N Wraxall 13–20; NSM from 20. *4 Kents Bottom, Yatton Keynell, Chippenham SN14 7BW* T: (01249) 782165 E: gillianparkin4@gmail.com

PARKIN, Mrs Jennifer Anne. b 47. Nene Coll Northn BEd 85. WMMTC 95. **d** 98 **p** 99. C Northampton St Alb *Pet* 98–02; P-in-c Ecton 02–07; P-in-c Wootton w Quinton and Preston Deanery 07–12; Chapl Cynthia Spencer Hospice 02–07; Warden of Past Assts *Pet* 06–10; rtd 12; Lay Voc Officer *Pet* 12–13; PtO from 13. *40 Pinewood Road, Northampton NN3 2RB* T: (01604) 244549 E: parkinjen@btinternet.com *or* jenny.johnparkin@gmail.com

PARKIN, Canon John Edmund. b 44. Open Univ BA 73. St Jo Coll Nottm 83. **d** 85 **p** 86. C Aberavon *Llan* 85–90; R Eglwysilan 90–01; P Missr Merthyr Tydfil Ch Ch 01–09; Hon Can Llan Cathl 09; rtd 09; PtO *Llan* from 12; *S & B* from 15. *2 Mount Pleasant, Penderyn Road, Hirwaun, Aberdare CF44 9RT*

PARKIN, Jonathan Samuel. b 73. La Sainte Union Coll BTh 95 Birm Univ MA 97. Qu Coll Birm 98. **d** 98 **p** 99. C Skegness and Winthorpe *Linc* 98–01; Chapl Leic Coll of FE 01–03; Chapl De Montfort Univ 04–07; Chapl Leic Cathl 01–07; TV Market Harborough and The Transfiguration etc 07–11; P-in-c Welham, Glooston and Cranoe and Stonton Wyville 07–11; C Branston w Nocton and Potterhanworth *Linc* 11–16; C Metheringham w Blankney and Dunston 11–16; Dioc Fresh Expressions Enabler 16; C S Grantham from 18; PtO *Ely* 16–21. *The Vicarage, 4 Station Road East, Grantham NG31 6HX* E: jonnie.parkin@gmail.com

PARKIN, Mrs Melanie Joanne. b 75. Wolv Univ BSc 97 Ox Brookes Univ BA 04. Westcott Ho Cam 16. **d** 18 **p** 19. C Grantham St Wulfram *Linc* 18–21; C Grantham, Manthorpe 18–21. *Address temp unknown* E: melparkin1@gmail.com

PARKIN, Melvyn Christopher. b 57. NEOC 99. **d** 02 **p** 03. NSM Boston Spa *York* 02–03; C Elvington w Sutton on Derwent and E Cottingwith 03–06; R Howardian Gp 06–11; V Gt and Lt Ouseburn w Marton cum Grafton etc *Leeds* 11–17; rtd 17; PtO *Leeds* from 17. *20 Forest Grove, Harrogate HG2 7JU* E: chrisandlindaparkin@yahoo.com

PARKINSON, Alan. See PARKINSON, Thomas Alan

PARKINSON, Alec. b 60. All SS Cen for Miss & Min 14. **d** 16 **p** 17. NSM Pemberton St Jo *Liv* 16–19; NSM Wigan from 20. *28 Townfields, Ashton-in-Makerfield, Wigan WN4 9LJ* T: (01942) 272838 E: alecp28@hotmail.co.uk

PARKINSON, Andrew. b 74. St Steph Ho Ox. **d** 01 **p** 02. C Lancaster Ch Ch *Blackb* 01–04; P-in-c Yarnton w Begbroke and Shipton on Cherwell *Ox* 04–05; TV Blenheim 05–12; P-in-c Kirkby Stephen w Mallerstang etc *Carl* 12–16; PtO *Dur* from 16. *Address withheld by request*

PARKINSON, Daniel James. b 86. Trin Coll Cam BA 17 Wadh Coll Ox MA 18. Westcott Ho Cam 15. **d** 18 **p** 19. C Doncaster St Geo *Sheff* from 18. *13 Osborne Road, Doncaster DN2 5BX* M: 07816-891584 E: danparkinson1@gmail.com

PARKINSON, David Thomas. b 42. Linc Th Coll 77. **d** 79 **p** 80. C Yate New Town *Bris* 79–82; TV Keynsham *B & W* 82–88; R Bleadon 88–07; rtd 07; PtO *B & W* from 08. *Sherwell Court, 48 Old Church Road, Uphill, Weston-super-Mare BS23 4UP* T: (01934) 708125 M: 07951-239778 E: dtparkinson@talktalk.net

PARKINSON, Frances Anne. b 66. Cen Lancs Univ BA 96. Cumbria Chr Learning 16. **d** 19 **p** 20. NSM High Westmorland *Carl* from 19. *Studfold Farmhouse, Ravenstonedale, Kirkby Stephen CA17 4LP* T: (015396) 23393 M: 07500-876761 E: curate.hwparishes@gmail.com

PARKINSON, Francis Wilson. b 37. Open Univ BA 80. St Aid Birkenhead 59. **d** 62 **p** 63. C Monkwearmouth St Andr *Dur* 62–64; C Speke All SS *Liv* 64–67; CF 67–92; PtO *Ox* 92–20. *9 Priory Mead, Longcot, Faringdon SN7 7TJ* T: (01793) 784406

PARKINSON, Canon Ian Richard. b 58. Dur Univ BA 79 Lon Univ BD 84. Wycliffe Hall Ox 80. **d** 83 **p** 84. C Hull St Jo Newland *York* 83–86; C Linthorpe 86–92; V Saltburn-by-the-

Sea 92–01; V Marple All SS *Ches* 01–15; Hon Can Ches Cathl 12–15; Leadership Specialist CPAS from 16; PtO *Sheff* from 16; Assoc Adn Sheff and Rotherham from 21. *CPAS, Unit 3, Sovereign Court 1, Sir William Lyons Road, University of Warwick Science Park, Coventry CV4 7EZ* E: iparkinson@cpas.org.uk

PARKINSON, John Reginald. b 32. Qu Coll Birm 79. d 81 p 82. NSM Catshill and Dodford *Worc* 81–85; C Knightwick w Doddenham, Broadwas and Cotheridge 85–88; C Martley and Wichenford 85–88; P-in-c Berrow w Pendock and Eldersfield 88–89; R Berrow w Pendock, Eldersfield, Hollybush etc 89–97; RD Upton 95–97; rtd 97; PtO *Glouc* from 97; *Worc* 97–08. *8 Glebe Close, Stow on the Wold, Cheltenham GL54 1DJ* T: (01451) 830822

PARKINSON, Nicholas John. b 46. FCCA 75 Cranfield Inst of Tech MBA 85. St Alb Minl Tr Scheme 92. d 95 p 96. NSM Woburn Sands *St Alb* 95–98; NSM Westoning w Tingrith 98–01; NSM Woburn Sands 01–15; rtd 15; PtO *St Alb* from 15. *Thornbank House, 7 Church Road, Woburn Sands, Milton Keynes MK17 8TE* T: (01908) 583397 E: nickp@thornbank.com

PARKINSON, Richard Duncan. b 51. UMIST BSc 72 S Bank Univ MA 01 Nottm Trent Univ PGCE. ERMC 04. d 07 p 08. NSM Leverington, Newton and Tydd St Giles *Ely* 07–11; NSM Wisbech St Mary and Guyhirn w Ring's End etc 11–21; P-in-c 17–21; rtd 21; PtO *Ely* 21. *Colegate House, 166 Leverington Common, Leverington, Wisbech PE13 5BP* T: (01945) 465818 E: rykparkinson@btinternet.com

PARKINSON, Richard Francis. b 76. Cranmer Hall Dur. d 10 p 11. C Ilkley All SS *Bradf* 10–13; R Cherry Burton *York* from 13; C Etton w Dalton Holme 13–19; P-in-c from 19; Chapl Bp Burton Coll York from 13; RD Beverley *York* from 17. *The Rectory, Main Street, Cherry Burton, Beverley HU17 7RF* T: (01964) 503036 E: richard@poiema.co.uk *or* rector@stmichaelscherryburton.org.uk

PARKINSON, Mrs Sarah Kathryn Rachel. b 80. Trin Coll Ox MMath 02. Ripon Coll Cuddesdon BA 06. d 07 p 08. NSM Steeple Aston w N Aston and Tackley *Ox* 07–10; Chapl HM Pris Bullingdon 05–08; Manager Relig Affairs Campsfield Ho Immigration Removal Cen 08–12; PtO *Carl* 12–16; *Ripon* 13–14; *Leeds* 14–16; Chapl HM YOI Deerbolt 16–17; Chapl HM Pris Low Newton from 17. *HM Prison Low Newton, Finchale Avenue, Brasside, Durham DH1 5YA* T: 0191-386 1141 E: sarah.parkinson@justice.gov.uk

PARKINSON, Thomas Alan. b 40. St Jo Coll York CertEd 61. NW Ord Course 75. d 78 p 79. NSM Sheff St Cecilia Parson Cross 78–82; NSM Goldthorpe w Hickleton 82–90; C Cantley 90–01; Dioc RE and Worship Adv 93–04; V Ryecroft St Nic 02–10; rtd 10; PtO *Sheff* 10–21; CMP from 00. *40 South Street, Rawmarsh, Rotherham S62 5RG* T: (01709) 525654

PARKMAN, Christopher Charles. b 67. Selw Coll Cam MA 88 Birm Univ MSc 92. Wycliffe Hall Ox 14. d 16 p 17. C Bris St Steph w St Jas and St Jo w St Mich etc 16–19; PtO *Eur* from 19. *Domaine des Courmettes, Route des Courmettes, 06140 Tourrettes-sur-Loup, France* T: (033) 4 92 11 02 32 E: rev.chris.parkman@gmail.com

PARKMAN, Mrs Michelle Joy. b 77. SS Mark & Jo Univ Coll Plymouth BA 00. Trin Coll Bris BA 08. d 08 p 09. C Nailsea H Trin *B & W* 08–13; PtO *Truro* from 16; Chapl Univ of St Mark and St Jo from 19. *16 Home Park Road, Saltash PL12 6BH* M: 07740-366597 E: mparkman@hotmail.co.uk

PARMENTER, Canon Deirdre Joy. b 45. EAMTC 91. d 94 p 95. C Ipswich St Aug *St E* 94–97; P-in-c Haughley w Wetherden 97–00; V Haughley w Wetherden and Stowupland 00–07; RD Stowmarket 99–05; Bp's Chapl 07–10; Dioc Adv for Women's Min 08–10; Hon Can St E Cathl 03–10; rtd 10; PtO *St E* from 10; Dioc Warden of Readers 10–13; RD Loes 14–15. *Avalon, Marlesford Road, Campsea Ashe, Woodbridge IP13 0QG* T: (01728) 748145 E: deirdreparmenter@gmail.com

PARNELL, Bryan Donald. b 38. JP. DipEd 88. Chich Th Coll 66. d 69 p 70. C Lewisham St Jo Southend *S'wark* 69–72; Asst Chapl Cooleg Sch of St Pet Australia 72–76; R Angaston 76–78; Chapl RAN 78–88; R Edwardstown 89–02; rtd 02. *PO Box 2131, Unit 19, Manson Towers, 13 Moseley Street, Glenelg SA 2035, Australia* M: (0061) 41-469 2340 E: trinitas@senet.com.au

PARNELL, Michael Gordon. b 61. Yorks Min Course 15. d 17. NSM Doncaster St Jas *Sheff* from 17. *25 Bramworth Road, Doncaster DN4 0HZ* T: (01302) 855475 E: mikegp2003@yahoo.co.uk

PARR, Mrs Anne Patricia. b 38. Nottm Univ CertEd 59. d 07 p 08. OLM Penistone and Thurlstone *Wakef* 07–14; OLM Penistone and Thurlstone *Sheff* 14–15; PtO from 15. *7 Rydal Close, Penistone, Sheffield S36 8HN* T: (01226) 764490 M: 07971-513301 E: mail@anneparr.co.uk

PARR, Clive William. b 41. FCIS FHA. WEMTC 02. d 03 p 04. NSM Evesham w Norton and Lenchwick *Worc* 03–07; NSM

Hampton w Sedgeberrow and Hinton-on-the-Green 07–14; Bp's Health Service Adv 08–12; PtO 14–19; *Heref* from 19. *Nimrod, Church Lane, Bridgnorth WV16 4NW* T: (01746) 767023 M: 07801-820006 E: cw.parr@btinternet.com

PARR, Frank. b 35. Nottm Univ BCombStuds 82 Lanc Univ MA 86. Linc Th Coll 79. d 82 p 83. C Padiham *Blackb* 82–85; P-in-c Accrington St Andr 85–88; V Oswaldtwistle Immanuel and All SS 88–96; V Tunstall w Melling and Leck 96–01; rtd 01; PtO *Blackb* from 01; *Bradf* 02–14; *Leeds* from 14. *1 Bank View, Burton Road, Lower Bentham, Lancaster LA2 7DZ* T: (015242) 61159 E: f.parr207@btinternet.com

PARR, Jeffrey John. b 48. FCA 73. EMMTC 03. d 06 p 07. NSM Bassingham Gp *Linc* 06–09; NSM Claypole 09–10; LtO from 10. *17 Honeysuckle Road, Witham St Hughs, Lincoln LN6 9ZG* M: 07785-281215 E: jparr@chesapeake.co.uk

PARR, Canon John. b 53. St Edm Hall Ox BA 74 MA 87 Lon Univ BD 79 Sheff Univ PhD 90. Trin Coll Bris 75. d 79 p 80. C Gt Crosby St Luke *Liv* 79–82; C Walton St Mary 82–84; V Ince St Mary 84–87; Tutor and Lect Ridley Hall Cam 87–95; Chapl 87–93; Dir Studies 93–95; CME Officer *Ely* 95–99; P-in-c Harston w Hauxton 95–99; P-in-c Newton 97–99; Can Res and CME Officer *St E* 99–00; PtO 06–09; TR Bury St Edmunds All SS w St Jo and St Geo 09–12; Dir Min Educn and Tr 12–16; C Hadleigh, Layham and Shelley 16–18; Min Formation Adv 18–19; Hon Can St E Cathl 15–19; rtd 19; PtO *St E* from 19. *18 Victoria Street, Bury St Edmunds IP33 3BB* E: johnparr53@gmail.com

PARR, Mabel Ann. b 37. CBDTI 07. d 07 p 08. NSM Bentham *Bradf* 07–10; PtO *Blackb* from 10; *Bradf* 12–14; *Leeds* from 14. *1 Bank View, Burton Road, Lower Bentham, Lancaster LA2 7DZ* T: (015242) 61159 E: f.parr207@btinternet.com

PARR, Vanessa Caroline. *See* CONANT, Vanessa Caroline

PARRATT, Dennis James. b 53. Glos Coll of Art & Design BA 74. St Steph Ho Ox 82. d 84 p 85. C Cainscross w Selsley *Glouc* 84–88; C Old Shoreham and New Shoreham *Chich* 88–91; PtO *Glouc* 01–08. *11 Millbrook Gardens, Cheltenham GL50 3RQ* T: (01242) 525730 E: djparratt@hotmail.co.uk

PARRETT, Mrs Mary Margaret. b 42. Shenstone Coll of Educn DipEd 63. St Alb Minl Tr Scheme 86. d 98 p 99. NSM Barton-le-Cley w Higham Gobion and Hexton *St Alb* 98–06; PtO from 06; NSM Officer Bedford Adnry 10–14. *49 Manor Road, Barton-le-Clay, Bedford MK45 4NP* T: (01582) 883089 E: mary.parrett@btinternet.com

PARRETT, Mrs Rosalind Virginia. b 43. Ox Brookes Univ MTh 02. Cant Sch of Min 84. d 87 p 94. NSM Selling w Throwley, Sheldwich w Badlesmere etc *Cant* 87–91; Asst Chapl Cant Hosp 87–91; Par Dn Stantonbury and Willen *Ox* 91–94; TV 94–96; P-in-c Owlsmoor 96–98; V 98–03; rtd 03; PtO *Cant* 03–04; Hon C Faversham 04–11; Hon C Preston next Faversham, Goodnestone and Graveney 04–10; PtO from 11. *16 Hilton Close, Faversham ME13 8NN* T: (01795) 530380 M: 07881-788155 E: revros@talktalk.net

PARRETT, Stephen. b 65. Cant Ch Ch Univ Coll BA 96. d 07 p 08. OLM Herne Bay Ch Ch *Cant* 07–14; NSM 14–19; NSM Reculver and Herne Bay St Bart and Hoath from 19. *1 Birkdale Gardens, Herne Bay CT6 7TS* T: (01227) 360139 M: 07742-439563 E: stephenparrett48@yahoo.com

PARRIS, Mrs Alison Louise. b 54. d 14 p 15. NSM Camelot Par *B & W* from 14. *76 Combe Park, Yeovil BA21 3BE* T: (01935) 476412 M: 07710-539855

PARRISH, Ian Robert. b 62. SEITE 05. d 09 p 10. C Kingsnorth and Shadoxhurst *Cant* 09–10; C Maidstone St Paul 11–14; P-in-c Maidstone All SS and St Phil w Tovil 14–20; P-in-c Temple Ewell w Lydden from 20. *The Rectory, Green Lane, Temple Ewell, Dover CT16 3AS* T: (01304) 279673 E: revd.irp@gmail.com

PARRISH, Robert Carey. b 57. St Steph Ho Ox 89. d 91 p 92. C Abington *Pet* 91–94; C Leckhampton SS Phil and Jas w Cheltenham St Jas *Glouc* 94–97; PV Llan Cathl 97–02; R Merthyr Dyfan 02–16; TV Barry from 16. *9 Glas y Llwyn, Barry CF63 1DD* T: (01446) 748527

PARROTT, David Wesley. b 58. Univ of Wales (Cardiff) LLM 01. Oak Hill Th Coll BA. d 84 p 85. C Thundersley *Chelmsf* 84–87; C Rainham 87–89; P-in-c Heydon w Gt and Lt Chishill 89–90; P-in-c Chrishall 89–90; P-in-c Elmdon w Wendon Lofts and Strethall 89–90; R Heydon, Gt and Lt Chishill, Chrishall etc 91–96; R Rayleigh 96–00; TR 00–04; RD Rochford 02–04; Barking Area CME Adv 04–09; C Hornchurch St Andr 05–09; Hon Can Chelmsf Cathl 07–09; V St Lawr Jewry *Lon* from 09. *St Lawrence Jewry Vicarage, Guildhall Yard, London EC2V 5AA* T: (020) 7600 9478 E: dwparrott01@aol.com

PARROTT, George. b 37. Leeds Univ BA 61. Bps' Coll Cheshunt 61. d 63 p 64. C Lower Mitton *Worc* 63–65; C-in-c Fairfield St Rich CD 65–68; Zambia 68–70; C Cleethorpes *Linc* 70–75; R Withern 75–80; P-in-c Gayton le

Marsh 76–80; P-in-c Strubby 76–80; P-in-c Authorpe 76–80; P-in-c Belleau w Aby and Claythorpe 76–80; P-in-c N and S Reston 76–80; P-in-c Swaby w S Thoresby 76–80; R Withern 80–90; V Reston 80–90; V Messingham 90–93; P-in-c Fincham *Ely* 95–02; P-in-c Marham 95–02; P-in-c Shouldham 95–02; P-in-c Shouldham Thorpe 95–02; rtd 02; PtO *Linc* from 03. *8 Anson Close, Skellingthorpe, Lincoln LN6 5TH* T: (01522) 694417 E: george.parrott15@gmail.com

PARROTT, Canon Gerald Arthur. b 32. St Cath Coll Cam BA 56 MA 60. Chich Th Coll. **d** 58 **p** 59. C Ashington *Newc* 58–61; C Brighton St Pet *Chich* 61–63; V Leeds St Wilfrid *Ripon* 63–68; R Lewisham St Jo Southend *S'wark* 69–73; TR Catford (Southend) and Downham 73–77; RD E Lewisham 75–77; Can Res and Prec S'wark Cathl 77–88; TR Wimbledon 88–95; rtd 95; PtO *Chich* from 95. *10 Palings Way, Fernhurst, Haslemere GU27 3HJ* T: (01428) 641533

PARROTT, Joanna Joy. b 78. Trin Coll Bris 17. **d** 19 **p** 20. C Halstead Area *Chelmsf* from 19. *47 Tidings Hill, Halstead CO9 1BL* E: halsteadcuratejop@gmail.com

PARROTT, Martin William. b 57. Keele Univ BA 79 K Coll Lon MA 93 W Lon Inst of HE PGCE 80. Ripon Coll Cuddesdon 82. **d** 85 **p** 86. C Birchfield *Birm* 85–88; Chapl Univ Coll Medical Sch *Lon* 88–93; Chapl SOAS 88–93; P-in-c Univ Ch Ch the K 90–93; V Hebden Bridge *Wakef* 93–01; Asst Chapl Pinderfields and Pontefract Hosps NHS Trust 01–02; Chapl Calderdale and Huddersfield NHS Trust 02–11; V Crosland Moor and Linthwaite *Wakef* 11–12; rtd 12; P-in-c Todmorden w Cornholme and Walsden *Leeds* 16–19. *16 Upper Bell Hall, Halifax HX1 3AQ* T: (01422) 363386 M: 07905-444872 E: martinwilliamparrott@gmail.com

PARRY, Canon Alfred Charles Ascough. b 37. Natal Univ BA 58. Westcott Ho Cam 59. **d** 61 **p** 62. C E Ham w Upton Park *Chelmsf* 61–63; C Durban St Martin S Africa 63–64; R Newcastle H Trin 64–70; Dir Chr Educn Kloof 70–76; Sub Dean Pietermaritzburg 76–81; R Estcourt S Africa 81; Adn N Natal 81–85; R Kloof S Africa 86–93; R Berea 93–98; Hon Can Pietermaritzburg from 86; Sen Asst Min Hornchurch St Andr *Chelmsf* 99–04; C Furze Platt *Ox* 04–05; Hon C 05–07; rtd 05; PtO *St Alb* 08–18; *Glouc* from 19. *16 Capel Court, The Burgage, Prestbury, Cheltenham GL52 3EL* T: (01242) 352992

PARRY, Andrew Martyn. b 64. Witwatersrand Univ BA 81 MBA 91 Open Univ BSc 04 Birkbeck Coll Lon MSc 16. Ox Min Course 06. **d** 09 **p** 10. NSM Horton and Wraysbury *Ox* 09–12; NSM Stoke Poges 12–19; P-in-c Wexham 19–20; R from 20. *2 Pennylets Green, Stoke Poges, Slough SL2 4BT* M: 07972-142073 E: andrewmparry@icloud.com

PARRY, Benjamin. See PARRY, Owen Benjamin

PARRY, Canon Bryan Horace. b 33. St Mich Coll Llan 65. **d** 67 **p** 68. C Holyhead w Rhoscolyn w Llanfair-yn-Neubwll *Ban* 67–71; TV 71–73; P-in-c Small Heath St Greg *Birm* 73–78; V 78–80; V Perry Barr 80–94; RD Handsworth 83–91; P-in-c Kingstanding St Luke 86–92; Hon Can Birm Cathl 87–94; rtd 94; PtO *Nor* from 94. *St Seiriol, Old Crown Yard, Walsingham NR22 6BU* T: (01328) 820019

PARRY, Charles. See PARRY, Alfred Charles Ascough

PARRY, David Alan. b 62. Bris Univ BSc 83 Univ of Wales (Cardiff) CQSW 88. Trin Coll Bris. **d** 94 **p** 95. C Withywood *Bris* 94–98; P-in-c Litherland St Phil *Liv* 98–02; V 02–06; Hon Chapl to the Deaf 00–05; AD Bootle 02–05; Dioc Dir of Ords 05–16; V Toxteth Park Ch Ch and St Mich w St Andr 06–16; Hon Can Liv Cathl 03–05 and 12–16; V Bro Celynnin *Ban* from 16. *The Vicarage, Rose Hill Street, Conwy LL32 8LD* T: (01492) 593402 M: 07403-635510 E: davidparry@esgobaethbangor.net

PARRY, David Thomas Newton. b 45. Selw Coll Cam BA 67 MA 71 Victoria Univ Man MPhil 91 Linacre Coll Ox MSt 07 Linc Coll Ox DPhil 15. Lambeth STh 76 Cuddesdon Coll 67. **d** 69 **p** 70. C Oldham St Mary w St Pet *Man* 69–73; C Baguley 73–74; Tutor Sarum & Wells Th Coll 74–78; V Westleigh St Pet *Man* 78–88; TR E Farnworth and Kearsley 88–97; TR Deanshanger *St Alb* 97–03; V Blackbird Leys *Ox* 03–11; rtd 11; PtO *Llan* from 11. *32 Barry Road, Pontypridd CF37 1HY* T: (01443) 650549 E: david@parsonage.org.uk

PARRY, Denis. b 34. Sarum & Wells Th Coll 83. **d** 85 **p** 86. C Hubberston w Herbrandston and Hasguard etc *St D* 85–88; C Herbrandston and Hasguard w St Ishmael's 89; P-in-c 89–90; R 90–99; Dioc RE Adv 89–99; rtd 99; PtO *Heref* 99–20; *St D* 10–17. *Mayfield, 33 Mill Street, Kington HR5 3AL* T: (01544) 230550

PARRY, Canon Dennis John. b 38. Univ of Wales (Lamp) BA 60. St Mich Coll Llan 60. **d** 62 **p** 63. C Caerphilly *Llan* 62–64; C Aberdare St Fagan 64–67; Miss at Povungnituk Canada 67–69; R Gelligaer *Llan* 69–75; V Llanwnnog and Caersws w Carno *Ban* 75–89; V Llanidloes w Llangurig 89–01; RD Arwystli 89–01; Hon Can Ban Cathl 90–01; Can Cursal Ban Cathl 97–01; rtd 02; PtO *Ban* 02–17. *Lock*

Cottage, Groesfford, Brecon LD3 7UY T: (01874) 665400 E: dj519@btinternet.com

PARRY, Gordon Martyn Winn. b 47. Down Coll Cam BA 68 MA 70 Univ Coll Chich MA 02. **d** 04 **p** 05. NSM Turners Hill *Chich* 04–07; NSM E Grinstead St Swithun 07–11; NSM Worth, Pound Hill and Maidenbower from 11. *31A Mount Close, Crawley RH10 7EF* M: 07802-432398 E: gordonmwparry@btinternet.com

PARRY, Jane. See PARRY, Patricia Jane

PARRY, Canon Kenneth Charles. b 34. Ripon Hall Ox 56. **d** 58 **p** 59. C Stoke *Cov* 58–61; Chapl RN 61–65; V Cradley *Worc* 65–70; V Gt Malvern H Trin 70–83; RD Malvern 74–83; Hon Can Worc Cathl 80–83; V Budleigh Salterton *Ex* 83–91; Can Res and Prec Ex Cathl 91–00; rtd 00; PtO *Ex* from 04. *Brook Cottage, Pye Corner, Kennford, Exeter EX6 7TB* T: (01392) 832767 E: kc.parry@btinternet.com

PARRY, Lily Jacqueline Nicola. b 58. All SS Cen for Miss & Min 15. **d** 17 **p** 18. C Gt Crosby St Luke *Liv* from 17; Chapl Liv Women's NHS Foundn Trust from 18; Chapl Wirral Univ Teaching Hosp NHS Foundn Trust from 19. *Liverpool Women's NHS Foundation Trust, Crown Street, Liverpool L8 7SS* T: 0151-708 9988

PARRY, Manon Ceridwen. See JAMES, Manon Ceridwen

PARRY, Canon Marilyn Marie. b 46. W Coll Ohio BA 68 Man Univ MA 77 PhD 00. Episc Th Sch Cam Mass 68 Gilmore Ho 76. **dss** 79 **d** 87 **p** 94. Westleigh St Pet *Man* 78–85; Chapl Asst N Man Gen Hosp 85–90; Tutor NOC 90–97; Dir Studies 91–97; Lic Preacher *Man* 90–94; Hon C E Farnworth and Kearsley 94–97; Nat Adv for Pre-Th Educn and Selection Sec Min Division Abps' Coun 97–01; Public Preacher *St Alb* 98–01; Can Res Ch Ch *Ox* 01–11; Dioc Dir of Ords 01–10; IME Officer 10–11; rtd 11; PtO *Llan* from 11. *32 Barry Road, Pontypridd CF37 1HY* T: (01443) 650549 M: 07952-309667 E: marilyn@parsonage.org.uk

PARRY, Mrs Olwen Margaret. b 45. Cardiff Coll of Educn CertEd 67. Llan Dioc Tr Scheme 88. **d** 92 **p** 97. NSM Newcastle *Llan* 92–04; NSM Llansantffraid, Bettws and Aberkenfig 04–15; rtd 15; PtO *Llan* from 15. *17 Wernlys Road, Bridgend CF31 4NS* T: (01656) 721860

PARRY, Owen Benjamin. b 42. St As Minl Tr Course 99. **d** 01 **p** 02. C Llangollen w Trevor and Llantysilio *St As* 01–07; rtd 07; C-in-c Pradoe *Lich* 09–11; PtO *St As* from 09; *Lich* 14–19. *Fairways, Halton, Chirk, Wrexham LL14 5BD* T: (01691) 778484

PARRY, Mrs Patricia Jane. b 54. Liv Univ BTh 99. NOC 97. **d** 99 **p** 00. C Wilmslow *Ches* 99–03; V Baddiley and Wrenbury w Burleydam 03–08; V Alderley Edge 08–16; RD Knutsford 13–16; V Tranmere St Paul w St Luke 16–20; rtd 20; PtO *Ches* from 20. *School House, Kingsley Road, Crowton, Northwich CW8 2RW* T: (01928) 890259 E: schoolhousecrowton@outlook.com

PARRY, Peter John. b 42. Westmr Coll Ox BTh 99 Sarum Coll MA 14. EAMTC 99. **d** 01 **p** 02. NSM Montreux w Gstaad *Eur* 01–06; PtO *Pet* from 05. *Forge House, Church Road, Hargrave, Wellingborough NN9 6BQ* E: phwparry@btinternet.com

PARRY, Robin Allinson. b 69. Qu Foundn (Course) 17. **d** 18 **p** 19. NSM Worc SE from 18. *12 Whitewood Way, Worcester WR5 2LN*

PARRY, Miss Violet Margaret. b 30. Selly Oak Coll 53. **dss** 82 **d** 87. W Kilburn St Luke w St Simon and St Jude *Lon* 82–83; St Marylebone St Mary 83–86; Stamford All SS w St Jo *Linc* 86–90; C 87–90; rtd 90; PtO *Linc* 90–03; *Leic* 03–16. *2 Stuart Court, High Street, Kibworth Beauchamp, Leicester LE8 0LR* T: 0116-279 6858

PARRY-JENNINGS, Christopher William. b 34. Lon Coll of Div 57. **d** 60 **p** 62. C Claughton cum Grange *Ches* 60–63; C Folkestone H Trin w Ch Ch *Cant* 63–67; V Lincoln NZ 67–72; Chapl Cant Univ 68–72; V Riccarton St Jas 72–88; V Heathcote Mt Pleasant 88–96; First Gen Sec SPCK (NZ) 89–90; P Asst Upper Riccarton St Pet NZ from 96. *22 Ambleside Drive, Burnside, Christchurch 8053, New Zealand* T/F: (0064) (3) 358 9304 E: chpj@globe.net.nz

PARRY JONES, Dylan Caradog. **d** 18 **p** 19. C Dyffryn Clwyd Miss Area *St As* 18–21; P-in-c Wrexham from 21. *The Vicarage, Vicarage Hill, Rhostyllen, Wrexham LL14 4AR* E: dcparryjones@gmail.com

PARRY-JONES, Leonard. b 29. Univ of Wales (Ban) BA 52. St Mich Coll Llan 52. **d** 54 **p** 55. C Newtown w Llanllwchaiarn w Aberhafesp *St As* 54–58; C Abergele 58–60; V Pennant, Hirnant and Llangynog 60–65; V Llanynys w Llanychan 65–71; V Brynymaen w Trofarth 71–94; RD Rhos 77–94; rtd 94; PtO *Lich* 15. *29 Pengwern Court, Longden Road, Shrewsbury SY3 7JE*

PARSELLE, Stephen Paul. b 53. Univ of Wales (Cardiff) MTh 06. St Jo Coll Nottm. **d** 82 **p** 83. C Boscombe St Jo *Win* 82–86; CF 86–05; Dir of Ords 02–05; Chapl RN

05–08; PtO *Win* from 09. *11 Southbourne Overcliff Drive, Bournemouth BH6 3TE*   T: (01202)   433858   M: 07711-017282 E: parselle@aol.com

PARSONAGE, Robert Hugh. b 55. Nottm Trent Univ BSc 78. Trin Coll Bris BA 97. **d** 97 **p** 98. C Chell *Lich* 97–01; R Poringland *Nor* from 01; RD Loddon 10–16. *The Rectory, Rectory Lane, Poringland, Norwich NR14 7SL*   T: (01508) 492215 E: rector@poringland-benefice.org.uk

PARSONS, Andrew David. b 53. UEA BA 74 Fitzw Coll Cam BA 77 MA 81. Westcott Ho Cam 75. **d** 78 **p** 79. C Hellesdon *Nor* 78–82; C Eaton 82–85; P-in-c Burnham Thorpe w Burnham Overy 85–87; R Burnham Sutton w Burnham Ulph etc 85–87; R Burnham Gp of Par 87–93; P-in-c Wroxham w Hoveton and Belaugh 93; R 93–07; RD St Benet 99–07; V Old Catton 07–21; rtd 21. *The Thatched Cottage, St Swithin's Alley, Norwich NR2 4TX* E: adp07@btinternet.com

PARSONS, Canon Christopher Kelly. b 75. Simon Fraser Univ BC BA 99. Vancouver Sch of Th MDiv 03. **d** 03 **p** 04. C Ch Ch Cathl Victoria Canada 04–05; R Victoria St Martin in the Fields and St Columba 06–11; C Victoria Three Saints 10–12; R Cordova Bay and Lakehill 12–15; P-in-c Freiburg-im-Breisau *Eur* 15–20; R Newmarket Canada from 20. *162 Banbrooke Crescent, Newmarket ON L3X 2W6, Canada* E: ckparsons@protonmail.com

PARSONS, Christopher Paul. b 58. EAMTC 01. **d** 04 **p** 05. C Pakefield *Nor* 04–08; P-in-c Kenwyn w St Allen *Truro* 08–16; R from 16. *The Vicarage, Kenwyn Church Road, Truro TR1 3DR*   T: (01872) 263015 E: vicarkenstallen@gmail.com

PARSONS, David Norman. b 39. Glos Univ BA 06 FCIB 83. Trin Coll Bris 92. **d** 94 **p** 95. NSM Swindon Dorcan Bris 94–03; PtO *Glouc* 03–15; *Carl* from 15. *24 Helme Lodge, Natland, Kendal LA9 7QA*   T: (01539)   727183 E: davidnparsons39@btinternet.com

PARSONS, Preb Deborah Anne. b 66. Surrey Univ BA 87. STETS 04. **d** 07 **p** 08. C Goodrington *Ex* 07–11; TV Totnes w Bridgetown, Berry Pomeroy etc from 11; RD Totnes from 18; Dioc Interfaith Adv from 19; Preb Ex Cathl from 20. *St John's Vicarage, Crosspark, Totnes TQ9 5BQ*   T: (01803) 840113 E: d.a.parsons@btinternet.com

PARSONS, Geoffrey Fairbanks. b 35. Trin Coll Cam BA 58 MA 68. Ridley Hall Cam 59. **d** 61 **p** 62. C Over St Chad *Ches* 61–64; C Heswall 64–69; V Congleton St Steph 69–75; V Weaverham 75–94; P-in-c Backford and Capenhurst 94–00; R 00–01; rtd 01; PtO *Ches* from 02. *28 Springcroft, Parkgate, South Wirral CH64 6SE*   T: 0151-336 3354

PARSONS, Canon Jennifer Anne. b 53. Univ of Wales (Lamp) BA 76 MA 78 Jes Coll Cam PhD 90. Westcott Ho Cam 92. **d** 94 **p** 95. C Halesowen *Worc* 94–97; TV Worc St Barn w Ch Ch 97–04; R Matson *Glouc* 04–12; Hon Can Glouc Cathl 07–12; Asst Dean of Women Clergy 09–11; rtd 12; PtO *St D* from 12; Dioc Officer for Soc Resp 15–16. *Lan Fach, Cefnypant, Whitland SA34 0TS*   T: (01994) 419808 E: jeniparsons7@gmail.com

PARSONS, Jeremy Douglas Adam. b 64. Worc Coll Ox BA 87 MA 88. Ridley Hall Cam. **d** 09 **p** 11. NSM Cambridge St Martin *Ely* 09–13; PtO *S'well* 13–14; TV Saffron Walden and Villages *Chelmsf* 14–17; R St Edm Way *St E* 17–21; TV Cherwell Valley *Ox* from 21. *The Vicarage, 44 Forge Place, Fritwell, Bicester OX27 7QQ* M: 07980-016974

PARSONS, Canon John Banham. b 43. Selw Coll Cam BA 65 MA 68. Ridley Hall Cam 65. **d** 67 **p** 68. C Downend Bris 67–71; Public Preacher Withywood LEP 71–77; P-in-c Hengrove 77–78; V 78–85; V Letchworth St Paul w Willian *St Alb* 85–94; P-in-c Barking St Marg w St Patr *Chelmsf* 94–98; TR 98–04; RD Barking and Dagenham 00–04; P-in-c Hornchurch H Cross 04–09; RD Havering 04–08; Hon Can Chelmsf Cathl 01–09; rtd 09; PtO *St Alb* from 09. *8 Pound Close, Upper Caldecote, Biggleswade SG18 9AU*   T: (01767) 315285 E: j.parsons986@btinternet.com

PARSONS, Canon Marlene Beatrice. b 43. Wilson Carlile Coll. **dss** 76 **d** 87 **p** 94. Coulsdon St Jo *S'wark* 76–79; Hill *Birm* 79–86; Dioc Lay Min Adv 80–90; Vice Prin WMMTC 86–90; Dioc Dir of Ords *Birm* 90–04; Dean of Women's Min 90–04; Hon Can Birm Cathl 89–04; rtd 04; PtO *Birm* 04–18. *20 Copperbeech Close, Birmingham B32 2HT*   T: 0121-427 2632

PARSONS, Michael. b 46. Open Univ BA 84. SWMTC 05. **d** 08 **p** 09. NSM Boscastle w Davidstow *Truro* 08–15; NSM Boscastle and Tintagel Gp 15–16; rtd 16; PtO *Truro* from 16. *2 Penally Terrace, Boscastle PL35 0HA*   T: (01840) 250625 E: mike@2penally.co.uk

PARSONS, Canon Michael William Semper. b 47. St Cath Coll Ox BA 69 MA 74 DPhil 74 Selw Coll Cam BA 77 MA 81. Ridley Hall Cam 75. **d** 78 **p** 79. C Edmonton All SS *Lon* 78–81; SPCK Research Fell Dur Univ 81–84; Hon Lect Th 84–85; SPCK Fell N of England Inst for Chr Educn 84–85;

P-in-c Derby St Aug 85–95; TR Walbrook Epiphany 95–96; Dioc Voc Adv 86–96; P-in-c Hempsted *Glouc* 96–00; Dir of Ords 96–04; Dir Curates' Tr 00–04; Prin WEMTC *Glouc* 04–11; Prin Lect Glos Univ 09–11; P-in-c Coney Hill 11–15; rtd 15; PtO *Glouc* from 15; Clergy Retirement Officer from 17; Hon Can Glouc Cathl from 03. *6 Spa Villas, Montpellier, Gloucester GL1 1LB*   T: (01452) 308227 E: mwsp@btinternet.com

PARSONS, Canon Robert Martin. b 43. Qu Coll Cam BA 65 MA 69. ALCD 68. **d** 68 **p** 69. C Chapeltown *Sheff* 68–71; C Sheff St Jo 71–75; V Swadlincote *Derby* 75–91; RD Repton 81–91; P-in-c Gresley 82–86; R Etwall w Egginton 91–93; Can Res Derby Cathl 93–98; Hon Can Derby Cathl 98–09; P-in-c Belper 98–03; V 03–09; Jt P-in-c Ambergate and Heage 06–09; rtd 09; Hon C Bicton, Montford w Shrawardine and Fitz *Lich* 09–18; Hon C Leaton and Albrighton w Battlefield 09–18; PtO 18–21. *43 Steepside, Shrewsbury SY3 6DS*   T: (01743)   365845 E: canonparsons@btinternet.com

PARSONS, Mrs Samantha Jayne. b 69. Aber Univ MA 93 N Coll of Educn PGCE 95 St Jo Coll Dur BATM 16. Cranmer Hall Dur 14. **d** 16 **p** 17. C Horncastle Gp *Linc* 16–19; V Grantham, Harrowby w Londonthorpe from 19. *The Vicarage, Edinburgh Road, Grantham NG31 9QZ* E: rev.samparsons@gmail.com

PARSONS, Stephen Christopher. b 45. Keble Coll Ox BA 67 MA 72 BLitt 78. Cuddesdon Coll 68. **d** 70 **p** 71. C Whitstable All SS *Cant* 70–71; C Croydon St Sav 71–74; PtO Ox 74–76; C St Laur in Thanet *Cant* 76–79; V Lugwardine w Bartestree and Weston Beggard *Heref* 79–87; V Lechlade *Glouc* 87–03; R Edin St Cuth 03–10; rtd 10; PtO *Carl* 12–19; Newc from 16. *3 Church Road, Greystoke, Penrith CA11 0TW*   T: (01768) 483221 E: parsvic2@gmail.com

PARSONS, Stephen Drury. b 54. Qu Mary Coll Lon BSc 76 CCC Cam MSc 79. Westcott Ho Cam 79. **d** 82 **p** 83. C Stretford All SS *Man* 82–85; C Newton Heath All SS 85–86; V Ashton St Jas 86–90; PtO 97–13; TR Turton Moorland 13–19; rtd 19. *174 Bolton Road, Turton, Bolton BL7 0AH*

PARSONS, Mrs Susan Catherine. b 60. SWMTC 06 ERMC 08. **d** 09 **p** 10. NSM Oakham, Ashwell, Braunston, Brooke, Egleton etc *Pet* 09–11; NSM Polden Wheel *B & W* 12–14; PtO 14–19. *Greystones, Broadway, Chilton Polden, Bridgwater TA7 9DJ*   T: (01278) 723885 E: susie.parsons@hotmail.co.uk

PARSONS, Thomas James. b 74. K Coll Lon BMus 97 LRAM 96. Oak Hill Th Coll BA 06. **d** 06 **p** 07. C Hensingham *Carl* 06–10; V Sidcup Ch Ch *Roch* from 10. *The Vicarage, 16 Christchurch Road, Sidcup DA15 7HE*   T: (020) 8308 0835   M: 07960-944287 E: tjparsons@tiscali.co.uk

PARTINGTON, The Ven Brian Harold. b 36. OBE 02. St Aid Birkenhead 60. **d** 63 **p** 64. C Barlow Moor *Man* 63–66; C Deane 66–68; V Patrick *S & M* 68–96; Bp's Youth Chapl 68–77; RD Peel 76–96; P-in-c German St Jo 77–78; V 78–96; P-in-c Foxdale 77–78; V 78–96; Can St German's Cathl 85–96; Adn of Man 96–05; V Douglas St Geo 96–04; rtd 04. *Brambles, Patrick Village, Peel, Isle of Man IM5 3AH*   T: (01624) 844173 E: bpartington@mcb.net

PARTINGTON, John. *See* PARTINGTON, Peter John

PARTINGTON, Canon Kevin. b 51. Huddersfield Poly BA 73. St Jo Coll Nottm 91. **d** 93 **p** 94. C Salterhebble All SS *Wakef* 93–96; V Pontefract All SS 96–03; TR Dewsbury 03–14; *Leeds* 14–15; Hon Can Wakef Cathl 07–15; RD Dewsbury Wakef 13–14; AD Leeds 14–15; rtd 15; PtO Leeds from 15. *46 Larch Road, Huddersfield HD1 4JG*   T: (01484) 614767   M: 07563-513632 E: kevin.partington@aol.co.uk

PARTINGTON, Peter John. b 57. Peterho Cam MA. St Jo Coll Nottm 79. **d** 81 **p** 82. C Cov H Trin 81–85; C Woking St Jo *Guildf* 85–87 and 94–99; R Busbridge 87–94; Dir of Ords 94–03; P-in-c Winchcombe, Gretton, Sudeley Manor etc *Glouc* 03–05; TR Winchcombe 05–15; TV S Cotswolds 15–19; rtd 19; PtO Ox from 20. *32 The Slade, Charlbury, Chipping Norton OX7 3SJ*   T: (01608) 810657 E: john@pjohnp.me.uk

PARTON, Mrs Michelle Elizabeth. b 82. Univ of Wales (Abth) BA 05 Newman Univ BA(Theol) 17. Qu Coll Birm 12. **d** 15 **p** 16. C Wythall *Birm* 15–19; C Willand, Uffculme, Kentisbeare etc *Ex* from 19. *5 Cotters Close, Kentisbeare, Cullompton EX15 2DJ*   T: (01884)   266741 E: revmichelleparton@gmail.com

PARTRIDGE, Alan Christopher. b 55. Thames Poly BA 77 Ex Univ PGCE 78. St Jo Coll Nottm MA 00. **d** 00 **p** 01. C Woking St Jo *Guildf* 00–03; C Ely 03–08; TV 08–09; P-in-c Sawston 09–18; V 19–20; P-in-c Babraham 09–18; V 19–20; rtd 20; PtO *Ely* from 21. *Address temp unknown* E: a.partridge7@ntlworld.com

PARTRIDGE, Mrs Bryony Gail. b 51. St Anne's Coll Ox BA 72 MA 76 Ox Univ PGCE 73 Leeds Univ BA 11. Yorks Min Course 09. **d** 11 **p** 12. NSM Oakworth *Bradf* 11–14; Leeds from 14. *New House Farm, Oakworth, Keighley BD22 7JW*   T: (01535) 643206 E: geraldandbryony@hotmail.com

PARTRIDGE, Ian Starr. b 36. Linc Th Coll 87. **d** 89 **p** 90. C Barton upon Humber *Linc* 89–92; P-in-c Barkwith Gp 92–97; R 97–02; rtd 02; PtO *Linc* from 02; RD Calcewaithe and Candleshoe 03–05. *Altair, 4 Thames Street, Louth LN11 7AD* T: (01507) 600398 E: ian@altair.org.uk

PARTRIDGE, Preb Michael John. b 61. St Edm Hall Ox BA 83 MA 89 St Jo Coll Dur BA 86. Cranmer Hall Dur 84. **d** 87 **p** 88. C Amington *Birm* 87–90; C Sutton Coldfield H Trin 90–93; P-in-c W Exe *Ex* 93–01; RD Tiverton 96–00; V Tiverton St Geo and St Paul 01–06; P-in-c Pinhoe and Broadclyst 06–13; P-in-c Aylesbeare, Rockbeare, Farringdon etc 06–13; TR Broadclyst, Clyst Honiton, Pinhoe, Rockbeare etc 13–17; R Alphington, Shillingford St George and Ide from 17; Preb Ex Cathl from 12. *The Rectory, 6 Lovelace Gardens, Exeter EX2 8XQ* T: (01392) 491476 M: 07751-725306 E: rev.mike.partridge@gmail.com

PARTRIDGE, Richard Bruce. b 65. Kingston Poly BA 87. STETS 10. **d** 12 **p** 13. NSM Christchurch *Win* 12–16; C from 16. *The Paddocks, Holly Lane, Walkford, Christchurch BH23 5QQ* T: (01425) 279043 E: richardpartridge310@btinternet.com

PARTRIDGE, Ronald Malcolm. b 49. Bris Bapt Coll LTh 74 Cuddesdon Coll 74. **d** 75 **p** 76. C Bris St Andr Hartcliffe 75–78; C E Bris 78–82; V Easton All Hallows 82–85; TV Brighton St Pet w Chpl Royal and St Jo *Chich* 85–86; TV Brighton St Pet and St Nic w Chpl Royal 86–88; C-in-c Bermondsey St Hugh CD *S'wark* 88–90; Asst Chapl Gt Ormond Street Hosp for Children NHS Trust 91–97; PtO *Chich* 13–17. *29 All Saints Street, Hastings TN34 3BJ* T: (01424) 715219

PARTRIDGE, Ronald William. b 42. Shimer Coll Illinois BA 64 K Coll Lon MA 09. Cant Sch of Min 93 SEITE 94. **d** 96 **p** 97. NSM Upchurch w Lower Halstow *Cant* 96–12; NSM Newington w Hartlip and Stockbury 96–12; NSM Iwade 96–12; Chapl HM Pris Standford Hill 00–08; Chapl Medway NHS Foundn Trust 10–20; PtO *Roch* from 10; *Cant* from 12. *4 The Green, Lower Halstow, Sittingbourne ME9 7DT* T: (01795) 842007 M: 07570-404706 E: revdron.partridge@gmail.com

PARTRIDGE, Canon Sarah Mercy. b 59. SEITE 04. **d** 07 **p** 08. NSM Tunbridge Wells K Chas *Roch* from 07; Hon Can Roch Cathl from 18. *Long Hedges, Station Road, Rotherfield, Crowborough TN6 3HP* T: (01892) 853451 E: sm.partridge@outlook.com

PARTRIDGE, Stephen Hugh. b 70. Bath Univ BSc 91 Univ of Wales (Swansea) PGCE 92. St Jo Coll Nottm MTh 13. **d** 13 **p** 14. C Canford Magna *Sarum* 13–16; TV The Lytchetts and Upton from 16. *The Rectory, Jennys Lane, Lytchett Matravers, Poole BH16 6BP* E: revspartridge@gmail.com

PARTRIDGE, Timothy David. b 85. Bath Univ BSc 07. Oak Hill Th Coll BA 18. **d** 18 **p** 19. C Plymouth St Andr and Stonehouse *Ex* from 18. *The Rectory, 6 Underhill Road, Plymouth PL3 4BP* M: 07709-491261 E: timothydpartridge@gmail.com

PARTRIDGE, Canon Timothy Reeve. b 39. Lon Univ BSc 60 AKC 60. Wells Th Coll 60. **d** 62 **p** 63. C Glouc St Cath 62–65; C Sutton St Nicholas *Linc* 65–74; R Bugbrooke *Pet* 74–95; R Bugbrooke w Rothersthorpe 95–04; RD Daventry 81–88; Can Pet Cathl 83–04; Warden of Par Ev 96–02; rtd 04; PtO *Ox* 06–20. *419 St Crispin Retirement Village, St Crispin Drive, Northampton NN5 4RA* T: (01604) 591329 E: tim.partridge39@tiscali.co.uk

PASCHAL, Brother. See WORTON, David Reginald Paschal

PASCOE, Preb Caroline Elizabeth Alice. b 62. **d** 08 **p** 09. NSM Ewenny w St Brides Major *Llan* 08–10; NSM Ross w Walford and Brampton Abbotts *Heref* from 15; Lay Development Officer from 10; Preb Heref Cathl from 17. *Diocese of Hereford, Unit 8-9, The Business Quarter, Eco Park Road, Ludlow SY8 1FD* T: (01584) 871086 E: c.pascoe@hereford.anglican.org

PASCOE, Lorraine Eve. See SUMMERS, Lorraine Eve

PASCOE, Michael Lewis. b 43. **d** 99 **p** 00. OLM Crowan and Treslothan *Truro* 99–02; C 02–13; OLM Penponds 01–02; C 02–13; P-in-c 13–14; rtd 14; PtO *Truro* from 14. *Genesis, Bosparva Lane, Leedstown, Hayle TR27 6DN* T: (01736) 850425 E: revdmike@supanet.com

PASHLEY, Howard Thomas. b 47. Kent Univ MSc 85 Keele Univ PGCE 71 ARIC 70. **d** 06 **p** 07. OLM Sandwich *Cant* 06–12; OLM Sandwich and Worth 12–17; rtd 17; PtO *Cant* from 18. *56 New Street, Sandwich CT13 9BB* T: (01304) 612018

PASK, Howard. b 54. St Jo Coll Nottm. **d** 99 **p** 00. C Todmorden *Wakef* 99–02; P-in-c Hebden Bridge 02–03; P-in-c Heptonstall 02–03; V Hebden Bridge and Heptonstall 03–14; *Leeds* 14–18; rtd 18. *PO Box 122, Ctra de Cartáma L1, 29120 Alhaurín el Grande (Málaga), Spain* M: 07581-403148 *or* (0034) 686 400 244 E: howie120@msn.com

PASK (formerly THURTELL), Canon Victoria Ann. b 59. St Jo Coll Dur BSc 82 Univ of Wales (Lamp) BA 11 PGCE 96. STETS 02. **d** 05 **p** 06. C Chickerell w Fleet *Sarum* 05–08; TV Dorchester 08–14; TV Dorchester and the Winterbournes 14–15; Can Res and Prec Ex Cathl 15–17; PtO 17–19; Chapl Greycoat Hosp Sch 18–19; V Bromley St Mark *Roch* from 19; AD Bromley from 21. *St Mark's Vicarage, 51 Hayes Road, Bromley BR2 9AE* T: (020) 8460 6220 E: paskvictoria@gmail.com

PASKETT, Ms Margaret Anne. b 45. Northd Coll of Educn CertEd 67 York Univ BSc 81 Leeds Univ MEd 83. NEOC 84. **d** 87 **p** 94. Par Dn Marske in Cleveland *York* 87–91; C 92–96; Dioc Adv for Diaconal Mins 92–96; P-in-c Hemingbrough and Tr Officer (York Adnry) 96–05; rtd 06; PtO *York* from 07. *15 Hubert Street, York YO23 1EF* T: (01904) 626521 E: annepaskett62@gmail.com

PASKINS, David James. b 52. Univ of Wales (Lamp) BA 73 Trin Hall Cam BA 76 MA 81. Westcott Ho Cam 74. **d** 77 **p** 78. C St Peter-in-Thanet *Cant* 77–82; C Swanage *Sarum* 80–82; R Waldron *Chich* 82–92; R Bere Ferrers *Ex* 92–96; V Lockerley and E Dean w E and W Tytherley *Win* 96–03; R Cranborne w Boveridge, Edmondsham etc *Sarum* 03–15; rtd 15; PtO *Nor* from 16. *8 Blackthorn Avenue, Holt NR25 6TY* T: (01263) 715905 E: david@paskins.eclipse.co.uk

PASTERFIELD, Laura Sophia. See FERGUSON, Laura Sophia

PATCH, Simon John. b 63. Aus Nat Univ BA 88 Southn Univ BTh 95 Univ of S Qld MEd 15. Chich Th Coll 92 Westcott Ho Cam 94. **d** 95 **p** 96. C Ifield *Chich* 95–99; C Stepney St Dunstan and All SS *Lon* 03–06; Hong Kong from 07. *Flat 3/A, Tower 20, Hong Kong Gold Coast, 1 Castle Peak Road, Castle Peak Bay, Hong Kong, Hong Kong, China* E: simon_patch@yahoo.com.au

PATCHELL, Miss Gwendoline Rosa. b 49. Goldsmiths' Coll Lon BA 69 TCert 70. Trin Coll Bris 90. **d** 92 **p** 94. C Ashton-upon-Mersey St Mary Magd *Ches* 92–98; TV Hemel Hempstead *St Alb* 98–06; P-in-c Kirkby in Ashfield *S'well* 06–11; R 11–14; rtd 14; PtO *S'well* from 16. *21 Leivers Close, East Leake, Loughborough LE12 6PQ* E: revdwendypatchell@gmail.com

PATCHING, Julian Francis. b 65. Colchester Inst BA 87 Liv Inst of HE PGCE 88. Ushaw Coll Dur 88. **d** 93 **p** 94. In RC Ch 93–09; C Langdon Hills *Chelmsf* 13–19; P-in-c Hornchurch H Cross from 19. *Holy Cross Vicarage, 260 Hornchurch Road, Hornchurch RM11 1PX* M: 07860-119450 E: jfp65@hotmail.co.uk *or* holycrosschurch1409@gmail.com

PATE, Barry Emile Charles. b 50. NE Lon Poly BA 80 CQSW 80. S'wark Ord Course 85. **d** 88 **p** 89. NSM E Dulwich St Jo *S'wark* 88–92; C Farnborough *Roch* 92–94; C Broxbourne w Wormley *St Alb* 94–00; V Wilbury 00–19; rtd 19; PtO *Ely* from 20. *31 Greengarth, St Ives PE27 5QS* E: b.pate@ntlworld.com

PATEL, Jitesh Krisnakant. b 82. Jes Coll Ox MPhys 04 Kellogg Coll Ox PGCE 06. Wycliffe Hall Ox BA 09 MA 09. **d** 10 **p** 11. C Abingdon *Ox* 10–13; C N Abingdon 13–15; C Southsea St Jude *Portsm* 15–18; C Leic H Trin w St Jo from 18; Dioc Dir Contextual Tr 18–19; Asst Dir St Mellitus E Midl from 19. *46 Brading Road, Leicester LE3 9BG* T: 0116-254 8981 E: jpatel@htl.church

PATEMAN, Miles Thomas. b 89. Swansea Univ BA 12 Sheff Univ MA 19. Coll of Resurr Mirfield BA 17. **d** 18 **p** 19. C Stanground and Farcet *Ely* 18–19; C Fulbourn 19–21; C Lt Wilbraham 19–21; C Gt Wilbraham 19–21; TV Aberavon *Llan* from 21. *62 Mariners Point, Port Talbot SA12 6DN* M: 07936-261144 E: rev.miles@outlook.com

PATERNOSTER, Canon Michael Cosgrove. b 35. Pemb Coll Cam BA 59 MA 63. Cuddesdon Coll 59. **d** 61 **p** 62. C Surbiton St Andr *S'wark* 61–63; Chapl Qu Coll Dundee 63–68; Dioc Supernumerary *Bre* 63–68; Chapl Dundee Univ 67–68; Sec Fellowship of SS Alb and Sergius 68–71; R Dollar *St And* 71–75; R Stonehaven *Bre* 75–90; Hon Can St Paul's Cathl Dundee 81–12; R Aberdeen St Jas *Ab* 90–00; rtd 00; PtO *B & W* from 00. *12 Priest Row, Wells BA5 2PY*

PATERSON, Canon Alan Michael. b 64. **d** 06 **p** 07. SSF 87–11; NSM Bartley Green *Birm* 06–10; V Cowgate *Newc* from 10; P-in-c Newbiggin Hall from 18; Hon Can Newc Cathl from 19. *St Peter's Vicarage, Druridge Drive, Newcastle upon Tyne NE5 3LP* T: 0191-286 9913 E: fatheralan64@btinternet.com

PATERSON (née SOAR), Mrs Angela Margaret. b 58. Aston Univ MSc 81 MCIPD 82. SAOMC 97. **d** 00 **p** 01. NSM Icknield *Ox* from 00. *86 Hill Road, Watlington OX49 5AF* T: (01491) 614033 E: angie.paterson@btinternet.com

PATERSON, Douglas Monro. b 30. Em Coll Cam BA 54 MA 57. Tyndale Hall Bris 55. **d** 57 **p** 58. C Walcot *B & W* 57–60; C Portman Square St Paul *Lon* 60–62; Lect Oak Hill Th Coll 60–62; Min Hampstead St Jo Downshire Hill Prop Chpl *Lon* 62–65; Lect All Nations Chr Coll Ware 62–65; Rwanda 67–73; C Edin St Thos 73–75; Lect Northumbria Bible Coll 73–94; PtO *Edin* 75–94; LtO *Newc* 76–94; rtd 94;

PtO *Ox* 94–10; *York* from 10. *8 Dulverton Hall, Esplanade, Scarborough YO11 2AR* T: (01723) 340108

PATERSON, Geoffrey Gordon. b 45. Cant Univ (NZ) LTh 69. **d** 69 **p** 70. C Linwood NZ 69–71; C Belfast-Redwood 71–76; V Mayfield Mt Somers 76–78; P-in-c Astwood Bank w Crabbs Cross *Worc* 78–80; V Halswell-Prebbleton NZ 80–87; Chapl Sunnyside Hosp 87–95. *19 Ridder Place, Christchurch 8025, New Zealand* T: (0064) (3) 322 7787 *or* (3) 365 3211 E: geoffpat@xtra.co.nz

PATERSON, Mrs Jennifer Ann. b 49. Brooklands Tech Coll 69. S Dios Minl Tr Scheme 85. **d** 88 **p** 95. C Hale *Guildf* 88–92; PtO 94–95; NSM Seale, Puttenham and Wanborough 95–01; rtd 01; PtO *Guildf* 01–16. *4 St George's Close, Badshot Lea, Farnham GU9 9LZ* T: (01252) 316775 E: ja.paterson@btinternet.com

PATERSON, Michael Séan. b 61. Heythrop Coll Lon BD 89 MA 95 Univ of Wales (Lamp) MMin 04. **d** 04 **p** 05. C Stonehaven *Bre* 04–05; C Arbroath 05–06; C Edin Ch Ch 06–08; Chapl St Andr Hospice Airdrie 08–09; Chapl St Columba's Hospice 09–13; Dir Inst Past Supervision and Reflective Practice from 08; PtO *St And* from 16. *8 Greenmount Road North, Burntisland KY3 9JQ* E: michael@ipsrp.org.uk

PATERSON, Paul Philip. b 49. St Jo Coll Dur BA 11 MA 13. Cranmer Hall Dur. **d** 18 **p** 19. NSM Hawthorn and Murton *Dur* 18–21; NSM Hawthorn from 21. *The Old Rectory, The Village, Hawthorn, Seaham SR7 8SG* T: 0191-527 1908 M: 07834-348580 E: p@ulpaterson.net

✠**PATERSON, The Rt Revd Robert Mar Erskine.** b 49. St Jo Coll Dur BA 71 MA 82. Cranmer Hall Dur. **d** 72 **p** 73 c 08. C Harpurhey St Steph and Harpurhey Ch Ch *Man* 72–73; C Sketty *S & B* 73–78; R Llangattock and Llangynidr 78–83; V Gabalfa *Llan* 83–94; TR Cowbridge 94–00; Prin Officer Ch in Wales Coun for Miss and Min 00–06; Metrop Can 04–08; Abp's Chapl and Researcher *York* 06–08; Bp S & M 08–16; Dean St German's Cathl 08–10; rtd 16; Hon Asst Bp Worc from 17; Hon Asst Bp Heref 17–20. *Cedar House, 63 Greenhill, Evesham WR11 4LX* T: (01386) 247105 M: 07979-600627 E: mar.erskine@me.com

PATERSON, Robin Fergus (Robert). b 32. Moore Th Coll Sydney 83. **d** 87 **p** 89. Singapore 87–88; NSM Crieff *St And* 88–92; NSM Comrie 88–92; R Dunkeld 93–98; R Strathtay 93–98; rtd 98; LtO *St And* from 98; PtO *Eur* 98–21. *1 Corsiehill House, Corsiehill, Perth PH2 7BN* T: (01738) 446621 E: robinatcorsie@talktalk.net

PATERSON, Robin Lennox Andrew. b 43. NOC 84. **d** 87 **p** 88. C Manston *Ripon* 87–91; P-in-c Leeds All So 91–95; V 95–98; V Middleton St Mary 98–08; rtd 08; PtO *Leeds* from 17; *York* 18–20. *22 Manston Way, Leeds LS15 8BR* M: 07778-860178 E: rlap@mypostoffice.co.uk

PATERSON, Rodney John. b 62. Keele Univ BA 84. St Jo Coll Nottm MA 98. **d** 98 **p** 99. C Huddersfield H Trin *Wakef* 98–01; P-in-c Charlton Kings H Apostles *Glouc* 01–14; V 14–18; P-in-c Cheltenham St Mich 14–18; R W Cheltenham from 18. *St Mark's Vicarage, Fairmount Road, Cheltenham GL51 7AQ*

PATERSON, Mrs Shirley Anne. b 56. Reading Univ BA 78 Ex Univ PGCE 79. SWMTC 11. **d** 14 **p** 15. NSM Barnstaple *Ex* 14–17; NSM Barnstaple H Trin and Goodleigh from 17. *Elm Cottage, Ladywell, Barnstaple EX31 1QS* T: (01271) 346095 M: 07971-251707 E: shirley.p@live.co.uk

PATERSON, Mrs Susan Ann. b 57. St Hilda's Coll Ox MA 84. EMMTC 92. **d** 95 **p** 96. NSM Evington *Leic* 95–98; C Humberstone 98–03; TV Melton Mowbray 03–09; P-in-c Ab Kettleby and Holwell w Asfordby 09–15; V Deeping St James *Linc* 15–18; R Whippingham w E Cowes *Portsm* from 18. *The Rectory, 69 Victoria Grove, East Cowes PO32 6DL* E: revspaterson@gmail.com

PATMORE, Hector Michael. b 81. Trevelyan Coll Dur BA 03 MA 05. St Jo Coll Dur PhD 08. Ripon Coll Cuddesdon MTh 17. **d** 16 **p** 17. NSM Lisvane *Llan* 16; Dir Studies St Geo Coll Jerusalem 16–17; PtO Jerusalem 18–19; PtO *Eur* from 19. *Katholieke Universiteit Leuven, Faculteit Theologie en Religiewetenschappen, Sint-Michielsstraat4 - bus 3100 B-3000 Leuven, The Netherlands* T: (0031) (32) 1632 3695 E: hec_uk@yahoo.co.uk

✠**PATON, The Rt Revd Ian James.** b 57. Jes Coll Cam MA 78 PGCE 79 Edin Univ MTh 07. Westcott Ho Cam MA 81. **d** 82 **p** 83 **c** 18. C Whitley Ch Ch *Ox* 82–84; Bp's Dom Chapl 84–86; Chapl Wadh Coll Ox 86–90; C Ox St Mary V w St Cross and St Pet 86–90; Can and Vice Provost St Mary's Cathl Edin 90–94; R Edin St Mary 90–94; R Haddington and Dunbar 94–97; R Edin Old St Paul 97–18; Can St Mary's Cathl 04–18; Hon Chapl Edin Univ 11–18; Bp St And from 18. *28A Balhousie Street, Perth PH1 5HJ* T: (01738) 580428 E: bishop@standrews.anglican.org

PATON, Canon John William Scholar. b 52. Mert Coll Ox BA 74 MA 95. St Steph Ho Ox 93. **d** 95 **p** 96. C Sherborne w Castleton and Lillington *Sarum* 95–98; Succ S'wark Cathl 98–01; Chapl Medical and Dental Students K Coll Lon 98–01; P-in-c Purley St Mark S'wark 01–07; P-in-c Purley St Swithun 05–07; Prec Ch Ch Ox 07–17; P-in-c Sulhamstead Abbots and Bannister w Ufton Nervet *Ox* from 17; Hon Can Ch Ch from 18. *The Rectory, Sulhamstead Road, Ufton Nervet, Reading RG7 4DH* M: 07790-498175 E: sunrector@outlook.com

PATON-WILLIAMS, David Graham. b 58. Warwick Univ BA 81 Selw Coll Cam BA 86 MA 90 Newc Univ MA 92. Ridley Hall Cam 84. **d** 87 **p** 88. C S Westoe *Dur* 87–90; C Newton Aycliffe 90–91; TV 91–93; Chapl Univ Coll of Ripon and York St Jo 93–98; Min Can Ripon Cathl 93–98; R Bedale 98–02; P-in-c Leeming 98–02; R Bedale and Leeming 03–08; P-in-c Thornton Watlass 07–08; R Bedale and Leeming and Thornton Watlass 08; AD Wensley 05–08; V Roundhay St Edm 08–14; *Leeds* 14–16; Hon Can Ripon Cathl 11–16; R Edin St Columba from 16. *28 Castle Terrace, Edinburgh EH1 2EL*

PATRICIA, Sister. See PERKINS, Patricia Doris

PATRICK, Andrew. b 83. Hull Univ BA 06. St Jo Coll Nottm 09. **d** 12 **p** 13. C Harrogate St Mark *Leeds* 12–16; TV Bilton from 16. *8 Pecketts Way, Harrogate HG1 3EW* M: 07966-360437 E: mrandrewpatrick@gmail.com

PATRICK, Charles. See PATRICK, Peter Charles

PATRICK, Hugh Joseph. b 37. TCD BA 62 MA 66. **d** 63 **p** 64. C Dromore Cathl *D & D* 63–66; C Lurgan Ch the Redeemer 66–70; C Rothwell *Ripon* 70–73; V Thurnscoe St Hilda *Sheff* 73–78; V Wales 78–82; P-in-c Thorpe Salvin 78–82; RD Laughton 93–98; rtd 02; PtO *Sheff* 02–10. *5 Fairfax Avenue, Worksop S81 7RH* T: (01909) 477622 E: hughpatrick@sky.com

PATRICK, Canon John Andrew. b 62. St Jo Coll Dur BA 84. Ripon Coll Cuddesdon 87. **d** 89 **p** 90. C Frankby w Greasby *Ches* 89–92; Lect Boston *Linc* 92–95; P-in-c Graffoe Gp 95–97; R 97–02; P-in-c New Sleaford 02–12; P-in-c Kirkby Laythorpe 10–12; RD Lafford 08–12; Can and Preb Linc Cathl 07–12; Can Res and Subdean Linc Cathl from 12. *The Subdeanery, 18 Minster Yard, Lincoln LN2 1PX* T: (01522) 561600 E: japatrick1@btinternet.com *or* subdean@lincolncathedral.com

PATRICK, Canon Peter Charles. b 64. Leeds Univ BA 86 Fitzw Coll Cam BA 91 MA 95. Ridley Hall Cam 89. **d** 92 **p** 93. C Barton upon Humber *Linc* 92–96; TV Gt Grimsby St Mary and St Jas 96–03; RD Grimsby and Cleethorpes 99–03; R Middle Rasen Gp 03–15; P-in-c Barkwith Gp 07–15; R Horncastle Gp from 15; Can and Preb Linc Cathl from 18. *9 Langton Drive, Horncastle LN9 5AJ* E: pcp941@yahoo.co.uk

PATTEN (*née* STARNS), Mrs Helen Edna. b 43. St Hilda's Coll Ox BA 65 Maria Grey Coll Lon CertEd 70. Trin Coll Bris 73 Oak Hill Th Coll 81. **dss** 82 **d** 87 **p** 94. Tunbridge Wells St Jo *Roch* 82–86; Patcham *Chich* 86–91; Par Dn 87–91; Par Dn Eckington w Handley and Ridgeway *Derby* 91–94; C 94–95; TV 95–98; Chapl St Mich Hospice St Leonards-on-Sea 98–03; rtd 03; Hon C Fairlight and Pett *Chich* from 04. *Address temp unknown*

PATTEN, The Ven Ruth Janet. b 72. Roehampton Inst BA 94 Goldsmiths' Coll Lon MMus 98. Westcott Ho Cam 08. **d** 10 **p** 11. C Witham *Chelmsf* 10–14; P-in-c Gt Dunmow and Barnston 14–19; Adn Colchester from 19. *63 Powers Hall End, Witham CM8 1NH* T: (01376) 513130 E: a.colchester@chelmsford.anglican.org

PATTEN, Sarah Kathleen. b 72. Liv Univ BA 94 UMIST BSc 98 PGCE 95. Wycliffe Hall Ox BA 05. **d** 05 **p** 06. C W Ealing St Jo w St Jas *Lon* 05–08; V Blockhouse Bay NZ 08–19; Prin Wellbeing and Min Development S'well from 19. *Discipleship and Ministry Team, Jubilee House, Westgate, Southwell NG25 0JH* T: (01636) 814331 E: sarah.patten@southwell.anglican.org

PATTENDEN, Mrs Alison Margaret. b 53. Eastbourne Tr Coll CertEd 75 Sussex Univ BEd 76 Glyndŵr Univ MA 16. St Steph Ho Ox 04. **d** 06 **p** 07. C Goring-by-Sea *Chich* 06–10; P-in-c Amberley w N Stoke and Parham, Wiggonholt etc 10–14; V 14–16; rtd 16. *16 Crowborough Court, Elverlands Close, Ferring, Worthing BN12 5QF* E: revapattenden@btinternet.com

PATTERSON, Alfred Percy. b 85. **d** 85 **p** 87. NSM Aghalee *D & D* 85–91; C Gilford 91–93; Bp's C 93–95; I 95–00; rtd 00. *Brookdale, 723 Upper Newtownards Road, Belfast BT4 3NU* T: (028) 9029 4741 E: revap.patterson@ntlworld.com

PATTERSON, Andrew John. b 56. Master Mariner 85. Qu Coll Birm 85. **d** 88 **p** 89. C Newc St Phil and St Aug 88–92; Chapl Hunter's Moor Hosp 91–92; Asst Chapl R Victoria Infirmary Newc 92–96; V Whitley *Newc* from 96; Chapl Hexham Gen Hosp from 96; AD Hexham *Newc* from 21.

The Vicarage, Whitley, Hexham NE46 2LA T: (01434) 673379
E: revdocpatt@doctors.org.uk

PATTERSON, Anthony. b 43. Moore Th Coll Sydney BTh 82. **d** 83 **p** 83. Australia 83–91; C Darfield *Sheff* 91–94; TR Marfleet *York* 94–99; TV Heeley and Gleadless Valley *Sheff* 99–04; TR 04–10; AD Attercliffe 04–10; rtd 11; PtO *York* 11–13; P-in-c Bempton w Flamborough, Reighton w Speeton 13–17. *56 Highcliffe Drive, Sheffield S11 7LU* T: 0114-263 0790 E: tonypatterson1@gmail.com

PATTERSON, Colin Hugh. b 52. St Pet Coll Ox MA 77 Univ of Wales (Cardiff) MPhil 90 CertEd 75. Trin Coll Bris. **d** 87 **p** 88. C Blackb Sav 87–90; C Haughton le Skerne *Dur* 90–93; Adult Educn Adv 93–05; Asst Dir Bridge Builders Min 05–17; NSM Dur St Nic 05–17; rtd 17; PtO *Dur* from 18. *24 Monks Crescent, Durham DH1 1HD*

PATTERSON, Colin Peter Matthew. b 62. Newc Poly BA 84. St Steph Ho Ox 92. **d** 94 **p** 95. C Cullercoats St Geo *Newc* 94–97; Shrine P Shrine of Our Lady of Walsingham 97–99; P-in-c Harlow St Mary Magd *Chelmsf* 99–00; V 00–09; V Willesden Green St Andr and St Fran *Lon* from 09; CMP from 97. *The Clergy House, 4 St Andrew's Road, London NW10 2QS* T: (020) 8459 2670

PATTERSON, Mrs Diane Rosemary. b 46. WMMTC 88. **d** 91 **p** 94. C Hill *Birm* 91–95; PtO 95–96; C Shottery St Andr *Cov* 96–01; C Hunningham 01–13; C Wappenbury w Weston under Wetherley 01–13; C Long Itchington and Marton 01–13; C Offchurch 01–13; RD Southam 02–08; rtd 13; PtO *Cov* from 13. *169A Clopton Road, Stratford-upon-Avon CV37 6TF* T: (01789) 266453 E: revdianepatterson@yahoo.co.uk

PATTERSON, Hugh John. b 38. Southn Univ MPhil 76. AKC 63. **d** 64 **p** 65. C Epsom St Martin *Guildf* 64–65; Chapl Ewell Coll 65–68; Asst Chapl and Lect Bp Otter Coll Chich 68–71; Lect Dudley Coll of Educn 71–77; Lect Wolv Poly 77–92; Wolv Univ 92–00; Chapl 89–00; rtd 01; Hon C Morville w Aston Eyre *Heref* 82–08; Hon C Upton Cressett w Monk Hopton 82–08; Hon C Acton Round 82–08; PtO 08–20. *6 Victoria Road, Bridgnorth WV16 4LA* T: (01746) 765298

PATTERSON, John. *See* PATTERSON, Norman John

PATTERSON, Marjorie Jean. *See* BROWN, Marjorie Jean

PATTERSON, Neil Sydney. b 79. BNC Ox BA 00 MA 04 Ox Univ BD 17 FRSA 21. Ripon Coll Cuddesdon BA 03. **d** 04 **p** 05. C Cleobury Mortimer w Hopton Wafers etc *Heref* 04–08; TV Ross 08; R Ariconium 08–15; Dioc Dir Voc and Dir of Ords from 15; RD Heref 18–20. *Diocesan Office, The Palace, Palace Yard, Hereford HR4 9BL* T: (01432) 373320 E: pattersonneil@hotmail.com *or* ddvo@hereford.anglican.org

PATTERSON, Norman John. b 47. Peterho Cam BA 69 ALCD. St Jo Coll Nottm 70. **d** 73 **p** 74. C Everton St Ambrose w St Tim *Liv* 73–74; C Everton St Pet 74–78; TV 79–84; C Aigburth 84–92; Dioc Adv for Past Care and Counselling 84–92; V Gt Crosby All SS 92–04; Crosslinks Uganda 05–09; rtd 12; PtO *Ches* from 11. *6 Brookside, Great Boughton, Chester CH3 5TL* T: (01244) 314613 E: johnpatterson6098@yahoo.com

PATTERSON, Scott Robert. b 71. GTCL 92. Oak Hill Th Coll 07. **d** 09 **p** 10. C Newton Tracey, Horwood, Alverdiscott etc *Ex* 09–13; P-in-c Curry Rivel w Fivehead and Swell *B & W* 13–18; R from 18. *The Rectory, Church Street, Curry Rivel, Langport TA10 0HQ* M: 07973-139092 E: scottr.patterson@btinternet.com

PATTERSON, Susan Margaret. b 48. Otago Univ BA 71 BD 89 PhD 92. Knox Coll Dunedin 84. **d** 88 **p** 89. C Dunedin St Martin NZ 88–91; Tutor Otago Univ and Knox Coll 89–91; USA 91–92; Assoc P Hawke's Bay NZ 92–96; Lect Trin Coll Bris 97–00; I Kildallon w Newtowngore and Corrawallen *K, E & A* 00–04; I Killala w Dunfeeny, Crossmolina, Kilmoremoy etc *T, K & A* 04–10; Dean Killala 05–10; Sen Lect and Registrar Bishopdale Th Coll NZ from 10. *Bishop Eaton House, 30 Vanguard Street, PO Box 100, Nelson 7040, New Zealand* T: (0064) (3) 548 8785 E: sue.patterson@bishopdale.ac.nz

PATTIMORE, Daniel James. b 64. Nottm Univ MEng 88 Lon Bible Coll BA 94. Wycliffe Hall Ox 97. **d** 99 **p** 00. C Charlesworth and Dinting Vale *Derby* 99–03; NSM Norley, Crowton and Kingsley *Ches* 03–04; P-in-c Heanor *Derby* 04–14; P-in-c Langley Mill and Aldercar 07–14; NSM Kirkby Thore w Temple Sowerby and Newbiggin *Carl* 14–17; NSM Heart of Eden from 14. *The Rectory, Kirkby Thore, Penrith CA10 1UR* T: (017683) 62655 M: 07973-406022 E: danpattimore@gmail.com

PATTIMORE (née GORDON), Mrs Kristy. b 72. Leeds Univ BA 94 Newc Univ PGCE 95. Wycliffe Hall Ox 98. **d** 01 **p** 02. C Hallwood *Ches* 01–04; NSM Heanor *Derby* 04–14; NSM Kirkby Thore w Temple Sowerby and Newbiggin *Carl* 14–17;

NSM Heart of Eden from 14. *The Rectory, Kirkby Thore, Penrith CA10 1UR* T: (017683) 62655 E: kristy@pattimore.com

PATTINSON, Christine Brodie. b 43. Darlington Tr Coll CertEd 64. **d** 06 **p** 07. OLM Chertsey, Lyne and Longcross *Guildf* 06–13; PtO from 13. *32 Twynersh Avenue, Chertsey KT16 9DE* E: cbpattinson@btinternet.com

PATTINSON, Rhobert James. St Mich Coll Llan. **d** 04 **p** 05. C Llanelli *St D* 04–07; TV Dewisland 07–10; V Llanegwad w Llanfihangel Uwch Gwili 10–19; V Bro Dinefwr from 19; Min Can St D Cathl from 07. *Y Ficerdy, Clos y Myrtwydd, Nantgaredig, Carmarthen SA32 7LT* T: (01267) 290142

PATTINSON, Richard Clive. b 46. Keble Coll Ox BA 68 MA 84. CBDTI 98. **d** 00 **p** 01. C Hesket-in-the-Forest and Armathwaite *Carl* 00–04; C Inglewood Gp 04–05; P-in-c Dacre 05–12; TV Penrith w Newton Reigny and Plumpton Wall 05–12; TV Gd Shep TM 10–12; rtd 12; PtO *Carl* 12–16; Bris from 17. *Hall Floor, South Parade Mansions, 47 Oakfield Road, Bristol BS8 2BA* T: 0117-973 1947 E: clivepattinson@btinternet.com

PATTISON, Prof George Linsley. b 50. Edin Univ MA 72 BD 77 Dur Univ PhD 83 DD 04. Edin Th Coll 74. **d** 77 **p** 78. C Benwell St Jas *Newc* 77–80; P-in-c Kimblesworth *Dur* 80–83; R Badwell Ash w Gt Ashfield, Stowlangtoft etc *St E* 83–91; Dean of Chpl K Coll Cam 91–01; Lect Aarhus Univ Denmark 01–04; Lady Marg Prof Div Ox Univ 04–13; Can Res Ch Ch Ox 04–13; Prof Div Glas Univ from 13. *School of Divinity, University of Glasgow, University Avenue, Glasgow G12 8QQ*

PATTISON, Stephen Bewley. b 53. Selw Coll Cam BA 76. Edin Th Coll 76. **d** 78 **p** 80. C Gosforth All SS *Newc* 78–79; NSM St Nic Hosp Newc 78–82; Hon C Newc St Thos Prop Chpl 80–82; Chapl Edin Th Coll 82–83; Lect Past Studies Birm Univ 83–88; PtO *Birm* 83–86 and 87–00 and from 17; Hon C Moseley St Mary 86–87. *11A Salisbury Road, Moseley, Birmingham B13 8JS* M: 07951-145989 E: stephenbpattison@gmail.com

PATTLE (née OLIVER), Mrs Suzanne Marie. b 66. LMH Ox BA 88 SSEES Lon MA 91. Trin Coll Bris BTS 03. **d** 03 **p** 04. C Rainham *Roch* 03–07; P-in-c Gillingham St Mary 07–14; V Colehill *Sarum* from 14. *The Vicarage, Smugglers Lane, Colehill, Wimborne BH21 2RY* T: (01202) 883721 M: 07971-073093 E: vicar.stmichaels.colehill@gmail.com

PATTON (née GRAVELING), Mrs Hannah. b 79. Univ Coll Lon BSc 03 MSc 10 Murray Edwards Coll Cam BTh 14. Ridley Hall Cam 12. **d** 14 **p** 15. C Colchester St Jo *Chelmsf* 14–19; P-in-c Goole *Sheff* from 19. *St John the Evangelist Church, Church Street, Goole DN14 5BA* T: (01405) 766058 E: hannah@stjohnsgoole.org.uk

PAUL, Ian Benjamin. b 62. St Jo Coll Ox BA 84 MA 88 Southn Univ MSc 85 Nottm Univ BTh 91 PhD 98. St Jo Coll Nottm 89. **d** 96 **p** 97. C Longfleet *Sarum* 96–00; NSM 00–04; Visiting Lect Trin Coll Bris 00–01; Th Adv Dioc Bd of Min *Sarum* 00–04; Tutor Sarum OLM Scheme 00–04; Visiting Lect STETS 00–04; Dir Partnership Development St Jo Coll Nottm 04–05; Dean of Studies 05–13; NSM Nottingham St Nic S'well from 13. *102 Cator Lane, Beeston, Nottingham NG9 4BB* M: 07974-351502 E: editor@grovebooks.co.uk

PAUL, John Matthew. b 61. K Coll Lon BA 82 Fitzw Coll Cam BA 88 MA 92 FRSA 06. Westcott Ho Cam 86. **d** 89 **p** 90. C Writtle w Highwood *Chelmsf* 89–94; Min Can and Chapl St Paul's Cathl *Lon* 94–96; Min Can and Sacr St Paul's Cathl 96–99; V Winchmore Hill St Paul 99–09; AD Enfield 04–09; PtO from 09; *Portsm* from 18. *4 Woodcroft Mews, Station Road, Petersfield GU32 3FE* M: 07800-606555 E: jm.paul@virgin.net *or* john.paul@london.anglican.org

PAUL, Naunihal Chand (Nihal). b 40. Allahabad Univ MA. Bangalore Th Coll BD. **d** 69 **p** 70. C Simla Ch Ch India 69–70; V Kangra w Dharamsala 70–74; C Urmston *Man* 75–77; P-in-c Farnworth St Pet 77–80; TV E Farnworth and Kearsley 80–83; TV Laindon St Martin and St Nic w Nevendon *Chelmsf* 83–90; R Laindon w Dunton 90–05; rtd 05; PtO *Chelmsf* from 06. *3 Wellstye Green, Basildon SS14 2SR* T: (01268) 293965 E: nihalpaul@live.co.uk

PAUL, Roger Philip. b 53. Clare Coll Cam BA 74 MA 88 CertEd 76 Open Univ PhD 98. Westcott Ho Cam 78. **d** 81 **p** 82. C Coventry Caludon *Cov* 81–85; R Warmington w Shotteswell and Radway w Ratley 85–98; R Kirkby Stephen w Mallerstang etc *Carl* 98–08; Nat Adv (Unity in Miss) Coun for Chr Unity 08–17; rtd 17; PtO *Ox* 11–19; *Lich* 18–21. *3 Farm Lane, Tetchill, Ellesmere SY12 9AT* T: (01961) 623066

PAUL, Canon Rosalind Miranda. b 53. Man Univ BA 74 Bris Univ PGCE 77 Paris Univ LèsL 86 Open Univ MBA 95. Ripon Coll Cuddesdon 05. **d** 07 **p** 08. C Budock *Truro* 07–09; C Mawnan 07–09; R Higham, Holton St Mary, Raydon and Stratford *St E* 09–18; Can Res Wells Cathl *B & W* from

18; PtO *Chelmsf* from 13. *2 The Liberty, Wells BA5 2SU*
E: pastor@wellscathedral.uk.net
PAVEY, Canon Angela Mary. b 55. Hull Univ BA 77 Nottm
Univ BCombStuds 84 Univ of Wales (Lamp) MA 06. Linc
Th Coll 81. **dss** 84 **d** 87 **p** 94. Linc St Faith and St Martin
w St Pet 84–86; Chapl Boston Coll of FE 87–95; Asst Min
Officer *Linc* 89–95; C Birchwood 95–97; Dioc Dir of Ords
97–07; P-in-c Linc St Faith and St Martin w St Pet 07–13;
Chapl Lincs Partnership NHS Foundn Trust 07–20; Can and
Preb Linc Cathl from 00. *The Gatehouse, Long Leys Road,
Lincoln LN1 1EJ* T: 01522 518500
PAVLOU, Michael. b 55. St Jo Coll Nottm BA. **d** 06 **p** 07.
C Woodside Park St Barn *Lon* 06–10 and from 12; C
Wandsworth St Mich w St Steph *S'wark* 10–12. *53 Gallants
Farm Road, East Barnet, Barnet EN4 8ER* M: 07956-573217
E: mikepavlou@stbarnabas.co.uk
PAVLOU, Paul Christopher. b 87. Brunel Univ BA 08 Middx
Univ PGCE 10 Dur Univ BA 18. Ridley Hall Cam 15.
d 18 **p** 19. C Bletchley *Ox* from 18. *1 Ashburnham Close,
Bletchley, Milton Keynes MK3 7TR* M: 07525-534250
E: paulpav2@gmail.com
PAVYER, Jennifer Elizabeth. *See* FENNELL, Jennifer Elizabeth
PAWSON (née ROYLE), Mrs Gillian Mary. b 57. Kingston
Univ BA 79 Roehampton Inst PGCE 82. SEITE 99. **d** 02
p 03. C Wimbledon *S'wark* 02–06; P-in-c Merton St Jo
06–09; P-in-c Colliers Wood Ch Ch 06–09; TV Merton
Priory 09; PtO 10–12; C Putney St Mary 12–14; PtO *Eur*
from 18. *20 Beaumont Gardens, Poulton-le-Fylde FY6 7NX*
E: gillypawson@gmail.com
PAWSON, John. b 66. Moorlands Th Coll BA 00. Wycliffe Hall
Ox. **d** 02 **p** 03. C Bursledon *Win* 02–06; P-in-c Sway 06–12;
V 12–18; P-in-c Bursledon from 18. *The Vicarage, School
Road, Bursledon, Southampton SO31 8BW* M: 07762-246947
E: john.pawson@bursledonparish.org
PAWSON, Preb John Walker. b 38. Kelham Th Coll 58. **d** 63
p 64. C N Hull St Mich *York* 63–67; C Lower Gornal *Lich*
67–70; V Tipton St Jo 70–78; V Meir Heath 78–03; RD
Stoke 88–98; Preb Lich Cathl 93–03; rtd 03; PtO *Nor* from
03. *39 Runton Road, Cromer NR27 9AT* T: (01263) 511715
E: pawson.meirton@btinternet.com
PAXON, Robin Michael Cuninghame. b 46. St Jo Coll Dur
BA 69. Westcott Ho Cam 69. **d** 71 **p** 72. C Croydon St Pet S
End *Cant* 71–77; C Saffron Walden w Wendens Ambo and
Littlebury *Chelmsf* 77–80; P-in-c Plaistow St Mary 80–83;
TV Plaistow 83–89; TV Dovercourt and Parkeston 90–95;
rtd 95. *20 Park Road, Harwich CO12 3BJ* T: (01255) 551139
E: r.paxon@btinternet.com
PAXTON, Elizabeth Glynis. b 53. Salford Univ BSc 74.
St Mellitus Coll BA 12. **d** 13 **p** 14. NSM Sible Hedingham
w Castle Hedingham *Chelmsf* 13–16; C Upper Colne
16–17; C Sible Hedingham w Castle Hedingham 16–17; C
The Hedinghams and Upper Colne 17–18; R from 18; AD
Hinckford from 21. *The Old Stables, The Street, Stoke by Clare,
Sudbury CO10 8HP* T: (01787) 277270 M: 07932-160594
E: liz@paxtonconsulting.co.uk
PAXTON, John Ernest. b 49. Ex Univ BA 71. Westcott Ho
Cam 74. **d** 74 **p** 75. C Redditch St Steph *Worc* 74–77; UAE
77–81; C Bolton St Pet *Man* 81–91; Ind Missr 81–91; TV
Southampton (City Cen) *Win* 91–96; R S'wark Ch Ch 96–03;
Sen Chapl S Lon Ind Miss 96–03; Adv to Bd of Soc Resp *Worc*
03–11; Miss Development Officer 11–13; rtd 13; PtO *Chich*
from 15. *8 Bridge Road, Chichester PO19 7NW* T: (01243)
931318 E: johnpaxton@talktalk.net
PAXTON, William Neil. b 60. Brunel Univ BSc 88 MA 90.
Ripon Coll Cuddesdon 02. **d** 04 **p** 05. C Camberwell St Geo
S'wark 04–08; TV Southend *Chelmsf* 08–20; V Southend All
SS from 21. *All Saints' Vicarage, 1 Sutton Road, Southend-on-
Sea SS2 5PA* E: neil.paxton@blueyonder.co.uk
PAY, Norman John. b 50. St Jo Coll Dur BA 72. Cranmer
Hall Dur. **d** 74 **p** 75. C S Moor *Dur* 74–78; C Rawmarsh w
Parkgate *Sheff* 78–80; C in-c New Cantley CD 80–82; V New
Cantley 82–89; V Doncaster St Leon and St Jude 89–17;
P-in-c Moorends 11–17; Asst Clergy In-Service Tr Officer
90–93; rtd 17; PtO *Sheff* from 17. *13 Market Street, Goldthorpe,
Rotherham S63 9HB* E: njpay@btinternet.com
PAYNE, Alan. *See* PAYNE, Kenneth Alan
PAYNE, Mrs Anne Margaret. b 52. Bris Univ BA 73 Southn
Univ PGCE 74. STETS 11. **d** 14 **p** 15. NSM Worplesdon
Guildf 14–18; PtO 18–19. *3 Gibbetts, Langton Green, Tunbridge
Wells TN3 0DG* T: (01892) 331524 M: 07796-420382
E: annempayne3@gmail.com
PAYNE, Arthur Edwin. b 37. K Alfred's Coll Win TCert 59.
St Mich Coll Llan 86. **d** 87 **p** 88. C Swansea St Gabr *S & B*
87–90; Chapl Univ of Wales (Swansea) 87–90; V Brynmawr
90–91; TV Wickford and Runwell *Chelmsf* 91–94; Chapl
Runwell Hosp Wickford 91–94; P-in-c Wraxall *B & W* 94–95;

PtO 95–97; V Rhymney *Mon* 97–98; rtd 98; PtO *B & W*
from 99. *4 Villa Rosa, Shrubbery Road, Weston-super-Mare
BS23 2JB* T: (01934) 615522 E: aepayne630@btinternet.com
PAYNE, Daniel David John. b 81. Worc Univ BA 17
Ox Univ BA 21. Ripon Coll Cuddesdon 19. **d** 21. C
Stafford St Mary and Marston *Lich* from 21; C Stafford
St Chad from 21. *1 Navigation Loop, Stone ST15 8YU*
E: danny.payne@staffordchurches.uk
PAYNE, David Charles. b 62. Univ of Wales (Abth) BLib 84.
St Jo Coll Nottm MA 95. **d** 95 **p** 96. C Horncastle w Low
Toynton *Linc* 95–99; V Metheringham w Blankney and
Dunston 99–04; Chapl Sherwood Forest Hosps NHS Trust
04–06; R Standon and The Mundens w Sacombe *St Alb*
06–14; C Vale *Ox* 14–15; TV Vale of Belvoir *Leic* 15–20;
P-in-c Silsoe, Pulloxhill and Flitton *St Alb* from 20. *The
Vicarage, Fir Tree Road, Silsoe, Bedford MK45 4EA* M: 07985-
922553 E: revdpayne24@gmail.com
PAYNE, Mrs Glenys. b 53. **d** 14 **p** 15. NSM Llanelli *St D*
14–17; NSM Bro Lliedi from 17. *7 Pemberton Park, Llanelli
SA14 8NN* T: (01554) 777997 E: revglen@btinternet.com
PAYNE, Mrs Joanna Nicola. b 72. Liv Univ BA 93 Homerton
Coll Cam PGCE 95. Trin Coll Bris BA 00 MA 01. **d** 01 **p** 02. C
Chislehurst St Nic *Roch* 01–06; C The Mitre Benefice *Nor* from
17. *15 Nursery Lane, Costessey, Norwich NR8 5BU* T: (01603)
745792 M: 07958-598145 E: joanna.payne@hotmail.com
PAYNE, John. b 58. Glas Univ BSc 80 Edin Univ BD 84. Edin
Th Coll 81. **d** 90 **p** 90. C Dur St Nic 90–94; Australia from 94;
Chapl Toorak Coll Melbourne from 02. *11 Feathertop Chase,
Burwood East, Melbourne Vic 3151, Australia* T: (0061) (3)
9887 8748 E: johnpayne@rabbit.com.au
PAYNE, John Rogan. b 44. Episc Th Coll São Paulo. **d** 78
p 79. Brazil 78–86; C Ilkley All SS *Bradf* 86–88; R Elvington
w Sutton on Derwent and E Cottingwith *York* 88–94.
*Manor Farm House, East Flotmanby Road, Muston, Filey
YO14 0HX* T: (01723) 513969
PAYNE, Julia Kathleen. *See* PEATY, Julia Kathleen
PAYNE, Canon Kenneth Alan. b 45. Pemb Coll Ox BA 68
MA 71. Qu Coll Birm 71. **d** 74 **p** 74. Hon C Perry Barr
Birm 74–78; Hon C Ruislip Manor St Paul *Lon* 78–79; C
Hawksworth Wood *Ripon* 79–84; R Stanningley St Thos
84–94; TR Kippax w Allerton Bywater 94–00; AD Whitkirk
95–00; P-in-c Lambley *S'well* 00–09; Dioc Min Development
Adv 00–09; Dioc Dir of Min 02–09; Hon Can S'well Minster
06–09; rtd 10; PtO *York* from 10. *Fern Cottage, 2 Gladstone
Terrace, Thornton Dale, Pickering YO18 7SS* T: (01751)
476243 E: alanpayne203@gmail.com
PAYNE, Leonard John. b 49. St Jo Coll Nottm 93. **d** 95 **p** 96.
C Trimley *St E* 95–98; TV Sole Bay 98–09; P-in-c Wrentham,
Covehithe w Benacre etc 09–15; V 15–16; rtd 16. *3 Chartwell
Avenue, Wingerworth, Chesterfield S42 6SR* M: 07777-636808
E: rev.leonard.payne@gmail.com
PAYNE, Mark David. b 73. Univ of Wales (Ban) BD 95. All SS
Cen for Miss & Min 15. **d** 17 **p** 18. C Bocking St Mary and
Panfield *Chelmsf* 17–19; TV Halstead Area from 19. *20 Swallow
Field, Earls Colne, Colchester CO6 2RW* T: (01787) 220347
E: markdpayne@outlook.com *or* colnesvicar@gmail.com
PAYNE, Matthew Charles. b 62. Ex Univ LLB 85 All Nations
Chr Coll BA 95 Solicitor 89. Oak Hill Th Coll 99. **d** 01
p 02. C Angmering *Chich* 01–05; V Lowestoft Ch Ch
Nor 05–20. *76 Girton Road, Girton, Cambridge CB3 0LN*
E: revmattpayne@gmail.com
PAYNE, Michael Frederick. b 49. St Jo Coll Nottm 81. **d** 83
p 84. C Hyson Green *S'well* 83–86; P-in-c Peckham St Mary
Magd *S'wark* 86–90; V 90–05; Hon C Chenies and Lt
Chalfont, Latimer and Flaunden *Ox* 05–09; P-in-c Tollerton
S'well 09–11; R 11–14; rtd 14; PtO *S'well* from 15. *100
Denison Street, Beeston, Nottingham NG9 1DQ* T: 0115-808
6506 M: 07961-515840 E: mikefpayne@hotmail.com
PAYNE, Michael Jeffrey. b 75. Hull Univ MA 00 Cant
Ch Ch Univ MA 08 Open Univ PGCE 09. St Steph
Ho Ox 13. **d** 15 **p** 16. C Northfleet and Rosherville
Roch 15–18; C Perry Street 15–18; V Gravesend St Aid
from 18. *The Vicarage, St Gregory's Crescent, Gravesend
DA12 4JL* E: frmichael.anglican@gmail.com *or*
vicar.staidans@gmail.com
PAYNE, Mrs Norma. b 48. Bris Univ BA 70 Homerton
Coll Cam PGCE 71. STETS 98. **d** 01 **p** 02. NSM Cley Hill
Warminster *Sarum* 01–04; TV 04–07; R Cley Hill Villages
07–13; rtd 13; PtO *Sarum* from 13. *2 The Mews, Newport,
Warminster BA12 8BX* E: revnpayne@btinternet.com
PAYNE, Mrs Penelope Kenward. b 42. LGSM 64. Bp Otter
Coll 94. **d** 94 **p** 98. NSM Portsea N End St Mark *Portsm*
94–05; NSM S Hayling 05–12; rtd 12; PtO *Portsm* from 12. *38
Allcot Road, Portsmouth PO3 5DF* E: pennie@ppayne.f9.co.uk
PAYNE, Philip John. b 56. Warwick Univ BA 77 UMIST
MSc 94. Westcott Ho Cam 09. **d** 11 **p** 12. C Bury St Edmunds

All SS w St Jo and St Geo *St E* 11–14; P-in-c Coddenham w Gosbeck and Hemingstone w Henley 14–19; P-in-c Crowfield w Stonham Aspal and Mickfield 14–19; P-in-c The Creetings and Earl Stonham w Stonham Parva 14–19; R N Bosmere from 19. *The Rectory, The Street, Stonham Aspal, Stowmarket IP14 6AQ* T: (01449) 711684 E: revphilippayne@btinternet.com

PAYNE, Mrs Priscilla Mary. b 40. **d** 04 **p** 05. NSM Ditton *Roch* 04–15; PtO 15–19; *Leeds* 15–16. *5 Snowdon Gardens, Churchdown, Gloucester GL3 1JL* T: (01452) 324411 E: priscillapayne@outlook.com

PAYNE, Preb Robert Christian. b 42. MBE 12. St Mich Coll Llan. **d** 65 **p** 66. C Charlton Kings St Mary *Glouc* 65–69; C Waltham Cross *St Alb* 69–71; V Falfield *Glouc* 71–72; P-in-c Rockhampton 71–72; V Falfield w Rockhampton 72–76; Chapl HM Det Cen Eastwood Park 71–76; Chapl HM Borstal Everthorpe 76–79; Chapl HM YOI Glen Parva 79–85; Pris Service Chapl Tr Officer 85–88; Chapl HM Pris Swinfen Hall 85–88; Asst Chapl Gen of Pris 88–02; rtd 02; Sessional Chapl HM YOI Stoke Heath 02–06; Sessional Chapl HM Pris Swinfen Hall 05–12; Sessional Chapl HM Pris Foston Hall 06–08; Preb Lich Cathl 05–12; PtO 13–21. *Address temp unknown* E: r.payne126@btinternet.com

PAYNE, Robert Harold Vincent. b 44. St Jo Coll York CertEd 69. St Jo Coll Nottm 77. **d** 79 **p** 80. C Didsbury St Jas *Man* 79–80; C Didsbury St Jas and Emm 80–83; V Southchurch Ch Ch *Chelmsf* 83–90; P-in-c Charles w Plymouth St Matthias *Ex* 90–94; Warden Lee Abbey 94–02; R Thorley *St Alb* 02–14; rtd 14; PtO *Sarum* from 15. *131 Stour View Gardens, Corfe Mullen, Wimborne BH21 3TN*

PAYNE, Robert Sandon. b 48. Reading Univ BSc 69 MRICS 72. Ripon Coll Cuddesdon 77. **d** 80 **p** 81. C Bridgnorth, Tasley, Astley Abbotts and Oldbury *Heref* 80–83; P-in-c Wistanstow 83–92; P-in-c Acton Scott 86–92; P-in-c Dorrington 92–94; P-in-c Leebotwood w Longnor 92–94; P-in-c Smethcott w Woolstaston 92–94; P-in-c Stapleton 92–94; R Dorrington w Leebotwood, Longnor, Stapleton etc 94–11; rtd 11; PtO *Heref* from 11. *6 Clun Road, Aston-on-Clun, Craven Arms SY7 8EW* T: (01588) 661008 E: robert.payne48@btinternet.com

PAYNE, Stephen Michael. b 55. Plymouth Univ BSc 00. Wilson Carlile Coll 83. **d** 03 **p** 04. C Plymouth Em, St Paul Efford and St Aug *Ex* 03–10; TV Plymstock and Hooe 11–13; TR 13–17; PtO *Truro* 17–19; P-in-c St Breoke and Egloshayle from 20. *14 St Cleer Drive, Wadebridge PL27 6DU* M: 07400-429416 E: spayne55@live.co.uk

PAYNE, Mrs Tania Louise. b 61. St Mellitus Coll 17. **d** 19 **p** 20. NSM Buckhurst Hill *Chelmsf* from 19. *176 Hale End Road, Woodford Green IG8 9LZ* T: (020) 8418 5960 M: 07723-337616 E: tlpayne@hotmail.co.uk

PAYNE, Mrs Trudy. b 48. K Coll Lon BA 66 Lon Inst of Educn PGCE 73. **d** 04 **p** 05. OLM Clapham Park St Steph *S'wark* 04–06; NSM Telford Park 06–09; NSM Mitcham St Barn 09–18; PtO from 18. *6 Clarence Road, Croydon CR0 2EN* T: (020) 8689 5857 E: paynetrudy@hotmail.com

PAYNTER, Stephen Denis. b 59. Bath Univ BSc 82 CertEd 82. Trin Coll Bris BA 89. **d** 89 **p** 90. C Nailsea Ch Ch *B & W* 89–92; C Farnborough *Guildf* 92–97; TV N Farnborough 97–98; V Ealing St Mary *Lon* from 98. *11 Church Place, London W5 4HN* T: (020) 8567 0414 *or* 8579 7134 F: 8840 4534 E: steve.paynter@stmarysealing.org.uk

PAYTON, Paul John. b 59. Middx Poly MA 90 LRAM 79 GRSM 80. Ripon Coll Cuddesdon. **d** 05 **p** 06. C Lancaster St Mary w St John and St Anne *Blackb* 05–08; P-in-c Leeds Gipton Epiphany *Ripon* 08–13; TR Leeds All So and St Aid 13–14 and 14–15; rtd 15; PtO *Blackb* 15–19 and 20–21; *Eur* from 18; V Briercliffe *Blackb* 19–20; Hon C Burnley St Pet and St Steph from 21. *Address withheld by request*

PEABODY, Anthony John. b 43. St Cuth Soc Dur BSc 64 MSc 67 Surrey Univ PhD 82 Huddersfield Univ MA 18 CBiol 82 MRSB 82. Cuddesdon Coll 08. **d** 08. NSM Sulhamstead Abbots and Bannister w Ufton Nervet *Ox* 08–14; PtO from 14; *Eur* from 14. *Blackberries, 29 Woodlands Avenue, Burghfield Common, Reading RG7 3HU* T: 0118-983 2491 E: pisumcorporum@gmail.com

PEACE, Brian. b 38. St Jo Coll Nottm 90. **d** 92 **p** 93. C Huddersfield H Trin *Wakef* 92–95; R Cheswardine, Childs Ercall, Hales, Hinstock etc *Lich* 95–00; TR 00–03; RD Hodnet 00–03; rtd 03; PtO *Ches* from 03. *2 Mouldsworth Close, Northwich CW9 8FT* T: (01606) 333013

PEACE, Stuart Vaughan. b 47. **d** 04 **p** 05. OLM Dorking w Ranmore *Guildf* 04–14; rtd 14; PtO *Guildf* from 14. *95 Ashcombe Road, Dorking RH4 1LW* T: (01306) 883002 E: revdstuartpeace01@gmail.com

PEACH, Malcolm Thompson. b 31. St Chad's Coll Dur BA 56. Sarum Th Coll 56. **d** 58 **p** 59. C Beamish

Dur 58–61; Chapl Dur Univ 61–65; NE England Sec SCM 61–65; C-in-c Stockton St Mark CD *Dur* 65–72; P-in-c Bishopwearmouth St Nic 72–81; V 81–85; V S Shields St Hilda w St Thos 85–95; Hon Chapl Miss to Seamen 85–95; P-in-c S Shields St Aid w St Steph *Dur* 92–95; rtd 95; PtO *Dur* from 95. *116 Mount Road, Sunderland SR4 7QD* T: 0191-522 6216 E: peachestwo20@hotmail.co.uk

PEACHEY, Elizabeth Ann. b 70. St Mellitus Coll 14. **d** 17 **p** 18. C Knowle *Birm* 17–20; PtO from 20; C The Bridge, Cov from 20. *126 Dorridge Road, Dorridge, Solihull B93 8BN*

PEACOCK, Canon David. b 39. Liv Univ BA 61 Lanc Univ MA 71 Univ of the South (USA) Hon DD 00 FRSA 95. Westcott Ho Cam 84. **d** 84 **p** 85. Prin Lect St Martin's Coll Lanc 81–85; Hon C Lancaster St Mary *Blackb* 84–85; Prin Whitelands Coll *S'wark* 85–00; Pro Rector Surrey Univ *Guildf* 93–00; Hon C Roehampton H Trin *S'wark* 85–92; Hon C Putney St Mary 92–00; Hon Can S'wark Cathl 97–00; PtO *Blackb* 00–20. *Orchard House, 11 Parsonage Fold, Beetham, Milnthorpe LA7 7RJ* T: (015395) 63032 E: keersidecowshed@aol.com

PEACOCK, Mrs Kate Rebecca. b 78. Hatf Coll Dur BA 00. Westcott Ho Cam 01. **d** 03 **p** 04. C Cambridge Ascension *Ely* 03–07; C Three Rivers Gp 07–12; P-in-c Hormead, Wyddial, Anstey, Brent Pelham etc *St Alb* 12–13; R 13–18; RD Buntingford 16–18; Dean of Women's Min 17–18; Ch Growth Officer from 18. *Address withheld by request* E: kate.peacock@btopenworld.com

PEAL, Jacqueline. b 46. MCSP 70. Cant Sch of Min 88. **d** 91 **p** 94. NSM Bexley St Jo *Roch* 91–97; NSM Crayford 91–94; C 94–97 and 00–01; C Dartford H Trin 97–00; Hon C Ash 01–11; Asst Chapl Thames Gateway NHS Trust 01–11; Chapl Wisdom Hospice 04–11; rtd 11; PtO *Chich* from 17. *9 Crescent Rise, Thakeham, Pulborough RH20 3NB* T: (01903) 743083 E: peal@btinternet.com

PEAL, John Arthur. b 46. K Coll Lon BD 70 AKC. **d** 71 **p** 72. C Portsea All SS w St Jo Rudmore *Portsm* 71–74; C Westbury *Sarum* 74–77; V Borstal *Roch* 77–82; Chapl HM Pris Cookham Wood 78–82; V Erith Ch Ch *Roch* 82–91; P-in-c Erith St Jo 86–91; V Bexley St Jo 91–00; Chapl Erith and Distr Hosp 82–90; R Ash *Roch* 00–11; R Ridley 00–11; RD Cobham 08–11; rtd 11; PtO *Roch* from 11; *Chich* from 17. *9 Crescent Rise, Thakeham, Pulborough RH20 3NB* T: (01903) 743083 M: 07919-410438 E: peal@btinternet.com

PEALL, Mrs Linda Grace. b 66. Westmr Coll Ox BEd 88. EAMTC 99. **d** 02 **p** 03. NSM Blackwell All SS and Salutation *Dur* 02–04; C Darlington H Trin 04–07; Chapl Co Durham and Darlington NHS Foundn Trust 05–10; Chapl Basildon and Thurrock Univ Hosps NHS Foundn Trust 10–20; Chapl E Suffolk and N Essex NHS Foundn Trust from 20. *Spiritual Care and Chaplaincy, Ipswich Hospital, Heath Road, Ipswich IP4 5PD* T: (01206) 712233 ext 6101 M: 07923-241334 E: linda.peall@btopenworld.com *or* linda.peall@esneft.nhs.uk

PEARCE, Adrian Francis. b 55. Westmr Coll Ox BTh 05. S Dios Minl Tr Scheme 92. **d** 95 **p** 96. NSM Jersey St Luke w St Jas *Win* 95–13; NSM Jersey St Mary 01–13; P-in-c Bournemouth St Ambrose from 13; P-in-c Bournemouth St Fran 13–16. *72A West Cliff Road, Bournemouth BH4 8BE* T: (01202) 911569 E: afpear2@gmail.com

PEARCE, Mrs Angela Elizabeth. b 36. K Coll Lon BSc 58 CertEd 59 BD 79 AKC 79. **dss** 77 **d** 87. Chapl Raines Foundn Sch Tower Hamlets Lon 79–97; Homerton St Barn w St Paul *Lon* 79–85; Upper Chelsea St Simon 85–89; Hon Par Dn 87–89; Hon Par Dn Limehouse 89–97; PtO *St E* 97–17. *41 Cross Penny Court, Cotton Lane, Bury St Edmunds IP33 1XY* T: (01284) 760016

PEARCE, Canon Brian Edward. b 39. Kelham Th Coll 59. **d** 64 **p** 65. C Smethwick St Matt *Birm* 64–68; C Kings Norton 68–72; TV 73–80; TR Swindon Dorcan *Bris* 80–91; Min Withywood CD 91–94; V Withywood 94–98; V Fishponds All SS 98–05; RD Bedminster 92–98; Hon Can Bris Cathl 97–05; rtd 05; PtO *Heref* 09–19; *Mon* from 15. *32 Brook Estate, Monmouth NP25 5AW* T: (01600) 716057 E: brianpearce777@btinternet.com

PEARCE, Mrs Catherine Elizabeth. b 64. Birm Univ BSc 86. Ox Min Course 18. **d** 21. C N Buckingham w Stowe *Ox* from 21. *2 Temple Close, Buckingham MK18 1JB* T: (01280) 821976 E: cathy.pearce25@icloud.com

PEARCE, Daniel. *See* PEARCE, William Philip Daniel

PEARCE, Mrs Janet Elizabeth. b 49. Somerville Coll Ox BA 72 MA 76 CertEd 74. NOC 85. **d** 88 **p** 94. Par Dn Helsby and Dunham-on-the-Hill *Ches* 88–94; C 94–96; C Norley, Crowton and Kingsley 96–06; Dioc Adv in Spirituality 02–06; R Llanfair Mathafarn Eithaf w Llanbedrgoch *Ban* 06–11; TR Bangor 11–13; rtd 13; PtO *Ban* 13–16; *Roch* from 15. *2 Egdean Walk, Sevenoaks TN13 3UQ* T: (01732) 464598

PEARCE, Jonathan. b 55. St Jo Coll Nottm BTh 85. **d** 85 **p** 86. C Gt Chesham *Ox* 85–89; C Newport Pagnell w Lathbury and Moulsoe 89–93; TV Waltham H Cross *Chelmsf* 93–07; R Gt Totham and Lt Totham w Goldhanger 07–17; rtd 17; PtO *Chelmsf* 18–19. *15 Mill Close, Roxwell, Chelmsford CM1 4PG* E: revdjpearce@aol.com

PEARCE, Neville John Lewis. b 33. CBIM 88 Leeds Univ LLB 53 LLM 54. Trin Coll Bris 90. **d** 91 **p** 92. NSM Bath Walcot *B & W* 91–93; P-in-c Bath St Sav w Swainswick and Woolley 93–98; PtO from 98. *Penshurst, Weston Lane, Bath BA1 4AB* T: (01225) 426925 E: nevillepearce@tiscali.co.uk

PEARCE, Robert John. b 47. GLCM LLCM 72 Birm Univ PGCE 73. Ripon Coll Cuddesdon 79. **d** 82 **p** 83. C Broseley w Benthall *Heref* 82–83; C Kington w Huntington, Old Radnor, Kinnerton etc 83–85; R Westbury 85–94; R Yockleton 85–94; V Gt Wollaston 85–94; V Gwersyllt *St As* 94–99; V Northop 99–03; P-in-c Cerrigydrudion w Llanfihangel Glyn Myfyr etc 08–15; Hon C Henllan and Llannefydd and Bylchau 15–17; rtd 17; PtO *St As* from 17. *14 Trinity Avenue, Llandudno LL30 2SJ* T: (01492) 874340

PEARCE, Sacha John Tremain. b 64. Reading Univ BA 92 Ches Univ DProf 18 RGN 86. Ripon Coll Cuddesdon. **d** 00 **p** 01. C Tisbury *Sarum* 00–01; C Nadder Valley 01–04; V Seend, Bulkington and Poulshot 04–09; Chapl Plymouth Hosps NHS Trust from 09; LtO *Ex* from 09; PtO *Truro* from 14. *Derriford Hospital, Derriford Road, Plymouth PL6 8DH* T: (01752) 792022 E: sacha.pearce@nhs.net *or* sjtpearce@gmail.com

PEARCE, Shirley May. b 60. St Mellitus Coll BA 18. **d** 18 **p** 19. C Basildon St Andr w H Cross *Chelmsf* from 18. *12 Holden Gardens, Basildon SS14 3LF* T: (01268) 984913 E: revshirleym@gmail.com

PEARCE, Simon David. b 81. Univ of E Lon BSc 07. St Mellitus Coll BA 18. **d** 18 **p** 19. C Springfield All SS *Chelmsf* 18–21; C Chelmsf St Andr from 21. *12 Matfield Close, Chelmsford CM1 7TP* M: 07544-126990 E: revdsimonpearce@outlook.com

PEARCE, Mrs Susan Elizabeth. b 44. NEOC 03. **d** 06 **p** 07. NSM Pannal w Beckwithshaw *Ripon* 06–11; NSM High Harrogate St Pet 11–14; *Leeds* 14–17; PtO from 17. *8 Wheatlands Grove, Harrogate HG2 8JH* E: sue.pearce56@btopenworld.com

PEARCE, Valerie Olive. b 46. Whitelands Coll Lon CertEd 67 Roehampton Univ Hon BEd 17. SEITE 96. **d** 97 **p** 98. CSC 77–04; LtO *S'wark* 97–04; PtO from 09; *Cant* 15–20; *Roch* from 20. *10 Bromley College, London Road, Bromley BR1 1PE* T: (020) 8290 6662 E: revdval@gmail.com

PEARCE, William Philip Daniel. b 26. Stanford Univ BA 48 Leeds Univ CertEd 64 MA 75. Cuddesdon Coll 54. **d** 56 **p** 57. USA 56–60; CR 60–84; C St Geo-in-the-East w St Paul *Lon* 84–86; USA from 86; rtd 02. *1037 Olympic Lane, Seaside CA 93955-6226, USA* T: (001) (831) 393 2176

PEARKES, Nicholas Robin Clement. b 49. Ex Univ BA. Linc Th Coll. **d** 82 **p** 83. C Plymstock *Ex* 82–85; P-in-c Weston Mill 85–86; TV Devonport St Boniface and St Phil 86–99; R Broadhempston, Woodland, Staverton etc 99–14; rtd 14; PtO *Ex* from 14. *The Old Post Office, 128-130 Fore Street, Barton, Torquay TQ2 8DP* E: nicholaspearkes1@yahoo.com

PEARL, Mrs Sandra Ruth. b 47. SRN 69. LCTP 15. **d** 16. NSM N Westmorland *Carl* from 16. *Upper Orchard, Morland, Penrith CA10 3AX* T: (01931) 714564 E: sandra.pearl@btinternet.com

PEARMAIN, Brian Albert John. b 34. Lon Univ BD 68. Roch Th Coll 63. **d** 66 **p** 67. C Shirley St Jo *Cant* 66–69; C Selsdon St Jo w St Fran 69–73; P-in-c Louth H Trin *Linc* 73–75; TV Louth 75–79; R Scartho 79–97; RD Grimsby and Cleethorpes 89–94; Can and Preb Linc Cathl 94–97; rtd 97; PtO *Linc* 00–07; *Bradf* 07–14; *Leeds* from 14. *11 Ivy Garth, Church Lane, Chapel Allerton, Leeds LS7 4LY* M: 07944-675321

PEARMAN, Mrs Barbara Elizabeth Anne. b 48. RGN 69 RHV 72. ERMC 07. **d** 09 **p** 10. NSM E Marshland *Ely* 09–18; PtO from 18. *Rambles, 8 School Road, Tilney All Saints, King's Lynn PE34 4RS* T: (01553) 828808 M: 07946-348744 E: barbarapearman@hotmail.com

PEARS, Anthony John. b 58. Ripon Coll Cuddesdon 00. **d** 02 **p** 03. C Watton w Carbrooke and Ovington *Nor* 02–05; R Northanger *Win* from 05. *The Rectory, Gaston Lane, Upper Farringdon, Alton GU34 3EE* T: (01420) 588398 E: the96@btinternet.com

PEARSE, Andrew George. b 46. Wycliffe Hall Ox 71. **d** 74 **p** 75. C Homerton St Luke *Lon* 74–77; C Chadderton Em *Man* 77–81; R Collyhurst 81–89; Area Sec (NE, E Midl and Scotland) SAMS 89–03; rtd 03; Chapl Co-ord St Leon Hospice York 03–11; PtO *York* 11–16; Hon C Knaresborough *Leeds* 14–18; PtO *S'well* from 21. *48 Brixworth Way, Retford DN22 6TT* E: tarvethecurkey@yahoo.co.uk

PEARSE, Christopher George. b 84. Surrey Univ BA 06 Spurgeon's Coll Lon MA 14. Ridley Hall Cam 14. **d** 16

p 17. C Wollaton *S'well* 16–19; P-in-c Farnsfield from 19; P-in-c Kirklington w Hockerton from 19; P-in-c Maplebeck from 19; P-in-c Winkburn from 19. *The Vicarage, Beck Lane, Farnsfield, Newark NG22 8ER* M: 07505-963759 E: chris.pearse04@gmail.com

PEARSE, Jeffery Alun. **d** 16 **p** 17. C Abergavenny St Mary w Llanwenarth Citra *Mon* from 16; C Abergavenny H Trin from 16. *St Mary's Priory Church, Monk Street, Abergavenny NP7 5ND* M: 07985-241700 E: jeff.pearse@hotmail.co.uk

PEARSON, Andrew John. b 59. Westcott Ho Cam 86. **d** 89 **p** 90. C Knaresborough *Ripon* 89–92; C Wetherby 92–94; P-in-c Hunslet Moor St Pet and St Cuth 94–96; V 96–01; V Hawksworth Wood 01–06; Dioc Environment Officer 97–06; P-in-c Oulton w Woodlesford and Methley w Mickletown 06–13; P-in-c Wyther 13–14; *Leeds* from 14. *Beeston Vicarage, 16 Town Street, Beeston, Leeds LS11 8PN* T: 0113-272 3337 E: revajp@btinternet.com

PEARSON, Andrew Michael. b 54. Univ of Wales (Ban) BTh 10 Solicitor 77. **d** 07 **p** 08. OLM Shere, Albury and Chilworth *Guildf* 07–12; C from 12. *The Forge, The Street, Albury, Guildford GU5 9AG* M: 07887-360061 E: minister@alburychurches.org *or* rev.a.m.pearson@btinternet.com

PEARSON, Mrs Béatrice Levasseur. b 53. Sorbonne Univ Paris LèsL 74 MèsL 75 Lon Inst of Educn PGCE 76. Ripon Coll Cuddesdon 01. **d** 03 **p** 04. C Easthampstead *Ox* 03–06; TV Loddon Reach 06–13; rtd 13. *1 Northanger Court, Grove Street, Bath BA2 6PE* T: (01225) 571344 M: 07981-462145

PEARSON, Ms Brenda Elizabeth Frances (Brandy). b 51. SEITE 00. **d** 03 **p** 04. NSM Finsbury Park St Thos *Lon* 03–07; C Acton Green 07–15; NSM W Acton St Martin 15–20; rtd 20. *14 Bromley College, London Road, Bromley BR1 1PE* E: therevvedbee@hotmail.co.uk

PEARSON, Canon Brian William. b 49. Brighton Poly BSc 71 City Univ MSc 80 Westmr Coll Ox MTh 94 FHSM. S'wark Ord Course & Clapham Ord Scheme 76. **d** 79 **p** 80. Hon C Plumstead All SS *S'wark* 79–81; PtO *Chich* 81–83; Hon C Broadwater St Mary 83–88; Bp's Research and Dioc Communications Officer *B & W* 88–90; Dioc Missr 91; Abp's Officer for Miss and Evang and Tait Missr *Cant* 91–97; Abp's Dioc Chapl 91–97; Hon Prov Can Cant Cathl 92–97; Gen Dir CPAS 97–00; P-in-c Leek Wootton and Dioc Officer for OLM *Cov* 00–06; Assoc Dir of Voc *B & W* from 11; PtO 18–19. *Woodspring, Northfield, Somerton TA11 6SL* T: (01458) 274360 E: brian@vividclouds.com

PEARSON, Christopher John. b 49. GRSM LRAM ARCM. Oak Hill NSM Course 81. **d** 84 **p** 85. NSM Barton Seagrave w Warkton *Pet* 84–86; C Kettering St Andr 86–88; V Nassington w Yarwell and Woodnewton 88–91; V Pet St Mark 91–03; P-in-c Gt Doddington and Wilby 03–12; P-in-c Ecton 07–12; R Gt Doddington and Wilby and Ecton 12–15; rtd 15; PtO *Pet* 15–19; Hon C Northampton Em from 19; PtO *Eur* from 17. *10 Ashley Way, Westone, Northampton NN3 3DZ* T: (01604) 947861 E: c.pearson1@homecall.co.uk

PEARSON, Christopher William. b 56. Univ Coll Ox MA. St Jo Coll Nottm 07. **d** 09 **p** 10. C Norton St Mary and Stockton St Chad *Dur* 09–11; P-in-c Easington and Easington Colliery 11–14; TR Gt Aycliffe 14–16; rtd 16; PtO *Leeds* from 17. *1 The Paddock, Appleton Wiske, Northallerton DL6 2BE* T: (01609) 881872 E: revcwpearson@gmail.com

PEARSON, David. *See* PEARSON, James David

PEARSON, Fergus Tom. b 58. Middx Poly BA 81 Moore Th Coll Sydney MA 98. Oak Hill Th Coll BA 95. **d** 92 **p** 93. C Mildmay Grove St Jude and St Paul *Lon* 92–95; Australia 96–98; C Heatherlands St Jo *Sarum* 98–03; V Hensingham *Carl* from 03; C Mirehouse from 19. *St John's Vicarage, Egremont Road, Hensingham, Whitehaven CA28 8QW* T: (01946) 692822 E: fpe@rson.justbrowsing.com *or* fergus@stjohnshensingham.org.uk

PEARSON, Geoffrey Charles. b 49. Imp Coll Lon BSc 70 ARCS. Oak Hill Th Coll 80. **d** 82 **p** 83. C Folkestone St Jo *Cant* 82–86; V Ramsgate St Luke 86–93; Chapl to People at Work in Cam *Ely* 93–01; Co-ord Chapl HM Pris Chelmsf 01–07; rtd 07; PtO *Cant* from 08. *6 Lichfield Avenue, Canterbury CT1 3YA* M: 07890-808739 E: pearsongeoff@hotmail.co.uk

✠**PEARSON, The Rt Revd Geoffrey Seagrave.** b 51. St Jo Coll Dur BA 72. Cranmer Hall Dur 72. **d** 74 **p** 75 **c** 06. C Kirkheaton *Wakef* 74–77; C-in-c Blackb Redeemer 77–82; V 82–85; Asst Home Sec Gen Syn Bd for Miss and Unity 85–89; Hon C Forty Hill Jes Ch *Lon* 85–89; Exec Sec BCC Evang Cttee 86–89; V Roby *Liv* 89–06; AD Huyton 02–06; Hon Can Liv Cathl 03–06; Suff Bp Lancaster *Blackb* 06–17; C Ellel w Shireshead 08–16; C Shireshead 16–17; rtd 17; Hon Asst Bp Ches from 19. *10 Elderswood, Rainhill, Prescot L35 4QY* M: 07809-618385 E: geoff.s.pearson@outlook.com

PEARSON, Canon Henry Gervis. b 47. Mansf Coll Ox BA 72 MA 76. St Jo Coll Nottm 72. **d** 74 **p** 75. C Southgate *Chich* 74–76; TV 76–82; V Debenham w Aspall and Kenton *St E* 82–91; Chapl to Suffolk Fire Service 88–91; RD Loes 89–91; TR Marlborough *Sarum* 91–02; RD 94–02; R Queen Thorne 02–12; P-in-c Gifle Valley 10–12; RD Sherborne 04–11; Chapl Savernake Hosp Marlborough 91–94; Chapl E Wilts Health Care NHS Trust 99–94; Chapl Wilts and Swindon Healthcare NHS Trust 99–12; Can and Preb Sarum Cathl 99–12; rtd 12; PtO *Sarum* from 12. *1 Morris Road, Marlborough SN8 1TJ* T: (01672) 511788 E: henryandjudith@btinternet.com

PEARSON, Ian. b 49. Liv Univ BA 71. S'wark Ord Course 79. **d** 82 **p** 83. Archivist USPG 82–85; Archivist Nat Soc 85–91; NSM Lavender Hill Ascension *S'wark* 82–84; LtO *Lon* 84–86 and 88–90; NSM Westmr St Matt 86–88; PtO *S'wark* 85–90; *St Alb* 90–91; C Chesterfield St Mary and All SS *Derby* 91–95; R Bengeo *St Alb* 95–04; P-in-c Worc City St Paul and Old St Martin etc 04–06; R Worc City 06–10; rtd 10; PtO *B & W* from 10; *Sarum* from 16. *7 Rosedale Walk, Frome BA11 2JH* T: (01373) 469739 E: ianandlizpearson@waitrose.com

PEARSON, Miss Jacqueline Susan. b 86. Univ of Wales (Abth) BSc 08 Lucy Cavendish Coll Cam BTh 18. Ridley Hall Cam 16. **d** 19 **p** 20. C Boreham *Chelmsf* from 19. *124 Fairway Drive, Chelmsford CM3 3FH* M: 07704-777511 E: jacqui.pearson07@hotmail.co.uk *or* jacqui@borehamchurch.org.uk

PEARSON, James David. b 51. Cape Town Univ BSocSc 74. St Paul's Coll Grahamstown 76. **d** 78 **p** 79. C St Geo Cathl Cape Town S Africa 78–80; R Caledon H Trin 80–84; R Tristan da Cunha St Mary 84–86; R Camps Bay St Pet 86–89; R Kuruman St Mary-le-Bourne w Wrenchville 89–91; R Amalinda Ch Ch 92–96; Asst P Cambridge St Mark 96–98; Asst P-in-c Kidds Beach St Mary & St Andr 99; C Prittlewell St Steph *Chelmsf* 00–04; TV Barking St Marg w St Patr 04–09; P-in-c Hornchurch H Cross 09–18; rtd 18. *28 Victory Lane, Rochford SS4 3AN* E: revdavidpearson@outlook.com

PEARSON, Joanna Ruth. *See* SEABOURNE, Joanna Ruth

PEARSON, Mrs Katherine Elizabeth. b 77. Birm Univ LLB 99 MSc 08. Qu Coll Birm. **d** 12 **p** 13. C Brandwood *Birm* 12–15; C Brandwood and Weoley Castle 12–15; Chapl Warw Univ *Cov* 15–21; V St Alb St Mary Marshalswick from 21. *Address temp unknown* M: 07890-648008 E: kate.e.pearson@me.com

✠**PEARSON, The Rt Revd Kevin.** b 54. Leeds Univ BA 75 Edin Univ BD 79. Edin Th Coll 76. **d** 79 **p** 80 **c** 11. C Horden *Dur* 79–81; Chapl Leeds Univ *Ripon* 81–87; R Edin St Salvador 87–93; Chapl Edin Napier Univ 88–92 and 92–94; Dioc Dir of Ords 90–95; Prov Dir of Ords 91–11; Assoc R Edin Old St Paul 93–94; P-in-c Linlithgow *Edin* 94–95; R Edin St Mich and All SS 95–11; Can St Mary's Cathl 03–11; Dean Edin 04–10; Bp Arg 11–20; Provost Cumbrae Cathl 11–20; Bp Glas from 20. *Bishop's Office, Diocesan Centre, 5 St Vincent Place, Glasgow G1 2DH* T: 0141-221 6911 E: bishop@glasgow.anglican.org

PEARSON, Lewis Nicholas. b 82. Sarum Coll 14. **d** 17 **p** 18. C Poole *Sarum* 17–20; V Winterborne Valley and Milton Abbas from 20. *The Rectory, Back Street, Winterborne Strickland, Blandford Forum DT11 0NL* M: 07922-137348 E: revlewispearson@gmail.com

PEARSON, Lindsay Hildegard Anna. b 82. Coll of Resurr Mirfield. **d** 16 **p** 17. C Wirksworth *Derby* 16–19; C Chesterfield SS Aug 19–20; P-in-c Blackpool St Mary *Blackb* from 20; Chapl St Geo Sch Blackpool from 20. *71 Harrington Avenue, Blackpool FY4 1QD* T: (01253) 345995 E: revd.l.h.pearson@gmail.com

PEARSON, Ms Lindsey Carole. b 61. Cov Poly BA 86 CQSW 86. Westcott Ho Cam 86. **d** 89 **p** 94. C High Harrogate St Pet *Ripon* 89–93; C Moor Allerton 93–96; Chapl St Gemma's Hospice 94–96; TV Seacroft *Ripon* 96–04; World Development Officer 97–04; Area Co-ord (N and W Yorks) Chr Aid 04–07; PtO *Ripon* 04–07; P-in-c Swillington 07–13; NSM Kippax w Allerton Bywater 12–13; P-in-c Beeston 13–14; TR *Leeds* from 14; AD Armley from 20. *Beeston Vicarage, 16 Town Street, Beeston, Leeds LS11 8PN* T: 0113-272 3337 M: 07961-016052 E: revlcp@btinternet.com

PEARSON, Nigel Hetley Allan. b 45. Fitzw Coll Cam BA 67 MA 87. EMMTC 04. **d** 06 **p** 07. NSM Papworth *Ely* 06–15; rtd 15; PtO *Ely* from 15. *The House behind the Hedge, 71 Caxton End, Bourne, Cambridge CB23 2SS* T: (01954) 719351 M: 07713-639928 E: njfarm@gmail.com

PEARSON, Pauline Hilary. b 54. Newc Poly BA 77 PhD 88 RN 77 RHV 79. NEOC 02. **d** 05 **p** 06. NSM Denton *Newc* 05–10; NSM Newc St Geo and St Hilda 10–19; TV Ch the King 19–20; TR from 21. *St Columba's Vicarage, West View, Wideopen, Newcastle upon Tyne*

NE13 6NH T: 0191-236 2280 M: 07753-744349 E: pauline.pearson@northumbria.ac.uk

PEARSON, Mrs Priscilla Dawn. b 45. Oak Hill Th Coll BA 90. **d** 90 **p** 94. Par Dn Stanford-le-Hope w Mucking *Chelmsf* 90–94; C 94; C Colchester St Jo 94–96; Hon C Woking St Jo *Guildf* 03–05; rtd 10. *Talywain Cottage, Shop Road, Cwmavon, Pontypool NP4 7RU* T: (01495) 774132 E: priscillapearson@btinternet.com

PEARSON, Raymond Joseph. b 44. AKC 71. St Aug Coll Cant 71. **d** 72 **p** 73. C Wetherby *Ripon* 72–75; C Goring-by-Sea *Chich* 75–77; C Bramley *Ripon* 77–82; V Patrick Brompton and Hunton 82–94; V Crakehall 82–94; V Hornby 82–94; World Miss Officer 88–94; RD Wensley 92–94; V Bardsey 94–09; rtd 09; PtO *York* from 09. *7 St George's Croft, Bridlington YO16 7RW* T: (01262) 424332 E: r.pearson121@btinternet.com

PEARSON, Robert James Stephen. b 52. Cov Poly BA 74. St Steph Ho Ox 85. **d** 87 **p** 88. C Stoke Newington St Mary *Lon* 87–90; C Haggerston All SS 90–97; C Dalston H Trin w St Phil and Haggerston All SS 97–98; Chapl HM Pris Wandsworth 98–02; Chapl HM Pris Pentonville 02–07; PtO *Lon* 07–21; *Roch* from 21. *14 Bromley College, London Road, Bromley BR1 1PE* E: ahjay@hotmail.co.uk

PEARSON, Robert Lyon. b 57. St Jo Coll Nottm 90. **d** 92 **p** 93. C Netherton *Liv* 92–96; V Woolston 96–02; V Highfield 02–19; P-in-c E Widnes from 19. *St Matthew's Vicarage, Billinge Road, Wigan WN3 6BL* T: (01942) 222121 M: 07904-320542

PEARSON, Preb Roy Barthram. b 35. K Coll Lon 56. **d** 60 **p** 61. C Brookfield St Mary *Lon* 60–64; C St Marylebone St Cypr 64–70; V Tottenham All Hallows from 70; AD E Haringey 95–00; Preb St Paul's Cathl from 96. *The Priory, Church Lane, London N17 7AA* T: (020) 8808 2470

PEARSON-GEE, William Oliver Clinton. b 61. Wycliffe Hall Ox 04. **d** 06 **p** 07. C Ox St Andr 06–10; R Buckingham from 10. *The Rectory, 8 Aris Way, Buckingham MK18 1FX* T: (01280) 830221 E: rector@buckinghambenefice.org.uk

PEARSON-HICKS, John Michael. b 67. Crewe & Alsager Coll BA 89 K Coll Lon MA 01 K Alfred's Coll Win PGCE 90. NTMTC 02. **d** 05 **p** 06. NSM Grosvenor Chpl *Lon* 05–09; NSM Westmr St Steph w St Jo 09–15; P-in-c Pimlico St Barn from 15. *167 John Ruskin Street, London SE5 0PQ* T: (020) 7277 2383 M: 07540-062413 E: frhicks@me.com *or* john.pearson-hicks@london.anglican.org

PEARSON-SMITH, Mrs Danielle Alanna. b 82. SEITE BA 15. **d** 16 **p** 17. C Welling *Roch* 16–19; R Snodland All SS w Ch Ch from 19. *The Rectory, 11 St Katherine's Lane, Snodland ME6 5EH* T: (01634) 240232 E: revpearsonsmith@gmail.com

PEART, John Graham. b 36. Bps' Coll Cheshunt 65. **d** 68 **p** 69. C Cheshunt *St Alb* 68–70; C St Alb St Pet 70–73; R Hunsdon 73–76; R Widford 73–76; Ind Chapl 76–82; Chapl St Geo Hosp Stafford 82–87; Chapl Stafford Distr Gen Hosp 82–87; Chapl Qu Eliz Hosp Gateshead 87–89; Chapl Bensham Hosp Gateshead 87–89; Chapl Garlands Hosp 89–94; P-in-c Cotehill and Cumwhinton *Carl* 89–94; V Irthington, Crosby-on-Eden and Scaleby 94–98; rtd 98; Chapl Douglas MacMillan Hospice Stoke-on-Trent 98–01; P-in-c Salt and Sandon w Burston *Lich* 01–02; TV Mid Trent 02–03; PtO 04–07; *Eur* 07–13; *Lich* 15–16; *St E* 17–21. *Skinners End, Skinners Lane, Metfield, Harleston IP20 0LH* T: (01379) 586089 E: johnpeart@hotmail.co.uk

PEASE, Alexander Michael. b 56. Mansf Coll Ox MA. St Mellitus Coll BA 12. **d** 12 **p** 13. NSM Itchen Valley *Win* 12–18; P-in-c 18–21; rtd 21; PtO *Win* from 21. *The Mill House, Lower Chilland Lane, Martyr Worthy, Winchester SO21 1EB* T: (01962) 791010 M: 07931-380321 E: rev@ampease.co.uk

PEAT, Mrs Ann Kathleen. b 40. TCert 60. **d** 98 **p** 99. OLM Brumby *Linc* 98–14; PtO *Newc* from 15. *Ashgrove, Church Lane, Longframlington, Morpeth NE65 8HR* T: (01665) 570564

PEAT, David William. b 37. Clare Coll Cam MA 59 PhD 62 FRAS 63. Westcott Ho Cam 72. **d** 75 **p** 76. C Chesterton St Andr *Ely* 75–77; Chapl Univ Coll of Ripon and York St Jo 77–83; V E Ardsley *Wakef* 83–87; Prin Willesden Min Tr Scheme 87–94; NSM Headingley *Ripon* 94–14; P-in-c 06–12; Research Lect Leeds Univ 94–12; rtd 12; PtO *Leeds* from 12. *12 North Grange Mews, Headingley, Leeds LS6 2EW* T: 0113-275 3179 E: dw.peat@btinternet.com

PEAT, Canon Matthew. b 71. Bradf and Ilkley Coll BA 97. Ripon Coll Cuddesdon BTh 03. **d** 03 **p** 04. C Walney Is *Carl* 03–06; C Barrow St Matt 06–08; TR 08–10; TR N Barrow 10–13; RD Barrow 11–12; P-in-c Whitkirk *Leeds* 13–18; V from 18; AD from 18; Hon Can Ripon Cathl from 19. *Whitkirk Vicarage, 386 Selby Road, Leeds LS15 0AA* T: 0113-264 5790 M: 07772-560014 E: matthewpeat@talktalk.net *or* vicar@whitkirkchurch.org.uk

PEATMAN, Michael Robert. b 61. Keble Coll Ox BA 85 MA 89 St Jo Coll Dur BA 89 Lanc Univ MA 06. Cranmer Hall Dur 87. **d** 90 **p** 91. C Greasley *S'well* 90–94; P-in-c Whitley *Cov* 94–02; Dio Stewardship Adv 94–02; Sen Chapl St Martin's Coll *Blackb* 02–07; Sen Chapl Cumbria Univ 07–09; P-in-c Poulton-le-Sands w Morecambe St Laur 09–11; R 11–18; AD Lancaster and Morecambe 10–14; V Beverley St Nic *York* from 18; Tr Officer E Riding from 18. *St Nicholas' Vicarage, 72 Grovehill Road, Beverley HU17 0ER* T: (01482) 881458 E: mikepeatman@gmail.com

PEATTIE, The Ven Colin Hulme Reid. b 39. Natal Univ BSc 59. Ripon Hall Ox 61. **d** 63 **p** 64. C Belmont *Lon* 63–65; R Durban St Columba S Africa 65–69; R Dundee St Jas 69–72; Chapl St Andr Sch Bloemfontein 72–76; R Pietermaritzburg St Alphege 76–83; V S Ossett *Wakef* 83–85; R York-cum-Ravensworth S Africa 85–93; R Stranger All SS 93–96; R Umhlali All So 96–05; Adn N Coast 01–05; rtd 05. *PO Box 222, Salt Rock, 4391 South Africa* T: (0027) (32) 525 4004 M: (0027) 84-206 1093 E: cpeattie@absamail.co.za

PEATY, Canon Julia Kathleen. b 53. Salford Univ BSc 75 Glos Univ BA 07. STETS 96. **d** 99 **p** 00. NSM E Grinstead St Swithun *Chich* from 99; RD E Grinstead 10–19; Dean of Women's Min 13–17; Dean of Self-Supporting Min from 18; Acting Adn Horsham 20–21; Can and Preb Chich Cathl from 10. *15 Overton Shaw, East Grinstead RH19 2HN* T: (01342) 322386 E: julia@peaty.net

PEBERDY (née GARNETT), Mrs Alyson Susan. b 48. Trevelyan Coll Dur BA 69 Reading Univ MA 75. Ox Min Course 95. **d** 96 **p** 97. C New Windsor *Ox* 96–99; V Brockley Hill St Sav *S'wark* 99–18; P-in-c Perry Hill St Geo 00–01; P-in-c Forest Hill St Aug 00–02; Adv Women's Min Woolwich Area 10–18; Dean of Women's Min 12–17; rtd 18; PtO *Ox* from 18. *77 Lonsdale Road, Oxford OX2 7ES* M: 07552-958257 E: aspeberdy@aol.com

PECK, Christopher Wallace. b 49. UEA BA 72 Lon Bible Coll BA 75 Ches Coll of HE.MTh 96. Ripon Coll Cuddesdon 10. **d** 11 **p** 12. C Abington *Pet* 11–15; R Guilsborough and Hollowell and Cold Ashby etc 15–20; rtd 20; Lay Voc Officer *Pet* from 20. *14 Pine Court, Little Brington, Northampton NN7 4EZ* M: 07505-253096 E: revchrispeck@hotmail.co.uk

PECK, Kay Margaret. b 51. Milton Keynes Coll of Ed BEd 76. Ox Min Course 04. **d** 07 **p** 08. NSM Swan *Ox* 07–09; NSM The Claydons and Swan 09–10; NSM Lenborough 11–17; PtO from 17. *21 Beamish Way, Winslow, Buckingham MK18 3EU* T: (01296) 714253 E: kmpeck@btinternet.com

PECKHAM, Richard Graham. b 51. Sarum & Wells Th Coll 84. **d** 86 **p** 87. C Bishop's Cleeve *Glouc* 86–89; TV Ilfracombe, Lee, Woolacombe, Bittadon etc *Ex* 89–96; TV Sidmouth, Woolbrook, Salcombe Regis, Sidbury etc 96–12; RD Ottery 98–02; P-in-c Dunkeswell, Luppitt, Sheldon and Upottery 12–16; C Broadhembury, Payhembury and Plymtree 12–16; R Broadhembury, Dunkeswell, Luppitt, Plymtree, Sheldon, and Upottery 17; Hon Chapl ATC 98–17; rtd 17; PtO *B & W* from 17. *Ossory, Silvermead, Minehead TA24 6AP* E: rikpeckham@btinternet.com

PEDLAR, Canon John Glanville. b 43. Ex Univ BA 68 De Montfort Univ Hon MA 06. St Steph Ho Ox 68. **d** 70 **p** 71. C Tavistock and Gulworthy *Ex* 70–73; Prec Portsm Cathl 74–77; Prec St Alb Abbey 77–81; V Redbourn 81–98; V Bedford St Paul 98–13; PV Westmr Abbey 87–04; Hon Can St Alb 06–13; rtd 13; P-in-c Bris Ch Ch w St Ewen, All SS and St Geo 16–21. *1 Priory Dene, Bristol BS9 3EG* E: johnpedlar@btinternet.com

PEDLEY, Canon Betty. b 49. Ripon Coll of Educn CertEd 70 Leeds Univ BEd 71 ALCM 78. NOC 85. **d** 88 **p** 03. Par Dn Sowerby *Wakef* 88–92; Par Educn Adv and Youth Chapl 92–03; P-in-c Luddenden w Luddenden Foot 03–08; P-in-c Norland 06–08; Hon Can Wakef Cathl 00–08; rtd 08; PtO *Wakef* 08–14; *Leeds* from 14. *7 Ogden View Close, Halifax HX2 9LY* T: (01422) 252014 E: bettypedley@aol.com

✠**PEDLEY, The Rt Revd Geoffrey Stephen.** b 40. Qu Coll Cam BA 64 MA 67. Cuddesdon Coll 64. **d** 66 **p** 67 **c** 98. C Liv Our Lady and St Nic 66–69; C Cov H Trin 69–71; P-in-c Kitwe Zambia 71–77; P-in-c Stockton H Trin *Dur* 77–83; V Stockton St Pet 77–88; Chapl to The Queen 84–98; R Whickham *Dur* 88–93; Can Res Dur Cathl 93–98; Suff Bp Lancaster *Blackb* 98–05; Hon Can Blackb Cathl 98–05; rtd 05. *The Blue House, Newbrough, Hexham NE47 5AN* T: (01434) 674238

PEDLEY, Nicholas Charles. b 48. DipSW 75. Qu Coll Birm 88. **d** 90 **p** 91. C Stafford St Jo and Tixall w Ingestre *Lich* 90–93; C Kingswinford St Mary *Worc* 93–96; TV 96–97; C Cheswardine, Childs Ercall, Hales, Hinstock etc *Lich* 97–99; Chapl HM YOI Stoke Heath 97–99; rtd 99; PtO *Worc* from 00; *Lich* from 15. *1 Brindley Heath Cottages, Enville Road, Kinver, Stourbridge DY7 5LU* T: (01384) 877219 E: nickpedley48@gmail.com

PEDLEY, Simon David. b 76. Imp Coll Lon BSc 98 ARCS 98. Oak Hill Th Coll BA 10. **d** 10 **p** 11. C St Helen Bishopsgate w St Andr Undershaft etc *Lon* 10–14; C Fulwell from 18. *106 Fulwell Road, Teddington TW11 0RQ* T: (020) 8241 0761 M: 07713-897991 E: simon@stmichaelsfulwell.co.uk

PEDLOW, Henry Noel. b 37. QUB BA 59. **d** 61 **p** 62. C Belfast St Phil *Conn* 61–66; C Belfast St Nic 66–70; I Eglantine 70–82; I Kilkeel *D & D* 82–89; I Belfast St Donard 89–03; rtd 03. *8 Old Mill Dale, Dundonald, Belfast BT16 1WG* T: (028) 9048 5416

PEEBLES, David Thomas. b 64. Bris Univ BA 85 St Chad's Coll Dur PGCE 86 Man Univ MA 94 Heythrop Coll Lon MA 04 K Coll Lon DThMin 17. Coll of Resurr Mirfield 90. **d** 90 **p** 91. C Crewe St Andr *Ches* 90–93; Lect and Asst Dir Studies Mirfield 93–95; Chapl Qu Mary Univ of Lon 95–00; P-in-c Bethnal Green St Matt w St Jas the Gt 97–99; Chapl LSE 00–10; R Bloomsbury St Geo w Woburn Square Ch Ch from 10; Bp's Adv on New Relig Movements from 01. *The Rectory, 6 Gower Street, London WC1E 6DP* T: (020) 7580 4010 M: 07838-388074 E: rector@stgb.org.uk

PEEK, Alan Nicholas. b 65. Ridley Hall Cam 02. **d** 04 **p** 05. C Much Woolton *Liv* 04–08; I Derg w Termonamongan *D & R* 08–14; I Movilla *D & D* from 14. *The Rectory, 34 Hollymount Road, Newtownards BT23 7DL* T: (028) 9181 0787 or 9181 9794 E: rev.al@sky.com

PEEK, John Richard. b 51. Bris Univ BSc 72 Nottm Univ BA 75. St Jo Coll Nottm. **d** 76 **p** 77. C Hebburn St Jo *Dur* 76–78; C Dunston 78–81; R Armthorpe *Sheff* 81–86; RE Teacher K Edw VI Sch Southn 87–88; Chapl and Hd RE Casterton Sch Lancs 89; Teacher Furze Platt Comp Sch Berks 89–90; Chapl Bearwood Coll Wokingham 96–97; Teacher K Manor Sch Guildf 97–98; Teacher Stowford Coll Sutton 98–08; Teacher Ryde Sch w Upper Chine 08–09; PtO *Portsm* 08–11. *41 North Road, Shanklin PO37 6DE* T: (01983) 719631

PEEL, Mrs Christine Mary. b 44. Whitelands Coll Lon CertEd 66. Portsm Dioc Tr Course. **d** 90. NSM Sheet *Portsm* 90–03; PtO *York* from 03. *11 Whiteoak Avenue, Easingwold, York YO61 3GB* T: (01347) 823548 E: peel3gb@btinternet.com

PEEL, Canon David Charles. b 41. AKC 75. St Aug Coll Cant 75. **d** 76 **p** 77. C Tynemouth Cullercoats St Paul *Newc* 76–79; C Tynemouth St Jo 79–84; Ldr Cedarwood Project 84–88 and 91–11; Warden Communicare Ho 89–91; Min Killingworth 89–91; Hon Can Newc Cathl 08–11; rtd 11; PtO *Newc* 11–20. *47 Brock Farm Court, North Shields NE30 2BH* T: 0191-272 8743 E: peeldc524@gmail.com

PEEL, Derrick. b 50. Open Univ BA 82. Linc Th Coll 75. **d** 78 **p** 79. C Otley *Bradf* 78–82; V Shelf 82–94; P-in-c Buttershaw St Aid 89–94; TR Shelf w Buttershaw St Aid 94–95; V E Crompton *Man* 95–05; V Ware St Mary *St Alb* 05–15; rtd 15; PtO *Chelmsf* from 15. *10 Thornwood Close, West Mersea, Colchester CO5 8BU*

PEELING, Mrs Pamela Mary Alberta. b 44. Oak Hill Th Coll 83. **dss** 86 **d** 87 **p** 94. NSM Moulsham St Luke *Chelmsf* 86–88; NSM N Springfield 88–95; C Basildon St Martin 95–97; TV Grays Thurrock 97–05; rtd 05; PtO *St E* from 05. *4 Heron Road, Saxmundham IP17 1WR* T: (01728) 604584 E: ppeeling@freebie.net

PEER, Charles Scott. b 69. Bris Univ BSc 91 PGCE 94 Ex Univ MA 05. Trin Coll Bris BA 02. **d** 02 **p** 03. C Dawlish *Ex* 02–05; P-in-c Kea *Truro* 05–12; Miss Development Officer *Portsm* 12–16; Hd of Strategic Progr *B & W* from 16. *Diocesan Office, The Old Deanery, Wells BA5 2UG* E: charlie.peer@bathwells.anglican.org

PEERS, Esther Louise. b 76. St Mellitus Coll 15. **d** 18 **p** 19. C Leamington Spa H Trin *Cov* from 18. *18 Arlington Avenue, Leamington Spa CV32 5UD*

PEERS, Michael John. b 65. SS Paul & Mary Coll Cheltenham BA 86. Ripon Coll Cuddesdon 88. **d** 91 **p** 92. C Birstall and Wanlip *Leic* 91–94; C Leic St Marg and All SS 94–96; TV The Abbey Leic 96–00; P-in-c Langley Park *Dur* 00–01; V 01–21; P-in-c Esh 00–01; V 01–11; P-in-c Hamsteels 00–01; V 01–11; V Esh and Hamsteels 11–21; P-in-c Waterhouses 00–01; V 01–21; TV Dur N from 21. *The Vicarage, Church Street, Langley Park, Durham DH7 9TZ* T: 0191-373 3110 E: mjpeers@aol.com

PEERS, Conan Richard Charles. b 65. K Alfred's Coll Win BEd 88 Lon Inst of Educn MA 05. Chich Th Coll BTh 93. **d** 93 **p** 94. C Grangetown *York* 93–95; C Portsea St Mary *Portsm* 95–97; Dep Hd Emsworth Primary Sch 97–01; Hon Chapl Portsm Cathl 01–03; Chapl St Luke's Sch Southsea 01–03; Dep Hd Ch Sch Richmond 03–06; Chapl Abp Tenison's Sch Kennington 06–08; Headmaster Trin Sch Lewisham 08–16; Hon C Earlsfield St Andr *S'wark* 06–11; Hon C Blackheath All SS 11–13; Hon C Lewisham St Mary 13–16; Dir Educn *Liv* 16–20; Lic Preacher 16–20; PtO *Lich* from 16; Can Res and Sub-Dean Ch Ch *Ox* from 20. *Christ Church, St Aldates, Oxford OX1 1DP* E: richard.peers@chch.ox.ac.uk

PEET, John Christopher. b 56. Oriel Coll Ox BA 80 MA 83 Clare Coll Cam BA 82 MA 87 Leeds Univ MA 98 PhD 10. Ridley Hall Cam 80. **d** 83 **p** 84. C Menston w Woodhead *Bradf* 83–86; C Prenton *Ches* 86–89; V Harden and Wilsden *Bradf* 89–97; V Cononley w Bradley 97–14; *Leeds* 14–17; rtd 17; PtO *Leeds* from 17. *19 Main Street, Cononley, Keighley BD20 8LR*

PEET, Ruth Marie. b 59. **d** 15 **p** 16. C Plaistow St Mary *Roch* 15–19; V Aylesford from 19. *The Vicarage, Vicarage Close, Aylesford ME20 7BB* T: (01622) 717434 E: ruthmpeet@gmail.com

PEETERS, Erik Christian. b 75. Pretoria Univ BA 98 Leeds Univ MA 04 PhD 07. St Hild Coll 15. **d** 17 **p** 18. C Lupset *Leeds* 17–20; C Thornes 17–20; P-in-c Battyeford from 20; Lay Tr Officer from 20. *107A Stocks Bank Road, Mirfield WF14 9QT* T: (01924) 493277 M: 07761-919564 E: erik.peeters@leeds.anglican.org

PEGG, Danny Lee. b 89. Kent Univ BA 11 Cam Univ BTh 17 MPhil 18. Westcott Ho Cam 15. **d** 18 **p** 19. C Stone Cross St Luke w N Langney *Chich* from 18. *Address withheld by request* M: 07939-497002 E: revdpegg@gmail.com

PEGG, Josephine Anne. *See* ROBERTSON, Josephine Anne

PEGLER, Mrs Eve Charlotte. b 73. Cheltenham & Glouc Coll of HE BSc 95. Ridley Hall Cam 05. **d** 07 **p** 08. C Hullavington, Norton and Stanton St Quintin *Bris* 07–10; C Sherston Magna, Easton Grey, Luckington etc 07–10; TV Shaftesbury *Sarum* 10–14; Chapl Port Regis Sch 10–14; C Gillingham and Milton-on-Stour *Sarum* 14–19; C Gillingham, Milton-on-Stour and Silton from 19. *The Vicarage, 49 Fern Brook Lane, Gillingham SP8 4FL* T: (01747) 851442 E: evepegler@gmail.com

PEIRCE, John. b 35. Worc Coll Ox BA 59 MA 64 Kent Univ MA 96. Wycliffe Hall Ox 59. **d** 61 **p** 62. C Brompton H Trin *Lon* 61–64; C Wareham w Arne *Sarum* 64–68; V Sturminster Newton and Hinton St Mary 68–74; V Kingswood *Bris* 74–79; Dir Coun Chr Care *Ex* 79–89; Public Preacher 89–92; NSM Hackney *Lon* 90–94; NSM St Botolph Aldgate w H Trin Minories 94–02; Co-ord Ch Action on Disability 90–98; PtO *Ex* 92–98. *Danes View, Lyme Road, Axminster EX13 5BQ* E: peircejohn@aol.com

PEIRCE, Canon John Martin. b 36. Jes Coll Cam BA 59 MA 65. Westcott Ho Cam 65. **d** 66 **p** 67. C Croydon St Jo *Cant* 66–70; C Fareham H Trin *Portsm* 70–71; TV 71–76; TR Langley Marish *Ox* 76–85; RD Burnham 78–82; Dir of Ords and Post-Ord Tr 85–01; Can Res Ch Ch *Ox* 87–01; rtd 01; PtO *Ox* from 08. *8 Burwell Meadow, Witney, Oxford OX28 5JQ* T: (01993) 200103

PELHAM, Thomas John. b 87. Bris Univ BA 09 MA 11. Ripon Coll Cuddesdon BA 18. **d** 18 **p** 19. C Canford Cliffs and Sandbanks *Sarum* from 18. *4 Haven Heights, 22 Birchwood Road, Parkstone, Poole BH14 9ND* M: 07922-849982 E: revthomaspelham@gmail.com

PELLEREAU, Kate Louise Elizabeth. b 86. Buckm Univ BA 07 Univ of Wales (Trin St Dav) MA 16 PGCE 11. Wycliffe Hall Ox 18. **d** 20 **p** 21. C Buckingham *Ox* from 20. *5 Chandos Close, Buckingham MK18 1AW* M: 07791-065627 E: pellereau@hotmail.co.uk

PELLY, Mrs Elizabeth Wigram (Lulu). b 52. Bris Univ BA 73. ERMC 05. **d** 08 **p** 09. C Towcester w Caldecote and Easton Neston etc *Pet* from 08. *Pear Tree Cottage, Spring Lane, Alderton, Towcester NN12 7LW* T: (01327) 811488 M: 07723-604316 E: lulupelly@yahoo.com

PELLY, Margaret Helen. b 50. ERMC. **d** 11 **p** 12. OLM Stebbing and Lindsell w Gt and Lt Saling *Chelmsf* from 11; RD Dunmow and Stansted from 20. *Purples Farmhouse, Bardfield Saling, Braintree CM7 5EJ* T: (01371) 810369

PEMBERTON, Anthony Thomas Christie (Chris). b 57. BA. Cranmer Hall Dur 82. **d** 84 **p** 85. C Maidstone St Luke *Cant* 84–88; Chapl Ox Pastorate 88–98; V Cant St Mary Bredin 98–09; Tr Dir New Wine 09–16; PtO *Chelmsf* from 13; Tutor Ridley Hall Cam from 16; PtO *Eur* from 18. *Newhouse Farm, Walden Road, Radwinter, Saffron Walden CB10 2SP* T: (01799) 599977 E: atcp2@cam.ac.uk

PEMBERTON, Crispin Mark Rugman. b 59. St Andr Univ MTheol 83. St Steph Ho Ox 84. **d** 86 **p** 87. C Acton Green *Lon* 86–90; C Leckhampton SS Phil and Jas w Cheltenham St Jas *Glouc* 90–93; V Tuffley 93–97; RE Teacher and Boarding Housemaster Cheltenham Coll Jun Sch 97–02; RE Teacher Tormead Sch Guildf 02–05; Hd of Middle Sch and RE Clifton High Sch 05–08; PtO *Heref* 13–16; P-in-c Brampton 16–17; R StowCaple from 17. *Jenny Penny Whites, Little Dewchurch, Hereford HR2 6PR* M: 07824-444655 E: crispinpemberton@yahoo.co.uk

PEMBERTON FORD, Carrie Mary. b 55. St Hilda's Coll Ox BA 78 Cam Univ PGCE 82 Leeds Univ MA 92 Newnham Coll Cam PhD 98. Cranmer Hall Dur 83 NEOC 84. **dss** 86 **d** 87 **p** 94. NSM Leeds St Geo *Ripon* 86–87; Miss Partner CMS and Dir Women's Studies Angl Th Inst Zaïre 87–91; PtO *Pet* 92–94; NSM Bourn and Kingston w Caxton and Longstowe *Ely* 94–99; TV Elsworth w Knapwell 99; Min Cambourne LEP 00–01; PtO 01–07; Relig Manager Yarlswood Immigration and Detention Cen 01–03; Chief Exec CHASTE 04–08; Chief Exec Officer and Founding Dir Cam Cen for Applied Research in Human Trafficking from 07; PtO *Ely* 16–21. *Rectory Farm, Hildersham, Cambridge CB21 6DD* T: (01223) 891765 E: carrie@ccarht.org *or* carrieford@cantab.net

✠**PENBERTHY, The Rt Revd Joanna Susan.** b 60. Newnham Coll Cam BA 81 MA 85 St Jo Coll Nottm MTh 84. Cranmer Hall Dur 83. **dss** 84 **d** 87 **p** 97 **c** 16. Haughton le Skerne *Dur* 84–85; Llanishen and Lisvane *Llan* 85–89; NSM 87–89; NSM Llanwddyn and Llanfihangel-yng-Nghwynfa etc *St As* 89–93; NSM Llansadwrn w Llanwrda and Manordeilo *St D* 93–95; Prov Officer Div for Par Development Ch in Wales 94–99; P-in-c Cynwyl Gaeo w Llansawel and Talley *St D* 99–01; V 01–10; Dioc Adult Educn Officer 01–02; Warden of Readers 02–10; Can St D Cathl 07–10; P-in-c Charlton Musgrove, Cucklington and Stoke Trister *B & W* 10–11; R 11–15; R Glan Ithon *S & B* 15–16; Bp St D from 16. *Llys Esgob, Abergwili, Carmarthen SA31 2JG* T: (01267) 236597

PENDENQUE, Mrs Susan Mary. b 68. Nottm Poly BEd 90. St Hild Coll 17. **d** 19 **p** 20. C Sherwood *S'well* from 19. *152 Perry Road, Nottingham NG5 1GL* M: 07932-242398 E: sue.pendenque@gmail.com

PENDLEBURY, Richard Norman. MBE. **d** 16 **p** 17. OLM Bris St Matt and St Nath 16–20; NSM from 20. *27 Stanley Avenue, Bishopston, Bristol BS7 9AH* E: olm.rich@stmatthews-bristol.org.uk

PENDLEBURY, Stephen Thomas. b 50. Southn Univ BSc 73 ACA 78. Ridley Hall Cam 86. **d** 88 **p** 89. C Birkenhead St Jas w St Bede *Ches* 88–91; V 91–00; V Ches St Paul 00–16; P-in-c Huntington 12–16; rtd 16; PtO *Ches* 16–19; Hon C Cornerstone *Sheff* from 18. *The Vicarage, Stone Moor Road, Bolsterstone, Sheffield S36 3ZN* T: 0114-283 1238 E: stpendleby@aol.com

PENDORF, Canon James Gordon. b 45. Drew Univ New Jersey BA 67. Episc Th Sch Cam Mass STB 71. **d** 71 **p** 71. V Newark St Greg USA 71–76; V Colne H Trin *Blackb* 76–80; Sen Dioc Stewardship Adv *Chelmsf* 80–83; Dioc Sec *Birm* 83–95; P-in-c Highgate 95–97; V 97–04; Dioc Stewardship Adv 95–04; AD Birm City Cen 96–02; Hon Can Birm Cathl 90–04; Par Resources Adv and Chapl St Nic Ch Cen *St E* 04–13; NSM Holbrook, Stutton, Freston, Woolverstone etc 05–13; P-in-c Capel St Mary w Lt and Gt Wenham 13–19; rtd 19; PtO *St E* from 19. *10 Joseph Close, Hadleigh, Ipswich IP7 5FH* T: (01473) 484619 M: 07879-816549 E: canonpendorf@aol.com

PENDUCK, Joshua Paul James. b 87. Birm City Univ BMus 09 St Jo Coll Dur BA 13 MA 15. Cranmer Hall Dur 11. **d** 14 **p** 15. C Lich St Chad 14–17; C Newcastle w Butterton 17–19; R from 19. *The Rectory, St Giles Church, Seabridge Road, Newcastle ST5 2HS* T: (01782) 620322 E: revpenduck@gmail.com

PENFOLD, Brian Robert. b 54. Lon Univ BSc 75 Bris Univ PGCE 77. Oak Hill Th Coll BA 84. **d** 84 **p** 85. C Norwood St Luke *S'wark* 84–88; C Rayleigh *Chelmsf* 88–92; V New Barnet St Jas *St Alb* 92–08; V Worthing St Geo *Chich* 08–19; rtd 19. *Haversham House, 12 Nevill Avenue, Eastbourne BN22 9PU* M: 07753-680839

PENFOLD, Christopher James. b 68. St Aug Coll of Th 15. **d** 18. C Sittingbourne w Bobbing *Cant* from 18. *The Rectory, 9 Portland Avenue, Sittingbourne ME10 3QY*

PENFOLD, Colin Richard. b 52. St Pet Coll Ox BA 74 MA 78. Ridley Hall Cam 81. **d** 84 **p** 85. C Buckhurst Hill *Chelmsf* 84–87; C Greenside *Dur* 87–90; V Cononley w Bradley *Bradf* 90–97; P-in-c Shipley St Paul and Frizinghall 97; V Shipley St Paul 98–08; P-in-c Gt Harwood *Blackb* 08–12; V 12–18; AD Whalley 17–18; rtd 18. *10 Parkwood Road, Shipley BD18 4SS* M: 07553-255419 E: colinpenfold45@gmail.com

PENFOLD, Julian Oliver Kevin. b 56. Cliff Coll MA 13. All SS Cen for Miss & Min. **d** 15 **p** 16. NSM Alfreton *Derby* from 15; NSM Riddings and Ironville from 15; NSM Somercotes from 19. *Shirland Park Farm, Park Lane, Shirland, Alfreton DE55 6AX* T: (01773) 833242 M: 07932-564888 E: jokpenfold@gmail.com

PENFOLD, Kizzy Anna. b 90. Sussex Univ BA 12. Trin Coll Bris 18. **d** 21. C Ore Ch *Chich* from 21; C Ore St Helen and St Barn from 21. *266 Elphinstone Road, Hastings TN34 2AG* E: revkpenfold@outlook.com

PENFOLD, Marion Jean. b 49. NEOC 96. **d** 99 **p** 00. NSM Lesbury w Alnmouth *Newc* 99–02; C 02–03;

NSM Longhoughton w Howick 99–02; C 02–03; TV N Tyne and Redesdale 03–11; TV Glendale Gp 11–17; V Chatton w Chillingham, Eglingham and S Charlton and Ingram 17–19; rtd 19; PtO *Newc* from 21. *16 Meadow Lands, Tweedmouth, Berwick-upon-Tweed TD15 2FW* E: marion.penfold@btinternet.com

PENFOLD, Canon Susan Irene. b 52. York Univ BA 73 Bris Univ PhD 77 Selw Coll Cam BA 83 MA 87. Ridley Hall Cam 81. **dss** 84 **d** 87 **p** 94. Buckhurst Hill *Chelmsf* 84–87; Hon C Greenside *Dur* 87–90; Hon C Cononley w Bradley *Bradf* 90–97; Assoc Dioc Dir of Ords 96–01; Hon C Shipley St Paul 97–00; PtO 00–08; Dir of Ords and CME Officer *Wakef* 01–03; Dir of Ords and Dean of Min 03–08; Hon Can Wakef Cathl 04–08; Can Res Blackb Cathl 08–15; Dir of Min 08–18; rtd 18. *10 Parkwood Road, Shipley BD18 4SS* M: 07753-987977 E: sue.penfold@gmail.com

PENGELLY, Canon Geoffrey. b 50. Oak Hill Th Coll 86. **d** 88 **p** 89. C Redruth w Lanner and Treleigh *Truro* 88–91; TV Bolventor 91–92; V Egloskerry, N Petherwin, Tremaine, Tresmere etc 92–20; RD Trigg Major 04–10; Hon Can Truro Cathl 03–20; rtd 20. *Address temp unknown*

PENISTAN, Richard Luke. *See* PENNYSTAN, Richard Luke

PENMAN, Robert George. b 42. St Jo Coll Auckland LTh 66. **d** 65 **p** 66. C Mt Roskill NZ 65–68; C Henderson 69–70; V Glen Innes 71–72; C Alverstoke *Portsm* 73–74; CF 74–77; C Bridgwater St Mary w Chilton Trinity *B & W* 77–80; P-in-c Haselbury Plucknett w N Perrott 80–81; P-in-c Misterton 80–81; V Haselbury Plucknett, Misterton and N Perrott 81–89; P-in-c Appleton *Ox* 89–97; P-in-c Besselsleigh w Dry Sandford 89–00; P-in-c Besselsleigh 00–07; rtd 07; PtO *Ox* from 07. *31 High Street, Sherington, Newport Pagnell MK16 9NU* T: (01908) 611838 E: penman298@btinternet.com

PENN, Christopher Francis. b 34. ACII 63. Wells Th Coll 68. **d** 70 **p** 71. C Andover w Foxcott *Win* 70–72; C Odiham w S Warnborough 72–75; C Keynsham *B & W* 75–76; TV 76–82; R Chilcompton w Downside and Stratton on the Fosse 82–87; RD Midsomer Norton 84–86; V Bathford 87–90; V Avonmouth St Andr *Bris* 90–96; Ind Chapl 90–96; rtd 96; PtO *B & W* from 96; *Bris* 96–01. *53 Caernarvon Road, Keynsham, Bristol BS31 2PF* T: 0117-986 6831 E: c.s.penn@talktalk.net

PENN, Christopher Wilson. b 60. Cranmer Hall Dur 98. **d** 00 **p** 01. C Wrockwardine Deanery *Lich* 00–03; P-in-c Llanyblodwel and Trefonen 03–07; P-in-c Llanymynech 03–07; P-in-c Morton 03–07; R Llanyblodwel, Llanymynech, Morton and Trefonen 07–13; Rural Officer (Salop Adnry) 08–13; P-in-c Holsworthy w Hollacombe and Milton Damerel *Ex* 13–15; R Holsworthy, Hollacombe, Pyworthy etc 15–17; RD Holsworthy 15–17; P-in-c Bradworthy w Benthall, Jackfield, Linley etc *Heref* 17–19; R from 19; RD Telford Severn Gorge from 21. *All Saints' Rectory, Church Street, Broseley TF12 5DA* T: (01952) 882647 M: 07941-735318 E: crispy50@hotmail.co.uk *or* rector@broseleyparishes.org.uk

PENN, Ms Jane Rachel. b 52. ERMC 07. **d** 10 **p** 11. NSM Orton Longueville w Bottlebridge *Ely* 10–13; NSM Tadley w Pamber Heath and Silchester *Win* 13–17; P-in-c Worlingham w Barnby and N Cove *St E* 17–19; NSM Broadhembury, Dunkeswell, Luppitt, Plymtree, Sheldon, and Upottery *Ex* from 19. *The Rectory, Broadhembury, Honiton EX14 3LT* M: 07792-220156 E: janepenn@hotmail.co.uk

PENN, Mrs Jennifer Anne. b 64. Imp Coll Lon BEng 84 Leeds Univ BA 07. NOC 04. **d** 07 **p** 08. C Halliwell St Pet *Man* 07–10; TV New Bury w Gt Lever 10–14; P-in-c Reigate St Phil *S'wark* 14–18; V from 18; Chapl St Bede's Sch Reigate from 14. *The Parsonage, 102A Nutley Lane, Reigate RH2 9HA* T: (01737) 244542 E: jenpenn@virginmedia.com

PENN, Mrs Sarah Jane. b 56. City Univ BSc 83 Chelsea Coll Lon PGCE 84 Dur Univ BA 18. Lindisfarne Regional Tr Partnership 10. **d** 14 **p** 15. OLM St John Lee *Newc* 14–18; OLM Warden w Newbrough 14–18; P-in-c Bempton w Flamborough, Reighton w Speeton *York* from 18. *The Vicarage, Church Street, Flamborough, Bridlington YO15 1PE* M: 07747-865747 E: janepenn11@gmail.com

PENN-ALLISON, Mrs Nicola Alison. b 69. Man Univ BSc 99 Open Univ MBA 11 St Jo Coll Dur BA 14 Ox Brookes Univ PGCE 04. Cranmer Hall Dur. **d** 14 **p** 15. C Redcar *York* 14–17; P-in-c Saxilby Gp *Linc* 17–21; P-in-c Stow Gp 17–21. *The Old Post Office, West Lutton, Malton YO17 8TA* M: 07918-941656 E: nicky.allison@outlook.com

PENNAL, David Bernard. b 37. Ripon Hall Ox 64. **d** 67 **p** 68. C Moseley St Mary *Birm* 67–71; C Bridgwater St Mary w Chilton Trinity *B & W* 71–73; P-in-c Hilton w Cheselbourne and Melcombe Horsey *Sarum* 73–76; R Milton Abbas, Hilton w Cheselbourne etc 76–78; P-in-c Spetisbury w Charlton Marshall 78–88; R Spetisbury w Charlton Marshall etc

89–00; rtd 00. *11 High Street, Wicken, Ely CB7 5XR* T: (01353) 624295 M: 07778-120668 E: dbipennal1@gmail.com

PENNANT, David Falconer. b 51. Trin Coll Cam MA 73. Trin Coll Bris BD 84 PhD 88. **d** 86 **p** 87. C Bramcote *S'well* 86–88; C Woking St Jo *Guildf* 88–93. *30 Oriental Road, Woking GU22 7AW* T: (01483) 768055 E: df.pennant@ntlworld.com

PENNANT, Rachel Elizabeth Burrows. b 74. Ex Univ BA 95 Sheff Univ PhD 01. Trin Coll Bris MA 12. **d** 12 **p** 13. C Biggleswade *St Alb* 12–16; V Hoddesdon from 16. *The Vicarage, 11 Oxenden Drive, Hoddesdon EN11 8QF* T: (01992) 462627 M: 07811-774192 E: rpennant@btinternet.com

PENNELL, Ms Pamela. EAMTC 94. **d** 97 **p** 98. NSM Moulsham St Luke *Chelmsf* 97–98; NSM Writtle w Highwood 98–00; PtO 01–04; NSM Gt Waltham w Ford End 04–06; PtO 06–08; P-in-c Sandon 08–10; P-in-c E Hanningfield 08–13; rtd 13; PtO *Chelmsf* from 14. *Address withheld by request*

PENNELLS, David Malcolm Benedict. b 56. Leeds Univ BA 11 CQSW 80. Coll of Resurr Mirfield 09. **d** 11 **p** 12. C Kennington St Jo w St Jas *S'wark* 11–15; V Mitcham SS Pet and Paul from 15. *The Vicarage, 11 Vicarage Gardens, Mitcham CR4 3BL* T: (020) 8646 0666 E: fatherdavid@btinternet.com

PENNEY, David Richard John. b 39. St Jo Coll Dur BA 63. Cranmer Hall Dur 63. **d** 67 **p** 68. C Chilvers Coton w Astley *Cov* 67–70; C Styvechale 70–72; P-in-c Shilton w Ansty 72–77; P-in-c Withybrook w Copston Magna 74–77; R Easington w Liverton *York* 77–85; Dir Soc Resp *Sarum* 85–93; PtO *Blackb* 93–02; rtd 01; PtO *Blackb* from 16. *Highfield, 21 Keighley Road, Colne BB8 0LP* M: 07809-363290 E: davepenney75@gmail.com

PENNEY, William Affleck. b 41. MBIM 75 FRSA 91. K Coll Lon BD 63 AKC 63 St Boniface Warminster 65. **d** 66 **p** 67. C Chatham St Steph *Roch* 66–70; Ind Chapl 70–77; P-in-c Bredhurst 70–72; Hon C S Gillingham 72–74; Hon C Eynsford w Farningham and Lullingstone 74–77; Bp's Dom Chapl 74–88; Hon Ind Chapl 77–88; Hon C Balham St Mary and St Jo *S'wark* 89–91; PtO *St Alb* 91–94; Hon C Bushey 94–05; rtd 05. *3 Byron Close, Abingdon OX14 5PA* T: (01235) 206366 E: wpenney@btconnect.com

PENNIE, Mrs Fiona Clare. b 64. All SS Cen for Miss & Min 12. **d** 15 **p** 16. NSM Grassendale *Liv* 15–18; P-in-c Dovecot 18–19; PtO 19–20; C Walton-on-the-Hill from 20. *Address temp unknown* M: 07941-652488 E: revpennie@gmail.com

PENNIECOOKE, Dorothy Victoria. b 45. Dioc OLM tr scheme 97. **d** 00 **p** 01. NSM Balham Hill Ascension *S'wark* 00–15; PtO from 15. *56 Lysias Road, London SW12 8BP* T: (020) 8673 0037 E: dotty.pcooke@gmail.com

PENNINGTON, Edward Francis Quentin. b 76. G&C Coll Cam BA 97 MA 01 Birm Univ MSc 98. Oak Hill Th Coll BTh 04. **d** 04 **p** 05. C Moulton *Pet* 04–07; C Fulwood *Sheff* 07–18; LtO from 18. *237 Bannerdale Road, Sheffield S11 9FD* T: 0114-221 9393 M: 07743-942931 E: efqpennington@hotmail.com *or* ed@endcliffechurch.co.uk *or* ed.pennington@sheffield.anglican.org

PENNINGTON, Canon Emma Louise. b 71. Ex Univ BA 92 Kent Univ MA 96 Ox Univ DPhil 14. Ripon Coll Cuddesdon BA 00. **d** 00 **p** 01. C Shepperton *Lon* 00–03; Chapl Worc Coll Ox 03–08; TV Wheatley *Ox* 08–14; V Garsington, Cuddesdon and Horspath 14–19; AD Aston and Cuddesdon 18–19; Can Res Cant Cathl from 19. *15 The Precincts, Canterbury CT1 2EL* E: emmapennington153@gmail.com

PENNINGTON, James Edward. b 78. Essex Univ BA 00. St Jo Coll Nottm 12. **d** 14 **p** 15. C Nailsea H Trin *B & W* 14–18; R Passenham *Pet* from 18. *The Rectory, Wicken Road, Deanshanger, Milton Keynes MK19 6JP* T: (01908) 262371 M: 07736-299889 E: jepennington@hotmail.com

PENNINGTON, Ms Nicola Gail. b 67. Nottm Univ BA 88 Leic Univ MA 93 Cumbria Univ MA 18 CQSW 93. LCTP 10. **d** 13 **p** 14. C Maryport, Netherton and Flimby *Carl* 13–17; Team Ldr Cumbria Chr Learning 17–18; P-in-c Crosslacon *Carl* from 19. *The Vicarage, Trumpet Road, Cleator CA23 3EF* T: (01946) 451257 M: 07462-194549 E: revnickipennington@gmail.com

PENNOCK, Canon Christine. b 48. Bp Grosseteste Coll BEd 71 Leeds Univ PGCE 94 Teesside Univ PGDE 95. NEOC 98. **d** 01 **p** 02. C Crowland *Linc* 01–05; P-in-c Ruskington Gp 05–13; P-in-c Leasingham 09–13; P-in-c Cranwell 11–13; R N Lafford Gp 13–19; RD Lafford 12–19; Can and Preb Linc Cathl 15–19; rtd 19. *6 Hilda Close, Quarrington, Sleaford NG34 8UW* T: (01529) 304997 M: 07854-847280 E: revpennock77@btinternet.com

PENNY, Alexander Stuart Egerton. b 52. Wolv Art Coll BA 75. Ridley Hall Cam MA 00. **d** 00 **p** 01. C Uttoxeter Area *Lich* 00–03; V Crosthwaite Keswick *Carl* 03–17; RD Derwent 16–17; rtd 17; PtO *Lich* 17–21; *Eur* from 18. *51 Armoury Gardens, Shrewsbury SY2 6PJ*

PENNY, David Roy. b 67. Wilson Carlile Coll 89 NOC 00. **d** 03 **p** 04. C Hey and Waterhead *Man* 03–05; V Chadderton St Matt w St Luke from 05; AD Oldham W 09–17. *St Matthew's Vicarage, Mill Brow, Chadderton, Oldham OL1 2RT* T: 0161-624 8600 E: revdpenny@btinternet.com

PENNY, Diana Eleanor. b 51. Open Univ BA 87 MSc 13 Birm Univ DipEd 96. Nor Ord Course 87. **d** 89 **p** 94. NSM Gillingham w Geldeston, Stockton, Ellingham etc *Nor* 89–93; NSM Upton St Leonards *Glouc* 93–97; NSM Stiffkey and Cockthorpe w Morston, Langham etc *Nor* 97–03; NSM Stiffkey and Bale 03–04; C Lowestoft St Marg 04–06; V E Marshland *Ely* 06–10; rtd 10; PtO *Ely* 10–16 and from 18; Hon C Blanchland w Hunstanworth and Edmundbyers etc *Newc* 16–18. *Hibiscus, 33 Church Drove, Outwell, Wisbech PE14 8RH* E: dep451@btinternet.com

PENNY, Edwin John. b 43. Leeds Univ BA 64. Coll of Resurr Mirfield 64. **d** 66 **p** 67. C Acocks Green *Birm* 66–69; C Wombourne *Lich* 69–71; C Wednesbury St Paul Wood Green 71–74; V Kingshurst *Birm* 74–79; Chapl All Hallows Convent Norfolk 79–82; Hon Chapl Overgate Hospice Yorkshire 82–84; Hon C Raveningham *Nor* 84–90; All Hallows Hosp Nor Past Team 90–93; P-in-c Upton St Leonards *Glouc* 93–97; Dioc Communications Officer 93–97; P-in-c Stiffkey and Cockthorpe w Morston, Langham etc *Nor* 97–03; P-in-c Gunthorpe w Bale w Field Dalling, Saxlingham etc 99–03; R Stiffkey and Bale 03–04; rtd 04; PtO *Nor* from 04; *Ely* 08–16 and from 18; RD Wisbech Lynn Marshland 09–11; PtO *Dur* 17–18. *Hibiscus, 33 Church Drove, Outwell, Wisbech PE14 8RH* E: noakhillpupil@dialstart.net

PENNY, Michael John. b 36. Linc Th Coll 78. **d** 80 **p** 81. C Knighton St Mary Magd *Leic* 80–83; TV Leic Resurr 83–85; V Blackfordby 85–95; V Blackfordby and Woodville 95–00; RD Akeley W 88–93; rtd 00; PtO *Nor* from 00. *15 Sarah's Road, Hunstanton PE36 5PA* T: (01485) 534957

PENNY, Stuart. *See* PENNY, Alexander Stuart Egerton

PENNYSTAN, Richard Luke. b 74. Newc Univ BA 97 St Jo Coll Cam BA 02. Ridley Hall Cam 00. **d** 03 **p** 04. C E Twickenham St Steph *Lon* 03–06; C Fulham Ch Ch 06–11; V Romiley *Ches* from 11. *18 Chadkirk Road, Romiley, Stockport SK6 3JY* T: 0161-285 7748 M: 07971-663129 E: vicar@stchadsromiley.co.uk

PENRITH, Suffragan Bishop of. *Vacant*

PENTELOW, Mrs Ysmena Rachael. b 73. St Andr Univ BD 96 MLitt 99. EAMTC 01. **d** 03 **p** 04. C Stevenage H Trin *St Alb* 03–06; P-in-c Langleybury St Paul 06–13; V 13–16; Dioc CME Officer 06–16; V Ware St Mary from 16. *The Vicarage, 31 Thunder Court, Ware SG12 0PT* T: (01920) 464817 M: 07798-654194 E: vicar@stmarysware.co.uk

PENTLAND, The Ven Raymond Jackson. b 57. CB 13. Wm Booth Memorial Coll CertEd 79 Open Univ BA 90 Westmr Coll Ox MTh 02. St Jo Coll Nottm 86. **d** 88 **p** 89. C Nottingham St Jude *S'well* 88–90; Chapl RAF 90–05; Command Chapl RAF 05–06; Adn RAF 06–14; Chapl-in-Chief RAF 09–14; QHC 06–14; Can and Preb Linc Cathl 06–14; rtd 14; PtO *Ox* 14–19; *Lon* 14–19; NSM Walton H Trin *Ox* 19–21; PtO *Lich* from 21. *31 Lakesedge, Stone ST15 0BF* E: rjp57@me.com

PEOPLES, Mervyn Thomas Edwards. b 53. Open Univ BA 88. CITC 03. **d** 06 **p** 07. NSM Raphoe w Raymochy and Clonleigh *D & R* 06–09; NSM Clooney w Strathfoyle from 09. *29 Dunnalong Road, Magheramason, Londonderry BT47 2RU* T: (028) 7184 1416 E: mervynpeoples@hotmail.com

PEPPER, David Reginald. b 50. Lon Bible Coll. St Alb Minl Tr Scheme 89. **d** 92 **p** 93. NSM Cheshunt *St Alb* 92–95; NSM Bengeo 06–08; NSM Hertford 08–21; PtO from 21. *Bramley Cottage, 414 Ware Road, Hertford SG13 7EW* E: davidpepper2@yahoo.co.uk

PEPPIATT, Martin Guy. b 33. Trin Coll Ox BA 57 MA 60. Wycliffe Hall Ox 57. **d** 59 **p** 60. C St Marylebone All So w SS Pet and Jo *Lon* 59–63; Kenya 65–69; V E Twickenham St Steph *Lon* 69–96; rtd 96; PtO *Ox* from 06. *Pipers Cottage, East End, North Leigh, Witney OX29 8ND* T: (01993) 883001 E: mcpeppiatt@hotmail.com

PERCIVAL, Darren James. b 70. Yorks Min Course 09. **d** 12 **p** 13. NSM Dodworth *Wakef* 12–14; *Leeds* 14–16; NSM W Barnsley 16–17; P-in-c Hunslet w Cross Green 17–18; P-in-c Cross Green 18–21; P-in-c Leeds Richmond Hill 17–21; V Cross Green and Richmond Hill from 21. *8 High Keep Fold, Hall Green, Wakefield WF4 3QL* T: (01924) 253045 M: 07960-555609 E: percivalfamily1@gmail.com *or* darren.percival@leeds.anglican.org

PERCIVAL, James Frederick. b 74. New Coll Ox BA 96 MA 01 Barrister-at-Law (Middle Temple) 99. Ripon Coll Cuddesdon MA 02. **d** 03 **p** 04. C Redhill St Matt *S'wark* 03–06; TV Sanderstead 06–13; TR Limpsfield and Tatsfield 13–20;

PtO *Portsm* 20–21; P-in-c Ryde All SS 21; P-in-c Swanmore St Mich 21; Chapl RN from 21. *Royal Naval Chaplaincy Service Headquarters, Tanner Building, HMS Excellent, Whale Island, Portsmouth PO2 8ER* T: 03001-577544 E: james.percival7@gmail.com

PERCIVAL, Joanna Vèra. b 52. Univ of San Francisco BA 87. Ch Div Sch of Pacific MDiv 94. **d** 94 **p** 94. Asst R Almaden USA 94–95; NSM Ockham w Hatchford *Guildf* 95–96; C Cobham 96–00; Dioc Spirituality Adv 00–02; V Weston 02–06; PtO *Lon* 06–07; *S'wark* 06–07; *S & B* 07–08; Chapl Univ Hosp Southn NHS Foundn Trust 08–16; Chapl R Surrey Co Hosp NHS Foundn Trust 16–18; rtd 18; PtO *Sarum* from 19. *74 Hamilton Road, Salisbury SP1 3TQ* E: joanna.percival@btinternet.com

PERCIVAL, John Harry. b 83. Pemb Coll Cam MA 08. Wycliffe Hall Ox BA 10 Oak Hill Th Coll MA 12. **d** 12 **p** 13. C Eastbourne All So *Chich* 12–16; PtO *Ely* from 16; Lect Oak Hill Coll from 20. *58 Montague Road, Cambridge CB4 1BX* M: 07818-028494 E: john.percival@cantab.net

PERCIVAL, Canon Kathryn Janet. b 74. St Hilda's Coll Ox BA 95 MA 01 ARCM 89 Barrister-at-Law (Lincoln's Inn) 98. Ripon Coll Cuddesdon MTh 10. **d** 10 **p** 11. C Purley St Mark and Purley St Swithun *S'wark* 10–13; P-in-c Lingfield and Crowhurst 13–15; C Dormansland 13–15; V Lingfield and Dormansland 15–18; AD Tandridge 16–19; Can Res Portsm Cathl from 19; Vice Dean Portsm Cathl from 19. *Portsmouth Cathedral Office, Cathedral House, 63-68 St Thomas's Street, Portsmouth PO1 2HA* T: (023) 9282 3300 ext 229 M: 07985-272437 E: kathrynpercival@btinternet.com *or* kathryn.percival@portsmouthcathedral.org.uk

PERCIVAL, Martin Eric. b 45. Lon Univ BSc 66 Linacre Coll Ox BA 70 MA 74. Wycliffe Hall Ox 67. **d** 70 **p** 71. C Anfield St Marg *Liv* 70–73; C Witney *Ox* 73–74; TV Bottesford w Ashby *Linc* 74–76; TV Grantham 76–80; R Coningsby w Tattershall 80–82; P-in-c Coleford w Holcombe *B & W* 82–83; V 83–84; Chapl Rossall Sch Fleetwood 84–88; Chapl Woodbridge Sch 88–02; R Downham w S Hanningfield *Chelmsf* 02–05; P-in-c Ramsden Crays w Ramsden Bellhouse 02–05; P-in-c Leiston *St E* 05–13; rtd 13; PtO *St E* 13–18; P-in-c Upper Alde from 18. *1 Oak Drive, Aldringham, Leiston IP16 4FN* T: (01728) 598455 E: revmepercival@gmail.com

PERCIVAL, Patricia Anne. b 52. SEITE 03. **d** 06 **p** 07. NSM Footscray w N Cray *Roch* 06–10; NSM Blendon from 10. *31 Collindale Avenue, Sidcup DA15 9DN* T: (020) 8302 9754 E: mppercival@gmail.com

PERCY, Brian. b 34. **d** 93 **p** 94. OLM Walton *St E* 93–00; OLM Walton and Trimley 00–04; rtd 04; PtO *St E* 04–20. *16 Lynwood Avenue, Felixstowe IP11 9HS* T: (01394) 286782

PERCY, Christopher. *See* HEBER PERCY, Christopher John

PERCY, Canon Emma Margaret. b 63. Jes Coll Cam BA 85 MA 89 St Jo Coll Dur BA 89 Nottm Univ PhD 12. Cranmer Hall Dur 87. **d** 90 **p** 94. C Bedford St Andr *St Alb* 90–94; Chapl Anglia Poly Univ *Ely* 94–97; P-in-c Millhouses H Trin *Sheff* 97–03; V 03–04; Chapl Trin Coll Ox from 05; Hon Can Ch Ch Ox from 19. *The Deanery, Christ Church, St Aldates, Oxford OX1 1DP* T: (01865) 276162 E: emma.percy@trinity.ox.ac.uk

PERCY, Gordon Reid. b 46. St Jo Coll Dur BA 68. Cranmer Hall Dur 69. **d** 71 **p** 72. C Flixton St Jo *Man* 71–76; C Charlesworth *Derby* 76–77; P-in-c 77–87; P-in-c Dinting Vale 80–87; V Long Eaton St Jo 87–98; RD Ilkeston 92–98; R Torquay St Matthias, St Mark and H Trin *Ex* 98–12; rtd 12; PtO *Ex* from 13. *13 Wembury Drive, Torquay TQ2 8DT* E: gordonpercy@minister.com

PERCY, The Very Revd Prof Martyn William. b 62. Bris Univ BA 84 K Coll Lon PhD 92 Sheff Univ MEd. Cranmer Hall Dur 88. **d** 90 **p** 91. C Bedford St Andr *St Alb* 90–94; Chapl and Dir Th and RS Ch Coll Cam 94–97; Dir Th and RS SS Coll Cam 95–97; Dir Linc Th Inst Man Univ 97–04; Hon C Millhouses H Trin *Sheff* 97–04; Hon Can Sheff Cathl 97–04; Can Th Sheff Cathl 04–10; Sen Lect Relig and Soc Sheff Univ 97–00; Reader 00–02; Reader Man Univ 02–04; Prof Th and Min Hartford Sem Connecticut USA 02–07; Prin Ripon Coll Cuddesdon 04–14; Prin Ox Min Course 06–14; Dean Ch Ch *Ox* from 14; Prof Th Educn K Coll Lon from 04; Can and Preb Sarum Cathl 09–14; PtO *Ox* from 18. *The Deanery, Christ Church, St Aldates, Oxford OX1 1DP* T: (01865) 276161 E: pa.dean@chch.ox.ac.uk

PERCY, Mrs Pauline. b 62. Sheff City Poly BSc 84 Sheff Univ BA 14. Yorks Min Course 11. **d** 14 **p** 15. NSM Crathorne *York* 14–18; NSM Kirklevington w Picton, and High and Low Worsall 14–18; NSM Rudby in Cleveland w Middleton 14–18; NSM Sowerby from 18; NSM Sessay from 18; NSM Thirkleby w Kilburn and Bagby from 18; Chapl Qu Mary's Sch Baldersby Park from 19. *The Vicarage, Kilburn, York YO61 4AH* E: revd.pauline.percy@gmail.com

PEREIRA, Alwyn Antonio Basilio. b 63. Trin Coll Bris. **d** 11 **p** 12. C Sea Mills *Bris* 11–15; NSM Abbots Leigh w Leigh Woods 17; V Aldershot St Mich *Guildf* from 18. *The Vicarage, 120 Church Lane East, Aldershot GU11 3SS* **M:** 07767-702094 **E:** alwynper@googlemail.com

PEREIRA, Melvyn Christopher. b 52. Oak Hill Th Coll BA 04. **d** 04 **p** 05. C Kettering Ch the King *Pet* 04–07; Min Gleneagles CD 07–13; V Gleneagles 13–20; Warden of Par Ev 10–18; rtd 20. *Address temp unknown* **M:** 07810-816744

PERERA, Ms Chandrika Kumudhini. b 61. Qu Coll Birm. **d** 03 **p** 04. C Luton All SS w St Pet *St Alb* 03–07; TV Hemel Hempstead 07–14; V Stevenage St Hugh and St Jo from 14. *St Hugh's House, 4 Mobbsbury Way, Stevenage SG2 0HL* **T:** (01438) 727577 **E:** chandy.perera@btinternet.com

PERERA, George Anthony. b 51. Edin Univ BD 74. Linc Th Coll 74. **d** 76 **p** 77. Chapl Mabel Fletcher Tech Coll Liv 76–79; C Wavertree H Trin *Liv* 76–79; TV Maghull 79–94; V Hunts Cross 94–04; Chapl Park Lane Hosp Maghull 79–89; Asst Chapl Ashworth Hosp Maghull 89–04; Chapl R Liverpool and Broadgreen Univ Hosps NHS Trust from 05; CF (TA) 06–11; CF (ACF) from 12. *Broadgreen Hospital, Thomas Drive, Liverpool L14 3LB* **T:** 0151-425 4001 **M:** 07803-129501 **E:** padre.yacf@gmail.com

PEREZ CRIADO, Samuel. b 87. Granada Univ Lic 10 Cam Univ BTh 21. Westcott Ho Cam 19. **d** 21. C St Ives *Ely* from 21. *4 Adams Drive, St Ives PE27 6TD* **M:** 07714-133838 **E:** samuel.samperez@gmail.com *or* curate@stivesparishchurch.org.uk

PERKIN, Jonathan Guy. b 52. Westmr Coll Ox BEd 76. Trin Coll Bris 89. **d** 91 **p** 92. C Cullompton *Ex* 91–96; C Ashtead *Guildf* 96–01; V Egham 01–05; V Churchdown *Glouc* 05–21; Hon Can Glouc Cathl 17–21; rtd 21. *Victoria House, Hurstbourne Tarrant, Andover SP11 0BD* **E:** jjperkin@btconnect.com

PERKIN, Paul John Stanley. b 50. Ch Ch Ox BA 71 MA 75 K Coll Lon CertEd. Wycliffe Hall Ox 78. **d** 80 **p** 81. C Gillingham St Mark *Roch* 80–84; C Brompton H Trin w Onslow Square St Paul *Lon* 84–87; P-in-c Battersea Rise St Mark *S'wark* 87–92; V 92–20; P-in-c Battersea St Pet and St Paul 00–12; rtd 20; TV Limpsfield and Tatsfield *S'wark* from 20. *St Andrew's House, Kent Hatch Road, Oxted RH8 0TB* **T:** (01883) 412454 **E:** paul.perkin6@gmail.com

PERKINS, Barnaby Charles Rudolf. b 80. Peterho Cam BA 08 MPhil 10. Ridley Hall Cam 06 Ven English Coll Rome 08. **d** 10 **p** 11. C Guildf St Nic 10–13; Chapl St Jo Sch Leatherhead 12–13; R E and W Clandon *Guildf* from 13. *The Rectory, The Street, West Clandon, Guildford GU4 7RG* **T:** (01483) 222573 **E:** barnaby.perkins@cantab.net

PERKINS, Colin Blackmore. b 35. FCII 65. Lon Coll of Div 68. **d** 70 **p** 71. C Hyson Green *S'well* 70–73; V Clarborough w Hayton 73–79; P-in-c Cropwell Bishop 79–84; P-in-c Colston Bassett 79–84; P-in-c Granby w Elton 79–84; P-in-c Langar 79–84; V Tithby w Cropwell Butler 79–84; R Cropwell Bishop w Colston Bassett, Granby etc 84–94; P-in-c Sutton Bonington w Normanton-on-Soar 94–01; rtd 01; PtO *Newc* from 01. *6 Ravensmede, Alnwick NE66 2PX* **T:** (01665) 510445 **E:** cperk68836@aol.com

PERKINS, Canon David. b 51. Sarum & Wells Th Coll. **d** 87 **p** 88. C New Mills *Derby* 87–90; V Marlpool 90–95; P-in-c Turnditch 95–02; Min in charge Belper Ch Ch and Milford 95–02; V Belper Ch Ch w Turnditch 02–09; Jt P-in-c Ambergate and Heage 06–09; RD Duffield 97–09; Chapl Derbyshire Mental Health Services NHS Trust 95–09; Can Res Derby Cathl 09–13; rtd 13; P-in-c Beeley and Edensor *Derby* 13–15; V from 15. *The Vicarage, Edensor, Bakewell DE45 1PH* **T:** (01246) 386385 **E:** revdaveperkins@aol.com

PERKINS, David John Elmslie. b 45. Dur Univ BA 66 ATII 75. Cranmer Hall Dur 66. **d** 69 **p** 70. C Wadsley *Sheff* 69–71; C Shortlands *Roch* 71–73; PtO *Lon* 76–78; *B & W* 78–80 and from 02; LtO 80–02; rtd 02. *Rainbow's End, Montacute Road, Stoke-sub-Hamdon TA14 6UQ* **T:** (01935) 823314 **M:** 07840-598220 **E:** perkinsdavid@talktalk.net

PERKINS, John Everard. b 47. SEITE 04. **d** 06 **p** 07. NSM Speldhurst w Groombridge and Ashurst *Roch* 06–10; NSM Tonbridge St Steph 10–18; rtd 18; PtO *Roch* from 18. *25 Northfields, Speldhurst, Tunbridge Wells TN3 0PN* **T:** (01892) 863239 **E:** revjohnp@outlook.com

PERKINS, Miss Julia Margaret. b 49. Linc Th Coll 85. **d** 87 **p** 94. Par Dn Owton Manor *Dur* 87–89; Par Dn Leam Lane 89–94; C 94; P-in-c Stockton St Chad 94–96; V 96–00; C Eppleton and Hetton le Hole 00–06; C Heworth St Mary 06–11; rtd 11; PtO *Pet* from 14. *12 Portman Close, Peterborough PE3 9RJ* **T:** (01733) 262240

PERKINS, Julian John. b 67. Southn Univ BSc 90 MSc 92. Trin Coll Bris BA 00 MPhil 03. **d** 01 **p** 02. C Thornbury *Glouc* 01–02; C Thornbury and Oldbury-on-Severn w Shepperdine 02–04; C Tewkesbury w Walton Cardiff

and Twyning 04–07; P-in-c Crosland Moor *Wakef* 07–08; P-in-c Linthwaite 07–08; V Crosland Moor and Linthwaite 08–10; Chapl Sheff Teaching Hosps NHS Foundn Trust 11–17; Chapl Waikato Hosp NZ from 17. *47 Edgeview Crescent, Fitzroy, Hamilton 3206, New Zealand* **M:** (0064) 204-124   6555   **E:** julianjperkins@gmail.com *or* julianperkins@rocketmail.com

PERKINS, Kenneth Ronald. b 57. **d** 16 **p** 17. NSM Gidea Park *Chelmsf* 16–19; NSM Cranham Park from 19. *7 Laburnham Gardens, Upminster RM14 1HU* **E:** kenperkins28@gmail.com

PERKINS, Michael James. b 89. Dur Univ BA 18. Ridley Hall Cam 15. **d** 18 **p** 19. C York St Mich-le-Belfrey from 18. *3 Maida Grove, York YO10 4EU* **M:** 07515-464780 **E:** mikeperkins89@hotmail.com

PERKINS, Patricia Doris (Sister Patricia). b 29. Gilmore Ho 60. **dss** 73 **d** 87. CSA from 71; Sherston Magna w Easton Grey *Bris* 73–75; Cant St Martin and St Paul 76–78; Kilburn St Aug w St Jo *Lon* 80–84; Abbey Ho Malmesbury 84–87; Hon Par Dn Bayswater *Lon* 87–94; Chapl St Mary's Hosp Praed Street Lon 88–89; Chapl St Chas Hosp Ladbroke Grove 88–89; Dean of Women's Min *Lon* from 89; Dioc Dir of Ords 90–94; Hon Par Dn St Olave Hart Street w All Hallows Staining etc 94–01. *St Mary's Convent and Nursing Home, Burlington Lane, London W4 2QF*

PERKINTON, Keith Glyn. b 61. Humberside Poly BA 83 Leeds Univ BA 92 Brighton Poly PGCE 86. Coll of Resurr Mirfield 93. **d** 93 **p** 94. C Knowle H Nativity *Bris* 93–97; TV Brighton Resurr *Chich* 97–05; P-in-c Hangleton 05–07; V 07–21; RD Hove 10; rtd 21. *10 Nab Lane, Mirfield WF14 9BN* **M:** 07796-084210 **E:** keithperkinton1@hotmail.co.uk

PERLMAN, Francesca Jane Andrea. b 64. St Geo Lon MB, BS 89 City Univ Lon MSc 01 Univ Coll Lon PhD 06. St Aug Coll Cant 19. **d** 21. NSM Cheam *S'wark* from 21. *17 Well House, Woodmansterne Lane, Banstead SM7 3AA* **E:** francesca@cheamparish.org.uk

PERREAU, Mrs Deborah. b 57. **d** 16 **p** 17. NSM Ilminster and Whitelackington *B & W* 16–20; Deanery Miss P Ilminster from 20. *Croft House, Combe St Nicholas, Chard TA20 3NA* **T:** (01460) 67168 **E:** deborah@perreau.co

PERRETT, David Thomas. b 48. Cranmer Hall Dur 80. **d** 82 **p** 83. C Stapleford *S'well* 82–86; V Ollerton 86–87; P-in-c Boughton 86–87; V Ollerton w Boughton 87–93; V Winklebury *Win* 93–05; P-in-c Gresley *Derby* 05–10; V 10–13; RD Repton 11–13; rtd 13; PtO *Pet* from 14. *14 Dunbar Court, Kettering NN15 5DN* **T:** (01536) 659065 **E:** davdotp2405@sky.com

PERRETT (formerly ROWE), Canon Vanda Sheila. b 63. STETS 95. **d** 98 **p** 99. C Marlborough *Sarum* 98–01; TV Pewsey and Swanborough 01–06; TR Bourne Valley 06–14; C Salisbury St Fran and Stratford sub Castle 09–14; RD Alderbury 06–14; Can and Preb Sarum Cathl 12–14; P-in-c St Buryan, St Levan and Sennen *Truro* 14–15; R 15–21; RD Penwith 17–19; Chapl HM YOI Werrington from 21. *HM Youth Custody Centre, Werrington, Stoke-on-Trent ST9 0DX* **T:** (01782) 463300 **E:** canonvanda@gmail.com

PERRICONE, Vincent James. b 50. Connecticut Univ BA 74 Pontifical Univ Rome STB 88 STL 90 Glas Univ PhD 98. **d** 90 **p** 90. In RC Ch 89–94; C Glas St Mary 94–95; P-in-c Glas All SS and Glas H Cross 95–03; USA 03–04; PtO *Eur* 04–08; Asst Chapl Florence w Siena 08–09; LtO *Ab* from 10; C Kincardine O'Neil 10–12; Chapl Grampian Univ Hosp NHS Trust 10–12; P-in-c Devizes St Pet *Sarum* 14–15; V 15–16; Chapl Hants Hosps NHS Foundn Trust from 16. *Basingstoke and North Hampshire Hospital, Aldermaston Road, Basingstoke RG24 9NA* **T:** (01256) 473202 **M:** 07733-740372 **E:** vjperricone@googlemail.com

PERRIN, Andrew. **d** 12 **p** 13. C Morriston *S & B* 12–14; C Upper Ithon Valley 14–15; P-in-c 16–17; C Lower Ithon Valley 14–15; P-in-c 16–17; P-in-c Ithon Valley 17; R Glan Ithon from 17. *7 Rock House Court, Llandrindod Wells LD1 6AX* **T:** (01597) 829356 **E:** revperrin@btinternet.com

PERRIN, Bruce Alexander. b 72. Birm Univ BSc 94 MSc 96. St Jo Coll Nottm 08. **d** 09 **p** 10. C Marple All SS *Ches* 09–12; P-in-c Hollingworth w Tintwistle 15–20; V from 20. *6 Taylor Street, Hollingworth, Hyde SK14 8PB* **M:** 07914-211376 **E:** rev.bruce.perrin@gmail.com

PERRINS, Christopher Neville. b 68. St Steph Ho Ox 01. **d** 03 **p** 04. C Warrington St Elphin *Liv* 03–08; TV Walton-on-the-Hill 08–12; C Rainhill 12–15; PtO from 17. *1 Wesley Place, Liverpool L15 8JB* **T:** 0151-733 7930 **E:** revdcnperrins@btinternet.com

PERRIS, Preb Anthony. b 48. Univ of Wales (Abth) BSc 69 Selw Coll Cam BA 76 MA 79. Ridley Hall Cam 74. **d** 77 **p** 78. C Sandal St Helen *Wakef* 77–80; C Plymouth St Andr w St Paul and St Geo *Ex* 80–87; TV Yeovil *B & W* 87–88; V Preston Plucknett 88–16; RD Yeovil 06–16; Preb Wells Cathl

11–16; rtd 16; PtO *Ox* from 19. *Meadow Cottage, Meadow Lane, Shipton-under-Wychwood, Chipping Norton OX7 6BW* E: antonyperris@yahoo.com

PERRIS, Mrs Jocelyn Clare. b 69. Surrey Univ BSc 91. ERMC 08. **d** 11 **p** 12. C St Alb St Pet 11–17; Chapl Aldenham Sch Herts from 17; NSM Langelei *St Alb* from 21. *Aldenham School, Aldenham Road, Elstree, Borehamwood WD6 3AJ* M: 07979-590480 E: josperris@aol.com

PERRIS, John Martin. b 44. Liv Univ BSc 66. Trin Coll Bris 69. **d** 72 **p** 73. C Sevenoaks St Nic *Roch* 72–76; C Bebington *Ches* 76–79; V Redland *Bris* 79–97; RD Horfield 91–97; R Barton Seagrave w Warkton *Pet* 97–09; rtd 09; PtO *Carl* from 11. *3 Old Myse, Storth, Milnthorpe LA7 7HQ* T: (01539) 564446 E: martin.perris@hotmail.co.uk

PERRY, Alan David. b 64. Greenwich Univ BA 86 Lon Inst of Educn PGCE 87 Greenwich Univ MA 99. NTMTC 01. **d** 03 **p** 04. NSM Romford St Edw *Chelmsf* 03–08; Hd Teacher St Edw C of E Sch Havering 08–16; Public Preacher *Chelmsf* 08–16; TV Sole Bay *St E* from 16. *The Vicarage, 45A Wangford Road, Reydon, Southwold IP18 6PZ* T: (01502) 453624 M: 07946-730291 E: adperry64@gmail.com

PERRY, Andrew John. b 65. St Steph Ho Ox BTh 00. **d** 00 **p** 01. C Southwick St Mich *Chich* 00–03; P-in-c Upper St Leonards St Jo 03; R 03–13; P-in-c Portslade St Nic and St Andr and Mile Oak 13–16; V 16–17; V E Preston w Kingston from 17. *The Vicarage, 33 Vicarage Lane, East Preston, Littlehampton BN16 2SP* T: (01903) 783318 M: 07545-185358 E: revakperry@btinternet.com

PERRY, Canon Andrew Nicholas. b 62. Westmr Coll Ox BA 86. Trin Coll Bris MA 91. **d** 91 **p** 92. C Bath Weston All SS w N Stoke *B & W* 91–93; C Bath Weston All SS w N Stoke and Langridge 93–95; P-in-c Longfleet *Sarum* 95–00; V from 00; Can and Preb Sarum Cathl from 12. *The Vicarage, 2 Twemlow Avenue, Poole BH14 8AN* T: (01202) 253527 *or* 338720 F: 253527 E: andrew.perry@smlpoole.org

PERRY, Andrew William. b 44. MRAC 65. WMMTC 91. **d** 94 **p** 95. NSM Redmarley D'Abitot, Bromesberrow, Pauntley etc *Glouc* 94–14; PtO *Heref* 05–12; rtd 14; PtO *Glouc* from 14; *Heref* 17–19. *Rye Cottage, Broomsgreen, Dymock GL18 2DP* T: (01531) 890489 E: aperry9381@aol.com

PERRY, Anthony Henry. b 54. Leic Univ BA 76. Aston Tr Scheme 89 Linc Th Coll 93. **d** 93 **p** 94. C Bartley Green *Birm* 93–97; V Bearwood 97–21; AD Warley 06–13; rtd 21; PtO *Birm* from 21. *52 Rufford Road, Stourbridge DY9 7LT* M: 07846-516699 E: trinity20@hotmail.co.uk

PERRY, David. b 62. Newman Coll Birm BEd 86. Sarum Coll 15. **d** 18 **p** 19. NSM Clarendon *Sarum* from 18. *11 St Lawrence Close, Stratford sub Castle, Salisbury SP1 3LW* T: (01722) 328342 M: 07749-199453 E: bumbledp@gmail.com

PERRY, Edward John. b 35. AKC 62. **d** 63 **p** 64. C Honicknowle *Ex* 63–65; C Ashburton w Buckland-in-the-Moor 65–70; V Cornwood 70–92; Asst Dir of Educn 71–92; Chapl Moorhaven Hosp 91–93; V Ermington and Ugborough *Ex* 92–00; rtd 00; PtO *Ex* from 01. *32 Finches Close, Elburton, Plymouth PL9 8DP* T: (01752) 405364 E: perry.retvie@blueyonder.co.uk

PERRY, James Marcus. b 71. Ridley Hall Cam 02. **d** 04 **p** 05. C Cen Wolverhampton *Lich* 04–07; TV Tettenhall Regis 07–19; V Sydenham St Bart *S'wark* from 19. *The Vicarage, 4 Westwood Hill, London SE26 6QR* T: (020) 8776 5722 E: revjimperry@mailfence.com

✠**PERRY, The Rt Revd John Freeman.** b 35. Lon Coll of Div MPhil 86 ALCD 59. **d** 59 **p** 60 **c** 89. C Woking Ch Ch *Guildf* 59–62; C Chorleywood Ch Ch *St Alb* 62; Min Chorleywood St Andr 63–66; V 66–77; RD Rickmansworth 72–77; Warden Lee Abbey 77–89; RD Shirwell *Ex* 80–84; Hon Can Win Cathl 89–96; Suff Bp Southampton 89–96; Bp Chelmsf 96–03; rtd 03; Hon Asst Bp *B & W* from 11; PtO from 19. *8 The Firs, Bath BA2 5ED* T: (01225) 833987 E: jperry8@btinternet.com

PERRY, John Walton Beauchamp. b 43. Ex Coll Ox BA 64 Sussex Univ MA 67. EAMTC 82 Westcott Ho Cam 84. **d** 85 **p** 86. C Shrewsbury St Chad w St Mary *Lich* 85–89; V Batheaston w St Cath *B & W* 89–99; V Milborne Port w Goathill 99–07; P-in-c Charlton Horethorne w Stowell 06–07; V Milborne Port w Goathill etc 07–09; rtd 09; PtO *Heref* from 10. *67 Steventon New Road, Ludlow SY8 1JY* T: (01584) 873755 E: jwbperry@gmail.com

PERRY, Lesley Anne. b 52. K Coll Lon BA 73 MCIPR 99. SEITE 96. **d** 99 **p** 00. NSM Fulham All SS *Lon* 99–07; NSM Kensington St Mary Abbots w Ch Ch and St Phil 07–16; NSM Earl's Court Road St Phil from 17. *39A Gunter Grove, London SW10 0UN* T: (020) 7938 1357 E: lesley.perry@specr.org

PERRY, Lynne Janice. b 48. **d** 90 **p** 97. NSM Llanfair Mathafarn Eithaf w Llanbedrgoch *Ban* 90–97; C Bangor 97–99; TV 99–05; V Tregarth 04–05; V Tregarth and Llandygai and Maes y Groes 05–09; AD Ogwen 02–07; C Ogwen

Deanery 09–10; Hon Chapl Ban Cathl 10–12; Hon Can 11–12; rtd 12; PtO *B & W* from 15. *32 Adams Close, Highbridge TA9 3DX* M: 07817-518337 E: lynne.pcc@btinternet.com

PERRY, Mark Colin. b 71. K Alfred's Coll Win BA 97 Portsm Univ MA 20 Homerton Coll Cam PGCE FRSA 14 FCollT 15 FCMI 15. Regent's Park Coll Ox 02 Ripon Coll Cuddesdon 09. **d** 10 **p** 11. In Bapt Min 05–09; C Bourne Valley *Sarum* 10–11; C Iwerne Valley 11–13; Asst Chapl Shaftesbury Sch 11–13; Res Chapl Port Regis Sch 13–15; CF (ACF) 12–15; Chapl RAF from 15; P Assoc Shrine of Our Lady of Walsingham from 11; Hon Chapl Sarum Cathl 13–17; Bp's Ecum Officer (Dorset) 13–15; Hon Chapl Cottesmore Sch Crawley 15–20; PtO *Lon* from 17; *Ely* from 21. *Chaplaincy Services (RAF), HQ Air Command, RAF High Wycombe HP14 4UE* T: (01494) 496800 E: mark.perry725@mod.gov.uk

PERRY, Martin Herbert. b 43. Cranmer Hall Dur 66. **d** 70 **p** 71. C Millfield St Mark *Dur* 70–74; C Haughton le Skerne 74–77; V Darlington St Matt and St Luke 77–84; TR Oldland *Bris* 84–91; V 91–01; rtd 01; C Wellington and Distr *B & W* 12–16; PtO from 19. *51 Rockwell Green, Wellington TA21 9BZ* T: (01823) 652683 M: 07814-501261 E: bask4faith@yahoo.co.uk

PERRY, Michael James Matthew. b 66. Bris Univ BSc 87 MSc 89 PhD 93. Trin Coll Bris BA 99. **d** 99 **p** 00. C Keynsham *B & W* 99–03; R Cam Vale 03–13; V Woodford Valley w Archers Gate *Sarum* from 13. *The Vicarage, Middle Woodford, Salisbury SP4 6NR* T: (01722) 782310 E: mikeperry@posteo.net

PERRY, Michael Leonard. b 47. Univ of W Ontario BA 68 Wilfred Laurier Univ MA 90 Ottawa Univ PhD 00. Huron Coll Ontario MDiv 82. **d** 82 **p** 83. C London St Steph Canada 82–83; R Tyrconnell 83–84; R Dorchester 84–88; R Point Edward 90–93; P-in-c Quebec 93–95; R Ottawa All SS 95–97; P-in-c Hull St Jas 97–00; R Capreol and Garson 01–04; P-in-c Menton *Eur* 09. *701-99 Holland Avenue, Ottawa ON K1Y 0Y1, Canada* E: michaelperry47@gmail.com

PERRY, Nicholas Charles. b 07 **p** 08. NSM Ebbw Vale *Mon* 07–10; R Blaina and Nantyglo 10–13; TR Upper Ebbw Valleys 13–18; TR Cwmbran from 18. *The Rectory, Clomendy Road, Cwmbran NP44 3LS* E: nick.perry1@btinternet.com

PERRY, Valerie Evelyn. b 39. Southn Univ CertEd 59. S'wark Ord Course 82. **dss** 85 **d** 87 **p** 94. NSM Romford St Edw *Chelmsf* 85–89; Par Dn 89–91; Asst Chapl Middx Hosp Lon 92–93; Asst Chapl Univ Coll Lon Hosps NHS Trust 94; Chapl S Kent Hosps NHS Trust 94–98; Hon C Aylesham w Adisham *Cant* 98–00; Hon C Nonington w Wymynswold and Goodnestone etc 98–00; rtd 99; PtO *Truro* from 01. *115 Century Close, St Austell PL25 3UZ* T: (01726) 68075 E: vep10@hotmail.com

PERRY, Canon William Francis Pitfield. b 61. Keble Coll Ox BA 84 MA 87. Ripon Coll Cuddesdon 94. **d** 96 **p** 97. C Brockworth *Glouc* 96–01; P-in-c Millbrook *Win* 01–18; V Hawley H Trin *Guildf* from 18; V Minley from 18; Can Ruvuma Tanzania from 14. *Hawley Vicarage, Fernhill Road, Blackwater, Camberley GU17 9BN* E: fr.will@icxc.org

PERRY, William Luke. b 89. St Jo Coll Dur BA 14. St Mellitus Coll MA 20. **d** 20 **p** 21. C Onslow Square and S Kensington St Aug *Lon* from 20. *Flat 10, 46 Tregunter Road, London SW10 9LE* M: 07771-621814 E: willperry89@hotmail.co.uk *or* will.perry@htb.org

PERRYMAN, Preb David Francis. b 42. Brunel Univ BSc 64. Oak Hill Th Coll 74. **d** 76 **p** 77. C Margate H Trin *Cant* 76–80; R Ardingly *Chich* 80–90; V Bath St Luke *B & W* 90–07; RD Bath 96–03; Preb Wells Cathl 01–07; PtO *Win* from 08. *Treetops, Upper Froyle, Alton GU34 4JH* T: (01420) 520647 E: david.perrypeople@gmail.com

PERRYMAN, Graham Frederick. b 56. Southn Univ BA 78 Reading Univ PGCE 80. Aston Tr Scheme 90 Trin Coll Bris 92. **d** 94 **p** 95. C Hamworthy *Sarum* 94–98; P-in-c Moreton and Woodsford w Tincleton 98–02; R 02–04; TV Melbury 04–06; TR 06–15; RD Sherborne 12–14; P-in-c Upper Stour 15–19; rtd 19; PtO *Sarum* from 19; *B & W* from 19. *42 Combe Park, Yeovil BA21 3BD* E: revgfp@btopenworld.com

PERRYMAN, James Edward. b 56. Lon Bible Coll BA 85. Oak Hill Th Coll 86. **d** 88 **p** 89. C Gidea Park *Chelmsf* 88–91; C Becontree St Mary 91–94; Chapl Lyon *Eur* 94–00; R Allington and Maidstone St Pet *Cant* 00–08; Dioc Ecum Officer 02–08; P-in-c Stoneleigh w Ashow *Cov* 08–13; V Leek Wootton from 20; PtO *Eur* from 16. *The Vicarage, 4 Hill Wootton Road, Leek Wootton, Warwick CV35 7QL* T/F: (01926) 850610 E: vicar@leekwoottonchurch.org

PERRYMAN, Canon John Frederick Charles. b 49. Mert Coll Ox BA 71 MA 74 MInstGA 98. Ridley Hall Cam 72. **d** 74 **p** 75. C Shortlands *Roch* 74–78; Asst Chapl St Geo Hosp Lon 78–82; Chapl Withington Hosp Man 83–94; Chapl Univ Hosp of S Man NHS Foundn Trust 94–09; Hon Can Man Cathl

00–09; rtd 09; PtO *Man* 09–19. *50 Maudlin Drive, Teignmouth TQ14 8SB* T: (01626) 439109 E: jd_perryman@lineone.net

PERSSON, Matthew Stephen. b 60. Dundee Univ BSc 82 Bris Univ MA 98. Wycliffe Hall Ox 88. **d** 91 **p** 92. C Bath Twerton-on-Avon *B & W* 91–94; Chapl HM Pris Shepton Mallet 94–97; PtO *B & W* 97–98; C Shepton Mallet w Doulting 98–00. *Grange Farm, Fair Place, West Lydford, Somerton TA11 7DN* T: (01963) 240024

PERTH, Provost of. *See* FARQUHARSON, The Very Revd Hunter Buchanan

✠**PERUMBALATH, The Rt Revd John.** b 66. Calicut Univ BA 86 Union Bibl Sem Pune BD 90 Osmania Univ Hyderabad MA 93 NW Univ S Africa PhD 07. Serampore Th Coll MTh 93. **d** 94 **p** 95 **c** 18. C Calcutta St Jo India 94–95; V Calcutta St Jas 95–00; V Calcutta St Thos 00–01; C Beckenham St Geo *Roch* 02–05; TV Northfleet and Rosherville 05–08; V Perry Street 08–13; Dioc CUF Link Officer 08–13; Adn Barking *Chelmsf* 13–18; Area Bp Bradwell from 18. *Bishop's House, Orsett Road, Horndon-on-the-Hill, Stanford-le-Hope SS17 8NS* T: (01375) 673806 E: b.bradwell@chelmsford.anglican.org

PESCE, Fabrizio. b 73. Universidad del Salvador Buenos Aires BA MA 03 MD 09. St Steph Ho Ox 14. **d** 02 **p** 03. In RC Ch 02–09; C Bedford Park *Lon* from 15; C Acton Green from 15. *206 St Albans Avenue, London W4 5JU* M: 07713-444382

PESCOD, John Gordon. b 44. Leeds Univ BSc 70. Qu Coll Birm. **d** 72 **p** 73. C Camberwell St Geo *S'wark* 72–75; Chapl R Philanthropic Soc Sch Redhill 75–80; P-in-c Nunney w Wanstrow and Cloford *B & W* 80–84; R Nunney and Witham Friary, Marston Bigot etc 84–87; R Milverton w Halse and Fitzhead 87–93; V Frome St Jo and St Mary 93–00; V Frome St Jo 01; V Woodlands 93–01; RD Frome 97–01; V Castle Cary w Ansford 01–09; rtd 09. *32 Churchfield Drive, Castle Cary BA7 7LA*

PESKETT, Richard Howard. b 42. Selw Coll Cam BA 64 MA 67. Ridley Hall Cam 64. **d** 68 **p** 69. C Jesmond H Trin *Newc* 68–71; Lect Discipleship Tr Cen Singapore 71–76; Dean 76–86; Lect Coll of SS Paul and Mary Cheltenham 86–87; Research Dir OMF 88–91; Tutor Trin Coll Bris 91–06; Vice-Prin 98–06; Scholars Dir Langham Partnership 06–08; rtd 07; PtO *Truro* 06–08; Hon C Penzance St Mary w St Paul and St Jo 08–13; RD Penwith 08–13; PtO from 16. *7 North Parade, Penzance TR18 4SH* T: (01736) 362913 E: howard.peskett@btinternet.com

PESKETT, Canon Timothy Lewis. b 64. St Kath Coll Liv BA 86. Chich Th Coll BTh 90. **d** 90 **p** 91. C Verwood *Sarum* 90–91; C Southsea H Spirit *Portsm* 91–95; TV Burgess Hill St Jo w St Edw *Chich* 95–00; V Burgess Hill St Edw 00–05; R Felpham 05–14; R Whyke w Rumboldswhyke and Portfield 14–20; V W Worthing St Jo from 20; P-in-c Worthing St Andr from 20; Can and Preb Chich Cathl from 15. *St John's Vicarage, 15 Reigate Road, Worthing BN11 5NF* T: (01903) 247340 E: tpeskett@gmail.com

PESTELL, Miss Josephine Frances. b 72. Leeds Univ BSc 93 Bris Univ MPhil 17. Trin Coll Bris MA 14. **d** 16 **p** 17. C Cheltenham Network Ch and S Cheltenham *Glouc* 16–19; V Glouc St Cath from 19. *The Vicarage, 5 Kenilworth Avenue, Gloucester GL2 0QJ* T: (01452) 542205 E: jpestell@stcatharine.org.uk

PESTELL, Robert Carlyle. b 54. Aston Tr Scheme 89 Linc Th Coll 91. **d** 93 **p** 94. C Matson *Glouc* 93–97; P-in-c Charfield 97–01; R Charfield and Kingswood 02–06; P-in-c Cheltenham St Mich 06–13; P-in-c Cheltenham St Luke and St Jo 06–12; Chapl Leckhampton Court Hospice from 13. *Leckhampton Court Hospice, Church Road, Leckhampton, Cheltenham GL53 0QJ* T: (01242) 246290

PESTELL, Mrs Susan Beryl. b 56. Hull Coll of Educn CertEd 77. **d** 19 **p** 20. OLM The Guitings, Cutsdean, Farmcote etc *Glouc* from 19. *135 Gretton Road, Winchcombe, Cheltenham GL54 5EL* T: (01242) 609223 E: susan.pestell@gmail.com

PESTRIDGE, Vanessa. b 77. Ex Univ BA 98. St Mellitus Coll 18. **d** 20. C Ex St Matt w St Sidwell from 20. *Milbury End, Milbury Lane, Exminster, Exeter EX6 8AE* E: vanessa@stmattsexeter.org

PETCH, Canon Douglas Rodger. b 57. Nottm Univ BSc 79. St Jo Coll Nottm MA 96. **d** 94 **p** 94. C Vom Nigeria 94–95; C Pendleton *Man* 96–98; P-in-c Werneth and C Oldham St Paul 98–03; CMS Nigeria 03–07; Hon Can Jos from 05; TV Halliwell *Man* 07–11; TV W Bolton from 11; AD Bolton 10–15. *101 Cloister Street, Bolton BL1 3HA* T: (01204) 842627 M: 07837-423501 E: rodgerpetch@yahoo.co.uk

PETCH, Michelle Diane. b 68. Leeds Univ BA 89 Dur Univ BA 17. St Hild Coll 15. **d** 17 **p** 18. C Halifax H Trin and St Jude *Leeds* 17–21; V Rastrick from 21. *Address temp unknown* E: michelle.petch2@btinternet.com

PETER, Christopher Javed. b 51. Peshawar Univ BA 75. Qu Coll Birm 94. **d** 96 **p** 97. C Darwen St Pet w Hoddlesden *Blackb* 96–98; C Accrington 98–99; C Burnley St Andr w

St Marg and St Jas 99–05; Chapl R Liverpool and Broadgreen Univ Hosps NHS Trust from 05. *Royal Liverpool University Hospital, Prescot Street, Liverpool L7 8XP* T: 0151-706 2826 E: christopher.peter@rlbuht.nhs.uk

PETER DOUGLAS, Brother. *See* NEEDHAM, Peter Douglas

PETERBOROUGH, Bishop of. *See* ALLISTER, The Rt Revd Donald Spargo

PETERBOROUGH, Dean of. *See* DALLISTON, The Very Revd Christopher Charles

PETERS, Ann Margaret. *See* PETERS-WOTHERSPOON, Ann Margaret

PETERS, Carl Richard. b 62. Ripon Coll Cuddesdon 95. **d** 97 **p** 98. C Coventry Caludon *Cov* 97–01; V Gt Grimsby St Andr w St Luke and All SS *Linc* 01–02; TV Leek and Meerbrook *Lich* 02–14; P-in-c Brandon and Ushaw Moor *Dur* from 14. *The Clergy House, Sawmills Lane, Brandon, Durham DH7 8NS* T: 0191-378 0845 E: revpeters28@gmail.com

PETERS, Miss Carole Jean. b 61. Ripon Coll Cuddesdon 07. **d** 09 **p** 10. C Ivinghoe w Pitstone and Slapton and Marsworth *Ox* 09–11; C Aston Clinton w Buckland and Drayton Beauchamp 12–13; R Astwell Gp *Pet* 13–18; Dioc Dir Communications *Sarum* from 18; LtO from 19. *Church House, Crane Street, Salisbury SP1 2QB* M: 07710-128859 E: carolepeters@aol.com

PETERS, David. b 62. Reading Univ BSc 83. Wycliffe Hall Ox 11. **d** 14 **p** 15. NSM Wonersh w Blackheath *Guildf* 14–21; V from 21. *Rushtons, 15 Longdown Road, Guildford GU4 8PP* T: (01483) 575906 E: david.peters@knightfrank.com

PETERS, David Alexander. b 72. K Coll Lon BA 94. St Steph Ho Ox BA 98 MA 08. **d** 99 **p** 00. C Paddington St Jas *Lon* 99–03; PV Westmr Abbey 01–13; V Reading H Trin and Reading St Mark *Ox* 03–08; Asst Chapl Tonbridge Sch 08–11; Sen Chapl from 11. *Tonbridge School, High Street, Tonbridge TN9 1JP* T: (01732) 365555 E: dap@tonbridge-school.org

PETERS, Diane Rosemary. b 48. Ox Brookes Univ BA 18 Southn Univ CertEd 70. **d** 16 **p** 17. OLM Westborough *Guildf* 16–21; PtO from 21. *10 Weston Road, Guildford GU2 8AS* T: (01483) 532796 E: dianerpeters@netscape.net

PETERS, Heather. b 63. St Aug Coll of Th 15. **d** 17 **p** 18. NSM Brixton St Paul w St Sav *S'wark* 17–18; NSM Herne Hill 18–20; LtO from 20. *53 Stambourne Way, London SE19 2PY* M: 07885-569464 E: heather-peters@hotmail.co.uk

PETERS, Mrs Helen Elizabeth. b 67. Qu Marg Coll Edin BSc 88. Ox Min Course 08. **d** 11 **p** 12. NSM Hughenden *Ox* from 11. *Boundary House, Missenden Road, Great Kingshill, High Wycombe HP15 6EB* T: (01494) 716772 E: helen.peters@peters-research.com

PETERS, Mrs Jane Elisabeth. b 48. Kent Univ BA 08. **d** 08 **p** 09. NSM Shortlands *Roch* from 08. *27 The Gardens, Beckenham BR3 5PH* T: (020) 8650 5986 E: revjane@virginmedia.com

PETERS, John Peter Thomas. b 63. Keble Coll Ox BL 85. Wycliffe Hall Ox BA 91. **d** 95 **p** 96. C Brompton H Trin w Onslow Square St Paul *Lon* 95–99; P-in-c Bryanston Square St Mary w St Marylebone St Mark 00–04; R from 04. *13 Chomeley Crescent, London N6 5EZ* T: (020) 7258 5042

PETERS, John Thomas. b 58. Connecticut Univ BA 80. St Jo Coll Nottm 84. **d** 87 **p** 88. C Virginia Water *Guildf* 87–93; R Grand Rapids Ch Ch USA 93–00; R Eden Prairie St Alb from 00. *14434 Fairway Drive, Eden Prairie MN 557344-1904, USA* E: johnpeters@isd.net

PETERS, Malcolm John. b 71. Leic Univ BA 92. Oak Hill Th Coll BA 03. **d** 03 **p** 04. C Braintree *Chelmsf* 03–06; C Hull St Jo Newland *York* 06–09; P-in-c High Ongar w Norton Mandeville *Chelmsf* 09–18; PtO from 18. *1 Borromeo Way, Brentwood CM14 4GU* E: malcolm.peters892@btinternet.com *or* malcolm@stratfordtalks.org

PETERS, Preb Marilyn Ann. b 49. Open Univ BA 90. Qu Coll Birm 96. **d** 98 **p** 99. C Blakenall Heath *Lich* 98–01; TV Cen Telford 01–05; TR 05–13; Preb Lich Cathl 09–13; rtd 13; PtO *Lich* 15–16; Hon C Mease Valley 16–17; Hon C Yoxall 17–18; Hon C Kings Bromley, The Ridwares and Yoxall 18–19; PtO 19–21. *40 Campion Way, Uttoxeter ST14 7TB* T: (01889) 624127 M: 07889-372275 E: marilynpeters@talktalk.net

PETERS, Muriel. b 50. Lindisfarne Regional Tr Partnership. **d** 16 **p** 17. NSM Haswell and Shotton *Dur* from 16. *1 Tudor Court, Shotton Colliery, Durham DH6 2RE* T: 0191-526 1671 M: 07971-577715 E: muriel-at.the.lodge@live.co.uk

PETERS, Rebecca Jane. b 76. St Hilda's Coll Ox MPhys 98 St Cross Coll Ox PGCE 99. Wycliffe Hall Ox 06. **d** 08 **p** 09. C Roxeth *Lon* 08–11; P-in-c Drayton St Pet (Abingdon) *Ox* 11–16; LtO from 16; Min Peachcroft Chr Cen LEP from 16. *14 Boxhill Road, Abingdon OX14 2EU* T: (01235) 530227 M: 07821-710285 E: rebecca.a.peters@gmail.com *or* minister@peachcroftcc.org

PETERS, Samuel Benjamin Stuart. b 92. St Pet Coll Ox BA 14. Westcott Ho Cam 16. **d** 18 **p** 19. C Loughton St Jo *Chelmsf* from 18. *2 Doubleday Road, Loughton IG10 2AT* M: 07930-676260 E: revdpeters@outlook.com

PETERS-WOTHERSPOON, Ann Margaret. b 48. Lon Univ BD 84 Open Univ MA 95 UEA EdD 05 Anglia Ruskin Univ MA 09. ERMC 05. **d** 07 **p** 08. NSM Somersham w Pidley and Oldhurst and Woodhurst *Ely* 07–11; NSM Tweedmouth *Newc* 11–16; NSM Spittal 11–16; NSM Scremerston 11–16; NSM Upper Coquetdale 16–21. *Burleigh House Maisonette, High Street, Rothbury, Morpeth NE65 7TB* E: ann_m_peters@hotmail.com

PETERSEN, Jennifer Elizabeth. b 55. Aus Nat Univ BA 78. Moore Th Coll Sydney BTh 82 Wycliffe Hall Ox 92. **d** 94 **p** 95. C Elloughton and Brough w Brantingham *York* 94–96; C Ealing St Mary *Lon* 96–00; Chapl Thames Valley Univ 96–00; Chapl Qu Mary Univ of Lon 00–15; PV Westmr Abbey 16–17; Min Can and Chapl 17–21; PtO *Lon* 17–19; V Crockenhill All So *Roch* from 21. *The Vicarage, Eynsford Road, Crockenhill, Swanley BR8 8JS* T: (01322) 662157 E: crockenhillvicar@gmail.com

PETERSON, David Gilbert. b 44. Sydney Univ BA 65 MA 74 Lon Univ BD 68 Man Univ PhD 78. Moore Th Coll Sydney ThL 68. **d** 68 **p** 69. C Manly St Matt Australia 68–70; Lect Moore Th Coll 71–75; C Cheadle *Ches* 75–78; Sen Can and R Wollongong Cathl Australia 80–84; Lect Moore Th Coll 84–96; Prin Oak Hill Th Coll 96–07; PtO *Lon* 96–07; *St Alb* 96–07; Research Fell Moore Th Coll Australia from 07; rtd 09. *1 Vista Street, Belrose NSW 2085, Australia* E: davidandlesleypeterson@gmail.com

PETERSON, David Nwabueze Nwogbe. b 87. St Mellitus Coll 15. **d** 12 **p** 17. NSM Harlesden All So *Lon* 15–19; TV Grays Thurrock *Chelmsf* from 19. *Wendover Vicarage, College Avenue, Grays RM17 5UW* M: 07985-647897 E: rev.david@gttm.org

PETERSON, Elise Michelle. b 70. San Jose State Univ BA 93 W Sem MA 12 St Jo Coll Dur MA 18. Cranmer Hall Dur 16. **d** 17 **p** 18. NSM Chigwell and Chigwell Row *Chelmsf* 17–18; C 18–19; C Vale of Roding 19–20; R Rainham w Wennington from 20. *73 Lake Avenue, Rainham RM13 9SG* E: revelisepeterson@outlook.com

PETERSON, Paul John. b 67. Trin Coll Bris 94. **d** 97 **p** 98. C Burney Lane *Birm* 97–01; C-in-c Bradley Stoke N CD *Bris* 01–10; C Downend from 10. *15 Glendale, Bristol BS16 6EQ* T: 0117-330 7673 E: paulpeterson@christchurchdownend.com

PETFIELD, Bruce Le Gay. b 34. FHA. NEOC 76. **d** 79 **p** 80. NSM Morpeth *Newc* 79–86; C Knaresborough *Ripon* 86–87; V Flamborough *York* 87–94; V Bempton 87–94; rtd 94; PtO *York* 94–20. *36 Maple Road, Bridlington YO16 6TE* T: (01262) 676028 E: revb1980@gmail.com

PETHERAM, Louise Anne Miranda. b 62. Nottm Univ BSc 84 PGCE 85. Qu Coll Birm 09. **d** 12 **p** 13. NSM Upper Soar *Leic* 12–15; PtO *Derby* 15–17; P-in-c Youlgreave, Middleton, Stanton-in-Peak etc 17–20; P-in-c Hope, Castleton and Bradwell from 20. *The New Vicarage, Church Street, Bradwell, Hope Valley S33 9HJ* T: (01433) 621918 E: rev.louise.p@gmail.com

PETHERICK, Mrs Karen Elizabeth. b 64. Victoria Univ Man BSc 85. Qu Foundn Birm 12. **d** 14 **p** 15. OLM Hanley H Ev *Lich* 14–18; C Bradwell and Porthill 18–21; P-in-c Milton and Norton from 21. *The Vicarage, Baddeley Green Lane, Stoke-on-Trent ST2 7EY* M: 07941-725459 E: karenpetherick@ntlworld.com

PETIT, Andrew Michael. b 53. Em Coll Cam MA 78. Trin Coll Bris. **d** 83 **p** 84. C Stoughton *Guildf* 83–87; C Shirley *Win* 87–92; V Cholsey *Ox* 92–04; C Streatley w Moulsford 03–04; V Cholsey and Moulsford from 04; Chapl W Berks Priority Care Services NHS Trust 92–03. *The Vicarage, Church Road, Cholsey, Wallingford OX10 9PP* T: (01491) 651216 M: 07855-745220 E: andrewpetit@virginmedia.com

PETITT, Mrs Lydia Ann. b 81. St Mellitus Coll BA 16. **d** 16 **p** 17. C Loughton St Mary *Chelmsf* 16–19; V Loughton St Mich from 19. *St Michael's House, Roding Road, Loughton IG10 3EJ* M: 07769-694907 E: lydia@stmichaelsloughton.com

PETITT, Mark Peter. b 81. Trin Coll Bris BA 12. **d** 12 **p** 13. C Langdon Hills *Chelmsf* 12–16; PtO 16–19; NSM Loughton St Mich from 19. *St Michael's House, Roding Road, Loughton IG10 3EJ* M: 07900-466373 E: mark@stmichaelsloughton.com

PETRIE, Alistair Philip. b 50. Fuller Th Sem California DMin 99. Oak Hill Th Coll 76. **d** 76 **p** 77. C Eston *York* 76–79; P-in-c Prestwick *Glas* 79–81; R 81–82; Canada from 82. *PO Box 25103, Kelowna BC V1W 3Y7, Canada* T: (001) (250) 764 8590 F: 656 3298 E: alistair@partnershipministries.org

PETRIE, Ian Robert (Eric). b 53. Avery Hill Coll PGCE 84 Oak Hill Th Coll BA 83. Qu Coll Birm 93. **d** 95 **p** 96. C Sedgley All SS *Worc* 95–98; P-in-c Salwarpe and Hindlip w Martin Hussingtree 98–08; Co-ord Chapl W Mercia Police 98–08; rtd 08; PtO *B & W* from 12. *100 Highbridge Road, Burnham-on-Sea TA8 1LW* T: (01278) 787402 E: revdericpetrie@outlook.com

PETRIE, Ms Jane Margaret. b 85. LMH Ox MA 10 St Jo Coll Dur BA 15 MA 17. Cranmer Hall Dur 13. **d** 16 **p** 17. C Wallington Springfield Ch *S'wark* 16–20; TV E Greenwich from 20. *37 Becquerel Court, West Parkside, London SE10 0QQ* M: 07488-599786 E: petrie.jane@icloud.com *or* jane@holytrinitygreenwichpeninsula.org.uk

PETRINE, Andrei Anatolievich. b 73. St Jo Coll Dur BA 05. Cranmer Hall Dur 02. **d** 05 **p** 06. C Hounslow H Trin w St Paul and St Mary *Lon* 05–08; PtO 08–09; P-in-c Greensted-juxta-Ongar w Stanford Rivers etc *Chelmsf* 09–15; Chapl Russian Community *Lon* 09–14; P-in-c Laindon w Dunton *Chelmsf* from 15. *38 Claremont Road, Basildon SS15 5PZ* M: 07723-026925 E: a.petrine@mac.com

PETTENGELL, Ernest Terence. b 43. Ex Univ MA 98. K Coll Lon 65. **d** 69 **p** 70. C Chesham St Mary *Ox* 69–72; C Farnborough *Guildf* 72–75; Asst Master K Alfred Sch Burnham-on-Sea 75–78; C Bishop's Cleeve *Glouc* 78–80; Chapl Westonbirt Sch 80–85; P-in-c Shipton Moyne w Westonbirt and Lasborough *Glouc* 80–85; V Berkeley w Wick, Breadstone and Newport 85–92; TV Weston-super-Mare Cen Par *B & W* 92–95; P-in-c Weston super Mare Em 96–99; Chapl Staffs Univ *Lich* 99–03; V Douglas All SS and St Thos *S & M* 03–07; rtd 07; PtO *Ox* from 09; Ld Chapl Ripon Coll Cuddesdon 15–18. *3 Rushall Road, Thame OX9 3TR* T: (01844) 216298 E: ernest.pettengell@gmail.com

PETTER, Oliver Robert Hugh. b 80. St Edm Hall Ox BA 05. St Steph Ho Ox 11. **d** 14 **p** 15. C Old St Pancras *Lon* 14–17; C Ox St Barn and St Paul w St Thos 17–18; Chapl Missr Pusey Ho 17–18; R Yarnton w Begbroke and Shipton-on-Cherwell *Ox* from 18. *The Rectory, 26 Church Lane, Yarnton, Kidlington OX5 1PY* E: oliver.petter@gmail.com

PETTERSEN, Canon Alvyn Lorang. b 51. TCD BA 73 Dur Univ BA 75 PhD 81. Sarum & Wells Th Coll 78. **d** 81 **p** 82. Chapl Clare Coll Cam 81–85; Fell and Chapl Ex Coll Ox 85–92; Research Fell Linc Coll Ox 92–93; V Frensham *Guildf* 93–02; Can Res Worc Cathl 02–18; rtd 19; PtO *Ox* from 19. *1 Plantation Road, Oxford OX2 6JD*

PETTET, Christopher Farley. b 54. Ox Univ BEd 78. St Jo Coll Nottm 87. **d** 90 **p** 91. C Luton St Mary *St Alb* 90–93; C Fawley *Win* 93–97; P-in-c Amport, Grateley, Monxton and Quarley 97–09; TV Portway and Danebury 09–12; V E w W Wellow and Sherfield English 12–21; rtd 21. *3 Morley College, Market Street, Winchester SO23 9LF* E: cpettet@btinternet.com

PETTIFER, Bryan George Ernest. b 32. Qu Coll Cam BA 55 MA 59 Bris Univ MEd 74. Wm Temple Coll Rugby 56 Ridley Hall Cam 57. **d** 59 **p** 60. C Attercliffe w Carbrook *Sheff* 59–61; C Ecclesall 61–65; Chapl City of Bath Tech Coll 65–74; Adult Educn Officer *Bris* 75–80; Dir Past Th Sarum & Wells Th Coll 80–85; Can Res St Alb 85–92; Prin St Alb Minl Tr Scheme 85–92; Prin Ox Area Chr Tr Scheme 92–94; PtO 94–98; Min and Deployment Officer/Selection Sec ABM 94–97; rtd 97; PtO *Bris* 98–20; *Glouc* 98–00; *Sarum* 98–; *B & W* 02–05; Rtd Clergy Officer Malmesbury Adnry *Bris* 04–11. *23 Curlew Drive, Chippenham SN14 6YG* T: (01249) 659823

PETTIFER, Mrs Anne Elizabeth. b 64. Man Univ BSc 85 FIA 99. LCTP 10. **d** 14 **p** 15. NSM Kirkby Lonsdale *Carl* 14–18; TV from 18; RD Kendal from 18. *Stonebeck, Fairbank, Kirkby Lonsdale, Carnforth LA6 2DU* T: (015242) 73530 M: 07973-869475 E: anne.pettifor@btinternet.com

PETTIFOR, Canon David Thomas. b 42. Ripon Coll Cuddesdon 78. **d** 81 **p** 82. C Binley *Cov* 81–84; P-in-c Wood End 84–88; V 88–92; V Finham 92–98; TV Coventry Caludon 98–07; Hon Can Cov Cathl 04–07; rtd 07; PtO *Cov* from 08. *8 Austin Edwards Drive, Warwick CV34 5GW* T: (01926) 498736 E: davidtpettifor@yahoo.co.uk

PETTINGELL, Hubert. b 32. ACA 54 FCA 65 AKC 58. **d** 59 **p** 60. C Mansfield SS Pet and Paul *S'well* 59–61; CMS Iran 61–66; C Wellington w W Buckland and Nynehead *B & W* 67–68; Warden Student Movement Ho Lon 68–69; R Holywell w Needingworth *Ely* 69–71; Dir Finance WCC 80–96; PtO *Eur* 94–18; rtd 97. *chemin du Pommier 22, CH-1218 Le Grand Saconnex, Geneva, Switzerland* T: (0041) (22) 798 8586 E: hpettingell@hotmail.com

PETTIT, Canon Anthony David. b 72. Univ of Cen England in Birm BA 94 MA 95 St Jo Coll Dur BA 01. Cranmer Hall Dur 98. **d** 01 **p** 02. C Gt Malvern St Mary *Worc* 01–04; P-in-c Cradley 04–05; TV Halas 05–10; P-in-c Paget St Paul Bermuda from 10; Dioc Communications Officer 13–17; Dioc Dir Tr and Discipleship from 16; Hon Can Bermuda from 19. *PO Box*

HM 2941, Hamilton HM MX, Bermuda T: (001) (441) 236 5880 E: revant@anglican.bm

PETTIT, James Lee. b 78. Lon Bible Coll BA 01 MA 03. Ox Min Course 07. **d** 09 **p** 10. C Faversham *Cant* 09–13; TV Sittingbourne w Bobbing 13–17; PtO *S'wark* from 17. *17 Martingales Close, Richmond TW10 7JJ* E: jamesthemonk@gmail.com

PETTITT, Canon Robin Adrian. b 50. Newc Univ BA 77 MRTPI 79. St Steph Ho Ox 81. **d** 83 **p** 84. C Warrington St Elphin *Liv* 83–87; C Torrisholme *Blackb* 87–93; P-in-c Charnock Richard 93–00; Dioc Par Development Officer 93–98; Sec Dioc Adv Cttee for the Care of Chs 98–99; C Broughton 00–01; rtd 01; PtO *Liv* from 03; *Eur* from 17; Hon Can Wiawso Ghana from 13. *Urb El Aspre, Carrer Les Fonts 19, 03790 Orba (Alicante), Spain* T: (0034) 965 583 447 M: (0034) 677 638 449

PETTMAN, Mrs Hilary Susan. b 45. STETS 99. **d** 02 **p** 03. NSM Shottermill *Guildf* 02–08; PtO from 08. *Stacey's Farm Cottage, Thursley Road, Elstead, Godalming GU8 6DG* T: (01252) 703217 E: hilarypettman@btinternet.com

PETTS, Mrs Anna Carolyn. b 44. St Mich Coll Sarum CertEd 65. STETS 00. **d** 03 **p** 04. NSM Hordle *Win* 03–11; NSM NW Hants 11–15; rtd 15; PtO *Win* from 16. *8 Woodland Way, New Milton BH25 5RT* E: carolynpetts@tiscali.co.uk

PETTY, Alicia Christina Margaret. *See* DRING, Alicia Christina Margaret

PETTY, Brian. b 34. Man Univ BA 90. St Aid Birkenhead 59. **d** 62 **p** 63. C Meole Brace *Lich* 62–65; Chapl RAF 65–69; Australia 70–75; P-in-c Kimbolton w Middleton-on-the-Hill *Heref* 76–79; P-in-c Pudleston-cum-Whyle w Hatfield, Docklow etc 76–79; P-in-c Haddenham *Ely* 79–80; V 80–84; V Fairfield *Derby* 84–90; Chapl St Geo Sch Ascot 90–93; TR Sampford Peverell, Uplowman, Holcombe Rogus etc *Ex* 93–99; RD Cullompton 95–99; rtd 99; PtO *Ex* 99–02; Hon C Diptford, N Huish, Harberton, Harbertonford etc 02–13. *23 Gracey Court, Woodland Road, Broadclyst, Exeter EX5 3GA* E: petty245@btinternet.com

PETTY, Duncan. *See* PETTY, William Duncan

PETTY, Capt Stuart. b 56. Chich Th Coll 91. **d** 93 **p** 94. CA from 88; C W Bromwich St Andr w Ch Ch *Lich* 93–96; Asst Chapl Walsall Hosps NHS Trust 96–00; Sen Chapl Walsall Healthcare NHS Trust 00–03; Chapl Team Ldr R Wolv Hosps NHS Trust 03–08; Sen Chapl York Hosps NHS Foundn Trust 08–14; Asst Chapl R Wolv NHS Trust 14–19; Chapl from 19. *New Cross Hospital, Wolverhampton Road, Heath Town, Wolverhampton WV10 0QP* T: (01902) 307999

PETTY, William Duncan. b 55. Ex Univ BSc 76 Leic Univ PGCE 77. Oak Hill Th Coll 97. **d** 99 **p** 00. C Burscough Bridge *Liv* 99–04; Min Tanhouse The Oaks CD 04–21; AD Ormskirk 16–19; rtd 21. *7 Roseland Park, Camborne TR14 8LU* M: 07812-723567 E: duncanpetty@hotmail.co.uk

PETZER, Garth Stephen. MBE 99. Rhodes Univ BTh 95. St Paul's Coll Grahamstown. **d** 88 **p** 91. C Queenstown St Mich S Africa 88–89; C E London St Sav 90–93; R E London St Martin 93–95; Chapl RN 96–03 and 04–07; CF 03–04; rtd 07; PtO *Nor* 04–07. *43 Damask Way, Warminster BA12 9PP* M: 07803-436897 E: petzeggs@hotmail.com

PETZSCH, Hugo Max David. b 57. Edin Univ MA 79 BD 83 PhD 95 FRSCM. Edin Th Coll 80. **d** 83 **p** 84. C Dollar *St And* 83–86; NZ 86–90; P-in-c Alyth, Blairgowrie and Coupar Angus *St And* 90–91; Chapl Glenalmond Coll 91–98; Dep Headmaster Benenden Sch 99–12; rtd 12. *3 Baxley Court, Campion Square, Dunton Green, Sevenoaks TN14 5FE*

PEVERELL, Canon Paul Harrison. b 57. Hull Univ BA 80. Ripon Coll Cuddesdon. **d** 82 **p** 83. C Cottingham *York* 82–85; V Middlesbrough St Martin 85–93; V Gt Ayton w Easby and Newton under Roseberry from 93; P-in-c Nunthorpe 17–18; Hon Can Ho Ghana from 04. *The Vicarage, Low Green, Great Ayton, Middlesbrough TS9 6NN* T: (01642) 722333 E: revpev@btinternet.com

✠**PEYTON, The Rt Revd Nigel.** b 51. JP 87. Edin Univ MA 73 BD 76 Lanc Univ PhD 09. Union Th Sem (NY) STM 77 Edin Th Coll 73. **d** 76 **p** 77 **c** 11. Chapl St Paul's Cathl Dundee *Bre* 76–82; Dioc Youth Chapl 76–85; Chapl Invergowrie 79–82; P-in-c 82–85; Chapl Univ Hosp Dundee 82–85; V Nottingham All SS *S'well* 85–91; P-in-c Lambley 91–99; Chapl Bluecoat Sch Nottm 90–92; Dioc Min Development Adv *S'well* 91–99; Adn Newark 99–11; Bp Bre 11–17; Bp Miss to Seafarers Scotland 13–17; rtd 17; Hon Teaching Fell Lanc Univ *Blackb* 10–18; Hon Scholar Liv Univ from 18; Hon Can Iowa USA from 12; Hon Asst Bp Linc from 17; PtO *S'well* from 18. *8 Bishops Place, Welton, Lincoln LN2 3FR* T: (01673) 862174 M: 07974-402449 E: nigel@peytons.org

PEYTON JONES, Mrs Dorothy Helen. b 58. LMH Ox BA 79 MPhil 80 DipSW 02. Trin Coll Bris 84. **dss** 86 **d** 87 **p** 94. W Holloway St Luke *Lon* 86–89; Par Dn 87–89; C Glas

St Oswald 89–92; NSM Drumchapel 92–98; PtO *Ely* 98–03; NSM Chesterton St Andr from 03; Ind Chapl 09–12. *71 Humberstone Road, Cambridge CB4 1JD* T: (01223) 523485 *or* 311727 M: 07503-746520 E: dorothypj@ntlworld.com *or* dorothy@peytonjones.org

PHAIR, Neal David Stewart. b 70. Limerick Univ BA 98 UCD HDipEd 99 TCD MPhil 02. CITC 99. **d** 02 **p** 03. C Ballymena w Ballyclug *Conn* 02–05; I Ballintoy w Rathlin and Dunseverick 05–07; Chapl Dub Inst of Tech 07–10; R Cherbury w Gainfield *Ox* 10–14; I Ballybay w Mucknoe and Clontibret *Clogh* 14–19; I Swords w Donabate and Kilsallaghan *D & G* from 19. *The Rectory, Church Road, Swords, Co Dublin, Republic of Ireland* E: nealphair@gmail.com

PHARAOH, Carol Helen. b 63. Preston Poly BTech 84. Cranmer Hall Dur 96. **d** 98 **p** 99. C Heaton Ch Ch *Man* 98–02; TV Walkden and Lt Hulton 02–09; P-in-c E Farnworth and Kearsley 09–10; TR Farnworth, Kearsley and Stoneclough 10–19; TR Blackrod, Daisy Hill, Westhoughton and Wingates from 19. *The Rectory, Market Street, Westhoughton, Bolton BL5 3AZ* T: (01942) 859251 E: carol.pharaoh@gmail.com

PHELPS, Canon Arthur Charles. b 26. St Cath Coll Cam BA 50 MA 55. Ridley Hall Cam 51. **d** 53 **p** 54. C Kirkdale St Lawr *Liv* 53–56; C Rainham *Chelmsf* 56–60; Min Collier Row St Jas CD 60–65; V Collier Row St Jas 65–75; R Thorpe Morieux w Preston and Brettenham *St E* 75–84; R Rattlesden w Thorpe Morieux and Brettenham 84–90; Hon Can *St E* 84–90; rtd 90; PtO *Truro* 90–00; *St E* from 01. *8 Northfield Court, Aldeburgh IP15 5LU* T: (01728) 454772

PHELPS, Ian Ronald. b 28. Lon Univ BSc 53 PhD 57 FLS 58. Chich Th Coll 57. **d** 59 **p** 60. C Brighton Gd Shep Preston *Chich* 59–61; C Sullington 62–64; C Storrington 62–64; R Newtimber w Pyecombe 64–68; V Brighton St Luke 68–74; TV Brighton Resurr 74–76; V Peacehaven 76–94; rtd 94; PtO *Chich* from 94. *2 Kingston Green, Seaford BN25 4NB* T: (01323) 899511 E: prescote1849@outlook.com *or* prescote1849@outlook.com

PHENNA, Timothy Peter. b 69. Ridley Hall Cam BTh 01. **d** 01 **p** 02. C Woodseats St Chad *Sheff* 01–04; USA from 04. *965 Colorow Road, Golden CO 80401, USA* E: timphenna@yahoo.co.uk

PHILBRICK, Craig Edward. b 86. Win Univ BA 11 Dur Univ BA 19. Wycliffe Hall Ox 16. **d** 19 **p** 20. C N Stoneham and Bassett *Win* 19–20; C Win Ch Ch from 20. *Address temp unknown* M: 07539-408004

PHILBRICK, Canon Gary James. b 57. Southn Univ BA 78 K Alfred's Coll Win CertEd 79 MA(Theol) 00 Edin Univ BD 86. Edin Th Coll 83. **d** 86 **p** 87. C Southampton Maybush St Pet *Win* 86–90; R Fawley 90–00; P-in-c Swaythling 00–04; V 04–13; AD Southampton 07–13; P-in-c Fordingbridge and Breamore and Hale etc 13–17; R Fordingbridge and Hyde and Breamore etc from 17; AD Christchurch from 13; Hon Can Win Cathl from 09. *The Rectory, 71 Church Street, Fordingbridge SP6 1BB* T: (01425) 839622 *or* 653163 E: gary.philbrick@dsl.pipex.com *or* rector@avonvalleychurches.org.uk

PHILIP, Andrew. b 75. Edin Univ MA 98. Scottish Episc Inst BA 18. **d** 18 **p** 19. Chapl Edin St Mary from 18. *28 Braehead Drive, Linlithgow EH49 6EG* T: 0131-225 6293 M: 07593-905473 E: chaplain@cathedral.net

PHILIP, Mathew. b 54. Leeds Univ BSc 77 MSc 78 PhD 83 Surrey Univ BA 05. STETS 02. **d** 05 **p** 06. NSM Patcham *Chich* 05–20; NSM Brighton Gd Shep Preston from 20. *Hillside Lodge, 76 Redhill Drive, Brighton BN1 5FL* T: (01273) 883726 M: 07756-005331 E: m.philip1968r@gmail.com

PHILIP BARTHOLOMEW, Brother. *See* KENNEDY, Philip Bartholomew

PHILLIP, Ms Gail Ann. b 72. Trevelyan Coll Dur BA 95 Sheff Univ MA 09. St Jo Coll Nottm 14. **d** 16 **p** 17. C Kenilworth St Jo Cov 16–19; V Exhall from 19. *36 St Giles Road, Coventry CV7 9HA* M: 07794-643335 E: revgailphillip@outlook.com

PHILLIP, Isaiah Ezekiel. b 59. Univ of W Indies BA 88. Codrington Coll Barbados 85. **d** 88 **p** 89. C St Jo Cathl Antigua 88–91; R St Geo Dominica 91–96; R All SS Antigua 96–01; P-in-c Handsworth St Mich *Birm* 02–05; V Basseterre St Kitts-Nevis from 05. *St Peter's Rectory, PO Box 702, Basseterre, St Kitts, West Indies* T: (001869) (465) 2774 E: phillipisaiah@hotmail.com

PHILLIPS, Mrs Adele. b 59. Newc Univ LLB 84. NEOC 04. **d** 07 **p** 08. NSM Gateshead *Dur* from 07; PtO *Newc* from 15. *47 Blackstone Court, Blaydon NE21 4HH* T: 0191-414 0955 M: 07752-325736 E: revadele@gmail.com

PHILLIPS, Alison Claire. b 72. St Edm Hall Ox BA 93 Univ Coll Lon MA 99. St Mellitus Coll 15. **d** 18 **p** 19. NSM Edmonton All SS w St Mich *Lon* from 18. *33 Orpington Road, London N21 3PD* T: (020) 8882 8874 M: 07910-315918 E: alisonphillips2@gmail.com

PHILLIPS, Anne Jacqueline. d 17 **p** 17. NSM Matlock Bank and Tansley *Derby* 17–21; PtO from 21. *Tagg Hill Cottage, 43 Church Street, Matlock DE4 3BY* T: (01629) 583281 E: annejphillips@icloud.com

PHILLIPS, Canon Anthony Charles Julian. b 36. Lon Univ BD 63 AKC 63 G&C Coll Cam PhD 67 St Jo Coll Ox MA 75 DPhil 80. Coll of Resurr Mirfield 66. **d** 66 **p** 67. C-in-c Chesterton Gd Shep CD *Ely* 66–69; Dean, Chapl and Fell Trin Hall Cam 69–74; Hon Bp's Chapl *Nor* 70–71; Chapl and Fell St Jo Coll Ox 75–86; Lect Th Jes Coll Ox 75–86; Lect Th Hertf Coll Ox 84–86; Hd Master K Sch Cant 86–96; Hon Can Cant Cathl 87–96; Can Th Truro Cathl 86–02; PtO 02–10; rtd 01. *47 Warwick Street, Oxford OX4 1SZ* T: (01865) 244871 E: a.phillips920@btinternet.com

PHILLIPS, Benjamin Guy. b 75. Wycliffe Hall Ox. **d** 02 **p** 03. C Cockermouth w Embleton and Wythop *Carl* 02–05; V Stanwix 05–12; Chapl Rio de Janeiro Ch Ch Brazil 12–15; R Streetsville Canada 15–19; P-in-c Dalston w Cumdivock, Raughton Head and Wreay *Carl* from 19; C Inglewood Gp from 21. *The Vicarage, Townhead Road, Dalston, Carlisle CA5 7JF*

PHILLIPS, Benjamin Lambert Meyrick. b 64. K Coll Cam BA 86 MA 90. Ridley Hall Cam 87. **d** 90 **p** 91. C Wareham *Sarum* 90–94; C Chipping Barnet w Arkley *St Alb* 94–96; V Bodicote *Ox* 96–12; AD Deddington 05–10; V Towcester w Caldecote and Easton Neston etc *Pet* 12–19; V Goring and Streatley w S Stoke *Ox* from 19. *The Vicarage, Manor Road, Goring, Reading RG8 9DR* E: vicarofgsandss@yahoo.com

PHILLIPS, Mrs Brenda. b 41. St Hugh's Coll Ox BA 63 MA 68. **d** 04 **p** 05. OLM Sherborne w Castleton, Lillington and Longburton *Sarum* 04–11; rtd 11; PtO *Sarum* from 11. *5 Earls Close, Sherborne DT9 3RS* E: revd.brenda@btinternet.com

PHILLIPS, Brian Edward Dorian William. b 36. Bris Univ BA 58. Ripon Hall Ox 58. **d** 60 **p** 61. C Ross *Heref* 60–64; Chapl RAF 64–68; Hon C Fringford w Hethe and Newton Purcell *Ox* 68–73; Chapl Howell's Sch Denbigh 73–76; C Cleobury Mortimer w Hopton Wafers *Heref* 76–80; V Dixton 80–02; rtd 02; PtO *Heref* from 02. *37 Duxmere Drive, Ross-on-Wye HR9 5UW* T: (01989) 562993 M: 07712-071558 E: pastorprint@gmx.co.uk

PHILLIPS, Caroline Jill. b 80. Nottm Univ BA 02 Man Univ MA 04 Birm Univ ThD 16. Qu Coll Birm 07. **d** 10 **p** 11. C Ollerton w Boughton *S'well* 10–13; P-in-c Mansfield St Aug 13–15; P-in-c Pleasley Hill 13–15; V Mansfield St Aug and Pleasley Hill 15–19; V Mansfield St Mark from 19; V Mansfield SS Pet and Paul from 19. *The Vicarage, Lindhurst Lane, Mansfield NG18 4JE* E: revcarolinephillips@gmail.com

PHILLIPS, Christopher Peter. b 82. St Jo Coll Dur BA 00 Ox Univ BA 12. Ripon Coll Cuddesdon 10. **d** 13 **p** 14. C Ilkley St Marg *Leeds* 13–16; V Willesden St Mary *Lon* from 16. *110 Ellesmere Road, London NW10 1JS* M: 07917-798285 E: frchrisphillips@gmail.com

PHILLIPS, David Arthur. b 36. S Dios Minl Tr Scheme 90. **d** 94 **p** 95. NSM Canford Magna *Sarum* 94–06; rtd 06; PtO *Sarum* from 14. *32 Lynwood Drive, Wimborne BH21 1UG* T: (01202) 880262 E: dphillips581@btinternet.com

PHILLIPS, David Gordon. b 60. Toronto Univ BASc 82. Wycliffe Coll Toronto MDiv 95. **d** 94 **p** 95. R Kawawachikamach Canada 94–99; Exec Adn Prince Albert 99–03; R Petite Riviere and New Dublin 04–09; Chapl Palermo *Eur* 10–13; Chapl Utrecht w Zwolle 13–21; PtO from 21. *Address temp unknown* E: revdgphillips@hotmail.com

PHILLIPS, David Keith. b 61. New Coll Ox MA 90 St Jo Coll Dur BA 90. Cranmer Hall Dur 88. **d** 91 **p** 92. C Denton Holme *Carl* 91–94; C Chadderton Ch Ch *Man* 94–98; Gen Sec See Ch Soc 98–11; Public Preacher *St Alb* 98–11; V Chorley St Jas *Blackb* from 11. *St James's Vicarage, St James's Place, Chorley PR6 0NA* T: (01257) 233714 E: vicar@stjameschorley.org

PHILLIPS, David Thomas. b 47. NEOC 03. **d** 05 **p** 06. NSM Gt and Lt Driffield *York* 05–06; C Elloughton and Brough w Brantingham 06–10; rtd 11; P-in-c Vernet-les-Bains *Eur* from 11. *Lot 22, Cams de Baille, 66360 Olette, France* E: dphill9590@yahoo.co.uk

PHILLIPS, Eldon. b 50. Univ of Wales (Cardiff) BEd 85 MEd 92. St Mich Coll Llan. **d** 90 **p** 91. NSM Merthyr Cynog and Dyffryn Honddu etc *S & B* 90–94; LtO *St D* 94–99; NSM Ystradgynlais *S & B* 95–99; Chapl Trin Coll Carmarthen 95–99; P-in-c Llanrhidian w Llanmadoc and Cheriton *S & B* 99–05; Dioc Press Officer from 02; NSM Burry Port and Pwll *St D* 07–15; PtO *S & B* from 13; *St D* from 15. *2 Gerddi Glasfryn, Llanelli SA15 3LL* T: (01554) 744770 E: reveldon@btinternet.com

PHILLIPS, Mrs Emma Catharine. b 62. St Anne's Coll Ox BA 84. Trin Coll Bris BA 99. **d** 99 **p** 00. C Shawbury *Lich* 99–01; C Moreton Corbet 99–01; C Stanton on Hine Heath 99–01; C Cen Telford 01–02; TV 03–07; PtO 07–09; NSM Cen Telford 09–13; Chapl Severn Hospice from 09; PtO *Lich* 14–16; *Heref* from 16. *The Rectory, Pleasly Lane, Longden, Shrewsbury SY5 8ET* T: (01743) 861003

PHILLIPS (née PULLEN), Frances Jill. b 54. Birm Univ MB, ChB 76. WEMTC 10. **d** 13 **p** 14. NSM St Weonards *Heref* from 13. *New House, Garway Hill, Hereford HR2 8EZ* T: (01981) 240032 E: franjphillips@gmail.com

PHILLIPS, Geoffrey Clarke. b 50. SWMTC 94. **d** 96 **p** 97. NSM Georgeham *Ex* 96–98; Chapl HM YOI Huntercombe and Finnamore 99–00; Chapl HM Pris Shepton Mallet 01–03; Chapl Children's Hospice SW 07–15; rtd 15; PtO *Ex* 15–19. *8 Putsborough Close, Georgeham, Braunton EX33 1JX* T: (01271) 890346 E: geoffjancroyde@yahoo.co.uk

PHILLIPS, Ms Gillian. b 44. EMMTC 07. **d** 10 **p** 12. NSM Old Brampton and Great Barlow and Loundsley Green *Derby* 10–11; NSM Wrockwardine Deanery *Lich* 12–14; rtd 14. *78 Lawley Gate, Telford TF4 2NZ* T: (01952) 506038

PHILLIPS, Graham Donald. b 57. Magd Coll Cam BA 79 MA 83 Goldsmiths' Coll Lon PGCE 90. Qu Coll Birm 08. **d** 12 **p** 13. C Madeley *Heref* 12–15; R Gt Hanwood and Longden and Annscroft etc from 15. *The Rectory, Pleasly Lane, Longden, Shrewsbury SY5 8ET* T: (01743) 861003 E: revgrahamphillips@gmail.com

PHILLIPS, Ivor Lyn. b 44. Leeds Univ BA 70. Cuddesdon Coll 69. **d** 71 **p** 72. C Bedlinog *Llan* 71–73; C Roath 73–77; TV Wolverhampton All SS *Lich* 77–78; TV Wolverhampton 78–81; Chapl Charing Cross Hosp Lon 81–91; Chapl Milan w Genoa and Lugano *Eur* 91–94; C Hampstead St Jo *Lon* 95–00; V Whitton St Aug 00–09; rtd 09; PtO *S'wark* 10–11; *Newc* from 12; *Eur* from 18. *10 Northumberland Avenue, Berwick-upon-Tweed TD15 1JZ* T: (01289) 305075 M: 07702-022501 E: lyn.phillipsuk@gmail.com

PHILLIPS, Jason Paul Benedict Blezard. b 73. Man Metrop Univ BA 95 CertEd 95 PhD 05 FCollT 09. Ripon Coll Cuddesdon MA 09. **d** 09 **p** 10. C Mid Trent *Lich* 09–14; C Stafford St Mary and Marston 14–15; C Blakenall Heath 15; V Whittington w Weeford 15–20; TR Mid Trent from 20; Dioc Voc Adv from 14. *The Rectory, Stafford Road, Weston, Stafford ST18 0HX* E: revdjason@fastmail.co.uk

PHILLIPS (née LANGLEY), Mrs Jean. b 52. St Mary's Coll Chelt CertEd 73. WEMTC 03. **d** 06 **p** 07. NSM Bishop's Cleeve *Glouc* 06–08; NSM Bishop's Cleeve and Woolstone w Gotherington etc 08–13; rtd 13. *3 St Nicholas Drive, Cheltenham GL50 4RY* T: (01242) 237683 E: jeanp52@btinternet.com

PHILLIPS, John. b 50. ACIB 74. NOC 01. **d** 04. NSM Wavertree H Trin *Liv* 04–18; rtd 18. *12 Montclair Drive, Liverpool L18 0HA* T: 0151-722 2542 E: jpipps@hotmail.com

PHILLIPS, John David. b 29. G&C Coll Cam BA 50 MA 54 CertEd 69. SWMTC 85. **d** 87 **p** 88. NSM St Martin w E and W Looe *Truro* 87–88; NSM St Merryn 88–94; rtd 94; PtO *Truro* from 94. *Restings, Plaidy, Looe PL13 1LF* T: (01503) 262121

PHILLIPS, John Eldon. b 50. Univ of Wales (Cardiff) BEd 85 MEd 92. St Mich Coll Llan. **d** 90 **p** 91. NSM Merthyr Cynog and Dyffryn Honddu etc *S & B* 90–94; LtO *St D* 94–99; NSM Ystradgynlais *S & B* 95–99; Chapl Trin Coll Carmarthen 95–99; P-in-c Llanrhidian w Llanmadoc and Cheriton *S & B* 99–05; Dioc Press Officer from 02; NSM Burry Port and Pwll *St D* 07–15; PtO *S & B* from 13; *St D* from 15. *2 Gerddi Glasfryn, Llanelli SA15 3LL* T: (01554) 744770 E: reveldon@btinternet.com

PHILLIPS, Jonathan Richard. b 79. Liv Univ BA 01 Cam Univ BTh 13. Ridley Hall Cam 10. **d** 13 **p** 14. C Lache cum Saltney *Ches* 13–17; P-in-c Chester St Pet 17–21; V from 21. *20 Lime Wood Close, Chester CH2 2HD* T: (01244) 403634 M: 07813-709035 E: pioneerministerpic@chesterstpeter.org.uk

PHILLIPS, Lamont Wellington Sanderson. b 33. S'wark Ord Course 73. **d** 76 **p** 78. NSM Tottenham St Paul *Lon* 76–83; P-in-c Upper Clapton St Matt 83–88; V 88–97; rtd 98. *24 Berkshire Gardens, London N18 2LF* T: (020) 8807 7025

PHILLIPS, Mrs Lena. b 61. STETS 12. **d** 15 **p** 16. NSM Shirley *Win* from 15. *11 Clifton Road, Southampton SO15 4GU* T: (023) 8077 4307 E: lena@stjamesbythepark.org

PHILLIPS, Lyn. See PHILLIPS, Ivor Lyn

PHILLIPS, Mark. b 66. STETS 10. **d** 13 **p** 14. C Portland *Sarum* 13–16; V Charminster and Stinsford 16–17; P-in-c Bradford Peverell, Stratton, Frampton etc 16–17; R Charminster, Stinsford and the Chalk Stream villages from 17. *The Vicarage, Mill Lane, Charminster, Dorchester DT2 9QP* E: revdmarkphillips@outlook.com

PHILLIPS, Mary Alice. See ILSLEY, Mary Alice

PHILLIPS, Matthew Paul. b 89. Trin Coll Cam BA 11 BTh 17 MPhil 18. Ridley Hall Cam 15. **d** 18 **p** 19. C Ely 18–21; P-in-c Dunton w Wrestlingworth and Eyeworth *St Alb* from 21; Tutor Local Min Progr *Guildf* from 21. *29 Fen Reach, Dunton, Biggleswade SG18 8RZ* T: (01767) 512122 E: matt@dwe.org.uk

PHILLIPS, Michael John. b 54. JP . Trent Poly BA 77. Sarum & Wells Th Coll 78. **d** 81 **p** 82. C Killay *S & B* 81–83; C Treboeth 83–85; Hong Kong 85–88; Japan 88–91; TR Is of Scilly *Truro* 91–95; TR Cwmbran *Mon* 95–15; AD Pontypool 12–15; R Jersey St Pet *Win* from 15. *The Rectory, La Rue du Presbytere, St Peter, Jersey JE3 7ZH* T: (01534) 481805 E: mj-phillips1@hotmail.co.uk

PHILLIPS, Michael Thomas. b 46. CQSW 81. Linc Th Coll 89. **d** 90 **p** 91. C Hyson Green *S'well* 90–91; C Basford w Hyson Green 91–93; Chapl HM Pris Gartree 93–99; Chapl HM Pris Nottm 99–08; rtd 08; Hon C Radford All So and St Pet *S'well* 08–12; PtO from 12. *12 Edgbaston Gardens, Aspley, Nottingham NG8 5AY* T: 0115-929 7029 E: bigviola@hotmail.com

PHILLIPS, Noel William. b 70. Lanc Univ BSc 92 PhD 99 St Martin's Coll Lanc PGCE 97. Ox Min Couse 14. **d** 17 **p** 18. C Coventry Caludon *Cov* 17–19; C Wyken 19–20; R Curdworth, Middleton and Wishaw *Birm* from 20. *The Rectory, Glebe Fields, Curdworth, Sutton Coldfield B76 9ES* M: 07779-244174 E: n.w.phillips@live.com

PHILLIPS, Mrs Patricia. b 45. Glouc Sch of Min 83. **dss** 86 **d** 87 **p** 94. Newent and Gorsley w Cliffords Mesne *Glouc* 86–95; C 87–95; P-in-c Childswyckham w Aston Somerville, Buckland etc 95–97; R 97–00; R Redmarley D'Abitot, Bromesberrow, Pauntley etc 00–10; rtd 10; PtO *Glouc* from 14. *5 Freemans Orchard, Newent GL18 1TX* T: (01531) 828444

PHILLIPS, Miss Pauline. b 54. **d** 96 **p** 97. OLM Mossley *Man* 96–16; rtd 16. *82 Waterton Lane, Mossley, Ashton-under-Lyne OL5 0NQ* T: (01457) 832151 M: 07484-838332 E: pauline.phillips2015@gmail.com

PHILLIPS, Peter Miles Lucas. b 44. Reading Univ BA 66 QUB DipEd 69 Univ of Wales (Cardiff) MEd 88 Bris Univ MA 07 Cardiff Univ PhD 14. St Mich Coll Llan 90. **d** 92 **p** 93. Dep Hd Teacher Dynevor Sch 82–96; NSM Llangyfelach *S & B* 92–96; Dep Chapl HM Pris Liv 96–97; Chapl HM Pris Usk and Prescoed 97–01; Chapl HM Pris Bris 01–04; rtd 04; PtO Bris 04–12; Chapl Wesley Coll Bris 08–11. *Gwalia, Felindre, Swansea SA5 7PQ* T: (01792) 772523 E: revdpeterphillips@yahoo.co.uk

PHILLIPS, Rachel Susan. b 64. Newnham Coll Cam BA 86 MA 90 Nottm Univ MPhil 11 Solicitor 89. St Jo Coll Nottm 04. **d** 07 **p** 08. C Eastcote St Lawr *Lon* 07–10; P-in-c Northaw and Cuffley *St Alb* 10–13; V 13–17; RD Cheshunt 13–17; Can Res Roch Cathl 17–19; TR Dunstable *St Alb* from 19. *The Priory Office, Chew's House, 77 High Street South, Dunstable LU6 3SF* E: revrachelphillips@gmail.com

PHILLIPS, Richard Matthew. b 76. St Cath Coll Cam BA 98 MA 02. Ripon Coll Cuddesdon 11. **d** 13 **p** 14. C Walton H Trin *Ox* 13–16; V Long Crendon w Chearsley and Nether Winchendon from 16. *The Vicarage, 84A High Street, Long Crendon, Aylesbury HP18 9AL* M: 07541-197220 E: reverend.richard.phillips@gmail.com

PHILLIPS, Richard Paul. b 76. Man Univ BA 08. Trin Coll Bris 09. **d** 11 **p** 12. C Kingston upon Hull St Aid Southcoates *York* 11–14; V from 14. *St Aidan's Vicarage, 139 Southcoates Avenue, Hull HU9 3HF* M: 07944-541968 E: rich.phillips76@gmail.com

PHILLIPS, Robert Gareth. b 82. Bris Univ BSc 04. Oak Hill Th Coll BA 16 MA 18. **d** 17 **p** 18. C Eastrop *Win* 17–21; R from 21. *Eastrop Rectory, 2A Wallis Road, Basingstoke RG21 3DW* T: (01256) 357745 M: 07807-907461 E: rob_phil1@hotmail.com *or* rob.phillips@stmarys-basingstoke.org.uk

PHILLIPS, Robin Michael. b 33. AKC 58. **d** 59 **p** 60. C Hanwell St Mellitus *Lon* 59–61; C St Margaret's-on-Thames 61–64; C Hangleton *Chich* 64–68; V Mellor *Derby* 68–95; RD Glossop 89–93; rtd 95; Hon C Bridekirk *Carl* 95–96. *102 Elleray Gardens, Windermere LA23 1JE* T: (015394) 88841

PHILLIPS, Timothy Leo. b 72. Bris Univ BSc 95 PhD 99. Trin Coll Bris BA 01 MA 02. **d** 02 **p** 03. C Leic H Trin w St Jo 02–05; TV Ashby-de-la-Zouch and Breedon on the Hill from 05. *Holy Trinity Vicarage, 1 Trinity Close, Ashby-de-la-Zouch LE65 2GQ* T: (01530) 412339

PHILLIPS, Wayne. b 45. **d** 10 **p** 11. NSM Pontefract All SS *Wakef* 10–14; *Leeds* 14–19; NSM Pontefract from 19. *16 Maple Walk, Knottingley WF11 0PU* T: (01977) 678024 E: wayne.phillips16@btinternet.com

PHILLIPSON (née MACKAY), Alison. b 62. Teesside Univ BA 00. NEOC 01. **d** 04 **p** 05. C Stokesley w Seamer *York* 04–08; P-in-c Cosby *Leic* 08–09; P-in-c Whetstone 08–09; V Coatham and Dormanstown *York* 09–14; R Guisborough from 14. *The Rectory, Church Street, Guisborough TS14 6BS* E: alisonphillipson@aol.com

PHILLIPSON-MASTERS, Miss Susan Patricia. b 52. Sussex Univ CertEd 73 K Alfred's Coll Win BEd 81 Leeds Univ MA 04 Glos Univ MA 09 FIST 76 ACP 80. Trin Coll Bris 86. **d** 89 **p** 95. C Saltford w Corston and Newton St Loe *B & W*

89–94; C Uphill 94–97; C Nailsea Ch Ch w Tickenham 97–98; P-in-c Tredington and Darlingscott w Newbold on Stour *Cov* 98–00; P-in-c The Stanleys *Glouc* 00–11; Chapl Wycliffe Prep Sch 07–11; rtd 11; PtO *Glouc* 16–19; Hon C Cromhall, Tortworth, Tytherington, Falfield etc from 19. *Recsretreat, 1 Oakleaze Road, Thornbury, Bristol BS35 2LG* T: (01454) 600674 E: suepm@sky.com

PHILLPOT, Donald John. b 27. St Jo Coll Dur BA 53. **d** 55 **p** 56. C Southmead *Bris* 55–60; C Brislington St Luke 60–63; R Stapleton *Heref* 63–68; V Dorrington 63–68; P-in-c Astley Abbotts 68–78; R Bridgnorth w Tasley 68–78; V Lillington *Cov* 78–92; rtd 92; PtO *Glouc* from 92. *22 Williams Orchard, Highnam, Gloucester GL2 8EL* T: (01452) 386844

PHILP (née **NOBLE), Canon Ann Carol.** b 42. Sarum Dioc Tr Coll CertEd 63 Southn Univ MA(Ed) 89 MCIPD. S Dios Minl Tr Scheme 93. **d** 95 **p** 96. Dir Sarum Chr Cen 93–98; Chapl Sarum Cathl 95–02; Dioc NSM Officer 98–02; P-in-c Woodford Valley w Archers Gate 02–12; Dioc Dir of Ords 02–07; Bp's Dom Chapl 07–12; Can and Preb Sarum Cathl 05–12; rtd 12; PtO *Sarum* from 12. *55 The Close, Salisbury SP1 2EL* T: (01722) 555178 E: acphilp55@virginmedia.com

PHILPOTT, Barbara May. *See* WILKINSON, Barbara May

PHILPOTT, Canon John David. b 43. Leic Univ BA 64. Trin Coll Bris 69. **d** 72 **p** 73. C Knutsford St Jo and Toft *Ches* 72–75; C Bickenhill w Elmdon *Birm* 75–79; V Birm St Luke 79–91; RD Birm City 83–88; Hon Can Birm Cathl 89–91; V Chilvers Coton w Astley *Cov* 91–00; RD Nuneaton 95–00; Hon Can Cov Cathl 96–00; P-in-c Prague *Eur* 00–08; rtd 08; PtO *Eur* from 08; *Ex* from 09; *Birm* 17–20. *2 Portland Court, 1 Portland Avenue, Exmouth EX8 2DJ* T: (01395) 225044 E: jamphilpott@yahoo.com

PHILPOTT, Jonathan Mark. b 76. Chelt & Glouc Coll of HE BA 98. Trin Coll Bris BA 06 MA 10. **d** 07 **p** 08. C Lydney *Glouc* 07–10; P-in-c By Brook *Bris* 10–16; P-in-c Colerne w N Wraxall 10–11; C 11–16; P-in-c Berrow and Breane *B & W* 16–21; R from 21; RD Axbridge from 20. *1 Manor Way, Berrow, Burnham-on-Sea TA8 2RG* T: (01278) 751806 E: rev.jonathanphilpott@gmail.com

PHILPOTT, Preb Samuel. b 41. MBE 12. Kelham Th Coll 60. **d** 65 **p** 66. C Swindon New Town *Bris* 65–70; C Torquay St Martin Barton *Ex* 70–73; TV Withycombe Raleigh 73–76; V Shaldon 76–78; P-in-c Plymouth St Pet 78–80; V 80–09; RD Plymouth Devonport 86–93 and 95–01; Preb Ex Cathl 91–09; rtd 09; P-in-c Plymouth St Pet and H Apostles *Ex* 09–13; PtO from 15; *Truro* from 16. *21 Plaistow Crescent, Plymouth PL5 2EA* T: (01752) 298502 E: prebphilpott@gmail.com

PHILPOTT-HOWARD, John Nigel. b 54. Univ of Wales Coll of Medicine MB, BCh 77 FRCPath 83. SEITE 99. **d** 02 **p** 03. NSM Shooters Hill Ch Ch *S'wark* 02–11; PtO 11–15; NSM E Greenwich from 15. *80 Charlton Road, London SE7 7EY* T: (020) 8858 4692 M: 07789-985415 E: philpotthoward@aol.com

PHILPS, Mark Seymour. b 51. Worc Coll Ox BA 73 MA 78 Lon Univ MA 75 Nottm Univ BA 79. St Jo Coll Nottm 77. **d** 80 **p** 81. C Chadwell Heath *Chelmsf* 80–83; C Woodford Wells 83–87; V Tipton St Matt *Lich* 87–02; TV Roxeth *Lon* 02–03; TR 03–11; V 11–15; rtd 15; PtO *Sarum* 16–21. *1 White Horse Road, Marlborough SN8 2FE* E: marksphilps@gmail.com

PHIPPS, David John. b 46. Bris Univ BSc 68 Ex Univ PhD 93 Nottm Univ PGCE 69. Trin Coll Bris 75. **d** 78 **p** 79. C Madron w Morvah *Truro* 78–80; C Kenilworth St Jo *Cov* 80–83; TV Barnstaple *Ex* 83–95; I Abercraf w Callwen w Capel Coelbren *S & B* 95–02; P-in-c Gulval and Madron *Truro* 02–05; rtd 05. *11 Walton Way, Barnstaple EX32 8AE* T: (01271) 349746

PHIPPS, Eluned Clare. b 77. Univ of Wales (Abth) BA 99 Univ Coll Chich PGCE 01. All Nations Chr Coll BA 06 Sarum Coll 18 SCTEI 18. **d** 20 **p** 21. C Win St Bart and St Lawr w St Swithun from 20. *1 Wolvesey Cottages, College Street, Winchester SO23 9NB* M: 07516-637485 E: eluned@threesaints.org.uk

PHIPPS, Mathew Jamie David. b 76. Univ of Wales (Abth) LLB 98 All Nations Chr Coll BA 08 Barrister 99 Solicitor 04. ERMC 13. **d** 15 **p** 17. C Madrid *Eur* 15–16; Bp's Dom Chapl *Win* from 16; Dep Dioc Registrar 19–20. *Wolvesey, Winchester SO23 9ND* T: (01962) 897082 E: mat.phipps@winchester.anglican.org

PHIZACKERLEY, The Ven Gerald Robert. b 29. Univ Coll Ox BA 52 MA 56. Wells Th Coll 52. **d** 54 **p** 55. C Carl St Barn 54–57; Chapl Abingdon Sch 57–64; R Gaywood, Bawsey and Mintlyn *Nor* 64–78; RD Lynn 68–78; Hon Can Nor Cathl 75–78; Hon Can Derby Cathl 78–96; P-in-c Ashford w Sheldon 78–96; Adn Chesterfield 78–96; rtd 96; PtO *Derby* 96–18; *Cov* from 96. *Archway Cottage, Hall Road, Leamington Spa CV32 5RA* T: (01926) 332740 E: phizleam@yahoo.co.uk

PHOEBE, Sister. *See* HANMER, Phoebe Margaret

PHYPERS, David John. b 39. Leic Univ BA 60 CertEd 61 Lon Univ BD 65. Linc Th Coll 76. **d** 78 **p** 79. NSM Normanton *Derby* 78–80; NSM Sinfin 80–87; LtO 87–88; P-in-c Denby 88–00; P-in-c Horsley Woodhouse 88–00; P-in-c Wormhill, Peak Forest w Peak Dale and Dove Holes 00–07; Adv for Chr Giving 00–07; rtd 07; PtO *Derby* from 07; Sec Rtd Clergy Assn 11–18. *15 Albert Road, Chaddesden, Derby DE21 6SL* T: (01332) 239134 E: david@phypers.co.uk

PICKARD, Mrs Patricia Anne. b 44. **d** 04 **p** 05. NSM Ovenden *Wakef* 04–14; *Leeds* 14; rtd 14; PtO *Leeds* from 14. *8 Chapel Lane, Oakworth, Keighley BD22 7HY*

⊕**PICKARD, The Rt Revd Stephen Kim.** b 52. Newc Univ Aus BCom 74 Van Mildert Coll Dur PhD 90. Melbourne Coll of Div BD 79 St Jo Coll Morpeth 77. **d** 80 **p** 80 **c** 07. C Singleton Australia 80–82; C Dur St Cuth 82–84; Chapl Van Mildert Coll Dur 84–90; Chapl Trev Coll Dur 84–90; Lect United Th Coll Sydney Australia 91–97; Dir St Mark's Nat Th Cen 98–06; Assoc Prof and Hd Th Chas Sturt Univ 99–06; Asst Bp Adelaide 07–10; Adn The Port Australia 07–10; Visiting Fell Ripon Coll Cuddesdon 10–11; Dir Ox Cen for Ecclesiology and Practical Th 10–11; Six Preacher Cant Cathl 11–12; Chief Exec Anglicare NSW Australia 12–13; Asst Bp Canberra and Goulburn from 12; Prof Chas Sturt Univ Australia from 13. *15 Blackall Street, Barton ACT 2600, Australia* T: (0061) (4) 7864 8751 E: s.k.pickard@gmail.com

PICKEN, David Anthony. b 63. Lon Univ BA 84 Kent Univ PGCE 85 Nottm Univ MA 96. Linc Th Coll 87. **d** 90 **p** 91. C Worth *Chich* 90–93; TV Wordsley *Worc* 93–97; TR 97–04; RD Kingswinford 01–04; TR High Wycombe *Ox* 04–12; AD Wycombe 07–11; Hon Can Ch Ch 11–12; Adn Newark *S'well* 12–20; Adn Lancaster *Blackb* from 20. *Shireshead Vicarage, Whinney Brow, Forton, Preston PR3 0AE* E: david.picken@blackburn.anglican.org

PICKERING, David Arthur Ashley. b 67. G&C Coll Cam BA 89. Wycliffe Hall Ox BTh 06. **d** 06 **p** 07. C Hornchurch H Cross *Chelmsf* 06–09; P-in-c Fyfield w Tubney and Kingston Bagpuize *Ox* 09–16; V from 16. *1 Oxford Road, Kingston Bagpuize, Abingdon OX13 5FZ* T: (01865) 820451 E: vicar.kbsft@gmail.com

PICKERING, Canon David Colville. b 41. Kelham Th Coll 61. **d** 66 **p** 67. C Chaddesden St Phil *Derby* 66–70; C New Mills 70–72; C Buxton 72–74; V Chesterfield SS Aug 74–90; R Whittington 90–99; P-in-c Hathersage 99; P-in-c Bamford 99; R Hathersage w Bamford and Derwent 00–06; Hon Can Derby Cathl 05–06; rtd 06; PtO *Derby* 06–18. *Les Chênes Verts, Chemin de St Laurent, Le Rang, 84750 Viens, France* T: (0033) 4 90 74 68 55 M: 6 33 84 95 86 E: pickport@gmail.com

PICKERING, John Alexander. b 41. TCD BA 63 MA 66. CITC 65. **d** 65 **p** 66. C Magheralin *D & D* 65–67; C-in-c Outeragh *K, E & A* 67–68; I 68–71; Deputation Sec Hibernian Bible Soc 71–74; C-in-c Drumgoon w Dernakesh, Ashfield etc *K, E & A* 74–80; I Keady w Armaghbreague and Derrynoose *Arm* 80–83; I Drumcree 83–07; rtd 07. *25 Twinem Court, Portadown, Craigavon BT63 5FH* T: (028) 3833 5704 M: 07752-339558

PICKERING, Mrs Kathleen Patricia. b 70. Victoria Univ (BC) BA 92. St Hild Coll 18. **d** 20 **p** 21. C Linc St Geo Swallowbeck from 20. *20 Swallowbeck Avenue, Lincoln LN6 7HA* M: 07980-604412 E: choicewords.kp@gmail.com

PICKERING, Mark Penrhyn. b 36. Liv Univ BA 59 St Cath Coll Ox BA 62 MA 67. Wycliffe Hall Ox 60. **d** 63 **p** 64. C Claughton cum Grange *Ches* 63–67; C Newland St Jo *York* 67–72; TV Marfleet 72–76; V Kingston upon Hull St Nic 76–85; V Elloughton and Brough w Brantingham 85–88; Chapl R Hull Hosps NHS Trust 88–99; Chapl Hull and E Yorks Hosps NHS Trust 99–01; PtO *York* 02–20. *43 Lowerdale, Elloughton, Brough HU15 1SD* T: (01482) 662102

PICKERING, Mrs Maureen Anne. b 46. Man Univ CertEd 67 Open Univ BA 88 MA 93 Leeds Univ MA 07. NOC 04. **d** 07 **p** 08. NSM Ches St Mary 07–15; PtO from 15. *Curzon Cottage, 2A Curzon Park South, Chester CH4 8AB* T: (01244) 677352 M: 07966-409404 E: mapickering@btinternet.com

PICKERING, Sally Ann. b 64. St Hild Coll 16. **d** 19 **p** 20. C Starbeck *Leeds* from 19. *6 Florin Drive, Knaresborough HG5 0WG* E: sally.pickering@leeds.anglican.org

PICKERSGILL, James Richard. b 74. Brunel Univ BA 96. Trin Coll Bris 11. **d** 13 **p** 14. C Winchcombe *Glouc* 13–17; C Market Harborough and The Transfiguration etc *Leic* from 17. *Ashtree House, 38 Alvington Way, Market Harborough LE16 7NF* T: (01858) 465876 E: james@harborough-anglican.org.uk

PICKETT, Brian Laurence. b 48. Reading Univ BA 70 Qu Coll Birm BA 73 MA 77. Ripon Coll Cuddesdon. **d** 88 **p** 88. C Highcliffe w Hinton Admiral *Win* 88–91; P-in-c Colbury 91–01; P-in-c W End 01–04; V 04–12; rtd 12; PtO *Win*

from 12. *6 Woodlands Gardens, Romsey SO51 7TE* T: (01794) 523463

PICKETT, David. b 65. MBE 99. Leeds Univ BA 11. Coll of Resurr Mirfield 09. **d** 11 **p** 12. C Edenham w Witham on the Hill and Swinstead *Linc* 11–14; R Guiseley w Esholt *Leeds* from 14. *The Rectory, The Green, Guiseley, Leeds LS20 9BB* T: (01943) 874321 M: 07916-825465 E: daipickett@hotmail.co.uk

PICKETT, Ms Joanna Elizabeth. b 53. Leic Univ BA 74 MA 80 Lon Univ MTh 95. Wycliffe Hall Ox 87. **d** 89 **p** 94. Chapl Southn Univ *Win* 89–94; C N Stoneham 94–95; NSM Colbury 97–01; NSM W End 01–12; PtO from 12. *6 Woodlands Gardens, Romsey SO51 7TE* T: (01794) 523463 E: liz.pickett@btinternet.com

PICKETT, Mark William Leslie. b 60. Westhill Coll Birm BEd 84. Trin Coll Bris 93. **d** 95 **p** 96. C Hellesdon *Nor* 95–98; TV Thetford 98–03; R Clitheroe St Jas *Blackb* from 03; P-in-c Clitheroe St Paul Low Moor 15–17. *The Rectory, Woone Lane, Clitheroe BB7 1BJ* T: (01200) 423608 E: rector@stjamesclitheroe.co.uk

PICKETT, Peter Leslie. b 28. Guy's Hosp Medical Sch LDS 52. S Dios Minl Tr Scheme 83. **d** 86 **p** 87. NSM Eastbourne H Trin *Chich* 86–88; P-in-c Danehill 88–93; rtd 93; PtO *Chich* from 93. *Springfield, 76 Meads Road, Eastbourne BN20 7QJ* T: (01323) 731709 M: 07733-090957 E: pjpickett@btinternet.com

PICKFORD (*née* PACKER), The Ven Catherine Ruth. b 76. Nottm Univ BA 97 Anglia Poly Univ MA 00. Westcott Ho Cam MA 00. **d** 00 **p** 01. C Gosforth All SS *Newc* 00–04; TV Benwell 04–09; TR 09–15; TR Benwell and Scotswood 15; P-in-c Stannington 15–20; Dioc CMD Officer 15–20; Adn Northolt *Lon* from 20. *9 Sheridan Gardens, Harrow HA3 0JT* M: 07341-485070 E: catherine_pickford@yahoo.co.uk or archdeacon.northolt@london.anglican.org

PICKLES, Julia Clare. See BALDWIN, Julia Clare

PICKSTONE, Canon Charles Faulkner. b 55. BNC Ox BA 77 MA 81 Leeds Univ BA 80. Coll of Resurr Mirfield 78. **d** 81 **p** 82. C Birkenhead Priory *Ches* 81–84; Chapl Paris St Geo *Eur* 84; C Camberwell St Giles w St Matt *S'wark* 84–89; V Catford St Laur from 89; Asst RD E Lewisham 92–99; Hon Can S'wark Cathl from 13. *St Laurence's Vicarage, 31 Bromley Road, London SE6 2TS* T: (020) 8698 2871 or 8698 9706 E: st.laurence@btconnect.com

PICOT, Katherine Frances. b 73. Ox Brookes Univ BA. Ridley Hall Cam. **d** 09. C Houston St Martin USA 09–14; Dir Harnhill Cen of Chr Healing from 14. *Harnhill Centre of Christian Healing, Harnhill Manor, Harnhill, Cirencester GL7 5PX* T: (01285) 850283 E: director@harnhillcentre.org.uk

PIDGEON, Warner Mark. b 68. Trin Coll Bris 00. **d** 02 **p** 03. C Fair Oak *Win* 02–06; TV Billericay and Lt Burstead *Chelmsf* 06–14; V Carshalton Beeches *S'wark* 14–16. *19 Station Road, Netley Abbey, Southampton SO31 5DU* E: revwmp@aol.co.uk

PIDOUX, Ian George. b 32. Univ Coll Ox BA 55 MA 60. Coll of Resurr Mirfield 54. **d** 57 **p** 58. C Middlesbrough All SS *York* 57–60; C Haggerston St Aug w St Steph *Lon* 60–62; C Aylesford *Roch* 80–81; TV Rye *Chich* 81–84; P-in-c Bridgwater St Jo *B & W* 84–86; V 86–98; Chapl Bridgwater Hosp 91–98; rtd 98; PtO *B & W* 98–15; *St Alb* from 15. *21 Hollybush Avenue, St Albans AL2 3AE* M: 07746-615854 E: igsepidoux@btinternet.com

PIDSLEY, Preb Christopher Thomas. b 36. ALCD 61. **d** 61 **p** 62. C Enfield Ch Ch Trent Park *Lon* 61–66; C Rainham *Chelmsf* 66–70; V Chudleigh *Ex* 70–98; RD Moreton 86–91; Preb Ex Cathl 92–98; rtd 98. *Bellever, Shillingford Abbot, Exeter EX2 9QF* T: (01392) 833588

PIERCE, Alan. b 57. St Mark & St Jo Coll Lon TCert 68 Southlands Coll Lon BEd 75 K Coll Lon MA 85 Lambeth STh 11. NOC 89. **d** 92 **p** 93. NSM Bolton St Thos *Man* 92–98; NSM Halliwell 98–00; NSM Bolton Breightmet St Jas 00–06; NSM Leverhulme 06–15; rtd 15; PtO *Man* from 15. *3 Astley Road, Bolton BL2 4BR* T: (01204) 300071 F: 401556 E: alan_pierce@hotmail.com

⊕**PIERCE, The Rt Revd Anthony Edward.** b 41. Univ of Wales (Swansea) BA 63 Linacre Coll Ox BA 65 MA 71. Ripon Hall Ox 63. **d** 65 **p** 66 **c** 99. C Swansea St Pet *S & B* 65–67; C Swansea St Mary and H Trin 67–74; Chapl Univ of Wales (Swansea) 71–74; V Llwynderw 74–92; P-in-c Swansea St Barn 92–96; Dioc Dir of Educn 93–96; Can Brecon Cathl 93–99; Adn Gower 95–99; V Swansea St Mary w H Trin 96–99; Bp S & B 99–08; rtd 08. *2 Coed Ceirios, Swansea Vale, Swansea SA7 0NU* T: (01792) 790258

PIERCE, Bruce Andrew. b 58. TCD BBS 80 BTh 89 Dub City Univ MA 99 MA 02. CITC 86. **d** 89 **p** 90. C Raheny w Coolock *D & G* 89–92; C Taney 92–93; I Lucan w Leixlip 93–98; Chapl Adelaide and Meath Hosp Dublin 98–02;

C Haarlem *Eur* 02–03; Chapl Toronto Gen Hosp Canada 03–04; Chapl Princess Marg Hosp Toronto 04–05; Supervisor (Assoc) Kerry Gen Hosp 06–08; Dir Educn St Luke's Home Mahon *C, C & R* from 08. *Aquila, Church Road, Blackrock, Cork, Republic of Ireland* T: (00353) (21) 435 8914 *or* (21) 435 9444 ext 507 F: 435 9450 E: bruapierce@hotmail.com *or* bruce.pierce@stlukeshome.ie

PIERCE, Christopher Douglas. b 61. Middle Tennessee State Univ BSc 95 Covenant Th Sem St Louis MA 96. Asbury Th Sem Kentucky 92. **d** 08 **p** 09. C St Jo Cathl Antigua 08–10; I Clondehorkey w Cashel *D & R* 10–18; R Grand Cayman St Alb W Indies 18–20; Ed English Churchman from 21; PtO *Conn* from 20. *231 Orby Drive, Belfast BT5 6BE* T: 07795-042031 E: revcdp@gmail.com

PIERCE, Daniel Charles. b 78. Redcliffe Coll Glouc BA 01 St Jo Coll Dur MA 12. Cranmer Hall Dur 10. **d** 12 **p** 13. C Stockton St Jas *Dur* 12–15; C Stockton St Jo 12–15; TV Billericay and Lt Burstead *Chelmsf* 15–18; C Boreham from 18; C Broomfield from 18; C The Chignals w Mashbury from 18; C Gt and Lt Leighs and Lt Waltham from 18; C Gt Waltham w Ford End from 18; C Pleshey from 18; C Springfield All SS from 18; C N Springfield from 18. *2 Fairway Drive, Chelmsford CM3 3FH* M: 07790-558579 E: todanpierce@yahoo.co.uk

PIERCE, David. *See* PIERCE, Thomas David Benjamin

PIERCE, David Richard. b 49. York St Jo Univ Hon BEd 19. **d** 15 **p** 16. OLM Prittlewell St Pet w Westcliff St Cedd *Chelmsf* 15–18; OLM Prittlewell St Steph 16–18; PtO from 18. *52 Teigngrace, Shoeburyness, Southend-on-Sea SS3 8AH* E: david@revdavidpierce.net

PIERCE, Jeffrey Hyam. b 29. Chelsea Coll Lon BSc 51 FBIM 80. Ox NSM Course 86. **d** 88 **p** 89. NSM Gt Missenden w Ballinger and Lt Hampden *Ox* 88–93; NSM Penn 93–97; rtd 97; PtO *Ox* 97–15. *Glebe Cottage, Manor Road, Penn, High Wycombe HP10 8HY* T: (01494) 817179 E: jeff@revjeff.co.uk

PIERCE, Roderick Martin. b 52. Univ of Wales (Ban) BTh 09 ACIB 75. Guildf Dioc Min Course 03. **d** 06 **p** 07. OLM Guildf H Trin w St Mary from 06. *18 Blackwell Avenue, Guildford GU2 8LU* T: (01483) 505816 M: 07751-152640 E: ann.rodpierce@ntlworld.com

PIERCE, Thomas David Benjamin. b 67. Ulster Univ BA 88. Oak Hill Th Coll BA 94. **d** 94 **p** 95. C Cromer *Nor* 94–97; C Belfast St Donard *D & D* 97–99; C Holywood 99–00; I Kilwarlin Upper w Kilwarlin Lower 00–17; rtd 18. *2 Broomhill Grove, Magheralin, Craigavon BT67 0GY* T: (028) 3834 7242 M: 07787-741254

PIERCE-JONES, Alan. b 74. Coll of Ripon & York St Jo BA 98. St Mich Coll Llan 98. **d** 00 **p** 01. C Port Talbot St Theodore *Llan* 00–02; TV Neath 02–05; V Lt Marsden w Nelson St Mary and Nelson St Bede *Blackb* 05–10; C W Burnley All SS 10; C Burnley St Mark 10; Chapl HM YOI Lanc Farms and HM Pris Lanc Castle 10–11; Chapl HM Pris Kennet 11–17; Chapl HM Pris Liv 13–14; Chapl HM Pris Berwyn from 17; PtO *Man* 14–17. *HM Prison Berwyn, Bridge Road, Wrexham Industrial Estate, Wrexham LL13 9QE* E: alan.pierce-jones@justice.gov.uk

PIERCY, Elizabeth Claire. *See* FRANCE, Elizabeth Claire

PIERPOINT, The Ven David Alfred. b 56. **d** 86 **p** 88. NSM Athboy w Ballivor and Killallon *M & K* 86–88; NSM Killiney Ballybrack *D & G* 88–89; NSM Narraghmore and Timolin w Castledermot etc 89–91; Chan V St Patr Cathl Dublin 90–96; C Dublin St Patr Cathl Gp *D & G* 92–95; V Dublin Ch Ch Cathl Gp from 95; Can Ch Ch Cathl Dublin from 95; Adn Dublin from 04. *The Vicarage, 30 Phibsborough Road, Dublin 7, Republic of Ireland* T: (00353) (1) 830 4601 M: 87-263 0402 E: pierpoint.david@gmail.com

PIERPOINT, Nigel John. TCD MTh 16. CITC 12. **d** 15 **p** 16. Taney *D & G* 15–16; C from 16. *Church Lodge, 21 Taney Road, Dundrum, Dublin 14, Republic of Ireland* T: (00353) (1) 295 1895 M: 87-638 8238 E: nigel.pierpoint@gmail.com

PIERSSENÉ, Frances Jane. *See* GRIEVE, Frances Jane

PIGGOT, Alan Robert Lennox. b 62. Peterho Cam BA 84 MA 88 Ox Univ DPhil 04. Westcott Ho Cam 00. **d** 02 **p** 03. C Dalston H Trin w St Phil and Haggerston All SS *Lon* 02–04; C Stoke Newington St Mary 04–05; P-in-c Hackney Wick St Mary of Eton w St Aug 05–10; PtO 14–16; NSM Grosvenor Chpl from 16; NSM Hanover Square St Geo from 16. *20 Ascott Road, Aylesbury HP20 1HX* E: alan.piggot@btinternet.com

PIGGOTT, The Ven Andrew John. b 51. Qu Mary Coll Lon BSc(Econ) 72. St Jo Coll Nottm 83. **d** 86 **p** 87. C Dorridge *Birm* 86–89; TV Kidderminster St Geo *Worc* 89–94; V Biddulph *Lich* 94–99; Min and Voc Adv CPAS 99–01; Patr Sec 01–05; Adn Bath and Preb Wells Cathl *B & W* 05–17; rtd 17. *19 Sheraton Drive, Kidderminster DY10 3QR*

PIGGOTT, Clive. b 47. St Luke's Coll Ex CertEd 69. **d** 96 **p** 97. Hd of RE Beverley Boys' Sch 69–05; OLM Malden St Jas

S'wark 96–18; PtO from 18. *84 Manor Drive North, New Malden KT3 5PA* T: (020) 8337 0801 E: cliveoldmalden@aol.com

PIGOTT, Graham John. b 44. Lon Bible Coll BD 73 Nottm Univ MPhil 84 MEd 92 Lon Inst of Educn PGCE 74. St Jo Coll Nottm 79. **d** 81 **p** 82. C Beeston *S'well* 81–84; P-in-c W Bridgford 84–88; V Wilford Hill 88–09; AD W Bingham 97–04; Hon Can S'well Minster 04–09; rtd 09; PtO *Derby* from 09; *Sheff* from 15. *Tanner's House, 5A Goatscliff Cottages, Grindleford, Hope Valley S32 2HG* T: (01433) 639641 E: graham.pigott@btinternet.com

PIGOTT, Nicholas John Capel. b 48. Qu Coll Birm 75. **d** 78 **p** 79. C Belmont *Dur* 78–79; C Folkestone St Sav *Cant* 79–82; C Birm St Geo 82–85; V Stevenage St Hugh and St Jo *St Alb* 85–91; TV Totnes w Bridgetown, Berry Pomeroy etc *Ex* 91–02; Asst P 02–04; rtd 04. *27 Croft Road, Ipplepen, Newton Abbot TQ12 5SS* T: (01803) 813664

PIGREM, Terence John (Tim). b 39. Middx Univ BA 97 MA 01. Oak Hill Th Coll 66. **d** 69 **p** 70. C Islington St Andr w St Thos and St Matthias *Lon* 69–73; C Barking St Marg w St Patr *Chelmsf* 73–75; TV 75–76; C W Holloway St Luke *Lon* 76–79; V 79–95; P-in-c Abbess Roding, Beauchamp Roding and White Roding *Chelmsf* 95–96; R S Rodings 96–07; RD Dunmow 97–02; rtd 07; PtO *Chelmsf* from 08. *96 Vicarage Lane, Great Baddow, Chelmsford CM2 8JB* T: (01245) 471878 E: pigrem@btinternet.com

PIIR, The Very Revd Gustav Peeter. b 61. St Olaf Coll Minnesota BA 83 Saskatchewan Univ MDiv 86. **p** 88. Asst Toronto St Pet Canada 88–92; Asst Chas Ch Tallinn Estonia 92–95; R Tallinn H Spirit from 95; Dean Tallinn from 99; P-in-c Tallinn SS Tim and Titus *Eur* from 00. *Pühavaimu 2, Tallinn 10123, Estonia* T: (00372) 646 4430 F: 644 1487 M: 51-76159 E: praost@hot.ee

PIKE, Mrs Amanda Shirley Gail. b 69. Cranmer Hall Dur 99. **d** 01 **p** 02. C Boston Spa *York* 01–03; C Elloughton and Brough w Brantingham 03–05; P-in-c Eggleston and Middleton-in-Teesdale w Forest and Frith *Dur* 05–08; TV Bosworth and Sheepy Gp *Leic* 08–11; C Nailstone and Carlton w Shackerstone 08–11; P-in-c Elmton and Whitwell *Derby* 11–13; P-in-c Cheddleton *Lich* 13–14; P-in-c Horton, Lonsdon and Rushton Spencer 13–14; V Cheddleton, Horton, Longsdon and Rushton Spencer 14–19; TV Cen Wolverhampton 19–21; P-in-c Baddiley and Wrenbury w Burleydam *Ches* from 21. *The Vicarage, The Green, Wrenbury, Nantwich CW5 8EY* M: 07738-988767 E: amanda@ichthos.me.uk

PIKE, David Frank. b 35. BA Lon Univ TCert CEng MIMechE. S Dios Minl Tr Scheme 82. **d** 85 **p** 86. NSM Lancing w Coombes *Chich* 85–88; R Albourne w Sayers Common and Twineham 88–94; V Wisborough Green 94–04; rtd 04; PtO *Chich* from 15. *42 Greenoaks, Lancing BN15 0HE* T: (01903) 766209 E: davidf.pike@outlook.com

PIKE, Nicholas Keith. b 52. Warwick Univ BA 74 Brunel Univ MA 80 Cardiff Univ DSW 13 CQSW 80. Ox NSM Course 10. **d** 12 **p** 13. NSM Cogges and S Leigh *Ox* 12–20; NSM N Leigh 12–20; rtd 20; PtO *Ox* from 20. *The Old Nursery, 29 Bridge Street, Witney OX28 1DA* T: (01993) 705578 M: 07962-623310 E: revnick@btinternet.com

PIKE, Paul Alfred. b 38. Bognor Regis Coll of Educn CertEd 58 MIL 88. Wycliffe Hall Ox 83. **d** 84 **p** 85. C Penn Fields *Lich* 84–89; OMF Internat Japan 89–03; rtd 03; PtO *Bris* 03–11; *B & W* from 09; *Ex* from 19. *26 Gracey Court, Woodland Road, Broadclyst, Exeter EX5 3GA* T: (01392) 469753 E: papike@btinternet.com

PIKE, Canon Timothy David. b 68. Collingwood Coll Dur BA 90 Leeds Univ BA 94. Coll of Resurr Mirfield 92. **d** 95 **p** 96. C Owton Manor *Dur* 95–98; C Old St Pancras w Bedford New Town St Matt *Lon* 98–03; CR 03–04; P-in-c Hornsey H Innocents *Lon* 04–07; V 07–16; C Stroud Green H Trin 04–16; P-in-c Harringay St Paul 10–16; AD W Haringey 06–11; V Croydon St Mich w St Jas *S'wark* from 16; Hon Can S'wark Cathl from 20; CMP from 98; Warden 05–12. *St Michael's Vicarage, 39 Oakfield Road, Croydon CR0 2UX* T: (020) 8680 2848 E: fathertimpike@hotmail.com *or* michaels.church@btinternet.com

PILAVACHI, Canon Michael. b 58. MBE 20. St Mellitus Coll. **d** 12 **p** 13. Soul Survivor Watford St Pet *St Alb* from 12; Hon Can St Alb from 16. *37 Maytree Crescent, Watford WD24 5NJ*

PILCHER, Mrs Jennifer Anne. b 42. **d** 04 **p** 05. OLM Eastry and Northbourne w Tilmanstone etc *Cant* 04–12; rtd 12; PtO *Cant* 12–21. *1 Long Close, Church Street, Eastry, Sandwich CT13 0HN* T: (01304) 611472 E: jenniferpilcher@btinternet.com

PILGRIM, Canon Colin Mark. b 56. BA 77. Westcott Ho Cam 81. **d** 84 **p** 85. C Chorlton-cum-Hardy St Clem *Man* 84–87; C Whitchurch *Bris* 87–89; V Bedminster Down 89–95; Dioc Youth Officer 95–01; Hon C Stoke Bishop

96–01; V Henleaze from 01; AD Bris W 06–16; Hon Can Bris Cathl from 09. *St Peter's Vicarage, 17 The Drive, Henleaze, Bristol BS9 4LD* T: 0117-962 0636 *or* 962 3196 E: markpilgrimis@aol.com

PILGRIM, Ms Judith Mary. b 44. Westcott Ho Cam 88. **d** 90 **p** 94. C Probus, Ladock and Grampound w Creed and St Erme *Truro* 90–94; C Nottingham All SS *S'well* 94–97; Asst Chapl to the Deaf 94–97; PtO 97–00; *Ox* 00–01; P-in-c Zennor and Towednack *Truro* 02–06; rtd 06. *356 Bennett Street, Long Eaton, Nottingham NG10 4JD* T: 0115-972 5805

PILGRIM, Kenneth George. b 49. Lon Univ BEd 77 Kent Univ MA 94. **d** 01 **p** 02. OLM Alkham w Capel le Ferne and Hougham *Cant* 01–03; PtO *Nor* 04–05; NSM E Dereham and Scarning 05–06; NSM Swanton Morley w Beetley w E Bilney and Hoe 05–06; NSM Dereham and Distr 06–20; Bp's Officer for Wholeness and Healing 10–12; rtd 20; PtO *Nor* from 20. *16 Litcham Road, Gressenhall, Dereham NR20 4AR* T: (01362) 861265 E: kenpilgrim@btinternet.com

PILGRIM, Mark. *See* PILGRIM, Colin Mark

PILKINGTON, Miss Anne. b 57. Aston Tr Scheme 88 NOC 90. **d** 93 **p** 94. C Wythenshawe Wm Temple Ch *Man* 93–96; P-in-c 96–99; TV Wythenshawe 99–06; P-in-c Didsbury Ch Ch 06; P-in-c Withington St Chris from 06; R W Didsbury and Withington St Chris from 06. *Christ Church Rectory, 35 Darley Avenue, Manchester M20 2ZD* T: 0161-445 4152 E: anne@christchurchdidsbury.org.uk

PILKINGTON, David Stuart. b 70. St Mellitus Coll 17. **d** 19 **p** 20. C Old Ford St Paul and St Mark *Lon* from 19. *58 Chisenhale Road, London E3 5QZ* M: 07491-956861 E: dave@stpauloldford.com

PILKINGTON, Canon Timothy William. b 54. Nottm Univ BA 85 Univ of Wales (Lamp) MA 09. Linc Th Coll 82. **d** 85 **p** 86. C Newquay *Truro* 85–88; C Cockington *Ex* 88–91; R St John w Millbrook *Truro* 91–97; V Northampton St Matt *Pet* 97–02; TR Solihull *Birm* 02–14; AD 09–13; Hon Can Birm Cathl 06–14; TR Gt Berkhamsted, Gt and Lt Gaddesden etc *St Alb* 14–20; rtd 20. *8 Ponsvale, Ponsanooth, Truro TR3 7RQ* E: twill@timpilk.plus.com

PIMENTA, Valmor Alves. b 78. **d** 03 **p** 03. USA 03–13; NSM Harlesden All So *Lon* 14–16; C Bedford St Martin *St Alb* 16–18; V 18–19; PtO *Lon* 16–19; V Northolt St Jos from 19; PtO *St Alb* from 19. *St Joseph's Vicarage, 430 Yeading Lane, Northolt UB5 6JS* M: 07950-897771 E: pr.valmor@hotmail.com

PIMM, Robert John. b 57. Bris Univ BA 78 ACIB 82. Trin Coll Bris 92. **d** 94 **p** 95. C Long Benton *Newc* 94–98; TV Bath Twerton-on-Avon *B & W* from 98. *Ascension Vicarage, 35A Claude Avenue, Bath BA2 1AG* T: (01225) 405354 M: 07505-470815 E: robert@ascensionbath.org.uk *or* robertjpimm@gmail.com

PINCHBECK, Caroline Rosamund. b 70. Hatf Coll Dur BA 93. Wesley Ho Cam MA 00. **d** 02 **p** 03. C Mawnan *Truro* 02–06; C Budock 03–06; P-in-c Eastling w Ospringe and Stalisfield w Otterden *Cant* 06–11; Communities and Partnership Exec Officer 11–19; Rural Life Adv 06–19; Rural Life Adv *Roch* 06–11; C Blean *Cant* 12–19; Hon Can Cant Cathl 11–19; R Goodmanham *York* from 19; V Market Weighton 19–21; R Weighton Wold from 21; V Sancton from 19; RD S Wold from 19. *38 Cliffe Road, Market Weighton, York YO43 3BN* T: (01430) 879996 E: vicarmwgs627@btinternet.com

PINDER, Mrs Christine Alison. b 61. Birm Univ BSc 83 MSc 84. **d** 18 **p** 19. NSM Martlesham w Brightwell *St E* from 18. *3 Mayfields, Martlesham Heath, Ipswich IP5 3TU* M: 07555-748345 E: christine.pinder@btinternet.com

PINDER, Canon John Ridout. b 43. Peterho Cam BA 65 MA 69. Cuddesdon Coll 65. **d** 73 **p** 74. C Leavesden *St Alb* 73–76; Gen Sec Melanesian Miss 77–89; P-in-c Harpsden *Ox* 82–89; R Farlington *Portsm* 89–02; R Liss 02–09; RD Portsm 96–01; Hon Can Portsm Cathl 01–09; rtd 09; P-in-c Stapleford *Ely* 09–15; PtO from 15. *12A Granta Road, Sawston, Cambridge CB22 3HT* T: (01223) 502450 E: johnpinder@waitrose.com

PINDER-PACKARD, John. b 47. Lon Univ BSc. NOC 81. **d** 84 **p** 85. NSM Mosborough *Sheff* 84–85; C Norton 85–88; V New Whittington *Derby* 88–04; P-in-c Newbold and Gt Barlow 99–00; Chapl Whittington Hall Hosp 88–04; R Barlborough and Renishaw *Derby* 04–09; P-in-c Clowne 05–09; rtd 09; PtO *Leeds* from 17. *1 Great Common Close, Barlborough, Chesterfield S43 4SY* E: packards@tiscali.co.uk

PINE, David Michael. b 41. Lich Th Coll 68. **d** 71 **p** 72. C Northam *Ex* 71–74; R Toft w Caldecote and Childerley *Ely* 74–80; R Hardwick 74–80; V Ipswich St Andr *St E* 80–84; P-in-c Hazelbury Bryan w Stoke Wake etc *Sarum* 84–91; R Hazelbury Bryan and the Hillside Par 91–93; V Steep and Froxfield w Privett *Portsm* 93–00; rtd 00; PtO *Portsm* 07–11. *62 Carisbrooke Road, Newport PO30 1BW* T: (01983) 872939 E: davidmpine@hotmail.co.uk

PINFIELD, Leslie Arthur. b 57. Birm Univ BMus 79. St Steph Ho *Ox* 92. **d** 94 **p** 95. C Bath Bathwick *B & W* 94–98; TV Swindon New Town *Bris* 98–07; P-in-c Huddersfield All SS and St Thos *Wakef* 07–14; *Leeds* 14–15; V from 15; Bp's Adv on Inter-Faith Issues *Wakef* 07–14; *Leeds* from 14. *The Vicarage, 17 Cross Church Street, Paddock, Huddersfield HD1 4SN* T: (01484) 428253 E: frleslie@btopenworld.com

PINNEGAR, Alan Edward. b 58. SEITE 09. **d** 12 **p** 13. C Bearsted w Thurnham *Cant* 12–15; R Tunstall and Bredgar from 15. *The Rectory, Tunstall, Sittingbourne ME9 8DU* T: (01795) 471483 M: 07402-717325 E: aepinnegar@gmail.com

PINNELL (*formerly* **ALLEN**)**, Ms Beverley Carole.** b 52. Ch Ch Coll Cant CertEd 74 Open Univ BA 91. Sarum Th Coll 93. **d** 96 **p** 97. NSM Ruislip Manor St Paul *Lon* 96–12; PtO 12–16; *Ox* 14–17; Chich from 16. *10 Shipley Mill Close, Stone Cross, Pevensey BN24 5PY* T: (01323) 740283 E: revbev@tiscali.co.uk

PINNELL, George. b 39. NTMTC 96. **d** 99 **p** 00. NSM Hillingdon St Jo *Lon* 99–16; Chapl Heathrow Airport 08–16; PtO *Chich* from 16. *10 Shipley Mill Close, Stone Cross, Pevensey BN24 5PY* T: (01323) 740283 M: 07951-124976 E: pinneg@tiscali.co.uk

PINNER, Mrs Cheri Lee. b 36. Marietta Coll (USA) BA 59. **d** 07 **p** 08. C Greytown NZ 07–10; P-in-c Whaley Bridge *Ches* 10–12; rtd 12; PtO *Glouc* 16–18. *The Maple, Westend, Wickwar, Wotton-under-Edge GL12 8LB* M: 07889-796020 E: cheri.pinner@mac.com

PINNER, John Philip. b 37. K Coll Lon BA 59 AKC 59 Lon Inst of Educn PGCE 60. Westcott Ho Cam 69. **d** 71 **p** 72. C Dover St Mary *Cant* 71–74; Chapl Felsted Sch 74–81; Chapl Rathkeale Coll NZ 81–02; P-in-c Greytown St Luke 04–08; rtd 10; Hon C Whaley Bridge *Ches* 10–12; PtO *Glouc* 16–18. *The Maple, Westend, Wickwar, Wotton-under-Edge GL12 8LB* E: johnpinner1@icloud.com

PINNER, Canon Terence Malcolm William. b 35. Southn Univ MA 89. AKC 59. **d** 60 **p** 61. C Eltham St Barn *S'wark* 60–64; C Grahamstown Cathl S Africa 64–67; USPG 67–69; R King William's Town S Africa 69–72; R Beacon Bay 72–74; Sec for Home Affairs Conf of Br Miss Socs 74–76; P-in-c Hinstock *Lich* 76–79; Adult Educn Officer 76–79; Adult RE Officer 79–83; Chapl Southn Univ *Win* 83–88; Dioc Dir of Ords 88–98; Tutor S Dios Minl Tr Scheme 88–92; P-in-c Old Alresford and Bighton *Win* 93–00; Dir Old Alresford Place 93–00; Hon Can Win Cathl 92–00; rtd 00; PtO *Win* from 00. *11 Sorrell Way, Highcliffe, Christchurch BH23 4LY* M: 07889-177203

PINNINGTON, Mrs Gillian. b 59. St Kath Coll Liv BEd 81 Ches Coll of HE BTh 02. NOC 99. **d** 02 **p** 03. C Roby *Liv* 02–06; TV Speke St Aid 06–17; R Speke St Aid w All SS 17–18; V Coalville w Bardon Hill and Ravenstone *Leic* from 18; AD NW Leics from 20. *Christ Church Vicarage, 28 London Road, Coalville LE67 3JA* T: (01530) 810655 E: pinny@supanet.com

PINNOCK, Martyn Elliott. b 47. Linc Th Coll 91. **d** 93 **p** 94. C Fordingbridge *Win* 93–97; V St Minver *Truro* 97–01; P-in-c Luray Ch Ch USA 01–02; V Steeton *Bradf* 02–05; P-in-c Scottsville USA 05–08; rtd 09; P-in-c Tregony w St Cuby and Cornelly *Truro* 13–14; PtO from 14; Chapl Cornwall Partnership NHS Foundn Trust from 15. *Neyth Golvan, 149 Treffry Road, Truro TR1 1WE* T: (01872) 264578 M: 07817-036655 E: martyn.pinnock@nhs.net *or* martynpinnock@aol.com

PINTO, James Neil. b 82. Ex Univ BA 04 UEA PGCE 06. Oak Hill Th Coll BA 19. **d** 19 **p** 20. C Heigham H Trin *Nor* from 19. *14 Trinity Street, Norwich NR2 2BQ* M: 07739-582349 E: jamesnpinto@hotmail.com *or* james.pinto@trinitynorwich.org

PIPER, Canon Andrew. b 58. Magd Coll Ox BA 79 MA 83. Chich Th Coll 80. **d** 83 **p** 84. C Eastbourne St Mary *Chich* 83–88; TV Lewes All SS, St Anne, St Mich and St Thos 88–93; TR Worth 93–03; Can Res and Prec Heref Cathl from 03. *1 The Close, Hereford HR1 2NG* T: (01432) 266193 F: 374220 E: precentor@herefordcathedral.org

PIPER, Calum Lewis. b 91. Ches Univ BTh 12. St Jo Coll Nottm 12. **d** 14 **p** 15. C Wallasey St Hilary *Ches* 14–18; C Cheadle Deanery 18–19; V Bramhall *Ches* from 19. *The Vicarage, 66 St Michael's Avenue, Bramhall, Stockport SK7 2PG* M: 07890-977064 E: calum.piper14@gmail.com *or* calum.piper@bramhall.church

PIPER, Canon Clifford John. b 53. Moray Ord Course 91. **d** 93 **p** 94. C Invergordon St Ninian *Mor* 93–96; P-in-c 00–03; NSM Tain 96–98; P-in-c 98–03; P-in-c Forres 03–09; R 09–16; Can St Andr Cathl Inverness 00–09; Dean Mor 09–14; rtd 16; Hon Can St Andr Cathl Inverness *Mor* from 14. *17 Craig Crescent, Tain IV19 1JW* T: (01862) 892593 M: 07895-105104

PIPER, Gary Quentin David. b 42. Nottm Coll of Educn TCert 65 Maria Grey Coll Lon DipEd 71. Oak Hill Th Coll 75. d 78 p 79. NSM Fulham St Matt *Lon* 78–85; V 85–13; AD Hammersmith 86–92; AD Hammersmith and Fulham 06–12; rtd 13; PtO *Lon* from 13. *St Michael's Church, 60 Elmwood Road, London W4 3DZ* E: revgarypiper@hotmail.com

PIPER, Graham. b 58. Southn Univ BTh 91. Chich Th Coll 88. d 91 p 92. C Horsham *Chich* 91–94; TV Haywards Heath St Wilfrid 94–99; Dioc Voc Adv 96–99; V Bamber Bridge St Aid *Blackb* 99–04; V Hawes Side and Marton Moss 04–17; rtd 17; PtO *Blackb* 17–18; Hon C Accrington St Andr, St Mary and St Pet and Church Kirk 18–19; P-in-c Mitcham St Olave *S'wark* from 19. *All Saints' Vicarage, 10 Deburgh Road, London SW19 1DX* M: 07816-525843 E: fathergraham@live.co.uk

PIPER, Jessica Ann. b 92. Ches Univ BTh 13. St Mellitus Coll 15. d 17 p 18. C Bowdon *Ches* 17–20; C Stockport and Brinnington from 20. *The Vicarage, 66 St Michael's Avenue, Bramhall, Stockport SK7 2PG* M: 07854-185860 E: jessica.a.piper@outlook.com *or* jess@bowdonchurch.org

PIPPEN, Canon Brian Roy. b 50. St D Coll Lamp. d 73 p 74. C Maindee Newport *Mon* 73–77; TV Cwmbran 77–84; V Newport Ch Ch 84–90; R Pontypool 90–17; AD 98–08; Can St Woolos Cathl 01–17; rtd 17; PtO *Mon* from 17. *37 Thistle Court, Ty Canol, Cwmbran NP44 6JD* T: (01633) 869303

PIRET, Michael John. b 57. State Univ NY BA 79 Univ of Michigan MA 80 PhD 91 Mert Coll Ox MLitt 89. Edin Th Coll 90. d 92 p 93. C St Andr Cathl Inverness *Mor* 92–94; Dean of Div and Fell Magd Coll Ox 94–16; R Oyster Bay USA from 16. *65 East Main Street, Oyster Bay NY 11771, USA* E: rector@christchurchoysterbay.org

PITCHER, Canon David John. b 33. Ely Th Coll 55. d 58 p 59. C Kingswinford St Mary *Lich* 58–61; C Kirkby *Liv* 61–66; R Ingham w Sutton *Nor* 66–72; V Lakenham St Jo 72–76; R Framlingham w Saxtead *St E* 76–91; RD Loes 82–89; Hon Can St E Cathl 85–99; R Woodbridge St Mary 91–99; rtd 99; PtO *St E* from 00. *25 Coucy Close, Framlingham, Woodbridge IP13 9AX* T: (01728) 621580

PITCHER, George Martell. b 55. Birm Univ BA 77 Middx Univ BA 05. NTMTC 02. d 05 p 06. NSM St Bride Fleet Street w Bridewell etc *Lon* 05–13; P-in-c Waldron *Chich* from 13. *Culverwood, Little London Road, Cross in Hand, Heathfield TN21 0AX* T: (01435) 865376 M: 07778-917182 E: mail@georgepitcher.com

PITCHER, Canon Simon John. b 63. Reading Univ BA 85. Ridley Hall Cam 00. d 02 p 03. C Lightcliffe *Wakef* 02–05; P-in-c Heckmondwike 05–10; C Liversedge w Hightown 05–10; C Robertown w Hartshead 05–10; RD Birstall 08–10; TR Sole Bay *St E* from 10; RD Waveney and Blyth 11–20; Hon Can St E Cathl from 16. *The Vicarage, Gardner Road, Southwold IP18 6HJ* T: (01502) 725424 E: revsimon@talktalk.net

PITE, Sheila Reinhardt. *See* SWARBRICK, Sheila Reinhardt

PITHERS, Canon Brian Hoyle. b 34. Chich Th Coll 63. d 66 p 67. C Wisbech SS Pet and Paul *Ely* 66–70; V Fenstanton 70–75; V Hilton 70–75; V Habergham Eaves St Matt *Blackb* 75–85; P-in-c Habergham Eaves H Trin 78–85; V Burnley St Matt w H Trin 85–86; TR Ribbleton 86–92; V Torrisholme 92–00; Hon Can Blackb Cathl 97–00; rtd 01; PtO *Blackb* from 01. *37 Dallam Avenue, Morecambe LA4 5BB* T: (01524) 424786

PITKETHLY (née CHEVILL), Elizabeth Jane. b 65. Colchester Inst of Educn BA 86 K Coll Lon MMus 87 PhD 93 Warwick Univ BPhil 00 AKC 89 Lon Inst of Educn PGCE 91. Wycliffe Hall Ox MSt 04 MLitt 08. d 08 p 09. C Blackheath St Jo *S'wark* 08–11; PtO *Ox* 11–12; NSM Ox St Andr from 12; Chapl St Pet Coll Ox from 14. *24 Thorncliffe Road, Oxford OX2 7BB* T: (01865) 552571 M: 07952-024571 E: ejpitkethly@btinternet.com

PITKIN, James Mark. b 62. Man Univ BSc 83 Glos Univ BA(Theol) 03 MRAeS 90 CEng 90. STETS. d 99 p 00. C Chilworth w N Baddesley *Win* 99–03; V Thorngate from 03; P-in-c Somborne w Ashley 19–21; AD Romsey from 17; Corps Chapl ATC from 15. *The Vicarage, The Street, Lockerley, Romsey SO51 0JF* T: (01794) 340635 F: 08701-674691 M: 07931-736166 E: jamespitkin@priest.com

PITKIN, Mrs Janet Margaret. b 60. Man Univ BA 84 Surrey Univ BA 03. STETS 00. d 03 p 04. C Southampton Maybush St Pet *Win* 03–06; C Maybush and Southampton St Jude 06–09; Asst Chapl Southn Univ Hosps NHS Trust 09–10; Trust Chapl Univ Hosp Southn NHS Foundn Trust from 10. *The Vicarage, The Street, Lockerley, Romsey SO51 0JF* T: (01794) 340635 M: 07906-027042 E: suepitkin@minister.com

PITMAN, Mrs Janet Elizabeth. b 65. Salford Univ BEng 90 Open Univ BA 99. All SS Cen for Miss & Min 12. d 15 p 16. C Oldham St Paul and Werneth *Man* 15–19; V Milnrow and New Hey from 19. *St Thomas's Vicarage, Church*

Street, Newhey, Rochdale OL16 3QS M: 07985-971022 E: hildaofwhitby67@gmail.com

PITMAN, Jessica. b 62. Newton Park Coll Bath BEd 85. STETS 07. d 10 p 11. C Langport Area *B & W* 10–17; R Aller, High w Low Ham and Huish Episcopi cum Langport from 17. *Vicarage, Huish Episcopi, Langport TA10 9QR* T: (010458) 251489 E: jessicapitman@aol.com

PITMAN, Roger Thomas. b 64. St Mich Coll Llan BTh 00. d 00 p 01. C Caerphilly *Llan* 00–02; C Coity w Nolton 02–07; P-in-c Llanharry 07–12; P-in-c Llangeinor and the Garw Valley from 12; Chapl Pontypridd and Rhondda NHS Trust 07–10. *The Vicarage, 2 Waun Wen, Bettws Road, Llangeinor, Bridgend CF32 8PH* T: (01656) 870280 E: vicar@the-vicarage.net

PITT, George. b 52. QUB BD 79 MTh 88. CITC 81. d 81 p 82. C Belfast St Mary *Conn* 81–86; CMS 86–92; Zaïre 88–92; V Penycae *St As* 92–98; I Killesher *K, E & A* 98–01; Educn Adv Ch of Ireland Bps' Appeal 01–03; PtO *Bradf* 04–06; Chapl HM Pris Moorland 06–13; rtd 13. *20 Thornsbank, Sedbergh LA10 5LF* T: (01539) 622095

PITT, Karen Lesley Finella. *See* TIMMIS, Karen Lesley Finella

PITT, Canon Trevor. b 45. Hull Univ BA 66 MA 69 Open Univ DipEd 91. Linc Th Coll 68 Union Th Sem (NY) STM 70. d 70 p 71. C Sheff St Geo 70–74; TV Gleadless Valley 74–78; TR 78–79; P-in-c Elham *Cant* 79–82; V Elham w Denton and Wootton 82–91; Vice Prin Cant Sch of Min 81–91; Six Preacher Cant Cathl 85–91; Prin NEOC *Newc* 91–10; Hon Can Newc Cathl 91–10; PtO *York* 91–20; *Ripon* 91–14; *Leeds* 14–16; rtd 10; PtO *Newc* from 10; Hon C Escomb *Dur* 12–15; Hon C Etherley 12–15; Hon C Witton Park 12–15; Hon C Hamsterley and Witton-le-Wear 12–15; PtO from 15. *Green View House, Hamsterley, Bishop Auckland DL13 3QF* T: (01388) 488898 E: trevorpitt@aol.com

PITT, Mrs Valerie. b 55. Liv Univ BA 77. STETS 02. d 05 p 06. NSM Oxshott *Guildf* 05–09; NSM Meole Brace *Lich* from 09. *4 Meole Hall Gardens, Shrewsbury SY3 9JS* T: (01743) 270102 E: valerie.pitt@trinitychurches.org

PITTARIDES, Renos. b 62. Surrey Univ BA 85. d 07 p 08. OLM Cobham and Stoke D'Abernon *Guildf* 07–15; P-in-c E Horsley 15–17; R from 17. *The Rectory, Ockham Road South, East Horsley, Leatherhead KT24 6RL* E: renosp@gmail.com

PITTIS, Canon Stephen Charles. b 52. Sheff Univ MA 01. Oak Hill Th Coll. d 76 p 77. C Win Ch Ch 76–79; Chapl Dorset Inst of HE and Bournemouth and Poole Coll of FE *Sarum* 79–84; V Woking St Paul *Guildf* 84–97; Dir of Faith Development *Win* 97–09; Dioc Missr and Can Res Win Cathl 09–11; R Michelmersh and Awbridge and Braishfield etc 11–19; Hon Can Win Cathl 13–19; rtd 19; PtO *Win* from 20. *38 Beverley Road, Dibden Purlieu, Southampton SO45 4HS* T: (023) 8178 1274 E: pittisinc@gmail.com

PITTMAN, Louisa. b 76. Coll of Charleston (USA) BSc 06 Bris Univ MA 09 PhD 15 Cam Univ BTh 18. Westcott Ho Cam 16. d 18 p 19. C Wymondham *Nor* 18–19; C Barnham Broom and Upper Yare from 19. *The Vicarage, Honingham Road, Barnham Broom, Norwich NR9 4DB*

PITTS, Canon Evadne Ione (Eve). b 50. Qu Coll Birm. d 89 p 94. C Bartley Green *Birm* 89–93; Team Dn Kings Norton 93–94; TV 94–98; P-in-c Highters Heath 98–00; V 00–09; P-in-c Birchfield 09–14; V from 14; Hon Can Birm Cathl from 05. *Holy Trinity Vicarage, 213 Birchfield Road, Birmingham B20 3DG* T: 0121-356 4241 E: blackuhru@aol.com

PITTS, The Very Revd Michael James. b 44. Worc Coll Ox BA 66 Worc Coll of Educn MA 69. Qu Coll Birm 67. d 69 p 70. C Pennywell St Thos and Grindon St Oswald *CD Dur* 69–72; C Darlington H Trin 72–74; Chapl Dunkerque w Lille Arras etc Miss to Seamen *Eur* 74–79; V Tudhoe *Dur* 79–81; Chapl Helsinki w Moscow *Eur* 81–85; Chapl Stockholm 85–88; Hon Can Brussels Cathl 87–88; Hon Chapl Miss to Seafarers Canada from 88; R Montreal St Cuth 88–91; Dean Ch Ch Cathl Montreal 91–09; Can Res Montreal St Ignatius from 09; rtd 09. *3279 rue Gariepy RR4, Sainte Julienne QC J0K 2T0, Canada* T: (001) (450) 834 2956 E: michael.pitts@worc.oxon.org

PIX, Stephen James. b 42. Ex Coll Ox BA 64 MA 68 Univ of Wales (Cardiff) LLM 97. Clifton Th Coll 66. d 68 p 69. C St Helens St Helen *Liv* 68–71; LtO *S'wark* 71–76; Hon C Wallington 76–84; V Osmotherley w E Harlsey and Ingleby Arncliffe *York* 84–89; V Ox St Mich w St Martin and All SS 89–01; rtd 01; PtO *St E* 01–07; Ox from 07. *10 Cadogan Park, Woodstock OX20 1UW* T: (01993) 812473

PIZZEY, Canon Lawrence Roger. b 42. Dur Univ BA 64. Westcott Ho Cam 65. d 67 p 68. C Bramford *St E* 67–71; Tutor Woodbridge Abbey 71–77; Asst Chapl Woodbridge Sch 71–77; P-in-c Flempton w Hengrave and Lackford *St E* 77–85; R Culford, W Stow and Wordwell 77–85; P-in-c Acton w Gt Waldingfield 85–89; V 89–95; P-in-c Sudbury and

Chilton 95–98; R 98–07; RD Sudbury 96–06; Hon Can St E Cathl 00–07; rtd 07; PtO *St E* from 07. *9 Constable Road, Bury St Edmunds IP33 3UQ* T: (01284) 762863 E: lrp.sudbury@virgin.net

PLACE, Rodger Goodson. b 37. St Chad's Coll Dur BA 60. d 62 p 63. C Pontesbury I and II *Heref* 62–65; C Heref St Martin 65–68; V Ditton Priors 68–75; R Neenton 68–75; P-in-c Aston Botterell w Wheathill and Loughton 69–75; P-in-c Burwarton w N Cleobury 69–75; P-in-c Dacre w Hartwith *Ripon* 75–76; V 76–82; V Wyther 82–92; P-in-c Roundhay St Jo 92–97; V 97–00; rtd 00; PtO *York* 00–21. *72 Field Lane, Thorpe Willoughby, Selby YO8 9FL* T: (01757) 703174

PLACKETT-FERGUSON, Jane Louise. b 85. St Jo Coll Nottm 12. d 15 p 16. NSM Aston on Trent, Elvaston, Weston on Trent etc *Derby* 15–19; Pioneer Min Derwent Ward 15–19; C Houston St Martin USA from 19. *717 Sage Road, Houston TX 77056, USA* E: janeplackettferguson@gmail.com

PLAISTER, Keith Robin. b 43. K Coll Lon BD 65 AKC 65. d 66 p 67. C Laindon w Basildon *Chelmsf* 66–71; V Gt Wakering 71–78; V Gt Wakering w Foulness 78–90; C Witham 91–94; TV 94–99; P-in-c Sandon and E Hanningfield 99–08; rtd 08; PtO *Chelmsf* from 10. *118 Maldon Road, Great Baddow, Chelmsford CM2 7DH* T: (01245) 473135 E: keithplaister@hotmail.com

PLANT, Miss Elizabeth Bowers. b 48. Westf Coll Lon BA 70 Man Univ PGCE 71. d 08 p 09. OLM Deane *Man* 08–18; rtd 18; PtO *Man* from 18. *25 Kintyre Drive, Bolton BL3 4PE* T: (01204) 63730 E: eplant@supanet.com *or* eplant225@gmail.com

PLANT, Mrs Glenys. b 49. ALA 71. EMMTC 95. d 98 p 99. C Allestree *Derby* 98–01; rtd 01; PtO *Derby* from 01. *3 Stoodley Pike Gardens, Allestree, Derby DE22 2TN* T: (01332) 552697

PLANT, John Frederick. b 61. Man Univ BA 82 MEd 95. Qu Coll Birm 83. d 85 p 86. C Kersal Moor *Man* 85–88; Chapl Aston Univ *Birm* 88–94; TR Market Bosworth, Cadeby w Sutton Cheney etc *Leic* 94–00; P-in-c The Sheepy Gp 98–00; TR Bosworth and Sheepy Gp 00–12; P-in-c Nailstone and Carlton w Shackerstone 04–12; Ch Relns Manager Chr Aid 12–20; Nat Ch Relns Lead from 20; PtO *Leic* from 12. *Brookfield Barn, Sibson Lane, Shenton, Nuneaton CV13 6DA* T: (01455) 212334

PLANT, Katharine Jill. b 66. Leeds Univ BA 88 Bradf and Ilkley Coll PGCE 94. Coll of Resurr Mirfield 14. d 16 p 17. C Holbeach *Linc* 16–19; P-in-c Breadsall *Derby* from 19; P-in-c Morley and Smalley from 19. *The Rectory, 57 Rectory Lane, Breadsall, Derby DE21 5LL* M: 07975-774170 E: kateplant2610@gmail.com

PLANT, Michael Ian. b 47. Man Univ MEd 85 GNSM 68. St Jo Coll Nottm 97. d 99 p 00. NSM St D Cathl 99–01; NSM Dewisland 01–18; NSM Gtr Dewisland from 18. *Pencnwc Cottages, 1 Spring Gardens, Castle Morris, Haverfordwest SA62 5ER* T: (01348) 841390 E: mikeandvalplant@btinternet.com

PLANT, Nicholas. b 58. Sarum Coll MA 15 MAAT 87. SAOMC 95. d 98 p 99. OLM W Slough *Ox* 98–04; OLM Burnham w Dropmore, Hitcham and Taplow 04–08; NSM Taplow and Dropmore 08–09; C The Cookhams 09–14; V from 14. *The Vicarage, Churchgate, Sutton Road, Cookham, Maidenhead SL6 9SP* T: (01628) 529183 E: fr.nick@ymail.com

PLANT, Nicholas. See PLANT, Richard George Nicholas

PLANT, Richard. b 41. Open Univ BSc 93. Qu Coll Birm 88. d 90 p 91. C Skelmersdale St Paul *Liv* 90–93; R Golborne 93–00; R Hesketh w Becconsall *Blackb* 00–07; rtd 07; PtO *Blackb* from 07. *12 Granville Avenue, Hesketh Bank, Preston PR4 6AH* T: (01772) 815257 E: richard.plant1@yahoo.co.uk

PLANT, Richard George Nicholas. b 45. Man Univ BA 67. Coll of Resurr Mirfield 68. d 71 p 72. C Cleckheaton St Jo *Wakef* 71–74; P-in-c Adel *Ripon* 74–78; V Ireland Wood 78–82; V Armley w New Wortley 82–92; R Garforth 92–08; rtd 08; PtO *York* from 08. *3 Holman Avenue, Garforth, Leeds LS25 1HU* T: 0113-287 6064 E: nick.plant@tiscali.co.uk

PLANT, Stephen John. b 64. Birm Univ BA 86 Fitzw Coll Cam PhD 93. ERMC 10. d 11 p 11. Dean and Fell Trin Hall Cam from 10; NSM Cambridge St Jas *Ely* 11–13. *Trinity Hall, Cambridge CB2 1TJ* T: (01223) 241169 *or* 332548 M: 07824-835199 E: sjp27@cam.ac.uk

PLANT, Thomas Richard. b 79. St Andr Univ MA 01 Bris Univ MPhil 05 Selw Coll Cam PhD 13. Westcott Ho Cam 08. d 12 p 13. C Gt Berkhamsted, Gt and Lt Gaddesden etc *St Alb* 12–16; TV Old St Pancras *Lon* 16–17; Chapl Lich Cathl Sch 17–21; PV and Subchanter Lich Cath 17–21; Chapl Rikkyo Univ Japan from 21; CF(V) from 14. *4-15-7-17B Nishi-Ikebukuro, Toshima-ku, Tokyo 171-0021, Japan* M: 07766-283546 E: tomplant@mac.com

PLATT, Anne Cecilia. See HOLMES, Anne Cecilia

PLATT, Damian Edward. b 82. Ox Brookes Univ BA 04. Oak Hill Th Coll BA 12. d 12 p 13. C Bispham *Blackb* 12–15; V Thornton-le-Fylde from 15. *Christ Church Vicarage, Meadows Avenue, Thornton-Cleveleys FY5 2TW* T: (01253) 855099 M: 07875-311929 E: damian@theplattfamily.org

PLATT, Mrs Jane Marie. b 54. Westhill Coll Birm CertEd 76 Open Univ BA 90. Qu Coll Birm 05. d 08 p 09. NSM Quinton Road W St Boniface *Birm* 08–15; PtO 15–18; P-in-c Frankley from 18. *39 Richmond Road, Rubery, Rednal, Birmingham B45 9UN* T: 0121-453 3035 E: janeplatt@onetel.com

PLATTEN, Canon Aidan Stephen George. b 76. Ripon Coll Cuddesdon BTh 03. d 03 p 04. C Woodbridge St Mary St E 03–06; Bp's Chapl *Glouc* 06–11; Hon Min Can Glouc Cathl 09–11; V St Marylebone St Mark Hamilton Terrace *Lon* 11–17; Prec and Can Res Nor Cathl from 17. *33 The Close, Norwich NR1 4DZ* T: (01603) 218314 E: canonprecentor@cathedral.org.uk

PLATTEN, Canon Gregory Austin David. b 78. Worc Coll Ox BA 00 MA 08 Ox Univ MTh 05 Linc Coll Ox DPhil 13. Ripon Coll Cuddesdon 01. d 03 p 04. C St John's Wood *Lon* 03–07; Chapl Linc Coll Ox 07–13; Hon C Ox St Mich w St Martin and All SS 07–13; V Friern Barnet All SS *Lon* 13–20; AD Cen Barnet 16–20; AD W Barnet 18–20; Can Res and Chan Lich Cathl from 20. *23 The Close, Lichfield WS13 7LD* M: 07891-124478 E: gregory@priest.com

✠**PLATTEN, The Rt Revd Stephen George.** b 47. Lon Univ BEd 72 Trin Coll Ox BD 03 UEA Hon DLitt 03 Huddersfield Univ Hon DUniv 12 Hon FGCM 12. Cuddesdon Coll 72. d 75 p 76 c 03. C Headington *Ox* 75–78; Chapl and Tutor Linc Th Coll 78–83; Can Res Portms Cathl and Dir of Ords *Portsm* 83–89; Abp's Sec for Ecum Affairs *Cant* 90–95; Hon Can Cant Cathl 90–95; Dean Nor 95–03; Bp Wakef 03–14; rtd 14; R St Mich Cornhill w St Pet le Poer etc *Lon* 14–16; Hon Asst Bp Lon from 14; Hon Asst Bp Newc from 14; Asst Bp S'wark from 14; Hon Can Musoma from 08. *22 Quay Walls, Berwick-upon-Tweed TD15 1HB* T: (01289) 305067 E: stephen.platten@icloud.com

PLATTIN, Miss Darleen Joy. b 63. Oak Hill Th Coll BA 94. ERMC 04. d 07 p 08. C Barnham Broom and Upper Yare *Nor* 07–10; P-in-c Easton, Colton, Marlingford and Bawburgh 10–14; P-in-c Gt and Lt Plumstead w Thorpe End and Witton 14–18; P-in-c Rackheath and Salhouse 18; R Gt and Lt Plumstead, Rackheath w Salhouse and Witton from 18. *The Rectory, 56 Green Lane West, Rackheath, Norwich NR13 6PG* E: darleenplattin@btinternet.com

PLATTS, Anthony Russell. b 41. Qu Coll Birm. d 08 p 09. NSM Hill *Birm* 08–11; PtO from 11. *14 Wheatcroft Close, Four Oaks, Sutton Coldfield B75 5SU* M: 07984-817564 E: a_platts1@sky.com

PLATTS, Mrs Hilary Anne Norrie. b 60. K Coll Lon BD 85 AKC 85 SRN 81. Ripon Coll Cuddesdon 86. d 88 p 94. C Moulsham St Jo *Chelmsf* 88–90; Chapl Reading Univ *Ox* 90–99; C Calcot 90–92; NSM Reading Deanery 99–00; PtO *Birm* 00–07; Chapl Birm Community Healthcare NHS Foundn Trust 01–07; Chapl Cov and Warks Partnership NHS Trust 03–07; PtO *Birm* 07–09; Adv for Women's Min (Colchester Area) from 08; Chapl Colchester Hosp Univ NHS Foundn Trust 09–18; Chapl E Suffolk and N Essex NHS Foundn Trust 18–20; Chapl Essex Partnership Univ NHS Foundn Trust from 20. *11 West Lodge Road, Colchester CO3 3NL* E: hilaryplatts@gmail.com

PLATTS, Timothy Caradoc. b 61. LMH Ox BA 83 MA 88 St Cross Coll Ox DPhil 88. Ripon Coll Cuddesdon 87. d 89 p 90. C Whitley Ch Ch *Ox* 89–95; P-in-c Earley St Nic 95–98; V 98–00; V Four Oaks *Birm* 00–07; P-in-c Elmstead *Chelmsf* 07–14; Chapl to Bp Colchester 07–14; P-in-c Greenstead w Colchester St Anne 14–20; PtO from 20. *11 West Lodge Road, Colchester CO3 3NL* E: dogwalker2512@gmail.com

PLAYER, Leslie Mark. b 65. Ridley Hall Cam 92. d 95 p 96. C Belper *Derby* 95–98; C Hamworthy *Sarum* 98–03; R W Downland from 03. *The Rectory, 91 Mill End, Damerham, Fordingbridge SP6 3HU* T: (01725) 518642 E: leslieplayer@hotmail.com

PLAYLE, Ms Merrin Laura. b 58. Univ of Wales (Swansea) BSc 79. Ridley Hall Cam 99. d 01 p 02. C Haslemere and Grayswood *Guildf* 01–05; V E Ham St Paul *Chelmsf* from 05. *St Paul's Vicarage, 227 Burges Road, London E6 2EU* T: (020) 8552 9955 E: merrin.playle@btinternet.com

PLEDGER, Mrs Nicola. b 55. Lon Bible Coll BA 94. SAOMC 99. d 01 p 02. C Ware Ch Ch *St Alb* 01–05; PtO 05–11; V Hitcham *Ox* 11–16; rtd 16; PtO *Ox* from 16; *St Alb* from 17. *132 Quickley Lane, Chorleywood, Rickmansworth WD3 5PQ* T: (01923) 283200 E: npledger77@gmail.com

PLIMLEY, Canon William. b 17. St Aid Birkenhead 50. d 52 p 53. C Norbury *Ches* 52–55; V Laisterdyke *Bradf* 55–83; RD Calverley 65–78; Hon Can Bradf Cathl 67–83; rtd 83; PtO

Bradf 83–14; *Leeds* from 14. *18 Holden Grange, 31 Holden Lane, Baildon, Shipley BD17 6JF*

PLIMMER, Wayne Robert. b 64. St Chad's Coll Dur BA 85 Leeds Univ MA 07. St Steph Ho Ox 86. **d** 88 **p** 89. C Cockerton *Dur* 88–91; C Poulton-le-Fylde *Blackb* 91–93; V Darton *Wakef* 93–06; P-in-c Cawthorne 04–06; V Beeston *S'well* from 06. *The Vicarage, Middle Street, Beeston, Nottingham NG9 1GA* T: 0115-925 4571 E: wplimmer125@gmail.com

PLOWMAN, Richard Robert Bindon. b 38. Solicitor 61. Ridley Hall Cam 76. **d** 78 **p** 79. C Combe Down w Monkton Combe *B & W* 78–81; C Combe Down w Monkton Combe and S Stoke 81–83; V Coxley w Godney, Henton and Wookey 83–03; RD Shepton Mallet 95–01; rtd 03; PtO *B & W* from 04. *Hyland House, Lower Rudge, Frome BA11 2QE* T: (01373) 831316

PLOWS, Jonathan. b 57. Warwick Univ BA 79 Homerton Coll Cam PGCE 80 Birkbeck Coll Lon MSc 85. STETS BA 07. **d** 07 **p** 08. NSM Salisbury St Thos and St Edm *Sarum* 07–19; P-in-c Wylye and Till Valley from 19. *The Rectory, Duck Street, Steeple Langford, Salisbury SP3 4NH* E: jonplows@aol.com

PLUMB, Gordon Alan. b 42. Leeds Univ BA 64. Sarum & Wells Th Coll. **d** 82 **p** 83. C Biggleswade *St Alb* 82–86; TV Grantham *Linc* 86–95; P-in-c Saxby All Saints 95–97; R 97–07; P-in-c Bonby 95–97; V 97–07; P-in-c Horkstow 95–97; V 97–07; P-in-c S Ferriby 95–97; R 97–07; P-in-c Worlaby 95–97; V 97–07; rtd 07; PtO *Linc* from 08. *Ingham House, 45A Dam Road, Barton-upon-Humber DN18 5BT* T: (01652) 636445 E: gplumb2000@aol.com

PLUMB, Nicola Louise. *See* MOY, Nicola Louise

PLUMB, Capt Stephen Paul. b 59. Wilson Carlile Coll. **d** 15 **p** 17. C The Six *Cant* 15–18; NSM Homerton *Lon* from 18. *All Souls' Vicarage, 44 Overbury Street, London E5 0AJ* M: 07905-040119 E: revcaptainplumby@hotmail.com

PLUMB, Stuart Peter. b 81. Ox Brookes Univ BA 04. Trin Coll Bris MA 14. **d** 14 **p** 15. C Kingston Hill St Paul *S'wark* 14–17; C Ealing St Paul *Lon* from 17; C Hanwell St Mellitus w St Mark from 17. *St Mellitus' Vicarage, 1 Church Road, London W7 3BA* M: 07598-335324 E: stuplumb@gmail.com *or* stu@stmellitushanwell.com

PLUMB, Canon Valerie Isabelle Dawn Frances. b 69. Ripon Coll Cuddesdon BTh 02. **d** 01 **p** 02. C Newport St Andr *Mon* 01–03; C Monmouth w Overmonnow etc 03–06; TV By Brook *Bris* 06–09; TV Colerne w N Wraxall 06–09; OCM 06–09; R Quantock Towers *B & W* 09–15; Area Dean for Rural Miss and Development Buckm Adnry *Ox* from 15; RD Mursley from 19; Hon Can Ch Ch from 21. *Westfields, Church Lane, Ludgershall, Aylesbury HP18 9NU* T: (01844) 239347 M: 07825-877722 E: val.plumb@oxford.anglican.com

PLUMLEY, Paul Jonathan. b 42. St Jo Coll Nottm 71. **d** 74 **p** 75. C Mile Cross *Nor* 74–77; P-in-c Wickham Skeith *St E* 77–79; P-in-c Stoke Ash, Thwaite and Wetheringsett 77–79; Assoc Min Woodbridge St Jo 80–81; Chapl RAF 81–86; PtO *Roch* 86–95; R Hever, Four Elms and Mark Beech 95–00; Sen Chapl Maidstone and Tunbridge Wells NHS Trust 00–07; rtd 07; PtO *Roch* from 08; PV Roch Cathl from 12. *4 Cedar Ridge, Tunbridge Wells TN2 3NX* T: (01892) 514499 M: 07925-615601 E: pauljplumley@gmail.com *or* paulplumley@outlook.com

PLUMMER, Ángela. b 59. Linc Sch of Th and Min. **d** 13 **p** 14. C Melbourne, Ticknall, Smisby and Stanton *Derby* 13–17; P-in-c Kenton Ascension *Newc* 17–21; rtd 21. *11 The Links, Whitley Bay NE26 1PS* M: 07721-023339 E: aplummer@live.co.uk

PLUMMER, Miss Anne Frances. b 36. Bedf Coll Lon BA 57. S'wark Ord Course 79. **dss** 82 **d** 87 **p** 94. NSM Salfords S'wark 82–06; Dean MSE (Croydon) 97–02; PtO from 06. *50 Park View Road, Salfords, Redhill RH1 5DN* T: (01293) 785852

PLUMMER, Canon Deborah Ann. b 49. St Hugh's Coll Ox BA 71 MA 75. St Alb Minl Tr Scheme 82. **dss** 85 **d** 87 **p** 94. Ickenham *Lon* 85–88; Par Dn 87–88; C Northolt St Mary 88–92; Chapl Lee Abbey 92–95; P-in-c Kintbury w Avington *Ox* 95–01; Lect Bolton St Pet *Man* 01–07; P-in-c Prestwich St Marg 07–14; C Prestwich St Gabr 10–14; AD Radcliffe and Prestwich 09–13; Hon Can Man Cathl 12–14; rtd 14; PtO *Man* from 15; *Leeds* from 17. *Meadow View, 7 Church Terrace, Berry Brow, Huddersfield HD4 7NB* T: (01484) 667661 M: 07593-837343 E: debberry@mail.com

PLUMPTON, Paul. b 50. Keble Coll Ox BA 72 MA 76. St Steph Ho Ox 72. **d** 74 **p** 75. C Tonge Moor *Man* 74–76; C Atherton 76–79; V Oldham St Jas 79–99; V Oldham St Jas w St Ambrose 99–17; rtd 17. *6 Hallet Court, Hughes Hallet Street, Sliema SLM 3142, Malta GC* T: (00356) 2783 6339 E: theplookes@gmail.com

PLUNKETT, Michael Edward. b 38. MBE 04. Leeds Univ BSc 61. Ely Th Coll 61. **d** 63 **p** 64. C Kirkby *Liv* 63–68; Lect Stockton-on-Tees 68–72; LtO *Dur* 72–73; TV Stockton 73–75;

V Cantril Farm *Liv* 75–81; Soc Resp Officer 81–89; V Melling 81–91; TR Speke St Aid 91–04; rtd 04; PtO *Heref* from 04. *1 The Ridge, Bishops Castle SY9 5AB* T: (01588) 630018 E: m.plunkettzzl@btinternet.com

PLUNKETT, Canon Peter William. b 30. Oak Hill Th Coll. **d** 61 **p** 62. C Fazakerley Em *Liv* 61–64; C St Helens St Mark 64–68; V Kirkdale St Paul N Shore 68–79; P-in-c Bootle St Mary w St Jo 77–79; V Bootle St Mary w St Paul 79–81; V Goose Green 81–89; V W Derby St Jas 89–98; Hon Can Liv Cathl 97–98; rtd 98. *50 Trinity Crescent, West Shore, Llandudno LL30 2PQ* T: (01492) 872109

PLYMING, Philip James John. b 74. Rob Coll Cam BA 96 St Jo Coll Dur BA 00 Edin Univ PhD 08. Cranmer Hall Dur 98. **d** 01 **p** 02. C Chineham *Win* 01–06; V Claygate *Guildf* 06–17; AD Emly 12–17; Warden Cranmer Hall Dur from 17. *St John's College, 3 South Bailey, Durham DH1 3RJ* T: 0191-334 3894 E: cranmer.warden@durham.ac.uk

PLYMOUTH, Archdeacon of. *See* SHUTT, The Ven Nicholas Stephen

PLYMOUTH, Suffragan Bishop of. *See* MACKINNEL, The Rt Revd Nicholas Howard Paul

PNEMATICATOS, Nicholas Peter Anthony. b 59. N Lon Univ BA 92 Lon Univ MA 93. Ripon Coll Cuddesdon 93. **d** 95 **p** 96. C Yeovil St Mich *B & W* 95–98; Chapl Yeovil Coll 95–96; Chapl RN 98–02; Chapl RAF 02–08; P-in-c Mill End and Heronsgate w W Hyde *St Alb* 08–10; rtd 16. *c/o Crockford, Church House, 27 Great Smith Street, London SW1P 3AZ* M: 07703-566787 E: nicholaspeteranthony59@protonmail.com

POARCH, Canon John Chilton. b 30. Bris Univ BA 54. Ridley Hall Cam 54. **d** 56 **p** 57. C Swindon Ch Ch *Bris* 56–59; C Corsham 59–61; R Praslin Seychelles 61–63; V Brislington St Cuth *Bris* 63–69; Adn Seychelles 69–72; R St Paul's Cathl Mahé 69–72; V Warmley *Bris* 72–86; R Syston 72–86; RD Bitton 79–85; P-in-c 80–86; Hon Can Bris Cathl 82–95; P-in-c Langley Fitzurse 86–94; Dioc Dir of Ords 86–94; Dir Ord Tr 94–95; P-in-c Draycot Cerne 87–94; rtd 95; PtO *Bris* 95–19; *B & W* 98–01; Officer for the Welfare of Rtd Mins Bris Adnry from 01; Dioc Convenor Rtd Clergy Assn from 01. *16 Norley Road, Bristol BS7 0HP* T: 0117-329 4496

POCOCK, Lynn Elizabeth. b 48. Coll of Wooster Ohio BA 69 CertEd 71. Qu Coll Birm 73. **dss** 82 **d** 87 **p** 94. Gleadless *Sheff* 82–85; Thorpe Hesley 85–92; Par Dn 87–92; NSM Ribbesford w Bewdley and Dowles *Worc* 92–03; PtO 03–15; *Sheff* from 15. *149 Crimicar Lane, Sheffield S10 4FD* M: 07985-160470 E: lynn_pocock@yahoo.com

POCOCK, Canon Nigel John. b 47. Lon Univ BSc 68 Birm Univ MA 83 Lambeth STh 78 Univ of Wales (Lamp) MMin 11. Oak Hill Th Coll 69. **d** 72 **p** 73. C Tunbridge Wells St Jas *Roch* 72–75; C Heatherlands St Jo *Sarum* 75–78; V Leic St Chris 78–83; R Camborne *Truro* 83–97; RD Carnmarth N 91–96; Hon Can Truro Cathl 92–97; V Old Windsor *Ox* 97–09; rtd 09; PtO *Liv* from 17. *19 Epping Drive, Woolston, Warrington WA1 4QL* T: (01925) 555996 E: njpoc@tiscali.co.uk

PODD, Alexandra Frances Grace. b 96. Birm Univ BSc 17 Dur Univ BA 21. Trin Coll Bris 18. **d** 21. C Alwalton and Chesterton *Ely* from 21; C The Ortons from 21. *Address withheld by request* E: revdalexandra@gmail.com

PODGER, Richard Philip Champeney. b 38. K Coll Cam BA 61 MA 66. Cuddesdon Coll 62. **d** 64 **p** 65. C Doncaster St Geo *Sheff* 64–68; C Orpington All SS *Roch* 68–74; W Germany 76–88; Chapl Kassel *Eur* 83–88; TV Whitstable *Cant* 88–94; PtO 95–12; Chapl E Kent NHS and Soc Care Partnership Trust 02–06; Chapl Kent and Medway NHS and Soc Care Partnership Trust 06–10; PtO *S & B* from 12. *Dros y Sir, Pen Cantref, Cantref, Brecon LD3 8LT* T: (01874) 622160 E: podger38@gmail.com

⚥POGGO, The Rt Revd Anthony Dangasuic. b 64. Univ of Juba BSc 88 Nairobi Internat Sch of Th MA 94 Ox Brookes Univ MBA 01. **d** 95 **p** 96 **c** 07. C Moyo Town Uganda 95–96; C Nairobi St Luke Kenya 96–07; Bp Kajo-Keji S Sudan 07–16; Abp's Adv for Angl Communion Affairs *Cant* from 16; Hon Asst Bp Lon from 17; Hon Asst Bp S'wark from 17. *Lambeth Palace, London SE1 7JU* T: (020) 7898 1218 M: 07765-090963 E: anthony.poggo@lambethpalace.org.uk

POGMORE, Canon Edward Clement. b 52. Sarum & Wells Th Coll 76. **d** 79 **p** 80. C Calne and Blackland *Sarum* 79–82; TV Oakdale 82–89; Min Creekmoor LEP 82–89; Chapl Geo Eliot Hosp Nuneaton 89–94; Chapl Nuneaton Hosps 89–94; Chapl Geo Eliot Hosp NHS Trust Nuneaton 94–14; Chapl Co-ord for N Warks 94–14; PtO *Leic* from 91; Hon Can Cov Cathl 00–14; rtd 14; Chapl Abbeyfield Binley Cov from 14. *1 Bowman Green, Burbage, Hinckley LE10 2QY* T: (01455) 611492 M: 07721-510221 E: edpog@hotmail.com

POINTS, John David. b 43. Qu Coll Birm 78. **d** 80 **p** 81. C Wednesbury St Paul Wood Green *Lich* 80–85; V 93–01; V Sedgley St Mary 85–93; TR Wednesfield 01–08; AD

Wolverhampton 03–08; rtd 08; PtO *St As* from 09. *13 Oldcastle Avenue, Guilsfield, Welshpool SY21 9PA* T: (01938) 552092 E: jd.spoints@gmail.com

POLASHEK, Miss Stella Christine. b 44. Leic Poly MA 85. EMMTC 92. **d** 95 **p** 96. NSM Appleby Gp *Leic* 95–08; NSM Woodfield 08–10; Chapl Leic Gen Hosp NHS Trust 99–00; Chapl Univ Hosps Leic NHS Trust 00–10; rtd 10; PtO *Leic* 11–19. *85 Parkfield Crescent, Appleby Magna, Swadlincote DE12 7BW* T: (01530) 272707 E: stella.85@btinternet.com

POLE, David John. b 46. Bath Academy of Art BA 72. Trin Coll Bris 84. **d** 86 **p** 87. C Bris St Mary Redcliffe w Temple etc 86–90; V Alveston 90–98; V Alveston and Littleton-on-Severn w Elberton 98–15; C Pilning w Compton Greenfield 11–15; rtd 15. *18 Nelson House, Nelson Place West, Bath BA1 2TL* T: (01225) 333427 E: davepole@gmail.com

POLE, Francis John Michael. b 42. FRSA 64 MInstTA 00 CQSW 74 MCMI 99. St Jo Sem Wonersh 62. **d** 67 **p** 68. In RC Ch 67–75; NSM Walthamstow St Pet *Chelmsf* 75; NSM Penge Lane H Trin *Roch* 76–77; NSM Shirley St Jo *Cant* 77–79; Assoc Chapl The Hague *Eur* 79–83; V Norbury St Steph and Thornton Heath *Cant* 83–84; S'wark 85–00; Sen Dioc Police Chapl 95–00; Sen Chapl Sussex Police 00–03; Nat Co-ord Police Chapl 00–04; Sen Chapl Sussex Ambulance Service 04–06; Co-ord Chapl SE Coast Ambulance Service 06–12; TV Crawley *Chich* 00–12; Chapl to People at Work 00–12; Sen Chapl SE Coast Ambulance Service NHS Foundn Trust from 12; PtO *Chich* from 13. *35 Turnpike Place, Crawley RH11 7UA* T: (01293) 513264 M: 07764-752608 E: francis.pole@virgin.net

POLHILL, Mrs Christine. b 46. Nottm Coll of Educn CertEd 67 Qu Coll Birm BA 00. St Alb Minl Tr Scheme 81. **dss** 84 **d** 87 **p** 94. St Alb St Mary Marshalswick 84–94; Hon Par Dn 87–94; C Cottered w Broadfield and Throcking 94–96; C Ardeley 94–96; P-in-c 96–99; C Weston 94–96; PtO *Lich* 99–00; C Lich St Mich w St Mary and Wall 00–06; rtd 06; LtO *Lich* 06–12; PtO 12–13; Hon C Hints 13–14; PtO from 16. *Address withheld by request*

POLITT, Robert William. b 47. ARCM LGSM 68. Oak Hill Th Coll 73. **d** 76 **p** 77. C Bexleyheath St Pet *Roch* 76–82; TV Southgate *Chich* 82–90; Chapl N Foreland Lodge Sch Basingstoke 90–98; R Sherfield-on-Loddon and Stratfield Saye etc *Win* 98–13; P-in-c Bramley 10–13; rtd 13; PtO *Ely* from 15. *53 Somerset Road, Histon, Cambridge CB24 9JS* E: bobpolitt@btinternet.com

POLKINHORN, Mrs Judith Edith Elizabeth. b 47. Wolv Univ MBA 04. ERMC 13. **d** 14 **p** 15. NSM Lordsbridge *Ely* 14–16; PtO 16–21; *Carl* from 16. *Robridding, Kaber, Kirkby Stephen CA17 4ER* E: judypolkinhorn@gmail.com

POLL, Canon Martin George. b 61. Kent Univ BA 83. Ripon Coll Cuddesdon 84. **d** 87 **p** 88. C Mill Hill Jo Keble Ch *Lon* 87–90; Chapl RN 90–10; Prin Angl Chapl and Adn for the RN 10–12; QHC 10–12; Hon Can Portsm Cathl 11–12; Can Windsor and Chapl in Windsor Gt Park from 12. *1 The Cloisters, Windsor Castle, Windsor SL4 1NJ* T: (01753) 848713 E: martin.poll@stgeorges-windsor.org

POLLARD, Adrian. *See* POLLARD, James Adrian Hunter

POLLARD, Mrs Ann Beatrice. b 46. **d** 03 **p** 04. NSM Mirfield *Wakef* 03–10; NSM Dewsbury 10–14; *Leeds* 14–18; PtO from 18. *9 Manor Drive, Mirfield WF14 0EF* T: (01924) 495322 M: 07513-152864 E: revdannpollard@gmail.com

POLLARD, Mrs Christine Beryl. b 45. NOC 86. **d** 89 **p** 94. Par Dn Ingrow w Hainworth *Bradf* 89–94; C Nuneaton St Nic *Cov* 94–98; P-in-c Bourton w Frankton and Stretton on Dunsmore etc 98–07; C Leam Valley 06–07; rtd 07; PtO *Cov* 08–18. *9 Overberry Orchard, Leamington Spa CV33 9SJ* T: (01926) 832053 E: cbpollard@talktalk.net

POLLARD, David John Athey. b 44. ACP 74 Culham Coll Ox CertEd 69. St Jo Coll Nottm LTh 88. **d** 88 **p** 89. C Illogan *Truro* 88–91; R Roche and Withiel 91–95; TV Maidstone St Martin *Cant* 95–97; C Parkwood CD 95–97; R Lanreath *Truro* 97–99; V Pelynt 97–99; R Lanreath, Pelynt and Bradoc 99–03; rtd 03; PtO *Truro* 14–21. *Melyn Brea, 11 Mill Hill, Lostwithiel PL22 0HB* T: (01208) 871541 E: dave@melynbrea.co.uk

POLLARD, Eric John. b 43. Chich Th Coll 83. **d** 85 **p** 86. C Brighton St Matthias *Chich* 85–90; C E Grinstead St Swithun 90–96; C Hove 96–00; P-in-c Brighton St Matthias 00–13; rtd 13; PtO *Chich* 14–17. *30 Pondsyde Court, Sutton Drove, Seaford BN25 3ET* E: eric.pollard@btinternet.com

POLLARD, James Adrian Hunter. b 48. St Jo Coll Nottm BTh 78. **d** 78 **p** 79. C Much Woolton *Liv* 78–81; CMS 81–84; V Toxteth Park Ch Ch *Liv* 85–90; CF 90–09; rtd 09; PtO *Sarum* 09–12; Hon C Upper Wylye Valley 12–14; PtO from 14. *Horwood House, 80 Boreham Road, Warminster BA12 9JW* E: ade.pollard@gmail.com

POLLARD, Mrs Judith Mary. b 56. Westcott Ho Cam 09. **d** 11 **p** 12. C Newark w Coddington *S'well* 11–14; C Gayton,

Gayton Thorpe, E Walton, E Winch etc *Nor* 14–15; TV Ashwicken w Leziate, Bawsey etc from 15. *The Rectory, Watery Lane, Grimston, King's Lynn PE32 1BQ* M: 07852-257734 E: wotzpollard@aol.com

POLLARD, Matthew Rupert. b 66. Qu Coll Ox BA 88 MA 92. St Jo Coll Nottm. **d** 03 **p** 04. C Huddersfield St Pet *Wakef* 03–07; Asst Chapl Huddersfield Univ 03–07; P-in-c Rastrick St Matt 07–08; P-in-c Rastrick St Jo 07–08; V Rastrick 08–13; R Bridlington Priory *York* from 13; RD Bridlington from 17. *The Rectory, Church Green, Bridlington YO16 7JX* T: (01262) 672221 E: matthewrpollard@btinternet.com

POLLARD, Stephen. b 59. Coll of Resurr Mirfield 96. **d** 98 **p** 99. C Lt Lever *Man* 98–02; P-in-c Westleigh St Pet 02–10; P-in-c Westleigh St Paul 08–10; I Rosebud w McCrae Australia 10–21; I Newtown w Geelong W from 21. *15 Talbot Street, Newtown, Victoria 3220, Australia* E: fatherstephenpollard@gmail.com

POLLARD (née RAMSBOTTOM), Mrs Susan Elizabeth. b 56. Trin Coll Bris BD 79. Qu Coll Birm 06. **d** 09 **p** 10. NSM Warndon St Nic *Worc* 09–16; NSM Bowbrook N 16–18; NSM Bowbrook S 16–18; NSM Stoke Prior, Wychbold and Upton Warren 16–18; NSM Claines St Jo from 18; NSM Worc St Geo w St Mary Magd from 18. *5 Falmouth, Worcester WR4 0TE* T: (01905) 759214 E: suepollard2610@hotmail.com

POLLARD, Canon Vaughan. b 59. Aston Tr Scheme 88 Trin Coll Bris 90. **d** 92 **p** 93. C Nailsea H Trin *B & W* 92–95; C Acomb St Steph and St Aid *York* 95–97; P-in-c Moldgreen *Wakef* 97–99; P-in-c Rawthorpe 97–99; V Moldgreen and Rawthorpe 99–07; C Spalding and Spalding St Paul *Linc* 07–11; V Clayton *Bradf* 11–14; *Leeds* from 14; P-in-c Fairweather Green from 21; AD Bowling and Horton 14–16; AD Outer Bradf 17–21; Hon Can Wakef Cathl from 19. *The Vicarage, Clayton Lane, Clayton, Bradford BD14 6AX* T: (01274) 880373 E: vaughan.pollard@leeds.anglican.org

POLLINGER (née WHITFORD), Canon Judith. b 41. Ex Univ TCert 78 BEd 79. SWMTC 92. **d** 95 **p** 96. NSM St Endellion w Port Isaac and St Kew *Truro* 95–12; NSM St Minver 07–12; NSM N Cornwall Cluster 12–15; Convenor Bp's Gp for Min of Healing 04–11; Hon Can Truro Cathl 10–18; Preb St Endellion 12–18; rtd 15; PtO *Truro* from 15. *4 Marshalls Way, Trelights, Port Isaac PL29 3TE* T: (01208) 880181 E: rev.judith@btinternet.com

POLLINGTON, Miss Ann Elizabeth Jane. b 56. Univ Coll Chich BA 00. Ripon Coll Cuddesdon 00. **d** 02 **p** 03. C Honiton, Gittisham, Combe Raleigh, Monkton etc *Ex* 02–07; P-in-c St Ippolyts *St Alb* 07–10; R St Ippolyts w Gt and Lt Wymondley 07–10; R St Ippolyts w Gt and Lt Wymondley 10–15; RD Hitchin 11–15; V Cranbrook *Cant* from 15; AD Weald 17–19. *The Vicarage, Waterloo Road, Cranbrook TN17 3JQ* T: (01580) 388173 E: ann.pollington@btinternet.com

POLLIT, Preb Michael. b 30. Worc Coll Ox BA 54 MA 58. Wells Th Coll 54. **d** 56 **p** 57. C Cannock *Lich* 56–59; C Codsall 59–62; V W Bromwich St Pet 62–67; R Norton in the Moors 67–76; RD Leek 72–76; V Shrewsbury St Chad 76–87; V Shrewsbury St Chad w St Mary 87–95; Preb Lich Cathl 81–95; P-in-c Shrewsbury St Alkmund 91–95; rtd 95; PtO *Heref* 96–20. *Pentreheyling House, Churchstoke, Montgomery SY15 6HU* T: (01588) 620273

POLLIT, Ruth Mary. *See* LILLINGTON, Ruth Mary

POLLITT, Graham Anthony. b 48. BA 79. Oak Hill Th Coll 76. **d** 79 **p** 80. C Rusholme H Trin *Man* 79–82; TV Southgate *Chich* 82–83; C Burgess Hill St Andr 83–86; Chapl St Martin's Coll of Educn *Blackb* 86–90; Chapl Cheltenham and Glouc Coll of HE 90–98; PtO *Glouc* 98–99; C Bispham *Blackb* 99–04; P-in-c Caton w Littledale 04–17; rtd 17; PtO *Blackb* from 18. *12 Haydock Road, Lancaster LA1 4NB* E: grahamapollitt@gmail.com

POLLOCK, Christopher John. b 62. TCD BTh 89 QUB BD. CITC 86. **d** 89 **p** 90. C Agherton *Conn* 89–91; C Ballymoney w Finvoy and Rasharkin 91–93; I Derryvolgie 93–03; I Saintfield *D & D* from 03. *The Vicarage, 11 Lisburn Road, Saintfield, Ballynahinch BT24 7AL* T: (028) 9751 0286 E: chris.pollock3@btinternet.com

POLLOCK, Duncan James Morrison. b 54. QGM 75 MBE 95. Nottm Univ BCombStuds 83. Linc Th Coll 80. **d** 83 **p** 84. C Folkestone St Mary and St Eanswythe *Cant* 83–85; CF 85–98; R Broughton, Bossington, Houghton and Mottisfont *Win* 98–00; I Groomsport *D & D* from 00. *22 Sandringham Drive, Bangor BT20 5NA* T: (028) 9146 4476 E: duncanjmpollock@btinternet.com

POLLOCK, James Colin Graeme. b 53. St Chad's Coll Dur BA 76. Ripon Coll Cuddesdon 77. **d** 78 **p** 79. C Hartlepool St Oswald *Dur* 78–81; C Hartlepool St Aid 81–84; V Dawdon 84–05; V Seaham Harbour 03–05; TV S Shields All SS 05–13;

rtd 13; PtO *Dur* from 13. *25 Knocklofty Court, Belfast BT4 3NF*
E: graeme.pollock@hotmail.co.uk

POND, Canon Geraldine Phyllis. b 53. SRN 74 HVCert 75.
St Jo Coll Nottm MA 97. **d** 97 **p** 98. C Ancaster Wilsford Gp
Linc 97–01; P-in-c Harlaxton Gp 01–07; Chapl Linc Distr
Healthcare NHS Trust 01–07; P-in-c Ashbourne St Oswald
w Mapleton *Derby* 07–14; V 14–15; P-in-c Ashbourne St Jo
07–15; P-in-c Clifton 09–15; P-in-c Norbury w Snelston
09–15; Asst Dir of Ords 08–09; Dioc Dir of Ords 09–15;
Hon Can Derby Cathl 10–19; Dioc Voc Dir 15–19; Warden
of Readers 17–19; rtd 19; Chapl Derby Cathl 19–20; Chapl
to The Queen from 18. *Holy Cross House, Old Lincoln Road,
Caythorpe, Grantham NG32 3DF* M: 07736-196323

POND, Nigel Peter Hamilton. b 40. AKC 65. **d** 66 **p** 67.
C E Dereham w Hoe *Nor* 66–69; C Chapl RN 69–85; TR
Woughton *Ox* 85–93; Chapl Milton Keynes Gen Hosp
85–93; RD Milton Keynes *Ox* 90–93; R Olney w Emberton
93–97; R Olney 97–03; rtd 03. *4 Constantine Way, Bancroft
Park, Milton Keynes MK13 0RA* E: nigelphpond84@gmail.com

PONSONBY, Simon Charles Reuben. b 66. Bris Univ MLitt 96.
Trin Coll Bris BA 94. **d** 95 **p** 96. C Thorpe Edge *Bradf* 95–98;
Pastorate Chapl Ox St Aldate 98–05; C from 05. *St Aldate's
Parish Centre, 40 Pembroke Street, Oxford OX1 1BP* T: (01865)
254800 F: 201543 E: simon.ponsonby@staldates.org.uk

PONTEFRACT, Archdeacon of. *See* TOWNLEY, The Ven Peter
Kenneth

POOBALAN, The Very Revd Isaac Munuswamy. b 62.
RGN 84 Edin Univ BD 94 MTh 97 Aber Univ MPhil 98. Edin
Th Coll 91. **d** 94 **p** 95. C Edin St Pet 94–97; P-in-c Aberdeen
St Clem *Ab* 97–01; R Aberdeen St Jo 01–15; P-in-c Aberdeen
St Pet 04–15; Can St Andr Cathl 06–15; Chapl Robert Gordon
Univ from 08; Provost St Andr Cathl from 15; R Aberdeen
St Andr from 15. *St Andrew's Cathedral, 28 King Street, Aberdeen
AB4 5AX* T: (01224) 640119 E: aipoobalan@btinternet.com
or isaac.poobalan@standrewsaberdeen.org

POODHUN, Canon Lambert David. b 30. Natal Univ BA 53.
Edin Th Coll 54. **d** 56 **p** 57. C Durban St Aidan S Africa
56–60; P-in-c Pietermaritzburg St Paul 60–64; R 64–67; R
Overport 67–76; Adn Durban 75–76; C Upton cum Chalvey
Ox 77–80; Chapl Kingston Hosp Surrey 80–81; Chapl
Tooting Bec Hosp Lon 81–84; Chapl Hurstwood Park Hosp
Haywards Heath 84–91; Chapl St Fran Hosp Haywards Heath
84–94; Chapl Mid Sussex NHS Trust 94–01; Can and Preb
Chich Cathl 93–95; Hon C Haywards Heath St Rich from
01. *8 Nursery Close, Haywards Heath RH16 1HP* T: (01444)
440938 E: lambertpoodhun@gmail.com

POOLE, Clifford George. b 36. Keble Coll Ox BA 61 MA 65
Lon Univ PGCE 75. S'wark Ord Course 83. **d** 86 **p** 87. C W
Dulwich All SS and Em *S'wark* 86–90; Chapl Luxembourg
Eur 90–02; rtd 02; P-in-c Alderton, Gt Washbourne,
Dumbleton etc *Glouc* 02–05; TV Winchcombe 05–08; PtO
S'wark from 09; *Truro* from 15; *Lon* from 17; *Eur* from 09.
11 Berwyn Road, London SE24 9BD T: (020) 8674 3369
E: poole_clifford@yahoo.co.uk

POOLE, Canon Denise June. b 49. Leic Univ BSc 70 Bradf and
Ilkley Coll DipAdEd 85. NOC 90. **d** 93 **p** 94. C Horton and
Bradf St Oswald Chapel Green 93–97; Chapl Co-ord Bradf
Hosps NHS Trust 97–00; V Bradf St Aug Undercliffe 00–06;
Dioc Dir of Ords 01–06; Bp's Dom Chapl 06–14; Min and
Miss Officer 14–16; Hon Can Bradf Cathl 07–16; rtd 16; Hon
C Heaton St Barn *Leeds* 17–18; Hon C Girlington, Heaton
and Manningham 18–19; PtO from 19. *23 Leylands Lane,
Bradford BD9 5PX* T: (01274) 401679 *or* 545414 F: 544831
E: denise.poole@leeds.anglican.org

POOLE, Edward John. b 53. Hull Univ BA 81 Heythrop Coll
Lon MA 04. St Steph Ho Ox 81. **d** 83 **p** 84. C Stevenage
St Andr and St Geo St Alb 83–86; Tutor St Paul's Th Coll
Madagascar 86–88; V Weston and P-in-c Ardeley *St Alb*
88–96; P-in-c Cottered w Broadfield and Throcking
94–96; Chapl Bucharest w Sofia *Eur* 96–98; Chapl HM Pris
Lewes 98–03; Chapl HM Pris Featherstone 03–09; R York,
Beverley w Brookton and Quairading Australia 09–12; PtO
Heref 12–16; *Lon* 13–16; P-in-c Tenerife Sur *Eur* from 16.
*Residencial Sonia 17, Calle El Mojon, Callao Salvaje, 38678
Adeje, Santa Cruz de Tenerife, Spain* T: (0034) 922 742 045
E: john_poole_uk@yahoo.co.uk

POOLE, Helen Margaret. b 39. SRN. SWMTC. **d** 94 **p** 95. NSM
Ludgvan *Truro* 94–97; NSM Paul 97–02; NSM St Buryan,
St Levan and Sennen 02–04; rtd 04; PtO *Truro* 05–08;
Guildf from 12. *12 Lansdown, Guildford GU1 2LY* T: (01483)
546234 E: helenbob@stlevan.eclipse.co.uk

POOLE, Ian Richard Morley. b 52. Birm Univ MB, ChB 85
MRCGP 90. St Jo Coll Nottm MTh 02. **d** 02 **p** 03.
C Willenhall H Trin *Lich* 02–06; TV Bushbury
06–17; TR from 17. *St Mary's Vicarage, Bushbury*

Lane, Wolverhampton WV10 8JP T: (01902) 788151
E: woodchipper@btinternet.com

POOLE, James Christopher. b 73. Peterho Cam BA 94
MA 98. Aston Tr Scheme 96 Wycliffe Hall Ox 97. **d** 00 **p** 01.
C Wimbledon Park St Luke *S'wark* 00–04; Miss Partner
Crosslinks 04–07; Kenya 05–07; C Cambridge H Sepulchre
Ely 07–14; Exec Dir Wycliffe Bible Translators from 14; PtO
Ox 14–15; NSM Ox St Ebbe w H Trin and St Pet from 15.
28 Horseman Close, Headington, Oxford OX3 0NT T: (01865)
513268 E: james@poolehouse.org

POOLE, Miss Joan Wendy. b 37. Sarum Dioc Teacher Tr Coll
CertEd 57 Trin Coll Bris 86. **d** 87 **p** 94. Par Dn Longfleet
Sarum 87–89; Par Dn Hamworthy 89–94; C 94–97; rtd 97;
PtO *Sarum* 97–22. *35 Borley Road, Poole BH17 7DT* T: (01202)
256377 E: jwendypoole@virginmedia.com

POOLE, John. *See* POOLE, Edward John

POOLE, Mark. b 68. Westmr Coll of Educn BEd 90. St Hild
Coll 17. **d** 20 **p** 21. C Rural E York from 20. *Bede House,
Heslington Lane, Heslington, York YO10 5ED* T: (01904)
426522 M: 07854-446368 E: markpoole68@gmail.com

POOLE, Martin Bryce. b 59. Reading Univ BSc 80. St Jo Coll
Nottm 81. **d** 87 **p** 88. NSM Tulse Hill H Trin and St Matthias
S'wark 87–99; NSM Hove *Chich* 00–01; PtO 01–10;
P-in-c Prestonville St Luke 10–13; V from 13. *St Luke's Vicarage,
64A Old Shoreham Road, Brighton BN1 5DD* T/F: (01273)
557772 E: martin@stlukesonline.co.uk

POOLE, Martin Ronald. b 59. Aston Univ BSc 81 Leeds
Univ BA 86. Coll of Resurr Mirfield 84. **d** 87 **p** 88. C Sheff
St Cath Richmond Road 87–90; C W Hampstead St Jas *Lon*
90–94; V Colindale St Matthias 94–06; V Munster Square
Ch Ch and St Mary Magd 06–16; rtd 16; PtO *Lon* from
16. *17B Brodie Road, Enfield EN2 0EU* T: (020) 7388 3095
E: martin@martlondon.plus.com

POOLE, Nigel John Graydon. b 53. **d** 15 **p** 16. C Penge St Jo
Roch 15–17; P-in-c 17–19; PtO 20; C Beckenham Ch Ch from
20. *37 Groveland Road, Beckenham BR3 3PU* T: (020) 8663
1344 M: 07849-609486 E: nigel_poole@hotmail.co.uk

POOLE, Peter William. b 35. St Pet Hall Ox BA 59 MA 63.
Wells Th Coll 59. **d** 61 **p** 62. C Cheriton Street *Cant*
61–64; C Birchington w Acol 64–67; V Newington 67–73;
P-in-c Lower Halstow 72–73; V Bearsted 73–76; V Lane End
w Cadmore End *Ox* 84–89; R Chalfont St Giles 89–99; rtd
99; PtO *Guildf* from 99. *Primrose Cottage, St Nicholas Avenue,
Cranleigh GU6 7AQ* T: (01483) 272703

POOLE, Stuart. b 33. Lon Univ BScEng 55 Man Univ
MSc 76 CEng 65 FIEE 85. **d** 91 **p** 92. NSM Cheadle
Ches 91–03; PtO from 03. *1 Dene House, 3 Green
Pastures, Stockport SK4 3RB* T/F: 0161-432 6426
E: stuart.poole33@tiscali.co.uk

POOLE, Wendy. *See* POOLE, Joan Wendy

POOLEY, Clifford Russell. b 48. Glos Univ BA 03. WEMTC 08.
d 09 **p** 10. NSM Coberley, Cowley, Colesbourne and
Elkstone *Glouc* 09–14; NSM Churn Valley 14–21; rtd
21; PtO *Glouc* from 21. *8A Salterley Grange, Leckhampton
Hill, Cheltenham GL53 9QW* T: (01242) 243981
E: cliff.pooley@btinternet.com

POOLEY, Clive Nicholas. b 51. Lon Univ BEd 74. NTMTC 96.
d 99 **p** 00. C Barking St Marg w St Patr *Chelmsf* 99–02; V
Barking St Erkenwald 02–14; rtd 14; PtO *Chelmsf* from 14.
Bethel, 68 Tolkien Road, Eastbourne BN23 7AQ M: 07986-
451671 E: clive.n.pooley@gmail.com

POOLMAN, Alfred John. b 46. K Coll Lon BD 69 AKC 69.
St Aug Coll Cant 69. **d** 70 **p** 71. C Headingley *Ripon* 70–74;
C Moor Allerton 75–78; C Monk Bretton *Wakef* 78–80; V
Copley and Chapl Halifax Gen Hosp 80–90; R Llanfynydd
St As 90–06; P-in-c 06–10; rtd 11; PtO *St As* from 14. *The
Rectory, Llanfynydd, Wrexham LL11 5HH* T: (01978) 762304
E: johnpoolman@btinternet.com

POOLMAN, Mrs Carole Margaret. b 53. St As & Ban Minl
Tr Course 98. **d** 01 **p** 02. NSM Pontblyddyn *St As* 01–06;
P-in-c 06–16; P-in-c Llanfynydd 10–14; P-in-c Treuddyn
w Nercwys 15–16; I Mold Miss Area from 17. *The Rectory,
Llanfynydd, Wrexham LL11 5HH* T: (01978) 762304
E: cc.sm@btinternet.com

POOLTON, Martin Ronald. b 60. Kingston Poly BSc 81
Salford Univ MSc 83 Bp Grosseteste Coll PGCE 85 FRGS 81.
Ripon Coll Cuddesdon 95. **d** 97 **p** 98. C Penzance St Mary
w St Paul *Truro* 97–99; C Northampton St Matt *Pet* 99–01;
R Jersey St Pet *Win* 01–15. *Address withheld by request*
E: poolton2608@gmail.com

POON, Michael Nai-Chiu. b 53. Univ of BC BSc 75
MSc 77. Wycliffe Coll Toronto MDiv 80 DPhil 84. **d** 86
p 87. C St Steph Hong Kong Hong Kong 86–90; V Macau
St Mark 90–99; P-in-c Morrison Chpl 90–04; Dir Cen for
Story of Christianity Singapore Singapore 04–14; Hon
Can Singapore from 07; PtO *Lon* 14–19. *5 Avalon Close,*

London W13 0BJ T: (020) 8998 4525 M: 07779-537601
E: mncpoon@gmail.com

POPE, Preb Charles Guy. b 48. AKC 70. St Aug Coll Cant 70. d 71 p 72. C Southgate Ch Ch *Lon* 71–74; C N St Pancras All Hallows 74–77; C Hampstead St Steph 74–77; V New Southgate St Paul 77–86; V Brookfield St Mary 86–17; P-in-c Brookfield St Anne, Highgate Rise 88–99; AD S Camden 95–00; Preb St Paul's Cathl 04–17; rtd 17; PtO *Lon* 17–18. *6 Horsham Avenue, London N12 9BE* M: 07770-693435 E: cguypope@gmail.com

POPE, Miss Elizabeth Mercy. b 51. Man Univ BSc 73 Ex Univ PGCE 74. Trin Coll Bris 99. d 01 p 02. C Bardsley *Man* 01–05; P-in-c Oldham St Paul 05–08; P-in-c Denton St Lawr 08–17; C Audenshaw St Steph 13–17; C Denton Ch Ch 13–17; C Haughton St Anne 13–17; rtd 17; PtO *Ban* from 17. *33 Lon Gardener, Valley, Holyhead LL65 3DN* T: (01407) 740972 M: 07754-059364 E: elizabeth@mpope.plus.com

POPE, Guy. *See* POPE, Charles Guy

POPE, Miss Laura Elizabeth Hodgkinson. b 87. Kent Univ BA 09 Cam Univ PGCE 13 Dur Univ BA 20. Westcott Ho Cam 17. d 20 p 21. C Bury St Edmunds St Mary *St E* from 20. *18 Vinery Road, Bury St Edmunds IP33 2JR* E: laura.e.pope2020@gmail.com

POPE, Stephen Paul. b 49. Liv Univ MB, ChB 73 FRCA. Yorks Min Course 15. d 16 p 17. NSM Coxwold and Husthwaite *York* 16–20; NSM Crayke w Brandsby and Yearsley 16–20; NSM Alne 17–20; NSM Brafferton w Pilmoor, Myton-on-Swale etc 17–20; NSM Easingwold w Raskelf 17–20; NSM Skelton w Shipton and Newton on Ouse 17–20; NSM Strensall 17–20; NSM Forest of Galtres 17–20. *Bishop's Cottage, Church Hill, Crayke, York YO61 4TA* M: 07816-168735 E: stephenrevdoc@gmail.com

POPHAM, Neil Andrew. b 69. Trin Coll Ox BA 91 DPhil 96 MA 05 St Jo Coll Dur BA 05. Cranmer Hall Dur 03. d 05 p 06. C Quarry Bank *Worc* 05–07; C Brierley Hill 07–09; P-in-c Kirkby in Ashfield St Thos *S'well* 09–11; V 11–19; P-in-c Kirkby in Ashfield 15–19; TV Stantonbury and Willen *Ox* from 19. *Church House, 1A Atterbrook, Bradwell, Milton Keynes MK13 9EY* E: thepophams@talktalk.net *or* revneilpopham.mk@gmail.com

POPP, Miss Julia Alice Gisela. b 45. Univ of BC BA 71. St Jo Coll Nottm 78. dss 81 d 87 p 94. Woking St Mary *Guildf* 81–83; Hornsey Rise St Mary w St Steph *Lon* 83–87; Par Dn Hornsey Rise Whitehall Park Team 87–91; Par Dn Sutton St Nic *S'wark* 91–94; C 94–98; Missr Sutton Town Cen 91–98; rtd 05; PtO *Ely* 06–21. *32 Regatta Court, Oyster Row, Cambridge CB5 8NS* T: (01223) 350164 E: juliapopp16@gmail.com

POPPE, Andrew Nils. b 60. NE Lon Poly BSc 83. STETS 08. d 11 p 12. C Clarendon *Sarum* 11–15; V Cowes H Trin and St Mary *Portsm* from 15. *The Vicarage, Church Road, Cowes PO31 8HA* T: (01983) 292509 M: 07729-322616 E: stmarysvicarage@outlook.com

POPPLETON, Julian George. b 63. St Chad's Coll Dur BA 85 PGCE 86 Surrey Univ BA 02. STETS 99. d 02 p 03. NSM Harnham *Sarum* from 02; Chapl K Edw VI Sch Southn 02–20; Bp's Adv for Assoc Min *Sarum* from 20. *19 Thompson Close, Salisbury SP2 8QU* M: 07926-165189 E: revdjulian@gmail.com

POPPLEWELL, Andrew Frederick. b 53. St Jo Coll Dur BA 75. Wycliffe Hall Ox 76. d 78 p 79. C Clifton *York* 78–81; C Lich St Chad 82–84; V Laisterdyke *Bradf* 84–99. *Clifton, 210A Leeds Road, Eccleshill, Bradford BD2 3JU* T: (01274) 637651

PORT, Mrs Betty Anne. b 50. Univ of W Indies BA 71 Open Univ MA 93. STETS BA 10. d 10 p 11. NSM Preston w Sutton Poyntz, Littlemoor etc *Sarum* 10–14; NSM Wyke Regis 14–20; PtO from 20. *68 Mellstock Avenue, Dorchester DT1 2BQ* T: (01305) 263058 E: betty.port@which.net

PORTER, Andrew William. b 69. Bris Univ BSc 91 BA 01 PGCE 94. Trin Coll Bris 98. d 01 p 02. C Ipsley *Worc* 01–04; V Fairfield *Liv* 04–10; P-in-c Liv St Phil w St Dav 08–10; V Liv All SS 11–13; V S'well H Trin from 13. *Holy Trinity Vicarage, Westhorpe, Southwell NG25 0NB* E: awporter9@gmail.com

✠**PORTER, The Rt Revd Anthony.** b 52. Hertf Coll Ox BA 74 MA 78 Fitzw Ho Cam BA 76 MA 80. Ridley Hall Cam 74. d 77 p 78 c 06. C Edgware *Lon* 77–80; C Haughton St Mary *Man* 80–83; P-in-c Bacup Ch Ch 83–87; V 87–91; R Rusholme H Trin 91–06; Hon Can Man Cathl 04–06; Suff Bp Sherwood *S'well* 06–20; Hon Can S'well Minster 06–20; rtd 20; Hon Asst Bp Blackb from 20. *Address withheld by request* E: tprtrev@gmail.com

PORTER, Anthony. *See* PORTER, David Anthony

PORTER, Anthony David. b 79. Univ of Wales (Swansea) BS 03 BSc 04. St Mich Coll Llan 14. d 16 p 17. NSM Morriston *S & B* 16–17; C Llangyfelach from 17. *The Vicarage, 8 Maes y Dderwen, Llangyfelach, Swansea SA6 6ET* T: (01792) 790606 M: 07989-572837 E: a-porter38@sky.com

PORTER, Barbara Judith. *See* JEAPES, Barbara Judith

PORTER, Brian Meredith. b 39. Monash Univ Aus BA 66 Trin Hall Cam BA 75 MA 79 New England Univ NSW BLitt 79 MLitt 85 ACT ThD 01. Cuddesdon Coll 68. d 68 p 71. C Kew Australia 68–69; K Sch Parramatta 70–73; Chapl Canberra Gr Sch 75–82; Chapl Ivanhoe Gr Sch 83–97; Sen Chapl Melbourne Gr Sch 98–05; Chapl Brighton Gr Sch from 05. *4 Fairholme Grove, Camberwell Vic 3124, Australia* T: (0061) (3) 9882 8740 E: bmporter@comcen.com.au

PORTER (née RICHARDSON), Mrs Catherine Elisabeth. b 75. Edge Hill Coll of HE BA 96 Trin Coll Bris BA 99 MA 01. SNWTP 07. d 08 p 09. NSM Fairfield *Liv* 08–10; NSM Liv All SS 11–13; PtO S'well from 13. *Holy Trinity Vicarage, Westhorpe, Southwell NG25 0NB*

PORTER, Damian Michael. b 66. Linc Th Coll BTh 92. d 92 p 93. C Pelsall *Lich* 92–96; V Greenlands *Blackb* 96–00; V St Annes St Anne 00–09; AD Kirkham 06–09; P-in-c Warton St Oswald w Yealand Conyers 09–11; V 11–17; AD Tunstall 14–16; V Torrisholme from 17. *The Vicarage, 63 Michaelson Avenue, Morecambe LA4 6SF* T: (01524) 732946 E: fatherd@btinternet.com

PORTER, Canon David Anthony (Tony). b 34. Wycliffe Hall Ox 73. d 75 p 76. C Watford St Luke *St Alb* 75–78; C Worting *Win* 78–81; V Snettisham *Nor* 81–82; P-in-c Ingoldisthorpe 81–82; C Fring 81–82; R Snettisham w Ingoldisthorpe and Fring 82–84; Chapl Asst Colchester Gen Hosp 87–88; Chapl Maidstone Hosp 88–94; Chapl Mid Kent Healthcare NHS Trust 94–98; Hon Can Cant Cathl 97–98; rtd 98; PtO *Nor* from 98; *Ely* from 98. *The Greys, 12 Hawthorn Close, Watlington, King's Lynn PE33 0HD* T: (01553) 811301 E: daporter7985@btinternet.com

PORTER, David Michael. b 37. Coll of Ripon & York St Jo BA 88. Ely Th Coll 61. d 64 p 65. C Clun w Chapel Lawn *Heref* 64–67; C Scarborough St Mary w Ch Ch, St Paul and St Thos *York* 67–69; C Fulford 69–71; V Strensall 71–78; Chapl Claypenny and St Monica's Hosps 78–91; V Easingwold w Raskelfe *York* 78–91; TR York All SS Pavement w St Crux and St Martin etc 91–97; R York All SS Pavement w St Crux and St Mich 97–02; rtd 02; PtO *York* 02–21. *10 Ashwood Glade, Haxby, York YO32 3GQ* T: (01904) 769823

PORTER, David Rowland Shelley. b 46. City of Liv Coll of HE CertEd 69. STETS 00. d 03 p 04. NSM Whitehawk *Chich* 03–16; rtd 16; PtO *Chich* from 16. *3 Spring Cottages, Amberley Road, Storrington, Pulborough RH20 4JD* M: 07733-418755 E: porter@davejanera.co.uk

PORTER, Howard. b 56. S Glam Inst HE CertEd 78. St Mich Coll Llan 99. d 01 p 02. C Maindee Newport *Mon* 01–05; TV Aberystwyth *St D* 05–09. *21 Gwalch y Penwaig, Barry CF62 5AG*

PORTER, James Richard. b 73. Lon Univ BMedSci 97 MB, BS 98. Oak Hill Th Coll MTh 05. d 05 p 06. C Cromer *Nor* 05–09; R W Horsley *Guildf* 09–15; V Cromer *Nor* 15–19; C Jersey St Helier *Win* from 19. *The Vicarage, 8 Fairways, Plat Douet Road, St Clements, Jersey JE2 6PN* E: jamestherector@yahoo.co.uk

PORTER, Joanna Kathryn. b 73. Open Univ BA 10. Cranmer Hall Dur 15. d 17 p 18. C Ashington *Newc* 17–21; C Cannings and Redhorn *Sarum* 19–21; P-in-c Beercrocombe w Curry Mallet, Hatch Beauchamp etc *B & W* from 21. *11 Vickery Close, Bridgwater TA6 7JU* M: 07377-423884 E: joanna@sevensowers.org

PORTER, Mrs Linda Mary. b 55. St Mellitus Coll BA 13. d 13 p 14. NSM Walton le Soken *Chelmsf* 13–16; NSM Harwich Peninsula 16–17; PtO from 17; *Portsm* 18–19; NSM W Wight 19–20; rtd 20. *Sarum House, Moortown Lane, Brighstone, Newport PO30 4AN* M: 07854-156077 E: lindamporter@yahoo.co.uk

PORTER, Malcolm Derek. b 53. BSc. NTMTC. d 05 p 06. C Woodford Wells *Chelmsf* 05–09; NSM from 10; V Highams Park All SS from 19. *The Vicarage, All Saints' Church, Castle Avenue, London E4 9QD* T: (020) 8531 5107 M: 07779-146892 E: thoseporters@aol.com *or* malcolm@asww.org.uk

PORTER, Matthew James. b 69. Nottm Univ BA 90 Sheff Univ MA 01. Wycliffe Hall Ox BTh 93. d 96 p 97. C Dore *Sheff* 96–00; V Woodseats St Chad 00–09; Dir C Tr 05–08; C York St Mich-le-Belfrey 09–10; V from 10. *St Barnabas' Vicarage, Jubilee Terrace, York YO26 4YZ* T: (01904) 624190 E: matthew.porter@belfrey.org

PORTER, Canon Michael Edward. b 44. Trin Coll Bris 75. d 77 p 78. C Corby St Columba *Pet* 77–81; C Rainham *Chelmsf* 81–82; TV 82–92; P-in-c S Hornchurch St Jo and St Matt 92–95; V Anerley *Roch* 95–09; TR 09; AD Beckenham 05–09; Hon Can Roch Cathl 09; rtd 09; PtO *Nor* from 10. *20 Park Lane, Wymondham NR18 9BG* T: (01953) 602708 E: mike@porterfamily.freeuk.com

PORTER, Nigel Jonathan. b 58. Sunderland Univ BEd 90 Portsm Univ MPhil 99 PhD 05. STETS MA 10. d 10 p 11. C Lower Sandown St Jo *Portsm* 10–14; PtO 14–15; P-in-c Whitwell 15–16; V 16–21; P-in-c Niton 15–16; R 16–21; P-in-c St Lawrence 15–16; R 16–21; P-in-c Chale 15–16; R 16–21; rtd 21. *2 Amberley, 47 Victoria Avenue, Shanklin PO37 6LT* M: 07533-394043 E: nigel.porter6@btinternet.com

PORTER, Raymond John. b 43. Worc Coll Ox BA 66 MA 70 Wycliffe Hall Ox MPhil 93 FRAS 93. d 06 p 07. Dir World Miss Studies Oak Hill Th Coll 06–13; Visiting Lect Oak Hill Coll from 13; PtO *St Alb* from 07; *Ely* from 11; *Ox* 16–21. *24 Bevington Way, Eynesbury, St Neots PE19 2HQ* T: (01480) 211839   M: 07976-753822   E: porterray@me.com   or rayp@oakhill.ac.uk

PORTER-BABBAGE, Michelle Louise. b 64. EN(G) 86 RGN 04. Ridley Hall Cam 12. d 14 p 15. C Bourton-on-the-Water w Clapton etc *Glouc* 14–18; PtO 18–19; C Warfield *Ox* from 19. *Glen Lossie, Gough's Lane, Bracknell RG12 2PL* M: 07387-912920 E: michelle.porter-babbage@warfield.org.uk

PORTER-PRYCE, Preb Julia Frances. b 57. Man Univ BA 78 Leic Univ MPhil 94. NTMTC 93. d 96 p 97. C Stoke Newington Common St Mich *Lon* 96–99; C Is of Dogs Ch Ch and St Jo w St Luke 99–02; V De Beauvoir Town St Pet 02–21; AD Hackney 09–14; Preb St Paul's Cathl 17–21; rtd 21; PtO *Lon* from 21. *26 The Village, Clyro, Hereford HR3 5SF* E: juliap@freeuk.com

PORTEUS, Canon James **Michael**. b 31. Worc Coll Ox BA 55 MA 58. Cuddesdon Coll. d 57 p 58. C Fleetwood St Pet *Blackb* 57–60; C Ox St Mary V 60–62; Staff Sec SCM Ox 60–62; Chapl Chicago Univ USA 62–65; Chapl Bryn Mawr, Haverford and Swarthmore Colls 62–65; Chapl Lon Univ 69–74; V Hampstead Garden Suburb 74–86; Chapl Arizona Univ USA 86–91; Min Livingston LEP *Edin* 91–96; rtd 96; P-in-c Portree *Arg* 96–05; Hon Can Cumbrae from 06; PtO *Truro* from 09. *Triskele, Rinsey, Ashton, Helston TR13 9TS* T: (01736) 761870

PORTEUS, Canon Robert John Norman. b 50. TCD BA 72 MA 76. CITC 75. d 75 p 76. C Portadown St Mark *Arm* 75–79; I Ardtrea w Desertcreat 79–83; I Annaghmore 83–98; I Derryloran from 98; Can Arm Cathl from 98; Preb from 01. *Derryloran Rectory, 13 Loy Street, Cookstown BT80 8PZ* T/F: (028) 8676 2261 E: rector@derryloran.com

PORTLOCK, John Anthony. b 37. RIBA. WMMTC 96. d 99 p 00. NSM Lyddington w Stoke Dry and Seaton etc *Pet* 99–07; NSM Bulwick, Blatherwycke w Harringworth and Laxton 05–07; rtd 07; PtO *Pet* from 08. *7 Chestnut Close, Uppingham, Oakham LE15 9TQ* T: (01572) 823225 E: jandmportlock@gmail.com

PORTSDOWN, Archdeacon of. *See* ROWLEY, The Ven Jennifer Jane Elisabeth

PORTSMOUTH, Bishop of. *Vacant*

PORTSMOUTH, Dean of. *See* CANE, The Very Revd Anthony William Nicholas Strephon

POSKITT, Mark Sylvester. b 63. Loughb Univ BSc 84. St Jo Coll Nottm MA 95. d 97 p 98. C Brigg, Wrawby and Cadney cum Howsham *Linc* 97–00; TV Howden *York* 00–09; P-in-c Barnsley St Edw *Wakef* 09–14; *Leeds* 14–16; P-in-c Gawber *Wakef* 09–14; *Leeds* 14–16; P-in-c Bosworth and Sheepy Gp *Leic* 16–19; R Bosworth from 19; AD Sparkenhoe W from 19. *The Rectory, Park Street, Market Bosworth, Nuneaton CV13 0LL* T: (01455) 291152 E: rev.markp63@talktalk.net

POSS, Steven Keith. b 78. St Mellitus Coll BA 13. d 13 p 14. NSM Leigh-on-Sea St Aid *Chelmsf* 13–16; C 16–17; P-in-c Bradwell on Sea and St Lawrence from 17; P-in-c Tillingham from 17; P-in-c Dengie w Asheldham from 17. *6 Bakery Close, Tillingham, Southminster CM0 7TT* M: 07830-150713 E: stevenposs@hotmail.com

POST, David Charles William. b 39. Jes Coll Cam BA 61 MA 65. Oak Hill Th Coll 61. d 63 p 64. C Orpington Ch Ch *Roch* 63–66; C Fulwood *Sheff* 66–68; V Lathom *Liv* 68–75; V Poughill *Truro* 75–78; V Braddan and Santan *S & M* 78–79; Dioc Missr 78–79; V Sherburn in Elmet *York* 79–91; P-in-c Kirk Fenton 84–85; V Thornthwaite cum Braithwaite and Newlands *Carl* 91–93; R Wheldrake w Thorganby *York* 93–04; P-in-c Elvington w Sutton on Derwent and E Cottingwith 03–04; rtd 04; PtO *Linc* 15–18. *Cheviot, 5 Mayfield Crescent, Middle Rasen, Market Rasen LN8 3UA* T: (01673) 843388 E: davidcwpost@googlemail.com

POST, Oswald Julian. b 48. Derby Lonsdale Coll BEd 79. EMMTC. d 84 p 85. Travelling Sec Ruanda Miss 79–89; Hon C Hulland, Atlow, Bradley and Hognaston *Derby* 84–89; V Wormhill, Peak Forest w Peak Dale and Dove Holes 89–99; P-in-c Youlgreave, Middleton, Stanton-in-Peak etc 99–09; rtd 09; UK Ambassador AE Evangelisic Enterprise Ltd from

10; PtO *Lich* 13–21. *Rose Cottage, Hulland Village, Ashbourne DE6 3EP* T: (01335) 370285 E: ossiepost@icloud.com

POSTILL, John Edward. b 35. Oak Hill Th Coll 64. d 67 p 68. C Southgate *Chich* 67–70; C Bowling St Jo *Bradf* 70–74; TV Winfarthing w Shelfanger *Nor* 74–79; R Slaugham *Chich* 79–97; C Busbridge and Hambledon *Guildf* 97–03; rtd 03; PtO *Guildf* 04–20. *Dora Cottage, Beech Hill, Hambledon, Godalming GU8 4HL* T: (01428) 687968 E: j.epostill@gmail.com

POSTILL, Canon Richard Halliday. b 37. Hull Univ BSc 59. Westcott Ho Cam 66. d 68 p 69. C Wylde Green *Birm* 68–72; C Kingswinford St Mary *Lich* 72–76; V Yardley Wood *Birm* 76–86; V Acocks Green 86–02; AD Yardley 93–00; Hon Can Birm Cathl 99–02; rtd 02; PtO *Birm* from 03. *32 Longmore Road, Shirley, Solihull B90 3DY* T: 0121-744 6217

POSTON, Jonathan David. b 59. Ches Coll of HE MTh 05. NOC 01. d 04 p 05. C Prestwich St Marg *Man* 04–10; PtO 10–14; *Derby* 10–12; NSM Spondon 12–14; R Wingerworth from 14. *The Rectory, Longedge Lane, Wingerworth, Chesterfield S42 6PU* T: (01246) 279932 M: 07754-517797 E: jont.post@gmail.com

POTE, Thomas Gerald Edward. b 90. R Holloway Coll Lon BA 15 MA 17. CCC Cam BA 18. Westcott Ho Cam 16. d 19 p 20. C Guildf H Trin w St Mary from 19. *27 Pewley Way, Guildford GU1 3PX* M: 07578-502420 E: tom_pote@hotmail.co.uk

POTTAGE, Timothy Lindsay. b 65. d 15 p 16. C Galmington *B & W* from 15. *Midfields, Comeytrowe Lane, Taunton TA1 5BJ* T: (01823) 256152 M: 07971-010710 E: timpottage@hotmail.com

POTTEN, Rosemary Elizabeth. b 48. St Mellitus Coll 12. d 13 p 14. OLM Barkingside H Trin *Chelmsf* 13–17; NSM from 17. *51 Greenleafe Drive, Barkingside, Ilford IG6 1LH* T: (020) 8551 2011 E: rosemaryp@hotmail.co.uk

POTTER, Mrs Anne Mary. b 57. Open Univ BA 92 Newman Univ MA 18 Chich Coll PGCE 96. Qu Coll Birm 09. d 11 p 12. C Badsey w Aldington and Offenham and Bretforton *Worc* 11–15; TV Worcs W Rural from 15; C Worc Dines Green St Mich and Crown E, Rushwick 15–21; RD Martley and Worc W 19–21. *The Rectory, Leigh, Worcester WR6 5LE* M: 07783-711665 E: revannepotter@gmail.com

POTTER, The Ven Christopher Nicholas Lynden. b 49. Leeds Univ BA 71. St As Minl Tr Course 90. d 93 p 94. C Flint *St As* 93–96; V Llanfair DC, Derwen, Llanelidan and Efenechtyd 96–01; Dean and Lib St As Cathl 01–11; V St As 01–03; TR 03–11; R Caerwys and Bodfari 11–14; Adn St As 11–14; rtd 14; PtO *St As* from 14. *Bryn Celyn, Willow Street, Llangollen LL20 8HH* T: (01978) 861831

POTTER, Clive Geoffrey. b 55. Aston Tr Scheme 88 Sarum & Wells Th Coll 90. d 92 p 93. C Epsom Common Ch Ch *Guildf* 92–97; TV Westborough 97–98; TR 98–07; V Milford from 07; AD Godalming 12–19. *The New Vicarage, Milford Heath, Milford, Godalming GU8 5BX* T: (01483) 414710 E: milfordvicarage@gmail.com

POTTER, Harry Drummond. b 54. Em Coll Cam BA 76 MA 79 MPhil 81 LLB 92 Barrister 93. Westcott Ho Cam 79. d 81 p 82. C Deptford St Paul *S'wark* 81–84; Chapl Selw Coll Cam 84–87; Chapl Newnham Coll Cam 84–87; Chapl HM Pris Wormwood Scrubs 87–88; Chapl HM YOI Aylesbury 88–93; NSM Camberwell St Giles w St Matt *S'wark* 93–03; PtO 03–07. *19 Dobell Road, London SE9 1HE* T: (020) 7067 1500 E: tuahousis@hotmail.com

POTTER, John Dennis. b 39. Ealing Tech Coll. S Dios Minl Tr Scheme 92. d 94 p 95. NSM Box w Hazlebury and Ditteridge *Bris* 94–98; PtO *B & W* 06–19. *Avalon, Bucks Cross, Bideford EX39 5DX* T: (01237) 431750 M: 07745-873759 E: johndpotter@talktalk.net

POTTER, Mrs Judith Anne. b 46. Rolle Coll CertEd 68. d 05 p 06. OLM Shere, Albury and Chilworth *Guildf* 05–12; NSM 12–16; Chapl Birtley Ho Bramley 08–12; PtO from 16. *3 Bank Terrace, Gomshall Lane, Shere, Guildford GU5 9HB* T: (01483) 203352 F: 202077 E: judyp@btopenworld.com

POTTER, Mrs Leisa Caroline. b 69. Plymouth Univ BSc 92. SWMTC. d 14 p 15. C Ottery St Mary, Alfington, W Hill, Tipton etc *Ex* 14–18; P-in-c Brighstone and Brooke w Mottistone *Portsm* 18–19; P-in-c Shorwell w Kingston 18–19; P-in-c Calbourne w Newtown 18–19; P-in-c Shalfleet 18–19; P-in-c Thorley 18–19; P-in-c Freshwater 18–19; P-in-c Yarmouth 18–19; P-in-c Totland Bay 18–19; TV W Wight from 19. *The Vicarage, Alum Bay New Road, Totland Bay PO39 0ES* T: (01983) 753078 M: 07732-120233 E: revleisa@btinternet.com

POTTER, Mrs Linda. b 47. Cranmer Hall Dur 92. d 94 p 95. C Shildon w Eldon *Dur* 94–98; P-in-c Castleside 98–04; TR Gt Aycliffe 04–12; rtd 12; PtO *Ripon* 14; *Leeds* from 14. *32 Knaresborough Road, Harrogate HG2 7LU*

POTTER, Malcolm Emmerson. b 48. Bedf Coll Lon BSc 70. St Jo Coll Nottm. **d** 75 **p** 76. C Upton (Overchurch) *Ches* 76–78; CPAS Staff 78–84; Development Officer St Jo Coll Nottm 84–86; P-in-c Wellington All SS w Eyton *Lich* 86–95; V 95–06; Preb Lich Cathl 99–06; Membership Development Manager Age Concern 06–07; Chapl Shropshire Co Primary Care Trust 07–12; rtd 12. *2 Barns Green, Shrewsbury SY3 9QB* T: (01743) 235430 E: malcolm@kerameus.co.uk

POTTER, Mark Richard Anthony. b 77. Sheff Univ BA 99 Sheff Hallam Univ PGCE 00. St Mellitus Coll MA 19. **d** 19 **p** 20. C Wisley w Pyrford *Guildf* from 19. *Church House, Coldharbour Road, Woking GU22 8SP* M: 07776-341648 E: markpotter@btinternet.com

POTTER, Neil John. b 63. **d** 12 **p** 13. NSM Redruth w Lanner and Treleigh *Truro* 12–15; NSM Camborne and Tuckingmill 15–16; NSM Penponds 15–16; NSM Camborne, Tuckingmill and Penponds from 16. *Strawberry Bank, 2 Dam Bungalows, Carn, Stithians, Truro TR3 7AW* M: 07539-593684 E: neilpotter@talktalk.net

POTTER, The Ven Peter Maxwell. b 46. Univ of Wales (Swansea) BA 69 Univ of BC MA 71. Sarum & Wells Th Coll 83. **d** 85 **p** 86. C Bradford-on-Avon H Trin *Sarum* 85–88; C Harnham 88–91; P-in-c N Bradley, Southwick and Heywood 91–96; V Sale St Anne *Ches* 96–00; R Largs *Glas* 00–08; Chapl Berne *Eur* 08–16; Switzerland 09–16; rtd 16; PtO *St And* from 16; *Eur* from 18. *Lynnaren, Haining, Dunblane FK15 0AP*

POTTER, Phillip. b 54. Stirling Univ BA 75. Trin Coll Bris 82. **d** 84 **p** 85. C Yateley *Win* 84–88; V Haydock St Mark *Liv* 88–07; Dir Pioneer Min 07–14; C Haydock St Mark 07–09; P-in-c Southport St Phil and St Paul 12–14; Hon Can Liv Cathl 03–14; Abps' Missr and Team Ldr Fresh Expressions *Cant* from 14; NSM Bowdon *Ches* 15–19; PtO from 19. *Chapel House, Chester Road, Tabley, Knutsford WA16 0HN* T: (01565) 634327 E: phil.potter@freshexpressions.org.uk

POTTER, Canon Sharon Jane. b 63. UEA BSc 96 K Coll Lon MSc 00 RGN 91. Dioc OLM tr scheme 00. **d** 04 **p** 05. OLM Ipswich All Hallows *St E* 04–06; NSM Ipswich St Helen, H Trin, and St Luke 07–12; R Bradfield St Clare, Bradfield St George etc from 12; Hon Can St E Cathl from 20. *The Rectory, Howe Lane, Cockfield, Bury St Edmunds IP30 0HA* T: (01284) 828599 M: 07825-086063 E: revsharon@btinternet.com

POTTER, Simon Jonathan. b 76. Southn Univ BA 98 Ex Univ PGCE 99. Trin Coll Bris MA 14. **d** 14 **p** 15. C Ox St Andr 14–18; C Stoke Bishop *Bris* from 18. *3 Hollybush Lane, Bristol BS9 1BH* M: 07837-843229 E: potterjsimon@gmail.com

POTTER, Stephen Michael. b 55. Oak Hill Th Coll 93. **d** 95 **p** 96. C Chesterfield H Trin and Ch Ch *Derby* 95–99; P-in-c S Normanton 99–01; R from 01. *The Rectory, Church Street, South Normanton, Alfreton DE55 2BT* T: (01773) 811273 E: stephen.potter55@gmail.com

POTTER, Timothy John. b 49. Bris Univ BSc 71. Oak Hill Th Coll 73. **d** 76 **p** 77. C Wallington *S'wark* 76–79; C Hampreston *Sarum* 79–81; TV Stratton St Margaret w S Marston etc *Bris* 81–87; P-in-c Hatfield Heath *Chelmsf* 87–89; P-in-c Sheering 87–89; R Hatfield Heath and Sheering 90–09; P-in-c Gt Hallingbury and Lt Hallingbury 06–09; RD Harlow 07–09; Hon Can Chelmsf Cathl 02–09; rtd 09. *Redcott, 91 High Street, Dunmow CM6 1AF* E: tim.potter1@btinternet.com

POTTERTON, David Steven. b 59. Ox Min Course 13. **d** 15 **p** 16. C Romsey *Win* 15–18; P-in-c Lyndhurst and Emery Down and Minstead from 18. *The Vicarage, Forest Gardens, Lyndhurst SO43 7AF* M: 07827-994083 E: david.potterton@btinternet.com

POTTINGER, Justin Charles Edward. b 82. Keble Coll Ox BA 03 Ox Brookes Univ PGCE 04. STETS 05 Ripon Coll Cuddesdon 07. **d** 08 **p** 09. C Devizes St Jo w St Mary *Sarum* 08–11; Chapl Clayesmore Sch Blandford 11–14; V Red Post *Sarum* from 15; RD Milton and Blandford from 20. *The Vicarage, East Morden, Wareham BH20 7DW* T: (01929) 459244 E: redpostbenefice@gmail.com

POTTS, Heather Dawn. *See* BUTCHER, Heather Dawn

POTTS, Mrs Jill. b 46. Open Univ BA 89. STETS 02. **d** 05 **p** 06. NSM Corfe Mullen *Sarum* 05–07; NSM Grantham, Manthorpe *Linc* 07–13; rtd 13; PtO *Linc* from 13. *18 Dallygate, Great Ponton, Grantham NG33 5DP* T: (01476) 530361 E: jilldallygate@gmail.com

POTTS, Mrs Susan Pamela. b 54. Huddersfield Poly BA 76 Lanc Univ PGCE 77. ERMC 09. **d** 12 **p** 13. NSM Raddesley Gp *Ely* 12–14; NSM Three Rivers Gp 14–21; rtd 21. *Address temp unknown* M: 07851-184295 E: revd.sue@icloud.com

POULARD, Christopher. b 39. FCA 64. Ridley Hall Cam 82. **d** 84 **p** 85. C N Walsham w Antingham *Nor* 84–86; C Oulton Broad 86–90; TV Raveningham 90–94; R Raveningham Gp 94–99; RD Loddon 98–99; PtO *Chelmsf* from 99; rtd 04. *Cuddington, Colam Lane, Little Baddow,*

Chelmsford CM3 4SY T: (01245) 224221 F: 221394 E: chris@poulard.org.uk

POULSON, Anna Louise. b 73. Univ Coll Dur BA 94 K Coll Lon MA 97 PhD 06. Ridley Hall Cam 98. **d** 02 **p** 03. C Ealing St Mary *Lon* 02–06; C Southall Green St Jo 11–14; V from 15. *St John's Vicarage, Church Avenue, Southall UB2 4DH* T: (020) 8571 3027 M: 07795-595915 E: annapoulson@btinternet.com

POULSON, Canon Mark Alban. b 63. Bath Coll of HE BEd 86 Anglia Poly Univ MA 03. Ridley Hall Cam. **d** 00 **p** 01. C Alperton *Lon* 00–03; P-in-c Southall Green St Jo 03–06; V 06–14; Adv for Inter Faith Matters 14–18; Abp's Sec for Inter-Relig Affairs *Cant* 15–18; Dioc Co-ord for Presence and Engagement *Lon* from 18; Can for Interfaith Relns St Paul's Cathl from 18; Hon Can Bradf Cathl *Leeds* from 17. *St John's Vicarage, Church Avenue, Southall UB2 4DH* T: (020) 8571 9877 E: mpoulson@btinternet.com

POULTNEY, Andrew Timothy. b 68. K Coll Lon MA 03. St Paul's Th Cen Lon 06. **d** 08 **p** 09. C Collier Row St Jas and Havering-atte-Bower *Chelmsf* 08–17; P-in-c Sheff St Paul from 18; C Sheff St Cecilia Parson Cross from 18; C Sheff St Leon Norwood from 18. *98 Chaucer Close, Sheffield S5 9QE* M: 07903-112599 E: andypoultneypxpioneerminister@gmail.com

POULTNEY, Ann Josephina. b 76. Southn Univ BSc 97. St Mellitus Coll BA 17. **d** 17 **p** 18. C Aldenham, Radlett and Shenley *St Alb* 17–18; C Attleborough *Cov* 18–20; TV Bedworth from 20. *2 Bryony Close, Bedworth CV12 0GF* T: (024) 7636 4961

POULTNEY, David Elis. b 73. Loughb Univ BEng 96 CEng 97. Trin Coll Bris 07. **d** 09 **p** 10. C Luton Lewsey St Hugh *St Alb* 09–13; C Bushey 13–18; TR Bedworth *Cov* from 18; AD Nuneaton from 19. *2 Bryony Close, Bedworth CV12 0GF* T: (024) 7631 0688 E: dave.poultney@outlook.com

POULTON, Neville John. b 48. STETS. **d** 02. NSM Portsea St Cuth *Portsm* 02–07. *18 Belgravia Road, Portsmouth PO2 0DX* T: (023) 9236 1104 M: 07768-661796 E: moandnev@ntlworld.com

POUNCEY, Christopher Michael Godwin. b 52. Reading Univ BSc 74 Wycliffe Hall Ox BA 77 MA. SWMTC 03. **d** 04 **p** 05. NSM S Molton w Nymet St George, High Bray etc *Ex* 04–16; NSM S Molton w Nymet St George, Chittlehamholt etc from 16. *Brightley Barton, Umberleigh EX37 9AL* T: (01769) 540405 M: 07977-930045

POUND, Canon Keith Salisbury. b 33. St Cath Coll Cam BA 54 MA 58. Cuddesdon Coll 55. **d** 57 **p** 58. C St Helier *S'wark* 57–61; Tr Officer Hollowford Tr and Conf Cen Sheff 61–64; Warden 64–67; R S'wark H Trin 68–74; P-in-c Newington St Matt 68–74; R S'wark H Trin w St Matt 74–78; RD S'wark and Newington 73–78; TR Thamesmead 78–86; Sub-Dean Woolwich 84–86; RD Greenwich 85–86; Hon Can S'wark Cathl 85–86; Chapl Gen of Pris 86–93; Chapl to The Queen 88–03; Chapl HM Pris Grendon and Spring Hill 93–98; rtd 98; PtO *Chich* from 99. *1 Sinnock Square, Hastings TN34 3HQ* T: (01424) 428330

POUNTAIN, Thomas Iain. b 86. Ex Univ BA 07. Moore Th Coll Sydney BTh 17. **d** 18 **p** 19. C W Hampstead St Luke *Lon* 18–20; R Ross River Australia from 21. *Ross River Church, 154 Ross River Road, Townsville, QLD 4812, Australia* E: t.pountain@gmail.com

POUT, John Robert. b 61. Salford Univ BA 83. WEMTC 09. **d** 12 **p** 14. NSM Moreton-in-Marsh w Batsford, Todenham etc *Glouc* 12–16; C 16–17; V Paignton Ch Ch and Preston St Paul *Ex* from 17. *The Vicarage, Locarno Avenue, Paignton TQ3 2DH* M: 07739-500913 E: johnpout@icloud.com

POVALL, David Justin. b 66. Birkbeck Coll Lon LLB 99 Barrister-at-Law 00. St Aug Coll of Th 17. **d** 20 **p** 21. C Clapham St Paul *S'wark* from 20. *19 Fernwood Avenue, London SW16 1RD* T: (020) 8696 7643 M: 07947-736228 E: davidpovall@23es.com *or* djpovall@hotmail.com

POVEY, William Peter. b 36. JP 85. Man Univ MSc 82 MRCS 61 LRCP 61 FFPH 79 FRIPH HonFChS. NOC 90. **d** 93 **p** 94. Dioc Drug Liaison Officer *Ches* 93–01; NSM Latchford Ch Ch 93–00; NSM Daresbury 00–03; rtd 03; PtO *Ches* from 03; *Ex* from 04. *Applebrook House, 4 Trinnicks Orchard, Ugborough, Ivybridge PL21 0NX* T: (01752) 691654 E: povey.peter@googlemail.com

POWDRILL, Penelope Anne. b 47. Lon Univ BSc 69 PGCE 71 Birm Univ MEd 77. WEMTC 10. **d** 11 **p** 12. OLM Wye Brooks Benefice *Heref* 11–19; OLM Wye Reaches Gp 11–19; NSM from 19. *Homebush, Lower Prospect Road, Osbaston, Monmouth NP25 3HS* T: (01600) 714096 E: pennypowdrill@btinternet.com

POWE, David James Hector. b 50. Wycliffe Hall Ox 88. **d** 90 **p** 91. C Ventnor St Cath *Portsm* 90–92; Chapl HM

Pris Belmarsh 93–94 and 98–04; Chapl HM Pris Lewes 94–97; Chapl HM Pris Bris 04–17; PtO *B & W* 13–18; *Bris* 13–19; *Glouc* from 17. *St John's Church Centre, Wickwar Road, Chipping Sodbury, Bristol BS37 6BQ* T: (01454) 313159 E: davidpowe@ymail.com

POWELL, Canon Anthony James. b 51. Sarum & Wells Th Coll 78. **d** 79 **p** 80. C Larkfield *Roch* 79–83; C Leybourne 79–83; V Borough Green 83–16; Hon Can Roch Cathl 04–16; rtd 16. *Address withheld by request*

POWELL, Carolyne Yolanda. b 80. Ridley Hall Cam 17. **d** 19 **p** 20. C Cov St Geo 19–20; C Allesley Park and Whoberley from 20. *52 Haynestone Road, Coventry CV6 1GJ* M: 07842-751065 E: revcarolynepowell@gmail.com

POWELL, Charles David. b 38. St Pet Coll Saltley CertEd 61 ACP 74. SAOMC 96. **d** 99 **p** 00. NSM Ampthill w Millbrook and Steppingley *St Alb* 99–04; PtO from 05; RD Ampthill 03–08. *33 Putnoe Heights, Bedford MK41 8EB* T: (01234) 345020 M: 07811-260675 E: rev.davidpowell@btinternet.com

POWELL, Christopher John. b 71. K Coll Lon BA 94 AKC 94. Coll of Resurr Mirfield 95. **d** 97 **p** 98. C Botley *Portsm* 97–01; C Portsea N End St Mark 01–05; P-in-c Clayton w Keymer *Chich* 05–13; R 13–16; V Wivelsfield from 16. *The Vicarage, Church Lane, Wivelsfield, Haywards Heath RH17 7RD* E: christopher.powell123@btinternet.com

POWELL, David. *See* POWELL, Charles David

POWELL, Mrs Diane. b 41. SWMTC 85. **d** 88 **p** 94. Hon C St Merryn *Truro* 88–92; Dn-in-c Gerrans w St Anthony in Roseland 92–94; P-in-c 94–00; Asst Chapl R Cornwall Hosps Trust 00–05; rtd 05; PtO *Truro* from 05. *Pendower, 15 Fairfield, St Merryn, Padstow PL28 8FQ* T: (01841) 521610 E: dianepowell389@gmail.com

POWELL, Dudley John. b 44. Tyndale Hall Bris 65. **d** 69 **p** 70. C Blackb Sav 69–71; C Rodbourne Cheney *Bris* 71–74; P-in-c Kingsdown 74–79; V 79–80; V Stoke Gifford 80–90; TR 90–91; Ancient World Outreach Albania 91–03; PtO *Bris* 91–03; Win 03–13; rtd 09. *30 Homechurch House, 31 Purewell, Christchurch BH23 1EH* T: (01202) 481379

POWELL, Eleanor Ann. b 55. Univ of Wales BA 82 Leeds Univ MA 06 Gwent Coll Newport CertEd 76. Qu Coll Birm 82. **d** 83 **p** 94. C Caereithin *S & B* 83–86; C Bishopston 86–88; Dioc Children's Officer *Glouc* 88–94; Dioc Adv for Women's Min 94–01; P-in-c The Edge, Pitchcombe, Harescombe and Brookthorpe 94–00; V Churchdown St Jo 00–01; Hon Can Glouc Cathl 94–01; Chapl Univ Hosps Bris NHS Foundn Trust 01–06; Lead Chapl Cwm Taf Univ Health Bd 06–18; PtO *Llan* from 18. *Park Farm Lodge, The Legar, Langattock, Crickhowell NP8 1HH* T: (01873) 811355 E: epowell97@gmail.com

POWELL, Preb Frank. b 29. AKC 52. **d** 53 **p** 54. C Stockingford *Cov* 53–56; C Netherton St Andr *Worc* 56–60; P-in-c W Bromwich St Jo *Lich* 60–66; C W Bromwich Gd Shep w St Jo 60–66; V 66–69; V Bilston St Leon 69–76; P-in-c Hanbury 76–82; V Hanbury w Newborough 83–86; V Basford 86–92; Preb Lich Cathl 87–92; rtd 92; PtO *Ches* from 92. *39 Wright Court, London Road, Nantwich CW5 6SE* T: (01270) 618679 E: fjpowell1@aol.com

POWELL, Jason Corrin. b 79. St Mellitus Coll. **d** 16 **p** 17. C Middleton and Thornham *Man* 16–20; V Norden w Ashworth and Bamford from 20. *6 Westbrook Close, Rochdale OL11 2XY* T: (01706) 631050 M: 07968-482058 E: jasoncorrinpowell@gmail.com

POWELL, John. b 44. St Luke's Coll Ex CertEd 66 Univ of Wales (Lamp) MA 02. Glouc Sch of Min 81. **d** 84 **p** 85. NSM Stroud and Uplands w Slad *Glouc* 84–89; Chapl Eliz Coll Guernsey 89–92; C Llandudno *Ban* 92–93; TV 94–96; V Dwygyfylchi 96–02; V Cardigan w Mwnt and Y Ferwig w Llangoedmor *St D* 02–10; rtd 10; P-in-c Llangrannog w Llandysiliogogo w Penbryn *St D* 10–11; PtO 11–12; P-in-c Maenordeifi Gp 12–14; PtO from 14. *Crud yr Haul, 12 Maes y Dderwen, Cardigan SA43 1PE* T: (01239) 621512 E: parchjohnpowell@btinternet.com

POWELL, John Keith Lytton. b 52. S Dios Minl Tr Scheme 91. **d** 94 **p** 95. NSM Bridgwater H Trin *B & W* 94–97; P-in-c Hatch Beauchamp w Beercrocombe, Curry Mallet etc 97–02; P-in-c Staple Fitzpaine, Orchard Portman, Thurlbear etc 97–02; R Beercrocombe w Curry Mallet, Hatch Beauchamp etc 02–05; P-in-c Exford, Exmoor, Hawkridge and Withypool 05–09; P-in-c Middlezoy and Othery and Moorlinch 09–11; P-in-c Greinton 09–11; R Middlezoy w Othery, Moorlinch and Greinton 11–17; Dioc Renewal Adv from 06. *Honeywood, East Lyng, Taunton TA3 5AU* E: jill.powell3@googlemail.com

POWELL, Kelvin. b 49. Wycliffe Hall Ox 71. **d** 74 **p** 75. C Prescot *Liv* 74–77; C Ainsdale 77–79; V Bickershaw 79–85; R Hesketh w Becconsall *Blackb* 85–99; PtO Ox 03–14; rtd 14; PtO *Leic* 14–19; *Blackb* from 19. *17 Fosbrooke House, 8 Clifton Drive, Lytham St Annes FY8 5RQ*

POWELL, Laurence James. b 86. Win Univ BA 08. Ripon Coll Cuddesdon 10. **d** 13 **p** 14. C Strood St Nic w St Mary *Roch* 13–16; V Tunbridge Wells K Chas from 16; P-in-c Tunbridge Wells St Mark from 19. *The Vicarage, Rodmell Road, Tunbridge Wells TN2 5ST* T: (01892) 525455

POWELL, Canon Mark. b 57. Bath Univ BSc 78 PhD 81. Ripon Coll Cuddesdon BA 84 MA 88. **d** 85 **p** 86. C Evesham *Worc* 85–88; V Exhall *Cov* 88–96; V Leavesden *St Alb* 96–00; V Ealing St Pet Mt Park *Lon* 00–11; V Melbourne, Ticknall, Smisby and Stanton *Derby* 11–16; Can Windsor from 16. *6 The Cloisters, Windsor Castle, Windsor SL4 1NJ* T: (01753) 848709 E: mark.powell@stgeorges-windsor.org

POWELL, Martin. b 71. St Steph Ho Ox BTh 00. **d** 00 **p** 01. C Caterham *S'wark* 00–03; V New Addington 03–14; R Aldingbourne, Barnham and Eastergate *Chich* 14–18; P-in-c Moulsecoomb w Bevendean and Coldean 18–20. *Address temp unknown* E: frmartinpowell@gmail.com

POWELL, Canon Pamela. b 56. Univ of Wales BEd 79 Goldsmiths' Coll Lon MA 82. St As Minl Tr Course 00. **d** 03 **p** 04. C Wrexham *St As* 03–06; P-in-c Llansantffraid-ym-Mechain and Llanfechain 06–08; V 08–15; AD Llanfyllin 11–12; AD Caereinion and Llanfyllin 12–14; V Brymbo w Bwlchgwyn 15–16; TV Alyn Miss Area 17–18; P-in-c Borderlands Miss Area from 18; Dir Lay Min from 10; Chan St As Cathl from 14. *The Vicarage, 8 Whiteoaks, Bwlchgwyn, Wrexham LL11 5UJ* T: (01978) 721083 M: 07711-053565 E: pampowell@microplusmail.co.uk

POWELL, Patricia Mary. b 46. STETS. **d** 03 **p** 04. NSM Woodford Valley *Sarum* 03–09; NSM Tidworth, Ludgershall and Faberstown 09–12; NSM Woodford Valley w Archers Gate 13–16; NSM Amesbury 13–16; rtd 16; PtO *Sarum* 16–18. *Hawthorne Cottage, Great Durnford, Salisbury SP4 6AZ* T: (01722) 782546 E: p.powell22@btinternet.com

POWELL, Peter John. b 57. G&C Coll Cam MA 80 MB, BChir 83. Coll of Resurr Mirfield 17. **d** 18 **p** 19. C Workington St Mich *Carl* from 18. *St Michael's Rectory, Dora Crescent, Workington CA14 2EZ* M: 07952-372435 E: ppowellhome@gmail.com *or* stmichaelsworkington@btinternet.com

POWELL, Canon Ralph Dover. b 49. ARMCM 70. Chich Th Coll 71. **d** 74 **p** 75. C Coppenhall *Ches* 74–77; C Heref H Trin 77–80; V Crewe St Barn *Ches* from 80; Hon Can Ches Cathl from 14. *St Barnabas' Vicarage, West Street, Crewe CW1 3AX* T: (01270) 212418 E: stbarnabascrewe@outlook.com

POWELL, Richard Graham. b 88. Glos Univ BA 11. Oak Hill Th Coll BA 19. **d** 19 **p** 20. C Kensington Ch Ch *Lon* from 19. *Flat 1, 94 Warwock Gardens, London W14 8PR* M: 07854-550778 E: richpowell938@gmail.com *or* rich@christchurchkensington.com

POWELL, Robert John. b 65. Trin Coll Bris BA 92. **d** 92 **p** 93. C Biggin Hill *Roch* 92–95; C Edgware *Lon* 95–01; Area Sec SAMS (NW England and N Wales) 01–04; TV Upper Holloway *Lon* 04–12; V Whitehall Park 12–13; TR Furzedown *S'wark* from 13. *St James's Rectory, 236 Mitcham Lane, London SW16 6NT* T: (020) 8677 3947 *or* 8696 0728

POWELL, Roger Roy. b 68. Thames Poly BSc 91. Ripon Coll Cuddesdon BTh 94. **d** 94 **p** 95. C Leic St Jas 94–98; C The Abbey Leic 98–00; TV 00–05; P-in-c Leic St Paul 01–05; Youth Chapl 98–05; P-in-c Ridgeway *Sarum* 05–10; R from 10; RD Marlborough from 18. *The Rectory, 3 Butts Road, Chiseldon, Swindon SN4 0NN* T: (01793) 740369 E: rectorofridgeway@gmail.com

POWELL, Stuart William. b 58. K Coll Lon BD 80 AKC 80. Ripon Coll Cuddesdon 86. **d** 88 **p** 89. C Horden *Dur* 88–90; C Northolt Park St Barn *Lon* 90–93; V Castle Vale St Cuth *Birm* 93–00; V Stockland Green 00–11; P-in-c Rough Hills *Lich* 11–15; P-in-c Wolverhampton St Steph 11–15; V Wolverhampton St Martin and St Steph 15–19; PtO from 19; CF (ACF) from 08; Corps Chapl Sea Cadet Corps from 20. *16 Belvidere Road, Walsall WS1 3AU* T: (01922) 900722 M: 07905-760964 Pager: 07336-734456 E: spowell.t21@btinternet.com

POWER, Canon David Michael. b 56. BEM 16. BA 81 BEd. Oak Hill Th Coll. **d** 81 **p** 82. C Warblington w Emsworth *Portsm* 81–84; C-in-c Hartplain CD 84–88; V Hartplain 88–91; Adv in Evang 91–97; V Portsea St Cuth 97–18; Hon Can Portsm Cathl 13–18; rtd 18; Hon Can Ho Ghana from 19; PtO *Portsm* from 19. *22 Ashling Park Road, Denmead, Waterlooville PO7 6EH* E: davidmpower@ntlworld.com

POWER, James Edward. b 58. Nottm Univ BSc 81 Leeds Univ BA 85. Coll of Resurr Mirfield 83. **d** 86 **p** 87. C Cadoxton-juxta-Barry *Llan* 86–89; Chapl Harrow Sch from 89; V Harrow St Mary *Lon* from 15; PtO C, C & R from 18. *35 West Street, Harrow HA1 3EG* T: (020) 8872 8234 *or* 8423 4014 E: jep@harrowschool.org.uk

POWER, Canon Jeanette. b 57. Oak Hill Th Coll BA 81. **dss** 82 **d** 87 **p** 94. Warblington w Emsworth *Portsm* 82–84; Hartplain CD 84–87; Hon C Hartplain 87–91; Community Mental Health Chapl Havant and Petersfield Child and Adolescent Mental Health Service 91–01; Team Chapl Portsm Hosps NHS Trust 01–16; NSM Wickham *Portsm* 93–97; NSM Portsea St Cuth 97–18; PtO from 18; Hon Can Ho Ghana from 19. *22 Ashling Park Road, Denmead, Waterlooville PO7 6EH* T: (023) 9234 2044 E: jeanettepower1@virginmedia.com

POWER, Mrs Lynn Diane. b 59. K Coll Lon BA 81 PGCE 82 AKC 81. STETS 10. **d** 13 **p** 14. NSM N Hants Downs *Win* 13–16; NSM Alton from 16; Chapl Treloar Coll of FE 16–19. *Sanctuary House, 28 Vicarage Hill, Alton GU34 2BT* T: (01420) 83372 M: 07850-232995 E: revlynnpower@outlook.com

POWER, Canon Michael Andrew. b 61. Westcott Ho Cam. **d** 12 **p** 13. C Romford St Edw *Chelmsf* 12–15; V 15–20; P-in-c Romford Ascension Collier Row 19–20; AD Havering 18–20; NSM Bowers Gifford w N Benfleet from 20; Miss and Stewardship Adv Bradwell Area from 20; Hon Can Chelmsf Cathl from 19. *101 London Road, Bowers Gifford, Basildon SS13 2DU* M: 07793-463640 E: mikeapower@aol.com

POWER, Richard Victor John. b 80. Oak Hill Th Coll 13. **d** 15 **p** 16. C Banbury St Paul *Ox* 15–19; C Harold Wood *Chelmsf* from 19. *8 Archibald Road, Romford RM3 0RH* T: (01708) 348406 M: 07925-394122 E: rvjpower@gmail.com

POWIS, Amy Victoria. *See* ADENIRAN, Amy Victoria

POWIS, Canon Michael Ralph. b 63. St Jo Coll Nottm BTh 95. **d** 95 **p** 96. C Dibden *Win* 95–00; V Hedge End St Luke 00–09; Adult Discipleship and Evang Tr Officer 09–11; P-in-c Bournemouth St Clem 11–17; P-in-c Pokesdown All SS 11–18; V from 18; Hon Can Win Cathl from 20. *All Saints' Vicarage, 14 Stourwood Road, Bournemouth BH6 3QP* T: (01202) 423747 E: mikepowischurch@gmail.com

POWLES, Charles Anthony. b 39. EAMTC. **d** 88 **p** 89. NSM Hemsby *Nor* 88–93; NSM Bradwell 01–07; PtO from 07. *94 Winifred Way, Caister-on-Sea, Great Yarmouth NR30 5PE* T: (01493) 720096 E: charles.powles@btinternet.com

POWLES, Michael Charles. b 34. Reading Univ BSc 56 Lon Univ PGCE 83. Qu Coll Birm. **d** 60 **p** 61. C Goodmayes All SS *Chelmsf* 60–65; C Surbiton St Matt *S'wark* 65–78; Lect Woolwich Coll 79–99; rtd 99. *Spring Cottage, 3 Rushett Close, Thames Ditton KT7 0UR* T: (020) 8398 9654

POWLEY, Miss Julia Hodgson. b 55. St Andr Univ MA 77 Anglia Ruskin Univ MA 10 FCA 80. Ridley Hall Cam 07. **d** 09 **p** 10. C Carl H Trin and St Barn 09–12; P-in-c Harrington 12–18; P-in-c Distington 12–18; R Harrington and Distington from 18. *The Rectory, Rectory Close, Harrington, Workington CA14 5PN* T: (01946) 830215 M: 07765-217335 E: julia@powley.plus.com

POWLEY, Canon Mark Thomas. b 75. Nottm Univ BA 96 Birm Univ PGCE 98. Wycliffe Hall Ox 01. **d** 03 **p** 04. C Addiscombe St Mary Magd w St Martin *S'wark* 03–06; C Hammersmith St Paul *Lon* 06–09; TV Leeds St Geo *Ripon* 10–14 and 14–15; Prin Yorks Min Course from 15; Prin St Hild Coll from 17; Hon Can Ripon Cathl *Leeds* from 17. *11 Brookfield Road, Leeds LS6 4EJ* E: principal@ymc.org.uk

POWLEY, Canon Robert Mallinson. b 39. Fitzw Coll Cam MA 65. Ridley Hall Cam 61. **d** 63 **p** 64. C Bermondsey St Mary w St Olave, St Jo etc *S'wark* 63–67; C Moseley St Anne *Birm* 67–69; LtO *Man* 72–77; Hon C Walshaw Ch Ch 77–88; V Prestwich St Gabr 88–94; Bp's Dom Chapl 88–94; P-in-c Hargrave *Ches* 94–05; Exec Officer Bd for Soc Resp 94–05; Hon Can Ches Cathl 00–05; rtd 05; PtO *Ban* 05–12; *Leeds* from 17. *39A Bentley Lane, Leeds LS6 4AJ* T: 0113-275 9876 E: powley915@btinternet.com

POWNALL, Lydia Margaret. *See* HURLE, Lydia Margaret

POWNALL-JONES, Timothy William. b 79. Univ of Wales (Cardiff) BD 00 MTh 02. Trin Coll Bris 04. **d** 06 **p** 07. C Newark w Coddington *S'well* 06–10; Chapl Farndon Unit 08–10; Chapl N Notts Coll of FE *S'well* 10–11; Hon C Bassetlaw and Bawtry Deanery from 11; Tutor All SS Cen for Miss and Min 12–20; Chapl Notts Healthcare NHS Foundn Trust from 15; Chapl Sherwood Forest Hosps NHS Foundn Trust 17–18. *Rampton Hospital, Retford DN22 0PD* M: 07837-630005 E: t_pownall_jones@hotmail.com

POYNER, David Roy. b 61. WEMTC 15. **d** 18 **p** 19. NSM Highley w Billingsley, Glazeley etc *Heref* from 18. *136 Hoo Road, Kidderminster DY10 1LP* T: (01562) 686638 E: d.r.poyner@aston.ac.uk

POYNTZ, Jocelin Georgina Massey. b 58. Ridley Hall Cam. **d** 13 **p** 14. C Stanford-le-Hope w Mucking *Chelmsf* 13–17; TV Harlow Town Cen w Lt Parndon from 17. *4A The Drive, Harlow CM20 3QD* M: 07743-124181 E: rev.jokey.poyntz@gmail.com

PRADELLA, Henry. b 54. St Mary's Coll Twickenham BEd 78. NTMTC 97. **d** 00 **p** 01. NSM Hainault *Chelmsf* 00–04; C Romford Gd Shep 04–06; R Rainham w Wennington 06–18; rtd 18. *Address withheld by request* E: pradfam@outlook.com

PRAGNELL, Sandra Ann. b 53. Hull Univ BA 75 TCD BTh 01 Dub City Univ MA 04. CITC 98. **d** 01 **p** 02. C Castleknock and Mulhuddart w Clonsilla *D & G* 01–05; PV Ch Ch Cathl Dublin 03–05; I Dundalk w Heynestown *Arm* 05–12; I Ballymascanlan w Creggan and Rathcor 05–12; Dean Limerick and Ardfert *L & K* 12–17; I Limerick City 12–17; rtd 17. *c/o Robbins, Drynachan, Invergarry PH35 4HL* E: sandrapragnell@eircom.net *or* revsandrapragnell@gmail.com

PRANCE, Robert Penrose. b 47. Southn Univ BTh 73. Sarum & Wells Th Coll 69. **d** 72 **p** 73. C Gillingham and Fifehead Magdalen *Sarum* 72–76; P-in-c Edmondsham 76–80; P-in-c Woodlands 76–80; P-in-c Wimborne St Giles 76–80; P-in-c Cranborne 77–80; R Cranborne w Boveridge, Edmondsham etc 80–83; Chapl Sherborne Sch 83–93; Asst Dir of Ords *Sarum* 76–86; V Stoke Gabriel and Collaton *Ex* 93–99; Dep PV Ex Cathl 95–99; Chapl Shiplake Coll Henley 99–09; Chapl St Edm Sch Cant 09–10; rtd 10; PtO *Ox* 09–12; *Sarum* from 11. *Sedgehill House, 9 Wyndham Road, Salisbury SP1 3AA* T: (01722) 329289 E: robertprance@live.co.uk

PRASADAM, Canon Madhu Smitha. b 64. Leeds Univ BA 87 Birm Univ MA 04 LTCL 88. Qu Coll Birm. **d** 03 **p** 04. C Blackheath *Birm* 03–07; V Hamstead St Paul 07–18; Chapl Denmark *Eur* from 18; Hon Can from 21. *St Alban's Church, Tuborgvej 82, 2900 Hellerup, Copenhagen, Denmark* T: (0045) 2232 5227 E: chaplain@st-albans.dk

PRATT, Basil David. b 38. Westmr Coll of Educn TCert 59. Ripon Hall Ox 64. **d** 67 **p** 68. C Lewisham St Jo Southend *S'wark* 67–68; C Caterham Valley 68–70; CF 70–93; PtO *Glas* from 08. *St Michael's, Bankend Road, Dumfries DG1 4AL* T: (01387) 267933

PRATT, Edward Andrew. b 39. Clare Coll Cam BA 61 MA 65. Clifton Th Coll 63. **d** 66 **p** 67. C Southall Green St Jo *Lon* 66–69; C Drypool St Columba w St Andr and St Pet *York* 69–71; P-in-c Radbourne *Derby* 71–74; R Kirk Langley 71–78; V Mackworth All SS 71–78; V Southsea St Simon *Portsm* 78–97; rtd 97; PtO *Sarum* from 97. *7 Bay Close, Swanage BH19 1RE*

PRATT, Mrs Janet Margaret. b 40. Herts Coll BEd 78. St Alb Minl Tr Scheme 78. **dss** 81 **d** 87 **p** 94. High Wych and Gilston w Eastwick *St Alb* 81–89; Hon Par Dn 87–89; Par Dn Histon *Ely* 89–94; C 94–97; Par Dn Impington 89–94; C 94–97; R Bardney *Linc* 97–07; PtO *Ely* 08–18; *St Alb* 08–19. *26 Stamford Avenue, Royston SG8 7DD* T: (01763) 243508 E: janetmpratt99@yahoo.com

PRATT, Michael. *See* HARRIS, Michael

PRATT, The Ven Richard David. b 55. Linc Coll Ox BA 77 MA 81 Birm Univ PhD 01 Nottm Univ BCombStuds 84. Linc Th Coll 81. **d** 84 **p** 85. C Wellingborough All Hallows *Pet* 84–87; TV Kingsthorpe w Northampton St Dav 87–92; V Northampton St Benedict 92–97; Dioc Communications Officer *Carl* from 97; P-in-c Carl St Cuth w St Mary 97–08; Adn W Cumberland from 09; Hon Can Carl Cathl from 02. *50 Stainburn Road, Stainburn, Workington CA14 1SN* T: (01900) 66190 E: archdeacon.west@carlislediocese.org.uk

PRATT, Stephen Samuel. b 67. Univ Coll Ches BA 88 Keele Univ PGCE 89. Oak Hill Th Coll BA 00. **d** 00 **p** 01. C Goodmayes All SS *Chelmsf* 00–03; TV Chell *Lich* 03–07; P-in-c 07–08; V 08–15; CF(V) 05–15; CF from 15. *c/o MOD Chaplains (Army)* T: (01264) 383430 F: 381824 E: stephen_pratt@sky.com

PRATTEN, Miss Susan Avarina. b 60. Birm Univ BA 81 Univ Coll of Swansea PGCE 82. St Mich Coll Llan 10. **d** 12 **p** 13. C Caerphilly *Llan* 12–15; C Eglwysilan and Caerphilly 15–18; V Caerleon and Llanfrechfa *Mon* from 18. *The Vicarage, High Street, Caerleon, Newport NP18 1AZ* T: (01633) 421485 M: 07979-742198 E: s.pratten@btinternet.com

PRECIOUS, Christopher. b 78. Open Univ BSc 01. Cranmer Hall Dur 14. **d** 16 **p** 17. C Alrewas *Lich* 16–19; C Wychnor 16–19; R Kinnerley w Melverley, Knockin w Maesbrook and Maesbury from 19. *The Rectory, Vicarage Lane, Kinnerley, Oswestry SY10 8DE* T: (01691) 682351 E: revdchrisprecious@gmail.com

PRECIOUS, Sally Joanne. *See* WRIGHT, Sally Joanne

PREECE, Barry Leslie. b 48. Lich Th Coll 68. **d** 71 **p** 72. C Ewell *Guildf* 71–74; C York Town St Mich 75–77; P-in-c Ripley 77–81; Chapl HM Det Cen Send 77–81; V Cuddington *Guildf* 81–88; V Cobham 88–03; R E and W Clandon 03–13; rtd 13; PtO *Cant* from 13. *1 Collard Place, Hawkinge, Folkestone CT18 7TY* E: rev.preece@btinternet.com

PREECE, Canon Colin George. b 51. Bernard Gilpin Soc Dur 71 Chich Th Coll 72. **d** 75 **p** 76. C Upper Gornal *Lich*

75–78; C Wednesbury St Paul Wood Green 78–81; V Oxley 81–89; V Kennington *Cant* 89–03; RD E Charing 92–98; P-in-c Ashford 03–15; Hon Can Cant Cathl 08–15; rtd 15; PtO *Ex* from 15; Hon Can Toliara Madagascar from 13. *Bowood House, 2 Bishop Court, Colyton EX24 6RQ* T: (01297) 552154 E: colinpreece@btinternet.com

PREECE, David Nathan. b 87. Ox Brookes Univ BA 11 K Coll Lon PGCE 12. Trin Coll Bris MA 17. **d** 17 **p** 18. C Busbridge and Hambledon *Guildf* 17–21; P-in-c Saxmundham w Kelsale cum Carlton *St E* from 21. *The Rectory, 6 Manor Gardens, Saxmundham IP17 1ET* E: dnpreece@hotmail.co.uk

PREECE, Mrs Jill Annette. b 58. Bp Otter Coll BEd 79. SEITE 08. **d** 11 **p** 12. NSM Eastbourne St Elisabeth *Chich* 11–15; NSM Eastbourne St Jo from 15. *17 Rowsley Road, Eastbourne BN20 7XS* T: (01323) 638020 M: 07742-655986 E: jill@stjm.org.uk

PREECE, Canon Mark Richard. b 61. St Paul's Coll Chelt BA 85. Linc Th Coll 85. **d** 87 **p** 88. C Coity w Nolton *Llan* 87–89; C Penarth w Lavernock 89–92; V Ewenny w St Brides Major 92–99; V Canton St Luke 99–02; TR Canton Cardiff 02–19; AD Cardiff 08–13; Can Llan Cathl 14–19; Prec and Can Llan Cathl from 19. *2 White House, The Cathedral Green, Cardiff CF5 2EB* T: (029) 2056 8842 E: precentor@llandaffcathedral.org.uk

PREECE, The Ven Roger Martin Howell. b 64. Imp Coll Lon BSc 86 FRSA 96. St Steph Ho Ox BA 05 MA 10. **d** 06 **p** 07. C Marple All SS *Ches* 06–08; V Bowdon 08–15; Adn St Helens and Warrington *Liv* 15–19; Master R Foundn of St Kath in Ratcliffe from 19. *The Royal Foundation of St Katharine, 2 Butcher Row, London E14 8DS* T: 03001-111147 E: roger.preece@gmail.com *or* roger.preece@rfsk.org.uk

PREMRAJ, Deborah Devashanthy. b 66. Bangalore Univ BSc 87 BEd 92 Serampore Univ BD 91. United Th Coll Bangalore 87. **d** 96 **p** 97. Deacon Vedal India 96-97; Presbyter Madurantakam 97–02; PtO *S'wark* 02–05; C Battersea Fields 05–06; Presbyter St Geo Cathl Chennai India 06–11; Presbyter Chennai St Mary 06–11; Presbyter Chennai Emmanuel 11–14; Presbyter Chennai Redeemer 12–17; Presbyter Chennai Inba Yesu Aalayam 17–19; C New Addington *S'wark* from 20. *St Edward's Vicarage, Cleves Crescent, New Addington, Croydon CR0 0DL*

PREMRAJ, Dhanaraj Charles. b 63. Madras Univ BA 86 MA 88 Heythrop Coll Lon MTh 03. United Th Coll Bangalore BD 92. **d** 93 **p** 94. India 93–02; PtO *S'wark* 02–05; C Battersea Fields 05–06; Presbyter St Geo Cathl Chennai India 06–11; Presbyter Chennai Redeemer 11–17; Presbyter Chennai Inba Yesu Aalayam 17–19; P-in-c New Addington *S'wark* from 19. *St Edward's Vicarage, Cleves Crescent, New Addington, Croydon CR0 0DL* T: (01689) 845588 M: 07942-755011 E: prem_rajcsi@yahoo.com

PRENDERGAST, Mrs Sally Elizabeth. b 67. Portsm Univ BA 05. SCTEI 16. **d** 19 **p** 20. NSM Wendover and Halton *Ox* from 19. *Wylderne, Bridge Street, Great Kimble, Aylesbury HP17 9TW* T: (01844) 761206 M: 07876-515098 E: sallyprendergast22@gmail.com

PRENTICE, Mrs Heike. b 67. St Mellitus Coll BA 18. **d** 18 **p** 19. C Hammersmith St Pet *Lon* 18–21; PtO from 21; R Coggeshall, Markshall, Cressing etc *Chelmsf* from 21. *The Vicarage, 4 Church Green, Coggeshall, Colchester CO6 1UD* M: 07752-308048

PRENTICE, Mark Neil. b 73. Ex Univ BA 94. Wycliffe Hall Ox MTh 00. **d** 00 **p** 01. C Tulse Hill H Trin and St Matthias *S'wark* 00–04; C Langham Place All So *Lon* 04–13; P-in-c Ipswich St Jo *St E* 13–19; P-in-c Ipswich St Andr 14–19; V Ipswich St Jo w St Andr from 19. *St John's Vicarage, Cauldwell Hall Road, Ipswich IP4 4QE* T: (01473) 721070 E: mark@stjohnsipswich.org.uk *or* mark@mie.org.uk

PRENTIS, Calvert Clayton. b 62. St Jo Coll Nottm 95. **d** 97 **p** 98. C Wood End *Cov* 97–00; TV Leeds St Geo *Ripon* 00–05; Asst Dioc Dir of Ords 02–05; P-in-c Huddersfield H Trin *Wakef* 05–07; V 07–12; Asst Dioc Dir of Ords 09–12; TR Horley *S'wark* 12–15; Asst Dir of Ords Croydon Area 13–15; Dioc Minority Ethnic Voc Champion 14–15; P-in-c Gt Ilford St Jo *Chelmsf* 15–18; Asst Dioc Dir of Ords 15–18; Dioc Dir of Ords and Voc Development *Birm* from 18. *Diocesan Office, 1 Colmore Row, Birmingham B3 2BJ* T: 0121-426 0400 M: 07505-036602 E: calvertprentis93@gmail.com

PRENTIS, Canon Sharon Teresa. b 64. Cov Univ BA 93 Keele Univ MSc 97 Leeds Univ PhD 05 Sheff Univ MA 13. Yorks Min Course 10. **d** 13 **p** 14. NSM Redhill St Matt *S'wark* 13–15; NSM Gt Ilford St Jo *Chelmsf* 15–18; Lect St Mellitus Coll 15–18; Intercultural Miss Enabler and Dean of Black, Asian and Minority Ethnic Affairs *Birm* 18–21; Hon Can Birm Cathl 21; Dean of Min St Mellitus Coll from 21; PtO *Birm* from 18; *Lich* from 20; Can Th Lich Cathl from 21. *St Mellitus College,*

192-194 Mansfield Road, Nottingham NG1 3HX T: (020) 7052 0573 E: sharon.prentis@stmellitus.ac.uk

PRESCOTT, David Anthony. b 62. Univ of Wales (Lamp) BA 84 Coll of Ripon & York St Jo PGCE 85. Ripon Coll Cuddesdon MTh 07. **d** 07 **p** 08. C W Heref 07–10; TV Burrington, Chawleigh, Cheldon, Chulmleigh etc *Ex* 10–12; Chapl Warminster Sch 12–18; Hon C River Were *Sarum* 17–19; Chapl Wycliffe Coll Glos from 19. *Wycliffe College, Bath Road, Stonehouse GL10 2JQ* T: (01453) 852831 M: 07779-588619 E: revd.david.prescott@gmail.com *or* david.prescott@wycliffe.co.uk

PRESCOTT, David John. b 51. St Kath Coll Liv BEd 73. NOC 00. **d** 03 **p** 04. C Southport Em *Liv* 03–07; P-in-c Birchwood 07–11; rtd 11. *90 Halsall Lane, Ormskirk L39 3AX* T: (01695) 574602 M: 07762-943138 E: prezzy@hotmail.co.uk

PRESCOTT, Thomas Robert. b 41. St Mich Coll Llan 93. **d** 95 **p** 96. C Abertillery w Cwmtillery w Six Bells *Mon* 95–99; V Llanhilleth 99–03; rtd 03. *70 Glandwr Street, Abertillery NP13 1TZ* T: (01495) 216782

PRESCOTT, William Allan. b 57. ACIS 87. Sarum & Wells Th Coll 91. **d** 93 **p** 94. C Horsell *Guildf* 93–98; R Guernsey St Sav Win 98–08; P-in-c Guernsey St Marguerite de la Foret 98–08; Chapl Guernsey Airport 08; R Compton, Hursley, and Otterbourne *Win* from 08. *The Rectory, Kiln Lane, Otterbourne, Winchester SO21 2EJ* T: (01962) 714551

PRESS, Richard James. b 45. Southn Univ CertEd 67. Sarum & Wells Th Coll 92. **d** 92 **p** 93. C Bradford-on-Avon H Trin *Sarum* 92–95; P-in-c Rowde and Poulshot 95–98; R Rowde and Bromham 98–01; Chapl Wilts and Swindon Healthcare NHS Trust 98–00; P-in-c Chickerell w Fleet *Sarum* 01–07; R 07–11; P-in-c Abbotsbury, Portesham and Langton Herring 09–11; rtd 11; PtO *Sarum* 12–21. *10 Carrick Close, Dorchester DT1 2SB* T: (01305) 262130 E: rjpress@gmail.com

PRESS, Canon William John. b 72. QUB MEng 94 TCD BTh 99 QUB MTh 04. **d** 99 **p** 00. C Knockbreda *D & D* 99–03; C Dundonald 03–05; I Annalong 05–14; I Knockbreda from 14; Can Down Cathl from 20. *Knockbreda Rectory, 69 Church Road, Newtownbreda, Belfast BT8 7AN* T: (028) 9064 1493 E: billclaire.press@gmail.com

PREST, Ms Deborah Ann. b 56. Leeds Univ BA 77 Ches Univ BTh 13 Man Univ PGCE 98. SNWTP 07. **d** 10 **p** 11. C Timperley *Ches* 10–14; P-in-c Greenlands *Blackb* from 14; P-in-c Blackpool St Paul from 14. *Address withheld by request* T: (01253) 353900 E: deborahprest@icloud.com

PREST, Hilary Irene. **d** 15 **p** 16. NSM Bassaleg *Mon* 15–18; NSM Magor from 18. *6 Silure Way, Langstone, Newport NP18 2NU* T: (01633) 412803 E: hilprest@aol.com

PRESTIDGE, Colin Robert. b 58. W Sussex Inst of HE BEd 86 Open Univ BA 01. STETS 01. **d** 04 **p** 05. NSM Crofton *Portsm* from 04; Asst Chapl E Hants Primary Care Trust 04–08. *96 Titchfield Road, Stubbington, Fareham PO14 2JB* T: (01329) 664375 E: colin@prestidge.org.uk

PRESTNEY, Canon Patricia Christine Margaret. b 49. UEA BEd 94. Oak Hill Th Coll 84. **d** 87 **p** 94. NSM Lawford *Chelmsf* 87–95; Chapl Benenden Sch 95–97; Chapl St Jo Coll Ipswich 97–00; R Lawford *Chelmsf* 00–10; Hon Can Chelmsf Cathl 09–10; rtd 10; PtO *Chelmsf* 11–13; P-in-c Gt Bentley 13–15; PtO 15–16; Hon C Colchester Ch Ch w St Mary V 16–19; PtO 20–21. *36 Inglis Road, Colchester CO3 3HU* T: (01206) 574287 M: 07825-222780 E: patprestney@yahoo.com

PRESTON, David Francis. b 50. BNC Ox BA 72 MA 78. St Steph Ho Ox 72. **d** 74 **p** 75. C Beckenham St Jas *Roch* 74–79; C Hockley *Chelmsf* 81–83; C Lamorbey H Redeemer *Roch* 83–89; V Gillingham St Barn 89–00; PtO 00–11. *103 High Street, Kirkcudbright DG6 4JG* T: (01557) 330650 E: d.preston.347@btinternet.com

PRESTON, Mrs Deborah Anne. b 46. GTCL 67. CBDTI 01. **d** 04 **p** 06. OLM Kirkby Lonsdale *Carl* 04–06; NSM Old Hutton and New Hutton and Crosscrake 06–10; NSM Kirkby Lonsdale 10–16; rtd 16; PtO *Carl* from 16. *The Old Schoolhouse, Kirkby Lonsdale, Carnforth LA6 2DX* T: (015242) 72509 M: 07799-246380 E: deborahpreston@gmail.com

PRESTON, John Michael. b 40. K Coll Lon BD 63 AKC 63 Lon Univ BA 81 Southn Univ PhD 91 Univ of Wales (Lamp) MA 09. St Boniface Warminster. **d** 65 **p** 66. C Heston *Lon* 65–67; C Northolt St Mary 67–72; Trinidad and Tobago 72–74; P-in-c Aveley *Chelmsf* 74–78; V 78–82; C Eastleigh *Win* 82–84; C-in-c Boyatt Wood CD 84–87; V W End 87–00; P-in-c Newton Valence, Selborne and E Tisted w Colemore 00–03; rtd 03; Chapl SSB from 03; PtO *Portsm* from 03; *Win* from 09. *10 Trent Way, Lee-on-the-Solent PO13 8JF* T: (023) 9263 7673 M: 07801-553233 E: john.preston1508@gmail.com

PRESTON, Michael Christopher. b 47. Hatf Coll Dur BA 68. Ripon Coll Cuddesdon 75. **d** 78 **p** 79. C Epsom St Martin *Guildf* 78–82; C Guildf H Trin w St Mary

82–86; V Epsom St Barn 86–14; rtd 14. *1 Madeira Court, Clifton Crescent, Folkestone CT20 2ER* T: (01303) 211605 E: rev.retired@m-c-preston.org.uk

PRESTON, Oliver Robert. b 88. Ox Brookes Univ BA 10 St Jo Coll Dur BA 17. Cranmer Hall Dur 14. **d** 17 **p** 18. C Halliwell St Pet *Man* 17–20; C Bridlington Ch Ch w Bessingby and Ulrome *York* from 20. *Bessingby Vicarage, Kent Road, Bridlington YO16 4RR* M: 07912-622646

PRESTON, Mrs Paula Ann. b 65. St Jo Coll Nottm 10. **d** 12 **p** 13. C Cambridge St Martin *Ely* 12–16; TV Chigwell and Chigwell Row *Chelmsf* 16–19; TV Vale of Roding from 19. *All Saints' Vicarage, Romford Road, Chigwell IG7 4QD* T: (020) 8501 5226 E: revpaulapreston@gmail.com

PRESTON, The Very Revd Reuben James. b 65. York Univ BSc 86 MEng 87 Univ of Cen England in Birm MA 05 Birm Univ PGCE 97. Westcott Ho Cam 88. **d** 91 **p** 92. C Weoley Castle *Birm* 91–94; TV Malvern Link w Cowleigh *Worc* 94–96; PtO *Birm* 96–99; C Bordesley St Benedict 99–07; PtO *Portsm* 07–08; Hon C Portsea St Sav 08; Hon C Portsea St Alb 08; P-in-c Bridgemary 08–11; Chapl Bridgemary Community Sports Coll 08–11; Chapl HM Pris Kingston (Portsm) 08–11; V Hackney Wick St Mary of Eton w St Aug *Lon* 11–16; R Sharnbrook, Felmersham and Knotting w Souldrop *St Alb* 16–18; R Johnstone *Glas* from 18; R Renfrew from 18; Dean Glas from 20. *29 Gleniffer Road, Renfrew PA4 0RD* T: 0141-883 1398 M: 07971-895897 E: rjp@reubenjamespreston.co.uk *or* dean@glasgow.anglican.org

PRESTWOOD, James Anthony. b 78. York Univ BSc 99 K Coll Lon MA 03. St Mellitus Coll BA 11. **d** 11 **p** 12. C Tollington *Lon* 11–14; P-in-c Linc St Swithin 14–18; V from 18; P-in-c Linc St Faith and St Martin w St Pet from 21. *41 Mercer Drive, Lincoln LN1 1AG* E: jimprestwood@me.com

PRESTWOOD, Ms Jayne Marie. b 64. Man Univ BA 86 Nottm Univ MA 93. Linc Th Coll MA 94. **d** 94 **p** 95. C Reddish *Man* 94–98; Dioc Drugs Misuse Project Worker 98–00; P-in-c N Reddish 00–04; P-in-c Haughton St Anne 04–06; Tr Officer for Reader Tr 04–06; Vice Prin Dioc Reader and OLM Schemes 06–12; Chapl Man Univ 12–16; Chapl Man Metrop Univ 12–16; Chapl RNCM 12–16; Dioc Officer for Lay Voc and Min *Chich* from 17. *Church House, 211 New Church Road, Hove BN3 4ED* T: (01273) 421021 E: jayne.prestwood@chichester.anglican.org *or* jprestwood@sky.com

PRETT, Alan. b 39. **d** 05 **p** 06. OLM Styvechale *Cov* 05–12; PtO 12–13; *St And* from 13. *Meikleour Lodge, Meikleour, Perth PH2 6DY* T: (01250) 883304 E: alanprett@btinternet.com

PRETTY, John Leslie. b 51. **d** 10 **p** 11. OLM Draycott-le-Moors w Forsbrook *Lich* 10–15; OLM Walsall Wood 16–18; PtO from 18. *14 Shire Ridge, Walsall Wood, Walsall WS9 9RB* T: (01543) 820194

PREUSS-HIGHAM, Mrs Margaret. b 56. STETS 07. **d** 10 **p** 11. NSM Bridport *Sarum* 10–15; NSM Abbotsbury, Portesham and Langton Herring from 15. *The Rectory, Church Lane, Portesham, Weymouth DT3 4HB* T: (01305) 873978 E: margaret.preusshigham@gmail.com

PREVETT, Mark Norman. b 59. Univ of Wales (Cardiff) BD 88. St Mich Coll Llan 85. **d** 88 **p** 89. C Brynmawr *S & B* 88–90; C Bassaleg *Mon* 90–92; R Blaina and Nantyglo 92–97; TV Halas *Worc* 97–04; RD Dudley 00–04; TR Totton *Win* 04–13; P-in-c Merthyr Tydfil St Dav and Abercanaid *Llan* from 13; P-in-c Merthyr Tydfil Ch Ch 18–21. *6 Llwyncelyn Lane, Merthyr Tydfil CF48 1AL* T: (01685) 553529 E: prevtherev@sky.com

PREVITÉ, Anthony Michael Allen. b 41. CITC 85. **d** 88 **p** 89. C Galway w Kilcummin *T, K & A* 88–91; I Omey w Ballynakill, Errislannan and Roundstone 91–93; Dean Tuam 93–96; I Tuam w Cong and Aasleagh 93–96; Adn Tuam and Can Tuam Cathl 96–06; I Omey w Ballynakill, Errislannan and Roundstone 96–06; rtd 06. *Oldchapel, Oughterard, Co Galway, Republic of Ireland* T: (00353) (91) 552126 E: amaprevite@gmail.com

PREWER, Dennis. b 30. Kelham Th Coll 50. **d** 54 **p** 55. C Stockport St Thos *Ches* 54–58; C Gt Grimsby St Mary and St Jas *Linc* 58–62; V Gt Harwood St Jo *Blackb* 62–64; V Scarcliffe *Derby* 64–70; Org Sec CECS 70–92; Dios Liv, Ban and St As 70–78; Dio Man 78–92; LtO *Ches* 70–92; PtO *Man* 78–96; rtd 92; PtO *Ches* 92–10. *10 Langton Close, Grimsby DN33 1HG*

PRICE, Alan John. b 48. Wilson Carlile Coll 69. **d** 08 **p** 08. P-in-c Charlesworth and Dinting Vale *Derby* 08–11; rtd 11; LtO *Mor* 12–17. *28 Manor Road, Belper DE56 1NT* M: 07785-723952 E: alan@alanprice.me.uk

PRICE, Alison Jane. *See* DOBELL, Alison Jane

PRICE, Alison Jean. b 50. Man Univ BSc 71 Open Univ MA 93 Kellogg Coll Ox DPhil 01 PGCE 89. Ox Min Course 05. **d** 08 **p** 09. NSM Marston w Elsfield *Ox* 08–16; rtd 16; PtO *Ox* from 17. *31 Holliers Close, Thame OX9 2EN* T: (01844) 214942 M: 07792-460923 E: alisonjeanprice@gmail.com

PRICE, Mrs Alison Mary. b 48. K Alfred's Coll Win CertEd 69. **d** 01. Par Dn Magor *Mon* 01–11; PtO 11–12; rtd 13. *103 Bawnmore Road, Bilton, Rugby CV22 6EJ* T: (01788) 879738 E: alisonprice@talktalk.net

PRICE, Alun Huw. b 47. MBE 91. St D Coll Lamp. **d** 70 **p** 71. C Carmarthen St Dav *St D* 70–73; V Betws Ifan 73–77; CF 77–03; PtO *St D* from 02. *Bryn Seion, Llyn y Fran Road, Llandysul SA44 4JW* T: (01559) 363954 E: alun47@sky.com

PRICE, Anthony Ronald. b 49. Linc Coll Ox BA 71 MA 83 St Jo Coll Dur BA 78. **d** 79 **p** 80. C St Alb St Paul 79–81; C Wootton 81–85; C Lydiard Millicent w Lydiard Tregoz *Bris* 85–86; TV The Lydiards 86–91; V Marston *Ox* 91–95; V Marston w Elsfield 95–16; RD Cowley 97–02; rtd 16; PtO *Ox* from 17. *31 Holliers Close, Thame OX9 2EN* T: (01844) 214942 M: 07584-492225 E: tonyprice01@gmail.com

PRICE, Carol Ann. b 46. St Jo Coll Nottm 02. **d** 03 **p** 04. NSM Derby St Alkmund and St Werburgh 03–04; NSM Charlesworth and Dinting Vale 04–11; rtd 11; LtO *Mor* 12–17. *28 Manor Raod, Belper DE56 1NT* M: 07787-522127 E: carol@carolprice.me.uk

PRICE, Mrs Christine Janice. b 45. Sarum & Wells Th Coll 83. **dss** 86 **d** 87 **p** 94. Roxbourne St Andr *Lon* 86–90; NSM 87–90; NSM Roxeth Ch Ch and Harrow St Pet 90–93; C Roxeth 93–96; C Costessey *Nor* 96–98; rtd 98; PtO *Nor* 98–05; *Ox* 06–16. *49 Turner Road, Marple, Stockport SK6 7NJ* M: 07702-818256 E: chrisjpri@aol.com

PRICE, Canon Clive Stanley. b 42. ALCD 69. **d** 69 **p** 70. C Chenies and Lt Chalfont *Ox* 69–75; R Upper Stour *Sarum* 75–79; C-in-c Panshanger CD *St Alb* 79–82; TV Digswell and Panshanger 82–86; P-in-c St Oswald in Lee w Bingfield *Newc* 86–07; Dioc Ecum Officer 86–07; Hon Can Newc Cathl 97–07; AD Bellingham 00–06; rtd 07; PtO *Newc* from 07. *24 Castlegate Court, Berwick-upon-Tweed TD15 1BU*

PRICE, David. b 27. Wycliffe Hall Ox 61. **d** 63 **p** 64. C Bucknall and Bagnall *Lich* 63–67; C Abingdon w Shippon *Ox* 67–76; Warden Stella Carmel Conf Cen Haifa Israel 76–80; Dir Israel Trust of the Angl Ch and R Jerusalem 80–84; V S Kensington St Luke *Lon* 84–92; P-in-c S Kensington St Jude 88–92; rtd 92; Hon C Hordle *Win* 92–97; PtO 97–98; *Worc* 98–07. *16 Masefield Avenue, Ledbury HR8 1BW* T: (01531) 634831

PRICE, David Gareth Michael. b 64. Ex Univ BA 86 Kent Univ MA 87 FSS. Wycliffe Hall Ox BTh 94. **d** 97 **p** 98. C Godalming *Guildf* 97–00; Min Elvetham Heath LEP 00–12; V Heatherlands St Jo *Sarum* from 12. *St John's Vicarage, 21 Crescent Road, Poole BH14 9AS* T: (01202) 740235 E: mail@pricefamilypoole.plus.com

PRICE, Canon David Rea. b 39. St Aid Birkenhead 61. **d** 63 **p** 64. C Green Street Green *Roch* 63–66; C Gillingham St Mary 66–69; C New Windsor St Jo *Ox* 69–72; V Winkfield 72–80; RD Bracknell 78–86; V Sunningdale 80–86; TR Wimborne Minster and Holt *Sarum* 86–96; R Wimborne Minster 96–01; RD Wimborne 88–98; Can and Preb Sarum Cathl 92–01; P-in-c Witchampton, Stanbridge and Long Crichel etc 00–01; Chapl Wimborne Hosp 86–01; rtd 01; PtO *Ex* 01–14; RD Aylesbeare 11–13; PtO *Sarum* 14–21. *161 Sopwith Crescent, Wimborne BH21 1SR* T: (01202) 885488 E: rea@14broadway.eclipse.co.uk

PRICE, Canon David Trevor William. b 43. Keble Coll Ox BA 65 MA 69 Univ of Wales (Trin St Dav) Hon DD 18 MEHS 79 FRHistS 79 FSA 95. Sarum & Wells Th Coll 72. **d** 72 **p** 73. Lect Univ of Wales (Lamp) *St D* 70–87; Sen Lect 87–97; Chapl 79–98; Dean of Chpl 90–91; Public Preacher 72–86; Dioc Archivist 82–98; P-in-c Betws Bledrws 86–97; Hon Can St D Cathl 90–92; Can St D Cathl 92–00; V Cydweli and Llandyfaelog 97–00; P-in-c Myddle and Broughton *Lich* 00–08; P-in-c Loppington w Newtown 02–08; rtd 08; PtO *St As* 01–17; *Lich* 08–21; RD Wem and Whitchurch 14–15; Can St Helena from 18. *57 Kynaston Drive, Wem, Shrewsbury SY4 5DE* T: (01939) 234777 M: 07811-712911 E: williamprice@talktalk.net

PRICE, Derek Henry. b 51. Trin Coll Bris BA 98. **d** 98 **p** 99. C Bayston Hill *Lich* 98–02; R Barrow St Paul *Carl* 02–18; rtd 18. *15 Langford Drive, Boldon Colliery NE35 9LJ* E: dh.price@virgin.net

PRICE, Canon Derek William. b 27. St Pet Hall Ox BA 51 MA 55. Qu Coll Birm 51. **d** 53 **p** 54. C St Marylebone St Mark w St Luke *Lon* 53–57; C Stevenage *St Alb* 57–63; Jamaica 63–67; R Bridgham and Roudham *Nor* 67–80; R E w W Harling 69–80; Hon Can Nor Cathl 75–92; RD Thetford and Rockland 76–86; P-in-c Kilverstone 80–87; P-in-c Croxton 80–87; TR Thetford 80–87; R Castleacre w Newton, Rougham and Southacre 87–92; PtO 92–99 and from 00; P-in-c Easton w Colton and Marlingford 99–00. *c/o*

Mrs Broadhurst, 2 Croft View, Ovingham, Pudhoe NE42 6AN
E: pricefourways@Gmail.com

PRICE, Canon Edward Glyn. b 35. Univ of Wales (Lamp) BA 55. Ch Div Sch of the Pacific (USA) BD 58. **d** 58 **p** 59. C Denbigh *St As* 58–65; V Llanasa 65–76; V Buckley 76–91; Dioc RE Adv 77–88; RD Mold 86–91; Can St As Cathl from 87; Preb and Sacr from 95; V Llandrillo-yn-Rhos 91–00; rtd 00; PtO *St As* from 09. *7 Rhodfa Criccieth, Bodelwyddan, Rhyl LL18 5WL* T: (01745) 571286 *or* 582912 E: glynandfreda@gmail.com

PRICE, Elizabeth Anne. b 49. **d** 17. OLM Loughton St Mich *Chelmsf* 17–21; NSM from 21. *6 The Plains, 3 Crescent Road, London E4 6AU*

PRICE, Frederick Leslie. b 30. Oak Hill Th Coll 59. **d** 61 **p** 62. C Hougham in Dover Ch Ch *Cant* 61–64; R Plumbland and Gilcrux *Carl* 64–95; rtd 95; PtO *Carl* 98–14. *29 Cumwhinton Road, Carlisle CA1 3LA* T: (01228) 596445 E: flprice@btinternet.com

PRICE, Geoffrey David Gower. b 46. Oak Hill Th Coll. **d** 83 **p** 84. C Gt Baddow *Chelmsf* 83–86; C Hampreston Sarum 86–88; TV 88–93; P-in-c Drayton in Hales *Lich* 93–97; V 97–99; P-in-c Adderley and Moreton Say 93–97; R Ipswich St Helen, H Trin, and St Luke *St E* 99–05; V E Bedfont *Lon* 05–14; TV Cherwell Valley *Ox* 14–19; rtd 19; PtO *Glouc* from 20; *Ox* from 20. *21 Beauchamp Close, Fairford GL7 4LP* E: geoffandhope@yahoo.com

PRICE, Glyn. *See* PRICE, Edward Glyn

PRICE, Gregory Philip. b 54. Cranmer Hall Dur. **d** 83 **p** 84. C Gt Crosby St Luke *Liv* 83–86; PtO *Derby* 12–13; *S'well* 12–15; V Tuxford w Weston, Markham Clinton etc from 15. *The Vicarage, 30 Lincoln Road, Newark NG22 0HP* T: (01777) 872917 M: 07850-182951 E: revdgregprice@gmail.com

PRICE, Iorwerth Meirion Rupert. b 68. Univ of Wales (Lamp) BA 92 SOAS Lon MA 93 Greenwich Univ PGCE 97. SEITE 05 WEMTC 07. **d** 08 **p** 09. C Heref S Wye 08–10; C Woodford Valley w Archers Gate *Sarum* 10–12; CF (TA) 10–13; CF from 13. *c/o MOD Chaplains (Army)* T: (01264) 383430 F: 381824 M: 07886-273827 E: frioriprice@gmail.com *or* iorwerth.price397@mod.gov.uk

PRICE, Janice Amanda. b 58. Huddersfield Univ BA 80 K Coll Lon MA 96 MSc 07. St Aug Coll Cant 18. **d** 21. NSM Surbiton St Andr and St Mark *S'wark* from 21. *69 Selwood Road, Chessington KT9 1PT* M: 07790-708877 E: janice.price3@btopenworld.com

PRICE, Janine Susan Grace. b 51. **d** 18 **p** 19. NSM Pakenham w Norton, Tostock etc *St E* from 18. *Honeysuckle Cottage, Bobby Hill, Wattisfield, Diss IP22 1NL* T: (01359) 251268 E: jsgprice@aol.com

PRICE, Jonathan Michael. b 88. **d** 20 **p** 21. C King's Lynn St Jo the Ev *Nor* from 20. *45 Jarvis Street, King's Lynn PE30 2EQ* M: 07542-435094 E: jonathanmprice@protonmail.com

PRICE, Mrs Katherine Ann Magdalene. b 83. Mert Coll Ox BA 04 MA MSt 05 Sheff Univ BA 13. Coll of Resurr Mirfield 11. **d** 14 **p** 15. C Gt Grimsby St Mary and St Jas *Linc* 14–17; Chapl Qu Coll Ox from 17. *The Queen's College, High Street, Oxford OX1 4AW* E: katherine.price@queens.ox.ac.uk

PRICE, Laurence Martin. b 81. Ex Coll Ox BA 03 Cam Univ BTh 16. Westcott Ho Cam 14. **d** 16 **p** 17. C Waltham Gp *Linc* 16–19; Chapl Qu Coll Ox 19; PtO *Ox* from 19. *24B Leopold Street, Oxford OX4 1PS* M: 07753-466761

PRICE, Preb Lawrence Robert. b 43. LlCeram 71. Cranmer Hall Dur 76. **d** 78 **p** 79. C Harlescott *Lich* 78–80; C Cheddleton 80–83; Chapl St Edward's Hosp Cheddleton 80–83; P-in-c Calton, Cauldon, Grindon and Waterfall *Lich* 83–84; R 85–88; P-in-c Kingsley 95–00; R Kingsley and Foxt-w-Whiston 01–07; P-in-c 00–01; C Alton w Bradley-le-Moors and Oakamoor w Cotton 06–07; RD Cheadle 98–07; Preb Lich Cathl 00–08; rtd 08; P-in-c Cheddleton *Lich* 07–13; PtO 13–16; Hon C Alstonfield, Butterton, Ilam etc 16–18; RD Cheadle 16–18; PtO 18–21. *3 Beech Close, Leek ST13 7AF* E: preblrprice@btinternet.com

PRICE, Leslie. *See* PRICE, Frederick Leslie

PRICE, Canon Mari Josephine. b 43. St Hugh's Coll Ox BA 65 Ox Univ MA 69 DipEd 66. Llan Dioc Tr Scheme 93. **d** 97 **p** 98. NSM Lisvane *Llan* 97–02; NSM Roath 02–03; Hon Chapl Llan Cathl 03–14; Hon Can Llan Cathl 11–14. *23 Ty Draw Road, Roath, Cardiff CF23 5HB* T: (029) 2045 6757 M: 07850-019883 E: mari.price23@gmail.com

PRICE, Martin Randall Connop. b 45. Lon Univ BSc 71 Fitzw Coll Cam BA 75 MA 79 Univ of Wales (Swansea) PhD 02 Solicitor 71. Ridley Hall Cam 73. **d** 76 **p** 77. C Keynsham *B & W* 76–79; Ind Chapl *Sheff* 79–83; V Wortley 79–83; R Hook Norton w Gt Rollright, Swerford etc *Ox* 83–91; V Shiplake w Dunsden 91–03; P-in-c Harpsden 02–03; R Shiplake w Dunsden and Harpsden 03–09; rtd 09; PtO *Heref* 10–20. *Address withheld by request*

PRICE (née ALDERTON), Mrs Mary Louise. b 54. Nottm Univ BSc 75 IPFA 87. EAMTC 02. **d** 05 **p** 06. NSM Melbourn *Ely* from 05; NSM Meldreth from 05. *4 Barrons Green, Shepreth, Royston SG8 6QN* T: (01763) 261569 E: maryprice9486@gmail.com

PRICE, Matthew James. b 78. BEM 20. Selw Coll Cam BA 99 MA 03. Wycliffe Hall Ox 14. **d** 16 **p** 17. C Bradwell *Nor* 16–18; P-in-c Gorleston St Mary 18–19; V from 19. *The Vicarage, 41 Nuffield Crescent, Gorleston, Great Yarmouth NR31 7LL* T: (01493) 494248 E: revmatthewprice@gmail.com

PRICE, Michael Graham. b 62. Ex Coll Ox BA 84. Linc Th Coll 84. **d** 86 **p** 87. C Salford St Phil w St Steph *Man* 86–90; R Man Gd Shep 90–95; V Netherton St Andr *Worc* 95–99; Chapl Bloxham Sch 00–14; Dep Hd from 14; PtO *Ox* from 14. *Bloxham School, Bloxham, Banbury OX15 4PQ* T: (01295) 720222

PRICE, Morris John. b 39. **d** 03 **p** 04. OLM Gt Wyrley *Lich* 03–19; PtO 19–21. *42 Huthill Lane, Walsall WS6 6PB* T: (01922) 412846

PRICE, Norman. *See* PRICE, William Norman

✠**PRICE, The Rt Revd Peter Bryan.** b 44. Redland Coll of Educn CertEd 66. Oak Hill Th Coll 72. **d** 74 **p** 75 **c** 97. C Portsdown *Portsm* 74–78; Chapl Scargill Ho 78–80; P-in-c Addiscombe St Mary *Cant* 80–81; V 81–84; V Addiscombe St Mary *S'wark* 85–88; Can Res and Chan S'wark Cathl 88–92; Gen Sec USPG 92–97; Area Bp Kingston *S'wark* 97–02; Bp B & W 02–13; rtd 13; Hon Asst Bp Sarum 16–18. *86 Whitgift House, 76 Brighton Road, South Croydon CR2 6AB* E: peter@peterlongways.myzen.co.uk

PRICE, Philip Huw. b 84. Essex Univ BA 05 Dur Univ BA 18. Ridley Hall Cam 15. **d** 18 **p** 19. C Earley St Pet *Ox* 18–20; C Tilehurst St Cath and Calcot from 20. *33 Clevedon Drive, Earley, Reading RG6 5XF* M: 07960-947068 E: curate@earleystpeters.org.uk

PRICE, Rachel Anne. *See* JACKSON, Rachel Anne

PRICE, Ramon Philip. *See* PRICE, Gregory Philip

PRICE, Raymond Francklin. b 30. Wycliffe Hall Ox 61. **d** 62 **p** 63. C Bilston St Leon *Lich* 62–67; C Keighley Bradf 67–70; V Mangotsfield *Bris* 70–79; Ind Chapl *Birm* 79–86; C Birm St Martin 84–85; C Birm St Martin w Bordesley St Andr 85–86; V Edgbaston St Aug 86–99; PtO *Birm* 00–19. *35 Middle Park Road, Selly Oak, Birmingham B29 4BH* T: 0121-475 4458 E: raymondprice@virginmedia.com

PRICE, Sarah Anne. b 68. Roehampton Inst BA 89 Otago Univ BTheol 07 Ex Univ PGCE 94. **d** 07 **p** 08. C Opawa St Martin NZ 07–09; V Ellesmere 09–18; C Christchurch St Mich 14–17; P-in-c 17–18; Chapl Cathl Gr Sch 14–17; Chapl St Mich Ch Sch 16–17; PtO *Cant* from 19. *Bowley Oast East, Bowley Lane, Sandway, Maidstone ME17 2BG* T: (01622) 924963 M: 07988-355685 E: bowleyoast@hotmail.com

PRICE, Steven Albert. b 68. Brunel Univ BSc 90 CEng 95. Oak Hill Th Coll BTh 06. **d** 06 **p** 07. C New Borough and Leigh *Sarum* 06–09; C Loose *Cant* 09–11; P-in-c 11–14; V from 14. *The Vicarage, 17 Linton Road, Loose, Maidstone ME15 0AG* T: (01622) 745882 E: steveandhelenprice@btinternet.com

PRICE, Timothy Fry. b 51. CQSW. St Jo Coll Nottm 85. **d** 87 **p** 88. C Church Stretton *Heref* 87–91; V Sinfin *Derby* 91–00; Regional Adv (SW) CMJ 00–03; Nat Field Co-ord 03–05; PtO *Glouc* 01–05; *B & W* 01–05; *Bris* 01–05; V Chaffcombe, Cricket Malherbie etc *B & W* 06–16; PtO *Ex* 06–09; Dioc Ecum Miss Enabler *B & W* 17–21; PtO from 17. *65 Herne Rise, Ilminster TA19 0HH* T: (01460) 929282 E: pricetf@aol.com

PRICE, Victor John. b 35. Oak Hill Th Coll 62. **d** 65 **p** 66. C Rainham *Chelmsf* 65–70; V Dover St Martin *Cant* 70–78; V Madeley *Heref* 78–90; P-in-c Derby St Pet and Ch Ch w H Trin 90–91; V 91–96; P-in-c Morley 96–00; P-in-c Smalley 96–00; rtd 00; PtO *S'well* 00–21. *4 Holmefield, Farndon, Newark NG24 3TZ* T: (01636) 611788

PRICE, William. *See* PRICE, David Trevor William

PRICE, William Norman. b 52. GRNCM 73. NOC 86. **d** 89 **p** 90. C Lower Broughton Ascension *Man* 89–91; Min Can and Succ St E Cathl 92–96; Prec 94–96; V Par *Truro* 96–00; V Musbury *Blackb* 00–06; rtd 06; PtO *Man* 06–16; *Liv* from 14. *5 Lower Drake Fold, Westhoughton, Bolton BL5 2RE* T: 07071-299999

PRIDDIN, Emma. *See* YOUNG, Emma

PRIDDIN, Mrs Maureen Anne. b 46. Leeds Univ BA 67 Nottm Univ DipEd 68. EMMTC 82. **dss** 85 **d** 87 **p** 94. Mickleover St Jo *Derby* 85–11; Hon Par Dn 87–94; Hon C 94–06; P-in-c 06–11; Hon C Mickleover All SS 06–11; Dioc World Development Officer 87–90; rtd 11. *7 Portland*

Close, Mickleover, Derby DE3 9BZ T: (01332) 513672
E: mpriddin@ntlworld.com

✠**PRIDDIS, The Rt Revd Anthony Martin.** b 48. CCC Cam
BA 69 MA 73 New Coll Ox MA 75. Cuddesdon Coll 69.
d 72 **p** 73 **c** 96. C New Addington *Cant* 72–75; Chapl Ch Ch
Ox 75–80; TV High Wycombe *Ox* 80–86; P-in-c Amersham
86–90; R 90–96; RD 92–96; Hon Can Ch Ch 95–96; Suff Bp
Warw and Hon Can Cov Cathl 96–04; Bp Heref 04–13; rtd
13; Hon Asst Bp Worc from 13; Hon Asst Bp Glouc from 14;
PtO *Heref* from 15. *Round Oak Cottage, Bridstow, Ross-on-Wye
HR9 6QJ* T: (01989) 218503 E: anthony@priddis.me

PRIDEAUX, Humphrey Grevile. b 36. CCC Ox BA 59 MA 63
Birm Univ CertEd 66 Lon Univ DipEd 73 Open Univ BA 87.
Linc Th Coll 59. **d** 61 **p** 62. C Northampton St Matt *Pet*
61–62; C Milton *Portsm* 62–65; PtO *Birm* 65–66; Hd of RE
Qu Mary's Gr Sch Walsall 66–69; Lect St Martin's Coll Lanc
69–80; PtO *Portsm* 80–86; Hon C Fareham H Trin 86–87;
Hon C Bishop's Waltham 87–94; NSM P-in-c W Meon
and Warnford 94–03. *6 Rectory Close, Alverstoke, Gosport
PO12 2HT* T: (023) 9250 1794

PRIDIE, William Raleigh. b 49. Bris Univ BEd 72 ACP 82
FCollP 83. SWMTC 90. **d** 93 **p** 94. C Kingstone w Clehonger,
Eaton Bishop etc *Heref* 93–96; P-in-c Kimbolton w Hamnish
and Middleton-on-the-Hill 96–97; P-in-c Bockleton w
Leysters 96–97; CME Officer 96–00; TV Leominster 97–00;
R Fownhope w Mordiford, Brockhampton etc 00–10; rtd
11; PtO *Heref* 11–20. *64 Bargates, Leominster HR6 8EY*
E: wpridie365@waitrose.com

PRIDMORE, John Stuart. b 36. Nottm Univ BA 62 MA 67 Lon
Inst of Educn PhD 00. Ridley Hall Cam 62. **d** 65 **p** 66. C
Camborne *Truro* 65–67; Tutor Ridley Hall Cam 67–68; Chapl
68–71; Asst Chapl K Edw Sch Witley 71–75; Chapl 75–86;
Tanzania 86–88; Angl Chapl Hengrave Hall Cen 88–89; C
St Martin-in-the-Fields *Lon* 89–95; TR Hackney 95–03; R
St John-at-Hackney 03–06; rtd 06. *Flat 2, 3 Palmeira Square,
Hove BN3 2JA*

PRIEST, Richard Mark. b 63. Oak Hill Th Coll BA 90.
d 90 **p** 91. C Okehampton w Inwardleigh *Ex* 90–94; CF
94–20; rtd 20; PtO *Bris* from 20. *Twynholm, Plough Lane,
Kington Langley, Chippenham SN15 5PR* M: 07789-977802
E: rmpriest@hotmail.com

PRIEST, Richard Philip. b 52. WEMTC 08. **d** 10 **p** 11. NSM
Frome Valley *Heref* 10–17; V Stour Vale *Sarum* from 17. *The
Vicarage, Kington Magna, Gillingham SP8 5EW* T: (01747)
838494 M: 07717-132896 E: richard@allegro.co.uk

PRIESTLEY, Adam James. b 80. Wolv Univ BA 11. St Jo Coll
Nottm MTh 15. **d** 14 **p** 15. C W Bessacarr *Sheff* 14–16; C
Doncaster St Geo 16–17; C Doncaster St Mary and St Paul
from 17. *278 Thorne Road, Doncaster DN2 5AJ* M: 07883-
851700 E: adampriestley@hotmail.co.uk *or*
adam.priestley@sheffield.anglican.org

PRIESTLEY, Mandy. b 65. **d** 11 **p** 12. C Broughton w
Loddington and Cransley etc *Pet* 11–13; C Shepton Mallet
w Doulting *B & W* 13–15; C Beacon Trinity from 15. *The
Rectory, Fosse Road, Oakhill, Radstock BA3 5HU* T: (01749)
840239 E: priestleymandy@me.com

PRIESTLEY, Richard Allan. b 63. Ridley Hall Cam 07. **d** 09
p 10. C Broughton w Loddington and Cransley etc *Pet* 09–12;
P-in-c Beacon Trinity *B & W* from 13; C Shepton Mallet
w Doulting 13–21; Encourager of New Chr Communities
from 21. *The Rectory, Fosse Road, Oakhill, Radstock
BA3 5HU* T: (01749) 840239 E: vicar@beacontrinity.church
or richard.priestley@bathwells.anglican.org

PRIESTLEY, Rosemary Jane. *See* LAIN-PRIESTLEY, Rosemary
Jane

PRIESTNER, Hugh. b 45. Nottm Univ BTh 75. Linc Th Coll 71.
d 75 **p** 76. C Seaton Hirst *Newc* 75–78; C Longbenton
St Bart 78–81; P-in-c Glendale Gp 81–82; TV 83–88; Chapl
Stafford Acute Hosps 88–89; Tr Co-ord W Cumberland Hosp
89–92; Chapl Fair Havens Hospice 94–98; Chapl Walsgrave
Hosps NHS Trust 98–00; Chapl Team Ldr Univ Hosps Cov
and Warks NHS Trust 00–17; PtO *Cov* 10–17; V Offchurch
Gp from 17. *Address temp unknown* M: 07568-166910
E: hugh.priestner@btinternet.com

PRIGG, Patrick John. b 53. K Coll Lon BD 82. Sarum & Wells
Th Coll 89. **d** 92 **p** 93. C Wavertree St Mary *Liv* 92–96;
Chapl Sandown Coll 92–96; P-in-c Glemsford, Hartest w
Boxted, Somerton etc *St E* 96–99; R from 99. *The Rectory, 6
Lion Road, Glemsford, Sudbury CO10 7RF* T: (01787) 282164
E: revpatrick@btinternet.com

PRIME, David Alan. b 54. Chelt & Glouc Coll of HE BEd 98.
Wesley Coll Bris 82. **d** 12 **p** 13. NSM Trellech and Penallt
Mon 12–15; PtO 15–17. *The Rectory, 1 Rectory Drive, St Athan,
Barry CF62 4PD* T: (01446) 750273 M: 07870-216995
E: prime.family@yahoo.com

PRIME, Mrs Kathryn Rhian. d 12 **p** 13. NSM Trellech and
Penallt *Mon* 12–15; PtO 15–17; TV Llantwit Major *Llan*
17–18; TV Glamorgan Heritage Coast from 18. *The Rectory,
1 Rectory Drive, St Athan, Barry CF62 4PD* T: (01446) 750273
E: rhianprime1960@gmail.com

PRIMROSE, Preb David Edward Snodgrass. b 55. St Jo
Coll Cam MA 80. Trin Coll Bris BA 92. **d** 87 **p** 92. Pakistan
87–89; C Glouc St Paul 92–96; R Badgeworth, Shurdington
and Witcombe w Bentham 96–03; V Thornbury and
Oldbury-on-Severn w Shepperdine 03–10; AD Hawkesbury
04–09; Dir Transforming Communities *Lich* 10–21;
Preb Lich Cathl from 20; rtd 21. *Hill House, Vicarage
Lane, Bednall, Stafford ST17 0SE* T: (01785) 748976
E: david.primrose@lichfield.anglican.org

PRINCE, Alastair. b 76. Nottm Univ BSc 99 SS Coll Cam
BTh 06. Westcott Ho Cam 03. **d** 06 **p** 07. C Toxteth Park
Ch Ch and St Mich w St Andr *Liv* 06–09; V Croxteth
Park 09–17; Voc and Strategy Development Adv *Dur*
from 17. *20 Murphy Close, Crook DL15 9GL* M: 07732-
489424 E: alastairprince@hotmail.com *or*
alastair.prince@durham.anglican.org

PRINCE (*née* RUMBLE), Mrs Alison Merle. b 49. Surrey Univ
BSc 71. Trin Coll Bris BA 89. **d** 89 **p** 94. Par Dn Willesden
Green St Gabr *Lon* 89–91; Par Dn Cricklewood St Gabr and
St Mich 92; Par Dn Herne Hill *S'wark* 92–94; C 94–95; Chapl
Greenwich Healthcare NHS Trust 95–96; TV Sanderstead All
SS *S'wark* 97–03; TV Kegworth, Hathern, Long Whatton,
Diseworth etc *Leic* 04–09; rtd 09; PtO *Leic* 13–21. *23
Grangefields Drive, Rothley, Leicester LE7 7ND* T: 0116-237
5530

PRINCE, Mrs Melanie Amanda. b 71. St D Coll Lamp BA 92
Univ of Wales (Cardiff) MPhil 93. St Mich Coll Llan 96.
d 98 **p** 99. C Aberavon *Llan* 98–01; C Gabalfa 01–08; TV
Llantwit Major 08–13; P-in-c Porthkerry and Rhoose 13–20;
P-in-c Porthkerry, Rhoose and Penmark from 21; Voc
Adv from 13. *The Vicarage, 6 Milburn Close, Rhoose, Barry
CF62 3EJ* T: (01446) 719734 E: maprince77@gmail.com

PRINCE, Penelope Ann. b 46. SWMTC 96. **d** 99 **p** 00. NSM
Halsetown *Truro* 99–02; P-in-c Breage w Godolphin and
Germoe 02–12; rtd 12; Hon C Is of Scilly *Truro* 13–16;
PtO from 16; *Ex* 17–19. *1 Angel Place, Coinagehall Street,
Helston TR13 8EF* T: (01326) 574924 M: 07535-202855
E: revpenp@gmail.com

PRINCE, Roderick Hubert. b 63. All SS Cen for Miss & Min 17.
d 18 **p** 19. NSM Wirksworth *Derby* from 18. *Red Lion House,
Red Lion Hill, Brassington, Matlock DE4 4HA* T: (01629)
540475

PRING, Althon Kerrigan. b 34. AKC 58. **d** 59 **p** 60. C
Limehouse St Anne *Lon* 59–61; C Lt Stanmore St Lawr
61–64; C Langley Marish *Ox* 64–68; P-in-c Radnage 68–72;
P-in-c Ravenstone w Weston Underwood 72–75; P-in-c Stoke
Goldington w Gayhurst 72–75; R Gayhurst w Ravenstone,
Stoke Goldington etc 75–85; P-in-c 85–86; RD Newport
78–80; TV Woughton 86–90; P-in-c Nash w Thornton,
Beachampton and Thornborough 90–94; R 94–96; rtd
96; PtO *Ox* 99–07. *Kingsmead, 9 Malting Close, Stoke
Goldington, Newport Pagnell MK16 8NX* T: (01908) 551345
E: kerriganpring@btinternet.com

PRINGLE, The Ven Cecil Thomas. b 43. TCD BA 65. CITC 66.
d 66 **p** 67. C Belfast St Donard *D & D* 66–69; I Cleenish
Clogh 69–73; I Cleenish w Mullaghdun 78–80; I Rossorry
80–08; Bp's C Drumkeeran w Templecarne and Muckross
08–18; Preb Clogh Cathl 86–89; Adn Clogh 89–14; rtd
18. *35 Station Road, Derryscobe, Letterbreen, Enniskillen
BT74 9FB* M: 07742-516188 E: cecilpringle@hotmail.com

PRINGLE, Graeme Lindsley. b 59. St Cath Coll Cam
BA 81 MA 85. St Jo Coll Nottm 92. **d** 94 **p** 95. C Binley
Cov 94–99; V Allesley Park and Whoberley 99–11; Dir
Dioc Projects and Communications Officer 11–16; Dir
Projects and Communications from 16; PtO 11–16; Hon
C Leamington Priors St Paul from 16; Gen LtO from 18.
The Rectory, Ryton Road, Bubbenhall, Coventry CV8 3BL
E: graeme.pringle@covcofe.org

PRINGLE, Margaret Brenda. b 49. CITC. **d** 05 **p** 06. NSM
Clogh w Errigal Portclare 05–13; NSM Carrickmacross
w Magheracloone 13–15; NSM Ematris w Rockcorry,
Aghabog and Aughnamullan from 15. *Rawdeer Park, Clones,
Co Monaghan, Republic of Ireland* T: (00353) (47) 51439
E: margaretpringle14@gmail.com

PRINGLE, Richard John. b 55. Lon Univ AKC 76 CertEd 77
Open Univ BA 84. Chich Th Coll 78. **d** 78 **p** 79. C
Northampton St Matt *Pet* 78–81; C Delaval *Newc* 81–84; V
Newsham 84–18; RD Bedlington 93–98; rtd 18; PtO *Newc*
18–21. *72 Goschen Street, Blyth NE24 1NL* T: (01670) 797736
E: father.pringle@blythchurches.co.uk

PRINT, Michael Guy. b 81. Sheff Univ BA 02. Wycliffe Hall Ox BTh 15. **d** 15 **p** 16. C Padiham w Hapton and Padiham Green *Blackb* 15–19; V Chorley St Geo from 19. *St George's Vicarage, Letchworth Place, Chorley PR7 2HJ* T: (01257) 263064 E: vicar@stgeorgechorley.co.uk

PRIOR, Adam Phillip. b 72. Cen Lancs Univ BA 94 K Coll Lon MA 05. Ridley Hall Cam. **d** 08 **p** 09. NSM Watford St Pet *St Alb* 08–15; LtO from 15; Min Stevenage Oak Ch BMO from 20. *31 Harefield, Stevenage SG2 9NG* M: 07931-896750

PRIOR, Carla. See VICENCIO PRIOR, Carla Alexandra Torres Lopes

PRIOR *(née* **CHIUMBU), Esther Tamisa.** b 73. Univ of Zimbabwe BSc 95. Trin Coll Bris BA 02 MA 07. **d** 03 **p** 04. NSM Redland *Bris* 03–05; C Deptford St Jo w H Trin and Ascension *S'wark* 05–08; Chapl Blackheath Bluecoat C of E Sch 08–09; Chapl HM Pris Cookham Wood 10–11; TV Cove St Jo *Guildf* 11–18; V Egham from 18. *Mauley Cottage, 13 Manorcrofts Road, Egham TW20 9LU* T: (01784) 432066 E: esthertj@yahoo.com

PRIOR, Gregory Stephen. b 68. Geo Whitefield Coll S Africa BTh 90. **d** 95 **p** 96. In C of E in S Africa 95–01; Min for Miss Muswell Hill St Jas w St Matt *Lon* 01–04; P-in-c Wandsworth All SS *S'wark* 04–06; V from 06; AD Wandsworth 13–18. *Wandsworth Vicarage, 11 Rusholme Road, London SW15 3JX* T: (020) 8788 7400

PRIOR, Canon Ian Graham. b 44. Lon Univ BSc(Econ) 71. Oak Hill Th Coll 78. **d** 80 **p** 81. C Luton Ch Ch *Roch* 80–83; TV Southgate *Chich* 83–93; V Burgess Hill St Andr 93–09; RD Hurst 98–04; Can and Preb Chich Cathl 03–09; rtd 09; PtO *Chich* from 14. *5 Chestnut Walk, Worthing BN13 3QL* T: (01903) 830127 E: ian3gl@btinternet.com

PRIOR, Ian Roger Lyndon. b 46. St Jo Coll Dur BA 68. Lon Coll of Div 68. **d** 70 **p** 71. C S Croydon Em *Cant* 70–73; PtO *S'wark* 73–85; Dir Overseas Personnel TEAR Fund 73-79; Dep Dir 79–83; Fin and Admin Dir CARE Trust and CARE Campaigns 85–92; Dir Careforce 92–12; NSM New Malden and Coombe *S'wark* 85–12; rtd 12; PtO *S'wark* from 12. *39 Cambridge Avenue, New Malden KT3 4LD* T: (020) 8949 0912 E: ianrlprior@gmail.com

PRIOR, James Murray. b 39. Edin Univ BCom 64. St And Dioc Tr Course 85. **d** 90 **p** 91. NSM Kirriemuir *St And* 90–02; NSM Forfar 90–02; NSM Dundee St Jo and Dundee St Ninian *Bre* 02–10; rtd 10. *Naughton Lodge, Balmerino, Newport-on-Tay DD6 8RN* T: (01382) 330132 E: ham.prior@tiscali.co.uk

PRIOR, Jonathan Roger Lyndon. b 74. Trin Coll Ox BA 95 MA 99 K Coll Lon PGCE 96. Wycliffe Hall Ox 07. **d** 09 **p** 10. C Elworth and Warmingham *Ches* 09–11; C Elworth 11–12; Chapl City of Lon Freemen's Sch from 12; C Ashtead *Guildf* 12–16. *15 Post House Lane, Bookham, Leatherhead KT23 3EA* M: 07957-220650

PRIOR, Matthew Thomas. b 74. Rob Coll Cam BA 97 MA 00. Trin Coll Bris BA 04 MA 05. **d** 05 **p** 06. C Deptford St Jo w H Trin and Ascension *S'wark* 05–08; P-in-c Borstal *Roch* 08–11; PtO *Guildf* 11–13; NSM Cove St Jo 13–18; NSM Egham From 18; Chapl Abp Tenison's C of E High Sch Croydon 13–14; Adult Discipleship and Learning Adv *Guildf* from 15. *Mauley Cottage, 13 Manorcroft Road, Egham TW20 9LU* T: (01784) 432066 E: mprior36@gmail.com *or* matt.prior@cofeguildford.org.uk

PRIOR, Nigel John. b 56. Bris Univ BA 78 Chich Univ MA 09. Westcott Ho Cam 79. **d** 81 **p** 82. C Langley All SS and Martyrs *Man* 81–82; C Langley and Parkfield 82–84; C Bury St Jo w St Mark 84–87; R Man Clayton St Cross w St Paul 87–99; P-in-c Mark Cross *Chich* 99–00; V Mayfield 99–20; R Woodbridge w Gt Bealings *St E* from 20. *St Mary's Rectory, 11 Church Street, Woodbridge IP12 1DS* E: nigelprior1@btinternet.com

PRIOR, Mrs Rachel Elizabeth Mary. b 93. Ch Coll Cam BA 14. Trin Coll Bris 15. **d** 17 **p** 18. C Saffron Walden and Villages *Chelmsf* 17–21; V Black Notley, Gt Notley and Rayne from 21. *The Rectory, 265C London Road, Black Notley, Braintree CM77 8QQ* E: revrachelprior@gmail.com

PRIOR, Canon Stephen Kenneth. b 55. Rhode Is Coll (USA) BA 78. Wycliffe Hall Ox 79. **d** 82 **p** 83. C Aberavon *Llan* 82–85; P-in-c New Radnor and Llanfihangel Nantmelan etc *S & B* 85–86; R 86–90; V Llansamlet 90–94; P-in-c Chester le Street *Dur* 94–96; R 96–01; R Caldbeck, Castle Sowerby and Sebergham *Carl* 01–09; Dir of Ords 04–08; R Rushden St Mary w Newton Bromswold *Pet* from 09; RD Higham 14–19; Can Pet Cathl from 16. *The Rectory, Rectory Road, Rushden NN10 0HA* T: (01933) 312554 E: sprior@toucansurf.com

PRIORY, Barry Edwin. b 44. Open Univ BA 81 FCIS. Qu Coll Birm 84. **d** 86 **p** 87. C Boldmere *Birm* 86–89; C Somerton w Compton Dundon, the Charltons etc *B & W* 89–93; R Porlock and Porlock Weir w Stoke Pero etc 93–08; RD Exmoor 97–03; rtd 08; PtO *B & W* from 08; Chapl Somerset

Partnership NHS Foundn Trust from 09. *Dove Cottage, Moor Road, Minehead TA24 5RX* T: (01643) 706808 M: 07811-092416 E: barry.priory@btinternet.com

PRITCHARD, Andrew James Dunn. See PRITCHARD-KEENS, Andrew James Dunn

PRITCHARD, Antony Robin. b 53. Van Mildert Coll Dur BSc 74 SS Paul & Mary Coll Cheltenham CertEd 75. St Jo Coll Nottm. **d** 84 **p** 85. C Desborough *Pet* 84–87; C Rushden w Newton Bromswold 87–91; R Oulton St Mich *Nor* 91–17; rtd 17; PtO *Nor* from 19. *17 West End Avenue, Costessey, Norwich NR8 5BA* T: (01603) 748903 E: robinpritchard925@btinternet.com

PRITCHARD, Brian James. Open Univ BA 05 ACIS 85. SAOMC 99. **d** 01 **p** 02. NSM Newbury *Ox* 01–06; V Billingshurst *Chich* 06–16; rtd 16; PtO *St D* from 05; Win from 16; AD Alton from 17. *15 Blackberry Lane, Four Marks, Alton GU34 5BN* T: (01420) 561394 E: brianpritchard15@gmail.com

PRITCHARD, Mrs Carol Sandra. b 52. St Aid Coll Dur BA 74 Bris Univ PGCE 75. EAMTC 96. **d** 99 **p** 00. NSM Oulton St Mich *Nor* 99–17; rtd 17; PtO *Nor* 18–20; NSM Earlham from 20; Bp's Adv for SSM from 20. *17 West End Avenue, Costessey, Norwich NR8 5BA* T: (01603) 748903 E: carolpritchard3@btinternet.com

PRITCHARD, Colin Wentworth. b 38. K Coll Lon 59 St Boniface Warminster 59. **d** 63 **p** 64. C Putney St Marg *S'wark* 63–67; C Brixton St Matt 67–70; C Milton *Portsm* 70–74; V Mitcham St Mark *S'wark* 74–82; R Long Ditton 82–94; V Earlsfield St Andr 94–03; RD Wandsworth 98–03; rtd 03; PtO *Chich* from 03. *38 Hartfield Road, Seaford BN25 4PW* T: (01323) 894899 E: colin.pritchard@gmx.co.uk

PRITCHARD, Canon David Paul. b 47. Newc Univ BA 68 Em Coll Cam PGCE 69 LTCL 70 FRCO 72. Wycliffe Hall Ox 80. **d** 82 **p** 83. C Kidlington *Ox* 82–84; P-in-c Marcham w Garford 84–85; V 86–96; RD Abingdon 91–96; R Henley w Remenham 96–04; Can Res Ely Cathl 04–14; Pastor 04–14; Prec 04–08; Vice Dean 08–14; Acting Dean 11–12; Rtd Clergy Officer *Ely* from 13; rtd 15; PtO *Ely* from 14. *2 Chapel Lane, Little Downham, Ely CB6 2TN* T: (01353) 698831 M: 07470-072322 E: dpp123@cantab.net

PRITCHARD, John Anthony. b 74. Ripon Coll Cuddesdon BTh 07. **d** 07 **p** 08. C Gt Berkhamsted, Gt and Lt Gaddesden etc *St Alb* 07–11; C St Marylebone All SS *Lon* 11–13; P-in-c Upper Norwood St Jo *S'wark* 13–17; V from 17. *The Vicarage, 2 Sylvan Road, London SE19 2RX* T: (020) 8771 6686

✠**PRITCHARD, The Rt Revd John Lawrence.** b 48. St Pet Coll Ox BA 70 MA 73 Dur Univ MLitt 93. Ridley Hall Cam 70. **d** 72 **p** 73 **c** 02. C Birm St Martin 72–76; Asst Dir RE *B & W* 76–80; Youth Chapl 76–80; P-in-c Wilton 80–88; Dir Past Studies Cranmer Hall Dur 89–93; Warden 93–96; Adn Cant and Can Res Cant Cathl 96–02; Suff Bp Jarrow *Dur* 02–07; Bp Ox 07–14; rtd 14; Hon Asst Bp Leeds from 15; Hon Asst Bp Dur from 15; PtO from 15. *42 Bolton Avenue, Richmond DL10 4BA* T: (01748) 850854 E: johnlpritchard@btinternet.com

PRITCHARD, Jonathan Llewelyn. b 64. Edin Univ MA 87 Leeds Univ MA 89 PhD 99. Ripon Coll Cuddesdon 98. **d** 00 **p** 01. C Skipton H Trin *Bradf* 00–04; P-in-c Keighley All SS 04–16; P-in-c Thwaites Brow 06–16; TV Keighley *Leeds* 16–21; TR Witham and Villages *Chelmsf* from 21. *The Rectory, 7 Chippingdell, Witham CM8 2JX* E: jllpritchard@icloud.com

PRITCHARD, Kathryn Anne. b 60. St Cath Coll Ox MA K Coll Lon MA 10 Win Univ PhD. Cranmer Hall Dur. **d** 87. Par On Addiscombe St Mary *S'wark* 87–90; CPAS Staff 90–92; PtO *Cov* 92–95; Producer Worship Progr BBC Relig Broadcasting 94–99; Publicity Manager Hodder & Stoughton Relig Books 99–01; Commissioning and Product Development Manager Ch Ho Publishing 01–09; Project Manager and Research Fell Templeton Project Abps' Coun from 15. *Mission and Public Affairs, Church House, 27 Great Smith Street, London SW1P 3AZ* E: kathryn.pritchard@churchofengland.org *or* k.pritchard410@btinternet.com

PRITCHARD, Kenneth John. b 30. Liv Univ BEng 51. NW Ord Course 72. **d** 74 **p** 75. C Ches 74–78; Miss to Seamen 78–84; V Runcorn St Jo Weston *Ches* 78–84; V Gt Meols 84–98; rtd 98; PtO *Ches* 99–14; *Liv* from 99. *13 Fieldlands, Scarisbrick, Southport PR8 5HQ* T: (01704) 514600 E: kennethpritchard@btinternet.com

PRITCHARD, Malcolm John. b 55. Bradf Univ BA 85 CQSW 85. St Jo Coll Nottm 86. **d** 88 **p** 89. C Peckham St Mary Magd *S'wark* 88–93; V Luton St Matt High Town *St Alb* 93–16; PtO from 17; CMS Uganda from 17. *Church Mission Society, Watlington Road, Cowley, Oxford OX4 6BZ* E: malcolmpritchard@outlook.com

PRITCHARD, Martin Dale. d 16 **p** 17. C Bro Deiniol *Ban* 16–17; C Bro Celynnin 17–18; C Llandudno 18–20; P-in-c Denbigh Miss Area *St As* from 20. *Trigfan, Ochr y Bryn, Henllan, Denbigh LL16 5AT* E: martinpritchard@esgobaethbangor.net

PRITCHARD, Michael Owen. b 49. Trin Coll Carmarthen CertEd 71. St Mich Coll Llan 71. **d** 73 **p** 74. C Conwy w Gyffin *Ban* 73–76; TV Dolgellau w Llanfachreth and Brithdir etc 76–78; Dioc Children's Officer 77–86; V Betws y Coed and Capel Curig 78–83; V Betws-y-Coed and Capel Curig w Penmachno etc 83–86; CF (VR) from 79; Chapl Claybury Hosp Woodford Bridge 86–96; Chapl Team Leader Forest Healthcare NHS Trust Lon 96–01; Chapl Team Leader NE Lon Foundn Trust 01–12; rtd 12. *1 St James Court, 71 Aldersbrook Road, London E12 5DL* T: (020) 8989 3813 M: 07852-194967 E: mopritchard@hotmail.com

PRITCHARD, Paul John. b 74. Wycliffe Hall Ox 16. **d** 18 **p** 19. C Barnton *Ches* 18–20; C Northwich St Luke 18–20; C Bro Dyfri *St D* from 20. *42 Broad Street, Llandovery SA20 0AY* M: 07810-264764 E: revpaulpritchard@protonmail.com

PRITCHARD, Paul Martin. b 46. **d** 13 **p** 14. OLM Mickleover All SS *Derby* 13–14; OLM Mickleover St Jo 13–14; OLM Mickleover from 14. *11 Gisborne Close, Mickleover, Derby DE3 9LU* T: (01332) 512530

PRITCHARD, Peter Humphrey. b 47. Univ of Wales (Ban) BA 70 MA 98 Liv Univ PGCE 73. Qu Coll Birm 85. **d** 87 **p** 88. C Llanbeblig w Caernarfon and Betws Garmon etc *Ban* 87–90; R Llanberis w Llanrug 90–94; R Llanfaethlu w Llanfwrog and Llanrhuddlad etc 94–99; R Llanfair Mathafarn Eithaf w Llanbedrgoch 99–05; rtd 05. *4 Penlon Gardens, Bangor LL57 1AQ*

PRITCHARD, Robin. *See* PRITCHARD, Antony Robin

PRITCHARD, Simon Geraint. b 61. Coll of Ripon & York St Jo BA 85 Ex Univ PGCE 88. Cranmer Hall Dur 98. **d** 00 **p** 01. C Heysham *Blackb* 00–01; C Morecambe St Barn 01–03; C Standish 03–06; V Haigh and Aspull *Liv* 06–15; TV Wigan All SS 15–19; R Stamford Bridge Gp *York* from 19; P-in-c Wilberfoss w Kexby from 21. *The Rectory, 8 Viking Road, Stamford Bridge, York YO41 1BR* T: (01759) 372468 E: s.pritchard41@btinternet.com

PRITCHARD, Thomas James Benbow. b 47. St Paul's Coll Chelt CertEd 69 Univ of Wales (Cardiff) BEd 79 MSc 85 Ex Univ BTh 08. SWMTC 96. **d** 99 **p** 00. NSM St Enoder *Truro* 99–01; P-in-c Roche and Withiel 01–05; V Llangollen w Trevor and Llantysilio *St As* 05–06; P-in-c Mylor w Flushing *Truro* 06–07; rtd 07; PtO *Truro* from 15. *Suncot, Short Cross Road, Mount Hawke, Truro TR4 8DU* T: (01209) 891766 E: thms_pritchard@yahoo.co.uk

PRITCHARD, The Ven Thomas William. b 33. Keele Univ BA 55 DipEd 55 Univ of Wales (Cardiff) LLM 94. St Mich Coll Llan 55. **d** 57 **p** 58. C Holywell *St As* 57–61; C Ruabon 61–63; V 77–87; R Pontfadog 63–71; R Llanferres, Nercwys and Eryrys 71–77; Dioc Archivist 76–98; Can St As Cathl 84–98; RD Llangollen 86–87; Adn Montgomery 87–98; V Berriew and Manafon 87–98; rtd 98; PtO *St As* from 09. *32B Glynne Way, Hawarden, Deeside CH5 3NL* T: (01244) 538381

PRITCHARD-KEENS, Andrew James Dunn. b 57. Van Mildert Coll Dur BSc 79 Ch Ch Ox PGCE 80. Wycliffe Hall Ox 07. **d** 09 **p** 10. C Cogges and S Leigh *Ox* 09–12; C N Leigh 09–12; TV Wheatley 12–14; V Beckley, Forest Hill, Horton-cum-Studley and Stanton St John 14–18; R Olney from 18; Chapl Thames Valley Police from 14. *The Rectory, 9 Orchard Rise, Olney MK46 5HB* T: (01234) 241721 E: andrewjdp@yahoo.co.uk

PRITCHETT, Antony Milner. b 63. Kent Univ BA 86 York Univ MA 15. Westcott Ho Cam 96. **d** 98 **p** 99. C Broughton Astley and Croft w Stoney Stanton *Leic* 98–02; V Gawber *Wakef* 02–08; Chapl Barnsley Hospice 02–08; P-in-c Pickering w Lockton and Levisham *York* 08–12; V 12–19; PtO *York* from 19. *1 Allenby Road, Helmsley, York YO62 5BB*

PRITCHETT, Mrs Beryl Ivy. b 48. Worc Coll of Educn TCert 69. WMMTC 02. **d** 05 **p** 06. NSM Brockmoor *Worc* 05–07; NSM Brierley Hill from 07. *7 Muirville Close, Wordsley, Stourbridge DY8 5NR* T: (01384) 271470 M: 07790-563479 E: berylpritchett@hotmail.co.uk

PRITCHETT, Edward Robert. b 87. Cant Ch Ch Univ BA 09 Wolfs Coll Cam BTh 16. Westcott Ho Cam 14. **d** 17 **p** 18. C Beckenham St Geo and St Barn *Roch* 17–21; V Haywards Heath St Wilfrid *Chich* from 21. *The Rectory, St Wilfrid's Way, Haywards Heath RH16 3QH* E: edward.pritchett@cantab.net *or* revedwardpritchett@outlook.com

PRIVETT, Peter John. b 48. Qu Coll Birm 75. **d** 78 **p** 79. C Moseley St Agnes *Birm* 78–81; V Kingsbury 81–87; P-in-c Dilwyn and Stretford *Heref* 87–90; Dioc Children's Adv 87–01; TV Leominster 90–98; NSM 98–05; Dioc Millennium Officer 98–01; PtO 05–07; *Cov* 07–09; C Rugby 09–13; C Rugby St Andr w St Pet and St John 13–17; rtd

18. *166 Lower Hillmorton Road, Rugby CV21 3TJ* T: (01788) 570332 E: peter.privett@yahoo.co.uk

PROBERT, Beverley Stuart. b 42. **d** 01 **p** 02. OLM Canford Magna *Sarum* 01–12; rtd 13; PtO *Sarum* 13–19. *Blaenafon, 102 Knights Road, Bournemouth BH11 9SY* T: (01202) 571731 E: bevprobert@tiscali.co.uk

PROBERT, Christopher John Dixon. b 54. Univ of Wales (Ban) BTh 95 MTh 97. St Mich Coll Llan 74. **d** 78 **p** 79. C Aberdare St Fagan *Llan* 78–79; C Cadoxton-juxta-Barry 79–81; R Llanfynydd *St As* 81–84; V Gosberton Clough and Quadring *Linc* 84–86; TV Coventry Caludon *Cov* 86–88; V Llanrhian w Llanhywel and Llanreithan *St D* 88–91; LtO 91–93; Chapl and Tutor St D NSM Course Tregaron Hosp 91–93; V Betws-y-Coed and Capel Curig w Penmachno etc *Ban* 93–96; Warden of Readers 96–98; Examining Chapl 96–98; V Lt Drayton *Lich* 98–04; P-in-c Lezant w Lawhitton and S Petherwin w Trewen *Truro* 04–10; R Three Rivers 10–11; rtd 11; PtO *Eur* from 12. *La Haudiardiere, Heusse, 50640 Le Teilleul, France* T: (0033) (2) 33 61 35 82 E: cjdprobert@gmail.com

PROBERT, Canon Edward Cleasby. b 58. St Cath Coll Cam BA 80 MA 84. Ripon Coll Cuddesdon BA 84. **d** 85 **p** 86. C Esher *Guildf* 85–89; V Earlsfield St Andr *S'wark* 89–94; V Belmont 94–04; Can Res and Chan Sarum Cathl from 04. *24 The Close, Salisbury SP1 2EH* T: (01722) 555193 E: chancellor@salcath.co.uk

PROCTER, Andrew David. b 52. St Jo Coll Ox BA 74 MA 86. Trin Coll Bris 74. **d** 77 **p** 78. C Barnoldswick w Bracewell *Bradf* 77–80; P-in-c Kelbrook 80–82; V 82–87; V Heaton St Barn 87–93; V Swanley St Paul *Roch* 93–07; R Shipbourne w Plaxtol 07–16; rtd 16. *6 Grange Road, Platt, Sevenoaks TN15 8NF* M: 07963-943524 *or* 07872-597953 E: a.procter@live.co.uk

PROCTER, Nicholas Jonathan. b 59. Liv Univ BVSc 84 MRCVS 84. LCTP 06. **d** 09 **p** 10. NSM Leyland St Jo *Blackb* 09–14; PtO 14–15; NSM Bamber Bridge St Aid 15–20; NSM Walton-le-Dale St Leon 15–20; NSM Bamber Bridge St Aid and Walton-le-Dale St Leon 20; rtd 20; PtO *Blackb* from 20. *23 Regents Way, Euxton, Chorley PR7 6PG* T: (01257) 241927 E: n.r.procter@btinternet.com

PROCTOR, Michael John. b 59. Cranmer Hall Dur 93. **d** 93 **p** 94. C Leatherhead *Guildf* 93–98; V Henlow and Langford *St Alb* 98–01; V Marton-in-Cleveland *York* 01–13; Min Coulby Newham LEP 03–13; V S Cave and Ellerker w Broomfleet from 13; RD Howden from 15. *The Vicarage, 10 Station Road, South Cave, Brough HU15 2AA* E: revmikeproctor@gmail.com

PROCTOR, Canon Michael Thomas. b 41. Ch Ch Ox BA 65 MA 67. Westcott Ho Cam 63. **d** 65 **p** 66. C Monkseaton St Mary *Newc* 65–69; Pakistan 69–72; C Willington *Newc* 72–77; TV 77–79; Ed Sec Nat Soc 79–84; P-in-c Roxwell *Chelmsf* 79–84; Bp's Ecum Officer 85–00; Dir of Miss and Unity 85–94; P-in-c Gt Waltham w Ford End 94–00; Hon Can Chelmsf Cathl 85–00; rtd 00; Dir Chelmsf Counselling Foundn from 00. *Claremont, South Street, Great Waltham, Chelmsford CM3 1DP* E: mtproctor@lineone.net

PROCTOR, Nicholas Jonathan. *See* PROCTER, Nicholas Jonathan

PROCTOR, Canon Noel. b 30. MBE 93. St Aid Birkenhead 62. **d** 64 **p** 65. C Haughton le Skerne *Dur* 64–67; R Byers Green 67–70; Chapl HM Pris Eastchurch 70–74; Chapl HM Pris Dartmoor 74–79; Chapl HM Pris Man 79–95; Hon Can Man Cathl 91–95; rtd 95; PtO *Man* from 95. *Mizpah, 64 Barton Road, Swinton, Manchester M27 5LP* T: 0161-794 6040 E: berylproctor@talktalk.net

PROSSER, Jean. b 40. MBE 10. Open Univ BA 84 Surrey Univ PhD 94. **d** 02 **p** 05. NSM Grosmont and Skenfrith and Llangattock etc *Mon* 02–16; P-in-c 09–16. *Yew Tree Farm, Llangattock Lingoed, Abergavenny NP7 8NS* T: (01873) 821405 E: revjean.prosser@btinternet.com

PROTHERO, Brian Douglas. b 52. St Andr Univ MTheol 75 Dundee Univ CertEd 77. Linc Th Coll 84. **d** 86 **p** 87. C Thornbury *Glouc* 86–89; V Goodrington *Ex* 89–04; R Weybridge *Guildf* from 04; Chapl Sam Beare Hospice from 06. *The Rectory, 3 Churchfields Avenue, Weybridge KT13 9YA* T: (01932) 842566 M: 07715-364389 E: brian.prothero@talktalk.net

PROTHERO, John Martin. b 32. Oak Hill Th Coll 64. **d** 66 **p** 67. C Tipton St Martin *Lich* 66–69; C Wednesfield Heath 69–72; Distr Sec BFBS 72–85; LtO *S'well* 73–86; Hon C Gedling 73; R Willoughby-on-the-Wolds w Wysall and Widmerpool 86–97; rtd 98. *The Elms, Vicarage Hill, Aberaeron SA46 0DY* T: (01545) 570568

PROTHEROE, Canon Rhys Illtyd. b 50. St D Coll Lamp. **d** 74 **p** 75. C Pen-bre *St D* 74–76; C Carmarthen St Dav 76–78; V Llanegwad 78–79; V Llanegwad w Llanfynydd 79–82; V Gors-las 82–95; RD Dyffryn Aman 94–95; V Llan-llwch w Llangain and Llangynog 95–15; Hon Can St D Cathl 13–15;

rtd 15; PtO *St D* from 15. *69 Meysydd y Coleg, Carmarthen SA31 3GR* T: (01267) 232427 E: parch.rhys@gmail.com

PROTHEROE, Canon Robin Philip. b 33. St Chad's Coll Dur BA 54 MA 60 Nottm Univ MPhil 75 Ox Univ DipEd 62. **d** 57 **p** 58. C Roath *Llan* 57–60; Asst Chapl Culham Coll Abingdon 60–64; Sen Lect RS Trent (Nottm) Poly *S'well* 64–84; PtO 64–66; LtO 66–84; P-in-c Barton in Fabis 70–73; P-in-c Thrumpton 70–73; Dir of Educn *Bris* 84–98; Hon Can Bris Cathl 85–98; Capitular Can Bris Cathl 01–07; PtO 98–10; *Chich* from 10. *20 Prestonville Court, Dyke Road, Brighton BN1 3UG* T: (01273) 709829 E: rpprotheroe@gmail.com

✠**PROUD, The Rt Revd Andrew John.** b 54. K Coll Lon BD 79 AKC 79 SOAS Lon MA 01. Linc Th Coll 79. **d** 80 **p** 81 **c** 07. C Stansted Mountfitchet *Chelmsf* 80–83; TV Borehamwood *St Alb* 83–90; C Bp's Hatfield 90–92; R E Barnet 92–01; Chapl Adis Ababa St Matt Ethiopia 02–07; Area Bp Ethiopia and Horn of Africa 07–11; Area Bp Reading *Ox* 11–19; rtd 19; Hon Asst Bp Pet from 19. *21 Clarence Avenue, Northampton NN2 6NX*

PROUD, David John. b 56. Leeds Univ BA 77 Dur Univ CertEd 78. Ridley Hall Cam 85. **d** 88 **p** 89. C Lindfield *Chich* 88–91; TV Horsham 91–97; V Ware Ch Ch *St Alb* 97–10; RD Hertford and Ware 04–10; Chapl E Herts NHS Trust 97–00; Chapl E and N Herts NHS Trust 00–06; R Bedhampton *Portsm* 10–18; rtd 18; PtO *Portsm* from 18. *33 Pine Road, Bishop's Waltham, Southampton SO32 1EJ*

PROUDFOOT (née BLACKBURN), Mrs Jane Elizabeth. b 66. Lanc Univ BA 88 St Martin's Coll Lanc PGCE 93 Leeds Univ BA 09. NOC 06. **d** 09 **p** 10. C Stockton Heath *Ches* 09–12; R Grappenhall from 12; RD Gt Budworth from 20. *The Rectory, 17 Hill Top Road, Stockton Heath, Warrington WA4 2ED* T: (01925) 661546 E: revdproudfoot@hotmail.co.uk

PROUDLEY, Sister Anne. b 38. Edin Univ BSc 60. SAOMC 97. **d** 00 **p** 01. CSJB from 00; NSM Blackbird Leys *Ox* 00–04; LtO 04–11; Chapl to the Homeless 05–11; NSM Blenheim 11–12; PtO from 12. *Harriet Monsell House, Ripon College, Cuddesdon, Oxford OX44 9EX* E: annecsjb@csjb.org.uk

PROUDLOVE, Lee Jason. b 70. Lon Bible Coll BA 94. Trin Coll Bris MA 01. **d** 01 **p** 02. C Morden *S'wark* 01–04; CMS Philippines 05–08; P-in-c W Bridgford *S'well* 08–11; R from 11. *The Rectory, 86 Bridgford Road, West Bridgford, Nottingham NG2 6AX* T: 0115-981 1112 E: rector@stgilesparish.com

PROUDLOVE, Stephen. b 81. SS Coll Cam BA 02 MA 05. Ridley Hall Cam 12. **d** 14 **p** 15. C Ilkley All SS *Leeds* 14–17; V Menston w Woodhead from 17; Asst Dir of Ords from 17. *The Vicarage, 12 Fairfax Gardens, Menston, Ilkley LS29 6ET* T: (01943) 872433 M: 07794-678268 E: stephen.proudlove@leeds.anglican.org or vicar@stjohnmenston.org.uk

PROUSE, Ms Carole Maureen. b 45. NOC. dss 86 **d** 87 **p** 95. NSM Coalville and Bardon Hill *Leic* 87–90; PtO 90–95; NSM Thorpe Acre w Dishley 95–96; P-in-c Packington w Normanton-le-Heath 96–01; Chapl HM Pris Low Newton 01–04; Asst Chapl 04–10; rtd 10; PtO *Nor* from 13. *1 Acacia Grove, Sheringham NR26 8PA* T: (01263) 479781 E: carole.prouse@btinternet.com

PROVOST, Ian Keith. b 47. CA Tr Coll IDC 73 Ridley Hall Cam 91. **d** 93 **p** 94. C Verwood *Sarum* 93–97; P-in-c Redlynch and Morgan's Vale 97–02; TV Plymstock and Hooe *Ex* 02–10; rtd 10; PtO *Ex* from 10. *8 Larkhall Rise, Plymouth PL3 6LY* T: (01752) 319528 E: ian.provost17@gmail.com

PROWSE, Mrs Barbara Bridgette Christmas. b 41. R Holloway Coll Lon BA 62. **d** 91 **p** 94. C Kingsthorpe w Northampton St Dav *Pet* 91–97; V Northampton St Jas 97–02; rtd 02; PtO *Truro* from 02. *36 Carn Basavern, St Just, Penzance TR19 7QX* T: (01736) 787994 E: vicarette.prowse@btinternet.com

PRUEN, Canon Edward Binney. b 56. K Coll Lon BD 77 AKC 77. St Jo Coll Nottm 78. **d** 79 **p** 80. C Kidderminster St Mary *Worc* 79–82; C Woking St Jo *Guildf* 82–84; Chapl Asst R Marsden Hosp 84–86; C Stapleford *S'well* 86–88; Min Winklebury CD *Win* 88; V Winklebury 88–93; Chapl Treloar Sch and Coll Alton 93–09; Hon Can Win Cathl 05–09; Can Res *S'well* Minster 09–12; P-in-c St Columb Major *Truro* 12–16; P-in-c St Mawgan w St Ervan and St Eval 12–16; R Lann Pydar 16; P-in-c Bentworth, Lasham, Medstead and Shalden *Win* 16–21; rtd 21. *19 Church Road, Lydney GL15 5EA* M: 07752-569794 E: edpruen@yahoo.co.uk

PRYCE, Donald Keith. b 35. Man Univ BSc. Linc Th Coll 69. **d** 71 **p** 72. C Heywood St Jas *Man* 71–74; P-in-c 74–75; V 75–86; R Ladybarn 86–06; Chapl S Man Coll 87–06; Chapl Christie Hosp NHS Trust Man 93–06; rtd 06; PtO *Ches* from 06; *Man* from 06. *62 Belmont Road, Gatley, Cheadle SK8 4AQ* T: 0161-286 9985 E: donaldpryce@hotmail.com

PRYCE, Canon Robin Mark. b 60. Sussex Univ BA 82 Cam Univ MA 94 Birm Univ DPT 15. Westcott Ho Cam 84 United Th Coll Bangalore 85. **d** 87 **p** 88. C W Bromwich All SS *Lich* 87–90; Chapl Sandwell Distr Gen Hosp 90; Chapl and Fell CCC Cam 90–02; Tutor 92–02; Dean of Chpl 96–02; V Smethwick *Birm* 02–06; Bp's Adv for Clergy CME from 06; Dir Min from 17; Hon Can Birm Cathl from 11; Chapl to The Queen from 17. *1 Colmore Row, Birmingham B3 2BJ* T: 0121-426 0430 E: markp@cofebirmingham.com

PRYCE, Mrs Yvonne. **d** 16 **p** 17. NSM Alyn Miss Area *St As* from 16. *Hazeldene, King Street, Acrefair, Wrexham LL14 3RH* T: (01978) 824891 E: yvonnepryce2@aol.com

PRYKE, Jonathan Justin Speaight. b 59. Trin Coll Cam BA 80 MA 85. Trin Coll Bris BD 85. **d** 85 **p** 86. C Corby St Columba *Pet* 85–88; C Jesmond Clayton Memorial *Newc* from 88. *15 Lily Avenue, Newcastle upon Tyne NE2 2SQ* T: 0191-281 9854

PRYOR, William Lister Archibald. b 39. Trin Coll Cam BA 67 MA 69 DipEd 68. Ox NSM Course 72. **d** 75 **p** 90. NSM Summertown *Ox* from 75; PtO *Nor* 93–04 and from 09. *23 Harbord Road, Oxford OX2 8LH* T: (01865) 515102

PRYS, Deiniol. b 53. Univ of Wales (Ban) BTh 91. St Mich Coll Llan 82. **d** 83 **p** 84. C Llanbeblig w Caernarfon and Betws Garmon etc *Ban* 83–86; TV Amlwch 86–88; V Llanerch-y-medd 89–92; R Llansadwrn w Llanddona and Llaniestyn etc 92–11; LtO from 11. *Bryn Celyn, Llansadwrn, Menai Bridge LL59 5SU* T: (01248) 810534 M: 07740-541316

PRYSE, Preb Hugh Henry David. b 58. St Chad's Coll Dur BA 81 SS Coll Cam PGCE 82 K Coll Lon MA 96. St Steph Ho Ox 94. **d** 96 **p** 97. C Branksome St Aldhelm *Sarum* 96–00; Chapl St Edw Sch Poole 98–00; TV Hove *Chich* 00–05; R Ex St Jas from 05; Asst Dioc Dir of Ords from 09; Preb Ex Cathl from 17. *The Rectory, 45 Thornton Hill, Exeter EX4 4NR* T: (01392) 431297 or 420407 E: henry.pryse@blueyonder.co.uk

PRYSOR-JONES, John Glynne. b 47. Heythrop Coll Lon MA 94 Leeds Metrop Univ BSc 05 Man Univ DCouns 15 CQSW 73. Westcott Ho Cam 88. **d** 90 **p** 91. C Mitcham St Mark *S'wark* 90–93; V Dudley St Fran *Worc* 93–99; R Woodchurch *Ches* 99–01; Hd Past Care Services Chorley and S Ribble NHS Trust and Preston Acute Hosps NHS Trust 01–02; Hd Past Care Services Lancs Teaching Hosps NHS Trust 02–06; PtO *Ban* from 16. *Bryn-y-Mor, St John's Park, Penmaenmawr LL34 6NE* T: (01492) 622515

PRZESLAWSKI, Maria Christina. b 50. Nottm Univ MA 91. EMMTC 08. **d** 10 **p** 11. NSM Wilne and Draycott w Breaston *Derby* 10–17; rtd 17; PtO *Derby* from 17. *9 Holmes Road, Breaston, Derby DE72 3BT* T: (01332) 874480 E: maria.9@btinternet.com

PRZYWALA, Karl Andrzej. b 63. Univ Coll Dur BA 85 Chas Sturt Univ NSW BTh 04. St Mark's Nat Th Cen Canberra 01. **d** 04 **p** 05. C Huntingdale Spring *Dur* 04–05; C Chester le Street 05–07; P-in-c Whatton w Aslockton, Hawksworth, Scarrington etc *S'well* 07–11; V 11–14; R Vancouver H Trin Canada from 14. *908 - 1755 West 14th Avenue, Vancouver V6J 2J6, Canada* T: (001) (604) 731 3221 E: karl_sydney@yahoo.co.uk

PUDGE, Mark Samuel. b 67. K Coll Lon BD 90 AKC 90 Heythrop Coll Lon MA 99. Ripon Coll Cuddesdon 91. **d** 93 **p** 94. C Thorpe Bay *Chelmsf* 93–96; TV Wickford and Runwell 97–00; Management Consultant Citizens' Advice Bureau 00–04; Consultant Legal Services Commn 04–06; Dir Voluntary Action Westmr 06–10; Hon C Paddington St Jo w St Mich *Lon* 03–10; PtO *Eur* from 13. *Finca La Maroma, Cerro Panadero s/n, 29715 Sedella (Málaga), Spain* E: markpudge@hotmail.com

PUDNEY, Malcolm Lloyd. b 48. SEITE 99. **d** 01 **p** 02. NSM S Nutfield w Outwood *S'wark* 01–06; P-in-c Woodham Mortimer w Hazeleigh and Woodham Walter *Chelmsf* 06–10; P-in-c Lurgashall and N Chapel w Ebernoe *Chich* 10–13; rtd 13; PtO *Chich* from 14. *26 Cuckfield Crescent, Worthing BN13 2ED* M: 07860-464836 E: yenduptoo@madasafish.com

PUGH, Harry. b 48. K Coll Lon BD 70 AKC 71 Lanc Univ MA 89. **d** 72 **p** 73. C Milnrow *Man* 72–75; P-in-c Rochdale Gd Shep 75–78; TV Rochdale 78–79; PtO *Liv* 79–82; C Darwen St Cuth *Blackb* 82–85; C Darwen St Cuth w Tockholes St Steph 85–86; V Burnley St Steph 86–93; R Hoole 93–01; P-in-c Porthleven w Sithney *Truro* 01–13; rtd 13; PtO *Blackb* from 16. *17 Cavendish Road, Blackpool FY2 9JR* T: (01253) 594016

PUGH, Lynda. b 49. Man Univ BSocSc 93 MA 96 PhD 04. Ripon Coll Cuddesdon 07. **d** 09 **p** 10. C Glen Gp *Linc* 09–12; P-in-c Ringstone in Aveland Gp 12–17; rtd 17; PtO *Ches* from 18. *8 Patch Lane, Bramhall, Stockport SK7 1JB* M: 07775-660081 E: dr.lynda.pugh@gmail.com

PUGH, Stephen Gregory. Southn Univ BEd 77. Linc Th Coll 85. **d** 87 **p** 88. C Harpenden St Nic *St Alb* 87–90; C

Stevenage All SS Pin Green 90–93; V Stotfold and Radwell 93–00; V Gt Ilford St Marg and St Clem *Chelmsf* from 00. *The Vicarage, 70 Brisbane Road, Ilford IG1 4SL* T: (020) 8554 7542 M: 07910-395925 E: stephenpugh@waitrose.com

PUGH, Miss Wendy Kathleen. b 48. Newnham Coll Cam BA 69 MA 75. Trin Coll Bris 93. **d** 95 **p** 96. C Hailsham *Chich* 95–99; C Frimley *Guildf* 99–07; Hon C Chertsey, Lyne and Longcross 07–12; rtd 13; PtO *Sarum* from 14. *39 Elizabeth Court, Crane Bridge Road, Salisbury SP2 7UX* T: (01722) 326680 E: wkpugh@aol.com

PUGMIRE, Canon Alan. b 37. Tyndale Hall Bris 61. **d** 64 **p** 65. C Islington St Steph w St Bart and St Matt *Lon* 64–66; C St Helens St Mark *Liv* 66–71; R Stretford St Bride *Man* 71–82; R Burnage St Marg 82–02; C Heaton Norris Ch w All SS 88–89; P-in-c Heaton Mersey 92–93; AD Heaton 88–98; Hon Can Man Cathl 98–02; rtd 02; PtO *Man* from 02. *20 Shortland Crescent, Manchester M19 1SZ* T: 0161-431 3476 E: alan.pugmire@tiscali.co.uk

PUGSLEY, Anthony John. b 39. ACIB. Oak Hill Th Coll 89. **d** 90 **p** 91. C Chadwell *Chelmsf* 90–94; P-in-c Gt Warley Ch Ch 94–01; V Warley Ch Ch and Gt Warley St Mary 01–04; rtd 04; PtO *Chelmsf* from 07. *3 Southcliffe Court, Southview Drive, Walton on the Naze CO14 8EP* T: (01255) 850967 E: revtonp@aol.com

PULESTON, Mervyn Pedley. b 35. K Coll Lon BD 60 AKC 60. **d** 61 **p** 62. C Gt Marlow *Ox* 61–65; P Missr Blackbird Leys CD 65–70; V Kidlington 70–85; R Hampton Poyle 70–85; TR Kidlington w Hampton Poyle 85–86; Chapl Geneva *Eur* 86–92; TV Dorchester *Ox* 92–00; rtd 00; PtO *Ox* from 00. *55 Benmead Road, Kidlington OX5 2DB* T: (01865) 372360 E: mpuleston@aol.com

PULFORD, John Shirley Walter. b 31. Jes Coll Cam BA 55 MA 59. Cuddesdon Coll 55. **d** 57 **p** 58. C Blackpool St Steph *Blackb* 57–60; N Rhodesia 60–63; V Newington St Paul *S'wark* 63–68; C Seacroft *Ripon* 68–70; Chapl HM Pris Liv 70–72; Chapl HM Pris Linc 72–73; Student Cllr Linc Colls of Art and Tech 73–79; Cam Univ Counselling Service 79–96; Dir 82–96; rtd 96. *59 Cromer Road, North Walsham NR28 0HB* T: (01692) 404320 E: jpulford@btinternet.com

PULKO, Susan Helen. b 55. Imp Coll Lon BSc 77 Nottm Univ PhD 81 Sheff Univ BA 14 CEng 88. Yorks Min Course 11. **d** 14 **p** 15. NSM Market Weighton *York* 14–18; NSM Goodmanham 14–18; NSM Sancton 14–18; P-in-c Hedon, Paull, Sproatley and Preston 18–20; R from 20. *The Vicarage, Staithes Road, Preston, Hull HU12 8TD* E: s.h.pulko@emeritus.hull.ac.uk

PULLEN, Adam William. b 73. Univ of Wales (Abth) BSc 97. St Jo Coll Nottm 03. **d** 06 **p** 07. C Swansea St Pet *S & B* 06–09; C Swansea St Thos and Kilvey 09–10; I Ballisodare w Collooney and Emlaghfad *T, K & A* 10–15; Dom Chapl to Bp Tuam 12–15; I Stranorlar w Meenglas and Kilteevogue *D & R* from 15. *The Rectory, The Glebe, Stranorlar, Co Donegal, F93 C8Y8, Republic of Ireland* M: (00353) 87-682 9627 E: adam.pullen@googlemail.com

PULLEN, Frances Jill. *See* PHILLIPS, Frances Jill

PULLEN, Roger Christopher. b 43. Lon Univ BSc 65 PGCE 90. Wells Th Coll 65. **d** 67 **p** 68. C S w N Hayling *Portsm* 67–69; C Farlington 69–73; V Farington *Blackb* 73–80; V Chorley All SS 80–83; V Kingsley *Ches* 83–92; R Cilcain and Nannerch and Rhydymwyn *St As* 92–99; Dioc MU Admin *Guildf* 99–02; Hon C Bramley and Grafham 99–02; PtO 99–02; *Chich* from 03. *16 East Way, Selsey, Chichester PO20 0SL* T: (01243) 603425 M: 07909-954772 E: pullenselsey@gmail.com

PULLEN, Timothy John. b 61. BNC Ox BA 84 St Jo Coll Dur MA 96. Cranmer Hall Dur 93. **d** 96 **p** 97. C Allesley *Cov* 96–00; V Wolston and Church Lawford 00–08; Can Res Cov Cathl 08–13; Sub-Dean 10–13; R Wollaton *S'well* from 13. *St Leonard's Rectory, 143 Russell Drive, Nottingham NG8 2BD* T: 0115-928 9963 M: 07974-007665 E: pullen1961@gmail.com

PULLIN, Andrew Eric. b 47. Kelham Th Coll 67 Linc Th Coll 71. **d** 73 **p** 74. C Pershore w Pinvin, Wick and Birlingham *Worc* 73–77; TV Droitwich 77–80; V Woburn Sands *St Alb* 80–85; PtO *B & W* 85–87. *85 Weymouth Road, Frome BA11 1HJ* T: (01373) 472170 E: a.pullin@talktalk.net

PULLIN, Canon Christopher. b 56. St Chad's Coll Dur BA 77 Heythrop Coll Lon MA 04. Ripon Coll Cuddesdon 78 Ch Div Sch of Pacific 79. **d** 80 **p** 81. C Tooting All SS *S'wark* 80–85; V New Eltham All SS 85–92; V St Jo in Bedwardine *Worc* 92–08; RD Martley and Worc W 03–08; Hon Can Worc Cathl 07–08; Can Res and Chan Heref Cathl from 08. *2 Cathedral Close, Hereford HR1 2NG* T: (01432) 374273 F: 374220 E: chancellor@herefordcathedral.org

PULLIN, Rebecca. *See* CLARKE, Kathleen Jean Rebecca

PULLIN, The Ven Stephen James. b 66. S Bank Univ BEng 89 Open Univ MBA 98. Trin Coll Bris BA 04. **d** 04 **p** 05. C Soundwell *Bris* 04–07; P-in-c Stapleton 07–14;

C Frenchay and Winterbourne Down 07–14; Bp's Adv for Deliverance Min 10–14; P-in-c Reading St Mary the Virgin *Ox* 14–15; V 15–20; AD Reading 14–17; Hon Can Ch Ch 19; Adn Berks from 20. *25 Wilderness Road, Earley, Reading RG6 7RU* T: (01635) 552820 M: 07435-798846 E: archdeacon.berkshire@oxford.anglican.org

PULLINGER, Mrs Catherine Ann. b 54. York Univ BA 76. Oak Hill Th Coll 91. **d** 93 **p** 97. NSM Luton St Paul *St Alb* 93–99; NSM Luton Lewsey St Hugh 99–11; P-in-c Woodside 11–17; V 17–21; rtd 21; PtO *St Alb* from 21. *52B Wheatfield Road, Luton LU4 0TR* E: cathy@rwh.org.uk

PULLINGER, Ian Austin. b 61. Oak Hill Th Coll. **d** 96 **p** 97. C Weston *Win* 96–00; TV The Ortons, Alwalton and Chesterton *Ely* 00–10; TV Alwalton and Chesterton 10–12; C-in-c Orton Goldhay LEP 12–13; V Corby St Columba *Pet* from 13; RD Corby from 13. *St Columba's Vicarage, 157 Studfall Avenue, Corby NN17 1LG* T: (01536) 400225 E: ianpullinger@btinternet.com

PULLINGER, Peter Mark. b 53. Heythrop Coll Lon MA 97. Ridley Hall Cam 01. **d** 03 **p** 04. C Clapham Park St Steph *S'wark* 03–06; C Telford Park 06–07; TV Sutton 07–15; P-in-c Merstham, S Merstham and Gatton 15–16; TR from 16. *The Rectory, Battlebridge Lane, Merstham, Redhill RH1 3LH* T: (01737) 642647 E: mark@pullinger.net *or* mplarksong@aol.co.uk *or* rector.mgteam@btinternet.com

PULMAN, John. b 34. EMMTC 78. **d** 81 **p** 82. NSM Mansfield SS Pet and Paul *S'well* 81–83; C Mansfield Woodhouse 83–86; V Flintham 86–99; R Car Colston w Screveton 86–99; Chapl HM YOI Whatton 87–90; Chapl HM Pris Whatton 90–99; rtd 99; PtO *S'well* 99–21; *Derby* 00–18. *101 Ling Forest Road, Mansfield NG18 3NQ* T: (01623) 474707

PUMFREY (*née* CERRATTI), **Canon Christa Elisabeth.** b 54. Wycliffe Hall Ox 94. **d** 97 **p** 98. C Chipping Norton *Ox* 97–00; P-in-c Lavendon w Cold Brayfield, Clifton Reynes etc 00–08; R from 08; R Gayhurst w Ravenstone, Stoke Goldington etc from 08; Deanery Youth Co-ord from 00; AD Newport 06–12; Hon Can Ch Ch from 11. *The New Rectory, 7A Northampton Road, Lavendon, Olney MK46 4EY* T: (01234) 240013 E: christa.pumfrey@btinternet.com

PUNSHON, Carol Mary. *See* BRENNAN, Carol Mary

PUNSHON, Canon Keith. b 48. JP TD 92. Jes Coll Cam BA 69 MA 73 Birm Univ MA 77. Qu Coll Birm 71. **d** 73 **p** 74. C Yardley St Edburgha *Birm* 73–76; Chapl Eton Coll 76–79; V Hill *Birm* 79–86; CF (VR) from 79; V S Yardley St Mich *Birm* 86–96; Can Res Bradf Cathl 96–14; *Leeds* 14; Acting Dean Ripon 13–14; rtd 14; PtO *Leeds* from 19. *4 Willow Bridge Lane, Dalton, Thirsk YO7 3QQ*

PURCELL, Mrs Helen Elizabeth. b 65. All SS Cen for Miss & Min 17. **d** 20 **p** 21. C Liv All SS from 20. *36 Bingley Road, Liverpool L4 2TB* M: 07867-117981 E: cc.wb@live.com

PURCELL SMITH, Geoffrey. b 45. Bernard Gilpin Soc Dur 65 Sarum Th Coll 66. **d** 69 **p** 70. C Hatfield *Sheff* 69–71; C Bolton St Pet *Man* 71–74; V Lt Hulton 74–78; P-in-c Newc St Andr and Soc Resp Adv *Newc* 78–87; Hon Can Newc Cathl 84–87; Dir Cen for Applied Chr Studies 87–91; Team Ldr Home Office Birm Drug Prevention Unit 91–93; Public Preacher *Birm* 87–93; C Brampton and Farlam and Castle Carrock w Cumrew *Carl* 93–96; ACUPA Link Officer 94–96; Can Res Bradf Cathl 96–00; Nat Dir Toc H 00–07; PtO *Ox* 00–02; Hon C Biddenham *St Alb* 02–07; rtd 07; PtO *Carl* from 07; *Eur* from 07; P-in-c Shotley *Newc* from 18. *St John's Vicarage, Shotley Bridge, Consett DH8 9TL* T: 05602-231702 *or* (01207) 255577 E: canongeoff@me.com

PURDY, Canon John David. b 44. Leeds Univ BA 65 MPhil 76. Coll of Resurr Mirfield 72. **d** 75 **p** 76. C Marske in Cleveland *York* 75–78; C Marton-in-Cleveland 78–80; V Newby 80–87; V Kirkleatham 87–95; V Kirkbymoorside w Gillamoor, Farndale etc 95–09; RD Helmsley 99–09; rtd 09; P-in-c Fylingdales and Hawsker cum Stainsacre *York* 10–12; Can and Preb York Minster 98–17; PtO 12–21. *16 Dulverton Hall, Esplanade, Scarborough YO11 2AR* M: 07504-428713 E: david.purdy@virgin.net

PURLE, Joanne Louise. b 70. Surrey Univ BSc 92. Trin Coll Bris 14. **d** 17 **p** 18. C Folkestone St Jo *Cant* 17–21. *2 Chalk Close, Folkestone CT19 5TD* M: 07790-342718 E: purleyjo@gmail.com *or* revjop@virginmedia.com

PURNELL, Mrs Laura Louise. b 75. Southn Univ BA 96. Ridley Hall Cam 16. **d** 18 **p** 19. C Gaywood *Nor* from 18. *170 Wootton Road, Gaywood, King's Lynn PE30 4BU* M: 07787-975408 E: laurapurnell@hotmail.com

PURNELL, Marcus John. b 75. Ridley Hall Cam 07. **d** 09 **p** 10. C Northampton St Benedict *Pet* 09–12; V Cottesmore and Burley, Clipsham, Exton etc 12–18; TV March *Ely* 18–20. *Address temp unknown* M: 07535-639915 E: revmarcuspurnell@gmail.com

PURSER, Alec. d 10 **p** 11. NSM Abbeyleix w Ballyroan etc *C, F & O* 10–14; P-in-c Stradbally w Ballintubbert, Coraclone etc from 14. *The Rectory, Main Street, Stradbally, Co Laois, Republic of Ireland* T: (00353) (57) 862 5173 M: (00353) 87-923 2694 E: alecpurser@gmail.com

PURVEY-TYRER, Neil. b 66. Leeds Univ BA 87 MA 88. Westcott Ho Cam 88. **d** 90 **p** 91. C Denbigh and Nantglyn *St As* 90–92; Chapl Asst Basingstoke Distr Hosp 92–95; TV Cannock *Lich* 95–99; V Northampton H Sepulchre w St Andr and St Lawr *Pet* 99–02; Dioc Co-ord for Soc Resp 99–03; TR Duston 02–08; Chapl St Andr Hosp Northn 08–12; Hd of Chapl 12–19; Past Care and Counselling Adv *Pet* 10–13; Chapl Kettering Gen Hosp NHS Foundn Trust from 19; Bp's Adv for Healthcare Chapl *Pet* from 19. *Kettering General Hospital NHS Trust, Rothwell Road, Kettering NN16 8UZ* T: (01536) 492000

PURVIS, Sandra Anne. *See* TAUSON, Sandra Anne

PURVIS, Canon Stephen. b 48. AKC 70. **d** 71 **p** 72. C Peterlee *Dur* 71–75; Dioc Recruitment Officer 75–79; V Stevenage All SS Pin Green *St Alb* 79–88; TR Borehamwood 88–00; RD Aldenham 94–98; V Leagrave 00–13; RD Luton 07–12; Hon Can St Alb 02–13; rtd 13; PtO *St Alb* 13–18; *Bris* from 14; *B & W* from 19. *23 Almeda Road, Bristol BS5 8RY* T: 0117-967 0507 E: stephen.purvis48@gmail.com

PURVIS-LEE, Lynn. b 58. St Jo Coll Dur BA 97. Cranmer Hall Dur 94. **d** 98 **p** 99. C Gt Aycliffe *Dur* 98–02; Chapl N Tees and Hartlepool NHS Foundn Trust 02–14; R Penhill *Leeds* 14–18; rtd 19; Chapl OHP from 20. *10 Church Bank, Eggleston, Barnard Castle DL12 0AH* E: lynnhome28@gmail.com

PUSEY, Canon Ian John. b 39. Sarum Th Coll 69. **d** 71 **p** 72. C Waltham Abbey *Chelmsf* 71–75; TV Stantonbury *Ox* 75–80; P-in-c Bletchley 80–84; R 84–00; AD Milton Keynes 96–00; P-in-c Lamp 00–06; AD Newport 04–06; Hon Can Ch Ch 06; rtd 06; PtO *Ex* from 07. *16 Gussiford Lane, Exmouth EX8 2SF* T: (01395) 275549 E: ian.pusey@btinternet.com

PUTNAM, Mrs Gillian. b 43. WEMTC 00. **d** 02 **p** 03. NSM Milton *B & W* 02–09; NSM Milton and Kewstoke 09–13; PtO 13–18. *c/o All Saints' Vicarage, Tresawls Road, Truro TR1 3LD* E: revgillputnam@gmail.com

PUTNAM, Jeremy James. b 76. Ripon Coll Cuddesdon 09. **d** 11 **p** 12. C Portishead *B & W* 11–15; P-in-c Highertown and Baldhu *Truro* from 14. *All Saints' Vicarage, Tresawls Road, Truro TR1 3LD* M: 07477-921397 E: jeremyjputnam@gmail.com

PUTT, Thomas David. b 83. Loughb Univ BEng 05. Oak Hill Th Coll BA 11. **d** 11 **p** 12. C Kirk Ella and Willerby *York* 11–15; Chapl Yeovil Coll *B & W* 15–19; C Yeovil w Kingston Pitney 15–19; V Burford w Fulbrook, Taynton, Asthall etc *Ox* from 19. *The Vicarage, Church Lane, Burford OX18 4SD* E: tomputt@burfordchurch.org

✠**PWAISIHO, The Rt Revd William Alaha.** b 48. OBE 04. Bp Patteson Th Coll (Solomon Is) 71. **d** 74 **p** 75 **c** 81. Solomon Is 74–76; NZ 78–79; Solomon Is 79–95; Dean Honiara 80–81; Bp Malaita 81–89; C Sale St Anne *Ches* 97–99; R Gawsworth 99–14; R Gawsworth w North Rode 14–19; Hon Asst Bp Ches 97–19; rtd 19; PtO *Ches* from 19. *1 Williams Way, Henbury, Macclesfield SK11 9NR* M: 07711-241625 E: bishop.gawsworth@hotmail.co.uk

PYBUS, Antony Frederick. b 54. Birm Univ BA 77. Cranmer Hall Dur 78. **d** 81 **p** 82. C Ches H Trin 81–84; C W Hampstead St Jas *Lon* 84–89; V Alexandra Park St Andr 89–93; V Alexandra Park 93–21; rtd 21. *Address temp unknown* E: antony.pybus@prolepsis.net

PYE, Alexander Frederick. b 61. St Mich Coll Llan 93. **d** 95 **p** 96. C Griffithstown *Mon* 95–97; P-in-c Bistre St As 97–99; P-in-c Penmaen and Crumlin *Mon* 99–00; V 00–02; R Govilon w Llanfoist w Llanellen 02–09; V Beguildy and Heyope and Llangynllo and Bleddfa *S & B* 09–12; V Swansea St Pet 12–17; P-in-c Gowerton 17–21; V Pont Gors Fawr from 21. *The Vicarage, 14 Church Street, Gowerton, Swansea SA4 3EA* T: (01792) 927158 E: afp.vic13@gmail.com

PYE, Canon Allan Stephen. b 56. Univ of Wales (Lamp) BA 78 Lanc Univ MPhil 86. Westcott Ho Cam 79. **d** 81 **p** 82. C Scotforth *Blackb* 81–85; C Oswaldtwistle Immanuel 85–87; C Oswaldtwistle All SS 85–87; V Wrightington 87–91; P-in-c Hayton St Mary *Carl* 91–93; V Hayton w Cumwhitton 93–98; RD Brampton 95–98; P-in-c Hawkshead and Low Wray w Sawrey 98–03; V Hawkshead and Low Wray w Sawrey and Rusland etc 03–06; V Keswick St Jo 06–15; P-in-c Cross Fell Gp 15–18; R from 18; Hon Can Carl Cathl from 17. *1 Low Farm, Langwathby, Penrith CA10 1NH* T: (01768) 881212 E: allans.pye@gmail.com

PYE, Mrs Gay Elizabeth. b 46. RN 67 RM 68. Trin Coll Bris BD 73. **d** 96 **p** 96. NSM Castle Church *Lich* 96–00; Asst Chapl HM Pris Stafford 96–97; Chapl HM Pris Shrewsbury 97–00; Regional Manager Bible Soc 00–06; NSM Upper Derwent *Carl* 06–15; rtd 15; PtO *Lich* 16–20. *5 Thorneyfields Lane,*

Stafford ST17 9YS T: (01785) 212348 M: 07414-230922 E: gay.pye@gmail.com

PYE, James Timothy. b 58. Oak Hill Th Coll BA 90. **d** 90 **p** 91. C Normanton *Derby* 90–94; R Talke *Lich* 94–04; R Knebworth *St Alb* 04–21; C Kingsdown, Creekside and High Downs *Cant* from 21. *Address temp unknown* E: revpye@gmail.com

PYE, Joseph Terence Hardwidge. b 41. MRICS 64. Trin Coll Bris 70. **d** 73 **p** 74. C Blackb Ch Ch 73–76; OMF 77–90; Korea 77–90; V Castle Church *Lich* 90–06; rtd 06; PtO *Carl* 07–15; *Lich* 16–20. *5 Thorneyfields Lane, Stafford ST17 9YS* T: (01785) 212348 E: terry.pye@gmail.com

PYE, Michael Francis. b 53. New Coll Ox BA 75 MA 78 DPhil 78. STETS 97. **d** 00 **p** 01. C Fareham H Trin *Portsm* 00–07; V Portsea All SS 07–18; rtd 18; PtO *Portsm* from 19. *22 Harvey Crescent, Warsash, Southampton SO31 9TA* E: revmikepye@btinternet.com

PYE, Nicholas Richard. b 62. Univ Coll Lon BA 84 Man Univ PGCE 87 Anglia Poly Univ MA 03. Ridley Hall Cam 95. **d** 98 **p** 99. C Epsom Common Ch Ch *Guildf* 98–01; C Harrow Trin St Mich *Lon* 01–03; V Finchley St Paul and St Luke from 03. *St Paul's Vicarage, 50 Long Lane, London N3 2PU* T: (020) 8346 8729 or 8349 3792 E: vicar@stpaulsfinchley.org.uk or revpye1@gmail.com

PYE, Robin. b 63. Clare Coll Cam BA 86 Man Univ PGCE 97. All SS Cen for Miss & Min 12. **d** 15 **p** 16. C Hale and Ashley *Ches* 15–17; V Alderley Edge from 17. *The Vicarage, Church Lane, Alderley Edge SK9 7UZ* M: 07794-122602 E: revrobinpye@gmail.com

PYE, Sandra Anne. *See* ELLISON, Sandra Anne

PYE, Stephen. *See* PYE, Allan Stephen

PYKE, Alan. b 37. Trin Coll Bris BA 87. **d** 87 **p** 88. CA 58–87; C Ipswich St Mary at Stoke w St Pet *St E* 87–90; R The Creetings and Earl Stonham w Stonham Parva 90–98; C S Trin Broads *Nor* 98–02; rtd 03; PtO *Nor* 03–08; *Leic* from 14. *29 Stuart Court, High Street, Kibworth Beauchamp, Leicester LE8 0LR* T: 0116-279 0113 E: alan.pyke@o2.co.uk

PYKE, Canon Barry John. b 62. Qu Mary Coll Lon BSc 84 Southn Univ BTh 94 Open Univ MA 96 FGS 84. Sarum & Wells Th Coll 91. **d** 94 **p** 95. C Bengeworth *Worc* 94–96; C Worc City St Paul and Old St Martin etc 96–99; R Chipping Ongar w Shelley *Chelmsf* 99–06; RD Ongar 04–06; R Hinderwell, Roxby and Staithes etc *York* 06–16; RD Whitby 13–16; Can Res Ripon Cathl *Leeds* from 16; AD Ripon 16–17. *16 Primrose Drive, Ripon HG4 1EY* T: (01765) 603462 or 600427 E: canonbarry@riponcathedral.org.uk

PYKE, Canon Richard Ernest. b 50. Sarum & Wells Th Coll. **d** 82 **p** 83. C Bushey *St Alb* 82–85; C Gt Berkhamsted 85–89; V St Alb St Mary Marshalswick 89–00; TR Bp's Hatfield 00–05; TR Bishop's Hatfield, Lemsford and N Mymms 05–16; RD Welwyn Hatfield 03–16; Hon Can St Alb 12–16; rtd 16; PtO *St Alb* from 16. *The Rectory, 135 High Street, Barkway, Royston SG8 8ED* T: (01763) 848756 E: richard50pyke@tiscali.co.uk

PYKE, Canon Ruth Cheryl. b 56. Bath Coll of HE BA 78 W Lon Inst of HE PGCE 80. SAOMC 95. **d** 98 **p** 99. C Leavesden *St Alb* 98–02; C St Alb St Steph 02–06; P-in-c Caddington 06–12; Bedfordshire Area Children's Work Adv 06–12; Dioc Children's Work Adv 12–15; R Barkway, Barley, Reed and Buckland from 15; RD Buntingford from 19; Hon Can St Alb from 18. *The Rectory, 135 High Street, Barkway, Royston SG8 8ED* T: (01763) 848756 M: 07787-112376

PYKE, Thomas Fortune. b 62. St Chad's Coll Dur BA 85 Fitzw Coll Cam BA 88. Ridley Hall Cam 86. **d** 89 **p** 90. C Hitchin *St Alb* 89–94; Chapl Aston Univ *Birm* 94–99; V Birm St Paul 99–06; Ind Chapl 01–06; Th Ecum Officer Birm Bd for Miss 01–06; V Is of Dogs Ch Ch and St Jo w St Luke *Lon* from 06. *Christ Church Vicarage, Manchester Road, London E14 3BN* T: (020) 7538 1766 M: 07753-616499 E: tom.pyke@parishiod.org.uk

PYM, David Pitfield. b 45. Nottm Univ BA 65 Ex Coll Ox DPhil 68. Ripon Hall Ox 66. **d** 68 **p** 69. C Nottingham St Mary S'well 68–72; Chapl RN 72–76 and 79–84; Chapl Worksop Coll Notts 76–79; R Avon Dassett w Farnborough and Fenny Compton *Cov* 84–07; rtd 07; PtO *Cov* from 07; Cov from 08. *Sunrise, Bury Court Lane, Shotteswell, Banbury OX17 1JA* T: (01295) 738948 E: davidpym@lineone.net

PYMBLE, Adam Oliver James. b 79. **d** 11 **p** 12. C Lindfield *Chich* 11–14; C Clerkenwell St Mark *Lon* 14–15; C Hornsey Ch Ch 15–19; V from 19. *The Vicarage, 32 Crescent Road, London N8 8AX* E: adam@crouchend.church

PYNE-BAILEY, Mrs Sarian Iyamide Remilekun. b 40. Sierra Leone Th Hall 99. **d** 03 **p** 05. Sierra Leone 06–10; PtO *Chelmsf* from 11. *17 Maple Court, 16 Angelica Drive, London E6 6NX* T: (020) 8279 4221 M: 07415-995370 E: iyamidepb@ymail.com

PYNN, Catherine. b 45. Reading Univ BSc 67. SAOMC 93. **d** 96 **p** 97. NSM Caversham St Pet and Mapledurham etc *Ox*

96–03; NSM Aldermaston w Wasing and Brimpton 03–06; NSM Woolhampton w Midgham and Beenham Valance 05–06; Chapl Bradfield Coll Berks 00–06; NSM Kintbury w Avington *Ox* 06–11; NSM W Woodhay w Enborne, Hampstead Marshall etc 06–11; NSM Walbury Beacon 11–13; PtO from 13; *Win* from 13. *27 Silchester Road, Pamber Heath, Tadley RG26 3ED* T: 0118-970 1007 M: 07863-968624 E: cathy.pynn@btinternet.com

PYNN, David Christopher. b 47. Trin Coll Cam MA 70 Cam Inst of Educn CertEd 69. NOC 06. **d** 08 **p** 09. NSM Scalby *York* 08–11; NSM Scarborough St Luke 08–17; RD Scarborough 11–16; NSM Hackness w Harwood Dale 14–17; NSM Ravenscar and Staintondale 14–17; PtO from 17. *6 Stepney Drive, Scarborough YO12 5DH* T: (01723) 369687 M: 07980-922208 E: davidpynn12@aol.com

PYRKE, Adam Lee Julien. b 79. St Mellitus Coll 17. **d** 19 **p** 20. C Roch St Justus from 19. *18 Kings Avenue, Rochester ME1 3DS* M: 07419-901676 E: aljpyrke@hotmail.com

⊕**PYTCHES, The Rt Revd George Edward** David**.** b 31. Bris Univ BA 54 Nottm Univ MPhil 84. Tyndale Hall Bris 51. **d** 55 **p** 56 **c** 70. C Ox St Ebbe 55–58; C Wallington *S'wark* 58–59; Chile 59–77; Suff Bp Valparaiso 70–72; Bp Chile, Bolivia and Peru 72–77; V Chorleywood St Andr *St Alb* 77–96; rtd 96; PtO *St Alb* 96–19. *5 Churleswood Court, Shire Lane, Chorleywood, Rickmansworth WD3 5NH*

PYTCHES, Preb Peter Norman Lambert. b 32. Lon Univ BD 57 Bris Univ MLitt 67 Southn Univ PhD 81 K Coll Lon MA 00 Potchefstroom Univ MTh 03 Open Univ MPhil 06 Lambeth STh 74. Tyndale Hall Bris 53. **d** 57 **p** 58. C Heatherlands St Jo *Sarum* 57–61; C Cromer *Nor* 61–63; V Plymouth St Jude *Ex* 63–71; V Heatherlands St Jo *Sarum* 71–76; Dir Past Tr Oak Hill Th Coll and Registrar Oak Hill NSM Course 76–81; V Finchley Ch Ch *Lon* 81–91; AD Cen Barnet 86–91; V Forty Hill Jes Ch 91–97; Preb St Paul's Cathl 92–97; rtd 97; PtO *Lon* from 98. *25 Weardale Gardens, Enfield EN2 0BA* T/F: (020) 8366 5126 E: peterpytches@gmail.com

Q

QUAK-WINSLOW, Mrs Kimberley. b 82. Huddersfield Univ BSc 09. Trin Coll Bris MA 17. **d** 17 **p** 18. C Sutton, Wincle, Wildboarclough and Bosley *Ches* 17–19; Youth Chapl and Min Can St Alb 19–21; P-in-c Whetstone St Jo *Lon* from 21; P-in-c Friern Barnet All SS from 21. *St John the Apostle Vicarage, 1163 High Road, London N20 0PG*

QUANRUD, Nicholas James. b 89. Brunel Univ BSc 12 Clare Coll Cam BTh 18. Westcott Ho Cam 16. **d** 19 **p** 20. C Kennington St Jo w St Jas *S'wark* from 19. *96 Vassall Road, London SW9 6JA* E: njquanrud@gmail.com

QUANTRILL, Mrs Sarah Ellen. b 67. Newnham Coll Cam BA 90 MA 93 UEA PGCE 92. Westcott Ho Cam 13. **d** 15 **p** 16. C Oulton Broad *Nor* 15–18; P-in-c New Catton St Luke w St Aug 18–20; P-in-c Carlton Colville and Mutford from 20. *The Rectory, Rectory Road, Carlton Colville, Lowestoft NR33 8BB* E: sarah.quantrill@cantab.net

QUARMBY, David John. b 43. St Jo Coll Dur BA 64 Lon Univ CertEd 70 Man Univ MEd 89 Sheff Univ MA 99. Ridley Hall Cam 65. **d** 67 **p** 68. C Bournville *Birm* 67–71; V Erdington St Chad 71–73; LtO *Blackb* 73–83; PtO *Man* 83–90; C Oldham St Paul 90–98; Hon C 98–14; Hon C Oldham St Paul and Werneth from 14; Cllr Huddersfield Poly 90–92; Huddersfield Univ 92–01; Prin Adult Psychotherapist Hyndburn Community Mental Health Team from 00; Sen Cllr Blackb and Darwen Primary Care Trust 01–08. *6 Windy Bank, Port Sunlight, Wirral CH62 5EA* T: 0161-626 2771 E: david.quarmby@zen.co.uk

QUARTON, Robert Edward. b 43. Wilson Carlile Coll 64 EMMTC 84. **d** 87 **p** 88. C Gresley *Derby* 87–88; C Clay Cross 88–90; C N Wingfield, Clay Cross and Pilsley 90–91; R Darley 91–10; P-in-c S Darley, Elton and Winster 03–10; RD Wirksworth 03–08; rtd 10. *12 Blenheim Avenue, Swanwick, Alfreton DE55 1PQ* T: (01773) 605766 E: robertquarton@uwclub.net

QUASH, Canon Jonathan Ben**.** b 68. Peterho Cam BA 90 MA 94 PhD 99. Westcott Ho Cam 91. **d** 95 **p** 96. NSM Cambridge St Mary Less *Ely* 95–96; Asst Chapl Peterho Cam 95–96; Chapl Fitzw Coll Cam 96–99; Fell 98–99; Tutor Wesley Ho Cam 96–99; Fell and Dean Peterho Cam 99–07; Prof K Coll Lon from 07; Can Th Cov Cathl from 04; Can Th Bradf Cathl 13–14; *Leeds* from 14. *King's College London, Strand, London WC2R 2LS* T: (020) 7848 2336 F: 7848 2255 E: ben.quash@kcl.ac.uk

QUAYLE, Margaret Grace. b 28. Gipsy Hill Coll of Educn TCert 48 Lon Univ BA 53 Liv Univ MPhil 78. **d** 98 **p** 99. OLM Gt Crosby St Luke *Liv* 98–03; PtO from 03. *Clwyd, 9 Myers Road West, Liverpool L23 0RS* T: 0151-924 1659

QUAYLE, Martin Stuart. b 60. Lon Hosp BDS 82 Birkbeck Coll Lon BA 98 Leeds Univ BA 08 Open Univ MA 11. Coll of Resurr Mirfield 06. **d** 08 **p** 09. C Basingstoke *Win* 08–11; PtO *Heref* 12–14; NSM Diddlebury w Munslow, Holdgate and Tugford 14–17; PtO 17–19; NSM Cleobury Mortimer w Hopton Wafers etc 19–21; P-in-c Middle Marches from 21. *The Rectory, Weston Road, Bucknall SY7 0BA* M: 07976-664872 E: martinsquayle@icloud.com

QUIBELL, Mrs Susan Elizabeth. b 50. **d** 03 **p** 04. OLM Aldridge *Lich* 03–20; rtd 20; PtO *Lich* from 20. *20 Summer Lane, Walsall WS4 1DS* T: (01922) 744205 E: s.quibell@googlemail.com

QUICK, John Michael. b 46. N Counties Coll Newc TCert 68 Birkbeck Coll Lon BSc 73 FRGS 70. SAOMC 97. **d** 00 **p** 01. OLM New Windsor *Ox* 00–16; PtO from 16. *White Roses, 45 York Road, Windsor SL4 3PA* T: (01753) 865557 M: 07977-754822 E: littlefrquick@aol.com

QUICK, Roger Aelfred Melvin Tricquet. b 55. Leeds Univ BA 79 BA 96 PGCE 81. Coll of Resurr Mirfield 94. **d** 96 **p** 97. C Chapel Allerton *Ripon* 96–00; C Ireland Wood 00–04; Chapl Strathallan Sch 04–11; R Pitlochry *St And* 11–13; R Kilmaveonaig 11–13; R Kinloch Rannoch 11–13; Chapl St Geo Crypt Leeds from 13. *17 Wensleydale Court, Stainbeck Lane, Leeds LS7 3SA* T: 0113-245 9061 M: 07762-159047 E: father@priest.com

QUIGLEY, Adam. **d** 03 **p** 04. NSM Castlerock w Dunboe and Fermoyle *D & R* from 03. *41 Queens Park, Coleraine BT51 3JS* T: (028) 7035 5191 E: adam.quigley@hotmail.co.uk

QUIGLEY, Donna Maree. b 40. Ulster Univ BEd BTh. **d** 01 **p** 02. C Portadown St Columba *Arm* 01–03; I Derryvolgie *Conn* 04–09. *284 Tennent Street, Belfast BT13 3GG* E: donna_quigley@yahoo.co.uk

QUIGLEY, John Christopher. b 41. Pontifical Lateran Univ STL 68. **d** 67 **p** 68. P-in-c N Bersted *Chich* 03–08; rtd 08; P-in-c Lyminster *Chich* 11–15; PtO from 16. *West House, 6 Hillview Crescent, East Preston, Littlehampton BN16 1RD* T: (01903) 417501 M: 07792-718875 E: quigs41@sky.com

QUILL, Andrew Thomas Edward. b 67. Heriot-Watt Univ BArch 91. Uganda Chr Univ 05. **d** 05 **p** 07. Dioc Co-ord Community Health Empowerment Uganda 05–06; C Drumragh w Mountfield *D & R* 06–09; I Kinawley w H Trin *K, E & A* 09–16; Dioc Communications Officer 10–16; I Dromore *Clogh* from 16. *The Rectory, 19 Galbally Road, Dromore, Omagh BT78 3EE* T: (028) 8289 8246 M: 07738-960707 E: holytrinitydromore@gmail.com

QUILL, John Stephen. b 51. Linc Th Coll 76. **d** 79 **p** 80. C Sawbridgeworth *St Alb* 79–81; C Watford Ch Ch 81–85; Dioc Soc Services Adv *Worc* 85–90; Adv to Bd of Soc Resp 90–95; PtO *St Alb* 07–14; Chapl R Masonic Sch for Girls Rickmansworth from 14; PtO *S & B* from 13. *35 Kingfisher Drive, Hemel Hempstead HP3 9DD* T: (01442) 266369 *or* 266369 *or* 773168 E: johnsquill@btopenworld.com

QUILL, Walter Paterson. b 35. MBE. **d** 60 **p** 61. C Glendermott *D & R* 60–63; I Kilbarron 63–66; I Kilcronaghan w Ballynascreen 66–81; I Derg w Termonamongan 81–07; Can Derry Cathl 89–07; Preb Howth St Patr Cathl Dublin 94–07; rtd 07; P-in-c Clondevaddock w Portsalon and Leatbeg *D & R* 09–11. *1 University Gardens, Coleraine BT52 1JT* T: (028) 7035 2114 E: wquill@btinternet.com

QUILTER, Mrs Sharon Deloris. b 62. MIIA 02 CMIIA 10 MICA 13. St Mellitus Coll 17. **d** 20 **p** 21. NSM Halstead Area *Chelmsf* from 20. *The Coach House, Colne Green Farm, Halstead Road, Earls Colne, Colchester CO6 2NG* M: 07944-517456 E: colnescurate@gmail.com *or* shazquilter@hotmail.com

QUIN, David Christopher. b 42. SAOMC 97. d 00 p 01. NSM Blunham, Gt Barford, Roxton and Tempsford etc *St Alb* 00–06; rtd 06; PtO *Glouc* from 15. *16 Beceshore Close, Moreton-in-Marsh GL56 9NB* T: (01608) 651571 M: 07867-664924 E: davidcquin@aol.com

QUIN, John James Neil. b 31. Ox Univ MA DipEd 53. Qu Coll Birm 61. d 63 p 64. C Cannock *Lich* 63–68; V Sneyd Green 68–78; V Stafford St Paul Forebridge 78–90; TV Tettenhall Regis 90–98; rtd 98; PtO *Ex* from 00. *Watcombe House, 28 Barnpark Road, Teignmouth TQ14 8PN* T: (01626) 772525

QUINE, Christopher Andrew. b 38. St Aid Birkenhead 61. d 64 p 65. C Hunts Cross *Liv* 64–67; C Farnworth and C-in-c Widnes St Jo 67–71; V Clubmoor 71–78; V Formby H Trin 78–99; V Arbory and Santan *S & M* 99–03; rtd 03; PtO *Liv* from 16. *31 Trinity Lodge, 103 Lonsdale Road, Formby, Liverpool L37 3AA* M: 07963-588332 E: chris.quine@googlemail.com

QUINN, Canon Arthur Hamilton Riddel. b 37. TCD BA 60 MA 64 BD 67. d 61 p 62. C Belfast H Trin *Conn* 61–63; C Belfast St Mary Magd 63–64; Chapl Hull Univ *York* 64–69; Chapl Keele Univ *Lich* 69–74; P-in-c Keele 72–74; V Shirley St Jo *Cant* 74–84; V Shirley St Jo S'wark 85–06; RD Croydon Addington 95–04; Hon Can S'wark Cathl 03–06; rtd 06; PtO S'wark from 06. *23 Eden Road, Croydon CR0 1BB* T: (020) 8680 3049 E: quinncanon@btinternet.com

QUINN, John James. b 46. TCD BA 70 PhD 76. St Jo Coll Nottm. d 81 p 82. C Gorleston St Andr *Nor* 81–84; R Belton 84–90; R Burgh Castle 84–90; R Belton and Burgh Castle 90–10; rtd 10; PtO *Nor* from 10. *23 Wren Drive, Bradwell, Great Yarmouth NR31 8JW* T: (01493) 718634 E: johnjquinn@lineone.net

QUINN, Naomi Caroline. d 11 p 12. C Derg w Termonamongan *D & R* 11–20; I Errigle Keerogue w Ballygawley and Killeshil *Arm* from 20. *24 Old Omagh Road, Dungannon BT70 2AA* E: revnaomi@outlook.com

QUINNELL, Peter Francis. b 48. St Steph Ho Ox 93. d 95 p 96. C Tewkesbury w Walton Cardiff *Glouc* 95–99; R Stratton, N Cerney, Baunton and Bagendon 99–08; AD Cirencester 06–08; R Whitewater *Win* 08–14; rtd 14; Hon C Tetbury, Beverston, Long Newnton etc *Glouc* 14–15; Hon C Avening w Cherington 14–15; TV Stroud Team 15–17; Hon C S Cheltenham 17–21; PtO from 21. *4 Foxgrove Drive, Cheltenham GL52 6TQ* T: (01242) 227112 M: 07752-341916 E: quinnell708@btinternet.com

QUINTON, Mrs Jane. b 63. Ridley Hall Cam 15. d 17 p 18. C Chipping Ongar w Shelley etc *Chelmsf* from 17. *49 Kettlebury Way, Ongar CM5 9HA* M: 07973-295492 E: janequinton@hotmail.com

QUINTON, Rosemary Ruth. See BRABY, Rosemary Ruth

QUIREY, Mrs Edith. b 56. CITC 98. d 01 p 02. Aux Min Belfast St Mich *Conn* 01–05; P-in-c Belfast St Steph w St Luke 05–07; Bp's C 07–09; I 09–15; P-in-c Hodnet *Lich* from 15; P-in-c Moreton Corbet 16–17; P-in-c Shawbury 16–17; P-in-c Stanton on Hine Heath 16–17; C Edstaston, Fauls, Prees, Tilstock and Whixall 18–20; C Prees, Edstaston and Whixall 20; C Cen Telford 21. *The Rectory, Abbots Way, Hodnet, Market Drayton TF9 3NQ* T: (01630) 685491 E: e.quirey@btinternet.com

QUIST, Ms Frances Buckurel. NTMTC BA 09. d 09 p 10. C E Ham w Upton Park and Forest Gate *Chelmsf* 09–12; P-in-c Matson *Glouc* 12–18. *Address withheld by request* M: 07734-711929 E: francesquist@btinternet.com

R

RAAFF, Trevor Howard. b 74. Cape Town Univ BBS 97. Ridley Hall Cam 10. d 12 p 13. C Biddulph *Lich* 12–16; P-in-c Linby w Papplewick *S'well* from 16. *The Rectory, Main Street, Linby, Nottingham NG15 8AE* T: 0115-963 2346 M: 07847-660618 E: revraaff@gmail.com

RABJOHNS, Benjamin Thomas. b 86. Ex Univ BA 07 Cardiff Univ BA 11. St Mich Coll Llan 08. d 11 p 12. C Aberavon *Llan* 11–14; TV 14–16; P-in-c Penrhiwceiber, Matthewstown and Ynysboeth from 16. *The Vicarage, Winifred Street, Mountain Ash CF45 3YF* T: (01443) 473716 E: b.t.rabjohns@gmail.com

RABLEN, Christine Mary. b 52. Trevelyan Coll Dur BA 74 Hull Univ BA 92 Leeds Univ MA 94. NOC 00. d 02 p 03. C Sutton St Mich *York* 02–05; V Roxbourne St Andr *Lon* 05–11; V Leyton St Mary w St Edw and St Luke *Chelmsf* 11–18; AD Waltham Forest 17–18; Hon Can Chelmsf Cathl 17–18; P-in-c Offerton *Ches* from 18. *The Vicarage, 1A Salcombe Road, Stockport SK2 5AG* T: 0161-480 3773 E: cmrablen@gmail.com

RABY, Malcolm Ernest. b 47. St Jo Coll York BEd 73. NOC 81. d 84 p 85. NSM Chadkirk *Ches* 84–88; Consultant E England CPAS 88–94; C Ely 94–96; TV 96–98; Dioc Adv in Miss and Evang 98–13; P-in-c Over 98–13; P-in-c Long Stanton w St Mich 02–13; rtd 13; Hon C Leatherhead and Mickleham *Guildf* 13–17; PtO from 17. *3 Greenbank Court, Sherwood Way, Epsom KT19 8LQ* T: (01372) 729757 E: rm.raby007@btinternet.com

RACE, Canon Alan. b 51. Bradf Univ BTech 73 Birm Univ MA 82. Ripon Coll Cuddesdon 73. d 76 p 77. C Tupsley *Heref* 76–79; Asst Chapl Kent Univ *Cant* 79–84; Dir Studies S'wark Ord Course 84–94; R Aylestone St Andr w St Jas *Leic* 94–07; P-in-c Leic St Phil 07–11; Hon Can Leic Cathl 07–11; R Lee St Marg *S'wark* 11–17; rtd 17; PtO *Leic* 19–21; *Ox* from 21. *5 Mardy, Caversham, Reading RG4 7NY* E: alan2race@gmail.com

RACE, Andrew James. b 68. Birm Univ BA 92 Man BA 93. Ripon Coll Cuddesdon MTh 15. d 15 p 16. C Littleover *Derby* 15–19; V Castle Donington and Lockington cum Hemington *Leic* from 19. *The Vicarage, 6 Delven Lane, Castle Donington, Derby DE74 2LJ* T: (01332) 810364

RACE, Christopher Keith. b 43. St Paul's Coll Grahamstown 76. d 78 p 80. Angl Chapl Stellenbosch Univ S Africa 79–81; R Kalk Bay 81–83; P-in-c E Kalahari, Dioc Admin Botswana and Personal Asst to Abp Cen Africa 83–86; V Tanworth St Patr Salter Street *Birm* 86–96; P-in-c Rothiemurchus *Mor*

96–01; PtO *Glouc* 02–03; P-in-c Kemble, Poole Keynes, Somerford Keynes etc 03–04; R 04–06; Prin Tutor and Lect Cant Ch Ch Univ 06–08; rtd 08; PtO *Eur* from 09; P-in-c St Matt St Helena 15–16; PtO *Cov* from 20. *c/o the Revd S P Race, 22 Elmwood Way, Barnsley S75 1EY* M: 07866-585973 E: ck.race@gmail.com

RACE, Canon Stephen Peter. b 69. SS Hild & Bede Coll Dur BA 93. St Steph Ho Ox MTh 03. d 02 p 03. C Wigton *Carl* 02–05; V Dodworth *Wakef* 05–14; P-in-c Barnsley St Mary Leeds 14–18; P-in-c Barnsley St Edw 17–18; P-in-c Gawber 17–18; R Cen Barnsley 18–19; P-in-c Barnsley St Geo 18–19; R Cen Barnsley from 19; Asst Dioc Dir of Ords *Wakef* 05–09; Dir from 09; AD Barnsley *Leeds* from 09; Hon Can Wakef Cathl from 11. *22 Elmwood Way, Barnsley S75 1EY* M: 07549-876505 E: stephen.race@leeds.anglican.org

RACKLYEFT, Emma Joy. b 79. Univ Coll Chich BA 01. Wycliffe Hall Ox BTh 13. d 13 p 14. C Thame *Ox* 13–17; V Denmead *Portsm* from 17; Asst Dir of Ords from 20. *The Vicarage, Ludcombe, Denmead, Waterlooville PO7 6TL* M: 07837-845420 E: emma@theracklyefts.co.uk

RACTLIFFE, Dudley John. b 38. Man Univ BA 62. Ridley Hall Cam 63. d 66 p 67. C Radford *Cov* 66–68; C Haslemere *Guildf* 69–73; V Perry Beeches *Birm* 73–78; V Worle *B & W* 78–88; Dioc Ecum Officer and R Dowlishwake w Kingstone, Chillington etc 88–93; TR Swanage and Studland *Sarum* 93–01; rtd 01; PtO *B & W* 02–19. *12 Sid Lane, Sidmouth EX10 9AN* T: (01395) 579712

RADCLIFFE, Canon Albert Edward. b 34. Lon Univ BD 63. St Aid Birkenhead Ch Div Sch of the Pacific (USA) 61. d 62 p 63. C Knotty Ash St Jo *Liv* 62–64; C Blundellsands St Nic 64–66; Chapl Haifa St Luke Israel 66–69; V Tonge w Alkrington *Man* 69–77; R Ashton St Mich 77–91; AD Ashton-under-Lyne 87–91; Can Res Man Cathl 91–00; rtd 00; PtO *Man* from 01. *26 St Chad's Road, Withington, Manchester M20 4WH* T: 0161-445 1327 E: albertradcliffe34@gmail.com

RADCLIFFE, David Jeffrey. b 52. Linc Th Coll 77. d 79 p 80. C Poulton-le-Fylde *Blackb* 79–84; V Ingol 84–88; R Lowther and Askham *Carl* 88–96; R Lowther and Askham and Clifton and Brougham 96–06; R Upton-on-Severn, Ripple, Earls Croome etc *Worc* 06–11; P-in-c W Preston *Blackb* 11–15; rtd 15; PtO *Blackb* 16–17 and from 20. *39 Naze Lane, Freckleton, Preston PR4 1RH* M: 07552-440755 E: revjeffradcliffe@hotmail.co.uk

RADCLIFFE, Eileen <u>Rose</u>. b 54. Carl Dioc Tr Inst 92. **d** 95 **p** 96. NSM Gt Salkeld w Lazonby Carl 95–96; NSM Dacre 99–02; PtO 02–06; Worc 06–08; NSM Upton-on-Severn, Ripple, Earls Croome etc 08–11; PtO Blackb 11–19 and from 20. 39 Naze Lane, Freckleton, Preston PR4 1RH M: 07468-413864 E: rosieradcliffe@hotmail.com

RADCLIFFE, James Scotson. b 75. Rob Coll Cam MA 98. Oak Hill Th Coll BA 08. **d** 08 **p** 09. C Hove Bp Hannington Memorial Ch Chich 08–13; R Lavant 13–15; C Linc St Pet in Eastgate 15–21; Chapl K Edw Sch Witley from 21. King Edward's School, Petworth Road, Wormley, Godalming GU8 5SG M: 07941-248213 E: jamesradcliffe@gmail.com

RADCLIFFE, Jeffrey. See RADCLIFFE, David Jeffrey

RADCLIFFE, John Frederick. b 39. **d** 01 **p** 02. OLM Meltham Wakef 01–14; Leeds from 14. 13 Orchard Close, Meltham, Huddersfield HD9 4EG   T: (01484) 348806 E: johnandenid@yahoo.com

RADCLIFFE, Robert Mark. b 63. St Jo Coll Dur BA 08. Cranmer Hall Dur 05. **d** 08 **p** 09. C Welling Roch 08–11; P-in-c Erith St Jo 11–12; V 12–19; V Malew and Santan S & M from 19. Malew Vicarage, Crossag Road, Ballasalla, Isle of Man IM9 3EF E: markradcliffe@msn.com

RADCLIFFE, Mrs Rosemary. b 45. SWMTC 87. **d** 90 **p** 94. NSM Devoran Truro 90–93; Dn-in-c N Newton w St Michaelchurch, Thurloxton etc B & W 93–94; P-in-c 94–00; Chapl to the Deaf 96–96; P-in-c Whipton Ex 00–01; rtd 01; PtO Truro from 03. 76 Upland Crescent, Truro TR1 1NE   T: (01872) 273906

RADCLIFFE, Rosie. See RADCLIFFE, Eileen Rose

RADCLIFFE, Timothy Simon. b 81. Surrey Univ BSc 04. St Mellitus Coll BA 20. **d** 20 **p** 21. C Ealing St Paul Lon from 20. 23A Culmington Road, London W13 9NJ E: tim.radcliffe81@btinternet.com

RADFORD, Andrew James. b 67. St Mellitus Coll BA 16. **d** 16 **p** 17. C Much Woolton Liv 16–19; TV Halewood and Hunts Cross from 19. 7 Kingsmead Drive, Liverpool L25 0NG M: 07966-033648 E: radfordandy67@gmail.com or revandyhhc@gmail.com

RADFORD, Blair William. St Steph Ho Ox 15. **d** 18 **p** 19. C Monk Bretton Leeds 18–21; P-in-c Barnsley St Pet and St Jo from 21; P-in-c Lundwood from 21. The Vicarage, 1 Osbourne Mews, Barnsley S70 1UU   T: 07951-171094 E: blair.radford@leeds.anglican.org

RADFORD, Georgina Margaret. b 55. R Free Hosp Sch of Medicine MB, BS 79 FFPH 97 FRCP 02. ERMC 14. **d** 16 **p** 17. NSM Anglesey Gp Ely 16–19; TV Buckfastleigh, Dean Prior, Littlehempston etc Ex from 19. The Vicarage, Hillside, South Brent TQ10 9AN E: gina.radford@btinternet.com

RADFORD, Mrs Janet. b 58. Chelt & Glouc Coll of HE BSc 00 RN 79. Ripon Coll Cuddesdon 11. **d** 14 **p** 15. NSM Harwell w Chilton Ox 14–21; Chapl Ox Univ Hosps NHS Foundn Trust 14–21; rtd 21. 1 The Croft, Marcham, Abingdon OX13 6NF   T: (01865) 391282 M: 07956-448011 E: janradford@yahoo.com

RADFORD, Vincent Arthur. b 45. Ches Coll of HE CertEd 69. **d** 05 **p** 06. OLM Westhoughton and Wingates Man 05–13; OLM Daisy Hill, Westhoughton and Wingates 13–15; rtd 15; PtO Man from 16. 64 Molyneux Road, Westhoughton, Bolton BL5 3EU   T: (01942) 790091 E: revrad1@virginmedia.com

RADLEY, Richard Brian. b 68. St Jo Coll Nottm 02. **d** 04 **p** 05. C Utley Bradf 04–08; P-in-c Doncaster St Mary Sheff 09–10; P-in-c Wheatley Park 09–10; V Doncaster St Mary and St Paul 10–15; TV Billingham Dur from 15. 68 Wolviston Road, Billingham TS22 5ET E: revrichardr@gmail.com

RADMALL, Andre. **d** 07 **p** 08. NSM Woodside Park St Barn Lon 07–17; PtO 17–18; St Alb 17–18; NSM St Alb St Paul from 18. 11 Kenerne Drive, Barnet EN5 2NW   T: (020) 8440 2138 E: andreradwriter@gmail.com

RAE, Stephen Gordon. b 65. AGSM 87. Oak Hill Th Coll BA 09. **d** 09 **p** 10. C Danehill Chich 09–13; V Westgate St Jas Cant 13–21; C Fulwood Sheff from 21. 65 Whirlow Park Road, Sheffield S11 9NH

RAE SMITH, Tristram Geoffrey. b 57. Clare Coll Cam BA 79 MA 83 St Jo Coll Dur BA 04. Cranmer Hall Dur 02. **d** 04 **p** 05. C Bradford-on-Avon Ch Ch Sarum 04–08; C Westwood and Wingfield 04–08; R Camelot Par B & W from 08; C Bruton and Distr 08–12. The Rectory, 6 The Close, North Cadbury, Yeovil BA22 7DX   T: (01963) 440585 M: 07751-306272 E: tristramraesmith@gmail.com

RAFFAY, Julian Paul. b 60. Stirling Univ BSc 84 St Jo Coll Dur BA 90 Cardiff Univ MTh 12 Dur Univ DThM 18. Cranmer Hall Dur 87. **d** 90 **p** 91. C Adel Ripon 90–93; C Leeds Halton St Wilfrid 93–95; Asst Chapl S Derbys Mental Health NHS Trust 95–97; TV Gleadless Sheff 97–01; V Deepcar 01–07; Mental Health Chapl Team Ldr Sheff Care Trust 07–14; Specialist Research Chapl Mersey Care NHS Foundn Trust 14–19; TR 4Saints Team Liv 19–20; Dir Studies St Padarn's Inst

from 20. St Padarn's Institute, 54 Cardiff Road, Llandaff, Cardiff CF5 2YJ M: 07957-298073 E: julian.raffay@stpadarns.ac.uk

RAFFAY, Marie Josephine. b 63. Nottm Univ BA 85. All SS Cen for Miss & Min 16. **d** 18 **p** 19. C Mossley Hill Liv 18–20; C Allerton All Hallows 20–21; V Huyton St Mich from 21. St Michael's Vicarage, Bluebell Lane, Huyton L36 7SA M: 07853-796270 E: marie.huyton@outlook.com

RAGAN, Mrs Jennifer Mary. b 39. Linc Th Coll 71. **dss** 80 **d** 87 **p** 94. Hackney Lon 80–84; Hornchurch St Andr Chelmsf 84–88; Par Dn 87–88; Par Dn Ingrave St Steph CD 88–90; Par Dn Gt Parndon 90–94; C 94–99; TV 99–07; rtd 07; PtO Chelmsf 07–13; St E 07–20. 18 Holme Oaks Court, 50 Cliff Lane, Ipswich IP3 0PE   T: (01473) 213577 E: revjenniferragan@btinternet.com

RAGGETT, Anita Jane. b 56. NOC. **d** 07 **p** 08. C Gomersal Wakef 07–10; C Cleckheaton St Jo 08–10; P-in-c Lepton 10–14; Leeds 14–16; Chapl Huddersfield Univ 10–16; P-in-c Walton Ches 16–20; V from 20. 13 Hillfoot Crescent, Stockton Heath, Warrington WA4 6SB   T: (01925) 262939 E: anitaraggett138@gmail.com

RAIKES, Miss Gwynneth <u>Marian</u> Napier. b 51. Somerville Coll Ox MA 72 Lon Univ BD 81. Trin Coll Bris 79. **dss** 81 **d** 98 **p** 98. Asst Chapl Bris Poly 81–86; Beckenham Ch Ch Roch 86–00; C 98–00; Dean of Women and Oak Hill Th Coll 00–13; 14; PtO Lon 03–13; Ely from 02. 28 Pilgrims Way, Ely CB6 3DL E: gmnrpilgrim@gmail.com

RAIKES, Canon Peter. b 37. St Mich Coll Llan 78. **d** 80 **p** 81. C Roath Llan 80–82; V Resolven 82–86; V Resolven w Tonna 86–92; RD Neath 89–01; V Skewen 92–02; Can Llan Cathl 97–02; rtd 02; PtO Llan 04–18. 2 Kennedy Drive, Pencoed, Bridgend CF35 6TW   T: (01656) 862317

RAIKES, Robert Laybourne. b 32. Wells Th Coll 59. **d** 61 **p** 62. C Poplar All SS w St Frideswide Lon 61–66; C Grendon Underwood w Edgcott Ox 66–68; C Swan 68–71; V Whitchurch Canonicorum w Wooton Fitzpaine etc Sarum 71–81; P-in-c Branksome St Aldhelm 81–82; V 82–91; I Pitminster w Corfe B & W 91–92; rtd 92; Chapl Madeira Eur 93–95; PtO Glouc 95–98; Hon C Broadwell, Evenlode, Oddington, Adlestrop etc 98–01; LtO Eur 02–19; PtO Chelmsf 09–13; S'wark 10–19. The College of St Barnabas, Blackberry Lane, Lingfield RH7 6NJ   T: (01342) 872826

RAILTON, David James. b 66. Bradf Univ BPharm 89. EMMTC 06. **d** 08 **p** 09. C Melbourne, Ticknall, Smisby and Stanton Derby 08–11; V Hazelwood, Holbrook and Milford 11–15; Bp's Asst Chapl 11–15; V Blackwell All SS and Salutation Dur 15–19; AD Darlington 17–19; R Dunoon Arg from 19; R Rothesay from 19. The Rectory, Kilbride Road, Dunoon PA23 7LN   T: (01369) 702444 E: davidrailton@gmail.com or dunoonrector@gmail.com

RAILTON, John Robert Henry. b 45. Reading Univ BSc 68 Lon Univ LLB PhD 82 FCIB 79. S Dios Minl Tr Scheme 82. **d** 85 **p** 86. NSM Wickham Portsm 85–89; C Bridgemary 89–90; V 90–96; TR Ridgeway Sarum 96–02; TR Whitton 02–08; rtd 08; P-in-c Purton Bris 11–12; PtO 13–18 and from 19; Ox 16–19; Sarum from 16. 20 Baileys Way, Wroughton, Swindon SN4 9AH   T: (01793) 814162 E: john.railton@icloud.com

RAILTON, Malcolm. b 60. Lindisfarne Regional Tr Partnership 17. **d** 19 **p** 20. NSM Tynemouth Priory Newc from 19. St Peter's Old Rectory, North Terrace, Wallsend NE28 6PY M: 07880-945095 E: railtontownfield@btinternet.com

RAILTON, Ray. b 44. ERMC 13. **d** 15 **p** 16. NSM Wellingborough St Barn Pet 15–18; NSM Wellingborough St Andr and St Barn from 18. Saltbox Cottage, 10 Buckwell End, Wellingborough NN8 4LR M: 07502-510545 E: ray.railton@btinternet.com

RAILTON, Sandra. b 46. S Dios Minl Tr Scheme 82. **dss** 85 **d** 87 **p** 94. Catherington and Clanfield Portsm 85–86; Lee-on-the-Solent 86–89; C 87–89; Par Dn Burnham w Dropmore, Hitcham and Taplow Ox 89–94; TV Wallingford w Crowmarsh Gifford etc 94–98; TV Wallingford 98; Dioc Dir Ords (OLM) Berks 96–99; TV Ridgeway Sarum 98–02; Dioc Voc Adv 99–02; TV Whitton 02–08; RD Marlborough 04–08; rtd 08; PtO Bris from 10; Ox from 16; Sarum from 16. 20 Baileys Way, Wroughton, Swindon SN4 9AH   T: (01793) 814162 E: sandyrailton@btinternet.com

RAILTON-CROWDER, Mrs Mary. b 51. Luton Univ BA 96 RN 72 RM 91 MIOSH 93. SAOMC 98. **d** 01 **p** 02. C Elstow St Alb 01–04; Chapl De Montford Univ 02–04; C Douglas All SS and St Thos S & M 04–07; P-in-c Birchencliffe Wakef 07–08; V Birkby and Birchencliffe 08–14; Leeds 14–16; AD Huddersfield 10–15; rtd 16; PtO Ches from 16. Thorn Villa, 36 Newton Park Road, Wirral CH48 9XF   T: 0151-384 2482 E: maryrailtoncrowder@gmail.com

RAINBIRD, Ms Ruth Patricia. b 40. SRN 62. **d** 01 **p** 02. OLM Limpsfield and Titsey S'wark 01–10; PtO from 10.

73 Stoneleigh Road, Oxted RH8 0TP T: (01883) 713683 E: ruthrainbird@btinternet.com

RAINE, Alan. b 49. NEOC 92. **d** 95 **p** 96. NSM Jarrow *Dur* 95–05; Chapl S Tyneside Coll 95–05; V Leam Lane *Dur* 05–20; rtd 20; PtO *Dur* from 20. *6 Coquet Street, Jarrow NE32 5SW* E: alanraine@virginmedia.com

RAINE, David. b 58. Dur Univ MBA 96 Open Univ BSc 96 MCIM 99 MCIPD 03. NEOC 01. **d** 04 **p** 05. NSM N Wearside *Dur* 04–06; NSM Millfield St Mary 06–17; NSM Bishopwearmouth Gd Shep 06–17; V Grangetown from 17. *St Aidan's Vicarage, Ryhope Road, Sunderland SR2 9RS* E: farvad@sky.com

RAINE, Stephen James. b 49. Sheff Poly BA 80. NOC 85. **d** 86 **p** 87. C Cottingham *York* 86–90; V Dunscroft Ch Ch *Sheff* 90–92; V Dunscroft St Edwin 92–96; V Kettering St Mary *Pet* 96–08; P-in-c Ipswich St Mary at the Elms *St E* 08–14; Chapl Ipswich Hosp NHS Trust 08–14; rtd 14. *20 rue du Château, 16190 Montmoreau-St-Cybard, France* T: (0033) 5 45 61 74 43 E: evangelist24@hotmail.com

RAINER, John Charles. b 54. Ex Univ BA 76 CertEd 78 Hull Univ MBA 02. St Jo Coll Nottm 86. **d** 88 **p** 89. C Fletchamstead *Cov* 88–94; V Leic H Apostles 94–03; V Shipley St Pet *Bradf* 03–14; Leeds from 14. *The Vicarage, 2 Glenhurst Road, Shipley BD18 4DZ* T: (01274) 584488 *or* 400381 E: john.rainer@leeds.anglican.org *or* johnrainer@btinternet.com

RAINES, Mrs Gisela Rolanda. b 58. Groningen Univ Kandidaats 80. K Coll Lon BD 83. dss 84 **d** 87 **p** 94. Charlton St Luke w H Trin *S'wark* 84–87; Par Dn 87; Chapl Imp Coll *Lon* 87–91; Hon C Birch w Fallowfield *Man* 94–95; P-in-c Withington St Chris 95–03; C Man St Ann 03–10; R Withington St Paul 10–18; rtd 18; PtO *Blackb* from 18. *15 Powis Road, Ashton-on-Ribble, Preston PR2 1AD* E: revgisela@btinternet.com

RAINES, William Guy. b 46. Lon Univ BSc 69 MSc 70 Ox Univ BA 80. Ripon Coll Cuddesdon 78. **d** 81 **p** 82. C W Drayton *Lon* 81–84; C Charlton St Luke w H Trin *S'wark* 84–87; Chapl K Coll Lon 87–94; Chapl Imp Coll 91–94; P-in-c Birch w Fallowfield *Man* 94–95; R 95–12; rtd 12; PtO *Man* from 13; *Blackb* from 18. *15 Powis Road, Ashton-on-Ribble, Preston PR2 1AD* M: 07908-758804 E: wraines@btinternet.com

RAINFORD, Robert Graham. b 55. Lanc Univ CertEd 76 BEd 77. St Steph Ho Ox 81. **d** 83 **p** 84. C Burnley St Cath w St Alb and St Paul *Blackb* 83–86; C-in-c Hawes Side St Chris CD 86–89; V Hawes Side 89–03; P-in-c Marton Moss 01–03; AD Blackpool 00–03; Hon Can Blackb Cathl 00–03; Sen Chapl to Bp Dover *Cant* 03–05; P Admin Upper Chelsea H Trin *Lon* 05–08; PtO 08–11; Hon C Upper Chelsea H Trin and St Sav 11–15; PtO from 15; Hd RS Sussex Ho Sch from 15. *Sussex House School, 68 Cadogan Square, London SW1X 0EA* E: gr@sussexhouseschool.co.uk

RAINSFORD, Peter John. b 31. FCP 72. Qu Coll Birm 75. **d** 77 **p** 78. Hon C Lich St Chad 77–81; C 82; C Coseley Ch Ch 82–84; V Wednesbury St Bart 84–91; Chapl Sandwell Distr Gen Hosp 89–91; rtd 91; PtO *Lich* 91–20. *34 Pegasus Court, 155 Chester Road, Streetly, Sutton Coldfield B74 3NW* E: ppr157@hotmail.co.uk

RAISTRICK, Brian. b 38. St Paul's Coll Chelt TCert 60 Ex Univ AdDipEd 68 Newc Univ MEd 76 UEA PhD 86. Westcott Ho Cam 92. **d** 93 **p** 94. C Haverhill w Withersfield, the Wrattings etc *St E* 93–95; P-in-c Horringer cum Ickworth 95–02; P-in-c Risby w Gt and Lt Saxham and Westley 99–02; P-in-c Chevington w Hargrave and Whepstead w Brockley 00–02; R Horringer 02; RD Thingoe 99–01; rtd 03; PtO *St E* 03–21. *Greenways, Westwood, Great Barton, Bury St Edmunds IP31 2SF* T: (01284) 787372 *or* 747372 E: braistrick@btinternet.com

RAISTRICK, Mrs Tracey Ann. b 65. Coll of Resurr Mirfield 13. **d** 15 **p** 16. C Utley *Leeds* 15–16; C Keighley from 16; P-in-c Ingrow w Hainworth from 19. *St John's Vicarage, Oakfield Road, Keighley BD21 1BT* M: 07850-940079 E: rev.tracey@outlook.com

RAISTRICK, Tulo Dirk. b 69. Jes Coll Ox BA 91. SEITE 08. **d** 11 **p** 12. C Telford Park *S'wark* 11–14; V Earlsdon *Cov* from 14. *St Barbara's Vicarage, 24 Rochester Road, Coventry CV5 6AG* T: (024) 7501 7889 M: 07552-948068 E: tulo@raistricks.com

RAITT, Derek. b 41. K Coll Lon BD 63 AKC 63. **d** 64 **p** 65. C Blackb St Jas 64–67; C Burnley St Pet 67–69; V Foulridge 69–74; V Euxton 74–91; V Penwortham St Mary 91–00; P-in-c Halton w Aughton 00–06; rtd 06; PtO *Blackb* from 06. *84 Lymm Avenue, Lancaster LA1 5HR* E: draitt@wightcablenorth.net

RAITT, Hannah Elizabeth. b 92. Homerton Coll Cam BA 13 MA 17 St Jo Coll Dur BA 17 MA 18. Cranmer Hall Dur 15. **d** 18 **p** 19. C Bankfoot and Bowling St Steph

Leeds from 18. *St Matthew's Vicarage, Carr Bottom Road, Bradford BD5 9AA* E: hannah.e.raitt@gmail.com *or* hannah.raitt@leeds.anglican.org

RAJ-SINGH, Reji. b 52. Sidney Webb Coll of Educn CertEd 79 N Lon Poly BEd 90 Heythrop Coll Lon MA 02. SAOMC 02. **d** 05 **p** 06. NSM Paddington St Jas *Lon* 05–11; NSM Paddington St Mary Magd and St Pet 11–17; PtO from 17; *Sarum* 18–21; NSM Dorchester and the Winterbournes from 21. *29 Peverell Avenue East, Poundbury, Dorchester DT1 3RH* M: 07983-430050 E: reji4@btinternet.com

RAJA, Canon John Christopher Joshva. b 65. Serampore Coll MTh 93 Leic Univ MA 96. **d** 93 **p** 94. India 93–95; Hon C Leic H Spirit 95–96; Hon C Edin H Cross 96–99; Tutor Qu Foundn Birm 00–12; R Curdworth, Middleton and Wishaw *Birm* 12–18; Hon Can Birm Cathl 18; Academic Co-ord Barnabas Fund from 18; NSM Wellsprings *Sarum* 18–21; Hd Internat Bible Advocacy Cen from 21. *Address temp unknown* E: joshvajohn@yahoo.co.uk

RAJKOVIC, Michael. b 52. Sheff Univ BMet 74 MMet 75 PhD 79 St Jo Coll Nottm MA 95 Lon Bible Coll MPhil 03. **d** 95 **p** 96. C Harrow Weald All SS *Lon* 95–98; C Woodford Wells *Chelmsf* 98–02; V Bricket Wood *St Alb* 02–15; TR Maltby *Sheff* from 15; P-in-c Thurcroft 15–21; P-in-c Laughton-en-le-Morthen and Throapham from 18. *The Rectory, 69 Blyth Road, Maltby, Rotherham S66 7LF* T: (01709) 814914 E: mikerajkovic@btinternet.com *or* michael.rajkovic@sheffield.anglican.org

RAKE, David John. b 47. Nottm Univ BA 68 PhD 73. Wycliffe Hall Ox 73. **d** 74 **p** 75. C Radcliffe-on-Trent *S'well* 74–77; P-in-c Upwell St Pet *Ely* 77–79; P-in-c Outwell 77–79; Chapl Warw Univ *Cov* 79–86; V Kenilworth St Nic 86–98; P-in-c Tintagel *Truro* 98–03; Bp's Adv on Spiritual Formation 98–03; Dioc Adv 03–08; rtd 08; PtO *Truro* from 09. *The Old Vicarage, Zennor, St Ives TR26 3BY* T: (01736) 796955

RALPH, Brian Charles. b 66. St Steph Ho Ox 89. **d** 92 **p** 93. C Yeovil St Mich *B & W* 92–95; TV St Jo on Bethnal Green *Lon* 95–01; P-in-c Bethnal Green St Barn 01–03; V from 03. *12 Chisenhale Road, London E3 5TG* T: (020) 7247 1448 *or* 8983 3426 *or* 8806 4130 E: brianralph@btinternet.com *or* frbrianralph@gmail.com

RALPH, Ms Caroline Susan. b 60. Birm Univ BA 81 UWE LLM 98. Westcott Ho Cam 04. **d** 06 **p** 07. C Crediton, Shobrooke and Sandford etc *Ex* 06–10; V Harborne St Pet *Birm* 10–13; R Dunster, Carhampton, Withycombe w Rodhuish etc *B & W* from 13; RD Exmoor from 17. *The Rectory, Church Lane, Carhampton, Minehead TA24 6NT* E: caroline@249ralph.eclipse.co.uk

RALPH, Canon Nicholas Robert. b 63. Lanc Univ BSc 85 Trin Coll Cam BA 91. Westcott Ho Cam 89. **d** 92 **p** 93. C Fareham H Trin *Portsm* 92–95; C Portsea St Cuth 95–96; V Hayling Is St Andr 96–03; V N Hayling St Pet 96–03; Soc Resp Adv 03–06; Hd Miss and Soc from 06; Hon Can Portsm Cathl 06–09; Can Res Portsm Cathl from 09. *First Floor, Peninsular House, Wharf Road, Portsmouth PO2 8HB* T: (023) 9289 9674 E: nick@ralphy.org *or* nick.ralph@portsmouth.anglican.org

RALPH, Richard Gale. b 51. Pemb Coll Ox BA 73 MA 78 DPhil 78 FRSA 90. S Dios Minl Tr Scheme 84. **d** 87 **p** 88. NSM St Leonards Ch Ch and St Mary etc *Chich* from 87; NSM St Pancras H Cross w St Jude and St Pet *Lon* 87–94; Prin Westmr Coll Ox 96–00. *St Alban, 11 The Mount, St Leonards-on-Sea TN38 0HR* T: (01424) 422722 E: wea@nildram.co.uk

RALPHS, Sharon Ann. *See* SIMPSON, Sharon Ann

RAMPTON, Paul Michael. b 47. St Jo Coll Dur BA 69 MA 73 K Coll Lon PhD 85 Westmr Coll Ox MTh 99 AKC 20. Wycliffe Hall Ox 72. **d** 73 **p** 74. C Folkestone H Trin w Ch Ch *Cant* 73–77; P-in-c Ringwould w Oxney 77–79; P-in-c Kingsdown 77–79; R Ringwould w Kingsdown 79–83; V Maidstone St Paul 83–88; V Maidstone St Martin 88–95; V Steyning *Chich* 95–12; R Ashurst 95–12; RD Storrington 99–03; rtd 12; Dioc Warden of Readers *Chich* from 12; Chapl Gen CSP from 20. *54 Greenacres, Shoreham-by-Sea BN43 5WY* T: (01273) 271488

RAMPTON, Canon Valerie Edith. b 41. Nottm Univ BSc 63 MSc 66 BA 79. Gilmore Course 78. dss 82 **d** 87 **p** 94. Sneinton St Chris w St Phil *S'well* 80–87; Par Dn 87–88; Par Dn Stapleford 88–93; Dioc Adv on Women in Min 90–01; Dn-in-c Kneesall w Laxton and Wellow 93–94; V 94–02; Hon Can S'well Minster 97–02; rtd 02; PtO *Linc* from 02; *S'well* from 02. *Tansy Cottage, Hillside, Beckingham, Lincoln LN5 0RQ* T: (01636) 626665 E: valerie.rampton@waitrose.com

RAMSARAN, Susan Mira. b 49. K Coll Lon BA 70 Univ Coll Lon MA 72 PhD 78. Ripon Coll Cuddesdon 82. **d** 93 **p** 94. C Selling w Throwley, Sheldwich w Badlesmere etc *Cant* 93–97; P-in-c Shipbourne *Roch* 97–99; P-in-c Plaxtol 97–99; R Shipbourne w Plaxtol 99–06; RD Shoreham 01–06;

TR N Tyne and Redesdale *Newc* 06–20; AD Bellingham 06–16; rtd 20; PtO *Newc* 20–21. *West View, Wark, Hexham NE48 3LG* E: smramsaran@aol.com

RAMSAY, Canon Alan Burnett. b 34. AKC 62. **d** 63 **p** 64. C Clapham H Trin *S'wark* 63–67; C Warlingham w Chelsham and Farleigh 67–71; P-in-c Stockwell St Mich 71–78; V Lingfield 78–85; P-in-c Crowhurst 83–85; V Lingfield and Crowhurst 85–92; RD Godstone 88–92; V Mitcham St Mark 92–00; Hon Can S'wark Cathl 93–00; rtd 00; PtO *Cant* 00–21; *S & B* from 10. *Kent House, 9 Scotton Street, Wye, Ashford TN25 5BU* T: (01233) 813730 E: aramsay@talktalk.net

RAMSAY, Christopher. b 68. St Jo Coll Dur BA 90 Heythrop Coll Lon MA 09. Wycliffe Hall Ox BTh 94. **d** 97 **p** 98. C Cricklewood St Gabr and St Mich *Lon* 97–01; P-in-c Southall St Geo 01–06; V from 06; AD Ealing 10–15; Dir of Ords Willesden Area 18–20; Dir of Miss from 20. *1 Lancaster Road, Southall UB1 1NP* T: (020) 8574 1876 M: 07818-444894 E: christopher.ramsay@btinternet.com

RAMSAY, James Anthony. b 52. Wadh Coll Ox BA 75 MA. **d** 86 **p** 87. C Olney w Emberton *Ox* 86–89; V Blackbird Leys 89–02; Chapl Bucharest w Sofia *Eur* 02–05; P-in-c Lt Ilford St Barn *Chelmsf* 05–10; V 10–17; Chapl E Lon Univ 05–17; rtd 17; PtO *Nor* from 17. *Lawn Cottage, Edgefield Road, Briston, Melton Constable NR24 2HX* T: (01263) 502309 M: 07985-993191 E: ramsay.jas@gmail.com

RAMSAY, Kerry. *See* TUCKER, Kerry

RAMSAY, Max Roy MacGregor. b 34. Ball Coll Ox MA 58. Qu Coll Birm 82. **d** 84 **p** 85. C Hale *Ches* 84–86; C Nantwich 87; V Haslington w Crewe Green 87–91; P-in-c Dunham Massey St Marg and St Mark 92–95; rtd 95; PtO *Ches* 95–14. *6 Comber Way, Knutsford WA16 9BT* T: (01565) 632362 E: mrm.ramsay@ntlworld.com *or* maxtmramsay@gmail.com

RAMSBOTTOM, David James. b 48. **d** 12 **p** 13. NSM Crowthorne *Ox* 12–18; PtO from 18. *15 Corbett Road, Carterton OX18 3LG* M: 07986-852970 E: d.j.ramsbottom@btinternet.com

RAMSBOTTOM, Canon Julie Frances. b 54. Trevelyan Coll Dur BA 76. S'wark Ord Course 88. **d** 91 **p** 94. Par Dn Bray and Braywood *Ox* 91–94; C 94–97; R W Woodhay w Enborne, Hampstead Marshall etc 97–11; P-in-c Kintbury w Avington 05–11; R Finchampstead and California 11–20; AD Sonning 13–18; Hon Can Ch 16–20; rtd 20. *15 Corbett Road, Carterton OX18 3LG* E: julie.ramsbottom@talk21.com

RAMSBOTTOM, Susan Elizabeth. *See* POLLARD, Susan Elizabeth

RAMSBURY, Area Bishop of. *See* RUMSEY, The Rt Revd Andrew Paul

✠**RAMSDEN, The Rt Revd Peter Stockton.** b 51. Univ Coll Lon BSc 74 Leeds Univ MA 92. Coll of Resurr Mirfield 74. **d** 77 **p** 78 **c** 07. C Houghton le Spring *Dur* 77–80; C S Shields All SS 80–83; Papua New Guinea 83–90 and 93–96; P-in-c Micklefield *York* 90–93; V Long Benton *Newc* 96–07; Bp Port Moresby 07–14; rtd 14; Hon Asst Bp Carl from 15. *Brampton Fell Cottage, Tarn Road, Brampton CA8 1HN* T: (016977) 41851 E: bishopramsden@gmail.com

RAMSDEN, Raymond Leslie. b 49. Open Univ BA 86. **d** 78 **p** 79. C Greenhill St Jo *Lon* 78–85; C Staines St Mary and St Pet 85–90; V Hounslow St Steph 90–19; rtd 19; PtO *St E* from 19. *58 Castle Brooks, Framlington, Woodbridge IP13 9SF*

RAMSEY, Christopher John. b 76. St Jo Coll Nottm BA 07. **d** 07 **p** 08. C Saxmundham w Kelsale cum Carlton *St E* 07–10; V Gt Cornard from 10; C Sudbury w Ballingdon and Brundon from 19; RD Sudbury from 21. *The Vicarage, 95 Bures Road, Great Cornard, Sudbury CO10 0JE* T: (01787) 376293 E: revchrisramsey@gmail.com

RAMSEY, The Ven Victoria Claire. b 71. **d** 11 **p** 12. C Ex St Mark, St Sidwell and St Matt 11–18; Ch Growth and Planting Enabler *S'well* 18–21; Adn Newark from 21. *Goverton Hill, Goverton, Bleasby, Nottingham NG14 7FN* M: 07803-431069 E: victoria.ramsey@southwell.anglican.org

RAMSEY-HARDY, Stuart John Andrew. b 46. St Jo Coll Dur BA 69. Wycliffe Hall Ox 69. **d** 74 **p** 75. C Stoke Newington St Mary *Lon* 74–77; C Hersham *Guildf* 78–79; Hon C Thames Ditton 79–83; rtd 11. *Villa Tristana, 83040 Guardia dei Lombardi AV, Italy* T: (0039) (389) 486 2681 E: ramsey.hardy@gmail.com

RANCE, Canon Eleanor Jane. b 72. K Coll Lon BA 93 AKC 93 St Jo Coll Dur MA 96. Cranmer Hall Dur 94. **d** 96 **p** 97. C Barnes *S'wark* 96–99; Chapl RAF 99–10; PtO *Blackb* 10–13; P-in-c Wylye and Till Valley *Sarum* 13; V Salisbury Plain from 14; RD Stonehenge from 15; Can and Preb Sarum Cathl from 16. *The Rectory, Chapel Lane, Shrewton, Salisbury SP3 4BX* T: (01980) 620580 E: reveleanorrance@gmail.com

RAND, Stacey Elizabeth. b 82. Qu Coll Cam BA 04 MA 08 Dur Univ BA 19 Kent Univ PhD 20. SEITE 13. **d** 16 **p** 17. NSM Hackington *Cant* 16–19; NSM Herne from

19; NSM Kent Univ from 19. *Address withheld by request* E: staceyelizabethrand@hotmail.com

RANDALL, Benjamin Thomas. b 84. St Andr Univ MA 06 Bradf Univ MA 08. Ridley Hall Cam 11. **d** 14 **p** 15. C Pudsey St Lawr and St Paul *Leeds* from 14; V McMinnville St Matt USA from 17. *105 Edgewood Avenue, McMinnville TN 37110, USA* T: (001) (931) 473 8233 E: benjamin.t.randall@hotmail.com

RANDALL, Bernard Charles. b 72. St Andr Univ MA 95 Edin Univ MSc 97 Man Univ PhD 04. St Steph Ho Ox BA 06. **d** 06 **p** 07. C Bury St Mary *Man* 06–07; C Atherton and Hindsford w Howe Bridge 07–09; C Sale St Paul *Ches* 09–11; Chapl Ch Coll Cam 11–15; Chapl Trent Coll Nottm 15–20. *2 Brecon Close, Long Eaton, Nottingham NG10 4JW* T: 0115-972 3971

RANDALL, Colin Antony. b 57. SS Paul & Mary Coll Cheltenham BEd 78. Trin Coll Bris BD 84. **d** 84 **p** 85. C Denton Holme *Carl* 84–87; C Brampton RD 87–90; R Hanborough and Freeland *Ox* 90–99; P-in-c Croglin *Carl* 99–09; P-in-c Holme Eden 99–05; P-in-c Wetheral w Warwick 99–05; R Holme Eden and Wetheral w Warwick 05–09; RD Brampton 05–09; Hon Can Carl Cathl 08–09; P-in-c Barrow *Ches* 09–10; R 10–14; Dioc Worship Adv 09–14; P-in-c Sevenhampton w Charlton Abbots, Hawling etc *Glouc* from 14; R from 16. *The Rectory, Station Road, Andoversford, Cheltenham GL54 4LA* T: (01242) 820631 E: carandall93@gmail.com

RANDALL, Preb Colin Michael Sebastian. b 50. Aston Univ BSc 72. Qu Coll Birm 72. **d** 75 **p** 76. C Tonge w Alkrington *Man* 75–78; C Elton All SS 78–82; P-in-c Bridgwater H Trin *B & W* 82–86; V 86–90; V Bishops Hull 90–00; Chapl St Marg Hospice Taunton 90–00; TR Wellington and Distr *B & W* 00–12; Preb Wells Cathl 05–12; rtd 12; PtO *Ex* from 13. *16 The Rosemullion, Cliff Road, Budleigh Salterton EX9 6LA* E: colin.randall@outlook.com

RANDALL, Elizabeth Nicola. *See* BILLETT, Elizabeth Nicola

RANDALL, Evelyn. b 49. **d** 10 **p** 11. NSM Dormansland *S'wark* 10–15; NSM Lingfield and Dormansland 15–16; NSM Godstone and Blindley Heath 16–17; PtO from 17. *58 Hickmans Close, Godstone RH9 8EB* T: (01883) 742751

RANDALL, Gordon Charles. b 58. STETS BA 11. **d** 11 **p** 12. NSM Chineham *Win* 11–19; C Alton from 19. *The Vicarage, 7 Church Lane, Holybourne, Alton GU34 4HD* M: 07913-742208

RANDALL, Ian Neville. b 39. Oriel Coll Ox BA 62 MA 65. St Steph Ho Ox 62. **d** 65 **p** 66. C Perivale *Lon* 65–68; C Fulham St Jo Walham Green 68–73; C Cowley St Jas *Ox* 73–79; TV 79–82; V Didcot St Pet 82–93; P-in-c Clewer St Andr 93–04; rtd 04. *12 Westmead Road, Fakenham NR21 8BL* T: (01328) 862443 E: iandfrandall@tiscali.co.uk

RANDALL, Canon John Terence. b 29. St Cath Coll Cam BA 52 MA 59. Ely Th Coll 52. **d** 54 **p** 55. C Luton Ch Ch *St Alb* 54; C Dunstable 54–57; C Ely 57–60; C March St Jo 60–62; Area Sec (S Midl) UMCA 62–64; Area Sec USPG Birm and Cov 65–76; P-in-c Avon Dassett w Farnborough *Cov* 76–78; P-in-c Fenny Compton 76–78; R Avon Dassett w Farnborough and Fenny Compton 78–84; V New Bilton 84–94; RD Rugby 89–94; Hon Can Cov Cathl 93–94; rtd 94; PtO *Cov* from 94; *Pet* from 94; *Leic* 96–21. *52 Cymbeline Way, Rugby CV22 6LA* T: (01788) 816659 E: fatherjohnrandall@gmail.com

RANDALL, Jonathan Aubrey. b 64. Bris Univ BSc 85. Ridley Hall Cam 04. **d** 06 **p** 07. C Hemingford Grey *Ely* 06–09; C Hemingford Abbots 06–09; V Yaxley and Holme w Conington 09–18; P-in-c Farcet Hampton 09–12; Jt RD Yaxley 16–18; C Huntingdon St Barn and the Riptons 18–19; C Huntingdon All SS w St Jo St Mary etc 18–19; R Huntingdon from 19; Bp's Change Officer w Resp for Market Towns from 21. *St Barnabas' Vicarage, Coneygear Road, Huntingdon PE29 1RQ* E: huntingdon.vicar@gmail.com

RANDALL, Julian Adrian. b 45. Open Univ BA 78 Stirling Univ MSc 94 St Andr Univ PhD 01 MCIPD. St Jo Sem Wonersh 68. **d** 70 **p** 71. Asst P Mortlake w E Sheen *S'wark* 71–72; Asst P Welling 72–74; Asst P Tunbridge Wells H Trin w Ch Ch *Roch* 74–79; NSM Dunfermline *St And* 96–98; P-in-c Elie and Earlsferry 98–03; P-in-c Pittenweem 98–03; Asst P St Andrews St Andr 03–05; Dir Progr Business Sch St Andr Univ 03–05; Sen Lect Aber Univ *Ab* from 05. *Flat D, 10 Shearwater Crescent, Dunfermline KY11 8JX* T: (01224) 273571 E: drjulianrandall@gmail.com

RANDALL, Kelvin John. b 49. JP 80. K Coll Lon BD 71 AKC 71 Birm Univ PGCE 72 Trin Coll Carmarthen MPhil 97 Univ of Wales (Ban) PhD 00. St Jo Coll Nottm 73. **d** 74 **p** 75. C Peckham St Mary Magd *S'wark* 74–78; C Portsdown *Portsm* 78–81; C-in-c Crookhorn Ch Cen CD 81–82; R Bedhampton 82–90; Bp's Chapl for Post-Ord Tr 84–89; RD Havant 87–89; P-in-c Bournemouth St Jo w St Mich *Win* 90–94; V 94–97; Chapl Talbot Heath Sch Bournemouth 90–94; Research Fell

Trin Coll Carmarthen 97–00; C Portswood St Denys *Win* 00–02; P-in-c 02–15; rtd 15; Visiting Research Fell Glyndŵr Univ from 10; PtO *Win* from 16. *28 Ravenshall, 19-21 West Cliff Road, Bournemouth BH4 8AT* T: (01202) 244818 E: k.randall@glyndwr.ac.uk *or* kelvinjohnrandall@gmail.com

RANDALL, Mrs Lynda Lorraine. b 44. Sarum & Wells Th Coll 89. **d** 91 **p** 94. Par Dn Chesterton St Andr *Ely* 91–94; C 94–95; C Linton 95–96; TV 96–99; R Byfield w Boddington and Aston le Walls *Pet* 99–10; rtd 10; PtO *Pet* from 12; *Ox* from 16. *14 Smithland Court, Greens Norton, Towcester NN12 8DA* T: (01327) 350203

RANDALL, Miss Marian Sally. b 49. Trin Coll Bris 75. dss 80 **d** 87 **p** 94. Peckham St Mary Magd *S'wark* 80–83; Sutton Ch Ch 83–97; Par Dn 87–94; C 94–97; P-in-c S Merstham 97–08; rtd 08; PtO *Cant* 09–12; *S'wark* from 14. *4 Vision Place, 8 Oxford Road, Redhill RH1 1QE* T: (01737) 764169 E: marian.randall@btinternet.com

RANDALL, Martin Trevor. b 51. St Jo Coll Dur BA 74. Trin Coll Bris 74. **d** 77 **p** 78. C Ashton-upon-Mersey St Mary Magd *Ches* 77–80; C Everton St Sav w St Cuth *Liv* 80–82; V W Derby Gd Shep 82–91; P-in-c Toxteth Park Ch Ch 91–94; P-in-c Toxteth Park St Bede 91–94; V Toxteth Park Ch Ch w St Bede 95–97; Chapl HM Pris Altcourse 97–07; PtO *Liv* 07–18; *Ab* from 19. *7 Greenwell, Gott, Shetland ZE2 9UL* T: (01595) 840784 M: 07717-845518 E: martinrandall51@gmail.com

RANDLE-BISSELL, Alexander Paul. b 71. **d** 12 **p** 13. C E Green *Cov* 12–15; P-in-c Pastrow *Win* 15–20; V from 20. *The Rectory, Chalkcroft Lane, Penton Mewsey, Andover SP11 0RD* M: 07717-778853 E: revdalex@me.com

RANDOLPH-HORN, David Henry. b 47. Nottm Univ BA 69 CQSW 71 Leeds Beckett Univ PhD 15. Qu Coll Birm 80. **d** 82 **p** 83. C Hamstead St Paul *Birm* 82–84; V Aston St Jas 84–94; Hon C Leytonstone H Trin and St Aug Harrow Green *Chelmsf* 93–99; Sec Inner Cities Relig Coun 94–99; Assoc Dir Leeds Ch Inst 99–07; P-in-c Heptonstall *Wakef* 99–02; Hon C Farnley *Ripon* 03; Leeds St Marg and All Hallows 07–18. *23 Spencer Place, Leeds LS7 4DQ* T: 0113-229 7546 E: davidhrh23@outlook.com

RANGER, Keith Brian. b 34. Down Coll Cam BA 58 MA 63. Glas NSM Course 58. **d** 81 **p** 82. OMF Internat 81–99; Ethnic Min Co-ord 90–99; Hong Kong 81–89; PtO *Ches* 89–93; *Man* 93–99; rtd 99; PtO *Ches* 99–02 and 06–17; Hon C Macclesfield Team 02–06; PtO *York* from 17. *12 Dulverton Hall, Esplanade, Scarborough YO11 2AR* T: (01723) 350307 M: 07779-528997 E: keithranger73@gmail.com

RANKIN, John. *See* RANKIN, William John Alexander

RANKIN, Stephen Brian. b 65. Salford Univ BSc 88. Trin Coll Bris 95. **d** 97 **p** 98. C Ashton-upon-Mersey St Mary Magd *Ches* 97–06; V from 06. *St Mary's Vicarage, 20 Beeston Road, Sale M33 5AG* T: 0161-973 5118 E: srankin@stmarysaom.org

RANKIN, Canon William John Alexander. b 45. Van Mildert Coll Dur BA 68 Fitzw Coll Cam BA 73 MA 77. Westcott Ho Cam 71. **d** 74 **p** 75. C St John's Wood *Lon* 74–78; Chapl Clifton Coll Bris 78–86; P-in-c The Claydons *Ox* 86–91; R 91–93; R Clare w Poslingford, Cavendish etc *St E* 93–04; R Stour Valley 04–10; Hon Can St E Cathl 05–10; rtd 10; PtO *St E* 10–20; *Pet* from 11. *12 Hawthorn Drive, Uppingham, Oakham LE15 9TA* T: (01572) 822180 E: therankins123@gmail.com

RANKINE, Christopher Barry. b 66. Portsm Poly BA 88. Linc Th Coll BTh 93. **d** 93 **p** 95. C Farlington *Portsm* 93–96; C Alverstoke 96–98; C Romsey *Win* 98–00; P-in-c W Andover 00–09; TR Portway and Danebury 09–13; V Eastcote St Lawr *Lon* 13–19; V Walham Green St Jo w St Jas from 19. *St John's Vicarage, 40 Racton Road, London SW6 1LP* T: (020) 7385 7634 M: 07766-475743 E: chris.rankine@icloud.com

RANSLEY, Steven Edward. b 82. Cardiff Univ LLB 03. Oak Hill Th Coll BA 15. **d** 16 **p** 17. C Cornerstone Team *Leic* 16–19; TV from 19. *The Rectory, 18 Main Street, Houghton-on-the-Hill, Leicester LE7 9GD* T: 0116-241 6895 M: 07977-298838 E: steve@houghtonchurch.co.uk

RANSOM, Adam John. b 85. Chich Univ BA 07 Sheff Univ MA 15. Coll of Resurr Mirfield 13. **d** 15 **p** 16. C Eastbourne Ch Ch and St Phil *Chich* from 15; P-in-c Hampden Park and The Hydneye from 18. *60 Brassey Avenue, Eastbourne BN22 9QH* T: (01323) 502738 E: fradamransom@beneficeofhampdenpark.co.uk

RANSOM, Nigel Lester. b 60. Leeds Univ BA 81. Wycliffe Hall Ox 83 SE Asia Sch of Th MTh 83. **d** 85 **p** 86. C Gidea Park *Chelmsf* 85–88; C Widford 88–91; Chapl St Jo Hosp Chelmsf 88–91; V Eastwood *Chelmsf* 91–10; PtO *St E* from 10; *Nor* from 10; *Ely* from 16. *86 Nunnery Drive, Thetford IP24 3EP* T: (01842) 820922 E: nlran@btinternet.com

RANSON, Canon Arthur Frankland. b 50. St Jo Coll Dur BA 73. Wycliffe Hall Ox 73. **d** 75 **p** 76. C Bare *Blackb* 75–78; C Scotforth 78–81; V Leyland St Ambrose 81–02; AD Leyland 96–02; P-in-c Blackb St Silas 02–15; Hon

Can Blackb Cathl 00–15; rtd 15; PtO *Blackb* from 15. *6 Hazlewood, Silverdale, Carnforth LA5 0TQ* T: (01524) 702959 E: arthur.ranson@ntlworld.com

RANYARD, Michael Taylor. b 43. Nottm Univ BTh 74. Linc Th Coll 71. **d** 74 **p** 75. C Sutton in Ashfield St Mary *S'well* 74–76; Hon C Lewisham St Mary *S'wark* 76–77; C Rushmere *St E* 77–79; R Hopton, Market Weston, Barningham etc 79–83; Chr Educn and Resources Adv *Dur* 83–93; Prin Adv to Dioc Bd of Educn *Blackb* 93–98; Asst P Blackb Cathl 98–99; rtd 99; PtO *Heref* from 99. *72 Wyedean Rise, Belmont, Hereford HR2 7XZ* T/F: (01432) 355452 E: sm@ranyard.plus.com

RAO, Norma Ruoman. b 63. Westmr Coll Ox BTh 97 Anglia Ruskin Univ MA 05. Westcott Ho Cam 99. **d** 01 **p** 02. C Endcliffe *Sheff* 01–04; C Rotherham 04–08; R Rossington 08–15; V W Acklam *York* from 15. *The Vicarage, 50 Church Lane, Middlesbrough TS5 7EB* E: norma.rao@btinternet.com

RAPHOE, Archdeacon of. *See* HUSS, The Ven David Ian

RAPHOE, Dean of. *Vacant*

RAPLEY, Mrs Joy Naomi. b 41. Portsm Poly CertEd 63 Open Univ BA 79. Sarum & Wells Th Coll 87. **d** 89 **p** 94. Par Dn Welwyn Garden City *St Alb* 89–92; Chapl S Beds Community Healthcare Trust 92–98; C Wilbury *St Alb* 94–95; NSM St Mary's Bay w St Mary-in-the-Marsh etc *Cant* 98–02; NSM New Romney w Old Romney and Midley 98–02; Asst Chapl E Kent NHS and Soc Care Partnership Trust 99–02; P-in-c Clopton w Otley, Swilland and Ashbocking *St E* 02–08; PtO 08–17; *Cant* from 18. *20 Rogersmead, Tenterden TN30 6LF* T: (01580) 762391 E: revraps@aol.com

RAPSEY, Preb Peter Nigel. b 46. K Coll Lon BD 68 AKC 68. St Boniface Warminster. **d** 69 **p** 70. C Walton-on-Thames *Guildf* 69–73; C Fleet 73–77; P-in-c The Collingbournes and Everleigh *Sarum* 77–79; TV Wexcombe 79–84; R Wokingham St Paul *Ox* 84–93; Chapl Warminster Sch 93–96; V Frome Ch Ch *B & W* 96–04; P-in-c Evercreech w Chesterblade and Milton Clevedon 04–11; RD Frome 01–03; Dir of Ords 03–11; Preb Wells Cathl 04–11; rtd 11; PtO *Ex* from 12. *3A Saxon Close, Crediton EX17 3DS* T: (01363) 774068 E: peter.rapsey@btinternet.com

RAPSON, Jonathan David. b 95. Wycliffe Hall Ox 16. **d** 19 **p** 20. C Gt Stanmore *Lon* from 19. *Church House Cottage, Old Church Lane, Stanmore HA7 2QX* M: 07557-808527 E: jonny.rapson@hotmail.com

RAPSON, Tina Angela. b 62. **d** 16 **p** 17. NSM Uxbridge *Lon* from 16. *30 Station Road, Uxbridge UB8 3AA* T: (01895) 813923 M: 07867-557472 E: tina.rapson247@hotmail.co.uk

RATCLIFF, Canon David William. b 37. Edin Th Coll 59. **d** 62 **p** 63. C Croydon St Aug *Cant* 62–65; C Selsdon St Jo w St Fran 65–69; V Milton Regis St Mary 69–75; Hon Min Can Cant Cathl 75–91; Asst Dir of Educn 75–91; Dioc Adv in Adult Educn and Lay Tr 75–91; Hon Pres Protestant Assn for Adult Educn in Eur 82–88; Chapl Frankfurt-am-Main 91–98; Adn Scandinavia *Eur* 96–05; Chapl Stockholm w Gävle and Västerås 98–02; rtd 05; PtO *Cant* from 02; *Eur* from 19. *9 The Orchards, Elham, Canterbury CT4 6TR* T: (01303) 840624 F: 840871 E: archdeacon.david@zen.co.uk

RATCLIFF, Paul Ronald. b 62. Univ Coll Lon BSc 83 Leic Univ MSc 84 PhD 89 FRAS MInstP. SEITE 05. **d** 09 **p** 10. C Cant St Martin and St Paul 09–12; R King's Wood 12–19; AD W Bridge 14–19; P-in-c Stonegate *Chich* 19–20; P-in-c Tidebrook 19–20; P-in-c Wadhurst 19–20; V Wadhurst, Tidebrook and Stonegate from 20. *The Vicarage, High Street, Wadhurst TN5 6AA* E: pr.ratcliff@gmail.com

RATCLIFFE, Elizabeth Clare. b 65. Leeds Univ BSc 87 York Univ DPhil 91. Ox Min Course 12. **d** 15 **p** 16. C Reading Ch Ch *Ox* 15–18; R Tilehurst St Mich from 18. *Tilehurst Rectory, Routh Lane, Tilehurst, Reading RG30 4JY* M: 07752-388707 E: liz-ratcliffe@live.co.uk *or* office@stmichaelstilehurst.org.uk

RATCLIFFE, Canon Michael David. b 43. Lon Univ BSc 65 Southn Univ PGCE 67 Lon Univ BA 75 Lanc Univ MA 84. Cranmer Hall Dur 75. **d** 77 **p** 78. C Blackpool St Thos *Blackb* 77–81; V Oswaldtwistle St Paul 81–10; RD Accrington 97–03; Hon Can Blackb Cathl 00–10; rtd 10; PtO *Blackb* from 10. *8 Stanhill Road, Oswaldtwistle, Accrington BB5 4PP* E: mratossy@tiscali.co.uk

RATCLIFFE, Nicholas Hugh Bernard. b 61. **d** 12 **p** 13. NSM Chartham *Cant* 12–14; NSM Chartham and Upper Hardres w Stelling 14–15; C Cliftonville 15–19; C Aylesham from 19. *The Rectory, Dorman Avenue North, Aylesham, Canterbury CT3 3BL* T: (01304) 274959 M: 07599-406059 E: nick.ratcliffe@outlook.com

RATCLIFFE, Peter Graham Bruce. St Mich Coll Llan. **d** 08 **p** 09. C Carmarthen St Pet *St D* 08–09; C E Carmarthen 09–10; P-in-c Llanpumsaint w Llanllawddog 10–15; P-in-c Cilgerran w Bridell and Llantwyd and Eglwyswrw 15–18; P-in-c Bro Teifi from 18. *The Rectory, Penllyn, Cilgerran, Cardigan SA43 2RZ* T: (01239) 612511 E: peter@revpeter.plus.com

RATE, Susan. *See* LEIGHTON, Susan

RATHBAND, The Very Revd Kenneth William. b 60. Edin Univ BD 86. Edin Th Coll 82. **d** 86 **p** 87. C Dundee St Paul *Bre* 86–88; TV Dundee St Martin 88–89; C Edin SS Phil and Jas 90–91; R Alyth *St And* 91–18; R Blairgowrie 91–18; R Coupar Angus 91–18; R Dunfermline from 18; R Lunan Head from 18; Can St Ninian's Cathl Perth from 05; Dean St Andr from 07. *17 Ardeer Place, Dunfermline KY11 4YX* E: krathband@btinternet.com *or* abcsaints@btinternet.com

RATHBONE, Mrs Isobel. b 48. Girton Coll Cam MA 70 Leeds Univ MA 02 Solicitor 81. NEOC 02. **d** 05 **p** 06. NSM Moor Allerton *Ripon* 05–08; NSM Hooe and Ninfield *Chich* 08–09; NSM Guiseley w Esholt *Bradf* 10–13; P-in-c Batheaston w St Cath *B & W* 13–18; rtd 18; PtO *B & W* from 18. *Meadowcroft House, Draughton, Skipton BD23 6EB* M: 07775-656257 E: isobel.rathbone@gmail.com

RATHBONE, Paul. b 36. BNC Ox BA 58 MA 62. Wycliffe Hall Ox 58. **d** 60 **p** 61. C Carl St Jo 60–63; C Heworth w Peasholme St Cuth *York* 63–68; V Thorganby w Skipwith and N Duffield 68–83; V Bishopthorpe and Acaster Malbis 83–01; rtd 01; PtO *York* from 01. *12 Whitelass Close, Thirsk YO7 1FG* T: (01845) 523347 E: paul2rathbone@btinternet.com

RATHBONE, Stephen Derek. b 61. Wycliffe Hall Ox. **d** 00 **p** 01. C W Kirby St Bridget *Ches* 00–03; P-in-c Rainow w Saltersford and Forest 03–10; V 10–20; rtd 20. *Address temp unknown*

RATTENBERRY, Christopher James. b 59. York Univ BA 80 Solicitor. St Jo Coll Nottm 91. **d** 93 **p** 94. C Porchester *S'well* 93–98; P-in-c Daybrook 98–04; V 04–06; AD Nottm N 01–05; P-in-c Ravenshead 06–11; V 11–17; rtd 17; P-in-c Danby w Castleton and Commondale *York* 18–19; P-in-c Moorsholm 18–19; P-in-c Westerdale 18–19; TV Oakham, Ashwell, Braunston, Brooke, Egleton etc *Pet* from 19. *45 Trent Road, Oakham LE15 6HE* E: revdcjr@aol.com

✠RATTERAY, The Rt Revd Alexander Ewen. b 42. Codrington Coll Barbados 61. **d** 65 **p** 66 **c** 96. C S Kirkby *Wakef* 66–68; C Sowerby St Geo 68–71; V Airedale w Fryston 71–80; Bermuda 80–08; Adn Bermuda 94–96; Bp Bermuda 96–08; rtd 08; PtO *York* from 09. *PO Box HM 2021, Hamilton HM JX, Bermuda* E: bishopratteray@logic.bm

RATTIGAN, Canon Paul Damian. b 61. Reading Univ BSc 87 Liv Hope MA 00 Sussex Univ PGCE 88. Qu Coll Birm 93. **d** 95 **p** 96. C Parr *Liv* 95–99; P-in-c St Helens St Matt Thatto Heath 99–01; V 01–05; P-in-c Boldmere *Birm* 05–08; V 08–13; Can Res Liv Cathl 13–19; Can Res and Chan Leic Cathl from 19; Dir of Ords from 19. *Leicester Cathedral, St Martin's House, 7 Peacock Lane, Leicester LE1 5PZ* T: 0116-261 5200

RATTUE, James. b 69. Ball Coll Ox BA 91 MA 04 Leic Univ MA 93. St Steph Ho Ox 03. **d** 05 **p** 06. C Weybridge *Guildf* 05–08 and 09; C Englefield Green 08–09; R Farncombe from 09. *The Rectory, 38 Farncombe Hill, Godalming GU7 2AU* T: (01483) 860709 M: 07952-615499 E: jamesrattue@hotmail.com

RAVALDE, Canon Geoffrey Paul. b 54. St Cuth Soc Dur BA 76 SS Coll Cam BA 86 MA 90 Lon Univ MTh 91 Barrister 78. Westcott Ho Cam 84. **d** 87 **p** 88. C Spalding St Mary and St Nic *Linc* 87–91; P-in-c Wigton *Carl* 91–92; V from 92; P-in-c Thursby from 10; RD Carl 95–00; Hon Can Carl Cathl from 96; Chapl to The Queen from 14. *The Vicarage, Longthwaite Road, Wigton CA7 9JR* T: (016973) 42337 E: gpravalde@yahoo.co.uk

RAVEN, Ann. *See* GURNER, Margaret Ann

RAVEN, Canon Barry. b 48. Sarum & Wells Th Coll 69. **d** 72 **p** 73. C Henbury *Bris* 72–76; P-in-c S Marston w Stanton Fitzwarren 76–78; TV Stratton St Margaret w S Marston etc 78–80; P-in-c Coalpit Heath 80–84; V 84–91; R Ashton Keynes, Leigh and Minety 07–13; RD N Wilts 99–06; Hon Can Bris Cathl 12–13; rtd 13; PtO *Bris* from 14; *Glouc* from 14. *10 Springfields, Tetbury GL8 8EN* T: (01666) 505616 E: barry@deanery.org.uk

RAVEN, Canon Charles Frank. b 58. Magd Coll Ox BA 80 MA 86 St Jo Coll Dur BA 87 ACIB 84. Cranmer Hall Dur 85. **d** 88 **p** 89. C Heckmondwike *Wakef* 88–92; TV Kidderminster St Jo and H Innocents *Worc* 92–02; Abp's Officer for Angl Communion Affairs Kenya from 12; Hon Can All SS Cathl Nairobi from 16; PtO *Dur* 13–19. *Anglican Church of Kenya, PO Box 40502-00100, Nairobi, Kenya* T: (00254) (20) 2711 4755 M: 00254-716-835315 *or* 07789-934836 E: charlesraven@gafcon.org

RAVEN, Margaret Ann. *See* GURNER, Margaret Ann

RAVEN, Tony. b 39. Garnett Coll Lon CertEd 65. SAOMC 94. **d** 97 **p** 98. NSM Lt Berkhamsted and Bayford, Essendon etc *St Alb* 97–01; P-in-c Lt Hadham w Albury 01–05; rtd 05; Hon C Hazelbury Bryan and the Hillside Par *Sarum* 07–11; PtO *Ex*

from 11. *33 Liberty Way, Exeter EX2 7AS* T: (01392) 875150 E: tony@theravens.org *or* tonyraven39@john-lewis.com

RAVENSCROFT, Avril Shirley. b 46. **d** 11 **p** 12. NSM Prestbury *Ches* 11–21; NSM Upton Priory from 21. *17 Legh Road, Prestbury, Macclesfield SK10 4HX* T: (01625) 820041 E: avril.ravenscroft@zen.co.uk

RAWDING, Andrew. b 70. Cranmer Hall Dur 00. **d** 02 **p** 03. C Enfield St Andr *Lon* 02–05; Hon C Arm St Mark 05–07; Chapl RN 08–11; I Brackaville w Donaghendry and Ballyclog *Arm* from 11. *Holy Trinity Rectory, 82 Dungannon Road, Coalisland, Dungannon BT71 4HT* T: (028) 8774 0243 M: 07771-851838 E: andrewrawding@gmail.com *or* rectorcoalisland@gmail.com

RAWDON-MOGG, Timothy David. b 45. St Jo Coll Dur BA 76. Cuddesdon Coll 75. **d** 77 **p** 78. C Wotton St Mary *Glouc* 77–80; C Ascot Heath *Ox* 80–82; V Woodford Halse w Eydon *Pet* 82–88; V Shrivenham w Watchfield and Bourton *Ox* 88–00; R Horsted Keynes *Chich* 00–08; rtd 08; PtO *Heref* from 12; *Lich* 13–21. *Stone Cottage, The Bog, Minsterley, Shrewsbury SY5 0NJ* T: (01743) 792073 E: timrm@mail.com

RAWLING, Miss Jane Elizabeth. b 51. Birm Univ BSc 73 St Jo Coll York CertEd 75. St Jo Coll Nottm 81. **dss** 84 **d** 87 **p** 94. Southsea St Jude *Portsm* 84–88; C 87–88; C St Paul's Cray St Barn *Roch* 88–91; Hon C from 91; SE Regional Co-ord BCMS Crosslinks 91–01; Sec for Bps' Selection Conf and CME Sec Min Division 01–07. *89 Beddington Road, Orpington BR5 2TE* T: (020) 8309 2987 E: j.rawling@outlook.com

RAWLINGS, Elizabeth. b 66. Nottm Univ BSc 96 RGN 87. St Jo Coll Nottm 04. **d** 06 **p** 07. C Derby St Alkmund and St Werburgh 06–07; C Walbrook Epiphany 07–10; Min Hamilton CD *Leic* 10–19; Warden Past Assts 11–14; AD City of Leic 18–19; Discipleship and Voc Adv from 19. *12 Anstey Lane, Groby, Leicester LE6 0DA* M: 07947-533739 E: liz.rawlings@leccofe.org

RAWLINGS, Helen. b 54. **d** 13. NSM Brighton Gd Shep Preston *Chich* 13–18; NSM Helmsley *York* from 18; NSM Upper Ryedale from 18. *The Rectory, Old Byland, York YO62 5LG*

RAWLINGS, The Ven John Edmund Frank. b 47. AKC 69. St Aug Coll Cant 69. **d** 70 **p** 71. C Rainham *Roch* 70–73; C Tattenham Corner and Burgh Heath *Guildf* 73–76; Chapl RN 76–92; V Tavistock and Gulworthy *Ex* 92–05; Chapl Kelly Coll Tavistock 93–02; RD Tavistock *Ex* 97–02; Preb Ex Cathl 99–14; Adn Totnes 06–14; PtO from 15. *9 Rosemount Lane, Honiton EX14 1RJ* T: (01404) 43404 E: rawlings1@btinternet.com

RAWLINGS, Canon Philip John. b 53. St Jo Coll Nottm BTh 83. **d** 83 **p** 84. C Blackley St Andr *Man* 83–87; C Halliwell St Pet 87–93; R Old Trafford St Bride 93–11; AD Stretford 95–05; Borough Dean Trafford 10–11; Interfaith Officer Oldham from 11; Hon Can Man Cathl from 04. *68 Dudley Road, Manchester M16 8DE* T: 0161-232 0413 E: philjr053@gmail.com

RAWLINS, Mrs Nicola Jane Phillips. b 60. Newc Poly BA 86 Cant Ch Ch Univ BSc 10. St Aug Coll of Th BA 18. **d** 18 **p** 20. NSM Gillingham St Aug *Roch* from 18. *3 Marble Close, Gillingham ME7 2RB* T: (01634) 787660 E: nicky.rawlins@hotmail.co.uk

RAWLINSON, Curwen. b 32. MBE 73. Leeds Univ CertEd 55 Man Univ DipEd 56 Open Univ BA 80. Sarum Th Coll 59. **d** 61 **p** 62. C Wigan St Mich *Liv* 61–63; CF 63–78; Dep Asst Chapl Gen 78–80; Asst Chapl Gen 80–85; QHC 83–98; R Uley w Owlpen and Nympsfield *Glouc* 85–98; RD Dursley 89–96; rtd 98; PtO *Glouc* 98–19; Sessional Chapl HM Pris Glouc 02–13. *Cark House, 6 Groves Place, Fairford GL7 4BJ* T: (01285) 711009

RAWLINSON, Preb James Nigel. b 56. Em Coll Cam BA 77 MB, BCh 80 FRCSE 86 FFAEM 98. WMMTC 95. **d** 98 **p** 99. NSM Bath Weston All SS w N Stoke and Langridge *B & W* 98–16; Chapl Bath Univ from 16; PtO *Bris* 98–19; Consultant Bris R Infirmary from 99; Preb Wells Cathl *B & W* from 15. *The Chaplain's House, The Avenue, Claverton Down, Bath BA2 7AX* T: (01225) 386458 M: 07722-005452 E: email@nigelrawlinson.co.uk

RAWLINSON, John. b 47. Guy's Hosp Medical Sch BSc 67 MB, BS 71 MRCS. EAMTC 89. **d** 92 **p** 93. NSM Tilbrook *Ely* 92–05; NSM Covington 92–05; NSM Catworth Magna 92–05; NSM Keyston and Bythorn 92–05; Chapl Chu Coll Cam from 98. *The Malt House, 42 Stonely, Huntingdon PE28 0EH* T: (01480) 860263 F: 861590 E: jr338@cam.ac.uk

RAWSON, Canon Michael Graeme. b 62. York Univ BA 84. St Steph Ho Ox BA 88. **d** 89 **p** 90. C Brighouse St Martin *Wakef* 89–92; C Brighouse and Clifton 92–93; V Gomersal 93–04; Bp's Dom Chapl and Publicity Officer 04–07; Can Res Wakef Cathl 07–14; Can Res S'wark Cathl from 14; Vice Dean S'wark from 14; Min Bermondsey

St Hugh CD from 14. *73 St George's Road, London SE1 6ER*
E: michael.rawson@southwark.anglican.org

RAY, John Mead. b 28. OBE 79. St Andr Univ MA 50 DipEd 51. CMS Tr Coll Chislehurst 60. **d** 70 **p** 71. Miss Partner CMS 70–95; C Sparkhill St Jo *Birm* 87–90; C Sparkbrook Em 87–90; C Sparkhill w Greet and Sparkbrook 90; Deanery Missr 90–95; rtd 95; PtO *Birm* 95–14; *Sheff* 15–20. *2 Birchfield, Hook, Goole DN14 5NJ* T: (01405) 475238 M: 07506-563239 E: hardyraycj@gmail.com

RAY, Robin John. b 44. Sarum & Wells Th Coll 72. **d** 74 **p** 75. C Bourne Valley *Sarum* 74–78; P-in-c Dilton's-Marsh 78–82; V 82–87; V Taunton Lyngford *B & W* 87–93; R Exford, Exmoor, Hawkridge and Withypool 93–04; ACORA Link Officer and Rural Affairs Officer 93–04; rtd 04; PtO *B & W* from 04; RD Glastonbury 09–11. *Leigholt Farm, Somerton Road, Street BA16 0SU* T: (01458) 841281 M: 07772-563597 E: robinray@btinternet.com

RAYBOULD, James Clive Ransford. b 37. Wolv Univ BSc 62 Anglia Poly Univ MBA 94 PhD 01. Cranmer Hall Dur 81. **d** 83 **p** 84. C Cannock *Lich* 83–86; P-in-c Leek Wootton *Cov* 86–89; Dioc Tr Advr 86–89; TV Cannock *Lich* 89; Assoc Lect Anglia Ruskin Univ *Chelmsf* from 90; rtd 00. *29 Greystones, Bromham, Chippenham SN15 2JT* T: (01380) 859623

✠**RAYFIELD, The Rt Revd Lee Stephen.** b 55. Southn Univ BSc 78 Lon Univ PhD 81 SOSc 95. Ridley Hall Cam 93. **d** 93 **p** 94 **c** 05. C Woodford Wells *Chelmsf* 93–97; P-in-c Furze Platt *Ox* 97–05; AD Maidenhead and Windsor 00–05; Suff Bp Swindon *Bris* from 05. *Mark House, Field Rise, Swindon SN1 4HP* T: (01793) 538654 F: 525181 E: bishop.swindon@bristoldiocese.org

RAYMENT, Alexander Louis. b 88. Ox Brookes Univ BA 10. St Mellitus Coll 14. **d** 17 **p** 18. C Onslow Square and S Kensington St Aug *Lon* 17–20; P-in-c Penny Lane *Liv* from 20. *Springwood Vicarage, 499 Mather Avenue, Liverpool L19 4TF* M: 07530-861537 E: alexlrayment@gmail.com

RAYMENT, Andrew David. b 55. Univ of Wales (Lamp) BA 68 Univ of Wales (Abth) MA 70 Nottm Univ PhD 06. Ridley Hall Cam 78. **d** 80 **p** 81. C Costessey *Nor* 80–83; C Earlham St Anne 83–90; V Old Catton 90–96; PtO *Pet* 00–11; Min Partnership Development Officer 04–11; Adult Educn Officer (CME and Min Partnership) 05–11; rtd 11; P-in-c Ketton, Collyweston, Easton-on-the-Hill and Tinwell *Pet* 11–17; P-in-c Ketton and Tinwell 17–18. *Pyghtle Piece, Latchmoor Lane, Ludham, Great Yarmouth NR29 5QY* T: (01692) 678820 M: 07752-648537 E: andrew-rayment2010@hotmail.co.uk

RAYMER, Victoria Elizabeth. b 46. Wellesley Coll (USA) BA 68 Harvard Univ MA 69 JD 78 PhD 81. St Steph Ho Ox BA 86 Qu Coll Birm 88. **d** 89 **p** 94. Par Dn Bushey *St Alb* 89–94; C Eaton Socon 94–98; V Milton Ernest, Pavenham and Thurleigh 98–01; Tutor Westcott Ho Cam from 01; Dir Studies 01–14; PtO *St Alb* from 08; *Ely* 16–21. *Westcott House, Jesus Lane, Cambridge CB5 8BP* T: (01223) 272967 E: ver21@cam.ac.uk

RAYMOND, The Very Revd Walter Harvey. b 49. **d** 92 **p** 93. OGS from 93; C Willowdale All So Canada 92–94; Chapl H Trin Sch Toronto 94–99; Dean and R H Trin Cathl Quebec 99–07; Chapl Monte Carlo *Eur* 08–17; rtd 17; PtO from 17. *25 rue Saint Louis, Standon QC G0R 4L0, Canada* T: (001) (418) 951 3307 E: wraymond@ogs.net

RAYMOND, Philip Richard. b 56. Univ of Qld BA 79 BEdSt 86 Melbourne Univ MEd 00 Cam Univ PhD 05 MACE. **d** 04 **p** 09. Asst Chapl Selw Coll Cam 04–07; PtO *Ely* 07–09; Sen Chapl Guildford Gr Sch Australia 09–21. *Address temp unknown*

RAYNER, Angela Claire. Rob Coll Cam BA 02 MPhil 03 MA 06 Heythrop Coll Lon MTh 04. Westcott Ho Cam 16. **d** 18 **p** 19. C King's Lynn St Marg w St Nic *Nor* from 18. *Pilot Hoy, 10 Pilot Street, King's Lynn PE30 1QL* M: 07480-051148 E: fr.angela.rayner@gmail.com

RAYNER, Canon George Charles. b 26. Bps' Coll Cheshunt 50. **d** 52 **p** 53. C Rowbarton *B & W* 52–56; V Taunton H Trin 56–63; Chapl Taunton and Somerset Hosp 60–63; V Lower Sandown St Jo *Portsm* 63–69; R Wootton 69–89; Hon Can Portsm Cathl 84–89; rtd 89; PtO *B & W* 89–92; *Portsm* 98–15; P-in-c Six Pilgrims *B & W* 93–02. *The Bungalow, 1 Alresford Road, Shanklin PO37 6HX* T: (01983) 867304 E: rennergc@hotmail.com

RAYNER, Michael John. b 55. Magd Coll Ox BA 78 DPhil 85. Ox Min Course 04. **d** 07 **p** 08. Dir Br Heart Foundn Health Promotion Research Gp from 94; NSM Ox St Matt from 07. *198 Marlborough Road, Oxford OX1 4LT* T: (01865) 289244 M: 07871-758745 E: mike.rayner@dph.ox.ac.uk

RAYNER, Paul Anthony George. b 39. Dur Univ BA 60 Lon Univ BD 68 Cape Town Univ MA 79. Lon Coll of Div 65. **d** 68 **p** 69. C Crookes St Thos *Sheff* 68–72; P-in-c Diep River St Luke S Africa 72–79; P-in-c S Shoebury *Chelmsf* 80–84;

R 84–97; V Loughton St Mich 97–04; rtd 04; PtO *Chelmsf* from 04; *Eur* from 08. *36 Amberley Road, Buckhurst Hill IG9 5QW* T: (020) 8504 7434 E: prayner@globalnet.co.uk

RAYNER, Miss Rosemary Jane. b 54. ERMC 12. **d** 15 **p** 16. NSM Nor Lakenham St Jo and All SS and Tuckswood 15–20; PtO from 20. *7 St Andrew's Close, Poringland, Norwich NR14 7TB* T: (01508) 495650 E: rosemaryrayner@btinternet.com

RAYNER, Mrs Shirley Christine. b 54. SEITE BA 08. **d** 05 **p** 06. C S Croydon St Pet and St Aug *S'wark* 05–09; C Carew *St D* 09–11; TV 11–14; P-in-c Carew and Cosheston and Nash and Redberth 14; Dioc Lay Development Officer 11–14; rtd 14; PtO *St D* 14–15 and 17–18 and from 19; Hon C St Issell's and Amroth w Crunwere and Marros 15–17; Hon C Begelly w Ludchurch and E Williamston 18–19. *Address withheld by request*

RAYNER, Stewart Leslie. b 39. St Jo Coll Dur BA 61 MA 73. Cranmer Hall Dur. **d** 67 **p** 68. C Whiston *Sheff* 67–70; C Doncaster St Geo 70–74; Chapl Doncaster R Infirmary 70–74; R Adwick-le-Street *Sheff* 74–85; V Totley 85–91; Asst Chapl Pastures Hosp Derby 91–94; Asst Chapl Kingsway Hosp Derby 91–94; Asst Chapl S Derby Mental Health Services 91–94; P-in-c Etwall w Egginton *Derby* 94–99; R 99–08; RD Longford 96–01; rtd 09. *26 Lawn Avenue, Etwall, Derby DE65 6JB* T: (01283) 736079 E: stewart.rayner37@googlemail.com

RAYNER-WILLIAMS, Gareth Wynn. b 67. St D Coll Lamp BA 88 Hull Univ MA 89 Trin Coll Carmarthen PGCE 06. Westcott Ho Cam 89. **d** 91 **p** 92. C Mold *St As* 91–93; TV Hawarden 93–95; Ecum Chapl Glam Univ *Llan* 95–99; Lect Cardiff Univ from 99; Dir Academic Studies St Mich Coll Llan 99–04; Vice-Prin 02–04; V Roath *Llan* 04–05; PtO from 05; Hd RS Hawthorn Comp Sch Pontypridd 06–08; Chapl Bp of Llan High Sch 08–18; Hd RE 12–18; Asst Hd Teacher 15–18; Sen Teacher St Teilo's High Sch Cardiff from 19. *12 Fairwater Grove West, Llandaff, Cardiff CF5 2JQ* T: (029) 2056 9581 E: garethrw@icloud.com

RAYNES, Canon Andrew. b 60. R Holloway Coll Lon BA 83 Ches Univ MTh 14. Wycliffe Hall Ox 93. **d** 95 **p** 96. C Crowborough *Chich* 95–99; V Blackb Ch Ch w St Matt from 99; AD Blackb and Darwen 03–16; Hon Can Blackb Cathl from 10. *The Vicarage, Brandy House Brow, Blackburn BB2 3EY* T: (01254) 56292 E: andrewraynes@btopenworld.com

RAYNHAM, Mrs Penelope Anne. b 44. SWMTC 97. **d** 00 **p** 01. OLM S Hill w Callington *Truro* 00–15; rtd 15. *Bramblings, Honicombe Corner, Harrowbarrow, Callington PL17 8JN* T: (01822) 833065 E: penny@bramvista.co.uk

RAYNOR, Duncan Hope. b 58. Ex Coll Ox MA 80 MA 82 Birm Univ PGCE 88 MLitt 93. Qu Coll Birm 82. **d** 84 **p** 85. C Kings Heath *Birm* 84–87; Hd of RE Alderbrook Sch Solihull 88–94; Chapl K Edw Sch Birm 94–18; rtd 18. *29 Edenhall Road, Quinton, Birmingham B32 1DA* T: 0121-684 3407

RAYNOR, Lynn Mary. b 52. HCIMA 00. St Jo Coll Nottm 12. **d** 13 **p** 14. NSM Ravenshead *S'well* 13–16; NSM Epperstone, Gonalston, Oxton and Woodborough from 17; Chapl Nottm Univ Hosp NHS Trust from 16. *18 Park Drive, Hucknall, Nottingham NG15 7LQ* T: 0115-953 5949 M: 07855-648410 E: rev.raynorshine@virginmedia.com

RAYNOR, Michael. b 53. Lanc Univ BA 74 MSc 75. Ripon Coll Cuddesdon BA 84 MA 99. **d** 85 **p** 86. C Gt Crosby St Faith *Liv* 85–88; V Warrington St Barn 88–97; V Orford St Andr 97–20; AD Warrington 90–05; Hon Can Liv Cathl 03–05; rtd 20; PtO *Ches* from 20. *41 Park Road North, Newton-le-Willows WA12 9TA* E: mjraynor@care4free.net

RAZZALL, Charles Humphrey. b 55. Worc Coll Ox BA 76 MA 81 Qu Coll Cam BA 78. Westcott Ho Cam 76. **d** 79 **p** 80. C Catford (Southend) and Downham *S'wark* 79–83; V Crofton Park St Hilda w St Cypr 83–87; UPA Officer 87–92; TV Oldham *Man* 87–01; AD 92–99; Hon Can Man Cathl 98–01; R Coppenhall *Ches* 01–19; V N Thornaby *York* from 19; RD Middlesbrough 20–21. *St Paul's Vicarage, 60 Lanehouse Road, Thornaby, Stockton-on-Tees TS17 8EA* T: (01642) 613335 M: 07506-570680 E: razzall@angelfields.eclipse.co.uk

REA, Simon William John. b 60. G&C Coll Cam MA Victoria Univ Wellington MA Liv Univ BTh 07 Univ of Wales (Ban) PGCE. Ridley Hall Cam 02. **d** 04 **p** 05. C Moreton *Ches* 04–08; C Edgware *Lon* from 08. *9 Lacey Drive, Edgware HA8 8GH* T: (020) 8958 6939 M: 07905-699185 E: simonrea@gmx.net *or* simon.rea@london.anglican.org

READ, Barbara Ann. b 50. **d** 16 **p** 17. OLM Loughton St Jo *Chelmsf* 16–19; NSM from 19. *20 Theydon Bower, Bower Hill, Epping CM16 7AB* E: barb_and_dave@talktalk.net *or* barbara@loughtonchurch.org.uk

READ, Benjamin Stanley. b 85. Univ of Wales (Cardiff) BA 07. St Mich Coll Llan BTh 12. **d** 12 **p** 13. C Carmarthen St Pet *St D* 12–14; C Carmarthen St Pet and Abergwili etc 14–16; V Kingsclere and Ashford Hill w Headley *Win* from 16. *The Vicarage, Fox's Lane, Kingsclere, Newbury RG20 5SL* T: (01635) 298471 E: readben@hotmail.com

READ, Charles William. b 60. Man Univ BA 81 MPhil 95 Man Poly PGCE 82. St Jo Coll Nottm 86. **d** 88 **p** 89. C Oldham *Man* 88–90; C Urmston 90–94; P-in-c Broughton St Jas w St Clem and St Matthias 94–96; TV Broughton 96–99; Lect Cranmer Hall Dur 99–06; Dir Studies 00–06; Teacher Dur Sch 06–07; Vice-Prin and Dir Studies Nor Dioc Min Course 07–13; Reader Tr Co-ord from 13; Dir Liturgy and Worship ERMC from 13; Dep Warden of Readers *Nor* from 14. *42 Heigham Road, Norwich NR2 3AU* T: (01603) 660824 *or* 632041 E: charles.read@dioceseofnorwich.org

READ, Geoffrey Philip. b 61. Bris Univ LLB 82 Spurgeon's Coll MTh 04 York St Jo Univ MA 13. Wycliffe Hall Ox 85. **d** 88 **p** 89. C Dorking St Paul *Guildf* 88–92; TV Westborough 92–97; TR 97–98; Chapl Basle *Eur* 98–13; P-in-c Freiburg-im-Breisau 98–01; CMD Adv Colchester Area *Chelmsf* 13–18; Public Preacher 13–16; C Colchester St Jo 16–18; Chapl Luxembourg *Eur* from 18. *5 In der Acht, Steinsel, 7302 Luxembourg* T: (00352) 621 199 242 E: chaplain@anglican.lu

READ, James Arthur. b 51. Nottm Coll of Educn BEd 74. EMMTC 84. **d** 87 **p** 88. C Weoley Castle *Birm* 87–91; C W Smethwick 91–92; TV Atherton *Man* 92–97; P-in-c Facit 97–00; V Whitworth w Facit 00–08; P-in-c Royton St Anne 08–15; C Heyside 12–15; V Heyside and Royton 15–20; rtd 20; PtO *Man* from 20. *Address temp unknown*

READ, Mrs Julie Margaret. b 61. Keble Coll Ox BA 82 Univ of Wales (Ban) PGCE 83. WEMTC 97. **d** 00 **p** 01. C Bishop's Castle w Mainstone, Lydbury N etc *Heref* 00–03; R Pembridge w Moor Court, Shobdon, Staunton etc 03–11; PtO 11–12; C Bredenbury 12–13; C Kingsland w Eardisland, Aymestrey etc 13; P-in-c from 13. *The Rectory, Kingsland, Leominster HR6 9QW* T: (01568) 708255 E: rev.julie@btinternet.com

READ, Maureen Elizabeth. b 52. Man Metrop Univ BEd 93 Ches Coll of HE BTh 99. NOC 95. **d** 98 **p** 99. NSM Leesfield *Man* 98–99; C 99–02; TV Heywood 02–09; V Meltham *Wakef* 09–14; *Leeds* 14–17; P-in-c Petton w Cockshutt, Welshampton and Lyneal etc *Lich* from 17. *The Rectory, Cockshutt, Ellesmere SY12 0JQ* E: maureen.read09@btinternet.com

READ, Michael Antony. b 75. Lanc Univ BA 99 St Jo Coll Dur BA 01. Cranmer Hall Dur 99. **d** 02 **p** 03. C Stanley *Liv* 02–05; P-in-c Lowton St Luke 05–11; P-in-c Sudden and Heywood All So *Man* 11–16; V from 16. *St Aidan's Vicarage, 41 Harold Lees Road, Heywood OL10 4DW* T: (01706) 360693 E: revmikeread@yahoo.co.uk

READ, Nicholas George. b 51. Chelsea Coll Lon BSc 72 PhD 81. SEITE 97. **d** 00 **p** 01. NSM Beckenham St Jo *Roch* 00–03; P-in-c Penge Lane H Trin 03–09; V 09–21; Hon Can Roch Cathl 18–21; rtd 21. *15 Roslyn Road, Hathersage, Hope Valley S32 1BY* M: 07904-317488 E: hancompro@aol.com

READ, Preb Nicholas John. b 59. OBE 99. Keble Coll Ox BA 81 MSc 82 MA 85. Ox Min Course 92. **d** 95 **p** 96. NSM Charlbury w Shorthampton *Ox* 95–98; Dir Rural Stress Information Network 96–00; Chapl for Agric *Heref* 98–11; Assoc from 11; Preb Heref Cathl from 21. *The Rectory, Kingsland, Leominster HR6 9QW* T: (01568) 708255 E: nick.read@brightspacefoundation.org.uk

READ, Canon Robert Edgar. b 47. Kelham Th Coll 66. **d** 70 **p** 71. C Harton Colliery *Dur* 70–75; C Wilmslow *Ches* 76–80; V Gatley 80–92; V Offerton 92–06; RD Stockport 00–05; V Newton 06–07; P-in-c Gatley 07–10; V 10–14; Hon Can Ches Cathl 14; rtd 14; PtO *Ches* from 14; *Cov* 17–19. *Address temp unknown* E: reread@btinternet.com

✠**READE, The Rt Revd Nicholas Stewart.** b 46. Leeds Univ BA 70. Coll of Resurr Mirfield 70. **d** 73 **p** 74 **c** 04. C Coseley St Chad *Lich* 73–75; C Codsall 75–78; V Upper Gornal 78–82; V Mayfield *Chich* 82–88; RD Dallington 82–88; V Eastbourne St Mary 88–97; RD Eastbourne 88–97; Can and Preb Chich Cathl 90–97; Min The Hydneye CD 91–93; Adn Lewes and Hastings 97–04; Bp Blackb 04–12; rtd 12; Hon Asst Bp Eur from 13; Hon Asst Bp Chich from 13. *5 Warnham Gardens, Bexhill-on-Sea TN39 3SP* E: nicholas.reade@btinternet.com

READE, Richard Barton. b 66. Wolv Poly BA 88. Ripon Coll Cuddesdon BA 91 MA 97. **d** 92 **p** 93. C Wilnecote *Lich* 92–96; C Penkridge 96–98; P-in-c Basford 98–04; P-in-c Matlock Bank *Derby* 04–11; V Matlock Bank and Tansley from 11. *2 Portway Drive, Matlock DE4 3TS* T: (01629) 581233 E: richardreade@btinternet.com

READER, John. b 53. Trin Coll Ox BA 75 MA 79 Man Univ MPhil 87 Univ of Wales (Ban) PhD 02. Ripon Coll Cuddesdon 76. **d** 78 **p** 79. C Ely 78–80; C Baguley *Man* 80–83; TV Kirkby Lonsdale *Carl* 83–86; V Lydbury N

Heref 86–89; P-in-c Hopesay w Edgton 86–89; R Lydbury N w Hopesay and Edgton 89–90; Tutor Glouc Sch for Min 86–88; Vice-Prin 88–90; Dir Past Th Sarum & Wells Th Coll 90–92; P-in-c Elmley Lovett w Hampton Lovett and Elmbridge etc *Worc* 92–07; Assoc Tr and Educn Officer 92–02; Ind Chapl 01–07; P-in-c Chelford w Lower Withington and Dioc Rural Officer *Ches* 07–09; R Ironstone *Ox* 09–20; rtd 20; PtO *Glouc* from 20. *6 Mickleton Road, Honeybourne, Evesham WR11 7PN* T: (01386) 830569 E: drjohnreader@hotmail.co.uk

READER, The Ven Trevor Alan John. b 46. Lon Univ BSc 68 MSc 70 Portsm Poly PhD 72. S Dios Minl Tr Scheme 83. **d** 86 **p** 87. C Alverstoke *Portsm* 86–89; P-in-c Hook w Warsash 89–95; V 95–98; P-in-c Blendworth w Chalton w Idsworth 98–03; Dioc Dir NSM 98–03; Adn Is of Wight 03–06; Adn Portsdown 06–13; Bp's Liaison Officer for Pris 03–06; Bp's Liaison Officer for Hosps 06–13; rtd 13; PtO *Portsm* from 13. *54 David Newberry Drive, Lee-on-the-Solent PO13 8FE* M: 07826-846133 E: trevor.reader@hotmail.co.uk

READING, Glenn Thomas. b 76. Staffs Univ BSc 98. Ripon Coll Cuddesdon 07. **d** 09 **p** 10. C Horninglow *Lich* 09–13; TV Redditch Ch the K *Worc* from 13. *The Vicarage, 16 Church Road, Astwood Bank, Redditch B96 6EH* T: (01527) 894436 M: 07964-282278 E: glenn.reading@gmail.com

READING, Lesley Jean. *See* ARMSTRONG, Lesley Jean

READING, Michael Dudley. b 66. Leeds Univ BEd 90 Nottm Trent Univ MA 98. Wycliffe Hall Ox MTh 17. **d** 17 **p** 18. C Thame *Ox* 17–20; TR from 20. *St Mary's Church Office, Church Road, Thame OX9 3AJ* T: (01844) 213491 E: mike@stmarysthame.org.uk

READING, Area Bishop of. *See* GRAHAM, The Rt Revd Olivia Josephine

REAGON, Darrol Franklin. b 46. St Mich Coll Llan 74. **d** 76 **p** 77. C Llandrillo-yn-Rhos *St As* 76–78; C Hawarden 78–81; V Northwich St Luke and H Trin *Ches* 81–85; V Moulton *Linc* 85–91; V Scunthorpe Resurr 91–92; P-in-c Branston 92–94; R Branston w Nocton and Potterhanworth 94–07; rtd 07; PtO *Win* from 09. *17 Wessex Avenue, New Milton BH25 6NG* T: (01425) 613622 E: revddarrol@btinternet.com

REAKES, Richard Frank. b 68. STETS 02. **d** 05 **p** 06. NSM Shepton Mallet w Doulting *B & W* 05–09; NSM Evercreech w Chesterblade and Milton Clevedon 09–14; TV Bishop's Cleeve and Woolstone w Gotherington etc *Glouc* 14–21; R Four Saints *Leic* from 21. *The Vicarage, 102A Station Road, Countesthorpe, Leicester LE8 5TB* E: richard.vicarage@gmail.com

REAKES-WILLIAMS, Canon Gordon Martin. b 63. St Cath Coll Cam BA 86 MA 89 St Jo Coll Dur BA 90. Cranmer Hall Dur. **d** 91 **p** 92. C Harold Wood *Chelmsf* 91–94; Chapl Leipzig *Eur* from 95; Hon Can from 17. *Shakespearestrasse 53, 04107 Leipzig, Germany* T: (0049) (341) 302 7951 M: 177-240 4207 E: pastor@leipzig-english-church.de

REANEY, Mrs Beverly Jane. b 58. Nottm Univ BA 81. S Wales Ord Course 00. **d** 03 **p** 04. NSM Llanharry *Llan* 03–11; NSM Llangynwyd w Maesteg 11–13; P-in-c Glyncorrwg and the Upper Afan Valley etc from 13. *12 Cwrt y Fedwen, Maesteg CF34 9GH* T: (01656) 734142 E: bevreaney1158@btinternet.com

REANEY, Christopher Thomas. b 60. Univ of Wales (Lamp) BA 82. St Mich Coll Llan. **d** 85 **p** 86. C Maindee Newport *Mon* 85–87; C Griffithstown 88–89; V Treherbert w Treorchy *Llan* 89–99; V Treorchy and Treherbert 99–02; R Llanfabon 02–11; V Troedrhiwgarth from 11. *12 Cwrt y Fedwen, Maesteg CF34 9GH* T: (01656) 734142 E: c.reaney350@btinternet.com

REAST, Eileen Joan. *See* BANGAY, Eileen Joan

REAVLEY, Cedric. b 51. Lon Univ BPharm 73. **d** 05 **p** 06. OLM Burford w Fulbrook, Taynton, Asthall etc *Ox* 05–21; rtd 21; PtO *Glouc* from 19; *Ox* from 21. *5 Swan Lane, Burford OX18 4SP* T: (01993) 823957 E: cedric.reavley51@gmail.com

RECORD, John. b 47. St Chad's Coll Dur BA 71. Westcott Ho Cam 71. **d** 73 **p** 74. C Paddington St Jo w St Mich *Lon* 73–75; C Witney *Ox* 75–78; P-in-c Lt Compton and Chastleton 78–80; R Lt Compton w Chastleton, Cornwell etc 80–83; V Hawkhurst *Cant* 83–97; RD W Charing 89–95; Hon Can Cant Cathl 96–97; P-in-c Devizes St Jo w St Mary *Sarum* 97–07; P-in-c Devizes St Pet 00–04; RD Devizes 98–07; Can and Preb Sarum Cathl 02–07; V Hammersmith St Pet *Lon* 07–14; rtd 15; PtO *Lon* from 15. *135 Watchfield Court, Sutton Court Road, London W4 4NE* M: 07802-716630 E: jrecord47@gmail.com

REDDIN, Mrs Christine Emily. b 46. Essex Univ BA 67. STETS 01. **d** 04 **p** 05. NSM Burpham *Guildf* 04–10; rtd 11; PtO *Guildf* from 11. *1 New Cottages, Sutton Green Road, Sutton Green, Guildford GU4 7QD* T: (01483) 714708 M: 07764-677898 E: c.reddin@sky.com

REDDING, Roger Charles. b 45. Chich Th Coll 87. **d** 89 **p** 90. C Yeovil St Mich *B & W* 89–93; P-in-c Salisbury St Mark *Sarum* 93–94; LtO 94–96; TV Chalke Valley 96–12; Chapl to Travelling People 02–12; rtd 12; PtO *Bris* 02–14; *B & W* from 03; *Win* 12–16. *46 Queen Street, Tintinhull, Yeovil BA22 8PQ* T: (01935) 825057 E: mail@rogerredding.co.uk

REDEYOFF, Neil Martyn. b 69. St Jo Coll Nottm BA 01. **d** 01 **p** 02. C Grange St Andr and Runcorn H Trin *Ches* 01–04; R Darfield *Sheff* 04–08; P-in-c Finningley w Auckley 08–10; R from 10; AD W Doncaster 11–15. *The Rectory, Rectory Lane, Finningley, Doncaster DN9 3DA* T: (01302) 770240 E: neil.redeyoff@sheffield.anglican.org

REDFEARN, James Jonathan. b 62. Newc Univ BA 83 PGCE 89. Cranmer Hall Dur 95. **d** 95 **p** 96. C Kidsgrove *Lich* 95–97. *56 Holly Avenue, Jesmond, Newcastle upon Tyne NE2 2QA* T: 0191-281 9046 E: jonathan.redfearn@church.org.uk

REDFEARN, Michael. b 42. Open Univ BA 78 Hull Univ MA 84 BA 86. St Aid Birkenhead 64. **d** 68 **p** 69. C Bury St Pet *Man* 68–71; C Swinton St Pet 71–74; Ind Chapl *Bris* 74–79 and 80–81; Ind Chapl Australia 79–80; Ind Chapl *York* 81–86; V Southill and Course Dir St Alb Minl Tr Scheme 86–93; Dep Chapl HM Pris Wandsworth 94; Chapl HM YOI and Rem Cen Feltham 94–97; Chapl HM YOI Aylesbury 97–02; rtd 02; Asst Chapl Palma de Mallorca *Eur* 04–10. *19 Old Railway Close, Lechlade GL7 3FS* E: mandsfearn42@gmail.com

✠**REDFERN, The Rt Revd Alastair Llewellyn John.** b 48. Ch Ch Ox BA 70 MA 74 Trin Coll Cam BA 74 MA 79 Bris Univ PhD 01. Westcott Ho Cam 72 Qu Coll Birm 75. **d** 76 **p** 77 **c** 97. C Tettenhall Regis *Lich* 76–79; Tutor Ripon Coll Cuddesdon 79–87; Hon C Cuddesdon *Ox* 83–87; Can Res Bris Cathl 87–97; Dioc Dir Tr 91–97; Suff Bp Grantham *Linc* 97–05; Dean Stamford 98–05; Can and Preb Linc Cathl 00–05; Bp Derby 05–18; rtd 18; PtO *Sarum* from 19; *B & W* from 19; Hon Asst Bp Sarum from 19; Hon Asst Bp B & W from 20. *Manor Farm, Claverton, Bath BA2 7BP* E: bishopalastair.redfern@gmail.com

REDFERN, Lisa. b 67. Man Univ MB, ChB 94 Salford Univ MA 10. All SS Cert for Miss & Min 12. **d** 15 **p** 16. NSM Broadheath *Ches* from 15. *St Alban's Church Office, Lindsell Road, West Timperley, Altrincham WA14 5NX*

REDFERN, Paul. b 48. Ulster Univ BA 88. CITC BTh 94. **d** 94 **p** 95. C Belfast St Aid *Conn* 94–97; I Belfast St Mark 97–03; I Kilbride 03–16; rtd 16. *25 Beechview, Ballyclare BT39 9XT* T: (028) 9332 2895

REDGERS, Brian. b 42. St Jo Coll Dur BA 65 Keswick Hall Coll PGCE 75. Westcott Ho Cam 65. **d** 67 **p** 68. C Rushmere *St E* 67–73; LtO 73–15; PtO *Ely* from 15. *Two Acres, Downham Road, Salters Lode, Downham Market PE38 0AY* T: (01366) 387666 E: revredgers@live.co.uk

REDGRAVE, Christine Howick. b 50. AIAT 73. Trin Coll Bris 75. dss 78 **d** 87 **p** 94. Watford *St Alb* 78–83; Maidenhead St Andr and St Mary *Ox* 83–85; Bracknell 85–96; Par Dn 87–94; TV 94–96; P-in-c Woolhampton w Midgham and Beenham Valance 96–04; Asst Dir of Ords 95–04; Dir of Ords (Reading and Dorchester) 04–10; Hon Can Ch Ch 00–10; C Yoxmere *St E* 10–14; V 14–19; RD Saxmundham 12–18; rtd 19. *17 Cheyney Green, Darsham, Saxmundham IP17 3FA* M: 07774-905491 E: redgrave460@btinternet.com

REDHOUSE, Mark David. b 67. Oak Hill Th Coll BA 94. **d** 94 **p** 95. C Fulham St Mary N End *Lon* 94–96; C Hove Bp Hannington Memorial Ch *Chich* 96–01; V Horam 01–10; RD Dallington 04–07; V Eastbourne All So from 10. *All Souls Vicarage, 53 Susans Road, Eastbourne BN21 3TH* T: (01323) 727033

REDMAN, Anthony James. b 51. Reading Univ BSc 72 Anglia Ruskin Univ MA 05 FRICS 95. EAMTC 01. **d** 03 **p** 04. NSM Bury St Edmunds All SS w St Jo and St Geo *St E* 03–06; NSM Blackbourne 06–21; rtd 21; Bp's Adv for Self-Supporting Min *St E* from 16; Asst Dioc Dir of Ords from 17; PtO from 21. *The Cottage, Great Livermere, Bury St Edmunds IP31 1JG* T: (01359) 269335 F: (01284) 704734 E: tony@theredmans.co.uk

REDMAN, Julia Elizabeth Hithersay. *See* WHITE, Julia Elizabeth Hithersay

REDMAN, Michael John. b 52. St Jo Coll Ox BA 76 MA 80 Heythrop Coll Lon MA 13 SOAS Lon MA 19 Solicitor 86. NTMTC 04. **d** 06 **p** 07. NSM St Marylebone St Paul *Lon* 06–19; PtO from 19; *Chelmsf* from 20. *8 Bryanston Mews West, London W1H 2DD* T: (020) 7723 7407 E: redman.michaelj@gmail.com

REDPARTH, Paul Robert. b 58. Open Univ BSc 97 K Coll Lon PhD 01. Westcott Ho Cam 04. **d** 06 **p** 07. C Roughey *Chich* 06–09; C Forest Row 09–11; P-in-c Kirdford 11–16; P-in-c Crowborough St Jo 16–17; V 17–20; rtd 20. *Address temp unknown*

REDPATH, Mrs Grace. b 53. TISEC 12. **d** 15 **p** 16. C Duns *Edin* 15–18; C Kelso from 18. *12 Bowmont Court, Heiton,*

Kelso TD5 8JY T: (01573) 450752 M: 07768-456671 E: grace.redpath@btconnect.com

REDSHAW, Mrs Alison Janet. b 58. EMMTC 08. **d** 10 **p** 11. NSM Crich and S Wingfield *Derby* 10–13; C and Missr for Retirement Communities Repton 13–16; C Swadlincote *Derby* 16–19; C Hartshorne and Bretby 16–19; C Swadlincote and Hartshorne from 20. *107 Ashby Road, Burton-on-Trent DE15 0NX* M: 07986-527293 E: revalisonr@gmail.com

REECE, Donald Malcolm Hayden. b 36. CCC Cam BA 58 MA 62. Cuddesdon Coll 58. **d** 60 **p** 61. C Latchford St Jas *Ches* 60–63; C Matlock and Tansley *Derby* 63–67; C-in-c Hackenthorpe Ch Ch CD 67–70; C Salisbury Cathl Rhodesia 70–73; V Leic St Pet 74–82; V Putney St Marg *S'wark* 82–91; Home Sec Coun for Chr Unity 92–97; Hon C Wandsworth St Anne *S'wark* 94–97; V Shepherd's Bush St Steph w St Thos *Lon* 97–04; rtd 04; PtO *Ox* from 05. *8 Lamarsh Road, Oxford OX2 0LD* T: (01865) 792678 E: dmh.reeve@gmail.com

REECE, Paul Michael. b 60. Southn Univ BA 81. Coll of Resurr Mirfield 83. **d** 85 **p** 86. C Borehamwood *St Alb* 85–89; C Potters Bar 89–92; R Lt Stanmore St Lawr *Lon* from 92; AD Harrow 97–02; Chapl R Nat Orthopaedic Hosp NHS Trust from 20. *Whitchurch Rectory, St Lawrence Close, Edgware HA8 6RB* T: (020) 8952 0019 F: 8537 0547 M: 07860-690503 E: paul.reece@london.anglican.org

REECE, Roger Walton Arden. b 56. **d** 00 **p** 01. OLM Chadderton St Luke *Man* 00–04; OLM Chadderton St Matt w St Luke 04–08; NSM 08–09; C Ashton 09–16; PtO from 16; Chapl HM Pris Buckley Hall from 08; PtO *Leeds* from 17. *HM Prison Buckley Hall, Buckley Hall Road, Rochdale OL12 9DP* T: (01706) 514300 M: 07904-078901 E: roger.reece@ntlworld.com

REED, Adam Michael Frederick. b 73. Humberside Univ BA 95. Cranmer Hall Dur 96. **d** 99 **p** 00. C Northallerton w Kirby Sigston *York* 99–03; R Middleton, Newton and Sinnington 03–11; V Saltburn-by-the-Sea from 11; V New Marske from 14. *The Vicarage, Greta Street, Saltburn-by-the-Sea TS12 1LS* T: (01287) 622007 E: bilpop@btinternet.com

REED, Canon Annette Susan. b 54. Birm Univ BA 76 CQSW 78. Qu Coll Birm 84. **d** 87 **p** 94. C Churchover w Willey *Cov* 89–92; C Clifton upon Dunsmore and Newton 89–92; C Walsgrave on Sowe 92–95; C Cov E 92–95; C Burbage w Aston Flamville *Leic* 95–98; C Hinckley St Mary 95–98; C The Sheepy Gp 98–00; TV Bosworth and Sheepy Gp 00–06; V The Paxtons w Diddington *Ely* 06–15; V The Paxtons w Diddington and Southoe from 15; RD St Neots 07–19; Hon Can Ely Cathl from 14. *The Vicarage, 24 St James's Road, Little Paxton, St Neots PE19 6QW* T: (01480) 211048 E: canonannettereed@gmail.com

REED, Brian. b 43. Bris Univ BSc 65. Linc Th Coll 73. **d** 76 **p** 77. C S Ashford Ch Ch *Cant* 76–78; C Spring Park 78–83; V Barming Heath 83–13; rtd 13; PtO *Cant* 14–20. *8 The Thatchers, Maidstone ME16 0XA* T: (01622) 298164 M: 07759-620502

REED, Christopher John. b 42. Selw Coll Cam BA 64 MA 68. Cranmer Hall Dur 64. **d** 67 **p** 68. C Gt Ilford St Andr *Chelmsf* 67–70; P-in-c Bordesley St Andr *Birm* 70–72; V 72–80; V Crofton St Paul *Roch* 80–98; V Yalding w Collier Street 98–08; RD Paddock Wood 01–06; rtd 08; PtO *Roch* from 09. *66 Willow Park, Otford, Sevenoaks TN14 5NG* T: (01959) 523439 E: rev.chris.reed@sky.com

REED, Colin. *See* REED, Matthew Colin

REED, Colin Bryher. b 58. York Univ BA 80 RGN 86. Ridley Hall Cam 93. **d** 95 **p** 96. C Grays North *Chelmsf* 95–99; Chapl Plymouth Hosps NHS Trust 99–02; Hd Chapl Services Norfolk and Nor Univ Hosps NHS Foundn Trust 02–09; Asst RD Ingworth *Nor* 10–11; TR High Oak, Hingham and Scoulton w Wood Rising 11–16; R 16–21; RD Humbleyard 18–21; rtd 21; PtO *Nor* from 21. *7 Sunningdale, Norwich NR4 6AQ* M: 07825-559132 E: rev-colinreed@btconnect.com

REED, Mrs Elizabeth Christine. b 43. Lon Bible Coll Lon Univ BD 65. WMMTC 95. **d** 97 **p** 98. NSM Ledbury *Heref* 97–17; Chapl Bromsgrove Sch 99–06; PtO *Heref* from 17. *The Old Barn, Perrystone Hill, Ross-on-Wye HR9 7QX* T: (01989) 780439 E: 34831@oldbarnperrystone.co.uk

REED, Ethel Patricia Ivy. *See* WESTBROOK, Ethel Patricia Ivy

REED, Harvey. *See* REED, William Harvey

REED, The Ven John Peter Cyril. b 51. BD 78 AKC 78. Ripon Coll Cuddesdon 78. **d** 79 **p** 80. C Croydon St Jo *Cant* 79–82; Prec St Alb Abbey 82–86; R Timsbury and Priston *B & W* 86–93; Chapl Rural Affairs Bath Adnry 87–93; P-in-c Ilminster w Whitelackington 93–94; TR Ilminster and Distr 94–99; Adn Taunton 99–16; rtd 16; PtO *Ex* from 06; *Truro* from 17. *11 Morwellham, Tavistock PL19 8JL* T: (01822) 834105 E: john.morwellham@hotmail.com

REED, John William. b 57. Sussex Univ BSc 79. NOC 95. d 97 p 98. C Padgate *Liv* 97–99; C Orford St Marg 99–01; V 01–08; P-in-c Golborne 08–13; TV Lowton and Golborne 13–17; P-in-c Gt Crosby St Faith and Waterloo Park St Mary from 17. *St Faith's Vicarage, Milton Road, Waterloo, Liverpool L22 4RE* E: reed926@btinternet.com

REED (née McCARTHY), Mrs Lorraine Valmay. b 52. Birm Univ CertEd 73 Univ of Wales (Ban) BA 95 MTh 97 LGSM 82. SNWTP 09. d 11 p 12. NSM Middlewich w Byley *Ches* from 11; Asst Dir of Ords from 14. *1 Douglas Close, Hartford, Northwich CW8 1SH* T: (01606) 781071 M: 07711-379339 E: revlvreed@gmail.com

REED, Malcolm Edward. b 45. Graduate Soc Dur MSc 75. Yorks Min Course 08. d 10 p 11. NSM Hoylandswaine and Silkstone w Stainborough *Wakef* 10–14; NSM Ryhill 14; *Leeds* 14–17; Bp's Hon Asst Chapl *Wakef* 11–14; *Leeds* 14–17; rtd 17; PtO from 18; *Sheff* from 18. *Clough Cottage, Cathill, Hoylandswaine, Sheffield S36 7JB* T: (01226) 767328 M: 07803-031199 E: cathillreed@btinternet.com

REED, Matthew Colin. b 50. Edin Univ BD 82. Edin Th Coll 72. d 84 p 85. C Edin St Pet 84–87; P-in-c Linlithgow 87–94; P-in-c Bathgate 87–91; Chapl HM YOI Polmont 91–94; R Motherwell *Glas* 94–97; R Wishaw 94–97; Hon Asst P Edin St Fillan 00–14; Chapl HM Pris Edin 02–13; Hon C Edin Old St Paul 14–17; P-in-c Edin St Marg 14–20; rtd 20. *48 Braeside Road South, Gorebridge EH23 4DL* M: 07713-775435 E: colinmcreed@aol.com

REED, Canon Pamela Kathleen. b 38. EMMTC. dss 84 d 87 p 94. Cambridge Ascension *Ely* 84–88; Par Dn 87–88; Par Dn Cherry Hinton St Andr 88–90; C 91–95; C Teversham 91–95; V Chesterton St Geo 95–04; Hon Can Ely Cathl 00–04; rtd 04; PtO *Ely* from 04. *17 Woodland Road, Sawston, Cambridge CB22 3DT* T: (01223) 832571 E: pamkreed@hotmail.com

REED, Simon John. b 63. Trin Coll Ox BA 86 MA 90 K Coll Lon MPhil 05. Wycliffe Hall Ox BA 90. d 91 p 92. C Walton H Trin *Ox* 91–96; P-in-c Hanger Hill Ascension and W Twyford St Mary *Lon* 96–01; V from 01. *The Ascension Vicarage, Beaufort Road, London W5 3EB* T/F: (020) 8566 9920 E: simonreed@ascensionealing.org

REED, Tomos Lodwick. b 79. Em Coll Cam BA 02 MSc 02 MA 04. Westcott Ho Cam 17. d 19 p 20. C S Dulwich St Steph *S'wark* from 19. *18 Talisman Square, London SE26 6XY* M: 07779-092405 E: tomos.l.reed@gmail.com

REED, William Harvey. b 47. K Coll Lon BD 69 AKC 69. St Aug Coll Cant 69. d 70 p 71. C Stockton St Mark CD *Dur* 70–72; C Billingham St Cuth 72–76; C S Westoe 76–79; V Chilton Moor 79–87; R Hutton *Chelmsf* 87–95; V Hullbridge 95–10; C Rawreth w Rettendon 06–10; V Rettendon and Hullbridge 10–12; rtd 12; PtO *Nor* from 12. *117 Lloyds Avenue, Kessingland, Lowestoft NR33 7TT* T: (01502) 741881 E: whreed@btinternet.com

REEDER, Michael William Peter. b 58. Wilson Carlile Coll 84. d 09 p 10. Chapl St Luke's Hospice Sheff from 07; Hon C Sheff Cathl 09–12; Min Can from 12; Liturg Chapl to Bp Doncaster from 12. *5 Brookhouse Court, 92 Brookhouse Hill, Sheffield S10 3TE* M: 07947-706256 E: m.reeder@hospicesheffield.co.uk

REES (née HOLDER), Ms Adèle Claire. b 76. Luton Univ BSc 97 Sheff Univ Th 03. Ripon Coll Cuddesdon 04. d 07 p 08. C Hill *Birm* 07–10; C Hatcham St Jas *S'wark* 10–17; Chapl Goldsmiths' Coll Lon 10–17; Ecum Adv Woolwich Area 13–17; CF from 21. *c/o MOD Chaplains (Army)* M: 07841-640974 E: adelerees@yahoo.co.uk

REES, Anthony John. b 49. St Jo Coll Dur BA 72 MA 77 Man Univ MEd 89 MPhil 07. d 74 p 75. C Smethwick St Matt w St Chad *Birm* 74–77; C Bolton St Pet *Man* 77–80; R Cheetham St Mark 80–88; V Mottram in Longdendale w Woodhead *Ches* 88–93; V Mottram in Longdendale 93–02; V Chirk *St As* 02–14; rtd 14; PtO *Blackb* 14–20. *31 Redhills Road, Arnside, Carnforth LA5 0AR* T: (01524) 761478 E: tonyandmary75@btinternet.com

REES, Canon Brian Allison. b 48. McGill Univ Montreal BA 74 St Andr Univ BD 76 PhD 80. Montreal Dioc Th Coll 76. d 80 p 81. C Montreal St Jas and Chapl Concordia Univ Canada 80–82; R Rawdon Ch Ch 82–85; Chapl Bedford Sch 85–92; Hd Master Bedford Prep Sch 92–97; Hd Master Pilgrims' Sch 97–11; rtd 11; Hon Can Win Cathl from 11. *39 Grange Close, Winchester SO23 9RS* T: (01962) 853508 E: brianarees@aol.com

REES, Celia Pamela. b 48. St D Coll Lamp BA 70. d 98 p 99. OLM Leominster *Heref* 98–18; rtd 19; PtO *Heref* from 19. *Rivendell, 50 Oldfields Close, Leominster HR6 8TL* T: (01568) 616581 or 612124

REES, Mrs Christine Deryn Irving. b 57. Nottm Univ BSc Sheff Univ MA. Qu Coll Birm. d 00 p 01. NSM Astwood Bank *Worc* 00–01; C 01–03; TV Dronfield w Holmesfield *Derby* 03–11; PtO 11–18; *Sheff* 16–19; NSM Gleadless from 19; NSM Hackenthorpe from 19; NSM Woodhouse St Jas from 19. *54 Wake Road, Sheffield S7 1HG* T: 0114-250 7619 E: revdchristine.rees@btopenworld.com

REES, Christopher John. b 40. Dur Univ BA 62. Ridley Hall Cam 62. d 64 p 65. C Wilmslow *Ches* 64–70; C Birkenhead St Pet w St Matt 70–74; V Lostock Gralam 75–83; R Davenham 83–96; P-in-c Aldford and Bruera 96–05; rtd 05; PtO *Ches* from 05. *15 Chapel Close, Comberbach, Northwich CW9 6BA* T: (01606) 891366 E: christopherrees954@btinternet.com

REES, David Richard. b 60. St Mich Coll Llan. d 84 p 85. C Llanstadwel *St D* 84–86; C Carmarthen St Dav 86–91; V Llanrhian w Llanhywel and Carnhedryn etc 91–99; V Spittal w Trefgarn and Ambleston w St Dogwells 99–19; P-in-c Daugleddau LMA from 19. *The Vicarage, Spittal, Haverfordwest SA62 5QP* T: (01437) 741505 E: rev.rees@btinternet.com

REES, Ms Diane Eluned. b 61. Univ of Wales (Ban) BSc 82 Univ of Wales (Swansea) MEd 87 K Coll Lon DThMin 13 Em Coll Cam PGCE 83 CPsychol 87 AFBPsS 84. St Jo Coll Nottm BTh 95 MA 96. d 96 p 97. C Hall Green St Pet *Birm* 96–00; P-in-c Bozeat w Easton Maudit *Pet* 00–03; C Putney St Mary *S'wark* 03–04; TV 04–05; Asst Dir of Min and Tr *Roch* 06–09; PtO 09–15; V Shoreham from 15; Chapl St Mich Sch Otford 15–20. *The Vicarage, Station Road, Shoreham, Sevenoaks TN14 7SA* T: (01959) 522363 M: 07764-678661 E: revdrdi@outlook.com

REES, Emma Louise. *See* REES-KENNY, Emma Louise

REES, Mrs Helen. b 78. Univ of Wales (Cardiff) BD 99 MTh 10. St Mich Coll Llan 07. d 09 p 10. NSM Penarth All SS *Llan* 09–10; NSM Llandrindod w Cefnllys and Disserth *S & B* 10–13; NSM Gowerton 13–16; C Cen Swansea 16–21; Dioc Dir of Educn 11–17; Tutor St Padarn's Inst from 17. *10 Cassia Drive, Usk NP15 1TZ* E: helenrees78@gmail.com

REES, The Ven Ian Kendall. b 66. St Mich Coll Llan 98. d 00 p 01. C Barry All SS *Llan* 00–03; Assoc P Grangetown 03–05; P-in-c Pyle w Kenfig 05–10; R Llandrindod w Cefnllys and Disserth *S & B* 10–13; V Gowerton 13–16; V Cen Swansea 16–21; Bp's Officer for Lay Min 14–18; Dioc Dir for Ords and Voc 18–21; Hon Can Brecon Cathl 16–17; Can Res Brecon Cathl 17–21; Adn Mon from 21; Dir Min and Discipleship from 21. *10 Cassia Drive, Usk NP15 1TZ* E: ianrees@churchinwales.org.uk

REES, Jane Elizabeth. b 70. K Coll Lon BD 92. Westcott Ho Cam 12 ERMC 13. d 14 p 15. NSM Wisbech St Mary and Guyhirn w Ring's End etc *Ely* 14–17; NSM March from 17. *49 Gresley Way, March PE15 8QA* E: revjanerees@gmail.com

REES, Jennifer Mary. *See* MORRELL, Jennifer Mary

REES, Joanna Mary. *See* STOKER, Joanna Mary

REES, John. *See* REES, Vivian John Howard

REES, John Nigel. b 58. Derby Lonsdale Coll BCombStuds 79 Coll of Ripon & York St Jo PGCE 80. STETS 03. d 06 p 07. NSM Broad Blunsdon and Highworth w Sevenhampton and Inglesham etc *Bris* 06–10; P-in-c Rowde and Bromham *Sarum* 10–16; R Canalside Benefice from 16; Chapl Wilts Air Ambulance from 18. *The Rectory, 22 Warren Road, Staverton, Trowbridge BA14 8UZ* M: 07912-503267 E: canalsiderector@gmail.com

REES, Canon John Philip Walford. b 41. St D Coll Lamp BA 62 Linacre Coll Ox BA 64 MA 69 Univ of Wales (Cardiff) BD 72. Wycliffe Hall Ox 62. d 64 p 65. C Reading St Jo *Ox* 64–67; V Patrick *S & M* 67–68; C Pontypool *Mon* 68–70; Area Sec CMS Glouc, Heref and Worc 70–75; V Bream *Glouc* 75–91; Team Ldr Ichthus Chr Fellowship 91–96; TV Glyncorrwg w Afan Vale and Cymmer Afan *Llan* 96–99; R Llandogo and Tintern *Mon* 99–00; R Llandogo w Whitebrook Chpl and Tintern Parva 00–07; AD Monmouth 02–06; Hon Can St Woolos Cathl 05–07; rtd 07; PtO *Glouc* from 15. *Sparrow Cottage, The Narth, Monmouth NP25 4QG* T: (01600) 869194

REES, Canon Judith Margaret. b 39. Southn Univ BTh 89. dss 86 d 87 p 94. Sanderstead All SS *S'wark* 86–87; Par Dn 87; Dir Cottesloe Chr Tr Progr *Ox* 89–99; Par Dn Gt Horwood 89–91; Par Dn Winslow w Gt Horwood and Addington 91–94; C 94–99; RD Claydon 96–99; Hon Can Ch Ch 97–99; rtd 99; PtO *Sarum* from 01. *10 Hadrians Close, Salisbury SP2 9NN* T: (01722) 410050

REES, Canon Michael Lloyd. b 51. St D Coll Lamp. d 74 p 75. C Cardigan w Mwnt and Y Ferwig *St D* 74–77; Min Can St D Cathl 77–81; TV Aberystwyth 81–83; Dioc Children's Adv 83–92; V Pen-boyr 83–88; V Henfynyw w Aberaeron and Llanddewi Aberarth 88–99; RD Glyn Aeron 95–99; V Gors-las 99–13; V Betws w Ammanford 13–15; AD Dyffryn Aman 07–14; Can St D Cathl 09–15; rtd 15; PtO *St D* from 15; *Ban* from 18; *Eur* from 18. *3 Clôs Y Drindod, Buarth Road,*

Aberystwyth SY23 1LR T: (01970) 627593 M: 07972-602620 E: michaelrees2013@outlook.com *or* mlr1@hotmail.co.uk

REES (*née* **CURREY), Mrs Pauline Carol.** b 46. WMMTC 94. **d** 98 **p** 99. OLM Leominster *Heref* 98–16; rtd 17; PtO *Heref* from 17. *Crossways Cottage, Leysters, Leominster HR6 0HR* T: (01568) 750300 *or* 612124 E: rees.crossways@btinternet.com

REES, Philip. *See* REES, John Philip Walford

REES, Mrs Sally Elizabeth. b 14 **p** 20. NSM Crickhowell *S & B* 14–15; NSM Gtr Brecon from 16; Bp's Officer for Min to Older People from 18. *Curlews, Tretower, Crickhowell, NP8 1RG* T: (01873) 811332 E: sallyrees50@gmail.com

REES, Stephen Philip. b 70. St Luke's Coll Ex BA. Oak Hill Th Coll BA 03. **d** 03 **p** 04. C Moreton-in-Marsh w Batsford, Todenham etc *Glouc* 03–06; P-in-c Lt Heath *St Alb* 06–12; V 12–16; V Crowborough *Chich* from 16. *All Saints Vicarage, Church Road, Crowborough TN6 1ED* T: (01892) 652081 M: 07970-619469 E: steve@allsaintscrowborough.org

REES, Miss Susan Mary. b 61. Univ of Wales (Cardiff) BSc 82 Ox Univ BTh 05. Ripon Coll Cuddesdon 00. **d** 02 **p** 03. C Penarth All SS *Llan* 02–05; C Roath 05–08; P-in-c Eglwysilan 08–14; P-in-c Pontyclun w Talygarn 14–19; P-in-c Llanharry 14–19. *108 Fishguard Road, Llanishen, Cardiff CF14 5PS* T: (029) 2075 8021 E: susanmrees@hotmail.com

REES, Canon Vivian John Howard. b 51. Southn Univ LLB 72 Ox Univ BA 79 MA 84 Leeds Univ MPhil 89. Wycliffe Hall Ox 76. **d** 79 **p** 80. C Moor Allerton *Ripon* 79–82; Sierra Leone 82–86; LtO *Ox* 86–21; Jt Dioc Reg 98–21; Dep Prov Reg 98–00; Prov Reg 00–21; Legal Adv ACC 98–21; Hon Prov Can Cant Cathl 01–21; Hon Can Ch Ox 17–21; Chapl to The Queen 14–21; rtd 21; LtO *Ox* from 21. *36 Cumnor Hill, Oxford OX2 9HB* T: (01865) 865875

REES-JONES, Mrs Diana Mary. b 58. St Jo Coll Dur BA 80 Anglia Ruskin Univ MA 07 Hughes Hall Cam PGCE 81. Ridley Hall Cam 04. **d** 07 **p** 08. C Ness Gp *Linc* 07–09; Asst Chapl Oundle Sch 09–13; PtO *Pet* 13–14; C Northampton St Giles 14–19; rtd 19; Hon C Ilkley All SS *Leeds* from 20. *7 Olicana Park, Ilkley LS29 0AW* E: reesjones.diana@gmail.com

REES-KENNY, Mrs Emma Louise. b 79. Univ of Wales (Abth) BTh 01. St Mich Coll Llan MTh 11. **d** 11 **p** 12. C Barry All SS *Llan* 11–15; V Llansantffraid-ym-Mechain and Llanfechain *St As* 15–16; TV Vyrnwy Miss Area 17–18; TV Canton Cardiff *Llan* from 18. *The New Rectory, 3A Romilly Road, Canton, Cardiff CF5 1FH* T: (01691) 829307 E: reverendemma@gmail.com

REESE, Preb John David. b 49. Cuddesdon Coll 73. **d** 76 **p** 77. C Kidderminster St Mary *Worc* 76–81; Malaysia 81–85; V Bishop's Castle w Mainstone *Heref* 85–91; RD Clun Forest 87–91; V Tupsley 91–93; P-in-c Hampton Bishop and Mordiford w Dormington 91–93; V Tupsley w Hampton Bishop 93–08; RD Heref City 96–02; Preb Heref S Wye 08–14; Preb Heref Cathl 96–14; rtd 14; PtO *Cov* 15–21. *32 Burns Road, Leamington Spa CV32 7EL* T: (01926) 833389

REEVE, Canon Brian Charles. b 36. Lon Univ BSc 57 BD 60. Tyndale Hall Bris 58. **d** 61 **p** 62. C Eccleston St Luke *Liv* 61–63; C Upton (Overchurch) *Ches* 63–65; C Pemberton St Mark Newtown *Liv* 65–68; V Macclesfield Ch Ch *Ches* 68–74; V Stone Ch Ch *Lich* 74–84; RD Trentham 77–84; V Hoole *Ches* 84–94; Chapl Ches City Hosp 84–91; P-in-c Alderley *Ches* 94–01; Dioc Warden of Readers 94–00; Hon Can Ches Cathl 94–01; rtd 01; PtO *Ches* 02–14; *Lich* 09–19. *18 Mount Crescent, Stone ST15 8LR* T: (01785) 749178 E: reeveinleek@talktalk.net

REEVE, David Michael. b 44. St Cath Coll Cam BA 67 MA 71. Coll of Resurr Mirfield 68. **d** 70 **p** 71. C Willingdon *Chich* 70–73; C Hove All SS 73–76; C Moulsecoomb 76–80; R Singleton and V E and W Dean 80–90; R Hurstpierpoint 90–99; R Kingston Buci 99–05; rtd 05; PtO *Cant* from 06; Clergy Widows Officer Cant Adnry from 09. *11 Wells Avenue, Canterbury CT1 3YB* T: (01227) 478446

REEVE, John Richard. b 65. Southn Univ BA 86 La Sainte Union Coll PGCE 88. Ripon Coll Cuddesdon 95. **d** 97 **p** 98. C Hale w Badshot Lea *Guildf* 97–00; TV Totton *Win* 00–21; P-in-c Copythorne 11–21; R Copythorne and Netley Marsh from 21. *The Vicarage, Ringwood Road, Woodlands, Southampton SO40 7GX* T: (023) 8066 3267 E: johnreeve6@aol.com

REEVE, Kenneth John. b 42. Sarum & Wells Th Coll 91. **d** 93 **p** 94. C Thorpe St Matt *Nor* 93–96; P-in-c S Lynn 96–99; PtO 03–04; P-in-c Gt and Lt Ellingham, Rockland and Shropham etc 04–11; RD Thetford and Rockland 09–11; rtd 11; PtO *Nor* from 11. *1 The Hop Kilns, Eardiston, Tenbury Wells WR15 8JH* E: kenreeve@btinternet.com

REEVE, Michael. *See* REEVE, David Michael

REEVE, Rebecca Louise Elizabeth. b 74. Univ Coll Lon BA 96 Lanc Univ PGCE 98 Univ of Wales (Cardiff) MA 03 Dur Univ MA 21. Coll of Resurr Mirfield 19. **d** 21. C Walbrook

---

Epiphany Derby from 21. *27 Clarence Road, Derby DE23 6LN* E: becky.haigh@hotmail.co.uk

REEVE, Richard Malcolm. b 64. Reading Univ BSc 85. Trin Coll Bris BA 92. **d** 92 **p** 93. C Northolt St Mary *Lon* 92–95; C Acton Green 95–98; V Hayes St Edm 98–08; TR Tettenhall Regis *Lich* from 08. *The Rectory, 2 Lloyd Road, Tettenhall, Wolverhampton WV6 9AU* T: (01902) 742801 E: richardmreeve@aol.com

REEVE, Sally Ann. *See* EPPS, Sally Ann

REEVES, David Eric. b 46. Sarum Th Coll 68. **d** 71 **p** 72. C Guildf H Trin w St Mary 71–74; C Warmsworth *Sheff* 74–78; V Herringthorpe 78–90; V Cleveleys *Blackb* 90–12; RD Poulton 94–00; rtd 12; PtO *Blackb* from 12. *443 North Drive, Thornton-Cleveleys FY5 3AP* T: (01253) 864636

REEVES, Donald St John. b 34. Qu Coll Cam BA 57 MA 61 Lambeth MLitt 03. Cuddesdon Coll 62. **d** 63 **p** 64. C Maidstone All SS w St Phil *Cant* 63–65; Bp's Dom Chapl S'wark 65–68; V St Helier 69–80; R Westmr St Jas *Lon* 80–98; Dir Soul of Eur Project from 98; rtd 98; PtO *Ex* from 00. *The Coach House, Church Street, Crediton EX17 2AQ* T: (01363) 775100 F: 773911 E: donalreeve@aol.com *or* donaldnunn34@gmail.com

REEVES, Elizabeth Anne. *See* THOMAS, Elizabeth Anne

REEVES, George Edward Charles. b 70. Dundee Univ MA 92. St Jo Coll Nottm 11. **d** 13 **p** 14. C Ashton Man 13–17; R Levenshulme from 17. *The Rectory, 27 Errwood Road, Manchester M19 2PN* M: 07484-310276 E: revgeorgereeves@outlook.com

REEVES, Gillian Patricia. b 46. S'wark Ord Course 87. **d** 90 **p** 94. Par Dn Shirley St Geo *S'wark* 90–94; C 94–96; C Caterham 96–98; TV 98–12; rtd 12. *3 Kynaston Court, Underwood Road, Caterham CR3 6BB* E: revgill99@hotmail.com

REEVES, Graham. b 65. Southn Univ BTh 94 Univ Coll Chich MA 04. Chich Th Coll 91. **d** 94 **p** 95. C Cardiff St Mary and St Steph w St Dyfrig etc *Llan* 94–95; C Roath 95–98; Chapl Sussex Weald and Downs NHS Trust 98–02; Chapl W Sussex Health and Soc Care NHS Trust 02–08; Chapl Sussex Partnership NHS Foundn Trust from 08; NSM Aldingbourne, Barnham and Eastergate *Chich* from 18; OSB from 11. *2 Abbottsbury, Bognor Regis PO21 4RX* T: (01243) 265209 E: graham.reeves@sussexpartnership.nhs.uk

REEVES, Helen Marie. b 68. SEITE BA 15. **d** 15 **p** 16. NSM Gravesend St Geo *Roch* 15–18; R Ash from 18; R Ridley from 18. *The Rectory, 11 Lambardes, New Ash Green, Longfield DA3 8HX* T: (01474) 872209 E: ashandridleyrector@gmail.com

REEVES, Karen Susan. b 56. Bris Univ BA 78. Ripon Coll Cuddesdon 02. **d** 05 **p** 07. C De Beauvoir Town St Pet *Lon* 05–06; C Islington St Jas w St Pet 06–08; Chapl Frimley Park Hosp NHS Foundn Trust 08–09; NSM Frimley *Guildf* 08–09; Chapl Milton Keynes Hosp NHS Foundn Trust 09–10; TV Coventry Caludon *Cov* 10–13; Min Stoke Aldermoor CD 13–15; P-in-c Moston St Jo *Man* 15–16; P-in-c Moston St Chad from 15; V Walsall Pleck and Bescot *Lich* 16–18; Chapl Epsom and St Helier Univ Hosps NHS Trust 18–21; P-in-c St Margarets-at-Cliffe w Westcliffe etc *Cant* from 21. *The Vicarage, Sea Street, St Margarets-at-Cliffe, Dover CT15 6AR* E: newvicar@gmail.com

REEVES, Mrs Katharine Vive. b 66. Derbys Coll of HE BEd 89. St Jo Coll Nottm 11. **d** 13 **p** 14. C Denton St Lawr *Man* 13–14; C Droylsden St Mary 14–17; PtO from 18. *The Rectory, 27 Errwood Road, Manchester M19 2PN* M: 07484-194681 E: revkatiereeves@hotmail.co.uk

REEVES, Kenneth William. b 38. TCD 67. **d** 69 **p** 70. C Killowen *D & R* 69–70; I Ardara 70–75; TV Quidenham *Nor* 76–81; V Swaffham 81–86; Chapl Nor City Coll of F&HE 86–91; P-in-c Lakenham St Alb 86–91; rtd 92; PtO *Nor* 92–98 and from 05; P-in-c Trowse 99–03; P-in-c Nerja and Almuñécar Eur 03–04. *Address temp unknown* E: revkenn@btinternet.com

REEVES, Maria Elizabeth Ann. *See* COULTER, Maria Elizabeth Ann

REEVES, Nicholas John Harding. b 44. Glos Univ BA 99 Nottm Univ MA 02 Dur Univ DThM 14. ALCD 69. **d** 69 **p** 70. C Upton (Overchurch) *Ches* 69–72; C Woodlands *Sheff* 72–74; C-in-c Cranham Park CD *Chelmsf* 74–79; V Cranham Park 79–88; rtd 89; PtO *Lich* 17–19. *Trefonen Cottage, Trefonen, Oswestry SY10 9DZ* T: (01691) 590172 M: 07400-340668 E: the7reeves@aol.com

REEVES, Pamela Lindsay. b 49. Ridley Hall Cam 06. **d** 07 **p** 08. C Immingham, Habrough Gp and Keelby Gp *Linc* 07–09; C Scawby, Redbourne and Hibaldstow 09–10; C Bishop Norton, Waddingham and Snitterby 09–10; C Kirton in Lindsey w Manton 09–10; C Grayingham 09–10; S Wolds Community Chapl from 10; C Wolds Gateway Group from

17. *Maple Cottage, Aylesby, Grimsby DN37 7AW* M: 07756-852907 E: pamcostin@yahoo.co.uk

REEVES, Mrs Sasha Louise. b 95. Dur Univ BA 21. Trin Coll Bris 17. **d** 21. C Didcot All SS *Ox* from 21. *23 The Avenue, Didcot OX11 6AW* M: 07955-754951 E: curate@didcotallsaints.org.uk

REGAN, Brian. b 46. MBIM 80. WMMTC 88. **d** 91 **p** 92. C Cov St Jo 91–94; V Tile Hill 94–09; rtd 09; PtO *Cov* from 09. *160 Ansley Road, Nuneaton CV10 8NU* M: 07766-721837 E: brianregan32@hotmail.com

REGAN, Canon Noel Henry Likely. b 49. **d** 99 **p** 00. Aux Min Cloonclare w Killasnett, Lurganboy and Drumlease *K, E & A* 99–06; Dioc C and P-in-c Garrison w Slavin and Belleek *Clogh* 06–11; I Clogh w Errigal Portclare 11–16; Prec Clogh Cathl 11–16; rtd 16; P-in-c Skreen w Kilmacshalgan and Dromard *T, K & A* from 18. *Gurteen Farm, Cliffoney, Co Sligo, Republic of Ireland* T: (00353) (71) 916 6253 M: 86-887 5714

REGAN, Paul John. b 67. Southn Univ BA 88 PhD 96 St Jo Coll Dur BA 98. Cranmer Hall Dur 96. **d** 99 **p** 00. C St Alb St Pet 99–03; TV Smestow Vale *Lich* 03–09; Chapl Trevelyan Coll *Dur* 09–14; Chapl Dur Univ 09–14; C Dur St Oswald and Shincliffe 09–14; Tutor Cranmer Hall Dur from 14. *Cranmer Hall, St John's College, 3 South Bailey, Durham DH1 3RJ* T: 0191-334 3893 E: cran.udos@durham.ac.uk

REICH, Joachim. b 66. St Patr Coll Maynooth 89 ERMC 18. **d** 96 **p** 99. C Berlin *Eur* from 19. *St George's Anglican Church, Preussenallee 17–19, 14052 Berlin, Germany* T: (0049) (30) 304 1280 E: reich.joachim@email.de

REID, Alison Margaret. *See* WADSWORTH, Alison Margaret

REID, Amanda Joy. *See* MARRIOTT, Amanda Joy

REID, Andrew John. b 58. Thames Poly BA 90. Trin Coll Bris 09. **d** 11 **p** 12. C Chorleywood St Andr *St Alb* 11–15; R Musselburgh *Edin* from 15. *12 Windsor Gardens, Musselburgh EH21 7LP* T: 0131-653 4809 *or* 665 3585 M: 07854-049875 E: revreidserving@gmail.com

REID, Andrew John. b 47. Birm Univ BEd 70 Man Univ MEd 76. S'wark Ord Course 88. **d** 88 **p** 89. NSM Westerham *Roch* 88–90; Chapl Abp Tenison's Sch Kennington 90–05; PtO *Roch* from 05. *12 Westways, Westerham TN16 1TT* T: (01959) 561428

REID, Andrew Kieran. b 67. Coll of SS Mark and Jo Plymouth BA 90. Trin Coll Bris 10. **d** 12 **p** 13. C Addlestone *Guildf* 12–15; C Woking Ch Ch 15–19; V New Haw from 19. *The Vicarage, 149 Woodham Lane, New Haw, Addlestone KT15 3NJ* M: 07799-883412 E: andykreid@outlook.com *or* newhawvicar@gmail.com

REID, Angus David Ingvar. b 77. K Coll Lon LLB 99 Nottm Univ MA 14 Dur Univ PhD 19. Westcott Ho Cam 14. **d** 18 **p** 19. C Hove All SS *Chich* from 18. *28 Lyndhurst Road, Hove BN3 6FA* T: (01273) 959158 M: 07884-207270 E: angusreid40@hotmail.com

REID, Catherine Elizabeth. b 79. Hull Univ BA 00 MA 02 St Petersburg State Univ PhD 07. Coll of Resurr Mirfield MA 14. **d** 14 **p** 15. C Ingleby Barwick *York* 14–17; V Ampleforth w Oswaldkirk, Gilling E etc 17–20; Chapl York Univ from 20. *The Vicarage, School Lane, Heslington, York YO10 5EE* E: crcatherinereid@gmail.com

REID, Christopher Jason. b 69. Glos Univ BA 08. Trin Coll Bris 01. **d** 03 **p** 04. C Woodley *Ox* 03–07; V Selby St Jas *York* from 07. *St James's Vicarage, 14 Leeds Road, Selby YO8 4HX* T: (01757) 702861 E: cjasonreid@hotmail.com

REID, Canon Colin Guthrie. b 30. **d** 56 **p** 57. C Kendal St Thos *Carl* 56–59; C Crosthwaite Keswick 59–60; R Caldbeck w Castle Sowerby 60–76; RD Wigton 69–70; P-in-c Sebergham 75; R Caldbeck, Castle Sowerby and Sebergham 76–93; Hon Can Carl Cathl 88–93; rtd 93; PtO *Carl* 93–20. *Mellbreak, Longthwaite Road, Wigton CA7 9JR* T: (016973) 45625

REID, David Graham. b 78. Hatf Coll Dur BSc 00. Wycliffe Hall Ox BTh 09. **d** 09 **p** 10. C Ox St Ebbe w H Trin and St Pet 09–18; PtO from 18. *50 Ramsay Road, Headington, Oxford OX3 8AY* T: (01865) 430965 E: davereid78@gmail.com

REID, Mrs Diane Mary. b 73. Lanc Univ BMus 94 Huddersfield Univ PGCE 98. Trin Coll Bris BA 04. **d** 04 **p** 05. C Reading St Agnes w St Paul and St Barn *Ox* 04–07; PtO *York* 11–12; Hon C Selby St Jas from 12. *St James's Vicarage, 14 Leeds Road, Selby YO8 4HX* T: (01757) 702861 E: dianereid2003@hotmail.com

REID, Donald. b 58. Glas Univ LLB 79 Pemb Coll Ox MPhil 81 Edin Univ BD 85. Edin Th Coll 82. **d** 85 **p** 86. C Greenock *Glas* 85–88; C Baillieston 88–91; R 91–95; C Glas St Serf 88–91; R 91–95; Chapl Glas Univ 89–00; Chapl Glas Caledonian Univ 89–00; Chapl Strathclyde Univ 89–00; TP Glas St Mary 95–00; Assoc P 00–04; C Edin St Jo 04–13; Chapl St Columba's Hospice Edin 13–16; PtO *Edin* 15–17. *Address temp unknown* E: dreid212@me.com

REID, Eileen. b 54. **d** 12 **p** 13. NSM Westward, Rosley-w-Woodside and Welton *Carl* 12–18; P-in-c from 18; NSM Caldbeck, Castle Sowerby and Sebergham 12–18; P-in-c from 18. *Ceardach, Brackenthwaite, Wigton CA7 8AS* T: (01697) 343089 E: ereid2002@yahoo.co.uk

REID, Gareth McEwan. b 82. Univ of Wales (Abth) BA 03. St Mich Coll Llan BTh 10. **d** 10 **p** 11. C Dewisland *St D* 10–13; P-in-c Llandysul w Bangor Teifi and Llanfairollwyn etc 13–20; P-in-c Dyffryn Teifi from 20; AD from 20; Dioc Warden Ords 14–15. *The Vicarage, Tanyfron, Well Street, Llandysul SA44 4DR* T: (01559) 363874 E: garethmreid@googlemail.com

✠**REID, The Rt Revd Gavin Hunter.** b 34. OBE 00. K Coll Lon BA 56. Oak Hill Th Coll 56. **d** 60 **p** 61 **c** 92. C E Ham St Paul *Chelmsf* 60–63; C Rainham 63–66; Publications Sec CPAS 66–71; Hon C St Paul's Cray St Barn *Roch* 68–71; Ed Sec USCL 71–74; Hon C Woking St Jo *Guildf* 72–92; Sec for Evang CPAS 74–92; Consultant Missr CPAS and BMU Adv 90–92; Suff Bp Maidstone *Cant* 92–00; Six Preacher Cant Cathl 92–97; rtd 00; PtO *Nor* from 00; *St E* from 00; Hon Asst Bp St E from 08. *Furzefield, 17 Richard Crampton Road, Beccles NR34 9HN* T: (01502) 717042 M: 07941-770549 E: gavin@reids.org

REID, Geraldine Felicity (Jo). b 47. RGN 69. EMMTC 95. **d** 98 **p** 99. NSM Skellingthorpe w Doddington *Linc* 98–02; NSM Hykeham from 02. *Tol Pedn, Monson Park, Skellingthorpe, Lincoln LN6 5UE* T: (01522) 828402 *or* 828403 E: tolpedn@ntlworld.com

REID, James. b 46. Strathclyde Univ BSc 69. WMMTC 88. **d** 91 **p** 92. C Attleborough *Cov* 91–95; V Walsall Pleck and Bescot *Lich* 95–99; TR Chell 99–06; rtd 06; PtO *Cov* from 08. *22 St Ives Way, Nuneaton CV11 6FR* T: (024) 7634 2264 E: jimoreid@gmail.com

REID, Jason. *See* REID, Christopher Jason

REID, Jo. *See* REID, Geraldine Felicity

REID, Joanne. b 68. St Mich Coll Llan 08. **d** 10 **p** 11. C Brize Norton and Carterton *Ox* 10–14; TV Savernake *Sarum* from 14. *The Vicarage, Church Street, Collingbourne Ducis, Marlborough SN8 3EL* T: (01264) 850385 E: jo.reid185@btinternet.com

REID, Kirrilee Anne. b 70. Canberra Univ BTh 06. St Mark's Coll Canberra. **d** 06 **p** 07. C Canberra St Jo Australia 06–07; C Chapman 09–10; Youth Min Course Co-ord Chas Stuart Univ 07–10; R Glencarse *Bre* 10–18; Dioc Dir of Ord 12–16; Dioc Min Officer 14–18; Chapl and Refugee Project Officer Nord Pas de Calais *Eur* 18–20. *The Bield Retreat Centre, Blackruthven House, Tibbermore, Perth PH1 1PY* T: (01738) 583238 E: kirrilee.reid@gmail.com

REID, Miss Margaret Patricia. b 41. Hull Univ BSc 62 Leeds Univ MA 07. Yorks Min Course 09. **d** 10 **p** 11. NSM Ilkley All SS *Bradf* 10–14; *Leeds* 14–16; PtO from 17; *Dur* from 21. *2 Bishopbek Hall, Lee Hill Court, Lanchester, Durham DH7 0QE* E: pat.reid29@btinternet.com

REID, Mrs Pauline Ann. b 57. Anglia Ruskin Univ MA 10. EAMTC 00. **d** 03 **p** 04. C Silverstone and Abthorpe w Slapton etc *Pet* 03–07; P-in-c Raddesley Gp *Ely* 07–14; P-in-c Cley Hill Villages *Sarum* 14–19; R from 19; RD Heytesbury from 15. *The Rectory, 6 Homefields, Longbridge Deverill, Warminster BA12 7DQ* T: (01985) 841290 M: 07586-358162 E: revpauline@btinternet.com

REID, Roderick Andrew Montgomery. b 80. Brunel Univ BSc 01 Trin Hall Cam BTh 10. Westcott Ho Cam 08. **d** 11 **p** 12. C Waltham H Cross *Chelmsf* 11–14; P-in-c Bocking St Mary 14–16; C Panfield and Rayne 16; P-in-c Bocking St Mary and Panfield from 16; RD Braintree from 20. *The Deanery, Deanery Hill, Braintree CM7 5SR* T: (01376) 324887 M: 07799-734898 E: rod.a.reid@gmail.com

REID, Stewart Thomas. b 45. Liv Hope MA 01. Oak Hill Th Coll 66. **d** 70 **p** 71. C Normanton *Derby* 70–73; C Leyland St Andr *Blackb* 73–78; V Halliwell St Luke *Man* 78–95; V Southport Ch Ch *Liv* 95–16; rtd 16; PtO *Liv* from 16. *1 Sanderling Drive, Banks, Southport PR9 8RY* T: (01704) 226400 E: stewartreid1945@icloud.com

REID, Stuart Alexander. York Univ MEng. CITI. **d** 17 **p** 19. Faughanvale *D & R* 17–19; NSM Ballymoney w Finvoy and Rasharkin *Conn* from 19. *41 Millburn Road, Coleraine BT52 1QT* M: 07951-723619 E: streid@tcd.ie *or* stuandgwyn@me.com

REIDE, Susannah Louise Court. b 69. Clare Coll Cam BA 91. Trin Coll Bris BA 04. **d** 04 **p** 05. C Marlborough *Sarum* 04–08; TV Cowley St Jas *Ox* 08–11; PtO 11–18; Chapl Harris Manchester Coll Ox from 18; C Ox St Mary V w St Cross and St Pet 20–21. *96 Cricket Road, Oxford OX4 3DJ* T: (01865) 401439 E: sr@reide.plus.com

REIGATE, Archdeacon of. *See* ASTIN, The Ven Moira Anne Elizabeth

REILLY, Thomas Gerard. b 38. d 64 p 64. In RC Ch 64–73; Hon C Clapton Park All So *Lon* 73–76; Hon C Haggerston All SS 76–78; Hon C Walthamstow St Sav *Chelmsf* 79–85; P-in-c Forest Gate Em w Upton Cross 85–89; V 89–92; V Chaddesden St Phil *Derby* 92–01; RD Derby N 95–00; rtd 01; PtO *B & W* 01–12 and from 17; *Eur* from 17. *High Beech, East Street, Crewkerne TA18 7AG* T: (01460) 76246 E: grryreilly@yahoo.co.uk

REILY, Jacqueline Estelle. b 61. Oak Hill Th Coll BA 84. ERMC 08. d 11 p 12. C Rayleigh *Chelmsf* 11–14; Chapl Scargill Ho from 14; Community Ldr St Oswald's Community Sleights from 20. *Scargill House, Kettlewell, Skipton BD23 5HU* T: (01756) 761236 M: 07580-114641 E: admin@scargillmovement.org *or* jackie@reily.co.uk *or* jackie.reily@scargillmovement.org

REILY, Paul Alan. b 59. UEA BA 81. St Jo Coll Nottm MA 92. d 92 p 93. C Westcliff St Mich *Chelmsf* 92–96; P-in-c Barkingside St Cedd 96–98; V 98–01; V Leyton St Cath and St Paul 01–11; AD Waltham Forest 04–07; PtO 11–14; *Leeds* from 17; Community Ldr St Oswald's Community Sleights from 20. *Scargill House, Kettlewell, Skipton BD23 5HU* T: (01756) 761236 M: 07967-977115 E: paul@reily.co.uk

REINDORP, David Peter Edington. b 52. TD 05 DL 14. Trin Coll Cam BA 82 MA 86 CQSW 77. Westcott Ho Cam 79. d 83 p 84. C Chesterton Gd Shep *Ely* 83–85; C Hitchin *St Alb* 85–88; R Landbeach and V Waterbeach *Ely* 88–97; OCM 88–97; CF(V) 92–12; RD Quy *Ely* 94–97; V Cherry Hinton St Jo 97–06; RD Cambridge 04–06; Hon Can Ely Cathl 05–06; V Chelsea All SS *Lon* 06–21; AD Chelsea 11–17. *2 Old Church Street, London SW3 5DQ* T: (020) 7352 5627 E: david.reindorp@talk21.com

REINDORP, Canon Michael Christopher Julian. b 44. Trin Coll Cam BA 67 MA 70 K Coll Lon MA 99. Cuddesdon Coll 67 United Th Coll Bangalore 68. d 69 p 70. C Poplar *Lon* 69–74; V Chatham St Wm *Roch* 74–84; R Stantonbury *Ox* 84–87; TR Stantonbury and Willen 87–92; P-in-c Richmond St Mary w St Matthias and St Jo *S'wark* 92–95; TR 96–09; Hon Can *S'wark* Cathl 03–09; rtd 09; PtO *Lon* from 10; *S'wark* from 11. *10 Alpha Road, Teddington TW11 0QG* T: (020) 8614 6800 E: julianreindorp@hotmail.co.uk

REISS, Prof Michael Jonathan. b 58. Trin Coll Cam BA 78 MA 82 PhD 82 Open Univ MBA 02 PGCE 83 FIBiol 90 FISSR 13. EAMTC 87. d 90 p 91. Lect Cam Univ 88–94; Sen Lect and Reader 94–00; NSM Comberton *Ely* 94–00; NSM Deanery of Bourn 94–96; NSM 99–00; P-in-c Boxworth and Elsworth w Knapwell 96–99; PtO 99–03; Prof Science Educn Inst of Educn Lon Univ from 01; NSM Toft w Caldecote and Childerley *Ely* 03–10; P-in-c 03–05; NSM Lordsbridge from 10. *Institute of Education, University College London, 20 Bedford Way, London WC1H 0AL* T: (020) 7612 6800 E: m.reiss@ucl.ac.uk

REISS, Canon Peter Henry. b 62. Hertf Coll Ox BA 85 MA 91 Natal Univ MA 95. St Jo Coll Nottm 95. d 95 p 96. C Sherwood *S'well* 95–00; TV Bestwood 00–03; V Bestwood Park w Rise Park 03–04; Tr Officer CME and Laity Development *Man* 04–06; Dir Discipleship and Min Tr 06–19; TR Turton Moorland from 19; Hon Can Man Cathl from 11. *St Anne's Vicarage, High Street, Turton, Bolton BL7 0EH* E: peter.reiss@yahoo.co.uk

REISS, Canon Robert Paul. b 43. Trin Coll Cam BA 67 MA 71 Lambeth PhD 12. Westcott Ho Cam 67. d 69 p 70. C St John's Wood *Lon* 69–73; Bangladesh 73; Chapl Trin Coll Cam 73–78; Selection Sec ACCM 78–85; Sen Selection Sec 83; TR Grantham *Linc* 86–96; RD 92–96; Adn Surrey and Hon Can Guildf Cathl 96–05; Can Westmr Abbey 05–13; rtd 13; Min and Tr Consultant *S'wark* 13–14; PtO from 13. *35 Addington Square, London SE5 7LB* M: 07545-178192 E: bobreiss@hotmail.co.uk

REITH, David Robert. b 82. Oak Hill Th Coll 14. d 17 p 18. C Weldon w Deene *Pet* 17–20; R Brixworth w Holcot from 20. *The Vicarage, Station Road, Brixworth, Northampton NN6 9DF* T: (01604) 880139 E: revdavidreith@gmail.com

REITH, Robert Michael. b 55. Oak Hill Th Coll BA 83. d 83 p 84. C Kendal St Thos *Carl* 83–87; C Leyland St Andr *Blackb* 87–92; V Leyland St Jo 92–94; TR Dagenham *Chelmsf* 94–03; V 03–14; rtd 14. *1 Coneygreave Drive, Drakelow, Burton-on-Trent DE15 9UL* T: (01283) 509118 M: 07595-303023 E: mikereith@me.com

RENAUT, Vanessa Anne. *See* HERRICK, Vanessa Anne

RENDALL, Canon John Albert. b 43. Hull Univ BTh 84 MA 89. Ripon Hall Ox 65. d 68 p 69. C Southsea St Simon *Portsm* 68–71; C Wallington *S'wark* 71–77; P-in-c Rufforth w Moor Monkton and Hessay *York* 77–79; R 79–08; P-in-c Long Marston 77–79; R 79–08; RD New Ainsty 85–97; P-in-c Healaugh w Wighill, Bilbrough and Askham Richard 02–08; P-in-c Tockwith and Bilton w Bickerton 03–08; Can

and Preb York Minster 94–08; Chapl Purey Cust Nuffield Hosp 82–04; rtd 08; PtO *York* from 09. *5 Wains Road, York YO24 2TP* T: (01904) 778764 E: canjohnrendall@aol.com

RENDALL, Richard John. b 54. Wadh Coll Ox BA 76 LLB 76 MA 92 Solicitor 78. Wycliffe Hall Ox 90. d 92 p 93. C Heswall *Ches* 92–98; R High Ongar w Norton Mandeville *Chelmsf* 98–04; R Broadwell, Evenlode, Oddington, Adlestrop etc *Glouc* 04–21; rtd 21. *Address temp unknown* E: rendalls@talk21.com

RENDALL, Mrs Susan. b 49. Northumbria Univ MA 94. Lindisfarne Regional Tr Partnership 13. d 13 p 14. NSM Kenton Ascension *Newc* 13–18; NSM Weetslade from 18. *5 Fawdon Walk, Brunton Bridge, Newcastle upon Tyne NE13 7AW* T: 0191-286 5090 E: irendall@btinternet.com

RENDELL, Jason. b 68. d 05 p 09. Chapl to Bp Stepney *Lon* 05–07; NSM Clerkenwell H Redeemer 06–07; NSM Clerkenwell St Mark 06–07; Min Can and Succ St Paul's Cathl 07–09; Min Can and Sacr St Paul's Cathl 09–13; Chapl to Bp Chich 13–14; V Kingsbury St Andr *Lon* from 14. *St Andrew's Vicarage, 28 Old Church Lane, London NW9 8RZ* T: (020) 8205 7447

RENDLE, Graham Barton. b 40. d 99 p 00. OLM Rougham, Beyton w Hessett and Rushbrooke *St E* 99–10; rtd 10; PtO *St E* 10–16 and 20–21. *Appletrees, Bury Road, Beyton, Bury St Edmunds IP30 9AB* T: (01359) 270924 E: graham.rendle@tiscali.co.uk

RENDLE, Lesley Joy. b 17. d 17 p 18. NSM Bro Tysilio *Ban* from 17. *Hafod Rhug, Llandonna, Beaumaris LL58 8UR* T: (01248) 810965 E: lesley.rendle@gmail.com

RENFREY, Edward Donald John-Baptist. b 53. ACT. d 76 p 77. C Naracoorte Australia 76–77; P-in-c Kingston w Robe 78–81; R 81–84; Chapl RN 84–00; Chapl R Aus Navy Australia 00–10; rtd 10. *4 Coconut Grove, Kuranda QLD 4872, Australia* T: (0061) (7) 4093 7296 M: 45-893 7222 E: edwardrenfrey@hotmail.com

RENGERT, Mrs Helen Caroline. b 70. Open Univ BSc 97 Anglia Ruskin Univ MA 14 RGN 92. ERMC 10. d 13 p 14. C Thorpe St Matt *Nor* 13–17; C Reepham and Wensum Valley 17–18; TV 18–20; R from 20; Chapl Reepham High Sch and Coll from 19. *The Rectory, Station Road, Reepham, Norwich NR10 4LJ* T: (01603) 871263 *or* 879275 E: helen.rengert@dioceseofnorwich.org *or* revdhelenrwv@gmail.com

RENGERT, Keith Alan Francis. b 67. RGN 92. Ripon Coll Cuddesdon 07. d 09 p 10. C N Walsham and Edingthorpe *Nor* 09–12; R Horsham St Faith, Spixworth and Crostwick 12–17; TR Reepham and Wensum Valley 17–20; TV from 20; RD Ingworth and Sparham from 19; Chapl Reepham High Sch and Coll from 19; Hon PV Nor Cathl 14–20; Chapl E of England Ambulance Service from 16; Chapl E Anglian Air Ambulance from 16. *The Rectory, Station Road, Reepham, Norwich NR10 4LJ* T: (01603) 879275 M: 07796-607649 E: revdkeith@gmail.com

RENISON, Simon James. b 88. St Mellitus Coll BA 18. d 18 p 19. C Southport Ch Ch *Liv* 18–20; C Parr Mount 20–21; C Warrington E from 21. *105 Hallfields Road, Warrington WA2 8DS* M: 07891-323291 E: renison.s@hotmail.co.uk

RENNARD, Margaret Rose. b 49. CertEd 75. Linc Th Coll 76. dss 80 d 87 p 94. C Fairfield St Matt *Linc* 87–88; C Hykeham 88–00; Chapl HM Pris Morton Hall 91–00; Asst Chapl HM Pris Blundeston 00–01; Asst Chapl HM Pris Hollesley Bay from 01; Chapl Allington NHS Trust 00–01; PtO *St E* from 00. *The Rectory, Highfield Road, Halesworth IP19 8SJ* T: (01986) 872602 E: edward.rennard@btinternet.com

RENNIE, John Aubery. b 47. Lon Univ MB, BS 70 FRCS 75. SEITE 04. d 06 p 07. NSM Melbury *Sarum* 06–10; NSM Sherborne w Castleton, Lillington and Longburton 10–12; Deanery Missr Sherborne 12–16; rtd 16; P-in-c Upper Dever Win from 19. *10 Pigeonhouse Field, Sutton Scotney, Winchester SO21 3NJ* M: 07552-034225 E: johnrennie40@hotmail.com

RENNISON, Mrs Patricia Elinor. b 46. d 11 p 12. OLM Shilbottle *Newc* 11–16; rtd 16; PtO *Newc* from 16. *8 The Crescent, Shilbottle, Alnwick NE66 2UU* T: (01665) 575686 E: patriciarennison983@btinternet.com

RENNIX, Raymond Latham. b 37. QUB BTh 02. CITC 00. d 03 p 04. NSM Killaney w Carryduff *D & D* 03–08; NSM Glencraig 08–12; rtd 12. *5 Brompton Court, Dromara, Dromore BT25 2DQ* T: (028) 9753 3167 M: 07977-584053 E: r.rennix@btinternet.com

RENSHAW, Mrs Anne-Marie Louise. b 71. St Hilda's Coll Ox MA 96 Fitzw Coll Cam BA 97. Ridley Hall Cam 95. d 98 p 99. C Norton *St Alb* 98–02; TV Borehamwood 02–05; TV Elstree and Borehamwood 05–11; P-in-c Tolleshunt Knights w Tiptree and Gt Braxted *Chelmsf* 11–13; TR Thurstable and Winstree from 13. *The Rectory, Rectory Road, Tiptree, Colchester CO5 0SX* T: (01621) 815260 E: amlrenshaw@btinternet.com

RENSHAW, Mrs Claire Louise. b 80. Yorks Min Course 12. **d** 15 **p** 16. C Knaresborough *Leeds* 15–18; P-in-c Walkingham Hill 18–19; R from 19. *The Rectory, Main Sreet, Staveley, Knaresborough HG5 9LD* T: (01423) 341957 M: 07912-104442 E: claire.renshaw@sky.com *or* claire.renshaw@leeds.anglican.org

RENSHAW, David William. b 59. Oak Hill Th Coll BA 85. **d** 85 **p** 86. C Shawbury *Lich* 85–88; V Childs Ercall and R Stoke upon Tern 88–92; V Stoneleigh *Guildf* 92–97; RD Epsom 95–97; Chapl Scarborough and NE Yorks Healthcare NHS Trust 97–99; Chapl St Cath Hospice Scarborough 97–99; R Meppershall w Campton and Stondon *St Alb* 99–01; C Bedford St Andr 02; PtO *Chich* 05–06; Hon C Bexhill St Pet 06; TV Rye 09–11; P-in-c Lynch w Iping Marsh and Milland 11–12; R 12–14; PtO 16–18; P-in-c Worthing Ch Ch 18–19; V from 19. *102 Wallace Avenue, Worthing BN11 5QA* T: (01903) 244283 E: renshaw221@btinternet.com

RENSHAW, Canon Susan Kathryn. b 55. Shenstone Coll of Educn CertEd 77. WMMTC 99. **d** 02 **p** 03. C Sedgley All SS *Worc* 02–05; C Gornal and Sedgley 05–06; V Eckington 06–18; V Defford w Besford 06–18; C Overbury w Teddington, Alstone etc 09–18; RD Pershore 11–18; Hon Can Worc Cathl 15–18; rtd 18. *41 Myatt Road, Offenham, Evesham WR11 8SB* T: (01386) 421580 E: canonsusan@btinternet.com

RENYARD, Paul Holmwood. b 42. K Coll Lon BD 65 AKC 65. **d** 66 **p** 67. C Croydon St Aug *Cant* 66–69; C Farnham *Guildf* 69–72; V Capel 72–78; Asst Dir RE 72–78; Asst Dir RE *Roch* 78–83; Hon C Roch St Pet w St Marg 78–83; V Holdenhurst *Win* 83–95; V Pennington 95–07; rtd 07; PtO *Win* from 07; *Sarum* 07–22. *53 Scarf Road, Poole BH17 8QJ* T: (01202) 682460 E: vandprenyard@gmail.com

RENZ, Thomas. b 69. Freie Theologische Akademie Giessen MA 93 Chelt & Glouc Coll of HE PhD 97. Coll of Resurr Mirfield 09. **d** 09 **p** 10. C Highgate St Mich *Lon* 09–12; R Monken Hadley from 12. *The Rectory, Hadley Common, Barnet EN5 5QD* T: (020) 8449 9441 M: 07933-073692 E: thomas.renz@gmail.com

REPATH, John Richard. b 48. St Mich Coll Llan 72. **d** 75 **p** 76. C Canton St Jo *Llan* 75–79; C Burghclere w Newtown and Ecchinswell w Sydmonton *Win* 80–83; R Bewcastle and Stapleton *Carl* 83–88; P-in-c Kirklinton w Hethersgill and Scaleby 86–88; R Bewcastle, Stapleton and Kirklinton etc 88–97; P-in-c New Galloway *Glas* 97–18; rtd 18; PtO *Heref* from 19. *9 The Meads, Kington HR5 3DQ* T: (01544) 239245 E: johnrepath@btinternet.com

REPTON, Suffragan Bishop of. *See* MACNAUGHTON, The Rt Revd William Malcolm

RESCH, Colin Ernst. b 67. Trin Coll Bris 04. **d** 06 **p** 07. C Highley w Billingsley, Glazeley etc *Heref* 06–10; P-in-c Stottesdon w Farlow, Cleeton St Mary etc 10–14; P-in-c Mountsorrel Ch Ch and St Pet *Leic* from 14. *Christ Church Vicarage, 4 Rothley Road, Mountsorrel, Loughborough LE12 7JU* E: colin@godstuff.org.uk

RESCH, Mrs Elizabeth Barbara. b 66. Edge Hill Coll of HE BEd 88 Cant Ch Ch Univ BA 16. SEITE 10. **d** 13 **p** 14. C Sittingbourne w Bobbing *Cant* 13–21; PtO *Leeds* 21. *The Vicarage, Wheatlands Road, Harrogate HG2 8AZ* M: 07454-242679 E: lizresch@me.com

RESCH, Michael Johann. b 63. NTMTC 96. **d** 99 **p** 00. C Cullompton, Willand, Uffculme, Kentisbeare etc *Ex* 99–03; P-in-c Sittingbourne H Trin w Bobbing *Cant* 03–12; TR Sittingbourne w Bobbing 12–21; AD Sittingbourne 15–21; V Harrogate St Mark *Leeds* from 21. *The Vicarage, Wheatlands Road, Harrogate HG2 8AZ* M: 07967-771231 E: mikeresch@me.com

RESTALL, Miss Susan Roberta. b 45. MSc. Sarum & Wells Th Coll 79. **dss** 82 **d** 87 **p** 94. Dorchester *Sarum* 82–84; Portland All SS w St Pet 84–87; Par Dn 87; Team Dn Yate New Town *Bris* 87–94; TV 94–95; Chapl Birm Heartlands and Solihull NHS Trust 95–01; rtd 01; PtO *Birm* from 03. *45 Fentham Road, Hampton-in-Arden, Solihull B92 0AY* E: suerestall@gmail.com

REUSS, Nathanael. b 76. Ballarat Univ BSc 98. St Jo Coll Nottm MA(MM) 12. **d** 11 **p** 12. C Ripley *Derby* 11–13; C Brailsford w Shirley, Osmaston w Edlaston etc 13–14; C Launceston St Jo Australia 15–17; P-in-c Onkaparinga Valley 17–19; C Norwood from 19. *PO Box 4231, South Norwood SA 5067, Australia* M: (0061) 44-829 7863 E: nathanaelreuss@gmail.com

REVELEY, Canon James Stewart. b 69. Goldsmiths' Coll Lon BMus 92 Ox Univ BA 95 MA 00. Ripon Coll Cuddesdon Ch Div Sch of the Pacific (USA) 95. **d** 96 **p** 97. C Goldington *St Alb* 96–00; C Harpenden St Nic 00–04; V Boxmoor St Jo 04–13; V Bedford St Andr 13–20; Can Res Ely Cathl from 20. *The Black Hostelry, The College, Ely CB7 4DL* T: (01353) 660302 E: j.reveley@elycathedral.org

REVELL, Roger Lawson. b 82. Wycliffe Hall Ox BTh 11. Vancouver Sch of Th MTh 16. **d** 15 **p** 15. PtO *Ely* 18–21. *Selwyn College, Cambridge CB3 9DQ* E: roger.revell@theology.oxon.org

REW, Eric Malcolm. b 63. UEA BSc 84 PGCE 89. Qu Coll Birm 98. **d** 00 **p** 01. C Shepshed *Leic* 00–04; TV Kingsthorpe *Pet* 04–16; Chapl Northants Police 07–16; Chapl HM Pris Gartree 16–18; PtO *Leic* from 18. *14 Brampton Way, Brixworth, Northampton NN6 9BD* T: (01604) 883573

REY, Joshua Barnabas. b 65. Ball Coll Ox BA 03 MA 10. Ripon Coll Cuddesdon BA 11 MSt 12. **d** 12 **p** 13. C Streatham St Leon *S'wark* 12–16; Bp's Chapl 16–20; V Roehampton H Trin from 20; Hon Min Can S'wark Cathl from 16. *Holy Trinity Vicarage, 7 Ponsonby Road, London SW15 4LA* T: (020) 3726 8580 M: 07525-421681 E: mail@joshuarey.com

REYNISH, David Stuart. b 52. Nottm Univ BEd 75. Linc Th Coll 72. **d** 77 **p** 78. C Boston *Linc* 77–80; C Chalfont St Peter *Ox* 80–84; V Thursby *Carl* 84–88; R Iver Heath *Ox* 88–03; V Kelvedon and Feering *Chelmsf* 03–13; TR Bexhill St Pet *Chich* 13–20; rtd 20; PtO *Glouc* from 21. *34 Ben Grazebrook Well, Stroud GL5 1DL*

REYNOLDS, Alan Thomas William. b 43. Lon Univ BSc 64. Linc Th Coll 64. **d** 66 **p** 67. C Leic St Pet 66–70; C Huntington *York* 70–72; R Darliston Jamaica 72–76; V Stechford *Birm* 76–83; Chapl E Birm Hosp 76–83; P-in-c Hampton in Arden *Birm* 83–86; V 87–93; Chapl Parkway Hosp Solihull 83–93; V Moseley St Anne *Birm* 93–02; Chapl Moseley Hall Hosp Birm 93; Chapl Birm Community Healthcare NHS Foundn Trust 94–02; V Kerry, Llanmerewig, Dolfor and Mochdre *St As* 02–08; AD Cedewain 03–08; rtd 08; PtO *Lich* 08–21; *St As* from 09. *49 Gittin Street, Oswestry SY11 1DU* T: (01691) 680416 E: robbie.reynolds1@btinternet.com

REYNOLDS, Mrs Angela Heather. b 46. Wye Coll Lon BSc 66 Birm Univ CertEd 67. EAMTC 94. **d** 97 **p** 98. NSM Barnham Broom *Nor* 97–99; C Easton w Colton and Marlingford 99–00; P-in-c Easton, Colton, Marlingford and Bawburgh 00–09; rtd 09; PtO *Nor* from 09; Hon PV Nor Cathl from 14. *26 Clickers Road, Norwich NR3 2DD* T: (01603) 402688 E: angord@btinternet.com

REYNOLDS, David James. b 48. TD 03. St Jo Coll Dur BA 72 Lanc Univ MA 85 Univ of Wales (Trin St Dav) MMin 13. Cranmer Hall Dur 69. **d** 73 **p** 74. C Formby H Trin *Liv* 73–77; P-in-c Widnes St Paul 77–80; V Southport St Paul 80–87; P-in-c Mawdesley *Blackb* 87–91; R 91–14; P-in-c Croston and Bretherton 06–13; R 13–14; CF (TA) 87–03; Chapl Derian Ho Children's Hospice 93–97; rtd 14; PtO *Blackb* from 14; *Liv* from 16. *Holly Mount, Rufford Road, Bispham, Ormskirk L40 3SA* T: (01704) 821684 E: rectordavid@hotmail.co.uk

REYNOLDS, Mrs Emily Jane. b 84. Lanc Univ BA 05. Westcott Ho Cam 11. **d** 15 **p** 16. C Walsall St Paul *Lich* 15–19; V Walsall Pleck and Bescot from 19. *St John's Vicarage, Vicarage Terrace, Walsall WS2 9HB* M: 07964-598760

REYNOLDS, Gordon. b 42. Sarum & Wells Th Coll 71. **d** 72 **p** 73. C Tunstall *Lich* 72–74; USPG Zambia 75–88; C Southmead *Bris* 88–90; rtd 07. *78 William Bentley Court, Graiseley Lane, Wolverhampton WV11 1QW* T: (01902) 730381

REYNOLDS, Hannah Claire. b 67. Kingston Univ MBA 95. St Steph Ho Ox BTh 09. **d** 06 **p** 07. C Twickenham All Hallows *Lon* 06–09; P-in-c Hanworth All SS 09–13; P-in-c Didcot St Pet *Ox* from 13. *The Vicarage, 47A Newlands Avenue, Didcot OX11 8QA* T: (01235) 812114 M: 07981-981493 E: hcreynolds@hotmail.co.uk

REYNOLDS, Canon John Lionel. b 34. JP . Westmr Coll Ox MTh 00. Chich Th Coll 58. **d** 61 **p** 62. C Whitkirk *Ripon* 61–64; C Tong *Bradf* 64–68; V Chisledon and Draycot Foliatt *Sarum* 68–74; TR Ridgeway 74–76; RD Marlborough 74–76; V Calne and Blackland 76–89; RD Calne 77–84; Can and Preb Sarum Cathl 80–02; V Woodford Valley 89–02; rtd 02; PtO *Sarum* 02–10; *Win* from 03. *St Edmund, 21 New Road, Romsey SO51 7LL* T: (01794) 516349 E: carolannreynolds@aol.com

REYNOLDS, Mandy Elizabeth. b 59. NTMTC 99. **d** 02 **p** 03. NSM Wembley St Jo *Lon* 02–04; CF 04–15; R Alde River *St E* 15–16; Chapl Ipswich Hosp NHS Trust 16–18; Chapl E Suffolk and N Essex NHS Foundn Trust 18–19; TV Wilford Peninsula *St E* from 19; PtO *Chelmsf* from 18. *The Vicarage, 11 Walnut Tree Avenue, Rendlesham, Woodbridge IP12 2GG* T: (01394) 420129 E: revmandy.rendlesham@yahoo.co.uk

REYNOLDS, Marion. b 49. Chelmer Inst of HE CertEd 84. STETS 04. **d** 06 **p** 07. NSM Quantock Towers *B & W* 06–07; NSM Shelswell *Ox* 07–11; P-in-c Pattishall w Cold Higham and Gayton w Tiffield *Pet* 12–16; R 16–17; V Fulford w Hilderstone *Lich* 17–21; rtd 21. *Address temp unknown* M: 07834-062268 E: marion.reynolds2@btopenworld.com

REYNOLDS, Michael. *See* REYNOLDS, Richard Michael

REYNOLDS, Michelle Angela. b 70. Ridley Hall Cam 02. d 04 p 05. C Hoddesdon *St Alb* 04–07; TV Grays Thurrock *Chelmsf* 07–18; rtd 18; PtO *Chelmsf* from 18. *3B Bower Grove, West Mersea, Colchester CO5 8GJ* M: 07854-055660 E: michellea_reynolds@hotmail.com

REYNOLDS, Paul Andrew. b 57. BA 86. Trin Coll Bris 83. d 86 p 87. C Reading St Jo *Ox* 86–90; C Dorridge *Birm* 90–95; TV Riverside *Ox* 95–06; R Beercrocombe w Curry Mallet, Hatch Beauchamp etc *B & W* 06–18; rtd 18; PtO *Ex* from 19. *Nutshell Cottage, South Knighton, Newton Abbot TQ12 6NT*

REYNOLDS, Paul Frederick. b 56. St Jo Coll Nottm 90. d 92 p 93. C Hyde St Geo *Ches* 92–96; P-in-c Delamere 96–00; Asst Dir Par Support and Development 96–98; Acting Dir 98–00; V Handforth *Ches* 00–07; P-in-c Bramcote *S'well* 07–11; V from 11. *The Vicarage, Moss Drive, Bramcote, Beeston NG9 3NF* T: 0115-922 9600 E: vicar@bramcoteparishchurch.com

REYNOLDS, Philip Delamere. b 53. Leeds Univ CertEd 74 Nottm Univ BCombStuds 82. Linc Th Coll 79. d 82 p 83. C Huddersfield St Jo *Wakef* 82–85; C Barkisland w W Scammonden 85–87; P-in-c Skelmanthorpe 87–14; *Leeds* 14–18; V 18–19; rtd 19. *St Aidan's Vicarage, Radcliffe Street, Skelmanthorpe, Huddersfield HD8 9AF* T: (01484) 863232

REYNOLDS, Raymond Ernest. b 29. Nottm Univ MPhil 89. Lambeth STh 84 CA Tr Coll 50 Chich Th Coll 58. d 60 p 61. C Leeds St Marg *Ripon* 60–62; C Beeston *S'well* 62–64; R Farnley *Ripon* 64–76; R Higham-on-the-Hill w Fenny Drayton *Leic* 76–81; R Higham-on-the-Hill w Fenny Drayton and Witherley 81–90; V Sutton *Ely* 90–94; R Witcham w Mepal 90–94; rtd 94; C Nantwich *Ches* 94–96; PtO 96–14. *4 St Alban's Drive, Nantwich CW5 7DW* T: (01270) 623534 E: syl.rayreynolds@gmail.com

REYNOLDS, Richard Michael. b 42. St Steph Ho Ox 65. d 67 p 68. C Kidderminster St Mary *Worc* 67–70; Guyana 70–73; TV N Creedy *Ex* 73–80; R Holsworthy w Hollacombe 80–86; R Holsworthy w Hollacombe and Milton Damerel 86–12; Chapl N Devon Healthcare NHS Trust 94–12; rtd 12. *Blagrove, Germansweek, Beaworthy EX21 5BH* T: (01837) 871226 E: michaelreynolds64@hotmail.co.uk

REYNOLDS, Roderick Bredon (Rory). b 58. Man Univ BA 80. Ripon Coll Cuddesdon 93. d 95 p 96. C Hitchin *St Alb* 95–98; C Stevenage St Andr and St Geo 98–00; P-in-c High Wych and Gilston w Eastwick 00–06; TV Plaistow and N Canning Town *Chelmsf* 06–10; Chapl S Lon and Maudsley NHS Foundn Trust 10–12; Chapl SW Lon and St George's Mental Health NHS Trust 12–13; Chapl St Geo Healthcare NHS Trust Lon from 13; PtO *S'wark* from 16. *63B South Croxted Road, London SE21 8BA* M: 07515-353456 E: roryreynolds@mac.com

REYNOLDS, Mrs Rosemary Joan. b 46. WMMTC 00. d 03 p 04. NSM Brandwood *Birm* 03–16; rtd 16; PtO *Birm* 16–20. *23 Chanston Avenue, Birmingham B14 5BD* T: 0121-444 7015 E: rosemary560@btinternet.com

REYNOLDS, Stephen Paul. b 52. d 08 p 09. NSM Cannock *Lich* 08–09; NSM Heath Hayes 09–16; NSM Cannock and Huntington 13–18; NSM Hatherton 16–18; rtd 19; PtO *Lich* from 19. *4 Harebell Close, Cannock WS12 3XA* T: (01543) 270940

RHOADES, Andrew Craig. b 56. Hatf Poly BSc 79 CEng 84 MIET 84 AMIMechE 84. St Jo Coll Nottm MTh 09. d 09 p 10. C Hexagon *Leic* 09–12; P-in-c Broom Leys 12–17; V 17–19; rtd 19; PtO *Leic* from 20; RD Guthlaxton from 21. *6 Almond Way, Lutterworth LE17 4XJ* T: (01455) 552050 M: 07531-121145 E: acrhoades@cheerful.com *or* rhoades_mail@btinternet.com

RHOADES, Mrs Abigail Louise. b 75. St Pet Coll Ox BA 98 MA 03 FLCM 05. St Mellitus Coll 17. d 19 p 20. C Finham *Cov* from 19. *St Martin-in-the-Fields Church, 136 Green Lane, Coventry CV3 6EA* T: (024) 7669 2358 E: revabbyrhodes@gmail.com

RHOADES, Canon Adrian Michael. b 48. K Coll Lon BD 71 AKC 71. Qu Coll Birm 71. d 72 p 73. C Bury St Jo *Man* 73–75; Chapl N Man Gen Hosp 75–77; C Crumpsall *Man* 75–77; Chapl Walsall Manor and Bloxwich Hosps 77–83; Chapl Walsall Gen Hosp 81–83; Chapl Man R Infirmary 83–94; Chapl St Mary's Hosp Man 83–94; Chapl Man R Eye Hosp 83–94; Chapl Cen Man Healthcare NHS Trust 94–00; PtO *Man* 00–08; Hon Can Man Cathl from 08; PtO from 18. *58 Errwood Road, Burnage, Manchester M19 2QH* T: 0161-224 1739 M: 07753-677422 E: adrian@rhodes.net

RHODES, Mrs Amanda Louise. b 63. Leeds Univ BA 07. NOC 04. d 07 p 08. C Kippax w Allerton Bywater *Ripon* 07–11; P-in-c Lofthouse 11–14; *Leeds* 14–15; TV Rothwell, Lofthouse, Methley etc from 15. *The Vicarage, 8 Church Farm Close, Lofthouse, Wakefield WF3 3SA* T: (01924) 823286 M: 07464-541628 E: revmac63@googlemail.com

RHODES, Ann. b 56. d 13 p 14. NSM Hackenthorpe *Sheff* 13–17; NSM Gleadless from 17. *1 Ormes Meadow, Owlthorpe, Sheffield*

S20 6TE T: 0114-247 8749 E: treble20jr@hotmail.com *or* ann.rhodes@sheffield.anglican.org

RHODES, Anthony John. b 27. Mert Coll Ox BA 50 MA 53. St Steph Ho Ox 52. d 54 p 55. C Northampton St Alb *Pet* 54–57; C Oakham 57–60; P-in-c S Queensferry *Edin* 60–74; V Mitcham St Olave *S'wark* 74–81; V Owston *Linc* 81–92; V W Butterwick 81–92; rtd 92; PtO *Leic* 14–17. *12 Stuart Court, High Street, Kibworth Beauchamp, Leicester LE8 0LR* T: 0116-279 3674

RHODES, Arthur. b 31. Dur Univ BA 58. Cranmer Hall Dur 57. d 59 p 60. C Kirkdale St Lawr *Liv* 59–61; C Litherland St Phil 61–64; V St Helens St Matt Thatto Heath 64–67; V Samlesbury *Blackb* 67–79; LtO 80–01; PtO 01–20. *76 The Pennines, Fulwood, Preston PR2 9GB* T: (01772) 712212 E: ajbrhodes@hotmail.co.uk

RHODES, Benjamin. b 71. Portsm Univ BSc 93 Heythrop Coll Lon MA 10. Westcott Ho Cam 94. d 97 p 98. C Upminster *Chelmsf* 97–01; Asst Chapl Lewisham Hosp NHS Trust 01–05; Sen Chapl Barts and The Lon NHS Trust 05–08; Lead Chapl 08–10; Lead Chapl Tower Hamlets Primary Care Trust 08–10; Spiritual Care Lead and Chapl Team Ldr King's Coll Hosp NHS Foundn Trust 10–18; Hd Chapl Services Leeds Teaching Hosps NHS Trust from 18; NSM St Bart Less *Lon* 05–07; Bp's Adv for Healthcare Chapl Stepney Area 08–10; Bp's Adv for Hosp Chapl *S'wark* 15–18; Hon Can *S'wark* Cathl 15–18; Bp's Adv for Healthcare Chapl *Leeds* from 18. *The Chaplaincy, Leeds Teaching Hospitals NHS Trust, St James's University Hospital, Beckett Street, Leeds LS9 7TF* T: 0113-206 4658 M: 07786-510292 E: benrhodes@nhs.net

RHODES, Mrs Caroline Laura. b 66. Bath Univ BPharm 87 K Coll Lon MSc 91. Ripon Coll Cuddesdon 08. d 10 p 11. C Allestree St Edm and Darley Abbey *Derby* 10–14; C Wirksworth 14–15; V Guilsfield w Buttington and Pool Quay *St As* 15–17; P-in-c Pool Miss Area from 18. *The Vicarage, Guilsfield, Welshpool SY21 9NF* T: (01938) 554245 E: revcarolinerhodes@me.com

RHODES, Christine. *See* RHODES, Lois Christine

RHODES, David George. b 45. Univ of Wales (Abth) BA 66. Trin Coll Bris 83. d 85 p 86. C Brinsworth w Catcliffe *Sheff* 85–89; V Mortomley St Sav 89–90; V Mortomley St Sav High Green 90–99; V Totley 99–11; rtd 11; PtO *Sheff* from 11; rtd 11. *12 Sheards Close, Dronfield Woodhouse, Dronfield S18 8NJ* T: (01246) 767838 E: drhodes@toucansurf.com

RHODES, David Grant. b 43. Ex Univ BA 66 Leeds Univ DipAdEd 75. Sarum & Wells Th Coll 69. d 72 p 73. C Mirfield *Wakef* 72–75; V Batley St Thos 75–80; Dioc Adult Educn Officer 76–80; Hon C Huddersfield St Jo 85–86; Dir BRF 86–87; V Robert Town *Wakef* 87–94; Project Worker 'Faith in Leeds' 94–99; Hon C Potternewton *Ripon* 95–99; Chapl Missr Children's Soc 99–03; Hon C Leeds City *Ripon* 99–03; rtd 03; PtO *York* 00–08. *2 Moorland Road, York YO10 4HF* T: (01904) 651749 M: 07712-006930 E: rhodes@freeuk.com

RHODES, John. *See* RHODES, Anthony John

RHODES, John Andrew. b 61. Teesside Poly GRSC 82 Univ of Wales (Swansea) PhD 91. WEMTC 11. d 14 p 15. NSM Ledbury *Heref* 14–17; NSM Cider Churches 17–19; Chapl 2gether NHS Foundn Trust 19; PtO *Ex* from 20. *Lower Bealy Court Orchard, Chulmleigh EX18 7EG* E: john.a.rhodes@btinternet.com

RHODES, Jonathan Peter. b 69. Coll of Ripon & York St Jo BA 96. NOC 01. d 04 p 05. C High Harrogate Ch Ch *Ripon* 04–08; P-in-c Hartlepool St Aid and St Columba *Dur* 08–11; R Brotton Parva *York* from 11. *St Margaret's Rectory, 9 Crispin Court, Brotton, Saltburn-by-the-Sea TS12 2XL* T: (01287) 201961

RHODES, Mrs Laura Clare. b 82. Ripon Coll Cuddesdon 13. d 15 p 16. C Wilmslow *Ches* 15–17; NSM Ches St Mary from 17; Chapl Ches Univ from 18. *78 Ringway, Waverton, Chester CH3 7NR* M: 07875-657784 E: lauracrhodes@gmail.com

RHODES, Lois Christine. b 34. Lon Univ BSc 61. Glouc Sch of Min 84. d 87 p 94. NSM Weobley w Sarnesfield and Norton Canon *Heref* 87–92; NSM Letton w Staunton, Byford, Mansel Gamage etc 87–92; Chapl Asst Heref Hosps NHS Trust 93–07; PtO *Heref* from 06. *Bellbrook, Bell Square, Weobley, Hereford HR4 8SE* T: (01544) 318410 *or* (01432) 355444

RHODES, Canon Matthew Ivan. b 66. Bris Univ BA 89 Birm Univ MPhil 95 PhD 05. Qu Coll Birm BD 93. d 94 p 95. C Willenhall H Trin *Lich* 94–97; Chapl Maadi St Jo Egypt 97–00; P-in-c Middleton *Birm* 00–07; P-in-c Wishaw 00–07; P-in-c Curdworth 05–07; R Curdworth, Middleton and Wishaw 07–11; P-in-c Maney 11; V 11–18; AD Sutton Coldfield 06–13; Dioc Chapl MU 11–18; Hon Can Birm Cathl 16–18; V Ranmoor *Sheff* from 18; C Walkley from 21; AD Hallam from 18. *The Vicarage, 389A Fulwood Road, Sheffield S10 3GA* T: 0114-230 1199 M: 07754-068391 E: matthew.rhodes@stjohnsranmoor.org.uk

RHODES, Robert George. b 41. Man Univ BSc 62. Ripon Hall Ox 72. d 74 p 75. C Banbury Ox 74–77; TV 77–81; P-in-c Long Horsley and Adult Educn Adv Newc 81–86; TR Wolverton Ox 86–97; P-in-c Bledlow w Saunderton and Horsenden 97–98; TV Risborough 98–02; Warden of Readers 97–02; USPG Miss Belize 02–06; rtd 06; PtO Derby from 07. *3 China House Yard, St Mary's Gate, Wirksworth, Matlock DE4 4DQ* T: (01629) 823623 E: bandjrhodes@hotmail.com

RHYDDERCH, David Huw. b 48. St Mich Coll Llan 70. d 73 p 74. C Gelligaer Llan 73–76; C Penarth All SS 76–78; V Resolven 78–81; V Ystrad Rhondda w Ynyscynon 81–93; RD Rhondda 89–93; R St Andrews Major w Michaelston-le-Pit 93–13; rtd 13; PtO Llan from 13. *34 Holly Road, Cardiff CF5 3HJ* T: (029) 2055 5597

RICE, David. b 57. Nottm Univ BA 79. Ripon Coll Cuddesdon 80. d 82 p 83. C Cirencester Glouc 82–86; R Theale and Englefield Ox 86–00; TR Wallingford from 00; AD from 17. *The Rectory, 22 Castle Street, Wallingford OX10 8DW* T: (01491) 202188

RICE, John Leslie Hale. b 38. Lon Univ BScEng 60 BD 68 FCMI. EMMTC 73. d 76 p 77. NSM Allestree St Nic Derby 76–90; LtO 90–08; PtO 08–18. *14 Gisborne Crescent, Allestree, Derby DE22 2FL* T: (01332) 557222 E: j.rice.t21@btinternet.com

RICE-OXLEY, John Richard. b 44. Keble Coll Ox BA 66 MA 69 Dur Univ MA 85. Lon Coll of Div 68. d 70 p 71. C Eastwood S'well 70–73; Youth Adv CMS 73–78; V Mansfield St Jo S'well 78–82; P-in-c Thornley Dur 82–85; P-in-c Darlington St Matt and St Luke 85–87; V 87–98; V Hornsea w Atwick York 98–06; P-in-c Aldbrough, Mappleton w Goxhill and Withernwick 05–06; rtd 06; PtO York 07–17; Linc 16–19. *34 Arnhem Way, Bourne PE10 9UD* E: richardriceoxley@gmail.com

RICE-OXLEY, Mrs Sylvia Jeanette Kathleen. b 48. d 08 p 09. C Aldbrough, Mappleton w Goxhill and Withernwick York 08–11; P-in-c 11–13; rtd 13; PtO Linc 16–19. *34 Arnhem Way, Bourne PE10 9UD* E: sylviariceoxley@gmail.com

RICH, Brian John. b 49. Reading Univ BSc 70. Guildf Dioc Min Course 94. d 97 p 98. OLM Stoke Hill Guildf 97–12; PtO Win 12–15. *2 Boon Way, Basingstoke RG23 7BS* T: (01256) 783111 E: btrich@talktalk.net

RICH, Paul Michael. b 36. OBE 87. Sarum Th Coll 62. d 65 p 66. C Woodbridge St Mary St E 65–68; C W Wycombe Ox 68–70; CF 70–88; LtO S & B 88–90; V Crondall and Ewshot Guildf 91–05; rtd 05; PtO Win 08–13. *The Firs, The Street, Binsted, Alton GU34 4PF* T: (01420) 525302 E: padrerich@btinternet.com

RICH, Peter Geoffrey. b 45. Oak Hill Th Coll 74. d 77 p 78. C Blackheath St Jo S'wark 77–80; C Surbiton St Matt 80–87; V St Alb St Luke 87–98; V Gravesend St Aid Roch 98–10; rtd 11; P-in-c Stone w Dinton and Hartwell Ox 11–16; PtO from 16. *8 Broadmarsh Close, Grove, Wantage OX12 0NH* E: angela_richuk@yahoo.co.uk

RICHARDS, Canon Anne. b 69. d 10 p 11. NSM N Hull St Mich York 10–15; Chapl Abp Sentamu Academy Hull from 14; PtO York from 18; Can and Preb York Minster from 21. *42 Riplingham Road, Kirk Ella, Hull HU10 7TP* M: 07947-160455 E: richards.a1@sentamuacademy.org or personal@anne-richards.com

RICHARDS, Mrs Anne Maria. b 54. Wolv Poly CertEd 88 HCIMA 83. Qu Coll Birm 08. d 11 p 12. OLM Fletchamstead Cov 11–18; P-in-c Whitley from 18; Chapl Cov Univ from 18. *2 Farthing Walk, Coventry CV4 8GR* T: (024) 7646 8660 M: 07769-943019 E: anne.richards_uk@yahoo.co.uk

RICHARDS, Mrs April Deborah. b 42. Man Univ BSc 63. S Dios Minl Tr Scheme 82. dss 85 d 87 p 94. Catherington and Clanfield Portsm 85–89; C 87–89; C E Meon and Langrish 89–95; Chapl Portsm Hosps NHS Trust 92–95; P-in-c Blackmoor and Whitehill Portsm 95–98; V 98–05; RD Petersfield 99–04; rtd 05; PtO Pet 06–08; Hon C Brington w Whilton and Norton etc 08–12; PtO from 12. *6 Burrows Vale, Brixworth, Northampton NN6 9US* T: (01604) 882230 E: aprilrichards@btinternet.com

RICHARDS, Christopher Mordaunt. b 40. New Coll Ox BA 63 MA 72 Bris Univ MB, ChB 72. Cuddesdon Coll 63. d 65 p 81. C Bris St Mary Redcliffe w Temple etc 65–66; PtO 66–72; Hon C Keynsham B & W 81–90; PtO 90–93; Bris from 03. *Garden Flat, 124 Redland Road, Bristol BS6 6XY* T: 0117-974 4062

RICHARDS, Daniel James. b 40. Bernard Gilpin Soc Dur 62 St D Coll Lamp 63. d 66 p 67. C Kingswinford H Trin Lich 66–69; C Banbury Ox 69–71; C Aylesbury 71–73; C-in-c Stoke Poges St Jo Manor Park CD 73–78; R W Slough 78–80; R Ilchester w Northover, Limington, Yeovilton etc B & W 80–90; RD Ilchester 81–91; RD Martock 89–91; TR Bruton and Distr 90–97; R Axbridge w Shipham and Rowberrow 97–04; rtd 04; PtO B & W from 05; Co-ord Clergy Retirement and Widows' Officer 06–14. *29 Sexey's Hospital, Bruton BA10 0AS* M: 07762-189958 E: revdanrich@btinternet.com

RICHARDS, Daniel Michael Hamilton. b 79. Man Univ BA 02. Cranmer Hall Dur 05. d 07 p 08. C Bury St Jo w St Mark Man 07–08; C Tonge w Alkrington 08–11; Asst Chapl Salford Univ 09–11; Chapl Cov Univ 11–13; P-in-c Braddan S & M 13–14; V from 14. *The Vicarage, Saddle Road, Braddan, Douglas, Isle of Man IM4 4LB* T: (01624) 675523 E: thecollar@outlook.com

RICHARDS, David Arnold. b 56. Wycliffe Hall Ox 76. d 81 p 82. C Skewen Llan 81–84; C Barking St Marg w St Patr Chelmsf 84–85; TV 85–90; Chapl Barking Hosp 87–88; P-in-c Stratford St Jo and Ch Ch w Forest Gate St Jas Chelmsf 90–97; V Stratford St Jo w Ch Ch 97–21; P-in-c W Ham St Matt 13–15; C 15–21; rtd 21. *1 Marsh Way, Swanage BH19 2TE* M: 07779-079844 E: revdave456@gmail.com

RICHARDS, David Gareth. b 60. Hull Univ BA 83. Qu Coll Birm 89. d 92 p 93. C Knowle Birm 92–96; Assoc R Edin St Paul and St Geo 96–00; R from 00. *10 Broughton Street, Edinburgh EH1 3RH* T: 0131-332 3904 or 556 1355 F: 556 0492 E: dave@pandgchurch.org.uk

RICHARDS, Mrs Delyth Anne. b 63. d 13 p 14. NSM Carmarthen St Dav St D 13–18; C 18–19; P-in-c Bro Caerfyrddin from 19; Dioc Schools Officer from 18. *36 Meysydd y Coleg, Carmarthen SA31 3GU* T: (01267) 229134 E: delyth.richards@icloud.com

RICHARDS, Mrs Glenys Heather. b 51. SEN 73. d 06 p 07. OLM Heatons Man 06–16; PtO from 16. *32 Lomas Close, Manchester M19 1TE* T: 0161-282 7831

RICHARDS, James Johnston. b 59. Lon Bible Coll BA 90 Dur Univ MA 97 Solicitor 84. Cranmer Hall Dur 90. d 92 p 93. C Harrow Trin St Mich Lon 92–95; C Kendal H Trin Carl 95–99; R Windermere St Martin from 99; RD Windermere 10–16; C Windermere St Mary and Troutbeck from 19; C Staveley, Ings and Kentmere from 19. *The Rectory, Longlands Road, Bowness-on-Windermere, Windermere LA23 3AS* T: (015394) 43063 E: rector@stmartin.org.uk

RICHARDS, Canon Jane Susan. b 64. Univ of E Lon MSc 03. St Mellitus Coll BA 14. d 14 p 15. NSM S Woodham Ferrers Chelmsf 14–17; NSM Woodham Ferrers and Bicknacre 14–17; Asst Chapl Mid-Essex Hosp Services NHS Trust 15–17; V Basildon St Andr w H Cross Chelmsf from 17; RD Basildon from 19; Hon Can Chelmsf Cathl from 20. *St Andrew's Vicarage, 3 The Fremnells, Basildon SS14 2QX* T: (01268) 520519 M: 07702-808408 E: revjanerichards2@gmail.com

RICHARDS, Mrs Jane Valerie. b 43. Westf Coll Lon BA 64 Birm Univ CertEd 65. S Dios Minl Tr Scheme 84. d 87 p 94. NSM Locks Heath Portsm 87–90; Chapl Qu Alexandra Hosp Portsm 90–92; Chapl Portsm Hosps NHS Trust 92–95; Asst to RD Fareham Portsm 95–96; C Locks Heath 95–96; Chapl Southn Univ Hosps NHS Trust 96–03; rtd 03; PtO Portsm from 97; Win 03–06. *16 Lodge Road, Locks Heath, Southampton SO31 6QY* T: (01489) 573891 E: revjane.richards@btinternet.com

RICHARDS, Mrs Joanna Sue. b 67. Univ Coll Lon MSc 96. SEITE BA 18. d 14 p 15. C Cant St Martin and St Paul 14–18; R Cant St Dunstan, St Mildred and St Pet from 18. *The Benefice Office, St Dunstan's Church Hall, 80 London Road, Canterbury CT2 8LS* M: 07824-155355 E: rev.jorichards@gmail.com

RICHARDS, Preb John Francis. b 37. Dur Univ BA 61. Wells Th Coll 61. d 63 p 64. C Sherwood S'well 63–67; C Bishopwearmouth St Mich Dur 67–69; C Cegg Buckland Ex 69–75; CF (ACF) 72–02; V Plymouth St Jas Ham Ex 75–83; V Plympton St Mary 83–02; RD Plymouth Moorside 88–93 and 96–01; Preb Ex Cathl 91–07; rtd 02; PtO Ex from 02; Clergy Widow(er)s Officer 02–13. *24 Trewithy Drive, Plymouth PL6 5TY* T: (01752) 214442 E: jfr-sjr@blueyonder.co.uk

RICHARDS, John George. b 48. Qu Coll Birm 87. d 89 p 90. C Acocks Green Birm 89–92; TV Shirley 92–96; P-in-c Yardley Wood 96–00; V 00–13; rtd 13; PtO Birm from 13; Dioc Retirement Officer 16. *60 Alderney Gardens, Birmingham B38 8YW* T: 0121-603 0801 E: rev.johnrichards@virginmedia.com

RICHARDS, John Michael. b 53. Coll of Ripon & York St Jo TCert 76 Open Univ BA 81. Cranmer Hall Dur 93. d 93 p 94. C Wath-upon-Dearne Sheff 93–95; R Warmsworth 95–01; R Sprotbrough 01–10; P-in-c Barningham w Hutton Magna and Wycliffe Ripon 10–14; Leeds 14–15; P-in-c Gilling and Kirkby Ravensworth Ripon 10–14; Leeds 14–15; AD Richmond Ripon 12–14; Leeds 14–15; rtd 15; PtO Leeds 17–21. *Meadow View, 10 Reighton Court, Reighton, Filey YO14 9BL* T: (01723) 639799 E: johnmr1953@talk21.com

RICHARDS (née WOOLLEY), Ms Justine Clare. b 73. Plymouth Univ BSc 95 SS Mark & Jo Coll Chelsea PGCE 98. Cranmer Hall Dur 03. d 05 p 06. C Dulverton and Brushford B & W 05–10; PtO 10–16; Chapl Wellington Sch Somerset 16–19; V Galmington B & W from 19. *1 Comeytrowe Lane, Taunton TA1 5PA* M: 07821-536460 E: rev.justine.richards@gmail.com

RICHARDS, Keith David. b 50. Didsbury Coll of Educn CertEd 72. S'wark Ord Course 79. **d** 82 **p** 83. NSM Walworth *S'wark* 82–85; Chapl Derbyshire Coll of HE 85–87; V Rottingdean *Chich* 87–93; TR Crawley 93–97; V Arundel w Tortington and S Stoke 97–07; RD Arundel and Bognor 04–07; Can and Preb Chich Cathl 07; V Selby Abbey *York* 07–10; P-in-c Hove St Barn and St Agnes *Chich* 10–13; RD Hove 11–13; rtd 13; P-in-c Durrington *Chich* 14–15; P-in-c Worthing St Andr 16; PtO 17–19; R Balcombe 19–21; PtO *Nor* from 15. *13 Fakenham Road, Great Ryburgh, Fakenham NR21 7AW* T: (01553) 769200 E: keithdrichards2@btinternet.com

RICHARDS, Kelvin. b 58. Univ of Wales (Abth) BSc 80 MA 88. Ripon Coll Cuddesdon BA 82. **d** 83 **p** 84. C Killay *S & B* 83–86; C Morriston 86–89; R Llangattock and Llangyndir 89–15; P-in-c The Beacons from 15; P-in-c Llyn Safaddan from 15; AD Crickhowell 02–14. *The Rectory, Talybont-on-Usk, Brecon LD3 7UX* T: (01874) 676146 E: kelvin.richards@btinternet.com *or* kelvin@beaconssafaddan.plus.com

RICHARDS (née Norfolk), Kirsten. b 85. **d** 16 **p** 17. C Ludgvan, Marazion, St Hilary and Perranuthnoe *Truro* 16–20; C Helston and Wendron from 20; C W Kerrier from 20. *The Vicarage, Breage, Helston TR13 9PN*

RICHARDS, Mrs Mary Edith. b 33. SWMTC 85. **d** 87 **p** 94. NSM Kea *Truro* 87–88; Asst Chapl Bris Poly 88–91; C E Clevedon and Walton w Weston w Clapton *B & W* 91–96; rtd 96; Hon C Probus, Ladock and Grampound w Creed and St Erme *Truro* from 97; Mental Health Chapl Cornwall Healthcare NHS Trust 97–01; PtO *Truro* from 16. *62 Midway Drive, Uplands Park, Truro TR1 1NQ* T: (01872) 277556 E: revdmary@hotmail.co.uk

RICHARDS, Norman John. b 47. BSc. Ridley Hall Cam. **d** 83 **p** 84. C Luton St Fran *St Alb* 83–86; R Aspenden and Layston w Buntingford 86–95; P-in-c Westmill 94–95; R Aspenden, Buntingford and Westmill 95–08; rtd 09; PtO *St Alb* from 09; Hon Chapl Stansted Airport *Chelmsf* from 09. *Gardeners Cottage, Hare Street, Buntingford SG9 0DY* T: (01763) 289720 E: nrichardsvic@btinternet.com

RICHARDS, Poppy. See THORPE, Eleanor Poppy

RICHARDS, Rebecca Mary. b 66. **d** 14 **p** 15. C Stafford St Jo and Tixall w Ingestre *Lich* 14–18; TR Cheswardine, Childs Ercall, Hales, Hinstock etc from 18. *3 High Street, Cheswardine, Market Drayton TF9 2RS* T: (01630) 661204 M: 07905-891869 E: beckyrichards@hotmail.co.uk

RICHARDS, Robert Graham. b 42. St Jo Coll Nottm 77. **d** 80 **p** 81. C Radipole and Melcombe Regis *Sarum* 80–83; TV Billericay and Lt Burstead *Chelmsf* 84–91; UK Dir CMJ 91–95; Chief Exec Nat Bibl Heritage Cen Ltd Trust 95–97; C Chorleywood St Andr *St Alb* 97–00; Chapl Lee Abbey 02–05; rtd 05; PtO *Sarum* from 05. *33 Stowell Crescent, Wareham BH20 4PT* T: (01929) 552174 E: rev_rob_richards@yahoo.co.uk

RICHARDS, Simon Granston. b 47. St Jo Coll Nottm BTh 72 ALCD 72. **d** 72 **p** 73. C Waltham Abbey *Chelmsf* 72–77; TV Basildon St Martin w H Cross and Laindon etc 77–80; V Grayshott *Guildf* 80–88; V Eccleston Ch Ch *Liv* 88–92; V Berkeley w Wick, Breadstone and Newport *Glouc* 92–02; P-in-c Stone w Woodford and Hill 99–02; V Berkeley w Wick, Breadstone, Newport, Stone etc 02–05; RD Dursley 96–02; Chapl Severn NHS Trust 94–05; V Bisley, Chalford, France Lynch, and Oakridge *Glouc* 05–12; AD Bisley 06–08; rtd 12; PtO *Heref* from 14. *1 Wynyard Close, Leominster HR6 8HH* T: (01568) 616602 E: sgranston@gmail.com

RICHARDS, Stephen. b 51. Bris Univ BSc 72 Birm Univ MEd 77 Maria Grey Coll Lon PGCE 73. STETS 07. **d** 10 **p** 11. NSM Corfe Mullen *Sarum* 10–16; PtO *Ex* from 20. *Longacre, Buzzacott Lane, Combe Martin, Ilfracombe EX34 0LB* T: (01271) 883566 M: 07767-066321 E: richards.steve@btinternet.com

RICHARDS, Stuart Anthony. b 70. K Coll Lon BA 92 AKC 92 Keble Coll Ox BA 97 MA 02. St Steph Ho Ox MTh 02. **d** 99 **p** 00. C Reading All SS *Ox* 99–02; C Solihull *Birm* 02–05; Deanery P Handsworth 06–07; CF from 07. *c/o MOD Chaplains (Army)* T: (01264) 383430 F: 381824

RICHARDS, Terence David. b 43. Trin Coll Carmarthen DipEd 64 Open Univ BA 73 Magd Coll Ox MSc 83. Ox Min Course 04. **d** 07 **p** 08. NSM Chenderit *Pet* 07–13; rtd 13; PtO *Pet* from 13; *Ox* 15–20. *11 Portway Drive, Croughton, Brackley NN13 5NA* T: (01869) 811251 E: tasker1@btinternet.com

RICHARDS, Tony Benjamin. b 48. STETS. **d** 09 **p** 10. NSM Sandown Ch Ch *Portsm* from 09; NSM Lower Sandown St Jo from 09. *Abbotsford Lodge, Cliff Bridge, Shanklin PO37 6QJ* T: (01983) 863607

RICHARDS, Canon William Neal. b 38. ALCD 63. **d** 63 **p** 64. C Otley *Bradf* 63–65; C Leamington Priors St Mary *Cov*

65–67; CMS 67–69; Kenya 69–74; Asst Provost and Can Res Nairobi 70–74; V Gt Malvern St Mary *Worc* 74–86; Chapl Kidderminster Health Distr 86–91; RD Kidderminster *Worc* 89–91; R Martley and Wichenford, Knightwick etc 91–01; rtd 01; PtO *Worc* 01–20. *7 Grenfell Road, Hereford HR1 2QR* T: (01432) 508721 M: 07976-317987

RICHARDSON, Ms Alison Mary. b 63. Leic Univ BSc 84 St Jo Coll Dur BA 09. Cranmer Hall Dur 07. **d** 09 **p** 10. C Spennymoor and Whitworth *Dur* 09–11; C Upper Skerne 11–13; P-in-c Blackhall, Castle Eden and Monkhesleden 13–16; C Peterlee 13–16; P-in-c Kelloe and Coxhoe 16–19; P-in-c Chilton 16–19; Chapl Tudor Hall Sch from 19. *Tudor Hall School, Wykham Lane, Banbury OX16 9UR* T: (01295) 263434 M: 07873-596164 E: arichardson2102@gmail.com

RICHARDSON, Andrew Edward John. b 75. St Andr Univ BD 97. TISEC 04. **d** 06 **p** 07. C Dundee St Mary Magd *Bre* 06–09; Hon Chapl Dundee Univ 07–09; R Glas E End 09–15; Chapl St Botolph Aldgate w H Trin Minories *Lon* 15–19; Hon Chapl St Paul's Cathl from 19. *8A Amen Court, London EC4M 7BU* T: (020) 7248 6115 E: aejrichardson@hotmail.com *or* chaplain@stbotolphs.org.uk

RICHARDSON, Miss Ann. b 72. Leeds Univ BA 94. Trin Coll Bris BA 10. **d** 10 **p** 11. C Bromley St Mark *Roch* 10–14; V Gillingham H Trin 14–19; P-in-c Gillingham St Barn 16–19; RD Gillingham 15–19; AD Aston and Sutton Coldfield *Birm* from 19. *St Mark's Vicarage, Bleak Hill Road, Birmingham B23 7EL* M: 07341-733553 E: ad.astonandsuttoncoldfield@cofebirmingham.com

RICHARDSON, Anne Charlotte. b 84. Warwick Univ BA 05. St Mellitus Coll BA 18. **d** 18 **p** 19. C Styvechale *Cov* 18–21; C Cove St Jo *Guildf* from 21. *15 The Copse, Farnborough GU14 0QD* M: 07973-221635 E: talktoanne@gmail.com *or* anne@parishofcove.org.uk

RICHARDSON, Carol Margaret. b 47. Leeds Univ BA 07. NOC 04. **d** 07 **p** 08. Sessional Chapl HM Pris Stafford 03–17; NSM Upper Tean *Lich* 07–11; R Kingsley and Foxt-w-Whiston and Oakamoor etc 11–17; rtd 17; PtO *Lich* 17–21. *The Woodlands, Spicerstone Estate, Leek ST13 7DS* T: (01538) 372082 E: crichardson@spicerstone.plus.com

RICHARDSON, Catherine Elisabeth. See PORTER, Catherine Elisabeth

RICHARDSON, Christopher Edward. b 72. STETS 12. **d** 15 **p** 16. C Alverstoke *Portsm* 15–19; V Camberley St Martin Old Dean *Guildf* from 19. *St Martin's Vicarage, Hampshire Road, Camberley GU15 4DW* M: 07584-308877 E: vicarstmartinscamberley@gmail.com

RICHARDSON, David. b 71. Edin Univ MA 93 QUB PhD 98 K Coll Lon MA 14 Cardiff Univ MTh 20 Stranmillis Coll PGCE 94. CITC BTh 02. **d** 02 **p** 03. C Coleraine *Conn* 02–06; Chapl RAF from 06. *Chaplaincy Services (RAF), HQ Air Command, RAF High Wycombe HP14 4UE* T: (01494) 496309

RICHARDSON, David John. b 50. MA LLB FCIArb. S'wark Ord Course. **d** 85 **p** 86. NSM S Croydon Em *S'wark* 85–06; PtO 06–13. *20 Hurst View Road, South Croydon CR2 7AG* T: (020) 8688 4947 *or* 8688 6676 E: richardsonhome@blueyonder.co.uk

RICHARDSON, Edward John. b 39. Westmr Coll Ox MTh 98 Chich Univ PhD 17. Chich Th Coll 62. **d** 65 **p** 66. C Chessington *Guildf* 65–70; TV Trunch *Nor* 70–75; V Stoneleigh *Guildf* 75–79; PtO *S'wark* 92–94; Hon C Kingston All SS w St Jo 94–99; C 99–04; rtd 04; PtO *S'wark* from 04; P-in-c Burpham *Chich* 05–09; PtO *Guildf* from 09. *3 Westways, Epsom KT19 0PH* T: (020) 8393 3648 E: revdejr@gmail.com

RICHARDSON (née WOOD), Elaine Mary. b 51. SRN 74. SEITE 00. **d** 03 **p** 04. C Hythe *Cant* 03–06; C Folkestone Trin 06–07; V Herne 07–16; Jt AD Reculver 12–16; rtd 16. *Kenora, St Arvans, Chepstow NP16 6EZ* T: (01291) 622300 E: elaine.longview@virgin.net *or* elaine.kenora@gmail.com

RICHARDSON, Mrs Elizabeth Rosalind. b 54. STETS 05. **d** 08 **p** 09. NSM Ewell St Fran *Guildf* 08–11; TV Surrey Weald from 11. *54 The Street, Capel, Dorking RH5 5LE* T: (01306) 711260 E: liz@hostmyserver.co.uk *or* vicar@stjohnthebaptistcapel.org.uk

RICHARDSON, Geoffrey Stewart. b 47. St Jo Coll Ox BA 69 MA 73. St Steph Ho Ox 70. **d** 72 **p** 73. C Roxbourne St Andr *Lon* 72–75; C Woodford St Barn *Chelmsf* 75–80; V Goodmayes St Paul 80–87; R Stow in Lindsey *Linc* 87–92; P-in-c Coates 87–92; P-in-c Willingham 87–92; R Stow Gp 92–01; RD Corringham 93–00; R Shaldon, Stokeinteignhead, Combeinteignhead etc *Ex* 01–12; rtd 12; PtO *Ex* from 12. *167 Westhill Road, Torquay TQ1 4NS*

RICHARDSON, Graeme James. b 75. Oriel Coll Ox BA 97. Ripon Coll Cuddesdon MPhil 02. **d** 03 **p** 04. C Hatfield Hyde *St Alb* 03–06; Chapl BNC Ox 06–14; V Harborne St Pet *Birm* 14–19. *Frauenplan 8, 99423 Weimar, Germany*

RICHARDSON, Hannah Mary. b 90. Dur Univ MA 20. Westcott Ho Cam 17. **d** 20 **p** 21. C Soham *Ely* from 20. *12 Shocksham Terrace, Townsend, Soham, Ely CB7 5QN* M: 07922-836224 E: hannahmarysoham@gmail.com

RICHARDSON, Mrs Jacqueline Ann. b 61. Ox Brookes Univ BA 14. **d** 10 **p** 11. OLM Walton-on-Thames *Guildf* 10–16; C Weston 16–19; V Hersham from 19. *The Vicarage, 5 Burwood Road, Hersham, Walton-on-Thames KT12 4AA* M: 07787-445272 E: jackier6161@gmail.com *or* vicar@stpetershersham.com

RICHARDSON, Canon James John. b 41. OBE 07. Hull Univ BA 63 Sheff Univ DipEd 64 FRSA 91. Cuddesdon Coll 66. **d** 69 **p** 70. C Wolverhampton St Pet *Lich* 69–72; P-in-c Hanley All SS 72–75; R Nantwich *Ches* 75–82; Hon Can Ripon Cathl 82–88; V Leeds St Pet 82–88; Exec Dir Coun of Chrs and Jews 88–92; P-in-c Brington w Whilton and Norton *Pet* 93–96; P-in-c Brington w Whilton and Norton and Brockhall 96; P-in-c Church Brampton, Chapel Brampton, Harleston etc 94–96; TR Bournemouth St Pet w St Swithun, H Trin etc *Win* 96–08; P-in-c Bournemouth St Aug 01–08; rtd 09; Hon C Sherborne w Castleton, Lillington and Longburton *Sarum* 09–14; PtO *B & W* 14–18; *Sarum* 14–19. *23 Mount Pleasant, Clerk Bank, Leek ST13 5HB* T: (01538) 383856 E: canonrichardson@gmail.com

RICHARDSON, John. b 55. Lon Univ BEd BD Kent Univ MA. St Steph Ho Ox. **d** 83 **p** 84. C Thornbury *Glouc* 83–86; C Sheff St Cecilia Parson Cross 86–87; C Clacton St Jas *Chelmsf* 87–90; R Gt and Lt Tey w Wakes Colne and Chappel 90–20; rtd 20; PtO *Chelmsf* from 20. *19 The Greenways, Coggeshall, Colchester CO6 1QH* T: (01376) 563297 E: john.richardson195@btinternet.com

RICHARDSON, John. b 47. Linc Th Coll 78. **d** 80 **p** 81. C Keighley St Andr *Bradf* 80–83; V Hugglescote w Donington *Leic* 83–84; V Hugglescote w Donington-le-Heath and Ellistown 84–86; TR Hugglescote w Donington, Ellistown and Snibston 86–97; RD Akeley S 87–96; Chapl ATC 84–97; R Hallaton w Horninghold, Allexton, Tugby etc *Leic* 97–00; Rural Officer (Leic Adnry) 97–00; rtd 00; PtO *Pet* 04–05; P-in-c Fylingdales and Hawsker cum Stainsacre *York* 05–09; C Alton w Bradley-le-Moors and Denstone etc *Lich* 09–17. *All Saints House, 10 Bennion Grove, Denstone, Uttoxeter ST14 5EZ* T: (01889) 590266 E: allsaints2012@btinternet.com

RICHARDSON, John. b 41. Qu Coll Birm 69. **d** 72 **p** 73. C Ormskirk *Liv* 72–74; C Doncaster St Geo *Sheff* 74–77; R Hemsworth *Wakef* 77–79; V Penallt *Mon* 79–85; R Amotherby w Appleton and Barton-le-Street *York* 85–89; P-in-c Hovingham 86–89; P-in-c Slingsby 86–89; TR Street 89–90; R Skelton w Shipton and Newton on Ouse 90–93; V Alsager St Mary *Ches* 93–96; V Grangetown *York* 96–00; V E Coatham 00–02; V Coatham and Dormanstown 02–04; P-in-c York St Lawr w St Nic 04–06; rtd 06; Chapl Castle Howard 06–13; PtO *York* from 06. *27 Park Road, Norton, Malton YO17 9DZ* T: (01653) 690146 E: johnrichardson841@btinternet.com

RICHARDSON, John. See RICHARDSON, Edward John

✠**RICHARDSON, The Rt Revd John Henry.** b 37. Trin Hall Cam BA 61 MA 65. Cuddesdon Coll 61. **d** 63 **p** 64 **c** 94. C Stevenage *St Alb* 63–66; C Eastbourne St Mary *Chich* 66–68; V Chipperfield St Paul *St Alb* 68–75; V Rickmansworth 75–86; RD 77–86; V Bishop's Stortford St Mich 86–94; Hon Can St Alb 87–94; Suff Bp Bedford 94–02; rtd 02; Hon Asst Bp Carl from 03; Hon Asst Bp Newc from 03. *The Old Rectory, Bewcastle, Carlisle CA6 6PS* T: (01697) 748389

RICHARDSON, John Malcolm. b 39. Glas Univ MA 60 BD 63 Andover Newton Th Coll STM 65. Edin Th Coll 84. **d** 84 **p** 85. C Edin Old St Paul 84–86; R Leven *St And* 86–90; R Newport-on-Tay 90–96; R Tayport 90–96; Can St Ninian's Cathl Perth 93–07; rtd 07; LtO *St And* from 07; LtO *Edin* from 13. *14 Chewton Road, Thornton, Kirkcaldy KY1 4AZ* T/F: (01592) 775133

RICHARDSON, John Stephen. b 50. Southn Univ BA 71. St Jo Coll Nottm 72. **d** 74 **p** 75. C Bramcote *S'well* 74–77; C Radipole and Melcombe Regis *Sarum* 77–80; P-in-c Stinsford, Winterborne Came w Whitcombe etc 80–83; Asst Dioc Missr 80–83; V Nailsea Ch Ch *B & W* 83–90; Adv on Evang 86–90; Provost Bradf 90–00; Dean Bradf 00–01; V Wye w Brook and Hastingleigh etc *Cant* 01–09; P-in-c 04–09; C Mersham w Hinxhill and Sellindge 08–09; AD W Bridge 03–09; Chapl Wye Coll Kent *Lon* 01–09; P-in-c Margate H Trin *Cant* 09–13; V 13–16; rtd 16; C Romney Marsh *Cant* from 16. *135 Hight Street, Dymchurch, Romney Marsh TN29 0LD* E: vicarjohnsrichardson@googlemail.com

RICHARDSON, Canon John Stuart. b 46. Trin Coll Ox BA 68 MA 71 DPhil 73 FRSE 96. **d** 79 **p** 80. NSM St Andrews St Andr *St And* 79–87; Chapl St Andr Univ 80–87; Prof Classics Edin

Univ 87–02; TV Edin St Columba 87–16; PtO from 16; Hon Can St Mary's Cathl from 00. *Marketgate Farmhouse, Main Street, Ormiston, Tranent EH35 5HT* E: j.richardson@ed.ac.uk

RICHARDSON, John Thandule. b 49. Bradf and Ilkley Coll BSc 80 Lanc Univ MA 97. CBDTI 94. **d** 97 **p** 98. NSM Lea *Blackb* 97–02; NSM Broughton 02–04; NSM Lanercost, Walton, Gilsland and Nether Denton *Carl* 04–05; PtO *Blackb* 06–09; C Preston Risen Lord 09–12; Chapl Preston Coll 09–11; TV Costa Blanca *Eur* 12–13; PtO *Leeds* 15–16; NSM Guiseley w Esholt from 16. *17 Queens Terrace, Otley LS21 3JE* T: (01943) 969402 M: 07769-716861 E: johntr123@aol.com

RICHARDSON, Katherine Ruth. b 50. **d** 15 **p** 16. NSM Cirencester *Glouc* 15–20. *1 Chesterton Terrace, 16 Watermoor Road, Cirencester GL7 1JW* T: (01285) 652576 E: revkatie@cirenparish.co.uk

RICHARDSON, Canon Laurence Leigh. b 71. Trin Coll Carmarthen BA 92 PGCE 93 Univ of Wales (Cardiff) BTh 97 FGMS 04. St Mich Coll Llan 94. **d** 97 **p** 98. C Carmarthen St Pet *St D* 97–01; Chapl Carmarthenshire Coll 99–01; P-in-c Abergwili w Llanfihangel-uwch-Gwili etc *St D* 01–03; V 03–09; TV E Carmarthen 09–10; TR 10–12; P-in-c Carmarthen St Pet 12–14; P-in-c Carmarthen St Pet and Abergwili etc 14–18; AD Carmarthen 09–18; Dioc Warden Ords 15–18; Can St D Cathl from 15; Sub Dean from 18. *Brecon House, The Close, St Davids , Haverfordwest SA62 6PE* T: (01437) 720456 E: landcat10a@aol.com *or* subdean@stdavidscathedral.org.uk

RICHARDSON, Malcolm. See RICHARDSON, John Malcolm

RICHARDSON, Preb Neil. b 46. Southn Univ BTh 83 SS Mark & John Univ Plymouth Hon BEd 19. Sarum & Wells Th Coll 71. **d** 74 **p** 75. C Oldham St Mary w St Pet *Man* 74–77; C-in-c Holts CD 77–82; R Greenford H Cross *Lon* 82–13; Preb St Paul's Cathl 02–13; rtd 13; PtO *Chelmsf* from 14. *27 Hatchfields, Great Waltham, Chelmsford CM3 1AJ* E: neilandmarion49@btinternet.com

RICHARDSON, Canon Paul. b 58. Univ of Wales (Cardiff) BSc 80. Ridley Hall Cam 81. **d** 84 **p** 85. C Stanwix *Carl* 84–87; Ind Chapl 87–89; Staff P Dalton-in-Furness 87–89; V Marton Moss *Blackb* 89–95; P-in-c Prestwich St Gabr *Man* 95–00; Bp's Dom Chapl 95–00; V Westbury *Sarum* 00–02; TR White Horse 02–07; RD Heytesbury 04–07; R Devizes St Jo w St Mary 07–20; Can and Preb Sarum Cathl 07–20; RD Devizes 10–11 and 15–20; PtO *Eur* from 18; Hon C Shrivenham and Ashbury *Ox* from 20. *St Mary's House, 8 Chapel Lane, Ashbury, Swindon SN6 8LS* T: (01793) 710241 M: 07801-365280 E: rcpr07@outlook.com

RICHARDSON, Pauline Kate. See JENKINS, Pauline Kate

RICHARDSON, Philip David. b 82. Reading Univ BA 04. St Mellitus Coll BA 17. **d** 17 **p** 18. C E Green *Cov* 17–21; C Cove St Jo *Guildf* from 21. *15 The Copse, Farnborough GU14 0QD* M: 07747-776230 E: revphilrichardson@gmail.com

RICHARDSON, Scott Gordon. b 67. Open Univ BA 14 Nottm Univ MA 17. All SS Cen for Miss & Min 18. **d** 20 **p** 21. C Newchurch *Man* from 20. *221 Turf Lane, Royton, Oldham OL2 6ET* T: 0161-633 6299 M: 07739-095866 E: revsrichardson@outlook.com *or* sr221@btinternet.com

RICHARDSON, Simon Kay Caoimhin. b 74. St Jo Coll Dur BA 96 Cant Ch Ch Univ MA 10 QUB MTh 13. Wycliffe Hall Ox 01. **d** 03 **p** 04. C Folkestone Trin *Cant* 03–06; C Hillsborough *D & D* 06–08; I 08–11; C Holywood 11–14; I Glencraig 14–18; Min Can Belf Cathl 15–18; V Kempston Transfiguration *St Alb* 18–20; PtO *Nor* from 21. *2 Marlpit Close, Mill Road, Banham, Norwich NR16 2HU* M: 07875-514431 E: simonkcr@gmail.com

RICHARDSON, Miss Susan. b 58. Cranmer Hall Dur. **d** 87 **p** 94. Par Dn Stokesley *York* 87–91; Par Dn Beverley St Nic 91–94; P-in-c Cloughton 94–97; V Cloughton and Burniston w Ravenscar etc 97–99; V Middlesbrough St Oswald 99–10; P-in-c Middlesbrough St Chad 09–10; V Middlesbrough St Oswald and St Chad from 10; Tr Officer E Riding from 94. *St Oswald's Vicarage, Lambton Road, Middlesbrough TS4 2RG* T: (01642) 816156 E: sue.richardson3@btinternet.com

RICHBOROUGH, Suffragan Bishop of (Provincial Episcopal Visitor). See BANKS, The Rt Revd Norman

RICHERBY, Canon Glynn. b 51. K Coll Lon BD 73 AKC 73. St Aug Coll Cant 73. **d** 74 **p** 75. C Weston Favell *Pet* 74–78; Prec Leic Cathl 78–81; V Glen Parva and S Wigston 81–93; V Leic St Jas 93–16; Dir Post-Ord Tr 86–95; Dir CME 95–16; Hon Can Leic Cathl 98–16; rtd 17. *115 Bath Road, Worcester WR5 3AF* T: (01905) 355757

RICHES, Malcolm Leslie. b 46. St Jo Coll Nottm 92. **d** 94 **p** 95. C Swaythling *Win* 94–97; P-in-c Boldre w S Baddesley 97–01; V 01–03; V Ellingham and Harbridge and Hyde w Ibsley 03–11; rtd 11; Hon C Caldbeck, Castle Sowerby and Sebergham *Carl* 11–16; PtO from 16. *13 Edmondson Close, Brampton CA8 1GH*   M: 07968-139851 E: malcolm.l.riches@gmail.com

RICHEUX, Marc Stephen. b 66. Man Univ BA 89. Trin Coll Bris BA 00. **d** 00 **p** 01. C Plumstead St Jo w St Jas and St Paul *S'wark* 00–04; V Streatham Park St Alb 04–12; TV Furzedown from 12. *St Alban's Vicarage, 5 Fayland Avenue, London SW16 1SR*   T: (020) 8677 4521 *or* 8769 5415

RICHMOND, Patrick Henry. b 69. Ball Coll Ox BA 90 Green Coll Ox MA 94 DPhil 94. Wycliffe Hall Ox BA 96. **d** 97 **p** 98. C Leic Martyrs 97–01; Chapl and Fell St Cath Coll Cam 01–07; Dean of Chpl 06–07; V Eaton Ch Ch *Nor* from 07; RD Nor S from 19. *161 Newmarket Road, Norwich NR4 6SY*   T: (01603) 250844 E: phr@eatonparish.com

RICHMOND, Peter James. b 54. Cant Ch Ch Univ MSc 07 Ex Univ PGCE 95. St Jo Coll Nottm. **d** 80 **p** 81. C Ogley Hay *Lich* 80–83; C Trentham 83–85; P-in-c Wolverhampton St Jo 85–89; P-in-c Loppington w Newtown 89–93; P-in-c Edstaston 89–93; PtO *Ex* 94–95; P-in-c Weston Zoyland w Chedzoy *B & W* 95–03; Chapl Somerset Partnership NHS and Soc Care Trust 97–03; Lead Chapl E Kent NHS and Soc Care Partnership Trust 03–06; Lead Chapl Kent and Medway NHS and Soc Care Partnership Trust 06–13; Hon C St Nicholas at Wade w Sarre and Chislet w Hoath *Cant* 04–10; rtd 13; PtO *Cant* 13–16 and from 20. *41 The Rope Walk, Canterbury CT1 2FY*   T: (01227) 379229

RICHMOND AND CRAVEN, Archdeacon of. *See* GOUGH, The Ven Jonathan Robin Blanning

RICHMOND TULLOCH, Yvonne Lorraine. *See* TULLOCH, Yvonne Lorraine

RICKARDS, Bruce Walter. b 69. NTMTC 98. **d** 01 **p** 02. NSM St Marg Lothbury and St Steph Coleman Street etc *Lon* 01–06; NSM Wimbledon *S'wark* 06–09; C 09–18; AD Merton 17–18; C S Wimbledon St Andr from 19; PtO *Lon* 20–21; Chapl Heathrow Airport from 21. *18 Marian Lodge, 5 The Downs, London SW20 8HJ*   M: 07850-655102 E: byrickards@btinternet.com

RICKETTS, Mrs Diane. b 54. NTMTC 98. **d** 01 **p** 02. NSM Nazeing and Roydon *Chelmsf* 01–06; R Laindon w Dunton 06–14; rtd 14. *8 Tots Gardens, Barrow Hill, Acton, Sudbury CO10 0DJ*

RICKETTS, Canon Kathleen Mary. b 39. Southlands Coll Lon TCert 59 Univ of W Aus BA 79. Westcott Ho Cam 81. **dss** 83 **d** 87 **p** 94. All Hallows by the Tower etc *Lon* 83–88; C 87–88; C Hall Green Ascension *Birm* 88–91; Chapl Birm Children's Hosp 91–94; Chapl Birm Children's Hosp NHS Trust 94–99; Hon Can Birm Cathl 96–99; rtd 99; PtO *Birm* from 00. *22 Holly Drive, Birmingham B27 7NF*   T: 0121-706 1087

RICKETTS, Mrs Linda Elizabeth. b 52. RNMH 85. EAMTC 98. **d** 01 **p** 02. C Loddon, Sisland, Chedgrave, Hardley and Langley *Nor* 01–05; V Gorleston St Mary 05–17; rtd 17; PtO *Nor* from 19. *17 Muriel Kenny Court, Hethersett, Norwich NR9 3EZ*   T: (01603) 814964 E: l.ricketts787@btinternet.com

RICKETTS, Theresa Lesley. b 76. Greyfriars Ox BA 00 Kingston Univ PGCE 07 Cam Univ BTh 14. Westcott Ho Cam 12. **d** 14 **p** 15. C Weybridge *Guildf* 14–17; P-in-c Cuddington from 17. *St Mary's Vicarage, St Mary's Road, Worcester Park KT4 7JL*   M: 07949-769580 E: theresaricketts@hotmail.co.uk

RIDDEL, Robert John. b 37. CITC 65. **d** 68 **p** 69. C Derryloran *Arm* 68–74; I Keady w Armaghbreague and Derrynoose 74–80; I Cleenish w Mullaghdun *Clogh* 80–84; I Cleenish 80–84; I Fivemiletown 84–05; Can Clogh Cathl 95–05; Preb Donaghmore St Patr Cathl Dublin 95–05; rtd 05. *9 Coolcrannel Square, Maguiresbridge, Enniskillen BT94 4RE*   T: (028) 6772 3199 E: riddel.r.j@btinternet.com

RIDDING, George. b 24. Oriel Coll Ox BA 50 MA 57. Wells Th Coll 60. **d** 61 **p** 62. C Wear *Ex* 61–62; Chapl Ex Sch 62–64; India 64–68; Hd Master W Buckland Sch Barnstaple 68–78; USPG 78–82; P-in-c Broadhembury w Payhembury *Ex* 82–83; P-in-c Plymtree 82–83; R Broadhembury, Payhembury and Plymtree 83–89; rtd 89; PtO *Sarum* 89–09. *The College of St Barnabas, Blackberry Lane, Lingfield RH7 6NJ*   T: (01342) 872821 E: georgeridding@gmail.com

RIDDLESTONE, Mrs Jennifer Jane. b 83. Warwick Univ BSc 05 St Jo Coll Dur BATM 15. Cranmer Hall Dur 12. **d** 15 **p** 16. C Egham *Guildf* 15–19; V Shottermill from 19. *The Vicarage, Vicarage Lane, Haslemere GU27 1LQ* E: vicar@shottermillparish.org.uk

RIDER, Andrew. b 62. Nottm Univ BTh 90 K Coll Lon MA 96 RMN 85. Aston Tr Scheme 85 St Jo Coll Nottm 87. **d** 90 **p** 91. C Luton Ch Ch *Roch* 90–93; C w resp for Clubhouse Langham Place All So *Lon* 93–03; P-in-c Spitalfields Ch Ch w All SS 03–04; R 04–20; AD Tower Hamlets 12–20; Dean of Miss Stepney Area from 20; C Bow w Bromley St Leon from

20. *13 Eaton Terrace, Aberavon Road, London E3 5AJ*   T: (020) 7247 0790   F: 7247 5921

RIDER, Canon Dennis William Austin. b 34. St Aid Birkenhead 58. **d** 61 **p** 62. C Derby St Aug 61–64; C Sutton *Liv* 64–67; R Stiffkey w Morston, Langham Episcopi etc *Nor* 67–71; V Buxton w Oxnead 71–79; R Lammas w Lt Hautbois 72–79; R Gaywood, Bawsey and Mintlyn 79–91; RD Lynn 89–91; Hon Can Nor Cathl 90–99; R E Dereham and Scarning 91–98; TR 98–99; RD Dereham in Mitford 95–98; rtd 99; PtO *Nor* 01–08; C Litcham w Kempston, E and W Lexham, Mileham etc 08–09; C Gt and Lt Dunham w Gt and Lt Fransham and Sporle 08–09; C Foulsham, Guestwick, Stibbard, Themelthorpe etc 10–11; PtO from 15. *37A Holt Road, Fakenham NR21 8BW*   T: (01328) 856018

RIDER, Geoffrey Malcolm. b 29. Selw Coll Cam BA 53 MA 56 Lon Inst of Educn PGCE 68. Coll of Resurr Mirfield 53. **d** 55 **p** 56. C S Elmsall *Wakef* 55–60; C Barnsley St Mary 60–63; V Cleckheaton St Jo 63–67; Public Preacher *S'wark* 67–92; rtd 92; Succ Kimberley Cathl S Africa 92–95; PtO *S'wark* 95–03; Chapl and Hon Min Can Ripon Cathl 04–14; *Leeds* from 14. *26 Riverside House, Williamson Close, Ripon HG4 1AZ*   T: (01765) 690517   E: geoffrey.rider2016@gmail.com   *or* geoffreyr547@gmail.com

RIDER, Paul Gill. b 57. Univ of Arkansas BA 81 MA 85. Nashotah Ho MDiv 89. **d** 89 **p** 90. R Fourche and Sturgis USA 89–93; R Minot 93–00; Can Minneapolis Cathl 00–02; R Mankato 02–17; P-in-c Nor Lakenham St Jo and All SS and Tuckswood from 18. *Old Lakenham Vicarage, Harwood Road, Norwich NR1 2NG*   M: 07745-846770 E: prider57@man.com

RIDGE, The Ven James Scott. b 77. Ex Univ BSc 99 Selw Coll Cam BTh 05. Westcott Ho Cam 02. **d** 05 **p** 06. C Halstead Area *Chelmsf* 05–09; C Bocking St Pet 09; Chapl HM Pris *Chelmsf* 09–16; Chapl HM Pris Wayland 16–18; Chapl Gen of Pris and Adn to HM Pris from 18. *HMPPS Chaplaincy HQ, Post Point 8.34, Ministry of Justice, 102 Petty France, London SW1H 9AJ*   M: 07394-715223 E: james.ridge@justice.gov.uk

RIDGE, Jennifer Karen. b 64. St Hild Coll 14. **d** 17 **p** 18. NSM Leic H Trin w St Jo 17–19; C 19–21; NSM Leic H Apostles 17–19; C 19–21; P-in-c from 21. *96 Highway Road, Leicester LE5 5RF*   T: 0116-298 3218

RIDGEWAY, David. b 59. St Chad's Coll Dur BSc 80 Cam Univ CertEd 81. Ripon Coll Cuddesdon 84. **d** 87 **p** 88. C Kempston Transfiguration *St Alb* 87–90; C Radlett 90–95; P-in-c Heath and Reach 95–98; V 98–01; V St Alb St Steph 01–15; RD St Alb 05–15; R Castor w Upton and Stibbington etc *Pet* from 15. *The Rectory, 5 Church Hill, Castor, Peterborough PE5 7AU*   T: (01733) 380244   F: 07092-109111 E: davidridgeway@btinternet.com

RIDGEWELL, Miss Mary Jean. b 54. Dur Univ BA 76 PGCE 77. Ridley Hall Cam 89. **d** 91 **p** 94. Par Dn Trowbridge St Jas *Sarum* 91–94; C 94–95; Chapl Lee Abbey 95–96; NSM Bradford Peverell, Stratton, Frampton etc *Sarum* 96–97; Chapl HM Pris and YOI Guys Marsh 97–12; rtd 12; PtO *Sarum* 12–22. *11 Gower Road, Shaftesbury SP7 8RU* E: rewarmedgilly@gmail.com

RIDGWAY, Mrs Janet Elizabeth Knight. b 40. St Alb Minl Tr Scheme 83. **dss** 86 **d** 87 **p** 94. Tring *St Alb* 86–87; Hon Par Dn 87–94; Hon C 94–05; rtd 05; PtO *St Alb* from 06. *Barleycombe, Trooper Road, Aldbury, Tring HP23 5RW*   T/F: (01442) 851303 E: rev.j.ridgway@breathe.com

RIDGWELL, Graham Edgar Charles. b 46. LGSM 71 Open Univ BA 82 Leeds Univ MA 04. **d** 02 **p** 03. NSM Whitby w Aislaby and Ruswarp *York* 02–05; Hon TV Linton *Ely* 05–15; PtO *Chelmsf* from 15; *Ely* 15–20. *76 Swan Street, Sible Hedingham, Halstead CO9 3HT*   T: (01799) 584545 E: gecridgwell@googlemail.com *or* ridgwell@onetel.com

RIDING, Pauline Alison. *See* BICKNELL, Pauline Alison

RIDINGS, Neil Arthur. b 66. Man Poly BEd 90. St Jo Coll Nottm 01. **d** 01 **p** 02. C Holyhead *Ban* 01–05; TV 05–07; R Valley w Llechylched and Caergeiliog 07–14; R Bro Cwyfan 14–18; C Bro Cybi from 18. *Y Ficerdy, Trearddur House Mews, Lon St Ffraid, Trearddur Bay, Holyhead LL65 2UD*   T: (01407) 861663 E: revridings@gmail.com

RIDLEY, Andrew Roy. b 55. St Pet Coll Ox BA 77. Ripon Coll Cuddesdon 78. **d** 79 **p** 80. C Bollington St Jo *Ches* 79–83; V Runcorn St Mich 83–94; Dioc Chapl MU 92–98; RD Frodsham 94–98; V Helsby and Dunham-on-the-Hill 94–98; P-in-c Alvanley 94–98; R Whitchurch *Lich* 98–11; RD Wem and Whitchurch 01–06; V Barton under Needwood w Dunstall and Tatenhill 11–19; V Witton *Ches* from 19; P-in-c Lostock Gralam from 19. *The Vicarage, 61 Church Road, Northwich CW9 5PB*   T: (01606) 42943   M: 07772-214966 E: arridley1@gmail.com

RIDLEY, David Gerhard. b 60. Southn Univ BSc 82 Bath Univ PGCE 83. Qu Coll Birm 91. **d** 93 **p** 94. C Faversham *Cant* 93–97; Min Folkestone St Aug CD 97–01; V Dover St Mary

01–13; P-in-c Whitfield w Guston 02–12; P-in-c Guston 13; AD Dover 06–11; R Eastry and Woodnesborough 13–21; TV Sittingbourne w Bobbing from 21. *32 Valenciennes Road, Sittingbourne ME10 1EN* T: (01795) 426753 M: 07887-880272 E: davidridley@btopenworld.com

RIDLEY, Derek. b 40. Newc Univ BSc 74. Cranmer Hall Dur 75. **d** 78 **p** 79. C Upperby St Jo *Carl* 78–81; C Penrith w Newton Reigny 81; C Penrith w Newton Reigny and Plumpton Wall 81–82; TV 82–86; V Cadishead *Man* 86–99; R Asfordby and P-in-c Ab Kettleby Gp *Leic* 99–02; P-in-c Old Dalby and Nether Broughton 99–01; rtd 02; PtO *Carl* 08–20. *32 Carleton Place, Penrith CA11 8LW* T: (01768) 890676 E: lesley.ridley@me.com

RIDLEY, Jay. b 41. Birm Univ BA 63. St Steph Ho Ox 63. **d** 65 **p** 66. C Woodford St Mary *Chelmsf* 65–67; C Prittlewell St Mary 67–70; C-in-c Dunscroft CD *Sheff* 70–74; Asst Chapl HM Pris Wormwood Scrubs 75–77; Chapl HM Rem Cen Ashford 77–84; Chapl HM YOI Feltham 84–91; Chapl HM Pris Ashwell 91–00; C Oakham, Hambleton, Egleton, Braunston and Brooke Pet 00; rtd 11; PtO *Chich* from 16. *11 Ramsay Hall, 9-13 Byron Road, Worthing BN11 3HN* T: (01903) 210224 E: jay.ridley@hotmail.co.uk

RIDLEY, Mrs Jennifer Mary. b 62. **d** 14 **p** 15. NSM Sudbury w Ballingdon and Brundon *St E* 14–17; NSM Gt Cornard from 17; NSM Sudbury w Ballingdon and Brundon from 19; NSM Sudbury and Chilton from 19. *67 Acton Lane, Sudbury CO10 1QW* T: (01787) 375974 E: jennie67mr@gmail.com

RIDLEY, Mrs Lesley. b 46. Cranmer Hall Dur 75. **dss** 78 **d** 87 **p** 94. Upperby St Jo *Carl* 78–81; Penrith w Newton Reigny and Plumpton Wall 81–86; Cadishead *Man* 86–99; Par Dn 87–94; C 94–99; C Asfordby and Ab Kettleby Gp *Leic* 99–02; rtd 02; PtO *Carl* 08–20. *32 Carleton Place, Penrith CA11 8LW* T: (01768) 890676 E: lesley.ridley@me.com

RIDLEY, Michael Laurence. b 59. BA 81. Ripon Coll Cuddesdon 81. **d** 83 **p** 84. C Bollington St Jo *Ches* 83–88; V Thelwall 88–95; V Weaverham 95–05; RD Middlewich 99–05; V Stockton Heath from 05; P-in-c Latchford St Jas from 19. *12 Melton Avenue, Walton, Warrington WA4 6PQ* T: (01925) 261396 E: stocktonheathvicar@tiscali.co.uk

RIDLEY, Peter John. b 39. Keble Coll Ox BA 61 MA 97. Tyndale Hall Bris 61. **d** 63 **p** 64. C Clifton Ch Ch w Em *Bris* 63–67; C Lambeth St Andr w St Thos *S'wark* 67–69; V W Hampstead St Cuth *Lon* 69–77; V Eynsham *Ox* 77–85; RD Woodstock 82–84; V Nicholforest and Kirkandrews on Esk *Carl* 85–96; P-in-c E Knoyle, Semley and Sedgehill *Sarum* 96–04; rtd 04; PtO *Carl* from 05. *The Castle, Castle Street, Hilton, Appleby-in-Westmorland CA16 6LX* T: (017683) 51682 E: peterandsally.ridley@btinternet.com

RIDLEY, Stephen James. b 57. St Pet Coll Ox BA 80 MA 83 Dur Univ EdD 13. Ripon Coll Cuddesdon 80. **d** 82 **p** 83. C Heald Green St Cath *Ches* 82–85; Chapl Ches Coll 85–90; Dioc Press Officer 85–90; Lect St Deiniol's Lib Hawarden 85–90; Chapl Birkenhead Sch 90–96; LtO *Ches* 90–96; Chapl and Dep Hd Barnard Castle Sch 96–14; Teacher Dur High Sch for Girls 14–21; PtO *Dur* 15–21. *7 Oakfields Grove, Spondon, Derby DE21 7ST* E: stephen.ridley3@btinternet.com

RIDLEY, Stewart Gordon. b 47. K Coll Lon AKC 72. St Aug Coll Cant 72. **d** 73 **p** 74. C Armley w New Wortley *Ripon* 73–77; C Hawksworth Wood 77–79; C Rothwell w Lofthouse 79–81; R Whitwood *Wakef* 81–87; R Ingoldmells w Addlethorpe *Linc* 87–92; RD Calcewaithe and Candleshoe 89–92; V Settle *Bradf* 92–05; C Bolton by Bowland w Grindleton 05–07; P-in-c Hurst Green and Mitton 05–07; P-in-c Waddington 05–07; rtd 07; PtO *York* 09–14; Chapl S Tees Hosps NHS Foundn Trust 11–14; PtO *Leeds* from 14. *18 Brough Meadows, Catterick, Richmond DL10 7LQ* T: (01748) 519359 M: 07952-584138 E: stewartridley@uwclub.net

RIDLEY, Vic. *See* RIDLEY, David Gerhard

RIDOUT, Canon Christopher John. b 33. K Coll Lon BD 57 AKC 57 MA 92. St Gabr 58 **p** 59. C Roxeth Ch Ch *Lon* 58–62; CMS 62–63; Kenya 63–75; C Gt Malvern St Mary *Worc* 75–79; R Bredon w Bredon's Norton 79–98; RD Pershore 91–97; Hon Can Worc Cathl 92–98; rtd 98; PtO *Glouc* 98–18. *5 Belworth Drive, Hatherley, Cheltenham GL51 6EL* T: (01242) 231765 E: shirleyjohn@tiscali.co.uk

RIDPATH, Ms Vivienne Elizabeth Theresa. b 54. Aber Univ BSc 77 UEA PGCE 94. ERMC 16. **d** 19 **p** 20. OLM Belton and Burgh Castle *Nor* from 19. *30 North Denes Road, Great Yarmouth NR30 4LU* M: 07523-717810 E: vivridpath@aol.com

RIEM, Canon Roland Gerardus Anthony. b 60. St Chad's Coll Dur BSc 82 Kent Univ PhD 86 Heythrop Coll Lon MA 99. St Jo Coll Nottm 86. **d** 89 **p** 90. C Deal St Leon and St Rich and Sholden *Cant* 89–92; Sen Chapl Nottm Univ *S'well* 92–98; Dir Min STETS 98–05; Can Res Win Cathl from 05. *5A The Close, Winchester*

SO23 9LS T: (01962) 857216 *or* 857239 F: 857201 E: roland.riem@winchester-cathedral.org.uk

RIENSTRA, Bruce Elliot. b 59. Ohio Univ (USA) BA 83 Ches Univ MA 18. St Jo Coll Nottm 11. **d** 13 **p** 14. C Warsop *S'well* 13–16; R Inkberrow w Cookhill and Kington w Dormston *Worc* from 16. *The Vicarage, High Street, Inkberrow, Worcester WR7 4DU* T: (01386) 792222 M: 07742-172333 E: b.e.rienstra@gmail.com

RIESS, Trevor William. b 54. Down Coll Cam MA 76 CertEd 77. St Jo Coll Nottm 84. **d** 86 **p** 87. C Stainforth *Sheff* 86–88; Chapl St Jas Choir Sch Grimsby 89; C Lowestoft and Kirkley *Nor* 89–90; TV 90–94; TV Lowestoft St Marg 94–95; Chapl Lothingland Hosp 90–95; V Gorleston St Mary *Nor* 95–05; P-in-c Scole, Brockdish, Billingford, Thorpe Abbots etc 05–11; R Gunton St Pet 11–19; rtd 20. *26 Bellflower Road, Grimsby DN33 3AZ* E: trevorriess@btinternet.com

RIGBY, Anthony Paul. **d** 20 **p** 21. NSM Elworth *Ches* from 20. *Address temp unknown*

RIGBY, William. b 51. Leic Univ BSc(Econ) 72 Newc Poly BSc 82. Cranmer Hall Dur 86. **d** 88 **p** 89. C Morpeth *Newc* 88–92; R St John Lee 92–00; Chapl to the Deaf 92–08; P-in-c Chapel House 00–08; V Bywell and Mickley 08–16; rtd 16; PtO *Dur* from 16. *1 Bromley Close, High Shincliffe, Durham DH1 7TZ* M: 07734-068668 E: bill.rigby1@btopenworld.com

RIGELSFORD, Mrs Anne Catharina (Ank). b 44. BEM 21. EAMTC 99. **d** 02 **p** 03. NSM Cambridge H Cross *Ely* 02–06; NSM Cambridge Ascension 06–15; PtO from 15. *19 Clare Street, Cambridge CB4 3BY* T: (01223) 368150 M: 07932-846395 E: ank1@btinternet.com

RIGLIN, Ms Jacqueline Anne. b 57. ERMC 13. **d** 16 **p** 17. NSM Chesterton St Geo *Ely* from 16. *30 Lavender Road, Cambridge CB4 2PU* T: (01223) 660144 M: 07513-331783 E: jackie.riglin@gmail.com

✠**RIGLIN, The Rt Revd Keith Graham.** b 57. Lon Inst of Educn BEd 80 Regent's Park Coll Ox BA 83 MA 86 Heythrop Coll Lon MTh 85 Birm Univ ThD 08 FRSA 09 AKC 16 MSSTh 20. Westcott Ho Cam 06. **d** 08 **p** 08 c 21. In Bapt Union 83–96; in URC 97–08; C Notting Dale St Clem w St Mark and St Jas *Lon* 08–11; PtO 12–16; *S'wark* 12–13; *Arg* 12–21; Chapl K Coll Lon 12–21; Visiting Lect 16–19; Asst Dean 17–20; Vice Dean 20–21; Visiting Research Fell from 21; NSM Soho St Anne w St Thos and St Pet 16–21; NSM St Mary le Strand w St Clem Danes 17–21; Dir of Ords Two Cities Area 19–21; Hon Can St Jo Cathl Oban *Arg* 20–21; Bp Arg from 21. *Diocesan Centre, Croft Avenue, Oban PA34 5JJ* T: (01631) 570870 M: 07946-871850 E: kgr23@cam.ac.uk *or* bishop@argyll.anglican.org

RILEY, Alison Mary. b 70. Warwick Univ BSc 91 St Martin's Coll Lanc PGCE 98. St Mellitus Coll 15. **d** 17 **p** 18. C Whitehaven *Carl* 17–19. *8 Spruce Grove, Whitehaven CA28 6NP* T: (01946) 65451 M: 07787-508391 E: alidunnuk@yahoo.co.uk

RILEY, David Leo. b 51. S Bank Univ MSc 95. Dioc OLM tr scheme 97. **d** 00 **p** 01. NSM Bellingham St Dunstan *S'wark* from 00. *117 Whitefoot Lane, Bromley BR1 5SB* T: (020) 8516 4544 E: driley3020@aol.com

RILEY, John Graeme. b 55. St Jo Coll Dur BA 78. Trin Coll Bris 79. **d** 81 **p** 82. C Hensingham *Carl* 81–84; C Preston St Cuth *Blackb* 84–87; V Blackb Ch Ch w St Matt 87–98; Chapl Qu Park Hosp Blackb 87–94; V Shevington *Blackb* 98–04; V Euxton 04–14; P-in-c Gosforth w Nether Wasdale and Wasdale Head *Carl* 14–17; P-in-c Beckermet St Jo and St Bridget w Ponsonby 14–17; R Seatallan from 17. *The Rectory, Gosforth, Seascale CA20 1AZ* T: (01946) 725251 E: lesleyjohn.riley@gmail.com

RILEY, The Very Revd Kenneth Joseph. b 40. OBE 03. Univ of Wales BA 61 Linacre Ho Ox BA 64 MA 68. Wycliffe Hall Ox 61. **d** 64 **p** 65. C Fazakerley Em *Liv* 64–66; Chapl Brasted Place Coll Westerham 66–69; Chapl Oundle Sch 69–74; Chapl Liv Cathl 74–75; Chapl Liv Univ 74–93; V Mossley Hill St Matt and St Jas 75–83; RD Childwall 82–83; Can Res and Treas Liv Cathl 83–87; Can Res and Prec Liv Cathl 87–93; Dean Man 93–05; rtd 05. *4 Lindisfarne Road, Alnwick NE66 1AU*

RILEY, Mrs Lesley Anne. b 54. Totley Thornbridge Coll TCert 75. Trin Coll Bris. **dss** 81 **d** 87 **p** 98. Hensingham *Carl* 81–84; Preston St Cuth *Blackb* 84–87; Hon Par Dn Blackb Ch Ch w St Matt 87–98; Asst Dir of Ords 96–00; Dir of Ords and Dir IME 4-7 00–05; Hon C Shevington 98–04; Hon C Whittle-le-Woods 06–07; Resources Co-ord Dioc Bd of Educn 07–14; NSM Gosforth w Nether Wasdale and Wasdale Head *Carl* 14–17; NSM Beckermet St Jo and St Bridget w Ponsonby 14–17; NSM Seatallan 17–19; PtO from 19. *The Rectory, Gosforth, Seascale CA20 1AZ* T: (01946) 725251

RILEY, Linda. *See* RILEY-DAWKIN, Linda

RILEY, Martin Shaw. b 47. Selw Coll Cam BA 71 MA 75 Cam Univ CertEd 72. Sarum & Wells Th Coll 85. **d** 87 **p** 88.

C Tuffley *Glouc* 87–91; Hon Min Can Glouc Cathl from 88; P-in-c Barnwood 91–94; V 94–99; P-in-c Highnam, Lassington, Rudford, Tibberton etc 99–04; R 04–06; Chapl Glos Hosps NHS Foundn Trust 06–12; rtd 12; PtO *Eur* from 17. *61 Kingsholm Road, Gloucester GL1 3BA* T: (01452) 417337

RILEY, Michael Charles. b 57. Ball Coll Ox BA 79 MA 83 Ex Univ CertEd 80. Edin Th Coll 84. **d** 86 **p** 87. C Newc St Geo 86–89; C Chiswick St Nic w St Mary *Lon* 89–90; V Chiswick St Paul Grove Park from 90. *St Paul's Vicarage, 64 Grove Park Road, London W4 3SB* T: (020) 8987 0312 E: michaelc.riley@virgin.net

RILEY, Preb Patrick John. b 39. Leeds Univ BA 62. Coll of Resurr Mirfield 62. **d** 64 **p** 65. C Rowbarton *B & W* 64–72; P-in-c Farleigh Hungerford w Tellisford 72–73; P-in-c Rode Major 72–73; R 73–85; RD Frome 78–85; V Glastonbury w Meare and W Pennard 85–01; Preb Wells Cathl 90–01; rtd 01; PtO *Sarum* 02–22. *30 St James Street, Shaftesbury SP7 8HE* T: (01747) 850361 E: andy.blows@phonecoop.coop

RILEY-BRALEY, Robert James. b 57. Ch Ch Ox BA 82 MA 82 Down Coll Cam BA 83 MA 87 K Coll Lon MA 98 Surrey Univ PGCE 92. Ridley Hall Cam 81. **d** 84 **p** 85. C Thames Ditton *Guildf* 84–87; C Gravesend St Geo *Roch* 87–91; PtO *Lon* 91–92; *Blackb* 92–95; *S'wark* 95–00; C Stevenage St Mary Shephall w Aston *St Alb* 02–08; P-in-c Croxley Green St Oswald 08–12; V from 12. *St Oswald's Vicarage, 159 Baldwins Lane, Croxley Green, Rickmansworth WD3 3LL* T: (01923) 332244

RILEY-DAWKIN, Mrs Linda. b 67. St Jo Coll Nottm BA 00. **d** 00 **p** 01. C Ince Ch Ch *Liv* 00–06; Chapl Knowsley Community Coll 06–08; V Ditton St Mich w St Thos *Liv* from 08. *339 Ditchfield Road, Widnes WA8 8XR* T: 0151-420 4963 M: 07932-038443 E: revlin.riley@btinternet.com

RIMMER, Alan Howard. b 88. Ch Ch Ox MA 10. St Steph Ho Ox BA 18. **d** 19 **p** 21. C Tottenham St Mary *Lon* 19–21; C S Kensington St Steph from 20. *Flat 4, 47 Marloes Road, London W8 6LA* M: 07582-399967 E: alanhowardrimmer@gmail.com

RIMMER, Andrew Malcolm. b 62. Magd Coll Cam BA 84 MA 88. Wycliffe Hall Ox 86. **d** 88 **p** 89. C Romford Gd Shep *Chelmsf* 88–92; C Hazlemere *Ox* 92–97; V Crookhorn *Portsm* 97–05; TV Canford Magna *Sarum* 05–17; V S Mimms Ch Ch *Lon* from 17. *Christ Church Vicarage, St Albans Road, Barnet EN5 4LA* E: andy@rimmerteam.com *or* vicar@ccbarnet.org.uk

RIMMER, Canon David Henry. b 36. Ex Coll Ox BA 60 MA 65. Linc Th Coll 62. **d** 64 **p** 65. C Liv Our Lady and St Nic 64–66; C Daybrook *S'well* 66–69; Chapl St Mary's Cathl *Edin* 69–71; R Kirkcaldy *St And* 71–78; R Haddington *Edin* 78–83; R Dunbar 79–83; R Edin Gd Shep 83–01; Hon Can St Mary's Cathl 98–01; rtd 01; LtO *Edin* from 01. *28/25 Roseburn Place, Edinburgh EH12 5NX* T: 0131-237 3070 E: ehhdhome@icloud.com

RIMMER, Mrs Margaret. b 55. St Jo Coll Dur BA 05 SRN 77 SCM 78. Cranmer Hall Dur 00. **d** 02 **p** 03. C Aysgarth and Bolton cum Redmire *Ripon* 02–06; V Gt and Lt Ouseburn w Marton cum Grafton etc 06–11; P-in-c Lostock Hall and Farington Moss *Blackb* 10–12; V 12–16; rtd 16; PtO *Blackb* from 16. *28 Hampson Avenue, Leyland PR25 5TH* T: (01772) 512109 E: margaretrimmer.rev@gmail.com

RIMMER, Rebecca Mary. b 91. **d** 20 **p** 21. C Highbury Ch Ch w St Jo and St Sav *Lon* from 20. *18 Athenaeum Court, Highbury New Park, London N5 2DN* M: 07983-478907

RINDL, Antony William. b 64. St Jo Coll Nottm 97. **d** 99 **p** 00. C Syston *Leic* 99–03; TV Colne and Villages *Blackb* 03–08; TR 08–13; P-in-c Brierfield 10–13; AD Pendle 05–13; V Watford *St Alb* from 13. *The Vicarage, 14 Cassiobury Drive, Watford WD17 3AB* T: (01923) 819152 E: tony.rindl@googlemail.com

RINGER, Philip James. b 47. Ox Min Course 88. **d** 91 **p** 92. NSM Chalfont St Peter *Ox* 91–95; P-in-c Lynton, Brendon, Countisbury, Lynmouth etc *Ex* 95–96; TV Combe Martin, Berrynarbor, Lynton, Brendon etc 96–03; Chapl Devon and Cornwall Constabulary 00–03; R Wriggle Valley *Sarum* 03–08; rtd 08; PtO *Sarum* from 08; Chapl SW Dorset Primary Care Trust from 08; Chapl Dorset Police from 10. *7 Wanderwell Farm Lane, Bridport DT6 4JW* T: (01308) 425774 E: philipringer@aol.com

RINGLAND, Tom Laurence. b 61. SS Hild & Bede Coll Dur BSc 83. Trin Coll Bris BA 89. **d** 89 **p** 90. C Southgate *Chich* 89–92; C Polegate 92–96; P-in-c Coalville and Bardon Hill *Leic* 96–98; V 98–06; TR Kirby Muxloe 06–15; C Desford and Peckleton w Tooley 13–15; R Desford and Kirby Muxloe 15–19; AD Sparkenhoe E 16–19; R Penhill *Leeds* from 19. *The Vicarage, Carperby, Leyburn DL8 4DQ* E: tringland@aol.com *or* tom.ringland@leeds.anglican.org

RINK, Caroline Natalie. b 82. Ex Univ BA 06. Coll of Resurr Mirfield BA 19. **d** 19 **p** 20. C Kilburn St Mary w

All So and W Hampstead St Jas *Lon* from 19. *3 St James's House, Sherriff Road, London NW6 2AP* M: 07740-336829 E: rev.caroline.rink@gmail.com

RINK, Pamela Rosemary. b 56. Kent Univ BA 05. SEITE 08. **d** 10 **p** 12. NSM E Malling, Wateringbury and Teston *Roch* 10–16; Guardian Pilsdon at Malling Community 11–15; TV Shaftesbury *Sarum* from 16. *The Vicarage, Bittles Green, Motcombe, Shaftesbury SP7 9NX* T: (01747) 590712 M: 07881-786526 E: pam.rink@gmail.com

RINSLER, Miriam Philippa. b 58. Cam Univ BA 80 Lon Univ MA 82 Lon Inst of Educn PGCE 86. St Mellitus Coll 19. **d** 20 **p** 21. NSM Hendon St Mary and Ch Ch *Lon* from 20. *63A Dresden Road, London N19 3BG* M: 07946-481993 E: mimpol@hotmail.com

RIOCH, Mrs Wenda Jean. b 35. Sarum & Wells Th Coll 84. **d** 87 **p** 94. Par Dn Basingstoke *Win* 87–91; Par Dn Catshill and Dodford *Worc* 91–94; C 94–98; TV Ottery St Mary, Alfington, W Hill, Tipton etc *Ex* 98–05; rtd 05; PtO *Win* from 08; *Sarum* from 09. *76 Gardeners Green, Shipton Bellinger, Tidworth SP9 7TA* T: (01980) 842334 E: wrioch123@aol.com

RIORDAN, Sean Charles. b 67. Loughb Univ BA 89. St Jo Coll Nottm MA 98 LTh 99. **d** 99 **p** 00. C Ockbrook *Derby* 99–03; Asst Chapl Tervuren *Eur* 03–08; C Woodley *Ox* 08–18; V Woodley Em from 18. *171 Hurricane Way, Woodley, Reading RG5 4UH* T: 0118-375 3718 E: sean@emmanuelwoodley.org.uk

RIPLEY, Gordon. b 48. SWMTC 03. **d** 06 **p** 07. NSM Torquay St Matthias, St Mark and H Trin *Ex* 06–10; NSM Timsbury w Priston, Camerton and Dunkerton *B & W* 10–17; rtd 17. *42 Ampney Drive Kingsway, Quedgeley, Gloucester GL2 2HR* E: gordon.ripley364@btinternet.com

RIPON, Dean of. *See* DOBSON, The Very Revd John Richard

RIPON, Suffragan Bishop of. *See* HARTLEY, The Rt Revd Helen-Ann Macleod

RISBRIDGER, Jeffrey Edward. b 58. K Alfred's Coll Win BA 80 PGCE 81. Ripon Coll Cuddesdon 12. **d** 14 **p** 15. C Waterloo St Jo w St Andr *S'wark* 14–18; C Ludgvan, Marazion, St Hilary and Perranuthnoe *Truro* from 18; RD Penwith 19–21. *Meadowcroft, Relubbus Lane, St Hilary, Penzance TR20 9EF* M: 07711-019590 E: fatherjeffrey@icloud.com

RISBY, John. b 40. Lambeth STh 82. Oak Hill Th Coll 64. **d** 67 **p** 68. C Fulham Ch Ch *Lon* 67–68; C Ealing St Mary 68–70; C Chitts Hill St Cuth 70–73; C Hove Bp Hannington Memorial Ch *Chich* 73–76; V Islington St Jude Mildmay Park *Lon* 76–82; P-in-c Islington St Paul Ball's Pond 78–82; V Mildmay Grove St Jude and St Paul 82–84; R Hunsdon w Widford and Wareside *St Alb* 84–05; RD Hertford 91–96; rtd 05; PtO *St Alb* 06–20; *Chelmsf* from 06. *1 Pilgrim Close, Great Chesterford, Saffron Walden CB10 1QG* T: (01799) 530232 E: john.risby179@btinternet.com

RISDON, Mrs Caroline Louise. b 79. Cape Town Univ BSocSc 01 Univ Coll Lon MA 11 Chu Coll Cam BTh 14. Westcott Ho Cam 12. **d** 14 **p** 15. C Greenwich St Alfege *S'wark* 14–21; V Eltham St Jo from 21. *32 Kings Orchard, London SE9 5TJ* M: 07899-916089 E: vicar@elthamchurch.org.uk

RISDON, John Alexander. b 42. Clifton Th Coll 66. **d** 68 **p** 69. C Ealing Dean St Jo *Lon* 68–72; C Heref St Pet w St Owen 72–74; Ord Cand Sec CPAS and Hon C Bromley Ch Ch *Roch* 74–77; TV Cheltenham St Mary, St Matt, St Paul and H Trin *Glouc* 77–86; R Stapleton *Bris* 86–00; R Bedhampton *Portsm* 00–09; rtd 09; PtO *Glouc* from 10. *10 St Margarets Road, Gloucester GL3 3BP* T: (01452) 372702 M: 07719-460991 E: john.risdon65@btinternet.com

RISHTON, Mrs Tracy Jane. b 67. St Jo Coll Nottm 01. **d** 04 **p** 05. C Earby *Bradf* 04–07; C Kelbrook 04–07; C Cross Roads cum Lees 07–09; Area Missr S Craven Deanery 07–09. *Hovland, 4389 Vikesa, Norway* E: tracy@rishton.info

RITCHIE, Canon Angus William Mark. b 74. Magd Coll Ox BA 94 BPhil 96 MA 98. Westcott Ho Cam 96. **d** 98 **p** 99. C Plaistow and N Canning Town *Chelmsf* 98–02; TV 02–04; Dir Contextual Th Cen R Foundn of St Kath in Ratcliffe 05–16; Fells' Chapl Magd Coll Ox from 05; Hon C Gt Ilford St Luke *Chelmsf* 05–08; Chapl E Lon Univ 08–11; Asst Chapl Keble Coll Ox 11–12; Hon C Bethnal Green St Pet w St Thos *Lon* 12–15; NSM St Geo-in-the-East w St Paul from 15; P-in-c 15–18; Hon Can Worc Cathl from 15. *St George-in-the-East Church, 14 Cannon Street Road, London E1 0BH* T: (020) 7481 1345 M: 07841-362786 E: angus@stgeorgeintheeast.org *or* director@theology-centre.org

RITCHIE, David John Rose. b 48. St Jo Coll Dur BA 72. Cranmer Hall Dur. **d** 74 **p** 75. C Harold Wood *Chelmsf* 74–79; TV Ipsley *Worc* 79–84; Chapl Vevey w Château d'Oex and Villars *Eur* 84–93; V Stoke Bishop *Bris* 93–13; rtd 13; PtO *Worc* from 15. *The Old Stores, Forty Green, Lowbands, Redmarley, Gloucester GL19 3SL* E: davidritchie@live.co.uk

RITCHIE, Canon David Philip. b 60. Hatf Coll Dur BA 85. Wycliffe Hall Ox 85. **d** 87 **p** 88. C Chadwell *Chelmsf* 87–90; C Waltham H Cross 90–94; TV Becontree W 94–98; TR 98–01; Lay Tr Officer 01–11; C Lt Waltham 02–05; C Gt and Lt Leighs and Lt Waltham 05–11; Dir Lay Min Studies NTMTC 06–11; TR Gt Baddow *Chelmsf* 11–20; Miss and Min Adv Colchester Area from 20; Hon Can Chelmsf Cathl from 09. *50 Colchester Road, White Colne, Colchester CO6 2PP* E: dpritchie1@gmail.com

RITCHIE, Miss Jean. b 30. Lon Univ CertEd 51. Trin Coll Bris 77. **dss** 79 **d** 87 **p** 94. Ox St Ebbe w H Trin and St Pet 79–87; Par Dn 87–91; rtd 91; PtO *B & W* 91–94 and 96–18; NSM Clevedon St Andr and Ch Ch 94–96. *63 Holland Road, Clevedon BS21 7YJ* T: (01275) 871762

RITCHIE, June. *See* FAULKNER, June

RITCHIE, Philip. *See* RITCHIE, David Philip

RITCHIE, Philip Simon James. b 68. Man Univ BA 90 Sussex Univ MA 98 Leeds Univ MA 01 Man Metrop Univ PGCE 92. Coll of Resurr Mirfield 99. **d** 01 **p** 02. C Brighton St Nic *Chich* 01–04; P-in-c Chich St Wilfrid 04–08; P-in-c Hove 08–10; V Hove All SS 10–15; V Cowley St Jo *Ox* from 15. *Redwood House, 276A Cowley Road, Oxford OX4 1UR* E: philipsj68@gmail.com *or* philipsj@gmail.com

RITCHIE, William James. b 62. TCD MA 84. CITC. **d** 86 **p** 87. C Enniscorthy w Clone, Clonmore, Monart etc *C, F & O* 86–89; Asst Chapl Alexandria Egypt 89–91; Bp's C Kells Gp *C, F & O* 91–92; I Kells Union *M & K* 92–99; Warden of Readers 93–97; Dioc Ecum Officer 97–99; Min Can St Patr Cathl Dublin 97–99; I Clondehorkey w Cashel *D & R* 99–00; I Dublin St Bart w Leeson Park *D & G* 00–04; I Tullow w Shillelagh, Aghold and Mullinacuff *C, F & O* 04–08; Warden of Readers 05–08; PtO *Lon* 08–12; P-in-c Newport All SS *Mon* 12–15; P-in-c Abertillery w Cwmtillery w Llanhilleth etc 15–16. *73 Cae'r Wern, Merthyr Tydfil CF48 1AF* E: duwillo@yahoo.co.uk

RITSON, Canon Gerald Richard Stanley (Bill). b 35. CCC Cam BA 59 MA 63. Linc Th Coll 59. **d** 61 **p** 62. C Harpenden St Jo *St Alb* 61–65; C Goldington 65–69; R Clifton 69–76; Sec to Dioc Past Cttee and P-in-c Aldenham 76–87; Hon Can St Alb 80–87; Can Res St Alb 87–00; rtd 00; PtO *S'wark* 00–16; *Lon* 04–09. *Terry's Cross House, Brighton Road, Woodmancote, Henfield BN5 9SX* T: (01273) 494215

RITTMAN, Mrs Margaret. b 52. C F Mott Coll of Educn CertEd 73 Trent Poly BEd 80. Ripon Coll Cuddesdon MA 11. **d** 11 **p** 12. NSM Knight's Enham and Smannell w Enham Alamein *Win* 11–13; NSM Martlesham w Brightwell *St E* from 13. *Woodlea, The Street, Martlesham, Woodbridge IP12 4RG* M: 07914-771061 E: mgtritt@me.com

RIVIERE, Canon Jonathan Byam Valentine. b 54. LVO 15. Cuddesdon Coll. **d** 83 **p** 84. C Wymondham *Nor* 83–88; TV Quidenham 88–94; P-in-c Somerleyton w Ashby, Fritton and Herringfleet 94; R Somerleyton, Ashby, Fritton, Herringfleet etc 95–03; R Sandringham w W Newton and Appleton etc from 03; P-in-c Castle Rising 03–11; R from 11; P-in-c Hillington 03–11; R from 11; RD Heacham and Rising 13–17; Dom Chapl to The Queen from 03; Chapl to The Queen from 07; Hon Can Nor Cathl from 14. *The Rectory, Sandringham PE35 6EH* T: (01485) 540587 E: rector.sandringham@gmail.com

RIZZELLO, Karen Margaret. b 56. **d** 16 **p** 17. C Whitton *Sarum* from 16. *Brindley House, Vastern Wharf, Royal Wootton Bassett, Swindon SN4 7PD* T: (01793) 850945 E: karen@rizzello.co.uk

ROACH, Preb Jason O'Neale. b 77. Guy's Hosp Medical Sch BSc 98 K Coll Lon MB, BS 02 St Mary's Coll Twickenham MA 05. Oak Hill Th Coll MTh 10. **d** 10 **p** 11. C St Helen Bishopsgate w St Andr Undershaft etc *Lon* 10–21; Bp's Adv on Policy and Strategy 19–21; Dir Min Lon City Miss from 21; PtO *S'wark* from 19; Preb St Paul's Cathl *Lon* from 21. *London City Mission, Nasmith House, 175 Tower Bridge Road, London SE1 2AH* M: 07957-473507 E: revdrjroach@gmail.com

ROACHE, Anthony. b 60. Nazarene Th Coll Man BA 98. Qu Coll Birm 98. **d** 99 **p** 00. C Bury St Mary *Man* 99–02; P-in-c Ringley w Prestolee 02–06; Voc Adv 04–06; CF(V) 03–06; CF 06–19; P-in-c Darlington St Hilda and St Columba *Dur* from 19; P-in-c Darlington St Jo from 19. *239 Parkside, Darlington DL1 5TG* M: 07740-102733

ROAKE, Anthony Richard Garrard. b 52. Keble Coll Ox BA 75 MA 80. Wycliffe Hall Ox 75. **d** 77 **p** 78. C Clifton *S'well* 77–80; V Lapley w Wheaton Aston *Lich* 80–86; V Bournemouth St Andr *Win* 86–98; V Fernhurst *Chich* 98–07; Chapl The Hague *Eur* 07–12; R Nailsea Ch Ch w Tickenham *B & W* 12–19; NSM Timsbury w Priston, Camerton and Dunkerton from 19. *The Rectory, Skinners Hill, Camerton, Bath BA2 0PU* E: tonyrgr@gmail.com

ROBARTS, Mrs Freda Margaret. b 43. Open Univ BA 86. St As Minl Tr Course 98. **d** 04 **p** 06. NSM Berriew *St As* 04–06; P-in-c Llansilin w Llangadwaladr and Llangedwyn 06–09; rtd

09; PtO *St As* 09–16. *23 Fordwich Close, St Arvans, Chepstow NP16 6EL*

ROBB, Ian Archibald. b 48. K Coll Lon 68. **d** 72 **p** 73. C E Ham w Upton Park *Chelmsf* 72–74; C Leckhampton SS Phil and Jas w Cheltenham St Jas *Glouc* 74–79; P-in-c Cheltenham St Mich 79–90; V Lower Cam w Coaley 90–14; rtd 14; PtO *Glouc* from 14. *19 Pear Tree Close, Hardwicke, Gloucester GL2 4TL* T: (01452) 676059 E: ia_jdr@lineone.net

ROBB, Timothy Simon. b 72. Cant Univ (NZ) BMus 94 LTCL 94 Lon Bible Coll BTh 98. Trin Coll Bris MA 03. **d** 03 **p** 04. C Bedford Ch Ch *St Alb* 03–07; Chapl De Montford Univ 05–07; V Eaton Socon from 07. *St Mary's Vicarage, 34 Drake Road, Eaton Socon, St Neots PE19 8HS* T: (01480) 212219 E: vicar@eatonsocon.org

ROBBIE, James Neil. b 68. Strathclyde Univ BEng 90. Oak Hill Th Coll BTh 02. **d** 05 **p** 06. C Wolverhampton St Luke *Lich* 05–09; V W Bromwich H Trin from 09. *Holy Trinity Vicarage, 1 Burlington Road, West Bromwich B70 6LF* T: 0121-525 3595 E: neilrobbie208@gmail.com

ROBBINS, Angela Mary. *See* TOWNSHEND, Angela Mary

ROBBINS, David Ronald Walter. b 47. Sarum & Wells Th Coll 85. **d** 87 **p** 88. C Meir Heath *Lich* 87–89; C Collier Row St Jas and Havering-atte-Bower *Chelmsf* 89–93; C Tamworth *Lich* 93–97; P-in-c Hulland, Atlow, Kniveton, Bradley and Hognaston *Derby* 97–98; R 98–02; R Widford *Chelmsf* 02–12; rtd 12; PtO *Lich* from 18. *65 The Lawns, Rollston-on-Dove, Burton-on-Trent DE13 9DD* T: (01283) 814051 E: dave@robbinsdrw.plus.com

ROBBINS, Mrs Janet Carey. b 41. LMH Ox BA 63 MA 95 Nôtre Dame Coll Bearsden PGCE 81. St D Dioc Tr Course 96. **d** 98 **p** 99. NSM Llanfihangel Ystrad and Cilcennin w Trefilan etc *St D* 98–01; NSM Quantock Towers *B & W* 02–03; rtd 03; Hon C Bro Teifi Sarn Helen *St D* 08–11; PtO 11–14; *Worc* from 14. *Gothic House, 48 Bridge Street, Pershore WR10 1AT* T: (01386) 555709 E: revdjcr@gmail.com

ROBBINS, The Ven Stephen. b 53. K Coll Lon BD 74 AKC 74. St Aug Coll Cant 75. **d** 76 **p** 77. C Tudhoe Grange *Dur* 76–80; C-in-c Harlow Green CD 80–84; V Gateshead Harlow Green 84–87; CF 87–97; Sen CF 97–01; Chapl R Memorial Chpl Sandhurst 01–02; Asst Chapl Gen 02–07; Dep Chapl-Gen 07–09; Chapl-Gen 08–11; Adn for the Army 04–11; QHC 05–11; Can and Preb Sarum Cathl 07–11; PtO 11–16; Bp's Chapl 12–15; Bp's Adv for Deliverance Min from 15; PtO *Newc* from 12. *Mill Leat, Gomeldon, Salisbury SP4 6JY* E: venstephen@gmail.com

ROBBINS, Walter. b 35. **d** 72 **p** 73. Argentina 73–82; Adn N Argentina 80–82; C Southborough St Pet w Ch Ch and St Matt *Roch* 82–86; V Sidcup St Andr 86–95; V Grain w Stoke 95–00; rtd 00; PtO *Roch* 00–13; *Cant* 01–09. *Mariners, Imperial Avenue, Minster on Sea, Sheerness ME12 2HG* T: (01795) 876588

ROBERT, Brother. *See* ATWELL, Robert Ronald

ROBERTS, Alan Moss. b 39. CEng 68 MIMechE 68 MIMarEST 68. St Jo Coll Nottm 77. **d** 79 **p** 80. C Bromsgrove St Jo *Worc* 79–83; C Edgbaston St Germain *Birm* 83–89; R Broadhembury, Payhembury and Plymtree *Ex* 89–06; rtd 06; PtO *Ex* 06–21. *8 Oakleigh, Sheldon, Honiton EX14 4QT* T: (01404) 841358

ROBERTS, Mrs Alison Jane. b 51. Luton Univ MSc 97. Ripon Coll Cuddesdon 13. **d** 16 **p** 17. OLM Aston Clinton w Buckland and Drayton Beauchamp *Ox* from 16. *Dormers, Buckland, Aylesbury HP22 5HY* T: (01296) 630256 M: 07702-268157 E: alisonroberts999@btinternet.com

ROBERTS, Allen. b 47. Trin Coll Ox MA 72 Warwick Univ MA 74 PhD 79 Wolv Univ LLM 99. Qu Coll Birm 06. **d** 07 **p** 09. NSM Tettenhall Regis *Lich* 07–19; PtO from 19. *11 Grosvenor Court, Lime Tree Avenue, Wolverhampton WV6 8HB* T: (01902) 765741 M: 07885-341540 E: allen.roberts1@btinternet.com

ROBERTS, Preb Andrew Alexander. b 49. Open Univ BA 75. Bp Otter Coll CertEd 70 Sarum & Wells Th Coll 76. **d** 80 **p** 81. NSM Dorchester *Sarum* 80–85; C Swanage and Studland 85–87; TV 87–94; TR Bridgnorth, Tasley, Astley Abbotts, etc *Heref* 94–09; P-in-c Morville w Aston Eyre 08–09; P-in-c Acton Round 08–09; P-in-c Upton Cressett w Monk Hopton 08–09; RD Bridgnorth 05–09; Preb Heref Cathl 03–09; rtd 09; PtO *Sarum* from 11. *Quayway Cottage, 2 Cliff Place, Swanage BH19 2PL* T: (01929) 424324

ROBERTS, Anne Judith. b 44. CertEd 65 DipEd 78 Open Univ BA 82. S Dios Minl Tr Scheme 86. **d** 89 **p** 94. Hon Par Dn S Kensington H Trin w All SS *Lon* 89–92; NSM Barnes *S'wark* 92–14; S'wark OLM Scheme 98–04; PtO *S'wark* from 14. *5 Avenue Gardens, London SW14 8BP* T: (020) 8878 5642 M: 07715-041212 E: revjr@blueyonder.co.uk

ROBERTS, Anne Marie. b 55. York Univ BA 77. St Jo Coll Nottm 80 WMMTC 93. **d** 96 **p** 97. NSM Meole Brace *Lich*

96–08; Chapl Robert Jones/Agnes Hunt Orthopaedic NHS Trust 98–00; Chapl Prestfelde Sch Shrewsbury 99–08; Dioc Healing Adv *Carl* 09–13; Dioc Dir of Ords 10–11; Chapl N Cumbria Univ Hosps NHS Trust 11–16; Palace Pastor B & W 16–18; PtO *Lich* 19–20; C Cen Telford from 20. *9 Bickerton Grove, Telford TF3 5JL* M: 07470-400301 E: revsroberts55@gmail.com

ROBERTS, Anthony. *See* ROBERTS, John Anthony Duckworth

ROBERTS, Barrie Moelwyn Antony. b 43. RN Coll Dartmouth 63 Trin Coll Carmarthen CertEd 70 Birm Poly BA 83. Qu Coll Birm 00. **d** 04 **p** 05. NSM Bartley Green *Birm* 04–12; NSM Rowley Regis 12–13; PtO from 13. *34 Wheats Avenue, Harborne, Birmingham B17 0RJ* T: 0121-426 2501 E: b.roberts@lineone.net

ROBERTS, Barry. *See* ROBERTS, Ronald Barry

ROBERTS, Brian David. b 44. Ball Coll Ox BA 66 Univ of Wales (Ban) BTh 06 FRSA 00. **d** 03 **p** 04. OLM Guildf H Trin w St Mary 03–14; PtO from 14. *Risby, Upper Guildown Road, Guildford GU2 4EZ* T: (01483) 570556 F: (020) 7631 6224 M: 07979-766471 E: brianroberts2012@gmail.com

ROBERTS, Bryan Richard. b 55. Univ of Wales (Cardiff) BD 80. St Mich Coll Llan 78. **d** 80 **p** 81. C Finham *Cov* 80–83; Asst Youth Officer *Nor* 83–86; R N and S Creake w Waterden 86–91; P-in-c E w N and W Barsham 86–91; Chapl Epsom Coll 91–01; Chapl Gresham's Sch Holt 01–20; rtd 20; PtO *Nor* from 21. *6 Kelling Close, Holt NR25 6RU* T: (01263) 713817

ROBERTS, Carol Susan Butler. b 63. Univ of Wales (Ban) BA 84 MTh 99 MPhil 02 PhD 05. Ban Ord Course 06. **d** 07 **p** 08. NSM Bangor *Ban* 07–10; C 10–11; P-in-c Llanberis, Llanrug and Llandinorwig 11–15; V Bro Eryri 15–18; PtO from 18; P-in-c Penedeyrn Miss Area *St As* 18–21. *Address temp unknown* E: parchcarolroberts@yahoo.co.uk

ROBERTS, Charles Richard Meyrick. b 53. Huddersfield Poly BA 75 ARCM 75. St Paul's Coll Grahamstown 89. **d** 92 **p** 92. C Lansdowne St Aidan S Africa 92–93; C Claremont St Sav 93–94; C Bath Abbey w St Jas *B & W* 94–98; P-in-c Chew Magna w Dundry 98–00; R Chew Magna w Dundry and Norton Malreward 00–10; R Chew Magna w Dundry, Norton Malreward etc 10–19; P-in-c Chew Stoke w Nempnett Thrubwell 03–19; rtd 19; PtO *B & W* from 20. *14 Bourke Road, Shepton Mallet BA4 4FS* M: 07876-451376 E: chewrector@gmail.com

ROBERTS, Christopher Michael. b 39. Man Univ DipAE 79. Qu Coll Birm 62. **d** 64 **p** 65. C Milton next Gravesend Ch Ch *Roch* 64–68; C Thirsk w S Kilvington *York* 68–69; V Castleton *Derby* 69–75; TV Buxton w Burbage and King Sterndale 75–79; PtO 84–87; NSM Marple All SS *Ches* 87–90; Chapl Asst St Helens Hosp Liv 90–91; Chapl Asst Whiston Co Hosp Prescot 90–91; Chapl Asst Rainhill Hosp Liv 90–91; Chapl R United Hosp Bath 91–94; Chapl R United Hosp Bath NHS Trust 94–99; Sen Chapl Birm Children's Hosp NHS Trust 99–04; rtd 04; PtO *Birm* 04–12. *6 Myring Drive, Sutton Coldfield B75 7RZ* T: 0121-329 2547

ROBERTS, Canon Cyril. b 41. St Deiniol's Hawarden. **d** 84 **p** 85. C Maltby *Sheff* 84–86; TR Gt Snaith 86–12; AD Snaith and Hatfield 03–11; Hon Can Sheff Cathl 05–12; rtd 12; PtO *Sheff* from 12; *York* from 13. *28 Broadacres, Carlton, Goole DN14 9NF* T: (01405) 947328 M: 07979-949485 E: cyrilroberts@hotmail.co.uk

ROBERTS, David Alan. b 38. Open Univ BA 82. Ripon Hall Ox 71. **d** 73 **p** 74. C W Bridgford *S'well* 73–77; V Awsworth w Cossall 77–82; V Oxclose *Dur* 82–94; P-in-c New Seaham 94–04; rtd 04; PtO *Dur* 13–16. *8 Hazel Road, Gateshead NE8 2EP* T: 0191-460 9919

ROBERTS, David Geoffrey. b 97. Dur Univ BA 21. Trin Coll Bris 18. **d** 21. NSM Andover *Win* from 21. *2 Madrid Road, Andover SP10 1JR* M: 07770-681578 E: david.roberts@stmarysandover.org *or* dgroberts.97@gmail.com

ROBERTS, Preb David Henry. b 38. St Chad's Coll Dur BA 60. Qu Coll Birm. **d** 62 **p** 63. C Stonehouse *Glouc* 62–65; C Hemsworth *Wakef* 65–69; V Newsome 69–76; R Pontesbury I and II *Heref* 76–03; RD Pontesbury 83–93; Preb Heref Cathl from 85; rtd 03; PtO *Heref* from 03. *14 Beaconsfield Park, Ludlow SY8 4LY* T: (01584) 878568 E: dhroberts38@gmail.com

ROBERTS, Canon David John. b 36. Man Univ BSc 58. St D Coll Lamp 65. **d** 67 **p** 68. C Rhosllannerchrugog *St As* 67–70; R Cerrigydrudion w Llanfihangel Glyn Myfyr etc 70–75; R Llanrwst and Llanddoget 75–76; R Llanrwst 76–77; R Llanrwst and Llanddoget and Capel Garmon 77–84; RD Llanrwst 77–84; V Abergele 84–01; RD Rhos 94–00; Hon Can St As Cathl 95–96; Can Cursal St As Cathl 96–01; rtd 01; PtO *St As* from 09. *21 Lowther*

Court, Bodelwyddan, Rhyl LL18 5YG T: (01745) 798604 E: david.roberts608@uwclub.net

ROBERTS, David Ross. b 86. St Jo Coll Ox MEng 08 Clare Coll Cam BTh 19. Ridley Hall Cam 17. **d** 20 **p** 21. C Hounslow H Trin *Lon* from 20. *56 Whitton Dene, Hounslow TW3 2JT* M: 07852-263719 E: davrrob@gmail.com

ROBERTS, Dean Aaron. b 91. Cardiff Univ BA 12. Trin Coll Bris MA 17. **d** 16 **p** 17. C Bedwas w Machen w Michaelston-y-Fedw w Rudry *Mon* 16–20; R from 20. *The Rectory, Michaelston-y-Fedw, Cardiff CF3 6XS* T: (01633) 309691 E: rev.roberts@vicar.email

ROBERTS, Mrs Deryn Anne. b 49. Nottm Univ TCert 70 BEd 71. SWMTC 04. **d** 07 **p** 08. C St Teath and Lanteglos by Camelford w Advent *Truro* 07–12; NSM P-in-c Altarnon w Bolventor, Laneast and St Clether 14–15; C Boscastle w Davidstow 14–15; R Moorland Gp 15–19; rtd 19. *11 Cambeak Close, Crackington Haven, Bude EX23 0PE* M: 07977-318589 E: stnonnas@gmail.com

ROBERTS, Canon Dewi James Llewelyn. b 63. United Th Coll Abth 83. **d** 96 **p** 97. C Llandudno *Ban* 96–02; C Bodedern w Llanfaethlu 99–02; V Newcastle Emlyn and Llandyfriog etc *St D* 02–19; AD Emlyn 12–19; P-in-c Bro Cydweli from 19; Can St D Cathl from 13. *The Vicarage, Llanddarog, Carmarthen SA32 8PA* T: (01267) 275556 E: dewi44@googlemail.com

ROBERTS, Diane. b 45. Bris Univ CertEd 66 BEd 82. STETS 02. **d** 05 **p** 06. NSM Kinson and W Howe *Sarum* 05–13; NSM Salisbury St Mark and Laverstock 13–15; rtd 15; PtO *Sarum* from 15. *6 Herbert Road, Woodfalls, Salisbury SP5 2LF* T: (01725) 510894 E: robertsdiane1@aol.com

ROBERTS, Edward Mark. b 68. **d** 07 **p** 08. OLM Droylsden St Mary *Man* 07–10; P-in-c Blackley St Paul from 10; P-in-c Blackley St Pet from 10; P-in-c Blackley St Andr from 16; Assoc Dir of Ords from 15; AD N Man 17–21. *14 Hill Lane, Blackley, Manchester M9 6PE* T: 0161-264 9982 M: 07792-419103 E: eddie@blackleycofe.org

ROBERTS, Canon Edward Owen. b 38. K Coll Lon BD 63 AKC 63. **d** 64 **p** 65. C Auckland St Andr and St Anne *Dur* 64–67; C Cheltenham St Paul *Glouc* 67–68; Asst Master Colne Valley High Sch Linthwaite 69–71; V Meltham Mills *Wakef* 71–75; R Emley 75–88; RD Kirkburton 80–88; V Huddersfield H Trin 88–04; RD Huddersfield 89–99; Hon Can Wakef Cathl 92–04; rtd 04; PtO *York* 04–18. *2B Queen Street, Filey YO14 9HB* T: (01723) 515535

ROBERTS, Garry Peter. b 77. Ripon Coll Cuddesdon 12. **d** 14 **p** 15. C Fareham H Trin *Portsm* 14–18; C Chandler's Ford *Win* 18–19; V Sholing from 19. *St Mary's Church, St Monica Road, Southampton SO19 8ES* T: (023) 8044 8337 M: 07554-142729 E: vicar@sholing.church

ROBERTS, Gillian Susan. b 54. **d** 13 **p** 14. C Napton-on-the-Hill, Lower Shuckburgh etc *Cov* 13–16; P-in-c from 16; C Priors Hardwick, Priors Marston and Wormleighton 13–16; P-in-c from 16. *Sycamore Lodge, Church Street, Stockton, Southam CV47 8JG* T: (01926) 815831 E: gillian@thebridgesgroup.org.uk

ROBERTS, Graham Miles. b 59. Open Univ BA 95. Trin Coll Bris 90. **d** 92 **p** 93. C Charles w Plymouth St Matthias *Ex* 92–96; Chapl Plymouth Univ 92–94; TV Liskeard, St Keyne, St Pinnock, Morval etc *Truro* 96–99; P-in-c Bournemouth St Andr *Win* 99–04; V 04–21; rtd 21. *Green Ways, Newquay Road, St Columb Road, St Columb TR9 6PY* E: grahamroberts@talktalk.net

ROBERTS, Gregory Stephen. b 64. St Chad's Coll Dur BSc 86 PGCE 87 CPhys 95. Ripon Coll Cuddesdon 08. **d** 10 **p** 11. C Kettering SS Pet and Paul 10–14; Asst Chapl St Andr Healthcare 12–13; P-in-c Pet All SS 14–16; V 16–21; R Ford, Gt Wollaston and Alberbury w Cardeston *Heref* from 21. *The Vicarage, Ford, Shrewsbury SY5 9LZ* T: (01743) 851806 E: therevdgregroberts@outlook.com

ROBERTS, Gwyneth. *See* WATKINS, Gwyneth

ROBERTS, James. *See* ROBERTS, William James

ROBERTS, Jane Elizabeth. b 53. SEITE 98. **d** 01 **p** 02. NSM Mitcham Ascension *S'wark* 01–17; PtO from 17; NSM Midhurst *Chich* from 19. *23 Downsview Drive, Midhurst GU29 9LW* M: 07790-703710 E: janeroberts40@gmail.com

ROBERTS, Canon Janet Lynne. b 56. Trin Coll Bris 76. **dss** 82 **d** 87 **p** 94. Dagenham *Chelmsf* 82–86; Huyton St Mich *Liv* 86–91; Par Dn 87–91; C Aughton Ch Ch 91–98; TV Parr 98–05; TR 05–13; P-in-c Blundellsands St Nic 13–19; V 19; Hon Can Liv Cathl 13–19; rtd 19. *8 Rothwell Close, Ormskirk L39 3ND* T: (01695) 571965 E: rovingrector@btinternet.com

ROBERTS, Mrs Jasmine Cynthia. b 46. Can Sch of Min 88. **d** 91. NSM Sandwich *Cant* 91–13; Asst Dir of Ords 02–09; PtO from 14. *The Rectory, Knightrider Street, Sandwich CT13 9ER* T/F: (01304) 613138

ROBERTS, Ms Jeanette. b 67. RMHN 00. Cranmer Hall Dur 07. d 09 p 10. C Todmorden *Wakef* 09–12; P-in-c Sowerby 12–13; P-in-c Norland 12–13; V Ryburn 13–14; *Leeds* from 14. *Sowerby Vicarage, Sowerby, Sowerby Bridge HX6 1JJ* T: (01422) 646371 E: revdjeanetteroberts@gmail.com

ROBERTS, Jennifer. *See* GRAY, Jennifer

ROBERTS, John Anthony Duckworth. b 43. K Coll Lon BD 65 AKC 65. St Boniface Warminster 65. d 66 p 67. C Wythenshawe Wm Temple Ch CD *Man* 66–69; C Bradford-on-Avon H Trin *Sarum* 69–72; Chapl Dauntsey's Sch Devizes 72–73; CF 73–77; P-in-c Verwood *Sarum* 77–81; V 81–86; V Clitheroe St Mary *Blackb* 86–97; R Paget St Paul Bermuda 97–03; rtd 03; PtO *Glouc* from 14; *Win* from 17. *The Old Coach House, Forwood, Minchinhampton, Stroud GL6 9AB* T: (01453) 835811 E: anthilr@hotmail.com

ROBERTS, John Charles Welch. b 39. UMIST BSc 60. Oak Hill NSM Course 91 SWMTC 92. d 94 p 95. NSM Washfield, Stoodleigh, Withleigh etc *Ex* 94–19; PtO *Lich* 21. *Bridge Cottage, Ford, Shrewsbury SY5 9LJ* E: jcwr.sidborough@gmail.com

ROBERTS, Canon John Hugh. b 42. K Alfred's Coll Win CertEd 72 Open Univ BA 75. Wells Th Coll 65. d 67 p 68. C Wareham w Arne *Sarum* 67–70; C Twyford *Win* 70–72; Asst Teacher Rawlins Sch Leics 72–74; V Nassington w Yarwell *Pet* 74–77; Asst Teacher Sponne Sch Towcester 78–92; RD Brackley *Pet* 94–03; P-in-c Helmdon w Stuchbury and Radstone etc 93–03; P-in-c Weedon Lois w Plumpton and Moreton Pinkney etc 02–03; R Astwell Gp 03–05; Can Pet Cathl 01–05; rtd 05; PtO *Pet* from 05; Chapl to Retired Clergy and Clergy Widows' Officer 08–10. *Pimlico House, Pimlico, Brackley NN13 5TN* T: (01280) 850378 E: johnpimlicohouse@gmail.com

ROBERTS, Canon John Mark Arnott. b 54. AKC 75 CertEd 76. Chich Th Coll 77. d 77 p 78. C Ashford *Cant* 77–82; V St Mary's Bay w St Mary-in-the-Marsh etc 82–91; R Sandwich 91–12; P-in-c Woodnesborough w Worth and Staple 04–12; P-in-c Eastry and Northbourne w Tilmanstone etc 10–12; R Sandwich and Worth from 12; AD Sandwich 00–06; Hon Can Cant Cathl from 03. *The Rectory, Knightrider Street, Sandwich CT13 9ER* T/F: (01304) 613138 E: revdmarkroberts@supanet.com

ROBERTS, John Victor. b 40. GIPE 61. Qu Coll Birm 83. d 85 p 86. C Ludlow *Heref* 85–89 and 92–93; P-in-c Coreley w Doddington 89–92; P-in-c Knowbury 89–92; TV Ludlow, Ludford, Ashford Carbonell etc 93–02; rtd 02; PtO *Heref* from 02. *Carwood, 16 Stretton Farm Road, Church Stretton SY6 6DX* T: (01694) 723164

ROBERTS, Jonathan Christopher. b 82. Reading Univ BA 09. Ripon Coll Cuddesdon BA 15. d 15 p 16. C Dorchester *Ox* 15–19; V Southmead *Bris* from 19. *St Stephen's Vicarage, Wigton Crescent, Bristol BS10 6DR* M: 07980-929302 E: revjonroberts@gmail.com

ROBERTS, Jonathan George Alfred. b 60. Lon Univ BD 82 Dur Univ MA 93. Qu Coll Birm. d 84 p 85. C Shepshed *Leic* 84–86; C Braunstone 86–87; Dioc Youth Adv *Dur* 88–92; Nat Youth Officer Gen Syn Bd of Educn 92–94; P-in-c Washington *Dur* 94–95; R 95–99; Regional Co-ord for Community Work Assessment Consortium for the NE 99–03; Sen Lect Teesside Univ *York* 03–14; PtO *Dur* 99–14; *Newc* 01–14; Par Development Adv Woolwich Area *S'wark* from 14; Chapl Ark All SS Academy Camberwell from 14; PtO *S'wark* 14–15; P-in-c Camberwell St Mich w All So w Em 15–20; V from 20. *128 Bethwin Road, London SE5 0YY* T: (020) 7701 2231 M: 07530-003368 E: jonathan.roberts@southwark.anglican.org

ROBERTS, Jonathan Peter Higham. b 76. St Jo Coll Dur BA 97 PGCE 98. St Jo Coll Nottm 09. d 12 p 13. C Cotes Heath and Standon and Swynnerton etc *Lich* 12–15; R Draycott-le-Moors w Forsbrook from 15. *The Rectory, Cheadle Road, Blythe Bridge, Stoke-on-Trent ST11 9PW* T: (01782) 437600 E: jonathanroberts@talktalk.net

ROBERTS, Joseph Samuel. b 86. Birm Univ BA 16 Anglia Ruskin Univ MA 16. Westcott Ho Cam 14. d 16 p 17. C Marston Green *Birm* 16–19; TV Gt Berkhamsted, Gt and Lt Gaddesden etc *St Alb* from 19. *The Vicarage, Church Road, Potten End, Berkhamsted HP4 2QY* M: 07966-175803 E: josephroberts11@hotmail.com *or* revjoeroberts@hotmail.com

ROBERTS, Judith. *See* ABBOTT, Judith

ROBERTS, Judith. *See* ROBERTS, Anne Judith

ROBERTS, Preb Kathleen Marie. b 50. Th Ext Educn Coll 94. d 00 p 01. S Africa 00–02; C Crediton, Shobrooke and Sandford etc *Ex* 03–05; P-in-c Black Torrington, Bradford w Cookbury etc 05–08; R 15–19; RD Holsworthy 11–15; Dean of Women's Min 15–19; Preb Ex Cathl 15–19; rtd 19; PtO *Ex* from 19. *Mill House, Thorverton, Exeter EX5 5LX* T: (01392) 861444 E: robertskm8@aol.com

ROBERTS, Keith Mervyn. b 55. St Pet Coll Birm CertEd 76 LGSM 78 GMus 78. Qu Coll Birm 89. d 91 p 92. C Hall Green St Pet *Birm* 91–95; TV Warwick *Cov* 95–00; P-in-c Bishop's Tachbrook 00–09; Dir Communications 03–04 and 04–09; Relig Affairs Correspondent BBC W Midl 95–01; Presenter/Producer 01–09; Hon Can Cov Cathl 07–09; TR Godalming *Guildf* 09–16. *15 Anderson Avenue, Rugby CV22 5PE* E: mervynrob@aol.com *or* revmervyn@gmail.com

ROBERTS, The Ven Kevin Thomas. b 55. Qu Coll Cam BA 78 MA 82 Nottm Univ BA 82. St Jo Coll Nottm 80. d 83 p 84. C Beverley Minster *York* 83–86; C Woodley St Jo the Ev *Ox* 86–91; V Meole Brace *Lich* 91–09; RD Shrewsbury 98–08; Preb Lich Cathl 02–08; Adn Carl and Can Res Carl Cathl 09–16; Can Res Carl Cathl 09–16; RD Brampton 15–16; Dir ReSource from 16; Adn Wells *B & W* 16–17; Public Preacher 16–19; Public Preacher *Lich* from 19. *9 Bickerton Grove, Telford TF3 5JL* T: (01952) 371300 M: 07880-762868 E: revsroberts55@gmail.com *or* kevinroberts@resource-arm.net

ROBERTS, Canon Leanne Kelly. b 74. St Hilda's Coll Ox BA 95 MA 02 Em Coll Cam BA 01 MA 05 Hertf Coll Ox MSt 08. Westcott Ho Cam 99. d 02 p 03. C Hampton All SS *Lon* 02–05; Chapl Hertf Coll Ox 05–11; Voc Adv *Ox* 07–11; Chapl Ox and Bucks Mental Health Trust 10–11; Can Res and Treas S'wark Cathl from 11; Dioc Dir of Ords from 11. *Trinity House, 4 Chapel Court, London SE1 1HW* T: (020) 7939 9400 F: 7939 9468 E: leanne.roberts@southwark.anglican.org

ROBERTS, Mark. *See* ROBERTS, John Mark Arnott

ROBERTS, Martin Vincent. b 53. Birm Univ BA 76 MA 77 PhD 82 LRAM 72. Ripon Coll Cuddesdon 76. d 78 p 79. C Perry Barr *Birm* 78–81; Sen Chapl and Lect W Sussex Inst of HE 81–86; Leic Poly 86–92; Sen Chapl De Montfort Univ 92–95; TV Leic H Spirit 86–89; TR 89–95; V Baswich *Lich* 95–01; V Selly Oak St Mary *Birm* 01–08; rtd 08; PtO *Birm* 08–18. *14 Hartley Place, Vicarage Road, Edgbaston, Birmingham B15 3HS* T: 0121-454 5180

ROBERTS, Mervyn. *See* ROBERTS, Keith Mervyn

ROBERTS, Michael Brian. b 46. Oriel Coll Ox BA 68 MA 72 St Jo Coll Dur BA 73. Cranmer Hall Dur 71. d 74 p 75. C St Helens St Helen *Liv* 74–76; C Goose Green 76–78; C Blundellsands St Nic 78–80; V Fazakerley St Nath 80–87; V Chirk *St As* 87–01; V Cockerham w Winmarleigh and Glasson *Blackb* 01–13; rtd 13; PtO *Blackb* 13–16 and from 19; P-in-c Woodplumpton 16–19. *35 Worcester Avenue, Garstang PR3 1FJ* T: (01995) 603787 E: michaelroberts@btinternet.com

ROBERTS, Michael Frederick. b 46. Sarum Th Coll 86. d 88 p 89. C Reading St Matt *Ox* 88–91; NSM Douglas St Geo and St Barn *S & M* 91–93; V Malew 93–11; rtd 11. *Rose Cottage, St Mary's Road, Port Erin, Isle of Man IM9 6JL* E: revroberts@manx.net

ROBERTS, Michael Graham Vernon. b 43. Keble Coll Ox BA 65. Cuddesdon Coll 65 Ch Div Sch of the Pacific (USA) BD 67. d 67 p 68. C Littleham w Exmouth *Ex* 67–70; Chapl Clare Coll Cam 70–74; V Bromley St Mark *Roch* 74–79; Tutor Qu Coll Birm 79–85; TR High Wycombe *Ox* 85–90; Vice-Prin Westcott Ho Cam 90–93; Prin 93–06; Hon Can Ely Cathl 04–06; rtd 06; PtO *B & W* from 17; *Ex* from 20. *Chatter Box Cottage, 16-18 Chudleigh Road, Exeter EX2 8TU* T: (01392) 211080

ROBERTS, Neil Charles. b 72. K Coll Lon BA 94 AKC 94 Kent Univ BA(ThM) 10 Cant Ch Ch Univ MA 14 Homerton Coll Cam PGCE 95 FGMS 01 MCollT 10 FNMSM 16 LGSM 19. SEITE. d 10 p 11. C Bletchingley and Nutfield *S'wark* 10–14; V Steyning *Chich* 14–16; R Ashurst 14–16; Boarders' Chapl Steyning Gr Sch 14–16; Chapl Repton Sch Derby 16–21; R Guildf St Nic from 21. *The Rectory, 3 Flower Walk, Guildford GU2 4EP* T: (01483) 504895

ROBERTS, Nia Wyn. *See* MORRIS, Nia Wyn

ROBERTS, Nicholas John. b 47. Lon Univ BD 70 AKC 70 MTh 78 Surrey Univ MSc 93 K Coll Lon PhD 15. St Aug Coll Cant 70. d 71 p 72. C Tividale *Lich* 71–74; C St Pancras H Cross w St Jude and St Pet *Lon* 74–76; C Camberwell St Giles *S'wark* 76–78; Chapl Ch Coll Cam 78–82; V Kingstanding St Luke *Birm* 82–85; Chapl St Chas Hosp Ladbroke Grove 85–96; Chapl Princess Louise Hosp Lon 85–96; Chapl Paddington Community Hosp 85–96; Chapl Cen Middx Hosp NHS Trust 96–99; Chapl St Mary's NHS Trust Paddington 99–04; Chapl CSC 04–10; rtd 10; PtO *S'wark* from 10; *Lon* from 14. *183 Dukes Avenue, Richmond TW10 7YH* T: (020) 8940 5504 M: 07946-243660 E: n.roberts7@homecall.co.uk

ROBERTS, Mrs Patricia Frances. b 62. Roehampton Inst BEd 85. Trin Coll Bris 93. d 96 p 97. NSM Buckhurst Hill *Chelmsf* 96–99; NSM Gt Baddow 99–07; NSM W Swindon and the Lydiards *Bris* 11–18; NSM NW Swindon and Lydiard Millicent from 18; Chapl HM Pris Bris from 21. *HM*

Prison, Cambridge Road, Bristol BS7 8PS T: 0117-372 3100 E: tricia.f.roberts@gmail.com

ROBERTS, Paul Carlton. b 57. Worc Coll Ox BA 78 MA 85 Lon Univ PGCE 79. St Jo Coll Nottm 84. **d** 87 **p** 88. C Hazlemere *Ox* 87–91; C Woodley St Jo the Ev 91–92; TV Woodley 92–03; R Coulsdon St Jo *S'wark* from 03; RD Croydon S from 16. *The Rectory, 232 Coulsdon Road, Coulsdon CR5 1EA* T/F: (01737) 552152 E: rev.paul.c.roberts@gmail.com

ROBERTS, Paul John. b 60. Man Univ BA 82 PhD 91 Man Poly PGCE 83. St Jo Coll Nottm 83. **d** 85 **p** 86. C Burnage St Marg *Man* 85–88; Tutor Trin Coll Bris 88–00; V Cotham St Sav w St Mary and Clifton St Paul *Bris* 00–08; Hon Can Bris Cathl 06–08; Dean Non-Res Tr St Mich Coll Llan 09–10; Dir Angl Formation and Tutor Trin Coll Bris from 10. *Trinity College, Stoke Hill, Bristol BS9 1JP* T: 0117-968 0267 E: p.roberts@trinitycollegebristol.ac.uk

ROBERTS, Paul Matthew. b 78. Leeds Univ BA 00 UWE MA 07. Ripon Coll Cuddesdon. **d** 15 **p** 16. C Bartestree Cross *Heref* 15–18; R Maund Gp from 18. *The Vicarage, Bodenham, Hereford HR1 3JX* M: 07735-430335 E: revdpaulroberts@gmail.com

ROBERTS, Peter Francis. b 59. N Illinois Univ BSc 81 Leeds Univ BA 87. Coll of Resurr Mirfield 85. **d** 88 **p** 89. C Leeds All So *Ripon* 88–92; Asst Dioc Youth Chapl 91–92; USPG Belize 92–94; V Collingham w Harewood *Ripon* 95–01; World Miss Officer 95–01; Chapl Dubai and Sharjah w N Emirates 01–03; R Merritt Is USA 03–19; R Monk Fryston and S Milford *York* from 19. *The Rectory, Main Street, Hillam, Leeds LS25 5HH* E: frpeterroberts@gmail.com

ROBERTS, Peter Reece. b 43. Chich Th Coll 73. **d** 75 **p** 76. C Cadoxton-juxta-Barry *Llan* 75–79; C Brixham w Churston Ferrers *Ex* 79–81; C Bexhill St Pet *Chich* 81–84; R Heene 84–14; RD Worthing 89–97; rtd 14; PtO *Chich* from 14. *7 Mayfair Court, 21 Parchment Street, Chichester PO19 3RA* T: (01243) 778543 E: revp.roberts@btinternet.com

ROBERTS, Philip Anthony. b 50. St Jo Coll Dur BA 73. Wycliffe Hall Ox 75. **d** 77 **p** 78. C Roby *Liv* 77–79; C Ainsdale 79–80; C Pershore w Pinvin, Wick and Birlingham *Worc* 80–83; Chapl Asst Radcliffe Infirmary Ox 83–88; John Radcliffe and Littlemore Hosps Ox 83–88; Chapl R Victoria Hosp Bournemouth 88–91; Chapl R Bournemouth Gen Hosp 88–91; Chapl Heref Co Hosp 91–94; Chapl Wye Valley NHS Trust 94–12; rtd 12. *More House, More, Bishop's Castle SY9 5HH* E: philipandsueroberts@gmail.com

ROBERTS, Mrs Rebecca Helena. b 80. Salford Univ BA 01. Trin Coll Bris BA 12. **d** 12 **p** 13. C Penwortham St Mary *Blackb* 12–16; TV Warrington E *Liv* 16–21; V Lower Darwen St Jas *Blackb* from 21; P-in-c Over Darwen St Jas and Hoddlesden from 21. *Address temp unknown* M: 07511-142197 E: revrebecca@hotmail.com

ROBERTS, Miss Rebecca Mary. b 71. Glam Univ BA 92 Chelt & Glouc Coll of HE PGCE 93. Qu Coll Birm BA 02 MA 03. **d** 03 **p** 04. C Greenstead w Colchester St Anne *Chelmsf* 03–06; PtO *Win* 06–10; NSM Southampton (City Cen) 10–13; V Harnham *Sarum* from 13. *The Vicarage, Old Blandford Road, Salisbury SP2 8DQ* M: 07727-154234 E: reverendbecky@gmail.com

ROBERTS, Ronald Barry. b 40. S Dios Minl Tr Scheme 80. **d** 83 **p** 85. NSM Wedmore w Theale and Blackford *B & W* 83–85; C Odd Rode *Ches* 85–87; V Eaton and Hulme Walfield 87–04; Chapl Cheshire Agric Soc 91–04; rtd 04; PtO *Ches* from 04. *Iona, 8 Belmont Avenue, Sandbach CW11 1BX* T: (01270) 766124 E: barryroberts@uwclub.net

ROBERTS, Mrs Rosamunde Mair. b 58. RN 80. STETS 98. **d** 01 **p** 02. C Farnham *Guildf* 01–04; C Fleet 04–08; V Lenborough *Ox* from 08; AD Buckingham from 17. *The Vicarage, Thornborough Road, Padbury, Buckingham MK18 2AH* T: (01280) 813162 E: lenborough.vicar@gmail.com

ROBERTS, Mrs Rosanne Elizabeth. b 51. Glouc Sch of Min 85. **d** 88 **p** 94. NSM Charlton Kings St Mary *Glouc* 88–93; C Leckhampton SS Phil and Jas w Cheltenham St Jas 93–96; R Ashchurch 96–08; R Ashchurch and Kemerton 08–13; rtd 13; PtO *Glouc* from 16. *25 Buckles Close, Charlton Kings, Cheltenham GL53 8QT* T: (01242) 248194 E: rosanne.roberts@btinternet.com

ROBERTS, Mrs Sharon. b 56. **d** 11 **p** 12. OLM Amersham on the Hill *Ox* 11–18; NSM Beaconsfield 18–19; TV from 19. *St Michael's Parsonage, 3 St Michael's Green, Beaconsfield HP9 2BN* E: sharon.roberts433@gmail.com

ROBERTS, Stephen Bradley. b 66. K Coll Lon BD 90 Heythrop Coll Lon MA 03 PhD 11. Wycliffe Hall Ox 89. **d** 91 **p** 92. C W Hampstead St Jas *Lon* 91–94; TV Uxbridge 94–98; Chapl Brunel Univ 98–04; Vice Prin St Mich Coll Llan 04–12; PtO *Llan* from 12. *122 Pwllmelin Road, Cardiff CF5 3NA* E: drsbroberts@gmail.com

ROBERTS, Stephen John. b 58. K Coll Lon BD 81 Heythrop Coll Lon MTh 99. Westcott Ho Cam. **d** 83 **p** 84. C Riverhead w Dunton Green *Roch* 83–86; C St Martin-in-the-Fields *Lon* 86–89; Warden Trin Coll Cen Camberwell 89–99; V Camberwell St Geo *S'wark* 89–99; RD Camberwell 97–99; Treas and Can Res S'wark Cathl 00–05; Sen Dioc Dir of Ords 00–05; Adn Wandsworth 05–15; P-in-c Upper Tooting H Trin w St Aug 10–11; Dep Dioc Sec 15–20; Public Preacher 15–20; Hon Can S'wark Cathl 15–20; rtd 20. *49 Upper Kings Drive, Eastbourne BN20 9AW* M: 07791-315302 E: sjrwillingdon@outlook.com

ROBERTS, Preb Susan Emma. b 60. La Sainte Union Coll BTh 93. St Steph Ho Ox 94. **d** 96 **p** 97. C Petersfield *Portsm* 96–00; P-in-c Ashprington, Cornworthy and Dittisham *Ex* 00–04; TV Totnes w Bridgetown, Berry Pomeroy etc 04–06; RD Totnes 03–06; TR Honiton, Gittisham, Combe Raleigh, Monkton etc 06–20; TR Honiton w Monkton, Awliscombe, Buckerell etc from 21; RD Honiton 07–13; Preb Ex Cathl from 06. *The Rectory, Rookwood Close, Honiton EX14 1BH* T: (01404) 42925 E: sue41260@gmail.com

ROBERTS, Mrs Sylvia Ann. b 40. Stockwell Coll Lon TCert 60. S Dios Minl Tr Scheme 81. **dss** 84 **d** 87 **p** 94. Crookhorn *Portsm* 84–88; Hon Par Dn Bedhampton 88–89; Par Dn Southampton (City Cen) *Win* 89–91; Team Dn 91–94; TV 94–96; V Merton St Jo *S'wark* 96–06; P-in-c Colliers Wood Ch Ch 01–06; rtd 06; PtO *Portsm* from 07. *16 Bramble Road, Petersfield GU31 4HL* T: (01730) 301501 E: annarobb40@hotmail.com

ROBERTS, Terry Harvie. b 45. Sarum & Wells Th Coll 87. **d** 89 **p** 90. C Weymouth H Trin *Sarum* 89–93; TV Basingstoke *Win* 93–98; P-in-c Win St Barn 98–10; rtd 10; PtO *Win* from 10; *Sarum* from 16. *1 Poulner Park, Ringwood BH24 1TZ* T: (01425) 471206

ROBERTS, Timothy Frank. b 85. Univ of Wales BA 11. St Jo Coll Nottm MTh 16. **d** 16 **p** 17. C Clayton *Leeds* 16–19; C Preston St Jo and St Geo *Blackb* from 19. *8 Kings Drive, Fulwood, Preston PR2 3HN* M: 07825-542312 E: 1rev.roberts@gmail.com

ROBERTS, Tudor Vaughan. b 58. Newc Univ BA 81. All Nations Chr Coll 91 Trin Coll Bris BA 94. **d** 96 **p** 97. C Buckhurst Hill *Chelmsf* 96–99; TV Gt Baddow 99–07; TV W Swindon and the Lydiards *Bris* 07–18; V NW Swindon and Lydiard Millicent from 18. *The Vicarage, The Butts, Lydiard Millicent, Swindon SN5 3LR* T: (01793) 772417 E: tudorandtricia@btinternet.com

ROBERTS, Tunde. *See* ROBERTS, Vincent Akintunde

ROBERTS, Canon Vaughan Edward. b 65. Selw Coll Cam BA 88 MA 91. Wycliffe Hall Ox 89. **d** 91 **p** 92. C Ox St Ebbe w H Trin and St Pet 91–95; Student Pastor 95–98; R from 98; Hon Can Ch Ch from 16. *St Ebbe's Rectory, 2 Roger Bacon Lane, Oxford OX1 1QE* T: (01865) 240438

ROBERTS, Vaughan Simon. b 59. Univ of Wales (Ban) BA 80 Bath Univ PhD 99. McCormick Th Sem Chicago MA 82 Westcott Ho Cam 83. **d** 85 **p** 86. C Bourne *Guildf* 85–89; Chapl Phyllis Tuckwell Hospice Farnham 88–89; Chapl Bath Univ *B & W* 89–96; NSM Bath Ch Ch Prop Chpl 90–96; P-in-c 92–96; P-in-c Chewton Mendip w Ston Easton, Litton etc 96–03; Dioc Voc Adv 99–03; Dir of Ords 99–03; TR Warwick *Cov* from 03. *St Mary's Vicarage, The Butts, Warwick CV34 4SS* T: (01926) 492909 E: vaughan.roberts@btinternet.com

ROBERTS, Preb Vincent Akintunde (Tunde). b 55. Kingston Poly BA(Econ) 81. S'wark Ord Course. **d** 91 **p** 92. Hon C Brixton Road Ch Ch *S'wark* 91–96; C Mitcham St Barn 96–99; P-in-c Stoke Newington St Olave *Lon* 99–03; V from 03; P-in-c Stoke Newington St Andr 06–12; P-in-c Upper Clapton St Matt 08–12; Preb St Paul's Cathl from 07. *St Olave's Vicarage, Woodberry Down, London N4 2TW* T/F: (020) 8800 1374

ROBERTS, Vivian Phillip. b 35. Univ of Wales BD 78. St D Coll Lamp 57. **d** 60 **p** 61. C Cwmaman *St D* 60–64; R Puncheston, Lt Newcastle and Castle Bythe 64–72; V Brynamman 72–77; V Brynaman w Cwmllynfell 77–83; V Pen-bre 83–00; rtd 00. *40 New Road, Llanelli SA15 3DR* T: (01554) 755506

ROBERTS, William James (Jim). b 55. Lon Bible Coll BA 77 Hughes Hall Cam PGCE 78. NEOC 92. **d** 94 **p** 95. NSM York St Mich-le-Belfrey from 94; Chapl Pocklington Sch 06–15; PtO *Eur* from 16. *12 Bishop's Way, York YO10 5JG* T: (01904) 413479 E: roberts.jim@talk21.com

ROBERTSHAW, Mrs Eleanor Elizabeth Mary. b 77. Univ of Wales (Ban) BA 98 MTh 00 Leeds Univ MA 10 PGCE 99. Yorks Min Course 08. **d** 10 **p** 11. C Stainforth *Sheff* 10–13; TR Gt Snaith from 13. *The Orchard, Pontefract Road, Snaith, Goole DN14 9JS* T: (01405) 860866 M: 07718-123138 E: eleanor.robertshaw@sheffield.anglican.org

ROBERTSHAW, Canon John Sean. b 66. York St Jo Coll BA 12 Cardiff Univ MTh 17. Cranmer Hall Dur 90. d 93 p 94. C Morley St Pet w Churwell *Wakef* 93–96; TV Upper Holme Valley 96–01; TR 01–14; *Leeds* from 14; CF (VR) from 98; Hon Can Wakef Cathl *Leeds* from 11. *The Vicarage, Kirkroyds Lane, New Mill, Holmfirth HD9 1LS* T/F: (01484) 683375 M: 07980-289727 E: revsean@tiscali.co.uk *or* revsean10@gmail.com

ROBERTSHAW, Mrs Kina Perrira Njamba. b 75. Anglia Ruskin Univ BA 13. Ridley Hall Cam 10. d 16 p 17. C Bromyard and Stoke Lacy *Heref* from 16. *12 Lower Thorn, Bromyard HR7 4AZ* M: 07917-664182 E: robertshawkina@yahoo.co.uk

ROBERTSHAW, Sean. *See* ROBERTSHAW, John Sean

ROBERTSON, Ms Beverley Ann. b 57. Qu Coll Birm 98. d 01 p 02. C Sutton Coldfield H Trin *Birm* 01–05; C Portsea N End St Mark *Portsm* 05–06; TV 06–10; P-in-c Bromsgrove All SS *Worc* 10–12; C Catshill and Dodford 10–12; TV Bromsgrove from 12. *20 Burcot Lane, Bromsgrove B60 1AE* T: (01527) 578297 E: bevrobertson.church@gmail.com

ROBERTSON, Charles Peter. b 57. Aston Tr Scheme 92 Linc Th Coll 94. d 96 p 97. C Holbeach *Linc* 96–99; C S Lafford 01–03; P-in-c 03–13; P-in-c Bicker 13–14; P-in-c Donington 13–14; P-in-c Swineshead 13–14; P-in-c Sutterton and Wigtoft 13–14; V Haven Gp from 14. *The Rectory, Church Lane, Swineshead, Boston PE20 3JA* T: (01205) 820223 E: charles.robertson2@btopenworld.com

ROBERTSON, Mrs Claire Mary. b 63. Ridley Hall Cam 15. d 17 p 18. C Two Rivers *Chelmsf* 17–21; TV Lordsbridge *Ely* from 21. *The New Vicarage, Broad Lane, Haslingfield, Cambridge CB23 1JF* E: claire.cann@yahoo.co.uk

ROBERTSON, David John. b 54. Sheff Univ BA 76. Ridley Hall Cam 77. d 79 p 80. C Downend *Bris* 79–83; C Yate New Town 83–85; TV 85–87; TV High Wycombe *Ox* 87–97; RD Wycombe 91–97; P-in-c Haley Hill *Wakef* 97–99; V Ovenden 97–11; V S Ossett 11–14; *Leeds* 14–21; rtd 21. *18 Greenfields, Earith, Huntingdon PE28 3QH* E: rev.d.robertson@gmail.com

ROBERTSON, Douglas Laurence. b 52. St Edm Hall Ox MA 75. SEITE 04. d 07 p 08. C Roch St Pet w St Marg 07–11; V Pembury 11–18; rtd 18; PtO *York* from 19; Chapl Castle Howard from 19. *3 Damson Avenue, Malton YO17 7FR* E: dlrobertson@btinternet.com

ROBERTSON, Mrs Elizabeth Mary. b 60. Cam Univ BA 82 MA 86 ACA 85 FCA 95. SEITE 03. d 06 p 07. NSM Fawkham and Hartley *Roch* 06–13; NSM Ash from 13; NSM Ridley from 13. *58 Redhill Wood, New Ash Green, Longfield DA3 8QP* T: (01474) 874144 E: robertem@supanet.com

ROBERTSON, Fiona Jane. *See* GREGSON, Fiona Jane Robertson

ROBERTSON, Iain Michael. b 67. Trin Coll Bris 03. d 05 p 06. C E Clevedon w Clapton in Gordano etc *B & W* 05–09; TV Salter Street and Shirley *Birm* 09–11; P-in-c Heanton Punchardon w Marwood *Ex* 11–15; R Heanton Punchardon, Marwood and W Down 15–16; P-in-c Southway 16–17; TV Tamerton Foliot and Southway from 17. *16 Southway Lane, Plymouth PL6 7DH* E: reviain@hotmail.co.uk

ROBERTSON, Canon James Alexander. b 46. Ox Univ MTh 99. Sarum & Wells Th Coll 72. d 75 p 76. C Monkseaton St Pet *Newc* 75–78; C Prudhoe 78–79; TV Brayton *York* 79–84; V Redcar 84–93; V Selby Abbey 93–96; V Monkseaton St Pet *Newc* 96–11; AD Tynemouth 98–09; V Whittingham and Edlingham w Bolton Chapel 11–15; AD Alnwick 11–15; Hon Can Newc Cathl 05–15; rtd 15; PtO *Newc* 15–21. *4 Greenrigg Place, Shiremoor, Newcastle upon Tyne NE27 0GA* T: 0191-253 7637 E: canjamesrobertson@outlook.com

ROBERTSON, James Macaulay. b 51. St Jo Coll Dur BA 73. Oak Hill Th Coll. d 00 p 01. C Holdenhurst and Iford *Win* 00–04; V Marden *Cant* 04–11; R Holwell, Ickleford and Pirton *St Alb* 11–16; rtd 16; PtO *Win* from 17. *23 Wick Point Mews, Christchurch BH23 1NZ* E: jmrobertson91@gmail.com

ROBERTSON, Mrs Jane Elizabeth. b 58. Bp Grosseteste Coll BA 04. Linc Sch of Th and Min 13. d 16 p 17. C Boston *Linc* 16–19; TV from 19. *The Vicarage, Church Lane, Swineshead, Boston PE20 3JA* T: (01205) 820223 E: janeyrob@btopenworld.com

ROBERTSON, Jane Lesley. *See* TRENHOLME, Jane Lesley

ROBERTSON, Canon John Charles. b 61. St Pet Coll Ox BA 81 Trin Coll Cam BA 89. Ridley Hall Cam 87. d 90 p 91. C Kenilworth St Jo *Cov* 90–94; Chapl York Univ 94–00; V Grove Ox 00–12; RD Wantage 09–12; Dir Ecum Miss Milton Keynes from 12; Hon Can Ch Ch from 11. *16 Clover Close, Loughton, Milton Keynes MK5 8HA* T: (01908) 660338 E: jcrdem@gmail.com

ROBERTSON (née PEGG), Mrs Josephine Anne. b 51. Lon Univ CertEd 72 Ch Ch Coll Cant BSc 91. d 02 p 03. OLM Folkestone H Trin w Ch Ch *Cant* 02–06; Chapl Dover Coll 02–05; C Sandgate St Paul w Folkestone St Geo *Cant* 05–06; C Folkestone Trin 06–10; C Wingham w Elmstone and Preston w Stourmouth 10–12; C Canonry 12–15; PtO 15–19; P-in-c Cheriton w Newington from 19. *100 Surrenden Road, Folkestone CT19 4AQ* T: (01303) 277330 M: 07905-954504 E: jo.robertson@ntlworld.com

ROBERTSON, Kathryn. b 58. Leeds Univ BA 05. NOC 02. d 05 p 06. C Dewsbury *Wakef* 05–08; TV 08–14; *Leeds* 14–17; C Wakef St Andr and St Mary 17–18; C Wakefield St Andr and St Mary and Belle Vue from 18. *St Andrew's Vicarage, Johnston Street, Wakefield WF1 4DZ* M: 07967-909560 E: revkathyrob@gmail.com

ROBERTSON, Mrs Linda Margaret. b 51. Somerville Coll Ox BA 71 MA 76 Aber Univ MSc 73. STETS 00. d 03 p 04. NSM Ampfield *Win* 03–08; NSM Totton 08–15; TV 10–15; R Cocking w W Lavington, Bepton and Heyshott *Chich* 15–20; rtd 20. *22 Greenfields, Liss GU33 7EH* M: 07802-955133 E: revlindarob@yahoo.co.uk

ROBERTSON, Neil Matthew John. b 78. Bournemouth Univ BSc 10. Trin Coll Bris BA 17. d 17 p 18. C Blandford Forum and Langton Long *Sarum* 17–20; Chapl RN from 20; PtO *Sarum* from 20. *Royal Navy Chaplaincy Service Headquarters, Tanner Building, HMS Excellent, Whale Island, Portsmouth PO2 8ER* T: 0300-157 7544 M: 07809-149606 E: neilmjr@yahoo.co.uk

ROBERTSON, Canon Paul Struan. b 45. St Jo Coll Dur BA 73 Newc Univ Aus BEdSt 79 MA 95. d 72 p 73. C Chester le Street *Dur* 72–73; C Hamilton Australia 73–77; C Cessnock 77–79; R Scone 79–88; V Collierley w Annfield Plain *Dur* 88–89; R New Lambton Australia 89–10; AD Newc W 96–10; Lect St Jo Coll Morpeth 97–06; Can Newc Cathl 01–10; rtd 10. *40 Cromwell Street, New Lambton NSW 2305, Australia* T: (0061) (2) 4957 2795 E: paulstruanrobertson@gmail.com

ROBERTSON, Philip Stuart. b 55. Newc Univ BA 77 BArch 80. Oak Hill Th Coll BA 07. d 07 p 08. C Woking St Jo *Guildf* 07–11; V Wolverhampton St Jude *Lich* from 11; P-in-c Wolverhampton St Andr 15–18. *St Jude's Vicarage, St Jude's Road, Wolverhampton WV6 0EB* T: (01902) 827214 E: philipsrobertson@virginmedia.com

ROBERTSON, Rachel Heather. b 75. Dur Univ BA 96. Trin Coll Bris MA 18. d 17 p 18. C Tupsley w Hampton Bishop *Heref* 17–21; Chapl Bp's Bluecoat Sch 18–20; Asst Dir of Ords *Heref* 19–21; V Goudhurst w Kilndown *Cant* from 21. *The Church Office, Back Lane, Goudhurst, Cranbrook TN17 1AN* T: (01580) 211739

ROBERTSON (née OWEN), Mrs Sally Ann. b 68. New Hall Cam BA 89. Ox Min Course 07. d 10 p 11. NSM Purley *Ox* 10–13; NSM Haydon Wick *Bris* 13–17; P-in-c N Swindon St Andr from 17. *15 Rackham Close, Tadpole Garden Village, Swindon SN25 2QT* M: 07588-594410 E: sally.robertson27@btinternet.com

ROBERTSON, Simon John. b 76. Bournemouth Univ BSc 09. Ridley Hall Cam 14. d 16 p 17. C Hordle *Win* 16–19; C Andover 19–21; V Bitterne Park from 21. *Bitterne Park Vicarage, 7 Thorold Road, Southampton SO18 1HZ* M: 07592-888940 E: simon.robers2@gmail.com

ROBERTSON, Stephen Andrew. b 60. Strathclyde Univ BSc 82. Trin Coll Bris 90. d 92 p 93. C Vange *Chelmsf* 92–96; R Creeksea w Althorne, Latchingdon and N Fambridge 96–06; R Downham w S Hanningfield 06–11; V Downham w S Hanningfield and Ramsden Bellhouse 11–19; TR Eden, Gelt and Irthing *Carl* from 19. *St Martin's Vicarage, Main Street, Brampton CA8 1SH* T: (01697) 741304 E: stephen.robertson15@btinternet.com *or* teamrectoregi@gmail.com

ROBERTSON, Stuart Lang. b 40. Glas Univ MA 63 Edin Univ MTh 97. St Jo Coll Nottm 72. d 75 p 76. C Litherland St Jo and St Jas *Liv* 75–78; C Edin St Thos 78–81; Chapl Edn Univ and C Edin St Pet 81–83; R Edin St Jas 83–91; Miss to Seamen 83–91; Crosslinks 91–05; Hon Chapl St Petersburg *Eur* 93–98; Chapl Warsaw 98–04; Asst Chapl Barcelona 04–05; rtd 05; PtO *Edin* from 17. *3 Pentland Villas, Juniper Green EH14 5EQ* T: 0131-453 4755 E: langs.robertson2@gmail.com

ROBILLIARD (née DE GARIS), Mrs Juliette Elizabeth Charmaine. b 58. STETS 11. d 13 p 14. NSM Guernsey Ste Marie du Castel *Win* 13–16; NSM Guernsey St Matt 13–16; NSM Guernsey St Andr from 16; Chapl Guernsey Financial Services Commn from 18. *Le Petit Gree, Torteval, Guernsey GY8 0RD* T: (01481) 264344 E: revrob151@gmail.com

ROBINS, Christopher Charles. b 41. St Mich Coll Llan 66. d 68 p 69. C Bideford *Ex* 68–71; C Dawlish 71–74; V Laira 74–81; P-in-c Dodbrooke 81–83; P-in-c Churchstow w Kingsbridge 81–83; R Kingsbridge and Dodbrooke 83–06; rtd 07; PtO *Ex* from 17. *26 Brownings Walk, Ogwell, Newton Abbot TQ12 6YR* T: (01626) 331366

ROBINS, Canon Douglas Geoffrey. b 45. Open Univ BA 90. Ex & Truro NSM Scheme. **d** 81 **p** 83. NSM Kenwyn *Truro* 81–84; Public Preacher 84–00; NSM Truro St Paul and St Clem 00–04; P-in-c Gerrans w St Anthony-in-Roseland and Philleigh 04–08; P-in-c Veryan w Ruan Lanihorne 08–16; Hon Can Truro Cathl 09–16; rtd 16; PtO *Truro* from 16. *Caladrick Barn, Veryan Green, Truro TR2 5QQ* T: (01872) 501788 E: fatherdougrobins@outlook.com

ROBINS, Ian Donald Hall. b 28. K Coll Lon BD 51 AKC 51 Lanc Univ MA 74. **d** 52 **p** 53. C Heyhouses on Sea *Blackb* 52–55; C Clitheroe St Mary 55–57; V Trawden 57–66; Hd of RE St Chris C of E Sch Accrington 67–75; P-in-c Hugill *Carl* 75–82; Asst Adv for Educn 75–82; Chapl St Martin's Coll of Educn *Blackb* 82–86; V St Annes St Marg 86–91; rtd 91; PtO *Blackb* 91–20; *Bradf* 05–14; *Leeds* 14–16. *33 Manorfields, Whalley, Clitheroe BB7 9UD* T: (01254) 824930

ROBINS, Canon Wendy Sheridan. b 56. Lanc Univ BA 77. EAMTC 93. **d** 93 **p** 94. Dir Communications and Resources *S'wark* 92–20; NSM Walthamstow St Pet *Chelmsf* 93–02; Dir Discipleship, Lay Min and CMD *S'wark* from 20; Hon C S'wark Cathl 02–20; Hon Can S'wark Cathl 08–20; Can Res and Chan S'wark Cathl from 20. T: (020) 8523 0016 *or* 7403 8686 F: 7403 4770 E: wendy.s.robins@southwark.anglican.org

ROBINSON, Alison Jane. b 55. WEMTC 99. **d** 02 **p** 03. C Bishop's Cleeve *Glouc* 02–06; P-in-c Meysey Hampton w Marston Meysey and Castle Eaton 06–08; TV Fairford Deanery 09–10; rtd 10. *19 Marsh Drive, Cheltenham GL51 9LN* T: (01242) 698759 M: 07773-721238 E: alicesonrobinson@virginmedia.com

ROBINSON, Andrew David. b 61. St Cath Coll Ox BA 84 MA 01 RMN 89. Trin Coll Bris 97. **d** 02 **p** 08. C Southmead *Bris* 02–03; C Kington St Michael and Chippenham St Paul w Hardenhuish etc 03–04; NSM Barlby and Riccall *York* 05–10; P-in-c Ledsham w Fairburn 10–20; Chapl HM Pris Full Sutton from 20. *HM Prison Full Sutton, York YO41 1PS* T: (01579) 475100 E: andy.robinson@justice.gov.uk

ROBINSON, Canon Andrew Nesbitt. b 43. AKC 67. **d** 68 **p** 69. C Balsall Heath St Paul *Birm* 68–71; C Westmr St Steph w St Jo *Lon* 71–75; Chapl Sussex Univ *Chich* 75–12; Chapl Brighton Poly 75–92; Chapl Brighton Univ 92–93; P-in-c Stanmer w Falmer 80–12; Can and Preb Chich Cathl 98–12; rtd 12; PtO *Chich* 12–17. *Appleberry Cottage, Newhaven Road, Kingston, Lewes BN7 3NE* T: (01273) 757797 E: goretti_uk@yahoo.co.uk

⌖**ROBINSON, The Rt Revd Anthony William.** b 56. CertEd. Sarum & Wells Th Coll. **d** 82 **p** 83 **c** 02. C Tottenham St Paul *Lon* 82–85; TV Leic Resurr 85–89; TR 89–97; RD Christianity N 92–97; P-in-c Belgrave St Pet 94–95; Hon Can Leic Cathl 94–97; Adn Pontefract *Wakef* 97–03; Suff Bp Pontefract 02–15; Suff Bp Wakef *Leeds* from 15; Can Res Wakef Cathl 05–13. *Pontefract House, 181A Manygates Lane, Sandal, Wakefield WF2 7DR* T: (01924) 250781 E: bishop.tony@leeds.anglican.org

ROBINSON, Mrs Arabella Mary Milbank. b 87. New Coll Ox BA 10 MSt 11 Em Coll Cam PhD 18 MPhil 19. Westcott Ho Cam 17. **d** 18 **p** 19. C Louth *Linc* from 18. *The Rectory, Westgate, Louth LN11 9YE* M: 07734-871159

ROBINSON, Arthur Robert Basil. b 32. ACP 67 St Jo Coll Dur BA 56 Bradf Univ MA 84. Wycliffe Hall Ox 56. **d** 58 **p** 59. C Pemberton St Mark Newtown *Liv* 58–62; CF 62–65; Asst Master Colne Valley High Sch Linthwaite 65–69; Asst Chapl HM Pris Man 69; Chapl HM Borstal Roch 69–74; Peru 74–77; V Golcar *Wakef* 77–83; Admin Sheff Fam Conciliation Service 84–91; Warden St Sampson's Cen York 91–00; rtd 00. *Morangie, 2A Brecksfield, Skelton, York YO30 1YD* T: (01904) 470558

ROBINSON, Arthur William. b 35. Dur Univ BSc 60. Clifton Th Coll 60. **d** 62 **p** 63. C Ox St Clem 62–65; Chile 65–77; V Hoxton St Jo w Ch Ch *Lon* 78–88; TV Gateacre *Liv* 88–00; rtd 00; PtO *Liv* from 00. *86 Kingsthorne Park, Liverpool L25 0QS* T: 0151-486 2588 E: arthelrob@frasani.com

ROBINSON, Mrs Christine. b 50. Nottm Univ BA 71. EAMTC 01. **d** 04 **p** 05. NSM Prittlewell St Pet w Westcliff St Cedd *Chelmsf* 04–13; NSM Hadleigh St Jas 13–19; NSM Hadleigh St Barn 13–19; rtd 20; PtO *Chelmsf* from 20. *Pasadena, St John's Road, Benfleet SS7 2PT* T: (01702) 557000 E: crrob75@aol.com

ROBINSON (née KILCOOLEY), Mrs Christine Margaret Anne. b 59. K Coll Lon BA 05. SEITE 06. **d** 07 **p** 08. C Notting Hill St Pet *Lon* 07–10; V Belmont from 10. *St Anselm's Vicarage, Ventnor Avenue, Stanmore HA7 2HU* T: (020) 8907 3186 E: xtinerob@googlemail.com

ROBINSON, Christopher Gordon. b 49. Ridley Hall Cam. **d** 82 **p** 83. C Stanton *St E* 82–85; C Lawshall 85–86; P-in-c Lawshall w Shimplingthorne and Alpheton 86–89; TV

Oakdale *Sarum* 89–99; V Easton H Trin w St Gabr and St Lawr and St Jude *Bris* 99–05; C S Molton w Nymet St George, High Bray etc *Ex* 05–12; C Shirwell, Loxhore, Kentisbury, Arlington, etc 12–14; rtd 14. *22 John Street, Bargoed CF81 8PG*

ROBINSON, Christopher James. b 52. St Pet Coll Birm CertEd 74. OLM course 97. **d** 99 **p** 00. OLM Wilnecote *Lich* 99–16; PtO from 16. *55 Sycamore, Wilnecote, Tamworth B77 5HB* T: (01827) 282331 E: chrisrobinson55@hotmail.co.uk

ROBINSON, Christopher Mark Scott. b 83. Warwick Univ BSc 04. Ridley Hall Cam 06. **d** 09 **p** 10. C S Hartismere *St E* 09–12; R Rattlesden w Thorpe Morieux, Brettenham etc from 12; RD Lavenham from 17. *The Rectory, High Street, Rattlesden, Bury St Edmunds IP30 0RA* T: (01449) 737197 M: 07789-772024 E: tifferrobinson@gmail.com

ROBINSON, Daffyd Charles. b 48. Qu Coll Birm 77. **d** 80 **p** 85. C Abington *Pet* 80–82; C Immingham *Linc* 85–90; R Willoughby 90–13; rtd 13; PtO *Linc* 17–20. *57 Weelsby Avenue, Grimsby DN32 0AU* T: (01472) 753862 E: d_m@post.com

ROBINSON, Mrs Danielle Georgette Odette. b 47. SEITE 98. **d** 01 **p** 02. NSM Reigate St Mary *S'wark* 01–17; Chapl Surrey and Sussex Healthcare NHS Trust 01–15; PtO *Chich* from 01; *S'wark* from 17. *1 Chandler Way, Dorking RH5 4GA* T: (01306) 883947 *or* (01293) 600300 ext 3141 E: daniellerobinson@uwclub.net

ROBINSON, David. b 42. Sarum & Wells Th Coll. **d** 82 **p** 83. C Billingham St Cuth *Dur* 82–86; V Longwood *Wakef* 86–94; C Athersley 94–97; P-in-c Brotherton 97–02; rtd 02; PtO *York* 03–13. *5 High Street, Stanhope, Bishop Auckland DL13 2UP*

ROBINSON, Canon David Hugh. b 47. Linc Th Coll 76. **d** 79 **p** 80. C Bulkington *Cov* 79–82; C Whitley 82–87; Chapl Whitley, Gulson & Cov and Warks Hosp 82–87; Chapl Walsgrave Hosp Cov 87–97; Hon Can Cov Cathl 92–98; Succ 00–05; PtO *Cov* 97–00 and 05–07; P-in-c Cov St Mary 07–10; rtd 10; PtO *Ex* 11–16. *23A Crockwells Road, Exminster, Exeter EX6 8DH* T: (01392) 833135 M: 07947-023888

ROBINSON, David Mark. b 55. Univ Coll Dur BSc 76 Leic Univ MA 80 CQSW 80. Cranmer Hall Dur 86. **d** 88 **p** 89. C Shipley St Pet *Bradf* 88–92; P-in-c Ingrow w Hainworth 92–97; V Bramhope *Ripon* 97–05; V Chapel Allerton 05–14; *Leeds* 14–21; rtd 21. *602 King Lane, Leeds LS17 7AN* T: 0113-440 1109

ROBINSON, David Michael Wood. *See* WOOD-ROBINSON, David Michael

ROBINSON, Denis Hugh. b 53. SS Mark & Jo Univ Coll Plymouth CertEd 75. S Dios Minl Tr Scheme 88. **d** 91 **p** 92. NSM Bisley and W End *Guildf* 91–18; Hd RS Gordon's Sch Woking 80–12; Asst Chapl 91–94; Chapl 94–17; rtd 17; P-in-c Sparkwell *Ex* 18–19; P-in-c Cornwood 18–19; C Ivybridge, Cornwood, Harford and Sparkwell 19–21. *Mistledown, Dousland, Yelverton PL20 6NA* E: steviedenrob@aol.com

ROBINSON, Dennis Winston. b 42. QUB BScEng 68. CITC. **d** 88 **p** 89. NSM Mullavilly *Arm* 88–92; NSM Arm St Mark 92–95; C Portadown St Mark 95–98; I Aghavea *Clogh* 98–10; Preb Clogh Cathl 06–10; rtd 10. *Oakridge, 31 Snowhill Road, Beagho, Lisbellaw, Enniskillen BT94 5FY* T: (028) 6638 5858 E: dw.robinson@btopenworld.com

ROBINSON, Derek Charles. b 43. S'wark Ord Course 91. **d** 94 **p** 95. NSM Abbey Wood *S'wark* 94–13; PtO from 13. *19 Silverdale Road, Bexleyheath DA7 5AB* T: (01322) 523870

ROBINSON, Dorothy Ann. b 50. Cranmer Hall Dur 05. **d** 07 **p** 08. NSM Tynemouth Priory *Newc* 07–17; NSM N Shields from 17. *57 Millview Drive, North Shields NE30 2QD* T/F: 0191-257 0980 E: dottirobinson@hotmail.com

ROBINSON, Douglas. b 48. Nottm Univ BEd 70 Lon Univ BD 74 Union Th Sem Virginia MA 75. **d** 75 **p** 76. C Southport Ch Ch *Liv* 75–78; V Clubmoor 78–85; Chapl Epsom Coll 85–88; Chapl Dauntsey's Sch Devizes 89–95; PtO *Eur* 00–20. *Im Grünen Weg 1, Hangen Wiesheim 55234, Germany* T: (0049) (6375) 941575 E: douglasrobinson@t-online.de

ROBINSON, Elizabeth Carole Lesley. b 67. CITC 99. **d** 02 **p** 03. Aux Min Clonfert Gp *L & K* 02–06; Aux Min Roscrea w Kyle, Bourney and Corbally 06–11; Dioc C 11–13; I Dublin Clontarf *D & G* from 13. *The Rectory, 15 Seafield Road West, Clontarf, Dublin 3, Republic of Ireland* T: (00353) (1) 833 1181 M: 87-909 1561 E: clontarf@dublin.anglican.org

ROBINSON, Eric Charles. b 47. Lon Univ BD 71 Lanc Univ MA 97. CBDTI 94. **d** 97 **p** 98. NSM Carl St Cuth w St Mary 97–99; C Kendal H Trin 99–01; P-in-c Arthuret 01–07; P-in-c Nicholforest and Kirkandrews on Esk 01–07; R Arthuret w Kirkandrews-on-Esk and Nicholforest 07–08; P-in-c Kendal H Trin 08–10; rtd 10; PtO *Carl* 10–13; C York H Trin Micklegate 14–18; P-in-c Erpingham w Calthorpe, Ingworth, Aldborough etc *Nor* 19. *Address temp unknown* M: 07964-061810 E: revecrobinson@aol.com

ROBINSON, Fiona. b 69. Yorks Min Course 15. **d** 17 **p** 18. NSM Sutton Park *York* 17–18; NSM Wawne 17–18; NSM Sutton Park and Wawne from 18. *13 Wivern Road, Hull HU9 4HS* T: (01482) 703038 M: 07533-767016 E: revd-robinson@outlook.com

ROBINSON, Fiona Heather Anne. b 61. SNWTP 14. **d** 17 **p** 18. NSM Chelford and Lower Withington w Marthall *Ches* from 17; P-in-c from 20. *1 Drumble Field, Chelford, Macclesfield SK11 9BT* T: (01625) 860679 E: fionarobinson61@btinternet.com

ROBINSON, Frank. *See* ROBINSON, John Francis Napier

ROBINSON, Gareth James. b 74. Sheff Univ BA 95 Sheff Hallam Univ PGCE 96 K Coll Lon MA 13. St Mellitus Coll 13. **d** 13 **p** 14. C Marple All SS *Ches* 13–16; V Salford St Phil w St Steph *Man* from 16. *6 Encombe Place, Salford M3 6FJ* T: 0161-839 9709 M: 07825-413430 E: gareth.r@saintphilips.org.uk

ROBINSON, Hannah Ruth. b 82. Moorlands Th Coll BA 04 Ridley Hall Cam 18. **d** 20 **p** 21. C S Shoebury *Chelmsf* from 20. *56 Wakering Road, Shoeburyness, Southend-on-Sea SS3 9SY* E: rev.hannah.robinson@outlook.com

ROBINSON, Mrs Hazel. b 61. RGN 83 RSCN 83. St Jo Coll Nottm 02. **d** 04 **p** 05. C Toton *S'well* 04–09; P-in-c Blidworth w Rainworth 09–11; V 11–19; P-in-c Annesley w Newstead and Kirkby Woodhouse from 19. *The Vicarage, Annesley Cutting, Annesley, Nottingham NG15 0AJ* E: haze.rob@btopenworld.com

ROBINSON, Canon Ian. b 57. Nottm Univ BTh 87 MA 97. Linc Th Coll 84. **d** 87 **p** 88. C Bottesford w Ashby *Linc* 87–90; TV 90–95; P-in-c Caistor w Clixby 95–00; P-in-c Grasby 95–00; P-in-c Searby w Owmby 95–00; V Caistor Gp 00–18; V Caistor from 18; RD W Wold 01–17; Can and Preb Linc Cathl from 07. *3 Spa Top, Caistor, Market Rasen LN7 6RB* T: (01472) 851339 E: revianrobinson@tiscali.co.uk

ROBINSON, Ian Christopher. b 63. Hull Univ BSc 84 Leeds Univ MA 10 ACMA. Yorks Min Course 07. **d** 10 **p** 11. C New Malton *York* 10–13; PtO from 20. *Skewsby Grange, Skewsby, York YO61 4SG* T: (01347) 889232 M: 07983-505917 E: ian.robinson@tutanota.com

ROBINSON, Ian Morgan. b 53. Lanc Univ BA 08 CEng 86 MCIBSE 86. CBDTI 05. **d** 08 **p** 09. NSM Askrigg w Stallingbusk *Ripon* 08–12; NSM Hawes and Hardraw 09–12; R Bedale and Leeming and Thornton Watlass 12–14; *Leeds* 14–18; rtd 18; PtO *York* from 20. *High Dalby House, Dalby, Pickering YO18 7LP* M: 07801-657988 E: revrobbo@btinternet.com

ROBINSON, James Edward. b 85. Univ of Wales (Swansea) BA 09 Linc Coll Ox MSt 10 St Jo Coll Cam BA 14. Westcott Ho Cam 12. **d** 15 **p** 16. C Grantham St Wulfram *Linc* 15–18; C Grantham, Manthorpe 15–18; V Legbourne and Wold Marsh from 18; RD Louthesk from 21. *The Rectory, Westgate, Louth LN11 9YE* M: 07500-829413 E: jrobinson@stwulframs.com *or* jerobinson7980@gmail.com

ROBINSON, Mrs Jane Hippisley. b 41. Somerville Coll Ox MA 66 K Coll Lon PGCE. S Dios Minl Tr Scheme 88. **d** 91. NSM Ealing St Pet Mt Park *Lon* 91–96; NSM N Acton St Gabr 96–00; PtO 00–21. *Address temp unknown*

ROBINSON, Jean. *See* CLARK, Jean Robinson

ROBINSON, Mrs Jean Anne. b 50. Lon Univ BPharm 72 MRPharmS 73 Southn Univ BTh 98. STETS 95. **d** 98 **p** 99. NSM Frimley *Guildf* 98–03; NSM Worplesdon 03–05; NSM Egham Hythe 05–07; C Woodham 07–14; Chapl Surrey and Borders Partnership NHS Foundn Trust 05–14; Chapl Alpha Hosp Woking 06–14; NSM E Clevedon w Clapton in Gordano etc *B & W* 14–17; rtd 17; PtO *Guildf* from 17. *8 Westfield Avenue, Woking GU22 9PH* E: revjar95@yahoo.co.uk

ROBINSON, Jennifer Elizabeth. b 53. Sheff Hallam Univ BA 96. NOC 01. **d** 04 **p** 06. NSM Fishlake w Sykehouse and Kirk Bramwith etc *Sheff* 04–08; PtO 08–11; Chapl Rotherham, Doncaster and S Humber NHS Foundn Trust 13–19; rtd 19. *14 Thorncliffe Drive, Stainforth, Doncaster DN7 5PX* E: jerobinson@hotmail.co.uk

ROBINSON, Joan. b 62. **d** 13 **p** 14. NSM Blaydon and Swalwell *Dur* 13–16; Chapl Gateshead Health NHS Foundn Trust from 16. *9 Rose Avenue, Whickham, Newcastle upon Tyne NE16 4NA* T: 0191-420 1572 E: jrdallas@hotmail.co.uk

ROBINSON, Ms Joanne Sally. b 65. Warwick Univ BA 86. Trin Coll Bris 18. **d** 20 **p** 21. C Hardington Vale *B & W* from 20. *3 Manor Barn, The Barton, Norton St Philip, Bath BA2 7NE* T: (01373) 834643 M: 07821-464215 E: 321jorobinson@gmail.com

ROBINSON, John Francis Napier (Frank). b 42. St Edm Hall Ox BA 64 MA 68. Clifton Th Coll 65. **d** 68 **p** 69. C Southport Ch Ch *Liv* 68–71; C Coleraine *Conn* 71–74; Deputation Sec (Ireland) BCMS 74–76; TV Marfleet *York* 76–81; V Yeadon St Jo *Bradf* 81–95; P-in-c Rounds Green *Birm* 95–00; V 00–02;

rtd 02; PtO *S'well* from 03; *Derby* 03–18. *61 Clumber Avenue, Beeston, Nottingham NG9 4BH* T: 0115-922 1704

ROBINSON, Judith Lee Hughes. b 83. NW Univ Illinois BA 05 Wycliffe Hall Ox MTh 16. St Mellitus Coll 16. **d** 18 **p** 19. C W Hampstead Trin *Lon* 18–19. *46 Aberdare Gardens, London NW6 3QA* M: 07895-820540 E: judy.lh.robinson@gmail.com

ROBINSON, Katharine Mary. *See* McATEER, Katharine Mary

ROBINSON, Kathryn Elizabeth. b 55. Hull Univ BA 76 K Coll Lon MSc 86 St Hilda's Coll Ox PGCE 77. NTMTC 03. **d** 05 **p** 06. NSM Leytonstone St Jo *Chelmsf* 05–12; PtO from 12. *80 Carr Road, London E17 5EN* M: 07956-658450 E: krobinsonrev14@gmail.com

ROBINSON, Kenneth Borwell. b 37. Lon Univ BA 62. Ridley Hall Cam 68. **d** 70 **p** 71. C Walthamstow St Jo *Chelmsf* 70–74; P-in-c Becontree St Alb 74–78; P-in-c Heybridge w Langford 78–84; TV Horley *S'wark* 84–98; C Oxted and Tandridge 98–02; rtd 02; PtO *Portsm* 03–15; *S'wark* from 16. *8 Master Close, Oxted RH8 9NA* E: kennethrobinson@hotmail.co.uk

ROBINSON, Kevan John. b 63. Chich Univ BA 09. SEITE 08. **d** 10 **p** 11. NSM Southbourne w W Thorney *Chich* 10–14; P-in-c E Dean, Singleton, and W Dean 14–19; Chapl Chich Coll from 14; P-in-c Bexhill St Steph *Chich* from 19. *St Stephen's Vicarage, Woodsgate Park, Bexhill-on-Sea TN39 4DL* T: (01424) 211186 M: 07757-122446 E: k.robinson275@btinternet.com

ROBINSON, Lesley. *See* ROBINSON, Elizabeth Carole Lesley

ROBINSON, Leslie. b 31. St Aid Birkenhead 56. **d** 59 **p** 60. C Hugglescote w Donington *Leic* 59–61; C Greenside *Dur* 61–63; C-in-c New Cantley CD *Sheff* 63–66; V Choral Heref Cathl 66–67; R Easton-on-the-Hill *Pet* 67–69; Hon Min Can Pet Cathl 68–69; C Weston-super-Mare St Jo *B & W* 69–70; V Winkleigh *Ex* 70–72; V Thorpe Acre w Dishley *Leic* 72–78; V Cloughton *York* 78–79; V Hedon w Paull 79–81; V Bywell *Newc* 81–86; V Wymeswold and Prestwold w Hoton *Leic* 86–97; rtd 97; PtO *Leic* 97–98. *16 Victoria Road, Oundle, Peterborough PE8 4AY* T: (01832) 275048

ROBINSON, Linda Ann. b 53. **d** 12 **p** 13. NSM Newington w Hull St Andr *York* 12–18; PtO from 18. *153 Boothferry Road, Hessle HU13 9BA* E: robinson.linda28@yahoo.co.uk

ROBINSON, Linda Anne. b 54. Westf Coll Lon BA 75 Man Univ MEd 05 Ches Univ DProf 15. Yorks Min Course. **d** 14 **p** 15. NSM Bedale and Leeming and Thornton Watlass *Leeds* 14–18; rtd 18; PtO *York* from 20. *High Dalby House, Dalby, Pickering YO18 7LP* M: 07736-771216 E: lindarobinson@talk21.com

ROBINSON, Matthew Jamie. b 72. St Steph Ho Ox 13. **d** 15 **p** 16. C Sevenoaks St Jo *Roch* 15–19; V King's Sutton and Newbottle and Charlton *Pet* from 19. *The Vicarage, Church Avenue, King's Sutton, Banbury OX17 3RJ* T: (01295) 811364

ROBINSON, Matthew John. b 91. St Jo Coll Dur BA 20. Cranmer Hall Dur 17. **d** 20 **p** 21. C Layton and Staining *Blackb* from 20. *18 Burwood Drive, Blackpool FY3 8NS* M: 07913-110493 E: robinsonmatthew67@gmail.com

ROBINSON, Canon Michael Thomas Edward. b 87. Magd Coll Cam BA 08 MA 12. Westcott Ho Cam 13. **d** 16 **p** 17. C Walworth St Pet *S'wark* 16–20; Bp's Chapl *St E* from 20; Can Th St Edmundsbury Cathl from 20. *264 Norwich Road, Ipswich IP1 4BT* T: (01473) 252829 E: michael.robinson@cantab.net

ROBINSON, Monica Dorothy. b 40. SAOMC 99. **d** 01 **p** 02. NSM Bedford St Andr *St Alb* 01–10; PtO from 10. *Shoyswell, Radwell Road, Milton Ernest, Bedford MK44 1RY* T: (01234) 824366 E: mdrobinson@btopenworld.com

ROBINSON, Neil. b 66. Trin Coll Bris 13. **d** 16 **p** 17. C Bemerton *Sarum* 16–19; Chapl to the Deaf from 16; PtO *Win* from 20. *4 Ash Crescent, Bishopdown, Salisbury SP1 3GY* M: 07717-055219 E: coolie66smiley@gmail.com

ROBINSON, Mrs Norma Georgina. b 57. Edge Hill Coll of HE BEd 78 RGN 03. SNWTP 10. **d** 12 **p** 13. NSM Hyde St Geo *Ches* 12–14; NSM Macclesfield St Jo w Henbury 14–20; NSM Tilston and Shocklach from 20. *41 Inveresk Road, Tilston, Malpas SY14 7ED*

ROBINSON, Oliver Patrick Kilcooley. b 88. Heythrop Coll Lon BA 10 MA 11. Wycliffe Hall Ox MTh 15. **d** 15 **p** 17. C Cricklewood St Gabr and St Mich *Lon* 15–16; C W Hampstead Trin 16–19; PtO 19–20. *Ground Floor Flat, 46 Aberdare Gardens, London NW6 3QA* M: 07904-531036 E: opk.robinson@gmail.com

ROBINSON, Mrs Patricia May. b 51. Man Poly BEd 92 St Jo Coll Nottm MA 16. All SS Cen for Miss & Min 15. **d** 16 **p** 17. NSM Rostherne w Bollington *Ches* from 16; NSM High Legh from 16; NSM Over Tabley from 16. *The Vicarage, Rostherne Lane, Rostherne Village, Knutsford WA16 6RZ* T: (01565) 830595 M: 07854-418488 E: pmrobinson51@gmail.com

ROBINSON, Capt Paul Andrew. b 68. Hull Univ MBA 09. **d** 09 **p** 10. OLM Royton St Anne *Man* 09–12; NSM Medlock

Head 12–17; CF (R of O) from 13. *19 Dorchester Drive, Royton, Oldham OL2 5AU* T: 0161-628 9019 M: 07984-938393 E: paul@nomoreproblems.co.uk

ROBINSON, Paul Anthony. b 60. Wolv Univ LLB 81 Barrister-at-Law 85. St Aug Coll of Th 16. **d** 19 **p** 20. NSM S Chatham H Trin *Roch* from 19. *Address withheld by request* M: 07306-023483 E: revphtsc@btinternet.com

ROBINSON, Paul Leslie. b 65. St Steph Ho Ox 95. **d** 97 **p** 98. C Upholland *Liv* 97–01; V Lydiate and Downholland 01–08; P-in-c Halsall 04–08; R Halsall, Lydiate and Downholland 08–20; P-in-c Cork St Ann's Union *C, C & R* from 20; Chapl St Luke's Home Mahon from 20. *49 Ard Na Loi, Montenotte, Cork, T23 A8R5, Republic of Ireland* T: (00353) (21) 241 1879 M: 85-268 7009 E: paulrobinson407@gmail.com

ROBINSON, Canon Paul Leslie. b 46. Dur Univ BA 67. Linc Th Coll 71. **d** 74 **p** 75. C Poynton *Ches* 74–76; C Prenton 76–78; V Seacombe 78–88; V Stalybridge St Paul 88–00; P-in-c Wallasey St Hilary 00–04; R 04–10; Urban Min Officer 96–00; Hon Can Ches Cathl 98–10; P-in-c E and W Tilbury and Linford *Chelmsf* 10–16; R 16; PtO from 16. *37 Clyde Crescent, Rayleigh SS6 7SX* T: (01268) 963911 E: canonrobinson@outlook.com

ROBINSON, Paula Patricia. b 50. Man Univ MEd 83 TCD BTh 94. **d** 94 **p** 95. C Killala w Dunfeeny, Crossmolina, Kilmoremoy etc *T, K & A* 94–97; I Crosspatrick Gp *C, F & O* 97–00; R Leonardtown St Andr USA 00–09; P-in-c Tockwith and Bilton w Bickerton *York* 09–11; P-in-c Rufforth w Moor Monkton and Hessay 09–11; P-in-c Healaugh w Wighill, Bilbrough and Askham Richard 09–11; P-in-c Long Marston 09–11; PtO *Man* 12–15; NSM Heaton Reddish 15–16; NSM N Reddish 15–16; rtd 16; PtO *Man* from 16. *3 Lea Court, Heaton Moor Road, Stockport SK4 4PZ* T: 0161-975 0986 E: revpaularobinson@gmail.com

ROBINSON, Peter Charles. b 53. Open Univ BA 83. Oak Hill Th Coll 85. **d** 87 **p** 88. C Nottingham St Ann w Em *S'well* 87–89; C Worksop St Anne 89–92; V S Ramsey St Paul *S & M* 92–99; Can St German's Cathl 98–99; P-in-c Goostrey and Dioc Dir of Ords *Ches* 99–03; P-in-c Aldeburgh w Hazlewood *St E* 03–04; C Arbory *S & M* 05–06; V Arbory 05–13; C Santan 05–06; V 06–13; C Castletown 05–06; V 06–13; RD Castletown and Peel 08–12; Hon Can St German's Cathl 09–12; Can and Bp's Chapl 12–13; V Malton and Old Malton *York* 13–18; rtd 18; PtO *York* 19. *1 Shaftesbury Avenue, Hornsea HU18 1LX* T: (01964) 751291

ROBINSON, Peter Edward Barron. b 40. Open Univ BSc 99. Sarum & Wells Th Coll 76. **d** 78 **p** 79. C Petersfield w Sheet *Portsm* 78–82; R Bentworth and Shalden and Lasham *Win* 82–88; R W Horsley *Guildf* 88–00; rtd 00; PtO *B & W* from 01; *Ex* from 21. *34 Manleys Lane, Dunkeswell, Honiton EX14 4XQ* T: (01404) 890080 E: peter@robinsonp.co.uk

ROBINSON, The Very Revd Peter John Alan. b 61. St Jo Coll Cam BA 83 MA 87 St Jo Coll Dur BA 92 PhD 97. Cranmer Hall Dur 90. **d** 95 **p** 96. C N Shields *Newc* 95–99; P-in-c Byker St Martin 99–08; P-in-c Byker St Mich w St Lawr 01–08; Hon Can Newc Cathl 07–08; Adn Lindisfarne 08–20; Dean Derby from 20. *The Deanery, 27A Penny Long Lane, Derby DE22 1AX* T: (01332) 341201 E: dean@derbycathedral.org

ROBINSON, Philip. b 38. S Dios Minl Tr Scheme 88. **d** 91 **p** 92. NSM Ickenham *Lon* 91–95; P-in-c 95–04; P-in-c Hayes St Anselm 98–99; P-in-c Harlington 98–00; AD Hillingdon 97–03; rtd 04; PtO *Eur* from 04; *Lon* from 04. *Résidence Stella Maris A, 7 Chemin des Myrtes, 06310 Beaulieu-sur-Mer, France* T: (0033) 4 93 04 75 11 E: philiprobinson208@gmail.com

ROBINSON, Philip John. b 50. St Luke's Coll Ex CertEd 71 Leeds Univ BA 07. NOC 04. **d** 06 **p** 07. NSM Macclesfield Team *Ches* 06–09; P-in-c Rostherne w Bollington 09–13; V from 13; P-in-c High Legh from 15; P-in-c Over Tabley from 15; rtd 22. *The Vicarage, Rostherne Lane, Rostherne Village, Knutsford WA16 6RZ* T: (01565) 830595 E: robinsonpj50@gmail.com

ROBINSON, Robert James. **d** 14 **p** 15. Drumglass w Moygashel *Arm* 14–15; C Drumragh w Mountfield *D & R* 15–18; CF from 18. *c/o MOD Chaplains (Army)* T: (01264) 383430 F: 381824 E: robertjamesrobinson3@gmail.com

ROBINSON, Prof Simon John. b 51. Edin Univ MA 72 PhD 89 Ox Univ BA 77. Wycliffe Hall Ox 75. **d** 78 **p** 79. C Haughton le Skerne *Dur* 78–81; Chapl Asst N Tees Hosp Stockton-on-Tees 81–83; C Norton St Mary *Dur* 81–83; Chapl Heriot-Watt Univ *Edin* 83–90; R Dalmahoy 83–90; Chapl Leeds Univ *Ripon* 90–04; P-in-c Leeds Em 90–04; Prof Ethics Leeds Metrop Univ 04–14; NSM Leeds City 05–14 and from 14; Prof Ethics Leeds Beckett Univ from 14. *42 Woodside Avenue, Meanwood, Leeds LS7 2UL* T: 0113-285 7440 M: 07931-916381 E: s.j.robinson@leedsmet.ac.uk *or* s.j.robinson@leedsbeckett.ac.uk

ROBINSON, Simon Joseph. b 67. Warwick Univ BA 89. STETS. **d** 12 **p** 13. C Freshford, Limpley Stoke and Hinton Charterhouse *B & W* 12–15; V Minehead from 15. *7 Paganel Road, Minehead TA24 5ET* M: 07825-925243 E: sijorobinson@me.com

ROBINSON, Steven Paul. b 65. Roehampton Univ BEd 89 Oak Hill Th Coll BA 05. St Mellitus Coll MA 13. **d** 10 **p** 11. C Perranzabuloe and Crantock w Cubert *Truro* 10–13; R St Illogan from 13. *The Rectory, Robartes Terrace, Illogan, Redruth TR16 4RX* T: (01209) 843938 M: 07813-324148

ROBINSON, Canon Teresa Jane. b 56. SAOMC 98. **d** 01 **p** 02. OLM The Cookhams *Ox* 01–08; NSM Maidenhead St Luke 08–21; Angl Communion Office 14–19; Hon Can Ch Ch *Ox* from 18; LtO from 21. *7 Golden Ball Lane, Maidenhead SL6 6NW* T: (01628) 634107 E: terrie.robinson2702@gmail.com

ROBINSON, Tiffer. *See* ROBINSON, Christopher Mark Scott

ROBINSON, Timothy. b 56. Hull Univ BSc 78 Liv Univ PhD 83 St Jo Coll Dur BA 07 FGA 86. Cranmer Hall Dur 05. **d** 07 **p** 08. C Nantwich *Ches* 07–10; V Stalybridge St Paul 10–14; V Macclesfield St Jo w Henbury 14–20; R Tilston and Shocklach from 20. *41 Inveresk Road, Tilston, Malpas SY14 7ED* M: 07981-108779 E: trtimrobinson@gmail.com

ROBINSON, Timothy James. b 59. Middx Poly BA 84 Open Univ MA 13 Coll of Ripon & York St Jo PGCE 00. St Steph Ho Ox 88. **d** 91 **p** 92. C W Acklam *York* 91–95; P-in-c N Ormesby 95–96; V 96–99; PtO *Ripon* 99–02; Teacher Hall Garth Sch Middlesbrough 00–10; Tutor NEOC 02–09; P-in-c Helmsley *York* 10–11; V 11–21; P-in-c Upper Ryedale 10–11; R 11–21; AD N Ryedale 11–21; Can and Preb York Minster 21; rtd 21; PtO *York* from 21. *6 Petersway, York YO30 6AR* E: tim.robinson123@btinternet.com

ROBINSON-BROWN, Jarel Adrian. b 91. Cardiff Univ BTh 17 Dur Univ MA 21 ALCM 14. Wesley Ho Cam 10 St Melitus Coll 20. **d** 21. In Methodist Ch 13–21; C St Botolph Aldgate w H Trin Minories *Lon* from 21. *St Mary's Vicarage, 134A Abbey Road, London NW6 4SN* M: 07842-588457 E: jarelrb@gmail.com

ROBINSON-MULLER, Ank. *See* MULLER, Ank

ROBOTTOM, David Leonard Douglas. b 40. Qu Coll Birm 80 Sarum & Wells Th Coll 81. **d** 83 **p** 84. C Uppingham w Ayston and Wardley w Belton *Pet* 83–87; TV Sidmouth, Woolbrook and Salcombe Regis *Ex* 87–91; TV Sidmouth, Woolbrook, Salcombe Regis, Sidbury etc 91–95; R Bradninch and Clyst Hydon 95–10; RD Cullompton 03–08; rtd 10; PtO *Ex* from 15. *2 Bridge Meadow Close, Lapford, Crediton EX17 6FH* T: (01363) 884495 E: david@serafim.eclipse.co.uk

ROBSON, Claire English. b 62. Middx Poly BEd 88. Westcott Ho Cam 96. **d** 99 **p** 00. C Dorchester *Sarum* 99–02; C Kilburn St Mary w All So and W Hampstead St Jas *Lon* 02–04; Min Can and Chapl St Paul's Cathl 04–09; C Bath Abbey w St Jas *B & W* 09–18; Dioc Dir of Ords *Newc* from 18; NSM Hexham 18–20; NSM Humshaugh w Simonburn and Wark from 20. *20 Chesters Meadow, Humshaugh, Hexham NE46 4BF* T: 0191-270 4154 M: 07741-849651 E: clairerobson@clara.net

ROBSON, Howard. *See* ROBSON, John Howard

ROBSON, James Edward. b 65. Pemb Coll Ox BA 88 Middx Univ PhD 05. Wycliffe Hall Ox 91. **d** 94 **p** 95. C Enfield Ch Ch Trent Park *Lon* 94–98; C Oakwood St Thos 98–00; Tutor Oak Hill Th Coll 00–09; Tutor Wycliffe Hall Ox 09–10; Sen Tutor 10–17; Min Dir Keswick Min from 17; NSM Hartford *Ches* from 19. *Keswick Ministries, Skiddaw Street, Keswick CA12 4BY* T: (017687) 80075 M: 07454-865670 E: james.robson@keswickministries.org

ROBSON, Miss Jane. b 69. Nottm Univ BPharm 90 Dur Univ MSc 15. Cranmer Hall Dur 18. **d** 20 **p** 21. C Gt Ayton w Easby and Newton under Roseberry *York* from 20. *42 Blantyre Road, Middlesbrough TS6 0EY* M: 07762-052302 E: revjanerob@gmail.com

ROBSON, John Howard. b 60. Newc Univ BA 81 ACIB 87. Cranmer Hall Dur 98. **d** 00 **p** 01. C Hethersett w Canteloff w Lt and Gt Melton *Nor* 00–04; R Brooke, Kirstead, Mundham w Seething and Thwaite 04–13; V Littleport *Ely* 13–20; RD Ely 14–19; TR Cottesloe *Ox* from 20. *The Vicarage, 27B Aylesbury Road, Wing, Leighton Buzzard LU7 0PD* E: therevhowward@outlook.com

ROBSON, John Phillips. b 32. LVO 99. St Edm Hall Ox. AKC 58. **d** 59 **p** 60. C Huddersfield SS Pet and Paul *Wakef* 59–62; Asst Chapl Ch Hosp Horsham 62–65; Chapl 65–80; Sen Chapl Wellington Coll Berks 80–89; Chapl to RVO and Qu Chpl of the Savoy 89–02; Chapl to The Queen 93–02; rtd 02; Extra Chapl to The Queen from 02. *Charterhouse, Charterhouse Square, London EC1M 6AN* T: (020) 7253 1591 E: johnrevolt@gmail.com

ROBSON, Mrs Julie. b 52. d 12 p 13. NSM Corbridge w Halton and Newton Hall *Newc* 12–17; rtd 17; PtO *Newc* from 18. *Address temp unknown* E: j-r@talktalk.net

ROBSON, Martin Douglas. b 62. St Andr Univ MTheol 85 Cam Univ PGCE 88 Edin Univ MTh 94. Edin Th Coll 92. d 94 p 95. C Perth St Ninian *St And* 94–97; P-in-c Lockerbie *Glas* 97–01; P-in-c Moffat 97–01; R Edin St Hilda 01–06; R Edin St Fillan 01–14; R Edin St Mich and All SS from 14. *203 Gilmore Place, Edinburgh EH3 9PN* T: 0131-923 1179 E: rector@stmichaelandallsaints.org

ROBSON, Nolan Daniel Rhyl. b 77. Bath Univ BSc 99 Sheff Univ DipArch 02. Oak Hill Th Coll BA 13. d 13 p 14. C Kilnhurst *Sheff* 13–16; R Thrapston, Denford and Islip Pet from 16. *The Rectory, 48 Oundle Road, Thrapston, Kettering NN14 4PD* T: (01932) 734614 M: 07740-700899 E: nolanrobson@me.com

ROBSON, Pamela Jean. b 44. STETS 94. d 97 p 98. NSM W Ewell *Guildf* 97–01; P-in-c Wotton and Holmbury St Mary 02–14; rtd 14; PtO *St E* from 15. *Old Guildhall, The Street, Badwell Ash, Bury St Edmunds IP31 3DP* T: (01359) 258939 E: robsonpam@btinternet.com

ROBSON, Canon Patricia Anne. b 40. MBE 99. CertEd 60. SWMTC 85. d 87 p 94. Dioc Youth Officer *Truro* 87–92; Hon C Paul 87–92; Hon C Kenwyn St Geo 88–92; Dn-in-c St Enoder 92–94; P-in-c 94–05; P-in-c Newlyn St Newlyn 03–05; Hon Can Truro Cathl 98–05; RD Pydar 02–03; rtd 05; P-in-c St Goran w Caerhays *Truro* 06–09; PtO from 16. *Mill Cottage, Mill Lane, Grampound, Truro TR2 4RU* T: (01726) 882366 E: intercelt@aol.com

ROBSON, Paul Coutt. b 37. Leeds Univ BA 60. Coll of Resurr Mirfield 63. d 64 p 65. C Stokesay *Heref* 64–66; C St Geo Cathl Cape Town S Africa 66–68; R Roodebloem All SS 68–70; Chapl HM Pris Man 70–71; Chapl HM Borstal Feltham 71–74; Chapl HM Borstal Hollesley Bay 74–78; Chapl HM Pris Grendon and Spring Hill 78–85; Chapl HM Pris Nor 85–92; Chapl HM YOI and Remand Cen Brinsford 92–99; rtd 99; PtO *Heref* 00–01 and 04–20; P-in-c Wistanstow 01–04. *Pilgrims, Henley Common, Church Stretton SY6 6RS* T: (01694) 781221 E: robson718@btinternet.com

ROBSON, Peter. b 58. Leeds Univ BEd 80. Cranmer Hall Dur 05. d 07 p 08. C Bishopwearmouth St Gabr *Dur* 07–11; PtO 16–18; Hon C Shildon from 18. *1 Broad Oak, Bishop Middleham, Ferryhill DL17 9BW* E: peterpoprobson@aol.co.uk

ROBSON, Thomas Iain. b 83. Ridley Hall Cam 10. d 13 p 14. C Angmering *Chich* 13–16; P-in-c Lyminster and Wick 16–17; V from 17. *The Vicarage, 40 Beaconsfield Road, Wick, Littlehampton BN17 6LN* T: (01903) 714838 E: tom.robson@allsaintswick.org.uk

ROBSON, William. b 34. FCIS 66 FCCA 80. Sarum & Wells Th Coll 77. d 79 p 80. C Lymington *Win* 79–81; CF 81–93; V Barton Stacey and Bullington etc *Win* 93–98; rtd 98; Hon C Knaresborough *Ripon* 98–01; PtO *Newc* 03–04; Hon C Barrow upon Soar w Walton le Wolds *Leic* 04–07; Hon C Wymeswold and Prestwold w Hoton 04–07; PtO *Glouc* from 18. *30 Capel Court, The Burgage, Prestbury, Cheltenham GL52 3EL* T: (01242) 226001 M: 07914-829885

ROBUS, Keith Adrian. b 59. Heythrop Coll Lon MA 01 MHCIMA 82. Chich Th Coll 85. d 88 p 89. C Greenhill St Jo *Lon* 88–92; C Willesden St Matt 92–02; V N Acton St Gabr 02–09; Chapl RN 09–19; P-in-c Stoke Damerel and Devonport St Aubyn *Ex* 19; R Stoke Damerel from 19. *The Rectory, 6 Underhill Road, Plymouth PL3 4BP* T: (01752) 509724 M: 07801-069997 E: keith.robus@btinternet.com

ROCHDALE, Archdeacon of. *See* SHARPLES, The Ven David John

ROCHE, Miss Alison Mary. b 70. Man Univ BSc 91 Nottm Univ PGCE 94. St Jo Coll Nottm MA 00. d 01 p 02. C Leic Martyrs 01–05; P-in-c Leic St Chris 05–09; V 09–16; PtO from 18. *Knighton Vicarage, 5 Church Lane, Leicester LE2 3WG* T: 0116-270 4268 M: 07901-621250

ROCHE, Barry Robert Francis. b 40. Lon Univ BD 66 Ox Univ MTh 93. Clifton Th Coll 63. d 68 p 69. C Beckenham Ch Ch *Roch* 68–72; C Chester le Street *Dur* 72–74; C-in-c N Bletchley CD *Ox* 74–78; R Luton Ch Ch *Roch* 78–92; Chapl All SS Hosp Chatham 78–92; TR Glascote and Stonydelph *Lich* 92–99; RD Tamworth 95–99; V Oulton Broad *Nor* 99–05; rtd 05; PtO *S & B* from 06. *24 Lakeside Close, Nantyglo, Ebbw Vale NP23 4EG* T: (01495) 311048 E: roche440@btinternet.com

ROCHE, David Michael. b 71. Redcliffe Coll Glouc MA 14. d 16 p 16. P-in-c Beirut All SS Lebanon 16–18; P-in-c Whitchurch w Tufton and Litchfield *Win* from 18; AD Whitchurch from 20. *The Vicarage, Church Street, Whitchurch RG28 7AS* M: 07783-506944 E: david.roche@hotmail.com

ROCHE, Philip Edmund. b 70. SCRTP 14. d 17 p 18. C Milford *Guildf* 17–18; C Seale, Puttenham and Wanborough from 18. *130 Ockford Road, Godalming GU7 1RG* E: rev.phil@outlook.com

ROCHELL, Stephen Peter. b 56. Open Univ MA 95 Sheff Univ BA 14. Yorks Min Course 11. d 14 p 15. NSM Hartshead, Hightown, Roberttown and Scholes *Leeds* from 14. *55 Greenside Road, Mirfield WF14 0AU* T: (01924) 521121 M: 07707-763689 E: stephen.rochell@ntlworld.com

ROCHESTER, Archdeacon of. *See* WOODING JONES, The Ven Andrew David

ROCHESTER, Bishop of. *Vacant*

ROCHESTER, Dean of. *See* HESKETH, The Very Revd Philip John

ROCK, Mrs Jean. b 37. Gilmore Course 76. dss 79 d 87 p 97. Douglas St Matt *S & M* 79–81; Marown 81–83; Chapl Asst Oswestry and Distr Hosp 83–87; Oswestry St Oswald *Lich* 83–90; Par Dn 87–90; C-in-c Pont Robert and Pont Dolanog *St As* 90–97; V 97; rtd 97; PtO *Lich* 99–13; *St As* from 09. *Burnet Cottage, Church Lane, St Martins, Oswestry SY11 3AP* T: (01691) 773766

ROCK, Rebecca Mary. b 78. Newc Univ BA 00. Linc Sch of Th and Min 18 St Hild Coll 19. d 21. C Quarrington w Old Sleaford *Linc* from 21. *16 Dove Close, Seaford NG34 7UT* E: revdrebeccarock@gmail.com

ROCKEY, Antony Nicolas. b 65. Kingston Poly BEng 89 Cumbria Univ MA 12. CBDTI 02. d 05 p 06. C Cockermouth Area *Carl* 05–09; P-in-c Fernhurst *Chich* 09–11; PtO *Ex* 15–16; TR Burrington, Chawleigh, Cheldon, Chulmleigh etc from 16. *The Rectory, Chulmleigh EX18 7BY* T: (01769) 581712 E: rector@littledartchurches.org.uk

ROCKS, James Anthony. b 82. Trin Coll Bris BA 10. d 11 p 12. C Stoke Gifford *Bris* 11–15; CMS Brazil from 15. *Address temp unknown* M: 07786-034993 E: jimmyrocks1@gmail.com

RODD, Philip Rankilor. b 60. Ex Univ BA 79 K Coll Lon PGCE 85. Ridley Hall Cam 03. d 05 p 06. C Heigham H Trin *Nor* 05–08; V Eaton St Andr from 08. *The Vicarage, 210 Newmarket Road, Norwich NR4 7LA* T: (01603) 455778

RODD, Susan Eleanor. b 46. d 10 p 11. NSM Whitton *Sarum* 10–14; TV from 14. *16 The Garlings, Aldbourne, Marlborough SN8 2DT* T: (01672) 541571 E: revsuerodd@btinternet.com

RODDAM, Helen Margaret. *See* BAILEY, Helen Margaret

RODDY, Keith Anthony. b 67. Leic Univ BA 89. Oak Hill Th Coll BA 09. d 09 p 10. C Chesterton *Lich* 09–12; V Springfield H Trin *Chelmsf* from 12. *The Vicarage, 61 Hill Road, Chelmsford CM2 6HW* T: (01245) 359299 M: 07986-903110 E: keitharoddy@googlemail.com

RODEL, Mark Neil. b 71. Southn Univ BA 96 Win Univ MA 11. STETS 02. d 05 p 06. C Southsea St Jude *Portsm* 05–08; C Portsea St Luke 08–12; V Lady Bay w Holme Pierrepont and Adbolton *S'well* 12–19; Tutor St Jo Coll Nottm 12–19; Dioc Fresh Expressions Adv *Ely* from 19. *Ely Diocesan Office, Bishop Woodford House, Barton Road, Ely CB7 4DX* T: (01353) 652701 E: mark.rodel@elydiocese.org

RODEN, Jo. *See* LOVERIDGE, Joan Margaretha Holland

RODEN, John Michael. b 37. St Jo Coll York CertEd 64 Open Univ BA 82 MA 92 York Univ DPhil 96. Ripon Hall Ox 71. d 73 p 74. C Saltburn-by-the-Sea *York* 73–77; Chapl St Pet Sch York 77–82; Warden Marrick Priory *Ripon* 83; Hon C Appleton Roebuck w Acaster Selby *York* 84–85; P-in-c 86–03; Youth Officer 86–91; Sen Chapl Selby Coalfield Ind Chapl 96–03; rtd 03; PtO *York* from 03; *Eur* from 10. *Ebor Cottage, 8 Copmanthorpe Grange, Copmanthorpe, York YO23 3TN* T: (01904) 744826 E: j.m.roden@btinternet.com

RODEN, Canon Michael Adrian Holland. b 60. Birm Univ MA 03. Ripon Coll Cuddesdon 82. d 85 p 86. C S Lambeth St Anne and All SS *S'wark* 85–88; C Wandsworth St Paul 88–90; C Ox St Mary V w St Cross and St Pet 90–94; Chapl Wadh Coll Ox 90–94; R Steeple Aston w N Aston and Tackley *Ox* 94–02; TR Hitchin *St Alb* 02–16; P-in-c St Paul's Walden 10–16; TR Hitchin and St Paul's Walden 16–19; RD Hitchin 07–15; Hon Can St Alb from 14; Can Res Bris Cathl 19–20; Chapl The Hague *Eur* from 20. *St John and St Philip, Ary van der Spuyweg 1, 2585 HA The Hague, The Netherlands* T: (0031) (70) 322 7941 E: chaplain@stjohn-stphilip.org

RODERICK, Philip David. b 49. Univ of Wales (Swansea) BA 70 Univ of Wales (Abth) BD 77 Lon Univ CertEd 71. Linc Th Coll 80. d 80 p 81. C Llanfair-is-gaer and Llanddeiniolen *Ban* 80–82; TV Holyhead w Rhoscolyn w Llanfair-yn-Neubwll 82–84; Chapl and Lect Th Univ of Wales (Ban) 84–88; Warden Angl Chapl Cen 84–88; Prin Bucks Chr Tr Scheme *Ox* 88–94; Dir Chiltern Chr Tr Progr 88–94; Dir Quiet Garden Trust from 92; Dir The Well Inst from 96; V Amersham on the Hill *Ox* 96–04; Ldr Contemplative Fire from 04; Bp's Adv in Spirituality *Sheff* 10–16; Chapl Whirlow Grange Conf Cen Sheff 10–15; rtd 16. *16 Chorley Avenue, Saltdean, Brighton BN2 8AQ* T: (01273) 275352 E: philiproderick@btinternet.com

RODGER, Mark David. b 83. St Mellitus Coll BA 20. d 20 p 21. C Lyminster and Wick *Chich* from 20. *70 Cornwall Road, Littlehampton BN17 6EQ* M: 07920-850814 E: markrodger83@gmail.com

RODGER, Canon Raymond. b 39. Westmr Coll Ox MTh 93. Bps' Coll Cheshunt 62. d 63 p 64. C Frodingham *Linc* 63–66; Asst Chapl St Geo Hosp Lon 66–69; C Waltham *Linc* 69–73; V Nocton 73–86; P-in-c Potter Hanworth 74–86; P-in-c Dunston 77–86; RD Graffoe 81–92; Can and Preb Linc Cathl from 85; V Nocton w Dunston and Potterhanworth 86–92; Bp's Dom Chapl 92–05; Gen Preacher 92–05; rtd 05. *13 Lupin Road, Lincoln LN2 4GB* T: (01522) 536723 M: 07803-123975 E: canrod@hotmail.com

RODGERS, Alasdair Martin. b 75. Lon Bible Coll BA 96 Ches Univ PhD 19. St Jo Coll Nottm 13. d 15 p 16. C Bebington *Ches* from 15. *22 Woodhey Road, Wirral CH63 8PD* T: 0151-645 8375 M: 07790-270060 E: al@kateandal.com *or* al@standrewsbebington.org.uk

RODGERS, Daniel Christopher. b 88. Open Univ BA 10. St Mellitus Coll 14. d 16 p 17. C Buckingham *Ox* 16–19; V Loudwater from 19. *St Peter's Vicarage, Treadaway Hill, Loudwater, High Wycombe HP10 9QL* T: (01628) 526087 M: 07814-243193 E: danny.youth@gmail.com

RODGERS, Eamonn Joseph. b 41. QUB BA 63 PhD 70. TISEC 04. d 05 p 06. NSM Glas St Ninian 05–12; LtO from 12. *4 Albert Drive, Glasgow G73 3RT* T: 0141-583 6949 M: 07586-302613 E: er8907@ntlworld.com

RODGERS, Preb Frank Ernest. b 46. Tyndale Hall Bris 68. d 71 p 72. C Madeley *Heref* 71–74; C Littleover *Derby* 74–77; V Clodock and Longtown w Craswell and Llanveyno *Heref* 77–79; P-in-c St Margaret's w Michaelchurch Eskley and Newton 77–79; V Clodock and Longtown w Craswell, Llanveynoe etc 79–10; RD Abbeydore 90–96; Preb Heref Cathl 96–10; rtd 10; PtO *Heref* from 10. *Thorneyglatt Cottage, Didley, Hereford HR2 9DA* T: (01981) 570629

RODGERS, Matthew. b 87. Cliff Coll BA 13. St Mellitus Coll MA 20. d 19 p 20. C Linc St Swithin from 19. *c/o 4 Cooper Lane, Laceby, Grimsby DN37 7AX* T: (01472) 277892 M: 07476-950414 E: matt.rodgers@stmarksgrimsby.org.uk

RODGERS, Richard Thomas Boycott. b 47. Lon Univ MB, BS 70 FRCS 81. St Jo Coll Nottm. d 77 p 78. C Littleover *Derby* 77–80; Lect Birm St Martin w Bordesley St Andr 89–90; PtO from 90; rtd 12. *63 Meadow Brook Road, Birmingham B31 1ND* T: 0121-476 0789 E: dick@rodgars.org.uk

RODHAM, The Ven Morris. b 59. Hatf Coll Dur BA 81 St Jo Coll Dur PGCE 85. Trin Coll Bris MA 93. d 93 p 94. C New Milverton *Cov* 93–97; V Leamington Priors St Mary 97–10; RD Warwick and Leamington 06–09; Adn Missr 10–19; Adn Warwick 10–19; P-in-c Patterdale *Carl* from 19. *The Rectory, Patterdale, Penrith CA11 0NL* T: (017684) 82209 M: 07929-861233

RODLEY, Ian Tony. b 48. Open Univ BA 08. Qu Coll Birm 77. d 80 p 81. C Baildon and Dioc Children's Adv *Bradf* 80–85; V Bradf St Wilfrid Lidget Green 85–90; Chapl to the Deaf 88–90; V Otley 90–98; C Wolverton *Ox* 98–03; TR Bramley *Ripon* 03–13; rtd 13. *4 Beadon Avenue, Huddersfield HD5 8QZ* E: ianrod@clara.co.uk

RODLEY, James William Eric. b 66. SS Hild & Bede Coll Dur BA 86 ACA 89. St Steph Ho Ox BTh 11. d 09 p 10. C Pokesdown All SS and Bournemouth St Clem *Win* 09–13; P-in-c Harlow St Mary Magd *Chelmsf* 13–18; V from 18; P-in-c N Weald Bassett 13–18. *The Vicarage, 3 Oaklands Drive, Harlow CM17 9BE* T: (01279) 451065 E: jwerodley@yahoo.co.uk

RODRIGUEZ, Luis Mario. b 64. Occidental Coll (USA) BA 86 S California Univ MA 93. St Steph Ho Ox MTh 99. d 98 p 99. C Battersea Ch Ch and St Steph S'wark 98–02; C Pimlico St Pet w Westmr Ch Ch Lon 02–05; PtO S'wark 07–08; R Hanford USA from 08. *510 N Douty Street, Hanford CA 93230, USA* T: (001) (559) 584 7706 F: 584 7710 E: luis@smeltern.com

RODRIGUEZ, Miguel. *See* SANCHEZ RODRIGUEZ, Miguel

RODWELL, Barry John. b 39. Birm Univ CertEd 59 Cam Univ DipAdEd 77. Ridley Hall Cam 67. d 70 p 71. C Sudbury St Greg and St Pet *St E* 70–73; Hd RE Hedingham Sch 73–80; R Sible Hedingham *Chelmsf* 80–85; RE Adv 85–93; V Gt Burstead 93–00; rtd 00; PtO *Nor* 00–07 and from 15. *The Nutshell, 11 Filbert Road, Loddon, Norwich NR14 6LW* T: (01508) 522949

RODWELL, Mrs Helen. b 70. WEMTC. d 09 p 10. NSM Forest of Dean Ch Ch w English Bicknor *Glouc* 09–16; PtO from 19. *The Other House, English Bicknor, Coleford GL16 7PD* T: (01594) 860205 E: rev.rodwell@icloud.com

RODWELL (née VINCENT), Mrs Jacqueline Margaret. b 59. Glos Univ BA 04. WEMTC 01. d 04 p 05. NSM Cheltenham St Mark *Glouc* 04–08; NSM Cheltenham Em

w St Steph 08–09; NSM S Cheltenham 10–14; PtO from 14. *7 Winchester House, Malvern Road, Cheltenham GL50 2NN* E: the.rodwells@blueyonder.co.uk

RODWELL, Canon John Stanley. b 46. Leeds Univ BSc 68 Southn Univ PhD 74. Cuddesdon Coll 71. d 74 p 75. Hon C Horfield H Trin *Bris* 74–75; Hon C Skerton St Luke *Blackb* 75–77; LtO 77–16; Hon Can Blackb Cathl 03–16; rtd 16; PtO *Blackb* from 16. *7 Derwent Road, Lancaster LA1 3ES* T: (01524) 62726 E: johnrodwell@tiscali.co.uk

ROE, Mrs Caroline Ruth. b 57. Birm Univ BA 80 PGCE 93. Wycliffe Hall Ox 81. dss 84 d 87 p 96. Olveston *Bris* 84–87; Par Dn 87; NSM Alveley and Quatt *Heref* 87–94; Bp's Voc Officer 90–94; Hon C Loughborough Em and St Mary in Charnwood *Leic* 97–98; C Hathern, Long Whatton and Diseworth w Belton etc 98–00; PtO 01–04; Chapl Univ Hosps Leic NHS Trust 04–07; Lead Chapl 07–13. *4 John's Lee Close, Loughborough LE11 3LH* T: (01509) 260217 *or* 0116-258 5487 E: roe_caroline@hotmail.com

ROE, Daniel Cameron. b 84. Ball Coll Ox BA 05. Oak Hill Th Coll MTh 10. d 10 p 11. C Clifton *York* 10–15; PtO from 17. *Shincliffe Hall, Hall Lane, Shincliffe, Durham DH1 2SY* M: 07778-572928 E: daniel.roe@balliol.oxon.org *or* daniel.c.roe@gmail.com

ROEMMELE, Canon Michael Patrick. b 49. TCD BA 72 MA 76. d 73 p 74. C Portadown St Columba *Arm* 73–77; C Drumachose *D & R* 77–80; Bahrain 79–83; Cyprus 79–83; Chapl RAF 83–00; CF 00–07; I Camus-juxta-Bann *D & R* 07–17; Can Derry Cathl 14–17; rtd 18. *30 Drumrane Road, Limavady BT49 9LB* T: (028) 7776 3554 M: 07977-239863 E: mproemmele@gmail.com

ROESCHLAUB, Robert Friedrich. b 39. Purdue Univ BSc 63. Berkeley Div Sch MDiv 66. d 66 p 66. USA 66–77; Hon C Tilehurst St Cath *Ox* 78–79; Hon C Tilehurst St Mich 79–82; P-in-c Millom H Trin w Thwaites *Carl* 82–85; P-in-c Millom 85–89; R Dunstall w Rangemore and Tatenhill *Lich* 89–93; rtd 94; PtO *Carl* 98–20; *Lich* 02–16. *20 Pannatt Hill, Millom LA18 5DB* T: (01229) 772185 E: hoosier@btconnect.com

ROEST, Canon Wilma. b 62. Utrecht Univ MA 88 Roehampton Inst PGCE 92. SEITE 96. d 99 p 00. C Merton St Mary *S'wark* 99–02; TV N Lambeth 02–06; P-in-c Balham St Mary and St Jo 06–10; V 10–16; AD Tooting 09–16; TR Richmond St Mary w St Matthias and St Jo from 16; Hon Can S'wark Cathl from 20. *The Vicarage, Ormond Road, Richmond TW10 6TH* T: (020) 8940 0362 E: rector@richmondteamministry.org

ROFF, Andrew Martin. b 42. Bede Coll Dur BSc 65. Westcott Ho Cam 65. d 70 p 71. C Ches St Mary 70–73; Min Can Blackb Cathl 73–76; P-in-c Blackb St Jo 74–75; V Longton 76–81; Chapl Trin Coll Glenalmond 82–83; R Allendale w Whitfield *Newc* 83–92; V Gosforth St Nic 92–97; Dioc Supernumerary *Mor* 01–07; LtO from 08. *Rowan Glen, Upper Braefindon, Culbokie, Dingwall IV7 8GY* T: (01349) 877762 E: martin@roff-rowanglen.co.uk

ROFF, Canon John Michael. b 47. St Chad's Coll Dur BSc 69. Westcott Ho Cam 70. d 72 p 73. C Lancaster St Mary *Blackb* 72–75; C Dronfield *Derby* 75–76; TV 76–80; TR N Wingfield, Pilsley and Tupton 80–85; V Ilkeston St Mary 85–90; V Stockport St Geo *Ches* 90–94; TR Stockport SW 94–00; RD Stockport 95–00; Dioc Ecum Officer 92–99; Hon Can Ches Cathl 98–00; Can Res Ches Cathl 00–04; rtd 04; PtO *Ches* 05–06; *Blackb* from 05. *12 Westbourne Road, Lancaster LA1 5DB* T: (01524) 841621 E: roff@roff.org.uk

ROGERS, Anne Frances. *See* ILSLEY, Anne Frances

ROGERS, Brian Victor. b 50. Trin Coll Bris 75. d 78 p 79. C Plumstead St Jo w St Jas and St Paul *S'wark* 78–83; P-in-c Gayton *Nor* 83–85; P-in-c Gayton Thorpe w E Walton 83–85; P-in-c Westacre 83–85; P-in-c Ashwicken w Leziate 83–85; R Gayton Gp of Par 85–91; R Rackheath and Salhouse 91–96; P-in-c Warmington, Tansor, Cotterstock and Fotheringhay *Pet* 96–97; V Warmington, Tansor and Cotterstock etc 97–15; rtd 15. *Gortatlea, Mastergeehy, Killarney, Kerry, Republic of Ireland* E: bvictorr@hotmail.co.uk

ROGERS, Christopher Antony. b 47. NOC 79. d 81 p 82. C Chesterfield SS Aug *Derby* 81–84; C Chaddesden St Phil 84–86; R Whitwell 86–95; V W Burnley All SS *Blackb* 95–01; V Ashford St Hilda *Lon* 01–17; rtd 17; PtO *Lon* from 17; *St Alb* from 17. *17 Lochnell Road, Northchurch, Berkhamsted HP4 3QD* M: 07931-685100 E: chris1947rogers@gmail.com

ROGERS, Christopher Ian. b 79. Trin Coll Bris BA 01. K Coll Lon MA 05. d 07 p 08. NSM Roxeth *Lon* 07–10; C Shadwell St Paul w Ratcliffe St Jas from 10; C Bromley by Bow All Hallows 10–14; P-in-c 14–15; R from 15. *All Hallows' Rectory, Devons Road, London E3 3PN* T: (020) 7538 9756 M: 07974-371418 E: revcrisrogers@me.com

ROGERS, Christopher Thomas Augustine. b 80. CCC Cam MA 06 K Coll Lon MA 13 Barrister-at-Law 04. Westcott Ho Cam 15. d 18 p 19. Dep Chan *Ox* from 16; C Catford

(Southend) and Downham *S'wark* 18–21; C Kensington St Mary Abbots *Lon* from 21. *Cottage 1, St Mary Abbots Vicarage, Vicarage Gate, London W8 4HW* T: (020) 7937 2419 E: frchristopherrogers@outlook.com

ROGERS, Clive Trevor Thorne. b 49. SAOMC 02. **d** 05 **p** 06. NSM Beaconsfield *Ox* 05–10; PtO *Ex* 11–16 and from 21; NSM Kingsbridge, Dodbrooke, and W Alvington 16–21. *Leeward House, West Charleton, Kingsbridge TQ7 2AB* T: (01548) 531109 E: clivettrogers@gmail.com

ROGERS, Canon Clive William. b 62. Selw Coll Cam BA 83 MA 87 MEng 93 Southn Univ BTh 90. Chich Th Coll 87. **d** 90 **p** 91. C Leic St Aid 90–93; P-in-c Ryhall w Essendine *Pet* 93–94; LtO *Ely* 94–03; PtO 03–04; LtO *Sarum* 04–06; Hon C Forest and Avon 06–20; PtO from 20; Can and Preb Sarum Cathl 17–20. *Address temp unknown* E: bill@billrogers.info

ROGERS, Cyril David. b 55. Birm Univ BA 76 BTheol. Sarum & Wells Th Coll 80. **d** 83 **p** 84. C Leagrave *St Alb* 83–87; TV Langtree *Ox* 87–97; R Ballaugh *S & M* 97–12; V Michael 97–12; R Andreas, Ballaugh, Jurby and Sulby 12–16; RD Ramsey 12; Hon Can St German's Cathl 12–16; rtd 16; PtO *Win* from 17. *23 Chantry Mews, Basingstoke RG22 4UE* T: (01256) 359827 E: cdr851392@gmail.com

ROGERS, Damon. b 66. Cov Univ BEng 92 Wolv Univ PGCE 94 Warwick Univ BPhil 02. Cranmer Hall Dur 01. **d** 03 **p** 04. C Heigham St Thos *Nor* 03–06; R Freethorpe, Wickhampton, Halvergate etc 06–13; V Lowestoft St Andr from 13; Jt RD Lothingland 18–20; Asst Dioc Dir of Ords from 21. *51 Beresford Road, Lowestoft NR32 2NQ* T: (01502) 511521 E: damon.rogers@romanhill.org.uk

ROGERS, David Alan. b 55. City of Lon Poly BA 77 MCIT 82. Linc Th Coll 88. **d** 90 **p** 91. C Kingston upon Hull St Nic *York* 90–93; P-in-c Kingston upon Hull St Mary 93–96; N Humberside Ind Chapl 93–02; Dir Leeds Ch Inst *Ripon* 02–04; Chief Officer Hull Coun for Voluntary Service 04–12; TR Marfleet *York* 12–21; NSM Escrick and Stillingfleet w Naburn from 21; NSM Bubwith w Skipwith from 21. *The Vicarage, 19 Ings Road, Wilberfoss, York YO41 5NG*

ROGERS, David Barrie. b 46. S Dios Minl Tr Scheme 89. **d** 93. NSM Old Alresford and Bighton *Win* 93–96; Dep Warden Dioc Retreat Ho (Holland Ho) Cropthorne *Worc* 96–98; Warden Stacklands Retreat Ho W Kingsdown 98–03; Hon C Kingsdown *Roch* 98–03; Warden St Pet Bourne Cen 03–13; rtd 13. *16 Quay Road, Newton Abbott TQ12 2BU* E: adecon.dr@gmail.com

ROGERS, Mrs Gail. b 77. Qu Foundn Birm 16. **d** 18 **p** 19. C Bournville *Birm* from 18. *117 Sellywood Road, Birmingham B30 1XA* T: 0121-243 2199 M: 07941-765727 E: gailrogers18@outlook.com

ROGERS, Canon George Hutchinson. b 51. Windsor Univ Ontario BSW 75. Wycliffe Coll Toronto MDiv 78. **d** 78 **p** 78. C Victoria St Matthias Canada 78–81; R Cobble Hill and Cowichan Station 81–86; I Vancouver St Matthias 86–97; Hon C Vancouver St Helen 97–98; C Tonbridge SS Pet and Paul *Roch* 99–03; V Werrington *Pet* 03–21; Can Pet Cathl 18–21; rtd 21. *36 Fraserburgh Way, Orton Southgate, Peterborough PE2 6SS* E: george@revgeorgerogers.plus.com

ROGERS, George Michael Andrew. b 69. Yale Div Sch MDiv 95. **d** 99 **p** 99. C Brant Lake St Paul USA 99–00; C New York St Thos 00–03; C Pelham Ch Ch 03–10; C Staines *Lon* 10–13; P-in-c Milton next Sittingbourne Cant 13–16; P-in-c Murston w Bapchild and Tonge 13–16; V Milton Regis w Murston, Bapchild and Tonge 16–20; V Orpington All SS *Roch* from 20. *The Vicarage, 1A Keswick Road, Orpington BR6 0EU* M: 07527-746060 E: george.rogers3@gmail.com

ROGERS, Hayley. b 67. Reading Univ LLB 88. St Mellitus Coll 19. **d** 21. C Ashingdon w S Fambridge, Canewdon and Paglesham *Chelmsf* from 21. *St George's Vicarage, Rushbottom Lane, Benfleet SS7 4DN* M: 07773-700453 E: hayleyrogers@hotmail.co.uk

ROGERS, Jane. *See* LISVANE, Constance Jane

ROGERS, John. b 61. St Jo Coll Nottm 03. **d** 05 **p** 06. C Otley *Bradf* 05–08; V Oakworth 08–14; *Leeds* 14–19; V Meanwood from 19. *15 Parkside Green, Leeds LS6 4NY* E: john.rogers@leeds.anglican.org

ROGERS, John Arthur. b 47. MBIM. Edin Dioc NSM Course 90. **d** 92. C Middlesbrough St Martin *York* 92–93; NSM The Trimdons *Dur* 00–05; NSM Upper Skerne 05–07; R Tilehurst St Mich *Ox* 07–17; rtd 17; PtO *B & W* from 18. *Bow Cottage, Selworthy Green, Selworthy, Minehead TA24 8TP* T: (01643) 863100 E: rogj8@aol.com

ROGERS, John Howard. b 47. Ripon Coll Cuddesdon. **d** 09 **p** 09. NSM Southgate Ch Ch *Lon* 09–12; NSM Highgate All SS from 12; NSM Highgate St Mich from 12. *48 Twisden Road, London NW5 1DN* T: (020) 7485 6376 E: hrogers442@aol.com

ROGERS, John Robin. b 36. St Alb Minl Tr Scheme 78. **d** 81 **p** 82. NSM Digswell and Panshanger *St Alb* 81–84; C Welwyn w Ayot St Peter 85–92; R Wilden w Colmworth and Ravensden 92–99; rtd 99; PtO *St Alb* 99–02; *Heref* 03–19. *37 The Birches, Shobdon, Leominster HR6 9NG* T: (01568) 708903

ROGERS, Canon Kathleen. b 56. Open Univ BA 93 Leeds Univ BA 07. NOC 04. **d** 07 **p** 08. Sen Resources Officer *Liv* 93–09; NSM Formby H Trin 07–09; C 09–12; P-in-c Thornton and Crosby 12–13; V 13–21; Hon Can Liv Cathl 19–21; rtd 21. *24 Bronshill, The Serpentine South, Liverpool L23 6XG*

ROGERS, Canon Kathleen Anne. b 54. **d** 08 **p** 09. C Machynlleth w Llanwrin and Penegoes *Ban* 08–11; P-in-c 11–12; P-in-c Machynlleth w Corris w Llanwrin and Penegoes 12–14; P-in-c Bro Cyfeiliog and Mawddwy 14–18; rtd 18; PtO *Ban* from 18. *30 Tregarth, Machynlleth SY20 8HU* T: (01654) 702961 E: kathleenrogers@hotmail.co.uk

ROGERS, Kevin. b 62. Ridley Hall Cam 13. **d** 15 **p** 16. C Parkstone St Luke *Sarum* 15–19; R Abbas and Templecombe, Henstridge and Horsington *B & W* from 19; RD Bruton and Cary from 20. *The Vicarage, Church Street, Henstridge, Templecombe BA8 0QE* M: 07979-932241 E: revkrogers@gmail.com

ROGERS, Leon James. b 83. St Andr Univ MTheol 06. Qu Coll Birm MA 09. **d** 09 **p** 10. C E Darlington *Dur* 09–12; P-in-c Hartlepool St Aid and St Columba 12–17; R Creston Ch Ch Canada from 17. *430 7th Avenue North, Creston BC V0B 1G4, Canada* T: (001) (250) 428 4248 M: 07714-354771 E: lnrgrs@gmail.com

ROGERS, Canon Llewelyn. Univ of Wales (Lamp) BA 59. St Mich Coll Llan. **d** 61 **p** 62. C Holywell *St As* 61–64; C Hawarden 64–70; R Bodfari 70–73; V Rhosymedre 73–78; V Llansantffraid-ym-Mechain 77–83; V Llansantffraid-ym-Mechain and Llanfechain 83–98; RD Llanfyllin 84–88; V Pont Robert, Pont Dolanog, Garthbeibio etc 98–01; Can St As Cathl 98–01; rtd 01; PtO *Lich* 02–19; *St As* from 09. *17 Orchard Green, Llanymynech SY22 6PJ* T: (01691) 839920

ROGERS, Mrs Lynne Rosemary. b 49. CITC 00. **d** 03 **p** 04. Aux Min Ferns w Kilbride, Toombe, Kilcormack etc *C, F & O* 03–06; Aux Min Gorey w Kilnahue, Leskinfere and Ballycanew 06–07; P-in-c New w Old Ross, Whitechurch, Fethard etc 07–11; NSM Chartham *Cant* 11–14; NSM Stone Street Gp 11–14; C Chartham and Upper Hardres w Stelling 14–16; rtd 16; PtO *Sarum* from 17. *1 Boyte Road, Pimperne, Blandford Forum DT11 8UY* T: (01258) 456202 E: lynnerogers123@gmail.com

ROGERS, Malcolm Dawson. b 63. SS Hild & Bede Coll Dur BA 84 Selw Coll Cam BA 88. Ridley Hall Cam 86. **d** 89 **p** 90. C Ipswich St Jo *St E* 89–93; CMS Russia 93–95; C Holloway St Mary Magd *Lon* 95–97; V 97–05; V Bury St Edmunds St Mary *St E* 05–17; Hon Can St E Cathl 13–17; Chapl Moscow *Eur* from 17. *8/5 Voznesensky Pereulok, Moscow 125009, Russia* T: (007) (495) 629 0990 E: malcolm.d.rogers@gmail.com

ROGERS, Canon Malcolm Kenneth. b 72. MBE 16. Liv Inst of Educn BA 93. St Jo Coll Nottm MA 95 LTh 96. **d** 96 **p** 97. C W Derby St Luke *Liv* 96–00; V Huyton Quarry from 00; AD Huyton from 18; Hon Can Liv Cathl from 13. *St Gabriel's Vicarage, 2 St Agnes Road, Huyton, Liverpool L36 5TA* T: 0151-489 2688 E: malcolm.rogers@huytondeanery.org

ROGERS, Mark James. b 64. Univ of Wales (Lamp) BA. Qu Coll Birm. **d** 89 **p** 90. C Dudley St Aug Holly Hall *Worc* 89–93; C Worc St Barn w Ch Ch 93–94; TV 94–97; USPG Belize 97–00; R Montreal St Columba Canada from 00. *4020 Hingston Avenue, Montreal QC H4A 2J7, Canada* T: (001) (514) 486 1753

ROGERS, Martin Brian. b 53. **d** 92 **p** 93. OLM Collyhurst *Man* from 92. *8 Greenford Road, Crumpsall, Manchester M8 0NW* T: 0161-740 4614 E: m.rogers17@ntlworld.com

ROGERS, Michael Andrew. b 47. OBE 91. FRAeS 96. Ripon Coll Cuddesdon. **d** 01 **p** 02. C Bromsgrove St Jo *Worc* 01–04; R Berrow w Pendock, Eldersfield, Hollybush etc 04–13; rtd 13; PtO *Ches* from 14. *York House, Wyche Lane, Bunbury, Tarporley CW6 9PD* T: (01829) 261682 E: mandmrogers@btinternet.com

ROGERS, Michael Ernest. b 34. Open Univ BA 20. Sarum & Wells Th Coll 83. **d** 85 **p** 86. C Roehampton H Trin *S'wark* 85–88; V Ryhill *Wakef* 88–94; V S Elmsall 94–00; rtd 00; PtO *Derby* from 00. *The Willows, 49 Main Street, Weston-on-Trent, Derby DE72 2BL* T: (01332) 706654 E: michaelrogers1398@gmail.com

ROGERS, Michael Hugh Walton. b 52. K Coll Lon BD 73 AKC 73. St Aug Coll Cant 74. **d** 75 **p** 76. C Eastbourne St Andr *Chich* 75–78; C Uppingham w Ayston *Pet* 78–82; V Eye 82–90; R Cottesmore and Barrow w Ashwell and Burley

90–04; C 04–09; C Greetham and Thistleton w Stretton and Clipsham 01–05; P-in-c 05–09; C Empingham and Exton w Horn w Whitwell 06–09; RD Rutland 95–00; Can Pet Cathl 01–09; Bp's Adv for Min of Healing 05–09; P-in-c Ilfracombe SS Phil and Jas w W Down *Ex* 09–15; R Ilfracombe SS Phil and Jas 15–18; rtd 18. *7 Meadow Park, Molland, South Molton EX36 3ND* E: mhwrogers76@gmail.com

ROGERS, Mrs Patricia Anne. b 54. Lon Univ BD. Trin Coll Bris. d 87 p 94. Hon C Gayton Gp of Par *Nor* 87–91; Hon C Rackheath and Salhouse 91–96; Chapl to the Deaf 91–96; Chapl to the Deaf *Pet* 96–00; Visual Communications 00–11; TR Binsey *Carl* 11–19; Min Kendal Methodist Chs 19–20; Disability Adv *Carl* from 19; C Beacon TM 19–20; P-in-c from 20. *Church House, 19-24 Friargate, Penrith CA11 7XR* T: (01768) 807777

ROGERS, Patricia Gladys Sylvia. b 48. d 13 p 14. NSM Llanrhian and Mathry w Grandstone etc *St D* 13–14; NSM Letterston w Llanfair Nant-y-Gof etc 14–18. *Crud yr Awel, Wolfscastle, Haverfordwest SA62 5LT* T: (01437) 741338 E: raprogers@btinternet.com *or* parishoffice@stgileslet.plus.com

ROGERS, Pauline Ann. *See* GODFREY, Pauline Ann

ROGERS, Philip John. b 52. Univ of Wales CertEd 74. St Jo Coll Nottm BTh 79. d 79 p 80. C Stretford St Bride *Man* 79–84; P-in-c Plumstead St Jo w St Jas and St Paul *S'wark* 84–85; V 85–20; rtd 20. *17 Crocus Avenue, Minster on Sea, Sheerness ME12 3GX* T: (01795) 876507 E: philipjrogers@aol.co.uk

ROGERS (née GOLDER), Mrs Rebecca Marie (Beki). b 71. Brunel Univ BA 94. Trin Coll Bris BA 02. d 02 p 03. C Short Heath *Birm* 02–05; Dir Faith Willesden Area *Lon* from 05; NSM Roxeth 05–10; NSM Bromley by Bow All Hallows from 10; Prin St Edm Course from 18; Dir Lon Cen for Spiritual Direction from 19. *All Hallows' Rectory, Devons Road, London E3 3PN* T: (020) 7538 9756 E: bekirogers@gmail.com *or* beki.rogers@london.anglican.org

ROGERS, Richard Anthony. b 46. Ex Coll Ox BA 69. Qu Coll Birm 70. d 71 p 72. C Shirley *Birm* 71–74; Chapl Solihull Sch 74–78; Hon C Cotteridge *Birm* 78–84; Hon C Hill 84–93; Hd RE Kings Norton Girls' Sch 93–05; rtd 05; PtO *Birm* 93–07. *4 Byron House, Belwell Place, Sutton Coldfield B74 4AY* T: 0121-308 0310

ROGERS, Canon Robert. b 42. Bernard Gilpin Soc Dur 66 St Aid Birkenhead 67 Ridley Hall Cam 69. d 70 p 71. C Childwall St Dav *Liv* 70–73; C Huntington *York* 73–76; TR Brayton 76–89; RD Selby 84–89; V New Malton 89–98; RD Bulmer and Malton 97–98; Sen Chapl York Hosps NHS Foundn Trust 98–08; Can and Preb York Minster 03–08; rtd 08; PtO *York* from 08; Succ Canonicorum York Minster 11–18. *Tabgha, 9 Middlecave Drive, Malton YO17 7BB* T: (01653) 699469 E: bob.jacqui@btinternet.com

ROGERS, Robert Charles. b 55. Warwick Univ MA 99 St Pet Coll Birm CertEd 77. St Jo Coll Nottm 87. d 89 p 90. C Wellesbourne *Cov* 89–93; R Bourton w Frankton and Stretton on Dunsmore etc 93–97; Specialist Support Teacher Warks LEA 98–18; LtO *Cov* 98–20; NSM Rugby 07–13; PtO from 20; *Pet* from 20. *18 Waring Way, Dunchurch, Rugby CV22 6PH* T: (01788) 817361 E: rob.rogers@talktalk.net

ROGERS, Robin. *See* ROGERS, John Robin

ROGERS, Ryder Rondeau. b 44. Lon Bible Coll 62. d 08 p 08. In Bapt Min 68–04; NSM Bride Valley *Sarum* 08–16; PtO from 16. *Stonehaven, 25 Bindbarrow Road, Burton Bradstock, Bridport DT6 4RG* T: (01308) 897780

ROGERS, Ms Sally Jean. b 54. Univ of Wales (Lamp) BA 77 Nottm Univ BTh 87. Linc Th Coll 84. d 87 p 94. Par Dn Bris St Mary Redcliffe w Temple etc 87–90; Par Dn Greenford H Cross *Lon* 90–94; C 94–96; TV Hemel Hempstead *St Alb* 96–02; Development Worker Changing Attitude 03–06; Chapl R Holloway and Bedf New Coll *Guildf* 06–10; R Petryal and Betws yn Rhos *St As* 10–16; TV Aled Miss Area 17–18; rtd 18. *1 Warren Road, Deganwy, Conwy LL31 9SU*

ROGERS, Sarah Ann. b 73. York Univ BSc 94 Univ of Wales (Cardiff) PhD 98. St Mich Coll Llan BA 09. d 09 p 10. C Caerphilly *Llan* 09–12; P-in-c Abercynon 12–17; Dom Chapl Bp Llan from 17. *The Maisonette, Pendinas, The Cathedral Green, Cardiff CF5 2EB* T: (029) 2056 2400 E: sarahrogers@churchinwales.org.uk

ROGERS, Timothy Harold. b 73. Sheff Univ BEng 94 Aston Univ Dur BSc 95. Ridley Hall Cam 14. d 16 p 17. NSM Redenhall w Scole *Nor* 16–20; V Yoxmere *St E* from 20. *The Rectory, The Street, Darsham, Saxmundham IP17 3QA* M: 07887-352564 E: timrogers197@gmail.com

ROGERS, Valentine Hilary. b 48. UCD BA 68. St Columban's Coll Navan 65. d 71 p 72. C Dandenong Australia 88–89; P-in-c Eltham 89–92; I 92–96; C Dublin Ch Ch Cathl Gp and PV Ch Ch Cathl Dublin *D & G* 96–97; I Armadale H Advent Australia 98–09; I Aughaval w Achill, Knappagh, Dugort etc

T, K & A 09–19; Can Tuam Cathl 14–19; Can Killala Cathl 14–19; rtd 19. *1 Riverside, Castlebar Road, Newport, Westport, Co Mayo, F28 VW40, Republic of Ireland* M: (00353) 87-147 5597 E: valandjorogers@gmail.com *or* revdvalrogers@gmail.com

ROGERS, William. *See* ROGERS, Clive William

ROGERS, William John. b 71. SEITE 07. d 10 p 11. C Wimbledon Park St Luke *S'wark* 10–14; V Fulham St Matt *Lon* from 14. *St Matthew's Vicarage, 2 Clancarty Road, London SW6 3AB* T: (020) 7731 3272 M: 07879-084321 E: william@stmf.org.uk

ROGERSON, Anthony Carroll. b 37. Trin Coll Ox BA 59 MA 63 MCIPD 92. SAOMC 96. d 98 p 99. NSM Radley and Sunningwell *Ox* 98–02; PtO from 02. *9 Selwyn Crescent, Radley, Abingdon OX14 3AW* T: (01235) 550214

✠ROGERSON, The Rt Revd Barry. b 36. Leeds Univ BA 60 Bris Univ Hon LLD 93. Wells Th Coll 60. d 62 p 63 c 79. C S Shields St Hilda w St Thos *Dur* 62–65; C Bishopwearmouth St Nic 65–67; Lect Lich Th Coll 67–71; Vice-Prin 71–72; Lect Sarum & Wells Th Coll 72–74; V Wednesfield St Thos *Lich* 75–79; TR Wednesfield 79; Suff Bp Wolverhampton 79–85; Bp Bris 85–02; rtd 02; Hon Asst Bp B & W from 03. *Flat 2, 30 Albert Road, Clevedon BS21 7RR* T: (01275) 541964 E: barry.rogerson@blueyonder.co.uk

ROGERSON, Colin Scott. b 30. St Andr Univ MA 55. Edin Th Coll. d 57 p 58. C Byker St Ant *Newc* 57–59; C Newc St Geo 59–63; C Wooler 63–67; V Tynemouth St Aug 67–75; C Dur St Marg 75–88; P-in-c Hebburn St Jo 88–95; rtd 95; PtO *Dur* 95–17. *6 Edlingham Road, Durham DH1 5YS* T: 0191-386 1956

ROGERSON, Canon Ian Matthew. b 45. Open Univ BA 76 Bede Coll Dur CertEd 67. Oak Hill Th Coll. d 83 p 84. C Haughton St Mary *Man* 83–86; V Ramsbottom St Andr 86–05; P-in-c Edenfield and Stubbins 04–05; TR Ramsbottom and Edenfield 05–10; AD Bury 96–05; Hon Can Man Cathl 04–10; rtd 10; PtO *Man* 10–14; *St D* from 10; *Llan* from 17. *16 Heol Erwin, Cardiff CF14 6QP* T: (029) 2062 1849 E: ian@rogerson.org.uk

ROLAND, Andrew Osborne. b 45. Mert Coll Ox BA 66 St Jo Coll Dur BA 84. Cranmer Hall Dur. d 84 p 85. C Streatham St Leon *S'wark* 84–87; C Kingston All SS w St Jo 87–94; P-in-c Hackbridge and Beddington Corner 94–06; V 06–15; rtd 15; PtO *Lon* from 16. *Flat 2, 100 Philbeach Gardens, London SW5 9ET* T: (020) 7370 7431 E: aoroland@gmail.com

ROLES, John William. b 54. Middx Poly BA 76 Whitelands Coll Lon PGCE 77. Ripon Coll Cuddesdon 11. d 12 p 13. NSM Ilfracombe, Lee, Woolacombe, Bittadon etc *Ex* 12–16; P-in-c 16–20; TR from 20. *The New Vicarage, St Brannock's Road, Ilfracombe EX34 8EG* T: (01271) 863350 E: johnroles@talk21.com

ROLFE, Joseph William. b 37. Qu Coll Birm 78. d 81 p 82. NSM Tredington and Darlingscott w Newbold on Stour *Cov* 81–91; NSM Brailes from 91; NSM Sutton under Brailes from 91; NSM Shipston Deanery from 98. *35 Manor Lane, Shipston-on-Stour CV36 4EF* T: (01608) 661737

ROLFE, Paul Douglas. b 46. MIBC 90. NOC 90. d 93 p 94. C Urmston *Man* 93–96; V Lawton Moor 96–03; P-in-c Burnage St Nic 03–07; Sen Chapl Costa Blanca *Eur* 07–08; P-in-c Mellor *Blackb* 09–11; P-in-c Balderstone 09–11; rtd 12; PtO *Leeds* from 17. *51A Westfield Lane, Scholes, Cleckheaton BD19 6DR* T: (01274) 690476 E: paul.d.rolfe@btinternet.com

ROLFE, Mrs Susan Margaret. b 58. Man Univ BA 81. ERMC 05. d 08 p 09. NSM Pet Ch Carpenter 08–11; NSM Paston 11–12; NSM Pet St Paul 13; rtd 13; NSM Wellingborough St Mark *Pet* 15–17; PtO from 17; Chapl HM Pris Littlehey from 17; PtO *Ely* from 21. *11 Wansford Road, Elton, Peterborough PE8 6RZ* E: susan.m.rolfe@btinternet.com

ROLLETT, Robert Henry. b 39. Leeds Univ BA 61 Leic Univ CertEd 62. Linc Th Coll 77. d 79 p 80. C Littleport *Ely* 79–82; P-in-c Manea 82–83; V 83–85; P-in-c Wimblington 83–85; R 83–85; V Thorney Abbey 85–93; P-in-c The Ramseys and Upwood 93–94; TR 94–99; rtd 99; P-in-c Scalford w Goadby Marwood and Wycombe etc *Leic* 99–00; PtO *Pet* 01–05. *2 Stockerson Crescent, Uppingham, Oakham LE15 9UB* T: (01572) 823685 E: r.rollett@btinternet.com

ROLLINGS, Mrs Tina Petula. b 51. St Mellitus Coll 12. d 13 p 14. OLM Chingford SS Pet and Paul *Chelmsf* 13–17; PtO 17–18; *Ox* from 18. *Address temp unknown* E: tinaprollings@aol.com

ROLLINS, David. b 65. De Montfort Univ BA 98. St Steph Ho Ox 99. d 01 p 02. C Leic St Aid 01–05; P-in-c Corringham *Chelmsf* 05–10; P-in-c Fobbing 05–10; R Corringham and Fobbing from 10. *The Rectory, Church Road, Corringham, Stanford-le-Hope SS17 9AP* T: (01375) 673074 E: drollins@btinternet.com

ROLLINS, Deborah Mary. *See* FLACH, Deborah Mary Rollins

ROLLINSON, James Christopher. b 50. **d** 13 **p** 14. NSM Carmarthen St Pet and Abergwili *etc St D* 13–14; C Cynwyl Elfed w Newchurch and Trelech a'r Betws 14–17; rtd 18. *Ysgubor Fawr, Pencader SA39 9BU* E: jim.rollinson@gmail.com

ROLLS (*née* **Jobling**), **Mary.** b 77. Aachen University BPharm 99 Derby Univ MSc 03. Cranmer Hall Dur 13. **d** 15 **p** 16. C Cayton w Eastfield *York* 15–17; C Eastfield 17–19; 20s-40s Team Ldr from 19; C Thirsk from 19. *6 Turkhan Close, Thirsk YO7 1GA* E: maryjobling@hotmail.com

ROLLS, Miss Pamela Margaret. b 59. **d** 10 **p** 11. OLM Harwell w Chilton *Ox* from 10. *15 Elderfield Crescent, Chilton, Didcot OX11 0RY* T: (01235) 834475 E: pamrolls@tiscali.co.uk

ROLLS, Peter. b 40. Leeds Inst of Educn CertEd. NOC 80. **d** 83 **p** 84. NSM Meltham *Wakef* 83–14; *Leeds* from 14. *14 Heather Road, Meltham, Huddersfield HD7 3EY* T: (01484) 340342 E: p.c.rolls@hotmail.com

ROLT (*formerly* **SHARPLES**), **Mrs Jean.** b 37. Padgate Coll of Educn TCert 58. **d** 04 **p** 05. NSM Gerrans w St Anthony-in-Roseland and Philleigh *Truro* 04–08; NSM St Just-in-Roseland and St Mawes 05–08; rtd 08; PtO *Truro* from 14. *Tregear Vean Farmhouse, St Mawes, Truro TR2 5AB* T: (01326) 270954 M: 07840-567933 E: revjeanrolt@mac.com

ROLTON, Patrick Hugh. b 49. Sarum & Wells Th Coll 72. **d** 74 **p** 75. C Roch St Pet w St Marg 74–79; C Edenbridge 79–81; R N Cray 81–97; rtd 97. *71 The Grove, Sidcup DA14 5NG* E: pcrolton@virginmedia.com

ROMANIS, Adam John Aidan. b 57. Pemb Coll Ox BA 78 MA 83. Westcott Ho Cam 81. **d** 84 **p** 85. C Northfield *Birm* 84–88; TV Seaton Hirst *Newc* 88–93; V Newc Ch Ch w St Ann 93–99; V Cowley St Jo *Ox* 99–14; V Perry Beeches *Birm* 14–20; P-in-c Heslington *York* from 20; P-in-c York St Lawr w St Nic from 20. *The Vicarage, 11 Newland Park Close, York YO10 3HW* E: adam.romanis@btinternet.com

RONCHETTI, Canon Quentin Marcus. b 56. Ripon Coll Cuddesdon 79. **d** 80 **p** 81. C Eastbourne St Mary *Chich* 80–83; C Moulsecoomb 83–85; TV 85–90; V Findon Valley *Chich* 90–97; V Shoreham Beach 97–07; V Midhurst 07–12; Chapl Costa Blanca *Eur* 12–15; Sen Chapl from 15; Hon Can from 21. *Partida Cuxarret 20C, 03710 Calpe (Alicante), Spain* T: (0034) 965 874 166 *or* 603 259 769 E: marcusronchetti@yahoo.co.uk

ROOKE, James Templeman. b 43. Saltley Tr Coll *Birm* CertEd 65. EMMTC 79. **d** 84 **p** 85. NSM Bassingham *Linc* 84–89; NSM Hykeham 89–94; Sub Chapl HM Pris Morton Hall 94; P-in-c Borrowdale *Carl* 94–97; Chapl Keswick Sch 94–95; NSM Hykeham *Linc* 97–02; Sub Chapl HM Pris Morton Hall 97–00; CF (ACF) 00–08; NSM Swinderby *Linc* from 02. *The Chestnuts, Main Street, Norton Disney, Lincoln LN6 9JU* T: (01522) 788315 E: jim.rooke@lincoln.anglican.org

✠**ROOKE, The Rt Revd Patrick William.** b 55. Open Univ BA 85 TCD MPhil 04. Sarum & Wells Th Coll 75. **d** 78 **p** 79 **c** 11. C Mossley *Conn* 78–81; C Ballywillan 81–83; I Craigs w Dunaghy and Killagan 83–88; I Ballymore *Arm* 88–94; Asst Prov and Dioc Registrar 92–94; Hon V Choral Arm Cathl 93–94; I Agherton *Conn* 94–06; Preb and Can Conn Cathl 01–06; Adn Dalriada 05–06; Dean Arm and Keeper of Public Lib 06–11; Bp T, K & A 11–21; rtd 21. *18 Dundooan Road, Coleraine BT52 1SF* E: rooke59@hotmail.com

ROOKWOOD, Colin John. b 40. TCD BA 64 MA 66 SS Mark & Jo Coll Chelsea PGCE 66. Clifton Th Coll 67. **d** 70 **p** 71. C Eccleston Ch Ch *Liv* 70–75; V Penge St Jo *Roch* 75–82; V Childwall All SS *Liv* 82–91; Chapl Bethany Sch Goudhurst 91–03; rtd 03; PtO *Roch* 01–10; *Ches* 11–14 and 19–21. *11 Coppice Road, Poynton, Stockport SK12 1SL* T: 0161-877 540 M: 07803-507673 E: colinrookwood@icloud.com

ROOKWOOD (*née* **TASH**), **Elizabeth.** b 82. Leeds Univ BA 05 St Jo Coll Dur MATM. Cranmer Hall Dur 12. **d** 15 **p** 16. C Morpeth *Newc* 15–19; Bp's Adv for Pioneer Min from 19. *1 Barns Farm, Netherwitton, Morpeth NE61 4NW* M: 07793-964392

ROOMS (*née* **JONES**), **Canon Karen Sheila Frances.** b 61. Bris Univ BA 82. St Jo Coll Nottm MTh 06. **d** 06 **p** 07. C Hyson Green and Forest Fields *S'well* 06–09; P-in-c Nottingham St Ann w Em 09–11; V 11–16; AD Nottm S 13–16; Can Res Leic Cathl from 16; P-in-c Leic H Spirit 16–21; Women's Min Enabler from 19. *St Andrew's Church Vicarage, 53B Jarrom Street, Leicester LE2 7DH* M: 07906-899611 E: roomskaren@gmail.com *or* karen.rooms@leccofe.org

ROOMS, Canon Nigel James. b 60. Leeds Univ BSc 81 Nottm Univ MA 95 Birm Univ ThD 08 CEng 86 MIChemE 86. St Jo Coll Nottm 87. **d** 90 **p** 91. C Chell *Lich* 90–94; Min Moshi St Marg Tanzania 94–01; Dir Th Educn by Ext 94–01; Hon Can Arusha from 01; Dioc Dir of Tr *S'well* 01–07; Assoc Dir Practical Th 07–10; P-in-c Basford St Leodegarius 07–09; Dir Min and Miss 10–16; C Bestwood Park w Rise Park 10–16; Ldr Partnership for Missional Ch UK CMS from 16; NSM

Braunstone Park *Leic* from 17. *St Andrew's Church Vicarage, 53B Jarrom Street, Leicester LE2 7DH* M: 07920-292956 E: nigel.rooms@churchmissionsociety.org

ROONEY, Andrew John. b 59. Univ Coll Ox MA 81. St Mellitus Coll BA 15. **d** 15 **p** 16. NSM Hammersmith H Innocents and St Jo *Lon* 15–19; NSM White City from 19. *123 Duke Road, London W4 2BX* T: (020) 8994 3216 M: 07788-414408 E: andy@rooneyw4.net

ROOSE, Lucy Josephine. b 71. Man Univ BA 92. Sarum Coll 18. **d** 21. C Crondall and Ewshot *Guildf* from 21. *17 Conifer Close, Church Crookham, Fleet GU52 6LR* M: 07496-909828 E: lucyroosey@gmail.com

ROOSE-EVANS, James Humphrey. b 27. St Benet's Hall Ox BA 52 MA 56. **d** 81 **p** 81. NSM Kington and Weobley *Heref* 81–05; NSM Primrose Hill St Mary w Avenue Road St Paul *Lon* 82–97; PtO *Heref* 05–13; *S & B* 07–13; *Lon* from 97. *26B Upper Park Road, London NW3 2UT* T: (020) 7586 6507 E: j.rooseevans@btinternet.com

ROOT, Preb John Brereton. b 41. Lon Univ BA 64 Em Coll Cam BA 66 MA. Ridley Hall Cam 64. **d** 68 **p** 69. C Harlesden St Mark *Lon* 68–73; C Lower Homerton St Paul 73–76; Chapl Ridley Hall Cam 76; Vice-Prin 76–79; V Alperton *Lon* 79–95; AD Brent 95–00; Preb St Paul's Cathl 01–11; rtd 11; Licensed Preacher Under Seal Lic Preacher *Lon* from 12. *42 Newlyn Road, London N17 6RX* M: 07723-033831 E: stjames.john@gmail.com

ROOTES, William Brian. b 44. St And NSM Tr Scheme 88. **d** 91. NSM Auchterarder *St And* 91–97; NSM Muthill 91–97; Dioc Sec 98–00; Treas Action of Chs Together in Scotland 01–06; LtO *St And* from 06. *The Old School House, Fowlis Wester, Crieff PH7 3NL* T: (01764) 683772 E: w.rootes77@btinternet.com

ROOTHAM, Gerald Raymond. b 47. **d** 02 **p** 03. OLM Mattishall and the Tudd Valley *Nor* 02–10; C 10–14; rtd 15; PtO *Nor* from 15; *Eur* from 18. *8 Burgh Lane, Mattishall, Dereham NR20 3QW* T: (01362) 858533 E: geraldrootham@outlook.com

ROPER, David John. b 53. St Steph Ho Ox 93. **d** 95 **p** 96. C Hunstanton St Mary w Ringstead Parva *etc Nor* 95–98; TV E Dereham and Scarning 98–00; R Barham w Bishopsbourne and Kingston *Cant* 00–08; C Nonington w Wymynswold and Goodnestone *etc* 00–08; AD E Bridge 01–08; P-in-c Broadstairs 08–11; R 11–14; AD Thanet 08–09; P-in-c St Peter-in-Thanet 10–11; Hon Min Can Cant Cathl 03–08; Hon Can Cant Cathl 08–14; R Ch Ch Cathl and the Falkland Is 14–15; R Poppyland *Nor* 15–18; Hon PV Nor Cathl 16–18; rtd 18; PtO *Nor* from 19; Chapl Monte Carlo *Eur* from 21. *Chaplain's House, 22 avenue de Grande-Bretagne, MC 98000, Monaco* T: (0033) 6 40 61 03 85 M: 07464-693701   E: davidjroper53@gmail.com *or* chaplain@stpaulsmonaco.com

ROPER, Glenn. b 51. York Univ MA 91 Caerleon Coll of Educn CertEd 73. **d** 04 **p** 05. NSM Ovenden *Wakef* 04–14; *Leeds* from 14. *113 Meadow Drive, Halifax HX3 5JZ* T: (01422) 368086 E: glennroperhfx@gmail.com

ROPER, Mrs Joan. b 49. **d** 10 **p** 11. NSM Newport w Longford, and Chetwynd *Lich* 10–12; NSM Tong, Shifnal and Sheriffhales 12–13; NSM Gt and Lt Ouseburn w Marton cum Grafton *etc Leeds* 13–19; PtO 21. *11 Back Lane, Whixley, York YO26 8BG* T: (01423) 331661 E: revjoanroper@outlook.com

ROPER, Michael Darwin Alston. b 66. Leeds Univ BA 03. Coll of Resurr Mirfield 01. **d** 03 **p** 04. C Mortlake w E Sheen *S'wark* 03–07; P-in-c Egham Hythe *Guildf* 07–16; P-in-c Epsom St Barn 16–19; V Malden St Jo *S'wark* from 19. *The Vicarage, 5 Vicarage Close, Worcester Park KT4 7LZ* E: gore_lodge@yahoo.co.uk *or* stjohnsmaldenoffice@gmail.com

ROSAMOND, Derek William. b 49. Linc Th Coll 87. **d** 89 **p** 90. C Coventry Caludon *Cov* 89–93; Urban Regeneration Chapl S Tyneside *Dur* 93–96; TV Sunderland 96–04; P-in-c Stockton St Paul 04–15; Community P SW Stockton 04–15; rtd 15. *28 Stoneybrough Lane, Thirsk YO7 2LS* E: derekrosamond@hotmail.com

ROSBOROUGH, Mrs Rachel Claire. b 76. Anglia Poly Univ BA 00 Ches Univ MA 14. St Jo Coll Nottm 06. **d** 08 **p** 09. C Charlton Kings H Apostles *Glouc* 08–11; R Bourton-on-the-Water w Clapton *etc* 11–17; P-in-c Cambridge St Mark *Ely* 17–20; V from 20; P-in-c Grantchester 17–20; V from 20; RD Cambridge S from 21; Chapl Wolfs Coll Cam from 17; Past Tutor Ridley Hall Cam from 18. *The Vicarage, 44 High Street, Grantchester, Cambridge CB3 9NF* T: (01223) 845634 E: rachelrosborough@hotmail.com

ROSCOE, David John. b 64. UEA BA 87 Selw Coll Cam BA 93. Aston Tr Scheme 89 Westcott Ho Cam 91. **d** 94 **p** 95. C Ditton St Mich *Liv* 94–98; TV Kirkby 98–99; V Wigan St Steph 99–03; Jt P-in-c Aspull and New Springs 02–03; V New Springs and Whelley and Chapl Wrightington, Wigan and Leigh NHS Foundn Trust 03–10; P-in-c Feniscowles *Blackb* from 10; C Blackb St Fran and St Aid 13–14; P-in-c Feniscliffe from 14. *The Vicarage, 732 Preston Old Road, Feniscowles, Blackburn BB2 5EN* T: (01254) 201236

ROSE (*née* **ARDLEY), Annette Susan.** b 68. SEITE 01. **d** 04 **p** 05. C Barham w Bishopsbourne and Kingston *Cant* 04–07; P-in-c Wingham w Elmstone and Preston w Stourmouth 07–09; P-in-c New Eltham All SS *S'wark* 09–10; V from 10. *All Saints' Vicarage, 22 Bercta Road, London SE9 3TZ* T: (020) 8850 0374 E: revannette.rose@btinternet.com

ROSE, Anthony James. b 47. Trin Coll Bris BD 72. **d** 73 **p** 74. C Hallwell St Pet *Man* 73–76; CF 76–94; R Colchester Ch Ch w St Mary V *Chelmsf* 94–01; RD Colchester 98–01; P-in-c Boreham 01–06; rtd 06; PtO *Chelmsf* from 06. *30 The Mill Apartments, East Street, Colchester CO1 2QT* T: (01206) 616739 E: aj.rose@talktalk.net

ROSE, Anthony John. b 53. Birm Univ BA 79. Trin Coll Bris 84. **d** 86 **p** 87. C The Quinton *Birm* 86–90; R Abbas and Templecombe w Horsington *B & W* 90–98; V New Thundersley *Chelmsf* 98–19; rtd 19; PtO *Sarum* from 20. *1 Freeman Road, Devizes SN10 3FF*

ROSE, Canon Bernard Frederick. b 47. **d** 91 **p** 92. OLM Ipswich St Thos *St E* 91–09; P-in-c Somersham w Flowton and Offton w Willisham 09–15; P-in-c Ringshall w Battisford, Barking w Darmsden etc 09–15; Hon Can St E Cathl from 05; rtd 15; PtO *St E* from 15. *84 Chesterfield Drive, Ipswich IP1 6DN* T: (01473) 462390 E: holy-rose@supanet.com

ROSE, Christopher John. b 66. Edin Univ BSc 88. EAMTC 97. **d** 00 **p** 01. NSM Cambridge St Paul *Ely* from 00; NSM All Hallows Lon Wall 07–14; P-in-c St Clem Eastcheap w St Martin Orgar 14–19; PtO from 21. *6 Montreal Road, Cambridge CB1 3NP* T: (01223) 511241 M: 07758-650512 E: chris@amostrust.org

ROSE, Miss Eileen Cynthia. b 64. Univ of E Lon MA 02. St Mellitus Coll 16. **d** 19 **p** 20. NSM Leyton Em *Chelmsf* from 19. *57 Belvedere Road, London E10 7NW* T: (020) 8923 9477 M: 07930-269877 E: eileen.rose64@btinternet.com

ROSE, Miss Geraldine Susan. b 47. Trin Coll Bris BD 78. dss 78 **d** 87 **p** 94. Tonbridge St Steph *Roch* 78–80; Littleover *Derby* 80–88; Par Dn 87–88; Par Dn Wombwell *Sheff* 88–94; C 94–96; rtd 96; PtO *Sheff* from 96. *5 Wheatcroft, Conisbrough, Doncaster DN12 2BL* T: (01709) 867761

ROSE, Harry. See ROSE, Lionel Stafford Harry

ROSE, Ms Helen Anita. b 63. STETS 09. **d** 12 **p** 13. C Shoreham Beach *Chich* 12–14; C New Shoreham and Shoreham Beach 14–16; C Chich St Paul and Westhampnett 16–17; P-in-c Woodingdean 17–19; V from 19. *The Vicarage, 2 Downsway, Brighton BN2 6BD* M: 07971-779284 E: revrosyrosy@gmail.com

ROSE, Ingrid Elizabeth. b 57. Univ of Wales (Abth) BA 78 DipEd 79. Trin Coll Carmarthen 84. **d** 87 **p** 01. NSM Ysbyty Cynfyn w Llantrisant and Eglwys Newydd *St D* 87–90 and 92–95; NSM to Adn Cardigan 00–03; NSM Grwp Bro Ystwyth a Mynach 03–13; PtO from 13. *Ystwyth Villa, Pontrhydygroes, Ystrad Meurig SY25 6DS* T: (01974) 282728 E: ingridrose@btinternet.com

ROSE, John Clement Wansey. b 46. New Coll Ox BA 71 MA 72. Ripon Hall Ox 70. **d** 72 **p** 73. C Harborne St Pet *Birm* 72–76; TV Kings Norton 76–81; V Maney 81–02; R Condover w Frodesley, Acton Burnell etc *Heref* 02–12; rtd 12; PtO *Lich* from 13. *32 Park Lane, High Ercall, Telford TF6 6AY* T: (01952) 770243

ROSE, Jonathan Graham. b 47. Leeds Univ BA 72 Birm Univ PGCE 73 MEd 83 Ex Univ MA 08 Bris Univ MPhil 17 FRSA 97 MCIPD 03. STETS 10. **d** 11 **p** 12. NSM Quantock Towers *B & W* 11–17; RD Quantock 15–17; PtO from 17; *Ex* from 19. *Rosemount, Cottington Mead, Sidmouth EX10 8HB* T: (01395) 512094 M: 07969-008091 E: revjonrose@gmail.com

ROSE, Judith Barbara. b 51. TCert 72. SAOMC 96. **d** 99 **p** 00. OLM Stantonbury and Willen Ox 99–11; PtO from 11. *16 Runnymede, Giffard Park, Milton Keynes MK14 5QL* T/F: (01908) 618634

ROSE, The Ven Kathleen Judith. b 37. Lon Bible Coll BD 73 St Mich Ho Ox 64. dss 76 **d** 87 **p** 94. Leeds St Geo *Ripon* 76–81; Bradf Cathl 81–85; S Gillingham *Roch* 85–87; Par Dn 87–90; RD Gillingham 88–90; Bp's Dom Chapl 90–95; Asst Dir of Ords 90–95; Hon Can Roch Cathl 93–02; Acting Adn Tonbridge 95–96; Adn Tonbridge 96–02; rtd 02; PtO *B & W* from 03. *47 Hill Lea Gardens, Cheddar BS27 3JH* T: (01934) 744871 M: 07719-670954 E: rose.gwyer@btinternet.com

ROSE, Lionel Stafford Harry. b 38. MBE 93. Wells Th Coll 69. **d** 71 **p** 72. C Minchinhampton *Glouc* 71–73; C Thornbury 73–75; R Ruardean 75–80; V Whiteshill 80–84; CF 84–93; Chapl HM Pris Kirkham 93–95; Chapl HM Pris Wymott 95–01; Chapl HM Pris Rye Hill 01; rtd 01; PtO *Ely* 02–17. *4 Samian Close, Highfield, Caldecote, Cambridge CB23 7GP* E: revdrose@gmail.com

ROSE, Mrs Lynda Kathryn. b 51. Ex Univ BA 73 Barrister-at-Law (Gray's Inn) 81. Wycliffe Hall Ox BA 86. **d** 87 **p** 94. C Highfield *Ox* 87–88; C Ox St Clem 89–93; Dir Anastasis Min 93–99; NSM Ambrosden w Merton and Piddington *Ox* 94–99. *14 Scholar Mews, Marston Ferry Road, Oxford OX2 7GY* T: (01865) 554421 E: lyndarose2000@yahoo.co.uk

ROSE, Michael Mark. b 63. Hull Univ BA 04. Westcott Ho Cam 07. **d** 09 **p** 10. C Linc St Nic w St Jo Newport 09–10; C Boultham 10–12; V Carr Dyke Gp 12–18; PtO from 18; *Cant* from 20; Hon Chapl Miss to Seafarers from 19. *The Vicarage, Bull Lane, Bethersden, Ashford TN26 3HA* T: (01233) 820266 M: 07846-601141 E: mikeredrose63@hotmail.com

ROSE, Michele Claire. See KITTO, Michele Claire

ROSE, Mrs Nadine Jayne. b 64. Ripon Coll Cuddesdon 13. **d** 16 **p** 17. C Wychert Vale *Ox* 16–19; C Wendover and Halton from 19. *Heathlands, Marriotts Avenue, South Heath, Great Missenden HP16 9QL* T: (01494) 866339 M: 07834-771008 E: nadinerose1987@outlook.com

ROSE, Mrs Pamela Inneen. b 49. Hull Univ BSc 71 Moray Ho Coll of Educn PGCE 72. **d** 06 **p** 07. OLM Stow Gp *Linc* 06–16; PtO 17–20. *Daisy Cottage, 16-18 Grange Lane, Willingham by Stow, Gainsborough DN21 5LB* T: (01427) 787578 E: pam.i.rose@hotmail.co.uk

ROSE, Robert Alec Lewis. b 41. Man Univ BSc 64. Wycliffe Hall *Ox* 85. **d** 87 **p** 88. C Vange *Chelmsf* 87–91; C Langdon Hills 91–94; P-in-c Bentley Common 94–00; P-in-c Kelvedon Hatch 94–00; P-in-c Navestock 94–00; R Bentley Common, Kelvedon Hatch and Navestock 00–08; rtd 08; PtO *St E* 09–21. *47 High Street, Wickham Market, Woodbridge IP13 0HE* T: (01728) 748199 E: robdaphnerose@btinternet.com

ROSE, Susan. See ROSE, Geraldine Susan

ROSE, Preb Susan Margaret. b 59. Westmr Coll of Educn BEd 81. SAOMC 95. **d** 98 **p** 99. C N Petherton w Northmoor Green *B & W* 98–01; P-in-c 01–03; P-in-c N Newton w St Michaelchurch, Thurloxton etc 01–03; R Alfred Jewel 03–09; RD Sedgemoor 06–09; P-in-c Cheddar 09–11; P-in-c Rodney Stoke w Draycott 09–11; R Cheddar, Draycott and Rodney Stoke 11–15; RD Axbridge 14–15; Dir of Voc from 15; Dir IME 4-7 from 15; Preb Wells Cathl from 17. *25 Wood Close, Wells BA5 2GA* T: (01749) 938449 E: rev.suerose@virgin.net

ROSE, Miss Susan Mary. b 36. TCert 56. Dalton Ho Bris 68 Trin Coll Bris 74. dss 81 **d** 87 **p** 94. Brinsworth w Catcliffe *Sheff* 75–77; Scargill Ho 77–83; Netherthorpe *Sheff* 83–87; Tutor Trin Coll Bris 87–96; V Normanton *Wakef* 96–01; rtd 01; PtO *Sheff* from 01. *23 Kendal Vale, Worsborough Bridge, Barnsley S70 5NL* T: (01226) 771590 E: s.rose2012@icloud.com

ROSE, Suzanne Elaine. b 59. Cant Ch Ch Univ MA 00. Westcott Ho Cam 15 Sewanee Sch of Th 16. **d** 17 **p** 18. C Boston *Linc* 17–20; R Bethersden w High Halden and Woodchurch *Cant* from 20. *The Vicarage, Bull Lane, Bethersden, Ashford TN26 3HA* T: (01233) 820266 M: 07748-982128 E: revsuerose@outlook.com

ROSE, Timothy Edward Francis. b 72. Univ of Wales (Cardiff) BD 93 MA 95 K Coll Lon PhD 98. Wycliffe Hall Ox MTh 03. **d** 01 **p** 02. C Jesmond H Trin and Newc St Barn and St Jude 01–04; Chapl R Holloway and Bedf New Coll *Lon* 04–06; C Farnham *Guildf* 06–09; P-in-c Stanford in the Vale w Goosey and Hatford *Ox* 09–12. *13 Nea Road, Christchurch BH23 4NA* M: 07709-722325 E: tefrose@gmail.com

ROSE, Timothy Mark. b 77. Luton Univ BA 98. St Mellitus Coll BA 10. **d** 10 **p** 11. C Upper Sunbury St Sav *Lon* 10–13; C Shepperton and Littleton 13–20; V Littleton from 20. *Littleton Rectory, Rectory Close, Shepperton TW17 0QE* T: (01932) 562249 M: 07966-031432 E: tm_rose@hotmail.co.uk

ROSE-CASEMORE, Preb Claire Pamela. b 63. St Paul's Coll Chelt BA 84 St Luke's Coll Ex PGCE 85 Anglia Poly Univ MA 02. Ridley Hall Cam 95. **d** 97 **p** 98. Par Dn Kingsthorpe w Northampton St Dav *Pet* 97–98; C 98–01; TV Daventry, Ashby St Ledgers, Braunston etc 01–10; P-in-c Bideford, Northam, Westward Ho!, Appledore etc *Ex* 10–17; TR Bideford, Landcross, Littleham etc from 17; Preb Ex Cathl from 19. *The Rectory, Abbotsham Road, Bideford EX39 3AB* T: (01237) 475765 E: clairerc@btopenworld.com

ROSE-CASEMORE, Canon Penelope Jane. b 56. Bris Univ CertEd 77 BEd 78. Westcott Ho Cam 83. dss 85 **d** 87 **p** 94. Waterloo St Jo w St Andr *S'wark* 85–87; Par Dn 87–88; Asst Chapl Gt Ormond Street Hosp for Sick Children Lon 88–90; Par Dn Balham St Mary and St Jo *S'wark* 90–94; C 94–96; Par Dn Upper Tooting H Trin 90–94; C 94–96; V Clapham Team 96–01; V Clapham Ch Ch and St Jo from 02; AD Lambeth N 05–10; Dir Ords Kingston Area from 13; Hon Can S'wark Cathl from 17. *Christchurch Vicarage, 39 Union Grove, London SW8 2QJ* T/F: (020) 7622 3552 E: penny@christchurchstjohn.com

ROSEDALE, Johnny Richard (John). b 54. Leeds Univ BA 05. NOC 02. **d** 05 **p** 06. NSM Hadfield *Derby* 05–10; TV Saddleworth *Man* from 10. *Friarmere Vicarage, 1 Coblers Hill, Delph, Oldham OL3 5HT* T: (01457) 874209

ROSENTHAL, Canon James Milton. b 51. **d** 07 **p** 09. Dir Communications Angl Communion Office 89–09; NSM All Hallows by the Tower etc *Lon* 07–12; C Wantsum Gp *Cant* 12–16; P-in-c Merton St Jas *S'wark* 16–19; V 19–21; P-in-c Salfords from 21. *44 Cockshot Hill, Reigate RH2 8AN* M: 07742-856149 E: james.rosenthal@gmail.com

ROSENTHAL, Sheila. b 57. Warwick Univ BA 81 MA 95. Ripon Coll Cuddesdon 04. **d** 06 **p** 07. C Worc SE 06–09; Asst Chapl St Richard's Hospice Worc 09–19; Chapl Worcs Health and Care NHS Trust 10–19; PtO *Glouc* 16–19; Asst Chapl Oslo w Bergen, Trondheim and Stavanger *Eur* from 19. *St Edmund's Church, c/o British Embassy, 0244 Oslo, Norway* T: (0047) 9486 2604 E: trondheimchaplain@osloanglicans.no

ROSIE, James Robert. b 78. Leeds Univ BA 08. Coll of Resurr Mirfield 08. **d** 10 **p** 11. C Kingston upon Hull St Alb *York* 10–14; R Cheadle w Freehay *Lich* 14–17; TV Dereham and Distr *Nor* from 17. *The Vicarage, Woodgate Lane, Swanton Morley, Dereham NR20 4NS* T: (01362) 637311 E: jamesrosie952@gmail.com

ROSINGH, Anna Clara Abena. *See* THOMASSON-ROSINGH, Anna Clara Abena

ROSKELLY, James Hereward Emmanuel. b 57. BSc ACSM 80. Cranmer Hall Dur 83. **d** 86 **p** 87. C Dunster, Carhampton and Withycombe w Rodhuish *B & W* 86–90; C Ealing St Mary *Lon* 90–93; Chapl R Marsden Hosp 93–95; CF 95–03; TV Rayleigh *Chelmsf* 03–10; R Dickleburgh and The Pulhams *Nor* 10–16. *Address withheld by request* M: 07989-442434 E: jamesroskelly@btinternet.com

ROSS, Alexander. *See* ROSS, David Alexander

ROSS, Alexander John. b 84. Melbourne Univ BEd 08 BA 09 Melbourne Coll of Div BTh 10 Aus Catholic Univ MA 11 Ox Univ MTh 13 Em Coll Cam PhD 18. Trin Coll Melbourne 09 Ripon Coll Cuddesdon 11. **d** 13 **p** 13. C S Yarra Ch Ch Australia 13–15; Asst Chapl Em Coll Cam 15–18; Assoc Dean and Bye-Fell 18–19; Tutor Westcott Ho Cam 18–19; NSM Cambridge St Clem *Ely* 18–19; V E Malvern St Jo Australia from 19. *7 Finch Street, East Malvern VIC 3145, Australia* M: (0061) 43-130 8703 E: vicar@saintjohns.org.au

ROSS, Canon Anthony McPherson. b 38. OBE. Univ of Wales (Lamp) BA 60 Lon Univ BD 63. St Mich Coll Llan 60. **d** 61 **p** 62. C Gabalfa *Llan* 61–65; Chapl RN 65–93; QHC 89–93; P-in-c Coln St Aldwyns, Hatherop, Quenington etc *Glouc* 93–95; V 95–08; RD Fairford 96–04; rtd 08; Bp's Adv on Deliverance Min *Glouc* from 08; Hon Can Glouc Cathl from 02. *Rowan Tree Cottage, Ampney Crucis, Cirencester GL7 5RY* T: (01285) 851410 E: tonyrosstssf468@gmail.com

ROSS (née BENSON), Ashley Dawn. b 85. **d** 14 **p** 15. C Everton St Geo *Liv* 14–17; PtO from 17; C Hamworthy *Sarum* from 20. *Address temp unknown*

ROSS, Daniel James. b 87. Bath Univ BSc 09 Open Univ BA 12. Ridley Hall Cam 14. **d** 17 **p** 18. C Upper Armley *Leeds* from 17. *27 Hough End Lane, Leeds LS13 4EY* T: 0113-255 7679 M: 07410-411453 E: revdanross@gmail.com

ROSS, David Alexander. b 46. Oak Hill Th Coll 73. **d** 75 **p** 76. C Northwood Em *Lon* 75–80; R Eastrop *Win* 80–86; V Hove Bp Hannington Memorial Ch *Chich* 86–93; V Muswell Hill St Jas w St Matt *Lon* 93–07; rtd 07; Hon C S Tottenham St Ann *Lon* 07–11; PtO *Ox* from 11. *8 Windrush Court, 175 The Hill, Burford OX18 4RE* T: (01993) 824871 E: alexlynne.ross@googlemail.com

ROSS, Douglas. b 58. SEITE 12. **d** 15 **p** 16. NSM Salfords *S'wark* from 15. *40 Brockham Lane, Brockham, Betchworth RH3 7EH* M: 07717-665007 E: revdoug@squarepeg.com

ROSS, Preb Duncan Gilbert. b 48. Lon Univ BSc 70. Westcott Ho Cam 75. **d** 78 **p** 79. C Stepney St Dunstan and All SS *Lon* 78–84; V Hackney Wick St Mary of Eton w St Aug 84–95; P-in-c Bow Common 95–03; V 03–13; Preb St Paul's Cathl 95–13; rtd 13; PtO *Lon* from 14. *35 Aberavon Road, London E3 5AR* M: 07957-235078 E: duncan.ross5@btopenworld.com

ROSS, Frederic Ian. b 34. Man Univ BSc 56. Westcott Ho Cam 58. **d** 62 **p** 63. C Oldham *Man* 62–65; Sec Th Colls Dept SCM 65–69; Teacher Man Gr Sch 69–84; V Shrewsbury H Cross *Lich* 84–02; rtd 02; PtO *Heref* 02–19; *Lich* 02–13. *The Paddock, Plealey Road, Annscroft, Shrewsbury SY5 8AN* T: (01743) 860327 E: mail@fiross.plus.com

ROSS, Canon Helen Jane. b 61. Moray Ho Coll of Educn PGCE 87 St Andr Univ BSc 84 Aber Univ DipEd 90 MTh 12 SOSc 10. TISEC DipTheol 09. **d** 09 **p** 10. C Aberdeen St Clem *Ab* 09–12; P-in-c 12; R Prestwick *Glas* from 12; Can St Mary's Cathl from 18. *St Ninian's Rectory,*

175 Obree Avenue, Prestwick KA9 2NT M: 07579-048645 E: rector@stniniansprestwick.org.uk

ROSS, John. b 41. Wells Th Coll 66. **d** 69 **p** 70. C Newc St Gabr 69–71; C Prudhoe 71–75; Hon C Shotley 75–87; Hon C Whittonstall 75–87; P-in-c Wallsend St Pet 93–94. *20 Holburn Gardens, Ryton NE40 3DZ* E: rossj41@blueyonder.co.uk

ROSS, John Colin. b 50. Oak Hill Th Coll 84. **d** 86 **p** 87. C Stowmarket *St E* 86–89; C Wakef St Andr and St Mary 89–91; R Gt and Lt Whelnetham w Bradfield St George *St E* 91–94; V Newmarket All SS 94–02; V Erith St Paul *Roch* 02–04; P-in-c Combs and Lt Finborough *St E* 04–13; rtd 13; PtO *St E* from 14. *23 Pinner's Way, Bury St Edmunds IP33 3JN* T: (01284) 706776 M: 07904-124227 E: john@johnross.org

ROSS, Mrs Kirsty Leanne. b 88. Trin Coll Melbourne BTh 10 Qu Coll Ox PGCE 13. Ripon Coll Cuddesdon 11. **d** 13 **p** 13. C Toorak Australia 13–15; Chapl Trin Coll Cam 15–19; Chapl Melbourne Girls Gr Sch Australia from 19. *86 Anderson Street, South Yarra VIC 3121, Australia* M: (0061) 43-576 1880 E: kirstylross@hotmail.com *or* chaplain@mggs.vic.edu.au

ROSS, Oliver Charles Milligan. b 58. SOAS Lon BA 80 St Edm Ho Cam BA 86 K Coll Lon MA 17 Whitelands Coll Lon PGCE 81. Ridley Hall Cam 84. **d** 87 **p** 88. C Preston St Cuth *Blackb* 87–90; C Paddington St Jo w St Mich *Lon* 90–95; V Hounslow H Trin w St Paul and St Mary 95–06; P-in-c Isleworth St Mary 01–02; R St Olave Hart Street w All Hallows Staining etc 06–18; P-in-c St Kath Cree 06–18; P-in-c St Clem Eastcheap w St Martin Orgar 12–14; P-in-c St Marg Pattens 14–18; AD The City 09–18; V Malmesbury and Upper Avon *Bris* from 18. *The Vicarage, Holloway, Malmesbury SN16 9BA* M: 07879-490139 E: ocmross@me.com

ROSS, Ms Rachel Anne. b 64. York Univ BSc 85 SS Coll Cam PGCE 86 Sheff Univ MA 97 Coll of Ripon & York St Jo MA 00. NOC 97. **d** 00 **p** 01. C Pendleton *Man* 00–04; P-in-c Salford Ordsall St Clem 03–04; P-in-c Salford St Ignatius and Stowell Memorial 03–04; R Ordsall and Salford Quays 04–07; P-in-c Loughborough All SS w H Trin *Leic* 07–08; R 08–14; Bp's NSM Officer 10–13; Chapl Qu Anne's Sch Caversham from 15; NSM Caversham Thameside and Mapledurham *Ox* from 15. *The Rectory, 20 Church Road, Caversham, Reading RG4 7AD* T: 0118-947 9505 M: 07884-371688 E: rachelross@tiscali.co.uk

ROSS (née FAIRWATER), Mrs Sally Helen. b 69. St Hilda's Coll Ox BA 91. Cranmer Hall Dur 94. **d** 97 **p** 98. C Illingworth *Wakef* 97–01; Warden H Rood Ho and C Thirsk *York* 01–02; Chapl Northallerton Health Services NHS Trust 01–02; C Sheff St Mark Broomhill 02–04; Mental Health Chapl Sheff Care Trust 04–08; Mental Health Chapl Sheff Health and Social Care NHS Foundn Trust from 08. *40 Bents Drive, Sheffield S11 9RP* T: 0114-235 1652 E: sally.ross@shsc.nhs.uk

ROSS, The Ven Vernon. b 57. Portsm Poly BSc 79 RGN 86 York St Jo Univ MA 13. Trin Coll Bris 89. **d** 91 **p** 92. C Fareham St Jo *Portsm* 91–94; P-in-c Witheridge, Thelbridge, Creacombe, Meshaw etc *Ex* 94–00; TR Barnstaple 00–08; P-in-c Fyfield, Moreton w Bobbingworth etc *Chelmsf* 08–16; NSM Chigwell and Chigwell Row 16–17; Miss Min Adv Barking Area 12–17; Adn Westmorland and Furness *Carl* from 17. *The Vicarage, Windermere Road, Lindale, Grange-over-Sands LA11 6LB* T: (01539) 534717 E: archdeacon.south@carlislediocese.org.uk

ROSS-McCABE, Mrs Philippa Mary Seton. b 63. Natal Univ BA 83 HDipEd 86 Bris Univ BA 01. Trin Coll Bris 99. **d** 01 **p** 02. C Burpham *Guildf* 01–05; LtO 05–06; C Wisley w Pyrford 06–08; Tutor Local Min Progr from 06; Hon C Byfleet from 09. *The Rectory, 81 Rectory Lane, Byfleet, West Byfleet KT14 7LX* T: (01932) 342374 E: p.rossmccabe@btinternet.com

ROSS-McNAIRN, Jonathon Edward. b 73. Sheff Univ LLB 95 Solicitor 98. St Mellitus Coll BA 11. **d** 11 **p** 12. C Hucclecote *Glouc* 11–12; C Glouc St Geo w Whaddon 12–14; Chapl Trin Sch Teignmouth 14–19; Managing Chapl Plymouth Univ *Ex* 19–20; Lead Chapl Devon and Cornwall Police from 21. *Address temp unknown* E: jonathonrossm@yahoo.co.uk

✠**ROSSDALE, The Rt Revd David Douglas James.** b 53. Westmr Coll Ox MA 91 Surrey Univ MSc 01 K Coll Lon MSc 10. Chich Th Coll 80. **d** 81 **p** 82. C 00. C Upminster *Chelmsf* 81–86; V Moulsham St Luke 86–90; V Cookham *Ox* 90–00; RD Maidenhead 94–00; Hon Can Ch Ch 99–00; Suff Bp Grimsby *Linc* 00–13; rtd 13; Can and Preb Linc Cathl from 00; Hon Asst Bp Linc from 13. *Home Farm, Fen Lane, East Keal, Spilsby PE23 4AY* T: (01790) 752163 E: rossdale@btinternet.com

ROSSETER, Miss Susan Mary. b 46. Man Univ BA 67 Edin Univ DASS 71. St Jo Coll Nottm LTh 84. **d** 87 **p** 94. Par Dn Bromley Common St Aug *Roch* 87–88; C Pudsey St Lawr and

St Paul *Bradf* 88–95; C Haughton le Skerne *Dur* 95–00; C Wilnecote *Lich* 00–11; rtd 11. *14 Meadowsway, Upton, Chester CH2 1HZ* E: sue.rosseter@btinternet.com

ROSSITER, Canon Gillian Alice. b 56. SRN 75 RSCN 75. NOC 98. **d** 01 **p** 02. C Neston *Ches* 01–06; P-in-c Gt Meols 06–09; V from 09; RD Wirral N 08–15; Hon Can Ches Cathl from 15. *The Vicarage, 1 Stanley Road, Hoylake, Wirral CH47 1HL* T: 0151-632 3897 E: grossiter1956@outlook.com

ROSSITER, Paul Albert. b 55. Leeds Univ BA 06. NOC 03. **d** 06 **p** 07. NSM Wallasey St Nic w All SS *Ches* 06–12; V Hoylake from 12. *The Vicarage, 1 Stanley Road, Hoylake, Wirral CH47 1HL* T: 0151-632 3897 E: p.a.rossiter@uwclub.net

ROSSLYN SMITH, Mrs Katherine Dorothy Nevill. b 40. STETS 97. **d** 00 **p** 01. NSM Tisbury *Sarum* 00–01; NSM Nadder Valley 01–03; NSM Chalke Valley 03–06; rtd 06; PtO *Sarum* 06–16 and from 18. *The Old School House, Church Street, Bowerchalke, Salisbury SP5 5BE* T: (01722) 780011 E: katersinthevalley@gmail.com

ROSSLYN-SMITH, Mrs Kirsten Louise. b 73. Nottm Trent Univ BA 96. St Jo Coll Nottm MTh 05. **d** 05 **p** 06. C Tunbridge Wells St Jas *Roch* 05–10; V Stoke Hill *Guildf* from 10. *St Peter's Church House, 37 Hazel Avenue, Guildford GU1 1NP* T: (01483) 451908

ROSTILL, Brian. b 50. K Alfred's Coll Win BTh 00. Cranmer Hall Dur 01. **d** 03 **p** 04. C Knight's Enham and Smannell w Enham Alamein *Win* 03–07; P-in-c Boyatt Wood 07–09; V 09–12; Hon C Jersey St Mary 12–13; R 13–18; NSM Tamworth *Lich* from 18. *The Parsonage, Church Drive, Hopwas, Tamworth B78 3AL* T: (01827) 311750 E: brianrostill@gmail.com

ROSTRON, Derek. b 34. St Mich Coll Llan 65. **d** 67 **p** 68. C Morecambe St Barn *Blackb* 67–70; C Ribbleton 70–72; V Chorley All SS 72–79; C Woodchurch *Ches* 79–80; V Audlem 80–03; RD Nantwich 87–97; rtd 04; PtO *Lich* 04–06; *Ches* 04–06. *30 St Matthew's Drive, Derrington, Stafford ST18 9LU* T: (01785) 246349

ROTH, Jill Marie. b 61. Ox Min Course 07. **d** 10 **p** 11. NSM Flackwell Heath *Ox* 10–16; NSM Gerrards Cross and Fulmer from 16. *White Cottage, Hay Lane, Fulmer, Slough SL3 6HJ* T: (01753) 663181 M: 07985-945990 E: jillroth@btinternet.com

ROTH, Johannes. b 66. Ridley Hall Cam. **d** 13 **p** 14. C Northwood Em *Lon* 13–16; P-in-c Cambridge St Martin *Ely* 16–20; V from 20. *St Martin's Vicarage, 127 Suez Road, Cambridge CB1 3QD* T: (01223) 665848 M: 07810-373891 E: vicar@stm.org.uk

ROTHERHAM, Eric. b 36. Clifton Th Coll 63. **d** 67 **p** 68. C Gt Crosby St Luke *Liv* 67–69; C Sutton 69–71; V Warrington St Paul 72–79; LtO 79–80; PtO from 80; *Ches* 80–10. *7 Paul Street, Warrington WA2 7LE* T: (01925) 633048

ROTHERY, Robert Frederick (Fred). b 34. Lon Coll of Div 67. **d** 69 **p** 70. C Burscough Bridge *Liv* 69–72; C Chipping Campden *Glouc* 72–75; P-in-c Didmarton w Oldbury-on-the-Hill and Sopworth 75–77; R Boxwell, Leighterton, Didmarton, Oldbury etc 77–83; R Stow on the Wold 83–00; RD Stow 90–99; rtd 00; PtO *Sarum* 06–18. *12 Phillips Road, Marnhull, Sturminster Newton DT10 1LF* T: (01258) 820668 E: woodyperson@gmail.com

ROTHWELL, Canon Bryan. b 60. St Edm Hall Ox BA 81 MA 85. Trin Coll Bris. **d** 85 **p** 86. C Carl St Jo 85–88; C Ulverston St Mary w H Trin 88–90; P-in-c Preston St Mary *Blackb* 90–96; P-in-c St John's in the Vale w Wythburn *Carl* 96–99; R St John's-in-the-Vale, Threlkeld and Wythburn 99–11; Warden Dioc Youth Cen 96–11; RD Derwent 05–10; TR Solway Plain 11–18; R from 18; Hon Can Carl Cathl from 08. *The Vicarage, Wigton Road, Silloth, Wigton CA7 4NJ* T: (016973) 31413 E: bryan@therothwells.co.uk

ROTHWELL, Edwin John. b 53. Lanc Univ BA 74 PhD 79. Sarum & Wells Th Coll 88. **d** 90 **p** 91. C Malvern Link w Cowleigh *Worc* 90–94; R Bowbrook N 94–00; Asst Chapl Swindon and Marlborough NHS Trust 00–03; Chapl Yeovil Distr Hosp NHS Foundn Trust 03–14; Chapl Somerset Partnership NHS Foundn Trust 14–16; rtd 16; PtO *Sarum* from 15; *B & W* from 16. *c/o Crockford, Church House, 27 Great Smith Street, London SW1P 3AZ* M: 07811-304350 E: johnrothwell@phonecoop.coop

ROTHWELL, Steven. b 68. Roehampton Inst BA 99 Open Univ MA 02. Westcott Ho Cam 00. **d** 02 **p** 03. C Chesterton Gd Shep *Ely* 02–06; R Gamlingay and Everton 06–16; P-in-c Cambridge St Jas 16–21; V from 21; IME Tr Officer from 16. *St James's Vicarage, 110 Wulfstan Way, Cambridge CB1 8QJ* T: (01223) 246419 E: s.rothwell3@btinternet.com

ROTHWELL-JACKSON, Christopher Patrick. b 32. St Cath Soc Ox BA 58 MA 61 Bris Univ PGCE 66. St Steph Ho Ox 55. **d** 59 **p** 60. C E Clevedon All SS *B & W* 59–62; C Midsomer Norton 62–65; Asst Teacher St Pet Primary Sch Portishead 66–68; Clevedon Junior Sch 68–72; Dep

Hd Clevedon All SS Primary Sch 72–75; Hd Master Bp Pursglove Sch Tideswell 75–90; rtd 90; PtO *Ex* 95–13. *Rosedale, Hookway, Crediton EX17 3PU* T: (01363) 772039 E: crothwelljackson@gmail.com

ROUCH, David Vaughan. b 36. Oak Hill Th Coll 67. **d** 69 **p** 70. C Denton Holme *Carl* 69–74; V Litherland St Jo and St Jas *Liv* 74–95; V Pemberton St Mark Newtown 95–06; P-in-c Wigan St Barn Marsh Green 03–06; rtd 06; PtO *Lich* 07–18. *16 Parrs Lane, Bayston Hill, Shrewsbury SY3 0JS* T: (01743) 873800 E: drouch@sky.com

ROUCH, Peter Bradford. b 66. BNC Ox MA 87 Peterho Cam MA 99 Man Univ PhD 05. Westcott Ho Cam 96. **d** 99 **p** 00. C E Dulwich St Jo *S'wark* 99–02; Jun Research Fell St Steph Ho Ox 02–04; Chapl St Jo Coll Ox 03–04; P-in-c Man Apostles w Miles Platting 05–11; Hon Research Fell Man Univ 07–11; Adn Bournemouth *Win* 11–20; Prin External Consultant (Transforming Effectiveness) 20–21; Chief Exec CA from 21; PtO *Sheff* from 21. *Church Army, Wilson Carlile Centre, 50 Cavendish Street, Sheffield S3 7RZ* T: 03001-232113 E: peter.rouch@churcharmy.org

ROULSTON (née MAYLES), Helena Rosemary Laura. b 84. Nottm Univ BA 06. Westcott Ho Cam 12. **d** 14 **p** 15. C Over St Chad *Ches* 14–17; Chapl Sheff Hallam Univ from 18. *20 Rydal Road, Sheffield S8 0US* T: 0114-225 3153 E: h.roulston@shu.ac.uk

ROULSTON, Joseph Ernest. b 52. BNC Ox BA 74 MA 78 Lon Univ PhD 81 FRSC 86 FLS 94 FIBiol 01 FRCPath 01 CSci 04. Edin Dioc NSM Course 83. **d** 86 **p** 87. C Edin St Hilda 86–88; C Edin St Fillan 86–88; NSM Edin St Mich and All SS 88–97; Dioc Chapl Gen from 96; Assoc P Roslin (Rosslyn Chpl) 99–07; P-in-c from 07. *Whitehill Villa, 1 Eldindean Road, Bonnyrigg EH19 2HE* M: 07903-969698 E: revjoeroulston@gmail.com

ROUND, Canon Malcolm John Harrison. b 56. Lon Univ BSc 77 BA 81. Oak Hill Th Coll. **d** 81 **p** 82. C Guildf St Sav w Stoke-next-Guildford 81–85; C Hawkwell *Chelmsf* 85–88; R Balerno *Edin* from 88; Hon Chapl Heriot-Watt Univ from 12; Can St Mary's Cathl from 21. *St Mungo's Ministry Centre, 46B Bavelaw Road, Balerno EH14 7AE* T: 0131-449 9907 E: malcolm.round@stmungos.org

ROUNDHILL, The Ven Andrew (John). b 65. CCC Cam BA 87. Ripon Coll Cuddesdon BTh 93. **d** 93 **p** 94. C Lancaster Ch Ch w St Jo and St Anne *Blackb* 93–97; Chapl Loretto Sch Musselburgh 97–02; Chapl Hong Kong Cathl 02–04; Sub-Dean 04–06; R Aspley w Albany Creek Australia 06–07; AD Brisbane NW 07–08; Adn Lilley from 08. *30 Ridley Road, Bridgeman Downs QLD 4035, Australia* T: (0061) (7) 3263 9254 *or* (7) 3263 3518

ROUNDTREE, James Clabern (Clay). b 75. Oklahoma Univ BFA 98 York Univ MA 00. St Steph Ho Ox BA 02. **d** 03 **p** 04. C Yarm *York* 03–07; V Ingleby Barwick 07–21; Acting Adn Cleveland 19–20; RD Stokesley 20–21; C Grantham St Wulfram *Linc* from 21. *Address temp unknown* E: clayroundtree@hotmail.com

ROUNTREE, Richard Benjamin. b 52. NUI BA 73. CITC 76. **d** 76 **p** 77. C Orangefield *D & D* 76–80; C Dublin Zion Ch *D & G* 80–83; I Dalkey St Patr 83–97; I Powerscourt w Kilbride 97–18; Dioc Dir Decade of Evang 90–96; Can Ch Ch Cathl Dublin 92–18; Treas Ch Ch Cathl Dublin 04–09; Dioc Dir Lay Min 05–09; Adn Glendalough 09–18; rtd 18. *8 Blacklion Manor, Greystones, Co Wicklow, Republic of Ireland* M: (00353) 87-276 7564 E: rbrountree@gmail.com

ROUSE, Graham. b 58. Sheff City Coll of Educn CertEd 79 Leic Univ DipEd 84. Cranmer Hall Dur 90. **d** 92 **p** 93. C Longridge *Blackb* 92–96; P-in-c Fairhaven 96–97; V 97–07; P-in-c Blackpool St Mary 07–10; P-in-c S Shore St Pet 07–10; P-in-c S Shore H Trin 08–10; PtO 10–17. *36 Canterbury Street, Chorley PR6 0LN* T: (01257) 265996

ROUSELL, Ian Douglas. b 64. Trin Coll Bris 11. **d** 13 **p** 14. C Keynsham *B & W* 13–17; P-in-c Westfield from 17. *85 Beauchamp Avenue, Midsomer Norton, Radstock BA3 4FW* M: 07896-598830 E: rev.ian.stpeters@gmail.com

ROUT, Thomas. b 78. Univ Coll Lon BA 02. Wycliffe Hall Ox BA 10. **d** 11 **p** 12. C Rothley *Leic* 11–15; P-in-c Ipswich St Helen, H Trin, and St Luke *St E* 15–21; Chapl Suffolk Univ and Suffolk New Coll 15–20; P-in-c Stanford-le-Hope w Mucking *Chelmsf* from 21. *The Rectory, The Green, Stanford-le-Hope SS17 0EP* M: 07791-122331

ROUTH, Canon Eileen Rosemary. b 41. Cant Sch of Min 82. dss 85 **d** 87 **p** 94. Folkestone St Sav *Cant* 85–90; Par Dn 87–90; Par Dn Woodnesborough w Worth and Staple 90–91; Dn-in-c 91–94; V 94–96; V Maidstone St Martin 96–99; Hon Can Cant Cathl 99; rtd 99; PtO *Cant* from 00. *4C St John's Hospital, Northgate, Canterbury CT1 1BG* T: (01227) 464052

ROUTH, Canon William John. b 60. Magd Coll Ox BA 81 MA 92. Ripon Coll Cuddesdon 93. **d** 95 **p** 96. C Longton *Blackb* 95–99; V Sutton Coldfield St Chad *Birm* 99–06; P-in-c 06–11; P-in-c Sutton Coldfield H Trin 06–11; R from 11; Hon Can Birm Cathl from 21. *Holy Trinity Rectory, 5 Broome Gardens, Sutton Coldfield B75 7JE* T: 0121-311 0474 E: john.routh.htsc@gmail.com

ROUTLEDGE, Christopher Joseph. b 78. Keele Univ BSc 99 SS Mark & Jo Univ Coll Plymouth PGCE 01. Oak Hill Th Coll BA 08. **d** 08 **p** 09. C Tiverton St Geo and St Paul *Ex* 08–12; P-in-c Egg Buckland 12–17; C Estover 12–17; V Eggbuckland w Estover from 17; C Plymouth Crownhill Ascension 12–17; C Bickleigh and Shaugh Prior 12–17. *The Vicarage, 100 Church Hill, Eggbuckland, Plymouth PL6 5RD* T: (01752) 781564 E: chrisroutledge829@btinternet.com

ROUTLEDGE, Christopher Simon Bruce. b 73. Southn Univ BA 94. Ripon Coll Cuddesdon BTh 12. **d** 11 **p** 12. C Northfleet and Rosherville *Roch* 11–15; V Bradwell and Porthill *Lich* from 15; Chapl Staffs and Stoke on Trent Partnership NHS Trust 15–16; Chapl Univ Hosps of N Midl NHS Trust from 16. *St Barnabas' Vicarage, Oldcastle Avenue, Newcastle ST5 8QG* T: (01782) 929216 M: 07837-177571 E: rev.chrisr73@gmail.com

ROWAN, Canon Nicholas Edward. b 76. Essex Univ BA. Trin Coll Bris. **d** 06 **p** 07. C Rayleigh *Chelmsf* 06–10; TV 10–18; P-in-c Hawkwell 18–21; R from 21; AD Rochford from 18; Hon Can Chelmsf Cathl from 19. *The Rectory, 53 Hawkwell Road, Hockley SS5 4DE* T: (01702) 543514 M: 07795-245212 E: nickrowan@btinternet.com *or* nick.rowan@hawkwellparishchurch.org

ROWBERRY, Christopher Michael. b 58. Univ of Wales (Lamp) MA 04 CQSW 85. Qu Coll Birm 94. **d** 96 **p** 97. C Lytchett Minster *Sarum* 96–00; TV Totton *Win* 00–10; V Hedge End St Jo from 10. *The Vicarage, Vicarage Drive, Hedge End, Southampton SO30 4DU* T: (01489) 789578 E: chrisrow@btopenworld.com

ROWBERRY, Michael James. b 46. Sussex Univ BA 74. Edin Th Coll 85. **d** 87 **p** 92. C Wolvercote w Summertown *Ox* 87–88; NSM Cov St Fran N Radford 91–95; PtO 95–98; C Doncaster Intake and Doncaster H Trin *Sheff* 98–00; C-in-c St Edm Anchorage Lane CD 00–06; C Doncaster St Geo 06–12; rtd 12; PtO *Leic* 16–21. *5 Thorntree Close, Leicester LE3 9QS* T: 0116-319 5469 E: microbert@talktalk.net

ROWBORY, Simon Michael. b 84. Grey Coll Dur BSc 06. Westcott Ho Cam 10. **d** 13 **p** 14. C Leic Martyrs 13–16; P-in-c Mill Hill Jo Keble Ch *Lon* from 16. *1A Church Close, Edgware HA8 9NS* M: 07799-300771 E: simon.rowbory@gmail.com

ROWE, Andrew Robert. b 64. Westmr Coll Ox BA 85 PGCE 86. Ridley Hall Cam 93. **d** 95 **p** 96. C Broadheath *Ches* 95–99; V E Ardsley *Wakef* 99–06; Chapl HM Pris Wakef 06–13; Chapl HM YOI Wetherby from 13. *HM Young Offender Institution, York Road, Wetherby LS22 5ED* T: (01937) 544200 E: andyrowe@uwclub.net

ROWE, Canon Bryan. b 50. Carl Dioc Tr Course 87. **d** 90 **p** 91. C Kells *Carl* 90–93; P-in-c Aspatria w Hayton 93–02; R Workington St Mich 02–15; P-in-c Distington 06–08; P-in-c Westfield St Mary 10–12; RD Solway 99–08 and 11–15; Hon Can Carl Cathl 99–15; rtd 15. *7 Berwick Street, Workington CA14 3EN* E: bryan.rowe50@yahoo.com

ROWE, Christine Elizabeth. b 55. Southn Univ BEd 77. Ripon Coll Cuddesdon 83. **dss** 86 **d** 87 **p** 94. Denham *Ox* 86–89; Par Dn 87–89; Par Dn Aylesbury 89–93; NSM Caversham St Jo 93–99; Chapl HM Pris Reading 93–98; Chapl MU 95–00; Chapl R Berks and Battle Hosps NHS Trust 96–00; P-in-c Vancouver St Thos Canada 00–01; R 01–04; Adn Burrard 04–06; R N Vancouver St Cath 06–15; C Kerrisdale St Mary from 15. *1062 Ridgewood Drive, North Vancouver BC V7R 1H8, Canada* T: (001) (604) 987 6307 *or* (604) 985 0666 F: 980 3868 E: christinerowe86@gmail.com

ROWE, The Very Revd David Brian. b 58. Trin Coll Bris 80. **d** 83 **p** 84. C Radipole and Melcombe Regis *Sarum* 83–86; C Cranham Park *Chelmsf* 86–88; Assoc Min and Par Missr Eastrop *Win* 88–92; P-in-c Arborfield w Barkham *Ox* 92–97; Asst Dioc Adv in Evang *S'well* 97–02; P-in-c Wilford 00–06; R 06–08; Warden Lee Abbey 08–15; P-in-c Win Ch Ch 15–18; V 18; Dean Wellington NZ from 18. *Wellington Cathedral of St Paul, PO Box 12-044, Thorndon, Wellington 6144, New Zealand* T: (0064) (4) 472 0286 M: 07787-522307 E: davidrowe3@sky.com *or* admin@wellingtoncathedral.org.nz

ROWE, Geoffrey Lewis. b 44. Univ of Wales (Lamp) BA. Ripon Coll Cuddesdon 80. **d** 82 **p** 83. C Milber *Ex* 82–84; TV Withycombe Raleigh 84–90; R Clyst St Mary, Clyst St George etc 90–08; rtd 08. *33 Sandringham Drive, Preston, Paignton TQ3 1HU*

ROWE, George William. b 36. K Alfred's Coll Win CertEd 64 BEd 82 Win Univ Hon BA 15. **d** 07 **p** 08. NSM Week St Mary Circle of Par *Truro* 07–11; PtO 11–15; *Guildf* from 15. *Tanglewood, 5 Crofts Close, Chiddingfold, Godalming GU8 4SG* T: (01428) 288078 M: 07970-186038 E: jwellar05@gmail.com

ROWE, Miss Joan Patricia. b 54. Trin Coll Bris BA 87. **d** 88 **p** 94. C Radstock w Writhlington *B & W* 88–92; C Nailsea H Trin 92–96; P-in-c Shapwick w Ashcott and Burtle 96–07; Master St Jo Hosp Bath 07–09; PtO *Liv* 10–11; P-in-c Westbury *Heref* 11–13; P-in-c Worthen 11–13; P-in-c Yockleton 11–13; R Westbury, Worthen and Yockleton 13–17; rtd 17; PtO *B & W* from 18. *14 Waverley Road, Backwell, Bristol BS48 3LP* T: (01275) 463214 E: j.rowe91@btinternet.com

ROWE, Jonathan. b 67. Bath Univ BSc 89 Open Univ BA 96 MA 97 St Andr Univ PhD 09. **d** 19 **p** 20. Dir Min *Truro* from 17; Jt Prin SWMTC 17–20; NSM Chacewater w St Day and Carharrack *Truro* from 19; NSM Devoran from 19; NSM Feock from 19; NSM St Stythians w Perranarworthal and Gwennap from 19. *Address withheld by request* M: 07754-616611 E: jonathan.rowe@truro.anglican.org *or* jonathan@thewatersidechurches.com

ROWE, Mrs Pauline Frances. b 58. **d** 13 **p** 14. NSM Wigan All SS and St Geo *Liv* 13–15; C Wigan All SS 15–16; TV Parr 16–21; rtd 21. *67 Middlewich Road, Winsford CW7 3NH* M: 07960-102862 E: pauline.rowe2@btinternet.com

ROWE, Philip William. b 57. Southn Univ BSc 78 Lambeth STh 86. Trin Coll Bris 82. **d** 85 **p** 86. C Tooting Graveney St Nic *S'wark* 85–89; V Abbots Leigh w Leigh Woods *Bris* 89–96; V Almondsbury 96–98; P-in-c Littleton on Severn w Elberton 96–98; V Almondsbury and Olveston 98–19; C Pilning w Compton Greenfield 10–18; P-in-c 18–19; V S Severnside from 19; AD Bris W 00–06. *The Vicarage, 3 Sundays Hill, Almondsbury, Bristol BS32 4DS* T: (01454) 613223 E: office@stmaryssevernside.org.uk

ROWE, Shiela. *See* JOHNSON, Shiela

ROWE, Stephen Mark Buckingham. b 59. SS Mark & Jo Univ Coll Plymouth BA 81. Ripon Coll Cuddesdon 83. **d** 86 **p** 87. C Denham *Ox* 86–89; C Aylesbury 89–90; TV 90–93; V Caversham St Jo 93–00; Canada from 00; Sen Chapl Miss to Seafarers 00–01; P-in-c Surrey Epiphany Canada 01–02; R from 02; Adn Fraser 07–17. *962 29th Street East, North Vancouver BC V7K 1B8, Canada* T: (001) (604) 987 6307 *or* (604) 588 4511 F: (604) 588 4511 E: rowesmb@aol.com

ROWE, Vanda Sheila. *See* PERRETT, Vanda Sheila

ROWELL, Canon Alan. b 50. Lon Univ BSc 71 AKC 71. Trin Coll Bris. **d** 75 **p** 76. C W Hampstead St Cuth *Lon* 75–78; C Camborne *Truro* 78–81; V Pendeen 81–84; V Pendeen w Morvah 85–15; Hon Can Truro Cathl 03–15; rtd 15. *34 Penhaligon Court, Truro TR1 1YB* E: canonrowell@outlook.com

ROWELL, Mrs Gillian Margaret. b 56. Lon Bible Coll BA 96. SAOMC 97. **d** 99 **p** 00. NSM The Lee *Ox* 99–04; NSM Hawridge w Cholesbury and St Leonard 99–04; TV Cottesloe 13–18; V Tilehurst St Cath and Calcot from 18. *The Vicarage, Wittenham Avenue, Tilehurst, Reading RG31 5LN* T: 0118-942 7786 E: gillrowell@tiscali.co.uk

ROWELL, William Kevin. b 51. Reading Univ BSc 71. Linc Th Coll 78. **d** 80 **p** 81. C Cannock *Lich* 80–83; Ind Chapl 83–86; C Ketley and Oakengates 83–86; R Norton in the Moors 86–93; RD Leek 91–93; P-in-c Minsterley and Habberley *Heref* 93–01; RD Pontesbury 99–01; Miss Adv USPG Heref, Worc and Glouc 01–03; NSM Wenlock *Heref* 02–03; R Llandysilio and Penrhos and Llandrinio etc *St As* 04–08; R Welshpool, Castle Caereinion and Pool Quay 08–11; Can Cursal St As Cathl 08–11; rtd 11; PtO *Heref* 15–18; V Chirbury, Marton, Middleton and Trelystan etc from 18; RD Pontesbury from 20. *17 Croft Road, Welshpool SY21 7QD* T: (01938) 552064 M: 07711-298104 E: wkrowell@btinternet.com

ROWETT, Canon David Peter. b 55. Univ Coll Dur BA 76. Ripon Coll Cuddesdon 82. **d** 84 **p** 85. C Yeovil *B & W* 84–88; C Yeovil St Mich 88–89; V Fairfield St Matt *Linc* 89–05; P-in-c Barton upon Humber 05–10; V from 10; R Saxby All Saints from 10; V Horkstow from 10; R S Ferriby from 10; RD Yarborough from 11; Can and Preb Linc Cathl from 18. *The Vicarage, Beck Hill, Barton-upon-Humber DN18 5EY* T: (01652) 632202

ROWLAND, Canon Andrew John William. b 60. STETS 98. **d** 01 **p** 02. C Verwood *Sarum* 01–06; V W Moors 06–18; R Wimborne Minster and Villages from 18; RD Wimborne from 16; Can and Preb Sarum Cathl from 19. *The Rectory, 17 King Street, Wimborne BH21 1DZ* E: ajwrowland@tiscali.co.uk

ROWLAND, Ms Dawn Jeannette. b 38. RSCN 61 RGN 63. S'wark Ord Course 81. **dss** 84 **d** 87 **p** 94. Par Dn Croydon H Sav *S'wark* 84–89; NSM Riddlesdown 89–08; PtO from 08. *18 Le Personne Road, Caterham CR3 5SU*

ROWLAND, Jennifer Norah. b 48. Worc Coll of Educn CertEd 70 Open Univ BA 83 Worc Univ Hon BA 12 ACIB. WMMTC 96. **d** 99 **p** 00. C Stratford-upon-Avon, Luddington etc *Cov* 99–03; P-in-c Ditton Priors w Neenton, Burwarton etc *Heref* 03–12; R 12–14; rtd 14; PtO *Cov* from 15. *19 Farnell Drive, Stratford-upon-Avon CV37 9DJ* T: (01789) 415548 E: jennyrowlandsoa@gmail.com

ROWLAND, Mrs June Mary. b 46. SRN 67. EMMTC 03. **d** 05 **p** 06. NSM Grantham St Wulfram *Linc* from 05; Chapl United Lincs Hosps NHS Trust from 06. *73 Harlaxton Road, Grantham NG31 7AE* M: 07710-455379 E: junerowlandhome@aol.com

ROWLAND, Matthew John. b 80. UWE BA 02 Bris Univ PGCE 03. Wycliffe Hall Ox 11. **d** 14 **p** 15. C Ex St Leon w H Trin 14–18; R Modbury, Bigbury, Ringmore etc from 18. *The Vicarage, Church Lane, Modbury, Ivybridge PL21 0QN* M: 07818-422449 E: m.rowland@oxon.org

ROWLAND, Canon Robert William. b 51. Birm Univ BA 72. St Mich Coll Llan 72. **d** 74 **p** 75. C Connah's Quay *St As* 74; C Shotton 74–76; C Llanrhos 76–81; V Dyserth and Trelawnyd and Cwm 81–17; P-in-c Bryn a Mor Miss Area 18; AD St As 94–10; Hon Can St As Cathl 08–11; Can Cursal St As Cathl 11–18; rtd 18. *17 Abbey Road, Rhos on Sea, Colwyn Bay LL28 4NW* T: (01492) 330283

ROWLAND, Sally Margaret. *See* MARCHANT, Sally Margaret

ROWLAND JONES, The Very Revd Sarah Caroline. b 59. LVO 93 OBE 97. Newnham Coll Cam BA 80 MA 84 Nottm Univ PhD 11. St Jo Coll Nottm BTh 98. **d** 99 **p** 00. C Wrexham *St As* 99–02; S Africa 02–13; P-in-c Cardiff City Par *Llan* 13–18; Dean St D from 18. *The Deanery, The Pebbles, St David's, Haverfordwest SA62 6RD* T: (01437) 720202 E: dean@stdavidscathedral.org.uk

ROWLANDS, Alison Mary. b 51. **d** 06 **p** 07. OLM Redland *Bris* 06–12; rtd 12; PtO *Glouc* from 20. *Calico House, Back of Avon, Tewkesbury GL20 5BA* M: 07789-535355

ROWLANDS, Alun Geoffrey. b 51. Open Univ MBA 02. **d** 12 **p** 13. OLM Mickleover All SS *Derby* 12–14; OLM Mickleover St Jo 12–14; OLM Mickleover 14–16; NSM 16–21; rtd 21; PtO *Derby* from 21. *117 Western Road, Mickleover, Derby DE3 9GR* T: (01332) 517964 E: alunrowlands@btinternet.com

ROWLANDS, The Ven Emyr Wyn. b 42. St Mich Coll Llan 69. **d** 70 **p** 71. C Holyhead w Rhoscolyn *Ban* 70–71; C Holyhead w Rhoscolyn w Llanfair-yn-Neubwll 71–74; V Bodedern w Llechgynfarwy and Llechylched etc 74–88; R Machynlleth and Llanwrin 88–97; R Machynlleth w Llanwrin and Penegoes 97–03; AD Cyfeiliog and Mawddwy 96–10; Can Ban Cathl 97–03; Can and Preb Ban Cathl 03–10; Adn Meirionnydd 04–10; rtd 10; PtO *Ban* from 10. *2 Ffordd Meillion, Llangristiolus, Bodorgan LL62 5DQ* T: (01248) 750148

ROWLANDS, Preb Graeme Charles. b 53. K Coll Lon BD 74 AKC 74. St Aug Coll Cant 75. **d** 76 **p** 77. C Higham Ferrers w Chelveston *Pet* 76–79; C Gorton Our Lady and St Thos *Man* 79–81; C Reading H Trin *Ox* 81–89; P-in-c Kentish Town St Silas *Lon* 89–92; V 92–98; P-in-c Haverstock Hill H Trin w Kentish Town St Barn 93–98; V Kentish Town St Silas and H Trin w St Barn from 98; Preb St Paul's Cathl from 16. *St Silas's House, 11 St Silas's Place, London NW5 3QP* T: (020) 7485 3727

ROWLANDS, Mrs Jacqueline Adèle. b 43. Golds Coll Lon CertEd 65 BEd 72 Heythrop Coll Lon MA 05. St Alb Minl Tr Scheme 82. **dss** 85 **d** 87 **p** 05. Bromham w Oakley *St Alb* 85–88; Par Dn 87–88; Stagsden 85–88; Par Dn 87–88; Par Dn Bromham w Oakley and Stagsden 88–89; Chapl Bromham Hosp 85–89; PtO *St Alb* 04–05 and from 13; Hon C Bedford St Andr 05–13; PtO *Chich* from 18. *20 Anvil Close, Portslade, Brighton BN41 2HT* M: 07793-045203 E: sienajar@hotmail.com

ROWLANDS, Canon John Henry Lewis. b 47. Univ of Wales (Lamp) BA 68 Magd Coll Cam BA 70 MA 74 Dur Univ MLitt 86. Westcott Ho Cam 70. **d** 72 **p** 73. C Aberystwyth *St D* 72–76; Chapl Univ of Wales (Lamp) 76–79; Youth Chapl 76–79; Dir Academic Studies St Mich Coll Llan 79–84; Sub-Warden 84–88; Warden 88–97; Lect Univ of Wales (Cardiff) *Llan* 79–97; Asst Dean 81–83; Dean 93–97; Dean of Div 91–95; Dir of Ords 85–88; V Whitchurch 97–02; TR 02–17; Hon Can Llan Cathl 90–97; Can Llan Cathl 97–02; Chan Llan Cathl 02–17; Chapl Cardiff and Vale Univ Health Bd 97–17; Fell Woodard Corp 89–17; Hon Fell from 17; rtd 17. *Llys y Coed, Bwlch Gwynt, New Quay SA45 9QS* T: (01545) 560143 M: 07343-579466 E: johnrowlands1915@outlook.com

ROWLANDS, Marc Alun. b 62. Univ of Wales (Abth) BSc 84 St D Coll Lamp MPhil 89 PhD 95. Wycliffe Hall Ox 97. **d** 99 **p** 00. C Betws w Ammanford *St D* 99–01; C Carmarthen St Pet 01–02; P-in-c Llanpumsaint w Llanllawddog 02–05; TV Cwm Gwendraeth 06–10; TR Trisant 10–18; P-in-c Lampeter w Maestir and Silian and Llangybi and Betws Bledrws 18–19; P-in-c Lampeter from 19; AD from 19. *The Vicarage, Maesllan, Lampeter SA48 7EN* E: revdocrock@yahoo.com

ROWLANDS, Robert. b 31. Roch Th Coll. **d** 68 **p** 69. C Hooton *Ches* 68–71; V Stretton 71–88; P-in-c Appleton Thorn and Antrobus 87–88; V Stretton and Appleton Thorn 88–00; rtd 00; PtO *Carl* 01–20. *Uplands, Redhills Road, Arnside, Carnforth LA5 0AS* T: (01524) 761612

ROWLANDS, Simon David. b 66. **d** 99 **p** 00. C St Peter-in-Thanet *Cant* 99–03; Chapl Cant Ch Ch Univ 03–06; V Bridge *Cant* 07–13; P-in-c Faversham 13–17; C The Brents and Davington w Oare and Luddenham 13–14; C Eastling w Ospringe and Stalisfield w Otterden 13–14; P-in-c The Brents and Davington 14–17; C Ospringe 14–17; P-in-c Preston-next-Faversham 16–17; V Faversham from 17. *The Vicarage, 16 Newton Road, Faversham ME13 8DY* T: (01795) 532592

ROWLANDS, Mrs Valerie Christine. b 54. St As Minl Tr Course 99. **d** 02 **p** 03. NSM Llanbedr DC w Llangynhafal, Llanychan etc *St As* 02–04; Chapl St As Cathl 04–14; TV St As 06–14; V Llanrhaeadr-yng-Nghinmeirch and Prion w Nantglyn 14–16; TV Denbigh Miss Area from 17. *The Rectory, Llandyrnog, Denbigh LL16 4LT* T: (01824) 790777

ROWLANDSON, Diana Mary. b 56. Ox Min Course 10. **d** 13 **p** 14. NSM Gerrards Cross and Fulmer *Ox* 13–18; R Earlham *Nor* from 18; C The Mitre Benefice from 18. *The Vicarage, Bluebell Road, Norwich NR4 7LP* T: (01603) 501713 M: 07831-265806 E: earlhamparish@gmail.com *or* di.rowlandson@earlhamparish.org

ROWLES, Mrs Elizabeth Clare. b 68. RGN 90. All SS Cen for Miss & Min 15. **d** 18 **p** 19. C Droylsden St Andr and St Martin *Man* from 18. *23 Oak Drive, Denton, Manchester M34 2JR* T: 0161-336 1214 M: 07535-923176 E: revlizrowles@gmail.com

ROWLEY, Ms Anne Christine. b 50. Lanc Univ BA 96 Leeds Univ MA 10 Huddersfield Univ PGCE 99. Yorks Min Course 07. **d** 10 **p** 11. NSM Dunnington *York* 10–12; Chapl York Hosps NHS Foundn Trust from 12; NSM Rural E York 12–14; NSM York All SS Pavement w St Crux and St Mich 14; NSM York St Olave w St Giles 14; NSM York St Helen w St Martin 14; NSM York St Denys 14; Chapl York St Jo Univ 14–19; PtO *York* from 19. *2 Lady Hewley's Cottages, St Saviourgate, York YO1 8NW* T: (01904) 651189 *or* 876606

ROWLEY, Preb Christopher Francis Elmes. b 48. St Jo Coll Dur BA 70 St Luke's Coll Ex PGCE 71. St Steph Ho Ox 76. **d** 78 **p** 79. C Parkstone St Pet w Branksea and St Osmund *Sarum* 78–81; TV 82–85; P-in-c Chard Gd Shep Furnham B & W 85–89; P-in-c Dowlishwake w Chaffcombe, Knowle St Giles etc 88–89; R Chard, Furnham w Chaffcombe, Knowle St Giles etc 89–91; V Stoke St Gregory w Burrowbridge and Lyng 91–04; RD Taunton 01–04; TV Wellington and Distr 04–13; RD Tone 07–12; Preb Wells Cathl 09–13; rtd 13; PtO *B & W* from 14. *39 Cornlands, Sampford Peverell, Tiverton EX16 7UA* T: (01884) 799011 E: christopherrowley@uwclub.net

ROWLEY, David Michael. b 39. NOC 87. **d** 90 **p** 91. C Stainland *Wakef* 90–93; V Hayfield *Derby* 93–99; P-in-c Chinley w Buxworth 98–99; V Glossop 99–04; RD 96–04; rtd 04; PtO *Derby* 04–18. *8 Weavers Close, Belper DE56 0HZ* T: (01773) 882690

ROWLEY, The Ven Jennifer Jane Elisabeth. b 61. LMH Ox BA 84 MA 92. EAMTC 99. **d** 02 **p** 03. C Kingsthorpe w Northampton St Dav *Pet* 02–04; C Kettering SS Pet and Paul 04–06; P-in-c Nettleham *Linc* 06–13; P-in-c Welton and Dunholme w Scothern 10–13; R Selsdon St Jo w St Fran *S'wark* 13–20; AD Croydon Addington 15–20; Adn Portsdown *Portsm* from 20. *Diocesan Office, First Floor, Peninsular House, Wharf Road, Portsmouth PO2 8HB* E: jenny.rowley@portsmouth.anglican.org

ROWLEY, Mrs Susan. b 49. **d** 01 **p** 02. OLM Fazeley *Lich* 01–11; rtd 11; PtO *Lich* from 12. *137 Reindeer Road, Fazeley, Tamworth B78 3SP* T: (01827) 250431 *or* 289414 E: s.rowley2@sky.com

ROWLING, Canon Catherine. b 55. Man Poly BEd 77 Dur Univ MA 04. Westcott Ho Cam 83 NEOC 85. **dss** 86 **d** 87 **p** 94. Gt Ayton w Easby and Newton-in-Cleveland *York* 86–89; Par Dn 87–89; Chapl Teesside Poly 89–92; Chapl Teesside Univ 92–96; Dean of Women's Min 96–08; Co Dir of Ords 96–05; Dioc Dir of Ords 05–09; Dioc Moderator Reader Tr 99–04; Dir Reader Studies 05–09; Can and Preb York Minster 01–09; Prin Lindisfarne Regional Tr Partnership 09–17; PtO *York* 09–15; *Leeds* 20–21. *Address withheld by request* M: 07714-052282 E: cathyrowling0408@gmail.com

ROWLING, Canon Richard Francis. b 56. BA. Westcott Ho Cam. **d** 84 **p** 85. C Stokesley *York* 84–87; C Stainton-in-Cleveland 87–90; V New Marske 90–96; V Wilton 92–96;

P-in-c Ingleby Greenhow w Bilsdale Priory, Kildale etc 96–98; V 98–03; R Thirsk 03–16; Abp's Adv for Rural Affairs 98–16; RD Mowbray 04–14; Can and Preb York Minster 10–16; Chapl HM Pris Northd 16–17; rtd 17; PtO *York* from 20. *c/o Crockford, Church House, 27 Great Smith Street, London SW1P 3AZ* E: richard.f.rowling@gmail.com

ROWNTREE, Peter. b 47. St D Coll Lamp BA 68 Univ of Wales (Cardiff) MA 70. St Steph Ho Ox 70. **d** 72 **p** 73. C Stanwell *Lon* 72–75; C Northolt St Mary 75–79; Chapl Ealing Gen Hosp 79–83; Chapl Cherry Knowle Hosp Sunderland 83–87; Chapl Ryhope Hosp Sunderland 83–87; Chapl Ealing Gen Hosp 87–90; Chapl Ealing Hosp NHS Trust 91–94 and 94–99; Chapl W Lon Healthcare NHS Trust 94–99; Sen Co-ord Chapl Univ Coll Lon Hosps NHS Foundn Trust 99–08; rtd 08; PtO *Nor* from 08. *Address withheld by request*

✠**ROWTHORN, The Rt Revd Jeffery William.** b 34. Ch Coll Cam BA 57 MA 62 Union Th Sem (NY) BD 61 Oriel Coll Ox BLitt 72 Berkeley Div Sch DD 87. Cuddesdon Coll 61. **d** 62 **p** 63 **c** 87. C Woolwich St Mary w H Trin *S'wark* 62–65; R Garsington *Ox* 65–68; Chapl and Dean Union Th Sem NY USA 68–73; Assoc Prof Past Th Yale and Berkeley Div 73–87; Suff Bp Connecticut 87–93; Bp in Charge Convocation of American Chs in Eur 94–01; Asst Bp Eur 95–01; Asst Bp Spain 97–01; Asst Bp Portugal 97–01; rtd 01. *17 Woodland Drive, Salem CT 06420-4023, USA* T: (001) (860) 859 3377 E: jefferyrowthorn@yahoo.com

ROXBY, Gordon George. b 39. Lon Univ BSc 61. Coll of Resurr Mirfield 61. **d** 63 **p** 64. C Fleetwood St Pet *Blackb* 63–66; C Kirkham 66–68; V Runcorn St Jo Weston *Ches* 68–78; R Monkton St Chad *Man* 78–86; V Bury St Pet 86–99; AD Bury 86–96; Hon Can Man Cathl 97–99; V Sandiway *Ches* 99–05; Initial Minl Tr Officer 99–04; rtd 05; PtO *Ches* from 05. *16 St Joseph's Way, Nantwich CW5 6TE* T: (01270) 619898 E: gordon@roxbylife.org.uk

ROY, Jennifer Pearl. *See* DREW, Jennifer Pearl

ROYDEN, Canon Charles. b 60. Wycliffe Hall Ox BA 86 MA 91. **d** 87 **p** 88. C Bidston *Ches* 87–91; V N Brickhill and Putnoe *St Alb* 91–92; V Bedf St Mark from 93; Hon Can St Alb from 13. *The Vicarage, Calder Rise, Bedford MK41 7UY* T: (01234) 309175 F: 342613 M: 07973-113861 E: vicar@thisischurch.com

ROYDEN, Eric Ramsay. b 29. St Deiniol's Hawarden 75. **d** 77 **p** 78. Hon C Tranmere St Paul w St Luke *Ches* 77–81; C Eastham 81; V New Brighton All SS 81–95; P-in-c 95–97; rtd 95; PtO *Ches* 97–07; St Alb from 07. *84 Asgard Drive, Bedford MK41 0UT* T: (01234) 294496 E: eroyden@googlemail.com

ROYDEN, Ross Eric. b 55. Lon Bible Coll BA 77 Nottm Univ MTh 82. Wycliffe Hall Ox 79. **d** 81 **p** 82. C Moreton *Ches* 81–84; Chapl and Tutor Bedf Coll of HE *St Alb* 84–93; R Banchory *Ab* 93–00; R Kincardine O'Neil 93–00; V Kowloon Tong Ch Ch Hong Kong from 00. *Christ Church Vicarage, 2 Derby Road, Kowloon Tong, Kowloon, Hong Kong* T: (00852) 2338 4433 F: 2338 8422 E: rossroyden@gmail.com

ROYLANCE, Mrs Margaret. b 47. St Mary's Coll Chelt CertEd 68. Cant Sch of Min 93. **d** 96 **p** 97. Chapl Ashford Sch 96–10; NSM Tenterden and Smallhythe *Cant* 96–16; NSM Rother and Oxney 13–16; NSM Tenterden, Rother and Oxney 16–17; rtd 17; PtO *Cant* from 17. *5 Southgate Road, Tenterden TN30 7BS* T: (01580) 762332 F: 765267 E: johnsroylance@gmail.com

ROYLE, Antony Kevan. b 50. Lon Univ BSc 71 FIA 76. Trin Coll Bris 76. **d** 79 **p** 80. C Chell *Lich* 79–82; C Leyland St Andr *Blackb* 82–86; V Blackb Sav 86–95; Chapl Blackb R Infirmary and Park Lee Hosp 86–95; Chapl E Lancs Hospice 86–95; TR Walton H Trin *Ox* 95–01; NSM Wendover Deanery 01–17; PtO *B & W* from 17. *20 Earlesfield, Nailsea, Bristol BS48 4SF* M: 07796-143905 E: kevanroyle@gmail.com

ROYLE, Gillian Mary. *See* PAWSON, Gillian Mary

ROYLE, Canon Peter Sydney George. b 34. K Coll Lon BD 57 AKC 57. **d** 58 **p** 59. C St Helier *S'wark* 58–62; C Alice Springs Australia 62–63; R 63–68; Can Darwin 68; P-in-c Sydenham St Phil *S'wark* 69–72; V Leigh Park *Portsm* 72–85; RD Havant 77–82; V S w N Hayling 85–96; V S Hayling 96–97; Hon Can Portsm Cathl 95–97; rtd 97; PtO *Ex* 97–06; *Sarum* from 06. *The Lodge, Easton Farm, Bishop's Canning, Devizes SN10 2LR* T: (01380) 862900 E: george.royle.1@btinternet.com

ROYLE, Canon Roger Michael. b 39. AKC 61 Lambeth MA 90. **d** 62 **p** 63. C Portsea St Mary *Portsm* 62–65; C St Helier *S'wark* 65–68; Succ S'wark Cathl 68–71; Warden Eton Coll Dorney Par Project *Ox* 71–74; Conduct Eton Coll 74–79; LtO *S'wark* 79–90; Chapl Ld Mayor Treloar Coll Alton 90–92; Hon C Froyle and Holybourne *Win* 90–92; Hon Can and Chapl S'wark Cathl 93–99; PtO from 99; rtd 04. *Address withheld by request*

ROYSTON, Virginia Helen. b 53. Bris Univ BSc 76 MB, ChB 79. STETS 09. **d** 12 **p** 13. NSM Cotham St Sav w St Mary and Clifton St Paul *Bris* from 12. *14 Grove Avenue, Coombe Dingle, Bristol BS9 2RP* T: 0117-968 6622 M: 07813-692852

RUBIE, William Edward. b 80. Ox Univ BA 03 Oak Hill Th Coll BA 12. St Mellitus Coll 18. **d** 19 **p** 20. C Heatons *Man* from 19. *112 Crescent Park, Stockport SK4 2JE* E: will@stms.org.uk

RUDALL, Mark Edward. b 53. Regent's Park Coll Ox BA 80 MA 84. Ripon Coll Cuddesdon 00. **d** 01 **p** 02. In Bapt Min 80–00; C Wallingford *Ox* 01–03; Dioc Dir Communications *Guildf* 04–13; rtd 13; PtO *Win* 13–21; *Guildf* from 13. *108 Prospect Road, Farnborough GU14 8NS* T: (01252) 645486 M: 07779-654975 E: mark.rudall@ntlworld.com

RUDD, Carl Nigel. b 71. Salford Univ BSc 93 PhD 97. Trin Coll Bris BA 06. **d** 06 **p** 07. C Whitstable *Cant* 06–10; C Penn Fields *Lich* 10–18; R Stafford St Jo and Tixall w Ingestre from 18. *The Rectory, Westhead Avenue, Stafford ST16 3RP* T: (01785) 253493 E: carl.rudd@gmail.com

RUDD, Colin Richard. b 41. AKC 64. **d** 65 **p** 66. C N Stoneham *Win* 65–70; V Rotherwick, Hook and Greywell 70–74; R Hook w Greywell 74–78; Toc H 78–89; V Buckland *Ox* 89–98; V Littleworth 89–98; R Pusey 89–98; R Gainfield 98–99; RD Vale of White Horse 96–99; rtd 99; PtO *B & W* 06–21. *Alcudia, Bilbrook, Minehead TA24 6HE* T: (01984) 640021 E: colinrudd70@gmail.com

RUDD, Robert Arthur. b 33. ALCD 60. **d** 60 **p** 61. C Blackb Sav 60–63; C Huyton St Geo *Liv* 63–65; V Bickershaw 65–72; Asst Chapl HM Pris Liv 72–73; Birm 73-78; Parkhurst 78-86; Camp Hill 86–92; Chapl St Mary's Hosp Newport 92–95; rtd 95; PtO *Portsm* from 95. *The Elms, 13 Horsebridge Hill, Newport PO30 5TJ* T: (01983) 524415

RUDD, Mrs Sonia Winifred. b 44. Nottm Univ BSc 66 Leeds Univ MSc 68. Ox Min Course 92. **d** 94 **p** 95. NSM Ox St Andr 94–96; C Buckland 96–99; PtO *B & W* 06–21. *Alcudia, Bilbrook, Minehead TA24 6HE* T: (01984) 640021 M: 07886-451743 E: soniarudd67@gmail.com

RUDDICK, David Mark. b 76. Pemb Coll Cam BA 98 Homerton Coll Cam PGCE 99. Oak Hill Th Coll BA 09. **d** 09 **p** 10. C Elmswell *St E* 09–12; TV Morden *S'wark* from 12. *140 Stonecot Hill, Sutton SM3 9HQ* T: (020) 8330 6566 M: 07761-320736 E: davidruddick09@gmail.com

RUDDLE, Canon Donald Arthur. b 31. MBE 04. Linc Th Coll 64. **d** 66 **p** 67. C Kettering SS Pet and Paul 66–70; V Earlham St Anne *Nor* 70–79; V E Malling *Roch* 79–95; RD Malling 84–93; Hon Can Roch Cathl 88–95; Chapl Nord Pas de Calais *Eur* 95–98; rtd 98; PtO *Eur* from 98; *Cant* from 05. *Sycamore Lodge, 5 Windmill Lane, Faversham ME13 7GT* T: (01795) 533461 E: don.ruddle@talktalk.net

RUDDOCK, Brian John. b 45. Dur Univ BA 66 Nottm Univ MEd 91. Westcott Ho Cam 67. **d** 69 **p** 70. C Ross *Heref* 69–72; C Kettering SS Pet and Paul 72–75; P-in-c Colchester St Steph *Chelmsf* 75–77; TR Colchester St Leon, St Mary Magd and St Steph 77–84; R March St Pet *Ely* 84–89; R March St Mary 84–89; RD March 87–89; Bp's Officer for Unemployment *Sheff* 89–94; Resource and Development Officer Chs Community Work Alliance 96–02; LtO *Sheff* 96–07; PtO *Sarum* 07–15; rtd 09. *10 Holly Drive, Wick, Littlehampton BN17 6LB* T: (01903) 721467 E: brianjruddock@btinternet.com

RUDDOCK, Bruce. *See* RUDDOCK, Reginald Bruce

RUDDOCK, Canon Edgar Chapman. b 48. St Jo Coll Dur BA 70 MA 76. Cranmer Hall Dur 70. **d** 74 **p** 75. C Birm St Geo 74–78; R 78–83; Dir Tr Dio St Jo S Africa 83–86; P-in-c Mandini 86–87; Prov Dir Tr 88–91; Hon Can Zululand from 95; TR Stoke-upon-Trent *Lich* 91–02; Dir Internat Relns United Soc 03–14; Dep Gen Sec 05–14; rtd 14; PtO *Guildf* 04–14; *Win* from 15. *2 Talbot Road, Dibden Purlieu, Southampton SO45 4PP* T: (023) 8194 4047 E: edgar.ruddock@gmail.com

RUDDOCK, Kenneth Edward. b 30. TCD BA 52 QUB MTh 79. CITC 53 TCD Div Sch Div Test. **d** 53 **p** 54. C Ballymena *Conn* 53–56; C Belfast St Thos 56–60; I Tomregan w Drumlane *K, E & A* 60–68; I Belfast St Luke *Conn* 68–80; Miss to Seamen 80–96; I Whitehead and Islandmagee *Conn* 80–96; Can Lisburn Ch Ch Cathl 90–96; Dioc Info Officer from 90; Chan Conn Cathl 96; rtd 96; Dioc C *Conn* 98–18. *24 Fourtowns Manor, Ahoghill, Ballymena BT42 1RS* T: (028) 2587 8966

RUDDOCK, Canon Leonard William. b 58. CITC 90. **d** 94 **p** 95. NSM Roscrea w Kyle, Bourney and Corbally *L & K* 94–06; C Stillorgan w Blackrock *D & G* 06–08; I Blessington w Kilbride, Ballymore Eustace etc from 08; Can Ch Ch Cathl Dublin from 18. *The Rectory, 13 Ashton, Blessington, Co Wicklow, Republic of Ireland* T: (00353) (45) 865178 M: 87-764 3296 E: leonardruddock@gmail.com

RUDDOCK, Canon Reginald Bruce. b 55. AGSM 77. Chich Th Coll 80. **d** 83 **p** 84. C Felpham w Middleton *Chich* 83–86; C Portsea St Mary *Portsm* 86–88; P-in-c Barnes St Mich *S'wark*

88–95; Dir Angl Cen Rome 95–99; Hon Can American Cathl Paris from 96; Can Res Worc Cathl 99–04; Can Res Pet Cathl 04–17; Liturg Officer 04–12; rtd 17; Chapl Chich Cathl from 18; Custos St Mary's Hosp Chich from 18; Chapl to The Queen from 08. *6 Priory Road, Chichester PO19 1NS* E: rbruddock@outlook.com

RUDGE, Colin. b 48. Open Univ BA 04 Chich Univ BA 13. Wilson Carlile Coll 96 SEITE 08. **d** 10 **p** 11. C Hollington St Jo *Chich* 10–12; C Seaford w Sutton 12–16; rtd 16; PtO *Chich* from 16. *10 Harrow Close, Seaford BN25 3PE* T: (01323) 898739 M: 07967 778765 E: colin.rudge@gmail.com

RUDGE, Susannah Mary. *See* BRASIER, Susannah Mary

RUDKIN, Simon David. b 51. Bradf Univ BA 74 K Coll Lon BD 77 AKC 77. Coll of Resurr Mirfield 77. **d** 78 **p** 79. C Flixton St Mich *Man* 78–81; C Atherton 81–84; V Lever Bridge 84–91; P-in-c Pennington w Lindal and Marton *Carl* 91–96; P-in-c Pennington and Lindal w Marton and Bardsea 96–00; R Morland, Thrimby, Gt Strickland and Cliburn 00–09; P-in-c Kirkby Thore w Temple Sowerby and Newbiggin 04–07; P-in-c Bolton and Crosby Ravensworth 05–09; R Bedale and Leeming and Thornton Watlass *Ripon* 09–11; V The Thorntons and The Otteringtons *York* 11–16; Chapl N Yorks Police 11–16; rtd 16. *4 Templars Court, Temple Sowerby, Penrith CA10 1SR* T: (01768) 362059 E: sd.rudkin@btinternet.com

RUDMAN, Preb David Walter Thomas. b 48. Oak Hill Th Coll BD 72. **d** 72 **p** 73. C Plymouth St Jude *Ex* 72–75; C Radipole *Sarum* 76; C Radipole and Melcombe Regis 77; Warden St Geo Ho Braunton 77–03; R Georgeham *Ex* 88–03; Dioc Adv in Adult Tr 97–03; TV S Molton w Nymet St George, High Bray etc 03–13; Dioc Adv in OLM 03–13; Preb Ex Cathl 09–13; rtd 13. *Greendale Farm, Pill Lane, Barnstaple EX32 9EQ* E: rudman1604@gmail.com

RUE, Kenneth Gordon. TCD BBS 75. **d** 10 **p** 11. NSM Powerscourt w Kilbride *D & G* 10–11; NSM Wicklow w Killiskey from 11; OLM Co-ord Ch of Ireland from 19. *Shancarrig, Cronroe, Ashford, Co Wicklow, Republic of Ireland* M: 87-276 6590 E: krue@eircom.net

RUEHORN, Eric Arthur. b 33. St Aid Birkenhead 58. **d** 61 **p** 62. C Harpurhey Ch Ch *Man* 61–65; V Roughtown 65–74; V Hawkshaw Lane 74–99; rtd 99; PtO *Man* from 00. *101 Bankhouse Road, Bury BL8 1DZ* T: 0161-761 3983 E: e.ruehorn@btopenworld.com

RUFF, Brian Chisholm. b 36. Lon Univ BD 66 ACA 60 FCA 70. Oak Hill Th Coll 63. **d** 67 **p** 68. C Cheadle *Ches* 67–72; Educn and Youth Sec CPAS 72–76; V New Milverton *Cov* 76–90; V Westbourne Ch Ch Chpl *Win* 90–01; rtd 02; PtO *Win* 02–19; *Sarum* 03–18. *19 Hardy Road, West Moors, Wimborne BH22 0EX* T: (01202) 868733 E: bandjruff@yahoo.co.uk

RUFF, Michael Ronald. b 49. K Coll Lon BD 72 AKC 72 Ch Coll Cant PGCE 77. St Aug Coll Cant 72. **d** 73 **p** 74. C Old Shoreham *Chich* 73–76; Chapl Ellesmere Coll 77–81; Chapl Grenville Coll Bideford 81–87; Chapl Stamford Sch 87–06; P-in-c Stamford St Mary and St Martin *Linc* 06–13; rtd 11; PtO *Linc* 17–20; *Pet* from 17. *3 Baxters Lane, Easton on the Hill, Stamford PE9 3NH* T: (01780) 766567 E: michael.ruff342@btinternet.com

RUFFLE, Preb John Leslie. b 43. ALCD 66. **d** 66 **p** 67. C Eastwood *S'well* 66–70; C Keynsham w Queen Charlton *B & W* 70–75; P-in-c Weston-super-Mare Em 75; TV Weston-super-Mare Cen Par 75–84; V Yatton Moor 84–91; TR 91–98; P-in-c Chew Stoke w Nempnett Thrubwell 98–03; Dioc Adv in Past Care and Counselling 03–06; rtd 06; Preb Wells Cathl *B & W* 97–13; PtO 06–14. *52 Highbridge Road, Burnham-on-Sea TA8 1LN* T: (01278) 788322 E: john.ruffle01@btinternet.com

RUFFLE, Wendy Ann. b 56. WEMTC 07. **d** 10 **p** 11. C Tewkesbury w Walton Cardiff and Twyning *Glouc* from 10; Pioneer Min from 13. *89 York Road, Tewkesbury GL20 5HE* M: 07768-182769 E: rev.wendy@icloud.com

RUGEN, Peter. b 60. Crewe & Alsager Coll BEd 86. Trin Coll Bris MA 00. **d** 00 **p** 01. C Shipley St Pet *Bradf* 00–04; P-in-c Riddlesden and Morton St Luke 04–08; P-in-c Norley, Crowton and Kingsley *Ches* 08–11; V 11–18; RD Frodsham 11–18; V Plas Newton from 18. *St Michael's Vicarage, 22 Plas Newton Lane, Chester CH2 1PA* T: (01244) 319677 E: peterugen@gmail.com

RUGG, Andrew Philip. b 47. Kent Univ BA 82. Sarum & Wells Th Coll 83. **d** 85 **p** 86. C Harlesden All So *Lon* 85–90; TV Benwell *Newc* 90–97; V Weetslade 97–00; rtd 00; PtO *York* 00–12. *2 Ellen Wilson Cottages, Lawrence Street, York YO10 3WP* M: 07980-390051

RUGG, Christopher James McTeer. b 75. St Jo Coll Dur BSc 97. Trin Coll Bris 06. **d** 08 **p** 09. C Week St Mary Circle of Par *Truro* 08–11; USA from 11. *4104 Tiffany Lane, Redding CA 96002, USA* T: (001) (503) 233 3833

RUGMAN, Mrs Hazel. b 47. R Holloway Coll Lon BA 68 ACIS 89. NOC 01. **d** 03 **p** 04. NSM Sandbach *Ches* 03–06; NSM Crewe St Andr w St Jo 06–17; NSM Crewe Ch Ch 07–13; rtd 18; PtO *Ches* from 18. *High Trees, 157 Sandbach Road North, Alsager, Stoke-on-Trent ST7 2AX* T: (01270) 876386 F: 883737 M: 07762-706120 E: hazelrugman@btinternet.com

RUITERS, Ivan John. b 61. Coll of Transfiguration Grahamstown 94. **d** 96 **p** 97. C Berea S Africa 96–00; R Maidstone 00–01; R Newlands 02–07; I Killesher *K, E & A* 07–16; Can Kilmore Cathl 14–16; V Milnrow and New Hey *Man* 16–18; R Karkloof S Africa 18–21; I Kinneigh Union *C, C & R* from 21. *The Rectory, Derrigra, Ballineen, Co Cork, P47 X672, Republic of Ireland* E: ivanruiters@yahoo.com

✠**RUMALSHAH, The Rt Revd Munawar Kenneth (Mano).** b 41. Punjab Univ BSc 60 Serampore Coll BD 65 Karachi Univ MA 68 Homerton Coll Cam PGCE 88. Bp's Coll Calcutta 62. **d** 65 **p** 66 **c** 94. C H Trin Cathl Karachi Pakistan 65–69; C Roundhay St Edm *Ripon* 70–73; Area Sec and Asst Home Sec CMS 73–78; Educn Sec BCC 78–81; P-in-c Southall St Geo *Lon* 81–88; Lect Edwardes Coll Peshawar Pakistan 89–94; Bp Peshawar 94–99 and 03–07; Gen Sec USPG and Hon Asst Bp S'wark 99–03; rtd 07. *81 Bantry Road, Slough SL1 5FD*

RUMBALL, William Michael. b 41. Surrey Univ BSc 63 Hon BUniv 11 Birm Univ PhD 66 MA 11 Open Univ BA 75. Wycliffe Hall Ox 78. **d** 80 **p** 81. C S Molton, Nymet St George, High Bray etc *Ex* 80–83; V S Hetton w Haswell *Dur* 83–90; V S Wingfield and Wessington *Derby* 90–99; rtd 99; Hon C Brailsford w Shirley and Osmaston w Ednaston *Derby* 01–03; PtO 03–10; *Lich* 08–10; *B & W* 10–14; *Glouc* 14–19; *Worc* from 19; *Heref* from 21. *61 Arosa Drive, Malvern WR14 3QE* T: (01684) 491141 E: wm.rumball@gmail.com

RUMBLE, Alison Merle. *See* PRINCE, Alison Merle

RUMBLE, Sarah Victoria. b 74. Newc Univ BA 96 St Martin's Coll Lanc PGCE 97. SCTEI 17. **d** 19 **p** 20. C Portswood St Denys *Win* from 19. *The Vicarage, 54 Whitworth Crescent, Southampton SO18 1GD* M: 07818-857239 E: serarumble@gmail.com

RUMENS, Ms Katharine Mary. b 53. UEA BEd 76. Westcott Ho Cam 90. **d** 92 **p** 94. Par Dn E Ham w Upton Park and Forest Gate *Chelmsf* 92–94; C 94–95; C Waterloo St Jo w St Andr *S'wark* 95–00; Chapl S Bank Cen and Chapl Lon Weekend TV 95–00; R St Giles Cripplegate w St Bart Moor Lane etc *Lon* 00–21; rtd 21; PtO *Lon* from 21. *20 Constable Way, Salisbury SP2 8LN* M: 07544-384452 E: katharine.rumens@gmail.com

✠**RUMSEY, The Rt Revd Andrew Paul.** b 68. Reading Univ BA 89 K Coll Lon DThMin 16. Ridley Hall Cam MA 98. **d** 97 **p** 98 **c** 19. C Harrow Trin St Mich *Lon* 97–01; V Gipsy Hill Ch Ch *S'wark* 01–11; R Oxted and Tandridge 11–14; TR Oxted 14–19; Area Bp Ramsbury *Sarum* from 19. *Ramsbury House, Bath Road, Marlborough SN8 4HS* E: bishop.ramsbury@salisbury.anglican.org

RUMSEY, Ian Mark. b 58. Van Mildert Coll Dur BSc 79 St Jo Coll Dur BA 89. Cranmer Hall Dur 87. **d** 90 **p** 91. C Dalston *Carl* 90–94; C Wreay 92–94; TV Cockermouth w Embleton and Wythop 94–04; Adv for Post-Ord Tr 97–00; V Hurdsfield *Ches* 04–12; Par Development Officer 12–16; V Bowdon from 16. *The Vicarage, Church Brow, Bowdon, Altrincham WA14 2SG* T: 0161-928 2468 E: ian@bowdonchurch.org

RUNCORN, David Charles. b 54. BA 77. St Jo Coll Nottm 77. **d** 79 **p** 80. C Wealdstone H Trin *Lon* 79–82; Chapl Lee Abbey 82–87; C Ealing St Steph Castle Hill *Lon* 89–90; V 90–96; Dir Past and Evang Studies Trin Coll Bris 96–03; Dir Min Development *Lich* 03–08; Tutor St Jo Coll Nottm 08–12; Public Preacher *Glouc* from 12; Assoc Dioc Dir of Ords 15–19; Warden of Readers 15–19; PtO *Ex* from 18. *32 The Avenue, Tiverton EX16 4HW* M: 07870-331537 E: davidruncorn@mac.com

RUNCORN, Jacqueline Ann. *See* SEARLE, Jacqueline Ann

RUNDELL, Gerard Kenneth Bate. b 85. Goldsmiths' Coll Lon BMus 08 RCM MPerf 11 St Jo Coll Dur BA 18. Cranmer Hall Dur 15. **d** 18 **p** 19. C Alnwick *Newc* 18–21; P-in-c Ch the King from 21. *60 Barmoor Drive, Newcastle upon Tyne NE3 5RG* M: 07394-792277 E: gerard.rundell@gmail.com

RUNDELL, Simon Philip. b 67. Univ of N Lon BSc 95 Leeds Univ MA 01 RGN 90. Coll of Resurr Mirfield 99. **d** 01 **p** 02. C Southsea H Spirit *Portsm* 01–04; P-in-c Elson 04–09; V 09–12; P-in-c Bickleigh and Shaugh Prior *Ex* from 12; C Egg Buckland 12–17; C Estover 12–17; C Plymouth Crownhill Ascension 12–17. *33 Leat Walk, Roborough, Plymouth PL6 7AT* E: simon@rundell.org.uk

RUNDELL-EVANS, Benjamin Oscar. b 94. Sarum Coll MA 21. Ripon Coll Cuddesdon BA 16. **d** 16 **p** 17. C Devizes St Jo w St Mary *Sarum* 16–20; P-in-c Upper Stour from 20. *The Rectory,*

Portnells Lane, Zeals, Warminster BA12 6PG T: (01747) 840221 E: revben@upperstour.co.uk

RUNDLE, Hilary. *See* WONG, Hilary

RUNNACLES, Ms Jasmine Celine Leweston. b 47. Lon Bible Coll BA 75 RN 68. STETS 05. d 08 p 09. NSM Burpham *Guildf* 08–17; PtO from 18; Chapl N Surrey Primary Care Trust from 11. *Chydham Cottage, Maybury Hill, Woking GU22 8AF* T/F: (01483) 765239 M: 07774-171818 E: jclrunnacles@virginmedia.com

RUOFF, Mark Frederick John. b 76. K Coll Lon BA 98. St Mellitus Coll BA 15. d 15 p 16. C Onslow Square and S Kensington St Aug *Lon* 15–17; C Hammersmith St Paul from 17. *147 Lavenham Road, London SW18 5EP* M: 07919-403853 E: markfjruoff@gmail.com *or* mark.ruoff@sph.org

RUOFF, Tandy. b 79. St Mellitus Coll BA 20. d 20 p 21. NSM HM Pris Bronzefield from 20. *HM Prison Bronzefield, Woodthorpe Road, Ashford TW15 3JZ* M: 07886-631978 E: tandyruoff@gmail.com

RUSCOE, Canon John Ernest. b 32. Dur Univ BA 57. Qu Coll Birm 57. d 59 p 60. C Jarrow St Paul *Dur* 59–63; C Whitburn 63–65; V S Hylton 65–10; Hon Can Dur Cathl 85–10; rtd 10; PtO *Dur* 10–21. *Address temp unknown*

RUSDELL-WILSON, Arthur Neville. b 43. Lon Univ BScEng 65 Linacre Coll Ox BA 70 MA 74. St Steph Ho Ox 68. d 71 p 72. C Whitton St Aug *Lon* 71–73; C Chiswick St Nic w St Mary 73–76; C Littlehampton St Jas *Chich* 76–81; C Littlehampton St Mary 76–81; C Wick 76–81; V Whitworth St Bart *Man* 81–88; V Shaw 88–98; rtd 03. *21 Fairview Avenue, Goring-by-Sea, Worthing BN12 4HT* T: (01903) 242561 E: arthur@go-forward.co.uk

RUSH, Paul Andrew. b 57. Lon Bible Coll BA 79 Anglia Poly Univ MA 01. Ridley Hall Cam 98. d 00 p 01. C Bar Hill *Ely* 00–03; Dioc Evang Officer *Leic* 03–06; Adv in Evang and Par Development *Bris* 06–13; C W Sheppey *Cant* from 13. *2 St Peter's Close, Minster on Sea, Sheerness ME12 3DD* T: (01795) 663661 M: 07906-118810 E: revdpaulrush@gmail.com

RUSH, Miss Shan Elizabeth. b 64. RGN 86 RSCN 86. Yorks Min Course 07. d 10 p 12. NSM Sheff St Mark Broomhill from 10; Chapl Bluebell Wood Children's Hospice 14–16. *28 Rivelin Street, Sheffield S6 5DL* M: 07598-156817 E: shan.rush@sheffield.anglican.org

RUSHFORTH, Colin Stephen. b 53. Chich Th Coll 74. d 77 p 78. C Moulsecoomb *Chich* 77–79; C Rumboldswyke 79–81; C Whyke w Rumboldswhyke and Portfield 81–82; V Friskney *Linc* 82–84; P-in-c Thorpe St Peter 82–84; TV Leic H Spirit 84–87; Chapl Leic R Infirmary 87–94; Chapl Leic R Infirmary NHS Trust 94–98; PtO *Leic* 08–12; P-in-c Sneinton St Steph w St Matthias *S'well* 12–16; P-in-c Nottingham St Geo w St Jo 12–16; rtd 16. *24 Holly Tree Avenue, Birstall, Leicester LE4 4LF* M: 07960-649191 E: colinrushforth@hotmail.co.uk

RUSHFORTH, Richard Hamblin. b 40. Keble Coll Ox BA 62 MA 71. Chich Th Coll 62. d 64 p 65. C St Leonards Ch Ch *Chich* 64–79; Org Sec Fellowship of St Nic 79–81; V Portslade St Nic and St Andr *Chich* 81–12; Min Portslade Gd Shep CD 88–89; rtd 12; PtO *Chich* 12–17. *12 Upper Church Road, St Leonards-on-Sea TN37 7AT* E: rhrushforth@btinternet.com

RUSHOLME, Susan. b 53. Leeds Univ BA 10. Yorks Min Course 07. d 10 p 11. NSM Chapel Allerton *Ripon* 10–14; *Leeds* from 14. *71 Eaton Hill, Leeds LS16 6SE* T: 0113-261 2913 M: 07504-880199 E: revsue.rusholme@virginmedia.com

RUSHTON, Charlotte Louise. d 17 p 18. C Merthyr Tydfil St Dav and Abercanaid *Llan* 17–21; Min Area Ldr Pontypridd from 21. *Address withheld by request* T: (01685) 385884 E: rev.rushton@gmail.com

RUSHTON, Christopher John. b 54. JP 89. LBIPP 93. Qu Coll Birm 10. d 11 p 12. OLM Hartshill, Penkhull and Trent Vale *Lich* 11–14; NSM 14–15; R from 15; Dioc Lay Min Adv from 12. *The School House, Vicarage Road, Hartshill, Stoke-on-Trent ST4 7NL* T: (01782) 410011 E: church@chrisrushton.co.uk

RUSHTON, David William. b 70. St Chad's Coll Dur BA 96 Cardiff Univ MTh 19. St Steph Ho Ox. d 98 p 99. C Hornsey St Mary w St Geo *Lon* 98–01; C Thamesmead *S'wark* 01–02; Asst Chapl King's Coll Hosp NHS Trust 02–04; Chapl King's Coll Hosp NHS Foundn Trust 04–10; Lead Chapl and Hospitaller Barts and The Lon NHS Trust 10–14; Lead Chapl R Free London NHS Foundn Trust 14–17; Chapl St Chad's Coll *Dur* from 17. *St Chad's College, 18 North Bailey, Durham DH1 3RH* T: 0191-334 3352 E: david.rushton@durham.ac.uk

RUSHTON, Gavin Michael. b 77. St Jo Coll Nottm 14. d 16 p 17. C Kendal St Thos *Carl* 16–19; P-in-c Oxclose *Dur* from 19. *37 Brancepeth Road, Washington NE38 0LA* M: 07976-701454 E: gavin.rushton@yahoo.co.uk

RUSHTON, Canon James David. b 39. Dur Univ BA 61. Cranmer Hall Dur. d 64 p 65. C Upper Armley *Ripon* 64–67; C Blackpool Ch Ch *Blackb* 67–70; V Preston St Cuth 70–79; V Denton Holme *Carl* 79–96; P-in-c Preston All SS *Blackb* 96–00; V 00–04; AD Preston 98–03; Hon Can Blackb Cathl 00–04; rtd 04; PtO *Blackb* from 04. *1 Stable Mews, Fleetwood Road, Thornton-Cleveleys FY5 1SQ* T: (01253) 820402

RUSHTON, Ms Janet Maureen. b 46. Keele Univ BA 68 Leic Univ PGCE 69. Wycliffe Hall Ox BTh 94. d 94 p 95. C Harrow St Mary *Lon* 94–98; C Putney St Mary *S'wark* 98–02; P-in-c Wolvercote w Summertown *Ox* 02–07; P-in-c Summertown 07–11; rtd 11; PtO *Lon* from 11; *S'wark* from 19. *20 Harvard Court, Honeybourne Road, London NW6 1HJ* T: (020) 7431 4606 E: jan.rushton5@gmail.com

RUSHTON, Canon Matthew John. b 75. St Anne's Coll Ox BA 96 MA 01 Linc Univ MA 13 Solicitor 01. Ripon Coll Cuddesdon 07. d 09 p 10. C Nettleham *Linc* 09–12; Hon PV Linc Cathl 11–12; Abp's Chapl *Cant* 12–13; Chapl to Bp Dover 12–13; C Cant St Dunstan w H Cross and Cant St Pet w St Alphege and St Marg etc 12–13; Prec Cant Cathl 13–17; Can Res Roch Cathl from 17. *East Canonry, 2 Kings Orchard, Rochester ME1 1TG* E: matthew.rushton@rochestercathedral.org

RUSHTON, Patricia Mary. *See* DUFFETT-SMITH, Patricia Mary

RUSHTON, The Ven Samantha Jayne. b 65. St Hilda's Coll Ox MA 87. Trin Coll Bris BA 05. d 05 p 06. C Highworth w Sevenhampton and Inglesham etc *Bris* 05–08; C Broad Blunsdon 05–08; Dioc Adv for Local Min 08–15; C Chippenham St Paul w Hardenhuish etc 08–15; C Kington St Michael 08–15; Warden of Readers 11–15; AD Chippenham 13–15; Adn Cleveland *York* 15–19; Adn York from 19. *1 New Lane, Huntington, York YO32 9NU* M: 07906-376036 E: adyk@yorkdiocese.org

RUSHTON, Mrs Susan Elizabeth. b 44. Univ of Wales (Cardiff) BA 65. Bris Sch of Min 83. dss 86 d 87 p 94. Westbury-on-Trym H Trin *Bris* 86–87; Hon Par Dn 87–91; C Wotton St Mary *Glouc* 91–94; P-in-c Frampton Cotterell *Bris* 94–07; Chapl United Bris Healthcare NHS Trust 94–98; P-in-c Iron Acton *Bris* 98–07; rtd 07; PtO *York* from 08. *9 Lime Avenue, Heworth, York YO31 1BT* T: (01904) 410363 E: rushton.sue.e@gmail.com

RUSHTON, Mrs Valerie Elizabeth Wendy. b 40. Birm Univ BSocSc 62. WMMTC 86. d 89 p 94. C Nuneaton St Nic *Cov* 89–93; C Stockingford 93–96; TV Watling Valley *Ox* 96–01; rtd 02; PtO *Ox* 02–20. *106 Moreton Road, Buckingham MK18 1PW* T: (01280) 824942

RUSS, Canon Timothy John. b 41. AKC 64. Sarum Th Coll 66. d 66 p 67. C Walthamstow St Pet *Chelmsf* 66–70; C Epping St Jo 70–73; C Stepney St Dunstan and All SS *Lon* 73–75; Youth Officer 75–79; Tutor YMCA Nat Coll Walthamstow 79–84; Hon C St Botolph Aldgate w H Trin Minories *Lon* 82–89; Selection Sec ACCM 84–89; Dir St Marylebone Healing and Counselling Cen 89–92; Gen Sec Inst of Relig and Medicine 89–92; Hon C Hoxton St Anne w St Columba *Lon* 90–92; P-in-c St Dennis *Truro* 92–06; Par Development Adv 92–99; Dioc Dir Minl Tr 99–06; Hon Can Truro Cathl 01–06; rtd 06. *7 The Cedars, Truro TR1 2FD* T: (01872) 272286

RUSSELL, Adrian Camper. b 45. Chich Th Coll 79. d 81 p 82. C Marton *Blackb* 81–84; C Haslemere *Guildf* 84–85; V Hartlepool H Trin *Dur* 85–89; P-in-c Cornforth 89–94; R Auchterarder *St And* 94–97; R Muthill 94–97; P-in-c Kenton Ascension *Newc* 97–07; rtd 07; PtO *Newc* from 17. *23 Lambley Avenue, North Shields NE30 3SL* T: 0191-280 9552 E: acr26682@blueyonder.co.uk

RUSSELL, Andrea. b 64. K Coll Lon LLB 86 Nottm Univ BA 04 MA 05 PhD 10. EMMTC 08. d 10 p 11. C Sherwood *S'well* 10–12; Dir of Studies St Jo Coll Nottm 12–14; Tutor Qu Foundn Birm 14–20; PtO *Birm* from 16; Dir Formation for Min *Ox* from 21; LtO from 21. *Church House Oxford, Langford Locks, Kidlington OX5 1GF* T: (01865) 208200 E: andrea.russell@oxford.anglican.org

RUSSELL, Ms Anne. b 66. Man Univ BA(Econ) 88. LCTP 06. d 11 p 12. C Kendal H Trin *Carl* 11–14; TR Bentham, Burton-in-Lonsdale, Chapel-le-Dale etc *Leeds* from 14; AD Bowland and Ewecross 19–21. *The Rectory, 1 Moons Acre, Bentham, Lancaster LA2 7BL* T: (01524) 261609 M: 07528-572072 E: revanne.ingleborough@gmail.com

✠**RUSSELL, The Rt Revd Anthony John.** b 43. St Chad's Coll Dur BA 65 Trin Coll Ox DPhil 71. Cuddesdon Coll 65. d 70 p 71 c 88. C Hilborough w Bodney *Nor* 70–73; P-in-c Preston-on-Stour w Whitchurch *Cov* 73–76; P-in-c Atherstone on Stour 73–76; V Preston on Stour and Whitchurch w Atherstone 77–88; Can Th Cov Cathl 77–88; Chapl Arthur Rank Cen 73–82; Dir 83–88; Chapl to The Queen 83–88; Area Bp Dorchester *Ox* 88–00; Bp Ely 00–10;

rtd 10; Hon Asst Bp Ox 11–18. *Lye Hill House, Holton, Oxford OX33 1QF* T: (01865) 876415

RUSSELL, The Ven Brian Kenneth. b 50. Trin Hall Cam BA 73 MA 76 Birm Univ MA 77 PhD 83. Cuddesdon Coll 74. **d** 76 **p** 77. C Redhill St Matt *S'wark* 76–79; Dir Studies NEOC 79–83; P-in-c Merrington *Dur* 79–83; Dir of Studies and Lect Linc Th Coll 83–86; Selection Sec and Sec Cttee for Th Educn ABM 86–93; Bp's Dir for Min *Birm* 93–05; Adn Aston 05–14; Hon Can Birm Cathl from 99; Sen Chapl Oslo w Bergen, Trondheim and Stavanger *Eur* 14–17; PtO *Birm* from 14; *Eur* from 17. *1 Plover Close, Stratford-upon-Avon CV37 9EN* T: (01789) 299923 E: b-russell5@sky.com

RUSSELL, Bruce Harley. b 57. Ch Ch Ox BA 79 Roehampton Inst PGCE 80. Ripon Coll Cuddesdon. **d** 99 **p** 00. C Bracknell *Ox* 99–03; TV Langley Marish 03–17; Min Can and Succ Windsor 17–19. *58A Alexandra Road, Windsor SL4 1HU*

RUSSELL, Clive Phillip. b 61. Ridley Hall Cam 04. **d** 06 **p** 07. C High Ongar w Norton Mandeville *Chelmsf* 06–09; V Grays North from 09. *St John's Vicarage, 8A Victoria Avenue, Grays RM16 2RP* T: (01375) 372101 E: crussell.main@gmail.com

RUSSELL, Canon David John. b 57. Sarum & Wells Th Coll BTh 94. **d** 94 **p** 95. C Glouc St Geo w Whaddon 94–98; P-in-c Wickwar w Rangeworthy 98–01; R Wickwar, Rangeworthy and Hillesley 02–11; R Charfield and Kingswood w Wickwar etc from 11; AD Wotton from 15; Hon Can Glouc Cathl from 17. *The Rectory, 75 High Street, Wickwar, Wotton-under-Edge GL12 8NP* T: (01454) 294267 E: davidrussell@gmx.com

RUSSELL, David John Timothy. b 75. Oak Hill Th Coll. **d** 09 **p** 10. C Padiham w Hapton and Padiham Green *Blackb* 09–13; V Woodford *Ches* from 13. *The Vicarage, 531 Chester Road, Woodford, Stockport SK7 1PR* T: 0161-439 2286 E: revdavidrussell@yahoo.com

RUSSELL, Canon Derek John. b 30. St Pet Hall Ox BA 54 MA 58. Qu Coll Birm 54. **d** 56 **p** 57. C Boxley *Cant* 56–59; C Whitstable All SS 59–63; Chapl HM Pris Wormwood Scrubs 63–65; Chapl HM Pris Stafford 65–69; Chapl HM Pris Pentonville 70; Chapl HM Pris Wormwood Scrubs 71–89; SE Regional Chapl 74–81; Chapl HM Rem Cen Latchmere Ho 74–77; Asst Chapl Gen of Pris 81–83; Dep 83–90; Hon Can Cant Cathl 86–90; rtd 90; PtO *Cant* 90–16. *25 Pier Avenue, Whitstable CT5 2HQ* T: (01227) 276654 E: derekandlizrussell@tiscali.co.uk

RUSSELL, Ms Elizabeth Marilyn Vivia. b 50. LRAM 72 GRSM 72. Westcott Ho Cam 95. **d** 97 **p** 98. C Alton St Lawr *Win* 97–01; C St Martin-in-the-Fields *Lon* 01–08; P-in-c S Kensington H Trin w All SS 08–20; Dir of Ords Two Cities Area 08–20; rtd 20; PtO *Lon* from 20. *5 Aldwyn House, Davidson Gardens, London SW8 2HX* T: (020) 7498 5623 E: erussell101@btinternet.com

RUSSELL, Eric Watson. b 39. FCA 76. Clifton Th Coll 66. **d** 69 **p** 70. C Kinson *Sarum* 69–73; C Peckham St Mary Magd *S'wark* 73–77; TV Barking St Marg w St Patr *Chelmsf* 77–82; V Lozells St Paul and St Silas *Birm* 82–95; RD Aston 89–94; P-in-c Barston and C Knowle 95–04; I Kells Union *M & K* 04–09; rtd 09; PtO *St E* 15–19. *Address temp unknown* E: ericandjoan@uwclub.net

RUSSELL, Gary William Algernon. b 64. Ripon Coll Cuddesdon 04. **d** 06 **p** 07. C Harpenden St Nic *St Alb* 06–09; P-in-c St Alb St Mary Marshalswick 09–14; rtd 14; Hon Chapl ATC from 07. *183A Victoria Road, Ferndown BH22 9HY* E: moreteavicar@hotmail.co.uk

RUSSELL, Ms Isoline Lucilda (Lyn). b 41. **d** 03 **p** 04. OLM Camberwell St Giles w St Matt *S'wark* 03–11; PtO from 11. *124 Hindman's Road, London SE22 9NH* T: (020) 8299 4431

RUSSELL, James Anthony Tomkins. *See* TOMKINS-RUSSELL, James Anthony

RUSSELL, Canon Janet Mary. b 53. Univ of Wales BSc 74 BArch 76. Ox Min Course 91. **d** 94 **p** 95. C Watlington w Pyrton and Shirburn *Ox* 94–97; C Icknield 97–98; TV Wallingford 98–05; Par Development Adv (Berks) 05–11; Dir Miss *S & B* 11–16; Hon Can Brecon Cathl 12–15; Can Res Brecon Cathl 15–16; PtO from 16; *Heref* from 17; *Leeds* from 19. *The Mill, Rhosgoch, Builth Wells LD2 3JY* M: 07894-821828 E: janetrussell@churchinwales.org.uk

RUSSELL, John Bruce. b 56. Ripon Coll Cuddesdon 93. **d** 95 **p** 96. C Newport Pagnell w Lathbury and Moulsoe *Ox* 95–98; P-in-c Wing w Grove 98–03; AD Mursley 02–03; PtO *St Alb* 08–10; TV Gt Berkhamsted, Gt and Lt Gaddesden etc 10–20; TR from 20. *St John's Vicarage, Pipers Hill, Great Gaddesden, Hemel Hempstead HP1 3BY* T: (01442) 214898 E: john_russell@live.co.uk

RUSSELL, John Graham. b 35. G&C Coll Cam BA 58 MA 62. Westcott Ho Cam 59. **d** 61 **p** 62. C Durleigh *B & W* 61–66; C Bridgwater St Mary w Chilton Trinity 61–66; C Far Headingley St Chad *Ripon* 66–72; P-in-c Leeds St Matt Lt

London 72–79; V Rowley Regis *Birm* 79–84; V Hall Green Ascension 84–95; Deanery P Warley Deanery 95–00; rtd 01; PtO *Birm* from 01. *1 Stapylton Avenue, Harborne, Birmingham B17 0BA* T: 0121-426 4529

RUSSELL, John Richard. b 53. Westmr Coll Ox MTh 01 FRSA 02. Spurgeon's Coll 77 Ripon Coll Cuddesdon 01. **d** 01 **p** 02. Hon C St Mary le Strand w St Clem Danes *Lon* 01–02; Chapl RAF 02–08; PtO *Chelmsf* from 09. *32 Feeches Road, Southend-on-Sea SS2 6TD* T: (01702) 300978 E: revjohnrussell@virginmedia.com

RUSSELL, Canon Jonathan Vincent Harman. b 43. K Coll Lon 68. **d** 69 **p** 70. C Addington *Cant* 69–73; C Buckland in Dover w Buckland Valley 73–76; P-in-c Selling 76–85; P-in-c Throwley w Stalisfield and Otterden 79–85; R Selling w Throwley, Sheldwich w Badlesmere etc 85–95; Hon Min Can Cant Cathl 83–94; RD Ospringe 90–95; P-in-c Elham w Denton and Wootton 95–01; V 01–08; Hon Can Cant Cathl 94–08; rtd 08; PtO *Cant* from 08. *Kirkella, Goodwin Road, St Margaret's Bay, Dover CT15 6ED* T: (01304) 852811 M: 07702-314865 E: jvhrussell@btinternet.com

RUSSELL, Jonathan Wingate. b 55. Newc Univ BSc 76. St Jo Coll Nottm BA 83. **d** 84 **p** 85. C Southsea St Jude *Portsm* 84–87; P-in-c Shorwell w Kingston 87–92; V 92–06; P-in-c Gatcombe 87–92; R 92–06; P-in-c Chale 89–92; R 92–06; RD W Wight 96–01; R Allendale w Whitfield *Newc* 06–20; AD Hexham 11–16; rtd 20. *25 Otter's Holt, Culgaith, Penrith CA10 1SG* E: cuthbertallendale@gmail.com

RUSSELL, Lyn. *See* RUSSELL, Isoline Lucilda

RUSSELL, Madeleine. b 41. Pargau Teacher Tr Coll Switzerland TDip 62. **d** 04 **p** 05. NSM Halifax H Trin and St Jude *Wakef* 04–13; rtd 13; PtO *Leeds* from 13. *Hillcroft, 12 Westborough Drive, Halifax HX2 7QN*

RUSSELL, Marion Elisabeth. b 54. Glas Univ BEd 75 Jordanhill Coll Glas TCert 75. CBDTI 03. **d** 06 **p** 07. NSM Altham w Clayton le Moors *Blackb* 06–10; Chapl Trin Academy Halifax 10–12; C Huddersfield St Pet *Wakef* 12–14; V Rastrick *Leeds* 14–20; AD Brighouse and Elland 16–20; Jt AD Calder Valley 18–19; Jt AD Halifax and Calder Valley 20; V Embsay w Eastby from 20; Hon Can Ripon Cathl 19–20; Clergy Development Officer Ripon Area from 20. *21 Shires Lane, Embsay, Skipton BD23 6SB* E: revd.marion@gmail.com or marion.russell@leeds.anglican.org

RUSSELL, Martin Christopher. b 48. St Jo Coll Dur BA 70. Coll of Resurr Mirfield 72. **d** 74 **p** 75. C Huddersfield St Pet *Wakef* 74–77; Trinidad and Tobago 78–85; V S Crosland *Wakef* 86–00; P-in-c Helme 86–00; P-in-c Halifax H Trin 00–02; V Halifax St Jude 00–02; V Halifax H Trin and St Jude 02–13; rtd 13; PtO *Leeds* from 17. *Hillcroft, 12 Westborough Drive, Halifax HX2 7QN*

RUSSELL, Canon Neil. b 47. EMMTC 78. **d** 81 **p** 82. NSM Wyberton *Linc* 81–84; C 84–85; V Frampton 85–93; Agric Chapl and Countryside Officer 88–93; P-in-c Stamford All SS w St Jo 93–97; R 97–08; RD Aveland and Ness w Stamford 00–06; Warden Sacrista Prebend Retreat Ho *S'well* 08–10; Can and Preb Linc Cathl 02–10; rtd 10; PtO *Dur* 11–17. *Clare Cottage, 4 The Paddocks, Gainford, Darlington DL2 3GA* T: (01325) 733140 M: 07730-403630 E: canonneilrussell@yahoo.co.uk

RUSSELL, Mrs Noreen Margaret. b 39. Man Univ BA 60 Lon Univ PGCE 61 BD 66. WMMTC 90. **d** 91 **p** 94. NSM Swynnerton and Tittensor *Lich* 91–97; C Draycott-le-Moors w Forsbrook 97–06; rtd 06; PtO *Lich* 06–20. *40 Old Road, Barlaston, Stoke-on-Trent ST12 9EQ* T: (01782) 372992 E: norrenbungalow40@gmail.com

RUSSELL, The Ven Norman Atkinson. b 43. Chu Coll Cam BA 65 MA 69 Lon Univ BD 70. Lon Coll of Div 67. **d** 70 **p** 71. C Clifton Ch Ch w Em *Bris* 70–74; C Enfield Ch Ch Trent Park *Lon* 74–77; R Harwell w Chilton *Ox* 77–84; P-in-c Gerrards Cross 84–88; P-in-c Fulmer 85–88; R Gerrards Cross and Fulmer 88–98; Hon Can Ch Ch 95–98; RD Amersham 96–98; Adn Berks 98–13; rtd 13; PtO *Ox* from 13; *Guildf* from 14. *47A Theobalds Way, Frimley, Camberley GU16 9RF* E: ven.narussell@gmail.com

RUSSELL, Paul Selwyn. b 38. ALCD 61. **d** 61 **p** 62. C Gillingham St Mark *Roch* 61–64; SAMS 64–84; Chile, Peru and Bolivia 64–84; V Brinsworth w Catcliffe *Sheff* 84–91; R Brinklow *Cov* 91–04; R Harborough Magna 91–04; V Monks Kirby w Pailton and Stretton-under-Fosse 91–04; rtd 04. *19 Larchfields, Wolston, Coventry CV8 3JL* T: (024) 7654 3906 E: paul.russell024@yahoo.com

RUSSELL, Peter Richard. b 60. Ch Ch Coll Cant BA 99. SEITE 02. **d** 05 **p** 06. NSM Margate All SS and Westgate St Sav *Cant* 05–08; Chapl St Lawr Coll Ramsgate 09–19; rtd 19; PtO *Cant* from 19. *40 Dane Road, Birchington CT7 9PT* E: minnisbay@hotmail.com

RUSSELL, Richard Alexander. b 44. Univ of Wales (Abth) BA 65 McMaster Univ Ontario MA 67 Bris Univ MA 73 PGCE 74 MEd 76. Trin Coll Bris 79. **d** 82 **p** 83. C Hartlepool St Paul *Dur* 82–85; P-in-c Bath Widcombe *B & W* 85–88; V 88–00; rtd 00; PtO *B & W* from 09. *76 Waterside Way, Radstock, Bath BA3 3YQ* T: (01761) 433217 E: therealrichardrussell@gmail.com

RUSSELL, Roger Geoffrey. b 47. Worc Coll Ox BA 69 MA 73. Cuddesdon Coll 70. **d** 72 **p** 73. C Anlaby Common St Mark *York* 72–75; C Wilton Place St Paul *Lon* 75–86; R Lancing w Coombes *Chich* 86–12; RD Worthing 97–05; rtd 13; PtO *Chich* 13–17. *32 Lime Grove, Angmering, Littlehampton BN16 4HA*

RUSSELL, Canon William Warren. b 52. QUB BSocSc 74. CITC 74. **d** 77 **p** 78. C Agherton *Conn* 77–79; C Lisburn Ch Ch Cathl 79–83; I Magheradroll *D & D* from 83; Treas Dromore Cathl from 08; Dioc C from 11. *The Rectory, 18 Church Road, Ballynahinch BT24 8LP* T: (028) 9756 2289 M: 07810-222906 E: rev_wwrussell@hotmail.com *or* revwwrussell@gmail.com

RUSSELL GRANT, Julia Rosalind. b 45. **d** 11 **p** 12. OLM Layer de la Haye and Layer Breton w Birch etc *Chelmsf* 11–13; OLM Thurstable and Winstree 13–15; NSM 15–18; rtd 18; PtO *Chelmsf* 18–21. *8 Heath House, Crayes Green, Layer Breton, Colchester CO2 0PN* T: (01206) 330235 E: church@hatfield-broad-oak.net *or* julia@bretonheath.me.uk

RUSSELL-SMITH, Mark Raymond. b 46. New Coll Edin MTh 91 St Jo Coll Dur BA 71. Cranmer Hall Dur. **d** 72 **p** 73. C Upton (Overchurch) *Ches* 72–75; C Deane *Man* 75–77; UCCF Travelling Sec 77–80; LtO *York* 78–81; BCMS Kenya 81–92; P-in-c Slaidburn *Bradf* 92–11; P-in-c Long Preston w Tosside 97–11; rtd 11; PtO *York* from 12. *11 Osprey Close, York YO24 2YE* T: (01904) 792154 E: mars4654@uwclub.net

RUST, Mrs Alison Theresa (Tessa). Auckland Univ BA 76. St Mellitus Coll BA 11. **d** 11 **p** 12. C W Ealing St Jo w St Jas *Lon* 11–14; Chapl Heathrow Airport from 14. *The Chapel of St George, Central Terminal Area, London Heathrow Airport, Hounslow TW6 1BP* M: 07979-627714 E: tessarust@gmail.com

RUST, Jonathan Kenneth. b 62. Reading Univ BSc 84 St Mellitus Coll MA 14. Ridley Hall Cam. **d** 00 **p** 01. C Holloway St Mary Magd *Lon* 00–16; Dir Miss Development Kensington Area from 16; Public Preacher from 16. *10 Eversley Crescent, Isleworth TW7 4LS* E: jonathan.rust@london.anglican.org

RUSTED, Amanda Giselle. b 61. Liv Univ MA Ches Univ BTh. All SS Cen for Miss & Min 17. **d** 19 **p** 20. NSM Dunham Massey St Marg and St Mark *Ches* 19–20; NSM Hale and Ashley from 20; Mental Health Chapl Manchester Mental Health and Soc Care Trust from 19; Chapl Pennine Care NHS Foundn Trust from 19. *Spode Cottage, Coe Lane, Little Bollington, Altrincham WA14 3SH* T: (01565) 830697 M: 07714-959180 E: gisellerusted@outlook.com

RUSTED, Mrs Mary Elizabeth. b 44. **d** 00 **p** 01. OLM Mildenhall *St E* 00–10; rtd 10; PtO *St E* from 10. *3 Ford Close, West Row, Bury St Edmunds IP28 8NR* T: (01638) 715054 E: maryrusted@hotmail.com

RUSTELL, Canon Anthony Christopher. b 77. Ch Ch Ox BA 98 MSt 01 MA 02 Keble Coll Ox DPhil 07. St Steph Ho Ox 98. **d** 01 **p** 02. NSM Ox St Barn and St Paul 01–04; P-in-c N Hinksey and Wytham 04–10; P-in-c Ox St Frideswide w Binsey 09–10; R Osney 10–11; Dir Minl Tr *Llan* 11–14; P-in-c Tongwynlais 11–14; Can Res Portsm Cathl from 14; Hd Miss, Discipleship and Min from 14. *1 Pembroke Close, Portsmouth PO1 2NX* T: (023) 9289 9654 E: acrustell@btinternet.com *or* anthony.rustell@portsmouth.anglican.org

RUTHERFORD, Anthony Richard. b 37. Culham Coll Ox TCert 62 Sussex Univ MA 77. S'wark Ord Course 83. **d** 86 **p** 87. Hon C Tunbridge Wells St Luke *Roch* 86–88; C Bromley SS Pet and Paul 88–90; V Wragby *Linc* 90–94; Asst Min Officer 90–94; V Penge Lane H Trin *Roch* 94–02; rtd 02; PtO *Roch* from 03; *Chich* from 16; *Eur* 16–19. *6 Ashley Gardens, Tunbridge Wells TN4 8TY* T: (01892) 541009 E: tony.rutherford37@icloud.com

RUTHERFORD, Daniel Fergus Peter. b 65. Hatf Coll Dur BA 86 CertEd 87. Ridley Hall Cam 88. **d** 90 **p** 91. C Harold Wood *Chelmsf* 90–94; C Hove Bp Hannington Memorial Ch *Chich* 94–97; Chapl City of Lon Freemen's Sch 97–11; Chapl Strathallan Sch 12–15; Asst Hd (Past) Dulwich Prep Sch Cranbrook from 15; PtO *Cant* from 16. *Dulwich Preparatory School, Coursehorn, Golford Road, Cranbrook TN17 3NP* T: (01580) 712179 E: drutherford@dulwichprepcranbrook.org

RUTHERFORD, Emma Catherine. Ulster Univ BA. St Jo Coll Nottm MTh. **d** 11 **p** 12. C Coleraine *Conn* 12–13; Dioc C 13–17; I Stormont *D & D* from 17. *St Molua's Rectory, 3 Rosepark, Belfast BT5 7RG* T: (028) 9048 2292 M: 07753-117838 E: revecr@gmail.com

✠**RUTHERFORD, The Rt Revd Graeme Stanley.** b 43. Cranmer Hall Dur BA 77 MA 78 ACT 66. **d** 66 **p** 67 **c** 00. C Bendigo Cathl Australia 66–70; V Pyramid Hill 70–73; C Holborn St Geo w H Trin St Bart *Lon* 73–74; C Dur St Nic 74–77; R Kyabram Australia 77–82; I Malvern 82–87; I Camberwell St Jo 87–00; Can Melbourne Cathl 91–00; Asst Bp Newcastle 00–08; rtd 08. *3/68 Campbell Road, Hawthorn East VIC 3123, Australia* T: (0061) (3) 9813 4185 M: 40-837 4847 E: gcruth@bigpond.com

RUTHERFORD, Ian William. b 46. Univ of Wales (Lamp) BA 68. Cuddesdon Coll 68. **d** 70 **p** 71. C Gosforth All SS *Newc* 70–72; C Prestbury *Glouc* 73–76; Chapl RN 76–93; TV Redruth w Lanner and Treleigh *Truro* 93–94; V Paulsgrove *Portsm* 94–99; V Leeds Belle Is St Jo and St Barn *Ripon* 99–11; rtd 11; CMP from 93; PtO *Portsm* from 11; *Eur* from 15; *Win* from 15. Flat 12, 27-29 St Simons Road, Southsea PO5 2QE T: (023) 9229 7492

RUTHERFORD, Janet Elizabeth. b 37. S'wark Ord Course 86. **d** 89. NSM Plaistow St Mary *Roch* 89–90; NSM Linc St Botolph 91–93. *6 Ashley Gardens, Tunbridge Wells TN4 8TY* T: (01892) 541009

RUTHERFORD, Peter Marshall. b 57. St Andr Univ MTheol 81 Ulster Univ MA 96. CITC 83. **d** 83 **p** 84. C Stormont *D & D* 83–85; CF 85–01; Asst Chapl Gen 01–02; Asst Chapl Milan w Genoa and Varese *Eur* 03–04; I Castlepollard and Oldcastle w Loughcrew etc *M & K* 04–10; I Julianstown and Colpe w Drogheda and Duleek 10–15; Dioc Dir of Ords 05–15; Warden of Readers 12–15; I Kinsale Union *C, C & R* from 15; Dir of Ords from 21. *The Rectory, 3 Abbeycourt, Kinsale, Co Cork, Republic of Ireland* T: (00353) (21) 477 2220 E: peterrutherford@me.com

RUTHERFORD (née ERREY), Ms Rosalind Elisabeth. b 52. St Hugh's Coll Ox BA 74 Surrey Univ BA 02 Goldsmiths' Coll Lon PGCE 78. STETS 99. **d** 02 **p** 03. C Earley St Pet *Ox* 02–06; TV Basingstoke *Win* 06–18; rtd 18; PtO *Ox* from 18. *7 Godwyn Close, Abingdon OX14 1BU* E: revrosalind@btinternet.com

RUTLEDGE, Canon Christopher John Francis. b 44. Lon Univ BSc 67 Univ of Wales MPhil 94 PhD 99 Glyndŵr Univ MSc 15 Lon Inst FETC 80. Sarum Th Coll 67 Clare Coll Cam 69. **d** 70 **p** 71. C Birm St Pet 70–73; C Calne and Blackland *Sarum* 73–76; P-in-c Derry Hill 76–78; V 78–81; P-in-c Talbot Village 81–82; V 82–10; Can and Preb Sarum Cathl 95–10; Chapl Talbot Heath Sch Bournemouth 04–09; rtd 10; PtO *Sarum* from 10. *48 Wollaton Road, Ferndown BH22 8QY* T: (01202) 895116 E: christopher.rutledge@talktalk.net

RUTT-FIELD, Benjamin John. b 48. Chich Th Coll. **d** 90 **p** 91. C Wickford and Runwell *Chelmsf* 90–94; V Goodmayes St Paul 94–14; rtd 14; PtO *Lon* from 14; *Chelmsf* from 17. *33 Hillcourt Avenue, London N12 8EY* T: (020) 8446 3457 E: benruttfield@outlook.com

RUTTER, Canon Allen Edward Henry (Claude). b 28. Qu Coll Cam BA 52 MA 56. Cranmer Hall Dur. **d** 59 **p** 60. C Bath Abbey w St Jas *B & W* 59–60; C E Dereham w Hoe *Nor* 60–64; R Cawston 64–69; Chapl Cawston Coll 64–69; P-in-c Felthorpe w Haveringland *Nor* 64–69; R Gingindhlovu S Africa 69–73; P-in-c Over and Nether Compton, Trent etc *Sarum* 73–80; RD Sherborne 77–87; P-in-c Oborne w Poyntington 79–80; P-in-c Queen Thorne 80–86; Can and Preb Sarum Cathl 86–96; rtd 96; PtO *B & W* 98–99 and from 00; P-in-c Thorncombe w Winsham and Cricket St Thomas 99; C Chard and Distr 99–00. *Home Farm, Chilson, South Chard, Chard TA20 2NX* T: (01460) 221368

RUTTER, Graham Piers. b 77. St Jo Coll Dur BSc 98 PhD 03 Liv Univ MSc 99 FHEA 17. St Jo Coll Nottm MTh 08. **d** 08 **p** 09. C Wellington All SS w Eyton *Lich* 08–12; P-in-c Swadlincote *Derby* 12–19; C Hartshorne and Bretby 13–19; C Gresley 18–19; C Newhall 18–19; RD Repton 13–18; AD Mercia 18–19; Tutor and Lect St Mellitus NW from 19; NSM Aughton Ch Ch *Liv* from 20. *St Mellitus College North West, The St Aidan's Centre, Liverpool Cathedral, St James Road, Liverpool L1 7AZ* E: graham.rutter@stmellitus.ac.uk

RUTTER, John Edmund Charles. b 53. Qu Coll Cam MA 76. St Jo Coll Nottm MA 93. **d** 93 **p** 94. C Penge St Jo *Roch* 93–97; Bp's C Bangor Primacy *D & D* 97–04; I Glenavy w Tunny and Crumlin *Conn* 04–19; rtd 19. *57 Drumnabreeze Road, Donaghcloney, Craigavon BT66 7NT* M: 07917-376023 E: jec.rutter@gmail.com

RUTTER, Preb Martin Charles. b 54. Wolv Poly BSc 75 Southn Univ BTh 81. Sarum & Wells Th Coll 76. **d** 79 **p** 80. C Cannock *Lich* 79–82; C Uttoxeter w Bramshall 82–86; V W Bromwich St Jas 86–97; P-in-c W Bromwich St Paul 89–97; V W Bromwich St Jas w St Paul 97–02; RD W Bromwich 94–02; V Gt Barr from 02; RD Walsall 10–15; Preb Lich Cathl from

16. *St Margaret's Vicarage, Chapel Lane, Great Barr, Birmingham B43 7BD* T: 0121-357 1390 E: martincrutter@gmail.com

RUTTER, Michael. b 75. Trin Coll Bris BA 06 Coll of Resurr Mirfield 99. **d** 07 **p** 08. C Dudley Wood *Worc* 07–10; TV Halas 10–15; V Darby End and Netherton 15–18; CF from 18. *c/o MOD Chaplains (Army)* T: (01264) 383430 E: fr.mike.rutter@gmail.com

RYALL, Michael Richard. b 36. TCD BA 58 MA 65 HDipEd 66. TCD Div Sch Div Test 58. **d** 58 **p** 59. C Dublin St Geo and St Thos, Finglas and Free Ch *D & G* 58–62; Chapl Mountjoy Pris 58–62; CF 62–65 and 68–90; CF (TAVR) 67–68; C Dublin Rathmines *D & G* 65–66; R Yardley Hastings, Denton and Grendon etc *Pet* 90–01; Chapl HM Pris Wellingborough 92–93; rtd 01; PtO *St D* from 07; P-in-c Mayland *Chelmsf* 08–12. *59 Pill Road, Hook, Haverfordwest SA62 4LX* M: 07828-763567 E: michaelryall36@michaelryall36.plus.com

RYALLS, Craig James. b 74. Bris Univ BA 96 Peterho Cam BA 01. Ridley Hall Cam 99. **d** 02 **p** 03. C Bearsted w Thurnham *Cant* 02–06; C Woking Ch Ch *Guildf* 06–14; R Fisherton Anger *Sarum* from 14. *St Paul's Church Centre, Fisherton Street, Salisbury SP2 7QW* T: (01722) 334005 E: craig@wearestpauls.church

RYAN, Alan John. b 57. SWMTC. **d** 09 **p** 10. C Fremington, Instow and Westleigh *Ex* 09–11; C Whitchurch 11–13; V Winterborne Valley and Milton Abbas *Sarum* 13–19; TV Brixton, Newton Ferrers, Revelstoke etc *Ex* 19–20; TR from 20; C Holbeton 19–20; P-in-c from 20; RD Ivybridge from 20. *The Vicarage, Bowden Hill, Yealmpton, Plymouth PL8 2JX* T: (01752) 880257

RYAN, Mrs Barbara. b 56. **d** 12 **p** 13. NSM Hessle *York* 12–16; NSM Bilton St Pet 16–18; NSM Sutton St Mich 16–18; NSM Spofforth w Kirk Deighton *Leeds* from 18. *The Rectory, Church Lane, Spofforth, Harrogate HG3 1AF* E: revbryan@hotmail.com

RYAN, David Peter. b 64. Aston Univ BSc 86. Linc Th Coll BTh 94. **d** 94 **p** 95. C Horsforth *Ripon* 94–97; C Bedale 97–98; P-in-c Startforth and Bowes and Rokeby w Brignall 98–00; V 00–04; P-in-c Warndon St Nic *Worc* 04–13; Chapl Worcs Acute Hosps NHS Trust from 13; Dioc Ecum Officer *Worc* from 04. *The Alexandra Hospital, Woodrow Drive, Redditch B98 7UB* T: (01527) 503030 E: david.ryan@cofe-worcester.org.uk *or* david.ryan5@nhs.net

RYAN, Mrs Diane Thérèse Hazel. b 69. Lanc Univ BA 90. St Hild Coll 14. **d** 17 **p** 18. C Gt Snaith *Sheff* 17–21; P-in-c Blaydon *Dur* from 21; P-in-c High Spen and Rowlands Gill from 21. *Address temp unknown* M: 07501-271754 E: diane_ryan@btinternet.com

RYAN, Graham William Robert (Gregg). b 51. CITC 90. **d** 93 **p** 94. NSM Clonsast w Rathangan, Thomastown etc *M & K* 93–97; Dioc Communications Officer 96–97; Press Officer from 97; Dioc C *M & K* 97–16; P-in-c Clane w Donadea and Coolcarrigan 16–18; rtd 18. *Millicent Hall, Millicent South, Sallins, Naas, Co Kildare, Republic of Ireland* T: (00353) (45) 879464 F: 875173 E: gwr.ryan@gmail.com

RYAN, James Francis. b 47. Surrey Univ BSc. St Jo Coll Nottm. **d** 83 **p** 84. C Littleover *Derby* 83–86; C Chipping Sodbury and Old Sodbury *Glouc* 86–89; V Pype Hayes *Birm* 89–99; R W Winch w Setchey, N Runcton and Middleton *Nor* 99–12; rtd 12; PtO *Chich* from 13. *30 Rook Way, Horsham RH12 5FR*

RYAN, Maureen Sheila. **d** 98 **p** 99. NSM Tuam w Cong and Aasleagh *T, K & A* 98–16; Preb Kilmactalway St Patr Cathl Dublin 01–09; Can Tuam Cathl *T, K & A* 05–16; Provost Tuam 14–16; Can Killala Cathl 13–16; rtd 16. *Marshal's Park, Rinville, Oranmore, Galway, Republic of Ireland* T/F: (00353) (91) 794599

RYAN, Robert Lloyd. b 65. Warwick Univ BA 87. SEITE 05. **d** 08 **p** 09. C Roch Cathl 08–12; NSM Gillingham St Mark 12–15; TV E Greenwich *S'wark* 15–18; Chapl Ch Ch and St Mary Magd Primary Schs 15–18; P-in-c Lt Ilford St Barn *Chelmsf* from 18. *St Barnabas' Vicarage, 153C Browning Road, London E12 6PB* T: (020) 8472 2777 M: 07595-354007 E: rob.ryan@mac.com *or* stbarnabasmanorpark@gmail.com

RYAN, Roger John. b 47. Lon Bible Coll BA 79 Surrey Univ MA 00 St Pet Coll Ox DPhil 06 Univ Coll Lon MA 09. Oak Hill Th Coll 79. **d** 80 **p** 81. C Luton St Fran *St Alb* 80–83; R Laceby *Linc* 83–88; V Summerstown *S'wark* 88–17; rtd 17; PtO *S'wark* from 18. *7 Beechwood Court, West Street Lane, Carshalton SM5 2PZ* T: (020) 3802 8978 E: rogerryan307@hotmail.com

RYAN, Mrs Saffron Mandy. b 77. Surrey Univ BA 99. St Mellitus Coll BA 17. **d** 17 **p** 18. C Hornchurch St Andr *Chelmsf* 17–20; C Stratford St Paul and St Jas from 20. *42 Villiers Gardens, London E20 1GW* M: 07557-309979 E: saffron@jjssp.co.uk

RYAN, Canon Stephen John. b 49. Univ of Wales (Swansea) BA 70. Sarum & Wells Th Coll 70. **d** 73 **p** 74. C Llantrisant *Llan* 73–77; V Treherbert w Treorchy 77–89; Youth Chapl 80–85; RD Rhondda 84–89; V Aberdare St Fagan 89–02; RD

Cynon Valley 97–02; TR Neath 02–18; P-in-c Llansawel, Briton Ferry 16–18; AD Neath 04–10 and 15–17; Can Llan Cathl 02–18; rtd 18. *191 Fitzroy House, Trawler Road, Maritime Quarter, Swansea SA1 1XX* M: 07967-345853 E: ryanstephen1949@gmail.com

RYCRAFT, Andrew George. b 48. Ox Brookes Univ BA 12 FRICS 94. Wycliffe Hall *Ox* 02 SAOMC 04. **d** 06 **p** 07. NSM Ray Valley *Ox* 06–07 and 09–15; P-in-c Exning St Martin w Landwade *St E* 15–18; rtd 18; PtO *St E* from 18; *Ely* from 21. *19 Cardigan Street, Newmarket CB8 8HZ* E: andrew.rycraft@gmail.com

RYCRAFT, Mrs Rosemary Ives Stewart. b 49. Westmr Coll Ox BTh 00 SRN 72 SCM 74. SAOMC 00. **d** 03 **p** 04. NSM New Marston *Ox* 03–07; TV Aylesbury 07–11; PtO 11–12; C Mildenhall *St E* 12–17; P-in-c Dalham, Gazeley, Higham, Kentford and Moulton 17–20; rtd 20; PtO *St E* from 20; *Ely* from 21. *19 Cardigan Street, Newmarket CB8 8HZ* E: rosemaryrycraft121@gmail.com

RYCROFT, Alistair John. b 79. St Cath Coll Ox BA 01 Fitzw Coll Cam BA 08 Ox Brookes Univ PGCE 02. Ridley Hall Cam 06. **d** 09 **p** 10. C York St Mich-le-Belfrey 09–13; C York St Thos w St Maurice 14–15; P-in-c from 15; P-in-c Heworth St Wulstan CD from 21. *157 Haxby Road, York YO31 8JL* T: (01904) 341979 E: info@stthomasyork.org.uk

RYDEN, Huw Deiniol. b 73. Cardiff Univ BTh 17. St Mich Coll Llan 15. **d** 17 **p** 18. C Littleham-cum-Exmouth w Lympstone *Ex* 17–20; CF from 20. *c/o MOD Chaplains (Army)* T: (01264) 887064 M: 07549-284038

RYDER, Elaine Lesley. b 52. Lindisfarne Regional Tr Partnership 16. **d** 18 **p** 19. NSM N Tyne and Redesdale *Newc* 18–21; NSM Hexham from 21. *The Vicarage, Otterburn, Newcastle upon Tyne NE19 1NP* T: (01830) 520212 E: revelaine212@gmail.com

RYDER, John Merrick. b 55. Natal Univ BA 75 BA 77. St Pet Coll Natal 81. **d** 82 **p** 83. C Rosebank St Martin S Africa 84–86; R Mayfair Ch Ch 86–88; V Hutt's Gate St Matt w St Mark St Helena 88–91; C Havant *Portsm* 91–95; P-in-c Godshill 95–99; V 99–20; P-in-c Wroxall 99–02; rtd 20; PtO *St E* from 20. *177 Dover Road, Ipswich IP3 8JJ* T: (01473) 806619 E: johnmryder@mac.com

RYDER, Judith Ruth. b 55. St Jo Coll Ox BA 98 MPhil 02 DPhil 06 FRHistS 12. Ripon Coll Cuddesdon 13. **d** 16 **p** 17. C Caversham Thameside and Mapledurham *Ox* 16–20. *5 Briar Close, Kidlington OX5 2DD* M: 07890-114456 E: judith.ryder@wolfson.ox.ac.uk *or* judith@ctmparish.org.uk

RYDER, Lisle Robert Dudley. b 43. Selw Coll Cam BA 68 MA 72. Sarum Th Coll 69. **d** 71 **p** 72. C Lowestoft St Marg *Nor* 71–75; Chapl Asst Oxon Area HA 76–79; C Littlehampton St Jas *Chich* 79–85; C Littlehampton St Mary 79–85; C Wick 79–85; Chapl Worc R Infirmary 85–94; Chapl Worc R Infirmary NHS Trust 94–00; Chapl Worcs Acute Hosps NHS Trust 00–03; Hon Can Worc Cathl 89–04; P-in-c Pyworthy, Pancrasweek and Bridgerule *Ex* 04–08; rtd 08; PtO *Leeds* from 17. *Little Appleton, 3 Lumley Terrace, Newton le Willows, Bedale DL8 1SS* T: (01677) 450180 E: lisleryder@gmail.com

RYDER, Oliver Hugh Dudley. b 74. UEA BA 98. Ridley Hall Cam 05. **d** 07 **p** 08. C Tollington *Lon* 07–10; C Kensal Rise St Mark and St Martin 10–11; V Kensal Rise St Mark 11–16; P-in-c Charles w Plymouth St Matthias *Ex* from 16. *St Matthias Vicarage, 6 St Lawrence Road, Plymouth PL4 6HN* M: 07963-580242 E: oliver.ryder@gmail.com

RYDINGS, Donald. b 33. Jes Coll Ox BA 57 MA 61. Linc Th Coll 57. **d** 59 **p** 60. C Poulton-le-Fylde *Blackb* 59–62; C Ox St Mary V 62–66; Staff Sec SCM 62–66; C-in-c Bourne End St Mark CD *Ox* 66–74; R Hedsor and Bourne End 74–76; P-in-c Gt Missenden w Ballinger and Lt Hampden 76–93; RD Wendover 79–89; V Gt Missenden w Ballinger and Lt Hampden 93–02; rtd 02; PtO *Ox* 02–19. *16 Marroway, Weston Turville, Aylesbury HP22 5TQ* T: (01296) 612281

RYELAND, John. b 58. K Coll Lon BD 80 AKC 80 Lon Sch of Th MA 09. Linc Th Coll 80. **d** 81 **p** 82. C Enfield St Jas *Lon* 81–84; C Coulsdon St Andr *S'wark* 84–87; C-in-c Ingrave St Steph CD *Chelmsf* 87–97; Dir Chr Healing Miss from 97; PtO *Lon* from 21. *24 Watermans Road, Henley-on-Thames RG9 1EX* T: (020) 7603 8118 E: chm@healingmission.org

RYLANCE, Wendy Sheila. b 52. Lon Univ MB, BS 78 MRCGP 82 DRCOG 89. WEMTC 11. **d** 13 **p** 14. NSM Highley w Billingsley, Glazeley etc *Heref* 13–18; rtd 19; PtO *Heref* from 19. *Roughton Farmhouse, Roughton, Bridgnorth WV15 5HE* T: (01746) 716399 M: 07523-352210 E: wendyrylance@aol.com

RYLANDS, Preb Amanda Craig. b 52. Homerton Coll Cam CertEd 75. Trin Coll Bris 83. **dss** 85 **d** 87 **p** 94. Chippenham St Andr w Tytherton Lucas *Bris* 85–87; Par Dn Stockport St Geo *Ches* 87–91; Par Dn Acton and Worleston, Church

688

Minshull etc 91–94; C 94–97; Dioc Adv for Min Among Children 95–97; NSM Langport Area *B & W* 97–98 and 99–01; TV 98–99; Asst Dioc Voc Adv 00–01; PtO *Ex* 02–03; C Tedburn St Mary, Whitestone, Oldridge etc 04–05; Dioc Dir of Ords 05–09; Bp's Adv for Women in Min 06–09; Preb Ex Cathl 08–09; PtO *Lich* 10–13; NSM Shrewsbury St Chad, St Mary and St Alkmund 13–17; Rep for Women in Min Shrewsbury Area 13–17; SSM Officer 13–17; rtd 17; PtO *Lich* 17–18; *Ex* 18–19 and from 20; RD Moreton 19–20. *The Rectory, Copperwood Close, Ashburton, Newton Abbot TQ13 7JQ* T: (01364) 716309 E: rylandsamanda@gmail.com

✠RYLANDS, The Rt Revd Mark James. b 61. SS Hild & Bede Coll Dur BA 83 Sheff Univ MA 06. Trin Coll Bris BA 87. d 87 p 88 c 09. C Stockport St Geo *Ches* 87–91; V Acton and Worleston, Church Minshull etc 91–97; TR Langport Area *B & W* 97–02; Dioc Missr and Can Res Ex Cathl 02–09; Area Bp Shrewsbury *Lich* 09–18; P-in-c Ashburton, Bickington, Buckland in the Moor etc *Ex* from 18; Asst Bp Ex from 18. *The Rectory, Copperwood Close, Ashburton, Newton Abbot TQ13 7JQ* T: (01364) 716309 E: mark.rylands@mmuk.net

RYLETT, Adam Geoffrey. b 78. Southn Univ MEng 00 Ox Brookes Univ BA 04. Trin Coll Bris 10. d 12 p 13. C S

Croydon Em *S'wark* 12–15; C Barnes 15–18; V Kingston Hill St Paul from 18. *St Paul's Vicarage, 33 Queens Road, Kingston upon Thames KT2 7SF* T: (020) 8549 8597 *or* 8549 5444 M: 07595-345480 E: adam@rylett.co.uk *or* adam.rylett@stpaulskingston.org.uk

RYLEY, Canon Patrick Macpherson. b 30. Pemb Coll Ox BA 54 Lon Univ BD 56. Clifton Th Coll 54. d 56 p 57. C Ox St Clem 56–59; Burma 60–66; Kenya 68–75; V Lynn St Jo *Nor* 76–92; V King's Lynn St Jo the Ev 92–95; RD Lynn 78–83; Hon Can Nor Cathl 90–95; rtd 95; PtO *Bradf* 95–11. *12 Green End, Denton, Manchester M34 7PU*

RYLEY, Timothy Patrick. b 64. Man Univ BA 86. St Jo Coll Nottm MA 93. d 93 p 94. C Pendlebury St Jo *Man* 93–97; P-in-c Norris Bank 97–01; Age Concern from 01; PtO *Man* 09–21. *12 Green End, Denton, Manchester M34 7PU*

RYRIE, Alexander Crawford. b 30. Edin Univ MA 52 BD 55 Glas Univ MLitt 75. New Coll Edin 52 Union Th Sem (NY) STM 56. d 83 p 83. Hon C Edin St Mary 83–85; R Jedburgh 85–95; rtd 95. *Boisils, Bowden, Melrose TD6 0ST* T: (01835) 823226 E: sandyryrie@googlemail.com

---

S

SABELL, Michael Harold. b 42. Open Univ BA 78 Surrey Univ MSc 84 Cam Univ MA 05. Sarum & Wells Th Coll 77. d 80 p 81. NSM Shirley *Win* 80–82; NSM Finham *Cov* 82–85; Chapl to the Deaf *Win* 81–82; PtO *Cov* 82–85; *Sheff* 85–89; Chapl to the Deaf 85–89; PtO *Lich* 89–96; Sen Chapl to the Deaf 89–96; PtO *St Alb* 96–01; Chapl to the Deaf 96–01; P-in-c Gt and Lt Wymondley 96–01; R Ingoldsby *Linc* 01–04; R Old Somerby 01–04; R Ropsley 01–04; R Sapperton w Braceby 01–04; rtd 04; PtO *Lich* 05–08 and 10–12; P-in-c Muchalls *Bre* 08–10; PtO *S & B* 12–18; *Leeds* from 18. *Halwyn Lodge, 152 Moorview Way, Skipton BD23 2LN* M: 07935-776656 (text only) E: sabell42117@gmail.com

SABEY-CORKINDALE, Charmaine Clare. b 58. SROT 87. SAOMC. d 02 p 03. NSM St Ippolyts *St Alb* 02–03; C Hitchin 03–05; TV 05–13; PtO 16–18 and from 18. *5 Lavender Way, Hitchin SG5 2LU* T: (01462) 435497 E: c.sabeycorkindale@btinternet.com

SABINE WILLIS, Anthony Charles. See WILLIS, Anthony Charles Sabine

SABLAN (*née* Howarth), Lucy Hope. b 94. Trin Coll Bris 16. d 19 p 20. C Philadelphia St Thos *Sheff* from 19. *St Paul's and St Leonard's Vicarage, 458B East Bank Road, Sheffield S2 2AD* M: 07758-208105 E: lucysablan@ncsheffield.org

SACHS, Andrew James. b 73. Reading Univ BSc 94 Kingston Univ PGCE 96. Wycliffe Hall Ox BTh 05. d 05 p 06. C Upper Sunbury St Sav *Lon* 05–08; C E Twickenham St Steph 08–12; P-in-c Colchester St Jo *Chelmsf* from 12. *St John's Vicarage, Evergreen Drive, Colchester CO4 0HU* T: (01206) 843232 M: 07808-886996 E: andy.sachs@stjohnscolchester.org.uk

SACKLEY (*née* WITT), Mrs Caroline Elizabeth. b 51. Surrey Univ BSc 84. STETS 02. d 05 p 06. C Graffoe Gp *Linc* 05–08; P-in-c W Meon and Warnford *Portsm* 08–12; rtd 12; P-in-c The Vendée *Eur* 13–16; Hon C E Clevedon w Clapton in Gordano etc *B & W* from 17. *5 Chestnut Grove, Clevedon BS21 7LA* E: revcarosack1@gmail.com

SACRE, Phillip Daniel. b 83. Essex Univ BSc 04. Oak Hill Th Coll BA 14. d 14 p 15. C Gt Clacton *Chelmsf* 14–19. *Address temp unknown* E: phillip.sacre@gmail.com

SADDINGTON, Mrs Jean. b 53. Bournemouth Univ BSc 02 Cant Ch Ch Univ PGCE 04. STETS 05. d 08 p 12. NSM Dorchester *Sarum* 08–14; NSM Dorchester and the Winterbournes from 14. *The Rectory, Martinstown, Dorchester DT2 9JZ* E: jean.saddington@hotmail.co.uk

SADGROVE, The Very Revd Michael. b 50. Ball Coll Ox BA 71 MA 75. Trin Coll Bris 72. d 75 p 76. LtO *Ox* 75–77; Tutor Sarum & Wells Th Coll 77–82; Vice-Prin 80–82; V Alnwick *Newc* 82–87; Vice-Provost, Can Res and Prec Cov Cathl 87–95; Provost Sheff 95–00; Dean Sheff 00–03; Dean Dur 03–15; rtd 16; PtO *Newc* from 16. *12 Burswell House, 27 Church Street, Haydon Bridge, Hexham NE47 6JG* T: (01434) 688675 M: 07828-516198 E: sadgrove@outlook.com

SADLER, Ann Penrith. See IRVINE, Ann Penrith

SADLER, Michael Stuart. b 57. Wycliffe Hall Ox 78. d 81 p 82. C Henfynyw w Aberaeron and Llanddewi Aberarth *St D* 81–88; V Llanddewi Rhydderch w Llangattock-juxta-Usk etc *Mon* 88–09; V Llandeilo Fawr and Taliaris *St D* from 09. *The New Vicarage, Thomas Terrace, Llandeilo SA19 6NN* T: (01558) 823862 E: mssadler@macunlimited.net

SAGE, Canon Andrew George. b 58. Univ Coll Chich BA 99. Chich Th Coll 83. d 85 p 86. C Rawmarsh w Parkgate *Sheff* 85–87; C Fareham SS Pet and Paul *Portsm* 87–89; C Southsea H Spirit 89–91; P-in-c Nuthurst *Chich* 91–93; R 93–95; V Hangleton 95–04; Chapl Worthing and Southlands Hosps NHS Trust 01–04; Chapl W Sussex Health and Soc Care NHS Trust 02–04; V Blackpool St Steph *Blackb* from 04; Warden Whalley Abbey 08–10; Hon Can Blackb Cathl from 08. *The Vicarage, St Stephen's Avenue, Blackpool FY2 9RB* T: (01253) 351484 E: vicar@ststephenblackpool.co.uk

SAGOVSKY, Canon Nicholas. b 47. CCC Ox BA 69 St Edm Ho Cam PhD 81. St Jo Coll Nottm BA 73. d 74 p 75. C Newc St Gabr 74–77; C Cambridge Gt St Mary w St Mich *Ely* 81–82; Vice-Prin Edin Th Coll 82–86; Dean Clare Coll Cam 86–97; Wm Leech Prof Fell Newc Univ 97–02; Liv Hope Univ Coll 02–04; Can Westmr Abbey 04–11; rtd 11; PtO *Newc* from 11; *S'wark* 12–17; *Lon* from 16. *92 Tyndale Mansions, Upper Street, London N1 2XG* T: (020) 7682 3287 E: nsagovsky@gmail.com

SAID, Yazid. b 75. Hebrew Univ Jerusalem BA 96 CCC Cam BA 99 MA 03 MPhil 05 PhD 10. Westcott Ho Cam 97. d 99 p 01. Chapl Ch Ch Sch Nazareth Israel 99–00; Chapl to Bp Jerusalem 00–02; C St Geo Cathl 00–04; Acting Dean 02–04; Asst Chapl CCC Cam 04–09; PtO *Ely* 08–11; Research Fell McGill Univ Canada 10–11; Israel 11–12; Lect Dublin City Univ *D & G* 13–14; Lect Free Univ Berlin from 15; Research Fell Tübingen Univ 15–16; Lect Liv Hope Univ from 16; PtO *Liv* from 16. *Liverpool Hope University College, Hope Park, Taggart Avenue, Liverpool L16 9JD* E: yazeed.said@gmx.net

SAINSBURY, Peter Donald. b 67. K Coll Lon MA 04. Ridley Hall Cam 98. d 00 p 01. C Longfleet *Sarum* 00–04; Chapl Glos Univ 04–08; V Summerfield *Birm* 08–19; PtO from 19; TV Marlborough *Sarum* from 20. *Preshute Vicarage, 7 Golding Avenue, Marlborough SN8 1TH* T: (01672) 512364 M: 07717-414787 E: revpetesainsbury@gmail.com

✠SAINSBURY, The Rt Revd Roger Frederick. b 36. Jes Coll Cam BA 58 MA 62. Clifton Th Coll. d 60 p 61. C Spitalfields Ch Ch w All SS *Lon* 60–63; Missr Shrewsbury Ho Everton *Liv* 63–74; P-in-c Everton St Ambrose w St Tim 67–74; Warden Mayflower Family Cen Canning Town *Chelmsf* 74–81; P-in-c Victoria Docks St Luke 78–81; V Walsall *Lich* 81–87; TR 87–88; Adn W Ham *Chelmsf* 88–91; Area Bp Barking 91–02; Moderator Ch's Commn for Racial Justice 99–02; rtd 02; Hon Asst Bp B & W from 03. *Abbey Lodge, Battery Lane, Portishead, Bristol BS20 7JD* T: (01275) 847082 E: bishoproger@talktalk.net

SAINT, Richard John. b 85. Edin Univ BSc 07 Qu Coll Cam PhD 13. Wycliffe Hall Ox 16. **d** 19 **p** 20. C Southbroom *Sarum* from 19. *14 Stockwell Road, Devizes SN10 2DP* M: 07773-028907 E: richardjsaint@gmail.com

ST ALBANS, Archdeacon of. *See* MAINWARING, The Ven Jane Frances

ST ALBANS, Bishop of. *See* SMITH, The Rt Revd Alan Gregory Clayton

ST ALBANS, Dean of. *See* KELLY-MOORE, The Very Revd Joanne

ST ANDREWS, DUNKELD AND DUNBLANE, Bishop of. *See* PATON, The Rt Revd Ian James

ST ANDREWS, DUNKELD AND DUNBLANE, Dean of. *See* RATHBAND, The Very Revd Kenneth William

ST ASAPH, Bishop of. *See* CAMERON, The Rt Revd Gregory Kenneth

ST ASAPH, Dean of. *See* WILLIAMS, The Very Revd Nigel Howard

ST DAVIDS, Archdeacon of. *See* MACKNESS, The Ven Paul Robert

ST DAVIDS, Bishop of. *See* PENBERTHY, The Rt Revd Joanna Susan

ST DAVIDS, Dean of. *See* ROWLAND JONES, The Very Revd Sarah Caroline

ST EDMUNDSBURY AND IPSWICH, Bishop of. *See* SEELEY, The Rt Revd Martin Alan

ST EDMUNDSBURY, Dean of. *See* HAWES, The Very Revd Joseph Patricius

ST GERMANS, Suffragan Bishop of. *See* NELSON, The Rt Revd Hugh Edmund

ST JOHN, Christopher George. b 66. Open Univ BA 98 MA 02 MA 05 Hull Univ MEd 05 Ulster Univ PhD 14. CITI 14. **d** 16 **p** 17. Woodburn H Trin *Conn* 16–17; C Dundela St Mark *D & D* 17–21; I Carrickfergus *Conn* from 21. *Address temp unknown* M: 07463-745105 E: christopher.stjohn@btinternet.com

ST JOHN NICOLLE, Jason Paul. b 66. Mert Coll Ox BA 88 Called to the Bar (Inner Temple) 95. Ripon Coll Cuddesdon 01. **d** 04 **p** 05. C Kidlington w Hampton Poyle *Ox* 04–08; R The Churn from 08; AD Wallingford 12–17; AD Wantage 13–20; AD Vale of White Horse from 18. *The Rectory, Church End, Blewbury, Didcot OX11 9QH* T: (01235) 850267 E: office@churnchurches.co.uk

SAKAKINI, Gillian Cudmore. b 63. St Mellitus Coll 16. **d** 18 **p** 19. C Tadley w Pamber Heath and Silchester *Win* 18–21; Pioneer Min *B & W* from 21. *The Old Dairy, Manor Farm, West Cranmore, Shepton Mallet BA4 4QL* E: gilly.sak@gmail.com

SALA, Kuabuleke Meymans. b 68. **d** 08 **p** 09. C Edmonton All SS w St Mich *Lon* 08–16; C Wood Green St Mich w Bounds Green St Gabr etc 16–18; Chapl Mid-Essex Hosp Services NHS Trust from 18. *Mid Essex Hospital NHS Trust, Broomfield Hospital, Chelmsford CM1 7ET* T: (01245) 515244 E: smeymans@hotmail.com

SALAMAN, Paul William. b 71. York Univ BSc 92 PGCE 94 Edin Univ MSc 12. St Mellitus Coll 18. **d** 20 **p** 21. C Probus, Ladock and Grampound w Creed and St Erme *Truro* from 20. *The Rectory, Tresillian, Truro TR2 4AA* M: 07511-965595 E: salaman_pandc@yahoo.co.uk

SALEH, Mrs Carey Jane. b 62. Sheff Univ BA 94 RGN 83. Qu Coll Birm 11. **d** 13 **p** 14. C Bromsgrove *Worc* 13–17; V Stourport and Wilden from 17. *The Vicarage, Church Avenue, Stourport-on-Severn DY13 9DD* T: (01299) 822041 M: 07933-744107 E: revcareysaleh@gmail.com

SALES, Canon Patrick David. b 43. K Coll Lon AKC 68 BD 74 Kent Univ MA 00. **d** 69 **p** 70. C Maidstone All SS w St Phil *Cant* 69–71; C Maidstone All SS w St Phil and H Trin 71–72; C Chart next Sutton Valence 72–74; C Birchington w Acol 75–77; V Boughton under Blean w Dunkirk 77–83; V Herne 83–03; P-in-c St Nicholas at Wade w Sarre and Chislet w Hoath 98–03; TV Whitstable 03–06; Hon Min Can Cant Cathl 83–01; Hon Can Cant Cathl 01–06; RD Reculver 86–92; AD 01–06; Dioc Adv in Liturgy 00–06; rtd 06; Dioc Adv *Chich* from 14. *The Well House, South Lane, Dallington, Heathfield TN21 9NJ* T: (01435) 830194 M: 07585-269588 E: patricksales@btinternet.com

SALFORD, Archdeacon of. *See* BURGESS, The Ven Jean Ann

SALISBURY, Anne Ruth. b 37. Dalton Ho Bris 63. **d** 87 **p** 94. C Harrow Trin St Mich *Lon* 87–98; C Paddington Em and W Kilburn St Luke w St Simon and St Jude 99–03; rtd 03. *c/o Crockford, Church House, 27 Great Smith Street, London SW1P 3AZ* M: 07986-868667

SALISBURY, Matthew Robert Cheung. b 84. Toronto Univ BA 07 Worc Coll Ox MSt 08 DPhil 11 FHEA 14 FRHistS 15. Blackfriars Studium Ox 17 Wycliffe Hall Ox 20. **d** 21. Nat Liturgy and Worship Adv Abps' Coun from 15; NSM Ox St Barn and St Paul w St Thos from 21; Asst Chapl Worc Coll

Ox from 21. *23 Wellington Street, Oxford OX2 6BB* M: 07425-322125 E: matthew.salisbury@churchofengland.org

SALISBURY, Canon Peter Brian Christopher. b 58. UMIST BSc 80 MBCS 85. Sarum & Wells Th Coll BTh 92. **d** 92 **p** 93. C Stanmore *Win* 92–95; V Chilworth w N Baddesley 95–05; V Lymington from 05; AD Lyndhurst from 13; Hon Can Win Cathl from 17. *The Vicarage, Grove Road, Lymington SO41 3RF* T: (01590) 673847 E: vicar@lymingtonchurch.org

SALISBURY, Canon Roger John. b 44. Lon Univ BD 67. Lon Coll of Div 66. **d** 68 **p** 69. C Harold Wood *Chelmsf* 68–73; V Dorking St Paul *Guildf* 73–82; R Rusholme H Trin *Man* 82–90; TR Gt Chesham *Ox* 90–06; RD Amersham 98–04; Hon Can Ch Ch 02–06; C Langham Place All So *Lon* 06–11; rtd 11; Sec Ch Patr Trust 06–15; Sec Peache Trustees 11–19; PtO *B & W* from 12. *6 Church Street, Widcombe, Bath BA2 6AZ* T: (01225) 489076 E: rogerandhilda.salisbury@gmail.com

SALISBURY, Canon Tobias. b 33. Em Coll Cam BA 60. Ripon Hall Ox 60. **d** 62 **p** 63. C Putney St Mary *S'wark* 62–65; C Churchdown St Jo *Glouc* 65–67; V Urchfont w Stert *Sarum* 67–73; R Burton Bradstock w Shipton Gorge and Chilcombe 73–79; P-in-c Long Bredy w Lt Bredy and Kingston Russell 75–79; TR Bride Valley 79–86; V Gt and Lt Bedwyn and Savernake Forest 86–97; Can and Preb Sarum Cathl 92–98; rtd 98; PtO *B & W* from 98. *Anfield, Hayes Lane, Compton Dundon, Somerton TA11 6PB* T: (01458) 274459

SALISBURY, Bishop of. *Vacant*

SALISBURY, Dean of. *See* PAPADOPULOS, The Very Revd Nicholas Charles

SALMON, Canon Andrew Ian. b 61. St Jo Coll Nottm BTh 88. **d** 88 **p** 89. C Collyhurst *Man* 88–92; P-in-c Pendleton St Ambrose 92–95; TV Pendleton 95–99; TR 99–04; P-in-c Salford Sacred Trin and St Phil 04–16; V Salford Sacred Trin from 16; AD Salford 06–13; Borough Dean Salford 13–18; Hon Can Man Cathl from 10. *Sacred Trinity Rectory, 52 George Leigh Street, Manchester M4 5DG* T: 0161-839 1180 M: 07436-532408 E: revandysalmon@gmail.com *or* andy@sacredtrinity.org.uk

SALMON, Andrew Meredith Bryant. b 30. Jes Coll Cam BA 54 MA 58. Ridley Hall Cam 54. **d** 56 **p** 57. C Enfield Ch Ch Trent Park *Lon* 56–58; Chapl Monkton Combe Sch Bath 58–71; Chapl Milton Abbey Sch Dorset 71–89; TV Bride Valley *Sarum* 89–96; rtd 97; PtO *Sarum* 97–22. *Heatherland, Barnhill Road, Wareham BH20 5BD* T: (01929) 554039 E: amsalmonbh20@gmail.com

SALMON, Mrs Constance Hazel. b 25. R Holloway Coll Lon BSc 46. Lon Bible Coll 66 Gilmore Course 71. **dss** 80 **d** 87 **p** 96. Sidcup St Andr *Roch* 80–88; NSM 87–88; PtO 88–96; NSM Eynsford w Farningham and Lullingstone 96–05. *43 Old Mill Close, Eynsford, Dartford DA4 0BN* T: (01322) 866034

SALMON, Jonathan. b 66. Univ Coll of Swansea BSc(Econ) 88 Sussex Univ MA 95 MPhil 95. Wycliffe Hall Ox 01. **d** 03 **p** 04. C Bowling St Jo *Bradf* 03–07; P-in-c Earley Trin *Ox* 07–14; V from 14. *Trinity Church House, 15 Caraway Road, Earley, Reading RG6 5XR* T: 0118-986 9798 M: 07840-494072 E: jon.salmon@trinityearley.org.uk

SALMON, Karen Elizabeth. **d** 18. Lurgan Ch the Redeemer *D & D* 18–19; C Willowfield from 19. *8 Jocelyn Gardens, Belfast BT6 9BA* M: 07842-015355 E: salmonk@tcd.ie

SALMON, Michael John. b 77. **d** 13. NSM Bishopston and St Andrews *Bris* 13–14. *40 Fenner Square, London SW12 2HQ* M: 07779-107841 E: michaelsalmon@mac.com *or* michael@it-games.co.uk

SALMON, Philip John. b 63. Oak Hill Th Coll 96. **d** 98 **p** 99. C Kington w Huntington, Old Radnor, Kinnerton etc *Heref* 98–02; TV Radipole and Melcombe Regis *Sarum* 02–18; P-in-c Pitsmoor Ch Ch *Sheff* from 18; C Sheff St Cuth from 18; C Ellesmere St Pet from 18; AD Ecclesfield from 20. *The Vicarage, 257 Pitsmoor Road, Sheffield S3 9AQ* M: 07799-944436 E: revpip@yahoo.com *or* pip.salmon@sheffield.anglican.org

SALMON, Richard Harold. b 35. Fitzw Ho Cam BA 57. Clifton Th Coll 57. **d** 59 **p** 60. C Blackheath Park St Mich *S'wark* 59–61; C St Alb St Paul 61–63; OMF 63–65; C Telok Anson St Luke Malaysia 63–65; V Kuanton Pehang Epiphany 65–75; P-in-c March St Wendreda *Ely* 75–76; R 76–85; V Congresbury w Puxton and Hewish St Ann *B & W* 85–00; rtd 00; PtO *Truro* 00–01; *B & W* from 02. *2 Wisteria Avenue, Hutton, Weston-super-Mare BS24 9QF* T: (01934) 813750 M: 07966-038543 E: richardandhelensalmon@gmail.com

SALMON, William John. b 50. Lon Univ BSc 72 DipEd 73. Cranmer Hall Dur 76. **d** 79 **p** 80. C Summerstown *S'wark* 79–81; C Hampreston *Sarum* 81–86; V Sundon *St Alb* 86–90; Dep Chapl HM Young Offender Inst Glen Parva 90–91; Chapl HM Pris Whitemoor 91–95; Chapl HM Pris Blundeston 95–04 and 07–14; Chapl HM Pris Belmarsh

04–07; Chapl HM Pris and YOI Warren Hill 14–17; Chapl HM Pris Wayland 17–20; rtd 20; PtO *Nor* from 16. *Address withheld by request*

SALMON, Mrs Yvonne Delysia. b 40. Cant Sch of Min 00. **d** 03 **p** 04. OLM Boughton Monchelsea *Cant* 03–10; PtO from 11. *Elderden Farm Cottage, Maidstone Road, Staplehurst, Tonbridge TN12 0RN* T: (01622) 842598

SALOP, Archdeacon of. *See* THOMAS, The Ven Paul Wyndham

SALT, David Thomas Whitehorn. b 32. K Coll Lon AKC 56 BD 57. **d** 57 **p** 58. Chapl Torgil Girls' Sch Aoba New Hebrides 57–59; Warden Catechist Coll Lolowai 59–63; Prin St Andr Coll Guadalcanal Solomon Is 63–66; C Hawley H Trin *Guildf* 66–68; V Shelf *Bradf* 68–73; R Checkendon *Ox* 73–81; RD Henley 78–84; TR Langtree 81–84; V Hungerford and Denford 84–89; Chapl Hungerford Hosp 84–89; P-in-c Harpsden *Ox* 89–95; Gen Sec Melanesian Miss 89–95; rtd 95; PtO *Sarum* 95–05; *Guildf* 06–15; *Win* 06–12; *Portsm* from 16. *1 Victoria Court, 19 Beach Road, Hayling Island PO11 0AB* T: (023) 9246 4764 E: dtwsalt@gmail.com

SALT, Jeremy William. b 56. St Mellitus Coll. **d** 11 **p** 12. NSM Ingatestone w Fryerning *Chelmsf* 11–15; P-in-c Buckden w the Offords *Ely* 15–21; Dioc Social Justice Co-ord 15–21; C Empingham, Edith Weston, Lyndon, Manton etc *Pet* from 21. *The Rectory, 5A Audit Hall Road, Empingham, Oakham LE15 8PH* E: jes.salt@btinternet.com

SALT, Neil. b 64. Univ of Wales (Ban) BA 85 New Coll Edin BD 89 Man Metrop Univ BSc 97. Edin Th Coll 86. **d** 89 **p** 90. C Stretford All SS *Man* 89–93; V Smallbridge and Wardle 93–94; PtO *Wakef* 94–01; Hon C Ripponden and Barkisland w W Scammonden 01–06; Chapl Rishworth Sch Ripponden 02–05; V Thornton-le-Fylde *Blackb* 06–14; PtO 14–17; V Grimsargh from 17. *6 Douglas Lane, Grimsargh, Preston PR2 5JF* T: (01772) 796854 E: vicar.grimsargh@gmail.com

SALT, Mrs Susan. b 64. Imp Coll Lon MB, BS 89 Man Univ PhD 10. All SS Cen for Miss & Min 17. **d** 19 **p** 20. C Fellside Team *Blackb* from 19. *6 Douglas Lane, Grimsargh, Preston PR2 5JF* M: 07730-197656 E: sdsalt93@gmail.com

SALTER, Arthur Thomas John. b 34. TD 88. AKC 60. **d** 61 **p** 62. C Ealing St Pet Mt Park *Lon* 61–65; C Shepherd's Bush St Steph w St Thos 65–66; C Holborn St Alb w Saffron Hill St Pet 66–70; P-in-c Barnsbury St Clem 70–77; P-in-c Islington St Mich 70–77; V Pentonville St Silas w All SS and St Jas 70–00; CF (VR) from 75; Gen Sec Angl and E Chs Assn from 76; Chmn from 90; P-in-c St Dunstan in the West *Lon* 79–99; rtd 00. *1 St James's Close, Bishop Street, London N1 8PH* T: (020) 7359 0250 E: salteralexis@aol.com

SALTER, Christopher. *See* SALTER, Nigel Christopher Murray

SALTER, David Whitton. b 69. Bris Univ BEng 90. Trin Coll Bris 06. **d** 08 **p** 09. C Eynsham and Cassington *Ox* 08–11; TV Chipping Norton from 11; AD from 21. *6 The Grange, Kingham, Chipping Norton OX7 6XY* T: (01608) 658852 M: 07768-582285 E: david.w.salter@btinternet.com

SALTER, Janet Elizabeth. b 48. Leeds Univ CertEd 69. SWMTC 92. **d** 95 **p** 98. C Coleshill *Birm* 95–97; Hon C St Dennis *Truro* 97–00; TV Gillingham *Sarum* 00–04; V Stour Vale 04–11; rtd 11; PtO *Truro* from 14. *6 Maple Close, St Columb TR9 6SL* T: (01637) 881552 E: jansalter552@gmail.com

SALTER, John. *See* SALTER, Arthur Thomas John

SALTER, Canon John Frank. b 37. Dur Univ BA 62. Cranmer Hall Dur 62. **d** 64 **p** 65. C Bridlington Priory *York* 64–67; Travelling Sec IVF 67–70; V Stoughton *Guildf* 70–02; RD Guildf 89–94; Hon Can Guildf Cathl 99–02; rtd 03; PtO *Guildf* from 03. *7 Aldershot Road, Guildford GU2 8AE* T: (01483) 511165 E: johnsalter37@gmail.com

SALTER, Nigel Christopher Murray. b 46. Loughb Univ BTech. Ripon Coll Cuddesdon 79. **d** 81 **p** 82. C Glouc St Aldate 81–84; C Solihull *Birm* 84–88; V Highters Heath 88–97; Asst Chapl Greenwich Healthcare NHS Trust 97–01; Asst Chapl Qu Eliz Hosp NHS Trust 01–03; P-in-c Leaton and Albrighton w Battlefield *Lich* 03–06; rtd 06; PtO *Win* from 12. *4 Maple Close, Alton GU34 2AY* T: (01420) 85412

SALTER, Roger John. b 45. Trin Coll Bris 75. **d** 79 **p** 80. C Bedminster St Mich *Bris* 79–82; C Swindon Ch Ch 82–84; V Bedminster Down 84–89; P-in-c Northwood *Portsm* 89–93; P-in-c W Cowes H Trin 89–92; V Cowes H Trin and St Mary 92–94; USA from 94; rtd 10. *1300 Panorama Drive, Vestavia Hill AL 35216-3032, USA* T: (001) (1) 205 7967 E: salter.roger@gmail.com

SALTMARSH, Philip. b 71. Keele Univ MA 03 RN 93. SNWTP 08. **d** 11 **p** 12. NSM Grassendale *Liv* 11–14; C Liv All SS 14–19; AD Liv N 18–19; R Speke St Aid w All SS from 19. *9 Rivenhall Square, Liverpool L24 1WD* M: 07365-279983 E: philsaltmarsh@aol.com or speke.rector@gmail.com

SAMBROOK, Kenneth Henry. b 42. NOC 04. **d** 05 **p** 06. NSM Wistaston *Ches* 05–15; rtd 15; PtO *Ches* from 15. *6 Westfield*

Drive, Wistaston, Crewe CW2 8ES T: (01270) 662455 E: revd.ken@stmaryswistaston.org.uk

SAMMÉ, Raymond Charles. b 50. Anglia Poly Univ MA 03 St Andr Univ MLitt 08 CBiol 80 MIBiol 80. Oak Hill Th Coll 85. **d** 87 **p** 88. C Holmer w Huntington *Heref* 87–90; C Derby St Alkmund and St Werburgh 90–93; V Romford Gd Shep *Chelmsf* 93–08; P-in-c Swanley St Paul *Roch* 08–16; rtd 17. *18 Sevenoaks Avenue, Derby DE22 4HU* E: ray.samme@gmail.com

SAMMON, Canon Helen Mary Kirkman. b 57. Newnham Coll Cam MA 79 Bris Univ MB, ChB 82 MRCGP 98 Qu Foundn for Ecum Th Educn MA 10. WEMTC 00. **d** 03 **p** 04. NSM Painswick, Sheepscombe, Cranham, The Edge etc *Glouc* 03–07; P-in-c Tuffley 07–12; Public Preacher 12–16; P-in-c Highnam, Tibberton w Rudford etc 16–21; CMD Officer 15–21; Hon Can Glouc Cathl 13–21; rtd 21. *Windycot, Cranham, Gloucester GL4 8HZ*

SAMMONS, Elizabeth Mary. *See* SLATER, Elizabeth Mary

SAMPLE, Mrs Fiona Jean. b 55. Dur Univ BA 11. Lindisfarne Regional Tr Partnership 02. **d** 08 **p** 09. Chapl Mowden Hall Sch 06–17; OLM Bolam w Whalton and Hartburn w Meldon *Newc* 08–14; NSM 14–17; C 17–21; P-in-c from 21; OLM Nether Witton 08–14; NSM 14–17; C 17–21; P-in-c from 21. *South Middleton Farm, Middleton, Morpeth NE61 4EB* T: (01670) 774245 M: 07486-364582 E: f.sample@btinternet.com

SAMPLE, Thomas Ian. b 92. Lindisfarne Coll of Th 17. **d** 20 **p** 21. C Berwick H Trin and St Mary *Newc* from 20. *1 Windsor Crescent, Berwick-upon-Tweed TD15 1NT* T: (01289) 298521 M: 07305-592637 E: thomasisample@outlook.com

SAMPSON, Brian Andrew. b 39. **d** 94 **p** 95. C Glemsford, Hartest w Boxted, Somerton etc *St E* 94–96; C Pentlow, Foxearth, Liston and Borley *Chelmsf* 96–97; P-in-c 97–03; P-in-c N Hinckford 03–04; C 04–09; rtd 09. *4 Friars Court, Edgworth Road, Sudbury CO10 2TG* T: (01787) 371529 E: captainbrianca@waitrose.com

SAMPSON, Clive. b 38. St Jo Coll Cam BA 61 MA 64. Ridley Hall Cam 63. **d** 65 **p** 66. C Tunbridge Wells St Jo *Roch* 65–69; Travelling Sec Scripture Union 69–79; V Maidstone St Luke *Cant* 79–94; rtd 98; PtO *Win* from 17. *108 Bure Homage Gardens, Christchurch BH23 4DR* T: (01425) 279029 E: clive.sampson12@gmail.com

SAMPSON, Gemma Sophia Marie. b 75. Huddersfield Univ BA 96 Leic Univ MA 05 Sheff Univ BA 15. Coll of Resurr Mirfield 13. **d** 15 **p** 16. C Hartlepool St Aid and St Columba *Dur* 15–19; P-in-c 19–21; P-in-c Beaconsfield Australia from 21. *St Paul's Rectory, 162 Hampton Road, Beaconsfield, Perth WA 6162, Australia* M: 07780-675322 E: revdgemma@gmail.com

SAMPSON, Julian Robin Anthony. b 78. St D Coll Lamp BA 00. St Steph Ho *Ox* 01. **d** 03 **p** 04. C Notting Hill All SS w St Columb *Lon* 03–04; C Staines and Asst Chapl HM Pris Bronzefield 04–07; Chapl HM Pris Birm 07–13; V Handsworth St Mich *Birm* 13–18; P-in-c Birm Bp Latimer w All SS 14–18; V Small Heath from 18. *The Clergy House, 85 Jenkins Street, Birmingham B10 0PQ* T: 0121-772 0621 M: 07801-944520 E: vicarhandsworth@hotmail.com *or* julians@cofebirmingham.com

SAMPSON, Terence Harold Morris. b 41. ACA 64 FCA 75. Bps' Coll Cheshunt 64. **d** 67 **p** 68. C Penrith St Andr *Carl* 67–72; V Carl St Barn 72–80; TR Carl H Trin and St Barn 80–84; Chapl Cumberland Infirmary 83–84; R Workington St Mich *Carl* 84–01; Hon Can Carl Cathl 89–01; RD Solway 90–95; PtO 02–16; *Eur* from 03. *Edificio Balcon de San Miguel, Avenida de Alicante 17/19, 03193 San Miguel de Salinas (Alicante), Spain* T: (0034) 677 237 496 M: 07775-683275 E: terenceandmargaret@hotmail.co.uk

SAMS, Mrs Jacqueline. b 53. Open Univ BA 82 St Osyth Coll of Educn CertEd 74. NTMTC BA 10. **d** 10 **p** 11. NSM Colchester Ch Ch w St Mary V *Chelmsf* 10–14; PtO 14–16; NSM Berechurch St Marg w St Mich 16–20; rtd 20; PtO *Chelmsf* from 20. *17 Chestnut Avenue, Colchester CO2 0AL* T: (01206) 530586 E: revjackiesams@gmail.com

SAMS, Michael Charles. b 34. FCA 62. Ox NSM Course 81. **d** 84 **p** 85. NSM Abingdon *Ox* 84–92 and 99–04; P-in-c Shippon 92–99; PtO 04–20. *23 Charney Avenue, Abingdon OX14 2NZ* T: (01235) 529084 E: michael-gwenda@uwclub.net

SAMSON, Canon Hilary Lynn. b 50. SWMTC. **d** 03 **p** 04. NSM St Agnes and Mithian w Mount Hawke *Truro* 03–06; P-in-c St Enoder 06–18; P-in-c Newlyn St Newlyn 06–18; RD Pydar 13–18; Hon Can Truro Cathl 16–18; rtd 18. *The Stable, 12 Newton Road, Troon, Camborne TR14 7SJ* E: hilarysamson@btinternet.com

SAMSON, Mrs Susan Mary. b 52. Southn Univ BA 73. **d** 09 **p** 10. OLM Sittingbourne w Bobbing *Cant* from 09. *11*

Adelaide Drive, Sittingbourne ME10 1YB   T: (01795) 478635
E: suesamson@sky.com
SAMUEL, Brother. *See* DOUBLE, Richard Sydney
SAMUEL, Fiaz. *See* SAMUEL, Luther Fiaz
SAMUEL, John Shafi. b 71. Middx Univ BA 14. St Mellitus
Coll 19. **d** 21. C Foleshill St Laur   *Cov* from 21. *20
Dragonfly Drive, Coventry CV2 1UG*   M: 07886-745310
E: johnfrom12@yahoo.co.uk *or* johnshafi@icloud.com
SAMUEL, Kerry Jay. b 71. Nottm Univ BA 92 Hughes Hall
Cam PGCE 93 K Coll Lon PhD 07. NTMTC 05. **d** 07 **p** 08.
C Twickenham St Mary *Lon* 07–10; PtO *Glouc* 13–15; Chapl
Cheltenham Coll from 13; Chapl All SS Academy Cheltenham
from 13. *Chandos Lodge, Thirlestaine Road, Cheltenham
GL53 7AA*   M: 07717-470403 E: kerrysamuel@hotmail.com
SAMUEL, Luther Fiaz. b 47. Karachi Univ BA 83. St Thos
Th Coll Karachi BTh 88. **d** 88 **p** 89. Pakistan 88–96; Oman
96–03; PtO *Lich* 03–04; NSM Walsall St Matt 04–15; Minority
Ethnic Angl Concerns Officer 04–05; Asian Missr 05–13; rtd
13; PtO *Lich* 15–17; *Nor* from 17. *3 Charlotte Drive, Costessey,
Norwich NR8 5HJ*   M: 07736-761754
SAMUELS, Canon Anne Elizabeth. b 51. Birm Univ BA 73
CertEd 74. Trin Coll Bris 85. **d** 87 **p** 94. Par Dn Moreton
Ches 87–91; Par Dn Halton 91–94; C 94–03; Bp's Adv for
Women in Min 94–96; Asst Dir of Ords 94–03; RD Frodsham
99–03; Chapl Halton Gen Hosp NHS Trust 99–00; Chapl N
Cheshire Hosps NHS Trust 01–03; V Higher Bebington *Ches*
03–14; Hon Can Ches Cathl 01–14; rtd 14; Chapl Foxhill
Retreat and Conf Cen *Ches* from 16. *10 West Heath Court,
Gerard Road, West Kirby, Wirral CH48 4ES*   T: 0151-625 3492
E: annesamuels47@btinternet.com
SAMUELS, Canon Christopher William John. b 42. AKC 66.
d 67 **p** 68. C Kirkholt *Man* 67–72; C-in-c Houghton Regis
St Thos CD *St Alb* 72–76; R Tarporley *Ches* 76–83; R Ches
St Mary 83–05; RD Ches 95–02; Hon Can Ches Cathl 97–05;
rtd 05; Chapl to The Queen 01–12; LtO *St As* from 05;
PtO *Ches* from 07; *St As* from 16; *Eur* from 09. *Long View,
Mannings Lane, Hoole Village, Chester CH2 2PB*   M: 07929-
420423 E: cwjsamuels@gmail.com
SAMUELS, Canon Raymond John. b 49. Qu Mary Coll Lon
BSc 73 Ex Univ PGCE 74. Trin Coll Bris 85. **d** 87 **p** 88. C
Moreton *Ches* 87–91; V Halton 91–02; Dioc Dir of Ords
03–14; rtd 14; V Alvanley *Ches* 14–18; Hon Can Ches
Cathl 16–18; PtO from 18. *10 West Heath Court, Gerard
Road, West Kirby, Wirral CH48 4ES*   T: 0151-625 3492
E: raysamuels47@btinternet.com
SAMUELS, Mrs Sheila Tarona. b 70. St Mellitus Coll
MA 19. **d** 19 **p** 20. C Godalming *Guildf* from 19. *49
Coopers Rise, Godalming GU7 2NH*   M: 07951-215260
E: s.samuels70@hotmail.com
SAMWAYS, Denis Robert. b 37. Leeds Univ BA 62. Coll of
Resurr Mirfield 62. **d** 64 **p** 65. C Clun w Chapel Lawn *Heref*
64–69; C Pocklington w Yapham-cum-Meltonby, Owsthorpe
etc *York* 69–71; C Millington w Gt Givendale 69–71; R
Hinderwell w Roxby 71–76; Hon C 80–91; Hon C Loftus
76–80; V Boosbeck w Moorsholm 91–95; R Kirby Misperton
w Normanby, Edston and Salton 95–02; rtd 02; PtO *Glas*
from 16. *7 High Street, Gatehouse of Fleet, Castle Douglas
DG7 2HR*   T: (01557) 814095 E: dennissamways71@sky.com
SAMWAYS, John Feverel. b 44. BA. Trin Coll Bris 81. **d** 83 **p** 84.
C Patcham *Chich* 83–86; C Ox St Aldate w St Matt 86–94; R Ox
St Matt 95–97; TR Keynsham *B & W* 97–09; rtd 09; PtO *B & W*
from 10. *9 Newland Gardens, Frome BA11 1PN*   T: (01373)
454047 E: john.samways@btinternet.com
SANCHEZ RODRIGUEZ, Miguel. b 66. Deusto Univ MA 95.
Coll of Resurr Mirfield 12. **d** 14 **p** 15. C Elland *Leeds* 14–17;
C Barnsley St Edw 17–18; C Barnsley St Mary 17–18; C
Gawber 17–18; C Cen Barnsley from 18. *The Vicarage,
Church Street, Gawber, Barnsley S75 2RL*   M: 07761-501229
E: msanrod@gmail.com
SANDAY, Robert Ward. b 55. Sarum & Wells Th Coll 89.
d 91 **p** 92. C Swindon Ch Ch *Bris* 91–94; V Lyddington and
Wanborough and Bishopstone etc 94–00; Chapl to the Deaf
Portsm and *Win* 00–20; V Southampton Lord's Hill and
Lord's Wood 10–15; P-in-c Hound 15–20; C Bursledon 15–20;
C Hamble le Rice 15–20; Portsm Dioc Disability Adv 15–20;
rtd 20. *Address temp unknown* E: robertsanday12@gmail.com
SANDBERG, Canon Peter John. b 37. Lon Univ LLB 59.
Lon Coll of Div 67. **d** 69 **p** 70. C Hailsham *Chich* 69–72;
C Billericay St Mary *Chelmsf* 72–77; TV Billericay and Lt
Burstead 77–83; R Thundersley 83–02; RD Hadleigh 90–00;
Hon Can Chelmsf Cathl 00–02; rtd 02; PtO *Chelmsf* from 02.
Hethersett, School Road, Pentlow, Sudbury CO10 7JR   T: (01787)
281006 E: peterandcelia@talktalk.net
SANDELLS-REES, Kathy Louise. *See* JONES, Kathy Louise
SANDER, Thomas William. b 87. Westcott Ho Cam.
d 11 **p** 12. C Sharnbrook, Felmersham and Knotting w

Souldrop *St Alb* 11–14; V Flamstead and Markyate Street
14–21; RD Wheathampstead 20–21; R St Giles-in-the-
Fields *Lon* from 21. *15A Gower Street, London WC1E 6HW*
E: thomas.william.sander@gmail.com
SANDER-HEYS, Mrs Jemma Joan. b 79. Ex Univ BA 02
Leeds Univ BA 11 Sheff Univ MA 12. Coll of Resurr
Mirfield 09. **d** 12 **p** 13. C R Wootton Bassett *Sarum* 12–15;
TV Gt Yarmouth *Nor* from 15. *1 Osborne Avenue, Great
Yarmouth NR30 4EE*   T: (01493) 304609   M: 07811-480438
E: jemmajsanders@hotmail.com
SANDERCOCK-PICKLES, Deborah Sharon Agnes. b 62. Coll
of Ripon & York St Jo BSc 84 Man Metrop Univ MSc 96
Crewe & Alsager Coll PGCE 87. SNWTP 09. **d** 12 **p** 13. C
Chadderton St Matt w St Luke *Man* 12–15; P-in-c Prestwich
St Marg 15–18; V from 17; AD Radcliffe and Prestwich
18–19. *St Margaret's Vicarage, 2 St Margaret's Road, Prestwich,
Manchester M25 2QB*   T: 0161-773 2698   M: 07871-760107
E: deborah.sandercock@hotmail.co.uk
SANDERS, Mrs Alexandra Jane. b 58. Ex Univ BA 80 Leeds
Univ MA 09. NOC 06. **d** 09 **p** 10. NSM Tarporley *Ches* 09–12;
C Acton and Worleston, Church Minshull etc 11–12; V
Mellor 12–18; rtd 18; PtO *Ches* from 18. *2 The Orchards,
Sadlers Wells, Bunbury, Tarporley CW6 9SG*   M: 07813-
326313 E: alex@oftheriver.com
SANDERS, Bryant John. **d** 15 **p** 16. C S Molton w Nymet
St George, High Bray etc *Ex* 15–16; C S Molton w Nymet
St George, Chittlehamholt etc from 16. *Shears Cottage, Kings
Nympton, Umberleigh EX37 9SP*   T: (01769) 581420
SANDERS, Canon Hilary Clare. b 57. Hull Univ BA 79
UEA CertEd 81. EAMTC 83. **dss** 85 **d** 87 **p** 94. Haverhill
w Withersfield, the Wrattings etc *St E* 85–87; Hon Par Dn
Melton 87–94; Hon C 94–99; Dioc Dir Educn (Schools)
88–99; P-in-c Earl Soham w Cretingham and Ashfield 99–05;
P-in-c Boulge w Burgh, Grundisburgh and Hasketon 05–13;
R Carlford 13–20; Dioc Adv for Women's Min 10–20; RD
Woodbridge 11–20; Hon Can St E Cathl from 04; rtd 20;
Hon C Craven Arms *Heref* from 21. *3 Nursery Fields, Rushbury
Road, Rushbury, Church Stretton SY6 7DY*   T: (01694) 771775
E: revclaresanders@tiscali.co.uk
SANDERS, Canon Mark. b 57. Hull Univ BA 79 Cam Univ
BA 82. Westcott Ho Cam 80. **d** 83 **p** 84. C Haverhill w
Withersfield, the Wrattings etc *St E* 83–87; P-in-c Melton
87–91; R 91–98; Dioc Dir Post-Ord Tr 97–14; Asst Dioc Dir of
Ords 98–99; Dioc Dir of Ords 99–14; Dioc Dir of CME 99–01;
R Framlingham w Saxtead 14–20; RD Loes 15–20; Hon Can
St E Cathl 01–20; rtd 20; Hon C Craven Arms *Heref* from
21. *3 Nursery Fields, Rushbury Road, Rushbury, Church Stretton
SY6 7DY*   T: (01694) 771775 E: revmarksanders@tiscali.co.uk
SANDERS, Michael Barry. b 45. Fitzw Coll Cam BA 67 MA 71
Lon Univ BD 71. St Jo Coll Nottm 68 Lon Coll of Div. **d** 71
p 72. C Ashtead *Guildf* 71–74; Chapl St Jo Coll Cam 75–79; V
Dorridge *Birm* 79–89; TR Walsall *Lich* 89–01; Preb Lich Cathl
97–01; Chapl The Hague *Eur* 01–07; P-in-c Kemble, Poole
Keynes, Somerford Keynes etc *Glouc* 07–12; rtd 12; PtO *Glouc*
from 15; Clergy Retirement Officer 16–20; PtO *Eur* from 12.
1 Rowena Cade Avenue, Cheltenham GL50 2LA   T: (01242)
515631 E: mbsanders45@gmail.com
SANDERS (née SHAW), Mrs Pamela Joyce. b 54. Liv Univ
BA 76. WEMTC 02. **d** 05 **p** 06. C Leominster *Heref* 05–09;
V Kirklevington w Picton, and High and Low Worsall
York 09–17; V Rudby in Cleveland w Middleton 09–17;
R Crathorne 09–17; rtd 17. *1 Grain Court, Junction Road,
Kirkwall KW15 1AX* E: pj.notsaunders@gmail.com
SANDERS, Susan Rachel. *See* COLLINGRIDGE, Susan Rachel
SANDERS, Canon Wendy Elizabeth. b 49. Carl Dioc Tr
Course 87. **d** 90 **p** 94. NSM Bampton w Mardale *Carl* 90–92; C
Walney Is 92–94; C Stanwix 94–98; TV Chippenham St Paul
w Hardenhuish etc *Bris* 98–03; TV Kington St Michael 98–03;
RD Chippenham 99–03; TR Cockermouth Area *Carl* 03–14;
Hon Can Carl Cathl 10–14; rtd 14; RD Derwent *Carl* 11–16.
23 Lowscales Drive, Cockermouth CA13 9DR   T: (01900)
823269 E: revdwes@gmail.com
SANDERS, William John. b 48. Liv Inst of Educn BA 80.
Wycliffe Hall Ox 81. **d** 83 **p** 84. C Netherton *Liv*
83–87; P-in-c Wavertree St Bridget 87–97; V Wavertree
St Bridget and St Thos 97–14; P-in-c 14–18; rtd 14;
PtO *Liv* 19–21. *14 Nightingale Road, Liverpool L12 0QF*
E: billandalice@virginmedia.com
SANDERSON, Colin James. b 54. Univ of Wales (Cardiff)
MA 95 SEN 70 RGN. St Mich Coll Llan 85. **d** 87 **p** 88.
C Merthyr Dyfan *Llan* 87–90; C Cadoxton-juxta-Barry
90–91; V Llangeinor 91–99; LtO 04–10; V Congleton St Jas
Ches from 10; Chapl Mid Cheshire Hosps NHS Foundn
Trust 11–12; Lead Chapl from 12. *St James's Vicarage, 116
Holmes Chapel Road, Congleton CW12 4NX*   T: (01260)

408203 *or* (01270) 255141   M: 07713-742365 E: cjsanderson2005@hotmail.com

SANDERSON, Daniel. b 40. AKC 66. **d** 67 **p** 68. C Upperby St Jo *Carl* 67–72; V Aldingham 72–75; V Ireleth w Askam 75–02; C Dalton-in-Furness and Ireleth-with-Askam 02–05; Hon Can Carl Cathl 95–05; RD Furness 01–04; rtd 05; PtO *Carl* 13–20. *52 Parklands Drive, Askam-in-Furness LA16 7JP* T: (01229) 463018

SANDERSON, Canon Gillian. b 47. Cranmer Hall Dur 80. dss 82 **d** 87 **p** 94. Allesley *Cov* 82–86; Warwick 86–00; C 87–94; TV 94–00; Hon Can Cov Cathl 94–00; PtO 00–15. *17 Marlborough Drive, Leamington Spa CV31 1XY* T: (01926) 459749 M: 07714-193776 E: gillian7647@gmail.com

SANDERSON, Paul. b 59. Univ of Wales (Abth) BSc 80 Man Univ MEd 92 Ches Coll of HE PGCE 81. **d** 05 **p** 06. OLM Bury St Jo w St Mark *Man* 05–10; OLM Walmersley Road, Bury 10–19; P-in-c Elton St Steph from 19. *22 Birley Street, Bury BL9 5DT* E: paul270159@gmail.com

SANDERSON, Timothy. b 68. York Univ BSc 89 Glos Univ BA 03 St Jo Coll Dur MATM 09. Cranmer Hall Dur 07. **d** 09 **p** 10. C Newc St Barn and St Jude 09–17; C Jesmond H Trin 09–20; V from 20. *13 Glastonbury Grove, Newcastle upon Tyne NE2 2HA* M: 07592-720879 E: tim@htj.org.uk

SANDES, Denis Lindsay. b 46. CITC BTh 86. **d** 89 **p** 90. C Bandon Union *C, C & R* 89–92; I Kells Gp *C, F & O* 92–97; Can Leighlin Cathl 03–07; I Omey w Ballynakill, Errislannan and Roundstone *T, K & A* 07–13; Can Tuam Cathl 08–11; Provost Tuam 10–13; rtd 13. *Ballyhasty, Cloughjordan, Co Tipperary, Republic of Ireland* T: (00353) (76) 604 5868 M: 86-647 5056 E: revdlsandes@gmail.com

SANDFORD, Nicholas Robert. b 63. Kent Univ BA 84 Univ of Wales (Cardiff) BD 87. St Mich Coll Llan 84. **d** 87 **p** 88. C Neath w Llantwit *Llan* 87–90; C Cardiff St Jo 90–94; R Cilybebyll 94–97; Chapl HM Pris Swansea 95–97; Chapl HM Pris Parc (Bridgend) 97–04; Chapl HM Pris Usk and Prescoed 04–13; Chapl HM Pris Swansea 13–16; Chapl HM Pris Cardiff from 16; PtO *Llan* from 14. *HM Prison, Knox Road, Cardiff CF40 0UG* T: (029) 2092 3100 E: nick.r.sandford@justice.gov.uk

SANDFORD, Paul Richard. b 47. Em Coll Cam BA 69 MA 73. Wycliffe Hall Ox 72. **d** 75 **p** 76. C Upper Holloway St Pet *Lon* 75–77; C Finchley St Paul Long Lane 77–81; Ind Chapl *Newc* 81–88; TV Cramlington 81–88; P-in-c Elmsett w Aldham *St E* 89–92; P-in-c Kersey w Lindsey 89–92; R Esigodini *Zimbabwe* 92–96; Sub Dean Harare 97; Chapl Algarve *Eur* 98–00; V Castle Bromwich St Clem *Birm* 00–09; P-in-c Yardley St Edburgha 09–11; V from 11. *49 Vicarage Road, Yardley, Birmingham B33 8PH* E: williamsands123@btinternet.com

SANER-HAIGH, Canon Robert James. b 73. Birm Univ BA 94 MPhil 98. Wycliffe Hall Ox BA 04 MA 08. **d** 05 **p** 06. C Appleby *Carl* 05–07; Bp's Dom Chapl and C Dalston w Cumdivock, Raughton Head and Wreay 07–10; Officer for IME 4-7 07–08; Dir of Ords 08–10; P-in-c Kendal H Trin 10–20; Dir Min and Miss *Newc* from 20; Can Res Newc Cathl from 20. *Church House, St John's Terrace, North Shields NE29 6HS* T: 0191-270 4100 M: 07826-405972 E: r.sanerhaigh@newcastle.anglican.org

SANGSTER, Andrew. b 45. K Coll Lon BD 67 AKC 67 BA 71 MA 84 Lon Inst of Educn MPhil 93 LLB 97 UEA PhD 14 FCollP. St Boniface Warminster. **d** 69 **p** 70. C Aylesford *Roch* 69–72; C Shirley *Win* 73–76; V Woolston 76–79; Prov Youth Chapl Ch in Wales 79–82; Chapl Collegiate Sch NZ 82–89; Chapl Eton Coll 89–92; Hd Master St Edm Sch Hindhead 92–96; Hd Thos Day Schs Lon 96–99; V Ormesby St Marg w Scratby, Ormesby St Mich etc *Nor* 99–04; Chapl Bromley Coll 04–10; rtd 10; PtO *Nor* 10–15; Bp's Officer for Rtd Clergy from 15; Hon PV Nor Cathl from 14. *10 Harvey Lane, Norwich NR7 0BQ* T: (01603) 437402 E: asangster666@btinternet.com

SANKEY, Julian. b 52. Qu Coll Ox BA 74 MA 79. St Jo Coll Nottm 84. **d** 86 **p** 87. C New Barnet St Jas *St Alb* 86–89; C Mansfield SS Pet and Paul *S'well* 89–94; Chapl St Luke's Hospice Sheff 94–07. *29 Grindlow Close, Sheffield S14 1PE* T: 0114-264 9988

SANSBURY, Canon Christopher John. b 34. Peterho Cam BA 57 MA. Westcott Ho Cam 58. **d** 59 **p** 60. C Portsea N End St Mark *Portsm* 59–63; C Weeke *Win* 63–71; V N Eling St Mary 71–78; R Long Melford *St E* 78–00; P-in-c Lawshall w Shimplingthorne and Alpheton 98–00; Hon Can St E Cathl 97–00; rtd 00; PtO *St E* 00–18. *2 Deacon's Close, Lavenham, Sudbury CO10 9TT* T: (01787) 248068

SANSOM, John Reginald. b 40. St Jo Coll Nottm 73. **d** 75 **p** 76. C Ipswich St Marg *St E* 75–79; P-in-c Emneth *Ely* 79–85; P-in-c Hartford 85–86; TV Huntingdon 86–91; R Sawtry 91–97; R Sawtry and Glatton 97–99; TV Ely 99–05; rtd 05; PtO *Ely* from 06. *77 St Ovins Green, Ely CB6 3AW* T: (01353) 614913 E: johnjudysansom@ntlworld.com

SANSOM, Canon Michael Charles. b 44. Bris Univ BA 66 St Jo Coll Dur PhD 74. Cranmer Hall Dur 68. **d** 72 **p** 73. C Ecclesall *Sheff* 72–76; LtO *Ely* 76–88; Dir of Studies Ridley Hall Cam 76–88; Vice-Prin 78–88; Dir of Ords *St Alb* 88–10; Can Res St Alb 88–10; rtd 10; PtO *Ex* from 16. *101 Churchfields Drive, Bovey Tracey, Newton Abbot TQ13 9QZ* T: (01626) 836773 E: michaelsansom123@btinternet.com

SANSUM, Canon David Henry. b 31. Bris Univ BA 52 MA 63. St Aid Birkenhead 54. **d** 56 **p** 57. C Henleaze *Bris* 56–59; C Stratton St Margaret 59–60; C Stoke Bishop 60–64; V Stechford *Birm* 64–76; V Ashbourne St Oswald w Mapleton *Derby* 76–98; P-in-c Fenny Bentley, Thorpe and Tissington 77–83; V Ashbourne St Jo 81–98; RD Ashbourne 91–98; Hon Can Derby Cathl 95–98; rtd 98; PtO *Glouc* 98–15; *Bris* 98–15. *60 Mile End Road, Newton Abbot TQ12 1RW* E: davidsansum@btinternet.com

SANTANA, Levy. *See* CAMPOS DE SANTANA, Levy Henrique

✠**SANTER, The Rt Revd Mark.** b 36. Qu Coll Cam BA 60 MA 64 Lambeth DD 99. Westcott Ho Cam. **d** 63 **p** 64 **c** 81. Tutor Cuddesdon Coll 63–67; C Cuddesdon *Ox* 63–67; Fell and Dean Clare Coll Cam 67–72; Tutor 68–72; Prin Westcott Ho Cam 73–81; Hon Can Win Cathl 78–81; Area Bp Kensington *Lon* 81–87; Bp Birm 87–02; rtd 02; Hon Asst Bp Worc from 02 and Birm from 03. *81 Clarence Road, Kings Heath, Birmingham B13 9UH* T: 0121-441 2194

SAPWELL, Mrs Lynette Lilian. b 51. Sussex Univ BEd 73 Middx Univ BA 03. NTMTC 00. **d** 03 **p** 04. NSM Rochford *Chelmsf* 03–07; P-in-c Appleton *Ox* 07–16; P-in-c Besselsleigh 07–16; rtd 16; PtO *Ox* 16–17; *Bris* from 16. *The Old Post Office, 45 Queens Road, Hannington, Swindon SN6 7RP* T: (01793) 764418 E: lynsapwell@gmail.com

SARALIS, Preb Christopher Herbert. b 34. Univ of Wales BA 54 St Cath Coll Ox BA 56 MA 60. Wycliffe Hall Ox. **d** 57 **p** 58. C Abergavenny St Mary w Llanwenarth Citra *Mon* 57–61; C Bridgwater St Mary w Chilton Trinity *B & W* 61–65;

Left column second entries:

SANDHAM, Daniel Paul. b 82. St Chad's Coll Dur BA 05. St Steph Ho Ox BA 09 MA 14. **d** 09 **p** 10. C Hendon St Mary and Ch Ch *Lon* 09–12; V Brownswood Park 12–18; P-in-c Winchmore Hill St Paul 18–19; V from 19. *St Paul's Vicarage, Church Hill, London N21 1JA* T: (020) 8886 3545 E: vicar@spwh.org

SANDHAM, Stephen McCourt. b 41. K Coll Lon BD 65 AKC 65. **d** 66 **p** 67. C Stockton St Pet *Dur* 66–69; C Bishopwearmouth Gd Shep 69–71; C Bishopwearmouth St Mich w St Hilda 71–75; V Darlington St Mark w St Paul 75–82; P-in-c Sunderland St Chad 82–87; R Shincliffe 87–98; P-in-c 98–06; rtd 06; Chapl Sherburn Hosp Dur 98–07; PtO *Dur* from 07. *21 Hill Meadows, High Shincliffe, Durham DH1 2PE* E: stephensandham@yahoo.co.uk

SANDIFORD, Mrs Christine Krogh. b 44. Smith Coll (USA) BA 66 Wesleyan Univ Connecticut MA 68 Man Univ PGCE 87. SNWTP 11. **d** 12 **p** 13. OLM Didsbury St Jas and Em *Man* 12–17; PtO from 17. *330 Lapwing Lane, Manchester M20 6UW* T: 0161-434 1343 E: cksandiford@hotmail.com

SANDLAND, Richard Julian Matthew. b 65. Lon Univ BA 01. Qu Foundn Birm 18. **d** 21. C Bromsgrove *Worc* from 21; C Dodford from 21. *2 Verona Road, Bromsgrove B60 2SS* M: 07970-068150 E: richardjsandland@btinternet.com

SANDLE, Lynne Kirsty. b 75. Paisley Univ BA 98. St Mellitus Coll 15. **d** 18 **p** 19. C Chellington *St Alb* from 18. *The Rectory, Bamfords Lane, Turvey, Bedford MK43 8DS* T: (01234) 881654 M: 07967-509314

SANDOM, Miss Carolyn Elizabeth. b 63. Homerton Coll Cam BEd 85. Wycliffe Hall Ox BTh 93. **d** 94. C St Helen Bishopsgate w St Andr Undershaft etc *Lon* 94–96; C Cambridge H Sepulchre *Ely* 96–05; PtO *Chelmsf* 05–06; NSM Mayfair Ch Ch *Lon* 06–11; NSM Tunbridge Wells St Jo *Roch* 11–18. *57 Green Way, Tunbridge Wells TN2 3HJ* T: (01892) 671629

SANDOVER, Cherry Elizabeth. b 57. Essex Univ BA 98 MA 00 PhD 04 PGCE 04. St Mellitus Coll 14. **d** 15 **p** 16. NSM Leigh St Clem *Chelmsf* from 15; NSM Southend 19–20; NSM Westcliff St Alban and Southend St Mark from 21. *7B Victoria Drive, Leigh-on-Sea SS9 1SF* T: (01702) 715845 M: 07859-911997 E: revcherrysandover@gmail.com

SANDS, William James. b 55. Nottm Univ LTh 83 Birm Univ MA 99. St Jo Coll Nottm 80. **d** 83 **p** 84. C St Mary-at-Latton *Chelmsf* 83–86; R Mvurwi Zimbabwe 86–87; C-in-c Barkingside St Cedd *Chelmsf* 87–89; C Woodford St Mary w St Phil and St Jas 87–89; P-in-c Elmsett w Aldham *St E* 89–92; P-in-c Kersey w Lindsey 89–92; R Esigodini *Zimbabwe* 92–96; Sub Dean Harare 97; Chapl Algarve *Eur* 98–00; V Castle Bromwich St Clem *Birm* 00–09; P-in-c Yardley St Edburgha 09–11; V from 11. *49 Vicarage Road, Yardley, Birmingham B33 8PH* E: williamsands123@btinternet.com

V Berrow 65–72; R Berrow and Breane 72–76; RD Burnham 72–76; V Minehead 76–92; RD Exmoor 80–86; Preb Wells Cathl 84–92; V Bovey Tracey SS Pet, Paul and Thos w Hennock *Ex* 92–99; rtd 99; PtO *B & W* 99–19. *17 George Maher Court, Shudrick Lane, Ilminster TA19 0BP* T: (01460) 52416 E: christophersaralis@talktalk.net

SARGANT, John Raymond. b 38. CCC Cam BA 61 MA 70. Westcott Ho Cam 64 Harvard Div Sch 66. d 67 p 68. C Croydon St Jo *Cant* 67–72; Sec Zambia Angl Coun 72–75; P-in-c Bradford-on-Avon Ch Ch *Sarum* 76–81; V 81–90; TV Marlborough 90–03; Dioc Inter-Faith Adv 90–00; Can and Preb Sarum Cathl 92–01; rtd 03. *48 Summerhill Road, Lyme Regis DT7 3DT* T: (01297) 445922

✠SARGEANT, The Rt Revd Frank Pilkington. b 32. St Jo Coll Dur BA 55. Cranmer Hall Dur 57. d 58 p 59 c 84. C Gainsborough All SS *Linc* 58–62; C Gt Grimsby St Jas 62–66; V Hykeham 66–73; Dir In-Service Tr and Adult Educn *Bradf* 73–84; Can Res Bradf Cathl 73–77; Adn Bradf 77–84; Suff Bp Stockport *Ches* 84–94; Bp at Lambeth (Hd of Staff) *Cant* 94–99; rtd 99; Hon Asst Bp Eur 99–07; Hon Asst Bp Man from 99; PtO *Ches* from 99. *32 Brotherton Drive, Trinity Gardens, Salford M3 6BH* T: 0161-839 7045 E: franksargeant68@outlook.com

SARGENT, Ann. b 65. d 98 p 99. C Bris St Andr Hartcliffe 98–01; P-in-c Flax Bourton *B & W* 01–09; P-in-c Barrow Gurney 01–09; P-in-c Long Ashton 05–09; R Long Ashton w Barrow Gurney and Flax Bourton 09–19; Dioc Dir of Ords *Glouc* from 19; Warden of Readers from 19. *4 College Green, Gloucester GL1 2LR* T: (01452) 835547

SARGENT, Charles Edward. b 68. K Coll Lon BD 89 Leeds Univ MA 96. Coll of Resurr Mirfield 94. d 96 p 97. C Notting Dale St Clem w St Mark and St Jas *Lon* 96–00; P-in-c S Kensington St Aug 00–04; Chapl Imp Coll 00–04; Chapl Brunel Univ 04–10; PtO *S'wark* 05–16; NSM The Windmill from 16; PtO *Truro* 11–16. *Westlands Farm, Antlands Lane, Shipley Bridge, Horley RH6 9TE* T: (01342) 842232 E: charles.sargent@priest.com

SARGENT, Canon David Gareth. b 63. Sheff Univ BA 85 St Jo Coll Dur BA 96. Cranmer Hall Dur 93. d 96 p 97. C Norbury *Ches* 96–01; V Hooton 01–06; TR Penrith w Newton Reigny and Plumpton Wall *Carl* from 06; RD Penrith from 14; Hon Can Carl Cathl from 18. *The Rectory, 3 Lamley Gardens, Penrith CA11 9LR* T: (01768) 863000

SARGENT, Mrs Janet. b 54. d 07 p 08. OLM Birchencliffe *Wakef* 07–08; OLM Birkby and Birchencliffe 08–12; NSM Huddersfield St Pet 12–14; *Leeds* 14–20; NSM Golcar and Longwood from 20. *11 Kirkwood Drive, Huddersfield HD3 3WA* T: (01484) 650390

SARGENT, Miss Philippa Mary. b 68. Oriel Coll Ox MA 94. Ripon Coll Cuddesdon 13. d 15 p 16. C Kempsey and Severn Stoke w Croome d'Abitot *Worc* 15–18; P-in-c Marnhull *Sarum* from 18; V Sturminster Newton, Hinton St Mary and Lydlinch from 18. *The Vicarage, Church Street, Sturminster Newton DT10 1DB* T: (01258) 473905 M: 07963-273221 E: philippa.sargent@me.com

SARGENT, Trevor Harold. TCD BEd 81 MTh 18. CITI. d 17 p 18. Tullow w Shillelagh, Aghold and Mullinacuff *C, F & O* 17–18; C Waterford w Killea, Drumcannon and Dunhill 18–20; I Bunclody w Kildavin, Clonegal and Kilrush from 20. *The Rectory, Ryland Upper, Bunclody, Co Wexford, Republic of Ireland* M: (00353) 87-254 7836 E: sargentt@tcd.ie

SARMEZEY, George Arpad. b 61. Qu Mary Coll Lon BA 83 Goldsmiths' Coll Lon PGCE 86. Westcott Ho Cam 89. d 92 p 93. C Eastville St Anne w St Mark and St Thos *Bris* 92–94; C Stratton St Margaret w S Marston etc 94–97; Asst Chapl Northn Gen Hosp NHS Trust 97–00; Sen Chapl from 00. *Northampton General Hospital, Billing Road, Northampton NN1 5BD* T: (01604) 545773 *or* 634700 F: 544608 E: george.sarmezey@ngh.nhs.uk

SARUM, Archdeacon of. *See* JEANS, The Ven Alan Paul

SARVANANTHAN, Sudharshan. b 70. Trin Coll Bris 06. d 08 p 09. C Heart of Eden *Carl* 08–12; P-in-c Clifton, Dean and Mosser 12–17; C Brigham, Gt Broughton and Broughton Moor 14–17; P-in-c Brigham, Clifton, Dean and Mosser 17–19; Network Youth Ch Ldr 12–19; R Wyberton *Linc* from 19; V Frampton from 19. *The Rectory, Church Lane, Wyberton, Boston PE21 7AF* M: 07785-334804 E: rev.sudharshan@googlemail.com

SASSER, Canon Howell Crawford. b 37. Maryland Univ BA 72 Geo Mason Univ Virginia MA 74 Westmr Coll Ox MTh 97. Washington Dioc Course 75. d 77 p 78. W Germany 77–80; Somalia 80–83; Cyprus 84–92; Chapl Montreux w Gstaad *Eur* 92–97; Chapl Oporto 97–05; Adn Gib 02–05; Bp's Chapl and Research Asst 05–06; rtd 06. *5225 Wilson Lane, Apt 3119, Mechanicsburg PA 17055, USA* E: hcrawfordsasser@aol.com

SATHYARAJ, Canon Rajkumar Reuben. Bangalore Univ BSc Karnatak Univ MA. Trin Th Coll Singapore MDiv. d 97. Egypt 01–11; C Seagoe *D & D* 11–18; P-in-c Kilwarlin Upper w Kilwarlin Lower from 18; Hon Can All SS Cathl Cairo from 05. *Kilwarlin Rectory, 9 St John's Road, Hillsborough BT26 6ED* M: 07927-938185 E: revraj@hotmail.com

SATKUNANAYAGAM, Kuhan. b 76. St Jo Coll Dur BSc 01 BA 11 Univ of E Lon MSc 06 PsychD 08. Cranmer Hall Dur 09. d 11 p 12. C Leatherhead and Mickleham *Guildf* 11–15; C Long Ditton from 15. *The Rectory, 5 Church Meadow, Long Ditton, Surbiton KT6 5EP* T: (020) 8398 1583 M: 07957-293907 E: kuhan@dunelm.org.uk

SAUM, Rachel Elizabeth. b 78. Edin Univ BSc 00 K Coll Lon MA 11. St Mellitus Coll BA 16. d 16 p 17. C Chesterton *Cov* 16–20; C Lighthorne 16–20; C Newbold Pacey w Moreton Morrell 16–20; PtO 20–21; P-in-c Newnham w Awre and Blakeney *Glouc* from 21. *The Vicarage, 1 Whetstones, Unlawater Lane, Newnham GL14 1BT* M: 07815-793625 E: revrachelsaum@gmail.com

SAUNDERS, Alan William. b 67. St Mellitus Coll. d 13 p 14. C Halliwell St Pet *Man* 13–16; V Pennington from 16. *Christ Church Vicarage, Schofield Street, Leigh WN7 4HT* T: (01942) 673619 M: 07767-643444 E: alan@alongside.me.uk

SAUNDERS, Andrew Vivian. b 44. Leeds Univ BA 65. Coll of Resurr Mirfield 66. d 68 p 69. C Goodmayes St Paul *Chelmsf* 68–71; C Horfield H Trin *Bris* 71–75; C Oldland 75–77; Ind Chapl *B & W* 77–80; P-in-c Buckland Dinham w Elm, Orchardleigh etc 77–78; P-in-c Buckland Dinham 78–80; V Westfield 80–90; R Clutton w Cameley 90–99; C Christchurch *Win* 99–05; rtd 05; PtO *B & W* from 06. *8 Mill House Court, Willow Vale, Frome BA11 1BG* T: (01373) 467683 E: andrewvsaunders@gmail.com

SAUNDERS, Barry. *See* SAUNDERS, John Barry

SAUNDERS, Bridget Frances. b 57. De Montfort Univ BA 04 SRN 78 SCM 81. Qu Foundn Birm 18. d 20 p 21. NSM Fosse Team *Leic* from 20. *19 Blackfriars Road, Syston, Leicester LE7 2DS* T: 0116-210 0423 M: 07597-921051 E: biddys0909@gmail.com

SAUNDERS, Canon Bruce Alexander. b 47. St Cath Coll Cam BA 68 MA 72. Cuddesdon Coll 68. d 71 p 72. C Westbury-on-Trym H Trin *Bris* 71–74; Hon C Clifton St Paul 74–78; Asst Chapl Bris Univ 74–78; TV Fareham H Trin *Portsm* 78–84; TR Mortlake w E Sheen *S'wark* 84–97; RD Richmond and Barnes 89–94; Can Missr for Ch in Soc 97–03; Can Res S'wark Cathl 03–14; Sub Dean 12–14; C-in-c Bermondsey St Hugh CD *S'wark* 03–14; rtd 14; PtO *Bris* from 15. *10 Reedley Road, Bristol BS9 3ST* T: 0117-373 2123

SAUNDERS, David Anthony. b 48. Trin Coll Bris 76. d 78 p 79. C Bath Walcot *B & W* 78–80; Asst Dir RE 80–83; Youth Chapl 80–83; C Long Ashton 83–84; V Bath St Bart 84–90; OCM 84–90; V Cullompton *Ex* 90–97; R Kentisbeare w Blackborough 90–97; Dir Shiloh Min USA from 97; rtd 13. *605 Tuscan Valley Drive, Oxford MS 38655, USA* E: dasaunders@mac.com

SAUNDERS, David James. b 63. Ripon Coll Cuddesdon 18. d 21. C Ascot Heath *Ox* from 21. *43 Hitherhooks Hill, Binfield, Bracknell RG42 4QW* M: 07834-459672 E: saundersdave2@aol.com

SAUNDERS, Gareth John McKeith. b 71. St Andr Univ BD 93 Edin Univ MTh 99. TISEC 99. d 99 p 00. C Inverness St Andr *Mor* 99–03; C Edin St Salvador and Edin Gd Shep 03–06; LtO *St And* from 07; Hon C St Andrews All SS from 10. *14 Balcomie Green, Crail, Anstruther KY10 3UX* M: 07732-356123 E: gareth@garethjmsaunders.co.uk

SAUNDERS, Ivor John. b 37. Wolv Poly CQSW 81. d 04 p 05. OLM Wolverhampton St Jude *Lich* 04–17; PtO 17–21. *34 Wrottesley Road, Wolverhampton WV6 8SF* T: (01902) 751162

SAUNDERS, James Benedict John. b 72. St Aid Coll Dur BA 93 St Jo Coll Cam PhD 97 St Jo Coll Dur BA 00. Cranmer Hall Dur 98. d 01 p 02. C Sole Bay *St E* 01–04; P-in-c Teigh w Whissendine and Market Overton *Pet* 04–09; Asst Chapl HM Pris Ashwell 04–07; Chapl Uppingham Sch from 09. *Pentire, 48 High Street West, Uppingham, Oakham LE15 9QD* T: (01572) 829934 E: jbjs@uppingham.co.uk

SAUNDERS, Mrs Joan Mary (Jo). b 44. Univ Coll Lon BA 66 PGCE 67. EAMTC 00. d 03 p 04. NSM Gt and Lt Casterton w Pickworth and Tickencote *Pet* 03–05; P-in-c 09–16; P-in-c Castle Bytham w Creeton *Linc* 05–09; Hon C Ketton, Collyweston, Easton-on-the-Hill and Tinwell *Pet* 09–16; rtd 17; PtO *Pet* 17–19; P-in-c Ryhall w Essendine and Carlby from 19. *Mellstock, Bourne Road, Essendine, Stamford PE9 4LH* T: (01780) 480479 E: revjosaunders@live.co.uk

SAUNDERS, John Barry. b 40. Chich Th Coll. d 83 p 84. C St Breoke *Truro* 83–84; C St Breoke and Egloshayle 84–87; V Treverbyn 87–96; RD St Austell 91–96; V Perranzabuloe

96–03; rtd 03; PtO *Truro* from 04. *48 Cormorant Drive, St Austell PL25 3BA* T: (01726) 71994

SAUNDERS, Canon John Michael. b 40. Brasted Th Coll 66 Clifton Th Coll 68. **d** 70 **p** 71. C Homerton St Luke *Lon* 70–74; SAMS Brazil 74–91; P-in-c Horsmonden *Roch* 91–97; Area Sec (SE England) SAMS 91–97; V Gillingham St Mark *Roch* 97–08; rtd 08; Hon C Newton Longville, Mursley, Swanbourne etc *Ox* 08–15; rtd 15; PtO *Ox* 15–19; *Cant* from 19. *The Rectory, Roman Road, Aldington, Ashford TN25 7EF* M: 07732-682472 E: canonjohnsaunders@aol.com

SAUNDERS, Mrs Margaret Rose. b 49. Newnham Coll Cam BA 71 St Jo Coll York PGCE 72. St Alb Minl Tr Scheme 85. **d** 88 **p** 94. Hon Par Dn Gt Berkhamsted *St Alb* 88–90; Hon Chapl Asst Gt Ormond Street Hosp for Sick Children Lon 88–90; Asst Chapl Aylesbury Vale HA 90–92; Chapl Milton Keynes Gen NHS Trust 92–98; Chapl Milton Keynes Community NHS Trust 92–98; C Newport Pagnell w Lathbury and Moulsoe *Ox* 98–01; TV Grantham *Linc* 01–02; P-in-c Grantham, Manthorpe 02–04; Chapl United Lincs Hosps NHS Trust 01–14; rtd 14; Gen Preacher *Linc* 15–16; PtO *St Alb* from 16. *7 Applecroft, Northchurch, Berkhamsted HP4 3RX* T: (01442) 874955 E: margar3t.saunders@gmail.com

SAUNDERS, Mark Richard. *See* VASEY-SAUNDERS, Mark Richard

SAUNDERS, Martin Paul. b 54. K Coll Lon BD 76 AKC 76 Univ of Northumbria at Newc DipSW 96. Westcott Ho Cam 77. **d** 78 **p** 79. C Seaton Hirst *Newc* 78–81; Regional Chapl Hong Kong Miss to Seamen 81; C Egglescliffe *Dur* 81–82; Chapl to Arts and Recreation 81–84; C Jarrow *Dur* 82–84; TV 84–88; V Southwick St Columba 88–94; PtO from 94. *55 The Meadows, Burnopfield, Newcastle upon Tyne NE16 6QW* T: (01207) 271242 M: 07817-964538 E: martinsaunders18@gmail.com

SAUNDERS, Martyn Leonard John. b 69. Magd Coll Cam MEng 92. Wycliffe Hall Ox BA 97. **d** 98 **p** 99. C Quinton Road W St Boniface *Birm* 98–02; TV Barnsbury *Lon* 02–10; V Chatham St Phil and St Jas *Roch* from 10. *The Vicarage, 139 Sussex Drive, Walderslade, Chatham ME5 0NR* T: (01634) 861108 E: martyn.saunders@pipnjims.co.uk

SAUNDERS, Michael. b 38. Charing Cross Hosp Medical Sch MB, BS 62 FRCPEd 74 FRCP 78 MSOSc 84. NEOC 82. **d** 84 **p** 85. LtO *York* 84–92; Tutor NEOC 84–93; NSM Stokesley *York* 92–93; C Ripon Cathl 93–95; PtO *York* 93–13; NSM Gt and Lt Ouseburn w Marton cum Grafton etc *Ripon* 95–02; NSM Masham and Healey 02–08; PtO 08–14; *Leeds* from 14. *College Grove, College Lane, Masham, Ripon HG4 4HE* T: (01765) 688306 M: 07711-567160

SAUNDERS, Michael Walter. b 58. Grey Coll Dur BSc 79 CChem MRSC 84. Wycliffe Hall Ox 86. **d** 89 **p** 90. C Deane *Man* 89–93; TV Eccles 93–02; Chapl Eccles Sixth Form Coll 96–02; Dioc Adv on Evang *Man* 98–02; C Yateley and Eversley *Win* 02–06; P-in-c Darby Green 05–06; V Darby Green and Eversley 06–16; V Hungerford and Denford *Ox* from 16. *The Vicarage, Parsonage Lane, Hungerford RG17 0JB* M: 07713-810811 E: mike@mikethevicar.co.uk

SAUNDERS, Moira Ruth Forbes. *See* FORBES, Moira Ruth

SAUNDERS, Richard George. b 54. BNC Ox BA 76 MA 81. St Jo Coll Nottm 82. **d** 85 **p** 86. C Barrow St Mark *Carl* 85–89; C Cranham Park *Chelmsf* 89–97; TV Kinson *Sarum* 97–00; TR Kinson and W Howe 00–12; V Sheet *Portsm* 12–21; rtd 21. *13 Tatham Road, Abingdon OX14 1QB*

SAUNDERS, Ronald. b 37. St Pet Coll Birm CertEd 62 Memorial Univ Newfoundland CertEd 80 Columbia Univ MA 82 PhD 87 ACP 67. Sarum Th Coll 69. **d** 68 **p** 70. Lic to Offic Malawi 68–70; C Blantyre 71–72; C Kensington St Mary Abbots w St Geo *Lon* 72–73; C Bournemouth St Fran *Win* 73–75; I Twillingate Canada 75–76; Lic to Offic 77–81; C Gt Marlow *Ox* 81–82; Area Org Leprosy Miss 82–85; V Penycae *St As* 85–87; TV Wrexham 87–89; LtO *Ox* 90–97; Chapl Morden Coll Blackheath 91–97; Master Wyggeston's Hosp Leic 97–03; P-in-c Nerja and Almuñécar *Eur* 05–07. *Barrio San Isidro 92, 18830 Huescar (Granada), Spain* E: ron1937uk@hotmail.co.uk

SAUNDERS (née CORNWALL), Valerie Cecilia. b 40. Bedf Coll Lon BSc 62 Lon Inst of Educn PGCE 63. Scottish Chs Open Coll 96. **d** 03 **p** 04. NSM Dingwall *Mor* from 03; NSM Strathpeffer from 03. *Chessbury, 12 Firthview, Dingwall IV15 9PF* T: (01349) 865445 M: 07747-066993 E: valeriestj@btopenworld.com

SAUNDERS, Ms Wendy Jennifer. b 49. S'wark Ord Course 86. **d** 95 **p** 96. C Thamesmead *S'wark* 95–98; P-in-c Eltham St Sav 98–15; rtd 15; PtO *S'wark* from 15; *Nor* from 15. *Thistle Barn, Reepham Road, Felthorpe, Norwich NR10 4DU* M: 07802-603754 E: revwendy@tiscali.co.uk

SAUSBY, John Michael. b 39. AKC. **d** 63 **p** 64. C Crosland Moor *Wakef* 63–65; C Halifax St Jo Bapt 65–67; V Birkby 67–77; V Holmfirth 77–89; TR Upper Holme Valley 89–01;

rtd 01; PtO *Wakef* 04–14; *Leeds* 14–16. *15 River Holme View, Brockholes, Huddersfield HD9 7BP* T: (01484) 667228

SAUVEN, Edward Paul. b 82. St Jo Coll Nottm 14. **d** 16 **p** 17. C Tewkesbury w Walton Cardiff and Twyning *Glouc* from 16. *126 Queens Road, Tewkesbury GL20 5ER* M: 07727-241370

SAVAGE, Andrew Michael. b 67. Wye Coll Lon BSc 89 Cranfield Inst of Tech MSc 91. Wycliffe Hall Ox BTh 96. **d** 96 **p** 97. C Ecclesall *Sheff* 96–99; TV Kirk Ella and Willerby *York* 99–06; Chapl Kingham Hill Sch 06–21; Chapl Lambrook Sch Bracknell from 21. *Lambrook School, Winkfield Row, Bracknell RG42 6LU* T: (01344) 882717

SAVAGE, Canon Christopher Marius. b 46. Hull Univ MA 94. Bernard Gilpin Soc Dur 65 Bps' Coll Cheshunt 66 Qu Coll Birm 68. **d** 70 **p** 71. C Battersea St Luke *S'wark* 70–75; TV Newbury *Ox* 75–80; R Lich St Mary w St Mich 80–85; V Chessington *Guildf* 85–91; Ind Chapl *Win* 91–00; V Newc Ch Ch w St Ann 00–07; Team Ldr Chapl to People at Work in Cam *Ely* 07–12; rtd 12; PtO *Sarum* from 12. *22 Burcombe Lane, Wilton, Salisbury SP2 0ES* M: 07769-856481 E: chrismsavage@gmail.com

SAVAGE, Helen. b 55. Birm Univ BA 76 Dur Univ BA 82 MA 90 Newc Univ MLitt 83 Dur Univ PhD 05. Cranmer Hall Dur 80. **d** 83 **p** 84. C Newc St Gabr 83–86; Adult Educn Adv 86–94; V Bedlington 94–04; PtO 09–15; V Slaley, Healey and Whittonstall from 15; R Blanchland w Hunstanworth and Edmundbyers etc from 15. *Slaley Vicarage, Hexham NE47 0AA* T: (01434) 673609 E: helensavage1@gmail.com

SAVAGE, Mrs Hilary Linda. b 48. RGN 71 RM 86. WMMTC 89. **d** 92 **p** 94. C Quinton Road W St Boniface *Birm* 92–96; P-in-c Edgbaston SS Mary and Ambrose 96–01; V 01–02; TV Cramlington *Newc* 02–10; R Eckington and Ridgeway *Derby* 10–14; rtd 14; PtO *Ban* from 14. *Ein ty Noddfa, 4 Belle Vue, Ffestiniog, Blaenau Ffestiniog LL41 4NU* T: (01766) 762383 E: hilarysavage@hotmail.com

SAVAGE, Mrs Jennifer Anne. b 52. CertEd 73. NOC 96. **d** 99 **p** 00. C Haworth *Bradf* 99–02; R 02–09; P-in-c Cross Roads cum Lees 07–09; P-in-c Thornton in Lonsdale w Burton in Lonsdale 09–13; Steeton *Leeds* 13–16; V 16–18. *13 Currer Walk, Steeton, Keighley BD20 6TL*

SAVAGE, Lucy Jane. *See* WORMSLEY, Lucy Jane

SAVAGE, Paul Andrew. b 78. Univ of Wales (Ban) BA 00 Ches Univ MTh 15. St Jo Coll Nottm 10. **d** 12 **p** 13. C Bawtry w Austerfield and Misson *S'well* 12–15; C Bawtry w Austerfield, Misson, Everton and Mattersey 15; P-in-c Humberstone and Thurnby Lodge *Leic* from 15. *73 Thurnby Lodge, Nursery Road, Leicester LE5 2HQ* T: 0116-241 9526 E: revsavage2013@gmail.com

SAVEGE, Timothy Michael. b 38. **d** 00 **p** 01. OLM Blyth Valley *St E* 00–05; OLM Bury St Edmunds St Mary 05–09; PtO *Chelmsf* 09–20. *2 Chequer Square, Bury St Edmunds IP33 1QZ* T: (01284) 728041 E: tim.savege@btinternet.com

SAVIDGE, Graham John. b 47. Univ of Wales (Ban) BSc 69 PhD 78. CITC 89. **d** 92 **p** 94. LtO *D & D* 92–10; NSM Down Cathl 94–97; NSM Lecale Gp 97–10; PtO from 10. *7 Cedar Grove, Ardglass, Downpatrick BT30 7UE* T: (028) 4461 3101

SAVIGEAR, Miss Elfrida Beatrice. b 49. Wye Coll Lon BSc 71 Bath Univ MSc 85 Lambeth STh 94. Ridley Hall Cam 91. **d** 93 **p** 94. C Ross w Brampton Abbotts, Bridstow, Peterstow etc *Heref* 93–97; P-in-c Butlers Marston and the Pillertons w Ettington *Cov* 97–99; P-in-c Alderminster and Halford 97–99; P-in-c Bicknoller w Crowcombe and Sampford Brett *B & W* 99–00; P-in-c Stogumber w Nettlecombe and Monksilver 99–00; R Quantock Towers 00–08; C Darlington H Trin *Dur* 08–11; rtd 11; Hon C Beaminster Area *Sarum* 11–19; PtO from 19. *7 Trinity Way, Bridport DT6 3XJ* T: (01308) 424031

SAVILL (née LANE), Jessica. b 93. Ches Univ BA 14 R Cen Sch Speech & Drama MA 15. St Mellitus Coll BA 20. **d** 20 **p** 21. C Aspley *S'well* from 20; C Bilborough and Strelley from 20. *St Martin's Rectory, St Agnes Close, Nottingham NG8 4BJ* M: 07857-714017 E: jessmlane93@gmail.com

SAVILLE, Andrew. b 66. Worc Coll Ox BA 92 MA 92 Cov Univ PhD 00. Wycliffe Hall Ox. **d** 95 **p** 96. C Tonbridge SS Pet and Paul *Roch* 95–99; NSM Bromley Ch Ch 99–03; Dir Bromley Chr Tr Cen 99–03; C Fordham *Chelmsf* 03–10; V Laleham *Lon* from 10; AD Spelthorne 14–20. *The Vicarage, The Broadway, Laleham, Staines TW18 1SB* T: (01784) 455524 E: andy@savilles.org.uk

SAVILLE, Canon Edward Andrew. b 47. Leeds Univ CertEd 70 Open Univ BA 75. Carl Dioc Tr Inst. **d** 90 **p** 91. C Accrington St Jo w Huncoat *Blackb* 90–93; C Standish 93–95; V Brierfield 95–09; P-in-c 09–10; Hon C 10–13; AD Pendle 98–05 and 13–18; Lead Officer Dioc Bd for Soc Resp 09–19; Hon Can Blackb Cathl 11–19; PtO from 19. *6 Blea Close, Burnley BB12 7TP* M: 07912-227144 E: e.saville@btinternet.com

SAVILLE (née McCULLAGH), Mrs Elspeth Jane Alexandra. b 68. Man Univ BSc 90. Wycliffe Hall Ox BTh 95. **d** 95

p 96. C Huddersfield H Trin *Wakef* 95–98; NSM Tonbridge SS Pet and Paul *Roch* 98–99; NSM Bromley Ch Ch 99–03; NSM Fordham *Chelmsf* 03–07; PtO *Lon* 19–20; NSM Laleham from 20. *The Vicarage, The Broadway, Laleham, Staines TW18 1SB* T: (01784) 455524

SAVILLE, Mrs Margaret. b 46. SWMTC 93. **d** 94 **p** 95. C Over St Chad *Ches* 94–98; V Crewe All SS and St Paul 98–05; P-in-c Helsby and Dunham-on-the-Hill 05–12; V 12; rtd 12; Hon C Devoran *Truro* 12–15; Hon C Feock 12–15; PtO from 15. *Coombe Lodge, Church Coombe, Redruth TR16 6RT* T: (01872) 863116 E: margaretsaville@rocketmail.com

SAWYER, Andrew William. b 49. AKC 71 St Aug Coll Cant 71. **d** 72 **p** 73. C Farnham *Guildf* 72–75; C Dawlish *Ex* 75–78; R Colkirk w Oxwick, Whissonsett and Horningtoft *Nor* 78–82; R Colkirk w Oxwick w Pattesley, Whissonsett etc 82–90; V Hungerford and Denford *Ox* 90–15; rtd 15; PtO *York* from 19. *22 Lowdale Lane, Sleights, Whitby YO22 5BU* T: (01947) 229123

SAWYER, Derek Claude. b 33. ALCD 58. **d** 58 **p** 59. C Kirby Muxloe *Leic* 58–60; C Braunstone 60–65; R Vacoas St Paul Mauritius 65–68; V Knighton St Mich *Leic* 68–82; Chapl Kifissia *Eur* 82; LtO *Glouc* 85–87; V Glouc St Aldate 87–01; P-in-c Capisterre St Paul and St Jo St Kitts-Nevis 01–08; LtO 09; P-in-c Roseau w Portsmouth Dominica 09–11; LtO St Kitts-Nevis 11–15; Hon C Cayon w Nichola Town from 15. *Rawlins Ground, St Paul's Village, PO Box 4031, Sandy Point, St Kitts 00265, St Kitts and Nevis* T: (001) (869) 466 2773 M: 669 5697 E: derekcsawyer@gmail.com

SAWYER, Frank Denzil. b 71. Toronto Univ BA 93 MDiv 97 Ch Div Sch of the Pacific (USA) DMin 04. **d** 97. C Toronto St Clem Canada 97–99; USA 99–16; P-in-c Corfu *Eur* 14–15; USA 15–16; Chapl Gtr Lisbon *Eur* 16–19. *619 Barnwell Avenue NW, Aiken SC 29801, USA*

SAWYER, James Thomas Lawrence. b 66. Middx Poly BA 88. ERMC 12. **d** 15 **p** 16. NSM Baldock w Bygrave *St Alb* 15–17; C 17–18; R Hormead, Wyddial, Anstey, Brent Pelham etc from 18. *The Vicarage, Great Hormead, Buntingford SG9 0NT* M: 07733-368776 E: rev.j.sawyer@btinternet.com *or* rev.j.sawyer@quintetchurches.com

SAX, Ms Katharine Margaret. b 50. Ripon Coll Cuddesdon. **d** 03 **p** 06. NSM Pokesdown All SS and Southbourne St Chris *Win* 04–05; C Swaythling 06–09; Ecum Officer (Wilts Area) *Sarum* 09–11; P-in-c Churchill and Langford *B & W* 11–16; rtd 16; PtO *Win* 16–19; Hon C Aisholt, Enmore, Goathurst, Nether Stowey etc *B & W* from 19. *The Rectory, Church Road, Spaxton, Bridgwater TA5 1DA* M: 07733-442476 E: kate.kinkiizi@gmail.com

✠**SAXBEE, The Rt Revd John Charles.** b 46. Bris Univ BA 68 St Jo Coll Dur PhD 74. Cranmer Hall Dur 68. **d** 72 **p** 73 **c** 94. C Compton Gifford *Ex* 72–77; P-in-c Weston Mill 77–80; V 80–81; TV Cen Ex 81–87; Jt Dir SWMTC 81–92; Preb Ex Cathl 88–92; Adn Ludlow *Heref* 92–01; Preb Heref Cathl 92–01; P-in-c Wistanstow 92–94; P-in-c Acton Scott 92–94; Suff Bp Ludlow 94–01; Bp Linc 01–11; rtd 11; PtO *St D* from 11. *22 Shelley Road, Priory Park, Haverfordwest SA61 1RX* T: (01437) 768918 E: john.saxbee@btinternet.com

SAXBY, Canon Martin Peter. b 52. St Jo Coll Dur BA 77. Cranmer Hall Dur 74. **d** 78 **p** 79. C Peckham St Mary Magd *S'wark* 78–81; C Ramsey *Ely* 81–84; P-in-c Mattishall w Mattishall Burgh *Nor* 84–89; P-in-c Welborne 84–89; P-in-c Yaxham 84–89; R Mattishall w Mattishall Burgh, Welborne etc 89–90; V Rugby St Matt *Cov* 90–07; V Rugby W 08–13; RD Rugby 06–13; Healthy Churches Development Mentor 13–17; Hon Can Cov Cathl 11–17; rtd 17; PtO *Cov* from 13. *13 Ambleside, Rugby CV21 1JB* M: 07961-316555

SAXBY, Canon Steven Michael Paul. b 70. Fitzw Coll Cam BA 98 MA 02 Heythrop Coll Lon MA 05 Univ Coll Lon MA 08 K Coll Lon PhD 20. Aston Tr Scheme 92 Linc Th Coll 94 Westcott Ho Cam 95. **d** 98 **p** 01. C E Ham w Upton Park and Forest Gate *Chelmsf* 98–00; C Barking St Marg w St Patr 00–02; Waltham Forest Deanery Development Worker 02–07; NSM Walthamstow 02–03; V Walthamstow St Pet 03–09; P-in-c Walthamstow St Barn and St Jas Gt 09–14; V 14–20; P-in-c Walthamstow St Sav 11–13; RD Waltham Forest 07–12; Exec Officer Lon Chs Soc Action 13–19; Hon Can Manila Philippines from 14. *49 Soldene Court, Georges Road, London N7 8HQ* M: 07855-551050 E: stevensaxby@btinternet.com

SAXON, John. b 61. Ridley Hall Cam 15. **d** 17 **p** 18. NSM Saffron Walden and Villages *Chelmsf* 17–20; TV from 20. *The Rectory, Mill Road, Debden, Saffron Walden CB11 3LB* E: debdenwimbishcurate@gmail.com

SAXTON, James. b 54. Lanc Univ BEd 77 Hull Univ MEd 85. Linc Th Coll 84. **d** 86 **p** 87. C Moor Allerton *Ripon* 86–90; C Knaresborough 90–92; TV Seacroft 92–95; V Ireland Wood 95–00; TV Becontree S *Chelmsf* 02–09; C Camberwell St Geo

S'wark 09–12; Chapl S Lon and Maudsley NHS Foundn Trust 09–12; rtd 12; PtO *S'well* from 18. *11 Stannier Way, Watnall, Nottingham NG16 1GL* E: james_saxton@outlook.com

SAYER, The Ven Penelope Jane. b 59. Newc Univ BA 80 Open Univ BA 93. SEITE 04. **d** 07 **p** 08. NSM Upper St Leonards St Jo *Chich* 07–10; TR Becontree S *Chelmsf* 10–16; NSM Woodham Mortimer w Hazeleigh 16–18; NSM Woodham Walter 16–18; Turnaround Min (Bradwell Area) 16–18; Adn Sherborne *Sarum* from 18. *Aldhelm House, West Stafford, Dorchester DT2 8AB* T: (01305) 269074 M: 07729-372996 E: adsherborne@salisbury.anglican.org

SAYER, Simon Benedict. b 59. Man Univ BA 07. St Steph Ho Ox MTh 11. **d** 10 **p** 11. C Hollinwood and Limeside *Man* 10–13; V Tipton St Jo *Lich* 13–20; V Shrewsbury All SS w St Mich from 20; CMP from 13. *All Saints' Vicarage, 5 Liney Close, Shrewsbury SY1 2UN* T: (01743) 357862 M: 07754-100845 E: simonsayer@icloud.com

SAYER, Vivienne Rosina. b 56. Univ of Wales (Cardiff) BA 78 Trin Coll Carmarthen MA 04 Cardiff Univ BTh 15 PGCE 85. St Mich Coll Llan 13. **d** 15 **p** 16. C Newcastle Emlyn and Llandyfriog etc *St D* 15–19; P-in-c Bro Dyfri from 19; AD from 20. *The Vicarage, Llanwrda SA19 8HD* T: (01550) 777200 E: revd.viv.sayer@gmail.com

SAYERS, Karen Jane. *See* GARDINER, Karen Jane

SAYERS, Susan. *See* HILL, Susan

SAYLE, Philip David. b 61. Nottm Univ BA 98. St Jo Coll Nottm 92. **d** 94 **p** 95. C Helston and Wendron *Truro* 94–97; R St Stephen in Brannel 97–00; R Kenwyn w St Allen 00–06; V Upton Ascension *Ches* 06–15; P-in-c Diptford, N Huish, Harberton, Harbertonford etc *Ex* 15–18; P-in-c Ermington and Ugborough 15–18; R Diptford w N Huish, Ermington, Halwell etc from 18. *The Rectory, Diptford, Totnes TQ9 7NY* T: (01548) 821199 M: 07484-847672 E: parish_sayle@me.com

SCAMMAN (née BEWES), Mrs Helen Catherine. b 71. Leeds Univ BA 94 York Univ PGCE 95 Cam Univ BA 01. Ridley Hall Cam 99. **d** 02 **p** 03. C Win Ch Ch 02–06; NSM 06–07; PtO *Ely* 07–10; *Blackb* 10–14; C Lancaster St Thos from 14. *St Thomas's Vicarage, 33 Belle Vue Terrace, Lancaster LA1 4TY* T: (01524) 590410 E: helen@st.tees.org.uk

SCAMMAN, Jonathan Leitch. b 73. St Andr Univ MA 96 Ex Coll Ox MPhil 98 Cam Univ MA 01. Ridley Hall Cam 99. **d** 02 **p** 03. C Win Ch Ch 02–07; C Cambridge St Barn *Ely* 07–10; P-in-c Lancaster St Thos *Blackb* 10–11; V from 11. *St Thomas's Vicarage, 33 Belle Vue Terrace, Lancaster LA1 4TY* T: (01524) 590410 E: scampersons@yahoo.com

SCAMMELL, Canon Frank. b 56. Cam Univ MA. St Jo Coll Nottm BA 83. **d** 82 **p** 83. C Stapenhill w Cauldwell *Derby* 82–86; TV Swanage and Studland *Sarum* 86–92; Min Southgate LEP *St E* 92–03; V Stoughton *Guildf* from 03; AD Guildf 11–17; Hon Can Guildf Cathl from 16. *Stoughton Vicarage, 3 Shepherds Lane, Guildford GU2 9SJ* T: (01483) 560560 E: frankpippa@hotmail.com

SCANLAN, Helen Tracy. b 66. Dioc OLM tr scheme 06. **d** 09 **p** 10. NSM Heaton Reddish *Man* 09–11; C Heatons 11–12; TV 12–21; AD Heaton 18–21; C N Reddish from 21; AD Man N and E from 21. *The Vicarage, 42 Lea Road, Stockport SK4 4JU* T: 0161-432 1227 E: helen.scanlan@btinternet.com

SCARD, Canon Linda Joyce. b 52. STETS 11. **d** 14 **p** 15. NSM N Hants Downs *Win* 14–21; rtd 21; Hon Can Win Cathl from 20; PtO from 21. *Adams Farm, The Street, North Warnborough, Hook RG29 1BL* T: (01256) 703294 M: 07801-039717 E: linda.scard@btinternet.com

SCARGILL, Christopher Morris. b 57. UEA BA 79 York Univ MA 81 Leeds Univ CertEd 81 Nottm Univ BTh 89. Linc Th Coll 86. **d** 89 **p** 90. C Desborough and Brampton Ash w Dingley and Braybrooke *Pet* 89–92; C Buxton w Burbage and King Sterndale *Derby* 92–93; TV 93–98; V Ipstones w Berkhamsytch and Onecote w Bradnop *Lich* 98–09; RD Alstonfield 08–09; Local Min Adv (Stafford) 07–09; Sen Chapl Torrevieja *Eur* 09–14; V St Annes St Thos *Blackb* from 14; PtO *Eur* from 14. *The Vicarage, 2 St Thomas Road, Lytham St Annes FY8 1JL* T: (01253) 725551 E: revdcms@gmail.com

SCARGILL, Mrs Claire Frances. b 49. Birkbeck Coll Lon BSc 83 Heythrop Coll Lon MA 06. St Mellitus Coll 13. **d** 14 **p** 15. OLM Mistley w Manningtree and Bradfield *Chelmsf* from 14. *Mistley Lodge, 32 New Road, Mistley, Manningtree CO11 2AQ* T: (01206) 395417 M: 07714-752100 E: revclairescargill@gmail.com

SCARISBRICK, Canon Helen. b 60. Sheff Univ BA 81 Sheff Poly PGCE 82 Ches Coll of HE BTh 99. NOC 97. **d** 99 **p** 00. C Norbury *Ches* 99–03; P-in-c Cheadle Heath 03–07; C Edgeley and Cheadle Heath 07–09; V Broadheath 09–18; P-in-c Gee Cross from 18; RD Mottram 18–21; Hon Can Ches Cathl from 19. *8 Kensington Street, Hyde*

SK14 5QD T: 0161-366 7243 E: hscarisbrick@btinternet.com *or* info@holytrinitychurch-gx.org.uk

SCARLATA, Mark. b 72. **d** 13 **p** 14. NSM Cambridge St Mark *Ely* 13–16; Chapl Cam St Edw from 16; Tutor St Mellitus Coll from 16. *10 Roseford Road, Cambridge CB4 2HD* T: (01223) 977345 *or* 655399 E: mwscar@gmail.com

SCARR, Mrs Hazel Anne. b 44. SAOMC. **d** 00 **p** 01. NSM Adderbury w Milton *Ox* 00–04; NSM Chadlington and Spelsbury, Ascott under Wychwood 04–05; NSM Hardington Vale *B & W* 05–07; NSM Hook Norton w Gt Rollright, Swerford etc *Ox* 07–10; PtO 11–17 and from 21; Chapl Green Pastures Chr Nursing Home 17–20. *Betula House, Barford Road, Bloxham, Banbury OX15 4EZ* T: (01295) 720022 E: revhazel@yahoo.co.uk

SCEATS, Preb David Douglas. b 46. Ch Coll Cam BA 68 MA 72 Bris Univ MA 71. Clifton Th Coll 68. **d** 71 **p** 72. C Cambridge St Paul *Ely* 71–74; Lect Trin Coll Bris 74–83; V Shenstone *Lich* 83–86; Dioc Tr Officer 86–91; P-in-c Colton 86–90; Dir Local Min Development 91–98; Warden of Readers 91–96; C Lich St Chad 94–98; Dioc Board of Min Team Ldr 96–98; Preb Lich Cathl 96–98; Prin NTMTC 99–07; Preb St Paul's Cathl *Lon* 02–07; P-in-c Selkirk *Edin* 07–11; rtd 11; Hon C Selkirk *Edin* from 11. *11 Shawpark Road, Selkirk TD7 4DS* T: (01750) 779278 E: dsceats@gmail.com *or* d-sceats@sky.com

SCHAEFER, Carl Richard. b 67. Coll of Resurr Mirfield 91. **d** 94 **p** 95. C Ribbleton *Blackb* 94–98; V Blackb St Thos w St Jude 98–08; P-in-c Blackb St Mich w St Jo and H Trin 03–08; V Goldthorpe w Hickleton *Sheff* from 08; P-in-c Bolton-upon-Dearne from 16. *Goldthorpe Presbytery, Lockwood Road, Goldthorpe, Rotherham S63 9JY* T: (01709) 898426 E: frcschaefer@outlook.com *or* carl.schaefer@sheffield.anglican.org

SCHARF, Brian Howard. b 39. Alberta Univ BA 60. Trin Coll Toronto 60 Coll of Resurr Mirfield 61. **d** 63 **p** 65. C Vancouver St Faith Canada 63–65; C Broadstairs *Cant* 65–68. *3236 Robinson Road, North Vancouver BC V7J 3E9, Canada* T: (001) (604) 987 0219 E: brianscharf@shaw.ca

SCHEFFER (née SQUIRES), Mrs Rachel Louise Squires. b 79. Coll of Ripon & York St Jo BA 00. Ripon Coll Cuddesdon MA 07. **d** 07 **p** 08. C Alnwick *Newc* 07–12; C Monkseaton St Pet 13–15; P-in-c Stamfordham w Matfen from 15; Dioc Development Officer for Youth Work from 15; P-in-c Heddon-on-the-Wall from 21. *St Mary's Vicarage, Stamfordham, Newcastle upon Tyne NE18 0QQ* T: (01661) 886853 E: rlsscheffer@gmail.com

SCHEMANOFF, Ms Natasha Anne. b 50. CertEd 71. Trin Coll Bris 94. **d** 96 **p** 97. C Freshford, Limpley Stoke and Hinton Charterhouse *B & W* 96–99; TV Worle 99–00; V Kewstoke w Wick St Lawrence 00–07; Bp's Adv for Racial Justice 00–07; rtd 07; PtO *Truro* 97–16; *Newc* from 17. *30 Green Batt, Alnwick NE66 1TU* T: (01665) 603815

SCHILD, John. b 38. ALCD 64. **d** 64 **p** 65. C Cheltenham Ch Ch *Glouc* 64–67; Area Sec CMS Sheff and S'well 67–73; Area Sec CMS Chelmsf and St Alb 73–76; V Lt Heath *St Alb* 76–88; R Bedford St Pet w St Cuth 88–94; P-in-c King's Walden and Offley w Lilley 94–98; V 98–03; rtd 03; PtO *Truro* 17–21. *Trenarren, St Cleer, Liskeard PL14 5DN* T: (01579) 347047 E: john@schild.demon.co.uk

SCHLEGER, Ms Maria Francesca. b 57. LSE BA 78 SS Coll Cam BA 84 MA 89. Westcott Ho Cam 82. **dss** 85 **d** 87 **p** 94. De Beauvoir Town St Pet *Lon* 85–90; Par Dn 87–90; Team Dn Bow H Trin and All Hallows 90–94; Dean of Women's Min (Stepney Area) 90–94; PtO *Birm* 94–98; NSM Stepney St Dunstan and All SS *Lon* 99–03; Chapl Mildmay Miss Hosp 03–12; PtO *Lon* from 12. *75 Lansdowne Drive, London E8 3EP* T: (020) 7683 0051

SCHLOSS, Mrs Sandra Vanessa. b 63. Cant Ch Ch Univ BA 13. **d** 13 **p** 14. NSM Addiscombe St Mildred *S'wark* 13–17; C Camberwell St Luke 17–20; P-in-c 20–21; V from 21. *30 Commercial Way, London SE15 5JQ* M: 07743-497156 E: sandra.stlukespeckham@gmail.com

SCHLUTER, Nathaniel David. b 71. Pemb Coll Ox BA 93 MA 97 Green Coll Ox DPhil 98. Wycliffe Hall Ox BA. **d** 00 **p** 01. C Gerrards Cross and Fulmer *Ox* 00–05; Prin Johannesburg Bible Coll S Africa from 05; PtO *Ox* from 14. *PO Box 374, Auckland Park, 2006 South Africa*

SCHMAUS, Miss Christine. b 84. Ripon Coll Cuddesdon 18. **d** 20 **p** 21. C Helston and Wendron *Truro* from 20. *38 Bosnoweth, Helston TR13 8FR* T: (01326) 573837 E: curatehelstonwendron@gmail.com

SCHMIDT, Canon Karen Rosemarie. b 48. Surrey Univ BSc 70 Solicitor 76. STETS 06. **d** 99 **p** 00. NSM Lee-on-the-Solent *Portsm* 99–05; P-in-c Purbrook 05–06; V 06–09; rtd 09; Bp's Dom Chapl *Portsm* 09–12; Hon C Brighstone and Brooke w Mottistone 13–14; Hon C Shorwell w Kingston 13–14;

Hon C Chale 13–14; PtO *Glouc* from 15. *31 Truscott Avenue, Swindon SN25 2GR* T: (01793) 753457 M: 07990-518541 E: karenrschmidt@yahoo.co.uk

SCHMUCKI, Manuela Marianne. b 87. St Mellitus Coll 18. **d** 21. C Leic Cathl from 21. *216A London Road, Leicester LE2 1NE* M: 07392-922711 E: schmuckimanuela@gmail.com

SCHNYDER, Cécile. b 76. Ausbildungs Schule Bern BA 97 Roehampton Univ MA 10. Westcott Ho Cam BTh 15. **d** 15 **p** 16. C Sutton *S'wark* 15–18; P-in-c Dulwich St Clem w St Pet 18–21; V from 21; Chapl Jas Allen's Girls' Sch Dulwich from 18. *The Vicarage, 140 Friern Road, London SE22 0AY* T: (020) 8693 1890 E: cecile.schnyder@cantab.net

SCHOFIELD, Andrew Thomas. b 47. K Coll Lon BD 70 AKC 71 Win Univ MA 16 Ch Ch Coll Cant PGCE 72. St Aug Coll Cant 70. **d** 81 **p** 82. C Whittlesey *Ely* 81–84; C Ramsey 84–87; P-in-c Ellington, Grafham, Easton and Spaldwick w Barham and Woolley 87–94; R March St Jo 94–05; P-in-c Duxford 05–09; P-in-c Hinxton 05–09; P-in-c Ickleton 05–09; rtd 09; P-in-c Beetham *Carl* 09–12; PtO from 12; *Blackb* from 12. *Holker House, Whittington, Carnforth LA6 2NX* T: (01524) 274391 E: atschofield@outlook.com

SCHOFIELD, Mrs Carol Anne. b 62. Coll of Resurr Mirfield BA 19. **d** 19 **p** 20. C Wythenshawe *Man* from 19. *8 Devoke Road, Wythenshawe, Manchester M22 1TY* M: 07875-660379 E: revcarol11@gmail.com

SCHOFIELD, David Leslie. b 40. MISM 89. EMMTC 98. **d** 01 **p** 02. NSM Derby St Mark 01–04; PtO *Man* from 05; P-in-c Dukinfield St Luke *Ches* 07–12; rtd 12. *72 Bromley Cross Road, Bromley Cross, Bolton BL7 9LT* T: (01204) 303137 M: 07855-906987 E: fatherschofield@aim.com *or* fatherschofield@gmail.com

SCHOFIELD, Gary. b 64. Ripon Coll Cuddesdon 97. **d** 99 **p** 00. C Exhall *Cov* 99–02; V Wales *Sheff* from 02; P-in-c Harthill and Thorpe Salvin from 08; P-in-c Todwick 12–13; AD Laughton 11–14. *The Vicarage, Manor Road, Wales, Sheffield S26 5PD* T: (01909) 771111 E: gary.schofield@sheffield.anglican.org

SCHOFIELD, John Martin. b 47. Selw Coll Cam BA 69 MA 73. St Steph Ho Ox 70. **d** 72 **p** 73. C Palmers Green St Jo *Lon* 72–75; C Friern Barnet St Jas 75–80; V Luton St Aug Limbury *St Alb* 80–89; V Biddenham and Dir CME 89–94; Dir Minl Tr *Guildf* 94–99; Can Res Guildf Cathl 95–99; PtO 03–05; Dir Dioc Min Course 05–09; rtd 09. *81 Pickmere Road, Sheffield S10 1GZ*

SCHOFIELD, Canon Nigel Timothy. b 54. Dur Univ BA 76 Nottm Univ BCombStuds 83 FRCO. Linc Th Coll 80. **d** 83 **p** 84. C Cheshunt *St Alb* 83–86; TV Colyton, Southleigh, Offwell, Widworthy etc *Ex* 86–94; V Seaton 94–03; P-in-c Beer and Branscombe 01–03; V Seaton and Beer 03–06; RD Honiton 99–03; Can Res Chich Cathl 06–20; rtd 20. *Address temp unknown*

SCHOFIELD, Ruth Elizabeth. b 65. Imp Coll Lon BEng 87. STETS 06. **d** 09 **p** 10. NSM Botley, Curdridge and Durley *Portsm* 09–12; TV Fareham H Trin 12–17; Asst Chapl Portsm Hosps NHS Trust 11–17; P-in-c Rowde and Bromham *Sarum* 17–18; R from 18. *The Rectory, High Street, Bromham, Chippenham SN15 2HA* M: 07738-858909 E: revrschofield@gmail.com

SCHOFIELD, Preb Sarah. b 70. Man Univ BA 95 Birm Univ MPhil 99. Qu Coll Birm 95. **d** 97 **p** 98. C Longsight St Luke *Man* 97–02; Tutor (Man Ho) Westcott Ho Cam 00–04; P-in-c Gorton St Phil *Man* 02–06; P-in-c Abbey Hey from 04; TV Cen Wolverhampton *Lich* 06–18; Rep for Women in Min Wolverhampton Area 15–18; Bp's Adv for Women's Min 18–20; Lead Chapl Wolv Univ from 18; Preb Lich Cathl from 16. *27 Adelaide Walk, Wolverhampton WV2 1DX* M: 07500-780494 E: sarah.schofield@wlv.ac.uk

SCHOFIELD, Simon Whitworth. b 64. Birm Univ BA 88. SNWTP 10. **d** 13 **p** 14. NSM Stretford St Matt *Man* from 13. *20 Langshaw Street, Manchester M16 9LR* T: 0161-227 8285 M: 07761-636751 E: simon_schodog@yahoo.co.uk

SCHOFIELD, Timothy. See SCHOFIELD, Nigel Timothy

SCHOFIELD, Mrs Victoria Louise. b 56. Liv Poly BSc 88 Liv Univ PGCE 91. Wycliffe Hall Ox BTh 05. **d** 02 **p** 03. C Hattersley *Ches* 02–05; P-in-c Runcorn St Mich 05–06; V 06–19; rtd 19; PtO *Ches* from 19. *16 Braemore Road, Wallasey CH44 2BL* E: vicki_schofield@hotmail.com

SCHOLES, Jade Eleanor. b 74. Birm Univ BN 96. Ripon Coll Cuddesdon 17. **d** 20 **p** 21. NSM Churchdown St Jo and Innsworth *Glouc* from 20. *3 Mead Road, Cheltenham GL53 7DU* T: (01242) 512686 M: 07767-890058

SCHOLES, Ms Victoria Prichard. b 68. Man Univ BSc 89. St Jo Coll Nottm 97. **d** 00 **p** 01. C Macclesfield St Jo *Ches* 00–02; NSM 02–03; PtO 03–14. *87B Gawsorth Road, Macclesfield SK11 8UF* T: (01625) 425049

SCHOLEY, Michael. b 66. d 10. NSM Staincross *Wakef* 10–13; Grimethorpe w Brierley *Leeds* from 20; NSM Ryhill from 20; NSM S Kirkby from 20. *8 Croft Close, Mapplewell, Barnsley S75 6FN* T: (01226) 386173 E: michael.scholey@virgin.net

SCHOLLAR, Canon Pamela Mary. b 39. Southn Univ DipEd 80. S Dios Minl Tr Scheme 89. d 92 p 94. NSM Bournemouth St Andr *Win* 92–94; NSM Pokesdown St Jas 94–09; Hon Can Win Cathl 02–09; PtO from 10. *22 Bethia Road, Bournemouth BH8 9BD* T: (01202) 397925

SCHOLZ, Terence Brinsley. b 44. St Martin's Coll Lanc MA 98. CBDTI 94. d 97 p 98. NSM Ashton St Thos *Blackb* 97–01; NSM Broughton 01–02; PtO 02–04; NSM Freckleton 04–12; rtd 12; PtO *Blackb* 12–21. *14 Further Ends Road, Freckleton, Preston PR4 1RL* T: (01772) 632966 M: 07989-931909 E: tbscholz@btinternet.com

SCHOOLING, Bruce James. b 47. Rhodes Univ BA 73. St Paul's Coll Grahamstown 76. d 76 p 77. C Rondebosch St Thos S Africa 76–79; C St Geo Cathl Cape Town 79–83; R Malmesbury 83–86; C Wanstead St Mary *Chelmsf* 87–90; V Leigh-on-Sea St Jas 90–04; PtO from 05; rtd 07. *249 Woodgrange Drive, Southend-on-Sea SS1 2SQ* T: (01702) 613429 M: 07710-208476 E: b.schooling@btinternet.com

SCHRIMSHAW, Angela Anna Violet. b 51. SRN 73 SCM 76 Hull Univ HVCert 93 BSc 98. NEOC 01. d 04 p 05. NSM Welton w Melton *York* 04–16; Chapl HM Pris Humber 16–18; PtO *York* from 18; Sheff from 21. *22 Bricknell Avenue, Hull HU5 4JS* T: (01482) 446609 E: schrim@schrim.karoo.co.uk

SCHRODER, Edward Amos. b 41. Cant Univ (NZ) BA 64. Cranmer Hall Dur. d 67 p 68. C St Marylebone All So w SS Pet and Jo *Lon* 67–71; Dean Gordon Coll and C Hamilton Ch Ch USA 71–76; Can Missr and Asst to Bp Florida 76–79; R Orange Park Grace Ch 79–86; R San Antonio Ch Ch 86–00; Chapl Amelia Plantation Chpl 00–06; rtd 06. *15 Hickory Lane, Amelia Island FL 32034, USA* T: (001) (904) 277 6752 F: 277 8323 E: tschroder100@gmail.com

SCHUIL-BREWER, Miss Sophie Victoria. b 76. Greenwich Univ LLB 98 Cam Univ BTh 18. Westcott Ho Cam 16. d 18 p 19. C Kensal Rise St Martin *Lon* from 18; V Kingsbury H Innocents from 21. *Kingsbury Vicarage, 54 Roe Green, London NW9 0PJ* M: 07771-514691 E: sophie.s-b@hotmail.co.uk

SCHUMAN, Andrew William Edward. b 73. Birm Univ BA 95 MSc 96 Bris Univ PhD 00 FRGS 02. Trin Coll Bris BA 03 MA 04. d 04 p 05. C Shirehampton *Bris* 04–08; C Bris Ch the Servant Stockwood 08–13; P-in-c Brislington St Chris from 13; Partnership P Bris S from 08. *23 First Avenue, Bristol BS4 4DU* T: 0117-909 4235 E: andrewschuman@me.com

SCHÜNEMANN, Canon Bernhard George. b 61. K Coll Lon BD 86 AKC 86 Keble Coll Ox MSt 88 LRAM 93. Ripon Coll Cuddesdon 88. d 90 p 91. C Kirkby *Liv* 90–93; C St Martin-in-the-Fields *Lon* 93–97; Chapl Br Sch of Osteopathy 93–97; P-in-c Littlemore *Ox* 97–06; V S Dulwich St Steph *S'wark* from 06; Dir Ords Woolwich Area from 13; Hon Can Tamale Ghana from 13. *St Stephen's Vicarage, 111 College Road, London SE21 7HN* T: (020) 8693 3797 M: 07775-737082 E: bernhardgeorgeschunemann@gmail.com

SCHWIER, Paul David. b 55. d 96 p 97. OLM Pulham Market, Pulham St Mary and Starston *Nor* 96–99; OLM Dickleburgh and The Pulhams from 99. *Street Farm, Pulham Market, Diss IP21 4SP* T: (01379) 676240 E: paulschwier@hotmail.co.uk

SCHWIER, Peter Andrew. b 52. d 91 p 92. NSM Fressingfield, Mendham, Metfield, Weybread etc *St E* 91–13; NSM Sancroft from 13. *Valley Farm, Metfield, Harleston IP20 0JZ* T: (01379) 586517

SCLATER, Jennifer. b 44. TISEC. d 02 p 04. Par Dn Elgin w Lossiemouth *Mor* 02–04; NSM from 04. *77 Wards Road, Elgin IV30 1TE* M: 07950-830017 E: jenny@sclater.com

SCLATER, John Edward. b 46. Nottm Univ BA 68 St Edm Hall Ox CertEd 71. Cuddesdon Coll 69. d 71 p 72. C Bris St Mary Redcliffe w Temple etc 71–75; Chapl Bede Ho Staplehurst 75–79; Chapl Warw Sch 79; P-in-c Offchurch *Cov* 79–80; Belgium 81–89; Willen Priory 89–91; C Linslade *Ox* 91–94; P-in-c Hedsor and Bourne End 94–02; rtd 02; PtO *B & W* from 03. *3 East Court, South Horrington Village, Wells BA5 3HL* T: (01749) 671349 M: 07896-893432 E: john.jes007@yahoo.co.uk

SCOFFIELD, Catherine Rosemary. b 61. d 16 p 17. NSM Barnstaple *Ex* 16–17; NSM Newport and Bishops Tawton from 17. *8 Church Grove, Barnstaple EX32 9DJ* E: cathy.scoffield@exeter.anglican.org

SCOONES, Roger Philip. b 48. Trin Coll Bris. d 82 p 83. C Childwall All SS *Liv* 82–85; Bradf Cathl 85–90; V Congleton St Pet *Ches* 90–96; P-in-c Congleton St Steph 94–96; R Stockport St Mary 96–16; PtO *Man* 14–16; rtd 16; PtO *Glouc* from 16; *Eur* from 17. *3 Warwick Close, Fairford GL7 4LR* T: (01285) 711864 M: 07821-878678 E: roger.scoones@icloud.com

SCORER, Canon John Robson. b 47. Westcott Ho Cam 73. d 75 p 76. C Silksworth *Dur* 75–78; C Newton Aycliffe 78–82; V Sherburn 82–83; V Sherburn w Pittington 83–89; P-in-c Croxdale 89–93; Chapl Dur Constabulary 89–11; Chapl Dur Police Tr Cen 93–05; Hon Can Dur Cathl 04–11; rtd 11; PtO *Dur* from 11. *45 Norwich Road, Durham DH1 5QA*

SCOTCHMER, Michael Leslie. b 48. d 14 p 15. OLM Chingford St Anne *Chelmsf* from 14. *142 Kings Avenue, Woodford Green IG8 0JQ* T: (020) 8504 7497 M: 07802-483147 E: mls@milesconsulting.co.uk

SCOTFORD, Bethan Lynne. b 44. Univ of Wales (Cardiff) BA 67 PGCE 68. St As Minl Tr Course 95. d 99 p 00. Fieldworker (Wales) USPG 98–11; C Guilsfield w Pool Quay *St As* 99–02; V Corwen w Llangar, Glyndyfrdwy etc 02–11; rtd 11; PtO *St As* 11–16 and from 17. *7 Fairview Avenue, Guilsfield, Welshpool SY21 9NE* T: (01938) 555153 M: 07802-656607 E: bscotford@toucansurf.com

SCOTLAND, Nigel Adrian Douglas. b 42. Gordon-Conwell Th Sem MDiv 70 McGill Univ Montreal MA 71 Aber Univ PhD 75 PGCE 75 Bris Univ MLitt 85 LTh 74. ALCD 66. d 66 p 67. C Harold Wood *Chelmsf* 66–69; LtO Dio Massachusetts USA 69–70; R Lakefield Canada 70–72; LtO *Ab* 72–75; Chapl and Lect St Mary's Coll Cheltenham 75–79; Sen Lect 77–79; Chapl and Sen Lect Coll of SS Paul and Mary Cheltenham 79–84; NSM Cheltenham St Mark *Glouc* 85–92; Ldr Glenfall Fellowship 90–03; Field Chair RS Cheltenham and Glouc Coll of HE 89–01; Field Chair Glos Univ 01–05; Prin Lect 96–08; Research Fell from 08; LtO *Glouc* 90–03; PtO from 03; Tutor Trin Coll Bris 06–17; Tutor Bris Univ 09–12; LtO from 07; Lect Cuddesdon: Glouc and Heref from 19; PtO *Eur* from 12. *8 The Rowans, Woodmancote, Cheltenham GL52 4RL* T: (01242) 676969 E: nigelad.scotland@gmail.com

SCOTLAND, Primus of the Episcopal Church in. See STRANGE, The Most Revd Mark Jeremy

SCOTT, Adam. b 47. TD 78 OBE 08. Ch Ch Ox BA 68 MA 72 City Univ MSc 79 MBA 11 St Andr Univ PhD 10 Barrister 72 FRSA 95 CEng 81 MIEE 81 FIEE 94 FIET 06. S'wark Ord Course 73. d 75 p 76. MSE Blackheath Park St Mich *S'wark* 75–17; Dean for MSE, Woolwich from 90; Prof Fell St Andr Univ *St And* 96–97; Sen Res Fell 98–12; Pto *Lon* from 11; *S'wark* from 17; OCM 16–21; Hon CF from 21. *19 Blackheath Park, London SE3 9RW* T: (020) 8852 3286 E: adam.scott@btinternet.com

SCOTT, Canon Barrie. b 63. Birm Univ BA 85 Goldsmiths' Coll Lon PGCE 86. St Steph Ho Ox 93. d 95 p 96. C Tilehurst St Mich *Ox* 95–98; PtO *Birm* 98–15; V Perry Barr from 15; Hon Can Birm Cathl from 19. *The Vicarage, Church Road, Perry Barr, Birmingham B42 2LB* T: 0121-356 7998 M: 07841-202408 E: vicar@st-johns-perry-barr.org.uk

SCOTT, Basil John Morley. b 34. Qu Coll Cam BA 59 Banaras Hindu Univ MA 65. Ridley Hall Cam 58. d 60 p 61. C Woking St Pet *Guildf* 60–63; India 63–83; TR Kirby Muxloe *Leic* 83–89; Asian Outreach Worker (Leic Martyrs) 89–95; Derby Asian Chr Min Project 95–00; rtd 00; PtO *Ely* from 00. *14 Scotsdowne Road, Trumpington, Cambridge CB2 9HU* T: (01223) 476565 E: basil.scott2@ntlworld.com

SCOTT, Charles Geoffrey. b 32. St Jo Coll Cam BA 54 MA 58. Cuddesdon Coll 56. d 58 p 59. C Brighouse *Wakef* 58–61; C Bathwick w Woolley *B & W* 61–64; V Frome Ch Ch 64–78; R Winchelsea *Chich* 78–93; R Winchelsea and Icklesham 93–95; rtd 95; PtO *Chich* from 95. *Hickstead, Main Street, Iden, Rye TN31 7PT* T: (01797) 280096

SCOTT, Christopher Stuart. b 48. Surrey Univ BA 92 MBPsS 92. Sarum & Wells Th Coll 79. d 81 p 82. C Enfield Chase St Mary *Lon* 81–82; C Coalbrookdale, Iron-Bridge and Lt Wenlock *Heref* 82–86; P-in-c Breinton 86–89; Chapl Hickey's Almshouses Richmond 89–01; PtO *S'wark* 06–16; Chapl Richmond Charities Almshouses 08–16; rtd 16; PtO *Win* from 17. *10 King Alfred Terrace, Winchester SO23 7DE* M: 07734-747750 E: revchrisscott@outlook.com

SCOTT, Claude John. b 37. Qu Mary Coll Lon BSc 60 PhD 64 Lon Inst of Educn PGCE 61 FRSA 94. EAMTC 88. d 91 p 92. NSM Heigham H Trin *Nor* 91–98; PtO from 98. *26 The Pastures, Blakeney, Holt NR25 7LY* T: (01263) 740573 E: claudescott@icloud.com

SCOTT, Colin. b 32. Dur Univ BA 54. Coll of Resurr Mirfield 58. d 60 p 61. C Wallsend St Pet *Newc* 60–64; C Seaton Hirst 64–68; C Longbenton St Bart 68–70; V Benwell St Aid 70–77; V Sleekburn 77–89; P-in-c Cambois 77–88; V Longhoughton w Howick 89–96; rtd 96; PtO *Newc* from 96. *Pele Cottage, Hepple, Morpeth NE65 7LH* T: (01669) 640258

SCOTT, Daniel Mark. b 82. Trin Coll Cam BA 05 MEd 08. St Mellitus Coll 16. d 19 p 20. C Stratford St Jo w Ch Ch *Chelmsf* from 19. *3 Riverside Road, London E15 2RG* M: 07859-053933 E: dmscott46@gmail.com *or* dan@christchurchthreemills.co.uk

SCOTT, David. b 40. Rhodes Univ BA 63. St Paul's Coll Grahamstown LTh 65. d 65 p 66. C Pietermaritzberg St Pet

S Africa 66–67; C Durban N St Martin-in-the-Fields 68; R Harding 69; R Newcastle H Trin 70–75; R Bellair 76–78; R Kabega Park All SS 79–87; Chapl Port Elizabeth Univ 88–91; TV Cheltenham St Mark *Glouc* 92–96; R Swanscombe *Roch* 96–10; rtd 10; PtO *Roch* from 11. *103 Hillside Avenue, Gravesend DA12 5QN* T: (01474) 248735 M: 07949-069019 E: scottrev@uwclub.net

SCOTT, David. *See* SCOTT, Timothy David

SCOTT, Canon David Victor. b 47. St Chad's Coll Dur BA 69 Lambeth DLitt 08. Cuddesdon Coll 69. d 71 p 72. C St Mary-at-Latton *Chelmsf* 71–73; Chapl Haberdashers' Aske's Sch Elstree 73–80; V Torpenhow *Carl* 80–91; V Allhallows 80–91; R Win St Lawr and St Maurice w St Swithun 91–10; Warden Sch of Spirituality Win 91–10; Hon Can Win Cathl 02–10; rtd 10; Hon Fell Win Univ from 05. *2 Sunnyside, Kendal LA9 7DJ* T: (01539) 728650 E: davidandmiggyscott@hotmail.com

SCOTT, Mrs Erica Jane. b 58. Trin Coll Bris BA 02. d 02 p 03. C Ilminster and Distr *B & W* 02–05; C Nailsea Ch Ch w Tickenham 05–07; P-in-c Whitchurch *Bris* 07–08; PtO *S & M* 09–12; Chapl K Wm's Coll Is of Man from 12. *King William's College, Castletown, Isle of Man IM9 1TP* T: (01624) 820400 E: rev.ericaj@gmail.com *or* chaplain@kwc.im

SCOTT, Francis Richard. b 63. St Jo Coll Dur BA 85 Selw Coll Cam PGCE 86. St Jo Coll Nottm MA 02. d 00 p 01. C Huntington *York* 00–03; TV 03–09; V Swanland from 09. *The Vicarage, St Barnabas Drive, Swanland, North Ferriby HU14 3RL* T: (01482) 631271 E: fandfscott@aol.com *or* francis@stbchurch.org.uk

SCOTT, Gary James. b 61. Edin Univ BD 87 Heriot-Watt Univ PGCE 98. Edin Th Coll 85. d 87 p 88. C Edin St Cuth 87–90; R Peebles 90–96; P-in-c Innerleithen 92–96; R Penicuik 96–98; R W Linton 96–98; Sen Chapl ACF 98–08; LtO *Edin* 98–10; Hd Master Tweedbank Sch 06–10; CF from 10; Chapl Chigwell Sch Essex from 17. *The White House, Radleys Yard, 121A High Road, Chigwell IG7 6QQ* T: (020) 7998 8308 M: 07710-600953 E: shamrock.racing@btinternet.com *or* garyscott999@btinternet.com

SCOTT, Geoffrey. *See* SCOTT, Charles Geoffrey

SCOTT, Guy Charles. b 61. Coll of Resurr Mirfield. d 00 p 01. C Abington *Pet* 00–03; P-in-c Mullion *Truro* 03–07; C Cury and Gunwalloe 03–07; R Is of Scilly 07–10; P-in-c Biggleswade *St Alb* 10–13; V 13–20; RD 18–20; V Midsomer Norton w Clandown *B & W* from 20. *The Vicarage, 42 Priory Close, Midsomer Norton, Radstock BA3 2HZ* T: (01761) 412904 M: 07928-745543 E: vicarmsnstjohns@gmail.com

SCOTT, Mrs Inez Margaret Gillette. b 26. St Alb Minl Tr Scheme 76. dss 79 d 87 p 94. Preston w Sutton Poyntz, Littlemoor etc *Sarum* 83–86; Dorchester 86–96; Par Dn 87–88; NSM 88–96; rtd 88; PtO *Sarum* 96–15. *21 Chesil Place, Somerleigh Road, Dorchester DT1 1AF* T: (01305) 267145 E: pandiscott@googlemail.com

SCOTT, Canon Janice Beasant. b 44. Cam Th Federation MA 08 MCSP 66. EAMTC 89. d 92 p 94. NSM Fakenham w Alethorpe *Nor* 92–95; C Eaton 95–99; R Dickleburgh and The Pulhams 99–09; RD Redenhall 03–06; PtO 09–13; P-in-c Trowse 13–19; Hon Can Nor Cathl from 08. *21 School Row, Prudhoe NE42 5FE* M: 07450-480023 E: rockingrector@gmail.com

SCOTT, John. b 54. Heriot-Watt Univ BA 76 Leeds Univ BA 97 Heythrop Coll Lon MA 05. Coll of Resurr Mirfield 95. d 97 p 98. C Bethnal Green St Matt w St Jas the Gt *Lon* 97–00; Asst Chapl Qu Mary Univ of Lon 97–00; C Heston 00–04; Inter-Faith Adv 00–05; USA 06–11; PtO Win 06–08; rtd 11. *Lakeview, Church Street, St Mary Bourne, Andover SP11 6BN* T: (01264) 738972 M: 07889-977593 E: absalom1662@yahoo.co.uk

SCOTT, John. *See* SCOTT, William John

SCOTT, John Peter. b 47. Open Univ BA 80 Lambeth STh 81 AKC TCert. St Aug Coll Cant 74. d 75 p 76. C Dartford St Alb *Roch* 75–78; C-in-c Goring-by-Sea *Chich* 78–81; Chapl Wells Hosp 81–86; Chapl Meare Manor Hosp 81–86; CF (TAVR) 82–90; Chapl Pangbourne Coll 86–90; Min Reigate St Phil CD *S'wark* 90–92; P-in-c Reigate St Phil 92–14; Chapl St Bede's Sch Reigate 90–13; rtd 14; CF (Army Reserve) from 04; Chapl RNR from 18; PtO *S'wark* from 14. *5 Haine Close, Horley RH6 9SU* E: johnpeterscott@gmail.com

SCOTT, John Vickers. b 48. Open Univ BA 88 MCIOB 81. CBDTI 02. d 05 p 06. NSM Penwortham St Leon *Blackb* 05–09; P-in-c Chipping and Whitewell 09–15; rtd 15; PtO *Blackb* 15–21. *10 Cuerden Rise, Lostock Hall, Preston PR5 5YD* T: (01772) 335555 M: 07875-895354 E: frjohn.chipping@btinternet.com

SCOTT, Julie Elizabeth. b 68. Ripon Coll Cuddesdon 16. d 18 p 19. C Wellington and Distr *B & W* 18–20; C Bridgwater St Jo from 20. *9 Park Avenue, Bridgwater TA6 7EF* M: 07935-812736 E: revjuliescott@hotmail.com

SCOTT, Mrs June Christine. b 43. SRN 64 RM 66 RHV 84. d 11 p 12. OLM Foremark and Repton w Newton Solney *Derby* from 11; Dioc Clergy Widows' and Widowers' Officer 16–21. *32 Hillcrest Avenue, Burton-on-Trent DE15 0TZ* T: (01283) 565074 E: jcscott242@gmail.com

SCOTT, Katharine Jane. b 65. Warwick Univ BA 88 Univ of Wales (Trin St Dav) LTh 12 Dur Univ MA 17 PGCE 89. ERMC 14. d 17 p 18. C Elstow *St Alb* 17–20; PtO *B & W* 20–21; Asst Chapl Somerset NHS Foundn Trust from 21. *The Vicarage, 42 Priory Close, Midsomer Norton, Radstock BA3 2HY* T: (01761) 412904 M: 07922-487705 E: k.j.scott@outlook.com

SCOTT (née GOLDIE), Canon Katrina Ruth. b 76. Fitzw Coll Cam BA 97 MPhil 00 MA 01. Westcott Ho Cam 98. d 00 p 01. C Cov E 00–04; V Willenhall 04–15; Dioc Adv for Women's Min 06–10; Dean Women's Min 10–15; Hon Can Cov Cathl 10–15; R The Guitings, Cutsdean, Farmcote etc *Glouc* from 15; AD N Cotswold from 15; Hon Can Glouc Cathl from 18. *The Rectory, Copse Hill Road, Lower Slaughter, Cheltenham GL54 2HY* T: (01451) 821777 E: krgscott@hotmail.com

SCOTT, Keith Brounton de Salve. b 55. QUB BD. d 83 p 84. C Belfast St Matt *Conn* 83–87; I Ardclinis and Tickmacrevan w Layde and Cushendun 87–01; CMS 02–09; P-in-c Rathkeale w Askeaton, Kilcornan and Kilnaughtin *L & K* 09–16; CMS Ireland 16–17; CMS Zambia from 17. *Church Mission Society, Watlington Road, Oxford OX4 6BZ* T: 08456-201799 E: kbs16355@gmail.com

SCOTT, Kenneth James. b 46. Bris Univ BA 68. Trin Coll Bris 71. d 73 p 74. C Illogan *Truro* 73–76; C Camberley St Paul *Guildf* 76–81; R Bradford Peverell, Stratton, Frampton etc *Sarum* 81–08; RD Dorchester 95–99; rtd 08; PtO *St E* from 09. *2 Fir Close, Wickham Market, Woodbridge IP13 0UB* T: (01728) 747232

SCOTT, Kevin Francis. b 51. Peterho Cam MA Mert Coll Ox DPhil 76 CChem MRSC. Wycliffe Hall Ox BA 83. d 83 p 84. C Ox St Ebbe w H Trin and St Pet 83–86; P-in-c Prestonpans *Edin* 86–93; R Musselburgh 86–93; R Edin SS Phil and Jas 93–08. *Kirklands, Craigend Road, Stow, Galashiels TD1 2RJ* T: 0131-208 0402 E: drkfs@aol.com

SCOTT, Kevin Willard. b 53. Open Univ BA 96 Glos Univ MA 03. Linc Th Coll 92. d 92 p 93. C Walton-on-Thames *Guildf* 92–97; R Matson *Glouc* 97–03; RD Glouc City 01–03; V Malden St Jo *S'wark* 03–18; AD Kingston 05–09; Chapl MU 12–16; rtd 18. *43 Henty Road, Worthing BN14 7HE* E: kevinwscott@btinternet.com

SCOTT (née CURRELL), Mrs Linda Anne. b 62. K Alfred's Coll Win BEd 84. Trin Coll Bris BA 92. d 92 p 94. Par Dn Tunbridge Wells St Mark *Roch* 92–94; C 94–97; TV Walthamstow *Chelmsf* 97–02; PtO 02–04; *S'wark* 05–14; *B & W* 14–16; Chapl Yeovil Distr Hosp NHS Foundn Trust from 16. *42 High Street, Yatton, Bristol BS49 4HJ* T: (01934) 838960 M: 07823-324979 E: scottlinda125@gmail.com

SCOTT, Mrs Lissa Melanie. b 58. Birm Univ BA 79 PGCE 80. SAOMC 98. d 01 p 02. C Risborough *Ox* 01–06; Chapl Bucks Hosps NHS Trust 05–07; TV Monkwearmouth *Dur* 07–11; V Heighington and Darlington St Matt and St Luke from 11. *9 Pinewood Crescent, Heighington Village, Newton Aycliffe DL5 6RR* T: (01325) 312134

SCOTT, Canon Malcolm Kenneth Merrett. b 30. ACA 53 FCA 64. Clifton Th Coll 56. d 58 p 59. C Highbury Ch Ch *Lon* 58–60; CMS 60–61; Uganda 61–74; V Sunnyside w Bourne End *St Alb* 74–90; V Clapham 90–95; rtd 95; PtO *Lich* 96–14. *10 The Ring, Little Haywood, Stafford ST18 0TP* T: (01889) 881464

SCOTT, Canon Paul Malcolm. b 57. Sheff City Poly BA 79 CPFA 85. Ripon Coll Cuddesdon 98. d 00 p 01. C N Shields *Newc* 00–03; V Shiremoor 03–12; V Alnwick from 12; AD 15–18; Hon Can Newc Cathl from 16. *St Michael's Vicarage, Howling Lane, Alnwick NE66 1DH* T: (01665) 602184 E: paulscott1957@btinternet.com

SCOTT, Canon Pauline Claire Michalak. b 55. St Anne's Coll Ox BA 77 MA 82 Dur Univ PGCE 78. TISEC 98. d 01 p 02. NSM Papworth *Ely* 01–05; TV Ely 05–09; P-in-c Alresford *Chelmsf* 09–10; P-in-c Gt Bentley and Frating w Thorrington 09–10; V Alresford and Frating w Thorrington 10–17; P-in-c Elmstead 16–17; V Tenpenny Villages 17–18; AD St Osyth 16–18; Hon Can Chelmsf Cathl 17–18; rtd 18; PtO *Chelmsf* from 19. *19A Belle Vue Road, Wivenhoe, Colchester CO7 9LD* T: (01206) 823172 M: 07872-968323 E: pauline@pscott.eclipse.co.uk

SCOTT, Peter Lindsay. b 29. Keble Coll Ox BA 54 MA 58. Linc Th Coll 54. d 56 p 57. C Weston-super-Mare St Sav *B & W* 56–59; C Knowle H Nativity *Bris* 59–61; P-in-c Glas St Pet 61–63; V Heap Bridge *Man* 63–73; V Rochdale St Geo w St Alb 73–86; R Droylsden St Andr 86–94; rtd 94; PtO *Man* from 94;

Ches from 14. *3 Rothesay Crescent, Sale M33 4NL* T: 0161-972 0139

SCOTT, Prof Peter Manley. b 61. Birm Univ BA 83 MA 84 Bris Univ PhD 91. All SS Cen for Miss & Min 12. **d** 14 **p** 15. NSM Old Trafford St Jo *Man* 14–18; NSM Man Apostles w Miles Platting from 18. *19 Victoria Road, Fallowfield, Manchester M14 6AQ* M: 07932-688503 E: petermanleyscott@outlook.com

SCOTT, Simon James. b 65. Ch Ch Ox BA 87 MA 90. Wycliffe Hall Ox 87. **d** 91 **p** 92. C Cheadle All Hallows *Ches* 91–95; Scripture Union 95–98; C Cambridge H Sepulchre *Ely* 98–05; R Lt Shelford from 05. *The Rectory, 2 Manor Road, Little Shelford, Cambridge CB22 5HF* T: (01223) 841998 M: 07739-984323 E: simonjscott1965@btinternet.com

SCOTT, Simon Lee. b 74. **d** 16 **p** 17. NSM Halifax *Leeds* 16–17; NSM Halifax w Siddal 17–18; NSM Tain *Mor* from 18; NSM Brora from 19. *Big Barns, Dunrobin, Golspie KW10 6SF* T: (01408) 633614 E: ihssimonscott@gmail.com

SCOTT, The Ven Terence. b 56. QUB BSc 77. CITC 77. **d** 80 **p** 81. C Ballymena w Ballyclug *Conn* 80–83; C Antrim All SS 83–85; P-in-c Connor w Antrim St Patr 85–88; I Magherafelt *Arm* from 88; Hon V Choral Arm Cathl 95–06; Can Arm Cathl from 06; Adn Arm from 14. *The Rectory, 1 Churchwell Lane, Magherafelt BT45 6AL* T: (028) 7963 2365 M: 07590-894529 E: terryscott123@btinternet.com *or* terencescott41@gmail.com

SCOTT, Canon Theresa Anne. b 53. Bris Univ BSc 75 Lon Univ PGCE 76. Ox Min Course 89. **d** 92 **p** 94. NSM Wickham Bishops w Lt Braxted *Chelmsf* 92–93; NSM Drayton St Pet (Abingdon) *Ox* 94–01; NSM Convenor (Berks) 97–01; Bp's Officer for NSM 98–01; P-in-c Hurley and Stubbings 01–02; V Burchetts Green 02–08; AD Maidenhead and Windsor 05–07; TR Bicester w Bucknell, Caversfield and Launton 08–13; Hon Can Ch Ch 05–13; rtd 13; PtO *Ox* from 13. *24 High Street, Thame OX9 2BZ* T: (01844) 218730 E: theresa.scott@driftway.co.uk

SCOTT, Timothy Charles Nairne. b 61. Ex Univ BA 83. Westcott Ho Cam 84. **d** 87 **p** 88. C Romford St Edw *Chelmsf* 87–89; Community Priest 89–94; P-in-c Leytonstone H Trin and St Aug Harrow Green 94–97; V 97–02; Educn and Tr Adv (Bradwell Area) 02–04; R S'wark Ch Ch 04–13; PtO 13–14; TR Yatton Moor *B & W* from 14. *42 High Street, Yatton, Bristol BS49 4HJ* E: timcnscott@gmail.com

SCOTT, Timothy David. b 68. Girton Coll Cam BA 89 Warw Univ PGCE 91. Ridley Hall Cam 13. **d** 15 **p** 16. C Romford Gd Shep *Chelmsf* 15–18; C Northwood Em *Lon* from 18. *4 Church Close, Northwood HA6 1SG* M: 07766-793959 E: dave.scott@ecn.org.uk

SCOTT, Trevor Ian. b 57. Culham Coll Ox CertEd 79. EAMTC 97. **d** 98 **p** 99. NSM Waltham H Cross *Chelmsf* from 98; PtO *Eur* from 16. *Hartland Villas, 208 High Road, Broxbourne EN10 6QF* T: (01992) 420376 E: trevor.scott2@ntlworld.com

SCOTT, William John. b 46. MBE 14. TCD BA 70. CITC. **d** 71 **p** 72. C Bangor St Comgall *D & D* 71–74; C Holywood 74–80; Dioc Min of Healing Team from 75; I Carnalea 80–90; N Ireland Wing Chapl ATC from 80; I Seapatrick *D & D* 90–11; Treas Dromore Cathl 02–08; Adn Dromore 05–11; rtd 11. *61 The Rowans, Banbridge BT32 4DQ* T: (028) 4062 5853 M: 07803-147751 E: john@scottsfamily.co.uk

SCOTT-BROMLEY, Ms Deborah Joan. b 58. Open Univ BA 96 Surrey Univ BA 01 K Coll Lon MA 11 AKC 12. STETS 98. **d** 01 **p** 02. C Hale w Badshot Lea *Guildf* 01–05; V Bordon 05–20. *Address temp unknown*

SCOTT-DEMPSTER, Canon Colin Thomas. b 37. Em Coll Cam BA 65 MA 68. Cuddesdon Coll 64. **d** 66 **p** 67. C Caversham *Ox* 66–69; Chapl Coll of SS Mark and Jo Chelsea 69–73; V Chieveley w Winterbourne and Oare *Ox* 73–02; RD Newbury 77–98; Hon Can Ch Ch 90–02; rtd 02; PtO *St And* from 10. *Whiligh, New Fowlis, Crieff PH7 3NH* T: (01764) 683779 E: colinscottdempster@gmail.com

SCOTT-GARNETT, Linda. b 44. **d** 07 **p** 08. NSM Bermondsey St Hugh CD *S'wark* 07–14; rtd 14; PtO *S'wark* from 14. *6 Bromley College, London Road, Bromley BR1 1PE* T: (020) 3689 0939 M: 07425-135804 E: revlindasg@gmail.com

SCOTT-THOMPSON, Ian Mackenzie. b 57. Ch Ch Ox BA 78. St Jo Coll Nottm BA 82. **d** 83 **p** 84. C Hartley Wintney, Elvetham, Winchfield etc *Win* 83–85; C Bitterne 85–89; V Iford 89–99; P-in-c Holdenhurst 95–99; TR Cove St Jo *Guildf* 99–06; RD Aldershot 03–06; V Wonersh w Blackheath 06–10; P-in-c Marks Tey and Aldham *Chelmsf* from 10. *The Rectory, Church Lane, Marks Tey, Colchester CO6 1LW* T: (01206) 215772 E: ian.scott-thompson@virgin.net

SCRACE, Canon David Peter. b 46. Sarum & Wells Th Coll 79. **d** 81 **p** 82. C Abbots Langley *St Alb* 81–85; TV Chippenham St Paul w Hardenhuish etc *Bris* 85–91; P-in-c Harnham *Sarum* 91–99; V 99–11; RD Salisbury 93–98; Can and Preb Sarum

Cathl 10–11; rtd 11; C Budleigh Salterton, E Budleigh w Bicton etc *Ex* 12–14; PtO from 14. *14 Roselands, Sidmouth EX10 8PD* T: (01395) 708239 E: d.scrace@btopenworld.com

SCRASE-FIELD, Edward Fraser Austin Longmer. b 76. Aber Univ BSc 98 Man Univ PhD 04 Cam Univ BA 07. Ridley Hall Cam 05. **d** 08 **p** 09. C Denton Holme *Carl* 08–11; C Cheadle *Ches* 11–15; V Blackheath St Jo *S'wark* from 15. *146 Langton Way, London SE3 7JS* T: (020) 8305 0520 M: 07730-514074 E: eddie@stjohnsblackheath.org.uk

✠**SCREECH, The Rt Revd Royden.** b 53. K Coll Lon BD 74 AKC 74. St Aug Coll Cant 75. **d** 76 **p** 77 **c** 00. C Hatcham St Cath *S'wark* 76–80; V Nunhead St Antony 80–87; P-in-c Nunhead St Silas 82–87; RD Camberwell 83–87; V New Addington 87–94; Selection Sec ABM 94–97; Sen Selection Sec Min Division Abps' Coun 97–00; Suff Bp St Germans *Truro* 00–11; rtd 12; PtO *Truro* from 15. *61 Edgcumbe Road, St Austell PL25 5DX* E: royscreech@yahoo.com

SCREETON, Kirsty Hayley. b 86. Newman Univ MA 20. Qu Foundn Birm BA 15. **d** 16 **p** 17. C Blackrod, Daisy Hill, Westhoughton and Wingates *Man* 16–20; V Heywood St Jo and St Luke from 20. *St John's Vicarage, Manchester Road, Heywood OL10 2EQ* T: (01706) 416279 M: 07786-578776 E: revkirstyscreeton@gmail.com

✠**SCRIVEN, The Rt Revd Henry William.** b 51. Sheff Univ BA 72. St Jo Coll Nottm 73. **d** 75 **p** 76 **c** 95. C Wealdstone H Trin *Lon* 75–79; SAMS Argentina 79–82; USA 82–83; SAMS Spain 84–90; Chapl Madrid w Bilbao *Eur* 90–95; Suff Bp Eur 95–02; Dean Brussels 95–97; Dir of Ords 97–02; Asst Bp Pittsburgh USA 02–08; Miss Dir for S America SAMS / CMS 09–17; Hon Asst Bp Ox from 09; Hon Asst Bp Win from 13; PtO *Eur* from 18. *16 East St Helen Street, Abingdon OX14 5EA* T: (01235) 536607 M: 07789-635260 E: henry.scriven@gmail.com

SCRIVEN, Hugh Alexander. b 59. Trin Coll Cam BA 80. Cranmer Hall Dur 81. **d** 84 **p** 85. C Pudsey St Lawr and St Paul *Bradf* 84–87; C Madeley *Heref* 87–91; TV 91–00; V Edgbaston St Germain *Birm* 00–18; P-in-c Accrington St Jo w Huncoat *Blackb* from 18. *36 Bluebell Way, Huncoat, Accrington BB5 6TD* T: (01254) 872911 E: hughscriven@outlook.com

SCRIVENER, Margaret Thelma. b 47. RN. STETS. **d** 12 **p** 13. NSM E Win 12–17; rtd 17; PtO *Win* 17–18; Ex from 18. *Rose Cottage, Lower Budleigh, East Budleigh, Budleigh Salterton EX9 7DL* M: 07867-556225 E: marscriv@gmail.com

SCRIVENER, Robert Allan. b 54. Nottm Univ BEd 78 Hull Univ BTh 98 De Montfort Univ Leic MA 99 Huddersfield Univ BA 03. Linc Th Coll 79. **d** 80 **p** 81. C Sherwood *S'well* 80–83; C Burghclere w Newtown and Ecchinswell w Sydmonton *Win* 83–86; TV Hemel Hempstead *St Alb* 86–93; V Kingston upon Hull St Nic *York* 93–03; V Mansfield Woodhouse *S'well* 03–17; rtd 17. *26 Eastwood Grove, Rugby CV21 4DP* E: allan.scrivener@virginmedia.com

SCRIVENS, Mrs Elaine. b 53. TCert 74 Man Univ BEd 75. NEOC. **d** 00 **p** 01. NSM E Coatham *York* 00–02; NSM Coatham and Dormanstown 02–04; Chapl Ven Bede Sch Ryhope 04–10; P-in-c Bishop's Tachbrook *Cov* 10–21; rtd 21. *14 Wheatlands Park, Redcar TS10 2PD* M: 07766-083666 E: elaine.scrivens@gmail.com

SCROGGIE, Canon Felicity Marie-Louise. b 62. Pemb Coll Ox BA 86 St Andr Univ MPhil 87. STETS BTh 99. **d** 99 **p** 00. C Brondesbury St Anne w Kilburn H Trin *Lon* 99–02; V Sudbury St Andr 02–13; AD Brent 10–13; TR Kidlington w Hampton Poyle *Ox* from 13; Bp's Adv for Women in Ord Min from 18; Hon Can Ch Ch from 20. *The Rectory, 19 Mill Street, Kidlington OX5 2EE* T: (01865) 372230 E: felicityscroggie@gmail.com

SCULLY, Kevin John. b 55. NIDA BDA 96. St Steph Ho Ox 91. **d** 93 **p** 94. C Stoke Newington St Mary *Lon* 93–97; C Stepney St Dunstan and All SS 97–00; Dir of Ords and Voc Adv 97–00; P-in-c Bethnal Green St Matt w St Jas the Gt 00–02; R 02–18; Warden Coll of St Barn Lingfield 18–21; rtd 21; PtO *S'wark* from 21. *The Bungalow, Claridge House, Dormans Road, Dormansland, Lingfield RH7 6QH* E: revkevwrites@outlook.com

SCURR, Capt David. b 54. Wilson Carlile Coll 98 SAOMC 05. **d** 05 **p** 06. C Thatcham *Ox* 05–08; P-in-c Farndon and Coddington *Ches* 08–12; V from 12. *The Vicarage, Church Lane, Farndon, Chester CH3 6QD* T/F: (01829) 270270 E: revdscurr@gmail.com

SEABOURNE, Che Royce. b 84. York Univ BSc 06 Leeds Univ PhD 11. St Hild Coll MA 20. **d** 20 **p** 21. NSM Leeds St Geo from 20. *The Rectory, 1 Vicarage View, Leeds LS5 3HF* T: 0113-230   7115   E: che.seabourne@leeds.anglican.org   *or* che.seabourne@stgs.org.uk

SEABOURNE (née PEARSON), Mrs Joanna Ruth. b 76. St Hilda's Coll Ox BA 97 PGCE 98 St Jo Coll Dur BA 05 MA 09. Cranmer Hall Dur 03. **d** 06 **p** 07. C Leeds St Geo *Ripon* 06–10; TV from 10; P-in-c Woodhouse and Wrangthorn 12–18; Dir Dioc Interns from 18; AD Headingley from 18. *The Rectory, 1 Vicarage View, Leeds LS5 3HF* T: 0113-243 8498 *or* 230 7115 M: 07712-590991 E: joanna.seabourne@stgeorgesleeds.org.uk

SEABRIGHT, Preb Elizabeth Nicola. b 52. SRN 73. WEMTC 01. **d** 04 **p** 05. NSM Ledbury *Heref* 04–17; NSM Hop Churches from 17; PtO *Worc* from 05; Preb Heref Cathl from 16. *The Grove Cottage, Fromes Hill, Ledbury HR8 1HP* T: (01531) 640252 M: 07977-016683 E: revdnick@gmail.com

SEABROOK, Alan Geoffrey. b 43. ALCD 65. **d** 66 **p** 67. C Bethnal Green St Jas Less *Lon* 66–70; C Madeley *Heref* 70–73; V Girlington *Bradf* 74–80; P-in-c Abdon w Clee St Margaret *Heref* 80–83; R Bitterley 80–83; P-in-c Cold Weston 80–83; P-in-c Hopton Cangeford 80–83; P-in-c Stoke St Milburgh w Heath 80–83; R Bitterley w Middleton, Stoke St Milborough etc 83–08; RD Ludlow 01–05; rtd 08; PtO *Heref* from 08; RD Bromyard 12–17. *Penhope House, Ballhurst, Bromyard HR7 4EF* T: (01885) 482184

SEABROOK, Paul. b 60. Univ of Wales (Cardiff) BA 81 Glos Univ BA 08 Nottm Univ PGCE 82. Ridley Hall Cam 01. **d** 03 **p** 04. C Wimborne Minster *Sarum* 03–07; R Taverham *Nor* 07–16; R Taverham w Ringland from 16. *The Rectory, 173 Taverham Road, Taverham, Norwich NR8 6SG* T: (01603) 868217 E: vicartaverham@gmail.com

SEABROOK, Mrs Penelope Anne. b 56. Hertf Coll Ox BA 77 K Coll Lon MA 98. SEITE 00. **d** 03 **p** 04. C Southfields St Jas Less *Lon* 03–08; NSM 03–07; C Fulham All SS *Lon* 08–19; V from 19. *All Saints' Vicarage, 70 Fulham High Street, London SW6 3LG* T: (020) 7736 3264 M: 07985-108541 E: pennyseabrook@hotmail.com *or* vicar@allsaints-fulham.org.uk

SEABROOK, Richard Anthony. b 68. Southn Univ BTh 92. Chich Th Coll 92. **d** 92 **p** 93. C Cottingham *York* 92–94; C Hawley H Trin *Guildf* 94–98; V Hockley *Chelmsf* 98–05; R Benalla Australia 05–09; R Mount Barker 09–15; Adn The Murray 09–14; Adn The Murray-Riverland 14–15; Dioc Admin The Murray 10–13; P-in-c Torrevieja *Eur* 15–20; Chapl from 20. *calle Manuel de Falla 240, 03169 Algorfa (Alicante), Spain* T: (0034) 966 840 136 E: frras@blackwater.org.au *or* frras@c-of-e-torrevieja.com

SEAFORD, The Very Revd John Nicholas. b 39. Dur Univ BA 67. St Chad's Coll Dur 68. **d** 68 **p** 69. C Bush Hill Park St Mark *Lon* 68–71; C Stanmore *Win* 71–73; V N Baddesley 73–76; V Chilworth w N Baddesley 76–78; V Highcliffe w Hinton Admiral 78–93; RD Christchurch 90–93; Hon Can Win Cathl 93–05; Dean Jersey and R Jersey St Helier 93–05; Angl Adv Channel TV 93–05; Chapl Jersey Airport 98–00; Chapl HM Pris La Moye 03–05; rtd 05; PtO *Sarum* 05–22; *Win* 05–14. *Claremont, Buffetts Road, Sturminster Newton DT10 1DZ* T: (01258) 471479 E: jolen.claremont@tiscali.co.uk

SEAGO, Aled Niclas. b 88. Lanc Univ BA 09. Oak Hill Th Coll BA 17. **d** 18 **p** 19. C Poynton *Ches* 18–21; P-in-c Dunham Massey St Marg and St Mark from 21. *St Margaret's Vicarage, Dunham Road, Altrincham WA14 4AQ* E: rev.a.seago@outlook.com *or* vicar@dunhamchurch.org

SEAGO, Timothy Paul. b 59. Ripon Coll Cuddesdon 06. **d** 08 **p** 09. C Marlborough *Sarum* 08–12; P-in-c Totteridge *St Alb* 12–17; V from 17; AD Barnet 18–20. *St Andrew's Vicarage, 78 Greenway, London N20 8EJ* M: 07772-809136 E: revdtim@seago.org.uk

SEAL, Canon Nicholas Peter. b 57. Ex Univ BA. Linc Th Coll 81. **d** 83 **p** 84. C Wareham *Sarum* 83–87; Chapl K Alfred Coll *Win* 87–91; V Stanmore 91–01; P-in-c Win St Matt 01–10; R 10–21; RD Win 99–07; Chapl Peter Symonds Coll Win 01–21; Hon Can Win Cathl 13–21; rtd 21. *4 Folly Lane, Wareham BH20 4HH* M: 07856-507178 E: peterseal64@gmail.com

SEAL (*formerly* **MILLER), Mrs Rosamund Joy.** b 56. R Holloway Coll Lon BSc 77 Whitelands Coll Lon PGCE 80. EMMTC 89. **d** 94 **p** 96. NSM Grantham *Linc* 94–96; C Stamford All SS w St Jo 96–00; C Spalding St Mary and St Nic 00–05; P-in-c Moulton 05–13; V Holbeach 13–21; RD Elloe E 09–21; RD Elloe W 09–13; rtd 21. *Address temp unknown* E: rosamund.seal@btinternet.com

SEALY, Stephen. b 52. K Coll Lon BD 86 AKC 86. Linc Th Coll 86. **d** 88 **p** 89. C Botley *Portsm* 88–91; Min Can and Prec Cant Cathl 91–96; V Pembury *Roch* 96–04; V Sidcup St Jo 04–17; P-in-c Footscray w N Cray 16–17; AD Sidcup 08–13; C Wymondham *Nor* 17–20; rtd 20; V Lt Malvern *Worc* from 20. *3 Royal Well Court, West Malvern Road, Malvern WR14 4EW* E: sealynk@btconnect.com

SEAMAN, Christopher Robert. b 34. St Jo Coll Ox BA 58 MA 74. Solicitor 62. Ox Min Course 92 SAOMC 94. **d** 95 **p** 96. NSM Watlington w Pyrton and Shirburn *Ox* 95–97; NSM Icknield 97–98; PtO 98–99 and 05–20; Hon C Shippon

99–04. *5 Curtyn Close, Abingdon OX14 1SE* T: (01235) 520380

SEAMAN, John. *See* SEAMAN, Robert John

SEAMAN, Miss Miranda Kate. b 66. Univ Coll Lon BSc 88 Solicitor 90. EAMTC 02. **d** 05 **p** 06. NSM S Weald *Chelmsf* 05–08; NSM Ingatestone w Fryerning 08–10; NSM Downham w S Hanningfield 10–11; NSM Downham w S Hanningfield and Ramsden Bellhouse 11–21; NSM Stock Harvard from 21; NSM W Hanningfield from 21. *Copt Hall, 2 High Street, Stock, Ingatestone CM4 9BW* T: (01277) 841921 M: 07909-522763 E: seamanyoung@btinternet.com

SEAMAN (*née* **HEWLINS), Mrs Pauline Elizabeth.** b 47. Lon Univ BD 68 AKC. Ox Min Course 93. **d** 96 **p** 97. NSM Radley and Sunningwell *Ox* 96–99; NSM Shippon 99–09; P-in-c 06–09; Chapl SS Helen and Kath Sch Abingdon 96–04; Chapl SW Oxon Primary Care Trust 05–07; PtO *Ox* from 09. *5 Curtyn Close, Abingdon OX14 1SE* T: (01235) 520380

SEAMAN, Robert John. b 44. Glos Univ BA 04 Newland Park Teacher Tr Coll DipEd 69 ACP 84. EAMTC 84. **d** 84 **p** 85. NSM Downham Market w Bexwell *Ely* 84–90; V Southea w Murrow and Parson Drove 90–97; V Guyhirn w Ring's End 90–97; V Newnham w Awre and Blakeney *Glouc* 97–08; AD Forest N 04–08; Hon C Whitwick, Thringstone and Swannington *Leic* 08–11; rtd 11; PtO *Leic* 11–19; *Pet* from 11. *6 Hiawatha, Wellingborough NN8 3SH* T: (01933) 382165 E: shipmates2@hotmail.co.uk

SEAMER, Stephen James George. b 50. AKC 73. Ridley Hall Cam 74. **d** 75 **p** 76. C Rustington *Chich* 75–78; C Bulwell St Jo *S'well* 78–79; P-in-c Camber and E Guldeford *Chich* 79–80; TV Rye 80–83; V Knowle *Birm* 83–87; Assoc Chapl Brussels Cathl *Eur* 87–88; P-in-c Tervuren 88–94; Chapl 94–98; P-in-c Liège 90–98; V Tonbridge SS Pet and Paul *Roch* 98–06; Chapl Düsseldorf *Eur* 06–14; rtd 14; PtO *Nor* from 15. *Low Wood, The Street, Erpingham, Norwich NR11 7QB* T: (01263) 768125 E: cromerclifftops@gmail.com

SEAR, Benjamin William. b 84. Southn Univ BSc 07. Oak Hill Th Coll BA 15. **d** 15 **p** 16. C Patcham *Chich* 15–19; R Maresfield from 19; V Nutley from 19. *Crystals Rest, High Street, Maresfield, Uckfield TN22 2EH* E: benjamin.w.sear@gmail.com *or* vicar.maresfieldandnutley@protonmail.com

SEAR, Mrs Julie Anne Caradoc. b 61. Trin Coll Bris 08. **d** 10 **p** 11. C Ashington, Washington and Wiston w Buncton *Chich* 10–13; R Hartfield w Coleman's Hatch from 13. *The Rectory, Church Street, Hartfield TN7 4AG* T: (01892) 770436 M: 07840-021909 E: revjuliesear1@gmail.com

SEAR, Peter Lionel. b 49. Ex Univ BA 72. Linc Th Coll 72. **d** 74 **p** 75. C Sheldon *Birm* 74–77; C Caversham *Ox* 77–81; C Caversham St Pet and Mapledurham etc 81–85; TR Thatcham 85–98; V Castle Cary w Ansford *B & W* 98–00; rtd 00; PtO *B & W* from 03. *Plumtree Cottage, 1 Rodmore Road, Evercreech, Shepton Mallet BA4 6JL* T: (01749) 838843 E: peter@knowlecottage.eclipse.co.uk

SEARE, Mrs Janice Mae. b 48. SEN. STETS 99. **d** 02 **p** 03. C Holdenhurst and Iford *Win* from 02. *Wood Farm, Holdenhurst Village, Bournemouth BH8 0EE* T: (01202) 302468 F: 391281 E: peter.seare@sky.com

SEARLE, Anthony Miles. b 76. Univ of Wales (Abth) BSc 98 PGCE 99 SS Coll Cam BTh 10. Westcott Ho Cam 98. **d** 10 **p** 11. C Bishop's Stortford St Mich *St Alb* 10–13; Asst Chapl Oundle Sch 13–16; P-in-c Corby SS Pet and Andr from 16; P-in-c Gt and Lt Oakley from 16. *The Vicarage, 40 Beanfield Avenue, Corby NN18 0EH* M: 07785-357562 E: asearle76@googlemail.com

SEARLE, David William. b 37. MASI 89 ACIOB 98. **d** 99 **p** 00. OLM E Bergholt and Brantham *St E* 99–07; rtd 07; PtO *St E* from 07. *Rowan House, Elm Road, East Bergholt, Colchester CO7 6SG* T: (01206) 298932

✠**SEARLE, The Rt Revd Jacqueline Ann.** b 60. Whitelands Coll Lon BEd 82 Bris Univ MA 01. Trin Coll Bris 90. **d** 92 **p** 94 **c** 18. Par Dn Roxeth *Lon* 92–94; C Ealing St Steph Castle Hill 94–96; Tutor and Dean of Women Trin Coll Bris 96–03; P-in-c Littleover *Derby* 03–04; V 04–12; RD Derby S 10–12; Hon Can Derby Cathl 11–12; Adn Glouc 12–18; Can Res Glouc Cathl 12–18; Suff Bp Crediton *Ex* from 18. *32 The Avenue, Tiverton EX16 4HW* T: (01884) 250002 E: bishop.of.crediton@exeter.anglican.org

SEARLE, John Francis. b 42. OBE 98. Lon Univ MB, BS 66 FRCA 70 FRSocMed 84. SWMTC 92. **d** 95 **p** 96. NSM Ex St Leon w H Trin 95–03; Assoc Staff Member SWMTC from 03; Can Res Ex Cathl 15–16; PtO from 15. *Belle Isle Lodge, Belle Isle Drive, Exeter EX2 4RY* T: (01392) 432153 M: 07814-712921 E: j.f.searle@btinternet.com

SEARLE, Mark Robin. b 73. Cen Sch Speech & Drama BA 94. Trin Coll Bris BA 03. **d** 03 **p** 04. C Cant St Mary Bredin 03–07; C Ashtead *Guildf* 07–10; P-in-c Upton *Ex* 10–17; R Bath Weston All SS w N Stoke and Langridge *B & W*

from 17. *The Rectory, Church Street, Weston, Bath BA1 4BU*
E: revmarksearle@gmail.com

SEARLE, Michael Westran. b 47. Leeds Univ LLB 68. Cuddesdon Coll 69. **d** 71 **p** 72. C Norton St Mary *Dur* 71–74; C Westbury-on-Trym H Trin *Bris* 74–77; V Bedminster Down 77–84; V Bris Ch the Servant Stockwood 84–88; Dir of Tr *York* 88–00; R Dunnington 00–07; rtd 07; PtO *Truro* from 16. *Lamorna Vean, Lamorna, Penzance TR19 6NY* T: (01736) 810218 E: mike.lamornavean@btinternet.com

SEARLE, Philip Robert. b 67. Westcott Ho Cam. **d** 95 **p** 96. C Plymstock *Ex* 95–97; C Plymstock and Hooe 97–98; TV Stoke-upon-Trent *Lich* 98–10; PtO 10–21. *164 Vicarage Gardens, Plymouth PL5 1LJ* E: phil.hairetic@hotmail.co.uk

SEARLE-BARNES, Belinda Rosemary. b 51. Lon Univ MA 93 ARCM 72 GRSM 73. Sarum Th Coll 93. **d** 96 **p** 97. NSM Pimperne, Stourpaine, Durweston and Bryanston *Sarum* 96–00; Asst Par Development Adv 98–00; Asst Chapl Bryanston Sch 98–00; TV Southampton (City Cen) *Win* 00–04; Chapl Godolphin Sch 04–07; P-in-c Winslow w Gt Horwood and Addington *Ox* 07–08; R 08–14; rtd 14; PtO *Win* 14–19; *St Alb* from 17; SSM Officer Bedford Adnry from 19. *3 Ravensden Grange, Sunderland Hill, Ravensden, Bedford MK44 2SH* T: (01234) 771112 E: belinda@searle-barnes.com *or* ssmobeds@stalbans.anglican.org

SEARS, Jacqueline Isabella. SRN 69. NTMTC 95. **d** 99 **p** 00. NSM Hanwell St Mellitus w St Mark *Lon* 99–02; Asst Chapl Essex Rivers Healthcare NHS Trust 03; Chapl 04–06; C Ipswich St Matt *St E* 04–06; C Triangle, St Matt and All SS 06–10; rtd 10; PtO *St E* from 10. *4 Woodward Close, Ipswich IP2 0EA* T: (01473) 214125 E: jackie@jbsears.com

SEATON, Christopher Charles. **d** 10 **p** 11. C St Andrews Major w Michaelston-le-Pit *Llan* 10–15; C Cadoxton-juxta-Barry 15–16; C Barry from 16. *13 Hillside Close, Barry CF63 2QP* T: (01446) 747541 E: chris.c.seaton@hotmail.co.uk

SEATON-BURN, Paul Simon. b 70. Ex Univ BA 92. St Jo Coll Nottm MTh 06. **d** 06 **p** 07. C Broughton w Loddington and Cransley etc *Pet* 06–09; P-in-c Desborough, Brampton Ash, Dingley and Braybrooke 09–11; P-in-c Chagford, S Tawton, Drewsteignton etc *Ex* 11–13; TR Chagford, Gidleigh, Throwleigh etc from 13; RD Okehampton from 20. *The Rectory, Chagford, Newton Abbot TQ13 8BW* T: (01647) 432880 E: paulsburn@btinternet.com

SEBBAGE, Lynda Anne. b 54. ERMC 16. **d** 17 **p** 18. NSM Stour Valley *St E* 17–20; P-in-c Barrow from 20. *The Rectory, Barrow, Bury St Edmunds IP29 5BA* T: (01284) 811280 M: 07870-640074 E: revlyndasebbage@gmail.com

SEBER, Derek Morgan. b 43. Man Poly MA 87 Man Metrop Univ MPhil 96. Oak Hill Th Coll 71. **d** 73 **p** 74. C Collyhurst *Man* 73–76; C Radcliffe St Thos and St Jo 76–77; Ind Missr 77–89; P-in-c Hulme St Geo 77–83; Hon C Moss Side St Jas w St Clem 83–96; Project Officer Linking Up 89–96; Lic Preacher *Man* 90–96; P-in-c Cheetham St Jo 97; P-in-c Thornton Hough *Ches* 97–05; V 05–08; Ind Chapl 97–05; rtd 08; PtO *Ches* 08–12; *Blackb* from 12. *3 Castle Park, Hornby, Lancaster LA2 8SB* T: (015242) 22011 E: derek.seber@sky.com

SEDANO, Juan Daniel. b 83. Liv Univ BA 05 Man Univ MA 08. St Mellitus Coll BA 20. **d** 20 **p** 21. C Frankby w Greasby *Ches* from 20. *2 Summertrees Avenue, Wirral CH49 2QD* M: 07730-561940 E: jdsedano@hotmail.com

SEDDON, Mrs Carol Susan. b 44. ARCM 63 GNSM 66 Man Univ DipEd 67. Ripon Coll Cuddesdon 05. **d** 05 **p** 06. NSM Alsager St Mary *Ches* 05–08; Asst Chapl HM YOI Stoke Heath 05–08; V Northwich St Luke and H Trin *Ches* 08–17; rtd 17; PtO *Ches* 15–18; P-in-c Northwich H Trin from 18. *The Vicarage, 1 Tall Trees Close, Northwich CW8 4YA* T: (01606) 74632 M: 07973-737038 E: carol_seddon@hotmail.com

SEDDON, Ernest Geoffrey. b 26. Man Univ MA 85 ARIBA 51. St Deiniol's Hawarden 80. **d** 80 **p** 81. C Dunham Massey St Marg *Ches* 80–83; P-in-c Warburton 82–87; P-in-c Dunham Massey St Mark 85–86; V 86–92; rtd 92; PtO *Ches* 92–06. *7 Colwyn Place, Llandudno LL30 3AW* T: (01492) 547639 *or* 642107

SEDDON, Philip James. b 45. Jes Coll Cam BA 68 MA 71 Birm Univ MPhil 01. Ridley Hall Cam 67. **d** 70 **p** 71. C Tonge w Alkrington *Man* 70–74; CMS Nigeria 74–78; Lect St Jo Coll Nottm 78–79; LtO *Ely* 79–85; Chapl Magd Coll Cam 79–85; Lect Bibl Studies Selly Oak Colls 86–00; LtO *Birm* 87–05; Lect Th Birm Univ 00–05; Dir Min STETS 05–10; rtd 10; PtO *Sarum* from 11. *6 Beech Close, Porton, Salisbury SP4 0NP* T: (01980) 619104 E: philipjseddon@gmail.com

SEDEN, Martin Roy. b 47. Man Univ MSc Salford Univ PhD. EMMTC 79. **d** 82 **p** 83. NSM Knighton St Mary Magd *Leic* 82–07; NSM Rutland Deanery *Pet* 08–20; SSM Officer Oakham Adnry 18–20; rtd 20. *5 Aldous Close, East Bergholt, Colchester CO7 6SQ* M: 07806-940407 E: rseden@gmail.com

SEDGEWICK, Clive Malcolm. b 56. Loughb Univ BSc 78 UEA MA 92 PGCE 79. SAOMC 00. **d** 04 **p** 05. NSM High Harrogate Ch Ch *Ripon* 04–13; P-in-c Bardsey 13–14; *Leeds* 14–17; TR Axminster, Chardstock, All Saints etc *Ex* 17–20; TR Axminster, All Saints, Axmouth, Chardstock etc from 20. *The Rectory, Church Street, Axminster EX13 5AQ* M: 07903-326053 E: clivesedgewick@yahoo.com

SEDGLEY, Mrs Jean. b 41. Open Univ BA 03 Whitelands Coll Lon CertEd 63. S Dios Minl Tr Scheme 92. **d** 95 **p** 96. NSM Haywards Heath St Wilfrid *Chich* 95–01; NSM Cuckfield 01–09; rtd 09; PtO *Chich* from 14. *10 St Nicholas Court, Lindfield, Haywards Heath RH16 2EY* T: (01444) 413974 E: jean@sedgley.org

SEDGLEY, Canon Timothy John. b 42. St Jo Coll Ox BA 63 MA 68. Westcott Ho Cam 64. **d** 66 **p** 67. C Nor St Pet Mancroft 66–70; V Costessey 70–79; RD Nor N 75–79; V Walton-on-Thames *Guildf* 79–05; RD Emly 86–91; Hon Can Guildf Cathl 86–05; Dir OLMs and NSMs 93–05; rtd 05; PtO *Glouc* from 06. *6 St Paul's Court, Moreton-in-Marsh, Gloucester GL56 0ET* T: (01608) 652696 E: timsedgley@hotmail.com

SEDGWICK, Canon Jonathan Maurice William. b 63. BNC Ox BA 85 MA 89 Leeds Univ BA 88. Coll of Resurr Mirfield 86. **d** 89 **p** 90. C Chich St Paul and St Pet 89–91; Dean of Div and Chapl Magd Coll Ox 91–94; PtO *S'wark* 97–99; Hon C E Dulwich St Jo 99–11; Hon C Walworth St Chris 11–14; P-in-c S'wark St Geo w St Alphege and St Jude 14–18; R from 18; AD S'wark and Newington from 20; Hon Can Asante Mampong Ghana from 20. *St George's Rectory, Manciple Street, London SE1 4LW* M: 07585-113773 E: jonathan@stgeorge-themartyr.co.uk

SEDGWICK, Canon Peter Humphrey. b 48. Trin Hall Cam BA 70 Dur Univ PhD 83. Westcott Ho Cam 71. **d** 74 **p** 75. C Stepney St Dunstan and All SS *Lon* 74–77; P-in-c Pittington *Dur* 77–79; Lect Th Birm Univ 79–82; Hon C The Lickey *Birm* 79–82; Th Consultant for NE Ecum Gp *Dur* 82–88; Lect Th Westcott Ho Cam 88–94; Abp's Adv on Ind Issues *York* 88–94; Vice-Prin Westcott Ho Cam 94–96; Asst Sec Abps' Coun Bd for Soc Resp 96–04; NSM Pet St Barn 96–98; Prin St Mich Coll Llan 04–14; Internal Examr from 06; PtO *Llan* from 14. *Church House, Grand Avenue, Cardiff CF5 4HX* T: (029) 2067 9833 E: peter.sedgwick2@btinternet.com

SEEAR, Ms Louise. b 57. St Mary's Coll Dur BA 78. Ripon Coll Cuddesdon 09. **d** 12 **p** 13. NSM N Lambeth *S'wark* 12–15; Asst Chapl King's Coll Hosp NHS Foundn Trust 13–19; Chapl Lewisham and Greenwich NHS Trust from 19; NSM Hythe *Cant* 16–20; Asst Dir of Ords from 16. *Address temp unknown* M: 07813-615150 E: revlouseear@gmail.com

SEED, Richard Edward. b 55. UNISA BTh 86 Westmr Coll Ox MEd. Kalk Bay Bible Inst S Africa. **d** 80 **p** 81. S Africa 80–85 and 87–89; Zimbabwe 85–87; Asst Chapl Kingham Hill Sch Oxon 89–90; C Beckenham Ch Ch *Roch* 90–95; Chapl Düsseldorf *Eur* 96–00; CMS from 00. *CMS, PO Box 1799, Oxford OX4 9BN* T: 08456-201799

SEED, The Ven Richard Murray Crosland. b 49. Leeds Univ MA 91. Edin Th Coll 69. **d** 72 **p** 73. C Skipton Ch Ch *Bradf* 72–75; C Baildon 75–77; Chapl HM Det Cen Kidlington 77–80; TV Kidlington *Ox* 77–80; V Boston Spa *York* 80–99; P-in-c Newton Kyme 84–85; P-in-c Clifford 89–99; P-in-c Thorp Arch w Walton 98–99; Chapl Martin House Hospice for Children Boston Spa 85–99; RD New Ainsty *York* 97–99; Adn *York* 99–12; R York H Trin Micklegate 00–12; rtd 12; PtO *York* from 12. *74 Palace Road, Ripon HG4 1UN* T: (01765) 698609 E: randjseed@gmail.com

SEED, Susan Mary. b 61. **d** 14 **p** 15. C Lancaster Ch Ch *Blackb* 14–18; R Slyne w Hest and Halton w Aughton from 18. *The Vicarage, 2 Summerfield Drive, Slyne, Lancaster LA2 6AQ* T: (01524) 822128 E: revsusan.seed@btinternet.com

SEEL, Richard Malcolm. b 45. **d** 04 **p** 05. OLM Bacton w Edingthorpe w Witton and Ridlington *Nor* 04–07; OLM Happisburgh, Walcott, Hempstead w Eccles etc 04–07; NSM Loddon, Sisland, Chedgrave, Hardley and Langley 07–15; PtO 16–18. *31 Hillside, Chedgrave, Norwich NR14 6HZ* T: (01508) 521938 M: 07923-266403 E: richard@emerging-church.org

SEELEY, Jutta. *See* BRUECK, Jutta

✠**SEELEY, The Rt Revd Martin Alan.** b 54. Jes Coll Cam BA 76 MA 79. Ripon Coll Cuddesdon 76 Union Th Sem (NY) STM 78. **d** 78 **p** 79 **c** 15. C Bottesford w Ashby *Linc* 78–80; USA 80–90; Selection Sec ABM 90–96; Sec for Continuing Minl Educn 90–96; V Is of Dogs Ch Ch and St Jo w St Luke *Lon* 96–06; Prin Westcott Ho Cam 06–15; Hon Can Ely Cathl 08–15; Bp St E from 15; Hon Asst Bp Ely from 15; PtO *Eur* from 17. *The Bishop's House, 4 Park Road, Ipswich IP1 3ST* T: (01473) 252829 E: bishop.martin@cofesuffolk.org

SEEVARATNAM, Mohan Surenda. b 64. St Mellitus Coll 12. **d** 15 **p** 16. NSM W Harrow St Pet *Lon* 15–17; NSM Southall

St Geo 17–19; PtO 19–20; NSM S Harrow St Paul 20–21; C from 21. *64 Wilson Gardens, Harrow HA1 4DZ* T: (020) 8422 3422 M: 07975-973982 E: mohan@stpaulsharrow.org.uk *or* barakams@aol.com

SEGGAR, Jennifer Mary. b 63. Open Univ PGCE 01. **d** 05 **p** 06. OLM Bildeston w Wattisham and Lindsey etc *St E* 05–09; C Sudbury and Chilton 09–11; P-in-c Bramford 11–19; Spiritual Dir Cursillo 16–19; R Holbrook, Stutton, Freston, Woolverstone etc from 19. *15 Denmark Gardens, Ipswich Road, Holbrook, Ipswich IP9 2BG* E: revjseggar@outlook.com

SEGGIE, Karen Angela. *See* NELSON, Karen Angela

SEGRAVE-PRIDE, Mrs Philippa Louise. b 73. Westhill Coll Birm BTh 96. Ripon Coll Cuddesdon 97. **d** 99 **p** 00. C Harborne St Pet *Birm* 99–02; TV Tring *St Alb* 02–04; TV Bishop's Hatfield, Lemsford and N Mymms 04–09; P-in-c Harpenden St Jo 09–12; V 12–13; Canada from 13. *1281 Durant Drive, Coquitlam, British Columbia V3B 6K8, Canada* T: (001) (778) 838 3132 E: philippa@segrave.net

SELBY, Canon Carole Janis. b 50. Chelsea Coll of Physical Educn CertEd 71 Sussex Univ BEd 72 K Coll Lon MA 03. Westcott Ho Cam 93. **d** 95 **p** 96. C Worc St Barn w Ch Ch 95–99; Min Turnford St Clem CD *St Alb* 99–08; TV Cheshunt 08–17; RD 04–12; Hon Can St Alb 13–17; rtd 17. *6 Perrings, Wymondham NR18 0JR* T: (01953) 600635

SELBY, Michael Ernest. b 59. Preston Poly BEd 80. Ripon Coll Cuddesdon 14. **d** 16 **p** 17. C Ealing St Pet Mt Park *Lon* 16–19; V Ruislip Manor St Paul from 19. *St Paul's Vicarage, Thurlstone Road, Ruislip HA4 0BP* M: 07795-187164 E: revmselby@gmail.com

SELBY, Peter Leslie. b 54. Down Coll Cam BA 75 MA 79 MB, BChir 79 MD 90 FRCP. All SS Cen for Miss & Min 16. **d** 18 **p** 19. NSM Cheadle Hulme St Andr *Ches* from 18. *22 Nevill Road, Bramhall, Stockport SK7 3ET* T: 0161-439 4735 M: 07721-539081 E: peter@theselbys.org *or* peter@standrewscheadlehulme.org.uk

✠**SELBY, The Rt Revd Peter Stephen Maurice.** b 41. St Jo Coll Ox BA 64 MA 67 Episc Th Sch Cam Mass BD 66 K Coll Lon PhD 75 Birm Univ Hon DD 07. Bps' Coll Cheshunt 66. **d** 66 **p** 67 **c** 84. C Queensbury All SS *Lon* 66–69; C Limpsfield and Titsey *S'wark* 69–77; Assoc Dir of Tr 69–73; Vice-Prin S'wark Ord Course 70–72; Asst Dioc Missr *S'wark* 73–77; Dioc Missr *Newc* 77–84; Can Res Newc Cathl 77–84; Suff Bp Kingston *S'wark* 84–91; Area Bp 91–92; Wm Leech Prof Fell Dur Univ 92–97; Asst Bp Dur and Newc 92–97; Bp Worc 97–07; Hon Prof Univ Coll Worc from 98; Bp HM Pris 01–07; rtd 07; Pres Nat Coun Ind Monitoring Boards 08–13; Hon Asst Bp Portsm 08–11; Hon Co-Dir St Paul's Inst 12–14; Hon Asst Bp S'wark from 11; Visiting Prof K Coll Lon from 08. *57 Girton Road, London SE26 5DJ* T: (020) 3538 0220 E: petarselby1941@gmail.com

SELBY, Philip James. b 82. Nottm Univ BSc 04 Derby Univ PGCE 06. Oak Hill Th Coll BA 15. **d** 15 **p** 16. C Buxton Trin Prop Chpl *Derby* 15–19; R Stanton-by-Dale w Dale Abbey and Risley from 19. *The Rectory, Stanhope Street, Stanton-by-Dale, Ilkeston DE7 4QA* M: 07910-321576 E: philselby82@gmail.com

SELBY-BOOTHROYD, Richard George. b 46. SWMTC. **d** 09 **p** 10. NSM St Illogan *Truro* 09–11; NSM Lyneham w Bradenstoke *Sarum* 11–18; P-in-c 15–18; NSM R Wootton Bassett *Sarum* 11–15; NSM Woodhill 11–18; rtd 19; PtO *Ox* from 19; *Bris* from 20; *Sarum* from 21. *8 St Josephs Way, Lyneham, Chippenham SN15 4FA* E: rsb@priest.com

SELBY, Suffragan Bishop of. *See* THOMSON, The Rt Revd John Bromilow

SELDON, Francis Peter. b 58. St Jo Coll Nottm 98. **d** 00 **p** 01. C Styvechale *Cov* 00–02; C Cheylesmore 02–04; V 04–11; V Chilvers Coton w Astley from 11; AD Nuneaton 16–18. *Chilvers Coton Vicarage, Coventry Road, Nuneaton CV11 4NJ* T: (024) 7638 3010 *or* 7634 6413

SELDON, Mrs Miranda Damaris. Ripon Coll Cuddesdon 17. **d** 20 **p** 21. NSM Northchurch and Wigginton *St Alb* from 20. *Address withheld by request* T: (01442) 877975 M: 07761-165871 E: revmseldon@outlook.com

SELF, Canon David Christopher. b 41. Toronto Univ BSc 62 MA 64 K Coll Lon BD 68 AKC 68. **d** 69 **p** 70. C Tupsley *Heref* 69–73; Chapl Van Mildert and Trevelyan Colls Dur 73–78; TV Southampton (City Cen) *Win* 78–84; TR Dunstable *St Alb* 84–95; RD 90–91; TR Bris St Paul's 95–06; RD Bris City 98–99; AD City 99–03; Hon Can Bris Cathl 99–06; rtd 06; PtO *Bris* from 07; *Glouc* from 16. *3 Shannon Court, Thornbury, Bristol BS35 2HN* T: (01454) 418006 E: david@dcself.plus.com

SELFE, John Ronald. b 41. EMMTC 85. **d** 95 **p** 96. OLM Mid Marsh Gp *Linc* from 95. *Bookend, 236 Eastgate, Louth LN11 8DA* T: (01507) 603809

SELLER, Prof Mary Joan. b 40. Qu Mary Coll Lon BSc 61 Lon Univ PhD 64 DSc 82. S'wark Ord Course 89. **d** 91

p 94. NSM Hurst Green *S'wark* 91–10; rtd 10; PtO *S'wark* from 10. *11 Home Park, Oxted RH8 0JS* T: (01883) 715675 E: maryjseller0@gmail.com

SELLER, Timothy John. b 46. Qu Mary Coll Lon BSc 67 Lon Univ PhD 71. **d** 08 **p** 09. OLM Ewhurst *Guildf* 08–16; PtO 16–17; rtd 17. *Long Barn, Back Street, Ilmington, Shipston-on-Stour CV36 4LJ* M: 07845-192041 E: tim.seller@outlook.com

SELLERS, Canon Anthony. b 48. Southn Univ BSc 71 PhD 76. Wycliffe Hall Ox 84. **d** 86 **p** 87. C Luton St Mary *St Alb* 86–90; V Luton St Paul 90–16; Hon Can St Alb 12–16; rtd 16; PtO *St Alb* from 16. *Address withheld by request*

SELLERS, Joseph Matthew Christopher. b 81. Trin Coll Bris 16. **d** 18 **p** 19. C Chorleywood St Andr *St Alb* 18–21; V St Margaret's-on-Thames *Lon* from 21. *295 St Margaret's Road, Twickenham TW1 1PN* T: (020) 8891 6820

SELLERS, Mrs Rosalind April. b 48. Liv Univ MA 77. SWMTC 06. **d** 09 **p** 11. NSM Cannington, Otterhampton, Combwich and Stockland *B & W* 09–10; NSM Puriton and Pawlett 10–18; PtO from 18. *1 St Mary's Crescent, North Petherton, Bridgwater TA6 6RA* T: (01278) 661279 M: 07759-405485 E: rosalind.sellers153@gmail.com

SELLERS, Warren John. b 43. Bp Otter Coll Chich TCert 73 W Sussex Inst of HE DipAdEd 88. K Coll Lon 63 Sarum Th Coll 65. **d** 68 **p** 69. C Guildf H Trin w St Mary 68–72; Hon C Chich St Paul and St Pet 72–73; C Epping St Jo *Chelmsf* 73–76; Hon C Pulborough *Chich* 76–90; Hon C Fleet *Guildf* 90–92; Teacher Waltham Abbey St Lawr and H Cross Schs Essex 73–76; Teacher Pulborough St Mary, Easebourne and Bp Tuffnell Schs 76–89; Hd Teacher St Pet Jun Sch Farnborough 90–92; TV Upper Kennet *Sarum* 92–95; TR 95–03; rtd 03. *71 Bay Crescent, Swanage BH19 1RD* T: (01929) 425322 E: wjandmjs27@btinternet.com

SELLERS, Wendy. b 62. Leeds Univ BA 84 Herts Univ PGCE 00. ERMC 16. **d** 18 **p** 19. NSM Hertford *St Alb* 18–21; V Sandridge from 21. *2 Anson Close, Sandridge, St Albans AL4 9EN* T: (01727) 301542 E: revwendy55@gmail.com

SELLEY, Paul Edward Henry. b 47. Bris Univ BEd 70 ALCM 67 LTCL 87. Sarum Th Coll 93. **d** 96 **p** 97. C Swindon Dorcan *Bris* 96–00; V Ashton Keynes, Leigh and Minety 00–07; rtd 07; PtO *Sarum* from 07. *5 Miles Gardens, Weymouth DT3 5NH* T: (01305) 814948 E: paul.selley@which.net

SELLGREN, Eric Alfred. b 33. AKC 61. **d** 62 **p** 63. C Ditton St Mich *Liv* 62–66; V Hindley Green 66–72; V Southport St Paul 72–80; Warden Barn Fellowship Winterborne Whitchurch 80–86; V The Iwernes, Sutton Waldron and Fontmell Magna *Sarum* 86–98; rtd 98; PtO *Sarum* from 98. *19 Savoy Court, Shaftesbury SP7 8BN* T: (01747) 853327 E: revsellgren@gmail.com

SELLICK, Canon Peter James. b 67. Wadh Coll Ox BA 89. Edin Th Coll BD 94. **d** 94 **p** 95. C Kippax w Allerton Bywater *Ripon* 94–97; C Stanningley St Thos 97–02; C W Bromwich All SS *Lich* 02–12; Ind Chapl Black Country Urban Ind Miss 02–12; Development Dir Chs and Ind Gp Birm and Solihull from 12; PtO *Lich* from 15; Hon Can Birm Cathl from 16. *41 Wheatley Road, Oldbury B68 9HW* T: 0121-423 4334 *or* 426 0425 M: 07746-299676 E: peters@cofebirmingham.com

✠**SELLIN, The Rt Revd Deborah Mary.** b 64. St Andr Univ MA 86. STETS 04. **d** 07 **p** 08 **c** 19. NSM Guildf St Sav 07–10; V Wonersh w Blackheath 10–19; AD Cranleigh 15–19; Hon Can Guildf Cathl 18–19; Suff Bp Southampton *Win* from 19. *39 Hook Road, Ampfield, Romsey SO51 9DB* T: (01962) 737315 E: bishop.debbie@winchester.anglican.org

SELLIN, Jacqueline Mary. b 67. Sarum Coll 14. **d** 17 **p** 18. NSM Southampton (City Cen) *Win* 17–18; NSM Southampton St Mich 18–20; PtO from 20. *50 Bullar Road, Southampton SO18 1GS*

SELLIX, Mrs Pamela Madge. b 47. Lon Univ BA 68 PGCE 68. SWMTC 00. **d** 04 **p** 05. NSM Saltash *Truro* from 04. *Farthings, Quarry Road, Pensilva, Liskeard PL14 5NT* T: (01579) 363464

SELMAN, Laura Margaret. b 81. **d** 15 **p** 16. C Surbiton St Andr and St Mark *S'wark* 15–17; C Bury St Edmunds All SS w St Jo and St Geo *St E* 17–19; C Lark Valley 17–19; C Lark Valley and N Bury 19–20; TV Sidmouth, Woolbrook, Salcombe Regis, Sidbury etc from 20. *The Rectory, Glen Road, Sidmouth EX10 8RW* E: laura.selman@sidvalley.org.uk

SELMAN, Matthew Robert. b 81. Leic Univ BA 03 SOAS Lon MA 06 St Edm Coll Cam BTh 17. Westcott Ho Cam 17. **d** 17 **p** 18. C Bury St Edmunds All SS w St Jo and St Geo *St E* 17–19; C Lark Valley 17–19; C Lark Valley and N Bury 19–20; TV Sidmouth, Woolbrook, Salcombe Regis, Sidbury etc *Ex* from 20. *The Rectory, Glen Road, Sidmouth EX10 8RW* E: matt.selman@sidvalley.org.uk

SELMAN, Michael Richard. b 47. Sussex Univ BA 68 Bris Univ MA 70. Coll of Resurr Mirfield 71. **d** 73 **p** 74. C Hove All SS *Chich* 73–74; C Horfield H Trin *Bris* 74–78; P-in-c Landkey *Ex* 78–79; C Barnstaple and Goodleigh

78–79; TV Barnstaple, Goodleigh and Landkey 79–82; TR 82–84; P-in-c Sticklepath 83–84; TR Barnstaple 85; RD 83–85; TR Cen Ex 85–00; Chapl Aquitaine *Eur* 00–08; Partnership P E Bris 08–12; rtd 12; PtO *Eur* from 16; *Ex* from 18. *1 Millwey Court, Axminster EX13 5GD* M: 07735-499920 E: revmichael.selman@gmail.com

SELMES, Brian. b 48. Nottm Univ BTh 74 Dur Univ MA 97. Linc Th Coll 70. **d** 74 **p** 75. C Padgate *Liv* 74–77; C Sydenham St Bart *S'wark* 77–80; Chapl Darlington Memorial and Aycliffe Hosps 80–98; Co-ord Chapl S Durham Healthcare NHS Trust 98–02; Sen Chapl Co Durham and Darlington NHS Foundn Trust 02–12; rtd 12. *19 The Avenue, Richmond DL10 7AZ* T: (01748) 821873 E: bmselmes@outlook.com

SELVARATNAM, Christian Nathan. b 68. Warwick Univ BSc 90. Cranmer Hall Dur 06 Asbury Th Sem Kentucky DMin 20. **d** 08 **p** 09. NSM York St Mich-le-Belfrey 08–21; Tutor St Hild Coll 19–21; Dir Ch Planting and Revitalisation from 21; PtO *York* from 21. *St Hild College, The Mirfield Centre, Stocks Bank Road, Mirfield WF14 0BW* T: (01924) 481925 M: 07773-784728 E: christian.selvaratnam@sthild.org

SELVEY, Canon John Brian. b 33. Dur Univ BA 54. Cuddesdon Coll 56. **d** 58 **p** 59. C Lancaster St Mary *Blackb* 58–61; C Blackb Cathl 61–65; Cathl Chapl 64–65; V Foulridge *Blackb* 65–69; V Walton-le-Dale 69–82; V Cleveleys 82–89; Hon Can Bloemfontein Cathl from 88; V Slyne w Hest *Blackb* 89–97; Hon Can Blackb Cathl 93–97; rtd 97; PtO *Carl* 98–19. *Low Quietways, Borrowdale Road, Keswick CA12 5UP* T: (01768) 773538 E: jselvey7@btinternet.com

SELWOOD, Michael. b 40. Oak Hill Th Coll BA 91. **d** 91 **p** 92. Canada 91–95; P-in-c Sherborne, Windrush, the Barringtons etc *Glouc* 95–07; rtd 07; PtO *Glouc* from 16. *17 Croft Holm, Moreton-in-Marsh GL56 0JH* T: (01608) 812384 E: mselwood@btinternet.com

SELWYN, David Gordon. b 38. Clare Coll Cam BA 62 MA 66 DD New Coll Ox MA 66 MEHS. Ripon Hall Ox 62. **d** 64 **p** 65. C Ecclesall *Sheff* 64–65; Asst Chapl New Coll Ox 65–68; Lect Univ of Wales (Lamp) *St D* 68–98; Reader 98–05; PtO *St D* 68–05. *62A Swiss Valley, Llanelli SA14 8BT* T: (01554) 773983

SEMPER, Jocelyn Rachel. *See* WALKER, Jocelyn Rachel

SEMPLE, Henry Michael. b 40. K Coll Lon BSc 62 Birkbeck Coll Lon PhD 67 CMath FIMA FCMI FRSA. S Dios Minl Tr Scheme. **d** 87 **p** 88. NSM Steyning *Chich* 87–91; PtO *Guildf* 87–91; *Linc* 92–93; NSM Linc Cathl 93–99; TR Headley All SS *Guildf* 99–02; R 02–10; rtd 10; PtO *Guildf* 10–12; *Chich* from 11. *10 North Walls, Chichester PO19 1DB* T: (01243) 784211 E: michael.semple1@outlook.com

SEMPLE, Sean Alexander John. b 71. Natal Univ BSocSc 93 BTh 03 UNISA BTh 97 Kwazulu-Natal Univ MTh 14. **d** 09 **p** 11. C Hillcrest H Trin S Africa 09–10; Asst P Pinetown St Jo 10–12; Asst P Larnaca Cyprus 13–15; V Weobley w Sarnesfield and Norton Canon *Heref* 15–19; R Letton w Staunton, Byford, Mansel Gamage etc 15–19; R Ross w Walford and Brampton Abbotts from 19; RD Ross and Archenfield from 21. *The Rectory, Church Street, Ross-on-Wye HR9 5HN* T: (01989) 562175 E: sean@rawchurch.org.uk

SEMPLE, Studdert Patrick. b 39. TCD BA 66. CITC 66. **d** 67 **p** 68. C Orangefield *D & D* 67–70; USA 70–71; I Stradbally *C, F & O* 71–82; Ch of Ireland Adult Educn Officer 82–88; I Donoughmore and Donard w Dunlavin *D & G* 88–96; Bp's C Dublin St Geo and St Thos 96–99; Chapl Mountjoy Pris 96–99; Chapl Mater Hosp 96–99; rtd 99. *49 Richmond Park, Monkstown, Co Dublin, Republic of Ireland* T: (00353) (1) 214 0843 M: 86-375 3207 E: naturesplaythings@gmail.com

SEN, Arani. b 61. R Holloway Coll Lon BA 84 St Martin's Coll Lanc PGCE 86 Open Univ MA 94 Fitzw Coll Cam BA 98 MA 02. Ridley Hall Cam 96. **d** 99 **p** 00. C Mildmay Grove St Jude and St Paul *Lon* 99–02; C-in-c Southall Em CD 02–06; V Southall Em 06–08; V Upper Armley *Ripon* 08–14; *Leeds* 14–19; AD Armley *Ripon* 13–14; *Leeds* 14–19; Hon Can Bradf Cathl 17–19; R St Olave Hart Street w All Hallows Staining etc *Lon* from 19; Dir Min Two Cities Area from 19; Dean of Cultural Diversity from 20. *St Olave's Rectory, 8 Hart Street, London EC3R 7NB* T: (020) 8091 3677 E: arani.sen@london.anglican.org or rector@stolave.com

SENIOR, Canon Brian Stephen. b 55. Brighton Coll of Educn CertEd 76. Oak Hill Th Coll 91. **d** 93 **p** 94. C Hildenborough *Roch* 93–98; TV Tunbridge Wells St Jas w St Phil 98–04; V Tunbridge Wells St Phil 04–15; RD Tunbridge Wells 07–14; TR S Gillingham from 15; AD Gillingham from 19; Hon Can Roch Cathl from 16. *The Vicarage, 4 Drewery Drive, Rainham, Gillingham ME8 0NX* T: (01634) 231071 E: revbriansenior@gmail.com

SENIOR, David John. b 47. Oak Hill Th Coll. **d** 82 **p** 83. C Market Harborough *Leic* 82–85; TV Marfleet *York* 85–91; R Desford and Peckleton w Tooley *Leic* 91–96; P-in-c Hall Green

Ascension *Birm* 96–99; V 99–12; P-in-c Gospel Lane St Mich 97–03; AD Shirley 10–12; rtd 12; Hon C Londesborough Wold *York* 12–15; Hon C Pocklington Wold 12–15; PtO *Carl* 15–17; *York* from 18. *9 Knott Lane, Easingwold, York YO61 3LX* T: (01347) 822295 E: davidsenior3@gmail.com

SENIOR, David Norman. b 59. Cam Univ MA 82. St Mellitus Coll 12. **d** 15 **p** 17. NSM Howell Hill *Guildf* from 15; Dioc Miss Adv from 19. *65 Higher Drive, Banstead SM7 1PW* M: 07710-313749

SENIOR, Mrs Lisa Elaine. b 65. Leeds Univ BA 09. NOC 06. **d** 09 **p** 10. C Dewsbury *Wakef* 09–14; *Leeds* 14; R Colne Blackb 14–20; Chapl HM Pris and YOI New Hall from 20. *HM Prison and Young Offenders Institution New Hall, New Hall Way, Flockton, Wakefield WF4 4XX*

SENIOR, Patrick Nicolas Adam. b 63. Univ of Wales (Ban) BA 86. Trin Coll Bris BA 94. **d** 94 **p** 95. C Derringham Bank *York* 94–98; V Brownhill *Wakef* 98–14; R Burnley St Pet and St Steph *Blackb* 14–21; AD Burnley 19–20; C Drighlington and Gildersome *Leeds* from 21. *2A Church Street, Gildersome, Morley, Leeds LS27 7AF* E: patricksenior24@gmail.com

✠**SENTAMU, The Rt Revd and Rt Hon Lord (John Tucker Mugabi).** b 49. Makerere Univ Kampala LLB 71 Selw Coll Cam BA 76 MA MPhil 79 PhD 84. Ridley Hall Cam. **d** 79 **p** 79 **c** 96. Chapl HM Rem Cen Latchmere Ho 79–82; C Ham St Andr *S'wark* 79–82; C Herne Hill St Paul 82–83; P-in-c Tulse Hill H Trin 83–84; V Upper Tulse Hill St Matthias 83–84; V Tulse Hill H Trin and St Matthias 85–96; P-in-c Brixton Hill St Sav 87–89; Hon Can S'wark Cathl 93–96; Area Bp Stepney *Lon* 96–02; Bp Birm 02–05; Abp York 05–20; rtd 20. *Address withheld by request*

SENTAMU, Lady (Margaret Nightingale Mugabi). b 51. **d** 19 **p** 20. NSM York St Chad 19–20; NSM Norham and Duddo *Newc* from 20; NSM Cornhill w Carham from 20; NSM Branxton from 20. *c/o Crockford, Church House, 27 Great Smith Street, London SW1P 3AZ*

SENTAMU BAVERSTOCK, The Hon Grace Kathleen Nabanja. b 75. Nottm Univ BA 96 Selw Coll Cam BTh 10. Ridley Hall Cam 06. **d** 10 **p** 11. C Watford St Luke *St Alb* 10–14; V Leagrave from 14. *St Luke's Vicarage, High Street, Luton LU4 9JY* T: (01582) 592361 E: gracesenba@gmail.com

SEPHTON, Mrs Jacqueline Ann Driscoll. b 46. RGN 67. **d** 10 **p** 11. OLM Stoke by Nayland w Leavenheath and Polstead *St E* 10–13; NSM 13–16; rtd 16. *12 Highlands Road, Hadleigh, Ipswich IP7 5HU* T: (01473) 810072

SEPHTON, John. b 43. **d** 01 **p** 02. OLM Newburgh w Westhead *Liv* from 01; Asst Chapl HM Pris Risley 02–09. *37 Brighouse Close, Ormskirk L39 3NA* T: (01695) 576774 E: johnsephton@postmaster.co.uk

SEPPALA, Christopher James. b 59. St Jo Coll Dur BA 82 Ch Ch Coll Cant CertEd 92. Chich Th Coll 83. **d** 85 **p** 86. C Whitstable *Cant* 85–88; C S Ashford Ch Ch 88–91; PtO 01–16. *2 The Briars, Long Reach Close, Whitstable CT5 4QF* T: (01227) 282622

SERBUTT, Rita Eileen. b 33. Man Univ BA 54 Univ of Wales (Cardiff) DipEd 56 FRSA 94. **d** 01 **p** 02. OLM Balham St Mary and St Jo *S'wark* 01–03; rtd 03; PtO *S'wark* from 03. *56 Manville Road, London SW17 8JL* T: (020) 8767 8383 E: eileen.serbutt@btinternet.com

SERGENT, Jean-Luc James. b 78. Paris Univ MSc 02. St Mellitus Coll BA 15. **d** 15 **p** 18. C The Hague *Eur* 15–17; C Kensington St Barn *Lon* from 17. *17 Devonport Road, London W12 8NZ* M: 07528-731953 E: jeanluc.sergent@gmail.com

SERJEANT, Frederick James. b 28. Lon Inst of Educn BEd 77. AKC 53 St Boniface Warminster 53. **d** 54 **p** 55. C Leytonstone St Marg w St Columba *Chelmsf* 54–58; C Parkstone St Pet w Branksea *Sarum* 58–59; V Reigate St Luke S Park *S'wark* 59–65; V Battersea St Pet 65–71; C-in-c Battersea St Paul 67–71; V W Mersea *Chelmsf* 71–73; P-in-c E Mersea 71–73; R W w E Mersea 73–75; rtd 93. *9 Howard Close, Bothenhampton, Bridport DT6 4SR* T: (01308) 424510 E: f.serjeant@gmail.com

SERJEANT, Heather Faith. *See* SMITH, Heather Faith

SERMON, Michael John. b 61. Univ of Cen England in Birm ACIB 85. Qu Coll Birm BA 98 MA 99. **d** 99 **p** 00. C W Heath Birm 99–03; V Blackheath 03–21; P-in-c Rounds Green 11–21; AD Warley and Edgbaston from 21. *64 Selwyn Road, Birmingham B16 0SW* E: mike@mikesermon.co.uk

SERTIN, Jonathan Paul Bartlett. b 67. **d** 14 **p** 15. NSM Earlsfield St Andr *S'wark* from 14. *1 Glebe House, Waynflete Street, London SW18 3QG* M: 07970-159090 E: johnny@becomingconsulting.com

SERVANT, Canon Alma Joan. b 51. Nottm Univ BA 76. Westcott Ho Cam 83. **dss** 85 **d** 87 **p** 94. Ordsall *S'well* 85–88; Par Dn 87–88; Par Dn Man Whitworth 88–94; TV 94–96; Chapl Man Poly 88–92; Chapl Man Metrop Univ 92–96; P-in-c Heaton Norris St Thos 96–00; P-in-c Hulme Ascension

00–05; R 05–14; C Man Cathl 14–15; C Man St Ann 14–15; Hon Can Man Cathl 02–15; rtd 15; PtO *Man* from 15. *10 Stoneyfield Close, Manchester M16 8GT*

SESSFORD, Canon Alan. b 34. Bps' Coll Cheshunt 65. **d** 66 **p** 67. C Highcliffe w Hinton Admiral *Win* 66–69; C Minehead *B & W* 70; C Chandler's Ford *Win* 70–73; V Burton and Sopley 73–00; RD Christchurch 93–98; Hon Can Win Cathl 98–00; rtd 00; PtO *Win* from 00; Chapl R Bournemouth and Christchurch Hosps NHS Foundn Trust 01–20. *4 Benson Close, Bransgore, Christchurch BH23 8HX* T: (01425) 673412

SETTERFIELD, Canon Nicholas Manley. b 63. Colchester Inst of Educn BA 89. St Steph Ho Ox 89. **d** 92 **p** 93. C Prestbury *Glouc* 92–96; R Letchworth *St Alb* 96–03; V Northampton St Matt *Pet* from 03; Can Pet Cathl from 17. *St Matthew's Vicarage, 30 East Park Parade, Northampton NN1 4LB* T: (01604) 604412 E: vicar@stmatthews-northampton.org.uk

SETTERFIELD, Pauline Jane. b 58. Huddersfield Univ BA 79. Ripon Coll Cuddesdon 18. **d** 20 **p** 21. C Tetbury, Beverston, Long Newnton etc *Glouc* from 20. *Stone Cottage, The Barton, Hawkesbury Upton, Badminton GL9 1AX* T: (01454) 238307 E: pleensetterfield@hotmail.com

SETTIMBA, John Henry. b 52. Nairobi Univ BSc 78 Leeds Univ MA 91. Pan Africa Chr Coll BA 78. **d** 78 **p** 80. Kenya 78–81; Uganda 81–85; C Allerton *Bradf* 86–87; C W Ham *Chelmsf* 87–91; C-in-c Forest Gate All SS 91–94; P-in-c 94–96; TV Hackney *Lon* 96–02; rtd 07. *63 Belvedere Court, Upper Richmond Road, London SW15 6HZ* T: (020) 3722 0279 E: henrysettimba@outlook.com

SEVILLE, Thomas Christopher John. b 57. Trin Hall Cam MA 80. Coll of Resurr Mirfield 87. **d** 89 **p** 90. C Knowle *Bris* 89–93; CR from 93. *House of the Resurrection, Stocks Bank Road, Mirfield WF14 0BN* T: (01924) 483315 E: tseville@mirfield.org.uk

SEWARD, Jolyon Frantom. b 57. Univ of Wales (Cardiff) BA 81. Chich Th Coll 83. **d** 86 **p** 87. C Llanblethian w Cowbridge and Llandough etc *Llan* 86–88; C Newton Nottage 88–93; Dioc Children's Officer 88–98; V Penyfai w Tondu 93–01; TV Heavitree and St Mary Steps *Ex* from 01. *St Lawrence's Vicarage, 36 Lower Hill Barton Road, Exeter EX1 3EH* T: (01392) 466302 *or* 677152 E: frjolyon@blueyonder.co.uk

SEWARD, Kristian Robert. b 68. Cranmer Hall Dur 18. **d** 20 **p** 21. C Clipston, Haselbech, Kelmarsh, Marston Trussell etc *Pet* from 20. *The Vicarage, 35 The Leys, Welford, Northampton NN6 6HS* E: krisseward@me.com *or* curate@nasebygroup.org

SEWARD, Nicholas. b 70. Imp Coll Lon BEng 97 Jo Coll Dur BA 96 MA 98. Cranmer Hall Dur 94. **d** 98 **p** 99. C Bearsted w Thurnham *Cant* 98–02; Chapl and Hd RS Magd Coll Sch Ox 02–08; Hd Kingham Hill Sch from 08. *Kingham Hill School, Kingham, Chipping Norton OX7 6TH* T: (01608) 658999 E: n.seward@kingham-hill.oxon.sch.uk

SEWELL, Andrew. *See* SEWELL, John Andrew Clarkson

SEWELL, The Ven Andrew William. b 61. Nottm Univ BSc 83. St Jo Coll Nottm 93. **d** 93 **p** 94. C Adel *Ripon* 93–96; C Far Headingley St Chad 96–98; Asst Dioc Missr 96–98; P-in-c Otham w Langley *Cant* 98–01; R 01–10; P-in-c Maidstone St Paul 10–20; AD Maidstone 10–20; Hon Can Cant Cathl 11–20; Adn Maidstone from 20. *The Archdeaconry, 267 Boxley Road, Penenden Heath, Maidstone ME14 2AE* T: (01622) 203529 E: andrew@asewell.plus.com

SEWELL, Canon Elizabeth Jill. b 56. Reading Univ BSc 77. Trin Coll Bris BA 97. **d** 97 **p** 98. C Rothley *Leic* 97–01; TV Market Harborough and The Transfiguration etc 01–07; RD Gartree I 06–07; TR Knaresborough *Ripon* 07–13; P-in-c Nidd 11–13; Can Res Ripon Cathl 13–16; rtd 16. *1 The Green, Bewerley, Harrogate HG3 5HU* E: jsewell13@gmail.com

SEWELL, Jacqueline. b 57. Auckland Univ BMus 80 LTh 85 K Coll Lon MA 00 PhD 15. St Jo Coll Auckland. **d** 84 **p** 85. C Warkworth NZ 84–85; P-in-c 85–86; TV Glenfield 87–91; Dioc Youth Facilitator 92–03; Dir Amaze Cen 02–05; Dir Field Educn St Jo Coll Auckland 05–12; Tutor Cuddesdon: Glouc and Heref from 15; Dioc Dir Reader Tr *Heref* from 15. *Diocesan Office, The Palace, Hereford HR4 9BL* T: (01432) 373300 E: jacky.sewell@rcc.ac.uk

SEWELL, John Andrew Clarkson. b 58. Aston Tr Scheme 93 Ripon Coll Cuddesdon 95. **d** 97 **p** 98. C Horsham *Chich* 97–99; C Cleobury Mortimer w Hopton Wafers etc *Heref* 99–01; R 01–03; TV Ludlow, Ludford, Ashford Carbonell etc 03–04; Chapl Shropshire's Community NHS Trust 03–04; Lead Chapl ChAT (Weston-super-Mare Chapl About Town) *B & W* 05–10; Hon C Weston super Mare St Jo 06–07; P-in-c Westbury sub Mendip w Easton 07–09; Retail Chapl Bris City Cen 10–17; Min Can Bris Cathl 15–17; R Redmarley D'Abitot, Bromesberrow, Pauntley etc *Glouc* 17–18. *Address temp unknown* E: rectorandy@icloud.com

SEWELL, Canon Richard Michael. b 62. Birm Univ BA 84. SEITE 99. **d** 02 **p** 03. C Putney St Mary *S'wark* 02–05; TV

Wimbledon 05–10; TR Barnes 10–18; Dir IME Kingston Area 12–18; Dean St Geo Coll Jerusalem from 18; Hon Can S'wark Cathl from 19. *St George's College, PO Box 1248, Jerusalem 91000, via Israel* T: (00972) (2) 626 4704 M: 07714-265864 E: richardsewell4@virginmedia.com

SEWELL, Miss Sarah Frances. b 61. Wycliffe Hall Ox 87. **d** 91 **p** 94. C Binley *Cov* 91–94; Asst Chapl Derriford Hosp Plymouth 94–96; Chapl Stoke Mandeville Hosp NHS Trust 96–00; Chapl R Marsden NHS Foundn Trust 00–05; Chapl Team Ldr Epsom and St Helier Univ Hosps NHS Trust 05–07; Sen Co-ord Chapl 07–13; Lead Chapl 13–18; C Sutton *S'wark* 14–18; Lead Chapl Ox Univ Hosps NHS Foundn Trust from 18. *Chaplaincy Office, John Radcliffe Hospital, Headley Way, Headington, Oxford OX3 9DU* T: (01865) 857921 M: 07552-262974

SEXTON, Canon Michael Bowers. b 28. SS Coll Cam BA 52 MA 56. Wells Th Coll 52. **d** 54 **p** 55. C Miles Platting St Luke *Man* 54–57; C Bradford cum Beswick 57–58; C-in-c Oldham St Chad Limeside CD 58–62; R Filby w Thrigby w Mautby *Nor* 62–72; P-in-c Runham 67–72; P-in-c Stokesby w Herringby 68–72; R Hethersett w Canteloff 72–85; V Ketteringham 73–84; RD Humbleyard 81–86; Hon Can Nor Cathl 85–93; R Hethersett w Canteloff w Lt and Gt Melton 85–86; V Hunstanton St Mary w Ringstead Parva, Holme etc 86–93; rtd 94; PtO *Nor* from 94. *3 Forge Close, Poringland, Norwich NR14 7SZ* T: (01508) 493885

SEYMOUR, Canon David Raymond Russell. b 56. Keble Coll Ox BA 79 MA 88. St Steph Ho Ox 79. **d** 81 **p** 82. C Tilehurst St Mich *Ox* 81–85; TV Parkstone St Pet w Branksea and St Osmund *Sarum* 85–91; V Bradford-on-Avon Ch 91–01; P-in-c Sturminster Newton and Hinton St Mary 01–02; V Sturminster Newton, Hinton St Mary and Lydlinch 02–18; C Hazelbury Bryan and the Hillside Par 08–18; C Okeford 08–18; P-in-c Marnhull 15–18; RD Blackmore Vale 08–16; Can and Preb Sarum Cathl 13–18; P-in-c Blisland w Temple, St Breward and Helland *Truro* 18–19; P-in-c St Tudy w St Mabyn and Michaelstow 18–19; R Camelside from 19. *The Rectory, Glebe Parc, St Tudy, Bodmin PL30 3AS* T: (01208) 850088 E: drrseymour@hotmail.co.uk

SEYMOUR, John. b 73. Bris Univ BSc 95 MB, ChB 98 Heythrop Coll Lon MA 03 Trin Coll Cam BA 05. Westcott Ho Cam 03. **d** 06 **p** 07. C Poplar *Lon* 06–09; Chapl Twyford C of E High Sch Acton 09–17; Tutor St Aug Coll of Th 17–19; PtO *Lon* 17–20; C Eastcote St Lawr from 20; Public Preacher *S'wark* from 17; PtO *St Alb* from 19. *The Vicarage, 2 Bridle Road, Pinner HA5 2SJ* T: (020) 7939 9400 or 8996 9350 M: 07535-049710 E: john.seymour@london.anglican.org

SEYMOUR, John Anthony. b 46. SWMTC. **d** 08 **p** 09. NSM Carbis Bay w Lelant *Truro* 08–11; P-in-c 11–13; rtd 13; PtO *Truro* from 16. *5 Station Hill, Lelant, St Ives TR26 3DJ* T: (01736) 449794 E: tonyseymour@talktalk.net

SEYMOUR, Canon John Charles. b 30. Oak Hill Th Coll 51 and 55 Wycliffe Coll Toronto 54. **d** 57 **p** 58. C Islington St Andr w St Thos and St Matthias *Lon* 57–60; C Worthing St Geo *Chich* 60–63; V Thornton *Leic* 63–70; R Kirby Muxloe 70–81; TR 81–83; RD Sparkenhoe I 83–88; R Market Bosworth w Shenton 83–87; TR Market Bosworth, Cadeby w Sutton Cheney etc 87–93; RD Sparkenhoe W 89–92; Hon Can Leic Cathl 82–93; rtd 93; PtO *Leic* 15–18. *56 William House, Wyggestons, 160 Hinkley Road, Leicester LE3 0UX* T: 0116-254 8295 E: jams56@btinternet.com

SEYMOUR, Paul Edward. b 62. Humberside Univ BA 92. St Jo Coll Nottm 01. **d** 03 **p** 04. C Ingleby Barwick *York* 03–07; C Hatfield Hyde *St Alb* 07–10; P-in-c Stevenage All SS Pin Green 10–13; V 13–16; TV Bishop's Hatfield, Lemsford and N Mymms 16–21; V Panshanger from 21. *69 Hardings, Welwyn Garden City AL7 2HA* M: 07809-839773 E: revpaulseymour@icloud.com *or* revpaulseymour@gmail.com

SEYMOUR-JONES, Michael D'Israeli. b 37. **d** 09. OLM Shiplake w Dunsden and Harpsden *Ox* 09–12; PtO from 13. *6 Heathfield Close, Binfield Heath, Henley-on-Thames RG9 4DS* T: 0118-947 8632 E: m.seymour_jones@btinternet.com

SEYMOUR-WHITELEY, Ms Alison. b 51. City of Lon Poly MA 90 Homerton Coll Cam PGCE 95. CITC 04. **d** 07 **p** 08. LtO *Clogh* 07–11; Chapl HM Pris Morton Hall 11–12; Chapl Notts Healthcare NHS Foundn Trust 12–15; P-in-c Templemore w Thurles and Kilfithmone *C, F & O* 15–20; rtd 20. *The Rectory, The Square, Rathdowney, Co Laois, Republic of Ireland* M: (00353) 85-141 3354 E: alisonsw@hotmail.co.uk

SHACKELL, Daniel William. b 42. **d** 95 **p** 96. Dir Spires Cen S'wark 93–06; OLM Streatham St Leon *S'wark* 95–99; LtO 99–06; rtd 07; PtO *Guildf* 01–09; *Sarum* from 09. *Wynways, 146 West Bay Road, Bridport DT6 4AZ* T: (01308) 426514 M: 07818-808249 E: danshackell@gmail.com

SHACKERLEY, The Very Revd Albert Paul. b 56. K Coll Lon MA 97 Sheff Univ PhD 07. Chich Th Coll 91. d 93 p 94. C Harlesden All So *Lon* 93–96; P-in-c Chelmsf All SS 96–98; V 98–02; Can Res Sheff Cathl 02–09; Vice Dean 05–09; V Doncaster St Geo 10–14; Hon Can Sheff Cathl 10–14; Dean Brecon *S & B* from 14. *The Cathedral Office, Cathedral Close, Brecon LD3 9DP* T: (01874) 623857   E: paul_shackerley@btinternet.com   *or* dean@breconcathedral.org.uk

SHACKLADY, Mrs Thelma. b 38. Liv Univ BA 60. St Alb Minl Tr Scheme 89. d 92 p 94. NSM Luton St Andr *St Alb* 92–96; NSM Luton All SS w St Pet 96–03; PtO from 03; *Ox* from 06. *45 Lilly Hill, Olney MK46 5EZ* T: (01234) 712997 E: thelma.shacklady@gmail.com

SHACKLETON, Canon Alan. b 31. Sheff Univ BA 53. Wells Th Coll 54. d 56 p 57. C Ladybarn *Man* 56–58; C Bolton St Pet 58–61; V Middleton Junction 61–70; V Heywood St Luke 70–84; AD Rochdale 82–92; Hon Can Man Cathl 84–97; V Heywood St Luke w All So 85–86; TV Rochdale 86–91; TR 91–97; rtd 97; PtO *Man* 97–17. *28 Taunton Avenue, Rochdale OL11 5LD* T: (01706) 645335

SHAFTO, Robert James. b 38. Univ of Wales (Ban) BTh 06 Heythrop Coll Lon MA 10 FCA 61. OLM course 96. d 99 p 00. NSM W Dulwich All SS *S'wark* 99–07; rtd 07; PtO *S'wark* from 08. *46 Cedar Close, London SE21 8HX* T: (020) 8761 7395 E: bob.shafto46@gmail.com

SHAKESHAFT, Mrs Petra Jayne. b 60. Anglia Ruskin Univ BA 97 Cam Univ BTh 14. Westcott Ho Cam 12. d 14 p 15. C Cherry Hinton St Jo *Ely* 14–17; P-in-c Duxford 17–19; P-in-c Hinxton 17–19; P-in-c Ickleton 17–19; P-in-c Pampisford 17–19; P-in-c Whittlesford 17–19; PtO from 20. *20 Paddock Way, Sawston, Cambridge CB22 3JS* M: 07847-307416 E: petra_paul.shakeshaft@ntlworld.com

SHAKESPEARE, James Douglas Geoffrey. b 71. Fitzw Coll Cam BA 93 MA 97 Man Univ MA 96. Westcott Ho Cam 97. d 99 p 00. C Cherry Hinton St Jo *Ely* 99–02; Bp's Chapl and Policy Adv *Leic* 02–05; P-in-c Birstall and Wanlip 05–09; R 09–10; NSM Market Harborough and The Transfiguration etc 10–11; TV 11–17; P-in-c Cherry Hinton St Jo *Ely* 17–21; V from 21; Asst Dir of Ords from 19. *St John's Vicarage, 9 Luard Road, Cambridge CB2 8PJ* T: (01223) 241815 *or* 241316 E: jshakespeare@btinternet.com

SHAKESPEARE, Steven. b 68. CCC Cam BA 89 PhD 94. Westcott Ho Cam 93. d 96 p 97. C Cambridge St Jas *Ely* 96–99; V Endcliffe and Chapl Sheff Hallam Univ 99–03; Chapl Liv Hope Univ from 03; PtO *Liv* from 16. *Anglican Chaplaincy, Hope Park, Taggart Avenue, Liverpool L16 9JD* T: 0151-291 3545 E: shakess@hope.ac.uk

SHALLOE, Jacqueline. St Mellitus Coll 15. d 18 p 19. NSM Hillingdon St Jo *Lon* 18–19; NSM Greenford H Cross 19–21; V Preston from 21. *319 Preston Road, Harrow HA3 0QQ* M: 07543-975577

SHAMEL-WOOD, Mrs Sorrel May. b 87. Dur Univ BA 09 Homerton Coll Cam PGCE 10 MEd 11. Ripon Coll Cuddesdon BA 19 MSt 20. d 20. C Dorchester *Ox* from 20. *26 Windrush Road, Berinsfield, Wallingford OX10 7PF* T: (01865) 341427 E: revdsorrelshamelwood@gmail.com

SHAND, Brian Martin. b 53. Univ Coll Lon BA 76 PhD 82. St Steph Ho Ox 85. d 87 p 88. C Uxbridge St Marg *Lon* 87–88; C Uxbridge 88–90; C Worplesdon *Guildf* 90–94; Relig Affairs Producer BBC Radio Surrey 90–94; V Weston *Guildf* 94–01; V Witley 01–14; rtd 14; PtO *Guildf* from 17. *Tan Cottage, Garden Close, Shamley Green, Guildford GU5 0UW* T: (01483) 894066

SHANKS, Canon Robert Andrew Gulval. b 54. Ball Coll Ox BA 75 G&C Coll Cam BA 79 Leeds Univ PhD 90. Westcott Ho Cam 77. d 80 p 81. C Potternewton *Ripon* 80–83; C Stanningley St Thos 84–87; Lect Leeds Univ 87–91; Teaching Fell Lanc Univ *Blackb* 91–95; Research Fell in Th Cheltenham and Glouc Coll of HE 95–96; NSM Leeds City *Ripon* 95–96; P-in-c Upper Ryedale and CME Officer Cleveland Adnry *York* 97–04; Can Res Man Cathl 04–14; rtd 14; PtO *York* from 14; *Eur* from 16. *39 Derwent Mews, York YO10 3DN* T: (01904) 500253 E: shanks.york@gmail.com

SHANNON, Alexander David John. b 86. Ch Coll Cam BA 07 MMath 08 PhD 13 Peterho Cam MPhil 16. Westcott Ho Cam 2013. d 16 p 17. C St Ives *Ely* 16–20; P-in-c Finchingfield and Cornish Hall End etc *Chelmsf* from 20. *The Vicarage, Bardfield Road, Finchingfield, Braintree CM7 4JR* M: 07483-878659 E: rev.alex.shannon@gmail.com

SHANNON, Helen Louise. b 68. NTMTC 07. d 10 p 12. C Woodside Park St Barn *Lon* from 10. *24 Stable Walk, London N2 9RD* T: (020) 8883 7450 M: 07866-507609 E: helenshannon@stbarnabas.org.uk

SHANNON, Canon Trevor Haslam. b 33. Selw Coll Cam BA 57 MA 61 Lon Univ BD 69. Westcott Ho Cam 57. d 59 p 60. C Moss Side Ch Ch *Man* 59–62; V Woolfold 62–66;

Chapl Forest Sch Snaresbrook 66–80 and 87–88; V Gt Ilford St Marg *Chelmsf* 88–90; TR Gt Ilford St Clem and St Marg 90–96; V 96–99; RD Redbridge 90–95; Hon Can Chelmsf Cathl 93–99; rtd 99; PtO *Nor* from 00. *Honeysuckle Cottage, Clubbs Lane, Wells-next-the-Sea NR23 1DP* T: (01328) 711409 E: tshannon409@btinternet.com

SHARKEY, Philip Michael. b 50. York Univ BA 73 MA 08 CQSW 78. ERMC 06. d 08 p 09. NSM Shingay Gp *Ely* 08–13; NSM Duxford 13–21; NSM Hinxton 13–21; NSM Ickleton 13–21; Chapl Cam Univ Hosps NHS Foundn Trust from 19. *23 Priory Drive, Royston SG8 7DL* T: (01763) 221284 M: 07917-619124 E: sharkey_phil@yahoo.co.uk

SHARLAND, Canon Marilyn. b 40. City of Birm Coll CertEd 61. Oak Hill Th Coll 84. d 87 p 94. Barkingside St Laur *Chelmsf* 86–88; Hon Par Dn Hucclecote *Glouc* 88–89; C Coney Hill 89–98; P-in-c Tuffley 98–99; V 99–06; Hon Can Glouc Cathl 02–06; rtd 06. *51 Lynmouth Road, Hucclecote, Gloucester GL3 3JD* E: canon.marilyn@gmail.com

SHARLAND, Ms Sarah Jane. b 65. Sussex Univ BSc 89. Trin Coll Bris BA 18. d 18 p 19. C Plympton *Ex* 18–20; C Pennycross from 20. *22 Priory Mill, Plympton, Plymouth PL7 1WR* T: (01752) 941612 M: 07527-443241 E: s.j.sharland@outlook.com

SHARP, Alexander Mark. b 87. Univ Coll Falmouth BA 08. Oak Hill Th Coll BA 17. d 18 p 19. C St Illogan *Truro* from 18. *14 Glenfeadon Terrace, Portreath, Redruth TR16 4JX* M: 07717-748353 E: alexsharp353@gmail.com

SHARP, Mrs Barbara Elaine. b 52. Open Univ BA 84. Ripon Coll Cuddesdon 01. d 03 p 04. C Timperley *Ches* 03–06; P-in-c Lostock Gralam 06–11; V Sale St Paul 11–21; rtd 21. *2 Beech Grove, Warrington WA4 1EG* E: revbarb@hotmail.co.uk

SHARP, Brian Phillip. b 48. Kent Univ MA 07. Cant Sch of Min 85. d 88 p 89. C S Ashford Ch Ch *Cant* 88–92; C St Laur in Thanet 92–96; V Margate St Jo 96–13; P-in-c Margate All SS 09–13; PtO *Cant* from 14. *32 The Hawthorns, Broadstairs CT10 2NG* T: (01843) 579871 E: brianthevic@yahoo.co.uk

SHARP, Mrs Hazel Patricia. b 39. Qu Eliz Coll Lon BSc 61. SWMTC 05. d 06 p 07. NSM St Merryn and St Issey w St Petroc Minor *Truro* 06–09; rtd 09; PtO *B & W* 10–11; Chapl Somerset Partnership NHS Foundn Trust 11–14; PtO *B & W* from 14. *22 Bekynton Avenue, Wells BA5 3NF* T: (01749) 674397 M: 07751-258558 E: hh.psharp@btinternet.com

SHARP (née BROWN), Mrs Jane Madeline. b 54. d 97 p 98. C Aylestone St Andr w St Jas *Leic* 97–00; NSM Knighton St Mary Magd 00–08; NSM Leic St Jas from 08; Chapl Leic Coll of FE from 14. *10 St Mary's Road, Leicester LE2 1XA* T: 0116-270 6002

SHARP, Mrs Janice Anne. b 54. Aston Tr Scheme 91 NOC 93. d 96 p 97. C Skipton H Trin *Bradf* 96–00; V Buttershaw St Paul 00–02; Chapl Hull and E Yorks Hosps NHS Trust 02–17; Hon C Patrington w Hollym, Welwick and Winestead *York* 07–14; Hon C Easington w Skeffling, Keyingham, Ottringham etc from 14. *3 Ringrose Cottages, Northside Road, Hollym, Withernsea HU19 2RS* T: (01964) 612548 E: jas5000.js@googlemail.com

SHARP, Nicholas Leonard. b 64. Grey Coll Dur BA 85. St Jo Coll Nottm MA 95. d 95 p 96. C Oakwood St Thos *Lon* 95–99; TV N Farnborough *Guildf* 99–05; Chapl Farnborough Sixth Form Coll 01–05; P-in-c Lt Amwell *St Alb* 05–08; TV Hertford 08–18; V Rye Park St Cuth from 18. *The Vicarage, 8 Ogard Road, Hoddesdon EN11 0NU* E: nicthevic@gmail.com

SHARP, Philip Paul Clayton. b 66. Open Univ BSc 97. Trin Coll Bris 04. d 06 p 07. C Liskeard and St Keyne *Truro* 06–11; P-in-c St Martin w Looe 11–17; C Duloe, Herodsfoot, Morval and St Pinnock 11–17; R Looe and Morval 17–21; RD W Wivelshire 13–18. *Address temp unknown* E: ppsharp@tiscali.co.uk

SHARP, Miss Sarah Elizabeth. b 67. Bp Otter Coll Chich BA 89 Anglia Poly Univ MA 00 K Coll Lon MA 11 Coll of Ripon & York St Jo PGCE 90. Westcott Ho Cam 98. d 00 p 01. C Ross *Heref* 00–03; R Lower Windrush *Ox* 03–13; V Bodicote from 13; AD Deddington from 19. *2 The Rydes, Bodicote, Banbury OX15 4EJ* T: (01295) 250282 E: ss550sharp@btinternet.com

SHARP, Thomas Matthew. b 91. St Cath Coll Cam BA 12 MA 16 St Jo Coll Dur BA 16 MA 19. Cranmer Hall Dur 14. d 17 p 18. C Chapel House *Newc* 17–18; C Newc Cathl from 18. *Flat 2, St Luke's Church House, Hugh Street, Wallsend NE28 6RL* M: 07769-737314 E: fr.tomsharp@gmail.com

SHARP, Trevor Andrew. b 63. Westcott Ho Cam. d 14 p 15. C St Mary-at-Latton *Chelmsf* 14–17; V Norton *St Alb* from 17. *The Vicarage, 17 Norton Way North, Letchworth Garden City SG6 1BY* M: 07970-284332 E: trevorann@hotmail.co.uk *or* revtrev08@gmail.com

SHARPE, Anthony Mark. b 67. Leeds Univ BA 01. Coll of Resurr Mirfield 99. d 01 p 02. C Acomb Moor *York* 01–02; C Norton juxta Malton 02–03; C W Buckrose 03–04; Chapl RN 04–05; R Teme Valley S *Worc* 05–09; rtd 09. *Old Rectory, Ceodana, Lannerch-y-Medd LL71 8EW* E: am67sharpe@aol.com

SHARPE, Canon Bruce Warrington. b 41. JP 88. Ely Th Coll 62 St Steph Ho Ox 64. **d** 65 **p** 66. C Streatham St Pet *S'wark* 65–67; C Castries St Lucia 67–68; Hon C Leic St Matt and St Geo 68–69; Hon C Catford St Laur *S'wark* 69–70; Hon C Deptford St Paul 70–75; Hon C Lamorbey H Redeemer *Roch* 76–83; PtO 83–88; Hon C Sidcup St Andr 88–99; PtO 99–01; Hon C Bickley 01–11; Locum Chapl Morden Coll Blackheath 98–08; PtO *Lon* 97–06; *S'wark* 98–10 and from 17; *Ex* from 09; Hon Can Windward Is from 01. *Walnut Cottage, Upper Braddons Hill Road, Torquay TQ1 1QE* E: canonbruce1@aol.com

SHARPE, David Francis. b 32. Ex Coll Ox BA 56 MA 59. St Steph Ho Ox 57. **d** 60 **p** 61. C Hunslet St Mary and Stourton *Ripon* 60–63; C Notting Hill St Jo *Lon* 63–68; V Haggerston St Mary w St Chad 68–78; P-in-c Haggerston St Aug w St Steph 73–78; V Haggerston St Chad 78–83; V Mill Hill St Mich 83–98; rtd 98; Chapl St Raphaël *Eur* 98–02; PtO *Lon* 02–13; *S'wark* from 11. *10 Up, The Quadrangle, Morden College, London SE3 0PW* T: (020) 8853 5104

SHARPE, Miss Jennifer Louise. b 74. St Jo Coll Nottm BA 15. **d** 15 **p** 16. C Mansfield St Jo w St Mary *S'well* 15–16; C Warsop 16–19; P-in-c Stockton Christchurch *Dur* from 19. *243 Darlington Lane, Stockton-on-Tees TS19 8AA* T: (01642) 602036 E: jenniesharpe2305@gmail.com *or* revdjenniesharpe@gmail.com

SHARPE, Miss Joan Valerie. b 33. EMMTC 73. **dss** 84 **d** 88 **p** 94. Hon Par Dn Warsop *S'well* 88–94; Hon C 94–98; rtd 98; PtO *S'well* 04–18. *1 Forest Court, Eakring Road, Mansfield NG18 3DP* T: (01623) 424051

SHARPE, Canon John Edward. b 50. St Jo Coll Dur BSc 72. Cranmer Hall Dur 73. **d** 76 **p** 77. C Woodford Wells *Chelmsf* 76–79; C Ealing St Mary *Lon* 79–83; Min Walsall St Martin *Lich* 83–87; TV Walsall 87–96; R Glenfield *Leic* 96–15; AD Sparkenhoe E 03–11; Hon Can Leic Cathl 10–15; rtd 15; PtO *Glouc* from 16; Clergy Retirement Officer from 20. *18 Bramble Chase, Bishops Cleeve, Cheltenham GL52 8WN* T: (01242) 677057 E: jesharpe1@btinternet.com

SHARPE, The Ven Kenneth William. b 40. Univ of Wales (Lamp) BA 61. Sarum Th Coll 61. **d** 63 **p** 64. C Hubberston *St D* 63–71; TV Cwmbran *Mon* 71–74; Dioc Children's Adv 72–82; Dioc Youth Chapl 74–82; V Dingestow and Llangovan w Penyclawdd and Tregaer 74–82; V Newport St Mark 82–97; Chapl Alltyryn Hosp Gwent 83–97; RD Newport *Mon* 93–97; Can St Woolos Cathl 94–08; Adn Newport 97–08; rtd 08; PtO *St D* from 09. *27 Incline Way, Saundersfoot SA69 9LX* T: (01834) 813674

SHARPE, Lance Roland. b 68. Birm Chr Coll MA 10. Birm Bible Inst 91. **d** 16 **p** 17. NSM Morriston *S & B* 16–19; Sen Chapl Abertawe Bro Morgannwg Univ Health Bd 16–19; P-in-c Gwastedyn *S & B* from 19. *Rhayader Vicarage, Dark Lane, Rhayader LD6 5DA* M: 07938-762570 E: lancersharpe@gmail.com

SHARPE, Mrs Margaret Joy. b 43. Qu Coll Birm. **d** 09 **p** 10. OLM Bilton *Cov* 09–12; NSM 12–18; rtd 18; PtO *Cov* from 18. *60 Cymbeline Way, Bilton, Rugby CV22 6LA* T: (01788) 810794

SHARPE, Mrs Margaret Therèsa. b 48. Man Univ BEd 70. Cranmer Hall Dur 72 WMMTC 90. **d** 91 **p** 94. C W Bromwich H Trin *Lich* 91–96; Asst Chapl Glenfield Hosp NHS Trust Leic 96–99; Chapl 99–00; Chapl Univ Hosps Leic NHS Trust 00–04; Chapl Team Ldr 04–12; rtd 12; PtO *Leic* 13–16; *Glouc* from 16. *18 Bramble Chase, Bishops Cleeve, Cheltenham GL52 8WN* T: (01242) 677057 E: mtsharpe@btinternet.com

SHARPE, Mark. *See* SHARPE, Anthony Mark

SHARPE, Peter Richard. b 55. Salford Univ BSc 76 ACIB 81. STETS 98. **d** 01 **p** 02. C Ex St Jas 01–04; R S Hill w Callington *Truro* 04–12; C St Ive and Pensilva w Quethiock 09–12; P-in-c Linkinhorne and Stoke Climsland 10–12; RD E Wivelshire 11–12; P-in-c St Keverne 12–16; P-in-c St Ruan w St Grade and Landewednack 12–16; R St Keverne, St Ruan w St Grade and Landewednack 16–20; rtd 20. *10 Siskin Chase, Cullompton EX15 1UD* E: peter@isaiah504.org

SHARPE, Richard Gordon. b 48. Birm Univ BA 69. St Jo Coll Nottm BA 74. **d** 75 **p** 76. C Hinckley H Trin *Leic* 75–78; C Kingston upon Hull H Trin *York* 78–85; Chapl Marston Green Hosp Birm 85–88; Chapl Chelmsley Hosp Birm 86–88; TV Chelmsley Wood *Birm* 85–88; P-in-c Dosthill 88–93; V 93–97; R Desford and Peckleton w Tooley *Leic* 97–12; rtd 12; PtO *York* from 17. *17 Elmslac Road, Helmsley, York YO62 5AW* T: (01439) 770031 E: sharpeselmslac@hotmail.com

SHARPE, Canon Roger. b 35. TCD BA 60 MA 63. Qu Coll Birm 60. **d** 62 **p** 63. C Stockton H Trin *Dur* 62–64; C Oakdale

St Geo *Sarum* 64–68; V Redlynch and Morgan's Vale 68–86; RD Alderbury 82–86; V Warminster St Denys 86–88; R Upton Scudamore 86–88; V Horningsham 86–88; R Warminster St Denys, Upton Scudamore etc 88–95; Can and Preb Sarum Cathl 89–00; RD Heytesbury 89–95; Chmn Dioc Assn for Deaf 91–98; P-in-c Corsley *Sarum* 92–95; TR Cley Hill Warminster 95–00; rtd 00; PtO *Sarum* from 01. *Woodside, Bugmore Lane, East Grimstead SP5 3SA* T: (01722) 712753 E: rsharpe@macline.co.uk

SHARPE, William Wilberforce. b 62. **d** 05 **p** 06. NSM Brixton St Matt w St Jude *S'wark* 05–10; NSM Tulse Hill H Trin and St Matthias from 10; Chapl Guy's and St Thos' NHS Foundn Trust 08–18; Sen Chapl and Dep Team Ldr from 18. *1D Lovelace Road, London SE21 8JY* T/F: (020) 8761 8539 M: 07912-205414 E: sharpeww@aol.com *or* william.sharpe@gstt.nhs.uk

SHARPLES, Catherine Ruth. b 70. Nottm Univ BSc 92 Nottm Trent Univ PhD 96. Trin Coll Bris 11. **d** 13 **p** 14. C Stevenage St Pet Broadwater *St Alb* 13–17; V from 17. *St Peter's Vicarage, 1 The Willows, Stevenage SG2 8AN* T: (01438) 217526 M: 07505-459157 E: revkatesharples@gmail.com

SHARPLES, The Ven David John. b 58. Lon Univ BD 81 AKC 81. Coll of Resurr Mirfield. **d** 82 **p** 83. C Prestwich St Mary *Man* 82–87; V Royton St Anne 87–02; AD Tandle 94–02; Dir of Ords from 02; Adn Salford 09–20; Adn Rochdale from 20; Hon Can Man Cathl from 06; Can Res Man Cathl from 17. *2 The Walled Gardens, Swinton, Manchester M27 0FR* T: 0161-794 2331 *or* 708 9366 F: 794 2411 M: 07909-231278 E: ddo@bishopscourt.manchester.anglican.org *or* archsalford@manchester.anglican.org

SHARPLES, Gregory Stephen. b 80. **d** 14 **p** 15. C S Widnes *Liv* 14–17; TV 17–21; V Widnes St Jo and St Paul from 21. *St Mary's Vicarage, St Mary's Road, Widnes WA8 0DN* M: 07730-512603

SHARPLES, Jean. *See* ROLT, Jean

SHARPLES, Jonathan David. b 65. Lon Bible Coll BA 95. Wycliffe Hall Ox 03. **d** 05 **p** 06. C Ashton-upon-Mersey St Mary Magd *Ches* 05–09; R Astbury and Smallwood 09–14. *Address withheld by request* E: jonsharples@hotmail.com

SHAVE, Canon Norman Rossen. b 60. G&C Coll Cam BA 82 MA 95 Newc Univ MB, BS 85 MRCGP 90. Cranmer Hall Dur 98. **d** 00 **p** 01. C Preston on Tees *Dur* 00–03; C Preston-on-Tees and Longnewton 03–04; V Norton St Mary 04–12; P-in-c Stockton St Chad 04–12; P-in-c Stranton 12–16; V from 16; P-in-c Hartlepool St Luke from 19; Hon Can Dur Cathl from 19. *The Vicarage, 34A Westbourne Road, Hartlepool TS25 5RE* T: (01429) 233609

SHAW, Alan Taylor. b 52. Sarum & Wells Th Coll 88. **d** 90 **p** 91. C Beeston *Ripon* 90–93; C Stanningley St Thos 93–96; TV Seacroft 96–98; V Ryhill *Wakef* 98–02; rtd 03; PtO *Wakef* 04–14; *Leeds* from 14. *65 Hollingthorpe Avenue, Hall Green, Wakefield WF4 3NP* T: (01924) 255210

SHAW, Alan Walter. b 41. TCD BA 63 BAI 63 Chu Coll Cam MSc 66. **d** 94 **p** 95. NSM Drumcliffe w Kilnasoolagh *L & K* 94–97; NSM Kenmare w Sneem, Waterville etc 97–09; Can Limerick Cathl 07–09; rtd 09. *22 Ceann Mara Court, Pairc na Gloine, Kenmare, Co Kerry, Republic of Ireland* T: (00353) (64) 664 0626 M: 87-678 8700 E: shawa@eircom.net

✠**SHAW, The Rt Revd Alexander Martin.** b 44. AKC 67. **d** 68 **p** 69 **c** 04. C Glas St Oswald 68–70; C Edin Old St Paul 70–75; Chapl K Coll Cam 75–77; C St Marylebone All SS *Lon* 77–78; R Dunoon *Arg* 78–83; Succ Ex Cathl 81–83; Dioc Miss and Ecum Officer 83–89; TV Cen Ex 83–87; Can Res St E Cathl 89–04; Prec 96–04; Bp Arg 04–09; rtd 09; Hon Asst Bp Ex from 10; Can Res and Prec Ex Cathl 17–18. *11 Russell Terrace, Exeter EX4 4HX* T: (01392) 663511 M: 07801-549615 E: amartinshaw@gmail.com

SHAW, Mrs Alison Barbara. b 55. Open Univ BA 92. SWMTC 98. **d** 01 **p** 02. NSM St Breoke and Egloshayle *Truro* 01–03; C Bodmin w Lanhydrock and Lanivet 03–05; TV 05–10; TV Devonport St Boniface and St Phil *Ex* 10–14; V Devonport St Boniface 14–16; P-in-c Stoke Fleming, Blackawton and Strete 16–17; V Stoke Fleming, Blackawton, Strete and E Allington from 17; RD Woodleigh from 19. *The Rectory, Rectory Lane, Stoke Fleming, Dartmouth TQ6 0QB* T: (01803) 770868 E: alishaw2001@yahoo.co.uk

SHAW, Andrew James. b 54. MBE 12. York Univ MA 97 Cumbria Univ BA 10. LCTP 07. **d** 10 **p** 11. NSM Fleetwood St Dav and Fleetwood St Pet *Blackb* 10–13; NSM Waterside Par 13–15; V 15–19; NSM Stalmine w Pilling 13–15; V 15–19; V Over Wyre from 20. *St John's Vicarage, Lancaster Road, Pilling, Preston PR3 6AE* T: (01253) 799895 E: pillingrev@btconnect.com

SHAW, Anne. *See* MORRIS, Anne

SHAW, Ms Anne Lesley. b 50. SRN SCM. Linc Th Coll 77. **dss** 80 **d** 87 **p** 94. Camberwell St Luke *S'wark* 80–85; Chapl

Asst R Lon Hosp (Whitechapel) 85–90; Chapl Lewisham Hosp 90–94; Chapl Hither Green Hosp 90–94; Chapl Sydenham Childrens Hosp 90–94; Chapl Lewisham Hosp NHS Trust 94–10; rtd 10; PtO S'wark 11–13; Cant from 14. *54 Nutcroft Road, London SE15 1AF* T: (020) 7639 4031 E: shawpowell@hotmail.co.uk

SHAW, Anne Patricia Leslie. b 39. MB, BS 63 MRCS 63 LRCP 63. Qu Coll Birm 79. **dss** 81 **d** 87 **p** 94. Pinner Lon 81–84; Rickmansworth *St Alb* 84–09; NSM 87–09; rtd 09; PtO *St Alb* from 09. *37 Sandy Lodge Road, Moor Park, Rickmansworth WD3 1LP* T: (01923) 827663 E: anneshaw@doctors.org.uk

SHAW, Anthony Keeble. b 36. K Alfred's Coll Win CertEd 60 Birkbeck Coll Lon CPsychol 98. SWMTC 78. **d** 81 **p** 82. Hd Teacher Wolborough C of E Primary Sch 73–87; NSM E Teignmouth *Ex* 81–83; NSM Highweek and Teigngrace 83–87; Sub Chapl HM Pris Channings Wood 85–87; C Southbourne St Kath *Win* 87–89; Teaching 89–96; NSM Regent's Park St Mark *Lon* 93–96; P-in-c Winthorpe and Langford w Holme S'well 96–01; Dioc Chief Insp of Schs 96–01; rtd 01; PtO *Win* from 01. *Manlea Cottage, Centre Lane, Everton, Lymington SO41 0JP* T: (01590) 645451

SHAW, Craig Lee. b 72. Newc Univ LLB 94. Cranmer Hall Dur 12. **d** 14 **p** 15. C Penkridge *Lich* 14–17; PtO *Ches* from 18; P-in-c Essington *Lich* 19; P-in-c Shareshill 19; V Essington, Featherstone and Shareshill 19; Chapl Northn Gen Hosp NHS Trust from 19. *The Chaplaincy Department, Northampton General Hospital Trust, Cliftonville, Northampton NN1 5BD* T: (01604) 634700 M: 07443-505615 E: craig.shaw@ngh.nhs.uk

SHAW, David George. b 40. Lon Univ BD 64 MA 03. Tyndale Hall Bris 58. **d** 65 **p** 66. C Kirkdale St Lawr *Liv* 65–68; C Bebington *Ches* 68–70; V Swadlincote *Derby* 70–75; R Eyam 75–04; rtd 04; PtO *Sarum* 15–20. *7 Battle Walk, Lansdown, Bath BA1 9AX* T: (01225) 251473 E: berdavshaw@outlook.com

SHAW, Canon David Michael. b 61. Univ Coll Dur BA 83 Bris Univ BA 97. Trin Coll Bris 91. **d** 93 **p** 94. C Wotton-under-Edge w Ozleworth and N Nibley *Glouc* 93–97; P-in-c Jersey St Clem *Win* 97–98; R from 98; Can Mombasa from 11. *The Rectory, La rue du Presbytere, St Clement, Jersey JE2 6RB* T: (01534) 851992

SHAW, David Thomas. b 45. Open Univ BA 78. WMMTC 87. **d** 90 **p** 91. C Sheldon *Birm* 90–93; R Chelmsley Wood 93–02; TR Broughton Astley and Croft w Stoney Stanton *Leic* 02–10; rtd 10; PtO *Cov* from 11. *39 Orchard Way, Stretton on Dunsmore, Rugby CV23 9HP* T: (024) 7654 2036 E: davidshaw139@btinternet.com

SHAW, Mrs Felicity Mary. b 46. UEA BSc 67 MSc 68. NOC 88. **d** 91 **p** 94. Par Dn Benchill *Man* 91–94; C 94–95; TV E Farnworth and Kearsley 95–98; TR 98–03; V Woodhall *Bradf* 03–07; rtd 07; PtO *Man* 08–17; *St And* from 16. *20 The Sycamores, 16 Muirs, Kinross KY13 8GG* E: rev.fmshaw@btinternet.com

SHAW, Graham Lister. b 81. Fitzw Coll Cam BA 04 MA 08 Ox Brookes Univ MA 11. Wycliffe Hall Ox 05. **d** 07 **p** 08. C Camberley St Paul *Guildf* 07–11; V Ches Ch Ch 11–21. *57 Black Diamond Park, Chester CH1 3ET* T: (01244) 325302

SHAW, Canon Grahame David. b 44. Lich Th Coll 65. **d** 68 **p** 69. C Grange St Andr *Ches* 68–73; TV E Runcorn w Halton 73–74; TV Thamesmead *S'wark* 74–79; V Newington St Paul 79–13; S'wark Adnry Ecum Officer 90–13; RD S'wark and Newington 96–02; Hon Can S'wark Cathl 99–13; rtd 13; PtO *Sarum* 16–21. *2 St Peter's Close, Pimperne, Blandford Forum DT11 8UZ*

SHAW, Gregory. b 66. Chu Coll Cam MA 90 MEng 89. Ripon Coll Cuddesdon 09. **d** 12 **p** 13. NSM Yardley Hastings, Denton and Grendon etc *Pet* 12–15; NSM Earls Barton 15–17; PtO from 17. *114 Birchfield Road, Northampton NN1 4RH* T: (01604) 459954 E: gregnshaw@hotmail.com

SHAW, Mrs Irene. b 45. Gilmore Course 80 NEOC 82. **dss** 83 **d** 87 **p** 94. Elloughton and Brough w Brantingham *York* 83–86; Westborough *Guildf* 86–88; C 87–88; C Shottermill 88–91; C Lamorbey H Redeemer *Roch* 91–97; V Belvedere All SS 97–02; TV Em TM *Wakef* 02–05; rtd 05; PtO *York* from 07. *26 Brereton Close, Beverley HU17 7QE* T: (01482) 871095

SHAW, Prof Jane Alison. b 63. Ox Univ BA 85 MA 91 Harvard Div Sch MDiv 88 Univ of California Berkeley PhD 94. SAOMC 96. **d** 97 **p** 98. Fell Regent's Park Coll Ox 94–01; Dean 98–01; Hon Cathl Chapl Ch Ch Ox 00–10; Fell, Chapl and Dean of Div New Coll Ox 01–10; NSM Ox St Mary V w St Cross and St Pet 97–01; Hon Can Ch Ch 05–10; Can Th Sarum Cathl 07–12; Dean Grace Cathl San Francisco USA 10–14; Dean Relig Life and Prof RS Stanford Univ 14–18; Prin Harris Manchester Coll Ox from 18; Prof Hist of Relig and Pro-Vice-Chan Ox Univ from 18. *Harris Manchester College, Mansfield Road, Oxford OX1 3TD* T: (01865) 618082 E: jane.shaw@theology.ox.ac.uk

SHAW, Miss Jane Elizabeth. b 47. New Hall Cam BA 68 MA 72 Brunel Univ MPhil 79 Win Univ MA 14. NEOC 98. **d** 01 **p** 02. NSM Moor Allerton *Ripon* 01–05; Presbyter Bp Rockey Chpl Raiwind Pakistan 06–11; NSM Upper Wylye Valley *Sarum* 11–17; PtO from 17. *Manor Farm House, Corton, Warminster BA12 0SZ* T: (01985) 850141 E: shawjane2005@gmail.com

SHAW, Canon Jane Louise Claridge. b 66. Birm Poly BA 87. WMMTC 00. **d** 03 **p** 04. C Longbridge *Birm* 03–07; V Dosthill from 07; AD Polesworth 17–19; Jt AD Coleshill and Polesworth 19–20; AD from 20; Hon Can Birm Cathl from 19. *The Vicarage, 1 Church Road, Dosthill, Tamworth B77 1LU* T: (01827) 281349 E: louiseshaw6@yahoo.co.uk

SHAW, Judy Anne. b 57. Lon Metrop Univ BA 05. Linc Sch of Th and Min 12. **d** 17 **p** 18. NSM Nettleham *Linc* from 17. *122 Hermit Street, Lincoln LN5 8EG* T: (01522) 822649 M: 07594-670408 E: judeshaw.shaw3@gmail.com

SHAW, Keith Arthur. b 51. **d** 10 **p** 11. NSM Baswich *Lich* 10–21; Chapl S Staffs and Shropshire Healthcare NHS Foundn Trust 10–21; rtd 21; PtO *Lich* from 21. *44 Chasewood, Longford Road, Cannock WS11 1RJ*

SHAW, Kenneth James. b 36. St Jo Coll Nottm 85 Edin Th Coll 88. **d** 87 **p** 89. NSM Troon *Glas* 87–89; C Glas St Mary 89–90; R Lenzie 90–01; Warden of Readers 96–01; rtd 01; Hon C Glas St Mary 02–06; LtO from 08. *19 Mailerbeg Gardens, Moodiesburn, Glasgow G69 0JP* T: (01236) 873987 E: kenneth.shaw24@btinternet.com

SHAW, Louise. See SHAW, Jane Louise Claridge

SHAW, Malcolm. b 46. Trin Coll Bris. **d** 01 **p** 02. C Bolsover *Derby* 01–05; R Brimington 05–10; P-in-c Chelford w Lower Withington *Ches* 10–13; rtd 13; PtO *Ches* from 13. *85 Rochester Crescent, Crewe CW1 5YQ* T: (01270) 213317 M: 07713-624005 E: malcolmshaw238@btinternet.com

SHAW, Malcolm Roy. b 47. Lon Univ BA 69 CQSW 76. NEOC 03. **d** 05 **p** 06. NSM Hunmanby w Muston *York* 05–08; NSM Rufforth w Moor Monkton and Hessay 08–13; NSM Long Marston 08–13; NSM Healaugh w Wighill, Bilbrough and Askham Richard 08–13; NSM Tockwith and Bilton w Bickerton 08–13; NSM N Ainsty 13; V 13–17; rtd 17; PtO *York* from 18. *11 Privet Drive, Thorpe Willoughby, Selby YO8 9GD* T: (01757) 212360 E: revroytockwith@btinternet.com

SHAW, Canon Margaret Ann. b 58. Bp Otter Coll Chich BA 80 SS Paul & Mary Coll Cheltenham PGCE 81. EAMTC 00. **d** 03 **p** 04. C Langdon Hills *Chelmsf* 03–06; TV Basildon St Andr w H Cross 06–16; RD Basildon 10–16; TR Harwich Peninsula from 16; Hon Can Chelmsf Cathl from 15. *The Rectory, 51 Highfield Avenue, Harwich CO12 4DR* E: sh.ma@btinternet.com

SHAW, Martin. See SHAW, Alexander Martin

SHAW, Michael. See SHAW, Ralph Michael

SHAW, Neil Graham. b 61. St Jo Coll Nottm LTh 91. **d** 91 **p** 92. C Leamington Priors St Paul *Cov* 91–95; TV Bestwood S'well 95–99; Chapl HM YOI Thorn Cross 99–01; Chapl HM Pris Hindley 01–07; Chapl HM Pris Liv 07–14; TV Warrington E *Liv* 14–16; TR from 16; AD Warrington from 19. *The Rectory, 33 Station Road, Padgate, Warrington WA2 0PD* M: 07432-157443 E: rev.ngs1@gmail.com

SHAW, Neil James. b 79. Leeds Univ BA 00 K Coll Lon MA 11 Dur Univ MA 16. Westcott Ho Cam 14 Yale Div Sch 15. **d** 16 **p** 17. C Upper St Leonards St Jo *Chich* 16–17; C Chich St Paul and Westhampnett 17–20; R Stamford All SS w St Jo *Linc* from 20. *The Rectory, 18 Little Casterton Road, Stamford PE9 1BE* M: 07527-447615 E: njshaw1@icloud.com

SHAW, Norman William. b 46. Open Univ BA 94. **d** 13 **p** 14. OLM Glossop *Derby* from 13. *32 Duke Street, Glossop SK13 8DU* T: (01457) 867493

SHAW, Pamela Joyce. See SANDERS, Pamela Joyce

SHAW, Peter William. b 89. Wycliffe Hall Ox 14. **d** 17 **p** 18. C Wollaton S'well 17–19; C Aspley from 19; C Bilborough and Strelley from 19. *St John's Vicarage, Graylands Road, Nottingham NG8 4FD* M: 07706-047133 E: peter@stjnotts.org

SHAW, Ralph. b 38. Man Univ MEd 70. Sarum & Wells Th Coll 78. **d** 80 **p** 81. C Consett *Dur* 80–84; P-in-c Tanfield 84–88; V 88–97; R S Shields St Aid and St Steph 97–05; rtd 05. *10 Shipley Court, Gateshead NE8 4EZ* T: 0191-420 5137

SHAW, Ralph Michael. b 45. DipAdEd. Lich Th Coll 68. **d** 70 **p** 71. C Dewsbury All SS *Wakef* 70–75; TV Redcar w Kirkleatham *York* 75–76; Dioc Youth Officer *St Alb* 76–91; Chief Exec John Grooms 91–98; Team Ldr Workplace Min *St Alb* 08–10; rtd 10; PtO *St Alb* from 10. *18 Wyton, Welwyn Garden City AL7 2PF* T: (01707) 321813 M: 07710-465548 E: revmshaw@btinternet.com

SHAW, Preb Richard Tom. b 42. AKC 69. St Aug Coll Cant 69. **d** 70 **p** 71. C Dunston St Nic *Dur* 70–73; C Maidstone All SS w St Phil and H Trin *Cant* 73–75; Chapl RN 75–79; V Barrow-on-Humber *Linc* 79–83; V Linc St Faith and St Martin w St Pet 83–91; V Clun w Bettws-y-Crwyn and Newcastle *Heref* 91–11; P-in-c Hopesay 98–02; rtd 11; RD Clun Forest *Heref* 94–05 and 08–11; Preb Heref Cathl 02–11; PtO from 12. *The Granary, Newcastle Court, Newcastle, Craven Arms SY7 8QL* E: richard@rick-shaw.co.uk

SHAW, Canon Robert William. b 46. Lon Univ BD 69. St Aug Coll Cant 69. **d** 70 **p** 71. C Hunslet St Mary and Stourton *Ripon* 70–71; C Hunslet St Mary 71–74; C Hawksworth Wood 74–76; R Stanningley St Thos 76–84; V Potternewton 84–94; V Manston 94–02; P-in-c Beeston Hill H Spirit 02–04; P-in-c Hunslet Moor St Pet and St Cuth 02–04; V Beeston Hill and Hunslet Moor 04–11; Hon Can Ripon Cathl 08–11; rtd 11; PtO *Leeds* from 17. *23 St Chad's Rise, Leeds LS6 3QE* E: bobshaw46@hotmail.co.uk

SHAW, Mrs Rosemary Alice. b 44. CertEd 65 CQSW 78 Heythrop Coll Lon MA 96 MA 04. S'wark Ord Course 87. **d** 89 **p** 94. Par Dn Walworth *S'wark* 89–92; Par Dn E Dulwich St Jo 92–95; NSM 95–96; Eileen Kerr Mental Health Fell Maudsley Hosp 95–96; Chapl King's Healthcare NHS Trust 96–01; Sen Chapl Guy's and St Thos' NHS Foundn Trust 02–07; Chapl from 13; Hon C E Dulwich St Jo *S'wark* 96–12; Hon C Peckham St Sav 12–14; PtO from 14. *19 Scutari Road, London SE22 0NN* T: (020) 8693 6325 M: 07731-693247 E: rosemary.shaw1@ntlworld.com

SHAW, Roy. *See* SHAW, Malcolm Roy

SHAW, Sarah Louise Kate. b 71. **d** 14 **p** 15. C Edin St Cuth 14–17; R Falkirk from 17. *The Rectory, 33 Carronflats Road, Grangemouth FK3 9DG* T: (01324) 482438 M: 07943-405156 E: sarah.shaw0614@yahoo.co.uk

SHAW, Stewart James. b 64. Wilson Carlile Coll 97 NTMTC BA 07. **d** 07 **p** 08. C Hounslow H Trin w St Paul and St Mary *Lon* 07–09; Chapl RAF from 09. *Chaplaincy Services (RAF), HQ Air Command, RAF High Wycombe HP14 4UE* T: (01494) 496800

SHAW, William John. b 74. Edin Coll of Art BSc 96 Bradf Univ MSc 97 Internat Chr Coll BA 10. TISEC 10. **d** 12 **p** 13. Chapl St Mary's Cathl *Edin* 12–15; P-in-c Grangemouth 15–16; R from 16; P-in-c Bo'ness 15–16; R from 16. *The Rectory, 33 Carronflats Road, Grangemouth FK3 9DG* T: (01324) 482438 M: 07749-256547 E: stmarysandstcatharines@virginmedia.com

SHAW NOTICE, Mrs Clarice (Clarissa). b 58. Sarum Coll 14. **d** 16 **p** 17. NSM Frome H Trin *B & W* 16–20; P-in-c Deane Vale from 20. *6 Cole Close, Cotford St Luke, Taunton TA4 1NZ* M: 07956-784088 E: clarissashawnotice@outlook.com

SHAYLER-WEBB, Peter. b 57. Bath Univ BSc 81 BArch 83. Ripon Coll Cuddesdon 93. **d** 95 **p** 96. C Bedford St Paul *St Alb* 95–99; C Dorking w Ranmore *Guildf* 99–04; R Sherwood Australia from 04. *PO Box 107, Sherwood Qld 4075, Australia* T: (0061) (7) 3278 2498 *or* (7) 3379 3437 F: 3278 2048 E: psw5957@bigpond.net.au

SHEA, Martyn Paul Leathley. b 66. City Univ BSc 89. Wycliffe Hall Ox. **d** 00 **p** 01. C Ches Square St Mich w St Phil *Lon* 00–03; C Stamford St Geo w St Paul *Linc* 03–08; P-in-c Jersey St Mark *Win* 08–10; V 10–21; V Luton Lewsey St Hugh *St Alb* from 21. *St Hugh's Vicarage, 367 Leagrave High Street, Luton LU4 0ND* M: 07429-363598 E: martyn@sthughs.org.uk

SHEARCROFT, Sister Elizabeth Marion. b 57. SRN 76. **d** 94 **p** 95. CA from 84; NSM Margate H Trin *Cant* 94–98; Chapl Thanet Healthcare NHS Trust 94–98; Chapl E Kent Hosps NHS Trust 99–02; C Kendal H Trin *Carl* 02–05; V Streatham Immanuel and St Andr *S'wark* 05–19; V Taunton All SS *B & W* from 19. *All Saints' Vicarage, Outer Circle, Taunton TA1 2DE* T: (01823) 339269 E: liz@thekingfishery.co.uk

SHEARD, Andrew Frank. b 60. York Univ BA 81. St Jo Coll Nottm 92. **d** 94 **p** 95. C Uxbridge *Lon* 94–96; TV 96–99; P-in-c 99–01; TR 01–18; R Warblington w Emsworth *Portsm* from 18; Jt AD Havant from 20. *The Rectory, 20 Church Path, Emsworth PO10 7DP* E: andrewf.sheard@btinternet.com

SHEARD, Cindy Heather Shirley. b 67. Open Univ BA 05. Yorks Min Course 14. **d** 16 **p** 17. NSM Birstall *Leeds* 16–17; NSM Heckmondwike (w Norristhorpe) and Liversedge 17–20; NSM Mirfield from 20. *5 Ash Grove, Gomersal, Cleckheaton BD19 4SJ* T: (01274) 872615 E: cindy.sheard@hotmail.co.uk *or* cindy.sheard@leeds.anglican.org

SHEARD, Gillian Freda. *See* COOKE, Gillian Freda

SHEARD, Canon Michael Rowland. b 42. K Coll Lon BA Man Univ PhD. **d** 95 **p** 95. World Miss Officer Lich 86–09; TV Willenhall H Trin *Lich* 95–09; Preb Lich Cathl 99–09; rtd 09; Hon Can Kuala Lumpur from 10; PtO *Linc* 15–18. *9 Queen Street, Kirton Lindsay, Gainsborough DN21 4NS* T: (01652) 648846 M: 07711-541983 E: m.r.sheard@btinternet.com

SHEARLOCK, Revd David John. b 32. Birm Univ BA 55 FRSA 91 FRGS 92 ARSCM 98. Westcott Ho Cam 56. **d** 57 **p** 58. C Guisborough *York* 57–60; C Christchurch

Win 60–64; V Kingsclere 64–71; V Romsey 71–82; Dioc Dir of Ords 77–82; Hon Can Win Cathl 78–82; Dean Truro 82–97; R Truro St Mary 82–97; Chapl Cornwall Fire Brigade 91–97; rtd 98; PtO *Sarum* 98–22. *3 The Tanyard, Shadrack Street, Beaminster DT8 3BG* T: (01308) 863170 E: davidshearlock@gmail.com

SHEARN, Andrew William. b 43. Ex Univ BA 65. WMMTC 04. **d** 06 **p** 07. NSM Wellesbourne *Cov* 06–09; NSM Studley 10–13; NSM Spernall, Morton Bagot and Oldberrow 10–13; PtO 13–21. *58 St Fremund Way, Leamington Spa CV31 1AB* T: (01926) 930552 E: andy_shearn@hotmail.com

SHEATH, Allan Philip. b 48. SWMTC 95. **d** 98 **p** 99. NSM Tiverton St Pet and Chevithorne w Cove *Ex* 98–03; C Honiton, Gittisham, Combe Raleigh, Monkton and Cove; TV 04–11; C Tiverton St Andr 12–15; PtO from 15; *B & W* 16–21. *11 Fairfield, Sampford Peverell, Tiverton EX16 7DE* T: (01884) 820136 E: allan.sheath@gmail.com

SHEDD, Mrs Christine Elizabeth. b 49. City of Birm Coll CertEd 70 St Jo Coll York MA 02. NOC 02. **d** 04 **p** 05. C Thornton St Jas *Bradf* 04–07; TV Oakenshaw, Wyke and Low Moor 07–12; V Low Moor and Oakenshaw 12–13; Warden of Readers 09–13; rtd 14; PtO *Wakef* 14; *Leeds* from 14. *84 New Road, Huddersfield HD5 0HR* T: (01484) 511071 M: 07814-958919 E: c.shedd@btinternet.com

SHEDDEN, Canon Valerie. b 56. Ripon Coll of Educn CertEd 77. Cranmer Hall Dur 81. **dss** 84 **d** 87 **p** 94. Tudhoe Grange *Dur* 84–85; Whitworth w Spennymoor 85–91; Par Dn 87–91; Par Dn E Darlington 91–94; P-in-c Bishop Middleham 94–00; Dioc RE Adv 94–00; V Heworth St Mary 00–10; AD Gateshead 06–10; P-in-c Consett 10–20; Hon Can Dur Cathl 17–20; rtd 20. *Address temp unknown* E: val.shedden@talk21.com

SHEDLOCK, Hilary Ann. b 63. All SS Cen for Miss & Min 15. **d** 18 **p** 19. OLM Kersal Moor *Man* from 18. *5 Vernon Drive, Prestwich, Manchester M25 9RA*

SHEEHAN, Vincent Thomas Paul. b 77. **d** 16 **p** 17. NSM Enfield St Geo *Lon* from 16. *21 Forty Hill, Enfield EN2 9HT* T: (020) 8362 1213 E: vincentsheehan@talktalk.net

SHEEHY, Jeremy Patrick. b 56. Magd Coll Ox BA 78 MA 81 New Coll Ox DPhil 90. St Steph Ho Ox 78. **d** 81 **p** 82. C Erdington St Barn *Birm* 81–83; C Small Heath St Greg 83–84; Dean Div, Fell and Chapl New Coll Ox 84–90; V Leytonstone St Marg w St Columba *Chelmsf* 90–96; P-in-c Leytonstone St Andr 93–96; Prin St Steph Ho Ox 96–06; TR Swinton and Pendlebury *Man* from 06; AD Eccles 11–13. *St Peter's Rectory, Vicarage Road, Swinton, Manchester M27 0WA* T: 0161-794 1578

SHEEN, David Kenneth. b 70. Cov Univ BSc 95 Univ of Wales (Cardiff) BA 04 MA 08. St Mich Coll Llan 01. **d** 04 **p** 05. C Cowbridge *Llan* 04–07; C Penarth and Llandough 07–10; P-in-c Pwllgwaun and Llanddewi Rhondda 10–14; Warden of Readers 10–14; Chapl Cardiff Univ from 14. *The Anglican Chaplaincy, 61 Park Place, Cardiff CF10 3AT* T: (029) 2023 2550 E: sheend2@cardiff.ac.uk *or* dks101@mac.com

SHEFFIELD, Julia. b 55. MCSP 78 SRP 78. NTMTC BA 05. **d** 05 **p** 06. NSM Yiewsley *Lon* 05–09; Chapl Mid-Essex Hosp Services NHS Trust 09–12; Lead Chapl 12–18; rtd 18; PtO *Chelmsf* from 18. *Latton Vicarage, The Gowers, Harlow CM20 2JP* T: (01279) 423609 E: julishef@hotmail.co.uk

SHEFFIELD, Canon Michael Julian. b 53. Brentwood Coll of Educn CertEd. Sarum & Wells Th Coll 76. **d** 79 **p** 80. C Locks Heath *Portsm* 79–83; C Ryde All SS 83–86; P-in-c Ryde H Trin 86–92; V 92–96; P-in-c Swanmore St Mich 86–92; V 92–96; V W Leigh 96–04; V Waterlooville 04–17; Hon Can Portsm Cathl 16–17; rtd 17; PtO *Portsm* from 18. *21 David Newberry Drive, Lee-on-the-Solent PO13 8FF* M: 07818-031902 E: mikesheffield@btinternet.com

SHEFFIELD, Sean Andrew. b 70. Trin Coll Bris 15. **d** 17 **p** 18. C Dover Town *Cant* 17–20; P-in-c Bewsborough from 20. *The Vicarage, Bewsbury Cross Lane, Whitfield, Dover CT16 3EZ* M: 07710-423432 E: rev.sean.sheffield@gmail.com

SHEFFIELD AND ROTHERHAM, Archdeacon of. *See* CHAMBERLAIN, The Ven Malcolm Leslie

SHEFFIELD, Bishop of. *See* WILCOX, The Rt Revd Peter Jonathan

SHEFFIELD, Dean of. *See* THOMPSON, The Very Revd Abigail Laura

SHEGOG, Preb Eric Marshall. b 37. City Univ MA 88. Lich Th Coll 64. **d** 65 **p** 66. C Benhilton *S'wark* 65–68; Asst Youth Adv 68–70; V Abbey Wood 70–76; Chapl Sunderland Town Cen 76–83; C Bishopwearmouth St Mich w St Hilda *Dur* 76–83; Hd Relig Broadcasting IBA 84–90; PtO *Lon* 85–90; *St Alb* 85–89; Hon C Harpenden St Nic 89–97; Dir Communications for C of E 90–97; Dir Communications *Lon* 97–00; Preb St Paul's Cathl 97–00; Acting Dioc Gen

Sec 99; rtd 00; PtO *St Alb* from 00. *The Coach House, 7A High Street, Clophill, Bedford MK45 4AB* T: (01525) 864868 E: ericshegog37@gmail.com

SHEKERIE, Colleen Cecilia. b 66. Birm City Univ MA 00. Qu Foundn Birm 17. **d** 19 **p** 20. C Smethwick *Birm* from 19. *58 Lechlade Road, Birmingham B43 5NF* M: 07890-773454 E: revdcolleenoldchurch@hotmail.com

SHELDON, Jennifer Christine. b 43. K Coll Lon BA 99. NTMTC 00. **d** 02 **p** 03. NSM Poplar *Lon* from 02. *15 Townshend Road, Chislehurst BR7 6HP* T: (020) 8295 3107 E: jensheldon@aol.com

SHELDRAKE, Mrs Varlie Ivy. b 39. SRN 64 SCM 65. **d** 03 **p** 04. OLM E w W Harling, Bridgham w Roudham, Larling etc *Nor* 03–09; rtd 09; PtO *Nor* from 09. *12 Kemp's Barns, Garboldisham Road, East Harling, Norwich NR16 2TS* T: (01953) 717404 E: varlie@eastharling.com

SHELLARD-JAMES, Janet Elizabeth. b 64. Southn Univ BSc 85 Kingston Univ PGCE 92. Sarum Coll BA 17. **d** 17 **p** 18. C Wells St Thos w Horrington *B & W* 17–21; C Chewton Mendip w Ston Easton, Litton etc 17–21; P-in-c Coxley w Godney, Henton and Wookey from 21. *The Vicarage, Vicarage Lane, Wookey, Wells BA5 1JT* E: jansjames@hotmail.co.uk

SHELLEY, Catherine Jean. b 65. Down Coll Cam BA 88 LLM 89 MA 93 Man Univ PhD 11 Called to the Bar (Lincoln's Inn) 91 Solicitor 00. Westcott Ho Cam 08. **d** 10 **p** 11. C Kersal Moor *Man* 10–12; C W Didsbury and Withington St Chris 12–13; Chapl Birm Univ 13–15; PtO *S'wark* 16–17; V Mottingham St Edw from 17; PtO *Lon* 16–17; Dep Registrar Ely and Liv 16–17; AD Eltham and Mottingham *S'wark* from 20. *St Edward's Vicarage, St Keverne Road, London SE9 4AQ* T: (020) 8857 6278 M: 07711-611201 E: revdrcath@gmail.com

SHELLEY, Derrick Sydney David. b 38. Lon Univ LLB 60 AKC 65. Linc Th Coll 66. **d** 68 **p** 69. C Weybridge *Guildf* 68–72; Chapl Red Bank Schs 71–76; PtO *Blackb* 76–96; rtd 96; PtO *Truro* 96–03; *Lich* 04–09; *Blackb* 11–14. *57 Kenilworth Road, Lytham St Annes FY8 1LB* T: (01253) 780298

SHELLEY, Robin Arthur. b 34. CEng MIMechE. St Jo Coll Nottm 85. **d** 87 **p** 88. C Countesthorpe w Foston *Leic* 87–90; V Enderby w Lubbesthorpe and Thurlaston 90–00; rtd 00; PtO *Leic* 00–03; *York* from 02. *10 Old Pond Place, North Ferriby HU14 3JE* T: (01482) 637063 E: robin@shelley10.karoo.co.uk

SHELLEY, Rupert Harry. b 78. Bris Univ BSc 00. Wycliffe Hall Ox BTh 10. **d** 10 **p** 11. C Wimbledon Em Ridgway Prop Chpl *S'wark* 10–14; Ldr Forres Holidays Titus Trust from 14; PtO *Ox* 15–18; *Win* 15–18 and from 20. *Forres, 12 Lime Tree Mews, 2 Lime Walk, Oxford OX3 7DZ* T: (01865) 766155 M: 07956-914123 E: info@forresholidays.org or rupertshelley@hotmail.com

SHELTON, Canon Ian Robert. b 52. BEd 74 Lon Univ MA 79. Ripon Coll Cuddesdon BA 81 MA 90. **d** 82 **p** 83. C Wath-upon-Dearne w Adwick-upon-Dearne *Sheff* 82–86; TV Grantham *Linc* 86–93; P-in-c Waltham 93–97; R 97–11; P-in-c Barnoldby le Beck 93–97; R 97–11; RD Haverstoe 01–11; RD Grimsby and Cleethorpes 10–11; Can and Preb Linc Cathl 05–11; V Rowley Regis *Birm* 11–18; AD Warley 13–17; rtd 18; PtO *Leeds* from 18. *2 Mulberry Drive, Golcar, Huddersfield HD7 4FA*

SHELTON, Ms Pauline Mary. b 52. K Coll Lon BA 73. NOC 96. **d** 99 **p** 00. C Baswich *Lich* 96–02; TV Stoke-upon-Trent 02–06; Dioc OLM Course Ldr 06–10; Prin OLM and Reader Tr 10–19; rtd 19; PtO *Lich* from 20. *Dray Cottage, Cheadle Road, Draycott, Stoke-on-Trent ST11 9RQ* T: (01782) 388834

SHEMILT, Lisa. b 69. St Jo Coll Nottm 03. **d** 05 **p** 06. C Walton St Jo *Derby* 05–13; P-in-c Morley w Smalley and Horsley Woodhouse 13–14; V Morley and Smalley 14–16; Dir Studies Initial Reader Tr 13–16; C Heanor from 16; C Langley Mill and Aldercar from 16; C Marlpool from 16. *The Vicarage, 1B Mundy Street, Heanor DE75 7EB* E: revlisashemilt@hotmail.co.uk

SHENTON, Canon Brian. b 43. Chich Th Coll 73. **d** 75 **p** 76. C Mill Hill Jo Keble Ch *Lon* 75–78; C New Windsor *Ox* 78–81; TV 81–82; P-in-c Cherbury 82–83; V Calcot 83–89; V Reading St Mary the Virgin 89–13; P-in-c Reading St Matt 96–00; RD Reading 95–13; Hon Can Ch Ch 98–13; rtd 13; PtO *Ox* 13–17; Hon C Nettlebed w Bix, Highmoor, Pishill etc 17–19; Hon C Nuffield 17–19; PtO from 19. *73 Watlington Street, Reading RG1 4RQ* M: 07710-490250 E: canon@waitrose.com

SHEPHERD, Canon Anthony Michael. b 50. MBE 17. Em Coll Cam BA 72 MA 76. Westcott Ho Cam 72. **d** 74 **p** 75. C Folkestone St Mary and St Eanswythe *Cant* 74–79; Bp's Dom Chapl *Ripon* 79–87; Dioc Communications Officer 79–87; V High Harrogate St Pet 87–14; *Leeds* 14–15; Hon Can Ripon Cathl from 99; rtd 15; Chapl to The Queen

from 09. *3 Heatherdale Mews, Summerbridge, Harrogate HG3 4BQ* T: (01423) 500901 E: ashepherd@talktalk.net

SHEPHERD, Mrs Bridget Clare. b 76. Open Univ BSc 01 K Coll Lon MA 04. Trin Coll Bris BA 08. **d** 08 **p** 09. C S Croydon Em *S'wark* 08–14; V Lee Gd Shep w St Pet from 14. *The Vicarage, 47 Handen Road, London SE12 8NR* M: 07833-031258 E: bridget@goodpeter.org.uk

SHEPHERD, Mrs Clare Frances. b 75. Cov Univ BA 02. St Mellitus Coll BA 15. **d** 15 **p** 16. C Shottermill *Guildf* 15–18; R Ewhurst w Okewood and Forest Green from 18. *The Rectory, The Street, Ewhurst, Cranleigh GU6 7PX* T: (01483) 273604 E: revclareshepherd@gmail.com

SHEPHERD, Jack Eric Bloss. b 88. Edin Univ MA 12. Cranmer Hall Dur 15. **d** 17 **p** 18. C Skelmersdale St Paul *Liv* 17–20; C Up Holland and Dalton from 20. *6 Wilcove, Skelmersdale WN8 8NF* M: 07415-122370 E: jshepherd88@outlook.com

SHEPHERD, Miss Jayne Elizabeth. b 57. Reading Univ BA 78. Cranmer Hall Dur 79. dss 82 **d** 87 **p** 94. Wombourne *Lich* 82–85; Harlescott 85–90; Par Dn 87–90; Chapl Asst Qu Medical Cen Nottm Univ Hosp NHS Trust 90–97; Asst Chapl Cen Notts Healthcare NHS Trust 90–97; Chapl Pet Hosps NHS Trust 97–02; Chapl St Helens and Knowsley Hosps NHS Trust 02–08; V Knutsford St Cross *Ches* 08–15; P-in-c Alsager St Mary 15–18; rtd 18. *53 News Lane, Rainford, St Helens WA11 7JY* T: (01744) 601043 E: j.shepherd57@hotmail.com

SHEPHERD, John Martin. b 68. St Jo Coll Cam BA 90. Oak Hill Th Coll BA 96. **d** 96 **p** 97. C Rusholme H Trin *Man* 96–00; SAMS Brazil 00–03; TV Gt Chesham *Ox* 03–21; V Surbiton Hill Ch Ch *S'wark* from 21. *Christ Church, 8 Christ Church Road, Surbiton KT5 8JJ* T: (020) 8390 7215 E: john@theshepherds.org.uk

SHEPHERD, Canon John Michael. b 42. BNC Ox BA 63 MA 72. Coll of Resurr Mirfield 64. **d** 66 **p** 67. C Clapham H Spirit *S'wark* 66–69; C Kingston All SS 69–72; V Upper Tooting H Trin 73–80; V Wandsworth St Paul 80–90; P-in-c Mitcham SS Pet and Paul 90–92; V 92–97; RD Merton 96–97; V Battersea St Luke 97–07; RD Battersea 01–04; Hon Can S'wark Cathl 01–07; rtd 07; PtO *Portsm* from 08. *36 Lawrence Road, Southsea PO5 1NY* T: (023) 9283 7387 E: johnmshepherd36@gmail.com

SHEPHERD, Mrs Julie Margaret. b 37. **d** 03 **p** 04. OLM Halliwell *Man* 03–08; PtO from 08. *Apple Cottage, 16 Grove Street, Bolton BL1 3PG* T: (01204) 844508 M: 07742-667903 E: julieshepherd@hushmail.com

SHEPHERD, Keith Frederick. b 42. EMMTC 86. **d** 89 **p** 90. NSM Stocking Farm *Leic* 89–93; NSM Church Langton w Tur Langton, Thorpe Langton etc 93–99; TV Syston 99–07; rtd 07; PtO *Leic* 07–21. *57 Fielding Road, Birstall, Leicester LE4 3AG* T: 0116-267 4172 E: keithshepherd55@btinternet.com

SHEPHERD, Mrs Pauline. b 53. Stockwell Coll of Educn TCert 73. WMMTC 00. **d** 03 **p** 04. C Walsall Pleck and Bescot *Lich* 03–08; P-in-c Yoxall 08; rtd 09; PtO *Lich* 10–21; *Leeds* 21. *5 Newtons College, The Close, Lichfield WS13 7LF* T: (01543) 418451 M: 07814-680304 E: p.shepherd140@btinternet.com

SHEPHERD, Canon Peter William. b 48. Reading Univ BA 71 Lon Univ BD 80 Brighton Poly MPhil 87 Lanc Univ MA 94 Open Univ PhD 04. Chich Th Coll 77. **d** 80 **p** 81. NSM Eastbourne St Sav and St Pet *Chich* 80–82; NSM Clitheroe St Mary *Blackb* 82–14; LtO 14–19; Hd Master Wm Temple Sch Preston 83–88; Hd Master Canon Slade Sch Bolton 89–06; rtd 06; PtO *Man* 89–12; Hon Can Man Cathl from 06; PtO *Blackb* from 19. *Homestead, Eastham Street, Clitheroe BB7 2HY* T/F: (01200) 425053 M: 07507-287968 E: canonpetershepherd@gmail.com

SHEPHERD, Stephen. b 54. All SS Cen for Miss & Min 12. **d** 15 **p** 16. NSM Whitworth w Facit *Man* 15–18; NSM Castleton Moor from 18. *93 Rugby Road, Rochdale OL12 0DZ* T: (01706) 661572 E: stephenshep38@gmail.com

SHEPHERD, Thomas. b 52. Man Univ BA 79 Didsbury Coll Man PGCE 83 SRN 74. NOC 92. **d** 95 **p** 96. C Baguley *Man* 95–99; C Timperley *Ches* 99–03; V Sale St Paul 03–08; V Sandbach 08–19; rtd 19. *25 Greetwell Lane, Nettleham, Lincoln LN2 2PN*

SHEPHERDSON, Mrs Maria Thérèse. b 65. STETS. **d** 07 **p** 08. C Warmley, Syston and Bitton *Bris* 07–11; P-in-c Upper Kennet *Sarum* 11–13; R from 13. *The Rectory, 27 High Street, Avebury, Marlborough SN8 1RF* T: (01672) 539643 E: revmariashepherdson@outlook.com

SHEPPARD, Miss Barbara Ann. b 48. Portsm Poly BA 71 Southn Univ PGCE 72 St Paul's Coll Chelt CertEd 82. Trin Coll Bris 14. **d** 16 **p** 17. OLM Swindon All SS w St Barn *Bris* from 16. *8 Southbrook Street, Swindon SN2 1HF* T: (01793) 612682 M: 07785-267721 E: barbarasheppard@btinternet.com

SHEPPARD, David Owain. b 72. Sunderland Univ BA 95 Cam Univ PGCE 99. Westcott Ho Cam 16. **d** 18 **p** 19. C Ware St Mary *St Alb* 18–21; P-in-c Buckden w the Offords *Ely* from 21. *The Vicarage, Church Street, Buckden, St Neots PE19 5TL* M: 07792-128503 E: revd.d.sheppard@gmail.com

SHEPPARD, Ian Arthur Lough. b 33. Sarum & Wells Th Coll 71. **d** 74 **p** 75. C Bishop's Cleeve *Glouc* 74–77; Chapl RAF 77–81; V Gosberton *Linc* 81–87; V Leven Valley *Carl* 87–90; Deputation and Gen Appeals Org Children's Soc 90–98; rtd 98. *57 Seymour Grove, Eaglescliffe, Stockton-on-Tees TS16 0LE* T: (01642) 791612 E: ials@btopenworld.com

SHEPPARD, Canon Martin. b 37. Hertf Coll Ox BA 61 MA 65. Chich Th Coll 63. **d** 65 **p** 66. C N Hull St Mich *York* 65–68; C Hove St Jo *Chich* 68–71; V Heathfield St Rich 71–77; V New Shoreham and Old Shoreham 77–94; TR Rye 94–03; RD 95–02; Can and Preb Chich Cathl 02–03; rtd 03; PtO *Chich* from 03. *62 St Pancras Road, Lewes BN7 1JG* T: (01273) 474999

SHEPPARD, Roger Malcolm. b 47. Aston Univ MBA 86 Wolv Poly PGCE 88 Solicitor 74. WMMTC 98. **d** 01 **p** 02. NSM Castle Vale w Minworth *Birm* 01–07; NSM Four Oaks 08–13; P-in-c Wylde Green 13–16; P-in-c Bordesley St Benedict 16–21; CF(V) 07–16; rtd 21; PtO *Birm* from 21. *193 Dower Road, Sutton Coldfield B75 6SY* T: 0121-308 8850 M: 07775-281777 E: rmsheppard@hotmail.co.uk

SHEPPARD, Sam. b 92. Ripon Coll Cuddesdon BA 17. **d** 17 **p** 18. C Filwood Park *Bris* 17–20; C Hengrove 20–21; P-in-c from 21. *7A Novers Park Drive, Bristol BS4 1RF* M: 07949-949842 E: s-sheppard@hotmail.co.uk or christchurchhengrove@gmail.com

SHEPPARD, Preb Susan. b 59. Ex Univ BA 80 MA 99 SS Hild & Bede Coll Dur PGCE 81. SWMTC 95. **d** 98 **p** 99. NSM Stoke Canon, Poltimore w Huxham and Rewe etc *Ex* 98–01; Chapl St Pet High Sch Ex 99–06; Tutor SWMTC from 05; NSM Brampford Speke, Cadbury, Newton St Cyres etc *Ex* 08–20; C Moretonhampstead, Manaton, N Bovey and Lustleigh from 20; Preb Ex Cathl from 11. *The Rectory, 3 Grays Meadow, Moretonhampstead, Newton Abbot TQ13 8NB* T: (01392) 861022 E: moretonrector@gmail.com

SHEPTON, Robert Leonard McIntire. b 35. Jes Coll Cam BA 58 MA 61. Oak Hill Th Coll 59. **d** 61 **p** 62. C Weymouth St Jo *Sarum* 61–63; Boys' Ldr Cam Univ Miss Bermondsey 63–66; Warden Ox-Kilburn Club 66–69; Chapl St D Coll Llandudno 69–77; Chief Instructor Carnoch Outdoor Cen 77–80; Chapl Kingham Hill Sch Oxon 80–92; rtd 92. *Innis Free, Appin PA38 4BL* T: (01631) 730382 E: bobshepton1@gmail.com

SHER, Canon Falak. b 65. Coll of Resurr Mirfield. **d** 07 **p** 08. C Radcliffe *Man* 07–10; TV Gorton and Abbey Hey 10–14; P-in-c Chorlton-cum-Hardy St Werburgh 14–17; R 17–20; P-in-c Hulme Ascension 14–20; C Whalley Range St Edm and Moss Side etc 14–16; C Lower Broughton Ascension from 20; Hon Can Man Cathl from 16. *11 Belgrave Crescent, Eccles, Manchester M30 9AE* M: 07930-573624 E: falakfalak@hotmail.com

SHERBORNE, Archdeacon of. *See* SAYER, The Ven Penelope Jane

SHERBORNE, Area Bishop of. *See* GORHAM, The Rt Revd Karen Marisa

SHERBOURNE, Gloria. b 49. STETS 00. **d** 03 **p** 04. NSM Jersey St Brelade *Win* 03–10; Asst Chapl Jersey Gp of Hosps 03–04 and 05–10. *11 Iter Court, Bow, Crediton EX17 6BZ* T: (01363) 881240 E: gsherbourne@gmail.com

SHERCLIFF, Canon Elizabeth Ann. b 56. Salford Univ BSc 79 Open Univ MA 96. St Jo Coll Nottm 08. **d** 09 **p** 10. Dir of Studies for Readers *Ches* from 09; NSM Marple All SS 09–10; NSM Bredbury St Barn 10–11; NSM Gee Cross 11–13; Hon Can Ches Cathl from 20. *56 Ernocroft Road, Marple Bridge, Stockport SK6 5DY* M: 07515-633856 E: liz.shercliff@chester.anglican.org

SHERDLEY, Mrs Margaret Ann. b 46. Ches Coll of HE BTh 03. NOC 00. **d** 03 **p** 04. NSM Fellside Team *Blackb* 03–14; Chapl Myerscough Coll 06–11; rtd 11; PtO *Blackb* from 15. *Home Barn, Hollowforth Lane, Woodplumpton, Preston PR4 0BD* T: (01772) 691101 M: 07931-592787 E: m.sherdley@sky.com

SHERIDAN, Amy-Elizabeth. b 85. Salford Univ BA 16 MA 17. St Mellitus Coll BA 20. **d** 20 **p** 21. C Hey *Man* from 20; C Leesfield from 21. *15 Grotton Hollow, Grotton, Oldham OL4 4LN* M: 07879-880208 E: curate.amyelizabeth.stjohns@gmail.com

SHERIDAN, Canon Andrew Robert (Drew). b 61. Edin Univ MA 83 Jordanhill Coll Glas PGCE 86. TISEC 95. **d** 98 **p** 99. C Glas St Mary 98–01; R Greenock 01–16; P-in-c Gourock 06–16; R Lanark w Douglas from 16; Bp's Dom Chapl from 15; Can St Mary's Cathl from 15. *The Rectory, 1 Cleghorn Road, Lanark ML11 7QT* T: (01555) 663065 E: thecanteringcanon@outlook.com

SHERIDAN, Preb Deborah Jane. b 47. Kent Univ BA 69 ALA 73. WMMTC 90. **d** 93 **p** 94. NSM Lich St Chad 93–03; NSM The Ridwares and Kings Bromley 03–18; NSM Kings Bromley, The Ridwares and Yoxall 18–19; PtO from 19; Voc Educn Officer 06–18; Chapl St Giles Hospice Lich 98–14; Spiritual Companions Co-ord Wolverhampton Area *Lich* from 20; Preb Lich Cathl from 16. *45 High Grange, Lichfield WS13 7DU* T: (01543) 264363 or 416595 E: d.sheridan@postman.org.uk

SHERIDAN, Stephen Anthony. b 62. RMN 87 Chich Univ BA 11. SEITE 04. **d** 07 **p** 08. NSM Bexhill St Pet *Chich* 07–08; NSM Stone Cross St Luke w N Langney 08–12; NSM Shotton *St As* 12–13; PtO *Ches* 15–17; P-in-c Ches St Oswald and St Thos from 17. *The Vicarage, 33 Abbots Grange, Chester CH2 1AJ* T: (01244) 399990 M: 07770-629875 E: sheridan_steve@yahoo.com

SHERIFF (née WORRALL), Canon Suzanne. b 63. Trin Coll Bris BA 86. **d** 87 **p** 94. Par Dn Kingston upon Hull St Nic *York* 87–91; Par Dn Kingston upon Hull St Aid Southcoates 91–94; C 94–96; TV Marfleet 96–00; TR 00–07; V Tadcaster w Newton Kyme 07–14; P-in-c Kirk Fenton w Kirkby Wharfe and Ulleskelfe 10–14; V Tadcaster 14–19; P-in-c Heworth St Wulstan CD from 20; C Fulford 20–21; P-in-c from 21; Can and Preb York Minster from 01. *8 Abbotsway, York YO31 9LD* E: sue.sheriff8@gmail.com

SHERLOCK, Mrs Barbara Lee Kerney. b 48. Dur Univ PhD 07. Westcott Ho Cam. **d** 05 **p** 06. C Norton St Mary and Stockton St Chad *Dur* 05–07; P-in-c Newport and Widdington *Chelmsf* 07–11; V Barrow *St E* 11–18; rtd 18; PtO *St E* from 18. *Flat 2, 34 Southgate Street, Bury St Edmunds IP33 2AZ* E: barbara_sherlock@btinternet.com

SHERLOCK, Charles Patrick. b 51. New Coll Ox BA 73 MA 76 Open Univ MBA 00. Ripon Coll Cuddesdon 75. **d** 77 **p** 78. C Ashtead *Guildf* 77–81; Ethiopia 81–82; Chapl Belgrade w Zagreb *Eur* 82–84; USPG Ethiopia 84–91; R Dollar *St And* 91–97; Bursar Fistula Hosp Ethiopia 97–00; P-in-c Crieff *St And* 01–04; R 04–07; P-in-c Comrie 01–04; R 04–07; P-in-c Lochearnhead 01–04; R 04–07; PtO 07–13; Assoc Chapl Addis Ababa St Matt Ethiopia 07–13; P-in-c Hilborough w Bodney *Nor* 13–17; P-in-c Oxborough w Foulden and Caldecote 13–17; P-in-c Cockley Cley w Gooderstone 13–17; P-in-c Didlington 13–17; P-in-c Gt and Lt Cressingham w Threxton 13–17; C Mundford w Lynford 16–17; rtd 17; PtO *St And* from 18; Chapl Glenalmond Coll 19–20. *26 Hunter Street, Auchterarder PH3 1PA* T: (01764) 664429 M: 07740-981951 E: cpsherlock@msn.com

SHERLOCK, Helen Georgina. b 69. Southn Univ BEd 93. St Mellitus Coll BA 18. **d** 18 **p** 19. C Alphington, Shillingford St George and Ide *Ex* 18–21; Ldr Unlimited Ch from 21. *Glenn House, 96 Old Tiverton Road, Exeter EX4 6LD* M: 07919-405212 E: helen@sherlockfamily.co.uk

SHERLOCK, Baroness Maeve Christina Mary. b 60. OBE 00. St Mellitus Coll 16. **d** 18 **p** 19. NSM Dur St Nic from 18; PtO *Lon* from 20; *St E* 20–21. *House of Lords, London SW1A 0PW* E: curate.maeve@stnics.org.uk

SHERLOCK, Canon Thomas Alfred. b 40. Aux Course 87. **d** 90 **p** 91. NSM Kilmallock w Kilflynn, Kilfinane, Knockaney etc *L & K* 90–94; C Templemore w Thurles and Kilfithmone *C, F & O* 95–98; I 98–00; I Castlecomer w Colliery Ch, Mothel and Bilboa 00–11; Preb Ossory Cathl 05–11; rtd 11; Chapl Kingston Coll Mitchelstown from 13. *Castlequarter, Kildorrery, Co Cork, P67 EH74, Republic of Ireland* T: (00353) (22) 40677 M: 86-810 4463 E: hazelsherlock@eircom.net

SHERMAN, Cornelia. b 70. Win Univ MA 12. STETS 06. **d** 09 **p** 10. C Portchester *Portsm* 09–13; P-in-c Purbrook 13–18; C Crookhorn 13–18; C Portsdown 13–18; Chapl Portsm Univ from 18. *Portsmouth University Chaplaincy, Nuffield Centre, St Michael's Road, Portsmouth PO1 2ED* T: (023) 9284 3030 or 9284 3511 E: cornelia.sherman@port.ac.uk

SHERRATT, David Arthur. b 60. Univ of Wales (Lamp) BA 82 Leeds Univ BA 91. Coll of Resurr Mirfield 92. **d** 92 **p** 93. C St Jo on Bethnal Green *Lon* 92–95; C W Hampstead St Jas 95–98; V Abbey Wood *S'wark* from 98. *St Michael's Vicarage, 1 Conference Road, London SE2 0YH* T: (020) 8311 0377

SHERRED, Peter William. b 47. Kent Univ BA 69. SEITE 96. **d** 99 **p** 00. NSM Dover St Mary *Cant* 99–02; PtO from 02. *Copthorne, Dover Road, Guston, Dover CT15 5EN* T: (01304) 203548

SHERRING, Patrick. b 55. Trent Park Coll of Educn BEd 78 CertEd 77. Ridley Hall Cam 95. **d** 97 **p** 98. C Leyton St Mary w St Edw and St Luke *Chelmsf* 97–01; P-in-c Ingatestone w Buttsbury 01–04; C Fryerning w Margaretting 01–04; V Ingatestone w Fryerning 04–21; P-in-c Margaretting w

Mountnessing and Buttsbury 15–21; rtd 21. *18 Kingsford Drive, Chelmsford CM2 6YR*

SHERRING, Toby Bruce. b 76. Ex Univ BA 97 St Luke's Coll Ex PGCE 98. St Steph Ho Ox MTh 04. **d** 02 **p** 03. C W Derby St Jo *Liv* 02–05; Chapl St Hilda's Sch for Girls Perth Australia 06–16; Chapl The Peterborough Sch from 16; PtO *Ely* from 18. *The Peterborough School, Thorpe Road, Peterborough PE3 6AP* T: (01733) 343357

SHERRINGTON, Penelope. b 51. Kent Univ BA 11. SEITE 08. **d** 11 **p** 12. Chapl Gt Ormond Street Hosp NHS Foundn Trust from 11; NSM Godstone and Blindley Heath *S'work* 11–14; NSM Bletchingley and Nutfield from 14; PtO *Lon* from 14. *Little Granta, Godstone Road, Bletchingley, Redhill RH1 4PL* T: (01883) 744991 E: martinpenny012000@yahoo.com *or* penny.sherrington@gosh.nhs.uk

SHERWIN, Canon David Royston. b 56. St Jo Coll Nottm 84. **d** 89 **p** 90. C Conisbrough *Sheff* 89–95; V Wheatley Park and Dioc Adv for Evang 95–01; P-in-c Martley and Wichenford, Knightwick etc *Worc* 01–08; TR Worcs W Rural from 09; RD Martley and Worc W 08–19; Hon Can Worc Cathl from 15. *The Rectory, Martley, Worcester WR6 6QA* T/F: (01886) 888664 E: davidwin56@aol.com

SHERWIN, Miss Margaret Miriam. b 32. Ripon Coll Cuddesdon 81. **dss** 83 **d** 87 **p** 94. Holborn St Alb w Saffron Hill St Pet *Lon* 83–88; Par Dn 87–88; Par Dn Highgate St Mich 88–93; rtd 93; Hon C Purbrook *Portsm* 93–99; PtO from 99. *16 Lombard Court, Lombard Street, Portsmouth PO1 2HU* T: (023) 9283 8429

SHERWIN, Mrs Philippa Margaret. b 46. Lon Univ BDS 70 LDS 70. **d** 99 **p** 00. OLM Queen Thorne *Sarum* 99–08; rtd 08; PtO *Sarum* 08–15. Haycroft, Sandford Orcas, Sherborne DT9 4RP T: (01963) 220380 E: pm.sherwin@btinternet.com

SHERWOOD, David Charles. b 56. LRPS 94. WEMTC 98. **d** 01 **p** 02. C Taunton Lyngford *B & W* 01–05; P-in-c Hemyock w Culm Davy, Clayhidon and Culmstock *Ex* 05–11; P-in-c Ashburton, Bickington, Buckland in the Moor etc 11–17; RD Moreton 12–15; rtd 17. *Address withheld by request*

SHERWOOD, David James. b 45. Univ of Wales (Cardiff) LLM 94 Solicitor 69. St Steph Ho Ox 81. **d** 83 **p** 84. C Westbury-on-Trym H Trin *Bris* 83–85; C Corringham *Chelmsf* 85–87; V Hullbridge 87–94; V Kenton *Lon* 94–06; rtd 06; PtO *Chich* from 06; *Eur* from 98. *130 St Helens Road, Hastings TN34 2EJ* T: (01424) 254510 E: canddsherwood@aol.co.uk

SHERWOOD, Canon Ian Walter Lawrence. b 57. TCD BA 80. **d** 82 **p** 84. C Dublin St Patr Cathl Gp *D & G* 82–83; Chapl Billinge Hosp Wigan 83–86; C Orrell *Liv* 83–86; Chapl Bucharest w Sofia *Eur* 86–89; Chapl Istanbul w Moda from 89; Can Malta Cathl from 97; PtO from 92. *c/o FCO (Istanbul), King Charles Street, London SW1A 2AH* T: (0090) (212) 251 5616 F: 243 5702 E: anglicanistanbul1@gmail.com

SHERWOOD, Jane. *See* LEES, Jane

SHERWOOD, Kenneth Henry. b 37. CITC 90. **d** 93 **p** 94. NSM Malahide w Balgriffin *D & G* 93–96 and 04–15; NSM Castleknock and Mulhuddart w Clonsilla 96–97; NSM Leighlin w Grange Sylvae, Shankill etc *C, F & O* 97–04; NSM Holmpatrick w Balbriggan and Kenure *D & G* 15–18; NSM Swords w Donabate and Kilsallaghan 18–19; rtd 19. *49 Mountfield Park, Malahide, Co Dublin, Republic of Ireland* T: (00353) (1) 803 8485 M: 86-258 0002 E: kensherwood07@eircom.net

SHERWOOD, Suffragan Bishop of. *See* EMERTON, The Rt Revd Andrew Neil

SHEWAN, Alistair Boyd. b 44. Open Univ BA 83 BSc 95. Edin Th Coll 63. **d** 67 **p** 68. Prec St Andr Cathl Inverness *Mor* 67–69; C Shepherd's Bush St Steph w St Thos *Lon* 70–72; Hon C Edin St Mich and All SS 73–75; PtO 75–81; Hon C Edin Old St Paul 81–86; NSM Edin St Columba 87–91; Asst Dioc Supernumerary from 91; C Edin St Ninian 95–08. *Limegrove, High Street, Gifford, Haddington EH41 4QU* T: (01620) 810402 E: alistair315@btinternet.com

SHEWRING (née SMITH), Mrs Susan Helen. b 51. Univ of Cen England in Birm BEd 87 Warwick Univ PGDE 90. WMMTC 01. **d** 04 **p** 05. NSM Billesley Common *Birm* 04–07; Asst Chapl Univ Hosp Birm NHS Foundn Trust 07–14; rtd 14; PtO *Birm* from 14. *48 St Helens Road, Solihull B91 2DA* T: 0121-448 1846 M: 07914-434058 E: sue_shewring@yahoo.co.uk

SHIELD, Mrs Christine Ann. b 54. Lindisfarne Regional Tr Partnership 13. **d** 15 **p** 16. NSM Warkworth and Acklington *Newc* 15–19; NSM Warkworth, Acklington and Shilbottle from 19. *Godric's Hollow, 18 Watershaugh Road, Warkworth, Morpeth NE65 0TX* T: (01665) 711141 E: christineannshield@googlemail.com

SHIELDS, Dennis. b 50. Brighton Coll of Educn CertEd 72 Brighton Poly DipEd 84 Roehampton Inst MA 87 Sheff

Univ MA 16. **d** 05 **p** 06. NSM Meltham *Wakef* 05–14; Leeds from 14. *11 The Hollow, Meltham, Holmfirth HD9 5LA* T: (01484) 850074 F: 07812-349202 M: 07812-349202 E: dennis_shields@btinternet.com

SHIELDS, Mrs Jennifer Jill. b 39. Heref Coll of Educn CertEd 74. SAOMC 99. **d** 02 **p** 03. OLM Lenborough *Ox* 02–11; PtO from 11. *8 West Furlong, Padbury, Buckingham MK18 2BP* T: (01280) 814474

SHIELLS, Alex Alan Terry. b 94. Mattersey Hall BA 16 Dur Univ MA 19. St Hild Coll 17. **d** 19 **p** 20. C Worksop Ch Ch and Shireoaks *S'well* from 19. *27 Sunnyside, Worksop S81 7LN* M: 07591-982497 E: revalexshiells@gmail.com

SHIELS, Rosalinde Cameron. *See* WALSER, Rosalinde Cameron

SHILLAKER, Mrs Christine Frances. b 39. Gilmore Ho 74. **dss** 86 **d** 87 **p** 94. Colchester St Leon, St Mary Magd and St Steph *Chelmsf* 86–89; Par Dn 87–89; Par Dn Colchester, New Town and The Hythe 89–94; C 94–96; P-in-c Ramsey w Lt Oakley 96–02; rtd 02; PtO *Chelmsf* from 02. *21 Nelson Road, Colchester CO3 9AP* T: (01206) 570234

SHILLING, Ms Audrey Violet. b 26. Dur Univ BA 69. CA Tr Coll 51 Cranmer Hall Dur 66. **d** 87 **p** 94. CA from 53; NSM Gillingham H Trin *Roch* 87–93; NSM Rainham 94–96; PtO 96–10; *Guildf* 10–18. *Flat 14, Manormead, Tilford Road, Hindhead GU26 6RA* T: (01428) 601514 E: ashilling14@gmail.com

SHILLINGFORD, Brian. b 39. Lich Th Coll 65. **d** 68 **p** 69. C Lewisham St Swithun *S'wark* 68–71; C Godstone 71–75; TV Croydon St Jo *Cant* 75–81; TV N Creedy *Ex* 81–93; TR 93–05; rtd 05; PtO *Ex* from 05. *Lyndbank, Albert Road, Crediton EX17 2BZ* T: (01363) 772657 E: brianandkayshil@gmail.com

SHILLINGTON, Maureen Lesley. *See* BROWELL, Maureen Lesley

SHILLITO, Catherine Jayne. b 66. Man Metrop Univ BEd 90 Open Univ MA 00. Nazarene Th Coll Man MA 93 St Aug Coll Cant 18. **d** 21. C Longfield *Roch* from 21; C Fawkham and Hartley from 21; C Ash from 21; C Ridley from 21. *67 Main Road, Longfield DA3 7PQ* M: 07496-737020 E: jayne.shillito@btinternet.com

SHILSON-THOMAS, Mrs Annabel Margaret. b 60. Jes Coll Ox BA 82. Westcott Ho Cam 87. **d** 89 **p** 98. Par Dn Sydenham St Bart *S'wark* 89–93; Journalist CAFOD 95–03; Hon C Kingston All SS w St Jo *S'wark* 97–98; PtO *Ely* 00–03; Chapl Anglia Poly Univ 03–04; C Kingston All SS w St Jo *S'wark* 04–05; Spirituality Consultant CAFOD from 05; C Cambridge Gt St Mary w St Mich *Ely* 07–15; Tutor Westcott Ho Cam from 15; PtO *Ely* 15–20. *28 Fulbrooke Road, Cambridge CB3 9EE* T: (01223) 729475 E: ams94@cam.ac.uk

SHILSON-THOMAS, Canon Hugh David. b 64. Ex Coll Ox BA 86 MA 98 K Coll Lon MA 99. Westcott Ho Cam 87. **d** 89 **p** 90. C Sydenham All SS *S'wark* 89–92; C Lower Sydenham St Mich 89–92; Ecum Chapl Kingston Univ 93–98; Chapl Rob Coll Cam 98–03; Nat Adv for HE/Chapl Abps' Coun 03–08; Chapl and Dean of Chpl Selw Coll Cam from 08; Chapl Newnham Coll Cam from 08; Chapter Can Ely Cathl 10–18. *28 Fulbrooke Road, Cambridge CB3 9EE* T: (01223) 729475 *or* 335846 E: hds21@cam.ac.uk

SHIMWELL, Robert John. b 46. ARCM 65. Trin Coll Bris 75. **d** 78 **p** 79. C Richmond H Trin and Ch Ch *S'wark* 78–79; C Cullompton and Kentisbeare w Blackborough *Ex* 79–81; V S Cave and Ellerker w Broomfleet *York* 81–87; Chapl Lee Abbey 87–88; R Glas St Silas 88–94; V Upton (Overchurch) *Ches* 94–05; RD Wirral N 97–98; Hon Can Ches Cathl 02–05; V Lee St Mildred *S'wark* 05–11; rtd 11; PtO *S'wark* 11–15; *Roch* 12–16; *Ches* from 16. *12 The Oaks, Glossop SK13 6LD* T: (01457) 514601 E: rob.shimwell@gmail.com

SHIN, Beom Jin (Stephen). b 80. Kyung Hee Univ Korea BA 03 Univ Coll Lon MSc 08. St Steph Ho Ox 08. **d** 11 **p** 12. C Banbury *Ox* 11–15; PtO 16–17; Miss Partner CMS from 16. *Church Mission Society, Watlington Road, Cowley, Oxford OX4 6BZ* E: bjmonani@gmail.com

SHINE, Canon Ann Aisling. RGN SCM. **d** 03 **p** 04. Aux Min Dublin Drumcondra w N Strand *D & G* 03–10; Aux Min Clondalkin w Rathcoole from 05; Can Ch Ch Cathl Dublin from 10. *1 Roselawn Grove, Castleknock, Dublin 15, Republic of Ireland* T: (00353) (1) 820 1797 M: 87-239 7902 E: aislingshine@hotmail.com

SHINHMAR, Joshua Rajbir. b 68. Ridley Hall Cam 16. **d** 18 **p** 19. C Chesterton St Geo *Ely* 18–21; Chapl N Lon Hospice from 21. *5 Inkwell Close, London N12 8QQ* M: 07730-177765 E: rev.joshuashinhmar@gmail.com

SHINKINS, Pamela Mhairi. b 41. Leeds Univ BSc 62 Open Univ BA 84. TISEC 05. **d** 07 **p** 08. LtO *Mor* from 08. *Homelea, 7 Blair, Poolewe, Achnasheen IV22 2LP* T: (01445) 781346 E: pam.shinkins@btinternet.com

SHINTON, Bertram. b 41. WMMTC 95. **d** 98 **p** 99. NSM Broseley w Benthall, Jackfield, Linley etc *Heref* 98–12; PtO from 10; *Lich* 19–21. *Eve Cottage, 6 Carvers Road, Broseley TF12 5HP* T: (01952) 883534

SHIPLEY, Christopher John. b 44. Leeds Univ BSc 65 MSc 70 BA 72. Coll of Resurr Mirfield 70. **d** 73 **p** 74. C Preston St Jo *Blackb* 73–77; Chapl Lancs (Preston) Poly 75–77; V Blackb St Mich w St Jo 77–81; P-in-c Blackb H Trin 78–81; V Blackb St Mich w St Jo and H Trin 81–82; V Walthamstow St Pet *Chelmsf* 82–85; Gen Sec Mary Feilding Guild Lon 85–86; Org Waltham Forest Coun for Voluntary Service 86–89; Gen Sec Hull 89–91; Dir Grimsby and Cleethorpes 91; Teacher Upbury Manor High Sch Gillingham 92–94; Hd of Science 94–02; Teacher Whitstable Community Coll 02–03; Hd of Science Cheyne Middle Sch Sheerness 03–09; Team Ldr Science Is of Sheppey Academy 09–10; C Minster-in-Sheppey *Cant* 10–12; C Sheerness H Trin w St Paul 10–12; C Queenborough 10–12; C W Sheppey 12–14; C Eastchurch w Leysdown and Harty 10–12; P-in-c 12–14; R 14–16; PtO 17–20. *12 Cumberland Drive, Lower Halstow, Sittingbourne ME9 7JA* T: (01795) 841125 E: chrisshply@gmail.com

SHIPLEY, June Patricia. *See* ASQUITH, June Patricia

SHIPLEY, Ruth Mary. *See* HOWLETT-SHIPLEY, Ruth Mary

SHIPLEY, Canon Stephen Edwin Burnham. b 52. Univ Coll Dur BA 74. Westcott Ho Cam 85. **d** 87 **p** 88. C Ipswich St Marg *St E* 87–90; P-in-c Stuntney *Ely* 90–95; Min Can, Prec and Sacr Ely Cathl 90–95; Producer Worship Progr BBC Relig Broadcasting from 95; LtO *Derby* from 96; Hon Can Derby Cathl from 09. *21 Devonshire Road, Buxton SK17 6RZ* T: (01298) 78383 M: 07808-403812 E: sebshipley@gmail.com

SHIPP, Elizabeth Ann. *See* MURGATROYD-SHIPP, Elizabeth Ann

SHIPP, Susan. *See* HOLLINS, Patricia Susan

SHIPTON, Canon Andrew James. b 60. Leeds Univ BA 82 Univ of Northumbria at Newc MEd 99 Leeds Univ MPhil 06. Cranmer Hall Dur 83. **d** 85 **p** 86. C Fishponds St Jo *Bris* 85–88; C Gosforth All SS *Newc* 88–91; V Long Benton St Mary 91–96; Chapl Northumbria Univ 96–06; TV Ch the King 06–07; TR 07–14; V Gosforth All SS from 14; P-in-c Gosforth St Hugh from 17; Dioc Development Officer for Youth Work from 06; Hon Can Newc Cathl from 07. *All Saints' Vicarage, 33 Brackenfield Road, Newcastle upon Tyne NE3 4DX* T: 0191-284 5540 E: andrewshipton085@aol.com

SHIPTON, Eileen Kay. *See* OSGOOD, Eileen Kay

SHIPTON, Linda Anne. *See* GREEN, Linda Anne

SHIRES, Alan William. b 36. Lon Univ BA 60. Oak Hill Th Coll 57. **d** 61 **p** 62. C York St Paul 61–64; C Southgate *Chich* 64–67; V Doncaster St Mary *Sheff* 67–75; PtO *Portsm* 75–96; Student Cllr Portsm Poly 95–88; Hd Student Services Portsm Univ 88–94; rtd 96; PtO *Lich* 13. *15 Broomfield Road, Admaston, Wellington TF5 0AR* E: aw.shires@btinternet.com

SHIRES, Benjamin Crossley. b 90. Dur Univ BA 12 Middx Univ BA 21. Oak Hill Th Coll 18. **d** 21. C Kilnhurst *Sheff* from 21. *20 Canalside View, Kilnhurst, Mexborough S64 5SD* M: 07805-654448 E: bcshires@gmail.com

SHIRLEY, Gary Ronald. b 57. Wilson Carlile Coll 96 SWMTC 06. **d** 09 **p** 10. C Devonport St Budeaux *Ex* 09–12; C Yelverton, Meavy, Sheepstor and Walkhampton 12–16; C Yelverton, Meavy, Sheepstor, Walkhampton, Sampford Spiney and Horrabridge 16–19; rtd 19. *47 Hallsfield, Cricklade, Swindon SN6 6LR* E: gary.shirley2@btinternet.com

SHIRLEY, Valerie Joy. b 42. **d** 96 **p** 97. OLM Sydenham H Trin *S'wark* 96–07; OLM Sydenham H Trin and St Aug 07–12; PtO from 12. *9 Faircroft, 5 Westwood Hill, London SE26 6BG* T: (020) 8778 2551 E: valshirley@btinternet.com

SHIRRAS, Mrs Pamela Susan. b 41. St Andr Univ BSc 62 Brunel Univ PGCE 80. Wycliffe Hall Ox 04. **d** 05 **p** 06. NSM Marcham w Garford *Ox* 05–09; PtO 09; NSM Abingdon 09–11; PtO from 11. *4 Culham Close, Abingdon OX14 2AS* T: (01235) 553129 E: epshirras@aol.com

SHOCK, Rachel Alexandra. b 63. Nottm Trent Univ LLB 94. EMMTC 95. **d** 98 **p** 00. NSM Radford All So w Ch Ch and St Mich *S'well* 98–99; NSM Lenton Abbey 99–02; NSM Wollaton 02–08; Internet Chapl Development Worker 06–10; Workplace Chapl and NSM Nottingham All SS, St Mary and St Pet *S'well* 11–15; PtO from 15; Chapl Costa Brava *Eur* from 18. *Placa Firal 4, 17121 Corçà (Girona), Spain* E: chaplaincostabrava@gmail.com

SHODEINDE, Mrs Shavaun Veta. b 85. Birm Univ BSc 07. Coll of Resurr Mirfield 17. **d** 20 **p** 21. C Wandsworth Common St Mary *S'wark* from 20. *59 Fieldview, London SW18 3HF* M: 07983-414219 E: shavaunshodeinde@outlook.com *or* curate@smmwandsworth.org.uk

SHOESMITH (*née* HALL), Mrs Judith Frances. b 64. SS Coll Cam BA 85 MA 89 MEng 94 BTh 02 CEng 97. Ridley Hall Cam 99. **d** 02 **p** 03. C Drayton in Hales *Lich* 02–05; LtO *Liv* 05–11; TV Walthamstow *Chelmsf* 11–18; TV Wigan All SS *Liv* 18–19; TV Wigan from 20. *The Vicarage, 141 Whelley, Wigan WN1 3UE* M: 07505-126167 E: fshoesmith@gmail.com *or* hubleader.northeast@churchwigan.org

SHOESMITH, Canon Kathia Andree. b 64. Leeds Univ BA 08 RN 98. Coll of Resurr Mirfield 06. **d** 08 **p** 09. C Ripponden and Barkisland w W Scammonden *Wakef* 08–11; V Bradshaw and Holmfield 11–14; *Leeds* from 14; C Southowram and Claremount 17–19; AD Halifax 17–19; Jt AD Calder Valley 18–19; AD Halifax and Calder Valley from 20; AD Brighouse and Elland 20–21; Hon Can Bradf Cathl from 19. *The Vicarage, Pavement Lane, Bradshaw, Halifax HX2 9JJ* T: (01422) 244330 E: reverend.kathia@outlook.com

SHOKRALLA, Adel Salah Makar. b 75. Ain Shams Univ Cairo BSc 96. Alexandria Sch of Th 05 Trin Coll Bris MA 10. **d** 09 **p** 11. C Heavitree and St Mary Steps *Ex* 10–12; CMS Egypt 12–15; V Old Windsor *Ox* from 15. *The Vicarage, Church Road, Old Windsor, Windsor SL4 2PQ* T: (01753) 865778 M: 07729-772276

SHONE, Miss Ursula Ruth. b 34. Stirling Univ BA 75 Open Univ BPhil 88. dss 81 **d** 86 **p** 94. Bridge of Allan *St And* 81–85; Lochgelly 85–87; Chapl Cov Cathl 87–90; Ind Chapl 87–90; Par Dn Ainsdale *Liv* 90–94; Dioc Science Adv 90–99; C Ainsdale 94–96; C Childwall St Dav 96–99; rtd 99; NSM Brechin *Bre* 00–12; LtO *Edin* from 12. *5 Abbotsford Court, Kelso TD5 7SQ* T: (01573) 224210 E: u.shone@btinternet.com

SHOOTER, Philippa Margaret. b 49. Hull Univ BA 70 Nottm Univ MA 72 CQSW 72. NOC 04. **d** 06 **p** 07. NSM Fence-in-Pendle and Higham *Blackb* 06–11; Hon C Coppull and Coppull St Jo 11–13; rtd 13; PtO *York* from 13. *23 Nelson Street, Bridlington YO15 3BJ* T: (01262) 424802 E: philippashooter@btinternet.com

SHOOTER, Robert David. b 44. Lon Univ BSc 70 Lanc Univ MA 94 CQSW 72 LRAM 92. NOC 99. **d** 02 **p** 03. NSM Brierfield *Blackb* 02–04; NSM Briercliffe 04–09; PtO 09–13; *York* from 13. *23 Nelson Street, Bridlington YO15 3BJ* T: (01262) 424802 E: robertshooter@btinternet.com

SHOOTER, Susan. b 58. Nottm Univ BA 81 PGCE 82 K Coll Lon DThMin 11. St Jo Coll Nottm MA 96. **d** 96 **p** 98. C Dartford H Trin *Roch* 96–97; C Crayford 97–00; V Bostall Heath 00–09. *131 Pengelly, Delabole PL33 9AT* T: (01840) 213645 M: 07929-496942 E: shooter160@btinternet.com

SHOREY, Simon Daniel John. b 77. St Mellitus Coll 15. **d** 18 **p** 19. C Wivelsfield *Chich* from 18; C Mid-Sussex Network Ch from 18. *30 Haywards Road, Haywards Heath RH16 4JB* E: simon@thepointchurch.co.uk

SHORT, Bryan Raymond. b 37. Bris Univ BSc 59 CertEd 60. **d** 02 **p** 03. OLM Kirkheaton *Wakef* 02–09; PtO 09–14; *Leeds* from 14. *12 Bankfield Lane, Kirkheaton, Huddersfield HD5 0JG* T: (01484) 425832

SHORT, Ms Clare. b 50. Leic Univ BA 72 St Mary's Coll Twickenham PGCE 73. S Dios Minl Tr Scheme 89. **d** 92 **p** 94. NSM Horsham *Chich* 92–99; PtO *Newc* 04–15. *Hedgelea, South Road, Lowick, Berwick-upon-Tweed TD15 2TX* T: (01289) 389222

SHORT, David Keith. b 64. Nottm Univ MSci 01 Chu Coll Cam BTh 13 Warwick Univ PGCE 04. Ridley Hall Cam 10. **d** 13 **p** 14. C Chorleywood Ch Ch *St Alb* 13–16; V Furze Platt *Ox* from 16. *Address withheld by request* T: (01628) 621961 E: david@stpetersmaidenhead.org

SHORT, Eileen. b 45. Ex Univ BA 66. NOC 93. **d** 96 **p** 97. NSM Castleton Moor *Man* 96–98; NSM Chorlton-cum-Hardy St Clem 98–00; NSM Baguley 00–10; PtO 10–19; *Ches* from 16. *2 Netherwood Road, Northenden, Manchester M22 4BQ*

SHORT, Mrs Heather Mary. b 50. LWCMD 71 Cardiff Coll of Educn CertEd 72. WEMTC 98. **d** 01 **p** 02. C Heref S Wye 01–05; P-in-c Bodenham, Felton and Preston Wynne 05–12; P-in-c Marden w Amberley and Wisteston 05–12; P-in-c Sutton St Nicholas w Sutton St Michael 05–12; R Maund Gp 12–17; rtd 17; PtO *Heref* from 20. *24 Boraston Drive, Burford, Tenbury Wells WR15 8AG*

SHORT, Canon John Timothy. b 43. Kelham Th Coll 63. **d** 68 **p** 69. C St Marylebone Ch Ch w St Barn *Lon* 68–70; C Southgate Ch Ch 70–72; P-in-c Mosser and Dioc Youth Officer *Carl* 72–78; R Heyford w Stowe Nine Churches *Pet* 78–87; V Northampton St Jas 87–96; RD Wootton 88–96; TR Kingsthorpe w Northampton St Dav 96–08; Can Pet Cathl 97–08; rtd 08; PtO *Pet* from 09; *Derby* 14–18. *11 Cytringan Close, Kettering NN15 6GW* T: (01536) 310633 E: jtimshort@btinternet.com

SHORT, Kenneth Arthur. b 33. Tyndale Hall Bris 64. **d** 67 **p** 68. C E Twickenham St Steph *Lon* 67–71; C Paddock Wood *Roch* 71–74; SE Area Sec BCMS 74–82; Hon C Sidcup Ch Ch

Roch 74–82; V Tollington Park St Mark w St Anne Lon 82–86; V Holloway St Mark w Em 86–89; R Alfold and Loxwood Guildf 89–98; rtd 98; PtO Roch 00–13; Lon 02–13; S'wark from 15. *10 Montague Graham Court, Kidbrooke Gardens, London SE3 0PD* T: (020) 8858 8033 E: jukebox.short@gmail.com

SHORT, Martin Peter. b 54. Peterho Cam BA 77 MA 81. Wycliffe Hall Ox 77. **d** 79 **p** 80. C Shipley St Pet Bradf 79–82; C Becontree St Mary Chelmsf 82–86; V Bolton St Jas w St Chrys Bradf 86–92; Dioc Communications Officer 92–98; C Otley 92–98; Hd Media Tr Communications Dept Abps' Coun 98–05; Hon C and Hon Chapl Bradf Cathl 98–05; Chapl to Bp Dover Cant 06–12; Hon Min Can Cant Cathl 06–12; R Stow on the Wold, Condicote and The Swells Glouc 12–21; rtd 21. *11 Coach Road, Baildon, Shipley BD17 5JE* E: ms66uk@icloud.com

SHORT, Martin Ronald. b 57. Crewe & Alsager Coll CertEd 78 Leic Univ BEd 85 St Jo Coll Nottm MA 01. 93. **d** 93 **p** 94. C Frankby w Greasby Ches 93–97; TV Horwich and Rivington Man 97–02; TV Turton Moorland 02–08; P-in-c Rawtenstall St Mary 08–15; P-in-c Constable Lee 08–15; Borough Dean Rossendale 10–13; AD Rossendale 13–15; R Middleton and Thornham 15–18; V Honley Leeds from 18. *The Vicarage, St Mary's Road, Honley, Holmfirth HD9 6AZ* E: martin.short@leeds.anglican.org

SHORT, Canon Michael John. b 38. Univ of Wales (Lamp) BA 59. Sarum Th Coll 59. **d** 61 **p** 62. C Swansea St Nic S & B 61–64; C Oystermouth 64–69; V Merthyr Vale w Aberfan Llan 69–82; RD Merthyr Tydfil 76–82; R Caerphilly 82–08; RD 83–04; Can Llan Cathl 89–08; Prec 02–08; rtd 08; PtO Llan from 10. *238 Abercynon Road, Abercynon, Mountain Ash CF45 4LU* T: (01443) 742650 M: 07831-742515

SHORT, Neil Robert. b 58. Loughb Univ BSc 81 St Jo Coll Dur BA 86. Cranmer Hall Dur 83. **d** 86 **p** 87. C Whitfield Derby 86–90; C Bradf St Aug Undercliffe 90–96; V Burscough Bridge Liv 96–07; Pioneer Min Toxteth 07–09; V St Jas in the City 09–18; V Blundellsands St Mich from 18. *5 Ramleh Park, Liverpool L23 6YD* E: neil@theshorts.go-plus.net

SHORT, Mrs Patricia Ann (Pip). b 41. K Coll Lon BA 62 AKC 62. **d** 00 **p** 01. NSM Etwall w Egginton Derby 00–10; NSM Ashbourne St Jo 10–11; NSM Ashbourne St Oswald w Mapleton 10–11; NSM Clifton 10–11; NSM Norbury w Snelston 10–11; Chapl Asst Univ Hosps of Derby and Burton NHS Foundn Trust from 00; PtO Lich 05–09 and 14–15; Derby from 11; Lich 17–20. *Ivy Cottage, 19 Monk Street, Tutbury, Burton-on-Trent DE13 9NA* T: (01283) 813640 or (01332) 347141 F: (01283) 814373 M: 07711-823082 E: pip.short2011@gmail.com

SHORT, Robert Leslie. b 48. Em Coll Cam BA 70 MA 76. Wycliffe Hall Ox 87. **d** 92 **p** 92. Mexico 92–93; Chapl Repton Sch Derby 93–04; P-in-c Ibiza Eur 04–13; rtd 13; PtO Eur from 13; S'well from 13. *49 Manton Crescent, Beeston, Nottingham NG9 2GD* E: bobthevicar@gmail.com

SHORT, Stephen John. b 60. Salford Univ MSc 99. St Mellitus Coll 18. **d** 20 **p** 21. NSM Banbury St Paul Ox from 20. *30 Washle Drive, Middleton Cheney, Banbury OX17 2PY* T: (01295) 713942 M: 07768-492915 E: steveishome@gmail.com

SHORT, Stephen Timothy. b 71. Cheltenham & Glouc Coll of HE BA 96. Ripon Coll Cuddesdon 05. **d** 07 **p** 08. C Tewkesbury w Walton Cardiff and Twyning Glouc 07–11; P-in-c Clowne Derby 11–13; C Barlborough and Renishaw 11–13; R Barlborough and Clowne 13–17; V Melbourne, Ticknall, Smisby and Stanton from 17. *The Rectory, Church Square, Melbourne, Derby DE73 8JH* T: (01332) 864741 M: 07801-357612 E: stephen.short71@btinternet.com

SHORT, Timothy. See SHORT, John Timothy

SHORT, Vincent Charles. b 57. Oak Hill Th Coll 95. **d** 97 **p** 98. C Chatham St Phil and St Jas Roch 97–01; V Istead Rise 01–11; V New Beckenham St Paul 11–16; TV Limpsfield and Tatsfield S'wark from 16. *The Rectory, Ricketts Hill Road, Tatsfield, Westerham TN16 2NA* T: (01959) 577289

SHORTER, Mrs Anne Roberta. b 56. Edin Univ BA 77 Cam Univ BTh 09. Westcott Ho Cam 07. **d** 09 **p** 10. C Brackley St Pet w St Jas Pet 09–12; P-in-c Stanground Ely 13; P-in-c Farcet 13; V Stanground and Farcet 13–19; rtd 19. *1/7 St Vincent Place, Edinburgh EH3 5BQ* E: anne.shorter@btinternet.com

SHORTER, Robert Edward. b 48. Ripon Coll Cuddesdon 89. **d** 91 **p** 92. C Braunton Ex 91–94; C Bishopsnympton, Rose Ash, Mariansleigh etc 94–96; TV 96–98; P-in-c E w W Harptree and Hinton Blewett B & W 98–03; Dioc Ecum Officer 98–03; rtd 03. *Neduadd Bungalow, Dyffryn Road, Llandrindod Wells LD1 6AN* T: (01597) 829790 E: robertshorter@live.co.uk

SHOTLANDER, Lionel George. b 27. Cant Univ (NZ) BA 49 MA 51. **d** 51 **p** 52. NZ 51–58 and 60–74; C Southsea St Pet Portsm 58–60; V Curdridge 74–85; R Durley 79–85; V Twyford and Owslebury and Morestead Win 85–91; rtd 91;

PtO Win 91–20; Portsm from 91. *Cambria, High Street, Shirrell Heath, Southampton SO32 2JN* T: (01329) 832353

SHOTTON, Heather Margaret Elizabeth. d 18 **p** 19. NSM Wrexham St As from 18; NSM Offa Miss Area from 20. *10 Brynmally Park, Pentre Broughton, Wrexham LL11 6BP* T: (01978) 721666

SHOULER, Canon the Hon Margaret Fiona. b 55. Nottm Univ BEd 78. St Jo Coll Nottm MTh 03. **d** 01 **p** 02. C Sherwood S'well 01–06; P-in-c Selston 06–11; V from 11; AD Newstead 17–20; Hon Can S'well Minster from 17. *The Vicarage, 58 Church Lane, Selston, Nottingham NG16 6EW* T: (01773) 813777 E: fionashouler@hotmail.com

SHOULER, Simon Frederic. b 54. Pemb Coll Cam MA 79 FRICS 89. EMMTC 82. **d** 85 **p** 86. NSM Asfordby Leic 85–89; LtO from 89. *1 West End, Long Clawson, Melton Mowbray LE14 4PE* T: (01664) 822698

SHOWERS, Cyril Rotimi Sigismond. b 64. Fourah Bay Coll Freetown BA 89 DipAdEd 84. SEITE 09. **d** 12 **p** 13. NSM N Dulwich St Faith S'wark 12–16; PtO 16–18; Public Preacher 18–19; NSM Perry Street Roch 19–20; NSM Northfleet and Rosherville 19–20; P-in-c from 20. *St Mark's Vicarage, 123 London Road, Northfleet, Gravesend DA11 9NH* T: (01474) 535814 M: 07956-767718 E: spriestincharge@gmail.com

SHREEVE, The Ven David Herbert. b 34. St Pet Hall Ox BA 57 MA 61. Ridley Hall Cam 57. **d** 59 **p** 60. C Plymouth St Andr Ex 59–64; V Bermondsey St Anne S'wark 64–71; V Eccleshill Bradf 71–84; RD Calverley 78–84; Hon Can Bradf Cathl 83–84; Adn Bradf 84–99; rtd 99; PtO Bradf 99–14; Ripon 00–14; Leeds from 14. *26 Kingsley Drive, Harrogate HG1 4TJ* T: (01423) 886479

SHREEVES, Keir Laurence. b 82. Brunel Univ BA 04 K Coll Lon MA 16 Aber Univ PhD 19. St Mellitus Coll BA 13. **d** 13 **p** 14. C Turnham Green Ch Ch Lon 13–16; NSM Brighton St Pet Chich 16–19; Dioc Dir of Ords from 19. *Diocese of Chichester, Church House, 211 New Church Road, Hove BN3 4ED* T: (01273) 425019 E: keir.shreeves@chichester.anglican.org

SHREWSBURY, Area Bishop of. See BULLOCK, The Rt Revd Sarah Ruth

SHRIMPTON, Mrs Sheila Nan. b 32. Qu Mary Coll Lon BA 54 LSE CertSS 55. St Chris Coll Blackheath 57. **dss** 83 **d** 87 **p** 94. LtO B & W 83–90; NSM Barkston and Hough Gp Linc 90–97; Asst Local Min Officer 90–97; C Brant Broughton and Beckingham 97–98; P-in-c Churchstanton, Buckland St Mary and Otterford B & W 98–02; rtd 02; PtO B & W 03–14. *2 King William Mews, Church Street, Curry Rivel, Langport TA10 0HD* T: (01458) 259293

SHRINE, Mrs Susan Elaine Walmsley. b 56. NOC. **d** 02 **p** 03. C Bradshaw and Holmfield Wakef 02–04; TV Shelf w Buttershaw St Aid Bradf 04–10; P-in-c Queensbury 10–15; V 15–16; P-in-c Bredbury St Barn Ches from 16; P-in-c Queensbury Leeds from 14. *St Barnabas' Vicarage, Osborne Street, Bredbury, Stockport SK6 2AD* T: 0161-406 6569 E: sue.shrine780@btinternet.com

SHUKER, Linda Kathleen. b 56. Imp Coll Lon BSc 77 PhD 81. St Jo Coll Nottm 05. **d** 07 **p** 08. C Rothley Leic 07–11; R Birling, Addington, Ryarsh and Trottiscliffe Roch 11–21; rtd 21. *Broadmarsh, Horsey Road, West Somerton, Great Yarmouth NR29 4DW* E: dlshuker@aol.com

SHUKMAN, Ann Margaret. b 31. Girton Coll Cam BA 53 MA 58 LMH Ox DPhil 74. WMMTC 80. **dss** 84 **d** 92 **p** 94. Steeple Aston w N Aston and Tackley Ox 84–96; NSM 92–96; rtd 96; PtO Ox 96–01; Hon C Dumfries Glas from 01. *Elshnieshields Tower, Lockerbie DG11 1LY* T: (01387) 810280 E: revann@stjohnsdumfries.org or ann.shukman@gmail.com

SHULER, Patricia Ann Margaret. b 52. Anglia Ruskin Univ MA 08 Univ of Wales (Ban) BTh 08. Ridley Hall Cam 02. **d** 05 **p** 06. C Ipswich St Aug St E 05–09; C Woodbridge St Jo and Bredfield 09–12; P-in-c Martlesham w Brightwell 12–15; rtd 15; Rtd Clergy, Widows and Widowers Officer Ches from 15; PtO from 16. *27 The Beeches, Upton, Chester CH2 1PE* T: (01244) 318941 E: tricia.shuler@gmail.com

SHUTT, Anthony John. b 57. Brunel Univ BSc 79. Trin Coll Bris 87. **d** 89 **p** 90. C Epsom St Martin Guildf 89–95; P-in-c Send from 95. *St Mary's Vicarage, Vicarage Lane, Send, Woking GU23 7JN* T: (01483) 222193 E: tony@tonyshutt.co.uk

SHUTT, The Ven Nicholas Stephen. b 58. Qu Mary Coll Lon LLB 80 Univ of Wales (Cardiff) LLM 01 Plymouth Coll of Art BA 11 Solicitor 83. SWMTC 91. **d** 94 **p** 95. NSM Yelverton, Meavy, Sheepstor and Walkhampton Ex 94–08; P-in-c 08–16; R Yelverton, Meavy, Sheepstor, Walkhampton, Sampford Spiney and Horrabridge 16–19; Adn Plymouth from 19; Preb Ex Cathl from 11. *12 Blackbrook Close, Walkhampton, Yelverton PL20 6JP* T: (01822) 854653 or (01752) 858382 E: archdeacon.of.plymouth@exeter.anglican.org or nick.shutt@gmail.com

SHUTTLEWORTH, Caroline Elizabeth. b 59. K Coll Lon BA 92. St Mellitus Coll BA 16. d 16 p 17. C Islington St Mary Lon 16–21. *20 Ellesmere Road, London E3 5QX* M: 07986-064025 E: ceshuttleworth@aol.com *or* caroline.shuttleworth@stmaryislington.org

SHUTTLEWORTH (née Gaunt), Rachel. b 81. St Cuth Soc Dur BA 04. St Mellitus Coll BA 18. d 18 p 19. C Tanhouse The Oaks CD *Liv* 18–20; TV St Helens Town Cen from 20. *The Rectory, 51A Rainford Road, Dentons Green, St Helens WA10 6BZ* M: 07508-354019 E: revrachelshuttleworth@gmail.com

SIBANDA, The Very Revd Melusi Francis. b 72. Univ of Zimbabwe BSc 96 BA 99 St Martin's Coll Lanc MA 06. Bp Gaul Th Coll Harare 97. d 98 p 99. C Bulawayo Cathl Zimbabwe 98–01; R Bulawayo St Marg 01–03; C Colne and Villages *Blackb* 03–06; P-in-c Rednal *Birm* 06–12; V 12–16; AD Kings Norton 12–16; R Dunsborough Australia 16–19; Dean St Paul's Cathl Rockhampton from 19. *The Deanery, 164 Alma Lane, Rockhampton QLD 4700, Australia* E: melusi.sibanda@gmail.com

SIBANDA, Thabani Isaac. b 84. Cranmer Hall Dur 15. d 18 p 19. C Nor Heartsease St Fran 18–20; C Thorpe St Matt 19–20. *9 Pine Road, Norwich NR7 9LE* M: 07709-552157 E: thabo.i.sibanda@gmail.com

SIBBALD, Olwyn Eileen. See MARLOW, Olwyn Eileen

SIBLEY, Jonathan Paul Eddolls. b 55. Newc Univ BA 77. Westcott Ho Cam 78 Ripon Coll Cuddesdon 85. d 87 p 88. C Waltham Cross *St Alb* 87–90; C Chalfont St Peter *Ox* 90–96; P-in-c Sulhamstead Abbots and Bannister w Ufton Nervet 96–02; P-in-c Sutton St Mary *Linc* 02–11; V Long Sutton w Lutton etc from 11. *The Vicarage, Market Place, Long Sutton, Spalding PE12 9JJ* T/F: (01406) 362033 E: jonathan.sibley3@btinternet.com

SIBLEY, Peter Linsey. b 40. Selw Coll Cam BA 61 MA 63. Oak Hill Th Coll 79. d 81 p 82. C Crofton *Portsm* 81–84; TV Cheltenham St Mark *Glouc* 84–93; P-in-c Tewkesbury H Trin 93–96; V 96–05; RD Tewkesbury and Winchcombe 97–02; rtd 05; PtO *Glouc* from 14. *14 Griffiths Avenue, Cheltenham GL51 7BH* T: (01242) 514640 E: sibglos@aol.com

SIBSON, Canon Edward John. b 39. Brasted Th Coll 61 St Aid Birkenhead 63. d 65 p 66. C Gt Parndon *Chelmsf* 65–69; C Saffron Walden 69–72; P-in-c Colchester St Leon 72–77; TV Colchester St Leon, St Mary Magd and St Steph 77–80; Ind Chapl 72–80; V Layer de la Haye 80–90; R Chipping Ongar w Shelley 90–98; RD Ongar 94–98; P-in-c High and Gd Easter w Margaret Roding 98–04; P-in-c Gt Canfield w High Roding and Aythorpe Roding 02–04; Hon Can Chelmsf Cathl 01–04; rtd 04; PtO *Chelmsf* from 04. *73 Thaxted Road, Saffron Walden CB11 3AG* T: (01799) 520007 E: ejohnsibson@btinternet.com

SIBSON, Canon Robert Francis. b 46. Leeds Univ CertEd 68. Sarum & Wells Th Coll 78. d 80 p 81. C Watford St Mich *St Alb* 80–83; TV Digswell and Panshanger 83–90; Chapl Qu Eliz Hosp Welwyn Garden City 86–88; V Biggleswade *St Alb* 90–02; Chapl Bedford and Shires Health and Care NHS Trust 94–02; RD Biggleswade *St Alb* 96–01; V Sawbridgeworth 02–12; Hon Can St Alb 98–12; rtd 12; PtO *St Alb* from 12; *Ely* from 13; Asst Rtd Clergy Officer from 16. *35 High Street, Offord D'Arcy, St Neots PE19 5RF* T: (01480) 812756 M: 07711-705081 E: robert.sibson@btinternet.com

SICHEL, Stephen Mackenzie. b 59. UEA BA 80 Birm Univ MA 95 K Coll Lon DThMin 16. Ripon Coll Cuddesdon 87. d 90 p 91. C Tettenhall Regis *Lich* 90–95; C Camberwell St Giles w St Matt *S'wark* 95–01; P-in-c Brixton St Matt 01–02; P-in-c Brixton St Matt w St Jude 02–13; V from 13; AD Lambeth N 10–12. *The Vicarage, 5 St Matthew's Road, London SW2 1ND* T/F: (020) 7733 9605 E: sichel@tiscali.co.uk

SIDDALL, Canon Arthur. b 43. Lanc Univ MA 81 Surrey Univ PGCE 94 MCMI 96. ALCD 67. d 67 p 68. C Formby H Trin *Liv* 67–70; C Childwall All SS 70–72; CMS 72–77; Chapl Chittagong Ch Ch Bangladesh 74–77; V Clitheroe St Paul Low Moor *Blackb* 77–82; V Blackb St Gabr 82–90; Dep Gen Sec Miss to Seamen 90–93; Hon C Leatherhead *Guildf* 93–96; V Chipping and Whitewell *Blackb* 96–04; Rural Chapl 03–04; Chapl Naples w Sorrento, Capri and Bari *Eur* 04–07; Chapl Montreux w Anzere, Gstaad and Monthey 07–09; Adn Italy and Malta 05–09; Switzerland 07–09; rtd 09; PtO *Liv* from 16; *Blackb* 16–17; *Eur* 16–21. *73 Hillary Court, Freshfield Road, Formby, Liverpool L37 3PS*

SIDDALL, Mark. b 77. Southn Univ BSc 99 PhD 03 Univ of Bordeaux II MSc 98. St Mellitus Coll MA 18. d 18 p 19. C Draycot *Bris* from 18. *11 Aintree Drive, Chippenham SN14 0FA* M: 07482-316541 E: mr_mark_sid@yahoo.com

SIDEBOTTOM, Andrew John. See GRACE, Andrew John

SIDEBOTTOM, Susan Marie. b 60. Yorks Min Course. d 09 p 10. NSM Chesterton *Lich* 09–16; NSM Knutton from 16. *18 Leech Avenue, Newcastle ST5 7PN*

SIDHU, Rajiv Daniel. b 88. Wycliffe Hall Ox 18 Ripon Coll Cuddesdon 19. d 21. C Portsea St Cuth *Portsm* from 21. *102 Copnor Road, Portsmouth PO3 5AL* M: 07534-863451 *or* 07510-089692 E: rajiv@stcuthbertandstaidan.org.uk

SIDWELL, Elizabeth Sarah. b 57. Girton Coll Cam BA 79 MA 83 Univ of Wales (Swansea) MSc 94. Ripon Coll Cuddesdon 08. d 10 p 11. C Wells St Cuth w Wookey Hole *B & W* 10–14; PtO 14–15; R Bredenbury *Heref* from 15. *The Rectory, Bredenbury, Bromyard HR7 4TF* T: (01885) 482737 E: essidwell@yahoo.ie

SIEBER, Miss Samantha Lyn. b 81. Univ of Delaware BSc 04. Ridley Hall Cam 19. d 21. C Edgbaston St Germain *Birm* from 21. *5 Statham Drive, Birmingham B16 0TF* M: 07766-258950 E: samanthasieber@gmail.com *or* samantha@stgermains.org.uk

SIEBERT, Mrs Rosemary Clare. b 48. Solicitor 03. SEITE 99. d 08 p 09. NSM Folkestone St Mary, St Eanswythe and St Sav *Cant* 08–15; NSM Marcham w Garford and Shippon *Ox* from 16. *9 Sweetbriar, North Street, Marcham, Abingdon OX13 6PD* T: (01865) 392135 M: 07763-330113 E: rsiebert@btinternet.com

SIEJKOWSKI, Piotr Jan. See ASHWIN-SIEJKOWSKI, Piotr Jan

SIGRIST, Mrs Catherine Mary. b 55. Westcott Ho Cam. d 07 p 08. C Cheriton St Martin *Cant* 07–10; C Cheriton All So w Newington 07–10; R Ringwould w Kingsdown and Ripple etc 10–16; P-in-c Saltash *Truro* 16–20; P-in-c Landrake w St Erney and Botus Fleming 16–20; P-in-c King's Wood *Cant* from 20. *The Rectory, 3 Hambrook Close, Chiltham, Canterbury CT4 8EJ* T: (01227) 738046 E: rev.cathysigrist@gmail.com

SIGRIST, Richard Martin. b 46. Bernard Gilpin Soc Dur 67 Sarum Th Coll 68. d 71 p 72. C Yeovil St Mich *B & W* 71–74; Chapl RN 74–84; TV Sidmouth, Woolbrook and Salcombe Regis *Ex* 84–86; TR 86–91; TR Sidmouth, Woolbrook, Salcombe Regis, Sidbury etc 91–94; RD Ottery 90–94; USA 94–99; P-in-c Devonport St Bart *Ex* 99–02; V 02–07; V Devonport St Bart and Ford St Mark 08–11; RD Plymouth Devonport 01–11; rtd 11; PtO *B & W* from 11. *4 Brue Crescent, Burnham-on-Sea TA8 1LR* T: (01278) 780135 E: rmsigrist@hotmail.com

SIGSWORTH, David. b 61. York Univ BA 82 K Coll Lon MMus 83 Lon Inst of Educn PGCE 84. Trin Coll Bris 12. d 14 p 15. C Gt Bookham *Guildf* 14–18; V Lightwater from 18. *The Vicarage, 28 Broadway Road, Lightwater GU18 5SJ* T: (01276) 471016 E: david.sigsworth@allsaintslightwater.org.uk

SILCOCK, Donald John. b 30. AKC 59. d 60 p 61. C Hackney St Jo *Lon* 60–63; C-in-c Plumstead Wm Temple Ch Abbey Wood CD *S'wark* 63–68; C Felpham w Middleton *Chich* 68–74; R Ightham *Roch* 74–84; R Cliffe at Hoo w Cooling 84–92; RD Strood 85–91; rtd 92; PtO *Chich* from 92. *Puck's House, 26 Ancton Way, Bognor Regis PO22 6JN* T: (01243) 582883

SILINS, Jacqueline. See JOHNSON, Jacqueline

SILK, Canon Ian Geoffrey. b 60. Pemb Coll Cam BA 81 MA 85. Trin Coll Bris BA 89. d 89 p 90. C Linc St Giles 89–93; P-in-c Linc St Geo Swallowbeck 93–98; V 98–16; PV Linc Cathl from 01; Can and Preb Linc Cathl from 07. *5 The Brambles, Littleport, Ely CB6 1XH* M: 07944-688505 E: ian.silk@ntlworld.com

SILK, Stuart Charles. b 76. SS Mark & Jo Univ Coll Plymouth BA 99. Oak Hill Th Coll BA 10. d 10 p 11. C Southbourne w W Thorney *Chich* 10–13; C Lindfield from 13. *66 Finches Gardens, Lindfield RH16 2PB* T: (01444) 483547 M: 07866-487535 E: stuartcsilk@gmail.com *or* stuart@lindfield.info

SILLER, Canon James Robert William. b 44. Pemb Coll Ox BA 65 MA 70. Westcott Ho Cam 67. d 70 p 71. C Spring Grove St Mary *Lon* 70–73; C Leeds St Pet *Ripon* 73–77; P-in-c Leeds City 73–77; V Gilling and Kirkby Ravensworth 77–82; P-in-c Middleton Tyas and Melsonby 77–82; R Farnley 82–94; V Potternewton 94–05; Hon Can Ripon Cathl 99–05; rtd 05; PtO *York* 06–11. *1 Sandhill Oval, Leeds LS17 8EB* T: 0113-268 0014

SILLETT, Angela Veronica Isabel. See BERNERS-WILSON, Angela Veronica Isabel

SILLEY, Andrew. b 85. Bris Univ BSc 07. Wycliffe Hall Ox BTh 15. d 15 p 16. C Corby St Jo w Epiphany *Pet* 15–21; V Bransholme *York* from 21. *St John's Vicarage, Wawne Road, Sutton-on-Hull, Hull HU7 4YR* M: 07534-419072 *or* 07791-086899 E: andrewsilley@msn.com

SILLEY, Canon Michael John. b 48. Ripon Coll Cuddesdon 82. d 84 p 85. C Frodingham *Linc* 84–87; V Ingham w Cammeringham w Fillingham 87–96; R Aisthorpe w Scampton w Thorpe le Fallows etc 87–96; RD Lawres 92–96; P-in-c N w S Carlton 93–96; P-in-c Brigg 96–97; V Brigg,

Wrawby and Cadney cum Howsham 97–04; RD Yarborough 01–02; Bp's Dom Chapl 05–12; Gen Preacher 05–12; Can and Preb Linc Cathl 09–13; rtd 12; PtO *Linc* from 13. *46 Windsor Way, Broughton, Brigg DN20 0EL* T: (01652) 651055 E: michaelsilley48@outlook.com

SILLIS, Andrew Keith. b 66. Wolv Poly BSc 87. Aston Tr Scheme 91 Westcott Ho Cam 93. d 96 p 97. C Boyne Hill *Ox* 96–99; C Hayes St Nic CD *Lon* 99–00; C-in-c 00–05; V N Hayes St Nic 05–09; V Cuddington *Guildf* 09–12; Chapl Bonn w Cologne *Eur* 12–15; P-in-c Stourbridge St Thos *Worc* 15–18; V from 18; RD Stourbridge 17–21; Area Sub-Dean Gtr Dudley from 21. *St Thomas' Church, Market Street, Stourbridge DY8 1AQ* T: (01384) 394185 M: 07951-904122 E: vicar@stthomasstourbridge.org

SILLS, Canon Peter Michael. b 41. Nottm Univ BA 63 LLM 68 Kent Univ PhD 00 Barrister 76. S'wark Ord Course 78. d 81 p 82. C W Wimbledon Ch Ch *S'wark* 81–85; P-in-c Barnes H Trin 85–93; Wandsworth Adnry Ecum Officer 90–93; V Purley St Mark 93–00; Can Res Ely Cathl 00–08; rtd 08; PtO *Chich* from 08. *The Coach House, Keymer Road, Hassocks BN6 8JR* T: (01273) 842760 E: peter@peter-sills.co.uk

SILVA, Peter John. b 47. Rhodes Univ BA 73 HDipEd 77 BEd 79. St Paul's Coll Grahamstown 68. d 74 p 74. C Bloemfontein Cath S Africa 74–75; Chapl Dioc Sch for Girls Grahamstown 75–79; Lect Rhodes Univ 79–81; Dir Academic Support Services Natal Univ 81–85; Regional Manager Performance and Educn 86; Dir Tape Aids for the Blind 87; R Overport Ch Ch 88–89; Chapl Dioc Sch for Girls Grahamstown 89–95; Dir Educn Projects Grahamstown Foundn 95–98; TV Abingdon *Ox* 99–02; Chief Exec Officer Peers Early Educn Partnership 02–11; P-in-c Gt w Lt Tew and Over w Nether Worton *Ox* 11–13; rtd 12; PtO *Ox* from 13. *45 Spring Street, Chipping Norton OX7 5NN* T: (01608) 430234 M: 07980-264472 E: silvapete@gmail.com

SILVERSIDES, Mark. b 51. Lon Univ BD 73. St Jo Coll Nottm 74. d 76 p 77. C Hornchurch St Andr *Chelmsf* 76–80; P-in-c Becontree St Thos 80–85; TR Becontree W 85–86; CPAS Staff 86–92; New Media Producer from 92. *15 Glenhurst Drive, Whickham, Newcastle upon Tyne NE16 5SH* T: 0191-488 1937 E: marksilversides@gmail.com

SILVERTHORN, Alan. b 37. St Mich Coll Llan 62. d 65 p 66. C Machen and Rudry *Mon* 65–71; V New Tredegar 71–83; V Llanfrechfa and Llanddewi Fach w Llandegfeth 83–04; rtd 04; PtO *Llan* 05–17. *14 Davies Street, Ystrad Mynach, Hengoed CF82 8AD* T: (01443) 816649

SILVESTER, Christine. b 51. WMMTC 02. d 05 p 06. NSM Walsall Wood *Lich* 05–08; NSM Shelfield and High Heath 08–18; Chapl R Wolv NHS Trust 08–14; rtd 18. *Address withheld by request* E: silvesterchristine@hotmail.com

SILVESTER, David. b 59. Qu Mary Coll Lon BSc 80 Nottm Univ BCombStuds 85. Linc Th Coll 82. d 85 p 86. C Walthamstow St Mary w St Steph *Chelmsf* 85–90; TV Barking St Marg w St Patr 90–96; V Mildmay Grove St Jude and St Paul *Lon* 96–08; AD Islington 03–07; TR Hackney Marsh 08–11; V Studley *Cov* 11–13; P-in-c Spernall, Morton Bagot and Oldberrow 11–13; R Arden Marches 13–17; AD Alcester 14–17; rtd 17; PtO *Cov* 17–21; *Glouc* from 19. *2 Spiers Court, St Laurence Way, Bidford-on-Avon, Alcester B50 4LF* E: revdsilvester@btinternet.com

SILVESTER, Canon Stephen David. b 59. Chu Coll Cam BA 80 MA 83 K Coll Lon MSc 12 Man Univ PGCE 82. St Jo Coll Nottm 88. d 91 p 92. C Nottingham St Jude *S'well* 91–96; V Gamston and Bridgford 96–08; AD W Bingham 04–07; P-in-c Nottingham St Nic 08–11; R from 11; P-in-c Sneinton St Chris w St Phil 10–14; AD Nottm S 16–19; Hon Can S'well Minster from 13. *37 Lyme Park, West Bridgford, Nottingham NG2 7TR* T: 0115-982 0407

SIMESTER, Paul Stephen. b 57. Oak Hill Th Coll 97. d 99 p 00. C Branksome Park All SS *Sarum* 99–03; TV Wareham 03–07; PtO from 14. *27 Weyman's Avenue, Bournemouth BH10 7JR* T: (01202) 574995 E: psimester@gmail.com

SIMISTER, Norman Harold. b 39. Bris Univ BSc 60. d 93 p 94. OLM Wainford *St E* 93–09; PtO 10–21. *Romaine, 1 School Road, Ringsfield, Beccles NR34 8NZ* T: (01502) 715549

SIMMONDS, Paul Andrew Howard. b 50. Nottm Univ BSc 73. Trin Coll Bris 75. d 78 p 79. C Leic H Trin w St Jo 78–82; SW Regional Co-ord CPAS 83–86; Hd Adult Tr and Resources CPAS 86–95; Hon C Wolston and Church Lawford *Cov* from 88; Dioc Miss Adv 95–03; Research Dir Forward Vision 03–05; Team Ldr Foundations21 BRF from 05; Ind Chapl *Cov* from 08. *31 John Simpson Close, Wolston, Coventry CV8 3HX* T: (024) 7654 3188 E: paul@workcare.org

SIMMONDS, Canon Paul Richard. b 38. AKC 63. d 64 p 65. C Newington St Mary *S'wark* 64–67; C Cheam 68–73; P-in-c Stockwell Green St Andr 73–87; V 87–03; Hon Can S'wark Cathl 97–03; rtd 03; PtO *Chich* from 15. *Timbers, 37*

Ocean Drive, Ferring, Worthing BN12 5QP T: (01903) 242679 E: paulangela@hotmail.com

SIMMONDS, Robert William. b 52. Nottm Univ BTh 77. Linc Th Coll 72. d 80 p 81. C Roehampton H Trin *S'wark* 80–83; TV Hemel Hempstead *St Alb* 83–90; V S Woodham Ferrers *Chelmsf* 90–94; rtd 94; PtO *Cant* 03–06; *Blackb* 10–14; *Cant* 14–16. *70 Wynn Road, Whitstable CT5 2JN* T: (01227) 634919 E: bob.simmonds@zen.co.uk or writerbobsimmonds@gmail.com

SIMMONS, Andrew John. b 88. Van Mildert Coll Dur MChem 10. Oak Hill Th Coll BA 16. d 16 p 17. C Houghton Carl 16–19; C Toxteth St Philemon *Liv* from 19. *78 Pomfret Street, Liverpool L8 8ND* E: andrew@stphilemons.co.uk

SIMMONS, Ann. b 56. WMMTC 04. d 07 p 08. C Blackheath *Birm* 07–11; V Dordon 11–19; AD Polesworth 14–17; rtd 19; PtO *Birm* from 20. *Address withheld by request* E: anncsimmons3@gmail.com

SIMMONS, Canon Brian Dudley. b 35. Master Mariner. St Steph Ho *Ox* 62. d 64 p 65. C Bournemouth St Pet *Win* 64–67; Miss to Seamen 67–71; Hon C Milton next Gravesend w Denton *Roch* 67–70; Hon C Gravesend St Geo 70–71; V Lamorbey H Trin 71–90; R Hever w Mark Beech 90–93; P-in-c Four Elms 90–93; R Hever, Four Elms and Mark Beech 93–94; V Langton Green 94–01; Hon Can Roch Cathl 91–01; rtd 01; PtO *Roch* from 04. *17 Chancellor House, Mount Ephraim, Tunbridge Wells TN4 8BT* T: (01892) 617262 E: canonsimmons@gmail.com

SIMMONS, Canon Christopher John. b 49. Mert Coll Ox MA 77. NEOC 88. d 90 p 91. C Kirkleatham *York* 90–93; P-in-c Barlby 93–95; V Barlby and Riccall 95–02; RD Derwent 98–01; R Pocklington and Owsthorpe and Kilnwick Percy etc 02–08; P-in-c Burnby 06–08; P-in-c Londesborough 06–08; P-in-c Nunburnholme and Warter and Huggate 06–08; P-in-c Shiptonthorpe and Hayton 06–08; P-in-c Skirlaugh w Long Riston, Rise and Swine 08–12; C Brandesburton and Leven w Catwick 11–12; RD N Holderness 09–11; Can and Preb York Minster 08–12; rtd 12; Hon C Brandesburton and Leven w Catwick *York* 12–13; PtO *Newc* from 13. *22 Valebrook, Hexham NE46 2BL* E: chris@csimmons.plus.com

SIMMONS, Gary David. b 59. Trin Coll Bris BA 86. d 87 p 88. C Ecclesfield *Sheff* 87–90; Min Stapenhill Immanuel CD *Derby* 90–95; V Stapenhill Immanuel 97–98; R Slaugham *Chich* 98–10; P-in-c Staplefield Common 08–10; R Slaugham and Staplefield Common 10–16; RD Cuckfield 11–16; TR Glascote and Stonydelph *Lich* from 16; RD Tamworth from 20. *The Vicarage, 86 Bamford Street, Tamworth B77 2AS*

SIMMONS, John Graham. b 54. Westf Coll Lon BSc 75 Man Univ PGCE 76. NOC 89. d 92 p 93. C Thame w Towersey *Ox* 92–97; R Heydon, Gt and Lt Chishill, Chrishall etc *Chelmsf* 97–05; V Chadderton Ch Ch *Man* 05–20; rtd 20; PtO *Eur* 16–19. *Address withheld by request*

SIMMONS, John Harold. b 46. FCCA. Sarum & Wells Th Coll 86. d 89 p 90. NSM The Iwernes, Sutton Waldron and Fontmell Magna *Sarum* 89–01; NSM Iwerne Valley 01–17; RD Milton and Blandford 13–16; rtd 17; PtO *Sarum* 17–22. *Fourways, Frog Lane, Shroton, Blandford Forum DT11 8QL* T: (01258) 860515 E: john@fourways.plus.com

SIMMONS, Mrs Margaret Irene. b 49. Cov Univ BSc 02 RGN RSCN. d 08 p 09. NSM Leam Valley *Cov* 08–10; NSM Hillmorton 10–18; P-in-c 12–18; rtd 18; PtO *Cov* 18–19; Hon C Hillmorton from 19. *The Vicarage, 18 Hoskyn Close, Rugby CV21 4LA* T: (01788) 576279 E: mi.simmons@btinternet.com

SIMMONS, Ms Marion. b 45. NOC 95. d 98 p 99. NSM Stoneycroft All SS *Liv* 98–99; C 00–01; TV Fazakerley Em 01–08; TR 08–14; rtd 14; PtO *Liv* from 16. *1 Rainbow Drive, Melling, Liverpool L31 1BY* T: 0151-739 4367 E: marionrainbow1@yahoo.co.uk

SIMMONS, Peter Maurice. b 51. ERMC 10. d 11 p 12. C Kettering Ch the King *Pet* 11–15; V Penn Street *Ox* 15–19; rtd 19; PtO *Pet* from 20. *20 Wetherby Close, Corby NN18 8TF* M: 07824-618875 E: revpeter@live.co.uk

SIMMONS, Richard Andrew Cartwright. b 46. Trin Coll Bris 73. d 75 p 76. C Worting *Win* 75–80; R Six Pilgrims *B & W* 80–92; R Bincombe w Broadwey, Upwey and Buckland Ripers *Sarum* 92–15; rtd 15; PtO *Sarum* from 16. *36 Alma Road, Weymouth DT4 0AJ* T: (01305) 246660 E: richard.simmons46@gmail.com

SIMMS, Diane Marcia. b 65. Bath Univ BA 87 Bris Poly PGCE 90. Trin Coll Bris 19. d 21. C Fishponds All SS and St Mary *Bris* from 21. *53 Stonebridge Park, Bristol BS5 6RP* M: 07518-372950 E: diane.simms@blueyonder.co.uk

SIMMS, Miss Melanie Laura. b 73. Trin Coll Bris 06. d 08 p 09. C Southway *Ex* 08–13; C Rainham *Roch* 13–15; Chapl Peter Carnley Angl Community Sch Australia 15–18; P-in-c Bicton w Attadale 18–19; R from 19. *3 Champagny Way, Secret Harbour WA 6173, Australia* E: revmelaniesimms@hotmail.co.uk

SIMON, Brother. *See* BROOK, Peter Geoffrey

SIMON, Fiona Elizabeth. b 64. Bradf Univ BEng 86. STETS 06. **d** 09 **p** 10. C Stoke-next-Guildf *Guildf* 09–13; PtO 13–14; P-in-c New Haw 14–16; V 16–18; Asst Chapl Brussels *Eur* 18–20; R Bisley and W End *Guildf* from 20. *The Rectory, Clews Lane, Bisley, Wokng GU24 9DY* T: (01483) 473377 M: 07810-160254 E: fionasimon1964@gmail.com

SIMON, Frederick Fairbanks. b 42. Ripon Coll Cuddesdon 74. **d** 77 **p** 78. C Cheddleton *Lich* 77–79; C Woodley St Jo the Ev *Ox* 79–82; V Spencer's Wood 82–85; P-in-c Steventon w Milton 85–87; Chapl Grenville Coll Bideford 87–95; rtd 96; PtO *Ex* 96–04. *26 Castle Street, Calne SN11 0DX* E: fr.fred@btopenworld.com

SIMON, Haydn Henry England. See ENGLAND-SIMON, Haydn Henry

✠**SIMON, The Rt Revd Oliver.** b 45. Dur Univ BA 67 Sussex Univ MA 68 Sheff Univ MMinTheol 94 Lon Univ DMin 09 AKC 19. Cuddesdon Coll 69. **d** 71 **p** 72 **c** 12. C Kidlington *Ox* 71–74; C Bracknell 74–78; V Frodsham *Ches* 78–88; R Easthampstead *Ox* 88–00; Chapl Ripon Coll Cuddesdon 00–05; Chapl Community of St Mary V Wantage 00–05; Chapl Pemb Coll Ox 03–04; TV Rugby *Cov* 05–10; OLM Officer and Dir Studies 06–10; OLM Tutor Qu Foundn Birm 07–10; rtd 10; Dir Studies Dio Mauritius 10–12; Bp Antsiranana 12–15; PtO *Ex* from 15. *Colcombe Mill Cottage, Colyton EX24 6EU* T: (01297) 552870 E: oliversimon@dunelm.org.uk

SIMONS, Miss Christine. b 40. RGN 62 RM 64 RHV 69. St Jo Coll Nottm 82. **dss** 84 **d** 87 **p** 94. Claygate *Guildf* 84–87; C Camberley St Paul 87–93; NSM 93–99; C Woking Ch Ch 99–05; rtd 05; PtO *Guildf* from 05. *1 Petworth Court, 62-64 Portsmouth Road, Camberley GU15 1JN* T: (01276) 38810 E: chris@spaceagenow.co.uk

SIMONS, Preb John Trevor. b 34. Lon Univ BD 67. ALCD 66. **d** 67 **p** 68. C Becontree St Mary *Chelmsf* 67–71; V Cranham Park 71–78; P-in-c Nailsea H Trin *B & W* 78–83; R 83–97; Sen Asst P 97–99; Preb Wells Cathl 90–99; rtd 99; Nat Dir Crosswinds Prayer Trust from 97; PtO *B & W* from 99. *1 Gillmore Road, Weston-super-Mare BS22 8JG* T: (01934) 221537 M: 07449-984724 E: crosswinds@btopenworld.com *or* john@crosswinds.org.uk

SIMONS, Joseph Robert. b 62. Nottm Trent Univ BSc 86 FRICS. Ripon Coll Cuddesdon 17. **d** 20 **p** 21. C Cleobury Mortimer w Hopton Wafers etc *Heref* from 20. *5 New Road Gardens, Cleobury Mortimer, Kidderminster DY14 8AW* M: 07872-464276 E: joe_simons@icloud.com

SIMONS, Rachel Clare. b 72. ERMC 15. **d** 18 **p** 19. NSM Bedford St Pet w St Cuth *St Alb* from 18. *1 Soroptimist House, Green Lane, Clapham, Bedford MK41 6ER* E: curatestpeterdemerton@gmail.com

SIMONSON, Canon Juergen Werner Dietrich. b 24. Lon Univ BD 52. ALCD 52. **d** 52 **p** 53. C W Kilburn St Luke w St Simon and St Jude *Lon* 52–56; Nigeria 57–63; Chapl CMS Tr Coll Chislehurst 64–65; Vice-Prin 65–67; Prin CMS Tr Coll Chislehurst 67–69; V Putney St Marg *S'wark* 69–81; RD Wandsworth 74–81; Hon Can S'wark Cathl 75–90; R Barnes St Mary 81–90; rtd 90; PtO *Win* 90–15. *33 Barnhill Court, Barnhill Road, Chipping Sodbury, Bristol BS37 6FG* E: juergens@tiscali.co.uk

SIMPER, Rachel Dawn. See WATTS, Rachel Dawn

SIMPKINS, Canon Lionel Frank. b 46. UEA BSc 68 Lambeth STh 77. St Jo Coll Nottm ALCD 72 LTh 74. **d** 73 **p** 74. C Leic H Apostles 73–77; C Bushbury *Lich* 77–80; V Sudbury w Ballingdon and Brundon *St E* 80–96; Chapl Sudbury Hosps 80–96; RD Sudbury *St E* 88–96; V Ipswich St Aug 96–12; Warden of Readers 03–10; Hon Can *St E* Cathl 94–12; rtd 12; Widows Officer *St E* from 14; PtO from 12; *Chelmsf* from 18. *64A Nowton Road, Bury St Edmunds IP33 2BU* T: (01284) 725108 E: lionelsimpkins@hotmail.com

SIMPKINS, Matthew Jonathan. b 78. Oriel Coll Ox BA 99 MA 08 Essex Univ PGCE 08. Ripon Coll Cuddesdon MPhil 15. **d** 15 **p** 16. C Wickford and Runwell *Chelmsf* 15–18; Bp's Chapl 17–18; P-in-c Lexden from 18. *2 Wroxham Close, Colchester CO3 3RQ* E: revdmatthewsimpkins@gmail.com

SIMPKINS, Susan Carol. b 58. St Steph Ho Ox 03. **d** 05. NSM Ruislip St Martin *Lon* 05–11; PtO 12–13. *70 Park Avenue, Ruislip HA4 7UJ* T: (01895) 630170 M: 07742-912664 E: sue.simpkins@btopenworld.com

SIMPSON, Alan Eric. b 52. Ch Ch Ox BA 73 MA 77 Birm Univ PhD 77 Dur Univ MA 01 CPhys 77 MInstP 77. Cranmer Hall Dur 96. **d** 98 **p** 99. C Long Benton *Newc* 98–02; P-in-c Cresswell and Lynemouth 02–06; V 06–17; rtd 17; PtO *Newc* from 17; *Edin* from 18; *Mor* from 18. *Keeper's Cottage,*

8 High Street, Kirk Yetholm, Kelso TD5 8PH M: 07387-158747 E: alansimpson@dunelm.org.uk

SIMPSON, Alexander. b 31. Oak Hill Th Coll 74. **d** 76 **p** 77. Hon C Lower Homerton St Paul *Lon* 76–81; Hon C Homerton St Barn w St Paul 81–85; V Kensington St Helen w H Trin 87–97; rtd 97; PtO *Derby* 01–07; *Nor* from 08. *2 Ferndale Close, Norwich NR6 5SD* T: (01603) 443412

SIMPSON, The Very Revd Alison Jane. b 60. St Andr Univ BSc 83 BD 86 Princeton Univ MTh 87. **d** 99 **p** 99. C Ellon *Ab* 99–02; R Huntly *Mor* 02–09; R Keith 02–09; R Aberchirder 02–09; P-in-c Fochabers 04–09; R Nairn from 09; Can St Andr Cathl Inverness from 09; Dean Mor from 14. *The New Rectory, 3 Queen Street, Nairn IV12 4AA* T: (01667) 452458 M: 07548-230745 E: revalison433@btinternet.com *or* dean@moray.anglican.org

SIMPSON, Andrew Charles. b 65. NEOC 06. **d** 09 **p** 10. C Hessle *York* 09–12; V Skirlaugh, Catwick, Long Riston, Rise, Swine w Ellerby 12–20; P-in-c Sigglesthorne w Nunkeeling and Bewholme 12–20; V Barton under Needwood w Dunstall and Tatenhill *Lich* from 20. *Address temp unknown* E: andrew617simpson@hotmail.com

SIMPSON, Andrew John. b 48. Liv Univ BEng 69. Sarum Th Coll 83. **d** 86 **p** 87. NSM Canford Magna *Sarum* 86–15; rtd 15; PtO *Sarum* from 15. *17 Sopwith Crescent, Wimborne BH21 1SH* T: (01202) 883996 E: andrews.1248@gmail.com

SIMPSON (formerly MCGIVERN), Mrs Ann Margaret. b 49. Newc Poly BSc 79 MPhil 92 Newc Univ PGCE 80. Lindisfarne Regional Tr Partnership 10. **d** 11. NSM Long Benton *Newc* 11–15; NSM Balkwell 15–17; Chapl Newcastle upon Tyne Hosps NHS Foundn Trust 14–17; rtd 17; PtO *Newc* from 17; *Edin* from 18; *Mor* from 18. *Keeper's Cottage, 8 High Street, Kirk Yetholm, Kelso TD5 8PH* M: 07388-448208 E: annpope@hotmail.com

SIMPSON, Catherine Jane. **d** 14 **p** 15. Castledawson *D & R* 14–15; C Seapatrick *D & D* 15–19; I Glencraig from 19. *3 Seahill Road, Holywood BT18 0DA* T: (028) 9042 1691 E: revcatherinesimpson@icloud.com *or* catherine@holytrinityglencraig.org

SIMPSON, Charles Michael. b 38. St Cath Coll Cam MA 64 Campion Hall Ox MA 65 Heythrop Coll Lon STL 69 K Coll Lon PhD 71. **d** 68 **p** 69. Lect Th Lon Univ 72–84; Chapl Prince of Peace Community Greenwich 85–87; Retreat Dir St Beuno's Clwyd 87–91; P-in-c Selkirk *Edin* 91–94; P-in-c Offchurch *Cov* 94–96; Warden Offa Retreat Ho and Dioc Spirituality Adv 94–00; P-in-c Stoke Canon, Poltimore w Huxham and Rewe etc *Ex* 00–04; Dioc Adv in Adult Tr 00–04; rtd 04; PtO *Cov* 05–13; *Ex* from 12. *10 Applemede, Silverton, Exeter EX5 4JX* T: (01392) 861757 E: michaelandsharon@simpson4.plus.com

SIMPSON, Christine. b 52. **d** 07 **p** 08. OLM Drayton in Hales *Lich* 07–14; NSM Cheswardine, Childs Ercall, Hales, Hinstock etc from 14; RD Hodnet from 17. *18 Mortimer Road, Buntingsdale Park, Market Drayton TF9 2EP* T: (01630) 638794

SIMPSON, David Charles Edward. b 51. NEOC 02. **d** 05 **p** 06. NSM York St Chad 05–09; PtO 09–12; NSM York All SS Pavement w St Crux and St Mich from 12; NSM York St Helen w St Martin from 12; NSM York St Denys from 12; NSM York St Olave w St Giles from 12. *98 Brunswick Street, York YO23 1ED* T: (01904) 635085 E: davidcitycentre@outlook.com

SIMPSON, David John. b 61. Univ Coll Dur BA 85 Univ Coll Lon MA 11. Sarum & Wells Th Coll 85. **d** 91 **p** 92. C Selby Abbey *York* 91–94; C Romsey *Win* 94–97; Chapl Southn Univ 97–05; Chapl RN 05–21; V Romford St Edw *Chelmsf* from 21. *St Edward's Vicarage, 15 Oaklands Avenue, Romford RM1 4DB* T: (01708) 744973 E: office@stedwardsromford.org

SIMPSON, Derek John. b 59. Oak Hill Th Coll BA 89. **d** 89 **p** 90. C Alperton *Lon* 89–95; TR Brentford 95–17; AD Hounslow 02–15; R Thirsk *York* from 17. *The Rectory, Cemetery Road, Thirsk YO7 1PR* E: derek.simpson@btinternet.com

SIMPSON, Eleanor Elizabeth Mary. See ROBERTSHAW, Eleanor Elizabeth Mary

SIMPSON, Mrs Elizabeth Ann. b 59. Lon Bible Coll BA 80 Trin Coll Bris 84. **dss** 86 **d** 97 **p** 98. Thornbury *Glouc* 86–87; Beckenham Ch Ch *Roch* 87–90; Heydon, Gt and Lt Chishill, Chrishall etc *Chelmsf* 90–93; Shirwell, Loxhore, Kentisbury, Arlington, etc *Ex* 93–97; NSM S Molton w Nymet St George, High Bray etc 97–99; C 99–03; P-in-c W Buckingham *Ox* 03–11; R 11–19; V Adderbury w Milton from 19. *12 Round Close Road, Adderbury, Banbury OX17 3EE* T: (01295) 810159 E: addliz@outlook.com

SIMPSON, Jill. b 53. **d** 13 **p** 14. NSM Ferring *Chich* 13–21; NSM Sullington and Thakeham w Warminghurst from 21. *Greensward, 64 Lime Tree Avenue, Worthing BN14 0DP* T: (01903) 872746

SIMPSON, Canon John Bernard. b 40. St Paul's Coll Chelt CertEd 62 Ox Univ MTh 95 ACP 66. **d** 93 **p** 93. In URC 63–93; Asst to RD Lothingland *Nor* 93–94; RD 99–10; C Hopton w Corton 93–94; P-in-c 94–99; TR Lowestoft St Marg 99–10; Hon Can Nor Cathl 01–10; rtd 10; P-in-c Publow w Pensford, Compton Dando and Chelwood *B & W* 10–15; PtO *Heref* from 16. *34 Dorchester Way, Belmont, Hereford HR2 7ZP* T: (01432) 269241 M: 07905-013183 E: canonjohn145@btinternet.com

SIMPSON, Canon John Lawrence. b 33. DL 04. SS Coll Cam BA 55 MA 59 ARCM 60 UWE Hon MMus. Wells Th Coll 63. **d** 65 **p** 66. Chapl Win Cathl 65–66; C Win St Bart 65–69; Chapl Repton Sch Derby 69–71; Hd of RE Helston Sch 71–78; P-in-c Curry Rivel *B & W* 79–80; R Curry Rivel w Fivehead and Swell 80–86; V Tunbridge Wells K Chas *Roch* 86–89; Can Res Bris Cathl 89–99; rtd 99; PtO *B & W* from 00. *Yardes Cottage, Windmill Hill, Ilminster TA19 9NT* T: (01823) 480593 E: simpson.yardes@btinternet.com

SIMPSON, John Raymond. b 41. Univ of S Aus DipEd 92. Chich Th Coll 65. **d** 67 **p** 68. C Scarborough St Martin *York* 67–71; C Grangetown 71–72; Youth Chapl Bermuda 72–75; C Lewisham St Mary *S'wark* 76; C Albany Australia 76–78; R Carey Park 78–84; Chapl RAAChD 77–84; Chapl RAN 84–90; Chapl RAAF 90–99; Asst P Grace Cathl San Francisco USA 99–00; Chapl RANSR Australia from 00. *44/19 Oakleigh Drive, Erskine Grove, Erskine WA 6210, Australia* T: (0061) (8) 9586 4144 E: simpsonjohnr@googlemail.com

SIMPSON, John Verrent. b 68. Univ of Wales (Cardiff) BScEcon 93. Ripon Coll Cuddesdon BTh 98. **d** 98 **p** 99. C Cardiff St Jo *Llan* 98–00; C Cen Cardiff 00–01; C Upper Chelsea H Trin *Lon* 01–04; P-in-c Lt Missenden *Ox* from 05. *The Vicarage, Little Missenden, Amersham HP7 0RA* T: (01494) 862008 M: 07919-551614 E: vicar@lmchurch.org

SIMPSON, Kevin Gordon. b 54. QPM 02. Univ of Wales BEd 96 MCIPD 94. St Mich Coll Llan. **d** 02 **p** 03. NSM Llantwit Fardre *Llan* 02–16; PtO from 16; *St D* from 16. *St Ignatius, Caldey Island, Tenby SA70 7UJ* M: 07870-397494 E: kgsimpson4151@gmail.com

SIMPSON, Mrs Madeline Bridget. b 79. Newc Univ BA 01 Regent Coll Vancouver MA 09. St Mellitus Coll 17. **d** 19 **p** 20. C Ulverston St Mary w H Trin *Carl* from 19. *Trinkeld Vicarage, Main Road, Swarthmoor, Ulverston LA12 0RZ* M: 07502-315137 E: simpson.madi@gmail.com

SIMPSON, Miss Margery Patricia. b 36. SRN 57 SCM 59. Oak Hill Th Coll BA 86. **dss** 86 **d** 87 **p** 94. Rodbourne Cheney *Bris* 86–87; Par Dn 87–90; Par Dn Warmley 90–94; C Warmley, Syston and Bitton 94–95; TV Yate New Town 95–96; rtd 97; PtO *Sarum* 97–04; *Carl* 05–18. *19 Wentworth Park, Stainburn, Workington CA14 1XP* T: (01900) 61523

SIMPSON, Mark Lawrence. b 73. Oak Hill Th Coll BA 03. **d** 03 **p** 04. C Leyland St Andr *Blackb* 03–09; C-in-c Wellfield Propr Chpl from 09. *45 Westgate, Leyland PR25 2LX* T: (01772) 622446

SIMPSON, Martha Grace. b 83. **d** 14 **p** 15. C Chipping Norton *Ox* 14–20; PtO from 20. *15 Cross Leys, Chipping Norton OX7 5HG* M: 07828-921518

SIMPSON, Matthew John. b 76. Nottm Univ BA 98 Leic Univ MA 01. St Jo Coll Nottm 11. **d** 13 **p** 14. C The Quinton *Birm* 13–16; C Knowle 16–20; TR The Lytchetts and Upton *Sarum* from 20. *The Vicarage, New Road, Lytchett Minster, Poole BH16 6JQ* M: 07522-586254 E: revmattsimpson@gmail.com

SIMPSON, Michael. *See* SIMPSON, Charles Michael

SIMPSON, Morna Mary Heather. b 79. Cen Lancs Univ BA 00 St Martin's Coll Lanc PGCE 07. Ripon Coll Cuddesdon 15. **d** 17 **p** 18. C Stocking Farm and Beaumont Leys *Leic* 17–19; C Leic H Spirit 19–20; R Yardley Hastings, Denton and Grendon etc *Pet* from 20. *The Rectory, 14 The Leys, Denton, Northampton NN7 1DH* E: revmorna@gmail.com

SIMPSON, Peter Richard. b 53. Univ Coll Lon BSc(Econ) 74 Qu Mary Coll Lon MSc 75 FRSocMed 09. **d** 97. In RC Ch 97–11; NSM St Andr Cathl Inverness *Mor* 12–18; rtd 18; PtO *York* from 19. *32 Cardinal Court, Bishophill Junior, York YO1 6ES* T: (01904) 638572 M: 07710-123202 E: prs1@waitrose.com

SIMPSON, Philip Alexander. b 54. Keele Univ BA 79 Sunderland Univ MSc 03 CQSW 79. CMS Tr Coll Selly Oak 85. **d** 89 **p** 07. CMS 85–14; Pakistan 85–98; Regional Dir for Eurasia 98–14; PtO *Guildf* 06–07; NSM Woking Ch Ch from 07. *10 Horsell Park Close, Woking GU21 4LZ* T: (01483) 770510 E: phil_simpsoncms@mac.com

SIMPSON, Rachel Victoria. *See* BUNTING, Rachel Victoria

SIMPSON, Raymond James. b 40. Lon Coll of Div ALCD 63 LTh 74 K Coll Lon 63. **d** 63 **p** 64. C Longton St Jas *Lich* 64–68; C Upper Tooting H Trin *S'wark* 68–71; BFBS Distr

Sec E Anglia 71–77; C-in-c Bowthorpe CD *Nor* 78–84; V Bowthorpe 84–96; Team Ldr Bowthorpe Ecum Project 84–96; Guardian Community of Aid and Hilda 96–11; Founding Guardian from 11; PtO *Newc* from 96. *7 Wallace Green, Berwick-upon-Tweed TD15 1EB* T: (01289) 306771 E: revd.ray.simpson@btinternet.com

SIMPSON, The Ven Richard Lee. b 66. Keble Coll Ox BA 88 MPhil 91 Westmr Coll Ox PGCE 89. Wycliffe Hall Ox 91. **d** 93 **p** 94. C Newc St Gabr 93–97; P-in-c Jesmond H Trin 97–06; P-in-c Newc St Barn and St Jude 97–06; P-in-c Brancepeth *Dur* 06–18; Dir IME 4-7 Dur and Newc 06–09; Dir IME 4-7 Lindisfarne Coll of Th from 09; Adn Auckland and Can Dur Cathl from 18. *45 Milbank Road, Darlington DL3 9NL* T: (01325) 480444 M: 07867-802671 E: ricksimpson300@btinternet.com *or* archdeacon.of.auckland@durham.anglican.org

SIMPSON, Canon Robert Charles. b 46. Ridley Hall Cam. **d** 85 **p** 86. C Eastwood *S'well* 85–88; V Yardley St Cypr Hay Mill *Birm* 88–93; P-in-c Newent and Gorsley w Cliffords Mesne *Glouc* 93–95; R 95–05; Dioc Ecum Officer 04–05; P-in-c Glouc St Jas and All SS 05–10; V Glouc St Jas and All SS and Ch Ch 10–12; AD Glouc City 08–11; Hon Can Glouc Cathl 10–12; rtd 12; PtO *Glouc* 12–13; C St Briavels w Hewelsfield and Brockweir 13–19; PtO from 20. *27 Ryelands Road, Bream, Lydney GL15 6LD* T: (01594) 560202

SIMPSON, Robert David. b 61. Fitzw Coll Cam BA 83 MA 87 Bris Univ MLitt 94. Trin Coll Bris 85. **d** 87 **p** 88. C Beckenham Ch Ch *Roch* 87–90; C Heydon w Gt and Lt Chishill *Chelmsf* 90; C Chrishall 90; C Elmdon w Wendon Lofts and Strethall 90; C Heydon, Gt and Lt Chishill, Chrishall etc 91–93; TV Shirwell, Loxhore, Kentisbury, Arlington, etc *Ex* 93–97; TR S Molton w Nymet St George, High Bray etc 97–03; R Cranborne w Boveridge, Edmondsham etc *Sarum* from 16. *The Rectory, Grugs Lane, Cranborne, Wimborne BH21 5PX* T: (01725) 517232 E: quintetrector3@gmail.com

SIMPSON, Robert John. NUU BA PGCE. **d** 03 **p** 04. NSM Ballymoney w Finvoy and Rasharkin *Conn* 03–08; NSM Ballywillan 08–18; rtd 18. *28 Willowfield Park, Coleraine BT52 1RE* T: (028) 7035 8552 M: 07793-059858 E: rev.robertsimpson@gmail.com

SIMPSON, Canon Roger Westgarth. b 51. Lon Univ BSc 72. St Jo Coll Nottm 77. **d** 79 **p** 80. C St Marylebone All So w SS Pet and Jo *Lon* 79–85; R Edin St Paul and St Geo 85–95; R Vancouver H Trin Canada 95–99; V York St Mich-le-Belfrey 99–10; C 10–13; Hon C York St Barn 14–17; Abp's Evangelist 11–20; Can and Preb York Minster 10–20; Hon C Chipping Norton *Ox* 17–21; PtO from 21. *Juxon House, Little Compton, Moreton-in-Marsh GL56 0SE* E: rogerwestgarthsimpson@gmail.com

SIMPSON, Mrs Sarah Jamieson. b 80. Univ Coll Lon BA 03 K Coll Lon PGCE 04. St Mellitus Coll 15 MA 17. **d** 17 **p** 18. C Lee Gd Shep w St Pet *S'wark* 17–20; P-in-c Streatham Immanuel and St Andr 20–21; V from 21. *Immanuel House, 51A Guildersfield Road, London SW16 5LS* T: (020) 8679 6888 M: 07522-995607 E: mrssarahsimpson@gmail.com

SIMPSON (née RALPHS), Mrs Sharon Ann. b 55. St Mary's Coll Dur BA 77. Cranmer Hall Dur 81. **dss** 83 **d** 87 **p** 94. Caverswall *Lich* 83–87; Par Dn 87–89; Asst Dioc Officer for Minl Tr *St As* 90–91; NSM Selkirk *Edin* 91–94; C Offchurch *Cov* 94–96; Warden Offa Retreat Ho and Dioc Spirituality Adv 94–00; C Stoke Canon, Poltimore w Huxham and Rewe etc *Ex* 00–04; Dioc Adv in Adult Tr 00–04; rtd 04; PtO *Cov* 05–13; *Ex* from 12. *10 Applemede, Silverton, Exeter EX5 4JX* T: (01392) 861757 E: michaelandsharon@simpson4.plus.com

SIMPSON, Mrs Susan Fiona. b 67. Herts Univ BSc 89. ERMC 09. **d** 11 **p** 12. C Soham and Wicken *Ely* 11–14; V Somersham w Pidley and Oldhurst and Woodhurst from 14. *The Rectory, Rectory Lane, Somersham, Huntingdon PE28 3EL* T: (01487) 840676 M: 07775-828745 E: susan.charlotte@googlemail.com

SIMPSON, Mrs Susie Alexandra. b 58. Hertf Coll Ox BA 81. St Steph Ho Ox BA 98. **d** 99 **p** 00. C High Wycombe *Ox* 99–03; TV 03–08; Chapl HM YOI Roch 09–10; Managing Chapl HM Pris Isis 10–19; Managing Chapl HM Pris E Sutton Park 19–21; rtd 21. *Address withheld by request*

SIMPSON, Thomas William Newton. b 89. Ex Univ BA 10. Oak Hill Th Coll BA 17. **d** 17 **p** 18. C Fremington, Instow and Westleigh *Ex* 17–21; C Cambridge St Matt *Ely* from 21. *36 St Matthew's Street, Cambridge CB1 2LT* M: 07940-428313 E: twnsimpson@gmail.com

SIMPSON, Ursula Lucy. b 51. St Anne's Coll Ox MA 73 Leeds Univ MA 05. NOC 02. **d** 05 **p** 06. NSM York St Paul 05–10; P-in-c York St Barn 10–16; rtd 16; PtO *York* 16–19; NSM Chipping Norton *Ox* 17–21. *Juxon House, Little Compton, Moreton-in-Marsh GL56 0SE* E: ulsimpson@gmail.com

SIMPSON-GRAY, Lennox George (Rickey). b 64. S Bank Univ BA 93 FCMA 96. ERMC 11. **d** 14 **p** 15. NSM Hemel Hempstead *St Alb* 14–19; TV The Claydons and Swan *Ox* from 19. *The Rectory, Queen Catherine Road, Steeple Claydon, Buckingham MK18 2PY* M: 07783-027603 E: rev-rick@outlook.com

SIMS, Bernard David. b 40. Bath Univ BSc 66. Ox Min Course 91. **d** 94 **p** 95. NSM Beedon and Peasemore w W Ilsley and Farnborough *Ox* 94–98; TV Blakenall Heath *Lich* 98–10; rtd 10; PtO *Lich* 10–21. *2 March Way, Walsall WS9 8SG* E: reverenddavid98@gmail.com

SIMS, The Ven Christopher Sidney. b 49. Wycliffe Hall Ox 74. **d** 77 **p** 78. C Walmley *Birm* 77–80; V Yardley St Cypr Hay Mill 80–88; V Stanwix *Carl* 88–96; RD Carl 89–95; Hon Can Carl Cathl 91–95; P-in-c Bassenthwaite, Isel and Setmurthy 96–00; P-in-c Bolton w Ireby and Uldale 96–00; P-in-c Allhallows 96–00; P-in-c Torpenhow 96–00; TR Binsey 00–03; V Shrewsbury H Cross *Lich* 03–09; RD Shrewsbury 08–09; Adn Walsall 09–14; rtd 14; PtO *Carl* from 16. *4 Jubilee Lodge, Beacon Edge, Penrith CA11 7SQ* E: ven.csims@gmail.com

SIMS, James Henry. b 35. St Jo Coll Nottm 87. **d** 89 **p** 91. NSM Bangor Abbey *D & D* 89–93; C Holywood 93; Bp's C Kilbroney 93–01; Min Can Belf Cathl 99–09; P-in-c Clonallon w Warrenpoint *D & D* 01–09; Can Dromore Cathl 03–09; rtd 09. *7 Prior's Lea, Holywood BT18 9QW* T: (028) 9042 4360 E: jim.sims321@tiscali.co.uk

SIMS, Mrs Julia Mary Heaton. b 56. STETS 04. **d** 07 **p** 08. NSM Winscombe and Sandford *B & W* 07–11; Past Co-ord St Monica Trust Sandford Station 11–21; PtO *B & W* 11–15; C Banwell 15–17; C Banwell and Congresbury w Hewish, Puxton and W Wick 17–18; PtO from 18. *7 Round Oak Grove, Cheddar BS27 3BW* T: (01934) 740120 M: 07875-340291

SIMS, Ruth. b 40. **d** 06 **p** 07. NSM Alveley and Quatt *Heref* 06–10; PtO 10–20. *Church Farm House, Alveley, Bridgnorth WV15 6ND*

SIMS, Canon Vickie Lela. b 56. Iowa State Univ BA 79. Ripon Coll Cuddesdon 00. **d** 02 **p** 03. C Grantham St Wulfram *Linc* 02–05; P-in-c Coulsdon St Andr *S'wark* 05–11; V 11–14; Jt Dir of IME Croydon Area 09–14; Chapl Milan w Lake Como *Eur* from 14; Chapl Genoa 14–18; Adn Italy and Malta *Eur* 16–19; Hon Can from 19. *via Solferino 17, 20121 Milano, Italy* T: (0039) (02) 655 2258 E: allsaintspriest@hotmail.com *or* simstabbat@hotmail.com

SIMS-WILLIAMS, Robert James Alden (Robin). b 79. Trin Hall Cam MEng 02 MA 05 BTh 12. Westcott Ho Cam 10. **d** 13 **p** 14. C Paddington St Jo w St Mich *Lon* 13–17; P-in-c Hendon All SS Childs Hill from 17. *All Saints' Vicarage, Church Walk, London NW2 2TJ* T: (020) 7435 3182 M: 07812-167292 E: robin@cantab.net

SINCLAIR, Canon Arthur Alfred. b 46. **d** 87 **p** 89. Hon C St Andr Cathl Inverness *Mor* 87–92; C 93–97; Chapl Asst Inverness Hosp 87–89; Dioc Chapl *Mor* 87–89; NSM Culloden St Mary-in-the-Fields 89–92; P-in-c 93–12; P-in-c Inverness St Jo 93–12; Edin Th Coll 92–93; Chapl Raigmore Hosp NHS Trust Inverness from 93; Can St Andr Cathl Inverness *Mor* 05–12; rtd 12; LtO *Mor* from 12. *Rose Cottage, 8A Southside Place, Inverness IV2 3JF* T: (01463) 716288 E: arthurasinclair@btinternet.com

SINCLAIR, Craig Paul. b 82. Ridley Hall Cam 15. **d** 17 **p** 19. C Wulfric Benefice *B & W* 17–18; C Weston-super-Mare St Paul from 18. *15 Cornwall Road North, Weston-super-Mare BS23 4AT*

✠**SINCLAIR, The Rt Revd Gordon Keith.** b 52. Ch Ch Ox BA 75 MA 75 St Jo Coll Dur BA 84. Cranmer Hall Dur. **d** 84 **p** 85 **c** 08. C Summerfield *Birm* 84–88; V Aston SS Pet and Paul 88–01; AD Aston 00–01; Hon Can Birm Cathl 00–01; V Cov H Trin 01–07; Suff Bp Birkenhead *Ches* 07–21; rtd 21; Hon Asst Bp Man from 21. *50 Silverlace Avenue, Manchester M11 1GN* E: keithsinclair8307@gmail.com

SINCLAIR, Canon John Robert. b 58. Oak Hill Th Coll 90. **d** 92 **p** 93. C Ponteland *Newc* 92–96; V Long Benton St Mary 96–01; V Newburn 01–11; AD Newc W 07–11; Hon Can Newc Cathl 08–11; Can Res Newc Cathl 11–19; Dioc Adv in Local Evang 11–19; R Upper Coquetdale from 19; Hon Can Newc Cathl from 19. *The Rectory, Rothbury, Morpeth NE65 7TL* T: (01669) 620482 M: 07706-154383 E: rectorjohn@outlook.com

SINCLAIR, Keith. *See* SINCLAIR, Gordon Keith

✠**SINCLAIR, The Rt Revd Maurice Walter.** b 37. Nottm Univ BSc 59 Leic Univ PGCE 60. Tyndale Hall Bris 62 Nashotah Ho Hun DD 01. **d** 64 **p** 65 **c** 90. C Boscombe St Jo *Win* 64–67; SAMS 67–02; Argentina 67–78; Personnel Sec 79–83; Asst Gen Sec 83–84; Prin Crowther Hall CMS Tr Coll Selly Oak 84–90; Bp N Argentina 90–02; Primate of S Cone 95–02; rtd 02; Hon Asst Bp Birm from 02. *55 Selly Wick Drive, Birmingham B29 7JQ* T: 0121-471 2617

SINCLAIR, Peter. b 44. Oak Hill Th Coll. **d** 88 **p** 89. C Darlington H Trin *Dur* 88–91; C-in-c Bishop Auckland Woodhouse Close CD 91–98; P-in-c Consett 98–09; rtd 09; PtO *Dur* from 11. *16 Deanery View, Lanchester, Durham DH7 0NH* E: annandpetersinclair@talktalk.net

SINCLAIR, Peter Monteith. b 52. St Andr Univ BSc 73. NEOC. **d** 01 **p** 02. NSM Darlington St Cuth *Dur* 01–05; Hon Min Can Dur Cathl 05–12; V Woodhorn w Newbiggin *Newc* 12–17; rtd 17; PtO *Newc* 17–18; C Ch the King 18–20. *7 Haughton Green, Darlington DL1 2DD* T: (01325) 358424 M: 07710-017625 E: peter@aftersunday.org.uk

SINCLAIR, Reginald William. b 53. Wolv Poly BSc 77 CEng MIMechE. Man OLM Scheme 04. **d** 07 **p** 08. OLM Atherton and Hindsford w Howe Bridge *Man* 07–09; TV from 09; Borough Dean Wigan from 13. *Bumbles, 23 Millers Lane, Atherton, Manchester M46 9BW* T: (01942) 892996 M: 07530-162920 E: revreg@btinternet.com

SINDALL, Canon Christine Ann. b 42. ALA 69. EAMTC 84. **d** 87 **p** 94. NSM Sutton *Ely* 87–89; C Cambridge Ascension 89–94; TV 94–96; R Cheveley 96–07; R Ashley w Silverley 96–07; V Kirtling 96–07; V Wood Ditton w Saxon Street 96–07; RD Linton 01–07; Hon Can Ely Cathl 01–07; rtd 07; PtO *Newc* from 07. *9 East Moor, Longhoughton, Alnwick NE66 3JB* T: (01665) 572287 E: csindall@btinternet.com

SINGH, Jonathan James. *See* BAUER, Jonathan Nathaniel

SINGH, Vivian Soorat. b 30. Trin Coll Cam BA MA 53. Westcott Ho Cam 54. **d** 55 **p** 56. C Yardley Wood *Birm* 55–57; C Birm St Paul 57–59; Asst Master Framlingham Coll 59–72; Chapl 60–72; Chapl Wymondham Coll 72–75; Dep Hd Litcham High Sch 75–88; rtd 88; PtO *Nor* from 88. *Manor Cottage, Wendling Road, Longham, Dereham NR19 2RD* T: (01362) 687382

SINGLETON, David Brinley. b 59. St Steph Ho Ox. **d** 00 **p** 01. C Soham *Ely* 00–01; C Soham and Wicken 02–04; P-in-c Capel St Mary w Lt and Gt Wenham *St E* 04–08; R 08–13; RD Samford 10–13; R Bansfield 13–18; P-in-c Haughley w Wetherden and Stowupland from 18. *The Vicarage, The Folly, Haughley, Stowmarket IP14 3NS* E: brinsingleton@btinternet.com

SINNAMON, William Desmond. b 43. TCD BA 65 MA 80 MPhil 95. CITC 66. **d** 66 **p** 67. C Seapatrick *D & D* 66–70; C Arm St Mark w Aghavilly 70–74; V Choral Arm Cathl 73–74; I Ballinderry 75–80; I Dublin St Patr Cathl Gp *D & G* 80–83; Preb Tipperkevin St Patr Cathl Dublin 80–83; I Taney *D & G* 83–11; Can St Patr Cathl Dublin 91–11; Treas St Patr Cathl Dublin 91–96; Chan St Patr Cathl Dublin 96–11; rtd 11. *3 Botanic Avenue, Glasnevin, Dublin 9, Republic of Ireland* T: (00353) (1) 444 1616 M: 86-828 0003 E: dessinnamon@gmail.com

SINTON, Bernard. b 43. Leic Univ BSc 66. Sarum & Wells Th Coll 87. **d** 90 **p** 91. NSM Horsham *Chich* 90–19; PtO from 19. *Kinsale, 28 Kennedy Road, Horsham RH13 5DA* E: pa.sinton@outlook.com

SINTON, Mrs Patricia Ann. b 41. RGN 62 SCM 64. STETS 95. **d** 98 **p** 99. NSM Horsham *Chich* 98–01; P-in-c Shipley 01–19; rtd 19. *Kinsale, 28 Kennedy Road, Horsham RH13 5DA* E: pa.sinton@outlook.com

SINTON, Vera May. b 43. Somerville Coll Ox BA 65 MA 69 Bris Univ CertEd 66. Trin Coll Bris 79. **dss** 81 **d** 87 **p** 94. Broxbourne w Wormley *St Alb* 81–87; Hon Par Dn 87; Tutor All Nations Chr Coll Ware 81–87; Chapl St Hilda's Coll Ox 87–90; Tutor Wycliffe Hall Ox 87–98; NSM Ox St Clem 99–09; Tutor Ox Cen for Youth Min 01–04; rtd 09; PtO *Ox* from 09; *Leeds* from 10. *Rookhurst, West End, Gayle, Hawes DL8 3RT* T: (01969) 666948 E: vera@vsinton.co.uk

SIRCAR, Deepak Debchandan. b 46. Lon Hosp BDS 72 Leeds Univ BA 06. NOC 03. **d** 06 **p** 07. NSM Doncaster St Geo *Sheff* 06–10; NSM Bath Widcombe *B & W* 10–13; P-in-c Barnby Dun *Sheff* 13–17; rtd 17; PtO *Sheff* from 17. *5 Barnsdale Mews, Campsall, Doncaster DN6 9RH* M: 07768-830393 E: deepaksircar@btinternet.com

SIRR, John Maurice Glover. b 42. TCD BA 63. CITC 65. **d** 65 **p** 66. C Belfast St Mary *Conn* 65–68; C Finaghy 68–69; I Drumcliffe w Lissadell and Munninane *K, E & A* 69–87; Preb Elphin Cathl 81–87; Dean Limerick and Ardfert *L & K* 87–11; I Limerick City 87–11; Chapl Limerick Pris 87–11; rtd 11. *17A Knockhill, Ennis Road, Limerick, V94 CR24, Republic of Ireland* T: (00353) (61) 277372 M: (00353) 87-254 1121 E: maurice42sirr@gmail.com

SISTIG (née STEWART), Mrs Jennifer Jane. b 71. Urban Univ Rome STB 00. St Jos Th Inst Cedara BTh 00. **d** 99 **p** 00. C Kirby-Hilton S Africa 99–00; C Scottsville 00–01; R Woodlands-Montclair-cum-Yellowwood Park 01–05; R Hillcrest 05–08; NSM Fleet *Guildf* 08–13; Chapl Frimley Health NHS Foundn Trust from 13; Chapl St Geo Sch Ascot 10–18; PtO *Ox* from 12; *Guildf* from 19. *The*

Vicarage, 43 Church Road, Bagshot GU19 5EQ T: (01276) 473348 M: 07546-120844 E: jenniferjanesistig@gmail.com

SITWELL, Mrs Mary Elizabeth. b 49. Brighton Coll of Educn DipEd 71 Sussex Univ BEd 72. **d** 03 **p** 12. Chapl Roedean Sch Brighton 87–05; NSM Bishopstone *Chich* 03–06; rtd 05; NSM Alfriston w Lullington, Litlington and W Dean *Chich* 06–09; PtO 09–12 and from 16; NSM Iford w Kingston and Rodmell 12–13; NSM Iford w Kingston and Rodmell and Southease 13–16. *Chambles, Village Green, Piddinghoe, Newhaven BN9 9AP* T: (01273) 510183 E: isla.sitwell@btinternet.com

SIU, Leslie. b 87. City Univ BSc 09. Wycliffe Hall Ox BA 14. **d** 15 **p** 16. C Westlands St Andr *Lich* 15–18; V Wickham Market w Pettistree *St E* from 18; RD Loes from 21. *The Vicarage, Crown Lane, Wickham Market, Woodbridge IP13 0SA* T: (01728) 561572 E: leslie@wickhammarketchurch.org

SIVILL, David Neil. b 69. **d** 14. OLM Atherton and Hindsford w Howe Bridge *Man* from 14. *7 Kennet Way, Leigh WN7 1SN* M: 07535-753594 E: sivilld@manchesterfire.gov.uk

SIVYER, Steven Robert. b 74. RCM BMus 97 Leic Univ MSc 09 PhD 14 Dur Univ BA 18 Cant Ch Ch Univ PGCE 98. SEITE 12. **d** 15 **p** 16. C Marden *Cant* 15–17; C Boughton Monchelsea 17–18; P-in-c Marham w Bastwick, Thurne etc *Nor* from 18. *The Rectory, School Road, Marham, Great Yarmouth NR29 4PX* T: (01493) 740823 M: 07725-229841 E: steven@sivyer.org.uk

SIXSMITH, David. b 39. Lon Univ BD 66. **d** 97 **p** 98. NSM Castleacre w Newton, Rougham and Southacre *Nor* 97–99; OLM Narborough w Narford 97–99; OLM Pentney St Mary Magd w W Bilney 97–99; OLM Westacre 97–99; C Hunstanton St Mary w Ringstead Parva etc 99–01; P-in-c Foulsham w Hindolveston and Guestwick 01–06; P-in-c N Elmham w Billingford and Worthing 02–05; rtd 06; PtO *Nor* from 06. *Old Mill Cottage, Broadmeadow Common, Castle Acre, King's Lynn PE32 2BU* T: (01760) 755703 E: david.sixsmith@hotmail.co.uk

SIZER, Stephen Robert. b 53. Sussex Univ BA Ox Univ MTh 94. Trin Coll Bris 80. **d** 83 **p** 84. C St Leonards St Leon *Chich* 83–86; C Guildf St Sav w Stoke-next-Guildford 86–89; R Stoke-next-Guildf 89–97; V Virginia Water 97–17; rtd 17; PtO *Win* 17–18. *39 Bevan Close, Southampton SO19 9PE* M: 07970-789549 E: stephen@peacemakers.ngo

SKELTON, Beresford. b 52. St Chad's Coll Dur BA 74. Chich Th Coll 74. **d** 76 **p** 77. C Byker St Ant *Newc* 76–80; C Newc St Jo 80–82; Chapl Asst Newc Gen Hosp 80–81; Chapl Asst Freeman Hosp Newc 81–82; V Cresswell and Lynemouth *Newc* 82–88; P-in-c Millfield St Mary *Dur* 88–93; V from 93; P-in-c Bishopwearmouth Gd Shep from 04; CMP from 77; Warden from 12. *St Mary Magdalene's Vicarage, Wilson Street, Sunderland SR4 6HJ* T/F: 0191-565 6318

SKELTON (*née* BOXER), **Mrs Caroline Victoria.** b 46. Bradf Univ BA 69. Yorks Min Course 09. **d** 11 **p** 12. NSM Baildon *Bradf* 11–14; Leeds 14–16; Rtd Clergy and Widows Officer (Bradford) from 16. *2 Highfield Mews, Baildon, Shipley BD17 5PF* T: (01274) 582224 E: caroline.skelton46@gmail.com

SKELTON, Melvyn Nicholas. b 38. St Pet Coll Ox BA 61 MA 65 Selw Coll Cam BA 63 MA 68. Ridley Hall Cam 62. **d** 64 **p** 65. C St Marychurch *Ex* 64–66; C Bury St Edmunds St Mary *St E* 66–69; Hon C 69–78; LtO 78–08; PtO 09–21. *Milburn House, The Street, Moulton, Newmarket CB8 8RZ* T: (01638) 750563 E: melvynskelton@gmail.com

SKEPPER, Mrs Suzanne Jayne. b 63. Trin Coll Bris BA 09. **d** 09 **p** 10. C Wotton St Mary *Glouc* 09–13; V Twigworth, Down Hatherley, Norton, The Leigh etc 13–21; rtd 21. *173 Grange Road, Tuffley, Gloucester GL4 0NP* M: 07981-429259 E: suzanne.skepper@hotmail.co.uk

SKIDMORE, Iaen Macdonald. b 58. SNWTP 11. **d** 13 **p** 14. C Marown, Foxdale and Baldwin *S & M* 13–16; R Andreas, Ballaugh and Sulby from 16. *The Rectory, Churchtown, Ramsey, Isle of Man IM7 2AN* T: (01624) 897873 M: 07624-403945 E: revd.iaenskidmore@gmail.com

SKIDMORE (*née* CANNINGS), **Karen Rachel.** b 75. Nottm Univ MA 96. Ridley Hall Cam 04. **d** 06 **p** 07. C Pitsmoor Ch Ch *Sheff* 06–10; P-in-c Herringthorpe 10–15; V from 15; P-in-c Whiston from 21; C Clifton St Jas from 21. *The Vicarage, 493 Herringthorpe Valley Road, Rotherham S60 4LB* T: (01709) 836052 E: karen.skidmore@yahoo.co.uk *or* karen.skidmore@sheffield.anglican.org

SKIDMORE, Michael Anthony. b 38. **d** 98 **p** 99. NSM Rainworth and Blidworth *S'well* 98–00; P-in-c Basford St Leodegarius 00–05; P-in-c Willoughby-on-the-Wolds w Wysall and Widmerpool 05–07; NSM Carlton-in-the-Willows, Porchester and Woodthorpe 07–09; rtd 09; PtO *S'well* from 09. *11 Graveney Gardens, Arnold, Nottingham NG5 6QW* T: 0115-926 0773 E: mikeskidmore1@sky.com

SKIDMORE, Mrs Sheila Ivy. b 36. **d** 87 **p** 94. Hon Par Dn Leic Resurr 87–91; Par Dn Clarendon Park St Jo w Knighton St Mich 91–94; TV 94–01; rtd 01; PtO *Leic* 01–17. *15 School Lane, Birstall, Leicester LE4 4EA* T: 0116-267 3318 E: skidmore010@btinternet.com

SKIDMORE, Simon Peter. b 88. Univ of Wales (Ban) BD 10. Trin Coll Bris 12. **d** 14 **p** 15. C Wednesbury St Bart *Lich* 14–18; TV Bilston from 18. *The Vicarage, 8 Cumberland Road, Bilston WV14 6LT* M: 07919-800533 E: skiders180@hotmail.co.uk

SKILLEN, John Clifford Tainish. b 50. NUU BA 72 MA 82 TCD BTh 89 QUB DipEd 73. CITC 86. **d** 89 **p** 90. C Bangor Abbey *D & D* 89–92; I Kilwarlin Upper w Kilwarlin Lower 92–96; I Finaghy *Conn* 96–09; Asst Ed The Church of Ireland Gazette 99–15; Bp's Sen Dom Chapl *Conn* from 08. *25 Berkeley Hall Square, Lisburn BT27 5TB* T: (028) 9267 0257 M: 07740-553926 E: revcskillen25@gmail.com

SKILLING, Graham. b 57. **d** 12 **p** 13. NSM Kendal H Trin *Carl* from 12. *7 Danes Road, Staveley, Kendal LA8 9PW* T: (01539) 822695 E: gr36939@yahoo.co.uk

SKILTON, The Ven Christopher John. b 55. Magd Coll Cam BA 76 MA 80. Wycliffe Hall Ox 77. **d** 80 **p** 81. C Ealing St Mary *Lon* 80–84; C New Borough and Leigh *Sarum* 84–88; TV Gt Baddow *Chelmsf* 88–95; TR Sanderstead All SS *S'wark* 95–04; P-in-c Sanderstead St Mary 02–04; RD Croydon S 00–04; Adn Lambeth 04–13; P-in-c Kennington St Mark 08–09; Adn Croydon 13–20; rtd 20. *46 Downview Road, Worthing BN11 4QY* E: cskilton11@gmail.com

SKILTON, Joseph Laurence. b 41. Univ of Wales TCert 64 Murdoch Univ Aus BA 90 Aus Pacific Coll MA 93. St Mich Coll Llan. **d** 70 **p** 71. C Bicester *Ox* 71–73; C Shrewsbury St Chad *Lich* 73–76; V W Bromwich St Phil 76–80; Australia from 80; rtd 06. *37 Cosmo Crescent, Newstead, Launceston TAS 7250, Australia* E: pax2u2@gmail.com

SKINGLEY, Christopher George. b 49. K Coll Lon MA 98. Oak Hill Th Coll BA 90 Qu Coll Birm. **d** 00 **p** 01. C Enfield St Jas *Lon* 00–03; V Ramsgate St Mark *Cant* 03–15; rtd 15; PtO *Cant* from 16. *18 Royal Native Way, Whitstable CT5 4UE* T: (01227) 272508 E: chris.skingley@btinternet.com

✠**SKINNER, The Rt Revd Brian Antony.** b 39. Reading Univ BSc 60. Tyndale Hall Bris 66. **d** 67 **p** 68 **c** 77. C Woking St Pet *Guildf* 67–70; Chile 70–86; Adn Valparaiso 76–77; Suff Bp Valparaiso 77–86; C Chorleywood St Andr *St Alb* 87–96; V Iver *Ox* 96–06; rtd 06; PtO *Ox* from 08. *10 Benton Drive, Chinnor OX39 4DP* T: (01844) 353504 E: b.skinner@dsl.pipex.com

SKINNER, Mrs Elaine Teresa (Terri). b 55. Bath Univ BSc 78. EMMTC 99. **d** 02 **p** 03. NSM Whitwick St Jo the Bapt *Leic* 02–05; NSM Thorpe Acre w Dishley 05–10; P-in-c Leic St Theodore 10–17; rtd 17; PtO *Leic* from 18. *55 Rosslyn Road, Whitwick, Coalville LE67 5PU* T: (01530) 832676 M: 07810-241381 E: terri.skinner@btopenworld.com

SKINNER, Mrs Frances. b 54. Nottm Trent Univ BSc 02. Qu Foundn Birm 18. **d** 20 **p** 21. NSM Gt Meols *Ches* from 20. *3 Raby Park Close, Neston CH64 9XS* T: 0151-336 2922 M: 07784-915226 E: franskin54@gmail.com

SKINNER, Graeme John. b 57. Southn Univ BSc 79. Trin Coll Bris BA 86. **d** 86 **p** 87. C Bebington *Ches* 86–90; V Ashton-upon-Mersey St Mary Magd 90–06; V Upton (Overchurch) 06–18; P-in-c Holme Eden and Wetheral w Warwick *Carl* from 18. *The Rectory, Warwick Bridge, Carlisle CA4 8RF* T: (01228) 561358 E: graemevicarofeden@gmail.com

SKINNER, Mrs Jane Mary. b 59. Leeds Univ BA 81. Cranmer Hall Dur 82. **dss** 84 **d** 87 **p** 94. Chatham St Phil and St Jas *Roch* 84–87; Hon Par Dn Church Coniston *Carl* 87–91; Hon Par Dn Torver 87–91; NSM Dalton-in-Furness 91–97; Chapl HM Pris Haverigg 92–97; Chapl Carl Hosps NHS Trust 97–01; Chapl N Cumbria Acute Hosps NHS Trust 01–02; TV Carl H Trin and St Barn 98–02; Hon C W Swindon and the Lydiards *Bris* 02–09; Chapl Swindon and Marlborough NHS Trust 03–10; NSM Golden Cap Team *Sarum* 09–10; TV 10–18; TR Parkham, Alwington, Buckland Brewer etc *Ex* from 18. *The Rectory, Old Market Drive, Woolsery, Bideford EX39 5QF* T: (01237) 431622 E: rectorhartlandcoast@gmail.com

SKINNER, Canon Jean. b 47. Univ of Northumbria at Newc BA 03 RN 68 RM 70. NEOC 93. **d** 96 **p** 97. NSM Ch the King *Newc* 96–03; NSM Newc St Thos Prop Chpl 03–17; NSM City Cen Chapl 03–06; Dioc Child Protection Adv 07–17; NSM Newc Cathl 12–17; Hon Can Newc Cathl 16–17; rtd 17; PtO *Newc* from 17. *32 Easedale Avenue, Melton Park, Newcastle upon Tyne NE3 5TB* T: 0191-236 3474 E: revjeanskinner@yahoo.com *or* jeanskinner1@gmail.com

SKINNER, Preb John Cedric. b 30. Bris Univ BA 55. Tyndale Hall Bris 55. **d** 57 **p** 58. C St Leonard *Ex* 57–62; Univ Sec IVF 62–68; V Guildf St Sav 68–76; R Stoke next Guildf St Jo 74–76; R Guildf St Sav w Stoke-next-Guildford 76–84; R Ex St Leon w H Trin 84–98; Chapl R W of England Sch for the

Deaf 84–98; Preb Ex Cathl 92–98; rtd 98; PtO *Ex* from 00. *386 Topsham Road, Exeter EX2 6HE* T: (01392) 876540

SKINNER, Maurice Wainwright. b 30. St Jo Coll Ox BA 53 MA 59 FRSC 70. Ox NSM Course. **d** 86 **p** 87. NSM Furze Platt *Ox* 86–94; NSM Hurley and Stubbings 94–00; rtd 00; PtO *Ox* 00–21. *133 Beverley Gardens, Maidenhead SL6 6ST* T: (01628) 624875

SKINNER, Michael Thomas. b 39. Open Univ BA 88 BA 90 Heythrop Coll Lon MA 11. S'wark Ord Course 73. **d** 78 **p** 79. NSM Orpington St Andr *Roch* 78–82; P-in-c 99–09; NSM Orpington All SS 82–99; Assoc Bp's Officer for NSMs 90–98; Bp's Officer for NSMs *Roch* 98–09; rtd 09; PtO *Roch* from 09; *Lon* from 11; *S'wark* 02–05 and from 10; *Truro* from 12. *16 Ambleside Gardens, South Croydon CR2 8SF* T: (020) 8239 1973 E: mikeskinner2@virginmedia.com

SKINNER, Paul Anthony. b 35. RD . Sarum Th Coll. **d** 09 **p** 10. NSM Sixpenny Handley w Gussage St Andrew etc *Sarum* 09–14; PtO from 14. *6 Fleur de Lis, 41 High Street, Christchurch BH23 1AS* E: paulofpaskin@yahoo.com

SKINNER, Raymond Frederick. b 45. St Jo Coll Dur BA 67 Dur Univ MA 93. Cranmer Hall Dur. **d** 70 **p** 71. C High Elswick St Paul *Newc* 70–76; V Newbottle *Dur* 76–87; Ind Chapl 81–87; RD Houghton 84–87; Chapl Oman 87–90; TR Morden *S'wark* 90–13; rtd 13; Public Preacher *S'wark* 13–17; PtO from 17. *6 Lawrence Avenue, Bidborough, Tunbridge Wells TN4 0XB* T: (01892) 525913 E: skinhicks@tiscali.co.uk

SKINNER, Richard Lynn. b 50. Open Univ BA 88 Ches Coll of HE MEd 93. Qu Foundn Birm 18. **d** 20 **p** 21. NSM Hoylake *Ches* from 20. *3 Raby Park Close, Neston CH64 9XS* T: 0151-336 2922 M: 07784-915216 E: richskin7@gmail.com

SKINNER, Stephen John. b 52. Bris Univ BSc 74 St Jo Coll Dur BA 82 Dur Univ MLitt 88 AIA. Cranmer Hall Dur. **d** 83 **p** 84. C Chatham St Phil and St Jas *Roch* 83–87; P-in-c Church Coniston *Carl* 87–90; V 90–91; P-in-c Torver 87–90; R 90–91; V Dalton-in-Furness 91–97; TR Carl H Trin and St Barn 97–02; TR W Swindon and the Lydiards *Bris* 02–09; TR Golden Cap Team *Sarum* 09–18; rtd 18; PtO *Ex* 18–20; P-in-c Ashwater, Halwill, Beaworthy, Clawton etc 20; P-in-c Black Torrington, Bradford w Cookbury etc 20; R Ashwater, Halwill, Beaworthy, Clawton etc from 20. *The Rectory, Old Market Drive, Woolsery, Bideford EX39 5QF* T: (01237) 431622 E: sjmskinners@btinternet.com

SKINNER, Terri. *See* SKINNER, Elaine Teresa

SKIPPON, Kevin John. b 54. St Steph Ho Ox 78. **d** 81 **p** 82. C Gt Yarmouth *Nor* 81–84; C Kingstanding St Luke *Birm* 84–86; V Smethwick SS Steph and Mich 86–92; Chapl Derbyshire R Infirmary 92–94; Chapl Derbyshire R Infirmary NHS Trust 94–98; Chapl Derby Hosps NHS Foundn Trust 98–04 and 04–08; C Upminster *Chelmsf* 09–14; Chapl St Andr Healthcare 09–13; Chapl Havering Primary Care Trust 09–13; rtd 14; PtO *Heref* from 16. *Beech Cottage, 25 Banks Head, Bishops Castle SY9 5JL* T: (01588) 630777 E: kevin.skippon@asitis.me.uk

SKIPWORTH, Nicola Rachael. b 72. Southn Inst BA 95. Trin Coll Bris BA 01. **d** 01 **p** 02. C Bassaleg *Mon* 01–05; TV High Wycombe *Ox* 05–13; TV Carew *St D* 13–14; P-in-c Pembroke Dock 14–18; P-in-c Harworth *S'well* from 18. *The Vicarage, Tickhill Road, Harworth, Doncaster DN11 8PD* M: 07734-233742 E: nickythevicar@gmail.com

SKIRROW, Paul Richard. b 52. Hull Univ BA 82 Ches Coll of HE MTh 00. NOC 97. **d** 00 **p** 01. C St Luke in the City *Liv* 00–03; V Ditton St Mich w St Thos 03–07; Asst Dir CME 03–07; rtd 07; PtO *Ely* 10–15; *Leeds* from 17; *Eur* from 18. *2 The Crosskeys, Church Street, Pateley Bridge, Harrogate HG3 5LB* T: (01423) 712973 E: paul.skirrow@live.co.uk

SKRINE, Charles Walter Douglas. b 75. Qu Coll Ox BA 98. Oak Hill Th Coll BA 03. **d** 03 **p** 04. C St Helen Bishopsgate w St Andr Undershaft etc *Lon* 03–21; P-in-c St Mich Cornhill w St Pet le Poer etc 17–21; Asst Dir of Ords Two Cities Area 17–21; R Langham Place All So from 21. *12 Weymouth Street, London W1W 5BY* T: (020) 7580 3522 E: charlie.skrine@london.anglican.org

SKUSE, Anne Martha. CITC. **d** 09 **p** 10. NSM Kilmocomogue C, C & R 09–15; I Moviddy Union 15–17; Chapl Bandon Gr Sch from 17. *Westlands, Crossmahon, Bandon, Co Cork, Republic of Ireland* T: (00353) (23) 8884 4306 M: (00353) 86-023 9699 E: annemskuse@gmail.com

SLACK, Mrs Moira Elizabeth. b 52. Brunel Univ BTech 74 Leeds Univ BA 06. NOC 03. **d** 06 **p** 07. C Heaton Ch Ch *Man* 06–09; P-in-c Stretford All SS 09–14; C Bolton St Pet w St Phil 14–20; rtd 20; PtO *Man* from 20. *50 Devonshire Road, Bolton BL1 4PQ* T: (01204) 841865 E: moslack@btinternet.com

SLADDEN, Daniel John. b 69. K Coll Cam BA 91 MA 95. Yorks Min Course. **d** 12 **p** 13. NSM Ingleby Barwick *York* 12–16; Min Can Ripon Cathl *Leeds* from 16; PtO *York* from 18.

Ripon Cathedral Office, Liberty Courthouse, Minster Road, Ripon HG4 1QS T: (01765) 602072 E: dan@sladden.com

SLADDEN, John David. b 49. RN Eng Coll Plymouth BSc 74 St Edm Coll Cam MA 86. Ridley Hall Cam 80. **d** 83 **p** 84. C St Bees *Carl* 83–85; PtO *Lich* 85–87; Miss Co-ord Down to Earth Evangelistic Trust 85–87; V Doncaster St Jas *Sheff* 87–94; PtO *Ely* from 07. *9 Teal Close, Chatteris PE16 6PR* T: (01354) 694097 E: jds25@cantab.net

SLADE, Canon Adrian Barrie. b 47. K Alfred's Coll Win DipEd 68. St Jo Coll Nottm BTh 73 ALCD 72. **d** 73 **p** 74. C Streatham Immanuel w St Anselm *S'wark* 73–76; C Chipping Barnet *St Alb* 76–78; C Chipping Barnet w Arkley 78–80; V Sundon 80–85; Soc Resp Officer *Glouc* 86–12; Hon Can Glouc Cathl 91–12; rtd 12; PtO *Glouc* from 15. *16 Conway Road, Hucclecote, Gloucester GL3 3PL* T: (01452) 372468 E: glossr@star.co.uk

SLADE, Joanna Elisabeth. *See* STOBART, Joanna Elisabeth

SLADE, Michael John. b 55. Trin Coll Bris 94. **d** 96 **p** 97. C Blagdon w Compton Martin and Ubley *B & W* 96–99; V Winscombe and Sandford 99–10; RD Locking 05–08; V Chollerton w Birtley and Thockrington *Newc* 10–17; rtd 17; PtO *Newc* from 17. *Meadowfield, Church Lane, Wark, Hexham NE48 3LX* E: emjayslade@gmail.com

SLADE, Roland Gregory. b 88. Southn Univ BSc 09. Ridley Hall Cam 14. **d** 17 **p** 18. C Gt Marlow w Marlow Bottom, Lt Marlow and Bisham *Ox* from 17. *5 Pine Croft, Marlow SL7 3BJ* M: 07449-330581 E: rolandgslade@gmail.com

SLATER, Andrew Kenneth. b 62. Reading Univ BA 84 PGCE 85 Open Univ MA 99. ERMC 10. **d** 13 **p** 14. NSM Wymondham *Nor* 13–18; NSM Attleborough w Besthorpe from 18. *The Battle, 110 Norwich Road, Attleborough NR17 2JY* T: (01953) 455046 M: 07850-924575 E: joannaandandrewslater@gmail.com

SLATER, Canon Ann. b 46. Somerville Coll Ox BA 67 MA 71. WMMTC 92. **d** 95 **p** 96. C Northampton St Benedict *Pet* 95–99; TV Daventry, Ashby St Ledgers, Braunston etc 99–05; R Heyford w Stowe Nine Churches and Flore etc 05–14; RD Daventry 08–13; Can Pet Cathl 10–14; rtd 14; PtO *Pet* from 15. *34 Millway, Northampton NN5 6ES* T: (01604) 586014 E: annslater34@gmail.com

SLATER, Carol Ann. *See* COSLETT, Carol Ann

SLATER, Christopher Richard. b 69. Oak Hill Th Coll BA 08. **d** 08 **p** 09. C Rock Ferry *Ches* 08–12; C Tranmere St Cath 08–12; V Rock Ferry from 12. *The Vicarage, St Peter's Road, Birkenhead CH42 1PY* T: 0151-645 1622 M: 07899-807507 E: slater.cr@me.com

SLATER (*née* SAMMONS), Mrs Elizabeth Mary. b 71. RN 94 RHV 98. Wycliffe Hall Ox 03. **d** 05 **p** 06. C Stoke Gifford *Bris* 05–09; PtO 09–17; NSM Lawrence Weston and Avonmouth 17–18; Adv for Initial Minl Educn 17–18; TR Broadclyst, Clyst Honiton, Pinhoe, Rockbeare etc *Ex* 18–21; R Pinhoe w Poltimore from 21. *The Rectory, 9 Church Hill, Pinhoe, Exeter EX4 9ER* M: 07576-812951 E: teamrectorcmc@gmail.com

SLATER, Ian Stuart. b 47. St Jo Coll Nottm BA 07. **d** 04 **p** 05. NSM Gt Horton *Bradf* 04–11; P-in-c 11–12; C Fairweather Green 12–14; *Leeds* 14; PtO from 17. *Stable Cottage, 5 The Drive, Denholme, Bradford BD13 4DY* T: (01274) 831437 E: revianslater@gmail.com

SLATER, John Ralph. b 38. Kent Univ BA 90. Linc Th Coll 71. **d** 73 **p** 74. C S Hackney St Mich w Haggerston St Paul *Lon* 73–74; C Leytonstone St Marg w St Columba *Chelmsf* 74–77; C Whitstable All SS w St Pet *Cant* 77–80; V Gt Ilford St Alb *Chelmsf* 80–83; V Clipstone *S'well* 83–87; rtd 87. *4 Rowena Road, Westgate-on-Sea CT8 8NQ* T: (01227) 831593

SLATER, Canon Mark Andrew. b 56. ARCS 79 Imp Coll Lon BSc 79. Ridley Hall Cam 87. **d** 89 **p** 90. C Northampton St Giles *Pet* 89–92; C Stopsley *St Alb* 92–93; C-in-c Bushmead CD 93–99; V St Alb St Luke from 99; RD St Alb 15–20; Hon Can St Alb from 18. *St Luke's Vicarage, 46 Cell Barnes Lane, St Albans AL1 5QJ* T: (01727) 865399 F: 865399 E: mark.slater@saint-lukes.co.uk

✠**SLATER, The Rt Revd Paul John.** b 58. CCC Ox MA 83 St Jo Coll Dur BA 83. Cranmer Hall Dur 81. **d** 84 **p** 85 **c** 15. C Keighley St Andr *Bradf* 84–88; P-in-c Cullingworth and Dir Dioc Foundn Course 88–93; Bp's Personal Exec Asst 93–95; Warden of Readers 92–96; R Haworth *Bradf* 95–01; Bp's Officer for Min and Miss 01–15; Adn Craven 05–14; Adn Richmond and Craven *Leeds* 14–15; Suff Bp Kirkstall from 15. *4 Borrowdale Court, 5 Clifton Drive, Menston, Ilkley LS29 6FZ* T: 0113-284 4304 E: paul.slater@leeds.anglican.org *or* bishop.paul@leeds.anglican.org

SLATER, Paul John. *See* CAREY-SLATER, Paul John

SLATER, Robert Adrian. b 48. St Jo Coll Nottm 76. **d** 79 **p** 80. C Bedworth *Cov* 79–82; TV Billericay and Lt Burstead *Chelmsf* 82–88; V Rounds Green *Birm* 88–94; rtd 07.

11 Lewis Road, Birmingham B30 2SU T: 0121-689 2721
E: robslater@freeuk.com *or* skyblueteddy68@icloud.com
SLATER, Victoria Ruth. b 59. Hertf Coll Ox BA 82 MA 87
Selw Coll Cam BA 89 MA 94 Lon Univ MA 01 Anglia Ruskin
Univ DProf 13. Westcott Ho Cam 86. **d** 89 **p** 94. Chapl Asst
Man R Infirmary 89–90; Chapl 90–94; Chapl St Mary's
Hosp Man 90–94; Chapl Ox Radcliffe Hosp NHS Trust
94–97; Chapl Sir Michael Sobell Ho Palliative Care Unit
97–05; Asst Soc Resp Adv *Ox* 05–07; Chapl Care Co-ord N
Lon Hospice 07–08; Research and Development Officer Ox
Cen for Ecclesiology and Practical Th 09–13; Chapl Frimley
Health NHS Foundn Trust 14–15. *Address withheld by request*
E: slaterv2@btinternet.com
SLATER, Preb William Edward. b 51. Aston Tr Scheme 85
Oak Hill Th Coll 87. **d** 89 **p** 90. C Balderstone *Man* 89–94; V
Newchapel *Lich* 94–16; RD Stoke N 99–08 and 12–16; Preb
Lich Cathl 08–16; rtd 16; PtO *Lich* from 17; *Ches* from 18. *4
Gwyn Avenue, Knypersley, Stoke-on-Trent ST8 7BW* T: (01782)
518350
SLATER, Wiz. *See* SLATER, Elizabeth Mary
SLATER-CARR, Robert Alexander. b 76. Ripon Coll
Cuddesdon 18. **d** 20 **p** 21. C S'wark St Geo w St Alphege
and St Jude from 20. *St Alphege House, Pocock Street, London
SE1 0BJ* M: 07751-940234 E: rob@stgeorge-themartyr.co.uk
SLATTER, Barrie John. b 44. Nottm Univ BSc 66 Ban Univ
BTh 04 FRICS 97. **d** 00 **p** 01. OLM Hundred River *St E* 00–03;
C Alde River 03–06; R 06–14; rtd 14; PtO *St E* from 14. *Moor
Farm Barn, Kings Lane, Sotherton, Beccles NR34 8AF* T: (01986)
872100 M: 07802-924738 E: barrie.rectory@btinternet.com
SLATTERY, Maurice Michael. b 43. Southlands Coll Lon
TCert 73 Lon Inst of Educn BEd 74. S'wark Ord Course 91.
d 94 **p** 95. NSM Malden St Jas S'wark 94–97; NSM Niton,
Whitwell and St Lawrence *Portsm* 97–99; NSM Selsdon St Jo
w St Fran S'wark 99–03; PtO *Portsm* 03–04 and 07–08 and
from 09; P-in-c St Lawrence 04–06; NSM Clayton w Keymer
Chich 08–09; P-in-c Burpham 13–16; P-in-c Poling 13–16;
rtd 16. *1 Woodland Mews, East Hill Road, Ryde PO33 1QU*
E: mauricemslattery@hotmail.com
SLAUGHTER, Clive Patrick. b 36. St Paul's Coll Grahamstown.
d 77 **p** 78. S Africa 77–87; R Thorley w Bishop's Stortford H
Trin *St Alb* 87–90; R Thorley 90–01; RD Bishop's Stortford
96–01; rtd 01; PtO *St Alb* 01–03; P-in-c Much Hadham
03–04; P-in-c Braughing w Furneux Pelham and Stocking
Pelham 04–05; PtO 09–19. *53 High Street, Hunsdon, Ware
SG12 8QB* T: (01279) 844955 E: marcia.slaughter@virgin.net
SLAVIC, Jean-Sacha (Sacha). b 68. **d** 12 **p** 13. NSM Foleshill
St Laur *Cov* 12–14; NSM Cov Cathl from 15; Chapl Bablake
Sch Cov from 14. *1 Crown Green, Coventry CV6 6FA* T: (024)
7627 1200 M: 07714-288352 E: slavic@btinternet.com
SLAYEN, Karen Elizabeth. b 59. **d** 12 **p** 13. OLM Atherton
and Hindsford w Howe Bridge *Man* 12–16; NSM Westleigh
St Pet 16–18; NSM Westleigh St Paul 16–18; NSM Westleigh
St Pet and St Paul from 18; NSM Leigh St Mary from 16. *51
Treen Road, Astley, Tyldesley, Manchester M29 7HD* T: (01942)
891154 M: 07966-643950 E: karenslayen@aol.com
SLEDGE, The Ven Richard Kitson. b 30. Peterho Cam BA 52
MA 57. Ridley Hall Cam 52. **d** 54 **p** 55. C Compton Gifford
Ex 54–57; C Ex St Martin, St Steph, St Laur etc 57–63; V
Dronfield *Derby* 63–76; TR 76–78; RD Chesterfield 72–78;
Adn Huntingdon *Ely* 78–96; R Hemingford Abbots 78–89;
Hon Can Ely Cathl 78–99; rtd 96; Bp's Dom Chapl *Ely*
96–99; Rtd Clergy Officer 98–07; Asst (Huntingdon/Pet
Area) 07–16; PtO 99–19. *7 Budge Close, Brampton, Huntingdon
PE28 4PL* T: (01480) 380284 *or* (01353) 662749 F: (01480)
437789 E: rksledge@supanet.com
SLEDGE, Canon Timothy Charles Kitson. b 64. Coll of Ripon
& York St Jo BA 87 York Univ MA 88. Trin Coll Bris. **d** 95
p 96. C Huddersfield St Thos *Wakef* 95–98; V Luddenden w
Luddenden Foot 98–03; P-in-c Sowerby 02–03; Dioc Miss
Enabler *Pet* 03–08; V Romsey *Win* 08–17; AD 13–17; Hon
Can Win Cathl from 14. *Baker Court, 2A Fraser Road, Southsea
PO5 1EE* E: timsledge01@gmail.com
SLEE, John Graham. b 51. Brunel Univ BTech 73. Oak Hill Th
Coll 85. **d** 87 **p** 88. C St Columb Minor and St Colan *Truro*
87–91; R St Mawgan w St Ervan w St Eval 91–02; RD Pydar
93–95; P-in-c St Just-in-Roseland and St Mawes 02–07; rtd
07; PtO *Ox* 08–13; *Blackb* from 18. *209 Court View House,
Aalborg Place, Lancaster LA1 1AT* E: john@nbepiphany.co.uk
SLEEP, Benjamin Luke. b 78. Ridley Hall Cam 16. **d** 18 **p** 19. C
Eastbourne St Jo *Chich* from 18; C Eastbourne St Mich from
20. *12 Upper Dukes Drive, Eastbourne BN20 7XT*
SLEGG, John Martin. b 36. St Pet Coll Ox BA 62 MA 66.
Ridley Hall Cam 62. **d** 64 **p** 65. C Perranzabuloe *Truro* 64–66;
CF 66–86; V Lyminster and Poling *Chich* 86–05; rtd 06. *4
Bakers Meadow, Billingshurst RH14 9GG*

SLEIGHT, Gordon Frederick. b 47. AKC 69. St Aug Coll
Cant 69. **d** 70 **p** 71. C Boston *Linc* 70–74; P-in-c Louth
St Mich and Stewton 74; TV Louth 74–81; V Crosby 81–95;
P-in-c Nettleham 95–97; V 97–05; RD Lawres 04–05; rtd
05; LtO *Mor* from 05. *17 Kintail Place, Dingwall IV15 9RL*
E: gsassynt@gmail.com
SLENNETT, Mrs Jane Alison. b 57. St Mich Coll Llan. **d** 08.
NSM Aberavon *Llan* 08–18; LtO from 18. *42 Carlton Place,
Porthcawl CF36 3ET* T: (01656) 784840
SLINGSBY, Miss Philippa Jane. b 89. Birm Univ BSc 12
St Jo Coll Dur BA 18. Cranmer Hall Dur 15. **d** 18 **p** 19. C
Tong and Laisterdyke *Leeds* from 18. *207 Broadstone Way,
Bradford BD4 9BT* T: (01274) 4060425 M: 07576-484897
E: philippa.slingsby@leeds.anglican.org
SLIPPER, Charles Callan. b 55. Lanc Univ BA 77 PhD 84. S
Dios Minl Tr Scheme 91. **d** 93 **p** 94. Focolare Movement from
77; NSM N Acton St Gabr *Lon* 93–96; LtO 96–12; PtO from
12; Public Preacher *St Alb* from 12; Nat Ecum Officer Coun
for Chr Unity from 17. *Council for Christian Unity, Church
House, 27 Great Smith Street, London SW1P 3AZ* T: (01707)
339242 *or* (020) 7898 1479 E: callanslipper@gmail.com *or*
callan.slipper@churchofengland.org
SLIPPER, Robert James. b 64. St Jo Coll Cam BA 87 MA 91.
Wycliffe Hall Ox BA 92. **d** 92 **p** 93. C Southgate *Chich* 92–95;
C Stoughton *Guildf* 95–00; V Terrington St Clement *Ely* from
00. *The Vicarage, 27 Sutton Road, Terrington St Clement, King's
Lynn PE34 4PQ* T: (01553) 828430
SLOAN, William. b 49. Lanc Univ CertEd 78 BEd 79 Cumbria
Univ MA 11. CBDTI 04. **d** 07 **p** 08. NSM Croston and
Bretherton *Blackb* 07–10; NSM Hoole 10–11; PtO 11–13;
NSM Hesketh w Becconsall 13–15; rtd 15; PtO *Blackb* from
15. *5 Red House Lane, Eccleston, Chorley PR7 5RH* T: (01257)
453665 M: 07721-923001
SLOANE, The Very Revd Niall James. b 81. TCD BA 03 MA 06
MPhil 05. CITC 03. **d** 05 **p** 06. C Agherton *Conn* 05–07; C
Taney *D & G* 07–12; I Killiney H Trin 12–17; Abp's Dom Chapl
08–15; Min Can St Patr Cathl Dublin 08–15; Dean Limerick
L & K from 17; I Limerick City from 17; Can St Patr Cathl
Dublin from 15. *The Deanery, 7 Kilbane, Castletroy, Limerick,
Y94 Y4AX, Republic of Ireland* E: dean@limerick.anglican.org
SLOGGETT, Donald George. b 49. Trin Coll Bris 81. **d** 83
p 84. C Horfield H Trin *Bris* 83–86; C Highworth w
Sevenhampton and Inglesham etc 86–88; P-in-c Upavon
w Rushall *Sarum* 88–90; R Upavon w Rushall and Charlton
90–01; R Stoulton w Drake's Broughton and Pirton etc *Worc*
01–16; rtd 16; PtO *Worc* from 17. *1 Chevalier Close, Pershore
WR10 3EE* T: (01386) 244021 E: don.sloggett@gmail.com
SLOW, Leslie John. b 47. Liv Univ BSc 68 MSc 69. NOC 77.
d 80 **p** 81. NSM Gt Horton *Bradf* 80–07; PtO *York* from 08.
21 Mile End Park, Pocklington, York YO42 2TH T: (01759)
303888 E: les@theslows.plus.com
SLUMAN, Richard Geoffrey Davies. b 34. St Jo Coll Ox BA 68
MA 68. Sarum Th Coll 68. **d** 70 **p** 71. C Gt Yarmouth *Nor*
70–73; V Churchdown *Glouc* 73–82; P-in-c Blockley w Aston
Magna 82–83; V Blockley w Aston Magna and Bourton on
the Hill 83–94; rtd 94; PtO *Cov* 94–10. *21 Manor Farm Road,
Tredington, Shipston-on-Stour CV36 4NZ* T: (01608) 662317
SLUSAR (née WOODLEY), Priscilla Elizabeth. b 54. Univ
of Wales (Abth) BA 75 Homerton Coll Cam PGCE 76.
Westcott Ho Cam 08. **d** 10 **p** 11. C Codsall *Lich* 10–14; R
Bernwode Ox 14–20; rtd 20; PtO *Ely* from 20; RD Bourn from
21. *80 Canterbury Street, Cambridge CB4 3QE* T: (01223)
356906 M: 07812-851839
SLYFIELD, Mrs Margaret Medi. b 61. Linc Sch of Th and
Min 11. **d** 14 **p** 15. NSM Buxton w Burbage and King
Sterndale *Derby* from 14. *Asher House, Sherwood Road,
Tideswell, Buxton SK17 8HJ* E: mmslyfield@gmail.com
SMAIL, Richard Charles. b 57. CCC Ox BA 80 MA 83. Ox Min
Course 90. **d** 93 **p** 95. NSM Keble Coll Ox 93–96; Chapl, Fell
and Lect BNC Ox 97–02; PtO *Ox* 02–05; P-in-c Rousham from
05. *Top Flat, 256 Abingdon Road, Oxford OX1 4SP* T: (01865)
245553 E: richardsmail@supanet.com
SMAILES, Ian Collingwood. b 46. Brighton Poly BSc 71.
NTMTC BA 07. **d** 07 **p** 08. NSM Laleham *Lon* 07–16;
PtO from 16. *Gadebridge House, 211 Thames Side, Staines
TW18 1UF* T: (01784) 461195 E: ianandrosalind@gmail.com
SMALE, Ian Keith. b 53. Wycliffe Hall Ox 98. **d** 00 **p** 01. C
Overton w Laverstoke and Freefolk *Win* 00–04; P-in-c E
Dean w Friston and Jevington *Chich* 04–06; R 06–08;
P-in-c Overton w Laverstoke and Freefolk *Win* 08–18;
P-in-c N Waltham and Steventon, Ashe and Deane 11–18;
rtd 18; PtO *Win* from 18. *33 Mercia Avenue, Charlton, Andover
SP10 4EJ*
SMALE, Ian Stuart. b 49. **d** 07. NSM Chich Cathl 07–19;
rtd 19; PtO *Chich* from 19. *9 Canal Place, Chichester
PO19 8DR* M: 07973-747694 E: ishmael@ishmael.org.uk

SMALE, Irene Euphemia. b 52. Chich Univ BA Win Univ MA Southn Univ PhD 15. **d** 14. NSM Chich St Pancras and St Jo 14–17; Chapl Prebendal Sch Chich from 17. *9 Canal Place, Chichester PO19 8DR* T: (01273) 421021 M: 07980-617584 E: irene.smale@chichester.anglican.org

SMALING, Christopher James. b 72. Bath Univ BSc 93 K Coll Lon PGCE 95. STETS 11. **d** 14 **p** 15. NSM Aldersbrook *Chelmsf* from 14. *84 St James Road, London E15 1RN* M: 07977-564035

SMALL, Gary William. b 57. Witwatersrand Univ BSc 81 Stockholm Univ MSc 86 KTH R Inst of Tech Stockholm MSc 94. Qu Foundn (Course) 16. **d** 19 **p** 20. NSM Harlescott *Lich* from 19. *34 Queen Street, Shrewsbury SY1 2JX* T: (01743) 614803 M: 07891-690010 E: gwmsmall31@gmail.com

SMALL, Gordon Frederick. b 41. St Jo Coll Nottm 77. **d** 79 **p** 80. C Belper *Derby* 79–84; NSM Matlock Bath 90–91; C Ripley 91–93; TV Bucknall and Bagnall *Lich* 93–98; Assoc P Deal St Leon w St Rich and Sholden etc *Cant* 98–06; rtd 06; PtO *Bris* from 07. *10 Elmer Close, Malmesbury SN16 9UE* T: (01666) 823722 E: gordonsmall@talktalk.net

SMALL, Marcus Jonathan. b 67. Univ of Wales (Ban) BD 94 St Jo Coll Dur MA 13. Ripon Coll Cuddesdon 94. **d** 96 **p** 97. C Moseley St Mary *Birm* 96–99; TV Wenlock *Heref* 99–05; R Eardisley w Bollingham, Willersley, Brilley etc from 05; RD Kington and Weobley 12–14. *Church House, Church Road, Eardisley, Hereford HR3 6NN* T: (01544) 327440 E: rector@eardisleygroup.org.uk

SMALL, William. *See* SMALL, Gary William

SMALLDON, The Ven Keith. b 48. Open Univ BA 76 Newc Univ MA 94. St Mich Coll Llan. **d** 71 **p** 72. C Cwmbran *Mon* 71–73; C Chepstow 73–75; Dioc Youth Adv *Bradf* 75–79; P-in-c Woolfold *Man* 82–85; Dioc Youth and Community Officer 82–90; P-in-c Thursby *Carl* 90–94; Dir of Clergy Tr 90–94; TR Daventry, Ashby St Ledgers, Braunston etc *Pet* 94–98; Chapl Danetre Hosp 94–98; TR Llantwit Major *Llan* 98–03; Can Res Brecon Cathl *S & B* 03–11; Dioc Dir of Min 03–11; P-in-c Swansea St Barn 08–11; Adn St D 11–13; P-in-c Steynton 11–13; rtd 13; PtO *Ox* from 13. *41 Horsham Close, Banbury OX16 1XP* T: (01295) 269281 M: 07977-263690 E: keithsmalldon@btinternet.com

SMALLEY, The Very Revd Stephen Stewart. b 31. Jes Coll Cam BA 55 MA 58 PhD 79. Eden Th Sem (USA) BD 57 Ridley Hall Cam. **d** 58 **p** 59. C Portman Square St Paul *Lon* 58–60; Chapl Peterho Cam 60–63; Dean 62–63; Lect RS Ibadan Univ Nigeria 63–69; Lect Th Man Univ 70–77; Can Res and Prec Cov Cathl 77–87; Vice-Provost 86–87; Dean Ches 87–01; rtd 01; PtO *Glouc* 02–16. *30 Orchard Park, Elton, Chester CH2 4NQ*

SMALLMAN, Godfrey John. b 57. St Hild Coll 18. **d** 19 **p** 20. NSM Lodge Moor St Luke *Sheff* from 19. *26 Slayleigh Lane, Sheffield S10 3RH* T: 0114-230 9690

SMALLMAN, Miss Margaret Anne. b 43. Hull Univ BSc 64 Bris Univ CertEd 65. St Jo Coll Nottm. **dss** 83 **d** 87 **p** 94. Bromsgrove St Jo *Worc* 83–88; Par Dn 87–88; Par Dn Stoke Prior, Wychbold and Upton Warren 88–90; Team Dn Tettenhall Wood *Lich* 91–94; TV 94–99; P-in-c W Bromwich H Trin 99–08; C W Bromwich Gd Shep w St Jo 99–08; RD W Bromwich 04–08; rtd 08; PtO *Lich* 08–09 and 18–21; Hon C Wellington All SS w Eyton 09–18. *10 St Agatha's Close, Telford TF1 3QP* T: (01952) 253643

SMALLS, Peter Harry. b 34. FCCA. **d** 97 **p** 98. OLM Castleacre w Newton, Rougham and Southacre *Nor* 97–99; OLM Narborough w Narford 97–99; OLM Pentney St Mary Magd w W Bilney 97–99; OLM Westacre 97–99; OLM Narborough w Narford and Pentney 99–02; PtO from 03; *St E* 07–19. *Windward, Drapers Lane, Ditchingham, Bungay NR35 2JW* T: (01986) 894667 E: peter.smalls@outlook.com

SMALLWOOD, Nicola. b 76. Univ Coll Lon BSc 98 RVC (Lon) BVetMed 01. Win Sch of Miss 16. **d** 20 **p** 21. C Whitchurch w Tufton and Litchfield *Win* from 20. *12 Kingsley Park, Whitchurch RG28 7HA* T: (01256) 859281 M: 07775-903321 E: rev.nicky@ahwhitchurch.org.uk

SMALLWOOD, Simon Laurence. b 58. St Jo Coll Dur BSc 80. Cranmer Hall Dur 89. **d** 92 **p** 93. C Stapenhill w Cauldwell *Derby* 92–96; TV Dagenham *Chelmsf* 96–03; V Becontree St Geo 03–19. *Address temp unknown* E: smallwood164@gmail.com

SMART, Barry Anthony Ignatius. b 57. Lanc Univ BEd 79. St Steph Ho Ox 85. **d** 88 **p** 89. C Wantage *Ox* 88–91; C Abingdon 91–93; TV 93–95; C Princes Risborough w Ilmer 95–97; C Kingstanding St Luke *Birm* 97–00; V Small Heath 00–09; Chapl Compton Hospice 09–13; V Kingstanding St Luke *Birm* from 13. *The Clergy House, 49 Caversham Road, Birmingham B44 0LW* T: 0121-354 3281 M: 07952-663872 E: frbarrysmart@yahoo.co.uk

SMART, Mrs Cara Louise Jane. b 85. Ripon Coll Cuddesdon 17. **d** 20 **p** 21. C Wokingham St Paul *Ox* from

20. *13 Brook Close, Wokingham RG41 1ND* T: 0118-901 4365 M: 07812-349857 E: revcarasmart@gmail.com

SMART, Mrs Carol. b 45. SRN 67. S Dios Minl Tr Scheme 89. **d** 92 **p** 94. Chapl Isle of Wight Healthcare NHS Trust 92–99; NSM Shorwell w Kingston *Portsm* 99–02; NSM Gatcombe 92–02; NSM Chale 92–02; PtO 02–20. *20 Sydney Close, Shide, Newport PO30 1YG* T: (01983) 526242 E: revcarolsmart@gmail.com

SMART, Harry Gavin. b 67. St D Coll Lamp BA 90 Sheff Hallam Univ MA 06. Westcott Ho Cam 90. **d** 94 **p** 95. C Thirsk *York* 94–97; C Sheff St Leon Norwood 97–99; Mental Health Chapl Sheff Care Trust 99–06; Lead Mental Health Chapl Lincs Partnership NHS Foundn Trust 07–13; Chapl N Lincs and Goole NHS Foundn Trust 14–21; Sen Chapl from 21. *North Lincolnshire and Goole NHS Trust, Scunthorpe General Hospital, Cliff Gardens, Scunthorpe DN15 7BH* T: (03033) 302489

SMART, Mrs Hilary Jean. b 42. SOAS Lon BA 63. EMMTC 85. **d** 88 **p** 94. Par Dn Walsall Pleck and Bescot *Lich* 88–94; TV Sheff Manor 94–02; Bp's Ecum Officer 94–02; rtd 02; Chapl Compton Hospice 02–06; PtO *S'well* from 06. *77 Denton Drive, West Bridgford, Nottingham NG2 7FS* T: 0115-923 1097

SMART, Lorraine Ann. b 58. Wall Hall Coll Aldenham BEd 79. St Mellitus Coll 14. **d** 15 **p** 16. OLM Loughton St Mich *Chelmsf* 15–21; NSM Vale of Roding from 21. *30 Stonards Hill, Loughton IG10 3EG* T: (020) 8502 2017 E: lorraine.smart@btopenworld.com

SMART, Neil Robert. b 61. Bris Univ BVSc 84. Ridley Hall Cam 01. **d** 03 **p** 04. C Shirley *Win* 03–07; P-in-c Brockenhurst 07–11; V 11–18; P-in-c Boldre w S Baddesley 09–11; V 11–18; C Southsea St Jude *Portsm* from 18. *St Margaret's Vicarage, 13 Cousins Grove, Southsea PO4 9RP* E: somesmarts@btopenworld.com

SMART, Russell Martin. b 79. Moorlands Coll BA 06 Anglia Ruskin Univ MA 11. Ridley Hall Cam 09. **d** 11 **p** 12. C Romford Gd Shep *Chelmsf* 11–15; C N Farnborough *Guildf* 15–17; C Farnborough Gd Shep 17–18; V from 18. *The Parsonage, 45 Sand Hill, Farnborough GU14 8ER* T: (01252) 543789 E: russ@goodshepherdchurch.org.uk

SMEATON, William Brian Alexander. b 37. CITC 69. **d** 71 **p** 72. C Belfast St Luke *Conn* 71–81; I Tullyaughnish w Kilmacrennan and Killygarvan *D & R* 81–02; Bp's Dom Chapl 87–02; Can Raphoe Cathl 88–02; Dioc Radio Officer 90–02; rtd 02. *Bearna Ghaoithe, Drumcavney, Trentagh, Letterkenny, Co Donegal, Republic of Ireland* M: (00353) 74-913 7917 E: smeaton@indigo.ie

SMEDLEY, Christopher John. b 62. Trent Poly BSc 90. St Jo Coll Nottm MA 98. **d** 98 **p** 99. C Cotmanhay *Derby* 98–02; R Wilne and Draycott w Breaston from 02. *The Rectory, 68 Risley Lane, Breaston, Derby DE72 3AU* T: (01332) 872242 E: smedley7@btinternet.com

SMEDLEY, Paul Mark. b 59. Bris Univ BA 80 Lanc Univ MA 81. S Dios Minl Tr Scheme 89. **d** 92 **p** 93. NSM Acton St Mary *Lon* 92–08; PtO from 08; *S'wark* from 17; *Ex* from 15. *6 Media House, 32 Coin Street, London SE1 8YG* M: 07958-438712

SMEETON (*née* GRESHAM), Canon Karen Louise. b 75. Hull Univ LLB 96. Ripon Coll Cuddesdon BA 01. **d** 02 **p** 03. C Leesfield *Man* 02–05; V Hamer 05–11; P-in-c Spotland 11–13; C Oakenrod and Bamford 11–13; V Spotland and Oakenrod 13–21; C Norden w Ashworth and Bamford from 21; AD Rochdale from 17; Hon Can Man Cathl from 19. *13 Brooklands Court, Rochdale OL11 4EJ* T: (01706) 347163 M: 07504-960446 E: therevdksmeeton@gmail.com

SMEETON, Canon Nicholas Guy. b 74. Trin Hall Cam MA 99. Ripon Coll Cuddesdon BA 03. **d** 04 **p** 05. C Ashton Ch Ch *Man* 04–07; P-in-c Oldham St Steph and All Martyrs 07–11; TV Oldham 07–11; V Coldhurst and Oldham St Steph 11–17; Assoc Dir of Ords 15–17; Hon Can Man Cathl from 17; Dir of Ords from 17; PtO *Leeds* 20–21. *Bishopscourt, Bury New Road, Salford M7 4LE* T: 0161-708 9366 M: 07840-482280 E: frnicksmeeton@gmail.com

SMEJKAL, Yenda Marcel. b 68. Van Mildert Coll Dur BA 97. Coll of Resurr Mirfield 97. **d** 99 **p** 00. C S Shields All SS *Dur* 99–03; TV N Wearside 03–04; P-in-c Sundon *St Alb* from 04; P-in-c Luton St Sav from 12. *St Mary's Vicarage, 1 Selina Close, Luton LU3 3AW* T: (01582) 583076 E: yenda.smejkal@virgin.net

SMETHAM, Abigail Laura. *See* THOMPSON, Abigail Laura

SMETHURST, David Alan. b 36. Lon Univ BD 60 Man Univ MPhil 84. Tyndale Hall Bris 57. **d** 61 **p** 62. C Burnage St Marg *Man* 61–63; P-in-c Whalley Range St Marg 63–65; R Haughton St Mary 65–74; R Ulverston St Mary w H Trin *Carl* 74–87; Dean Hong Kong 87; Dir Acorn Chr Healing Trust Resource Cen 88–93; V Epsom St Martin *Guildf* 93–00; RD Epsom 97–00; rtd 01; PtO *Carl* 01–20. *16*

Helme Lodge, Natland, Kendal LA9 7QA T: (01539) 729997
E: friarsground@yahoo.com

SMETHURST, Gordon McIntyre. b 40. Man Univ BA 62 BD 69. Wells Th Coll 70. **d** 70 **p** 71. C Sandal St Helen *Wakef* 70–73; P-in-c Whitwood and Smawthorpe 73–75; Hd RE Goole Gr Sch 75–79; S Hunsley Sch Melton 80–00; V Anlaby Common St Mark *York* 00–03; P-in-c Roos and Garton w Tunstall, Grimston and Hilston 03–07; rtd 07. *266 Sigston Road, Beverley HU17 9PL* T: (01482) 863431 M: 07817-434209 E: revsmev@hotmail.com

SMILLIE, Linda Barbara. b 46. Oak Hill Th Coll 85. **d** 87 **p** 94. Par Dn Holloway St Mary w St Jas *Lon* 87–88; Par Dn Holloway St Mary Magd 88–90; Chapl W End Stores 90–91; C Holloway St Mark w Em 90–91; Hon C Islington St Mary 92–94; C-in-c Southall Em CD 95–01; rtd 01; PtO *Ox* 01–04; Hon C Hanger Hill Ascension and W Twyford St Mary *Lon* 04–07; PtO *Chich* 12–17. *20 Wyvern Place, Warnham, Horsham RH12 3QU* T: (01403) 273788

SMITH, Adrian Paul. b 73. Ches Coll of HE BA 94 Linc Univ MA 15. Cranmer Hall Dur 07. **d** 09 **p** 10. C Mablethorpe w Trusthorpe *Linc* 09–12; R Springline 12–15; R Owmby Gp 12–15; Dioc Communications Officer 15–18; Lic Preacher 15–18; V Linc St Mary Magd w St Paul and St Mich 18–20; Chapl HM Pris Linc from 20. *HM Prison, Greetwell Road, Lincoln LN2 4BD* T: (01522) 663000

SMITH, Adrian William Chase. b 62. **d** 18 **p** 18. C Watford St Luke *St Alb* 18–19; P-in-c Woodhouse and Wrangthorn Leeds from 19; TV Leeds St Geo from 19. *96 Becketts Park Drive, Leeds LS6 3PL*

SMITH, Aidan John. b 54. Leic Univ BA 76 Man Univ MBA 81 Heythrop Coll Lon MA 17. STETS 04. **d** 07 **p** 08. NSM St Martin Ludgate *Lon* 07–13; NSM Pinner 13–18; NSM Lilliput *Sarum* from 19. *4 Glenair Avenue, Poole BH14 8AD* T: (01202) 718434 E: smithanddenny@hotmail.com

⚭**SMITH, The Rt Revd Alan Gregory Clayton.** b 57. Birm Univ BA 78 MA 79 Univ of Wales (Ban) PhD 02. Wycliffe Hall Ox 79. **d** 81 **p** 82 **c** 01. C Pudsey St Lawr *Bradf* 81–82; C Pudsey St Lawr and St Paul 82–84; Chapl Lee Abbey 84–90; TV Walsall *Lich* 90–97; Dioc Missr 90–97; Adn Stoke-upon-Trent 97–01; Area Bp Shrewsbury 01–09; Bp St Alb from 09. *Abbey Gate House, 4 Abbey Mill Lane, St Albans AL3 4HD* T: (01727) 853305 F: 846715 E: bishop@stalbans.anglican.org

SMITH, Alan Leonard. b 51. Madeley Coll of Educn CertEd 72. Trin Coll Bris 93. **d** 95 **p** 96. C Taunton St Mary *B & W* 95–98; V Taunton Lyngford 98–07; RD Taunton 04–06; V Chatham St Steph *Roch* 07–14; RD Roch 11–14; rtd 14; PtO *Ex* from 14. *4 Elm Grove Drive, Dawlish EX7 0EU* T: (01626) 439983 E: revdalansmith@yahoo.co.uk

SMITH, Alan Thomas. b 35. Open Univ BA 78 Sussex Univ DipEd 79. Ridley Hall Cam 82. **d** 84 **p** 85. C Bedworth *Cov* 84–89; R Carlton Colville w Mutford and Rushmere Nor 89–97; rtd 97; PtO *Nor* from 01. *17 St Martins Gardens, New Buckenham, Norwich NR16 2AX* T: (01953) 860550 M: 07811-229493

SMITH, Alec John. b 29. AKC 53. **d** 54 **p** 55. C Charlton Kings St Mary *Glouc* 54–56; C-in-c Findon Valley CD *Chich* 56–57; V Viney Hill *Glouc* 57–65; V Churchdown St Jo 65–66; V Bishop's Cleeve *Sarum* 66–69; CF 69–88; V Douglas St Thos *S & M* 88–92; rtd 92; PtO *S & M* 92–05. *17 Saddle Mews, Douglas, Isle of Man IM2 1JA* T: (01624) 670093 E: padrealec@gmail.com

SMITH, Mrs Alice Elizabeth. b 87. Univ Coll Lon BSc 09. St Steph Ho Ox BA 13. **d** 14 **p** 15. C Moulsecoomb *Chich* 14–17; C E Grinstead St Swithun 17–18; V Brownswood Park *Lon* from 18. *St John's Vicarage, 2A Gloucester Drive, London N4 2LW* T: (020) 8809 6111 M: 07745-809669 E: alice.whalley@me.com

SMITH, Andrew. b 84. Southn Univ BSc 06 K Coll Lon MA 12. Wycliffe Hall Ox 06. **d** 09 **p** 10. C Lymington *Win* 09–13; P-in-c Bitterne Park 13–18; V 18–20; PtO from 20; Growing Younger Enabler *Carl* from 21; LtO from 21. *1 St John's Gate, Threlkeld, Keswick CA12 4TZ* E: revandysmith@gmail.com

SMITH, Andrew Clifford. b 67. Ridley Coll Melbourne BMin 00. **d** 01 **p** 01. C Clayton All SS Australia 01–03; C Gainsborough and Morton *Linc* 03–06; TV 06–08; P-in-c Woodhall Spa Gp 08–14; P-in-c Mt Dandelong Australia from 14. *PO Box 148, Kalorama VA 3766, Australia*

SMITH, Andrew David. b 62. All SS Cen for Miss & Min 15. **d** 18 **p** 19. NSM Blackley St Andr *Man* from 18; NSM Blackley St Paul from 18; NSM Blackley St Pet from 18. *5 Heathland Road, Salford M7 3GD* E: smudger1275@gmail.com

SMITH, Andrew Graham. b 81. St Mellitus Coll BA 14. **d** 14 **p** 15. C Basildon St Andr w H Cross *Chelmsf* 14–17; P-in-c Hutton 17–21; R from 21; AD Brentwood from 20. *The Rectory, 175 Rayleigh Road, Hutton, Brentwood*

CM13 1LX T: (01277) 514896 M: 07743-870851 E: fatherandysmith@gmail.com *or* andy@huttonparish.com

SMITH, Andrew John. b 53. Loughb Univ BTech 74. Lon Bible Coll 95 St Jo Coll Nottm MA 98. **d** 99 **p** 00. C Hailsham *Chich* 99–02; P-in-c Worc St Mich 02–03; TV Almondbury w Farnley Tyas *Wakef* 03–07; V Woolston NZ 07–11; C Remuera St Aidan 13–14; Jt P-in-c St Heliers Bay 14–15; Jt V Pahiatua and Eketahuna 15–18; PtO *Chich* from 18; *Guildf* from 21. *All Saints' Rectory, High Street, Headley, Bordon GU35 8PP* E: ajsinz211@gmail.com

SMITH, Andrew John. b 59. Birm Univ BSc 80 PhD 81. WMMTC 87 Qu Coll Birm 89. **d** 91 **p** 92. C Lower Mitton Worc 91–92; C Stourport and Wilden 92–95; TV Redditch, The Ridge 95–05; P-in-c Redditch St Steph 02–05; Ind Chapl 95–05; Chapl Redditch and Bromsgrove Primary Care Trust 01–05; V W Bromwich All SS *Lich* 05–15; RD W Bromwich 08–15; TR March *Ely* from 15; RD from 16. *St Peter's Rectory, 54 High Street, March PE15 9JR* E: andrew.marchurch@gmail.com

SMITH, Andrew Lewis. b 60. Bris Univ BSc 83 CEng 88 MIET 88. Trin Coll Bris BA 11. **d** 11 **p** 12. C E Dean w Friston and Jevington *Chich* 11–15; R Fetcham *Guildf* 15–20; Generous Giving Adv *Chich* from 21; LtO from 21. *20 Grove Road, Worthing BN14 9DG* E: revandrewsmith@hotmail.com *or* andrew.smith@chichester.anglican.org

SMITH, Andrew Perry Langton. b 56. Sheff City Poly BSc 79 Imp Coll Lon MSc 80 Qu Coll Birm MA 10. Trin Coll Bris 89. **d** 91 **p** 92. C Littleover *Derby* 91–95; TV Walsall *Lich* 95–09; Ind Chapl Black Country Urban Ind Miss 95–10; Hon C Walsall St Paul 05–09; Hon C Walsall Pleck and Bescot 05–09; Ecum Dean Telford Chr Coun 10–16; RD Telford 12–16; C Shawbury 16–18; P-in-c Kinnerley w Melverley, Knockin w Maesbrook and Maesbury 18–19; P-in-c Harlescott 19–20; rtd 21. *St Matthew's Vicarage, St George's Road, Donnington, Telford TF2 7NJ* T: (01952) 604239

SMITH, Mrs Angela. b 64. Portsm Poly BA 86 DipArch 89. Wycliffe Hall Ox 11. **d** 14 **p** 15. C Win Ch Ch 14–17; P-in-c Hartley Wintney, Elvetham, Winchfield etc 17–20; V from 20. *The Vicarage, Church Lane, Hartley Wintney, Hook RG27 8DZ* T: (01252) 842215 M: 07754-877575 E: angierosiesmith@gmail.com *or* angie.smith@stjohnshw.org.uk

SMITH, Angela Elisabeth. b 53. Southn Univ BA 75 Bp Grosseteste Coll PGCE 76. WEMTC 03. **d** 06 **p** 07. NSM Matson *Glouc* 06–09; NSM Glouc St Geo w Whaddon 09–15; NSM N Cheltenham 15–16; rtd 16; PtO *Nor* from 16. *The Rectory, 12 Pinewood Drive, Horning, Norwich NR12 8LZ* T: (01692) 630216 E: angela.draesmith2@btinternet.com

SMITH, Mrs Anita Elisabeth. b 57. Westhill Coll Birm BEd 79. Trin Coll Bris 85. **d** 88 **p** 94. Par Dn Bermondsey St Anne S'wark 88–92; Par Dn Brockley Hill St Sav 92–94; C 94–99; Miss Partner CMS Kenya 99–13; V Banbury St Hugh *Ox* from 14. *St Hugh's Vicarage, 4 Longfellow Road, Banbury OX16 9LB* T: (01295) 369021 E: anita.smith.nbi@gmail.com

SMITH, Ann Veronica. b 38. Doncaster Coll of Educn DipEd. Edin Dioc NSM Course 88. **d** 95 **p** 96. NSM S Queensferry *Edin* 95–99; NSM Falkirk 99–10; rtd 10; LtO *Edin* from 10. *16 Mannerston, Linlithgow EH49 7ND* T: (01506) 834361 E: avandmds@btinternet.com

SMITH, Anthony Cyril. b 40. K Coll Lon 65. **d** 69 **p** 70. C Crewkerne *B & W* 69–71; C Crewkerne w Wayford 71–74; TV Hemel Hempstead *St Alb* 74–76; Asst Chapl K Coll Taunton 76–80; Chapl 80–02; rtd 02; PtO *B & W* from 03. *1 Castle Street, Stogursey, Bridgwater TA5 1TG* T: (01278) 733577 E: kayandtony40@gmail.com

SMITH, Anthony James. b 57. Sheff Univ BA FCA. Ridley Hall Cam 83. **d** 86 **p** 87. C Woking St Pet *Guildf* 86–90; C Reigate St Mary *S'wark* 90–94; CMS Kenya 94–00; Finance Team Ldr World Vision UK 00–05; NSM Walton Milton Keynes *Ox* 10–12; PtO *Win* 12–20; Hd of Resource Development 13–20; P-in-c Burghclere w Newtown and Ecchinswell w Sydmonton from 20. *The Rectory, Well Street, Burghclere, Newbury RG20 9HS* T: (01635) 278470 M: 07521-222886 E: burghclere.rector@gmail.com

SMITH, Anthony James. b 80. Jes Coll Cam BA 02 MA 06 Sussex Univ MSc 03 DPhil 08 St Jo Coll Dur BA 18 MA 19. Cranmer Hall Dur 16. **d** 19 **p** 20. C Spennymoor and Whitworth *Dur* from 19. *34 Bluebell Drive, Spennymoor DL16 7YF* T: (01388) 304882 E: revdanthonysmith@gmail.com

SMITH, Mrs Antoinette. b 47. NTMTC 94. **d** 98 **p** 99. NSM Chigwell and Chigwell Row *Chelmsf* 98–02; TV 02–10; Chapl Haven Ho Children's Hospice 03–10; V Blackmore and Stondon Massey *Chelmsf* 10–15; RD Ongar 10–13; PtO *Pet* 15–17; R w Lt Harrowden and Orlingbury and Isham etc 17–21; rtd 21. *Address temp unknown* M: 07815-025242 E: reverend.tonismith@gmail.com

SMITH, Miss Audrey. b 47. S'wark Ord Course 89. **d** 92 **p** 94. NSM Croydon St Aug *S'wark* 92–98; P-in-c Redmarley D'Abitot, Bromesberrow w Pauntley etc *Glouc* 98–00; PtO 05–06; NSM Newent and Gorsley w Cliffords Mesne 06–08; Chapl Hartpury Coll 06–08; NSM Brampton St Thos *Derby* 08–10; rtd 10; PtO *Derby* from 15. *Fern Cottage, Stoney Way, Matlock DE4 3BW* M: 07583-109001 E: rev.audrey.s.21429@gmail.com

SMITH, Austin John Denyer. b 40. Worc Coll Ox BA 62. Cuddesdon Coll 64. **d** 66 **p** 67. C Shepherd's Bush St Steph w St Thos *Lon* 66–69; C W Drayton 69–72; Chapl Sussex Univ *Chich* 72–79; V Caddington *St Alb* 79–06; rtd 06; PtO *St Alb* from 07. *209 Bedford Road, Hitchin SG5 2UE* T: (01462) 437433 E: ajdsmith@waitrose.com

SMITH, Mrs Barbara Ann. b 56. SNWTP 07. **d** 10 **p** 11. NSM Liv St Chris Norris Green from 10. *25 Meadow Lane, Liverpool L12 5EA* T: 0151-226 3534 M: 07957-963546 E: basmith@blueyonder.co.uk

SMITH, Mrs Barbara Mary. b 47. Doncaster Coll of Educn CertEd 68. Cranmer Hall Dur 82. **dss** 85 **d** 87 **p** 94. Beverley St Nic *York* 85–87; Par Dn 87; NSM S'wark H Trin w St Matt 89–90; Ind Chapl Teesside *York* 91–95; Hon C Middlesbrough St Chad 94–95; PtO *St Alb* 96–02; Locum Chapl Anglia Poly Univ *Ely* 96–98; TV Linton 00–04; rtd 04; PtO *Newc* from 04; *Dur* from 10. *14 Glebelands, Corbridge NE45 5DS*

SMITH, Barry. b 41. Univ of Wales (Lamp) BA 62 Fitzw Ho Cam BA 64 MA 68 Man Univ MPhil 91. Ridley Hall Cam. **d** 65 **p** 66. C Rhyl w St Ann *St As* 65–70; Chapl Scargill Ho 70–72; C Flint *St As* 72–74; V Broughton 74–86; Dioc Ecum Officer 82–86; RD Wrexham 82–86; TR 86–95; Can Cursal St As Cathl 86–95; Chan 95; PtO *S'wark* 97–02. *1 Acorn Keep, Rowhills, Farnham GU9 9BL* T: (01252) 322111

SMITH, Barry Roy. b 46. STETS. **d** 00 **p** 04. NSM Blendworth w Chalton w Idsworth *Portsm* 00–05; Asst Chapl Portsm Hosps NHS Trust 03–05; Team Chapl Portsm Hosps Univ NHS Trust from 05; PtO *Portsm* 05–07 and from 09; NSM Blendworth w Chalton w Idsworth 07–09. *1 Kings Mews, Frimley Green, Camberley GU16 6HD* T: (01252) 444864 E: barry.roy.smith@googlemail.com

SMITH, Beverley Anne. b 56. Univ of Wales Coll of Medicine MSc 97 Univ of S Wales MSc 15 RN 78 RM 80 RHV 87 Univ of Wales PGCE 00. St Mich Coll Llan. **d** 05 **p** 06. NSM Whitchurch *Llan* 05–11; NSM Mynyddislwyn *Mon* 11–13; NSM Cyncoed from 15; Chapl Cardiff and Vale Univ Health Bd 08–11. *3 Solva Avenue, Cardiff CF14 0NP* M: 07841-707525 E: beverleyatciw@btinternet.com

SMITH, The Ven Brian. b 44. Westmr Coll Ox MTh 95. Sarum & Wells Th Coll 71. **d** 74 **p** 75. C Pennywell St Thos and Grindon St Oswald CD *Dur* 74–77; Chapl RAF 77–95; P-in-c Keswick St Jo *Carl* 95–96; V 96–05; RD Derwent 98–05; Hon Can Carl Cathl 99–05; Adn of Man *S & M* 05–11; V Douglas St Geo 05–11; rtd 11; PtO *Carl* from 12. *68 Greta Gardens, Crow Park Road, Keswick CA12 5EL* T: (017687) 75064 E: brian.smith157@btinternet.com

✠SMITH, The Rt Revd Brian Arthur. b 43. Edin Univ MA 66 Fitzw Coll Cam BA 68 MA 72 Jes Coll Cam MLitt 73. Westcott Ho Cam 66. **d** 72 **p** 73 **c** 93. Tutor and Lib Cuddesdon Coll 72–75; Dir of Studies Ripon Coll Cuddesdon 75–78; Sen Tutor 78–79; C Cuddesdon *Ox* 76–79; Dir Tr *Wakef* 79–87; P-in-c Halifax St Jo 79–85; Hon Can Wakef Cathl 81–87; Adn Craven *Bradf* 87–93; Suff Bp Tonbridge *Roch* 93–01; Hon Can Roch Cathl 93–01; Bp Edin 01–11; rtd 11; LtO *Edin* from 11; PtO *Ab* from 12. *Flat E, 2A Dean Path, Edinburgh EH4 3BA* T: 0131-220 6097 E: bishopsmith@btinternet.com

SMITH, Brian Michael. b 42. Kelham Th Coll 69. **d** 69 **p** 70. C Somers Town *Lon* 74–77; C Stamford Hill St Jo 74–75; C Stamford Hill St Bart 75–84; P-in-c Edmonton St Pet w St Martin 84–92; V 92–07; rtd 07. *9 Derwent Gardens, Derwent Avenue, Matlock DE4 3LX* T: (01629) 56559 E: bms.stple@gmail.com

SMITH, Canon Bridgid Mary. b 46. Bp Otter Coll CertEd 67. S Dios Minl Tr Scheme 88. **d** 91 **p** 94. C Pet H Spirit Bretton 91–95; P-in-c Silverstone and Abthorpe w Slapton 95–03; R Silverstone and Abthorpe w Slapton etc 03–09; Warden of Past Assts 00–06; Can Pet Cathl 01–09; rtd 09; PtO *S'well* from 10. *2 Merryweather Close, Southwell NG25 0BN* T: (01636) 812215 E: quickvic@lineone.net

SMITH, Carl Alexander. b 82. Glos Univ BA 05. Trin Coll Bris 13. **d** 13 **p** 14. C Burgess Hill St Andr *Chich* 13–17; R Slaugham and Staplefield Common from 17. *The Rectory, Brighton Road, Handcross, Haywards Heath RH17 6BU* M: 07816-979665 E: handcrossrectory@gmail.com

SMITH, Mrs Carol. b 55. SEITE 01. **d** 04 **p** 05. C Epping Distr *Chelmsf* 04–07; Chapl Epping Forest Primary Care Trust 05–07; V Moulsham St Luke *Chelmsf* 07–17; P-in-c Moulsham St Jo 13–17; C Galleywood Common 13–17; C Widford

13–17; Hon Can Chelmsf Cathl 13–17; Chapl Essex Co Coun 10–17; V Herne *Cant* from 17; AD Reculver from 19. *The New Vicarage, Herne Street, Herne Bay CT6 7HE* T: (01227) 636960 E: carolrevd@gmail.com

SMITH, Mrs Catherine Eleanor Louise. b 52. SAOMC 99. **d** 02 **p** 03. NSM Denham *Ox* 02–05; NSM Penn Street 05–15; NSM Beaconsfield 15–17; PtO from 17; Chapl Heatherwood & Wexham Park Hosps NHS Foundn Trust 05–14; Chapl Frimley Health NHS Foundn Trust from 14. *24 Westfield Road, Beaconsfield HP9 1EF* T/F: (01494) 670389 M: 07973-818998 E: catherinesmith52@btinternet.com

SMITH, Mrs Charlene. b 79. Coll of Resurr Mirfield 12. **d** 14 **p** 15. C Meltham *Leeds* 14–18; P-in-c Ackworth 18–20; R Ackworth and Badsworth from 21. *The Rectory, Cross Hill, Ackworth, Pontefract WF7 7EJ* T: (01977) 599979 E: revd.charlenesmith@gmail.com

SMITH, Charles Henry Neville. b 31. Nottm Univ BA 52 MA 65. Sarum Th Coll 55. **d** 57 **p** 58. C Thirsk w S Kilvington *York* 57–60; C Linthorpe 60–61; V Danby 61–66; Chapl United Camb Hosps 66–76; Chapl Lanc Moor Hosp 76–84; Hon Can Blackb Cathl 81–84; Asst Sec Gen Syn Hosp Chapl Coun 84–88; Hon C Lee St Marg *S'wark* 84–88; Chapl Guy's Hosp Lon 88–96; rtd 96; Hon Chapl S'wark Cathl from 96. *57 Belmont Park, London SE13 5BW* T: (020) 8318 9993 E: revnev@talktalk.net

SMITH, Canon Charles Rycroft. b 46. Sarum & Wells Th Coll 76. **d** 78 **p** 79. C Heref St Martin 78–81; C Southampton Maybush St Pet *Win* 81–83; R The Candover Valley 83–99; RD Alresford 90–99; P-in-c Guernsey St Andr 99–01; R 01–07; Vice-Dean Guernsey 02–07; P-in-c Beaulieu and Exbury and E Boldre 07–14; rtd 14; Hon Can Win Cathl from 14; PtO *Heref* 15–20. *Hope Cottage, 25B New Street, Ledbury HR8 2EA* T: (01531) 631104 E: rycs006@gmail.com

SMITH, Charlotte Emily. b 91. Warwick Univ BA 12 Univ Coll Lon MA 14. Ridley Hall Cam 18. **d** 21. C Richmond St Mary w St Matthias and St Jo *S'wark* from 21. *Church Cottage, 8 Church Walk, Richmond TW9 1SN* M: 07963-216722 E: charlotte-emily-smith@outlook.com

SMITH, Christine Lydia. *See* CARTER, Christine Lydia

SMITH, Mrs Christine Mary. b 53. Lanc Univ BA 75. Ox Min Course 13. **d** 15 **p** 16. NSM E Win from 15. *Pilgrim Cottage, Stoke Charity, Winchester SO21 3PF* T: (01962) 760309 M: 07751-303007 E: christine@hymnsam.co.uk

SMITH, Canon Christopher Blake Walters. b 63. Univ of Wales (Cardiff) BMus 84 BD 88 LLM 95. St Mich Coll Llan 85. **d** 88 **p** 89. C Aberdare *Llan* 88–93; V Tongwynlais 93–00; Dioc Dir Post-Ord Tr 95–05; Dom Chapl Bp Llan 01–07; Warden of Ords 01–07; Chapl to Abp Wales 03–07; Adn Morgannwg *Llan* 06–20; P-in-c Cwmbach 07–20; V Llanishen from 20; Metrop Can from 04. *Llanishen Vicarage, 2 The Rise, Cardiff CF14 0RA* T: (029) 2075 2545

SMITH, Canon Christopher Francis. b 46. K Coll Lon BD 68 AKC 68. St Aug Coll Cant 69. **d** 70 **p** 71. C Norwood All SS *Cant* 70–72; Asst Chapl Marlborough Coll 72–76; C Deal St Leon w Sholden *Cant* 77–81; P-in-c Benenden 81–83; V 83–07; P-in-c Sandhurst w Newenden 04–07; Hon Can Cant Cathl 03–07; AD Tenterden 05–07; Chapl Benenden Sch 81–92; Chapl Benenden Hosp 91–07; rtd 07; PtO *Cant* from 07. *34 Reynard Road, Whitstable CT5 3PH* T: (01227) 266569 E: christopherfrancissmith@yahoo.co.uk *or* cfsmith46@gmail.com

SMITH, Christopher James. b 72. Newc Univ BSc 94. Wycliffe Hall Ox BTh 01. **d** 02 **p** 03. C Cambridge H Trin *Ely* 02–04; Assoc R Manchester Zion Ch USA 04–08; R Chevening *Roch* 09–19; RD Sevenoaks 19; TR Marlborough *Sarum* from 19. *The Rectory, Rawlingswell Lane, St Martins, Marlborough SN8 1AU* E: revcjsmith@gmail.com

SMITH, Christopher John. b 81. Ridley Hall Cam 16. **d** 18 **p** 19. C Colchester St Luke *Chelmsf* from 18. *9 Asquith Drive, Highwoods, Colchester CO4 9FS*

SMITH, Christopher Matthew. b 67. New Coll Ox BA 89 MA 93 Open Univ LLB 07 Cardiff Univ LLM 09 Homerton Coll Cam PGCE 90 Called to the Bar (Gray's Inn) 10. St Steph Ho Ox BA 94. **d** 95 **p** 96. C Wantage *Ox* 95–99; Dom Chapl to Bp Horsham *Chich* 99–01; V Beckenham St Mich w St Aug *Roch* 01–11; V Holborn St Alb w Saffron Hill St Pet *Lon* from 11; AD S Camden 16–18. *St Alban's Clergy House, 18 Brooke Street, London EC1N 7RD* T: (020) 7405 1831 *or* 7430 2551

SMITH, Canon Christopher Milne. b 44. Selw Coll Cam BA 66. Cuddesdon Coll 67. **d** 69 **p** 70. C Liv Our Lady and St Nic 69–74; TV Kirkby 74–81; R Walton St Mary 81–91; Can Res Sheff Cathl 91–02; V Doncaster St Geo 02–10; Bp's Adv on the Paranormal 97–10; Hon Can Sheff Cathl 03–10; rtd 10; PtO *Sheff* 10–14; *Newc* from 10; Chapl to The Queen 04–14; PtO *Eur* 10–19. *14 Ravensdowne, Berwick-upon-Tweed TD15 1HX* T: (01289) 330375 E: smithrevcm@gmail.com

SMITH, Clifford. b 31. St Aid Birkenhead 59. **d** 61 **p** 62. C Limehouse St Anne *Lon* 61–63; C Ashtead *Guildf* 63–66; R Bromley All Hallows *Lon* 66–76; V Hillsborough and Wadsley Bridge *Sheff* 76–89; V Stainforth 89–96; rtd 96; Hon C Hurst *Ox* 97–12; Hon C Ruscombe and Twyford w Hurst 12–20; PtO from 20. *33 King Street Lane, Winnersh, Wokingham RG41 5AX* T: 0118-978 9453

SMITH, Clive Leslie. b 50. Leeds Univ BA 72 MA 03 Ch Coll Liv PGCE 73. Coll of Resurr Mirfield 75. **d** 77 **p** 78. C Goldington *St Alb* 77–81; C Cheshunt 81–84; V Watford St Pet 84–89; Chapl Leavesden Hosp Abbots Langley 89–94; Chapl St Alb and Hemel Hempstead NHS Trust 94–00; Chapl W Herts Hosps NHS Trust 00–01; Sen Chapl Doncaster and Bassetlaw Hosps NHS Foundn Trust 01–14; rtd 14; PtO *S'well* 02–17; *Sheff* 14–18; Chapl HM Pris Lindholme from 18. *HM Prison Lindholme, Doncaster DN7 6EE* T: (01302) 524870 E: clive.smith@justice.gov.uk

SMITH, Colin. b 39. MBE . Open Univ BA 80 LRSC 65 CChem 88 FRSC 88. NEOC 94. **d** 97 **p** 98. NSM Jesmond H Trin and Newc St Barn and St Jude 97–08; rtd 08; PtO *Newc* 08–21. *1 Cayton Grove, Newcastle upon Tyne NE5 1HL* T: 0191-267 9519 E: colinandevelyn@btopenworld.com

SMITH, Colin Graham. b 59. Hatf Poly BA 82 Westmr Coll Ox MTh 01 UNISA DTh 07 Hatf Poly CQSW 82. Trin Coll Bris BA 88. **d** 88 **p** 89. C Bermondsey St Jas w Ch Ch *S'wark* 88–92; V Brockley Hill St Sav 92–99; Miss Partner CMS Kenya 99–13; Dean Miss Educn CMS from 14; PtO *Ox* 14–17; NSM Banbury St Hugh from 17. *St Hugh's Vicarage, 4 Longfellow Road, Banbury OX16 9LB* T: (01295) 369021 E: colin.smith.nbi@gmail.com

SMITH, Colin Richard. b 53. Liv Poly BA 80 Liv Univ MTD 83. Oak Hill Th Coll 84. **d** 86 **p** 87. C Ormskirk *Liv* 86–89; V Wigan St Cath 89–94; C St Helens St Helen 94–99; TV 99–10; P-in-c St Helens St Mark 06–10; TV St Helens Town Cen 10–15; rtd 15; PtO *Liv* from 17. *5 Victoria Avenue, St Helens WA11 7BU*

SMITH, Mrs Corinne Anne. b 52. St Andr Univ MTheol 91. SAOMC 95. **d** 97. C Abingdon *Ox* 97–02; Chapl Pemb Coll Ox 02–03; Chapl Portsm Hosps NHS Trust 07–12; Chapl Sue Ryder Nettlebed Hospice 12–15; PtO *Portsm* 16–17; NSM Lake 17–20; C from 20; NSM Godshill 17–20; C from 20; NSM Shanklin St Sav 17–20. *Dovecote, 7 Culver Road, Shanklin PO37 6ER* T: (01983) 861581 M: 07775-628593 E: therevcozza@gmail.com

SMITH, Craig Philip. b 61. Sheff City Poly BA 86. St Jo Coll Nottm 90. **d** 93 **p** 94. C Bramley and Ravenfield w Hooton Roberts etc *Sheff* 93–97; C Rainham w Wennington *Chelmsf* 97–00; TV Gainsborough and Morton *Linc* 00–03; V Catshill and Dodford *Worc* 03–07; NZ 07–15; TR Gorton and Abbey Hey *Man* from 16; AD Ardwick 17–21. *The Rectory, 42-44 Wellington Street, Manchester M18 8LJ* T: 0161-231 7401 E: craig@gortonchurch.org

SMITH, Daniel Bradley. b 69. Harris Man Coll Ox BTh 05. St Steph Ho Ox 04. **d** 06 **p** 07. C Bexhill St Pet *Chich* 06–11; R W Blatchington 11–19; rtd 20. *2 Edgehill Way, Portslade, Brighton BN41 2PU*

SMITH, Canon Darren John Anthony. b 62. Nottm Univ BCombStuds 84. Linc Th Coll 84. **d** 86 **p** 87. C Leic Ascension 86–90; C Curdworth w Castle Vale *Birm* 90; C Castle Vale St Cuth 90–91; C Kingstanding St Luke 91–92; P-in-c 92–93; V 93–08; P-in-c Kingstanding St Mark 01–02; Gen Sec ACS from 08; Hon Can Ghana from 18. *Gordon Browning House, 8 Spitfire Road, Birmingham B24 9PB* T: 0121-382 5533 F: 382 6999 E: fr.smith@additionalcurates.co.uk

✠**SMITH, The Rt Revd David James.** b 35. AKC 58 FKC 99. **d** 59 **p** 60 **c** 87. C Gosforth All SS *Newc* 59–62; C Newc St Fran 62–64; C Longbenton St Bart 64–68; V Longhirst 68–75; V Monkseaton St Mary 75–82; RD Tynemouth 80–82; Hon Can Newc Cathl 81–87; Adn Lindisfarne 81–87; V Felton 82–83; Suff Bp Maidstone *Cant* 87–92; Bp HM Forces 90–92; Bp Bradf 92–02; rtd 02; Hon Asst Bp York from 02; Hon Asst Bp Eur from 02. *34 Cedar Glade, Dunnington, York YO19 5QZ* T: (01904) 481225 E: david@djmhs.force9.co.uk

SMITH, Canon David John. b 32. Goldsmiths' Coll Lon BA 76 LSE MSc 79. Lon Coll of Div 68. **d** 70 **p** 71. C Clerkenwell St Jas and St Jo w St Pet *Lon* 70–73; P-in-c Penge St Paul *Roch* 74–78; V 78–89; RD Beckenham 86–89; Chapl Bromley and Sheppard's Colls 90–97; PtO *S'wark* 90–97; Dioc Clergy Widows and Retirement Officer *Roch* 90–97; Hon Can Roch Cathl 95–97; rtd 98; PtO *St Alb* from 98; *Lon* from 99; *Ox* 09–19. *13 Park Way, Rickmansworth WD3 7AU* T: (01923) 775963

SMITH, David Robert. b 54. Southn Univ BSc 75 Loughb Univ MSc 86 CEng 84 MRAeS 84. WEMTC 02. **d** 05 **p** 06. C Matson *Glouc* 05–09; P-in-c Glouc St Geo w Whaddon

09–12; V 12–15; AD Glouc City 11–15; TR N Cheltenham 15–16; Hon Can Glouc Cathl 14–16; R Ashmanhaugh, Barton Turf etc *Nor* from 16. *The Rectory, 12 Pinewood Drive, Horning, Norwich NR12 8LZ* T: (01692) 630216 E: draesmith2@btinternet.com

SMITH, David Roy. b 74. Westcott Ho Cam 10. **d** 12 **p** 13. C Thorpe St Andr *Nor* 12–16; P-in-c E w W Harling, Bridgham w Roudham, Larling etc 16–20; P-in-c Raveningham Gp 20–21; P-in-c Gillingham w Geldeston, Stockton, Ellingham etc 20–21; R Waveney Marshlands from 21. *The Rectory, 60 The Street, Geldeston, Beccles NR34 0LN* E: revdavidrsmith@gmail.com

SMITH, David Stanley. b 41. Ox NSM Course. **d** 84 **p** 85. NSM Burghfield *Ox* 84–86; NSM Stratfield Mortimer 86–88; NSM Mortimer W End w Padworth 86–88; C St Breoke and Egloshayle *Truro* 88–93; V Penwerris 93–07; rtd 07; PtO *Ox* 09–10. *Emmaus, 1 Webster Close, Reading RG2 8BF* T: 0118-987 2597

SMITH, Mrs Deborah Louise. b 56. WEMTC 02 NOC 03. **d** 05 **p** 06. C Honley *Wakef* 05–07; Chapl HM Pris and YOI New Hall 05–07; NSM Woolston NZ 07–11; Chapl Nelson Hosps 11–12; C Remuera St Aidan 13–14; Jt P-in-c St Heliers Bay 14–15; Jt V Pahiatua and Eketahuna 15–18; P-in-c Tillington *Chich* 18–19; P-in-c Duncton 18–19; P-in-c Upwaltham 18–19; Chapl St Wilfrid's Hospice Eastbourne 19–21; C Churt and Hindhead *Guildf* from 21. *All Saints' Rectory, High Street, Headley, Bordon GU35 8PP* T: (01323) 434200 E: dlsinz211@gmail.com

SMITH, Mrs Decia Jane. b 47. ALAM 66. WMMTC 92. **d** 95 **p** 96. C Edgbaston St Germain *Birm* 95–99; P-in-c Abbots Leigh w Leigh Woods *Bris* 00–12; rtd 12; PtO *Bris* 13–19. *4 Kingsmill, Bristol BS9 1BZ* T: 0117-968 3511 E: revdecia@yahoo.co.uk

SMITH, Declan. See SMITH, Godfrey Declan Burfield

SMITH, Denis Richard. b 53. MA. St Jo Coll Nottm 83. **d** 85 **p** 86. C Hersham *Guildf* 85–88; C Thatcham *Ox* 88–91; V Shefford *St Alb* 91–02; P-in-c Tilehurst St Cath *Ox* 02–07; V Tilehurst St Cath and Calcot 07–16; rtd 16; PtO *Ox* from 16; *Win* from 17. *32 Basswood Drive, Basingstoke RG24 9SW* E: revdenissmith@hotmail.com

SMITH, Mrs Denise. b 46. Didsbury Coll of Educn CertEd 67. **d** 08 **p** 09. OLM Goodshaw and Crawshawbooth *Man* 08–16; rtd 16; PtO *Man* from 18. *Address temp unknown* M: 07551-361875 E: mrsbucket122@btinternet.com

SMITH, Dennis Austin. b 50. Lanc Univ BA 71 Liv Univ PGCE 72. NW Ord Course 74. **d** 77 **p** 78. NSM Seaforth *Liv* 77–83; NSM Gt Crosby St Faith 77–83; Hon C 83–98; Hon C Gt Crosby St Faith and Waterloo Park St Mary from 98; Asst Chapl Merchant Taylors' Sch Crosby 79–83; Chapl from 83. *16 Fir Road, Liverpool L22 4QL* T: 0151-928 5065

SMITH, Derek Graham. b 52. St Cath Coll Cam BA 74 MA 77. Westcott Ho Cam 74. **d** 76 **p** 77. C Weymouth H Trin *Sarum* 76–79; P-in-c Bradpole 79; TV Bridport 79–84; R Monkton Farleigh, S Wraxall and Winsley 84–98; TR Melksham 98–09; C Atworth w Shaw and Whitley 07–09; C Broughton Gifford, Gt Chalfield and Holt 07–09; RD Bradford 01–08; Chapl Wilts and Swindon Healthcare NHS Trust 00–02; Can and Preb Sarum Cathl 03–09; Chapl Limassol St Barn 09–17; rtd 17; PtO *B & W* from 18. *2 Underleaf Way, Peasedown St John, Bath BA2 8SY* T: (01761) 438976 E: revdgsmith52@gmail.com

SMITH, Donald Edgar. b 56. Oak Hill Th Coll 89. **d** 91 **p** 92. C Holloway St Mark w Em *Lon* 91–92; C Tollington 92–95; TV W Ealing St Jo w St Jas 95–08; R Frinton *Chelmsf* from 08. *The Rectory, 22 Queens Road, Frinton-on-Sea CO13 9BL* T: (01255) 674664 E: donthevic@btinternet.com

SMITH, Dorothea Violet. See EDWARDS, Dorothea Violet

SMITH, Edward George. b 61. Surrey Univ BSc 82 Cov Univ MSc 95 Anglia Ruskin Univ MA 15. Ox Min Course 06. **d** 09 **p** 10. NSM Aynho and Croughton w Evenley etc *Pet* 09–11; NSM Chenderit 11–14; R Cogenhoe and Gt and Lt Houghton w Brafield from 14; RD Wellingborough from 18. *The Rectory, Church Street, Cogenhoe, Northampton NN7 1LS* T: (01604) 891166 M: 07740-909756 E: eddie.smith@talk21.com

SMITH, Elizabeth Anne. See ETHERINGTON, Elizabeth Anne

SMITH, Miss Elizabeth Jane. b 50. Birm Univ BA 72. Trin Coll Bris 88. **d** 90 **p** 94. C Lowestoft and Kirkley *Nor* 90–94; TV Rugby *Cov* 94–01; C Shepton Mallet w Doulting *B & W* 01–03; R 03–10; Chapl Mendip Primary Care Trust 01–06; Chapl Somerset Primary Care Trust 06–10; rtd 10; PtO *Sarum* from 11; *B & W* from 15. *19 Alcock Crest, Warminster BA12 8ND* E: lizinwarminster@gmail.com

SMITH, Canon Elizabeth Marion. b 52. ACA 76 FCA 82. Carl Dioc Tr Inst 91. **d** 94 **p** 95. C Appleby *Carl* 94–98; P-in-c Hesket-in-the-Forest and Armathwaite 98–04; P-in-c Skelton and Hutton-in-the-Forest w Ivegill 98–04; R Inglewood Gp 04–12; RD Penrith 06–09; Hon Can Carl

Cathl 08–12; rtd 13; PtO *Carl* 13–16; Hon C Harraby from 16. *Tanglewood, Cumwhinton, Carlisle CA4 8DL* T: (01228) 560310 E: revdesmith@hotmail.com

SMITH, Esther. b 65. Coll of Ripon & York St Jo BA 86 York Univ PGCE 87. Trin Coll Bris BA 13. **d** 13 **p** 14. C Bath Walcot *B & W* 13–17; C Combe Down w Monkton Combe and S Stoke 17–18; R Chilcompton w Downside and Stratton on the Fosse from 18. *The Rectory, The Street, Chilcompton, Radstock BA3 4HN* T: (01761) 233401 E: esthersmith369@gmail.com

SMITH (*née* DAVIS), Felicity Ann. b 40. Bris Univ MB, ChB 63. Qu Coll Birm 83. **dss** 86 **d** 87 **p** 94. NSM Dioc Bd for Soc Resp *Cov* 86–96; NSM Leamington Spa H Trin from 96. *14 Oakwood Grove, Warwick CV34 5TD* T: (01926) 492452 E: felicity@fandi.me.uk

SMITH, Felix Arran Jerome. b 87. Edin Univ MA 11 Win Univ MA 17. Ripon Coll Cuddesdon MTh 13. **d** 13 **p** 15. C Dundee St Paul *Bre* 13–14; C Coplow *Leic* 14–17; V Lancing St Mich *Chich* from 17. *St Michael's Vicarage, 117 Penhill Road, Lancing BN15 8HD* T: (01903) 753653 M: 07818-407114 E: revfelixsmith@gmail.com

SMITH, Frances Mary. *See* KNIGHT, Frances Mary

SMITH, Francis Malcolm. b 44. Open Univ BA 82 FCMI ACIB 69. EAMTC 90. **d** 93 **p** 94. NSM Prittlewell St Mary *Chelmsf* 93–08; PtO 08–16; NSM N Shoebury 16–17; NSM Southchurch H Trin 16–17; PtO from 17. *24 St Augustine's Avenue, Southend-on-Sea SS1 3JH* T: (01702) 586680 F: 291166 E: franksmith44@hotmail.com

SMITH, Gavin Craig. b 71. Ridley Hall Cam 02. **d** 04 **p** 05. C Heatons *Man* 04–07; CF from 07. *c/o MOD Chaplains (Army)* T: (01264) 383430 F: 381824 M: 07919-354796 E: gavinsmith1971@hotmail.com

SMITH, Geoffrey. *See* PURCELL SMITH, Geoffrey

SMITH, Geoffrey Keith. b 37. Lon Coll of Div 57. **d** 60 **p** 61. C Leek St Luke *Lich* 60–63; C Trentham 63–66; V Lilleshall 66–84; P-in-c Sheriffhales w Woodcote 83–84; V Lilleshall and Sheriffhales 84–87; P-in-c Haughton 87–91; R Derrington, Haughton and Ranton 91–03; rtd 03; PtO *Lich* 03–21; CF (ACF) 73–02. *19 Meadow Drive, Haughton, Stafford ST18 9HU* T: (01785) 259076 E: geoffmar@btinternet.co.uk

SMITH, Geoffrey Raymond. b 49. AKC 71. St Aug Coll Cant 71. **d** 72 **p** 73. C Hendon St Alphage *Lon* 72–75; C Notting Hill St Mich and Ch Ch 75–78; P-in-c Isleworth St Fran 78–83; P-in-c Chipping Ongar *Chelmsf* 83–84; R 84–86; R Shelley 84–86; R Chipping Ongar w Shelley 86–89; RD Ongar 88–89; P-in-c Harlow St Mary Magd 89–90; V 90–98; R Woodford St Mary w St Phil and St Jas 98–08; TR Loughton St Jo 08–09; R 09–15; rtd 15; PtO *Chich* 16–18; R Laughton w Ripe and Chalvington from 18. *The Rectory, Church Lane, Laughton, Lewes BN8 6AH* T: (01323) 811898

SMITH, Georgina Leah. *See* HOLDING, Georgina Leah

SMITH, Gerald. b 36. Sarum Th Coll 61. **d** 63 **p** 64. C Menston w Woodhead *Bradf* 63–66; Chapl RAF 66–70; C Hoylake *Ches* 70–72; R Inverurie *Ab* 72–74; R Kemnay 72–74; TV Hucknall Torkard *S'well* 74–75; R Falkland Is 75–78; V Luddenden w Luddenden Foot *Wakef* 79–86; V Scopwick Gp *Linc* 86–94; P-in-c Leasingham 94–96; rtd 96; PtO *Ex* 96–21. *Ivy Cottage, Woolsery, Bideford EX39 5QS* T/F: (01237) 431298

SMITH (*née* McVeigh), Mrs Gillian. b 55. EAMTC 02. **d** 05 **p** 06. NSM Burwell w Reach *Ely* 05–09; P-in-c Potton w Sutton and Cockayne Hatley *St Alb* 09–13; R 13–19; rtd 19; PtO *Nor* from 20. *Abel Cottage, New Road, Ashwellthorpe, Norwich NR16 1HF* E: gillsmith.ash@gmail.com

SMITH, Gillian Angela. *See* SMITH RILEY, Gillian Angela

SMITH, Gillian Carol. *See* HUBBARD, Gillian Carol

SMITH, Godfrey Declan Burfield. b 42. TCD BA 64 MA 67 PGCE 65. Sarum Th Coll. **d** 69 **p** 70. Zambia 70–75; PtO *D & G* 81–02; S Regional Sec (Ireland) CMS 81–99; Overseas Sec 87–93; Miss Personnel Sec 93–99; I Donoughmore and Donard w Dunlavin *D & G* 02–11; rtd 11. *Moelvra, 1 Marlborough Road, Glenageary, Co Dublin, Republic of Ireland* M: (00353) 87-298 7364 E: declansmith14@gmail.com

SMITH, Graham. b 39. Univ of Wales (Ban) CertEd 60 Lon Univ DipEd 75. **d** 01 **p** 02. OLM Upper Holme Valley *Wakef* 01–05; NSM E Richmond *Ripon* 05–08; rtd 08; PtO *Derby* 08–18. *15 Church Street, Denby Village, Ripley DE5 8PA* T: (01332) 881324 M: 07402-285238 E: gsmith370@btinternet.com *or* revdgsmith@btinternet.com

SMITH, The Very Revd Graham Charles Morell. b 47. St Chad's Coll Dur BA 74. Westcott Ho Cam 74. **d** 76 **p** 77. C Tooting All SS *S'wark* 76–80; TV Thamesmead 80–87; TR Kidlington w Hampton Poyle *Ox* 87–97; RD Ox 89–95; TR Leeds City *Ripon* 97–04; Hon Can Ripon Cathl 97–04; Dean Nor 04–13; rtd 13; PtO *Ex* 13–17; P-in-c Ashreigney 17–18; P-in-c Broadwoodkelly 17–18; P-in-c Brushford

17–18; P-in-c Winkleigh 17–18. *Blacksmith's Cottage, Church Street, Ashreigney, Chulmleigh EX18 7LP* T: (01769) 520824 E: gcsmith@uwclub.net

SMITH, Graham David Noel. b 37. Oak Hill Th Coll 72. **d** 73 **p** 74. C Southborough St Pet w Ch Ch and St Matt *Roch* 73–76; C Bedworth *Cov* 76–79; R Treeton *Sheff* 79–84; V Riddlesden *Bradf* 84–96; RD S Craven 91–96; rtd 96; Hon C Ilkley All SS *Bradf* 97–03; PtO 03–14; *Leeds* from 14. *8 Bobbin Mill Court, Steeton, Keighley BD20 6PU* T: (01535) 654439

SMITH, Graham John. b 60. RN Eng Coll Plymouth BScEng 84 FHEA 11. Trin Coll Bris BA 90 St Jo Coll Nottm MA 00. **d** 90 **p** 91. C Herne *Cant* 90–93; Chapl RN 93–96; C Henfield w Shermanbury and Woodmancote *Chich* 96–98; Chapl Sussex Police 96–98; Chapl Portsm Hosps NHS Trust 98–00; P-in-c Cosham and Chapl Highbury Coll of FE Portsm 00–05; CME Officer *Portsm* 03–05; PtO from 06; *Guildf* from 16; Chapl SE Coast Ambulance Service NHS Foundn Trust from 16. *Ladymead, 6 Birtley Rise, Bramley, Guildford GU5 0HZ* T: (01483) 892792 M: 07923-574659 E: gjsmith@first-web.co.uk

SMITH, Graham Russell. b 60. New Coll Ox BA 81 MA 89 Lon Univ BD 89. Qu Coll Birm 02. **d** 04 **p** 05. C Yardley St Edburgha *Birm* 04–08; TV Bushbury *Lich* from 08. *The Good Shepherd Vicarage, 17 Goodyear Avenue, Wolverhampton WV10 9JX* T: (01902) 731713 M: 07746-994186 E: smith-graham32@sky.com

SMITH, Greg Peter. b 60. Warwick Univ BA 86 Qu Coll Birm BA 99. WMMTC 97. **d** 99 **p** 00. C Binley *Cov* 99–04; P-in-c E Green 04–15; V 15–21; AD Cov S 18–20; R Pontesbury I and II *Heref* from 21; R Minsterley, Habberley and Hope w Shelve from 21. *The Deanery, Main Road, Pontesbury, Shrewsbury SY5 0PS* E: rectorpontstip@gmail.com

SMITH, Gregory James. *See* CLIFTON-SMITH, Gregory James

SMITH, Mrs Gwendoline Anne. b 52. K Coll Lon BA 97. SEITE 97. **d** 99 **p** 00. C Erith St Paul *Roch* 99–02; V Hadlow 02–12; RD Paddock Wood 10–12; TV Bideford, Northam, Westward Ho!, Appledore etc *Ex* 12–17; rtd 17; PtO *B & W* from 17. *13 Dillons Road, Creech St Michael, Taunton TA3 5DS* E: gwensmith1252@gmail.com

SMITH, Miss Hannah Joy. b 82. Sheff Univ BA 03 K Coll Lon MA 10. St Mellitus Coll 08. **d** 12 **p** 13. C Leeds City *Ripon* 12–14; C Riverside Ch BMO 13–16; P-in-c Leeds Halton St Wilfrid 16–17; P-in-c Osmondthorpe 16–17; V Halton and Osmondthorpe from 17. *St Wilfrid's Vicarage, Selby Road, Leeds LS15 7NP* T: 0113-260 9154 E: hannah.smith@leeds.anglican.org

SMITH, Sister Hazel Ferguson Waide. b 33. Univ Coll Lon BA 55. **dss** 64 **d** 87 **p** 06. CSA 58–77; St Etheldreda's Children's Home Bedf 64–85; Bedford St Paul *St Alb* 85–92; Par Dn 87–92; rtd 92; PtO *St Alb* from 92; *Ox* 93–20; Assoc Sister CSA from 03. *Paddock House, 6 Linford Lane, Willen, Milton Keynes MK15 9DL* T: (01908) 397267 M: 07789-654881 E: sisterhazelsmith@gmail.com

SMITH, Heather Faith. b 60. Stirling Univ BSc 80 Ox Univ BTh 04 Heythrop Coll Lon MA 11. Ripon Coll Cuddesdon 00. **d** 02 **p** 03. C Caversham St Pet and Mapledurham *Ox* 02–06; PtO from 19; *Sarum* 19–20; C Rowde and Bromham from 21. *36 Greystones, Bromham, Chippenham SN15 2JT* T: (01380) 850729

SMITH, Henry Robert. b 41. Lanchester Poly Cov BSc 66. Qu Coll Birm 75. **d** 78 **p** 79. Hon C Hillmorton *Cov* 78–81; LtO *S'well* 81–85; Hon C Radcliffe-on-Trent and Shelford etc 85–89; C Sutton in Ashfield St Mary 89–92; P-in-c Forest Town 92–98; P-in-c Babworth w Sutton-cum-Lound 98–02; P-in-c Scofton w Osberton 98–02; P-in-c Babworth w Sutton-cum-Lound and Scofton etc 02–06; rtd 06; PtO *S'well* from 18. *15 Park Lane, Retford DN22 6TX* T: (01777) 949649 E: bobsmith@dircon.co.uk

SMITH, Howard Alan. b 46. St Jo Coll Dur BA 73. Cranmer Hall Dur. **d** 74 **p** 75. C Brighton St Matthias *Chich* 74–77; C Henfield w Shermanbury and Woodmancote 77–80; R Northiam 80–87; Chapl St Ebba's Hosp Epsom 87–94; Chapl Qu Mary's Hosp Carshalton 87–94; Chapl Merton and Sutton Community NHS Trust 94–99; Chapl Epsom and St Helier Univ Hosps NHS Trust 99–08; rtd 08; PtO *S'wark* from 08; Chapl Wandsworth Primary Care Trust 10–13. *72 Park Lane, Wallington SM6 0TL* T: (020) 8643 3300 E: howard_a_smith2003@yahoo.co.uk

SMITH, Howard Gilbert. b 48. Leeds Univ BA 69. St Steph Ho Ox BA 71 MA 75 Ridley Hall Cam 72. **d** 73 **p** 74. C Wallsend St Luke *Newc* 73–76; C Farnworth and Kearsley *Man* 76–77; P-in-c Farnworth All SS 77–78; TV E Farnworth and Kearsley 78–82; V Belfield 82–93; V Leesfield 93–04; V Northallerton w Kirby Sigston *York* 04–13; rtd 13; PtO *York* from 13; *Carl* from 18. *3 Kent Park Avenue, Kendal LA9 5JT* E: howardgsmith@tiscali.co.uk

SMITH, Howard Vincent. b 48. Trin Coll Bris 09. **d** 11 **p** 12. OLM Winterbourne *Bris* 11–16; OLM Coalpit Heath 12–13; OLM Frampton Cotterell and Iron Acton 12–16; OLM Frenchay and Winterbourne Down 12–16; OLM Fromeside 16–20; NSM from 20. *15 Winchcombe Road, Frampton Cotterell, Bristol BS36 2AG* T: (01454) 773817 M: 07504-435443 E: revd.hvs@gmail.com

SMITH, Canon Ian. b 62. Hull Univ BA 83 Man Univ MA 09. Oak Hill Th Coll BA 88. **d** 88 **p** 89. C W Hampstead St Luke *Lon* 88–90; C Woking St Pet *Guildf* 90–95; V Leyland St Jo *Blackb* 95–02; C Goole *Sheff* 02–03; P-in-c Sheff St Paul 03–12; R Warmsworth from 12; AD W Doncaster from 15; Hon Can Sheff Cathl from 12. *Warmsworth Rectory, 187 Warmsworth Road, Doncaster DN4 0TW* T: (01302) 853324 E: ian.smith@sheffield.anglican.org

SMITH, Ian. b 62. Qu Coll Birm. **d** 14 **p** 15. C Edgbaston St Germain *Birm* 14–18; V Blendon *Roch* from 18. *The Vicarage, 37 Bladindon Drive, Bexley DA5 3BS* T: (020) 8301 5387 M: 07841-615945 E: revd.iansmith@gmail.com

SMITH, Ian Martin. b 60. ERMC 14. **d** 17 **p** 18. NSM Silsoe, Pulloxhill and Flitton *St Alb* 17–20; NSM Renhold 20–21; P-in-c from 21. *The Vicarage, 46 Church End, Renhold, Bedford MK41 0LU*

SMITH, Canon Ian Walker. b 29. Leeds Univ BA 52. Coll of Resurr Mirfield 52. **d** 54 **p** 55. C Moulsecoomb *Chich* 54–61; Chapl K Sch Cant 61–62; C Crawley *Chich* 62–79; TV 79–81; R Clenchwarton *Ely* 81–94; RD Lynn Marshland 84–94; Hon Can Ely Cathl 88–94; PtO *Nor* 88–94; rtd 94; PtO *Ely* 94–09. *27 Jubilee Drive, Dersingham, King's Lynn PE31 6YA* T: (01485) 540203

SMITH, Mrs Irene Mary. b 43. Shenstone Coll of Educn CertEd 64 Lon Univ BD 77. OLM course 96. **d** 99 **p** 00. OLM Uttoxeter Area *Lich* 99–18; PtO 18–21. *16 Teanhurst Close, Tean, Stoke-on-Trent ST10 4NN* T: (01538) 722975 E: irene.smith0@btinternet.com

SMITH, Irene Victoria. *See* WATKINS, Irene Victoria

SMITH, Janet. *See* SMITH, Patricia Janet

SMITH, Mrs Janette Elizabeth. b 61. Sarum Coll 13. **d** 16 **p** 17. C Hartley Wintney, Elvetham, Winchfield etc *Win* 16–19; V Crookhorn *Portsm* from 19; C Purbrook from 19; C Portsdown from 19. *87 Perseus Place, Waterlooville PO7 8AW* M: 07708-730832 E: revjanettesmith@gmail.com *or* vicar@cogs.org.uk

SMITH, Janice Lilian. b 51. Open Univ BSc 98. NOC 98. **d** 01 **p** 02. NSM Yeadon St Jo *Bradf* 01–06; P-in-c Bramhope *Ripon* 06–14; *Leeds* 14–18; P-in-c Ireland Wood *Ripon* 09–12; rtd 18. *17 Silverdale Close, Guiseley, Leeds LS20 8BQ* E: revjanice.smith@gmail.com

SMITH, Janice Margaret. b 62. ERMC 18. **d** 20 **p** 21. NSM Hemingford Grey *Ely* from 20; Chapl among Deaf and Deafblind People from 20. *22 Buttermere, Huntingdon PE29 6UB* M: 07593-633774 E: smithjan312@gmail.com *or* cambsdeafchurch@gmail.com

SMITH, Canon Jeffry Bradford. b 56. Pitzer Coll BA 82. Ripon Coll Cuddesdon 83 Ch Div Sch of the Pacific (USA) MDiv 85. **d** 86 **p** 87. C Visalia USA 86–87; C Frimley *Guildf* 87–91; R E and W Clandon 91–03; Chapl HM Pris Send 94–96; Chapl HM Pris Channings Wood 03–04; Can Res Bermuda 04–07; TV Glendale Gp *Newc* 09–14; rtd 14; PtO *Newc* from 14; R Coldstream *Edin* from 15. *20 Tenter Hill, Wooler NE71 6DG* E: revcanonjsmith@gmail.com

SMITH, Mrs Jennifer Pamela. b 63. Girton Coll Cam BA 85 MA 88. Oak Hill Th Coll BA 91. **d** 91 **p** 94. C Rawdon *Bradf* 91–93; Chapl Bradf Cathl 93–96; P-in-c Kelbrook 96–00; Asst Chapl Airedale NHS Trust 01–07; Chapl Airedale NHS Foundn Trust from 07. *24 Greenacres, Skipton BD23 1BX* T: (01756) 790852 *or* (01535) 294088 E: jenny.smith@leeds.anglican.org

SMITH, Jeremy John Hawthorn. b 52. Birm Univ BSc 73 Lanc Univ MA 97. CBDTI 94. **d** 97 **p** 98. NSM Long Marton w Dufton and w Milburn *Carl* 97–00; NSM Hesket-in-the-Forest and Armathwaite 00–04; NSM Skelton and Hutton-in-the-Forest w Ivegill 00–04; NSM Ainstable 00–04; NSM Inglewood Gp 04–12; PtO 13–19. *Tanglewood, Cumwhinton, Carlisle CA4 8DL* T: (01228) 560310 E: revdesmith@hotmail.com

SMITH, Jesse Lee. b 70. Man Univ BA 93 Nottm Univ MA 96. Linc Th Coll 94 Westcott Ho Cam 95. **d** 96 **p** 97. C Gomersal *Wakef* 96–00; C Penarth All SS *Llan* 00–02; TV Cen Cardiff 02–03; V Hartlepool H Trin *Dur* 03–08; V Caerau w Ely *Llan* from 08. *The Vicarage, Cowbridge Road West, Cardiff CF5 5BQ* T: (029) 2056 32564 E: jesselsmith1970@gmail.com

SMITH, Jessica Clare. b 73. Ex Coll Ox BA 95 Ox Univ PGCE 96. Ridley Hall Cam 16. **d** 18 **p** 19. C Strood St Fran *Roch* 18–21; V Penge H Trin and St Jo from 21. *The Vicarage, 4 St John's Road, London SE20 7EQ* M: 07508-958802

SMITH, Joanne Sarah. b 79. Salford Univ BSc 01. St Jo Coll Nottm 14. **d** 16 **p** 17. C Horwich and Rivington *Man* 16–19; V Euxton *Blackb* from 19. *The Vicarage, Wigan Road, Euxton, Chorley PR7 6JH* T: (01257) 262102 M: 07026-279494 E: revdjosmith@hotmail.com

SMITH, John. *See* SMITH, Stephen John

SMITH, John Alec. b 37. Lon Coll of Div ALCD 62 BD 63. **d** 63 **p** 64. C Cromer *Nor* 63–66; C Barking St Marg *Chelmsf* 66–69; V Attercliffe *Sheff* 69–75; P-in-c Sheff St Barn and St Mary 76–78; V 78–89; Ind Chapl 78–89; RD Ecclesall 80–85; TR Chippenham St Paul w Hardenhuish etc *Bris* 89–00; V Kington St Michael 89–00; rtd 00. *The Willows, Salford Priors, Evesham WR11 8UU* T: (01789) 772072

SMITH, John Bartlett. b 50. St Chad's Coll Dur BA 73 ACIPD. Cuddesdon Coll 73. **d** 76 **p** 77. C Heref St Martin 76–86; NSM Isleworth St Mary *Lon* 86–89; NSM Millom *Carl* 89–92; NSM Balham St Mary and St Jo *S'wark* 92–04; PtO *Ox* 10–14. *91 Willowbourne, Fleet GU51 5BP* M: 07769-990391 E: j29bs@yahoo.com

SMITH, John Denmead. b 44. Keble Coll Ox BA 65 MA 69 St Jo Coll Ox DPhil 71. Coll of Resurr Mirfield 72. **d** 75 **p** 76. NSM Win St Lawr and St Maurice w St Swithun 75–80; Chapl Win Coll 75–04; Sen Chapl 04–06; rtd 06; Lect Uganda Chr Univ Mukono from 06. *56D North Bar Without, Beverley HU17 7AB* T: (01482) 865513 E: jds1000@gmail.com

SMITH, John Ernest. b 52. St Andr Univ MTheol 77. Wycliffe Hall Ox 78. **d** 79 **p** 80. C Bermondsey St Mary w St Olave, St Jo etc *S'wark* 79–87; P-in-c Whyteleafe 87–97; RD Caterham 96–98; P-in-c Merstham and Gatton 98–10; TR Merstham, S Merstham and Gatton 10–12; P-in-c Hoo St Werburgh *Roch* 12–19; rtd 19; PtO *Cant* from 21. *21 Bayfield, Painters Forstal, Faversham ME13 0EF* E: revjohn.e.smith@btinternet.com

SMITH, John Fenn. b 47. Murdoch Univ Aus BSc 89 BA 06 Notre Dame Univ Aus MA 06. Wollaston Th Coll 02. **d** 05. C Fremantle St Jo Australia 05–08; NSM Slindon, Eartham and Madehurst *Chich* 08–09; NSM Arundel w Tortington and S Stoke 09–11; Australia 11–17; PtO *Chich* from 17. *1 Matrons Cottages, Sea Road, East Preston, Littlehampton BN16 1JP* E: jhnf.smith@googlemail.com

SMITH, John Lawrence. b 43. Birm Univ BSc 65. Linc Th Coll 67. **d** 70 **p** 71. C Frodingham *Linc* 70–75; TV Gt Grimsby St Mary and St Jas 75–83; V Wolverhampton St Andr *Lich* 83–12; rtd 12; PtO *Ox* from 14. *75 Courtington Lane, Bloxham, Banbury OX15 4HS* T: (01295) 721709

SMITH, Canon John Leslie. b 44. Trin Coll Cam BA 65 MA 71. Ripon Coll Cuddesdon 79. **d** 81 **p** 82. C Ollerton *S'well* 81–84; P-in-c Farndon and Thorpe 84–88; P-in-c Winthorpe and Langford w Holme 88–95; Dioc Chief Insp of Schs 88–95; Dir of Educn *Pet* 95–99; P-in-c Cottingham w E Carlton 97–99; P-in-c Gretton w Rockingham and Cottingham w E Carlton 99; Dir of Educn *Roch* 99–10; Hon Can Roch Cathl 04–10; P-in-c Bredgar w Bicknor and Frinsted w Wormshill etc *Cant* 05–10; rtd 10; PtO *S'well* from 10; *Eur* from 19. *Whiteways, Low Road, Besthorpe, Newark NG23 7HJ* T: (01636) 894277 E: revcanjohn.smith@googlemail.com *or* revcanjohn.smith@me.com

SMITH, John Malcolm. b 36. ACIB 60. NOC 81. **d** 84 **p** 85. NSM Bury St Pet *Man* 84–06; rtd 06; PtO *Man* from 06. *46 Ajax Drive, Bury BL9 8EF* T: 0161-766 8378 E: jmalcolmsmith@btinternet.com

SMITH, John Rollin. b 43. **d** 11 **p** 17. OLM Penn and Tylers Green *Ox* 11–12; NSM Gt Marlow w Marlow Bottom, Lt Marlow and Bisham from 16. *The Knoll, Paul's Hill, Penn, High Wycombe HP10 8NZ* T: (01494) 815718 E: jsmithmpg@aol.com

SMITH, John Simon. b 46. Middx Hosp MB, BS 70 FRCGP 91. Ripon Coll Cuddesdon 05. **d** 06 **p** 07. NSM Kettering SS Pet and Paul 06–16; rtd 16; PtO *Pet* 16–21. *34 Poplars Farm Road, Barton Seagrave, Kettering NN15 5AG* T: (01536) 513786 E: john@poplarsfarm.org

SMITH, John Sydney. b 36. Lanc Univ MA 97 ALA 59 FLA 68 FISM 82. CBDTI 94. **d** 97 **p** 98. NSM Arthuret, Nicholforest and Kirkandrews on Esk *Carl* 97–02; rtd 02; PtO *Carl* 01–20. *The Jays, 3 White House, Walton, Brampton CA8 2DJ* T: (016977) 41114 E: johnandjill.thejays@btinternet.com

SMITH, John Thompson. b 30. Wycliffe Hall Ox 64. **d** 66 **p** 67. C Walsall *Lich* 66–69; V Stoke Prior *Worc* 69–75; Asst Gen Sec Red Triangle Club 75–85; R Tendring and Lt Bentley w Beaumont cum Moze *Chelmsf* 85–89; R Fairstead w Terling and White Notley etc 89–92; Chapl Heath Hosp Tendring 85–92; rtd 92; PtO *B & W* 92–12. *1 Harvey Close, Weston-super-Mare BS22 7DW* T: (01934) 514256

SMITH, John Trevor. b 47. GGSM. Coll of Resurr Mirfield 74. **d** 77 **p** 78. C Loughton St Jo *Chelmsf* 77–80; C Ruislip St Martin *Lon* 80–84; P-in-c Southall Ch Redeemer 84–91; V Kingsbury St Andr 91–13; rtd 13; PtO *Nor* from 13. *1*

All Saints Street, King's Lynn PE30 5AD T: (01553) 775250
E: johntsmith23@btinternet.com

SMITH, Jonathan Edward. b 78. Bradf Univ BSc 99. Wycliffe Hall Ox 16. **d** 18 **p** 19. C Bilton *Cov* from 18. *10 Monks Close, Cawston Grange, Rugby CV22 7FP* T: (01788) 842049 M: 07813-786261 E: curatebilton@icloud.com

SMITH, Jonathan Paul. b 60. Univ of Wales (Lamp) BA 81. Wycliffe Hall Ox 82. **d** 84 **p** 85. C Baglan *Llan* 84–88; C Gabalfa 88–90; R Llangammarch w Llanganten and Llanllconfel etc *S & B* 90–01; Dioc Missr 95–01; R Denbigh *St As* 01–15; AD 09–14; TV Wrexham from 15. *Llwyn, 3 Craigmillar Road, Wrexham LL12 7AR* T: (01978) 350797 E: jonathan@plwyfwrecsam.org.uk

SMITH, The Ven Jonathan Peter. b 55. K Coll Lon BD 77 AKC 77 Cam Univ PGCE 78. Westcott Ho Cam 79. **d** 80 **p** 81. C Gosforth All SS *Newc* 80–82; C Waltham Abbey *Chelmsf* 82–85; Chapl City Univ *Lon* 85–88; R Harrold and Carlton w Chellington *St Alb* 88–97; Chapl Beds Police 90–97; V Harpenden St Jo *St Alb* 97–08; RD Wheathampstead 99–04; Adn St Alb 08–20; rtd 20; PtO *St Alb* from 20. *Address temp unknown*

SMITH, Joseph Paul. b 87. Northn Univ BA 09. Trin Coll Bris BA 18. **d** 18 **p** 19. C Over St Chad *Ches* 18–21; P-in-c Bidston from 21. *6 Statham Road, Prenton CH43 7XS* M: 07702-425344 E: revjoesmith87@gmail.com

SMITH, Joseph Paul Tobias George. b 73. Ox Univ BTh 95 Ex Univ MA 97. **d** 08 **p** 09. OLM Talbot Village *Sarum* 08–11; NSM Branksome St Aldhelm 11–16; PtO 16–21; *Win* 16–21; *Ox* from 21. *14 Broad Platts, Slough SL3 7SA* M: 07376-794974 E: smithjoe91264316@aol.com

SMITH, Canon Joyce Mary. b 52. Lon Hosp BDS 74 Nottm Univ MMedSc 77 Lon Univ PhD 84 MCCDRCS 89. EAMTC. **d** 00 **p** 01. C Harlow St Mary and St Hugh w St Jo the Bapt *Chelmsf* 00–02; C Waltham H Cross 02–03; TV 03–10; NSM from 10; RD Epping Forest 10–13; RD Epping Forest and Ongar 13–18; Chapl St Clare Hospice 10–14; Hon Can Chelmsf Cathl from 15. *2 Takeley Close, Waltham Abbey EN9 1QH* T: (01992) 733655 E: revdjoyces@sky.com

SMITH, Miss Judith. b 74. SS Coll Cam BA 95 MA 98 PGCE 97 Sheff Univ MA 14. Trin Coll Bris BA 09. **d** 09 **p** 10. C Beeston *Ripon* 09–13; TV Abbeylands 13–14; *Leeds* 14–17; TR Moor Allerton and Shadwell 17–21; Dir Ch Revitalisation from 21. *Address temp unknown* E: revjudesmith@gmail.com

SMITH, Sister Judith Lillian. b 56. Cumbria Univ BA 13. All SS Cen for Miss & Min 15. **d** 17 **p** 18. NSM Hornby w Claughton and Whittington etc *Blackb* 17–20; PtO from 20. *St Joseph's House of Prayer, New Vicarage, Church Lane, Tunstall, Carnforth LA6 2RQ* T: (03330) 119563 E: sisterjudithocmm@gmail.com

SMITH, Julian William. b 64. Liv Univ BSc 85. Trin Coll Bris BA 93. **d** 93 **p** 94. C Henfynyw w Aberaeron and Llanddewi Aberarth *St D* 93–97; V Llansantffraed and Llanbadarn Trefeglwys etc 97–05; V Llansantffraed w Llanrhystud and Llanddeiniol 05–20; P-in-c Bro Wyre from 20; AD from 20. *The Vicarage, 11 Maes Wyre, Llanrhystud SY23 5AH* T: (01974) 202336 E: julian.debs@tiscali.co.uk

SMITH, Julie Lesley. b 64. **d** 14 **p** 15. C Saltburn-by-the-Sea *York* 14–17; V Barrowford and Newchurch-in-Pendle *Blackb* from 17. *The Vicarage, Wheatley Lane Road, Barrowford, Nelson BB9 6QS* E: jls446439@gmail.com

SMITH, Mrs Justine Lydia. b 69. **d** 12 **p** 13. C Elloughton and Brough w Brantingham *York* 12–16; P-in-c The Marshland *Sheff* from 16; AD Snaith and Hatfield from 20. *25 Prospect Close, Swinefleet, Goole DN14 8FB* T: (01405) 704626 E: justine.smith@sheffield.anglican.org

SMITH, Mrs Katharine Emma. b 85. Pemb Coll Cam MEng 08. Ridley Hall Cam 11. **d** 14 **p** 16. C Battersea St Pet and St Paul *S'wark* 14–19; C Underwood St Aug *Bris* from 19. *8 Figsbury Close, Swindon SN25 1UA* M: 07814-601366 E: kaf@patternchurch.org

SMITH, Mrs Katherine Jane. b 42. Sussex Univ BA 65. **d** 07 **p** 08. NSM Battersea St Luke *S'wark* 07–12; rtd 12; PtO *S'wark* from 12; *Chich* from 19. *74 Alfriston Road, London SW11 6NW* T: (020) 7228 3079 M: 07747-874970 E: katherine.smith42@btopenworld.com

SMITH, Keith. b 46. ACIB. S Dios Minl Tr Scheme 85. **d** 87 **p** 88. NSM W Worthing St Jo *Chich* 87–94; NSM Maybridge 94–96; C Durrington 96–01; V Pagham 01–11; rtd 11; PtO *Chich* from 11. *20 Trent Road, Worthing BN12 4EL* T: (01903) 534498 E: keith_smith_99@yahoo.com

SMITH, Kenneth Robert. b 48. K Coll Lon BD 75 AKC 75. St Aug Coll Cant 75. **d** 76 **p** 77. C Birtley *Dur* 76–80; V Lamesley 80–90; R Whitburn 90–13; rtd 13. *105 Sidecliffe Road, Sunderland SR6 9JR* T: 0191-549 7700

SMITH, Kevin. b 66. Westmr Coll Ox BA 89. Chich Th Coll 90. **d** 92 **p** 93. C Worksop Priory *S'well* 92–96; V New Cantley

Sheff 96–03; P-in-c Horden *Dur* 03–06; V 06–16; P Admin Shrine of Our Lady of Walsingham from 16. *The Shrine of Our Lady of Walsingham, The College, Knight Street, Walsingham NR22 6EF* T: (01328) 824204 E: ks.horden@btinternet.com *or* pr.adm@olw-shrine.org.uk

SMITH, Laurence Robert. b 91. UEA BA 12. Ridley Hall Cam 12. **d** 15 **p** 16. C Bury St Edmunds St Mary *St E* 15–18; V Woodley *Ox* from 18; V Southlake from 18. *St James's Vicarage, 97 Reading Road, Woodley, Reading RG5 3AE* T: 0118-969 3445 M: 07909-331350 E: revlaurencesmith@gmail.com

SMITH, Laurence Sidney. b 37. Sarum & Wells Th Coll 70. **d** 73 **p** 74. C Surbiton St Matt *S'wark* 73–76; C Horley 76–81; V W Ewell *Guildf* 81–90; V W Byfleet 90–02; rtd 02; PtO *Glouc* from 03. *Candlemill Cottage, Millbank, George Street, Nailsworth, Stroud GL6 0AG* T: (01453) 836432

SMITH, Lewis Shand. b 52. Aber Univ MA 74 Edin Univ BD 78 FRSA 00. Edin Th Coll 74. **d** 77 **p** 78. C Wishaw *Glas* 77–79; P-in-c 79–80; C Motherwell 77–79; P-in-c 79–80; R Lerwick *Ab* 80–00; P-in-c Burravoe 80–00; Can St Andr Cathl 93–00; R Dumfries *Glas* 00–05; Miss to Seamen 80–00; LtO *Edin* from 08. *Sandview, Bigton, Shetland ZE2 9JA* M: 07785-744610 E: shand.smith@talk21.com

SMITH, Mrs Linda Jean. b 61. Ripon Coll Cuddesdon 97. **d** 99 **p** 00. C St Martin w Looe *Truro* 99–03; P-in-c Talland 03–09; C Lanreath, Pelynt and Bradoc 03–09; TV Langtree *Ox* from 09; AD Henley 16–19. *The Vicarage, Reading Road, Woodcote, Reading RG8 0QX* T: (01491) 680979 E: woodcotevicarage@btinternet.com

SMITH, Miss Lorna Cassandra. b 43. Open Univ BA 76. Cant Sch of Min 82. **dss** 86 **d** 87 **p** 94. Birchington w Acol and Minnis Bay *Cant* 86–92; Par Dn 87–92; C Addlestone *Guildf* 92–97; V Englefield Green 97–05; rtd 05; PtO *Guildf* 05–18; *Lon* 08–13. *St Mary's Convent and Nursing Home, Burlington Lane, London W4 2QE* T: (020) 8994 4641 E: revlcs@aol.com

SMITH, Lorna Mary. See LAVARELLO-SMITH, Lorna Mary

SMITH, Mrs Lorna Rosalind. b 53. Oak Hill NSM Course 89. **d** 92 **p** 94. NSM Squirrels Heath *Chelmsf* 92–94; NSM Stanford-le-Hope w Mucking 94–97; P-in-c Fobbing 97–04; P-in-c Tillingham 04–15; rtd 15; PtO *Chelmsf* from 15. *33 Latchingdon Road, Cold Norton CM3 6JG* T: (01621) 828755 E: adrianlorna33@btinternet.com

SMITH, Lydia Jane. b 63. St Mellitus Coll BA 13. **d** 13 **p** 14. C Saffron Walden and Villages *Chelmsf* 13–16; TV Thurstable and Winstree 16–21; P-in-c Duxford *Ely* from 21; P-in-c Hinxton from 21; P-in-c Ickleton from 21. *The Rectory, 13 St John's Street, Duxford, Cambridge CB22 4RA* E: revlydiasmith@gmail.com

SMITH (née THORNTON), Magdalen Mary. b 69. Warwick Univ BA 90. Qu Coll Birm BD 95. **d** 96 **p** 97. C Kirkby *Liv* 96–98; C Birm St Martin w Bordesley St Andr 00–03; NSM Tilston and Shocklach *Ches* 03–08; C Wilmslow 08–17; Asst Dir of Ords 12–14; Dioc Dir of Ords 14–19; Nat Adv for Selection Abps' Coun 19–20; NSM Guildf Cathl 19–21; C Moseley St Mary and St Anne *Birm* from 21. *15 Park Hill, Birmingham B13 8DU* E: revmagssmith@btinternet.com

SMITH, Margaret Elizabeth. b 46. Bretton Hall Coll CertEd 67. NOC 85. **d** 88 **p** 94. Hon Par Dn Battyeford *Wakef* 88–89; Hon C Mirfield 89–91; Chapl HM Pris and YOI New Hall 90–95; Dn-in-c Flockton cum Denby Grange *Wakef* 91–94; P-in-c 94–96; V Scholes 95–01; P-in-c Buckden *Ely* 01–05; P-in-c Offord D'Arcy w Offord Cluny 01–05; R Buckden w the Offords 05–06; rtd 06; PtO *Bradf* 06–14; *Leeds* 14–16. *9 Bobbin Mill Court, Steeton, Keighley BD20 6PU* T: (01535) 654721

SMITH, Mrs Marion Elizabeth. b 51. Bris Univ CertEd 73 Middx Univ BA 99. NTMTC. **d** 98 **p** 99. NSM Cowley *Lon* 98–00; P-in-c Harlington 00–08; R 08–21; rtd 21. *46 Anderwood Drive, Sway, Lymington SO41 6AW* M: 07803-617509 E: marionsmith1@tiscali.co.uk

SMITH, Mark Alan. b 85. Peterho Cam BA 06 MA 10. Oak Hill Th Coll 14. **d** 17 **p** 18. C Frogmore *St Alb* 17–21; Bp's C Kildrumferton w Ballymachugh and Ballyjamesduff *K, E & A* from 21. *13 Parkview, Ballyjamesduff, Co Cavan, A82 XW65, Republic of Ireland* T: (00353) (49) 855 3222 M: (00353) 89-278 2540 E: revmarkasmith@gmail.com

SMITH, Mark Andrew. b 59. UNISA BA 86. St Paul's Coll Grahamstown. **d** 85 **p** 86. P Port Elizabeth St Mary Magd S Africa 88–89; R Cradock St Pet 89–92; R Alexandra Plurality 93; Chapl St Andr Coll Grahamstown 94–01; Chapl Denstone Coll Uttoxeter 02–07; NSM Alton w Bradley-le-Moors and Oakamoor w Cotton *Lich* 06–07; NSM Denstone w Ellastone and Stanton 06–07; NSM Mayfield 06–07; Chapl K Coll Taunton from 07. *King's College, South Road, Taunton TA1 3LA* T: (01823) 328211 *or* 328137 M: 07969-141242 E: masmith@kings-taunton.co.uk

SMITH, Mark David. See LAYNESMITH, Mark David

SMITH, Mark Gordon Robert Davenport. b 56. St Jo Coll Dur BA 77. Ridley Hall Cam 78. **d** 80 **p** 81. C Sheff St Jo 80–83; C Brightside w Wincobank 83–86; V Kimberworth Park 86–91; Consultant NE England CPAS 91–98; Nat Co-ord Cert in Evang Studies (CA) 98–04; Chapl for Deaf People *Derby* 04–15; V Rawdon *Leeds* from 15; Min in Deaf Community from 15. *The Vicarage, Layton Avenue, Rawdon, Leeds LS19 6QQ* T: 0113-391 0389 M: 07702-269608 E: mail@revmarksmith.com *or* mark@deafchurch.co.uk

SMITH, Mark Peter. b 61. Reading Univ BA 82 Open Univ BA 93 MA 97 Liv Univ MTh 02 Univ of Wales (Trin St Dav) PhD 12 Keele Univ PGCE 84. NOC 99. **d** 02 **p** 03. C Wingerworth *Derby* 02–06; TV Ex St Thos and Em 06–09; P-in-c Kingsteignton and Teigngrace 09–15; V from 15; RD Newton Abbot and Ipplepen 12–16. *The Vicarage, Daws Meadow, Kingsteignton, Newton Abbot TQ12 3UA* T: (01626) 355127 E: marksmith487@btinternet.com

SMITH, Mark Stephen. b 84. Peterho Cam BA 05 PGCE 06 MA 10 MPhil 12 PhD 16. Ridley Hall Cam 08. **d** 12 **p** 13. C Lt Shelford *Ely* 12–15; Chapl Peterho Cam 12–15; Chapl Ch Coll Cam 15–18; Fell and Dean Clare Coll Cam from 19; LtO *Ely* from 15. *Clare College, Trinity Lane, Cambridge CB2 1TL* T: (01223) 333240 E: mss53@cam.ac.uk

SMITH, Mark Winton. b 60. St Jo Coll Dur BA 81 Barrister-at-Law (Middle Temple) 82. SEITE 01. **d** 04 **p** 05. NSM E Wickham *S'wark* from 04. *16 Watersmeet Way, London SE28 8PU* T/F: (020) 8310 5063 E: revdmarksmith@aol.com

SMITH, Martin Stanley. b 53. Univ of Wales (Abth) BScEcon 75. STETS. **d** 99 **p** 00. NSM Woking Ch Ch *Guildf* from 99. *Brackenlea, 11 Heather Close, Horsell, Woking GU21 4JR* T: (01483) 714307 E: martin.wokingsmiffs@googlemail.com

SMITH, Canon Martin William. b 40. K Coll Lon BD 63 AKC 63. **d** 64 **p** 65. C Ashford St Hilda CD *Lon* 64–67; R Labuan Sabah Malaysia 67–69; R Likas Sabah 69–71; V Lakenham St Mark *Nor* 72–85; V N Walsham w Antingham 85–01; P-in-c Neatishead, Barton Turf and Irstead 94–95; RD Tunstead 91–96; RD St Benet 96–99; Hon Can Nor Cathl 93–05; V Waymondham 01–05; rtd 06; PtO *Nor* from 06. *Dragon House, 72 Besthorpe Road, Attleborough NR17 2NQ* T: (01953) 456003 E: smithdragonhouse@btinternet.com

SMITH, Martyn. b 52. CertEd 73. Oak Hill Th Coll BA 81. **d** 81 **p** 82. C Halliwell St Pet *Man* 81–86; V Cambridge St Martin *Ely* 86–89; Vineyard Chr Fellowship 89–15. *6 Rowan Court, Bolton BL1 7SL*

SMITH, Matthew. b 94. Trin Coll Bris 16. **d** 19 **p** 20. C Weston Favell *Pet* from 19. *5 Kestrel Close, Northampton NN3 3JG* E: revdmatthewsmith@gmail.com

SMITH, Matthew Gordon. b 71. Sarum Coll 18. **d** 20 **p** 21. C Corfe Mullen *Sarum* from 20. *6 Towers Way, Corfe Mullen, Wimborne BH21 3UB* T: (01202) 570449 M: 07973-410454

SMITH, The Ven Megan Rachel. Man Univ MB, ChB 94 Liv Univ MTh 00 Univ of Wales Coll of Medicine MSc 04 MRCP 97 FHEA 04 FRCPCH 05. EMMTC 06. **d** 07 **p** 08. C Wilford *S'well* 07–12; V Lenton 12–21; Chapl Nottm Univ 12–21; Adn Stoke-upon-Trent *Lich* from 21. *Address temp unknown*

SMITH, Melvyn. *See* SMITH, William Melvyn

SMITH (née Evans), Merewyn Abigail. b 80. Univ of Wales (Ban) BA 02 MTh 04 St Jo Coll Dur MATM 14 Warwick Univ PGCE 04. Cranmer Hall Dur 12. **d** 14 **p** 15. C Blurton and Dresden *Lich* 14–17; C Bucknall 17–18; R Newport w Longford, and Chetwynd from 18. *The Rectory, 10 Forton Glade, Newport TF10 8BP* M: 07982-239783 E: revmerry@outlook.com *or* merry.win.2012@gmail.com

SMITH, Merrick Thomas Jack. b 37. CEng 65 MCIBSE 65. Oak Hill NSM Course 90. **d** 92 **p** 93. NSM Isleworth St Mary *Lon* 92–94; PtO *Birm* 94–96; NSM Warfield *Ox* 96–98; TV Wallingford 98–01; P-in-c Tredington and Darlingscott w Newbold on Stour *Cov* 01–03; rtd 03; PtO *Sarum* from 03; P-in-c Ilsington *Ex* 06–11; PtO 13–16; B & W 16–21. *4 Parc Llwyfen, Llanymynech SY22 6FD* T: (01691) 831192 E: smith.merrick@btinternet.com

SMITH, Michael David. b 68. Trin Coll Bris BA 15. **d** 15 **p** 16. C Cheltenham Ch Ch *Glouc* 15–19; PtO 19–20; V Brockworth from 20. *St George's Vicarage, 42 Court Road, Brockworth, Gloucester GL3 4ET* T: (01452) 550554 M: 07415-089897 E: mdsmith.email@gmail.com *or* mike.smith@stgeorgebrockworth.uk

SMITH, Canon Michael David. b 57. BA 80. St Steph Ho Ox 81. **d** 83 **p** 84. C Beaconsfield *Ox* 83–87; V Wing w Grove 87–92; R Farnham Royal w Hedgerley 92–01; P-in-c Cookham 01–03; V The Cookhams 03–13; AD Maidenhead and Windsor 11–13; Can Res York Minster from 13. *4 Minster Yard, York YO1 7JD* T: (01904) 557211

SMITH, Michael Edward. b 69. MCIM. STETS 08. **d** 11 **p** 12. C Chandler's Ford *Win* 11–14; V Hatch Warren and Beggarwood 14–18; V Winton, Moordown and Charminster from 18. *31 Lonsdale Road, Bournemouth BH3 7LY* M: 07799-730362 E: frmichael.smith@gmail.com

SMITH, Michael Ian Antony. b 69. Warwick Univ BSc 91. Oak Hill Th Coll BA 95. **d** 95 **p** 96. C Cheadle *Ches* 95–98; C Hollington St Leon *Chich* 98–01; C Hartford *Ches* 01–04; V from 04. *The Vicarage, 7 The Green, Hartford, Northwich CW8 1QA* T: (01606) 77557 *or* 872255 E: mike@stjohnshartford.com

SMITH, Michael John. b 47. Kelham Th Coll 65. **d** 71 **p** 72. C Cov St Mary 71–75; Chapl RN 75–90; CF 90–95; R Lynch w Iping Marsh and Milland *Chich* 95–03; RD Midhurst 98–03; Community Chapl Bielefeld Station Germany 03–12; rtd 13; PtO *S'well* 14–21. *36 Sherwin Road, Stapleford, Nottingham NG9 8PQ* E: revmjsmith@hotmail.com

SMITH, Michael Keith John. b 66. Thames Poly BSc 88. Linc Th Coll BTh 95. **d** 95 **p** 96. C Birch St Agnes w Longsight St Jo w St Cypr *Man* 95–99; TV Pendleton 99–06; P-in-c Lower Kersal 03–06; Bp's Chapl and Policy Adv *Leic* 06–14; R Caversham Thameside and Mapledurham *Ox* from 14. *The Rectory, 20 Church Road, Caversham, Reading RG4 7AD* T: 0118-947 9505 E: mkjsmith@btinternet.com

SMITH, Michael Raymond. b 36. Qu Coll Cam BA 59 MA 63 ARCM 56 ARCO 56. Cuddesdon Coll 64. **d** 65 **p** 66. C Redcar *York* 65–70; V Dormanstown 70–73; Prec Worc Cathl 73–77; TR Worc St Barn w Ch Ch 77–83; RD Worc E 79–83; V Eskdale, Irton, Muncaster and Waberthwaite *Carl* 83–87; Chapl Uppingham Sch 87–93; P-in-c Stoke Lacy, Moreton Jeffries w Much Cowarne etc *Heref* 93–01; Dioc Schs Officer 93–03; rtd 01; PtO *Heref* 04–12; *Mon* from 10. *Upper House, Grosmont, Abergavenny NP7 8EP* T: (01981) 240790 E: michael.smith365@btinternet.com

SMITH, Michael Richard Guy. b 55. Man Univ BA 77. Ripon Coll Cuddesdon 88. **d** 90 **p** 91. C Wallasey St Hilary *Ches* 90–93; C Howden *York* 93–94; TV 94–97; V Gt and Lt Driffield 04–10; RD Harthill 08–10; Chapl Puerto de la Cruz Tenerife *Eur* 10–14; P-in-c Nailsworth w Shortwood, Horsley etc *Glouc* 14–15; V 15–18; AD Stroud 17–18; rtd 18; PtO *Glouc* 19–20. *64 Foxwhelp Way, Quedgeley, Gloucester GL2 4BY* M: 07840-260182 E: mike.davica@sky.com

SMITH, Neville. *See* SMITH, Charles Henry Neville

SMITH, Nicholas William. b 87. York Univ BA 10 Peterho Cam BA 16. Ridley Hall Cam 14. **d** 17 **p** 18. C Tulse Hill H Trin and St Matthias *S'wark* 17–20; TV Hitchin and St Paul's Walden St Alb from 20. *The Vicarage, St Mark's Close, Hitchin SG5 1UR* M: 07964-560195 E: nick.smith@stmarks-hitchin.org.uk

SMITH, Nicola Jane. b 85. Ox Brookes Univ BSc 08. St Mellitus Coll BA 17. **d** 17 **p** 18. C Sholing *Win* 17–20; C Bitterne Park 17–20; ICS 20–21; PtO *Win* from 20; Dir Min Development *Carl* from 21. *1 St John's Gate, Threlkeld, Keswick CA12 4TZ* E: revnickysmith@gmail.com

SMITH, Preb Olwen. b 44. Birm Univ BA 66. Selly Oak Coll 67. **d** 87 **p** 94. Ind Chapl Black Country Urban Ind Miss *Lich* 84–98; TV Cen Wolverhampton 94–10; Preb Lich Cathl 99–10; rtd 10; PtO *Lich* 10–13; *Ox* from 14. *75 Courtington Lane, Bloxham, Banbury OX15 4HS* T: (01295) 721709 E: smitholwen@btinternet.com

SMITH, Ms Pamela Jane Holden. b 56. Warwick Univ BA 78 Lon Inst of Educn PGCE 82. Qu Coll Birm BA 04. **d** 04 **p** 05. C Coventry Caludon *Cov* 04–08; NSM 04–06; PtO 08–21; Web Pastor i-church *Ox* from 08. *34 Styvechale Avenue, Coventry CV5 6DX* T: (024) 7667 2893 E: rev.pam.smith@gmail.com *or* webpastor@i-church.org

SMITH, Canon Patricia Janet. b 45. Oak Hill Th Coll 87. **d** 89 **p** 90. Canada 89–02; V Charminster and Stinsford *Sarum* 02–16; P-in-c Bradford Peverell, Stratton, Frampton etc 09–16; RD Dorchester 09–16; Can and Preb Sarum Cathl 10–16; rtd 16. *Sparrows, New Buildings, Charminster, Dorchester DT2 7SG* M: 07468-580196 E: plumsmith18@gmail.com

SMITH, Patricia Joanna. b 50. **d** 12 **p** 13. C Dumbarton *Glas* 12–14; C Johnstone 14–16; C Renfrew 14–18; C Helensburgh 18–21; PtO from 21. *21 Macleod Drive, Helensburgh G84 9QS* T: (01436) 671091 E: patsmithcurate@gmail.com

SMITH, Paul. b 52. **d** 98 **p** 99. OLM Leominster *Heref* from 98. *32 The Meadows, Leominster HR6 8RF* T: (01568) 615862 *or* 612124

SMITH, Paul. b 48. STETS 99. **d** 02 **p** 03. NSM Copthorne *Chich* 02–12; rtd 12; PtO *Chich* 12–17. *7 Heather Close, Copthorne, Crawley RH10 3PZ* T: (01342) 714308

SMITH, Paul Aidan. b 59. Birm Univ BA 82 Heythrop Coll Lon MA 09 K Coll Lon DThMin 19. Wycliffe Hall Ox 82. **d** 85 **p** 86. C Selly Park St Steph and St Wulstan *Birm* 85–88; C Kensal Rise St Mark and St Martin *Lon* 88–91;

V Water Eaton *Ox* 91–00; TR Hale w Badshot Lea *Guildf* 00–02; TV Stantonbury and Willen *Ox* 02–09; TR from 09. *2 Hooper Gate, Willen, Milton Keynes MK15 9JR* T: (01908) 606689 M: 07930-308644 E: smith.paul.a@icloud.com

SMITH, Paul Allan. b 66. Ch Coll Cam BA 88 MA 00 PhD 94. WMMTC 98 Ripon Coll Cuddesdon 99. **d** 00 **p** 01. C Moseley St Mary *Birm* 00–03; P-in-c Tilston and Shocklach *Ches* 03–08; Officer for Initial Min Tr 03–08; R Wilmslow 08–17; Can Res Guildf Cathl 17–20. *Address temp unknown* E: revpaulsmith@btinternet.com

SMITH, Canon Paul Andrew. b 55. St Chad's Coll Dur BA 76. Chich Th Coll 78. **d** 80 **p** 81. C Habergham Eaves St Matt *Blackb* 80–83; C Ribbleton 83–86; V Rishton 86–05; RD Whalley 95–01; R Cottingham *York* 05–19; AD Cen and N Hull 10–16; rtd 19; Hon Can Ho Ghana from 14; PtO *Blackb* from 20. *126 Holmfield Road, Blackpool FY2 9RE* T: (01253) 422467 M: 07908-892444 E: canonpaulsmithssc@hotmail.com

SMITH, Paul Anthony. b 66. Ripon Coll Cuddesdon. **d** 00 **p** 01. C Prestwood and Gt Hampden *Ox* 00–05; P-in-c W Leigh *Portsm* 05–06; V 06–10; TV Abingdon *Ox* from 10. *St Michael's Vicarage, Faringdon Road, Abingdon OX14 1BG* T: (01235) 534654 E: paul315smith@btinternet.com

SMITH, Preb Paul Gregory. b 39. Ex Univ BA 61. St Steph Ho Ox 61. **d** 63 **p** 64. C Walthamstow St Mich *Chelmsf* 63–66; C Devonport St Mark Ford *Ex* 66–69; C Hemel Hempstead *St Alb* 69–71; TV 71–83; R Bideford *Ex* 83–96; TR Bideford, Northam, Westward Ho!, Appledore etc 96; Chapl Bideford and Torridge Hosps 83–96; P-in-c Ex St Jas 96–98; R 98–03; rtd 03; Preb Ex Cathl 95–09; PtO from 09. *Valrose, Broad Lane, Appledore, Bideford EX39 1ND* T: (01237) 423513 E: pgsmith490@btinternet.com

SMITH, Miss Paula. b 57. Ox Min Course 14. **d** 17 **p** 18. NSM Deddington w Barford, Clifton and Hempton *Ox* 17–20; R W Buckingham from 20. *The Vicarage, Orchard Place, Westbury, Brackley NN13 5JT* M: 07818-053978 E: paulawoodcote@hotmail.co.uk

SMITH, Mrs Paula Mary. b 57. Sheff Poly BA 79 Qu Coll Birm BA 06. WMMTC 03. **d** 06 **p** 07. C Walsall *Lich* 06–10; P-in-c Donnington Wood from 10; Min Development Adv (Salop) 10–20. *St Matthew's Vicarage, St George's Road, Donnington, Telford TF2 7NJ* T: (01952) 604239 E: revdpaula@hotmail.co.uk

SMITH, Mrs Pauline Frances. b 37. Bris Univ BA 58 Lon Univ CertEd 59. Sarum & Wells Th Coll 87. **d** 90 **p** 94. C Cobham *Guildf* 90–96; P-in-c Lower Wylye and Till Valley *Sarum* 96–97; RD Stonehenge 01–03; rtd 03; PtO *Glouc* from 04. *267B London Road, Charlton Kings, Cheltenham GL52 6YG* T: (01242) 222810 E: panda.smith@talktalk.net

SMITH, Mrs Pauline Patricia. b 14 **p** 15. P-in-c Coity, Nolton and Bracklaw Coychurch *Llan* 14–18; TV Eglwysilan and Caerphilly from 18. *2 Clos Cae'r Wern, Caerphilly CF83 1SQ* T: (029) 2085 2356 E: paulinesmith5133@gmail.com

SMITH, Peter. b 36. Keele Univ BA 60. Cuddesdon Coll 73. **d** 75 **p** 76. C Shrewsbury St Chad *Lich* 75–80; V Burton St Chad 80–90; P-in-c Berwick w Selmeston and Alciston *Chich* 90–91; R 91–02; rtd 02; PtO *Sarum* from 03. *3 Olivier Place, Hart Close, Wilton, Salisbury SP2 0FW*

SMITH, Peter Alexander. *See* GRAYSMITH, Peter Alexander

SMITH, Peter Denis Frank. b 52. Local Minl Tr Course. **d** 81 **p** 83. OLM Camberwell St Mich w All So w Em *S'wark* 81–95; OLM Croydon St Jo 95–04; PtO from 10. *57 Alton Road, Croydon CR0 4LZ* T: (020) 8406 3557 E: peter.smith59@live.co.uk

SMITH, Peter Harold. b 53. Cumbria Univ BA 13. LCTP 07. **d** 10 **p** 11. NSM Euxton *Blackb* 10–15; C Chorley St Pet 15–17; V 17–21; rtd 21. *15 Howard Road, Chorley PR7 3NJ* T: (01257) 270411 M: 07412-624931 E: ordinand07@gmail.com

SMITH, Peter Henry. b 62. Bris Univ BA 83. SEITE 96. **d** 99 **p** 00. C Romford St Edw *Chelmsf* 99–02; V Aldersbrook 02–10; TR Waltham H Cross from 10. *The Rectory, Highbridge Street, Waltham Abbey EN9 1DG* T: (01992) 701352 E: peterhsmith@aol.com

SMITH, Peter Howard. b 57. St Jo Coll Dur BSc 78 Selw Coll Cam BA 82 MA 85. Ridley Hall Cam 80. **d** 83 **p** 84. C Welling *Roch* 83–87; C Hubberston w Herbrandston and Hasguard etc *St D* 87–88; C Hubberston 89–91; V Canley *Cov* 91–00; V Burney Lane *Birm* 00–06; P-in-c 06–07; P-in-c Ward End 06–07; P-in-c Bordesley Green 06–07; V Ward End w Bordesley Green 07–17; AD Yardley and Bordesley 05–12; V Penn Fields *Lich* from 17. *St Philip's Vicarage, Church Road, Bradmore, Wolverhampton WV3 7EJ* E: petersmith50@icloud.com

SMITH, Philip David. b 55. Shoreditch Coll Lon BEd 78. Oak Hill Th Coll BA 98. **d** 98 **p** 99. C Cheltenham St Mary, St Matt, St Paul and H Trin *Glouc* 98–03; TV Cheltenham

St Mark 03–18; PtO *Ox* 19–21; TV S Chilterns from 21. *7 Lammas Way, Lane End, High Wycombe HP14 3EX* T: (01494) 881250 E: philipdsmith1304@gmail.com

SMITH, Philip James. b 60. Imp Coll Lon BScEng 82 Fitzw Coll Cam BA 94. Ridley Hall Cam 92. **d** 95 **p** 96. C Aldborough w Boroughbridge and Roecliffe *Ripon* 95–99; V 99–14; *Leeds* 14–15; V E Bedfont *Lon* from 15. *9 Hatton Road, Bedfont, Feltham TW14 9JR* M: 07786-087389 E: revpsmith@gmail.com

SMITH, Philip Raymond. b 56. ERMC 08. **d** 11 **p** 12. NSM Farndon w Thorpe, Hawton and Cotham *S'well* 11–14; NSM E Trent 14–15; NSM Newark w Coddington 15–17; NSM Balderton, Barnby in the Willows and Coddington from 18. *Dart Cottage, 4 Lancaster Road, Coddington, Newark NG24 2TA* T: (01636) 703305 M: 07532-164314 E: dartcottage@btinternet.com

SMITH, Mrs Priscilla Elizabeth. b 48. Open Univ BSc 93 Nottm Univ MA 08. **d** 12 **p** 13. OLM Horncastle Gp *Linc* 12–19; OLM Hemingby Gp 12–19; OLM Asterby Gp 12–19; P-in-c from 19. *Evergreen, Upland Close, Horncastle LN9 5AR* T: (01507) 524611 M: 07798-695950 E: priscilla.smith926@btinternet.com *or* southwoldsgroup@btinternet.com

SMITH, Rachel Ross. *See* ROSS, Rachel Anne

SMITH, Raymond Charles William. b 56. K Coll Lon BD 78 AKC 78. Coll of Resurr Mirfield 79. **d** 80 **p** 81. C Iffley *Ox* 80–83; C Wallingford w Crowmarsh Gifford etc 83–86; V Tilehurst St Mary *Ox* 86–96; V Haywards Heath St Wilfrid *Chich* 96–08; V 08–20; rtd 20. *11 Bramber Mews, Caversham, Reading RG4 6NN*

SMITH, Raymond George Richard. b 38. Univ of Wales (Ban) BSc 61 MSc 65. WMMTC 91. **d** 94 **p** 95. NSM Edgmond w Kynnersley and Preston Wealdmoors *Lich* 94–97; Chapl Princess R Hosp NHS Trust Telford 95–03; V Llandegfan w Llandysilio *Ban* 03–08; rtd 09; PtO *Ban* 09–14; AD Tindaethwy 11–15; PtO from 15. *41 Cae Mair, Beaumaris LL58 8YN* T: (01248) 810032 E: rayandhazel41@btinternet.com

SMITH, Richard Harwood. b 34. Sarum Th Coll 57. **d** 59 **p** 60. C Kington w Huntington *Heref* 59–62; C Georgetown St Phil Br Guiana 62–64; C Kitty 64–65; V Mackenzie Guyana 65–69; C Broseley w Benthall *Heref* 69–70; Area Sec USPG Heref and Worc 70–76; R Wigmore Abbey *Heref* 76–84; V Eye w Braiseworth and Yaxley *St E* 84–96; P-in-c Bedingfield 84–96; P-in-c Occold 84–96; rtd 96. *30 Townsend Court, Green Lane, Leominster HR6 8TD* T: (01568) 616458

SMITH, Richard Keith. b 44. St Jo Coll Nottm. **d** 84 **p** 85. C Wirksworth w Alderwasley, Carsington etc *Derby* 84–87; R Hulland, Atlow, Bradley and Hognaston 87–96; P-in-c Long Compton, Whichford and Barton-on-the-Heath *Cov* 96–08; P-in-c Wolford w Burmington 97–08; P-in-c Cherington w Stourton 97–08; P-in-c Barcheston 97–08; R S Warks Seven Gp 08–09; RD Shipston 05–09; rtd 09; PtO *Cov* from 09. *12 Moreton Close, Stratford-upon-Avon CV37 7HB* T: (01789) 296712 E: rkvjsmith@gmail.com

SMITH, Richard Michael. b 52. Lon Univ BA 74. EAMTC 79. **d** 82 **p** 83. NSM Cambridge Ascension *Ely* 82–84; C Rainham *Roch* 84–88; V Southborough St Thos 88–96; P-in-c Lake *Portsm* 96–99; V 99–06; P-in-c Shanklin St Sav 96–99; V 99–06; V Southsea 06–15; rtd 15; PtO *York* from 16. *159 Prospect Road, Scarborough YO12 7LF*

SMITH, Robert Alfred William. b 53. **d** 08 **p** 09. OLM Withington St Paul *Man* 08–18; rtd 18; PtO *Man* from 18; *Ches* 15–18. *4 Brigsteer Walk, Manchester M40 8LW* M: 07896-967043 E: lowchenbob@gmail.com

✠**SMITH, The Rt Revd Robin Jonathan Norman.** b 36. Worc Coll Ox BA 60 MA 64. Ridley Hall Cam 60. **d** 62 **p** 63 **c** 90. C Barking St Marg *Chelmsf* 62–67; Chapl Lee Abbey 67–72; V Chesham St Mary *Ox* 72–80; RD Amersham 79–82; TR Gt Chesham 80–90; Hon Can Ch Ch 88–90; Suff Bp Hertford *St Alb* 90–01; rtd 01; Hon Asst Bp St Alb from 02. *7 Aysgarth Road, Redbourn, St Albans AL3 7PJ* T/F: (01582) 791964 E: bprobin@no7.me.uk

SMITH, Roger. *See* SMITH, Thomas Roger

SMITH, Roger Owen. b 50. Univ of Wales (Abth) BA 72 St Chad's Coll Dur CertEd 73 FRGS. S'wark Ord Course 84. **d** 87 **p** 88. NSM Nunhead St Antony w St Silas *S'wark* 87–91; NSM Forest Hill St Aug 91–98; NSM Crofton Park St Hilda w St Cypr 91–98; NSM Brockley Hill St Sav 91–98; NSM Camberwell St Giles w St Matt 98–00; PtO *Cant* 01–07; NSM Folkestone Trin from 07. *22 Wear Bay Road, Folkestone CT19 6BN* T: (01303) 259896 E: rohsmith@aol.com

SMITH, Canon Roger Stuart. b 41. Chich Th Coll 65. **d** 66 **p** 67. C Garforth *Ripon* 66–70; C Hilborough Gp Nor 70–73; TV 73–78; V Mendham w Metfield and Withersdale *St E* 78–89; P-in-c Fressingfield w Weybread and Wingfield

86–89; R Fressingfield, Mendham, Metfield, Weybread etc 90–91; RD Hoxne 86–91; R Kelsale-cum-Carlton, Middleton, Theberton etc 91–01; C Yoxmere Conf 01–04; RD Saxmundham *St E* 96–03; Hon Can St E Cathl 97–04; rtd 04; PtO *St E* from 04. *Rookery Nook, Wash Lane, St Margaret South Elmham, Harleston IP20 0PQ* T: (01986) 782465 E: rogerandmolly@mypostoffice.co.uk

SMITH, Roger William. b 48. Imp Coll Lon BSc 70. EAMTC. **d** 00 **p** 01. NSM Rothwell w Orton, Rushton w Glendon and Pipewell *Pet* 00–11; PtO *Eur* from 11. *14 rue du Parc, 34480 Autignac, France* T: (0033) 4 99 57 07 81 E: rogerwilliamsmith@gmail.com

SMITH, Ronald Eric. b 43. EMMTC 93. **d** 93 **p** 94. NSM Wingerworth *Derby* 93–99; NSM Newbold w Dunston 99–01; NSM Loundsley Green 01–05; rtd 05; PtO *Derby* 05–18; *York* from 06. *20 Oak Tree Lane, Haxby, York YO32 2YH* T: (01904) 767691 E: revronsmith@btinternet.com

SMITH, Preb Roy Leonard. b 36. Clifton Th Coll 63. **d** 66 **p** 67. C Clapham St Jas *S'wark* 66–70; C Kennington St Mark 70–74; C-in-c Southall Em CD *Lon* 74–83; V Stonebridge St Mich 83–06; Preb St Paul's Cathl 96–06; rtd 06; Hon C Kensal Rise St Mark and St Martin *Lon* 06–11; PtO from 11. *4 Biko House, 2 Barry Road, London NW10 8DW* T: (020) 8961 7312 E: prebroy@yahoo.co.uk

SMITH, Ruth. *See* YOUNG, Vivienne Ruth

SMITH, Rycroft. *See* SMITH, Charles Rycroft

SMITH, Mrs Sally Anne. b 63. Ches Univ BA 13 RN 85. St Jo Coll Nottm 07. **d** 09 **p** 10. C Stone St Mich and St Wulfad w Aston St Sav *Lich* 09–12; C Hanley H Ev 12–13; TV from 13; Dioc Officer for Vulnerable Adults from 12. *1 Poplar Avenue, Newcastle ST5 9HR* M: 07962-025659 E: revsally6@aol.com

SMITH, Mrs Sarah Elizabeth. b 67. Local Minl Tr Course 18. **d** 21. NSM Iver *Ox* from 21. *21 Clammas Way, Uxbridge UB8 3AN* M: 07972-680427 E: hisarah67@gmail.com

SMITH, Scott Anthony. b 73. K Alfred's Coll Win BA 99. Trin Coll Bris 08. **d** 10 **p** 11. C Clevedon St Andr and Ch Ch *B & W* 10–13; C Beckenham St Jo *Roch* from 13. *30 Ash Road, Croydon CR0 8HU* M: 07810-810313 E: smithscott@hotmail.com

SMITH, Sharon. b 56. Herts Univ BSc 98 PhD 02. ERMC 13. **d** 15 **p** 16. NSM Caddington *St Alb* 15–18; NSM Farley Hill St Jo 15–18; V Orpington Ch Ch *Roch* from 19. *The Vicarage, 165 Charterhouse Road, Orpington BR6 9EP* M: 07821-571283 E: revsharonsmith@outlook.com

SMITH, Mrs Shirley Ann. b 46. Sarum & Wells Th Coll 89. **d** 93 **p** 94. C Totton *Win* 93–96; Chapl Portsm Hosps NHS Trust 96–98; V Lord's Hill *Win* 98–01; TV Beaminster Area *Sarum* 01–05; rtd 05; PtO *Sarum* 05–08; P-in-c Hazelbury Bryan and the Hillside Par 08–11; P-in-c Okeford 08–11; PtO *B & W* 11–12 and 17–19; *Sarum* from 20; Chapl Yeovil Distr Hosp NHS Foundn Trust 12–16. *2 Franklyn Place, Kingsbury Episcopi, Martock TA12 6AZ* T: (01935) 508013 E: puddleduckwater@gmail.com

SMITH, Stephen. b 53. CQSW 78. Sarum & Wells Th Coll 87. **d** 89 **p** 90. C Redcar *York* 89–92; C Leeds St Aid *Ripon* 92–96; R Lanteglos by Camelford w Advent *Truro* 96–99; Chapl Hull and E Yorks Hosps NHS Trust 99–01; V Leeds St Marg and All Hallows *Ripon* 08–14; AD Headingley 09–13; P-in-c Mabe *Truro* 14–21; rtd 21. *3 Lemon Terrace, Bissoe, Truro TR4 8SS* E: revstevesmith53@gmail.com

SMITH, Stephen. b 60. Leeds Univ MA 07. Coll of Resurr Mirfield 02. **d** 04 **p** 05. C Burnley St Cath w St Alb and St Paul *Blackb* 04–07; C St Annes St Anne 07–10; PtO 10–17; V Chadderton St Mark *Man* from 17. *St Mark's Vicarage, Milne Street, Chadderton, Oldham OL9 0HR* M: 07898-301807

SMITH, Stephen John. b 55. Lon Univ BD 80. Trin Coll Bris 77. **d** 81 **p** 82. C Fulham St Matt *Lon* 81–86; C Stoke Gifford *Bris* 86–90; TV 90–01; rtd 01; PtO *Bris* from 01. *47 Saxon Way, Bradley Stoke, Bristol BS32 9AR* T: (01454) 616429 E: stevesmith334@btinternet.com

SMITH, Stephen John. b 46. Kelham Th Coll 65. **d** 69 **p** 70. C Warsop *S'well* 69–73; C Heaton Ch Ch *Man* 73–75; V Bolton St Bede 75–78; R Bilborough w Strelley *S'well* 78–84; R E Leake 84–92; P-in-c Costock 84–92; P-in-c Rempstone 84–92; P-in-c Stanford on Soar 84–92; R E and W Leake, Stanford-on-Soar, Rempstone etc 92–97; RD W Bingham 92–97; V Swaffham *Nor* 97–11; C Gt and Lt Dunham w Gt and Lt Fransham and Sporle 03–11; RD Breckland 02–06; Chapl NW Anglia Healthcare NHS Trust 99–11; rtd 11; PtO *Linc* 18–21; *Nor* from 19; *Ely* from 20. *15 Sandpiper Way, King's Lynn PE30 5DN* M: 07837-790712 E: revsjsmith@gmail.com

SMITH, Canon Stephen John Stanyon. b 49. Sussex Univ BA 81 Birm Univ MSocSc 83. Westcott Ho Cam 83. **d** 85 **p** 86. C Four Oaks *Birm* 85–89; Asst P Cheyenne River Reservation USA 89–91; Miss P Rosebud Reservation 91–94; Assoc R Ivoryton and Essex 94–98; Can St Paul's Cathl Buffalo

98–04; Asst P Buffalo St Andr from 04. *3105 Main Street, Buffalo NY 14214, USA* T: (001) (716) 834 9337 F: 836 0558 E: sjsmith6@buffalo.edu

SMITH, Stephen Thomas. b 55. Westcott Ho Cam 95. **d** 97 **p** 98. C Kempston Transfiguration *St Alb* 97–01; C Bromham w Oakley and Stagsden 01–05; TV Elstow from 05. *St Michael's Vicarage, Faldo Road, Bedford MK42 0EH* T: (01234) 266920

SMITH, Stephen Thomas. d 16 **p** 17. NSM Goetre w Llanover *Mon* 16–18; NSM Lower Islwyn Min Area from 18. *5 The Rise, Fairview, Blackwood NP12 3PL* T: (01443) 820872 M: 07523-719630 E: stephen.smith11@btinternet.com

SMITH, Steven Barnes. b 60. Cov Poly BSc 83 Leeds Univ BA 86 Middx Univ MSc 02 Essex Univ MA 05 Liv Jo Moores Univ PhD 18. Coll of Resurr Mirfield 84. **d** 87 **p** 88. C Darlington St Mark w St Paul *Dur* 87–89; C Prescot *Liv* 89–91; V Hindley Green 91–96; Asst Chapl Havering Hosps NHS Trust 96–98; Hd Multi-Faith Chapl Chelsea and Westmr Hosp NHS Foundn Trust 98–07; PtO *Lon* 07–13; *Ban* from 12. *Address withheld by request* E: sbsmith01@aol.com

SMITH, Steven Gerald Crosland. b 48. Linc Th Coll 82. **d** 84 **p** 85. Chapl St Jo Sch Tiffield 84–87; C Towcester w Easton Neston *Pet* 84–87; P-in-c Kings Heath 87–89; V 89–93; TV N Creedy *Ex* 93–06; TR 06–13; RD Cadbury 02–13; rtd 13; PtO *Ex* from 13. *5 Melhuish Close, Witheridge, Tiverton EX16 8AZ* E: stevengcsmith@aol.com

SMITH, Susan. b 48. FInstD 87. Ox Min Course 93. **d** 96 **p** 97. C Burnham w Dropmore, Hitcham and Taplow *Ox* 96–00; TV Whitton *Sarum* 00–02; TV W Slough *Ox* 02–08; V Cippenham 08–13; rtd 13; PtO *Ox* from 13. *Easter Cottage, 36 Britwell Road, Burnham, Slough SL1 8AG* T: (01628) 603046 E: suzone@hotmail.co.uk

SMITH, Miss Susan Ann. b 50. Bris Univ BA 72 St Jo Coll York PGCE 73. Ripon Coll Cuddesdon 97. **d** 99 **p** 00. C Swaffham *Nor* 99–02; R King's Beck 02–12; rtd 12; PtO *Nor* from 13. *9 Eagle Close, Erpingham, Norwich NR11 7AW* T: (01263) 761497

SMITH, Mrs Susan Elizabeth. b 53. Man Univ BSc 94 Brunel Univ MSc 98. SEITE 03. **d** 08 **p** 09. NSM Reigate St Mark *S'wark* 08–12; NSM Hoo St Werburgh *Roch* 12–19; rtd 19; PtO *Cant* from 21. *21 Bayfield, Painters Forstal, Faversham ME13 0EF* T: (01795) 532780

SMITH, Susan Helen. *See* SHEWRING, Susan Helen

SMITH, Mrs Susan Jennifer. b 52. MCIPD 90. SAOMC 94. **d** 97 **p** 98. C Ascot Heath *Ox* 97–01; P-in-c Flixton St Mich *Man* 01–10; P-in-c Altcar and Hightown *Liv* 10–14; P-in-c Hightown 14–16; rtd 16; PtO *Liv* from 16. *79 Greenlooms Drive, Formby, Liverpool L37 2LX* E: saxoncross@btinternet.com

SMITH, Mrs Susan Penelope Zoë. b 61. Ox Min Course 12. **d** 15 **p** 16. NSM Weston Turville *Ox* 15–17; NSM Broughton from 17; Chapl HM Pris Grendon and Spring Hill from 18. *HM Prison Grendon, Grendon Underwood, Aylesbury HP18 0TL* M: 07854-659756 E: suepzsmith@gmail.com

SMITH, Terence. b 38. Brunel Univ BSc 79 Cranfield Inst of Tech MSc 80. Tyndale Hall Bris 67. **d** 69 **p** 70. C Cheylesmore *Cov* 69–71; C Leamington Priors St Paul 71–74; V Halliwell St Paul *Man* 74–75; Lect Uxbridge Coll 80–86; R Medstead w Wield *Win* 86–99; P-in-c Kennington *Ox* 99–03; V 03–08; rtd 08. *15 Grove Road, Seaford BN25 1TP* E: ter.s@btinternet.com

SMITH, Terrence Gordon. b 34. TD 83. MCSP 58 SRN 60. St Mich Coll Llan 68. **d** 70 **p** 71. C Gelligaer *Llan* 70–73; CF (TA) 72–99; C Aberavon *Llan* 73–75; V Pontlottyn w Fochriw 75–77; V Kenfig Hill 77–84; V Dyffryn 84–99; rtd 99. *1 Gnoll Crescent, Neath SA11 3TF* T: (01639) 633460

SMITH, Canon Thomas Roger. b 48. Cant Sch of Min 77. **d** 80 **p** 81. NSM Folkestone St Sav *Cant* 80–82; NSM Lyminge w Paddlesworth, Stanford w Postling etc 82–85; Chapl Cant Sch of Min 82–91; R Biddenden and Smarden *Cant* 86–91; TR Totnes, Bridgetown and Berry Pomeroy etc *Ex* 91–96; P-in-c Haslingden w Grane and Stonefold *Blackb* 96–98; V 98–15; P-in-c Musbury 07–15; AD Accrington 03–13; Hon Can Blackb Cathl 08–15; rtd 15; PtO *Blackb* from 15; *Man* from 20. *150 Southwood Drive, Accrington BB5 2TU* T: (01254) 237581 E: rsmith9456@aol.com

SMITH, Timothy. b 58. Trin Coll Bris 00. **d** 02 **p** 03. C Warminster Ch Ch *Sarum* 02–06; P-in-c Plymouth St Jude *Ex* from 06. *St Jude's Vicarage, Knighton Road, Plymouth PL4 9BU* T: (01752) 224178 *or* 263163

SMITH, Timothy Stewart. b 90. Trin Coll Bris 14. **d** 17 **p** 18. C Northampton St Giles *Pet* 17–20; C Cambridge St Barn *Ely* from 20. *80 St Barnabas Road, Cambridge CB1 2DE* T: (01223) 519526 E: revdtimsmith@gmail.com

SMITH, Toni. *See* SMITH, Antoinette

SMITH (née WOOD), Mrs Valerie Rosemary. b 53. Warwick Univ BA 74. WEMTC 06. **d** 09 **p** 10. NSM Highley w Billingsley, Glazeley etc *Heref* from 09; Par

Giving Adv from 17. *20 Yew Tree Grove, Highley, Bridgnorth WV16 6DG* T: (01746) 861966 E: keithandvals@aol.com

SMITH, Mrs Virginia Jane. b 41. Nottm Univ BSc 63. Guildf Dioc Min Course 04. **d** 09 **p** 10. NSM Surrey Weald *Guildf* 09–13; rtd 13; PtO *Guildf* from 13. *Dove Cottage, 14 The Paddock, Westcott, Dorking RH4 3NT* T: (01306) 885349 E: virginia.smith@smartemail.co.uk *or* rev.virginia.smith@talktalk.net

SMITH, Mrs Wendy Patricia. b 60. **d** 10 **p** 11. OLM Walton and Trimley *St E* 10–13; NSM from 13. *12A Langley Avenue, Felixstowe IP11 2NA* T: (01394) 211755 M: 07708-597808 E: grannysmith57@hotmail.co.uk

SMITH, William Manton. b 64. Univ of Wales (Abth) LLB 85 St Jo Coll Dur PGCE 90. United Th Coll Abth BD 89 St Jo Coll Nottm MA 92. **d** 93 **p** 94. C Coventry Caludon *Cov* 93–97; V Exhall 97–09; TR Coventry Caludon 09–18; V Lillington and Old Milverton from 18. *Lillington Vicarage, Vicarage Road, Leamington Spa CV32 7RH* E: wms.smith@btinternet.com

SMITH, Canon William Melvyn. b 47. K Coll Lon BD 69 AKC 69 PGCE 70. St Aug Coll Cant 71. **d** 71 **p** 72. C Kingswinford H Trin *Lich* 71–73; Hon C Coseley Ch Ch 73–74; C Wednesbury St Paul Wood Green 75–78; V Coseley St Chad 78–91; TR Wordsley 91–93; RD Himley 83–93; TR Wordsley *Worc* 93–96; RD Himley 93–96; Stewardship and Resources Officer 97–10; Hon Can Worc Cathl 03–10; Asst Chapl Palma de Mallorca *Eur* 10–12; rtd 12; PtO *Worc* from 13; *Lon* 16–18; *Eur* from 17. *14 Beech Tree Close, Kingswinford DY6 7DR* T: (01384) 357062 E: wmelsmith@blueyonder.co.uk

SMITH-CAMERON, Canon Ivor Gill. b 29. Madras Univ BA 50 MA 52. Coll of Resurr Mirfield. **d** 54 **p** 55. C Rumboldswyke *Chich* 54–58; Chapl Imp Coll *Lon* 58–72; Dioc Missr *S'wark* 72–92; Can Res S'wark Cathl 72–94; C Battersea Park All SS 92–94; Hon C 94–96; Hon C Battersea Fields 96–05; Co-ord All Asian Chr Consultation 92–93; rtd 94; Chapl to The Queen 95–99; PtO *S'wark* from 05. *24 Holmewood Gardens, London SW2 3RS* T: (020) 8678 8977 E: ivorsmithcameron@yahoo.co.uk

SMITH-HOWARD, Vivian Alycia Mary. *See* TIMMIS, Vivian Alycia Mary

SMITH RILEY, Mrs Gillian Angela. b 39. RGN 60 RM 62. All Nations Chr Coll IDC 65. **d** 94 **p** 95. NSM Haydock St Mark *Liv* 94–96; PtO *Ely* 96–02; *Eur* 98–01; Hon C Milton *Win* 02–03; PtO *Ely* 03–11; *Chelmsf* 04–11; *York* from 11. *36 Homeyork House, Danesmead Close, York YO10 4QX* T: (01904) 864506 E: gill.rev@outlook.com

SMITH-WILDS, Mrs Deborah Jane. b 68. Kingston Poly BA 91. Ripon Coll Cuddesdon 18. **d** 20 **p** 21. C Uppingham w Ayston and Belton w Wardley *Pet* from 20. *18 Siskin Road, Uppingham, Oakham LE15 9UL* T: (01572) 822906 M: 07407-113312 E: curateofuppingham@gmail.com

SMITHAM, Ann. *See* HOWELLS, Elizabeth Ann

SMITHSON, Philip George Allan. b 55. Bede Coll Dur TCert 76 Open Univ BA 82. **d** 07 **p** 08. OLM Monkwearmouth *Dur* 07–21; rtd 21. *2 Sea View Gardens, Sunderland SR6 9PN* E: philipsmithson@talktalk.net

SMITHURST, Jonathan Peter. b 54. FInstLEx 81. EMMTC 91. **d** 94 **p** 95. NSM Bramcote *S'well* 94–03; NSM Attenborough 03–06; AD Beeston 99–06; P-in-c Everton, Mattersey, Clayworth and Gringley 06–11; V 11–14; AD Bassetlaw and Bawtry 09–14; P-in-c Attenborough 14; V 14–20; Dioc Ecum Officer 14–17; rtd 20. *46 Sandy Lane, Bramcote, Nottingham NG9 3GS* E: jonathansmithurst@gmail.com

SMYTH, Anthony Irwin. b 40. TCD BA 63 MA 66. Clifton Th Coll 64. **d** 66 **p** 67. C Worthing St Geo *Chich* 66–69; SAMS Chile 70–75; Dir Th Educn Valparaiso 72–75; C Woodley St Jo the Ev *Ox* 75–80; V St Leonards St Ethelburga *Chich* 80–93; R Stopham and Fittleworth 93–05; rtd 05; PtO *Chich* 05–20; *Portsm* from 05. *20 Grenehurst Way, Petersfield GU31 4AZ* T: (01730) 260370 E: anthony.smyth@btinternet.com

SMYTH, Elizabeth. *See* LEAVER, Lucinda Elizabeth Jane

SMYTH, Canon Gordon William. b 47. Open Univ BA. St Jo Coll Nottm 81. **d** 83 **p** 84. C St Keverne *Truro* 83–86; V Landrake w St Erney and Botus Fleming 86–95; RD E Wivelshire 94–95; V Highertown and Baldhu 95–14; Hon Can Truro Cathl 06–14; rtd 14; PtO *Truro* from 14; PV Truro Cathl 14–20. *3 Carnon Valley, Carnon Downs, Truro TR3 6LG* T: (01872) 870743 E: gordonsmyth58@gmail.com

SMYTH, Kenneth James. b 44. TCD BA 67 MA 72. **d** 68 **p** 69. C Bangor Abbey *D & D* 68–71; C Holywood 71–74; I Gilnahirk 74–82; I Newtownards w Movilla Abbey 82–88; I Newtownards 89–11; Preb Wicklow St Patr Cathl Dublin 93–11; rtd 11. *3 Mount Royal, Bangor BT20 3BG* T: (028) 9145 8706 E: kennethjsmith@aol.com *or* kennethjsmyth1944@gmail.com

SMYTH, Lucinda Elizabeth Jane. *See* LEAVER, Lucinda Elizabeth Jane

SMYTH, Peter Frederick. b 58. SNWTP. **d** 10 **p** 11. C Prescot *Liv* 10–13; TV Kirkby 13–17; V Childwall St Dav 17–20; V Dovecot from 20. *St Christopher's Vicarage, 58 Lorenzo Drive, Liverpool L11 1BQ* M: 07847-456025 E: frpeterfsmyth@gmail.com

SMYTH, The Very Revd Roderick Lindsay. Ulster Univ MEd QUB BMus PGCE Univ of Wales (Lamp) BTh. **d** 13 **p** 14. C Belfast Malone St Jo *Conn* 14–16; I Nenagh *L & K* from 16; Dean Killaloe and Clonfert from 20. *St Mary's Rectory, Church Road, Nenagh, Co Tipperary, Republic of Ireland* T: (00353) (67) 32598 M: 87-970 6479 E: rsmyth6582@btinternet.com

SMYTH, Trevor Cecil. b 45. Chich Th Coll 66. **d** 69 **p** 70. C Cookridge H Trin *Ripon* 69–73; C Middleton St Mary 73–75; C Felpham w Middleton *Chich* 75–78; P-in-c Wellington Ch *Ch Lich* 78–80; V 80–86; P-in-c W Wittering *Chich* 86; R W Wittering and Birdham w Itchenor 86–94; PtO 00; TV Withycombe Raleigh *Ex* 01–15; Hon C E Blatchington and Bishopstone *Chich* from 15. *St Andrew's House, 14 Marine Drive, Seaford BN25 2RS* T: (01323) 892972

SMYTH, William Richard Stephen. b 56. Cape Town Univ BA 77. **d** 90 **p** 92. S Africa 90–07; C Ballyholme *D & D* 09–12; I Kilmore and Inch from 12. *The Rectory, 22 Church Road, Crossgar, Downpatrick BT30 9HR* T: (028) 4483 0371 E: stephensmyth17@gmail.com

SMYTHE, Mrs Angela Mary. b 53. St Jo Coll Nottm 85. **d** 87 **p** 94. Par Dn Forest Town *S'well* 87–90; Dn-in-c Pleasley Hill 90–94; V 94–03; AD Mansfield 98–03; P-in-c Sneinton St Chris w St Phil 03–08; Chapl Qu Eliz Adademy and Samworth Ch Academy 08–13; rtd 13; PtO *S'well* from 13. *Address withheld by request* M: 07443-472401 E: angelasmythe1@sky.com

SMYTHE, Peter John Francis. b 32. Lon Univ LLB 56 Barrister-at-Law (Middle Temple) 76. Wells Th Coll 56. **d** 58 **p** 59. C Maidstone All SS *Cant* 58–62; V Barrow St Jo *Carl* 62–65; V Billesdon w Goadby and Rolleston *Leic* 65–71; rtd 97. *The Gables, 16 Geraldine Road, Malvern WR14 3PA* T: (01684) 573266

SNAITH, Bryan Charles. b 33. Univ of Wales BSc 55. St Mich Coll Llan 61. **d** 61 **p** 62. C Bargoed w Brithdir *Llan* 61–62; C Llanishen and Lisvane 62–71; Ind Chapl *Dur* 71–76; Ind Chapl *Worc* 76–81; P-in-c Stone 76–81; C Chaddesley Corbett 77–81; TV Colchester St Leon, St Mary Magd and St Steph *Chelmsf* 81–86; Ind Chapl 81–03; rtd 03; PtO *Chelmsf* from 04. *4 Wren Close, Stanway, Colchester CO3 8ZB* T: (01206) 767793 E: bryansnaith-colchester@msn.com

SNAPE, Paul Anthony Piper. b 44. **d** 98 **p** 99. OLM Tettenhall Wood and Perton *Lich* 98–10; rtd 10; PtO *Lich* 10–19. *24 Windsor Gardens, Castlecroft, Wolverhampton WV3 8LY* T: (01902) 763577 E: p-snape44@tiscali.co.uk *or* rev.ps@outlook.com

SNARE, Peter Brian. b 39. Cape Town Univ BSc 63. SEITE 99. **d** 02 **p** 03. NSM Dymchurch w Burmarsh and Newchurch *Cant* 02–09; NSM New Romney w Old Romney and Midley 07–09; NSM St Mary's Bay w St Mary-in-the-Marsh etc 07–09; PtO from 09. *35 Shepherds Walk, Hythe CT21 6PW* T: (01303) 269242 *or* (020) 7320 1701 E: peter.snare@btinternet.com

SNARES, Ian. b 68. Brunel Univ BEng 91. Ridley Hall Cam 09. **d** 11 **p** 12. C Ilfracombe, Lee, Woolacombe, Bittadon etc *Ex* 11–15; C Ilfracombe SS Phil and Jas w W Down 11–15; V Cowplain *Portsm* from 15; Jt AD Havant from 19. *The Vicarage, Padnell Road, Waterlooville PO8 8DZ* E: iansnares@gmail.com

SNASDELL, Canon Antony John. b 39. St Chad's Coll Dur BA 63. **d** 65 **p** 66. C Boston *Linc* 65–70; Hon C Worksop Priory *S'well* 71–82; P-in-c Gt Massingham *Nor* 82–84; P-in-c Lt Massingham 82–84; P-in-c Harpley 82–84; R Gt and Lt Massingham and Harpley 84–91; R Thorpe St Andr 91–04; Hon Can Nor Cathl 03–04; rtd 04; PtO *Nor* from 05. *1 Speedwell Road, Wymondham NR18 0XQ* T: (01953) 857509

SNEARY, Michael William. b 38. Brentwood Coll of Educn CertEd 71 Open Univ BA 79. Ely Th Coll 61. **d** 64 **p** 65. C Loughton St Jo *Chelmsf* 64–67; Youth Chapl 67–70; Hon C Ingrave 70–71; Teacher Harold Hill Gr Sch Essex 71–74; Ivybridge Sch 74–76; Coombe Dean Sch Plymouth 76–03; rtd 03. *The Lodge, 1 Lower Port View, Saltash PL12 4BY*

SNELL, Mrs Brigitte. b 43. BA 85. EAMTC 86. **d** 89 **p** 94. NSM Cambridge Gt St Mary w St Mich *Ely* 89–93; Par Dn Cambridge St Jas 91–94; C 94–95; V Sutton 95–03; R Witcham w Mepal 95–03; rtd 03; PtO *Ely* 05–16 and from 19. *45 London Road, Harston, Cambridge CB22 7QQ* T: (01223) 872839 E: brigittesnell@gmail.com

SNELL, Christiaan Steve. Potchefstroom Univ BA. Geo Whitefield Coll S Africa LTh. **d** 07. S Africa 07–12; Bp's C Kildrumferton w Ballymachugh and Ballyjamesduff *K, E & A* 12–17; P-in-c Mostrim w Granard, Clonbroney, Killoe etc from 17. *The Manse, Battery Road, Longford, Co Longford, Republic of Ireland* T: (00353) (43) 334 0769

SNELL, Colin. b 53. Trin Coll Bris 94. **d** 96 **p** 97. C Martock w Ash *B & W* 96–00; TV Wilton 00–08; V Galmington 08–18; rtd 18. *Mapperton House, Blind Lane, Bower Hinton, Martock TA12 6LR*

SNELLGROVE, Canon Martin Kenneth. b 54. City Univ BSc 77 CEng 80 MICE 84. Aston Tr Scheme 85 Ridley Hall Cam 87. **d** 89 **p** 90. C Four Oaks *Birm* 89–92; TV Wrexham *St As* 92–01; R Hope 01–13; AD Hawarden 03–10; V Corwen w Llangar w Glyndyfrdwy etc 13–17; I Valle Crucis Miss Area 18–21; AD Penllyn and Edeirnion 13–18; AD Valle Crucis 18–21; Can Cursal St As Cathl 13–21; rtd 21. *9 Meadow Gardens, Llandudno LL30 1UW*

SNELLING, Brian. b 40. **d** 69 **p** 70. C Slough *Ox* 69–72; C Hoole *Ches* 72–76; V Millbrook 76–80; V Homerton St Luke *Lon* 80–90; R Marks Tey w Aldham and Lt Tey *Chelmsf* 90–98; V Stebbing w Lindsell 98–04; V Stebbing and Lindsell w Gt and Lt Saling 04–05; rtd 05; PtO *Chelmsf* 06–16. *69 Reymead Close, West Mersea, Colchester CO5 8DN* T: (01206) 383717 E: revbrians@aol.com

SNELLING, Joseph David Griffith. b 90. Clare Coll Cam BA 12 MA 16. St Mellitus Coll 15. **d** 17 **p** 18. C Linc St Swithin 17–20; R Woodhall Spa Gp from 20. *The Vicarage, Alverston Avenue, Woodhall Spa LN10 6SN* M: 07585-845793 E: rev.joseph.snelling@gmail.com

SNELLING, Stephen Thomas. b 47. City of Lon Poly BA 73 Win Univ MA 19. SEITE 08. **d** 10 **p** 11. NSM Seal SS Pet and Paul *Roch* 10–11; NSM Nantwich *Ches* 12–18; PtO from 18; *St E* from 20. *Tailors Green House, Tailors Green, Bacton, Stowmarket IP14 4LL* T: (01449) 782970 M: 07775-833824 E: stephen.snelling@tailorsgreenhouse.com

SNOOK, Mrs Margaret Ann. b 41. S Dios Minl Tr Scheme. **d** 91 **p** 94. NSM Keynsham *B & W* 91–04; Chapl Univ Hosps Bris and Weston NHS Foundn Trust from 91; PtO *B & W* from 04. *32 Hurn Lane, Keynsham, Bristol BS31 1RS* T: 0117-986 3439 M: 07802-944528 E: snook926@btinternet.com

SNOW, Frank. b 31. Lon Univ BD 57. **d** 83 **p** 84. Hon C Tweedmouth *Newc* 83–86; Hon C Berwick H Trin 86–89; Hon C Berwick St Mary 86–89; Hon C Berwick H Trin and St Mary 89–90; R Gt Smeaton w Appleton Wiske and Birkby etc *Ripon* 90–97; rtd 97; PtO *Ripon* 97–14; *Leeds* 14–16; *Sheff* 02–20. *18D Abbey Lane Dell, Sheffield S8 0BZ* T: 0114-327 5067 E: fersnow@outlook.com

⚜**SNOW, The Rt Revd Martyn James.** b 68. Sheff Univ BSc 89. Wycliffe Hall Ox BTh 95. **d** 95 **p** 96 **c** 13. C Brinsworth w Catcliffe and Treeton *Sheff* 95–97; CMS Guinea 98–01; V Pitsmoor Ch Ch *Sheff* 01–10; P-in-c Stocksbridge 07–08; AD Ecclesfield 07–10; Adn Sheff and Rotherham 10–13; Suff Bp Tewkesbury *Glouc* 13–16; Bp Leic from 16. *12 Springfield Road, Leicester LE2 3BD* T: 0116-270 8985 E: bishop.leicester@leicestercofe.org

SNOW, Peter Richard. b 85. Qu Coll Cam MA 10. Oak Hill Th Coll BA 16. **d** 16 **p** 17. C St Helen Bishopsgate w St Andr Undershaft etc *Lon* 16–19; C Harringay St Paul 18–19; P-in-c from 19. *St Paul's Church House, 1 Wightman Road, London N4 1RW* T: (020) 8341 0390 E: pete@stpaulsharringay.com

SNOW, Rachel Elizabeth. b 71. Southn Univ BSc 93 PhD 99. St Mellitus Coll BA 20. **d** 20 **p** 21. C Letchworth St Paul w Willian *St Alb* from 20. *89 Howard Drive, Letchworth Garden City SG6 2BX* M: 07570-976954 E: snow41@sky.com

SNOW, Canon Richard John. b 57. Bris Univ BSc 80 K Coll Lon MA 05. **d** 90 **p** 91. C Preston Plucknett *B & W* 90–95; TV Stratton St Margaret w S Marston etc *Bris* 95–02; R Box w Hazlebury and Ditteridge 02–07; TR Kirkby Lonsdale *Carl* from 07; Hon Can Carl Cathl from 21. *The Rectory, Vicarage Lane, Kirkby Lonsdale, Carnforth LA6 2BA* T: (01524) 272044 E: rector@therainbowparish.org

SNOWBALL, Miss Deborah Jane. b 67. Middx Poly BEd 90. Ripon Coll Cuddesdon 02. **d** 04 **p** 05. C Sawbridgeworth *St Alb* 04–07; P-in-c Rickmansworth 07–12; V from 12; RD 11–16. *The Vicarage, Bury Lane, Rickmansworth WD3 1ED* T: (01923) 772627 E: vicar@stmarysrickmansworth.org.uk

SNOWBALL, Canon Dorothy Margaret. b 52. Sunderland Univ BA 98. NEOC 98. **d** 01 **p** 02. NSM Heworth St Mary *Dur* 01–07; P-in-c Eighton Banks 07–19; AD Gateshead 16–19; Hon Can Dur Cathl 17–19; rtd 19; PtO *Dur* from 20. *2 Oval Park View, Felling, Gateshead NE10 9DS* T: 0191-469 5059 E: dorothysnowball@btinternet.com

SNOWDEN (née HALL), The Ven Elizabeth. b 58. Plymouth Poly BSc 79 Birm Univ BA 01 Lon Inst of Educn PGCE 80. Qu Coll Birm 98. **d** 01 **p** 02. C Burntwood *Lich* 01–04; C and Youth Work Co-ord Ogley Hay 04–10; P-in-c Bestwood Em w St Mark *S'well* 10–11; V 11–16; AD Nottm N 13–16; Adn Chelmsf from 16. *The Archdeacon's Lodge,*

136 Broomfield Road, Chelmsford CM1 1RN T: (01245) 258257 M: 07954-690788 E: revesnowden@yahoo.co.uk *or* a.chelmsford@chelmsford.anglican.org

SNUGGS, Canon David Sidney. b 49. Keble Coll Ox BA 71 PGCE 72 MA 75. S Dios Minl Tr Scheme 89. **d** 92 **p** 93. C Bitterne *Win* 92–96; V Fair Oak 96–14; Hon Can Win Cathl 11–14; rtd 14; PtO *Win* from 14. *13 Cranbourne Park, Hedge End, Southampton SO30 0NX* M: 07875-733323

SNYDER, Miss Susanna Jane. b 78. Em Coll Cam BA 00 MA 05 Birm Univ PhD 09. Qu Coll Birm BA 04. **d** 05 **p** 06. C Brownswood Park and Stoke Newington St Mary *Lon* 05–08; PtO *Ox* 08–10 and from 14; USA 10–14; Dir Part-Time Pathway Ripon Coll Cuddesdon from 18. *Ripon College, Cuddesdon, Oxford OX44 9EX* T: (01865) 877400 E: susannajsnyder@gmail.com

SNYDER GIBSON, Catherine. *See* GIBSON, Catherine Snyder

SOADY, Mark. b 60. Univ of Wales BTh RMN 84 MCGI 11. St Mich Coll Llan 96. **d** 96 **p** 97. C Tenby *St D* 96–99; TV 99–03; Min Can St Woolos Cathl *Mon* 03–08; P-in-c Newport All SS 08–12; Chapl Univ of Wales (Newport) 08–12; V Abergavenny St Mary w Llanwenarth Citra 12–20; P-in-c Abergavenny H Trin 12–20; AD Abergavenny 14–20; CF(V) 98–12; Prior Holywell Community 14–20; Can St Woolos Cathl *Mon* 14–20; R Rufford and Tarleton *Blackb* from 20; Sec Angl Relig Communities in England from 20; Hon Fell Univ of Wales (Newport) *Mon* from 12. *92 Blackgate Lane, Tarleton, Preston PR4 6UT* M: 07968-753978 E: sec@arcie.org.uk

SOAR, Angela Margaret. *See* PATERSON, Angela Margaret

SOAR, Martin William. b 54. Wye Coll Lon BSc 78. Wycliffe Hall Ox 86. **d** 88 **p** 89. C Henfynyw w Aberaeron and Llanddewi Aberarth *St D* 88–91; C Hubberston 91–93; P-in-c Low Harrogate St Mary *Ripon* 93–95; V 95–06; Chapl Old Swinford Hosp Sch Stourbridge 06–18; C Kinver and Enville *Lich* 10–18; C Alton w Bradley-le-Moors, Ellastone w Stanton, and Mayfield from 18. *The Vicarage, Church Lane, Mayfield, Ashbourne DE6 2JR* E: msoar@oshsch.com *or* msoar54@gmail.com

SOBCZAK, Mrs Susan Clare. b 49. WEMTC 10. **d** 13 **p** 14. NSM Nailsworth w Shortwood, Horsley etc *Glouc* 13–19; rtd 19; PtO *Glouc* from 20. *1 Byways, Horsley, Stroud GL6 0PP* T: (01453) 833526 E: suesobczak@gmail.com

SOCHON, David Lomas Philipe. b 40. Univ Coll Lon BA 62. **d** 07 **p** 08. OLM Newton Flotman, Swainsthorpe, Tasburgh, etc *Nor* 07–15; RD Depwade 09–13; rtd 15; PtO *St E* 15–21; *Nor* from 15. *Greenacre, Stone Street, Spexhall, Halesworth IP19 0RN* T: (01986) 781151 E: davidsochon@gmail.com

SODADASI, David Anand Raj. b 63. Osmania Univ Hyderabad BCom 85 MA 99 Union Bibl Sem Pune BD 95 Univ of Wales PhD 12. United Th Coll Bangalore MTh 00. **d** 01 **p** 02. C Jabalpur Cathl India 01–04; Lect Leonard Th Coll 00–04; PtO *Ox* 04–05; NSM Ray Valley 05–10; R Cusop w Blakemere, Bredwardine w Brobury etc *Heref* 10–17; R Icknield Way Villages *Chelmsf* from 17. *The Rectory, 1 Hall Lane, Great Chishill, Royston SG8 8SG* E: anandsodadasi@hotmail.co.uk

SODERMAN, Claire Louise. b 71. Coll of Ripon & York St Jo BEd 92 St Jo Coll Dur BA 21. Cranmer Hall Dur 19. **d** 21. C Northallerton w Kirby Sigston *York* from 21. *Meadow Croft, Morton on Swale, Northallerton DL7 9RF* E: curate@cofe-northallerton.org.uk

SODOR AND MAN, Bishop of. *See* EAGLES, The Rt Revd Peter Andrew

SOER, Patricia Kathleen Mary. b 40. Hull Coll of Educn CertEd 61. **d** 99 **p** 00. OLM Deptford St Jo w H Trin *S'wark* 99–06; OLM Deptford St Jo w H Trin and Ascension 06–10; rtd 10; PtO *S'wark* from 10. *350 Wood Vale, London SE23 3DY* T: (020) 8699 4616

SOFIELD, Martin. b 60. **d** 02 **p** 03. OLM Clifton *Man* 02–10; NSM Ardrossan *Glas* 10–11; R 11–16; NSM Dalry 10–11; R 11–16; NSM Irvine St Andr LEP 10–11; I 11–16; LtO from 17. *44 Gooding Crescent, Stevenston KA20 4AU* M: 07710-428896 E: martin.sofield@btinternet.com

SOHAIL, Victor. b 67. All SS Cen for Miss & Min 14. **d** 17 **p** 18. C Gt Marsden w Nelson St Phil *Blackb* from 17. *3 Pinewood Drive, Nelson BB9 0WB*

SOKANOVIC (née HARRIS), Mrs Mary Noreen Cecily. b 58. Suffolk Coll BA 97 RGN 79 RN 96. EAMTC 02. **d** 05 **p** 06. NSM Whitton and Thurleston w Akenham *St E* 05–10; Bp's Chapl 10–15; C Ipswich St Mary-le-Tower 10–15; P-in-c Whitton and Thurleston w Akenham from 15; Bp's Adv for Healthcare Chapl 12–16. *Side View, School Road, Coddenham, Ipswich IP6 9PS* M: 07824-323073 E: marysokanovic@outlook.com

SOKOLOWSKI (née MAHON), Mrs Stephanie Mary. b 56. Liv Univ BSc 80 SRN 80 K Coll Lon BA 00. S'wark Ord Course 91. **d** 94 **p** 95. C Warlingham w Chelsham and Farleigh *S'wark*

94–97; C Godstone and Blindley Heath 97–04; C Shere, Albury and Chilworth *Guildf* 07–21; rtd 21. *6 Woolmer Hill House, Hatchetts Drive, Haslemere GU27 1LX* T: (01428) 652293 M: 07731-783924 E: ssokolowski@btinternet.com

SOLMAN, Mrs Fiona Barbara. b 53. SRN 75 RSCN 75 RHV 80. STETS 03. d 06 p 07. C Cottesmore and Barrow w Ashwell and Burley *Pet* 06–09; C Empingham and Exton w Horn w Whitwell 06–09; C Greetham and Stretton w Stretton and Clipsham 06–09; R Etwall w Egginton *Derby* 09–18; rtd 18; PtO *Linc* from 19. *The Gables, 21 Castleton Boulevard, Skegness PE25 2TU* T: (01754) 465698 E: fionasolman@aol.com

SOMASUNDRAM, Ian Mark. b 81. Man Univ MEng 04 Jes Coll Cam PhD 10. Oak Hill Th Coll BA 15. d 15 p 16. C Hebburn St Jo *Dur* 15–19; P-in-c from 19; C Jarrow Grange 15–19; P-in-c from 19. *23 St John's Avenue, Hebburn NE31 2TZ* M: 07742-319151 E: ian.m.somasundram@gmail.com

SOMERS-EDGAR, Carl John. b 46. Otago Univ BA 69. St Steph Ho Ox 72. d 75 p 76. C Northwood H Trin *Lon* 75–79; C St Marylebone All SS 79–82; V Liscard St Mary w St Columba *Ches* 82–85; V Caversham St Pet *NZ* 85–11; rtd 11. *32 Cole Street, Caversham, Dunedin 9012, New Zealand* T: (0064) (3) 487 9877 E: paratus@xtra.co.nz

SOMERS HESLAM, Peter. *See* HESLAM, Peter Somers

SOMERVILLE, John William Kenneth. b 38. St D Coll Lamp 60. d 63 p 64. C Rhosllannerchrugog *St As* 63–67; C Llangystennin 67–70; V Gorsedd 70–76; V Gorsedd w Brynford and Ysgeifiog 77–02; RD Holywell 96–02; rtd 02; PtO *St As* from 09. *15 Bryn Marl Road, Mochdre, Colwyn Bay LL28 5DT*

SOPER, Jonathan Alexander James. b 64. Univ Coll Dur BA 85. Wycliffe Hall Ox 94. d 96 p 97. C Bath Weston All SS w N Stoke and Langridge *B & W* 96–00; C Bryanston Square St Mary w St Marylebone St Mark *Lon* 00–04; LtO *Ex* from 07. *Church Office, 22 Southernhay West, Exeter EX1 1PR* T: (01392) 434311 E: jon@enc.uk.net

SOPP, Mrs Phyllis. b 62. Bucks Chilterns Univ Coll BSc 07. Ox Ord Course 17. d 20 p 21. NSM Maidenhead St Luke *Ox* from 20. *17 Halifax Road, Maidenhead SL6 5ER* T: (01628) 781390 M: 07833-221017 E: fourbeaus@btinternet.com

SORENSEN, Ms Anna Katrine Elizabeth. b 58. Man Univ BA 82 MPhil 94 Open Univ PGCE 95. Ripon Coll Cuddesdon 83. d 87 p 94. Par Dn Ashton H Trin *Man* 87–88; Asst Chapl St Felix Sch Southwold 89–90; Chapl 90–99; Hon Par Dn Reydon *St E* 89–92; Hon Par Dn Blythburgh w Reydon 92–94; Hon C 94–99; C Gislingham and Thorndon 99–03; P-in-c Billingborough Gp *Linc* 03–18; P-in-c N Beltisloe Gp 18–20; V N Beltisloe Par from 20. *The Rectory, 30 High Street, Ropsley, Grantham NG33 4BE* M: 07793-544238 E: sorensenanna8@gmail.com

SØRENSEN, Michaela Alexandra. b 70. Kent Univ BA 92 Univ of Div Vic BTheol 17. Dio of Newc NSW 17 ERMC 18. d 19 p 20. C Watton *Nor* from 19. *44 Jubilee Road, Watton, Thetford IP25 6BJ* M: 07554-542861 E: revkyla@gmail.com

SOTONWA, Canon Oladapo Oyegbola. b 56. Ibadan Univ Nigeria BEd 79 MEd 81 PhD 86. Immanuel Coll Ibadan 91. d 94 p 95. C Italupe Em Nigeria 94–95; V Egbeba All SS 95–03; V Simeon Ashiru Mem Ch 03–04; V Odogbondu St Pet 04–05; Hon Can Ijebu from 05; PtO *S'wark* 06–07; Hon C W Dulwich Em 07–11; Hon C S'wark H Trin w St Matt 11; Chapl HM Pris *Nor* from 11. *HM Prison Norwich, Knox Road, Norwich NR1 4LU* T: (01603) 708600 M: 07983-630658 E: oladaposotonwa@yahoo.co.uk *or* oladapo.sotonwa@justice.gov.uk

SOTONWA, Canon Thomas Bamidele Adegboyega. b 78. Ambrose Alli Univ Nigeria BMLS 05 Middx Univ MSc 11. d 05 p 06. Nigeria 05–13; PtO *Birm* 13–17; V Rednal from 17; Hon Can Ibadan Nigeria from 19. *St Stephen's Vicarage, Edgewood Road, Rednal, Birmingham B45 8SG* T: 0121-453 3347 M: 07837-421941 E: sotzi2002@gmail.com

SOULSBY, Canon Michael. b 36. Dur Univ BSc 57. Westcott Ho Cam 61. d 62 p 63. C Selly Oak St Mary *Birm* 62–66; C Kings Norton 66–72; TV 73–76; TR Sutton *Liv* 76–88; RD Prescot 84–88; P-in-c Orton Longueville *Ely* 88–96; RD Yaxley 92–02; TR The Ortons, Alwalton and Chesterton 96–04; Hon Can Ely Cathl 94–04; rtd 04; PtO *Ely* from 05; *Pet* from 14; *Ox* from 17. *8 Leiston Court, Eye, Peterborough PE6 7WL* T: (01733) 221124 E: m.soulsby@talk21.com

SOULT, Mrs Pamela Elizabeth. b 46. SNWTP. d 09 p 10. NSM Over Peover w Lower Peover *Ches* 09–11; NSM Goostrey w Swettenham 11–17; rtd 17; PtO *Ches* from 17; *Ely* from 19. *6 Thrapston Road, Kimbolton, Huntingdon PE28 0HW* E: pamelasoult@aol.com

SOUPPOURIS, Ms Gail Camilla. b 52. Essex Univ BA 75 Anglia Ruskin Univ MA 07. SEITE 02. d 05 p 06. C W Wickham St Fran and St Mary *S'wark* 05–08;

P-in-c Shoreham Beach *Chich* 08–14; rtd 14; PtO *Chich* from 16. *The Rotyngs, Rottingdean, Brighton BN2 7DX* T: (01273) 240420 M: 07950-665051 E: gail.souppouris@gmail.com

SOURBUT, Preb Philip John. b 57. Cam Univ BA MA. Cranmer Hall Dur BA. d 85 p 86. C Springfield All SS *Chelmsf* 85–88; C Roxeth Ch Ch and Harrow St Pet *Lon* 88–91; P-in-c Bath St Sav *B & W* 91–93; R Bath St Sav w Swainswick and Woolley 93–98; V Cullompton and R Kentisbeare w Blackborough *Ex* 98–01; TR Cullompton, Willand, Uffculme, Kentisbeare etc 01–09; Dioc Voc Development Officer 09–15; Tutor SWMTC 09–15; C Ex St Mark, St Sidwell and St Matt 09–15; Dioc Dir Miss and Min from 15; Jt Prin SWMTC 17–20; Preb Ex Cathl from 13. *The Old Deanery, The Cloisters, Cathedral Close, Exeter EX1 1HS* T: (01392) 294903 E: philip.sourbut@exeter.anglican.org

SOURBUT GROVES, The Ven Catherine Ann. b 67. Bath Univ BA 91 MSc 93 PhD 97. STETS MA 07. d 07 p 08. C Saltford w Corston and Newton St Loe *B & W* 07–11; P-in-c Bath St Barn w Englishcombe 11–16; V 16–20; Preb Wells Cathl 19–20; Adn Lindisfarne *Newc* from 20. *The Vicarage, Stannington, Morpeth NE61 6HL* T: 0191-270 4166 E: lindisfarne@newcastle.anglican.org

SOUTER, Ruth Rosemary. b 55. Dur Univ BEd 77. EMMTC 00. d 03 p 04. C Braunstone Park CD *Leic* 03–07; V Erdington Ch the K *Birm* from 07. *St Margaret's Vicarage, Somerset Road, Erdington, Birmingham B23 6NQ* T: 0121-373 9209 E: ruthsouter@yahoo.com

SOUTER, William Ewen Logan. b 66. Em Coll Cam BA 88 Univ Coll Lon PhD 93. Trin Coll Bris BA 94 MA 97. d 97 p 98. C Harborne Heath *Birm* 97–01; TV Horsham *Chich* 01–11; PtO *Llan* 13–19; P-in-c Urban Crofters CD from 19. *89 Claude Road, Cardiff CF24 3QD* T: (029) 2140 4356 M: 07807-384350 E: willsouter@hotmail.co.uk

SOUTH, Gerald Peter. b 45. d 09 p 10. NSM Limpsfield and Tatsfield *S'wark* 09–15; PtO from 15; P-in-c Avening w Cherington *Glouc* from 17. *9 Dr Crawford's Close, Minchinhampton, Stroud GL6 9EZ* T: (01453) 883456 E: gp.south@btopenworld.com

SOUTH, Gillian. *See* HARWOOD, Gillian

SOUTHAMPTON, Suffragan Bishop of. *See* SELLIN, The Rt Revd Deborah Mary

SOUTHCOMBE, Matthew Leonard. b 81. Surrey Univ BMus 04 Roehampton Univ MA 08. St Mellitus Coll BA 18. d 18 p 19. C Whitchurch St Aug *Bris* from 18; C Bedminster 18–20; C Bedminster and Southville from 20. *41 Birchall Road, Bristol BS6 7TT* M: 07714-754660 E: matt@stnicholasbristol.org

SOUTHEE, Mrs Sandra Margaret. b 43. EAMTC 97. d 00 p 01. NSM Galleywood Common *Chelmsf* 00–02; NSM Moulsham St Jo 02–06; Asst Chapl Mid-Essex Hosp Services NHS Trust 01–06; PtO *Chelmsf* 06–07; NSM Gt Baddow 07–12; rtd 12; PtO *Chelmsf* from 12. *6 Hampton Road, Chelmsford CM2 8ES* T: (01245) 475456 E: sandysouthee@hotmail.co.uk

SOUTHEND, Archdeacon of. *See* SNOWDEN, The Ven Elizabeth

✠**SOUTHERN, The Rt Revd Humphrey Ivo John.** b 60. Ch Ch Ox BA 82 MA 86. Ripon Coll Cuddesdon 83. d 86 p 87 c 07. C Rainham *Roch* 86–90; C Walton St Mary *Liv* 90–92; C Walton-on-the-Hill 92; V Hale *Guildf* 92–96; TR 96–97; TR Hale w Badshot Lea 97–99; Dioc Ecum Officer 92–99; TR Tisbury *Sarum* 99–01; TR Nadder Valley 01–07; RD Chalke 00–07; Can and Preb Sarum Cathl 06–07; Suff Bp Repton *Derby* 07–15; Warden of Readers 09–15; Prin Ripon Coll Cuddesdon from 15; Asst Bp Ox from 15. *Ripon College, Cuddeson, Oxford OX44 9EX* T: (01865) 877400 E: principal@rcc.ac.uk

SOUTHERN, John Abbott. b 27. Leeds Univ BA 47. Coll of Resurr Mirfield. d 51 p 52. C Leigh St Mary *Man* 51–55; C Gt Grimsby St Jas *Linc* 55–58; V Oldham St Jas *Man* 58–60; V Haigh *Liv* 60–75; V Pemberton St Jo 75–98; rtd 98; PtO *Liv* from 00. *145 Moor Road, Orrell, Wigan WN5 8SJ* T: (01942) 732132

SOUTHERN, Mrs Lindsay Margaret. b 70. Univ of Wales (Abth) BA 01 Reading Univ PGCE 04 St Jo Coll Dur BA 08. Cranmer Hall Dur 06. d 08 p 09. C Kirklington w Burneston and Wath and Pickhill *Ripon* 08–12; V Catterick *Leeds* from 12. *The Vicarage, High Green, Catterick, Richmond DL10 7LN* T: (01748) 811462 M: 07720-242468

SOUTHERN, Paul Ralph. b 48. Oak Hill Th Coll 85. d 87 p 88. C Chadwell Heath *Chelmsf* 87–91; P-in-c Tolleshunt D'Arcy w Tolleshunt Major 91–01; V Tolleshunt D'Arcy and Tolleshunt Major 01–08; rtd 08; PtO *Chelmsf* from 08; *Eur* from 19. *12 Guisnes Court, Back Road, Tolleshunt D'Arcy, Maldon CM9 8TW* T: (01621) 860380

SOUTHERTON, Kathryn Ruth. *See* TRIMBY, Kathryn Ruth

SOUTHERTON, Canon Peter Clive. b 38. MBE 01. Univ of Wales (Lamp) BA 59. Qu Coll Birm. **d** 61 **p** 62. C Llandrillo-yn-Rhos *St As* 61–68; Bermuda 68–71; V Esclusham *St As* 72–82; V Prestatyn 82–04; Hon Can St As Cathl 96–04; rtd 04; PtO *St As* from 09. *6 Llwyn Mesen, Prestatyn LL19 8NS* T: (01745) 853176 E: clivesoutherton@yahoo.co.uk

SOUTHGATE, Mrs Clair Mary. b 67. Trin Coll Bris 09. **d** 11 **p** 12. OLM Box w Hazlebury and Ditteridge *Bris* from 11; OLM Colerne w N Wraxall from 11. *6 Queens Square, Box, Corsham SN13 8EA* T: (01225) 743970 M: 07917-117644 E: meddling@tiscali.co.uk

SOUTHGATE, Graham. b 63. GlBiol 85 NE Surrey Coll of Tech PhD 89. Ripon Coll Cuddesdon BTh 93. **d** 93 **p** 94. C Tisbury *Sarum* 93–97; TV Chalke Valley 97–03; R Bratton, Edington and Imber, Erlestoke etc 03–11; TR Nadder Valley from 11; RD Chalke from 19. *The Rectory, Shaftesbury Road, Fovant, Salisbury SP3 5JA* T: (01722) 714826 E: grahamsouthgate63@hotmail.com

SOUTHGATE, Patricia Elizabeth. b 44. **d** 03 **p** 04. OLM Parkstone St Pet and St Osmund w Branksea *Sarum* from 03. *1 Dune Crest, 105 Banks Road, Poole BH13 7QQ* T: (01202) 700124 E: patsouthgate@btinternet.com

SOUTHGATE, Stephen Martin. b 61. Lanc Univ BA 83 St Martin's Coll Lanc PGCE 84. Cranmer Hall Dur 96. **d** 98 **p** 99. C Witton *Ches* 98–01; R Backford and Capenhurst 01–16; R Hambleden Valley *Ox* 16–20; P-in-c Ripponden *Leeds* from 20; P-in-c Barkisland w W Scammonden from 20. *The Vicarage, Ripponden, Sowerby Bridge HX6 4DF* T: (01422) 822239 E: stephen.southgate@leeds.anglican.org

SOUTHWARD, Canon James Fisher. b 57. St Martin's Coll Lanc BEd 80. Chich Th Coll 83. **d** 86 **p** 87. C Woodford St Barn *Chelmsf* 86–89; TV Crawley *Chich* 89–95; V Higham and Merston *Roch* 95–21; RD Strood 02–12; P-in-c Perry Street from 20; Hon Can Roch Cathl from 09. *36 Rosebank Gardens, Northfleet, Gravesend DA11 8RZ* E: allsts.perryst@gmail.com

SOUTHWARK, Archdeacon of. *Vacant*

SOUTHWARK, Bishop of. *See* CHESSUN, The Rt Revd Christopher Thomas James

SOUTHWARK, Dean of. *See* NUNN, The Very Revd Andrew Peter

SOUTHWELL, Peter John Mackenzie. b 43. New Coll Ox BA 64 MA 68. Wycliffe Hall Ox 66. **d** 67 **p** 68. C Crookes St Thos *Sheff* 67–70; Lect Sheff Univ 67–70; Sen Tutor Wycliffe Hall Ox 70–08; Chapl and Lect Qu Coll Ox 82–10; rtd 10; Lect Ox 10–11 and 15–18; PtO from 19. *The Queen's College, Oxford OX1 4AW* T: (01865) 279120 E: peter.southwell@queens.ox.ac.uk

SOUTHWELL AND NOTTINGHAM, Bishop of. *See* WILLIAMS, The Rt Revd Paul Gavin

SOUTHWELL, Dean of. *See* SULLIVAN, The Very Revd Nicola Ann

SOWDEN, Charles William Bartholomew. b 47. **d** 97 **p** 98. OLM Saxonwell *Linc* 97–06; NSM Metheringham w Blankney and Dunston 06–09; P-in-c Wyberton 09–17; P-in-c Frampton 09–17; rtd 17. *Address temp unknown* E: charles.sowden1@btinternet.com

SOWDEN, Geoffrey David. b 57. Kingston Poly BA 79. Wycliffe Hall Ox 95. **d** 97 **p** 98. C Ware Ch Ch *St Alb* 97–02; V Highworth w Sevenhampton and Inglesham etc *Bris* from 02; P-in-c Broad Blunsdon from 05. *The Vicarage, 10 Stonefield Drive, Highworth, Swindon SN6 7DA* T: (01793) 765554 E: the.sowdens@btinternet.com

SOWERBUTTS, Alan. b 49. Sheff Univ BSc 70 PhD 73 Qu Coll Cam BA 75 MA 79. Cranmer Hall Dur 74. **d** 76 **p** 77. C Salesbury *Blackb* 76–80; V Lower Darwen St Jas 80–84; V Musbury 84–93; P-in-c Brindle 93–98; Sec Dioc Adv Cttee for the Care of Chs 93–98; V Read in Whalley 98–14; rtd 14; PtO *Man* from 14; *Blackb* from 14. *9 Hapton Way, Rossendale BB4 8QG* T: (01706) 219279 M: 07849-722437 E: fralans@yahoo.co.uk

SOWERBUTTS, Philip John. b 67. Ches Coll of HE BEd 89 Edge Hill Coll of HE PGCE 99. Oak Hill Th Coll BA 03. **d** 03 **p** 04. C Kirk Ella and Willerby *York* 03–07; V Castle Church *Lich* from 07. *Castle Church Vicarage, 18 Castle Bank, Stafford ST16 1DJ* T: (01785) 607150 M: 07910-606876 E: vicar@castlechurch.org.uk

SOWERBY, Geoffrey Nigel Rake. b 35. St Aid Birkenhead 56. **d** 60 **p** 61. C Armley St Bart *Ripon* 60–63; Min Can Ripon Cathl 63–65; V Thornthwaite w Thruscross and Darley 65–69; V Leeds All SS 69–73; V Leyburn w Bellerby 73–81; R Edin Old St Paul 81–86; V Hawes and Hardraw *Ripon* 86–92; Dioc Adv in Deliverance Min 91–92; rtd 92; PtO *Dur* 92–13; *Ripon* 92–14; *Leeds* 14–16. *25 Greendale Court, Bedale DL8 1FB* T: (01677) 425860 M: 07749-229189 E: geoffreynsowerby@btinternet.com

✠SOWERBY, The Rt Revd Mark Crispin Rake. b 63. K Coll Lon BD 85 AKC 85 Lanc Univ MA 94. Coll of Resurr Mirfield 85. **d** 87 **p** 88 **c** 09. C Knaresborough *Ripon* 87–90; C Darwen St Cuth w Tockholes St Steph *Blackb* 90–92; V Accrington St Mary 92–97; Chapl St Chris High Sch Accrington 92–97; Chapl Victoria Hosp Accrington 92–97; Asst Dir of Ords *Blackb* 93–96; Voc Officer and Selection Sec Min Division 97–01; V Harrogate St Wilfrid *Ripon* 01–04; TR 04–09; Asst Dir of Ords 05–09; Area Bp Horsham *Chich* 09–19; Prin Coll of Resurr Mirfield from 19; Hon Asst Bp Leeds from 19. *College of the Resurrection, Stocks Bank Road, Mirfield WF14 0BW* T: (01924) 490441

SOWTER, Colin Victor. b 35. Ball Coll Ox BA 56 MA 59 DPhil 60. Oak Hill Th Course 88. **d** 91 **p** 92. NSM Cranleigh *Guildf* 91–93; NSM Wonersh 93–98; NSM Wonersh w Blackheath 98–05; rtd 05; PtO *Guildf* 05–21. *Hollycroft, Grantley Avenue, Wonersh Park, Guildford GU5 0QN* T: (01483) 892094 E: colin.sowter@btopenworld.com

SOWTON, Mrs Alison. b 62. Qu Coll Birm. **d** 09 **p** 10. C Oxhey All SS *St Alb* 09–13; TV Melksham *Sarum* from 13. *The Vicarage, 59 Linnet Lane, Melksham SN12 7FA* T: (01225) 434113 M: 07739-712548 E: alisonsowton@live.com

SPACKMAN (*née* MORRISON), Mrs Ailsa. b 40. Qu Univ Kingston Ontario BA 82. Montreal Dioc Th Coll. **d** 83 **p** 85. Canada 83–95; Dn Caspe 83–85; I Malbay Miss Par 85–92; Chapl Drummondville Penitentiary 92–93; rtd 93; PtO *Ex* from 99. *Cofton Lodge, Cofton Hill, Cockwood, Exeter EX6 8RB* T: (01626) 891584

SPACKMAN, Canon Peter John. b 37. Southn Univ BSc 60. Westcott Ho Cam 65. **d** 66 **p** 67. C Boxmoor St Jo *St Alb* 66–69; C Alnwick St Paul *Newc* 69–72; C-in-c Stewart Town Jamaica 72–74; I Sept-Iles Canada 74–77; R Baie Comeau 77–80; R Gaspe 80–92; Adn Gaspe 88–92; R Richmond and Hon Can Quebec Canada 92–94; PtO *Ex* 95–97; Hon C Kenton, Mamhead, Powderham, Cofton and Starcross 97–02; PtO 02–15. *Cofton Lodge, Cofton Hill, Cockwood, Exeter EX6 8RB* T: (01626) 891584

SPAIGHT, Robert George. b 45. Ridley Hall Cam. **d** 84 **p** 85. C St Columb Minor and St Colan *Truro* 84–87; C Worksop St Jo *S'well* 87–89; V Barlings *Linc* 89–13; rtd 13. *The Forge, Cross Roads, Riby, Grimsby DN37 8NH* T: (01469) 569768

SPANKIE, Mrs Susan Jane. b 61. Bp Grosseteste Coll BEd 90. SCRTP 12. **d** 15 **p** 17. NSM Hanborough and Freeland *Ox* 15–21; R Fremington, Instow and Westleigh *Ex* from 21. *19 Lane End Close, Instow, Bideford EX39 4LG* T: (01271) 861204 E: vicar@ttec.org.uk

SPANNER, Handley James. b 51. Lanchester Poly Cov BSc 73 BA. Oak Hill Th Coll 82. **d** 85 **p** 86. C Cov H Trin 85–89; V Rye Park St Cuth *St Alb* 89–01; V Colney Heath St Mark 01–12; rtd 12; PtO *Chich* from 13. *79 Old Manor Road, Rustington, Littlehampton BN16 3QF* E: jamesspanner@aol.com

SPAREY-TAYLOR, Mrs Rebecca-Elizabeth. b 76. Univ of Wales (Cardiff) BSc 99. St Padarn's Inst 12. **d** 17 **p** 18. C Wrexham *St As* 17–20; P-in-c Denbigh Miss Area 20–21; Miss Area Ldr from 21. *The Rectory, Trefnant, Denbigh LL16 5UG* T: (01978) 291621 E: revdrebecca@outlook.com

SPARGO, Anne Elizabeth. b 51. Newnham Coll Cam MB 76 BChir 77 MA 79. WEMTC 03. **d** 06 **p** 07. NSM Frampton on Severn, Arlingham, Saul etc *Glouc* 06–10; P-in-c 10–16; rtd 16; PtO *Heref* from 18. *Quilter, Walwyn Road, Upper Colwall, Malvern WR13 6PX* E: anne.spargo@btinternet.com

SPARHAM, Canon Anthony George. b 41. St Jo Coll Dur BA 69. Cranmer Hall Dur 66. **d** 71 **p** 72. C Bourne *Linc* 71–74; TV Tong *Bradf* 74–76; V Windhill 76–81; Dioc Dir of Educn *St E* 82–85; V Goostrey *Ches* 85–99; R Wilmslow 99–08; Jt Dir Lay Tr 85–97; Hon Can Ches Cathl 94–08; rtd 08; PtO *Ches* 08–17; *Lich* 08–11 and 14–17; Hon C Whittington and W Felton w Haughton 11–14; Hon C Grantown-on-Spey *Mor* from 16; Hon C Rothiemurchus from 16. *48 Strathspey Drive, Grantown-on-Spey PH26 3EY* T: (01479) 481151 E: t.sparham41@sky.com

SPARKES, Mrs Lynne. b 55. Chelt & Glouc Coll of HE BEd 96. WEMTC 06. **d** 09 **p** 10. NSM Barnwood *Glouc* 09–12; C Gt Malvern Ch Ch *Worc* 13–14; TV Malvern Chase from 14. *137 Madresfield Road, Malvern WR14 2HD* E: lynnesparkes@googlemail.com

SPARKS, Ian. b 59. Lanc Univ BSc(Econ) 81. Cranmer Hall Dur 94. **d** 96 **p** 97. C Bowdon *Ches* 96–00; V Chelford w Lower Withington 00–06; P-in-c Macclesfield St Jo 06–14; P-in-c Luddenden w Luddenden Foot *Leeds* from 14; C Ryburn from 14; P-in-c Greetland and W Vale from 20. *The Vicarage, 50 Carr Field Drive, Luddenden, Halifax HX2 6RJ* T: (01422) 884421 E: ian.sparks@leeds.anglican.org

SPARROW, Miss Elisabeth Joy. b 70. Nottm Univ BEng 94. Qu Coll Birm 11. **d** 11 **p** 12. C Bartley Green

Birm 11–15; P-in-c Bridgwater St Jo *B & W* 15–16; V from 16. *St John's Vicarage, Blake Place, Bridgwater TA6 5BA* T: (01278) 422540 E: lis.sparrow@gmail.com *or* revlisstjohnbridgwater@gmail.com

SPARROW, Michael Kenneth. St Jo Coll Dur BA 74. Coll of Resurr Mirfield 74. **d** 75 **p** 76. C N Hinksey *Ox* 75–78; C Portsea St Mary *Portsm* 78–85; V Midsomer Norton w Clandown *B & W* 85–93; Chapl Schiedam Miss to Seafarers *Eur* 93–03; Chapl Mombasa Miss to Seafarers Kenya 04–12; P-in-c N Ockendon *Chelmsf* 14–19; rtd 19; PtO *Chelmsf* from 19. *9 Carmelite Terrace, King's Lynn PE30 5AF* T: (01553) 766097 E: mksparrow13@gmail.com

SPEAKE, Emma Louise. b 81. Man Univ BA 12 Sheff Univ MA 16. Yorks Min Course 14. **d** 16 **p** 17. C W Kirby St Bridget *Ches* 16–18; V Grange St Andr from 18; Chapl St Chad's Catholic and C of E High Sch from 19. *The Vicarage, 37 Lime Grove, Runcorn WA7 5JZ* T: (01928) 830170 M: 07515-174597 E: rev.em@outlook.com

SPEAKMAN, Anthony Ernest. b 40. **d** 71 **p** 72. C Newtown w Llanllwchaiarn w Aberhafesp *St As* 71–72; C Holywell 72–75; C St Marylebone w H Trin *Lon* 75–77; V Camberwell St Phil and St Mark *S'wark* 77–80; LtO *Lon* 94–96; NSM Kensington St Jo 96–05; PtO 10–17. *26 Hughenden House, 33 Jerome Crescent, London NW8 8SH*

SPEAR, Andrew James Michael. b 60. Dur Univ BA 81. Ridley Hall Cam 83. **d** 86 **p** 87. C Haughton le Skerne *Dur* 86–90; C Eastbourne H Trin *Chich* 90–95; C Patcham 95–02; V Oldland *Bris* 02–16; P-in-c Longwell Green 13–16; rtd 16; PtO *Chich* 17–18; Hon C E Dean w Friston and Jevington from 18. *36 Summerdown Lane, East Dean, Eastbourne BN20 0LE* E: andrewjmspear@hotmail.com

SPEAR, Miss Jennifer Jane. b 53. Westhill Coll Birm BEd 76. Trin Coll Bris 82. **dss** 84 **d** 87 **p** 95. Reading St Jo *Ox* 84–90; Par Dn 87–90; Hon Par Dn Devonport St Barn *Ex* 90–91; Hon Par Dn Devonport St Mich 90–91; Par Dn Plymstock 91–94; C 94–97; TV Plymstock and Hooe 97–11; rtd 11; PtO *Ex* from 12. *69 Plymstock Road, Plymouth PL9 7PD* T: (01752) 405202

SPEAR, John Cory. b 33. Open Univ BA 87. Ridley Hall Cam 68. **d** 70 **p** 71. C Gerrards Cross *Ox* 70–73; TV Washfield, Stoodleigh, Withleigh etc *Ex* 73–79; R Instow 79–90; V Westleigh 79–90; RD Hartland 82–89; V Pilton w Ashford 90–97; TR Barnstaple 97–99; rtd 99; PtO *Ex* 00–18. *Abbots Lodge, Abbotsham Court, Abbotsham, Bideford EX39 5BH* T: (01237) 476607

SPEARS, Reginald Robert _Derek_. b 48. Trin Coll Ox BA 72 MA 75. Cuddesdon Coll 72. **d** 75 **p** 76. C Hampton All SS *Lon* 75–79; C Caversham *Ox* 79–81; C Caversham St Pet and Mapledurham etc 81–84; V Reading St Matt 84–94; V Earley St Pet 94–14; rtd 14; PtO *Ox* from 14. *65 Aborn Parade, West End Road, Mortimer Common, Reading RG7 3TQ* T: 0118-933   2722   E: derekspears@compuserve.com   *or* dspears.awb@gmail.com

SPECK, Ms Jane Elisabeth. b 72. Univ of Cen England in Birm BA 94 St Jo Coll Dur BA 01 MA 02. Cranmer Hall Dur 98. **d** 02 **p** 03. C Stourport and Wilden *Worc* 02–05; C N Lambeth *S'wark* 05–11; Chapl K Coll Lon 05–19; Dir Ords Kingston Area 13–19; NSM St Mary le Strand w St Clem Danes *Lon* 17–19; Chapl York St Jo Univ from 19. *St Wulfstan's Vicarage, 8 Abbotsway, York YO31 9LD* E: janespeck@hotmail.com

SPECK, Preb Peter William. b 42. Univ of Wales (Ban) BSc 64 Birm Univ BA 66 MA 71 Lambeth DM 12. Qu Coll Birm 64. **d** 67 **p** 68. C Rhosddu *St As* 67–71; C Wrexham 71–72; Asst Chapl United Sheff Hosps 72–73; Chapl N Gen Hosp Sheff 73–79; Chapl R Free Hosp Lon 79–95; Hon Sen Lect Sch of Med 87–95; Preb St Paul's Cathl *Lon* 92–95; Chapl Southn Univ Hosps NHS Trust 95–02; rtd 02; Public Preacher *Win* from 02; Visiting Fell Southn Univ 02–18; Hon Sen Research Fell and Hon Sen Lect K Coll Lon from 02. *22 The Harrage, Romsey SO51 8AE* T: (01794) 516937

SPECK, Raymond George. b 39. Oak Hill Th Coll 64. **d** 67 **p** 68. C Stretford St Bride *Man* 67–70; C Roxeth Ch Ch *Lon* 70–74; V Woodbridge St Jo *St E* 74–85; R Jersey St Ouen w St Geo *Win* 85–98; rtd 98; PtO *Win* from 98. *Rosevale Lodge, rue du Craslin, St Peter, Jersey JE3 7BU* T: (01534) 634987

SPEDDING, Clare. *See* FRYER-SPEDDING, Clare Caroline

SPEDDING, William Granville. b 39. Tyndale Hall Bris BD 60. **d** 62 **p** 63. C Man Albert Memorial Ch 62–65; Hd RE Whitecroft Sch Bolton 65–71; Co-ord Humanities Hayward Sch Bolton 71–93; PtO *Man* 65–67 and from 02; NSM New Bury 67–79; NSM Bolton St Paul w Em 79–86; NSM Pennington 86–02. *26 Milverton Close, Lostock, Bolton BL6 4RR* T: (01204) 841248 E: granvillespedding@ntlworld.com

SPEED-ANDREWS, Armynel _Belinda_. b 62. SWMTC 14. **d** 17 **p** 18. NSM Newton Tracey, Horwood, Alverdiscott etc *Ex* 17–20; NSM Ex St Dav from 20. *Swanview Suite,*

Riverside Centre, 13-14 Okehampton Street, Exeter EX4 1DU E: bspeedandrews@gmail.com

SPEEDY (née BRINDLEY), Mrs Angela Mary. b 44. Oak Hill Th Coll 93 NOC 99. **d** 00 **p** 01. C Handforth *Ches* 00–03; R Whaley Bridge 03–05; rtd 05; Hon C Barthomley *Ches* 07–18; PtO 18–19. *19 Church Lane, Sandbach CW11 2LG* T: (01270) 753303 E: darrelspeedy735@gmail.com

SPEEDY, Canon Darrel Craven. b 35. St Chad's Coll Dur BA 57. Wells Th Coll 57. **d** 59 **p** 60. C Frodingham *Linc* 59–63; V Heckington w Howell 63–71; V Barton upon Humber 71–79; R Tain *Mor* 79–85; Dioc Sec 82–85; Can St Andr Cathl Inverness 83–85; Syn Clerk 83–85; R Whaley Bridge *Ches* 85–01; RD Chadkirk 88–95; Hon Can Ches Cathl from 96; rtd 01; P-in-c Barthomley *Ches* 01–19; PtO from 19. *19 Church Lane, Sandbach CW11 2LG* T: (01270) 753303 E: darrelspeedy735@gmail.com

✠**SPEERS, The Rt Revd Samuel Hall.** b 46. TCD BA 70 MA 75. Cuddesdon Coll 70. **d** 73 **p** 74 **c** 19. C Boreham Wood All SS *St Alb* 73–76; Madagascar 76–88; Hon Can Antananarivo from 85; R S Lafford *Linc* 88–02; RD Lafford 96–02; TR Chipping Barnet *St Alb* 02–13; rtd 13; Hon C Chingford SS Pet and Paul *Chelmsf* 13–16; Bp Mahajanga Madagascar from 19. *Évêché Anglican, BP 365, 401 Mahajanga, Madagascar* T: (00261) (62) 23611 E: hallspeers@gmail.com

SPELLER, Shaun Lawrence. b 65. Birm Poly BA 88. Ripon Coll Cuddesdon 11. **d** 13 **p** 14. C Harpenden St Nic *St Alb* 13–17; V Henlow and Langford from 17. *The Vicarage, 65 Church Street, Langford, Biggleswade SG18 9QT* T: (01462) 700248 M: 07922-129361

SPENCE, Amanda Jane. b 70. St Aug Coll of Th 17. **d** 19 **p** 20. C Crayford *Roch* from 19. *1A Iron Mill Place, Crayford, Dartford DA1 4RT*

SPENCE, David Royston. b 80. St Jo Coll Cam MA 06 PhD 06. Trin Coll Bris 10. **d** 13 **p** 14. C Shill Valley and Broadshire *Ox* 13–16; C Kirk Ella and Willerby *York* 16–19; C Cogges and S Leigh *Ox* from 19. *7 Barleyfield Way, Witney OX28 1AA* T: (01993) 778611 M: 07754-299275 E: revdspence@gmail.com

SPENCE, James Andrew Deane. b 83. Loughb Univ BSc 06. Oak Hill Th Coll BA 17. **d** 17 **p** 18. C Rusholme H Trin *Man* 17–21; C Davyhulme Ch Ch and Urmston from 21. *St Clement's Vicarage, 24 Stretford Road, Urmston, Manchester M41 9JZ* T: 0161-748 9838 M: 07793-739115 E: james@plattchurch.org

SPENCE, Michael James. b 62. Sydney Univ BA 85 LLB 87 St Cath Coll Ox DPhil 96. St Steph Ho Ox. **d** 06 **p** 07. NSM Cowley St Jas *Ox* 06–08; Vice-Chan Sydney Univ Australia 08–21; Pres Univ Coll *Lon* from 21. *University College London, Gower Street, London WC1E 6BT*

SPENCE, Mrs Moira Joan. b 44. SAOMC 96. **d** 01 **p** 02. OLM Risborough *Ox* 01–06; NSM Ewenny w St Brides Major *Llan* 07–18. *Ty Bara, 33 Main Road, Ogmore-by-Sea, Bridgend CF32 0PD*

SPENCELEY, Douglas. b 49. Edin Univ MA 70 SS Mark & Jo Univ Coll Plymouth PGCE 71. ERMC 07. **d** 09 **p** 10. NSM Arthingworth, Harrington w Oxendon and E Farndon *Pet* 09–12; NSM Maidwell w Draughton, Lamport w Faxton 09–12; Bp's V for Ch Schs 12–20; NSM Billing 12–17; NSM Northampton Em from 17. *1 Russet Drive, Little Billing, Northampton NN3 9TF* T: (01604) 407977 E: dspenceley@lineone.net

SPENCELEY, Haydon du Garde. b 84. Nottm Univ BA 06 Leeds Univ MA 09. St Jo Coll Nottm 11. **d** 14 **p** 15. C Northampton Em *Pet* 14–17; TR from 17; Asst Dir Ords from 17. *24 The Nurseries, Northampton NN1 5HN* T: (01604) 244391 M: 07985-973773 E: haydon.spenceley@gmail.com

SPENCELEY, Malcolm. b 40. Open Univ BA 92 Dur Inst of Educn CertEd 72. Cranmer Hall Dur 78. **d** 80 **p** 81. C Redcar *York* 80–85; V Middlesbrough Ascension 85–93; V Newby 93–05; rtd 05; PtO *York* 06–21. *6 Tameside, Stokesley, Middlesbrough TS9 5PE* T: (01642) 710443

SPENCER, Andrew. b 47. St Matthias Coll Bris BEd 70 Univ of Wales (Ban) BTh 05. **d** 04 **p** 05. Moderator for Reader Tr *Guildf* 01–06; OLM Busbridge and Hambledon from 04; Tutor Local Min Progr from 07. *24 Park Road, Godalming GU7 1SH* T: (01483) 416333 E: andy.spencer@bhcgodalming.org

SPENCER, Antony Wade. b 50. Ridley Hall Cam 92. **d** 94 **p** 95. C Bury St Edmunds St Geo *St E* 94–96; PtO 96–97; C Rougham, Beyton w Hessett and Rushbrooke 97–99; TV Mildenhall 99–07; Dir Past Development Harborne Heath *Birm* 07–11; C 11–18; PtO from 18. *74 Croftdown Road, Birmingham B17 8RD* T: 0121-426 6228 M: 07704-324444 E: antonyspencer@stjohnsharborne.org

SPENCER, Miss Christine Patricia. b 66. Man Univ BSc 02. St Steph Ho Ox BTh 16. **d** 15 **p** 16. C Storrington *Chich* 15–18;

P-in-c Three Bridges 18–20; R Ifield from 20. *Ifield Rectory, Rusper Road, Ifield, Crawley RH11 0LR* M: 07980-617588 E: christine.spencer66@gmail.com *or* rector@ifieldparish.org

SPENCER, Christopher Graham. b 61. Magd Coll Cam BA 83 MA 87 Bath Univ MSc 84. St Jo Coll Nottm 93. d 93 **p** 94. C Ore St Helen and St Barn *Chich* 93–97; V Deal St Geo *Cant* from 97; AD Sandwich from 20. *The Vicarage, 8 St George's Road, Deal CT14 6BA* T: (01304) 372587 E: chris.spencer@stgdeal.org

SPENCER, Christopher Stuart. b 84. Bournemouth Univ BSc 05. St Jo Coll Nottm 08. d 12 **p** 20. C Southbroom *Sarum* 12–14; NSM Longwell Green *Bris* 15–19; NSM Oldland 15–19; C Aber-Morfa Miss Area *St As* from 19. *The Vicarage, 18B Dyserth Road, Rhyl LL18 4DP* T: (01745) 351449 M: 07960-232367 E: chris_spencer2000@yahoo.co.uk

SPENCER, David William. b 43. EAMTC 80. d 81 **p** 82. NSM Wisbech St Aug *Ely* 81–84; C Whittlesey 84–86; R Upwell Christchurch 86–90; R March St Pet and March St Mary 90–98; TV Stanground and Farcet 98–01; V Farcet 01–04; V Farcet Hampton 04–08; rtd 08; PtO *Ely* 08–10; P-in-c Elton w Stibbington and Water Newton 10–12; PtO from 13. *10 Hemingford Crescent, Peterborough PE2 8LL*

SPENCER, Derek Kenneth. b 67. St Jo Coll Nottm BA 98. d 03 **p** 05. Storrington Deanery Youth Missr *Chich* 01–06; C Steyning 05–06; P-in-c Sullington and Thakeham w Warminghurst 07–15; R 15–17; rtd 17. *Address withheld by request*

SPENCER, Miss Emily Jane. b 87. Man Univ BA 09 MA 10 Man Metrop Univ PGCE 11 Dur Univ BTh 20. Ridley Hall Cam 18. d 21. C Knowle *Birm* from 21. *St Anne's Cottage, 1713 High Street, Knowle, Solihull B93 0LN* M: 07825-651356 E: espencer48@gmail.com

SPENCER, Mrs Gail. b 57. STETS. d 03 **p** 04. NSM Wilton w Netherhampton and Fugglestone *Sarum* 03–06; NSM Radcliffe-on-Trent and Shelford *S'well* 06–07; Chapl Qu Medical Cen Nottm Univ Hosp NHS Trust from 07. *2 Gatcombe Close, Radcliffe-on-Trent, Nottingham NG12 2GG* T: 0115-933 6068 E: gailespencer@yahoo.co.uk

SPENCER, George. b 56. Cam Univ BA 77 MA 83 Leeds Metrop Univ DipSW 01. Coll of Resurr Mirfield 80. d 83 **p** 84. C Edin Old St Paul 83–85; P-in-c Edin St Ninian 85–92; Chapl Asst St Helens and Knowsley Hosps NHS Trust 92–93; Chapl 93–96; Chapl Calderdale and Huddersfield NHS Foundn Trust 12–20; PtO *Wakef* 08–14; *Leeds* 14–20; P-in-c Ravensthorpe and Thornhill Lees w Savile Town from 20. *7 Low Westwood, Golcar, Huddersfield HD7 4ER* E: hospitalgeorge@gmail.com *or* george.spencer@leeds.anglican.org

SPENCER, Canon Gilbert Hugh. b 43. Lon Univ BD 67. ALCD 66. d 67 **p** 68. C Bexleyheath Ch Ch *Roch* 67–73; C Bexley St Jo 73–76; P-in-c Bromley St Jo 76–78; V 78–81; R Chatham St Mary w St Jo 81–91; V Minster-in-Sheppey *Cant* 91–09; P-in-c Queenborough 99–05; AD Sittingbourne 94–00, 03-04 and 06–09; Hon Can Cant Cathl 99–09; Chapl Sheppey Community Hosp 91–98; Chapl Thames Gateway NHS Trust 98–09; rtd 09; PtO *Cant* from 09; Retirement Officer (Ashford Adnry) 11–18. *75 Acorn Close, Kingsnorth, Ashford TN23 3HR* T: (01233) 501774 M: 07961-545934 E: gilbert_spencer@hotmail.com

SPENCER, Graham Lewis. b 48. St Jo Coll Nottm 80. d 82 **p** 83. C Leic St Anne 82–85; P-in-c Frisby-on-the-Wreake w Kirby Bellars 85–86; TV Melton Gt Framland 86–93; V Upper Wreake 93–99; V Glen Magna cum Stretton Magna etc 99–05; rtd 05; PtO *Leic* from 05. *18 Chetwynd Drive, Melton Mowbray LE13 0HU* T: (01664) 564266 E: grahamandtrish@talktalk.net

SPENCER, Ian John. b 61. Qu Coll Birm 03. d 05 **p** 06. C Gt Malvern St Mary *Worc* 05–08; Warden Dioc Retreat Ho (Holland Ho) Cropthorne from 08. *Holland House, Main Street, Cropthorne, Pershore WR10 3NB* T: (01386) 860330 E: ian.spencer@hollandhouse.org

SPENCER, Joan. b 50. d 98 **p** 99. OLM Nor St Mary Magd w St Jas 98–20; PtO from 20. *94 Mousehold Avenue, Norwich NR3 4RS* T: (01603) 404471 E: revjoan@virginmedia.com

SPENCER, Jordan John Lyndon. b 95. Univ of Wales (Trin St Dav) BTh 20 FRSA 16. Ridley Hall Cam 17 St Padarn's Inst 19. d 20 **p** 21. C W Cemaes *St D* from 20. *6 Gwaun View, Fishguard SA65 9LF* T: (01348) 874144 E: revjordanspencer@gmail.com

SPENCER, Mrs Margot Patricia Winifred. b 48. Coll of St Matthias Bris CertEd 69. STETS 98. d 01 **p** 02. NSM Wonersh w Blackheath *Guildf* 01–05; NSM Busbridge and Hambledon from 05. *24 Park Road, Godalming GU7 1SH* T: (01483) 416333 E: margotspencer@btinternet.com

SPENCER, Peter Roy. b 40. CertEd. Sarum & Wells Th Coll 72. d 74 **p** 75. C Northampton St Alb *Pet* 74–77; TV Cov E 77–90; V Erdington St Barn *Birm* 90–02; TR Erdington 02–07;

Chapl John Taylor Hospice Birm 90–07; rtd 07; PtO *Birm* from 07. *15 Poplar Road, Smethwick B66 4AW* T: 0121-429 4514 E: p.r.spencer@btinternet.com

SPENCER, Richard Dennis. b 50. Imp Coll Lon BSc 71. NTMTC 93. d 96 **p** 97. C Leek and Meerbrook *Lich* 96–00; P-in-c Shrewsbury H Trin w St Julian 00–10; V 10–15; TV Saffron Walden and Villages *Chelmsf* 15–19; rtd 19; PtO *Chelmsf* from 20. *2 Cowlins, Harlow CM17 0FZ*

SPENCER, Robert. b 48. St Jo Coll Nottm. d 93 **p** 94. NSM Ellon *Ab* 93–95 and from 99; NSM Cruden Bay 93–95; NSM Fraserburgh w New Pitsligo 95–99; P-in-c Oldmeldrum from 09. *12 Riverview Place, Ellon AB41 9NW* T: (01358) 723193 E: revbob.spencer@btinternet.com

SPENCER, Canon Stephen Christopher. b 60. Ball Coll Ox BA 82 DPhil 90. Edin Th Coll 88. d 90 **p** 91. C Harlesden All So *Lon* 90–93; P-in-c Nyamandhlovu Zimbabwe 93–99; R Bulawayo All SS 96–99; V Caton w Littledale *Blackb* 99–03; Dep Prin CBDTI 99–03; Tutor NOC 03–08; Tutor Yorks Min Course 08–12; Co-ord Yorks Regional Tr Partnership 08–10; P-in-c Brighouse and Clifton *Wakef* 10; V 11–14; Tutor Yorks Min Course 14–17; Vice Prin St Hild Coll 17–18; Dir Th Educn Angl Communion Office from 18; Hon Can Musoma from 13; PtO *Bris* from 21. *Anglican Consultative Council, St Andrew's House, 16 Tavistock Crescent, London W11 1AP* T: (020) 7313 3900 E: stephenspencer8@me.com *or* stephen.spencer@aco.org

SPENCER, Stephen Nigel Howard. b 53. Pemb Coll Ox BA 75 MA 03 Jes Coll Cam PGCE 76. Trin Coll Bris 80. d 82 **p** 83. C Partington and Carrington *Ches* 82–85; C Brunswick *Man* 85–88; Chapl UEA *Nor* 88–92; rtd 92; PtO *Nor* 92–95; *Ely* from 19. *1 Forty Acre Road, Trumpington, Cambridge CB2 9AL*

SPENCER, Stephen Robert. b 61. NTMTC BA 08. d 08 **p** 09. C Langdon Hills *Chelmsf* 08–11; V Eastwood 11–19; V Bromley Common St Aug w St Luke *Roch* from 19. *The Vicarage, Southborough Lane, Bromley BR2 8AT* T: (020) 8467 1351 E: revsteve.spencer@btinternet.com

SPENCER, Canon Susan. b 47. EMMTC 87. d 90 **p** 94. Par Dn Cotgrave *S'well* 90–94; C 94–98; P-in-c Rolleston w Fiskerton, Morton and Upton 98–10; Asst Warden of Readers 98–07; AD S'well 07–10; Jt AD S'well and Newark 08–09; Hon Can S'well Minster 08–10; rtd 10; PtO *Linc* 16–19. *15 Cherry Avenue, Branston, Lincoln LN4 1UY* T: (01522) 823947 E: suespencer47@googlemail.com

SPENCER, Mrs Susan Lesley. b 55. d 00 **p** 01. OLM Middleton and Thornham *Man* from 00. *20 Chiltern Close, Shaw, Oldham OL2 7RL* E: suelspencer@yahoo.co.uk

SPENCER, Sylvia. d 98. Chapl Grampian Univ Hosp NHS Trust 98–03; Chapl NHS Grampian from 04; NSM Ellon *Ab* from 99. *12 Riverview Place, Ellon AB41 9NW* T: (01358) 723193 E: revsylvia.spencer@btinternet.com

SPENCER-THOMAS, Canon Owen Robert. b 40. MBE 08. Lon Univ BSc(Soc) 70 Westmr Univ DLitt 10 LGSM 96 MRTvS 76. Westcott Ho Cam 70. d 72 **p** 73. C S Kensington St Luke *Lon* 72–76; Lect RS S Kensington Inst 74–76; Dir Lon Chs Radio Workshop & Relig Producer BBC 76–78; Relig Producer Anglia TV 78–95; LtO *Lon* 76–87; NSM Cambridge Ascension *Ely* 87–07; Chapl St Jo Coll Sch Cam 93–98; Chapl St Bede's Sch Cam 96–97; Chapl Ch Coll Cam 97–01; Dioc Dir of Communications *Ely* 02–07; Bp's Press Officer 07–11; Hon Can Ely Cathl 04–11; PtO 11–21. *52 Windsor Road, Cambridge CB4 3JN* T: (01223) 358446 M: 07801-492151 E: owenst@btinternet.com

SPICER, David John. b 52. Sussex Univ BA 76 Lon Univ MTh 78. Westcott Ho Cam 77. d 79 **p** 80. C E Dulwich St Jo *S'wark* 79–82; C Richmond St Mary w St Matthias and St Jo 82–87; V Lewisham St Swithun 87–91; Chapl Community of All Hallows Ditchingham 91–17; rtd 17; PtO *Nor* from 18. *28 Pakefield Road, Lowestoft NR33 0HU* T: (01502) 580129

SPICER, Leigh Edwin. b 56. Birm Univ MA 02. Sarum & Wells Th Coll 78. d 81 **p** 82. C Harborne St Pet *Birm* 81–83; C Bloxwich *Lich* 83–87; Chapl RAF 87–11; PtO *S & B* from 12. *Dolyfelin, Llanbister Road, Llandrindod Wells LD1 6SP* T: (01597) 851109

SPICER, Canon Nicolas. b 61. Univ of Wales (Lamp) BA 84. Coll of Resurr Mirfield 84. d 86 **p** 87. C Westbury-on-Trym H Trin *Bris* 86–89; C Willesden Green St Andr and St Fran *Lon* 89–93; Chapl Asst Charing Cross Hosp Lon 93–94; Asst Chapl Hammersmith Hosps NHS Trust 94–97; R Ardleigh and The Bromleys *Chelmsf* 97–07; P-in-c Worksop Priory *S'well* 07–11; V from 11; P-in-c Worksop St Paul from 13; Hon Can S'well Minster from 17. *The Vicarage, Cheapside, Worksop S80 2HX* T: (01909) 472180 E: vicar@worksoppriory.co.uk

SPICER, Robert Patrick. b 39. FCA 68. SAOMC 94. d 97 **p** 98. NSM Riverside *Ox* 97–01; NSM Beaconsfield 01–07; PtO from 07. *16 Hayse Hill, Windsor SL4 5SZ* T: (01753) 864697 E: spicerrevrob@aol.com

SPIERS, The Ven Peter Hendry. b 61. St Jo Coll Dur BA 82. Ridley Hall Cam 83. **d** 86 **p** 87. C W Derby St Luke *Liv* 86–90; TV Everton St Pet 90–95; V Everton St Geo 95–05; P-in-c Gt Crosby St Luke 05–13; V 13–15; Adn Knowsley and Sefton from 15; Hon Can Liv Cathl from 06. *2A Monfa Road, Bootle L20 6BQ* E: pete.spiers@liverpool.anglican.org

SPIERS, Philip John. b 55. Reading Univ BSc 76. Ripon Coll Cuddesdon 10. **d** 13 **p** 14. NSM Darby Green and Eversley *Win* 13–17; NSM Minchinhampton w Box and Amberley *Glouc* from 17. *The Rectory, Amberley, Stroud GL5 5JG* T: (01453) 873176 E: spiersjohn@talk21.com

SPIKIN, Simon John Overington. b 48. Nottm Univ BTh 74 K Coll Lon MTh 80 Univ of Wales (Lamp) MA 11 NW Univ S Africa PhD 21. Linc Th Coll 70. **d** 75 **p** 76. C Sawbridgeworth *St Alb* 75–79; C Odiham w S Warnborough and Long Sutton *Win* 79–81; R Dickleburgh w Thelveton w Frenze and Shimpling *Nor* 81–82; P-in-c Dickleburgh w Thelveton, Frenze, Shimpling etc 81–82; R Dickleburgh, Langmere, Shimpling, Thelveton etc 82–96; rtd 96; PtO *Cant* 01–12. *Marley Court, Kingston, Canterbury CT4 6JH* T: (01227) 832405

SPILLER, Canon David Roger. b 44. St Jo Coll Dur BA 70 Fitzw Coll Cam BA 72 MA 76 Nottm Univ DipAdEd 80. Ridley Hall Cam 70. **d** 73 **p** 74. C Bradf Cathl 73–77; C Stratford-on-Avon w Bishopton *Cov* 77–80; Chapl Geo Eliot Hosp Nuneaton 80–90; V Chilvers Coton w Astley *Cov* 80–90; RD Nuneaton 84–90; Prin Aston Tr Scheme 90–97; C Kings Norton *Birm* 98–99; C Shirley 99–00; Dir of Min and Dioc Dir of Ords *Cov* 00–11; Hon Can Cov Cathl 04–11; rtd 11; PtO *Cov* from 12; *Worc* from 12. *Pear Tree Cottage, Wick Road, Little Comberton, Pershore WR10 3EG* T: (01386) 710725 E: rogerspiller@btinternet.com

SPINDLER, Miss Jane Diana. b 54. Southn Univ BA 75 CertEd 76. Wycliffe Hall Ox 87. **d** 89 **p** 94. C Bishopsworth *Bris* 89–93; C Brislington St Luke 93–94; rtd 95; PtO *Bris* from 95. *3 Crab Tree Close, Malmesbury SN16 0AF*

SPINK, Mrs Diana. b 40. Ex Univ BA 63 PGCE 64. SAOMC 97. **d** 00 **p** 01. NSM Hemel Hempstead *St Alb* 00–10; rtd 10; PtO *St Alb* from 10. *39 Garland Close, Hemel Hempstead HP2 5HU* T: (01442) 262133 M: 07808-184321 E: diana2spink@hotmail.com

SPINKS, Prof Bryan Douglas. b 48. St Chad's Coll Dur BA 70 BD 79 K Coll Lon MTh 72 Dur Univ DD 88 Yale Univ Hon MA 98 FRHistS 85. **d** 75 **p** 76. C Witham *Chelmsf* 75–78; C Clacton St Jas 78–79; Chapl Chu Coll Cam 80–97; Affiliated Lect Div Cam Univ 82–97; Prof Liturg Studies Yale Univ and Fell Morse Coll 98–07; Prof Liturg Studies and Past Th Yale Univ from 07; PtO *Ely* 02–20. *57 White Birch Drive, Guilford CT 06437, USA* E: bryan.spinks@yale.edu

SPINKS, Christopher George. b 53. Oak Hill Th Coll BA 88. **d** 88 **p** 89. C Hove Bp Hannington Memorial Ch *Chich* 88–92; Travelling Sec UCCF 92–95; Itinerant Min 95–98; Chapl Martlets Hospice Hove 98–11; TV Hove *Chich* 99–10; V Polegate from 11. *Withane, St John's Vicarage, The Thatchings, Polegate BN26 5DT* T: (01323) 485652 E: chrisgspinks@hotmail.com

SPINKS, John Frederick. b 40. Westmr Coll Ox MTh 97. Oak Hill Th Coll 79. **d** 82 **p** 83. NSM Roxbourne St Andr *Lon* 82–89; C Northwood H Trin 89–93; P-in-c Greenhill St Jo 93–96; V 96–04; rtd 04; PtO *Lon* from 04; *Ox* 04–20; *St Alb* from 04. *Woodpecker Cottage, 232 Northwood Road, Harefield, Uxbridge UB9 6PT* T: (01895) 822477 M: 07711-635199 E: woodpecker232@tiscali.co.uk

SPITTLE, Christopher Bamford. b 74. St Jo Coll Dur BA 95. Ridley Hall Cam 97. **d** 99 **p** 00. C Netherton *Liv* 99–03; TR Sutton 03–11; P-in-c Skelmersdale St Paul from 11. *The Vicarage, Church Road, Skelmersdale WN8 8ND* T: (01695) 722087

SPITTLE, Robin. b 57. St Jo Coll Nottm 84. **d** 86 **p** 87. C Ipswich St Fran *St E* 86–91; Min Shotley St Mary CD 91–92; R Shotley 92–99; P-in-c Copdock w Washbrook and Belstead 93–99; V Kesgrave 99–20; V Kesgrave w Lt Bealings and Playford from 21. *4 Wades Grove, Kesgrave, Ipswich IP5 2EF* T: (01473) 623388 E: robinspittle@btinternet.com

SPIVEY, Colin. b 35. ACII 61. Oak Hill Th Coll 74. **d** 76 **p** 77. C Egham *Guildf* 76–79; C Edgware *Lon* 79–83; R Haworth *Bradf* 83–95; Sub Chapl HM Pris Leeds 94–99; V Thorpe Edge *Bradf* 95–00; rtd 01; PtO *Ripon* 01–14; *Leeds* from 14. *12 Micklethwaite View, Wetherby LS22 5HB* T: (01937) 919438 E: cawetherby@live.co.uk

SPOKES, David Lawrence. b 57. Nottm Univ BCombStuds 85. Linc Th Coll 82. **d** 85 **p** 86. C Rushall *Lich* 85–89; TV Thornaby on Tees *York* 89–93; R Yardley Hastings, Denton and Grendon etc *Pet* 02–14; Rural Adv Northn Adnry 05–14; P-in-c Howden-le-Wear and Hunwick *Dur* 14–16; P-in-c Willington and Sunnybrow 14–16; V Hunwick

and Willington from 16; AD Stanhope from 18. *The Rectory, Willington, Crook DL15 0DE* T: (01388) 747914 E: vicar@hunwickandwillington.org.uk

SPONG, Bennett Jarod. b 49. Coll of Charleston (USA) BA 74 Thames Poly PGCE 87. **d** 05 **p** 06. OLM Charlton *S'wark* 05–20; PtO from 20. *10 Mayhill Road, London SE7 7JQ* T: (020) 8853 4457 E: bjspong@hotmail.com

SPONG, Mrs Hilary Vida. b 44. Ex Univ BTh 09 Sarum Coll MA 16. SWMTC 06. **d** 09 **p** 10. NSM St Stythians w Perranarworthal and Gwennap *Truro* 09–12; NSM Feock 11–12; NSM Devoran 11–12; NSM Perranzabuloe and Crantock w Cubert 12–14; rtd 14; PtO *Truro* from 14. *Nansough Manor, Ladock, Truro TR2 4PB* T: (01726) 883315 M: 07855-781134 E: hilaryspong@sent.com

SPONG, Terence John. See MESLEY-SPONG, Terence John

SPOOR, Nigel Christopher Oliver. b 51. Univ Coll Dur BA 73 Heythrop Coll Lon MA 16. **d** 18 **p** 19. C Prestwood and Gt Hampden *Ox* from 18. *30 Westwood Drive, Amersham HP6 6RJ* T: (01494) 765108 M: 07724-122981 E: nigel.spoor@talktalk.net *or* nigel@htprestwood.org.uk

SPRATT, Robert Percival. b 31. MBE 08. FCIOB MRSPH ACABE. Carl Dioc Tr Inst 84. **d** 87 **p** 88. NSM Kendal St Thos Carl 87–89; Chapl HM Pris Preston 89–96; Dir Miss to Pris from 96; Asst Chapl HM Pris Wymott 97–04; Sessional Chapl HM Pris Lanc 04–06; Asst Chapl HM Pris Haverigg from 06; PtO *Blackb* 96–20; *Carl* from 97. *Missions to Prisons, PO Box 37, Kendal LA9 6GF* T/F: (01539) 720475 E: bob@greenstones.org.uk

SPRAY, John William. b 29. Sarum & Wells Th Coll 71. **d** 73 **p** 74. C Clayton *Lich* 73–77; V Hartshill 77–82; P-in-c Aston 82–83; P-in-c Stone St Mich 82–83; P-in-c Stone St Mich w Aston St Sav 83–84; R 84–90; rtd 90; PtO *Lich* 90–16. *2 Belvoir Avenue, Trentham, Stoke-on-Trent ST4 8SY* T: (01782) 644959

SPRAY, Mrs Josephine Ann. b 44. Nottm Coll of Educn TCert 65. SAOMC 95. **d** 98 **p** 99. NSM Watford St Mich *St Alb* 98–02; P-in-c Turvey 02–10; rtd 11; PtO *St Alb* from 11; *Ox* from 11. *121 High Street, Olney MK46 4EF* T: (01234) 713726 E: jo-spray@sky.com

SPRAY, Mrs Karen Patricia. b 55. **d** 06 **p** 07. NSM Littleham w Exmouth *Ex* 06–07; C Honiton, Gittisham, Combe Raleigh, Monkton etc 07–09; P-in-c Clyst St Mary, Clyst St George etc 09–13; C Lympstone and Woodbury w Exton 09–13; C Aylesbeare, Rockbeare, Farringdon etc 09–13; V Aylesbeare, Clyst St George, Clyst St Mary etc 13–17; Hon C E w W Harptree and Hinton Blewett *B & W* 17–20. *20 Summerfield, Woodbury, Exeter EX5 1JF* E: unitedparish@revdkaren.org.uk

SPRAY, Richard Alan. b 43. EMMTC 85. **d** 88 **p** 89. NSM Cotgrave *S'well* 88–96; P-in-c Barton in Fabis 96–01; P-in-c Thrumpton 96–01; P-in-c Kingston and Ratcliffe-on-Soar 96–01; P-in-c Blyth 01–02; P-in-c Scrooby 01–02; V Blyth and Scrooby w Ranskill 02–10; AD Bawtry 06–09; rtd 11; PtO *Sheff* 12–20; *S'well* from 18. *Thorn Lea, Mattersey Road, Ranskill, Retford DN22 8ND* T: (01777) 816048 M: 07971-637670

SPREADBRIDGE, Alison Margaret. b 50. Open Univ BSc 96. SEITE 04. **d** 07 **p** 08. C Dartford St Edm *Roch* 07–11; P-in-c Gillingham H Trin 11–13; rtd 13. *16 Murhill Lane, Plymouth PL9 7FN* M: 07979-013559

SPREADBRIDGE, Paul Andrew. b 49. Greenwich Univ CertEd 02 Kent Univ BA 05. SEITE 98. **d** 98 **p** 03. In RC Ch 98–01; NSM Chatham St Steph *Roch* 02–04; C Orpington All SS 04–07; V Bexley St Mary 07–11; R Chelsfield 11–13; P-in-c Charlestown *Truro* 13–16; P-in-c Par 13–16; rtd 16; PtO *Truro* 16–17; C Stoke Damerel and Devonport St Aubyn *Ex* 17–18. *16 Murhill Lane, Plymouth PL9 7FN*

SPREADBURY, Canon Joanna Mary Magdalen (Jo). b 65. Magd Coll Ox BA 90 MA 93 K Coll Lon PhD 99. Westcott Ho Cam MA 99. **d** 99 **p** 00. C Watford St Mich *St Alb* 99–03; C Leavesden 03–06; V Abbots Langley 06–15; Can Res Portsm Cathl from 15. *51 High Street, Portsmouth PO1 2LU* T: 023-9282 3300 ext 226 E: jo.spreadbury@portsmouthcathedral.org

SPREDBURY, Mary Jane. b 59. Open Univ BA 99. STETS 03. **d** 06 **p** 07. NSM Acton St Mary *Lon* from 06. *6 St Catherine's Court, Bedford Road, London W4 1UH* T: (02) 8995 8879 M: 07803-759886 E: spredbury@btinternet.com

SPRIGGS, John David Robert. b 36. BNC Ox BA 58 MA 63. S'wark Ord Course 73. **d** 75 **p** 76. LtO *Ox* 75–97; Chapl Pangbourne Coll 95–97; PtO *Linc* 97–18; *Eur* from 18; *Cant* from 20. *20 The Rope Walk, Canterbury CT1 2FY* T: (01227) 451718

SPRINGATE, Paul Albert Edward. b 48. Oak Hill Th Coll 81. **d** 83 **p** 84. C Pennycross *Ex* 83–87; TV Sileby, Cossington and Seagrave *Leic* 87–96; Chapl and Warden Harnhill Healing Cen 96–13; Bp's Adv on Healing *Glouc* 03–13;

rtd 13; PtO *Glouc* from 17. *111 North Home Road, Cirencester GL7 1DU* M: 07748-846164

SPRINGBETT, John Howard. b 47. Pemb Coll Cam BA 70 MA 74. Ridley Hall Cam 70. d 72 p 73. C Ulverston St Mary w H Trin *Carl* 72–76; V Dewsbury Moor *Wakef* 76–84; V Hoddesdon *St Alb* 84–00; RD Cheshunt 94–00; TR Shelf w Buttershaw St Aid *Bradf* 00–03; V Woodford Bridge *Chelmsf* 03–14; rtd 14. *Walton Farmhouse, 68 Main Street, Walton, Street BA16 9QF* T: (01458) 899641 E: springbett25@hotmail.com

SPRINGER, Richard Kevin. b 76. Middx Univ BA 98 Birkbeck Coll Lon MSc 06 Cam Univ BTh 13. Westcott Ho Cam 11. d 13 p 14. C De Beauvoir Town St Pet *Lon* 13–16; C St Geo-in-the-East w St Paul 16–18; R from 18. *St George-in-the-East Rectory, 16 Cannon Street Road, London E1 0BH* T: (020) 7481 1345 M: 07730-597513 E: richard.springer@london.anglican.org or richard@stgeorgeintheeast.org

✠**SPRINGETT, The Rt Revd Robert Wilfred.** b 62. Nottm Univ BTh 89 Lon Univ MA 92. Linc Th Coll 86. d 89 p 90 c 16. C Colchester St Jas, All SS, St Nic and St Runwald *Chelmsf* 89–92; C Basildon St Martin w Nevendon 92–94; P-in-c Belhus Park and S Ockendon 94–01; RD Thurrock 98–01; R Wanstead St Mary w Ch Ch 01–10; AD Redbridge 08–10; Hon Can Chelmsf Cathl 08–10; Adn Cheltenham *Glouc* 10–16; Suff Bp Tewkesbury from 16. *Bishop's House, 3 Hill Road, Gloucester GL4 6ST* T: (01452) 489456 M: 07962-273544 E: btewkesbury@glosdioc.org.uk

SPRINGETT, Simon Paul. b 56. Warwick Univ LLB 78 Dur Univ MA 10 Plymouth Univ PGCE 07. Wycliffe Hall Ox 78. d 81 p 82. C Harlow St Mary and St Hugh w St Jo the Bapt *Chelmsf* 81–84; C Gt Clacton 84–86; R Rayne 86–91; Chapl RN 91–14; Chief Exec Officer Aggie Weston's 14–16; Chapl RNR from 14; PtO *Portsm* 14–16; *Ex* from 14. *99 Eggbuckland Road, Plymouth PL3 5JR* T: (01752) 248341 E: simonspringett@yahoo.com

SPRINGFORD, Patrick Francis Alexander. b 45. Wycliffe Hall Ox 71. d 74 p 75. C Finchley Ch Ch *Lon* 74–79; CF 79–00; Rtd Officer Chapl RAChD 00–12; PtO *Eur* from 12; *Cant* 13–17; *Glouc* from 18. *15 Grouse Gardens, Brockworth, Gloucester GL3 4SE* E: patrick.springford@live.co.uk

SPRINGTHORPE, Canon David Frederick. b 47. Open Univ BA. AKC 72. d 73 p 74. C Dartford St Alb *Roch* 73–77; C Biggin Hill 77–80; R Ash 80–89; R Ridley 80–89; R Eynsford w Farningham and Lullingstone 89–94; V Barnehurst 94–04; RD Erith 98–04; R Keston 04–12; Hon Can Roch Cathl 02–12; rtd 12; PtO *Roch* from 12; *Cant* from 13. *38 Alvis Avenue, Herne Bay CT6 8AR* T: (01227) 219853 E: david.springthorpe@btopenworld.com

SPROATS, Mrs Beverley Louise. b 73. St Cath Coll Ox BA 94 MA 98 Cam Univ BTh 13. Ridley Hall Cam 11. d 13 p 14. C Yeadon *Leeds* 13–17; R Jersey St Jo *Win* from 17. *St John's Rectory, La rue des Landes, St John, Jersey JE3 4AF* T: (01534) 861677 M: 07700-731114 E: beverleysproats@gmail.com

SPROSTON, Bernard Melvin. b 37. Cranmer Hall Dur 77. d 79 p 80. C Westlands St Andr *Lich* 79–82; P-in-c Heage *Derby* 82–87; V Heath 87–02; rtd 02; PtO *Derby* from 02. *2 Upwood Close, Holmehall, Chesterfield S40 4UP* T: (01246) 207401 E: bernel@hotmail.co.uk or bernel37@outlook.com

SPRY, Miss Elisabeth Roselie. b 47. Open Univ BA 82. d 06 p 07. OLM Stratton St Mary w Stratton St Michael etc *Nor* 06–16; OLM Long Stratton and Pilgrim TM 16–17; PtO from 17. *13 Whitehouse Drive, Long Stratton, Norwich NR15 2TD* T: (01508) 530478 E: erspry@yahoo.co.uk

SPURGEON, Michael Paul. b 53. Open Univ BA 02 MIEx. Linc Th Coll 83. d 85 p 86. C Lillington *Cov* 85–89; C Min Can Ripon Cathl 89–95; R Lower Nidderdale 95–14; *Leeds* from 14. *Lower Nidderdale Rectory, 6 Old Church Green, Kirk Hammerton, York YO26 8DL* T: (01423) 331142

SPURR, Andrew. b 58. St Jo Coll Dur BA 80. Qu Coll Birm 92. d 93 p 94. C Rainham *Roch* 93–96; C Stansted Mountfitchet *Chelmsf* 96; C Stansted Mountfitchet w Birchanger and Farnham 97; R 97–06; V Evesham w Norton and Lenchwick *Worc* from 06. *Church House, Market Place, Evesham WR11 4RW* T: (01386) 446219 E: vicar@evesham.church

SPURRELL, John Mark. b 34. CCC Ox BA 57 MA 61 FSA 87. Linc Th Coll 58. d 60 p 61. C Tilbury Docks *Chelmsf* 60–65; C Boston *Linc* 65–76; R Stow in Lindsey 76–85; P-in-c Willingham 76–85; P-in-c Coates 76–85; P-in-c Brightwell w Sotwell *Ox* 85–97; rtd 97; PtO *B & W* from 97. *10 The Liberty, Wells BA5 2SU* T: (01749) 678966 M: 07929-725502 E: mspurrell@gmail.com

SPURWAY, Christine Frances. b 54. Cuddesdon Coll 96. d 98 p 99. C Coulsdon St Andr *S'wark* 98–02; P-in-c Riddlesdown 02–05; V 05–16; RD Croydon S 04–16; rtd 16; PtO *S'wark* from 16; *Roch* from 17. *6 Highfield Close,*

Pembury, Tunbridge Wells TN2 4HQ T: (01892) 824563 E: rev.christine54@btinternet.com

SQUIRE, Geoffrey Frank. b 36. Ex & Truro NSM Scheme. d 83 p 84. NSM Barnstaple *Ex* 83–98; NSM Swimbridge w W Buckland and Landkey 98–11; PtO from 11. *Litchdon House, 20 Litchdon Street, Barnstaple EX32 8ND* T: (01271) 344935 E: gfsquire@yahoo.co.uk

SQUIRE, Susan Elizabeth. *See* WIGGINS, Susan Elizabeth

SQUIRES, John Wallace Howden. b 45. Sydney Univ BA 67 DipEd 68 MTh 97 PhD 05 Lon Univ BD 75. Moore Th Coll Sydney ThL 74. d 76 p 76. C Normanhurst Australia 76–78; C Luton St Mary *St Alb* 78–79; Chapl Home of Divine Healing Crowhurst 79–80; C-in-c Putney Australia 80–82; R Longueville 83–97; Dir Inst for Values Univ of NSW 97–02; Dir Aus Human Rights Cen Univ of NSW 03–05. *22 Moorehead Street, Redfern NSW 2016, Australia* T: (0061) (2) 9690 0206 or (2) 9385 3637 F: 9385 1778 M: 41-822 6976 E: j.squires@unsw.edu.au

SQUIRES, The Ven Malcolm. b 46. St Chad's Coll Dur BA 72. Cuddesdon Coll 72. d 74 p 75. C Headingley *Ripon* 74–77; C Stanningley St Thos 77–80; V Bradshaw *Wakef* 80–85; V Ripponden 85–89; V Barkisland w W Scammonden 85–89; V Mirfield 89–96; TR Wrexham *St As* 96–02; Hon Can St As Cathl 00–01; Adn Wrexham 01–10; R Llandegla 02–10; Bp's Chapl 10–11; Can Cursal St As Cathl 10–11; rtd 11; PtO *St As* from 11. *1A Penrhyn Park, Penrhyn Bay, Llandudno LL30 3HW* T: (01492) 544560 M: 07966-200894 E: malcolmsquires1a@gmail.com

SQUIRES, Rachel Louise. *See* SCHEFFER, Rachel Louise Squires

STABLES, Katharine Ruth. b 45. R Holloway Coll Lon BA 67. WMMTC 90. d 93 p 94. NSM Knutton *Lich* 93–05; NSM Silverdale and Alsagers Bank 93–96; Soc Resp Officer 96–99; Officer for NSMs 03–05; P-in-c Startforth and Bowes and Rokeby w Brignall *Ripon* 05–09; rtd 10; PtO *Dur* from 10; *Leeds* from 17. *15 Greenbank, Eggleston, Barnard Castle DL12 0BQ* T: (01833) 650006 E: ruthstables@gmail.com

STACE, Michael John. b 44. Open Univ MA 80. SEITE 94. d 97 p 98. NSM Cant St Dunstan w H Cross 97–01; NSM Cant All SS 01–06; P-in-c 06–14; rtd 14; PtO *Cant* 15–21. *124 St Stephen's Road, Canterbury CT2 7JS* T: (01227) 451169 F: 455627 M: 07831-174900 E: michaelstace31@gmail.com

STACEY, Gillian. *See* STILL, Gillian

STACEY, Graham John. b 68. Lon Bible Coll BA 97. Ripon Coll Cuddesdon 05. d 08 p 09. C Beedon and Peasemore w W Ilsley and Farnborough *Ox* 08–10; C E Downland 10–11; PtO 12–18; *Glouc* from 19. *The Vicarage, 58 Cashes Green Road, Stroud GL5 4RA* M: 07753-687389 E: graham@thestaceys.tv

STACEY, Kate Elizabeth. b 73. Lon Bible Coll BTh 97. Ripon Coll Cuddesdon 05. d 08 p 09. C E Downland *Ox* 08–11; V Wychwood 11–18; TR Stroud *Glouc* from 18. *The Vicarage, 58 Cashes Green Road, Stroud GL5 4RA* T: (01453) 840006 E: rector@stroudparishchurches.org

STACEY, Rosalind Ruth. *See* LA STACEY, Rosalind Ruth

STACEY (née O'BRIEN), Mrs Shelagh Ann. b 55. RGN 83 Bedf Coll Lon BSc 77. NOC 89. d 92 p 94. Par Dn S Elmsall *Wakef* 92–94; C 94–95; C Carleton 95–97; P-in-c 97–99; C E Hardwick 95–97; P-in-c 97–99; V Carleton and E Hardwick 99–14; *Leeds* from 14. *The Vicarage, 10 East Close, Pontefract WF8 3NS* T: (01977) 702478

STACY, Christine Rosemary. b 49. UEA BSc 70 Keswick Hall Coll PGCE 71 Univ of Wales (Ban) MSc 75 Northumbria Univ PhD 94. d 10 p 11. OLM Upper Coquetdale *Newc* 10–18; rtd 18; PtO *Newc* from 18. *Ovenstone, Sharperton, Morpeth NE65 7AT* T: (01669) 640382 E: rosie.stacy65@gmail.com

STAFF, Mrs Jean. b 44. CertEd 64. EMMTC 81. dss 84 d 87 p 94. Old Brumby *Linc* 84–88; C 87–88; C Gainsborough St Geo 88–91; Dn-in-c 91–94; P-in-c 94–96; P-in-c Haxey 96–97; P-in-c Owston 96–97; V Haxey 97–04; V Owston 97–04; rtd 04; PtO *Linc* 17–20. *5 South Furlong Croft, Epworth, Doncaster DN9 1GB* T: (01427) 871422

STAFF, Susan. *See* JACKSON, Susan

STAFFORD, Christopher James. b 67. Birm Univ BSc 88 PhD 92. St Jo Coll Nottm MA 98. d 99 p 00. C Westbrook St Phil *Liv* 99–03; R Newchurch Culcheth w Croft 03–14; TV Newton 14–16; TR from 16. *243 Crow Lane East, Newton-le-Willows WA12 9UB* T: (01925) 271421 E: chrisj.stafford@virginmedia.com

STAFFORD, Mark Anthony. b 64. Huddersfield Univ BSc 92. St Jo Coll Nottm MA 98. d 98 p 99. C Stafford St Jo and Tixall w Ingestre *Lich* 98–01; C W Retford *S'well* 01; TV Retford 02–09; P-in-c Babworth w Sutton-cum-Lound and Scofton etc 08–09; PtO *S'wark* 18–19; TV Kingston from 19. *30 Bloomfield Road, Kingston upon Thames KT1 2SE* T: (020) 8546 9542 M: 07730-799609 E: vicarstjohnskingston@gmail.com

STAFFORD, Matthew Charles. b 73. Wilson Carlile Coll 94 Ripon Coll Cuddesdon 99. **d** 99 **p** 00. C High Wycombe *Ox* 99–02; P-in-c Wrockwardine Wood *Lich* 02–04; R Oakengates and Wrockwardine Wood 04–15; TR Wenlock *Heref* from 15. *The Rectory, 1 New Road, Much Wenlock TF13 6EQ* T: (01952) 727396 M: 07889-376865 E: wenlockrectory@btinternet.com

STAFFORD, Canon Richard William. b 46. Ringsent Tech Inst TCert 69. CITC 96. **d** 99 **p** 00. NSM Annagh w Drumgoon, Ashfield etc *K, E & A* 99–07; P-in-c Drumgoon 07–12; Can Kilmore Cathl 08–12; rtd 12. *12 Cherrymount, Keadue Lane, Cavan, Co Cavan, Republic of Ireland* T: (00353) (49) 437 1173 M: 87-240 4630 E: rwstafford@yahoo.com

STAFFORD, Area Bishop of. *See* PARKER, The Rt Revd Matthew John

STAGG, Jeremy Michael. b 47. Leeds Univ BSc 69 Fontainebleau MBA 77 Southn Univ BTh 94. Sarum & Wells Th Coll 90. **d** 92 **p** 93. C Basing *Win* 92–96; P-in-c Barton, Pooley Bridge and Martindale *Carl* 96–99; Hon CMS Rep 96–99; C Burgh-by-Sands and Kirkbampton w Kirkandrews etc *Carl* 99–00; C Barony of Burgh 00–01; P-in-c Distington 01–05; Dioc Past Sec 00–05; TR Cheswardine, Childs Ercall, Hales, Hinstock etc *Lich* 05–10; RD Hodnet 06–11; rtd 10; PtO *Lich* 11–20. *27 Fishers Lock, Newport TF10 7ST* T: (01952) 813735

STAGG, Roy Ernest. b 48. **d** 01 **p** 02. OLM Birchington w Acol and Minnis Bay *Cant* 01–04; OLM St Laur in Thanet 04–05. *7 Minster Road, Acol, Birchington CT7 0JB* T: (01843) 841551 M: 07802-406066 E: roystagg@ymail.com

STAGG, Russell James. b 69. SEITE 08. **d** 11 **p** 12. NSM Haggerston St Chad *Lon* 11–12; C Holborn St Alb w Saffron Hill St Pet 12–15; P-in-c Roughey *Chich* 15–17; V Colgate and Roffey from 17. *Roffey Vicarage, 1 Forest Oaks, Horsham RH13 6RX* T: (01403) 252137 M: 07834-735002 E: father.russell@me.com *or* fr.russell@allsaintsroffey.org.uk

STAINER, David John. b 58. RCM BMus 80. St Mellitus Coll BA 11. **d** 11 **p** 12. NSM Collier Row St Jas and Havering-atte-Bower *Chelmsf* 11–15; NSM Rainham w Wennington from 15. *29 Cormorant Walk, Hornchurch RM12 5HE* T: (01708) 550053 M: 07870-820314 E: davidjstainer@hotmail.co.uk

STAINER, Helene Lindsay. b 59. SWMTC 01. **d** 04 **p** 05. NSM Ivybridge w Harford *Ex* 04–09; P-in-c Milverton w Halse and Fitzhead *B & W* 09–10; R Milverton w Halse, Fitzhead and Ash Priors from 10; RD Tone from 19. *The Vicarage, Parsonage Lane, Milverton, Taunton TA4 1LR* T: (01823) 400305 E: helenestainer@aol.com

STAINER, Canon Richard Bruce. b 62. Anglia Ruskin Univ MA 09. Linc Th Coll 92. **d** 94 **p** 95. C N Walsham w Antingham *Nor* 94–97; R Cogenhoe and Gt and Lt Houghton w Brafield *Pet* 97–14; RD Wootton 01–07; V Higham Ferrers w Chelveston 14–19; R Blisworth, Alderton, Grafton Regis etc from 19; Can Pet Cathl from 12. *The Rectory, 37 High Street, Blisworth, Northampton NN7 3BJ* E: canon.stainer@gmail.com

STAINES, Edward Noel. b 26. Trin Coll Ox BA 48 BSc 49 MA 52 MSc 85. Chich Th Coll 51 57. **d** 57 **p** 58. C Eastbourne St Mary *Chich* 57–61; V Amberley w N Stoke 61–70; V Forest Row 70–75; V Bexhill St Aug 75–79; TR Ovingdean w Rottingdean and Woodingdean 79–85; V Rottingdean 85–86; Chapl Gtr Lisbon *Eur* 88; Chapl Marseille 90; rtd 90; PtO *Worc* 86–09. *4 Little Penny Rope, Pershore WR10 1QN* T: (01386) 554382

STALEY, John Colin George. b 44. Hull Univ MA 83. Wycliffe Hall Ox 68. **d** 71 **p** 72. C Tinsley *Sheff* 71–73; C Slaithwaite w E Scammonden *Wakef* 73–75; V Wakef St Andr and St Mary 75–80; Warden Scargill Ho 80–82; P-in-c Macclesfield St Pet *Ches* 82–85; TV Macclesfield Team 85–86; Sen Ind Chapl 86–99; Hon Ind Chapl 99–02; PtO 10–14 and from 20. *2 Gleave Avenue, Bollington, Macclesfield SK10 5LX* T: (01625) 477771 M: 07824-736383 E: jojasta@outlook.com

STALKER, William John. b 49. NOC 89. **d** 91 **p** 92. C Formby H Trin *Liv* 91–94; V Stoneycroft All SS 94–03; Chapl R Liv Univ Hosp NHS Trust 94–03; P-in-c Lowton St Mary *Liv* 03–13; TR Lowton and Golborne 13–14; rtd 14. *Hilltop House, Oubas Hill, Ulverston LA12 7LB* E: flostalker@aol.com

STALLARD, The Ven Mary Kathleen Rose. b 67. Selw Coll Cam BA 88 Lon Inst of Educn PGCE 90. Qu Coll Birm 91. **d** 93 **p** 97. C Newport St Matt *Mon* 93–96; P-in-c Ysbyty Cynfyn w Llantrisant and Eglwys Newydd *St D* 96–97; V 97–02; Min Can and Chapl St As Cathl 02–03; Can Res St As Cathl 03–11; Dir of Ords and Co-ord of Minl Formation St As 10–11; Chapl St Jos High Sch Wrexham 11–18; Adn Ban from 18; C Llandudno from 18. *The Rectory, 27 Church Walks, Llandudno LL30 2HL* T: (01492) 876624 M: 07779-418007 E: faithdevwxm@gmail.com *or* archdeacon.bangor@churchinwales.org.uk

STALLEY, Brian Anthony. b 38. Oak Hill Th Coll 60. **d** 63 **p** 64. C Summerstown *S'wark* 63–70; Surrey BFBS Sec 70–73; Manager Action Cen BFBS 73–76; R Branston *Linc* 76–91; rtd 91; PtO *Linc* from 91. *6 Sunningdale Grove, Washingborough, Lincoln LN4 1SP* T: (01522) 794164 F: 794663 M: 07941-508445 E: patchyann104@gmail.com

STAMFORD, Dean of. *Vacant*

STAMP, Andrew Nicholas. b 44. Ex Univ BA 67. Sarum Th Coll 67. **d** 69 **p** 70. C S Beddington St Mich *S'wark* 69–73; Tutor Sarum & Wells Th Coll 73–76; Chapl RN 76–81; C-in-c W Leigh CD *Portsm* 81–82; V W Leigh 82–87; R Botley 87–95; V Curdridge and R Durley 94–95; P-in-c Compton, the Mardens, Stoughton and Racton *Chich* 95–08; P-in-c Stansted 95–08; Tutor Bp Otter Coll Chich 95–98; Dioc Rural Officer *Chich* 00–08; rtd 08; Hon C Arlington, Berwick, Selmeston w Alciston etc *Chich* 11–13; PtO *Portsm* from 15; *Chich* from 17. *36 Up Marden, Chichester PO18 9JR* T: (01243) 535010 E: a.stamp@btinternet.com

STAMP, Canon Ian Jack. b 47. Aston Tr Scheme 82 NOC 83. **d** 86 **p** 87. C Tonge w Alkrington *Man* 86–89; V Heywood St Marg 89–98; P-in-c Heywood St Luke w All So 96–98; TR Heywood 98–01; V Bury St Jo w St Mark 01–10; V Walmersley Road, Bury 10–12; Borough Dean Bury 10–12; Hon Can Man Cathl 11–12; rtd 12; PtO *Man* from 12. *10 Unity Crescent, Heywood OL10 3DW* T: (01706) 367788 M: 07816-425881 E: ianstamp10@btinternet.com

STAMP, Philip Andrew. b 53. Linc Th Coll 86. **d** 88 **p** 89. C Barton w Peel Green *Man* 88–91; R Blackley H Trin 91–19; P-in-c Lightbowne 04–19; rtd 19; PtO *Man* from 19. *29 Mough Lane, Chadderton, Oldham OL9 9PJ*

STAMPS, Canon Dennis Lee. b 55. Biola Univ (USA) BA 78 Trin Evang Div Sch (USA) MDiv 83 MA 87 Dur Univ PhD 95. Westcott Ho Cam 90. **d** 92 **p** 93. C Moseley St Mary *Birm* 92–96; Dir WMMTC 96–01; Dean Qu Coll Birm 01–02; Can Res St Alb 02–12; Minl Development Officer 02–12; Dir Min 11–12; R Harpenden St Nic from 12. *The Rectory, 9 Rothamsted Avenue, Harpenden AL5 2DD* T: (01582) 712202 E: dstampsuk@aol.com

⚜**STANCLIFFE, The Rt Revd David Staffurth.** b 42. Trin Coll Ox BA 65 MA 68 Lambeth DD 04. Cuddesdon Coll 65. **d** 67 **p** 68 **c** 93. C Armley St Bart *Ripon* 67–70; Chapl Clifton Coll Bris 70–77; Dir of Ords and Can Res Portsm Cathl 77–82; Provost Portsm 82–93; Bp Sarum 93–10; rtd 10; Hon Asst Bp Eur from 11; Hon Asst Bp Dur from 13; PtO from 13. *Butts House, 15 The Butts, Stanhope, Bishop Auckland DL13 2UQ* T: (01388) 526912 E: david.stancliffe@hotmail.com

STAND, Andrew George. b 68. St Jo Coll Dur BA 06. Cranmer Hall Dur 04. **d** 06 **p** 07. C Bromsgrove St Jo *Worc* 06–09; TV Gornal and Sedgley 09–16; TV Worc SE from 16. *The Vicarage, 11 Jasmine Close, Worcester WR5 3LU* T: (01905) 358150 E: andy.stand@sky.com

STANDEN, David Charles. b 68. K Coll Lon BA 91 AKC 91 PGCE 92 Lon Univ PhD 00. Westcott Ho Cam 01. **d** 03 **p** 04. C Prittlewell St Mary *Chelmsf* 03–07; P-in-c Stratton and Launcells *Truro* 07–11; P-in-c Bude Haven and Marhamchurch 09–11; R Edin St Mich and All SS 11–13; Chapl K Edw Sch Witley 13–19; Chapl HM Pris and YOI Doncaster from 21. *HM Prison and Young Offender Institution, Marsh Gate, Doncaster DN5 8UX* T: (01302) 764323 E: d.c.standen@btinternet.com

STANDEN, Canon Mark Jonathan. b 63. LMH Ox BA 85 Cam Univ BA 94 Barrister 86. Ridley Hall Cam 92. **d** 95 **p** 96. C Sevenoaks St Nic *Roch* 95–99; R Angmering *Chich* from 99; RD Arundel and Bognor from 08; Acting Adn Chich 18–19; Can and Preb Chich Cathl from 19. *The Rectory, Rectory Lane, Angmering, Littlehampton BN16 4JU* T: (01903) 896417 E: markstanden@stmargaretsangmering.church

STANDING, Victor. b 44. Lon Univ BMus 66 Clare Coll Cam PGCE 68 FRCO 67. Ripon Coll Cuddesdon 75. **d** 78 **p** 79. C Wimborne Minster *Sarum* 78–80; TV Wimborne Minster and Holt 80–83; R Ex St Sidwell and St Matt 83–94; Dep PV Ex Cathl 83–01; Chapl R Devon and Ex Hosp 83–94; Chapl W of England Eye Infirmary Ex 83–94; P-in-c Tedburn St Mary, Whitestone, Oldridge etc *Ex* 94–96; P-in-c Dunsford and Doddiscombsleigh 95–96; P-in-c Cheriton Bishop 95–96; TR Tedburn St Mary, Whitestone, Oldridge etc 96–01; RD Kenn 97–01; V New Shoreham *Chich* 01–11; V Old Shoreham 01–11; rtd 11; P-in-c Shanklin St Blasius *Portsm* 11–15; PtO *Lich* 17–19. *23 Abnalls Croft, Lichfield WS13 7BP* T: (01543) 418890 E: victor@victorstanding.plus.com

STANDRING, Rupert Benjamin Charles. b 68. Pemb Coll Ox BA 90 MA 99 Cam Univ BA 94. Ridley Hall Cam 92. **d** 95 **p** 96. C Bromley Ch Ch *Roch* 95–99; Tutor Cornhill Tr Course 99–04; Hon C W Hampstead St Luke *Lon* 99–04; PtO 04–05; Min Mayfair Ch Ch 05–09; Lic Preacher 09–10; P-in-c Fulham St Pet 10–11; V from 11.

56 Langthorne Street, London SW6 6JY T: (020) 7385 4950
E: rupert.standring@googlemail.com

STANES, The Ven Ian Thomas. b 39. Sheff Univ BSc 62
Linacre Coll Ox BA 65 MA 69. Wycliffe Hall Ox 63. d 65
p 66. C Leic H Apostles 65–69; V Broom Leys 69–76;
Warden Marrick Priory *Ripon* 76–82; Officer Miss, Min and
Evang Willesden Area *Lon* 82–92; CME Officer 82–92; Preb
St Paul's Cathl 89–92; Adn Loughborough *Leic* 92–05; rtd
05; PtO *Sarum* from 06. *192 Bath Road, Bradford-on-Avon
BA15 1SP* T: (01225) 309036 E: istanes@btinternet.com

STANESBY, Derek Malcolm. b 31. Leeds Univ BA 56 Man
Univ MEd 75 PhD 84 SOSc. Coll of Resurr Mirfield 56. d 58
p 59. C Lakenham St Jo *Nor* 58–61; C Welling *S'wark* 61–63;
V Bury St Mark *Man* 63–67; R Ladybarn 67–85; Can and
Steward Windsor 85–97; rtd 97; PtO *Leic* 00–15; *Pet* 00–07.
32 Elizabeth Way, Uppingham, Oakham LE15 9PQ T: (01572)
821298

STANFORD, Mark Roger. b 59. St Mellitus Coll MA 21.
Cranmer Hall Dur 96. d 98 p 99. C Aughton Ch Ch *Liv* 98–02;
TV Toxteth St Philemon w St Gabr and St Cleopas 02–11; TR
11–12; AD Toxteth and Wavertree 06–12; Chapl St Hilda's
Sch *Liv* 03–12; P-in-c Formby H Trin *Liv* 12–14; V Formby
H Trin and Altcar from 14; Hon Can Liv Cathl 06–12. *Holy
Trinity Vicarage, 2A Brows Lane, Liverpool L37 3HZ* T: (01704)
386464 E: mark-stanford@hotmail.co.uk

STANFORD, Timothy Charles. b 61. d 11 p 12. C Walton
Breck *Liv* 11–13; P-in-c Worksop St Jo *S'well* from 13.
St John's Vicarage, 1B Shepherds Avenue, Worksop S81 0JD
E: tcs227@gmail.com

STANFORTH, Coryn Hazel. b 71. Hull Univ BA 93 Anglia
Ruskin Univ BA 15 Dur Univ MA 20. Westcott Ho
Cam 18. d 20 p 21. C Newton Flotman, Swainsthorpe,
Tasburgh, etc *Nor* from 20. *The Rectory, Church Road,
Newton Flotman, Norwich NR15 1QB* M: 07436-992347
E: revdcoryn@btinternet.com

STANGHAN, Eileen. b 40. Whitelands Coll Lon CertEd 75.
d 98 p 99. OLM Reigate St Phil *S'wark* 98–10; rtd 10; PtO
S'wark from 10. *20 Saxon Way, Reigate RH2 9DH* T: (01737)
240920 *or* (01293) 430043 E: eileenstanghan@ntlworld.com

STANIER, Robert Sebastian. b 75. Magd Coll Ox BA 98 Selw
Coll Cam BA 05. Westcott Ho Cam 03. d 06 p 07. C Perry
Hill St Geo w Ch Ch and St Paul *S'wark* 06–09; Chapl Abp
Tenison's Sch Kennington 09–13; Hon C N Lambeth and
S Lambeth St Anne and All SS *S'wark* 09–13; V Surbiton
St Andr and St Mark from 13; AD Kingston from 18. *The
Vicarage, St Mark's Hill, Surbiton KT6 4LS* T: (020) 8399 0639
E: robertstanier@btinternet.com

STANIFORD, Canon Doris Gwendoline. b 43. Gilmore
Course IDC 79. Bp Otter Coll *Chich* 80–82. d 87 p 94. Hangleton *Chich* 80–82;
Durrington 82–89; Par Dn 87–89; Chich Th Coll 83–89; C
Crawley and Chapl Crawley Gen Hosp 89–97; Dioc Voc Adv
and Chapl St Cath Hospice Crawley 92–97; Asst Dir of Ords
Chich 97–12; C Southwick St Mich 97–99; Can and Preb
Chich Cathl 08–12; rtd 12; PtO *Chich* from 15. *23 Beechside,
Crawley RH10 6TL* E: staniforddoris@gmail.com

STANIFORTH, Julian Martin. b 59. Aston Univ BSc 82
ACMA 93. SEITE 07. d 10 p 11. C Herne *Cant* 10–14; V
The Six from 14; AD Sittingbourne from 21. *The Vicarage,
Church Lane, Newington, Sittingbourne ME9 7JU* T: (01795)
227329 M: 07879-626115 E: julian.staniforth@gmail.com

STANLEY, Arthur Patrick. b 32. TCD BA 54 Div Test 55 MA 64.
d 55 p 56. C Waterford H Trin *C, F & O* 55–57; CF 58–74;
Dep Asst Chapl Gen 74–83; USA 84–04; rtd 94; PtO *B & W*
05–12. *9 Westbourne Court, Cooden Drive, Bexhill-on-Sea
TN39 3AA* T: (01424) 539307 E: patnpaddy@hotmail.com

STANLEY, Belinda Susan. b 59. Southn Univ BM 82 MRCP 87
FRCP 98 FHEA 11. Qu Foundn Birm 18. d 21. NSM Carl
Cathl from 21. *The Old Vicarage, Dacre, Penrith CA11 0HH*

STANLEY, Canon John Alexander. b 31. OBE 99. Tyndale
Hall Bris. d 56 p 57. C Preston All SS *Blackb* 56–60; C
St Helens St Mark *Liv* 60–63; V Everton St Cuth 63–70;
P-in-c Everton St Sav 69–70; V Everton St Sav w St Cuth
70–74; V Huyton St Mich 74–18; Hon Can Liv Cathl
87–18; AD Huyton 80–92; Chapl to The Queen 93–01; rtd
18; PtO *Ches* from 19; *Liv* from 19. *14 Meadowfield Road,
Chester CH4 7QJ* T: (01244) 678903 M: 07740-621833
E: canonjohnstanley@jastanley.co.uk

STANLEY, Canon Nicola Vere. b 56. Surrey Univ BA 07
MCIPD 83. STETS 99. d 02 p 03. C Bedford Park *Lon* 02–06; V
Twickenham All Hallows 06–14; Asst Dir of Ords Kensington
Area 04–14; Can Res, Prec and Sacr Bris Cathl from 14. *Bristol
Cathedral, College Green, Bristol BS1 5TJ* T: 0117-926 4879
E: canon.precentor@bristol-cathedral.co.uk

STANLEY, Patrick. *See* STANLEY, Arthur Patrick

STANLEY, Peter Vincent. b 60. N Staffs Poly BSc 82. d 20
p 21. *15 St Anne's Close, Worksop S80 3QS* T: (01909)
477391 M: 07931-895939

STANLEY, Canon Simon Richard. b 44. Wells Th Coll 66.
d 69 p 70. C Foleshill St Laur *Cov* 69–71; C Hessle *York*
71–75; P-in-c Flamborough 75–80; R Dunnington 80–92;
P-in-c York St Barn 92–99; P-in-c York St Chad 99–14;
P-in-c York All SS Pavement w St Crux and St Mich 03–09;
P-in-c York St Denys 04–09; Relig Progr Producer BBC Radio
York 94–03; rtd 09; P-in-c York St Chad 09–14; Can and Preb
York Minster 05–14; PtO from 14. *69 Temple Avenue, York
YO10 3RS* M: 07946-466364 E: simonstanley@clara.net

STANLEY, Mrs Susan Dorothy Margaret. b 61. Ox Min
Course 14. d 17 p 18. C Potterspury w Furtho and
Yardley Gobion etc *Pet* 17–20; R Lambfold from 20.
*Hole in the Wall, Main Street, Upper Stowe, Northampton
NN7 4SH* T: (01327) 341307 M: 07745-765575
E: stanley.thehole@btinternet.com

STANLEY-SMITH, James. b 29. Hatf Coll Dur BA 54 DipEd 55.
S Dios Minl Tr Scheme 81. d 84 p 85. C Bournemouth St Jo w
St Mich *Win* 84–87; R Hale w S Charford 87–94; rtd 94; PtO
Win from 94. *10 Rownhams Way, Rownhams, Southampton
SO16 8AE* T: (023) 8073 2529

STANNARD, Miss Beryl Elizabeth. b 36. SRN 62 SCM 64.
Oak Hill Th Coll BA 92. d 92 p 94. Par Dn Streatham Park
St Alb *S'wark* 92–94; C 94–96; C Gerrards Cross and Fulmer
Ox 96–01; rtd 01; PtO *Ox* from 02. *31 Codmore Crescent,
Chesham HP5 3LZ*

STANNARD, Brian. b 46. MICE 71 MIStructE 71. Cranmer
Hall Dur 86. d 88 p 89. C Burnage St Marg *Man* 88–91;
V Walmersley 91–03; TV Westhoughton and Wingates
03–04; rtd 04; PtO *Liv* from 16. *Address temp unknown*
E: b.stannard@btinternet.com

STANNARD, The Ven Colin Percy. b 24. TD 66. Selw Coll
Cam BA 47 MA 49. Linc Th Coll 47. d 49 p 50. C St E Cathl
49–52; C-in-c Nunsthorpe CD *Linc* 52–55; CF (TA) 53–67; V
Barrow St Jas *Carl* 55–64; V Upperby St Jo 64–70; R Gosforth
70–75; RD Calder 70–75; P-in-c Natland 75–76; V 76–84;
RD Kendal 75–84; Hon Can Carl Cathl 75–84; Can Res Carl
Cathl 84–93; Adn Carl 84–93; rtd 93; PtO *Carl* 93–14. *Flat 4,
Manormead, Tilford Road, Hindhead GU26 6RA*

STANNARD, Neill David. b 74. Brunel Univ BA 99 Dur Univ
MA 19 Univ Coll Lon PGCE 00. Ridley Hall Cam 17. d 19
p 20. C Worthing St Matt *Chich* 19–20; C Goring-by-Sea
from 20. *16 St Michael's Road, Worthing BN11 4SD* M: 07368-
987103 E: rev.stannard@gmail.com

STANNARD, Canon Peter Graville. b 59. Univ of Wales (Abth)
BSc(Econ) 81. St Steph Ho Ox BA 85 MA 86. d 86 p 87. C
Worksop Priory *S'well* 86–89; Prin St Nic Th Coll Ghana
89–96; Hon Can Koforidua from 93; TR Shelf w Buttershaw
St Aid *Bradf* 96–99; P-in-c Heaton Norris St Thos *Man* 00–02;
TV Heatons 02–08; P-in-c S Shields St Hilda w St Thos
Dur 08–12; P-in-c S Shields St Aid and St Steph 08–12; C
Houghton le Spring 12–13; rtd 13; PtO *Dur* 13–15; *S'wark*
16–17; *St Alb* from 17; Chapl Luton and Dunstable Univ
Hosp NHS Foundn Trust from 21. *10 Johnson Court, Park Side
Drive, Houghton Regis, Dunstable LU5 5RQ* M: 07428-519778
E: petergstannard@gmail.com

STANNING (née CROMPTON), Mrs Gillian Kay. b 65. Univ
of Wales (Ban) BA 86 Homerton Coll Cam PGCE 87.
SNWTP 07. d 10 p 11. C Norley, Crowton and Kingsley *Ches*
10–13; V Sandbach Heath w Wheelock 13–17; C Borderlands
Miss Area *St As* from 17. *32 Well House Drive, Penymynydd,
Chester CH4 0LB* T: (01244) 541420 M: 07840-627725
E: gill.pioneerpriest@gmail.com

STANTON, Ms Angela. b 59. Loughb Univ BSc 80 Ch Coll
Liv PGCE 81. Westcott Ho Cam 03. d 05 p 06. C Atherton
and Hindsford w Howe Bridge *Man* 05–08; P-in-c Reddish
08–18; R from 18; Hon Assoc Dioc Dir of Ords from 10;
Borough Dean Stockport from 13. *St Elisabeth's Rectory,
28 Bedford Street, Stockport SK5 6DJ* T: 0161-432 3033
E: angiestanton27@yahoo.co.uk

STANTON, The Ven David John. b 60. St Andr Univ
MTheol 82 Ex Univ MA 00 FSAScot 89 FRSA 98. Ripon Coll
Cuddesdon 83. d 85 p 86. C Beckenham St Geo *Roch* 85–88;
Asst Chapl Shrewsbury Sch 88–90; Hon C Shrewsbury All
SS w St Mich *Lich* 88–90; P-in-c Abbotskerswell *Ex* 90–94;
Chapl Plymouth Univ 92–97; P-in-c Bovey Tracey St Jo,
Chudleigh Knighton etc 94–99; V Bovey Tracey St Jo w
Heathfield 99–05; Dioc Voc Adv 95–05; Warden of Readers
96–03; Acting Dioc Dir of Ords 03–05; RD Moreton 98–05;
Can Prec and Can Past Worc Cathl 05–13; Can and Treas
Westmr Abbey from 13; Sub Dean Westmr from 18; Adn
Westmr from 18. *1 Little Cloister, London SW1P 3PL* T: (020)
7654 4804 E: david.stanton@westminster-abbey.org

STANTON, Gregory John. b 47. Sarum & Wells Th Coll 84. d 86 **p** 87. C Willenhall H Trin *Lich* 86–89; C Plympton St Mary *Ex* 89–91; V Milton Abbot, Dunterton, Lamerton etc 91–13; rtd 13; P-in-c Bovey Tracey St Jo w Heathfield *Ex* 13–15; V 15–17. *The Granary, Rubbytown Farm, Tavistock PL19 8PA* E: frgregssc@gmail.com

STANTON, Ms Karen Janis. b 55. NOC 00. d 03 **p** 04. C Withington St Paul *Man* 03–04; C Urmston 04–07; TV Wythenshawe 07–12; R Kinver and Enville *Lich* 12–19; V Hale and Ashley *Ches* from 19. *1 Harrop Road, Hale, Altrincham WA15 9BU* T: 0161-928 4182 M: 07814-254744 E: kaz@thestantons.me.uk

STANTON, Richard Oliver. b 90. Pemb Coll Cam BA 11 MA 15 MPhil 12. Westcott Ho Cam 12. d 15 **p** 16. C Attleborough w Besthorpe *Nor* 15–19; P-in-c Nor St Jo w St Julian from 19. *The Rectory, 8 Kilderkin Way, Norwich NR1 1RD* T: (01603) 626104 E: richard_stanton@btinternet.com

STANTON-HYDE, Mrs Marjorie Elizabeth. b 37. TCert 58. Cranmer Hall Dur 86. d 88 **p** 94. Par Dn Elmley Lovett w Hampton Lovett and Elmbridge etc *Worc* 88–91; Par Dn Wilden 88–91; Par Dn Hartlebury 88–91; Dn-in-c 91–94; P-in-c 94–97; R 97–98; rtd 98; Hon C Gt Malvern St Mary *Worc* 99–02; Warden Jes Hosp Cant 02–05; Chapl Worcs Community and Mental Health Trust 05–12; PtO *Worc* from 12. *4 Severn Drive, Malvern WR14 2SZ* T: (01684) 569589 E: marjemoto@gmail.com

STANTON-SARINGER, Maurice Charles. b 49. Bris Univ BSc 71 PGCE 72 Fitzw Coll Cam BA 77 MA 81. Ridley Hall Cam 75. d 78 **p** 79. C Gerrards Cross *Ox* 78–80; C Bletchley 80–83; Chapl Stowe Sch 83–91; R Sherington w Chicheley, N Crawley, Astwood etc *Ox* 91–06; RD Newport 05–14; TR Loddon Reach 06–13; rtd 13; PtO *Ox* from 13. *23 Western Avenue, Buckingham MK18 1LJ* E: saringer@btinternet.com

STANWAY, Peter David. b 48. K Coll Lon BD 71. St Aug Coll Cant 72. d 73 **p** 74. C Maidstone All SS w St Phil and H Trin *Cant* 73–77; Canada 77–84; C Waterlooville *Portsm* 84–87; R Laughton w Ripe and Chalvington *Chich* 87–90; Chapl Witney Community Hosp 90–91; C Wheatley w Forest Hill and Stanton St John *Ox* 91–92; C Cowley St Jas 93–02; rtd 02; PtO *Ox* 14–20. *20 College Way, Gullane EH31 2BX* E: peterstroudley060@gmail.com

STAPLE, Miss Patricia Ann. b 54. Birm Univ BA 75. St Steph Ho Ox 00. d 02 **p** 05. C Dartmouth and Dittisham *Ex* 02–04; C Colyton, Musbury, Southleigh and Branscombe 04–07; V Athelney *B & W* 07–19; rtd 19. *1 Compton Close, Taunton TA2 7UD* M: 07731-931683 E: triciastaple1@gmail.com

STAPLEFORD, Robin Duncan. b 62. Aston Tr Scheme 92 St Jo Coll Nottm 94. d 96 **p** 97. C Evington *Leic* 96–99; TV Vale of Belvoir 99–08; R Upper Wensum Village Gp *Nor* from 08. *The Rectory, Market Hill, Colkirk, Fakenham NR21 7NU* T: (01328) 853226 E: upperwensumrector@btinternet.com

STAPLES, David. b 35. Jes Coll Ox BA 59 MA 63 BD 75. Linc Th Coll 59. d 61 **p** 62. C Kettering St Andr *Pet* 61–64; C Doncaster St Geo *Sheff* 64–66; Dioc Youth Chapl 66–71; V Mexborough 71–83; Chapl Montagu Hosp Mexborough 71–83; RD Wath *Sheff* 77–83; Hon Can Sheff Cathl 80–83; V W Haddon w Winwick *Pet* 83–88; RD Brixworth 83–89; V W Haddon w Winwick and Ravensthorpe 88–90; ACUPA Link Officer 90–00; rtd 00; PtO *Linc* from 00. *1 Sycamore Close, Bourne PE10 9RS* T: (01778) 423121 E: david.staples@talktalk.net

STAPLES, Jeffrey Joseph. b 61. St Jo Coll Nottm 97. d 99 **p** 00. C Prenton *Ches* 99–03; P-in-c Wallasey St Nic 03–04; P-in-c New Brighton All SS 03–04; V Wallasey St Nic w All SS from 04. *St Nicholas' Vicarage, 22 Groveland Road, Wallasey CH45 8JY* T: 0151-639 3589 E: jeffstaples4@hotmail.com

STAPLES, John Michael. b 45. STETS 94. d 97 **p** 98. C Tisbury *Sarum* 97–01; P-in-c Barford St Martin, Dinton, Baverstock etc 00–01; TV Nadder Valley 01–08; C Fovant, Sutton Mandeville and Teffont Evias etc 06–08; rtd 08; PtO *Sarum* from 08. *Crabstone Cottage, Locarno Road, Swanage BH19 1HY* T: (01929) 421715 E: john_staples@btinternet.com

STAPLES, John Wedgwood. b 42. Hertf Coll Ox BA 64 MA. Wycliffe Hall Ox 64. d 66 **p** 67. C Yardley St Edburgha *Birm* 66–69; C Knowle 69–74; R Barcombe *Chich* 74–81; V Old Windsor Ox 81–96; P-in-c Pangbourne w Tidmarsh and Sulham 96–99; R 99–07; rtd 07; PtO *Win* from 07. *6 Douglas Road, Bournemouth BH6 3ER* T: (01202) 425859 E: revdjohn.staples@gmail.com

STAPLES, Canon Peter Brian. b 38. Ely Th Coll 63 Brasted Th Coll 64 Bps' Coll Cheshunt 66. d 68 **p** 69. C Birkdale St Jas *Liv* 68–71; C Sevenoaks St Jo *Roch* 71–74; V Treslothan *Truro* 74–80; V Truro St Paul and St Clem 80–02; Hon Can Truro Cathl 98–02; rtd 02; PtO *St E* 03–20. *25 Osmund*

Walk, Bury St Edmunds IP33 3UU T: (01284) 760620 E: canonpeter@hotmail.com

STAPLETON, The Very Revd Henry Edward Champneys. b 32. MBE 09. FSA 74 Pemb Coll Cam BA 54 MA 58. Ely Th Coll 54. d 56 **p** 57. C York St Olave w St Giles 56–59; C Pocklington w Yapham-cum-Meltonby, Owsthorpe etc 59–61; R Seaton Ross w Everingham and Bielby and Harswell 61–67; RD Weighton 66–67; R Skelton by York 67–75; V Wroxham w Hoveton *Nor* 75–81; P-in-c Belaugh 76–81; Can Res and Prec Roch Cathl 81–88; Dean Carl 88–98; rtd 98; PtO *Wakef* 98–14; *Leeds* from 14; *York* from 03. *Rockland House, 20 Marsh Gardens, Honley, Huddersfield HD9 6AF* T: (01484) 666629 E: hec.stapleton@talktalk.net

STAPLETON, Robert Vauvelle. b 47. St Jo Coll Dur BA 70. Cranmer Hall Dur. d 71 **p** 72. C Moreton *Ches* 71–73; C Monkwearmouth All SS *Dur* 73–76; C Stranton 76–79; P-in-c Kelloe 79–86; V New Shildon 86–96; R Stoke Albany w Wilbarston and Ashley etc *Pet* 96–04; P-in-c Somborne w Ashley *Win* 04–12; Dioc Rural Officer 04–12; rtd 12; PtO *York* from 12. *14 St Mary's Way, Thirsk YO7 1BS* T: (01845) 522676 E: robertstapleton@hotmail.com

STARES, Mrs Olive Beryl. b 33. Sarum Th Coll 83. dss 86 d 87 **p** 94. Crofton *Portsm* 86–87; Hon C 87–01; rtd 01; PtO *Portsm* from 05. *62 Mancroft Avenue, Hill Head, Fareham PO14 2DD* T: (01329) 668540 E: berylstares@hotmail.co.uk

STARK, Mrs Beverley Ann. b 52. Bp Otter Coll CertEd 73 EMMTC 92. d 92 **p** 94. Par Dn Bulwell St Jo *S'well* 92–94; C 94–97; TV Bestwood 97–03; V Bestwood Em w St Mark 03–04; R Ironstone Villages *Leic* 04–16; RD Framland 06–11; rtd 16; PtO *Linc* 17–20. *2 Church Walk, Great Hale, Sleaford NG34 9LL* E: beverley.stark@btinternet.com

STARK, Margaret Alison. b 46. Univ of Wales BA 70 BA 71. St Mich Coll Llan. d 90 **p** 97. C Llanishen and Lisvane *Llan* 90–93; C Llanishen 93–94; C Aberavon 94–98; R Llanfabon 98–01; rtd 01; PtO *Llan* from 04. *6 Alexandra House, Beach Road, Penarth CF64 1FN* T: (029) 2070 1303 E: stark545@btinternet.com

STARK TOLLER, Peter Sheridan. b 74. Pemb Coll Ox BA 96 MA Nottm Univ PGCE 97. Wycliffe Hall Ox 11. d 13 **p** 14. C Dibden *Win* 13–18; R from 18. *c/o St Andrew's Church, Beaulieu Road, Dibden Purlieu, Southampton SO45 4PT* M: 07758-006578 E: peter@starktoller.co.uk *or* rector@dibdenchurches.org

STARKEY, Michael Stuart. b 63. LMH Ox BA 85 Nottm Univ BTh 92 MA 93. St Jo Coll Nottm 90. d 93 **p** 94. C Ealing St Mary *Lon* 93–95; C Brownswood Park 95–97; P-in-c 97–01; V Twickenham Common H Trin 01–09; V Kennington St Mark *S'wark* 09–11; V Llanidloes w Llangurig *Ban* 11–13; Can Ban Cathl 12–13; Tutor Wilson Carlile Coll of Evang from 14; PtO *Man* from 14; Hd of Ch Growth from 19. *1 Princess Court, 38 Circular Road, Manchester M20 3LP* T: 0161-434 6306 M: 07870-281055 E: revstarkey@yahoo.co.uk

STARKEY, Ms Naomi Ernestine. b 65. LMH Ox BA 86. St Seiriol Cen 11. d 14 **p** 15. NSM Bro Cyfeiliog and Mawddwy *Ban* 14–15; C Bro Enlli 15–18; C Bro Dwynwen 18–19; Min Area Ldr Bro Padrig from 19; Pioneer Ev from 19. *The Rectory, Ffordd Caergybi, Llanfairpwllgwyngyll LL61 5SX* T: (01248) 713421 E: naomi.starkey@gmail.com

STARKEY, Susan Anne. b 52. St Jo Coll Nottm. d 97 **p** 98. C Watford St Luke *St Alb* 97–02; C Oxhey All SS 02–04; V Findern *Derby* 04–21; V Willington 04–21; rtd 21. *Address temp unknown* E: susan.starkey@btopenworld.com

STARKIE, Catherine Vivienne. b 54. Qu Foundn (Course) 14. d 17 **p** 18. OLM Mid Trent *Lich* from 17. *3 Old School Close, Weston, Stafford ST18 0HF* T: (01889) 271046

STARKINGS, Susan Anne. b 52. Kent Univ BSc 82 Sheff City Poly MSc 90 Punjab Univ PhD 93. SEITE 08. d 11 **p** 12. NSM G7 Benefice *Cant* 11–14; C King's Wood 14–19; rtd 19; PtO *Cant* from 20. *Stable Cottage, Polla House, Church Lane, Hothfield, Ashford TN26 1EL* T: (01233) 643497 E: sue.starkings@btinternet.com

STARLING, Deborah Mary Patricia. b 57. d 13 **p** 14. NSM Dawlish, Cofton and Starcross *Ex* 15–16; NSM Melton Mowbray *Leic* 17–18; PtO 18–21; Dioc Disability Awareness Adv 18–19. *23 Courtfield Close, Sudbrooke, Lincoln LN2 2QN* M: 07863-398707 E: debbiestarling@btinternet.com

STARLING, Timothy Gordon James. b 69. Ripon Coll Cuddesdon 16. d 18 **p** 19. C StowCaple *Heref* 18–21; P-in-c Wye Reaches Gp from 21. *28 Grange Park, Whitchurch, Ross-on-Wye HR9 6EA* M: 07980-204572 E: revtimstarling@gmail.com

STARNS, Helen Edna. *See* PATTEN, Helen Edna

STARR, Michael Richard. b 43. Sarum Th Coll 65. d 68 **p** 69. C Plymouth St Pet *Ex* 68–72; C Blackpool St Paul *Blackb* 72–74; V Burnley St Cuth 74–79; C Eastbourne St Mary

Chich 79–84; P-in-c Eastbourne Ch Ch 84–87; V 87–88; R Guernsey Ste Marie du Castel *Win* 88–01; V Guernsey St Matt 94–01; Vice-Dean Guernsey 99–01; P-in-c Win St Bart 01–08; rtd 09; PtO *Win* from 09. *62 Beresford Road, Chandler's Ford, Eastleigh SO53 2LY* T: (023) 8036 1505 E: michael_starr@hotmail.co.uk

STARTIN, Frank David. b 60. Qu Foundn (Course) 14. **d** 17 **p** 18. NSM Winshill *Derby* 17–19; NSM Hartshorne and Bretby 17–19; NSM Winshill and Bretby from 20. *91 Scalpcliffe Road, Burton-on-Trent DE15 9AB* T: (01283) 566736 E: frankstartin@gmail.com

STARTIN, Nicola Gail. b 57. K Coll Lon LLB 79. St Steph Ho Ox 88. **d** 90 **p** 96. C Wellingborough All SS *Pet* 90–92; NSM Pyle w Kenfig *Llan* 94–95; Asst Chapl Mid Kent Healthcare NHS Trust 95–97; Chapl HM Pris E Sutton Park 97–00; Chapl HM Pris Haslar 00–02; Chapl Haslar Immigration Removal Cen 02–18. *Address temp unknown*

STATHAM, Brian Edward. b 55. K Coll Lon MA AKC 76. St Steph Ho Ox 77. **d** 78 **p** 79. C Ches H Trin 78–81; C Birkenhead Priory 81–82; TV 82–86; V Newton 86–91; SSF 91–94; TV Horsham *Chich* 95–99; Chapl Horsham Gen Hosp 95–99; TV Ches 99–03; P-in-c Stockport St Matt 03–07; C Edgeley and Cheadle Heath 07–10; V Milton *Lich* 10–19; P-in-c Norton in the Moors 18–19; R Milton and Norton 19–20; RD Leek 15–20; rtd 20; PtO *Lich* from 20. *35 Meeanee Drive, Nantwich CW5 5JN* M: 07724-133215 E: brianstatham1955@btinternet.com

STATHER, Thomas William John. b 79. Van Mildert Coll Dur BSc 00. St Steph Ho Ox BTh 04. **d** 04 **p** 05. C Colchester St Jas and St Paul w All SS etc *Chelmsf* 04–08; P-in-c Tunstall *Lich* 08–10; V Goldenhill and Tunstall from 10. *Christ Church Vicarage, 26 Stanley Street, Tunstall, Stoke-on-Trent ST6 6BW* T: (01782) 838288 E: john_stather@hotmail.com

STATON, Preb Geoffrey. b 40. Wells Th Coll 64. **d** 66 **p** 67. C Wednesfield St Thos *Lich* 66–69; C Cannock 69–72; V Cheddleton 72–82; RD Leek 77–82; V Harlescott 82–90; TR Penkridge 90–05; rtd 05; C Colton, Colwich and Gt Haywood *Lich* 05–10; C Abbots Bromley, Blithfield, Colton, Colwich etc 11–13; Preb Lich Cathl 87–10; PtO 13–21. *5 Hunters Close, Great Haywood, Stafford ST18 0GF* T: (01889) 882081 M: 07971-016494 E: geoffrey.staton@virgin.net

STATTER, Ms Deborah Hilary. b 55. **d** 00 **p** 01. OLM Everton St Pet *Liv* 00–02; OLM Everton St Pet w St Chrys 02–04; C 04–08; P-in-c Netherton 08–14; TR 14–17; TR Netherton and Sefton from 17. *St Oswald's Vicarage, 183 St Oswald's Lane, Bootle L30 5SR* T: 0151-525 1882 M: 07952-105466 E: debbie.statter@btinternet.com

STAUNTON, Mrs Mary Provis. b 52. Leic Univ BSc 74. EMMTC 05. **d** 07 **p** 08. NSM Mickleover All SS *Derby* 07–14; NSM Mickleover St Jo 07–14; NSM Mickleover from 14. *165A Pastures Hill, Littleover, Derby DE23 4AZ* T: (01332) 510264 E: mps52@staunton.force9.co.uk

STAVERT, Miss Rachel Louise. b 66. Coll of Ripon & York St Jo BEd 88. Cranmer Hall Dur 10. **d** 12 **p** 13. C Penrith w Newton Reigny and Plumpton Wall *Carl* 12–16; TV Cartmel Peninsula from 16. *The Vicarage, Boarbank Lane, Allithwaite, Grange-over-Sands LA11 7QR* M: 07813-962740 E: revrachstav@gmail.com

STAVROU, Stephen Francis. b 83. St Jo Coll Cam BA 05 MA 09 Peterho Cam MPhil 09. Westcott Ho Cam 07. **d** 09 **p** 10. C Bedford Park *Lon* 09–13; Succ S'wark Cathl 13–16; Chapl K Coll Lon 13–16; TV Barnes from 16; Dir Ords Kingston Area from 17. *St Michael's Vicarage, 39 Elm Bank Gardens, London SW13 0NX* T: (020) 8878 7589 *or* 8876 5230 E: vicar@stmichaelbarnes.org

STAYNINGS, Margaret Rose. b 42. **d** 13 **p** 14. OLM Bris Lockleaze St Mary Magd w St Fran 13–16; P-in-c 15–16; PtO from 16. *5 Cotman Walk, Bristol BS7 9UG* T: 0117-935 4540 M: 07542-191959 E: davenmar@hotmail.co.uk

STAYTE, Miss Samantha Mary. b 71. Ex Coll Ox BA 92 MPhil 02 Ex Univ PGCE 95. Westcott Ho Cam 10. **d** 13 **p** 14. C Summertown *Ox* 13–17; P-in-c Combe Martin, Berrynarbor, Lynton, Brendon etc *Ex* 17–18; R Lynton, Brendon, Countisbury etc from 18. *The Rectory, 20 Lee Road, Lynton EX35 6BP* T: (01598) 752289 E: samanthastayte@hotmail.com *or* priest-in-charge@stmarylynton.uk

STAZIKER, Catherine. b 61. Hull Univ BA 84 Anglia Ruskin Univ BA 13. Westcott Ho Cam 10. **d** 12 **p** 13. C Millhouses H Trin *Sheff* 12–15; C Abbeydale St Jo 12–15; PtO 15–16 and from 18; TV Digswell and Panshanger *St Alb* 16–18; PtO *Roch* from 18; P-in-c Cloughton and Burniston *York* from 21; P-in-c Ravenscar and Staintondale from 21. *Address temp unknown* M: 07968-316812 E: catherinestaziker@btinternet.com

STEACY, William Leslie. b 59. UCD BAgrSc 82 MAgrSc 88 TCD BTh 06. CITC 03. **d** 06 **p** 07. C Dunboyne and Rathmolyon *M & K* 06–10; I Kingscourt w Syddan 10–18; I Athlone w Benown, Kiltoom and Forgney from 18. *The Rectory, Killyon Hill, Bonavalley, Athlone, Co Westmeath, N37 XP08, Republic of Ireland* T: (00353) (90) 647 9984 E: williamsteacy@eircom.net *or* williamlsteacy@gmail.com

STEAD, Canon Andrew Michael. b 63. BA 84 Heythrop Coll Lon MA 12. Coll of Resurr Mirfield 84. **d** 87 **p** 88. C Wellingborough All Hallows *Pet* 87–90; Chapl St Alb Abbey 90–94; Chapl Aldenham Sch Herts 94–04 and 12–13; Ho Master 01–08; Teacher 08–13; PtO *St Alb* 04–12; NSM St Alb Abbey 05–13; Chapl Lich Cathl Sch 13–17; Can Res Lich Cathl from 13; Prec from 17. *24 The Close, Lichfield WS13 7LD* T: (01543) 622510 E: rev.amstead@gmail.com *or* andrew.stead@lichfield-cathedral.org

STEAD, Philip John. b 60. Sheff Univ LLB 82 City of Lon Poly ACII 85. Linc Th Coll 95. **d** 95 **p** 96. C Warsop *S'well* 95–99; P-in-c Forest Town from 99; P-in-c Mansfield Oak Tree Lane from 07; P-in-c Mansfield St Lawr 13–19. *The Vicarage, Old Mill Lane, Forest Town, Mansfield NG19 0EP* T: (01623) 622177

STEADMAN, Mrs Gloria Ann. b 44. STETS BA 04. **d** 04 **p** 05. NSM Farlington *Portsm* 04–08; NSM W Leigh 08–15; PtO 15–16; *Linc* from 16. *56 Nettleham Road, Lincoln LN2 1RH* T: (01522) 402844 E: gloria@freshvisions.co.uk

STEADMAN, Mark John. b 74. Southn Univ LLB 95 Ch Coll Cam BA 01 MA 05 Barrister-at-Law (Inner Temple) 96. Westcott Ho Cam 99. **d** 02 **p** 03. C Portsea St Mary *Portsm* 02–05; P-in-c Camberwell St Phil and St Mark *S'wark* 05–12; AD Bermondsey 08–11; Bp's Chapl 11–15; Adn Stow and Lindsey *Linc* 15–21; Chief of Staff to Abp York from 21. *Bishopthorpe Palace, Bishopthorpe, York YO23 2GE* M: 07870-266553 E: mark.steadman@archbishopofyork.org

STEADMAN-ALLEN, Miss Barbara. b 53. Birm Univ BMus 77 Spurgeon's Coll Lon MTh 00 York Univ MA 21 Trent Park Coll of Educn CertEd 74 ARCM 83. Cranmer Hall Dur 88. **d** 90 **p** 94. C Chessington *Guildf* 90–94; C Chertsey 94–99; P-in-c Mickleham 99–01; C Leatherhead and Mickleham 01–04; Chapl Box Hill Sch 99–04; TV Surrey Weald *Guildf* 04–21; rtd 21. *Allen House, 11 North Street, Dorking RH4 1DN* M: 07711-884941 E: revdbsa@gmail.com

STEAR, Michael Peter Hutchinson. b 47. Goldsmiths' Coll Lon TCert 68. Wycliffe Hall Ox 71. **d** 74 **p** 75. C Streatham Vale H Redeemer *S'wark* 74–77; C-in-c Ramsgate St Mark *Cant* 77–82; V 82–83; Min Jersey St Paul Prop Chpl *Win* 83–94; TR Radipole and Melcombe Regis *Sarum* 94–00; Chapl Weymouth Coll 94–97; rtd 00; PtO *Sarum* from 01. *Flat 3, 5 Widcombe Street, Poundbury, Dorchester DT3 6BH* T: (01305) 520811 E: mphstear@gmail.com

STEBBING, Christopher Henry. b 64. G&C Coll Cam MEng 87 MA 90 St Jo Coll Dur MATM 09. Cranmer Hall Dur 98. **d** 00 **p** 01. C Malin Bridge *Sheff* 00–04; V Sheff St Jo 04–12; Dir IME 4-7 08–12; V Lodge Moor St Luke 12–21; C Crosspool 17–21; Assoc Adn Sheff and Rotherham from 21. *56 Lister Crescent, Sheffield S12 3FU* M: 07874-870159 E: chris.stebbing@sheffield.anglican.org

STEBBING, Michael Langdale (Nicolas). b 46. Univ of Zimbabwe BA 68 UNISA MTh 86. Coll of Resurr Mirfield. **d** 74 **p** 75. C Borrowdale Rhodesia 74–75; P-in-c Chikwaka 76–77; S Africa 79–86; CR from 80; PtO *Leeds* 19–21. *House of the Resurrection, Stocks Bank Road, Mirfield WF14 0BN* T: (01924) 494318 E: nstebbing@mirfield.org.uk

STEDMAN, Preb Michael Sydney. b 34. MRICS 58. Clifton Th Coll 62. **d** 65 **p** 66. C Lindfield *Chich* 65–68; C Gt Baddow *Chelmsf* 68–73; TV Ashby w Thurton, Claxton and Carleton *Nor* 73–75; P-in-c 75–85; TV Rockland St Mary w Hellington 73–75; P-in-c 75–85; TV Framingham Pigot 73–75; P-in-c 75–85; TV Bramerton w Surlingham 73–75; P-in-c 75–85; TV Bergh Apton w Yelverton 73–75; P-in-c 75–85; R Church Stretton *Heref* 85–99; RD Condover 88–96; Preb Heref Cathl 94–99; rtd 99; PtO *St E* 00–21. *44 The Mowbrays, Framlingham, Woodbridge IP13 9DL* T: (01728) 564253 E: michael.gillstedman@yahoo.co.uk

STEED, Christopher Denis. b 55. Lon Univ BD 92 Bris Univ MSc 03 Ex Univ PGCE 01 EdD 05. Sarum Th Coll 05. **d** 06 **p** 07. C Yatton Moor *B & W* 06–10; P-in-c Combe Martin, Berrynarbor, Lynton, Brendon etc *Ex* 11–15; TR Totton *Win* 15–20; rtd 20; PtO *Sarum* from 20; *Win* from 21. *7A Milton Road, Bournemouth BH8 8LP* T: (01202) 097547 M: 07704-138433 E: chrissteed2012.cs@gmail.com

STEED, Mrs Helene. b 70. Uppsala Univ MDiv 95. Past Inst Uppsala 95. **p** 96. C Stora Melby Sweden 96–97; TV Essunga 97–04; Dean's V Cork Cathl *C, C & R* 04–08; I Clones w Killeevan *Clogh* 08–16; Preb Clogh Cathl 11–16; Adn Clogh

14–16; I Dundela St Mark *D & D* from 16. *St Mark's Rectory, 4 Sydenham Avenue, Belfast BT4 2DR* M: (00353) 86-860 3112 E: helenesteed@yahoo.com *or* dundela@down.anglican.org

STEEL, Christine Susan. b 58. All SS Cen for Miss & Min 16. **d** 19 **p** 20. NSM Hey *Man* from 19; NSM Leesfield from 21. *164 Elmsfield Avenue, Rochdale OL11 5XA* T: (01706) 558744 E: csteel58@hotmail.com

STEEL, Coralie Mary. b 47. Bedf Coll Lon BA 69 Solicitor 73. St Mich Coll Llan 98. **d** 01 **p** 02. NSM Llangunnor w Cwmffrwd *St D* 01–12; rtd 12; PtO *St D* from 12. *Llwyn Celyn, 24 Picton Terrace, Carmarthen SA31 3BX* T: (01267) 236369

STEEL, Graham Reginald. b 51. Cam Univ MA. Trin Coll Bris 80. **d** 83 **p** 84. C Gt Parndon *Chelmsf* 83–86; C Barking St Marg w St Patr 86–89; P-in-c Westcliff St Cedd 89–96; P-in-c Prittlewell St Pet 92–96; Chapl Southend Health Care NHS Trust 89–92; V Prittlewell St Pet w Westcliff St Cedd *Chelmsf* 96–07; P-in-c S Trin Broads *Nor* 07–08; R 08–16; rtd 16. *5 Tide Way, Bracklesham Bay, Chichester PO20 8FE* E: grahamrsteel@tiscali.co.uk

STEEL, Leslie Frederick. b 34. Webster Univ Geneva MA 88. St Jo Coll Auckland 57 LTh 65. **d** 59 **p** 60. C Roslyn NZ 59–62; V Waimea Plains 62–69; CF 70–73; Singapore 72–73; V Dunstan NZ 74–81; Adn Otago 77–82; V Anderson's Bay and Chapl Police Force 82–86; Can Dunedin Cathl 82–85; Adn Dunedin 85–86; Hon C Geneva *Eur* 87–90; Chapl Lausanne 90–97; PtO *Pet* 98–99; P-in-c Potterspury, Furtho, Yardley Gobion and Cosgrove 99–02; R Potterspury w Furtho and Yardley Gobion etc 02–04; rtd 04; Hon C Warkworth NZ 04–10; P-in-c Wellsford 10–14; PtO Auckland 14–21. *14 Kaspar Street, Warkworth 0910, New Zealand* T: (0064) (9) 422 2560 E: lfsteel55@gmail.com

STEEL, Norman William. b 53. Sarum & Wells Th Coll 85. **d** 87 **p** 88. C S Woodham Ferrers *Chelmsf* 87–91; R Woolavington w Cossington and Bawdrip *B & W* 91–99; P-in-c Pitminster w Corfe 99–02; Chapl Richard Huish Coll Taunton 99–05; PtO *B & W* 02–05. *49 The Fairways, Sherford, Taunton TA1 3PA*

STEEL, Richard John. b 57. Dur Univ BA 79 Cam Univ MA 86 Edin Univ MTh 97. Ridley Hall Cam 81. **d** 84 **p** 85. C Hull St Jo Newland *York* 84–87; Relig Broadcasting Officer *Derby* 88–92; Dioc Communications Officer *Blackb* 92–97; Communication Dir CMS 97–05; NSM Stoke-next-Guildf *Guildf* 00–05; R Kirkheaton *Wakef* 05–14; Leeds 14–16; RD Almondbury *Wakef* 06–14; AD Leeds 14–16; Miss Team Ldr Linc from 16. *9 Loweswater Close, Waddington, Lincoln LN5 9PU* M: 07900-216363 E: richardsteel03@icloud.com *or* richard.steel@lincoln.anglican.org

STEEL, Thomas Molyneux. b 39. Man Univ BA 61. Ripon Hall Ox 61. **d** 63 **p** 64. C Newc H Cross 63–66; P-in-c Man St Aid 66–71; R Failsworth St Jo 71–79; P-in-c Farnham Royal *Ox* 79–81; P-in-c Hedgerley 80–81; R Farnham Royal w Hedgerley 81–91; V Prescot *Liv* 91–03; rtd 03; PtO *Lon* from 04. *20 Barnet Way, London NW7 3BH* T: (020) 8906 0271 E: t.steel@virgin.net

STEELE, Edwin Harry. b 80. Mattersey Hall BA 05 Anglia Ruskin Univ MA 08. Ridley Hall Cam 06. **d** 08 **p** 09. C Ecclesall *Sheff* 08–11; P-in-c Greenhill 11–15; V 15–16; P-in-c Doncaster St Mary and St Paul 16–18; Bp's Interim Min 18–19; Ch Growth Officer *St Alb* from 19; R Therfield w Kelshall from 20. *The Rectory, Church Lane, Therfield, Royston SG8 9QD* E: rev.harry.steele@gmail.com

STEELE, The Ven Gordon John. b 55. Kent Univ BA 76 Worc Coll Ox BA 82 MA 87. Coll of Resurr Mirfield 82. **d** 84 **p** 85. C Greenhill St Jo *Lon* 84–88; TV Uxbridge 88–94; V Northampton St Alb *Pet* 94–01; V Pet St Jo 01–12; RD Pet 04–10; Adn Oakham 12–21; Can Pet Cathl 04–21; rtd 21. *15 Sutherland Avenue, Shirley, Solihull B90 3HA*

STEELE, Peter Gerald. b 44. Bournemouth Tech Coll BSc 67 Essex Univ MSc 69. Sarum & Wells Th Coll 91. **d** 93 **p** 94. C Beaminster Area *Sarum* 93–97; P-in-c Aldermaston w Wasing and Brimpton *Ox* 97–08; P-in-c Woolhampton w Midgham and Beenham Valance 05–08; R Aldermaston and Woolhampton 08–10; AD Bradfield 07–10; rtd 10; PtO *Sarum* 14–20; *Win* from 18. *19 Tolme Way, Picket Piece, Andover SP11 6FF* T: (01264) 393288 E: petesteele@btinternet.com

STEELE, Canon Terence. b 54. Linc Th Coll 85. **d** 87 **p** 88. C New Sleaford *Linc* 87–90; V Cowbit 90–95; P-in-c Burgh le Marsh 95–97; V 97–06; P-in-c Orby 95–97; V 97–06; P-in-c Bratoft w Irby-in-the-Marsh 95–97; R 97–06; P-in-c Welton-le-Marsh w Gunby 95–97; R 97–06; R Burgh Gp from 06; RD Calcewaithe and Candleshoe 05–17; Can and Preb Linc Cathl from 07. *The Vicarage, Glebe Rise, Burgh le Marsh, Skegness PE24 5BL* T: (01754) 810216 E: father.terry@btclick.com

STEELE-PERKINS, Mrs Barbara Anita. b 46. Whitelands Coll Lon CertEd 68 Spurgeon's Coll MTh 98. STETS 99. **d** 01 **p** 02. Tutor Local Min Progr *Guildf* from 95; NSM Wisley w

Pyrford 01–04; NSM Haslemere and Grayswood 04–18; rtd 18; PtO *Guildf* from 18. *68 Church Road, Milford, Godalming GU8 5JD* T: (01483) 351467 E: barbarasp46@gmail.com

✠**STEEN, The Rt Revd Jane Elizabeth.** b 64. Newnham Coll Cam BA 88 MA 90 PhD 92 Cardiff Univ LLM 18. Westcott Ho Cam 93. **d** 96 **p** 97 **c** 21. C Chipping Barnet w Arkley *St Alb* 96–99; Chapl and Personal Asst to Bp S'wark 99–05; Hon Chapl S'wark Cathl 00–05; Chan and Can Th and Dir Min Tr 05–13; Adn S'wark 13–21; Suff Bp Lynn *Nor* from 21. *Lynn House, Commercial Road, Dereham NR19 1AE* T: (01362) 709200 E: bishop.lynn@dioceseofnorwich.org

STEER, Andrew David. b 67. Huddersfield Univ BA 97 PGCE 98 RGN 88 RM 92. Ridley Hall Cam 14. **d** 16 **p** 17. C Almondbury w Farnley Tyas *Leeds* 16–19; P-in-c Gargrave w Coniston Cold 19–21; P-in-c Kirkby-in-Malhamdale 19–21; V Upper Aire from 21. *The Vicarage, Church Lane, Gargrave, Skipton BD23 3NQ* E: adsteer@icloud.com *or* andrew.steer@leeds.anglican.org

STEER, Norman William. b 35. MBE 00. SRN 57. EAMTC 01. **d** 03 **p** 04. NSM Dickleburgh and The Pulhams *Nor* 03–14; PtO from 14. *Brook Cottage, Harleston Road, Starston, Harleston IP20 9NL* T: (01379) 854245 M: 07941-473255 E: steernorman@gmail.com

STEER, Philip Lloyd. b 36. Ex Coll Ox BA 60. Ripon Hall Ox 60. **d** 62 **p** 63. C Ilkeston St Mary *Derby* 62–65; C Eckington 65–67; V Woodville 67–72; P-in-c Stiffkey w Morston and Langham Episcopi *Nor* 72–74; rtd 96. *15 Front Street, Binham, Fakenham NR21 0AN*

STEER, Simon Morrison. b 58. York Univ BA 81. Princeton Th Sem MDiv 87 Westmr Th Sem (USA) PhD 02. **d** 12 **p** 13. Chapl Abingdon Sch from 12; NSM N Abingdon *Ox* 12–18; PtO from 18. *29 Park Road, Abingdon OX14 1DA* T: (01235) 536529 M: 07758-850086 E: simon.steer@abingdon.org.uk

STEERS, Alan James. *See* COOK, Alan James

STEIN, Mrs Ann Elizabeth. b 57. Loughb Univ BSc 78 Liv Hope MA 01. NOC 05. **d** 07 **p** 08. C Ormskirk *Liv* 07–11; P-in-c Abram 11–17; P-in-c Bickershaw 11–17; TV Chapelfields 17–19; TV Wigan 20–21; rtd 21. *Address temp unknown* E: revannstein@yahoo.com

STEINBERG, Eric Reed (Joseph). b 65. Trin Coll Bris BA 94. **d** 94 **p** 95. C Chigwell and Chigwell Row *Chelmsf* 94–99; Dir Y2000 99–00; Dir Jews for Jesus UK 00–05; Dir CMS from 05; PtO *Ox* from 12. *47 New Bridge Street, Witney OX18 1YA* T: (01865) 787400 E: kosherjoe@mac.com

STENTIFORD, Canon Pauline Cecilia Elizabeth. b 48. EAMTC 98. **d** 00 **p** 01. NSM Gt and Lt Bealings w Playford and Culpho *St E* 00–03; P-in-c 03–13; RD Woodbridge 05–11; Hon Can St E Cathl 08–13; rtd 14; PtO *St E* from 14. *Sheepstor, Boyton, Woodbridge IP12 3LH* T: (01394) 411469 E: pauline@stentiford.com

STEPHEN, Canon Kenneth George. b 47. Strathclyde Univ BA 69 Edin Univ BD 72. Edin Th Coll 69. **d** 72 **p** 73. C Ayr *Glas* 72–75; R Renfrew 75–80; R Motherwell 80–93; R Wishaw 80–93; R Kilmarnock 93–06; R Dalbeattie 06–14; Syn Clerk 87–12; Can St Mary's Cathl 87–12; Hon Can St Mary's Cathl 12–14; rtd 14; LtO Glas from 14. *32 Dalmellington Road, Ayr KA7 3PY* T: (01292) 267065

STEPHENS, Canon Anthony Wayne. b 54. Surrey Univ BSc 80. St Jo Coll Nottm 02. **d** 04 **p** 05. C Preston w Sutton Poyntz, Littlemoor etc *Sarum* 04–08; Pioneer Min Weymouth Town Cen 08–13; P-in-c S Hill w Callington *Truro* 13–16; P-in-c Stoke Climsland 13–16; P-in-c Linkinhorne 13–16; R Callington Cluster 16–20; Chapl Duchy Coll 15–20; Hon Can Truro Cathl 18–20; rtd 20. *13 Hollow Lane, Hayling Island PO11 9AA* E: revtonystephens@icloud.com

STEPHENS, Canon Harold William Barrow. b 47. Lon Univ BEd 71. S Dios Minl Tr Scheme 80. **d** 82 **p** 83. NSM Heytesbury and Sutton Veny *Sarum* 82–83; NSM Bishopstrow and Boreham 83–91; Dep Hd Master Westwood St Thos Sch Salisbury 91–99; P-in-c Market Lavington and Easterton *Sarum* 99–03; P-in-c W Lavington and the Cheverells 02–03; R The Lavingtons, Cheverells, and Easterton 03–07; TR Dorchester 07–13; P-in-c The Winterbournes and Compton Valence 09–13; Can and Preb Sarum Cathl 09–13; rtd 13; PtO *Sarum* from 13. *40 Ashley Place, Warminster BA12 9QJ* T: (01985) 301137 E: rectoryh@googlemail.com

STEPHENS, Mrs Jean. b 46. St As Minl Tr Course. **d** 89 **p** 97. NSM Gwernaffield and Llanferres *St As* 89–02 and 04–09; NSM Hawarden 02–04; NSM Cilcain, Gwernaffield, Llanferres etc 09–12; rtd 13; PtO *St As* from 14. *Noddfa, Pen y Fron Road, Pantymwyn, Mold CH7 5EF* T: (01352) 740037 E: jean.noddfa@btinternet.com

STEPHENS, Jill. *See* STEPHENS, Rosemary Jill

STEPHENS, Mrs Joanna Louise. b 69. St Jo Coll Nottm BA 08. **d** 08 **p** 09. C Bramcote *S'well* 08–10; C Attenborough 10–12; C Toton 10–12; TV Hucknall Torkard 12–19; V W

Hucknall 19–20. *Address temp unknown* M: 07890-385133
E: joke.stephens@talktalk.net

STEPHENS, John Michael. b 29. MRICS 52. Lich Th Coll 62.
d 64 **p** 65. C Birchington w Acol *Cant* 64–70; V Tovil 70–79;
V Brabourne w Smeeth 79–94; RD N Lympne 87–94; rtd 94;
PtO *York* from 94. *Southacre, Kirby Mills, Kirkbymoorside, York
YO62 6NR* T: (01751) 432766

STEPHENS, Martin Nicholas. b 64. Brunel Univ BSc 88 Nottm
Univ MTh 01. St Jo Coll Nottm 99. **d** 01 **p** 02. C Newchapel
Lich 01–04; TV Bucknall 04–16; TR Macclesfield Team *Ches*
from 16. *85 Beech Lane, Macclesfield SK10 2DY* T: (01625)
426110 E: teamrector.macc@gmail.com

STEPHENS, Michael. *See* STEPHENS, John Michael

STEPHENS, Paul. b 53. AGSM 73 Newton Park Coll Bath
PGCE 74. Trin Coll Bris 91. **d** 93 **p** 94. C S Molton w Nymet
St George, High Bray etc *Ex* 93–97; R Norton Fitzwarren
B & W 97–99; Chapl St Aug Sch Taunton 97–99; Chapl
Monkton Combe Sch Bath 99–08; P-in-c Winford w Felton
Common Hill *B & W* 08–19; rtd 19; PtO *B & W* from 20.
Foxcombe House, 38 Crocombe, Timsbury, Bath BA2 0JS

STEPHENS, Canon Penny Clare. b 60. St Anne's Coll Ox
BA 83 Lon Inst of Educn PGCE 85. Oak Hill Th Coll. **d** 99
p 00. C Turnham Green Ch Ch *Lon* 99–03; P-in-c Brasted
Roch 03–10; PtO from 10; Chapl St Joseph's Hospice Hackney
13–17; Chapl Hospice in the Weald from 17; Hon Can Roch
Cathl from 21. *The Oast House, Forest Farm, Pembury Road,
Tonbridge TN11 0ND* T: (01732) 358208 *or* (01892) 820500
E: pennystephens@btinternet.com

STEPHENS, Canon Peter John. b 42. Oriel Coll Ox BA 64
MA 67. Clifton Th Coll 63. **d** 68 **p** 68. C Lenton *S'well*
68–71; C Brixton Hill St Sav *S'wark* 71–73; P-in-c 73–82; TV
Barnham Broom *Nor* 82–89; V Gorleston St Mary 89–94;
RD Flegg (Gt Yarmouth) 92–94; P-in-c High Oak 94–97;
RD Humbleyard 95–98; C Hingham w Wood Rising w
Scoulton 96–97; TR High Oak, Hingham and Scoulton
w Wood Rising 97–05; Hon Can Nor Cathl 99–05; rtd
05; PtO *St Alb* 12–16. *15 Church Row, Wootton, Bedford
MK43 9HQ* T: (01234) 765403 M: 07768-425349 *or* 07973-
322513 E: peterstephens@aol.com

STEPHENS, Mrs Rebecca Louise. b 76. Birm Univ BSc 97
PGCE 98. Qu Coll Birm 12. **d** 14 **p** 15. C Coleshill *Birm*
14–17; C Maxstoke 14–17; R The Whitacres, Lea Marston,
and Shustoke 17–20; Jt AD Coleshill 18–19; Jt AD Coleshill
and Polesworth 19–20; V Maney from 20; Bp's Adv
for Women's Min from 17. *Address withheld by request*
E: revbeckys@gmail.com

STEPHENS, Mrs Rosemary Jill. b 46. SRN 68. WEMTC 96.
d 08 **p** 13. NSM Goodrich, Marstow, Welsh Bicknor,
Llangarron etc *Heref* 08–17; NSM Wye Reaches Gp
08–17; PtO from 17. *Sunnyside Cottage, Coppett Hill,
Goodrich, Ross-on-Wye HR9 6JG* T: (01600) 890975
E: jill.stephens1@btinternet.com

STEPHENS, Canon Simon Edward. b 41. OBE 97. Qu Coll
Birm PhD 80. Bps' Coll Cheshunt 63. **d** 67 **p** 68. C Cov
St Mark 67–71; C Lillington 71–76; C-in-c Canley CD 76–79;
V Canley 79–80; Chapl RN 80–97; Asst Chapl Menorca *Eur*
97–98; Chapl 98–99; Chapl Moscow 99–14; Hon Can Malta
Cathl 01–14; Chapl Solomon Is 14–15; P-in-c Tangier
Eur 16–17; PtO from 17. *119 Hoe Court, Citadel Road,
Plymouth PL1 2RN* E: apokosar@gmail.com

STEPHENS, Mrs Tessa. b 74. Leeds Univ BA 97. St Jo Coll
Nottm MTh 10. **d** 10 **p** 11. C Hipswell *Ripon* 10–14; C
Linthorpe *York* 14–18; Chapl Teesside Univ 14–18; V
Nunthorpe from 18; RD Stokesley from 21. *114 Gypsy
Lane, Nunthorpe, Middlesbrough TS7 0DR* M: 07944-302344
E: tessa.stephens@btinternet.com

STEPHENSON, David. b 76. Huddersfield Univ BMus 98. Qu
Coll Birm 12. **d** 14 **p** 15. C Darwen St Pet *Blackb* 14–18;
C Haslingden w Grane and Stonefold 18; V from 18; C
Musbury 18; V from 18. *The Rectory, Sawley Road, Grindleton,
Clitheroe BB7 4QS* E: frdavidstephenson@gmail.com

STEPHENSON, David John. b 65. Bris Univ BSc(Soc) 87 Dur
Univ BA 91. Cranmer Hall Dur 92. **d** 92 **p** 93. C Wickham
Dur 92–94; C Sunderland Pennywell St Thos 94–97; V
Stockton St Jo 97–06; V Stockton St Jas 99–06; V W Dulwich
All SS *S'wark* 06–18; P-in-c Streatham Hill St Marg 14–16; AD
Lambeth S 13–18; V Cotham St Sav w St Mary and Clifton
St Paul *Bris* from 18. *12 Belgrave Road, Bristol BS8 2AB*

STEPHENSON, Canon Eric George. b 41. Bede Coll Dur
CertEd 63. Qu Coll Birm. **d** 66 **p** 67. C Wakef St Jo 66–69; C
Seaham w Seaham Harbour *Dur* 69–73; C Cockerton 73–75;
LtO 75–85; V E Boldon 85–08; AD Jarrow 92–01; Hon Can
Dur Cathl 93–08; rtd 08; Chapl to The Queen 02–11; PtO *Dur*
14–17. *39 Haversham Park, Sunderland SR5 1HW* T: 0191-
549 5278 E: ericgstephenson@googlemail.com

STEPHENSON, James Alexander. b 77. Hatf Coll Dur BSc 00
Ox Univ BTh 15. Ripon Coll Cuddesdon 09. **d** 11 **p** 12.
Chapl Canford Sch and C N Poole Ecum Team *Sarum*
11–12; PtO *Ox* 13; Zambia 13–18; Chapl St Paul's Colleg Sch
Hamilton NZ 15–18; Chapl Blue Coat Sch Reading 18–19;
Zambia from 19. *Address temp unknown* M: 07809-125657
E: jxstevo@hotmail.com

STEPHENSON, Mrs Jane Eleanor. b 50. Leeds Univ BA 72
PGCE 73. **d** 05 **p** 06. NSM Bunbury and Tilstone Fearnall
Ches 05–09; P-in-c Tilston and Shocklach 09–13; R 13–19;
Educn and Tr Officer 07–09; Past Worker Tr Officer 06–10;
rtd 19; PtO *Ches* from 19; *Lich* from 21. *The Mount,
Hobb Hill, Tilston, Malpas SY14 7DU* T: (01829) 250249
E: stephenson256@btinternet.com

STEPHENSON (*née* BRYAN), Judith Claire. b 57. Aston Univ
BSc 79 PhD 82 Trent Poly PGCE 83. St Jo Coll Nottm BTh 94
LTh 95. **d** 95 **p** 96. C Wolverhampton St Matt *Lich* 95–99;
Chapl Hull Univ *York* 99–08; Chapl W Lon YMCA 08–14;
PtO *Lon* 14–18; Chapl HM Pris Wormwood Scrubs 18–20.
Address temp unknown E: stephenson414@btinternet.com

STEPHENSON, Juliet. b 69. St Jo Coll Dur BA 05. Cranmer
Hall Dur 03. **d** 05 **p** 06. C Retford *S'well* 05–08; V Newnham
w Awre and Blakeney *Glouc* 08–13; V Chapel House *Newc*
13–18; Dir Good Funerals Co from 18; NSM Toxteth St Marg
Liv from 19. *42J Central Avenue, Liverpool L24 0TP* T: 0151-
486 3990 E: juliet_stephenson@hotmail.com

STEPHENSON, Canon Martin Woodard. b 55. St Cath
Coll Cam BA 77 MA 82. Westcott Ho Cam 78. **d** 81 **p** 82.
C Eastleigh *Win* 81–85; C Ferryhill *Dur* 85–87; Asst Dir of
Ords 87–89; Chapl St Chad's Coll 87–89; TR Clarendon
Park St Jo w Knighton St Mich *Leic* 89–98; P-in-c Hall Green
St Pet *Birm* 98–99; V from 99; P-in-c Hall Green St Mich
from 16; Warden of Readers 08–17; Hon Can Birm Cathl
from 14; Dioc Chapl MU from 19. *St Peter's Vicarage, 33
Paradise Lane, Birmingham B28 0DY* T: 0121-777 1935
E: martin.stephenson@cantab.net

STEPHENSON, Norman Keith. b 62. St Jo Coll Cam MA 88
Strathclyde Univ MBA 91. NEOC 04. **d** 07 **p** 08. NSM
Kingston upon Hull H Trin *York* 07–08; NSM Ealing St Pet
Mt Park *Lon* 08–13; PtO from 13. *25B Montpelier Road,
London W5 2QT* T: (020) 8991 9134 M: 07880-602577
E: n.k.stephenson@btinternet.com

STEPHENSON, Canon Robert. b 36. St Chad's Coll Dur BA 58.
d 60 **p** 61. C Whickham *Dur* 60–63; C Gateshead St Mary
63–65; PC Low Team 65–67; R Stella 67–74; V Comberton
Ely 74–04; RD Bourn 94–97; P-in-c Dry Drayton 97–01; Hon
Can Ely Cathl 01–04; rtd 04; PtO *Ely* 04–18. *1 Porthmore
Close, Highfields, Caldecote, Cambridge CB23 7ZR* T: (01954)
210638 E: robert1pc@yahoo.co.uk

STEPHENSON, Simon George. b 44. St Jo Coll Dur BA 67.
Trin Coll Bris 74. **d** 76 **p** 77. C Hildenborough *Roch*
76–82; C Bishopsworth *Bris* 82–85; C-in-c Withywood
CD 85–90; TV Wreningham *Nor* 90–97; P-in-c Tasburgh
w Tharston, Forncett and Flordon 94–97; rtd 05; Asst
Chapl HM Pris Wayland 98–09; PtO *Nor* from 09. *7
Swanton Avenue, Dereham NR19 2HJ* T: (01362) 699537
E: paulineandsimon@talktalk.net

STEPNEY, Area Bishop of. *See* GRENFELL, The Rt Revd Joanne
Woolway

STERLING, Anne. *See* HASELHURST, Anne

STERLING, John Haddon. b 40. Pemb Coll Cam BA 62
MA 66. Cuddesdon Coll 63. **d** 65 **p** 66. C Pretoria Cathl
S Africa 65–69; Lic to Offic Natal 69–70; Chapl Bris Cathl
71–74; Member Dioc Soc and Ind Team 71–74; Ind Chapl
Linc 74–87; Ind Chapl *Ripon* 87–92; TV Hanley H Ev *Lich*
92–97; Min in Ind 92–97; P-in-c Hixon w Stowe-by-Chartley
97–02; P-in-c Fradswell, Gayton, Milwich and Weston
97–02; TR Mid Trent 02–06; rtd 06; PtO *Lich* 07–21. *10
Newquay Avenue, Stafford ST17 0EB* T: (01785) 662870
E: dojo.sterling@gmail.com

STERRY, Christopher. b 54. K Coll Lon BD 77 AKC 77.
Episc Sem Austin Texas 78 St Jo Coll Nottm 79. **d** 80
p 81. C Huddersfield St Jo *Wakef* 80–84; V Middlestown
84–89; Chapl and Tutor NOC 89–94; Lect Ches Coll
of HE 93–94; NSM Padgate *Liv* 92–94; Bp's Dom Chapl
Blackb 94–97; Chapl Whalley Abbey 94–97; Warden
97–04; V Whalley 97–09; P-in-c Sabden and Pendleton
07–09; C Colne and Villages 09–12; P-in-c Huntley and
Longhope, Churcham and Bulley *Glouc* 12–17; C Abenhall
w Mitcheldean 12–17; C Westbury-on-Severn w Flaxley,
Blaisdon etc 12–17; Warden of Readers 13–15; rtd 17. *3
Woodlands, Newland, Malvern WR13 5AX* M: 07947-753791
E: woodlandschris2017@gmail.com

STEVEN, Canon David Bowring. b 38. AKC 64. **d** 64 **p** 65. C
Grantham St Wulfram *Linc* 64–68; C Kimberley St Cypr S
Africa 68–71; R Mafeking 71–75; C Bramley *Ripon* 76–77; V

Sutton Valence w E Sutton and Chart Sutton *Cant* 77–82; P-in-c Littlebourne 82–86; Warden of Readers 82–86; V Mansfield Woodhouse *S'well* 86–98; P-in-c Mullion *Truro* 98–03; RD Kerrier 01–03; rtd 03; Hon Can Truro Cathl 03–07; PtO 03–19. *5 Guinea Port Parc, Wadebridge PL27 7BY* T: (01208) 815393

STEVEN, Canon James Henry Stevenson. b 62. CCC Cam BA 84 MA 87 St Jo Coll Dur BA 87 K Coll Lon PhD 99. Cranmer Hall Dur 84. **d** 87 **p** 88. C Welling *Roch* 87–91; C Bournemouth St Jo w St Mich *Win* 91–94; TV Bournemouth St Pet w St Swithun, H Trin etc 94–00; Chapl Bournemouth and Poole Coll of FE 94–00; Tutor Trin Coll Bris 00–08; Lect K Coll Lon 08–11; Dir Liturgy and Worship Sarum Coll 11–21; Can Th Glouc 14–21; PtO *Bris* 12–21. *6 Green Dell Close, Bristol BS10 7RG* E: jhssteven@btinternet.com

STEVEN, Richard John. b 54. Oak Hill Th Coll BA 99. **d** 99 **p** 01. C Bluff Pt Australia 00–03; P-in-c Horsmonden *Roch* 04–09; Chapl HM Pris Blantyre Ho 05–09; Australia 09–11; P-in-c Herstmonceux and Wartling *Chich* from 11. *The Rectory, West And, Herstmonceux, Hailsham BN27 4NY* T: (01323) 833124 E: ra_steven@hotmail.com

STEVENETTE, Canon Simon Melville. b 62. Hull Univ BA 83. Wycliffe Hall Ox 84. **d** 87 **p** 88. C Carterton *Ox* 87–90; C Keynsham *B & W* 90–91; TV 91–98; Chapl Keynsham Hosp Bris 92–98; V Swindon Ch Ch *Bris* from 98; AD Swindon 11–17; Hon Can Bris Cathl from 13. *Christ Church Vicarage, 26 Cricklade Street, Swindon SN1 3HG* T: (01793) 522832 *or* 529166 M: 07902-239936 E: simon.stevenette@gmail.com

STEVENS, Alan Robert. b 55. Warwick Univ BA 77. St Jo Coll Nottm 87. **d** 89 **p** 90. C Ex St Leon w H Trin 89–92; TV Rugby *Cov* 92–97; P-in-c N w S Kilworth and Misterton *Leic* 97–00; PtO 13–19. *Address withheld by request* E: hattersbarmyarmy@googlemail.com

STEVENS, Andrew. *See* STEVENS, John David Andrew

STEVENS, Canon Andrew Graham. b 54. BEd MA. Coll of Resurr Mirfield. **d** 83 **p** 84. C Leigh Park *Portsm* 83–87; TV Brighton Resurr *Chich* 87–94; V Plumstead St Nic *S'wark* from 94; Hon Can S'wark Cathl from 14. *St Nicholas's Vicarage, 64 Purrett Road, London SE18 1JP* T: (020) 8854 0461 E: frandrew@dircon.co.uk

STEVENS, Anne Helen. b 61. Warwick Univ BA 82 Fitzw Coll Cam BA 90 MA 94 Heythrop Coll Lon MTh 99. Ridley Hall Cam 88. **d** 91 **p** 94. Par Dn E Greenwich Ch Ch w St Andr and St Mich *S'wark* 91–94; Chapl Trin Coll Cam 94–99; P-in-c Battersea St Mich *S'wark* 99–07; V 07–12; Dir Readers' Tr 99–12; Hon Can S'wark Cathl 05–12; V St Pancras w St Jas and Ch Ch *Lon* from 12; Dean of Women's Min Edmonton Area 15–20. *St Pancras Vicarage, 6 Sandwich Street, London WC1H 9PL* T: (020) 7388 1461 E: vicar@stpancraschurch.org

STEVENS, Anthony Harold. b 46. CEng 71 MIStructE 71 FIStructE 87 MICE 75 FICE 92. St Mich Coll Llan 94. **d** 95 **p** 96. C Cardiff St Jo *Llan* 95–98; TV Cowbridge 98–01; R Eglwysilan 01–08; R Gelligaer 08–12; AD Caerphilly 04–10; rtd 13; PtO *Llan* from 13; *Mon* from 14. *2 Falcon Grove, Penarth CF64 5FB* T: (029) 2070 7745 E: anthony.stevens@btinternet.com

STEVENS, Brian Henry. b 45. Open Univ BA 80. S Dios Minl Tr Scheme 81. **d** 84 **p** 85. NSM S Malling *Chich* 84–86; C Langney 86–87; TV Wolverton *Ox* 87–88; V Welford w Sibbertoft and Marston Trussell *Pet* 88–91; V Hardingstone and Horton and Piddington 91–11; Chapl Northants Police 06–11; rtd 11. *2C Manor Road, Kingsthorpe, Northampton NN2 6QJ* M: 07710-207201 E: fr.brian@talktalk.net

STEVENS, David John. b 45. Bris Univ BA 67. Clifton Th Coll. **d** 70 **p** 71. C Ex St Leon w H Trin 70–75; P-in-c Lt Burstead *Chelmsf* 75–77; TV Billericay and Lt Burstead 77–81; P-in-c Illogan *Truro* 81–83; R St Illogan 83–96; RD Carnmarth N 96; V Highworth w Sevenhampton and Inglesham etc *Bris* 96–01; P-in-c Constantine *Truro* 01–10; RD Kerrier 03–10; rtd 10; PtO *Truro* from 10; RD Penwith 14–17. *Bede House, Primrose Hill, Goldsithney, Penzance TR20 9JR* T: (01736) 719090 E: djstevens121@btinternet.com

STEVENS, Douglas George. b 47. Lon Univ BA 69. Westcott Ho Cam 69. **d** 72 **p** 73. C Portsea St Geo CD *Portsm* 72–75; C Portsea N End St Mark 75–79; Chapl NE Lon Poly *Chelmsf* 79–83; C-in-c Orton Goldhay CD *Ely* 83–87; V Elm 87–91; V Coldham 87–91; V Friday Bridge 87–91; R Woodston 91–98; P-in-c Fletton 94–98; rtd 98. *28 Francis Gardens, Peterborough PE1 3XX* T: (01733) 755430

STEVENS, Miss Gillian. b 51. K Alfred's Coll Win CertEd 72. EAMTC 98. **d** 01 **p** 02. C March St Mary and March St Pet *Ely* 01–03; C Whittlesey, Pondersbridge and Coates 03–05; TV 05–16; rtd 16; PtO *Nor* from 17; *Ely* from 17. *21 Lighthouse Lane, Hunstanton PE36 6EN* E: gill.stevens8@btinternet.com

STEVENS, James Anthony. b 47. Worc Coll Ox MA 69. Trin Coll Bris 78. **d** 80 **p** 81. C Heref St Pet w St Owen and St Jas 80–84; C Lowestoft and Kirkley *Nor* 84–85; TV 85–89; V Dorridge *Birm* 89–05; AD Shirley 02–05; R Sarratt and Chipperfield *St Alb* 05–12; rtd 12; PtO *Roch* from 13. *17 Prospect Park, Southborough, Tunbridge Wells TN4 0EQ* T: (01892) 670954 E: revjim@virginmedia.com

STEVENS, Jane. *See* KRAFT, Jane

STEVENS, John David Andrew. b 44. Wycliffe Hall Ox. **d** 68 **p** 69. C Standish *Blackb* 68–71; C Stonehouse *Glouc* 71–76; P-in-c Closworth *B & W* 76–77; P-in-c Barwick 76–77; TV Yeovil 77–80; R Chewton Mendip w Ston Easton, Litton etc 80–94; R Quantoxhead 94–07; RD Quantock 95–01; rtd 07; PtO *B & W* from 07. *Amberwell, Holywell Road, Edington, Bridgwater TA7 9LE* T: (01278) 722327 E: andrewstevens@zetnet.co.uk

STEVENS, Jonathan Mark. b 76. St Mellitus Coll 16. **d** 19 **p** 20. NSM Soul Survivor Watford *St Alb* from 19; NSM Soul Survivor St Alb Abbey from 19. *18 Rutherford Way, Bushey Heath, Bushey WD23 1NJ* M: 07798-700685 E: jstevens@soulsurvivorwatford.co.uk

STEVENS, Norman William. b 38. St Chad's Coll Dur BA 61. **d** 63 **p** 99. C Wingate Grange *Dur* 63–64; NSM Bulkington w Shilton and Ansty *Cov* 99–08; PtO from 08. *60 Clinton Lane, Kenilworth CV8 1AT* T: (01926) 858090 *or* (024) 7622 7597 E: norstevens@hotmail.com

STEVENS, Canon Olive. b 48. Ex Univ BA 04. SWMTC 01. **d** 04 **p** 05. C Camborne *Truro* 04–13; C Redruth w Lanner and Treleigh 11–14; TV 14–15; R Camborne and Tuckingmill 15–16; P-in-c Penponds 15–16; R Camborne, Tuckingmill and Penponds 16–18; RD Carnmarth N 08–16; Hon Can Truro Cathl 14–18; rtd 18. *Hideaway, The Square, Portreath, Redruth TR16 4LA* T: (01209) 842372 E: olivestevens@aol.com

STEVENS, Penelope Ann. *See* PRINCE, Penelope Ann

STEVENS, Philip Terence. b 55. MBE 07. Man Univ BSc 76 Lon Univ BD 81 St Jo Coll Dur MA 86. Cranmer Hall Dur 81. **d** 83 **p** 84. C Withington St Paul *Man* 83–86; C Middleton 86–88; V Saddleworth 88–92; V Sheff St Paul 93–96; TR Sheff Manor 96–00; PtO 00–06; *Newc* 06–08; *B & W* 09–10; P-in-c Bleadon and Weston-super-Mare St Andr Bournville 10–13; PtO *York* 13–18; P-in-c Laceby and Ravendale Gp *Linc* 14; P-in-c Keelby Gp 14; V Wolds Gateway Group 14–20; RD Haverstoe 14–20; rtd 20. *Address temp unknown* M: 07914-357544 E: philiptstevens@gmail.com

STEVENS, Richard William. b 36. AKC 59. St Boniface Warminster 59. **d** 60 **p** 61. C Greenhill St Jo *Lon* 60–63; Chapl RAF 63–79; CF 79–01; rtd 01; PtO *Cant* 02–10. *The Old Vicarage, Stockbury, Sittingbourne ME9 7UN* T: (01795) 844891

STEVENS, Robin George. b 43. Leic Univ BA 65. Cuddesdon Coll 74. **d** 74 **p** 75. C Hemel Hempstead *St Alb* 74–77; Chapl K Coll Sch Wimbledon 77–03; TV Wimbledon *S'wark* 98–08; rtd 09; PtO *S'wark* 11–13; *Sarum* from 13. *34 Long Street, Devizes SN10 1NT*

STEVENS, Mrs Sara-Jane. b 72. Southn Univ BEd 97. SEITE 12. **d** 15 **p** 16. C Worthing St Matt *Chich* from 15; P-in-c Sullington and Thakeham w Warminghurst from 18. *The Rectory, The Street, Thakeham, Pulborough RH20 3EP* T: (01798) 813121 M: 07923-420834 E: revsj@btinternet.com

STEVENS, Mrs Susan Marjorie Earlam. b 52. RGN 74. WMMTC 97. **d** 00 **p** 01. NSM Harborne St Faith and St Laur *Birm* 00–02; NSM Publow w Pensford, Compton Dando and Chelwood *B & W* 03–12; Chapl R United Hosp Bath NHS Trust 06–12; rtd 12; PtO *B & W* from 15. *The Coach House, Woodeaton, Oxford OX3 9TN* E: smestevens@hotmail.co.uk

STEVENS, Timothy David. b 80. Leeds Univ BA 01 Sheff Univ MA 16. Yorks Min Course 13. **d** 16 **p** 17. C Wakef Cathl *Leeds* 16–19; V Darton w Staincross and Mapplewell from 19. *The Vicarage, 6 Jacobs Hall Court, Darton, Barnsley S75 5LY* M: 07979-854727 E: tim.stevens@leeds.anglican.org *or* fr.tim.vicar@hotmail.com

✠**STEVENS, The Rt Revd Timothy John.** b 46. CBE 16. Selw Coll Cam BA 68 MA 72. Ripon Coll Cuddesdon 75. **d** 76 **p** 77. **c** 95. C E Ham w Upton Park and Forest Gate *Chelmsf* 76–80; TR Canvey Is 80–88; Dep Dir Cathl Cen for Research and Tr 82–84; Bp's Urban Officer 87–91; Hon Can Chelmsf Cathl 87–91; Adn W Ham 91–95; Suff Bp Dunwich *St E* 95–99; Bp Leic 99–15; rtd 15; Hon Asst Bp St E from 16; PtO *Ely* from 20. *62 Horringer Road, Bury St Edmunds IP33 2DR* T: (01284) 768321 M: 07860-692258 E: tjs46@icloud.com

STEVENSON, Canon Alastair Rice. b 42. Open Univ BA 78. Ripon Coll Cuddesdon 78. **d** 80 **p** 81. C Bexhill St Pet *Chich* 80–82; C Brighton St Matthias 82–84; C Swindon Ch Ch *Bris* 84–87; Bp's Soc and Ind Adv 87–97; P-in-c Swindon All SS w St Barn 97–01; V 01–11; P-in-c Swindon St Aug 04–11; Hon Can Bris Cathl 02–11; rtd 11; PtO *Bris* 12–17. *17 Kelly Gardens, Swindon SN25 4YH* T: (01793) 336587 M: 07880-710172 E: al@stair.me.uk

STEVENSON, Alistair Philip. b 84. Sheff Univ BA 07. Yorks Min Course 13. **d** 16 **p** 17. C Ecclesall *Sheff* 16–20; P-in-c Greystones from 18. *The Vicarage, 1 Cliffe Farm Drive, Sheffield S11 7JW* T: 0114-266 7686 M: 07769-213581 E: alistair@acstevenson.net *or* alistair.stevenson@sheffield.anglican.org *or* vicar@saintgs.co.uk

STEVENSON, Canon Andrew James. b 63. IEng AMICE MIAT. SWMTC 94. **d** 97 **p** 98. NSM Highertown and Baldhu *Truro* 97–08; NSM Mylor w Flushing from 08; Hon Can Truro Cathl from 15. *31 Nansavallon Road, Truro TR1 3JU* T: (01872) 241880 E: theblackstuff@sky.com

STEVENSON, Beaumont. *See* STEVENSON, Frank Beaumont

STEVENSON, Bernard Norman. b 57. Kent Univ BA 78 Fitzw Coll Cam BA 81 MA 86. Ridley Hall Cam. **d** 82 **p** 83. C Mortlake w E Sheen *S'wark* 82–84; C Kensal Rise St Martin *Lon* 84–88; C Headstone St Geo 88–90; V Worfield *Heref* 90–95; R Hutton *B & W* 95–07; RD Locking 04–05. *High Ridge, 7 Lauderdale, Barnstaple EX32 8DU* T: (01271) 321972 E: bstevenson@clara.net

STEVENSON, Brian. b 34. JP 66. NW Ord Course 76. **d** 79 **p** 80. C Padiham *Blackb* 79–82; V Clitheroe St Paul Low Moor 82–89; V Blackb St Silas 89–01; rtd 01; PtO *Blackb* 01–20. *1 Chatburn Close, Great Harwood, Blackburn BB6 7TL* T: (01254) 885051

STEVENSON, Brian. *See* STEVENSON, Robert Brian

STEVENSON, Christopher James. b 43. TCD BA 65 MA 73 Em Coll Cam BA 69 MA 73. Westcott Ho Cam 68. **d** 70 **p** 71. C Newc H Cross 70–72; C Arm St Mark w Aghavilly 72–73; C Dublin Crumlin *D & G* 73–76; Hon Clerical V Ch Ch Cathl Dublin 75–76; C-in-c Appley Bridge All SS CD *Blackb* 76–82; P-in-c Appley Bridge 82–91; Bp's C Cloonclare w Killasnett, Lurganboy and Drumlease *K, E & A* 91–12; rtd 12. *7 Merchants Quarter, Cathcart Square, 14 Dublin Road, Enniskillen BT74 6HJ* T: (028) 6632 8512 M: 07982-262862

STEVENSON, David Andrew. b 60. Trin Coll Bris BA 92. **d** 92 **p** 93. C Nottingham St Sav *S'well* 92–96; P-in-c Darlaston All SS and Ind Chapl Black Country Urban Ind Miss *Lich* 96–00; C Darlaston St Lawr 99–00; TV Broadwater *Chich* 00–08; P-in-c Eastwood *S'well* from 08; P-in-c Brinsley w Underwood from 09. *The Rectory, 5A Woodland Way, Eastwood, Nottingham NG16 3BU* T: (01773) 710770 E: revdavidstevenson@sky.com

STEVENSON, David Eugene. b 66. Luton Univ BA 02. St Steph Ho Ox 06. **d** 08 **p** 09. C Nor St Jo w St Julian 08–11; P-in-c Watford St Jo *St Alb* 11–13; V from 13. *St John's Vicarage, 9 Monmouth Road, Watford WD1 1QW* T: (01923) 25775 M: 07980-315534 E: rev.davidstevenson@googlemail.com

STEVENSON, Donald Macdonald. b 48. Lon Univ BSc(Econ) 70 Leeds Univ MA 72 Univ of Wales (Abth) PGCE 73 Warwick Univ MEd 78 MBACP 11. Oak Hill Th Coll BA 88. **d** 88 **p** 89. C Gt Malvern St Mary *Worc* 88–92; Chapl Bedford Sch 92–98; Sen Chapl 96–98; PtO *St Alb* 99–02; rtd 13; PtO *St Alb* from 17. *94 Curlew Crescent, Bedford MK41 7HZ* T: (01234) 217013 E: don_xmcds9@gmx.co.uk

STEVENSON, Elizabeth. *See* STEVENSON, Margaret Elizabeth Maud

STEVENSON, Canon Frank Beaumont. b 39. Duke Univ (USA) BA 61 MInstGA. Episc Th Sch Harvard MDiv 64. **d** 64 **p** 64. USA 64–66; Zambia 66–68; Lect Th Ox Univ from 68; Bp's Tr Officer *Ox* 69–70; Chapl Keble Coll Ox 71–72; Chapl Oxon Mental Healthcare NHS Trust 75–07; Officer for CME *Ox* from 90; Dioc Adv Past Care from 90; Hon Can Ch Ch 98–19; PtO 19–21. *The School House, Wheatley Road, Stanton St John, Oxford OX33 1ET* T: (01865) 351635 E: beaumont.stevenson@gmail.com

STEVENSON, Gerald Ernest. b 35. S'wark Ord Course 80. **d** 83 **p** 84. NSM Eltham Park St Luke *S'wark* 83–88; Asst Chapl HM Pris Wormwood Scrubs 88–98; PtO *S'wark* 88–99; rtd 99; Hon C Eltham St Barn *S'wark* 99–04. *7 Moira Road, London SE9 1SJ* T: (020) 8850 2748

STEVENSON, Graham. b 82. Ex Coll Ox MBiochem 04 K Coll Lon MA 15. St Mellitus Coll BA 14. **d** 14 **p** 15. NSM Stamford Hill St Thos *Lon* 14–16; C 17–18; C Clapton St Jas 16–17; Chapl Fitzw Coll Cam from 18. *Fitzwilliam College, Storey's Way, Cambridge CB3 0DG* T: (01223) 332000 M: 07954-409472 E: stevenson_g@hotmail.com *or* chaplain@fitz.cam.ac.uk

STEVENSON, John. b 39. Glas Univ MA 64 Jordan Hill Coll Glas TCert 65. St Jo Coll Nottm Edin Th Coll. **d** 87 **p** 88. NSM Moffat *Glas* 87–92; P-in-c Eastriggs 92–95; P-in-c Gretna 92–95; P-in-c Langholm 92–95; Israel 95–01; P-in-c Thurso

and Wick *Mor* 01–06; rtd 06; LtO *Glas* from 07. *Hoppertitty, Beattock, Moffat DG10 9PJ* T: (01683) 300164 M: 07588-342060 E: hoppertitty@msn.com

STEVENSON, John William. b 44. Salford Univ BSc 66 UNISA BTh 89. St Paul's Coll Grahamstown 84. **d** 87 **p** 87. C St Mary's Cathl Johannesburg S Africa 87–88; R Bezuidenhout Valley 88–93; V Broom Leys *Leic* 93–11; rtd 11; PtO *Pet* from 12. *5 Roman Way, Daventry NN11 0RW* T: (01327) 700119 E: johnandrene@btinternet.com

STEVENSON, The Ven Leslie Thomas Clayton. b 59. TCD BA MPhil. **d** 83 **p** 84. C Dundela St Mark *D & D* 83–87; I Kilmore and Inch 87–92; R Donaghadee 92–99; I Portarlington w Cloneyhurke, Lea etc *M & K* from 99; Can Meath from 08; Can Kildare Cathl from 08; Adn Meath from 09; Adn Kildare from 09. *The Rectory, Portarlington, Co Laois, Republic of Ireland* T: (00353) (57) 864 0117 E: lesliestevenson53@gmail.com

STEVENSON, Miss Margaret Elizabeth Maud. b 49. Stranmillis Coll CertEd 70 Ulster Univ BEd 86. CITC 07. **d** 10 **p** 11. NSM Drumglass w Moygashel *Arm* from 10. *The Rubrics, 1 Derrycaw Lane, Portadown, Craigavon BT62 1TW* T: (028) 3885 1503 E: elizabethstevenson431@btinternet.com

STEVENSON, Michael Richard Nevin. b 52. Univ Coll Lon MA 77. CITC. **d** 86 **p** 87. C Clooney w Strathfoyle *D & R* 86–89; CF 89–12; I Bunclody w Kildavin, Clonegal and Kilrush *C, F & O* 12–20; Can Ferns Cathl 16–20; rtd 20. *Claymore House, 3 Church Street, Hingham, Norwich NR9 4HL* T: (01953) 851989

STEVENSON, Nikki James Blanton. b 79. **d** 16 **p** 17. C Northampton St Mary *Pet* 16–19; 20s-40s Team Ldr *York* from 19; C Ingleby Barwick from 19. *11 Bodiam Close, Ingleby Barwick, Stockton-on-Tees TS17 5GQ* M: 07701-024843 E: nikthevic@icloud.com

STEVENSON, Miss Pamela Mary. b 35. CQSW 74. **d** 97 **p** 98. OLM Mitcham Ascension *S'wark* 97–05; PtO from 05; Retirement Officer Kingston Area from 08. *7 Robin Hood Close, Mitcham CR4 1JN* T: (020) 8764 8331 M: 07702-928204 E: revpamstevenson@gmail.com

STEVENSON, Robert. b 52. UWIST BSc 73 Cant Ch Ch Univ MA 11 MRTPI 78 MCIM 89. SEITE 03. **d** 05 **p** 06. NSM Woodnesborough w Worth and Staple *Cant* 05–12; NSM Eastry and Woodnesborough from 12; Managing Dir Dioc Architects from 11. *The Old Rectory, 5 Cowper Road, Deal CT14 9TW* T: (01304) 366003 E: rev.rob.stevenson@btinternet.com

STEVENSON, Canon Robert Brian. b 40. QUB BA 61 Qu Coll Cam BA 67 MA 71 Pemb Coll Ox BA 69 BD 76 MA 76 Birm Univ PhD 70. Cuddesdon Coll 69. **d** 70 **p** 71. C Lewisham St Jo Southend *S'wark* 70–73; C Catford (Southend) and Downham 73–74; Lect and Dir Past Studies Chich Th Coll 74–81; Acting Vice-Prin 80–81; V W Malling w Offham *Roch* 81–10; RD Malling 93–02; Hon Can Roch Cathl 98–10; rtd 10; PtO *Roch* from 10; *Cant* from 18. *Michaelmas Cottage, Stan Lane, West Peckham, Maidstone ME18 5JT* T: (01622) 817693 E: woolystevenson@yahoo.co.uk

STEVENSON, Sheila Reinhardt. *See* SWARBRICK, Sheila Reinhardt

STEVENSON, Canon June Lesley. b 61. Aston Tr Scheme 86 Sarum & Wells Th Coll BTh 91. **d** 91 **p** 94. Par Dn Chatham St Steph *Roch* 91–94; C 94–96; PtO *York* 96–97; Liv 97–00; V Abram 00–10; V Bickershaw 00–10; P-in-c Winwick 10–15; R 15–20; P-in-c Burtonwood 14–15; V 15–20; R Warrington St Elphin from 20; Hon Can Liv Cathl from 06. *The Rectory, 129 Church Street, Warrington WA1 2TL* E: june.steventon123@btinternet.com

STEVENTON, Kenneth. b 59. Cuddesdon Coll 94. **d** 96 **p** 97. C Spalding St Mary and St Nic *Linc* 94–99; R Sutterton, Fosdyke, Algarkirk and Wigtoft 99–05; P-in-c Evenwood *Dur* 05–09; P-in-c Ingleton 05–21; P-in-c Staindrop 05–21; rtd 21. *3 Mansion Court, Bedlington NE22 5LE* E: revken@freeuk.co.uk

STEVINSON, Harold John Hardy. b 34. Selw Coll Cam BA 57 MA 61. Qu Coll Birm. **d** 59 **p** 60. C Bris St Mary Redcliffe w Temple 59–63; C Caversham *Ox* 63–73; Soc Resp Officer *Dur* 74–82; Sec Dioc Bd for Miss and Unity 82–88; P-in-c Croxdale *Dur* 82–88; P-in-c Leamington Hastings and Birdingbury *Cov* 88–96; rtd 96; PtO *Cov* 96–00; *Glouc* from 96. *8 Greenways, Winchcombe, Cheltenham GL54 5LG* T: (01242) 602195 E: jstevinsons@gmail.com

STEWARD, Mrs Linda Christine. b 46. NE Lon Poly CQSW 82. S'wark Ord Course 85. **d** 88 **p** 94. NSM E Ham w Upton Park and Forest Gate *Chelmsf* 88–91; Chapl Newham Healthcare NHS Trust Lon 91–98; NSM Plaistow *Chelmsf* 91–96; NSM Plaistow and N Canning Town 96–98; P-in-c Rawreth w Rettendon 98–06; rtd 06. *2 Belfairs Park Close, Leigh-on-Sea SS9 4TR* T: (01702) 525638 E: lindasteward123@gmail.com

STEWARDSON, Enid Joyce. b 53. d 11 p 12. OLM Heath Hayes *Lich* 11–15; PtO 15–21. *Highfield House, 20 Highfield Road, Cannock WS12 2DX* T: (01543) 279817 E: joycestewa@aol.com

STEWART, Alan. *See* STEWART, Hugh Alan

STEWART, Alan Valentine. b 47. Univ Coll Galway BA 98. d 97 p 98. NSM Mullingar, Portnashangan, Moyliscar, Kilbixy etc *M & K* 97–00; NSM Clane w Donadea and Coolcarrigan 00–05; NSM Dunboyne Union 05–06; NSM Portarlington w Cloneyhurke, Lea etc 06–17; NSM Navan w Kentstown, Tara, Slane, Painestown etc from 17. *Casteway, Baltrasna, Ashbourne, Co Meath, Republic of Ireland* T: (00353) (1) 835 0997 M: 87-279 3197 E: casteway@hotmail.com

STEWART, Alistair Charles. b 60. St Andr Univ MA 83 Birm Univ PhD 92. Qu Coll Birm 86. d 89 p 90. C Stevenage St Andr and St Geo *St Alb* 89–92; C Castle Vale St Cuth *Birm* 92–93; Lect Codrington Coll Barbados 93–97; C Hanley H Ev *Lich* 97–98; Prof Gen Th Sem NY USA 98–01; V Bridge Par *Sarum* 01–10; C Sherborne w Castleton, Lillington and Longburton 10–12; TV Upton cum Chalvey *Ox* from 13. *St Peter's Vicarage, 52 Montem Lane, Slough SL1 2QJ* T: (01753) 520725

STEWART, Andrew Thomas. b 83. d 16 p 17. C Wilford Hill *S'well* 16–19; PtO from 19; TV Walthamstow *Chelmsf* from 21. *St Gabriel's Vicarage, 17 Shernhall Street, London E17 3EU* M: 07510-719636 E: revandrewstewart@outlook.com

STEWART (née BARBER), Mrs Anne Louise. b 71. QUB BA 93 PGCE 94. CITC 97. d 00 p 01. NSM Belfast Malone St Jo *Conn* 00–09; NSM Finaghy 09–11; I from 11. *St George's Rectory, 6 Royal Lodge Park, Belfast BT8 7YP* T: (028) 9070 1350 *or* 9029 2980 M: 07724-067547

STEWART, Mrs Brenda Alice. b 60. ERMC. d 09 p 10. C Abbots Ripton w Wood Walton *Ely* 09–12; C Kings Ripton 09–12; C Houghton w Wyton 09–12; R W Leightonstone 12–18; R Holkham w Egmere w Warham etc *Nor* from 18. *The Rectory, 19 Home Piece Road, Wells-next-the-Sea NR23 1PX* T: (01328) 710628 E: bas@con-brio.uk

STEWART, Brian. b 59. TCD BTh 91. CITC 88. d 91 p 92. C Ballywillan *Conn* 91–94; I Belfast St Geo from 94. *St George's Rectory, 6 Royal Lodge Park, Belfast BT8 7YP* T: (028) 9070 1350 M: 07902-792080 E: bstewart1662@gmail.com

STEWART, Charles. b 55. St Jo Coll Cam BA 77 MA 81 CertEd 79. Wycliffe Hall Ox 85. d 87 p 88. C Bowdon *Ches* 87–90; C Bath Abbey w St Jas *B & W* 90–94; Can Res, Prec and Sacr Win Cathl 94–06; V Walton-on-Thames *Guildf* 06–15; P-in-c Christchurch *Win* 15–19; V from 19. *The Vicarage, 13A Church Street, Christchurch BH23 1BW* T: (01202) 485804 E: vicar@christchurchpriory.org

STEWART, Charles Michael. b 50. Ball Coll Ox MA 82 K Coll Lon BA 05 AKC 05 MA 07 FCA 82. Ripon Coll Cuddesdon 06. d 07 p 08. NSM Leatherhead and Mickleham *Guildf* 07–11; PtO from 13. *Rickstones, Punchbowl Lane, Dorking RH5 4BN* T: (01306) 884153 M: 07936-524152 E: carolandmikestewart@outlook.com

STEWART, Ms Dorothy Elaine. b 51. Man Metrop Univ BA 93 Bradf Univ MA 98. Coll of Resurr Mirfield 08. d 10 p 11. C Potternewton *Ripon* 10–14; Leeds 14; V Fairweather Green 14–21; rtd 21. *Address temp unknown* M: 07826-107049 E: dotelartuna@hotmail.com

STEWART, Gregor. b 77. St Mellitus Coll 17. d 20 p 21. C Eccleston *Liv* from 20. *St Luke's Vicarage, 31 Mulberry Avenue, St Helens WA10 4DE* T: (01744) 738401 M: 07946-880180 E: revgregor@outlook.com

STEWART, Hugh Alan. b 67. Lon Inst BA 91 Middx Univ BA 03. NTMTC 00. d 03 p 04. C Gt Stanmore *Lon* 03–06; P-in-c Hertford St Andr *St Alb* 06–08; P-in-c Hertingfordbury 06–08; TV Hertford from 08. *St Andrew's Rectory, 7 Elizabeth Close, Hertford SG14 2DB* T: (01992) 582726 E: h.alanstewart1@gmail.com

STEWART, James. *See* STEWART, Malcolm James

STEWART, Canon James Patrick. b 55. Keele Univ BA 77 Birm Univ MA 78. Ridley Hall Cam 86. d 88 p 89. C Boulton *Derby* 88–91; C Cove St Jo *Guildf* 91–92; TV 92–97; TR Tunbridge Wells St Jas w St Phil *Roch* 97–04; V Tunbridge Wells St Jas from 04; RD Tunbridge Wells 99–07 and 15–18; Hon Can Roch Cathl from 05. *The Vicarage, 12 Shandon Close, Tunbridge Wells TN2 3RE* T: (01892) 530687 *or* 521703 E: jpstewart4@googlemail.com

STEWART, James William. b 71. Selw Coll Cam BA 92 MA 96 Anglia Ruskin Univ MA 12. Westcott Ho Cam 09 Yale Div Sch 10. d 11 p 12. C Gt Yarmouth *Nor* 11–14; Bp's Chapl 14–16; Hon PV Nor Cathl from 14; R Thorpe St Andr from 16. *The Rectory, 21A South Avenue, Norwich NR7 0EY* T: (01603) 927291 M: 07986-839583 E: jstewart1971@googlemail.com

STEWART, Mrs Janet Margaret. b 41. Roehampton Inst CertEd 62. Cranmer Hall Dur 67. d 87 p 94. Hon Par Dn Oulton Broad *Nor* 87–94; Hon C 94–97; Chapl Lowestoft Hosp 94–97; PtO *B & W* 97–98; C Quidenham Gp *Nor* 98–01; Chapl Norfolk and Nor Univ Hosps NHS Foundn Trust from 00; Chapl Norfolk Community Health and Care NHS Trust from 04. *30 St Joseph's Road, Sheringham NR26 8JA* T: (01263) 824497 E: janet.stewart10@btinternet.com

STEWART, Jennifer Jane. *See* SISTIG, Jennifer Jane

STEWART, John. b 39. Oak Hill Th Coll 75. d 77 p 78. C Accrington Ch Ch *Blackb* 77–79; TV Darwen St Pet w Hoddlesden 79–86; R Coppull St Jo 86–04; rtd 04; PtO *Blackb* 05–11. *83 Regents Way, Euxton, Chorley PR7 6PG*

STEWART, John Wesley. b 52. QUB BD 76 TCD 76. d 77 p 78. C Seagoe *D & D* 77–79; C Lisburn Ch Ch *Conn* 79–85; I Ballybay w Mucknoe and Clontibret *Clogh* 85–90; I Derryvullen S w Garvary 90–18; Bp's Dom Chapl 95–00; Glebes Sec 95–18; Dioc Registrar 98–17; Exam Can Clogh Cathl 98–00; Preb 00–18; Chan Clogh Cathl 14–18; rtd 18. *Address withheld by request* E: jva.stewart@hotmail.co.uk

STEWART, Kathryn Susan. b 57. Coll of Ripon & York St Jo BA 79 Glyndŵr Univ BA 17. d 18 p 19. NSM Mold Miss Area *St As* 18–20; P-in-c from 20. *16 Ffordd Trem y Foel, Mold CH7 1NG* T: (01352) 753374 M: 07500-936985 E: kathy12oct@sky.com

STEWART, Keith Malcolm Morris. b 45. d 08 p 09. OLM Stalybridge *Man* 08–14; PtO from 14; *Ches* from 14. *6 Hillside Close, Weston, Crewe CW2 5FZ* T: (01270) 829044 E: julkeith@btinternet.com

STEWART, Kim Deborah. *See* MATHERS, Kim Deborah

STEWART, Louise. *See* STEWART, Anne Louise

STEWART, Malcolm James. b 44. TD 78. York Univ BA 66 K Coll Lon MA 68 Lon Inst of Educn PGCE 69 Solicitor 79. NEOC 89. d 93 p 94. NSM Upper Nidderdale *Ripon* 93–95; C Fountains Gp 95–98; V Catterick 98–03; P-in-c Culmington w Onibury, Bromfield etc *Heref* 03–06; TV Ludlow 06–10; RD 07–10; rtd 10; PtO *Heref* from 11; *Worc* from 17. *3 Leadon Place, Ledbury HR8 2GD* T: (01531) 630237 E: james.mjs@btinternet.com

STEWART, Michael. *See* STEWART, Charles Michael

STEWART, Michael James. b 86. Ripon Coll Cuddesdon 18. d 20 p 21. C Shottery St Andr *Cov* from 20. *54 Grove Road, Stratford-upon-Avon CV37 6PB* M: 07826-856446 E: revdmikestewart@outlook.com

STEWART, Ms Monica Frances Ethel. b 35. RGN 57 RM 59. d 08 p 12. NSM Stamford Hill St Thos *Lon* from 08. *2 The Heights, 165 Mountview Road, London N4 4JU* T: (020) 8340 4746 M: 07947-026297 E: monica.f.stewart@googlemail.com

STEWART, Philip John. b 76. Glas Univ MB, ChB 99 MRCGP 03 Westmr Th Sem California MA 16. Ridley Hall Cam 18. d 19 p 20. NSM Upper Chelsea St Simon *Lon* from 19. *Pepperdine University, 56 Princes Gate, London SW7 2PG* M: 07967-310796 E: drphilstewart@mac.com

STEWART, The Very Revd Raymond John. b 55. TCD BA 79 MA 82. CITC Div Test 77. d 79 p 80. C Clooney *D & R* 79–82; I Dunfanaghy 82–87; I Gweedore Union 85–87; Dioc Youth Adv 83–87; Bp's Dom Chapl 85–87; I Castledawson 87–03; I Tamlaght O'Crilly Upper w Lower 03–17; Ed D & R Dioc News 89–93; Dioc Glebes Sec *D & R* 93–17; Stewardship Adv 98–17; Can Derry Cathl 99–17; Dean Derry from 17; I Templemore from 17. *The Deanery, 30 Bishop Street, Londonderry BT48 6PP* T: (028) 7126 2746 M: 07761-585412 E: deanofderry@stcolumbs.net

STEWART, Stephen John. b 62. Oak Hill Th Coll. d 99 p 00. C Mile Cross *Nor* 99–04; TV Cove St Jo *Guildf* 04–20; C 20–21; R Hanborough and Freeland *Ox* from 21. *The Rectory, Swan Lane, Long Hanborough, Witney OX29 8BT* T: (01993) 881270 E: rector@hanboroughparish.com

STEWART, Susan Catherine. *See* BELL, Susan Catherine

STEWART-DARLING, Preb Fiona Lesley. b 58. Kingston Poly GRSC 79 Lon Univ PhD 82 K Coll Lon MA 99. Trin Coll Bris BA 91. d 91 p 94. C Cirencester *Glouc* 91–94; Chapl Cheltenham and Glouc Coll of HE 94–97; Chapl Portsm Univ 97–04; Hon Chapl Portsm Cathl 97–04; Bp's Chapl in Docklands *Lon* from 04; PV Westmr Abbey from 13; Preb St Paul's Cathl *Lon* from 21. *Canary Wharf Multifaith Chaplaincy, 1 Canada Square, London E14 5AB* T: (020) 7477 1073 M: 07739-461090 E: fiona@canarywharfchaplaincy.co.uk

STEWART SMITH, Mrs Alison Mary. b 74. St Andr Univ MA 96 St Jo Coll Dur BA 15 Homerton Coll Cam PGCE 97. Cranmer Hall Dur 13. d 15 p 16. C Swaledale *Leeds* 15–20; P-in-c Winlaton *Dur* from 20; P-in-c Ryton from 20. *St Paul's Rectory, Scotland Head, Blaydon-on-Tyne NE21 6PL* E: alisonmstewartsmith@gmail.com

STEWART-SYKES, Teresa Melanie. b 64. Bris Univ BA 85. Qu Coll Birm 87. **d** 89 **p** 16. Par Dn Stevenage St Andr and St Geo *St Alb* 89–92; PtO *Birm* 92–93; Par Dn St John H Cross Barbados 93–97; C Meir Heath *Lich* 97–98; USA 98–00; NSM Dorchester *Sarum* 12–14; NSM Dorchester and the Winterbournes 14–19; TV Dorchester *Ox* from 19. *The Vicarage, Cherwell Road, Berinsfield, Wallingford OX10 7PB* M: 07823-809112 E: revteresa@outlook.com

STIBBE, Mrs Hazel Mary. d 99 **p** 00. NSM Wolverhampton St Andr *Lich* 99–02; LtO *St As* 03–08; rtd 08; PtO *St As* from 09. *Braemar, Kerry Street, Montgomery SY15 6PG* T: (01686) 668912 E: hazel.stibbe@gmail.com

STICKINGS, James Edmund de Garis. b 76. Magd Coll Ox BA 98 MA 08. Ripon Coll Cuddesdon 08. **d** 12 **p** 13. C Headington Quarry *Ox* 12–16; R Rotherfield Peppard and Kidmore End etc from 16. *The Rectory, Kidmore End, Reading RG4 9AY* M: 07522-042735 E: revjstickings@gmail.com

STICKLAND, David Clifford. b 44. Surrey Univ BA 01 CPFA 68 MAAT 77 FCCA 80. STETS 98. **d** 01 **p** 02. NSM Greatham w Empshott and Hawkley w Prior's Dean *Portsm* 01–05; NSM Petersfield and Buriton 05–10; rtd 10; PtO *Portsm* from 11. *14 Captains Row, Portsmouth PO1 2TT* M: 07836-282561 E: david_stickland.t21@btinternet.com

STICKLAND, Geoffrey John Brett. b 42. Open Univ BSc 96. St D Coll Lamp. **d** 66 **p** 67. C Aberavon H Trin *Llan* 66–69; C-in-c Llanrumney CD *Mon* 69–72; C Tetbury w Beverston *Glouc* 72–75; V Hardwicke 75–82; R Hardwicke, Quedgeley and Elmore w Longney 82–98; V Quedgeley 98–11; rtd 11. *19 Tai Cae Mawr, Llanwrtyd Wells LD5 4RJ* T: (01591) 610701 E: geoffstickland@googlemail.com

STICKLEY (née BRAGG), Mrs Annette Frances. b 44. Chich Th Coll 97. **d** 00. NSM Worth *Chich* 00–06; PtO from 06. *14 Elmstead Park Road, West Wittering, Chichester PO20 8NQ* T: (01243) 514619 E: annettestickley@talktalk.net

STIFF, Canon Derrick Malcolm. b 40. Lich Th Coll 69. **d** 72 **p** 73. C Cov St Geo 72–75; R Benhall w Sternfield *St E* 75–79; P-in-c Snape 75–79; V Cartmel *Carl* 79–87; R Sudbury and Chilton *St E* 87–94; P-in-c Lavenham 94–95; P-in-c Preston 94–95; R Lavenham w Preston 95–03; Min Can St E Cathl 90–00; Hon Can St E Cathl 00–03; RD Lavenham 95–03; rtd 03; PtO *St E* 03–19; *Sarum* 03–11. *8 Keats Close, Saxmundham IP17 1WJ* T: (01728) 652964 E: canonstiff@outlook.com

STILEMAN, William Mark Charles. b 63. Selw Coll Cam BA 85 MA 89 PGCE 86. Wycliffe Hall Ox. **d** 91 **p** 92. C Ox St Andr 91–95; TV Gt Chesham 95–03; P-in-c Maidenhead St Andr and St Mary 03–04; V from 04; C White Waltham from 19. *St Mary's Vicarage, 14 Juniper Drive, Maidenhead SL6 8RE* T: (01628) 624908 E: will.stileman@stmarysmaidenhead.org

STILL, Colin Charles. b 35. Selw Coll Cam BA 67 MA 71 United Th Sem Dayton STM 69. Cranmer Hall Dur 67. **d** 69 **p** 70. C Drypool St Columba w St Andr and St Pet *York* 69–72; Abp's Dom Chapl 72–75; Recruitment Sec ACCM 76–80; P-in-c Ockham w Hatchford *Guildf* 76–80; R 80–90; Can Missr and Ecum Officer 80–90; PtO *Chich* from 92; rtd 96. *Flat 9, 16 Lewes Crescent, Brighton BN2 1GB* T: (01273) 686014

STILL (née STACEY), Mrs Gillian. b 53. SWMTC 94. **d** 97 **p** 98. NSM Peter Tavy, Mary Tavy, Lydford and Brent Tor *Ex* 97–06; C Abbotskerswell 06–15; C Totnes w Bridgetown, Berry Pomeroy etc from 15; Chapl Rowcroft Hospice Torquay from 01. *The Vicarage, School Hill, Stoke Gabriel, Totnes TQ9 6QX* M: 07971-412511 E: gillstill@yahoo.co.uk

STILL, Canon Jonathan Trevor Lloyd. b 59. Ex Univ BA 81 Qu Coll Cam BA 84 MA 88. Westcott Ho Cam 82. **d** 85 **p** 86. C Weymouth H Trin *Sarum* 85–88; Chapl for Agric *Heref* 88–93; V N Petherton w Northmoor Green *B & W* 93–00; V The Bourne and Tilford *Guildf* 00–11; RD Farnham 05–10; V Buckland Newton, Cerne Abbas, Godmanstone etc *Sarum* from 11; RD Dorchester 16–20; Can and Preb Sarum Cathl from 18; Chapl RNR from 19. *The Vicarage, 4 Back Lane, Cerne Abbas, Dorchester DT2 7JW* T: (01300) 341251 E: cernevicar@gmail.com

STILL, Michael John. b 63. Reading Univ BSc 84 S Bank Univ PGCE 96. St Mellitus Coll 16. **d** 19 **p** 20. NSM Kenton *Lon* from 19; Chapl Quainton Hall Sch Harrow from 19. *12A Radnor Road, Harrow HA1 1RY* T: (020) 8863 8540 M: 07870-952274 E: mikestill63@gmail.com

STILWELL, Malcolm Thomas. b 54. Coll of Resurr Mirfield 83. **d** 86 **p** 87. C Workington St Mich *Carl* 86–90; P-in-c Flimby 90–93; PtO 93–95; NSM Westfield St Mary 95–11; NSM Workington St Jo 11–21; NSM Maryport, Netherton, Flimby and Broughton Moor 17–21; NSM Solway Plain 17–21; rtd 21. *18 Moorfield Avenue, Workington CA14 4HJ* T: (01900) 66757 E: info@thestilwellstudio.co.uk

STILWELL, Mrs Susan May. b 59. Herts Univ MA 96. ERMC 08. **d** 11 **p** 12. NSM Bishop's Hatfield, Lemsford and N Mymms *St Alb* from 11. *Field View, Kimpton Road, Welwyn AL6 9NN* T: (01438) 716338 E: susan.stilwell@clara.co.uk

STILWELL, Timothy James. b 65. Birm Univ BA 87. Wycliffe Hall Ox 96. **d** 98 **p** 99. C Clifton Ch Ch w Em *Bris* 98–02; C Hammersmith St Paul *Lon* 02–05; V Fulham St Dionis from 05; AD Hammersmith and Fulham 15–20. *St Dionis' Vicarage, 18 Parson's Green, London SW6 4UH* T: (020) 7731 1376 E: tim@stdionis.org.uk

STIMPSON, Nigel Leslie. b 60. St Martin's Coll Lanc BA 92 Lanc Univ MA 99. Coll of Resurr Mirfield 94. **d** 94 **p** 95. C Heyhouses on Sea *Blackb* 94–96; C Torrisholme 96–99; V Ravensthorpe and Thornhill Lees w Savile Town *Wakef* 99–05; TR Ribbleton *Blackb* 05–12; R 12–13; Chapl Gtr Lisbon *Eur* 13–14; Asst Chapl Palma de Mallorca 14–19; Chapl Costa del Sol E from 19. *Casa Esperanza, Calle Virgen del Carmen 3, 29640 Fuengirola (Málaga), Spain* T: (0034) 952 472 140 M: 07790-319798 E: nigel.stimpson13@gmail.com *or* vicar.costadelsol@gmail.com

STINSON, Andrew James. b 80. Newc Univ MEng 04 St Jo Coll Dur BA 11. Cranmer Hall Dur 09. **d** 12 **p** 13. C Oxton *Ches* 12–15; R Barrow from 15; Dioc Worship Adv from 15. *The Rectory, Mill Lane, Great Barrow, Chester CH3 7JF* T: (01829) 740263 M: 07847-948976 E: revandystinson@gmail.com

STIRLING, Canon Christina Dorita (Tina). b 48. Lon Univ BEd 73. Wycliffe Hall Ox 87. **d** 89 **p** 94. Par Dn Thame w Towersey *Ox* 89–94; C 94–98; P-in-c Brill, Boarstall, Chilton and Dorton 98; R Bernwode 98–13; AD Aylesbury 05–10; Hon Can Ch Ch 09–13; rtd 13; PtO *Ox* 13–16; *Sarum* 16–19. *Sherborne House, Tower Hill, Iwerne Minster, Blandford Forum DT11 8NH* T: (01747) 811451 E: tinadstirling@aol.com

STIRLING TROY, Mrs Margaret Ann. b 63. St Hilda's Coll Ox BA 85 MA Win Univ MA 15. STETS 10. **d** 13 **p** 14. C Farncombe *Guildf* 13–21; Chapl HM Pris Send 17–21; rtd 21. *3 Parkfield Way, Topsham, Exeter EX3 0DP* E: mstirling1@hotmail.co.uk

STOBART (formerly SLADE), Joanna Elisabeth. b 70. Leeds Univ BA 91 MA 92 Coll of Ripon & York St Jo PGCE 93. Sarum Coll BA 16. **d** 16 **p** 17. C Yatton Moor *B & W* 16–19; V Ilminster and Whitelackington from 19. *21 Higher Beacon, Ilminster TA19 9AJ* M: 07765-110266 E: joannaslade@aol.com

STOBART, Stuart Malcolm. b 64. Glos Univ BA 07 Leeds Univ MA 12. Yorks Min Course 07. **d** 09 **p** 10. C Clayton *Bradf* 09–12; P-in-c Hellifield 12–14; *Leeds* 14–15; P-in-c Long Preston w Tosside *Bradf* 12–14; *Leeds* 14–15; V Hellifield and Long Preston 15–20; V Halifax H Trin and St Jude from 20; PtO *Eur* from 17. *Holy Trinity Vicarage, 9 Love Lane, Halifax HX1 2BQ* M: 07545-631387 E: stuart.stobart@yahoo.co.uk *or* stuart.stobart@leeds.anglican.org

STOBER, Ms Brenda Jacqueline. Liv Univ BSc 79 Leeds Univ BA 08 Cranmer Hall Dur MA 19 Leeds Univ PGCE 80. NOC 04. **d** 07 **p** 08. C Southport Em *Liv* 07–11; C Wavertree H Trin 11–13; V Denton *Newc* 13–18; P-in-c Kirk Langley *Derby* from 18; P-in-c Mackworth All SS from 18; P-in-c Mugginton and Kedleston from 18; RD Duffield 18; RD Longford 18; AD Dove and Derwent from 18; Asst Dir of Ords from 20. *4 Church Lane, Kirk Langley, Ashbourne DE6 4NG* T: (01332) 824792 E: bjstober@yahoo.com

STOCK, Edward Christopher James. b 85. Heythrop Coll Lon BA 12. Ridley Hall Cam 12. **d** 14 **p** 15. C Eastwood *Chelmsf* 14–17; C Sydenham H Trin and St Aug *S'wark* 17–19; P-in-c Sydenham H Trin and Forest Hill 19–21. *Address temp unknown* M: 07838-156835 E: reveddstock@gmail.com

STOCK, Katharine Victoria Hannah. b 90. Heythrop Coll Lon BA 12 K Coll Lon MA 13. St Mellitus Coll. **d** 21. C Birm St Luke from 21. *41 Gas Street, Birmingham B1 2JT* M: 07943-813589 E: katie.vh.stock@gmail.com

STOCK, Lionel Crispian. b 58. Nottm Univ BTh 94 ACMA 85 ACIS 94. Linc Th Coll. **d** 94 **p** 95. C Preston w Sutton Poyntz, Littlemoor etc *Sarum* 94–97; P-in-c Stalbridge 97–00; Hon C Hillingdon All SS *Lon* 01–04; NSM Kendal H Trin *Carl* 04–10; PtO *Win* 10–12; Min Can Win Cathl 12–13; PtO *Eur* 10–13; P-in-c W Meon and Warnford *Portsm* 13–18; rtd 18; PtO *Eur* from 18; *Ex* from 19. *46 Butts Road, Ottery St Mary EX11 1EL* M: 07814-935715 E: revlstock@hotmail.com

STOCK, Nigel. See STOCK, William Nigel

STOCK, Miss Ruth Vaughan. b 51. Birkbeck Coll Lon BA 79 MA 85. Wycliffe Hall Ox 91. **d** 93 **p** 94. Par Dn Toxteth St Philemon w St Gabr and St Cleopas *Liv* 93–94; C 94–97; TV 97–10; TV St Luke in the City 10–13; C 13–16; rtd 16; PtO *Liv* from 17. *88 South Quay, Wapping Quay, Liverpool L3 4BW* E: ruthstock@ymail.com

STOCK, The Very Revd Victor Andrew. b 44. OAM 02. AKC 68 FRSA 95. **d** 69 **p** 70. C Pinner *Lon* 69–73; Chapl

Lon Univ 73–79; R Friern Barnet St Jas 79–86; R St Mary le Bow w St Pancras Soper Lane etc 86–02; P-in-c St Mary Aldermary 87–98; Dean Guildf 02–12; rtd 12; PV Westmr Abbey from 12; PtO *Lon* from 13. *62 Bramwell House, Churchill Gardens, London SW1V 3DS* T: (020) 7828 4921 E: vastock@btinternet.com

✠STOCK, The Rt Revd William **Nigel.** b 50. St Cuth Soc Dur BA 72. Ripon Coll Cuddesdon. **d** 76 **p** 77 **c** 00. C Stockton St Pet *Dur* 76–79; Papua New Guinea 79–84; V Shiremoor *Newc* 85–91; TR N Shields 91–98; RD Tynemouth 92–98; Hon Can Newc Cathl 97–98; Can Res Dur Cathl 98–00; Chapl Grey Coll Dur 99–00; Suff Bp Stockport *Ches* 00–07; Bp St E 07–13; Bp at Lambeth *Cant* 13–17; Hon Asst Bp S'wark from 13; Lon 13–18; B & W from 16; Bp Falkland Is 14–17; Bp HM Forces 14–17; rtd 17; PtO *B & W* from 14. *18 Trendle Lane, Bicknoller, Taunton TA4 4EG*

STOCKER, David William George. b 37. Bris Univ BA 58 Lon Univ CertEd. Qu Coll Birm 58. **d** 60 **p** 61. C Sparkhill St Jo *Birm* 60–64; C Keighley *Bradf* 64–66; V Grenoside *Sheff* 66–83; V Sandbach *Ches* 83–01; rtd 01; PtO *Ches* 01–16; *Sheff* from 19; *Leeds* 19–21. *3 Ivy Bank Close, Ingbirchworth, Penistone, Sheffield S36 7GT* T: (01226) 953415 E: davidwgstocker@gmail.com

STOCKER, John Henry. b 48. Cov Univ BSc 71 Sheff Univ BEd 81 ACP 88. St Mich Coll Llan 01. **d** 04 **p** 05. NSM E Radnor *S & B* 04–06; NSM Irfon Valley 06–09; rtd 09; PtO *S & B* from 10. *1 Tai Cae Mawr, Llanwrtyd Wells LD5 4RJ* T: (01592) 610231 M: 07891-086631 E: stocker65@btinternet.com

STOCKER, Rachael Ann. *See* KNAPP, Rachael Ann

STOCKING, Clifford **Brian.** b 67. Trin Coll Bris 08. **d** 10 **p** 11. C Hadlow *Roch* 10–13; P-in-c March St Wendreda *Ely* 13–15; P-in-c March St Jo 13–15; TV March 15–17; V Margate H Trin *Cant* from 17; Jt AD Thanet 18–21. *5 Devonshire Gardens, Margate CT9 3AF* M: 07941-056237 E: clifford2567@gmail.com

STOCKITT, Robin **Philip.** b 56. Liv Univ BA 77 St Andr Univ MLitt 16 Tübingen Univ DrTheol 10 Crewe & Alsager Coll PGCE 78. Ridley Hall Cam 95. **d** 97 **p** 98. C Billing *Pet* 97–01; P-in-c Freiburg-im-Breisau *Eur* 01–14; Asst Chapl Basle 01–14; I Donagheady *D & R* 14–21; rtd 21. *5 Glenbank Flats, Seacourt Lane, Bangor BT20 3TQ* T: (028) 7139 8017 M: 07538-243138 E: robin.stockitt@gmail.com

STOCKLEY, Mrs Alexandra Madeleine Reuss. b 43. Cranmer Hall Dur 80 Carl Dioc Tr Inst. **dss** 84 **d** 87 **p** 94. Upperby St Jo *Carl* 84–89; Par Dn 87–89; Dn-in-c Grayrigg, Old Hutton and New Hutton 90–94; P-in-c 94–95; P-in-c Levens 95–03; rtd 03; PtO *Carl* from 03. *Crowberry, Ulpha, Broughton-in-Furness LA20 6DZ* T: (01229) 716875

STOCKPORT, Suffragan Bishop of. *See* CORLEY, The Rt Revd Samuel Jon Clint

STOCKS, Simon **Paul.** b 68. Rob Coll Cam BA 89 MA 93 Man Univ PhD 11. Trin Coll Bris BA 03 MPhil 06. **d** 04 **p** 05. C Coulsdon St Jo *S'wark* 04–07; Hon C 07–13; Hon C Purley Ch Ch from 13; Tutor St Aug Coll of Th from 11. *316 Coulsdon Road, Coulsdon CR5 1EB* T: (01737) 553190 E: s.stocks@staugustinescollege.ac.uk

STOCKTON, Canon Ian **George.** b 49. Selw Coll Cam BA 72 MA 76 Hull Univ PhD 90. St Jo Coll Nottm PGCE 74. **d** 75 **p** 76. C Chell *Lich* 75–78; C Trentham 78–80; R Dalbeattie *Glas* 80–84; P-in-c Scotton w Northorpe *Linc* 84–88; Asst Local Min Officer 84–88; Local Min Officer and LNSM Course Prin 88–97; TR Monkwearmouth *Dur* 97–11; Can Res and Chan Blackb Cathl 11–17; rtd 17. *13 Longdales Road, Lincoln LN2 2JR* E: ian.g.stockton@gmail.com

STODDART, David **Easton.** b 36. K Coll Dur BSc 60 PhD 66 CEng 66 MIMechE 66 FCMI 72 FIQA 76. WEMTC 92. **d** 95 **p** 96. OLM Stroud H Trin *Glouc* 95–99; OLM Woodchester and Brimscombe 99–00; NSM 00–08; Jt Angl Chapl Severn NHS Trust 99–05; Jt Angl Chapl Glos Primary Care Trust 05–11; rtd 11; PtO *Glouc* from 08. *Woodstock, Hampton Green, Box, Stroud GL6 9AD* T: (01453) 885338 E: stoddart@david-isabel.co.uk

STODDART, Mrs Hazel Elizabeth **Jane.** b 92. Cranmer Hall Dur 17. **d** 19 **p** 21. C Salford St Phil w St Steph *Man* from 19. *42 Vancouver Quay, Salford M50 3TU* E: hazelej92@gmail.com

STOKE-ON-TRENT, Archdeacon of. *See* SMITH, The Ven Megan Rachel

STOKER, **Andrew.** b 64. Coll of Ripon & York St Jo BA 86. Coll of Resurr Mirfield 87. **d** 90 **p** 91. C Horton *Newc* 90–92; C Clifford *York* 92–96; P-in-c Cawood 96–98; P-in-c Ryther 96–98; P-in-c Wistow 96–98; R Cawood w Ryther and Wistow 98–04; P-in-c York St Clem w St Mary Bishophill Senior 04–05; R York St Clem w St Mary Bishophill 05–19; rtd 19; PtO *York* from 20. *4 Dyon Walk, Bubwith, Selby YO8 6LQ*

STOKER, Canon Howard **Charles.** b 62. Linc Th Coll BTh 93. **d** 93 **p** 94. C Hessle *York* 93–96; C Richmond w Hudswell

Ripon 96–99; C Downholme and Marske 96–99; R Holt w High Kelling *Nor* from 99; RD Holt 05–11; Hon Can Nor Cathl from 13. *The Rectory, 11 Church Street, Holt NR25 6BB* T: (01263) 712048 F: 711397 E: holtrectory@tiscali.co.uk

STOKER, Canon Joanna **Mary.** b 57. Leic Univ BA 79 Nottm Univ BCombStuds 83. Linc Th Coll 80. **dss** 83 **d** 87 **p** 94. Greenford H Cross *Lon* 83–87; Par Dn 87–89; Par Dn Farnham Royal w Hedgerley *Ox* 89–92; Dn-in-c Seer Green and Jordans 92–94; P-in-c 94–97; TV Stantonbury and Willen 97–03; TR Basingstoke *Win* from 03; Hon Can Win Cathl from 08. *The Rectory, Church Street, Basingstoke RG21 7QT* T: (01256) 326654 E: jostoker@dsl.pipex.com

STOKES, Colin Arthur (**Ted**). b 59. Birm Univ BDS 82. WEMTC 00. **d** 03 **p** 04. NSM Bromyard *Heref* 03–08; NSM Bromyard and Stoke Lacy 09–18; PtO from 18. *Solmor Paddocks, Linley Green Road, Whitbourne, Worcester WR6 5RE* T: (01886) 821625

STOKES, Dawn **Ann.** b 63. **d** 16 **p** 17. C Daventry *Pet* 16–19; P-in-c from 19. *28 Osprey Drive, Daventry NN11 0XP* E: revdawn63@gmail.com

STOKES, Roger **Sidney.** b 47. Clare Coll Cam BA 68 MA 72. Sarum & Wells Th Coll 69. **d** 72 **p** 73. C Keighley *Bradf* 72–74; C Bolton St Jas w St Chrys 74–78; V Hightown *Wakef* 78–85; Dep Chapl HM Pris Wakef 85–87; Chapl HM Pris Full Sutton 87–89; PtO *Wakef* 92–95; P-in-c Carlinghow 95–99; P-in-c Bedford St Martin *St Alb* 99–14; rtd 14; PtO *St Alb* from 14. *88 Sovereigns Quay, Bedford MK40 1TF* T: (01234) 261812 E: r.s.stokes@cantab.net

STOKES, Canon Simon **Colin.** b 62. Nene Coll Northn BSc 83 Anglia Ruskin Univ MA 12. Ridley Hall Cam 89. **d** 92 **p** 93. C New Catton Ch Ch *Nor* 92–96; P-in-c King's Lynn St Jo the Ev 96–06; P-in-c Bowthorpe 06–11; Chapl Coll of W Anglia 01–06; R Sprowston w Beeston *Nor* from 11; C New Catton Ch 13–19; P-in-c from 20; RD Nor N from 16; Hon Can Nor Cathl from 06. *The Vicarage, 2 Wroxham Road, Norwich NR7 8TZ* T: (01603) 426492 E: simon@simonstokes.co.uk *or* vicar@sprowston.org.uk

STOKES, Simon **Jeremy.** b 63. St Anne's Coll Ox BA 86 MA 90 Mass Inst of Tech SM 88 Univ of Wales (Cardiff) LLM 97 Solicitor 92. NTMTC BA 08. **d** 08 **p** 09. NSM Clerkenwell H Redeemer *Lon* 08–13; NSM St Marylebone St Cypr 13–17. *4 Stable Court, Charterhouse, 15 Charterhouse Square, London EC1M 6AU* M: 07722-048110

STOKES, **Ted.** *See* STOKES, Colin Arthur

STOKES, Terence **Harold.** b 46. Open Univ BA 89. Sarum & Wells Th Coll 71. **d** 73 **p** 74. C Blakenall Heath *Lich* 73–75; C Walsall Wood 75–78; C Northampton St Alb *Pet* 78–81; TV Swinton St Pet *Man* 81–85; V Daisy Hill 85–92; rtd 09; PtO *Blackb* 09–12; Hon C Chorley St Laur from 12; PtO *Man* 13–14. *17 St John's Court, Chorley Road, Westhoughton, Bolton BL5 3WG* M: 07899-040781 E: revthstokes@aim.com

STOKES-HARRISON, David Neville **Hurford.** b 41. FCA 65 FCCA 67 FInstM 68. Qu Coll Birm 97. **d** 00 **p** 01. NSM Walsall *Lich* 00–07; NSM Edgmond w Kynnersley and Preston Wealdmoors 07–18; NSM Tibberton w Bolas Magna and Waters Upton 07–18; rtd 18; PtO *Lich* 18–19. *The Rectory, Mill Lane, Tibberton, Newport TF10 8NL* T: (01952) 551063 E: stokesharrison@btinternet.com

STOKOE, Wayne **Jeffrey.** b 56. Coll of Resurr Mirfield 94. **d** 96 **p** 97. C Sheff St Cath Richmond Road 96–99; V Edlington 99–09; P-in-c Doncaster H Trin 09–10; P-in-c New Cantley 09–10; V from 10. *St Hugh's House, Levet Road, Doncaster DN4 6JQ* T: (01302) 371256 E: wjs56@live.co.uk

STOLTZ, Christopher **Barry.** b 76. St Olaf Coll Minnesota BA 99. Concordia Th Sem Indiana MDiv 03. **d** 06 **p** 07. C Highgate St Mich *Lon* 06–09; Chapl Trin Coll Cam 09–14; Min Can Westmr Abbey 14–20; Succ 14–15; Prec 15–20; PV Westmr Abbey from 20; Chapl Haileybury Coll from 20. *The Deanery, Haileybury and Imperial Service College, Hertford SG13 7NU* T: (01992) 706200

STONE, Preb Adrian **Gordon.** b 68. Trent Poly BSc 89 Nottm Univ PGCE 92. St Jo Coll Nottm 01. **d** 03 **p** 04. C Bayston Hill *Lich* 03–06; R Stafford St Jo and Tixall w Ingestre 06–17; V Trentham from 17; Preb Lich Cathl from 20. *The Vicarage, Trentham Park, Stoke-on-Trent ST4 8AE* T: (01782) 691948 M: 07739-043709 E: adrianstone@me.com

STONE, Albert **John.** b 44. Loughb Univ BTech 67 BSc. Sarum & Wells Th Coll 83. **d** 85 **p** 86. C Plymstock *Ex* 85–88; P-in-c Whitestone 88–92; P-in-c Oldridge 88–92; P-in-c Holcombe Burnell 88–92; R Tedburn St Mary, Whitestone, Oldridge etc 93–94; P-in-c Yarcombe w Membury and Upottery 94; P-in-c Cotleigh 94; V Yarcombe, Membury, Upottery and Cotleigh 95–99; P-in-c Bampton, Morebath, Clayhanger and Petton 99–10; rtd 10; PtO *Ex* from 10. *9 Castle Park, Hemyock, Cullompton EX15 3SA* T: (01823) 681459 E: ajstone@orpheusmail.co.uk

STONE, Christopher. See STONE, John Christopher
STONE, Christopher John. b 49. Lanc Univ MA 89 Keele Univ MA 92. Lambeth STh 84 Linc Th Coll 78. **d** 81 **p** 82. C Bromley St Mark *Roch* 81–84; R Burgh-by-Sands and Kirkbampton w Kirkandrews etc *Carl* 84–89; Chapl N Staffs R Infirmary Stoke-on-Trent 89–93; Co-ord Staff Support Services N Staffs Hosp 93–09; rtd 09. *Coppers Nest, Fore Street, Milton Abbot, Tavistock PL19 0PA* T: (01822) 870721 E: stonecj49@btinternet.com
STONE, Christopher Martyn Luke. b 78. Glam Univ BA 99. St Steph Ho Ox 99. **d** 02 **p** 03. C Merthyr Tydfil Ch Ch *Llan* 02–07; TV Bassaleg *Mon* 07–13; TR from 13. *The Vicarage, 1 Church View, Caerphilly Road, Bassaleg, Newport NP10 8ND* T: (01633) 378354 E: vicchris78@sky.com
STONE, Canon David Adrian. b 56. Oriel Coll Ox BA 78 MA 83 BM, BCh 83. Wycliffe Hall Ox 85. **d** 88 **p** 89. C Holborn St Geo w H Trin and St Bart *Lon* 88–91; C S Kensington St Jude 91–93; V 93–02; AD Chelsea 96–02; TR Newbury *Ox* 02–10; Can Res and Prec Cov Cathl from 10; Sub-Dean from 14. *55 Cotswold Drive, Coventry CV3 6EZ* M: 07973-215927 E: david@dandb.org.uk
STONE, Elizabeth Karen Forbes. See FORBES STONE, Elizabeth Karen
STONE, The Ven Godfrey Owen. b 49. Ex Coll Ox BA 71 MA 75 W Midl Coll of Educn PGCE 72. Wycliffe Hall Ox BA 78. **d** 81 **p** 82. C Rushden w Newton Bromswold *Pet* 81–87; Dir Past Studies Wycliffe Hall Ox 87–92; TR Bucknall and Bagnall *Lich* 92–02; RD Stoke 98–02; Adn Stoke-upon-Trent 02–13; P-in-c Edensor 04–07; rtd 13; PtO *Ox* from 14. *12 William Lucy Way, Oxford OX2 6EQ* E: stonegodfrey03@gmail.com
STONE, Ian Matthew. b 72. Ox Univ BTh 08 St Mellitus Coll MA 20. Ripon Coll Cuddesdon 03. **d** 05 **p** 06. C Hammersmith St Pet *Lon* 05–08; V Queensbury All SS 08–14; R Gt Stanmore from 14. *14 Chambers Walk, Stanmore HA7 4FN* T: (020) 8954 3876 M: 07950-891883 E: rector@stjohnschurchstanmore.org.uk
STONE, Jeffrey Peter. b 34. Nottm Univ TCert 72 BEd 73. Lich Th Coll 58. **d** 61 **p** 62. C Newark St Mary *S'well* 61–65; C Sutton in Ashfield St Mich 65–69; Robert Smyth Sch Market Harborough 72–89; R Waltham on the Wolds, Stonesby, Saxby etc *Leic* 90–96; rtd 96; PtO *Leic* 99–17. *71 Redland Road, Oakham LE15 6PH* T: (01572) 756842
STONE, John. See STONE, Albert John
STONE, John Anthony. b 46. Univ of Wales (Lamp) MA 05. St Chad's Coll Dur BA 68. **d** 69 **p** 70. C New Addington *Cant* 69–72; C Tewkesbury w Walton Cardiff *Glouc* 72–76; C-in-c Dedworth CD *Ox* 76–82; V Dedworth 82–86; TV Chipping Barnet w Arkley *St Alb* 86–95; R Baldock w Bygrave 95–03; R Ches H Trin 03–11; rtd 11; PtO *St As* from 12; *Ban* from 14. *4 Carpenter Avenue, Llandudno LL30 1YW* E: jastone@dunelm.org.uk
STONE, Canon John Christopher. b 53. Newc Univ BA 74 Birkbeck Coll Lon MA 77 MSTSD 74 LGSM 73 MCIPR FRSA. Oak Hill NSM Course 89. **d** 92 **p** 93. NSM Southfleet *Roch* 92–07; Dioc Communications Officer 96–03; Chapl Univ of Greenwich 98–99; Hon Can Roch Cathl 02–18; Bp's Dom Chapl 03–07; Bp's Media Adv 03–07; Bp's Communications Consultant 07–18; R Gravesend St Geo 07–18; rtd 18. *37 The Old Yews, Longfield DA3 7JS*
STONE, Martyn. See STONE, Christopher Martyn Luke
STONE, Matthew. See STONE, Ian Matthew
STONE, Nigel John. b 57. Bedf Coll Lon BSc 82 Lon Bible Coll MA 95. St Jo Coll Nottm 82. **d** 85 **p** 86. C Battersea Park St Sav *S'wark* 85–87; C Battersea St Sav and St Geo w St Andr 87–89; P-in-c Brixton St Paul 89–92; V 92–97; Adult Educn and Tr Officer 97–09; Dioc Olympic Adv 10–12; Par Support P Kingston Area 10–13; Hon Chapl S'wark Cathl 97–13; V Mitcham St Mark from 13. *St Mark's Vicarage, Locks Lane, Mitcham CR4 2JX* T: (020) 8648 2397 *or* 8640 1035 E: nigelstone6@btinternet.com
STONE, Peter Jonathan Michael. b 71. Ripon Coll Cuddesdon 08. **d** 10 **p** 11. C Charminster and Stinsford *Sarum* 10–14; TV Bridport from 14. *The Vicarage, 5 Garden Close, Bridport DT6 3AJ* T: (01308) 426459 M: 07971-425889 E: revpetestone@yahoo.co.uk *or* pete@bridport-team-ministry.org
STONE, Canon Philip William. b 58. Ridley Hall Cam 85. **d** 88 **p** 89. C Hackney Marsh *Lon* 88–97; V Kensal Rise St Mark and St Martin 97–04; TR 04–10; AD Brent 03–10; Dir Scargill Ho from 10; Hon Can Bradf Cathl *Leeds* from 19. *Scargill House, Kettlewell, Skipton BD23 5HU* T: (01756) 761240 E: phil@scargillmovement.org
STONE, Robert David. b 65. St Mellitus Coll 14. **d** 16 **p** 17. NSM Bocking St Pet *Chelmsf* 16–20; P-in-c S Rodings from 20; P-in-c Gt Canfield w High Roding and Aythorpe

Roding from 20; P-in-c High Easter and Good Easter w Margaret Roding from 20. *The Rectory, Stortford Road, Leaden Roding, Dunmow CM6 1GY* M: 07726-719288 E: robertstone1965@gmail.com
STONEHOUSE, Ian Michael. b 66. Westhill Coll Birm BPhil 97. St Mellitus Coll BA 16. **d** 16 **p** 17. C Leatherhead and Mickleham *Guildf* 16–20; PtO 20–21. *Address temp unknown* M: 07775-681884 E: rev.stonehouse@icloud.com
STONESTREET, George Malcolm. b 38. MBE 05. AKC 61. **d** 62 **p** 63. C Leeds St Pet *Ripon* 62–64; C Far Headingley St Chad 64–67; V Askrigg w Stallingbusk 67–82; V Bramley 82–85; TR 85–94; V Eskdale, Irton, Muncaster and Waberthwaite *Carl* 94–03; rtd 03; PtO *Carl* from 09. *Northside, Grange, Keswick CA12 5UQ* T: (01768) 777671 E: malcolm@dip.edi.co.uk *or* malcolmstonestreet@gmail.com
STONHAM, Emma Jane. See GRAEME, Emma Jane
STONIER, Mrs Mary. b 56. **d** 09 **p** 10. OLM Crowle Gp *Linc* 09–18; NSM Bottesford w Ashby from 18. *28 Windsor Road, Crowle, Scunthorpe DN17 4ES* T: (01724) 710900 E: mary.stonier@tiscali.co.uk
STOPFORD, John Thomas. b 44. AIMLS 67. **d** 16 **p** 17. NSM Whitegate w Lt Budworth *Ches* from 16; Chapl Asst St Luke's Cheshire Hospice 16–19; Chapl from 19. *7 Pinner Avenue, Winsford CW7 1LA* T: (01606) 558802 M: 07710-228336 E: jstopford801@btinternet.com
STORDY, Canon Richard Andrew. b 64. St Jo Coll Ox BA 86 Univ of Wales MTh 10 Barrister 86. Cranmer Hall Dur BA 97. **d** 98 **p** 99. C Gt Horton *Bradf* 98–02; V Chapeltown *Sheff* from 02; AD Ecclesfield 10–14; Hon Can Sheff Cathl from 21. *St John's Vicarage, 23 Housley Park, Chapeltown, Sheffield S35 2UE* T: 0114-257 0966 M: 07812-924926 E: rick@rastordy.plus.com
STORER, Alison. b 62. Qu Foundn (Course) 16. **d** 18 **p** 19. NSM Penn *Lich* from 18. *12 Foxlands Avenue, Wolverhampton WV4 5LX* T: (01902) 330662 M: 07734-069355 E: alisonjohnson540@btinternet.com
STORER, Rachael. **d** 16 **p** 17. NSM Gwastedyn *S & B* 16–17; C Ithon Valley from 17. *The Rectory, Crossgates, Llandrindod Wells LD1 6RU* T: (01597) 851204 E: ithonvalleyrectory@googlemail.com
STOREY, Earl. See STOREY, William Earl Cosbey
STOREY, Mrs Elizabeth Mary. b 37. Man Univ BA 84. Local Minl Tr Course 81. **dss** 84 **d** 87 **p** 94. Liv All So Springwood 84–91; Par On 87–91; C St Helens St Helen 91–94; C Garston 94–97; Asst Chapl Liv Univ 94–98; C Mossley Hill St Matt and St Jas 97–03; Asst Chapl Liv Coll 98–03; rtd 03; PtO *Liv* from 16. *27 Mentmore Road, Mossley Hill, Liverpool L18 4PU* T: 0151-724 2075
STOREY, Gerard Charles Alfred. b 57. Thames Poly BSc 80 Lon Univ PhD 84 GRSC 80. Wycliffe Hall Ox 84. **d** 87 **p** 88. C Broadwater *Chich* 87–92; TV 92–95; Chapl Northbrook Coll of Design and Tech 90–95; Oman 95–99; P-in-c Guernsey H Trin *Win* 99–01; V 01–07; P-in-c Bream *Glouc* 07–12; V 12–14; Tanzania 14–19; Public Preacher *Glouc* 14–19; PtO *Chich* from 16. *22 Mayfield Road, Bognor Regis PO21 5NA* E: gerardstorey@yahoo.co.uk
STOREY, Canon Michael. b 36. Chich Th Coll 73. **d** 75 **p** 76. C Illingworth *Wakef* 75–78; V Rastrick St Jo 78–87; V Crosland Moor 87–06; Hon Can Wakef Cathl 00–06; rtd 06; PtO *Wakef* 07–14; *Leeds* from 14. *198 Healey Wood Road, Brighouse HD6 3RW* T: (01484) 713663 E: mickthevic@googlemail.com
✠**STOREY, The Most Revd Patricia Louise.** b 60. TCD MA 83. CITC BTh 94. **d** 97 **p** 98 **c** 13. C Ballymena w Ballyclug *Conn* 97–00; C Glenavy w Tunny and Crumlin 00–04; I Londonderry St Aug *D & R* 04–13; Bp M & K from 13. *Bishop's House, Moyglare, Maynooth, Co Kildare, Republic of Ireland* T: (00353) (1) 628 9825 *or* (1) 629 2163 E: patriciastorey56@yahoo.co.uk *or* bishop@meath.anglican.org
STOREY, Timothy. b 60. Trin Coll Bris 92. **d** 94 **p** 95. C Bath Weston St Jo w Kelston *B & W* 94–98; C Shirley *Win* 98–03; R Blandford Forum and Langton Long *Sarum* 03–14; TR Cen Telford *Lich* 14–20; RD Telford 16–20; R Yateley *Win* from 20. *The Vicarage, 99 Reading Road, Yateley GU46 7LR* T: (01252) 901213 E: revtimstorey@gmail.com
STOREY, William Earl Cosbey. b 58. Kent Univ BA MPhil. CITC. **d** 82 **p** 83. C Drumglass w Moygashel *Arm* 82–86; I Crinken *D & G* 86–96; I Glenavy w Tunny and Crumlin *Conn* 94–04; Dioc Communications Officer *D & R* from 07; Ed Church of Ireland Gazette from 17; Chapl Defence Forces from 20. *Bishop's House, Moyglare, Maynooth, Co Kildare, Republic of Ireland* T: (00353) (1) 628 9354 *or* (1) 628 9825 E: earl@topstorey.org *or* dco@derry.anglican.org
STORK BANKS, Daniel John. b 78. Reading Univ MBA 11 Univ of Wales (Abth) BScEcon 02. Ripon Coll Cuddesdon 13.

d 15 **p** 16. C Cheswardine, Childs Ercall, Hales, Hinstock etc *Lich* 15–19; V Chobham w Valley End *Guildf* from 19. *Chobham Vicarage, Bagshot Road, Chobham, Woking GU24 8BY* M: 07825-951659 E: danstorkbanks@gmail.com

STORY, Victor Leonard. b 45. St Mark & St Jo Coll Lon TCert 66 Brighton Poly BSc 74 LIMA 74 SS Mark & John Univ Plymouth Hon BEd 19. Ripon Coll Cuddesdon 80. **d** 81 **p** 82. C Evesham *Worc* 81–85; P-in-c Ilmington w Stretton on Fosse and Ditchford *Cov* 85–90; P-in-c Ilmington w Stretton-on-Fosse etc 90–96; Chapl Vlissingen (Flushing) Miss to Seamen *Eur* 96–97; Chapl Rotterdam Miss to Seafarers 97–99; Rotterdam 99; R Gt w Lt Milton and Gt Haseley *Ox* 99–15; rtd 15; PtO *Ox* from 15. *66 Rowell Way, Chipping Norton OX7 5BD* E: victor.story@btinternet.com

STOTE, Mrs Judith Ann. b 50. Qu Coll Birm 07. **d** 09 **p** 10. OLM Studley *Cov* 09–12; NSM 12–13; NSM Spernall, Morton Bagot and Oldberrow 12–13; NSM Arden Marches 13–15; rtd 15; PtO *Cov* from 15. *6 Dunstall Close, Redditch B97 5UY* T: (01527) 852515 E: judy@ardenmarches.com

STOTE, Mrs Pamela Anne. b 49. Dudley Coll of Educn TCert 70 Open Univ BA 83. WMMTC 97. **d** 00 **p** 01. NSM Cov St Geo 00–03; NSM Whitley 03–13; P-in-c 05–13; rtd 13; PtO *Cov* 14–15; NSM Allesley Park and Whoberley 15–19. *22 Chetwode Close, Coventry CV5 9NA* M: 07905-230924 E: pamstote49@gmail.com

STOTER, David John. b 43. MBE 02. K Coll Lon AKC 66. **d** 67 **p** 68. C Reading St Giles *Ox* 67–71; C Luton Lewsey St Hugh *St Alb* 71–73; Chapl Chelsea and Westmr Hosp Lon 73–79; Convenor of Chapls Notts Distr HA 79–94; Chapl Univ Hosp Nottm 79–94; Chapl Nottm Gen Hosp 79–02; Sen Chapl Qu Medical Cen Nottm Univ Hosp NHS Trust 94–02; Sen Chapl Notts Healthcare NHS Trust 94–02; Manager Chapl and Bereavement Services 94–02; R Gedling *S'well* 02–06; rtd 06; OCM 06–08; PtO *St And* 06–08; Hon C Nettlebed w Bix, Highmoor, Pishill etc *Ox* 08–10; PtO *Ches* from 11; *Heref* 19–21. *3 Brookdale Rise, Bramhall, Stockport SK7 3HG* E: david.stoter@yahoo.co.uk

STOTESBURY, Robert John. **d** 06 **p** 07. NSM Ferns w Kilbride, Toombe, Kilcormack etc *C, F & O* 06–10; NSM Enniscorthy w Clone, Clonmore, Monart etc 10–16; NSM Ardamine w Kiltennel, Glascarrig etc 16–18; P-in-c Killeshin w Cloydagh and Killabban from 18. *Croneyhorn, Carnew, Arklow, Co Wicklow, Republic of Ireland* T: (00353) (53) 942 6300 M: 87-988 2507 E: rstotesbury@hotmail.com

STOTHERS, Neil. b 60. Liv Hope BA PGCE. Coll of Resurr Mirfield 11. **d** 13 **p** 14. C Southport Em *Liv* 13–17; P-in-c S Croxton Gp *Leic* from 17; P-in-c Burrough Hill Pars from 18. *19 Main Street, South Croxton, Leicester LE7 3RJ* T: (01664) 841278 E: revneilstothers@yahoo.co.uk

STOTT, Andrew David. b 61. NOC 03. **d** 05 **p** 06. C Walton Breck *Liv* 05–09; P-in-c W Derby St Luke 09–14; TR 4Saints Team 14–18; AD Huyton 17–18; P-in-c Orrell Hey St Jo and St Jas 18; TR Litherland and Orrell Hey from 19; AD Sefton S from 19. *St Phillip's Vicarage, Orrell Road, Liverpool L21 8NG* M: 07510-222374

STOTT, Christopher John. b 45. Lon Univ BD 68. Tyndale Hall Bris. **d** 69 **p** 70. C Croydon Ch Ch Broad Green *Cant* 69–72; Ethiopia 73–76; Area Sec (SW) BCMS 76–78; Tanzania 78–84; R Harwell w Chilton *Ox* 85–10; RD Wallingford 91–95; rtd 10; Chapl Berks Healthcare NHS Foundn Trust from 10; PtO *Ox* from 10. *1 Dibleys, Blewbury, Didcot OX11 9PT* T: (01235) 850070

STOTT, Mrs Debra Ann. b 60. Univ of Wales (Ban) BA 81 Open Univ BSc 00. All SS Cen for Miss & Min 12. **d** 14 **p** 15. NSM Moreton *Ches* from 14. *20 Broomleigh Close, Wirral CH63 2RH* T: 0151-608 3364 M: 07879-851796 E: debbi.stott@outlook.com *or* debbi.stott@christchurchmoreton.org.uk

STOTT, Jonathan Robert. b 67. Ripon Coll Cuddesdon 99. **d** 01 **p** 02. C Anfield St Columba *Liv* 01–05; V Dovecot 05–10; Chapl HM Pris Risley 10; P-in-c Dovecot *Liv* 10–13; TR Lowton and Golborne from 15. *St Luke's Vicarage, 246 Slag Lane, Lowton, Warrington WA3 2ED* E: frjonathan@btinternet.com

STOTT, Miss Teresa. b 57. Linc Th Coll 94. **d** 94 **p** 95. C Lee-on-the-Solent *Portsm* 94–97; C Spalding St Jo w Deeping St Nicholas *Linc* 97–98; P-in-c Freiston w Butterwick 98–99; R Freiston w Butterwick and Benington 99–03; R Freiston, Butterwick w Bennington, and Leverton 03–04; C-in-c Cleethorpes St Fran CD 04–09; TV Gt and Lt Coates w Bradley 09–11; Chapl Matthew Humberston Sch 04–11; Chapl St Andr Hospice Grimsby 06–11; Chapl Wherry Village *Guildf* 11–15; V Skerton St Luke *Blackb* 15–17; rtd 17; PtO *Linc* 17–20. *22 Park Mews, Sandown PO36 9BL* E: stott145@btinternet.com

STOW, John Mark. b 51. Selw Coll Cam BA 73 MA 77. Linc Th Coll 76. **d** 78 **p** 79. C Harpenden St Jo *St Alb* 78–82; TV Beaminster Area *Sarum* 82–87; P-in-c Hawkchurch 87–88; P-in-c Marshwood Vale 87–88; TR 88–91; Past Co-ord Millfield Jun Sch 93–98; Manager Somerset Rural Youth Project 99–12; Regional Development Manager Learning SW from 12; PtO *B & W* 09–13; Hon C Somerton w Compton Dundon, the Charltons etc 13. *54 Etsome Terrace, Somerton TA11 6LS* E: stowjm@gmail.com

STOW, Peter John. b 50. Oak Hill Th Coll. **d** 89 **p** 90. C Forest Gate St Mark *Chelmsf* 89–94; V 94–18; rtd 18; PtO *Chelmsf* from 18. *21 Cecily Avenue, Braintree CM7 2BA* T: (01376) 348146 E: pj.stow@btinternet.com

STOW, Archdeacon of. *Vacant*

STOWE, Mrs Katharine Elizabeth. b 78. Birm Univ BA 01 PGCE 02 Trin Coll Cam BA 06. Westcott Ho Cam 04. **d** 07 **p** 08. C Salter Street and Shirley *Birm* 07–11; Bp's Dom Chapl 11–20; P-in-c Harborne St Pet from 20. *St Peter's Church and Parish Office, Old Church Road, Harborne, Birmingham B17 0BB* T: 0121-681 1940 E: revdkate@gmail.com

STOWE, Canon Rachel Lilian. b 33. Qu Coll Birm 79. **dss** 83 **d** 87 **p** 94. Dean w Yelden, Melchbourne and Shelton *St Alb* 82–87; Pertenhall w Swineshead 82–87; Bp's Officer for NSMs and Asst Dir of Ords 87–93; rtd 93; NSM The Stodden Churches *St Alb* 87–96; Hon Can St Alb 92–96; Convenor Dioc Adv Gp for Chr Healing *Ripon* 98–03; PtO 97–14; *Leeds* from 14; *York* 98–19. *Preston Cottage, East Cowton, Northallerton DL7 0BD* T/F: (01325) 378173 M: 07860-618600 E: rachelstowe2106@outlook.com

STOWELL, Ms Jody. b 75. Spurgeon's Coll BD 09. Ridley Hall Cam 09. **d** 11 **p** 12. C Harrow Weald All SS *Lon* 11–14; V Harrow Weald St Mich from 14. *74 Bishop Ken Road, Harrow HA3 7HR* M: 07940-269148 E: revjody@virginmedia.com

STRACHAN, Robert John. b 90. Ex Coll Ox BA 12. Oak Hill Th Coll BA 17. **d** 18 **p** 19. C Cambridge H Sepulchre *Ely* from 18. *9 Victoria Street, Cambridge CB1 1JP* M: 07900-202168 E: robbiejstrachan@gmail.com

STRADLING, Penelope Joy. b 79. Surrey Univ BA 02. **d** 20. C S Widnes *Liv* 20–21; C Widnes St Jo and St Paul from 21. *3 Motherwell Close, Widnes WA8 9DU* M: 07791-340294 E: pennystradling@gmail.com

STRAFFORD, Nigel Thomas Bevan. b 53. Univ of Wales (Lamp) BA 80. Sarum & Wells Th Coll 80. **d** 82 **p** 84. C Kidderminster St Mary *Worc* 82; C Kidderminster St Mary and All SS, Trimpley etc 82–83; Hon C Stockton St Mark *Dur* 84–86; Asst P Longwood *Wakef* 86–94; V Athersley 94–97; P-in-c Ferrybridge 97–03; P-in-c Holme and Seaton Ross Gp *York* 03–04; R 04–13; rtd 13; PtO *Dur* 14–20. *5 High Street, Stanhope, Bishop Auckland DL13 2UP* T: (01388) 526405

STRAIN, Benjamin Michael. b 90. **d** 16 **p** 17. C Ealing St Paul *Lon* from 16. *23 Littlewood Close, London W13 9XH* T: (020) 8579 9444 M: 07598-389614 E: ben@stpaulsealing.com

STRAIN, Canon Christopher Malcolm. b 56. Southn Univ LLB 77 Solicitor. Wycliffe Hall Ox 83. **d** 86 **p** 87. C Werrington *Pet* 86–89; C Broadwater *Chich* 89–94; TV Hampreston *Sarum* 94–00; P-in-c Parkstone St Luke 00–03; V from 03; Can and Preb Sarum Cathl from 18. *The Vicarage, 2 Birchwood Road, Parkstone, Poole BH14 9NP* T: (01202) 741030 E: cmstrain@tiscali.co.uk

STRAIN, John Damian. b 49. Keele Univ BA 72 Birkbeck Coll Lon MSc 83 PhD 89 AFBPsS 89. STETS BTh 00. **d** 00 **p** 01. NSM Hindhead *Guildf* 00–03; NSM Churt and Hindhead 03–09; Work Economy and Business Adv 08–12; P-in-c Compton, the Mardens, Stoughton and Racton *Chich* 09–12; P-in-c Stansted 09–12; R Octagon 12–16; rtd 16; PtO *Guildf* 17–19. *Pinewoods, Church Lane, Grayshott, Hindhead GU26 6LY*

STRAINE, Gillian Kathleen. b 79. Imp Coll Lon BSc 00 PhD 05. Ripon Coll Cuddesdon BA 08. **d** 09 **p** 10. C Kidlington w Hampton Poyle *Ox* 09–13; PtO *Lon* from 14; Dir Guild of Health and St Raphael from 16. *23 The Close, Lichfield WS13 7LD* M: 07398-164477 E: gillian.straine@btinternet.com *or* director@gohealth.org.uk

STRANACK, Canon David Arthur Claude. b 43. Chich Th Coll 65. **d** 68 **p** 69. C Forest Gate St Edm *Chelmsf* 68–69; C Colchester St Jas, All SS, St Nic and St Runwald 69–74; V Brentwood St Geo 74–82; V Nayland w Wiston *St E* 82–99; R Hadleigh 99–02; V Hadleigh, Layham and Shelley 02–08; Dean Bocking 99–08; RD Hadleigh 99–07; Hon Can St E Cathl 94–08; rtd 08; PtO *St E* from 08. *12 Sandy Lane, Sudbury CO10 7HG* T: (01787) 881657 E: david.stranack@btinternet.com

STRANACK, Canon Richard Nevill. b 40. Leeds Univ BA 63. Coll of Resurr Mirfield 63. **d** 65 **p** 66. C Bush Hill Park St Mark *Lon* 65–68; C Brighton St Martin *Chich* 68–72; P-in-c Toftrees w Shereford *Nor* 72–74; V 74–81; P-in-c Pensthorpe 72–74; R 74–81; V Hempton and Pudding Norton 72–81; RD Burnham and Walsingham 78–81; V Par *Truro* 81–94; P-in-c St Blazey 87–91; Hon Chapl Miss to Seafarers from 81; V Stratton and Launcells *Truro* 94–06; RD Stratton 02–05; Chapl Cornwall Healthcare NHS Trust 97–02; Chapl N and E Cornwall Primary Care Trust 02–06; rtd 06; P-in-c Duloe, Herodsfoot, Morval and St Pinnock *Truro* 06–08; Hon Can Truro Cathl 98–08. *8 Sunwine Place, Exmouth EX8 2SE* T: (01395) 225638 E: rnstranack@yahoo.co.uk

STRAND, Mrs Christine Ann. b 56. Sussex Univ CertEd 78. Yorks Min Course 13. d 15 p 16. NSM Bridlington Priory *York* from 15. *Ranamana, Georgian Way, Bridlington YO15 3TB* T: (01262) 679056 E: christine@thestrands.plus.com

STRAND, Matthew David. b 87. Northumbria Univ BSc 08. St Jo Coll Nottm MA 12. d 12 p 13. C Linthorpe *York* 12–16; V Kirkleatham from 16. *Kirkleatham Vicarage, 130 Mersey Road, Redcar TS10 4DF* T: (01642) 482073 M: 07825-585965 E: matthewstrand@hotmail.com

STRAND, Mrs Sarah Elizabeth. b 90. Ex Univ BA 11. St Jo Coll Dur BA 13 MA 14. Cranmer Hall Dur 11. d 14 p 15. C Stokesley w Seamer *York* 14–17; C Coatham and Dormanstown 17–18; Tutor Cranmer Hall Dur from 17; PtO *York* from 18. *130 Mersey Road, Redcar TS10 4DF* E: revsarahstrand@outlook.com

STRAND, Tyler Alan. b 51. Augustana Coll (USA) AB 73 Gen Th Sem NY MDiv 78. St Steph Ho Ox 74. d 77 p 78. C Barrington St Mich USA 77–80; R Whitewater St Luke 80–85; R Frankfurt am Main Ch the K W Germany 85–90; Chapl Helsinki w Moscow *Eur* 90–93; Chapl H Cross Greek Orthodox Sch USA 94–95; V Hoffman Estates H Innocents 96–99; Dean Makati Philippines 00–08; R Healdsburg St Paul USA from 08. *319 North Street Apt 3, Healdsburg CA 95448, USA* T: (001) (707) 433 2107 E: tylerastrand@yahoo.co.uk

STRANG, Martin Guthrie. b 55. Bris Univ BSc 76 Paisley Coll of Tech MSc 83 MIMechE 85. St Jo Coll Nottm 07. d 09 p 10. C Trowell, Awsworth and Cossall *S'well* 09–12; P-in-c Stafford St Paul Forebridge *Lich* 12–13; P-in-c Castle Town 12–13; V Stafford St Paul and St Thos from 13. *St Thomas's Vicarage, Doxey, Stafford ST16 1EQ* T: (01785) 258796 M: 07908-995450 E: mstrang12@btinternet.com

STRANGE, Canon Alan Michael. b 57. Pemb Coll Ox BA 79 MA 89 Bris Univ MPhil 13. Wycliffe Hall Ox BA 84. d 84 p 85. C York St Paul 84–87; Asst Chapl Brussels Cathl *Eur* 87–91; Assoc Chapl 91–95; P-in-c Heigham H Trin *Nor* 95–99; R 99–16; RD Nor S 09–16; Hon Can Nor Cathl 10–16; Chapl Amsterdam w Den Helder and Heiloo *Eur* 16–20; Chapl Amsterdam 20–21; Bp's Chapl from 21. *rue Capitaine Crespel 47 - boite 49, 1050 Brussels, Belgium* T: (0032) (2) 213 7480 M: (0031) 62-494 0884 E: alan.strange@churchofengland.org *or* alan.strange@europan.anglican.org

STRANGE, Malcolm. b 58. Westmr Coll Ox MTh 95 Bris Univ PGCE 02. Sarum & Wells Th Coll 82. d 85 p 86. C Seaton Hirst *Newc* 85–88; C Ridgeway *Sarum* 88–89; TV 89–91; TV Newbury *Ox* 91–98; TR Bideford, Northam, Westward Ho!, Appledore etc *Ex* 98–01; RD Hartland 99–01; NSM Winterbourne *Bris* 08–16; NSM Frampton Cotterell and Iron Acton 08–16; C Fromeside 16–17; P-in-c 17–21; R from 21. *Orchard House, 70 High Street, Winterbourne, Bristol BS36 1JQ* T: (01454) 775529 M: 07792-275237

✠**STRANGE, The Most Revd Mark Jeremy.** b 61. Aber Univ LTh 82. Linc Th Coll 87. d 89 p 90 c 07. C Worc St Barn w Ch Ch 89–92; V Worc St Wulstan 92–98; R Elgin w Lossiemouth *Mor* 98–07; P-in-c Dufftown 04–07; P-in-c Aberlour 04–07; Can St Andr Cathl Inverness 00–07; Syn Clerk 03–07; Bp Mor from 07; Provost St Andr Cathl Inverness from 14; Primus from 17. *Bishop's House, St John's, Arpafeelie, North Kessock, Inverness IV1 3XD* T: (01463) 811333 E: bishop@moray.anglican.org

STRANGE, Oliver John. b 81. Wycliffe Hall Ox 16. d 18 p 19. C Burford w Fulbrook, Taynton, Asthall etc *Ox* 18–21; P-in-c Broadwell, Evenlode, Oddington, Adlestrop etc *Glouc* from 21. *The Rectory, Broadwell, Moreton-in-Marsh GL56 0TU*

STRANGE, Canon Peter Robert. b 48. Univ Coll Lon BA 69 Ex Coll Ox BA 71 MA 76. Cuddesdon Coll 71. d 72 p 73. C Denton *Newc* 72–74; C Newc St Jo 74–79; Chapl for Arts and Recreation 79–90; R Wallsend St Pet 79–86; Can Res Newc Cathl 86–11; Angl Adv Tyne Tees TV 90–10; Asst Dioc Dir of Ords *Newc* 94–98; rtd 11; PtO *Newc* from 11. *4 Woodthorne Road, Jesmond, Newcastle upon Tyne NE2 3PB* T: 0191-284 4468 M: 07712-594950 E: p.strange119@btinternet.com

STRANGE, Preb Robert Lewis. b 45. Sarum & Wells Th Coll 72. d 74 p 75. C Walthamstow St Barn and St Jas Gt *Chelmsf* 74–77; C Wickford 77–80; P-in-c Treverbyn *Truro*

80–83; V 83–86; Asst Stewardship Adv 82–96; V Newlyn St Pet 86–10; Preb Trehaverock 94–10; rtd 10; Hon Chapl Miss to Seafarers from 86. *The Old School House , Carrallack Lane, St Just, Penzance TR19 7LZ* T: (01736) 786598 E: strange643@btinternet.com

STRANGE, The Ven William Anthony. b 53. Qu Coll Cam BA 76 MA 80 Ox Univ DPhil 89 K Alfred's Coll Win CertEd 77. Wycliffe Hall Ox 79. d 82 p 83. Tutor Wycliffe Hall Ox 82–87; C Aberystwyth *St D* 87; TV 87–91; V Llandeilo Fawr and Taliaris 91–96; Hd of Th and RS Trin Coll Carmarthen 96–01; V Carmarthen St Pet *St D* 03–09; AD Carmarthen 06–09; V Pencarreg and Llanycrwys 09–19; Adn Cardigan 09–19; rtd 19; PtO *Glouc* from 19. *Mistletoe Cottage, Station Road, Andoversford, Cheltenham GL54 4LA* T: (01242) 820378 E: will.a.strange@gmail.com

STRANRAER-MULL, The Very Revd Gerald Hugh. b 42. AKC 69. St Aug Coll Cant 69. d 70 p 71. C Hexham *Newc* 70–72; C Corbridge w Halton 72; R Ellon *Ab* 72–08; R Cruden Bay 72–08; Can St Andr Cathl 81–08; Dean Ab 88–08; P-in-c Peterhead 02–04; rtd 08; P-in-c Strathnairn St Paul *Mor* 09–12; Hon C Inverness St Mich from 11; Dioc Dir of Ords 14–16; PtO *Ab* from 19. *4 Lochlann Avenue, Culloden, Inverness IV2 7LT* T: (01463) 793943 E: stranraermull@btinternet.com

STRAPPS, Canon Robert David. b 28. St Edm Hall Ox BA 52 MA 56. Wycliffe Hall Ox 52. d 54 p 55. C Low Leyton *Chelmsf* 54–57; C Ox St Aldate w H Trin 57–60; V Sandal St Helen *Wakef* 60–94; RD Chevet 81–93; Hon Can Wakef Cathl 92–94; rtd 94; PtO *Wakef* 94–98; *Glouc* 94–12; *Worc* 94–12. *Brookside, Hill Road, Kemerton, Tewkesbury GL20 7JN* T: (01386) 725515

STRASZAK, Edmund Norman. b 57. Coll of Resurr Mirfield 88. d 90 p 91. C Adlington *Blackb* 90–93; C Harrogate St Wilfrid and St Luke *Ripon* 93–95; V Chorley All SS *Blackb* from 95. *All Saints' Vicarage, Moor Road, Chorley PR7 2LR* T: (01257) 265665 E: enstraszak@gmail.com

STRATFORD, Mrs Anne Barbara. Southn Univ CertEd 58 Ox Univ MTh 99. Qu Coll Birm 88. d 91 p 94. Officer Dioc Bd of Soc Resp (Family Care) *Lich* 85–97; NSM Kinnerley w Melverley and Knockin w Maesbrook 91–95; Chapl Robert Jones and Agnes Hunt Orthopaedic Hosp 95–97; NSM Maesbury *Lich* 95–96; P-in-c 96–97; Chapl Moreton Hall Sch from 96; P-in-c Ford *Heref* 97–02; V 02–05; P-in-c Alberbury w Cardeston 97–02; V 02–05; rtd 05; PtO *Lich* 05–20; *St As* from 05. *Pentre Cleddar, Hengoed, Oswestry SY10 7AB* T: (01691) 650469

STRATFORD, Niall Ralph. CITC. d 07. NSM Killiney Ballybrack *D & G* 09–17; NSM Powerscourt w Kilbride 17–19; NSM Narraghmore and Timolin w Castledermot etc from 19. *8 Hermitage Downs, Grange Road, Rathfarnham, Dublin 16, Republic of Ireland* T: (00353) (1) 493 7535 M: 86-607 8290 E: vanstratford@eircom.net

STRATFORD, Terence Stephen. b 45. Chich Th Coll 67. d 69 p 70. C Old Shoreham *Chich* 69–73; C New Shoreham 69–73; C Uckfield 73–75; C Lt Horsted 73–75; C Isfield 73–75; P-in-c Waldron 76–80; R 80–82; V Blacklands Hastings Ch Ch and St Andr 82–89; P-in-c Ovingdean 89–95; Dioc Ecum Officer 89–95; P-in-c Staplefield Common 95–00; Sussex Ecum Officer 95–01; V Ferring *Chich* 00–08; C New Shoreham and Old Shoreham 08–11; P-in-c Kingston Buci 11–15; Hon C New Shoreham and Shoreham Beach 15–18; RD Hove 14–18; rtd 18. *Tudor Croft, 3 Tudor Close, Seaford BN25 2LU* T: (01273) 453768 E: terry.stratford@yahoo.co.uk

STRATFORD, The Very Revd Timothy Richard. b 61. York Univ BSc 82 Sheff Univ PhD 08. Wycliffe Hall Ox 83. d 86 p 87. C Mossley Hill St Matt and St Jas *Liv* 86–89; C St Helens St Helen 89–91; Bp's Dom Chapl 91–94; V W Derby Gd Shep 94–03; TR Kirkby 03–12; Adn Leic 12–18; Dean Ches from 18. *The Deanery, 7 Abbey Street, Chester CH1 2JF* T: (01244) 500956 *or* 500971 E: tim.stratford@chestercathedral.com

STRATHIE, Duncan John. b 58. Heythrop Coll Lon MA 01. Cranmer Hall Dur BA 97. d 97 p 98. C Yateley *Win* 97–01; V Kempshott 01–07; Min Tr Officer 07–14; Dioc Convenor of Voc Advisers 03–14; PtO 14–15; Co-ord for Learning and Discipleship *Sarum* 14–15; V Moseley St Mary and St Anne *Birm* from 15. *18 Oxford Road, Moseley, Birmingham B13 9EH* M: 07515-313242 E: duncan@strathie.net

STRATON, Christopher James. b 46. d 93 p 94. Chapl Miss to Seamen S Africa 93–96; Asst P Gingindlovu All SS 97–99; R 99–00; P-in-c Tyldesley w Shakerley *Man* 00–06; TV Astley, Tyldesley and Mosley Common 06–11; rtd 11; PtO *Liv* from 16. *2 Scarisbrick Court, Scarisbrick New Road, Southport PR8 6QF* E: chris.straton@sky.com

STRATTA, Antony Charles. b 36. ACIS. S'wark Ord Course 82. d 85 p 86. C Southborough St Pet w Ch Ch and St Matt *Roch* 85–88; R Gt Mongeham w Ripple and Sutton by Dover

Cant 88–96; rtd 96; PtO *St E* 96–17; *Ex* from 17. *11 Gracey Court, Woodland Road, Broadclyst, Exeter EX5 3GA* T: (01392) 464950 E: antonystratta@btinternet.com

STRATTON, Mrs Anne Margaret. b 58. JP 98. Nottm Univ BEng 79. EMMTC 03. **d** 06 **p** 07. NSM Bradgate Team *Leic* 06–10; P-in-c Belper *Derby* 10–13; V from 13. *St Peter's Vicarage, 6 Chesterfield Road, Belper DE56 1FD* T: (01773) 821323 *or* 839560 M: 07773-076555 E: rev.annestratton@gmail.com

STRATTON, Henry William. b 39. Bris Univ CertEd 74 BEd 75. Glouc Sch of Min 80. **d** 83 **p** 84. NSM Cainscross w Selsley *Glouc* 83–87; C Codd Rode *Deene* 87–92; V Runcorn H Trin 92–96; V Lostock Gralam 96–05; rtd 05; PtO *Ches* from 05. *63 Hollymere, New Grosvenor Road, Ellesmere Port CH65 2HH* T: 0151-355 3423

STRAUGHAN, Prof Keith. b 60. Imp Coll Lon BSc 81 Lon Univ PhD 87 Imp Coll Lon ARCS 81 CPhys 87 MInstP 87 Trin Coll Cam BA 97 MA 00. Westcott Ho Cam 94. **d** 97 **p** 98. C Abbots Langley *St Alb* 97–00; Fell SS Coll Cam 00–08; Chapl 00–03; Dean 03–05; Sen Tutor 05–08; Dean Univ Cen Milton Keynes 08–17; NSM Milton Keynes *Ox* from 11; PtO *St Alb* from 17. *21 Watercress Way, Broughton, Milton Keynes MK10 7AJ* T: (01908) 200730

STRAW, Mrs Juliet Lesley. b 49. Univ of Wales (Ban) BA 70 Leeds Univ PGCE 71. SAOMC 00. **d** 03 **p** 04. NSM Stratfield Mortimer and Mortimer W End etc *Ox* 03–10; P-in-c Wymering *Portsm* 10–11; V 11–17; P-in-c Cosham 10–11; V 11–17; rtd 17; PtO *Ox* from 19. *Clive Cottage, 68 Windmill Road, Mortimer Common, Reading RG7 3RL* E: juliet.straw@btinternet.com

STRAWBRIDGE, Canon Jennifer Ruth. b 78. Washington & Lee Univ BA 01 Ox Univ MSt 02 DPhil 14. Yale Div Sch MDiv 04. **d** 04 **p** 04. C New Haven Ch Ch and Chapl Bridgeport Hosp USA 04–05; C Arlington St Mary 05–09; Asst Chapl Keble Coll Ox 09–10; Chapl and Fell 10–16; Assoc Prof NT Ox Univ from 16; LtO *Ox* from 10; NSM Headington from 18; Wiccamical Preb Chich Cathl from 18; Can Th Blackb from 20. *Mansfield College, Mansfield Road, Oxford OX1 3TF* M: 07578-296948 E: jennifer.strawbridge@theology.ox.ac.uk

STREATFEILD, Peter Michael Fremlyn. b 53. Newc Univ BSc 77 St Jo Coll Dur BA 03. Cranmer Hall Dur 00. **d** 03 **p** 04. C Solway Plain *Carl* 03–08; TV Binsey 08–18; rtd 18; PtO *Carl* from 18. *10 The Island, Anthorn, Wigton CA7 5AN* E: peterstreatfeild@btinternet.com

STREET, Anthony James. b 57. Trin Coll Bris 79. **d** 85 **p** 87. SAMS 85–95; C Temuco H Trin Chile 85–87; V Temuco St Matt 87–95; P-in-c Warley *Wakef* 96–99; V 99–14; *Leeds* 14; P-in-c Halifax St Hilda *Wakef* 10–14; *Leeds* 14; R Sawley *Derby* from 14. *The Rectory, 561 Tamworth Road, Long Eaton, Nottingham NG10 3FB* T: 0115-973 4900 E: familiastreet@btinternet.com

STREET, David. b 72. St Jo Coll Nottm. **d** 10 **p** 11. C Bucknall *Lich* 10–13; TV 13–18; TR from 18. *The Rectory, 151 Werrington Road, Stoke-on-Trent ST2 9AQ* T: (01782) 937113 E: revdavestreet@gmail.com

STREET, Peter Jarman. b 29. K Coll Lon BD 59 AKC 59. **d** 59 **p** 60. C Highters Heath *Birm* 59–60; C Shirley 60–62; Lect Cheshire Coll of Educn 62–66; St Pet Coll of Educn Birm 66–70; RE Adv Essex Co Coun 70–92; Hon C Gt Dunmow *Chelmsf* 78–85; Sen Insp RE and Humanities 74–92; R Gt w Lt Yeldham *Chelmsf* 85–92; RD Belchamp 90–92; rtd 92; PtO *Chelmsf* from 92. *18 Jubilee Court, Great Dunmow CM6 1DY* T: (01371) 876871

STREET, Philip. b 47. Lon Univ BPharm 68. NW Ord Course 75. **d** 78 **p** 79. C Heaton St Barn *Bradf* 78–81; C Evington *Leic* 82–84; R Wymondham w Edmondthorpe, Buckminster etc 84–88; V Gosberton Clough and Quadring *Linc* 88–95; Asst Local Min Officer 88–95; V Buttershaw St Paul *Bradf* 95–99; P-in-c Gt and Lt Casterton w Pickworth and Tickencote *Pet* 99–04; R 04–09; C Empingham and Exton w Horn w Whitwell 02–06; rtd 09; PtO *Pet* from 09; *Cov* 18–21. *43 Barton Road, Rugby CV22 7PT* E: p.street08@btinternet.com

STREETER, Brian Thomas. b 68. Reading Univ BSc 89. Ridley Hall Cam 05. **d** 08 **p** 09. C Windermere St Mary and Troutbeck *Carl* 08–12; Par Missr 13–15; P-in-c Egton-cum-Newland and Lowick and Colton *Carl* 15–19; P-in-c Coniston and Torver 18–19; R Coniston and the Crake Valley from 19. *The Vicarage, Penny Bridge, Ulverston LA12 7RQ* T: (01229) 861668 M: 07505-048736 E: vicar@conistonandcrakechurches.co.uk

STREETER, Christine Mary. *See* HADDON-REECE, Christine Mary

STRENGHOLT, Jozef Martinus. b 59. Utrecht Univ MA 87 PhD 08. **d** 07 **p** 08. Egypt 07–17; PtO *Eur* 17–20; Chapl Arnhem from 20. *Livingstonelaan 1068, 3526 JR Utrecht, The Netherlands* T: (0031) (641) 021346 E: jos@strengholt.info

STRETCH, Richard Mark. b 53. **d** 93 **p** 94. OLM Stowmarket *St E* 93–13; NSM from 13. *91 Kipling Way, Stowmarket IP14 1TS* T: (01449) 676219

STRETTON, Reginald John. b 37. Man Univ BSc 62 Nottm Univ PhD 65 MRPharmS 63 CBiol 70 MRSB 70. EMMTC 88. **d** 91 **p** 92. NSM Loughb Gd Shep *Leic* 91–94; P-in-c Burrough Hill Pars 94–02; rtd 02; PtO *Leic* from 02; *S'well* 02–14; *Derby* 05–14. *19 Paddock Close, Quorn, Loughborough LE12 8BJ* T: (01509) 412935 E: reginaldstretton@btinternet.com

STRETTON, Robert John. b 45. Kelham Th Coll. **d** 69 **p** 70. C Hendon *Dur* 69–73; C Middlesbrough St Thos *York* 73–77; OSB 77–78; V Brandon *Dur* 78–85; SSM from 85; LtO *Dur* 85–91; Tr in Evang Ch in Wales 91–94; PtO *S'wark* 94–01; Lesotho 01–05; PtO *S'wark* from 14. *86B Vassall Road, London SW9 6JA* E: ssmlondon@yahoo.co.uk *or* robssm@icloud.com

STREVENS, Brian Lloyd. b 49. St Jo Coll Dur BA 70. Ripon Hall Ox 70. **d** 73 **p** 74. C Old Trafford St Jo *Man* 73–76; C Bolton St Pet 76–78; Org Sec Southn Coun of Community Service 78–92; PtO *Win* 82–86 and 92–95 and 01–16; Hon C Bitterne Park 86–92; Hon C N Stoneham 95–01. *186 Hill Lane, Southampton SO15 5DB* T: (023) 8033 3301 E: brianstrevens@btinternet.com

STRICKLAND (née CUTTS), Mrs Elizabeth Joan Gabrielle. b 61. St Jo Coll Dur BA 83. Westcott Ho Cam 87. **d** 90 **p** 94. C Cayton w Eastfield *York* 90–92; NSM Biggin Hill *Roch* 93–96; PtO *Ox* 96–00; *Ely* 00–02; P-in-c Holywell w Needingworth 02–07; NSM Hartford and Houghton w Wyton from 15. *Windswept, Holywell, St Ives PE27 4TQ* T: (01480) 495275 *or* 460107 E: epstrickland@ukonline.co.uk *or* epstrickland@yahoo.co.uk

STRIDE, Clifford George. b 58. Win Univ BA 11. STETS 08. **d** 11 **p** 12. NSM Ampfield, Chilworth and N Baddesley *Win* 11–16; TV Upper Wylye Valley *Sarum* from 16. *Ashton Gifford Rectory, Green Lane, Codford, Warminster BA12 0NY* T: (01985) 850941 E: cgstride@btinternet.com

STRIDE, John David. b 46. Ex Univ BSc 68. Oak Hill Th Coll 86. **d** 88 **p** 89. C Ashtead *Guildf* 88–96; V Lodge Moor St Luke *Sheff* 96–11; rtd 11; PtO *Sheff* from 11. *11 Blenheim Mews, Sheffield S11 9PR* T: 0114-235 6220 E: john@jonjax.net

STRIDE, John Michael. b 48. Oak Hill Th Coll BA 77. **d** 80 **p** 81. C Edmonton All SS *Lon* 80–82; C Edmonton All SS w St Mich 82–83; C Wembley St Jo 83–85; P-in-c Hockering *Nor* 85–89; R Hockering, Honingham, E and N Tuddenham 89–91; V Tuckswood 91–93; Chapl HM Pris Leeds 93–94; Chapl HM Pris Littlehey 94–96; V Heeley *Sheff* 96–99; TR Heeley and Gleadless Valley 99–04; AD Attercliffe 02–04; V Goole 04–06; Chapl Combined Courts 06–11; Hon C Darfield 07–11; V Ludham, Potter Heigham, Hickling and Catfield *Nor* 11–16; rtd 16; PtO *Nor* from 17. *51 Mileham Drive, Aylsham, Norwich NR11 6WD* T: (01263) 479855 E: johnmo.stride@gmail.com

STRIDE, Simon Paul. b 85. Nazarene Th Coll Man BA 13 St Mellitus Coll MA 20. **d** 20 **p** 21. C Stalybridge H Trin and Ch Ch *Ches* from 20. *8 Richmond Close, Stalybridge SK15 2HU* M: 07392-079356 E: simonstride@hotmail.com

STRIKE, Maurice Arthur. b 44. FRSA 66. Sarum & Wells Th Coll 85. **d** 87 **p** 88. C Chippenham St Andr w Tytherton Lucas *Bris* 87–91; R Corfe Castle, Church Knowle, Kimmeridge etc *Sarum* 91–04; R Guernsey St Philippe de Torteval *Win* 04–13; R Guernsey St Pierre du Bois 04–13; rtd 13; PtO *Nor* from 13; *Win* 13–18. *The Flint House, 49 Mundesley Road, Overstrand, Cromer NR27 0NB* T: (01263) 576805 E: mstrike@hotmail.co.uk

STRINGER, Adrian Nigel. b 60. Univ of Wales (Cardiff) BD 82 Essex Univ PhD 09 Lanc Univ PGCE 83. Sarum & Wells Th Coll 86. **d** 88 **p** 89. C Barrow St Matt *Carl* 88–92; TV Westhoughton *Man* 92–94; I Inver w Mountcharles, Killaghtee and Killybegs *D & R* 94–96; V Tuckingmill *Truro* 96–01; Chapl R Alexandra and Albert Sch Reigate 01–03; I Desertlyn w Ballyeglish *Arm* from 03. *The Rectory, 24 Cookstown Road, Moneymore, Magherafelt BT45 7QF* T: (028) 8674 8200 E: blackdogmaverick@yahoo.co.uk

STRINGER, Harold John. b 36. Peterho Cam BA 58. Ripon Hall Ox 62. **d** 64 **p** 65. C Hackney St Jo *Lon* 64–68; C Roehampton H Trin *S'wark* 68–71; P-in-c Southampton St Mich w H Rood, St Lawr etc *Win* 71–73; TV Southampton (City Cen) 73–82; Ind Chapl 77–82; V Notting Hill St Jo *Lon* 82–87; V Notting Hill St Pet 82–87; V Notting Hill St Jo and St Pet 87–01; AD Kensington 98–01; rtd 02; PtO *Lon* from 03. *56 Mountfield Road, London W5 2NQ* T: (020) 8998 8049 E: mail@haroldstringer.co.uk

STROEBEL, Mrs Stephanie Suzanne. b 47. Middx Univ BA 06. NTMTC 03. **d** 06 **p** 07. NSM Ashingdon w S Fambridge *Chelmsf* 06–08; NSM S Woodham Ferrers 08–10; P-in-c Woodham Mortimer w Hazeleigh 10–15;

P-in-c Woodham Walter 10–15; rtd 15; PtO *Chelmsf* 15–17; Hon C Hockley from 17. *27 Orchard Avenue, Hockley SS5 5BA* T: (01702) 200901 M: 07930-105163 E: s.stroebel135@gmail.com *or* s.stroebel@btinternet.com

STRONG, Christopher Patteson. b 43. Ridley Hall Cam. **d** 83 **p** 84. C Dalton-in-Furness *Carl* 83–87; V Wootton *St Alb* 87–02; RD Elstow 94–02; R Fowlmere, Foxton, Shepreth and Thriplow *Ely* 02–08; rtd 08; PtO *St Alb* from 08. *Kiln Farm, Priory Road, Campton, Shefford SG17 5PG* T: (01462) 819274 E: christopherpstrong@hotmail.com

STRONG, John. *See* STRONG, William John Leonard

STRONG, Matthew John. b 60. Lon Univ BA 81 Cam Univ BA 84 MA 89. Ridley Hall Cam 82. **d** 85 **p** 86. C Houghton *Carl* 85–89; C Hirwaun *Llan* 89–91; V Troedyrhiw w Merthyr Vale 91–95; Tutor Llan Ord Course 91–95; PtO *Birm* from 14. *22 Birch Lane, Oldbury B68 0NZ* T: 0121-421 5978

STRONG, Rowan Gordon William. b 53. Victoria Univ Wellington BA 76 Edin Univ PhD 92 Melbourne Coll of Div ThM 88. St Jo Coll (NZ) LTh 80. **d** 77 **p** 78. C Kapiti NZ 77–83; C Palmerston N St Pet 79–81; V Shannon 81–83; Assoc P E Hill Australia 83–89; NSM Edin Old St Paul 89–92; Tutor Edin Univ 91–92; Lect Murdoch Univ Australia from 92; Sen Lect from 02. *150 George Street, East Fremantle WA 6158, Australia* T: (0061) (8) 9339 0643 *or* (8) 9360 6470 F: 9360 6480 M: 439-988896 E: r.strong@murdoch.edu.au

STRONG, Capt William John Leonard. b 44. CA Tr Coll 64 Chich Th Coll 87. **d** 89 **p** 90. CA from 66; C Mayfield *Chich* 89–92; C Seaford w Sutton 92–94; V Crawley Down All SS 94–97; rtd 01. *21 Carroll Close, Poole BH12 1PL* M: 07944-670125

STROUD, Daniel Joseph Shine. **d** 14 **p** 14. C Whitemarsh USA 14–17; TV Mold Miss Area *St As* from 17. *The New Rectory, Rectory Lane, Llanferres, Mold CH7 5SR* T: (01352) 810694 E: djstroud@gmail.com

STROUD, David Alan. b 74. Kent Univ BA 96 Ch Ch Coll Cant PGCE 95. Westcott Ho Cam 02. **d** 04 **p** 05. C Liss *Portsm* 04–08; Asst Chapl Cant Ch Ch Univ 08–12; Chapl from 12. *Canterbury Christ Church University, North Holmes Road, Canterbury CT1 1QU* T: (01227) 922538 E: david.stroud@canterbury.ac.uk

STROUD, Lara Christina Shine. b 83. Appalachian State Univ (USA) BMus 07. Virginia Th Sem MDiv 12. **d** 12 **p** 12. C Omaha All SS USA 12–13; C Rehoboth Beach and Harbeson 13–14; C Whitemarsh 14–17; C Estuary and Mountain Miss Area *St As* 17–19; Chapl St Jos High Sch Wrexham from 19. *The New Rectory, Rectory Lane, Llanferres, Mold CH7 5SR* T: (01352) 810694 E: motherlara@gmail.com

✠**STROYAN, The Rt Revd John Ronald Angus.** b 55. St Andr Univ MTheol 76 Univ of Wales (Lamp) MA 07 Birm City Univ Hon PhD 15. Qu Coll Birm 81 Bossey Ecum Inst Geneva 82. **d** 83 **p** 84 **c** 05. C Cov E 83–87; V Smethwick St Matt w St Chad *Birm* 87–94; V Bloxham w Milcombe and S Newington *Ox* 94–05; AD Deddington 02–05; Suff Bp Warw *Cov* from 05. *Warwick House, School Hill, Offchurch, Leamington Spa CV33 9AL* E: bishop.warwick@covcofe.org

STRUDWICK, Caroline Mary Easdeale. b 55. Solicitor 84. STETS 12. **d** 15 **p** 16. NSM Upper Itchen *Win* 15–19; PtO from 19; *Ex* from 21. *Combe House, 3 Forest Hill, Bideford EX39 5HS* T: (01237) 477594 E: carolinestrudwick@carolinestrudwick.co.uk

STRUDWICK, Paul Alan. **d** 99 **p** 00. USA 99–04; Canada 04–13; P-in-c Menorca *Eur* from 13. *Apartado de Correos 102, 07720 Es Castell, Menorca, Spain* T: (0034) 617 222 382 E: rev.strudwick@gmail.com

STRUDWICK, Canon Vincent Noel Harold. b 32. Nottm Univ BA 59 DipEd Lambeth DD 09. Kelham Th Coll 52. **d** 59 **p** 60. Tutor Kelham Th Coll 59–63; Sub-Warden 63–70; C Crawley *Chich* 70–73; Adult Educn Adv 73–77; R Fittleworth 73–77; Planning Officer for Educn Milton Keynes 77–80; Dir of Educn *Ox* 81–89; Hon Can Ch Ch from 81; Continuing Minl Educn Adv 85–89; Dir Dioc Inst for Th Educn 89–97; Prin Ox Min Course 89–94; Prin SAOMC 94–96; Fell and Tutor Kellogg Coll Ox 94–00; Hon Fell from 07; C Aylesbury *Ox* 97–98; PtO 98–16. *31 The Square, Brill, Aylesbury HP18 9RP* T: (01844) 237748 E: vincent.strudwick@kellogg.ox.ac.uk

STRUTT, Peter Edward. b 40. SAOMC 94. **d** 97 **p** 98. NSM Penn Street *Ox* 97–02; PtO from 02; *St Alb* from 10. *59 King's Ride, Penn, High Wycombe HP10 8BP* T: (01494) 812418 E: pestrutt@pennweb.uk

STRUTT, Preb Susan. b 45. Glouc Sch of Min 87. **d** 90 **p** 94. NSM Eye, Croft w Yarpole and Lucton *Heref* 90–94; C Leominster 94–96; Hon Chapl RAF 94–96; P-in-c Bosbury w Wellington Heath etc *Heref* 96–98; TV Ledbury 98–14; Dioc Adv on Women in Min 99–03; Preb Heref Cathl 07–14; rtd 14; PtO *Nor* 16–18; Hon C Gt and Lt Ellingham, Rockland

and Shropham etc from 18. *25 Edenside Drive, Attleborough NR17 2EL* E: prebsue@hotmail.com

STUART, Sister Ann-Marie Lindsay. b 41. Westmr Coll Lon CertEd 69 Kent Univ BA 80 Univ of Wales (Lamp) MA 03. Franciscan Study Cen 76. **d** 99 **p** 00. NSM Sherborne w Castleton and Lillington *Sarum* 99–01; TV Golden Cap Team 01–05; TR 05–08; rtd 08; Hon C Crosslacon *Carl* 08–11; NSM Brigham, Gt Broughton and Broughton Moor 11–12; Dioc Adv for Spirituality 09–12; PtO *Truro* 13–14; *Sarum* 14–18; C Kilcolman w Kiltallagh, Killorglin, Knockane etc *L & K* from 18. *Seaview House, Gurrane West, Sunhill, Killorglin, Co Kerry, V93 T2C1, Republic of Ireland* T: (00353) (66) 979 0359 E: revamls87@gmail.com

STUART, Brother. *See* BURNS, Stuart Maitland

STUART, Prof Elizabeth Bridget. b 63. Jes Coll Ox BA 84 St Hugh's Coll Ox MA 88 DPhil 88. SCTEI 17. **d** 19 **p** 20. NSM Win St Matt from 19. *5 Wychwood Place, Winchester SO22 6BE* T: (01962) 856501 M: 07711-607234 E: liz@stmatthewstpaul.org

STUART-BLACK, Veronica. *See* CAROLAN, Veronica

STUART-BOURNE, Mrs Rona. b 67. Surrey Univ BSc 89. Ripon Coll Cuddesdon 09. **d** 11 **p** 12. C Freshwater *Portsm* 11–12; C Yarmouth 11–12; C Southsea St Luke and St Pet 12–14; P-in-c Greatham w Empshott and Hawkley w Prior's Dean 14–15; V Empshott and Hawkley w Priors Dean 16–18; R Merrow *Guildf* from 18. *The Rectory, 232 Epsom Road, Guildford GU4 7AA* E: revrona@gmail.com

STUART-LEE, Nicholas Richard. b 54. Wycliffe Hall Ox. **d** 83 **p** 84. C Costessey *Nor* 83–85; TV Dewsbury *Wakef* 85–90; R Rowlands Castle *Portsm* 90–00; V Nottingham St Jude *S'well* 00–03; TR Thame *Ox* 03–07. *69 Harefields, Oxford OX2 8NR* T: (01865) 511044

STUART-LEE, William James. b 80. Somerville Coll Ox BA 01. Wycliffe Hall Ox BA 20. **d** 20 **p** 21. C Ox St Aldate from 20. *230 Headington Road, Headington, Oxford OX3 7PS* M: 07971-669756 E: will.stuartlee@gmail.com

STUART-MARTIN, Rosanna. b 60. Bris Univ BA 81. Wycliffe Hall Ox 89. **d** 92 **p** 94. Par Dn Stanford in the Vale w Goosey and Hatford *Ox* 92–94; C 94–96; C Abingdon 96–00; PtO 00–04; P-in-c Uffington, Shellingford, Woolstone and Baulking 04–14; PtO 15–21. *7 Limetrees, Chilton, Didcot OX11 0HW* T: (01235) 821861 E: rosanna.martin@btinternet.com

STUART-SMITH, David. b 36. St Pet Coll Ox BA 61 MA 65. Tyndale Hall Bris. **d** 63 **p** 64. C Tooting Graveney St Nic *S'wark* 63–67; C Richmond H Trin 67–70; LtO 70–74; NSM Canonbury St Steph *Lon* 70–74; Travelling Sec IVF 70–74; Bangladesh 74–79; V Clapham Park St Steph *S'wark* 79–95; RD Streatham 83–87; Chapl Wye Coll Kent 95–99; Chapl Wye Campus Imp Coll *Lon* 99–01; P-in-c Wye w Brook *Cant* 95–01; P-in-c Hastingleigh 00–01; rtd 01; PtO *Cant* 01–07 and 16–19; *Lon* 07–15. *100 North Street, Biddenden, Ashford TN27 8AE* T: (01580) 292615 E: speakup5@yahoo.com

STUART-WHITE, Canon William Robert. b 59. Ox Univ BA. Trin Coll Bris BA. **d** 86 **p** 87. C Upper Armley *Ripon* 86–91; P-in-c Austrey *Birm* 91–92; P-in-c Warton 91–92; V Austrey and Warton 92–98; R Camborne *Truro* 98–06; P-in-c Stoke Climsland 06–09; P-in-c Linkinhorne 06–09; P-in-c St Breoke and Egloshayle 09–12; Hon Can Truro Cathl 09–12 and from 18; adn Cornwall 12–18; P-in-c Falmouth All SS from 18; P-in-c Falmouth K Chas from 20. *5 St Nazaire Close, Falmouth TR11 5JP* T: (01326) 219246 E: wstuartwhite@gmail.com

STUBBINGS, Mrs Paulette Joanne. b 71. Kent Univ BA 92. SEITE 12. **d** 15 **p** 16. C Boughton-under-Blean w Dunkirk etc *Cant* 15–18; TV Whitstable from 18. *26 Ladysmith Grove, Seasalter, Whitstable CT5 4BE* E: paulettejstubbings@gmail.com

STUBBS, Ian Kirtley. b 47. Man Univ DipAE 90. Kelham Th Coll 66. **d** 70 **p** 71. C Chandler's Ford *Win* 70–75; C Farnham Royal *Ox* 75–80; Ind Chapl 75–80; Ind Chapl *Man* 81–86; TV Oldham 81–86; TR Langley and Parkfield 86–88; Community Work Officer Dioc Bd of Soc Resp 88–90; Dir Laity Development 90–96; Nat Adv in Adult Learning C of E Bd of Educn 97–02; V Stalybridge *Man* 02–11; P-in-c Glossop *Derby* 11–14; V 14–16; C Hadfield 11–14; C Charlesworth and Dinting Vale 11–14; V Dinting Vale 14–16; rtd 16; PtO *Ches* 17–18. *9 Carisbrooke Close, Wistaston, Crewe CW2 8JD* T: (01270) 381391 M: 07712-451710 E: iks1647@gmail.com

STUBBS, Stanley Peter Handley. b 23. Lon Univ BD 52 Lille 3 Univ MèsL 82. Ely Th Coll 55. **d** 55 **p** 56. C Fletton *Ely* 55–58; Hon Min Can Pet Cathl 56–58; C Hounslow Heath St Paul *Lon* 58–63; CF (TA) 59–78; V Northampton St Alb *Pet* 63–76; R Brondesbury Ch Ch and St Laur *Lon* 76–93; rtd 93; PtO *Lon* 93–18. *3 Westbury Lodge Close, Pinner HA5 3FG* T: (020) 8868 8296 E: peter.stubbsuk@gmail.com

STUBBS, Trevor Noel. b 48. AKC 70. St Aug Coll Cant 73. **d** 74 **p** 75. C Heckmondwike *Wakef* 74–77; C Warwick Australia 77–80; V Middleton St Cross *Ripon* 80–89; R Wool and E Stoke *Sarum* 89–95; TR Bridport 95–09; RD Lyme Bay 06–09; rtd 09; Admin Bp Gwynne Th Coll Sudan from 09; LtO *Sarum* 09–15; PtO *Bris* from 15; *B & W* from 15; Can and Preb Sarum Cathl 03–15. *15 Cleeve Grove, Keynsham, Bristol BS31 2HF* T: 0117-986 9664 E: revtrev.stubbs@gmail.com

STUBENBORD, Jess William. b 48. BA 72. Trin Coll Bris 75. **d** 78 **p** 79. C Cromer *Nor* 78–82; C Gorleston St Mary 82–85; P-in-c Saxthorpe and Corpusty 85–89; P-in-c Blickling 86–89; R Saxthorpe w Corpusty, Blickling, Oulton etc 89–93; P-in-c Mulbarton w Kenningham 93–97; P-in-c Mulbarton w Bracon Ash, Hethel and Flordon 94–97; P-in-c Wreningham 95–97; R Mulbarton w Bracon Ash, Hethel and Flordon 98–13; rtd 13; PtO *Nor* from 13. *Haven Cottage, 13 Cromer Road, Overstrand, Cromer NR27 0NT* T: (01263) 578230 E: jamstubenbord@gmail.com

STUCHFIELD, Nicolas John. b 60. ERMC 15. **d** 17 **p** 18. NSM Saxmundham w Kelsale cum Carlton *St E* from 17. *Address withheld by request* E: nic@stuchfield.com *or* nic@saxstjohns.org.uk

STUCKES, Stephen. b 62. Trin Coll Bris BA 99. **d** 96 **p** 97. C Dunster, Carhampton and Withycombe w Rodhuish *B & W* 96–00; V Alcombe 00–17; RD Exmoor 09–17; Preb Wells Cathl 12–17; Chapl Berne *Eur* 17–18; C Alfriston w Lullington, Litlington, W Dean and Folkington *Chich* 18; R from 18. *The Rectory, Sloe Lane, Alfriston, Polegate BN26 5UP* E: stephen1962@btinternet.com

STUCKEY, Mrs Ann Marie. b 54. STETS 10. **d** 13 **p** 14. NSM Seaton and Beer *Ex* 13–17; PtO from 17. *7 West Acres, Seaton EX12 2HP* T: (01297) 23016 M: 07814-078710

STUDDERT-KENNEDY, Andrew Geoffrey. b 59. Ch Ch Ox BA 80 MA 86. Ripon Coll Cuddesdon BA 88. **d** 89 **p** 90. C Wimbledon *S'wark* 89–94; V Norbury St Oswald 94–02; RD Croydon N 99–02; TR Marlborough *Sarum* 02–18; RD 09–18; Can and Preb Sarum Cathl 12–18; TR Uxbridge *Lon* from 18; Chapl to The Queen from 17. *St Andrew's Vicarage, Nursery Waye, Uxbridge UB8 2BJ* T: (01895) 239055 E: andrewsk1959@btinternet.com

STUDHOLME, Muriel Isabel. b 25. **d** 96. NSM Bromfield w Waverton *Carl* 96–02; NSM Solway Plain 02–09. *New Tree Cottage, Dundraw, Wigton CA7 0DP* T: (01697) 342506

STUDMAN, Tom Lucas. b 79. Leic Univ BSc 00 Man Metrop Univ PGCE 01. St Mellitus Coll BA 19. **d** 19 **p** 20. C W Didsbury and Withington St Chris *Man* from 19. *354 Wilbraham Road, Manchester M21 0UX* T: 0161-860 6003 E: tomstudman@hotmail.co.uk

STUPPLE, Mrs Angela Mary. b 60. St Aug Coll of Th 16. **d** 20 **p** 21. NSM Dover Town *Cant* from 20. *2 Hamilton Mews, 107 London Road, Temple Ewell, Dover CT16 3BY* T: (01304) 729870 M: 07966-056940 E: angiestupple@yahoo.co.uk

STURCH, Richard Lyman. b 36. Ch Ch Ox BA 58 MA 61 DPhil 70 Lon Univ BSc 06. Ely Th Coll. **d** 62 **p** 63. C Hove All SS *Chich* 62–65; C Burgess Hill St Jo 65–66; C Ox St Mich w St Martin and All SS 67–68; Tutor Ripon Hall Ox 67–71; Lect Univ of Nigeria 71–74; Lect Lon Bible Coll 75–80; TV Wolverton *Ox* 80–86; R Islip w Charlton on Otmoor, Oddington, Noke etc 86–01; rtd 01; PtO *Ox* 02–18. *128 Stoke Gifford Retirement Village, Edward Parker Road, Bristol BS16 1YE* E: sturchrichard@gmail.com

STURGEON, Mrs Susan Gerrie. b 53. Man Univ MBA 02. Yorks Min Course 16. **d** 17. NSM Abbeydale and Millhouses *Sheff* 17–20; PtO *Lon* from 21. *123B Dartmouth Road, London NW2 4ES* E: sgerriesturgeon@gmail.com

STURROCK, Marian Elizabeth. b 46. Westmr Coll Ox BTh 97. St Mich Coll Llan 97. **d** 99 **p** 00. C Swansea St Pet *S & B* 99–03; Chapl Swansea NHS Trust 00–03; R Thundersley *Chelmsf* 03–16; Chapl Lt Havens Hospice Benfleet 03–16; rtd 16; PtO *St D* from 16; *S & B* from 17. *29 Cleviston Park, Llandennech, Llanelli SA14 9UW* T: (01554) 821648 E: mariansturrock@gmail.com

STURT, Mrs Rachel Caroline. b 60. Open Univ BSc 03 RGN 81. STETS 08. **d** 11 **p** 12. NSM Wrecclesham *Guildf* 11–15; NSM Alton *Win* from 17; PtO *Guildf* 15–17. *14 Arthur Road, Farnham GU9 8PB* T: (01252) 710968 E: rachelsturt@btopenworld.com *or* rachel.annachaplain@hotmail.com

STURT, Rock André Daniel. b 56. Liv Univ BSc 79 Lon Inst of Educn CertEd 80. Oak Hill Th Coll BA 88. **d** 88 **p** 89. Chapl St Bede's Sch Cam 88–91; C Cambridge St Martin *Ely* 88–91; P-in-c Alwalton and Chesterton 91–96; TV The Ortons, Alwalton and Chesterton 96–03; R Gravesend St Geo *Roch* 03–06; Chapl HM YOI Roch 13–14; Chapl HM Pris Pentonville 14–18; V Mildmay Grove St Jude and St Paul

Lon 18–19. *11 Langdale Walk, Market Harborough LE16 9LG* E: sturtrock672@gmail.com

STUTTARD, Ms Anna. b 64. Newc Univ BA 86 Heythrop Coll Lon MA 14 Cam Univ BTh 17. Westcott Ho Cam 15. **d** 17 **p** 18. C Hornsey St Mary w St Geo *Lon* 17–20; V Edmonton St Aldhelm from 20. *St Aldhelm's Vicarage, 2 Windmill Road, London N18 1PA* T: (020) 8348 4968 *or* 8807 5336 M: 07941-121748 E: stuttard.tempest@btopenworld.com *or* vicar@aldhelms.co.uk

STYLER, Jamie Cuming. b 36. Sarum & Wells Th Coll 70. **d** 72 **p** 73. C Whipton *Ex* 72–75; C Paignton St Jo, St Andr and St Boniface 76–78; V Topsham 78–88; V Plymouth St Simon 88–01; Chapl Plymouth Community Services NHS Trust 94–01; rtd 01; PtO *Ex* 01–18. *Drey House, 27 Langham Way, Ivybridge PL21 9BX* T: (01752) 691592

STYLES, Charlie Adam Mark. b 81. St Hild Coll Dur BA 04. Oak Hill Th Coll 06. **d** 09 **p** 10. C Britwell *Ox* 09–11; C Stoke Poges 11–13; P-in-c Lutterworth w Cotesbach and Bitteswell *Leic* 13–16; R from 16. *The Rectory, Coventry Road, Lutterworth LE17 4SH* E: charliestyles@dunelm.org.uk *or* charlie.styles@lutterworthchurch.org

STYLES, Christopher James. b 60. Univ Coll Lon BA 94. Wycliffe Hall Ox 10. **d** 12 **p** 13. C Chich St Pancras and St Jo 12–16; C Polegate from 16. *St Wilfrid's House, 90 Broad Road, Eastbourne BN20 9RA* T: (01323) 370560 M: 07990-433020 E: cjstyles@talk21.com

STYLES, Mary Elise. b 60. Southn Univ BM 85 Univ Coll Lon MSc 97 Anglia Ruskin Univ BA 12. ERMC 09. **d** 12 **p** 13. C Rome *Eur* 12–16; R S Quantock *B & W* from 16. *The Vicarage, Kingston St Mary, Taunton TA2 8HW* T: (01823) 451189 E: styles@alice.it *or* revmarye@gmail.com

STYLES, Ross. **d** 15 **p** 17. C Greystones *D & G* 15–17; C Ch Ch Cathl Dublin 17–21; I Newcastle w Newtownmountkennedy and Calary from 21. *The Rectory, Church Lane, Newcastle, Greystones, Co Wicklow, Republic of Ireland* E: stylesross@gmail.com

SUART, Geoffrey Hugh. b 49. Man Univ BSc 70 Nottm Univ PGCE 71. Oak Hill Th Coll. **d** 83 **p** 84. C Ogley Hay *Lich* 83–86; TV Wenlock *Heref* 86–90; TR Kirby Muxloe *Leic* 90–04; RD Sparkenhoe E 99–03; R Snettisham w Ingoldisthorpe and Fring *Nor* 04–14; Chapl Norfolk Hospice 11–14; rtd 14. *285 Station Road, Bagworth, Coalville LE67 1BL* E: geoffsuart.t21@btinternet.com

SUBARAN, Ajennie. b 53. St Mellitus Coll 16. **d** 19 **p** 20. OLM Forest Gate Em w Upton Cross *Chelmsf* from 19. *67 Wyatt Road, London E7 9ND* M: 07956-134438 *or* 07930-165777 E: ajennie.subaran@btinternet.com

SUCH, Colin Royston. b 62. UEA LLB 83. Ripon Coll Cuddesdon 94. **d** 97 **p** 98. C Streetly *Lich* 97–00; P-in-c Wednesfield St Greg 00–04; V Rushall from 04; P-in-c Walsall St Pet 08–13. *Rushall Vicarage, 10 Tetley Avenue, Walsall WS4 2HE* T: (01922) 624677 E: suchcol@aol.com

SUCH, Canon Howard Ingram James. b 52. Southn Univ BTh 81 Lon Univ MA 97. Sarum & Wells Th Coll 77. **d** 81 **p** 82. C Cheam *S'wark* 81–84; Prec Cant Cathl 84–91; V Borden 91–03; Hon Min Can Cant Cathl 84–03; AD Sittingbourne 00–03; Can Res and Prec Sheff Cathl 03–07; Warden St Barn Coll Lingfield *S'wark* 07–18; Public Preacher from 18; Hon Can S'wark Cathl from 16; Superior Soc of Retreat Conductors 05–11; PtO *Chich* from 15; *Cant* 18–21; Hon Min Can Cant Cathl from 18. *6 Thundersland Road, Herne Bay CT6 6JT*

SUCH, Miss Nicola Jane. b 73. Roehampton Inst BA 95. Trin Coll Bris 12. **d** 14 **p** 15. C Wroughton and Wichelstowe *Bris* 14–18; P-in-c Kempshott *Win* 18–19; V from 19. *St Mark's Vicarage, 171 Kempshott Lane, Basingstoke RG22 5LF*

SUCKLING, Keith Edward. b 47. CChem FRSC Darw Coll Cam PhD 71 Liv Univ BSc 87 DSc 89. Oak Hill NSM Course 91. **d** 94 **p** 95. NSM Digswell and Panshanger *St Alb* 94–14; P-in-c Fraserburgh *Ab* 14–21; rtd 21. *6 Crimond Court, Fraserburgh AB43 9QW* T: (01346) 518158 E: keith.suckling@cantab.net

SUDBURY, Archdeacon of. *See* JENKINS, The Ven David Harold

SUDDABY, Susan Eveline. b 43. Bedf Coll of Educn CertEd 64. S'wark Ord Course 93. **d** 96 **p** 97. NSM Rusthall *Roch* 96–00; C Northfleet 00–02; PtO 03–06; P-in-c N Chapel w Ebernoe *Chich* 06–08; rtd 08; PtO *Chich* from 08; *S'wark* from 11. *54 Garden Wood Road, East Grinstead RH19 1JX* T: (01342) 313042

SUDELL, Philip Henry. b 61. Thames Poly BScEng 84 Lon Univ PGCE 85. Wycliffe Hall Ox 89. **d** 92 **p** 93. C Worthing Ch the King *Chich* 92–96; C Muswell Hill St Jas w St Matt *Lon* 96–05; LtO 05–14; P-in-c Chitts Hill St Cuth 14–15; AD W Haringey 14–20; Public Preacher 15–19; P-in-c Friern Barnet St Pet le Poer from 19; PtO *Eur* from 18. *163*

Colney Hatch Lane, London N10 1HA T: (020) 8883 7417
E: philip.sudell@gracech.org.uk
SUDRON, David Jeffrey. b 78. Univ Coll Dur BA 99 MA 00.
St Steph Ho Ox 01. **d** 03 **p** 04. C Gt Grimsby St Mary and
St Jas *Linc* 03–08; Min Can Dur Cathl 08–12; R Wallsend St Pet
and St Luke *Newc* 12–19; NSM Whorlton Gp *York* from 19.
18 Church Lane, Swainby, Northallerton DL6 3EA T: (01642)
700321 E: david.sudron@dunelm.org.uk
SUDWORTH, Frank. b 43. Open Univ BA 92. Oak Hill Th
Coll. **d** 78 **p** 79. C Deane *Man* 78–81; C Worksop St Jo *S'well*
82–85; V Wollaton Park 85–90; P-in-c Lenton Abbey 85–86;
V 86–90; V Upper Armley *Ripon* 90–97; RD Armley 92–95;
Dep Chapl HM Pris *Liv* 97–98; P-in-c Low Moor H Trin *Bradf*
98–03; V Low Moor 03; P-in-c Wyke 03–05; TR Oakenshaw,
Wyke and Low Moor 06–07; rtd 07; PtO *Blackb* 07–20. *12
Brampton Avenue, Thornton-Cleveleys FY5 2JY* T: (01253)
858377
SUDWORTH, Richard John. b 68. Leeds Univ LLB 90
Spurgeon's Coll MTh 05. Qu Coll Birm 05. **d** 10 **p** 11. C
Sparkbrook Ch Ch and Tyseley *Birm* 10–13; P-in-c Sparkbrook
Ch Ch 13–18; Tutor Qu Foundn Birm 13–17; Abp's Sec for
Inter-Relig Affairs *Cant* from 18; PtO *Birm* 18–21. *Lambeth
Palace, London SE1 7JU* T: (020) 7898 1247 M: 07891-
635664 E: suddy@blueyonder.co.uk
SUDWORTH, Timothy Mark. b 70. St Martin's Coll Lanc
BA 93 K Coll Lon MA 00 Anglia Ruskin Univ BA 08. St Paul's
Th Cen Lon 06. **d** 08 **p** 09. NSM Egham *Guildf* 08–16;
Chapl Strode's Coll 08–16; PtO *Guildf* 15–16; Min Oak Tree
Angl Fellowship *Lon* from 16. *100 Creffield Road, London
W3 9PX* T: (020) 3624 9184 *or* 8993 2060 M: 07964-760259
E: timsudworth@btinternet.com *or* tims@oaktree.org.uk
SUEKARRAN, Hannah Louise. Pemb Coll Cam MA 12
St Jo Coll Dur BA 15. Cranmer Hall Dur 13. **d** 16 **p** 17.
C Harton *York* 16–20; C Brayton 20; PtO from 21. *16
Hollytree Way, Brayton, Selby YO8 9SS* M: 07846-527021
E: hannahsuekarran@gmail.com
SUEKARRAN, Robert Patrick. b 84. Bradf Univ BSc 06
St Jo Coll Dur BA 15 Keele Univ PGCE 08. Cranmer
Hall Dur 12. **d** 15 **p** 16. C Strensall *York* 15–19; 20s-40s
Team Ldr from 19; C Brayton from 19. *16 Hollytree
Way, Brayton, Selby YO8 9SS* M: 07944-592355
E: robert_suekarran@hotmail.com
SUFFERN, Richard William Sefton. b 57. Reading Univ
BSc 79. Trin Coll Bris 88. **d** 90 **p** 91. C Radipole and
Melcombe Regis *Sarum* 90–94; TV Cheltenham St Mark
Glouc 94–99; R Whitnash *Cov* from 99; AD Warwick and
Leamington from 20. *St Margaret's Rectory, 2 Church Close,
Whitnash, Leamington Spa CV31 2HJ* T: (01926) 425070
E: revrwss@gmail.com
SUFFOLK, Archdeacon of. *See* GOSNEY, The Ven Jeanette
Margaret
SUGDEN, Charles Edward. b 59. Magd Coll Cam PGCE 82
MA 83. Trin Coll Bris 89. **d** 91 **p** 92. C Gidea Park *Chelmsf*
91–94; TV Melksham *Sarum* 94–01; NSM Poole 02–08;
V Locks Heath *Portsm* 08–15; P-in-c Frenchay and
Winterbourne Down *Bris* 15–16; P-in-c Stapleton 15–16; R
Frenchay and Stapleton from 16. *21 Park Road, Stapleton,
Bristol BS16 1AZ* T: 0117-965 4872 M: 07729-027969
SUGDEN, Canon Christopher Michael Neville. b 48. St Pet
Coll Ox BA 70 MA 74 Westmr Coll Ox PhD 88. St Jo Coll
Nottm MPhil 74. **d** 74 **p** 75. C Leeds St Geo *Ripon* 74–77;
Assoc P Bangalore St Jo India 77–83; Registrar and Dir
Academic Affairs Ox Cen for Miss Studies 83–01; Exec Dir
01–04; Exec Sec Angl Mainstream Internat 04–13; LtO *Ox*
83–13; Sec Ox Cen for Relig and Public Life from 13; PtO
Ox from 13; Hon Can Jos from 00; Hon Can Sunyani
Ghana from 12. *OCRPL, 21 High Street, Eynsham, Oxford
OX29 4HE* M: 07808-297043 E: csugden@ocrpl.org
SULLIVAN, Mrs Charlotte Lucy. b 66. ERMC 12. **d** 15 **p** 18.
C Aquitaine *Eur* 15–20; Chapl Maisons-Laffitte from 20.
15 avenue Carnot, 78600 Maisons-Laffitte, France T: (0033)
1 39 62 34 97 E: chaplain@htcml.com
SULLIVAN, Canon Julian Charles. b 49. Lon Univ BSc 74
CertEd 75. Wycliffe Hall Ox 80. **d** 83 **p** 84. C Southall Green
St Jo *Lon* 83–87; C Wells St Cuth w Wookey Hole *B & W*
87–90; V Sheff St Barn and St Mary 90–91; V Sheff St Mary w
Highfield Trin 91–95; V Sheff St Mary and Melbourne Lane 95–16;
P-in-c Endcliffe 04–07; AD Ecclesall 01–06; Bp's Urban Adv
05–16; Hon Can Sheff Cathl 01–16; rtd 16; PtO *Sheff* from
16. *64 Kingfield Road, Sheffield S11 9AU* T: 0114-258 3087
SULLIVAN, Mrs Linda Mary. b 45. **d** 14 **p** 15. OLM
Malmesbury w Westport and Brokenborough *Bris* 14–16;
OLM Malmesbury and Upper Avon 16–20; PtO from 20. *48
Bonners Close, Malmesbury SN16 9UF* T: (01666) 822281
SULLIVAN, Miss Lucy. b 87. Chich Univ BSc 10 Sheff
Univ BA 17. Coll of Resurr Mirfield 15. **d** 18 **p** 19. C

Rottingdean *Chich* 18–20; C Bosham from 20. *19 Willowhale
Avenue, Bognor Regis PO21 4AU* M: 07882-244320
E: mthr.lucysullivan@gmail.com
SULLIVAN, The Very Revd Nicola Ann. b 58. SRN 81 RM 84.
Wycliffe Hall Ox BTh 95. **d** 95 **p** 96. C Earlham St Anne *Nor*
95–99; Assoc V Bath Abbey w St Jas *B & W* 99–02; Chapl
R Nat Hosp for Rheumatic Diseases NHS Trust 99–02; Bp's
Chapl and Past Asst *B & W* 02–07; Sub-Dean and Preb
Wells Cathl 03–07; Adn Wells and Can Res Wells Cathl
07–16; Dean S'well from 16. *The Residence, Vicars Court,
Church Street, Southwell NG25 0HP* T: (01636) 817282
E: dean@southwellminster.org.uk
SULLY, Andrew Charles. b 67. Southn Univ BA 88 Birm Univ
MPhil 95. Qu Coll Birm 90. **d** 93 **p** 94. C Maindee Newport
Mon 93–96; V Llanfihangel w Llanafan and Llanwnnws
etc *St D* 96–02; TV St As 03–06; PV St As Cathl 02–06; V
Llangollen w Trevor and Llantysilio 06–17; P-in-c Valle
Crucis Miss Area 18; AD Llangollen 10–12; V Llandudno
Ban from 18. *The Rectory, 27 Church Walks, Llandudno
LL30 2HL* T: (01978) 860231
SUMMERFIELD, Mrs Nina Mary Joyner. b 59. Leic Univ
BSc 80 Wye Coll Lon MSc 82. WEMTC 13. **d** 16 **p** 17.
NSM Lydney *Glouc* 16–19; NSM Woolaston w Alvington
and Aylburton 16–19; NSM Lydney, Woolaston,
Alvington and Aylburton 19–20; NSM Bourton-on-the-
Water w Clapton etc from 20. *6 De Havilland Road, Upper
Rissington, Cheltenham GL54 2NZ* M: 07747-560351
E: nina.summerfield@hotmail.co.uk
SUMMERS, Aimée Louise (Jaimée). b 94. Selw Coll Cam
BA 16. Ripon Coll Cuddesdon MA 20. **d** 20 **p** 21. C Epping
Distr *Chelmsf* from 20. *Vicarage Cottage, Hartland Road, Epping
CM16 4PD* M: 07761-440450 E: summersaimee@gmail.com
SUMMERS, Canon Alexander William Mark. b 75. Leic Univ
BA 98 MA 00 Fitzw Coll Cam BTh 09 Dur Univ MA 20 Open
Univ PGCE 01. Westcott Ho Cam 07. **d** 09 **p** 10. C Chingford
SS Pet and Paul *Chelmsf* 09–12; P-in-c Walthamstow St Mich
12–13; V 13–18; AD Waltham Forest 15–16; Public Preacher
from 18; V W Ham 18–20; C Woodford St Mary w St Phil
and St Jas 20–21; C Walthamstow St Pet from 21; CMD Adv
Barking Area from 18; Hon Can Chelmsf Cathl from 15. *The
Vicarage, 9 Palmerston Road, London E17 6PQ* T: (020) 8509
3895 M: 07434-918410 E: awm.summers@icloud.com *or*
asummers@chelmsford.anglican.org
SUMMERS, Graham. b 50. SCRTP 12. **d** 15 **p** 16. NSM Penn
and Tylers Green *Ox* from 15. *43 Kings Ride, Penn, High
Wycombe HP10 8BP* T: (01494) 814347 M: 07866-920341
E: gandcsummers@icloud.com
SUMMERS, Jaimée. *See* SUMMERS, Aimée Louise
SUMMERS, Jeanne. *See* SUMMERS, Ursula Jeanne
SUMMERS, John Emrys. b 80. G&C Coll Cam LLM 03 Univ
Coll Ox MA 07 Barrister 04. Westcott Ho Cam 13. **d** 16 **p** 17.
C Three Valleys *Sarum* 16–19; Chapl Trin Coll Cam from
19. *Trinity College, Cambridge CB2 1TQ* T: (01223) 766327
E: john.summers@trin.cam.ac.uk
SUMMERS (née PASCOE), Mrs Lorraine Eve. b 51.
SAOMC 98. **d** 01 **p** 02. NSM Sandon, Wallington and
Rushden w Clothall *St Alb* 01–06; P-in-c Kimpton w
Ayot St Lawrence 06–14; Asst Chapl E and N Herts NHS
Trust 06–14; rtd 14; PtO *Nor* from 15. *Trafoi, Banham
Road, Kenninghall, Norwich NR16 2ED* T: (01953) 888389
E: lorrainesummers51@gmail.com
SUMMERS, Neil Thomas. b 58. Roehampton Inst BA 93 K
Coll Lon MA 94 St Mary's Coll Strawberry Hill PGCE 95.
SEITE 97. **d** 00 **p** 01. NSM Richmond St Mary w St Matthias
and St Jo *S'wark* 00–14; TV from 14. *2 Ravensbourne Road,
Twickenham TW1 2DH* T: (020) 8892 8313 M: 07540-
974702 E: neil.summers@richmondteamministry.org
SUMMERS, Canon Raymond John. b 41. Univ of Wales
TCert 63 Open Univ BA 75. St Mich Coll Llan 77. **d** 77 **p** 78.
NSM Mynyddislwyn *Mon* 77–81; NSM Abercarn 81–82;
P-in-c 82–89; V 89–91; V Mynyddislwyn 91–95; TR 95–08;
RD Bedwellty 93–04; Can St Woolos Cathl 01–08; rtd 08.
12A Maple Gardens, Risca, Newport NP11 6AR T: (01633)
613676
SUMMERS, Canon Stephen Bruce. b 63. St Andr Univ
MTheol 95 Chich Univ PhD 08. STETS 98. **d** 00 **p** 01.
C Bishop's Waltham *Portsm* 00–02; R Farlington 02–09;
Prin Local Min Progr *Guildf* from 09; Hon Can Guildf
Cathl from 18. *Church House, 20 Alan Turing Road, Surrey
Research Park, Guildford GU2 7YF* T: (01483) 790319
E: steve.summers@cofeguildford.org.uk
SUMMERS, Preb Ursula Jeanne. b 35. Birm Univ BA 56
Liv Univ CertEd 57. Glouc Sch of Min. **dss** 85 **d** 87 **p** 94.
Fownhope *Heref* 85–87; Hon C 87; Brockhampton w
Fawley 85–87; Hon C 87; C Marden w Amberley and
Wisteston 88–94; P-in-c 94–02; RD Heref Rural 93–99;

P-in-c Wellington w Pipe-cum-Lyde and Moreton-on-Lugg 96–02; Preb Heref Cathl 96–02; rtd 02; PtO *Heref* 02–20. *33 St Botolph's Green, Leominster HR6 8ER* T: (01568) 617456 E: roland.summers@yahoo.co.uk

SUMNER, Angela Diane. b 56. Brighton Poly BSc 78 Sussex Univ PGCE 92 Coll of SS Mark and Jo Plymouth MA 02 Ex Univ BTh 15 MRPharmS. SWMTC 10. **d** 12 **p** 13. NSM Totnes w Bridgetown, Berry Pomeroy etc *Ex* from 12; Asst Chapl S Devon Healthcare NHS Foundn Trust 12–13; Chapl 13–15; Chapl Torbay and S Devon NHS Foundn Trust from 15. *9 Wayside, Brixham TQ5 8PY* T: (01803) 853959 E: angela.sumner@outlook.com

SUMNER, Mrs Judith Elizabeth. b 68. Ox Poly BEd 90. Ripon Coll Cuddesdon 13. **d** 16 **p** 17. OLM Reading St Mary the Virgin *Ox* from 16. *97 Warborough Avenue, Tilehurst, Reading RG31 5LF* T: 0118-377 3286 M: 07866-614836 E: judithsumner29@gmail.com

SUMPTER, Guy. b 60. Leic Univ BA 01 PhD 08. Ripon Coll Cuddesdon 09. **d** 11 **p** 12. C Brentwood St Thos *Chelmsf* 11–14; R Eye *St E* from 14. *The Vicarage, 41 Castle Street, Eye IP23 7AW* T: (01379) 871986 E: fatherguy@btinternet.com

SUMSION, Paul Henry. b 74. UMIST BSc 97. Trin Coll Bris BA 03 MA 06. **d** 04 **p** 05. C Hawkshaw Lane *Man* 04–08; P-in-c 08; C Holcombe 04–08; P-in-c 08; R Holcombe and Hawkshaw from 09; Chapl Bury Coll of FE 05–07; CF (VR) from 11. *St Mary's Vicarage, Bolton Road, Hawkshaw, Bury BL8 4JN* T: (01204) 888060 E: paul@holcombehawkshaw.org

SUNDERLAND, Archdeacon of. *See* COOPER, The Ven Robert Gerard

SUNLEY, Carol. b 49. Leeds Univ BA 12. Yorks Min Course 10. **d** 12. NSM N Ormesby *York* 12–15; NSM Ormesby 15–16; rtd 17; PtO *York* from 18. *21 Norfolk Crescent, Middlesbrough TS3 0LZ* T: (01642) 503468 E: pcsunley@ntlworld.com

SURMAN, Malcolm Colin. b 48. Birm Univ CertEd 72 Southn Univ BTh 88 Worc Univ BA 12. Sarum & Wells Th Coll 76. **d** 78 **p** 79. C Basingstoke *Win* 78–81; P-in-c Alton All SS 81–85; V 85–01; Chapl N Hants Loddon Community NHS Trust 84–01; P-in-c Burton and Sopley *Win* 01–14; rtd 14; PtO *Win* from 14; *Ox* from 15. *31 Van Diemens Close, Chinnor OX39 4QE* T: (01844) 761717 E: mcsurman@me.com

SURREY, Mrs Maureen. b 53. Man OLM Scheme 98. **d** 01 **p** 03. OLM Davyhulme Ch Ch *Man* 01–02; OLM Walkden and Lt Hulton 03–09; OLM Flixton St Jo 09–21; PtO from 21. *56 Abingdon Road, Urmston, Manchester M41 0GN* T: 0161-748 3961 E: sidandmo@hotmail.com

SURREY, Archdeacon of. *See* DAVIES, The Ven Richard Paul

SURRIDGE, Jonathan Mark. b 67. Leic Poly BSc 88. Ripon Coll Cuddesdon 10. **d** 12 **p** 13. C Hinckley St Mary *Leic* 12–16; P-in-c Leic St Phil 16–20; P-in-c Leic Presentation 16–20; R Highfield St Pet and Leic St Phil from 20. *15 Castle Street, Leicester LE1 5WN* T: 0116-318 0680 E: jmsurridge@gmail.com

SUTCH, The Ven Christopher David. b 47. TD 92. AKC 69. St Aug Coll Cant 69. **d** 70 **p** 71. C Bris St Andr Hartcliffe 70–75; C Swindon Dorcan 75–78; TV 78–79; P-in-c Alveston 79–83; V 83–89; RD Westbury and Severnside 86–89; CF (TA) 80–03; TR Yate New Town *Bris* 89–99; RD Stapleton 95–99; V Cainscross w Selsley *Glouc* 99–07; AD Stonehouse 04–07; Chapl Costa del Sol E *Eur* 07–13; Adn Gib 08–13; rtd 13; PtO *Glouc* from 14; *Eur* from 16. *5 Mostyn Place, Brockworth, Gloucester GL3 4BA*

SUTCLIFFE, Crispin Francis Henry. b 48. Keble Coll Ox BA 69. Sarum & Wells Th Coll 73. **d** 74 **p** 75. C Truro St Paul 74–77; C St Jo Cathl Umtata S Africa 77–80; P-in-c Treslothan *Truro* 80–85; V 85–91; R Ilchester w Northover, Limington, Yeovilton etc *B & W* 91–11; rtd 11. *57 Wilbert Road, Beverley HU17 0AJ* T: (01482) 864674

SUTCLIFFE, Howard Guest. b 44. Fitzw Coll Cam BA 66 MA 70 Birm Univ MA 75. Westcott Ho Cam 73. **d** 74 **p** 75. C Chorlton-cum-Hardy St Clem *Man* 74–77; Chapl Chetham's Sch of Music 77–80; V Oldham St Paul *Man* 80–94; Co-ord Werneth and Freehold Community Development Project 94–06; PtO 94–09; Hon C Saddleworth *Man* 09–14; PtO from 16. *27 Spurn Lane, Diggle, Oldham OL3 5QP* T: (01457) 879640 E: howardguestsutcliffe@yahoo.co.uk

SUTCLIFFE, Ian. b 31. Surrey Univ BSc 69. Qu Coll Birm 61. **d** 63 **p** 65. C W Wimbledon Ch Ch *S'wark* 63–65; C Battersea St Phil 65–66; C Kingston Hill St Paul 71–73; LtO *Carl* 75–96; rtd 96. *42 Hill Street, Arbroath DD11 1AB*

SUTCLIFFE, John Leslie. b 35. Liv Univ BA 56. Sarum Th Coll 58. **d** 60 **p** 61. C Lytham St Cuth *Blackb* 60–62; C Altham w Clayton le Moors 62–65; C-in-c Penwortham St Leon CD 65–71; Ind Chapl *Liv* 71–74; V Orford St Andr 74–79; V Burnley St Cuth *Blackb* 79–88; Bp's Adv on UPA *Ripon* 88–94; Hon C Leeds Gipton Epiphany 88–94; I Carrickmacross w Magheracloone *Clogh* 94–01; rtd 01; PtO

Blackb from 02; *Bradf* 13–14; *Leeds* 14–16. *1 Beckside, Barley, Burnley BB12 9JZ* T: (01282) 449687

SUTCLIFFE, Richard John. b 67. ACMA 03. Ripon Coll Cuddesdon 09. **d** 12 **p** 13. NSM Hurstbourne Priors, Longparish etc *Win* from 12. *2 Applegate, St Mary Bourne, Andover SP11 6DT* T: (01264) 738288 M: 07976-672733 E: rev.sutcliffe@btinternet.com

SUTCLIFFE, Stephen Alan. b 71. Ripon Coll Cuddesdon 16. **d** 18 **p** 19. C Gurnard w Cowes St Faith *Portsm* 18–21; C Northwood 18–21; TV Newport and Carisbrooke from 21; C Gatcombe from 21. *The Vicarage, 56 Castle Road, Newport PO30 1DP* M: 07800-907300 E: steve.alan.sutcliffe@icloud.com

SUTER (née RENNIE), Mrs Margot Mardelle. b 63. Univ of Wales (Swansea) BSc 84. Ripon Coll Cuddesdon 13. **d** 16 **p** 17. NSM Flackwell Heath *Ox* 16–19; NSM Beaconsfield from 19. *46 Butlers Court Road, Beaconsfield HP9 1SG* T: (01494) 676952 M: 07779-803519 E: margotsuter@hotmail.com

SUTER, Canon Richard Alan. b 48. Rhodes Univ BA 72 St Jo Coll Dur BA 74. Cranmer Hall Dur 72. **d** 75 **p** 76. C Darlington H Trin *Dur* 75–77; C Wrexham *St As* 77–82; R Llansantffraid Glan Conwy and Eglwysbach 82–87; V Broughton 87–92; RD Wrexham 90–97; V Rossett 92–04; V Holt, Rossett and Isycoed 04–09; V Rossett and Isycoed 09–11; Hon Can St As Cathl 11; rtd 11; PtO *St As* from 11. *64 Leaches Lane, Mancot, Deeside CH5 2BL* T: (01244) 534374 E: etsuterra1@gmail.com

SUTHERLAND, Alan. b 55. Sarum & Wells Th Coll. **d** 80 **p** 81. C Hessle *York* 80–83; USA from 83; rtd 10. *18417 Black Bear Trail, Norman OK 73072-9604, USA* E: alansutherland@att.net

SUTHERLAND, Mrs Elaine Anita. b 64. EMMTC 95 Moorlands Bible Coll 86. **d** 10 **p** 11. C Leic H Trin w St Jo 10–20; V from 20. *104 Sports Road, Glenfield, Leicester LE3 8AJ* T: 0116-254 8981 M: 07747-466865 E: esutherland@htl.church

SUTHERLAND, Lesley Ann. b 61. **d** 16 **p** 17. C Cornforth and Ferryhill *Dur* 16–19; P-in-c Lanchester and Burnhope from 19; P-in-c Harelaw and Annfield Plain from 19. *The Vicarage, 1 Lee Hill Court, Lanchester, Durham DH7 0QE* M: 07548-249098 E: lesley.suthrland61@gmail.com

SUTHERLAND, Robert. b 78. Newc Univ BA 00 St Jo Coll Dur MATM 09 SS Hild & Bede Coll Dur PGCE 01 Sheff Univ MA 15. Cranmer Hall Dur 05 Coll of Resurr Mirfield 08. **d** 09 **p** 10. C Morley *Wakef* 09–12; V Mixenden and Illingworth 12–14; *Leeds* from 14. *37 Hops Lane, Halifax HX3 5FB* T: (01422) 353929 E: robb@priest.com

SUTHERLAND, Sophie Louisa. b 85. **d** 12 **p** 13. NSM Chevening *Roch* 12–17; NSM Bromley SS Pet and Paul from 17; Chapl King's Coll Hosp NHS Foundn Trust from 17. *Brasted Place, High Street, Brasted, Westerham TN16 1JE* T: (01959) 565611 M: 07962-136673 E: sophie.sutherland@gmail.com or sophie.sutherland1@nhs.net

SUTTIE, Miss Jillian. b 53. Ex Univ BA 75 PGCE 76. ERMC 05. **d** 08. NSM Colney Heath St Mark *St Alb* from 08; SSMs' Officer St Alb Adnry from 21. *51 West Riding, Bricket Wood, St Albans AL2 3QE* T: (01923) 662772 E: jillsuttie@ukgateway.net

SUTTLE, Neville Frank. b 38. Reading Univ BSc 61 Aber Univ PhD 64. **d** 76 **p** 77. NSM Penicuik *Edin* from 76. *44 St James's Gardens, Penicuik EH26 9DU* T/F: (01968) 673819 E: suttle_hints@hotmail.com

SUTTON, Charles Edwin. b 53. Bris Univ CertEd 76 BEd 77 Birkbeck Coll Lon MSc 00 PhD 07. Ripon Coll Cuddesdon 77. **d** 80 **p** 81. C Stanwix *Carl* 80–84; Warden Marrick Priory *Ripon* 84–88; Fell Birkbeck Coll *Lon* 00–10; PtO *Bris* 12–13; NSM Clifton All SS w St Jo 13–15; V from 15; Bp's Adv for SSM from 14; AD Bris W from 19. *All Saints' Vicarage, 68 Pembroke Road, Clifton, Bristol BS8 3ED* T: 0117-907 8088 or 974 1355 M: 07785-912663 E: charleses@me.com

SUTTON, Christopher David. b 69. Kent Univ BSc 90 FIA 93. SEITE 11. **d** 14 **p** 15. NSM Slaugham and Staplefield Common *Chich* 14–17; NSM Ardingly from 17. *Coppers, 19A Denmans Lane, Lindfield, Haywards Heath RH16 2LA* M: 07903-068366 E: christopher.sutton@yahoo.com

SUTTON, David Robert. b 49. Birm Univ BA 69 Leeds Beckett Univ MA 15 Ox Univ CertEd 72. St Steph Ho Ox 70. **d** 72 **p** 73. C Clitheroe St Mary *Blackb* 72–75; C Fleetwood St Pet 75–78; V Calderbrook *Man* 78–88; V Winton 88–08; Chapl Salford Mental Health Services NHS Trust 92–08; Chapl Gtr Man W Mental Health NHS Foundn Trust 08–17; rtd 17; PtO *Man* from 14; *Ches* from 14; *Blackb* from 16; *Liv* from 18. *42 Lulworth Road, Eccles, Manchester M30 8NP* T: 0161-707 3040 E: frlinedancer@talktalk.net

SUTTON, James William. b 41. Oak Hill Th Coll 81. **d** 84 **p** 85. NSM Chorleywood St Andr *St Alb* 84–06; PtO *Eur* 06–18; Hon Min Can Res Gibraltar Cathl from 11; PtO *St Alb* from 18. *7 Hillside Road, Chorleywood, Rickmansworth WD3 5AP* T: (01923) 282806 E: jsuttonsnr@outlook.com

SUTTON, Jeremy John Ernest. b 60. Ridley Hall Cam 83. **d** 86 **p** 87. C Seacombe *Ches* 86–88; C Northwich St Luke and H Trin 88–90; TV Birkenhead Priory 90–94; V Over St Chad 94–01; V Dunham Massey St Marg and St Mark 01–19; PtO from 19; CF from 19. *c/o MOD Chaplains (Army)* T: (01264) 383430 F: 381824 M: 07584-522897 (01785) 787355 E: jeremyjsutton@outlook.com *or* jeremy.sutton990@mod.gov.uk

SUTTON, Canon John. b 47. St Jo Coll Dur BA 70. Ridley Hall Cam 70. **d** 72 **p** 73. C Denton St Lawr *Man* 72–77; R 77–82; V High Lane *Ches* 82–88; V Sale St Anne 88–96; V Timperley 96–12; RD Bowdon 03–12; Hon Can Ches Cathl 01–12; rtd 12; PtO *Ches* from 12. *6 Walton Road, Sale M33 4AD* T: 0161-283 8914 E: jfsuttontimp@aol.com

SUTTON, John Stephen. b 33. Em Coll Cam BA 57 MA 61. Wycliffe Hall Ox 57. **d** 59 **p** 60. C Dagenham *Chelmsf* 59–62; C Bishopwearmouth St Gabr *Dur* 62–63; V Over Kellet *Blackb* 63–67; V Darwen St Barn 67–74; V Walthamstow St Jo *Chelmsf* 74–84; V Stebbing w Lindsell 84–98; RD Dunmow 94–98; rtd 98; PtO *Chich* from 98. *20 Firwood Close, Eastbourne BN22 9QL* T: (01323) 504654 E: johnsutton33@hotmail.co.uk

SUTTON, Canon John Wesley. b 48. Rolle Coll CertEd 71. All Nations Chr Coll. **d** 76 **p** 77. Chile 76–77; Peru 79–84; Area Sec SAMS 84–88; Youth Sec 88-91; Personnel Sec and Asst Gen Sec 91–03; Gen Sec 03–09; Dir Strategic Partnerships and Miss Nationwide Chr Trust 09–10; C Hornchurch St Andr *Chelmsf* 10–14; rtd 14; Hon Can Peru from 93. *Apt 1D, Block A Royal Golf, Sev Ballesteros, Mijas Costa, 29649 Málaga, Spain* E: johnsutton2104@gmail.com

SUTTON, Kingsley Edwin. b 70. TCD BTh 94. **d** 97 **p** 98. C Belfast St Matt *Conn* 97–99; C Willowfield *D & D* 99–02; I Newry 02–16; I Kilgariffe Union *C, C & R* from 16. *The Rectory, Gullanes, Clonakilty, Co Cork, Republic of Ireland* T: (00353) (23) 883 3357 E: rev.sutton@gmail.com

SUTTON, Mrs Monica Rosalind. b 48. Sheff Hallam Univ MSc 99 Leeds Univ BA 09. Yorks Min Course. **d** 09 **p** 10. NSM Sheff St Cuth 09–20; P-in-c 16–20; rtd 20; PtO *Sheff* from 20. *124 Dalewood Road, Sheffield S8 0EF* T: 0114-236 4399 E: monica_r_sutton@yahoo.com

SUTTON, Paul David. b 88. Ch Coll Cam BA 09 MA 13. Oak Hill Th Coll BA 19 MA 20. **d** 20. C Ex St Leon w H Trin from 20. *27 Barnardo Road, Exeter EX2 4ND* M: 07828-023492 E: paul.sutton@stleonards.church

SUTTON, The Ven Peter Allerton. b 59. Ex Univ BA 85. Linc Th Coll 85. **d** 87 **p** 88. C Fareham H Trin *Portsm* 87–90; C Alverstoke 90–93; Chapl HM Pris Haslar 90–93; V Lee-on-the-Solent *Portsm* 93–12; Warden of Readers 96–00; RD Gosport 06–09; Hon Can Portsm Cathl 09–12; Adn Is of Wight 12–18; P-in-c Empshott and Hawkley w Priors Dean 18; V Greatham, Empshott and Hawkley w Priors Dean from 18; IME Officer 4-7 12–20. *The Vicarage, Hawkley, Liss GU33 6NF* T: (01730) 827459 E: peter.sutton@portsmouth.anglican.org

SUTTON, Philip Frank. b 55. SAOMC 92. **d** 95 **p** 96. NSM Akeman *Ox* 95–00; Chapl Ox Radcliffe Hosps NHS Trust 96–00; Sen Chapl R United Hosp Bath NHS Trust 00–07; Dioc Adv Hosp Chapl *Ox* 04–07; Chapl Team Ldr Ox Radcliffe Hosps NHS Trust 07–12; Chapl Team Ldr Ox Univ Hosps NHS Foundn Trust 12–16; NSM Ox St Matt 16–18; C DAMASCUS from 18. *23 Harding Vale, Steventon, Abingdon OX13 6GF* T: (01235) 635476 M: 07507-378737 E: revpsutton@btinternet.com

SUTTON, Wesley Alan. b 55. Staffs Univ MA 14 Brentwood Coll of Educn CertEd 77. **d** 16 **p** 17. NSM Grayshott *Guildf* 16–20; NSM Churt and Hindhead from 20. *347 St Annes Hill, Midhurst GU29 9NN* T: (01420) 478121 M: 07734-870291 E: wsutton@acornchristian.org

SWABEY, Brian Frank. b 44. BA. Oak Hill Th Coll 79. **d** 82 **p** 83. C Clapham St Jas *S'wark* 82–84; C Wallington 84–88; Chapl Mt Gould Hosp Plymouth 88–89; V Plymouth St Jude *Ex* 88–92; Chapl RN 92–99; V Penn Fields *Lich* 99–01; rtd 01; PtO *Ex* 01–09; *Truro* from 15. *30 Treskewes Estate, St Keverne, Helston TR12 6RA* T: (01326) 281168 E: brian@swabey.org

SWABY, Desrene. b 42. SEITE 00. **d** 03 **p** 04. NSM S'wark St Geo w St Alphege and St Jude 03–09; NSM Camberwell St Mich w All So w Em 09–16; PtO from 16. *36 Gabriel House, 10 Odessa Street, London SE16 7HQ* T: (020) 7231 9834 E: desrene.s@hotmail.co.uk

SWAIN, John Edgar. b 44. Lich Th Coll 67. **d** 69 **p** 70. C E Dereham w Hoe *Nor* 69–73; V Haugh *Linc* 73–74; R S Ormsby w Ketsby, Calceby and Driby 73–74; R Harrington w Brinkhill 73–74; R Oxcombe 73–74; R Ruckland w Farforth and Maidenwell 73–74; R Somersby w Bag Enderby 73–74; R Tetford and Salmonby 73–74; R Belchford 73–74; V W Ashby 73–74; C Attleborough *Nor* 74–78; P-in-c Oxford Cen w Eastwood & Princeton Canada 78–84; P-in-c Oldcastle

w Colchester N 84–90; P-in-c Kirton w Falkenham *St E* 90–95; Chapl Suffolk Constabulary 90–01; P-in-c Gt and Lt Whelnetham w Bradfield St George 95–01; P-in-c Lawshall w Shimplingthorne and Alpheton 98–01; R Wawa w White River and Hawk Junction Canada 01–09; rtd 09. *70 Mosher Road, RR #2, Iron Bridge ON P0R 1H0, Canada* E: jswain@ontera.net

SWAIN, Preb Peter John. b 44. Sarum & Wells Th Coll 86. **d** 88 **p** 89. C Beaminster Area *Sarum* 88–92; P-in-c W Newton and Bromfield w Waverton *Carl* 92–98; Member Rural Life and Agric Team 93–96; Ldr 96–98; RD Solway *Carl* 95–98; Hon Can Carl Cathl 96–98; TR Leominster *Heref* 98–05; RD 98–05; Preb Heref Cathl 03–05; rtd 05; PtO *Heref* from 12. *10 Market Hall Street, Kington HR5 3DP* T: (01544) 230999 E: pandpswain@btinternet.com

SWAIN, Mrs Sharon Juanita. b 46. Sussex Univ BA 75 CertEd 76 Heythrop Coll Lon MA 04. Glouc Sch of Min 81. **dss** 84 **d** 87 **p** 94. Upton St Leonards *Glouc* 84–88; C 87–88; Children's Officer *Worc* 88–95; Min Can Worc Cathl 94–95; V Hanley Castle, Hanley Swan and Welland 95–01; R E Bergholt and Brantham *St E* 01–06; RD Samford 01–06; TR Solway Plain *Carl* 06–10; rtd 10; C Carew *St D* 13–14. *Selemat, Jameston, Tenby SA70 8QJ* T: (01834) 871381 E: rev.s.swain@googlemail.com

SWAINE, Judith Ann. b 55. STETS. **d** 09 **p** 10. C Portsea All SS *Portsm* 09–13; PtO *Win* 13–16; Chapl HM Pris Is of Wight from 14. *HM Prison Albany, 55 Parkhurst Road, Newport PO30 5RS* T: (01983) 556573

SWALES, David James. b 58. Warwick Univ BA 79. Cranmer Hall Dur 81. **d** 84 **p** 85. C Eccleshill *Bradf* 84–88; C Prenton *Ches* 88–92; V Oakworth *Bradf* 92–00; V Bolton St Jas w St Chrys 00–09; V Haughley w Wetherden and Stowupland *St E* 09–17; P-in-c Pott Shrigley *Ches* from 17. *The Vicarage, Spuley Lane, Pott Shrigley, Macclesfield SK10 5RS* T: (01625) 575846 E: rev.david@btinternet.com *or* vicar@pottshrigleychurch.org

SWALES, Peter. b 52. ACIB 78 Open Univ BA 99. Ridley Hall Cam 85. **d** 87 **p** 88. C Allestree *Derby* 87–91; P-in-c Horsley 91–99; RD Heanor 97–99; V Heckmondwike *Wakef* 99–03; V Chellaston *Derby* 03–10; rtd 10. *18 Kerry Drive, Smalley, Ilkeston DE7 6ER* T: (01332) 881752 E: pasta.swales@gmail.com

SWALLOW, Mrs Alice Gillian. b 51. Birm Univ BA 72 CertEd 73. NEOC 82. **dss** 84 **d** 87 **p** 94. Morpeth *Newc* 84–86; Uttoxeter w Bramshall *Lich* 86–88; Par Dn 87–88; Par Dn Rocester 88; Chapl to the Deaf *Man* 88–90; Par Dn Goodshaw and Crawshawbooth 88–93; C Barkisland w W Scammonden *Wakef* 93–95; V Ripponden 95–97; rtd 97; PtO *Wakef* 02–14; *Leeds* from 14. *22 Scholes Lane, Scholes, Cleckheaton BD19 6NR* T: (01274) 875529 E: jill_swallow@yahoo.co.uk

SWALLOW, John Brian. b 36. Trent Poly 78. **d** 84 **p** 85. C Cleveleys *Blackb* 84–87; V Blackpool St Mark 87–93; P-in-c Burnley St Steph 93–98; V 98–01; RD Burnley 97–00; rtd 01; PtO *Dur* from 01. *6 Chichester Walk, Haughton-le-Skerne, Darlington DL1 2SG* E: swallowj2@hotmail.co.uk

SWAMY, Muthuraj. b 76. Serampore Coll BTh 97 BD 01 MTh 05 Edin Univ PhD 12 Madurai Univ MA 13. **d** 20 **p** 21. Dir Cam Cen for Christianity Worldwide from 18; NSM Cherry Hinton St Jo *Ely* from 20. *The Cambridge Centre for Christianity Worldwide, Westminster College, Madingley Road, Cambridge CB3 0AA* T: (01223) 330641 M: 07856-297053 E: director@cccw.cam.ac.uk

SWAN, Canon Duncan James. b 65. Imp Coll Lon BSc 88 SS Coll Cam BA 91 MA 95 K Coll Lon MA 04 MPhil 18. Ridley Hall Cam 89. **d** 92 **p** 93. C Stevenage St Andr and St Geo *St Alb* 92–95; C Harpenden St Nic 95–99; V Redbourn 99–06; C Caterham *S'wark* 06–18; AD 11–16; Deaneries Development Adv from 18; Hon C Merton Priory from 18; Hon Can S'wark Cathl from 16. *St John's Vicarage, 135 High Path, London SW19 2JY* M: 07513-337585 E: duncpen@hotmail.com

SWAN, Judith Mary. b 77. Trin Coll Bris 19. **d** 21. C Ilminster and Whitelackington *B & W* from 21. *The Old Post Office, Waterrow, Taunton TA4 2AX* M: 07464-317608 E: swan.judith@outlook.com

SWAN, Philip Douglas. b 56. Wye Coll Lon BSc 78 Qu Coll Cam MA 81 CertEd 81. St Jo Coll Nottm 86. **d** 88 **p** 89. C Birm St Martin w Bordesley St Andr 88–92; C Selly Park St Steph and St Wulstan 92–96; P-in-c The Lickey 96–98; V 98–10; Dir World Miss *Lich* from 10; C Penn 12–14; C Hanley H Ev from 14. *Christ Church Vicarage, 10 Emery Street, Stoke-on-Trent ST6 2JJ*

SWAN, Preb Ronald Frederick. b 35. St Cath Coll Cam BA 59 MA. Coll of Resurr Mirfield. **d** 61 **p** 62. C Staveley *Derby* 61–65; Chapl Lon Univ 65–72; C St Martin-in-the-Fields 72–77; V Ealing St Barn 77–88; V Ealing St Steph Castle Hill 81–88; AD Ealing E 84–88; V Harrow St Mary 88–97; AD Harrow 89–94; Preb St Paul's Cathl 91–06; Master R Foundn of St Kath in Ratcliffe 97–06; rtd 06; PtO *Lon* from 10. *8 Moat

Lodge, London Road, Harrow HA1 3LU T: (020) 8864 4625
E: ronaldswan@btinternet.com

SWANBOROUGH, Alan William. b 38. Southn Univ BEd 75. Sarum & Wells Th Coll 77. d 80 p 81. NSM Ventnor H Trin *Portsm* 80–85; NSM Ventnor St Cath 80–85; Chapl Upper Chine Sch Shanklin 85–94; Chapl Ryde Sch w Upper Chine 94–03; NSM Shanklin St Blasius *Portsm* 91–10; P-in-c 93–10; rtd 10; PtO *Portsm* from 10. *6 The Cambria, 32 Broadway, Sandown PO36 9BY* T: (01983) 402686 E: a.swanborough38@btinternet.com

SWANN, Ms Anne Barbara. b 49. St Mich Coll Llan BTh 07 MTh 08. d 08 p 09. Hon C Peterston-super-Ely w St Brides-super-Ely *Llan* 08–10; PtO 10–12; C Glan Ely 12–15; rtd 14; PtO *Llan* from 15. *19 Fairways Crescent, Cardiff CF5 3DZ* T: (029) 2056 2641 M: 07810-798465 E: revdanne@live.co.uk

SWANN, Edgar John. b 42. TCD BA 66 MA 70 BD 77 HDipEd 80. CITC 68. d 68 p 69. C Crumlin *Conn* 68–70; C Howth *D & G* 70–73; I Greystones 73–08; Can Ch Ch Cathl Dublin 90–08; Adn Glendalough 93–08; rtd 09. *Noah's Ark, 4 Mount Haven, New Road, Greystones, Co Wicklow, Republic of Ireland* T: (00353) (1) 255 7572 M: 87-255 7032

SWANN, Paul David James. b 59. Ch Ch Ox BA 81 MA 88. St Jo Coll Nottm 87. d 90 p 91. C Old Hill H Trin *Worc* 90–94; V 94–02; C Worc City and Chapl Worc Tech Coll 02–09; rtd 09; PtO *Worc* from 12. *26 Knotts Avenue, Worcester WR4 0HZ* T: (01905) 619339 E: pdjswann@gmail.com

SWANNACK, David Joseph. b 65. d 11 p 12. C Frodingham and New Brumby *Linc* 11–15; V Messingham 15–16; P-in-c Scotter w E Ferry 15–16; P-in-c Scotton w Northorpe 15–16; R Messingham w E Butterwick, Scotter w E Ferry and Scotton w Northorpe from 16; RD Manlake from 20. *The Rectory, Church Lane, Scotter, Gainsborough DN21 3RZ* T: (01724) 647789 E: daveswannack@gmail.com

SWANSEA AND BRECON, Bishop of. *Vacant*

SWANTON, Canon John Joseph. b 61. Bradf and Ilkley Coll BA 84 Univ of Wales (Ban) BTh 10 MCIH 89. S Dios Minl Tr Scheme 92. d 95 p 96. NSM Shalford *Guildf* 95–99; NSM Compton w Shackleford and Peper Harow 99–11; TV S Cotswolds *Glouc* 11–14; TR from 14; Hon Can Glouc Cathl from 19. *The Rectory, Ampney Crucis, Cirencester GL7 5RY* T: (01285) 851309 E: john@swanton.plus.com

SWARBRICK, Miss Emma Jayne. b 83. St Martin's Coll Lanc BA(QTS) 05. Trin Coll Bris 16. d 18 p 19. C S Shore H Trin *Blackb* 18–20; C S Shore St Pet 18–20; C Blackpool St Thos from 20. *1 Windermere Road, Blackpool FY4 2BX* T: (01253) 348194 E: emmaswarbrick@outlook.com

SWARBRICK (née PITE), Mrs Sheila Reinhardt. b 60. St Jo Coll Dur BA 82 Nottm Univ MA 98. Oak Hill Th Coll BA 88. d 88 p 94. Par Dn Derby St Aug 88–92; C Brampton St Thos 92–95; PtO *St Alb* 95–96; P-in-c The Stodden Churches 96–98; Chapl Papworth Hosp NHS Trust 98–99; TV Braunstone *Leic* 99–02; P-in-c 02–07; PtO *Ex* 07–08; Hon C Cen Ex 08–14; P-in-c from 14; Asst Chapl R Devon and Ex NHS Foundn Trust from 09. *7 Lower Kings Avenue, Exeter EX4 6JT* T: (01392) 438866 E: sheila.pite@cooptel.net *or* s.swarbrick@nhs.net

SWARBRIGG, David Cecil. b 42. TCD BA 64 MA 67. d 65 p 66. C Lisburn Ch Ch *Conn* 65–67; C Thames Ditton *Guildf* 72–76; Chapl Hampton Sch Middx 76–97; rtd 97. *39 Harefield, Hinchley Wood, Esher KT10 9TY* T/F: (020) 8398 3950 E: d.swarbrigg@btinternet.com

SWART-RUSSELL, Phoebe. b 58. Cape Town Univ BA 79 MA 82 DPhil 88. Ox NSM Course 89. d 90 p 94. C Riverside *Ox* 90–95; Hon C Chenies and Lt Chalfont, Latimer and Flaunden 96–00; PtO from 10. *The Rectory, Latimer, Chesham HP5 1UA* T: (01494) 762281

SWARTZ, Clifford Robert. b 71. Trin Coll Connecticut BA 92 Trin Coll Cam BA 99 MA 03. Ridley Hall Cam 97. d 00 p 01. C Kirk Ella *York* 00–03; Regional Dir FOCUS USA 03–08; Hon C Tariffville Trin Ch 03–08; C New York Ch Ch USA 08–11; P-in-c St Bees *Carl* 11–12; V 12–15; Chapl St Bees Sch 11–15; PtO *Ox* 15–16; Chapl Haberdashers' Monmouth Schs from 16; PtO *Heref* from 17. *Lancaster House, 26 Hereford Road, Monmouth NP25 3HJ* E: clifford.swartz@gmail.com *or* swartz.clifford@habsmonmouth.org

✠**SWARTZ, The Rt Revd Oswald Peter Patrick.** b 53. St Paul's Coll Grahamstown 76. d 80 p 80 c 07. C Welkom St Matthias S Africa 80–81; R Heidedal 81–87; R Mafikeng 87–92; Adn Mafikeng 89–92; Bp's Exec Officer Kimberley and Kuruman 93–94; Sub-Dean Kimberley 94–96; Dioc Sec and Bp's Exec Officer 96–00; Can Kimberley from 93; USPG 01–06; Hon Chapl S'wark Cathl 01–06; Dean Pretoria 06–07; Bp Kimberley and Kuruman 07–20; rtd 20. *Chez Mason, 33 Via Appia, San Remo, Strandfontein, Cape Town, 7798 South Africa* E: oppswartz@onetel.com

SWATTRIDGE, Elliot Samuel Tom. b 93. Cliff Coll BA 14. Trin Coll Bris MA 18. d 18 p 19. C Heref St Pet w St Owen and St Jas from 18. *26 Clive Street, Hereford HR1 2SB* M: 07957-724965 E: curate@spsj.org.uk

SWAYNE, Jeremy Michael Deneys. b 41. Worc Coll Ox BA 63 BM, BCh 67 MRCGP 71 FFHom 91. d 00 p 01. NSM Fosse Trinity *B & W* 00–04; P-in-c 04–05; rtd 05; PtO *B & W* from 05. *Tanzy Cottage, Rimpton, Yeovil BA22 8AQ* T: (01935) 850031 E: jem.swayne@btinternet.com

SWAYZE, Margaret. b 69. d 11 p 12. OLM Diss *Nor* 11–19; rtd 19; PtO *Nor* from 19. *32 Croft Lane, Diss IP22 4NA* T: (01379) 644701 E: maggiecroftlane@live.co.uk

SWEATMAN, John. b 44. Open Univ BA 89. Bernard Gilpin Soc Dur 67 Oak Hill Th Coll 68. d 71 p 72. C Rayleigh *Chelmsf* 71–73; C Seaford w Sutton *Chich* 73–77; Chapl RN 77–82; CF 82–95; V Hellingly and Upper Dicker *Chich* 85–90; Hon C Mayfield 95–96; P-in-c Malborough w S Huish, W Alvington and Churchstow *Ex* 96–02; V Ash w Westmarsh *Cant* 02–11; P-in-c Wingham w Elmstone and Preston w Stourmouth 10–11; AD E Bridge 08–11; rtd 11; Chapl St Edm Sch Cant 12; PtO *Cant* 12–16; *Sarum* 16–21; *Ex* from 21; Prov Chapl MU 16–20. *12 Sarlsdown Road, Exmouth EX8 2HY* T: (01395) 227698 E: johnsrev@btinternet.com

SWEED, John William. b 35. Bernard Gilpin Soc Dur 58 Clifton Th Coll 59. d 62 p 63. C Shrewsbury St Julian *Lich* 62–64; C Sheff St Jo 64–70; V Doncaster St Jas 70–79; V Hatfield 79–00; RD Snaith and Hatfield 84–93; rtd 00; PtO *Sheff* 00–20. *21 The Oval, Tickhill, Doncaster DN11 9HF* T: (01302) 743293 E: john@thesweeds.com

SWEENEY, Andrew James. b 61. Wycliffe Hall Ox 96. d 96 p 97. C Bladon w Woodstock *Ox* 96–99; C Coleraine *Conn* 99–02; V Cogges and S Leigh *Ox* 02–12; V N Leigh 09–12; AD Witney 07–08; I Ballymoney w Finvoy and Rasharkin *Conn* from 12. *The Rectory, 4 Queen Street, Ballymoney BT53 6JA* T: (028) 2766 2149 M: 07720-472556 E: ballymoneyrector@sky.com

SWEENEY, Andrew John. b 59. Ripon Coll Cuddesdon 09. d 11 p 12. C Clapham Ch Ch and St Jo *S'wark* 11–15; P-in-c Hythe *Cant* 15–20. *Address temp unknown*

SWEENEY, Robert Maxwell. b 38. Ch Ch Ox BA 63 MA 66 Birm Univ MA 78. Cuddesdon Coll 63. d 65 p 66. C Prestbury *Glouc* 65–68; C Handsworth St Andr *Birm* 68–70; Asst Chapl Lancing Coll 70–73; V Wotton St Mary *Glouc* 74–79; V Ox St Thos w St Frideswide and Binsey 79–03; Chapl Magd Coll Ox 82–88; rtd 03. *22 Park House, 39 Park Place, Cheltenham GL50 2RF* T: (01242) 254028

SWEENEY, William David. b 89. St Jo Coll Nottm BA 13 LTh 14. d 14 p 15. C Ex St Thos and Em 14–17; C Plympton 17–18; TV 18–20; Chapl RN from 20. *Royal Naval Chaplaincy Service Headquarters, Tanner Building, HMS Excellent, Whale Island, Portsmouth PO2 8ER* T: 0300-157 7544 M: 07909-830621 E: fr.willsweeney@aol.co.uk

SWEERTS-VERMEULEN, Mrs Evelyn Harriet Elisabeth. b 75. Bris Univ BA 96 MA 98 PGCE 99. ERMC 16. d 19 p 20. NSM Luxembourg *Eur* from 19. *8 rue de Jardins, Hassel, 5762 Luxembourg* T: (00352) 2667 1135 E: evelyn.sweerts@outlook.com

SWEET, Reginald Charles. b 36. Open Univ BA 74. Ripon Hall Ox 61. d 62 p 63. C Styvechale *Cov* 62–65; Chapl RN 65–69 and 74–93; R Riddlesworth w Gasthorpe and Knettishall *Nor* 69–74; R Brettenham w Rushford 69–74; PtO 93–96; Chapl Miss to Seamen 96–99; rtd 99; Chapl St Cross Hosp 99–12; Master 12–20. *The Chaplain's Lodge, The Hospital of St Cross, St Cross Road, Winchester SO23 9SD* T: (01962) 853525 M: 07889-375085 E: master@hospitalofstcross.co.uk

SWEET, Stephen Paul. b 92. Southn Univ BA 14 Middx Univ BA 21. Oak Hill Th Coll 18. d 21. C Cornerstone Team *Leic* from 21. *270 Humberstone Lane, Leicester LE4 9JN* M: 07557-919392 E: stevesweet21@outlook.com

SWEET, Preb Vaughan Carroll. b 46. Aston Univ BSc 69 MSc 70. Linc Th Coll 89. d 91 p 92. C Uttoxeter w Bramshall *Lich* 91–95; P-in-c Hadley 95–98; V 98–07; P-in-c Wellington Ch Ch 03–07; V Hadley and Wellington Ch Ch 07–11; RD Telford 00–11; RD Telford Severn Gorge *Heref* 00–03; Preb Lich Cathl 05–11; rtd 12; PtO *Lich* 12–18; *St As* from 12. *64 Queens Park Flats, Queens Park Close, Mablethorpe LN12 2XA*

SWEETING, David Charles. b 67. Nottm Univ BSc 89. STETS 04. d 08 p 09. C Holbeach *Linc* 08–12; V Glen Gp from 12. *The Vicarage, 19 Spalding Road, Pinchbeck, Spalding PE11 3UD* T: (01775) 725698 M: 07973-841799 E: david@davidsweeting.orangehouse.co.uk

SWEETING, Paul Lee. b 68. Lanc Univ BSc 90 St Martin's Coll Lanc PGCE 92. Cranmer Hall Dur BA 99. d 99 p 00. C Blackb St Gabr 99–03; R Ch Ch Cathl and the Falkland Is

03–06; Chapl Sedbergh Sch from 06; Chapl RAuxAF from 15. *Greenrigg, Loftus Hill, Sedbergh LA10 5SQ* M: 07794-737886 E: sweeting.paul@googlemail.com

SWEETING, Miss Susan. b 57. Lindisfarne Coll of Th 17. **d** 21. C Sunderland St Mary and St Pet *Dur* from 21. *84 Stratford Avenue, Sunderland SR2 8RZ* M: 07539-917633 E: susansweeting3@gmail.com

SWEETMAN (née BURNIE), Ms Judith. b 57. Leic Univ BA 79. Westcott Ho Cam 05. **d** 07 **p** 08. C Coggeshall w Markshall *Chelmsf* 07–10; P-in-c Boxford, Edwardstone, Groton etc *St E* 10–18; rtd 18; PtO *Nor* 18–20; Hon C Reepham and Wensum Valley from 20. *15 The Dial, Reepham, Norwich NR10 4LX*

SWEETNAM, Joe. b 78. Trin Coll Bris 18. **d** 20 **p** 21. C Valley Park *Win* from 20. *45 Pantheon Road, Chandler's Ford, Eastleigh SO53 2PD* M: 07962-058221 E: joesweetnam@btinternet.com

SWENSSON, Sister Gerd Inger. b 51. Lon Univ MPhil 65 Uppsala Univ 70. **dss** 74 **d** 87. In Ch of Sweden 74–75; Notting Hill *Lon* 75–77; CSA from 75; Abbey Ho Malmesbury *Bris* 77–79; R Foundn of St Kath in Ratcliffe 79–81; Notting Hill All SS w St Columb *Lon* 81–84; Kensington St Mary Abbots w St Geo 85–89; C Bedford Park 91–95; Sweden from 95. *Christens Gård, Pl 8, St Slågarp, S-231 95 Trelleborg, Sweden* T/F: (0046) (40) 487059 M: 708-743994 E: tedeum@telia.com

SWIFT, Ainsley Laird. b 56. Liv Univ BEd 80. Ripon Coll Cuddesdon. **d** 94 **p** 95. C Prescot *Liv* 94–98; TV New Windsor *Ox* 98–01; P-in-c 01–15; TR 15–18; V Bray and Braywood from 18; AD Maidenhead and Windsor from 18. *The Vicarage, The Churchyard, Bray, Maidenhead SL6 2UB* T: (01628) 621527

✠**SWIFT, The Rt Revd Andrew Christopher.** b 68. Edin Univ BEng 90 Aber Univ MSc 97. Ripon Coll Cuddesdon BTh 05. **d** 07 **p** 08 **c** 18. C Glouc St Cath 07–10; P-in-c Dunoon *Arg* 10–16; R 16–18; P-in-c Rothesay 10–16; R 16–18; P-in-c Tighnabruaich 10–11; Dean Arg 12–18; Can Cumbrae 13–18; Can St Jo Cathl Oban 13–18; Bp Bre from 18. *Bishop's House, 5 Ballumbie View, Dundee DD4 0NQ* T: (01382) 800458 *or* 459569 E: rev.andrew@familyswift.org.uk *or* bishop@brechin.anglican.org

SWIFT, Andrew Christopher. b 87. K Coll Lon LLB 08. St Steph Ho Ox BTh 12. **d** 12 **p** 13. C Hendon St Mary and Ch Ch *Lon* 12–15; C Smallthorne *Lich* 15–19; P-in-c 19–20; P-in-c Burslem St Werburgh 19–20; TR N Potteries from 20. *The Vicarage, Ford Green Road, Smallthorne, Stoke-on-Trent ST6 1NX* T: (01782) 827889 M: 07792-809334 E: fr.andrew.c.swift@gmail.com

SWIFT, Christopher James. b 65. Hull Univ BA 86 Man Univ MA 95 Sheff Univ PhD 06. Westcott Ho Cam 89. **d** 91 **p** 92. C Longton *Blackb* 91–94; TV Chipping Barnet w Arkley *St Alb* 94–97; Chapl Wellhouse NHS Trust 97–98; Chapl Dewsbury Health Care NHS Trust 98–01; Hd Chapl Services Leeds Teaching Hosps NHS Trust 01–17; Dir Chapl and Spirituality Methodist Homes for the Aged from 17; PtO *Leeds* 17–20; *Sheff* 17–20; *York* from 20. *MHA, Epworth House, 3 Stuart Street, Derby DE1 2EQ* T: (01332) 221875 M: 07711-485773 E: chris.swift@mha.org.uk *or* chris.swift@cswift.net

SWIFT, Christopher John. b 54. Linc Coll Ox BA 76 MA Selw Coll Cam BA 80. Westcott Ho Cam 79. **d** 81 **p** 82. C Portsea N End St Mark *Portsm* 81–84; C Alverstoke 84–87; V Whitton SS Phil and Jas *Lon* 87–94; R Shepperton 94–08; R Shepperton and Littleton 08–20; AD Spelthorne 98–04; rtd 20. *Address temp unknown*

SWIFT, Ian John Edward. b 46. NTMTC 99. **d** 02 **p** 03. NSM Basildon St Martin *Chelmsf* 02–06; C Vange 06–11; Ind Chapl 06–11; Chapl Essex Police 06–11; P-in-c Crosscrake *Carl* 11–16; rtd 16; PtO *Carl* from 17. *4 Wilkinson View, Backbarrow, Ulverston LA12 8RE* M: 07725-037680 E: ijeswift@googlemail.com

SWIFT, Jessica Suzanne. b 75. Univ of New Brunswick BSc 99. Wycliffe Hall Ox 99. **d** 02 **p** 03. C Islington St Mary *Lon* 02–05; C Mildmay Grove St Jude and St Paul 05–09; C Barnsbury 09–19; Stepney Area from 14; AD Islington 17–19; V S Tottenham St Ann from 19; Dean of Women's Min Edmonton Area from 20. *St Ann's Vicarage, Quernmore Road, London N15 5QG* T: (020) 8211 8710 M: 07769-338624 E: swift_jessica@hotmail.com

SWIFT, Ms Pamela Joan. b 47. Liv Univ BSc 68. NEOC 85. **d** 88 **p** 94. Par Dn Bermondsey St Jas w Ch Ch *S'wark* 88–91; Par Dn Middleton St Cross *Ripon* 91–92; C Leeds All So and Dioc Stewardship Adv 92–95; TR Bramley 95–99; Miss Adv USPG Blackb, Bradf, Carl and Wakef 99–01; Hon C Kildwick *Bradf* 99–01; R Community P Glas St Matt 01–05; rtd 05; Hon C Lanercost, Walton, Gilsland and Nether Denton *Carl* 06–10; Chapl N Cumbria Acute Hosps NHS Trust 06–08; PtO *Newc* 11–14; Chapl Northumbria Healthcare NHS Foundn Trust 14–15; P-in-c Glazebury w Hollinfare *Liv* 15;

P-in-c New Galloway *Glas* from 19. *The Rectory, Kenbridge Road, New Galloway, Castle Douglas DG7 3RP* T: (01644) 420467 M: 07833-938843 E: pam.swift@live.co.uk

SWIFT, Sarah Jane. b 65. St Aid Coll Dur BSc 88 Nottm Univ MA 10. St Jo Coll Nottm 05. **d** 06 **p** 07. C Wealdstone H Trin *Lon* 06–10; Chapl Chr Healing Miss 10–19; V Harlow St Mary and St Hugh w St Jo the Bapt *Chelmsf* from 20. *The Vicarage, 5 Staffords, Harlow CM17 0JR* T: (01279) 450633 E: sarah@sarahswift.org.uk

SWIFT, Stanley. b 47. Open Univ BA 86 Kent Univ MA 95 ACIS 71. Linc Th Coll 71. **d** 74 **p** 75. C Heaton St Barn *Bradf* 74–77; C Bexhill St Pet *Chich* 77–81; R Crowland *Linc* 81–86; RD Elloe W 82–86; R Upminster *Chelmsf* 86–95; P-in-c N Ockendon 94–95; V Rush Green 95–02; V Gt Burstead 02–11; V Gt Burstead w Ramsden Crays 11–13; rtd 13; PtO *Chelmsf* from 14; *Lich* from 21. *7 Parrys Close, Bayston Hill, Shrewsbury SY3 0HP* T: (01743) 874567 E: stanswift@hotmail.com

SWINBANK, Jennifer. *See* WOOD, Anne Jennifer

SWINDELL, Anthony Charles. b 50. Selw Coll Cam BA 73 MA 77 Leeds Univ MPhil 77 PhD 07 Lambeth DD 12. Ripon Hall Ox 73. **d** 75 **p** 76. C Hessle *York* 75–78; P-in-c Litlington w W Dean *Chich* 78–80; Adult Educn Adv E Sussex 78–80; TV Heslington *York* 80–81; Chapl York Univ 80–81; R Harlaxton *Linc* 81–91; RD Grantham 85–90; C Jersey St Sav *Win* 91–15; PtO *Nor* 93–96; rtd 15. *Annakisha, 4 Troed y Garth, Y Fan, Llandiloes SY18 6NA* E: anthonyswindell@aol.co.uk

SWINDELL, Brian. b 35. St Jo Coll Nottm 86. **d** 88 **p** 89. C Wombwell *Sheff* 88–91; V Brinsworth w Catcliffe 91–93; TR Brinsworth w Catcliffe and Treeton 93–99; rtd 99; PtO *S'well* from 00. *36 Wasdale Close, West Bridgford, Nottingham NG2 6RG* T: 0115-914 1125

SWINDELL, Richard Carl. b 45. Open Univ BA 73 Leeds Univ MEd 86 Didsbury Coll Man CertEd 67. Qu Coll Birm 77 NOC 79. **d** 82 **p** 83. Hd Teacher Moorside Jun Sch 78–96; NSM Halifax St Aug *Wakef* 82–92; NSM Huddersfield H Trin 92–10; Family Life and Marriage Officer 96–00; PtO *Leeds* from 10. *13 Moor Hill Court, Laund Road, Salendine Nook, Huddersfield HD3 3GQ* T: (01484) 640473 M: 07946-761364 E: rswin25004@aol.com

SWINDELLS, Mrs Tracy Jane. b 67. Open Univ BA 01 Warwick Univ MA 09 Man Metrop Univ PGCE 03. LCTP 10. **d** 12 **p** 13. NSM Lostock Hall and Farington Moss *Blackb* 12–14; NSM Leyland St Jas 14–16; V Langho Billington from 16. *1 Higherfield, Langho, Blackburn BB6 8HQ* T: (01254) 247039 E: revtswindells@aol.com

SWINDLEHURST, Christine Frances. *See* SPURWAY, Christine Frances

SWINDON, Suffragan Bishop of. *See* RAYFIELD, The Rt Revd Lee Stephen

SWINERD, Emily Rose Mary. b 86. Ches Univ BTh 08. Trin Coll Bris 17. **d** 19 **p** 20. C Highworth w Sevenhampton and Inglesham etc *Bris* from 19. *14 Brookfield, Highworth, Swindon SN6 7HY* M: 07837-820747 E: emily.swinerd86@gmail.com

SWINHOE, John Robert. b 68. **d** 10 **p** 14. NSM Horton *Newc* 10–18; NSM Blyth St Mary 15–18; C Seaton Hirst from 18; Chapl Northd Fire and Rescue Service from 11. *St Andrew's Vicarage, Hawthorn Road, Ashington NE63 9AU* E: johnswinhoe19@gmail.com

SWINHOE, Terence Leslie. b 49. Man Univ BA 71 PGCE 72 Lon Univ BD 95. NOC. **d** 84 **p** 85. C Harborne St Pet *Birm* 84–87; V Warley *Wakef* 87–96; V Rastrick St Matt 96–06; P-in-c Greetland and W Vale 06–14; *Leeds* 14; rtd 14; PtO *Leeds* from 06. *6 Bent Lea, Huddersfield HD2 1QW* T: (01484) 429767 E: swinfam@aol.com

SWINNEY, Shawn Douglas. b 76. Oak Hills Chr Coll (USA) BA 01 Regent Coll Vancouver MA 04. Ox Min Course 07. **d** 09 **p** 10. C Gerrards Cross and Fulmer *Ox* 09–13; C Surbiton Hill Ch Ch *S'wark* 13–18; V Combe Down w Monkton Combe and S Stoke *B & W* from 18. *81 Church Road, Combe Down, Bath BA2 5JJ* M: 07508-078058 E: shawnswinney@hotmail.com

SWINTON, Garry Dunlop. b 59. SS Mark & Jo Univ Coll Plymouth BA 81 CertEd 82. Ripon Coll Cuddesdon 85. **d** 88 **p** 89. C Surbiton St Andr and St Mark *S'wark* 88–92; Succ S'wark Cathl 92–97; P-in-c Wandsworth St Faith 97–01; Chapl YMCA Wimbledon 97–01; Chapl Westmr City Sch 01–20; Chapl Greycoat Hosp Sch 01–18; PV Westmr Abbey from 06; PtO *Truro* from 17; *Lon* from 20. *4 Greenham Close, London SE1 7RP* M: 07961-422303 E: garry.swinton@gmail.com

SWINTON, Julie Debra. b 67. ERMC 18. **d** 21. C The Ch in the Woottons *Nor* from 21. *28 Persimmon, King's Lynn PE30 4SS* T: (01553) 772208 M: 07957-128263 E: juliedswinton@hotmail.co.uk

SWIRES-HENNESSY, Matthew. b 81. Lon Sch of Th BA 06. Wycliffe Hall Ox MTh 10. **d** 09 **p** 10. C Luton St Fran *St Alb* 09–12; C N Farnborough *Guildf* 12–17; C Farnborough St Pet

17–20; V Poynton *Ches* from 20. *The Vicarage, 41 London Road North, Poynton, Stockport SK12 1AF* M: 07803-928006 E: revd.msh@gmail.com

SWITHINBANK, Mrs Penelope Jane. b 53. St Andr Univ MTheol 74 Hughes Hall Cam PGCE 75. Ridley Hall Cam 00. **d** 02 **p** 03. Dir Connections Falls Ch Virginia USA 02–07; R Johns Island Ch of Our Sav 07–08; Chapl St Mellitus Coll *Lon* from 08; PtO *Bris* 13–18; *B & W* from 18. *Lanston House, 81 Fortescue Street, Norton St Philip, Bath BA2 7PE* M: 07870-497365 E: penelope@ministriesbydesign.org

SWITZERLAND, Archdeacon of. *See* KELHAM, Canon Adèle Mary

SWORD, Bernard James. b 46. **d** 04 **p** 05. NSM Millbrook *Ches* 04–07; P-in-c Bredbury St Barn 07–14; rtd 15; PtO *Ches* 16–18; C Sandbach Heath w Wheelock 18–19; V Sandbach Heath w Hassall Green from 19. *17 Woodlands Park, Wash Lane, Allostock, Knutsford WA16 9LG* T: (01565) 722168 M: 07866-446681 E: revdbsword@gmail.com

SWYER, David Martin. b 64. Univ of Wales (Abth) BA 87 PGCE 89. St Mich Coll Llan 89. **d** 91 **p** 92. C Killay *S & B* 91–93; C Newton St Pet 93–95; R Albourne w Sayers Common and Twineham *Chich* 95–13; Hon C Haywards Heath St Rich 16; Hon C Portslade St Nic and St Andr and Mile Oak 16–17; P-in-c from 17. *18 Amesbury Crescent, Hove BN3 5RD* T: (01273) 425695 E: davidswyer64@gmail.com

SWYER (née HARRIS), Canon Rebecca Jane. b 67. Univ of Wales (Lamp) BA 88 Univ of Wales (Cardiff) MPhil 93. St Mich Coll Llan 89. **d** 91. C Sketty *S & B* 91–95; PtO *Chich* 95–02; LtO from 02; Lect Th Chich Univ 97–09; Min Development Officer *Chich* from 09; Can and Preb Chich Cathl from 10; Dir Dept Apostolic Life from 15. *18 Amesbury Crescent, Hove BN3 5RD* T: (01273) 425695 E: rebecca.swyer@chichester.anglican.org

SYDNEY, Archbishop of. *See* DAVIES, Glenn Naunton

SYER, Mrs Angela. b 48. ARCM 69 Philippa Fawcett Coll CertEd 71. Qu Coll Birm. **d** 00 **p** 01. C Oakdale *Sarum* 00–04; P-in-c Coxley w Godney, Henton and Wookey *B & W* 04–13; rtd 13; PtO *Sarum* from 13. *The Old Inn, Stalbridge Weston, Sturminster Newton DT10 2LA* T: (01963) 362830 E: angelasyer@hotmail.com

SYKES, Alan Roy. b 53. Sheff Univ BA 75. Dioc OLM Tr Scheme 05. **d** 08 **p** 09. NSM Richmond St Mary w St Matthias and St Jo *S'wark* 08–18; PtO from 18. *251 King's Road, Kingston upon Thames KT2 5JH* T: (020) 8549 3887 E: alan.sykes@richmondteamministry.org

SYKES, Christine Virginia. b 55. **d** 07 **p** 08. NSM Castle Church *Lich* from 07. *18 Delamere Lane, Stafford ST17 9TL* T: (01785) 240529 E: curate@castlechurch.co.uk *or* chris@castlechurch.org.uk

SYKES, Mrs Clare Mary. b 61. Open Univ BA 10. WEMTC 93. **d** 96 **p** 97. C Tupsley w Hampton Bishop *Heref* 96–01; NSM Bromyard and Stanford Bishop, Stoke Lacy, Moreton Jeffries w Much Cowarne etc 01–08; NSM Bromyard and Stoke Lacy 09–12; RD Bromyard 05–12; R Osney *Ox* from 12. *Osney Rectory, 81 West Way, Oxford OX2 9JY* T: (01865) 242345 E: revclare@btinternet.com

SYKES, Cynthia Ann. b 41. **d** 05 **p** 06. OLM Em TM *Wakef* 05–14; Newsome and Armitage Bridge and S Crosland *Leeds* from 14. *The Old Dairy, Parkhead Farm, Birdsedge, Huddersfield HD8 8XW* T: (01484) 603894

SYKES, Mrs Emma Caroline Mary. b 75. Warwick Univ BA 96. St Jo Coll Nottm 06. **d** 08 **p** 09. C Birm St Martin w Bordesley St Andr 08–14; PtO 14–15; NSM Boldmere 15–20; Leadership Specialist CPAS 16–20; Asst Dioc Dir of Ords *Birm* 18–20; V Erdington St Barn from 20. *The Vicarage, Don Road, Erdington, Birmingham B24 9AX* M: 07859-066510 E: emmarsykes@hotmail.com

SYKES, Gerald Alfred. b 58. Univ of Wales (Abth) BSc 79 PhD 83 Univ of Wales (Cardiff) BD 98. St Mich Coll Llan 95. **d** 98 **p** 99. C Cardigan w Mwnt and Y Ferwig w Llangoedmor *St D* 98–01; P-in-c Brechfa w Abergorlech etc 01–08; P-in-c Alverthorpe *Wakef* 08–14; *Leeds* 14–17; P-in-c Westgate Common *Wakef* 08–14; *Leeds* 14–17; V Highgate *Birm* from 17; Chapl St Alb Academy from 17. *St Alban's Vicarage, 120 Stanhope Street, Birmingham B12 0XB* E: frgerrysykes@gmail.com

SYKES, Graham Timothy Gordon. b 59. ACIB 89. St Jo Coll Nottm BTh 92. **d** 92 **p** 93. C Kington w Huntington, Old Radnor, Kinnerton etc *Heref* 92–95; C Breinton 95–97; TV W Heref 97–98; Dioc Co-ord for Evang 95–01; V Bromyard 01–08; P-in-c Stanford Bishop, Stoke Lacy, Moreton Jeffries w Much Cowarne etc 01–08; V Bromyard and Stoke Lacy 09–12; Bp's Dom Chapl *Ox* 13–16; Chapl Sobell Ho Hospice from 17. *Sobell House, Churchill Hospital, Old Road, Oxford OX3 7LE* T: (01865) 225860 E: graham.sykes@ouh.nhs.uk

SYKES, Ian. b 44. Leic Univ DipEd. Ripon Coll Cuddesdon 84. **d** 85 **p** 86. In Bapt Min 64–84; C Headington *Ox* 85–88;

TV Bourne Valley *Sarum* 88–97; R Peter Tavy, Mary Tavy, Lydford and Brent Tor *Ex* 97–07; Hon C 07–10; PtO *Win* 11–17. *Pineview, Woodside Avenue, Granton-on-Spey PH26 3JR* T: (01479) 870394 E: iansforgery@btinternet.com

SYKES, James Clement. b 42. Keble Coll Ox BA 64 MA 71. Westcott Ho Cam 65. **d** 67 **p** 68. C Bishop's Stortford St Mich *St Alb* 67–71; Chapl St Jo Sch Leatherhead 71–73; Bermuda 74–79; V Northaw *St Alb* 79–87; Chapl St Marg Sch Bushey 87–98; R Guernsey St Sampson *Win* 99–07; rtd 07; PtO *Win* from 07. *Petit Robinet, Rue de Bouverie, Castel, Guernsey GY5 7UA* T: (01481) 256381 M: 07781-111459 E: jimandsue@cwgsy.net

SYKES, Miss Jean. b 45. Leeds Univ BA 66 Bris Univ CertEd 67. Ripon Coll Cuddesdon 86. **d** 88 **p** 94. C N Huddersfield *Wakef* 88–91; Team Dn 91–93; TV Kippax w Allerton Bywater *Ripon* 93–13; AD Whitkirk 05–09; rtd 13; PtO *Leeds* from 17. *21 Dearne Hall Road, Barugh Green, Barnsley S75 1LU* T: (01226) 388709

SYKES, Jeremy Gordon. b 63. Hull Univ BA 85. St Alb Minl Tr Scheme 92 Ripon Coll Cuddesdon 97. **d** 99 **p** 00. C Ipswich St Mary-le-Tower *St E* 99–02; P-in-c Briston w Burgh Parva and Melton Constable *Nor* 02–06; P-in-c Briston, Burgh Parva, Hindolveston etc 06–17; R 17–21; RD Holt 11–17 and 19–20; P-in-c Aylmerton, Runton, Beeston Regis and Gresham from 21. *The Rectory, Cromer Road, West Runton, Cromer NR27 9QT* T: (01263) 837761 E: jeremy.sykes@dioceseofnorwich.org

SYKES, Jeremy Jonathan Nicholas. b 61. Girton Coll Cam BA 83 MA 86. Wycliffe Hall Ox BA 88 MA 91. **d** 89 **p** 90. C Knowle *Birm* 89–92; Asst Chapl Oakham Sch 92–98; Chapl Giggleswick Sch 98–06; Hd Master Gt Walstead Sch 06–10; Chapl Hurstpierpoint Coll 10–20; V Hellingly and Upper Dicker *Chich* from 20. *The Vicarage, 14 Orchard Grange, Lower Dicker, Hailsham BN27 3PA* T: (01323) 441872 M: 07714-426286 E: revjeremysykes@icloud.com

SYKES, Canon John. b 39. Man Univ BA 62. Ripon Hall Ox 61. **d** 63 **p** 64. C Heywood St Luke *Man* 63–67; C Bolton H Trin 67–71; Chapl Bolton Colls of H&FE 67–71; R Reddish *Man* 71–78; V Saddleworth 78–87; TR Oldham 87–04; Hon Can Man Cathl 91–04; rtd 04; PtO *Man* from 04; Chapl to The Queen 95–09. *53 Ivy Green Drive, Springhead, Oldham OL4 4PR* T: 0161-678 6767 M: 07968-382075 E: sykesjohn76@gmail.com

SYKES, John Harold. b 50. Van Mildert Coll Dur BA 71 K Coll Lon BD 73 AKC 74 MTh 75 Linc Coll Ox MSc 89 ALAM 71 FRSA 92. S'wark Ord Course 75. **d** 09 **p** 09. NSM Ashburnham w Penhurst *Chich* from 09; PtO *Cant* from 19. *Woodlands, Dorothy Avenue, Cranbrook TN17 3AL* T: (01580) 712793

SYKES, Sandra. b 51. St Mellitus Coll 13. **d** 14 **p** 15. OLM Gt and Lt Leighs and Lt Waltham *Chelmsf* 14–17; NSM from 17; OLM Gt Waltham w Ford End 15–17; NSM from 17; OLM The Chignals w Mashbury 15–17; NSM from 17. *141 Main Road, Great Leighs, Chelmsford CM3 1NP* T: (01245) 362701 E: sandra.sykes59@btinternet.com

SYLVESTER, Jeremy Carl Edmund. b 56. Cape Town Univ BA 78 HDipEd 79. Coll of Resurr Mirfield 84. **d** 87 **p** 88. C St Cypr Cathl Kimberley S Africa 87–89; C Ganyesa 89–92; Chapl Informal Settlements Johannesburg 92–96; P-in-c Stoke Newington St Olave *Lon* 96–98; TV Plymouth Em, St Paul Efford and St Aug *Ex* 98–01; CMS 01–06; V Nether w Upper Poppleton *York* 06–20; TR Darlaston and Moxley *Lich* from 20. *The Rectory, Victoria Road, Wednesbury WS10 8AA* T: 0121-526 2240 E: jeremysylvester@btinternet.com *or* stlawdarlo@gmail.com

SYMCOX, Ms Caroline Jane. b 80. Keble Coll Ox BA 01 MSt 02 MLitt 10. Ripon Coll Cuddesdon 09. **d** 11 **p** 12. C Amersham *Ox* 11–14; TV S Cotswolds *Glouc* from 14. *The Vicarage, The Croft, Fairford GL7 4BB* T: (01285) 712467 M: 07811-212370 E: carolinesymcox@googlemail.com

SYMES-THOMPSON, Hugh Kynard. b 54. Peterho Cam BA 76 MA 81. Cranmer Hall Dur. **d** 79 **p** 80. C Summerfield *Birm* 79–82; C Harlow New Town w Lt Parndon *Chelmsf* 82–83; Australia 84–89; TV Dagenham *Chelmsf* 89–95; R Cranfield and Hulcote w Salford *St Alb* 95–19; Chapl Cranfield Univ 02–19; rtd 19; PtO *Truro* from 20. *23 Brewery Drive, St Austell PL25 4EH* T: (01726) 75062 E: revhugh.st@gmail.com

SYMINGTON, Patricia Ann. *See* TURNER, Patricia Ann

SYMMONS, Canon Roderic Paul. b 56. Chu Coll Cam BA 77 MA 81 Oak Hill Th Coll BA 83 Fuller Th Sem California DMin 90. **d** 83 **p** 84. C Ox St Aldate w St Matt 83–88; Lic to Offic LA USA 89–90; R Ardingly *Chich* 90–99; RD Cuckfield 95–99; P-in-c Redland *Bris* 99–14; V 14–18; PtO 18–20; Tutor Trin Coll Bris 99–10; AD City *Bris* 14–20; Adv for Min Development from 20; P-in-c Bradley Stoke from 20; Hon

Can Bris Cathl from 15. *18 Machin Road, Bristol BS10 7HQ* E: rod.symons@bristoldiocese.org

SYMON, Canon Roger Hugh Crispin. b 34. St Jo Coll Cam BA 59. Coll of Resurr Mirfield 59. **d** 61 **p** 62. C Westmr St Steph w St Jo *Lon* 61–66; P-in-c Hascombe *Guildf* 66–68; Chapl Surrey Univ 66–74; V Paddington Ch Ch *Lon* 74–78; V Paddington St Jas 78–79; USPG 80–87; Abp Cant's Acting Sec for Angl Communion Affairs 87–94; Can Res Cant Cathl 94–02; rtd 02; PtO *Glouc* 02–20. *5 Bath Parade, Cheltenham GL53 7HL* T: (01242) 700645 E: rogersymon@blueyonder.co.uk

SYMONDS, Alan Jeffrey. b 56. Ridley Hall Cam 93. **d** 95 **p** 96. C Bath St Luke *B & W* 95–99; R Abbas and Templecombe w Horsington 99–06; P-in-c Somerton w The Charltons and Kingsdon from 06. *Rosemount, Sutton Road, Somerton TA11 6QP* T: (01458) 272029 E: somerton.vicar@btinternet.com

SYMONDS, James Henry. b 31. Ripon Hall Ox 67. **d** 69 **p** 70. C Southampton (City Cen) *Win* 69–71; CF 71–78 and 79–90; P-in-c Arrington *Ely* 78–79; P-in-c Orwell 78–79; P-in-c Wimpole 78–79; P-in-c Croydon w Clopton 78–79; (R of O) 90–96; rtd 96; P-in-c Coughton, Spernall, Morton Bagot and Oldberrow *Cov* 99–02; PtO *Lich* 00–16; *Cov* 02–15; *Worc* from 13. *Thimble Cottage, Kings Coughton, Alcester B49 5QD* T: (01789) 764609 E: jim.marie@btinternet.com

SYMONS, Mrs Susannah Mary. b 59. LMH Ox BA 81 La Sainte Union Coll PGCE 94. STETS 02. **d** 05 **p** 06. C Nadder

Valley *Sarum* 05–09; TV Beaminster Area 09–11; R Bradeley, Church Eaton, Derrington and Haughton *Lich* 11–18; R Kingsley and Foxt-w-Whiston and Oakamoor etc from 18. *The Rectory, Holt Lane, Kingsley, Stoke-on-Trent ST10 2BA* E: sue.symons@btinternet.com

SYMS, Richard Arthur. b 43. Ch Coll Cam BA 66 MA 71. Wycliffe Hall Ox 66. **d** 68 **p** 69. C New Eltham All SS *S'wark* 68–72; Chapl to Arts and Recreation *Dur* 72–73; C Hitchin St Mary *St Alb* 73–76; TV Hitchin 77–78; PtO 78–97; P-in-c Datchworth 97–03; rtd 03; PtO *Lon* from 03; *St Alb* from 03. *8 Lytton Fields, Knebworth SG3 6AZ* T: (01438) 811933 M: 07900-241470 E: richard.syms@sky.com

SYNNOTT, Alan Patrick Sutherland. b 59. **d** 85 **p** 86. C Lisburn Ch Ch *Conn* 85–88; CF 88–95; I Galloon w Drummully *Clogh* 95–01; I Monkstown *Conn* 01–04; PtO 04–09; I Skreen w Kilmacshalgan and Dromard *T, K & A* 09–17; Adn Killala 10–17; Can Killala Cathl 10–17; Can Achonry Cathl 10–17; Dioc Dir of Ords 12–17; Can Tuam Cathl 13–17; I Camlough, Mullaglass and Ballymoyer *Arm* from 17. *The Rectory, 2 Maytown Road, Bessbrook, Newry BT35 7LY* T: (028) 3083 7448 M: (00353) 86-848 4924 E: alanpsynnott@gmail.com

SZEJNMANN, Claus-Christian Werner (Chris). b 65. R Holloway Coll Lon BA 90 K Coll Lon PhD 94 SFHEA 14. St Mellitus Coll 17. **d** 19 **p** 20. C Leic H Trin w St Jo from 19. *Holy Trinity Church, 2 Upper King Street, Leicester LE1 6XE* T: 0116-254 8981 E: cszejnmann@htl.church

T

TABER-HAMILTON, Nigel John. b 53. Univ of Wales (Ban) BA 75. Qu Coll Birm Ch Div Sch of Pacific 77. **d** 78 **p** 81. C W Wimbledon Ch Ch *S'wark* 78–79; C Berkeley St Mark USA 79–81; C Bloomington H Trin 81–90; and 92–94; Interim R Crawfordsville St Jo 90–91; Interim R New Harmony St Steph 91–92; V Seymour All SS 94–00; R St Aug in-the-Woods from 00. *PO Box 11, Freeland WA 98249, USA* T: (001) (360) 331 4887 F: 331 4822 E: rector@whidbey.com

TABOR, John Tranham. b 30. Ball Coll Ox BA 56 MA 58. Ridley Hall Cam 55. **d** 58 **p** 59. C Lindfield *Chich* 58–62; Tutor Ridley Hall Cam 62–63; Chapl 63–68; Warden Scargill Ho 68–75; R Berkhamsted St Mary *St Alb* 75–96; rtd 96; PtO *St Alb* 96–16; *Ox* 99–00. *1 The Downs, Aldbourne, Marlborough SN8 2RZ* T: (01672) 540640 E: johnttabor@yahoo.co.uk

TAFESSE, Bogale Tiruneh. b 68. **d** 84 **p** 85. PtO *Birm* from 17. *137 Rodney Close, Birmingham B16 8DJ* M: 07534-220148 E: bogye2003@yahoo.com

TAFFINDER, Dawn Anne. b 66. WEMTC 13. **d** 16 **p** 17. NSM Madeley *Heref* 16–20; V Sutton Hill and Woodside from 21. *5 Reynards Meadow, Sutton Hill, Telford TF4 4NQ* M: 07393-295727 E: dawn.taffinder@gmail.com

TAFT, Mrs Janet Anne. b 59. Sheff Univ BA 80 Wolv Univ PGCE 82. Wycliffe Hall Ox 06. **d** 08 **p** 09. NSM Abingdon *Ox* 08–12; Chapl SS Helen and Kath Sch Abingdon 10–13; C Warfield *Ox* 13–16; PtO from 16. *9 The Chestnuts, Abingdon OX14 3YN* T: (01344) 566390 M: 07929-543626

TAGGART, Terence. b 57. Linc Univ BA 13. Linc Sch of Th and Min 09. **d** 13 **p** 14. NSM Fen and Hill Gp *Linc* 13–15; P-in-c Stornoway *Arg* 15–18; P-in-c Eoropaidh 15–18; R Aberdeen St Mary *Ab* from 18. *The Rectory, 28 Stanley Street, Aberdeen AB10 6UR* M: 07768-219984 E: terry_t_2000_uk@yahoo.co.uk

TAGGART, Canon William Joseph. b 54. **d** 85 **p** 86. C Belfast St Mich *Conn* 85–90; I Belfast St Kath from 90; Dioc Registrar from 06; Can Conn Cathl from 12. *St Katharine's Parish Office, 2-4 Dunlambert Park, Belfast BT15 3NJ* M: 07933-588355 E: st.katharine@btinternet.com

TAGUE, Russell. b 59. Aston Tr Scheme 90 Linc Th Coll 92. **d** 94 **p** 95. C Astley Man 94–97; Chapl HM YOI Swinfen Hall 97–00; Chapl HM Pris Risley 00–05; TV Kirkby *Liv* 05–08; R Arthuret w Kirkandrews-on-Esk and Nicholforest *Carl* 08–17; rtd 17. *159 Hillock Lane, Woolston, Warrington WA1 4PJ* E: taguejosh@yahoo.co.uk

TAILBY, Ms Jane Dorothy. b 56. Culham Coll of Educn BEd 79. WEMTC 01. **d** 04 **p** 05. NSM Frampton Cotterell and Iron Acton *Bris* 04–09; NSM Winterbourne and Frenchay and Winterbourne Down 08–09; TV Nadder Valley *Sarum* 09–16; V Nassington, Apethorpe, Thornhaugh etc *Pet* from 16. *The*

Vicarage, 34 Station Road, Nassington, Peterborough PE8 6QB E: jdtailby@aol.com

TAILBY, Peter Alan. b 49. Chich Th Coll 83. **d** 85 **p** 86. C Stocking Farm *Leic* 85–88; C Knighton St Mary Magd 88–90; P-in-c Thurnby Lodge 90–98; P-in-c W Molesey *Guildf* 98–05; V 05–16; rtd 16. *6 Parkside Close, Leicester LE4 1EP* E: ptailby@virginmedia.com

TAIT, Philip Leslie. b 52. Ex Univ BA 73 Hull Univ PGCE 74. NEOC 87. **d** 90 **p** 91. NSM Osbaldwick w Murton *York* 90–92; Chapl and Hd RS Berkhamsted Sch Herts 93–97; P-in-c Woodhorn w Newbiggin *Newc* 98; Chapl HM Pris Wolds 98–00; Chapl R Russell Sch Croydon 00–05; Chapl Hurstpierpoint Coll 05–07; TV Upper Skerne *Dur* 07–13; P-in-c Ashley w Silverley *Ely* 13–18; P-in-c Cheveley 13–18; P-in-c Kirtling 13–18; P-in-c Wood Ditton w Saxon Street 13–18; rtd 19. *51 Farro Drive, York YO30 6QQ* M: 07852-943244 E: philiptait548@btinternet.com

TAIT (née DAVIS), Canon Ruth Elizabeth. b 39. St Andr Univ MA 62 Moray Ho Coll of Educn DipEd 63. Moray Ord Course 89. **dss** 90 **d** 94 **p** 95. Elgin w Lossiemouth *Mor* 90–96; C 94–96; NSM Dufftown *Ab* 96–03; C Forres *Mor* 96–98; NSM Aberlour 98–03; Dioc Dir of Ords 02–08; NSM Elgin w Lossiemouth 04–08; rtd 08; LtO *Mor* from 10; Hon Can St Andr Cathl Inverness from 03. *Benmore, Burnbank, Birnie, Elgin IV30 8RW* T: (01343) 862808 E: ruth.e.tait@btinternet.com

TAIT, Ms Valerie Joan. b 60. Open Univ BA 96 SRN 82 RSCN 83. Trin Coll Bris 99. **d** 01 **p** 02. C W Heref 01–06; P-in-c Ford 06–13; P-in-c Gt Wollaston 08–13; P-in-c Alberbury w Cardeston 06–13; R Ford, Gt Wollaston and Alberbury w Cardeston 13–19; V Cider Churches from 19. *27 Hazle Close, Ledbury HR8 2XX*

TAJIMA, Ms Serena. b 82. K Alfred's Coll Win BA 03 Bournemouth Univ MSc 11. Westcott Ho Cam 15. **d** 17 **p** 18. C Reading St Luke w St Bart *Ox* 17–20; R Banbury from 20. *The Vicarage, 3 Edgcote Way, Banbury OX16 2DT* M: 07307-896501 E: rev.serenatajima@gmail.com

TALBOT, Derek Michael. b 55. St Jo Coll Dur BSc 77. St Jo Coll Nottm 84. **d** 87 **p** 88. C Rushden w Newton Bromswold *Pet* 87–90; C Barton Seagrave w Warkton 90–95; V Kettering Ch the King 95–02; V Northwood Em *Lon* 02–16; P-in-c Northolt St Jos 13–14; AD Harrow 02–07; Dir of Ords Willesden Area 10–16; Evang Enabler *Carl* 16–19; Dir Miss Community Development 19–21; P-in-c Harlington *Lon* from 21; P-in-c Harmondsworth from 21. *St Mary's Vicarage, High Street, Harmondsworth, West Drayton UB7 0AQ* M: 07767-763715 E: vicarmike@btinternet.com

TALBOT (née THOMSON), Mrs Elizabeth Lucy. b 74. Lanc Univ BA 96 Bris Univ BA 00 MA 01. Trin Coll Bris 98. d 01 p 02. C Bitterne *Win* 01–05; Chapl Dean Close Sch 05–15; C Edin St Paul and St Geo from 16. *St Paul's and St George's Church, 10 Broughton Street, Edinburgh EH1 3RH* T: 0131-556 1335 M: 07977-115923

TALBOT, George Brian. b 37. Qu Coll Birm 78. d 80 p 81. C Heref St Martin 80–83; R Bishop's Frome w Castle Frome and Fromes Hill 83–90; P-in-c Acton Beauchamp and Evesbatch w Stanford Bishop 83–90; R Burstow *S'wark* 90–02; rtd 02; PtO *Chich* from 16. *14 Locksash Close, West Wittering, Chichester PO20 8QP* T: (01243) 512454

TALBOT, James Edward. b 85. St Cuth Soc Dur BA 07. Trin Coll Bris 11. d 14 p 15. C Woodford Wells *Chelmsf* 14–17; C Broughton *Ox* from 17. *11 Turney Street, Aylesbury HP20 1AR* M: 07746-133438 E: james@broughtonchurch.org

TALBOT, John Herbert Boyle. b 30. TCD BA 51 MA 57. CITC 52. d 53 p 54. C Dublin St Pet *D & G* 53–57; Chan Vicar St Patrick's Cathl Dub 56–61; C Dublin Zion Ch *D & G* 57–61; Chapl Asst St Thos Hosp Lon 61–64; Min Can and Sacr Cant Cathl 64–67; R Brasted *Roch* 67–84; R Ightham 84–95; P-in-c Shipbourne 87–91; RD Shoreham 89–95; rtd 95; PtO *Roch* from 01. *12 Waterlakes, Edenbridge TN8 5BX* T: (01732) 865729 E: jbtalbot@waitrose.com

TALBOT, Mrs June Phyllis. b 46. Ripon Coll of Educn CertEd 67. NEOC 88. d 91 p 94. NSM Cleadon *Dur* 91–97; Dioc Voc Adv 94–16; NSM Bishopwearmouth St Gabr 97–16; PtO from 16. *66 Wheatall Drive, Whitburn, Sunderland SR6 7HQ* T: 0191-529 2265 E: talbot886@btinternet.com

TALBOT, Mair Josephine. See McFADYEN, Mair Josephine

TALBOT, Michael. See TALBOT, Derek Michael

TALBOT, Simon George Guy. b 79. Reading Univ BSc 01. Oak Hill Th Coll BA 07. d 07 p 08. C Ipswich St Marg *St E* 07–10; C Plymouth Em, St Paul Efford and St Aug *Ex* 10–11; TV 11–15; P-in-c Willand, Uffculme, Kentisbeare etc from 15; RD Tiverton and Cullompton from 17. *The Rectory, Old Village, Willand, Cullompton EX15 2RH* T: (01884) 562570 E: simon@thetalbots.org.uk

TALBOT, Susan Gabriel. b 46. Leeds Univ BA 69 Man Poly CertEd 70 Man Univ PhD 00. NOC 91. d 94 p 95. C Wythenshawe St Martin *Man* 94–98; P-in-c Cheetham St Jo 98–02; LtO 02–04; C Wilmslow *Ches* 04–05; Dioc Healing Adv 06–08; NSM Bowdon 06–11; PtO from 11. *34 Eaton Road, Bowdon, Altrincham WA14 3EH* T: 0161-233 0630 E: susangabriel@btinternet.com

TALBOT-PONSONBY, Preb Andrew. b 44. Coll of Resurr Mirfield 66. d 68 p 70. C Radlett *St Alb* 68–70; C Salisbury St Martin *Sarum* 70–73; P-in-c Acton Burnell w Pitchford *Heref* 73–80; P-in-c Frodesley 73–80; P-in-c Cound 73–80; Asst Dioc Youth Officer 73–80; P-in-c Bockleton w Leysters 80–81; V 81–92; P-in-c Kimbolton w Middleton-on-the-Hill 80–81; V Kimbolton w Hamnish and Middleton-on-the-Hill 81–92; P-in-c Wigmore Abbey 92–96; R 97–98; RD Leominster 97–98; Public Preacher 98–14; Warden of Readers 02–12; Preb Heref Cathl from 87; rtd 09; Rtd Clergy Officer *Heref* from 13; PtO from 14. *Well Cottage, 5 Quay Street, Hereford HR1 2NH* T: (01432) 264725 E: andrew@talbot-ponsonby.org

TALBOT-PONSONBY, Preb Gillian. b 50. Sarum & Wells Th Coll 89. d 91 p 94. C Leominster *Heref* 91–92; NSM Wigmore Abbey 92–98; Public Preacher 98–20; Asst Dioc Adv on Women in Min 99–03; Dioc Adv 03–15; Dioc Chapl MU 13–18; PtO *Heref* from 20; Preb Heref Cathl from 14. *Well Cottage, 5 Quay Street, Hereford HR1 2NH* T: (01432) 264725 E: jill@talbot-ponsonby.org

TALBOTT, Scott Malcolm. b 55. SAOMC 00. d 03 p 04. NSM Watford St Andr *St Alb* 03–10; PtO 10–15; NSM Rickmansworth from 15. *Elmhurst, 40 Berks Hill, Chorleywood, Rickmansworth WD3 5AH* T: (01923) 282370 M: 07802-244877 E: scott.talbott@talk21.com

TALBOTT, Canon Simon John. b 57. Pontifical Univ Maynooth BD 81. d 81 p 82. In RC Ch 81–87; C Headingley *Ripon* 88–91; V Gt and Lt Ouseburn w Marton cum Grafton 91–97; Chapl Qu Ethelburga's Coll York 91–97; P-in-c Markington w S Stainley and Bishop Thornton *Ripon* 97–01; AD Ripon 97–01; P-in-c Epsom St Martin *Guildf* 01–02; V 02–13; Chapl Univ for the Creative Arts 06–13; P-in-c Gt Shelford *Ely* 13–19; V from 19; P-in-c Stapleford 16–19; V from 19; P-in-c Harston w Hauxton and Newton 18–19; V from 19; RD Granta from 16; Hon Can Ely Cathl from 20. *The Vicarage, 12 Church Street, Great Shelford, Cambridge CB22 5EL* T: (01223) 847068 M: 07740-665210 E: simon@thetalbotts.co.uk

TALKS, David. b 57. Trin Hall Cam BA 78 MA 81. Trin Coll Bris BA 06. d 06 p 07. C Colchester St Jo *Chelmsf*

06–11; P-in-c Lynchmere and Camelsdale *Chich* 11–15; C 15–16; NSM Newton Longville, Mursley, Swanbourne etc *Ox* from 16. *The Rectory, Drayton Road, Newton Longville, Milton Keynes MK17 0BH* T: (01908) 366330 E: david.5parishes@btinternet.com

TALLANT, John. b 45. Edin Th Coll 86. d 88 p 89. C Cayton w Eastfield *York* 88–90; C N Hull St Mich 90–91; V Scarborough St Sav w All SS 91–93; V Fleetwood St Nic *Blackb* 93–99; P-in-c Sculcoates St Paul w Ch Ch and St Silas *York* 99–03; P-in-c Hull St Mary Sculcoates 99–03; P-in-c Hull St Steph Sculcoates 99–03; R Woldsburn 03–11; P-in-c Dunscroft St Edwin *Sheff* 11–15; rtd 15; PtO *York* 15–18 and from 19; P-in-c Kingston upon Hull St Mary 18–19. *36 Taylors Field, Kings Mill Road, Driffield YO25 6FQ* E: john.tallant@talktalk.net

TALLINN, Dean of. See PIIR, Gustav Peeter

TALLON, Jonathan Robert Roe. b 66. Rob Coll Cam BA 88 MA 92 Nottm Univ MPhil 07. St Jo Coll Nottm BTh 94. d 97 p 98. C Bury St Jo w St Mark *Man* 97–01; P-in-c Cadishead 01–08; V 08–09; Tutor N Bapt Learning Community from 09. *Luther King House, Brighton Grove, Manchester M14 5JP* T: 0161-249 2546 E: jonathan.tallon@northern.org.uk

TALLOWIN (née BOUDIER), Mrs Rosemary. b 57. St Mellitus Coll BA 11. d 11 p 12. C Colchester St Mich Myland *Chelmsf* 11–14; TV Harwich Peninsula 14–19; P-in-c Fen Drayton w Fenstanton *Ely* 19–20; R from 20. *The Vicarage, 16 Church Street, Fenstanton, Huntingdon PE28 9JL* E: rosie.tallowin@btinternet.com

TAMPLIN, Peter Harry. b 44. Sarum & Wells Th Coll 71. d 73 p 74. C Digswell *St Alb* 73–76; C Chesterton St Luke *Ely* 76–82; V Chesterton St Geo 82–95; R Durrington *Sarum* 95–07; rtd 07. *1 Gathorne Road, Bristol BS3 1LR* T: 0117-963 9628 E: phtamplin@yahoo.co.uk

TAMS, Adam Michael. b 85. Trin Coll Bris BA 17. d 17 p 18. C Leamington Priors St Paul *Cov* 17–20; V Southsea St Jude *Portsm* from 20. *7 Hereford Road, Southsea PO5 2DH* M: 07498-210355 E: vicar@sjs.church

TAMS, Paul William. b 56. Huddersfield Poly CertEd 77. EAMTC 87. d 90 p 91. NSM Mildenhall *St E* 90–93; NSM Brandon and Santon Downham w Elveden etc 93–17; V Lakenheath, Santon Downham and Elveden from 17. *2 Kitchener Close, Lakenheath, Brandon IP27 9FT* T: (01842) 861819 M: 07503-211323 E: paultams@sky.com

TAN (née MITCHELL), Mrs Sarah Rachel. b 79. Birm Univ BA 00 Fitzw Coll Cam BA 04. Westcott Ho Cam 02. d 05 p 06. C Reddal Hill St Luke *Worc* 05–08; Chapl HM Pris Wayland 08–13; PtO *Ely* from 08. *Address withheld by request* E: icklesaraht@gmail.com

TANCOCK, Steven John. b 73. Westmr Coll Ox BTh 01. St Steph Ho Ox 02. d 04 p 05. C Wincanton and Pen Selwood *B & W* 04–09; C Warren Park and Leigh Park *Portsm* 09–14; PtO *B & W* 14–17; C Alfred Jewel from 17. *3 St Mary's Crescent, North Petherton, Bridgwater TA6 6RA* E: stevethevic@gmail.com

TANNER, Benjamin Michael. b 84. Loughb Univ BEng 06. Oak Hill Th Coll BA 19. d 19 p 20. C Endcliffe *Sheff* from 19. *48 Renshaw Road, Sheffield S11 7PD* M: 07912-890512 E: b.m.tanner@me.com

TANNER, Canon Frank Hubert. b 38. St Aid Birkenhead 63. d 66 p 67. C Ipswich St Marg *St E* 66–69; C Mansfield SS Pet and Paul *S'well* 69–72; V Huthwaite 72–79; Chapl to the Deaf 79–92; Hon Can S'well Minster 90–92; Chapl Northn and Rutland Miss to the Deaf 92–01; rtd 01; PtO *Truro* 03–15. *Caldecote, 1A Garrick Road, Northampton NN1 5ND* T: (01604) 631709 E: franktanner@blue-earth.co.uk

TANNER, Leonard John. d 03 p 04. C Taney *D & G* 03–07; I Tullow from 07; Dioc Dir Lay Min from 09; Chan V St Patr Cathl Dublin 07–11. *Tullow Rectory, Brighton Road, Carrickmines, Dublin 18, Republic of Ireland* T: (00353) (1) 289 3144 M: 86-302 1376 E: tanner1@eircom.net

✠**TANNER, The Rt Revd Mark Simon Austin.** b 70. Ch Ch Ox BA 92 MA 96 St Jo Coll Dur BA 98 Liv Univ MTh 05. Cranmer Hall Dur 95. d 98 p 99 c 16. C Upton (Overchurch) *Ches* 98–01; V Doncaster St Mary *Sheff* 01–07; V Ripon H Trin 07–11; AD Ripon 09–11; Warden Cranmer Hall Dur 11–16; Vice-Prin St Jo Coll Dur 11–16; Hon Can Dur Cathl 15–16; Suff Bp Berwick *Newc* 16–20; Bp Ches from 20. *Bishop's House, 1 Abbey Street, Chester CH1 2JD* T: (01244) 350864 E: bpchester@chester.anglican.org

TANNER, Canon Mark Stuart. b 59. Nottm Univ BA 81. Sarum & Wells Th Coll. d 85 p 86. C Radcliffe-on-Trent *S'well* 85; C Radcliffe-on-Trent and Shelford etc 85–88; C Bestwood 88–89; TV 89–93; Bp's Research Officer 93–97; P-in-c S'well H Trin 93–98; V 98–13; AD S'well 01–06; Hon Can S'well Minster 07–13; V Hartley Wintney, Elvetham, Winchfield etc *Win* 13–17; RD Odiham 16–17; V Radcliffe-on-Trent and Shelford *S'well* from 17. *The Vicarage, 2 Vicarage Lane, Radcliffe-on-Trent, Nottingham NG12 2FB*

TANNER, Martin Philip. b 54. Univ Coll Lon BSc(Econ) 75. Ridley Hall Cam 79. **d** 82 **p** 83. C Bitterne *Win* 82–85; C Weeke 85–88; V Long Buckby w Watford *Pet* 88–96; P-in-c Desborough 96–97; R Desborough, Brampton Ash, Dingley and Braybrooke 97–08; P-in-c Drayton in Hales *Lich* 08–17; RD Hodnet 14–17; OCM 09–17; rtd 17; PtO *Pet* from 18. *16 Feast Field Close, Wollaston, Wellingborough NN29 7QG* T: (01933) 664246 E: mp.tanner@btinternet.com

TANSEY, Daniel Matthew Robert. b 74. Leeds Metrop Univ BA 97 Cam Univ BTh 17. Ridley Hall Cam 15. **d** 17 **p** 18. C The Ch in the Woottons *Nor* from 17. *34 Castle Rising Road, South Wootton, King's Lynn PE30 3JB* M: (07928-825060 *or* 07866-368272 E: dan@churchinthewoottons.net

TANSILL, Canon Derek Ernest Edward. b 36. Univ of Wales (Lamp) BA 61. Ripon Hall Ox 61. **d** 63 **p** 64. C Chelsea St Luke *Lon* 63–67; C-in-c Saltdean CD *Chich* 67–69; V Saltdean 69–73; V Billingshurst 73–82; R Bexhill St Pet 82–85; RD Battle and Bexhill 84–86; V Horsham 85–86; TR 86–06; RD 77–82 and 85–93; Can and Preb Chich Cathl 81–06; Chapl Chich Cathl from 06. *5 The Chantry, Canon Lane, Chichester PO19 1PZ* T: (01243) 775596 E: derektansill@gmail.com

TANSLEY, Romney. b 41. K Coll Lon BD 64. **d** 65 **p** 66. C Royton St Anne *Man* 65–68; Chapl St Hilda's Coll Br Honduras 68–70; R Stann Creek & Chapl Stann Creek High Sch 70–71; V Westleigh St Pet *Man* 72–77; rtd 06. *Apartment 301, 18 Leftbank, Manchester M3 3AJ* E: romney@tansley.co.uk

TANSWELL, Stuart Keith. b 79. Reading Univ BSc 01. Ripon Coll Cuddesdon BTh 08. **d** 08 **p** 09. C St Blazey *Truro* 08–11; C Luxulyan 08–11; C Tywardreath w Tregaminion 08–11; V N Holmwood *Guildf* 11–18; R Guernsey St Michel du Valle *Win* from 18. *Vale Church Rectory, L'Abbaye, Vale, Guernsey GY3 5SF* T: (01481) 244088 E: stuart@tanswell.net *or* rector@valechurch.org.uk

TAPLIN, Kim. b 58. Lon Bible Coll BA 79 Homerton Coll Cam PGCE 84 Regent's Park Coll Ox MTh 03. S Dios Minl Tr Scheme 94. **d** 94 **p** 95. C Sholing *Win* 94–97; P-in-c Rendcomb *Glouc* 97–00; Chapl Rendcomb Coll Cirencester 97–00; Chapl Clifton Coll Bris 01–13; V Clifton All SS w St Jo *Bris* 14–15; Chapl Malvern St Jas Girls' Sch from 15. *20 Manby Road, Malvern WR14 3BB* E: kimtaplin1@gmail.com

TAPP, Mrs Sarah Alison. b 73. St Mellitus Coll 16. **d** 19 **p** 20. C Woking St Mary *Guildf* from 19. *6 Rapley Lane, Knaphill, Woking GU21 2SN* M: 07889-049019 E: sarah@sarahtapp.co.uk

TAPPER, Canon John A'Court. b 42. FCA 64. Sarum & Wells Th Coll 89. **d** 91 **p** 92. C Ashford *Cant* 91–94; P-in-c Folkestone H Trin w Ch Ch 94–96; V 96–06; P-in-c Sandgate St Paul w Folkestone St Geo 01–06; V Folkestone Trin 06–07; AD Elham 00–05; Hon Can Cant Cathl 06–07; rtd 07; PtO *Cant* 07–08 and from 12; Retirement Officer (Maidstone Adnry) 07–08; Hon C Cranbrook 08–12. *Mill Cottage, Mill Lane, Sissinghurst, Cranbrook TN17 2HX* T: (01580) 713836 E: john.tapper@btinternet.com

TARGETT, Kenneth. b 28. Qu Coll Birm 54. **d** 57 **p** 58. C Mansfield Woodhouse *S'well* 57–59; C Skipton Ch Ch *Bradf* 59–62; V Bradf St Jo 62–65; PtO 65–82; Australia 82–87; V Old Leake w Wrangle *Linc* 87–94; rtd 94; PtO *Linc* from 00. *The Sloop, Sea Lane, Old Leake, Boston PE22 9JA* T: (01205) 871991

TARLETON, Canon Peter. b 46. TCD BA 72 MA 80 HDipEd 77. TCD Div Sch Div Test 73. **d** 73 **p** 74. C Cork St Luke w St Ann *C, C & R* 73–75; C Dublin Drumcondra *D & G* 75–77; I Limerick City *L & K* 77–82; I Drumgoon w Dernakesh, Ashfield etc *K, E & A* 82–85; Chapl HM YOI Hindley 85–89; Chapl HM Pris Lindholme 89–99; Hon Can Sheff Cathl 98–99; Chapl HM Pris Leeds 99–06; Chapl Lancs Teaching Hosps NHS Trust 08–11; Co-ord Chapl Southport and Ormskirk Hosp NHS Trust 11; I Killeshin w Cloydagh and Killabban *C, F & O* 11–18; Can Ossory Cathl 15–18; P-in-c Maryborough w Dysart Enos and Ballyfin from 18; Can Kilkenny Cathl from 18. *The Rectory, Coote Street, Portlaoise, Co Laois, Republic of Ireland* T: (00353) (57) 862 1154 M: 87-769 0050 E: peter.tarleton@hotmail.co.uk

TARLING, Matthew Paul. b 79. Nottm Univ MEng 03. Oak Hill Th Coll BA 09. **d** 09 **p** 10. C Blaydon and Swalwell *Dur* 09–13; V Spennymoor and Whitworth from 13; AD Auckland from 18. *30 Jubilee Close, Spennymoor DL16 6GA* T: (01388) 327603 M: 07714-212374 E: revmatttarling@gmail.com

TARLING, Preb Paul. b 53. Oak Hill Th Coll BA. **d** 85 **p** 86. C Old Hill H Trin *Worc* 85–89; V Walford w Bishopswood *Heref* 89–90; P-in-c Goodrich w Welsh Bicknell and Marstow

89–90; R Walford and St John w Bishopswood, Goodrich etc 90–96; RD Ross and Archenfield 95–96; P-in-c Kington w Huntington, Old Radnor, Kinnerton etc 96–00; R 00–08; RD Kington and Weobley 02–07; Preb Heref Cathl 07–08; rtd 08; PtO *S & B* from 11. *1 Alexandra Road, Llandrindod Wells LD1 5LT* T: (01597) 822615 E: revpt@yahoo.com

TARLTON, Simon John Deverill. b 63. WEMTC 14. **d** 16 **p** 17. NSM Ross w Walford and Brampton Abbotts *Heref* 16–17; C 17–19; R Bartestree Cross from 19. *The Vicarage, Lugwardine, Hereford HR1 4AE* M: 07462-893457 E: simon.tarlton@gmail.com

TÄRNEBERG, Helene. *See* STEED, Helene

TARPER, Miss Ann Jennifer. b 47. SRN 71 Nottm Univ BCombStuds 82. Linc Th Coll 79. **dss** 83 **d** 87 **p** 96. Stamford All SS w St Jo *Linc* 82–85; Witham *Chelmsf* 85–90; Par Dn 87–90; Min and Educn Adv to Newmarch Gp Min *Heref* 90–93; PtO 93–95; Chapl HM Pris Dur 95–97; PtO *Dur* 95–97; Chapl HM Pris Foston Hall 97–00; PtO *Lich* 97–02; C W End *Win* 02–05; V Slade Green *Roch* 05–16; rtd 16; PtO *Lich* 17–21. *5 Ivinson Way, Bramshall, Uttoxeter ST14 5BF* T: (01889) 592728 E: ajtarper@gmail.com

TARRAN, Mrs Susan Ann. b 63. CPFA 92. ERMC 08. **d** 11 **p** 12. NSM Bishop's Stortford *St Alb* 11–12; NSM Hockerill 12–21; NSM High Wych and Gilston w Eastwick from 21. *47 Church Manor, Bishop's Stortford CM23 5AF* M: 07970-952228 E: su.tarran@ntlworld.com

TARRANT, The Very Revd Ian Denis. b 57. G&C Coll Cam BA MA. St Jo Coll Nottm 81. **d** 84 **p** 85. C Ealing St Mary *Lon* 84–87; CMS Congo 88–98; Can Boga from 97; Sen Angl Chapl Nottm Univ *S'well* 98–09; R Woodford St Mary w St Phil and St Jas *Chelmsf* 09–20; Dean Gib *Eur* from 20. *The Cathedral Church of the Holy Trinity, Cathedral Square, Main Street, Gibraltar GX11 1AA* T: (00350) 200 75745 *or* 200 78377 E: dean.gib@europe.anglican.org

TARRANT, John Michael. b 38. St Jo Coll Cam BA 59 MA 63 Ball Coll Ox BA 62 MA 76. Ripon Hall Ox 60. **d** 62 **p** 63. C Chelsea All SS *Lon* 62–65; Chapl and Lect St Pet Coll Saltley 66–70; Belize 70–74; V Forest Row *Chich* 75–87; PtO *Heref* 93–99; NSM Ross 99–00; P-in-c Guilsborough w Hollowell and Cold Ashby *Pet* 00–08; Jt P-in-c Cottesbrooke w Gt Creaton and Thornby 00–08; P-in-c W Haddon w Winwick and Ravensthorpe 03–08; P-in-c Spratton 07–08; rtd 08; PtO *Sarum* from 11; *Win* 16–21; *Eur* 09–19. *16 Windsor Road, Salisbury SP2 7DX* T: (01722) 340058 E: jandmtarrant1988@gmail.com

TARRIS, Canon Geoffrey John. b 27. Em Coll Cam BA 50 MA 55. Westcott Ho Cam 51. **d** 53 **p** 54. C Abbots Langley *St Alb* 53–55; Prec St E Cathl 55–59; V Bungay H Trin w St Mary 59–72; RD S Elmham 65–72; V Ipswich St Mary le Tower 72–78; V Ipswich St Mary le Tower w St Lawr and St Steph 78–82; Hon Can St E Cathl 74–82; Can Res St E Cathl 82–93; Dioc Dir of Lay Min 82–87; Warden of Readers 82–87; Dioc Dir of Ords 87–93; rtd 93; PtO *Nor* 93–12; *St E* from 93; Hon PV Nor Cathl 94–12. *53 The Close, Norwich NR1 4EG* T: (01603) 622136

TARRIS, Philip Geoffrey. b 54. Univ of Wales (Swansea) BSc 76 Lon Univ MSc 78. ERMC. **d** 10 **p** 11. P-in-c Gt Dunmow and Barnston *Chelmsf* 10–14; P-in-c The Sampfords and Radwinter w Hempstead 14–17; P-in-c Thaxted 15–17; R Thaxted, The Sampfords, Radwinter and Hempstead 17–21; rtd 21. *41 Marlborough Road, Southwold IP18 6LS* E: pgtarris@gmail.com

TARRY, Canon Gordon Malcolm. b 54. Leeds Univ BSc 75 Lon Bible Coll BA 83. Ridley Hall Cam. **d** 85 **p** 86. C Gt Ilford St Andr *Chelmsf* 85–89; C Rainham 89–92; C Rainham w Wennington 92–93; V Gt Ilford St Jo 93–06; RD Redbridge 01–06; TR Barking St Marg w St Patr 06–11; V Leigh-on-Sea St Aid from 15. *St Aidan's Vicarage, 78 Moor Park Gardens, Leigh-on-Sea SS9 4PY* T: (01702) 512531 E: gordontarry@yahoo.co.uk

TASH, Elizabeth. *See* ROOKWOOD, Elizabeth

TASH, Stephen Ronald. b 56. Warw Univ BEd 79. WMMTC 88. **d** 91 **p** 92. C Studley *Cov* 91–95; P-in-c Salford Priors 95–09; Dioc Youth Officer 95–00; P-in-c Temple Grafton w Binton 00–09; P-in-c Exhall w Wixford 03–09; V Fulford *York* 09–11; rtd 11; PtO *Cov* from 14; Chapl Univ Hosps Cov and Warks NHS Trust from 17. *16 Eclipse Road, Alcester B49 5EH* T: (01789) 765319 E: stevetash@aol.com

TASSELL, Mrs Stella Venetia. b 39. RGN 60 RNT 63 RMN 66 RHV 72. **d** 01 **p** 02. OLM Woodham *Guildf* 01–09; PtO *Bradf* 10–14; *Leeds* 14–16; *Guildf* 12–20. *3 Park Gate Court, Constitution Hill, Woking GU22 7RW* T: (01483) 755481 M: 07790-521567 E: stellatassell@googlemail.com

TATE, Denis Steven. b 53. Lanc Univ MA 76. LCTP 09. **d** 11 **p** 12. NSM Ellel w Shireshead *Blackb* 11–15; TV Bentham, Burton-in-Lonsdale, Chapel-le-Dale etc *Leeds* from 15.

The Vicarage, 21 Manor Close, Burton in Lonsdale, Carnforth LA6 3NE   T: (01524) 61579   E: revden@hotmail.co.uk

TATE, James. b 56. Oak Hill Th Coll 93. **d** 95 **p** 96. C Hammersmith St Simon *Lon* 95–98; C N Hammersmith St Kath 98–99; P-in-c from 99. *St Katherine's Vicarage, Primula Street, London W12 0RF*   T: (020) 8746 2213 *or* 8743 3951   E: jim.stkats@gmail.com

TATE, John Robert. b 38. Dur Univ BA 61 MA 71. Cranmer Hall Dur. **d** 70 **p** 71. C Bare *Blackb* 70–73; V Over Darwen St Jas 73–81; V Caton w Littledale 81–98; rtd 98; PtO *Blackb* 98–18. *69 Otley Road, Skipton BD23 1HJ*   T: (01756) 709235

TATE, Lesley Carole. b 58. St Mellitus Coll 15. **d** 18 **p** 19. NSM N Hammersmith St Kath *Lon* from 18. *The Vicarage, Primula Street, London W12 0RF*   T: (020) 8746 2213   E: lestateuk@yahoo.co.uk

TATE, Toby James. b 74. Univ of Wales (Abth) BSc 96 Sheff Univ MEd 00 Warwick Univ PGCE 97. Ridley Hall Cam 11. **d** 13 **p** 14. C Triangle, St Matt and All SS *St E* 13–16; P-in-c Martlesham w Brightwell 16–20; R from 20. *The Rectory, 17 Lark Rise, Martlesham Heath, Ipswich IP5 3SA*   T: (01473) 612659   E: tobyjtate@gmail.com

TATHAM, Andrew Francis. b 49. Grey Coll Dur BA 71 K Coll Lon PhD 84 AKC 88 FBCartS 96. S'wark Ord Course 88. **d** 92 **p** 93. NSM Headley w Box Hill *Guildf* 92–02; TV Ilminster and Distr *B & W* 02–10; V Isle Valley 10–14; RD Crewkerne and Ilminster 07–12; RD Ilminster 12–14; rtd 14; Hon Can Quantock Coast *B & W* 14–19; PtO from 20. *61 West Street, Watchet TA23 0BH*   T: (01984) 633331   E: aftatham@btinternet.com

TATTERSALL, Canon John Hartley. b 52. Ch Coll Cam BA 73 MA 76 FCA 89. SEITE 04. **d** 07 **p** 08. NSM Wykeham *Ox* from 07; PtO *Lon* from 19; Hon Can Ch Ch *Ox* from 21. T: (01295) 780283 *or* (020) 7603 1053   M: 07711-733978 E: jhtatters@aol.com

TATTERSALL, Jonathan Mark. b 76. Lon Bible Coll BTh 99. St Jo Coll Nottm MA 16. **d** 16 **p** 17. C Dorridge *Birm* 16–19; C Harborne Heath from 19. *2 Milford Copse, Birmingham B17 9TF*   M: 07939-139036

TATTON-BROWN, Canon Simon Charles. b 48. Qu Coll Cam BA 70 MA 78 Man Univ CQSW 72. Coll of Resurr Mirfield 78. **d** 79 **p** 80. C Ashton St Mich *Man* 79–82; P-in-c Prestwich St Gabr 82–87; V 87–88; Bp's Dom Chapl 82–88; TR Westhoughton 88–96; TR Westhoughton and Wingates 97–00; V Chippenham St Andr w Tytherton Lucas *Bris* 00–13; RD Chippenham 03–06; Hon Can Bris Cathl 11–13; rtd 14; PtO *B & W* from 14. *259 Bloomfield Road, Bath BA2 2BA*   T: (01225) 835404   M: 07891-898472 E: simon@tattonbrown.myzen.co.uk

TATTUM, Ian Stuart. b 58. N Lon Poly BA 79 Fitzw Coll Cam BA 89. Westcott Ho Cam 87. **d** 90 **p** 91. C Beaconsfield *Ox* 90–94; C Bushey *St Alb* 94–96; P-in-c Pirton 96–01; P-in-c St Ippolyts 00–06; P-in-c Gt and Lt Wymondley 01–06; P-in-c Southfields St Barn *S'wark* 06–11; V from 11; P-in-c Earlsfield St Jo 17–19; AD Wandsworth from 18. *St Barnabas' Vicarage, 146A Lavenham Road, London SW18 5EP*   T: (020) 8480 2290 E: iantattum@gmail.com

TATTUM, Ruth Margaret. *See* LAMPARD, Ruth Margaret

TATUM, Mrs Josephine Gayle. b 56. St Jo Coll Nottm BATM 12. **d** 12 **p** 13. C Nottingham St Nic *S'well* 12–16; Ind Chapl from 16. *55 St Austell Drive, Nottingham NG11 7BT*   T: 0115-846 5760   M: 07525-641320 E: jo.tatum@southwell.anglican.org

TAULTY, Mrs Eileen. b 45. **d** 03. OLM Pemberton St Mark Newtown *Liv* 03–07; OLM Marsh Green w Newtown 08–14; OLM Newtown 14–15; rtd 15; PtO *Liv* from 15. *38 Alexandra Crescent, Wigan WN5 9JP*   T: (01942) 208021

TAUNTON, Archdeacon of. *See* HILL, The Ven Simon James

TAUNTON, Suffragan Bishop of. *See* WORSLEY, The Rt Revd Ruth Elizabeth

TAUSON (née PURVIS), Ms Sandra Anne. b 56. Univ Coll Ches BTh 01. NOC 98. **d** 01 **p** 02. C Blackpool St Jo *Blackb* 01–06; P-in-c Gt Harwood 06–08; Chapl Pennine Acute Hosps NHS Trust 08–17; V Chorley St Pet *Blackb* 11–14; NSM Rochdale *Man* 15–17; PtO *Blackb* 14–17; Chapl Univ Hosp Southn NHS Foundn Trust from 17. *University Hospital Southampton NHS Trust, Tremona Road, Southampton SO16 6YD*   T: (023) 8077 7222   M: 07967-136992

TAVERNER, Lorraine Dawn. *See* COLAM, Lorraine Dawn

TAVERNOR (née LLOYD), Mrs Eileen. b 50. FIBMS 74. NOC 88. **d** 91 **p** 94. C Heref St Martin w St Fran 91–95; P-in-c Bucknell w Chapel Lawn, Llanfair Waterdine etc 95–01; V 01–09; rtd 09; PtO *Heref* 09–15. *Froglands, Rosemary Lane, Leintwardine, Craven Arms SY7 0LP*   T: (01547) 540365

TAVINOR, The Very Revd Michael Edward. b 53. Univ Coll Dur BA 75 Em Coll Cam CertEd 76 K Coll Lon MMus 77 AKC 77 ARCO 77 Univ of Wales (Lamp) MTh 10. Ripon Coll Cuddesdon BA 81 MA 86. **d** 82 **p** 83. C Ealing St Pet Mt Park *Lon* 82–85; Min Can, Prec and Sacr Ely Cathl 85–90; P-in-c Stuntney 87–90; V Tewkesbury w Walton Cardiff *Glouc* 90–99; P-in-c Twyning 98–99; V Tewkesbury w Walton Cardiff and Twyning 99–02; Hon Can Glouc Cathl 97–02; Dean Heref 02–21; rtd 21. *Address temp unknown*

TAWN, Canon Andrew Richard. b 61. Trin Coll Cam BA 83 Ox Univ BA 88 Sheff Univ MA 14. Ripon Coll Cuddesdon 86. **d** 89 **p** 90. C Dovecot *Liv* 89–93; TV Dorchester *Ox* 93–98; Student Supervisor Cuddesdon Coll 93–98; R Addingham *Bradf* 98–12; Dir Clergy Development *Leeds* from 12; Hon Can Bradf Cathl from 15. *The Vicarage, Morton Lane, East Morton, Keighley BD20 5RS*   T: (01274) 567898   E: a.tawn@btinternet.com

TAYLER, Jeremy Charles. b 78. LSE BSc 00 Birkbeck Coll Lon MA 06. Westcott Ho Cam 13. **d** 15 **p** 16. C St John's Wood *Lon* 15–18; R Henley w Remenham *Ox* from 18. *St Mary's Rectory, Hart Street, Henley-on-Thames RG9 2AU*   E: jeremyctayler@gmail.com

TAYLER, Mrs Wendy Christian. b 76. **d** 13 **p** 14. C Neath *Llan* 13–16; TV 16–18; C Llansawel, Briton Ferry 16–18; C Caerleon and Llanfrechfa *Mon* from 18. *Ridgeways, Usk Road, Caerleon, Newport NP18 1LN*   M: 07808-147619   E: wcsanderson@hotmail.co.uk *or* wendy.stcadocs@gmail.com

TAYLEUR, Mrs Gillian Sarah. b 61. Bedf Coll Lon BSc 82. OLM course 05. **d** 08 **p** 09. NSM Herne Hill *S'wark* from 08. *27 Finsen Road, London SE5 9AX*   T: (020) 7737 1991   M: 07546-539737

TAYLOR, Alan Clive. b 48. Southn Univ BTh 79 DipEd 73. Sarum Th Coll 69. **d** 74 **p** 75. C Watford St Pet *St Alb* 74–78; C Broxbourne w Wormley 78–83; Chapl to the Deaf 83–91; V Shefford 83–91; R Portishead *B & W* 91–02; TR 02–08; rtd 08; PtO *Bris* from 09; *Sarum* from 15. *Larkhill, The Green, Dauntsey, Chippenham SN15 4HY*   T: (01666) 511169 E: padreact@gmail.com

TAYLOR, Canon Alan Leonard. b 43. Chich Th Coll 67. **d** 69 **p** 70. C Walton St Mary *Liv* 69–73; C Toxteth St Marg 73–75; V Stanley 75–83; V Leeds St Aid *Ripon* 84–11; V Leeds Richmond Hill 06–11; TR Leeds All So and St Aid 11–12; Hon Can Ripon Cathl 97–12; AD Allerton 08–12; rtd 13; PtO *Linc* 16–19. *Marsh Bank Cottage, Frampton Roads, Frampton, Boston PE20 1AY*   T: (01205) 722693 E: alantaylor43@btinternet.com

TAYLOR, Andrew David. b 58. Regent's Park Coll Ox BA 81 MA 86 Toronto Univ MDiv 92 K Coll Lon MTh 95 FRSA 08. Westcott Ho Cam 85. **d** 87 **p** 89. C Leckhampton SS Phil and Jas w Cheltenham St Jas *Glouc* 87–91; P-in-c Swindon w Uckington and Elmstone Hardwicke 92–93; C Highgate St Mich *Lon* 94–97; Chapl R Holloway and Bedf New Coll *Guildf* 97–03; Public Preacher 04; PtO 05–13; C Englefield Green 13; Research Assoc Ox Cen for Christianity and Culture from 12; Chapl Downe Ho Sch Berks 15–17; PtO *Eur* from 18; Min The Hague 19–20. *25 Great Norwood Street, Cheltenham GL50 2AW*   T: (01242) 511955   M: 07952-866581 E: andrew.taylor@regents.ox.ac.uk

TAYLOR, Ann. *See* TAYLOR, Margaret Ann

TAYLOR, Ms Anne Elizabeth. b 68. Ulster Univ BSc 91 MA 99. CITC BTh 94. **d** 94 **p** 95. C Dublin Rathfarnham *D & G* 94–14; Chapl Adelaide and Meath Hosp Dublin 01–03; Abp's Dom Chapl *D & G* 03–14; Children's Min Officer Sunday Sch Soc of Ireland 05–14; V Formby St Pet *Liv* from 14; AD Sefton N from 15. *St Peter's Vicarage, Cricket Path, Formby, Liverpool L37 7DP*   T: (01704) 872824 E: revannetaylor@gmail.com

TAYLOR, Arthur Alfred. b 32. Univ Coll Ox MA 56. Ox Min Course 80. **d** 83 **p** 84. NSM Monks Risborough *Ox* 83–96; NSM Aylesbury Deanery from 96. *9 Place Farm Way, Monks Risborough, Princes Risborough HP27 9JJ*   T: (01844) 347197 E: arthurtaylor16@btinternet.com

TAYLOR, Brian. b 42. St Deiniol's Hawarden 78. **d** 80 **p** 81. C Mold *St As* 80–84; V Bagillt 84–08; rtd 08; PtO *St As* from 09. *13 Bryn Awel, Pentre Halkyn, Holywell CH8 8JB*   T: (01352) 780744   M: 07779-913883 E: brian.taylor970@btinternet.com

TAYLOR, Brian. b 38. Bris Univ BA 60 Liv Univ BA 70 Southn Univ MA 90. Ridley Hall Cam 60. **d** 66 **p** 66. Chapl Victoria Coll Ondo Nigeria 66–72; PtO *Derby* 74–78; Chapl Newbury Coll 76–94; P-in-c Shaw cum Donnington *Ox* 89–90; R 90–08; rtd 08; PtO *Ox* 08–15; *Derby* from 15. *Fairview House Barn, The Moor, Tideswell, Buxton SK17 8LR*   M: 07925-126761 E: brian_harker_taylor@yahoo.co.uk

TAYLOR, Brian Lee. b 71. Mattersey Hall BA 97 MA 99. Coll of Resurr Mirfield 04. **d** 17 **p** 18. C Chingford SS Pet and Paul *Chelmsf* 17–19; P-in-c Lt Ilford St Mich from 19. *Little Ilford Rectory, 124 Church Road, London E12 6HA*   T: (020) 3686 1085   M: 07786-261792 E: frlee.littleilford@gmail.com

TAYLOR, Mrs Bryony Ruthellen. b 77. Leeds Univ BA 99 MA 05 St Jo Coll Dur BA 14. Cranmer Hall Dur 12. **d** 14 **p** 15. C Houghton le Spring *Dur* 14–18; R Barlborough and Clowne *Derby* from 18. *The Rectory, Church Street, Barlborough, Chesterfield S43 4EP* T: (01246) 813569 M: 07960-735352 E: bryony.taylor@gmail.com

TAYLOR, Mrs Caroline Mary. b 85. Nottm Univ BA 07 Kellogg Coll Ox MSc 11 St Jo Coll Dur BATM 18. Cranmer Hall Dur 15. **d** 18 **p** 19. C Hoxton St Jo w Ch Ch *Lon* 18–21; V Marton-in-Cleveland w Easterside *York* from 21. *The Vicarage, Stokesley Road, Marton-in-Cleveland, Middlesbrough TS7 8JU* M: 07312-091853 E: revcarolinetaylor@gmail.com

TAYLOR, Charles Derek. b 36. Trin Hall Cam BA 59 MA 62. Ripon Hall Ox 59. **d** 61 **p** 62. C Nottingham All SS *S'well* 61–64; C Binley *Cov* 64–67; C Stoke 67–70; R Purley *Ox* 70–74; V Milton *B & W* 74–93; RD Locking 86–87 and 90–93; V Wells St Cuth w Wookey Hole 93–98; rtd 98; PtO *Roch* 00–16; *B & W* from 19. *5 Banner Farm Road, Tunbridge Wells TN2 5EA* T: (01892) 526825 E: c.derektaylor5@yahoo.co.uk

TAYLOR, The Very Revd Charles William. b 53. Selw Coll Cam BA 74 MA 78. Cuddesdon Coll 74. **d** 76 **p** 77. C Wolverhampton *Lich* 76–79; Chapl Westmr Abbey 79–84; V Stanmore *Win* 84–90; R N Stoneham 90–95; Can Res and Prec Lich Cathl 95–07; Dean Pet 07–16; PtO *Win* from 17; *Newc* from 18; Assoc Can Res Sarum Cathl 17–18. *38 Rochester Drive, Felton, Morpeth NE65 9DS* M: 07754-893718 E: charles53taylor@outlook.com

TAYLOR, Christopher Drewett. b 58. Qu Coll Birm 06. **d** 09 **p** 10. C Shepshed and Oaks in Charnwood *Leic* 09–13; Chapl Loughb Univ from 13. *3 Brockington Building, Loughborough University, Loughborough LE11 3TU* T: (01509) 223742 M: 07946-763257 E: christaylor36beacon@msn.com *or* c.taylor2@lboro.ac.uk

TAYLOR, Christopher Vincent. b 47. Glas Univ MTh 10 PhD 17 R Cen Sch Speech & Drama DipEd 71. Cranmer Hall Dur 94. **d** 96 **p** 97. C Kendal St Geo *Carl* 96–99; TV Wheatley *Ox* 99–03; TV Leeds City *Ripon* 03–06; Chapl Arts and Recreation City of Leeds 03–06; rtd 06; Hon C Beacon TM *Carl* 08–15; PtO from 15; Dioc Chapl to the Arts 08–20; Hon C Wanstead St Mary w Ch Ch *Chelmsf* from 20. *13 Wanstead Place, London E11 2SW* M: 07583-209915 E: christaylor156@btinternet.com

TAYLOR, Colin. **d** 15 **p** 16. Dromara w Garvaghy *D & D* 15–16; C 16–19; I from 19. *The Rectory, 58 Banbridge Road, Dromara, Dromore BT25 2NE* T: (028) 9753 3919 M: 07852-130463 E: colintaylorc@btinternet.com

TAYLOR, Colin John. b 66. Witwatersrand Univ BCom 87 BTh 94. Wycliffe Hall Ox MTh 97. **d** 97 **p** 98. C Denton Holme *Carl* 97–01; Bp's Dom Chapl 01–06; Dir CME 1-4 00–06; V Felsted and Lt Dunmow *Chelmsf* from 06. *The Vicarage, Bury Chase, Felsted, Dunmow CM6 3DQ* T: (01371) 820242 E: ctaylor585@googlemail.com

TAYLOR, Canon David. b 53. St Jo Coll Dur BA 74 PGCE 75 Liv Univ MTh 04. Sarum & Wells Th Coll 91. **d** 93 **p** 94. C Cheadle Hulme All SS *Ches* 93–97; V Macclesfield St Jo 97–05; RD Macclesfield 03–05; TR Congleton 05–19; RD 08–13; Hon Can Ches Cathl 09–19; rtd 19; PtO *Ches* from 19. *12 Garnett Close, Stapeley, Nantwich CW5 7RF* T: (01270) 618936

TAYLOR, David Christopher Morgan. b 56. Leeds Univ BSc 77 Univ Coll Lon PhD 80 Univ Coll Ches MEd 96 SOSc MRSB. NOC 91. **d** 94 **p** 95. Tutor Liv Univ from 86; NSM Waterloo Ch Ch and St Mary 94–99; P-in-c Altcar 98–00; NSM Altcar and Hightown 03–14; NSM Formby H Trin and Altcar from 14. *20 Liverpool Road, Formby, Liverpool L37 4BW* T: (01704) 873304 F: 0151-794 5337 E: dcmt@liverpool.ac.uk *or* taylordcm@aol.com

TAYLOR, Derek. *See* TAYLOR, Charles Derek

TAYLOR, The Very Revd Derek John. b 31. Univ of Wales (Lamp) BA 52 Fitzw Ho Cam BA 54 MA 58 Ex Univ CertEd 70. St Mich Coll Llan 54. **d** 55 **p** 56. C Newport St Paul *Mon* 55–59; CF (TA) 57–59 and 62–64; CF 59–62; V Bettws *Mon* 62–64; V Exminster *Ex* 64–70; Hd of RE Heathcote Sch Tiverton 70–71; W Germany 71–75; Chapl R Russell Sch Croydon 75–79; Chapl St Andr C of E High Sch Croydon 79–84; P-in-c Croydon St Andr *Cant* 79–81; V 81–84; Chapl Bromsgrove Sch 84–89; Provost St Chris Cathl Bahrain 90–97; Hon Chapl Miss to Seamen 90–97; PtO *Worc* 92–00; P-in-c Bearsden w Milngavie *Glas* 00–03; PtO *Worc* 04–11; *Leeds* from 17. *22 Coxwold View, Wetherby LS22 7PU* T: (01937) 918534 M: 07904-205669 E: dervaltaylor@talktalk.net

TAYLOR, Garry Kenneth. b 53. Edin Univ BMus 75 Southn Univ BTh 81 Ch Ch Coll Cant PGCE 95. Sarum & Wells Th Coll 76. **d** 79 **p** 80. C Southsea H Spirit *Portsm* 79–82; C Croydon St Jo *Cant* 82–84; C Croydon St Jo *S'wark* 85–86; V Choral S'well Minster 86–90; V Portsea St Alb *Portsm* 90–94; NSM Hamble le Rice *Win* 96–97; P-in-c Southampton St Jude 97–04; V Highcliffe w Hinton Admiral 04–09; V Highcliffe 09–15; rtd 15. *Oriel Cottage, 2 Avon View, Castle Street, Salisbury SP1 3SY* T: (01722) 334153 M: 07454-569169 E: garry.k.taylor@btinternet.com

TAYLOR, Canon Gordon. b 46. AKC 68. St Aug Coll Cant 69. **d** 70 **p** 71. C Rotherham *Sheff* 70–74; P-in-c Brightside St Thos 74–79; P-in-c Brightside St Marg 77–79; V Brightside St Thos and St Marg 79–82; R Kirk Sandall and Edenthorpe 82–91; V Beighton 91–96; V Goole 96–03; AD Snaith and Hatfield 98–03; V Tickhill w Stainton 03–11; Hon Can Sheff Cathl 93–11; rtd 11; PtO *Sheff* from 11. *96 Whitton Close, Doncaster DN4 7RD* T: (01302) 533249 E: gordon.taylor809@btinternet.com

TAYLOR, Gordon Edward James. b 90. Collingwood Coll Dur BA 12 Selw Coll Cam BTh 17 St Aug Coll Cant MA 20. Ridley Hall Cam 15. **d** 18 **p** 19. C Tunbridge Wells Ch Ch *Roch* from 18. *14 Teise Close, Tunbridge Wells TN2 5JN* T: (01892) 522323 M: 07831-725960 E: gordon@cctw.org.uk *or* taylorgej@gmail.com

TAYLOR, Canon Graham Smith. b 70. TISEC 98. **d** 01 **p** 02. C Ellon, Cruden Bay and Peterhead *Ab* 01–04; P-in-c 04–06; R Aberdeen St Mary 06–14; Dioc Dir Ords 06–14; Can St Andr Cathl 08–14; R Aberdeen St Clem 09–12; R Perth St Jo *St Andr* from 14; Can St Ninian's Cathl Perth from 19. *St John's Rectory, 23 Comely Bank, Perth PH2 7HU* T: (01738) 245922 M: 07773-482174 E: revgraham@tiscali.co.uk

TAYLOR, Hugh Nigel James. b 43. MCMI FInstD. NTMTC 04. **d** 06 **p** 07. NSM Loughton St Mary *Chelmsf* 06–14; PtO from 14. *4 Twentyman Close, Woodford Green IG8 0EW* T: (020) 8504 8901 M: 07770-365255 E: revhnjt@gmail.com

TAYLOR, Iain William James. b 41. **d** 03 **p** 04. OLM Cant St Pet w St Alphege and St Marg etc 03–11; rtd 11; PtO *Cant* from 12. *30 Deans Mill Court, The Causeway, Canterbury CT1 2BF* T: (01227) 457711 E: revd.iain.taylor@talktalk.net

TAYLOR, Ian. b 53. Saltley Tr Coll Birm CertEd 75. **d** 95 **p** 96. OLM Heywood *Man* 95–10; OLM Sudden and Heywood All So 10–21; rtd 21; PtO *Man* from 21. *818A Edenfield Road, Rochdale OL12 7RB* T: (01706) 355738 E: reviantaylor@gmail.com

TAYLOR, Preb Jacqueline Margaret. b 56. Trin Coll Bris 02. **d** 04 **p** 05. C Bath St Luke *B & W* 04–08; Chapl Univ Hosps Bris NHS Foundn Trust 08–13; P-in-c Kingsbridge and Dodbrooke *Ex* 13–15; R Kingsbridge, Dodbrooke, and W Alvington from 15; RD Woodleigh 16–19; Preb Ex Cathl from 19; Dean of Women's Min from 19. *Dodbrooke Rectory, Church Street, Kingsbridge TQ7 1NW* T: (01548) 856231 E: jtaylor808@btinternet.com

TAYLOR, James. *See* TAYLOR, Nigel James

TAYLOR, James Richard. b 78. Bath Univ BSc 00. Trin Coll Bris BA 17. **d** 17 **p** 18. C Bridgwater H Trin and Durleigh *B & W* 17–20; PtO *Win* from 20; Chapl Univ Hosps Dorset NHS Foundn Trust from 21. *43 Kingston Road, Poole BH15 2LR* M: 07837-573874 E: jamestaylormail@gmail.com

TAYLOR, James Robert. b 92. Cumbria Univ BA 14. Cranmer Hall Dur 17. **d** 20 **p** 21. C Wigan *Liv* from 20. *217 Darlington Street East, Wigan WN1 3EA* M: 07864-562745 E: jrail@live.co.uk *or* curate.contact@churchwigan.org

TAYLOR, Jamie Alexander Franklyn. b 73. Kent Univ BA 95. Westcott Ho Cam. **d** 98 **p** 99. C Walton-on-Thames *Guildf* 98–02; C St Peter-in-Thanet *Cant* 02–08; Chapl E Kent NHS and Soc Care Partnership Trust 03–06; Chapl Kent and Medway NHS and Soc Care Partnership Trust 06–08; V Sonning *Ox* from 08. *The Vicarage, Thames Street, Sonning, Reading RG4 6UR* T: 0118-969 3298 E: revjaft@yahoo.co.uk

TAYLOR, Jane Suzanne. b 54. Ex Univ BA 73. SEITE 96. **d** 99 **p** 00. NSM Knaphill w Brookwood *Guildf* 99–00; C Frimley Green and Mytchett 00–04; PtO *Ex* from 04. *Rocknell Manor Farm, Westleigh, Tiverton EX16 7ES* T: (01884) 829000 E: janetaylor@millhouseretreats.co.uk

TAYLOR (née MAYOR), Mrs Janet Hilary. b 55. St Martin's Coll Lanc BA 96 Open Univ PGCE 98. LCTP 10. **d** 11 **p** 12. NSM Chorley St Laur *Blackb* 11–15; NSM Croston, Bretherton and Mawdesley w Bispham from 15. *Orchard House, Old Pope Lane, Whitestake, Preston PR4 4JQ* E: curatejanet@gmail.com

TAYLOR, Jason Victor. b 71. Lon Bible Coll BTh 01 St Jo Coll Dur MA 03. Cranmer Hall Dur 01. **d** 03 **p** 04. C Ripley *Derby* 03–07; TV Drypool *York* 07–13; Chapl Abp Sentamu Academy Hull 09–13; P-in-c Brampton *Ely* 13–16; P-in-c Graffham and Ellington 13–16; V E Leightonstone 17–20; Bp's Chapl *Glouc* from 20. *2 College Green, Gloucester GL1 2LR* T: (01452) 835513 M: 07395-855353 E: jtaylor@glosdioc.org.uk

TAYLOR, Miss Jean. b 37. Nottm Univ TCert 58. St Andr Coll Pampisford 62. **dss** 68 **d** 00 **p** 01. CSA 62–79; E Crompton *Man* 79–97; Chadderton St Luke 97–04; OLM

00–04; OLM Chadderton St Matt w St Luke 04–05; Warden Jes Hosp Cant 05–08; PtO *Cant* from 05. *7 Chantry Court, St Radigund's Street, Canterbury CT1 2AD* T: (01227) 761652 E: revjtay7@gmail.com

TAYLOR, Canon Jennifer Anne. b 53. Sussex Univ BEd 75 Surrey Univ BA 01 Win Univ MA 09. STETS 98. d 01 p 02. Chapl Salisbury Cathl Sch 01–13; NSM Salisbury St Thos and St Edm *Sarum* 01–09; NSM Chalke Valley 09–13; TV from 13; Can and Preb Sarum Cathl from 18. *27 Viking Way, Salisbury SP2 8TA* T: (01722) 503081 E: revjennytaylor@gmail.com

TAYLOR, Sister Jennifer Mary. b 41. CA Tr Coll IDC 65. dss 77 d 87 p 07. CA from 65; Chapl Asst HM Pris Holloway 75–79; Ho Mistress Ch Hosp Sch Hertf 78–79; Chapl Asst Rtd Officer Chapl RAChD 80–90; Germany 90–96; rtd 96; PtO *Eur* from 96; *Nor* 06–07 and from 11; Hon C Dereham and Distr 07–11. *4 Eckling Grange, Norwich Road, Dereham NR20 3BB* T: (01362) 692547

TAYLOR, Jeremy Christopher. b 75. Birm Univ BA 97. Oak Hill Th Coll BA 07. d 07 p 08. C Chell *Lich* 07–10; P-in-c Enderby w Lubbesthorpe and Thurlaston *Leic* 10–18; V from 18. *The Rectory, 16A Desford Road, Leicester LE9 7TE* T: (01455) 888679 M: 07787-514058 E: juneandjerry@btinternet.com

TAYLOR, Joanna Beatrice. *See* NEARY, Joanna Beatrice

TAYLOR, John. b 58. Aston Tr Scheme 94 Ripon Coll Cuddesdon 96. d 98 p 99. C Southport Em *Liv* 98–03; V Hindley All SS 03–09; R Yanchep Australia 09–20; Chapl St Jas Sch Alkimos from 21. *2 Graceful Boulevard, Alkimos WA 6038, Australia* T: (0061) (8) 9561 1357 or (8) 6336 8330 M: (0061) 43-831 8285 E: revj-tay@bigpond.com *or* jtaylor@stjames.wa.edu.au

TAYLOR, John Andrew. b 53. Linc Th Coll 86. d 88 p 89. C Stanley *Liv* 88–91; V Wigan St Jas w St Thos 91–04; AD Wigan W 99–04; V Prescot 04–21; AD Huyton 06–17; Hon Can Liv Cathl 03–04 and 07–21; rtd 21; Chapl to The Queen from 16. *2 Fulwood Road, Lowton, Warrington WA3 2AX* T: (01942) 568866

TAYLOR, Canon John Michael. b 30. St Aid Birkenhead 56. d 59 p 60. C Chorley St Jas *Blackb* 59–62; C Broughton 62–64; Chapl St Boniface Coll Warminster 64–68; V Altham w Clayton le Moors *Blackb* 68–76; RD Accrington 71–76; Can Res Blackb Cathl 76–96; Tutor CBDTI 88–96; rtd 96; PtO *Blackb* from 96. *8 Fosbrooke House, Clifton Drive, Lytham St Annes FY8 5RQ*

✠**TAYLOR, The Rt Revd John Mitchell.** b 32. Aber Univ MA 54. Edin Th Coll 54. d 56 p 57 c 91. C Aberdeen St Marg *Ab* 56–58; R Glas H Cross 58–64; R Glas St Ninian 64–73; R Dumfries and Chapl Dumfries and Galloway R Infirmary 73–91; Can St Mary's Cathl *Glas* 79–91; Bp Glas 91–98; rtd 98; Hon Asst Bp Glas from 99. *85 Lord Lyell Drive, Kirriemuir DD8 4LF* T: (01575) 573132

TAYLOR, John Porter. b 48. Ex Univ BA 71 MA 76. Cranmer Hall Dur 93. d 93 p 94. C Ossett cum Gawthorpe *Wakef* 93–96; R Crofton 96–02; Chapl Mid Yorks Hosps NHS Trust 03–06; Chapl Oakham Sch 06–13; rtd 13; PtO *Pet* 13–14; Hon C Empingham, Edith Weston, Lyndon, Manton etc 14–20. *9 Zouche Way, Bushby, Leicester LE7 9DT* E: jpt100948@gmail.com

TAYLOR, John Ralph. b 48. St Jo Coll Nottm BTh 74. d 74 p 75. C Clitheroe St Jas *Blackb* 74–77; C Kidsgrove *Lich* 77–79; C Hawkwell *Chelmsf* 79–82; V Linc St Geo Swallowbeck 82–92; rtd 92. *16 Rosedale Close, Cherry Willingham, Lincoln LN3 4RE*

TAYLOR, Jonathan Paul. b 74. Birm Univ BEng 97 Birm Chr Coll BA 05. Trin Coll Bris 07. d 11 p 12. C Coventry Caludon *Cov* 11–14; V Binley from 14. *St Bartholomew's Vicarage, 68 Brandon Road, Binley, Coventry CV3 2JF* E: jonandsu@gmail.com

TAYLOR, Joseph Robin Christopher. b 34. St Aid Birkenhead 58. d 61 p 62. C Aldershot St Mich *Guildf* 61–64; C Fleet 64–68; R Manaton *Ex* 69–74; R N Bovey 69–74; V Dawlish 74–87; P-in-c Christow, Ashton, Trusham and Bridford 87–88; R 88–95; PtO 95–98; rtd 99; PtO *St E* from 98. *35 Foster Court, Witham CM8 2TQ* T: (01376) 511587

TAYLOR, Julia May. *See* CODY, Julia May

TAYLOR, Kane Matthew. b 70. Open Univ BSc 04. Wycliffe Hall Ox 09. d 11 p 12. C Kettering St Andr *Pet* 11–14; P-in-c Weldon w Deene 14–17; R from 17. *The Rectory, 13 School Lane, Weldon, Corby NN17 3JN* T: (01536) 626361 E: kane.taylor@hotmail.co.uk *or* kane.taylor@virgin.net

TAYLOR, Kelvin John. b 53. Portsm Univ CertEd 94 BA 96. Trin Coll Bris 02. d 04 p 05. C Overton w Laverstoke and Freefolk *Win* 04–08; V Kempshott 08–17; rtd 17; PtO *Win* from 17. *31 Melrose Road, Southampton SO15 7PB*

TAYLOR, Kingsley Graham. b 55. Univ of Wales (Cardiff) BD 93. St Mich Coll Llan 90. d 93 p 94. C Llanelli *St D* 93–97; V Whitland w Cyffig and Henllan Amgoed etc 97–20; P-in-c E Landsker from 20; AD Pembroke 16–20;

AD E Landsker from 20. *The Vicarage, North Road, Whitland SA34 0BH* T: (01994) 240494 E: ktaylor559@aol.com

TAYLOR, Lee. *See* TAYLOR, Brian Lee

TAYLOR, Lee Anthony. b 77. Univ of Wales (Lamp) BA 02 Win Univ MA 12. Ripon Coll Cuddesdon 10. d 12 p 13. C Leigh-on-Sea St Marg *Chelmsf* 12–15; C Leigh St Clem 15; C Croydon St Jo *S'wark* 15–18; P-in-c Valle Crucis Miss Area *St As* from 18. *The Vicarage, Abbey Road, Llangollen LL20 8SN* E: frleetaylor@hotmail.co.uk

TAYLOR, Lynda Brigid. b 54. Man Univ BA Cam Univ PhD. ERMC. d 10 p 11. NSM Chesterton St Geo *Ely* 10–13; NSM Cambourne LEP 13–16; PtO from 17. *110 School Lane, Lower Cambourne, Cambridge CB23 5DJ* E: lyndabtaylor7@gmail.com

TAYLOR, Lyndon John. b 49. St Mich Coll Llan 92. d 95 p 96. NSM Swansea St Nic *S & B* 95–99; C Llwynderw 99–01; V Waunarllwydd 01–06; V Clydach 08–14; rtd 14; PtO *Mon* from 14; *Llan* 15–18. *85 Pen yr Alltwen, Alltwen, Pontardawe, Swansea SA8 3EA* T: (01792) 934999

TAYLOR, Lynne. b 51. Sheff Univ BMet 73 Salford Univ PhD 80. Man OLM Scheme 98. d 01 p 02. OLM Turton Moorland *Man* 01–11; rtd 11; PtO *Man* from 11; *Carl* from 12; *Blackb* 14–17. *1 Croich Bank, Hawkshaw, Bury BL8 4HW* M: 07776-208732 E: innoveras@hotmail.co.uk

TAYLOR, Margaret Ann. b 46. d 98 p 99. OLM Newcastle w Butterton *Lich* 98–17; rtd 17; PtO *Lich* 17–19. *12 Silverton Close, Bradwell, Newcastle ST5 8LU* T: (01782) 660174 E: revanntaylor@yahoo.co.uk

TAYLOR, Mark Edward. b 54. St Jo Coll Auckland LTh. d 78 p 79. C Claudelands NZ 78–80; C Taumarunui 80–81; V Te Aroha 81–86; Chapl RN 86–90; Chapl RN NZ 90–94; Can Wellington 94–96; P-in-c Albany Greehithe NZ 96–19; P-in-c Glen Eden 02–03; rtd 19. *Apartment 41, 182B Ladies Mille, Ellerslie, Auckland 1051, New Zealand* T: (0064) (9) 571 0281 M: 27-495 1767 E: chalice@xtra.co.nz

TAYLOR, Canon Mark Frederick. b 62. N Ireland Poly BA 84. CITC. d 87 p 88. C Ballymacarrett St Patr *D & D* 87–90; C Dundela St Mark 90–93; I Kilmore and Inch 93–02; I Whitehead and Islandmagee *Conn* from 02; Can Belf Cathl from 16. *St Patrick's Rectory, 72 Riverford, Whitehead, Carrickfergus BT38 9TS* T/F: (028) 9337 3300

TAYLOR, Mark John. b 73. St Andr Univ MTheol 99. Coll of Resurr Mirfield 01. d 03 p 04. C N Meols *Liv* 03–07; TV Sutton 07–18; P-in-c Alfreton *Derby* from 18; P-in-c Riddings and Ironville from 18; C Somercotes from 18. *13 Church Street, Alfreton DE55 7AH* T: (01773) 833280 E: mjtaylor513@gmail.com

TAYLOR, Canon Martyn Andrew Nicholas. b 66. d 96 p 97. C Stamford St Geo w St Paul *Linc* 96–03; R from 03; C Wittering from 07; P-in-c Stamford Ch Ch *Linc* 11–15; RD Stamford from 19; Can and Preb Linc Cathl from 15. *St George's Rectory, 16 St George's Square, Stamford PE9 2BN* T: (01780) 757343 *or* 481800 E: rector@stgeorgeschurch.net

TAYLOR, Matthew Anthony. b 87. Van Mildert Coll Dur BSc 08. Wycliffe Hall Ox BTh 16. d 17 p 18. C Sevenoaks St Nic *Roch* from 17. *40 South Park, Sevenoaks TN13 1EJ* M: 07917-441265 E: matt.taylor1987@gmail.com *or* matt.taylor@stnicholas-sevenoaks.org

TAYLOR, Matthew Timothy. b 62. NTMTC. d 11 p 12. C Rushden St Mary w Newton Bromswold *Pet* 11–17; V Finham *Cov* from 17; AD Cov S from 20. *The Vicarage, 136 Green Lane, Coventry CV3 6EA* E: matt_t_taylor@btinternet.com

TAYLOR, Mrs Maureen. b 36. Lon Bible Coll BTh 90 MA 94. d 97 p 98. NSM Borehamwood *St Alb* 97–00; NSM Radlett 00–05; rtd 06; PtO *St Alb* 06–19. *57A Loom Lane, Radlett WD7 8NX* T: (01923) 855197

TAYLOR, Michael. *See* TAYLOR, John Michael

TAYLOR, Michael Allan. b 50. Nottm Univ BTh 80. St Jo Coll Nottm 76. d 80 p 81. C Bowling St Jo *Bradf* 80–82; C Otley 82–85; P-in-c Low Moor St Mark 85–92; P-in-c Bris St Andr w St Bart 92–96; PtO *Llan* from 05. *19 Alexander Place, Abercanaid, Merthyr Tydfil CF48 1SJ* T: (01443) 691481 E: micktaylor61@gmail.com

TAYLOR, Michael Andrew James. b 40. Univ Coll Ches BTh 96. d 99 p 00. NSM Halliwell *Man* 99–11; TV 03–11; rtd 11; PtO *Man* from 11. *123 Smithills Dean Road, Bolton BL1 6JZ* T: (01204) 491503 E: majtaylor123@aol.com

TAYLOR, Michael Barry. b 38. Leeds Univ MA 96. Bps' Coll Cheshunt 63. d 65 p 66. C Leeds St Cypr Harehills *Ripon* 65–68; C Stanningley St Thos 68–70; V Hunslet Moor St Pet and St Cuth 70–78; V Starbeck 78–00; rtd 00; PtO *Leic* 00–16; *Glouc* from 16. *13 Capel Court, The Burgage, Prestbury, Cheltenham GL52 3EL* T: (01242) 517969

TAYLOR, Michael Frank Chatterton. b 30. St Aid Birkenhead 59. d 61 p 62. C Knighton St Jo *Leic* 61–65; V Briningham *Nor* 65–86; R Melton Constable w Swanton

Novers 65–86; P-in-c Thornage w Brinton w Hunworth and Stody 85–86; R Lyng w Sparham 86–90; R Elsing w Bylaugh 86–90; R Lyng, Sparham, Elsing and Bylaugh 90–95; RD Sparham 92–95; rtd 95; PtO *Portsm* from 95. *The Rhond, 33 Station Road, St Helens, Ryde PO33 1YF* T/F: (01983) 873531 M: 07989-274848 E: mfct@uwclub.net

TAYLOR, Michael John. b 50. **d** 07 **p** 08. OLM Went Valley *Wakef* 07–11; NSM Pontefract St Giles 11–14; *Leeds* 14–19; NSM Pontefract 19–20; rtd 20; PtO *Leeds* 20–21. *19 Windsor Rise, Pontefract WF8 4PZ* T: (01977) 702824 M: 07968-932135

TAYLOR, Canon Michael Joseph. b 49. Gregorian Univ Rome STB 72 PhL 74 Birm Univ MA 81 Nottm Univ PhD 05. English Coll Rome 67. **d** 72 **p** 73. In RC Ch 72–83; Hon C Newport Pagnell w Lathbury *Ox* 83–85; Hon C Newport Pagnell w Lathbury and Moulsoe 85–86; TV Langley Marish 86–90; Vice Prin EMMTC *S'well* 90–97; Prin 97–06; R Gedling 06–16; P-in-c Lambley 11–16; Hon Can S'well Minster 00–16; rtd 16; PtO *S'well* from 16. *55 Field Lane, Beeston, Nottingham NG9 5FF* T: 0115-925 9228

TAYLOR, Michael Noel. b 40. Leeds Univ BSc 62 PGCE 63. EMMTC 95. **d** 98 **p** 99. NSM Woodthorpe *S'well* 98–02; NSM Gedling Deanery 02–03; NSM Epperstone, Gonalston, Oxton and Woodborough 03–10; NSM Calverton 03–10; rtd 10; PtO *S'well* from 11. *16 Church Meadow, Calverton, Nottingham NG14 6HG* T: 0115-847 3718 F: 912 7671 M: 07713-125771 E: michael.taylor21@ntlworld.com

TAYLOR, Michael Stewart. b 58. St Mich Coll Llan BTh 91. **d** 91 **p** 92. C Llangunnor w Cwmffrwd *St D* 91–94; V Llansantffraed and Llanbadarn Trefeglwys etc 94–97; P-in-c Jersey St Andr *Win* 97–99; V 99–16; P-in-c Freshford, Limpley Stoke and Hinton Charterhouse *B & W* from 16. *The Rectory, Crowe Lane, Freshford, Bath BA2 7WB* T: (01225) 723570 E: vicarmike@gmail.com

TAYLOR, Michelle Deborah. b 67. Trin Coll Bris 16. **d** 18 **p** 19. C Trendlewood CD *B & W* from 18. *16 Briar Close, Nailsea, Bristol BS48 1QG* M: 07969-243222

TAYLOR, Mrs Monica. b 39. **d** 06 **p** 07. OLM Wyke *Guildf* 06–09; PtO 09–16; *Cant* from 17. *8 Lime Trees, Staplehurst, Tonbridge TN12 0SS* E: mrsmonicataylor@hotmail.com

TAYLOR, Neil Andrew. b 56. ERMC 13. **d** 15 **p** 16. NSM Chigwell and Chigwell Row *Chelmsf* 15–17; NSM Chipping Ongar w Shelley etc from 17. *The Rectory, 52 Epping Road, Toot Hill, Ongar CM5 9SQ*

TAYLOR, Canon Nicholas Hugh. b 63. Cape Town Univ BA 83 MA 87 Dur Univ PhD 91 Ox Univ MTh 07. **d** 96 **p** 97. Lect and Chapl Univ of Swaziland 95–98; Chapl St Mich Sch Manzini 96–98; Sen Lect Africa Univ Zimbabwe 98–01; Can Th Mutare Cathl from 99; Dioc Dir Th Educn Manicaland 99–01; R Penhalonga 00–01; Assoc Prof Pretoria Univ S Africa 02–03; R Pretoria St Hilda 02–03; R Pretoria N St Mary 03; Hon C Smithfield St Bart Gt *Lon* 04; Research Fell Univ of Zululand S Africa 04–17; Hon Tutor Ripon Coll Cuddesdon 04–05; Lect K Coll Lon 06; PtO *Nor* 04–12; *Ox* 05–07; R Clarkston *Glas* from 09; Tutor TISEC 10–14; Tutor Scottish Episc Inst from 18. *St Aidan's Rectory, 8 Golf Road, Clarkston, Glasgow G76 7LZ* T: 0141-638 3080 M: 07944-091132 E: n.h.taylor@ripon.oxon.org *or* rector.staidansclarkston@gmail.com

TAYLOR, Preb Nicholas James. b 46. St Chad's Coll Dur BA 67. **d** 69 **p** 70. C Beamish *Dur* 69–74; C Styvechale *Cov* 74–77; P-in-c Wilmcote w Billesley 77–79; P-in-c Aston Cantlow 77–79; V Aston Cantlow and Wilmcote w Billesley 79–87; V Cov St Fran N Radford 87–97; RD Cov N 93–97; V Wilton *B & W* 97–11; Preb Wells Cathl 08–11; rtd 11; PtO *B & W* from 15. *50 Summerlands Park Avenue, Ilminster TA19 9BT* T: (01460) 929392 M: 07761-437505 E: nickruthtaylor@gmail.com

TAYLOR, Nicholas John. b 48. Leeds Univ BSc 69. St Mich Coll Llan BTh 09. **d** 09 **p** 10. NSM Griffithstown *Mon* 09–13; NSM Panteg and Griffithstown 13–17; rtd 17. *Little Barton, Trelleck, Monmouth NP25 4PE* M: 07860-507258 E: revnjt@btinternet.com

TAYLOR, Nigel James. b 73. Lanc Univ BA 94. Trin Coll Bris BA 11. **d** 11 **p** 12. C Risborough *Ox* 11–15; C Idle *Leeds* 15–18; V from 18. *17 Greencroft Close, Idle, Bradford BD10 8XD* M: 07749-816265 E: revdjimtaylor@gmail.com

TAYLOR, Nigel Roy. b 63. Keele Univ MA 01 RGN 86 RMN 89. Qu Coll Birm 10. **d** 12 **p** 13. C Walsall St Paul *Lich* 12–15; C Walsall St Luke 12–15; TV Kidderminster Ismere *Worc* 15–18; TR from 18; Ind Chapl from 15. *42 Woodlands Road, Cookley, Kidderminster DY10 3TL* E: revnrt@icloud.com

TAYLOR, Nigel Thomas Wentworth. b 60. Bris Univ BA 82 Ox Univ BA 86. Wycliffe Hall Ox 84. **d** 87 **p** 88. C Ches Square St Mich w St Phil *Lon* 87–91; C Roxeth Ch Ch and Harrow St Pet 91–93; TV Roxeth 93–97; V S Mimms Ch Ch 97–16;

AD Cen Barnet 04–09; Dir Tr and Development Edmonton Area from 16. *3 Guildown Avenue, London N12 7DE* T: (020) 8445 8495 *or* 3837 5254 E: nigel.taylor@london.anglican.org

TAYLOR, Mrs Noelle Rosemary. b 58. NTMTC 02. **d** 05 **p** 06. C St Mary-at-Latton *Chelmsf* 05–08; TV Gt Parndon 08–14; V 14–15; P-in-c Chipping Ongar w Shelley 15–17; R Chipping Ongar w Shelley etc from 17. *The Rectory, Shakletons, Ongar CM5 9AT* T: (01277) 362173 E: noelletaylor@hotmail.com

TAYLOR, Norman Adrian. b 48. Ho of Sacred Miss 64 St D Coll Lamp 70. **d** 73 **p** 74. C Fleur-de-Lis *Mon* 73–75; C W Drayton *Lon* 75–79; C-in-c Hayes St Edm CD 79–85; V Hayes St Edm 85–87; V Pilton w Ashford *Ex* 87–89; V Sidley *Chich* 89–02; Chapl Hastings and Rother NHS Trust 00–02; V Durrington *Chich* 02–13; rtd 13; PtO *Chich* 13–17. *7 Guernsey Road, Ferring, Worthing BN12 5PN* T: (01903) 245939 E: frnormantaylor@gmail.com

TAYLOR, Mrs Patricia Anne. b 56. TCD BTh 05. CITC 03. **d** 05 **p** 06. C Wicklow w Killiskey *D & G* 05–10; TV Smestow Vale *Lich* 10–13; rtd 13; PtO *Lich* 13–16; *Wakef* 14; *Leeds* from 14. *2 Poplar Avenue, Shafton, Barnsley S72 8PU* E: patricia.taylor@gmail.com

TAYLOR, Patricia Mary. b 52. Goldsmiths' Coll Lon BEd 80. Wycliffe Hall Ox 06. **d** 09 **p** 10. NSM Upper Holloway *Lon* 09–12 and 12–13; NSM Wandsworth St Mich w St Steph *S'wark* from 13. *1 Beloe Close, London SW15 5RB* M: 07880-656395 E: patricia@stmikes-ststeves.org.uk *or* patricia-taylor@hotmail.co.uk

TAYLOR, Patrick James. b 72. Magd Coll Cam BA 96 MA 99 MEng 96 K Coll Lon MA 11. Ripon Coll Cuddesdon BA 00. **d** 01 **p** 02. C Kenilworth St Nic *Cov* 01–05; TV Solihull *Birm* 05–14; R Stratford-upon-Avon, Luddington etc *Cov* from 14. *The Vicarage, 7 Old Town, Stratford-upon-Avon CV37 6BG* T: (01789) 508155 E: vicar@stratford-upon-avon.org

TAYLOR, Paul. b 63. RGN 85. Sarum & Wells Th Coll 92 Linc Th Coll BTh 95. **d** 95 **p** 96. C Boultham *Linc* 95–98; C Ditton St Mich w St Thos *Liv* 98–00; V Bickerstaffe and Melling 00–06; TV N Meols 06–08; rtd 08; Chapl St Helens and Knowsley Hosps NHS Trust from 13. *139 Sussex Road, Southport PR8 6AF* T: (01704) 500617 E: paulandjotaylor@virginmedia.com

TAYLOR, Paul Jeremy. b 72. Brunel Univ BSc 96 Moorlands Coll MA 11. Ridley Hall Cam 02. **d** 04 **p** 05. C Longfleet Sarum 04–08; V Hordle *Win* 08–20; V Barnstaple Trin and Goodleigh *Ex* from 20. *Holy Trinity Vicarage, Victoria Road, Barnstaple EX32 9HP* M: 07776-425621 E: pjtaylorsurfing@hotmail.com

TAYLOR, The Ven Paul Stanley. b 53. Ox Univ BEd 75 MTh 98. Westcott Ho Cam. **d** 84 **p** 85. C Bush Hill Park St Steph *Lon* 84–88; Asst Dir Post Ord Tr Edmonton Episc Area 87–94; Dir Post Ord Tr 94-00 and 02–04; V Southgate St Andr *Lon* 88–97; V Hendon St Mary 97–01; V Hendon St Mary and Ch Ch 01–04; AD W Barnet 00–04; Adn Sherborne *Sarum* 04–18; Can and Preb Sarum Cathl 04–18; rtd 18; PtO *Birm* from 19; *Lich* 19–21. *2 Blackwell Lane, Redditch B97 6SS* T: (01527) 591699 M: 07796-691203 E: pstaylor53@gmail.com

TAYLOR, Peter. b 51. St Jo Coll Cam BA 72 MA 76. Ridley Hall Cam 73. **d** 76 **p** 77. C Roch St Pet w St Marg 76–79; PtO *Ely* 79–99 and 05–06; NSM Downham 99–05; P-in-c Coveney 06–17; RD Ely 09–14; Bp's Adv for Self-Supporting Min 10–14; PtO from 17. *Gravel Head Farm, Downham Common, Little Downham, Ely CB6 2TY* T: (01353) 698714 F: 699107 E: peter@taylormonroe.co.uk

TAYLOR, Canon Peter David. b 47. Liv Univ BEd 74 Man Univ MEd 78 Lanc Univ MA 88. NOC 78. **d** 81 **p** 82. C Formby H Trin *Liv* 81–84; V Stoneycroft All SS 84–91; Chapl St Kath Coll 91–96; Dioc RE Field Officer 91–96; Dioc Dir of Educn *Leic* 96–09; Hon Can Leic Cathl 98–09; Dir Operations Ch Academy Services Ltd *Pet* 09–11; rtd 11; PtO *Leic* from 09. *87 Main Street, Humberstone, Leicester LE5 1AE* T: 0116-220 1461 *or* (01733) 566575 E: peter.tay1947@gmail.com

TAYLOR, Peter David. b 38. FCA. NOC 77. **d** 80 **p** 81. C Penwortham St Mary *Blackb* 80–84; V Farington 84–92; V Euxton 92–04; rtd 04; PtO *Blackb* 04–20. *33 Aspendale Close, Longton, Preston PR4 5LJ* T: (01772) 614795

TAYLOR, The Ven Peter Flint. b 44. Qu Coll Cam BA 65 MA 69. Lon Coll of Div BD 70. **d** 70 **p** 71. C Highbury New Park St Aug *Lon* 70–73; C Plymouth St Andr w St Paul and St Geo *Ex* 73–77; V Ironville *Derby* 77–83; P-in-c Riddings 82–83; R Rayleigh *Chelmsf* 83–96; Chapl HM YOI Bullwood Hall 85–90; RD Rochford *Chelmsf* 89–96; Adn Harlow 96–09; rtd 09; PtO *Ex* from 09. *5 Springfield Terrace, Springfield Road, South Brent TQ10 9AP* T: (01364) 73427 E: peterftaylor@pjtmail.net

TAYLOR, Peter John. b 46. Tyndale Hall Bris 70. **d** 73 **p** 74. C Walshaw Ch Ch *Man* 73–75; C Rodbourne Cheney *Bris*

75–78; Asst Chapl HM Pris Pentonville 78–79; Chapl HM Borstal Roch 79–84; Chapl HM Pris Highpoint 84–90; Asst Chapl Gen of Pris 90–01; rtd 01. *The Old Butchery, The Street, Redgrave, Diss IP22 1RY* T: (01379) 890368 E: peterblowingrock@aol.com

TAYLOR, Peter John. b 40. Oak Hill Th Coll 62. **d** 65 **p** 66. C St Paul's Cray St Barn *Roch* 65–69; C Woking St Jo *Guildf* 69–77; R Necton w Holme Hale *Nor* 77–94; R Necton, Holme Hale w N and S Pickenham 95–05; RD Breckland 86–94; Hon Can Nor Cathl 98–03; rtd 05; PtO *Nor* from 05. *5 Starling Close, Aylsham, Norwich NR11 6XG* T: (01263) 731964

TAYLOR, Peter Joseph. b 41. Bps' Coll Cheshunt 66. **d** 68 **p** 69. C Wollaton *S'well* 68–71; C Cockington *Ex* 71–74; V Broadhembury 74–79; V Broadhembury w Payhembury 79–81; V Gt Staughton *Ely* 81–86; V Gt Paxton and R Offord D'Arcy w Offord Cluny 86–01; Chapl HM YOI Gaynes Hall 81–91; rtd 01; PtO *Ely* 01–18; *St Alb* 07–16. *9 Park Way, Offord Cluny, St Neots PE19 5RW* T: (01480) 811662 E: peter.taylor9@talktalk.net

TAYLOR, Mrs Rachel Sara. b 60. Univ Coll Lon BA 81. SEITE 98. **d** 01 **p** 02. C Wimbledon *S'wark* 01–05; V Motspur Park from 05; AD Merton from 19. *The Vicarage, 2 Douglas Avenue, New Malden KT3 6HT* T: (020) 8942 3117 E: holycrossvicarage@btinternet.com

TAYLOR, Ralph Urmson. Tulsa Univ MA 72 Man Coll of Educn DipEd 74 TCert 82. Kelham Th Coll. **d** 56 **p** 57. C Redcar *York* 57–59; C Bridlington Quay H Trin 59–62; C Sewerby w Marton 60–62; Asst P Tulsa H Trin USA 62–65; Chapl Holland Hall Sch 65–93; rtd 93; Sacr Tulsa H Trin USA 93–02. *43 East Cliffe, Lytham St Annes FY8 5DX*

TAYLOR, Raymond. b 34. Lon Coll of Div 62. **d** 65 **p** 66. C Pennington *Man* 65–70; P-in-c Wombridge *Lich* 70–80; R S Normanton *Derby* 80–88; RD Alfreton 86–88; V Youlgreave, Middleton, Stanton-in-Peak etc 88–98; rtd 99; PtO *Derby* 98–18. *4 Jeffries Avenue, Crich, Matlock DE4 5DU* T: (01773) 856845

TAYLOR, Raymond Montgomery. b 43. Oak Hill Th Coll 77. **d** 80 **p** 81. Hon C Cricklewood St Pet *Lon* 80–85; Hon C Golders Green 85–87; V New Southgate St Paul 87–00; AD Cen Barnet 96–00; V Thaxted *Chelmsf* 00–13; rtd 13; PtO *Chelmsf* 13–18. *2 Crescent Close, Dunmow CM6 1DE* T: (01371) 874809 E: vade.mecum@outlook.com

TAYLOR, Richard Godfrey. b 73. Pemb Coll Cam MA 99. Oak Hill Th Coll BA 00. **d** 00 **p** 01. C Brunswick *Man* 00–04; C Aldridge *Lich* 04–09; V Clapham Common St Barn *S'wark* from 09; AD Battersea from 16. *The Vicarage, 8 Lavender Gardens, London SW11 1DL* T: (020) 7223 5953 E: fatboytaylor@gmail.com

TAYLOR, Richard John. b 46. Ripon Coll Cuddesdon 85. **d** 85 **p** 86. C Moseley St Mary *Birm* 85–87; V Kingsbury 87–91; TR Hodge Hill 91–03; P-in-c 03–05; R Weston super Mare St Jo *B & W* 05–16; RD Locking 08–16; rtd 16; PtO *B & W* from 18. *2 Ringwood Grove, Weston-super-Mare BS23 2UA*

TAYLOR, Robert Ian. b 68. St Jo Coll Nottm. **d** 08 **p** 09. C Buttershaw St Paul *Bradf* 08–12; Chapl Bradf Academy 08–19; PtO *Leeds* 20–21. *52 Bowling Park Drive, East Bowling, Bradford BD4 7ES* T: (01274) 788722 E: robtlr@aol.com

TAYLOR, Robin. *See* TAYLOR, Joseph Robin Christopher

TAYLOR, Roger James Benedict. b 42. Glouc Sch of Min 89 WMMTC 95. **d** 96 **p** 97. NSM Cromhall w Tortworth and Tytherington *Glouc* 96–99; P-in-c Wistanstow *Heref* 99–01; Min Can Brecon Cathl *S & B* 01–07; Chapl Brecon War Memorial Hosp 01–07; Chapl St Oswald's Almshouses 08–12; rtd 12. *9 Jubilee Close, Bidford-on-Avon, Alcester B50 4ED* E: rogertaylor.burdon@gmail.com

TAYLOR, Rosemary Edith. *See* JENKINS, Rosemary Edith

TAYLOR, Roy William. b 37. Ch Coll Cam BA 61 MA 64. Clifton Th Coll 61. **d** 63 **p** 64. C Blackb Sav 63–66; C Hensingham *Carl* 66–68; CMS Taiwan 69–79; TV Bushbury *Lich* 79–85; OMF 85–93; Hon C Wolverhampton St Jude *Lich* 93–94; P-in-c Torquay St Jo and Ellacombe *Ex* 94–99; R Instow and V Westleigh 99–03; RD Hartland 01–03; rtd 03. *31 Shore Road, Millisle, Newtownards BT22 2BT* T: (028) 9186 2769 E: roy.31@btinternet.com

TAYLOR, Simon Dominic Kent. b 69. Surrey Univ BSc 90 W Sussex Inst of HE PGCE 91 Sussex Univ MA(Ed) 99. Trin Coll Bris BA 01. **d** 01 **p** 02. C Southgate *Chich* 01–04; TV 04–10; Dioc Officer for Emerging Leadership 04–10; R Busbridge and Hambledon *Guildf* from 10; AD Godalming from 19. *Spinney Copse, Hambledon Road, Godalming GU7 1PJ* T: (01483) 421267 E: simon.taylor@bhcgodalming.org

TAYLOR, Simon John. b 72. Worc Coll Ox BA 94 MPhil 96 MA 99 DPhil 00. St Mich Coll Llan 00 Ven English Coll Rome 01. **d** 02 **p** 03. C Cotham St Sav w St Mary and Clifton St Paul *Bris* 02–06; P-in-c Bris St Mary Redcliffe w Temple etc 06–12; CMD Officer and Can Res Derby Cathl 12–19; AD

Derby City 18–19; Hd of Min Development *Bris* from 19; Warden of Readers from 20. *Bristol Diocesan Board of Finance, Hillside House, Bristol Parkway North, Newbrick Road, Stoke Gifford, Bristol BS34 8YU* T: 0117-906 0100

TAYLOR, Simon Wheldon. b 62. **d** 12 **p** 13. NSM Tunbridge Wells St Phil *Roch* 12–15; NSM Stapleford *Ely* from 15. *The Vicarage, 43 Mingle Lane, Stapleford, Cambridge CB22 5SY* T: (01892) 782043 M: 07970-716163 E: st@cloisters.com

TAYLOR, Stephen Charles. b 53. St Edm Hall Ox BA 75 Ex Univ PGCE 78. WEMTC 05. **d** 08 **p** 09. NSM Highnam, Lassington, Rudford, Tibberton etc *Glouc* 08–13; P-in-c Westbury-on-Severn w Flaxley, Blaisdon etc 13–20; rtd 20; PtO *Glouc* from 21. *Address withheld by request* T: (01452) 760756 E: stevewillstay@gmail.com

TAYLOR, Stephen Gordon. b 35. Bris Univ BA 60. Ridley Hall Cam 60. **d** 62 **p** 63. C Gt Baddow *Chelmsf* 62–65; C Portsdown *Portsm* 65–69; P-in-c Elvedon *St E* 69–70; R 70–75; P-in-c Eriswell 69–70; R 70–75; P-in-c Icklingham 69–70; R 70–75; Chapl St Felix Sch Southwold 75–77; R Lt Shelford w Newton *Ely* 77–96; rtd 96; PtO *Ely* 96–17. *15 Church Close, Whittlesford, Cambridge CB22 4NY* T: (01223) 830461 E: sgt707@btinternet.com

TAYLOR, Stephen James. b 48. Chich Th Coll 70. **d** 73 **p** 74. C Tottenham St Paul *Lon* 73–76; St Vincent 78–85; C Grenada 85–88; C-in-c Hammersmith SS Mich and Geo White City Estate CD *Lon* 88–96; AD Hammersmith 92–96; P-in-c Hammersmith St Luke 94–96; USPG Brazil 96–08; PtO *Lon* from 14. *12 Bletchley Court, Wenlock Street, London N1 7NX* T: (020) 7253 8629 E: stephentaylor2001@hotmail.com

TAYLOR, Stephen Mark. b 65. City Univ BSc 87 Lon Univ PGCE 90. NTMTC 95. **d** 98 **p** 99. Chapl Bp Stopford's Sch Enfield 98–02 and 03–06; NSM Enfield Chase St Mary *Lon* 98–02; PtO *Eur* 02–03; C Hornsey St Mary w St Geo *Lon* 03–06; P-in-c March St Jo *Ely* 06–08; Hon Asst Dir of Ords 07–08; P-in-c Enfield St Mich *Lon* 08–13; V from 13. *The Vicarage, 2 Gordon Hill, Enfield EN2 0QP* T: (020) 8363 1063 M: 07711-559107 E: stephen.taylor@london.anglican.org

TAYLOR, Canon Stephen Ronald. b 55. MBE 09. Dur Univ MA 99. Cranmer Hall Dur 80. **d** 83 **p** 84. C Chester le Street *Dur* 83–87; V Newbottle 87–92; V Stranton 92–00; TR Sunderland 00–07; Provost Sunderland Minster 07–11; Hon Can Dur Cathl 06–11; Adn Maidstone *Cant* 11–20; Chapl to Bp Dover from 20; Hon Can Rift Valley Tanzania from 00; Hon Fell Sunderland Univ *Dur* from 09. *The Old Palace, The Precincts, Canterbury CT1 2EE*

TAYLOR, Stewart. b 51. Cranmer Hall Dur 74. **d** 77 **p** 78. C Norwood St Luke *S'wark* 77–81; C Surbiton Hill Ch Ch 81–91; V Cambridge St Phil *Ely* 91–21; rtd 21. *46 Thorn Lodge Park, Milton, Cambridge CB24 6UB* M: 07306-203689 E: stewarttaylor1@hotmail.co.uk

TAYLOR, Canon Stuart Bryan. b 40. St Chad's Coll Dur BA 64. **d** 66 **p** 67. C Portsea N End St Mark *Portsm* 66–70; C Epsom St Martin *Guildf* 70–76; Chapl Clifton Coll Bris 76–88; Dir Bloxham Project 88–93; Chapl Giggleswick Sch 93–95; Bp's Officer for Miss and Evang *Bris* 96–01; Bp's Adv for Past Care for Clergy and Families 01–10; Hon Min Can Bris Cathl 02–04; Chapl Bris Cathl Sch 01–09; Hon Can Bris Cathl 04–10; rtd 10; PtO *B & W* from 12; *Bris* from 14. *62 Providence Lane, Long Ashton, Bristol BS41 9DN* T: (01275) 393625 M: 07974-316489 E: sbtbristol@gmail.com

TAYLOR, Susan Ann. b 57. **d** 16 **p** 17. NSM Gillingham St Mary *Roch* 16–17; NSM Gillingham H Trin from 17. *14 Century Road, Gillingham ME8 0BG* T: (01634) 235058 M: 07910-701806 E: taylorlodge14@gmail.com

TAYLOR, Mrs Susan Mary. b 51. Ex Univ LLB 73 St Anne's Coll Ox BCL 75 Solicitor 78. SEITE 03. **d** 06 **p** 07. NSM Barkingside St Laur *Chelmsf* 06–12; Chapl Evelina Children's Hosp from 12; Chapl Guy's and St Thos' NHS Foundn Trust from 13; PtO *S'wark* 10–13; *Chelmsf* from 12. *Norwood, North End, Buckhurst Hill IG9 5RA* T: (020) 8504 9867 *or* 7188 7188 E: suetaylorathome@aol.com *or* sue.taylor@gstt.nhs.uk

TAYLOR, Mrs Teresa Mary. b 53. SRN 76 SCM 78. WEMTC 98. **d** 02 **p** 03. NSM Kingswood *Bris* 02–12; Chapl Freeways Trust from 07; P-in-c Mangotsfield *Bris* 12–13; V from 13. *19 Hicks Avenue, Emersons Green, Bristol BS16 7HA* E: revtmt@blueyonder.co.uk

TAYLOR, Thomas. b 33. Sarum & Wells Th Coll 77. **d** 80 **p** 81. NSM Heatherlands St Jo *Sarum* 80–82; TV Kinson 82–88; TV Shaston 88–98; Chapl Westmr Memorial Hosp Shaftesbury 88–98; rtd 98; PtO *Sarum* 98–12. *10 Hanover Lane, Gillingham SP8 4TA* T: (01747) 826569

TAYLOR, Thomas. b 42. St Jo Coll Dur BA 64 Leeds Univ MA 02. Linc Th Coll 64. **d** 66 **p** 67. C Clitheroe St Mary *Blackb* 66–69; C Skerton St Luke 69–71; C-in-c Penwortham

St Leon CD 71–72; V Penwortham St Leon 72–78; R Poulton-le-Sands 78–81; P-in-c Morecambe St Lawr 78–81; R Poulton-le-Sands w Morecambe St Laur 81–85; Chapl Lord Wandsworth Coll Hook 85–92; V Walton-le-Dale *Blackb* 92–94; P-in-c Samlesbury 92–94; V Walton-le-Dale St Leon w Samlesbury St Leon 95–96; RD Leyland 94–96; Hon C Tarleton 03–11; Hon C Rufford and Tarleton 11–12; PtO from 12. *52 Hesketh Lane, Tarleton, Preston PR4 6AQ* T: (01772) 813871 E: rustichouse@bigfoot.com

TAYLOR, Timothy Robert. b 62. W Midl Coll of Educn BEd 87 Cumbria Univ BA 10. LCTP 07. **d** 10 **p** 11. NSM Egremont and Haile *Carl* from 10. *42 Abbey Vale, St Bees CA27 0EF* T: (01946) 822255 E: timothy@trtaylor.co.uk

TAYLOR, Willam Goodacre Campbell. See CAMPBELL-TAYLOR, William Goodacre

TAYLOR, Capt William Thomas. b 61. Rob Coll Cam BA 83 BA 90. Ridley Hall Cam 88. **d** 91 **p** 92. C Bromley Ch Ch *Roch* 91–95; C St Helen Bishopsgate w St Andr Undershaft etc *Lon* 95–98; R from 98; R St Pet Cornhill from 01. *St Helen's Church, Great St Helens, London EC3A 6AT* T: (020) 7283 2231

TAYLOR-COOK, Andrew. b 62. ERMC. **d** 08 **p** 09. C Wirksworth *Derby* 08–12; Chapl amongst Deaf People *Ox* 12–13; Chapl amongst Deaf People *Pet* 12–15; C Guilsborough and Hollowell and Cold Ashby etc 13–15; P-in-c Codnor *Derby* 15–19; P-in-c Horsley and Denby 15–19; P-in-c Loscoe 15–19; P-in-c Horsley Woodhouse 15–19; V Denby Gp 19–20; R Innerleithen *Edin* from 20; R Peebles from 20. *Tweeddale Rectory, 45 Edderston Road, Peebles EH45 9DT* T: (01721) 588648 E: andrewtc@btinternet.com

TAYLOR-KENYON (née THOMPSON), Louise Margaret. b 61. Clare Coll Cam BA 83 MA 07 Homerton Coll Cam PGCE 84 Leeds Univ MA 07. NOC 04. **d** 07 **p** 08. C Skipton H Trin *Bradf* 07–10; C Skipton Ch Ch w Carleton 07–10; C Embsay w Eastby 10–14; V 14; *Leeds* 14–19; CME Officer 10–19; V Bamburgh, Belford and Lucker *Newc* from 19; AD Bamburgh and Glendale from 19. *20 Radcliffe Park, Bamburgh NE69 7AN* M: 07545-235362 E: revdlouisetk@greennet.org.uk

TEAL, Andrew Robert. b 64. Birm Univ BA 85 PhD 06 Ox Brookes Univ PGCE 05 Pemb Coll Ox MA 08. Ripon Coll Cuddesdon 86. **d** 88 **p** 89. C Wednesbury St Paul Wood Green *Lich* 88–92; TV Sheff Manor 92–97; Asst Post-Ord Tr Officer 93–98; Tutor Ripon Coll Cuddesdon 92–97; V Tickhill w Stainton *Sheff* 97–02; Warden of Readers 98–02; Hd of Th Plater Coll 02–03; Hd of Th and Past Studies 03–05; Chapl Pemb Coll Ox from 05; Fell from 08; Lect Ripon Coll Cuddesdon 08–20; Warden Sisters of the Love of God Ox from 09; Lect Th Ox Univ from 07. *Pembroke College, Oxford OX1 1DW* T: (01865) 286276 F: 276418 E: andrew.teal@theology.ox.ac.uk

TEALE, Adrian. b 53. Univ of Wales (Abth) BA 74 CertEd 77 MA 80 Univ of Wales (Cardiff) MTh 89. Wycliffe Hall Ox 78. **d** 80 **p** 81. C Betws w Ammanford *St D* 80–84; V Brynaman w Cwmllynfell 84–19; P-in-c Bro Aman from 19; RD Dyffryn Aman 95–01. *Y Dalar Deg, 10 Bryn Road, Upper Brynamman, Ammanford SA18 1AU* T: (01269) 822275 E: tinkerteale@googlemail.com

TEAR, Jeremy Charles. b 67. Westmr Coll Ox BA 89 Birm Univ MA 99 MCIPD 94. Aston Tr Scheme 95 Qu Coll Birm 97. **d** 99 **p** 00. C Timperley *Ches* 99–03; V Macclesfield St Paul 03–10; C Caversham Thameside and Mapledurham *Ox* 10–15; TV Warrington W *Liv* 15–17; TR from 17. *St Paul's Vicarage, 6 Poplar Avenue, Penketh, Warrington WA5 2EH* T: (01925) 485288 E: revjeremytear@gmail.com

TEARE, Adrian Jeremy. b 79. Van Mildert Coll Dur BA 01 G&C Coll Cam BA 10 MA 15. Westcott Ho Cam 08. **d** 12 **p** 14. C Tottenham St Paul *Lon* 12–13; C Kilburn St Mary w All So and W Hampstead St Jas 13–14; C Palmers Green St Jo 14–15; PtO 15–18; Chapl Chelsea and Westmr Hosp NHS Foundn Trust 15–18; Hon Chapl S Lon and Maudsley NHS Foundn Trust 16–18; Lead Chapl R Surrey NHS Foundn Trust from 18; CF (VR) from 20. *Address withheld by request* E: a.teare@nhs.net

TEARE, Mrs Marie. b 46. Open Univ BA 81 RSCN 67. NOC 95. **d** 98 **p** 99. C Brighouse and Clifton *Wakef* 98–01; V Waggoners *York* 01–08; RD Harthill 02–08; rtd 08; PtO *York* from 08; Eur 17–21. *Mayfield Lodge, Easingwold Road, Huby, York YO61 1HN* T: (01347) 811565 E: marie.teare@btinternet.com

TEARE, Canon Robert John Hugh. b 39. Bris Univ BSc 62. Coll of Resurr Mirfield 67. **d** 70 **p** 71. C Fareham SS Pet and Paul *Portsm* 70–73; Chapl K Alfred Coll Win 73–78; V Pokesdown St Jas 78–82; R Winnall 82–06; RD Win 89–99; Hon Can Win Cathl 92–06; rtd 06; Chapl CSMV 06–09; PtO Ox 09–11; P-in-c Hanney, Denchworth and E Challow 11–12; PtO

from 12. *29 Elizabeth Drive, Wantage OX12 9YA* T: (01235) 770966 E: robertteare@gmail.com

TEARNAN, John Herman Janson. b 37. Bris Univ BSc 59. Kelham Th Coll 62. **d** 66 **p** 67. C Kettering SS Pet and Paul 66–71; LtO 71–85; PtO St Alb 82–85; Pet 85–94; Chapl HM YOI Wellingborough 89–90; Chapl HM YOI Glen Parva 90–94; Guyana 94–03; rtd 03; PtO *Pet* from 05. *14 Rectory Walk, Barton Seagrave, Kettering NN15 6SP* T: (01536) 510629 E: jaytee1937@btinternet.com

TEARNE, Jonathan Philip. b 84. Goldsmiths' Coll Lon BA 06 Birkbeck Coll Lon MSc 12. Wycliffe Hall Ox BA 18. **d** 19 **p** 20. C Emmaus Par Team *Leic* 19–21; C Oadby from 21. *Address withheld by request*

TEAROE, Mrs Tammy Elizabeth. b 71. Ripon Coll Cuddesdon 19. **d** 21. C Olton *Birm* from 21. *90 Monyhull Hall Road, Birmingham B30 3QJ* M: 07482-166667 E: curateofolton@gmail.com

TEASDALE, Angela. b 67. St Hild Coll 16. **d** 18 **p** 19. NSM Wadworth w Loversall and Balby *Sheff* 18–20; C The Marshland from 20. *Fernwood View, Littleworth Lane, Rossington, Doncaster DN11 0HD* E: teasdaleangela@aol.com

TEASDEL, David Charles. b 77. Coll of Resurr Mirfield 05. **d** 08 **p** 09. C Ouzel Valley *St Alb* 08–11; TV Staveley and Barrow Hill *Derby* 11–14; P-in-c Sharlston *Leeds* 14–16; V from 16; P-in-c Altofts 14–16; V from 16. *The Vicarage, 72A Church Road, Normanton WF6 2QG* T: (01928) 893110 M: 07914-045419 E: fatherdavidteasdel@gmail.com

TEBBOTH, Mrs Jennifer Mary. b 61. Univ Coll Lon BSc 82 RGN 87 Ox Brookes Univ PGCE 05. Ox Min Course 12. **d** 15 **p** 16. NSM Chalfont St Giles, Seer Green and Jordans *Ox* from 15. *40 Gaviots Way, Gerrards Cross SL9 7DX* T: (01753) 892940 M: 07708-094532 E: jenny.tebboth@btopenworld.com

TEBBS, Richard Henry. b 52. Southn Univ BTh. Sarum & Wells Th Coll 75. **d** 78 **p** 79. C Cinderhill *S'well* 78–82; C Nor St Pet Mancroft w St Jo Maddermarket 82–85; TV Bridport *Sarum* 85–94; TR Yelverton, Meavy, Sheepstor and Walkhampton *Ex* 94–08; P-in-c Frankley *Birm* 08–13; R 13–17; rtd 17; PtO *Lich* 18–21. *Severn Villa, 14 Waterside, Burton-on-Trent DE15 9HE*

TEBBUTT, Canon Christopher Michael. b 55. ACA CTA. St Jo Coll Nottm BA 99. **d** 96 **p** 97. C Catherington and Clanfield *Portsm* 96–00; P-in-c Southbroom *Sarum* 00–07; V 07–09; TR Canford Magna 09–21; TV from 21; RD Wimborne 11–16; Can and Preb Sarum Cathl from 12. *The Rectory, Canford Magna, Wimborne BH21 3AF* T: (01202) 882270 M: 07917-190307 E: rev.christebbutt@gmail.com

TEBBUTT, Sandra Eileen. b 56. FBDO 78. STETS 96. **d** 99 **p** 00. NSM Blendworth w Chalton w Idsworth *Portsm* 99–00; Chapl Wilts and Swindon Healthcare NHS Trust 00–05; Regional Manager Bible Soc from 05; NSM Southbroom *Sarum* 04–09; NSM Canford Magna from 10. *The Rectory, Canford Magna, Wimborne BH21 3AF* T: (01202) 883382 E: sandra.tebbutt@biblesociety.org.uk

TEBBY, Ms Janet Elizabeth. b 52. Open Univ BA 88 Lady Spencer Chu Coll of Educn CertEd 73. ERMC 05. **d** 08 **p** 09. NSM Wootton w Quinton and Preston Deanery *Pet* 08–12; TV Oakham, Ashwell, Braunston, Brooke, Egleton etc 12–17; rtd 17; Hon C Yardley Hastings, Denton and Grendon etc *Pet* from 18. *3 The Drive, Wellingborough NN8 2DB* T: (01933) 384628 E: jtebby@gmail.com

TEDD, Christopher Jonathan Richard. See HOWITZ, Christopher Jonathan Richard

TEECE, David. b 54. MIET. **d** 06 **p** 07. OLM Normanton *Wakef* 06–07; NSM Stanley 07–10 and 13–14; *Leeds* 14–17; NSM Ackworth *Wakef* 10–13; Outwood, Stanley and Wrenthorpe *Leeds* 17–20; NSM N Wakefield from 20. *31 Glebe Street, Castleford WF10 4AJ* T: (01977) 318453 M: 07500-907635 E: davidteece@gmail.com or david.teece@leeds.anglican.org

TEGALLY, Narinder Jit Kaur. b 57. RGN 93. SAOMC 99. **d** 02 **p** 03. NSM Welwyn Garden City *St Alb* 02–05; Asst Chapl R Free Hampstead NHS Trust 05–07; Sen Chapl Guy's and St Thos' NHS Foundn Trust 07–12; TV Beaconsfield *Ox* 12–17; Lead Sen Chapl R United Hosps Bath NHS Foundn Trust from 17; Asst Dir of Ords *B & W* from 19. *Chaplaincy Department, Royal United Hospital, Combe Park, Bath BA1 3NG* T: (01225) 824039 M: 07940-580859 E: narinder.tegally@nhs.net

TEGGARTY, Samuel James Karl. b 53. Dundee Univ BSc 77. CITC 98. **d** 01 **p** 02. NSM Newry *D & D* 01–03; NSM Kilkeel 03–15; P-in-c Castlewellan 05–06; P-in-c Aghaderg w Donaghmore and Scarva 16–19; rtd 20. *79 Knockchree Avenue, Kilkeel, Newry BT34 4BP* T: (028) 4176 9076 E: karl.teggarty@btinternet.com

TELEMAN, Roxana. See TENEA TELEMAN, Roxana Irina

TELEN, Salvador Roberto Sabornido. b 66. **d** 89 **p** 90. C Notting Hill St Jo *Lon* 05–10; Hon C Walthamstow St Sav

Chelmsf 12–13; P-in-c 13–14; V from 14; Hon C Walthamstow St Barn and St Jas Gt 12–13; P-in-c from 21; PtO *Lon* from 16; *St Alb* from 19. *St Saviour's Vicarage, 210 Markhouse Road, London E17 8EP* T: (020) 8520 2036 M: 07874-888138 E: father.telen@btinternet.com

TELFER, Andrew Julian. b 68. Essex Univ BA 94 Lon Sch of Th MA 18. Wycliffe Hall Ox BTh 97. d 97 p 98. C Skelmersdale St Paul *Liv* 97–01; C Ashton-in-Makerfield St Thos 01–03; V Whiston from 03. *The Vicarage, 90 Windy Arbor Road, Prescot L35 3SG* T: 0151-426 6329 E: ajtelfer@btinternet.com

TELFER, Canon Frank Somerville. b 30. Trin Hall Cam BA 53 MA 58. Ely Th Coll 53. d 55 p 56. C Liv Our Lady and St Nic 55–58; Chapl Down Coll Cam 58–62; Bp's Chapl *Nor* 62–65; Chapl Kent Univ *Cant* 65–73; Can Res Guildf Cathl 73–95; rtd 96; PtO *Nor* from 96. *Holbrook, Glandford, Holt NR25 7JP* T: (01263) 740586 E: fandjtelfer@btinternet.com

TELFORD, Alan. b 46. St Jo Coll Nottm. d 83 p 84. C Normanton *Derby* 83–86; TV N Wingfield, Pilsley and Tupton 86–90; TV N Wingfield, Clay Cross and Pilsley 90–92; P-in-c Oakwood 92–94; V Leic St Chris 94–05; P-in-c Leic St Theodore 05–09; rtd 09; PtO *Derby* from 09. *2 Springfield Cottage, Newmarket Lane, Clay Cross, Chesterfield S45 9AR* T: (01246) 866988 M: 07854-937449 E: atelford@talktalk.net

TELFORD, John Anthony. b 72. Oak Hill Th Coll BA 96. d 13 p 14. C Anlaby St Pet *York* 13–20; C Anlaby Common St Mark 13–20; C Kirk Ella and Willerby from 20. *St Luke's Vicarage, 2A Chestnut Avenue, Willerby, Hull HU10 6PA* M: 07956-100383 E: john.telfs@gmail.com *or* telford@btinternet.com

TELFORD, Richard Francis. b 46. K Coll Lon 65. d 69 p 70. C Barkingside H Trin *Chelmsf* 69–72; C Wickford 72–77; P-in-c Romford St Jo 77–80; V 80–82; PtO 93–96; rtd 08. *Juglans, The Street, Wattisfield, Diss IP22 1NS* E: richard_telford@hotmail.com

TEMBEY, David. b 51. d 96 p 97. NSM Whitehaven *Carl* 96–00; NSM Holme Cultram St Cuth 00–02; NSM Holme Cultram St Mary 00–02; NSM Bromfield w Waverton 00–02; TV Solway Plain 02–15; V Marske in Cleveland *York* from 15; RD Guisborough from 19. *The Vicarage, 6 Windy Hill Lane, Marske-by-the-Sea, Redcar TS11 7BN* T: (01642) 473119 E: tembey6@btinternet.com

TEMPERLEY-BARNES, Mrs Lisa Caroline. Westcott Ho Cam 09. d 11 p 12. C Newbold de Verdun, Barlestone and Kirkby Mallory *Leic* 11–13; C Bosworth and Sheepy Gp 13–14; R Woodhouse, Woodhouse Eaves and Swithland from 14. *St Paul's Rectory, 11 Paterson Drive, Woodhouse Eaves, Loughborough LE12 8RL* T: (01509) 890972 E: revdlisatemperley@gmail.com

TEMPEST, Anna. See STUTTARD, Anna

TEMPLE, Mrs Sylvia Mary. b 48. Ex Univ BA 70 Univ of Wales (Abth) PGCE 71. St D Dioc Tr Course 93. d 94 p 97. NSM Tenby *St D* 94–99; C 99–00; V Martletwy w Lawrenny and Minwear etc 00–05. *Llwyn Onn, Trafalgar Road, Tenby SA70 7DW*

TEMPLEMAN (née WILLIAMS), Mrs Ann Joyce. b 50. St Hugh's Coll Ox BA 72 MA 75 PGCE 73. Cranmer Hall Dur 03. d 05 p 06. Headmistress Dur High Sch for Girls 98–11; NSM Peterlee Dur 05–11; P-in-c Theale and Englefield Ox 11–18; R Hoole *Blackb* from 18. *The Rectory, 69 Liverpool Old Road, Much Hoole, Preston PR4 4RB* M: 07877-659156 E: anntempleman@live.co.uk

TEMPLEMAN, Peter Morton. b 49. Ch Ch Ox BA 71 MA 75. Wycliffe Hall Ox MA 75. d 76 p 77. C Cheltenham St Mary, St Matt, St Paul and H Trin *Glouc* 76–79; Chapl St Jo Coll Cam 79–84; P-in-c Finchley St Paul Long Lane *Lon* 84–85; P-in-c Finchley St Luke 84–85; V Finchley St Paul and St Luke 85–99; V Peterlee *Dur* 99–11; C Theale and Englefield *Ox* 11–18; PtO *Blackb* from 18. *The Rectory, 69 Liverpool Old Road, Much Hoole, Preston PR4 4RB* E: anntempleman@live.co.uk

TEMPLETON, Iain McAllister. b 57. St Andr Coll Drygrange 80. d 85 p 86. In RC Ch 85–92; NSM Dornoch *Mor* 95; P-in-c Kirriemuir *St And* 95–99; R Eccleston *Blackb* 99–09; V Walsall St Andr *Lich* from 09. *St Andrew's Vicarage, 119 Hollyhedge Lane, Walsall WS2 8PZ* T: (01922) 721658 E: fatheriain@aol.com

TEMPLETON, Susan Prichard Molison. b 83. R Holloway Coll Lon BSc 05 MA 11. Ripon Coll Cuddesdon 15. d 18 p 19. C Woodley *Ox* from 18. *25 Dunbar Drive, Woodley, Reading RG5 4HA* M: 07834-818751 E: susie.templeton@gmail.com

TEN WOLDE, Christine Caroline. b 57. d 99 p 00. NSM Llanegryn w Aberdyfi w Tywyn *Ban* 99–12; NSM Tywyn w Llanegryn w Aberdyfi w Tywyn 12–13; NSM Bro Ystumanner from 13. *Abergroes, Aberdovey LL35 0RE* T: (01654) 767047 F: 767572 M: 07977-108438 E: curate@stpeterschurch.org.uk

TENEA TELEMAN, Roxana Irina. b 63. ERMC 16. d 19 p 21. NSM Nice w Vence *Eur* 19–20; C Marseille w Aix-en-Provence and the Luberon from 20. *All Saints, 4 rue de Belloi, 13006 Marseille, France* T: (0033) 7 67 09 87 71 E: curate.anglican.marseille@gmail.com

TENGE-HESLOP, Mrs Sabine Ulrike. b 59. Goethe Univ Frankfurt MSc 83. Lindisfarne Regional Tr Partnership 12. d 17 p 18. NSM Harelaw and Annfield Plain *Dur* 17–19; NSM Brancepeth 19–21; Chapl Sheff Univ from 21. *University of Sheffield Chaplaincy, Octagon Centre, Clarkson Street, Sheffield S10 2TQ* E: s.u.tenge-heslop@durham.ac.uk

TENNANT, Cyril Edwin George. b 37. Keble Coll Ox BA 59 MA 63 Lon Univ BD 61 Ex Univ MA 03 Univ of Wales PhD 11. Clifton Th Coll 59. d 62 p 63. C Stapleford *S'well* 62–65; C Felixstowe SS Pet and Paul *St E* 65–69; V Gipsy Hill Ch Ch *S'wark* 69–84; V Lee St Mildred 84–90; P-in-c Lundy Is *Ex* 90–92; V Ilfracombe SS Phil and Jas w W Down 90–01; rtd 01; PtO *Ex* 01–06; *Ox* 06–08 and 12–18. *27 Harvest Way, Witney OX28 1BX* T: (01993) 778977 E: cyril.tennant@yahoo.co.uk

TER HAAR, Roger Edward Lound. b 52. QC 92. Magd Coll Ox BA 73. d 06 p 07. OLM Bramley and Grafham *Guildf* 06–13; PtO 17–20; *St D* from 17. *Testers, Upperton, Petworth GU28 9BE* T: (020) 7797 8100 E: terhaar@crownofficechambers.com

TERAUDKALNS, Valdis. b 64. Univ of Latvia PhD 00. Grand Rapids Th Sem MThSt 94 ERMC 18. d 20 p 21. NSM Riga, Latvia *Eur* from 20. *Zaubes 1-4, Riga LV 1013, Latvia* T: (00371) 2955 2398 E: valdis.teraudkalns@lu.lv

TERRANOVA, Jonathan Rossano (Ross). b 62. Sheff Poly BA 85 Heythrop Coll Lon MA 17. Oak Hill Th Coll BA 88. d 88 p 89. C Carl St Jo 88–91; C Stoughton *Guildf* 91–94; R Ditton *Roch* from 94; RD Malling 02–07. *The Rectory, 2 The Stream, Ditton, Maidstone ME20 6AG* T: (01732) 842027

TERRELL, Richard Charles Patridge. b 43. Wells Th Coll 69. d 71 p 72. C Shepton Mallet *B & W* 71–76; P-in-c Drayton 76–77; P-in-c Muchelney 76–77; TV Langport Area 78–82; P-in-c Tatworth 82–89; V 89–96; R W Coker w Hardington Mandeville, E Chinnock etc 96–09; rtd 09; PtO *B & W* from 09. *2 Hamdon View, Norton sub Hamdon, Stoke-sub-Hamdon TA14 6SE* T: (01935) 881330 M: 07736-836004 E: revrichardterrell@gmail.com

TERRY, Canon Christopher Laurence. b 51. Heythrop Coll Lon MA 09 FCA 80. St Alb Minl Tr Scheme. d 83 p 84. Hon C Dunstable *St Alb* 83–89; C Abbots Langley 89–92; TV Chambersbury 92–99; Chapl Abbot's Hill Sch Herts 96–99; R Southwick St Mich *Chich* 99–03; RD Hove 00–03; Finance and Admin Sec Min Division Abps' Coun 04–09; TR Gt Yarmouth *Nor* 09–16; RD 11–16; Hon Can Nor Cathl 13–16; rtd 16; PtO *Nor* from 16; *Worc* from 20. *5 Coates Drive, Pinvin, Pershore WR10 2DH* T: (01386) 718189 E: cterry925@btinternet.com

TERRY, Colin Alfred. b 49. Trin Coll Bris 98. d 00 p 01. C Bexleyheath Ch Ch *Roch* 00–03; V Belvedere All SS 03–10; Chapl Bromley Coll 10–12; P-in-c Lamorbey H Redeemer *Roch* 12–17; AD Sidcup 13–16; rtd 17; PtO *Cant* 18–21. *48 Egremont Road, Bearsted, Maidstone ME15 8LX* E: colin.terry.49@btinternet.com

TERRY, Darcy. See CHESTERFIELD-TERRY, John Darcy Francis Malcolm

TERRY, Miss Helen Eve. b 76. Sheff Hallam Univ BA 04 PGCE 05. St Hild Coll BA 20. d 20 p 21. C Hillsborough and Wadsley Bridge *Sheff* from 20. *3 Willis Road, Sheffield S6 4FJ* T: 0114-418 2668 M: 07759-510185 E: helenterry_uk@yahoo.co.uk

TERRY, Mrs Hilary June. b 45. SEITE 08. d 11 p 13. NSM Uckfield *Chich* 11–15; rtd 15; PtO *Roch* from 15. *110 Townsend Road, Snodland ME6 5RL* M: 07947-923513 E: juneterry1@gmail.com

TERRY, Ian Andrew. b 53. St Jo Coll Dur BA 74 St Mary's Coll Twickenham MA 99 Surrey Univ PhD 05 Win Univ DTh 21 St Jo Coll York PGCE 75 FRSA 21. Coll of Resurr Mirfield 78. d 80 p 81. C Beaconsfield *Ox* 80–83; C N Lynn w St Marg and St Nic *Nor* 83–84; Chapl and Hd RE Eliz Coll Guernsey 84–89; Chapl St Jo Sch Leatherhead 89–92; R Bisley and W End *Guildf* 92–02; asst Chapl HM Pris Coldingley 99–02; Dioc Dir of Educn *Heref* 02–08; Hon TV W Heref 03–08; Chapl St Edm Sch Cant 08–09; TR Bournemouth Town Cen *Win* from 09. *St Peter's Rectory, 18 Wimborne Road, Bournemouth BH2 6NT* T/F: (01202) 554058 E: ianterry@live.co.uk

TERRY, James Richard. b 74. Linc Coll Ox BA 95. Oak Hill Th Coll BA 03. d 03 p 04. C Harold Wood *Chelmsf* 03–07; NSM Blackb Ch Ch w St Matt 07–13; V Tranmere St Cath *Ches* from 13. *St Catherine's Vicarage, 39 Westbank Road, Birkenhead CH42 7JP* T: 0151-652 7379 E: james_terry1@hotmail.com

TERRY, Janet Mary. b 62. Sarum Coll 19. **d** 21. NSM Salisbury St Fran and Stratford sub Castle *Sarum* from 21. *2 Willow CLose, Laverstock, Salisbury SP1 1QF* M: 07732-203452 E: janetmaryterry@gmail.com

TERRY, Jeffrey. *See* TERRY, Robert Jeffrey

TERRY, John Arthur. b 32. S'wark Ord Course. **d** 66 **p** 67. C Plumstead All SS *S'wark* 66–69; C Peckham St Mary Magd 69–72; V Streatham Vale H Redeemer 72–80; R Sternfield w Benhall and Snape *St E* 80–84; V Stevenage St Mary Shephall *St Alb* 84–86; V Stevenage St Mary Shephall w Aston 86–90; V Cople w Willington 90–97; Chapl Shuttleworth Agric Coll 90–97; rtd 97; PtO *St E* 98–18; *Nor* 98–04; *Ely* 03–16. *2 Kestrel Drive, Brandon IP27 0UA* T: (01842) 812055 E: jterry83@hotmail.com

TERRY, John Darcy Francis Malcolm. *See* CHESTERFIELD-TERRY, John Darcy Francis Malcolm

TERRY, John Michael. b 56. Ex Univ BSc 78 Southn Univ MSc 88 Anglia Ruskin Univ BA 09 CEng 93 MIMarEST 93. Ridley Hall Cam 06. **d** 09 **p** 10. NSM Fareham St Jo *Portsm* 09–13; NSM Hook w Warsash 13–14; Jt P-in-c from 14. *The Vicarage, 113 Church Road, Warsash, Southampton SO31 9GF* T: (01489) 808296 E: mike@terry-home.co.uk

TERRY, June. *See* TERRY, Hilary June

TERRY, Justyn Charles. b 65. Keble Coll Ox BA 86 St Jo Coll Dur BA 95 K Coll Lon PhD 03. Cranmer Hall Dur 92. **d** 95 **p** 96. C Paddington St Jo w St Mich *Lon* 95–99; V Kensington St Helen w H Trin 99–05; Assoc Prof Trin Episc Sch for Min USA 05–08; Dean and Pres 08–16; Dean Wycliffe Hall Ox from 17. *Wycliffe Hall, 52-54 Banbury Road, Oxford OX2 6PW* T: (01865) 274620 M: 07495-781795 E: justyn.terry@wycliffe.ox.ac.uk

TERRY, Marc David. b 78. Trin Coll Bris 08. **d** 10 **p** 11. C Margate H Trin *Cant* 10–14; C Aylesham w Adisham and Nonington 15–18; TR By Brook *Bris* from 18. *By Brook Rectory, 3 Church Farm, Yatton Keynell, Chippenham SN14 7FD* T: (01249) 782672 E: revmarcterry@gmail.com

TERRY, Neal John. b 66. **d** 17 **p** 18. NSM Long Benton St Mary *Newc* from 17. *4 Sandpiper Place, Newcastle upon Tyne NE12 8PE* T: 0191-266 5285 E: n.j.terry@btinternet.com

TERRY (née LEONARD), Mrs Nicola Susan. b 61. Keele Univ BA 85 Anglia Ruskin Univ BA 14. Ridley Hall Cam 07. **d** 09 **p** 10. NSM Alverstoke *Portsm* 09–13; NSM Hook w Warsash 13–14; Jt P-in-c from 14. *The Vicarage, 113 Church Road, Warsash, Southampton SO31 9GF* T: (01489) 808296 E: revnsterry@gmail.com

TERRY, Robert Jeffrey. b 52. Lon Univ LLB 75 City Univ MA 81 Barrister-at-Law 76 FCIArb 96. SWMTC 17. **d** 19 **p** 20. NSM Boscastle and Tintagel Gp *Truro* 19–20; NSM Week St Mary Circle of Par 19–20; NSM Camel-Allen from 20. *St Pirans, Trethevy, Tintagel PL34 0BE* E: stpiran@me.com

TERRY, Stephen John. b 49. K Coll Lon BD 72 AKC 74. **d** 75 **p** 76. C Tokyngton St Mich *Lon* 75–78; C Hampstead St Steph w All Hallows 78–81; V Whetstone St Jo 81–89; TR Aldrington *Chich* 89–07; R 07–17; rtd 17. *36 Church Mead, Hassocks BN6 8BN* E: stephenterry49@gmail.com

TETLEY, Miss Carol Ruth. b 51. Ches Coll of HE BA 84. NEOC 06. **d** 09 **p** 10. NSM Anlaby St Pet *York* 09–13; NSM Anlaby Common St Mark 11–13; NSM Hessle from 13; Chapl Hull and E Yorks Hosps NHS Trust from 13. *27 Cranberry Way, Hull HU4 7AQ* T: (01482) 351644 E: caroltetley@crt61.karoo.co.uk

TETLEY, The Ven Joy Dawn. b 46. St Mary's Coll Dur BA 68 Leeds Univ CertEd 69 St Hugh's Coll Ox BA 75 MA 80 Dur Univ PhD 88. NW Ord Course 77. **dss** 77 **d** 87 **p** 94. Bentley *Sheff* 77–79; Buttershaw St Aid *Bradf* 79–80; Dur Cathl 80–83; Lect Trin Coll Bris 83–86; Chipping Sodbury and Old Sodbury *Glouc* 83–86; Dn Roch Cathl 87–89; Hon Can 90–93; Assoc Dir of Post Ord Tr 87–88; Dir Post Ord Tr 88–93; Hon Par Dn Gravesend H Family w Ifield 89–93; Prin EAMTC *Ely* 93–99; Adn Worc and Can Res Worc Cathl 99–08; rtd 08; PtO *Ox* 08–11. *23 Cripley Road, Oxford OX2 0AH* T: (01865) 250209 E: briantetley@btinternet.com

TETLEY, Matthew David. b 61. Bucks Coll of Educn BSc 83. Sarum & Wells Th Coll BTh 89. **d** 87 **p** 88. C Kirkby *Liv* 87–90; C Hindley St Pet 90–93; TV Whorlton *Newc* 93–96; V Newbiggin Hall 96–01; P-in-c Longhorsley and Hebron 01–06; Chapl HM Pris Acklington 01–06 and 08–15; Chapl HM Pris Frankland 06–08; Chapl HM Pris Dur from 15; PtO *Newc* from 15; Public Preacher and Min Can Dur Cathl from 21. *HM Prison Durham, 19B Old Elvet, Durham DH1 3HU* T: 0191-332 3400 E: matthew.tetley@justice.gov.uk

TETLOW, John. b 46. St Steph Ho Ox 73. **d** 76 **p** 77. C Stanwell *Lon* 76–77; C Hanworth All SS 77–80; C Somers Town 80–83; TV Wickford and Runwell *Chelmsf* 83–90; P-in-c Walthamstow St Mich 90–96. *6A Bushwood, London E11 3AY* T: (020) 8989 9076

TETLOW, Richard Jeremy. b 42. Trin Coll Cam MA 66 Goldsmiths' Coll Lon CQSW 74. Qu Coll Birm 81. **d** 83 **p** 84. C Birm St Martin 83–85; C Birm St Martin w Bordesley St Andr 85–88; V Birm St Jo Ladywood 89–01; V Ladywood St Jo and St Pet 01–08; rtd 08; PtO *Birm* from 08. *26 Sovereign Way, Moseley, Birmingham B13 8AT* T: 0121-449 4892

TETT, Richard Colin. b 60. Qu Foundn Birm 14. **d** 16 **p** 17. C Eckington *Worc* 16–20; C Defford w Besford 16–20; TV Woodfield *Leic* from 20. *17 Rectory Lane, Appleby Magna, Swadlincote DE12 7BQ* M: 07712-706717 E: captrickt@hotmail.co.uk

TETZLAFF, Mrs Geraldine Vivienne. b 59. St Jo Coll Nottm 10. **d** 12 **p** 13. C Macclesfield Team *Ches* 12–15; V Chelford and Lower Withington w Marthall 15–19; P-in-c Birkenhead Ch Ch from 19. *Christ Church Vicarage, 7 Palm Grove, Prenton CH43 1TE* M: 07756-664622 E: gerri.tetzlaff@gmail.com

TETZLAFF, Silke. b 67. Friedrich Schiller Univ 87 K Coll Lon BA 97 AKC 97 Anglia Poly Univ MA 01. Westcott Ho Cam 99. **d** 01 **p** 02. C Leagrave *St Alb* 01–05; TV Baldock w Bygrave and Weston 05–11; C Sandon, Wallington and Rushden w Clothall 10–11; R Staplehurst *Cant* from 11. *The New Rectory, High Street, Staplehurst, Tonbridge TN12 0BJ* T: (01580) 891258 E: silke.tetzlaff@btinternet.com

TEWKESBURY, Suffragan Bishop of. *See* SPRINGETT, The Rt Revd Robert Wilfred

THACKER, Christine Mary. b 44. Simon Fraser Univ BC BA 90. Vancouver Sch of Th MDiv 93. **d** 92 **p** 93. R Kitimat Ch Ch Canada 93–00; C Boultham *Linc* 00–09; rtd 10; PtO *Nor* from 10; *Ex* from 20. *2 Case Gardens, Seaton EX12 2AP* E: chrism.thacker@gmail.com

THACKER, Ian David. b 59. Univ of Wales (Lamp) MA 13. Oak Hill Th Coll BA 91. **d** 91 **p** 92. C Illogan *Truro* 91–94; C Eglwysilan *Llan* 94–96; TV Hornsey Rise Whitehall Park Team *Lon* 96–97; TV Upper Holloway 97–01; Chapl HM YOI Huntercombe and Finnamore 01–11; Chapl HM Pris Huntercombe from 11. *HM Prison Huntercombe, Huntercombe Place, Nuffield, Henley-on-Thames RG9 5SB* T: (01491) 632212 M: 07864-095435 E: ian.thacker@justice.gov.uk

THACKER, Jonathan William. b 53. Lon Univ BA 74. Linc Th Coll 76. **d** 79 **p** 80. C Bromyard *Heref* 79–82; C Penkridge w Stretton *Lich* 82–87; V Brothertoft Gp *Linc* 87–96; RD Holland W 92–95; P-in-c Crosby 96–01; V 01–19; RD Manlake 11–14; RD Is of Axholme 11–14; Chapl Scunthorpe and Goole Hosps NHS Trust 99–01; rtd 19. *Church Cottage, Front Street, Barnby, Newark NG24 2SA* M: 07804-250459 E: pajidog2017@gmail.com

THACKRAY, John Adrian. b 55. Southn Univ BSc 76 ACIB 81. Coll of Resurr Mirfield 81. **d** 84 **p** 85. C Loughton St Jo *Chelmsf* 84–87; Chapl Bancroft's Sch Woodford Green 87–92; Sen Chapl K Sch Cant 92–01; Chapl Abp's Sch Cant 01–02; Sen Chapl K Sch Roch 02–15; P-in-c Ipswich St Mary at the Elms *St E* from 15; PtO *Chelmsf* from 92; Hon Min Can Cant Cathl from 93; Hon PV Roch Cathl 02–15; Bp's Ecum Adv *St E* from 16; P-in-c Ipswich St Mary at Stoke w St Pet and St Fran from 21. *The Vicarage, 68 Blackhorse Lane, Ipswich IP1 2EF* M: 07780-613754

THACKRAY, William Harry. b 44. Leeds Univ CertEd 66. Chich Th Coll 70. **d** 73 **p** 74. C Sheff St Cuth 73–76; C Stocksbridge 76–78; P-in-c Newark St Leon *S'well* 79–80; TV Newark w Hawton, Cotham and Shelton 80–82; V Choral S'well Minster 82–85; V Bawtry w Austerfield 85; P-in-c Misson 85; V Bawtry w Austerfield and Misson 86–93; RD Bawtry 90–93; P-in-c Balderton 93–03; P-in-c Coddington w Barnby in the Willows 98–03; V Biggleswade *St Alb* 03–09; RD 07–09; rtd 09; Hon C Lower Swale *Ripon* 09–14; *Leeds* 14; PtO *York* from 14. *8 Newsham Way, Northallerton DL7 8HT* T: (01609) 780102 E: williamhthackray@gmail.com

THAKE, Preb Terence. b 41. ALCD 65. **d** 66 **p** 67. C Gt Faringdon w Lt Coxwell *Ox* 66–70; C Aldridge *Lich* 70–73; V Werrington 73–82; Chapl HM Det Cen Werrington Ho 73–82; TR Chell *Lich* 82–94; Chapl Westcliff Hosp 82–94; RD Stoke N *Lich* 91–94; V Colwich w Gt Haywood 94–00; P-in-c Colton 95–00; R Colton, Colwich and Gt Haywood 00–04; RD Rugeley 98–06; Preb Lich Cathl 94–10; Dioc Environmental Adv *Derby* from 12; rtd 04; PtO *Lich* 15–16. *18 Middleton Avenue, Codnor, Ripley DE5 9SS* E: terry.thake@btinternet.com

THATCHER, Ms Catherine Mary. b 72. Em Coll Cam MA 97 City Univ MSc 01 Cam Univ BTh 14 ACCA 98. Westcott Ho Cam 12. **d** 14 **p** 15. C Bradf Cathl *Leeds* 14–17; V Oxenhope from 17; Clergy Development Officer Bradf Area from 17. *20 Gledhow Drive, Oxenhope, Keighley BD22 9SA* E: oxenhopecat@gmail.com

THATCHER, Stephen Bert. b 58. Greenwich Univ PGCE 04. St Jo Coll Nottm LTh 87 ALCD 87. **d** 87 **p** 88. C Bargoed and Deri w Brithdir *Llan* 87–89; C Llanishen and Lisvane 89–91;

V Llanwnda, Goodwick w Manorowen and Llanstinan *St D* 91–95; P-in-c Coberley, Cowley, Colesbourne and Elkstone *Glouc* 95–96; Dioc Rural Adv 95–96; R New Radnor and Llanfihangel Nantmelan etc *S & B* 96–00; Dioc Tourism Officer 96–99; Dioc Chs and Tourism Rep 97–00; CF 00–18; R Seale, Puttenham and Wanborough *Guildf* from 18. *The Rectory, Elstead Road, Seale, Farnham GU10 1JA* T: (01252) 783057 M: 07379-526555 E: stephen_thatcher@sky.com

THAXTER, Paul. b 58. d 94. Pakistan 94–13; Dir Transcultural Miss CMS from 13; PtO *Win* from 13. *57 St Edmunds Road, Southampton SO16 4FT* E: paul.thaxter@cmsuk.org

THEAKER, David Michael. b 41. d 68 p 69. C Folkingham w Laughton *Linc* 68–71; C New Cleethorpes 71–74; P-in-c Gt Grimsby St Andr and St Luke 74–77; P-in-c Thurlby 77–79; PtO *Ely* from 00. *11 Willow Way, Hauxton, Cambridge CB22 5JB* T: (01223) 873132 E: david_theaker@yahoo.co.uk

THEAKSTON, Canon Sally Margaret. b 62. UEA BSc 84 K Coll Lon MA 94. Ripon Coll Cuddesdon BA 89. d 89 p 94. Par Dn Hackney *Lon* 89–93; Par Dn Putney St Mary *S'wark* 93–94; C 94–96; Chapl RN 96–02; TR Gaywood *Nor* 02–09; TR Dereham and Distr 09–19; RD Dereham in Mitford 10–13; P-in-c Shipdham w Bradenham 15; Bp's Chapl from 19; Asst Dir of Ords from 16; Hon Can Nor Cathl from 10. *Bishop's House, Norwich NR3 1SB* T: (01603) 614172 M: 07904-070654 E: stheakston@aol.com or bishops.chaplain@dioceseofnorwich.org

THELWELL, The Ven John Berry. b 49. Univ of Wales (Ban) BD 72. Qu Coll Birm 73. d 73 p 74. C Minera *St As* 73–80; Dioc Youth Chapl 78–86; V Gwernaffield and Llanferres 80–93; Chapl Clwyd Fire Service 88–94; RD Mold *St As* 91–95; TR Hawarden 93–02; Can Cursal St As Cathl 95–02; Prec 98–02; Adn Montgomery *St As* 02–12; V Berriew 03–12; rtd 12; PtO *St As* from 13. *O'r Diwedd, 2 Bryn Road, Bryn-y-Baal, Mold CH7 6RY* T: (01352) 750962 E: john.thelwell@btinternet.com

THEOBALD, Graham Fitzroy. b 43. ALCD 67. d 67 p 68. C Crookham *Guildf* 67–71; C York Town St Mich 71–74; V Wrecclesham 74–83; Chapl Green Lane Hosp 74–81; R Frimley *Guildf* 83–85; Chapl Frimley Park Hosp 83–85; PtO *Ox* 90–92; C Easthampstead 92–97; Chapl E Berks NHS Trust 92–03; rtd 03; PtO *Ox* 03–12; PtO *Ox* 03–12; Hon C Ruscombe and Twyford w Hurst from 12. *50 Viking, Bracknell RG12 8UL* T: (01344) 428525 M: 07721-408740 E: witsend50gra@gmail.com

THEOBALD, Susan Ann. b 61. La Sainte Union Coll BEd 83. STETS 07. d 10 p 11. C Southsea St Jude *Portsm* 10–14; P-in-c Ryde St Jo Oakfield and H Trin from 14. *St John's Vicarage, Victoria Crescent, Ryde PO33 1DQ* E: theobald.sue.79@gmail.com

THETFORD, Suffragan Bishop of. *See* WINTON, The Rt Revd Alan Peter

THEULINGS, Dimitri Jan Antonius Hendrica. b 66. Ridley Hall Cam 20. d 21. C Triangle, St Matt and All SS *St E* from 21. *7 Stuart Close, Ipswich IP4 4BN* E: dimitri@tastypies.co.uk

THEWLIS, Andrew James. b 64. Man Univ BSc 86. Cranmer Hall Dur 87. d 90 p 91. C Walshaw Ch Ch *Man* 90–95; P-in-c Jersey St Jo *Win* 95–98; R 98–16; TV Savernake *Sarum* 16–18. *7 Flathouse, Linthwaite, Huddersfield HD7 5PR* T: (01484) 617357 M: 07747-114707 E: thewlisandy@gmail.com

THEWLIS, Canon John Charles. b 49. Van Mildert Coll Dur BA 70 PhD 75. NOC 78. d 81 p 82. NSM Hull St Mary Sculcoates *York* 81–83; C Spring Park *Cant* 83–84; C Spring Park All SS *S'wark* 85–86; V Eltham Park St Luke 86–01; R Carshalton 01–17; Hon Can S'wark Cathl 14–17; rtd 17; PtO *S'wark* from 17; Heref from 17. *Willow Cottage, The Marsh, Wellington, Hereford HR4 8DU* T: 05603-670746 E: jct@thewlis.org.uk

THEWSEY, Robert Sydney. b 65. Sarum Coll MA 18. Ripon Coll Cuddesdon 99. d 01 p 02. C Chorlton-cum-Hardy St Clem *Man* 01–04; P-in-c Stretford All SS 04–08; P-in-c Boscastle w Davidstow *Truro* 08–15; R Boscastle and Tintagel Gp 15–16; RD Stratton 11–16; R Shiplake w Dunsden and Harpsden *Ox* from 16; AD Henley from 19. *The Rectory, Shiplake, Henley-on-Thames RG9 4BS* T: 0118-940 3484 E: robert.thewsey@btinternet.com

THICKE, James Balliston. b 43. Sarum & Wells Th Coll 74. d 77 p 78. C Wareham *Sarum* 77–80; TV 80–83; Dioc Youth Adv *Dur* 83–87; C Portishead *B & W* 87–90; V Westfield 90–08; RD Midsomer Norton 98–04; Chapl Norton Radstock Coll of FE 00–08; rtd 08; PtO *B & W* from 09. *11 Welton Grove, Midsomer Norton, Radstock BA3 2TS* T: (01761) 411905 M: 07971-943654 E: jamesballiston@hotmail.co.uk

THIJS, Matthias Jozua. b 83. St Mellitus Coll MA 20. d 20 p 21. C Voorschoten *Eur* from 20. *Ambachtsgaard 23, 2251CP Voorschoten, The Netherlands* T: (0031) (6) 8566 1179 E: matt@stjames.nl

THIRLWELL, Miss Margaret. b 36. Bris Univ BA 59 St Aid Coll Dur DipEd 61. d 03 p 04. OLM Binfield *Ox* 03–09; PtO 09–17 and from 18. *70 Red Rose, Binfield, Bracknell RG42 5LD* T: (01344) 423920 E: margaret.thirlwell@gmail.com

THIRTLE, Ms Lucy Rachel. b 62. Ex Univ BA 85. Cranmer Hall Dur 97. d 99 p 00. C Basingstoke *Win* 99–04; P-in-c Kingsclere 04–06; P-in-c Ashford Hill w Headley 06; V Kingsclere and Ashford Hill w Headley 06–15; Hon C Ray Valley *Ox* from 15. *3 The Rise, Islip, Kidlington OX5 2TG* T: (01865) 379470 E: revlucy.islip@gmail.com

THISELTON, Prof Anthony Charles. b 37. Lon Univ BD 59 K Coll Lon MTh 64 Sheff Univ PhD 77 Dur Univ DD 93 Lambeth DD 02 FBA 10 FKC 10. Oak Hill Th Coll 58. d 60 p 61. C Sydenham H Trin *S'wark* 60–63; Tutor Tyndale Hall Bris 63–67; Sen Tutor 67–70; Lect Bibl Studies Sheff Univ 70–79; Sen Lect 79–85; Prof Calvin Coll Grand Rapids USA 82–83; Special Lect Th Nottm Univ 86–88; Prin St Jo Coll Nottm 86–88; Prin St Jo Coll w Cranmer Hall Dur 88–92; Prof Chr Th Nottm Univ from 92; Can Th Leic Cathl from 94; Can Th S'well Minster from 00. *Department of Theology, Nottingham University, University Park, Nottingham NG7 2RD* T: 0115-951 5852 F: 951 5887 E: thiselton@ntlworld.com

THISTLETHWAITE, Canon Nicholas John. b 51. Selw Coll Cam BA 73 MA 77 PhD 80 FSA 79. Ripon Coll Cuddesdon BA 78 MA 83. d 79 p 80. C Newc St Gabr 79–82; Chapl G&C Coll Cam 82–90; LtO *Ely* 82–90; V Trumpington 90–99; Can Res and Prec Guildf Cathl 99–16; Sub-Dean 06–16; rtd 17; PtO *Ely* from 17; Hon PV Ely Cathl from 17; Chapl to The Queen 14–21. *16 Douglas Court, Ely CB7 4SE* T: (01353) 663231 E: njt1789@gmail.com

THISTLEWOOD, Michael John. b 31. Ch Coll Cam BA 53 MA 57. Linc Th Coll 54. d 56 p 57. C N Hull St Mich *York* 56–59; C Scarborough St Mary 59–61; V Kingston upon Hull St Jude w St Steph 61–67; V Newland St Aug 67–72; Asst Master Bemrose Sch Derby 72–80; V Derby St Andr w St Osmund 80–82; LtO *Ox* 84–95; rtd 88; PtO *Carl* 88–98; *Derby* 98–05; *Carl* 05–08 and from 09. *44 Blackhall Croft, Blackhall Road, Kendal LA9 4UU* E: mjtblackhall@outlook.com

THODAY, Margaret Frances. b 38. d 03 p 04. OLM Roughton and Felbrigg, Metton, Sustead etc *Nor* 03–08; PtO from 08. *Flat 3, 4 Norwich Road, Cromer NR27 0AX* T: (01263) 510945

THODY, Charles Michael Jackson. b 62. Linc Th Coll BTh 94. d 94 p 95. C Immingham *Linc* 94–97; P-in-c Leasingham and Cranwell 97–01; P-in-c Bishop Norton, Waddingham and Snitterby 01–03; Chapl Doncaster and S Humber Healthcare NHS Trust 01–03; Chapl Notts Healthcare NHS Trust 03–09; Chapl Rotherham, Doncaster and S Humber NHS Foundn Trust 09–11; Sen Chapl N Lincs and Goole NHS Foundn Trust 12–20. *Address temp unknown*

THOM, Alastair George. b 60. G&C Coll Cam BA 81 MA 84 ACA 86. Ridley Hall Cam 88. d 91 p 92. C Lindfield *Chich* 91–94; C Finchley St Paul and St Luke *Lon* 94–98; P-in-c W Kilburn St Luke w St Simon and St Jude 98–13; P-in-c Paddington Em Harrow Road 98–13; V W Kilburn St Luke and Harrow Road Em from 13; AD Westmr Paddington 06–11. *The Vicarage, 19 Macroom Road, London W9 3HY* T: (020) 8962 0294 E: alastairthom@yahoo.co.uk

THOM, James. b 31. St Chad's Coll Dur BA 53. d 57 p 58. C Middlesbrough St Thos *York* 57–60; C Hornsea and Goxhill 60–62; C S Bank 62–63; V Copmanthorpe 63–75; V Coxwold 75–77; V Coxwold and Husthwaite 77–87; RD Easingwold 77–82; Spiritual Dir York Angl Cursillo 86–93; P-in-c Topcliffe 87–93; rtd 93; PtO *York* from 93; *Ripon* 93–14; *Leeds* 14–16. *34 Hell Wath Grove, Ripon HG4 2JT* T: (01765) 605083

THOMAS, Adam Douglas. b 68. All SS Cen for Miss & Min 15. d 18 p 19. C Lytham St Cuth *Blackb* 18–21; Dir Whalley Abbey from 21. *Whalley Lodge, Whalley Abbey, Whalley, Clitheroe BB7 9SS* M: 07968-434328 E: cathyandadam89@gmail.com

THOMAS, Adrian Leighton. b 37. Univ of Wales (Lamp) BA 62 Univ of Wales (Cardiff) PGCE 73. St D Coll Lamp. d 63 p 64. C Port Talbot St Theodore *Llan* 63–70; V Troedrhiwgarth 70–73; C Sandhurst *Ox* 73–77; V Streatley 77–84; P-in-c Moulsford 81–84; V Streatley w Moulsford 84–90; P-in-c Sutton Courtenay w Appleford 90–00; V 00–02; AD Abingdon 96–02; rtd 02; P-in-c Lugano *Eur* 02–06; PtO *Ox* from 07. *13 The Birches, Goring, Reading RG8 9BW* T: (01491) 872696 E: adrianleighton.thomas@gmail.com

THOMAS, Alan. *See* THOMAS, Thomas Alan

THOMAS, Aled Huw. b 59. Univ of Wales (Abth) BD 81. St Mich Coll Llan 84. d 85 p 86. C Llandeilo Fawr and Taliaris *St D* 85–86; P-in-c Llangrannog and Llandysiliogogo 86–88; Chapl RAF 88–92; R Ystradgynlais *S & B* 92–94; CF 94–08; Sen CF 08–10; V St Dogmael's w Moylgrove and Monington w Meline *St D* 10–11; V St Dogmael's and Monington and Nevern etc 11–12; rtd 12. *Y Bwthyn, 8 Church Street, Rhayader LD6 5AY* M: 07515-902067 E: padrealed@gmail.com

THOMAS, Mrs Alison Margaret. b 55. Birm Univ BSocSc 77. Qu Foundn Birm 13. **d** 16 **p** 17. NSM Stafford St Mary and Marston *Lich* 16–19; C 19; NSM Stafford St Chad 16–19; C 19; C Stafford St Paul and St Thos 19–21; V Basford from 21; P-in-c Wolstanton from 21. *211 Basford Park Road, Newcastle ST5 0PG* M: 07542-887924 E: revdalison@gmail.com

THOMAS, Andrew Nigel. b 75. Ox Brookes Univ BA 13. Westcott Ho Cam 08. **d** 10 **p** 11. C The Cookhams *Ox* 10–13; Chapl RN 13–14; R Dulverton w Brushford, Brompton Regis etc *B & W* 14–20; R Yelverton, Meavy, Sheepstor, Walkhampton, Sampford Spiney and Horrabridge *Ex* from 20. *The Rectory, St Paul's Church, Yelverton PL20 6AB* T: (01822) 854804 E: rectorwestdartmoor@gmail.com

THOMAS, Andrew Robert. b 80. G&C Coll Cam BA 03. Oak Hill Th Coll BA 09. **d** 09 **p** 10. C Angmering *Chich* 09–12; C Cambridge St Matt *Ely* 12–17; P-in-c Doncaster St Mary and St Paul *Sheff* from 17. *The Vicarage, 59 St Mary's Road, Doncaster DN1 2NR* T: (01302) 739593 E: andythomas196@yahoo.co.uk

THOMAS, Anina Jane. b 76. Ex Univ BA 97 Edge Hill Coll of HE PGCE 02. St Mellitus Coll 17. **d** 19 **p** 20. C Lache cum Saltney *Ches* from 19. *19 Capeland Close, Saltney, Chester CH4 8PU* M: 07582-199167 E: anina@stmarkssaltney.org.uk

THOMAS, Anne Valerie. *See* NOBLE, Anne Valerie

THOMAS, Barrie. *See* THOMAS, Illtyd Barrie

THOMAS, Canon Barry Wilfred. b 41. Univ of Wales (Cardiff) BD 75. St Mich Coll Llan 72. **d** 75 **p** 76. C Porthmadog *Ban* 75–78; V Llanegryn and Llanfihangel-y-Pennant etc 78–82; TR Llanbeblig w Caernarfon and Betws Garmon etc 82–94; Sec Dioc Coun for Miss and Unity 81–94; Can Ban Cathl 89–94; Chapl Monte Carlo *Eur* 95–00; V Llanfihangel Ystrad and Cilcennin w Trefilan etc *St D* 00–06; rtd 06; PtO *Eur* from 07. *46 Ezel Court, Heol Glan Rheidol, Cardiff CF10 5NS* E: barry.thomas379@btinternet.com

THOMAS, Bernard. *See* THOMAS, Edward Bernard Meredith

THOMAS, Bernard. *See* THOMAS, Elwyn Bernard

THOMAS, Brian. *See* THOMAS, David Brian

THOMAS, The Ven Charles Edward. b 27. Univ of Wales (Lamp) BA 51. Coll of Resurr Mirfield 51. **d** 53 **p** 54. C Ilminster w Whitelackington *B & W* 53–56; Chapl St Mich Coll Tenbury 56–57; C St Alb St Steph 57–58; V Boreham Wood St Mich 58–66; R Monksilver w Brompton Ralph and Nettlecombe *B & W* 66–74; P-in-c Nettlecombe 68–69; R S Petherton w The Seavingtons 74–83; RD Crewkerne 77–83; Adn Wells, Can Res and Preb Wells Cathl 83–93; rtd 93; PtO *St D* 93–17. *Geryfelin, Tregaron SY25 6ND* T: (01974) 298102

THOMAS, Charles Leslie. b 58. Qu Coll Birm 09. **d** 11 **p** 12. C Sevenhampton w Charlton Abbots, Hawling etc *Glouc* 11–15; V Worc St Wulstan 15–18; RD Worc E 16–18; PtO *Lich* 18–19; P-in-c Wolverhampton St Andr 19; V from 19. *The Vicarage, High Street, Albrighton, Wolverhampton WV7 3EQ* T: (01902) 373415 M: 07542-532662 E: revcharlesthomas@gmail.com

THOMAS, Charles Moray Stewart Reid. b 53. BNC Ox BA 74 MA 79. Wycliffe Hall Ox 75. **d** 78 **p** 79. C Bradf Cathl 78–81; C Barnsbury St Andr and H Trin w All SS *Lon* 81–90; TV Barnsbury 90–99; Chapl Lon Goodenough Trust 99–08; V Grayshott *Guildf* 08–18; rtd 18; PtO *Eur* from 16. *Jubilee Cottage, Hospital Road, Shirrell Heath, Southampton SO32 2JR* T: (01329) 833174 E: moray@thethomases.plus.com

THOMAS, Clive Alexander. b 49. Open Univ BA 77 St Luke's Coll Ex CertEd 71. STETS 94. **d** 97 **p** 99. NSM Southwick St Mich *Chich* 97–01; C Bridport *Sarum* 01–04; TV Shaston 04–09; TR Shaftesbury 09–14; rtd 14; PtO *Ex* from 20. *2 Marlborough Park, Ilfracombe EX34 8JB* T: (01271) 600089 E: rev.clivet@gmail.com

THOMAS, Daniel James. b 85. St Hild Coll 19. **d** 21. C Selby Abbey *York* from 21. *49 Woodville Terrace, Selby YO8 4AJ*

THOMAS, David. b 48. **d** 08 **p** 09. NSM Barnes *S'wark* 08–12; PtO 12–14; Asst Chapl Richmond Charities Almshouses 14–18; rtd 18. *8 Church Estate Almshouses, Richmond TW9 1UX* T: (020) 8948 4188 *or* 8940 7812 M: 07596-018177 E: david.thomas497@googlemail.com

THOMAS, David Brian. b 45. MIEEE. St D Dioc Tr Course 82. **d** 85 **p** 86. NSM Llandysul *St D* 85–87; NSM Lampeter Pont Steffan w Silian 88–92; NSM Lampeter and Ultra-Aeron 92–96; P-in-c Llanfihangel Genau'r-glyn and Llangorwen 96–97; V 97–10; AD Llanbadarn Fawr 00–10; rtd 10; PtO *Lich* 15–21. *5 Willowdene, St Martin's Road, Gobowen, Oswestry SY10 7GA* T: (01691) 662629 E: dbrianthomas@yahoo.com

THOMAS, David Edward. b 60. Univ of Wales (Lamp) BA 83. St Mich Coll Llan 85. **d** 86 **p** 87. C Killay *S & B* 86–89; P-in-c Newbridge-on-Wye and Llanfihangel Brynpabuan 89–90; V 90–91; V Brecon St David w

Llanspyddid and Llanilltyd 91–09; V Glasbury and Llowes w Clyro and Betws from 09. *The Vicarage, 4 The Birches, Glasbury, Hereford HR3 5NW* T: (01497) 847156 E: thomas3693@btinternet.com

THOMAS, David Godfrey. b 50. St Chad's Coll Dur BA 71 Fitzw Coll Cam BA 74 MA 78. Westcott Ho Cam 72. **d** 75 **p** 76. C Kirkby *Liv* 75–78; TV Cov E 78–88; TR Canvey Is *Chelmsf* 88–92; R Wivenhoe 92–09; R Shenfield 09–16; rtd 16; PtO *Chelmsf* 18–19. *6 Inglis Road, Colchester CO3 3HU* T: (01206) 576565 M: 07875-126953 E: davidgthomas66@gmail.com

THOMAS, David Jeffrey. **d** 15 **p** 16. NSM Bro Dyfri *St D* from 15. *Llwyncelyn, Manordeilo, Llandeilo SA19 7BP* T: (01550) 777758 E: djt292@btinternet.com

THOMAS, David John. b 34. Univ of Wales (Swansea) St D Coll Lamp. St D Dioc Tr Course 85. **d** 88 **p** 89. NSM Cwmaman *St D* 88–96; Public Preacher 96–11; PtO from 11. *9 New School Road, Garnant, Ammanford SA18 1LL* T: (01269) 823936

THOMAS, David Jonathan. b 80. **d** 19 **p** 20. C Hounslow St Paul and Gd Shep *Lon* from 19. *360 Beavers Lane, Hounslow TW4 6HJ* E: david@hwparish.org.uk

THOMAS, Prof David Richard. b 48. BNC Ox BA 71 MA 74 Fitzw Coll Cam BA 75 MA 80 Lanc Univ PhD 83. Ridley Hall Cam 73 Qu Coll Birm 79. **d** 80 **p** 81. C Anfield St Columba *Liv* 80–83; C Liv Our Lady and St Nic w St Anne 83–85; Chapl CCC Cam 85–90; V Witton *Blackb* 90–93; Bp's Adv on Inter-Faith Relns 90–93; Lect Cen for Study of Islam and Chr-Muslim Relns Selly Oak 93–04; Sen Lect Birm Univ 99–04; Reader 04–07; Prof Christianity and Islam from 07; PtO *Derby* 05–11; LtO 11–16; Hon Can Th Derby Cathl 11–16; PtO *B & W* from 17; Preb Wells Cathl from 18; Dioc Interfaith Adv from 21. *Department of Theology and Religion, University of Birmingham, Edgbaston, Birmingham B15 2TT* T: 0121-415 8373 E: d.r.thomas.1@bham.ac.uk

THOMAS, Canon David Thomas. b 44. St Cath Coll Cam BA 66 MA 70. Cranmer Hall Dur. **d** 71 **p** 72. C Chorlton-cum-Hardy St Clem *Man* 71–74; Chapl Salford Tech Coll 74–79; P-in-c Pendleton St Thos *Man* 75–77; V 77–80; TR Gleadless *Sheff* 80–90; RD Attercliffe 86–90; V Benchill *Man* 90–99; TV Wythenshawe 99–00; AD Withington 99–00; P-in-c Stretford St Matt 00–09; Hon Can Man Cathl 09; rtd 09; PtO *Man* from 09; *Carl* 10–15. *40 Longmead Road, Salford M6 7EU* T: 0161-737 5867 E: tom-hil@talk21.com

THOMAS (née THOMSON), Mrs Dorothy Lucille. b 39. Univ of Wales (Lamp). **d** 00 **p** 10. OLM Pontnewydd *Mon* 00–15; rtd 15. *Raldoro, Mount Pleasant Road, Pontnewydd, Cwmbran NP44 1BD* T: (01633) 771353

THOMAS, Edward. *See* THOMAS, Charles Edward

THOMAS, Edward Bernard Meredith. b 21. Leeds Univ BA 44 Univ of Qld BEd 68 BD 72. Coll of Resurr Mirfield 47. **d** 49 **p** 50. C St Mary-at-Lambeth *S'wark* 49–54; C Portsea N End St Mark *Portsm* 54–56; V Portsea All SS 56–64; R Woolloongabba Australia 64–72; Perm to Offic Brisbane 72–78; Miss Chapl 78–92; rtd 92. *33 Highfield Street, Durack QLD 4077, Australia* T: (0061) (7) 3372 3517 M: 41-622 7121 E: bernard_thomas@iinet.net.au

THOMAS (née REEVES), Mrs Elizabeth Anne. b 45. Sheff Univ BA 67 PGCE 75. SWMTC 87. **d** 90 **p** 94. Par Dn Stoke Damerel *Ex* 90–93; Dioc Children's Adv *Bradf* 93–01; Par Dn Baildon 93–94; C 94–96; P-in-c Denholme Gate 96–01; PtO 08; PtO *S'well* from 18. *The Lyrics, 113 The Oval, Retford DN22 7SD* T: (01777) 700047 E: liz.thomas@sky.com

THOMAS, The Ven Elwyn Bernard. b 45. Univ of Wales (Swansea) BSc 68. St Mich Coll Llan BD 71. **d** 71 **p** 72. C Aberdare St Fagan *Llan* 71–74; C Merthyr Dyfan 74–76; R Dowlais 76–86; V Llangynwyd w Maesteg 86–00; Can Llan Cathl 98–00; Adn St As 00–11; R Llandyrnog and Llangwyfan 00–11; P-in-c 11–14; rtd 11; PtO *St As* 15–17; P-in-c Bala 17; TV Penedeyrn Miss Area 18; PtO from 18. *11 Cae Glas, Trefnant, Denbigh LL16 5UB* T: (01745) 731732 E: ebernardthomas@aol.com

THOMAS, Ernest Keith. b 49. St Mich Coll Llan 73. **d** 76 **p** 77. C Swansea St Gabr *S & B* 76–79; C Killay 79–81; Prec Kimberley Cathl S Africa 81–84; R Kimberley St Aug 84–92; R Kimberley St Alb 89–92; Can Kimberley Cathl 86–92; V Aberdare Llan 93–96; Sub-Dean Bloemfontein Cathl S Africa 96–10; R Welkom from 10. *PO Box 231, Welkom, 9460 South Africa* T: (0027) (57) 352 3497 *or* (57) 352 5664 F: 352 2272 M: 83-700 0976 E: stmatt@global.co.za

THOMAS, Gabrielle Rachael. b 74. Bris Univ BA 95 Ches Univ MTh 13 Nottm Univ PhD 17. St Jo Coll Nottm 11. **d** 15 **p** 16. C Teddington St Mary w St Alb *Lon* 15–17; Research Assoc Dur Univ 17–19; Hon Min Can Dur Cathl 18–19; PtO from 19; Lect Yale Div Sch USA 19–21; Asst Prof Candler Sch of Th from 21. *Candler School of Theology, Rita Anne*

Rollins Building, 1531 Dickey Drive, Atlanta GA 30322, USA
E: gabrielle.rachael.thomas@emory.edu

THOMAS, Mrs Gail Lesley. b 71. Wolv Univ BA 96. Trin Coll Bris 15. **d** 17 **p** 18. C Yate *Bris* 17–21; P-in-c Milton and Kewstoke *B & W* from 21. *22 Hampden Close, Yate, Bristol BS37 5UW* M: 07746-050607 E: gail_l_thomas@hotmail.com

THOMAS, Gareth David. b 75. Sheff Univ BA 96 Ches Univ PGCE 03. All SS Cen for Miss & Min 10. **d** 13 **p** 14. C Ches St Paul 13–15; C Huntington 13–15; Chapl Ches Univ 14–17; NSM Chester St Pet from 17. *9A St David's House, 24 High Street, Mold CH7 1AZ* T: (01352) 753673 E: g-thomas@hotmail.co.uk *or* g.thomas@chester.ac.uk

THOMAS, Gareth Mark. b 72. Cranmer Hall Dur. **d** 10 **p** 11. C Atherton and Hindsford w Howe Bridge *Man* 10–13; TV Daisy Hill, Westhoughton and Wingates 13–16; TV Blackrod, Daisy Hill, Westhoughton and Wingates 16–17; V Hope St Jas and Pendlebury St Jo from 17. *91 Broomhall Road, Pendlebury, Swinton, Manchester M27 8XR* T: 0161-925 0059 M: 07947-389893 E: garethmthomas@hotmail.com

THOMAS, Geoffrey Brynmor. b 34. K Coll Lon BA 56 AKC 56. Ridley Hall Cam 58. **d** 60 **p** 61. C Harlow New Town w Lt Parndon *Chelmsf* 60–65; V Leyton All SS 65–74; V Haley Hill *Wakef* 74–82; R The Winterbournes and Compton Valence *Sarum* 82–89; TV Cheltenham St Mark *Glouc* 89–92; P-in-c Dowdeswell and Andoversford w the Shiptons etc 92–95; RD Northleach 92–95; rtd 95; PtO *B & W* 96–18. *48 Riverside Walk, Midsomer Norton, Radstock BA3 2PD* T: (01761) 414146 E: gbt34@btinternet.com

THOMAS, George. b 46. Leeds Univ BEd 69. Cranmer Hall Dur 75. **d** 78 **p** 79. C Highfield *Liv* 78–83; V Chorley St Jas *Blackb* 83–02; P-in-c Blackb St Gabr 02–08; rtd 08; PtO *Blackb* from 08. *80 Severn Drive, Walton-le-Dale, Preston PR5 4TE* T: (01772) 330152

THOMAS, Glen Robert. b 70. St Steph Ho Ox 18. **d** 20 **p** 21. C N Potteries *Lich* from 20. *St Werburgh's Presbytery, Haywood Road, Stoke-on-Trent ST6 7AH* T: (01782) 837582 E: frglen@anglocatholic.org.uk

THOMAS, Glyn. b 36. Lon Univ BPharm 61. St Deiniol's Hawarden 80. **d** 82 **p** 83. C Rhyl w St Ann *St As* 83–85; R Llanycil w Bala and Frongoch and Llangower etc 85–03; RD Penllyn 96–03; rtd 03; PtO *St As* from 09. *Blaen-y-Coed, 7 Lon Helyg, Abergele LL22 7JQ* T: (01745) 827725 E: thombala@aol.com

THOMAS, Gordon Herbert. b 43. Guildf Dioc Min Course 00. **d** 00 **p** 01. OLM Cove St Jo *Guildf* 00–13; rtd 13; PtO *Guildf* from 13. *13 Tay Close, Farnborough GU14 9NB* T: (01252) 512347 E: gh.thomas27@btinternet.com

THOMAS, Greville Stephen. b 64. Qu Coll Birm 94. **d** 96 **p** 97. C Hillingdon All SS *Lon* 96–99; C Acton Green 99–04; P-in-c Northolt St Mary 04–06; R 06–14; V Sudbury St Andr from 14. *St Andrew's Vicarage, 956 Harrow Road, Wembley HA0 2QA* T: (020) 8904 4016 E: greville.sudbury@gmail.com

THOMAS, Gudrun Mary. b 68. St Mellitus Coll 17. **d** 19 **p** 20. C Willand, Uffculme, Kentisbeare etc *Ex* from 19.

THOMAS, Canon Harald Daniel. b 34. FInstTT. **d** 97 **p** 05. Par Dn Pontnewydd *Mon* 97–05; NSM 05–16; NSM Cwmbran from 16; Hon Can St Woolos Cathl from 10. *Raldoro, Mount Pleasant Road, Pontnewydd, Cwmbran NP44 1BD* T: (01633) 771353

THOMAS, Miss Hilary Faith. b 43. Ex Univ BA 65 Southn Univ PGCE 66. Trin Coll Bris 90. **d** 94 **p** 95. C Yeovil w Kingston Pitney *B & W* 94–98; V Brislington St Luke *Bris* 98–07; rtd 07; PtO *B & W* 09–12; NSM Mark w Allerton 12–14; PtO from 15. *Brierley, Lower North Street, Cheddar BS27 3HH* T: (01934) 742207 E: hilarythomas@uwclub.net

THOMAS, Hugh Vivian. b 57. Kingston Poly LLB 80 Barrister-at-Law (Lincoln's Inn) 86. SEITE 02. **d** 05 **p** 06. NSM Knockholt w Halstead *Roch* 05–17; P-in-c St Marg Pattens *Lon* 12–14; NSM St Mich Cornhill w St Pet le Poer etc 14–15; PtO 16–17; NSM Tottenham St Paul 17–18; NSM W Hampstead St Cuth from 18. *5 The Meadows, Halstead, Sevenoaks TN14 7HD* T: (01959) 532664 E: hughvthomas@btopenworld.com

THOMAS, Huw. *See* THOMAS, William Huw

THOMAS, Huw Daniel. b 76. Qu Coll Birm. **d** 13 **p** 14. C Salford Sacred Trin and St Phil *Man* 13–16; P-in-c Flixton St Mich from 16. *348 Church Road, Urmston, Manchester M41 6HR* M: 07708-501527 E: huwcantona@yahoo.co.uk

THOMAS, Canon Huw Glyn. b 42. MBE 07. St D Coll Lamp BA 62 Linacre Coll Ox BA 65 MA 69. Wycliffe Hall Ox 62. **d** 65 **p** 66. C Oystermouth *S & B* 65–68; Asst Chapl Solihull Sch 68–69; Chapl and Hd Div 69–73; Selection Sec ACCM 73–78; C Loughton St Jo *Chelmsf* 73–77; V Bury St Jo *Man* 78–83; V Bury St Jo w St Mark 83–86; Dir of Ords 82–87; Can Res and Treas Liv Cathl 87–95; USPG 95–06; Chapl Addis

Ababa Ethiopia 95–97; Provost All SS Cathl Cairo 97–01; Can from 01; Prin Edwardes Coll Peshawar Pakistan 01–06; rtd 06; Hon Sen Fell Liv Hope Univ from 07; PtO *Lon* 07–12; *Blackb* 12–14 and 16–17; P-in-c Overton 14–16. *Flat 3, 36 Knowls Road, Heysham, Morecambe LA3 2PF* T: (01524) 852292 M: 07981-114255 E: huwapglyn@gmail.com

THOMAS, Ian Melville. b 50. Jes Coll Ox BA 71 MA 75 Open Univ BSc 00. St Steph Ho Ox 71. **d** 73 **p** 74. PV St D Cathl 73–77; Chapl RAF 77–95; Command Chapl RAF 95–00; QHC 98–01; V Llanelli *St D* 01–02; R 02–06; R Eccleston and Pulford *Ches* 06–15; rtd 15; PtO *Llan* from 16. *43 The Verlands, Cowbridge CF71 7BY* T: (01446) 773567 E: cestrian09@gmail.com

THOMAS, Ian William. b 53. Bedf Coll of Educn CertEd 74. Ox Min Course 89. **d** 92 **p** 93. NSM Fenny Stratford *Ox* from 92. *5 Laburnum Grove, Bletchley, Milton Keynes MK2 2JW* T: (01908) 644457

THOMAS, Illtyd Barrie. b 54. Nazarene Th Coll Man BA 02 MA 06. Cumbria Chr Learning 17. **d** 18 **p** 18. NSM Carl H Trin and St Barn 18–21; Ld Chapl N Cumbria Integrated Care NHS Foundn Trust from 20. *The Chaplaincy, Cumberland Infirmary, Infirmary Street, Carlisle CA2 7HY* T: (01228) 523444 M: 07443-549525 E: barriethomas@outlook.com

THOMAS, Jeffrey. *See* THOMAS, David Jeffrey

THOMAS, Jeffrey Malcolm. **d** 10 **p** 12. C Morriston *S & B* 10–11; C Swansea St Thos and Kilvey 12–14; P-in-c Porth Newydd *Llan* from 14; P-in-c Dinas w Penygraig from 18; C Tonypandy w Clydach Vale w Williamstown from 18. *4 Kimberley Way, Porth CF39 9HS* T: (01443) 551754 E: jeffreymthomas61@yahoo.com

THOMAS, Canon Jennifer Monica. b 58. Wilson Carlile Coll 79 Sarum & Wells Th Coll 91. **d** 93 **p** 94. Par Dn Wandsworth St Paul *S'wark* 93–94; C 94–97; V Forest Hill 97–02; V Mitcham Ascension from 02; Hon Can S'wark Cathl from 14. *The Vicarage, Sherwood Park Road, Mitcham CR4 1NE* T: (020) 8764 1258 E: ascensionchurch@btinternet.com

THOMAS, Jeremy Paul. b 63. Lanc Univ BSc 87. Trin Coll Bris 04. **d** 06 **p** 07. C Aughton Ch Ch *Liv* 06–10; P-in-c Ashton-in-Makerfield St Thos 10–15; V 15–19; TV Wigan from 20. *The Vicarage, 18 Warrington Road, Ashton-in-Makerfield, Wigan WN4 9PL* T: (01942) 727275 E: jeremy@holmacre.plus.com *or* hubleader.south@churchwigan.org

THOMAS, Mrs Joanna Sophie. b 67. Ex Univ BTh. SWMTC 12. **d** 16. NSM St Buryan, St Levan and Sennen *Truro* 16–20; NSM Gulval and Madron from 20. *7 Morrab Road, Penzance TR18 4EL*

THOMAS, John Thurston. b 28. Univ of Wales (Swansea) BSc 48 DipEd 49 Leeds Univ PhD 58 CChem FRSC 65. Glouc Sch of Min 88. **d** 90 **p** 91. NSM S Cerney w Cerney Wick and Down Ampney *Glouc* 90–96; PtO 96–01; *S & B* from 01. *15 Roman Court, Blackpill, Swansea SA3 5BL* T: (01792) 406671

THOMAS, Julian Mark. b 48. Ex Univ BA 05. SWMTC 00. **d** 03 **p** 04. C Okehampton w Inwardleigh, Bratton Clovelly etc *Ex* 03–07; C Essington *Lich* 07–12; rtd 12; PtO *Lich* 13–16. *9 New Minster House, Bird Street, Lichfield WS13 6PR* T: (01543) 253319 E: mark.thomas108@o2.co.uk

THOMAS, Katie Jane. b 71. **d** 14 **p** 15. C Stoke-next-Guildf *Guildf* 14–15; C Guildf H Trin w St Mary 15–18; P-in-c Malden St Jas *S'wark* 18–19; V from 19; Women's Min Adv Kingston Area from 20. *The Vicarage, 7 Bodley Road, New Malden KT3 5QD*

THOMAS, Keith. *See* THOMAS, Ernest Keith

THOMAS, Kimberley Ann. b 59. Cranmer Hall Dur 02. **d** 04 **p** 05. C Chesterton *Lich* 04–07; V Stretton w Claymills 07–16; R Mundaring Australia from 16. *11 Mann Street, Mundaring WA 6073, Australia* T: (0061) (8) 9295 1029 E: mundaringparish@westnet.com.au

THOMAS, Leighton. *See* THOMAS, Adrian Leighton

THOMAS, Canon Leslie Richard. b 45. Lon Coll of Div 65. **d** 69 **p** 70. C Knotty Ash St Jo *Liv* 69–72; C Sutton 72–74; TV 74–77; V Banks 77–82; V Gt Crosby All SS 82–92; P-in-c Marthall *Ches* 92–02; Chapl David Lewis Cen for Epilepsy 92–02; V Bickerton, Bickley, Harthill and Burwardsley 02–10; RD Malpas 04–10; Hon Can Ches Cathl 07–10; rtd 10; PtO *Liv* from 16. *7 Fairhaven Road, Southport PR9 9UJ* T: (01704) 227511 E: sandstone1945@gmail.com

THOMAS, Mark. *See* THOMAS, Julian Mark

THOMAS, Mark Gareth. b 82. Cam Univ BA 04 MPhil 13. **d** 15 **p** 16. C Battersea Rise St Mark *S'wark* 15–18; C Onslow Square and S Kensington St Aug *Lon* 18–20; C Swansea St Thos and Kilvey *S & B* from 20. *5 Kilvey Terrace, St Thomas, Swansea SA1 8BA* T: (01792) 455671 E: mark.thomas@sts.church

THOMAS, Preb Mark Wilson. b 51. Dur Univ BA 72 Hull Univ MA 89. Ripon Coll Cuddesdon 76. **d** 78 **p** 79. C Chapelthorpe *Wakef* 78–81; C Seaford w Sutton *Chich* 81–84; V Gomersal *Wakef* 84–92; TR Almondbury w Farnley

Tyas 92–01; RD Almondbury 93–01; Hon Can Wakef Cathl 99–01; P-in-c Shrewsbury St Chad w St Mary Lich 01–07; V Shrewsbury St Chad, St Mary and St Alkmund 07–13; RD Shrewsbury 09–13; Preb Lich Cathl 11–13; rtd 13; PtO Lich 14–17; Hon C Witney Ox from 17. *Mill Farmhouse, Black Bourton, Bampton OX18 2PE* T: (01993) 840368 E: markthomas51@hotmail.com

THOMAS, Martin Russell. b 66. Edin Univ BMus 88 UEA PhD 13 LRSM 02. Ripon Coll Cuddesdon BTh 05. **d** 03 **p** 04. C Wymondham *Nor* 03–06; P-in-c Fulham St Andr *Lon* 06–07; V 07–11; Can Res St E Cathl 11–12; P-in-c Kennington Park St Agnes *S'wark* 12–13; TR Plaistow and N Canning Town *Chelmsf* 14–15; TR Catford (Southend) and Downham *S'wark* 15–20; PtO *B & W* from 21. *Henley Barn, East Horrington, Wells BA5 3EA* T: (01749) 678064 M: 07460-257103 E: fathermartinthomas@gmail.com

THOMAS (formerly **WADE**)**, Mary Ruth.** b 70. Leeds Univ BA 92 Wolv Univ PGCE 94. Qu Coll Birm 10. **d** 12 **p** 13. C Albrighton, Boningale and Donington *Lich* 12–15; V from 15. *The Vicarage, High Street, Albrighton, Wolverhampton WV7 3EQ* T: (01902) 373415 or 373160 M: 07857-039641 E: revmarythomas@gmail.com

THOMAS, Michael Longdon Sanby. b 34. Trin Hall Cam BA 55 MA 60. Wells Th Coll 56. **d** 58 **p** 59. C Sandal St Helen *Wakef* 58–60; Chapl Portsm Cathl 60–64; V Shedfield 64–69; V Portchester 69–98; rtd 98. *188 Castle Street, Portchester, Fareham PO16 9QH* T/F: (023) 9242 0416 E: thomasfamily73@cwtv.net or anmithomas@gmail.com

THOMAS, Michael Rosser David. b 74. Kent Univ BA 96. St Steph Ho Ox BTh 02. **d** 02 **p** 03. C Aberavon *Llan* 02–05; Min Can Brecon Cathl *S & B* 05–07; Succ 07–17; P-in-c Brecon St Mary w Llanddew 08–11; P-in-c Brecon St Mary 11–13; Bp's Chapl 14–16; TV Old St Pancras *Lon* from 17. *The Rectory, 191 St Pancras Way, London NW1 9NH* T: (020) 7267 3962 E: fr.michael@posp.co.uk

THOMAS, Moray. See THOMAS, Charles Moray Stewart Reid

THOMAS, Ms Natasha Creighton. b 70. St Hild Coll BA 18. **d** 18 **p** 19. NSM Keighley *Leeds* 18–19; C from 19. *13 Westview Grove, Keighley BD20 6JJ* M: 07987-707221 E: natasha.thomas@leeds.anglican.com

THOMAS, Nigel Bruce. b 63. Univ of Wales BD 91. St Jo Coll Nottm MA 98. **d** 97 **p** 98. C Millom *Carl* 97–02; R Bentham *Bradf* 02–07; P-in-c St Breoke and Egloshayle *Truro* 07–08; TR Carew *St D* 08–12; PtO *Sarum* 12–22; Chapl HM Pris The Verne 15–18; Chapl HM YOI Portland 15–18; TV Yatton Moor *B & W* from 18. *The Vicarage, 1 Millier Road, Cleeve, Bristol DT11 7QJ* T: (01258) 459414 M: 07817-356651 E: nigelbthomas1@gmail.com

THOMAS, Nigel Clayton. b 52. Leeds Univ BA 76 Univ of Wales (Cardiff) PGCE 77. ERMC 08. **d** 11 **p** 12. C Madrid *Eur* 11–16; P-in-c Nerja and Almuñécar 16–19; Chapl from 19. *Church House, Paseo Tamango Hill 25, Adosado 7, 29793 Torrox Costa (Málaga), Spain* T: (0034) 951 815 736 M: (0034) 608 695 756 E: cofenerja@gmail.com or nigelthomasnta@gmail.com

THOMAS, Ms Pamela Sybil. b 38. Ripon Coll Cuddesdon 88. **d** 90 **p** 94. Par Dn Preston w Sutton Poyntz, Littlemoor etc *Sarum* 90–94; C 94–96; P-in-c Weymouth St Edm 96–05; P-in-c Abbotsbury, Portesham and Langton Herring 97–08; Chapl Westhaven Hosp Weymouth 96–08; rtd 08; Hon C Cullompton, Willand, Uffculme, Kentisbeare etc *Ex* 08–15; PtO *Sarum* 16–20. *Rosewood, 22 North Square, Chickerell, Weymouth DT3 4DX* T: (01305) 750903 E: rev.thomas@btinternet.com or revpsthomas22@gmail.com

THOMAS, Canon Patrick Hungerford Bryan. b 52. St Cath Coll Cam BA 73 MA 77 Leeds Univ BA 78 Univ of Wales PhD 82. Coll of Resurr Mirfield 76. **d** 79 **p** 80. C Aberystwyth *St D* 79–81; C Carmarthen St Pet 81–82; R Llangeitho and Blaenpennal w Betws Leucu etc 82–84; Warden of Ords 83–86; R Brechfa w Abergorlech etc 84–01; V Carmarthen St Dav 01–19; P-in-c Bro Caerfyrddin 19–21; Can St D Cathl 00–21; Chan 09–21; rtd 21. *40 Myrddin Crescent, Carmarthen SA31 1DX* T: (01267) 643437 E: canon.patrick@yahoo.co.uk

THOMAS, Paul Richard. b 75. Univ of Wales (Cardiff) BA 96 MA 99 Hon ARAM 11. Ripon Coll Cuddesdon BA 01 MA 06. **d** 02 **p** 03. C Wanstead St Mary w Ch Ch *Chelmsf* 02–06; C St Marylebone w H Trin *Lon* 06–11; V Paddington St Jas from 11; Chapl St Marylebone C of E Sch 08–11; Chapl R Academy of Music *Lon* 08–12; AD Westmr Paddington from 16; Acting Adn Charing Cross 17–19; Chapl Wellington Coll Berks 18–19. *St James's Vicarage, 6 Gloucester Terrace, London W2 3DD* T: (020) 7262 1265 M: 07967-753671 E: vicar@stjamespaddington.org.uk

THOMAS, Canon Paul Robert. b 42. OBE 02. NOC. **d** 82 **p** 83. C Hull St Jo Newland *York* 82–84; P-in-c Rowley 84–87;

Soc Resp Officer Hull 84–87; R Rowley w Skidby 87–88; TR Barking St Marg w St Patr *Chelmsf* 88–93; Gen Sec and Admin St Luke's Hosp for Clergy 93–03; Can and Preb Chich Cathl 98–03; P in O 99–12; rtd 03; PtO *Nor* 03–14; P-in-c Erpingham w Calthorpe, Ingworth, Aldborough etc 14–18; PtO from 18. *11 Cecil Road, Dereham NR20 4AN* E: synergyatwork@aol.com

THOMAS, The Ven Paul Wyndham. b 55. Oriel Coll Ox BA 76 BTh 78 MA 80. Wycliffe Hall Ox 77. **d** 79 **p** 80. C Llangynwyd w Maesteg *Llan* 79–85; TV Langport Area *B & W* 85–90; P-in-c Thorp Arch w Walton *York* 90–93; Clergy Tr Officer 90–04; V Nether w Upper Poppleton 93–04; P-in-c Castle Town *Lich* 04–11; RD Stafford 05–11; Local Par Development Adv Stafford Area 10–11; Adn Salop from 11; P-in-c Forton from 11. *The Vicarage, Tong, Shifnal TF11 8PW* T: (01902) 372622

THOMAS, Peter James. b 53. Lon Univ BSc 75. Trin Coll Bris 77. **d** 80 **p** 81. C Hucclecote *Glouc* 80–84; C Loughborough Em *Leic* 84–85; TV Parr *Liv* 85–92; V Eckington *Worc* 92–05; V Defford w Besford 92–05; RD Pershore 00–05; P-in-c Norton sub Hamdon, W Chinnock, Chiselborough etc *B & W* 05–17; P-in-c Stoke sub Hamdon 12–17; R Ham Hill Villages 17–19; RD Ivelchester 07–13; rtd 19; PtO *B & W* from 19. *8 Irwell Green, Taunton TA1 2TA* E: pthomas5@aol.com

THOMAS, Peter Rhys. b 37. TCD BA 59 MA 72 MInstPkg MCIPD. **d** 72 **p** 73. C Tuam w Cong, Ballinrobe and Aasleagh *T, K & A* 73–75; I 75–77; C Bingley All SS *Bradf* 77–79; V Shelf 79–81; Producer Relig Broadcasting Viking Radio 81–84; P-in-c Croxton *Linc* 81–82; P-in-c Ulceby 81–82; P-in-c Wootton 81–82; P-in-c Ulceby Gp 82; V 82–84; R E and W Tilbury and Linford *Chelmsf* 84–89; I Celbridge w Straffan and Newcastle-Lyons *D & G* 89–93; I Youghal Union *C, C & R* 93–99; Dioc Communications Officer (Cork) 95–99; Can Cork Cathl 97–99; Preb Cloyne Cathl 97–99; rtd 99; Rep Leprosy Miss Munster from 00. *Abina Cottage, Ballykenneally, Ballymacoda, Co Cork, Republic of Ireland* T/F: (00353) (24) 98082 E: prthomas@iol.ie

THOMAS, Peter Wilson. b 58. K Coll Lon BD 80 AKC 80. Ripon Coll Cuddesdon 80. **d** 82 **p** 83. C Stockton St Pet *Dur* 82–85; TV Solihull *Birm* 85–90; V Rednal 90–05; Chapl MG Rover 95–05; P-in-c Balsall Common 05–10; V from 10. *St Peter's House, Holly Lane, Balsall Common, Coventry CV7 7EA* T/F: (01676) 532721 E: frpeter@uwclub.net

THOMAS, Canon Philip Harold Emlyn. b 41. Cant Univ (NZ) BA 64 MA 77 Dur Univ PhD 82. Melbourne Coll of Div BD 68. **d** 68 **p** 69. C Adelaide H Trin Australia 68–71; Lic to Offic Dio Christchurch NZ 71–77; Fell and Chapl Univ Coll Dur 77–83; V Heighington *Dur* 84–10; AD Darlington 94–00; Hon Can Dur Cathl 07–10; rtd 10; PtO *Glouc* from 14. *2 Gloucester Street, Cirencester GL7 2DG* E: philip.thomas7@btinternet.com

THOMAS, Philip John. b 52. Liv Poly BSc 74. Trin Coll Bris 94. **d** 96 **p** 97. C Skelton w Upleatham *York* 96–97; C Acomb St Steph and St Aid 97–01; V Woodthorpe *S'well* 01–14; V Cinderhill 15–17; rtd 17; PtO *S'well* from 18. *28 Lambley Lane, Gedling, Nottingham NG4 4PA* M: 07897-003409 E: philipthomas323@gmail.com

THOMAS, Ramon Lorenzo. b 44. Victoria Univ Wellington BCA 73 Mass Inst of Tech MSc 80 CA 73. Oak Hill Th Coll 89. **d** 97 **p** 98. NSM Yateley *Win* 97–99; Chairman Judah Trust from 99; PtO *Chich* from 10. *58 Rock Gardens, Bognor Regis PO21 2LF* T: (01243) 825523 E: judahtrust@aol.com

THOMAS, Rhys. See THOMAS, Peter Rhys

THOMAS, Richard Nathan. b 76. Ch Ch Coll Cant BA 98. Ridley Hall Cam 11. **d** 13 **p** 14. C Ealing St Paul *Lon* 13–16; V Tunbridge Wells St Phil *Roch* from 16. *St Philip's Vicarage, Birken Road, Tunbridge Wells TN2 3TE* T: (01892) 512071 M: 07786-132897 E: richnthomas@gmail.com

THOMAS, Robert Graham. b 53. G&C Coll Cam BA 75 MA 79 Imp Coll Lon PhD 78 CEng 82 FIMechE 93. SAOMC 04. **d** 06 **p** 07. C Bathampton w Claverton *B & W* 06–10; P-in-c Trowbridge St Jas and Keevil *Sarum* 10–11; R 11–21; Chapl Wilts Coun 11–21; rtd 21. *Freelyn, The Cleave, Harwell, Didcot OX11 0EL* E: rob.thomas@cantab.net

⊕**THOMAS, The Rt Revd Roderick Charles Howell.** b 54. LSE BSc 75. Wycliffe Hall Ox 91. **d** 93 **p** 94 **c** 15. C Plymouth St Andr w St Paul and St Geo *Ex* 93–95; C Plymouth St Andr and Stonehouse 95–99; P-in-c Elburton 99–05; V 05–15; Preb Ex Cathl 12–15; Suff Bp Maidstone *Cant* from 15; Hon Asst Bp Lon, S'wark and Ex from 15; Chelmsf, Sheff Man, Nor, Ches, Ely and Roch from 16; Hon Asst Bp Lich, Bris and Birm from 17; Hon Asst Bp Ox from 18. *The Old Vicarage, 29 St John's Meadow, Blindley Heath, Lingfield RH7 6JU* T: (01342) 834140 M: 07906-331110 E: bishop@bishopofmaidstone.org

THOMAS, Mrs Ruth Alison Mary. b 57. York Univ BA 79 Dur Univ PGCE 80 MA 96. NEOC 07. **d** 09 **p** 10. NSM Dur St Giles 09–21; NSM Dur St Giles, Shadforth and Sherburn from 21; NSM Shadforth and Sherburn 09–12; Chapl Dur Cathl from 12. *68 Gilesgate, Durham DH1 1HY* T: 0191-386 0402 M: 07855-236063 E: ruth.thomas@stgilesdurham.org.uk

THOMAS, Mrs Sheila Mary Witton. b 49. STETS 06. **d** 09 **p** 10. NSM Marnhull *Sarum* 09–13; NSM Okeford 13–14; PtO 15–17; NSM W Parley 17–21; PtO from 21. *11A West Moors Road, Ferndown BH22 9SA* M: 07748-974206 E: sheila2is@yahoo.co.uk

THOMAS, Sonia Patricia. *See* BARRON, Sonia Patricia

THOMAS, Preb Stephen Blayney. b 35. St D Coll Lamp BA 62. Bp Burgess Hall Lamp. **d** 63 **p** 64. C Ledbury *Heref* 63–67; C Bridgnorth w Tasley 67–68; C Clun w Chapel Lawn, Bettws-y-Crwyn and Newcastle 68–73; C Clungunford w Clunbury and Clunton, Bedstone etc 68–73; V Worfield 73–84; RD Bridgnorth 81–83; R Kingsland 84–96; P-in-c Eardisland 84–96; P-in-c Aymestrey and Leinthall Earles w Wigmore etc 84–96; R Kingsland w Eardisland, Aymestrey etc 97–99; Preb Heref Cathl 85–01; rtd 99; PtO *Heref* 00–19; *Worc* from 00. *28 Castle Close, Burford, Tenbury Wells WR15 8AY* T: (01584) 819642 E: stephenbthomas@btinternet.com

THOMAS, Canon Stuart Grahame. b 54. Pemb Coll Cam BA 77 MA 81 Ban Univ MPhil 15 ATCL 97. Ridley Hall Cam 85. **d** 87 **p** 88. C Guildf H Trin w St Mary 87–91; V Churt 91–94; V Ewell St Fran 94–14; Dioc Ecum Officer 99–07; RD Epsom 07–14; R Frimley from 14; Hon Can Guildf Cathl from 12. *The Rectory, 3 Parsonage Way, Frimley, Camberley GU16 8HZ* T: (01276) 23291 E: revstuart.thomas@btinternet.com

THOMAS, Miss Susan. b 58. City of Liv Coll of HE BA 80 PGCE 81. SNWTP 10. **d** 13 **p** 14. C Formby H Trin and Altcar *Liv* 13–17; C Chapelfields 17–18. *19 Hampton Road, Formby, Liverpool L37 6EJ* T: (01704) 398990 E: thomass1109@aol.com

THOMAS, Susan Linda. b 60. SEITE 08. **d** 11 **p** 12. NSM Coulsdon St Jo *S'wark* from 11. *40 West Hill, South Croydon CR2 0SA*

THOMAS, Mrs Susan Margaret Ann. b 60. Liv Univ MEd 95. All SS Cen for Miss & Min 19. **d** 21. NSM Wigan *Liv* from 21. *The Vicarage, 18 Warrington Road, Ashton-in-Makerfield, Wigan WN4 9PL* T: (01942) 727275 M: 07877-704645 E: sue.thomas@churchwigan.org

THOMAS, Canon Sydney Robert. b 44. Univ of Wales (Swansea) BA 65 MA 83. St D Coll Lamp LTh 67. **d** 67 **p** 68. C Llanelli *St D* 67–77; V Pontyberem 77–01; TR Cwm Gwendraeth 01–08; RD Cydweli 94–05; Can St D Cathl 94–08; Chan St D Cathl 01–03; Treas St D Cathl 03–08; rtd 09; PtO *St D* from 09. *40 Waungoch, Upper Tumble, Llanelli SA14 6BX* T: (01269) 841677 E: sydvic@sydvic.plus.com

THOMAS, Thomas. b 68. Selw Coll Cam BA 90. Wycliffe Hall Ox 91. **d** 93 **p** 94. C Much Woolton *Liv* 93–97; V Carr Mill 97–10; C Springfield *Birm* 10–11; P-in-c 11–15; V from 15. *St Christopher's Vicarage, 172 Woodlands Road, Springfield, Birmingham B11 4ET* T: 0121-702 2745 M: 07980-650801 E: tom172thomas@btinternet.com

THOMAS, Thomas Alan. b 37. K Coll Lon BD 60 AKC 60. St Boniface Warminster 60. **d** 61 **p** 62. C Washington *Dur* 61–65; C Bishopwearmouth St Mary V w St Pet CD 65–70; V Ruishton w Thornfalcon *B & W* 70–82; R Hutton 82–94; V Frome Ch Ch 94–96; Chapl Victoria Hosp Frome 94–96; R Camerton w Dunkerton, Foxcote and Shoscombe *B & W* 96–00; rtd 00; PtO *B & W* from 00. *12 Farrington Way, Farrington Gurney, Bristol BS39 6US* T: (01761) 453434

THOMAS, Timothy Charles Rank. b 75. Trin Coll Bris. **d** 14 **p** 15. C Walkden and Lt Hulton *Man* 14–17; P-in-c Bowling St Jo *Leeds* from 17. *96 Lister Avenue, Bradford BD4 7QS* T: (01274) 681300 E: tim@stjohnsbowling.com

THOMAS, Virginia Jacqueline. b 48. UEA BA 70. Yale Div Sch MDiv 97. **d** 00 **p** 01. NSM Chelsea St Luke and Ch Ch *Lon* 00–04; NSM W Brompton St Mary w St Pet 04–06; P-in-c 05–06; P-in-c W Brompton St Mary w St Peter and St Jude 06–10; V 10–14; V Gt w Lt Tew and Heythrop *Ox* 14–21. *13 Coolidge Close, Headington, Oxford OX3 7NP* E: ginnytea@gmail.com *or* ginny.tewvicar@gmail.com

THOMAS, Vivian Ivor. b 52. S Bank Univ MSc 95 Regent Coll Vancouver MCS 97 K Coll Lon PhD 02. **d** 08 **p** 09. NSM Hammersmith St Paul *Lon* from 08. *76 Rannoch Road, London W6 9SP* T: (020) 7384 5954 M: 07767-777891 E: vivian.thomas@btinternet.com *or* viv.thomas@formation.org.uk

THOMAS, William Huw. b 65. Yorks Min Course 15. **d** 17 **p** 18. NSM Pitsmoor Ch Ch *Sheff* from 17. *140 Abbeyfield Road, Sheffield S4 7AY* M: 07525-688479 E: huw.thomas@sheffield.anglican.org

THOMAS, Wilson Hugo. b 40. **d** 01 **p** 05. Barbados 01–05; NSM Frimley *Guildf* 05–07. *3B Ansell Road, Frimley GU16 8BS* T: (01276) 681652 E: wilsonthomas56@googlemail.com

THOMAS ANTHONY, Brother. *See* DEHOOP, Thomas Anthony

THOMASSON, Keith Duncan. b 69. St Pet Coll Ox BA 91 MA 97 Sarum Coll MA 15 Lon Inst of Educn PGCE 92. Ripon Coll Cuddesdon BA 01 Bossey Ecum Inst Geneva. **d** 02 **p** 03. C Lancaster St Mary w St John and St Anne *Blackb* 02–04; C Longridge 04–06; Partnership P E Bris 06–11; Chapl Hants Colleg Sch 11–14; Hon C Romsey *Win* 11–14; Sen Chapl Alabaré Chr Care Centres 14–21; R Troon *Glas* from 21. *70 Bentinck Drive, Troon KA10 6HZ* M: 07500-788148

THOMASSON-ROSINGH, Mrs Anna Clara Abena (Anna-Claar). b 74. Ede Chr Coll BEd 97 Utrecht Univ MA 01 Man Univ PhD 09. Leiden Remonstrant Sem 98 Bossey Ecum Inst Geneva 01. **d** 14 **p** 15. Remonstrant Min 02–14; C Salisbury St Thos and St Edm *Sarum* 14–18; Dir Studies Sarum Coll 15–18; TV Chalke Valley *Sarum* 18–21. *70 Bentinck Drive, Troon KA10 6HZ* M: 07410-696332

THOMPSON (née SMETHAM), The Very Revd Abigail Laura. b 75. K Coll Lon BMus 97 Clare Coll Cam BA 05. Westcott Ho Cam 03. **d** 06 **p** 07. C Sheff Manor 06–10; P-in-c Clifton St Jas 10–15; V 15–18; Dean of Women's Min 15–18; Can Res and Sub-Dean St Alb 18–21; Dean Sheff from 21. *Address temp unknown* E: abi.thompson@sheffield-cathedral.org.uk

THOMPSON, Adrian David. b 68. Univ of Wales (Abth) BSc 93 PhD 97 Bris Univ PGCE 98. Wycliffe Hall Ox 93. **d** 05 **p** 06. C Blackb St Gabr 05–08; Chapl Abp Temple Sch Preston 09–11; TV Cockermouth Area *Carl* from 11. *The Rectory, Lorton Road, Cockermouth CA13 9DU* T: (01900) 821288 *or* 829926 E: adrian.cockermouth@gmail.com *or* adrian@cateam.org.uk

THOMPSON, Andrew David. b 68. MBE 11. Poly of Wales BSc 90 Nottm Univ MA 03 Glos Univ MA 20 Gilgal Bibl Sem UAE PhD 20. Wycliffe Hall Ox 98. **d** 00 **p** 01. C Oakwood *Derby* 00–04; Asst Chapl UAE 05–06; Chapl Kuwait 06–10; Chapl Abu Dhabi St Andr UAE 10–20; Hon Can Bahrain 11–20; TV Uxbridge *Lon* from 20. *29 Belmont Close, Uxbridge UB8 1RF* M: 07414-137835 E: canonathompson@gmail.com

THOMPSON, Andrew Robert William. **d** 13 **p** 14. Belfast St Donard *D & D* 13–14; C Donaghcloney w Waringstown 14–17. *8 Hatchley Close, Sutton Heath, Woodbridge IP12 3TX* M: 07803-062874 E: andrew7hompson@yahoo.co.uk

THOMPSON, Canon Anthony Edward. b 38. Bris Univ BA 61. Ridley Hall Cam 61. **d** 63 **p** 64. C Peckham St Mary Magd *S'wark* 63–66; SAMS Paraguay 67–72; C Otley *Bradf* 72–75; TV Woughton *Ox* 75–82; P-in-c Lower Nutfield *S'wark* 82–02; V S Nutfield w Outwood 02–03; RD Reigate 91–93; Local Min Adv Croydon Episc Area 93–03; Hon Can S'wark Cathl 03; rtd 03; PtO *Chich* from 04. *3 The Curlews, Shoreham-by-Sea BN43 5UQ* T: (01273) 440182 E: tonythompsonsbs@hotmail.com

THOMPSON, Benjamin Joseph Peter. b 79. Trin Coll Cam BA 00 MA 04 QUB PhD 21. Oak Hill Th Coll MTh 12. **d** 12 **p** 13. C Moreton-in-Marsh w Batsford, Todenham etc *Glouc* 12–16; NSM from 16. *32 Croft Holm, Moreton-in-Marsh GL56 0JH* T: (01608) 238628 M: 07912-675561 E: bjpthompson1@gmail.com

THOMPSON, Brian. b 34. MRICS 65 FRICS 75. St Jo Coll Nottm 81. **d** 84 **p** 85. C Bletchley *Ox* 84–87; V Steynly Green *Lich* 87–99; rtd 99; PtO *Lich* 99–11; *Leic* 12–21. *14 Stuart Court, High Street, Kibworth Beauchamp, Leicester LE8 0LR* T: 0116-319 7523 E: thompson.brian48@gmail.com

THOMPSON, Carrie Julia Lucy Jadwiga. b 77. Keble Coll Ox BA 99 MA 04. St Steph Ho Ox MA 06. **d** 04 **p** 05. C Camberwell St Giles w St Matt *S'wark* 04–08; V Forton *Portsm* 08–20; Chapl St Vincent Sixth Form Coll 08–20. *Address temp unknown*

THOMPSON, Christopher William. *See* OGILVIE THOMPSON, Christopher William

THOMPSON, Daniel Edward John. b 75. Staffs Univ BA 97 Birkbeck Coll Lon MA 06 Heythrop Coll Lon MTh 18 Brighton Univ PGCE 08. **d** 14 **p** 15. C Hadleigh, Layham and Shelley *St E* 14–17; R Icknield *Ox* from 17. *The Rectory, 10 Prospect Place, Watlington OX49 5AJ* T: (01491) 614218 E: tbfspace@hotmail.com

THOMPSON, David. *See* THOMPSON, John David

THOMPSON, David Arthur. b 37. Clifton Th Coll. **d** 69 **p** 70. C Finchley Ch Ch *Lon* 69–72; C Barking St Marg w St Patr *Chelmsf* 72–75; TV 75–81; V Toxteth Park St Clem *Liv* 81–91; TR Parr 91–03; rtd 03; PtO *Sarum* 03–10; *Liv* from

16. *Calm Haven, 21 Arklow Drive, Hale Village, Liverpool L24 5RN* T: 0151-425 2012

THOMPSON, David John. b 64. Cranmer Hall Dur 92. d 95 p 96. C Poulton-le-Sands w Morecambe St Laur *Blackb* 95–99; V Farington Moss 99–02; V Lea 02–09; Warden Past Assts 06–09; P-in-c Ringley w Prestolee *Man* 09–10; TV Farnworth, Kearsley and Stoneclough 10–13; V Walmersley Road, Bury from 13. *St John's Vicarage, 270 Walmersley Road, Bury BL9 6NH* T: 0161-797 7652 E: dvjt@outlook.com

THOMPSON, Derrick Lionel. b 65. Trin Coll Bris 13. d 15 p 16. NSM S Norwood H Innocents *S'wark* 15–18; P-in-c Thornton Heath St Paul 18–19; V from 19. *19 Oliver Avenue, London SE25 6TY* T: 020-8768 5387 M: 07342-923138 E: revd.derrick@gmail.com

THOMPSON (*née* WHEATLEY), Diane. b 59. Goldsmiths' Coll Lon BMus 80 Anglia Ruskin Univ MA 14 Birm Poly PGCE 81. Westcott Ho Cam 10. d 12 p 13. C Kings Heath *Birm* 12–16; TV Warwick *Cov* from 16. *All Saints' Vicarage, Vicarage Fields, Warwick CV34 5NJ* T: (01926) 492073 E: revdt.allsaints@gmail.com

THOMPSON, Ms Eileen Carol. b 46. Lon Univ BA 69. New Coll Edin MTh 92. d 96 p 97. Par Dn Dhaka St Thos Bangladesh 96–97; Presbyter Madras H Cross w St Mich India 97–99; Presbyter in charge Madras St Mary 99–02; V Pallikunu St Geo and Palla Ch Ch 02–04; Min Livingston LEP *Edin* 04–13; rtd 13; LtO *Edin* from 13. *4/2 Saxe Coburg Terrace, Edinburgh EH3 5BU* T: 0131-315 4928 E: eileencthompson@gmail.com

THOMPSON, Canon Elizabeth Gray McManus. d 06 p 07. NSM Garrison w Slavin and Belleek *Clogh* 06–07; NSM Rossorry 07–09; NSM Enniskillen 09–11; Bp's C Aghalurcher w Tattykeeran, Cooneen etc 11–13; NSM Donagh w Tyholland and Errigal Truagh 13–18; NSM Derryvullen S w Garvary from 18; Can Clogh Cathl from 19. *En-Rimmon, 6 Tullylammy Road, Irvinestown, Enniskillen BT94 1RN* T: (028) 6862 8258 E: thompson.clogher@btinternet.com

✠THOMPSON, The Rt Revd Geoffrey Hewlett. b 29. Trin Hall Cam BA 52 MA 56. Cuddesdon Coll 52. d 54 p 55 c 74. C Northampton St Matt *Pet* 54–59; V Wisbech St Aug *Ely* 59–66; V Folkestone St Sav *Cant* 66–74; Area Bp Willesden *Lon* 74–79 and 79–85; Bp Ex 85–99; rtd 99; Hon Asst Bp Carl from 99. *Low Broomrigg, Warcop, Appleby-in-Westmorland CA16 6PT* T: (01768) 341281

THOMPSON, Geoffrey Peter. b 58. St Pet Coll Ox BA 80 MA 82. SEITE 99. d 02 p 03. C Cheam *S'wark* 02–06; C Croydon St Jo 06–11; P-in-c Norbury St Steph and Thornton Heath 11–15; V from 15. *St Stephen's Vicarage, 9 Warwick Road, Thornton Heath CR7 7NH* T: (020) 8684 3820 E: gtchurch@waitrose.com

THOMPSON, Harold Anthony. b 41. NOC 84. d 87 p 88. C Leeds Belle Is St Jo and St Barn *Ripon* 87–90; V Leeds St Cypr Harehills 90–96; V Shadwell 96–06; rtd 06; PtO *Leeds* from 17. *551 Shadwell Lane, Leeds LS17 8AP* T: 0113-266 5913 E: tonythompson1941@gmail.com

THOMPSON, Hewlett. *See* THOMPSON, Geoffrey Hewlett

THOMPSON, Ian David. b 51. Hull Univ BSc 72. NOC 94. d 97 p 98. C Blackley St Andr *Man* 97–00; P-in-c 00–06; R Burnage St Marg 06–16; rtd 16; PtO *Man* from 16. *4 Kinross Avenue, Heywood OL10 3FX* M: 07747-614054 E: iandthompson@virginmedia.com

THOMPSON, Ian George. b 60. SEITE 99. d 02 p 03. NSM Walworth St Pet *S'wark* 02–05; NSM Dulwich St Clem w St Pet 05–07; Chapl HM Pris Pentonville 07–11; Chapl HM YOI Wetherby 11–13; Chapl HM Pris Coldingley 13–16; Chapl HM Pris Wormwood Scrubs 16–18; Chapl HM Pris Brixton from 18. *HM Prison Brixton, Jebb Avenue, London SW2 5XF* T: (020) 8588 6052 M: 07985-582257

THOMPSON, James Stewart. b 46. St Padarn's Inst 19. d 20 p 21. C Pool Miss Area *St As* 20–21; P-in-c from 21. *Lower House Farm, Llansantffraid SY22 6TE* T: (01691) 828438 E: lowhousefarm@hotmail.com *or* jamesthompson1@cinw.org.uk

THOMPSON, Jane Elspeth Christine. b 58. Sarum Coll 13. d 16 p 17. NSM Michelmersh and Awbridge and Braishfield etc *Win* from 16. *36 Five Elms Drive, Romsey SO51 5RN* T: (01794) 502035 E: jane.thompson@me.com

THOMPSON, Jeremy James Thomas. b 58. Sunderland Univ BEd 92. Cranmer Hall Dur 94. d 96 p 97. C Bedlington *Newc* 96–00; P-in-c Choppington 00–02; V 02–08; R St John Lee from 08; V Warden w Newbrough from 08; AD Hexham 16–21. *St John Lee Rectory, Acomb, Hexham NE46 4PE* T: (01434) 600268 E: revjjtt@gmail.com

THOMPSON, John David. b 40. Lon Univ BD 65 Ch Ch Ox DPhil 69. St Steph Ho Ox 65. d 67 p 68. C Solihull *Birm* 67–71; C Biddestone w Slaughterford *Bris* 71–73; Lect Sarum & Wells Th Coll 71–72; C Yatton Keynell *Bris* 71–73; C Castle

Combe 71–73; V Braughing *St Alb* 74–77; R Digswell 77–82; TR Digswell and Panshanger 82–98; rtd 00; PtO *Ab* from 15. *11 Russell Street, Boddam, Peterhead AB42 3NG* T: (01779) 472680

THOMPSON, Canon John Michael. b 47. Nottm Univ BTh 77. Linc Th Coll 73. d 77 p 78. C Old Brumby *Linc* 77–80; C Grantham 80–81; TV 81–84; V Holton-le-Clay 84–94; V Holton-le-Clay and Tetney 94–97; R Humshaugh w Simonburn and Wark *Newc* 97–14; Hon Can Newc Cathl 11–14; rtd 14; PtO *Newc* from 14. *2 Woodside Avenue, Corbridge NE45 5EL* E: corbridgemichael@outlook.com

THOMPSON, John Richard. b 62. Birm Univ BA 89. WEMTC 16. d 16 p 16. C Minchinhampton w Box and Amberley *Glouc* 16–17; C Stroudwater from 17; Chapl Glos Hosps NHS Foundn Trust from 13. *Hillgrove, Verney Road, Stonehouse GL10 2QD* T: (01453) 823349 E: cloudend@waitrose.com *or* john.thompson10@nhs.net

THOMPSON, John Turrell. b 57. Sheff Univ BA(Econ) 79 Southn Univ BTh 88. Sarum & Wells Th Coll 83. d 86 p 87. C Tavistock and Gulworthy *Ex* 86–90; TV Pinhoe and Broadclyst 90–95; P-in-c Northam w Westward Ho! and Appledore 95–96; TV Bideford, Northam, Westward Ho!, Appledore etc 96–00; rtd 00; PtO *Ex* from 00. *Brambles Patch, 39 Westermore Drive, Roundswell, Barnstaple EX31 3XU*

THOMPSON (*née* LILLIE), Mrs Judith Virginia. b 44. LMH Ox BA 66 Essex Univ MA 73 Univ of E Africa DipEd 67. Gilmore Course IDC 82. dss 82 d 87 p 94. Lawrence Weston Bris 82–85; E Bris 85–95; Hon Par Dn 87–95; Chapl HM Rem Cen Pucklechurch 87–91; Chapl Asst Southmead Hosp Bris 91–95; C Knowle St Barn *Bris* 95–02; Bp's Adv for Past Care for Clergy and Families 97–00; Community Th St Mich Coll Llan 00–05; Dir In-House Tr 02–05; Chapl Worcs Acute Hosps NHS Trust 05–09; rtd 09; PtO *Sarum* from 11. *Grove Cottage, Barton Lane, Mere, Warminster BA12 6JA* T: (01747) 860553 E: judithvthompson@aol.com

THOMPSON, Kevin. b 55. Sheff Univ BEd 77 Sheff Hallam Univ MSc 03. Oak Hill Th Coll. d 89 p 90. C Brinsworth w Catcliffe *Sheff* 89–92; V Kimberworth Park 92–97; V Grenoside 97–98; PtO 98–20. *30 Arnold Avenue, Charnock, Sheffield S12 3JB* T: 0114-239 6986 E: kevthompson007@gmail.com

THOMPSON, Miss Leah Judith. b 92. Leeds Univ BA 15. Trin Coll Bris 18. d 21. C Idle *Leeds* from 21. *33 Cavalier Drive, Apperley Bridge, Bradford BD10 0UF* M: 07522-896225 E: thompson.leahj@gmail.com

THOMPSON, Louise Margaret. *See* TAYLOR-KENYON, Louise Margaret

THOMPSON, Mark William. b 52. St Jo Coll Nottm 77. d 81 p 82. C Barnsbury St Andr and H Trin w All SS *Lon* 81–84; C Addiscombe St Mary *S'wark* 84–87; V Thorpe Edge *Bradf* 87–94; Chapl Colchester Hosp Univ NHS Foundn Trust 94–17; rtd 17; PtO *Chelmsf* from 18. *38 St John's Close, Colchester CO4 0HP* T: (01206) 841648 E: mark.thompson57@virginmedia.com

THOMPSON, Martin Eric. b 52. FCCA. Trin Coll Bris 95. d 97 p 98. C Heref St Pet w St Owen and St Jas 97–01; P-in-c Huntley and Longhope *Glouc* 01–02; R Huntley and Longhope, Churcham and Bulley 03–05; P-in-c Worfield *Heref* 05–10; V Twigworth, Down Hatherley, Norton, The Leigh etc *Glouc* 10–13; rtd 13; PtO *Heref* 14–19; *Glouc* 18–20. *1 Church Close, Ross-on-Wye HR9 5HS* T: (01989) 565575 E: revmthompson123@btinternet.com *or* mandft@hotmail.co.uk

THOMPSON, The Very Revd Matthew. b 68. CCC Cam BA 90 MA 94 MPhil 94. Ridley Hall Cam 91. d 94 p 95. C Hulme Ascension *Man* 94–97; C Langley and Parkfield 97–98; TV 98–00; P-in-c Man Clayton St Cross w St Paul 00–08; AD Ardwick 03–08; P-in-c Bolton St Pet 08–11; P-in-c Bolton St Phil 08–11; V Bolton St Pet w St Phil 11–17; Borough Dean Bolton 10–17; Hon Can Man Cathl 12–17; Dean Birm from 17. *38 Goodby Road, Birmingham B13 8NJ* T: 0121-262 1840 E: dean@birminghamcathedral.com

THOMPSON, Melvyn Rodney. b 46. K Coll Lon BD 69 MPhil 73 PhD 79 AKC 70. St Aug Coll Cant 69. d 70 p 71. C Tye Green w Netteswell *Chelmsf* 71–73; C W Brompton St Mary w St Pet *Lon* 73–77; rtd 11. *22 Grasmere Road, Thunderlsey, Benfleet SS7 3HF* T: (01268) 759268 M: 07963-112512 E: mel@mel-thompson.co.uk

THOMPSON, Mervyn Patrick. b 59. Wilson Carlile Coll 84 Coll of Resurr Mirfield 90. d 92 p 93. C Sheff St Cath Richmond Road 92–95; V Thurnscoe St Hilda 95–06; P-in-c Thurnscoe St Helen 99–06; R Thurnscoe 06–11; TR S Shields All SS *Dur* from 11. *The Rectory, Tyne Terrace, South Shields NE34 0NF* T: 0191-456 1851 E: mervynthompson@aol.com

THOMPSON, Michael. b 49. NEOC 83. d 86 p 87. C Ashington *Newc* 86–88; C Ponteland 88–91; TV Newc Epiphany 91–98; P-in-c Choppington 98–99; P-in-c Woldingham *S'wark*

99–02; TV Caterham 02–03; TV Saffron Walden w Wendens Ambo, Littlebury etc *Chelmsf* 03–08; R N Hartismere *St E* 08–14; RD Hartismere 13–14; TV Upper Skerne *Dur* 14–18; rtd 18; PtO *Dur* from 19. *6 Ebberston Court, Spennymoor DL16 6YT* E: frmichael.thompson@btinternet.com

THOMPSON, Michael Bruce. b 53. N Carolina Univ BA 75 Dallas Th Sem ThM 79 Virginia Th Sem 79 Ch Coll Cam PhD 88. d 80 **p** 81. Asst Min New Bern N Carolina 80–83; Chair Youth and Evang and Renewal in E Carolina 81–83; Lect Greek Cam Univ 87–88; Lect St Jo Coll Nottm 88–95; Lect NT and Dir of Studies Ridley Hall Cam 95–00; Vice-Prin 00–17; Assoc Prin 17–20; rtd 20; Development Assoc Ridley Hall Cam from 20. *1 Larchfield, Gough Way, Cambridge CB3 9LR* M: 07957-735860 E: mbt2@cam.ac.uk

THOMPSON, Mrs Michelle. b 68. Man Univ BA 89. Ripon Coll Cuddesdon 90. d 92 **p** 94. Par Dn Leigh St Mary *Man* 92–94; Asst Chapl HM Pris Full Sutton 95–97; V York St Hilda 97–00; Dir Reader Tr and Local Min Development *Man* 00–03; Chapl HM Pris Styal 04–13; Chapl Wrightington, Wigan and Leigh NHS Foundn Trust 13–17; PtO *Birm* from 18. *38 Goodby Road, Birmingham B13 8NJ* T: 0121-447 9788

THOMPSON, Navina Winifred. b 67. Open Univ BA 12. Near E Sch of Th 16. d 18 **p** 19. C Ammochostos and Chapl Famagusta Cyprus 18–19; PtO 19; NSM Ickenham *Lon* from 21. *29 Belmont Close, Uxbridge UB8 1RF* M: 07426-367839 E: navthompson@yahoo.co.uk

THOMPSON, Canon Neil Hamilton. b 48. SS Hild & Bede Coll Dur BEd 72 Leic Univ MA 75. S'wark Ord Course 77 Ven English Coll Rome. d 80 **p** 81. C Merton St Mary *S'wark* 80–82; C Dulwich St Barn 82–84; V Shooters Hill Ch Ch 84–87; V S Dulwich St Steph 87–96; Ldr Post Ord Tr Woolwich Area 94–96; R Limpsfield and Titsey 96–08; Can Res and Prec Roch Cathl 08–16; rtd 16; PtO *Roch* from 17. *23 Hathaway Court, Esplanade, Rochester ME1 1QX* T: (01634) 405265 E: neilthompson@houndofheaven.co.uk

THOMPSON, Patrick Arthur. b 36. Dur Univ BA 59. Qu Coll Birm. d 61 **p** 62. C W Wickham St Fran *Cant* 61–65; C Portchester *Portsm* 65–68; C Birchington w Acol *Cant* 68–71; V S Norwood St Mark 71–77; P-in-c Norbury St Oswald 77–81; V Norbury St Oswald *S'wark* 81–93; V Sutton New Town St Barn 93–00; rtd 00; LtO *Mor* 00–03 and from 10; Resident P Grantown-on-Spey 04–10. *Rose Cottage, 2 Market Street, Forres IV36 1EF* T: (01309) 675917

THOMPSON, Canon Paul. b 65. TCD BA 87. CITC 87. d 89 **p** 90. C Orangefield w Moneyreagh *D & D* 89–92; I Dromara w Garvaghy 92–97; I Ramoan w Ballycastle and Culfeightrin *Conn* 97–00; Dep Chapl HM Pris Liv 00–01; Chapl HM YOI Portland 01–13; Chapl HM Pris Erlestoke 14–17; I Derryvullen N w Castlearchdale *Clogh* from 17; Preb Clogh Cathl from 19. *The Rectory, 5 Enniskillen Road, Castle Irvine Demesne, Irvinestown, Enniskillen BT94 1BD* T: (028) 6862 1890 E: irvinestown@clogher.anglican.org

THOMPSON, Canon Paul. b 58. Ox Univ BA. Ripon Coll Cuddesdon 80. d 83 **p** 84. Chapl Fazakerley Hosp Liv 83–86; C Kirkby *Liv* 83–86; TV 86–89; Ind Chapl 86–89; Chapl Kirkby Coll of FE 86–89; CF 89–01; Sen Chapl Epsom Coll 01–19; Chapl St Teresa's Sch Effingham from 20; PtO *Guildf* from 19; Hon Can Guildf Cathl from 18. *The Studio, Dawes Green House, Tapners Road, Leigh, Reigate RH2 8NN* M: 07868-753251 E: paulthompson@aol.com

THOMPSON, Canon Paul Noble. b 54. Univ of Wales (Cardiff) BMus 77 Univ of Wales (Ban) MPhil 04 Glyndŵr Univ PhD 13. Coll of Resurr Mirfield. d 80 **p** 81. C Bargoed and Deri w Brithdir *Llan* 80–83; C Whitchurch 83–84; V Porth w Trealaw 84–90; V Llanharan w Peterston-super-Montem 90–97; Hon C Barry All SS 97–01; Dioc Youth Chapl 90–01; V Lisvane 01–09; Chapl Univ of St Mark and St Jo *Ex* 09–14; C St Woolos Cathl *Mon* from 14; Dioc Dir of Ords from 14; Can St Woolos Cathl from 17. *St Mark's Vicarage, 7 Gold Tops, Newport NP20 4PH* T: (01633) 252046 E: revpaulthompson.pt@gmail.com

THOMPSON, Canon Peter Alrick. b 79. QUB BA 01 TCD MPhil 03 ARIAM 99 FLCM 09 FGCM LTCL. CITC 01. d 03 **p** 04. C Clooney w Strathfoyle *D & R* 03–06; I Donaghmore w Donaghmore Upper *Arm* from 06; Hon V Choral Arm Cathl 06–11; Succ 11–18; Can Arm Cathl from 18; Dioc Liturg Officer from 09. *St Michael's Rectory, 66 Main Street, Castlecaulfield, Dungannon BT70 3NP* T: (028) 8776 1214 M: 07732-856306 E: donaghmore@armagh.anglican.org

THOMPSON, Mrs Rachel Mary. b 65. Roehampton Inst BA 87 Rolle Coll PGCE 88 Nottm Univ MA 08. EMMTC 04. d 07 **p** 08. NSM Wilne and Draycott w Breaston *Derby* 07–11; NSM Kirk Hallam 11–14; Missr Erewash Deanery 14–15; PtO *Linc* 15–18; *Pet* 18–19; C Oakham, Ashwell, Braunston, Brooke, Egleton etc from 19. *All Saints' Church, Church Street, Oakham*

LE15 6AA T: (01572) 724007 E: rev.rach@gmail.com *or* rachel@oakhamteam.org.uk

THOMPSON, Raymond Craigmile. b 42. Man Univ BTh. d 84 **p** 85. C Clooney *D & R* 84–86; I Urney w Sion Mills 86–92; I Derryvullen N w Castlearchdale *Clogh* 92–05; Chapl to Bp Clogh 02–05; Can Clogh Cathl 03–05; Dean Clogh 05–09; I Clogh w Errigal Portclare 05–09; rtd 09. *En-Rimmon, 6 Tullylammy Road, Irvinestown, Enniskillen BT94 1RN* T: (028) 6862 8258 E: thompson.clogher@btinternet.com

THOMPSON, Robert Craig. b 72. Univ Coll Dur BA 92. Westcott Ho Cam 94. d 96 **p** 97. C Wigan All SS *Liv* 96–00; P-in-c Ladybrook *S'well* 00–05; P-in-c Bengeo *St Alb* 05–08; TV Hertford from 08. *The Rectory, Byde Street, Hertford SG14 3BS* T: (01992) 413691 E: revrobert@ntlworld.com

THOMPSON, Robert George. b 71. K Coll Cam BA 93 MA 97. Ripon Coll Cuddesdon MTh 95. d 97 **p** 98. C Ruislip St Martin *Lon* 97–01; Chapl Parkside Community NHS Trust Lon 01–09; Chapl R Brompton and Harefield NHS Foundn Trust 09–16; Hon C Holland Park *Lon* 09–15; Hon C Notting Dale St Clem w St Mark and St Jas 15–18; V Kilburn St Mary w All So and W Hampstead St Jas from 18. *St Mary's Vicarage, 134A Abbey Road, London NW6 4SN* T: (020) 7221 3548 E: rgt71@icloud.com

THOMPSON, Roger Quintin. b 63. K Coll Lon BA 85 AKC 85 Nottm Univ PGCE 86 MTh 96. Aston Tr Scheme 92 St Jo Coll Nottm 94. d 96 **p** 97. C Easton H Trin w St Gabr and St Lawr and St Jude *Bris* 96–00; C Lisburn Ch Ch Cathl *Conn* 00–04; I Kilwaughter w Cairncastle and Craigy Hill 04–15; Partnership Co-ord CMS Ireland from 15. *79 Mill Green, Doagh, Ballyclare BT39 0PH* M: 07754-684662 E: rogerthompson@cmsireland.org

THOMPSON, Ross Edwards. b 42. Otago Univ BA 63 TDip 64. Coll of Resurr Mirfield 66. d 68 **p** 69. C Fareham SS Pet and Paul *Portsm* 68–71; C W Hackney St Barn *Lon* 71–72; C Northolt St Mary 72–75; P-in-c Wells St Thos w Horrington *B & W* 75–80; V 80–81; TR Cowley St Jas *Ox* 81–87; Gen Sec Ch Union 87–89; V Petts Wood *Roch* 89–94; rtd 04–21.

THOMPSON, Ross Keith Arnold. b 53. Sussex Univ BA 75 Bris Univ PhD 82. Coll of Resurr Mirfield 80. d 82 **p** 83. C Knowle *Bris* 82–85; TV E Bris 85–94; V Bris St Aid w St Geo 94–95; V Knowle St Barn and H Cross Inns Court 95–02; Tutor St Mich Coll Llan 02–05; rtd 09. *Grove Cottage, Barton Lane, Mere, Warminster BA12 6JA* T: (01747) 860553 E: rosskathompson@aol.com

THOMPSON, Ruth Jean. *See* GOSTELOW, Ruth Jean

THOMPSON, Mrs Shanthi Hazel Peiris. b 67. Cranmer Hall Dur 07. d 09 **p** 10. C Kirkby Lonsdale *Carl* 09–13; P-in-c Staveley, Ings and Kentmere from 13; C Windermere St Mary and Troutbeck from 19; C Windermere St Martin from 19. *The Vicarage, Kentmere Road, Staveley, Kendal LA8 9PA* T: (01539) 821267 M: 07931-446025 E: staveleyvicarage@gmail.com

THOMPSON, Stephen Peter. b 45. Lon Univ BSc 67 Lon Inst of Educn PGCE 71 K Coll Lon BD 77 AKC 77 SOAS Lon BA 82 Poona Univ MPhil 85 PhD 87 FRAS 91. Ripon Coll Cuddesdon. d 00. NSM Bedford Park *Lon* 00–01; NSM Isleworth St Fran 01–08; PtO from 08; *St E* from 21. *12 Minsterley Avenue, Shepperton TW17 8QT* T: (01932) 761956 E: drstephenp.thompson@gmail.com

THOMPSON, Thomas Michael. b 46. d 11 **p** 12. NSM Silverton, Butterleigh, Bickleigh and Cadeleigh *Ex* 11–20; PtO from 20. *Gable Cottage, Bickleigh, Tiverton EX16 8RD* T: (01884) 855309 M: 07866-133640 E: tmdfthompson@uwclub.net

THOMPSON, Timothy Charles. b 51. Lon Univ BSc 73 AKC. Westcott Ho Cam 75. d 78 **p** 79. C Ipswich St Mary at Stoke w St Pet etc *St E* 78–81; Ind Chapl *Nor* 81–88; C Lowestoft and Kirkley 81–83; TV 83–88; V Coney Hill *Glouc* 88–94; P-in-c Caister *Nor* 94–00; R 00–16; rtd 16; PtO *Ely* 16–21; PV Ely Cathl from 17. *110 Columbine Road, Ely CB6 3WN* T: (01353) 772131 E: tim@timthompson.plus.com

THOMPSON, Canon Timothy William. b 47. Open Univ BA 78 Bris Univ CertEd 70. EMMTC. d 88 **p** 89. C Scartho *Linc* 88–91; V Haxey 91–95; P-in-c Surfleet 95–00; Asst Local Min Officer 95–00; RD Elloe W 98–00; P-in-c Linc St Pet-at-Gowts and St Andr 00–09; P-in-c Linc St Botolph 00–09; RD Christianity 02–08; rtd 09; Can and Preb Linc Cathl from 02; PtO *Ex* from 21. *3 The Heights, Tavistock PL19 8HQ* T: (01822) 614955 M: 07885-238813 E: timwthompson@btinternet.com

THOMPSON-VEAR, Joanna Arthur. b 76. Sunderland Univ BA 98. St Steph Ho Ox BA 02 MA 06. d 03 **p** 04. C Plymouth Crownhill Ascension *Ex* 03–06; Chapl RN 06–08; TV Harrogate St Wilfrid *Ripon* 08–11; CF(V) 10–12. *17 Manor Gardens, Killinghall, Harrogate HG3 2DS* M: 07377-844888 E: revjatv@gmail.com

THOMPSTONE, Canon John Deaville. b 39. BNC Ox BA 63 MA 67. Ridley Hall Cam 63. **d** 65 **p** 66. C Hoole *Ches* 65–68; C Fulwood *Sheff* 68–71; V Skirbeck H Trin *Linc* 71–77; V Shipley St Pet *Bradf* 77–91; RD Airedale 82–88; V Poynton *Ches* 91–04; Hon Can Ches Cathl 02–04; rtd 04; PtO *Glouc* from 14. *Greyfriars, Broadway Road, Childswickham, Broadway WR12 7HP* T: (01386) 852930 E: johndthompstone@gmail.com

THOMSON, Alexander Keith. b 38. Cranmer Hall Dur BA 63. **d** 64 **p** 65. C Middleton *Man* 64–68; P-in-c Kinloch Rannoch *St And* 68–72; Chapl Rannoch Sch 68–72; Asst Chapl Oundle Sch 72–94; Chapl Laxton Sch 88–94; LtO *Pet* 73–94; PtO 94–01; rtd 98. *School House Cottage, Alderley Road, Chelford, Macclesfield SK11 9AP* T: (01625) 860996 E: randathomson@outlook.com

THOMSON, Andrew Maitland. b 43. CA(Z) 67. Westcott Ho Cam 78. **d** 80 **p** 81. C Harre Cathl Zimbabwe 80–82; R Kadoma and P-in-c Chegutu 82–87; R Malborough St Paul Harare 87–92; P-in-c E w N and W Barsham *Nor* 92–95; P-in-c N and S Creake w Waterden 92–94; P-in-c Sculthorpe w Dunton and Doughton 92–94; R N and S Creake w Waterden, Syderstone etc 95–11; rtd 11; C E w W Rudham, Helhoughton etc *Nor* 11–16; PtO from 16. *3 Charles Road, Fakenham NR21 8JX* T: (01328) 862557 E: pandathomson@btinternet.com

THOMSON, Anjam. b 58. STETS. **d** 12 **p** 13. NSM Fishponds St Mary *Bris* 12–17; Chapl HM Pris Ashfield from 17; PtO *Bris* from 17. *HM Prison Ashfield, Shortwood Road, Pucklechurch, Bristol BS16 9QJ* T: 0117-303 8000 M: 07742-968633 E: anjathomson@btinternet.com

THOMSON, Bruce. *See* THOMSON, Sydney Bruce

THOMSON, Miss Caitlin Elizabeth. b 90. Sheff Univ BA 12 MA 14 St Jo Coll Dur BA 17. Cranmer Hall Dur 14. **d** 17 **p** 18. C W Bessacarr *Sheff* 17–19; C Sheff St Mark Broomhill from 19. *26 Elgin Street, Sheffield S10 1UQ* M: 07742-296180 E: caitlin.e.thomson@gmail.com

THOMSON, Canon Celia Stephana Margaret. b 55. LMH Ox MA 83 Birkbeck Coll Lon MA 87 K Coll Lon MA 94. Sarum & Wells Th Coll 89. **d** 91 **p** 94. Par Dn Southfields St Barn *S'wark* 91–94; C 94–95; V W Wimbledon Ch Ch 95–03; Tutor SEITE 95–00; Voc Adv Lambeth Adnry 96–00; Can Res Glouc Cathl from 03. *3 Miller's Green, Gloucester GL1 2BN* T: (01452) 415824 E: cthomson@gloucestercathedral.org.uk

THOMSON, Charles Hector. b 85. UWE BA 07 Reading Univ MSc 08. St Mellitus Coll BA 16. **d** 16 **p** 17. C Upper Chelsea St Simon *Lon* 16–19; C Battersea Rise St Mark *S'wark* 19–21; TR Melksham *Sarum* from 21. *The Rectory, Canon Square, Melksham SN12 6LX* M: 07739-825099

THOMSON, Christopher Grant. b 71. Cam Univ BTh 07. Westcott Ho Cam 05. **d** 07 **p** 08. C Bletchingley and Nutfield *S'wark* 07–11; P-in-c Kenley 11–17; P-in-c Purley St Barn 11–17; Asst Dir of Ords Croydon Area 13–17; Public Preacher *Truro* 17–19; Tutor St Padarn's Inst from 20. *Address withheld by request* E: revdthomson@btinternet.com

THOMSON, Canon Cynthia Margaret. b 47. Univ of Wales (Ban) BTh 94. **d** 94 **p** 97. NSM Llanfairpwll w Penmynydd *Ban* 94–95; C Twrcelyn Deanery 95–96; C Knighton St Mary Magd *Leic* 96–99; P-in-c Higham-on-the-Hill w Fenny Drayton and Witherley 99–02; P-in-c Stoke Golding w Dadlington 01–02; R Fenn Lanes Gp 02–03; V Shepshed and Oaks in Charnwood 03–16; RD Akeley E 06–11; Hon Can Leic Cathl 13–16; rtd 16; PtO *Leic* 16–18; R Hallaton and Allexton, w Horninghold, Tugby etc 18–20. *3 Stonton Road, Church Langton, Market Harborough LE16 7SZ* M: 07740-433871 E: cynthia.hebden47@gmail.com

✠**THOMSON, The Rt Revd David.** b 52. Keble Coll Ox MA 78 DPhil 78 Selw Coll Cam BA 80 MA 84 FRSA 06 FSA 08 FRHistS 08. Westcott Ho Cam 78. **d** 81 **p** 82 **c** 08. C Maltby *Sheff* 81–84; TV Banbury *Ox* 84–94; Sec Par and People 84–93; TR Cockermouth w Embleton and Wythop *Carl* 94–02; Adn Carl and Can Res Carl Cathl 02–08; Suff Bp Huntingdon *Ely* 08–18; rtd 18; PtO *Heref* from 19; Hon Asst Bp Heref from 19. *31 Apple Grove, Hereford HR4 0EA* T: (01432) 353008 M: 07771-864550 E: david@skypilots.co.uk

THOMSON, David Francis. b 54. Salford Univ BA 81 CPFA 84. NOC 05. **d** 07 **p** 08. NSM New Bury w Gt Lever *Man* 07–10; P-in-c Ainsworth from 10; C Bury St Mary 13–14; Borough Dean Bury from 17; AD Radcliffe and Prestwich 19–21. *The Vicarage, Ainsworth Hall Road, Ainsworth, Bolton BL2 5RY* T: (01204) 398567 M: 07551-437368 E: thomsondf@hotmail.com

THOMSON, Dorothy Lucille. *See* THOMAS, Dorothy Lucille

THOMSON, The Very Revd Elizabeth Jane. b 64. Univ Coll Ox MA 85 DPhil 89 Trin Coll Cam BA 02 Moray Ho Coll of Educn PGCE 90. Westcott Ho Cam 00. **d** 03 **p** 04. C Pilton w Croscombe, N Wootton and Dinder *B & W* 03–07; TV

Witney *Ox* 07–14; Can Missr Derby Cathl 14–21; Sub-Dean Derby Cathl 18–21; Provost St Paul's Cathl Dundee *Bre* from 21. *4 Richmond Terrace, Dundee DD2 1BQ* T: (01382) 224486 E: provost@stpaulscathedral.net

THOMSON, Elizabeth Lucy. *See* TALBOT, Elizabeth Lucy

THOMSON, Hannah Nadka. b 84. Qu Foundn Birm 16. **d** 18 **p** 19. C Cant St Martin and St Paul from 18. *70 Thanington Road, Canterbury CT1 3XE* E: revhannaht@hotmail.com

THOMSON, James. b 39. St Andr Coll Melrose 58 Episc Sem Austin Texas 88. **d** 62 **p** 63. C Oklahoma City All So USA 89–90; R Oklahoma St Matt 90–95; Assoc R Oklahoma H Trin 95–05; P-in-c Pittenweem *St And* 06–09; P-in-c Elie and Earlsferry 06–09; rtd 09; LtO *St And* 09–11 and from 16; P-in-c Fraserburgh *Ab* 11–12. *41A South Street, St Andrews KY16 9QR* T: (01334) 479645 E: jim39@talktalk.net

THOMSON, James Maclaren. b 69. Grey Coll Dur BA 91 Univ Coll Lon MA 93. Wycliffe Hall Ox BA 99. **d** 00 **p** 01. C Oulton Broad *Nor* 00–04; V Chatteris *Ely* 04–13; Hon C 13–17; Chapl Qu Eliz Hosp King's Lynn NHS Foundn Trust 13–17; Chapl Kettering Gen Hosp NHS Foundn Trust 17–18; Chapl NW Anglia NHS Foundn Trust from 18. *Chaplaincy Department, Peterborough City Hospital, Bretton Gate, Bretton, Peterborough PE3 9GZ* T: (01733) 673115 E: james.thomson2@nhs.net

✠**THOMSON, The Rt Revd John Bromilow.** b 59. York Univ BA 81 Nottm Univ PhD 01. Wycliffe Hall Ox BA 84 MA 91. **d** 85 **p** 86 **c** 14. C Ecclesall *Sheff* 85–89; Tutor St Paul's Coll Grahamstown S Africa 89–92; Asst P Grahamstown St Bart 90–92; Asst Lect Rhodes Univ 91–92; V Doncaster St Mary *Sheff* 93–01; Dir Min 01–14; Hon Can Sheff Cathl 01–14; Suff Bp Selby *York* from 14. *Bishop's House, York Road, Barlby, Selby YO8 5JP* T: (01757) 429982 E: bishopofselby@yorkdiocese.org

THOMSON, Julian Harley. b 43. AKC 70. St Aug Coll Cant 70. **d** 71 **p** 72. C Wellingborough All Hallows *Pet* 71–74; Min Can, Prec and Sacr Ely Cathl 74–80; P-in-c Stuntney 76–80; V Arrington 80–91; R Croydon w Clopton 80–91; R Orwell 80–91; R Wimpole 80–91; V Linton 91–96; R Bartlow 91–96; P-in-c Castle Camps 91–96; TR Linton 96–01; RD 99–01; rtd 01; PtO *Nor* from 01. *Lavender Cottage, 7 Abbey Road, Great Massingham, King's Lynn PE32 2HN* T: (01485) 520721 E: thomson5816@btinternet.com

THOMSON, Keith. *See* THOMSON, Alexander Keith

THOMSON, Mark Stephen. b 57. Glas Univ MA 78. Ridley Hall Cam 10. **d** 12 **p** 13. C Market Deeping *Linc* 12–15; C Deeping St James 12–15; C Uffington Gp 15–16; R Quarrington w Old Sleaford from 16. *The Rectory, 6 Spire View, Sleaford NG34 7RN*

THOMSON, Penelope Jane. b 59. ERMC 14. **d** 17 **p** 18. NSM Bishop's Hatfield, Lemsford and N Mymms *St Alb* from 17. *74 Pine Grove, Brookmans Park, Hatfield AL9 7BW*

THOMSON, Richard William Byars. b 60. Birm Univ BA 86. Ripon Coll Cuddesdon 86. **d** 88 **p** 89. C Moulsecoomb *Chich* 88–90; P-in-c Kirriemuir *St And* 90–94; P-in-c Piddletrenthide w Plush, Alton Pancras etc *Sarum* 94–02; P-in-c Milborne St Andrew w Dewlish 94–02; Chapl Milton Abbey Sch Dorset 02–12; P-in-c Boxwell, Leighterton, Didmarton, Oldbury etc *Glouc* from 12. *Withymore Vicarage, Old Down Road, Badminton GL9 1EU* T: (01454) 219236 E: revrichardthomson@gmail.com

THOMSON, Robert Douglass. b 37. Lon Univ TCert 61 Newc Univ DAES 70 Dur Univ BEd 75. NEOC 76. **d** 79 **p** 80. NSM Shincliffe *Dur* 79–98; Chapl St Aid Coll Dur 93–99; PtO *Dur* 99–21. *11 Hill Meadows, High Shincliffe, Durham DH1 2PE* T: 0191-386 3358 E: rdthomson@btinternet.com

THOMSON, Robin Alexander Stewart. b 43. Ch Coll Cam MA 69 K Coll Lon MTh 72. SEITE 94. **d** 96 **p** 97. NSM Wimbledon Em Ridgway Prop Chpl *S'wark* 96–02 and 10–13; NSM Tooting Graveney St Nic 02–10; rtd 13; PtO *S'wark* from 13. *2 Coppice Close, London SW20 9AS* T: (020) 8540 7748 *or* 8770 9717 F: 8770 9747

THOMSON, Sydney Bruce. b 49. Fuller Th Sem California MA 91 ThM 92 Stirling Univ MLitt 98. Ripon Coll Cuddesdon 05. **d** 07 **p** 08. C Worcs W Rural *Worc* 07–10; TV Leominster *Heref* 10–19; rtd 19; PtO *Ex* from 20. *28 The Laurels, Sidmouth EX10 8UX* M: 07807-917206 E: beagle67@btinternet.com

THOMSON, Canon Wendy Leigh. b 64. Trin W Univ Vancouver BA 87. Wycliffe Hall Ox BTh 99. **d** 00 **p** 01. C Oulton Broad *Nor* 00–04; C Chatteris *Ely* 04–13; V from 13; Bp's Adv on Women's Min *Chelmsf* from 16; Hon Can Ely Cathl from 16. *The Vicarage, Church Lane, Chatteris PE16 6JA* T: (01354) 692173 E: wendy@chatteris.org

THORBURN, Canon Guy Douglas Anderson. b 50. Trin Coll Ox BA 74 MA 78. Ridley Hall Cam. **d** 83 **p** 84. C Putney St Marg *S'wark* 83–87; R Moresby *Carl* 87–97; V Gt Clacton *Chelmsf* 97–17; C Harwich Peninsula 15–16; AD St Osyth

07–16; AD Harwich 15–16; Hon Can Chelmsf Cathl 15–17; rtd 17; PtO *Chelmsf* 18–19. *51 Pole Barn Lane, Frinton-on-Sea CO13 9NQ* E: revguy.thorburn@virgin.net

THORBURN, Preb Simon Godfrey. b 51. Newc Univ BSc 73 Fitzw Coll Cam BA 77 MA 81 Sheff Univ MMinTheol 97. Westcott Ho Cam 75. **d** 78 **p** 79. C Stafford *Lich* 78–82; C Tettenhall Regis 82–83; TV 83–90; Soc Resp Officer *S'wark* 90–97; V Edgbaston St Geo *Birm* 97–09; AD Edgbaston 03–08; Chapl St Geo Sch Edgbaston 99–08; V Oswestry *Lich* 09–17; R Rhydycroesau 09–17; Preb Lich Cathl 16–17; rtd 17. *Key Farm, New Road, Far Forest, Kidderminster DY14 9TG* E: thorburnsimon@gmail.com

THORIUS, Mrs Lynn Christine. b 51. Leeds Univ BA 11. Yorks Min Course 08. **d** 11 **p** 12. NSM E Richmond *Ripon* 11–14; Bp's Chapl and Policy Adv 14–17; P-in-c Wiske Benefice *Leeds* 18–19; Hon Min Can Ripon Cathl 19; PtO from 20. *The Retreat, Hornby, Northallerton DL6 2JH* T: (01609) 881451 M: 07788-862397 E: lynnthorius12@btinternet.com

THORN *(formerly KINGS)*, **Mrs Jean Alison.** b 63. St Jo Coll Dur BA 90 Heythrop Coll Lon MTh RGN 85. Cranmer Hall Dur 88. **d** 91 **p** 94. Chapl Bris Poly 91–92; Chapl UWE 92–95; Hon C Bris Lockleaze St Mary Magd w St Fran 91–95; C Fishponds All SS 95–96; Hon C 96–97; V Bris Ch the Servant Stockwood 97–01; Hon C Whitchurch 01–04; LtO *Sarum* 04–21; PtO from 21. *12 Rosamond Avenue, Shipton Gorge, Bridport DT6 4LN*

THORN, Kevan. b 67. CBDTI 03. **d** 06 **p** 07. NSM Blackpool H Cross *Blackb* 06–10; NSM Kirkham 10–20; PtO from 20. *16 Bannistre Close, Lytham St Annes FY8 3HS* E: kevanthorn@btopenworld.com

THORN, Mrs Pamela Mary. b 46. Brentwood Coll of Educn BEd 78. EAMTC 01. **d** 04 **p** 05. NSM Waterbeach *Ely* 04–15; PtO from 15. *31 Lode Avenue, Waterbeach, Cambridge CB25 9PX* T: (01223) 864262 M: 07989-491557 E: pamandtrevorthorn@btinternet.com

THORN, Peter. b 50. Man Poly BEd 79. Ridley Hall Cam 82. **d** 84 **p** 85. C Aughton Ch Ch *Liv* 84–87; C Skelmersdale St Paul 87–90; Dioc Children's Officer 87–92; P-in-c Croft w Southworth 90–92; C Streatley *St Alb* 92–95; R Blofield w Hemblington *Nor* 95–96; P-in-c 96–99; Assoc Dioc Dir of Tr 97–99; V Sheff St Bart 99–01; P-in-c Shotley *St E* 01–07; P-in-c Tweedmouth *Newc* 07–09; P-in-c Claydon and Barham *St E* 09–15; C Gt and Lt Blakenham w Baylham and Nettlestead 09–15; P-in-c Flixton St Jo *Man* 15–17; Chapl Bolton NHS Foundn Trust 16–18; rtd 18; PtO *Liv* from 20. *Address temp unknown* M: 07810-363291 E: peterthorn15@hotmail.co.uk

THORN, Simon Alexander. b 66. Bris Univ BSc 89 PhD 92 FLS 98 FCollP 96. Ox Min Course 06. **d** 09 **p** 10. NSM Abingdon *Ox* 09–12; NSM Hermitage 12–19; Chapl Win Coll from 15; Foundn Chapl 15–19; PtO *Win* from 20; *Ox* from 20. *Florence Cottage, Bucklebury Alley, Cold Ash, Thatcham RG18 9NN* T: (01635) 203187 M: 07714-194591 E: simonathorn@gmail.com

THORNALLEY, Graham Paul. b 70. Coll of Resurr Mirfield 05. **d** 07 **p** 08. C Brumby *Linc* 07–09; C Frodingham 09–11; TV Howden *York* 11–17; V Kingston upon Hull St Alb from 17. *St Alban's Vicarage, 62 Hall Road, Hull HU6 8SA* T: (01482) 443566 E: gthornalley@me.com

THORNBOROUGH, Keith Ronald. b 64. Liv Jo Moores Univ BA 12. All SS Cen for Miss & Min 15. **d** 18 **p** 19. NSM Blundellsands St Nic *Liv* from 18. *Roscrea, Queens Road, Crosby, Liverpool L23 5TR* T: 0151-281 4459 E: keith174@aol.com

THORNBURGH, Richard Hugh Perceval. b 52. Sarum & Wells Th Coll. **d** 84 **p** 85. C Broadstone *Sarum* 84–87; TV Beaminster Area 87–95; TV Hanley H Ev *Lich* 96–01; R The Saints *St E* 01–17; C Bungay 14–17; rtd 17. *180 Holmfield Road, Blackpool FY2 9PU* T: (01253) 508850 E: rhpt@pharisaios.co.uk

THORNBY, Mrs Janet. b 40. **d** 06 **p** 07. OLM Cheriton All So w Newington *Cant* 06–10; PtO from 10. *11 Peene Cottages, Peene, Folkestone CT18 8BB* T: (01303) 271267 E: thornbyrobjan@aol.com

THORNE, Mrs Anita Dawn. b 46. Trin Coll Bris 84. dss 86 **d** 87 **p** 94. Asst Chapl Bris Poly 86–88; Par Dn Olveston 88–94; P-in-c 94–96; P-in-c Portland All SS w St Pet *Sarum* 96–05; P-in-c Clutton w Cameley *B & W* 05–10; R Clutton w Cameley, Bishop Sutton and Stowey 10–12; rtd 12; PtO *Sarum* 12–20; *B & W* 13–18. *2 Armada Way, Dorchester DT1 2TL* T: (01305) 265118 E: thorne391@btinternet.com

THORNE, Mrs Anne. b 55. SWMTC 95. **d** 98 **p** 99. C Crediton and Shobrooke *Ex* 98–01; C Beer and Branscombe 01–03; C Seaton and Beer 03–06; P-in-c Braunton 06–20; rtd 20; PtO *Ex* from 20. *Address temp unknown* E: vicarthorne@aol.com

THORNE, Joshua David. b 90. Lon Sch of Th BA 11 Wycliffe Hall Ox MTh 20. **d** 20 **p** 21. C Whitefriars Rushden *Pet* from 20. *6 Martin Close, Rushden NN10 6YZ* M: 07979-235007 E: joshuathorne2020@gmail.com

THORNE, Mrs Margaret. b 58. Kingston Poly BA 79 Heythrop Coll Lon MA 02 Sarum Coll MA 16 LGSM 78. Ox Min Course 05. **d** 08 **p** 09. C Earley St Pet *Ox* 08–12; V Headington St Mary 12–15; R Chinnor, Sydenham, Aston Rowant and Crowell 15–19; R Coity, Nolton and Brackla w Coychurch *Llan* from 19. *The Rectory, Merthyrmawr Road North, Bridgend CF31 3NH* M: 07512-951780 E: maggie53thorne@gmail.com

THORNE, Valerie Joan. b 60. Chelt & Glouc Coll of HE BA 96. Wycliffe Hall Ox 07. **d** 09 **p** 10. C Wotton-under-Edge w Ozleworth, N Nibley etc *Glouc* 09–10; C Sodbury Vale 10–12; R Brimpsfield w Birdlip, Syde, Daglingworth etc from 12. *The Rectory, Duntisbourne Leer, Cirencester GL7 7AS* T: (01285) 821040 M: 07882-882796 E: rev.val@btinternet.com

THORNETT, Joan. b 38. **d** 07 **p** 09. OLM Stickney Gp *Linc* 07–12; rtd 13; PtO *Linc* 15–18. *Gardeners Cottage, Harrington, Spilsby PE23 4NH* E: fctjw@btinternet.com

THORNEYCROFT, Preb Pippa Hazel Jeanetta. b 44. Ex Univ BA 65. WMMTC 85. **d** 88 **p** 94. NSM Albrighton *Lich* 88–90; NSM Beckbury, Badger, Kemberton, Ryton, Stockton etc 90–96; P-in-c Shareshill 96–09; P-in-c Essington 07–09; Dioc Adv for Women in Min 93–00; Preb Lich Cathl 99–09; RD Penkridge 01–05; rtd 09; C Tettenhall Wood and Perton *Lich* 10–12; C Hadley and Wellington Ch Ch 12–20; PtO from 21; Chapl to The Queen 01–14. *Manor Cottage, 21 High Street, Albrighton, Wolverhampton WV7 3JB* T: (01902) 375523 M: 07970-869011 E: pippa@thorneycroft.plus.com

THORNILEY, Canon Richard James Gordon. b 56. Portsm Poly BA 78. St Jo Coll Nottm MTh 95. **d** 97 **p** 98. C Bowbrook S *Worc* 97–01; R Church Lench w Rous Lench and Abbots Morton etc from 01; RD Evesham 15–21; Hon Can Worc Cathl from 17. *The Rectory, Station Road, Harvington, Evesham WR11 8NJ* T: (01386) 870527

THORNLEY, David Howe. b 43. Wycliffe Hall Ox 77. **d** 79 **p** 80. C Burgess Hill St Andr *Chich* 79–83; P-in-c Amberley w N Stoke 83–84; P-in-c Parham and Wiggonholt w Greatham 83–84; V Amberley w N Stoke and Parham, Wiggonholt etc 84–92; P-in-c S w N Bersted 92–99; V 99–08; rtd 08; PtO *Chich* from 14. *Spinaway Cottage, Church Hill, Slindon, Arundel BN18 0RD* M: 07941-834920 E: dhthornley@btinternet.com

THORNLEY, Edward Charles. b 84. Ex Univ BA 05 Anglia Ruskin Univ MA 10. Westcott Ho Cam 08 Yale Div Sch 09. **d** 10 **p** 11. C Dereham and Distr *Nor* 10–13; C St Marylebone w H Trin *Lon* 13–18; Chapl St Marylebone C of E Sch 13–18; Chapl R Academy of Music 13–18; Chapl Fort Worth All SS Episc Sch USA from 18. *All Saints' Episcopal School, 9700 Saints Circle, Fort Worth TX 76108, USA* M: 07709-674615 E: edward.thornley@gmail.com

THORNLEY, Nicholas Andrew. b 56. St Jo Coll Nottm BTh 81. **d** 81 **p** 84. C Frodingham *Linc* 81–84; P-in-c Belton 84–85; V 85–90; V Horncastle w Low Toynton 90–98; V High Toynton 98; R Greetham w Ashby Puerorum 98; RD Horncastle 94–98; TR Gainsborough and Morton 98–11; Can and Preb Linc Cathl 98–11; P-in-c Broughton and Duddon *Carl* 11–17. *Purt ny Shee, Marton Road, Willingham by Stow, Gainsborough DN21 5JU* E: nickthorn1456@gmail.com

THORNS, Mrs Joanne. b 64. Sunderland Univ BSc 86 MRPharmS. Cranmer Hall Dur 97. **d** 99 **p** 00. C Norton St Mary *Dur* 99–04; C Stockton St Chad 02–04; TV Dur N 04–14; Regional Officer NE Chs Acting Together from 14. *19 Lumley Road, Durham DH1 5NP* T: 0191-386 8049 M: 07932-513295 E: regionalofficer@necat.co.uk

THORNTON, Canon Darren Thomas. b 68. Wilson Carlile Coll 90 EAMTC 00. **d** 02 **p** 03. C E Dereham and Scarning *Nor* 02–05; P-in-c Nor St Giles 05–13; V 13–21; Chapl UEA 05–21; RD Nor E 14–20; Chapl Norfolk and Nor Univ Hosps NHS Foundn Trust from 21; Hon Can Nor Cathl from 17. *Norfolk and Norwich University Hospital, Colney Lane, Colney, Norwich NR4 7UY* T: (01603) 287470 E: darren.thornton@nnuh.nhs.uk

THORNTON, Dominic Oskari. b 83. Kent Univ BA 05 Jes Coll Cam BTh 14. Westcott Ho Cam 12. **d** 15 **p** 16. C Salisbury St Thos and St Edm *Sarum* 15–19; PtO *Win* from 19. *The Vicarage, Church Lane, Old Basing, Basingstoke RG24 7DJ* M: 07522-862973 E: revdominic@icloud.com

THORNTON, Jackie-Dee. b 80. St Mellitus Coll BA 17. **d** 17 **p** 18. C Gt and Lt Leighs and Lt Waltham *Chelmsf* 17–19; C Gt Waltham w Ford End 17–19; C The Chignals w Mashbury 17–19; NSM Chelmsf Cathl from 19; Chapl Anglia Ruskin Univ from 19. *13 Blackwater Close,*

Chelmsford CM1 7QJ T: (01245) 604223 M: 07415-033045 E: jaxdee@hotmail.com

THORNTON, Magdalen Mary. *See* SMITH, Magdalen Mary

THORNTON, Timothy Charles Gordon. b 35. Ch Ch Ox BA 58 MA 61. Linc Th Coll 60. **d** 62 **p** 63. C Kirkholt CD *Man* 62–64; Tutor Linc Th Coll 64–68; Chapl 66–68; Lect Pacific Th Coll Suva Fiji 69–73; Chapl Brasted Place Coll Westerham 73–74; Can Missr *Guildf* 74–79; P-in-c Hascombe 74–79; V Chobham w Valley End 79–84; V Spelsbury and Chadlington *Ox* 84–87; V Chadlington and Spelsbury, Ascott under Wychwood 87–00; rtd 00; PtO *Carl* 01–20. *13 Capel Court, The Burgage, Prestbury, Cheltenham GL52 3EL* T: (01242) 231614

✠**THORNTON, The Rt Revd Timothy Martin.** b 57. Southn Univ BA 78 K Coll Lon MA 97. St Steph Ho Ox 78. **d** 80 **p** 81 **c** 01. C Todmorden *Wakef* 80–82; P-in-c Walsden 82–85; Chapl Univ of Wales (Cardiff) *Llan* 85–86; Sen Chapl 86–87; Bp's Chapl *Wakef* 87–91; Dir of Ords 88–91; Bp's Chapl *Lon* 91–94; Dep P in O 92–01; Prin NTMTC 94–98; V Kensington St Mary Abbots w St Geo *Lon* 98–01; AD Kensington 00–01; Area Bp Sherborne *Sarum* 01–08; Bp Truro 08–17; Bp at Lambeth *Cant* 17–21; Bp HM Forces 17–21; Bp Falkland Is 17–21; rtd 21; Hon Asst Bp Lon from 17; Hon Asst Bp Portsm from 17; Hon Asst Bp S'wark from 17. *Lambeth Palace, London SE1 7JU* T: (020) 7898 1200

THOROGOOD, Preb John Martin. b 45. Birm Univ BA 68 PGCE 69. Ox NSM Course 82. **d** 85 **p** 86. NSM Sunningdale *Ox* 85–90; Chapl St Geo Sch Ascot 88–90; TV Camelot Par *B & W* 90–97; V Evercreech w Chesterblade and Milton Clevedon 97–03; RD Cary and Bruton 96–03; R Dulverton and Brushford 03–10; P-in-c Brompton Regis w Upton and Skilgate 08–10; R Dulverton w Brushford, Brompton Regis etc 10–13; RD Exmoor 05–09; Preb Wells Cathl 07–13; rtd 13; PtO *B & W* from 14. *Holden Cottage, 2 West Street, Withycombe, Minehead TA24 6PX* T: (01984) 641745 M: 07966-640771 E: johntvicar@btinternet.com

THOROLD, Alison Susan Joy. *See* HEALY, Alison Susan Joy

THOROLD, Canon Jeremy Stephen. b 59. **d** 04 **p** 05. OLM Gainsborough and Morton *Linc* 04–07; NSM Lanteglos by Camelford w Advent and St Teath *Truro* 07–09; P-in-c Menheniot and St Ive and Pensilva w Quethiock 09–11; Bp's Dom Chapl 11–16; Minl Development Review Admin 10–14; Bp's Adv for Deliverance Min 14–16; P-in-c Newquay from 16; C St Columb Minor and St Colan from 16; Hon Can Truro Cathl from 16. *Sea Breeze, 28B West Road, Quintrell Downs, Newquay TR8 4LD* M: 07545-961233 E: jem33wheel@aol.com

THOROLD, Canon John Stephen. b 35. Bps' Coll Cheshunt 61. **d** 63 **p** 64. C Cleethorpes *Linc* 63–70; V Cherry Willingham w Greetwell 70–77; P-in-c Firsby w Gt Steeping 77–79; R 79–86; R Aswardby w Sausthorpe 77–86; R Halton Holgate 77–86; R Langton w Sutterby 77–86; V Spilsby w Hundleby 77–86; R Lt Steeping 79–86; R Raithby 79–86; V New Sleaford 86–01; RD Lafford 87–96; Can and Preb Linc Cathl 98–01; rtd 01; PtO *Linc* from 01. *8 Ashwood Close, Horncastle LN9 5HA* T: (01507) 526562

THORP, Adrian. b 55. Clare Coll Cam BA 77 MA 80 Lon Univ BD 80. Trin Coll Bris 77. **d** 80 **p** 81. C Kendal St Thos *Carl* 80–83; C Handforth *Ches* 83–86; V Siddal *Wakef* 86–91; V Bishopwearmouth St Gabr *Dur* 91–05; C Upper Skerne 05–07; R Blaydon and Swalwell 07–17; P-in-c Dinsdale w Sockburn 17–20; P-in-c Hurworth 17–20; P-in-c Middleton St George 17–20; rtd 20. *Croft Cottage, 2 Tees View, Boldron, Barnard Castle DL12 9RN* M: 07759-947236 E: revathorp@gmail.com

THORP, Mrs Alison Claire. b 63. Kingston Poly BSc 85 Nottm Univ MA 10. EMMTC 06. **d** 09 **p** 10. NSM Bosworth and Sheepy Gp *Leic* 09–13; Chapl Geo Eliot Hosp NHS Trust Nuneaton 12–14; Chapl Burton Hosps NHS Foundn Trust from 14; PtO *Leic* 13–21. *Culloden Farm, Gopsall, Atherstone CV9 3QJ* T: (01530) 270350 E: alisonthorp@btconnect.com *or* alison.thorp@burtonft.nhs.uk

THORP, Mrs Helen Mary. b 54. Bris Univ BA 75 MA(Theol) 77 Dur Univ MA 98. Trin Coll Bris 78. **d** 87 **p** 94. NSM Siddal *Wakef* 87–91; NSM Bishopwearmouth St Gabr *Dur* 91–05; NSM Upper Skerne 05–07; NSM Blaydon and Swalwell 07–17; NSM Dinsdale w Sockburn 17–20; NSM Hurworth 17–20; NSM Middleton St George 17–20; Voc Adv 93–05; Tutor Cranmer Hall Dur 98–18; rtd 20; PtO *Dur* from 20. *Croft Cottage, 2 Tees View, Boldron, Barnard Castle DL12 9RN* E: h.m.thorp@durham.ac.uk

THORP, Mrs Maureen Sandra. b 47. Man OLM Scheme 92. **d** 95 **p** 96. OLM Heywood *Man* 95–01; P-in-c Shore and Calderbrook 01–06; V Tonge w Alkrington 06–15; Borough Dean Rochdale 12–16; rtd 15; PtO *Man* from 15. *4 Lyn*

Grove, Heywood OL10 4SS E: thorpmaureen@aol.com *or* maureensandrathorp@gmail.com

THORP, Norman Arthur. b 29. Tyndale Hall Bris 63. **d** 65 **p** 66. C Southsea St Jude *Portsm* 65–68; C Braintree *Chelmsf* 68–73; P-in-c Tolleshunt D'Arcy w Tolleshunt Major 73–75; V 75–83; R N Buckingham *Ox* 83–95; RD Buckingham 90–95; rtd 95; PtO *Ox* 97–20. *Address temp unknown*

THORP, Roderick Cheyne. b 44. Ch Ch Ox BA 65 MA 69. Ridley Hall Cam 66. **d** 69 **p** 70. C Reading Greyfriars *Ox* 69–73; C Kingston upon Hull St Martin *York* 73–76; C Heworth H Trin 76–79; C-in-c N Bletchley CD *Ox* 79–86; TV Washfield, Stoodleigh, Withleigh etc *Ex* 86–96; RD Tiverton 91–96; P-in-c Dolton 96–00; P-in-c Iddesleigh w Dowland 96–00; P-in-c Monkokehampton 96–00; rtd 00; P-in-c Etton w Dalton Holme *York* 00–08; PtO 09–19. *4 Stonegate Court, Stonegate, Hunmanby, Filey YO14 0NZ* T: (01723) 892628 E: aranjay@freeuk.com *or* aranjay@phonecoop.coop

THORP, Samuel Stephen. b 92. Lon Sch of Th BA 14. Cranmer Hall Dur 16. **d** 18 **p** 19. C Diss *Nor* from 18. *7 De Lucy Close, Diss IP22 4YL* M: 07506-474538 E: samuel.thorp@disssteamministry.org.uk

THORP, Stephen Linton. b 62. Trin Coll Bris BA 92. **d** 92 **p** 93. C Knutsford St Jo and Toft *Ches* 92–96; TV Newton Tracey, Horwood, Alverdiscott etc *Ex* 96–06; R Necton, Holme Hale w N and S Pickenham *Nor* from 06; RD Breckland from 18. *The Rectory, 7 School Road, Necton, Swaffham PE37 8HT* T: (01760) 722021 E: slthorp@outlook.com

THORP, Susannah Ruth. *See* CURTIS, Susannah Ruth

THORP, Timothy. b 65. St Steph Ho Ox BTh 93. **d** 96 **p** 97. C Jarrow *Dur* 96–99; P-in-c N Hylton St Marg Castletown 99–02; C Felpham and Missr Arundel and Bognor *Chich* 02–07; C Arundel w Tortington and S Stoke 07–08; P-in-c Ernesettle *Ex* 08–11; P-in-c Whitleigh 08–11; C Honicknowle 08–11; P-in-c Plymouth Crownhill Ascension from 11. *The Vicarage, 33 Tavistock Road, Plymouth PL5 3AF* T: (01752) 417618 E: fathertimt@bigfoot.com

THORPE, Preb Christopher David Charles. b 60. Cov Poly BA 83. Ripon Coll Cuddesdon 85. **d** 88 **p** 89. C Norton *St Alb* 88–92; TV Blakenall Heath *Lich* 92–99; TR Bilston 99–08; V Shifnal and Sheriffhales 08–16; P-in-c Tong 11–16; V Shifnal, Sheriffhales and Tong from 16; Preb Lich Cathl from 07. *The Vicarage, Manor Close, Shifnal TF11 9AJ* T: (01952) 463694 E: chris@christhorpe.org

THORPE, Donald Henry. b 34. St Aid Birkenhead 57. **d** 60 **p** 61. C Mexborough *Sheff* 60–64; C Doncaster St Leon and St Jude 64–67; V Doncaster Intake 67–74; V Millhouses H Trin 74–85; Prec Leic Cathl 85–89; TR Melton Gt Framland 89–93; rtd 93; PtO *Sheff* 93–21; S'well 93–11. *18 All Hallows Drive, Tickhill, Doncaster DN11 9PP* T: (01302) 743129 E: dsthorpe1@tiscali.co.uk

THORPE (*née* RICHARDS), Eleanor Poppy. b 93. Ches Univ BA 14. Cranmer Hall Dur 15. **d** 17 **p** 18. C Formby H Trin and Altcar *Liv* 17–20; C W Derby Gd Shep from 20. *The Vicarage, 132 Aintree Lane, Liverpool L10 8LE* T: 0151-280 3883 E: poppyreverend@gmail.com

THORPE, Canon Kerry Michael. b 51. Oak Hill Th Coll BD 78. **d** 78 **p** 79. C Upton (Overchurch) *Ches* 78–81; C Chester le Street *Dur* 81–84; V Fatfield 84–93; V Margate H Trin *Cant* 93–98; C 98–09; Dioc Missr 06–11; Min Harvest New Angl Ch 10–11; Dioc Miss and Growth Adv *Cant* 11–16; Hon Can Cant Cathl 08–16; rtd 16; PtO *Cant* from 17. *19 Chapman Fields, Cliffsend, Ramsgate CT12 5LB* T: (01843) 591637 E: kerryandeunice@gmail.com

THORPE, Martin Xavier. b 66. Collingwood Coll Dur BSc 87 Bris Univ MPhil 00 GRSC 87. Trin Coll Bris BA 94. **d** 94 **p** 95. C Ravenhead *Liv* 94–98; TV Sutton 98–02; V Westbrook St Phil 02–11; P-in-c Westbrook St Jas 11–14; TV Warrington W from 14; Asst Dir CME from 01. *St James's Vicarage, 302 Hood Lane North, Great Sankey, Warrington WA5 1UQ* T: (01925) 471559 E: martinthevicar@btinternet.com

THORPE, Nathan Andrew. b 93. Univ of Wales (Trin St Dav) BA 14 St Jo Coll Dur BA 17. Cranmer Hall Dur 14. **d** 17 **p** 18. C Formby St Pet *Liv* 17–20; V Aintree St Giles w St Pet from 20. *The Vicarage, 132 Aintree Lane, Liverpool L10 8LE* T: 0151-280 3883 M: 07505-234115 E: nathanthorpe1@hotmail.co.uk

THORPE, Poppy. *See* THORPE, Eleanor Poppy

✠**THORPE, The Rt Revd Richard Charles.** b 65. Birm Univ BSc 87 Ox Univ BTh 96. Wycliffe Hall Ox 93 Asbury Th Sem Kentucky DMin 20. **d** 96 **p** 97 **c** 15. C Brompton H Trin w Onslow Square St Paul *Lon* 96–05; P-in-c Shadwell St Paul w Ratcliffe St Jas 05–10; R 10–15; P-in-c Bromley by Bow All Hallows 10–14; Suff Bp Islington from 15; Hon Asst Bp S'wark from 18; P-in-c St Edm the King and St Mary Woolnoth etc *Lon* 17–18; R St Edm and St Mary Woolnoth etc from 18. *26 Canonbury Park South, London N1 2FN* M: 07776-204945 E: bishop.islington@london.anglican.org

THREADGILL, Steven Alan. b 59. Cant Univ (NZ) BA 84 MA 88 Christchurch Teachers' Coll Dip Teaching 88. STETS MA 08. **d** 08 **p** 09. C Lee-on-the-Solent *Portsm* 08–11; C Bundaberg Australia from 11. *8 Hodgetts Court, Bundaberg QLD 4670, Australia* T: (0061) (7) 4151 2621 *or* (7) 4151 3128 M: 40-769 3897 E: steventhreadgill@yahoo.co.uk

THRELFALL-HOLMES, Miranda. b 73. Ch Coll Cam BA 95 MA 97 Univ Coll Dur PhD 00 St Jo Coll Dur BA 02. Cranmer Hall Dur 00. **d** 03 **p** 04. C Newc St Gabr 03–06; Chapl and Fell Univ Coll Dur 06–12; Interim Prin Ustinov Coll Dur 11–12; V Belmont and Pittington *Dur* 12–17; AD Dur 16–17; TR St Luke in the City *Liv* from 17. *St Bride's Church, Percy Street, Liverpool L8 7LT* M: 07565-521309 E: miranda@threlfall-holmes.net *or* rector@stlukeinthecity.org.uk

THROUP, Ms Caroline Elizabeth. b 64. St Cath Coll Cam BA 86 MA 90 Man Univ MBA 94 Ches Univ MTh 13. St Jo Coll Nottm 08. **d** 10 **p** 11. C Burnage St Marg *Man* 10–13; R Levenshulme 13–16; Tutor Ridley Hall Cam 16–18; LtO *Ely* 17–18; PtO *Man* 17–18; R Wilmslow *Ches* from 18. *15 Parkway, Wilmslow SK9 1LS* E: caroline.throup@ntlworld.com

THROUP, Marcus. b 78. Nottm Univ PhD 14. **d** 04 **p** 05. Voc Adv and Dioc Dir of Ords *Win* from 16. *The Diocesan Office, Wolvesey Palace, Winchester SO23 9ND* T: (01962) 710984 E: marcus.throup@winchester.anglican.org

THROWER, Clive Alan. b 41. Sheff Univ BSc 62 CEng 90. EMMTC 76. **d** 79 **p** 80. C Derby Cathl 79–86; C Spondon 86–91; Soc Resp Officer 86–91; Faith in the City Link Officer 88–91; Dioc Rural Officer 91; P-in-c Ashford w Sheldon 91; V Ashford w Sheldon and Longstone 92–07; Dioc Rural and Tourism Officer 96–07; RD Bakewell and Eyam 04–07; rtd 07; PtO *Derby* from 07. *Longstone House, 5 Vernon Green, Bakewell DE45 1DT* T: (01629) 814863 E: clive@thrower.org.uk

THROWER, Philip Edward. b 41. Kelham Th Coll 61. **d** 66 **p** 67. C Hayes St Mary *Lon* 66–69; C Yeovil *B & W* 69–71; C Shirley St Jo *Cant* 71–77; P-in-c S Norwood St Mark 77–81; V 81–84; V S Norwood St Mark *S'wark* 85–97; V Malden St Jas 97–07; rtd 07; PtO *S'wark* from 07. *243 Chipstead Way, Banstead SM7 3JN* T: (01737) 218306

THUBRON, Thomas William. b 33. Edin Th Coll 62. **d** 65 **p** 66. C Gateshead St Mary *Dur* 65–66; C Shildon 66–67; E Pakistan 68–71; Bangladesh 71–80; V Wheatley Hill *Dur* 80–87; V Dur St Giles 87–98; rtd 98; PtO *Dur* 04–21. *The Old Vicarage, Gable Terrace, Wheatley Hill, Durham DH6 3RA* T: (01429) 823940 E: dthubron@yahoo.com

THURBURN-HUELIN, David Richard. b 47. St Chad's Coll Dur BA 69 Ex Univ MA 98. Westcott Ho Cam 69. **d** 71 **p** 72. C Poplar *Lon* 71–76; Chapl Liddon Ho Lon 76–80; R Harrold and Carlton w Chellington *St Alb* 81–88; V Goldington 88–95; Dir OLM *Truro* 95–00; P-in-c Shipston-on-Stour w Honington and Idlicote *Cov* 01–05; R 05–12; rtd 12; PtO *Cov* from 13; *Glouc* from 13. *19 The Firs, Lower Quinton, Stratford-upon-Avon CV37 8TJ* T: (01789) 720967 E: thurburn.huelins@btinternet.com

THURGILL, Sally Elizabeth. b 60. **d** 02 **p** 03. OLM Mattishall and the Tudd Valley *Nor* 02–18; NSM from 18. *3 Dereham Road, Yaxham, Dereham NR19 1RF* T: (01362) 692745 E: sally.thurgill@matvchurch.uk

THURLOW, Miss Miriam Grace. b 95. York Univ BA 14 St Jo Coll Dur BA 18. Cranmer Hall Dur 18. **d** 21. C Bridlington Ch Ch w Bessingby and Ulrome *York* from 21. *20 The Lawns, Bridlington YO16 6FL* M: 07972-489524 E: mgthurlow123@gmail.com

THURSBY, Mrs Olive Eleanor. b 47. Open Univ BA 91 MA 98 Liv Hope Univ BEd 19 ATCL 74. St Mellitus Coll 19. **d** 20 **p** 21. NSM Wanstead St Mary w Ch Ch *Chelmsf* from 20. *5 Chancery House, 27 The Avenue, London E11 2DJ* T: (020) 8989 9948 M: 07506-757728 E: olive.thursby@mail.com

THURSTON-SMITH, Trevor. b 59. Chich Th Coll 83. **d** 86 **p** 87. C Rawmarsh w Parkgate *Sheff* 86–87; C Horninglow *Lich* 87–91; Chapl for People affected by HIV *Leic* 05–11; P-in-c Broughton Astley and Croft w Stoney Stanton 11–14; V Wigston from 14. *8 Harrogate Way, Wigston LE18 3YB* E: trevor@thursmith.co.uk

THURTELL, Victoria Ann. *See* PASK, Victoria Ann

THWAITES, Robin James. b 82. Ripon Coll Cuddesdon 18. **d** 20 **p** 21. C Camelside *Truro* from 20. *Merrymeeting Farmhouse, Tresarrett, Bodmin PL30 4QH* M: 07754-459174 E: revrobinthwaites@gmail.com

TIBBO, George Kenneth. b 29. Reading Univ BA 50 MA 54. Coll of Resurr Mirfield 55. **d** 57 **p** 58. C W Hartlepool St Aid *Dur* 57–61; V Darlington St Mark 61–73; V Darlington St Mark w St Paul 73–75; R Crook 75–80; V Oldham St Chad Limeside *Man* 80–87; V Hipswell *Ripon* 87–95; OCM 90–95; rtd 95; P-in-c Nidd *Ripon* 95–01; PtO 02–04; Hon C Saddleworth *Man* 04–10; Hon C Denshaw

10–14; PtO *Dur* 14–16. *14 Greenside, Greatham, Hartlepool TS25 2HQ* T: (01429) 682854

TIBBOTT (née VINE), Mrs Carolyn Ann. b 63. Anglia Poly Univ BSc 04. NTMTC BA 07. **d** 07 **p** 08. C Gidea Park *Chelmsf* 07–11; V Broomfield from 11; C Gt Waltham w Ford End from 21. *Broomfield Vicarage, 10 Butlers Close, Chelmsford CM1 7BE* T: (01245) 440318 E: revcat@outlook.com

TIBBS, Simon John. b 71. **d** 08 **p** 09. C Edin Old St Paul 08–11; Lect Coll of Transfiguration Grahamstown S Africa 11–12; PtO *St Alb* 12–13; P-in-c Gt Crosby St Faith and Waterloo Park St Mary *Liv* 13–14; C 14–16; Lect Coll of Transfiguration Grahamstown S Africa from 16. *College of the Transfiguration, PO Box 77, Grahamstown, 6040 South Africa* T: (0027) (46) 622 3332 E: tibbs.simon@gmail.com

TICE, Richard Ian. b 66. Bris Univ BA 88. Wycliffe Hall Ox BTh 94. **d** 94 **p** 95. C Langham Place All So *Lon* from 94. *12 De Walden Street, London W1G 8RN* T: (020) 7580 8954 *or* 7580 3522 E: ricospa-grace@allsouls.org

TICKLE, Robert Peter. St Chad's Coll Dur BA 74. St Steph Ho Ox 74. **d** 76 **p** 77. *5 Bramley Court, Orchard Lane, Harrold, Bedford MK43 7BG* T: (01234) 721417

TICKNER, Canon Colin de Fraine. b 37. Chich Th Coll. **d** 66 **p** 67. C Huddersfield SS Pet and Paul *Wakef* 66–68; C Dorking w Ranmore *Guildf* 68–74; V Shottermill 74–91; RD Godalming 89–91; R Ockley, Okewood and Forest Green 91–97; Hon Can Guildf Cathl 96–97; rtd 97; Adv for Past Care *Guildf* 97–12; Chapl St Cath Sch Bramley 97–12; PtO *Guildf* 12–14. *11 Linersh Drive, Bramley, Guildford GU5 0EJ* T: (01483) 898161 E: colin.tickner@sky.com

TICKNER, Canon David Arthur. b 44. MBE 89. AKC 67. **d** 69 **p** 70. C Thornhill Lees *Wakef* 69–71; C Billingham St Aid *Dur* 71–74; TV 74–78; CF 78–98; PtO *Guildf* 96–98; R Heysham *Blackb* 98–13; Hon Can Blackb Cathl 12–13; rtd 13; P-in-c Turners Hill *Chich* from 13. *The Vicarage, Church Road, Turners Hill, Crawley RH10 4PB* T: (01342) 715278 E: david.tickner@gmail.com *or* stleonardth@gmail.com

TIDESWELL, Mrs Lynne Maureen Ann. b 49. NOC 02. **d** 05 **p** 06. NSM Stoke-upon-Trent *Lich* 05–10; NSM Knutton 10–17; P-in-c 14–17; rtd 17; PtO *Lich* from 17. *74 Grange Road, Cheddleton, Leek ST13 7NP*

TIDEY, Mark James. b 72. Trin Coll Bris 14. **d** 17 **p** 18. NSM Stratton St Margaret w S Marston etc *Bris* from 17. *8 Whitby Grove, Swindon SN2 1NA*

TIDSWELL, David Alan. b 42. CEng 73 FIEE 84 Univ Coll Chich BA 03. St Steph Ho Ox 99. **d** 00 **p** 01. NSM Forest Row *Chich* 00–07; P-in-c Fairwarp 07–10; P-in-c High Hurstwood 07; rtd 17. *Manapouri, Hammerwood Road, Ashurst Wood, East Grinstead RH19 3SA* T: (01342) 822808 E: datidswell@btinternet.com

TIERNAN, Paul Wilson. b 54. Man Univ BA 76. Coll of Resurr Mirfield 77. **d** 79 **p** 80. C Lewisham St Mary *S'wark* 79–83; V Sydenham St Phil from 83. *St Philip's Vicarage, 122 Wells Park Road, London SE26 6AS* T: (020) 8699 4930

TIERNEY, Miss Sarah. b 72. Bp Grosseteste Coll BA(QTS) 94. Trin Coll Bris 17. **d** 19 **p** 20. C Frodingham and New Brumby *Linc* from 19. *The Vicarage, 159 Warwick Road, Scunthorpe DN6 1HH* M: 07765-314456 E: pennine357@gmail.com

TIESEMA-SAMSOM, Mrs Astrid Leonore. b 61. Anglia Ruskin Univ BA 13. ERMC 09. **d** 13 **p** 14. C Harwich Peninsula *Chelmsf* 13–17; V Pill, Portbury and Easton-in-Gordano *B & W* from 17. *The Rectory, 17 Church Road, Easton-in-Gordano, Bristol BS20 0PQ* E: altsamsom@hotmail.com

TIGHE, Derek James. b 58. Ox Univ BTh 11. Ripon Coll Cuddesdon 05. **d** 07 **p** 08. C Wimborne Minster *Sarum* 07–12; V Dorking w Ranmore *Guildf* from 12. *St Martin's Vicarage, Westcott Road, Dorking RH4 3DN* T: (01306) 882875 E: revd.derek.tighe@btinternet.com

TIGWELL, Brian Arthur. b 36. S'wark Ord Course 74. **d** 77 **p** 78. C Purley St Mark *S'wark* 77–80; TV Upper Kennet *Sarum* 80–85; V Devizes St Pet 85–99; Wilts Adnry Ecum Officer 88–99; RD Devizes 92–98; rtd 99; PtO *Sarum* from 01; *B & W* 04–18. *15 Sudweeks Court, New Park Street, Devizes SN10 1DX*

TILBY, Canon Angela Clare Wyatt. b 50. Girton Coll Cam BA 72 MA 76. Cranmer Hall Dur 77. **d** 97 **p** 98. Tutor Westcott Ho Cam 97–11; Vice-Prin 01–06; Hon C Cherry Hinton St Jo *Ely* 97–06; V Cambridge St Benedict 07–11; CMD Officer and Can Res Ch Ch *Ox* 11–16; rtd 16; PtO *Portsm* from 16; Hon Can Portsm Cathl from 19. *51 High Street, Portsmouth PO1 2LU* T: (023) 9275 2335 M: 07966-132045 E: angela.tilby@btinternet.com

TILDESLEY, Edward William David. b 56. SS Hild & Bede Coll Dur BEd 79. SAOMC 93. **d** 96 **p** 97. Chapl Shiplake Coll Henley 96–99; NSM Emmer Green *Ox* 96–99; Chapl Oakham Sch 99–00; TV Dorchester *Ox* 00–05; C Aldershot St Mich *Guildf* 05–08; rtd 08; NSM Wyke Regis *Sarum* 10–17;

Chapl HM Pris Dorchester 13–20; Chapl HM Pris The Verne from 20; PtO *Sarum* from 17. *Address withheld by request* E: ewdtildesley@outlook.com

TILL, Anthony Richard. b 61. Qu Foundn (Course) 17. d 19 p 20. NSM Walbrook Epiphany *Derby* from 19. *51 Friary Avenue, Allenton, Derby DE24 9DD* T: (01332) 691354 M: 07801-097859 E: anthonytill@virginmedia.com

TILLBROOK, Canon Richard Ernest. b 50. St Mark & St Jo Coll Lon CertEd 71 ACP 76. NTMTC 96. d 99 p 00. Hd RE Davenant Foundn Sch Loughton 71–03; NSM High Laver w Magdalen Laver and Lt Laver etc *Chelmsf* 99–03; V Colchester St Barn from 03; Hon Can Ho Ghana from 19. *St Barnabas' Vicarage, 13 Abbot's Road, Colchester CO2 8BE* T: (01206) 797481 M: 07818-440530 E: fathercap@hotmail.com

TILLER, Edgar Henry Valentine. b 22. Ex Univ CertEd 69 Open Univ BA 78 ACP 71. Wells Th Coll 57. d 59 p 60. C Weston-super-Mare St Jo *B & W* 59–62; V Stoke Lane and Leigh upon Mendip 62–67; Asst Master Chaddiford Sch Barnstaple 69–81; PtO *Ex* 67–05; *Llan* 06–17; rtd 91. *42 Llys Pegasus, Ty Glas Road, Llanishen, Cardiff CF14 5ER*

TILLER, The Ven John. b 38. Ch Ch Ox BA 60 MA 64 Bris Univ MLitt 72. Tyndale Hall Bris 60. d 62 p 63. C Bedford St Cuth *St Alb* 62–65; C Widcombe *B & W* 65–67; Tutor Tyndale Hall Bris 67–71; Chapl 67–71; Lect Trin Coll Bris 71–73; P-in-c Bedford Ch Ch *St Alb* 73–78; Chief Sec ACCM 78–84; Hon Can St Alb 79–84; Can Res Heref Cathl 84–04; Chan 84–02; Dioc Dir of Tr *Heref* 91–00; Adn Heref 02–04; rtd 05; Local Miss and Min Adv (Shrewsbury Area) *Lich* 05–09; Hon C Meole Brace 09; PtO 10–20; Hon C Heref 17–19. *2 Pulley Lane, Bayston Hill, Shrewsbury SY3 0JH* T: (01743) 873595 E: canjtiller@btinternet.com

TILLETT, Leslie Selwyn. b 54. Peterho Cam BA 75 MA 79 Leeds Univ BA 80. Coll of Resurr Mirfield 78. d 81 p 82. C W Dulwich All SS and Em *S'wark* 81–85; R Purleigh, Cold Norton and Stow Maries *Chelmsf* 85–93; R Beddington *S'wark* 93–05; R Wensum Benefice *Nor* 05–14; RD Sparham 08–13; P-in-c Flegg Coastal Benefice 14–18; P-in-c Nor St Mary Magd w St Jas from 18. *St Mary Magdalene Vicarage, 10 Crome Road, Norwich NR3 4RQ* E: selwyn@tillett.org.uk

TILLETT, Luke David. b 88. Rob Coll Cam BTh 10. Ridley Hall Cam 07. d 10 p 11. C Guisborough *York* 10–15; Chapl to Bp Beverley 15; V Acomb Moor from 15; RD City of York from 19. *The Vicarage, 2 Sherringham Drive, York YO24 2SE* T: (01904) 706047 E: lukedavidtillett@gmail.com

TILLETT, Michael John Arthur. b 57. Ridley Hall Cam 96. d 98 p 99. C Framlingham w Saxtead *St E* 98–01; P-in-c Stoke by Nayland w Leavenheath and Polstead 01–03; R 03–10; RD Hadleigh 07–10; R Ipswich St Helen, H Trin, and St Luke 10–13. *4 Oak Eggar Chase, Pinewood, Ipswich IP8 3TJ* M: 07531-940870 E: revtillett@aol.com

TILLETT, Miss Sarah Louise. b 59. Regent Coll Vancouver MCS 00. Wycliffe Hall Ox 01. d 03 p 03. C Knowle *Birm* 03–07; P-in-c Bloxham w Milcombe and S Newington *Ox* 07–14; PtO 16–17; Chapl Chantilly *Eur* from 17. *7A Avenue du Bouteiller, 60500 Chantilly, France* E: sarah02tillett@gmail.com

TILLETT, Selwyn. *See* TILLETT, Leslie Selwyn

TILLEY, Canon David Robert. b 38. Kelham Th Coll 58. d 63 p 64. C Bournemouth St Fran *Win* 63–67; C Moulsecoomb *Chich* 67–70; C Ifield 70–75; TV Warwick *Cov* 76–85; P-in-c Alderminster and Halford 85–96; Dioc Min Tr Adv 85–90; CME Adv 90–04; Assoc Min Willenhall 96–04; Hon Can Cov Cathl 03–04; rtd 04; PtO *Cov* from 04. *13 Stuart Court, High Street, Kibworth Beauchamp, Leicester LE8 0LR* T: 0116-279 3568 E: david.r.tilley@gmail.com

TILLEY, Elizabeth Ann. b 45. Bris Univ BA 67 PGCE 68. All Nations Chr Coll 72 Lon Bible Coll MA 89. d 07 p 08. OLM Wonersh w Blackheath *Guildf* 07–15; rtd 15; PtO *Guildf* 15–18; Chapl Birtley Ho Bramley from 18. *9 Hullmead, Shamley Green, Guildford GU5 0UF* T: (01483) 891730 E: etilley945@btinternet.com

TILLEY, James Stephen. b 55. St Jo Coll Nottm BTh 84. d 84 p 85. C Nottingham St Jude *S'well* 84–88; C Chester le Street *Dur* 88–92; Tr and Ed CYFA (CPAS) 92–94; Hd 94–02; PtO *Cov* 92–06; C Nailsea H Trin *B & W* from 06; Min Trendlewood CD from 17; RD Portishead from 18; rtd 22. *29 Vynes Way, Nailsea, Bristol BS48 2UG* T: (01275) 543332 M: 07971-563229 E: steve.tilley@trendlewoodchurch.org.uk

TILLIER, Preb Jane Yvonne. b 59. New Hall Cam BA 81 PhD 85. Ripon Coll Cuddesdon BA 90. d 91 p 94. Par Dn Sheff St Mark Broomhill 91–94; C 94–95; Chapl Glouc Cathl 95–97; P-in-c Madeley *Lich* 97–03; P-in-c Betley 02–03; PtO 03–04; Chapl and Team Ldr Douglas Macmillan Hospice Blurton 04–08; P-in-c Barlaston *Lich* 08–14; Min Development Adv Stafford Area 10–14; Dioc Adv for Women in Min 11–17; Bp's Adv for Past Care and Wellbeing 14–21;

Preb Lich Cathl 11–21; rtd 21. *10 Plantation Park, University of Keele, Keele, Newcastle ST5 5NA* T: (01782) 639720 E: jane@atherton-tillier.co.uk

TILLOTSON, Simon Christopher. b 67. Lon Univ BA 90 Trin Coll Cam BA 93 MA 96. Ridley Hall Cam 91. d 94 p 95. C Paddock Wood *Roch* 94–98; C Ormskirk *Liv* 98–00; V Aylesford *Roch* 00–07; TV Whitstable *Cant* from 07. *The Vicarage, Church Street, Whitstable CT5 1PG* T: (01227) 272308 M: 07946-527471 E: tillotsons@gmail.com

TILLYER, Preb Desmond Benjamin. b 40. Ch Coll Cam BA 63 MA 67. Coll of Resurr Mirfield 64. d 66 p 67. C Hanworth All SS *Lon* 66–70; Chapl Liddon Ho Lon 70–74; V Pimlico St Pet w Westmr Ch Ch *Lon* 74–06; AD Westmr St Marg 85–92; Preb St Paul's Cathl 01–06; rtd 06; PtO *Nor* from 06; *Lon* from 13. *85 Claremont House, 14 Aerodrome Road, London NW9 5NW* T: (020) 8032 5402 E: deslannw9@gmail.com

TILSON, Canon Alan Ernest. b 46. TCD. d 70 p 71. C Londonderry Ch Ch *D & R* 70–73; I Inver, Mountcharles and Killaghtee 73–79; I Leckpatrick w Dunnalong 79–89; Bermuda 89–05; Hon Can Bermuda Cathl 96–05; I Tullyaughnish w Kilmacrennan and Killygarvan *D & R* 05–10; rtd 10. *Coquina, 28 Castle Way, Glencarse, Perth PH2 7NY* T: (01738) 860914 M: 07470-056227 E: canontilson@gmail.com

TILTMAN, Canon Alan Michael. b 48. Selw Coll Cam BA 70 MA 74. Cuddesdon Coll 71. d 73 p 74. C Chesterton Gd Shep *Ely* 73–77; C Preston St Jo *Blackb* 77–79; Chapl Lancs (Preston) Poly 77–79; TV Man Whitworth 79–86; Chapl Man Univ (UMIST) 79–86; V Urmston *Man* 86–99; Dir CME 99–03; C Salford Sacred Trin and St Phil 99–02; V Buckley St As 04–14; Chan St As Cathl 13–14; rtd 14; PtO *St As* from 14. *The Vicarage, Church Street, Rhosymedre, Wrexham LL14 3EA* T: (01978) 824087 E: a.tiltman@hotmail.com

TILTMAN, Canon Katherine Joan. b 53. St Hugh's Coll Ox MA 74 Man Metrop Univ MSc 02. St Mich Coll Llan 09. d 11 p 12. C Wrexham *St As* 11–14; C Ruabon and Rhosymedre 14; V 14–16; I Offa Miss Area 17–21; Hon Can St As Cathl from 19. *Address temp unknown* M: 07753-230644 E: katherinetiltman@gmail.com

TIMBRELL, Keith Stewart. b 48. Edin Th Coll 72. d 74 p 75. C Chorley St Pet *Blackb* 74–77; C Altham w Clayton le Moors 77–79; Chapl Whittingham Hosp Preston 79–95; Trust Chapl Dorset HealthCare University NHS Foundn Trust 95–08; rtd 08; PtO *Sarum* 09–19; *Win* from 10. *9 Whitecross Close, Poole BH17 9HN* T: (01202) 604985 M: 07788-907965 E: clerigo@btinternet.com

TIMINGS, Julie Elizabeth. *See* WILLINGHAM, Julie Elizabeth

TIMMINS, Miss Susan Katherine. b 64. Leic Univ BScEng 85 MICE 91. St Jo Coll Nottm MTh 94. d 96 p 97. C Iver *Ox* 96–00; P-in-c Pendlebury St Jo *Man* 00–06; V 06–15; Hon Assoc Dioc Dir of Ords 10–15; PtO 15–16; V Appley Bridge and Parbold *Blackb* from 16. *The Vicarage, 5 Tan House Lane, Parbold, Wigan WN8 7HG* T: (01257) 462350 M: 07969-837394 E: susanktimmins@aol.com

TIMMIS (née PITT), Mrs Karen Lesley Finella. b 62. Lon Univ BA 84. Chich Th Coll BTh 94. d 94 p 95. C Walton-on-the-Hill *Liv* 94–98; P-in-c Warrington St Barn 98–00; V from 00. *The Vicarage, 73 Lovely Lane, Warrington WA5 1TY* T: (01925) 633556

TIMMIS, Vivian Alycia Mary. b 67. Coll of H Cross (USA) BA 89 Birm Univ MA 90 PhD 97 Long Is Univ MSLIS 06. Ripon Coll Cuddesdon 15. d 17 p 18. C Warwick *Cov* 17–21; Chapl Warw Sch 18–21; P-in-c Northleach w Hampnett and Farmington etc *Glouc* from 21. *The Vicarage, Northleach, Cheltenham GL54 3HL* T: (01451) 860452 F: (01926) 328628 M: 07827-377625 E: vicar@northleachbenefice.org

TIMS, Brian Anthony. b 43. Solicitor 64. STETS 95. d 98 p 99. NSM Whitchurch w Tufton and Litchfield *Win* 98–02; NSM Shipton Bellinger 02; PtO 06–13 and from 15; *Ox* from 13. *Fern Bank, Bere Court Road, Pangbourne, Reading RG8 8JT* T: 0118-984 2335 E: brian@timsfamily.com

TINGAY, Kevin Gilbert Xavier. b 43. Sussex Univ BA 79. Chich Th Coll 79. d 80 p 81. C W Tarring *Chich* 80–83; TV Worth 83–90; R Bradford w Oake, Hillfarrance and Heathfield *B & W* 90–01; RD Tone 96–01; P-in-c Camerton w Dunkerton, Foxcote and Shoscombe 01–10; Bp's Inter Faith Officer 01–10; Bp's Adv for Regional Affairs 01–10; rtd 10; PtO *B & W* from 10. *82B Keyford, Frome BA11 1JJ* T: (01373) 455778 E: kgxt@btinternet.com

TINKER, Christopher Graham. b 78. Collingwood Coll Dur BA 00. Wycliffe Hall Ox 02. d 04 p 05. C Houghton *Carl* 04–08; NSM Terrington St Clement *Ely* 08–13; R Bradwell *Nor* 13–18. *Address temp unknown* E: christinkerwork@aol.co.uk *or* cornerstonebrighouse@outlook.com

TINNISWOOD, Ms Louise. b 71. Staffs Univ BA 96 Cliff Coll MA 11 Huddersfield Univ PGCE 97. St Jo Coll Nottm 10. d 12 p 13. C Finningley w Auckley *Sheff* 12–15; R Crofton

Leeds from 15; V Warmfield from 15. *The Vicarage, 2A Ashdene Approach, Crofton, Wakefield WF4 1LZ* M: 07989-862189 E: louise.tinniswood@talktalk.net

TINSLEY, Derek. b 31. ALCM 65 BTh 93 PhD 97. NW Ord Course 73. d 76 p 77. C Gt Crosby St Faith *Liv* 76–80; V Wigan St Anne 80–85; V Colton w Satterthwaite and Rusland *Carl* 85–93; rtd 93; PtO *Liv* from 93. *Lyndale, 43 Renacres Lane, Ormskirk L39 8SG*

TINSLEY, Preb Derek Michael. b 35. Lon Coll of Div ALCD 66 LTh. d 66 p 67. C Rainhill *Liv* 66–68; C Chalfont St Peter *Ox* 68–73; P-in-c Maids Moreton w Foxcote 73–74; P-in-c Akeley w Leckhampstead 73–74; P-in-c Lillingstone Dayrell w Lillingstone Lovell 73–74; R N Buckingham 74–82; RD Buckingham 78–82; P-in-c Alstonfield *Lich* 82–84; P-in-c Butterton 82–84; P-in-c Warslow and Elkstones 82–84; P-in-c Wetton 82–84; V Alstonfield, Butterton, Warslow w Elkstone etc 85–95; RD Alstonfield 82–95; Preb Lich Cathl 91–98; V Cheddleton 95–98; Chapl St Edward's Hosp Cheddleton 96–98; rtd 98; PtO *Lich* 98–12; *Derby* 98–17; *Ex* from 17. *30 Gracey Court, Woodland Road, Broadclyst, Exeter EX5 3GA* T: (01392) 466763 E: derekm.tinsley@btinternet.com

TIPLADY, Janet. b 56. Liv Univ BEd 79 St Kath Coll Liv TCert 78. ERMC 10. d 12 p 13. NSM Warboys w Broughton and Bury w Wistow *Ely* 12–16; NSM Long Stanton w St Mich 16–21; NSM Over 16–21; NSM 5folds from 21. *22 Locksgate, Somersham, Huntingdon PE28 3HZ* T: (01487) 840193 M: 07713-099346 E: janet.tiplady@gmail.com

TIPP (formerly **NORTHERN**), **Mrs Elaine Joy.** b 54. Leic Univ BSc 75. SEITE 00. d 03 p 04. C Snodland All SS w Ch *Roch* 03–08. *14 Church Road, Murston, Sittingbourne ME10 3RU* T: (01795) 472574 E: 2xp@talktalk.net

TIPP, James Edward. b 45. Heythrop Coll Lon MA 93. Oak Hill Th Coll 73. d 75 p 76. C St Mary Cray and St Paul's Cray *Roch* 75–78; C Southborough St Pet w Ch Ch and St Matt 78–82; R Snodland All SS w Ch Ch 82–08; RD Cobham 96–08; Hon Can Roch Cathl 01–08; rtd 08. *14 Church Road, Murston, Sittingbourne ME10 3RU* T: (01795) 472574 E: 2xp@talktalk.net

TIPPING, Canon John Woodman. b 42. AKC 65. d 66 p 67. C Croydon St Sav *Cant* 66–70; C Plaistow St Mary *Roch* 70–72; V Brockley Hill St Sav *S'wark* 72–83; P-in-c Sittingbourne St Mary *Cant* 83–86; V 86–94; P-in-c Mersham w Hinxhill 94–03; P-in-c Mersham w Hinxhill and Sellindge 03–07; P-in-c Sevington 94–07; P-in-c Brabourne w Smeeth 95–00; AD N Lympne 95–02; Hon Can Cant Cathl 03–07; rtd 07; PtO *St E* from 08. *5 Peace Place, Thorpeness, Leiston IP16 4NA* T: (01728) 454165 E: jwtipping@talk21.com

TIPPLE, Neil. b 58. Loughb Univ BTech 81 Aston Univ MSc 86. WMMTC 01. d 04 p 05. C Cov E 04–08; V Haywards Heath Ascension *Chich* 08–17. *27 The Warren, Burgess Hill RH15 0DU* M: 07792-198451 E: ginandwhisky@aol.com *or* neiltipple@sky.com

TISDALE, Mark-Aaron Buchanan. b 67. Pittsburgh Univ BA 94. Westcott Ho Cam 00. d 02 p 03. C Norton *St Alb* 02–05; P-in-c Clifton and Southill 05–11; Chapl St Edm Sch Cant 11–12; C Finchampstead and California *Ox* 12–17; V Glinton, Etton, Maxey, Peakirk and Northborough *Pet* from 17; CF (ACF) 10–18. *The Rectory, 11 Lincoln Road, Glinton, Peterborough PE6 7JR* T: (01733) 252359 E: 9bridgesrector@gmail.com

TITCOMB, Mrs Claire. b 35. SAOMC 95. d 98 p 99. OLM Witney *Ox* 98–17; PtO 17–20; Assoc P for Min Development from 01. *30 Beech Road, Witney OX28 6LW* T: (01993) 771234

TITCOMBE, Peter Charles. See JONES, Peter Charles

TITFORD, Richard Kimber. b 45. UEA BA 67. Ripon Coll Cuddesdon 78. d 80 p 80. C Middleton *Man* 80–83; P-in-c Edwardstone w Groton and Lt Waldingfield *St E* 83–90 and 95–02; R 90–94; P-in-c Boxford 00–02; C Assington w Newton Green and Lt Cornard 00–02; R Boxford, Edwardstone, Groton etc 02–03; rtd 03; PtO *St E* from 03; *S'wark* 10–13; *Chelmsf* from 13. *2 Chestnut Mews, Friars Street, Sudbury CO10 2AH* T/F: (01787) 880303 M: 07971-031793 E: richardtitford3@outlook.com

TITLEY, Caroline. See TITLEY, Sarah Caroline

TITLEY, Canon David Joseph. b 47. Ex Univ BSc Surrey Univ PhD. Wycliffe Hall Ox. d 82 p 83. C Stowmarket *St E* 82–85; C Bloxwich *Lich* 85–90; TV 90–95; V Prees 95–00; V Fauls 95–00; V Clacton St Paul *Chelmsf* 00–13; Hon Can Chelmsf Cathl 12–13; rtd 13; PtO *Chelmsf* from 14. *34 Turner Avenue, Lawford, Manningtree CO11 2LG* T: (01206) 396462 E: titleydj@gmail.com

TITLEY, James Gareth. Bp Grosseteste Coll BA 09 Dur Univ BA 19. Westcott Ho Cam 16. d 19 p 20. C Grantham, Manthorpe *Linc* from 19; C Grantham St Wulfram from

19. *Gardener's Cottage, 43 Castlegate, Grantham NG31 6SS* E: james.titley@stwulframs.com

TITLEY, Canon Robert John. b 56. Ch Coll Cam BA 78 MA 82 K Coll Lon PhD 95. Westcott Ho Cam. d 85 p 86. C Lower Sydenham St Mich *S'wark* 85–88; C Sydenham All SS 85–88; Chapl Whitelands Coll of HE 88–94; V W Dulwich All SS 94–06; RD Streatham 04–06; Dioc Dir of Ords and Can Res and Treas S'wark Cathl 06–10; Hon Can S'wark Cathl 10–15; TR Richmond St Mary w St Matthias and St Jo 10–15; Can Res and Treas Sarum Cathl from 15. *Wyndham House, 65 The Close, Salisbury SP1 2EN* T: (01722) 555186 E: r.titley@salcath.co.uk

TITLEY, Mrs Sarah Caroline. b 58. Newnham Coll Cam MA 83 FCIH 93. SEITE 14 Sarum Coll 15. d 17 p 18. NSM Wilton w Netherhampton and Fugglestone *Sarum* from 17. *23 The Close, Salisbury SP1 2EH* M: 07808-298137 E: caroline.titley165@btinternet.com

TIZZARD, Canon David John. b 40. LRAM. Sarum Th Coll 65. d 68 p 69. C Foley Park *Worc* 68–70; Hon C Gravesend St Geo *Roch* 70–73; Miss to Seamen 70–72; PV Truro Cathl 73–75; TV Bemerton *Sarum* 75–79; Dir Soc Resp 79–85; Chapl to the Deaf 79–85; Can and Preb Sarum Cathl 84–85; R S Hill w Callington *Truro* 85–87; P-in-c Linkinhorne 86–87; Relig Affairs Producer BBC Radio Solent 87–94; V Portswood St Denys *Win* 87–94; P-in-c Distington *Carl* 94–96; Soc Resp Officer 94–96; Hon Can Carl Cathl 94–96; TV Beaminster Area *Sarum* 96–99; rtd 99; PtO *Ex* 99–05; *St D* 05–13; P-in-c Cilgerran w Bridell and Llantwyd and Eglwyswrw 13–14. *Chy Trevor, 4 Cambrian Way, Blaenannerch, Cardigan SA43 2BW* T: (01239) 811178

TIZZARD, Peter Francis. b 53. Oak Hill Th Coll 88. d 90 p 91. C Letchworth St Paul w Willian *St Alb* 90–95; I Drumkeeran w Templecarne and Muckross *Clogh* 95–00; P-in-c Ramsgate Ch Ch *Cant* 00–02; V 02–21; rtd 21. *8 Rhondda Vale, Aylesham, Canterbury CT3 3LP*

TOAN, Robert Charles. b 50. Oak Hill Th Coll. d 84 p 85. C Upton (Overchurch) *Ches* 84–87; V Rock Ferry 87–99; RD Birkenhead 97–99; V Plas Newton 99–06; P-in-c Ches Ch Ch 03–06; V Plas Newton w Ches Ch Ch 07–09; RD Ches 02–08; Cambodia 09–15; rtd 15; PtO *Ches* 16–19. *19 Meadows Lane, Saughall, Chester CH1 6AY* T: (01244) 881573 E: bobtoan@gmail.com

TOBIN, Rebecca Louise. See AMOROSO, Rebecca Mary Louise

TOBIN, Robert Benjamin. b 70. Harvard Univ AB 93 TCD MPhil 98 Mert Coll Ox DPhil 04 Em Coll Cam BA 07 MA 11 Ox Univ MA 11. Westcott Ho Cam 04. d 07 p 08. C Beaconsfield *Ox* 07–09; Chapl Harvard Univ USA 09–10; Chapl Oriel Coll Ox 10–17; V Balham St Mary and St Jo *S'wark* 17–21; Dir of Ords Kingston Area 18–21. *62 Hyde Vale, London SE10 8HP* M: 07817-956068 E: rbtobin@cantab.net

TOBIN, Mrs Vanessa Joanne. b 69. Wolv Univ BA 90 Univ of Cen England in Birm PGCE 92. Qu Coll Birm 13. d 15 p 16. C Wednesfield *Lich* 15–17; C Tettenhall Wood and Perton 17–19; V Pensnett *Worc* from 19. *St Mark's Vicarage, Vicarage Lane, Brierley Hill DY5 4JH* M: 07854-773432 E: revnesstobin@aol.com

TODD, Mrs Abigail Jean. b 85. St Mellitus Coll BA 18. d 18 p 19. C Woodford Wells *Chelmsf* 18–20; C Wanstead H Trin Hermon Hill 20; P-in-c from 20. *Holy Trinity Vicarage, Hermon Hill, London E18 1QQ*

TODD, Andrew George. b 67. Worc Coll Ox BA 90 Sheff Univ MA 16 FCA. Coll of Resurr Mirfield 13. d 15 p 16. C Barbourne *Worc* 15–18; P-in-c from 18. *1 Beech Avenue, Worcester WR3 8PZ* M: 07806-892165 E: revandyt@outlook.com

TODD, Canon Andrew John. b 61. Univ Coll Dur BA 84 K Coll Lon MPhil 98 Cardiff Univ PhD 09. Coll of Resurr Mirfield 85. d 87 p 88. C Thorpe St Andr *Nor* 87–91; Chapl K Alfred Coll *Win* 91–94; Sen Asst P E Dereham and Scarning *Nor* 94–97; Dir Studies EAMTC *Ely* 94–01; Vice-Prin 97–01; CME Officer *St E* 01–06; Can Res St E Cathl 01–06; Sub Dean 04–06; Dean Chapl Studies St Mich Coll Llan 06–16; Dir Chapl Studies St Padarn's Inst 16–17; Hon Research Fell Cardiff Univ *Llan* from 07; Progr Dir Sarum Coll from 17; PtO *St E* from 06; *Sarum* from 17. *Sarum College, 19 The Close, Salisbury SP1 2EE* T: (01722) 424836 M: 07785-560558 E: atodd@sarum.ac.uk

TODD, Ms Claire Dianne. b 67. Dur Univ MA 04. Ridley Hall Cam 15. d 17 p 18. C Marton-in-Cleveland *York* 17–20; P-in-c Brookfield 20–21; V from 21; P-in-c Stainton w Hilton 20–21; V Stainton w Hemlington and Hilton from 21. *31 Grange Wood, Coulby Newham, Middlesbrough TS8 0RT* T: (01642) 294582 M: 07940-191383 E: revtoddy@gmail.com

TODD, Clive. b 57. Open Univ BSc 04 Linc Univ MA 11. Linc Th Coll 89. d 91 p 92. C Consett *Dur* 91–93; C Bensham 93–95; P-in-c S Hetton w Haswell 95–98; R Ebchester 98–04; V

Medomsley 98–04; P-in-c S Lawres Gp *Linc* 04–09; RD Lawres 06–07; P-in-c Thanington *Cant* 09–13; Dir of Ords 09–13; R Lower Swale *Leeds* 13–18; P-in-c Brighstone and Brooke w Mottistone *Portsm* 18–19; P-in-c Shorwell w Kingston 18–19; P-in-c Calbourne w Newtown 18–19; P-in-c Shalfleet 18–19; P-in-c Thorley 18–19; P-in-c Freshwater 18–19; P-in-c Yarmouth 18–19; P-in-c Totland Bay 18–19; TR W Wight 19–20; V Brothertoft Gp *Linc* from 20; V Sibsey w Frithville from 20. *The Vicarage, Vicarage Lane, Sibsey, Boston PE22 0RT* E: vicar.clive@gmail.com

TODD, Edward Peter. b 44. Cranmer Hall Dur 86. **d** 88 **p** 89. C Hindley All SS *Liv* 88–91; P-in-c Wigan St Steph 91–96; V 96–98; P-in-c N Meols 98–03; TR 03–05; rtd 05; P-in-c Scarisbrick *Liv* 10–12; PtO from 16. *1B Nixons Lane, Southport PR8 3ES* T: (01704) 570227 E: revtodd6@gmail.com

TODD, Michael Edward. b 62. Brighton Poly BA 84 Surrey Univ PGCE 85. SEITE 96 Ven English Coll Rome 98. **d** 99 **p** 05. C Farnham *Guildf* 99–00; Chapl Surrey Inst Art and Design 99–00; Development Officer Surrey Univ *Guildf* 00–02; Progr Manager and Lect Croydon Coll 02–05; Dep Dir City and Islington Coll 05–07; Hon C Camberwell St Giles w St Matt *S'wark* 04–05; Hon C Newington St Mary from 05; Hd of Sch S Thames Coll 07–10; Chapl Trin Sch Lewisham 11–14; Ch Engagement Manager (Regional) Children's Soc from 15. *The Children's Society, Whitecross Studios, 50 Banner Street, London EC1Y 8ST* T: (020) 7841 4415 M: 07960-517297 E: mike.todd@childrenssociety.org.uk

TODD, Nicholas Stewart. b 61. Open Univ BA 03 MA 08 Cardiff Univ MTh 12. Wycliffe Hall Ox 94. **d** 96 **p** 97. C Gt Wyrley *Lich* 96–99; V Leaton and Albrighton w Battlefield 99–02; R Holbrook, Stutton, Freston, Woolverstone etc *St E* 02–06; CF from 06. *c/o MOD Chaplains (Army)* T: (01264) 383430 F: 381824 E: nick@toddsrus.org

TODD, Sarah Jane. b 74. Newman Univ BA 19. Qu Foundn Birm 13. **d** 16 **p** 17. C Tuffley *Glouc* 16–20; V from 20; P-in-c Matson from 20. *St Barnabas' Vicarage, 200 Reservoir Road, Gloucester GL4 6SB* M: 07534-720160 E: sjwakefieldtodd@gmail.com

TOLHURST, David. b 72. Cranmer Hall Dur 07. **d** 09 **p** 10. C Middleton St George *Dur* 09–13; C Sadberge 09–13; V Silksworth 13–18; V Sunderland St Matt and St Wilfrid from 18; AD Wearmouth from 17. *St Matthew's Vicarage, Silksworth Road, New Silksworth, Sunderland SR3 2AA* T: 0191-523 9932 E: revtolhurst@btinternet.com *or* vicar@stmatthewsilksworth.org

TOLLEFSEN VAN DER LANS, Alida Thadden Maria (Alja). b 50. Utrecht Univ 89. St Steph Ho Ox 96. **d** 98 **p** 99. C Bramhall *Ches* 98–02; V Knutsford St Cross 02–07; Utrecht Old Catholic Ch *Eur* 07–12; Chapl E Netherlands 12–15; P-in-c Twente 15–18; PtO 18–21; Chapl Gothenburg w Halmstad, Jönköping etc from 21. *Norra Liden 15/1202, 411 18 Göteborg, Sweden* T: (0046) (31) 711 1915 E: aljatollefsen@gmail.com

TÖLLER, Elizabeth Margery. b 53. Leeds Univ BA 75. Ripon Coll Cuddesdon 84. **d** 87 **p** 00. Asst Chapl Leeds Gen Infirmary 87–90; PtO *Nor* 90–91; Chapl Lt Plumstead Hosp 92–93; Chapl Co-ord HM Pris Nor 93–95; Chapl Gt Yarmouth Coll 96–99; PtO *S'wark* 99–00 and 11–18; Hon C Wandsworth St Paul 00–11; Hon Asst Chapl St Chris Hospice Lon 03–10. *Roseneath Cottage, Isle of Iona PA76 6SJ* E: mtoller@gmx.de

TÖLLER, Heinz Dieter. b 52. NEOC 86. **d** 87 **p** 88. C Leeds Gipton Epiphany *Ripon* 87–90; R Coltishall w Gt Hautbois and Horstead *Nor* 90–99; V Wandsworth St Paul *S'wark* 99–18; AD Wandsworth 05–13; rtd 18; Warden Iona Community *Arg* from 18; PtO from 18. *The Cottage, Cnoc-cul-Phail, Isle of Iona PA76 6SW* T: (01681) 778165 M: 07872-574374 E: htoller@gmail.com

TOLLER, Peter Sheridan. *See* STARK TOLLER, Peter Sheridan

TOMALIN, Stanley Joseph Edward. b 66. Oak Hill Th Coll BA 93. **d** 96 **p** 97. C Bitterne *Win* 96–00; C Hailsham *Chich* 00; P-in-c Hawkswood CD 01–05; V Hawkswood 05–11; C Hailsham 11–16; RD Dallington 07–14; C Cheadle *Ches* from 16. *1 Warren Avenue, Cheadle SK8 1NB* T: 0161-491 6939 E: stantomalin@gmail.com

TOMBS, Kenneth Roberts. b 42. Open Univ BA 84. S Dios Minl Tr Scheme 92. **d** 95 **p** 96. Dep Hd Twyford C of E High Sch Acton 86–97; Chapl 98–02; rtd 02; NSM Ickenham *Lon* 95–12; PtO from 12. *91 Burns Avenue, Southall UB1 2LT* T: (020) 8574 3738 E: ken.tombs@btinternet.com

TOMKINS, Ian James. b 60. Univ of Wales (Cardiff) LLB 81 Aston Business Sch MBA 90. Ridley Hall Cam. **d** 00 **p** 01. C Bourton-on-the-Water w Clapton *Glouc* 00–04; P-in-c Broxbourne w Wormley *St Alb* 04–07; R 07–10; Adv for Minl Support *Bris* 10–18; Hon C Stoke Gifford 11–14; Hon C Redland 14–18; V Bris St Matt and St Nath from 18. *St Matthew's Church Office, Clare Road, Cotham, Bristol BS6 5TB* T: 0117-944 1598 E: vicar@stmatthews-bristol.org.uk

TOMKINS, James Andrew. b 66. R Holloway & Bedf New Coll Lon 88. SAOMC 01. **d** 04 **p** 06. C Lavendon w Cold Brayfield, Clifton Reynes etc *Ox* 04–05; C Risborough 05–08; TV 08–20. *7 Waxwing Close, Aylesbury HP19 0WT* E: jamestomkins@btinternet.com

TOMKINS, Jocelyn Rachel. *See* WALKER, Jocelyn Rachel

TOMKINS, Justin Mark. b 71. Chu Coll Cam BA 93 MA 97 PhD 98. Trin Coll Bris BA 10 MPhil 12. **d** 11 **p** 12. C Longfleet *Sarum* 11–18; C The Hedinghams and Upper Colne *Chelmsf* from 19. *The Rectory, Church Road, Great Yeldham, Halstead CO9 4PT* E: email@justintomkins.org

TOMKINS, Simon Charles Ross. b 83. St Jo Coll Dur BA 06 Cam Univ BA 12. Ridley Hall Cam 10. **d** 13 **p** 14. C Lt Shelford *Ely* 13–16; R Alsagers Bank, Audley and Talke *Lich* from 16. *The Vicarage, 1 Wilbrahams Walk, Audley, Stoke-on-Trent ST7 8HL*

TOMKINS-RUSSELL, James Anthony. b 67. Oak Hill Th Coll BA 99. **d** 99 **p** 00. C Chadwell *Chelmsf* 99–03; C Patcham *Chich* 03–07; P-in-c N Mundham w Hunston and Merston 07–18; R 18–19; RD Chich 15–19; R Overton w Laverstoke and Freefolk *Win* from 19; P-in-c N Waltham and Steventon, Ashe and Deane from 19. *The Rectory, 54 Lordsfield Gardens, Overton, Basingstoke RG25 3EW* T: (01256) 589614 E: russell.j760@gmail.com

TOMKINSON, Linda Margaret. b 76. QUB BD 97 St Jo Coll Dur MATM 13. Cranmer Hall Dur 10. **d** 12 **p** 13. C Blackpool St Jo *Blackb* 12–16; C Marton 16–19; C Blackpool St Wilfrid 16–19; P-in-c from 19. *St Wilfrid's Vicarage, Langdale Road, Blackpool FY4 4RT* M: 07784-325537 E: revlindat@hotmail.co.uk

TOMKINSON, Raymond David. b 47. Ox Brookes Univ MA 10 SRN 71 MSSCh 72. EAMTC 86. **d** 89 **p** 90. NSM Chesterton St Geo *Ely* 89–91; C Sawston 91–93; C Babraham 91–93; P-in-c Wimbotsham w Stow Bardolph and Stow Bridge etc 93–94; R 94–00; RD Fincham 94–97; Dir Old Alresford Place *Win* 00–06; P-in-c Old Alresford and Bighton 00–06; rtd 06; PtO *Leic* 07–20; *Pet* 07–17; Chapl Ripon Coll Cuddesdon 09–14. *8 Uppingham Road, Oakham LE15 6JD* T: (01572) 756844 E: raymondtomkinson@gmail.com

✠TOMLIN, The Rt Revd Graham Stuart. b 58. Linc Coll Ox BA 80 MA 83 Ex Univ PhD 96. Wycliffe Hall Ox BA 85. **d** 86 **p** 87 **c** 15. C Ex St Leon w H Trin 86–89; Chapl Jes Coll Ox 89–94; Tutor Wycliffe Hall Ox 89–98; Vice-Prin 98–05; Prin St Paul's Th Cen *Lon* 05–15; Dean St Mellitus Coll 07–15; Area Bp Kensington from 15. *Dial House, Riverside, Twickenham TW1 3DT* T: (020) 7932 1180 M: 07929-048720 E: bishop.kensington@london.anglican.org

TOMLIN, Keith Michael. b 53. Imp Coll Lon BSc 75. Ridley Hall Cam 77. **d** 80 **p** 81. C Heywood St Jas *Man* 80–83; C Rochdale 83–84; TV 84–85; Chapl Rochdale Tech Coll 83–85; R Benington w Leverton *Linc* 85–99; R Leverton 99–01; Chapl HM Pris N Sea Camp 97–01; P-in-c Fotherby *Linc* 01–06; Louthesk Deanery Chapl 06–10; rtd 13; Chapl United Lincs Hosps NHS Trust from 14; PtO *Linc* 18–21. *Address withheld by request* E: keithtomlin@live.co.uk

TOMLINE, Stephen Harrald. b 35. Dur Univ BA 57. Cranmer Hall Dur. **d** 61 **p** 62. C Blackley St Pet *Man* 61–66; V Audenshaw St Steph 66–90; V Newhey 90–01; rtd 01; PtO *Carl* 01–16. *3 Humphrey Cottages, Stainton, Kendal LA8 0AD* T: (01539) 560988

TOMLINSON, Anne Lovat. b 56. Edin Univ MA 78 PhD 85 MTh 98. St Jo Coll Nottm 84. **d** 93. Tutor TISEC 93–02; Dir Past Studies 98–00; Dioc Dir of Ords *Edin* 02–05; Prov Local Collaborative Min Officer 02–08; Min Development Officer *Glas* 09–14; Prin Scottish Episc Inst from 14. *Scottish Episcopal Church, General Synod Office, 21 Grosvenor Crescent, Edinburgh EH12 5EE* T: 0131-225 6357 M: 07729-054417 E: principal@scotland.anglican.org

TOMLINSON, Barry William. b 47. Clifton Th Coll 72. **d** 72 **p** 73. C Pennington *Man* 72–76; SAMS 76–80; Chile 77–80; C-in-c Gorleston St Mary CD *Nor* 80; V Gorleston St Mary 80–88; Chapl Jas Paget Hosp Gorleston 81–87; P-in-c Gt w Lt Plumstead *Nor* 88–89; R Gt w Lt Plumstead and Witton 89–93; R Gt and Lt Plumstead w Thorpe End and Witton 93–98; Chapl Lt Plumstead Hosp 88–94; Chapl Norwich Community Health Partnership NHS Trust 94–95; RD Blofield *Nor* 96–98; V Margate H Trin *Cant* 98–99; R Roughton and Felbrigg, Metton, Sustead etc *Nor* 99–02; PtO 02–10; P-in-c Brinton, Briningham, Hunworth, Stody etc 10–16; PtO from 17. *St David's Nursing Home, 52 Common Lane, Sheringham NR26 8PW* M: 07796-243436 E: barrywtomlinson@gmail.com

TOMLINSON, Canon David Robert. b 63. Open Univ BA 07 St Jo Coll Dur BA 09 Sarum Coll MA 14. Cranmer Hall Dur 07. **d** 09 **p** 10. C Shildon *Dur* 09–13; P-in-c 13–19; AD Auckland 15–18; Sen Ldr Resourcing Ch Network from 19; Public Preacher from 19; Hon Can Dur Cathl from 17. *The Vicarage, Brookside, Evenwood, Bishop Auckland DL14 9RA* M: 07546-596079 E: smileydavid63@gmail.com or david.tomlinson@durham.anglican.org

TOMLINSON, David Robert. b 60. Kent Univ BSc 82 Chelsea Coll Lon PGCE 83 Jes Coll Cam BA 92 MA 96. Ridley Hall Cam 90. **d** 93 **p** 94. C Godalming *Guildf* 93–98; V Grays North *Chelmsf* 98–08; RD Thurrock 03–08; TR Saffron Walden w Wendens Ambo, Littlebury etc 08–11; TR Saffron Walden and Villages 12–20; RD Saffron Walden 20; Hon Can Chelmsf Cathl 15–20; PtO *Birm* 20; V Birm St Paul from 20. *23 Carisbrooke Road, Birmingham B17 8NN* T: 0121-236 7858 E: david.tomlinson@stpaulsjq.church

TOMLINSON, David William. b 48. Lon Bible Coll MA 95 Westcott Ho Cam 97. **d** 97 **p** 98. NSM W Holloway St Luke *Lon* 97–00; P-in-c 00–01; V 01–18; rtd 18; PtO *S'wark* from 19. *65 Tremadoc Road, London SW4 7NA* E: revdavetomlinson@hotmail.com

TOMLINSON, Eric Joseph. b 45. Lich Th Coll 70 Qu Coll Birm 72. **d** 73 **p** 74. C Cheadle *Lich* 73–76; C Sedgley All SS 77–79; V Ettingshall 79–94; V Horton, Lonsdon and Rushton Spencer 94–12; rtd 12; PtO *Lich* 12–13. *4 Burgis Close, Cheddleton, Leek ST13 7NR* T: (01538) 361151

TOMLINSON, Helen. b 53. **d** 07 **p** 08. OLM Stretford All SS *Man* 07–12; NSM Blackley St Paul from 12; Chapl Christie NHS Foundn Trust Man 13–18; Chapl Salford Univ *Man* from 18. *118 Crab Lane, Manchester M9 8WD* T: 0161-795 8768 E: helentomlinson116@gmail.com

TOMLINSON, Mrs Jean Mary. b 32. K Coll Lon BEd 75. S Dios Minl Tr Scheme 84. **d** 87 **p** 94. Hon Par Dn Spring Park All SS *S'wark* 87–92; Chapl HM YOI Hatfield 92–98; PtO *S'well* from 92. *6 Cheyne Walk, Bawtry, Doncaster DN10 6RS* T: (01302) 711281

TOMLINSON (*née*** MILLS), The Ven Jennifer Clare.** b 61. Trin Hall Cam BA 82 MA 86. Ridley Hall Cam 88. **d** 91 **p** 94. C Busbridge *Guildf* 91–95; C Godalming 95–98; NSM Grays North *Chelmsf* 98–08; Chapl Thurrock Primary Care Trust 99–08; NSM Saffron Walden w Wendens Ambo, Littlebury etc *Chelmsf* 08–11; NSM Saffron Walden and Villages 12–19; NSM N Blackwater 17–18; Bp's Adv on Women's Min 08–19; Par Development Adv (Colchester Area) 11–19; Hon Can Chelmsf Cathl 12–19; Adn Birm from 19. *23 Carisbrooke Road, Birmingham B17 8NN* T: 0121-426 0441 E: jennyt@cofebirmingham.com

TOMLINSON, John Howard. b 54. Newc Univ BSc 76 MICE 83. Chich Th Coll 91. **d** 93 **p** 94. C Blewbury, Hagbourne and Upton *Ox* 93–96; C Cowley St Jas 96–97; TV 97–04; TR Upper Wylye Valley *Sarum* 04–15; RD Heytesbury 07–13; rtd 15; PtO *Cant* 15–21. *11 Castle Mews, Folkestone CT20 2BU* T: (01303) 488123 E: johntomlinson73@gmail.com

TOMLINSON, John William Bruce. b 60. Univ of Wales (Abth) BA 82 Man Univ MA 90 Birm Univ PhD 08 Nottm Trent Univ PGCE 11. Hartley Victoria Coll 87 Mar Thoma Th Sem Kottayam 90 Linc Th Coll 91. **d** 92 **p** 93. In Methodist Ch 90–91; C Sawley *Derby* 92–95; P-in-c Man Victoria Park 95–98; Dioc CUF Officer 95–98; Chapl St Anselm Hall Man Univ 96–98; V Shelton and Oxon *Lich* 98–04; Ecum Co-ord for Miss and Chief Exec Officer Lincs Chapl Services *Linc* 04–06; PtO 08–14; V Carrington *S'well* 14–17; Registrar and Dir of Studies St Jo Coll Nottm 16–20; Sen Researcher CA from 20; Lic Preacher *S'well* 17–21; PtO *Derby* from 18; *Eur* from 20; *Sheff* from 21. *128 Dobcroft Road, Sheffield S7 2LU* M: 07983-134597 E: dr.pelican@hotmail.co.uk

TOMLINSON, Martyn Craig. b 78. Coll of Resurr Mirfield 13. **d** 15 **p** 16. C Barnsley St Mary *Leeds* 15–18; C Cen Barnsley 18; V Royston and Felkirk from 18. *The Vicarage, Church Street, Royston, Barnsley S71 4QZ* M: 07523-260707 E: fr.craig@outlook.com

TOMLINSON, Matthew Robert Edward. b 61. St Chad's Coll Dur BA 83 Univ of Wales (Cardiff) BD 94. St Mich Coll Llan 92. **d** 94 **p** 95. C Abergavenny St Mary w Llanwenarth Citra *Mon* 94–96; PV Llan Cathl and Chapl Cathl Sch Llan 96–00; V Edgbaston St Aug *Birm* from 00. *St Augustine's Vicarage, 44 Vernon Road, Birmingham B16 9SH* T/F: 0121-454 0127 M: 07989-915499 E: matthewtomlinson@me.com

TOMPKINS, April. b 51. Man Univ BEd 75. EMMTC 05. **d** 07 **p** 08. NSM Belper *Derby* 07–19; rtd 19; PtO *Derby* from 19. *8 Derwent Grove, Alfreton DE55 7PB* T: (01773) 835122 E: april_tompkins@hotmail.com

TOMPKINS, David John. b 32. Oak Hill Th Coll 55. **d** 58 **p** 59. C Northampton St Giles *Pet* 58–61; C Heatherlands St Jo *Sarum* 61–63; V Selby St Jas and Wistow *York* 63–73;

V Retford St Sav *S'well* 73–87; P-in-c Clarborough w Hayton 84–87; V Kidsgrove *Lich* 87–90; V Tockwith and Bilton w Bickerton *York* 90–97; rtd 97; PtO *Pet* 00–03. *49 Wentworth Drive, Oundle, Peterborough PE8 4QF* T: (01832) 275176

TOMPKINS, Michael John Gordon. b 35. JP 76. Man Univ BSc 58 MPS 59. NOC 82. **d** 85 **p** 86. C Abington *Pet* 85–87; TV Daventry 87–92; P-in-c Braunston 87–92; TV Daventry, Ashby St Ledgers, Braunston etc 92–93; R Paston 93–98; rtd 00; PtO *Ches* 98–19. *19 Clarendon Close, Chester CH4 7BL* T: (01244) 659147 E: mjgtompkins@onetel.com

TOMS, Elizabeth Jane. b 66. **d** 13 **p** 14. OLM Crondall and Ewshot *Guildf* 13–18; Chapl Frimley Health NHS Foundn Trust 15–20; Chapl N Lincs and Goole NHS Foundn Trust from 20. *Northern Lincolnshire and Goole NHS Foundation Trust, Scunthorpe General Hospital, Cliff Gardens, Scunthorpe DN15 7BH* T: (01724) 282282

TOMS, Sheila Patricia. b 33. Cam Univ TCert 54 Univ of Wales (Cardiff) BEd 77. Llan Ord Course 90. **dss** 91 **d** 94 **p** 97. Canton St Luke *Llan* 91–94; NSM Peterston-super-Ely w St Brides-super-Ely 94–00; P-in-c Newport St Paul *Mon* 00–06; PtO 07–13; P-in-c Goetre w Llanover 13–14; PtO from 14. *26 Fairfax View, Raglan, Usk NP15 2DR* T: (01291) 690250 E: sheilaptoms@btinternet.com

TONBRIDGE, Archdeacon of. *Vacant*

TONBRIDGE, Suffragan Bishop of. *See* BURTON JONES, The Rt Revd Simon David

TONGE, Brian. b 36. St Chad's Coll Dur BA 58. Ely Th Coll 59. **d** 61 **p** 62. C Fleetwood St Pet *Blackb* 61–65; Chapl Ranby Ho Sch Retford 65–69; Hon C Burnley St Andr w St Marg *Blackb* 69–97; rtd 97; PtO *Blackb* 97–20. *50 Fountains Avenue, Simonstone, Burnley BB12 7PY* T: (01282) 776518

TONGE, The Very Revd Lister. b 51. K Coll Lon AKC 74 Loyola Univ Chicago MPS 95. St Aug Coll Cant 74. **d** 75 **p** 76. C Liv Our Lady and St Nic w St Anne 75–78; C Johannesburg Cathl S Africa 78–79; CR 79–91; Lic to Offic *Wakef* 83–91; PtO *Man* 89–94; USA 93–95; PtO *Liv* 95–96; Chapl Community of St Jo Bapt from 96; Chapl Ripon Coll Cuddesdon 05–09; Lic to Offic Newark USA from 08; Chapl New Coll Ox 10–11; Dean Mon 12–18; Dean Newport 18–20; V Newport St Woolos 12–14; V Newport St Woolos w St Mark 14–20; rtd 20. *120 The Albany, 8 Old Hall Street, Liverpool L3 9EL* E: listertonge@gmail.com

TONGUE, Canon Paul. b 41. St Chad's Coll Dur BA 63. **d** 64 **p** 65. C Dudley St Edm *Worc* 64–69; C Sedgley All SS *Lich* 69–70; V Amblecote *Worc* 70–07; Chapl Dudley Gp of Hosps NHS Trust 93–07; Hon Can Worc Cathl 93–07; RD Stourbridge 96–01; rtd 07; PtO *Worc* from 09. *99 Woolhope Road, Worcester WR5 2AP* T: (01905) 352052 E: paul_tongue@sky.com

TONKIN, Mrs Jacqueline Anne. b 50. Open Univ BSc 02 DipSW 02. Yorks Min Course. **d** 11 **p** 12. NSM Langtoft w Foxholes, Butterwick, Cottam etc *York* 11–19; NSM Gt and Lt Driffield 12–19; P-in-c Waggoners from 19; RD Harthill from 17. *The Vicarage, 4 Pulham Lane, Wetwang, Driffield YO25 9XT* T: (01377) 236785 E: jacki.tonkin1@btinternet.com

TONKINSON, Canon David Boyes. b 47. K Coll Lon BD 71 AKC 71. St Aug Coll Cant 71. **d** 72 **p** 73. C Surbiton St Andr *S'wark* 72–74; C Selsdon St Jo w St Fran *Cant* 75–81; V Croydon St Aug Cant 81–84; V Croydon St Aug *S'wark* 85–89; C Easthampstead and Ind Chapl *Ox* 89–96; Chapl Bracknell Coll 93–96; Soc Resp Adv *Portsm* 96–02; Hon Can Portsm Cathl 96–02; Ind Chapl *Win* 02–08; Hon C Heckfield w Mattingley and Rotherwick 06–07; Hon C Hook and Heckfield w Mattingley and Rotherwick 07–08; Soc Resp Partnership Development Officer *Guildf* 08–11; rtd 11. *17 Squirrel Close, Sandhurst GU47 9DL*

TOOBY, Anthony Albert. b 58. Sarum & Wells Th Coll 89. **d** 91 **p** 92. C Warsop *S'well* 91–95; C Ollerton w Boughton 95–98; V Girlington *Bradf* 98–10; P-in-c Mancetter *Cov* 10–17; V Blyth St Cuth *Newc* from 17. *29 Ridley Avenue, Blyth NE24 3BA* E: tonytooby@virginmedia.com

TOOGOOD, John Peter. b 73. Leeds Univ BA 95. Ripon Coll Cuddesdon 98. **d** 00 **p** 01. C Sherborne w Castleton and Lillington *Sarum* 00–03; P-in-c Chieveley w Winterbourne and Oare *Ox* 03–10; R E Downland from 10. *The Vicarage, Church Lane, Chieveley, Newbury RG20 8UT* T: (01635) 247566 E: edownlandrector@gmail.com

TOOGOOD, Katie Leanne. *See* WAKEMAN-TOOGOOD, Katie Leanne

TOOGOOD, Robert Charles. b 45. AKC 70. St Aug Coll Cant 70. **d** 71 **p** 72. C Shepperton *Lon* 71–74; C Kirk Ella *York* 74–76; P-in-c Levisham w Lockton 76–81; P-in-c Ebberston w Allerston 76–81; R Kempsey and Severn Stoke w Croome d'Abitot *Worc* 81–92; V Bramley *Win* 92–10; rtd 10; PtO *Win* 10–19. *14 Huntsmead, Alton GU34 2SE* T: (01420) 87007

TOOGOOD, Robert Frederick. b 43. St Paul's Coll Chelt CertEd 65 Open Univ BA 74. Trin Coll Bris 93. **d** 95 **p** 96. C Southbroom *Sarum* 95–99; TV Langport Area *B & W* 99–04; rtd 04; PtO *Ox* 05–17; *Sarum* from 05. *49 Barrow Close, Marlborough SN8 2BE* T: (01672) 511468

TOOKE, Mrs Sheila. b 44. EAMTC 89. **d** 91 **p** 94. NSM March St Wendreda *Ely* 91–95; P-in-c Upwell Christchurch 95–97; P-in-c Welney 95–97; P-in-c Manea 95–97; R Christchurch and Manea and Welney 97–03; rtd 03; PtO *Ely* from 03. *The Haven, 21 Wisbech Road, March PE15 8ED* T: (01354) 652844 E: stooke@havenmarch.plus.com

TOOKEY, Preb Christopher Tom. b 41. AKC 67. **d** 68 **p** 69. C Stockton St Pet *Dur* 68–71; C Burnham *B & W* 71–77; R Clutton w Cameley 77–81; V Wells St Thos w Horrington 81–06; RD Shepton Mallet 86–95; Chapl Bath and West Community NHS Trust 95–06; Preb Wells Cathl *B & W* 90–11; rtd 06; PtO *B & W* from 06. *47 Drake Road, Wells BA5 3LE* T: (01749) 676006 E: pretookey@gmail.com

TOOP, Preb Allan Neil. b 49. St Alb Minl Tr Scheme 79 Linc Th Coll 82. **d** 83 **p** 84. C Kempston Transfiguration *St Alb* 83–87; C Ludlow *Heref* 87–92; P-in-c Stokesay and Sibdon Carwood w Halford 92–01; P-in-c Acton Scott 96–01; RD Condover 96–00; V Minsterley 01–13; R Habberley 01–13; P-in-c Hope w Shelve 07–13; R Minsterley, Habberley and Hope w Shelve 13–15; Preb Heref Cathl 06–15; rtd 15; PtO *Lich* 16–21. *6 Longacre Mews, Bicton Heath, Shrewsbury SY3 5DT* E: trigger.milward@gmail.com

TOOP, Mrs Mary-Louise. b 55. Glouc Sch of Min 90. **d** 04 **p** 05. Dir of Ords *Heref* 00–15; NSM Minsterley 04–13; NSM Habberley 04–13; NSM Hope w Shelve 04–13; NSM Minsterley, Habberley and Hope w Shelve 13–15; Preb Heref Cathl 12–15; Dioc Adv on Women in Min 13–15; P-in-c Bicton, Montford w Shrawardine and Fitz *Lich* 15–21; P-in-c Leaton and Albrighton w Battlefield 15–21; rtd 21. *6 Longacre Mews, Bicton Heath, Shrewsbury SY3 5DT*

TOOTH, Nigel David. b 47. RMN 69. Sarum & Wells Th Coll 71. **d** 74 **p** 75. C S Beddington St Mich *S'wark* 74–77; C Whitchurch *Bris* 77–83; TV Bedminster 83–87; Chapl Dorchester Hosps 87–94; Chapl Herrison Hosp Dorchester 87–94; Chapl Dorset County Hosp NHS Foundn Trust 94–11; rtd 11. *5 Hope Terrace, Martinstown, Dorchester DT2 9JN* T: (01305) 889576 E: nigeltooth@hotmail.co.uk

TOOVEY, Rupert William. b 66. **d** 10 **p** 11. NSM Storrington *Chich* 10–15 and from 18; NSM Steyning 15–18; NSM Ashurst 15–18. *31 Downsview Avenue, Storrington, Pulborough RH20 4PS* T: (01903) 740466 M: 07802-203655

TOPALIAN, Canon Berj. b 51. Sheff Univ BA 72 PhD 77. Sarum Th Coll 95. **d** 97 **p** 98. NSM Clifton Ch Ch w Em *Bris* 97–98; C Bris St Mich and St Paul 98–99; C Cotham St Sav w St Mary and Clifton St Paul 99–01; V Pilning w Compton Greenfield 01–08; Chapl St Monica Home Westbury-on-Trym 08–16; Hon Min Can Bris Cathl 04–11; Hon Can Bris Cathl 11–16; rtd 16; PtO *Bris* from 16. *40 Fenshurst Gardens, Long Ashton, Bristol BS41 9AU*

TOPHAM, Benjamin Mark. b 84. Cliff Coll BA 05. Ridley Hall Cam 13. **d** 14 **p** 15. C Chalfont St Peter *Ox* 14–17; C Gerrards Cross and Fulmer 17–20; C Stamford St Geo w St Paul *Linc* from 20. *2 Highgrove Gardens, Stamford PE9 2GR*

TOPHAM, Kim. b 63. Qu Foundn Birm 18. **d** 20 **p** 21. NSM Belbroughton w Fairfield and Clent *Worc* from 20; NSM Hagley from 20. *White Gates, Walton Pool, Clent, Stourbridge DY9 9RR* T: (01562) 887441 M: 07952-162373 E: kimbotopham@outlook.com

TOPLEY (née BRANCHE), Caren Teresa. b 59. Avery Hill Coll BEd 81. SEITE 94. **d** 97 **p** 98. NSM Arlesey w Astwick *St Alb* 97–99; NSM Clifton and Southill 99–16; R from 16. *The Rectory, 8 Rectory Close, Clifton, Shefford SG17 5EL* T: (01462) 615499 E: rector@clifton-beds.co.uk

TOPPING, Kenneth Bryan Baldwin. b 27. Bps' Coll Cheshunt 58. **d** 59 **p** 60. C Fleetwood St Pet *Blackb* 59–63; V Ringley *Man* 63–70; V Cleator Moor w Cleator *Carl* 70–91; rtd 92; PtO *Blackb* 92–07. *28 Glebelands, Corbridge NE45 5DS* T: (01434) 634944 E: bryantopping93@gmail.com

TOPPING, Roy William. b 37. MBE 92. S Dios Minl Tr Scheme 91. **d** 92 **p** 93. Bahrain 89–94; Chapl Miss to Seamen Milford Haven 94–99; rtd 99; PtO *Sarum* 00–15; *Chich* 15–20. *25 Strand Court, Harsfold Road, Rustington, Littlehampton BN16 2NT* T: (01903) 778939

TORDOFF, Donald William. b 45. Nottm Univ BA 69. Qu Coll Birm 69. **d** 71 **p** 72. C High Harrogate Ch Ch *Ripon* 71–75; C Moor Allerton 75–80; V Bilton 80–92; R Spennithorne w Finghall and Hauxwell 92–01; rtd 01; PtO *Ripon* 02–14; *Leeds* 14–16; *York* from 10. *13 Dulverton Hall, Esplanade, Scarborough YO11 2AR* E: don@tordoffs.myzen.co.uk

TORDOFF (née PARKER), Mrs Margaret Grace. b 40. SRN 65 SCM 67. Cranmer Hall Dur 81. **dss** 83 **d** 87 **p** 94. Bilton *Ripon* 83–87; C 87–92; Chapl Spennithorne Hall 92; NSM Spennithorne w Finghall and Hauxwell 92–00; rtd 00; PtO *M & K* from 00; *Ripon* 00–14; *Leeds* 14–16; *York* 10–20. *13 Dulverton Hall, Esplanade, Scarborough YO11 2AR* E: margaret@tordoffs.myzen.co.uk

TORR, Stephen Charles. b 81. Birm Univ BA 05 PhD 12. Ridley Hall Cam 10. **d** 12 **p** 13. C Wilnecote *Lich* 12–13; C Abbots Bromley, Blithfield, Colton, Colwich etc 13–16; P-in-c Norton *Ches* 16–21; Tutor St Mellitus Coll 16–19. *36 Noctorum Dell, Prenton CH43 9UL*

TORRANCE, David Alan. b 91. Fitzw Coll Cam BA 12 MA 16 PhD 17 Edin Univ MTh 13. Ridley Hall Cam 14. **d** 17 **p** 18. C Portswood Ch Ch *Win* 17–21; C Portswood St Denys 19–21; PtO from 21; CMS from 21. *Address withheld by request* E: torrance@cantab.net

TORRENS, Marianne Rose. *See* ATKINSON, Marianne Rose

TORRENS, Robert Harrington. b 33. Trin Coll Cam BA 56 MA 61. Ridley Hall Cam 56. **d** 58 **p** 59. C Bromley SS Pet and Paul *Roch* 58–60; C Aylesbury *Ox* 60–63; V Eaton Socon *St Alb* 63–73; LtO 73–75; V Pittville All SS *Glouc* 75–84; Chapl Frenchay Hosp Bris 84–94; Chapl Manor Park Hosp Bris 84–94; Chapl St Pet Hospice Bris 94–98; P-in-c Chippenham *Ely* 98–01; P-in-c Snailwell 98–01; PtO from 01; *St E* 01–21. *68 Barons Road, Bury St Edmunds IP33 2LW* T: (01284) 752075 E: torrensatkinson@aol.com

TORRY, Malcolm Norman Alfred. b 55. St Jo Coll Cam BA 76 MA 80 K Coll Lon MTh 79 LSE MSc 96 Lon Univ BD 78 PhD 90 BA 01 BSc 10 Lambeth MPhil 18. Cranmer Hall Dur 79. **d** 80 **p** 81. C S'wark H Trin w St Matt 80–83; C S'wark Ch Ch 83–88; Ind Chapl 83–88; V Hatcham St Cath 88–96; V E Greenwich Ch Ch w St Andr and St Mich 96–97; TR E Greenwich 97–13; TV 13–14; RD Greenwich Thameside 98–01; rtd 14; PtO *S'wark* 15–16; Hon C Nunhead St Antony w St Silas from 16. *286 Ivydale Road, London SE15 3DF* T: (020) 7635 7916 E: malcolm@torry.org.uk

TOSTEVIN, Alan Edwin John. b 41. Trin Coll Bris BA 86. **d** 86 **p** 87. C Hildenborough *Roch* 86–89; TV Ipsley *Worc* 89–06; rtd 06; PtO *Worc* from 06; *Cov* 16–21. *3 Canterbury Close, Studley B80 7JF* T: (01527) 852636 E: artostevin@gmail.com

TOTNES, Archdeacon of. *See* DETTMER, The Ven Douglas James

TOTNEY (née YATES), Mrs Jennifer Clare. b 83. Dur Univ BA 04 MA 05 Selw Coll Cam BA 08 MA 13. Westcott Ho Cam 06. **d** 09 **p** 10. C White Horse *Sarum* 09–12; TV Vale of Pewsey 12–21; Lic Lay Min Tr Officer 16–19; Dir Contextual Tr Westcott Ho Cam from 21. *Westcott House, Jesus Lane, Cambridge CB5 8BP* E: jennifer.totney@gmail.com

TOTTEN, Andrew James. b 64. MBE 01. QUB BA 87 TCD BTh 90 Univ of Wales (Cardiff) MTh 07. CITC. **d** 90 **p** 91. C Newtownards *D & D* 90–94; CF from 94; QHC from 16. *c/o MOD Chaplains (Army)* T: (01264) 887064 E: andrewjtotten@hotmail.com

TOTTERDELL, Mrs Rebecca Helen. b 57. Lon Bible Coll BA 80 MA 00. Oak Hill Th Coll 88. **d** 91 **p** 94. C Broxbourne w Wormley *St Alb* 91–95; C Stevenage St Nic and Graveley 95–99; P-in-c Benington w Walkern 99–08; Asst Dir of Ords 03–08; Bp's Adv for Women in Min 03–07; Asst Dioc Dir of Ords *Ex* 09–10; Dioc Dir of Ords 10–18; NSM Bovey Tracey SS Pet, Paul and Thos w Hennock 09–17; Preb Ex Cathl 14–17; Can Res Ex Cathl 17–19; R Hemyock w Culm Davy, Clayhidon and Culmstock from 19. *The Rectory, Hemyock, Cullompton EX15 3RQ* E: ucvmissionrector@gmail.com

TOTTLE, Nicola Rachael. *See* SKIPWORTH, Nicola Rachael

TOUGH, Christine Violet. b 53. **d** 16 **p** 17. OLM Tettenhall Wood and Perton *Lich* 16–19; NSM Wrockwardine Deanery from 19. *12 Mere Oak Road, Wolverhampton WV6 7NB* E: christine.v.tough@gmail.com

TOVAR, Gillian Elaine. *See* NICHOLLS, Gillian Elaine

TOVEY, Canon Phillip Noel. b 56. Lon Univ BA 77 Lon Bible Coll BA 83 Nottm Univ MPhil 88 Lambeth STh 95 Ox Brookes Univ PhD 06. St Jo Coll Nottm 85. **d** 87 **p** 88. C Beaconsfield *Ox* 87–90; C Banbury 90–91; TV 91–95; Chapl Ox Brookes Univ 95–98; P-in-c Holton and Waterperry w Albury and Waterstock 95–97; TV Wheatley 97–98; Dioc Tr Officer 98–18; Dir Reader Tr 04–18; NSM Wootton and Dry Sandford 05–10; Lect Ripon Coll Cuddesdon 04–16; Dep Warden Readers 16–19; Warden Readers from 19; Prin Ox Local Min Pathway from 18; Hon Can Ch Ch from 20. *20 Palmer Place, Abingdon OX14 5LZ* T: (01235) 527077 E: phillip.tovey@oxford.anglican.org

TOWERS, Patrick Leo. b 43. AKC 68 Hull Univ CertEd 69. **d** 74 **p** 75. Japan 74–81; TV Bourne Valley *Sarum* 81–83; Dioc Youth Officer 81–83; Chapl Oundle Sch 83–86; I Rathkeale w Askeaton and Kilcornan *L & K* 86–89; I Nenagh 89–00;

Can Limerick, Killaloe and Clonfert Cathls 97–00; Provost Tuam *T, K & A* 00–09; Can Tuam Cathl 00–09; I Galway w Kilcummin 00–09; rtd 09. *Doonwood, Mountbellew, Co Galway, H53 Y821, Republic of Ireland* T: (00353) (90) 968 4547 M: 86-814 0649 E: towers.patrick@gmail.com

TOWLER, David George. b 42. Cranmer Hall Dur 73. **d** 76 **p** 77. C Newbarns w Hawcoat *Carl* 76–80; V Huyton St Geo Liv 80–98; V Newburgh w Westhead 98–07; AD Ormskirk 01–06; Hon Can Liv Cathl 03–07; rtd 07; PtO *Liv* from 16. *7 Padstow Close, Southport PR9 9RX* E: davidgtowler@gmail.com

TOWLER, John Frederick. b 42. Surrey Univ PhD 05. Bps' Coll Cheshunt 62. **d** 66 **p** 67. C Lowestoft St Marg *Nor* 66–71; R Horstead 71–77; Warden Dioc Conf Ho Horstead 71–77; Prec and Min Can Worc Cathl 77–81; rtd 02; Hon C Fordingbridge and Breamore and Hale etc *Win* 06–12; PtO from 12; *Sarum* from 17. *5 Mill Race View, The Borough, Downton, Salisbury SP5 3LU* M: 07940-855952

TOWNEND, John Philip. b 52. Southn Univ BTh 95. Sarum & Wells Th Coll 89. **d** 91 **p** 92. C Sherborne w Castleton and Lillington *Sarum* 91–95; P-in-c Wool and E Stoke 95–98; Sacr and Chapl Westmr Abbey 98–01; P-in-c Brightwalton w Catmore, Leckhampstead etc *Ox* 01–10; P-in-c Beedon and Peasemore w W Ilsley and Farnborough 05–10; R W Downland 10–17; rtd 17. *Can yr Afon, 1 Brookside, Glasbury, Hereford HR3 5NF* T: (01497) 847807 E: jptownend@btinternet.com

TOWNEND, The Ven Lee Stuart. b 65. St Jo Coll Dur MA 08. Cranmer Hall Dur 96. **d** 98 **p** 99. C Buxton w Burbage and King Sterndale *Derby* 98–01; V Loose *Cant* 01–08; P-in-c Ilkley All SS *Bradf* 08–12; Ch Growth Officer Chesterfield Adnry *Derby* 12–17; Adn Carl and Can Res Carl Cathl from 17; P-in-c Barton, Pooley Bridge, Martindale etc from 20. *The Vicarage, Pooley Bridge, Penrith CA10 2LT* M: 07458-016925 E: leethevicar@gmail.com *or* archdeacon.north@carlislediocese.org.uk

TOWNER, Canon Andrew Paul John. b 76. Bris Univ BSc 98 Surrey Univ Roehampton PGCE 02. Oak Hill Th Coll MTh 07. **d** 07 **p** 08. C St Helen Bishopsgate w St Andr Undershaft etc *Lon* 07–10; C Beckenham Ch Ch *Roch* 10–14; P-in-c Houghton *Carl* 14–19; V from 19; Hon Can Carl Cathl from 21. *12 Brunswick Close, Carlisle CA3 0HL* T: (01228) 515363 M: 07956-569983 E: andrew.towner@hkchurch.org.uk

TOWNER, Ms Catherine Mary. b 68. Qu Mary and Westf Coll Lon BA 91 Brighton Univ PGCE 05 Cam Univ BTh 20. Westcott Ho Cam 18. **d** 20 **p** 21. C Bocking St Mary and Panfield *Chelmsf* from 20. *6 Samuel Courtauld Avenue, Braintree CM7 5GJ* M: 07717-712084 E: caytowner@hotmail.com

TOWNER, Colin David. b 39. St Pet Coll Ox BA 61 MA 65 Lon Univ BD 63 ARCM 72 LRAM 73. Tyndale Hall Bris 61. **d** 64 **p** 65. C Southsea St Simon *Portsm* 64–67; C Penge St Jo *Roch* 67–70; V Leic St Chris 70–74; Hon C Southsea St Jude *Portsm* 75–82; PtO 86–90 and 00–01 and from 12; C Southsea St Pet 01–03; P-in-c 03–07; P-in-c Portsea St Luke 05–07; rtd 07; PtO *Ely* 08–12. *10 Ophir Road, Portsmouth PO2 9EN* E: sctowner@btinternet.com

TOWNER, Preb Paul. b 51. Bris Univ BSc 72 BTh 81. Oak Hill Th Coll 78. **d** 81 **p** 82. C Aspley *S'well* 81–84; R Gt Hanwood *Heref* 84–99; RD Pontesbury 93–99; P-in-c Heref St Pet w St Owen and St Jas 99–11; V 11–16; RD Heref City 07–10; RD Heref Rural 07–10; RD Heref 10–16; Preb Heref Cathl 96–16; rtd 16; PtO *Ches* from 17. *14 Bachefield Avenue, Huntington, Chester CH3 6DA* E: preb.paul@btinternet.com

TOWNLEY, The Ven Peter Kenneth. b 55. Sheff Univ BA 78. Ridley Hall Cam 78. **d** 80 **p** 81. C Ashton Ch Ch *Man* 80–83; C-in-c Holts CD 83–88; R Stretford All SS 88–96; V Ipswich St Mary-le-Tower *St E* 96–08; RD Ipswich 01–08; Hon Can St E Cathl 03–08; Adn Pontefract *Wakef* 08–14; *Leeds* from 14; Hon Can Ripon Cathl from 15; Dioc Chapl MU from 16; Clergy Development Officer Wakefield Area *Leeds* from 19. *The Vicarage, Kirkthorpe Lane, Kirkthorpe, Wakefield WF1 5SZ* T: (01924) 896327 *or* 434459 F: 896327 *or* 364834 E: peter.townley@leeds.anglican.org *or* archdeacon.pontefract@leeds.anglican.org

TOWNLEY, Robert Keith. b 44. TCD MPhil 04. St Jo Coll Auckland LTh 67. **d** 67 **p** 68. C Devonport H Trin NZ 67–70; C Lisburn Ch Ch *Conn* 71–74; C Portman Square St Paul *Lon* 75–80; Dean Ross and I Ross Union *C, C & R* 82–94; Chan Cork Cathl 82–94; Dean Kildare and I Kildare w Kilmeague and Curragh *M & K* 95–06; Chapl Defence Forces 95–06; rtd 06; LtO *Arm* from 06. *10 Beresford Row, Armagh BT61 9AU* T: (028) 3752 5667

TOWNS, Ms Claire Louise. b 69. Portsm Poly BA 90 Univ of Wales (Cardiff) MSc 93 St Jo Coll Nottm MA 01. EMMTC 06.

d 07 **p** 08. C Beeston *S'well* 07–12; V Swanmore St Barn *Portsm* 12–21; P-in-c Wells St Thos w Horrington *B & W* from 21; P-in-c Chewton Mendip w Ston Easton, Litton etc from 21. *The Vicarage, 94 St Thomas Street, Wells BA5 2UZ* M: 07766-541152 E: clairetowns@gmail.com

TOWNS, Paul Robert. b 69. Plymouth Univ BSc 92 Nottm Univ MA 04. Westcott Ho Cam 15. **d** 17 **p** 18. NSM Ab Kettleby and Holwell w Asfordby *Leic* from 17; NSM Old Dalby, Nether Broughton, Saxelbye etc from 17. *Harby Hall, 14 School Lane, Harby, Melton Mowbray LE14 4BZ* T: (01664) 444188 M: 07855-839629 E: prtowns@outlook.com

TOWNSEND, Allan Harvey. b 43. WMMTC 89. **d** 92 **p** 93. NSM Fenton *Lich* 92–96; C Tividale 96–98; P-in-c Saltley and Shaw Hill *Birm* 98–06; P-in-c Washwood Heath 01–06; V Saltley and Washwood Heath 06–09; rtd 09; PtO *Lich* 09–19; C Wolstanton 10; PtO *Derby* 13–18; *Birm* 14–19. *5 The Croft, Stoke-on-Trent ST4 5HT* T: (01782) 416333

TOWNSEND, Anne Jennifer. b 38. Lon Univ MB, BS 60 MRCS 60 LRCP 60. S'wark Ord Course 88. **d** 91 **p** 94. NSM Wandsworth St Paul S'wark 91–08; Chapl Asst St Geo Hosp Lon 91–92; Dean MSE *S'wark* 93–99; PtO 08–13; *Roch* from 13. *3 Bromley College, London Road, Bromley BR1 1PE* T: (020) 8460 3869 E: revdrannetow@yahoo.co.uk

TOWNSEND, Christopher Robin. b 47. St Jo Coll Nottm. **d** 74 **p** 75. C Gt Horton *Bradf* 74–77; C Heaton St Barn 77–78; C Wollaton *S'well* 78–80; V Slaithwaite w E Scammonden *Wakef* 80–14; *Leeds* 14–18; P-in-c Marsden 16–18; rtd 18. *9 Vineyard, Leymoor Road, Golcar, Huddersfield HD7 4RN*

TOWNSEND, Derek William. b 52. Fitzw Coll Cam BA 74 Man Univ PhD 89. St Jo Coll Nottm 91. **d** 91 **p** 92. C Hazlemere *Ox* 91–95; TV Banbury 95–98; V Banbury St Paul 98–01; PtO 11–21; rtd 21. *24 Lower Lodge Lane, Hazlemere, High Wycombe HP15 7AT* T: (01494) 715964 M: 07855-015519 E: bill.townsend@tiscali.co.uk

TOWNSEND, Mrs Diane Rosalind. b 45. Stockwell Coll of Educn CertEd 66 K Alfred's Coll Win BEd 88. Sarum Th Coll 93. **d** 96 **p** 97. NSM Botley, Durley and Curdridge *Portsm* 96–00; NSM Buriton 00–05; NSM Portsea N End St Mark 05–10; TV 06–10; rtd 10; PtO *Portsm* from 10. *9 Daisy Lane, Locks Heath, Southampton SO31 6RA* T: (01489) 574092 E: dirobdaisy@aol.com

TOWNSEND, Gary. b 65. Trin Coll Bris. **d** 00 **p** 01. C Minster-in-Sheppey *Cant* 00–04; C Tonbridge SS Pet and Paul *Roch* 04–10; V Henham and Elsenham w Ugley *Chelmsf* 10–21; R Mereworth, Wateringbury and W Peckham *Roch* from 21. *The Rectory, 72 The Street, Mereworth, Maidstone ME18 5NA* T: (01622) 814568 E: gary.rev@outlook.com

TOWNSEND, Peter. b 37. Open Univ BA 87. Wells Th Coll 67. **d** 69 **p** 70. C Desborough *Pet* 69–72; C Bramley *Ripon* 72–75; C-in-c Newton Hall LEP *Dur* 75–80; P-in-c Newton Hall 80–81; V Hartlepool St Luke 81–03; rtd 03; PtO *Dur* 03–20. *348 Stockton Road, Hartlepool TS25 2PW* T: (01429) 291651 E: townsend_peter@yahoo.co.uk

TOWNSEND, Philip Roger. b 51. Sheff Univ BA 78. Trin Coll Bris 78. **d** 80 **p** 81. C W Streatham St Jas *S'wark* 80–85; C Ardsley *Sheff* 85–88; V Crookes St Tim 88–17; AD Hallam 05–12; rtd 17; PtO *Sheff* from 17. *71A Palm Street, Sheffield S6 2XF*

TOWNSEND, Canon Robert William. b 68. Univ of Wales (Ban) BA 90. St Mich Coll Llan BTh 93. **d** 93 **p** 95. C Dolgellau w Llanfachreth and Brithdir etc *Ban* 93–94; Min Can Ban Cathl 94–96; P-in-c Amlwch 96–97; R 97–99; R Llanfair-pwll and Llanddaniel-fab etc 99–03; P-in-c Llanilar w Rhostie and Llangwyryfon etc *St D* 03–06; Dioc Schools Officer 03–06; R Llanberis, Llanrug and Llandinorwig *Ban* 06–11; P-in-c Llandwrog and Llanwnda 11–12; P-in-c Uwch Gwyrfai Beuno Sant 12–13; AD Arfon 12–15; AD Synod Bangor 15–18; Dioc Dir of Educn 10–15; Dioc Communications Officer 12–15; Dioc Dir of Communication 15–18; Bp's Communications Officer from 18; C Bro Eryri from 15; Hon Can Ban Cathl from 12. *12 Llys y Waun, Waunfawr, Caernarfon LL55 4ZA* T: (01286) 650262 M: 07855-492006 E: robert@townsend.cx

TOWNSEND, Robin. *See* TOWNSEND, Christopher Robin

TOWNSEND, Mrs Teresa Lee. b 70. Ox Brookes Univ BA 05. Ox Min Course 16. **d** 18 **p** 19. NSM W Swindon and Lydiard Tregoze *Bris* from 18. *Tryphena, 18 St John Road, Wroughton, Swindon SN4 9ED* T: (01793) 812734 M: 07818-044431 E: rev.teresa.townsend@gmail.com

TOWNSEND, William. *See* TOWNSEND, Derek William

TOWNSHEND (formerly WEAVER), Canon Angela Mary. b 48. WMMTC 92. **d** 95 **p** 96. C Hill *Birm* 95–99; V Hamstead St Paul 99–06; AD Handsworth 05–06; Hon Can Birm Cathl 05–06; Can Res Guildf Cathl 06–11; C-in-c Bath Ch Ch Prop Chpl *B & W* 11–15; PtO *Guildf* 15–17 and 18–21; Chapl Birtley Ho Bramley 17–18; Chapl Oak Hall Nursing Home Haslemere

18–20. *16 Kings Road, Shalford, Guildford GU4 8JU* M: 07791-551824 E: angelatownshend@btinternet.com

TOWNSHEND, Patricia Olwyn. b 53. Univ of Rhodesia BA 74 UNISA BTh MTh 08. Coll of Transfiguration Grahamstown 09. **d** 09 **p** 10. C Pinelands S Africa 09–11; R Factreton 11–17; V Dunchurch *Cov* from 17. *The Vicarage, 11 Critchley Drive, Dunchurch, Rugby CV22 6PJ* T: (01788) 461987 M: 07555-458484 E: revptownshend@gmail.com

TOY, Canon John. b 30. Hatf Coll Dur BA 53 MA 62 Leeds Univ PhD 82 FSA 13. Wells Th Coll 53. **d** 55 **p** 56. C Newington St Paul *S'wark* 55–58; S Sec SCM 58–60; Chapl Ely Th Coll 60–64; Chapl Gothenburg w Halmstad and Jönköping *Eur* 65–69; Asst Chapl St Jo Coll York 69–72; Sen Lect 72–79; Prin Lect 79–83; Can Res and Chan York Minster 83–99; rtd 99; PtO *Eur* 99–18; *S'well* 03–15; *York* from 15. *15 Dulverton Hall, Esplanade, Scarborough YO11 2AR* T: (01723) 340115 E: johntoy@talktalk.net

TOYNE, Mrs Marian Elizabeth Christina. b 63. Rolle Coll BA 84 Linc Univ BA 14 Swansea Coll of Educn PGCE 85 NPQH 11. Linc Sch of Th and Min 11. **d** 14 **p** 15. NSM Frodingham and New Brumby *Linc* 14–16; C 16–19; V Woldmoor Gp from 19. *The Vicarage, Grange Lane, North Kelsey, Market Rasen LN7 6EZ* T: (01652) 679057 E: marian.toyne63@gmail.com

TOZE, Lissa Melanie. *See* SCOTT, Lissa Melanie

TOZE, Stephen James. b 51. Birm Univ BA 79. Qu Coll Birm 76 Westcott Ho Cam 93. **d** 93 **p** 94. C Leominster *Heref* 93–94; R Gt Brickhill w Bow Brickhill and Lt Brickhill *Ox* 94–02; Rural Officer Buckm Adnry 95–02; V Wilshamstead and Houghton Conquest *St Alb* 02–21; Ecum Officer Buckm Adnry *Ox* 13–21; rtd 21. *Address temp unknown* E: s@steve777.plus.com

TRACEY, Mrs Caroline Patricia. b 56. SNWTP 10. **d** 13 **p** 14. OLM Horwich and Rivington *Man* from 13; Chapl Wrightington, Wigan and Leigh Teaching Hosps NHS Foundn Trust from 18. *4 Evanstone Close, Horwich, Bolton BL6 5SQ* T: (01204) 692303 E: caroline.tracey@wwl.nhs.uk *or* caroline.tracey@gmail.com

TRACEY-MacLEOD, Talisker Isobel Alaethea Tuesday. *See* MacLEOD, Talisker Isobel Alaethea Tuesday

TRAFFORD-ROBERTS, Rosamond Jane. b 40. Qu Coll Birm BA. **d** 95 **p** 96. C Ledbury *Heref* 95–00; Lect St Botolph Aldgate w H Trin Minories *Lon* 00–05; Chapl Ho of St Barn-in-Soho 03–05; rtd 05; PtO *Lon* from 05; *Heref* from 18. *9 Ledbury Park, Ledbury HR8 1LF* M: 07736-335959 E: revdros@hotmail.com

TRAILL, Geoffrey Conway. b 58. Ridley Coll Melbourne BA 81 BTh 87. **d** 85 **p** 85. C Frankston Australia 85–86; C Shrub End *Chelmsf* 87–88; P-in-c Corio w Balliang and Anakie Australia 89–92; Chapl HM Pris Barwon 90–92; I Corio and N Geelong 92–99; I Point Lonsdale St Jas 99–05; P-in-c Queenscliff St Geo 02–05; RAAChD from 04; Adn Essendon 07–09. *AHQ DGCHAP-A Victoria Barracks, Melbourne VIC 3001, Australia* T: (0061) (3) 5242 8261 M: (0061) 44-452 0045 E: geoffrey.traill@defence.gov.au

TRAIN, Paul Michael. b 57. Stellenbosch Univ BChD 82. SEITE 03. **d** 06 **p** 07. NSM Loughton St Jo *Chelmsf* 06–10. *5 Monkchester Close, Loughton IG10 2SN* T: (020) 8508 2937

TRAINOR, Mrs Lynn Joanna. b 65. Bris Univ BSc 87 Ex Univ PGCE 89. SAOMC 99. **d** 02 **p** 03. C Ascot Heath *Ox* 02–06; PtO 15–17; V Langton Green *Roch* from 17. *The Vicarage, The Green, Langton Green, Tunbridge Wells TN3 0JB* T: (01892) 862072 E: lynn@lynnie.co.uk *or* lynn@langtongreenchurch.org.uk

TRANTER, John. b 51. St Jo Coll Nottm. **d** 00 **p** 01. C Gt Wyrley *Lich* 00–04; V Altham w Clayton le Moors *Blackb* 04–14; R Chelsfield *Roch* 14–18; P-in-c 18–21; AD Orpington 14–18; C Green Street Green and Pratts Bottom 18–21; rtd 21. *4 Whittington Close, Shrewsbury SY1 4TG* E: revjohnt@talktalk.net

TRANTER, Stephen. b 61. Lanc Univ BA 81 RGN 87 RM 89. Trin Coll Bris BA 99. **d** 99 **p** 00. C Blackpool St Thos *Blackb* 99–03; P-in-c Blackb St Jas 03–10; P-in-c Blackb St Steph 04–10; Chapl Univ Hosps of Morecambe Bay NHS Trust 10–12; P-in-c Ellel w Shireshead *Blackb* 11–12; OLM Officer *Man* 12–16; TR W Bolton from 16. *St Matthew's Vicarage, Stowell Street, Bolton BL1 3RQ* T: (01204) 398552 E: stephentranter@msn.com

TRAPNELL, Mrs Hazel Joan. b 45. Trin Coll Bris. **d** 12 **p** 13. OLM Stoke Bishop *Bris* 12–20; NSM from 20. *30 Hazelwood Court, Hazelwood Road, Bristol BS9 1PU* T: 0117-968 7190 E: hazeltrapnell@blueyonder.co.uk

TRAPNELL, Canon Stephen Hallam. b 30. G&C Coll Cam BA 53 MA 57 Virginia Th Sem BD 56 MDiv 70 Hon DD 02. Ridley Hall Cam 53. **d** 56 **p** 57. C Upper Tulse Hill St Matthias *S'wark* 56–59; C Reigate St Mary 59–61; V

Richmond Ch Ch 61–72; P-in-c Sydenham H Trin 72–80; R Worting *Win* 80–92; Field Officer Decade of Evang 92–96; Can Shyogwe (Rwanda) from 93; rtd 96; PtO *Sarum* 93–19; *Win* 96–14. *Yew Tree House, Mill Lane, Shalbourne, Marlborough SN8 3XA* T: (01672) 870460 E: steptrap@btinternet.com

TRASK, Imtiaz Ashley James. b 58. **d** 13 **p** 14. NSM Frant w Eridge *Chich* from 13. *22 Yeoman Gardens, Paddock Wood, Tonbridge TN12 6TX* M: 07395-425507 E: ijohnat58@gmail.com

TRASK, Mrs Marion Elizabeth. b 54. Leic Univ BSc 75 Brunel Univ PGCE 76. Moorlands Bible Coll 82 Oak Hill Th Coll 93. **d** 96 **p** 97. C Bermondsey St Mary w St Olave, St Jo etc *S'wark* 96–00; C Peckham St Mary Magd 00–04; P-in-c Cowden w Hammerwood *Chich* 10–16; P-in-c Cowden 16–19; Chapl Qu Victoria Hosp NHS Foundn Trust East Grinstead 10–19; rtd 19. *22 Yeoman Gardens, Paddock Wood, Tonbridge TN12 6TX* M: 07931-144260 E: m.traskcwhd@btinternet.com

TRASLER, Canon Graham Charles George. b 44. Ch Ch Ox BA 65 MA 69. Cuddesdon Coll 66. **d** 68 **p** 69. C Gateshead St Mary *Dur* 68–71; P-in-c Monkwearmouth St Pet 71–79; R Bentley and Binsted *Win* 79–84; R New Alresford w Ovington and Itchen Stoke 84–01; RD Alresford 99–01; P-in-c Stockbridge and Longstock and Leckford 01–03; R 03–09; Hon Can Win Cathl 05–09; rtd 09; PtO *Win* from 09. *3 Langtons Court, Alresford SO24 9UE* T: (01962) 736062 M: 07810-693910 E: costadelanton@gmail.com

TRATHEN, Paul Kevin. b 69. York Univ BA 91 MA 93 Middx Univ BA 03 Jordanhill Coll Glas PGCE 94. NTMTC 00. **d** 03 **p** 04. C Wickford and Runwell *Chelmsf* 03–07; P-in-c Rawreth w Rettendon 07–10; P-in-c Rawreth 10–11; Adv for Faith in Action (Bradwell Area) 07–11; Bp's Chapl 11; Dioc Adv for Faith in the Public Square 11–12; V Walthamstow St Pet 12–20; P-in-c Leytonstone St Andr 16–18; Chapl Forest Sch Walthamstow 12–19; R Aston-le-Walls, Byfield, Boddington, Eydon etc *Pet* from 21. *The Rectory, 55 Church Street, Byfield, Daventry NN11 6XN* M: 07871-584997 E: paul.trathen@btopenworld.com

TRAVERS, Canon Colin James. b 49. St Pet Coll Ox BA 70 MA 74. Ridley Hall Cam 70. **d** 72 **p** 73. C Hornchurch St Andr *Chelmsf* 72–75; Youth Chapl 75–77; C Aldersbrook 75–77; V Barkingside St Laur 77–82; V Waltham Abbey 82–88; V S Weald 88–95; Co-ord NTMTC and Hon C Gt Warley and Ingrave St Nic 95–98; P-in-c Gt Canfield w High Roding and Aythorpe Roding 98–02; V Theydon Bois 02–09; Hon Can Chelmsf Cathl 01–09; rtd 09; PtO *Ely* from 10. *7 Springhead Lane, Ely CB7 4QY* T: (01353) 659732 E: revtravs@gmail.com

TRAVERS, John William. b 48. Open Univ BA 84 Hull Univ MA 86. Linc Th Coll 75. **d** 78 **p** 79. C Headingley *Ripon* 78–81; TV Louth *Linc* 81–89; P-in-c Shingay Gp *Ely* 89; R 90–95; V Hamble le Rice *Win* 95–12. *Los Falcones 3, D3-10 Los Balandros, Palm Mar, Arona 38632, Tenerife* E: jwtravers@gmail.com

TRAVES, Stephen Charles. b 44. Sheff City Coll of Educn CertEd 66 Open Univ BA 79. NOC 96. **d** 99 **p** 00. NSM Barnsley St Pet and St Jo *Wakef* 99–02; NSM Cudworth 02–07; NSM Lundwood 02–04; PtO 07–14; *Leeds* 14–21; *Eur* 08–18. *23 Ecklands Croft, Millhouse Green, Sheffield S36 9AJ* T: 0119-695 6001 E: fr.s.traves2@gmail.com

TRAYNOR, Neil Owen. b 70. Worc Coll Ox BA 91 MA 94 Leeds Univ BA 11 Reading Univ PGCE 94. Coll of Resurr Mirfield 09. **d** 11 **p** 12. C Barnsley St Mary *Wakef* 11–13; Bp's Dom Chapl 13–14; TV Witney *Ox* 14–17; C Holland Park *Lon* from 17; Chapl Guy's and St Thos' NHS Foundn Trust from 18. *25 Sheffield Terrace, London W8 7NQ* M: 07887-778757 E: neil.traynor@yahoo.com *or* associatevicar@hollandparkbenefice.org

TRAYNOR, Nigel Martin Arthur. b 58. St Jo Coll Nottm 94. **d** 96 **p** 97. C Wellington All SS w Eyton *Lich* 96–00; P-in-c Pype Hayes *Birm* 00–02; TV Erdington 02–16; V Pype Hayes 16–18; AD Aston 12–18; Miss Outreach Co-ord Mercy Air S Africa 18–21; PtO *Birm* from 21. *30 Conifer Court, Moor Green Lane, Birmingham B13 8NB* E: revnigel36@gmail.com

TREACY, Richard James. b 74. Aber Univ BD Univ of Wales (Cardiff) MTh 99. **d** 98 **p** 99. C Hillsborough *D & D* 98–02; R Washington St Brendan's in the City USA from 10. *5803 Norton Road, Alexandria VA 22303, USA* T: (001) (202) 494 5731 M: 07917-854222 E: richard.treacy@btinternet.com

TREANOR, Timothy Lyons Victor. b 62. St Jo Coll Cam BA 83 MA 87 K Coll Lon MA 95 Cranfield Univ MSc 01. Ripon Coll Cuddesdon BTh 08. **d** 08 **p** 09. C Tavistock and Gulworthy *Ex* 08–10; C Ottery St Mary, Alfington, W Hill, Tipton etc 10–13; TR Wellington and Distr *B & W* 13–21; PtO *Ex* from

21. *Trelawn, Bickington Road, Sticklepath, Barnstaple EX31 2JE* E: tlvtreanor@btinternet.com

TREASURE, Canon Andrew Stephen. b 51. Oriel Coll Ox BA 73 MA 77. St Jo Coll Nottm BA 76. **d** 77 **p** 78. C Beverley Minster *York* 77–81; C Cambridge H Trin *Ely* 81–84; C Cambridge H Trin w St Andr Gt 84–85; V Eccleshill *Bradf* 85–98; P-in-c Bradf St Oswald Chapel Green 98–04; P-in-c Horton 98–04; V Lt Horton 04–14; *Leeds* 14–21; C Bowling St Steph *Bradf* 05–14; *Leeds* 14–15; Hon Can Bradf Cathl 04–21; rtd 21; PtO *Leeds* 21; V The Thorntons and The Otteringtons *York* from 21. *4 Endican Lane, Thornton-le-Moor, Northallerton DL7 9FB*

TREASURE, Geoffrey. b 39. Hatf Coll Dur BA 61 Univ of Wales (Cardiff) DipEd 62. Oak Hill NSM Course 90. **d** 93 **p** 94. NSM Forty Hill Jes Ch *Lon* 93–95; Consultant SW England CPAS 95–02; PtO *B & W* 95–04; P-in-c Stoke St Gregory w Burrowbridge and Lyng 04–07; rtd 07; PtO *B & W* from 07. *Gable Cottage, West Lyng, Taunton TA3 5AP* T: (01823) 490458 E: geofftreasure@googlemail.com

TREASURE, James. b 75. Roehampton Inst BSc 99. Ripon Coll Cuddesdon 16. **d** 17 **p** 17. C Kidderminster St Jo and H Innocents *Worc* 17–18; C Dudley from 18. *St James's Vicarage, The Parade, Dudley DY1 3JA* M: 07747-110847 E: jtreasure@gmail.com

TREEBY, Stephen Frank. b 46. Man Univ LLB 67 Lambeth STh 01. Cuddesdon Coll 69 Bangalore Th Coll 70. **d** 71 **p** 72. C Ashbourne St Oswald w Mapleton *Derby* 71–74; C Boulton 74–76; Chapl Trowbridge Coll *Sarum* 76–79; TV Melksham 79–87; V Dilton's-Marsh 87–01; Chapl Westbury Hosp 87–91; Chapl Wilts and Swindon Healthcare NHS Trust 92–01; R Spetisbury w Charlton Marshall etc *Sarum* 01–11; rtd 11; PtO *Ex* from 12. *5 Walnut Road, Honiton EX14 2UG* T: (01404) 643312 E: stephentreeby@hotmail.com

TREETOPS, Ms Jacqueline. b 47. NEOC 83. **dss** 86 **d** 87 **p** 94. Low Harrogate St Mary *Ripon* 86–87; C Roundhay St Edm 87–95; C Potternewton 95–97; rtd 97; PtO *Ripon* 01–14; *Leeds* 14–16. *43 Lincombe Bank, Leeds LS8 1QG* T: 0113-237 0474 E: j.treetops@sky.com

TREFUSIS, Charles Rodolph. b 61. Hull Univ BA 83. Wycliffe Hall Ox 85. **d** 90 **p** 91. C Blackheath St Jo *S'wark* 90–94; V Purley Ch Ch 94–18; V Walton H Trin *Ox* from 18. *Walton Rectory, 42 Redwood Drive, Aylesbury HP21 7TN*

TREGALE, Diane Ruth. b 68. Spurgeon's Coll MTh 05. St Jo Coll Nottm 07. **d** 08 **p** 09. C Wilford *S'well* 08–11; C Sherborne w Castleton, Lillington and Longburton *Sarum* 11–21; Chapl Gryphon Sch Sherborne 11–21; C St Alb St Paul from 21. *The New Vicarage, 7 Brampton Road, St Albans AL1 4PN* E: diane@stpauls-stalbans.org

TREGALE, John Ernest. b 69. Ex Univ BSc 90 Sheff Univ MA 01. St Jo Coll Nottm 05. **d** 08 **p** 09. C Wilford *S'well* 08–11; C Sherborne w Castleton, Lillington and Longburton *Sarum* 11–16; TV 16–21; V St Alb St Paul from 21. *The New Vicarage, 7 Brampton Road, St Albans AL1 4PN* T: (01727) 836810 *or* 846281 E: jono@stpauls-stalbans.org

TREGENZA, Matthew John. b 69. Univ of Wales (Lamp) BA 92 BA(Theol) 08 SS Coll Cam PGCE 93 Lon Univ MA 01 FRGS 96. Westcott Ho Cam 01. **d** 03 **p** 04. C Marnhull *Sarum* 03–06; TV Mynyddislwyn *Mon* 06–08; P-in-c Blackwood 08–12; R Bishop's Lydeard w Lydeard St Lawrence etc *B & W* 12–19; RD Tone 14–19; R Crediton, Shobrooke and Sandford etc *Ex* from 19; RD Cadbury from 20. *The Rectory, Church Street, Crediton EX17 2AQ* T: (01363) 894038 E: matthew.tregenza@gmail.com

TREGUNNO, Timothy Frederick. b 79. St Andr Univ MTheol 02. St Steph Ho Ox 04. **d** 06 **p** 07. C St Leonards Ch Ch and St Mary *Chich* 06–10; P-in-c Turners Hill 10–12; Chapl Heathfield Sch Ascot 12–16; Chapl Oakham Sch from 16. *Oakham School, Chapel Close, Market Place, Oakham LE15 6DT* T: (01572) 758500 E: tft@oakham.rutland.sch.uk

TREHARNE, David Owen. b 73. Univ of Wales (Cardiff) BMus 94 MPhil 06 Bris Univ MEd 04 Bris Coll PGCE 00. Trin Coll Bris 94. **d** 99 **p** 04. NSM Bassaleg *Mon* 99–00; C Caerphilly *Llan* 04–08; P-in-c Porthkerry and Rhoose 08–12; Dioc Voc Adv 08–12; V Tidenham w Beachley and Lancaut *Glouc* from 12; P-in-c St Briavels w Hewelsfield and Brockweir from 12. *Tidenham Vicarage, Gloucester Road, Tutshill, Chepstow NP16 7DH* T: (01291) 760034 E: dtrevd@aol.com

TRELENBERG, Olaf. b 72. Ridley Hall Cam 06. **d** 08 **p** 09. C Scotforth *Blackb* 08–12; P-in-c Sandiacre *Derby* 12–14; R from 14. *St Giles's Rectory, Church Drive, Sandiacre, Nottingham NG10 5EE* T: 0115-939 7163 M: 07877-357332 E: olaf@aol.com

TREMBATH, Martyn Anthony. b 65. Leeds Univ BA 86. Ripon Coll Cuddesdon 88. **d** 90 **p** 91. C Bodmin w Lanhydrock and Lanivet *Truro* 90–91; C St Erth 92–96; C Phillack w Gwithian and Gwinear 94–96; Asst Chapl R Free

Hampstead NHS Trust 96–98; Sen Chapl R Cornwall Hosps Trust 98–10; NSM Godrevy *Truro* 08–10; TR 10–13; Hon Can Truro Cathl 09–13; Chapl Luton and Dunstable Univ Hosp NHS Foundn Trust 13–20; Bp's Adv for Hosp Chapl *St Alb* 16–20; PtO *Ox* 14–19; R Ayr *Glas* from 20. *Address temp unknown*

TREMLETT, The Very Revd Andrew. b 64. Pemb Coll Cam BA 86 MA 90 Qu Coll Ox BA 88 MA 95 Ex Univ MPhil 96. Wycliffe Hall Ox 86. **d** 89 **p** 90. C Torquay St Matthias, St Mark and H Trin *Ex* 89–92; Miss to Seamen 92–94; Asst Chapl Rotterdam *Eur* 92–94; Chapl 94–95; TV Fareham H Trin *Portsm* 95–98; Bp's Dom Chapl 98–03; V Goring-by-Sea *Chich* 03–08; Can Res Bris Cathl 08–10; Can Westmr Abbey and R Westmr St Marg 10–16; Adn Westmr 14–16; Dean Dur from 16. *The Deanery, The College, Durham DH1 3EQ* T: 0191-384 7500 E: dean@durhamcathedral.co.uk

TREMTHTHANMOR, Canon Chrys Mymmir Evnath Tristan. b 66. Univ of California BA 88. St Mich Coll Llan BA 05 MPhil 07. **d** 06 **p** 07. C Coity, Nolton and Brackla *Llan* 06–10; TV Daventry, Ashby St Ledgers, Braunston etc *Pet* 10–16; Tr Officer (CMD) 16–21; Clergy Tr Officer from 21; C Abington 16–19; C Northampton St Alb from 21; Can Pet Cathl from 21. *1 Bouverie Court, The Lakes, Northampton NN4 7YD* T: (01733) 887000 E: vicarwelton@o2.co.uk

TRENDALL, Matthew James. b 72. Oriel Coll Ox BA 93 MA 98. Trin Coll Bris BA 10. **d** 10 **p** 11. C Redland *Bris* 10–13; P-in-c Walton Milton Keynes *Ox* 13–14; R from 14. *The Rectory, Walton Road, Wavendon, Milton Keynes MK17 8LW* T: (01908) 582839 M: 07947-150396 E: matt.trendall.mk@gmail.com

TRENDALL, Peter John. b 43. Oak Hill Th Coll 66. **d** 69 **p** 70. C Beckenham Ch Ch *Roch* 69–73; C Bedworth *Cov* 73–76; V Hornsey Rise St Mary *Lon* 76–82; P-in-c Upper Holloway St Steph 80–82; V Hornsey Rise St Mary w St Steph 82–84; TR Walthamstow St Mary w St Steph *Chelmsf* 84–85 and 85–93; P-in-c Chigwell 93–94; TR Chigwell and Chigwell Row 94–08; rtd 08; PtO *St E* from 08. *27 Crick Court, Station Road, Southwold IP18 6DE* T: (01502) 722962 M: 07453-347862 E: peter.trendall@btinternet.com

TRENDER, Lawrence. b 37. Bps' Coll Cheshunt 64. **d** 66 **p** 67. C Petersham *S'wark* 66–71; C Malden St Jo 71–73; R Thornham Magna w Thornham Parva *St E* 73–81; R Thornhams Magna and Parva, Gislingham and Mellis 81–87; P-in-c Mellis 73–81; P-in-c Gislingham 73–81; RD Hartismere 85–87; R Skipsea w Ulrome and Barmston w Fraisthorpe *York* 92–01; rtd 01; PtO *York* from 01. *Stone Cottage, 5 Far Lane, Bewholme, Driffield YO25 8EA* T: (01964) 533020 E: trender@waitrose.com

TRENHOLME, Mrs Jane Lesley. b 54. Man Univ BSc 76 Leeds Univ BA 06. NOC 03. **d** 06 **p** 07. NSM Northowram *Wakef* 06–08; C Tong *Bradf* 08–14; *Leeds* 14; C Laisterdyke *Bradf* 08–10; P-in-c 10–14; *Leeds* 14; PtO 17–18; C Shelf w Buttershaw St Aid from 18; C Wibsey St Paul from 18. *Stretchgate, Rookes Lane, Halifax HX3 8PU* T: (01274) 693392 M: 07771-823281 E: jltrenholme@hotmail.co.uk

TRENHOLME, William Nicholas David. b 85. Grey Coll Dur MSci 08. Oak Hill Th Coll BA 13. **d** 13 **p** 14. C Wollaston w Strixton and Bozeat etc *Pet* 13–16; TV Bentham, Burton-in-Lonsdale, Chapel-le-Dale etc *Leeds* from 16. *St Mary's Vicarage, Main Street, Ingleton, Carnforth LA6 3HF* M: 07712-627243 E: nick.trenholme@gmail.com

TRENIER, Canon Andrew Peter Christopher. b 80. Univ of Wales (Swansea) BScEcon 02 Ox Univ BA 11. Ripon Coll Cuddesdon 09. **d** 12 **p** 13. C Derby Cathl 12–15; R Chingford SS Pet and Paul *Chelmsf* 15–19; Can Res, Prec and Sacr Win Cathl from 19. *8 The Close, Winchester SO23 9LS* M: 07786-868615 E: andytrenier@gmail.com

TRETHEWEY, The Ven Frederick Martyn. b 49. Lon Univ BA 70 Lambeth STh 79. Oak Hill Th Coll 75. **d** 78 **p** 79. C Tollington Park St Mark w St Anne *Lon* 78–82; C Whitehall Park St Andr Hornsey Lane 82–87; TV Hornsey Rise Whitehall Park Team 87–88; V Brockmoor *Lich* 88–93; V Brockmoor *Worc* 93–01; Chapl Russells Hall Hosp Dudley 88–91; Chapl Dudley Gp of Hosps NHS Trust 92–01; RD Himley *Worc* 96–01; Hon Can Worc Cathl 99–01; Adn Dudley 01–13; rtd 13; P-in-c Brittany *Eur* 13–16; PtO *Leic* 16–21; *Glouc* from 17. *Finlock Bungalow, Redesdale Place, Moreton-in-Marsh GL56 0EQ* T: (01608) 654121 E: fred@trethewey.org.uk

TRETHEWEY, Richard John. b 74. Jes Coll Ox MA 02. Wycliffe Hall Ox BA 02. **d** 02 **p** 03. C Biddulph *Lich* 02–06; C Knowle *Birm* 06–16; R Glenfield and Newtown Linford *Leic* from 16; AD Sparkenhoe E from 19. *The Rectory, Main Street, Glenfield, Leicester LE3 8DG* M: 07595-320563 E: richard@trethewey.org.uk

TRETT, Peter John. b 44. **d** 97 **p** 98. OLM High Oak, Hingham and Scoulton w Wood Rising *Nor* 97–14; PtO from 14. *Holly House, 35 Plough Lane, Hardingham, Norwich NR9 4AE* T: (01953) 850369 E: trett@nnbus.co.uk

TREVELYAN, Mrs Rosemary Elizabeth. b 43. Ex Univ CertEd 64 Open Univ BA 91. **d** 11. NSM Washingborough w Heighington and Canwick *Linc* 11–17. *6 Wyebank Place, Tutshill, Chepstow NP16 7EU* E: rtrev911@hotmail.com

TREVITHICK, Janet Anne. b 54. **d** 13. NSM Titchfield *Portsm* from 13. *34 Vicarage Lane, Fareham PO14 2LA* T: (01329) 668957 E: janettrevithick@msn.com

TREVOR, Canon Charles Frederic. b 27. Sarum Th Coll 54. **d** 56 **p** 57. C Sutton in Ashfield St Mich *S'well* 56–58; C Birstall *Leic* 58–61; V Prestwold w Hoton 61–66; V Thornton in Lonsdale w Burton in Lonsdale *Bradf* 66–74; V Kirkby Malham 74–85; P-in-c Coniston Cold 81–85; Hon Can Bradf Cathl 85–92; V Sutton 85–92; RD S Craven 86–91; rtd 92; PtO *Bradf* 92–14; *Leeds* 14–16. *6 Elbolton Flats, Hebden Road, Skipton BD23 5LH* T: (01756) 752640

TREW, Jeremy Charles. b 66. Univ of Wales (Abth) BSc 89 Leeds Univ MSc 92. St Jo Coll Nottm MA 94. **d** 97 **p** 98. C Roundhay St Edm *Ripon* 97–01; P-in-c Spofforth w Kirk Deighton 01–07; V Seaton and Beer *Ex* 07–21; RD Honiton 13–19; TR Saffron Walden and Villages *Chelmsf* from 21; RD Saffron Walden from 21. *The Rectory, Borough Lane, Saffron Walden CB11 4AG* T: (01799) 506024 E: saffronrector@gmail.com

TREW, Robin Nicholas. b 52. UWIST BSc 74 Open Univ MA 01. St Jo Coll Nottm 87. **d** 89 **p** 90. C Cov H Trin 89–93; V Snitterfield w Bearley 93–02; R Allesley 02–16; AD Cov N 10–15; rtd 16; PtO *Heref* from 17. *The Hollies, 10 Watling Street South, Church Stretton SY6 7BG*

TREWEEK, Guy Matthew. b 65. LSE BSc(Econ) 87 Peterho Cam BA 07 MA 12. Westcott Ho Cam 05 Yale Div Sch 07. **d** 08 **p** 09. C Hammersmith St Pet *Lon* 08–11; P-in-c St Andrby-the-Wardrobe w St Ann, Blackfriars 11–15; P-in-c St Jas Garlickhythe w St Mich Queenhithe etc 11–15; PtO 15–18; *Glouc* 15–17; Public Preacher from 17; Chapl HM Pris Eastwood Park from 17; Min Can Glouc Cathl from 17; Bp's Chapl 19–20. *Bishopscourt, Pitt Street, Gloucester GL1 2BQ* T: (01452) 524158 E: guy.treweek@gmail.com *or* gtreweek@glosdioc.org.uk

✠**TREWEEK** (*née* **MONTGOMERY**), **The Rt Revd Rachel.** b 63. Reading Univ BA 85. Wycliffe Hall Ox BTh 94. **d** 94 **p** 95 **c** 15. C Tufnell Park St Geo and All SS *Lon* 94–99; V Bethnal Green St Jas Less 99–06; CME Officer 99–06; Adn Northolt 06–11; Adn Hackney 11–15; Bp Glouc from 15; Bp HM Pris from 20. *Bishopscourt, Pitt Street, Gloucester GL1 2BQ* T: (01452) 835512

TREWEEKS, Mrs Angela Elizabeth. b 35. Gilmore Ho IDC 59. **d** 87 **p** 94. Chapl Asst St Nic Hosp Newc 85–87; Chapl 87; Hon C Newc St Geo 87–89; Chapl St Mary's Hosp Stannington 92–95; Hon C Rothbury *Newc* 94–96; rtd 95; PtO *Newc* from 96. *The Nook, Pondicherry, Rothbury, Morpeth NE65 7YS* T: (01669) 620393 E: angelatreweeks@talktalk.net

TRICK, Matthew John Harvey. Univ of Wales (Abth) BSc 02. St Mich Coll Llan BTh 08. **d** 08 **p** 09. C Cowbridge *Llan* 08–10; C Aberavon 10–11; TV 11–14; P-in-c Cambourne *Ely* 14–17; V Ringwood w Ellingham and Harbridge etc *Win* from 17. *The Vicarage, 65 Southampton Road, Ringwood BH24 1HE* T: (01425) 540951 M: 07903-156688 E: matthew.trick@ringwoodbenefice.org.uk

TRICKETT, Canon Judith. b 50. Open Univ BA 00. St Jo Coll Nottm 89. **d** 91 **p** 94. Par Dn Kimberworth *Sheff* 91–93; Dn-in-c Worsbrough Common 93–94; V 94–01; V Herringthorpe 01–10; R Firbeck w Letwell 10–15; V Woodsetts 10–15; Hon Can Sheff Cathl 08–15; rtd 15; Hon C Harthill and Thorpe Salvin *Sheff* 15–16; Hon C Aston cum Aughton w Swallownest and Ulley 16–17; PtO from 17. *9 St Alban's Court, Wickersley, Rotherham S66 1FG* T: (01709) 739666 M: 07974-404831 E: judith.trickett493@btinternet.com

TRICKEY, Christopher Jolyon. b 57. Jes Coll Cam BA 79 MA 83 Barrister-at-Law 80. Trin Coll Bris BA 90. **d** 90 **p** 91. C Chesham Bois *Ox* 90–94; R Busbridge *Guildf* 94–98; P-in-c Hambledon 97–98; R Busbridge and Hambledon 98–09; Chapl Godalming Coll 01–09; R Nailsea H Trin *B & W* 09–17; PtO *Guildf* from 19; Hon C Oxshott Trin *B & W* 09–17; PtO *Guildf* from 19; Hon C Oxshott from 19. *The Vicarage, Steels Lane, Oxshott, Leatherhead KT22 0QH* T: (01372) 842071 E: cjtrickey@gmail.com

TRICKEY, Mrs Frances Anne. b 59. Keele Univ BA 81 Lon Inst of Educn PGCE 82 Win Univ BA 11. STETS 08. **d** 11 **p** 12. NSM Wraxall *B & W* 11–17; V Oxshott *Guildf* from 17. *The Vicarage, Steels Lane, Oxshott, Leatherhead KT22 0QH* T: (01372) 842071 E: francestrickey@hotmail.co.uk *or* frances.trickey@standrewsoxshott.org.uk

TRICKEY, The Very Revd Frederick Marc. b 35. Dur Univ BA 62. Cranmer Hall Dur. **d** 64 **p** 65. C Alton St Lawr *Win* 64–68; V Win St Jo cum Winnall 68–77; Angl Adv Channel

TV from 77; R Guernsey St Martin *Win* 77–02; P-in-c Sark 02–03; Dean Guernsey 95–03; Hon Can Win Cathl 95–03; rtd 03; PtO *Win* from 03. *L'Esperance, La Route des Camps, St Martin, Guernsey GY4 6AD* T: (01481) 238441 E: fut@ewgsy.net

TRICKEY, Mrs Joanna Charlotte. b 85. Leeds Univ BA 07 Wycliffe Hall Ox BA 10. St Mellitus Coll 14. **d** 17 **p** 19. C Guildf Ch Ch from 17. *2 Ivor Close, Guildford GU1 2ET* M: 07534-908689 E: thejtrickeys@gmail.com *or* jo@christchurchguildford.com

TRICKLEBANK, Steven. b 56. Nottm Univ BTh 88 Keele Univ MA 97. Linc Th Coll 85. **d** 88 **p** 89. C Ditton St Mich *Liv* 88–91; C Wigan All SS 91–93; Chapl Aintree Hosps NHS Trust Liv 93–97; C-in-c St Edm Anchorage Lane CD *Sheff* 97–00; Chapl Doncaster R Infirmary and Montagu Hosp NHS Trust 97–00; V Stocksbridge *Sheff* 00–04; P-in-c Streatham Ch Ch *S'wark* 04–05; P-in-c Streatham Hill St Marg 04–05; V Streatham Ch Ch 05–20; rtd 20; PtO *Derby* from 21. *35 Whinfell Road, Chesterfield S41 8BF* E: steventricklebank@hotmail.com

TRIFFITT, Jonathan Paul. b 74. St Jo Coll Nottm BA 03. **d** 03 **p** 04. C W Kilburn St Luke w St Simon and St Jude *Lon* 03–06; C Paddington Em Harrow Road 03–06; C Sherborne w Castleton, Lillington and Longburton *Sarum* 06–10; Chapl Gryphon Sch Sherborne 06–10; V Southbroom *Sarum* 10–15; RD Devizes 11–15; R Blandford Forum and Langton Long from 15; RD Milton and Blandford 16–20; Dir of Min from 20. *31 St Paul's Close, Sherborne DT9 4DU* E: jonathantriffitt@icloud.com

TRIGG, Jeremy Michael. b 51. Open Univ BA 88. Ripon Coll Cuddesdon 80. **d** 81 **p** 82. C Roundhay St Edm *Ripon* 81–84; C Harrogate St Wilfrid and St Luke 84–87; TV Pocklington Team *York* 87–90; R Rowley w Skidby 90–97; TV Wolverton *Ox* 97–98; R 98–11; P-in-c Rothwell *Ripon* 11–14; *Leeds* 14–15; TR Rothwell, Lofthouse, Methley etc 15–17; rtd 17. *2 Deep Ghyll Walk, Ripon HG4 1RL* E: jeremy.trigg@gmail.com

TRIGG, Preb Jonathan David. b 49. Ex Coll Ox BA 71 MA 75 Dur Univ PhD 92. Cranmer Hall Dur BA 82. **d** 83 **p** 84. C Enfield St Andr *Lon* 83–87; V Oakwood St Thos 87–96; AD Enfield 92–96; V Highgate St Mich 96–17; P-in-c Highgate All SS 09–14; C 14–17; AD W Haringey 00–06; Dir of Ords Edmonton Area 08–17; Preb St Paul's Cathl 10–17; rtd 17; PtO *B & W* from 17. *2 Park Street, Taunton TA1 4DF* M: 07883-340239 E: jdtrigg@gmail.com

TRIGLE, Alan Neil. b 61. Hertf Coll Ox BA 84 MA 87. St Mellitus Coll BA 15. **d** 15 **p** 17. C Kensal Town St Thos w St Andr and St Phil *Lon* 15–16; C Chiswick St Nic w St Mary from 17. *1 Oldfield Road, London W3 7TD* M: 07711-623834 E: atrigle@icloud.com

TRILL, Barry. b 42. Chich Th Coll 65. **d** 68 **p** 69. C W Hackney St Barn *Lon* 68–73; TV Is of Dogs Ch Ch and St Jo w St Luke 73–78; P-in-c Hastings All So *Chich* 78–79; V 79–99; rtd 99. *17 School Place, Bexhill-on-Sea TN40 2PX* T: (01424) 217765

TRIM, Elizabeth Ann. *See* VARLEY, Elizabeth Ann

TRIMBLE, Eleanor Louise. b 69. Man Metrop Univ BSc 97. Yorks Min Course. **d** 09 **p** 10. C Old Trafford St Jo *Man* 09–13; P-in-c Man Apostles w Miles Platting from 13. *Church of the Apostles Rectory, Ridgway Street, Manchester M40 7FY* T: 0161-948 4197 M: 07887-601451 E: eleanor.trimble@btinternet.com

TRIMBLE, Thomas Henry. b 36. TCD BTh 90. CITC 79. **d** 82 **p** 83. C Seapatrick *D & D* 82–85; I Magheracross *Clogh* 85–90; Bp's Appeal Sec 89–90; I Donegal w Killymard, Lough Eske and Laghey *D & R* 90–01; Can Raphoe Cathl 93–01; rtd 01. *Tyrone House, 4 Old Golf Course Road, Tullycullion, Co Donegal, F94 F3C6, Republic of Ireland* T: (00353) (74) 974 0706 E: harry.trimble@virgin.net

TRIMBY (*née* **SOUTHERTON**), **Kathryn Ruth.** b 66. Univ of Wales (Lamp) BA 88. Sarum & Wells Th Coll 90. **d** 92 **p** 97. C Connah's Quay *St As* 92–97; R Halkyn w Caerfallwch w Rhesycae 97–04; I Tubbercurry w Killoran *T, K & A* 04–14; Can Achonry Cathl 11–14; Can Tuam Cathl 13–14; R Llanyblodwel, Llanymynech, Morton and Trefonen *Lich* from 14. *The Rectory, Rectory Lane, Pant, Oswestry SY10 9RA* T: (01691) 831211 E: kathsoutherton@hotmail.com

TRIMMER, Penelope Marynice. *See* DRAPER, Penelope Marynice

TRINDER, Miss Gillian Joyce. b 68. Birm Univ BA 90 Bp Grosseteste Coll PGCE 91. Westcott Ho Cam 09. **d** 11 **p** 12. C Whitkirk *Ripon* 11–13; C Starbeck 13–14; *Leeds* 14; NSM Bury St Edmunds All SS w St Jo and St Geo *St E* 16–17; NSM Lark Valley 16–17; Chapl Ypres *Eur* 17–19; PtO *St E* from 19. *40 Fair Close, Beccles NR34 9QR*

TRIST, Richard McLeod. b 55. Univ of NSW BSEd 76. Ridley Coll Melbourne BTh 86. **d** 87 **p** 87. C Camberwell St Jo

Australia 87–88; P-in-c Cranbourne 88–91; I 91–92; Sen Assoc Min Kew St Hilary 93–96; C Langham Place All So *Lon* 97–01; V Camberwell St Mark Australia from 01; AD Camberwell 03–05. *1 Canterbury Road, Camberwell Vic 3124, Australia* T: (0061) (3) 9897 1532 *or* (3) 9882 3776 F: 9882 6514 E: richard.trist@bigpond.com

TRISTRAM, Canon Catherine Elizabeth. b 31. Somerville Coll Ox BA 53 MA 57. **dss** 83 **d** 87 **p** 94. Holy Is *Newc* 84–01; Hon C 87–01; Hon Can Newc Cathl 94–01; PtO from 01. *4 Lewins Lane, Holy Island, Berwick-upon-Tweed TD15 2SB* T: (01289) 389306

TRISTRAM, Canon Michael Anthony. b 50. Ch Coll Cam BA 72 MA 76 Solicitor 76. Ripon Coll Cuddesdon 79. **d** 82 **p** 83. C Stanmore *Win* 82–85; R Abbotts Ann and Upper Clatford and Goodworth Clatford 85–92; V Pershore w Pinvin, Wick and Birlingham *Worc* 92–03; Hon Can Worc Cathl 00–03; Can Res Portsm Cathl 03–15; rtd 15; PtO *Portsm* from 15; *Eur* from 16. *39 Oakwood Road, Hayling Island PO11 9AY* T: (023) 9246 3170

TRIVASSE, Keith Malcolm. b 59. Man Univ BA 81 CertEd 82 MPhil 90 Dur Univ MA 98. Qu Coll Birm 84. **d** 86 **p** 87. C Prestwich St Marg *Man* 86–88; C Orford St Marg *Liv* 88–90; TV Sunderland *Dur* 90–91; P-in-c N Hylton St Marg Castletown 91–95; R Bothal and Pegswood w Longhirst *Newc* 95–97; P-in-c Bury Ch King *Man* 01–11; P-in-c Bury St Paul 01–03; C Bury, Roch Valley 11–15; rtd 15; PtO *Man* from 15. *Address withheld by request* T: 0161-258 0649

TRIVASSE, Ms Margaret. b 59. Dur Univ BA 80 MA 97 New Coll Dur PGCE 01 Liv Univ MTh 05. NOC 01. **d** 04 **p** 05. NSM Radcliffe *Man* 04–08; NSM Prestwich St Gabr from 08. *114 Valley Mill Lane, Bury BL9 9BY* T: 0161-258 0649 M: 07796-366220 E: margtriv@yahoo.co.uk

TRODDEN, Canon Michael John. b 54. K Coll Lon BD 77 AKC 77 CertEd. Wycliffe Hall Ox 79. **d** 80 **p** 81. C Woodford St Mary w St Phil and St Jas *Chelmsf* 80–87; V Aldborough Hatch 87–96; R Ampthill w Millbrook and Steppingley *St Alb* 96–19; Hon Can St Alb 18–19; rtd 19; PtO *St Alb* 19–21; *St E* from 21. *130 Abbot Road, Bury St Edmunds IP33 3UW*

TROLLOPE, David Harvey. b 41. BSc 63. Lon Coll of Div 66. **d** 68 **p** 69. C Bermondsey St Jas w Ch Ch *S'wark* 68–71; CMS Namibia 71–72; Uganda 72–77; Kenya 77–82; V Gt Crosby St Luke *Liv* 82–04; rtd 04; PtO *Ches* from 04. *26 Whitehouse Lane, Heswall, Wirral CH60 1UQ* T: 0151-342 2648 E: davidtrollope@btinternet.com

TROMANS, Judith Anne. *See* OLIVER, Judith Anne

TROMANS, Kevin Stanley. b 57. St Martin's Coll Lanc BEd 79 St Jo Coll Dur MA 12. Aston Tr Scheme 90 Coll of Resurr Mirfield 92. **d** 94 **p** 95. C Rawdon *Bradf* 94–96; C Woodhall 96–98; V Liversedge w Hightown *Wakef* 98–02; V Bierley *Bradf* 02–07; Chapl Co Durham and Darlington NHS Foundn Trust 07–12; Sen Chapl from 12; CF(V) 08–18. *University Hospital Durham, North Road, Durham DH1 5TW* T: 0191-333 2183 E: kevintromans@nhs.net

TROMBETTI, Lynda Joan. b 52. **d** 03 **p** 04. OLM Dorking w Ranmore *Guildf* 03–11; NSM 11–12; Chapl Epsom and St Helier Univ Hosps NHS Trust 05–12; PtO *Guildf* 12–15; P-in-c Walton-on-the-Hill 15–17; PtO *Portsm* from 15; Chapl Isle of Wight NHS Trust from 19. *5 Egypt Copse, Cowes PO31 8BA* M: 07968-629364 E: rev.lyndi@gmail.com

TROOD, James William. b 68. Cov Poly BSc 90 St Jo Coll Dur PGCE 91. St Jo Coll Nottm MTh 02. **d** 02 **p** 03. C Anchorsholme *Blackb* 02–06; TV Glascote and Stonydelph *Lich* 06–15; RD Tamworth 09–14; P-in-c Walsall St Matt 15–18; R from 18. *The Rectory, 48 Jesson Road, Walsall WS1 3AX* T: (01922)　626039　M: 07939-587208 E: rector@stmatthewswalsall.co.uk

TROTMAN, Michael Edwin. b 81. Univ of Wales (Cardiff) BSc 02 Kingston Univ PGCE 10. Wycliffe Hall Ox 16. **d** 18 **p** 19. C Fordingbridge and Hyde and Breamore etc *Win* 18–20; R Parkstone St Pet and St Osmund w Branksea *Sarum* from 20. *The Rectory, 19 Springfield Road, Poole BH14 0LG* M: 07525-662999 E: revdmike@stpetersparkstone.org.uk

TROTT, Daniel Mark. b 84. Hertf Coll Ox BA 08 MA 10 New Coll Ox MSt 10 DPhil 14 Fitzw Coll Cam BA 15 MA 20. Westcott Ho Cam 13. **d** 16 **p** 17. C Upper Norwood St Jo *S'wark* 16–20; TV Putney St Mary from 20. *21 Landford Road, London SW15 1AQ* T: (020) 8785 3951 E: daniel.trott@parishofputney.co.uk

TROTT, Stephen. b 57. Hull Univ BA 79 Fitzw Coll Cam BA 83 MA 87 Univ of Wales (Cardiff) LLM 03 FRSA 86. Westcott Ho Cam 81. **d** 84 **p** 85. C Hessle *York* 84–87; C Kingston upon Hull St Alb 87–88; R Pitsford w Boughton *Pet* from 88; Sec CME 88–97; Chapl Pitsford Sch from 91; RD Brixworth *Pet* 15–20; Hon Can Th Richmond Canada from 15. *The Rectory, Humfrey Lane, Boughton, Northampton NN2 8RQ* M: 07712-863000 E: revstephentrott@gmail.com

TROTTER, Robin Fenwick. b 56. Qu Foundn (Course) 16. **d** 18 **p** 19. OLM Burton St Modwen *Lich* from 18; OLM Burton St Aid and St Paul from 18. *4 Home Farm, Geary Lane, Bretby, Burton-on-Trent DE15 0QE* T: (01283) 702221 M: 07984-450761 E: robin.trotter@icloud.com

TROUT, Keith. b 49. Trin Coll Bris 90. **d** 92 **p** 93. C Pudsey St Lawr and St Paul *Bradf* 92–97; V Burley *Ripon* 97–14; *Leeds* 14; P-in-c 14–17; rtd 14. *8 South Street, Gargrave, Skipton BD23 3RT*

TROWSDALE,　James　Andrew.　b 61.　Yorks　Min Course 13. **d** 15 **p** 16. NSM Rudston, Boynton, Carnaby etc *York* 15–19; PtO from 19. *The Rectory, Rudston Road, Burton Agnes, Driffield YO25 4NE* T: (01262) 490148　　　　　E: james.trowsdale@hey.nhs.uk　　　　*or* revjamestrowsdale@gmail.com

TRUBY, Canon David Charles. b 57. Liv Poly BA 79. Linc Th Coll 79. **d** 82 **p** 83. C Stanley *Liv* 82–85; C Hindley St Pet 85–90; R Brimington *Derby* 90–98; Can Res Derby Cathl 98–03; TR Wirksworth from 03; RD 08–17; Hon Can Derby Cathl from 04. *The Rectory, Coldwell Street, Wirksworth, Matlock DE4 4FB* T: (01629) 822858 E: david.truby@outlook.com

TRUDGETT, Raymond John. b 46. Wilson Carlile Coll 86. **d** 04 **p** 05. Port Chapl and C Aqaba SS Pet and Paul Jordan 04–07; Chapl Medway and Thames Ports *Roch* 07–11; PtO *Cant* 07–11; *Chelmsf* 07–11; rtd 11; PtO *Nor* from 11. *9 Holly Road, Lowestoft NR32 3NH* T: (01502) 583668

TRUMAN, Miss Catherine Jane. b 64. Coll of Ripon & York St Jo BEd 88. St Jo Coll Nottm 01. **d** 03 **p** 04. C Owlerton *Sheff* 03–06; Hd Academic Progr Wilson Carlile Coll of Evang 06–12; Tr Manager 12–19; PtO *Sheff* from 19. *14 Park Avenue, Chapeltown, Sheffield S35 1WE*

TRUMAN, Miss Charlotte Jane. b 71. Birm Univ BPhil 96. Westcott Ho Cam 96. **d** 99 **p** 00. C High Harrogate Ch Ch *Ripon* 99–03; P-in-c Oulton w Woodlesford 03–06; Chapl HM YOI Northallerton 06–09; Chapl HM Pris and YOI New Hall 09–18; Chapl Huddersfield Univ *Leeds* 18–20; PtO *Ches* from 20. *14 Tarporley Road, Tarvin, Chester CH3 8ER* E: revcjt@hotmail.co.uk

TRUMPER, Roger David. b 52. Ex Univ BSc 74 K Coll Lon MSc 75 Ox Univ BA 80 MA 85. Wycliffe Hall Ox 78. **d** 81 **p** 82. C Tunbridge Wells St Jo *Roch* 81–84; C Slough *Ox* 84–87; TV Shenley and Loughton 87–88; TV Watling Valley 88–93; R Byfleet *Guildf* 93–05; TV Sidmouth, Woolbrook, Salcombe Regis, Sidbury etc *Ex* 05–16; rtd 16. *28 Gilbert Road, Yeovil BA21 5FN* E: nonnobis115@gmail.com

TRUNDLE, Christopher Philip. b 85. Trin Coll Cam BA 07 MA 10 PGCE 08. Coll of Resurr Mirfield 08. **d** 10 **p** 11. C Tottenham St Paul *Lon* 10–12; C Pimlico St Gabr 12–13; P-in-c Clerkenwell H Redeemer 13–14; V from 14; P-in-c Clerkenwell St Mark 13–14; V from 14. *The Clergy House, 24 Exmouth Market, London EC1R 4QE* T: (020) 7837 1861 E: chris.trundle@gmail.com *or* holyredeemerstmark@tiscali.co.uk

TRURO, Bishop of. *See* MOUNSTEPHEN, The Rt Revd Philip Ian

TRURO, Dean of. *See* BUSH, The Very Revd Roger Charles

TRUSCOTT, Stephen Alistair. b 49. **d** 06 **p** 07. OLM Bishopston and St Andrews *Bris* 06–14; OLM Redland 14–20; NSM from 20. *5 Kent Road, Bristol BS7 9DN* T: 0117-942 4248 E: steve@redland.org.uk

TRUSS, Canon Charles Richard. b 42. Reading Univ BA 63 Linacre Coll Ox BA 66 MA 69 K Coll Lon MPhil 79 Win Univ MA 16. Wycliffe Hall Ox 64. **d** 66 **p** 67. C Leic H Apostles 66–69; C Hampstead St Jo *Lon* 69–72; V Belsize Park 72–79; V Wood Green St Mich 79–82; TR Wood Green St Mich w Bounds Green St Gabr etc 82–85; R Shepperton 85–94; V Waterloo St Jo w St Andr *S'wark* 94–08; RD Lambeth 95–05; Hon Can S'wark Cathl 01–08; Sen Chapl Actors' Ch Union 04–08; rtd 08; PtO *S'wark* from 08; *Guildf* from 10. *12 Camden Cottages, Church Walk, Weybridge KT13 8JT* T: (01932) 702317 E: richard.truss@btinternet.com

TRUSTRAM, Canon David Geoffrey. b 49. Pemb Coll Ox BA 71 MA 76 Qu Coll Cam BA 73 MA 77. Westcott Ho Cam 74. **d** 75 **p** 76. C Surbiton St Mark *S'wark* 75–77; C Surbiton St Andr and St Mark 77–78; C Richmond St Mary w St Matthias and St Jo 78–82; P-in-c Eastry *Cant* 82–88; R Eastry and Northbourne w Tilmanstone etc 88–90; Chapl Eastry Hosp 82–90; V Tenterden St Mildred w Smallhythe *Cant* 90–10; P-in-c Tenterden St Mich 07–10; Hon Can Cant Cathl 96–10; AD Tenterden 99–05; rtd 10; PtO *Cant* from 11. *Hensmead, New Road, Headcorn, Ashford TN27 9SE* T: (01622) 892480 M: 07811-874806 E: trustram@btinternet.com

TSANG, Wing Man. b 52. Lon Univ BSc 74 MPhil 84 MCB 88 MRCPath 88 FRCPath 96. STETS 99. **d** 02 **p** 03. C Merthyr Tydfil Ch Ch *Llan* 02–05; TV Broadwater *Chich* 05–17;

rtd 17; PtO *Portsm* from 18. *47 Mulberry Avenue, Fareham PO14 2SN* M: 07961-839018 E: wing2699@hotmail.com

TSUKADA, John Jutaro. d 15. NSM Aberdeen St Ninian *Ab* from 15. *25 Ashwood Circle, Bridge of Don, Aberdeen AB22 8XU*

TUAM, Archdeacon of. *See* MACWHIRTER, The Ven Stephen Joseph

TUAM, Dean of. *See* GRIMASON, The Very Revd Alistair John

TUAM, KILLALA AND ACHONRY, Bishop of. *Vacant*

TUBBS, Preb Brian Ralph. b 44. AKC 66. **d** 67 **p** 68. C Ex St Thos 67–72; TV Sidmouth, Woolbrook and Salcombe Regis 72–77; R Ex St Jas 77–96; RD Christianity 89–95; V Paignton St Jo and Chapl S Devon Healthcare NHS Foundn Trust 96–09; Preb Ex Cathl 95–09; rtd 09; PtO *Eur* 10–20; *Ex* from 10. *58 Dorset Avenue, Exeter EX4 1ND* T: (01392) 200506 E: fathertubbs@aol.com

TUBBS, Gary Andrew. b 59. Univ of Wales (Swansea) BA 82 Bris Univ MSc 84 Bris Poly PGCE 84. Oak Hill Th Coll. **d** 00 **p** 01. C Stanwix *Carl* 00–02; C Carl H Trin and St Barn 02–08; P-in-c Pennington and Lindal w Marton and Bardsea 08–17; C Henham and Elsenham w Ugley *Chelmsf* 17–21; C Houghton *Carl* from 21. *Address temp unknown* E: gary.tubbs@hotmail.co.uk

TUCK, Canon Andrew Kenneth. b 42. Kelham Th Coll 63. **d** 68 **p** 69. C Poplar *Lon* 68–74; TV 74–76; V Walsgrave on Sowe *Cov* 76–90; R Farnham *Guildf* 90–12; Chapl Surrey Hants Borders NHS Trust 90–05; Chapl Surrey and Borders Partnership NHS Foundn Trust 05–12; RD Farnham *Guildf* 00–05; Hon Can Guildf Cathl 09–12; rtd 12; PtO *Guildf* 12–13; Dioc Spiritual Direction Co-ord 14–20. *7 Forge Close, Farnham GU9 9PX* T: (01252) 716119 E: andrew.tuck@cofeguildford.org.uk

TUCK, David John. b 36. St Cath Coll Cam BA 61 MA 65. Cuddesdon Coll 61. **d** 63 **p** 64. C Holt and Kelling w Salthouse *Nor* 63–68; Zambia 68–73; V Sprowston *Nor* 73–84; R Beeston St Andr 73–84; RD Nor N 81–84; V Pinner *Lon* 84–01; rtd 01; PtO *Lon* 02–04 and from 18; *St Alb* from 04; Hon C N Harrow St Alb *Lon* 04–17. *119 High Street, Northwood HA6 1ED* T: (01923) 825806 M: 07443-576905 E: dandtuck@btinternet.com

TUCK, Gillian. b 40. SRN 64 SCM 66. Llan Dioc Tr Scheme 93. **d** 97 **p** 98. NSM Pontypridd St Cath w St Matt *Llan* 97–01; P-in-c Pontypridd St Matt and Cilfynydd 01–05; NSM Pontypridd St Matt and Cilfynydd w Llanwynno 05–08; rtd 08; PtO *Llan* from 09. *4 Maes Glas, Coed y Cwm, Pontypridd CF37 3EJ* T: (01443) 791049

TUCK, Rebecca Jane. b 78. Lon Guildhall Univ BSc 99 Univ of E Lon PGCE 00. Ridley Hall Cam 16. **d** 18 **p** 19. C Horsham *Chich* from 18. *18 Queensway, Horsham RH13 5AY* M: 07905-315577 E: rebecca.tuck.rt@gmail.com

TUCK, Canon Ronald James. b 47. S'wark Ord Course 75. **d** 78 **p** 79. C Upper Holloway St Pet w St Jo *Lon* 78–81; P-in-c Scottow and Swanton Abbott w Skeyton *Nor* 81–88; R Bradwell 88–12; Hon Can Nor Cathl 10–12; rtd 12; PtO *Nor* from 12; *St E* from 12. *5 Gosford Heights, 47 Gosford Road, Beccles NR34 9SP* T: (01502) 717273 E: revtuck@btinternet.com

TUCKER, Canon Anthony Ian. b 50. CA Tr Coll 73 S'wark Ord Course 81. **d** 85 **p** 86. NSM E Ham w Upton Park and Forest Gate *Chelmsf* 85–86; NSM S'well Minster 86–90; C Rolleston w Fiskerton, Morton and Upton 90–93; P-in-c Teversal 93–96; Chapl Sutton Cen 93–96; P-in-c Norwell w Ossington, Cromwell and Caunton 96–04; Dioc Tourism Adv 96–04; V Balderton and Barnby-in-the-Willows 04–15; AD Newark 00–12; Jt AD S'well 08–12; Hon Can S'well Minster 08–15; rtd 15; PtO *Linc* 16–19; R Claypole from 20; RD Loveden from 19. *The Rectory, 6 Rectory Lane, Claypole, Newark NG23 5BH* T: (01636) 921161 E: tonytucker57@gmail.com *or* tony.tucker@lincoln.anglican.org

TUCKER, Ms Catherine Jane. b 62. Birkbeck Coll Lon BA 97 Jes Coll Cam MPhil 11. Westcott Ho Cam 09. **d** 11 **p** 12. C Forest Hill w Lower Sydenham *S'wark* 11–14; V Croydon H Sav 14–21; AD Croydon N 17–21; P-in-c Dover Town *Cant* from 21. *5 Church Street, Dover CT16 1LY* T: (01304) 213899 M: 07709-618063 E: doverttm@outlook.com

TUCKER, Ian Malcolm. b 46. S Dios Minl Tr Scheme 86. **d** 89 **p** 90. NSM Pill w Easton in Gordano and Portbury *B & W* 89–95; C Frome St Jo and St Mary 95–99; TV Redruth w Lanner and Treleigh *Truro* 99–04; P-in-c Par and Hon Chapl Miss to Seafarers 04–11; rtd 11. *4 Priory Road, Portbury, Bristol BS20 7TH* E: iandm@btinternet.com

TUCKER, Canon Jill. b 47. UMIST BSc 68 MSc 69 PhD 77. Qu Coll Birm 05. **d** 06 **p** 07. NSM Ilmington w Stretton-on-Fosse etc *Cov* 06–09; NSM Shipston-on-Stour w Honington and Idlicote from 09; AD Shipston 09–19; Dean of Self-Supporting Min from 11; Hon Can Cov Cathl from 14; PtO *Truro* from 16. *The Old House, Back Lane, Oxhill, Warwick*

CV35 0QN T: (01295) 680663 F: 688193 M: 07973-994800 E: revjill.tucker@tiscali.co.uk

TUCKER, (née RAMSAY), Kerry. b 59. Heythrop Coll Lon MA 94. Westcott Ho Cam 92. **d** 94 **p** 96. C Westville St Eliz S Africa 95–96; C Charlton St Luke w H Trin *S'wark* 96–99; C Cambridge Gt St Mary w St Mich *Ely* 99–04; V Sunninghill *Ox* 04–08; P-in-c S Ascot 07–08; PtO 08–15; Hon C Byfleet *Guildf* 09–10; Hon C E Horsley and Ockham w Hatchford and Downside 10–14; PtO *S'wark* from 15. *The Homestead, Castle Street, Bletchingley, Redhill RH1 4QA* T: (01883) 742226

TUCKER, Michael. b 33. **d** 84 **p** 85. NSM Sawston *Ely* 84–87; C Ely 87–90; P-in-c Barton Bendish w Beachamwell and Shingham 90–98; P-in-c Wereham 90–98; rtd 98; PtO *Nor* 99–04 and from 13; *Ely* 00–17. *2 Lighthouse Close, Hunstanton PE36 6EL* T: (01485) 298192 E: mandstucker@icloud.com

TUCKER, Canon Michael Owen. b 42. Lon Univ BSc 66 Surrey Univ PhD 69. Glouc Sch of Min 81. **d** 84 **p** 85. NSM Uley w Owlpen and Nympsfield *Glouc* 84–92; P-in-c Amberley 92–09; Dioc NSM Officer 94–09; Hon Can Glouc Cathl 98–09; RD Stonehouse 99–04; rtd 09. *18 Bownham Mead, Rodborough Common, Stroud GL5 5DZ* T: (01453) 873352 E: mike@tuckers.org.uk

TUCKER, Nicholas Harold. b 41. Reading Univ BSc 66. NOC 90. **d** 93 **p** 94. NSM Ilkley All SS *Bradf* 93–98; P-in-c Uley w Owlpen and Nympsfield *Glouc* 98–06; rtd 06; NSM Nailsworth w Shortwood, Horsley etc *Glouc* 07–08; PtO from 16. *The Rowans, 13 Priory Way, Tetbury GL8 8HT* T: (01666) 503188

TUCKER, Nicholas John Cuthbert. b 74. Birm Univ BSc 96. Oak Hill Th Coll MTh 04. **d** 04 **p** 05. C Bebington *Ches* 04–07; Research Fell Oak Hill Th Coll 07–15; PtO *St Alb* 08–19; V Edgbaston St Bart *Birm* from 15; AD Edgbaston 17–20; Co-AD Warley and Edgbaston 20–21. *The Vicarage, 1B Arthur Road, Edgbaston, Birmingham B15 2UW* T: 0121-454 5439 M: 07957-566714 E: nick@hellotuckers.com *or* nick@edgbastonoldchurch.org.uk

TUCKER, Richard Parish. b 51. Cam Univ BA 72 MA 76 Lon Univ BD 83 Birm Univ MA 07. Wycliffe Hall Ox 80. **d** 83 **p** 84. C Wellington w Eyton *Lich* 83–84; C Walsall 84–88; TV Dronfield *Derby* 88–90; TV Dronfield w Holmesfield 90–98; V Sutton Coldfield St Columba *Birm* 98–17; rtd 17; PtO *Birm* from 17; *Derby* from 17. *2 Hopton Cottages, Main Street, Youlgrave, Bakewell DE45 1UW* T: (01629) 636074 E: rev.richardtucker@gmail.com

TUCKER, Stephen Reid. b 51. New Coll Ox BA 72 MA 76. Ripon Coll Cuddesdon. **d** 77 **p** 78. C Hove All SS *Chich* 77–80; Lect Chich Th Coll 80–86; V Portsea St Alb *Portsm* 86–90; Chapl and Dean of Div New Coll Ox 90–95; P-in-c Ovingdean *Chich* 96–01; Bp's Adv on CME 96–01; V Hampstead St Jo *Lon* 01–16; AD N Camden 14–16; rtd 16; PtO *Sarum* from 17. *10 Beechcroft Road, Laverstock, Salisbury SP1 1PF* E: stucker957@btinternet.com

TUCKER, Preb Susan. b 53. Stockwell Coll of Educn CertEd 74. **d** 97 **p** 98. C Taunton St Andr *B & W* 97–01; V Bishops Hull 01–10; RD Taunton 06–10; Chapl St Marg Hospice Taunton 01–07; R Chard St Mary w Combe St Nicholas, Wambrook etc *B & W* 10–17; RD Ilminster 14–17; Preb Wells Cathl 15–17; rtd 17; PtO *Ex* from 18. *The Clock House, Buckerell, Honiton EX14 3QD* E: suetucker99@btinternet.com

TUCKER, Vivian Clive Temple. b 39. Univ of Wales (Swansea) BSc 60 Univ of Wales DipEd 61. St As Minl Tr Course 93. **d** 96 **p** 97. NSM Gresford w Holt *St As* 96–04; NSM Holt, Rossett and Isycoed 04–09; rtd 09; PtO *St As* from 09. *8 Snowdon Drive, Ty Gwyn, Wrexham LL11 2UY* T: (01978) 359226 E: geraldine.tucker26@icloud.com

TUCKETT, Prof Christopher Mark. b 48. Qu Coll Cam MA 71 Lanc Univ PhD 79. Westcott Ho Cam 71. **d** 75 **p** 76. C Lancaster St Mary *Blackb* 75–77; Chapl and Fell Qu Coll Cam 77–79; Lect NT Man Univ 79–89; Sen Lect 89–91; Prof Bibl Studies 91–96; Lect NT Ox Univ 96–00; Prof NT Studies 00–13; rtd 13; PtO *Ox* from 13. *1 Wallingford Road, Cholsey, Wallingford OX10 9LQ* T: (01491) 659091 E: christopher.tuckett@theology.ox.ac.uk

TUCKETT, Katherine Ann. b 76. Selw Coll Cam MA 98. SEITE 10. **d** 13 **p** 14. C Merton Priory *S'wark* 13–17; V N Harrow St Alb *Lon* 17–21; V Wolvercote and Wytham *Ox* from 21. *Wolvercote Vicarage, 1 Mere Road, Oxford OX2 8AN* M: 07410-978921 E: kate.a.tuckett@gmail.com

TUCKWELL, Jonathan David. b 77. St Jo Coll Cam MEng 00 MA 02. Oak Hill Th Coll BA 11. **d** 11 **p** 12. C Cambridge St Andr Less *Ely* 11–18; V Enfield Ch Ch Trent Park *Lon* from 18. *2A Chalk Lane, Cockfosters, Barnet EN4 9JQ* M: 07785-576939 E: jon.t@cockfosters.church

TUCKWELL, Richard Graham. b 46. SS Mark & Jo Univ Coll Plymouth TCert 67 Open Univ BA. **d** 07 **p** 08. NSM Tarvin *Ches* 07–09; P-in-c Alvanley 09–12; V 12–14;

rtd 14; PtO *Ches* from 14. *Iddesleigh, 5 Walkers Lane, Tarporley CW6 0BX* T: (01829) 732732 M: 07713-485318 E: richard.tuckwell@googlemail.com

TUDGE, Canon Paul Quartus. b 55. Leeds Univ BEd 78. Cranmer Hall Dur 84. **d** 87 **p** 88. C Roundhay St Edm *Ripon* 87–90; C Leeds City 91; V Woodside 91–99; Warden of Readers 96–99; V Ilkley All SS *Bradf* 99–08; RD Otley 02–08; P-in-c Farsley 08–11; V 11–14; *Leeds* 14–20; RD Calverley *Bradf* 10–14; AD N Bradford *Leeds* 14–16; rtd 20; Hon Can Bradf Cathl 13–14; *Leeds* 14–20; PtO 21. *10 Chandos Gardens, Leeds LS8 1LW* E: paul.tudge@leeds.anglican.org

TUDGEY, Stephen John. b 51. Nottm Univ BTh 81 Westmr Coll Ox MTh 00. St Jo Coll Nottm LTh 81. **d** 81 **p** 82. C Grays Thurrock *Chelmsf* 81–83; C Madeley *Heref* 84–87; R Chilcompton w Downside and Stratton on the Fosse *B & W* 87–03; P-in-c Falmouth K Chas *Truro* 03–19; Hon Chapl Miss to Seafarers 04–19; rtd 20; PtO *B & W* from 21. *6 Cheddon Close, Cheddon Fitzpaine, Taunton TA2 8GE* T: (01823) 57382145 E: stevetudgey11@gmail.com

TUDOR, Canon David St Clair. b 55. K Coll Lon BD 77 AKC 77 K Coll Lon MTh 89. Ripon Coll Cuddesdon 77. **d** 78 **p** 79. C Plumstead St Nic *S'wark* 78–80; C Redhill St Matt 80–83; C-in-c Reigate St Phil CD 83–87; Asst Sec Gen Syn Bd for Miss and Unity 87–88; PtO *S'wark* 94–97; TV Canvey Is *Chelmsf* 97–00; TR from 00; AD Hadleigh from 08; Hon Can Chelmsf Cathl from 15. *St Nicholas House, 210 Long Road, Canvey Island SS8 0JR* T: (01268) 682586 E: dstudor@tiscali.co.uk

TUDWAY, Stephen William. b 75. Ch Ch Ox MA 97. ERMC 14. **d** 17 **p** 18. NSM Flamstead and Markyate Street *St Alb* 17–19; P-in-c Kirkby Ireleth *Carl* from 20; P-in-c Broughton and Duddon from 20. *Keppleway Lodge, Kepplewray Hill, Broughton-in-Furness LA20 6BH* T: (01229) 715259 M: 07954-441991 E: stephen@kbdchurches.com

TUFFIN, Mrs Gillian Patricia. b 43. S Dios Minl Tr Scheme 91. **d** 94 **p** 95. C Gidea Park *Chelmsf* 94–98; TV Stoke-upon-Trent *Lich* 98–01; Admin and Prayer Co-ord Shalom Chr Healing Cen from 02; NSM Northolt Park St Barn *Lon* 02–08; PtO from 08. *76 Stowe Crescent, Ruislip HA4 7SS* T: (020) 8864 5394

TUFFNELL, Canon Nigel Owen. b 65. Teesside Poly BSc 90 UEA MSc 01. St Jo Coll Nottm 87. **d** 94 **p** 95. C Guisborough *York* 94–97; P-in-c Northwold *Ely* 97–98; P-in-c Stoke Ferry w Wretton 97–98; P-in-c Whittington 97–98; R Northwold and Wretton w Stoke Ferry etc 98–03; Bp's Adv on Environmental Issues 02–03; TR Kegworth, Hathern, Long Whatton, Diseworth etc *Leic* 03–06; PtO *Nor* 10; Hon C Hopton w Corton 10–12; P-in-c Scole, Brockdish, Billingford, Thorpe Abbots etc 12–14; P-in-c Redenhall, Harleston, Wortwell and Needham 12–14; R Redenhall w Scole from 14; RD Redenhall from 15; Hon Can Nor Cathl from 16. *The Rectory, 10 Swan Lane, Harleston IP20 9AN* T: (01379) 308905 M: 07443-937050 E: rector@7churches.org.uk

TUFNELL, Andrew Stephen Goodwin. b 83. Univ of Wales (Cardiff) BSc 05 PGCE 06. Ridley Hall Cam 12. **d** 15 **p** 16. C Gamston and Bridgford *S'well* 15–17; V Chilwell from 17. *8 College Road, Beeston, Nottingham NG9 4AS* M: 07410-541354 E: a.tufnell@gmail.com *or* andytufnell@ccchilwell.org.uk

TUFNELL, Christopher Edward David. b 89. Sheff Univ BA 11. Oak Hill Th Coll BA 17. **d** 17 **p** 18. C Fulwood *Sheff* 17–20; P-in-c Oughtibridge from 20. *The Vicarage, Church Street, Oughtibridge, Sheffield S35 0FU*

TUFNELL, Edward Nicholas Pember. b 45. Chu Coll Cam MA 68. St Jo Coll Nottm BA 73. **d** 73 **p** 74. C Ealing St Mary *Lon* 73–76; BCMS Tanzania 76–88; P-in-c Lt Thurrock St Jo *Chelmsf* 89–91; V Grays North 91–98; Chapl Thurrock Community Hosp Grays 89–98; P-in-c Bourton-on-the-Water w Clapton *Glouc* 98–05; R Bourton-on-the-Water w Clapton etc 05–11; AD Stow 09–10; rtd 11; PtO *St Alb* from 11. *9 Peterborough Road, Sheffield S10 4JD* T: 0114-453 4782 M: 07816-123470

TUFNELL, Michael. b 81. Imp Coll Lon BEng 05. St Mellitus Coll MA 10. **d** 10 **p** 11. C Enfield Ch Ch Trent Park *Lon* 10–14; C Turnham Green Ch Ch 14–18; TV Canford Magna *Sarum* 18–21; TR from 21. *359 Sopwith Crescent, Wimborne BH21 1XQ* M: 07977-139544 E: michaeltufnell@gmail.com

TUFT, Preb Patrick Anthony. b 31. Selw Coll Cam BA 56 MA 60. Edin Th Coll 56. **d** 58 **p** 59. C Keighley *Bradf* 58–63; PV Chich Cathl 63–68; Min Can St Paul's Cathl *Lon* 68–74; Hon Min Can St Paul's Cathl 74–94; V Chiswick St Nic w St Mary 74–06; PV Westmr Abbey 74–79; AD Hounslow *Lon* 87–93; P-in-c Chiswick St Paul Grove Park 88–90; Preb St Paul's Cathl 95–06; rtd 07; PtO *Lon* from 07. *68 Worple Road, Isleworth TW7 7HU* T: (020) 8581 3014 M: 07768-892099 E: patrick@tuft.co

TULK, Giles David. b 65. Leeds Univ BA 86. ERMC 06. **d** 09 **p** 10. C Stansted Mountfitchet w Birchanger and Farnham *Chelmsf* 09–11; C Bocking St Mary 11–13; TR Albury, Braughing, Furneux Pelham, Lt Hadham etc *St Alb* 13–16; R Minsterley, Habberley and Hope w Shelve *Heref* 16–20; RD Pontesbury 18–20; TR Wilford Peninsula *St E* from 20. *The Rectory, 109A Front Street, Orford, Woodbridge IP12 2LN* T: (01394) 450610 E: revgileswtr@gmail.com

TULL, Preb Christopher Stuart. b 36. Hertf Coll Ox BA 60 MA 64. Oak Hill Th Coll 60. **d** 62 **p** 63. C Stoodleigh *Ex* 62–71; C Washfield 62–71; TV Washfield, Stoodleigh, Withleigh etc 71–74; RD Tiverton 74–75; R Bishops Nympton w Rose Ash 75–77; V Mariansleigh 75–77; TR Bishopsnympton, Rose Ash, Mariansleigh etc 77–99; RD S Molton 80–87 and 95–99; Preb Ex Cathl 84–99; rtd 99; PtO *Ex* from 99; *B & W* from 04. *The Old Smithy, Challacombe, Barnstaple EX31 4TU* T: (01598) 763201

TULLETT, Paul Budworth. b 71. Lanc Univ BSc 92 Birm Univ MBA 00 Anglia Ruskin Univ BA 09. Ridley Hall Cam 07. **d** 09 **p** 10. C Taunton St Mary *B & W* 09–13; V Water Orton *Birm* from 13. *The Vicarage, Vicarage Lane, Water Orton, Birmingham B46 1RX* T: 0121-730 2081 M: 07581-544978 E: paulofwaterorton@hotmail.co.uk

TULLETT, Peter Watts. b 46. Qu Coll Birm 92. **d** 94 **p** 95. C Worle *B & W* 94–96; Chapl HM YOI Portland 96–01; PtO *B & W* 02–04 and 07–18; Hon C Uphill 04–06. *2 Ferry Lane, Lympsham, Weston-super-Mare BS24 0BT* T: (01934) 814284 M: 07803-330395 E: peter@valmagnolia.plus.com

TULLOCH, Richard James Anthony. b 52. Wadh Coll Ox BA 74 Selw Coll Cam BA 79. Ridley Hall Cam 76. **d** 79 **p** 80. C Morden *S'wark* 79–83; C Jesmond Clayton Memorial *Newc* 83–94; V New Borough and Leigh *Sarum* 94–11; TR Eden, Gelt and Irthing *Carl* 11–18; RD Brampton 16–18; rtd 18. *12C Grafton Square, London SW4 0DQ* E: rjatulloch@gmail.com

TULLOCH, Canon Yvonne Lorraine. b 63. Sheff Univ MA 07. WEMTC 96. **d** 99 **p** 00. NSM Magor *Mon* 99–00; NSM Kenilworth St Jo *Cov* 00–05; Chapl for Evang Cov Cathl 05–06; Can Res for Miss 06–09; Can for Development Birm Cathl 09–10; PtO *Lich* 10–13; *Lon* from 13; *S'wark* from 14; Bp's Officer for Clergy Bereavement from 17. *112 Salcott Road, London SW11 6DG* M: 07801-351947 E: yvonne@ataloss.org

TULLY, David John. b 56. St Jo Coll Dur BA 77 Nottm Univ PGCE 78. Ridley Hall Cam 81. **d** 84 **p** 85. C Gosforth St Nic *Newc* 84–86; C Newburn 86–90; TV Whorlton 90–96; V 96–00; R Gateshead Fell *Dur* 00–09; R Chester le Street 09–21; AD Chester le Street and Houghton 20–21; rtd 21. *4 Winchcombe Place, Newcastle upon Tyne NE7 7AX*

TULLY, Janet Florence. b 43. **d** 03 **p** 04. OLM Margate St Jo *Cant* 03–08; PtO *Nor* from 09. *4 Westgate Court, Wymondham NR18 0PX* M: 07866-839275

TUNBRIDGE, Genny Louise. b 64. Clare Coll Cam BA 85 St Cross Coll Ox DPhil 93. Qu Coll Birm BD 95. **d** 96 **p** 97. C Boston *Linc* 96–00; Lect 00–01; Prec Chelmsf Cathl 01–06; Can Res Chelmsf Cathl 02–06; V Gosforth All SS *Newc* 06–13; rtd 13; PtO *Birm* from 15. *The Old Rectory, 80 Hodge Hill Common, Birmingham B36 8AG* M: 07891-610868 E: genny.tunbridge@gmail.com

TUNGAY, Michael Ian. b 45. Oak Hill Th Coll 70. **d** 73 **p** 74. C Fulham St Mary N End *Lon* 73–75; C Hammersmith St Simon 76–79; P-in-c 79–84; PtO *S'wark* 09–11. *7 Lily Close, London W14 9YA* T: (020) 8748 3151 E: miketungay@uk2.net

TUNLEY, Timothy Mark. b 61. Ridley Hall Cam 89. **d** 92 **p** 93. C Aldborough w Boroughbridge and Roecliffe *Ripon* 92–95; C Knaresborough 95–98; V Swaledale 98–05; TV Seacroft 05–09; Dioc Adv for NSM 03–08; Chapl Miss to Seafarers from 09. *109 Avalon Gardens, Linlithgow Bridge, Linlithgow EH49 7PL* T: (01506) 842629 M: 07581-625941 E: timothy.tunley@mtsmail.org

TUNNICLIFFE, Canon Martin Wyndham. b 31. Keele Univ BA 56. Qu Coll Birm 59. **d** 60 **p** 61. C Castle Bromwich SS Mary and Marg *Birm* 60–65; V Shard End 65–73; R Over Whitacre w Shustoke 73–78; V Tanworth 78–98; RD Solihull 89–94; Hon Can Birm Cathl 91–98; rtd 98; PtO *Birm* 98–17. *202 Ralph Road, Shirley, Solihull B90 3LE* T: 0121-745 6522 E: mwtunnicliffe@gmail.com

TUNNICLIFFE, Mrs Siv. b 33. Stockholm Univ MPhil 58. SAOMC 94. **d** 97 **p** 98. OLM Wingrave w Rowsham, Aston Abbotts and Cublington *Ox* 97–12; OLM Wing w Grove 04–12; OLM Cottesloe 12–10; PtO 10–19; rtd 19; PtO *Ox* from 20. *Baldwey House, Leighton Road, Wingrave, Aylesbury HP22 4PA* T/F: (01296) 681374

TUNSTALL, Mrs Alyson Margaret. b 70. St Mellitus Coll BA 17. **d** 17 **p** 18. C Garston *Liv* 17–20; V from 20. *St Michael's Vicarage, 49 Harbour Drive, Liverpool L19 8AB* M: 07795-171269

TUPLIN, Mrs Josette. b 52. Liv Univ BA 73. St Mellitus Coll 18. d 19 p 20. NSM Woodchurch *Ches* from 19. *5 Beryl Road, Prenton CH43 9RS* T: 0151-677 2266 M: 07592-721399 E: josietuplin@gmail.com

TUPLING, Mrs Catherine Louise. b 74. Westhill Coll Birm BTh 96. Wycliffe Hall Ox 01. d 03 p 04. C Belper *Derby* 03–07; P-in-c Hathersage w Bamford and Derwent 07–08; P-in-c Hathersage w Bamford and Derwent and Grindleford 08–13; V Dore *Sheff* 13–19; P-in-c Totley 17–19; Dioc Disability Adv and Chapl amongst Deaf People *Ox* from 19. *1 Tithe Barn Court, Manor Way, Kidlington OX5 2BL* E: katie.tupling@oxford.anglican.org

TURAHIRWA, Jean-Bosco. b 40. ERMC 16. d 18 p 19. NSM Brussels *Eur* from 18. *Pro-Cathedral of the Holy Trinity, 29 rue Capitaine Crespel, 1050 Brussels, Belgium* T: (0032) (2) 511 7183

TURK, James Richard. b 72. WEMTC 14. d 17 p 18. C Upton St Leonards *Glouc* from 17. *53 Goshawk Road, Quedgeley, Gloucester GL2 4NU* T: (01452) 558990 M: 07758-225113 E: jamesturk@blueyonder.co.uk

TURLEY, Debra. b 67. Oak Hill Th Coll BA 91. LCTP 07. d 10 p 11. C Utley *Bradf* 10–14; Leeds 14–15; V Taunton Lyngford *B & W* from 14. *62 Eastwick Road, Taunton TA2 7HD* E: debbi.turley@sky.com

✠**TURNBULL, The Rt Revd Anthony Michael Arnold.** b 35. CBE 03 DL 05. Keble Coll Ox BA 58 MA 62 Greenwich Univ Hon DLitt 94 Dur Univ Hon DD 03. Cranmer Hall Dur. d 60 p 61 c 88. C Middleton *Man* 60–61; C Luton w E Hyde *St Alb* 61–65; Dir of Ords *York* 65–69; Abp's Dom Chapl 65–69; Chapl York Univ 69–76; V Heslington 69–76; Chief Sec CA 76–84; Can Res Roch Cathl 84–88; Adn Roch 84–88; Bp Roch 88–94; Bp Dur 94–03; rtd 03; Hon Asst Bp Cant, Eur and Roch from 03. *3 Gardeners Quay, Upper Strand Street, Sandwich CT13 9DH* T: (01304) 611389 E: amichaelturnbull@yahoo.co.uk

TURNBULL, Brian Robert. b 43. Chich Th Coll 71. d 74 p 75. C Norbury St Phil *Cant* 74–76; C Folkestone St Sav 76–77; Hon C Tong *Lich* 83–88; C Jarrow *Dur* 88–89; TV 89–94; P-in-c Hartlepool St Oswald 94–96; V 96–04; rtd 04; PtO *Dur* from 05; Newc from 05. *50 The Chare, Leazes Square, Newcastle upon Tyne NE1 4DD* T: 0191-221 2312 E: frbrian@onetel.com

TURNBULL, George William Warwick. b 47. Leeds Poly BEd 84 Bradf Univ MSc 06 Open Univ MA 11 Lon Univ TDip 68 CQSW 75. NOC 85. d 88. Chapl Asst Leeds Gen Infirmary 88–91; PtO *Ripon* 91–94; NSM Leeds All So and St Aid 15–16; NSM Potternewton w Lt London from 16. *11 North Parade, Leeds LS16 5AY* T: 0113-228 8584 M: 07714-720234 E: warwick.t@ntlworld.com

TURNBULL, James Awty. b 28. Solicitor Bradf Univ HonDLaws 97. Cranmer Hall Dur 89. d 89 p 90. NSM Bolton Abbey *Bradf* 89–98; PtO 98–14; Leeds 14–19. *1 Woodlands Close, Ilkley LS29 9BY*

TURNBULL (née WILKINSON), Mrs Marlene Sandra. b 45. SRN 71. Trin Coll Bris IDC 78. dss 78 d 93 p 94. Wrose *Bradf* 78–82; Chapl St Luke's Hosp Bradf 78–82; Past Tutor Aston Tr Scheme 79–81; W Yorkshire CECS 82–84; Westgate Common *Wakef* 84–86; E Ardsley 86–92; Wakef St Jo 92–94; NSM 93–94; TV Barrow St Geo w St Luke *Carl* 94–00; TV Darwen St Pet w Hoddlesden *Blackb* 00–02; rtd 03; PtO *Wakef* 10–14; *Bradf* 12–14; Leeds 14–16. *9 Victoria Drive, Horsforth, Leeds LS18 4PN* E: wilkingreen2014@gmail.com

TURNBULL, Michael. *See* TURNBULL, Anthony Michael Arnold

TURNBULL, Michael Francis. b 62. Liv Univ BTh 99. NOC 95. d 98 p 99. C Birkenhead Ch Ch *Ches* 98–02; P-in-c Leasowe 02–08; R Wistaston from 08; Asst Warden of Readers from 04. *The Rectory, 104 Church Lane, Crewe CW2 8ER* T: (01270) 665742 *or* 567119 M: 07595-908644 E: mfturnbull@gmail.com

TURNBULL, Michael Peter. b 56. Chich Univ BA 15. SEITE 09. d 12. NSM Sidley *Chich* 12–16; NSM Upper St Leonards St Jo from 16; Asst Chapl E Sussex Healthcare NHS Trust from 17. *17 Knebworth Road, Bexhill-on-Sea TN39 4JH* T: (01424) 221948 M: 07864-628081 E: mpt@michaelturnbull.co.uk

TURNBULL, Peter Frederick. b 64. SS Mark & Jo Univ Coll Plymouth BA 85. Sarum & Wells Th Coll BTh 91. d 91 p 92. C Upper Norwood All SS *S'wark* 91–95; Chapl HM Pris Dorchester 95–98; C Dorchester *Sarum* 95–98; NSM Melbury 98–99; C Maltby *Sheff* 99–02; TV 02–08; TV Crosslacon *Carl* 08–16; TV Chellington St Alb from 16; PtO *Ox* from 19; Chapl Chadwick Lodge Secure Hosp from 21. *The Rectory, 3 The Moor, Carlton, Bedford MK43 7JR* T: (01234) 720961 E: pfturnbull@gmail.com *or* chellingtonteam@gmail.com

TURNBULL, Richard Duncan. b 60. Reading Univ BA 82 St Jo Coll Dur BA 92 Dur Univ PhD 97 Ox Univ MA 05

MICAS 85 FRHistS. Cranmer Hall Dur 90. d 94 p 95. C Portswood Ch Ch *Win* 94–98; V Chineham 98–05; Prin Wycliffe Hall Ox 05–12; Dir Cen for Enterprise, Markets and Ethics from 12. *16A Woodstock Road East, Begbroke, Kidlington OX5 1RG* T: (01865) 371358 E: richard.turnbull@theceme.org

TURNBULL, Mrs Sally Elizabeth. b 55. Bp Grosseteste Coll BEd 78. d 11 p 12. OLM Owmby Gp *Linc* 11–17; R from 17. *Sunnymede, Faldingworth Road, Spridlington, Market Rasen LN8 2DF* T: (01673) 862764 M: 07594-432058 E: supersonicsal55@gmail.com

TURNBULL, Warwick. *See* TURNBULL, George William Warwick

TURNER, Alan James. b 40. Oak Hill Th Coll BA 81. d 81 p 82. C Bradley *Wakef* 81–84; C Sandal St Helen 84–86; P-in-c Sileby *Leic* 86–87; TR Sileby, Cossington and Seagrave 87–94; R Hollington St Leon *Chich* 94–01; R Frant w Eridge 01–08; rtd 08; PtO *York* 10–20. *4 The Limes, Helmsley, York YO62 5DT* T: (01439) 771957 E: rev.alanturner@gmail.com

TURNER, Albert Edward. b 41. Glouc Sch of Min 83. d 89 p 90. C Woodford St Mary w St Phil and St Jas *Chelmsf* 89–91; R Greatworth and Marston St Lawrence etc *Pet* 91–99; R Somersham w Pidley and Oldhurst *Ely* 99–02; rtd 02; PtO *St Alb* from 04; Chapl Asst Bedford Hosp NHS Trust 05–10; Chapl Asst Papworth Hosp NHS Foundn Trust 06–18; PtO *Ely* 15–20. *23 Brace Dein, Upper Cambourne, Cambridge CB23 6HT* T: (01954) 269525 M: 07950-097525 E: aet546@hotmail.com

TURNER, Andrew John. b 52. St Jo Coll Nottm. d 83 p 84. C Framlingham w Saxtead *St E* 83–86; P-in-c Badingham w Bruisyard and Cransford 86–88; P-in-c Dennington 86–88; R Badingham w Bruisyard, Cransford and Dennington 88–91; Chapl RAF 91–12; rtd 12; PtO *Truro* from 16. *2 Spitfire Row, St Eval, Wadebridge PL27 7TF* T: (01841) 540947 E: a.turner682@btinternet.com

TURNER, Ann. *See* TURNER, Patricia Ann

TURNER, Mrs Ann Elizabeth Hamer. b 38. Ex Univ BA 59 PGCE 60. Trin Coll Bris 84. dss 86 d 87 p 94. Bath St Luke *B & W* 86–91; Hon C 87–91; Chapl Dorothy Ho Foundn 89–91; C Bath Twerton-on-Avon *B & W* 91–94; TV 94–96; rtd 98; PtO *Ex* 00–06; Hon C Ottery St Mary, Alfington, W Hill, Tipton etc from 06. *4 Beech Park, West Hill, Ottery St Mary EX11 1UH* T: (01404) 813476 E: jandaturner@btinternet.com

TURNER, Anthony John. b 49. St Mich Coll Llan 89. d 91 p 92. C Coity w Nolton *Llan* 91–95; R Castlemartin w Warren and Angle etc *St D* 95–04; TV Monkton 04–07; TV Cwmbran *Mon* 07–13; OCM 95–00; rtd 13; PtO *Llan* from 13. *14 Dol Nant Dderwen, Bridgend CF31 5AA* T: (01656) 750713 E: rev.anthony.turner@gmail.com

TURNER, Carl Francis. b 60. St Chad's Coll Dur BA 81. St Steph Ho Ox 83. d 85 p 86. C Leigh-on-Sea St Marg *Chelmsf* 85–88; C Brentwood St Thos 88–90; TV Plaistow 90–95; P-in-c 95–96; TR Plaistow and N Canning Town 96–01; Prec and Can Res Ex Cathl 01–14; R New York St Thos USA from 14. *1 West 53rd Street, New York, NY 10019, USA* T: (001) (212) 757 7013 F: (212) 977 6582 E: rector@saintthomaschurch.org

TURNER, Carlton John. b 79. Univ of W Indies BA 05 Qu Coll Birm MA 09 Glos Univ PhD 15. d 05 p 06. C Bahamas St Greg Bahamas 05–06; C S Beach All SS & Asst Chapl Main Hosp 06–08; C Nassau Calvery Hill 08–10; TV Bloxwich *Lich* 10–17; Tutor Qu Foundn Birm from 17; PtO *Lich* from 17; Birm from 18. *Queen's College, Somerset Road, Edgbaston, Birmingham B15 2QH* T: 0121-454 1527 E: carltonturner07@hotmail.com *or* turnerc@queens.ac.uk

TURNER, Christina Caroline. *See* FFRENCH-HODGES, Christina Caroline

TURNER, Mrs Christine. b 42. EMMTC. d 94 p 95. Asst Chapl Qu Medical Cen Nottm Univ Hosp NHS Trust 94–97; NSM Hickling w Kinoulton and Broughton Sulney *S'well* 94–97; NSM Cotgrave 97–99; P-in-c Willoughby-on-the-Wolds w Wysall and Widmerpool 99–04; rtd 04; PtO *Ex* from 12. *166 Parsons Piece, Banbury OX16 9GW* T: (01295) 722330 E: revd.christine@care4free.net

TURNER, Mrs Christine Margaret. Regents Th Coll BA 13. St Mellitus Coll MA 20. d 20 p 21. NSM Seacombe w Poulton *Ches* from 20; NSM Liscard Resurr from 20. *Tweed Cottage, 39 Bidston Village Road, Prenton CH43 7QT* M: 07772-301468 E: revchristurner3@gmail.com

TURNER, Christopher Gilbert. b 29. New Coll Ox BA 52 MA 55. Ox Min Course 91. d 92 p 93. NSM Hook Norton w Gt Rollright, Swerford etc *Ox* 92–99; PtO 99–19. *Rosemullion, High Street, Great Rollright, Chipping Norton OX7 5RQ* T: (01608) 737359 E: rosemullion@cooptel.net

TURNER, Christopher James Shepherd. b 48. Ch Ch Ox BA 70 MA 74. Wycliffe Hall Ox 71. d 74 p 75. C Rusholme

H Trin *Man* 74–78; C Chadderton Ch Ch 78–80; V 80–89; V Selly Park St Steph and St Wulstan *Birm* 89–99; P-in-c Locking *B & W* 99–05; Chapl Weston Hospice 99–05; P-in-c The Quinton *Birm* 05–09; R 09–11; AD Edgbaston 08–10; PtO from 11. *10 Presthope Road, Birmingham B29 4NJ* T: 0121-603 7916 E: cjsturner@gmail.com

TURNER, Christopher Matthew. b 68. Brunel Univ BSc 90. Cranmer Hall Dur 01. d 03 p 04. C Hykeham *Linc* 03–06; P-in-c Mid Marsh Gp 06–14; R 14–17; P-in-c Saltfleetby 06–14; V 14–17; P-in-c Theddlethorpe 06–14; R 14–17; P-in-c Borough Green *Roch* from 17. *The Vicarage, 24 Maidstone Road, Borough Green, Sevenoaks TN15 8BD* T: (01732) 882447 E: reverendchristurner@gmail.com

TURNER, Mrs Claire Elizabeth. b 76. Plymouth Univ BA 99. Qu Coll Birm 08. d 11 p 12. C Wednesfield *Lich* 11–14; P-in-c Rubery *Birm* 14–15; V from 15. *St Chad's Vicarage, 160A New Road, Rubery, Rednal, Birmingham B45 9JA* T: 0121-238 3168 M: 07748-998227 E: revclaireturner@gmail.com

TURNER, Colin Peter John. b 42. Clifton Th Coll 63. d 66 p 67. C Kinson *Sarum* 66–68; C York St Paul 68–72; Org Sec (SE Area) CPAS 73–78; TV Radipole and Melcombe Regis *Sarum* 78–87; R Radstock w Writhlington *B & W* 90–07; R Kilmersdon w Babington 90–07; RD Midsomer Norton 04–07; rtd 07; PtO *B & W* 07–13; *Sarum* from 14. *12 Gainsborough Rise, Trowbridge BA14 9HX* E: colinpjt@blueyonder.co.uk

TURNER, Dylan Lawrence. b 72. Goldsmiths' Coll Lon BMus 96 SS Coll Cam BTh 08. Westcott Ho Cam 06. d 08 p 09. C Strood St Nic w St Mary *Roch* 08–12; P-in-c Longfield 12–19; Dioc Growth Enabler from 19; PV Roch Cathl from 13; PtO *Cant* from 20. *10 Ramsfield, Wye, Ashford TN25 5AD* M: 07779-225810 E: dylan.turner@cantab.net *or* dylan.turner@rochester.anglican.org

TURNER, Edward. *See* TURNER, Albert Edward

TURNER, Edward Nicholas. b 80. Birm Univ BA 01 Anglia Ruskin Univ MA 08. Westcott Ho Cam 06. d 08 p 09. C Winchmore Hill St Paul *Lon* 08–11; V Edmonton St Aldhelm 11–14; V Southgate St Andr from 14. *St Andrew's Vicarage, 184 Chase Side, London N14 5HN* T: (020) 8886 7523 M: 07788-782646 E: edd.turner@expertit.net

TURNER, Canon Edward Robert. b 37. Em Coll Cam BA 62 BTh 66 MA 67. Westcott Ho Cam 64. d 66 p 67. C Salford St Phil w St Steph *Man* 66–69; Chapl Tonbridge Sch 69–81; Adv for In-Service Tr *Roch* 81–89; Dir of Educn 81–96; Can Res Roch Cathl 81–00; Vice-Dean 88–00; Dioc Adv on Community Affairs 96–00; Consultant Rochester 2000 Trust and Bp's Consultant on Public Affairs 00–02; rtd 02; PtO *Nor* from 03. *Glebe House, Church Road, Neatishead, Norwich NR12 8BT* T: (01692) 631295 E: aandeturner@broadlandnet.co.uk

TURNER, Mrs Eileen Margaret. b 45. Goldsmiths' Coll Lon TCert 66 Ches Coll of HE MTh 02. NOC 90. d 93 p 94. C Sandal St Cath *Wakef* 93–96; P-in-c Hammerwich *Lich* 96–02; Dir OLM Course 96–02; Dir Ext Studies St Jo Coll Nottm 02–10; rtd 10; PtO *Sheff* 11–18; *S'wark* from 18. *Apartment 25, 4 Gaumont Place, London SW2 4GA* M: 07774-623769 E: eileenmturner@ymail.com

TURNER, Mrs Elaine. b 58. Birm Univ BSc 79 Anglia Ruskin Univ MA 17 CEng 84 MICE 84 MIStructE 85. d 04 p 05. OLM Walesby *Linc* 04–18; OLM Walesby Gp from 18. *Rose Cottage, Normanby-le-Wold, Market Rasen LN7 6SS* T: (01673) 828142

TURNER, Miss Elizabeth Jane. b 67. Leeds Univ BEng 88. Trin Coll Bris 93. d 96 p 97. C Eccles *Man* 96–00; P-in-c Barrow *Ches* 00–08; Dioc Ecum Officer 00–08; R Thurstaston from 08. *Thurstaston Rectory, 77 Thingwall Road, Wirral CH61 3UB* T: 0151-648 1816 E: rector@thurstaston.org.uk

TURNER, Canon Frederick Glynne. b 30. Univ of Wales (Lamp) BA 52. St Mich Coll Llan 52. d 54 p 55. C Aberaman *Llan* 54–60; C Oystermouth *S & B* 60–64; V Abercynon *Llan* 64–71; V Ton Pentre 71–73; TR Ystradyfodwg 73–77; R Caerphilly 77–82; V Whitchurch 82–96; Can Llan Cathl 84–96; Prec 95–96; rtd 96; PtO *Llan* from 96. *83 Newborough Avenue, Llanishen, Cardiff CF14 5DA* T: (029) 2075 4443

TURNER, Miss Gaynor. b 44. LNSM course 93. d 96 p 97. NSM Salford Sacred Trin *Man* 96–99; Asst Chapl among Deaf People from 96; Lic Preacher 99–07; PtO 07–15; NSM Broughton 15–17; PtO from 17. *19 Ellesmere Avenue, Worsley, Manchester M28 0AL* E: gturner157@btinternet.com

TURNER, Gemma Dee. b 78. Coll of Resurr Mirfield BA 16. d 16 p 17. C Hessle *York* 16–19; V from 19. *The Vicarage, 4 Chestnut Avenue, Hessle HU13 0RH* M: 07583-448163 E: darkangel@alias1.karoo.co.uk

TURNER, Geoffrey. b 51. Selw Coll Cam BA 75 MA 78 PGCE 84. NOC 90. d 93 p 94. C E Crompton *Man* 93–96; C Heywood St Luke w All Ss 96–98; TV Heywood 98–01; TR 01–08; TR Worsley 08–16; C Swinton H Rood 13–16; rtd

16; PtO *Carl* from 17. *25 Pear Tree Park, Holme, Carnforth LA6 1SD* E: gt1951@btinternet.com

TURNER, Geoffrey Edwin. b 45. Aston Univ BSc 68 Newc Univ MSc 69 PhD 72. Cranmer Hall Dur BA 74. d 75 p 76. C Wood End *Cov* 75–79; V Huyton Quarry *Liv* 79–86; Press and Communications Officer *Ely* 86–94; P-in-c Gt w Lt Abington 86–94; P-in-c Hildersham 86–94; V Letchworth St Paul w Willian *St Alb* 94–01; P-in-c Willingham *Ely* 01–02; R 02–08; P-in-c Rampton 01–02; R 02–08; rtd 08; PtO *Ripon* 09–14; *Leeds* from 14. *8 Wayside Crescent, Harrogate HG2 8NJ* T: (01423) 885668 E: geoffrey168@btinternet.com

TURNER, Geoffrey James. b 46. St Deiniol's Hawarden 85. d 87 p 88. C Loughor *S & B* 87–89; C Swansea St Pet 89–90; R New Radnor and Llanfihangel Nantmelan etc 90–96; V Ystalyfera 96–07; RD Cwmtawe 00–06; V Loughor 07–13; rtd 13; PtO *S & B* from 13. *35 Tawe Park, Ystradgynlais, Swansea SA9 1GU* T: (01639) 841760 E: geoffrey.turner2@sky.com

✠TURNER, The Rt Revd Geoffrey Martin. b 34. Oak Hill Th Coll 60. d 63 p 64 c 94. C Tonbridge St Steph *Roch* 63–66; C Heatherlands St Jo *Sarum* 66–69; V Derby St Pet 69–73; V Chadderton Ch Ch *Man* 73–79; R Bebington *Ches* 79–93; Hon Can Ches Cathl 89–93; RD Wirral N 89–93; Adn Ches 93–94; Suff Bp Stockport 94–00; rtd 00; PtO *Ches* 00–18; Hon Asst Bp Ches 02–18; PtO *Ex* from 16. *18 Gracey Court, Woodland Road, Broadclyst, Exeter EX5 3GA* T: (01392) 465269 E: geoff@theturners.eu

TURNER, Gerald Garth. b 38. Univ of Wales (Lamp) BA 61 St Edm Hall Ox BA 63 MA 67 Man Univ PhD 11. St Steph Ho Ox 63. d 65 p 66. C Drayton in Hales *Lich* 65–68; Chapl Prebendal Sch Chich 68–70; PV Chich Cathl 68–70; C Forest Row 70–72; V Hope *Derby* 72–78; Prec Man Cathl 78–86; Can Res Man Cathl 78–86; R Tattenhall and Handley *Ches* 86–04; rtd 04; PtO *S'well* 04–12; *Ches* from 15. *75 London Road, Nantwich CW5 6LN* T: (01270) 749415 E: ggarthturner@hotmail.com

TURNER, Mrs Heather Winifred. b 43. Open Univ BA 08 Win Univ MA 13 SRN 65. Cant Sch of Min 87. d 90 p 94. Par Dn Orpington All SS *Roch* 90–93; Chapl to the Deaf 93–00; P-in-c Wrotham 95–01; TV E Dereham and Scarning *Nor* 01–02; rtd 02; PtO *Nor* 02–04; C Darsham *St E* 04–06; C Middleton cum Fordley and Theberton w Eastbridge 04–06; C Westleton w Dunwich 04–06; C Yoxford, Peasenhall and Sibton 04–06; C Blyth Valley 06–07; TV 07; PtO 07–12; *Cov* 08–21; Chapl Shakespeare Hospice 14–15; PtO *Glouc* 16–17. *10 Pembroke Gardens, Wellesbourne, Warwick CV35 9PX* T: (01789) 842442 E: revhwturner@gmail.com

TURNER, James Alfred. b 34. MCIPS 76. Ox Min Course 91. d 94 p 95. NSM Kidlington w Hampton Poyle *Ox* 94–06; PtO 06–07. *11 St Mary's Close, Kidlington, Oxford OX5 2AY* T: (01865) 375562

TURNER, James Henry. b 51. NOC 99. d 02 p 03. NSM Middleton St Cross *Ripon* 02–13; Beeston *Leeds* 13–15; NSM Leeds Belle Is St Jo and St Barn 15–17; rtd 17; PtO *Leeds* from 17. *38 Acre Crescent, Middleton, Leeds LS10 4DJ* T: 0113-229 6865 E: jamesjpturner@aol.com

TURNER, Jane. *See* TURNER, Elizabeth Jane

TURNER, Jessica Mary. b 60. SS Coll Cam BA 81 PGCE 82. Trin Coll Bris 88. d 91 p 94. Par Dn Preston Em *Blackb* 91–94; C Bamber Bridge St Aid 94–95; Chapl Preston Acute Hosps NHS Trust 95–98; Chapl Blackpool Victoria Hosp NHS Trust 98–03; Hon Can Blackb Cathl 02–05; Chapl Ox Radcliffe Hosps NHS Trust 06–12; PtO *Ox* from 12. *33 Mayfield Road, Farmoor, Oxford OX2 9NY* T: (01865) 864435 M: 07966-016399 E: jessicatu196@gmail.com

TURNER, John William. b 43. Sheff Univ BSc 73. Wycliffe Hall Ox 86. d 88 p 89. C Clayton *Bradf* 88–91; C Horton 91–92; V Bankfoot 92–01; V Holland-on-Sea *Chelmsf* 01–05; rtd 05. *20 Grantley Drive, Harrogate HG3 2ST* T: (01423) 545994

TURNER, Canon Keith Howard. b 50. Southn Univ BA 71. Wycliffe Hall Ox 72. d 75 p 76. C Enfield Ch Ch Trent Park *Lon* 75–79; C Chilwell *S'well* 79–83; P-in-c Linby w Papplewick 83–90; R 90–15; Hon Can S'well Minster 02–13; rtd 15; PtO *S'well* from 15. *20 Northfield Avenue, Radcliffe-on-Trent, Nottingham NG12 2HX* T: 0115-933 1737 E: k.h.turner@btinternet.com

TURNER, Keith Stanley. b 51. ACIB 80. NTMTC 96. d 99 p 00. C S Hornchurch St Jo and St Matt *Chelmsf* 99–12; rtd 12; PtO *Chelmsf* 12–15; Hon C Romford Gd Shep from 15. *16 Wells Gardens, Rainham RM13 7LU* T: (01708) 554274 E: revkeitht@ntlworld.com

TURNER, Lorraine Elizabeth. b 67. Brunel Univ BSc 90 Open Univ MA 96 Anglia Ruskin Univ MA 10 DProf 17. Cranmer Hall Dur 01. d 03 p 04. C Birchwood *Linc* 03–06; TV Louth 06–14; P-in-c Legbourne and Wold Marsh 06–14; V 14–17; Chapl United Lincs Hosps NHS Trust 07–13; RD Louthesk

Linc 16–17; V Platt *Roch* from 17. *24 Maidstone Road, Borough Green, Sevenoaks TN15 8BD* E: rev.lorraine@btinternet.com

TURNER, Mark. b 60. Aston Tr Scheme 87 Sarum & Wells Th Coll BTh 92. **d** 92 **p** 93. C New Sleaford *Linc* 92–94; C Bottesford and Muston *Leic* 94–98; C Harby, Long Clawson and Hose 94–98; C Barkestone w Plungar, Redmile and Stathern 94–98; P-in-c Thurnby Lodge 98–00; C Aylestone Park CD 00–03; P-in-c Areley Kings *Worc* 03–05; R from 05; C Shrawley, Witley, Astley and Abberley from 15; RD Stourport 06–07 and 13–21. *14 Dunley Road, Stourport-on-Severn DY13 0AX* T: (01299) 829557 E: revmturner@tiscali.co.uk

TURNER, Mark Roy James. b 79. Ches Univ BTh 08 MA 19 Edge Hill Univ PGCE 10. All SS Cen for Miss & Min 13. **d** 15 **p** 16. NSM Burton and Shotwick *Ches* 15–16; NSM Eastham from 16; Chapl Birkenhead Sch from 17. *20 The Birches, Neston CH64 3SB* T: 0151-652 4014 M: 07493-793628 E: fathermarkturner@gmail.com *or* frmark.turner@birkenheadschool.co.uk

TURNER, Martin John. b 34. Trin Hall Cam BA 55 MA 59. Cuddesdon Coll 58. **d** 60 **p** 61. C Rugby St Andr *Cov* 60–65; C Cov Cathl 65–68; USA 68–70; V Rushmere *St E* 70–82; V Monkwearmouth St Pet *Dur* 82–90; V Bathford *B & W* 90–99; rtd 99; PtO *B & W* 00–07; *Truro* 97–16; *Newc* from 17. *30 Green Batt, Alnwick NE66 1TU* M: 07929-231167 E: turnerschemanoff@aol.com

TURNER, Mrs Maureen. Leeds Univ BA 78 MA 01. St Jo Coll Nottm 84. **d** 87 **p** 94. Par Dn Darlaston St Lawr *Lich* 87–91; C Stratford-on-Avon w Bishopton *Cov* 91–98; Chapl Myton Hamlet Hospice 98–01; NSM Leire w Ashby Parva and Dunton Bassett *Leic* 00–06; Chapl Team Ldr Univ Hosps Leic NHS Trust 01–07; Chapl Team Ldr Jersey Gp of Hosps 07–21; V Gt Coxwell w Buscot, Coleshill etc *Ox* from 21. *The Vicarage, Great Coxwell, Faringdon SN7 7NG* T: (01367) 240875

TURNER, Michael Andrew. b 34. K Coll Cam BA 59 MA 62. Cuddesdon Coll 59. **d** 61 **p** 62. C Luton St Andr *St Alb* 61–64; V 70–77; C-in-c Northolt St Jos *Lon* 64–70; Public Preacher *St Alb* 77–93; PtO *Lon* 85–93; Dep Hd and Chapl Greycoat Hosp Sch 85–93; P-in-c Shilling Okeford *Sarum* 93–99; Chapl Croft Ho Sch Shillingstone 93–99; Dioc Adv on New Relig Movements 97–12; rtd 99; PtO *Sarum* from 99; *Eur* from 99; V of the Close Sarum Cathl 02–07; Dioc Retirement Officer from 08. *12 Berkshire Road, Harnham, Salisbury SP2 8NY* T: (01722) 504000 E: sarum.turners@ntlworld.com

TURNER, Canon Michael John Royce. b 43. St Jo Coll Dur BA 65. Chich Th Coll 65. **d** 67 **p** 68. C Hodge Hill *Birm* 67–71; C Eling, Testwood and Marchwood *Win* 71–72; TV 72–77; R Kirkwall *Ab* 77–85; R Drumlithie *Bre* from 85; R Drumtochty from 85; R Fasque from 85; R Laurencekirk from 85; Hon Can St Paul's Cathl Dundee from 13. *Beattie Lodge, Laurencekirk AB30 1HJ* T/F: (01561) 377380 E: mjrturner@btinternet.com

TURNER, Canon Nicholas Anthony. b 51. Clare Coll Cam BA 73 MA 77 Keble Coll Ox BA 77 MA 81. Ripon Coll Cuddesdon 76. **d** 78 **p** 79. C Stretford St Matt *Man* 78–80; Tutor St Steph Ho Ox 80–84; V Leeds Richmond Hill *Ripon* 84–91; Offg Chapl RAF and V Ascension Is 91–96; Can Th St Helena Cathl from 94; V Raynes Park St Sav *S'wark* 96–01; P-in-c Broughton, Marton and Thornton *Bradf* 01–02; R 02–19; *Leeds* 14–19; rtd 19. *31 Raley Drive, Barnsley S75 1FL* T: (01226) 215826

TURNER (née SYMINGTON), Canon Patricia Ann. b 46. SRN 68 RMN 71 SCM 72. St Steph Ho Ox 82. **dss** 84 **d** 87. Buttershaw St Aid *Bradf* 84–87; TM Manningham 87–91; Ascension Is 91–96; Par Dn Raynes Park St Sav *S'wark* 96–01; Par Dn Broughton, Marton and Thornton *Bradf* 01–14; *Leeds* 14–19; AD Skipton 05–16; Assoc Dioc Dir of Ords *Bradf* 04–07; Dir of Ords 07–14; *Leeds* 14–16; Hon Can Bradf Cathl 09–16. *31 Raley Drive, Barnsley S75 1FL* T: (01226) 215826 E: canonannturner@gmail.com

TURNER, Peter Carpenter. b 39. Oak Hill Th Coll 63. **d** 66 **p** 67. C Chadwell *Chelmsf* 66–69; C Braintree 69–73; R Fyfield 73–87; P-in-c Moreton 77–83; P-in-c Fyfield and Moreton w Bobbingworth 83–87; C-in-c Bobbingworth 82–83; P-in-c Willingale w Shellow and Berners Roding 84–87; V E Ham St Geo 87–04; rtd 04; PtO *Lon* 05–20. *9 Llandovery House, Chipka Street, London E14 3LE* T: (020) 7987 5902

TURNER, The Ven Peter Robin. b 42. CB 98 DL 07. St Luke's Coll Ex PGCE 70 Open Univ BA 79 Westmr Coll Ox MTh 96 AKC 65. St Boniface Warminster 65. **d** 66 **p** 67. C Crediton *Ex* 66–69; PtO 69–70; Chapl RAF 70–88; Asst Chapl-in-Chief RAF 88–95; Chapl-in-Chief RAF 95–98; Can and Preb Linc Cathl 95–98; Chapl Dulwich Coll 98–02; Bp's Dom Chapl *S'well* 02–07; Hon Can S'well Minster 02–12; Chapl for Sector Min 07–12; rtd 12; QHC from 92; PtO *S'well* from

17. 12 Chimes Meadow, Southwell NG25 0GB T: (01636) 812250 M: 07890-633137 E: pr.turner1942@gmail.com

TURNER, Philip James. b 54. **d** 11 **p** 12. NSM Gt Sankey *Liv* 11–14; NSM Warrington W 14–15; Chapl Warrington and Halton Hosps NHS Foundn Trust from 14; NSM Gateacre *Liv* 15–19. *147 Cradley, Widnes WA8 7PN* T: 0151-424 0037 E: philip.turner4@nhs.net

TURNER, Ms Philippa Anne. b 64. Trevelyan Coll Dur BA 86 Yale Univ MDiv 88. **d** 94 **p** 95. Chapl New York Hosp USA 91–95; Assoc P New York Ch of Heavenly Rest 95–08; Chapl R Veterinary Coll *Lon* 08–17; Chapl R Free and Univ Coll Medical Sch 08–17; V Earl's Court Road St Phil from 17; PtO *St Alb* 12–17. *2 Pembroke Road, London W8 6NT* M: 07525-234382 E: pipturn@gmail.com

TURNER, Ricky Ronald. b 84. Middx Univ BA 05 Goldsmiths' Coll *Lon* PGCE 06. Qu Coll Birm 11. **d** 14 **p** 15. C Oxhey All SS *St Alb* 14–17; TV Dunstable from 17. *St Augustine's Vicarage, 83 Halfmoon Lane, Dunstable LU5 4AE* E: rickyturner@ntlworld.com

TURNER, Canon Roger Dyke. b 39. Trin Coll Bris 79. **d** 81 **p** 82. C Clevedon St Andr and Ch Ch *B & W* 81–85; R Freshford, Limpley Stoke and Hinton Charterhouse 85–88; V Kenilworth St Jo *Cov* 88–04; RD Kenilworth 90–98; Hon Can Cov Cathl 00–04; rtd 04; PtO *Birm* 04–05; *Cov* 04–21; P-in-c Barston *Birm* 05–11; PtO 12–18. *15 Caesar Road, Kenilworth CV8 1DL* T: (01926) 734330

TURNER, Ms Ruth Carpenter. b 63. Anglia Ruskin Univ BA 09 LLCM 83 GLCM 84. Ridley Hall Cam 07. **d** 09 **p** 10. C Brampton St Thos *Derby* 09–13; TV Dronfield w Holmesfield 13–18; C Battersea Fields *S'wark* from 18. *St Saviour's Vicarage, 351A Battersea Park Road, London SW11 4LH* M: 07855-714538 E: ruthturner2632@btinternet.com

TURNER, Stewart Gordon. b 54. Ex Univ BA 06. SWMTC 03. **d** 06 **p** 07. NSM Falmouth All SS *Truro* 06–09; C Mawnan 09–13; P-in-c 13–17; C Budock 09–13; P-in-c Constantine from 11. *The Vicarage, Chalbury Heights Brill, Constantine, Falmouth TR11 5UR* T: (01326) 340259 E: rev.stewart.turner@btinternet.com *or* rev.stewart@stconstantine.plus.com

TURNER (formerly BENBOW), Mrs Susan Catherine. b 47. Birm Univ BEd 70. St Alb Minl Tr Scheme 82. **dss** 85 **d** 87 **p** 94. Gt Wyrley *Lich* 85–87; Par Dn 87–88; Par Dn Whitstable *Cant* 88–92; Par Dn Eastry and Northbourne w Tilmanstone etc 92–94; C 94–96; P-in-c Gt Mongeham w Ripple and Sutton by Dover 96–98; rtd 98; PtO *Nor* 99–04; *Sarum* from 08. *9 Whitehill, Puddletown, Dorchester DT2 8SB* T: (01305) 849030 E: bands8turner@uwclub.net

TURNER, Sylvia Jean. b 46. Lon Univ 72 Open Univ BA 77. Westcott Ho Cam 93. **d** 95 **p** 96. C Whitstable *Cant* 95–99; R Wigmore Abbey *Heref* 99–09; P-in-c Pontesbury I and II 09–11; rtd 11; PtO *Heref* from 11. *Wheelwrights, Witton, Ludlow SY8 3DB* T: (01584) 890586 M: 07773-036994 E: sylviaturner812@btinternet.com

TURNER, Valerie Kay. b 50. SS Paul & Mary Coll Cheltenham BEd 72. WMMTC 97 Wycliffe Hall Ox 99. **d** 00 **p** 01. C Cheltenham St Luke and St Jo *Glouc* 00–04; P-in-c Forest of Dean Ch Ch w English Bicknor 04–12; P-in-c Lydbrook 04–05; rtd 12; PtO *Heref* from 12. *2 River Meadows, Hereford HR1 1TB* T: (01432) 273697

TURNER, Vivien Andree Elizabeth. b 53. **d** 13 **p** 17. NSM Banstead *Guildf* 13–18; P-in-c Graffham w Woolavington *Chich* from 18. *The Rectory, Graffham, Petworth GU28 0NL* E: reverendvivien@gmail.com

TURNER-CALLIS, Mrs Gillian Ruth. b 79. Aber Univ BD 03. Wycliffe Hall Ox MTh 05. **d** 05 **p** 06. C Shepshed and Oaks in Charnwood *Leic* 05–08; TR Kegworth, Hathern, Long Whatton, Diseworth etc 08–15; R W Hallam and Mapperley w Stanley *Derby* from 15; Asst Dir of Ords 18–19; Dep Dioc Dir of Ords from 19. *The Rectory, The Village, West Hallam, Ilkeston DE7 6GR* T: (01332) 388672 *or* 0115-932 4695 M: 07838-881307 E: gill.turner-callis@derby.anglican.org

TURNER-LOISEL, Canon Elizabeth Anne. b 57. Lanc Univ BA 79 MA 80 York Univ PGCE 81. EMMTC 96. **d** 99 **p** 00. Chapl Nat Sch Hucknall 99–04; P-in-c Annesley w Newstead *S'well* 04–11; V 11–14; Hon Can S'well Minster 13–14; V Hatfield *Sheff* from 14; AD Snaith and Hatfield 14–19. *The Vicarage, 2 Vicarage Close, Hatfield, Doncaster DN7 6HN* T: (01302) 459110 E: revd.liz@gmail.com *or* liz.turner-loisel@sheffield.anglican.org

TURNHAM, Mrs Dominique Emma. b 90. Homerton Coll Cam BA 11 MA 15. St Steph Ho Ox 13. **d** 15 **p** 16. C Dereham and Distr *Nor* 15–20. *Glenholme, 11 Brunswick Road, Norwich NR2 2HA* T: (01362) 697388 M: 07788-278460 E: dominiqueturnham@gmail.com

TURNOCK, Geoffrey. b 38. Leeds Univ BSc 61 PhD 64 MSOSc. EMMTC 84. **d** 87 **p** 88. NSM Oadby *Leic* 87–00; NSM Okeford

Sarum 00–04; PtO 04–18. *10 Billingsmoor Lane, Poundbury, Dorchester DT1 3WT* T: (01305) 757177

TURP, Paul Robert. b 48. Oak Hill Th Coll BA 79. **d** 79 **p** 80. C Southall Green St Jo *Lon* 79–83; V Shoreditch St Leon w St Mich 83–88 and 00–18; TR Shoreditch St Leon and Hoxton St Jo 88–00; rtd 18. *148 Woodcock Road, Norwich NR3 3TA* T: (01603) 418116 E: p.turp48@btinternet.com

TURPIN, Christine Lesley. *See* DICKSON, Christine Lesley

TURPIN, Canon John Richard. b 41. St D Coll Lamp BA 63 Magd Coll Cam BA 65 MA 70. Cuddesdon Coll 65. **d** 66 **p** 67. C Tadley St Pet *Win* 66–71; V Southampton Thornhill St Chris 71–85; V Ringwood 85–10; Hon Can Win Cathl 99–10; rtd 10; PtO *Win* 10–19. *111 Beaufort Road, Bournemouth BH6 5AU* T: (01202) 421321 E: john.turpin4@btinternet.com

TURPIN, Raymond Gerald. b 35. **d** 97 **p** 98. OLM Brockley Hill St Sav *S'wark* 97–05; PtO from 05; Retirement Officer Woolwich Area from 08. *60 Bankhurst Road, London SE6 4XN* T: (020) 8690 6877 *or* 8311 2000 E: rayturpin@talktalk.net

TURRELL, Peter Charles Morphett. b 47. **d** 01 **p** 02. NSM Carshalton Beeches *S'wark* 01–15; PtO from 15. *2 Stanley Park Road, Carshalton SM5 3HW* T: (020) 8669 0318 E: peterturrell@btinternet.com

TURRELL, Stephen John. b 35. S'wark Ord Course. **d** 83 **p** 84. NSM W Wickham St Jo *Cant* 83–84; NSM Addington *S'wark* 85–92; NSM Blendworth w Chalton w Idsworth *Portsm* 92–97; PtO 97–01; NSM Storrington *Chich* 01–06; rtd 06; PtO *Chich* 13–17; *B & W* from 19. *38 Beaconfield Road, Yeovil BA20 2JN* T: (01935) 479196 E: turrell567@gmail.com

TURTLE, Jessica Ellen. b 75. St Mellitus Coll 15. **d** 17 **p** 18. NSM Bagshot *Guildf* from 17. *1 The Mount, Trumpsgreen Road, Virginia Water GU25 4EJ*

TURTON, Douglas Walter. b 38. Kent Univ BA 77 Surrey Univ MSc 90 Univ of Wales (Ban) PhD 04 Glyndŵr Univ DMin 16 CQSW 70. Oak Hill Th Coll 77. **d** 78 **p** 79. C Cant St Mary Bredin 78–80; P-in-c Thornton Heath St Paul 80–81; V 81–84; V Thornton Heath St Paul *S'wark* 85–91; R Eastling w Ospringe and Stalisfield w Otterden *Cant* 91–00; rtd 00; PtO *Cant* from 13. *16 Weatherall Close, Dunkirk, Faversham ME13 9UL* T: (01227) 752244

TURVILLE, Mrs Janet Elizabeth. b 59. Matlock Coll of Educn BEd 82. Ripon Coll Cuddesdon 11. **d** 12 **p** 13. C Wirksworth *Derby* 12–16; P-in-c Walton-on-Trent w Croxall, Rosliston etc 16–17; P-in-c Stapenhill Immanuel 16–17; C Seale and Lullington w Coton in the Elms 16–17; TV Louth *Linc* 17–19; V Painswick, Sheepscombe, Cranham, The Edge etc *Glouc* from 19. *The Vicarage, Orchard Mead, Painswick, Stroud GL6 6YD* M: 07710-550396 E: janetturville@hotmail.co.uk *or* janetbeacon6@gmail.com

TUSCHLING, Ruth Mary Magdalen. b 65. Freiburg Univ MA 94 CCC Cam PhD 04. Westcott Ho Cam BA 97. **d** 98 **p** 99. C Hampstead St Jo *Lon* 98–01; PtO *Ely* 02–04; OSB 04–08; Warden Offa Retreat Ho and Dioc Spirituality Adv *Cov* 08–12; Dioc Spirituality Adv *Portsm* from 12. *50 Penny Street, Portsmouth PO1 2NL* T: (023) 9281 5044 E: ruth.tuschling@portsmouth.anglican.org

✠**TUSTIN, The Rt Revd David.** b 35. Magd Coll Cam BA 57 MA 61 Lambeth DD 98. Cuddesdon Coll 58. **d** 60 **p** 61 **c** 79. C Stafford St Mary *Lich* 60–63; C St Dunstan in the West *Lon* 63–67; Asst Gen Sec C of E Coun on Foreign Relns 63–67; V Wednesbury St Paul Wood Green *Lich* 67–71; V Tettenhall Regis 71–79; RD Trysull 76–79; Suff Bp Grimsby *Linc* 79–00; Can and Preb Linc Cathl 79–00; rtd 00; Hon Asst Bp Linc from 01. *The Ashes, Tunnel Road, Wrawby, Brigg DN20 8SF* T/F: (01652) 655584 E: tustindavid@hotmail.com

TUTTON, Jeffrey Richard. b 64. St Aug Coll of Th 14. **d** 17 **p** 18. NSM Ore Ch Ch *Chich* 17–19; NSM Battle 19–20. *Timber House, Main Street, Northiam, Rye TN31 6NB*

TUTTON, Canon John Knight. b 30. Man Univ BSc 51. Ripon Hall Ox 53. **d** 55 **p** 56. C Tonge w Alkrington *Man* 55–57; C Bushbury *Lich* 57–59; R Blackley St Andr *Man* 59–67; R Denton Ch Ch 67–95; Hon Can Man Cathl 90–95; rtd 95; Hon C Exminster and Kenn *Ex* 96–01; PtO 01–19. *Gracey Court, Woodland Road, Broadclyst, Exeter EX5 3GA* T: (01392) 468673 E: johnktutton@hotmail.com

TWEDDLE, David William Joseph. b 28. Dur Univ BSc 50 Open Univ BA 97 ATCL 56. Wycliffe Hall Ox 54. **d** 56 **p** 57. C Darlington H Trin *Dur* 56–60; P-in-c Prestonpans *Edin* 60–63; PV Linc Cathl 63–65; C Pet St Jo 65–71; Hon Min Can Pet Cathl 68–93; V Southwick w Glapthorn 71–83; P-in-c Benefield 80–83; R Benefield and Southwick w Glapthorn 83–93; RD Oundle 84–89; rtd 94; PtO *Ely* 94–07. *6 Barton Square, Ely CB7 4DF* T: (01353) 614393

TWEED, Andrew. b 48. Univ of Wales (Cardiff) BA 69 Trin Coll Carmarthen MA 97. St Deiniol's Hawarden. **d** 81 **p** 84.

NSM Llandrindod w Cefnllys *S & B* 81–86; NSM Llandrindod w Cefnllys and Disserth 87–15; NSM Glan Ithon 15–18; PtO from 18. *Gwenallt, Wellington Road, Llandrindod Wells LD1 5NB* T: (01597) 823671 E: andrewtweed1@aol.com

TWEEDIE-SMITH, Ian David. b 60. Newc Univ BA 83. Wycliffe Hall Ox 83. **d** 85 **p** 86. C Hatcham St Jas *S'wark* 85–89; C Bury St Edmunds St Mary *St E* 89–02; TV Woking St Pet *Guildf* 02–12; P-in-c Purton *Bris* 12–14; V from 14. *The Vicarage, 2 Kingsacre, Hyde Lane, Purton, Swindon SN5 4DU* T: (01793) 770077 E: vicarage@stmaryspurton.org.uk

TWEEDY, Andrew Cyril Mark. b 61. Man Univ BA(Econ) 81. SAOMC 98. **d** 01 **p** 02. C Carterton *Ox* 01–03; C Brize Norton and Carterton 03–04; V Bromham w Oakley and Stagsden *St Alb* 04–08; Chapl Barcelona *Eur* 08–14; R Lower Windrush *Ox* 14–19; TR Brize Norton and Carterton from 19. *The Rectory, 6 Burford Road, Carterton OX18 3AA* E: revdrew61@gmail.com

TWEEDY, Richard Walpole. b 67. **d** 12 **p** 13. C Worcs W Rural *Worc* 12–16; V Polden Wheel *B & W* from 16. *The Vicarage, Vicarage Lane, Shapwick, Bridgwater TA7 9LR* T: (01458) 211098 E: vicar@poldenwheel.co.uk

TWIDELL, Canon William James. b 30. St Mich Coll Llan 58. **d** 60 **p** 61. C Tonge w Alkrington *Man* 60–63; C High Wycombe All SS *Ox* 63–65; P-in-c Elkesley w Bothamsall *S'well* 65–66; V Bury St Thos *Man* 66–72; V Daisy Hill 72–84; R Flixton St Mich 84–00; AD Stretford 88–98; Hon Can Man Cathl 97–00; rtd 00; PtO *Man* from 00; *Ches* 00–10. *20 Denehyrst Court, York Road, Guildford GU1 4EA* T: (01483) 673280 M: 07534-462048

TWIGG (née LATKA), Mrs Allison. b 70. Nene Coll Northn BEd 93. Ripon Coll Cuddesdon 13. **d** 15 **p** 16. C Weston Favell *Pet* 15–18; C Guilsborough and Hollowell and Cold Ashby etc 18–20; R from 20. *The Vicarage, 2 Church Road, Spratton, Northampton NN6 8HR* T: (01604) 846099 M: 07759-835011 E: revallisontwigg@gmail.com

TWIGG, Mrs Joanne Mary. b 72. Luton Univ BA 94. St Hild Coll 18. **d** 20. C Penistone and Thurlstone *Sheff* from 20. *56 Folly Way, Barnsley S71 2SP* T: (01226) 210479 M: 07956-514756 E: jotwigg@hotmail.co.uk

TWINE, Mrs Jacqueline Ann. b 64. Middx Univ BA 11. Ripon Coll Cuddesdon 15. **d** 18 **p** 19. C Southsea St Luke and St Pet *Portsm* from 18. *68 Court Lane, Portsmouth PO6 2LR* T: (023) 9279 6318 M: 07922-867552 E: jackie.curate@stlukessouthsea.church

TWINLEY, Canon David Alan. b 66. Ox Univ BTh 00 Heythrop Coll Lon MA 10. St Steph Ho Ox 97. **d** 00 **p** 01. C Saffron Walden w Wendens Ambo, Littlebury etc *Chelmsf* 00–03; V Bury w Houghton and Coldwaltham and Hardham *Chich* 03–16; RD Petworth 10–16; V Arundel w Tortington and S Stoke from 16; Can and Preb Chich Cathl from 19. *The Vicarage, 26 Maltravers Street, Arundel BN18 9BU* T: (01903) 885209 E: frdavid@twinley.me.uk *or* vicar@stnicholas-arundel.co.uk

TWISLETON, John Fiennes. b 48. St Jo Coll Ox BA 69 MA 73 DPhil 73. Coll of Resurr Mirfield 73. **d** 76 **p** 77. C New Bentley *Sheff* 76–79; P-in-c Moorends 79–80; V 80–86; USPG 86–90; Prin Alan Knight Tr Cen Guyana 87–90; V Holbrooks *Cov* 90–96; Edmonton Area Missr *Lon* 96–01; Dioc Adv for Miss and Renewal *Chich* 01–09; C Haywards Heath St Rich 01–09; R Horsted Keynes 09–17; rtd 17; PtO *Chich* from 17; *Lon* from 21. *3 Marylands, New England Road, Haywards Heath RH16 3JZ* E: john@twisleton.co.uk

TWISS, Dorothy Elizabeth. Gilmore Ho 68 Linc Th Coll 70. **d** 87 **p** 94. Chapl Asst RAF 78–91; TV Pewsey *Sarum* 91–95; Chapl HM Pris Drake Hall 95–01; Chapl HM Pris Ford 01–03; rtd 03; PtO *Portsm* from 05. *41 Rosecott, Havant Road, Horndean, Waterlooville PO8 0XA* M: 07929-650284 E: dorothy.twiss371@btinternet.com

TWITCHEN, Ruth Kathleen Frances. *See* BUSHYAGER, Ruth Kathleen Frances

TWITTY, Miss Rosamond Jane. b 54. Univ of Wales (Ban) BSc 75 CertEd 76. Trin Coll Bris BA 89. **d** 90 **p** 94. Par Dn Lt Thurrock St Jo *Chelmsf* 90–94; C 94–95; C Upper Armley *Ripon* 95–08; TV Langport Area *B & W* 08–14; C 14–17; V Levels Arc 17–20; rtd 20. *16 Tyndale Road, Gloucester GL3 3PH* E: jane.twitty@btinternet.com

TWOMEY, David James Benedict. b 87. Sheff Univ BSc 08 Northumbria Univ PGCE 09. **d** 14 **p** 15. C Cullercoats St Geo *Newc* 14–18; P-in-c Seaton Hirst from 18. *St John's Vicarage, Newbiggin Road, Ashington NE63 0TQ* E: david.twomey@ymail.com

TYDEMAN, Rosemary. *See* WILLIAMS, Rosemary

TYE, Eric John. b 37. St Alb Minl Tr Scheme 78. **d** 81 **p** 82. NSM Rushden St Mary w Newton Bromswold *Pet* 81–07; PtO from 07. *29 Kingsmead Park, Bedford Road, Rushden NN10 0NF* T: (01933) 353274

TYE, John Raymond. b 31. Lambeth STh 64 Linc Th Coll 66. **d** 68 **p** 69. C Crewe St Mich *Ches* 68–71; C Wednesfield St Thos *Lich* 71–76; P-in-c Petton w Cockshutt 76–79; P-in-c Hordley 79; P-in-c Weston Lullingfield 79; R Petton w Cockshutt and Weston Lullingfield etc 79–81; V Hadley 81–84; R Ightfield w Calverhall 84–89; V Ash 84–89; R Calton, Cauldon, Grindon and Waterfall 89–96; RD Alstonfield 95–96; rtd 96; PtO *Lich* 05–14. *38 Aston Street, Wem, Shrewsbury SY4 5AU* T: (01939) 236218

TYERS, Philip Nicolas. b 56. Univ of Wales (Lamp) MA 04. St Jo Coll Nottm BTh 84. **d** 84 **p** 85. C Rugby St Matt *Cov* 84–88; TV Cov E 88–95; P-in-c Preston St Matt *Blackb* 95–96; TR Preston Risen Lord 96–06; Co-ord Chapl HM Pris Leeds 06–07; Co-ord Chapl HM Pris Wymott 07–16; Chapl HM Pris Liv from 16; PtO *Blackb* from 16. *Chaplain's Office, HM Prison, 68 Hornby Road, Liverpool L9 3DF* T: 0151-530 4000 E: ptyers@outlook.com *or* philip.tyers@justice.gov.uk

TYLDESLEY, Mrs Vera. b 47. Man Coll of Educn BEd 80. **d** 98 **p** 99. OLM Pendlebury St Jo *Man* 98–17; rtd 17; PtO *Man* from 17. *7 Kingsway, Swinton, Manchester M27 4JU* T: 0161-736 3845 E: vera.tyldesley4@ntlworld.com

TYLER, Canon Alan William. b 60. Ridley Hall Cam 84. **d** 86 **p** 87. C Bedwellty *Mon* 86–89; C St Mellons and Michaelston-y-Fedw 89–92; V Abersychan and Garndiffaith 92–97; Chapl Glan Hafren NHS Trust 97–99; Sen Chapl Gwent Healthcare NHS Trust from 99; Can St Woolos Cathl *Mon* from 08. *Chaplaincy Office, The Royal Gwent Hospital, Cardiff Road, Newport NP20 2UB* T: (01633) 234263 *or* 871457 E: alan.tyler@wales.nhs.uk

TYLER, Alison Ruth. b 51. Keele Univ BA 74 CQSW 78. S'wark Ord Course 93. **d** 95 **p** 96. NSM Hatcham St Cath *S'wark* 95–99; Dep Chapl HM Pris Brixton 99–02; Chapl HM Pris Wormwood Scrubs 02–07; Learning and Development Manager HM Pris Service Chapl 07–15; Hon Min Can S'wark Cathl from 06; PtO from 06; *Cov* 08–15. *Address withheld by request* E: ar.tyler@ntlworld.com

TYLER, Andrew. Univ of Wales (Lamp) BA 79 Warw Univ MA 80 Leeds Univ BA 85 Man Univ BD 86. Coll of Resurr Mirfield 83. **d** 87 **p** 88. C Glen Parva and S Wigston *Leic* 87–90; C Didcot All SS *Ox* 90–92; Asst Chapl Chu Hosp Ox 92–93; NSM Caversham St Andr *Ox* 93–97; Co-ord Tr Portfolio (Berks) 96–97; P-in-c Nor St Giles 97–99; P-in-c Nor St Mary Magd w St Jas 99–00; V 00–08; Hon C Eaton Ch Ch 09–12; Discipleship and Lay Ministry Development Officer *Linc* 09–12; PtO 09–12; C Cawston w Booton and Brandiston etc *Nor* 12–15; PtO from 15; P-in-c Ipswich All Hallows *St E* 17–18; Dir St Marylebone Healing and Counselling Cen from 18; PtO *Sarum* from 20. *Address withheld by request* M: 07768-581679 E: xatyler@aol.com

TYLER, Benjamin David Scott. b 88. Coll of Resurr Mirfield BA 20. **d** 20 **p** 21. C Wantage *Ox* from 20. *5 Barnard's Way, Wantage OX12 7EA* M: 07505-650754

TYLER, Capt Christopher Paul. b 54. Brighton Univ BA 11. CA Tr Coll 84. **d** 17 **p** 18. C Lavenham w Preston *St E* 17–20; P-in-c Birkby and Woodhouse *Leeds* from 20. *Address temp unknown* E: cpaultyler@hotmail.com

TYLER, Canon David Stuart. b 69. Hull Univ BSc 91 ACA 94. Wycliffe Hall Ox 01. **d** 03 **p** 04. C Ashby-de-la-Zouch St Helen w Coleorton *Leic* 03–05; C Ashby-de-la-Zouch and Breedon on the Hill 05–07; P-in-c Hanborough and Freeland *Ox* 07–11; R 11–20; AD Woodstock 12–17 and 18–20; Asst Adn Dorchester 18–20; Assoc Adn from 20; Hon Can Ch Ch from 20. *39 The Motte, Abingdon OX14 3NZ* M: 07961-726403 E: david.tyler@oxford.anglican.org

TYLER (née FOSTER), Mrs Frances Elizabeth. b 55. Linc Th Coll 81. **dss** 84 **d** 87 **p** 94. Hampton All SS *Lon* 84–87; Par Dn Brentford 87–91; NSM Walsgrave on Sowe *Cov* 91–21; Dioc Adv for Women's Min 97–05; Chapl S Warks NHS Foundn Trust 06–20; rtd 20; PtO *Cov* from 21. *The Vicarage, 4 Farber Road, Coventry CV2 2BG* T: (024) 7661 5152 E: frances.e.tyler@gmail.com

TYLER, Mrs Gaynor. b 46. Univ of Wales (Abth) BA 68. S'wark Ord Course 87. **d** 90 **p** 94. NSM Reigate St Luke S Park *S'wark* 90–97; Deanery NSM Maelienydd *S & B* 97–04; NSM Cwmdauddwr w St Harmon and Llanwrthwl 04–05; NSM Llanwrthwl w St Harmon, Rhayader, Nantmel etc 05–06; PtO from 06. *Dyffryn Farm, Llanwrthwl, Llandrindod Wells LD1 6NU* T: (01597) 811017

TYLER, John Thorne. b 46. Selw Coll Cam BA 68 MA 71. Sarum & Wells Th Coll 70. **d** 72 **p** 73. C Frome St Jo *B & W* 72–74; Chapl Richard Huish Coll Taunton 74–93; Hon C Stoke St Gregory w Burrowbridge and Lyng *B & W* 77–93; P-in-c Shepton Beauchamp w Barrington, Stocklinch etc 93–94; TV Ilminster and Distr 94–98; rtd 99; Hon C Quantock Towers *B & W* 99–01; P-in-c Stogursey w Fiddington 01–06; PtO 06–09; C Chard St Mary w Combe St Nicholas,

Wambrook etc 09–10; PtO from 11. *4 Summerlands Park Drive, Ilminster TA19 9BN* E: tyleruk@tiscali.co.uk

TYLER, Malcolm. b 56. Kent Univ BSc 77 Cam Univ BA 84. Ridley Hall Cam 82. **d** 85 **p** 86. C Twickenham St Mary *Lon* 85–88; C Acton St Mary 88–91; V Walsgrave on Sowe *Cov* from 91; AD Cov E 07–14; Assoc Dioc Dir of Ords from 15. *The Vicarage, 4 Farber Road, Coventry CV2 2BG* T: (024) 7661 5152 *or* 7661 8845 E: stmaryssowe@aol.com

TYLER, Paul. *See* TYLER, Christopher Paul

TYLER, Canon Paul Graham Edward. b 58. St Jo Coll Dur BA 79 Dur Univ PGCE 93. Cranmer Hall Dur 81. **d** 83 **p** 84. C Stranton *Dur* 83–86; C Collierley w Annfield Plain 86–89; V Esh and Hamsteels 89–92; Chapl HM Pris Frankland 09–16; NSM Cornforth and Ferryhill *Dur* from 16; Hon Can Dur Cathl from 16. *Address withheld by request* E: pgetyler@hotmail.com

TYNDALL, Canon Daniel Frank. b 61. Aston Tr Scheme 90 Sarum & Wells Th Coll BTh 93. **d** 93 **p** 94. C Wolverhampton *Lich* 93–96; C Bris St Mary Redcliffe w Temple etc 96–01; V Earley St Nic *Ox* 01–08; P-in-c Caversham St Pet and Mapledurham 08–10; P-in-c Caversham Thameside and Mapledurham 10–13; R Caversham Thameside and Mapledurham 10–13; V Bris St Mary Redcliffe w Temple etc from 13; Hon Can Bris Cathl from 19. *The Vicarage, 10 Redcliffe Parade West, Bristol BS1 6SP* T: 0117-231 0060 M: 07769-296220 E: dan.tyndall@stmaryredcliffe.co.uk

TYNDALL, Jeremy Hamilton. b 55. Birm Univ MPhil 01. St Jo Coll Nottm BTh 81 LTh 81. **d** 81 **p** 82. C Oakwood St Thos *Lon* 81–84; C Upper Holloway St Pet w St Jo 84–87; TV Halewood *Liv* 87–96; P-in-c Yardley St Edburgha *Birm* 96–99; V 99–01; R Eugene St Thos USA 01–08; Dean Cen Convocation 06–08; TR Cove St Jo *Guildf* 08–17; rtd 17; PtO *Newc* from 18. *1 Chevington Green, Hadston, Morpeth NE65 9AX* T: (01670) 946713 M: 07854-595129 E: jeremytyndall@hotmail.com

TYNDALL, Samuel Michael. b 87. York Univ BA 08. Yorks Min Course BA 16. **d** 16 **p** 17. C Linthorpe *York* 16–19; 20s-40s Team Ldr from 19; C Marton-in-Cleveland 19–21; C Marton-in-Cleveland w Easterside from 21. *Parish Centre, Stokesley Road, Marton-in-Cleveland, Middlesbrough TS7 8JU* M: 07562-593474 E: sam@stcuthbertmarton.org.uk

TYNDALL, Simon James. b 54. LSE BSc(Econ) 77 Open Univ MA 98 Lon Univ PGCE 82. St Jo Coll Nottm 88. **d** 90 **p** 91. C Yeovil w Kingston Pitney *B & W* 90–94; V Rastrick St Jo *Wakef* 94–01; TR Chippenham St Paul w Hardenhuish etc *Bris* 01–13; V Kington St Michael 01–13; AD Chippenham 08–13; Hon Can Bris Cathl 11–13; Chapl Tervuren *Eur* 13–19; rtd 19; PtO *Eur* from 20; Win from 20. *The Coach House, 11 McKinley Road, Bournemouth BH4 8AG* T: (01202) 778164 E: simonjtyndall@gmail.com

TYNDALL, Canon Timothy Gardner. b 25. Jes Coll Cam BA 50. Wells Th Coll 50. **d** 51 **p** 52. C Warsop *S'well* 51–55; R Newark St Leon 55–60; V Sherwood 60–75; P-in-c Bishopwearmouth St Mich w St Hilda *Dur* 75–85; RD Wearmouth 75–85; Hon Can Dur Cathl 83–90; Chief Sec ACCM 85–90; rtd 90; PtO *Lon* 90–18; S'wark 90–11. *Flat 16, 2B Bollo Lane, London W4 5LE* T: (020) 8994 4516

TYRER, Ms Jayne Linda. b 59. Goldsmiths' Coll Lon BA 81 CertEd 82. Sarum & Wells Th Coll 85. **d** 87 **p** 95. C Rochdale *Man* 87–88; Par Dn Heywood St Luke w All So 88–91; Hon Par Dn Burneside *Carl* 91–07; Hon Par Dn Beacon TM 07–20; Chapl Kendal Hosp 91–94; Chapl Westmorland Hosps NHS Trust 94–98; Chapl Univ Hosps of Morecambe Bay NHS Foundn Trust 98–20. *68A The Close, Salisbury SP1 2EL*

TYRER, Neil. *See* PURVEY-TYRER, Neil

TYRÉUS, Per Jonas Waldemar (Peter). b 45. Uppsala Univ 66. **p** 71. Sweden 71–00; C Pelton *Dur* 00–03; C Chester le Street 03–11; rtd 11. *27 Castle Riggs, Chester le Street DH2 2DL* E: petertyreus@googlemail.com

TYRRELL, John Patrick Hammond. b 42. Cranmer Hall Dur 62. **d** 65 **p** 66. C Edin St Jo 65–68; Chapl RN 68–72; Chapl St Jo Cathl Hong Kong 72–74; V Westborough *Guildf* 74–78; P-in-c Em Ch Pok Fu Lam Hong Kong and Area Sec SE Asia SOMA UK 78–82; C Yateley *Win* 82–83; C-in-c Darby Green CD 83–88; V Darby Green 88–96; V Chineham 96–97; rtd 02; PtO *Linc* from 06. *5 Blacksmith's Court, Metheringham, Lincoln LN4 3YQ* T: (01526) 322147 E: john_tyrrell42@hotmail.com

TYRRELL, Martyn Christopher. b 79. Trin Coll Bris 15. **d** 17 **p** 18. C Shirwell, Loxhore, Kentisbury, Arlington, etc *Ex* from 17. *The Rectory, Shirwell, Barnstaple EX31 4JU* T: (01271) 850844 E: martyntyrrell@hotmail.com

TYRRELL, Stephen Jonathan. b 39. Sheff Univ BA 62. Clifton Th Coll. **d** 65 **p** 66. C Rodbourne Cheney *Bris* 65–68; C Lillington *Cov* 68–72; P-in-c Bishop's Itchington 73–78; V 78–86; V Kingston upon Hull St Nic *York* 86–92; TV Cheltenham St Mary, St Matt, St Paul and H Trin *Glouc*

92–04; rtd 04; PtO *Glouc* from 05. *96A Fosseway Avenue, Moreton-in-Marsh GL56 0EA* T: (01608) 812350

TYSON, Mrs Frances Mary. b 44. Reading Univ BScAgr 68 Wolv Univ PGCE 91. St Jo Coll Nottm 01. **d** 02 **p** 03. NSM Walsall *Lich* 02–07; NSM Portswood Ch Ch *Win* 07–19; rtd 19; PtO *Win* from 19. *26 Reynolds Road, Southampton SO15 5GS*

TYSON, Jacqueline. b 56. **d** 16 **p** 17. NSM Wearmouth Deanery from 16; NSM Sunderland Minster *Dur* from

17. *Address withheld by request* M: 07866-426177 E: revjacquityson@sunderlandminster.org

TYSON, Mrs Nigella Jane. b 44. RGN 66 Kent Univ BA 95. SEITE 96. **d** 97 **p** 98. NSM Aylesham w Adisham, Nonington w Wymynswold and Goodnestone etc *Cant* 97–00; P-in-c Kingsland w Eardisland, Aymestrey etc *Heref* 00–04; R 04–09; rtd 09; PtO *Heref* from 10. *Fairview, Stoke Prior, Leominster HR6 0NE* T: (01568) 760610 E: revnigella@sky.com

U

UDAL, Canon Joanna Elizabeth Margaret. b 64. SS Hild & Bede Coll Dur BSc 86. Ripon Coll Cuddesdon BTh 94. **d** 97 **p** 98. C Whitton St Aug *Lon* 97–00; Asst to Abp Sudan 00–09; Abp's Sec for Angl Communion Affairs *Cant* 09–14; Hon Min Can S'wark Cathl from 11; PtO from 11; *Eur* 18–20; Sen Chapl Oslo w Bergen, Trondheim and Stavanger from 20; Can Juba S Sudan from 07. *Harald Hårfagresgt 2, 0363 Oslo, Norway* T: (0047) 2269 2214 M: (0047) 9947 2987 E: oslochaplain@osloanglicans.com

UDDIN, Mohan. b 52. Sussex Univ BA 74 PGCE 75 Lon Bible Coll MA 87 PhD 98 Anglia Poly Univ MA 02 Southn Univ MA 15. Ridley Hall Cam 99. **d** 03 **p** 04. C Hornchurch St Andr *Chelmsf* 03–07; PtO 08–11; *Win* 09–12; TV Newbury *Ox* 10–13; rtd 13; PtO *Win* from 13. *247 Oceana Boulevard, Lower Canal Walk, Southampton SO14 3JG* M: 07515-386301 E: mohan.uddin@btopenworld.com

UFFINDELL, Harold David. b 61. Down Coll Cam MA 87. Wycliffe Hall Ox BA 86 MA 91 Oak Hill Th Coll 86. **d** 87 **p** 88. C Kingston Hill St Paul *S'wark* 87–91; C Surbiton St Matt 91–98; V Sunningdale *Ox* 98–16; P-in-c Bracknell 15–16; AD 12–15; R Farnham *Guildf* from 16. *The Rectory, Upper Church Lane, Farnham GU9 7PW* T: (01252) 710129 E: daviduffindell@btconnect.com or rector@standrewsfarnham.org

UGWUNNA, The Ven Sydney Chukwunma. b 45. Nebraska Wesleyan Univ BSc 67 Univ of Nebraska, Linc MSc 70 Wayne State Univ PhD 79. Virginia Th Sem MDiv 96. **d** 96 **p** 97. C Alexandria Resurrection USA 96–97; C Knaresborough *Ripon* 98–02; Dean Trin Th Coll and Adn Umuahia Nigeria 03–06; R Alexandria Meade Memorial Ch USA 06–08; Visiting P Washington Cathl 09–10; R Earleville St Steph 10–11. *189 New Haw Road, Addlestone KT15 2DP*

ULOGWARA, Canon Obinna Chiadikobi. b 68. Univ of Nigeria BA(Ed) 98 Lagos Univ MEd 03. Trin Coll Umuahia 87. **d** 90 **p** 91. V Ahiara H Trin Nigeria 90–05; Chapl Secondary Schs Dio Mbaise 90–93; V Irete St Pet 93–95; Chapl Secondary Schs Dio Owerri 94–99; V Egbeada Em 99; V Sari Iganmu St Phil 00–01; V Igbobi St Steph 01–05; Hon Chapl to Abp Lagos 01–05; C Dublin Whitechurch *D & G* 05–10; Bp's C Dublin St Geo and St Thos 10–17. *96 Lower Drumcondra Road, Dublin 9, Republic of Ireland* M: (00353) 87-247 6339 E: binagwara@yahoo.com

UMPLEBY, Canon Mark Raymond. b 70. Trin Coll Bris BA 99. **d** 99 **p** 00. C Birstall *Wakef* 99–02; TV N Huddersfield 02–06; Dioc Voc Adv 04–06; Chapl David Young Community Academy Leeds 06–13; PtO *Wakef* 14; C Batley St Thos *Leeds* 14–16; C Hanging Heaton 14–16; C Batley from 16; Jt AD Dewsbury and Birstall 21; Hon Can Ripon Cathl from 19. *St Thomas's Vicarage, 16 Stockwell Drive, Batley WF17 5PA* E: markumpleby@hotmail.com

UNDERDOWN (*née* PARE), Margaret Jean. b 49. Univ of Wales (Abth) BSc 70. St Mich Coll Llan 06. **d** 08 **p** 09. Chapl HM Pris Cardiff 03–13; NSM Cathays *Llan* 13–19; PtO from 19. *22 Caerleon Road, Cardiff CF14 3DR* T: (029) 2033 1988

UNDERDOWN, Steven. b 52. Hull Univ BSc 75 CertEd 76 K Coll Lon PhD 02. **d** 88 **p** 04. CSWG 82–02; Chapl Brighton and Sussex Univ Hosps NHS Trust 03–15; NSM Hove Ch Ch 03–09; P-in-c Hove St Patr 09–15; Chapl Burrswood Chr Hosp *Roch* 15–19; PtO from 19. *Address temp unknown* M: 07981-423973 E: steven.underdown@hotmail.com

UNDERHILL, Edward James. b 88. Dur Univ BSc 10. Oak Hill Th Coll BA 20. **d** 20 **p** 21. C St Helen Bishopsgate w St Andr Undershaft etc *Lon* from 20. *110 Buckler Court, Eden Grove, London N7 8GQ* M: 07746-975141 E: ed@eustonchurch.com

UNDERHILL, John Samuel Leslie. b 92. Ex Univ BA 13 MA 14. Coll of Resurr Mirfield 14. **d** 16 **p** 17. C Eastbourne St Andr *Chich* 16–19; R Skirbeck St Nic *Linc* from 19. *Skirbeck Rectory, Fishtoft Road, Boston PE21 0DJ* T: (01205) 362734 E: skirbeckstnicholas@gmail.com

UNDERHILL, Stanley Robert. b 27. Cant Sch of Min. **d** 82 **p** 83. C New Addington *Cant* 82–84; C Cannock *Lich* 84–86; TV 86–88; R Dymchurch w Burmarsh and Newchurch *Cant* 88–92; rtd 92; Chapl Menorca *Eur* 92–94; PtO *Cant* 94–04; *Lon* 05–13. *Charterhouse, Charterhouse Square, London EC1M 6AN* T: (020) 7490 5059 M: 07970-954958 E: stanunder@aol.com

UNDERWOOD, Brian. b 35. Dur Univ BA 57 Keble Coll Ox PGCE 76 Dur Univ MA 72. Clifton Th Coll 57. **d** 59 **p** 60. C Blackpool Ch Ch *Blackb* 59–61; C New Malden and Coombe *S'wark* 61–64; Travel Sec Pathfinders 64–68; Chapl Chantilly *Eur* 68–69; Home Sec CCCS 69–71; P-in-c Gatten St Paul *Portsm* 71–72; Chapl Lyon w Grenoble and Aix-les-Bains *Eur* 72–75; Asst Chapl Trent Coll Nottm 76–80; Chapl Qu Eliz Gr Sch Blackb 80–85; R Bentham St Jo *Bradf* 85–92; V St Alb Ch Ch 92–00; rtd 00; PtO *St Alb* 00–14; *Guildf* 15–20. *2 Coombe Court, Station Approach, Tadworth KT20 5AL* T: (01737) 479965 E: brian.v255@yahoo.com

UNDERWOOD, David Richard. b 47. AKC 69 St Osyth Coll of Educn PGCE 72. St Aug Coll Cant 69. **d** 70 **p** 92. C Witham *Chelmsf* 70–71; Teacher 71–82; Hd Teacher Gt Heath Sch Mildenhall 82–91; NSM Chevington w Hargrave and Whepstead w Brockley *St E* 82–91; Par Dn Haverhill w Withersfield, the Wrattings etc 91–92; TV 92–94; P-in-c Bury St Edmunds St Jo 94–99; RD Thingoe 95–99; P-in-c Bury St Edmunds St Geo 98–99; Dioc Dir of Educn 99–04; Hon Can St E Cathl 03–04; rtd 07; NSM Godmanchester and Hilton *Ely* 11–18; PtO from 18; *St E* from 20. *Parkwood House, 15 Buregate Road, Felixstowe IP11 2DE* T: (01394) 672505 E: davidunderwood2@btinternet.com

UNDERWOOD, Mrs Susannah Lucy. b 72. Westmr Coll Ox BTh 98. ERMC 05. **d** 08 **p** 09. C Stevenage H Trin *St Alb* 08–11; TV Welwyn from 11. *The Rectory, Brook Bridge Lane, Datchworth, Knebworth SG3 6SU* T: (01438) 817183 E: team.vicar@welwyn.org.uk

UNSWORTH, Philip James. b 41. UEA BEd 82 Nottm Coll of Educn CertEd 63 Nottm Univ DipEd 72. EAMTC 94. **d** 97 **p** 98. NSM Hethersett w Canteloff w Lt and Gt Melton *Nor* 97–00; P-in-c Blofield w Hemblington 00–06; rtd 06; PtO *Nor* from 06. *55 Campbell Close, Hunstanton PE36 5PJ* T: (01485) 532436

UNSWORTH, Thomas Foster. b 28. Lon Univ BA 56. Lich Th Coll 60. **d** 62 **p** 63. C Northfield *Birm* 62–64; C The Lickey 64–66; V Forcett *Ripon* 66–68; V Bellerby and Leyburn 68–69; V Leyburn w Bellerby 69–73; Chapl Whittingham Hosp Preston 73–79; V Freckleton *Blackb* 79–83; V S Yardley St Mich *Birm* 83–86; V Sutton w Carlton and Normanton upon Trent etc *S'well* 86–90; Chapl from 90; St Raphaël *Eur* 90–97; PtO *Cant* from 99. *31 Broadlands Avenue, New Romney TN28 8JE* T: (01797) 361922 E: tom.unsworth@outlook.com

UNWIN, Barry. b 70. Sheff Univ BA 91. Oak Hill Th Coll BA 05. **d** 05 **p** 06. C Hebburn St Jo *Dur* 05–09; C Jarrow Grange 05–09; P-in-c New Barnet St Jas *St Alb* 09–13; V 13–16; P-in-c Hanley Castle, Hanley Swan and Welland *Worc* from 16; P-in-c Upton-on-Severn, Ripple, Earls Croome etc from 16. *Rose Bay, Tunnel Hill, Upton-upon-Severn, Worcester WR8 0QL* M: 07757-610345 E: barry@hopechurchfamily.org

UNWIN, Christopher Michael Fairclough. b 31. Dur Univ BA 57. Linc Th Coll 65. **d** 67 **p** 68. C S Shields St Hilda w St Thos *Dur* 67–73; R Tatsfield *S'wark* 73–81; RE Adv to Ch Secondary Schs 73–81; V Newc St Gabr 81–96; RD Newc E 96; rtd 96; PtO *Dur* 96–21; *Newc* 96–18. *2 The Cottage, West Row, Greatham, Hartlepool TS25 2HW* T: (01429) 872781 E: jcmfunwin@gmail.com

UPCHARCH, Sarah Louise. b 66. RGN 89 RSCN 95. SEITE BA 15. **d** 12 **p** 13. NSM Ardingly *Chich* 12–16; NSM Haywards Heath Ascension 16–18; C Worth, Pound Hill and Maidenbower from 18. *St Barnabas House, Crawley Lane, Crawley RH10 7EB* T: (01293) 524804 M: 07910-464404 E: vicarstb@worthparish.org

UPHILL, Ms Ann Carol. b 54. Westcott Ho Cam 95. **d** 97 **p** 98. C Strood St Nic w St Mary *Roch* 97–01; R Footscray w N Cray 01–14; rtd 14; PtO *Roch* from 16. *46 St Leonard's Rise, Orpington BR6 9NB* T: (01689) 637515 M: 07802-883121 E: ann.uphill@uwclub.net

UPSON-SMITH (née GOODWIN), Nicola. b 74. Univ of Wales (Lamp) BA 96 Trin Coll Carmarthen PGCE 98. Ripon Coll Cuddesdon 14. **d** 16 **p** 17. C Northampton St Alb *Pet* 16–19; V Chadsmoor *Lich* from 19. *St Aidan's Vicarage, Albert Street, Cannock WS11 5JD* M: 07807-542417 E: nicola.upsonsmith@yahoo.co.uk

UPTON, Anthony Arthur. b 30. Leic Univ MA 97 PhD 03. Wells Th Coll 61. **d** 63 **p** 64. C Milton *Portsm* 63–67; Chapl RN 67–83; V Foleshill St Laur *Cov* 83–91; rtd 91; PtO *Cov* 91–13. *Redlands Bungalow, Banbury Road, Lighthorne CV35 0AH*

UPTON, Caroline Tracey. *See* APPLEGATH, Caroline Tracey

UPTON, Mrs Christina Phoebe. b 61. Man Univ MB, ChB 85 Ches Univ MTh 04 MRCPsych 93. NOC 06. **d** 08 **p** 09. C W Kirby St Bridget *Ches* 08–12; R Ches H Trin from 12. *The Rectory, 50 Norris Road, Chester CH1 5DZ* T: (01244) 372721

UPTON, Christopher Martin. b 53. Bp Grosseteste Coll CertEd 74. EAMTC 94. **d** 97 **p** 98. NSM Gorleston St Andr *Nor* 97–05; NSM Bradwell from 05. *27 Curlew Way, Bradwell, Great Yarmouth NR31 8QX* T: (01493) 668184 E: rev.martin.upton@talk21.com

UPTON, Clement Maurice. b 49. Linc Th Coll 88. **d** 90 **p** 91. C Northampton St Alb *Pet* 90–93; V Laxey and Lonan *S & M* 93–96; V Hipswell *Ripon* 96–01; V Wellingborough St Andr *Pet* 01–10; Chapl Northants Police 05–10; rtd 10; PtO *B & W* 12–14; P-in-c Costa Azahar *Eur* 13–14; PtO *Leic* 15–20; *Eur* 18–19; Chapl Malta and Gozo from 19. *74 Rodolphe Street, Sliema 1273, Malta GC* E: sheclem26@yahoo.co.uk

UPTON, Canon Julie. b 61. Ripon Coll Cuddesdon 87. **d** 88 **p** 94. C Kirkstall *Ripon* 88–91; Par Dn E Greenwich Ch Ch w St Andr and St Mich *S'wark* 91–94; C 94; PtO 01–03; *St E* 02–03; NSM Manningham *Bradf* 03–04; TV Bramley *Ripon* 04–10; P-in-c Sheff Manor 10–12; TR 12–21; Jt AD Attercliffe 18–21; Assoc Adn – Transition Enabler from 21; Hon Can Sheff Cathl from 14. *The Rectory, Village Street, Adwick-le-Street, Doncaster DN6 7AD* M: 07469-852868 E: julie.upton1@gmail.com *or* julie.upton@sheffield.anglican.org

UPTON, Martin. *See* UPTON, Christopher Martin

UPTON, Mrs Susan Dorothy. b 53. Bp Grosseteste Coll CertEd 74 Nottm Univ BEd 75. EAMTC 99. **d** 02 **p** 03. NSM Bradwell *Nor* from 02. *27 Curlew Way, Bradwell, Great Yarmouth NR31 8QX* T: (01493) 668184 E: sue-upton@talk21.com

UPTON-JONES, Peter John. b 38. Selw Coll Cam BA 63 MA 67 Liv Univ CertEd 64. NOC 90. **d** 92 **p** 93. NSM Formby H Trin *Liv* 92–00; P-in-c Lezayre St Olave Ramsey *S & M* 00–03; V 03–08; P-in-c Kirkbride 00–03; R 03–08; rtd 08; PtO *S & M* from 09. *Clock Cottage, Glen Road, Colby, Isle of Man IM9 4NT* T: (01624) 830216 E: peteru_j@hotmail.com

UREN, Malcolm Lawrence. b 37. AKC 63. **d** 64 **p** 65. C Cant St Martin w St Paul 64–67; C Falmouth K Chas *Truro* 67–71; V St Blazey 71–79; P-in-c Tuckingmill 79–83; V 83–89; V Launceston St Steph w St Thos

89–92; V St Stephen by Launceston 92–96; rtd 00; PtO *Truro* from 00. *17 Forth An Tewennow, St Mary's Gardens, Phillack, Hayle TR27 4QE* T: (01736) 756619 E: malcolm.uren1@btinternet.com

URMSON-TAYLOR, Ralph. *See* TAYLOR, Ralph Urmson

✠**URQUHART, The Rt Revd David Andrew.** b 52. KCMG 18. Ealing Business Sch BA 77. Wycliffe Hall Ox 82. **d** 84 **p** 85 **c** 00. C Kingston upon Hull St Nic *York* 84–87; TV Drypool 87–92; V Cov H Trin 92–00; Hon Can Cov Cathl 99–00; Suff Bp Birkenhead *Ches* 00–06; Bp Birm from 06. *Bishop's Croft, Old Church Road, Birmingham B17 0BG* T: 0121-427 1163 E: bishop@cofebirmingham.com

URQUHART, Canon Edmund Ross. b 39. Univ Coll Ox BA 62 MA 68. St Steph Ho Ox 62. **d** 64 **p** 65. C Milton *Win* 64–69; C Norton *Derby* 69–73; V Bakewell 73–05; RD Bakewell and Eyam 95–04; Hon Can Derby Cathl 02–05; rtd 05; PtO *Derby* from 05; *Lich* 08–13. *1 Hambleton Close, Ashbourne DE6 1NG* T: (01335) 346454 E: edmund991@btinternet.com

URQUHART, Ian Garnham. b 46. Univ Coll Lon LLB 71. Wycliffe Hall Ox 98. **d** 99 **p** 00. C Barnston *Ches* 99–16; rtd 16; PtO *Ches* from 16. *The Corrie, 19 Gayton Parkway, Wirral CH60 3SZ* T: 0151-342 6710 M: 07709-351933

URSELL, Preb David John. b 45. MRAC 70 FRAgS. SWMTC 92. **d** 95 **p** 96. NSM Dolton *Ex* 95–15; Rural Convenor 95–15; Preb Ex Cathl 08–15. *P-in-c* from 16. *Windout Farm, Tedburn St Mary, Exeter EX6 6DR* T: (01647) 270061 E: dursell7@gmail.com

URSELL, Canon Philip Elliott. b 42. Univ of Wales BA 66 Ox Univ MA 82 Nashotah Ho Wisconsin DD 08. St Steph Ho Ox 66. **d** 68 **p** 69. C Newton Nottage *Llan* 68–71; Asst Chapl Univ of Wales (Cardiff) 71–77; Chapl Wales Poly 74–77; LtO *Llan* 77–07; Chapl Em Coll Cam 77–82; Prin Pusey Ho 82–03; Warden Ascot Priory 85–13; LtO *Ox* 82–13; Can Rio Grande from 05; PtO *Llan* from 15. *273 Hayes Apartments, The Hayes, Cardiff CF10 1BZ* T: (029) 2132 8359 E: peu@cantab.net

✠**URWIN, The Rt Revd Lindsay Goodall.** b 56. Heythrop Coll Lon MA 03 Nashotah Ho Wisconsin DD 11. Ripon Coll Cuddesdon 77. **d** 80 **p** 81 **c** 93. C Walworth *S'wark* 80–83; V N Dulwich St Faith 83–88; Dioc Missr *Chich* 88–93; Area Bp Horsham 93–09; Can and Preb Chich Cathl 93–09; P Admin Shrine of Our Lady of Walsingham 09–15; Hon Asst Bp *Nor* from 09; OGS from 91; Provost Woodard Corp (S Division) 06–15; R Brunswick Ch Ch Australia from 15; Bp for Angl Schs Melbourne from 15. *8 Glenlyon Road, Brunswick, VIC 3056, Australia* T: (0061) 39-380 1064 E: lindsayurwin1@gmail.com

✠**USHER, The Rt Revd Graham Barham.** b 70. Edin Univ BSc 93 CCC Cam BA 95 MA 00. Westcott Ho Cam 93 St Nic Th Coll Ghana 96. **d** 96 **p** 97 **c** 14. C Nunthorpe *York* 96–99; V N Ormesby 99–04; R Hexham *Newc* 04–14; AD 06–11; Suff Bp Dudley *Worc* 14–19; Hon Can Kumasi Ghana 07–14; Bp Nor from 19. *Bishop's House, Norwich NR3 1SB* T: (01603) 629001 E: bishop@dioceseofnorwich.org

USHER, Tracey Louise. b 86. Sunderland Univ BSc 11. Coll of Resurr Mirfield BA 18. **d** 18 **p** 19. C Newc St Gabr 18–19; C Berwick H Trin and St Mary from 19. *17 Governors Gardens, Berwick-upon-Tweed TD15 1JF* T: (01289) 783083 E: rev.tracey@icloud.com

UTTIN, Suzanne. *See* GRINDROD, Suzanne

UTTLEY, Mrs Valerie Gail. b 43. Man Univ BA 64. NOC 80. **dss** 83 **d** 87 **p** 94. Otley *Bradf* 83–87; Hon Par Dn 87–89; Par Dn Calverley 89–92; Ind Chapl *Ripon* 92–97; C Kirkstall 95–97; V Lofthouse 97–10; rtd 10; PtO *Newc* from 11. *1 Victoria Terrace, Alnwick NE66 1RE*

UZOIGWE, Austin Chuks. b 64. Qu Coll Birm 13. **d** 15 **p** 16. C Mardyke *Chelmsf* 15–19; TV Newton Flotman, Swainsthorpe, Tasburgh, etc *Nor* from 19. *The New Rectory, Church Hill, Tasburgh, Norwich NR15 1NB* M: 07778-135998 E: revaustinuzoigwe@aol.com

V

VACCARO, Canon Alexandra. b 64. Qu Coll Birm 07. **d** 10 **p** 11. NSM Kidderminster St Mary and All SS w Trimpley etc *Worc* 10–15; NSM Kidderminster Ismere 15–19; NSM Kidderminster St Jo and H Innocents from 19; Dean Self-Supporting Min from 18; Hon Can Worc Cathl from 17. *18*

Batham Road, Kidderminster DY10 2TN T: (01562) 515894 E: alex640213@gmail.com

VAIL, David William. b 30. Dur Univ BA 56 Sheff Univ DipEd 71. Oak Hill Th Coll 56. **d** 58 **p** 59. C Toxteth Park St Bede *Liv* 58–61; Kenya 61–77; Chapl Versailles *Eur* 77–82;

Gen Sec Rwanda Miss 82–88; V Virginia Water *Guildf* 88–96; rtd 96; PtO *Ox* from 98. *36 Silverthorne Drive, Caversham, Reading RG4 7NS* T: 0118-954 6667

VAIZEY, Martin John. b 37. AKC 64. **d** 65 **p** 66. C Bishopwearmouth Gd Shep *Dur* 65–69; C Darlington H Trin 69–72; V Easington Colliery 72–80; C-in-c Bishopwearmouth St Mary V w St Pet CD 80–85; V Sunderland Springwell w Thorney Close 85–88; V Burton Gilbert 88–96; P-in-c Wingate Grange 96–99; V Wheatley Hill and Wingate w Hutton Henry 99–07; rtd 07; PtO *Dur* from 13. *Elmside, 2 Etherley Lane, Bishop Auckland DL14 7QR* T: (01388) 450093 E: vaizeym@gmail.com

VALE, Thomas Stanley George. b 52. Chich Th Coll 85. **d** 87 **p** 88. C Leic St Phil 87–90; C Knighton St Mary Magd 90–93; P-in-c Leic St Chad 93–97; V 97–01; V Blackfordby and Woodville 01–17; rtd 17; PtO *Llan* from 17. *107 Springfield Gardens, Hirwaun, Aberdare CF44 9LQ*

VALENTINE, Daniel James. b 74. Lon Guildhall Univ LLB 98 Middx Univ LLM 05 Sheff Univ BA 16 Solicitor 04. Yorks Min Course 14. **d** 16 **p** 17. NSM Chorlton-cum-Hardy St Clem *Man* 16–19; P-in-c Crumpsall from 19; Chapl Man Airport from 18; CF (ACF) from 21. *St Matthew's Rectory, 30 Cleveland Road, Manchester M8 4QU* T: 0161-492 0387 M: 07966-224160 E: daniel@crumpsallchurch.co.uk

VALENTINE, Hugh William James. b 56. Bradf Univ BA 83 CQSW. S'wark Ord Course 86. **d** 89 **p** 90. NSM Stoke Newington Common St Mich *Lon* 89–92; NSM Westmr St Jas 92–20; Bps' Adv in Child Protection Stepney and Two Cities Areas 96–10; Bp's Adv in Child Protection *Ox* 96–05; PtO *Lon* from 20. *The Clerk's House, 127 Kennington Road, London SE11 6SF* M: 07760-176704 E: mail@hughvalentine.net

VALENTINE, John Harvey. b 63. Ch Ch Ox BA 85 MA 85 Asbury Th Sem Kentucky DMin 20. Ridley Hall Cam BA 92. **d** 93 **p** 94. C Heigham H Trin *Nor* 93–97; C Ches Square St Mich w St Phil *Lon* 97–00; C Brompton H Trin w Onslow Square St Paul 00–02; P-in-c Holborn St Geo w H Trin and St Bart 02–09; R 09–19; C St Edm and St Mary Woolnoth etc 19–20; PtO from 21. *26 Quarrendon Street, London SW6 3SU* M: 07736-066091

VALENTINE, Mrs Katherine Anne. b 58. Newc Poly BA 80 Anglia Ruskin Univ MA 12. ERMC 03. **d** 06 **p** 07. C Haughley w Wetherden and Stowupland *St E* 06–10; P-in-c Pakenham w Norton and Tostock 10–18; C Badwell and Walsham 15–18; R Pakenham w Norton, Tostock etc from 18; Asst Dioc Dir of Ords from 16; RD Ixworth from 17. *The Orwell, Woolpit Road, Norton, Bury St Edmunds IP31 3LU* T: (01359) 235095 E: kavalentine677@gmail.com

VALIANT, Mrs Lesley Jean. b 51. Whitelands Coll Lon CertEd 74 Univ Coll Chich BA 99. STETS 99. **d** 01 **p** 02. NSM Bedhampton *Portsm* 01–04; C Southsea St Jude 04–06; Asst to RD Portsm 04–06; TV Pewsey and Swanborough *Sarum* 06–09; TV Modbury, Bigbury, Ringmore, Kingston etc *Ex* 11–13; Chapl MU 14–20; PtO *Cant* 14–21. *Ryelands, Carkeel, Saltash PL12 6PH* T: (01752) 843670 M: 07751-168228 E: ljvaliant@gmail.com

VALLENTE-KERR, Susan Fiona. b 77. St Martin's Coll Lanc BA 98 Ch Ch Coll Cant PGCE 00 Moorlands Coll MA 08. St Mellitus Coll 08. **d** 11 **p** 12. C Frindsbury w Upnor and Chattenden *Roch* from 11; C Strood St Nic w St Mary from 17; C Strood St Fran from 17. *The Vicarage, 3 Central Road, Rochester ME2 3HF* T: (01634) 956910 M: 07940-161044 E: suziqvk@yahoo.co.uk

VALLINS, Canon Christopher. b 43. Hon FRSocMed 06. Lich Th Coll 63. **d** 66 **p** 67. C Cuddington *Guildf* 66–70; C Aldershot St Mich 70–73; V W Ewell 73–81; R Worplesdon and Chapl Merrist Wood Coll of Agric and Horticulture 81–89; RD Guildf 86–89; Chapl Epsom Health Care NHS Trust 89–99; Hd Past Care Epsom and St Helier Univ Hosps NHS Trust 99–07; Bp's Adv on Healing *Guildf* 97–07; Bp's Adv for Hosp Chapl 07–16; Hon Can Guildf Cathl 01–17; PtO *S'wark* from 07; *Guildf* from 16; *Ex* from 19. *Bramble Cottage, 22 Cotford Road, Sidbury, Sidmouth EX10 0SQ* T: (01395) 597418 M: 07917-337920 E: chrisvallins@yahoo.com

VAN BEVEREN, Mrs Susan Margaret. b 64. St Hugh's Coll Ox BA 85 MA 89. Trin Th Sch Melbourne 95. **d** 96 **p** 96. Ind Chapl Inter-Ch Trade and Ind Miss Australia 96–99; NSM Amsterdam w Den Helder and Heiloo *Eur* 00–03; Officer for Miss in Work and Economic Life *Ox* 03–07; Dioc Adv 08–13; NSM S Ascot 07–09; NSM Sunninghill and S Ascot 09–13; PtO 14–20; Chapl Heatherwood & Wexham Park Hosps NHS Foundn Trust 14–15; Head of Chapl Kingston Hosp NHS Foundn Trust Surrey from 15. *Kingston Hospital NHS Foundation Trust, Kingston Hospital, Galsworthy Road, Kingston-upon-Thames KT2 7QB* T: (020) 8546 7711 E: susanvanbeveren@gmail.com *or* susan.vanbeveren@nhs.net

VAN BLERK, Etienne. b 68. Pretoria Univ BA 91 Stellenbosch Univ BTh 92 Lebanese American Univ BA 96. Ox Min Course 07. **d** 09 **p** 10. C Bicester w Bucknell, Caversfield and Launton *Ox* 09–11; C Walton H Trin 11–13; Chapl Rossall Sch Fleetwood 13–19; PtO *Blackb* 19; P-in-c Carbis Bay w Lelant *Truro* from 19. *The Vicarage, Porthrepta Road, Carbis Bay, St Ives TR26 2LD* M: 07795-985942 E: vanblerketienne@gmail.com

VAN CARRAPIETT, Timothy Michael James. b 39. Chich Th Coll 60. **d** 63 **p** 64. C Sugley *Newc* 63–65; C Newc St Fran 65–69; P-in-c Wrangbrook w N Elmsall CD *Wakef* 69–74; P-in-c Flushing *Truro* 74–75; P-in-c Mylor w Flushing 75–76; P-in-c St Day 76–82; R Aldrington *Chich* 82–87; V Bexhill St Barn 87–01; rtd 01; PtO *St E* 01–13; *Chelmsf* from 08. *The College of St Barnabas, Blackberry Lane, Lingfield RH7 6NJ*

VAN DE KASTEELE, Peter John. b 39. Magd Coll Cam BA 61 MA 65. Clifton Th Coll 61. **d** 63 **p** 64. C Eastbourne H Trin *Chich* 63–66; C N Pickenham w S Pickenham etc *Nor* 66–70; R Mursley w Swanbourne and Lt Horwood *Ox* 70–80; Admin Sec Clinical Th Assn from 83; Gen Dir 88–99; PtO *Glouc* 83–16; Hon C Westcote w Icomb and Bledington 88–89; rtd 99. *68 Springfield Road, Southwell NG25 0BT*

van de WEYER, Robert William Bates. b 50. Lanc Univ BA 76. S'wark Ord Course 78. **d** 81 **p** 82. Warden Lt Gidding Community 77–98; Hon C Gt w Lt Gidding and Steeple Gidding *Ely* 81–83; P-in-c 83–93; P-in-c Winwick 83–93; P-in-c Hamerton 83–93; P-in-c Upton and Copmanford 83–93; PtO from 93; *St Alb* from 15. *4 Copse Way, Cambridge CB2 8BJ* E: robert@vandeweyer.co.uk

VAN DEN BERG, Jan Jacob. b 56. Sarum & Wells Th Coll 86. **d** 88 **p** 89. C Glouc St Aldate 88–91; C Ollerton w Boughton *S'well* 91–95; P-in-c Scrooby 95–00; P-in-c Blyth 97–00; C Brampton and Farlam and Castle Carrock w Cumrew *Carl* 00–02; TV Eden, Gelt and Irthing 02–05; P-in-c Rockcliffe and Blackford 05–20; rtd 20; PtO *Newc* from 21. *27 Windsor Terrace, Hexham NE46 3JR* E: jan.vandenberg@mypostoffice.co.uk

VAN DEN BERG-OWENS, Jayne. b 65. **d** 11 **p** 12. C Kirkby *Liv* 11–14; TV 4Saints Team from 14. *9 Birkdale Close, Huyton, Liverpool L36 4QW* M: 07828-701890 E: jayne.vdbo@gmail.com

VAN DEN BERGH, Victor Michael Cornelius. b 53. ALBC 92. SAOMC 01 Ridley Hall Cam 02. **d** 03 **p** 04. C Tamworth *Lich* from 03; Chapl Staffs Police from 05; CF(V) from 05. *St Francis's Vicarage, Masefield Drive, Tamworth B79 8JB* T: (01827) 65926 E: minister_stf@btinternet.com

van den HOF, Ariadne Rolanda Magdalena. b 71. Univ of Wales (Cardiff) MTh 96 Leiden Univ MA 05. Old Cath Sem Amersfoort 90 St Mich Coll Llan 98. **d** 99 **p** 00. C Dolgellau w Llanfachreth and Brithdir etc *Ban* 99–01; Min Can Ban Cathl 01–02; P-in-c Trefdraeth w Aberffraw, Llangadwaladr etc 02–03; R 03–06; R Llanffestiniog w Blaenau Ffestiniog etc 06–11; Rural Life Co-ord 04–11; V Shooters Hill *Ch S'wark* from 11. *Christ Church Vicarage, 1 Craigholm, Shooters Hill, London SE18 3RR* T: (020) 8856 5858 E: armvandenhof@gmail.com

VAN DER HART, Lucinda Diana MacLeod. b 81. Ox Univ MA 03 Univ of the Arts Lon CertEd 06. Wycliffe Hall Ox 01 St Mellitus Coll 20. **d** 21. NSM Fulham St Dionis *Lon* from 21. *11 Glentham Gardens, London SW13 9JN* M: 07870-159746 E: lucinda@stdionis.org.uk

VAN DER HART, William Richard. b 76. Homerton Coll Cam BEd 99. Wycliffe Hall Ox BTh 04. **d** 04 **p** 05. C Bryanston Square St Mary w St Marylebone St Mark *Lon* 04–08; TV Roxeth 08–11; V W Harrow St Pet 11–14; C Onslow Square and S Kensington St Aug 14–20; C Fulham St Dionis from 20. *Address temp unknown* M: 07968-132129

VAN DER LELY, Canon Janice Kay. b 55. Sheff Univ BA 76 Dur Univ PhD 79 Webster Univ (USA) MA 05 Ox Brookes Univ MA 10. Ripon Coll Cuddesdon 08. **d** 09 **p** 10. C Cirencester *Glouc* 09–12; V Thornbury and Oldbury-on-Severn w Shepperdine 12–19; Chan Llan Cathl from 19. *1 St Mary's, The Cathedral Green, Cardiff CF5 2EB* T: (029) 2115 6258 M: 07472-610101 E: janvanderlely@gmail.com *or* chancellor@llandaffcathedral.org.uk

VAN DER PUMP, Charles Lyndon. b 25. FRCM. S'wark Ord Course 86. **d** 88 **p** 89. NSM Primrose Hill St Mary w Avenue Road St Paul *Lon* 88–02; PtO 02–18. *48 Canfield Gardens, London NW6 3EB* T/F: (020) 7624 4517 E: lyndonvdp@waitrose.com

VAN DER TOORN, Canon Stephne. b 53. Natal Univ BA 73 Stellenbosch Univ HDipEd 75. Th Ext Educn Coll. **d** 93 **p** 95. NSM Pretoria St Mary S Africa 93–01; C Fawley *Win* 01–07; R E Bergholt and Brantham *St E* from 07; Hon Can St E Cathl from 13. *The Rectory, Rectory Lane, Brantham, Manningtree CO11 1PZ* T: (01206) 392646 E: revstephvdt@googlemail.com

van der VALK, Jesse. b 59. Nottm Univ BTh 84 Birm Univ MPhil 88 Avery Hill Coll PGCE 85. St Jo Coll Nottm 81. **d** 88 **p** 89. C Droitwich Spa *Worc* 88–92; V Hartshead and Hightown *Wakef* 92–96; R Woolwich St Mary w St Mich *S'wark* from 96; USPG (Lon Volunteers and Co-workers Team) from 97. *The Rectory, 43 Rectory Place, London SE18 5DA* T: (020) 8465 7307 *or* 8316 4338 E: jvdv09@aol.com

VAN KRIEKEN VANNERLEY, David. *See* VANNERLEY, David van Krieken

VAN LEER, The Ven Samuel Wall. b 67. Virginia Univ BA 90 California Univ MA 91 St Jo Coll Dur BA 01. Cranmer Hall Dur 99. **d** 02 **p** 03. C Berne w Neuchâtel *Eur* 02–05; Chapl E Netherlands 05–11; Hon Asst Chapl Utrecht w Zwolle 11–21; Adn NW Eur from 21; Can Gib Cathl from 21. *Tussenkoelen 16, 9753 KX Haren, The Netherlands* T: (0031) (50) 785 0703 E: samvanleer@europe.anglican.org

VAN LEEUWEN, Canon Dirk Willem. b 45. Utrecht Univ LLD 71. Th Faculty Brussels 71 S'wark Ord Course 80. **d** 82 **p** 83. Asst Chapl Brussels Cathl *Eur* 82–84; Chapl Haarlem 84–93; Chapl Antwerp St Boniface 94–06; Assoc Chapl 06–07; Chapl Charleroi 94–00; P-in-c Ypres 97–99; P-in-c Leuven 98–99; Can Brussels Cathl 96–07; Chapl Knokke 01–07; P-in-c Ostend 01–06; P-in-c Bruges 01–03; V Gen to Bp Eur 02–07; Adn NW Eur 05–07; rtd 08. *De Gouden Druyfftack, Damplein 21, 4331GC Middelburg, The Netherlands* T: (0031) (615) 494914 E: dlw@skhl.nl

VAN OMMEREN, Ms Gerda Maria Jacoba. b 76. Leiden Univ MA 99. St Mellitus Coll 17. **d** 19 **p** 20. C Goodrington and Collaton St Mary *Ex* from 19. *40 Steed Close, Paignton TQ4 7SN* M: 07787-127983 E: reverendgerda@outlook.com

VAN ROSSUM, Paul Anthony. b 53. Sheff Univ BScTech 74 Birm Univ PGCE 75 Open Univ MA 92. Trin Coll Bris 09. **d** 12 **p** 13. OLM Almondsbury and Olveston *Bris* 12–19; Bp's Chapl 16–18; rtd 19; Hon C S Severnside *Bris* from 20. *18 Townsend Lane, Almondsbury, Bristol BS32 4EQ* T: (01454) 626160 E: paulvanrossum@gmail.com

VAN STRAATEN, Christopher Jan. b 55. Bris Univ BA 77 Natal Univ HDipEd 78. Oak Hill Th Coll 90. **d** 92 **p** 93. C Woodley *Ox* 92–96; V Gillingham St Aug *Roch* 96–07; V Aylesford 07–16; V Sutton Park *York* 16–18; P-in-c Wawne 16–18; V Sutton Park and Wawne from 18; AD E Hull from 19. *11 Sovereign Way, Kingswood, Hull HU7 3JG* T: (01482) 838486 E: cjvanstraaten@gmail.com

van WENGEN, Rosemary Margaret. *See* KOBUS van WENGEN, Rosemary Margaret

VAN ZANDBERGEN, Karen. *See* BURNETT-HALL, Karen

VANE, Benjamin Christopher George. b 81. Bath Univ BSc 03. Oak Hill Th Coll BA 15. **d** 15 **p** 16. C Oakwood St Thos *Lon* 15–19; C Ox St Ebbe w H Trin and St Pet from 19. *14 Kelburne Road, Oxford OX4 3SJ* M: 07967-602513 E: ben.vane@gmail.com

✠**VANN, The Rt Revd Cherry Elizabeth.** b 58. ARCM 78 GRSM 80. Westcott Ho Cam 86. **d** 89 **p** 94 **c** 20. Par Dn Flixton St Mich *Man* 89–92; Chapl Bolton Inst of F&HE 92–98; Par Dn Bolton St Pet 92–94; C 94–98; TV E Farnworth and Kearsley 98–04; TR 04–08; Chapl among Deaf People 98–04; AD Farnworth 05–08; Adn Rochdale 08–20; Bp Mon from 20. *Bishopstow, Stow Hill, Newport NP20 4EA* T: (01633) 263510 M: 07587-132707 E: bishop.monmouth@churchinwales.org.uk

VANNERLEY, David van Krieken. b 50. Kent Univ BA 78 Cant Ch Ch Univ MPhil 07 MA 11 PhD 16 Ch Ch Coll Cant CertEd 71. SEITE 00. **d** 05 **p** 06. NSM St Laur in Thanet *Cant* 05–13; PtO *Roch* from 13; *Cant* 13–14; TV Whitstable 14–20; Organising Chapl Kent Critical Incident Chapl Service 10–20; rtd 20; PtO *Cant* from 20. *118 St Stephen's Road, Canterbury CT2 7JS* E: dvannerley@gmail.com

VANNOZZI, Peter. b 62. Lon Univ BA 83 Heythrop Coll Lon MA 06. Ripon Coll Cuddesdon BA 86 MA 91. **d** 87 **p** 88. C Kenton *Lon* 87–90; C Fleet *Guildf* 90–93; V Northwood Hills St Edm *Lon* 93–97; AD Harrow 95–97; V S Dulwich St Steph *S'wark* 97–05; RD Dulwich 02–05; Can Res Wakef Cathl 05–07; V Hampton Hill *Lon* 07–15; V Highgate St Aug 15–19; V Isleworth St Fran from 19. *Vicarage of St Francis of Assisi, 865 Great West Road, Isleworth TW7 5PD* T: (020) 8374 6985 E: revpetervannozzi@gmail.com

VANSTONE, Preb Walford David Frederick. b 38. Open Univ BA 81. AKC 69. **d** 70 **p** 71. C Feltham *Lon* 70–75; TV E Runcorn w Halton *Ches* 75–80; V Grange St Andr 80–82; V Hampton All SS *Lon* 82–05; P-in-c Teddington SS Pet and Paul and Fulwell 99–00; AD Hampton 95–03; Preb St Paul's Cathl 99–05; Chapl Richmond Coll 02–05; rtd 05; PtO *Lon* from 05. *13 Lammas Close, Staines TW18 4XT* E: wvanstone@aol.com

VARAH, Canon Paul Hugh. b 46. St Deiniol's Hawarden 83. **d** 85 **p** 86. C Prestatyn *St As* 85–87; P-in-c Hawarden 87–88;

TV 88–89; V Esclusham 89–96; V Connah's Quay 96–13; Can Cursal St As Cathl 08–13; rtd 13; PtO *St As* from 14. *4 New Road, Dobshill, Deeside CH5 3LU* T: (01244) 540728 E: paulhvarah@gmail.com

VARGESON, Canon Peter Andrew. b 53. Wycliffe Hall Ox 85. **d** 87 **p** 88. C Yateley *Win* 87–92; V Bursledon 92–17; AD Eastleigh 99–06 and 09–16; P-in-c Hound 07–15; C 15–17; rtd 17; PtO *Win* from 17; Hon Can Tororo Uganda from 99. *4 Knoll Gardens, St Ives, Ringwood BH24 2LW* T: (01425) 839343 E: peter.vargeson@gmail.com

VARLEY (*née* **TRIM), Elizabeth Ann.** b 52. Homerton Coll Cam BEd 75 Van Mildert Coll Dur PhD 85 St Jo Coll Dur BA 96. NEOC 94. **d** 96 **p** 97. C Sedgefield *Dur* 96–99; Dir Post-Ord Tr Stepney Area *Lon* 99–02; V Hipswell *Ripon* 02–07; Hon Can Ripon Cathl 05–07; R Bacton w Wyverstone, Cotton and Old Newton etc *St E* 07–15; C Bro Arwystli *Ban* 15–16; PtO *Portsm* from 17. *Society of the Sisters of Bethany, 7 Nelson Road, Southsea PO5 2AR* M: 07922-012703 E: lizpssb@gmail.com

VARLEY, Robert. b 36. St Jo Coll Cam BA 57 MA 64 Man Poly PGCE 92. NW Ord Course 71. **d** 74 **p** 75. C Wallasey St Hilary *Ches* 74–77; V Rock Ferry 77–81; PtO *Man* 82–83; Hon C E Farnworth and Kearsley 83–86; Hon C Walkden Moor 86–87; C 87–89; V Lt Hulton 89–90; PtO from 97. *66 Normanby Road, Worsley, Manchester M28 7TS* T: 0161-790 8420 M: 07801-064602 E: revrobvarley@hotmail.com

VARNEY, Peter David. b 38. Univ Coll Dur BA 61 MA 64. Qu Coll Birm 61. **d** 64 **p** 65. C Newington St Paul *S'wark* 64–66; C Camberwell St Mich w All So w Em 66–67; Perm to Offic Kuching Malaysia 67–68; Hon C Croxley Green All SS *St Alb* 69; Asst Sec Gen Syn Bd for Miss and Unity 69–72; PtO *Roch* 69–72 and 74–84; Asst Chapl CSJB 72–73; Asst Sec Chrs Abroad 74–79; Dir Bloxham Project 84–86; PtO *Cant* 84–85; *S'wark* 85–86; P-in-c Thornage w Brinton w Hunworth and Stody *Nor* 87–88; P-in-c Briningham 87–88; C Melton Constable w Swanton Novers 87–88; PtO from 88; Chapl Yare and Norvic Clinics and St Andr Hosp Nor 90–95; rtd 03. *280 The Pavilion, St Stephens Road, Norwich NR1 3SN* T: (01603) 760838 E: varney@waitrose.com

VARNEY, Stephen Clive. b 59. Qu Mary Coll Lon BSc 80 Sussex Univ MSc 82 Southn Univ BTh 88. Sarum & Wells Th Coll 83. **d** 86 **p** 87. C Riverhead w Dunton Green *Roch* 86–91; V Bostall Heath 91–99; V Bromley St Mark 99–19; rtd 19. *56 High Street, Overton, Basingstoke RG25 3HG* M: 07961-117578

VARNON, Nicholas Charles Harbord. b 45. St Luke's Coll Ex CertEd 71 Open Univ BA 83 BPhil 91 MA 94 Univ of Wales MPhil 00. St Mich Coll Llan 91. **d** 93 **p** 94. C Pontypridd St Cath w St Matt *Llan* 93–97; P-in-c Sutton St Nicholas w Sutton St Michael *Heref* 97–04; P-in-c Withington w Westhide 97–04; P-in-c Weybourne Gp *Nor* 04–06; R N Elmham, Billingford, Bintree, Guist etc 06–16; CF (ACF) 00–16; rtd 16; PtO *Nor* from 16. *Willow Lodge, Springwell Road, Whissonsett, Dereham NR20 5TU* E: nicholas.varnon@btinternet.com

VARQUEZ, Leo Bacleon. b 61. St Andr Th Sem Manila 82. **d** 86 **p** 86. P St Andr Philippines 86-91; P St Isidore 92–94; SSF 95–99; NSM Edin St Jo 98–99; NSM Mill End and Heronsgate w W Hyde *St Alb* 99–00; Asst Chapl HM Pris Featherstone 00–02; C Hednesford *Lich* 00–04; C Kingstanding St Luke *Birm* 04–06; Asst Chapl Univ Coll Lon Hosps NHS Foundn Trust 06–08; Chapl Univ Hosp of N Staffs NHS Trust from 08. *University Hospital of North Staffs, Newcastle Road, Stoke-on-Trent ST4 6QG* T: (01782) 676400 E: leo.varquez@uhns.nhs.uk

VARTY, John Eric. b 44. Tyndale Hall Bris 68. **d** 71 **p** 72. C Barrow St Mark *Carl* 71–74; C Cheadle *Ches* 74–82; V Cheadle All Hallows 82–89; V Alsager Ch Ch 89–06; rtd 06; Chapl to Bp Stockport *Ches* 07–14; C Acton and Worleston, Church Minshull etc 12–14; PtO from 14. *14 Gowy Close, Alsager, Stoke-on-Trent ST7 2HX* T: (01270) 877360 E: john.varty@homecall.co.uk

VASBY-BURNIE, Timothy Roy. b 79. Trin Coll Cam MA 00. Wycliffe Hall Ox BTh 07. **d** 07 **p** 08. C Stone Ch Ch and Oulton *Lich* 07–10; V Wednesbury St Bart 10–16; V Shrewsbury St Geo w Greenfields from 16. *The Vicarage, St George's Street, Shrewsbury SY3 8QA* E: tim@vasbyburnie.net

VASEY, Mrs Janet Mary. b 41. Margaret McMillan Coll of Educn CertEd 62. Local Minl Tr Course 11. **d** 11. NSM Gt Grimsby St Mary and St Jas *Linc* from 11. *34 Western Outway, Grimsby DN34 5EX* T: (01472) 753145 E: jan.vasey@btinternet.com

VASEY-SAUNDERS, Leah Beverley. b 77. Huddersfield Univ BMus 98 St Jo Coll Dur BA 03. Cranmer Hall Dur 00. **d** 03 **p** 04. C Whorlton *Newc* 03–04; Hon C Newc St Geo 05–08; TV Cannock *Lich* 08–09; TV Cannock and Huntington 09–10; V Heath Hayes 10–11; C Hednesford 08–11; PtO *S'well* 12–13; P-in-c Harworth 13–16; Can Prec Wakef Cathl *Leeds* 16–21; V Lancaster St Mary w St John and St Anne

Blackb from 21. *Priory Vicarage, Priory Close, Lancaster LA1 1YZ* E: leahvasey@gmail.com

VASEY-SAUNDERS, Mark Richard. b 74. Coll of Ripon & York St Jo BA 95 St Jo Coll Dur BA 00. Cranmer Hall Dur 98. **d** 01 **p** 02. C Ponteland *Newc* 01–04; Chapl Newc Univ 04–08; PtO *Lich* 10–11; TV Retford Area *S'well* 11–16; Tutor St Hild Coll from 17; PV Wakef Cathl *Leeds* from 17. *4 Cathedral Close, Margaret Street, Wakefield WF1 2DP* E: mark@vasey-saunders.co.uk

VAUGHAN, Canon Andrew Christopher James. b 61. Univ of Wales (Lamp) BA 82. Linc Th Coll 82. **d** 84 **p** 85. C Caerleon *Mon* 84–86; C Magor w Redwick and Undy 86–88; Ind Chapl 84–94; Linc Ind Miss 94–17; P-in-c Swinderby from 17; Can and Preb Linc Cathl from 05. *46 Post Mill Close, North Hykeham, Lincoln LN6 9HL* T: (01522) 687242 M: 07702-468549 E: revandrewvaughan@gmail.com

VAUGHAN, Andrew Kenneth. b 64. Cant Ch Ch Univ BA 10 ACIOB 90 MCIOB 01. Ridley Hall Cam 04. **d** 07 **p** 08. C Chislehurst Ch Ch *Roch* 07–11; V Istead Rise 11–21; C Chatham St Phil and St Jas from 21. *Address temp unknown* M: 07977-154809 E: andrewvaughan@akv64s.com

VAUGHAN, Brian John. b 38. Lich Th Coll 65. **d** 68 **p** 69. C Fisherton Anger *Sarum* 68–70; C Wareham w Arne 70–73; Asst P Mt Lawley Australia 73; R Dalwallinu 73–76; R Morawa 75–78; Field Officer Bible Soc of W Australia 78–81; Assoc P Mt Lawley 82–86; R Pinjarra 86–96; R Manjimup 96–00; rtd 00. *Milborne, 6 Steeple Retreat, Busselton WA 6280, Australia* T: (0061) (8) 9751 1225 M: (0061) 42-407 4414 E: sherton38@gmail.com

VAUGHAN, Carole Ann. b 47. Leeds Univ CertEd 68. STETS 95. **d** 98 **p** 99. NSM Oakley w Wootton St Lawrence *Win* 98–18; rtd 18; PtO *Sheff* from 19. *365 Fox Hill Road, Sheffield S6 1BG* E: carole@cjvaughan.co.uk

VAUGHAN, Miss Catherine Margaret. b 64. Bp Grosseteste Coll BEd 88 Moorlands Coll BA 05. STETS MA 12. **d** 12 **p** 13. C Bath Twerton-on-Avon *B & W* 12–15; V Owlsmoor *Ox* from 15. *The Vicarage, 107 Owlsmoor Road, Owlsmoor, Sandhurst GU47 0SS* M: 07879-498474

VAUGHAN, Charles Jeremy Marshall. b 52. Man Univ BSc 75. St Jo Coll Nottm 83. **d** 85 **p** 86. C Epsom Common Ch Ch *Guildf* 85–88; C Woking Ch Ch 88–93; R Worting *Win* 93–07; R Winklebury and Worting 07–10; R Oakley w Wootton St Lawrence 10–18; rtd 18; PtO *Sheff* from 19. *365 Fox Hill Road, Sheffield S6 1BG* E: jeremy@cjvaughan.co.uk

VAUGHAN, Craig Aaron. b 72. **d** 12 **p** 13. NSM Newton Nottage *Llan* 12–17; TV Llantwit Major 17–18; TV Glamorgan Heritage Coast from 18. *The Vicarage, Trepit Road, Wick, Cowbridge CF71 7QL* T: (01656) 890468 E: fathercraig.70@btinternet.com

VAUGHAN, Edward Michael. b 59. Univ of NSW BA 80 Sydney Univ DipEd 81. Moore Th Coll Sydney BTh 87. **d** 89 **p** 89. C Jannali Australia 89–91; C Rozelle 92–94; R Darling Street 95–05; I Crinken *D & G* 05–10; Australia from 10. *PO Box 465, Kings Cross NSW 1340, Australia* T: (0061) (2) 9360 6844 E: edwardv@ughan.net

VAUGHAN, Idris Samuel. b 46. Sarum Th Coll 70. **d** 72 **p** 73. C Workington St Jo *Carl* 72–76; C Foley Park *Worc* 76–79; V Hayton St Mary *Carl* 79–85; Chapl Asst Univ Hosp Nottm 85–90; Chapl Asst Nottm Gen Hosp 85–90; Chapl Stafford Distr Gen Hosp 90–94; Chapl Chase Hosp Cannock 90–94; Chapl Mid Staffs Gen Hosps NHS Trust 94–06; rtd 06; P-in-c Lanzarote *Eur* 06–10. *43 Silkmore Crescent, Stafford ST17 4JL*

VAUGHAN, Jeremy. See VAUGHAN, Charles Jeremy Marshall

VAUGHAN, Jonathan Michael. b 84. Bris Univ BSc 06. Wycliffe Hall Ox BTh 11. **d** 13 **p** 14. NSM Ox St Andr 13–17; V Wolvey, Copston Magna and Withybrook *Cov* from 17. *The Vicarage, School Lane, Wolvey, Hinckley LE10 3LH* T: (01455) 220385 E: revjonathanvaughan@gmail.com

VAUGHAN, Patrick Handley. b 38. TCD BA 60 BD 65 Selw Coll Cam BA 62 MA 66 Nottm Univ PhD 88. Ridley Hall Cam 61. **d** 63 **p** 64. Min Can Bradf Cathl 63–66; Uganda 67–73; P-in-c Slingsby *York* 74–77; Tutor NW Ord Course 74–77; P-in-c Hovingham *York* 74–77; Prin EMMTC *S'well* 77–90; Hon Can Leic Cathl 87–90; Assoc Lect Open Univ from 94. *113 Upperthorpe Road, Sheffield S6 3EA* T: 0114-272 2675 E: patrickvaughan38@yahoo.co.uk

VAUGHAN, Preb Roger Maxwell. b 39. AKC 62. **d** 63 **p** 64. C W Bromwich All SS *Lich* 63–65; C Wolverhampton 65–70; V Tunstall Ch Ch 70–79; V Abbots Bromley 79–86; P-in-c Blithfield 85–86; V Abbots Bromley w Blithfield 86–93; R Stafford St Jo and Tixall w Ingestre 93–04; Preb Lich Cathl 99–04; rtd 04; PtO *Lich* 04–20. *51 Crestwood Drive, Stone ST15 0LW* T: (01785) 812192

VAUGHAN, Trevor. b 41. TD 91. Cen Lancs Univ BA 91. Linc Th Coll 66. **d** 69 **p** 70. C Wyken *Cov* 69–72; C Stratford-on-

Avon w Bishopton 72–73; P-in-c Monks Kirby w Withybrook and Copston Magna 73–75; P-in-c Wolvey, Burton Hastings and Stretton Baskerville 73–77; P-in-c Withybrook w Copston Magna 73–77; V Heyhouses *Blackb* 77–80; CF (TA) 79–99; V Chorley St Geo *Blackb* 80–83; R Bolton by Bowland w Grindleton *Bradf* 83–89; V Settle 89–91; R Broughton, Marton and Thornton 91–00; V Morecambe St Barn *Blackb* 00–03; P-in-c Sabden and Pendleton 03–06; rtd 06; PtO *Leeds* from 17. *Throstle Nest Cottage, Old Road, Thornton in Craven, Skipton BD23 3TB* T: (01282) 842383 E: trevor.vaughan3@outlook.com

VAUGHAN-WILSON, Canon Jane Elizabeth. b 61. Magd Coll Ox MA 87. Cranmer Hall Dur. **d** 89 **p** 94. Par Dn Ormesby *York* 89–93; Dn-in-c Middlesbrough St Agnes 93–94; P-in-c 94–95; TV Basingstoke *Win* 95–03; PtO *Truro* from 03; Dioc Dir of Ords from 14; Hon Can Truro Cathl from 16. *4 Tolver Road, Penzance TR18 2AG* T: (01736) 351825 E: jvaughanwi@hotmail.co.uk

VENABLES, Deborah. b 70. **d** 12 **p** 13. NSM Presteigne w Discoed, Kinsham, Lingen and Knill *Heref* from 12. *17 Caenbrook Meadow, Presteigne LD8 2NE* T: (01544) 267663 E: revdebbiev@aol.com

VENABLES, Canon Margaret Joy. b 37. Bp Otter Coll CertEd 57. S Dios Minl Tr Scheme 86. **d** 89 **p** 94. NSM Wilton *B & W* 89–91; C Taunton St Andr 91–97; P-in-c Haynes *St Alb* 97–03; P-in-c Clophill 00–03; R Campton, Clophill and Haynes 03–06; RD Shefford 01–06; Hon Can St Alb 05–06; rtd 06; P-in-c Barnack w Ufford and Bainton *Pet* 06–10; PtO from 10. *The Cottage, Millstone Lane, Barnack, Stamford PE9 3ET* T: (01780) 749127 E: margsv@waitrose.com *or* margaretvenables@gmail.com

VENABLES, Philip Richard Meredith. b 58. Magd Coll Ox BA 79 CertEd 80. Wycliffe Hall Ox 85. **d** 88 **p** 89. C Gillingham St Mark *Roch* 88–93; V Penge St Jo 93–07; R Bebington *Ches* 07–12; V Whittle-le-Woods *Blackb* from 12. *The Vicarage, Preston Road, Whittle-le-Woods, Chorley PR6 7PS* T: (01257) 241291 E: philip.venables@ntlworld.com

VENESS, David Roger. b 48. Brunel Univ BTech 70. St Jo Coll Nottm 73. **d** 75 **p** 76. C Selly Hill St Steph *Birm* 75–80; V Colney Heath St Mark *St Alb* 80–98; RD Hatfield 88–93; rtd 13; PtO *St Alb* from 15. *125 Westfields, St Albans AL3 4JR* M: 07930-430033 E: 100drv@gmail.com

VENETUCCI, Lisa. *See* REDFERN, Lisa

VENN, Richard Frank. b 49. Leeds Univ BSc 72 Strathclyde Univ PhD 77 CChem FRSC 97. Ridley Hall Cam 04. **d** 05 **p** 06. C Margate H Trin *Cant* 05–08; P-in-c Len Valley 08–16; AD N Downs 15–16; rtd 16; PtO *Bris* from 17; *Eur* from 18. *27 Abbey Row, Malmesbury SN16 0AG* T: (01666) 238315 M: 07970-288669 E: richardfvenn@gmail.com

VENNELLS, Ms Paula Anne. b 59. CBE 19. Bradf Univ BA 81 FRSA 88. SAOMC 02. **d** 05 **p** 06. NSM Bromham w Oakley and Stagsden 05–21. *Rushey Ford House, West End Road, Kempston, Bedford MK43 8RU* T: (01234) 851594 M: 07786-174638 E: paula.vennells@gmail.com

✠**VENNER, The Rt Revd Stephen Squires.** b 44. DL 09. Birm Univ BA 65 Linacre Coll Ox BA 67 MA 71 Lon Univ PGCE 72 Birm Univ Hon DD 09 Cant Ch Ch Univ DUniv 10. St Steph Ho Ox 65. **d** 68 **p** 69 **c** 94. C Streatham St Pet *S'wark* 68–71; C Streatham Hill St Marg 71–72; C Balham Hill Ascension 72–74; V Clapham St Pet 74–76; Bp's Chapl to Overseas Students 74–76; P-in-c Studley *Sarum* 76; V 76–82; V Weymouth H Trin 82–94; RD Weymouth 88–93; Can and Preb Sarum Cathl 89–94; Suff Bp Middleton *Man* 94–99; Suff Bp Dover *Cant* 99–09; rtd 09; Bp Falkland Is 07–14; Bp HM Forces 09–14; Hon Asst Bp Eur from 11; Hon Asst Bp St Alb from 13. *81 King Harry Lane, St Albans AL3 4AS* T: (01727) 831704 M: 07980-743628 E: stephen@venner.org.uk

VENNING, Miss Alice Helen. b 83. St Mellitus Coll 12. **d** 15 **p** 16. C Blenheim *Ox* 15–17; C Woodstock and Bladon 17–19. *6 Warleigh, Bath BA1 8EE* M: 07966-977157 E: alice.venning@gmail.com

VENNING, Nigel Christopher. b 50. K Coll Lon BD 75 AKC 75. St Aug Coll Cant 75. **d** 76 **p** 77. C Minehead *B & W* 76–80; C Fawley *Win* 80–83; P-in-c Whitestaunton and Combe St Nicholas w Wambrook *B & W* 83–89; R Staplegrove 89–01; P-in-c Norton Fitzwarren 00–01; R Staplegrove w Norton Fitzwarren 01–03; R Blackdown 03–05; RD Taunton 96–01; rtd 05; PtO *B & W* from 05. *Crispin House, 5 Mendip Edge, Weston-super-Mare BS24 9JF* T: (01934) 814112 E: nigelvenning@hotmail.com

VERE NICOLL, Charles Fiennes. b 55. Solicitor 79. SAOMC 96. **d** 99 **p** 00. NSM Basildon w Aldworth and Ashampstead *Ox* 99–08; P-in-c St Barthélemy French W Indies 02–16; PtO *Ox* 08–10; *Lon* from 09. *61 Eaton Terrace, London SW1W 8TR* M: 07768-238128 E: cvn@cvnsbh.com

VEREKER, Jennifer Lesley. b 45. Totley Hall Coll CertEd 66. WMMTC 96. **d** 99 **p** 00. NSM Rugby *Cov* 99–03; TV Gt and Lt Coates w Bradley *Linc* 03–08; rtd 08; PtO *St E* from 08. *5 Chancellery Mews, Bury St Edmunds IP33 3AB* T: (01284) 701918 E: j.vereker@btinternet.com

VEREY, Christopher Douglas. b 46. St Chad's Coll Dur BA 68 MA 70. Ripon Coll Cuddesdon 02. **d** 04 **p** 05. NSM Yate New Town *Bris* 04–09; PtO 12–17; *Glouc* from 13. *3A Hillcrest, Thornbury, Bristol BS35 2JA* E: vereychris7@gmail.com

VERNON, Bryan Graham. b 50. Qu Coll Cam BA 72 MA 76. Qu Coll Birm 73. **d** 75 **p** 76. C Newc St Gabr 75–79; Chapl Newc Univ 79–91; Lect Healthcare Ethics 91–20; Chmn Newc Mental Health Trust 91–94; rtd 20; PtO *Newc* from 94. *34 Queens Road, Jesmond, Newcastle upon Tyne NE2 2PQ* T: 0191-281 3861 E: b.g.vernon@ncl.ac.uk

VERNON, John Christie. b 40. Imp Coll Lon BScEng 62. Linc Th Coll 63. **d** 65 **p** 66. C Barnard Castle *Dur* 65–69; CF 69–90; Asst Chapl Gen 90–92; Chapl Ellesmere Coll 92–99; PtO *Lich* 99–01; NSM Ellesmere Deanery 01–05 and 06–08; P-in-c Petton w Cockshutt, Welshampton and Lyneal etc 05–06; RD Ellesmere 02–08; PtO 08–19 and 21. *The Drift House, Lake House Mews, Grange Road, Ellesmere SY12 9DE* T: (01691) 623765 M: 07778-312226 E: revjcv@gmail.com

VERNON, Canon Matthew James. b 71. Collingwood Coll Dur BSc 93 Fitzw Coll Cam BA 96 MA 98. Westcott Ho Cam 94. **d** 97 **p** 98. C Guildf H Trin w St Mary 97–01; Chapl St Jo Cathl and P-in-c Pokfulam Em Hong Kong 01–09; Can Res St E Cathl from 09; Sub Dean from 12. *2 Abbey Precincts, Bury St Edmunds IP33 1RS* T: (01284) 748720 *or* 701472 E: canon.pastor@stedscathedral.co.uk

VERNON, Rachele Evie. **d** 16. NSM Croydon Ch S'wark 16–20. *49 Dron House, Adelina Grove, London E1 3AA*

VERNON, Robert Leslie. b 47. Northumbria Univ MA 00. Sarum & Wells Th Coll 73. **d** 76 **p** 77. C Hartlepool St Luke *Dur* 76–79; C Birm St Geo 79–82; V Bordesley Green 82–86; Dioc Youth Officer *Carl* 86–89; P-in-c Holme 86–89; Bp's Adv for Child Protection *Newc* 86–01; Dioc Youth Adv 89–95; V Ulgham and Widdrington 95–01; P-in-c Pokesdown St Jas *Win* 01–12; P-in-c Boscombe St Andr 09–12; rtd 12. *Killard, Doonbeg, Co Clare, Republic of Ireland* E: revbobvernon@hotmail.com

VERRALL-KELLY, Laura Joanne. b 91. Trin Coll Bris 16. **d** 19 **p** 20. C Knowle St Martin *Bris* from 19. *18 Hill Street, Totterdown, Bristol BS3 4TP* E: laurajverrall91@gmail.com

VERWEY, Mrs Eileen Susan Vivien. b 41. Open Univ BA 78 BA 93 Goldsmiths' Coll Lon PGCE 82. WEMTC 03. **d** 05 **p** 06. NSM Burghill *Heref* 05–11; NSM Stretton Sugwas 05–11; NSM Pipe-cum-Lyde and Moreton-on-Lugg 05–11; rtd 11; PtO *Heref* from 11. *Mill Croft House, Staunton-on-Wye, Hereford HR4 7LW* T: (01981) 500626

VESEY, Nicholas Ivo. b 54. Bris Univ BSc 73. Cranmer Hall Dur 95. **d** 97 **p** 98. C Tunbridge Wells St Mark *Roch* 97–01; V New Catton St Luke w St Aug *Nor* 01–14; Chapl Aspen Chpl Colorado USA from 14; PtO Dio Colarado from 14. *77 Meadowood Drive, Aspen CO 81611, USA* T: (001) (970) 355 4243 E: nicholas@vesey.net

VESSEY, Canon Andrew John. b 45. Bp Otter Coll CertEd 67. Sarum & Wells Th Coll 84. **d** 86 **p** 87. C Framlingham w Saxtead *St E* 86–89; V Catshill and Dodford *Worc* 89–94; P-in-c Areley Kings 94–95; R 95–02; RD Stourport 00–02; TV Kidderminster St Jo and H Innocents 02–05; TR Cen Swansea *S & B* 05–10; Hon Can Brecon Cathl 10; rtd 10; PtO *Nor* from 10; *St E* from 10. *3 The Laurels, Fressingfield, Eye IP21 5NZ* T: (01379) 588389 E: andrew.vessey@btinternet.com

VESSEY, Peter Allan Beaumont. b 36. ALCD 65. **d** 64 **p** 65. C Rayleigh *Chelmsf* 64–67; C Cambridge H Trin *Ely* 67–71; V Kingston upon Hull St Aid Southcoates *York* 71–80; V Swanwick and Pentrich *Derby* 80–94; PtO from 94; rtd 96; PtO *Portsm* from 15. *5 Aman Court, Granville Road, Totland Bay PO39 0BG* M: 07983-759048 *or* 07990-509455 E: pnuvessey@hotmail.co.uk

VESTERGAARD, David Andrew. b 64. Reading Univ BSc 86. Wycliffe Hall Ox 97. **d** 99 **p** 00. C Chadderton Ch Ch *Man* 99–02; V Wednesfield Heath *Lich* 02–13; AD Wolverhampton 07–11; RD 11–13; Preb Lich Cathl 12–13; R Bebington *Ches* from 13; RD Wirral N from 21. *The Rectory, Church Road, Bebington, Wirral CH63 3EX* E: david@vestergaard.co.uk

VEVERS, Canon Geoffrey Martin. b 51. Oak Hill Th Coll. **d** 82 **p** 83. C Wealdstone H Trin *Lon* 82–84; C Harrow Trin St Mich 84–88; V Wandsworth St Steph S'wark 88–96; V Battersea Fields 96–15; RD Battersea 04–10; Hon Can S'wark Cathl from 06; rtd 16; Hon C Furzedown S'wark from 16. *15 Ash Close, Malvern WR14 2WF* M: 07903-357092 E: g.vevers@pobroadband.co.uk

VIBERT (née GREEN), Imogen Elizabeth. b 73. Birm Univ BA 96 Cam Univ BTh 02. Westcott Ho Cam 99. **d** 02 **p** 03. C Poplar *Lon* 02–06; Hon C Upper Clapton St Matt 06–12; Hon C Stamford Hill St Thos 06–12; Chapl St Sav and St Olave's Sch Newington from 12; Chapl S'wark Cathl from 13. *St Saviour's and St Olave's School, New Kent Road, London SE1 4AN* T: (020) 7407 1843 M: 07799-101075 E: imogen.vibert@gmail.com

VIBERT, Simon David Newman. b 63. Glas Univ MTh 94 Reformed Th Sem (USA) DMin 02. Oak Hill Th Coll BA 89. **d** 89 **p** 90. C Houghton *Carl* 89–92; C-in-c Buxton Trin Prop Chpl *Derby* 92–99; V Wimbledon Park St Luke S'wark 99–07; Vice Prin Wycliffe Hall Ox 07–12; Acting Prin 12–13; Dir Sch of Preaching 08–17; V Virginia Water *Guildf* from 17. *Christchurch Vicarage, Callow Hill, Virginia Water GU25 4LD* T: (01344) 430230 E: simon.vibert@cc-vw.org

VICCAJEE, Rutton Behram. b 55. SCRTP 15. **d** 18 **p** 19. NSM Tongham *Guildf* 18–20; NSM Cranleigh from 20. *Salix House, 2 Willow Fields, Ash Green, Aldershot GU12 6HF* T: (01252) 910212 M: 07770-750248

VICENCIO PRIOR, Mrs Carla Alexandra Torres Lopes. b 70. Bath Univ BSc 93 SSEES Lon MA 97 Ches Univ MTh 15. St Jo Coll Nottm 12. **d** 15 **p** 16. C Kirk Hallam *Derby* 15–18; C Derby Cathl 18–19; TV Wirksworth from 19. *58 Yokecliffe Drive, Wirksworth, Matlock DE4 4EX* M: 07767-087530 E: revcarla@talktalk.net

VICKERMAN, Canon John. b 42. Chich Th Coll 69. **d** 72 **p** 73. C Horbury *Wakef* 72–76; C Elland 76–78; V Glass Houghton 78–89; V Bruntcliffe 89–96; V King Cross 96–11; RD Halifax 00–06; Hon Can Wakef Cathl 02–11; rtd 11; PtO *Worc* from 15. *6 St Barnabas, Newland, Malvern WR13 5AX* T: (01684) 563741 E: john.vickerman42@gmail.com

VICKERS, Dennis William George. b 30. RIBA 72 York Univ MA 91 IHBC 99. Glouc Th Course 83. **d** 86 **p** 87. NSM Stokesay *Heref* 86–88; NSM Bucknell w Chapel Lawn, Llanfair Waterdine etc 88–92; NSM Wigmore Abbey 93–01; PtO 01–19. *The Willows, Norbury, Bishops Castle SY9 5DX*

VICKERS, Mrs Janice Audrey Maureen. b 56. **d** 96 **p** 97. OLM Woking Ch Ch *Guildf* 96–06; OLM Ottershaw 06–18; NSM Goldsworth Park from 18. *7 Langdale Close, Woking GU21 4RS* T: (01483) 720873 E: janvickers1520@gmail.com

VICKERS, Mrs Mary Janet. b 57. Westmr Coll Ox MTh 97. St Jo Coll Nottm BTh 85. **dss** 85 **d** 87 **p** 99. Worc City St Paul and Old St Martin etc 85–89; Par Dn 87–89; World Miss Officer Worc 89–92; USPG 92–00; LtO *Eur* 95–99; PtO from 99; PtO Adnry of the Army from 97; NSM Cheswardine, Childs Ercall, Hales, Hinstock etc *Lich* 99–01; NSM Wrecclesham *Guildf* 01–02; NSM Pimperne, Stourpaine, Durweston and Bryanston *Sarum* 03–05; NSM Hipswell *Ripon* 05–06; NSM W Andover *Win* 07–09; NSM Portway and Danebury 09–10; Ind Chapl *Linc* 10–17. *2 Meadow Drive, Healing, Grimsby DN41 7RU* T: (01472) 280148 M: 07730-972403 E: vickers983@btinternet.com

VICKERS, Michael. b 60. Cranmer Hall Dur BA 98. **d** 98 **p** 99. C Monkwearmouth *Dur* 98–00; C Kowloon St Andr Hong Kong 00–07; V Cranham Park *Chelmsf* from 07. *St Luke's Vicarage, 201 Front Lane, Upminster RM14 1LD* T: (01708) 222562 F: 223253 E: revmichaelvickers@gmail.com

⌖**VICKERS, The Rt Revd Michael Edwin.** b 29. Worc Coll Ox BA 56 MA 56. Cranmer Hall Dur. **d** 59 **p** 60 **c** 88. C Bexleyheath Ch Ch *Roch* 59–62; Chapl Lee Abbey 62–67; V Hull St Jo Newland *York* 67–81; AD Cen and N Hull 72–81; Can and Preb York Minster 81–88; AD E Riding 81–88; Area Bp Colchester *Chelmsf* 88–94; rtd 94; Hon Asst Bp Blackb 94–13. *137 Canalside, Redhill RH1 2FH* T: (01737) 642984 E: micjan38@btinternet.com

VICKERS, Peter. b 56. St Jo Coll Nottm LTh 85. **d** 85 **p** 86. C Worc St Barn w Ch Ch 85–88; TV Kidderminster St Mary and All SS w Trimpley etc 88–92; Ind Chapl 88–92; CF 92–11; RD Grimsby and Cleethorpes *Linc* 11–13; RD Haverstoe 11–13; Ind Chapl 13–17. *2 Meadow Drive, Healing, Grimsby DN41 7RU* T: (01472) 280148 E: revd.p.vickers@hotmail.co.uk

VICKERS, Peter George. b 41. Local Minl Tr Course 90. **d** 93 **p** 94. OLM Cobham *Guildf* 93–04; OLM Cobham and Stoke D'Abernon 04–11; rtd 11; PtO *Guildf* from 11. *24 Station Road, Stoke D'Abernon, Cobham KT11 3BN* T: (01932) 862497 E: revpgv@googlemail.com

VICKERS, Randolph. b 36. Newc Univ MA 93 FCIM FInstD. St Alb Minl Tr Scheme 77. **d** 80 **p** 82. NSM Hitchin *St Alb* 80–87; NSM Luton Lewsey Sr Hugh 87–89; NSM Shotley Newc 89–01; rtd 01; PtO *Newc* from 01; *Dur* from 14. *4 The Paddock, Stocksfield NE43 7PH* T/F: (01661) 842364 E: rvickers@christian-healing.com

VICKERS, Timothy Hugh. b 81. Jes Coll Cam BA 03 MA 06 Birkbeck Coll Lon MA 10. Ox Min Course 14. **d** 16 **p** 17.

C Redbourn *St Alb* 16–19; C Bushey from 19. *60 Beechcroft Road, Bushey WD23 2JU* E: timvickers@hotmail.co.uk

VICKERSTAFF, John Joseph. b 60. Dur Univ BEd 82 Teesside Univ BA 84 MA 86 MPhil 88 Univ of Wales DTh 13 ARCO 92. Westcott Ho Cam 97. **d** 97 **p** 98. C Halesworth w Linstead, Chediston, Holton etc *St E* 97–99; C Blyth Valley 99–00; TV Ch the King *Newc* 00–05; P-in-c Doveridge, Scropton, Sudbury etc *Derby* 05–10; C Alkmonton, Cubley and Marston Montgomery 07–10; R S Dales from 11. *The Rectory, Main Road, Sudbury, Ashbourne DE6 5HS* T: (01283) 585098 E: drjohn.vickerstaff@gmail.com

VICKERY, Jonathan Laurie. b 58. Bretton Hall Coll BEd 80. Wycliffe Hall Ox 81. **d** 84 **p** 85. C Gorseinon *S & B* 84–86; P-in-c Whitton and Pilleth and Cascob etc 86–87; R 87–91; V Crickhowell w Cwmdu and Tretower 91–02; P-in-c Downend *Bris* 02–07; V 07–21; rtd 21. *14 Ivy House Estate, Gorsley, Ross-on-Wye HR9 7SN* M: 07948-711199

VICKERY, Robin Francis. b 48. K Coll Lon BD 73 AKC 73. **d** 74 **p** 75. C Clapham St Jo *S'wark* 74–77; C Clapham Ch Ch and St Jo 75–77; C Reigate St Luke S Park 77–79; Hon C Clapham H Spirit 80–87 and 02–10; Hon C Clapham Team 87–01; Hon C N Lambeth 10–18; PtO from 18. *13 Chelsham Road, London SW4 6NR* T: (020) 7622 4792 M: 07748-781376 E: rf.vickery@gmail.com

VIDAL-HALL, Roderick Mark. b 37. Sheff Univ BSc 60. Lich Th Coll 62. **d** 64 **p** 65. C Ilkeston St Mary *Derby* 64–67; C Nether and Over Seale 67–70; V Chellaston 70–84; C Marchington w Marchington Woodlands *Lich* 84–97; C Kingstone w Gratwich 85–97; TV Uttoxeter Area 97–01; rtd 01. *Le Perhou, 22630 Saint-Juvat, France* T: (0033) 2 96 88 16 34 E: mark@vidalhall.co.uk

VIGARS, Anthony Roy. b 54. St Jo Coll Dur BA 75. Trin Coll Bris 77. **d** 78 **p** 79. C Barking St Marg w St Patr *Chelmsf* 78–81; C Littleover *Derby* 81–84; C-in-c Stapenhill Immanuel CD 84–90; V Meltham *Wakef* 90–97; V Reading St Jo *Ox* 97–06; rtd 07; PtO *Ox* 07–08; *Ex* from 09. *15 Edgcumbe Drive, Tavistock PL19 0ET* T: (01822) 610539 E: tony.vigars@hotmail.com

VIGERS, Neil Simon. b 62. K Coll Lon BD 84 MTh 87. Linc Th Coll 88. **d** 90 **p** 91. C Chelsea St Luke and Ch Ch *Lon* 90–93; C Staines St Mary and St Pet 93–96; P-in-c Hook *Win* 96–02; R 02–07; PtO *Guildf* from 14; *S'wark* from 18. *St Andrew's House, 16 Tavistock Crescent, London W11 1AP* T: (020) 7313 3900 F: 7313 3999

VIGOR, Ms Margaret Ann. b 45. Ripon Coll Cuddesdon 85. **d** 87 **p** 96. Chapl Asst All SS Convent Ox 87–89; Par Dn Basildon St Martin w Nevendon *Chelmsf* 89–91; NSM Billingham St Cuth *Dur* 96–11; rtd 11; PtO *Dur* 11–20. *15 Mitchell Street, Hartlepool TS26 9EZ* T: (01429) 867458

VILASECA-BRUCH, John. b 89. Cam Univ BA 16. Westcott Ho Cam 14. **d** 16 **p** 17. C Berwick H Trin and St Mary *Newc* 16–19; V Tynemouth Cullercoats St Paul from 19. *53 Grosvenor Drive, Whitley Bay NE26 2JR* M: 07860-828852 E: vilaseca26@yahoo.es

VILES, Joan Mary. b 47. **d** 13 **p** 14. NSM Thornes *Wakef* 13–14; *Leeds* 14–17; PtO from 17. *4 Thornes Moor Close, Wakefield WF2 8QA* T: (01924) 383564 E: revjoanviles@sky.com

VILLAGE, Prof Andrew. b 54. Collingwood Coll Dur BSc 75 Edin Univ PhD 80 Bris Univ PhD 03. Trin Coll Bris BA 92. **d** 92 **p** 93. C Northampton St Giles *Pet* 92–95; R Middleton Cheney w Chacombe 95–04; Dir Cen for Min Studies Univ of Wales (Ban) *Ban* 04–07; Lect York St Jo Univ 07–15; Prof Practical and Empirical Th from 15; PtO *York* from 08. *York St John University, Lord Mayor's Walk, York YO31 7EX* T: (01904) 876723 M: 07749-484425 E: a.village@yorksj.ac.uk

VILLER, Canon Allan George Frederick. b 38. EAMTC 78. **d** 81 **p** 82. NSM Ely 81–85; V Emneth 85–92; V Littleport 92–03; RD Ely 98–03; rtd 03; Hon Can Ely Cathl 01–06; Hon C Barton Bendish w Beachamwell etc 03–06; PtO *Ely* 06–21; *Nor* from 07. *41 Westfields, Narborough, King's Lynn PE32 1SX* T/F: (01760) 337633 E: allan@viller.net

VINCENT, Beverley. b 56. St Mellitus Coll 16. **d** 18 **p** 19. NSM Halstead Area *Chelmsf* from 18; TV from 21. *The Rectory, Church Street, Great Maplestead, Halstead CO9 2RG* T: (01787) 460273 E: khvicar@gmail.com

VINCENT, Jacqueline Margaret. *See* RODWELL, Jacqueline Margaret

VINCENT, John Leonard. b 61. Univ of Wales (Lamp) BA 83 Southn Univ BTh 87 Cardiff Univ MTh 14. Chich Th Coll 84. **d** 87 **p** 88. C Hampton All SS *Lon* 87–90; C Shepperton 90–95; V Whitton SS Phil and Jas 95–03; CF from 03. *c/o MOD Chaplains (Army)* T: (01264) 383430 F: 381824 E: padrejohn@live.co.uk

VINCENT, Michael Francis. b 48. CertEd 70 Open Univ BA 83. Sarum & Wells Th Coll 85. **d** 87 **p** 88. C Nuneaton St Mary *Cov*

87–90; C Stockingford 90–91; P-in-c 91–99; V 99–14; rtd 14; PtO *Leic* 15–18. *11 Elmcroft Road, North Kilworth, Lutterworth LE17 6HX* T: (01858) 881194 E: mick.vincent@gmail.com

VINCENT, Roy David. b 37. Chich Th Coll 81. **d** 83 **p** 84. C Atherton *Man* 83–86; V E Crompton 86–95; P-in-c Burwash *Chich* 95–00; R 00–04; rtd 04; PtO *Carl* 05–11; *Mor* from 12. *24 Stewart Street, Portgordon, Buckie AB56 5QT* T: (01542) 834705

VINCER, Ms Louise Claire. b 69. Roehampton Inst BA 90 Edin Univ MTh 93. Westcott Ho Cam 97. **d** 00 **p** 01. C Waltham H Cross *Chelmsf* 00–04; C Perry Hill St Geo w Ch Ch and St Paul *S'wark* 04–06; C Bermondsey St Anne and St Aug 06–11; C Bermondsey St Jas w Ch Ch and St Crispin 06–11; Community P N Lincs *Linc* 11–13; Developing Discipleship Progr Co-ord 14–17; C Humberston 17–20; P-in-c Chartham and Upper Hardres w Stelling *Cant* from 20. *22 The Precincts, Canterbury CT1 2EP* T: (01227) 767540

VINE, Carolyn Ann. *See* TIBBOTT, Carolyn Ann

VINE, James David. b 67. Brighton Univ BSc 95. St Steph Ho Ox. **d** 00 **p** 01. C Eastbourne St Mary *Chich* 00–03; V Stone Cross St Luke w N Langney from 03. *The Vicarage, 8 Culver Close, Eastbourne BN23 8EA* T: (01323) 764473 E: jamesdavidvine@gmail.com

VINE, Michael Charles. b 51. Worc Coll Ox BA 73 MA 80. Cuddesdon Coll 73. **d** 76 **p** 77. C Wallsend St Luke *Newc* 76–79; C Denton 79–81; V Sugley 81–91; V Shiremoor 91–02; R Wallsend St Pet and St Luke 02–11; rtd 11; PtO *Newc* from 11. *26 Percy Street, North Shields NE30 4HA* T: 0191-257 4711 E: vinemichael@freeuk.co.uk

VINE, Canon Neville Peter. b 54. K Coll Lon BD 80 AKC 80. Linc Th Coll 80. **d** 81 **p** 82. C Peterlee *Dur* 81–86; Chapl Peterlee Coll 84–86; V Auckland St Pet *Dur* 86–89; PtO 89–91; R Easington 91–99; R Easington, Easington Colliery and S Hetton 99–03; AD Easington 98–03; V Auckland St Andr and St Anne 03–14; V Bishop Auckland 14–16; AD Auckland 03–15; Hon Can Dur Cathl 03–16; rtd 16; PtO *Dur* from 17. *3 Highsteads, Medomsley, Consett DH8 6QA* E: neville.vine@hotmail.com

VINEY, Christopher William. b 54. All SS Cen for Miss & Min 13. **d** 14 **p** 15. NSM Newton w Flowery Field *Ches* 14–16; C Millbrook from 17; C Dukinfield St Jo from 17. *7 Rochester Close, Dukinfield SK16 5DG* T: 0161-303 1244 M: 07880-343804 E: chrisviney@me.com *or* chris.viney@stjohnsdukinfield.com

VINEY, Peter. b 43. Ox NSM Course. **d** 76 **p** 77. NSM High Wycombe *Ox* from 76. *76 Westmead, Princes Risborough HP27 9HS* T: (01844) 275461

VIRDEN, Richard. b 40. K Coll Lon BSc 61 Univ Coll Lon MSc 62 PhD 66. **d** 04 **p** 05. OLM N Tyne and Redesdale *Newc* 04–10; PtO from 10. *Ingram Cottage, West Woodburn, Hexham NE48 2SB* T: (01434) 270334

VIVASH, Peter Henry. b 57. Hockerill Coll of Educn CertEd 78 CQSW 85. Cranmer Hall Dur 90. **d** 92 **p** 93. C Malpas *Mon* 92–95; R Bettws 95–01; P-in-c Upper Derwent *Carl* 01–16; Dioc Rep CMS 01–16; Warden of Readers *Carl* 05–16; V Acomb St Steph and St Aid *York* from 16. *The Vicarage, 32 Carr Lane, York YO26 5HX* E: peter.vivash@dsl.pipex.com

VIVIAN, Adrian John. b 42. K Coll Lon BD 65 AKC 66. St Denys Warminster 62. **d** 66 **p** 67. C Bromley St Andr *Roch* 66–69; C Egg Buckland *Ex* 69–73; PtO 73–84; P-in-c Newton Ferrers w Revelstoke 84–87. *9 Munro Avenue, Yealmpton, Plymouth PL8 2NQ*

VIVIAN, Simon John. b 70. Edin Univ BMus 96. Ripon Coll Cuddesdon 14. **d** 16 **p** 17. C Gt Berkhamsted, Gt and Lt Gaddesden etc *St Alb* 16–20; V Sawbridgeworth from 20. *The Vicarage, 144 Sheering Mill Lane, Sawbridgeworth CM21 9ND* T: (01279) 723719 E: vicar@sawbridgeworthchurch.org.uk

VIVIAN, Victor Ivan. b 38. Nottm Poly LLB 87. EMMTC 91. **d** 94 **p** 95. NSM Bestwood *S'well* 94–99; Korea 99–03; rtd 03; PtO *S'well* from 03. *12 Deepdale Road, Wollaton, Nottingham NG8 2FU* T: 0115-928 3954 E: vicvivian@icloud.com

VOCKINS, Preb Michael David. b 44. OBE 96. Univ of Wales (Abth) BSc 69. Glouc Sch of Min 85. **d** 88 **p** 89. NSM Cradley w Mathon and Storridge *Heref* 88–14; PtO from 14; RD Ledbury 02–13; PtO *Worc* from 88; Chapl Heref Sixth Form Coll 05–09; Bp's Adv for SSM *Heref* 06–15; Preb Heref Cathl 09–15; PtO *B & W* from 18. *The Chantry, Charlton Musgrove, Wincanton BA9 8HG* T: (01963) 34837 E: mdvockins@btinternet.com

VOLLAND, Michael John. b 74. Northumbria Univ BA 96 K Coll Lon MA 04 Dur Univ DThM 13. Ridley Hall Cam 04. **d** 06 **p** 07. Pioneer Min Glouc City 06–09; C Glouc Sch 07–09; Dir Miss Cranmer Hall Dur 09–15; P Missr E Dur Miss Project 14–15; AD Easington *Dur* 14–15; PtO *Ely* 15–20; Tutor Ridley Hall Cam 15–17; Prin from 17; CF (ACF) from 13.

Ridley Hall, Ridley Hall Road, Cambridge CB3 9HG T: (01223) 746585 E: mjv22@cam.ac.uk

VOLOSSEVICH, Alexander. b 55. St Mellitus Coll 15. d 18 p 19. NSM Ealing St Mary *Lon* from 18. *26 Beech Gardens, London W5 4AJ* M: 07743-602256 E: revav@outlook.com

VON FRAUNHOFER, Nicola Anne. b 63. Bris Univ MB, ChB 88 Lon Univ MSc 05 MRCPsych 88. SEITE 14. d 14 p 16. NSM Wandsworth St Paul *S'wark* from 14. *St Paul's Community Centre, 23 Inner Park Road, London SW19 6ED* T: (020) 8785 2341 E: nickyvonfr@yahoo.co.uk

VON MALAISÉ, Nicolas Axel Christoph. b 62. Univ Coll Ox BA 84 MA. Ripon Coll Cuddesdon BA 87. d 87 p 88. C Oxhey St Matt *St Alb* 87–90; C Northfield *Birm* 90–92; Asst Chapl Win Coll 92–05; V Bordesley St Benedict *Birm* 06–10; PtO *Win* 06–10. *27 Kensington Place, London W8 7PR* E: utunumsint7@aol.com

VOOGHT, Canon Michael George Peter. b 38. St Pet Hall Ox BA 61 MA 65. Chich Th Coll 61. d 63 p 64. C E Dulwich St Jo *S'wark* 63–66; C Prestbury *Glouc* 66–72; R Minchinhampton 72–85; RD Stonehouse 79–85; V Thornbury 85–02; Hon Can Glouc Cathl 86–02; rtd 02; PtO *Glouc* 03–20; Bris 05–18. *62 High Street, Thornbury, Bristol BS35 2AN* T: (01454) 414915

VOST, Mrs Jane. b 62. d 04 p 08. OLM Radcliffe *Man* 04–10; OLM Radcliffe St Andr 10–13; PtO from 13; Chapl Wrightington, Wigan and Leigh NHS Foundn Trust 12–16; Chapl Man Univ NHS Foundn Trust 16–19. *Address withheld by request* M: 07986-668144 E: jane.vost@hotmail.co.uk

VOTH HARMAN, Karin Lee. b 65. Virginia Univ BA 87 Sussex Univ MA 93 DPhil 99. Westcott Ho Cam 09. d 11 p 12. NSM King's Cliffe, Bulwick and Blatherwycke etc *Pet* 11–16; NSM Ketton, Collyweston, Easton-on-the-Hill etc 13–16; P-in-c Cherry Hinton St Andr *Ely* 16–21; V from 21. *The Vicarage, 2 Fulbourn Old Drift, Cambridge CB1 9NE* T: (01223) 242954 M: 07971-936253 E: karinvothharman@gmail.com

VOUSDEN, Canon Alan Thomas. b 48. K Coll Lon BSc 69. Qu Coll Birm. d 72 p 73. C Orpington All SS *Roch* 72–76; C Belvedere All SS 76–80; R Cuxton and Halling 80–86; V Bromley St Mark 86–98; Chapl Bromley Hosp 86–94; Chapl Bromley Hosps NHS Trust 94–98; V Rainham *Roch* 98–10; RD Gillingham 00–10; Bp's Dom Chapl 10–13; Hon Can Roch Cathl 99–13; rtd 13; PtO *Roch* from 13. *3 Fartherwell Avenue, West Malling ME19 6NG* E: alanvousden@btinternet.com

VOWLES, Ms Patricia. b 50. S'wark Ord Course 84. d 87 p 94. USPG 70–91; NSM Nunhead St Antony w St Silas *S'wark* 87–91; Par Dn Newington St Mary 91–94; Par Dn Camberwell St Mich w All So w Em 91–94; V 94–06; Chapl Cautley Ho Chr Cen 06–10; C Croydon St Jo *S'wark* 11–20; rtd 20; Hon C Croydon St Jo *S'wark* 20–21; Hon C Llantilio Pertholey w Bettws Chpl etc *Mon* from 21. *21 Greystones Avenue, Mardy, Abergavenny NP7 6JX* T: (01873) 852769 M: 07709-253496 E: revpatriciavowles@gmail.com

VOWLES, Canon Peter John Henry. b 25. MBE 09. Magd Coll Ox BA 50 MA 54. Westcott Ho Cam 50. d 52 p 53. C Kings Heath *Birm* 52–56; C Huddersfield St Pet *Wakef* 56–57; V Perry Beeches *Birm* 57–64 and 64–72; R Cottingham *York* 72–83; R Man St Ann 83–91; Hon Can Man Cathl 83–91; rtd 91; PtO *Man* 91–17. *10 Redshaw Close, Manchester M14 6JB* T: 0161-257 2065

VROLIJK, Canon Paul Dick. b 64. Delft Univ of Tech MSc 88. Trin Coll Bris BA 03 PhD 08. d 04 p 05. NSM Stoke Gifford *Bris* 04–08; Chapl Aquitaine *Eur* 09–15; Sen Chapl and Chan Brussels Cathl from 15; Adn NW Eur 16–20. *Rue Capitaine Crespel 29, B-1050 Brussels, Belgium* T: (0032) (2) 511 7183 M: (0032) 47-685 0744 E: paul.vrolijk@gmail.com *or* paul.vrolijk@holytrinity.be

VROOM, Richard Adriaan. d 88 p 88. Utrecht Old Catholic Ch *Eur* 88–07; V Llanegryn w Aberdyfi w Tywyn *Ban* 07–12; V Tywyn w Llanegryn w Aberdyfi w Pennal 12–13; V Bro Ystumanner 13–17; rtd 17. *Karveel, 15 38, 8231 AX, Lelystad, The Netherlands* E: ravroom@mac.com

VYE, Mrs Georgina Ann. b 57. SWMTC 06. d 09 p 10. C Littleham w Exmouth *Ex* 09–10; C Lympstone and Woodbury w Exton 09–10; C Ex St Thos and Em 10–14; C Chard St Mary w Combe St Nicholas, Wambrook etc *B & W* from 14. *57 Caraway Close, Chard TA20 1HP* T: (01460) 66159 M: 07950-989916 E: g.vye@btinternet.com

VYSE, James Michael Owen. b 72. Leeds Univ BA 95. St Steph Ho Ox 16. d 18 p 19. C Worksop Priory *S'well* from 18. *6 Conrad Close, Worksop S80 2EN* M: 07951-859911 E: curate@worksoppriory.co.uk

VYVYAN, Michael David. b 78. Loughb Univ BSc 02 De Montfort Univ PGCE 03. Westcott Ho Cam 12. d 15 p 16. C Camberwell St Phil and St Mark *S'wark* 15–19; P-in-c Brockley Hill St Sav from 19. *31 Siddons Road, London SE23 2JH* E: fathervyvyan@gmail.com

W

WAAKO, Samuel. b 80. Makerere Univ Kampala BA 05. St Mellitus Coll 15. d 18 p 19. C Woking St Pet *Guildf* from 18. *The Rectory, 28 High Street, Old Woking, Woking GU22 9ER* T: (01483) 673528 M: 07923-331108 E: samyul2000@yahoo.com *or* curate@stpeterwoking.org

WACHEPA, Mrs Mahalha Botomani. b 68. Mzuzu Teachers' Tr Coll Malawi TCert 93. Cranmer Hall Dur 18. d 20 p 21. C Dur N from 20. *25 Barnard Close, Durham DH1 5XN* T: 0191-384 3212 M: 07517-721786 E: mwachepa@hotmail.com

WADDELL, James William Boece. b 74. Trin Coll Bris 06. d 08 p 09. C Slagham *Chich* 08–11; C Slaugham and Staplefield Common 11–12; USA 12–13; V Leyton St Cath and St Paul *Chelmsf* 13–18; C Chanctonbury *Chich* from 18. *Fryern House, Fryern Park, Fryern Road, Storrington, Pulborough RH20 4FF* T: (01903) 740182 M: 07813-872871 E: jim.waddell@chanctonbury.org.uk

WADDELL, Peter Matthew. b 75. Keble Coll Ox BA 96 Fitzw Coll Cam MPhil 98 PhD 02. Westcott Ho Cam 98. d 02 p 03. C Oxton *Ches* 02–04; Chapl SS Coll Cam 05–10; Past Dean 10–12; Dean of Chpl Win Univ 12–16; P-in-c Abbots Langley *St Alb* from 16; RD Watford from 21. *26 Greenways, Abbots Langley WD5 0EU* E: vicar@abbotslangley.org.uk

WADDINGTON, Gary Richard. b 69. St Chad's Coll Dur BSc 91 Heythrop Coll Lon MA 05. St Steph Ho Ox BTh 96. d 96 p 97. C Southsea H Spirit *Portsm* 96–00; V Paulsgrove 00–10; TR Harrogate St Wilfrid *Ripon* 10–14; *Leeds* from 14. *St Wilfrid's Vicarage, 51B Kent Road, Harrogate HG1 2EU* M: 07920-464818 E: teamrector@stwilfrid.org

WADE, Canon Andrew John. b 50. Ex Univ BSc 71. Ripon Coll Cuddesdon 84. d 86 p 87. C St Keverne *Truro* 86–89; TV Probus, Ladock and Grampound w Creed and St Erme 89–92; V Constantine 92–00; P-in-c Ludgvan 00–01; P-in-c Marazion 00–01;

P-in-c St Hilary w Perranuthnoe 00–01; R Ludgvan, Marazion, St Hilary and Perranuthnoe 01–08; RD Penwith 03–08; TR Probus, Ladock and Grampound w Creed and St Erme 08–17; Hon Can Truro Cathl 08–17; Rural Link Officer from 12; rtd 17. *34 Gloucester Avenue, Carlyon Bay, St Austell PL25 3PT* T: (01726) 882746 E: andrewsanctuary@aol.com

WADE, Christopher John. b 54. Trent Poly BSc 81 MRICS 82 ACIArb 88. Aston Tr Scheme 88 Trin Coll Bris. d 92 p 93. C Barnsley St Geo *Wakef* 92–95; C Whittle-le-Woods *Blackb* 95–99; P-in-c Bulwell St Jo *S'well* 99–03; Dir Heavenfire Min from 03. *3 Brierdene Court, Whitley Bay NE26 3HP* T: 084516-65277 E: chris@heavenfire.com

WADE, Canon David Peter. b 65. St Jo Coll Nottm LTh 92. d 92 p 93. C Victoria Docks Ascension *Chelmsf* 92–95; P-in-c Victoria Docks St Luke 95–97; V 97–19; P-in-c Canning Town 18–19; AD Newham 07–15; Hd of New Chr Communities from 19; NSM W Ham from 19; Hon Can Chelmsf Cathl from 08. *94 Devenay Road, London E15 4AZ* M: 07958-906413 E: davenicky@hotmail.com

WADE, Geoffrey Adrian. b 61. Ripon Coll Cuddesdon. d 01 p 02. C Worc City St Paul and Old St Martin etc 01–02; C Wordsley 02–04; TV Ilminster and Distr *B & W* 04–10; V Winsmoor from 10; RD Crewkerne 18–20. *The Rectory, Shepton Beauchamp, Ilminster TA19 0LP* T: (01460) 240228 E: gw@winsmoor.plus.com *or* winsmoorbenefice@icloud.com

WADE, Mark John. b 84. St Mary's Coll Twickenham BA 06 St Jo Coll Dur BA 17. Cranmer Hall Dur 14. d 17 p 18. C Goose Green *Liv* 17–19; C Wigan 20; TV from 20. *2 Lockgate Place, Wigan WN3 5DP* T: (01942) 494906 M: 07827-811530 E: mark-wade@live.com *or* hubleader.west@churchwigan.org

WADE, Mary Ruth. *See* THOMAS, Mary Ruth

WADEY, Rachel Susan. *See* ALLEN, Rachel Susan

WADGE, Alan. b 46. Grey Coll Dur BA 68 MA 72. St Chad's Coll Dur. **d** 70 **p** 71. C Cockerton *Dur* 70–74; C Whitworth w Spennymoor 74–75; P-in-c Shipton Moyne w Westonbirt and Lasborough *Glouc* 75–80; Chapl Westonbirt Sch 75–80; V Dean Forest H Trin *Glouc* 80–83; Chapl Gresham's Sch Holt 83–91; R Ridgeway *Ox* 91–11; RD Wantage 95–01; rtd 11; PtO *Sarum* 12–20. *8 Underhill, Mere, Warminster BA12 6LU*

WADMAN, Vera Margaret. b 51. EAMTC 97. **d** 00 **p** 01. NSM Burnham *Chelmsf* 00–02; NSM Creeksea w Althorne, Latchingdon and N Fambridge 02–09; NSM Creeksea from 09; P-in-c from 10. *Fernlea Cottage, 8 Fernlea Road, Burnham-on-Crouch CM0 8EJ* T: (01621) 783963 E: vera.wadman@allsaintscreeksea.org.uk

WADSWORTH (née REID), Mrs Alison Margaret. b 36. Bris Univ CertEd 57. **d** 97 **p** 98. OLM Cley Hill Warminster *Sarum* 97–06; PtO from 06. *2 Saxon's Acre, Warminster BA12 8HT* T: (01985) 212510 E: awap@blueyonder.co.uk

WADSWORTH, Andrew James. b 56. St Jo Coll Dur BA 79 Cam Univ CertEd 80 Lambeth STh 95 FRSA 99. Sarum & Wells Th Coll 84 Chich Th Coll 86. **d** 87 **p** 88. NSM Forest Row *Chich* 87–89; NSM E Grinstead St Swithun 87–89; C Shrewsbury St Chad w St Mary *Lich* 89–91; TV Honiton, Gittisham, Combe Raleigh, Monkton etc *Ex* 91–97; V Bulkington w Shilton and Ansty *Cov* 97–06; P-in-c Bognor *Chich* 06–07; V 07–18; rtd 18. *3 Shaftesbury Place, Rustington, Littlehampton BN16 2GA* E: andrewwadsworth@btinternet.com

WADSWORTH, Andrew John. b 67. Reading Univ BSc 88 MRICS 90. Wycliffe Hall *Ox* 99. **d** 01 **p** 02. C Plymouth St Andr and Stonehouse *Ex* 01–05; C Enfield Ch Ch Trent Park *Lon* 05–13; Pioneer Min 13–18; R Trull w Angersleigh *B & W* from 18. *The New Rectory, Wild Oak Lane, Trull, Taunton TA3 7JT* T: (01823) 368084 E: wadsworth.andy@outlook.com

WADSWORTH, Jean. b 44. St Jo Coll Dur BA 71. Cranmer Hall Dur 85. **d** 87 **p** 94. Par Dn Thamesmead *S'wark* 87–92; Par Dn Rotherhithe H Trin 92–94; C 94–98; V New Eltham All SS 98–08; RD Eltham and Mottingham 01–05; rtd 08. *2 Peak Coach House, Cotmaton Road, Sidmouth EX10 8SY*

WADSWORTH, Canon Peter Richard. b 52. Qu Coll Ox BA 73 MA 77. Cuddesdon Coll 74 English Coll Rome 76. **d** 77 **p** 78. C High Wycombe *Ox* 77–81; C Farnham Royal w Hedgerley 81–84; Dioc Ecum Officer *Portsm* 84–90; V E Meon 84–96; V Langrish 84–96; V Elson 96–04; RD Gosport 96–02; V St Alb St Sav 04–17; Hon Can St Alb 16–17; rtd 17; PtO *York* from 17. *45 Normandy Avenue, Beverley HU17 8PF* T: (01482) 865662 E: peter.wadsworth52@gmail.com

WAGGETT, Geoffrey James. b 49. Sarum & Wells Th Coll 83. **d** 85 **p** 86. C Newton Nottage *Llan* 85–88; TV Glyncorrwg w Afan Vale and Cymmer Afan 88–89; R 89–99; V Glyncorrwg and Upper Afan Valley 99–00; TR Ebbw Vale *Mon* 00–13; TV Upper Ebbw Valleys 13–16; rtd 16; P-in-c Upper Ebbw Valleys *Mon* 16–17; PtO *Llan* from 17. *43 Rushfield Gardens, Bridgend CF31 1DF* T: (01656) 658635 E: geoffandjennifer@hotmail.co.uk

WAGNER, Mrs Alison Judith. b 74. Univ Coll Lon BSc 95. St Mellitus Coll BA 20. **d** 20 **p** 21. C Northampton St Giles *Pet* from 20. *18 The Avenue, Cliftonville, Northampton NN1 5BT* T: (01604) 635754 M: 07971-542597 E: curate@stgilesnorthampton.org.uk

WAGSTAFF (née JONES), Ms Alison. b 40. K Coll Dur BA 63 Man Univ CertEd 64. TISEC 95. **d** 98 **p** 99. C Edin St Cuth 98–00; Assoc P Edin St Columba from 00; Chapl St Columba's Hospice 01–05. *27 Cambridge Gardens, Edinburgh EH6 5DH* T: 0131-554 6702 M: 07766-383117 E: alisonwagtsaff09@gmail.com

WAGSTAFF, Canon Andrew Robert. b 56. K Coll Lon BD 79 AKC 79. Coll of Resurr Mirfield 81. **d** 83 **p** 84. C Newark w Hawton, Cotham and Shelton *S'well* 83–86; C Dublin St Bart w Leeson Park *D & G* 86–89; V Nottingham St Geo w St Jo *S'well* 89–95; V Worksop Priory 95–06; Chapl Antwerp St Boniface *Eur* from 06; Hon Can from 12. *Grétrystraat 39, 2018 Antwerp, Belgium* T: (0032) (3) 239 3339 E: chaplain@boniface.be

WAGSTAFF, The Ven Christopher John Harold. b 36. St D Coll Lamp BA 62. **d** 63 **p** 64. C Queensbury All SS *Lon* 63–68; V Tokyngton St Mich 68–73; V Coleford w Staunton *Glouc* 73–83; RD Forest S 76–82; Adn Glouc 83–00; Hon Can Glouc Cathl 83–00; Hon Can St Andr Cathl Njombe (Tanzania) from 93; rtd 00; PtO *Glouc* from 00. *Karibuni, Collafield, Littledean, Cinderford GL14 3LG* T: (01594) 825282 E: mc.wagstaff@btinternet.com

WAGSTAFF, Miss Joan. b 33. Gilmore Ho. **dss** 75 **d** 87 **p** 94. Ellesmere Port *Ches* 86–87; Par Dn 87–93; rtd 93; PtO *Ches* from 93. *41 Heywood Road, Great Sutton, South Wirral CH66 3PS* T: 0151-348 0884

WAGSTAFF, Ms Julie. b 48. Univ of Wales (Swansea) BA 93. St Mich Coll Llan 10. **d** 13 **p** 15. NSM Waunarllwydd *S & B* 13–18; rtd 18; PtO *S & B* from 18. *14 Bethania Road, Clydach, Swansea SA6 5DE* T: (01792) 845426 E: juliewagstaff1948@gmail.com

WAGSTAFF, Michael. b 59. R Holloway Coll Lon BA 81. Coll of Resurr Mirfield 86. **d** 89 **p** 90. C Worksop Priory *S'well* 89–92; C Ab Kettleby Gp *Leic* 92–94; TV Leic Resurr 94–00; Dioc Soc Resp Officer *Sheff* 00–08; Chapl RN from 08. *Royal Naval Chaplaincy Service Headquarters, Tanner Building, HMS Excellent, Whale Island, Portsmouth PO2 8ER* T: 0300-157 7544

WAGSTAFFE, Eric Herbert. b 25. St Aid Birkenhead 55. **d** 57 **p** 58. C Harpurhey Ch Ch *Man* 57–60; R 60–69; V Pendlebury St Jo 69–84; V Hoghton *Blackb* 84–91; rtd 91; PtO *Blackb* 91–02; *Man* 95–17. *3 Chelwood Close, Bolton BL1 7LN* T: (01204) 596048

WAIN, Phillip. b 54. Aston Tr Scheme 89 Linc Th Coll 93. **d** 93 **p** 94. C Witton *Ches* 93–97; R Lea Gp *Linc* 97–14 and from 14; RD Corringham from 13. *Oaktree House, Padmoor Lane, Upton, Gainsborough DN21 5NH* T: (01427) 639933 E: phillip.wain@btinternet.com

WAINAINA, Canon Francis Samson Kamoko. b 51. St Jo Coll Dur MA 89. Oak Hill Th Coll BA 84. **d** 84 **p** 85. Kenya 84–88; C Upton (Overchurch) *Ches* 89–92; V Ellesmere St Pet *Sheff* 92–95; C York St Mich-le-Belfrey 95–01; V Starbeck *Ripon* 01–14; *Leeds* 14–16; Hon Can Ripon Cathl 12–16; rtd 16; PtO *S'well* from 16. *40 Elder Street, Sutton-in-Ashfield NG17 3FE* E: francis.wainaina51@gmail.com

WAINE, The Very Revd Stephen John. b 59. Westcott Ho Cam 81. **d** 84 **p** 85. C Wolverhampton *Lich* 84–88; Min Can and Succ St Paul's Cathl *Lon* 88–93; V Romford St Edw *Chelmsf* 93–10; P-in-c Romford St Jo 02–10; Adn Dorset *Sarum* 10–15; Can and Preb Sarum Cathl 10–15; Dean Chich from 15. *The Deanery, Canon Lane, Chichester PO19 1PX* T: 812484 *or* (01243) 812494 E: dean@chichestercathedral.org.uk

WAINMAN, Mrs Caroline Sarah Elizabeth. b 65. Aston Univ BSc 88 Mansf Coll Ox PGCE 90. ERMC 14. **d** 17 **p** 18. C Hemel Hempstead St Alb 17–20; TV Schorne *Ox* from 20. *Address temp unknown* M: 07889-788864

WAINWRIGHT, John Pounsberry. b 42. St Steph Ho Ox 64. **d** 66 **p** 67. C Palmers Green St Jo *Lon* 66–70; C Primrose Hill St Mary w Avenue Road St Paul 70–71; P-in-c St John's Wood All SS 71–73; V Hendon All SS Childs Hill 73–17; PtO from 16; rtd 16. *55 Silkstream Road, Edgware HA8 0DD*

WAINWRIGHT, Mrs Kirsty Anne. b 73. ERMC 16. **d** 19 **p** 20. C St Alb St Steph from 19. *12 Tavistock Avenue, St Albans AL1 2NH* T: (01727) 857613

WAINWRIGHT, Malcolm Hugh. b 47. Man Univ BA 68 Nottm Univ MA 89 Cam Univ PGCE 69. St Jo Coll Nottm MA 98. **d** 98 **p** 99. NSM Cotgrave and Owthorpe *S'well* 98–02; P-in-c Plumtree and Tollerton 02–09; Hon C Burton Fleming w Fordon, Grindale etc *York* 09–11; P-in-c Skelton w Shipton and Newton on Ouse 11–21; C Alne 17–21; C Brafferton w Pilmoor, Myton-on-Swale etc 17–21; C Coxwold and Husthwaite 17–21; C Crayke w Brandsby and Yearsley 17–21; C Easingwold w Raskelf 17–21; C Strensall 17–21; C Forest of Galtres 17–21; rtd 21. *Address temp unknown* E: malcolm@mhwainwright.eclipse.co.uk

WAINWRIGHT, Mrs Margaret Gillian. b 45. Qu Mary Coll Lon BA 68. EAMTC 00. **d** 03 **p** 04. NSM Combs and Lt Finborough *St E* 03–05; NSM The Creetings and Earl Stonham w Stonham Parva 05–11; rtd 11; PtO *St E* 11–20. *The Cottage, Elmswell Road, Wetherden, Stowmarket IP14 3LN* T: (01359) 242653

WAINWRIGHT, Martin John. b 69. Loughb Univ BEng 92. Trin Coll Bris BA 98. **d** 98 **p** 99. C Chislehurst Ch Ch *Roch* 98–02; V Camberley St Mary *Guildf* 02–10; V Howell Hill 10–21; CF(V) 16–21; CF from 21. *c/o MOD Chaplains (Army)* T: (01264) 383430 E: martinjwainwright@gmail.com

WAINWRIGHT, Pauline Barbara. *See* FLORANCE, Pauline Barbara

WAINWRIGHT, Peter Anthony. b 45. K Coll Lon BD 73 MRICS 67. Ridley Hall Cam 73. **d** 75 **p** 76. C Ashtead *Guildf* 76–79; V Woking St Paul 79–84; PtO *Ox* 87–92 and 03–05; P-in-c Harston w Hauxton and Newton *Ely* 05–10; rtd 10; PtO *Ox* from 10. *19 Rosebery Avenue, High Wycombe HP13 7AL* T: (01494) 267913 M: 07814-835528 E: rev@peterwainwright.plus.com

WAINWRIGHT, Robert James David. b 86. St Jo Coll Dur BA 07 Ch Ch Ox MSt 08 DPhil 11. Wycliffe Hall Ox BA 14 MA 18. **d** 15 **p** 16. C Burford w Fulbrook, Taynton, Asthall etc *Ox* 15–17; NSM from 18; Chapl and Fell Oriel Coll Ox from 18. *Oriel College, Oriel Square, Oxford OX1 4EW* M: 07799-262056 E: robert.wainwright@chch.oxon.org

WAINWRIGHT, Robert Neil. b 52. NEOC 99. **d** 02 **p** 03. NSM Barlby and Riccall *York* 02–05; NSM Selby Abbey 05–12; TV Tenby *St D* 12–19; P-in-c Narberth and Tenby LMA 19–20; Fellowship of Voc Co-ord 14–20; NSM Ripon Cathl Benefice *Leeds* from 20. *The Vicarage, Knaresborough Road, Bishop Monkton, Harrogate HG3 3QQ* T: (01765) 676298 M: 07768-390060 E: robbwain@gmail.com

WAITE, Daniel Alfred Norman. b 42. **d** 04 **p** 05. OLM Gorleston St Andr *Nor* 04–12; PtO from 12. *15 Laburnum Close, Bradwell, Great Yarmouth NR31 8JB* T: (01493) 664591

WAITE, Julian Henry. b 47. Open Univ BA 98. Brasted Th Coll 68 Ridley Hall Cam 70. **d** 72 **p** 73. C Wollaton *S'well* 72–76; C Herne Bay Ch Ch *Cant* 76–79; P-in-c Mersham 79–87; Chapl Wm Harvey Hosp Ashford 79–87; V Marden *Cant* 87–93; Chapl HM Pris Blantyre Ho 90–93; Chapl HM Pris Swaleside 01–12; rtd 12; PtO *Cant* from 12. *31 Shearwater, Maidstone ME16 0DW* T: (01622) 664957

WAITE, Kathryn Joy. b 69. Univ Coll Lon BSc 92 MB, BS 95 MRCP 98 FRCR 03. ERMC 14. **d** 17 **p** 18. C Chesterton St Andr *Ely* 17–21; V Sawston from 21; V Babraham from 21. *The New Vicarage, Church Lane, Sawston, Cambridge CB22 3JR* M: 07826-835410 E: kathrynw@freenetname.co.uk

WAIZENEKER, Canon Ann Elizabeth. b 56. Southn Univ BSc 78. SEITE 05. **d** 08 **p** 09. C Chich St Paul and Westhampnett 08–12; P-in-c New Shoreham 12–14; V New Shoreham and Shoreham Beach from 14; P-in-c Old Shoreham 12–15; R Old Shoreham and Kingston Buci 15–19; Dean of Women's Min from 17; Can and Preb Chich Cathl from 15. *The Vicarage, Church Street, Shoreham-by-Sea BN43 5DQ* T: (01273) 965303 E: annwaizeneker@gmail.com

WAKE, Colin Walter. b 50. Oriel Coll Ox 72 MA. Cuddesdon Coll 74. **d** 75 **p** 76. C Sandhurst *Ox* 75–78; C Faversham *Cant* 79–80; TV High Wycombe *Ox* 80–89; R Weston Favell *Pet* 89–06; Chapl St Jo Hosp Weston Favell 89–06; rtd 06. *35 Greenhill, Royal Wootton Bassett, Swindon SN4 8EH*

WAKEFIELD, Allan. b 31. Qu Coll Birm 72. **d** 74 **p** 75. C Kingsthorpe w Northampton St Dav *Pet* 74–77; TV Clifton *S'well* 77–81; V Bilborough St Jo 81–85; R Bere Ferrers *Ex* 85–91; R Mevagissey and St Ewe *Truro* 91–96; rtd 96; PtO *Truro* 96–98; Hon C Malborough w S Huish, W Alvington and Churchstow *Ex* 98–02; PtO 01–11. *4 Eden Cottages, Exeter Road, Ivybridge PL21 0BL* T: (01752) 698724

WAKEFIELD, Anne Frances. b 58. St Aid Coll Dur BSc 79 Sheff Univ PGCE 80. NTMTC 94. **d** 97 **p** 98. NSM Danbury *Chelmsf* 97–98; NSM Sherburn w Pittington *Dur* 98–01; Asst Chapl HM Pris Dur 01–03; Chapl HM YOI Northallerton 03–05; Chapl HM Pris Low Newton 05–08; P-in-c Stamford Bridge Gp *York* 09–12; R 12–18; RD S Wold 12–17; P-in-c York St Hilda 18–21; rtd 21. *7 Ferens Close, Durham DH1 1JX* E: fran.wakfield@gmail.com

WAKEFIELD, David Kenneth. b 64. Ridley Hall Cam 02. **d** 04 **p** 05. C Bures w Assington and Lt Cornard *St E* 04–07; P-in-c Burlingham St Edmund w Lingwood, Strumpshaw etc *Nor* 07–09; R from 09. *The Rectory, Barn Close, Lingwood, Norwich NR13 4TS* T: (01603) 713880 E: revd.wake@btinternet.com

WAKEFIELD, Frances. *See* WAKEFIELD, Anne Frances

WAKEFIELD, Gavin Tracy. b 57. Van Mildert Coll Dur BSc 78 Sheff Univ CertEd 80 Kent Univ PhD 98. St Jo Coll Nottm 83. **d** 86 **p** 87. C Anston *Sheff* 86–89; C Aston cum Aughton and Ulley 89–91; TV Billericay and Lt Burstead *Chelmsf* 91–98; Dir Miss and Past Studies Cranmer Hall Dur 98–08; Dir Tr, Miss and Min *York* 09–21; NSM Stamford Bridge Gp 13–18; rtd 21. *7 Ferens Close, Durham DH1 1JX* E: gavin.wakefield@yorkdiocese.org

WAKEFIELD, Mark Jeremy. b 58. York Univ BA 77. NTMTC BA 07. **d** 07 **p** 08. NSM Primrose Hill St Mary w Avenue Road St Paul *Lon* from 07. *15 Evangelist Road, London NW5 1UA* T: (020) 7267 8202 M: 07899-668493 E: mark.wakefield@blueyonder.co.uk

WAKEFIELD, Peter. b 48. St Jo Coll Nottm BTh 72 ALCD 72. **d** 72 **p** 73. C Hinckley H Trin *Leic* 72–75; C Kirby Muxloe 75–78; V Barlestone 78–85; TV Padgate *Liv* 85–88; V Quinton w Marston Sicca *Glouc* 91–97; rtd 97. *295 Leach Green Lane, Rednal, Birmingham B45 8RB* T: 0121-453 6979

WAKEFIELD, Mrs Rachel Clare. b 72. Leeds Univ BA 94. St Mellitus Coll 18. **d** 20 **p** 21. C Welwyn Garden City *St Alb* from 20. *71 Haldens, Welwyn Garden City AL7 1DH* T: (01707) 892616 M: 07989-515540 E: rachwakefield@outlook.com

WAKEFIELD, Dean of. *See* COWLING, The Very Revd Simon Charles

WAKEFIELD, Suffragan Bishop of. *See* ROBINSON, The Rt Revd Anthony William

WAKEHAM, Ellen Liesel. *See* EAMES, Ellen Liesel

WAKEHAM-DAWSON, Andrew Whistler. b 65. Wye Coll Lon BSc 87 Open Univ PhD 94. STETS 98. **d** 01 **p** 02. NSM Paddington St Sav *Lon* 01–04; Chapl RAF from 04. *Chaplaincy Services (RAF), HQ Air Command, RAF High Wycombe HP14 4UE* T: (01494) 496264 E: andrew.wakeham-dawson519@mod.gov.uk

WAKELIN, Canon Brian Roy. b 53. Westf Coll Lon BSc 74 Trin Coll Bris MA 12. STETS 96. **d** 99 **p** 00. NSM Win Ch Ch from 99; Hon Can Win Cathl from 17. *11 Elm Court, Elm Road, Winchester SO22 5BA* T: (01962) 868679 *or* 857985 E: brian.wakelin@ccwinch.org.uk

WAKELING, Canon Bruce. b 50. Lon Univ BA 74. Westcott Ho Cam 74. **d** 77 **p** 78. C Weymouth H Trin *Sarum* 77–82; TV Oakdale 82–89; R Clopton w Otley, Swilland and Ashbocking *St E* 89–98; V Rushmere 98–16; Hon Can St E Cathl 14–16; rtd 16; PtO *St E* from 16. *1 Queech Place, Barham, Ipswich IP6 0GD* T: (01473) 835884

WAKELING, Miss Faith Georgina. b 65. Anglia Ruskin Univ BA 10. Westcott Ho Cam 08. **d** 10 **p** 11. C Loughton *St Jo Chelmsf* 10–14; C Plaistow and N Canning Town 14–17; PtO from 17; NSM Greenwich St Alfege *S'wark* from 18. *Address withheld by request* M: 07837-968967 E: faithwakeling@gmail.com

WAKELING, Hugh Michael. b 42. Cape Town Univ BSc 63. Wycliffe Hall Ox 71. **d** 74 **p** 75. C Kennington St Mark *S'wark* 74–78; C Surbiton Hill Ch Ch 78–80; NSM Richmond H Trin and Ch Ch 80–84; NSM California *Ox* 85–89 and 00–07; NSM Arborfield w Barkham 89–00; PtO 07–17; *Heref* from 18. *Sunnybank, Dunns Copse, Ledbury HR8 2HR*

WAKELING, Mrs Joan. b 44. Hockerill Coll Cam CertEd 65. S'wark Ord Course 76. **dss** 79 **d** 90 **p** 94. Surbiton Hill Ch Ch *S'wark* 79–80; Richmond H Trin and Ch Ch 80–84; California *Ox* 84–89; Arborfield w Barkham 89–00; NSM 90–00; Chapl Luckley-Oakfield Sch Wokingham 90–05; NSM Finchampstead *Ox* 00–05; P-in-c Raglan w Llandenny and Bryngwyn *Mon* 05–14; rtd 14; PtO *Heref* from 14. *28 Pound Meadow, Ledbury HR8 2EU* T: (01531) 633188 E: revdjwakeling@gmail.com

WAKELING, Rayner Alan. b 58. Portsm Poly BSc 79 Bris Univ PGCE 80. St Steph Ho Ox. **d** 01 **p** 02. C Willesden Green St Andr and St Fran *Lon* 01–05; V Greenhill St Jo 05–11; V Pentonville St Silas w All SS and St Jas from 11. *St Silas House, 45 Cloudesley Road, London N1 0EL* T: (020) 7837 4228 E: raynerwakeling@hotmail.com

WAKELY, Edna Clare. **d** 12 **p** 14. C Dublin Drumcondra w N Strand *D & G* 12–14; C Limerick City *L & K* 14–20; I Castlecomer w Colliery Ch, Mothel and Bilboa *C, F & O* from 20. *The Rectory, Riverside, The Square, Castlecomer, Co Kilkenny, R95 W138, Republic of Ireland* M: 86-357 4917 E: ednawakely@hotmail.com

WAKELY, Marcus. b 40. Solicitor 62 FRSA 88. EMMTC 84. **d** 87 **p** 88. NSM Carrington *S'well* 87–91; C Worksop Priory 91–95; V Sheff St Matt 95–01; rtd 01. *16 Park House Gates, Nottingham NG3 5LX* T: 0115-960 9038 E: marcopaulo.w@outlook.com

WAKEMAN, Canon Hilary Margaret. b 38. EAMTC. **dss** 85 **d** 87 **p** 94. Heigham St Thos *Nor* 85–90; C 87–90; C Nor St Mary Magd w St Jas 90–91; Dn-in-c Norwich-over-the-Water Colegate St Geo 90–91; Team Dn Norwich Over-the-Water 91–94; TV 94–96; Hon Can Nor Cathl 94–96; I Kilmoe Union *C, C & R* 96–01; Dir of Ords 99–01; rtd 01; PtO *C, C & R* 01–17; *Nor* from 17. *15 Sherwyn House, 61 St George's Street, Norwich NR3 1BL* M: 07548-313030 E: hilary.wakeman@gmail.com

WAKEMAN-TOOGOOD, Katie Leanne. b 80. Leic Univ BSc 02 Man Metrop Univ PGCE 04. Ripon Coll Cuddesdon 11. **d** 14 **p** 15. C Louth *Linc* 14–17; Chapl Blue Coat Sch Reading from 17; NSM Sonning *Ox* from 17. *6 Park View Drive South, Charvil, Reading RG10 9QX* M: 07447-478048 E: kltoogood@yahoo.com

WALDEN, Alan Howard. b 64. Bris Univ BSc 86 Lon Business Sch MBA 93. Trin Coll Bris BA 09. **d** 09 **p** 10. C Frimley *Guildf* 09–12; TV Madeley *Heref* 12–20; V from 20. *St Michael's Vicarage, Church Street, Madeley, Telford TF7 5BN* T: (01952) 586645 M: 07957-773043 E: ahwalden@gmail.com *or* alan.walden@tf7.org.uk

WALDEN, Mrs Jane. b 55. Cartrefle Coll of Educn CertEd 76 Chelt & Glouc Coll of HE BA 01. WEMTC 02. **d** 05 **p** 06. NSM Minchinhampton *Glouc* 05–09; NSM Minchinhampton w Box and Amberley 09–12; V Brockworth 12–19; rtd 19; PtO *Glouc* from 20. *13 Sheppard Way, Minchinhampton, Stroud GL6 9BZ* E: janewalden7255@gmail.com

WALDEN, John Edward Frank. b 38. FInstSMM. Oak Hill Th Coll 67. **d** 69 **p** 70. C Rainham *Chelmsf* 69–73; P-in-c Bris H Cross Inns Court 73–78; Conf and Publicity Sec SAMS 78–81; Hon C Southborough St Pet w Ch Ch and St Matt *Roch* 78–81; Exec Sec Spanish and Portuguese Ch Aid Soc

80–81; Hon C Tonbridge St Steph *Roch* 81–84; R Earsham w Alburgh and Denton *Nor* 84–89; PtO from 01. *2 Wentworth Drive, Harrogate HG2 7LA* E: revjefw@gmail.com

WALDSAX, Mrs Heather. b 58. Bris Univ BA 79 PGCE 80. STETS 06. **d** 08 **p** 09. NSM Canford Magna *Sarum* 08–17; NSM Wimborne Minster and Villages from 17. *60 Floral Farm, Canford Magna, Wimborne BH21 3AU* T: (01202) 889269 E: heather@waldsax.net

WALE (née BROWN), Wendy Anne. b 71. Homerton Coll Cam BEd 93. Trin Coll Bris BA 11. **d** 11 **p** 12. C Summerfield *Birm* 11–14; C Edgbaston St Germain 11–14; Chapl Wadh Coll Ox 14–18; 20s-40s Team Ldr *York* from 18; C Beverley Minster 18–20; C Beverley St Jo and St Martin w Routh All SS from 20. *28 Newton Drive, Beverley HU17 8NX* M: 07825-288779 E: wendy@beverleyminster.org.uk

WALES, David Neville. b 55. Rhodes Univ BA 78 Open Univ BSc 01. Coll of Resurr Mirfield 80. **d** 82 **p** 83. Zimbabwe 82–88; C Linslade *Ox* 89–91; P-in-c Weston Turville 91–07; R from 07; Voc Adv from 99. *The Rectory, Church Walk, Weston Turville, Aylesbury HP22 5SH* T: (01296) 613212 M: 07534-001044 E: d.wales512@btinternet.com

WALES, Janet Mary. b 56. Rhodes Univ MA 93 CTABRSM 98. Ox Min Course 11. **d** 14 **p** 15. NSM Ellesborough, The Kimbles and Stoke Mandeville *Ox* 14–17; PtO 17–19; P-in-c Ellesborough, The Kimbles and Stoke Mandeville from 19. *The Rectory, Church Walk, Weston Turville, Aylesbury HP22 5SH* T: (01296) 612936 E: revjanetwales231@btinternet.com

WALES, Archbishop of. *Vacant*

WALFORD, Mrs Angela. b 44. Whitelands Coll Lon CertEd 76. S Dios Minl Tr Scheme 85. **d** 92 **p** 94. NSM Boyatt Wood *Win* 92–99; Asst Chapl Epsom and St Helier Univ Hosps NHS Trust 99–07; PtO *S'wark* 07–13 and from 19. *58 Wolseley Road, Mitcham Junction, Mitcham CR4 4JQ* T: (020) 8646 2841 E: wols1@tiscali.co.uk

WALFORD, David. b 45. S'wark Ord Course 75. **d** 78 **p** 79. NSM Hackbridge and N Beddington *S'wark* 78–83; C Fawley *Win* 83–87; C-in-c Boyatt Wood CD 87–90; V Boyatt Wood 90–97; rtd 97; PtO *S'wark* 98–02; Assoc P S Beddington and Roundshaw 00–07; Hon Chapl Epsom and St Helier NHS Trust 00–03; Asst Chapl Epsom and St Helier Univ Hosps NHS Trust 03–10; PtO *S'wark* 10–13. *58 Wolseley Road, Mitcham Junction, Mitcham CR4 4JQ* T: (020) 8646 2841

WALFORD, James Nicholas. b 80. Bris Univ BSc 02. Wycliffe Hall Ox 11. **d** 14 **p** 15. C Clifton Ch Ch w Em *Bris* from 14; C Redland 18–20. *89 Kings Drive, Bishopston, Bristol BS7 8JQ* M: 07852-674317 E: jimw@emmanuelbristol.org.uk

WALFORD, Marc-Ashton. b 88. Aber Univ BSc 11. Wycliffe Hall Ox BTh 16. **d** 16 **p** 17. C Llanstadwel and Burton and Rosemarket *St D* 16–18; C Glamorgan Heritage Coast *Llan* 18–21; V Merthyr Tydfil Ch Ch from 21. *Mandian House, Brondeg Heolgerrig, Merthyr Tydfil CF48 1TW* T: (01656) 880328 M: 07535-015332 E: marc2k1@yahoo.com

WALFORD, Mrs Marion Gladys. b 54. NTMTC BA 08. **d** 08 **p** 09. C Canvey Is *Chelmsf* 08–12; TV from 12. *37 Ruskoi Road, Canvey Island SS8 9QN* T: (01268) 698991 E: revmarion@gmail.com

WALKER, Alan Robert Glaister. b 52. K Coll Cam BA 76 MA 79 New Coll Ox MA 84 Poly Cen Lon LLB 91 Heythrop Coll Lon MTh 93 Univ of Wales LLM 96. St Steph Ho Ox 82. **d** 84 **p** 85. C St John's Wood *Lon* 84–86; Chapl Poly Cen Lon 87–92; Chapl Univ of Westmr 92–94; Chapl Univ Ch Ch the K 87–94; V Hampstead Garden Suburb from 94. *The Vicarage, 1 Central Square, London NW11 7AH* T/F: (020) 8455 7206 M: 07956-491037 E: fatherwalker@aol.com

WALKER, Mrs Alison Mary. b 91. St Pet Coll Ox MChem 13. Trin Coll Bris MA 17. **d** 18 **p** 19. C Wenlock *Heref* from 18. *3 Grenville Drive, Much Wenlock TF13 6HB* M: 07467-603325

WALKER, Canon Allen Ross. b 46. Portsm Univ BA 94 MA 98. Chich Th Coll 86. **d** 88. C Cosham *Portsm* 88–91; Chapl Portsm Mental Health Community 91–97; Dn Portsm Deanery 91–97; Community Chapl Burnham and Slough Deanery *Ox* 97–12; AD Burnham and Slough 05–12; Hon Can Ch Ch 08–12; rtd 12; PtO *Sarum* from 19. *2 Juniper Gardens, Gillingham SP8 4RF* E: mrarwalker@aol.com

WALKER, Mrs Amanda Frances. b 62. Cen Sch Speech & Drama BSc 85 Qui Coll Lon MSc 94 Qu Coll Birm BA 09. WMMTC 06. **d** 09 **p** 10. C Stafford *Lich* 09–12; V Streetly from 12. *All Saints' Vicarage, 2 Foley Church Close, Sutton Coldfield B74 3JX* T: 0121-353 5875 M: 07811-326204 E: revdmandywalker@btinternet.com

WALKER, Andrew David. b 84. BSc 06. Trin Coll Bris BA 10. **d** 11 **p** 12. C S Dales *Derby* 11–15; R Eckington and Ridgeway from 15. *The Rectory, 17 Church Street,*

Eckington, Sheffield S21 4BG T: (01246) 432196 E: our.rector@eckingtonchurch.org.uk

WALKER, Andrew James. b 70. Liv Hope Univ BA 10. SNWTP 15. **d** 17 **p** 18. C Cotes Heath and Standon and Swynnerton etc *Lich* 17–19; C Caverswall and Weston Coyney w Dilhorne 19–21; Chapl HM Pris Dovegate from 21. *HM Prison Dovegate, Uttoxeter ST14 8XR* M: 07933-293528 E: ajw0212@gmail.com

WALKER, Andrew Stephen. b 58. St Chad's Coll Dur BA 80 Heythrop Coll Lon MA 99. St Steph Ho Ox 83. **d** 85 **p** 86. C Fareham SS Pet and Paul *Portsm* 85–87; C St John's Wood *Lon* 87–93; V Streatham St Pet *S'wark* 93–98; PtO *Bris* 98–00; *S'wark* 98–09; R St Edm the King and St Mary Woolnoth etc *Lon* 00–10; P-in-c Lewes St Mich and St Thos at Cliffe w All SS *Chich* 09–14; NSM Brighton St Mich and St Paul 14–15; C St Marylebone w H Trin *Lon* 15–17; V Pimlico St Mary Bourne Street from 17; PtO *Eur* from 16. *The Presbytery, 30 Bourne Street, London SW1W 8JJ* M: 07931-745853 E: andrew.walker@operamail.com

WALKER, Ms Angela Jean. b 55. St Jo Coll Nottm 03. **d** 05 **p** 06. C Kempshott *Win* 05–09; P-in-c Cobham w Luddesdowne and Dode *Roch* from 10. *The Vicarage, Battle Street, Cobham, Gravesend DA12 3DB* T: (01474) 814332 E: ahiangel@aol.com

WALKER, Anna Katriina. b 78. Diaconia Univ BA 02. St Mellitus Coll BA 21. **d** 21. C Bamber Bridge St Aid and Walton-le-Dale St Leon *Blackb* from 21. *39 Walnutwood Avenue, Bamber Bridge, Preston PR5 6DT* M: 07484-118564 E: anna@equestra.net

WALKER, Canon Anthony Charles St John. b 55. Trin Coll Ox MA 80. Wycliffe Hall Ox 78. **d** 81 **p** 82. C Bradf Cathl 81–84; C Nottingham St Ann w Em *S'well* 84–88; V Retford St Sav 88–01; TR Retford 02–11; TR Retford Area 11–17; AD Retford 00–09; Hon Can S'well Minster 04–11; V Morton and Riddlesden *Leeds* from 17. *The Vicarage, St Mary's Road, Riddlesden, Keighley BD20 5PA* E: tonywalker153@outlook.com

WALKER, Arthur Daniel. b 60. Nene Coll Northn BA 86 St Martin's Coll Lanc PGCE 90 Leeds Univ BA 10. Yorks Min Course 07. **d** 10 **p** 11. C Northallerton w Kirby Sigston *York* 10–14; V Birkenshaw w Hunsworth *Leeds* 14–19; P-in-c Easington w Liverton *York* from 19. *2 Grinkle Lane, Easington, Saltburn-by-the-Sea TS13 4NT* E: revdannywalker@outlook.com

WALKER (née JEYES), Mrs Caroline Helen. b 58. Wye Coll Lon BSc 81 Anglia Ruskin Univ MA 11. ERMC 08. **d** 10 **p** 11. NSM Desborough, Brampton Ash, Dingley and Braybrooke *Pet* 10–13; Chapl Kettering Gen Hosp NHS Foundn Trust 10–13; R Hardington Vale *B & W* from 13; RD Frome from 21. *The Rectory, Vicarage Lane, Norton St Philip, Bath BA2 7LY* T: (01373) 834258 E: carolinehwalker@btinternet.com

WALKER, Catherine Jane. b 76. Birm City Univ MA 08. Qu Foundn Birm 15. **d** 17 **p** 18. C Boldmere *Birm* 17–20; V Mottram in Longdendale *Ches* from 20. *The Vicarage, 30A Broadbottom Road, Mottram, Hyde SK14 6JB* M: 07803-718776 or 07484-111614 E: revvcath@gmail.com

WALKER, Ms Cherie Pauline. b 57. LCTP BA 15. **d** 15 **p** 16. C Broughton *Blackb* 15–19; C Ingol 18–19; P-in-c from 19. *St Margaret's Vicarage, 1A St Margaret's Close, Ingol, Preston PR2 3ZU* T: (01772) 727208 M: 07840-328846 E: revrie52@outlook.com

WALKER, Christopher James Anthony. b 43. Sarum & Wells Th Coll 85. **d** 87 **p** 88. Hon C Durrington *Sarum* 87–89; CF 87–98; MOD Civil Service Chapl 98–15; rtd 15; PtO *Sarum* from 99; *Win* from 99. *Horseshoe Meadow Farm, Cholderton, Salisbury SP4 0ED* T: (01980) 629234 E: horseshoewalkers@gmail.com

WALKER, Christopher John Deville. b 42. St Jo Coll Dur BA 69. Westcott Ho Cam 69. **d** 71 **p** 72. C Portsea St Mary *Portsm* 71–75; C Saffron Walden w Wendens Ambo and Littlebury *Chelmsf* 75–77; C St Martin-in-the-Fields *Lon* 77–80; V Riverhead w Dunton Green *Roch* 80–89; V Chatham St Steph 89–97; R Chislehurst St Nic 97–05; rtd 05; PtO *Heref* 05–19; *Lich* 06–07; Hon C Shrewsbury St Chad, St Mary and St Alkmund 07–13; PtO 13–21. *2 Springbank, Shrewsbury Road, Church Stretton SY6 6HA* T: (01694) 723444 E: scarletpimpernel75@gmail.com

WALKER, Christopher Simon John. b 87. **d** 19 **p** 20. NSM Padiham w Hapton and Padiham Green *Blackb* from 19. *14 Bendwood Close, Padiham, Burnley BB12 8RT* E: kit@padihamparish.org

WALKER, Mrs Claire Victoria. b 79. Van Mildert Coll Dur BA 03. Westcott Ho Cam 15. **d** 17 **p** 18. C Market Rasen *Linc* 17–20; V from 20; V Legsby from 20; R Linwood from 20; V Lissington from 20. *The Rectory, 3B*

Caistor Road, Market Rasen LN8 3HY   M: 07495-190310
E: claire.walker@lincoln.anglican.org
WALKER, Daniel. *See* WALKER, Arthur Daniel
WALKER, Canon David. b 48. Linc Th Coll 71. **d** 74 **p** 75.
C Arnold *S'well* 74–77; C Crosby *Linc* 77–79; V Scrooby
S'well 79–86; V Sutton in Ashfield St Mary 86–94;
P-in-c Sutton in Ashfield St Mich 89–94; TR Birkenhead
Priory *Ches* 94–05; RD Birkenhead 99–05; R Bromborough
05–13; Hon Can Ches Cathl 03–13; rtd 13; PtO *Newc*
from 14. *12 Mead Court, Newcastle upon Tyne NE12 9RF*
E: dave.walker48@outlook.com
WALKER, Canon David Andrew. b 52. St Andr Univ
MTheol 75 MA Hull Univ MPhil 00. Linc Th Coll 79. **d** 81
p 82. C Hessle *York* 81–84; C N Hull St Mich 84–86; V from
86; AD Cen and N Hull 99–10; RD Hull 00–10; Can and Preb
York Minster from 01. *St Michael's Vicarage, 214 Orchard Park
Road, Hull HU6 9BX* T: (01482) 803375
WALKER, David Andrew. b 76. Van Mildert Coll Dur BSc 97.
Oak Hill Th Coll MTh 07. **d** 07 **p** 08. C Cheadle All Hallows
Ches 07–11; V Finchley Ch Ch *Lon* from 11. *Christ Church
Vicarage, 616 High Road, London N12 0AA* T: (020) 8445
2532 M: 07980-360408 E: davasarahwava@yahoo.co.uk
WALKER, David Ian. b 41. Bernard Gilpin Soc Dur 64 Bps'
Coll Cheshunt 65. **d** 68 **p** 69. C Todmorden *Wakef* 68–72;
V Rastrick St Jo 72–77; V Crosland Moor 77–86; R Kirton in
Lindsey w Manton *Linc* 86–99; R Grayingham 86–99; OCF
88–99; V Clee *Linc* 99–06; rtd 07; PtO *Linc* 07–21; Asst Chapl
N Lincs and Goole Hosps NHS Trust 08–11. *48 Pretymen
Crescent, New Waltham, Grimsby DN36 4PB* T: (01472)
826958 M: 07783-604850 E: davidian83@virginmedia.com
WALKER, David John. b 69. Yorks Min Course. **d** 16 **p** 17.
NSM Dronfield w Holmesfield *Derby* from 16. *Foxlyn,
Owlthorpe Lane, Mosborough, Sheffield S20 5BA* M: 07802-
374763 E: walkerd2@btconnect.com
✠**WALKER, The Rt Revd David Stuart.** b 57. K Coll Cam
MA 81 Warwick Univ PhD 15. Qu Coll Birm. **d** 83 **p** 84
c 00. C Handsworth *Sheff* 83–86; TV Maltby 86–91; Ind
Chapl 86–91; V Bramley and Ravenfield 91–95; R Bramley
and Ravenfield w Hooton Roberts etc 95–00; Hon Can Sheff
Cathl 00; Suff Bp Dudley *Worc* 00–13; Bp Man from 13.
Bishopscourt, Bury New Road, Salford M7 4LE T: 0161-792
2096 E: bishop.david@manchester.anglican.org
WALKER, Derek Fred. b 46. Trin Coll Bris 71. **d** 74 **p** 75. C
St Paul's Cray St Barn *Roch* 74–78; C Rushden w Newton
Bromswold *Pet* 78–80; R Kirkby Thore w Temple Sowerby and
Newbiggin *Carl* 80–83; V Coppull *Blackb* 83–87; V New Ferry
Ches 87–96; R Akeman *Ox* 96–11; rtd 11; PtO *Nor* from 13.
34 Valley Rise, Dersingham, King's Lynn PE31 6PT T: (01485)
541124 E: derek.dersingham@yahoo.co.uk
✠**WALKER, The Rt Revd Edward William Murray (Dominic).**
b 48. DL 14. AKC 73 Heythrop Coll Lon MA 97 Brighton
Univ Hon DLitt 98 Univ of Wales LLM 05. **d** 72 **p** 72 **c** 97.
CGA 67–83; C Wandsworth St Faith *S'wark* 72–73; Bp's Dom
Chapl 73–76; R Newington St Mary 76–85; RD S'wark and
Newington 80–85; OGS from 83; Superior 90–96; V Brighton
St Pet w Chpl Royal and St Jo *Chich* 85–86; P-in-c Brighton
St Nic 85–86; TR Brighton St Pet and St Nic w Chpl Royal
86–97; RD Brighton 85–97; Can and Preb Chich Cathl
85–97; Area Bp Reading *Ox* 97–03; Bp Mon 03–13; rtd 13;
Hon Asst Bp S & B from 13; Hon Asst Bp Llan from 17. *2
St Vincent's Drive, Monmouth NP25 5DS* T: (01600) 772151
E: dwalker.ogs@btinternet.com
WALKER, Mrs Elizabeth. b 42. CQSW 85. NEOC 91. **d** 94 **p** 00.
NSM Stockton St Chad *Dur* 94–08; rtd 08; PtO *Dur* from 08.
29 Bramble Road, Stockton-on-Tees TS19 0NQ T: (01642)
615332
WALKER, Canon Elizabeth Margaret Rea. b 49. Ch Ch Coll
Cant CertEd 70. S'wark Ord Course 89. **d** 92 **p** 94. NSM
Ash and Ridley *Roch* 92–97; Chapl St Geo Sch Gravesend
92–97; P-in-c Burham and Wouldham *Roch* 97–05;
P-in-c Platt 05–12; V 12–15; Assoc Dir of Ords 97–15; Hon
Can Roch Cathl 09–15; rtd 15; PtO *Roch* from 16; *Cant*
from 18. *26 Howard Drive, Maidstone ME16 0QD* T: (01622)
759609 M: 07434-156563 E: revliz.walker@btinternet.com
WALKER, Gavin Russell. b 43. FCA 78. Coll of Resurr
Mirfield 76. **d** 78 **p** 79. C Wakef St Jo 78–81; C Northallerton
w Kirby Sigston *York* 81–83; V Whorlton w Carlton and
Faceby 83–85; P-in-c Brotherton *Wakef* 85–89; V Earl's
Heaton 89–97; TV Dewsbury 97–99; TV Egremont and Haile
Carl 99–04; rtd 04; PtO *Carl* from 05. *37 Fell View Park,
Gosforth, Seascale CA20 1HY* T: (019467) 25386 M: 07986-
505886 E: gavinstaffa@sky.com
WALKER, Gerald Roger. b 41. K Coll Lon BD 67 AKC 67. **d** 68
p 69. C High Elswick St Phil *Newc* 68–70; C Goring-by-Sea
Chich 70–75; R Selsey 75–81; V Hove St Andr Old Ch 81–91;
V Copthorne 91–95; rtd 95; NSM Streat w Westmeston

Chich 95–99; PtO 99–21; S'wark 00–15; Guildf 00–15.
104 Marine Crescent, Goring-by-Sea, Worthing BN12 4JH
E: clergyoncall@btinternet.com
WALKER, Ian Richard Stevenson. b 51. Univ of Wales (Lamp)
BA 73. Qu Coll Birm. **d** 76 **p** 77. C Stainton-in-Cleveland
York 76–79; C Fulford 79–81; C Kidderminster St Mary *Worc*
81–82; TV Kidderminster St Mary and All SS, Trimpley etc
82–86; R Keyingham w Ottringham, Halsham and Sunk Is
York 86–98; RD S Holderness 94–98; R Scartho *Linc* 98–08;
P-in-c Epworth Gp 08–12; R 12–17; RD Is of Axholme
14–17; rtd 17; PtO *York* 17–20; P-in-c Kingston upon Hull
St Mary from 20; Hon C Kingston upon Hull H Trin from
20. *The New Rectory, 105 Main Street, Brandesburton, Driffield
YO25 8RG* T: (01964) 259252 E: irsw@btinternet.com
WALKER, Jane. b 65. All SS Cen for Miss & Min. **d** 14 **p** 15.
NSM Man Cathl 14–18; NSM Gorton and Abbey Hey 18–19;
NSM Birch w Fallowfield from 19. *Address withheld by request*
WALKER, Mrs Jane Louise. b 63. STETS 03. **d** 06 **p** 07. NSM
Alton All SS *Win* 06–09; Chapl Phyllis Tuckwell Hospice
Farnham from 10; NSM Rowledge and Frensham *Guildf*
11–16; V Frensham from 16; AD Farnham from 17. *The
Vicarage, The Street, Frensham, Farnham GU10 3DT* T: (01252)
792137 E: revjanewalker@gmail.com
WALKER (formerly WARHAM), Mrs Jean. b 55. **d** 00 **p** 01.
OLM Newcastle w Butterton *Lich* from 00. *166 High Street,
Alsagers Bank, Stoke-on-Trent ST7 8BA* T: (01782) 721505
E: mrspopasmurf@hotmail.com
WALKER, Mrs Jillian Francesca. b 41. **d** 99 **p** 00. OLM
Blackbourne *St E* 99–11; PtO 11–21. *2 The Causeway,
Walsham-le-Willows, Bury St Edmunds IP31 3AB*
E: digger.walker@mac.com
WALKER (née SEMPER), Jocelyn Rachel. b 64. Univ of Wales
(Ban) BA 85 Man Univ PGCE 86. NOC 98. **d** 01 **p** 02. C
Chadderton St Matt *Man* 01–04; Chapl Asst Salford R
Hosps NHS Trust 04–07; P-in-c Maidstone St Martin *Cant*
07–14; Voc Officer 14–20; Dioc Dir of Ords 13–20; Hon
Can Cant Cathl 14–20; PtO from 20; Guardian Pilsdon at
Malling Community from 21. *Pilsdon at Malling Community,
25-27 Water Lane, West Malling ME19 6HH* T: (01732)
870279   E: pilsdon@pilsdonatmalling.org.uk   or
jocelyn.walker@hotmail.co.uk
WALKER, Canon John. b 51. Aber Univ MA 74 Edin Univ
BD 78. Edin Th Coll 75. **d** 78 **p** 79. C Broughty Ferry *Bre*
78–81; P-in-c Dundee St Jo 81–85; Ind Chapl 83–88; R
Dundee St Luke 85–95; R Alford *Ab* 95–02; R Inverurie 95–21;
R Auchindoir 95–21; P-in-c Kemnay 95–21; R Whiterashes
11–21; Syn Clerk 08–21; Can St Andr Cathl 01–21; rtd 21.
18 Craigpark Circle, Ellon AB41 9FF E: jwcan@btinternet.com
WALKER, John Anthony Patrick. b 58. Kent Univ PhD 12.
Trin Coll Bris BA 86. **d** 86 **p** 87. C Canford Magna *Sarum*
86–90; TV Glyncorrwg w Afan Vale and Cymmer Afan
Llan 90–96; Hd of RE Wentworth High Sch Eccles 97–99;
Community Chapl and C Gorton St Phil *Man* 00–03;
P-in-c Oldham St Paul 03–04; PtO 04–07; *Cant* 07–12;
Hon C Maidstone St Martin 12–14; TR Dover Town
15–20; AD Dover 16–17; Jt AD 17–18; P-in-c Folkestone
St Mary, St Eanswythe and St Sav from 20. *The Vicarage,
Priory Gardens, Folkestone CT20 1SW* M: 07980-692813
E: johnwalker_uk@btinternet.com
WALKER, John David. b 44. St Jo Coll Dur BA 76. Cranmer
Hall Dur 77. **d** 77 **p** 78. C Heworth H Trin *York* 77–81;
P-in-c Allerthorpe and Barmby on the Moor w Fangfoss
81–83; TV Pocklington Team 84–89; P-in-c Hovingham
89; TV Street 89–92; R Dunnington 92–99; V Thorne *Sheff*
99–03; rtd 03; PtO *York* from 03. *9 Bishop Blunt Close, Hessle
HU13 9NJ* T: (01482) 642110
WALKER, John Frank. b 53. Leeds Univ BEd 76 Ripon Coll
of Educn CertEd 75. NW Ord Course 78. **d** 81 **p** 82. NSM
Whitkirk *Ripon* 81–82; C 82–85; V Sutton Courtenay w
Appleford *Ox* 85–90; Dioc Children's Adv *S'wark* 90–94;
V Walworth St Jo from 94; Youth and Children's Officer
Woolwich Episc Area 95–99. *St John's Vicarage, 18 Larcom
Street, London SE17 1NQ* T: (020) 7703 4375
WALKER, John Howard. b 47. Brasted Th Coll 67 Clifton Th
Coll 69. **d** 72 **p** 73. C Upton (Overchurch) *Ches* 72–76; Asst
Chapl Liv Univ 76–79; V Everton St Chrys 79–82; C Parr Mt
83–86; SAMS 86–94; Area Sec (NE and E Midl) SAMS 86–89;
Paraguay 89–94; V Calverley *Bradf* 95–12; rtd 12; Hon C
Leeds St Geo *Ripon* 12–14 and from 14. *103 Harehills Avenue,
Leeds LS8 4HU* T: 0113-249 6239 M: 07903-836806
WALKER, Canon John Percival. b 45. CITC 68. **d** 71 **p** 72.
C Belfast St Clem *D & D* 71–74; C Magheraculmoney
Clogh 74–78; C Lisburn St Paul *Conn* 78–81; I Belfast
St Ninian 81–88; I Belfast St Mary w H Redeemer 88–12;
Preb Conn Cathl 98–12; Treas Conn Cathl 04–12; rtd 12.

4 Sprucefield Court, Lisburn BT27 5UL M: 07835-866914 E: walkerjohnpercival@googlemail.com

WALKER, John Richard. *See* WALKER, Richard John

WALKER, Judith Anne. *See* WALKER-HUTCHINSON, Judith Anne

WALKER, Julie Lorraine. b 68. Liv Univ BTh 05 Ches Univ MTh 09. St Jo Coll Nottm 10. **d** 12 **p** 13. C Wybunbury and Audlem w Doddington *Ches* 12–15; V Haslington w Crewe Green 15–18; V Eccleshall *Lich* 18–21; RD 18–21; TV Uttoxeter Area from 21. *13 Moisty Lane, Marchington, Uttoxeter ST14 8JY* M: 07581-540435 E: juleswalker68@gmail.com

WALKER, Keith. b 48. Linc Th Coll 82. **d** 84 **p** 85. C Whickham *Dur* 84–87; C Trimdon Station 87; P-in-c 87–89; V 89–90; R Penshaw 90–98; P-in-c Shiney Row 92–95; P-in-c Herrington 93–95; rtd 98; Hon C Jersey St Brelade *Win* 01–03; PtO *Dur* 03–20. *16 Westfields, School Aycliffe, Newton Aycliffe DL5 6PX* T: (01325) 495715 M: 07906-542095 E: revdkwalker@hotmail.com

WALKER, Kit. *See* WALKER, Christopher Simon John

WALKER, Canon Lesley Ann. b 53. Westmr Coll Ox MTh 00. S Dios Minl Tr Scheme 85. **d** 88 **p** 94. Par Dn Oakdale *Sarum* 88–92; Team Dn Bridgnorth, Tasley, Astley Abbotts, etc *Heref* 92–94; TV 94–03; Vice-Prin OLM Tr Scheme *Cant* 03–04; PtO 06–07; R Meneage *Truro* 07–17; RD Kerrier 10–17; Bp's Dom Chapl 17–19; Hon Can Truro Cathl 15–19; rtd 19. *Address temp unknown*

WALKER, Mrs Linda Joan. b 47. **d** 04 **p** 05. OLM Blurton *Lich* 04–11; OLM Blurton and Dresden 11–17; rtd 17; PtO *Lich* from 18. *6 Thackeray Drive, Blurton, Stoke-on-Trent ST3 2HE* T: (01782) 324895 E: linda.walker910@ntlworld.com

WALKER, Margaret Joy. b 44. Westhill Coll Birm TCert 66 Newc Univ MA 93. CA Tr Coll 80. **dss** 86 **d** 87 **p** 94. Scargill Ho 86–87; Hon Par Dn Monkwearmouth St Andr *Dur* 87; Hon Par Dn Chester le Street 87–93; Hon Chapl Wells Cathl *B & W* 93–01; PtO *Cant* 02–05; NSM Stone Street Gp 05–11; AD W Bridge 09–11; PtO 11–13; *Leeds* from 13. *109 Hurrs Road, Skipton BD23 2JF* T: (01756) 229056 E: margi.walker@scargillmovement.org

WALKER, Mark Alexander (Marcus). b 81. Oriel Coll Ox BA 02 MA 08 MSt 04. Ripon Coll Cuddesdon MA 10. **d** 11 **p** 12. C Winchmore Hill St Paul *Lon* 11–14; Assoc Dir Angl Cen Rome 14–18; R Smithfield Gt St Bart *Lon* from 18. *15 Wilmington Square, London WC1X 0ER* M: 07919-201244 E: marcus.walker@greatstbarts.com

WALKER, Lt Col Mark George. b 68. Univ of New England BProfStud 00 Canberra Univ MDefStud 00 Chas Sturt Univ NSW BTheol 07. **d** 06 **p** 07. C Albany St Jo Australia 06–08; PtO Perth 09; C Balga w Mirrabooka 09–11; NSM Frampton on Severn, Arlingham, Saul etc *Glouc* 11; P-in-c Lesmurdie Australia 12–13; PtO Perth 14; Chapl Ocean Reef Primary Sch from 14. *33 Semaphore Avenue, Burns Beach WA 6028, Australia* T: (0061) (4) 1415 4885 M: 07580-756141 E: markwalker68@me.com

WALKER, Martin John. b 52. Linc Coll Ox BA 73 PGCE 74 St Jo Coll Dur BA 78. Cranmer Hall Dur. **d** 79 **p** 80. C Harlow New Town w Lt Parndon *Chelmsf* 79–81; C Dorchester *Ox* 81–83; Chapl Bath Coll of HE 83–89; TV Southampton (City Cen) *Win* 89–91; Adv in RE and Resources *Sarum* 91–92; Hon C Northolt St Mary *Lon* 92–00; Chapl Bancroft's Sch Woodford Green 92–99; Chapl St Helen's Sch Northwood 99–18; Chapl Wellingborough Sch 00–18; R Wiveliscombe and the Hills *B & W* from 18. *The Rectory, South Street, Wiveliscombe, Taunton TA4 2LZ* E: revmjwalker@icloud.com

WALKER, Martin John. b 66. Brighton Univ MBA 00 Dur Univ BA 18 Greenwich Univ CertEd 98. St Mellitus Coll 15. **d** 18 **p** 19. C Crawley *Chich* from 18. *23 Smoke Lane, Reigate RH2 7HJ* T: (01293) 522692 M: 07768-774099 E: martin.john.walker@icloud.com

WALKER, Michael John. b 39. St D Coll Lamp BA 61. St Aid Birkenhead 61. **d** 63 **p** 64. C Clifton *York* 63–66; C Marfleet 66–69; V Salterhebble St Jude *Wakef* 69–83; V Llangollen w Trevor and Llantysilio *St As* 83–93; RD Llangollen 87–93; V Kerry and Llanmerewig and Dolfor 93–01; RD Cedewain 97–01; rtd 01; PtO *Ban* 01–17; *Heref* from 12. *41 Oldfields Close, Leominster HR6 8TL* T: (01568) 617472 E: margaretwalker299@gmail.com

WALKER, Michael Maynard. b 82. Imp Coll Lon MEng 05. Trin Coll Bris 16. **d** 18 **p** 19. C Westcliff St Mich *Chelmsf* 18–21; C Southend St Jo from 21. *144 Alexandra Road, Southend-on-Sea SS1 1HB* M: 07989-498412 E: mike@stjohnssouthend.org *or* michaelwalker.mw@gmail.com

WALKER, Canon Nigel Maynard. b 39. ALCD 66. **d** 67 **p** 68. C Southsea St Jude *Portsm* 67–70; C Addington S Africa 70–73; R 73–76; C Abingdon w Shippon *Ox* 76–80; V Upton (Overchurch) *Ches* 80–94; Chapl Brussels and Chan

Brussels Cathl *Eur* 94–04; P-in-c Leuven 02–04; rtd 05; PtO *Cant* 05–10; *Eur* from 05; *Portsm* from 10; *Win* 10–21; *Chich* from 12; *Guildf* from 13. *12 The Sands, Whitehill, Bordon GU35 9QW* T: (01420) 477323 E: nigelmwalker@gmail.com

WALKER, Paul Colin. b 77. Thames Valley Univ BMus 01 Roehampton Inst PGCE 02. Trin Coll Bris 16. **d** 18 **p** 19. C Gt Faringdon w Lt Coxwell *Ox* 18–21; V Dedworth from 21. *3 Pierson Road, Windsor SL4 5RJ* M: 07825-372527 E: revpaulwalker@icloud.com

WALKER, Paul Gary. b 59. Lon Univ BD. St Jo Coll Nottm 82. **d** 84 **p** 85. C Bowling St Steph *Bradf* 84–87; C Tong 87–90; P-in-c Oakenshaw cum Woodlands 90–97; V Wrose 97–13; P-in-c Bolton St Jas w St Chrys 10–13; RD Calverley 01–09; R Wortley and Farnley *Leeds* 16–18; V Drighlington and Gildersome 18–21; rtd 21. *17 Grosvenor Place, Guisborough TS14 6PD* M: 07907-802135 E: paulwalker71@blueyonder.co.uk *or* paulwalker71@me.com

WALKER, Paul Laurence. b 63. St Chad's Coll Dur BA 84. Chich Th Coll BTh 90. **d** 88 **p** 89. C Shildon w Eldon *Dur* 88–91; C Barnard Castle w Whorlton 91–93; C Silksworth 93–96; C-in-c Moorside St Wilfrid CD 96–99; V Norton St Mary 99–04; Chapl Manager Tees and NE Yorks NHS Trust 04–06; Chapl Manager Tees, Esk and Wear Valleys NHS Foundn Trust 06–16; Staff Engagement Lead from 16; Chapl 16–20; PtO *Dur* from 04. *Tees, Esk and Wear Valleys NHS Foundation Trust, Flatts Lane Centre, Flatts Lane, Middlesbrough TS6 0SZ* T: (01642) 451665 E: paul.walker8@nhs.net

WALKER, Mrs Pepita. b 35. **d** 07 **p** 08. OLM Kemble, Poole Keynes, Somerford Keynes etc *Glouc* 07–11; NSM 11–14; rtd 14; PtO *Glouc* from 14. *Woodstock, Frampton Mansell, Stroud GL6 8JE* T: (01285) 760211 E: pepita@pepitawalker.co.uk

WALKER, Percival. *See* WALKER, John Percival

WALKER, Peter Anthony. b 57. Pemb Coll Cam BA 79 MA 83 St Jo Coll Dur BA 86. Cranmer Hall Dur 84. **d** 87 **p** 88. C Chesham Bois *Ox* 87–90; Chapl Bradf Cathl 90–93; TV W Swindon and the Lydiards *Bris* 93–99; V Keresley and Coundon *Cov* 99–10; P-in-c Bidford-on-Avon 10–12; V 12–15; P-in-c Exhall w Wixford 10–15; P-in-c Salford Priors 10–15; P-in-c Temple Grafton w Binton 10–15; R Heart of England from 15. *The Vicarage, 5 Howard Close, Bidford-on-Avon, Alcester B50 4EL* T: (01789) 772217 E: peter@heartparishes.org.uk

WALKER, Canon Peter Anthony Ashley. b 46. Chich Th Coll 67. **d** 70 **p** 71. C Stamford Hill St Thos *Lon* 70–74; C Bethnal Green St Matt 74–77; V Hackney Wick St Mary of Eton w St Aug 77–84; Warden Rydal Hall *Carl* 84–95; P-in-c Rydal 84–95; P-in-c Porthleven w Sithney *Truro* 95–01; RD Kerrier 96–01; Can Res Truro Cathl 01–11; P-in-c Feock 01–10; Chapl Is of Scilly 10–12; rtd 12; PtO *Truro* from 13. *Ryancot, Wansford Meadows, Gorran Haven, St Austell PL26 6HU* T: (01726) 843621 E: petelynne@btinternet.com *or* peter.walker2@btinternet.com

WALKER, Peter Ronald. b 50. Southn Univ BA 72 K Alfred's Coll Win PGCE 73. WMMTC 02. **d** 05 **p** 06. NSM Hadley and Wellington Ch Ch *Lich* 05–10; Chapl Shrewsbury and Telford NHS Trust 09–10; TV Rhos-Cystennin *St As* 10–16; Asst P Aberconwy Miss Area 17–19; PtO *Ban* from 14. *The Rectory, Glyn y Marl Road, Llandudno Junction LL31 9NS* T: (01492) 583579

WALKER, Peter Sidney Caleb. b 50. St Mich Th Coll Crafers 76. **d** 80 **p** 81. C Devonport Australia 80–81; P-in-c Fingal Valley 81–84; R E Devonport and Spreyton 84–88; R Swallow *Linc* 88–94; R Selworthy, Timberscombe, Wootton Courtenay etc *B & W* 94–01; Chapl Costa del Sol W *Eur* 01–04; R Coxheath, E Farleigh, Hunton, Linton etc *Roch* 05–12; P-in-c Offwell, Northleigh, Farway, Cotleigh etc *Ex* 12–17; rtd 17; P-in-c Ashburnham w Penhurst *Chich* 17–21. *20 Cralves Mead, Tenbury Wells WR15 8EX* E: p.walker977@btinternet.com

WALKER, Canon Peter Stanley. b 56. SRN RMN Nottm Univ BCombStuds. Linc Th Coll 80. **d** 83 **p** 84. C Woodford St Barn *Chelmsf* 83–86; C Brentwood St Thos 86–88; V Colchester St Barn 88–94; P-in-c Colchester St Jas, All SS, St Nic and St Runwald 94–96; R Colchester St Jas and St Paul w All SS etc 96–17; Hon Can Chelmsf Cathl 09–17; rtd 17; PtO *Chelmsf* 17–21. *55 Sweet Briar Road, Stanway, Colchester CO3 0HH* T: (01206) 545192 M: 07867-972231 E: frpeterwalker@gmail.com

WALKER, Philip Kingsley. b 47. Ox Univ BA 70. St Mich Coll Llan. **d** 90 **p** 91. C Maindee Newport *Mon* 90–92; C Llanmartin 92–94; V Bishton 94–98; R Panteg 98–03; R Panteg w Llanfihangel Pontymoile 03–07; rtd 07. *Glan Aber, Lon Isallt, Trearddur Bay, Holyhead LL65 2UP*

WALKER, Richard David. b 45. Hull Univ BSc 68. S Dios Minl Tr Scheme 92. **d** 95 **p** 96. NSM Horfield St Greg *Bris*

95–98; NSM Lawrence Weston and Avonmouth 98–00; Chapl HM Pris Leic 00–01; Chapl HM Pris Usk and Prescoed 01–03; Hon C Cromhall, Tortworth, Tytherington, Falfield etc *Glouc* 04–07. *Ford House, Bronllys Road, Talgarth, Brecon LD3 0HH* T: (01874) 712292 E: richard-walker@live.co.uk

WALKER, Richard John. b 67. Humberside Coll of Educn BSc 88 Leeds Univ MSc(Eng) 97 St Jo Coll Dur BA 04 St Jo Coll Nottm MA 14. Cranmer Hall Dur 02. **d** 04 **p** 05. C Scarborough St Mary w Ch Ch and H Apostles *York* 04–08; V Elloughton and Brough w Brantingham 08–13; V Beverley St Nic 13–17; Asst Dioc Dir of Ords 11–17; Bps' Adv for Ord Selection from 15; V Scarborough St Mary w Ch Ch and H Apostles from 17. *The Vicarage, 1 North Cliff Gardens, Scarborough YO12 6PR* T: (01723) 371354 E: revrichardjwalker@gmail.com

WALKER, Richard Mark. b 63. York Univ BSc 84. St Jo Coll Nottm MA 00. **d** 00 **p** 01. C Ben Rhydding *Bradf* 00–04; P-in-c Yeadon St Jo 04–08; V Yeadon 08–14; *Leeds* from 14. *St John's Vicarage, Barcroft Grove, Yeadon, Leeds LS19 7XZ* T: 0113-250 2272 E: richard.walker@leeds.anglican.org

WALKER, Rie. *See* WALKER, Cherie Pauline

WALKER, Rodney Graham. b 59. St Hild Coll 14. **d** 17 **p** 18. NSM Pontefract St Giles *Leeds* 17–19; NSM Pontefract from 19. *11A Ashgap Lane, Normanton WF6 2DT* M: 07746-980727 E: rod@carletoncourt.co.uk

WALKER, Roger. *See* WALKER, Gerald Roger

WALKER, Mrs Ruth. b 51. MAAT 95. **d** 03 **p** 04. OLM Camberley St Mary *Guildf* 03–21; rtd 21. *73 Verran Road, Camberley GU15 2ND* T: (01276) 503551 E: tandr.walker@ntlworld.com

WALKER (née APPLETON), Mrs Ruth Elizabeth. b 58. St Jo Coll Dur BA 79 Hughes Hall Cam PGCE 80. St Jo Coll Nottm 86. **d** 88 **p** 94. Par Dn Princes Risborough w Ilmer *Ox* 88–90; C and Congr Chapl Bradf Cathl 90–93; C The Lydiards *Bris* 93–94; NSM W Swindon and the Lydiards 94–96; C Swindon St Jo and St Andr 96–98; PtO 98–99; C Keresley and Coundon *Cov* 99–10; AD Cov N 04–10; C Bidford-on-Avon 10–15; C Exhall w Wixford 10–15; C Salford Priors 10–15; C Temple Grafton w Binton 10–15; C Heart of England 15–16; Project Dir Calling Young Disciples *Worc* from 16. *The Vicarage, 5 Howard Close, Bidford-on-Avon, Alcester B50 4EL* T: (01789) 772217 E: ruth@heartparishes.org.uk

WALKER, Sharon Anne. b 60. Derby Univ BA 99. St Jo Coll Nottm. **d** 02 **p** 03. C Greetham and Thistleton w Stretton and Clipsham *Pet* 02–05; C Cottesmore and Barrow w Ashwell and Burley 02–05; P-in-c Pet St Mary Boongate 05–10; R Street w Walton and Compton Dundon *B & W* 10–19; P-in-c Compton Dundon 13–19; C W Cheltenham *Glouc* from 19. *111 Brooklyn Road, Cheltenham GL51 8DX* E: sharonannewalker@hotmail.com

WALKER, Mrs Sheila. b 45. Ex Univ MA 66 PGCE 66. SWMTC 12. **d** 14 **p** 15. NSM Whimple, Talaton, Clyst St Lawr and Clyst Hydon *Ex* 14–17; NSM Rotherfield Peppard and Kidmore End etc *Ox* from 17. *2 Priory Copse, Peppard Common, Henley-on-Thames RG9 5LH* T: 0118-972 4861 E: swalk2@btinternet.com

WALKER, Simon Glyn Nicholas. b 82. Trevelyan Coll Dur BA 03. Wycliffe Hall Ox BTh 11. **d** 11 **p** 12. C Hensingham *Carl* from 11. *The Vicarage, Oakfield Court, Whitehaven CA28 6TG* T: (01946) 63797 E: simon@stjohnshensingham.org.uk

WALKER, Stephen Michael Maynard. b 62. St Jo Coll Dur BA 84. Trin Coll Bris 86. **d** 88 **p** 89. C Eastwood *S'well* 88–92; CF 92–02; C Marple All SS *Ches* 02–06; P-in-c Tewkesbury H Trin *Glouc* 06–10; V from 10; AD Tewkesbury and Winchcombe from 19. *Holy Trinity Vicarage, 49 Barton Street, Tewkesbury GL20 5PU* T: (01684) 293233 E: vicar@trinitytewkesbury.org.uk

WALKER, Stephen Patrick. b 62. York Univ BSc 83 PGCE 84. St Jo Coll Nottm 87. **d** 90 **p** 91. C Hull St Jo Newland *York* 90–94; Min Grove Green LEP *Cant* 94–98; Children's Min Adv 96–98; TV Drypool *York* 98–99; TR 99–04; TR Binsey *Carl* 04–11; RD Derwent 10–11; P-in-c Theydon Bois and Theydon Garnon *Chelmsf* 11; V 11–16; R W Buckrose *York* from 16. *The Rectory, 2 Sudnicton Croft, Westow, York YO60 7NB* T: (01653) 619715 E: rectorwestbuckrose@icloud.com

WALKER, Susan Ann. b 57. All SS Cen for Miss & Min 16. **d** 18 **p** 19. NSM Prestwich St Marg *Man* from 18. *Bishopscourt, Bury New Road, Salford M7 4LE* E: sue256@gmail.com

WALKER, Mrs Susan Joy. b 52. Univ of Wales (Lamp) BA 73 Hull Univ MA 91. Qu Coll Birm 75. dss 83 **d** 87 **p** 94. Kidderminster St Mary and All SS, Trimpley etc *Worc* 83–86; Keyingham w Ottringham, Halsham and Sunk Is *York* 86–87; Hon Par Dn 87–94; Hon C 94–98; Chapl Hull Coll of FE 89–98; Chapl N Lindsey Coll *Linc* 98–10; Chapl John Leggott

Coll 98–12; V Burstwick, Burton Pidsea etc *York* 12–21; RD S Holderness 14–21; rtd 21; C N Holderness Deanery from 21. *The New Rectory, 105 Main Street, Brandesburton, Driffield YO25 8RG* E: susanwalkerfe@hotmail.co.uk

WALKER, Terry Edward. b 55. St Mellitus Coll 15. **d** 17 **p** 18. C W w E Mersea, Peldon, Gt and Lt Wigborough *Chelmsf* from 17; Chapl St Helena Hospice Colchester from 19. *26 Garden Farm, West Mersea, Colchester CO5 8ES* T: (01206) 383640 E: terryinmersea@live.co.uk

WALKER, Trevor John. b 51. Southn Univ BTh 80. Sarum & Wells Th Coll 75. **d** 78 **p** 79. C Standish *Blackb* 78–81; P-in-c N Somercotes *Linc* 81–82; P-in-c S Somercotes 81–82; V Somercotes 82–85; R Binbrook Gp 85–17; rtd 17. *1 Neville Turner Way, Waltham, Grimsby DN37 0YJ* E: priest1@compuserve.com

WALKER, Valerie Anne. b 57. Leeds Poly BSc 80 Leeds Univ MHSc 92. TISEC 07. **d** 10 **p** 11. C Dunfermline and Alloa *St And* 10–12.

WALKER, Yaroslav Sky. b 92. St Pet Coll Ox BA 15. St Steph Ho Ox 17. **d** 19 **p** 20. C Ruislip St Martin *Lon* from 19. *5 Wyteleaf Close, Ruislip HA4 7SP* M: 07719-167101 E: fr.yswalker@gmail.com

WALKER-HILL, Richard John. b 51. WMMTC 06. **d** 09 **p** 10. C Oakengates and Wrockwardine Wood *Lich* 09–13; V Gravelly Hill *Birm* 13–20; P-in-c Stockland Green 13–20; AD Aston 18–19; Jt AD Aston and Sutton Coldfield 19; rtd 20. *65 Trench Road, Trench, Telford TF2 6PF* E: revrichardwh@yahoo.com

WALKER-HUTCHINSON, Mrs Judith Anne. b 58. St Jo Coll Dur BA 07 CPFA 88. Cranmer Hall Dur 05. **d** 07 **p** 08. C Penhill *Ripon* 07–10; R Haddington *Edin* 10–11; rtd 11; PtO *Dur* from 11. *Westrill, Cotherstone, Barnard Castle DL12 9PF* T: (01833) 650396 M: 07977-507038 E: revjudith@outlook.com

WALKEY, Malcolm Gregory Taylor. b 44. Lon Univ. Kelham Th Coll 63. **d** 68 **p** 69. C Oadby *Leic* 68–72; TV Corby SS Pet and Andr w Gt and Lt Oakley 72–79; R Ashton w Hartwell 79–86; TR Halesworth w Linstead, Chediston, Holton etc *St E* 86–91; P-in-c Laxfield 93–01; rtd 01; PtO *St E* from 02. *4 Church View, Holton, Halesworth IP19 8PB* T: (01986) 872594 E: walkeys4446@gmail.com

WALL, Miss Elizabeth Anne. b 51. Birm Univ BDS 73 St Andr Univ MLitt 17. WMMTC 97. **d** 00 **p** 01. NSM Lich St Chad 00–14; NSM Alrewas from 14; NSM Wychnor from 14. *15 Gaia Lane, Lichfield WS13 7LW* T: (01543) 254891 M: 07711-557770 E: ayton265@gmail.com

WALL, John Caswallen. b 60. York Univ BA 83 MA 85. St Steph Ho Ox BA 89. **d** 89 **p** 90. C Ifield *Chich* 89–94; C Brighton St Pet and St Nic w Chpl Royal 94–97; C Brighton St Pet w Chpl Royal 97–98; TV Newbury *Ox* 98–05; P-in-c Moulsecoomb *Chich* 05–16; P-in-c Isfield 16–20; R from 20; P-in-c Isfield 16–20; R from 20; P-in-c Lt Horsted 16–20; R from 20. *The Rectory, 1 Sand Ridge, Ridgewood, Uckfield TN22 5ET* T: (01825) 371688 E: jocaswall@hotmail.com

WALL, Canon Márcia Zélia. b 59. NOC 04. **d** 07 **p** 08. C Oakenrod and Bamford *Man* 07–10; V Rhodes and Parkfield 10–16; Borough Dean Rochdale 12–16; Bp's Adv for Women's Min 13–16; AD Heywood and Middleton 15–16; Can Res Man Cathl from 16. *Manchester Cathedral, Victoria Street, Manchester M3 1SX* M: 07823-332110 E: revdmarciawall@hotmail.co.uk

WALL, Matthew William. b 74. Westcott Ho Cam 12. **d** 14 **p** 15. C Stoke Newington St Mary *Lon* 14–17; TV Poplar from 17. *St Nicholas' Vicarage, 2N Dee Street, London E14 0PT* T: (020) 7515 8405 M: 07764-823266 E: rev.matt.wall@gmail.com

WALL, Nicholas John. b 46. TD 01 MBE 02. Brasted Th Coll 69 Trin Coll Bris 71. **d** 73 **p** 74. C Morden *S'wark* 73–78; R Dunkeswell and Dunkeswell Abbey *Ex* 78–83; V Sheldon 78–83; P-in-c Upottery, Luppitt and Monkton 81–83; V Dunkeswell, Sheldon and Luppitt 83–03; V Dunkeswell, Luppitt, Sheldon and Upottery 03–11; rtd 11; CF(V) from 87. *The Glasshouse Flat, Old Sheldon Grange, Dunkeswell, Honiton EX14 4SE* M: 07811-105090

WALL, Richard David. b 78. Ch Ch Ox BA 99. St Steph Ho Ox 00. **d** 02 **p** 03. C Bocking St Mary *Chelmsf* 02–05; C Philadelphia St Clem USA 05–15; R Washington St Paul from 15. *St Paul's Parish, 2430 K Street NW, Washington DC 20037, USA* T: (001) (202) 337 2020 E: frrichardwall@pm.com *or* wall@stpauls-kst.com

WALL, Timothy. b 87. Van Mildert Coll Dur MMath 09 St Jo Coll Dur BA 14 MA 15. Cranmer Hall Dur 12. **d** 15 **p** 16. C Peterlee *Dur* 15–18; P-in-c Hetton-Lyons w Eppleton from 18. *The Rectory, Houghton Road, Hetton-le-Hole, Houghton le Spring DH5 9PH* T: 0191-903 8619 E: revtwall@gmail.com

WALLACE, Preb Alastair Robert. b 50. St Cath Coll Cam BA 71 MA 75 Lon Univ BD 75. Trin Coll Bris 72. **d** 75 **p** 76. C Ex St Leon w H Trin 75–79; Chapl Ridley Hall

Cam 79–80; R Bath St Mich w St Paul *B & W* 83–96; RD Bath 90–96; Sub-Dean Wells Cathl 96–99; Hon Asst Dioc Missr 96–99; TR Ilminster and Distr 99–10; V Ilminster and Whitelackington 10–12; rtd 12; Preb Wells Cathl *B & W* from 96; PtO from 12. *Houses Barton, Thurloxton, Taunton TA2 8RH* T: (01823) 412712 M: 07746-951191 E: alastair.wallace@btinternet.com

WALLACE, Ms Brenda Claire. b 52. Linc Th Coll 73 S'wark Ord Course 78. dss 80 d 87 p 94. Sutton at Hone *Roch* 80–83; Borstal 83–89; Hon Par Dn 87–89; HM Pris Cookham Wood 83–89; Asst Chapl 87–89; NSM Stansted Mountfitchet *Chelmsf* 89–96; NSM Stansted Mountfitchet w Birchanger and Farnham 97; C Hutton 97–13; P-in-c Rettendon and Hullbridge 13–17; rtd 17; Hon C Rawreth *Chelmsf* from 17; Hon C Rettendon and Hullbridge from 17. *Highfield, Church Road, Rawreth, Wickford SS11 8SH* E: brenda.wallace9@outlook.com

WALLACE, David Alexander Rippon. b 39. CEng MIET. Ox Min Course 94. d 96 p 97. NSM Haddenham w Cuddington, Kingsey etc *Ox* 96–97; NSM Worminghall w Ickford, Oakley and Shabbington 97–02; NSM Aylesbury Deanery 02–12; rtd 12; PtO *Ox* from 12. *11 Station Road, Haddenham, Aylesbury HP17 8AN* T/F: (01844) 290670 E: revd@wallaces.org

WALLACE, Mrs Edwina Margaret. b 49. EMMTC 00. d 03 p 04. C Broughton Astley and Croft w Stoney Stanton *Leic* 03–07; C Sutton Coldfield St Chad *Birm* 07–11; P-in-c 11; V 11–14; rtd 14; PtO *Birm* from 14; *Derby* from 14; *Leic* from 14. *The Hawthorns, Acresford Road, Donisthorpe, Swadlincote DE12 7PT* T: (01530) 274002 M: 07597-588113 E: edwinawallace41@gmail.com

WALLACE, Godfrey Everingham. *See* EVERINGHAM, Georgina Wendy

WALLACE, Heather. b 60. Lindisfarne Coll of Th 19. d 21. NSM Millfield St Mark and Pallion St Luke *Dur* from 21. *43 Plantation Road, Sunderland SR4 6RL* T: 0191-567 5439 E: hw.seder3@hotmail.com

WALLACE, Ian Malcolm. b 57. Southn Univ LLB 78 Solicitor 79. STETS 06. d 09 p 10. C Wisley w Pyrford *Guildf* 09–13; P-in-c Yate New Town *Bris* 13–14; TR Yate from 14. *The Rectory, 97 Canterbury Close, Yate, Bristol BS37 5TU* T: (01454) 311483 M: 07799-076697 E: rector@yateparish.org.uk

WALLACE, James Andrew. b 84. Cranmer Hall Dur 19. d 21. C Haydock St Mark *Liv* from 21. *303 Park Street, Haydock, St Helens WA11 0BG* M: 07736-068344 E: jawallace316@gmail.com

WALLACE, James Marchant. d 11 p 12. C Waterford w Killea, Drumcannon and Dunhill *C, F & O* 11–17. *Address temp unknown* M: (00353) 87-272 1789 E: wallace1.jim@gmail.com

WALLACE, Julie Michele. *See* BARRELL, Julie Michele

WALLACE, Mark David. b 76. Worc Coll Ox BA 98 MA 01. Oak Hill Th Coll 05. d 08 p 09. C Trull w Angersleigh *B & W* 08–12; P-in-c Colchester St Pet and St Botolph *Chelmsf* from 12; Chapl to Bp Maidstone *Cant* from 20. *St Peter's Vicarage, Balkerne Close, Colchester CO1 1NZ* T: (01206) 572641 M: 07772-615378 E: towncentrevicar@gmail.com

WALLACE, Mark George. b 72. Qu Coll Cam BA 94. Oak Hill Th Coll BA 08. d 08 p 09. C Guildf Ch Ch w St Martha-on-the-Hill 08–12; V Lightwater 12–17; AD Surrey Heath 16–17; V Woking St Mary from 17. *Bethany House, West Hill Road, Woking GU22 7UJ* M: 07469-170317 E: vicar@stmaryofbethany.org.uk

✠**WALLACE, The Rt Revd Martin William.** b 48. K Coll Lon BD 70 AKC 70. St Aug Coll Cant 70. d 71 p 72 c 03. C Attercliffe *Sheff* 71–74; C New Malden and Coombe *S'wark* 74–77; V Forest Gate St Mark *Chelmsf* 77–93; RD Newham 82–91; P-in-c Forest Gate Em w Upton Cross 85–89; Hon Can Chelmsf Cathl 89–03; P-in-c Forest Gate All SS 91–93; Dioc ACUPA Link Officer 91–97; P-in-c Bradwell on Sea 93–97; P-in-c St Lawrence 93–97; Ind Chapl Maldon and Dengie Deanery 93–97; Adn Colchester 97–03; Bp's Adv for Hosp Chapl 97–03; Suff Bp Selby *York* 03–13; rtd 13; Hon Asst Bp York from 13. *28 Alexandra Court, Bridlington YO15 2LB* T: (01262) 670265 E: mdw28@btinternet.com

WALLACE, Matt. b 75. Liv Univ BA 96. Trin Coll Bris BA 11. d 11 p 12. C Chase Terrace *Lich* 11–15; TV Burntwood, Chase Terrace etc from 15. *3 Chapel Street, Chase Terrace WS7 1NL* M: 07855-960179 E: matt.wallace@o2.co.uk

WALLACE (née ALEXANDER), Mrs Nancy Joan. b 42. Ox Brookes Univ BA 97 Keele Univ MA 06 Roehampton Inst TCert 64 PQCSW 97. SAOMC 95. d 98 p 99. NSM Worminghall w Ickford, Oakley and Shabbington *Ox* 02–12; NSM Aylesbury Deanery 02–12; rtd 12; PtO *Ox* from 12. *11 Station Road, Haddenham, Aylesbury HP17 8AN* T/F: (01844) 290670 E: revn@wallaces.org

WALLACE, Nicholas Robert. b 56. Trin Coll Bris 93. d 95 p 96. C Fishponds St Jo *Bris* 95–98; P-in-c Barton Hill St Luke w Ch Ch 98–99; P-in-c Barton Hill St Luke w Ch Ch and Moorfields 99–00; R Binstead *Portsm* 00–10; V Havenstreet St Pet 00–10; P Adelaide St Mary Australia 10–13; V Sorrento w Rye from 13. *The Vicarage, 3473 Point Nepean Road, Sorrento Vic 3943, Australia* E: nrwallace@hotmail.com

WALLACE, Robert. b 52. Sussex Univ BSc 73. Linc Th Coll 73. d 76 p 77. C Plaistow St Mary *Roch* 76–79; C Dartford H Trin 79–83; V Borstal 83–89; Chapl The Foord Almshouses 83–89; Chapl HM Pris Cookham Wood 83–89; P-in-c Farnham *Chelmsf* 89–96; V Stansted Mountfitchet 89–96; R Stansted Mountfitchet w Birchanger and Farnham 97; R Hutton 97–15; rtd 15; PtO *Roch* from 16. *30 Bromley College, London Road, Bromley BR1 1PE* T: (020) 8001 1055 M: 07950-613932 E: fatherbobwallace@hotmail.com

WALLACE, Canon Susan Marilyn. b 67. Ch Ch Coll Cant BA(Ed) 90 Leeds Univ MA 06 Sheff Univ MA 15. NOC 03. d 06 p 07. NSM Acomb St Steph and St Aid *York* 06–10; NSM York St Mich-le-Belfrey 10; TV Leeds City *Ripon* 10–13; Can Res, Prec and Sacr Win Cathl 14–18; Liturg Dir and Creative Worship Consultant Transcendence Trust from 19; PtO *Win* from 19; *Sarum* from 19. *111 London Road, Salisbury SP1 3HA* M: 07962-071621 E: sue@transcendence.org.uk or sue@abbess.org.uk

WALLACE-JONES, Sally. b 66. Man Univ BA 87 PhD 91 Lucy Cavendish Coll Cam BTh 17. Ridley Hall Cam 15. d 17 p 18. C High Oak, Hingham and Scoulton w Wood Rising *Nor* 17–21; V Hartshead, Hightown, Roberttown and Scholes *Leeds* from 21. *The Vicarage, Scholes Lane, Scholes, Cleckheaton BD19 6PA* E: revsamwj@gmail.com

WALLBANK, Alison Patricia. b 59. d 09 p 10. OLM Whitworth w Facit *Man* 09–14; NSM Norden w Ashworth and Bamford 13–14; NSM Eggleston *Dur* from 14; NSM Middleton-in-Teesdale w Forest and Frith from 14; NSM Lower Teesdale *Leeds* from 14. *The Vicarage, 1 Greta Place, Middleton-in-Teesdale, Barnard Castle DL12 0RD* T: (01833) 641302 M: 07800-955091 E: alisonwallbank59@gmail.com

WALLER, Allen Ranson. b 82. James Madison Univ USA BA 05. Wycliffe Hall Ox BTh 16. d 16 p 17. C Oxton *Ches* 16–19; R Raleigh St Tim USA from 19. *116 East Wind Lane, Cary NC 27518, USA*

WALLER, Annalu. b 63. Cape Town Univ BSc 83 MSc 88 Dundee Univ PhD 92. TISEC 01. d 04 p 05. Hon C Dundee St Marg *Bre* 04–13; Hon C Dundee St Martin 10–13; Hon Chapl Dundee Univ from 07. *9 Invergowrie Drive, Dundee DD2 1RD* T: (01382) 644570 *or* 388223 E: awaller@dundee.ac.uk

WALLER, The Ven David James. b 58. Whitelands Coll Lon BA 85 K Coll Lon MA 95 Heythrop Coll Lon MTh 02 Sarum Coll MA 16. Ripon Coll Cuddesdon 85. d 88 p 89. C Tettenhall Regis *Lich* 88–91; Chapl Greenwich Univ *S'wark* 92–97; P-in-c Yiewsley *Lon* 97–01; TR Plymstock and Hooe *Ex* 01–12; Chapl Palma de Mallorca *Eur* from 12; Hon Can from 19; Adn Italy and Malta from 20; Adn Gib from 20. *Calle Goleta 34, 07350 Binissalem, Balearic Islands, Spain* T: (0034) 971 737 279 *or* 600 400 600 E: david.waller@europe.anglican.org

WALLER, Canon Derek James Keith. b 54. Em Coll Cam BA 75 PGCE 76. Trin Coll Bris 88. d 91 p 92. C Church Stretton *Heref* 91–95; R Appleby Gp *Leic* 95–04; P-in-c Rushden St Pet *Pet* 04–07; V 08–14; RD Higham 11–14; Can Pet Cathl 13–14; CMS S Sudan 14–16; CMS Madagascar 17–20; PtO *Pet* from 17. *14 Birch Spinney, Mawsley, Kettering NN14 1QW* E: revdwaller@gmail.com

WALLER, Mrs Elizabeth Alison. b 49. Open Univ BA 89 Univ of Cen England in Birm MA 99 Wolfs Coll Cam PGCE 91. EAMTC 02. d 05 p 06. NSM Oundle w Ashton and Benefield w Glapthorn *Pet* 05–08; NSM Aldwincle, Clopton, Pilton, Stoke Doyle etc from 08. *Priory Cottage, 40 Church Street, Stilton, Peterborough PE7 3RF* T: (01733) 242412 E: eawaller@btinternet.com

WALLER, Gordon Robert. b 50. Jes Coll Cam BA 72 MA 75. d 03 p 05. OLM Tooting All SS *S'wark* from 03. *131 Ribblesdale Road, London SW16 6SP* T: (020) 8769 6733 E: gordon.waller2012@yahoo.co.uk

WALLER, John. b 60. Man Univ BA 84 Liv Univ MA 07. St Jo Coll Nottm 85. d 87 p 88. C Chorlton-cum-Hardy St Clem *Man* 87–90; R Openshaw 90–95; Chapl Ancoats Hosp Man 93–95; TV Watling Valley *Ox* 95–96; TR 96–03; R Brickhills and Stoke Hammond from 03; AD Mursley 06–11. *The Rectory, 10 Pound Hill, Great Brickhill, Milton Keynes MK17 9AS* T: (01525) 261062 E: rector@brickhillschurches.org

WALLER, Maxine Dawn. b 62. St Hild Coll 17. d 19 p 20. NSM Bridlington Priory *York* from 19. *15*

Queen Street, Bridlington YO15 2SF M: 07737-816894
E: maxinewaller@hotmail.co.uk

WALLER, Philip Thomas. b 56. Ex Coll Ox BA 78 MA 88 St Jo
Coll Dur BA 87. Cranmer Hall Dur 85. d 88 p 89. C Enfield
St Andr Lon 88–91; C Belper Derby 91–95; P-in-c Oakwood
95–05; P-in-c Long Eaton St Jo V 10–15; Asst Dir
of Ords 09–15; TV Welwyn St Alb from 15; Asst Dir of
Ords from 15. The Vicarage, 4 Bury Lane, Codicote, Hitchin
SG4 8XT T: (01438) 504318 E: vicar@stgiles-church.org.uk

WALLER, William John. b 38. Bps' Coll Cheshunt 66. d 68
p 69. C Luton Lewsey St Hugh St Alb 68–73; C Oxhey
All SS 73–75; C Henllys w Bettws Mon 75–77. Bell House
with Brodawel, Church Road, Llandegfedd Village, Newport
NP18 1HX

WALLEY, Mark Nathan. b 83. Ox Brookes Univ BA 06. Oak
Hill Th Coll 17. d 19 p 20. C Linthorpe York from 19. 45
Lothian Road, Middlesbrough TS4 2HS M: 07752-050746
E: markwalley@hotmail.com

WALLEY, Canon Peter Francis. b 60. Bris Univ BSc 82
CEng 89 MICE 89. Trin Coll Bris 96. d 98 p 99. C Ex
St Jas 98–01; Asst Chapl Brussels Eur 01–05; Bp's Dom
Chapl Lich 05–12; P-in-c Mickleover All SS Derby 12–14;
P-in-c Mickleover St Jo 12–14; V Mickleover from 14; RD
Derby S 15–16; Acting Adn Derby 21; C Boylestone, Church
Broughton, Dalbury, etc from 21; Hon Can Derby Cathl
from 17. All Saints' Vicarage, Etwall Road, Mickleover, Derby
DE3 0DL T: (01332) 513793 E: peterwalley@btinternet.com
or peter.walley@derby.anglican.org

WALLINGTON, Martin John. b 59. SAOMC 95. d 98 p 99.
NSM Chorleywood St Andr St Alb 98–03; P-in-c Wooburn
Ox 03–08; V 08–20; rtd 20. 24 Capell Road, Chorleywood,
Rickmansworth WD3 5HZ

WALLINGTON, Paul. b 62. Birm Univ BCom 83 ACA 86.
Trin Coll Bris BA 94. d 94 p 95. C Chorley St Laur Blackb
94–97; C Darwen St Pet w Hoddlesden 97–98; TV 98–00;
rtd 00; PtO Man from 13; Chapl Canon Slade Sch Bolton
08–16; Chapl St Swithun's Sch Win from 16. St Swithun's
School, Alresford Road, Winchester SO21 1HA T: (01962)
835700   E: thewallingtons@hotmail.com   or
wallingtonp@stswithuns.com

WALLIS, Anna Louise. b 73. Leic Univ BSc 95 PhD 99 Selw
Coll Cam 05 MA 09. Westcott Ho Cam 03. d 06 p 07.
C Huddersfield St Pet Wakef 06–09; Chapl Sheff Teaching
Hosps NHS Foundn Trust 09–11; PtO Sheff 11–12; NSM
Huddersfield St Pet Leeds 12–17; PtO 20–21. Address withheld
by request E: anna.wallis121@gmail.com

WALLIS, Benjamin John. b 55. Wimbledon Sch of Art BA 79.
Chich Th Coll 92. d 94 p 95. C Battersea Ch Ch and St Steph
S'wark 94–98; C Wood Green St Mich w Bounds Green
St Gabr etc Lon 98–03; V Barkingside St Geo Chelmsf from 03.
St George's Vicarage, Woodford Avenue, Ilford IG2 6XQ T: (020)
8550 4149 E: pam@herdom.com

WALLIS, David Peter. b 72. Ripon Coll Cuddesdon
BTh 03. d 03 p 04. C Eastbourne St Mary Chich 03–07;
P-in-c Ditchling, Streat and Westmeston 07–08; R from
08. St Margaret's Vicarage, 2 Charlton Gardens, Lewes
Road, Ditchling, Hassocks BN6 8WA T: (01273) 843165
E: revdavidwallis@yahoo.co.uk

WALLIS, Ian George. b 57. Sheff Univ BA 79 PhD 92 St Edm
Ho Cam MLitt 87. Ridley Hall Cam 88. d 90 p 91. C
Armthorpe Sheff 90–92; Chapl and Fell SS Coll Cam 92–95;
Hon C Chesterton Gd Shep Ely 93–95; R Houghton le Spring
Dur 95–07; AD Houghton 04–07; Tutor Aston Tr Scheme
93–97; Prin NOC 07–08; V Sheff St Mark Broomhill 09–14;
rtd 14; PtO Sheff from 14; Leeds from 17; Tutor St Hild
Coll from 16. Cat Hill Barn, Cat Hill Lane, Hoylandswaine,
Sheffield S36 7JB T: (01226) 893407 M: 07717-417760
E: ian.wallis@sero.co.uk

WALLIS, John Anthony. b 36. St Pet Coll Ox BA 60 MA 65.
Clifton Th Coll 60. d 62 p 63. C Blackpool St Mark Blackb
62–65; C Leeds St Geo Ripon 65–69; Korea 69–74; Nat
Sec (Scotland) OMF 75–78; Home Dir OMF 78–89; Hon
C Sevenoaks St Nic Roch 78–89; Chapl The Hague Eur
89–95; V Northwood Em Lon 95–01; rtd 01; PtO Nor
from 03; Ely from 13. Church Cottage, 61 Gayton Road,
Grimston, King's Lynn PE32 1BG T: (01485) 600336
E: johna.wallis@btinternet.com

WALLIS, Raymond Christopher. b 38. Moor Park Coll
Farnham 62 Sarum Th Coll 63. d 66 p 67. C Allerton Bradf
66–68; C Langley Marish Ox 68–69; C Caister Nor 69–73;
P-in-c E w W Bradenham 73–80; R Upwell St Pet and
Outwell Ely 80–84; V Bishopstone Chich 84–97; rtd 97; PtO
Chich from 97. Lanthorn, Park Lane, Bexhill-on-Sea TN39 4DS
E: wallis.raymond@yahoo.co.uk

WALLIS, Richard David. b 69. Herts Univ BA 96. SWMTC 15.
d 18 p 19. C Chacewater w St Day and Carharrack Truro from

18; C Devoran from 18; C Feock from 18; C St Stythians w
Perranarworthal and Gwennap from 18. The Vicarage, 2 Old
Vicarage Close, Stithians, Truro TR3 7DZ M: 07484-616499
E: rwallis1969@gmail.com

WALLMAN-GIRDLESTONE,   Jane   Elizabeth.   b 61.
Homerton Coll BEd 83. St Steph Ho Ox 89 Sarum
& Wells Th Coll BTh 92. d 93 p 94. C Woodbridge
St Mary St E 93–96; V Ipswich St Thos 96–00; Dir Past
Studies and Adv for Women's Min St Mich Coll Llandaff
00–02; Lect TISEC 03–07; Lect Qu Foundn Birm 04–05;
LtO Mor from 06. St Columba House, The Clattach,
Alturlie Point, Allanfearn, Inverness IV2 7HZ T: (01463)
230708   M: 07776-181824 E: janewallman@hotmail.co.uk
or janewallmangirdlestone@gmail.com

WALLS, Michael Peter. b 38. Cape Town Univ BA 57. Wells
Th Coll 59. d 61 p 62. C Morecambe St Barn Blackb 61–64; C
Birm St Paul 64–66; Ind Chapl 64–74; V Temple Balsall 66–74;
Chapl Wroxall Abbey Sch 72–74; V Kings Heath Birm 74–76;
Hon C Bordesley St Benedict 76–78; Sen Chapl Oakham Sch
78–83; P-in-c Leic St Sav 83–85; P-in-c Knossington and Cold
Overton 85–87; P-in-c Owston and Withcote 85–87; V Tilton
w Lowesby 85–87; P-in-c 87; V Whatborough Gp 87–90; Bp's
Adv on Relns w People of Other Faiths 89–93; Hon Can Leic
Cathl 89–93; V Leic St Mary 90–93; rtd 93; PtO Ban 02–17. 4
Partridge Way, Oakham LE15 6BX E: brompot01@gmail.com

WALMSLEY, Canon Derek. b 57. Oak Hill Th Coll 89. d 91
p 92. C Bletchley Ox 91–95; C Utley Bradf 95–00; V 00–15;
P-in-c Keighley St Andr 14–15; Hon Can Bradf Cathl 13–15;
Dir of Ords Leeds from 15; Can Res Wakef Cathl from 15.
14 Belgravia Road, Wakefield WF1 3JP T: (01924) 314284
or 371802 M: 07743-338690 E: dwalmsley9@aol.com or
derek.walmsley@leeds.anglican.org

WALMSLEY, Geoffrey Gwynne. d 17 p 18. C Dundalk w
Heynestown Arm 17–18; P-in-c 18–20; C Ballymascanlan w
Creggan and Rathcor 17–18; P-in-c 18–20; I Milltown from
20. The Rectory, 10 Derrylileagh Road, Portadown, Craigavon
BT62 1TQ E: jcwalmsley@btinternet.com

WALMSLEY, Jane. See LLOYD, Patricia Jane

WALMSLEY-McLEOD, Paul Albert. b 56. St Cuth Soc Dur
BA 82 Cam Univ CertEd 83. Westcott Ho Cam 85. d 87 p 88.
C Gt Bookham Guildf 87–90; Asst Chapl St Chris Hospice
Lon 90–93; Soc Care Team Member Phoenix Ho Fountain
Project 93–95; C Catford (Southend) and Downham S'wark
95–96; TV 96–99; P-in-c Downham St Barn 00–02; R Friern
Barnet St Jas Lon 02–20; AD Cen Barnet 10–16; rtd 20; PtO Ex
from 20. Braemar, Bradley Road, Bovey Tracey, Newton Abbot
TQ13 9EU

WALPOLE, Jennifer Emily Beatrice. b 81. Dur Univ BA 20.
Westcott Ho Cam 19. d 21. C Cant St Dunstan, St Mildred
and St Pet from 21. 1 The Old Palace, The Precincts, Canterbury
CT1 2EE M: 07706-926338 E: jebwalpole@gmail.com

WALPOLE, Neil Derek. b 63. St Hild Coll 17. d 18 p 19. C
Dewsbury Leeds from 18. St John's Vicarage, 68 Staincliffe
Road, Dewsbury WF13 4ED T: (01924) 451247 M: 07419-
334234

WALROND-SKINNER, Susan Mary. See PARFITT, Susan Mary

WALSALL, Archdeacon of. See FRANCIS, The Ven Julian
Montgomery

WALSER (née SHIELS), Mrs Rosalinde Cameron. b 47. Edin
Univ MA 68 Moray Ho Coll of Educn PGCE 69. NOC 92.
d 95 p 97. NSM Scarborough St Mary w Ch Ch and H
Apostles York 95–97; Chapl St Cath Hospice Scarborough
95–97; Chapl Scarborough Coll 95–97; P-in-c E Ayton York
97–06; rtd 06; PtO York from 07. 45 Newby Farm Road,
Scarborough YO12 6UJ

WALSH, Abigail Kathryn. b 83. Qu Foundn (Course) 15. d 18
p 19. C Cen Wolverhampton Lich from 18. 1B Claremont
Road, Wolverhampton WV3 0EA T: (01902) 422642

WALSH, Mrs Alexandra Mary (Gussie). b 50. Wycliffe
Hall Ox 06. d 08 p 09. C Penrith w Newton Reigny and
Plumpton Wall Carl 08–12; C Buckingham Ox 12–18; rtd 18;
PtO Guildf from 19. Farm View, Upper House Lane, Shamley
Green, Guildford GU5 0SX E: gussiewalsh@hotmail.com

WALSH, Carys Ruth. b 62. Ex Univ BA 83 MPhil 89 Heythrop
Coll Lon MA 00 PhD 11 Win Univ MA 15. STETS 10. d 13
p 14. Selection Sec Min Division Abps' Coun 07–14; C
Chelsea St Luke and Ch Ch Lon 13–16; Tutor St Mellitus
Coll 15–18; PtO Chelmsf 16–21; Pet 16–17; C Kettering SS Pet
and Paul from 17; C Kettering All SS from 19; C Tr Officer
18–21; Project Officer Nat Min Team Abps' Coun from 20.
The Rectory, Church Walk, Kettering NN16 0DJ T: (01604)
887054 M: 07707-556761 E: carys@peterandpaul.org.uk

WALSH, David Christopher. b 59. Warwick Univ BA 81.
St Jo Coll Nottm BA 83 Ripon Coll Cuddesdon 00. d 02
p 03. C Greenwich St Alfege S'wark 02–06; C Kensington
St Mary Abbots w Ch Ch and St Phil Lon 06–16; AD

Kensington 11–16; R Kettering SS Pet and Paul from 16; P-in-c Kettering All SS from 19. *The Rectory, Church Walk, Kettering NN16 0DJ* T: (01536) 513385 M: 07957-656643 E: rector@peterandpaul.org.uk

✠**WALSH, The Rt Revd Geoffrey David Jeremy.** b 29. Pemb Coll Cam BA 53 MA 58. Linc Th Coll 53. **d** 55 **p** 56 **c** 86. C Southgate Ch Ch *Lon* 55–58; SCM Sec Cam 58–61; C Cambridge Gt St Mary w St Mich *Ely* 58–61; V Moorfields *Bris* 61–66; R Marlborough *Sarum* 66–76; Can and Preb Sarum Cathl 73–76; Adn Ipswich *St E* 76–86; R Elmsett w Aldham 76–88; Surr Bp Tewkesbury *Glouc* 86–95; rtd 95; PtO *St E* from 95; Hon Asst Bp St E from 08. *6 Warren Lane, Martlesham Heath, Ipswich IP5 3SH* T: (01473) 620797 E: jandcwalsh61@gmail.com

WALSH, Geoffrey Malcolm. b 46. Sarum & Wells Th Coll 82. **d** 84 **p** 85. C Wellington and Distr *B & W* 84–87; TV Axminster, Chardstock, Combe Pyne and Rousdon *Ex* 87–90; Chapl RN 90–94; R Huntspill *B & W* 94–11; rtd 11; PtO *Sarum* 12–17; C Axminster, Chardstock, All Saints etc *Ex* 14–18; PtO from 18. *Thimbles, 70 Flax Meadow Lane, Axminster EX13 5FJ* T: (01297) 598361 E: geoffreywalsh@talktalk.net

WALSH, Gussie. *See* WALSH, Alexandra Mary

WALSH, Canon Neil-Allan. b 72. Cant Ch Ch Univ BA 03 Cape Town Univ DipEd 97. Westcott Ho Cam 06. **d** 08 **p** 09. C Lt Ilford St Mich *Chelmsf* 08–11; P-in-c Leytonstone St Marg w St Columba 11–20; V from 20; P-in-c Leytonstone H Trin and St Aug Harrow Green 14–19; Black and Minority Ethnic Adv to Bp Barking from 14; Hon Can Cape Town from 16. *St Margaret's Vicarage, 15 Woodhouse Road, London E11 3NG* T: (020) 8519 0813 M: 07903-652874 E: neilallanwalsh@yahoo.com

WALSH, Nicholas Sean. b 83. Moorlands Coll BA 07 K Coll Lon MA 13. St Mellitus Coll 11. **d** 13 **p** 14. C Luton Lewsey St Hugh *St Alb* 13–17; TV Catford (Southend) and Downham *S'wark* from 17. *233 Bellingham Road, London SE6 1EH* M: 07774-516204 E: nswalsh@gmail.com

WALSH, Peter. b 64. Liv Univ BA 86 Nottm Univ BTh 90. Linc Th Coll 87. **d** 90 **p** 91. C Cantley *Sheff* 90–93; C Poulton-le-Fylde *Blackb* 93–95; V Blackpool St Steph 95–03; TR Ches 03–05; V Ches St Oswald and St Thos 05–11; Min Can Ches Cathl 04–05; V W Kirby St Andr 11–19; Minl Development Review Officer 11–14; rtd 19. *Huntingtower, 6 Coronation Road, Kirkham, Preston PR4 2HE* E: frpeterwalsh@btinternet.com

WALSH, Sarah Elaine. b 60. LLCM(TD) 90 CTABRSM 95. NEOC 04. **d** 07 **p** 10. NSM Waggoners *York* 07–08; NSM Crookes St Tim *Sheff* 09–11; NSM Walkley 11–12; Chapl HM Pris Nottm 12–13; Chapl HM Pris Stocken 12–13; Chapl HM Pris Lindholme 13–19; Chapl HM Pris Moorland 13–19; NSM Doncaster St Geo *Sheff* 18–19; R Dickleburgh and The Pulhams *Nor* from 19. *The Rectory, Station Road, Pulham Market, Diss IP21 4TE* E: sarahwalsh967@btinternet.com

WALSHAW, Mrs Caroline Elaine. b 59. St Jo Coll Dur BA 81 Goldsmiths' Coll Lon PGCE 82. SEITE 13. **d** 15 **p** 16. NSM Pembury *Roch* 15–20; NSM Northanger Win from 20. *The Vicarage, The Plestor, Selborne, Alton GU34 3JQ* M: 07311-340043 E: canrwalshaw@outlook.com *or* revcarriewalshaw@gmail.com

WALSHE, Marie Sylvia. b 54. RGN RCNT. **d** 99 **p** 00. NSM Kilkeel *D & D* 99–00; NSM Down H Trin w Hollymount 00–08; NSM Rathmullan w Tyrella 00–08; NSM Newcastle 08–13; NSM Gilnahirk from 13. *8 Castle View, Dundrum, Newcastle BT33 0SA* T: (028) 4375 1757 E: walshemarie@hotmail.com

WALT, Canon Trevor William. b 52. MBE 03. RMN 74 RNT 79. Ox NSM Course 83. **d** 86 **p** 87. NSM Crowthorne *Ox* 86–89; Chapl Asst Broadmoor Hosp Crowthorne 86–89; Chapl 89–10; Hon Can Ch Ch *Ox* 00–07; Bp's Adv for Healing and Deliverance Min *Chelmsf* 11–17; Chapl St Helena Hospice Colchester 13–17; rtd 17; PtO *Chelmsf* from 10. *Address withheld by request*

WALTER, Giles Robert. b 54. Cam Univ MA 76. Cranmer Hall Dur 78. **d** 82 **p** 83. C Finchley Ch Ch *Lon* 82–86; C Cambridge H Sepulchre w All SS *Ely* 86–92; C Cambridge H Sepulchre 92–93; P-in-c Tunbridge Wells St Jo *Roch* 93–95; V 95–19; rtd 19; PtO *Ely* from 21. *36 Belvoir Road, Cambridge CB4 1JJ*

WALTER, Ian Edward. b 47. Edin Univ MA 69 Keble Coll Ox BA 71 MA 78. Cuddesdon Coll 71. **d** 73 **p** 74. C Greenock *Glas* 73–76; C Glas St Mary and Chapl Angl Students Glas 76–79; R Paisley St Barn 79–84; P-in-c Bolton St Phil *Man* 84–86; V 86–91; Dioc Ecum Officer 88–94; V Elton All SS 91–98; V Stalybridge *Man* 98–01; R Hawick *Edin* 01–08; rtd 08; Hon C Oban St Jo *Arg* from 08. *Balaclava, 56 Dalriach Road, Oban PA34 5JE* T: (01631) 564855 E: ian_walter@btinternet.com

WALTER, Noël. b 41. St D Coll Lamp. **d** 66 **p** 67. C Mitcham Ascension *S'wark* 66–71; C Caterham 71–74; OCM 71–74;

V Welling *S'wark* 74–82; C Warlingham w Chelsham and Farleigh 82–88; Chapl Warlingham Park Hosp Croydon 82–88; Chapl R Earlswood Hosp Redhill 88–90; Chapl Redhill Gen Hosp 88–91; Chapl E Surrey Hosp Redhill 88–96; Sen Chapl Gt Ormond Street Hosp for Children NHS Trust 96–06; rtd 06; PtO *Ex* 98–07; C Chagford, S Tawton, Drewsteignton etc 07–12; PtO from 13. *Whiddon View, 13 Bretteville Close, Chagford, Newton Abbot TQ13 8DW* T: (01647) 432610 E: panda.walter@icloud.com

WALTER, Robin. b 37. Univ Coll Dur BA 63 MA 90 Linacre Coll Ox BA 65 MA 69. Pontigny Seminary 65. **d** 66 **p** 68. C Peckham St Jo *S'wark* 66–69; Chapl Lon Univ 69–70; C Dur St Marg 70–74; R Burnmoor 74–79; Asst Master Barnard Castle Sch 79–97; NSM Barnard Castle Deanery 80-82 and 88–97; Hon C Whorlton *Dur* 82–83; Hon C Barnard Castle w Whorlton 83–88; P-in-c Redmarshall 97–01; R 01–03; P-in-c Bishopton w Gt Stainton 97–01; V 01–03; rtd 03; PtO *York* from 03; *Worc* from 04. *The Laurels, Worcester Road, Great Witley, Worcester WR6 6HR* T: (01299) 890190 E: rfw@myric.net

WALTERS, Christopher Rowland. b 47. Open Univ BA 78 Univ of Wales PGCE 94 MEd 95 Texas Wesleyan Univ PhD 02. **d** 02 **p** 10. Hd Master Mayflower Chr Sch Pontypool 90–05; OLM Abergavenny H Trin *Mon* 02–12; P-in-c Govilon w Llanfoist w Llanellen 12–20; P-in-c Blaenavon w Capel Newydd from 20; PtO *S & B* from 14. *The Rectory, Merthyr Road, Govilon, Abergavenny NP7 9PT* T: (01873) 831048 M: 07967-945320 E: chris@patchwork.co.uk

WALTERS, Daniel Geoffrey Thomas. b 81. K Coll Cam BA 02 MA 06. Coll of Resurr Mirfield BA 15. **d** 16 **p** 17. C High Crompton and Thornham *Man* 16–19; C Ox St Giles and SS Phil and Jas w St Marg from 19. *19A St Margaret's Road, Oxford OX2 6RX* M: 07469-738948 E: dgtwalters@outlook.com

WALTERS, David Allan. b 48. Southn Univ MA 87 Bath Univ MEd 95. **d** 09 **p** 10. OLM Wylye and Till Valley *Sarum* 09–12; NSM Lower Wylye and Till Valley 12–14; NSM Salisbury Plain 14–18; rtd 18; PtO *Sarum* from 18. *Hillside, Chapel Lane, Shrewton, Salisbury SP3 4BX* T: (01980) 620038 E: david.a.walters@hotmail.com

WALTERS, David Trevor. b 37. Ex Coll Ox BA 58 MA 62. St Steph Ho Ox 62. **d** 64 **p** 65. C Cardiff St Mary *Llan* 64–69; C Brecon w Battle *S & B* 69–73; Min Can Brecon Cathl 69–73; V Llanddew and Talachddu 73–78; V Cefncoed and Capel Nantddu 78–80; V Cefn Coed and Capel Nantddu w Vaynor etc 80–87; V Talgarth and Llanelieu 87–04; rtd 04. *16 Dan-y-Bryn, Glasbury, Hereford HR3 5NH* T: (01497) 842966 E: david.t.walters@hotmail.com

WALTERS, Mrs Felicity Ann. b 56. WEMTC. **d** 01 **p** 02. C Glouc St Geo w Whaddon 01–05; C Matson 05–06; P-in-c Huntley and Longhope, Churcham and Bulley 06–11; P-in-c Hadfield *Derby* 11–14; V from 14; V Charlesworth and Gamesley from 14. *St Andrew's Vicarage, 122 Hadfield Road, Hadfield, Glossop SK13 2DR* T: (01457) 852431 E: walters@revfelicity.plus.com

WALTERS, Ian Robert. b 51. ACA 74 FCA 81. **d** 85 **p** 86. OLM Ingoldsby *Linc* 85–92; NSM Grantham St Anne New Somerby and Spitalgate 92–94; NSM Ingoldsby 94–06; NSM Ropsley 94–06; NSM Old Somerby 94–06; NSM Sapperton w Braceby 94–06; P-in-c Gosberton, Gosberton Clough and Quadring 06–15; V from 15. *The Vicarage, 6 Wargate Way, Gosberton, Spalding PE11 4NH* T/F: (01775) 840694 M: 07831-645683 E: vicar@gosberton.org

WALTERS, Ivan. *See* WALTERS, William Ivan

WALTERS, Canon James Arthur. b 78. Selw Coll Cam BA 00 PhD 07. Westcott Ho Cam 03. **d** 07 **p** 08. C Hampstead St Jo *Lon* 07–10; Chapl LSE from 10; NSM Bloomsbury St Geo w Woburn Square Ch Ch 11–15; Can and Preb Chich Cathl from 16. *London School of Economics, Houghton Street, London WC2A 2AE* T: (020) 7955 7965 E: j.walters2@lse.ac.uk

WALTERS, Canon John Philip Hewitt. b 50. Bp Burgess Hall Lamp 69 Coll of Resurr Mirfield 72. **d** 73 **p** 74. C Llangiwg *S & B* 73–76; Min Can Brecon Cathl 76–79; C Brecon w Battle 76–79; V Merthyr Cynog and Dyffryn Honddu etc 79–83; V Llandeilo Tal-y-bont 83–15; Hon Can Brecon Cathl 12–15; PtO *St D* 14–15; rtd 15; PtO *S & B* from 15. *12 Coles Close, Swansea SA1 2GD* T: (01792) 455026 E: jphwalters12@gmail.com

WALTERS, Canon Michael William. b 39. Dur Univ BSc 61. Clifton Th Coll 61. **d** 63 **p** 64. C Aldershot H Trin *Guildf* 63–66; C Upper Armley *Ripon* 66–69; NE Area Sec CPAS 69–75; V Hyde St Geo *Ches* 75–82; V Knutsford St Jo and Toft 82–97; P-in-c Congleton St Pet 97–98; TR Congleton 98–05; rtd 05; Hon Can Ches Cathl 94–13; Hon C Davenham 05–13; PtO from 13. *27 Alvanley Rise, Northwich CW9 8AY* T: (01606) 333126 E: michael@alvanleyrise.co.uk

WALTERS, Nicholas Humphrey. b 45. K Coll Lon BD 67 AKC 67. **d** 68 **p** 69. C Weston *Guildf* 68–71; Chapl and Lect

NE Surrey Coll of Tech Ewell 71–77; Hon C Ewell *Guildf* 71–77; Warden Moor Park Coll Farnham 77–80; Tutor Surrey Univ *Guildf* from 80; Dir of Studies Guildf Inst from 82; Public Preacher *Guildf* 84–15. *9 Valley View, Godalming GU7 1RD* T: (01483) 415106 *or* 562142

WALTERS, Nicholas Rhys. b 88. St Steph Ho Ox 14. **d** 17 **p** 18. C Primrose Hill St Mary w Avenue Road St Paul *Lon* 17–20. *2 St John's Hall, St John's Wood High Street, London NW8 7NE* M: 07704-715367 E: nickrwalters@gmail.com

WALTERS, Mrs Sheila Ann Beatrice. b 37. Bris Univ DipEd 58. EMMTC 85. **d** 89 **p** 94. NSM Ashby-de-la-Zouch St Helen w Coleorton *Leic* 89–98; PtO 99–02; NSM Packington w Normanton-le-Heath 02–05; rtd 05; PtO *Sheff* 06–21. *8 Kensington Park, Sheffield S10 4NJ* T: 0114-229 5497

WALTERS, William Ivan. b 49. CBDTI 04. **d** 07 **p** 08. NSM Lea *Blackb* 07–14; rtd 14; PtO *Blackb* from 14. *9 Thornpark Drive, Lea, Preston PR2 1RE* T: (01772) 732573 E: ivanwalters@btinternet.com

WALTNER, Moise (Mike). b 75. ERMC 13. **d** 15 **p** 16. C Vienna *Eur* from 15. *Address withheld by request* E: rmwccv@gmail.com

WALTON, Mrs Alison Claire. b 59. Homerton Coll Cam BEd 82. Lon Bible Coll Oak Hill Th Coll BA 90 MPhil 92. **d** 92 **p** 98. C Bedford Ch Ch St Alb 92–94; PtO 94–95; *S'well* 95–98; NSM Lenton Abbey 98–99; Assoc Lect St Jo Coll Nottm 97–99; C Thorley *St Alb* 00–03; V Croxley Green St Oswald 03–07; Dir Ch Study and Practice Ridley Hall Cam 07–16; Public Preacher *Ely* 07–16; V Isleworth All SS *Lon* from 16. *Butterfield House, 63 Church Street, Isleworth TW7 6BE* T: (020) 8560 7511 E: ali.walton@cantab.net *or* ali.walton@allsaints-isleworth.org

WALTON, Ann Beverley. b 56. Huddersfield Poly BSc 78 Sheff Poly MPhil 84 Coll of Ripon & York St Jo MA 97. NOC 00. **d** 03 **p** 04. C Ecclesfield *Sheff* 03–06; R Adwick-le-Street w Skelbrooke 06–21; P-in-c Owston 14–20; rtd 21. *6 St Paul's Chambers, 6 St Paul's Parade, Sheffield S1 2JL*

WALTON, Brian. b 53. Sarum & Wells Th Coll 83. **d** 85 **p** 86. C Silksworth *Dur* 85–86; C Bishopwearmouth St Mich w St Hilda 86–88; Chapl RN 88–92; V Sugley *Newc* 92–95; Chapl Lemington Hosp 92–95; CF 95–13; Chapl Morden Coll Blackheath 13–17; rtd 18; PtO *Roch* from 14; *Dur* from 18. *Pennine Lodge, St John's Chapel, Bishop Auckland DL13 1QX* E: brianwalton284@gmail.com

WALTON, Mrs Camilla Iris. b 56. STETS 97. **d** 00 **p** 01. C Lyndhurst and Emery Down and Minstead *Win* 00–04; V Boldre w S Baddesley 04–08; TV Beaconsfield *Ox* 08–18; AD Amersham 12–17; rtd 18; PtO *Bris* from 19. *1A Fore Street, Ashton Keynes, Swindon SN6 6NP* E: camillawalton@gmail.com

WALTON, Mrs Catherine. b 66. Lindisfarne Regional Tr Partnership. **d** 15 **p** 16. NSM Norton St Mary *Dur* from 15; NSM Norton St Mich from 15. *23 Wadham Grove, Darlington DL1 2GJ* T: (01325) 260274 M: 07581-043061 E: revd.catherine@gmail.com *or* archdeacons.secretary@durham.anglican.org

WALTON, Deborah Ruth. b 68. Wolv Poly LLB 90 Barrister-at-Law 91 Solicitor 97. St Mellitus Coll BA 17. **d** 17 **p** 18. C Kinver and Enville *Lich* 17–20; V Prees, Edstaston and Whixall from 20. *The Vicarage, Church Street, Prees, Whitchurch SY13 2EE* T: (01948) 840193 M: 07954-338902 E: deborah.r.walton@me.com

WALTON, James Daniel. b 98. St Steph Ho Ox 19. **d** 21. C Shrewsbury All SS w St Mich *Lich* from 21. *Holy Trinity Vicarage, Greyfriars Road, Shrewsbury SY3 7EP* T: (01743) 360639 M: 07879-654092 E: fr.jw@outlook.com

WALTON, John Victor. b 45. Lon Univ BSc 67. Linc Th Coll 79. **d** 81 **p** 82. C Stevenage St Mary Shephall *St Alb* 81–85; TV Bourne Valley *Sarum* 85–95; P-in-c Puddletown and Tolpuddle 95–02; R Puddletown, Tolpuddle and Milborne w Dewlish 02–04; rtd 04; PtO *Sarum* from 12. *Serenity, Wootton Grove, Sherborne DT9 4DL* T: (01935) 814435 E: revjvw@hotmail.com

WALTON, Canon Kevin Anthony. b 64. St Chad's Coll Dur BA 87 Dur Univ PhD 99. Trin Coll Bris BA 91. **d** 92 **p** 93. C Stranton *Dur* 92–95; C Hartlepool H Trin 95–96; V Sunderland St Mary and St Pet 96–08; AD Wearmouth 05–08; Can and Chan St Alb from 08. *2 Sumpter Yard, St Albans AL1 1BY* T: (01727) 890242 E: canon@stalbanscathedral.org

WALTON, Luke. b 64. Leeds Univ LLB 87. Cranmer Hall Dur BA 94. **d** 97 **p** 98. C Didsbury St Jas and Em *Man* 97–02; C Clifton Ch Ch w Em *Bris* 02–06; Arts Development Officer Bible Soc from 06; PtO *Bris* from 06. *Bible Society, Stonehill Green, Westlea, Swindon SN5 7DG* T: (01793) 418100 F: 418118 M: 07799-414199

WALTON, Reginald Arthur. b 40. St Jo Coll Nottm 80. **d** 81 **p** 82. C Woodthorpe *S'well* 81–84; P-in-c Nottingham St Andr 84–85; V 85–91; R Moreton *Ches* 91–01; P-in-c Whatton w Aslockton, Hawksworth, Scarrington etc *S'well* 01–05; V 05–07; rtd 07; PtO *S'well* from 17. *19 The Maltsters, Newark NG24 4RU* T: (01636) 659869 E: regwalton40@gmail.com

WALTON, Richard James. b 55. UMIST BSc 77 Sheff Univ MEd 84 Leeds Univ PhD 98 MA 10 CPhys MInstP SFHEA 13. NOC 07. **d** 09 **p** 10. NSM Warmsworth *Sheff* 09–11; P-in-c Burghwallis and Campsall 11–21; Bp's Adv for SSM 14–21; AD Adwick 19–21; rtd 21; Asst Dioc Dir of Ords *Sheff* from 14. *6 St Paul's Chambers, 6 St Paul's Parade, Sheffield S1 2JL* M: 07931-526333 E: r.j.walton94@gmail.com

WALTON, Stephen James. b 71. Mert Coll Ox BA 92 MA 97. Oak Hill Th Coll BA 01. **d** 02 **p** 03. C Thurnby w Stoughton *Leic* 02–07; R Marbury w Tushingham and Whitewell *Ches* 07–15; Chapl Düsseldorf *Eur* from 15. *Mulvany House, Rotterdamer Strasse 135, 40474 Düsseldorf, Germany* T: (0049) (211) 452759 E: walton_stephen@hotmail.com *or* chaplain@christchurch.de

WALTON, Prof Stephen John. b 55. Birm Univ BSc 76 Fitzw Coll Cam BA 79 MA 82 Sheff Univ PhD 97. Ridley Hall Cam 77. **d** 83 **p** 84. C Bebington *Ches* 83–86; Voc and Min Adv CPAS 86–92; LtO *St Alb* 86–94; Public Preacher 00–04; Bp's Dom Chapl 94–95; Lect St Jo Coll Nottm 95–99; Lect Greek and NT Lon Sch of Th 99–03; Sen Lect Greek and NT 03–11; Prof NT 11–13; Hon Research Fell Tyndale Ho Cam 13–15; Affiliated Lect Div Cam Univ 13–17; Prof NT and Research Fell St Mary's Univ Twickenham *Lon* 13–17; Public Preacher *Ely* 12–16; Lic Preacher *Lon* from 16; Assoc Research Fell Trin Coll Bris from 18. *Butterfield House, 63 Church Street, Isleworth TW7 6BE* T: (020) 8560 7511 M: 07897-630462 E: steve.walton@cantab.net *or* s.walton@trinitycollegebristol.ac.uk

WALTON, Teresa Margaret. b 61. **d** 12 **p** 13. NSM Washington *Dur* 12–17; PtO *Newc* from 17; *Dur* from 19. *18 Wingate Grange, Houghton le Spring DH4 6GQ* E: twalton2207@gmail.com

WALTON, William Frederick. b 59. IEng 98 CEnv 05. Qu Foundn (Course) 16. **d** 18 **p** 19. NSM Cov H Trin 18–21; rtd 21. *1 Rookery Lane, Coventry CV6 4GL* T: (024) 7668 0137 M: 07771-555764 E: bill.walton@hotmail.co.uk

⊕**WAMBUNYA, The Rt Revd Timothy Livingstone (Amboko).** b 66. Simon of Cyrene Th Inst 93 Oak Hill Th Coll BA 94. **d** 97 **p** 98 **c** 13. C Southall Green St Jo *Lon* 97–00; TV Tollington 00–07; Prin Carlile Coll Nairobi Kenya 07–13; Bp Butere 13–20; V Slough *Ox* from 20; Hon Asst Bp Ox from 21. *The Vicarage, 196 Stoke Road, Slough SL2 5AY* T: (01753) 521497 E: t.wamb@virgin.net *or* vicar@stpaulsslough.org.uk

WANDREY, Bryce Philip. b 77. St Olaf Coll Minnesota BA 99. Concordia Th Sem Indiana MDiv 03 St Steph Ho Ox 07. **d** 08 **p** 09. C Highgate St Mich *Lon* 08–17; C Highgate All SS 09–14; P-in-c 14–17; Chapl Porter Gaud Sch USA from 17. *5 Fields Place, Charleston SC 92403, USA* E: brycepwandrey@gmail.com

WANDSWORTH, Archdeacon of. *See* KIDDLE, The Ven John

WANJIE, Lukas Macharia. b 50. Fitzw Coll Cam BA 79 MA 83 Birkbeck Coll Lon MSc 98. St Paul's Coll Limuru 72 Ridley Hall Cam 76. **d** 75 **p** 76. C Uthiru St Pet Kenya 75–76; C Mill End and Heronsgate w W Hyde *St Alb* 79; V Westlands St Mark Nairobi Kenya 80–84; Prin Trin Bible Coll Nairobi 85–91; C St Alb St Steph 91–94; PtO 94–95; Race Relations Adv Croydon *S'wark* 95–01; V Bermondsey St Kath w St Bart 01–12; rtd 13. *7 Bute Walk, Derby DE21 6BN* E: wanjiel@yahoo.co.uk

WANSTALL, Noelle Margaret. *See* HALL, Noelle Margaret

WANT, Mrs Angela Patricia. b 47. Kent Univ BA 68. EAMTC 02. **d** 05 **p** 06. NSM Newport and Widdington *Chelmsf* 05–10; NSM Saffron Walden and Villages 10–17; rtd 17; PtO *Chelmsf* 17–20. *3 Orchard Close, Newport, Saffron Walden CB11 3QT* T: (01799) 540051 E: angelapwant@btinternet.com

WARBRICK, Canon Quentin David. b 66. Jes Coll Ox BA 88. Cranmer Hall Dur 89. **d** 92 **p** 93. C Birm St Martin w Bordesley St Andr 92–96; C Handsworth St Jas 96–00; V Packwood w Hockley Heath 00–10; AD Shirley 05–10; P-in-c Kings Heath 10–14; V from 14; AD Moseley 17–20; Co-AD Kings Norton, Moseley and Shirley 20–21; Hon Can Birm Cathl from 14. *The Vicarage, 4 Vicarage Road, Kings Heath, Birmingham B14 7RA* T: 0121-444 0260 *or* 444 0760 E: info@davidwarbrick.co.uk

WARBURTON, Andrew James. b 44. Oak Hill Th Coll 64. **d** 69 **p** 70. C New Milverton *Cov* 69–72; C Fulham St Matt *Lon* 72–76; C Chesham St Mary *Ox* 76–80; TV Gt Chesham 80–94; Chapl Paris St Mich *Eur* 94–97; Asst Chapl Amsterdam w Heiloo 97–99; rtd 99; PtO *Carl* from 11. *Burnbrae, Riccarton, Newcastleton TD9 0SN* T: (01387) 376293 M: 07962-622740 E: borderwarburton@gmail.com

WARD, Alan William. b 56. Trin Coll Bris 80. **d** 81 **p** 82. C New Ferry *Ches* 81–86; Dioc Youth Officer 86–91; C Charlesworth and Dinting Vale *Derby* 91–96; V Mickleover All SS 96–11; C Mickleover St Jo 06–11; R Wallasey St Hilary *Ches* from 11; RD Wallasey from 18. *St Hilary's Rectory, Church Hill, Wallasey CH45 3NH* T: 0151-638 4771 E: rector@sthilarywallasey.org.uk

WARD, Mrs Alice Belinda. b 58. Dur Univ BSc 79 MA 01 MBACP 04. Cranmer Hall Dur 15. **d** 17 **p** 18. NSM Jesmond H Trin *Newc* 17–18; NSM Newc St Luke 18–20; P-in-c from 20. *1 Hawthorn Villas, Wallsend NE28 7NT* E: aliceward1@mac.com

WARD, Alistair William McKenzie. b 62. Ridley Hall Cam 16. **d** 18 **p** 19. C Linc St Pet in Eastgate 18–21. *15 Queensway, Lincoln LN2 4AJ* T: (01522) 520512 M: 07999-426560 E: alistairward@virginmedia.com

WARD (née WEIGHTMAN), Mrs Andrea Frances. b 66. Sheff Univ BA 87. Ridley Hall Cam 00. **d** 03 **p** 04. C Handforth *Ches* 03–07; V Blendon *Roch* 07–17; P-in-c Chatham St Paul w All SS 17–21. *2 Rose Cottage, High Lorton, Cockermouth CA13 9UQ* M: 07506-789806 E: andreaward72@gmail.com

WARD, Andrew John. b 65. Cliff Th Coll 85 Trin Coll Bris BA 99. **d** 99 **p** 00. C Belper *Derby* 99–03; TV Walbrook Epiphany 03–11; TR from 11; RD Derby S 12–15. *St Augustine's Rectory, 155 Almond Street, Derby DE23 6LY* T: (01332) 760846 M: 07860-418915 E: rector.walbrook@gmail.com

WARD, Canon Anthony Peter. b 46. Bris Univ BSc 67 Ox Univ DipEd 68. St Jo Coll Nottm. **d** 82 **p** 83. C Hellesdon *Nor* 82–85; P-in-c Nor St Aug w St Mary 85–91; P-in-c Norwich-over-the-Water Colegate St Geo 85–90; Norfolk Churches' Radio Officer 85–95; TV Norwich Over-the-Water 91–95; V Gorleston St Andr 95–11; RD Gt Yarmouth 98–02; Hon Can Nor Cathl 03–11; rtd 11. *20 The Butts, Belper DE56 1HX* T: (01773) 821639 E: revtw@btinternet.com *or* revtw@live.com

WARD, Arthur John. b 32. Lon Univ BD 57. St Aid Birkenhead 57. **d** 57 **p** 58. C Ecclesfield *Sheff* 57–60; C Fulwood 60–63; Tutor St Aid Birkenhead 63–66; R Denton St Lawr *Man* 66–74; CMS 74–82; TV Wolverhampton *Lich* 82–90; V Edgbaston SS Mary and Ambrose *Birm* 90–96; rtd 96; PtO *Heref* 97–19. *Bramble Cottage, 6 Lower Forge, Eardington, Bridgnorth WV16 5LQ* T: (01746) 764758 E: revjohnward@aol.com

WARD, Miss Beverley Jayne. b 61. Bolton Inst of Educn CertEd 97. St Steph Ho Ox 00. **d** 02 **p** 07. C Standish *Blackb* 02–07; C Thornton-le-Fylde 07–09; P-in-c Eccleston 09–12; V Cleveleys 12–20; rtd 20. M: 07811-907274 E: rev.jayneward@gmail.com

WARD, Brett Ernest. b 62. Univ of Wales MTh 06. ACT 86. **d** 89 **p** 89. C E Maitland Australia 89; Asst P 89–91; Asst P Singleton 91–92; P-in-c Weston 92–97; C Forton *Portsm* 97–99; P-in-c 99–05; V 05–07; P-in-c Eltham H Trin *S'wark* 07–10; V from 10; AD Eltham and Mottingham 13–20; Asst Dir of Ords Woolwich Area from 16. *Holy Trinity Vicarage, 59 Southend Crescent, London SE9 2SD* T: (020) 8850 1246 E: fr.brett@ht-e.org.uk

WARD, Canon Calvin. b 34. Univ of Wales BA 57 DipEd 60 Fitzw Ho Cam BA 63 MA 67. Westcott Ho Cam 61. **d** 64 **p** 65. C Handsworth St Mich *Birm* 64–66; C Shaw Hill 66–69; V Windhill *Bradf* 69–76; V Esholt 76–81; V Oakworth 81–91; V Allerton 91–99; Hon Can Bradf Cathl 94–99; rtd 99; PtO *Bradf* 99–14. *47 Wheatlands Drive, Bradford BD9 5JN* E: calvin.ward28@gmail.com

WARD, Daran. b 65. Brunel Univ BSc 88. St Jo Coll Nottm 07. **d** 09 **p** 10. C Hartley Wintney, Elvetham, Winchfield etc *Win* 09–13; V Bramley *Sheff* 13–19; P-in-c Thrybergh 13–19; V Alsager Ch Ch *Ches* from 19. *43 Church Road, Alsager, Stoke-on-Trent ST7 2HS* E: daran.ward@gmail.com

WARD, David. b 40. St Jo Coll Nottm 83. **d** 85 **p** 86. C Aspley *S'well* 85–89; V 89–04; rtd 04; PtO *S'well* from 06. *150 Robins Wood Road, Nottingham NG8 3LD* T: 0115-929 3231 M: 07971-092089

WARD, David Graham. b 51. CBDTI 03. **d** 06 **p** 07. OLM Higher Walton *Blackb* 06–07; NSM 07–10; P-in-c Brindle 10–11; R from 11. *Coppice Farm, Goose Foot Lane, Samlesbury, Preston PR5 0RQ* T: (01254) 852995 F: 851101

WARD, Canon David Robert. b 51. Oak Hill Th Coll 74. **d** 77 **p** 78. C Kirkheaton *Wakef* 77–81; V Earl's Heaton 81–88; V Bradley 88–14; *Leeds* 14–16; P-in-c Fixby and Cowcliffe *Wakef* 09–14; *Leeds* 14–16; Hon Can Wakef Cathl 02–16; rtd 16; PtO *Leeds* from 17. *32 Lyndhurst Avenue, Brighouse HD6 3RY* T: (01484) 400809 E: drwardxvic@gmail.com

WARD, Edward. *See* WARD, William Edward

WARD, Mrs Elisabeth. b 63. Trevelyan Coll Dur BA 85 St Mellitus Coll MA 18 Bath Spa Univ PGCE 99. Linc Sch of Th and Min 11. **d** 14 **p** 15. C Stamford St Geo w St Paul *Linc* 14–18; V Skirbeck H Trin from 18. *Holy Trinity Vicarage, 64 Spilsby Road, Boston PE21 9NS* T: (01205) 355172 M: 07768-814698 E: rev.lisward@holytrinity.org.uk

WARD, Elizabeth Joyce. *See* HOLMES, Elizabeth Joyce

WARD, The Very Revd Frances Elizabeth Fearn. b 59. St Andr Univ MTheol 83 Man Univ PhD 00 Bradf Univ MA 06 RGN 87. Westcott Ho Cam 87. **d** 89 **p** 94. Par Dn Westhoughton *Man* 89–93; Tutor Practical Th N Coll Man 93–98; Hon C Bury St Pet *Man* 93–98; C Unsworth 98–99; V Bury St Pet 99–05; C Leverhulme 05–06; Bp's Adv on Women in Min 02–04; Hon Can Man Cathl 04–06; Can Res Bradf Cathl 06–10; Dean St E 10–18; P-in-c Workington St Jo *Carl* from 20; P-in-c Workington St Mich from 20; Lic Th from 18. *St Michael's Rectory, Dora Crescent, Workington CA14 2EZ* M: 07791-165774 E: fefward@gmail.com

WARD, Frank Wyatt. b 30. Oak Hill NSM Course 84. **d** 92 **p** 94. NSM Paddington St Pet *Lon* 92–09; NSM Paddington St Mary Magd and St Pet 09–15; rtd 15; PtO *Lon* from 15. *82 Hill Rise, Greenford UB6 8PE* T: (020) 8575 5515

WARD, Garry William. b 67. Anglia Ruskin Univ MA 11 RGN 90 RM 92. Qu Coll Birm 01. **d** 03 **p** 04. C Wednesfield *Lich* 03–06; TV Wordsley *Worc* 06–11; V Claverley w Tuckhill *Heref* from 11. *The Vicarage, Lodge Park, Claverley, Wolverhampton WV5 7DP* T: (01746) 710304 E: vicar@garry.org.uk

WARD, Prof Graham John. b 55. Fitzw Coll Cam BA 80 Selw Coll Cam MA 83. Westcott Ho Cam 87. **d** 90 **p** 91. C Bris St Mary Redcliffe w Temple etc 90–92; Chapl Ex Coll Ox 92–94; Dean Peterho Cam 95–99; Prof Contextual Th Man Univ 99–12; Regius Prof Div Ox Univ from 12; Can Res Ch Ch *Ox* from 12; LtO from 18. *Christ Church, Oxford OX1 1DP* T: (01865) 276246 E: graham.ward@chch.ox.ac.uk

WARD, Helen Frances. b 48. EAMTC 02. **d** 04 **p** 05. NSM Gorleston St Andr *Nor* 04–11; rtd 11. *20 The Butts, Belper DE56 1HX* T: (01773) 821639 E: revhw@btinternet.com

WARD, Ian Stanley. b 62. K Coll Lon BD 83. Cranmer Hall Dur 84. **d** 86 **p** 87. C Moreton *Ches* 86–89; Chapl RAF 89–18; C Skirbeck H Trin *Linc* from 18. *Holy Trinity Vicarage, 64 Spilsby Road, Boston PE21 9NS* T: (01205) 355172

WARD, Canon Janice Ann. b 65. Univ of Wales (Lamp) BA 86. ERMC 05. **d** 08 **p** 09. C Haverhill w Withersfield *St E* 08–12; P-in-c Marown, Foxdale and Baldwin *S & M* 12–13; V from 13; Can St German's Cathl from 16. *Marown Vicarage, Main Road, Crosby, Isle of Man IM4 4BH* T: (01624) 851378 M: 07624-406084 E: revjaniceward@manx.net

WARD, Jason David. b 71. Glas Univ BSc 93 PhD 98. Oak Hill Th Coll BA 06. **d** 06 **p** 07. C Cheadle Hulme St Andr *Ches* 06–09; C Harold Wood *Chelmsf* 09–13; V Chaddesden St Mary *Derby* from 13. *The Vicarage, 133 Chaddesden Lane, Chaddesden, Derby DE21 6LL* T: (01332) 280924 M: 07866-361054 E: jasethebass@gmail.com *or* jason@chaddesdenchurch.org.uk

WARD, Jayne. *See* WARD, Beverley Jayne

WARD, John. *See* WARD, Arthur John

WARD, Canon John Frederick. b 55. St Mich Coll Llan 81. **d** 84 **p** 85. C Pembroke Dock *St D* 84–86; PV Llan Cathl 86–89; R St Brides Minor w Bettws 89–97; V Shard End *Birm* 97–04; V Twigworth, Down Hatherley, Norton, The Leigh etc *Glouc* 04–10; C Wotton-under-Edge w Ozleworth, N Nibley etc 10–12; C Charfield and Kingswood 10–11; C Charfield and Kingswood w Wickwar etc 11–12; V Quedgeley 12–20; Hon Can Glouc Cathl 18–20; rtd 20. *37A St Mary's Square, Gloucester GL1 2QT* M: 07967-636094 E: jfmw23@gmail.com

WARD, Prof John Stephen Keith. b 38. Univ of Wales (Cardiff) BA 62 Linacre Coll Ox BLitt 68 DD 98 Trin Hall Cam MA 72 DD 99 FBA 01. Westcott Ho Cam 72. **d** 72 **p** 73. Lect Philosophy of Relig Lon Univ 71–75; Hon C Hampstead St Jo 72–75; Dean Trin Hall Cam 75–82; Prof Moral and Soc Th K Coll Lon 82–85; Prof Hist and Philosophy of Relig 85–91; Regius Prof Div Ox Univ 91–03; Can Res Ch Ch *Ox* 91–03; rtd 03; PtO *Ox* 03–15 and 17–19; Professorial Research Fell Heythrop Coll Lon 10–18. *39 Coopers Lane, Abingdon OX14 5GU* T: (01235) 539799 E: keith.ward@chch.ox.ac.uk

WARD, Keith Raymond. b 37. Dur Univ BSc 60. Chich Th Coll 63. **d** 65 **p** 66. C Wallsend St Luke *Newc* 65–68; C Wooler 68–74; V Dinnington 74–81; V Bedlington 81–93; V Stannington 93–99; rtd 99; PtO *Newc* from 00. *2 Ethel's Close, Gloster Meadows, Amble, Morpeth NE65 0GD* T: (01665) 714357 E: raymond987@btinternet.com

WARD, Kevin. b 47. Edin Univ MA 69 Trin Coll Cam PhD 76. **d** 78 **p** 79. CMS 75–92; Uganda 76–90; Qu Coll Birm 91; PtO *Birm* 91; C Halifax *Wakef* 91–92; P-in-c Charlestown 92–95; NSM Headingley *Ripon* 95–14; *Leeds* 14–19; Lect Leeds Univ from 95; PtO *Leeds* 19–21. *8 North Grange Mews, Leeds LS6 2EW* T: 0113-278 7801 E: trskw@leeds.ac.uk

WARD, Laura Louise. b 88. Birm Univ BSc 09 Dur Univ BA 21. St Steph Ho Ox 17. **d** 20 **p** 21. C Perry Barr *Birm* from 20. *30 Maple Road, Sutton Coldfield B72 1JP* M: 07890-524380 E: motherlaura@st-johns-perry-barr.com

WARD, Ms Lois Georgina. b 87. Cen Lancs Univ BA 15 Sheff Univ BA 18. Coll of Resurr Mirfield 16. **d** 19 **p** 20. C Poulton Carleton and Singleton *Blackb* from 19.

WARD, Mark. b 62. Imp Coll Lon BScEng 84. Wycliffe Hall Ox BTh 93. **d** 93 **p** 94. C Parkham, Alwington, Buckland Brewer etc *Ex* 93–96; C S Molton w Nymet St George, High Bray etc 96–97; TV 97–05; TV Ottery St Mary, Alfington, W Hill, Tipton etc from 05; RD Ottery from 17. *The Vicarage, Newton Poppleford, Sidmouth EX10 0HB* T: (01395) 568390 E: revmarkward@btinternet.com

WARD, Matthew Alan James. b 69. Nottm Poly BSc 91 Dur Univ DThM 16. Ridley Hall Cam 94. **d** 97 **p** 98. C Birchwood *Linc* 97–00; Chapl Cov Univ 00–05; Chapl Leeds Univ 05–18; Chapl Leeds Beckett Univ 05–18. *6 Barony, Millgate, Cupar KY15 5ER*

WARD (née MASSEY), Michelle Elaine (Shellie). Plymouth Univ BA 00. Trin Coll Bris BA 04. **d** 04 **p** 05. C Barrowby and Gt Gonerby *Linc* 04–09; P-in-c Saxonwell 09–12; P-in-c Claypole 11–12; P-in-c Broadway w Wickhamford *Worc* from 12. *The Vicarage, Church Street, Broadway WR12 7AE* T: (01386) 852352 M: 07780-002565 E: broadwaycofe@gmail.com

WARD, Nathan James. b 80. St Cuth Soc Dur BA 01 Leic Univ MSc 12. SEITE 11. **d** 14 **p** 15. NSM S Chatham H Trin *Roch* 14–18; V Rainham from 18. *St Margaret's Vicarage, 80 Broadview Avenue, Gillingham ME8 9DE* M: 07917-473586 E: wardnathan@me.com *or* vicar@rainhamchurch.co.uk

WARD, Nigel Andrew. b 50. Peterho Cam BA 72 MA 76. Oak Hill NSM Course 89. **d** 92 **p** 93. NSM Frogmore *St Alb* from 92. *15 Park Street, St Albans AL2 2PE* T: (01727) 872667

WARD, Peter Macdonald. b 41. **d** 09 **p** 10. NSM Harrow Weald All SS *Lon* 09–21; rtd 21. *9 Kennet Gardens, Bradford-on-Avon BA15 1LT* M: 07733-001777 E: wardhatchend@hotmail.com

WARD, Peter Nicholas. b 59. Ban Ord Course 03. **d** 08 **p** 09. NSM Llanwnnog and Caersws w Carno *Ban* 08–11; NSM Bro Ddyfi Uchaf 11–14; NSM Bro Cyfeiliog and Mawddwy from 14. *Coed Cae, Clatter, Caersws SY17 5NW* T: (01686) 688034 E: peteandsand@btopenworld.com

WARD, Robert. b 60. Em Coll Cam BA 81 MA 85. Chich Th Coll. **d** 86 **p** 87. C Horfield H Trin *Bris* 86–90; C Stantonbury and Willen *Ox* 90; TV 90–96; V Knowle St Martin *Bris* 96–07; R Cradley w Mathon and Storridge *Heref* from 07; RD Ledbury from 13. *The Rectory, Cradley, Malvern WR13 5LQ* T: (01886) 880438 E: robert.ward776@gmail.com

WARD, Robert Arthur Philip. b 53. Lon Univ BD 82 Open Univ BA 88. Qu Coll Birm 77. **d** 79 **p** 80. C Balsall Heath St Paul *Birm* 79–82; Chapl RAF 82–98; TR Blakenall Heath *Lich* 98–01; PtO 05–07; V Ravensthorpe and Thornhill Lees w Savile Town *Wakef* 07–13; P-in-c St Marychurch *Ex* 13–20; rtd 20; PtO *B & W* from 21. *220 Old Church Road, Clevedon BS21 7UB* E: father.ward@gmail.com

WARD, Robert Charles Irwin. b 48. Leic Univ LLB 70 Madras Bible Sem DD 01 Called to the Bar (Inner Temple) 72. Cranmer Hall Dur 78. **d** 80 **p** 81. C Byker St Mich w St Lawr *Newc* 80–85; PtO 86–07; NSM Newc St Luke 07–20; Dir Clarence Trust and NE Area Revival Min from 86; Asst Chapl HM Pris Frankland 91–95; PtO *Newc* 21. *1 Hawthorn Villas, The Green, Wallsend NE28 7NT* T/F: 0191-234 3969 M: 07768-528181 E: rwarduk@mac.com

WARD, Canon Robin. b 66. Magd Coll Ox BA 87 MA 91 K Coll Lon PhD 03. St Steph Ho Ox 88. **d** 91 **p** 92. C Romford St Andr *Chelmsf* 91–94; C Willesden Green St Andr and St Fran *Lon* 94–96; V Sevenoaks St Jo *Roch* 96–06; Chapl Invicta Community Care NHS Trust 97–06; Hon Can Roch Cathl 04–06; Prin St Steph Ho Ox from 06. *St Stephen's House, 16 Marston Street, Oxford OX4 1JX* T: (01865) 613500 E: robin.ward@ssho.ox.ac.uk

WARD, Mrs Rosemary Clare. b 57. Westf Coll Lon BA 79 Liv Univ MA 80 MPhil 82. Trin Coll Bris BA 94. **d** 94 **p** 95. C Bris St Andr Hartcliffe 94–98; C Downend 98–02; P-in-c Broad Blunsdon 02–05; C Highworth w Sevenhampton and Inglesham etc 02–05; Dioc Lay Tr Adv 02–05; Leadership Development Adv CPAS 05–11; R Sawtry and Glatton *Ely* 12–16; rtd 16; PtO *Win* from 17. *24 Farnleys Mead, Lymington SO41 3TJ* T: (01590) 679651 E: wardrosie@btinternet.com

WARD, Mrs Sandra Elizabeth. b 53. Lady Spencer Chu Coll of Educn TCert 75 Anglia Ruskin Univ MA 07. LCTP 08. **d** 13 **p** 14. NSM Orton and Tebay w Ravenstonedale etc *Carl* 13–16; NSM Shap w Swindale and Bampton w Mardale 13–16; NSM High Westmorland 16–18; P-in-c Lorton and Loweswater w Buttermere 18–20. *The Vicarage, Loweswater,*

Cockermouth CA13 0RU T: (01900) 85237 M: 07946-633334 E: revd.sandra@btinternet.com

WARD, Mrs Sheena Mary. b 55. Newc Univ BA 76 PGCE 77. **d** 00 **p** 01. OLM Cramlington *Newc* 00–18; rtd 18; PtO *Newc* 18–21; *Man* from 21. *15 Mossdale Avenue, Bolton BL1 5YA* M: 07557-880277 E: reverendsheena@gmail.com

WARD, Canon Simon William James. b 71. Dur Univ BA 94 Westmr Coll Ox PGCE 96. Ripon Coll Cuddesdon 98. **d** 00 **p** 01. C Aldershot St Mich *Guildf* 00–03; TV Sole Bay *St E* 03–09; Bp's Chapl *Nor* 09–14; P-in-c Earlham 14–17; TR Gt Yarmouth from 17; RD from 21; Hon Can Nor Cathl from 17. *The Rectory, Town Wall Road, Great Yarmouth NR30 1DJ* E: revdsimon@msn.com

WARD, Mrs Susan Elizabeth. b 50. NOC 92. **d** 95 **p** 96. NSM Heyside *Man* 95–09; NSM Newhey 09–16; NSM Belfield from 09; NSM Milnrow 09–16; NSM Milnrow and New Hey from 16; Chapl Pennine Acute Hosps NHS Trust 04–16; PtO *Leeds* from 17. *12 Airedale Quay, Rodley, Leeds LS13 1NZ* T: 0113-229 3839 M: 07595-593605 E: sue.ward1950@live.co.uk

WARD, Timothy James. b 67. CCC Ox BA 90 MA 95 Edin Univ PhD 99. Oak Hill Th Coll BA 95. **d** 99 **p** 00. C Crowborough *Chich* 99–04; TV Hinckley H Trin *Leic* 04–10; R 10–13; Assoc Dir Cornhill Tr Course 13–16; PtO *Roch* 14–16; Tutor Oak Hill Coll from 16. *Oak Hill College, Chase Side, London N14 4PS* T: (020) 8449 0467

WARD, Timothy John Conisbee. b 62. New Coll Ox BA 85 MA 02 PGCE 86. Wycliffe Hall Ox BA 91. **d** 92 **p** 93. C Dorking St Paul *Guildf* 92–96; C Herne Hill *S'wark* 96–02; V Walberton w Binsted *Chich* from 02. *St Mary's Vicarage, The Street, Walberton, Arundel BN18 0PQ* T: (01243) 551488 E: tjcward@uwclub.net

WARD, Timothy William. b 49. Open Univ BA 74 Birm Univ BPhil(Ed) 93. St Deiniol's Hawarden 78. **d** 79 **p** 80. NSM Handsworth St Mary *Birm* 79–95; PtO 95–05; NSM Gt Barr *Lich* 95–19; PtO from 19. *3 Dale Close, Birmingham B43 6AS* T: 0121-358 1880 *or* 358 2807 E: curate.greatbarr@btinternet.com

WARD, Tracy. b 63. RGN RSCN 89. All SS Cen for Miss & Min 13. **d** 16 **p** 17. C Sale St Anne *Ches* 16–18; V Mellor from 18. *The Vicarage, 51 Church Road, Mellor, Stockport SK6 5LX* M: 07875-059113 E: revdtracyward@icloud.com

WARD, Preb William Edward. b 48. TD 04. FSAScot 71. AKC 71. **d** 72 **p** 73. C Heref St Martin 72–77; C Blakenall Heath *Lich* 77–78; TV 78–82; V Astley, Clive, Grinshill and Hadnall 82–91; R Edgmond w Kynnersley and Preston Wealdmoors 91–17; P-in-c Tibberton w Bolas Magna and Waters Upton 02–17; Chapl Harper Adams Univ Coll 91–17; Preb Lich Cathl 09–17; CF (TA) 87–05; CF (ACF) 05–10; rtd 17; Hon C Forton *Lich* from 18. *31 Fair Oak, Newport TF10 7LR* T: (01952) 814886 E: e.ward17@btinternet.com

WARDALE, Robert Christopher. b 46. Newc Univ BA 69 MA 93. Coll of Resurr Mirfield 77. **d** 79 **p** 80. C Cockerton *Dur* 79–84; P-in-c Hedworth 84–87; V 87–92; V Darlington H Trin 92–96; rtd 06; PtO *Newc* from 06; *Dur* from 12. *24 Beechcroft, Kenton Road, Newcastle upon Tyne NE3 4NB* T: 0191-285 5284 E: wardalerc@aol.com

WARDELL, Gareth Kevin. b 59. York Univ BA 81 MA 01. Ridley Hall Cam 03. **d** 05 **p** 06. C Selby Abbey *York* 05–08; C Kensington St Mary Abbots w Ch Ch and St Phil *Lon* 08–13; V Hampton All SS 13–20; V Notting Dale St Clem w St Mark and St Jas from 20. *The Vicarage, 12 St Ann's Villas, London W11 4RS* E: wardellgareth@hotmail.com *or* gareth.wardell@london.anglican.org

WARDEN, Richard James. b 57. Kent Univ BA 79 K Coll Lon MTh 86. Wycliffe Hall Ox 81. **d** 83 **p** 84. C Fulham St Mary N End *Lon* 83–85; CF 85–89; Chapl Wycombe Abbey Sch 89–01; Sen Chapl and Hd RS Wellington Coll Berks 01–04; P-in-c Finchampstead *Ox* 04–10; Chapl Mill Hill Sch Lon from 10. *Mill Hill School, The Ridgeway, London NW7 1QS* T: (020) 8959 1176 E: rjw@millhill.org.uk

WARDLE, John Argyle. b 47. St Jo Coll Dur BA 71 ARCM 67 CertEd 73. **d** 73 **p** 74. C Mansfield SS Pet and Paul *S'well* 73–77; Chapl St Felix Sch Southwold 77–87; TV Haverhill w Withersfield, the Wrattings etc *St E* 87–90; TV Choral S'well Minster 90–99; Bp's Adv on Healing 94–99; R Bridlington Priory *York* 99–08; RD Bridlington 03–08; rtd 08; PtO *York* 12–17. *27 First Avenue, Bridlington YO15 2JW* T: (01262) 400127 E: jawardle27@btinternet.com

WARDMAN, Canon Carol Joy. b 56. Lon Univ BA 79 Man Univ MPhil 02. NOC 91. **d** 94 **p** 95. NSM Hebden Bridge *Wakef* 94–97; NSM Sowerby 97–10; Dioc Adv for Older People's Issues 08–11; NSM Halifax 10–11; Bps' Adv for Ch and Soc Ch in Wales from 11; PtO *St As* from 12; Metrop Can Llan Cathl from 15. *39 Cathedral Road, Cardiff CF11 9XF* T: (029) 2034 8260 E: carol.wardman@gmail.com *or* carolwardman@churchinwales.org.uk

WARE, Canon John Lawrence. b 37. Nottm Univ BA 59. Ridley Hall Cam 59. **d** 62 **p** 63. C Attercliffe *Sheff* 62–66; C Ranmoor 66–68; R Liddington and Soc and Ind Chapl Bris 68–74; Bp's Soc and Ind Adv and C-in-c Bris St Thos 74–79; V Kingswood 79–88; RD Bitton 85–87; P-in-c Broad Blunsdon 88–94; P-in-c Blunsdon St Andrew 88–94; R The Blunsdons 94–01; RD Cricklade 88–94; Hon Can Bris Cathl 76–01; rtd 01; PtO *Bris* from 01; Chapl HM Pris Bris 03–07. *26 Dongola Road, Bishopston, Bristol BS7 9HP* T: 0117-924 1304 E: jlwdongola@gmail.com

WARE, Ms Judith Marian. b 52. St Hugh's Coll Ox BA 74 MA 78 PGCE 75. CBDTI 00. **d** 02 **p** 03. NSM Windermere St Mary and Troutbeck *Carl* 02–05; C Thornes and Lupset *Wakef* 05–10; Chapl Wakef Cathl Sch 05–06; R Crumpsall *Man* 10–17; rtd 17; PtO *Man* from 17. *22 Kingsway Close, Oldham OL8 1BE* T: 0161-971 6326 E: jmware30@gmail.com

WARE, Stephen John. b 55. Univ of Wales (Lamp) BA 76. Ripon Coll Cuddesdon 77. **d** 79 **p** 80. C Lighthorne *Cov* 79–82; Chapl RAF 82–00; Command Chapl RAF 00–05; Selection Sec Min Division 05; V Bloxham w Milcombe and S Newington *Ox* 05–06; Warden of Readers *Glouc* 06–12; Asst Dioc Dir of Ords 06–14. *25 Beauchamp Meadow, Lydney GL15 5NS* T: (01594) 842299

WARHAM, Jean. *See* WALKER, Jean

WARHURST (née HART), Mrs Jane Elizabeth. b 56. Sheff Univ BA 77. NOC 98. **d** 01 **p** 02. C Edge Hill St Cypr w St Mary *Liv* 01–06; V Toxteth St Bede w St Clem 06–14; V Irlam *Man* from 14; Dioc Ecum Officer 14–16; AD Eccles 20–21. *The Vicarage, Vicarage Road, Irlam, Manchester M44 6WA*

WARHURST, Richard. b 76. Univ Coll Chich BA 99. St Steph Ho Ox 00. **d** 02 **p** 03. C New Shoreham *Chich* 02–06; C Old Shoreham 02–06; R Chailey 06–10; Chapl Dorothy House Hospice Winsley 10–15; PtO *B & W* 11–15; R St Bartholomew *Sarum* 15–20. *Address temp unknown*

WARING, Jeffery Edwin. b 53. Trin Coll Bris 80. **d** 83 **p** 84. C Harpurhey Ch Ch *Man* 83–86; TV Eccles 86–92; P-in-c Hamworthy *Sarum* 92–04; P-in-c Red Post 04–13; rtd 13; Hon C Iwerne Valley *Sarum* 14–19. *Glen View, Church Lane, Sutton Waldron, Blandford Forum DT11 8PB* E: jeffwaring@btinternet.com

WARING, John Robert Huw. b 66. Dur Univ BA 21. St Hild Coll 19. **d** 21. NSM Filey *York* from 21. *3 Barden Place, Filey YO14 0DR* T: (01723) 639597 M: 07581-690778 E: fileycurate@gmail.com

WARING, Mrs Ruth Margaret. b 44. Keele Univ CertEd 65. SWMTC 86. **d** 90 **p** 94. Par Dn Tavistock and Gulworthy *Ex* 90–94; C 94–96; TV Axminster, Chardstock, All Saints etc 96–04; rtd 04; PtO *Ex* from 04. *13 Latches Walk, Axminster EX13 5DQ* T: (01297) 639112

WARLAND, Peter William. b 35. K Coll Lon 56. **d** 60 **p** 61. C Pemberton St Jo *Liv* 60–64; C Warrington St Elphin 64–66; V Farnworth All SS *Man* 66–71; Chapl RN 71–92; QHC 88–92; Chapl Greenbank and Freedom Fields Hosps *Ex* 92–00; Chapl St Luke's Hospice Plymouth 94–00; rtd 00; PtO *Ex* from 00. *5 Evans Court, 6 Craigie Drive, Plymouth PL1 3TP* T: (01752) 663274

WARMAN, Philip Noel. b 64. Roehampton Inst BSc 85 PGCE 86. Ridley Hall Cam 99. **d** 01 **p** 02. C Burney Lane *Birm* 01–06; C Luton St Mary *St Alb* 06–09; V Brightside w Wincobank *Sheff* from 09. *The Vicarage, 24 Beacon Road, Sheffield S9 1AD* T: 0114-281 9360 E: phil.warman@sheffield.anglican.org

WARMINGTON, Thomas Zane. b 82. Ridley Hall Cam 16. **d** 18 **p** 19. C Epping Distr *Chelmsf* 18–21; P-in-c Gt Dunmow and Barnston from 21. *The Vicarage, Charters, Dunmow CM6 2SJ* E: tomwarmit@gmail.com

WARNE, Miss Susan Annette. b 39. Man Univ BSc 61 Nottm Univ DipEd 62. **d** 00 **p** 01. OLM Yoxmere *St E* 00–09; PtO 09–21. *Wynkyns, 22 Oakwood Park, Yoxford, Saxmundham IP17 3JU* T: (01728) 668410

WARNER, Alan Winston. b 51. Lon Univ BSc 73. Coll of Resurr Mirfield 73. **d** 76 **p** 77. C Willenhall St Anne *Lich* 76–78; C Baswich 78–81; V Wednesfield St Greg 81–87; Chapl Frimley Park Hosp 87–94; Chapl Frimley Park Hosp NHS Trust 94–04; Team Ldr Shrewsbury and Telford NHS Trust 04–10; Bp's Adv on Hosp Chapl *Lich* 06–10; rtd 10; PtO *Nor* from 11. *7 Dolphin Close, Lowestoft NR33 0LA* E: alan.warner77@talktalk.net

WARNER, Canon Andrew Compton. b 35. Fitzw Ho Cam BA 58 MA 62. Westcott Ho Cam 59. **d** 60 **p** 61. C Addlestone *Guildf* 60–64; C-in-c Ash Vale CD 64–71; V Hinchley Wood 71–80; R Gt Bookham 80–00; RD Leatherhead 88–93; Hon Can Guildf Cathl 99–00; rtd 00; PtO *Win* from 00. *5 Pearman Drive, Andover SP10 2SB* T: (01264) 391325 E: dandawarner@yahoo.co.uk

WARNER, Clifford Chorley. b 38. Hull Univ MA 88. EMMTC 76. **d** 79 **p** 80. NSM Swanwick and Pentrich *Derby* 79–88; NSM Allestree 88–98; PtO 98–18. *3 Meadow Reach, Station Approach, Duffield, Belper DE56 4HT* T: (01332) 843389 E: cliffgwen@gmail.com

WARNER, David. b 80. Leic Univ BA 02 Sheff Univ BA 13. Coll of Resurr Mirfield 10. **d** 13 **p** 14. C Abbots Langley *St Alb* 13–16; V Mossley *Man* from 16. *St John's Vicarage, Carrhill Road, Mossley, Ashton-under-Lyne OL5 0SA* T: (01457) 237667 E: frdavidwarner@gmail.com *or* vicarofmossley@gmail.com

WARNER, David. b 40. AKC 63. **d** 64 **p** 65. C Castleford All SS *Wakef* 64–68; Warden Hollowford Tr and Conf Cen Sheff 68–72; R Wombwell *Sheff* 72–83; V Wortley w Thurgoland 83–95; RD Tankersley 88–93; V Worsbrough St Mary 95–00; P-in-c Bildeston w Wattisham *St E* 00–02; P-in-c Whatfield w Semer, Nedging and Naughton 00–02; R Bildeston w Wattisham and Lindsey etc 02–05; rtd 05; PtO *St E* 05–16. *10 Magdalen Street, Eye IP23 7AJ* T: (01379) 870459 M: 07050-111478

WARNER, David Leonard John. b 24. Kelham Th Coll 47. **d** 51 **p** 52. C Mill Hill St Mich *Lon* 51–54; C Pimlico St Sav 54–56; R Rustenburg S Africa 56–64; R Hillcrest St Wilfrid 64–68; V Bournemouth H Epiphany *Win* 68–78; V Whitchurch w Tufton and Litchfield 78–89; RD Whitchurch 79–89; rtd 89; PtO *Win* 89–15; Hon Chapl Win Cathl from 97. *17 Lions Hall, St Swithun Street, Winchester SO23 9HW* T: (01962) 867343

WARNER, Dennis Vernon. b 46. Lon Univ BA 68 K Coll Lon BD 71. **d** 72 **p** 73. C W Bromwich All SS *Lich* 72–75; C Uttoxeter w Bramshall 75–79; NSM Stretton w Claymills 79–16; NSM Burton St Chad 16; PtO 17–21. *90 Beech Lane, Stretton, Burton-on-Trent DE13 0DU* T: (01283) 548058

WARNER, Canon George Francis. b 36. Trin Coll Ox BA 60 MA 64 Qu Coll Cam BA 63. Westcott Ho Cam 61. **d** 63 **p** 64. C Birm St Geo 63–66; C Maidstone All SS w St Phil and H Trin *Cant* 66–69; Chapl Wellington Coll Berks 69–78; TR Coventry Caludon *Cov* 78–95; Hon Can Cov Cathl 85–02; RD Cov E 89–95; P-in-c Leamington Priors All SS 95–02; P-in-c Leamington Spa H Trin and Old Milverton 95–02; rtd 02; PtO *Cov* from 02. *Coll Leys Edge, Fant Hill, Upper Brailes, Banbury OX15 5AY* T: (01608) 685550 E: sandgwarner@btinternet.com

WARNER, John Philip. b 59. Keble Coll Ox BA 80 MA 84. St Steph Ho Ox 81. **d** 83 **p** 84. C Brighton Resurr *Chich* 83–87; C Paddington St Mary *Lon* 87–90; V Teddington St Mark and Hampton Wick 90–00; P-in-c Belgrade *Eur* 00–03; P-in-c St Magnus the Martyr w St Marg New Fish Street *Lon* 03–10; R from 10; P-in-c St Mary Abchurch 04–13; P-in-c St Clem Eastcheap w St Martin Orgar 08–11. *St Magnus the Martyr, Lower Thames Street, London EC3R 6DN* T: (020) 7626 4481 E: rector@stmagnusmartyr.org.uk

WARNER, Mrs Marjorie Anne. b 53. York Univ BA 74 York St Jo Univ MA 04. NEOC 06. **d** 09 **p** 10. NSM Masham and Healey *Leeds* 09–16; PtO from 17. *26 Larkhill Crescent, Ripon HG4 2HN* T: (01765) 606961 E: marjorieawarner@gmail.com

✠**WARNER, The Rt Revd Martin Clive.** b 58. St Chad's Coll Dur BA 80 MA 85 PhD 03. St Steph Ho Ox 82. **d** 84 **p** 85 **c** 10. C Plymouth St Pet *Ex* 84–88; TV Leic Resurr 88–93; Admin Shrine of Our Lady of Walsingham 93–02; P-in-c Hempton and Pudding Norton *Nor* 98–00; Hon Can Nor Cathl 00–02; C St Andr Holborn *Lon* 02–03; Can Res St Paul's Cathl 03–10; Suff Bp Whitby *York* 10–12; Bp Chich from 12; Master of Guardians Shrine of Our Lady of Walsingham 06–16. *The Palace, Chichester PO19 1PY* T: (01243) 782161 F: 531332 E: bishop@chichester.anglican.org

WARNER, Canon Mary. b 52. Univ of Wales (Swansea) BSc 73 Aber Univ PhD 77. NEOC 90. **d** 93 **p** 94. C Bensham *Dur* 93–96; Asst Chapl Newcastle upon Tyne Hosps NHS Trust 96–98; Chapl Hartlepool and E Durham NHS Trust 98–99; Chapl N Tees and Hartlepool NHS Trust 99–04; Chapl City Hosps Sunderland NHS Foundn Trust 04–15; Hon Can Dur Cathl 10–15; rtd 15; PtO *Dur* from 15; *Newc* from 16. *47 Wydon Park, Hexham NE46 2DA* T: (01434) 607931 E: marywarner123@hotmail.com

WARNER, Canon Michael John William. b 41. Ex Univ MPhil 06. Sarum Th Coll 68. **d** 71 **p** 72. C Plympton St Mary *Ex* 71–75; V St Goran w Caerhays *Truro* 75–78; V Bishops Tawton *Ex* 78–79; V Newport 78–79; PtO *Truro* 79–83; V St Stythians w Perranarworthal and Gwennap 83–93; Sec Dioc Adv Cttee 93–01; P-in-c Budock 93–97; P-in-c Tregony w St Cuby and Cornelly 97–03; C Probus, Ladock and Grampound w Creed and St Erme 02–03; Hon Can Truro Cathl 98–03; rtd 03; PtO *Truro* from 03. *98 Porthpean Road, St Austell PL25 4PN* T: (01726) 64130 E: m.j.w.w@btinternet.com

WARNER, Nigel Bruce. b 51. St Jo Coll Cam BA 72 MA 76 ALCM 67. Wycliffe Hall Ox 75. **d** 77 **p** 78. C Luton St Mary St Alb 77–80; Prec Dur Cathl 80–84; R St John Lee Newc 84–91; V Lamesley Dur 91–98; V Bishopwearmouth St Nic 98–11; AD Wearmouth 99–05; V Heworth St Mary 11–16; rtd 16; PtO Dur 17–21; Newc from 17. 47 Wydon Park, Hexham NE46 2DA T: (01434) 607931 E: nigelwarner275@btinternet.com

WARNER (née King), Penelope Ann. b 86. Cant Ch Ch Univ BA 07 Sheff Univ MA 13. Coll of Resurr Mirfield 11. **d** 13 **p** 14. C Reddish Man 13–16; TV Rossendale Middle Valley 16–17; V Newchurch 17–20; V Stalybridge from 20. St John's Vicarage, Carrhill Road, Mossley, Ashton-under-Lyne OL5 0SA T: (01457) 237667 E: revdpennyking@outlook.com

WARNER, Philip. See WARNER, John Philip

WARNER, Mrs Stephanie Patricia. b 49. Lon Inst BA 96. SEITE 05. **d** 07 **p** 08. NSM Mottingham St Andr w St Alban S'wark 07–11; PtO Lon from 20. 20 Millbrook Gardens, Chadwell Heath, Romford RM6 6RP T: (020) 8503 8379 M: 07365-181414 E: renwars@btinternet.com

WARNER, Terence. b 36. **d** 92 **p** 93. NSM Leek and Meerbrook Lich 92–98; NSM Odd Rode Ches 98–03; PtO Lich 03–15; NSM Brown Edge 15; rtd 15; PtO Lich 15–20. 36 Haig Road, Leek ST13 6BZ T: (01538) 371988

WARNES, Brian Leslie Stephen. b 40. Natal Univ BSocSc 76. Kelham Th Coll 59. **d** 67 **p** 68. C Tonge Moor Man 67–71; S Africa 71–87; V Blean Cant 87–94; V Te Awamutu St Jo NZ 94–98; Chapl to Bp Christchurch 98–04; rtd 05. 57 Killarney Avenue, Torbay, North Shore City 0630, New Zealand E: stephen.warnes@gmail.com

WARNES, David John. b 50. Jes Coll Cam BA 72 MA 76 PGCE 73. EAMTC 01. **d** 04 **p** 05. Chapl Ipswich Sch and NSM Ipswich St Mary-le-Tower St E 04–10; NSM Edin St Martin 10–19; rtd 19; LtO Edin from 19. 7E Devon Place, Edinburgh EH12 5HJ T: 0131-337 3574 M: 07732-654603 E: warnesdavid@googlemail.com

WARNKE, Daniel James. b 76. St Mellitus Coll 16. **d** 18 **p** 19. C Paddington St Jo w St Mich Lon 18–21; Chapl Westmr Sch from 21. Westminster School, 17 Dean's Yard, London SW1P 3PB T: (020) 7963 1128 E: dan.warnke@westminster.org.uk

WARR, Timothy Gerald. b 59. Trin Coll Bris BA 86. **d** 88 **p** 89. C Yateley Win 88–91; C Chapel Allerton Ripon 91–93; V Wortley-de-Leeds 93–01; TR Borehamwood St Alb 01–05; TR Elstree and Borehamwood from 05. The Rectory, 94 Shenley Road, Borehamwood WD6 1EB T: (020) 8207 6603 or 8905 1365 F: 8207 6603 E: tim.warr@btinternet.com

WARRELL (née Lester), Stephanie Helen. b 94. Ches Univ BA 16. St Mellitus Coll MA 18. **d** 18 **p** 19. C Upton (Overchurch) Ches 18–20; C Cen Telford Lich from 20. 18 Gresham Drive, Telford TF3 5ES M: 07503-128253 E: stephanie_helen_@hotmail.co.uk

WARREN, Mrs Gillian. b 53. Sheff Univ BA 74 PGCE 75. WMMTC 89. **d** 92 **p** 94. Par Dn Tettenhall Regis Lich 92–94; C 94–95; TV Bilston 95–00; R Lich St Chad 00–02; V Wednesbury St Paul Wood Green 02–10; V Albrighton, Boningale and Donington 10–14; rtd 14; PtO Lich 18–21. 12 Walsall Road, Aldridge, Walsall WS9 0JL

WARREN, James Randolph. b 54. St Paul's Coll Chelt CertEd 75 Bris Univ BEd 76 Birm Univ MEd 84. Ridley Hall Cam 90. **d** 92 **p** 93. C Boldmere Birm 92–95; V Torpoint Truro 95–01; Hon Chapl RN 98–01; V Shottery St Andr Cov 01–18; P-in-c Winnersh Ox 18–21; rtd 21. 20 Hicks Close, Probus, Truro TR2 4NE

WARREN, Malcolm Clive. b 46. St D Coll Lamp. **d** 74 **p** 75. C Newport St Andr Mon 74–78; C Risca 78–79; V St Hilary Greenway 79–84; TV Grantham Linc 84–90; Ind Chapl Linc 87-90 and Worc 90–05; P-in-c Dudley St Aug Holly Hall Worc 95–96; PtO 96–97; TV Kidderminster St Mary and All SS w Trimpley etc 97–05; Ind Chapl Bris 05–10; TV Pontypool Mon 10–16; rtd 16; PtO Mon from 16. 31 Overdene, Pontllanfraith, Blackwood NP12 2JS T: (01495) 741879 M: 07971-222739 E: malcolm.warren296@btinternet.com

WARREN, Preb Martin John. b 59. Ch Coll Cam BA 81 MA 85. St Jo Coll Nottm LTh 85. **d** 86 **p** 87. C Littleover Derby 86–90; C Hermitage and Hampstead Norreys, Cold Ash etc Ox 90–91; TV 91–97; TV Hermitage 97–02; P-in-c Shebbear, Buckland Filleigh, Sheepwash etc Ex 02–15; TR from 15; Preb Ex Cathl from 19. The Rectory, Shebbear, Beaworthy EX21 5RU T: (01409) 281424 E: martinwarren535@btinternet.com

WARREN, Michael Philip. b 62. Oak Hill Th Coll BA 91 MA 04. **d** 94 **p** 95. C Tunbridge Wells St Jo Roch 94–98; Assoc Min Heydon, Gt and Lt Chishill, Chrishall etc Chelmsf 98–04; V Tunbridge Wells St Pet Roch from 04. St Peter's Vicarage,

Bayhall Road, Tunbridge Wells TN2 4TP T: (01892) 530384 E: vicar@stpeterstw.com

WARREN, Canon Paul Kenneth. b 41. Selw Coll Cam BA 63 MA 67. Cuddesdon Coll 64. **d** 67 **p** 68. C Lancaster St Mary Blackb 67–70; Chapl Lanc Univ 70–78; V Langho Billington 78–83; Bp's Dom Chapl and Chapl Whalley Abbey 83–88; R Standish 88–01; P-in-c Silverdale 01–19; Hon Can Blackb Cathl 91–19; RD Chorley 92–98; AD Tunstall 08–14; PtO from 19. 13 Cove Orchard, Cove Road, Silverdale, Carnforth LA5 0BF E: paulkwarren@btinternet.com

WARREN, Peter. b 40. Hull Univ MA 90 FCA 64. Oak Hill Th Coll 77. **d** 79 **p** 80. C Newcastle w Butterton Lich 79–82; TV Sutton St Jas and Wawne York 82–87; V Ledsham w Fairburn 87–95; R Ainderby Steeple w Yafforth and Kirby Wiske etc Ripon 95–03; rtd 03; PtO York from 04; Sheff from 08. 5 Bridge Farm, Pollington, Goole DN14 0BF T: (01405) 862925 E: rabbitsever67@gmail.com

WARREN, Peter John. b 55. Worc Coll of Educn CertEd 76. Trin Coll Bris BA 86. **d** 86 **p** 87. C W Streatham St Jas S'wark 86–91; P-in-c Edin Clermiston Em 91–98; P-in-c Blackpool Ch Ch w All SS Blackb 98–03; V 03–09; Co-Pastor Internat Chr Fellowship Phnom Penh 09–11; Pastor 11–18. Block 484A, Choa Chu Kang Avenue 5, # 11-24, 681484 Singapore E: revpwarren@gmail.com

WARREN, Robert. b 54. TCD BA 78 MA 81. CITC 76. **d** 78 **p** 79. C Limerick City L & K 78–81; Dioc Youth Adv (Limerick) 79–86; I Adare w Kilpeacon and Croom 81–88; Bp's Dom Chapl 81–95; Dioc Registrar (Limerick etc) 81–12; Dioc Registrar (Killaloe etc) 86–12; I Tralee w Kilmoyley, Ballymacelligott etc 88–12; Can Limerick, Killaloe and Clonfert Cathls 95–96; Chan 97–12; Asst Dioc Sec L & K 90–12; Adn Limerick, Ardfert and Aghadoe L & K 10–12; I Taney D & G 12–21; Preb Taney St Patr Cathl Dublin 04–12; Preb Tipperkevin 12–21; rtd 21. Address temp unknown M: (00353) 87-252 1133

WARREN, Canon Robert Peter Resker. b 39. Jes Coll Cam BA 63 MA. ALCD 65. **d** 65 **p** 66. C Rusholme H Trin Man 65–68; C Bushbury Lich 68–71; V Crookes St Thos Sheff 71–90; TR 90–93; RD Hallam 78–83; Hon Can Sheff Cathl 82–93; Can Th Sheff Cathl 93–04; Nat Officer for Evang 93–04; Springboard Missr 98–04; rtd 04; PtO Leic 95–98; Ripon 03–10; Newc from 10. 2 The Fairway, High Hauxley, Morpeth NE65 0JW T: (01665) 714697 E: robertwarren27@yahoo.com

WARREN, William Frederick. b 55. Sarum & Wells Th Coll 83. **d** 86 **p** 87. C E Greenwich Ch Ch w St Andr and St Mich S'wark 86–91; C Richmond St Mary w St Matthias and St Jo 91–95; TV 96–97; V Putney St Marg 97–08; V S Croydon St Pet and St Aug 08–18; AD Croydon Cen 17–18; Chapl Morden Coll Blackheath from 18. Morden College, 19 St Germans Place, London SE3 0PW T: (020) 8463 8324 M: 07920-506421 E: chaplain@mordencollege.org.uk

WARREN, William John. b 86. Warwick Univ BA 08. Wycliffe Hall Ox BTh 13. **d** 13 **p** 14. C Heigham H Trin Nor 13–17; C Nor St Andr 17–18; Public Preacher 18–19; P-in-c Cromer 19–20; V from 20. The Vicarage, 42 Cromwell Road, Cromer NR27 0BE T: (01263) 511474 E: william.warren@cromer-church.org.uk

WARRICK, Mark. b 54. Aston Univ BSc 76 Nottm Univ BCombStuds 83. Linc Th Coll 80. **d** 83 **p** 84. C Grantham Linc 83–87; C Cirencester Glouc 87–91; V Over Ely 91–97; V Deeping St James Linc 97–09; P-in-c Stamford All SS w St Jo 09–13; R 13–19; RD Aveland and Ness w Stamford 06–09 and 10–14; RD Stamford 14–19; Dean Stamford 11–19; rtd 19. 2 The Old Builders Yard, Newboults Lane, Stamford PE9 1FA E: mark.warrick@lincoln.anglican.org

WARRILLOW, Brian Ellis. b 39. Linc Th Coll 81. **d** 83 **p** 84. C Tunstall Lich 83–85; C Shrewsbury H Cross 86–87; P-in-c Tilstock 88; P-in-c Whixall 88; V Tilstock and Whixall 89–92; TV Hanley H Ev 92–94; rtd 94; PtO Lich 01–02; P-in-c Menton Eur 02–05; Hon C Wolstanton Lich 07–10; PtO 14–19; Eur from 00. 12 Sutton Avenue, Silverdale, Newcastle ST5 6TB T: (01782) 700925 E: brian.warrillow@gmail.com

WARRILOW, Mrs Christine. b 42. Lanc Univ BA 86. NOC 86. **d** 89 **p** 94. C Netherton Liv 89–92; C Cantril Farm 92–94; V 94–96; V Hindley Green 96–02; rtd 02; PtO Liv 03–08; Hon C Stanley and Stoneycroft St Paul from 08; PtO Blackb 16–17. 10 Beacon View Drive, Upholland, Skelmersdale WN8 0HL

WARRINGTON, Archdeacon of. See FISHER, The Ven Simon John Plumley

WARRINGTON, Suffragan Bishop of. See MASON, The Rt Revd Beverley Anne

WARWICK, Gordon Melvin. b 31. NOC 79. **d** 80 **p** 81. NSM Darrington Wakef 80–87; TV Almondbury w Farnley Tyas 87–95; rtd 95; PtO Newc 95–09; Hon C Dumfries Glas from

11. *4 Glencaple Avenue, Dumfries DG1 4SJ* T: (01387) 731357 E: gordonwarwick1931@btinternet.com

WARWICK, Hugh Johnston. b 39. ARCM 63. SAOMC 97. **d** 00 **p** 01. NSM Rotherfield Peppard *Ox* 00–02; NSM Rotherfield Peppard and Kidmore End etc 02–08; rtd 08; PtO *Ox* 08–21; *Pet* from 08. *Witan House, 38 Wheeler's Rise, Croughton, Brackley NN13 5ND* T: (01869) 819577 *or* 819596 E: hugh@pukekos.co.uk

WARWICK, Canon John Michael. b 37. Fitzw Ho Cam BA 58 MA 62. Ely Th Coll 58. **d** 60 **p** 61. C Towcester w Easton Neston *Pet* 60–63; C Leighton Buzzard *St Alb* 63–64; C Boston *Linc* 64–66; P-in-c Sutterton 66–72; V 72–74; V Sutton St Mary 74–84; V Bourne 84–02; Can and Preb Linc Cathl 89–02; RD Aveland and Ness w Stamford 93–00; Chapl Bourne Hosps Lincs 84–93; Chapl NW Anglia Healthcare NHS Trust 93–98; rtd 02; PtO *Ox* 03–17. *24 Hurst Park Road, Twyford, Reading RG10 0EY* T: 0118-932 0649

WARWICK, The Ven Neil Michael. b 64. Nottm Univ BA 86. Ridley Hall Cam 03. **d** 05 **p** 06. C Towcester w Caldecote and Easton Neston etc *Pet* 05–09; V Earley St Nic *Ox* 09–19; Adn Bris from 19. *Bristol Diocesan Board of Finance, Hillside House, Bristol Parkway North, Newbrick Road, Stoke Gifford, Bristol BS34 8YU* T: 0117-906 0100 E: neil.warwick@bristoldiocese.org

WARWICK, Archdeacon of. *See* DUGMORE, The Ven Barry John

WARWICK, Suffragan Bishop of. *See* STROYAN, The Rt Revd John Ronald Angus

WASEY, Kim Alexandra Clare. b 77. Man Univ BA 99 Birm Univ MPhil 03. Qu Coll Birm 00. **d** 02 **p** 03. C Rochdale *Man* 02–04; Chapl Man Univ 04–06; Chapl Man Metrop Univ 04–06; Chapl Salford Univ 06–09; Hon C Man Victoria Park from 09; Chapl Salford Univ from 12. *St Chrysostom's Rectory, 38 Park Range, Manchester M14 5HQ* T: 0161-224 6971 M: 07944-155772 E: kim.wasey@gmail.com *or* k.wasey@salford.ac.uk

WASHBROOK, Mrs Mary. **d** 12 **p** 13. OLM Peak Forest and Dove Holes *Derby* 12–18; OLM Fairfield, Peak Forest and Dove Holes from 18. *22 Alexander Road, Dove Holes, Buxton SK17 8BN* T: (01298) 815187 E: maryatdove@gmail.com

WASHFORD, Mrs Rhonwen Richarde Foster. b 50. RGN 99. ERMC 05. **d** 08 **p** 09. NSM Stalham, E Ruston, Brunstead, Sutton and Ingham *Nor* 08–11; NSM Thorpe St Andr 11–15; rtd 15; PtO *Nor* from 15. *60B The Close, Norwich NR1 4EH* T: (01603) 302800 E: rhonwenwashford@hotmail.com

WASHINGTON, Canon Nigel Leslie. b 50. St Paul's Coll Chelt BEd 73 Lon Univ MA 83. SAOMC 97. **d** 00 **p** 01. NSM Westoning w Tingrith *St Alb* 00–07; P-in-c 07–14; V 14–21; V Harlington, Tingrith and Westoning from 21; Hon Can St Alb from 20. *3 Avenue Mews, Flitwick, Bedford MK45 1BF* T: (01525) 714442 M: 07794-754986 E: nigelwash@hotmail.com

WASSALL, Canon Keith Leonard. b 45. Bede Coll Dur TCert 67. Chich Th Coll 68. **d** 71 **p** 72. C Upper Gornal *Lich* 71–74; C Codsall 74–75; TV Hanley H Ev 75–79; Asst P Pembroke Bermuda 79–81; V Rickerscote *Lich* 81–92; P-in-c Coven 92–99; Asst Chapl HM Pris Featherstone 92–99; Can Res Bermuda 99–04; C Houghton le Spring *Dur* 04–06; C Eppleton and Hetton le Hole 04–06; C Lyons 04–06; C Millfield St Mark and Pallion St Luke 06–09; rtd 09; PtO *Dur* from 10. *28 Monteigne Drive, Bowburn, Durham DH6 5QB* T: 0191-377 8709 E: klwassall@tiscali.co.uk

WASTELL, Canon Eric Morse. b 33. St Mich Coll Llan. **d** 62 **p** 63. C Oystermouth *S & B* 62–65; C St Jo Cathl Antigua 65–66; R St Mary 66–73; R St Paul 73–74; Dioc Registrar 69–74; Hon Can Antigua 71–74; V Swansea St Gabr *S & B* 74–98; RD Clyne 88–96; Can Brecon Cathl 90–98; rtd 98. *Stella Maris Care Home, Eaton Crescent, Swansea SA1 4QR* T: (01792) 473453

WASTIE, Canon David Vernon. b 37. Open Univ BA 84. Chich Th Coll 79. **d** 81 **p** 82. C Bitterne Park *Win* 81–83; TV Chambersbury *St Alb* 83–87; V Jersey St Luke *Win* 87–94; P-in-c Jersey St Jas 87–93; V 93–94; V Jersey St Luke w St Jas 94–95; V Southbourne St Kath 95–99; Hon Can Bukavu Congo from 94; rtd 02; PtO *Derby* 05–08; *Win* 09–13; C Bournemouth St Fran 13–14; PtO *Sheff* from 16. *28 Cuthbert Cooper Place, Sheffield S9 4JS* T: 0114-242 1612 E: canonwastie@hotmail.com

WATCHORN, Canon Brian. b 39. Em Coll Cam BA 61 MA 65 Ex Coll Ox BA 62. Ripon Hall Ox 61. **d** 63 **p** 64. C Bolton St Pet *Man* 63–66; Chapl G&C Coll Cam 66–74; V Chesterton St Geo *Ely* 75–82; Fell Dean and Chapl Pemb Coll Cam 82–06; Hon Can Ely Cathl 94–04; Chapter Can 00–10. *34 Petersfield Mansions, Petersfield, Cambridge CB1 1BB* T: (01223) 322378 E: bw214@pem.cam.ac.uk

WATERFIELD, Preb Janet Lyn. b 60. Birm Univ BA 06. WMMTC 99. **d** 02 **p** 03. C Bilston *Lich* 02–07; TV 07–12; P-in-c Lich Ch Ch 12–15; P-in-c Longdon 12–15; V Lichfield and Longdon from 15; RD Lich from 18; Preb Lich Cathl from 20. *Christ Church Vicarage, 95 Christ Church Lane, Lichfield WS13 8AL* T: (01543) 410751 M: 07905-539111 E: janwaterfield@blueyonder.co.uk

WATERFORD, Dean of. *See* JANSSON, The Very Revd Maria Patricia

WATERMAN, Canon Albert Thomas. b 33. Roch Th Coll 61. **d** 64 **p** 65. C Dartford St Alb *Roch* 64–67; V Ilkeston St Jo *Derby* 67–75; V Mackworth St Fran 75–79; V Dartford St Alb *Roch* 79–98; RD Dartford 84–97; Hon Can Roch Cathl 96–98; rtd 98. *19 Beachfield Road, Bembridge PO35 5TN* T: (01983) 874286

WATERMAN, Mrs Jacqueline Mahalah. b 45. ALCM 71. Cant Sch of Min 82. dss 85 **d** 87 **p** 94. Wavertree H Trin *Liv* 85–90; Par Dn 87–90; Par Dn Anfield St Columba 90–94; C 94; P-in-c Walton St Jo 97–99; V 99–01; C Baildon *Bradf* 01–05; rtd 05; PtO *Bradf* 05–14; *Leeds* from 14. *5 Lansdowne Close, Baildon, Shipley BD17 7LA* T: (01274) 468556

WATERS (*née* MUNRO-SMITH), **Alison Jean.** b 73. Regent's Park Coll Ox MA 94. Wycliffe Hall Ox 02. **d** 04 **p** 05. C Lostwithiel, St Winnow w St Nectan's Chpl etc *Truro* 04–08; C Shepperton and Littleton *Lon* 08–12; C Sonning *Ox* 12–16; R Cannington, Otterhampton, Combwich and Stockland *B & W* from 16; RD Quantock from 20. *The Rectory, 27 Brook Street, Cannington, Bridgwater TA5 2HP* T: (01278) 652636 E: alwaters@hotmail.co.uk

WATERS, Brenda Mary. *See* COUZENS, Brenda Mary

WATERS, Mrs Carolyn Anne. b 52. St Jo Coll Nottm BA 02. **d** 00 **p** 01. NSM Frodsham *Ches* 00–02; C Penhill *Bris* 02–06; P-in-c Stopham and Fittleworth *Chich* 06–09; rtd 09; PtO *Newc* from 10. *5 Leybourne Avenue, Newcastle upon Tyne NE12 7AP* M: 07789-430317 E: carolyn.anne.waters@googlemail.com

WATERS, Geoffrey John. b 64. UMIST BSc 85 Trin Coll Bris BA 99 Qu Coll Birm MA 08 St Hild Coll Dur PGCE 86. WMMTC 06. **d** 08 **p** 09. NSM Northampton St Giles *Pet* 08–13; P-in-c Shirehampton *Bris* 13–15; C Oldland 15–19; PtO from 19; Chapl Partis Coll Bath from 19; Chapl MHA Stratton Ho Care Home from 20. *6 Rodney Road, Saltford, Bristol BS31 3HP* E: geoffreyjwaters@btinternet.com

WATERS, John Michael. b 30. Qu Coll Cam BA 53 MA 58. Ridley Hall Cam 53. **d** 55 **p** 56. C Southport Ch Ch *Liv* 55–57; C Farnworth 57–62; V Blackb H Trin 63–70; Sec Birm Coun Chr Chs 70–77; Chapl Birm Cathl 70–74; Dioc Ecum Officer 74–77; V Hednesford *Lich* 77–93; RD Rugeley 78–88; rtd 93; P-in-c Etton w Dalton Holme *York* 93–99; PtO 00–20. *Blacksmith's Cottage, Middlewood Lane, Fylingthorpe, Whitby YO22 4UB* T: (01947) 880422

WATERS, John Sangster. b 48. CQSW 75. St Mich Coll Llan 67. **d** 13 **p** 13. NSM Caerwent w Dinham and Llanvair Discoed etc *Mon* 13–14; NSM Wentwood from 14. *Cae Golwg, Mynyddbach, Shirenewton, Chepstow NP16 6RT* T: (01291) 641449 M: 07836-585250 E: john@transientwaters.com

WATERS, Kenneth Robert. b 51. ERMC 08. **d** 10 **p** 11. NSM Grimshoe *Ely* 10–19; R Wissey Valley 19–20; C Paphos Cyprus and the Gulf from 20. *Address temp unknown* E: ken.waters@btinternet.com

WATERS, Mark. b 51. Southn Univ BTh 85. Sarum & Wells Th Coll 79. **d** 82 **p** 83. C Clifton All SS w St Jo *Bris* 82–85; P-in-c Brislington St Anne 85–91; Dioc Soc Resp Officer *Sheff* 91–94; Community Org Citizen Organisation Foundn 94–00; NSM Rotherham *Sheff* 94–97; Hon C Gt Crosby St Faith and Waterloo Park St Mary *Liv* 97–00; NSM 05–09; TV Kirkby 00–04; Progr Manager Participation for Change Ch Action on Poverty 04–05; PtO *Man* 06–13; NSM Toxteth Park Ch Ch and St Mich w St Andr *Liv* 09–14; NSM St Luke in the City 12–14; TV 14–19; rtd 19. *30 Victoria Road West, Crosby, Liverpool L23 8UQ* E: marko.waters@gmail.com

WATERS, Stephen. b 49. Chich Th Coll 83. **d** 85 **p** 86. C Baildon *Bradf* 85–87; V Altrincham St Geo *Ches* 87–89; TV Ellesmere Port 89–91; P-in-c Crewe St Jo 91–93; V Mossley 93–98; TV Congleton 98–99; P-in-c Alvanley 99–02; V Penhill *Bris* 02–05; rtd 05; PtO *Newc* from 16. *5 Leybourne Avenue, Newcastle upon Tyne NE12 7AP* M: 07796-694139

WATERS, William Paul. b 52. Aston Tr Scheme 84 Chich Th Coll 86. **d** 88 **p** 89. C Tottenham St Paul *Lon* 88–91; C Stroud Green H Trin 91–95; TV Wickford and Runwell *Chelmsf* 95–98; Chapl Runwell Hosp Wickford 95–98; Chapl Qu Medical Cen Nottm Univ Hosp NHS Trust 98–10; C Ilkeston H Trin *Derby* 10–12; rtd 12; P-in-c Ilkeston St Jo *Derby* 15–16; C Kirk Hallam 15–16; C Spondon from 17. *22 Teesdale Court, Beeston, Nottingham NG9 5PJ* T: 0115-917 3429 E: paulwat04@gmail.com

WATERSON, Graham Peter. b 50. d 07 p 08. OLM Astley Bridge *Man* 07–10; NSM Thame *Ox* from 10. *The Rectory, 46 High Street, Tetsworth, Thames OX9 7AS* T: (01844) 281462 M: 07747-757657

WATERSTREET, Canon John Donald. b 34. Trin Hall Cam BA 58 MA 62. Lich Th Coll 58. d 60 p 61. C Blackheath *Birm* 60–64; C Aston SS Pet and Paul 64–67; R Sheldon 67–77; RD Coleshill 75–77; V Selly Oak St Mary 77–89; RD Edgbaston 84–89; Hon Can Birm Cathl 86–00; R The Whitacres and Shustoke 89–97; C Acocks Green 97–00; rtd 00; PtO *Birm* 00–12 and 15–18. *67 Rivendell Court, 1071 Stratford Road, Hall Green, Birmingham B28 8AT* E: jwaterstreet81@gmail.com

WATERSTREET, Mark Andrew. b 61. Qu Foundn (Course) 15. d 18 p 19. NSM Dosthill *Birm* 18–21; C from 21; C The Whitacres, Lea Marston, and Shustoke from 21. *The Rectory, Dog Lane, Nether Whitacre, Coleshill, Birmingham B46 2DU* M: 07976-800481 E: m.waterstreet@btopenworld.com

WATES, John Norman. b 43. JP 82 OBE 14. BNC Ox MA 65 Solicitor 72 FRSA 00 Hon FRAM 09. d 02 p 03. OLM Chipstead *S'wark* 02–13; PtO from 13. *Elmore, High Road, Chipstead, Coulsdon CR5 3SB* T: (01737) 557550 F: 552918 E: john.wates@btinternet.com

WATHERSTON, Peter David. b 42. Lon Univ BSc 69 FCA 76. Ridley Hall Cam 75. d 77 p 78. C Barnsbury St Andr *Lon* 77–81; Chapl Mayflower Family Cen Canning Town *Chelmsf* 81–96; PtO 96–16; Dir First Fruit Charity from 97; PtO *Dur* from 14. *Manor Stables, 2A Staindrop Road, West Auckland, Bishop Auckland DL14 9JX* T: (01388) 606357 M: 07913-694678 E: pwatherston@aol.com

WATKIN, David Glynne. b 52. Univ of Wales (Lamp) BA 74 PhD 78 Wolv Univ PGCE 87 MTS FRGS. d 02 p 03. OLM Wolverhampton St Matt *Lich* 02–09; OLM Bilston 09–12; Bp's Officer for OLM 07–11; V Heath Hayes 12–20; rtd 20; PtO *Lich* from 20. *3 Alderdale, Wolverhampton WV3 9JF* M: 07810-412377 E: revglynne@hotmail.co.uk

WATKIN, David William. b 42. FCA 70. Qu Coll Birm 84. d 86 p 87. C Tunstall *Lich* 86–89; Camberwell Deanery Missr *S'wark* 89–95; V Trent Vale *Lich* 95–01; V Milton 01–10; rtd 10; PtO *Lich* 10–21. *33 Station Grove, Stoke-on-Trent ST2 7EA* T: (01782) 253237 E: davidwwatkin@hotmail.com

WATKIN, Paulie Elliss. b 75. Anglia Ruskin Univ BA 08. Westcott Ho Cam 06. d 08 p 09. C Harwich Peninsula *Chelmsf* 08–11; P-in-c Rivenhall 11–14; TV Witham and Villages from 14. *Swallows, Western Lane, Silver End, Witham CM8 3SA* T: (01376) 583930 E: psgw100@aol.com

WATKIN, Prof Thomas Glyn. b 52. QC (Hon). Pemb Coll Ox BA 74 MA 77 BCL 75 FLSW Barrister-at-Law (Middle Temple) 76. Llan Dioc Tr Scheme 89. d 92 p 94. NSM Roath St Martin *Llan* 92–04; PtO from 04. *49 Cyncoed Road, Penylan, Cardiff CF23 5SB* T: (029) 2049 5662

WATKINS, Adrian Raymond. b 57. St Andr Univ MA 80 Ox Univ MTh 15. Lon Bible Coll 82 Ripon Coll Cuddesdon 12. d 07 p 08. Regional Manager (Asia) CMS 00–12; Lic to Offic Amritsar India from 07; PtO *St E* 08–12; C Newmarket All SS 12–15; R N Hartismere from 15. *The Rectory, Oakley, Diss IP21 4BW* T: (01379) 741949 M: 07958-617665 E: adrianrwatkins@gmail.com *or* rectornorthhartismere@gmail.com

WATKINS, Mrs Andrea. b 71. ERMC. d 08 p 09. C Heyford w Stowe Nine Churches and Flore etc *Pet* 08–11; R Blisworth, Alderton, Grafton Regis etc 11–19; R Brington w Whilton and Norton etc from 19; Tr Co-ord for Lic Ev from 11. *The Rectory, Main Street, Great Brington, Northampton NN7 4JB* E: andrealwatkins@hotmail.co.uk

WATKINS, Anthony John. b 42. St D Coll Lamp BA 64. St Steph Ho Ox 64. d 66 p 67. C E Dulwich St Jo *S'wark* 66–71; C Tewkesbury w Walton Cardiff *Glouc* 71–75; Prec and Chapl Choral Ches Cathl 75–81; R Brixworth w Holcot *Pet* 81–12; rtd 12. *20 Bromley College, London Road, Bromley BR1 1PE* T: (020) 8290 4700

WATKINS, Betty Anne. See MOCKFORD, Betty Anne

WATKINS, Charles Mark. b 57. Bradf Univ BTech 79. Westcott Ho Cam 06. d 08 p 09. C Almondbury w Farnley Tyas *Wakef* 08–11; TV Castleford 11–14; *Leeds* 14–18; C Smawthorpe *Wakef* 11–12; Pontefract All SS *Leeds* 18–19; C Pontefract St Giles 18–19; C Pontefract from 19. *Grenton, South Baileygate, Pontefract WF8 2JL* M: 07751-930968 E: wattycm@me.com

WATKINS, Christopher. b 43. Sarum & Wells Th Coll 88. d 90 p 91. C Abergavenny St Mary w Llanwenarth Citra *Mon* 90–94; TV Cwmbran 94–96; TV Wordsley *Worc* 00–09; rtd 09; PtO *Mon* 09–15; P-in-c Newport All SS from 15. *287 Malpas Road, Newport NP20 6WA* T: (01633) 556583 E: chriswat1943@gmail.com

WATKINS (*née* ROBERTS), **Mrs Gwyneth.** b 35. Univ of Wales (Swansea) BA MEd. St Mich Coll Llan 90. d 91 p 97. C Llanbadarn Fawr w Capel Bangor and Goginan *St D* 91–94; P-in-c Maenordeifi and Capel Colman w Llanfihangel etc 94–97; R 97–98; rtd 98; PtO *Win* 09–15. *17 Carlinford, 26 Boscombe Cliff Road, Bournemouth BH5 1JW* T: (01202) 391076 E: gwynethwatkins1@hotmail.com

WATKINS (*née* SMITH), **Mrs Irene Victoria.** b 45. SRN 66 SCM 69. d 03 p 04. OLM Lawton Moor *Man* 03–11; rtd 11; PtO *Man* from 11. *288 Wythenshawe Road, Manchester M23 9DA* T: 0161-998 4100 M: 07889-116856

WATKINS, John Graham. b 48. N Lon Poly CQSW 74. WEMTC 04. d 07 p 08. NSM Ledbury *Heref* 07–17; NSM Hop Churches 17–18; PtO from 19. *18 Pound Close, Tarrington, Hereford HR1 4AZ* T: (01432) 890595 E: john.watkins_48@yahoo.co.uk

WATKINS, Jonathan. b 58. Padgate Coll of Educn BEd 79. Trin Coll Bris 90. d 92 p 93. C Wallington *S'wark* 92–97; C Hartley Wintney, Elvetham, Winchfield etc *Win* 97–99; Chapl Win Univ 99–08; P-in-c Stockbridge and Longstock and Leckford *Win* 10–12; R Test Valley 12–17; P-in-c Knutton *Lich* 18; V from 18. *St Mary's Vicarage, Church Lane, Knutton, Newcastle ST5 6DU* T: (01782) 618367

WATKINS, Mark. See WATKINS, Charles Mark

WATKINS, Michael Morris. b 32. MRCS 60 LRCP 60. St Jo Coll Nottm 77. d 81 p 81. C Hornchurch St Andr *Chelmsf* 81–84; P-in-c Snitterfield w Bearley *Cov* 84–90; V 90–92; rtd 93; PtO *Cov* from 93. *Glaslyn, Riverside, Tiddington Road, Stratford-upon-Avon CV37 7BD* T: (01789) 298085 E: michaelwatkins@talktalk.net

WATKINS, Canon Peter. b 51. Oak Hill Th Coll BA. d 82 p 83. C Whitnash *Cov* 82–86; V Wolston and Church Lawford 86–99; RD Rugby 94–99; V Finham 99–10; Hon Can Cov Cathl 04–10; rtd 11; PtO *Cov* from 11; AD Rugby 13–17; PtO *S'well* from 16. *4 Medway Drive, Bingham, Nottingham NG13 8YD* T: (01949) 729525 M: 07772-001812 E: watkins51@icloud.com

WATKINS, Peter Gordon. b 34. St Pet Coll Ox BA 57 MA 61. Wycliffe Hall Ox 58. d 59 p 60. C Wolverhampton St Geo *Lich* 59–60; C Burton St Chad 60–61; C Westmr St Jas *Lon* 61–63; USA 63–65; V Ealing Common St Matt *Lon* 67–15; rtd 15. *Charterhouse Sutton's Hospital, The Charterhouse, Charterhouse Square, London EC1M 6AN*

WATKINS, Robert Henry. b 30. New Coll Ox BA 54 MA 60. Westcott Ho Cam 59. d 60 p 61. C Newc H Cross 60–63; C Morpeth 63–67; V Delaval 67–80; V Lanercost w Kirkcambeck and Walton *Carl* 80–90; rtd 90; PtO *Carl* 90–20. *Lowpark, Loweswater, Cockermouth CA13 0RU* T: (01900) 85242 E: bob@lowpark242.plus.com

WATKINS, Susan Jane. See HEIGHT, Susan Jane

WATKINSON, Adam John McNicol. b 68. Keble Coll Ox BA 89 MA 93 St Martin's Coll Lanc PGCE 90. NOC 01. d 03 p 04. NSM Croston and Bretherton *Blackb* 03–05; Chapl Ormskirk Sch 02–03; Chapl Liv Coll 03–06; Chapl Repton Sch Derby 06–16 and from 21; Asst Chapl Charterhouse Sch Godalming 16–21; PtO *Lich* 14–16 and from 20; *Carl* from 15; *Guildf* from 16. *Repton School, Willington Road, Repton, Derby DE65 6FH* E: awatkinson@repton.org.uk

WATKINSON, Mrs Denise. b 59. St Jo Coll Nottm 13. d 15 p 16. NSM Hyson Green and Forest Fields *S'well* 15–19; NSM Aspley from 19; NSM Basford St Leodegarius and St Aid from 19; NSM Bilborough and Strelley from 19; NSM Broxtowe from 19; NSM Cinderhill from 19. *51 Oxclose Lane, Arnold, Nottingham NG5 6FW* M: 07806-385621 E: denise.watkinson1@sky.com

WATKINSON, George Albion. b 87. Wycliffe Hall Ox 14. d 17 p 18. C Win Ch Ch 17–20; C Onslow Square and S Kensington St Aug *Lon* from 20. *87 Ullswater Crescent, London SW15 3RE* T: (020) 7052 0200

WATKINSON, Simon Thomas. b 89. Hatf Coll Dur BA 12 K Coll Lon MA 13 AKC 14. St Mellitus Coll MA 18. d 18 p 19. C Salford St Phil w St Steph *Man* from 18. *68 The Royal, Wilton Place, Salford M3 6FT* M: 07882-940280

WATMORE, Mrs Georgina Jane Ann. b 63. Univ Coll Ox BA 85 MA 92 Ox Brookes Univ BA 10. SNWTP 10. d 12 p 13. C Hale and Ashley *Ches* 12–15; R Tarporley 15–20; rtd 21. *47 Racecourse Road, Wilmslow SK9 5LG* M: 07926-654707 E: revgeorgina@me.com

WATSON, Adam Stewart. b 75. Southn Univ BA 99. St Jo Coll Nottm 08. d 10 p 11. C Alton *Win* 10–14; V Welton and Dunholme w Scothern *Linc* from 14. *The Vicarage, Holmes Lane, Dunholme, Lincoln LN2 3QT* E: watson_adam3@sky.com

WATSON, Canon Alan. b 34. Lon Univ LLB 58. Linc Th Coll 58. d 60 p 61. C Spring Park *Cant* 60–63; C Sheerness H Trin w St Paul 63–68; R Allington 68–73; P-in-c Maidstone St Pet 73; R Allington and Maidstone St Pet 73–99; Hon

Can Cant Cathl 85–99; RD Sutton 86–92; rtd 99; PtO B & W from 00; *Sarum* 00–10. *68 Southgate Drive, Wincanton BA9 9ET* T: (01963) 34368 E: arw68@mypostoffice.co.uk

WATSON, Alan. b 41. AKC 64. St Boniface Warminster. **d** 65 **p** 66. C Hendon St Ignatius *Dur* 65–68; C Sheff St Cecilia Parson Cross 68–70; C Harton Colliery *Dur* 70–72; TV 72–74; R Gorton Our Lady and St Thos *Man* 74–82; TR Swinton St Pet 82–87; TR Swinton and Pendlebury 87–89; R Rawmarsh w Parkgate *Sheff* 89–94; P-in-c Dunscroft St Edwin 96–99; V 99–09; rtd 10; PtO *Sheff* 10–15; Hon C Sheff St Matt from 15; CMP from 98. *28 Shrewsbury Hospital, Norfolk Road, Sheffield S2 2SU* T: 0114-270 0212 M: 07884-230859 E: alan.watson61945@gmail.com

WATSON, Albert Victor. b 44. Ridley Hall Cam 85. **d** 87 **p** 88. C Hornchurch St Andr *Chelmsf* 87–94; P-in-c Tye Green w Netteswell 94–95; R 95–12; RD Harlow 99–04; rtd 12; Hon C Fyfield, Moreton w Bobbingworth etc *Chelmsf* 12–15; PtO from 15. *107 The Hoo, Harlow CM17 0HS* T: (01279) 453224 E: revalbie1944@gmail.com

WATSON, Alice Lydia Joy. b 87. G&C Coll Cam MA 08 K Coll Lon MSc 11. Ripon Coll Cuddesdon BA 18 MA 19. **d** 19 **p** 20. C Kettering SS Pet and Paul from 19; C Kettering All SS from 19. *2 Moorhouse Way, Kettering NN15 7LX* E: revalicewatson@gmail.com

✠**WATSON, The Rt Revd Andrew John.** b 61. CCC Cam BA 82 MA 90. Ridley Hall Cam 84. **d** 87 **p** 88 **c** 08. C Ipsley *Worc* 87–91; C Notting Hill St Jo and St Pet *Lon* 91–96; V E Twickenham St Steph 96–08; AD Hampton 03–08; Suff Bp Aston *Birm* 08–14; Bp Guildf from 14. *Willow Grange, Woking Road, Guildford GU4 7QS* T: (01483) 590500 E: bishop.andrew@cofeguildford.org.uk

WATSON, Anne-Marie Louise. *See* RENSHAW, Anne-Marie Louise

WATSON, Beverly Anne. b 64. K Coll Cam BA 86 MA 90 ALCM 83. STETS MA 08. **d** 08 **p** 09. C Spring Grove St Mary *Lon* 08; C Aston and Nechells *Birm* 08–12; TV Salter Street and Shirley 12–15; V Guildf All SS from 15. *Willow Grange, Woking Road, Guildford GU4 7QS* T: (01483) 841970 *or* 563173 M: 07547-416721 E: beverlyannewatson@btinternet.com

WATSON, Bruce Maclaren. b 68. Wolv Poly BA 90 Birm Univ PGCE 91. St Mellitus Coll 17. **d** 19 **p** 20. C Ashford Town *Cant* from 19. *29 Hawthorn Road, Kingsnorth, Ashford TN23 3LT* T: (01304) 374139 M: 07790-538284 E: bruised@btinternet.com *or* bruce.watson@ashfordchurches.co.uk

WATSON, Cathryn Dawn. b 67. Man Poly BSc 88. Trin Coll Bris 15. **d** 17 **p** 18. C Tipton St Matt *Lich* 17–18; C Tipton St Matt w St Martin and St Paul 19–20; V Bradley St Martin from 20. *St Martin's Vicarage, King Street, Bradley, Bilston WV14 8PQ* T: (01902) 546460 M: 07885-965459 E: vicar@stmartinsbradley.co.uk

WATSON, Christopher Ian. b 52. St Cuth Soc Dur BA 92 PGCE 93. Lindisfarne Regional Tr Partnership 18. **d** 19 **p** 20. NSM Sunderland Minster *Dur* from 19. *138 Whitworth Park Drive, Houghton le Spring DH4 6GN* T: 0191-385 7312 M: 07467-416353 E: chris.elba@gmail.com *or* revchrisw@sunderlandminster.org

WATSON, David. **d** 12 **p** 18. NSM Honicknowle *Ex* 12–14; NSM Ernesettle, Whitleigh and Honicknowle from 14. *23 Norfolk Road, Plymouth PL3 6BS* T: (01752) 670207 E: david@compton-it.co.uk

WATSON, Miss Dawn Louise. b 79. Greenwich Univ BA(QTS) 01. Ripon Coll Cuddesdon 14. **d** 16 **p** 17. C Margate St Jo *Cant* 16–18; P-in-c from 18; C Margate All SS 16–18; P-in-c from 18. *24 St Peter's Road, Margate CT9 1TH* M: 07805-699519 E: dawnlouise_watson@hotmail.co.uk

WATSON, The Very Revd Derek Richard. b 38. Selw Coll Cam BA 61 MA 65. Cuddesdon Coll 62. **d** 64 **p** 65. C New Eltham All SS *S'wark* 64–66; Chapl Ch Coll Cam 66–70; Bp's Dom Chapl *S'wark* 70–73; V Surbiton St Mark 73–77; V Surbiton St Andr and St Mark 77–78; Can Res and Treas *S'wark* Cathl 78–82; Dioc Dir of Ords 78–82; P-in-c Chelsea St Luke *Lon* 82–85; R 85–87; P-in-c Chelsea Ch Ch 86–87; R Chelsea St Luke and Ch St 87–96; AD Chelsea 94–96; Dean Sarum 96–02; rtd 02; PtO *Lon* from 17. *83 Winchester Street, London SW1V 4NU* T: (020) 7828 7377 E: dandswatson@gmail.com

WATSON, Derek Stanley. b 54. NEOC 92. **d** 95 **p** 96. C W Acklam *York* 95–98; C-in-c Ingleby Barwick CD 98–00; V Ingleby Barwick 00–06; V Middlesbrough St Martin w St Cuth 06–11; rtd 12; PtO *Dur* 14–17. *3 The Brother House, Greatham, Hartlepool TS25 2HS* T: (01429) 872848 E: d.watson909@btinternet.com

WATSON, Mrs Diane Elsie. b 44. Ches Coll of HE MA 98. NOC 92. **d** 95 **p** 96. C Grange St Andr *Ches* 95–00; C Runcorn H Trin 96–00; R Thurstaston 00–07; rtd 07; C

Oxton *Ches* 08–11; PtO from 11. *32 School Lane, Prenton CH43 7RQ* T: 0151-652 4288 E: de.watson@outlook.com

WATSON, Geoffrey. b 48. Liv Univ BEd 71. Linc Th Coll 81. **d** 83 **p** 84. C Hartlepool St Luke *Dur* 83–87; P-in-c Shadforth 87–94; Soc Resp Officer 87–94; Dioc Rural Development Adv 90–94; V Staveley, Ings and Kentmere *Carl* 94–13; rtd 13. *15 Hawkins Way, Helston TR13 8FQ* T: (01326) 619984 E: geof_watson@talktalk.net

WATSON, Mrs Gillian Edith. b 49. Cov Coll of Educn CertEd 70. LCTP 06. **d** 09 **p** 10. NSM Standish *Blackb* 09–14; Chapl Wrightington, Wigan and Leigh NHS Foundn Trust 09–14; PtO *Blackb* from 14. *Newstead Farm, School Lane, Forton, Preston PR3 0AS* T: (01524) 792398 E: gillian.e.watson@gmail.com

WATSON, The Ven Ian Leslie Stewart. b 50. Wycliffe Hall Ox 79. **d** 81 **p** 82. C Plymouth St Andr w St Paul and St Geo *Ex* 81–85; TV Ipsley *Worc* 85–90; V Woodley St Jo the Ev *Ox* 90–92; TR Woodley 92–95; Chapl Amsterdam w Den Helder and Heiloo *Eur* 95–01; Chief Exec ICS 01–07; Can Gib Cathl *Eur* 02–07; Adn Cov 07–12; rtd 12; PtO *Linc* 16–19. *The Cottages, 43 Station Road, Hibaldstow, Brigg DN20 9DY* T: (01652) 651040 M: 07714-214790 E: i.watson44@btinternet.com

WATSON, James Valentine John Giles. b 65. Newc Univ BA 87 Ox Univ BA 91 MA 97 Buckingham Univ PGCE 15. Ripon Coll Cuddesdon 89. **d** 92 **p** 93. C Newc St Geo 92–95; TV Daventry, Ashby St Ledgers, Braunston etc *Pet* 95–00; V Woodplumpton *Blackb* 00–03; TR Wheatley *Ox* 03–10; Chapl Old Buckenham Hall Sch 10–15; Chapl Maidwell Hall Sch from 15; C Maidwell w Draughton, Lamport w Faxton *Pet* from 15; C Arthingworth, Harrington w Oxendon and E Farndon from 15. *The Rectory, 35 Main Street, Great Oxendon, Market Harborough LE16 8NE* T: (01858) 469808 M: 07881-577149 E: jvjgwatson1@gmail.com

WATSON, Mrs Joanna Margaret. b 57. All SS Cen for Miss & Min. **d** 14 **p** 15. NSM Norden w Ashworth and Bamford *Man* 14–16; NSM Chadderton St Matt w St Luke 16–17; NSM Whitworth w Facit from 17. *21 Westfield Close, Rochdale OL11 5XB* T: (01706) 524657 E: jo.mwatson@tiscali.co.uk

WATSON, John Calum. b 69. Spurgeon's Coll BD 96 K Coll Lon MA 14. Trin Coll Bris MA 03. **d** 03 **p** 04. C Richmond H Trin and Ch Ch *S'wark* 03–06; TV Deptford St Jo w H Trin and Ascension 06–08; V Tupsley w Hampton Bishop *Heref* 08–14; V Dulwich St Barn *S'wark* from 14; Dir Ords Woolwich Area from 17. *38 Calton Avenue, London SE21 7DG* E: vicar@stbarnabasdulwich.org

WATSON, Jonathan Ramsay George. b 38. Oriel Coll Ox BA 61 MA 65 DipEd 62. Ridley Hall Cam 88. **d** 90 **p** 91. C Locks Heath *Portsm* 90–94; V Erith St Paul *Roch* 94–01; rtd 01; PtO *Chich* from 01. *14 Park Crescent, Midhurst GU29 9ED* T: (01730) 816145

WATSON, Ms Joyce. b 46. Ilkley Coll TCert 68. TISEC 06. **d** 09 **p** 10. NSM Iona *Arg* 10–16; rtd 16; PtO *Arg* from 16. *Beannachd, Isle of Iona PA76 6SP* T: (01681) 700525 E: joyce@iona76.plus.com

WATSON, Mrs Julie Ann. b 61. UWE BA 95 SS Coll Cam BTh 12. Westcott Ho Cam 09. **d** 11 **p** 12. C Malvern Link w Cowleigh *Worc* 11–14; TR Worc St Barn w Ch Ch from 14. *St Barnabas' Rectory, Church Road, Worcester WR3 8NX* T: (01905) 23785 E: revjulieann@btinternet.com

WATSON, Julie Sandra. b 59. Liv Poly BSc 81 Teesside Poly PhD 86. NEOC 99. **d** 02 **p** 03. NSM Redcar *York* 02–12; NSM Selby Abbey from 12; Dean Self-Supporting Min from 09. *8 Sherwood Drive, Thorpe Willoughby, Selby YO8 9TN* E: julie301watson@btinternet.com

WATSON, Mrs Linda Marie. b 58. St Mich Coll Llan 14. **d** 15 **p** 16. C New Radnor and Llanfihangel Nantmelan etc *S & B* 15–16; C Colwyn from 17. *The Rectory, Llanelwedd, Builth Wells LD2 3TY* T: (01982) 553533 E: revlindawatson@gmail.com

WATSON, Mark Edward. b 68. Birm Univ BEng 91. St Jo Coll Nottm 07. **d** 09 **p** 10. C Higher Bebington *Ches* 09–13; P-in-c Frizinghall St Marg *Bradf* 13–14; P-in-c Windhill *Bradf* 13–14; *Leeds* 14–21; P-in-c E Ardsley from 21. *The Vicarage, 1 Church Lane, East Ardsley, Wakefield WF3 2LJ* M: 07838-441568 E: lordsmyshepherd@yahoo.co.uk

WATSON, Nicholas Edgar. b 67. St Cath Coll Cam BA 88 MA 92. Wycliffe Hall Ox BA 91. **d** 92 **p** 93. C Benfieldside *Dur* 92–95; C-in-c Stockton Green Vale H Trin CD 95; P-in-c Stockton H Trin 96–00; Chapl Ian Ramsey Sch Stockton 95–00; P-in-c Breadsall *Derby* 00–09; Warden of Readers 00–09; TR Wednesfield *Lich* 09–21; RD Wulfrun 14–21; C Flixton St Jo *Man* from 21; AD Man S and Stretford from 21. *The Rectory, 9 Vicarage Road, Wednesfield, Wolverhampton WV11 1SB* E: revnickwatson@gmail.com

WATSON, Prof Paul Frederick. b 44. MRCVS 69 RVC(Lon) BSc 66 BVetMed 69 Sydney Univ PhD 73 Lon Univ DSc 95. Oak Hill NSM Course 86. **d** 88 **p** 89. NSM Muswell Hill St Jas w St Matt *Lon* 88–96; NSM Edmonton St Aldhelm 96–01; PtO 01–09; *St Alb* from 01. *50 New Road, Ware SG12 7BY* T: (01920) 466941 E: pwatson@rvc.ac.uk

WATSON, Paul William. b 55. Huddersfield Poly BA. St Jo Coll Nottm. **d** 86 **p** 87. C Meltham Mills *Wakef* 86–89; C Meltham 89–90; TV Borehamwood *St Alb* 90–96; V Oswaldtwistle Immanuel and All SS *Blackb* 96–08; rtd 08. *214 Union Road, Oswaldtwistle, Accrington BB5 3EG* T: (01254) 381441

WATSON, Peter Begbie. b 61. Southn Univ BSc 82 ACA 85. St Padarn's Inst 16. **d** 20 **p** 21. NSM Pontypridd *Llan* from 20. *29 Drovers Way, Radyr, Cardiff CF15 8GG* M: 07854-278442 E: revpbw20@gmail.com

WATSON, Peter David. b 69. St Andr Univ MA 92 Westmr Coll Ox PGCE 93. Cranmer Hall Dur 04. **d** 06 **p** 07. C Boston Spa and Thorp Arch w Walton *York* 06–10; R Brayton from 10. *The Rectory, Doncaster Road, Brayton, Selby YO8 9HE* T: (01757) 704707 E: pete.d.watson@outlook.com

WATSON, Philip. b 60. RGN 83. Qu Coll Birm 86. **d** 89 **p** 90. C Ordsall *S'well* 89–93; TV Benwell *Newc* 93–99; V Stocking Farm *Leic* 99–10; R Barwell w Potters Marston and Stapleton from 10. *The Rectory, 14 Church Lane, Barwell, Leicester LE9 8DG* T: (01455) 446993 E: frpwatson@virginmedia.com

WATSON, Richard Francis. b 40. Yorks Min Course 08. **d** 09 **p** 10. NSM Ilkley All SS *Bradf* 09–14; *Leeds* from 14. *23 St Helen's Way, Ilkley LS29 8NP* T: (01943) 430108

WATSON, Canon Richard Frederick. b 66. Avery Hill Coll BA 87. Trin Coll Bris 91. **d** 93 **p** 94. C Kempston Transfiguration *St Alb* 93–97; TV Dunstable 97–03; R E Barnet 03–11; RD Barnet 05–11; Can Res and Sub-Dean St Alb 11–17; V St Alb St Sav from 17. *St Saviour's Vicarage, 25 Sandpit Lane, St Albans AL1 4DF* E: rf.watson@btopenworld.com *or* vicar.stsaviours@gmail.com

WATSON, Robert Bewley. b 34. Bris Univ BA 59. Clifton Th Coll 56. **d** 61 **p** 62. C Bebington *Ches* 61–65; C Woking St Jo *Guildf* 65–68; V Knaphill 68–98; rtd 98; PtO *Guildf* 98–20. *Endrise, 1 Wychelm Road, Lightwater GU18 5RT* T: (01276) 453822

WATSON, Roger Brian. b 45. Cranmer Hall Dur 67. **d** 70 **p** 71. C Sandylands *Blackb* 70–74; C Wallingford *Ox* 74–77; C Winchmore Hill St Paul *Lon* 77–83; rtd 10. *20 Ferndene Road, London SE24 0AQ*

WATSON, Mrs Sarah Louise. b 73. SS Hild & Bede Coll Dur BA 95 Sheff Univ MA 17 PGCE 96. St Hild Coll 15. **d** 17 **p** 18. C Walbrook Epiphany *Derby* 17–19; Pioneer Min from 19; C Spondon 19–21; C Chaddesden St Phil w Derby St Mark from 21; C Pride Park, Wilmorton, Allenton and Shelton Lock from 21. *Address withheld by request* M: 07966-548868 E: sarahwatson311@gmail.com

WATSON, The Ven Sheila Anne. b 53. St Andr Univ MA 75 MPhil 80 Kent Univ Hon DD 13. Edin Th Coll 79. **dss** 79 **d** 87 **p** 94. Bridge of Allan *St And* 79–80; Alloa 79–80; Monkseaton St Mary *Newc* 80–84; Adult Educn Officer *Lon* 84–87; Hon C Chelsea St Luke and Ch 87–96; Selection Sec ABM 92–93; Sen Selection Sec 93–96; Adv on CME *Sarum* 97–02; Dir of Min 98–02; Can and Preb Sarum Cathl 00–02; Adn Buckingham *Ox* 02–07; Adn Cant and Can Res Cant Cathl 07–16; PtO *Lon* from 16; Preacher Lincoln's Inn from 17; Chapter Can St Paul's Cathl *Lon* from 17. *83 Winchester Street, London SW1V 4NU* T: (020) 7828 7377 E: vensheilawatson@gmail.com

WATSON, Ms Stephanie Abigail. b 61. Heriot-Watt Univ BA 84. Cranmer Hall Dur 86. **d** 90 **p** 94. C Bishop's Castle w Mainstone *Heref* 90–93; Dep Chapl HM Pris Dur 93–95; Chapl HM Rem Cen Low Newton 95–98; V Chilton *Dur* 98–02; V Cornforth 98–02; Chapl Wrekin Coll Telford 02–04; PtO *Worc* from 04; Sessional Chapl HM Pris Hewell from 14. *The Chaplaincy, HM Prison Hewell, Hewell Lane, Redditch B97 6QS* T: (01527) 785000 E: revd.stephanie.watson@hotmail.com

WATSON, Mrs Susan Judith. b 50. Birm Univ BA 72. Qu Coll Birm 09. **d** 12 **p** 13. C Cen Wolverhampton *Lich* 12–16; TV Smestow Vale 17–18; PtO 18–19; C Smestow Vale from 19. *6 Newbridge Avenue, Wolverhampton WV6 0LW* T: (01902) 680689 M: 07932-175846 E: suewatson@telecomplus.org.uk *or* suewatson6@gmail.com

WATSON, Timothy Daniel. b 71. ERMC. **d** 11 **p** 12. C Liv Cathl 11–15; CME Officer *Chich* 15–18; Chemin Neuf Community P Hove 15–18; R Hackett H Cross Australia from 18. *PO Box 164, Dickson ACT 2602, Australia* T: (0061) (4) 9033 6409 E: rector@holycrosshackett.org.au

WATSON, Timothy James. b 79. Coll of Ripon & York St Jo BA 01 St Jo Coll Dur BA 10 MA 12 Homerton Coll Cam PGCE 02. Cranmer Hall Dur 08. **d** 11 **p** 12. C Nantwich

Ches 11–14; Pioneer Min 14–15; Pioneer Min *Portsm* 16–21; V Betley *Lich* from 21; V Madeley from 21. *The Vicarage, Vicarage Lane, Madeley, Crewe CW3 9PQ* M: 07713-276407 E: revtimwatson@hotmail.com

WATSON, Canon Timothy Patrick. b 38. ALCD 66. **d** 66 **p** 67. C Northwood Em *Lon* 66–70; TV High Wycombe *Ox* 70–76; Gen Sec ICS 76–82; R Bath Weston All SS w N Stoke *B & W* 82–93; R Bath Weston All SS w N Stoke and Langridge 93–94; TR Cheltenham St Mary, St Matt, St Paul and H Trin *Glouc* 94–03; rtd 03; PtO *Glouc* from 04; Can Kitgum from 05. *The Gateways, Farm Lane, Leckhampton, Cheltenham GL53 0NN* T: (01242) 514298 E: tigertimwatson@yahoo.co.uk

WATSON, William. b 36. Ripon Hall Ox 64. **d** 66 **p** 67. C Leamington Priors H Trin *Cov* 66–69; V Salford Priors 69–74; V Malin Bridge *Sheff* 74–79; Chapl Shrewsbury R Hosps 79–89; Chapl R Hallamshire Hosp Sheff 89–92; Chapl Cen Sheff Univ Hosps NHS Trust 92–93; P-in-c Alveley and Quatt *Heref* 93–96; Chapl N Gen Hosp NHS Trust Sheff 96–01; Chapl Weston Park Hosp Sheff 96–99; Chapl Cen Sheff Univ Hosps NHS Trust 99–01; rtd 96; PtO *Sheff* 01–07; *Liv* from 16. *7 Sandiway Court, Preston Road, Southport PR9 9EG* T: (01704) 541017 E: billandolwyn@outlook.com

WATSON, William Lysander Rowan. b 26. TCD BA 47 MA 50 Clare Coll Cam MA 52 St Pet Hall Ox MA 57. **d** 49 **p** 50. C Chapelizod and Kilmainham *D & G* 49–51; Tutor Ridley Hall Cam 51–55; Chapl 55–57; Chapl St Pet Coll Ox 57–93; Fell and Tutor 59–93; Sen Tutor 77–81; Vice Master 83–85; Lect Th Ox Univ 60–93; rtd 93. *Llandaff Barn, 11 Thames Street, Eynsham, Witney OX29 4HF* T: (01865) 464198 E: lysander.watson@ntlworld.com

WATSON LEE, Christopher James. Leic Univ BA 04 Anglia Ruskin Univ PGCE 05. Oak Hill Th Coll BA 16. **d** 17 **p** 18. NSM Loose *Cant* 17–18; C 19–21. *Address withheld by request*

WATT, John Cameron. b 67. Keele Univ BA 89. Linc Sch of Th and Min 12. **d** 15 **p** 16. C Linc St Nic w St Jo Newport 15–19; C Billingborough Gp 19–21; P-in-c Louth from 21; Adns' Nat Development Officer Min Division Abps' Coun from 19. *24 Roselea Avenue, Welton, Lincoln LN2 3RT* T: (01673) 860028 *or* (020) 7898 1779 M: 078887-802784 E: cameron.watt@aol.com *or* carmeron.watt@churchofengland.org

WATTERS, Mrs Kay. b 44. SAOMC 98. **d** 01 **p** 02. OLM Prestwood and Gt Hampden *Ox* 01–07; Chapl to Bp Buckingham 04–07; rtd 07; PtO *Ox* 07–19; Cyprus and the Gulf 07–15; PtO *Sarum* from 15. *17 Pasture Way, Bridport DT6 4DW* E: kay_watters@hotmail.com

WATTLEY, Jeffery Richard. b 57. Univ of Wales (Abth) BSc(Econ) 79. Trin Coll Bris BA 92. **d** 92 **p** 93. C Reading Greyfriars *Ox* 92–96; V Wonersh *Guildf* 96–98; V Wonersh w Blackheath 98–06; V Egham 06–17; RD Runnymede 13–16; R Jersey St Martin *Win* from 17. *The Vicarage, Le Mont Gabard, St Martin, Jersey JE3 6UA* T: (01534) 853255

WATTS, Mrs Aline Patricia. b 57. St Jo Coll Nottm 02. **d** 04 **p** 05. C Lache cum Saltney *Ches* 04–08; P-in-c Leasowe 08–17; rtd 17; PtO *Ches* 17–19. *9 Ash Close, Weston Rhyn, Oswestry SY10 7TW* E: enyakwatts@gmail.com

WATTS (née DUCKWORTH), Mrs Angela Denise. b 58. RN 95 RM 98. Ripon Coll Cuddesdon 05. **d** 07 **p** 08. C Malvern H Trin and St Jas *Worc* 07–10; PtO *Rock* 10–11; *S'wark* 11–12; *Portsm* from 11; *Win* 12; Chapl St Mich Hospice Basingstoke 12–13; Chapl Hants Hosps NHS Foundn Trust 13–15; Lead Chapl 15–17; rtd 17; PtO *Win* from 17; *Sarum* from 18. *6 Church Farm Close, North Waltham, Basingstoke RG25 2BN* T: (01256) 397626 E: angiewatts.tssf@gmail.com

WATTS, Canon Anthony George. b 46. K Coll Lon BD 69 AKC 69 Lon Univ CertEd 70. Sarum & Wells Th Coll 82. **d** 84 **p** 85. C Wimborne Minster and Holt *Sarum* 84–87; P-in-c Shilling Okeford 87–92; Chapl Croft Ho Sch Shillingstone 87–92; R W Parley *Sarum* 92–00; RD Wimborne 98–00; TR Cley Hill Warminster 00–06; Can and Preb Sarum Cathl 00–06; rtd 06; Chapl Warminster Sch 07–12; PtO *Sarum* from 13. *12 Freesia Close, Warminster BA12 7RL* T: (01985) 847302

WATTS, Anthony John. b 30. AKC 59. **d** 60 **p** 61. C Whitburn *Dur* 60–63; C Croxdale 63–65; V Warrington St Pet *Liv* 65–70; V Peel *Man* 70–78; P-in-c Bury St Mark 78–81; V Davyhulme Ch Ch 81–99; Chapl Trafford Gen Hosp 89–94; Chapl Trafford Healthcare NHS Trust 94–98; rtd 99; PtO *Ches* 00–19; *Man* 00–17. *11 Brackenfield Way, Winsford CW7 2UX* T: (01606) 590803

WATTS, Clive Roger. b 69. RGN 92. Ripon Coll Cuddesdon 14. **d** 16 **p** 17. C Wigston *Leic* 16–19; P-in-c Barrow upon Soar w Walton le Wolds from 19; P-in-c Wymeswold and Prestwold w Hoton from 19. *Holy Trinity Rectory, 27 Cotes Road,*

Barrow upon Soar, Loughborough LE12 8JP M: 07905-230857
E: fr.clive.watts@gmail.com

WATTS, Daniel John. b 70. Wycliffe Hall Ox 04. **d** 06 **p** 07. C Paddock Wood *Roch* 06–09; C Harrogate St Mark *Ripon* 09–14; *Leeds* from 14. *2 Rossett Beck, Harrogate HG2 9NT* M: 07977-126438 E: daniel.watts11@icloud.com

WATTS, Fraser Norman. b 46. Magd Coll Ox BA 68 MA 74 K Coll Lon MSc 70 PhD 75 CPsychol 89 FBPsS 80. Westcott Ho Cam 88. **d** 90 **p** 91. NSM Harston w Hauxton *Ely* 90–95; P-in-c 91–95; Fell Qu Coll Cam 94–13; Lect Cam Univ 94–13; Chapl Cam St Edw *Ely* 95–13; Hon Can Ely Cathl 08–13; rtd 13. *19 Grantchester Road, Cambridge CB3 9ED* T: (01223) 359223 F: 763003 E: fraser.watts@cantab.net

WATTS, Gordon Sidney Stewart. b 40. CITC 63. **d** 66 **p** 67. C Belfast St Steph *Conn* 66–69; CF 69–94; V Boldre w S Baddesley *Win* 94–96; P-in-c Warmfield *Wakef* 96–02; Sub Chapl HM Pris Wakef 97–02; Chapl Huggens Coll Northfleet 02–07; rtd 07; PtO *Ches* from 07. *8 Bramwell Avenue, Prenton CH43 0RH* T: 0151-200 0861 M: 07967-134101 E: gss.watts@ntlworld.com

WATTS, Graham Hadley Lundie. b 74. Man Metrop Univ BA 95. Ridley Hall Cam 98. **d** 02 **p** 03. C Camberley St Paul *Guildf* 02–06; C Northwood Em *Lon* 06–14; TV Gt Marlow w Marlow Bottom, Lt Marlow and Bisham *Ox* from 14. *165 Marlow Bottom, Marlow SL7 3PL* T: (01628) 473548 E: graham.watts@4u-team.org

WATTS, John Michael. b 45. **d** 04 **p** 10. OLM Ashtead *Guildf* 04–15; PtO from 15; Asst Chapl Guy's and St Thos' NHS Foundn Trust from 04; PtO *S'wark* from 05. *31 Broadhurst, Ashtead KT21 1QB* T: (01372) 275134 E: john.watts@gstt.nhs.uk

WATTS, John Robert. b 39. Leeds Univ BSc 60 MSc 63 DipEd 63. Oak Hill Th Coll 88. **d** 90 **p** 91. C Partington and Carrington *Ches* 90–93; P-in-c Tintwistle 93–98; V Hollingworth w Tintwistle 98–04; RD Mottram 99–03; rtd 04; PtO *Ches* from 04. *16 Norley Drive, Vicars Cross, Chester CH3 5PG* T: (01244) 350439 E: revrobwatts@hotmail.co.uk

WATTS, Jonathan Peter (Jonah). b 52. Lon Univ BA 74. Ripon Coll Cuddesdon BTh 11. **d** 08 **p** 09. C Crayford *Roch* 08–11; V Twyford and Owslebury and Morestead etc *Win* 11–17; rtd 17; PtO *Win* from 17; *Sarum* from 19. *6 Church Farm Close, North Waltham, Basingstoke RG25 2BN* T: (01256) 397626 E: jonah.watts1@icloud.com

WATTS, Mrs Mary Kathleen. b 31. Lon Univ BA 86. Gilmore Ho 73. **dss** 77 **d** 87 **p** 94. Lower Streatham St Andr *S'wark* 77–88; C 87–88; C Streatham Immanuel w St Anselm 87–88; C Streatham Immanuel and St Andr 90–91; rtd 91; PtO *S'wark* 91–94 and 05–06; Hon C Norbury St Oswald 94–05; PtO *Roch* 10–16; *Chich* from 16. *25 Ramsay Hall, 9-13 Byron Road, Worthing BN11 3HN*

WATTS, Matthew David. b 79. Clare Coll Cam BA 01 MA 04 MSci 01 St Jo Coll Dur BA 05. Cranmer Hall Dur 03. **d** 06 **p** 07. C Comberton and Toft w Caldecote and Childerley *Ely* 06–09; V Burnside-Harewood NZ 09–19; V Buller from 19. *13A Lyndhurst Street, Westport 7825, New Zealand* T: (0064) (3) 789 8348 E: matt@churchinwestport.co.nz

WATTS, Sir Philip Beverley. b 45. KCMG 02. Leeds Univ BSc 66 MSc 69 Ox Brookes Univ BA 11 FInstP 80 FEI 90 FGS 98 FRGS 98. Ox Min Course 09. **d** 11 **p** 12. NSM Binfield Ox 11–13; P-in-c Waltham St Lawrence 13–16; PtO from 16. *Sunnyridge, Hill Farm Lane, Binfield, Bracknell RG42 5NR* T: (01344) 305965 E: philbwatts@gmail.com

WATTS (née SIMPER), Rachel Dawn. b 67. K Coll Lon BD 89. Westcott Ho Cam 90. **d** 92 **p** 94. Par Dn Clitheroe St Mary *Blackb* 92–94; C 94–95; C Nor St Pet Mancroft w St Jo Maddermarket 95–97; V Slyne w Hest *Blackb* 97–04; V Briercliffe 04–11; Women's Min Adv 00–11; Hon Can Blackb Cathl 10–11; R Uppingham w Ayston and Belton w Wardley *Pet* from 11; Asst Dir Ords from 14. *The Rectory, 45 Lime Tree Avenue, Uppingham, Oakham LE15 9SS* T: (01572) 829956 E: rwatts789@btinternet.com *or* rectorofuppingham@gmail.com

WATTS, Ms Rebecca Harriet. b 61. St Cath Coll Cam BA 83 MA. Wycliffe Hall Ox 87. **d** 90 **p** 94. C Goldsworth Park *Guildf* 90–94; Chapl Wadh Coll Ox 94–97; C Ox St Mary V w St Cross and St Pet 94–97; Chapl Somerville Coll Ox 97–98; PtO *Newc* 98–99 and from 02. *7 Westfield Avenue, Newcastle upon Tyne NE3 4YH* T: 0191-285 9840 E: rebecca.h.watts@blueyonder.co.uk

WATTS, Robert. *See* WATTS, John Robert

WATTS, Roger Mansfield. b 41. Univ of Wales (Cardiff) BSc 63 CEng 76 MIET 76. Chich Th Coll 89. **d** 91 **p** 92. C Chippenham St Andr w Tytherton Lucas *Bris* 91–93; C Henfield w Shermanbury and Woodmancote *Chich* 93–96; R Jedburgh *Edin* 96–99; R Wingerworth *Derby* 99–06; rtd

06; PtO *Llan* 14–16; *St As* 16; Hon C Aled Miss Area 16–19. *Address temp unknown* E: revrwatts@gmail.com

WATTS, Ms Samantha Alison Lundie. b 70. Birm Univ BA 92 Cam Univ BA 01. Ridley Hall Cam 99. **d** 02 **p** 03. C Camberley St Paul *Guildf* 02–06; NSM Northwood Em *Lon* 06–14; TV Gt Marlow w Marlow Bottom, Lt Marlow and Bisham *Ox* from 14; Chapl St Geo Sch Ascot from 18. *165 Marlow Bottom, Marlow SL7 3PL* T: (01628) 473548 E: sami.watts@4u-team.org

WATTS, Scott Antony. b 67. JP 08. Anglia Ruskin Univ MA 18 FRSA 12. EAMTC 00. **d** 03 **p** 04. NSM Brampton *Ely* 03–07; Chapl St Jo Hospice Moggerhanger 07–09; Lead Chapl Hinchingbrooke Health Care NHS Trust 09–17; TV Vale and Cotswold Edge *Glouc* from 17. *The New Vicarage, Stratford Road, Honeybourne, Evesham WR11 7PP* T: (01386) 834946 E: revscottwatts@yahoo.com

WATTS, Thomas Annesley. b 79. K Coll Cam BA 01 MA 05. Oak Hill Th Coll MTh 08. **d** 08 **p** 09. C Wharton *Ches* 08–12; C Gt Chesham Ox 12–18; Min Hampstead St Jo Downshire Hill Prop Chpl *Lon* from 18. *64 Pilgrims Lane, London NW3 1SN* T: (020) 7099 9360 *or* 7435 3805 M: 07764-679210 E: tom@tomandsue.net

WATTS, Mrs Valerie Anne. b 44. UEA BEd 79. EAMTC 90. **d** 93 **p** 94. NSM N Walsham and Edingthorpe *Nor* 93–14; PtO from 15. *15 Millfield Road, North Walsham NR28 0EB* T: (01692) 405119 E: rev.valwatts@outlook.com

WATTS, William Henry Norbury. b 51. CertEd. St Jo Coll Nottm 87. **d** 89 **p** 90. C S Molton w Nymet St George, High Bray etc *Ex* 89–93; TV Swanage and Studland *Sarum* 93–10; P-in-c Basildon w Aldworth and Ashampstead *Ox* 10–14; V 14–19; P-in-c Sulhamstead Abbots and Bannister w Ufton Nervet 14–17; AD Bradfield 11–17; rtd 19. *1 Chervil Close, Gloucester GL4 6YJ* E: revwillwatts@btinternet.com

WAUDBY, Miss Christine. b 45. TCert 66. Trin Coll Bris. **d** 90 **p** 94. C Weston-super-Mare Ch Ch *B & W* 90–94; C Blackheath *Birm* 94–99; PtO 99–03; NSM Ipsley *Worc* 03–10; rtd 10; PtO *Heref* from 11. *2 Coppice Close, Withington, Hereford HR1 3PP*

WAUGH, Ian William. b 52. Bede Coll Dur DipEd 74 BEd 75. NEOC 99. **d** 02 **p** 03. NSM Benfieldside *Dur* 02–07; NSM Ebchester from 07; NSM Medomsley from 07. *36 Muirfield Close, Shotley Bridge, Consett DH8 5XE* T: (01207) 591923 M: 07808-412953 E: iwwaugh@btinternet.com

WAUGH, Nigel John William. b 56. TCD BA 78 MA 81. CITC 76. **d** 79 **p** 80. C Ballymena w Ballyclug *Conn* 79–82; C Ballyholme *D & D* 82–84; I Bunclody w Kildavin *C, F & O* 84–85; I Bunclody w Kildavin, Clonegal and Kilrush 86–91 and 91–98; Preb Ferns Cathl 88–91; Treas 91–96; Radio Officer (Cashel) 90–91; (Ferns) 92–98; Dioc Info Officer (Ferns) *C, F & O* 91–98; Prec Ferns Cathl 96–98; I Delgany *D & G* from 98. *The Rectory, 8 Elsinore, Delgany, Greystones, Co Wicklow, Republic of Ireland* T: (00353) (1) 287 4515 M: 86-102 8888 E: nigelwaugh@gmail.com

WAY, Miss Alison Janet. b 61. York Univ BSc 83 FIBMS 86. St Mich Coll Llan 02. **d** 04 **p** 05. C Basingstoke *Win* 04–08; P-in-c Woodhill *Sarum* 08–10; R 10–14; NSM R Wootton Bassett and Lyneham w Bradenstoke 11–14; P-in-c S Nutfield w Outwood *S'wark* 14–15; V S Nutfield 15–20; Officer for Lay Miss and Min Croydon Area 14–20; R Wincanton *B & W* from 20; R Pen Selwood from 20. *Dorset Heights, Common Road, Wincanton BA9 9HS* E: rector@wincantonparishchurch.co.uk

WAY, Andrew Lindsay. b 43. Linc Th Coll 76. **d** 78 **p** 79. C Shenfield *Chelmsf* 78–82; C Waltham *Linc* 82–84; V New Waltham 84–89; R Duxford *Ely* 89–94; V Hinxton 89–94; V Ickleton 89–94; P-in-c Doddington w Benwick 94–97; P-in-c Wimblington 94–97; R Doddington w Benwick and Wimblington 97–98; R Eythorne and Elvington w Waldershare etc *Cant* 98–09; AD Dover 00–03; rtd 09; PtO *Cant* from 09. *17 Chequer Lane, Ash, Canterbury CT3 2AX* E: albeway@clara.net

WAY, Mrs Barbara Elizabeth. b 47. Open Univ BA 82 Hull Univ PGCE 86. Linc Th Coll IDC 78. **dss** 78 **d** 87 **p** 94. Shenfield *Chelmsf* 78–82; Adult Educn Adv *Linc* 82–85; Dioc Lay Min Adv 85; New Waltham 82–89; Min 87–89; Tetney 86–89; Min 87–89; NSM Duxford, Ickleton and Hinxton *Ely* 89–94; Dir Past Studies EAMTC 91–94; Min Pampisford 92–94; P-in-c Coates 94–95; TV Whittlesey, Pondersbridge and Coates 95–98; Local Min Adv *Cant* 98–02; Dioc Dir of Reader Selection and Tr 00–02; Dioc Adv in Women's Min 02–04; P-in-c Whitfield w Guston 02–10; Chapl E Kent Hosps NHS Trust 06–08; rtd 10; PtO *Cant* 10–13; C Westgate St Sav 13–16; PtO from 16. *17 Chequer Lane, Ash, Canterbury CT3 2AX* E: belway@clara.net

WAY, Colin George. b 31. St Cath Coll Cam BA 55 MA 59 Lon Inst of Educn PGCE 58. EAMTC. **d** 84 **p** 85. NSM Hempnall *Nor* 84–87; C Gaywood, Bawsey and Mintlyn 87–90; R Acle w Fishley and N Burlingham 90–96; RD Blofield 95–96; rtd 96; PtO Nor 96–97 and from 02; P-in-c Pulham Market, Pulham St Mary and Starston 97–99; Hon C Eaton 99–02. *347 Unthank Road, Norwich NR4 7QG* T: (01603) 458363 E: colin.way@ntlworld.com

WAY, Matthew Paul. b 87. Univ of Wales (Newport) BA 09. St Mellitus Coll BA 18. d 18 p 19. C Hope Ch Islington *Lon* from 18. *28 Witherington Road, London N5 1PP* M: 07715-578198 E: mattway222@gmail.com or matt@hopechurchislington.org

WAY, Michael David. b 57. K Coll Lon BD 78 AKC 78. St Steph Ho Ox 79. d 80 p 83. C Bideford *Ex* 80–81; Hon C Wembley Park St Aug *Lon* 81–84; C Kilburn St Aug w St Jo 84–89; V Earlsfield St Jo *S'wark* 89–92; Past Dir CARA 92–99; Consultant Cen Sch for Counselling and Therapy 99–00; Dir RADICLE *Lon* 00–06; Safeguarding Consultant and Social/ Health Care Tr 06–18; PtO *Dur* 20; P-in-c Darlington St Jas from 20. *Address withheld by request* M: 07505-160164 E: michael.priest@stjamesdarlington.org

WEAKLEY, Susan Margaret. b 52. SEITE 05. d 08 p 09. NSM Merstham and Gatton *S'wark* 08–10; NSM Merstham, S Merstham and Gatton 10–13; NSM Reigate St Mark 13–16; P-in-c Charlwood 16–21; P-in-c Sidlow Bridge 16–21; rtd 21. *81 Parkhurst Road, Horley RH6 8EX* T: (01293) 773954 M: 07887-888372

WEARING, Miss Julie Ann. b 65. Cov Poly BSc 89 St Jo Coll Dur BA 12. Cranmer Hall Dur 10. d 12 p 13. C Upton cum Chalvey *Ox* 12–15; V Linc St Faith and St Martin w St Pet 15–20; V Crosby from 20. *St George's Vicarage, 87 Ferry Road, Scunthorpe DN15 8LY* M: 07368-514486

WEARING, Malcolm Jamieson. b 72. Salford Univ BEng 94 PhD 00. All SS Cen for Miss & Min 11. d 14 p 15. OLM Farnworth, Kearsley and Stoneclough *Man* 14–21; C Blackrod, Daisy Hill, Westhoughton and Wingates from 21. *16 Butterfield Road, Bolton BL5 1DU* T: (01204) 658334 E: malcolm@revmw.co.uk

WEARMOUTH, Alan Wilfred. b 54. Bris Univ BEd 76. Glouc Sch of Min 85. d 88 p 89. NSM Coleford w Staunton *Glouc* 88–06; C Coleford, Staunton, Newland, Redbrook etc 06–19; rtd 19; PtO *Glouc* from 19. *Windhover, 2 Broadwell Bridge, Broadwell, Coleford GL16 7GA* T: (01594) 832660 M: 07811-118736 E: alanw22uk@yahoo.co.uk

WEARN, Simon Joseph. b 76. Pemb Coll Cam BA 00 MEng 00. Oak Hill Th Coll BA 09. d 09 p 10. C Gt Faringdon w Lt Coxwell *Ox* 09–13; R Hinckley H Trin *Leic* from 13. *Holy Trinity Vicarage, 1 Cleveland Road, Hinckley LE10 0AJ* M: 07980-910104 E: sjwearn@gmail.com

WEATHERHOGG, Susanne. *See* JUKES, Susanne

WEATHERILL, Martha Grace. b 77. Brunel Univ BSc 00 K Coll Lon MSc 01 MPhil 06. St Steph Ho Ox 15. d 17 p 18. C Chich St Paul and Westhampnett 17–21; P-in-c Lavant from 21; RD Chich from 21. *The Rectory, Pook Lane, East Lavant, Chichester PO18 0AH* M: 07472-909011 E: jmweatherill@icloud.com

WEATHERSON, Timothy Andrew Patrick. b 59. Bedf Coll Lon BSc 81 UEA MSc 82 Anglia Ruskin Univ BA 12 Tilburg Univ PhD 16. ERMC 05. d 08 p 09. C Bowthorpe *Nor* 08–11; C Shipdham w Bradenham 11–12; TV Barnham Broom and Upper Yare 11–15; R from 15. *The Rectory, The Street, Reymerston, Norwich NR9 4AG* T: (01362) 858748 or 858021 M: 07967-190976 E: bb.office@btinternet.com or rector@group0f15.org.uk

WEAVER, Alan William. b 63. Linc Th Coll 95. d 95 p 96. C Seaford w Sutton *Chich* 95–98; C Langney 98–01; P-in-c The Haven CD 02–05; P-in-c Jarvis Brook 05–07; V from 07. *St Michael's Vicarage, Crowborough Hill, Crowborough TN6 2HJ* T: (01892) 661565 E: angyalanweaver@waitrose.com

WEAVER, Angela Mary. *See* TOWNSHEND, Angela Mary

WEAVER, David Sidney George. b 46. Univ of Wales (Cardiff) BA 67 MA 71 Goldsmiths' Coll Lon MA 01 Lon Univ CertEd 76. SEITE 07. d 09 p 10. NSM Hove All SS *Chich* 09–12; P-in-c Haywards Heath St Rich 12–16; V 16; rtd 16; PtO *Chich* 16–17; P-in-c Eastbourne St Mich 17–19. *123 Ringwood Road, Eastbourne BN22 8TG* M: 07811-145656 E: frdavidweaver@gmail.com

WEAVER, Mrs Diane Beverley. b 57. LCTP 06. d 09 p 10. C Steeton *Bradf* 09–13; V Barnoldswick w Bracewell *Leeds* 13–18; rtd 18. *5 Oakwood Close, Thornton-Cleveleys FY5 4EL* E: revdianeweaver@btinternet.com

WEAVER, Duncan Charles. b 60. St Jo Coll Nottm BA 99 Cardiff Univ MA 09 St Andr Univ MLitt 14. St Jo Coll Nottm 92. d 94 p 95. C Watford *St Alb* 94–98; TV Bourne Valley *Sarum* 98–01; CF 01–17; Chapl Bloxham Sch from 17. *Bloxham School, Banbury Road, Bloxham, Banbury OX15 4PE* T: (01295) 720222 E: dcweaver60@hotmail.com

WEAVER, Elaine. b 54. St Mellitus Coll 15. d 18 p 19. NSM Roxeth *Lon* from 18. *37 Yeading Avenue, Harrow HA2 9RL* T: (020) 8868 1081 M: 07964-748891 E: elaine_weaver37@hotmail.com

WEAVER, Fiona Margaret. b 61. Westcott Ho Cam 99. d 00 p 01. C Islington St Jas w St Pet *Lon* 00–03; Asst Chapl Univ of N Lon 00–02; Asst Chapl Lon Metrop Univ 01–03; Chapl 03–05; Lead Chapl 05–11; Family and Youth Work Adv 12–13; P-in-c Purley St Swithun *S'wark* 13–18; P-in-c Purley St Mark 13–18; V Purley St Mark and St Swithun from 18. *The Vicarage, 2 Church Road, Purley CR8 3QQ* T: (020) 8668 0063 E: revfionaweaver@gmail.com

WEAVER, Mrs Joyce Margaret. b 43. d 00 p 01. OLM Warrington St Ann *Liv* 00–13; rtd 13; PtO *Liv* from 16. *71 Orford Avenue, Warrington WA2 8PQ* T: (01925) 634993 E: joycearniew@aol.com

WEAVER, Martyn Graham. b 71. Salford Univ BEng 93 St Jo Coll Dur BA 12. Cranmer Hall Dur 10. d 12 p 13. C Selby Abbey *York* 12–16; V Bingley All SS *Leeds* from 16; PtO *York* 18–21. *26 Falcon Road, Bingley BD16 4DW* E: revm.weaver@virginmedia.com

WEAVER, Canon Michael Howard. b 39. Southn Univ MPhil 95 DipArch. Chich Th Coll 63. d 66 p 67. C Kidderminster St Jo *Worc* 66–69; Cathl Chapl and Dioc Architect Br Honduras 69–71; TV Droitwich *Worc* 71–76; V Arundel w Tortington and S Stoke *Chich* 76–96; P-in-c Clymping 84–87; RD Arundel and Bognor 88–93; Sub-Chapl HM Pris Ford 77–96; V Lymington *Win* 96–04; Chapl Southn Community Services NHS Trust 96–01; Chapl Southn City Primary Care Trust 01–04; rtd 04; Hon Can Enugu from 94; PtO *Win* 04–14; *Portsm* from 04; AD W Wight 10–12; PtO *Chich* from 14. *Tau Cottage, Crossbush, Arundel BN18 9PJ* T: (01903) 885087 E: junovicarage@hotmail.com

WEAVER, Canon William. b 40. Man Univ BA 63 BD 65. d 74 p 75. Lect Th Leeds Univ 67–91; Hon C Clifford *York* 82–86; Chapl K Edw Sch Birm 91–94; Provost Woodard Schs (Midl Division) 94–03; Hon Can Derby Cathl from 96; PtO 96–18; *Blackb* 18–21. *1 Douglas Avenue, Stalmine, Poulton-le-Fylde FY6 0NB* T: (01253) 700849 E: william.antheaweaver@btinternet.com

WEBB, Alwyn Charles. b 62. Oak Hill Th Coll BA 95 K Coll Lon PGCE 96 MA 13. St Mellitus Coll 11. d 13 p 14. C Richmond H Trin and Ch Ch *S'wark* 13–18; C Onslow Square and S Kensington St Aug *Lon* from 19. *26 Sherland Road, Twickenham TW1 4HD* T: (020) 8404 1112 E: alwynwebb87@hotmail.com or alwyn.webb@htb.org

WEBB, Amy Lavinia. b 75. STETS 12. d 15 p 16. C Botley *Portsm* 15–17; C Curdridge 15–17; C Durley 15–17; C Locks Heath 17–19; V Wymering from 19; V Cosham from 19. *Wymering Vicarage, Medina Road, Portsmouth PO6 3NH* E: vicar@coshamandwymering.org

WEBB, Arthur Robert. b 33. Lanc Univ MA 82 FRSA LCP 67. Wells Th Coll 69. d 70 p 70. C W Drayton *Lon* 70–72; Hd Master St Jas Cathl Sch Bury St Edmunds 72–86; Min Can St E Cathl 72–87; Succ St E Cathl 81–87; P-in-c Seend and Bulkington *Sarum* 87–88; V 88–91; R Heytesbury and Sutton Veny 91–96; rtd 96; PtO *B & W* from 96; *Sarum* from 98; *Bris* 00–04; P-in-c Las Palmas *Eur* 04–08; PtO 09–19. *27 Marlborough Buildings, Bath BA1 2LY* T: (01225) 484442

WEBB, Mrs Barbara Mary. b 39. Bedf Coll Lon BA 60 Cam Univ DipEd 61. Wycliffe Hall Ox 00. d 02 p 03. NSM Cumnor *Ox* 02–05; NSM Stanford in the Vale w Goosey and Hatford 05–09; P-in-c Shippon 09–10; rtd 10; PtO *Ox* 10–14; *Ches* from 14. *72A Station Road, Marple, Stockport SK6 6NY* T: 0161-221 2414 E: derry_barbara@msn.com

WEBB, Mrs Brenda Lynn. b 45. Stockwell Coll of Educn CertEd 66. EAMTC 97. d 00 p 01. NSM Saxmundham w Kelsale cum Carlton *St E* 00–10; Teacher Beacon Hill Sch 00–10; rtd 10; PtO *St E* from 12. *48 Pightle Close, Elmswell, Bury St Edmunds IP30 9EL* T: (01359) 242925 E: brenda.l.webb@gmail.com

WEBB, Catharine Rosemary Wheatley. b 39. d 05 p 06. OLM Redhill St Matt *S'wark* 05–09; PtO from 09. *6 Hurstleigh Drive, Redhill RH1 2AA* T/F: (01737) 769763 M: 07709-700602 E: webbcrw8@ntlworld.com

WEBB, Christopher Scott. b 70. Univ of Wales (Abth) BSc. Trin Coll Bris BA 96. d 96 p 97. C Dafen *St D* 96–98; C Cowbridge *Llan* 98–01; Officer for Renewal, Par Development and Local Ecum 01–04; V Llanfair Caereinion, Llanllugan and Manafon *St As* 04–07; President of Renovaré USA 07–12; V Lampeter *St D* 12–14; Dioc Spirituality Adv and Dep Warden Launde Abbey *Leic* from 14. *Launde Abbey, Launde Road, Launde, Leicester LE7 9XB* T: (01572) 717254 E: cw@launde.org.uk

WEBB, Dominic Mark. b 68. Oriel Coll Ox BA 91. Wycliffe Hall Ox BA 93. d 96 p 97. C Cradley *Worc* 96–99; C Leyton

Ch Ch *Chelmsf* 99–02; P-in-c St Helier *S'wark* 02–06; Hon C Stratford St Paul and St Jas *Chelmsf* 07–15; PtO 15–20. *32A Lister Road, London E11 3DS* T: (020) 8558 6354 E: webbdom@googlemail.com

WEBB, Mrs Eileen Marion. b 46. Bingley Coll of Educn CertEd. **d** 08 **p** 09. OLM Cheriton St Martin *Cant* 08–11; OLM Cheriton All So w Newington 08–11; OLM Cheriton w Newington 11–16; rtd 16; PtO *Cant* from 16. *4 Westfield Lane, Etchinghill, Folkestone CT18 8BZ* T: (01303) 864272 F: 864272 M: 07867-546929 E: bryleen@aol.com

WEBB, Mrs Gillian Anne. b 49. Whitelands Coll Lon CertEd 71 Heythrop Coll Lon MA 04. St Alb Minl Tr Scheme 83. **dss** 86 **d** 87 **p** 94. Kempston Transfiguration *St Alb* 86–96; NSM 87–96; NSM Kempston All SS 96–08; P-in-c Marston Morteyne w Lidlington 08–16; Hon C 16–19; PtO from 19. *2 Hillson Close, Marston Moretaine, Bedford MK43 0QN* T: (01234) 767256

WEBB, Mrs Glenda Marjorie. St Jo Coll Nottm BA 13 Sheff Univ MA 16. Yorks Min Course 13. **d** 15 **p** 16. NSM Brayton *York* 15–19; NSM Askham Bryan from 19; NSM Copmanthorpe from 19; NSM Bolton Percy from 19; Asst Chapl York Teaching Hosp NHS Foundn Trust from 16. *Rockside, Springfield, Boston Spa, Wetherby LS23 6EB* M: 07871-241933 E: glendamwebb@gmail.com

WEBB (née EDWARDS), Mrs Helen Glynne. b 57. SRN 79 RMN 81 Birkbeck Coll Lon MSc 94. Wycliffe Hall Ox 88. **d** 90 **p** 94. Par Dn Clapham St Jas *S'wark* 90–94; Chapl Asst Southmead Health Services NHS Trust 94–97; PtO *Bris* from 97. *13 The Green, Olveston, Bristol BS35 4DN* T/F: (01454) 615827 E: helenw13@gmail.com

WEBB, Ian. b 77. UWE BA 00. Trin Coll Bris 12. **d** 14 **p** 15. C Dronfield w Holmesfield *Derby* 14–18; P-in-c Clipstone *S'well* 18–20; P-in-c Edwinstowe 18–20; P-in-c Perlethorpe 18–20; TV Dronfield w Holmesfield *Derby* from 20. *Address temp unknown* M: 07795-030241 E: ian@webbhome.co.uk

WEBB, Mrs Janice Beryl. b 49. Dioc OLM tr scheme 05. **d** 08 **p** 09. NSM Stour Vale *Sarum* 08–11; NSM Barbourne *Worc* 11–17; rtd 17; PtO *Worc* from 17; *Heref* from 18. *Seaview, Upper House, Wolferlow, Bromyard HR7 4QA* T: (01886) 853096 E: jan.dorset@gmail.com

WEBB, Jennifer Rose. b 48. Leeds Univ BA 70 Bedf Coll Lon CQSW 72. **d** 96 **p** 97. OLM Ham St Rich *S'wark* 96–05; NSM March St Mary *Ely* 05–14; P-in-c 14–15; NSM March St Pet 05–14; P-in-c 14–15; NSM March 15–18; rtd 18; PtO *Ely* from 18. *3 Wherry Close, March PE15 9BX* T: (01354) 650855 E: revdjennywebb@btinternet.com

WEBB, John. *See* WEBB, William John

WEBB, John Christopher Richard. b 38. ACA 63 FCA 74. Wycliffe Hall Ox 64. **d** 67 **p** 68. C Hendon St Paul Mill Hill *Lon* 67–71; CF 71–93; R Bentworth and Shalden and Lasham *Win* 93–03; RD Alton 98–02; rtd 03; PtO *B & W* from 04. *Lower Farm Cottage, Church Street, Podimore, Yeovil BA22 8JE* T: (01935) 841465 E: john-cr.webb465@tiscali.co.uk

WEBB, Jonathan Paul. b 62. Bapt Th Coll Johannesburg BTh 98. **d** 02 **p** 03. NSM Linden S Africa 02–04; Asst P Bryanston 04–06; TV Bury St Edmunds All SS w St Jo and St Geo *St E* 07–10; V E Molesey *Guildf* 10–15; V Brighouse and Clifton *Leeds* from 15. *47 Bracken Road, Brighouse HD6 2HX* E: revpaulwebb@gmail.com

WEBB, Kenneth Gordon. b 47. Lon Univ MB, BS 71. Trin Coll Bris BA 92. **d** 93 **p** 94. C Cheltenham St Mark *Glouc* 93–97; Banchang Ch Ch Thailand 97–02; P-in-c Duns *Edin* 02–17; LtO from 18. *9/32 Western Harbour View, Edinburgh EH6 6PG* T: 0131-629 2102 M: 07990-866918 E: kenwebb275@icloud.com

WEBB, Mrs Linda. b 61. Qu Foundn (Course) 15. **d** 17 **p** 18. NSM Hulland, Atlow, Kniveton, Bradley and Hognaston *Derby* 17–21. *Address temp unknown* E: linwebb@btinternet.com

WEBB (née NAGEL), Mrs Lucy Mary. b 86. Bris Univ BA 07 PGCE 08 Anglia Ruskin Univ MA 15. Ridley Hall Cam 13. **d** 15 **p** 16. C Redland *Bris* 15–18; C Guildf St Sav from 18. *5B Artillery Terrace, Guildford GU1 4NL* M: 07813-405361 E: lucy.webb@st-saviours.org.uk

WEBB, Lyndon James Stuart. b 89. G&C Coll Cam BA 11 MPhil 12. Ripon Coll Cuddesdon BA 18. **d** 19 **p** 20. C Broadstone *Sarum* from 19. *1A Mission Road, Broadstone BH18 8JJ* M: 07805-582432 E: revlyndonwebb@gmail.com

WEBB, Michael David. b 59. K Coll Lon BD 82 PGCE 83. Ripon Coll Cuddesdon 88. **d** 90 **p** 91. C Broughton Astley *Leic* 90–93; C Hugglescote w Donington, Ellistown and Snibston 93–94; TV 94–98; R Castleford All SS and Whitwood *Wakef* 98–01; P-in-c Glass Houghton 98–01; TR Castleford 02; rtd 02; PtO *S'well* 06–16; *York* 13–18; *Leic* from 17. *31 Bramley Road, Birstall, Leicester LE4 4FH* T: 0116-212 8466 M: 07813-144645 E: michael@michaelshouse.co.uk

WEBB, Canon Michael John. b 49. Linc Coll Ox BA 70 MA 74. Linc Th Coll 70. **d** 72 **p** 73. C Tring *St Alb* 72–75; C Chipping Barnet 75–78; C Chipping Barnet w Arkley 78–82; TV Cullercoats St Geo *Newc* 82–89; V Newc H Cross 89–97; Chapl MU 96–02; V Newc St Gabr 97–06; AD Newc E 97–04; V Alnwick 06–11; Hon Can Newc Cathl 02–11; rtd 11; PtO *Carl* from 12. *Underne, 24 Wordsworth Street, Keswick CA12 4BZ* T: (01768) 771180 E: mjwebb446@gmail.com

WEBB, Mrs Michelle Dawn. b 83. Bp Grosseteste Coll BA 04 PGCE 05. St Hild Coll 18. **d** 20 **p** 21. C Linc St Giles from 20. *23 Montaigne Crescent, Lincoln LN2 4QN* M: 07939-454605 E: michellestgileslincoln@gmail.com

WEBB, Miss Miriam May. b 50. **d** 19 **p** 20. NSM Lark Valley and N Bury *St E* from 19. *Address withheld by request* T: (01284) 704593 E: webbmiriamm@gmail.com

WEBB, Nicholas John. b 81. Moorlands Bible Coll BA 03 Sarum Coll MA 20. **d** 20 **p** 21. C St Aldhelm *Sarum* from 20. *16 Court Road, Swanage BH19 1JE* M: 07866-546162 E: fulloflifegardens@gmail.com

WEBB, Norma Fay. b 39. K Coll Dur BDS 62. **d** 04 **p** 05. OLM Thornhill and Whitley Lower *Wakef* 04–09; PtO 09–14; *Leeds* from 14. *24 High Street, Thornhill, Dewsbury WF12 0PS* T: (01924) 463574 E: normafwebb@btinternet.com

WEBB, Patrick James. b 84. Moorlands Th Coll BA 11 Greenwich Univ PGCE 08. Wycliffe Hall Ox BA 19. **d** 19 **p** 20. C Bleadon and Bournville *B & W* from 19. *6 Burrington Avenue, Weston-super-Mare BS24 9LP* M: 07581-719116 E: p.j.webb1984@gmail.com

WEBB, Paul. *See* WEBB, Jonathan Paul

WEBB, Peter Henry. b 55. Nottm Univ BA 77. St Steph Ho Ox 77. **d** 79 **p** 80. C Lancing w Coombes *Chich* 79–82; C The Hydneye CD 82–84; C-in-c 84–86; Chapl Sunderland Distr Gen Hosp 86–94; Chapl City Hosps Sunderland NHS Foundn Trust 94–21; rtd 21. *Address temp unknown*

WEBB, Richard. b 38. Oak Hill NSM Course 91. **d** 94 **p** 95. NSM Hanwell St Mary w St Chris *Lon* 94–04; rtd 04; PtO *Cant* from 05. *1 Haffenden Meadow, Charing, Ashford TN27 0JR* T: (01233) 714663 E: revrichardwebb@googlemail.com

WEBB, Canon Richard Frederick. b 42. Cant Sch of Min. **d** 84 **p** 85. C Ipswich St Clem w H Trin *St E* 84–87; R Rougham and Beyton w Hessett 87–91; R Rougham, Beyton w Hessett and Rushbrooke 91–92; P-in-c Woodbridge St Jo 92–98; P-in-c Saxmundham 98–04; P-in-c Kelsale-cum-Carlton, Middleton, Theberton etc 02–04; R Saxmundham w Kelsale cum Carlton 04–10; RD Saxmundham 03–05; Hon Can St E Cathl 06–10; rtd 10; PtO *St E* from 10. *48 Pightle Close, Elmswell, Bury St Edmunds IP30 9EL* T: (01359) 242925 E: richard.webb380@btinternet.com

WEBB, Robert. *See* WEBB, Arthur Robert

WEBB, Rosemary. b 59. **d** 10 **p** 11. NSM Ascot Heath *Ox* 10–13; P-in-c Clewer St Andr 13–15; R from 15; C New Windsor 13–14. *St Andrew's Rectory, 16 Parsonage Lane, Windsor SL4 5EN* T: (01753) 852334 E: rosiewebb@btinternet.com

WEBB, Rosemary. *See* WEBB, Catharine Rosemary Wheatley

WEBB, Timothy Robert. b 57. Univ of Wales (Abth) BA 79 Univ of Wales (Ban) BTh 03 CQSW 89. **d** 03 **p** 04. C Machynlleth w Llanwrin and Penegoes *Ban* 03–06; C Deanery of Llyn and Eifionydd 07–14; R Bro Cymer from 14. *The Rectory, Brecynfer Road, Dolgellau LL40 2YW* M: 07748-962193 E: timbrocymer@outlook.com

WEBB, William John. b 43. Cuddesdon Coll 68. **d** 71 **p** 72. C Weston Favell *Pet* 71–73; C Newport w Longford *Lich* 74–77; C Baswich 77–79; P-in-c Stonnall and Wall 79–83; V Prees and Fauls 83–95; V St Martin's 95–06; rtd 06; PtO *Heref* from 06; *Lich* 09–20. *72 Market Street, Kingswinford DY6 9LH* T: (01384) 295856

WEBBER, Emma Katherine. b 78. Reading Univ BA 99. Ripon Coll Cuddesdon 19. **d** 21. C Pinner *Lon* from 21. *13 Marsh Road, Pinner HA5 5NJ* M: 07855-875619 E: emuworks@hotmail.com

WEBBER, John Arthur. b 45. Keble Coll Ox BA 67 MA 71 Gen Th Sem NY STM 85. Cuddesdon Coll 70. **d** 71 **p** 72. C Penarth All SS *Llan* 71–74; USPG Bangladesh 75–84; 85–91; USA 84–85; Asst P Stepney St Dunstan and All SS *Lon* 91–97; Bp's Adv Relns w People of Other Faiths 91–04; P-in-c Bethnal Green St Barn 97–00; Dir of Ords 00–04; P-in-c St Benet Paul's Wharf 02–04; TR Llantwit Major *Llan* 04–10; rtd 10; PtO *Llan* from 10. *2 Arundel Place, Cardiff CF11 8DP* T: (029) 2039 6400 M: 07745-874839 E: johnwebber342@btinternet.com

WEBBER, Lorna Violet. b 40. **d** 06 **p** 07. OLM Woodbridge St Jo and Bredfield *St E* 06–10; rtd 10; PtO *St E* 10–19. *Deo Gratias, 43 Through Duncans, Woodbridge IP12 4EA* T: (01394) 384634

WEBBER, Canon Michael Champneys Wilfred. b 48. Man Univ BA 71 MA(Theol) 78. Cuddesdon Coll 73. **d** 75 **p** 76. C Caterham *S'wark* 75–79; P-in-c Kidbrooke St Jas 79–84; TV 84–85; V Earls Barton *Pet* 87–09; RD Wellingborough 00–06; P-in-c Daventry, Ashby St Ledgers, Braunston etc 09–16; TR Daventry 16–19; RD 18; Can Pet Cathl 04–19; rtd 19; Hon C Weston Favell *Pet* from 19. *12 Rowlandson Close, Northampton NN3 3PB* T: (01604) 403499 E: michaelc.webber@btinternet.com

WEBBER, Raymond John. b 40. Linc Th Coll 84. **d** 85 **p** 86. C Helston *Truro* 85; C Helston and Wendron 85–90; TV 90–93; R Kenton, Mamhead, Powderham, Cofton and Starcross *Ex* 93–03; rtd 03; PtO *Truro* from 03. *1 Seton Gardens, Camborne TR14 7JS* T: (01209) 711360

WEBBER, Thomas George Edward. b 63. LSE BSc 84. Trin Coll Bris. **d** 98 **p** 99. C Churchdown *Glouc* 98–02; TV Stoke Gifford *Bris* 02–12; V Weston super Mare Ch Ch and Em *B & W* from 12. *The Cedar, Montpelier, Weston-super-Mare BS23 2RQ* T: (01934) 709343 E: vicar@ccwsm.org.uk

WEBBER, Toby Roderic. b 75. St Jo Coll Dur BA 96. Wycliffe Hall Ox BA 01. **d** 02 **p** 03. C Chorley St Laur *Blackb* 02–06; P-in-c Bamber Bridge St Aid 06–12; P-in-c Walton-le-Dale St Leon w Samlesbury St Leon 11–12; Bp's Dom Chapl 12–15; V Altham w Clayton le Moors from 15. *The Vicarage, Church Street, Clayton le Moors, Accrington BB5 5HT*

WEBBLEY, Ms Rachel Catharine. b 75. Hatf Coll Dur BA 98. Qu Coll Birm BA 03. **d** 04 **p** 05. C Bicester w Bucknell, Caversfield and Launton *Ox* 04–07; TV Whitstable *Cant* 07–18; TR from 18; Asst Dir of Ords from 20. *28A West Cliff, Whitstable CT5 1DN* T: (01227) 273329

WEBSTER, Dennis Eric. b 39. Fitzw Ho Cam BA 60 MA 64 Linacre Coll Ox MA 70 Lon Univ CertEd 61. Wycliffe Hall Ox 62. **d** 65 **p** 66. C Herne Bay Ch Ch *Cant* 65–68; V Tulse Hill H Trin *S'wark* 68–69; Missr Kenya 70–75; Chapl Pierrepont Sch Frensham 75–91; R Chiddingfold *Guildf* 91–02; rtd 02; PtO *Guildf* from 02. *Sylvan Cottage, 24 Longdown Road, Lower Bourne, Farnham GU10 3JL* T: (01252) 713919 E: denweb@talktalk.net

WEBSTER, Derek Herbert. b 34. FRSA 82 Hull Univ BA 55 Lon Univ BD 55 Leic Univ MEd 68 PhD 73. Lambeth STh 67 Linc Th Coll 76. **d** 76 **p** 77. Lect Hull Univ from 72; Reader from 97; NSM Cleethorpes *Linc* from 76. *60 Queen's Parade, Cleethorpes DN35 0DG* T: (01472) 693786 E: dwebster@edrev.demon.co.uk or revwebster@btinternet.com

WEBSTER, Canon Diane Margaret. b 43. Oak Hill NSM Course 91. **d** 94 **p** 95. NSM Welwyn Garden City *St Alb* 94–99; P-in-c Burley Ville *Win* 99–10; RD Christchurch 03–10; Hon Can Win Cathl 08–10; rtd 10; PtO *Win* from 10. *Burwood, The Rise, Brockenhurst SO42 7SJ* T: (01590) 624927 E: diane.mwebster@tiscali.co.uk

⌖WEBSTER, The Rt Revd Glyn Hamilton. b 51. SRN 73. Cranmer Hall Dur 74. **d** 77 **p** 78 **c** 13. C Huntington *York* 77–81; V York St Luke 81–92; Chapl York Distr Hosp 81–92; Sen Chapl York Health Services NHS Trust 92–99; Can and Preb York Minster 94–99; Can Res York Minster 99–13; RD City of York 97–04; Assoc Dioc Dir of Ords 05–10; Suff Bp Beverley (PEV) from 13; Hon Asst Bp Liv from 13; Hon Asst Bp Ches from 13; Hon Asst Bp Sheff 13–14; Asst Bp Sheff from 14; Hon Asst Bp Dur from 14; Hon Asst Bp Man from 14; Hon Asst Bp Leeds from 14; rtd 22. *Holy Trinity Rectory, Micklegate, York YO1 6LE* T: (01904) 628155 M: 07983-341323 E: office@seeofbeverley.org.uk or bishopofbeverley@yorkdiocese.org

WEBSTER, James. See WEBSTER, Robin James Cook

WEBSTER, The Ven Martin Duncan. b 52. Nottm Univ BSc 74. Linc Th Coll 75. **d** 78 **p** 79. C Thundersley *Chelmsf* 78–81; C Canvey Is 81–82; TV 82–86; V Nazeing 86–99; RD Harlow 88–99; TR Waltham H Cross 99–09; Hon Can Chelmsf Cathl 00–09; Adn Harlow 09–17; rtd 17; PtO *Sarum* from 17. *22 Ashlands, Ford, Salisbury SP4 6DY* E: martinwebster52@me.com

WEBSTER, Robin James Cook. b 62. Plymouth Poly BSc 86 Cranfield Inst of Tech MSc 87 Cranfield Univ PhD 06. St Jo Coll Nottm MTh 13. **d** 13 **p** 14. C Broxbourne w Wormley *St Alb* 13–16; V Langleybury St Paul from 16; Dioc Officer for IME (2) from 16. *The Vicarage, Langleybury Lane, Kings Langley WD4 8QQ* T: (01923) 270634 M: 07875-080949 E: stpaulslangleybury@gmail.com

WEBSTER, Rosamond Mary. See LATHAM, Rosamond Mary

WEBSTER, Sarah Vernoy. b 38. Univ of Georgia BSc 61. S'wark Ord Course 87. **d** 90 **p** 94. NSM Primrose Hill St Mary w Avenue Road St Paul *Lon* 90–01; Hon C Ann Arbor St Andr USA from 02. *4179 Eastgate Drive, Ann Arbor MI 48103, USA* T: (001) (734) 424 2750 E: revsallyweb@comcast.net

WEBSTER, Canon Stephen Jeremy. b 71. Leic Univ BA 92 PGCE 93. Wycliffe Hall Ox 05. **d** 07 **p** 08. C Oundle w Ashton and Benefield w Glapthorn *Pet* 07–14; R from 14; RD Oundle from 13; Can Pet Cathl from 19. *2 Herons Wood Close, Oundle, Peterborough PE8 4HW* T: (01832) 275634

WEDGBURY, John William. b 53. RMCS BSc 78. St Jo Coll Nottm 84. **d** 87 **p** 88. C Folkestone St Jo *Cant* 87–91; V Mangotsfield *Bris* 91–92; NSM Manselton *S & B* 00–02; P-in-c Caereithin 02–05; NSM Swansea St Thos and Kilvey 05–12; PtO 12–15. *4 Ffynone Drive, Swansea SA1 6DD* T: (01792) 464194

WEDGE, Christopher Graham. b 67. LSE BSc(Econ) 89 Huddersfield Univ PGCE 94. NOC 00. **d** 06 **p** 07. C Castleford *Wakef* 06–09; Dep Chapl Manager United Lincs Hosps NHS Trust 09–11; C Boston *Linc* 11–12; TV 12–14; P-in-c Prestwich St Mary *Man* 14–18; R 18–19; AD Bury 15–16; PtO from 19. *Address temp unknown* E: chrisshef@hotmail.com

WEDGEWOOD, Karsten Eric. b 77. **d** 12 **p** 13. C Davyhulme St Mary *Man* 12–13; C Farnworth, Kearsley and Stoneclough 13–15; P-in-c Pendeen w Morvah *Truro* from 15; P-in-c Sancreed 15–16; P-in-c St Just in Penwith from 15. *Ermelo, Pendeen, Penzance TR19 7SQ* M: 07525-831386 E: karstenwedgewood@gmail.com

WEDGEWORTH, Canon Michael John. b 40. MBE 10. Nottm Univ BSc 62. Wesley Ho Cam MA 66. **d** 93 **p** 94. In Methodist Ch 66–93; NSM Feniscowles *Blackb* 93–96; Sec DBF 95–05; Hon P Blackb Cathl from 95; LtO 96–05; PtO from 05; Hon Can Blackb Cathl 03–10. *Abbott House, 74 King Street, Whalley, Clitheroe BB7 9SN* T: (01254) 825694 E: mike.wedgeworth@blackburn.anglican.org.uk or michael_wedgeworth@hotmail.com

WEEDEN, Canon Simon Andrew. b 55. York Univ BA 79. Wycliffe Hall Ox 88. **d** 90 **p** 91. C Gt Chesham *Ox* 90–94; P-in-c Haversham w Lt Linford, Tyringham w Filgrave 94–97; R Lamp 97–99; P-in-c Bramshott and Liphook *Portsm* 99–00; R 00–10; RD Petersfield 04–09; TR Whitton *Sarum* 10–19; Can and Preb Sarum Cathl 16–19; rtd 19; PtO *Ox* from 20. *5 Newbolt Close, Newport Pagnell MK16 8ND* E: simon@weeden.plus.com

WEEKES, David John. b 34. Magd Coll Cam BA 59 MA 68 Lon Univ PGCE 68 Aber Univ MTh 79 St Andr Univ PhD 17 FSAScot FRHistS. Clifton Th Coll 62. **d** 64 **p** 65. C Cheadle *Ches* 64–68; Chapl Ntare Sch Mbarara Uganda 69–73; PtO *St And* 73–74; Chapl and Hd of RE Fettes Coll Edin 74–94; Warden and Chapl Lee Abbey Internat Students' Club Kensington 94–01; rtd 01; PtO *Lon* 94–03. *Loaning Hill House, Kilmany, Cupar KY15 4PT* T: (01382) 330183 M: 07855-761970

WEEKES, Robin Alasdair Rutley. b 73. Peterho Cam MA 94. Wycliffe Hall Ox BA 98 MA 98. **d** 99 **p** 00. C Wimbledon Em Ridgway Prop Chpl *S'wark* 99–03; Crosslinks India 03–10; Tutor Cornhill Tr Course 10–13; Min Wimbledon Em Ridgway Prop Chpl from 13. *Emmanuel Parsonage, 8 Sheep Walk Mews, London SW19 4QL* T: (020) 8946 4613 M: 07811-384350 E: robin.weekes@emmanuelwimbledon.org.uk

WEEKS, Ms Jane Anne. b 61. UEA BA 00. Aston Tr Scheme 95 EAMTC 97. **d** 00 **p** 01. C Hadleigh *St E* 00–02; C Hadleigh, Layham and Shelley 02–03; Chapl HM Pris Bullwood Hall 03–06; Chapl HM Pris Cookham Wood 06–08; PtO *Cant* 09–10; R Hever, Four Elms and Mark Beech *Roch* 10–16; P-in-c Elham w Denton and Wootton and Acrise *Cant* 16–19; P-in-c Lyminge w Paddlesworth, Stanford w Postling etc 18–19; R Elham Valley from 20; AD Elham from 19. *The Vicarage, Vicarage Lane, Elham, Canterbury CT4 6TT* T: (01303) 840219 E: revweeks@hotmail.com

WEEKS, Mrs Rachel Elizabeth (Kim). b 51. STETS 09. **d** 14. NSM Portsea N End St Mark *Portsm* from 14. *7 Kingfisher Court, Portsmouth PO3 5XE* T: (023) 9269 8969 M: 07878-299231 E: kimeweeks@gmail.com

WEEKS, Timothy Robert. b 47. SAOMC 03. **d** 08 **p** 09. NSM Royston *St Alb* 08–12; LtO 12–17; Chapl Princess Alexandra Hosp NHS Trust from 08; PtO *Chelmsf* 09–16; *St Alb* from 17. *6 Chantry Road, Bishop's Stortford CM23 2SF* T: (01279) 831404 or (01763) 243265 M: 07974-866016

WEETMAN, Mrs Dorothy. b 41. **d** 03 **p** 04. OLM Prudhoe *Newc* 03–09; rtd 09; PtO *Newc* from 09. *Station Gate East, Eltringham Road, Prudhoe NE42 6LA* T: (01661) 834538

WEETMAN, Canon John Charles. b 66. Qu Coll Ox BA 87 MA 92. Trin Coll Bris BA 91. **d** 91 **p** 92. C Hull St Jo Newland *York* 91–95; V Boosbeck w Moorsholm 95–02; V Redcar 02–11; RD Guisborough 99–11; V Selby Abbey from 11; Can and Preb York Minster from 05. *The Abbey Vicarage, 32A Leeds Road, Selby YO8 4HX* T: (01757) 705130 E: weetman217@btinternet.com

WEIGHTMAN, Andrea Frances. See WARD, Andrea Frances

WEIGHTMAN, David Courtenay. b 47. FRICS 88. **d** 04 **p** 05. OLM Oxted and Tandridge *S'wark* 04–14; OLM Oxted 14–17; PtO from 17. *13 Silkham Road, Oxted RH8 0NP* T: (01883) 715420 F: 717336 M: 07739-456947 E: davidcweightman@gmail.com

WEIL, Thomas James. b 53. K Coll Lon BSc 74 PhD 79 AKC 74. S Tr Scheme 95. **d** 97 **p** 99. NSM Stoughton *Guildf* 97–03; PtO *Lon* 03–13; *Guildf* 04–15; NSM Worplesdon from 15. *Address withheld by request*

WEIR, David Alexander. b 69. City Univ BSc 91 Fitzw Coll Cam BA 94 MA 99 Chich Univ BA 08 Sarum Coll MA 19. Westcott Ho Cam 92. **d** 95 **p** 97. C Locks Heath *Portsm* 95–96; C W Leigh 96–00; C Leigh Park and Warren Park 00–01; PtO 03–05; NSM Portsea St Mary 05–08; PtO *Truro* 08–09; P-in-c Exford, Exmoor, Hawkridge and Withypool *B & W* 09–12; P-in-c Exton and Winsford and Cutcombe w Luxborough 11–12; R Exmoor from 12; Warden of Readers Taunton Adnry 14–17. *The Rectory, Exford, Minehead TA24 7LX* T: (01643) 831330 E: david.weir122@btinternet.com

WEIR, Graham Francis. b 52. GSM LASI. NOC 88. **d** 91 **p** 92. NSM High Crompton *Man* 91–92; NSM Heyside 92–94; Asst Chapl Bolton Hosps NHS Trust 94–96; Chapl Bolton NHS Foundn Trust 96–12; Dep Hd of Chapl 04–12; PtO *Man* 13–18; Chapl OHP 13–17; rtd 17; PtO *York* from 17. *10 Field Close, Whitby YO21 3LR* E: gweir52@hotmail.co.uk

WEIR, John Michael Vavasour. b 48. K Coll Lon BD 72 AKC 72 MA 00. **d** 73 **p** 74. C Hatfield Hyde *St Alb* 73–76; C Watford St Mich 76–79; Asst Chapl Oslo St Edm *Eur* 80–81; V Bethnal Green St Pet w St Thos *Lon* 81–04; Chapl Qu Eliz Hosp for Children Lon 81–98; Chapl Team Ldr Toc H 01–10; Sen Chapl Dubai and Sharjah w N Emirates 04–10; rtd 10; PtO *Lon* from 13. *38 Belgrave Street, London E1 0NQ* T: (020) 7791 7957 E: jmvweir@gmail.com

WEIR, John William Moon. b 36. St Luke's Coll Ex CertEd 69 Ex Univ BEd 76. SWMTC 82. **d** 85 **p** 86. NSM Meavy, Sheepstor and Walkhampton *Ex* 85–87; NSM Yelverton, Meavy, Sheepstor and Walkhampton 87–05; Hd Master Princetown Primary Sch 86–94; Sub-Chapl HM Pris Dartmoor 86–94; PtO *Ex* from 05. *Goblin's Green, Dousland, Yelverton PL20 6ND* T: (01822) 852671

WEIR, Nicholas James. b 77. Pemb Coll Cam BA 98 MA 02 Green Coll Ox BM, BCh 01 MRCPsych 05. Oak Hill Th Coll MTh 11. **d** 11 **p** 12. C Eastrop *Win* 11–15; V Frogmore *St Alb* from 15. *The Vicarage, 39 Frogmore, St Albans AL2 2JU* T: (01727) 872172

WEIR, Ms Rachel Sian Shapland. b 66. Newnham Coll Cam BA 88 MA 91 Called to the Bar 91. Ripon Coll Cuddesdon MTh 07. **d** 07 **p** 08. Asst Nat Adv for Inter Faith Relns Abps' Coun 07–08; NSM Wolvercote *Ox* 07–08; NSM Headington Quarry 09–11; Chapl Highgate Sch Lon 14–18; Min Can St Paul's Cathl *Lon* 18–19; PtO *Ox* from 14; *Lon* from 20; NSM Reading St Mark and All SS *Ox* 20–21. *Blackhall Farm, Garford Road, Oxford OX2 6UY* M: 07815-729565 E: rachelssweir@yahoo.co.uk

WEIR, William Daniel Niall. b 57. UEA BA 79. Ripon Coll Cuddesdon 80. **d** 83 **p** 84. C Chelsea St Luke *Lon* 83–87; PV Westmr Abbey 85–89; C Poplar *Lon* 87–88; TV 88–93; P-in-c Forest Gate Em w Upton Cross *Chelmsf* 93–97; V 97–99; Asst Chapl Southn Univ Hosps NHS Trust 99–00; Trust Chapl 00–03; R W Hackney *Lon* from 03. *The Rectory, 306 Amhurst Road, London N16 7UE* T: (020) 7254 3235 E: niall.weir@mac.com

WEISSERHORN, Julian Timothy David Moritz. *See* GADSBY, Julian Timothy David Moritz

WEITZMANN, Benjamin Edward Albert. b 80. Surrey Univ BSc 03. St Steph Ho Ox BTh 15. **d** 15 **p** 16. C Boxmoor St Jo *St Alb* 15–18; TV Portsea N End St Mark *Portsm* from 18; P-in-c Portsea St Sav from 18; C Portsea Ascension 18–20; P-in-c from 20. *The Vicarage, 98 Kirby Road, Portsmouth PO2 0PW* M: 07887-484080 E: benjamin@weitzmann.co.uk

WELBORN, Miles Herbert John. b 94. Dur Univ BA 21. Ripon Coll Cuddesdon 18. **d** 21. C Bampton w Clanfield *Ox* from 21. *3 Park View Lane, Witney OX28 1FZ* M: 07919-663680 E: miles.welborn@outlook.com

WELBOURN, David Anthony. b 41. K Coll Lon BD 63 AKC 63. St Boniface Warminster 63. **d** 64 **p** 65. C Stockton St Chad *Dur* 64–67; C S Westoe 69–74; Ind Chapl 69–80; Ind Chapl *Nor* 80–90; Ind and Commerce Officer *Guildf* 90–06; rtd 06; PtO *Guildf* 06–17. *3 Windgates, Guildford GU4 7DJ* T/F: (01483) 825541 E: welbourn@ntlworld.com

✠**WELBY, The Most Revd and Rt Hon Justin Portal.** b 56. PC 13. Trin Coll Cam BA 78 MA 90 St Jo Coll Dur BA 91 Hon FCT. Cranmer Hall Dur 89. **d** 92 **p** 93 **c** 11. C Chilvers Coton w Astley *Cov* 92–95; R Southam 95–02; V Ufton 96–02; Can Res Cov Cathl 02–07; Co-Dir Internat Min 02–05; Sub-Dean

05–07; P-in-c Cov H Trin 07; Dean Liv 07–11; Bp Dur 11–13; Abp Cant from 13. *Lambeth Palace, London SE1 7JU* T: (020) 7898 1200 E: contact@lambethpalace.org.uk

WELBY, Peter Edlin Brown. b 34. Open Univ BA 75. Cranmer Hall Dur 75. **d** 77 **p** 78. C Auckland St Andr and St Anne *Dur* 77–79; C S Westoe 79–81; V Tudhoe 81–93; R Croxdale and Tudhoe 93–99; rtd 99; PtO *Dur* 04–21. *Blyth House, 9 Rhodes Terrace, Nevilles Cross, Durham DH1 4JW* T: 0191-384 8295

WELCH, Amanda Jane. b 58. **d** 04 **p** 05. OLM Worplesdon *Guildf* 04–17; rtd 17; PtO *Heref* from 18. *Oak Barn, Brinsop Court Park, Brinsop, Hereford HR4 7AX* E: revmandywelch@gmail.com

WELCH, Gordon Joseph. b 47. Man Univ BSc 68 MSc 69 PhD 72. NOC 84. **d** 87 **p** 88. NSM Upton Ascension *Ches* 87–98; LtO 99–00; NSM Backford and Capenhurst 00–02; NSM Ellesmere Port from 02; RD Wirral S 06–11. *6 St James's Avenue, Upton, Chester CH2 1NA* T: (01244) 382196 M: 07890-993948 E: gordonwelch@btinternet.com

WELCH, John Harry. b 52. Oak Hill Th Coll 85. **d** 87 **p** 88. C Parr *Liv* 87–90; V W Derby St Luke 90–00; V Eccleston Park 00–07; P-in-c St Helens St Matt Thatto Heath 06–07; TR Eccleston 07–17; Chapl Willowbrook Hospice 01–12; rtd 17. *10 Bobbin Mill, Spark Bridge, Ulverston LA12 8BS*

WELCH, Pamela Jean. b 47. Girton Coll Cam MA 76 K Coll Lon BD 79 AKC 79 PhD 05. Qu Coll Birm 79. **dss** 80 **d** 87. Tottenham H Trin *Lon* 80–84; Asst Chapl Bryanston Sch 84–87; PtO *Chich* 87–94; C Mornington St Mary NZ 02–09; PtO Dunedin from 08; PtO Christchurch from 18. *2A Church Street, Amberley, Amberley 7410, New Zealand*

WELCH, Paul Baxter. b 47. Lanc Univ BEd 74 MA 75. St Alb Minl Tr Scheme 80. **d** 83 **p** 84. NSM Heath and Reach *St Alb* 83–84; Bp's Sch Adv *Win* 84–89; P-in-c Clungunford w Clunbury and Clunton, Bedstone etc *Heref* 89–93; V Wellingborough All SS *Pet* 93–01; R Pulborough *Chich* 01–16; RD Storrington 04–11; TV Crawley 16–17; V Green 17–21; rtd 21. *6 Willowbrook, Bognor Regis PO22 6PD* M: 07759-695110 E: paulbwelch@live.co.uk

WELCH, Rebecca Anne. *See* JONES, Rebecca Anne

WELCH, Canon Sally Ann. b 62. Pemb Coll Ox MA 88. SAOMC 96. **d** 99 **p** 00. NSM Abingdon *Ox* 99–01; P-in-c Kintbury w Avington 01–05; R Cherbury w Gainfield 05–09; C Ox St Giles and SS Phil and Jas w St Marg 09–15; V Charlbury w Shorthampton from 15; AD Chipping Norton 15–21; Hon Can Ch Ch from 21. *The Vicarage, Church Lane, Charlbury, Chipping Norton OX7 3PX* M: 07974-439630 E: vicar@charlburychurch.uk

WELCH, The Ven Stephan John. b 50. Hull Univ BA 74 Lon Univ MTh 98. Qu Coll Birm 74. **d** 77 **p** 78. C Waltham Cross *St Alb* 77–80; P-in-c Reculver *Cant* 80–86; P-in-c Herne Bay St Bart 82–86; V Reculver and Herne Bay St Bart 86–92; V Hurley and Stubbings *Ox* 92–00; P-in-c Hammersmith St Pet *Lon* 00–06; AD Hammersmith and Fulham 01–06; Adn Middx 06–19; rtd 20; PtO *Lon* from 20. *29 Cleminson Gardens, Cottingham HU16 4RW* E: rabelais.welch@gmail.com

WELDON, Nicholas Patrick. b 77. UWE BSc 99. Oak Hill Th Coll BA 07. **d** 07 **p** 08. C Moreton-in-Marsh w Batsford, Todenham etc *Glouc* 07–11; P-in-c N Tawton, Bondleigh, Sampford Courtenay etc *Ex* 11–13; TV Chagford, Gidleigh, Throwleigh etc from 13; RD Okehampton 16–20. *The Rectory, Essington Close, North Tawton EX20 2EX* T: (01837) 880183 M: 07970-984190 E: npweldon@gmail.com

WELDON, Robert Price. b 57. Cant Ch Ch Univ BA 12. SEITE 06. **d** 09 **p** 10. NSM Caterham *S'wark* 09–13; C G7 Benefice *Cant* 13–16; V Folkestone Trin from 16. *The Trinity Benefice Vicarage, 21 Manor Road, Folkestone CT20 2SA* T: (01303) 253831 M: 07929-866879 E: revbob62@gmail.com

WELDON, William Ernest. b 41. TCD BA 62 MA 66. **d** 64 **p** 65. C Belfast Trin Coll Miss *Conn* 64–67; C Carnmoney 67–71; Chapl RN 71–96; QHC 93–96; Hon C Holbeton *Ex* 96–01; PtO 01–18. *3 Garden Close, Holbeton, Plymouth PL8 1NQ* T: (01752) 830139 E: billanddinahweldon@btopenworld.com

WELFORD, Gillian Margaret. b 44. Westf Coll Lon BA 65. Guildf Dioc Min Course 01. **d** 04 **p** 05. OLM Chiddingfold *Guildf* 04–14; PtO from 14. *15 Woodberry Close, Chiddingfold, Godalming GU8 4SF* T: (01428) 683620 E: gill@welford.myzen.co.uk

WELHAM, Mrs Clare. b 77. Univ Coll Dur BA 98 MA 00. WEMTC 09. **d** 12 **p** 13. C Stroud Team *Glouc* 12–14; Asst Chapl Harrogate Ladies' Coll 15–16; C High Harrogate Ch Ch *Leeds* 15–16; P-in-c Bishop's Sutton and Ropley and W Tisted *Win* from 17. *The Vicarage, Lyeway Lane, Ropley, Alresford SO24 0DW* T: (01962) 773075 E: clarewelham77@gmail.com

WELHAM, Clive Richard. b 54. d 80 p 81. C Bellingham St Dunstan *S'wark* 80–84; Chapl Goldsmiths' Coll Lon 84–95; V Plumstead Ascension 95–10; P-in-c Plumstead St Mark and St Marg 07–10; V Plumstead Common from 10; AD Plumstead 14–20. *The Vicarage, 42 Jago Close, London SE18 2TY* T: (020) 8854 3395

WELLBELOVE, Sophie Rebecca. *See* LOVESMITH, Sophie Rebecca

WELLER, Sophie Helen. b 74. Lon Bible Coll 97 St Mellitus Coll 18. d 21. C Tye Green w Netteswell *Chelmsf* from 21. *29 Durnell Way, Loughton IG10 1TG* T: (020) 8923 0434 M: 07583-762004 E: sofishies@hotmail.com

WELLER (née SPENCE), The Ven Susan Karen. b 65. Leeds Univ BSc 86 Liv Univ PhD 89. Wycliffe Hall Ox BA 95. d 96 p 97. C Caverswall and Weston Coyney w Dilhorne *Lich* 96–00; C Wilnecote 00–05; Dioc Adv for Women in Min 00–04; Brazil 05–11; PtO *Lich* 11–14; Adn Walsall 15–19; Adn Lich from 19. *Unit 1 Three Spires House, Station Road, Lichfield WS13 6HX* T: (01543) 306145 E: archdeacon.lichfield@lichfield.anglican.org

WELLINGTON, James Frederick. b 51. Leic Univ LLB 72 Fitzw Coll Cam BA 76 MA 11 Nottm Univ MPhil 91 Lambeth PhD 14. Ridley Hall Cam 74. d 77 p 78. C Mill Hill Jo Keble Ch *Lon* 77–80; C Wood Green St Mich w Bounds Green St Gabr etc 80–83; V Stocking Farm *Leic* 83–90; V Gt Glen, Stretton Magna and Wistow etc 90–98; Warden of Readers 91–97; RD Gartree II 96–98; TR Syston 98–07; RD Goscote 00–06; Hon Can Leic Cathl 94–07; R Keyworth and Stanton-on-the-Wolds and Bunny etc *S'well* 07–16; AD E Bingham 08–15; rtd 16; PtO *S'well* from 16. *Michaelmas House, 28 Dunholme Avenue, Newark NG24 4AR* T: (01636) 674490 E: jhcwelli@btinternet.com

WELLMAN, Mrs Karen Ann. b 62. BNC Ox BA 84. Ox Min Course 09. d 12 p 13. C Basingstoke *Win* 12–15; P-in-c Teddington St Mark *Lon* 15–17; V from 17. *The Vicarage, St Marks Road, Teddington TW11 9DE* E: revkarenwellman@btinternet.com

WELLS, Adrian Mosedale. b 61. SWMTC 96. d 99 p 00. NSM Kingskerswell w Coffinswell *Ex* 99–02; C Wolborough and Ogwell 02–13; TV Burrington, Chawleigh, Cheldon, Chulmleigh etc from 13; RD S Molton from 15. *The Vicarage, The Square, Witheridge, Tiverton EX16 8AE* T: (01884) 861383 E: vicaradrian@btinternet.com

WELLS, Andrew Peter. b 54. Birm Poly BEd 83 Birm Univ BPhil 86 Open Univ BA 92. Qu Foundn Birm 12. d 15 p 16. NSM The Quinton *Birm* from 15. *89 Upper Meadow Road, Quinton, Birmingham B32 1NR* T: 0121-689 0376 M: 07977-579894 E: apwells1954@hotmail.com

WELLS, Andrew Stuart. b 48. St Jo Coll Dur BA 71 Man Metrop Univ PGCE 04. Cranmer Hall Dur. d 74 p 75. C Walmsley *Man* 74–77; C Failsworth H Family 77–79; R Openshaw 79–90; V Hindsford 90–98. *1 Henry Street, Haslington, Crewe CW1 5PS* T: (01270) 585303 E: andrewwells@hotmail.com

WELLS, Antony Ernest. b 36. Oak Hill Th Coll 58. d 61 p 62. C Bethnal Green St Jas Less *Lon* 61–64; SAMS Paraguay 64–69; V Kirkdale St Athanasius *Liv* 69–73; SAMS Argentina 73–75; V Warfield *Ox* 75–81; V Fairfield *Liv* 81–83; C Rainhill 83–85; TV Cheltenham St Mark *Glouc* 85–89; P-in-c Forest of Dean Ch Ch w English Bicknor 89–95; rtd 97; C Pinhoe and Broadclyst *Ex* 02–04. *4 Case Gardens, Seaton EX12 2AP* T: (01297) 20482 E: gentonwells@btinternet.com

WELLS, Daniel Michael. b 74. Trin Coll Cam MA 95 Cam Inst of Educn PGCE 97. Wycliffe Hall Ox BTh 05. d 06 p 07. C Plymouth St Andr and Stonehouse *Ex* 06–09; C W Hampstead St Luke *Lon* 09–12; C Langham Place All So 12–18; V Richmond H Trin and Ch Ch *S'wark* from 18. *The Vicarage, Sheen Park, Richmond TW9 1UP* E: dan@wellsweb.org.uk *or* dan.wells@htrichmond.org.uk

WELLS, David. b 63. Imp Coll Lon BSc 85 ARCS 85. EAMTC 97. d 00 p 01. C Sprowston w Beeston *Nor* 00–03; P-in-c Drayton w Felthorpe 03–05; R Drayton 05–18; R Caister from 18. *The Rectory, Rectory Close, Caister-on-Sea, Great Yarmouth NR30 5EG* E: david.wells@btinternet.com

WELLS, Mrs Gillian Lesley. b 50. Anglia Ruskin Univ BA 14. Nor Ord Course 07. d 10 p 11. OLM Reepham, Hackford w Whitwell, Kerdiston etc *Nor* 10–15; C Dereham and Distr 15; TV 15–20; rtd 20; PtO *Nor* from 20. *30 Granary Way, Hingham, Norwich NR9 4FA* M: 07597-306414 E: gilliewells1@btinternet.com

WELLS, Jeremy Stephen. b 47. Nottm Univ BA 69 UWE MSc 97. Chich Th Coll 72. d 73 p 74. C S Yardley St Mich *Birm* 73–76; C St Marychurch *Ex* 76–78; P-in-c Bridgwater H Trin *B & W* 78–82; P-in-c Brent Knoll 82–84; P-in-c E Brent w Lympsham 82–84; R Brent Knoll, E Brent and Lympsham 84–99; PtO *Chich* 99–07; rtd 07. *15A Victoria Close, Burgess Hill RH15 9QS* T: (01444) 244275

✠**WELLS, The Rt Revd Joanne Caladine Bailey.** b 65. CCC Cam BA 87 MA 90 Univ of Minnesota MA 90 St Jo Coll Dur BA 92 PhD 97. Cranmer Hall Dur. d 95 p 96 c 16. Chapl Clare Coll Cam 95–98; Dean 98–01; Tutor Ridley Hall Cam 01–05; PtO *Ely* 95–05; Nor 99–04; Dir Angl Episc Ho of Studies Duke Div Sch N Carolina USA 05–12; Abp's Chapl Cant 13–16; Can Th Liv Cathl 15–16; Suff Bp Dorking *Guildf* from 16. *Church House, 20 Alan Turing Road, Surrey Research Park, Guildford GU2 7YF* T: (01483) 790343 E: bishop.jo@cofeguildford.org.uk

WELLS, John Charles. b 44. St Jo Coll Nottm 00. d 19. NSM Scarborough St Mary w Ch Ch and H Apostles *York* from 19. *38 Newby Farm Crescent, Scarborough YO12 6UW* T: (01723) 352777 M: 07812-707628 E: john@sllew.go-plus.net

WELLS, Judith Margaret. b 48. Whitelands Coll Lon CertEd 71. Trin Coll Bris 09. d 11 p 12. OLM Purton *Bris* from 11. *The Live and Let Live, 7 Upper Pavenhill, Purton, Swindon SN5 4DQ* T: (01793) 770627 M: 07760-400257

WELLS, Kirsty Julia. b 73. Coll of SS Mark and Jo Plymouth BEd 95. Sarum Coll BA 16. d 16 p 17. C Sturminster Newton, Hinton St Mary and Lydlinch *Sarum* 16–20; Chapl Taunton and Somerset NHS Foundn Trust 20; P-in-c Woolavington w Cossington and Bawdrip *B & W* from 21. *7 Vicarage Road, Woolavington, Bridgwater TA7 8DX* M: 07581-250608 E: revkirsty@hotmail.com

WELLS, Canon Leslie John. b 61. Univ of Wales (Ban) BTh 06. d 04 p 05. OLM St Helier *S'wark* 04–08; C Morden 08–10; TV 10–17; AD Merton 16–17; TR Horley from 17; Hon Can S'wark Cathl from 17. *4 Russells Crescent, Horley RH6 7DN* T: (01293) 782218 M: 07804-231492 E: leswells80@hotmail.com *or* parishoffice@stbartshorley.org

WELLS, Canon Lydia Margaret Debert. b 50. Dur Univ BA 72 Sheff Univ MPhil 92 Leeds Univ MA 00. NOC 97. d 00 p 01. C Adwick-le-Street w Skelbrooke *Sheff* 00–03; V Doncaster Intake 03–09; V Sheff St Pet and St Oswald 09–14; AD Ecclesall 12–14; Hon Can Sheff Cathl 12–14; rtd 14; PtO *Sheff* from 14. *Apartment 1, 17 Bluecoat Rise, Sheffield S11 9DW* T: 0114-258 3097 M: 07803-710573 E: lydmwells@gmail.com

WELLS, Michael John. b 46. Univ Coll Ox BA 68 MA 73 Solicitor 74. S Dios Minl Tr Scheme 92. d 95 p 96. NSM Brighton St Pet w Chpl Royal *Chich* 95–98; Sen C 99–04; NSM Brighton St Bart 98–99; rtd 04; PtO *Chich* 04–10; P-in-c Brighton Annunciation 10–16; PtO from 16. *35 Park Crescent, Brighton BN2 3HB* T: (01273) 600735

WELLS, Nicholas Anthony. b 60. Cranmer Hall Dur 88. d 91 p 92. C Accrington St Jo w Huncoat *Blackb* 91–94; C Douglas St Geo and St Barn *S & M* 94–95; C Douglas All SS and St Thos 95–97; V Onchan 97–03; V Netherton *Liv* 03–07; AD Bootle 05–07; P-in-c Maghull 07–09; TR Maghull and Melling 09–16; AD Ormskirk 10–16; V Lytham St Cuth *Blackb* from 16; P-in-c Lytham St Jo from 20; Hon Can Liv Cathl 05–16. *St Cuthbert's Vicarage, Church Road, Lytham, Lytham St Annes FY8 5PX* E: nick.the-vic@blueyonder.co.uk

WELLS, Canon Peter Robert. b 59. Wilson Carlile Coll 78 Sarum & Wells Th Coll 87. d 89 p 90. CA from 81; C Mortlake w E Sheen *S'wark* 89–93; Dir St Marylebone Healing and Counselling Cen 93–97; TV N Lambeth *S'wark* 97–00; Chapl Trin Hospice Lon 97–03; Chapl Brighton and Sussex Univ Hosps NHS Trust 03–19; Can and Preb Chich Cathl 10–19; rtd 19; PtO *Chich* from 19. *10 Lewes Mews, Arundel Place, Brighton BN2 1GR*

WELLS, Philip Anthony. b 83. UEA BA 04 Leeds Univ BA 07 MA 08. Coll of Resurr Mirfield 05. d 08 p 09. C Holt w High Kelling *Nor* 08–11; Bp's Dom Chapl *Wakef* 11–13; V Lamorbey H Trin *Roch* 13–19; AD Sidcup 16–19; V Wantage *Ox* from 19. *The Vicarage, The Cloisters, Wantage OX12 8AQ* T: (01235) 762214 E: vicar@wantageparish.com

WELLS, Canon Philip Anthony. b 57. BA MPhil. Coll of Resurr Mirfield. d 84 p 85. C Wylde Green *Birm* 84–87; Chapl and Succ Birm Cathl 87–91; Bp's Dom Chapl 91–97; V Polesworth from 97; Hon Can Birm Cathl from 16. *The Vicarage, 26 High Street, Polesworth, Tamworth B78 1DU* T: (01827) 892340 E: polesworthabbey@aol.com

WELLS, The Ven Roderick John. b 36. Dur Univ BA 63 Hull Univ MA 85. Cuddesdon Coll 63. d 65 p 66. C Lambeth St Mary the Less *S'wark* 65–66; C Kennington Cross St Anselm 66–68; P-in-c 68–71; R Skegness *Linc* 71–77; P-in-c Winthorpe 77; R Skegness and Winthorpe 77–78; TR Gt and Lt Coates w Bradley 78–89; RD Grimsby and Cleethorpes 83–89; Can and Preb Linc Cathl 86–01; Adn Stow 89–01; V Hackthorn w Cold Hanworth 89–93; P-in-c N w S Carlton 89–93; rtd 01; PtO *Linc* 01–17; *Pet* from 01; Leic from 10. *5 Wheatfield Way, Barleythorpe, Oakham LE15 7UD* T: (01572) 492778 E: venrjw@gmail.com

WELLS, Ruth Mary. b 80. Ox Brookes Univ BA 03. Ripon Coll Cuddesdon MA 17. **d** 17 **p** 18. C W Moors *Sarum* 17–20; Chapl Bournemouth Univ from 20; Chapl Arts Univ Bournemouth from 20; PtO *Win* from 21. *29 Venator Place, Wimborne BH21 1DQ* M: 07715-670319 E: ruthwells@rocketmail.com *or* rwells@bournemouth.ac.uk

WELLS, Mrs Sally Ursula. b 40. St Mark's Coll Canberra BTh 93 Ripon Coll Cuddesdon 96. **d** 97 **p** 98. Asst Chapl Vienna *Eur* 97–02; PtO 02–06; rtd 06; PtO *Sarum* from 11. *10 Park Street, Salisbury SP1 3AU* T: (01722) 322954 E: wellsfrance@gmail.com

WELLS, Canon Samuel Martin Bailey. b 65. Mert Coll Ox BA 87 MA 95 Edin Univ BD 91 Dur Univ PhD 96. Edin Th Coll 88. **d** 91 **p** 92. C Wallsend St Luke *Newc* 91–95; C Cherry Hinton St Andr *Ely* 95–97; C Teversham 95–97; P-in-c Earlham St Eliz *Nor* 97–03; RD Nor S 99–03; P-in-c Cambridge St Mark *Ely* 03–05; Can Th and Wiccamical Preb Chich Cathl from 04; Dean Duke Chpl Duke Univ N Carolina USA 05–12; V St Martin-in-the-Fields *Lon* from 12; Hon Can Th Guildf Cathl from 18. *6 St Martin's Place, London WC2N 4JJ* T: (020) 7766 1107 E: sam.wells@smitf.org

WELLS, Terry Roy John. b 45. EAMTC 89. **d** 92 **p** 93. C Martlesham w Brightwell *St E* 92–95; R Higham, Holton St Mary, Raydon and Stratford 95–00; TV Walton and Trimley 00–07; rtd 07; PtO *Chelmsf* 07–16; *St E* 07–21. *Apartment 2, 1 The Maltings, The Quayside Maltings, High Street, Mistley, Manningtree CO11 1AL* T: (01206) 392957 E: terry.wells987@gmail.com

WELLS, Archdeacon of. *See* GELL, The Ven Anne Elizabeth

WELLS, Dean of. *See* DAVIES, The Very Revd John Harverd

WELSBY, George Andrew. b 61. St Martin's Coll Lanc BA 82 Leeds Univ BA 98 De Montfort Univ BA 09. Coll of Resurr Mirfield 96. **d** 98 **p** 99. C W Derby St Jo *Liv* 98–02; V Nuneaton St Mary *Cov* 02–07; PtO *Lich* 08–10; V Willenhall St Giles 10–18; P-in-c Willenhall St Anne 10–14; V 14–18; V Haydock St Jas *Liv* 18–21; rtd 21. *Address temp unknown* E: andrew.welsby@hotmail.co.uk

WELSH, Jennifer Ann. b 48. Univ Coll Lon BA. **d** 81 **p** 98. NSM Newport St Matt *Mon* 81–85; NSM Risca 85–04; NSM Maindee Newport 04–09; PtO *Worc* from 12. *470 Caerleon Road, Newport NP19 7LW* T: (01633) 258287 E: mtrjen@btinternet.com

WELSH, Mrs Jennifer Lee. b 59. Calgary Univ BSc 81. Cam Episc Div Sch (USA) MDiv 87. **d** 87 **p** 88. C Calgary H Nativity Canada 87–89; Asst Chapl HM Pris Linc 89–94; Asst Chapl HM Pris Win 95–02; Chapl to Lutheran Students 03–08; PtO *Win* 95–02; *Lon* 03–08; Chapl Univ Coll 08–13; C St Pancras w St Jas and Ch Ch 08–13; C Kensington St Mary Abbots 13–17; V W Brompton St Mary w St Peter and St Jude from 17; AD Chelsea from 19. *St Mary's Vicarage, 24 Fawcett Street, London SW10 9EZ* E: vicar@stmarytheboltons.org.uk

WELSH, Philip Peter. b 48. Keble Coll Ox BA 69 MA 73 Selw Coll Cam BA 72 MA 76. Westcott Ho Cam 71. **d** 73 **p** 74. C W Dulwich All SS and Em *S'wark* 73–76; C Surbiton St Andr and St Mark 76–79; Lect St Steph Coll Delhi India 79–81; V Malden St Jo *S'wark* 81–87; Min Officer *Linc* 87–94; TR Basingstoke *Win* 94–02; V Westmr St Steph w St Jo *Lon* 02–13; rtd 13; PtO *Lon* from 13. *St Mary's Vicarage, 24 Fawcett Street, London SW10 9EZ* E: philipwelsh66@gmail.com

WELSH, Robert Leslie. b 32. Sheff Univ BA 54. St Jo Coll Dur. **d** 58 **p** 59. C S Westoe *Dur* 58–62; C Darlington St Cuth 62–66; CF (TA) 64–67; V E Rainton *Dur* 66–85; R W Rainton 66–85; R Wolsingham and Thornley 85–97; rtd 97; PtO *Dur* 97–17. *12 Lea Green, Wolsingham, Bishop Auckland DL13 3DU* T: (01388) 528529 E: r.l.welsh@btinternet.com

WELSMAN, Canon Derek Brian. b 65. Trin Coll Bris. **d** 99 **p** 00. C Ash *Guildf* 99–02; V Easebourne *Chich* 02–10; P-in-c Lurgashall, Lodsworth and Selham 08–10; V Easebourne, Lodsworth and Selham from 10; P-in-c Lynchmere and Camelsdale 15–16; RD Midhurst from 10; Acting Adn Horsham 20–21; Can and Preb Chich Cathl from 21. *Northgate, Dodsley Grove, Easebourne, Midhurst GU29 9BE* T: (01730) 812655 *or* 813341 E: derek.welsman@outlook.com *or* derek.welsman@chichester.anglican.org

WELTERS, Mrs Elizabeth Ann. b 49. Bris Univ BSc 70 Reading Univ PGCE 71. SAOMC 94. **d** 97 **p** 98. NSM Aylesbury *Ox* 97–03; NSM Schorne 03–10; rtd 10; PtO *Ox* from 11. *19 Scampton Close, Bicester OX26 4FF* T: (01869) 249481 E: lizwelters@yahoo.co.uk

WEMYSS, Canon Gary. b 52. Cranmer Hall Dur 79. **d** 80 **p** 81. C Blackb St Jas 80–83; C Padiham 83–86; V Stalmine 86–90; P-in-c Egton-cum-Newland and Lowick *Carl* 90–03; V Egton-cum-Newland and Lowick and Colton 03–14; RD Furness 04–10; Hon Can Carl Cathl 08–14; rtd 14; PtO *Carl* from

14. 5 Highfield Road, Sedbergh LA10 5DH T: (015396) 22021 E: gary@eandgwemyss.co.uk

WENHAM, David. b 45. Pemb Coll Cam BA 67 MA Man Univ PhD 70. Ridley Hall Cam 81. **d** 84 **p** 85. Tutor Wycliffe Hall Ox 84–07; Dean 02–05; Vice-Prin 05–06; NSM Shelswell *Ox* 96–02; NSM Cumnor 03–07 and 13–17; Tutor Trin Coll Bris 07–12; Vice Prin 08–12; PtO *Ox* from 17. *66 Pinnocks Way, Oxford OX2 9DQ* T: (01865) 682984 E: todavidwenham@gmail.com

WENHAM, Michael Timothy. b 49. Pemb Coll Cam MA 75. Wycliffe Hall Ox. **d** 86 **p** 87. C Norbury *Ches* 76–79; V Stanford in the Vale w Goosey and Hatford *Ox* 89–09; rtd 09; PtO *Ox* 09–19. *19 Churchward Close, Grove, Wantage OX12 0QZ* T: (01235) 760094 M: 07719-715640 E: michaeltwenham@gmail.com

WENHAM, Peter William. b 47. Pemb Coll Cam MA 73 MD 85 FRCS 76. St Jo Coll Nottm 98. **d** 01 **p** 02. NSM Wollaton Park *S'well* 01–06; NSM Nottingham W Deanery 06–07; P-in-c Edwalton *S'well* 07–12; rtd 12; PtO *S'well* from 13. *31 Sutton Passeys Crescent, Nottingham NG8 1BX* T: 0115-970 2481

✠**WENT, The Rt Revd John Stewart.** b 44. CCC Cam BA 66 MA 70. Oak Hill Th Coll 67. **d** 69 **p** 70 **c** 96. C Northwood Em *Lon* 69–75; V Margate H Trin *Cant* 75–83; Vice-Prin Wycliffe Hall Ox 83–89; Adn Surrey *Guildf* 89–96; Chmn Dioc Coun for Unity and Miss 90–96; Suff Bp Tewkesbury *Glouc* 96–13; Hon Can Glouc Cathl 96–13; rtd 13; Hon C Chenies and Lt Chalfont, Latimer and Flaunden *Ox* 13–18; Hon Asst Bp Ox 13–20; PtO *Lon* from 20. *31 Pandorea House, 35 Lismore Boulevard, London NW9 4DL*

WENZEL, Andreas. b 81. St Steph Ho Ox MTh 14. **d** 14 **p** 15. C Horbury w Horbury Bridge *Leeds* 14–17; Shrine P Shrine of Our Lady of Walsingham 17–20; Vic-Prin and Dir Past Studies St Steph Ho Ox from 20; LtO *Ox* from 20. *St Stephen's House, 16 Marston Street, Oxford OX4 1JX* T: (01865) 613515 E: frandreas.wenzel@gmail.com

WERNER, Canon Donald Kilgour. b 39. Univ of Wales BA 61 Linacre Coll Ox BA 64 MA 67. Wycliffe Hall Ox 61. **d** 64 **p** 65. C Wrexham *St As* 64–69; Chapl Brasted Place Coll Westerham 69–73; Chapl Bris Univ 73–76; Hon C Clifton St Paul 73–76; Chapl Keele Univ *Lich* 77–79; P-in-c Keele 77–79; C York St Mich-le-Belfrey 79–83; Dir of Evang 79–83; R Holborn St Geo w H Trin and St Bart *Lon* 83–02; Hon Can Bujumbura from 99; Prof and Dean Th Light Univ Burundi from 03; Lic Preacher *Lon* 02–04; Vice-Chan Bujumbura Chr Univ 14–17; PtO *York* from 17. *25 Dulverton Hall, Esplanade, Scarborough YO11 2AR* M: 07927-295371 E: donaldinburundi@hotmail.com

WERRETT, Olivia Margaret. b 50. Brighton Univ BA 08 Eastbourne Tr Coll FETC 82. **d** 03. NSM Bexhill St Pet *Chich* 03–19; rtd 19. *127 Pebsham Lane, Bexhill-on-Sea TN40 2RP* T: (01424) 214144 M: 07772-383084 E: owerrett@btinternet.com

WESSON, Preb John Graham. b 38. St Pet Coll Ox BA 62 MA 68. Clifton Th Coll 63. **d** 65 **p** 66. C Southport Ch Ch w St Andr *Liv* 65–68; C Ox St Ebbe w St Pet 68–71; Chapl Poly Cen *Lon* 71–76; C-in-c Edin St Thos 76–82; Dir Past Studies Trin Coll Bris 82–86; R Birm St Martin w Bordesley St Andr 86–96; RD Birm City 88–95; Hon Can Birm Cathl 91–96; Dir Local Min Development *Lich* 96–98; Team Ldr Min Division 99–03; Team Ldr Bd of Min 99–03; C Lich St Mich w St Mary and Wall 96–03; Preb Lich Cathl 99–03; rtd 03. *11 Gordon Drive, Abingdon OX14 3SW* T: (01235) 526088 E: john.gwesson1@gmail.com

WEST, Alan David. b 61. Southn Univ BTh 92 Thames Valley Univ MA 97. Aston Tr Scheme 87 Sarum & Wells Th Coll 89. **d** 92 **p** 93. C S'wark St Geo the Martyr w St Jude 92–94; C S'wark St Geo w St Alphege and St Jude 95–96; V Boscoppa *Truro* 96–02; Chapl Mt Edgcumbe Hospice 02–05; Chapl R Cornwall Hosps Trust 05–10; Public Preacher *Truro* 10–12; Hon C St Blazey 12–14; Hon C Lanlivery 12–14; Hon C Luxulyan 12–14. *c/o Crockford, Church House, 27 Great Smith Street, London SW1P 3AZ*

WEST, Andrew Victor. b 59. Wycliffe Hall Ox 87. **d** 90 **p** 91. C Leyland St Andr *Blackb* 90–94; C Blackpool St Jo 94–96; TV Bedworth *Cov* 96–98; Chapl Cheltenham and Glouc Coll of HE 98–01; Chapl Glos Univ 01–03; Chapl St Martin's Coll *Carl* 03–07; Chapl Cumbria Univ 07–10; C Carl St Jo 03–10; R Gateshead Fell *Dur* 10–17; P-in-c Gateshead St Geo 14–16; Chapl HM Pris Frankland from 17. *HM Prison Frankland, Brasside, Durham DH1 5YD* T: 0191-376 5000

WEST, Bryan Edward. b 39. Avery Hill Coll CertEd 69 BEd 80 Kent Univ MA 86. Cant Sch of Min 85. **d** 88 **p** 89. NSM Gravesend H Family w Ifield *Roch* 88–92; C Gravesend St Geo 92–95; NSM Hatcham Park All SS *S'wark* 95–98; NSM Stambridge and Ashingdon w S Fambridge *Chelmsf* 98–01; NSM Canvey Is 01–06; Chapl Southend Health Care NHS

Trust 99–06; PtO *Chelmsf* 06–13; *Truro* from 16. *4 Barton Court, Central Treviscoe, St Austell PL26 7PD* T: (01726) 823102 E: roadbuilder2013@gmail.com

WEST, Miss Caroline Elisabeth. b 61. RGN 84. Wycliffe Hall Ox 93. **d** 95. NSM Eastrop *Win* from 95. *19 Beaulieu Court, Riverdene, Basingstoke RG21 4DQ* T: (01256) 350389 *or* 464249 E: caroline.west@stmarys-basingstoke.org.uk

WEST, Mrs Christine Cecily. TCD BA 60 MA 63 HDipEd 61. CITC 91. **d** 94 **p** 95. NSM Bray *D & G* 94–96; NSM Kilternan 96–99; LtO from 99. *55 Beech Park Road, Foxrock, Dublin 18, Republic of Ireland* T: (00353) (1) 289 6374 E: johncecily@eircom.net

WEST, Christopher Nigel. b 95. TCD MTh 20. CITC 17. **d** 19 **p** 20. Killyman *Arm* 19–20; C Taney *D & G* from 20. *Church Cottage, 19 Taney Road, Dublin 14, D14 W2C9, Republic of Ireland* M: (00353) 85-856 2301 E: westch@tcd.ie

WEST, David Marshall. b 48. St Jo Coll Dur BA 70. **d** 73 **p** 74. C Wylde Green *Birm* 73–76; C Wokingham St Paul *Ox* 76–79; V Hurst 79–88; V Maidenhead St Luke 88–95; C Whitley Ch Ch 95–99; P-in-c Reading Ch Ch 99–05; V 05–12; rtd 13; PtO *Ox* from 18; *Heref* from 20. *The Old Tannery, Church Lane, Ledbury HR8 1DW* T: (01531) 636580 E: oldtannery@hotmail.co.uk

WEST, Derek Elvin. b 47. Hull Univ BA 69. Westcott Ho Cam 71. **d** 73 **p** 74. C Walthamstow St Pet *Chelmsf* 73–77; C Chingford SS Pet and Paul 77–80; TV W Slough *Ox* 80–88; Slough Community Chapl 88–95; TV Upton cum Chalvey 95–12; rtd 12; PtO *Lon* from 12. *35 Wallasey Crescent, Ickenham, Uxbridge UB10 8SA* M: 07957-158069 E: derekewest@gmail.com

WEST, Mrs Elizabeth Maxine. b 47. Liv Univ BA 69 Lon Inst of Educn PGCE 70 K Coll Lon BA 95 AKC. NTMTC. **d** 99 **p** 00. NSM Hornsey H Innocents *Lon* 99–00; NSM Highgate St Mich 00–03; C 03–11; rtd 12; PtO *Lon* from 13. *West Villa, Inderwick Road, London N8 9JU* T: (020) 8348 3042 E: maxineanddennis@hotmail.com

WEST, Canon Eric Robert Glenn. b 55. QUB BA 79 Man Univ DipEd 80. CITC BTh 92. **d** 92 **p** 93. C Enniskillen *Clogh* 92–95; I Lisbellaw 95–00; CF 00–03; I Annagh w Drumgoon, Ashfield etc *K, E & A* 03–06; I Derryvullen N w Castlearchdale *Clogh* 06–15; I Carnteel and Crilly *Arm* from 15; Can St Patr Cathl Dublin from 11. *St James's Rectory, 22 Carnteel Road, Aughnacloy BT69 6DU* M: 07969-332530 E: glenn.west55@hotmail.com

WEST, Mrs Heather June. b 55. Dur Univ BA 18. SWMTC 12. **d** 15 **p** 16. NSM Three Rivers *Truro* 15–17; C 17–19; P-in-c 19–20; C Moorland Gp 19–20; rtd 20; PtO *Truro* from 21. *Lowarth Duw, 29 Liskeard Road, Callington PL17 7JD* T: (01579) 384453 M: 07734-810664 E: pronter@btinternet.com

WEST, Canon Jeffrey James. b 50. OBE 06. Worc Coll Ox BA 72 BPhil 74 MA 76 FSA 11 FRSA 01. Ripon Coll Cuddesdon 05. **d** 07 **p** 08. NSM Banbury *Ox* from 07; AD Deddington 12–17; Hon Can Ch Ch from 17. *St Mary's Centre, Horse Fair, Banbury OX16 0AA* T: (01608) 811136 M: 07766-198484 E: jeff@banburystmary.org.uk

WEST, Jennifer. **d** 16 **p** 17. NSM Holton-le-Clay, Tetney and N Cotes *Linc* from 16. *11 Belmont, Holton-le-Clay, Grimsby DN36 5HQ* T: (01472) 453029 E: revjennywest@outlook.com

WEST (formerly WINDIATE), Mrs Mary Elizabeth. b 49. Linc Th Coll 94. **d** 94 **p** 95. C Loughton St Jo *Chelmsf* 94–98; P-in-c Ashingdon w S Fambridge 98–01; P-in-c Stambridge 98–01; TV Canvey Is 01–07; P-in-c Greenstead w Colchester St Anne 07–08; TR 08–13; rtd 13; PtO *Truro* from 14. *4 Barton Court, Central Treviscoe, St Austell PL26 7PD* T: (01726) 823102 E: m.west653@btinternet.com

WEST, Maxine. See WEST, Elizabeth Maxine

WEST, Canon Michael Brian. b 39. Bris Univ BSc 60. Linc Th Coll 64. **d** 66 **p** 67. C Bp's Hatfield *St Alb* 66–69; Ind Chapl 69–81; Sen Ind Chapl 71–81; Hon Can St Alb 78–81; Sen Ind Chapl and Hon Can Sheff Cathl 81–01; Dir Open Forum for Economic Regeneration 02–04; rtd 04; PtO *Sheff* from 02. *23 Walton Road, Sheffield S11 8RE* T: 0114-266 2188 E: mike.west23@tiscali.co.uk

WEST, The Ven Michael Frederick. b 50. Trin Coll Ox BA 72 MA 76 UEA PhD 96. Westcott Ho Cam 72. **d** 74 **p** 75. C Wolverhampton *Lich* 74–78; C Hanley H Ev 78–79; TV 79–82; Dioc Youth Officer *St E* 83–88; V Ipswich St Thos 88–95; Prin OLM Scheme 96–03; Hon Can St E Cathl 96–03; Can Res and Chan Linc Cathl 03–08; Dioc Dir Formation in Discipleship and Min 03–06; TR Wrexham *St As* 08–13; AD 08–13; Chan St As Cathl 11–13; Res Can Ban Cathl 13–14; Tr Adn from 14; CMD Officer from 13. *The Vicarage, Newgate Street, Y Felinheli LL56 4SQ* T: (01248) 671159 M: 07795-544332 E: mike.west@stpadarns.ac.uk

WEST, Canon Paul John Francis. b 66. Newc Univ Aus BA 87 DipEd 93. Westcott Ho Cam 04. **d** 06 **p** 07. C Albury Australia 06–08; C Dee Why 08–09; C King Street 09–10; P-in-c Wisbech SS Pet and Paul *Ely* 10–16; Chapl Wisbech Gr Sch 10–15; Chapl Newcastle Gr Sch Australia 16–17; Can Res Newcastle Cathl from 16; R Maitland from 17. *St Mary's Rectory, 68 Church Street, Maitland NSW 2320, Australia* E: fatherpjfwest@gmail.com

WEST, Paul Leslie. b 57. OLM course 96. **d** 99 **p** 00. OLM Kinnerley w Melverley and Knockin w Maesbrook *Lich* 99–16; OLM Kinnerley w Melverley, Knockin w Maesbrook and Maesbury from 16. *Braddan, Farm Hall, Kinnerley, Oswestry SY10 8EG* T: (01691) 682600

WEST, Penelope Ann. b 44. Chelt & Glouc Coll of HE MA 98 Univ of Wales (Lamp) MPhil 08 FIBMS 72. **d** 00 **p** 01. NSM Hartpury w Corse and Staunton *Glouc* 00–09; NSM Ashleworth, Corse, Hartpury, Hasfield etc 09–12; PtO from 13. *Catsbury Cottage, Corsend Road, Hartpury GL19 3BP* T: (01425) 700314 E: revpennywest@gmail.com

WEST, Peter Harcourt. b 29. **d** 59 **p** 60. C Histon *Ely* 59–60; C Hampreston *Sarum* 60–61; C Braintree *Chelmsf* 61–63; PtO from 72; rtd 94. *12A The Piccards, Chestnut Avenue, Guildford GU2 4DW* T: (01483) 389487

WEST, Philip William. b 48. Magd Coll Ox BA 70 MA 78. St Jo Coll Nottm BA 74. **d** 75 **p** 76. C Rushden w Newton Bromswold *Pet* 75–79; C Pitsmoor w Ellesmere *Sheff* 79–83; V Attercliffe 83–89; Ind Chapl 85–90; P-in-c Darnall 86–89; V Stannington 89–13; P-in-c Sheff St Bart 02–07; AD Hallam 96–02; Hon Can Sheff Cathl 01–13; rtd 13; PtO *Sheff* from 13; Hon Canon Burstwick, Burton Pidsea etc *York* from 16; Hon C Easington w Skeffling, Keyingham, Ottringham etc from 16; Hon C Hedon, Paull, Sproatley and Preston from 16. *The Rectory, Ottringham Road, Keyingham, Hull HU12 9RX* T: (01964) 603199 E: philipwest65@gmail.com

WEST, Richard Barry. b 47. Mather Coll of Educn TCert 72. **d** 16 **p** 17. NSM Whaley Bridge *Ches* 16–19; PtO from 19. *Beech House, Kettleshulme, High Peak SK23 7EJ* T: (01663) 734497 M: 07751-834832 E: rickangelawest@yahoo.co.uk

WEST, Roderic. See WEST, Thomas Roderic

WEST, Ruth. BSc BTh. **d** 09 **p** 10. C Waterford w Killea, Drumcannon and Dunhill *C, F & O* 09–12; I Inver w Mountcharles, Killaghtee and Killybegs *D & R* 12–17; I Killesher *K, E & A* from 17. *Killesher Rectory, 10 Mill Road, Tully, Florencecourt, Enniskillen BT92 1FN* M: (00353) 87-625 9077 E: ruthjwest@hotmail.com

WEST, Stephen Peter. b 52. Liv Univ CertEd 74. Oak Hill Th Coll 87. **d** 89 **p** 90. C Gateacre *Liv* 89–92; V Liv All So Springwood 92–02; TV Teignmouth, Ideford w Luton, Ashcombe etc *Ex* 02–18; rtd 18. *98 Mulberry Close, Paignton TQ3 3GD* E: spwest33@gmail.com

WEST, Mrs Suzanne Elizabeth. b 46. STETS 04. **d** 07 **p** 08. NSM Portsea St Geo *Portsm* 07–11; Asst to RD Gosport from 11; PtO from 18. *64 Melville Road, Gosport PO12 4QX* T: (023) 9278 8782 E: melville64@ntlworld.com *or* sue.melville64@ntlworld.com

WEST, The Ven Thomas Roderic. b 55. BTh 90. TCD Div Sch. **d** 86 **p** 87. C Dromore Cathl *D & D* 86–89; I Carrowdore w Millisle 89–95; I Moira 95–12; I Seapatrick from 12; Can Dromore Cathl from 05; Chan Dromore Cathl 08–12; Adn Dromore from 11. *The Rectory, 63 Lurgan Road, Banbridge BT32 4LY* T: (028) 4062 2612 *or* 4062 2744 E: roderic@bchurch.co.uk

WEST, Timothy Ralph. b 53. Bath Univ BSc 75. Ridley Hall Cam 82. **d** 85 **p** 86. C Mildenhall *St E* 85–88; TV Melbury *Sarum* 88–92; TR 92–98; TR Preston w Sutton Poyntz, Littlemoor etc 98–15; TR Weymouth Ridgeway 15–21; RD Weymouth and Portland 12–17; Can and Preb Sarum Cathl 17–21; rtd 21. *Address withheld by request*

WEST CUMBERLAND, Archdeacon of. See PRATT, The Ven Richard David

WEST HAM, Archdeacon of. See COCKETT, The Ven Elwin Wesley

WEST-LINDELL, Stein Erik. b 54. BA. Linc Th Coll 82. **d** 84 **p** 85. C Allington and Maidstone St Pet *Cant* 84–87; R Orlestone w Snave and Ruckinge w Warehorne 87–93; R Byfield w Boddington and Aston le Walls *Pet* 93–99; V Nor Lakenham St Alb and St Mark 99–17; V Nor Lakenham St Mark from 17. *2 Conesford Drive, Norwich NR1 2BB* T: (01603) 621843

✠**WESTALL, The Rt Revd Michael Robert.** b 39. Qu Coll Cam BA 62 MA 66. Cuddesdon Coll 63 Harvard Div 65. **d** 66 **p** 67 **c** 01. C Heref St Martin 66–70; Lect Bp's Coll Calcutta India 70–76; Vice Prin 76–79; Prin 79–83; Prin St Mark's Th Coll Dar-es-Salaam Tanzania 84–92; R Alfrick, Lulsley, Suckley, Leigh and Bransford *Worc* 93–00; Bp SW Tanganyika 01–06; rtd 06; P-in-c Torquay St Luke *Ex* 07–12; Hon Asst Bp *Ex* 07–12; Hon Asst Bp Heref from 12; PtO from 13.

Oak House, Kingstone, Hereford HR2 9ET T: (01981) 250259
E: michaelwestall39@gmail.com

WESTBROOK, Canon Colin David. b 36. Oriel Coll Ox BA 59.
St Steph Ho Ox MA 63. **d** 61 **p** 62. C Roath St Martin *Llan*
61–66; C Roath 66–74; V Llantarnam *Mon* 74–79; V Newport
St Jo Bapt 79–07; Hon Can St Woolos Cathl 88–91; Can
St Woolos Cathl from 91; Warden of Ords 91–99. *St John's
Vicarage, 62 Oakfield Road, Newport NP20 4LP* T: (01633)
265581 E: colinwestbrook@talktalk.net

WESTBROOK (née REED), Mrs Ethel Patricia Ivy. b 42. Bris
Univ CertEd 63. Cant Sch of Min 82. **dss** 84 **d** 87 **p** 94.
Fawkham and Hartley *Roch* 84–85; Asst Dir of Educn 84–86;
Cliffe at Hoo w Cooling 85–86; Corby SS Pet and Andr w Gt
and Lt Oakley 86–90; Par Dn 87–90; Par Dn Roch St Pet w
St Marg 90–94; C Rainham 94–99; V Joydens Wood St Barn
99–05; Dioc Chapl MU 01–05; rtd 05; Hon C Banstead *Guildf*
05–11; PtO *Roch* from 05; *Cant* 12–21. *5 Victoria Mews,
Station Road, Westgate-on-Sea CT8 8RQ* T: (01843) 836022
E: patriciawipe@yahoo.co.uk

WESTBY, Martyn John. b 61. Leeds Univ BA 83. Trin Coll
Bris 96. **d** 98 **p** 99. C Drypool *York* 98–01; P-in-c Cherry
Burton 01–13; Chapl Bp Burton Coll York 01–13; Assoc
Dioc Dir of Ords *York* 05–10; C Etton w Dalton Holme
11–13; TV Drypool from 13. *383 Southcoates Lane,
Hull HU9 3UN* T: (01482) 781090 M: 07791-694566
E: martynwestby@btinternet.com

WESTERMANN-CHILDS, Miss Emma Jane. b 71. Univ of Wales
(Ban) BA 93 Ox Univ MTh 99. Ripon Coll Cuddesdon 96.
d 98 **p** 99. C Launceston *Truro* 98–01; P-in-c St Stephen in
Brannel from 01. *The Rectory, 70 Rectory Road, St Stephen,
St Austell PL26 7RL* T: (01726) 822236

WESTERN, Canon Robert Geoffrey. b 37. Man Univ BSc 60.
Qu Coll Birm. **d** 62 **p** 63. C Sedbergh *Bradf* 62–65; PV Linc
Cathl 65–73; Hd Master Linc Cathl Sch 74–96; Can and
Preb Linc Cathl 74–96; rtd 97; PtO *Carl* from 05. *2 Guldrey
House, Guldrey Lane, Sedbergh LA10 5DS* T: (015396) 21426
E: robthel1@aol.com

WESTHAVER, George Derrick. b 68. St Mary's Univ Halifax
NS BA 92. Wycliffe Coll Toronto MDiv 98. **d** 97 **p** 98. C
Teversham and Cherry Hinton St Andr *Ely* 97–00; TV The
Ramseys and Upwood 00–03; Chapl Linc Coll Ox 03–06; C
Ox St Mich w St Martin and All SS 03–06; R Halifax St Geo
Canada 07–13; Prin Pusey Ho from 13; Fell St Cross Coll Ox
from 13. *Pusey House, St Giles, Oxford OX1 3LZ* T: (01865)
278415 E: gwesthaver@gmail.com

WESTLAKE, Michael Paul. b 34. Ex Coll Ox BA 56 MA 64.
Wells Th Coll 59. **d** 61 **p** 62. C Southmead *Bris* 61–67; V
Eastville St Thos 67–74; V Eastville St Thos w St Anne 74–83;
P-in-c Easton St Mark 79–83; V Marshfield w Cold Ashton
and Tormarton etc 83–01; rtd 01; PtO *Birm* 03–14. *65 Duxford
Road, Great Barr, Birmingham B42 2JD* T: 0121-358 7030

WESTLAND, Richard Theodore. b 27. **d** 87 **p** 88. OLM
Freiston w Butterwick *Linc* 87–97; rtd 97; PtO *Linc* from 97.
76 Brand End Road, Butterwick, Boston PE22 0JD T: (01205)
760572

WESTMACOTT, Rosemary Margaret. *See* FRANKLIN,
Rosemary Margaret

WESTMINSTER, Archdeacon of. *See* STANTON, The Ven
David John

WESTMINSTER, Dean of. *See* HOYLE, The Very Revd David
Michael

WESTMORLAND AND FURNESS, Archdeacon of. *See* ROSS,
The Ven Vernon

WESTON, Carol Nancy. b 57. Qu Foundn Birm 18. **d** 20
p 21. NSM Brierley Hill *Worc* from 20. *33 Rosemary Lane,
Stourbridge DY8 3EP* T: (01384) 837596 M: 07971-651841
E: carolnweston@hotmail.com

WESTON, Canon David Wilfrid Valentine. b 37. Lanc Univ
PhD 93. **d** 67 **p** 68. OSB 60–84; LtO *Ox* 67–84; Prior Nashdom
Abbey 71–74; Abbot 74–84; C Chorley St Pet *Blackb* 84–85;
V Pilling 85–89; Bp's Dom Chapl *Carl* 89–94; Can Res
Carl Cathl 94–05; Lib 95–05; Vice-Dean 00; rtd 05; PtO
Carl from 06. *The Pond House, Ratten Row, Dalston, Carlisle
CA5 7AY* T: (01228) 710673 E: helweston@gmail.com

WESTON, Evelyn Sarah. b 68. **d** 17 **p** 18. NSM Heswall
Ches 17–20; PtO from 20. *3 The Pipers, Heswall, Wirral
CH60 9LL* T: 0151-342 4472 E: lyn_weston@yahoo.co.uk

WESTON, Gary James. b 72. Westmr Coll Ox BTh 95.
Wycliffe Hall Ox 02. **d** 04 **p** 05. C Barrow St Paul *Carl*
04–08; C S Barrow 08–09; P-in-c Hinckley H Trin *Leic* 09–10;
V Hinckley St Jo from 10; AD Sparkenhoe W 15–19. *21
Windrush Drive, Hinckley LE10 0NY* T: (01455) 233552
E: gary@stjohnshinckley.org

WESTON, Mrs Judith. b 36. Open Univ BA 75 MSR 56. St Jo
Coll Nottm 84. **dss** 85 **d** 87 **p** 94. Huddersfield H Trin *Wakef*
85–87; Par Dn 87–91; Par Dn Wakef St Andr and St Mary

91–94; C 94–95; Chapl Huddersfield NHS Trust 95–98; rtd
96; PtO *Wakef* 98–14; *Leeds* 14–16. *Overcroft, 8A Newland
Road, Huddersfield HD5 0QT* T: (01484) 453591

WESTON, Mrs Katherine. b 48. Ripon Coll Cuddesdon 18.
d 19 **p** 20. NSM Basildon w Aldworth and Ashampstead
Ox from 19. *Willow Tree Cottage, Ashampstead, Reading
RG8 8RA* T: (01635) 201356 M: 07765-255569
E: westonkaty@hotmail.com *or* katy@thebenfice.uk

WESTON, Neil. b 51. Jes Coll Ox BA 73 MA 78. Ridley
Hall Cam 74. **d** 76 **p** 77. C Ealing St Mary *Lon* 76–80;
P-in-c Pertenhall w Swineshead *St Alb* 80–89; P-in-c Dean
w Yelden, Melchbourne and Shelton 80–89; R The Stodden
Churches 89–91; R Newhaven *Chich* 91–98; P-in-c Radcliffe-
on-Trent and Shelford etc *S'well* 98–04; R 04–05; V Radcliffe-
on-Trent and Shelford 06–09; R Kington w Huntington, Old
Radnor, Kinnerton etc *Heref* 09–14; rtd 14; PtO *Ox* from 14.
15 Longmead, Abingdon OX14 1JQ T: (01235) 204147

WESTON, Paul David Astley. b 57. Trin Hall Cam BA 80
MA 83 Westmr Coll Ox MPhil 92 K Coll Lon PhD 02.
Wycliffe Hall Ox 83. **d** 85 **p** 86. C New Malden and Coombe
S'wark 85–89; Lect Oak Hill Th Coll 89–97; Vice-Prin 97–00;
Gen Sec UCCF 00–01; Assoc Lect Ridley Hall Cam 02–03;
Tutor from 03; PtO *Ely* 01–06. *Ridley Hall, Ridley Hall
Road, Cambridge CB3 9HG* T: (01223) 746580 F: 746581
E: pdaw2@cam.ac.uk

WESTON, Phillip Richard. b 76. Bath Univ BSc 99 York Univ
MSc 02 Lon Sch of Th PhD 18. Wycliffe Hall Ox BA 09.
d 10 **p** 11. C Aughton Ch Ch *Liv* 10–14; P-in-c Gidea Park
Chelmsf 14–16; V 16–18; V Ashton Hayes *Ches* from 18;
Tutor St Mellitus NW from 18. *14 Dunns Lane, Ashton,
Chester CH3 8BU* T: (01829) 752272 M: 07939-129631
E: vicar@ashtonhayes.church

WESTON, Stephen John Astley. b 55. Aston Univ BSc 77.
Ridley Hall Cam 78. **d** 81 **p** 82. C Gt Chesham *Ox* 81–85; C
Southport Ch Ch *Liv* 85–87; P-in-c Gayhurst w Ravenstone,
Stoke Goldington etc *Ox* 87–91; R 91–96; RD Newport
92–95; V Chipping Norton 96–01; TR 01–13; AD 02–07;
Hon Can Ch Ch 06–13; P-in-c Ottery St Mary, Alfington,
W Hill, Tipton etc *Ex* 13–16; TR 17–20; rtd 20; PtO *Ex* from
21. *Highfield, Parker Road, Bigbury on Sea, Kingsbridge TQ7 4AT*

WESTON, Timothy Bernard Charles. b 48. **d** 03 **p** 04. OLM
Watton w Carbrooke and Ovington *Nor* 03–07; OLM Ashill,
Carbrooke, Ovington and Saham Toney 07–14; PtO from
14. *Sunset Barn, Morton Lane, Weston Longville, Norwich
NR9 5JL* T: (01603) 879115 E: reverendweston@gmail.com

WESTON, Ms Virginia Anne. b 58. UEA BSc 79. Wycliffe
Hall Ox 84. **d** 87 **p** 02. Par Dn New Malden and Coombe
S'wark 87–89; LtO *Lon* 89–01; Chapl to People at Work in
Cam *Ely* 02–06; Chapl Cam Univ Hosps NHS Foundn Trust
18–19; PtO *Ely* from 20. *22 Ravensworth Gardens, Cambridge
CB1 2XL* E: virginiaweston@yahoo.co.uk

WESTWOOD, Canon John Richard. b 55. Clare Coll Cam
BA 77 MA 81 Lambeth MA 98. Ripon Coll Cuddesdon 77.
d 79 **p** 80. C Oakham w Hambleton and Egleton *Pet* 79–81;
C Oakham, Hambleton, Egleton, Braunston and Brooke
81–83; V Gt w Lt Harrowden and Orlingbury 83–90; V
Wellingborough St Andr 90–97; RD Wellingborough
92–97; R Irthlingborough 99–10; P-in-c Rothwell w Orton,
Rushton w Glendon and Pipewell 10–18; R Rothwell w
Orton and Rushton w Glendon etc from 18; C Broughton
w Loddington and Cransley etc 10–18; Warden of
Readers 95–05; Can Pet Cathl from 97. *The Vicarage, High
Street, Rothwell, Kettering NN14 6BQ* T: (01536) 710268
E: revdjohn.westwood@gmail.com

WESTWOOD, Peter. b 38. Open Univ BA 76. AKC 65. **d** 65
p 66. C Acomb St Steph and St Aid *York* 65–68; Chapl HM
Youth Cust Cen Onley 69–73; Chapl HM Pris Leic 73–77;
Maidstone 77–81; Dur 81–87; Brixton 87–93; Wormwood
Scrubs 93–98; PtO *S'wark* from 98; rtd 99. *St Stephen's
Church, College Road, London SE21 7HN* T: (020) 8693 0082
E: westwood773@btinternet.com

WESTWOOD, Richard Andrew. b 64. Nottm Univ BSc 85
PGCE 86. St Jo Coll Nottm 02. **d** 04 **p** 05. C Gt Wyrley *Lich*
04–15; TV Burntwood, Chase Terrace etc from 15. *The Vicarage,
158A High Street, Chasetown, Burntwood WS7 3XG* T: (01543)
682336 E: westwood.richard@btinternet.com

WESTWOOD, Timothy. b 61. Wolv Poly MBA 91.
WMMTC 95. **d** 98 **p** 99. NSM Sedgley St Mary *Worc* from 98.
85 High Park Crescent, Dudley DY3 1QY T: (01902) 831078
E: twestwood@mac.com

WETHERALL, Canon Nicholas Guy. b 52. Lon Univ BMus 73
Ox Univ CertEd 75. Chich Th Coll 82. **d** 84 **p** 85. C
Cleobury Mortimer w Hopton Wafers *Heref* 84–87; TV
Leominster 87–92; V Cuckfield *Chich* 92–14; RD 99–03;
Can and Preb Chich Cathl 08–14; rtd 14. *3 Brookward*

Terrace, Heamoor, Penzance TR18 3QZ T: (01736) 368887
E: nick.4epnewlyn@gmail.com
WETHERELL, Ms Eileen Joyce. b 44. Westf Coll Lon BSc 66.
S Dios Minl Tr Scheme 89. **d** 92 **p** 94. Par Dn Southampton
Maybush St Pet *Win* 92–94; C 94–96; TV Totton 96–04;
V Hythe 04–12; Dioc Adv for Women's Min 02–12; rtd
12; PtO *Win* from 12. *3 Creighton Road, Southampton
SO15 4JF* T: (023) 8184 8598 E: ewetherell@tiscali.co.uk
WETHERELL, Philippa Clare. See LEA, Philippa Clare
WEYMONT, Martin Eric. b 48. St Jo Coll Dur BA 69 MA 74
Fitzw Coll Cam PGCE 73 Lon Inst of Educn PhD 89 Open
Univ BSc 96. Westcott Ho Cam 71. **d** 73 **p** 74. C Blackheath
Birm 73–76; Hon C Willesden St Matt *Lon* 76–77; Hon C
Belmont 77–79; P-in-c W Twyford 79–85; NSM Cricklewood
St Mich 85–88; Chapl St Pet Colleg Sch Wolv 88–91; Hon
C Wolverhampton *Lich* 88–91; NSM Bickershaw *Liv* 91–97;
P-in-c Mells w Buckland Dinham, Elm, Whatley etc *B & W*
97–15; rtd 15; PtO *Sarum* from 16; *B & W* from 16. *33 Ludlow
Close, Warminster BA12 8BJ*
WHAITE, Richard Patrick. b 80. Univ Coll Lon BSc 01 Man
Univ MPhil 04 K Coll Lon MA 10. Ripon Coll Cuddesdon
BA 14. **d** 14 **p** 15. C Fulham All SS *Lon* 14–17; Assoc Tutor
St Mellitus Coll 15–17; Chapl and Fell Dur Univ 17–19;
Chapl Cranmer Hall Dur 18–19; R Ches St Mary from 19.
10 Lower Park Road, Chester CH4 7BB M: 07857-776247
E: rector.stmaryschester@btconnect.com
WHALE, David. b 81. Univ of Wales (Ban) BSc 02 Glos Univ
PGCE 06. Wycliffe Hall Ox BTh 15. **d** 15 **p** 16. C Glouc
St Cath 15–18; P-in-c Chenies and Lt Chalfont, Latimer and
Flaunden *Ox* from 18. *The Rectory, Chenies, Rickmansworth
WD3 6ER* E: revdwhale@gmail.com
WHALE, Noel Raymond. b 41. Ox Univ 67. **d** 70 **p** 71. C
Amersham *Ox* 70–73; C Geelong Australia 73–76; P-in-c
Altona 76–79; I 79–85; I Ivanhoe 86–97; Prec and Min Can
St Paul's Cathl 97–01; I Bundoora St Pet 01–11. *Unit 1, 33-35
Ligar Street, Sunbury VIC 3429, Australia* T: (0061) (3) 9740
3315 M: 41-219 6127 E: jonahnoel@hotmail.com
WHALE, Peter Richard. b 49. Auckland Univ MA 72 BSc 73
Down Coll Cam BA 74 MA 79 Otago Univ BD 78 Ex Univ
PhD 90. St Jo Coll Auckland 75. **d** 77 **p** 78. C Takapuna
NZ 77–80; Chapl K Coll Auckland 81–85; TV Saltash *Truro*
85–90; Jt Dir SW Minl Tr Course 86–90; Preb St Endellion
Truro 89–90; Prin WMMTC 90–92; rtd 04. *6 Bluebell Walk,
Coventry CV4 9XR* T: (024) 7646 4894
WHALEY, Stephen John. b 57. York Univ BA 79. Cranmer
Hall Dur BA 85. **d** 86 **p** 87. C Selby Abbey *York* 86–90; V
Derringham Bank from 90; AD W Hull 98–00. *110 Calvert
Road, Hull HU5 5DH* T: (01482) 352175
WHALLEY, Alice Elizabeth. See SMITH, Alice Elizabeth
WHALLEY, Anthony Allen. b 41. Linc Th Coll 77. **d** 79 **p** 80.
C Upton cum Chalvey *Ox* 79–83; R Newton Longville w
Stoke Hammond and Whaddon 83–96; R Winslow w Gt
Horwood and Addington 99–06; rtd 06; PtO *Worc* from
07. *2 Charlock Road, Malvern WR14 3SR* T: (01684) 562897
E: tony.rosemary@btinternet.com
WHALLEY, Mrs Constance Mary. b 55. CBDTI 99. **d** 02
p 03. NSM Garstang St Helen and St Michaels-on-
Wyre *Blackb* 02–16; rtd 16; PtO *Blackb* 17–20. *4 Leicester
Avenue, Garstang, Preston PR3 1FH* T: (01995) 238206
E: cwwhalley56@gmail.com
WHALLEY, Edward Ryder Watson. b 31. G&C Coll Cam
BA 54 MA 59. Westcott Ho Cam 55. **d** 57 **p** 58. C Ashton-on-
Ribble St Andr *Blackb* 57–60; Chapl Magd Coll Cam 60–63;
C Arnold *S'well* 63–67; PtO *Lon* 03–18. *6 Cranleigh, 137-139
Ladbroke Road, London W11 3PX* T: (020) 7727 1985
WHALLEY, Eleanor Jean. b 72. **d** 14 **p** 15. C St Neots
Ely 14–16; P-in-c Soham and Wicken 16–18; R Soham
from 18. *The Vicarage, 27 The Oaks, Soham, Ely CB7 5FF*
E: eleanorjw@gmail.com
WHALLEY, George Peter. b 40. **d** 86 **p** 86. NSM Ellon *Ab*
from 86; NSM Cruden Bay from 86. *128 Braehead Drive,
Cruden Bay, Peterhead AB42 0NW* T: (01779) 812511
E: peter_whalley@btinternet.com
WHALLEY, Jonathan Peter Lambert. b 60. Wm Booth
Memorial Coll 87. St Jo Coll Nottm BA 97. **d** 97 **p** 98.
C Hattersley *Ches* 97–01; V The Marshland *Sheff* 01–09;
P-in-c Wolsingham and Thornley *Dur* from 09; P-in-c Satley,
Stanley and Tow Law from 09; CF(V) from 02. *The
Rectory, 14 Rectory Lane, Wolsingham, Bishop Auckland
DL13 3AJ* T: (01388) 527340
WHALLEY, Peter. See WHALLEY, George Peter
WHALLEY, Ryder. See WHALLEY, Edward Ryder Watson
✠**WHALON, The Rt Revd Pierre Welté.** b 52. Boston Univ
BMus 74 Duquesne Univ MMus 81. Virginia Th Sem
MDiv 85. **d** 85 **p** 85 **c** 01. R N Versailles All So USA 85–91;
R Philadelphia St Paul 91–93; R Fort Pierce St Andr 93–01;

Bp in Charge Convocation of Episc Chs in Eur 01–19;
Hon Asst Bp Eur from 02. *23 avenue George V, 75008 Paris,
France* T: (0033) 6 77 56 22 15 E: bppwhalon@aol.com
WHARTON, Canon Gillian Vera. b 66. TCD BTh 93 MPhil 99
HDipEd 02. CITC 90. **d** 93 **p** 94. C Glenageary *D & G* 93–96;
Hon PV Ch Ch Cathl Dublin from 96; Dioc Youth Officer
96–00; C Lucan w Leixlip 96–00; Chapl Rathdown Sch
00–04; I Dublin Booterstown *D & G* from 04; I Dublin Mt
Merrion from 04; Can St Patr Cathl Dublin from 17. *The
Rectory, Cross Avenue, Booterstown, Blackrock, Co Dublin, A94
W7R6, Republic of Ireland* T: (00353) (1) 288 7118 or (1) 283
5873 M: 87-230 0767 E: booterstown@dublin.anglican.org
or gillwharton@gmail.com
✠**WHARTON, The Rt Revd John Martin.** b 44. Van Mildert
Coll Dur BA 69 Linacre Coll Ox BTh 71 MA 76. Ripon Hall
Ox 69. **d** 72 **p** 73 **c** 92. C Birm St Pet 72–75; C Croydon St Jo
Cant 76–77; Dir Past Studies Ripon Coll Cuddesdon 77–83; C
Cuddesdon *Ox* 79–83; Sec to Bd of Min and Tr *Bradf* 83–92;
Dir Post-Ord Tr 84–92; Hon Can Bradf Cathl 84–92; Can
Res Bradf Cathl 92; Bp's Officer for Min and Tr 92; Area Bp
Kingston *S'wark* 92–97; Bp Newc 97–14; rtd 14; PtO *Dur* from
15; Hon Asst Bp Lon from 15; Hon Asst Bp Eur from 16; Hon
Asst Bp S'wark from 16. *20 Thamespoint, Fairways, Teddington
TW11 9PP* T: (020) 8977 8347
WHARTON, Canon Kate Elizabeth. b 78. Leeds Metrop
Univ BSc 00. Wycliffe Hall Ox BTh 05. **d** 05 **p** 06. C
W Derby St Luke *Liv* 05–09; P-in-c Everton St Geo
09–15; V 15–17; AD Liv N 13–17; V Roby from 17; Hon
Can Liv Cathl from 13. *St Bartholomew's Vicarage, 11
Church Road, Roby, Liverpool L36 9TL* T: 0151-489 1698
E: vicar@stbartholomewsroby.org.uk
WHARTON, Canon Richard Malcolm. b 69. Univ of Cen
England in Birm BA 91 PGCE 92. Ripon Coll Cuddesdon
BTh 98. **d** 98 **p** 99. C Weoley Castle *Birm* 98–01; C Hall
Green Ascension 01–04; P-in-c Hall Green St Mich 03–08;
Chapl Univ Hosp Birm NHS Foundn Trust from 08; Hon
Can Birm Cathl from 16. *18 Pineapple Grove, Birmingham
B30 2TJ* T: 0121-627 1627 ext 52599 or 443 1371
WHARTON, Susan Jane. b 58. Leeds Univ BSc 79 Coll of
Ripon & York St Jo MA 00 Win Univ MA 18. NOC 96.
d 99 **p** 00. C Bingley All SS *Bradf* 99–03; P-in-c Weston w
Denton 03–08; P-in-c Leathley w Farnley, Fewston and
Blubberhouses 03–08; C Washburn and Mid-Wharfe
08–09; P-in-c 09–12; P-in-c Bethersden w High Halden and
Woodchurch *Cant* 12–19; P-in-c Lower Beeding *Chich* 19–20;
P-in-c Cowfold 19–20; V Lower Beeding and Cowfold from
20. *The Vicarage, Handcross Road, Plummers Plain, Horsham
RH13 6NU* T: (01403) 891352 E: sue@whartons.org.uk
WHARTON, Thomas Geoffrey. b 72. Glas Univ BA 93.
Westcott Ho Cam 03. **d** 05 **p** 06. C Linton in Craven and
Burnsall w Rylstone *Bradf* 05–09; TV Knight's Enham and
Smannell w Enham Alamein *Win* 09–13; P-in-c W End
13–18; V Romsey from 18. *The Vicarage, Church Lane, Romsey
SO51 8EP* E: rev.thomaswharton@gmail.com
WHATELEY, Stuart David. b 44. Ripon Hall Ox 71. **d** 73
p 74. C Chilvers Coton w Astley *Cov* 73–76; Chapl Miss
to Seafarers from 76; PtO *Sheff* 03–17. *10 Merryman Garth,
Hedon, Hull HU12 8NJ* T: (01405) 764730 M: 07551-
777717 E: whateleysd@gmail.com
WHATELEY, Thomas Roderick (Rod). b 52. St Jo Coll
Nottm 94. **d** 96 **p** 97. C Willesborough *Cant* 96–99;
P-in-c Cliftonville 99–03; R Orlestone w Snave and Ruckinge
w Warehorne etc 03–13; R Saxon Shoreline 13–19; rtd 19;
PtO *Eur* from 16. *Address temp unknown*
WHATLEY, Roger James. b 49. Chich Th Coll 94. **d** 96
p 04. NSM Newport St Thos and Newport St Jo *Portsm*
96–11; Chapl Is of Wight Fire and Rescue Service from 11.
Beechcroft, 46 Trafalgar Road, Newport PO30 1QG T: (01983)
825938 E: whatleys138@uwclub.net
WHATMOUGH, Michael Anthony. b 50. ARCO 71 Ex Univ
BA 72. Edin Th Coll BD 81. **d** 81 **p** 82. C Edin St Hilda and
Edin St Fillan 81–84; C Salisbury St Thos and St Edm *Sarum*
84–86; R 86–93; RD Salisbury 90–93; V Bris St Mary Redcliffe
w Temple etc 93–04; PtO *Lich* 08–10; C Cannock and
Huntington 10–12; C Hatherton 10–12; P-in-c Headingley
Ripon 12–14; TR *Leeds* 14–20; rtd 20; PtO *Leeds* 20–21.
16 Moor Grange Rise, Leeds LS16 5BP M: 07711-335050
E: tony@whatmough.org.uk
WHATSON, Mark Edwin Chadwick. b 57. Southn Univ
BSc 79 CEng 83 MIMechE 83. NOC 86. **d** 88 **p** 91. NSM
Church Hulme *Ches* 88–91; NSM Goostrey 91–95; NSM
Hardwicke, Quedgeley and Elmore w Longney *Glouc* 95–98;
C Thornbury 98–01; Ind Chapl 99–01; P-in-c Freshwater *Portsm*
01–17; R Yarmouth 01–17; rtd 17; PtO *Portsm* from 18. *26
Albert Road, Sandown PO36 8AW* T: (01983) 406236
WHATTON, Joanna Nicola. See PAYNE, Joanna Nicola

WHAWELL, Arthur Michael. b 38. SRN 59. Sarum & Wells Th Coll 74. **d** 76 **p** 77. C Cottingham *York* 76–79; P-in-c Bessingby 79–84; P-in-c Carnaby 79–84; V Birchencliffe *Wakef* 84–87; Chapl Huddersfield R Infirmary 84–87; V St Bart Less and Chapl St Barts Hosp Lon 87–95; P-in-c Wormingford, Mt Bures and Lt Horkesley *Chelmsf* 95–00; V 00–03; rtd 03; PtO *Pet* from 03. *Cherry Trees, Benefield Road, Upper Glapthorn, Peterborough PE8 5BQ* T: (01832) 272500 E: amwhawell@rev0538michael.plus.com

WHEALE, Alan Leon. b 43. Hull Univ MA 92 AKC 69. St Aug Coll Cant 69. **d** 70 **p** 71. C Tamworth *Lich* 70–73; C Cheddleton 73–75; V Garretts Green *Birm* 75–78; V Perry Beeches 78–83; V Winshill *Derby* 83–84; Deputation Appeals Org (E Midl) CECS 84–86; C Arnold *S'well* 86–88; V Daybrook 88–96; R Clifton Campville w Edingale and Harlaston *Lich* 96–06; P-in-c Thorpe Constantine 96–06; P-in-c Elford 97–06; rtd 06; PtO *Lich* 06–08; Hon C Tamworth 08–11; PtO 12–14; Hon C Rolleston 14–15; Hon C Anslow 14–15; Hon C Hanbury, Newborough, Rangemore and Tutbury 14–15; PtO *Derby* from 15. *1 Redbrick Gardens, Swadlincote DE11 0WJ* T: (01283) 221022 M: 07748-741034 E: alan-wheale@supanet.com

WHEALE, Sarah Ruth. *See* BULLOCK, Sarah Ruth

WHEATLEY, Diane. *See* THOMPSON, Diane

WHEATLEY (*née* GRAHAM), Mrs Fiona Karen. b 57. Hull Univ BA 84 De Montfort Univ PGCE 94. SAOMC 03. **d** 06 **p** 07. C Stevenage St Hugh and St Jo St Alb 06–10; TV Bishop's Hatfield, Lemsford and N Mymms 10–14; R Kingswood from 14. *The Vicarage, Payne End, Sandon, Buntingford SG9 0QU* T: (01763) 284189 E: fkwheatley@gmail.com

WHEATLEY, The Ven Ian James. b 62. Chich Th Coll BTh 94. **d** 94 **p** 95. C Braunton *Ex* 94–97; Chapl RN 97–18; Prin Angl Chapl and Adn for the RN 12–14; Chapl of the Fleet and Adn for the RN 14–18; Hon Can Portsm Cathl 14–18; QHC 14–18; rtd 18. *Mennabroom Farm, Warleggan, Mount, Bodmin PL30 4HE* T: (01208) 821272 E: wheatos82@gmail.com

WHEATLEY, Jane. *See* WHEATLEY, Sarah Jane

WHEATLEY, The Ven Paul Charles. b 38. St Jo Coll Dur BA 61. Linc Th Coll 61. **d** 63 **p** 64. C Bishopston *Bris* 63–68; Youth Chapl 68–73; V Swindon St Paul 73–77; TR Swindon Dorcan 77–79; R Ross *Heref* 79–81; P-in-c Brampton Abbotts 79–81; RD Ross and Archenfield 79–91; TR Ross w Brampton Abbotts, Bridstow and Peterstow 81–91; Preb Heref Cathl 87–91; Adn Sherborne *Sarum* 91–03; P-in-c W Stafford w Frome Billet 91–03; rtd 03; PtO *Heref* 04–20. *The Farthings, Bridstow, Ross-on-Wye HR9 6QF* T: (01989) 566965 E: paulwheatley@buckcastle.plus.com

✠**WHEATLEY, The Rt Revd Peter William.** b 47. Qu Coll Ox BA 69 MA 73 Pemb Coll Cam BA 71 MA 75. Ripon Hall Ox 72. **d** 73 **p** 74 **c** 99. C Fulham All SS *Lon* 73–78; V St Pancras H Cross w St Jude and St Pet 78–82; P-in-c Hampstead All So 82–90; P-in-c Kilburn St Mary 82–90; P-in-c Kilburn St Mary w All So 90–95; V W Hampstead St Jas 82–95; Dir Post-Ord Tr 85–95; AD N Camden 88–93; Adn Hampstead 95–99; Area Bp Edmonton 99–14; rtd 15; Hon Asst Bp S'wark from 13; Hon Asst Bp Lon from 15; P-in-c St Leonards Ch Ch and St Mary etc *Chich* from 19. *47 Sedlescombe Road South, St Leonards-on-Sea TN38 0TB* T: (01424) 424814

WHEATLEY, Miss Sarah Jane. b 45. St Gabr Coll Lon Dip Teaching 67. St Alb Minl Tr Scheme 77. **d** 96 **p** 97. NSM Meppershall w Campton and Stondon *St Alb* 96–99; P-in-c Shillington 99–03; V Gravenhurst, Shillington and Stondon 03–12; rtd 12; PtO *St Alb* from 12. *16 Queen Street, Stotfold, Hitchin SG5 4NX* T: (01462) 731170 E: jane.wheatley5@btinternet.com

WHEATLEY PRICE, Canon John. b 31. Em Coll Cam BA 54 MA 58. Ridley Hall Cam 54. **d** 56 **p** 57. C Drypool St Andr and St Pet *York* 56–59; CMS 59–76; Uganda 60–74; Adn Soroti 72–74; Hon Can Soroti 78–97; Adn N Maseno Kenya 74–76; V Clevedon St Andr *B & W* 76–82; V Clevedon St Andr and Ch Ch 82–87; Chapl Amsterdam w Heiloo *Eur* 87–92; P-in-c Cromford *Derby* 92–95; P-in-c Matlock Bath 92–95; V Matlock Bath and Cromford 95–96; rtd 96; PtO *Sarum* 96–01; *Birm* 01–18. *2 Beausale Drive, Knowle, Solihull B93 0NS* T: (01564) 730067 E: jean@wheatleyprice.co.uk

WHEATON, Canon Christopher. b 49. St Jo Coll Nottm BTh 80. **d** 80 **p** 81. C Hatcham St Jas *S'wark* 80–83; C Warlingham w Chelsham and Farleigh 83–87; V Carshalton Beeches 87–13; AD Sutton 03–10; Hon Can S'wark Cathl 07–13; rtd 13; PtO *S'well* from 14. *70 Gordon Road, West Bridgford, Nottingham NG2 5LS* T: 0115-982 7192 E: christopherwheaton@btinternet.com

WHEATON, Patrick Edward. b 78. Ex Coll Ox BA 00. Trin Coll Bris BA 08. **d** 09 **p** 10. C Shill Valley and Broadshire *Ox* 09–13; C Cheltenham St Mary w St Matt and St Luke *Glouc* from 13; PtO *Eur* from 16. *38 College Road, Cheltenham GL53 7HX* M: 07974-986608

WHEELER, Preb Alexander Quintin Henry (Alastair). b 51. Lon Univ BA 73 MBACP 07. St Jo Coll Nottm 74. **d** 77 **p** 78. C Kenilworth St Jo *Cov* 77–80; C Madeley *Heref* 80–83; P-in-c Draycott-le-Moors *Lich* 83–84; P-in-c Forsbrook 83–84; R Draycott-le-Moors w Forsbrook 84–91; V Nailsea Ch Ch *B & W* 91–96; R Nailsea Ch Ch w Tickenham 96–10; RD Portishead 95–01; V Wells St Cuth w Wookey Hole 10–16; RD Shepton Mallet 11–16; Preb Wells Cathl 03–16; rtd 16; PtO *B & W* from 16; *Sarum* 16–21. *32 Windy Ridge, Beaminster DT8 3SR* T: (01308) 862093 E: aqhw02@gmail.com

WHEELER, Andrew Charles. b 48. CCC Cam BA 69 MA 72 Makerere Univ Kampala MA 72 Leeds Univ PGCE 72. Trin Coll Bris BA 88. **d** 88 **p** 88. CMS from 76; C Whitton *Sarum* 88–89; C All SS Cathl Cairo Egypt 89–92; Co-ord for Th Educn Sudan 92–00; C All SS Cathl Nairobi Kenya 92–00; Abp's Sec for Angl Communion Affairs *Cant* 00–01; C Guildf St Sav 02–16; rtd 16; Dioc World Miss Adv *Guildf* 06–19; Hon C Guildf H Trin w St Mary 18–19; PtO from 19. *16 Little Street, Guildford GU2 9QG* E: andy.wheeler2@gmail.com

WHEELER (*née* MILLAR), Mrs Christine. b 55. City of Lon Poly BSc 76 DipCOT 81. S Dios Minl Tr Scheme 84. **d** 87 **p** 94. NSM Kingston Buci *Chich* 87–89; Par Dn Merstham and Gatton *S'wark* 89–94; C 94–96; R Rockland St Mary w Hellington, Bramerton etc *Nor* 96–04; PtO from 04. *Church View, The Street, Foxley, Dereham NR20 4QP* T: (01362) 688796 E: emailcw@sky.com

WHEELER, David Ian. b 49. Southn Univ BSc 70 PhD 78. NOC 87. **d** 90 **p** 91. C Blackpool St Jo *Blackb* 90–94; R Old Trafford St Jo *Man* 94–05; P-in-c Irlam 05–08; V 08–13; rtd 13; PtO *Win* from 15; *Sarum* from 16. *22 Glamis Avenue, Northbourne, Bournemouth BH10 6DP* T: (01202) 577820

WHEELER, David James. b 49. Leeds Univ MA 95 CQSW 74. S Dios Minl Tr Scheme 87. **d** 90 **p** 91. C Hythe *Cant* 90–92; C Knaresborough *Ripon* 92–97; Asst Soc Resp Officer 94–97; P-in-c Gt and Lt Ouseburn w Marton cum Grafton etc 97–01; V 01–05; Jt AD Ripon 01–05; V Cobbold Road St Sav w St Mary *Lon* 05–12; rtd 12; PtO *St E* 13–18; Hon C Lower Wharfedale *Leeds* from 18. *The Vicarage, Old Pool Bank, Pool in Wharfedale, Otley LS21 1EJ* E: david.wheeler@phonecoop.coop

WHEELER, Mrs Helen Mary. b 38. Qu Coll Birm 04. **d** 06 **p** 07. NSM Smethwick Resurr *Birm* 06–12; rtd 12; PtO *Birm* from 12. *99 Brookfield Road, Birmingham B18 7JA* T: 0121-554 4721 M: 07804-450099 E: revhwheeler@hotmail.co.uk

WHEELER, James Albert. b 49. Sarum & Wells Th Coll 74. **d** 76 **p** 77. C Orpington All SS *Roch* 76–79; C Roch St Pet w St Marg 79–81; C Bexley St Jo 81–84; V Penge Lane H Trin 84–93; P-in-c Tunbridge Wells St Luke 93–99; V 99–09; P-in-c Southborough St Thos 09–15; rtd 15; PtO *Chich* from 16. *19 Plover Close, Eastbourne BN23 7SB* T: (01323) 767533 E: j.wheeler@mybroadbandmail.com

WHEELER, Julian Aldous. b 48. Nottm Univ BTh 74. Kelham Th Coll 70. **d** 75 **p** 76. C Bideford *Ex* 75–79; LtO 79–86; Hon C Parkham, Alwington, Buckland Brewer etc 86–03. *Manorfield, Mount Raleigh Avenue, Bideford EX39 3NR* T: (01237) 477271

WHEELER, Preb Madeleine. b 42. Gilmore Course 76. **dss** 78 **d** 87 **p** 94. Ruislip Manor St Paul *Lon* 78–92; Par Dn 87–91; Team Dn 91–92; Chapl for Women's Min (Willesden Episc Area) 86–95; P-in-c N Greenford All Hallows *Lon* 94–00; Preb St Paul's Cathl 95–00; rtd 00; PtO *St Alb* from 00; *Lon* from 02. *178A Harefield Road, Uxbridge UB8 1PP* T: (01895) 257274 E: mm.wheeler@tiscali.co.uk *or* mwheeler7442@gmail.com

WHEELER, Nicholas Charles. b 50. LVO 09. Leic Univ BA 72. SEITE 00. **d** 03 **p** 04. NSM Blackheath St Jo *S'wark* 03–08; PtO 08–11; NSM Eltham H Trin 11–16; NSM Chipping Barnet *St Alb* from 16. *St Peter's House, Barnet Road, Barnet EN5 3JF* E: teamvicar.arkley@gmail.com

WHEELER, Nicholas Gordon Timothy. b 59. BCombStuds 84. Linc Th Coll. **d** 84 **p** 85. C Hendon St Alphage *Lon* 84–87; C Wood Green St Mich w Bounds Green St Gabr etc 87–89; TV 89–93; R Cranford 93–02; V Ruislip St Mary 02–16; R Hayes St Mary from 16. *The Rectory, 170 Church Road, Hayes UB3 2LR* T: (020) 8845 3485 M: 07769-339529 E: frnicholaswheeler@virginmedia.com

WHEELER, Canon Nicholas Paul. b 60. Ox Univ BA 86 MA 91. Wycliffe Hall Ox 83. **d** 87 **p** 88. C Wood Green St Mich w Bounds Green St Gabr etc *Lon* 87–91; Chapl to Bp Edmonton 91–96; P-in-c Somers Town 96–03; P-in-c Old St Pancras w Bedford New Town St Matt 96–03; P-in-c Camden Town St Mich w All SS and St Thos 96–03; P-in-c Camden Square St Paul 96–03; TR Old St Pancras 03–08; Brazil 08–15; R Upper Chelsea H Trin and St Sav *Lon* from 15. *97A Cadogan Lane, London SW1X 9DU* T: (020) 7730 7270 E: nicholaspaulwheeler@gmail.com

WHEELER, Paul Kenneth. b 81. Coll of Resurr Mirfield 17. d 19 p 20. C Nantwich *Ches* from 19. *12 Hallams Drive, Nantwich CW5 7RN* E: paulwheeler508@gmail.com

WHEELER, Canon Richard Roy. b 44. K Coll Lon BD 72. St Aug Coll Cant. d 74 p 74. C Brixton St Matt *S'wark* 74–78; Dir St Matt Meeting Place Brixton 78–79; Sec BCC Community Work Resource Unit 79–82; TV Southampton (City Cen) *Win* 83–88; TR 88–98; Hon Can Win Cathl 94–98; Soc Resp Adv *St Alb* 98–09; Can Res St Alb 01–09; rtd 09; PtO *S'wark* from 16. *114 Well Hall Road, London SE9 6TS* T: (020) 8856 5271 E: canonrwheeler@btinternet.com

WHEELER, Richenda Mary Celia. b 71. St Mary's Coll Strawberry Hill BA 93. Ripon Coll Cuddesdon BTh 98. d 99 p 00. C Dalston H Trin w St Phil and Haggerston All SS *Lon* 99–02; Asst Chapl R Free Hampstead NHS Trust 02–05; Chapl Lon Metrop Univ 05–10; Chapl Derby Univ 10–14; Chapl Derby Cathl 10–14; PtO *S'wark* 15; V Dalston H Trin w St Phil and Haggerston All SS *Lon* 15–17; PtO 17–19; Chapl Hartpury Coll from 18. *Hartpury College, Hartpury House, Hartpury, Gloucester GL19 3BE* T: (01452) 702100 M: 07971-659534 E: richenda@leigh.me

WHEELER, Mrs Sally Ann Violet. b 59. Westmr Coll Ox BEd 81. SAOMC 94. d 97 p 98. NSM Chippenham St Paul w Hardenhuish etc *Bris* 97–01; C Gtr Corsham and Lacock 01–04; TV 04–12; P-in-c Marshfield w Cold Ashton and Tormarton etc 12–17; V from 17; AD Chippenham from 15. *The Vicarage, Church Lane, Marshfield, Chippenham SN14 8NT* T: (01225) 892180 E: marshfield.benefice@gmail.com

WHEELER-KILEY, Mrs Susan Elizabeth. b 47. d 06 p 07. NSM S Norwood St Mark *S'wark* 06–17; NSM S Norwood H Innocents from 15; PtO from 17. *35 St Luke's Close, London SE25 4SX* T: (020) 8656 9923 M: 07890-780572 E: fs.kiley@btinternet.com

WHEELHOUSE, Paul Andrew. b 72. Bradf Univ BEd 95 Ox Brookes Univ MA 11 St Jo Coll Dur BATM 12. Cranmer Hall Dur 10. d 12 p 13. C Burley in Wharfedale *Bradf* 12–16; Ilkley St Marg *Leeds* 16–18; V Bierley from 18. *Bierley Vicarage, Bierley Lane, Bradford BD4 6AA* M: 07832-892854 E: pawheelhouse@gmail.com

WHEELWRIGHT, Michael Harvey. b 39. Bps' Coll Cheshunt 64. d 67 p 68. C Glen Parva and S Wigston *Leic* 67–70; C Evington 70–74; V Leic St Eliz Nether Hall 74–79; Chapl Prudhoe Hosp Northd 79–99; PtO *Dur* from 79; *Newc* from 99; rtd 04. *6 Nunnykirk Close, Ovingham, Prudhoe NE42 6BP* T: (01661) 835749

WHELAN, Miss Patricia Jean. b 33. ACA 55 FCA 82. Dalton Ho Bris 58. dss 64 d 87 p 94. Stapleford *S'well* 62–69; Aylesbury *Ox* 69–75; Bushbury *Lich* 75–77; Patchway *Bris* 77–81; Trin Coll Bris 81–82; W Swindon LEP 82–86; High Wycombe *Ox* 86–87; Par Dn 87–91; Par Dn Ox St Ebbe w H Trin and St Pet 91–93; rtd 93. *81 Cogges Hill Road, Witney OX28 3XU* T: (01993) 779099 E: patwhelan81@btinternet.com

WHELAN, Peter Warwick Armstrong. b 34. Southn Univ BTh 80 Open Univ BA 80. Sarum Th Coll 69. d 71 p 72. C Salisbury St Mark *Sarum* 71–73; C Solihull *Birm* 73–77; TR Shirley 77–86; Chapl Whittington Hosp NHS Trust 86–99; Chapl Camden and Islington Community Health NHS Trust 86–99; rtd 99; PtO *Ex* 98–20. *5 Greenacres, Asheldon Road, Torquay TQ1 2QS* T: (01803) 212483 E: warwickw@talktalk.net

WHELAN, Raymond Keith. b 40. Cant Sch of Min 85. d 88 p 91. C Eastbourne St Andr *Chich* 88–93; C-in-c Parklands St Wilfrid CD 93–95; TV Chich 95–00; V Chich St Wilfrid 00–01; rtd 04; PtO *Chich* from 04. *9 Ruislip Gardens, Aldwick, Bognor Regis PO21 4LB* T: (01243) 264865 E: wdiosc@aol.com

WHERRY, Anthony Michael. b 44. Nottm Univ BA 65. WMMTC 88. d 91 p 92. NSM Worc City St Paul and Old St Martin etc 91–95; NSM Worc E Deanery 95–02; NSM Worc SE 02–16; PtO 16–17. *2 Thomas Stock Gardens, Abbeymead, Gloucester GL4 5GH* T: (01905) 358532 E: tonywherry@btinternet.com

WHETTER, Linda Carol. b 56. Dur Univ BA 18. d 16 p 17. NSM Probus, Ladock and Grampound w Creed and St Erme *Truro* from 16. *Pencoose Barn, Tregony, Truro TR2 5TR* T: (01872) 530265 E: lindaw23@outlook.com

WHETTINGSTEEL, Raymond Edward. b 44. S Dios Minl Tr Scheme 79. d 82 p 83. NSM Sholing *Win* 82–84; C Southampton Maybush St Pet 84–89; R Hatherden w Tangley, Weyhill and Penton Mewsey 89–09; rtd 09; PtO *Win* from 11. *Longbridge House, Membury, Axminster EX13 7TY* E: raywhetters@gmail.com

WHETTON, Nicholas John. b 56. Open Univ BA 94. St Jo Coll Nottm 83. d 86 p 87. C Hatfield *Sheff* 86–90; V Cornholme *Wakef* 90–96; P-in-c Livesey

Blackb 96–99; V 99–03; P-in-c Ewood 96–97; Chapl HM Pris Hull from 03. *The Chaplain's Office, HM Prison, Hedon Road, Hull HU9 5LS* T: (01482) 282200 E: nicholas.whetton@justice.gov.uk

WHIFFIN, Vanessa Janet. See BRUNNER-ELLIS, Vanessa Janet

WHINNEY, Nigel Patrick Maurice. b 43. Open Univ BA 91. SWMTC 95. d 97 p 98. NSM Ilminster and Distr *B & W* 97–08; Bp's Officer for Ord NSM (Taunton Adnry) 99–06; RD Crewkerne and Ilminster 01–07; rtd 08; PtO *B & W* 08–12; Perm to Offic Nelson NZ from 12. *376B Hardy Street, Nelson 7010, New Zealand* T: (0064) (354) 67765

WHINTON, William Francis Ivan. b 35. NOC 77. d 80 p 81. NSM Stockport St Mary *Ches* 80–82; NSM Disley 82–87; V Birtles 87–00; Dioc Officer for Disabled 89–00; rtd 00; Chapl for Deaf People *Ches* 00–04; PtO from 05; *Lich* 09–15. *Allmeadows Cottage, Wincle, Macclesfield SK11 0QJ* T: (01260) 227278

WHIPP, Antony Douglas. b 46. Leeds Univ BSc 68 Lanc Univ PhD 04. Ripon Coll Cuddesdon 84. d 86 p 87. C Dalston *Carl* 86–89; V Holme Cultram St Mary 89–96; V Holme Cultram St Cuth 89–96; V Kells 96–00; V Hartlepool St Aid *Dur* 00–05; R Ebchester 05–13; V Medomsley 05–13; rtd 13; PtO *Dur* 14–17. *34 Egglestone Drive, Consett DH8 7UB* T: (01207) 588407 E: tony.whipp@durham.anglican.org *or* tony.whipp@outlook.com

WHIPP, Canon Margaret Jane. b 55. LMH Ox BA 76 Sheff Univ MB, ChB 79 MRCP 82 FRCR 86 Hull Univ MA 99 Glas Univ PhD 08. NOC 87. d 90 p 94. NSM Wickersley *Sheff* 90–98; Tutor Cranmer Hall Dur 98–99; Dir Practical Th NEOC 00–04; Ecum Chapl Ox Brookes Univ 04–08; Lect Past Studies Ox Min Course 06–08; Dean of Studies Ripon Coll Cuddesdon 08–12; Chapl Ox Univ Hosps NHS Foundn Trust 13–19; Lead Chapl 16–18; rtd 19; PtO *Ox* from 19; Hon Can Ch Ch from 16. *2 All Saints Road, Oxford OX3 7AU* T: (01865) 765409 M: 07775-617129 E: margaretwhipp@btinternet.com

WHITAKER, Anthony. b 50. SS Mark & Jo Coll Chelsea CertEd 72 Middx Univ BA 02. NTMTC 99. d 02 p 03. C Blackmore and Stondon Massey *Chelmsf* 02–06; P-in-c St Keverne *Truro* 06–11; C Churt and Hindhead *Guildf* 11–15; rtd 15; Hon C Stow on the Wold, Condicote and The Swells *Glouc* 16–20; PtO from 20. *27 Mosedale, Moreton-in-Marsh GL56 0HP* T: (01608) 652415 E: tony_whitaker@btinternet.com

WHITAKER, Benjamin. See WHITAKER, Michael Benjamin

WHITAKER, Irene Anne. b 57. d 01 p 02. OLM Parr *Liv* 01–06; TV Bootle 06–18; TR 18–19; R 19–20; rtd 20. *Address temp unknown* M: 07771-581886

WHITAKER, Margaret Scott. b 45. Dioc OLM tr scheme 00 EAMTC 04. d 03 p 04. OLM Eaton *Nor* 03–05; C Sprowston w Beeston 05–07; C New Catton Ch Ch 07–11; R Horsford, Felthorpe and Hevingham 11–15; rtd 15; PtO *Nor* from 15. *West End Lodge, Norwich Road, Ludham, Great Yarmouth NR29 5PB* T: (01692) 678302 M: 07717-317900 E: mwhitaker1@btinternet.com

WHITAKER, Michael Benjamin. b 60. Nottm Univ BA 83. Sarum & Wells Th Coll 85. d 87 p 88. C Gt Grimsby St Mary and St Jas *Linc* 87–91; C Abingdon *Ox* 91–95; Chapl to the Deaf *Sarum* 95–00; PtO *Win* 97–00; Asst Chapl amongst Deaf People *Ox* from 00; Chapl HM Pris Grendon and Spring Hill from 07. *HM Prison Grendon, Grendon Underwood, Aylesbury HP18 0TL* T: (01865) 736100 E: whitakerben5@gmail.com

WHITAKER, Neil Robert. b 71. All SS Cen for Miss & Min 16. d 18 p 19. NSM Langley *Man* from 18. *43 Melverley Road, Manchester M9 0PD* E: revneilster@outlook.com

WHITBY, Raymond Thomas. b 57. d 14 p 15. NSM Wigan All SS *Liv* 15–17. *52 Coroners Lane, Widnes WA8 9JB* T: 0151-423 6375 E: ramonw57@sky.com

WHITBY, Suffragan Bishop of. See FERGUSON, The Rt Revd Paul John

WHITCROFT, Graham Frederick. b 42. Oak Hill Th Coll 64. d 66 p 67. C Cromer *Nor* 66–69; C Attercliffe *Sheff* 69–72; V Kimberworth Park 72–85; V Lepton *Wakef* 85–07; RD Kirkburton 98–05; rtd 07; PtO *Wakef* 07–14; *Leeds* from 14. *18 Far Croft, Lepton, Huddersfield HD8 0LS* T: (01484) 609868 E: gswhitcroft@yahoo.com

WHITE, Preb Alan. b 43. Ex Univ BA 65. Chich Th Coll 65. d 68 p 69. C Upper Clapton St Matt *Lon* 68–72; C Southgate Ch Ch 72–76; P-in-c Friern Barnet St Pet le Poer 76–79; V 79–85; TR Ex St Thos and Em 85–08; RD Christianity 99–03; Preb Ex Cathl 03–08; rtd 08; RD Newton Abbot and Ipplepen Ex 16–18; PtO from 18. *Flat 3, 7 Courtenay Road, Newton Abbot TQ12 1HP* T: (01626) 332451 E: revalanwhite@tiscali.com

✠**WHITE, The Rt Revd Alison Mary.** b 56. St Aid Coll Dur BA 78 Leeds Univ MA 94. Cranmer Hall Dur 83. dss 86 d 87 p 94 c 15. NSM Chester le Street *Dur* 86–89; Dioc

Adv in Local Miss 89–93; Hon Par Dn Birtley 89–93; Dir Past Studies Cranmer Hall Dur 93–98; Dir of Ords *Dur* 98–00; Springboard Missr 00–04; Adult Educn Officer *Pet* 05–10; Can Pet Cathl 09–10; Hon Can Th Sheff Cathl 10–15; P-in-c Riding Mill *Newc* 11–15; Adv for Spirituality and Spiritual Direction 11–15; Suff Bp Hull *York* from 15. *Hullen House, Woodfield Lane, Hessle HU13 0ES* T: (01482) 649019 F: 647449 E: alisonmarywhite@btinternet.com *or* bishopofhull@yorkdiocese.org

WHITE, Canon Andrew Paul Bartholomew. b 64. MIOT 85 ABIST 85. Ridley Hall Cam 86. **d** 90 **p** 91. C Battersea Rise St Mark *S'wark* 90–93; P-in-c Balham Hill Ascension 93–97; V 97–98; Dir Internat Min and Can Res Cov Cathl 98–05; Chapl Iraq 05–14; President Foundn for Relief and Reconciliation in the Middle E 05–16; Jerusalem Merit 18–20. *The Croft, 66 Shepherds Way, Liphook GU30 7HH* T: (01428) 723939 *or* (00964) (7901) 265723 E: apbw2@cam.ac.uk

WHITE, Anne Margaret. b 55. Nottm Univ BEd 78. STETS 07. **d** 10 **p** 11. NSM Guernsey St Andr *Win* 10–13; P-in-c Aldbrough, Mappleton w Goxhill and Withernwick *York* from 13; RD N Holderness 16–21. *The Vicarage, Carlton Drive, Aldbrough, Hull HU11 4SF* T: (01964) 527230 M: 07911-712274 E: white.anne19@gmail.com

WHITE, Camilla Elizabeth Zoë. b 56. Somerville Coll Ox BA 78 MA 83 Heythrop Coll Lon MA 06. Ripon Coll Cuddesdon 05. **d** 07 **p** 08. NSM Bramley and Grafham *Guildf* 07–17; P-in-c from 19; PtO 17–19. *Bramley Mill, Mill Lane, Bramley, Guildford GU5 0HW* T: (01483) 892645 E: camillawhite@waitrose.com

WHITE, Colin Davidson. b 44. St And Dioc Tr Course 86. **d** 88 **p** 89. NSM Glenrothes *St And* 88–89; P-in-c 89–90; P-in-c Leven 90–92; R 92–95; V Grimethorpe *Wakef* 95–01; P-in-c Kellington w Whitley 01–02; TV Knottingley and Kellington w Whitley 02–10; rtd 10. *42 Glendale Avenue North, Belfast BT8 6LB* T: (028) 9029 6037 M: 07973-795560 E: col_the_rev@hotmail.co.uk

WHITE, Crispin Michael. b 42. Southn Univ MA 98 PhD 06 FRSA 94. Bps' Coll Cheshunt 62. **d** 65 **p** 66. C S Harrow St Paul *Lon* 65–67; C Mill Hill St Mich 67–68; I Labrador St Clem Canada 68–71; Toc H Padre (W Region) 71–75; (E Midl Region) 75–82; Ind Chapl *Portsm* 82–98; P-in-c Hatfield Broad Oak and Bush End *Chelmsf* 98–04; Ind Chapl 98–07; Harlow 98–04; Lon Thames Gateway 04–07; rtd 07; PtO *Chich* 12–17. *6 Downlands, Firsdown Close, Worthing BN13 3BQ* T/F: (01903) 830785 M: 07962-057436 E: postmaster@crispinwhite.plus.com *or* postmaster@erispiwhite.plus.com

WHITE, Daniel Charles. b 69. St Mellitus Coll 15. **d** 18 **p** 20. NSM St Marg Lothbury and St Steph Coleman Street etc *Lon* 18–19; NSM St Jas Garlickhythe w St Mich Queenhithe etc from 19. *35 Wickenden Road, Sevenoaks TN13 3PL* M: 07479-657775 E: dcwhite39@btinternet.com

WHITE, Canon David Christopher. b 51. Lon Univ LLB 73. St Jo Coll Nottm 86. **d** 88 **p** 89. C Bulwell St Mary *S'well* 88–92; V Nottingham All SS 92–98; TR Clarendon Park St Jo w Knighton St Mich *Leic* 98–05; R Emmaus Par Team 05–07; P-in-c Fosse Team 07–12; TR 12–16; Bp's Nshlm Officer 02–08; Hon Can Leic Cathl 08–16; rtd 16; PtO *Leic* from 16; *S'well* from 17. *Lindum, 11 Gainsborough Road, Winthorpe, Newark NG24 2NN* E: davidwhite264@virginmedia.com

WHITE, David Martin. b 50. St Jo Coll Dur BA 72. Cranmer Hall Dur DipTh 73. **d** 74 **p** 75. C Ripley *Derby* 74–78; C Normanton 78–80; C-in-c Sinfin 78–80; P-in-c 80; V 80–88; P-in-c Belper 88–91; V 91–97; RD Duffield 96–97; rtd 11. *Water's Edge, 18 Clipper View, Birmingham B16 9DJ* T: 0121-454 2758 E: dmartinwhite@gmail.com

WHITE, David Patrick John. b 75. All Hallows Coll Dublin BA 09 Irish Sch of Ecum MPhil 10. St Jo Coll Nottm 10 CITC MTh 13. **d** 12 **p** 13. C Clonsast w Rathangan, Thomastown etc *M & K* 12–13; C Bandon Union *C, C & R* 13–16; I Carlow w Urglin and Staplestown *C, F & O* from 16. *The Rectory, Green Road, Carlow, Republic of Ireland* T: (00353) (59) 913 2565 E: revdavidwhite2018@gmail.com

WHITE, Canon David Paul. b 58. Oak Hill Th Coll. **d** 84 **p** 85. C Toxteth Park St Clem *Liv* 84–87; C Woodford Wells *Chelmsf* 87–89; C Woodside Park St Barn *Lon* 89–90; TV Canford Magna *Sarum* 90–93; V York St Mich-le-Belfrey 93–99; V St Austell *Truro* 99–10; Dioc Dir Miss 05–10; Hon Can Truro Cathl 05–10; V Chorleywood St Andr *St Alb* 10–16; Public Preacher *Truro* from 16. *74 Boxwell Park, Bodmin PL31 2BE* E: dprm58@hotmail.com

WHITE, David Peter. b 55. Anglia Ruskin Univ MA 07 AMICE 78. ERMC 09. **d** 12 **p** 13. NSM Felixstowe St Jo *St E* 12–16; NSM Bacton w Wyverstone, Cotton and Old Newton etc 16–18; PtO 19; NSM Felixstowe SS Pet and Paul from 19.

154 Colneis Road, Felixstowe IP11 9LQ M: 07982-003144 E: david.pwhite@icloud.com

WHITE, Derek. b 35. MBE 97. **d** 84 **p** 85. C St Marylebone St Cypr *Lon* 84–96; Bp's Chapl for the Homeless 87–01; P-in-c St Mary le Strand w St Clem Danes 96–01; rtd 01; PtO *S'wark* 04–18. *80 Coleraine Road, London SE3 7PE* T: (020) 8858 3622

WHITE, Douglas Richard Leon. b 49. Linc Th Coll 81. **d** 83 **p** 84. C Warsop *S'well* 83–88; V Kirkby in Ashfield St Thos 88–93; Asst Chapl Qu Medical Cen Nottm Univ Hosp NHS Trust 93–98; Chapl Cen Notts Healthcare NHS Trust 98–01; Chapl Mansfield Distr Primary Care Trust 01–02; Chapl Geo Eliot Hosp NHS Trust Nuneaton 02–06; Chapl Mary Ann Evans Hospice 02–06; Chapl Compton Hospice 06–08; Chapl Marie Curie Hospice Solihull 08–11; Chapl Primrose Hospice Bromsgrove from 08; PtO *Birm* 11–14; *Cov* 06–20. *1 Glebe Avenue, Bedworth CV12 0DP* T: (024) 7636 0417 E: rickwhite29@btinternet.com

WHITE, Duncan Ernest. b 45. **d** 07 **p** 08. OLM Tilehurst St Geo and Tilehurst St Mary *Ox* 07–11; PtO from 11. *56 Buckingham Terrace, Pegasus Court, Park Lane, Tilehurst, Reading RG31 5DB* T: 0118-942 0629 E: rev.duncan.white@gmail.com

WHITE, Mrs Elaine. b 63. Leeds Univ BA 85 Ches Univ PGCE 89. All SS Cen for Miss & Min 16. **d** 19. C Liscard Resurr *Ches* from 19; C Seacombe w Poulton from 19. *22 Elleray Park Road, Wallasey CH45 0LH* M: 07856-709714

✠**WHITE, The Rt Revd Francis.** b 49. Univ of Wales (Cardiff) BSc(Econ) 70. St Jo Coll Nottm. **d** 80 **p** 81 **c** 02. C Dur St Nic 80–84; C Chester le Street 84–87; Chapl Dur and Chester le Street Hosps 87–89; V Birtley *Dur* 89–97; RD Chester-le-Street 93–97; Adn Sunderland and Hon Can Dur Cathl 97–02; Suff Bp Brixworth *Pet* 02–10; Can Pet Cathl 02–10; Asst Bp Newc 10–16; rtd 16; Hon Asst Bp York from 17; P-in-c Kingston upon Hull H Trin 19–20. *Hullen House, Woodfield Lane, Hessle HU13 0ES* T: (01482) 649019 E: white6.francis1949@gmail.com

WHITE, Geoffrey Brian. b 54. Jes Coll Ox BA 76 MA 80 BD 16. St Steph Ho Ox 76. **d** 79 **p** 80. C Huddersfield St Pet *Wakef* 79–82; C Flixton St Mich *Man* 82–84; TV Westhoughton 84–91; V Stevenage St Mary Shephall w Aston St Alb 91–06; RD Stevenage 01–06; R Norton *Sheff* 06–19; C Norton Lees St Paul 17–19; C Greenhill 17–19; C Woodseats St Chad 17–19; rtd 19; PtO *Sheff* from 20. *37 Vernon Road, Sheffield S17 3QE* M: 07799-004542 E: geoffreywhite_333@hotmail.com

WHITE, Canon Geoffrey Gordon. b 28. Selw Coll Cam BA 50 MA 54. Cuddesdon Coll 51. **d** 53 **p** 54. C Bradford-on-Avon H Trin *Sarum* 53–56; C Kennington St Jo *S'wark* 56–61; V Leeds St Wilfrid *Ripon* 61–63; Chapl K Coll Hosp Lon 63–66; V Aldwick *Chich* 66–76; V Brighton Gd Shep Preston 76–93; Can and Preb Chich Cathl 90–93; rtd 93; Hon C Stepney St Dunstan and All SS *Lon* 94–10; PtO 13–19; *Leic* 15–20; *Pet* 17–22. *7 Lime Tree Place, Great Bowden, Market Harborough LE16 7JE* T: (01858) 465186

WHITE, George Trevor. b 93. Heythrop Coll Lon BA 15. St Mellitus Coll 15. **d** 18 **p** 19. C Lenton Abbey *S'well* from 18. *18 Boyce Gardens, Nottingham NG3 3FB* M: 07807-645583 E: georgetrevorwhite@icloud.com

WHITE, Gillian Margaret. b 57. Qu Eliz Coll Lon BSc 79 Sheff Univ MEd 96 PhD 02 Nottm Univ MA 07. EMMTC 05. **d** 07 **p** 08. NSM Derby St Paul 07–13; PtO 14–15; NSM Tideswell from 15. *The Vicarage, 6 Pursglove Drive, Tideswell, Buxton SK17 8PA* T: (01298) 871317 M: 07973-866848 E: gillianwhite470@gmail.com

WHITE, Graham John. b 76. Lon Bible Coll BTh 99 K Coll Lon MA 08. Ripon Coll Cuddesdon 13. **d** 15. C Tring *St Alb* 15–16. *14 Leach Road, Aylesbury HP21 8LG* M: 07963-584458

WHITE, Miss Hazel Susan. b 65. Nottm Univ BA 88 Birm Univ MPhil 11. Qu Coll Birm 05. **d** 07 **p** 08. C Woodfield *Leic* 07–12; C Moseley St Mary and St Anne *Birm* 12–20; V Selly Oak St Mary from 20. *St Mary's Vicarage, Bristol Road, Selly Oak, Birmingham B29 6ND* E: hazelwhite1@btinternet.com

WHITE, Ian Jeffrey. b 57. Leeds Univ BSc 80 PhD 86 BA 05 CChem 83 MRSC 83. Coll of Resurr Mirfield 03. **d** 05 **p** 06. C Stanningley St Thos *Ripon* 05–09; P-in-c Adel 09–14; *Leeds* 14–17; R 17–19; P-in-c Ireland Wood *Ripon* 12–14; *Leeds* 14–16; Dioc Environment Officer *Ripon* 06–09; rtd 19; LtO *Leeds* from 19. *17 Haven Gardens, Leeds LS16 6SN* T: 0113-267 2923 E: ian.white.uk@outlook.com

WHITE, Ian Terence. b 56. CertEd. Ripon Coll Cuddesdon 83. **d** 86 **p** 87. C Maidstone St Martin *Cant* 86–89; C Earley St Pet *Ox* 89–91; TV Schorne 91–96; V St Osyth *Chelmsf* 96–00; R The Suttons w Tydd *Linc* 00–04; rtd 04; PtO *Nor* from 06; *St E*

from 10. *9 Haling Way, Thetford IP24 1EY* T: (01842) 820180 E: revianwhite@aol.com

WHITE, James Robert. b 88. St Steph Ho Ox 14. d 18 p 19. NSM Ruislip St Martin *Lon* from 18. *20 Lymington Drive, Ruislip HA4 7EZ* M: 07716-086302 E: whitejr@hotmail.co.uk

WHITE, Miss Janice. b 49. Trin Coll Bris IDC 76. d 91 p 94. C Claygate *Guildf* 91–98; Assoc Min Stanford-le-Hope w Mucking *Chelmsf* 98–12; rtd 12; PtO *St E* from 12. *27 Canterbury Gardens, Hadleigh IP7 5BS* T: (01473) 808835 E: wheeze4god@talktalk.net

WHITE, Jo. *See* WHITE, Julia Mary

WHITE, Canon John Austin. b 42. LVO 04. Hull Univ BA 64. Coll of Resurr Mirfield 64. d 66 p 67. C Leeds St Aid *Ripon* 66–69; Asst Chapl Leeds Univ 69–73; Chapl NOC 73–82; Can and Prec Windsor 82–12; rtd 12. *24 Camm Avenue, Windsor SL4 4NW*

WHITE, John Christopher. b 62. Keble Coll Ox BA 84 Ex Univ MA 98 PhD 10. Wycliffe Hall Ox BA 88. d 89 p 90. C Southway *Ex* 89–93; TV Plymouth Em, St Paul Efford and St Aug 93–99; Hon C Abbotskerswell 99–05; PtO *Birm* 05–10; TV Kings Norton 10–14; P-in-c Kingsbury from 14; P-in-c Baxterley w Hurley and Wood End and Merevale etc from 14. *The Vicarage, Church Lane, Kingsbury, Tamworth B78 2LR* T: (01827) 874252 E: jwhite.harborne@live.co.uk

WHITE, John Cooper. b 58. K Alfred's Coll Win BEd 82 Lon Univ MA 92 LTCL 79. St Steph Ho Ox 86. d 89 p 90. C Christchurch *Win* 89–93; P-in-c Bournemouth St Alb 93–94; V 94–00; P-in-c Southbourne St Kath 00–04; V 04–15; P-in-c Beaulieu and Exbury and E Boldre 15–16; R from 16. *The Rectory, Palace Lane, Beaulieu, Brockenhurst SO42 7YG* E: johncwhite634@btinternet.com

WHITE, John David. b 77. Univ of Missouri BA 05. Trin Coll Bris 16. d 18 p 19. C Stoke Bishop *Bris* from 18. *9 Dorset Road, Westbury-on-Trym, Bristol BS9 4BJ* M: 07540-960254 E: johndwhite77@gmail.com

WHITE, John Emlyn. *See* HARRIS-WHITE, John Emlyn

WHITE, Canon John Francis. b 47. Qu Coll Cam BA 69 MA 73. Cuddesdon Coll 72. d 72 p 73. Sacr Wakef Cathl 72–73; Prec 73–76; V Thurlstone *Wakef* 76–82; P-in-c Hoyland Swaine 81–82; V Chapelthorpe 82–06; RD Chevet 96–05; V Lindley 06–10; Hon Can Wakef Cathl 00–10; rtd 10. *16 Thorne End Road, Staincross, Barnsley S75 6NR* T: (01226) 217440 E: john.white110@virginmedia.com

WHITE, John Malcolm. b 54. Aston Univ BSc 77. Trin Coll Bris BA 87. d 87 p 88. C Harborne Heath *Birm* 87–91; C S Harrow St Paul *Lon* 91–93; TV Roxeth 93–96; V Derby St Alkmund and St Werburgh 96–13; PtO *Sheff* 13–18. *284 Springvale Road, Sheffield S10 1LJ* T: 0114-263 1447 E: whitejm@globalnet.co.uk *or* johnemw@gmail.com

WHITE, John William. b 37. CEng 71 MIMechE 71. SAOMC 98. d 01 p 02. NSM Sandhurst *Ox* 01–10; PtO from 10. *21 Broom Acres, Sandhurst GU47 8PN* T: (01344) 774349

WHITE (née REDMAN), Mrs Julia Elizabeth Hithersay. b 43. St Alb Minl Tr Scheme 87 SAOMC 99. d 99 p 00. NSM Harpenden St Jo *St Alb* 99–13; PtO from 13. *The Folly, 71 Station Road, Harpenden AL5 4RL* T: (01582) 763869

WHITE, Julia Mary (Jo). b 52. Harris Coll CertEd 73 Man Univ BEd 85 MEd 87 PhD 92. NOC 00. d 03 p 04. C Ashbourne St Oswald w Mapleton *Derby* 03–07; R Wingerworth 07–13; R Thornton Dale w Allerston, Ebberston etc *York* 13–18; rtd 18; PtO *York* from 18. *31 Low Moorgate, Rillington, Malton YO17 8JW* T: (01944) 758875 E: jo@handjwhite.uk

WHITE, Justin Michael. b 70. Keble Coll Ox MEng 93 Warwick Univ MA 94 Trin Coll Cam BA 00. Westcott Ho Cam 98. d 01 p 02. C Chippenham St Andr w Tytherton Lucas *Bris* 01–04; Chapl SS Helen and Kath Sch Abingdon 04–06; Jun Chapl Win Coll 06–14; Can Res San Francisco USA 14–15; Chapl Dulwich Coll 15–18; Hon C Dulwich St Barn *S'wark* 15–18; Chapl Win Coll 18–20; Dean of Chpl from 20; PV Westmr Abbey from 16. *Winchester College, College Street, Winchester SO23 9NA* E: justin_white@me.com

WHITE, Keith Robert. b 48. Open Univ BA 88. St Jo Coll Nottm 82. d 84 p 85. C Erith St Paul *Roch* 84–88; Chapl Salisbury Coll of Tech *Sarum* 88; PtO *Roch* 11–13; V Crockenhill All So 13–20. *118 Knockhall Road, Greenhithe DA9 9ES* E: keith.acts101@gmail.com

WHITE, Kenneth Charles. b 26. Tyndale Hall Bris 48. d 54 p 56. Chapl Lotome Sch Karamoja Uganda 54–55; Lic to Offic Mombasa Kenya 55–57; C Morden *S'wark* 57–60; V Ramsey St Mary's w Ponds Bridge *Ely* 60–66; V Leyton Ch Ch *Chelmsf* 66–81; V Totland Bay *Portsm* 81–91; rtd 91; PtO *Lon* 91–07; *Lon* from 08. *286A Torbay Road, Harrow HA2 9QW* T: (020) 8868 2431

WHITE, Kirsty Jane. b 95. Regents Th Coll BA 16 Ridley Hall Cam 18. d 21. C Penny Lane *Liv* from 21. *31*

Deepfield Road, Liverpool L15 5BX M: 07734-490318 E: kirstyogrady22@hotmail.co.uk

WHITE, Louise Mary. b 62. Dur Univ MA 21. St Mellitus Coll BS 18 Cranmer Hall Dur 19. d 21. C Hull St Martin w Transfiguration *York* from 21. *St John's Vicarage, Clough Road, Hull HU6 7PA* E: louisemwhite@gmail.com

WHITE, Malcolm Robert. b 46. Man Univ BSc 68. Cranmer Hall Dur 74. d 77 p 78. C Linthorpe *York* 77–81; C Sutton St Jas and Wawne 81–83; V Upper Holloway St Pet w St Jo *Lon* 83–95; TV Burnham w Dropmore, Hitcham and Taplow *Ox* 95–00; CMS Jordan 00–07; rtd 07; PtO *Ox* 08–19; *Chich* from 19. *30 Grand Court, King Edward's Parade, Eastbourne BN21 4BX* E: whitesmv@gmail.com

WHITE, Matthew Peter. b 87. Lon Sch of Th BA 14 St Jo Coll Dur MA 18. Cranmer Hall Dur 16. d 18 p 19. C W Byfleet *Guildf* 18–20; C Chertsey, Lyne and Longcross from 20. *St Peter's Church, Windsor Street, Chertsey KT16 8AT* T: (01932) 563141

WHITE (née DUNCOMBE), Mrs Maureen Barbara. b 42. Bris Univ BA 63 Ox Univ DipEd 64. Oak Hill Th Coll 87. d 89 p 00. NSM Wallington *S'wark* 89–91; PtO *Win* 99–00; NSM Totton 00–07; rtd 07; PtO *Win* 07–16. *Address temp unknown* M: 07786-908961 E: maureen@dhandmbwhite.plus.com

WHITE, Michael Godfrey. b 46. SAOMC 98. d 02 p 03. OLM Shelswell *Ox* 02–07; NSM Fawley *Win* 07–13; rtd 13; PtO *Win* 13–15; *Ox* from 15. *32 Fortescue Drive, Chesterton, Bicester OX26 1UT* T: (01869) 572559 E: revmikewhite@yahoo.co.uk

WHITE, Mrs Natalie Jane. b 65. Ridley Hall Cam 13. d 15 p 16. C Corby St Columba *Pet* 15–18; TV Daventry from 18. *The Rectory, 71 High Street, Braunston, Daventry NN11 7HS* M: 07806-664495 E: revnatwhite@gmail.com

WHITE, Nicholas John. b 71. Southn Univ BA 93 Open Univ PGCE 95. Ripon Coll Cuddesdon 15. d 18 p 19. C St Helens Town Cen *Liv* from 18. *14 Alpine Close, St Helens WA10 4EY* M: 07562-560695

WHITE, Paul John. b 68. JP 10. Middx Univ LLB 90 Bris Univ LLM 92 Dur Univ MA 19 Solicitor 91. St Mellitus Coll BA 08. d 08 p 09. C Woodchurch *Cant* 08–12; V Hadlow *Roch* from 13. *The Vicarage, Maidstone Road, Hadlow, Tonbridge TN11 0DJ* T: (01732) 850238 M: 07970-072757 E: pauljohnwhite@gmail.com

WHITE, Philip Craston. b 59. York Univ BA 81 Nottm Univ PGCE 84. Trin Coll Bris. d 99 p 00. C Countesthorpe w Foston *Leic* 99–03; C-in-c Hamilton CD 03–09; C Leic H Trin w St Jo 09–12; V Broughton *Ox* from 12. *24 King Edward Avenue, Aylesbury HP21 7JD* T: (01296) 484555 M: 07725-339236 E: phil@broughtonchurch.org

WHITE, Philip William. b 53. Bede Coll Dur CertEd 75 Coll of Ripon & York St Jo MA 01. St Jo Coll Nottm 89. d 91 p 92. C Clifton *York* 91–95; TV Heworth H Trin 95–01; P-in-c Scarborough St Jas w H Trin 01–15; Tr Officer E Riding 01–13; P-in-c Cayton w Eastfield 13–15; P-in-c Thurgarton w Hoveringham and Bleasby etc *S'well* 15–17; P-in-c Rolleston w Fiskerton, Morton and Upton 15–17; V W Trent from 17. *The Vicarage, Southwell Road, Thurgarton, Nottingham NG14 7GP* M: 07720-010066 E: phil_07@btinternet.com

WHITE, Ms Philippa Jane. b 77. Bris Univ BSc 99 MSc 03. Trin Coll Bris 17. d 19 p 20. C Cotham St Sav w St Mary and Clifton St Paul *Bris* from 19. *9 Dorset Road, Westbury-on-Trym, Bristol BS9 4BJ* M: 07540-959522 E: pippakendall@hotmail.com

WHITE, Mrs Philippa Judith. b 86. CCC Cam BA 08 MA 12. Ripon Coll Cuddesdon BA 13. d 14 p 15. C Linc St Jo 14–18; C Linc Cathl 14–15; PV 15–18; Succ Ch Ch Ox from 18. *Christ Church, St Aldates, Oxford OX1 1DP* M: 07474-958658 E: revdpjwhite@gmail.com

WHITE, Canon Phillip George. b 33. Univ of Wales (Lamp) BA 54. St Mich Coll Llan 54. d 56 p 57. C Tongwynlais *Llan* 56–58; C Mountain Ash 58–60; C Aberavon 60–62; Area Sec (Middx) CMS 62–64; V Treherbert *Llan* 64–75; P-in-c Treorchy 75–76; V Treherbert w Treorchy 76–77; V Pyle w Kenfig 77–99; RD Margam 86–99; Can Llan Cathl 91–99; rtd 99. PtO *Llan* from 99. *8 Heol Fair, Porthcawl CF36 5LA* T: (01656) 786297

WHITE, Canon Priscilla Audrey. b 62. St Hugh's Coll Ox BA 84 MA 88 Birm Univ MA 12. Wycliffe Hall Ox 87. d 89 p 94. Par Dn Southway *Ex* 89–93; NSM Plymouth Em, St Paul Efford and St Aug 93–99; P-in-c Abbotskerswell 99–05; P-in-c Harborne St Faith and St Laur *Birm* 05–10; V from 10; AD Edgbaston 10–17; Hon Can Birm Cathl from 15. *The Vicarage, Church Lane, Kingsbury, Tamworth B78 2LR* T: (01827) 874252 *or* 0121-427 2410 E: priscillawhite.harborne@btinternet.com

WHITE, Richard. *See* WHITE, Douglas Richard Leon

WHITE, Richard Michael. b 84. Ox Brookes Univ BA 07 PGCE 08. St Mellitus Coll BA 16. d 16 p 17. C Cogges and S

Leigh *Ox* 16–19; TR Bath Twerton-on-Avon *B & W* from 19. *The Rectory, Watery Lane, Bath BA2 1RL* M: 07716-688681 E: richardwhite115@hotmail.com

WHITE, Richard Stanley. b 70. Trin Coll Bris BA 02. **d** 03 **p** 04. C Haydock St Mark *Liv* 03–06; Pioneer Min Dream Network 06–09; Can for Miss and Evang 09–18; Dir Making and Nurturing Disciples *York* 18–21; P-in-c Hull St Jo Newland from 21. *St John's Vicarage, Clough Road, Hull HU6 7PA* M: 07989-312758 E: revrichardwhite@outlook.com

WHITE, Canon Robert Charles. b 61. Mansf Coll Ox BA 83. St Steph Ho Ox 83. **d** 85 **p** 86. C Forton *Portsm* 85–88; C Portsea N End St Mark 88–92; V Warren Park 92–00; P-in-c Leigh Park 94–96; V 96–00; RD Havant 98–00; V Portsea St Mary from 00; P-in-c Portsea All SS 19–20; AD Portsm from 11; Hon Can Portsm Cathl from 97; Chapl to The Queen from 19. *St Mary's Vicarage, Fratton Road, Portsmouth PO1 5PA* T: (023) 9282 2687 *or* 9282 2990 F: 9235 9320 E: revrcwhite@gmail.com

WHITE, Robin Edward Bantry. b 47. TCD BA 70 BD 79. CITC 72. **d** 72 **p** 73. C Dublin Zion Ch *D & G* 72–76; Min Can St Patr Cathl Dublin 76–79; C Taney Ch Ch *D & G* 76–79; I Abbeystrewry Union *C, C & R* 79–89; I Douglas Union w Frankfield 89–02; I Moviddy Union 02–14; Can Cork Cathl 89–14; Can Ross Cathl 89–93; Adn Cork, Cloyne and Ross 93–14; Preb Castleknock St Patr Cathl Dublin 09–14; rtd 14. *Ardcairn, 26 Marble Court, Paulstown, Co Kilkenny, R95 KT22, Republic of Ireland* T: (00353) (59) 972 6089 M: 87-286 2178 E: robinbantrywhite@gmail.com

WHITE, Roderick Harry. b 55. Trin Coll Bris BA 86. **d** 86 **p** 87. C Northampton St Giles *Pet* 86–89; C Godley cum Newton Green *Ches* 89–93; P-in-c 93–99; R Northiam *Chich* from 99. *The Rectory, 24 High Meadow, Northiam, Rye TN31 6GA* T: (01797) 253118 E: rod@rodwhite.freeuk.com

WHITE, Roger David. b 37. Univ of Wales (Cardiff) BTh 91. St Mich Coll Llan. **d** 66 **p** 67. C Mountain Ash *Llan* 66–71; C Port Talbot St Theodore 71–74; V Caerhun w Llangelynin w Llanbedr-y-Cennin *Ban* 74–85; R Llanbedrog w Llannor w Llanfihangel etc 85–88; V Llangeinor *Llan* 88–90; V Spittal w Trefgarn and Ambleston w St Dogwells *St D* 90–98; V Abergwili w Llanfihangel-uwch-Gwili etc 98–00; rtd 00. *Tir Na Nog, 18 Bryn Cir, Llanerchymedd LL71 8EG* T: (01248) 470159

WHITE, Roger Ian Scott. b 41. Leeds Univ BA 62 Culham Coll Ox PGCE 70. Coll of Resurr Mirfield 62. **d** 64 **p** 65. C Wotton-under-Edge *Glouc* 64–69; NSM Rugby St Andr *Cov* 71–80; W Germany 80–82; P-in-c Brinklow *Cov* 82–86; R 86–90; P-in-c Harborough Magna 82–86; R 86–90; P-in-c Monks Kirby w Pailton and Stretton-under-Fosse 82–86; V 86–90; Germany 90–92; V Lydgate w Friezland *Man* 92–01; Chapl Hamburg *Eur* 01–11; rtd 11; PtO *Eur* 16–21. *Spannwisch 7, 22159 Hamburg, Germany* T: (0049) (40) 664316 E: roger.white@gmx.de

WHITE, Ronald Henry. b 36. Bris Univ BSc 58. SWMTC 82. **d** 85 **p** 86. C Ivybridge *Ex* 85–87; C Ivybridge w Harford 87–88; V Blackawton and Stoke Fleming 88–95; V Stoke Fleming, Blackawton and Strete 95–00; RD Woodleigh 95–99; rtd 00; PtO *Ex* from 02. *10 Hollingarth Way, Hemyock, Cullompton EX15 3XB* T: (01823) 681020 E: revron@btinternet.com

WHITE, Sandy Dulcie. b 44. **d** 98 **p** 99. OLM W Streatham St Jas *S'wark* 98–05; PtO *Wakef* 05–07; NSM Cornholme and Walsden 07–14; PtO *Leeds* from 14. *774 Rochdale Road, Todmorden OL14 7UA* T: (01706) 812007 E: revsandyd@gmail.com

WHITE, Sheelagh Mary. *See* ASTON, Sheelagh Mary

WHITE, Simon Inigo Dexter. b 58. York Univ BA 80 Nottm Univ PGCE 81. St Jo Coll Nottm 87. **d** 90 **p** 91. C Chadkirk *Ches* 90–94; C Stockport St Geo 94; TV Stockport SW 94–99; Chapl Stockport Gr Sch 94–99; P-in-c W Hallam and Mapperley *Derby* 99–02; P-in-c Stanley 99–02; R W Hallam and Mapperley w Stanley 02–13; V Tideswell from 13. *The Vicarage, 6 Pursglove Drive, Tideswell, Buxton SK17 8PA* T: 0115-932 4695 *or* (01298) 871317 E: inigodexter@me.com

WHITE, Simon James Hithersay. b 65. St Jo Coll Nottm 01. **d** 03 **p** 04. C Alnwick *Newc* 03–06; P-in-c Felton and Longframlington w Brinkburn 06–13; Dioc Youth Officer 06–13; R Morpeth from 13. *The Rectory, Cottingwood Lane, Morpeth NE61 1ED* T: (01670) 517716 M: 07749-866402 E: rev.simonjhwhite@gmail.com

WHITE, Simon John. b 60. Southn Univ BSc 82. ERMC 13. **d** 16. NSM Hadleigh, Layham and Shelley *St E* 16–19; NSM Bures w Assington and Lt Cornard from 19; PtO *Chelmsf* from 20. *20 The Street, Assington, Sudbury CO10 5LJ* T: (01787) 211228 M: 07572-418555 E: simon@sjwhite.co.uk

WHITE, Stephen Ross. b 58. Hull Univ BA 81 QUB PhD 94. Ripon Coll Cuddesdon BA 84. **d** 85 **p** 86. C Redcar *York*

85–88; P-in-c Gweedore, Carrickfin and Templecrone *D & R* 88–92; Bp's Dom Chapl 91–92; Dean Raphoe 92–02; I Raphoe w Raymochy and Clonleigh 93–01; Dean Killaloe and Clonfert *L & K* 02–12; Chan St Patr Cathl Dublin 11–12; P-in-c Dunsfold and Hascombe *Guildf* 12–19. *27 Patcham Court, 113 Brighton Road, Sutton SM2 5SL* E: stephenwhite14@btinternet.com

WHITE, Mrs Susan Margaret. b 48. Univ of E Lon BA 84 Brunel Univ MBA 94 Anglia Poly Univ MA 04. EAMTC 01. **d** 04 **p** 05. C Harwich Peninsula *Chelmsf* 04–08; P-in-c Alkham w Capel le Ferne and Hougham *Cant* 08–12; P-in-c Eythorne and Elvington w Waldershare etc 12; P-in-c Whitfield w Guston 12; R Bewsborough 13–18; AD Dover 11–16; rtd 18; PtO *Cant* from 20. *29 Mount Road, Canterbury CT1 1YD* E: revsuewhite@gmail.com

WHITE (née BUTLER), Mrs Valerie Joyce. b 58. EAMTC 99. **d** 02 **p** 03. NSM Southminster *Chelmsf* 02–06; Hon Chapl Miss to Seafarers Tilbury 05–06; C Bury St Edmunds All SS w St Jo and St Geo *St E* 06–08; TV Walton and Trimley 08–16; P-in-c Bacton w Wyverstone, Cotton and Old Newton etc 16–18; rtd 19; PtO *St E* from 19. *154 Colneis Road, Felixstowe IP11 9LQ* M: 07859-464932 E: valthevic@talktalk.net

WHITE, Canon Vernon Philip. b 53. Clare Coll Cam BA 75 MA 79 Oriel Coll Ox MLitt 80. Wycliffe Hall Ox. **d** 77 **p** 78. Tutor Wycliffe Hall Ox 77–83; Chapl and Lect Ex Univ 83–87; R Wotton and Holmbury St Mary *Guildf* 87–93; Dir of Ords 87–93; Can Res and Chan Linc Cathl 93–01; Prin STETS 01–11; Can Th Win Cathl 06–11; Can Th Westmr Abbey 11–18; Sub-Dean 16–18; Visiting Prof K Coll Lon 11–18; rtd 18; PtO *Sarum* from 20. *Yew Tree Cottage, Whitsbury Road, Odstock, Salisbury SP5 4JE* T: (01722) 327042

WHITE, William Frederick. b 30. St Jo Coll Nottm. **d** 02. NSM Hillingdon St Jo *Lon* 02–06; NSM Cowley 06–08; Asst Chapl Hillingdon Hosp NHS Trust 02–08; PtO *Lon* 08–18. *31A Copperfield Avenue, Hillingdon, Uxbridge UB8 3NU* T: (01895) 236746 M: 07754-234233 E: billwhite2004@hotmail.com

WHITE-DUNDAS, Maithre Cecilia. b 60. Nottm Univ PhD. CITI. **d** 17 **p** 19. Ballyholme *D & D* 17–19; NSM Belf Cathl from 19. *59 Sharman Road, Belfast BT9 5FX* M: 07921-567094 E: whitedum@tcd.ie *or* firedgenius@gmail.com

WHITEHALL, Adrian Leslie. b 53. Leeds Univ MB, ChB 76 Sheff Univ MMedSc 93 MRCGP 80. Ridley Hall Cam 04. **d** 06 **p** 07. C Todwick *Sheff* 06–09; Tanzania 10–11; PtO *Derby* from 12; CMS Tanzania 13–15; PtO *Eur* from 19. *Meadow House, Ashbourne Road, Belper DE56 2DA* T: (01773) 826410 M: 07866-454148 E: adrian.whitehall@gmail.com

WHITEHEAD, Alexander. *See* WHITEHEAD, Matthew Alexander

WHITEHEAD, Andrew Paul. b 77. Lanc Univ BA 01 Cam Univ BTh 12. Westcott Ho Cam 10. **d** 12 **p** 13. C Clitheroe St Mary *Blackb* 12–15; C Cawston w Booton and Brandiston etc *Nor* 15–17; TV Aylsham and Distr from 17; Dioc Chapl MU from 19. *The Rectory, Ames Court, Cawston, Norwich NR10 4QD* T: (01603) 872236 M: 07801-290649 E: a.p.whitehead@me.com

WHITEHEAD, Anwyl David. b 67. St Hild Coll 16. **d** 18 **p** 20. NSM Chapeltown *Sheff* from 18; Chapl Sheff Teaching Hosps NHS Foundn Trust from 20. *68 The Rookery, Deepcar, Sheffield S36 2NA*

WHITEHEAD, David. b 62. Newc Univ BSc 83 MSc 85 PhD 89. St Jo Coll Nottm BA 09. **d** 07 **p** 08. C Ambleside w Brathay *Carl* 07–10; TV Kirkby Lonsdale 10–14; P-in-c Whitehaven 14–15; Dioc Healing Adv 13–15; rtd 15; PtO *Carl* from 16. *Brandle Howe, Helm Road, Bowness-on-Windermere, Windermere LA23 3AA* T: (015394) 44393 E: davidcwhitehead@btopenworld.com

WHITEHEAD, David. *See* WHITEHEAD, Anwyl David

WHITEHEAD, Gordon James. b 42. Culham Coll of Educn DipEd 64. Clifton Th Coll 66. **d** 73 **p** 74. C Romford Gd Shep *Chelmsf* 73; SAMS Santiago Chile 74–87; C Coleraine *Conn* 87–94; I Errigle Keerogue w Ballygawley and Killeshil *Arm* 94–02; I Bright w Ballee and Killough *D & D* 02–07; rtd 07. *75 Kensington Manor, Dollingstown, Craigavon BT66 7HR* T: (028) 3831 7989 E: whitehead105@btinternet.com

WHITEHEAD, Ian Richard. b 63. St Jo Coll Nottm BA 95. **d** 95 **p** 96. C Hillmorton *Cov* 95–97; C Whitnash 97–99; R Rolleston *Lich* 99–18; V Anslow 99–18; C Hanbury, Newborough, Rangemore and Tutbury 14–18; R Anslow, Rolleston and Tutbury 18–19; P-in-c Crich and S Wingfield *Derby* from 19. *New Vicarage, Coasthill, Crich, Matlock DE4 5DS* T: (01773) 425077 E: cswvicar@gmail.com

WHITEHEAD, Mrs Jennifer Jane. b 45. St Jo Coll York CertEd 67. **d** 98 **p** 99. OLM Winterton Gp *Linc* from 98. *11 Queen Street, Winterton, Scunthorpe DN15 9TR* T: (01724) 734027 E: jennifer.whitehead@btinternet.com

WHITEHEAD, Mrs Joanne Louise. b 71. Hull Univ BA 92 PGCE 93 Nottm Univ MA 08. EMMTC 05. **d** 08 **p** 09. C Oakwood *Derby* 08–13; P-in-c Newhall 13–16; Lead Chapl Derbyshire Constabulary and Fire and Rescue Services 16–17; Dioc Enablement Officer 18–19; PtO *Derby* from 18. *4 Bromyard Drive, Chellaston, Derby DE73 6PF* T: (01332) 388650 M: 07816-281023

WHITEHEAD, John Stanley. b 38. Jes Coll Cam BA 63 MA 67 MPhil. Westcott Ho Cam 63. **d** 64 **p** 65. C Batley All SS *Wakef* 64–67; C Mitcham St Mark *S'wark* 67–70; C Frindsbury w Upnor *Roch* 70–72; TV Strood 72–75; R Halstead 75–82; V Betley *Lich* 82–85; V Betley and Keele 85–01; Asst Chapl Keele Univ 82–01; PtO *Ches* 02–09 and from 11; C Acton and Worleston, Church Minshull etc 10; PtO *Lich* 09–19. *Paddock House, Longhill Lane, Hankelow, Crewe CW3 0JG* T: (01270) 812607

WHITEHEAD, Canon Matthew Alexander. b 44. Leeds Univ BA 65 Birm Univ MA 75 St Chad's Coll Dur DipEd 66 Newc Univ MPhil 03. Qu Coll Birm. **d** 69 **p** 70. C Bingley All SS *Bradf* 69–72; C Keele and Asst Chapl Keele Univ *Lich* 72–74; Bp's Dom Chapl *Dur* 74–80; V Escomb and Witton Park 74–80; V Birtley 80–89; RD Chester-le-Street 84–89; V Stockton St Pet 89–00; V The Trimdons 00–03; Dioc Warden of Readers 94–03; Hon Can Dur Cathl 96–03; P-in-c Stow Gp *Linc* 03–09; rtd 09; Dioc Warden of Readers *Linc* 03–11; Can and Preb Linc Cathl 04–18; V Linc St Mary Magd w St Paul and St Mich 14–18. *77 Yarborough Crescent, Lincoln LN1 3NE* M: 07518-746643 E: alex.whitehead@lincoln.anglican.org

WHITEHEAD, Canon Nicholas James. b 53. Univ of Wales (Ban) BTh 07 ACIB. Ridley Hall Cam 86. **d** 88 **p** 89. C Bourne *Guildf* 88–92; V Hersham 92–10; RD Emly 06–10; P-in-c Shere, Albury and Chilworth 10–14; R 14–18; RD Cranleigh 13–15; Hon Can Guildf Cathl 12–18; rtd 18; PtO *Portsm* from 19. *Rowan House, Dean Lane, Bishops Waltham, Southampton SO32 1FX* M: 07946-389583

WHITEHEAD, Paul Conrad. b 60. St Jo Coll Nottm LTh 92. **d** 92 **p** 93. C Mansfield Woodhouse *S'well* 92–96; C Carlton-in-the-Willows 96–02; C Colwick 96–02; CF (VR) from 96; NSM Trowell, Awsworth and Cossall *S'well* from 04. *84 Hillside Road, Beeston, Nottingham NG9 3AT* T: 0115-919 7030 M: 07973-727221

WHITEHEAD, Canon Robin Lawson. b 53. Bris Univ BA 76 Lon Univ MA 96. St Steph Ho Ox 77. **d** 80 **p** 81. C Cheshunt *St Alb* 80–83; C E Grinstead St Swithun *Chich* 83–85; V Friern Barnet St Pet le Poer *Lon* 85–92; R Friern Barnet St Jas 92–95; C Wood Green St Mich w Bounds Green St Gabr etc 96–97; TR Leic Resurr 97–04; V Boston *Linc* 04–05; TR 05–13; RD Holland E 09–10; RD Holland W 09–10; RD Holland 10–13; Can and Preb Linc Cathl 09–13; rtd 13; PtO *Cant* 13–16; R Winchelsea and Icklesham *Chich* 13–17; PtO *Glas* from 17; *Bre* 18–19. *Maynard, 12 New Abbey Road, Dumfries DG2 7NA* T: (01387) 251480 E: robinwhitehead6@btinternet.com

WHITEHOUSE, Alan Edward. b 35. CEng 66. Glouc Sch of Min 89. **d** 92 **p** 93. NSM Evesham *Worc* 92–96; NSM Evesham w Norton and Lenchwick 96–02; rtd 02; PtO *Worc* from 03. *The Coppice, 56 Elm Road, Evesham WR11 3DW* T: (01386) 442427 M: 07789-081595 E: awhitehouse56@outlook.com

WHITEHOUSE, David Garner. b 70. Sheff Univ BEng 91. EAMTC 03. **d** 05 **p** 06. C Cheadle *Ches* 05–10; P-in-c Southport SS Simon and Jude w All So *Liv* 10–19; V Leyland St Andr *Blackb* from 19. *St Andrew's Vicarage, 1 Crocus Field, Leyland PR25 3DY* T: (01772) 622964 E: vicarage@standrewsleyland.org.uk

WHITEHOUSE, Nigel Andrew. b 57. St Mary's RC Sem Birm 75 Westcott Ho Cam 91. **d** 80 **p** 81. In RC Ch 81–87; C Whittlesey and Pondersbridge *Ely* 92–94; P-in-c Newton 94–98; R 98–03; P-in-c Gorefield 94–98; V 98–03; P-in-c Tydd St Giles 94–98; R 98–03; TR Whittlesey, Pondersbridge and Coates 03–20; Hon Asst Dir of Ords 09–12; RD March 09–15; P-in-c Upwell St Pet from 20; P-in-c Outwell from 20; RD Wisbech Lynn Marshland from 20. *Wesley Manse, 21 Town Street, Upwell, Wisbech PE14 9AD* E: revnigel.whitehouse@gmail.com

WHITEHOUSE, Mrs Sarah Alice. b 61. QC 14. St Andr Univ MA 83. St Aug Coll of Th 16. **d** 19 **p** 20. NSM Tooting All SS *S'wark* from 19. *21 Nottingham Road, London SW17 7EA* M: 07831-613358 E: sarah.whitehouse@6kbw.com

WHITEHOUSE, Canon Susan Clara. b 48. R Holloway Coll Lon BA 70. Westcott Ho Cam 87. **d** 89 **p** 94. Par Dn Farnley *Ripon* 89–93; Dioc Development Rep 92–03; C Bedale and Thornton Watlass w Thornton Steward 93–96; V Aysgarth and Bolton cum Redmire 96–06; R Penhill 06–13; Hon Can Ripon Cathl 02–13; AD Wensley 03–05; rtd 13; LtO

Edin from 14. *157 The Murrays, Edinburgh EH17 8UN* E: revsuewhitehouse@btinternet.com

WHITELEY, Capt Paul Nigel. b 64. **d** 18 **p** 19. C Spalding St Paul *Linc* 18–21; R Paston *Pet* from 21. *The Rectory, 236 Fulbridge Road, Peterborough PE4 6SN* M: 07758-555525 E: paulwhiteley1@btinternet.com

WHITELEY, Raewynne Jean. b 66. Melbourne Univ BA 89 MA 92 ACT BTh 95 BMin 95 Princeton Th Sem PhD 03. **d** 96 **p** 98. C Hunters Hill Australia 96–98; C Princeton Trin Ch USA 98–01; C Trin Cathl Trenton 01–02; V Swedesboro 02–06; R New York St Jas 07–17; Can Th Long Is 09–17; Dioc Discipleship and Voc Missr *S'wark* 18–19; Dep Dir Discipleship and Lay Min from 19; Hon C Sanderstead St Mary from 18. *Trinity House, 4 Chapel Court, Borough High Street, London SE1 1HW* M: 07426-903725 E: raewynne.whiteley@southwark.anglican.org

WHITELEY, Canon Robert Louis. b 28. Leeds Univ BA 48. Coll of Resurr Mirfield 50. **d** 52 **p** 53. C Hollinwood *Man* 52–55; Br Honduras 56–61; V Illingworth *Wakef* 61–68; V Westgate Common 68–75; Can Res Wakef Cathl 75–80; Hon Can Wakef Cathl 80–93; V Almondbury 80–82; TR Almondbury w Farnley Tyas 82–92; RD Almondbury 81–93; rtd 93; PtO *Wakef* 93–14; *Leeds* 14–16; *Ox* 98–10; *Guildf* 10–13; *Ox* from 13. *34 Elizabeth Court, Victoria Road, Wargrave, Reading RG10 8BP* E: r.whiteley505@btinternet.com

WHITELOCK, Mrs Susan Karen. b 62. STETS 98. **d** 01 **p** 06. NSM Portsea N End St Mark *Portsm* 01–06; NSM Portsea St Mary from 06. *404 Copnor Road, Portsmouth PO3 5EW* M: 07903-414029 E: sue.whitelock@ntlworld.com

WHITEMAN, Christopher Henry Raymond. b 51. Portsm Poly BA 73 Worc Coll of Educn PGCE 74 Open Univ BSc 97. St Jo Coll Nottm MA 99. **d** 90 **p** 91. C Rockland St Mary w Hellington, Bramerton etc *Nor* 90–93; P-in-c Gillingham w Geldeston, Stockton, Ellingham etc 93–94; R 94–04; R Culworth w Sulgrave and Thorpe Mandeville etc *Pet* 04–11; rtd 11. *28 Penterry Park, Chepstow NP16 5AZ* E: chrwhiteman@aol.com

WHITEMAN, The Ven Rodney David Carter. b 40. Ely Th Coll 61. **d** 64 **p** 65. C Kings Heath *Birm* 64–70; V Rednal 70–79; V Erdington St Barn 79–89; RD Aston 81–86 and 88–89; Hon Can Birm Cathl 85–89; Adn Bodmin *Truro* 89–00; Adn Cornwall 00–05; P-in-c Cardynham and Helland 89–94; Hon Can Truro Cathl 89–05; rtd 06; PtO *Truro* from 16. *22 Treverbyn Gardens, Sandy Hill, St Austell PL25 3AW* T: (01726) 879043 E: rodneywhiteman@talktalk.net

WHITFIELD, Joy Verity. *See* CHAPMAN, Joy Verity

WHITFIELD, Leslie Turnbull. b 43. Cardiff Univ LLM 10 CEng 72 MIET 72 MCMI 74. St Jo Coll Nottm MA 00. **d** 00 **p** 01. C Bottesford w Ashby *Linc* 00–03; P-in-c Mablethorpe w Trusthorpe 03–07; Ind Chapl 07–08; rtd 08; PtO *Linc* 17–20. *3 Burland Court, Washingborough, Lincoln LN4 1HL* T: (01522) 791195 M: 07913-247783 E: rev.les@tiscali.co.uk

WHITFIELD, Miss Vivien Elizabeth. b 46. Westhill Coll Birm CertEd 68. Open Th Coll BA 01 Lon Sch of Th MA 04. **d** 17 **p** 18. NSM Colchester St Jo *Chelmsf* 17–21. *21 Broad Oaks Park, Colchester CO4 0JX* M: 07752-888273 (text only) E: vivien.whitfield@talk21.com

WHITFIELD, William. b 47. Open Univ BA 80 Univ of Wales (Cardiff) LLM 95 FRSH 81. STETS 01. **d** 04 **p** 05. NSM Marchwood *Win* 04–08; NSM Millbrook 08–11; PtO from 11; *Portsm* from 13. *35 The Rowans, Marchwood, Southampton SO40 4YW* T: (023) 8086 0399 E: william.whitfield@btinternet.com

WHITFORD, Judith. *See* POLLINGER, Judith

WHITFORD (née FAULKNER), Mrs Margaret Evelyn. b 54. Goldsmiths' Coll Lon BEd 77. EAMTC 98. **d** 01 **p** 02. C Grays Thurrock *Chelmsf* 01–05; C Bradwell on Sea 05–08; C Bradwell on Sea and St Lawrence 08–11; C Brandon and Santon Downham w Elveden etc *St E* 11–15; rtd 15. *19 High Street, West Mersea, Colchester CO5 8QA* E: mandlz@btinternet.com

WHITFORD, William Laurence. b 56. Open Univ BA 92. NOC 92. **d** 95 **p** 96. C Hindley All SS *Liv* 95–99; P-in-c E and W Tilbury and Linford *Chelmsf* 99–04; R 04–05; P-in-c Bradwell on Sea 05–08; R Bradwell on Sea and St Lawrence 08–11; R Brandon and Santon Downham w Elveden etc *St E* 11–15; rtd 15. *19 High Street, West Mersea, Colchester CO5 8QA* E: mandlz@btinternet.com

WHITHAM, Ian Scott. b 66. Oak Hill Th Coll. **d** 01 **p** 02. C Yateley *Win* 01–03; C Yateley and Eversley 03–05; V W Ewell *Guildf* 05–15; P-in-c Hyde w Ellingham and Harbridge *Win* 15–17; C Ringwood w Ellingham and Harbridge etc 17–21. *Address temp unknown* M: 07403-061116 E: ianwhitham67@gmail.com

WHITING, Alison Ruth. b 73. STETS. **d** 14 **p** 15. NSM Dorchester and the Winterbournes *Sarum* 14–16. *10 Royal*

Mews, Princes Street, Dorchester DT1 1RL T: (01305) 751716
E: ally_whiting@hotmail.com

WHITING, Joseph Alfred. b 41. Oak Hill Th Coll 82. **d** 85 **p** 86. Hon C Sidcup St Andr *Roch* 85–88; C Southborough St Pet w Ch Ch and St Matt 88–92; C Aldridge *Lich* 92–97; TV Rye *Chich* 97–02; rtd 02; PtO *Roch* 02–14. *238 Ralph Perring Court, Stone Park Avenue, Beckenham BR3 3LX* T: (020) 3583 3431 E: whitings71@tiscali.co.uk *or* whitings71@talktalk.net

WHITING, Stephen. b 60. Cranmer Hall Dur 06. **d** 08 **p** 09. C Scarborough St Mary w Ch Ch and H Apostles *York* 08–12; TV Leverhulme *Man* 12–17; P-in-c Forest of Galtres from 17; C Alne from 17; C Brafferton w Pilmoor, Myton-on-Swale etc from 17; C Coxwold and Husthwaite from 17; C Crayke w Brandsby and Yearsley from 17; C Easingwold w Raskelf from 17; C Skelton w Shipton and Newton on Ouse from 17; C Stensall from 17; RD Easingwold from 19. *The Vicarage, Main Street, Sutton-on-the-Forest, York YO61 1DW* T: (01347) 810251 M: 07789-950881 E: revstevewhiting@gmail.com

WHITLEY, Brian. b 58. Dundee Univ BA 97 Portsm Univ MA(Ed) 00 RMN 84 RGN 84. STETS BA 07. **d** 07 **p** 08. C Easthampstead *Ox* 07–10; P-in-c Woodplumpton *Blackb* 10–15; PtO 15–17; P-in-c Cockfield *Dur* from 17; P-in-c Lynesack from 17; P-in-c Evenwood from 17. *The Rectory, 107 Front Street, Cockfield, Bishop Auckland DL13 5AA* T: (01388) 718584 M: 07825-487536 E: bwhitley2@btinternet.com

WHITLEY, Eric Keir. b 47. Salford Univ BSc 68. Trin Coll Bris 77. **d** 79 **p** 80. C Nottingham St Ann w Em *S'well* 79–83; V Donisthorpe and Moira w Stretton-en-le-Field *Leic* 83–91; V Thorpe Acre w Dishley 91–00; V Loughb Gd Shep 00–15; rtd 15; PtO *Leic* from 15. *4 Lamport Close, Loughborough LE11 2TT* T: (01509) 324821

WHITLEY, Ian Peter. b 61. Ox Min Course 16. **d** 17 **p** 18. C Banstead *Guildf* 17–21; P-in-c Lingfield and Dormansland *S'wark* from 21. *The Vicarage, Vicarage Road, Lingfield RH7 6HA* M: 07961-382293 E: kittyandwitty@aol.com *or* vicar.ubld@outlook.com

WHITLEY, John William. b 46. TCD BA 68. Cranmer Hall Dur BA 71. **d** 71 **p** 72. C Belfast St Mary Magd *Conn* 71–73; C Toxteth St Philemon w St Gabr *Liv* 73–78; P-in-c Toxteth Park St Cleopas 78–88; TV Toxteth St Philemon w St Gabr and St Cleopas 89–95; P-in-c Litherland St Paul Hatton Hill 95–02; V 02–16; rtd 16; PtO *Dur* from 17. *3 Bishop's Close, Durham DH1 2BU* T: 0191-386 0328 E: anthea.whitley@virgin.net

WHITLEY (née ALLISON), Rosemary Jean. b 45. LTCL 67. Trin Coll Bris 75 St Jo Coll Nottm 94. **d** 95 **p** 99. NSM Loughb Gd Shep *Leic* 95–98 and 00–15; NSM Thorpe Acre w Dishley 98–00; rtd 15; PtO *Leic* from 15. *4 Lamport Close, Loughborough LE11 2TT*

WHITLOCK, Canon James Frederick. b 44. Ch Coll Cam BA 75 MA 78. Westcott Ho Cam 73. **d** 76 **p** 77. C Newquay *Truro* 76–79; P-in-c St Mawgan w St Ervan and St Eval 79–81; R 81; Bp's Dom Chapl 82–85; Dioc Dir of Ords 82–85; V Leagrave *St Alb* 85–89; TR Probus, Ladock and Grampound w Creed and St Erme *Truro* 89–95; V Penzance St Mary w St Paul 95–00; P-in-c Penzance St Jo 97–00; Hon Can Truro Cathl 98–00; rtd 00. *10 Barlandhu, Newlyn, Penzance TR18 5QT* T: (01736) 330474

WHITMARSH, Mrs Pauline. b 45. **d** 04 **p** 05. OLM Bramshaw and Landford w Plaitford *Sarum* 04–06; OLM Forest and Avon 06–14; rtd 14; PtO *Sarum* from 14. *Address temp unknown* E: paulinewhitmarsh@gmail.com

WHITMORE, Preb Benjamin Nicholas. b 66. Imp Coll Lon BEng 88. Cranmer Hall Dur 89. **d** 92 **p** 93. C Gt Wyrley *Lich* 92–95; C Hednesford 95–00; V Walsall Pleck and Bescot 00–07; Hon C Walsall and Walsall St Paul 05–07; V Penn from 07; Preb Lich Cathl from 13. *St Bartholomew's Vicarage, 68 Church Hill, Penn, Wolverhampton WV4 5JD* T: (01902) 332351 M: 07742-020246 E: benjowhitmore@gmail.com

WHITMORE, Edward James. b 36. Lon Univ BD 66. Tyndale Hall Bris. **d** 68 **p** 69. Tutor St Phil Th Coll Kongwa Tanzania 68–72; LtO Cen Tanganyika 72–76; LtO *Blackb* 77–09. *74 Greencroft, Penwortham, Preston PR1 9LB* T: (01772) 746522

WHITMORE, Stephen Andrew. b 53. Sheff Univ BSc 74. St Jo Coll Nottm 89. **d** 91 **p** 92. C Newbury *Ox* 91–95; TV High Wycombe 95–16; rtd 16; PtO *Ox* from 16. *128 Templewood, Walters Ash, High Wycombe HP14 4UF* E: banjovicar@hotmail.com

WHITNEY, Charles Edward. b 46. Goldsmiths' Coll Lon BA 71 TCert 72 ACP 75 Glos Univ MA 18. WEMTC 01. **d** 04 **p** 05. NSM Tewkesbury w Walton Cardiff and Twyning *Glouc* 04–17; NSM Deerhurst and Apperley w Forthampton etc 10–17; rtd 17; PtO *Glouc* from 17. *Sarn Hill Lodge, Bushley Green, Bushley, Tewkesbury GL20 6AD* T: (01684) 296764 E: whitneyok@sky.com

WHITNEY, John Charles. b 59. St Jo Coll Dur BATM 11. Cranmer Hall Dur 09. **d** 11 **p** 12. C Kirkheaton *Wakef* 11–14; Leeds 14–15; V Alvaston *Derby* from 15. *The Vicarage, 8 Church Street, Alvaston, Derby DE24 0PR* T: (01332) 571143 E: rev_john@whitney.org.uk *or* rev_john@alvaston.church

WHITTAKER, Canon Angela. b 68. Birm Univ BA 89 St Martin's Coll Lanc PGCE 91. NEOC 98. **d** 00 **p** 01. C Houghton le Spring *Dur* 00–04; TV Kirkby Lonsdale *Carl* 04–09; P-in-c Natland from 09; P-in-c Old Hutton and New Hutton from 09; RD Kendal 12–18; Hon Can Carl Cathl from 14. *The Vicarage, Natland, Kendal LA9 7QQ* T: (01539) 560355 E: ang.whitt68@gmail.com

WHITTAKER, Brian Lawrence. b 39. Univ of Wales MTh 06. Clifton Th Coll 63. **d** 66 **p** 67. C Whitton and Thurleston w Akenham *St E* 66–69; C Normanton *Wakef* 69–74; P-in-c Castle Hall, Stalybridge and Dukinfield Ch Ch *Ches* 74–77; V Stalybridge H Trin and Ch Ch 77–83; TR Bucknall and Bagnall *Lich* 83–91; R Draycott-le-Moors w Forsbrook 91–05; rtd 05; PtO *Lich* 05–21. *6 Rubens Way, Stoke-on-Trent ST3 7GQ* T: (01782) 397765 E: brianlwhittaker@gmail.com

WHITTAKER, Mrs Diane Claire. b 57. Newc Poly BA 79 Thames Poly BSc 87 Univ of Wales (Abth) MA 92. ERMC 06. **d** 08 **p** 09. C Welwyn *St Alb* 08–12; P-in-c Potterspury w Furtho and Yardley Gobion etc *Pet* 12–15; R 15–20; R Astwell Gp from 20. *The Vicarage, The Green, Lois Weedon, Towcester NN12 8PN* T: (01327) 226245 E: diane.whittaker7@btinternet.com

WHITTAKER, Edward Geoffrey. b 59. Birm Univ BSc 82 Avery Hill Coll PGCE 85 Dur Univ MA 95. Westcott Ho Cam 97. **d** 99 **p** 00. C Neston *Ches* 99–02; V Rocester and Croxden w Hollington *Lich* 02–10; P-in-c Uttoxeter Area 07–11; TR 11–15; P-in-c Upper Team 13–14; RD Uttoxeter 04–11; P-in-c Shrawley, Witley, Astley and Abberley *Worc* from 15; P-in-c Teme Valley N from 15; RD Stourport 19–21. *The Rectory, 1 Chiltern Close, Great Witley WR6 6HL* T: (01299) 890100 M: 07791-484774 E: ted@clovermail.net

WHITTAKER, Garry. b 59. St Jo Coll Nottm 89. **d** 91 **p** 92. C Denton Ch Ch *Man* 91–95; P-in-c Waterhead 95–05; TR Bacup and Stacksteads 05–15; TV Fellside Team *Blackb* from 15. *The Vicarage, Church Lane, Bilsborrow, Preston PR3 0RL* T: (01995) 643245 E: braincapers59@aol.com

WHITTAKER, Helena Jane. b 69. Leic Univ BA 91 Open Univ MA 00. Qu Coll Birm 09. **d** 12 **p** 13. NSM Braunstone Park *Leic* 12–15; NSM Hinckley St Mary 15–18; Hon Chapl Leic Gr Sch 15–18; Chapl Ark Burlington Danes Academy London 18–19; Chapl Leic Gr Sch 19–20; Chapl Lady Margaret Sch from 20; P-in-c Earlsfield St Jo *S'wark* from 20. *17 Montserrat Road, London SW15 2LD* T: (020) 8735 4950 M: 07787-383282 E: helenajwhittaker@gmail.com

WHITTAKER, Mrs Jennifer Margaret. b 43. Glas Univ MA 64. SAOMC 00. **d** 03 **p** 04. NSM Martley and Wichenford, Knightwick etc *Worc* 03–08; NSM Worcs W Rural 09–13; PtO from 13. *The Key Barn, Half Key, Malvern WR14 1UP* T: (01886) 833897 E: jen.whittaker@tiscali.co.uk

WHITTAKER, Jeremy Paul. b 59. Ox Univ MA. Ripon Coll Cuddesdon 82. **d** 84 **p** 85. C Crowthorne *Ox* 84–87; C Westborough *Guildf* 87–88; TV 88–91; Chapl Pierrepont Sch Frensham 91–95; PtO *Guildf* from 95. *6 Springhaven Close, Guildford GU1 2JP*

WHITTAKER, John. b 69. Leic Univ BA 90 ACA 93. Ripon Coll Cuddesdon BTh 00. **d** 00 **p** 01. C Melton Mowbray *Leic* 00–03; P-in-c Barrow upon Soar w Walton le Wolds 03–11; P-in-c Wymeswold and Prestwold w Hoton 05–11; V Hinckley St Mary 11–18; TR Putney St Mary *S'wark* from 18. *17 Monserrat Road, London SW15 2LD* E: johnwhittaker2010@gmail.com *or* john.whittaker@parishofputney.co.uk

WHITTAKER, Canon Karl Paul. b 55. ATL. CITC BTh 95. **d** 95 **p** 96. C Killowen *D & R* 95–99; I Annaghmore *Arm* 99–04; P-in-c Sunbury St Mary Australia 04–05; I Errigal w Garvagh *D & R* 05–19; I Leckpatrick w Dunnalong from 19; Can Derry Cathl from 17. *The Rectory, 1 Lowertown Road, Ballymagorry, Strabane BT82 0LE* E: revpaul007@btinternet.com

WHITTAKER, Canon Peter Harold. b 39. AKC 62. **d** 63 **p** 64. C Walton St Mary *Liv* 63–67; C Ross *Heref* 67–70; R Bridgnorth St Mary 70–78; P-in-c Oldbury 70–78; TR Bridgnorth, Tasley, Astley Abbotts and Oldbury 78–81; RD Bridgnorth 78–81; Preb Heref Cathl 80–81; V Leighton Buzzard w Eggington, Hockliffe etc *St Alb* 81–92; RD Dunstable 84–85; R Barton-le-Cley w Higham Gobion and Hexton 92–04; Hon Can St Alb 92–04; rtd 04; PtO *Lich* 06–17. *11 Llewellyn Place, Shrewsbury SY3 8QY* T: (01743) 361736

WHITTAKER, Robert Andrew. b 49. Open Univ BA 75 Nottm Univ MA 83 DipEd. Linc Th Coll 85. **d** 87 **p** 88. C Mansfield Woodhouse *S'well* 87–90; V Norwell w Ossington, Cromwell and Caunton 90–95; Chapl Ranby Ho Sch Retford

95–03; rtd 06; PtO *S'well* 14–21. *23 Birchcroft Road, Retford DN22 7ZD* T: (01777) 470153

WHITTICK, Emma Louise. b 81. Univ of Wales (Abth) MSc 05 PhD 10 New Coll Ox PGCE 03. St Jo Coll Nottm 09. **d** 15 **p** 16. C Dafen and Felinfoel *St D* 15–17; C Bro Lliedi 17–18; Chapl Univ of Wales Trin St Dav from 18. *The Chaplaincy, Forest Road, Lampeter SA48 8AN* T: (01570) 424781 E: revdremmawhittick@gmail.com

WHITTING, Dominic Peter. b 85. Cant Ch Ch Univ BA 07. Ripon Coll Cuddesdon 07. **d** 10 **p** 11. C St Breoke and Egloshayle *Truro* 10–14; V Crowan and Treslothan 14–18; Chapl R Cornwall Hosps Trust from 18. *79 Egloshayle Road, Wadebridge PL27 6AF* T: (01208) 812726 E: domwhitting@hotmail.com

WHITTINGHAM, Janet Irene. *See* HULSE, Janet Irene

WHITTINGHAM, Peter. b 58. Sheff Univ BA 79 PGCE. St Jo Coll Nottm 88. **d** 90 **p** 91. C Northowram *Wakef* 90–93; C Airedale w Fryston 93–96; V Wrenthorpe 96–06; P-in-c Alvertthorpe 02–06; V Attercliffe and Darnall *Sheff* 06–11; Chapl Shrewsbury Hosp from 11. *The Chaplain's House, Shrewsbury Hospital, Norfolk Road, Sheffield S2 2SU* T: 0114-275 9997 M: 07734-807866 E: peter.whittingham@sheffield.anglican.org *or* pete.whittingham@btconnect.com

WHITTINGHAM, Ronald Norman. b 43. Linc Coll Ox BA 65 MA 68. Coll of Resurr Mirfield 65. **d** 67 **p** 68. C Horninglow *Lich* 67–69; C Drayton in Hales 69–70; C Uttoxeter w Bramshall 71–75; P-in-c Burton St Paul 75–80; V Shareshill 80–83; V Silverdale and Knutton Heath 83–89; P-in-c Alsagers Bank 83–89; V Silverdale and Alsagers Bank 89–92; V Honley *Wakef* 92–99; TV Hugglescote w Donington, Ellistown and Snibston *Leic* 99–02; TV Leic Presentation 02–07; C Leic St Chad 02–07; rtd 07; PtO *Lich* 08–21. *848 High Lane, Stoke-on-Trent ST6 6HG* T: (01782) 860460 E: ronwhittingham@ntlworld.com

WHITTINGTON, David John. b 45. OBE 01. Qu Coll Ox BA 67 MA 71. Coll of Resurr Mirfield 69. **d** 71 **p** 72. Chapl St Woolos Cathl *Mon* 71–72; Chapl Qu Coll and C Ox St Mary V w St Cross and St Pet 72–76; V Stockton *Dur* 77–98; Hon Can Dur Cathl 93–98; Can Res and Dioc Dir of Educn 98–03; Nat Sch Development Officer Abps' Coun 03–08; rtd 08. *La Grange de Serrelongue, Hameau de Serrelongue, 09300 Benaix, France* M: 07702-036344 E: dj.whittington@btinternet.com

WHITTINGTON, Peter Graham. b 68. Ox Poly BA 90 Ches Univ MA 14. Trin Coll Bris BA 95. **d** 95 **p** 96. C Gateacre *Liv* 95–99; V Huyton St Geo 99–05; V Orrell 05–16; Dir Studies 16–21; Tutor Em Th Coll from 21; C Wigan *Liv* from 21. *Address withheld by request*

WHITTINGTON, Richard Hugh. b 47. MBE 74. Sarum & Wells Th Coll. **d** 93 **p** 94. C Enfield St Jas *Lon* 93–96; P-in-c Ightham *Roch* 96–97; R 97–01; Chapl R Hosp Chelsea 01–13; PtO *Lon* from 13; *Ox* from 14. *60 Walker Drive, Faringdon SN7 7FZ* T: (01367) 243738 M: 07879-335536 E: rhw47@btinternet.com

WHITTINGTON, Mrs Sharon Ann. b 56. Leeds Univ BA 79 PGCE 80. NEOC. **d** 00 **p** 01. NSM The Street Par *York* 00–03; P-in-c York St Thos w St Maurice 03–05; NSM York St Olave w St Giles 03–09; NSM York St Helen w St Martin 04–09; PtO from 09; Chapl St Leon Hospice York from 11. *30 Marygate, York YO30 7BH* T: (01904) 627401 E: sa.whittington@btinternet.com

WHITTLE, Adam Charles. b 87. Liv Univ BA 09 MA 10. Trin Coll Bris 15. **d** 18 **p** 19. C Pennington *Man* 18–21; V Swinton H Rood from 21; TR Worsley from 21. *St Mark's Rectory, Walkden Road, Worsley, Manchester M28 2WH* M: 07919-382278 E: adamwhittle17@hotmail.com

WHITTLE, Ian Christopher. b 60. Univ Coll Dur BA 81 Fitzw Coll Cam BA 88 MA 91. Ridley Hall Cam 85. **d** 88 **p** 89. C S Petherton w The Seavingtons *B & W* 88–91; Asst Chapl The Hague *Eur* 91–97; P-in-c Gayton Gp of Par *Nor* 97–99; R Gayton, Gayton Thorpe, E Walton, E Winch etc 99–10; RD Lynn 02–08; R Stiffkey and Bale from 10. *The Rectory, Langham, Holt NR25 7BX* T: (01328) 830246

WHITTLE, Canon Naomi Clare. b 54. Colchester Inst of Educn BA 75 Lon Univ PGCE 76 Middx Univ MA(Theol) 99 LGSM 77. SEITE 95. **d** 98 **p** 99. C Catford (Southend) and Downham *S'wark* 98–02; P-in-c Shooters Hill Ch Ch 02; V 02–10; Chapl Oxleas NHS Foundn Trust 06–10; V Stockwell St Andr and St Mich *S'wark* 10–16; rtd 16; PtO *S'wark* 16–17; Public Preacher from 17; Dioc Retirement Officer from 19; Hon Can S'wark Cathl from 15. *163 Abbotsbury Road, Morden SM4 5JS* T: (020) 8640 5639 E: n.whittle954@btinternet.com

WHITTLE, Robin Jeffrey. b 51. Bris Univ BA 72 Leic Univ CQSW 75. Sarum & Wells Th Coll 85. **d** 87 **p** 88. C Henbury Bris 87–91; V Capel *Guildf* 91–96; Chapl among Deaf People 96–09; PtO *S'wark* 97–99; *Roch* 97–99; P-in-c Walton-

on-the-Hill *Guildf* 99–04; V Tattenham Corner 04–09; V Findon w Clapham and Patching *Chich* 09–13; rtd 13; PtO *Chich* from 13. *3 Hillside Road, Storrington, Pulborough RH20 3LZ* T: (01903) 740542 E: bobwhittle@btinternet.com

WHITTLE, Mrs Sheila Margaret. b 36. Glouc Th Course 83 NY Th Sem MA 88 Vancouver Sch of Th. **d** 90 **p** 90. R Bulkley Valley Canada 90–93; C Dunbar St Phil 93; P-in-c Maple Ridge St Jo the Divine 93–95; Lethbridge St Mary the Virgin 95–97; NSM Portsea N End St Mark *Portsm* 97–98; P-in-c Lezant w Lawhitton and S Petherwin w Trewen *Truro* 98–02; rtd 02; PtO *Glouc* from 03. *71 Graylag Crescent, Walton Cardiff, Tewkesbury GL20 7RR* T: (01684) 299981 E: sheilawhittle5@gmail.com

WHITTLESEA, Grahame Stanley Jack Hammond. b 37. Kent Univ LLM 95. **d** 05 **p** 06. OLM Blean *Cant* 05–09; rtd 09; PtO *Cant* from 09; Retirement Officer (Cant Adnry) from 10. *4 Eastbridge Hospital, High Street, Canterbury CT1 2BD* T: (01227) 472536 M: 07866-037774 E: gandawhittlesea@tiscali.co.uk

WHITTLEWORTH, Ann Marie. b 53. **d** 12 **p** 13. NSM Hillock *Man* 12–14; NSM Unsworth 12–14; NSM Hillock and Unsworth from 14; NSM Stand from 15. *10 North Avenue, Unsworth, Bury BL9 8AR* T: 0161-796 1856 E: awhittleworth@gmail.com

WHITTOCK (née MARBUS), Alida Janny. b 52. RGN 78. STETS 00. **d** 03 **p** 07. NSM Weymouth H Trin *Sarum* 03–09; NSM Abbotsbury, Portesham and Langton Herring 09–14; PtO from 14. *79 Clearmount Road, Weymouth DT4 9LE* T: (01305) 788045 E: adamarbus@aol.com

WHITTOCK, Carol Jean. b 51. Goldsmiths' Coll Lon BA 74 Univ of Wales (Abth) PGCE 76. WEMTC 07. **d** 10 **p** 11. C Gt Hanwood and Longden and Annscroft etc *Heref* 10–14; C Churchstoke w Hyssington and Sarn from 14. *The Vicarage, Church Stoke, Montgomery SY15 6AF* T: (01588) 620693 E: carolwhittock@btinternet.com

WHITTOCK, Preb Michael Graham. b 47. Hull Univ BA 69 Fitzw Coll Cam BA 71 MA 76. Westcott Ho Cam 69 Union Th Sem Virginia 71. **d** 72 **p** 73. C Kirkby *Liv* 72–76; C Prescot 76–79; R Methley w Mickletown *Ripon* 79–92; RD Whitkirk 88–92; V Morley St Pet w Churwell *Wakef* 92–01; R Gt Hanwood *Heref* 01–13; R Longden and Annscroft w Pulverbatch 01–13; R Gt Hanwood and Longden and Annscroft etc 13–14; RD Pontesbury 08–13; Asst Adn Ludlow 13–14; Preb Heref Cathl 10–14; rtd 14; PtO *Heref* from 15. *The Vicarage, Church Stoke, Montgomery SY15 6AF* T: (01588) 620693 E: mgwhittock@gmail.com

WHITTON, Alysoun. b 55. St Steph Ho Ox 09. **d** 10 **p** 11. NSM Hampstead Em W End *Lon* 10–14; PtO *Cant* 15–16; NSM W Hampstead St Cuth *Lon* 16–18; PtO *Cant* from 18. *5 St Christopher's Green, Broadstairs CT10 2SS* T: (01843) 579930 M: 07985-020203 E: alysoun.whitton@gmail.com

WHITWELL, Canon John Peter. b 36. Open Univ BA 07. Qu Coll Birm 62. **d** 65 **p** 66. C Stepney St Dunstan and All SS *Lon* 65–68; C Chingford SS Pet and Paul *Chelmsf* 68–71; V Walthamstow St Sav 71–78; P-in-c Lt Ilford St Mich 78–88; R 88–98; RD Newham 91–97; Hon Can Chelmsf Cathl 96–98; rtd 98; PtO *Ox* from 99. *152 Bath Road, Banbury OX16 0TT* T: (01295) 266243 E: jandawhitwell@aol.com

WHITWORTH, Benjamin Charles Battams. b 49. CCC Ox BA 71 MA 85. Linc Th Coll 83. **d** 85 **p** 86. C Swanborough *Sarum* 85–88; C Sherborne w Castleton and Lillington 88–91; V Milborne Port w Goathill *B & W* 91–98; rtd 98; PtO *B & W* from 00. *13 The Avenue, Taunton TA1 1EA* T: (01823) 272442 E: whitworth@talktalk.net

WHITWORTH, Canon Duncan. b 47. K Coll Lon BD 69 AKC 69. St Aug Coll Cant 69. **d** 70 **p** 71. C Tonge Moor *Man* 70–73; C Upper Norwood St Jo *Cant* 73–78; Asst Chapl Madrid *Eur* 78–82; Chapl Br Embassy Ankara 82–83; V Douglas St Matt *S & M* 84–12; RD Douglas 91–12; Can St German's Cathl 96–12; rtd 12. *24 Ballafurt Close, Port Erin, Isle of Man IM9 6HS* T: (01624) 837350 E: duncando@manx.net

WHITWORTH, Canon Patrick John. b 51. Ch Ch Ox BA 72 MA 76 St Jo Coll Dur MA 78. **d** 76 **p** 77. C York St Mich-le-Belfrey 76–79; C Brompton H Trin w Onslow Square St Paul *Lon* 79–84; V Gipsy Hill Ch Ch *S'wark* 84–95; R Bath Weston All SS w N Stoke and Langridge *B & W* 95–16; RD Bath 03–10; Preb Wells Cathl 12–16; rtd 16; PtO *Ox* from 17; Hon Can Bauchi from 95. *Elcot Lodge, Elcot, Newbury RG20 8NJ* E: pwhitworth@metronet.co.uk

WHITWORTH, Vincent Craig. b 80. Nottm Univ BA 01. St Jo Coll Nottm MTh 06. **d** 07 **p** 08. C Parr *Liv* 07–11; C Halliwell St Pet *Man* 11–19; AD Bolton 15–19; P-in-c Bolton St Bede 19–21; V from 21; TV Deane from 19; AD 19–21. *St Paul's Vicarage, Vicarage Lane, Halliwell, Bolton BL1 8BP* T: (01204) 849079 M: 07759-920922

WHORTON, Mrs Ailsa Claire. b 67. All SS Cen for Miss & Min 16. **d** 18 **p** 19. C Newton *Ches* 18–20; CF from 20. *c/o MOD Chaplains (Army)* T: (01264) 383430 E: ailsacwhorton@gmail.com

WHYBORN, Robert. b 42. NOC 87. **d** 90 **p** 91. NSM Milnrow *Man* 90–97; NSM Greenfield 97–03; NSM Saddleworth 03–05; rtd 05; PtO *Man* from 05. *6 Burnell Court, Heywood OL10 2NW* T: (01706) 369397 E: revrob8@aol.com

WHYBROW, Paul Andrew. b 59. St Paul's Coll Chelt BEd 80 Oak Hill Th Coll BA 90. Wycliffe Hall Ox 95. **d** 97 **p** 98. C Magor *Mon* 97–00; V Poughill *Truro* 00–18; rtd 18; PtO *Ex* from 19. *12 The Old Station, Horrabridge, Yelverton PL20 7RQ* T: (01822) 852577 E: pa.whybrow59@icloud.com

WHYMARK, James Philip. b 82. St Mellitus Coll 18. **d** 20 **p** 21. C Win Ch Ch from 20. *8 Juniper Close, Winchester SO22 4LU*

WHYSALL, Canon Joan. b 42. Lady Mabel Coll CertEd 64 Nottm Univ MA 01. EMMTC 98. **d** 01 **p** 02. NSM Trowell, Awsworth and Cossall *S'well* 01–06; P-in-c Cinderhill 06–14; Hon Can S'well Minster 10–12; rtd 14; PtO *S'well* from 15. *55 Trowell Park Drive, Trowell, Nottingham NG9 3RA* T: 0115-939 6903 E: joan.whysall@btinternet.com

WHYTE, Henry Lewis. b 38. ALCD 70 LTh 74. **d** 70 **p** 71. C Crawley *Chich* 70–74; V Bermondsey St Jas w Ch Ch *S'wark* 74–82; V Kingston Hill St Paul 82–94; V Blackheath Park St Mich 94–02; rtd 02; PtO *S'wark* from 03. *6 Horn Park Lane, London SE12 8UU* T: (020) 8318 9837 E: henrywhyte@hotmail.co.uk

WHYTE, Canon Robert Euan. b 44. St Pet Coll Ox BA 67. Cuddesdon Coll 67. **d** 69 **p** 70. C Blackheath Ascension *S'wark* 69–73; BCC 73–87; NSM Lewisham St Swithun *S'wark* 73–76; NSM Heston *Lon* 76–77; C Rusthall *Roch* 77–88; V 88–08; RD Tunbridge Wells 91–96; Hon Can Roch Cathl 00–08; rtd 08. *9 Thornhill Avenue, Belper DE56 1SH* T: (01773) 880531 E: whyterobert@hotmail.com

WHYTE, William Hadden. b 75. Wadh Coll Ox BA 97 MA 03 MSt 98 DPhil 02. SAOMC 03. **d** 06 **p** 07. NSM Kidlington w Hampton Poyle *Ox* 06–17; NSM Wolvercote and Wytham from 17. *St John's College, Oxford OX1 3JP* T: (01865) 277338 F: 277300 E: william.whyte@sjc.ox.ac.uk

WICK, Canon Patricia Anne. b 54. Lon Bible Coll BA 80 Redcliffe Coll Glouc MA 12. Oak Hill Th Coll 84. **dss** 86 **d** 87 **p** 94. Halliwell St Luke *Man* 86–87; Par Dn 87–91; Par Dn Drypool *York* 91–94; C 94–95; TV 95–97; CMS Sudan 98–14; PtO *York* 15; Pioneer Min from 15; Canon Maridi from 09. *14 Cherry Tree Close, Bilton, Hull HU11 4EZ* M: 07527-523098 E: patricia@rcs-communication.com

WICKENS, Andrew Peter. b 63. St Jo Coll Dur BA 85 Magd Coll Cam MEd 97 PGCE 95 Cardiff Univ LLM 20 ARCM 84 FRSA 14. Westcott Ho Cam 98. **d** 00 **p** 01. C Louth *Linc* 00–03; TV 03–07; Lect Boston 07–10; PV Linc Cathl 01–10; R Newton Heath *Man* from 11; P-in-c Moston St Chad and Moston St Jo 11–13; Min Can Man Cathl from 18. *All Saints' Rectory, 2 Culcheth Lane, Manchester M40 1LR* T: 0161-219 1807 E: andrew.wickens08@btinternet.com

WICKENS, Andrew St Lawrence John. b 63. Mert Coll Ox BA 85 Birm Univ MPhil 94 Dur Univ PGCE 86. Qu Coll Birm 89. **d** 92 **p** 93. C Birchfield *Birm* 92–96; PtO 96–97 and 00–01; Zambia 97–00; P-in-c St Mich Cathl Kitwe 99–00; Lect St Paul's United Th Coll Limuru Kenya 01–05; P-in-c Dudley St Jas *Worc* 05–09; TV Dudley 09–17; Educn Chapl 05–17; Hon Can Worc Cathl 15–17; TR Stoke-upon-Trent and Fenton *Lich* from 17. *172 Smithpool Road, Stoke-on-Trent ST4 4PP* T: (01782) 413915 E: astljwickens@gmail.com

WICKENS, Laurence Paul. b 52. Selw Coll Cam BA 74 MA 78 Leeds Univ PhD 90 CEng 80 MIET 80 MIMechE 81 EurIng 90. EAMTC 02. **d** 06 **p** 07. NSM Cambridge St Barn *Ely* 06–08; NSM Meole Brace *Lich* 08–11; PtO *Cov* from 13. *31 Paddocks Close, Wolston, Coventry CV8 3GW* T: (024) 7651 0305 M: 07811-551583 E: laurence.wickens@gmail.com

WICKENS, Moira. b 56. S Dios Minl Tr Scheme 91. **d** 94 **p** 08. NSM Ifield *Chich* 94–96; C Saltdean 96–03; C Ovingdean and Schs Liaison Officer 03–06; C Kingston Buci 06–08; P-in-c Applegram 10–21; Dioc Voc Adv 06–10; R New Fishbourne 10–21; P-in-c Appledram 10–21; Can and Preb Chich Cathl 12–21; rtd 21. *Address withheld by request*

WICKENS, Mrs Sandra Ruth. b 68. St Mellitus Coll BA 19. **d** 19 **p** 20. C Rotherfield w Mark Cross *Chich* from 19. *Church Settle, Church Road, Rotherfield, Crowborough TN6 3LE* M: 07395-106514 E: sandiwickens@gmail.com

WICKERT, Keith Frederick. b 59. Birkbeck Coll Lon BSc 84. STETS 09. **d** 12 **p** 13. NSM Fareham H Trin *Portsm* 12–16; NSM Bishop's Waltham from 16; NSM Upham from 16. *14 Denewulf Close, Bishops Waltham, Southampton SO32 1GZ* T: (01489) 809403 M: 07717-312426 E: wickertkeith@gmail.com

WICKETT, Prof Reginald Ernest Yeatman. b 43. Toronto Univ BA 65 MEd 71 EdD 78 Em Coll Saskatoon Hon DCnL 96. Trin Coll Toronto 65. **d** 00 **p** 01. NSM Saskatoon All SS Canada 00–02; NSM St Jo Cathl from 02; PtO *Ely* 12–15. *14-102 Willow Street, Saskatoon SK S7J 0C2, Canada* M: 07984-909693 E: reg.wickett@usask.ca *or* rw461@cam.ac.uk

WICKHAM, Mrs Jennifer Ruth. b 68. Univ of W Ontario BA 91. Cranmer Hall Dur BA 98. **d** 98 **p** 99. C Ponteland *Newc* 98–00; Assoc P Ottawa St Geo Canada 01–18; V Cov St Geo from 18. *101 Moseley Avenue, Coventry CV6 1HR* T: (024) 7659 1994 E: ajwickham@yahoo.com *or* vicarstgs@gmail.com

✠**WICKHAM, The Rt Revd Robert James.** b 72. Grey Coll Dur BA 94 K Coll Lon MA 12. Ridley Hall Cam 95. **d** 98 **p** 99 **c** 15. C Willesden St Mary *Lon* 98–01; C Somers Town 01–03; TV Old St Pancras 03–07; R St John-at-Hackney 07–15; AD Hackney 14–15; Area Bp Edmonton from 15. *27 Thurlow Road, London NW3 5PP* T: (020) 3837 5250 E: bishop.edmonton@london.anglican.org

WICKHAM, Timothy James. b 86. Oak Hill Th Coll 12. **d** 15 **p** 16. C Balderstone *Man* from 15; C Rusholme H Trin from 18. *229 Heald Place, Manchester M14 5NJ* M: 07595-919627 E: tjwickham1986@gmail.com

WICKINGS, Luke Iden. b 59. Sheff Poly BA 81 K Coll Lon PGCE 07. Oak Hill Th Coll BA 90. **d** 90 **p** 91. C Fulham St Mary N End *Lon* 90–94; C Bletchley *Ox* 94–00; V W Norwood St Luke *S'wark* 00–07; Hon C New Malden and Coombe 13–15; C Tolworth, Hook and Surbiton 15–16; TV from 16. *The Vicarage, 278 Hook Road, Chessington KT9 1PF* M: 07983-398984 E: lukewickings@gmail.com

WICKREMASINGHE, Rosemary Ethel. b 32. Reading Univ ATD 52 K Coll Lon BD 85 AKC 85. SAOMC 93. **d** 96 **p** 97. NSM Godrevy *Truro* 96–05; rtd 05; PtO *Truro* 05–21. *10 Glebe Row, Phillack, Hayle TR27 5AJ* T: (01736) 757850

WICKS, Christopher Blair. b 59. Oak Hill Th Coll BA 88. **d** 88 **p** 89. C Edmonton All SS w St Mich *Lon* 88–92; C Southborough St Pet w Ch Ch and St Matt etc *Roch* 92–96; TV 96–19; V High Brooms from 19. *72 Powder Mill Lane, Southborough, Tunbridge Wells TN4 9EJ* T: (01892) 529098 E: chris@stmattschurch.org.uk

WICKS, Joel Gregory. b 85. Kent Univ BA 07. Oak Hill Th Coll BA 20. **d** 20 **p** 21. C Hampton *Ely* from 20. *15 West Water Crescent, Hampton Vale, Peterborough PE7 8LT* M: 07941-651239 E: joelgwicks@gmail.com

WICKS, Victoria Louise. b 68. Liv Univ BA 91 Salford Univ MA 93. Trin Coll Bris 18. **d** 20 **p** 21. C Stoke Gifford *Bris* from 20. *13 Tybalt Way, Stoke Gifford, Bristol BS34 8XJ* T: 0117-969 5990 M: 07886-599533 E: vicky@stmichaelsbristol.org

WICKSTEAD, Canon Gavin John. b 46. St Chad's Coll Dur BA 67. Linc Th Coll 82. **d** 84 **p** 85. C Louth *Linc* 84–87; P-in-c E Markham and Askham *S'well* 87–89; P-in-c Headon w Upton 87–89; P-in-c Grove 87–89; R E Markham w Askham, Headon w Upton and Grove 90–92; P-in-c Skegness and Winthorpe *Linc* 92–97; R 97–01; V Holbeach 01–11; RD Elloe E 05–07; Can and Preb Linc Cathl 05–16; rtd 11; PtO *Linc* from 11; *Ely* 16–21. *1 Aspen Drive, Sleaford NG34 7GN* T: (01529) 410231 E: wickstead@btinternet.com

WIDDECOMBE, Roger James. b 70. Wycliffe Hall Ox 01. **d** 03 **p** 04. C Downend *Bris* 03–06; C Cheltenham St Mary, St Matt, St Paul and H Trin *Glouc* 06–07; TV Cheltenham H Trin and St Paul from 07. *85 Brunswick Street, Cheltenham GL50 4HA* T: (01242) 300110 E: roger@widde.com

WIDDESS, Jonathan Mark. b 73. Univ of Wales (Abth) BScEcon 95. Wycliffe Hall Ox 07 08. **d** 09 **p** 10. C Gabalfa *Llan* 09–13; P-in-c Bargoed and Deri w Brithdir 13–17; V Cumnor *Ox* from 17. *The Vicarage, Abingdon Road, Cumnor, Oxford OX2 9QN* T: (01865) 863702 M: 07595-996534 E: revjonathan@icloud.com *or* revjonathan@cumnor.org *or* vicar@cumnor.org

WIDDESS, Mrs Margaret Jennifer. b 48. Bedf Coll Lon BA 70 Clare Hall Cam PGCE 75 Lambeth MA 03. EAMTC 94. **d** 97 **p** 98. NSM Cambridge St Botolph *Ely* 97–16; rtd 16; PtO *Ely* from 17. *69 Gwydir Street, Cambridge CB1 2LG* T: (01223) 313908 E: mjwiddess@btinternet.com

WIDDOWS, David Charles Roland. b 52. Hertf Coll Ox BA 75 MA 79. St Jo Coll Nottm BA 77. **d** 79 **p** 80. C Blackley St Andr *Man* 79–83; P-in-c Rochdale Deeplish St Luke 83–84; V 84–92; TR Stoke Gifford *Bris* 92–06; Chapl Lee Abbey 06–10; P-in-c Wiveliscombe and the Hills *B & W* 10–11; R 11–17; rtd 17; PtO *Ex* from 18. *1 Butterleigh Drive, Tiverton EX16 4PN* M: 07890-758751

WIDDOWS, Heather Susan. b 45. BEM 15. Open Univ BA 76 BA 12. Moray Ord Course 91. **d** 96 **p** 97. NSM Kishorn *Mor* 96–15; NSM Poolewe 96–15; LtO from 15. *2 Fasaich, Strath, Gairloch IV21 2DH* T: (01445) 712176 E: heather_widdows@yahoo.co.uk

WIDDOWS, Nicholas John. b 82. Ex Coll Ox MEng 05 Cam Univ PhD 21 CA 09. Trin Coll Bris 10. **d** 12 **p** 13. C Fowey *Truro* 12–14; C St Sampson 12–14; Chapl Jes Coll Cam 14–15; Chapl Magd Coll Cam 15–18; V St Ives and Halsetown *Truro* from 18. *The Vicarage, St John's in the Fields, Hellesvean, St Ives TR26 2HG* T: (01736) 449382 M: 07789-680070 E: nickwiddows@hotmail.com

WIDDOWSON, Robert William. b 47. Linc Th Coll 83. **d** 85 **p** 86. C Syston *Leic* 85–88; R Husbands Bosworth w Mowsley and Knaptoft etc 88–93; R Asfordby 93–98; P-in-c Ab Kettleby Gp 93–98; P-in-c Old Dalby and Nether Broughton 95–98; P-in-c Charlton Musgrove, Cucklington and Stoke Trister *B & W* 98–03; P-in-c Ashwick w Oakhill and Binegar 03–12; Adv in Rural Affairs 98–12; rtd 12; PtO *B & W* 15–20. *23 The Leaze, Westfield, Radstock BA3 3YH* E: robvalwidd@gmail.com

WIECK, Malcolm Rayment. b 44. Solicitor 70. **d** 08 **p** 09. OLM Bratton, Edington and Imber, Erlestoke etc *Sarum* 08–12; NSM 12–14; PtO from 14. *Sandy Lane Cottage, 12 Westbury Road, Edington, Westbury BA13 4QD* T: (01380) 830256 M: 07805-990087 E: malcolm.wieck@btinternet.com

WIEGMAN, Mrs Jacqueline Anne Cecilia. b 52. ERMC 10. **d** 13 **p** 14. NSM Longthorpe *Pet* 13–16; NSM Pet H Spirit Bretton 13–16; Sen Chapl HM Pris Peterborough from 13. *HM Prison Peterborough, Saville Road, Peterborough PE3 7PD* T: (01733) 217500

WIFFEN, Ronald. b 38. Glos Univ BA 99. SEITE 99. **d** 01 **p** 02. NSM Canvey Is *Chelmsf* 01–04; P-in-c Bowers Gifford w N Benfleet 04–06; NSM SW Gower *S & B* 06–08; P-in-c Southport St Luke *Liv* 08–09; rtd 09; PtO *Chelmsf* 09–11; P-in-c Mundford w Lynford *Nor* 11–15; P-in-c Ickburgh w Langford 11–15; P-in-c Cranwich 11–15; P-in-c W Tofts and Buckenham Parva 11–15; PtO *Chelmsf* from 15. *Southwycke, 197 Southchurch Boulevard, Southend-on-Sea SS2 4UU* T: (01702) 585608 E: revdronaldwiffen@gmail.com

WIFFIN, Susan Elizabeth. *See* MACDONALD, Susan Elizabeth

WIGGEN, Richard Martin. b 42. Open Univ BA 78 Hull Univ MA 86 Leeds Univ MPhil 90. Qu Coll Birm 64. **d** 67 **p** 68. C Penistone w Midhope *Wakef* 67–70; C Leeds St Pet *Ripon* 70–73; Asst Youth Chapl *Glouc* 73–76; Youth Officer *Liv* 76–80; V Kirkstall *Ripon* 80–90; V Meanwood 90–07; rtd 07; PtO *Leeds* from 17. *19 Shadwell Lane, Leeds LS17 6DP* T: 0113-266 5241 E: wiggen@btopenworld.com

WIGGINS, Karl Patrick. b 38. MRICS 64 FRICS 87. Trin Coll Bris BD 72. **d** 72 **p** 73. C Hildenborough *Roch* 72–76; Hon C Reading St Barn *Ox* 76–78; Hon C Chieveley w Winterbourne and Oare 78–80; Hon C Earley St Nic 80–83; Hon C Reading St Jo 83–88; Hon C Beech Hill, Grazeley and Spencers Wood 88–98; rtd 98; PtO *Ox* 99; *Sarum* from 05; *B & W* 16–21. *Willow Cottage, 37 New Road, Bradford-on-Avon BA15 1AP* T: (01225) 867007 E: kk-wiggins@msn.com

WIGGINS, Robert Carl Wesley. b 51. All SS Cen for Miss & Min 12. **d** 14 **p** 15. NSM Beeston S'well from 14. *31 Woodbridge Avenue, Nottingham NG11 8GP* T: 0115-914 2513 M: 07906-664263 E: rob.wiggins@ntlworld.com

WIGGINS (née SQUIRE), Susan Elizabeth. b 53. St Mellitus Coll 13. **d** 14 **p** 15. OLM Holland-on-Sea *Chelmsf* from 14. *18 Southcliff Hall, 55-57 Marine Parade East, Clacton-on-Sea CO15 6AD* T: (01255) 427724 M: 07974-100069

WIGGLESWORTH, Canon Mark. b 60. Clare Coll Cam BA 82 MA 96 St Jo Coll Dur MA 14. Cranmer Hall Dur 89. **d** 92 **p** 93. C Brinsworth w Catcliffe *Sheff* 92–93; C Brinsworth w Catcliffe and Treeton 93–95; C Goole 95–96; V Askern 96–11; AD Adwick 05–11; Dir Miss and Pioneer Min 11–14; Miss Development Adv Doncaster Adnry from 14; Hon Can Sheff Cathl from 10. *177 Harlington Road, Mexborough S64 0QR* T: (01709) 322952 M: 07818-416424 E: mark.dmpm@gmail.com

WIGGS, Robert James. b 50. Pemb Coll Cam BA 72 MA CertEd. Qu Coll Birm 78. **d** 80 **p** 81. C Stratford St Jo and Ch Ch w Forest Gate St Jas *Chelmsf* 80–83; C E Ham w Upton Park and Forest Gate 83–86; TV 86–91; TR Grays Thurrock 91–99; PtO 99–16; NSM Maldon St Mary w Mundon from 16. *113 Moulsham Street, Chelmsford CM2 0JN* T: (01245) 359138 E: robwiggs@virginmedia.com

WIGHT, The Ven Dennis Marley. b 53. Southn Univ BTh 87. Sarum & Wells Th Coll 82. **d** 85 **p** 86. C Gillingham *Sarum* 85–87; Appeals Org CECS from 87; PtO *Birm* 89–90; V Coseley Ch Ch *Lich* 90–93; V Coseley Ch Ch *Worc* 93–94; R Stoke Prior, Wychbold and Upton Warren 94–02; RD Droitwich 96–99; V Dale and St Brides w Marloes *St D* 02–10; AD Roose 05–10; Dioc Warden Ords 09–11 and 12–14 and 15; Bp's Chapl 10–14; Dir of Min 10–18; Hon Can St D Cathl 09–18; Adn St D 13–18; P-in-c Wiston w Walton E and Clarbeston 15–18; C Llawhaden w Bletherston and

Uzmaston 15–18; rtd 18; PtO *St D* from 18. *6 Llys Holcwm, Ferryside SA17 5SY*

WIGHTMAN, William David. b 39. Birm Univ BA 61. Wells Th Coll 61. **d** 63 **p** 64. C Rotherham *Sheff* 63–67; C Castle Church *Lich* 67–70; V Buttershaw St Aid *Bradf* 70–76; V Cullingworth 76–83; R Peterhead *Ab* 83–91; R Strichen, Old Deer and Longside 90–91; Provost St Andr Cathl 91–02; R Aberdeen St Andr 91–02; P-in-c Aberdeen St Ninian 91–02; Hon Can Ch Ch Cathl Connecticut from 91; rtd 02; PtO *York* from 04. *66 Wold Road, Pocklington, York YO42 2QG* T: (01759) 301369 E: wightmandavid@sky.com

WIGLEY, Brian Arthur. b 31. Qu Coll Birm. **d** 82 **p** 83. C Houghton le Spring *Dur* 82–85; C Louth *Linc* 85–86; TV 86–89; Chapl City Hosp NHS Trust Birm 89–95; rtd 95; PtO *Ex* 95–09; *Leic* 13–16. *11 Stuart Court, High Street, Kibworth Beauchamp, Leicester LE8 0LR* T: 0116-279 3682 E: p-bwigley@tiscali.co.uk

WIGLEY, Graham Michael. b 88. Qu Foundn Birm BA 20. **d** 20 **p** 21. C Shenstone and Stonnall *Lich* from 20. *11 Icknield Close, Sutton Coldfield B74 3NN* M: 07960-905234 E: g.wigley@hotmail.co.uk

WIGLEY, Canon Harry Maxwell (Max). b 38. Bernard Gilpin Soc Dur 60 Oak Hill Th Coll 61. **d** 64 **p** 65. C Upton (Overchurch) *Ches* 64–67; C Gateacre *Liv* 67–69; C Chadderton Ch Ch *Man* 67; V Gt Horton *Bradf* 69–88; Hon Can Bradf Cathl 85–03; V Pudsey St Lawr and St Paul 88–96; V Yeadon St Jo 96–03; rtd 03; Hon Dioc Ev *Bradf* 04–10; PtO 10–14; *Leeds* 14–18; *Ox* from 18; *Pet* from 20. *1 Bluebell Close, Buckingham MK18 1FP* T: (01280) 309796 E: maxwigley@sky.com

WIGLEY, Canon Jennifer. b 53. Bris Univ BA 74 Birm Univ MA 75 Ox Univ CertEd 76. Qu Coll Birm 86. **d** 87 **p** 97. C Llangollen w Trevor and Llantysilio *St As* 87–89; C Swansea St Jas *S & B* 89–94; NSM Aberystwyth *St D* 95–98; Tutor St Mich Coll Llan 98–00; C Sketty *S & B* 98–00; Chapl Univ of Wales (Swansea) 00–02; Dep Dir S Wales Ord Course 02–18; TV Cen Cardiff *Llan* 03–06; R Radyr 06–18; AD Llan 10–15; Can Llan Cathl 11–18; rtd 18. *12 Llwyn-y-Grant Road, Penylan, Cardiff CF23 9ET* E: jennifer.wigley@btinternet.com

WIGLEY, Trudie Anne. Somerville Coll Ox BA 91 MA 12 ACIB 94. Ripon Coll Cuddesdon 09. **d** 11 **p** 12. C Swindon Ch Ch *Bris* 11–14; P-in-c Swindon Dorcan 14–19; R from 19; AD Swindon from 21. *23 Sedgebrook, Swindon SN3 6EY* M: 07505-652781 E: rev.trudie@wigley.org.uk

WIGMORE, John Anthony Kingsland. b 62. Oak Hill Th Coll 05. **d** 07 **p** 08. C Braintree *Chelmsf* 07–11; R Winklebury and Worting *Win* from 11. *The Rectory, Glebe Lane, Worting, Basingstoke RG23 8QA* T: (01256) 327305 E: rector@winkleburyandworting.org.uk

WIGMORE, Mrs Lisa Jayn. b 66. Trin Coll Bris 09. **d** 11 **p** 12. C Horfield H Trin *Bris* 11–15; Min Can Bris Cathl 15–16; P-in-c Soundwell from 16. *52 Gladstone Street, Staple Hill, Bristol BS16 4RF* T: 0117-957 4297 M: 07799-883790 E: lisawigmore@blueyonder.co.uk

WIGNALL, Daniel Robert Phillip. b 65. Ox Poly BEd 88. St Jo Coll Nottm MA 98. **d** 98 **p** 99. C Fletchamstead *Cov* 98–01; C Abingdon *Ox* 01–07; V Shottermill *Guildf* 07–18; Local Miss Adv from 18; PtO *Lon* from 21. *St Richard's Vicarage, 35 Forge Lane, Feltham TW13 6UN* E: danny.wignall@cofeguildford.org.uk

WIGNALL, Mrs Deborah. b 66. Ox Brookes Univ BSc 87 PGCE 04. St Mellitus Coll BA 17. **d** 17 **p** 18. C Aldershot H Trin *Guildf* 17–20; V Hanworth St Rich *Lon* from 20. *St Richard's Vicarage, 35 Forge Lane, Feltham TW13 6UN* M: 07958-352083 E: debswignall@strichardshanworth.church

WIGNALL, Canon Paul Graham. b 49. Lanc Univ BA 72 Qu Coll Cam BA 74 MA 78. Westcott Ho Cam 72. **d** 74 **p** 75. C Chesterton Gd Shep *Ely* 74–76; Min Can Dur Cathl 76–79; Tutor Ripon Coll Cuddesdon 80–84; P-in-c Aston Rowant w Crowell *Ox* 81–83; C Shepherd's Bush St Steph w St Thos *Lon* 84–85; P-in-c St Just-in-Roseland and St Mawes *Truro* 99–01; C St Agnes and Mithian w Mount Hawke 01–06; Dir Tr and Development 01–05; Dir Min and Miss Resources 05–06; Hon Can Truro Cathl 05–06; rtd 06; IME Adv *Cov* 08–12; Hon C Aston Cantlow and Wilmcote w Billesley 08–11; Hon C Baginton w Bubbenhall and Ryton-on-Dunsmore 11–12; P-in-c Clun w Bettws-y-Crwyn and Newcastle *Heref* 12–14; P-in-c Clungunford w Clunbury and Clunton, Bedstone etc 12–14; P-in-c Hopesay 12–14; V Clun Valley 14; C Edstaston, Fauls, Prees, Tilstock and Whixall *Lich* 14–18; Chapl Málaga *Eur* 18–19; Chapl Las Palmas 19–20; TV Dorchester *Ox* from 20. *The Vicarage, High Street, Long Wittenham, Abingdon OX14 4QQ* E: paul@box-tree.me.uk

WIGRAM, Andrew Oswald. b 39. Lon Univ BD 64. Bps' Coll Cheshunt 61. **d** 64 **p** 65. C Marton-in-Cleveland *York* 64–69; Kenya 69–82; Warden Trin Coll Nairobi 77–82;

V Westcliff St Mich *Chelmsf* 82–95; RD Southend 89–94; R Cropwell Bishop w Colston Bassett, Granby etc *S'well* 95–05; rtd 05; PtO *Dur* 05–20. *Address temp unknown* E: andrew.wigram@ntlworld.com

WIGRAM, Miss Ruth Margaret. b 41. CertEd 63. Cranmer Hall Dur 83. **dss** 84 **d** 87 **p** 94. Shipley St Paul and Frizinghall *Bradf* 84–90; Par Dn 87–90; Asst Dioc Dir of Ords 90–96; C Skipton H Trin 90–96; V Easby w Skeeby and Brompton on Swale etc *Ripon* 96–06; rtd 07; PtO *York* from 07; *Leeds* 17–20. *Address temp unknown* E: ruthwigram@hotmail.co.uk

WIKELEY, Canon John Roger Ian. b 41. AKC 64. **d** 65 **p** 66. C Southport H Trin *Liv* 65–69; C Padgate 69–71; TV 71–73; R 73–74; TR 74–85; TR W Derby St Mary 85–98; V 98–06; P-in-c W Derby St Jas 04–06; AD W Derby 89–06; Hon Can Liv Cathl 94–06; rtd 06; PtO *Eur* 07–19. *72 Carisbrooke Drive, Southport PR9 7JD* T: (01704) 225412 E: rogel4152@yahoo.co.uk *or* jriw4152@gmail.com

WIKNER, Richard Hugh. b 46. MSI. St Alb Minl Tr Scheme 79. **d** 94 **p** 95. NSM Lt Heath *St Alb* 94–04; PtO from 04. *Koinonia, 5 The Avenue, Potters Bar EN6 1EG* T: (01707) 650437 E: hughwikner@lineone.net

✠**WILBOURNE, The Rt Revd David Jeffrey.** b 55. Jes Coll Cam BA 78 MA 82. Westcott Ho Cam 79. **d** 81 **p** 82 **c** 09. C Stainton-in-Cleveland *York* 81–85; Chapl Asst Hemlington Hosp 81–85; R Monk Fryston and S Milford *York* 85–91; Abp's Dom Chapl 91–97; Dir of Ords 91–97; V Helmsley 97–09; P-in-c Upper Ryedale 09; Can and Preb York Minster 08–09; Asst Bp Llan 09–17; Dir of Min 10–15; Hon Asst Bp York from 17. *8 Bielby Close, Scarborough YO12 6UU* T: (01723) 362850 E: davidwilbourne1983@btinternet.com

WILBRAHAM, Canon David. b 59. MBE 20. Oak Hill Th Coll BA 88. **d** 88 **p** 89. C Ince Ch Ch *Liv* 88–91; Min St Helens St Helen 91–93; PtO *Guildf* 96–99; NSM Hindhead 99–00; V 00–03; V Churt and Hindhead 03–07; Chapl Thames Valley Police 07–17; Nat Police Chapl from 18; Hon Can Ch Ch *Ox* from 11. *28 Tyndalls, Hindhead GU26 6AP* T: (01428) 609665 M: 07973-367786 E: david.wilbraham@thamesvalley.pnn.police.uk

WILBY, Canon Wendy Ann. b 49. St Hugh's Coll Ox BA 71 MA 93 Leeds Univ MA 01 ARCM 69 LRAM 72. NEOC. **d** 90 **p** 94. Par Dn Barwick in Elmet *Ripon* 90–93; C High Harrogate St Pet 93–94; P-in-c Birstwith 94–01; AD Harrogate 00–01; Chapl St Aid Sch Harrogate 94–01; V Halifax *Wakef* 01–07; RD 06–07; Can Res Bris Cathl 07–13; Dean of Women's Min 11–13; rtd 13; Hon Min Can Ripon Cathl 13; PtO *Leeds* from 14. *Skelton Windmill, Ripon Road, Boroughbridge, York YO51 9DP* M: 07720-141548 E: wilbywindmill@gmail.com

WILCOCK, Mrs Linda Jane. b 46. Nottm Univ TDip 67. **d** 09 **p** 10. OLM Melbury *Sarum* 09–12; TV 12–19; PtO from 19. *4 Beech Tree Close, Cattistock, Dorchester DT2 0JN* T: (01300) 321112 M: 07788-618412 E: linda.wilcock@virgin.net

WILCOCK, Michael Jarvis. b 32. Dur Univ BA 54. Tyndale Hall Bris 60. **d** 62 **p** 63. C Southport Ch Ch *Liv* 62–65; C St Marylebone All So w SS Pet and Jas *Lon* 65–69; V Maidstone St Faith *Cant* 69–77; Dir Past Studies Trin Coll Bris 77–82; V Dur St Nic 82–98; rtd 98; PtO *Chich* from 98. *1 Tudor Court, 51 Carlisle Road, Eastbourne BN21 4JR* T: (01323) 417170

WILCOCK, Paul Trevor. b 59. BEM 13. Bris Univ BA Leeds Univ MA 93 Huddersfield Univ PhD 15 FHEA 08. Trin Coll Bris 83. **d** 87 **p** 88. C Kirkheaton *Wakef* 87–90; Chapl Huddersfield Poly 90–92; Chapl Huddersfield Univ 92–93; Dir Student Services 93–16; rtd 17; Chapl W Yorkshire Police from 02; NSM Huddersfield H Trin *Wakef* 92–09; NSM Bradley 09–14; PtO *York* from 13; *Leeds* from 14. *25 Mendip Avenue, Huddersfield HD3 3QG* T: (01484) 325232

WILCOCK, Terence Granville. b 50. Open Univ BA 82. EAMTC 99. **d** 02 **p** 03. NSM Oundle w Ashton and Benefield w Glapthorn *Pet* 02–04; NSM Crosscrake *Carl* 04–11; P-in-c 06–11; NSM Old Hutton and New Hutton 06–09; Asst Chapl Gtr Athens *Eur* 11–14; V Patterdale *Carl* 14–18; rtd 18; PtO *Carl* from 18. *17 Graythwaite Court, Fernhill Road, Grange-over-Sands LA11 7BN* T: (015395) 34004 E: terryatash@aol.com

WILCOCKSON, Michael Leslie. b 59. Ball Coll Ox BA 81 MA 84 Pemb Coll Cam PGCE 82. **d** 18 **p** 19. NSM Eton w Eton Wick, Boveney and Dorney *Ox* 18–19; Asst Chapl Eton Coll 18–19; C Linton *Ely* from 19. *Queen's House, 16 High Street, Linton, Cambridge CB21 4HS* T: (01223) 891005 M: 07929-451302 E: m.wilcockson@hotmail.com

WILCOCKSON, The Ven Stephen Anthony. b 51. Nottm Univ BA 73 Ox Univ BA 75 MA 81. Wycliffe Hall Ox 73. **d** 76 **p** 77. C Pudsey St Lawr *Bradf* 76–78; C Wandsworth All SS *S'wark* 78–81; V Rock Ferry *Ches* 81–86; V Lache cum Saltney 86–95; V Howell Hill w Burgh Heath *Guildf* 95–09; RD Epsom 00–07; Par Development Officer *Ches* 09–12; Adn Doncaster *Sheff* 12–19; rtd 20; PtO *Sheff* from 20. *4*

Ellis Close, Shavington, Crewe CW2 5SX T: (01270) 395868 E: stevewilcockson@yahoo.com

WILCOX, Allan Frank Carey. b 47. Birm Univ CertEd 70 BA 77 Univ of Wales (Ban) MA 09. St Padarn's Inst 16. **d** 17 **p** 18. NSM Bro Eryri *Ban* from 17. *Tyn y Ffynnon, near Peris, Caernarfon LL55 4UH* T: (01286) 872281 M: 07972-242118 E: afcwilcox@gmail.com

WILCOX, Anthony Gordon. b 41. ALCD 67. **d** 67 **p** 68. C Cheltenham Ch Ch *Glouc* 67–72; C Beccles St Mich *St E* 72–74; TV 74–81; V Ipswich All SS 81–06; rtd 06; PtO *St E* 08–21. *58 Sproughton Court Mews, Sproughton, Ipswich IP8 3AJ* T: (01473) 461561 E: tony.wilcox@caringhandsru.org

WILCOX, Brian Howard. b 46. Westcott Ho Cam 71. **d** 73 **p** 74. C Kettering SS Pet and Paul 73–78; V Eye 78–82; R Clipston w Naseby and Haselbech w Kelmarsh 82–90; V Hornsea w Atwick *York* 90–97; RD N Holderness 95–97; R Uckfield, Isfield and Lt Horsted *Chich* 97–11; rtd 11; PtO *Nor* from 12. *29 Sunningdale, Norwich NR4 6AQ* E: brian@wilcoxbh.plus.com

WILCOX, Canon Colin John. b 43. St Mich Coll Llan 84. **d** 86 **p** 87. C Newport St Andr *Mon* 86–88; C Llanmartin 88–90; TV 90–92; V Griffithstown 92–08; Hon Can St Woolos Cathl 07–08; rtd 08; PtO *Mon* from 08; *Llan* from 09. T: (029) 2025 4294 *or* (01600) 740680 E: colin.wilcox63@gmail.com

✠**WILCOX, The Rt Revd David Peter.** b 30. St Jo Coll Ox BA 52 MA 56. Linc Th Coll 52. **d** 54 **p** 55 **c** 86. C St Helier *S'wark* 54–56; C Ox St Mary V 56–59; Tutor Linc Th Coll 59–60; Chapl 60–61; Sub-Warden 61–63; India 64–70; R Gt w Lt Gransden *Ely* 70–72; Can Res Derby Cathl 72–77; Warden EMMTC 73–77; Prin Ripon Coll Cuddesdon 77–85; V Cuddesdon *Ox* 77–85; Suff Bp Dorking *Guildf* 86–95; rtd 95; Hon Asst Bp Chich from 95. *4 The Court, Hoo Gardens, Willingdon, Eastbourne BN20 9AX* T: (01323) 506108 E: davidandpam.wilcox@tiscali.co.uk

WILCOX, David Thomas Richard. b 42. Down Coll Cam BA 63 Regent's Park Coll Ox BA 66. **d** 95 **p** 96. C Bris St Mary Redcliffe w Temple etc 95–97; TV Yate New Town 97–02; Hon C 02–06; rtd 02; PtO *B & W* from 06. *26 Lethbridge Road, Wells BA5 2FN* T: (01749) 673689 E: davidtrwilcox@hotmail.co.uk

WILCOX, Graham James. b 43. Qu Coll Ox BA 64 MA 75 Lon Univ BD 97 MTh 02 Birm Univ PhD 11. Ridley Hall Cam 64. **d** 66 **p** 67. C Edgbaston St Aug *Birm* 66–69; C Sheldon 69–72; Asst Chapl Wrekin Coll Telford 72–74; C Asterby w Goulceby *Linc* 74–77; R 77–81; R Benniworth w Market Stainton and Ranby 77–81; R Donington on Bain 77–81; R Stenigot 77–81; R Gayton le Wold w Biscathorpe 77–81; V Scamblesby w Cawkwell 77–81; R Asterby Gp 81–88; V Sutton le Marsh 88–90; R Sutton, Huttoft and Anderby 90–98; R Fyfield, Moreton w Bobbingworth etc *Chelmsf* 98–07; rtd 07; PtO *Cov* from 07. *7 Swallow Close, Stratford-upon-Avon CV37 6TT* T: (01789) 551759 E: g.wilcox4@ntlworld.com

WILCOX, Haydon Howard. b 56. Sarum & Wells Th Coll. **d** 82 **p** 83. C Fishponds St Jo *Bris* 82–85; TV Hucknall Torkard *S'well* 85–91; R Bilsthorpe 91–99; R Eakring 91–99; P-in-c Maplebeck 91–99; P-in-c Winkburn 91–99; P-in-c Aldershot St Mich *Guildf* 99–03; V 03; PtO 03–09; Chapl CSP from 07; PtO *Guildf* from 21. *2 Audley House, 10 Swingate Road, Farnham GU9 8JJ* M: 07843-770234 E: haydonwilcox@mac.com

WILCOX, Heather Yvonne. b 72. ERMC 05. **d** 08 **p** 09. C Pakefield *Nor* 08–11; R Stratton St Mary w Stratton St Michael etc 11–16; P-in-c Bunwell, Carleton Rode, Tibenham, Gt Moulton etc 14–16; TR Long Stratton and Pilgrim TM from 16; RD Depwade from 16. *The Rectory, 8 Flowerpot Lane, Long Stratton, Norwich NR15 2TS* M: 07932-416233 E: rev.heather@btconnect.com

✠**WILCOX, The Rt Revd Peter Jonathan.** b 61. St Jo Coll Dur BA 84 MA 91 St Jo Coll Ox DPhil 93. Ridley Hall Cam BA 86. **d** 87 **p** 88 **c** 17. C Preston on Tees *Dur* 87–90; NSM Ox St Giles and St Phil and Jas w St Marg 90–93; TV Gateshead *Dur* 93–98; Dir Urban Miss Cen Cranmer Hall 93–98; P-in-c Walsall St Paul *Lich* 98–06; Hon C Walsall and Walsall Pleck and Bescot 05–06; Can Res Lich Cathl 06–12; Dean Liv 12–17; Bp Sheff from 17. *Bishopscroft, Snaithing Lane, Sheffield S10 3LG* T: 0114-230 2170 E: bishop@bishopofsheffield.org.uk

WILCOX, Stephen Charles Frederick. b 75. Qu Coll Ox BA 97 ACA 00. Oak Hill Th Coll 04. **d** 07 **p** 08. C Kirk Ella and Willerby *York* 07–11; V Anlaby St Pet from 11; V Anlaby Common St Mark from 11. *The Vicarage, Church Street, Anlaby, Hull HU10 7DG* T: (01482) 653024 E: scfwilcox@gmail.com

WILD, Canon Alan James. b 46. **d** 97 **p** 98. OLM Walworth St Pet *S'wark* 97–07; NSM 07–16; PtO from 16; Hon Can S'wark Cathl from 15. *67 Liverpool Grove, London*

SE17 2HP T: (020) 7708 1216 M: 07903-371769
E: therevajwild@googlemail.com
WILD, Hilda Jean. b 48. Linc Th Coll 95. **d** 95 **p** 96. C Newark
S'well 95–99; V Earlsdon *Cov* 99–13; rtd 13; PtO *Man* from
13. *8 Littondale Close, Royton, Oldham OL2 6PN* T: 0161-652
3790 M: 07580-837760 E: hildajw@virginmedia.com
WILD, Laura Ruth. b 78. Dur Univ BA 00 Teesside Coll of
Educn PGCE 03. St Hild Coll 17. **d** 19 **p** 20. C Nunthorpe
York from 19. *15 Ripon Road, Nunthorpe, Middlesbrough
TS7 0HX* E: lauraruth.wild@gmail.com
WILD, Roger Bedingham Barratt. b 40. Hull Univ MA 93.
ALCD 64. **d** 65 **p** 65. C Shipley St Pet *Bradf* 65–68; C
Pudsey St Lawr 68–71; P-in-c Rawthorpe *Wakef* 71–73;
V 73–78; V Ripon H Trin 78–93; RD Ripon 86–93; OCM
80–91; R Barwick in Elmet *Ripon* 93–01; Asst Chapl Trin
Th Coll Singapore 02–05; rtd 05; PtO *York* 06–21. *Saddlers
Cottage, 15 Chapel Street, Thirsk YO7 1LU* T: (01845) 524985
E: rbbwild@hotmail.com
WILDING, Canon Anita Pamela. b 38. MBE 01. Blackpool
and Fylde Coll of Further Tech TCert 61. CMS Tr Coll
Chislehurst 65. dss 89 **d** 92 **p** 93. Chapl Kabare Girls' High
Sch Kenya 92–04; Chapl St Andr Primary Boarding Sch
Kabare 92–04; rtd 04; PtO *Blackb* from 04. *5 The Fairways,
35 The Esplanade, Knott End-on-Sea, Poulton-le-Fylde
FY6 0AD* T: (01253) 810642 E: pamwilding@btinternet.com
WILDING, David. b 43. K Coll Lon BD 67 AKC 67. **d** 68 **p** 69. C
Thornhill *Wakef* 68–70; C Halifax St Jo Bapt 70–72; V Scholes
72–79; V Lightcliffe 79–97; rtd 97; PtO *Wakef* 97–14; *Leeds* from
14. *10 Stratton Park, Rastrick, Brighouse HD6 3SN* T: (01484)
387651 E: revd.d.wilding@blueyonder.co.uk
WILDING, Miss Erica Jane. b 70. Ripon Coll Cuddesdon. **d** 20
p 21. C Uxbridge *Lon* from 20. *2 Sylvana Close, Uxbridge
UB10 0BH* M: 07774-967718 E: erica.wilding@gmail.com
WILDING, Michael Paul. b 57. Chich Th Coll 82. **d** 85 **p** 86.
C Treboeth *S & B* 85–87; C Llangiwg 87–88; V Defynnog
w Rhydybriw and Llandeilo'r-fan 88–00; V Blaenwysg
from 00; AD Brecon 14–15. *Brynorsaf, Sennybridge, Brecon
LD3 8RR* T: (01874) 638927 E: frpwilding@btinternet.com
WILDING, Pamela. *See* WILDING, Anita Pamela
WILDS, Canon Anthony Ronald. b 43. Hatf Coll Dur BA 64.
Bps' Coll Cheshunt 64. **d** 66 **p** 67. C Newport Pagnell *Ox*
66–72; P-in-c Chipili Zambia 72–75; V Chandler's Ford *Win*
75–84; V Andover w Foxcott 85–97; RD Andover 89–94; Hon
Can Win Cathl 91–97; TR Solihull *Birm* 97–01; Hon Can
Birm Cathl 00–01; Adn Plymouth *Ex* 01–10; rtd 10; Hon
C Marnhull *Sarum* 15–18; PtO *B & W* from 19. *10 St Luke's
Road, Midsomer Norton, Radstock BA3 2EJ* M: 07759-463884
E: tonywilds@gmail.com
WILES, Mrs Cathryn. b 51. BEd. **d** 04 **p** 05. NSM Wandsworth
Common St Mary *S'wark* 04–11; Chapl SW Lon and
St George's Mental Health NHS Trust 06–13; rtd 13; Hon
C W Dulwich All SS *S'wark* from 14. *10 Waldeck Grove,
London SE27 0BE* T: (020) 8761 4017 M: 07837-407491
E: cathy.mail@virgin.net
WILES, Roger Kenneth. b 58. Witwatersrand Univ BA 80.
St Paul's Coll Grahamstown 81. **d** 83 **p** 84. C Johannesburg
St Gabr S Africa 83–84; C Belgravia St Jo 84–85; Chapl Jeppe
Boys' High Sch 85–86; Chapl Witwatersrand Univ 86–93; R
Edenvale Em 94–99; P-in-c Edin Clermiston Em 99–05; V
Poulton Lancelyn H Trin *Ches* from 05. *6 Chorley Way, Wirral
CH63 9LS* T: 0151-334 6780 or 334 9815
WILFORD (formerly GIBSON), Laura Mary. b 50. NOC 85.
d 88 **p** 94. Par Dn Foley Park *Worc* 88–90; Par Dn
Kidderminster St Jo and H Innocents 90–94; TV 94–96;
P-in-c Mamble w Bayton, Rock w Heightington etc 96–99;
TV Cartmel Peninsula *Carl* 99–01; Jt Dir of Ords 00–01;
P-in-c Worminghall w Ickford, Oakley and Shabbington
Ox 01–06; rtd 06; PtO *Leeds* from 17; *York* from 21. *16
Kingsclere, Huntington, York YO32 9SF* T: (01904) 764173
E: laura.wilford@gmail.com
WILKES, Elizabeth Ann. *See* FRANKLIN, Elizabeth Ann
WILKES, Jonathan Peter. b 66. Leic Poly BA 88 K Coll
Lon MA 00. Ripon Coll Cuddesdon BTh 96. **d** 96 **p** 97.
C Hackney *Lon* 96–00; P-in-c Paddington St Pet 00–06;
P-in-c Paddington St Mary Magd 04–06; P-in-c Kingston All
SS w St Jo *S'wark* 06–07; TR 07–12; TR Kingston from 12. *All
Saints' Vicarage, 15 Woodbines Avenue, Kingston upon Thames
KT1 2AZ* T: (020) 3132 8717 or 8546 5964
WILKES, Robert Anthony. b 48. Trin Coll Ox BA 70 MA 73.
Wycliffe Hall Ox 71. **d** 74 **p** 75. C Netherton *Liv* 74–77; V
77–81; Bp's Dom Chapl 81–85; CMS 85–98; Pakistan 85–86;
Regional Sec Middle E and Pakistan 87–98; PtO *S'wark*
87–90; *Ox* 90–98; P-in-c Mossley Hill St Matt and St Jas *Liv*
98–05; TR Mossley Hill 05–06; Hon Can Liv Cathl 03–06;
Dean Birm 06–09; P-in-c Ox St Mich w St Martin and All SS

09–13; V 13–17; rtd 17; PtO *Ox* from 17. *4 Dashwood Mews,
Kirtlington, Oxford OX5 3JX* E: revwilkes@btinternet.com
WILKIE, David Robert. b 83. Cardiff Univ MPhys 05 Bris Bapt
Coll BA 10. Trin Coll Bris 18. **d** 20 **p** 21. C Taunton St Jas
B & W from 20. *5 Redlake Drive, Taunton TA1 2RU* M: 07912-
352447 E: davidwilkie83@gmail.com
WILKIE, Mrs Donna Louise. b 81. Plymouth Univ BA 02
Leeds Univ MSc 04. Trin Coll Bris 12. **d** 15 **p** 16. C Clevedon
St Andr and Ch Ch *B & W* 15–18; C Clevedon Ch Ch
18. *5 Redlake Drive, Taunton TA1 2RU* M: 07789-771110
E: donnawilkie81@gmail.com
WILKIE, Mrs Erica Anne. Open Univ BSc 02. Ripon Coll
Cuddesdon 16. **d** 19. NSM Gosport Deanery from
19. *Address withheld by request* M: 07380-608803
E: reveriwilkie@hotmail.com
WILKIN, Ms Heather Julia. b 69. Sussex Univ BA 91 PGCE 17.
St Aug Coll of Th BA 20. **d** 20 **p** 21. C Henfield w Shermanbury
and Woodmancote *Chich* from 20. *41 Furners Mead, Henfield
BN5 9JA* M: 07958-540087 E: heather.wilkin@outlook.com
WILKIN, Paul John. b 56. Linc Th Coll 88. **d** 90 **p** 91. C
Leavesden *St Alb* 90–93; C Jersey St Brelade *Win* 93–97; V
Squirrels Heath *Chelmsf* 97–07; R Stansted Mountfitchet w
Birchanger and Farnham 07–20; rtd 20; PtO *Chelmsf* from
20. *8 Portsch Close, Carlton Colville, Lowestoft NR33 8TY*
WILKIN, Rose Josephine. *See* HUDSON-WILKIN, Rose
Josephine
WILKINS, Mrs Anne Louise. b 65. St Jo Coll Nottm
BTh 90. Wycliffe Hall Ox 94. **d** 95 **p** 96. C Wembley
St Jo *Lon* 95–98; NSM S Gillingham *Roch* 98–07; Jt P-in-c
Locking *B & W* 07–09; Jt P-in-c Hutton and Locking
09–13; P-in-c 13–15; R from 15. *The Vicarage, The Green,
Locking, Weston-super-Mare BS24 8DA* T: (01934) 823556
E: revannewilkins1@gmail.com
WILKINS, Graham Paul. b 82. York Univ MChem 05 Cam
Univ BTh 12. Ridley Hall Cam 09. **d** 12 **p** 13. C N w S
Wootton *Nor* 12–16; R Cringleford and Colney from 16;
RD Humbleyard from 21. *The Vicarage, 7A Newmarket Road,
Cringleford, Norwich NR4 6UE* E: revd.wilkins@gmail.com
WILKINS, Mrs Julia. Brighton Univ BA 96 UWE PGCE 04.
St Hild Coll 16. **d** 19 **p** 20. C Leeds St Geo from
19. *Kirkstall Vicarage, Vicarage View, Leeds LS5 3HF*
E: julia.wilkins@leeds.anglican.org
WILKINS, Michael Richard. b 71. W Sussex Inst of HE
BA 92. Trin Coll Bris 07. **d** 09 **p** 10. C Bath Walcot *B & W*
09–13; V Huddersfield H Trin *Wakef* 13–14; *Leeds* from 14.
2 Norfolk Close, Huddersfield HD1 5NJ T: (01484) 513213
E: mike@ladytrinityhuddersfield.com
WILKINS, Ralph Herbert. b 29. Lon Univ BD 61. St Aug Coll
Cant 72. **d** 73 **p** 74. C Epsom Common Ch Ch *Guildf* 73–76;
C Haslemere 77–79; P-in-c Market Lavington and Easterton
Sarum 79–82; V 82–90; P-in-c Puddletown and Tolpuddle
90–94; P-in-c Milborne St Andrew w Dewlish 92–94;
P-in-c Piddletrenthide w Plush, Alton Pancras etc 92–94; rtd
94; PtO *Ab* 94–01; *Heref* 02–15. *The Mill, Marton, Welshpool
SY21 8JY* T: (01938) 580566 E: rhwilkins@hotmail.co.uk
WILKINS, Miss Susan Stafford. b 47. Dur Univ BA. Sarum Th
Coll. dss 82 **d** 87 **p** 94. Redlynch and Morgan's Vale *Sarum*
82–88; Hon Par Dn 87–88; Hon Par Dn Bemerton 88–90;
Par Dn Hilperton w Whaddon and Staverton etc 90–94;
TV Worle *B & W* 94–99; P-in-c Hallwood *Ches* 99–04; V
Hallwood Ecum Par 04–11; RD Frodsham 06–11; rtd 11; PtO
Ches from 11. *84 Wallerscote Road, Weaverham, Northwich
CW8 3LY* T: (01606) 246039 E: suewilkins1@sky.com
WILKINSON, The Ven Adrian Mark. b 68. TCD BA 90 MA 94
BTh 94 NUI MA 00 HDipEd 91. CITC 91. **d** 94 **p** 95. C
Douglas Union w Frankfield *C, C & R* 94–97; I Dunboyne
Union *M & K* 97–02; Chapl NUI 97–02; Min Can St Patr
Cathl Dublin 97–02; I Rathmolyon w Castlerickard,
Rathcore and Agher *M & K* 01–02; I Douglas Union w
Frankfield *C, C & R* from 02; Adn Cork, Cloyne and Ross
from 14. *The Rectory, Carrigaline Road, Douglas, Cork, Republic
of Ireland* T: (00353) (21) 489 1539 *or* (21) 436 9578 M: 86-
166 4805 E: archdeacon@cork.anglican.org
WILKINSON, Canon Alan Bassindale. b 31. St Cath Coll Cam
BA 54 MA 58 PhD 59 DD 97. Coll of Resurr Mirfield 57. **d** 59
p 60. C Kilburn St Aug *Lon* 59–61; Chapl St Cath Coll Cam
61–67; V Barrow Gurney *B & W* 67–70; Asst Chapl and Lect
St Matthias's Coll Bris 67–70; Prin Chich Th Coll 70–74; Can
and Preb Chich Cathl 70–74; Warden Verulam Ho 74–75;
Dir of Aux Min Tr *St Alb* 74–75; Sen Lect Crewe and Alsager
Coll of HE 75–78; Hon C Alsager St Mary *Ches* 76–78; Dioc
Dir of Tr *Ripon* 78–84; P-in-c Thornthwaite w Thruscross
and Darley 84–88; Hon Can Ripon Cathl 84–88; Tutor Open
Univ 88–96; PtO *Portsm* from 88; Hon P Portsm Cathl 88–14;
Hon Dioc Th 93–01; Hon Chapl Portsm Cathl 94–01; rtd 96;
Visiting Lect Portsm Univ 98–05; Fell Geo Bell Inst Chich

Univ from 96. *8 Byron Court, Stockbridge Road, Chichester PO19 8ES* T: (01243) 839578

WILKINSON (née PHILPOTT), Canon Barbara May. b 48. Leeds Univ BA 69 CertEd 70 MA 90. NOC 90. **d** 93 **p** 94. NSM Carleton and Lothersdale *Bradf* 93–96; C Steeton 96–00; Asst Chapl Airedale NHS Trust 96–01; Hd Chapl Services 01–07; Hon Can Bradf Cathl 04–13; RD S Craven 04–07; rtd 13; PtO *York* 13–18. *Carlton House, Market Place, Easingwold, York YO61 3AN* T: (01347) 823620 E: bnkwilkinson@gmail.com

WILKINSON, Benjamin Michael. b 84. Warwick Univ BSc 05. Wycliffe Hall Ox BA 17. **d** 18 **p** 19. C Deane *Man* from 18; C Lostock St Thos and St Jo from 18. *9 Lowside Avenue, Bolton BL1 5XQ* M: 07737-240729 E: bmwpost@gmail.com

WILKINSON, Carol Ann. b 54. Lon Univ BD 88 Man Univ PhD 95. CBDTI 04. **d** 06 **p** 07. NSM Poulton Carleton and Singleton *Blackb* 06–09; LtO from 09. *52 Lowick Drive, Poulton-le-Fylde FY6 8HB* T: (01253) 350700 M: 07894-830305

WILKINSON, Mrs Christine Margaret. b 52. Man Univ BA 74 Neville's Cross Coll of Educn Dur PGCE 75 Birm Univ MEd 78. **d** 04 **p** 05. OLM Eythorne and Elvington w Waldershare etc *Cant* 04–11; C Littlebourne and Ickham w Wickhambreaux etc 11–16; rtd 16. *36 Coach Road, Acrise, Folkestone CT18 8LT*

WILKINSON, Dagmar Ludmila Veronica. b 80. Ostrava Univ MA 06 MA 09. Ripon Coll Cuddesdon 15. **d** 17 **p** 18. C Aston cum Aughton w Swallownest and Ulley *Sheff* 17–19; C Gleadless 19–21; C Hackenthorpe 19–21; C Woodhouse St Jas 19–21; Asst Chapl Sheff Univ 19–21; R Friern Barnet St Jas *Lon* from 21. *The Rectory, 147 Friern Barnet Lane, London N20 0NP* T: (020) 8455 7844 M: 07745-306954 E: dagmarvh@yahoo.com

WILKINSON, Mrs Deborah Michelle. b 77. RN 99. St Mellitus Coll 18. **d** 20 **p** 21. C Birkenhead Priory *Ches* from 20. *65 Statham Road, Prenton CH43 7XS* M: 07900-561400 E: debbiewilko@live.co.uk

WILKINSON, Edward. b 55. Cranmer Hall Dur 86. **d** 88 **p** 89. C Bishopwearmouth St Nic *Dur* 88–92; P-in-c Newbottle 92–96; V from 96; AD Houghton 08–14. *The Vicarage, Front Street, Newbottle, Houghton le Spring DH4 4EP* T: 0191-584 3244 E: wilkinson.edward.rev@gmail.com

WILKINSON, The Ven Elizabeth Mary. b 65. St Edm Hall Ox MA 91. NEOC 02. **d** 05 **p** 06. C Harlow Green and Lamesley *Dur* 05–09; P-in-c Burnmoor 09–16; AD Houghton 14–16; V Bishopwearmouth St Gabr 16–20; Hon Can Dur Cathl 19–20; Adn Dur and Can Res Dur Cathl from 20; Dir Miss, Min and Discipleship from 20; Hon Can Dur Cathl from 21. *21 Westhouse Avenue, Durham DH1 4FH* T: 0191-386 5342 E: archdeacon.of.durham@durham.anglican.org

WILKINSON, Gemma Louise. *See* DONNELL, Gemma Louise

WILKINSON, Geoffrey. *See* WILKINSON, Roy Geoffrey

WILKINSON, Canon Guy Alexander. b 48. CBE 12. Magd Coll Cam BA 69. Ripon Coll Cuddesdon 85. **d** 87 **p** 88. C Coventry Caludon *Cov* 87–90; P-in-c Ockham w Hatchford *Guildf* 90–91; R 91–94; Bp's Dom Chapl 90–94; V Small Heath *Birm* 94–99; Adn Bradf 99–04; Abp's Sec for Inter Faith Relns 05–11; Nat Adv for Inter Faith Relns 05–11; V Fulham St Andr *Lon* 12–15; AD Hammersmith and Fulham 12–15; rtd 15; PtO *Sarum* 16–21; *Heref* 16–19; NSM Eardisley w Bollingham, Willersley, Brilley etc from 19; RD Kington and Weobley from 19. *Church House, Almeley, Hereford HR3 6LD* T: (01722) 680057 M: 07515-327757 E: guy@gwilkinson.org.uk

WILKINSON, Miss Helen Mary. b 53. Homerton Coll Cam BEd 76. Trin Coll Bris 02. **d** 04 **p** 05. C Newbury *Ox* 04–08; C Northwood Em *Lon* 08–19; rtd 19. *28 Teme Avenue, Malvern WR14 2XA* T: (01684) 560082 M: 07790-262631

WILKINSON, James Daniel. b 73. Westmr Coll Ox BTh 95 Reading Univ MA 07 MBACP 04. St Steph Ho Ox 97. **d** 99 **p** 00. C Wantage *Ox* 99–02; P-in-c S Hinksey 02–13; V 13–18; Sec to Bp Ebbsfleet *Cant* 02–04; Chapl to Bp Fulham *Lon* from 18; C St Dunstan in the West 18–19; P-in-c from 19. *184A Fleet Street, London EC4A 2HD* T: (020) 7430 1365 E: frjwilkinson@gmail.com

WILKINSON, Canon John Andrew. b 59. Pemb Coll Ox BA 83 MA 87 St Jo Coll Dur BA 86. Cranmer Hall Dur 84. **d** 87 **p** 88. C Broadheath *Ches* 87–91; TV Worthing Ch the King *Chich* 91–97; Chapl Chantilly *Eur* 97–06; Asst Chapl Fontainebleau 06–11; Chapl 11–15; Assoc Chapl Brussels Cathl from 15; Can Malta Cathl from 10. *Pro-Cathedral of the Holy Trinity, 29 rue Capitaine Crespel, 1050 Brussels, Belgium* T: (0032) (2) 289 0928 *or* (2) 511 7183 E: john.wilkinson@holytrinity.be

WILKINSON, John Lawrence. b 43. Lon Coll Div BA 65 MA 69 Birm Univ MLitt 91. Qu Coll Birm 67 Gen Th Sem (NY) STB 69. **d** 69 **p** 70. C Braunstone *Leic* 69–71; C Hodge Hill *Birm* 71–74; P-in-c Aston St Jas 75–84; Tutor Qu Coll

Birm 85–95; Hon C Birm St Geo 86–95; V Kings Heath 95–08; Hon Can Birm Cathl 99–08; rtd 09; PtO *Birm* from 09; *Lich* 15–21. *203 Barclay Road, Smethwick B67 5LA* T: 0121-434 3526 E: jrwilkinson@dsl.pipex.com

WILKINSON, Jonathan Charles. b 61. Leeds Univ BA 83. Wycliffe Hall Ox 85. **d** 87 **p** 88. C Plymouth St Andr w St Paul and St Geo *Ex* 87–90; C Oulton Broad *Nor* 90–93; V Hallwood *Ches* 93–99; TR Gateshead *Dur* 99–17; C Chester le Street 17–20; rtd 20. *21 Westhouse Avenue, Durham DH1 4FH* T: 0191-386 5342 E: jonwilko@virginmedia.com

WILKINSON, Mrs Joyce Aileen. b 29. BSc(Econ) MA. **d** 99 **p** 00. NSM Bredon w Bredon's Norton *Worc* 99–04; rtd 04; PtO *Worc* 04–14. *Foxgloves, Back Lane, Bredon, Tewkesbury GL20 7LH* T: (01684) 773389

WILKINSON, Mrs Judith Felicity. b 64. St Mellitus Coll 16. **d** 19 **p** 20. NSM Southend St Sav Westcliff *Chelmsf* from 19. *188 Westcliff Park Drive, Westcliff-on-Sea SS0 9LR* T: (01702) 343528 E: judith.wilkinson@rocketmail.com

WILKINSON, Canon Keith Howard. b 48. Hull Univ BA 70 FRSA 94 MCT 99. Westcott Ho Cam 74. **d** 76 **p** 77. C Pet St Jude 76–79; Chapl Eton Coll 79–84; PtO *Pet* 82–94; Chapl Malvern Coll 84–89; Hd Master Berkhamsted Sch Herts 89–96; LtO *St Alb* 89–96; Hd Master K Sch Cant 96–07; Hon Can Cant Cathl 96–07; Sen Chapl Eton Coll 08–18; rtd 18. *Trinity Cottage, 24 Link Terrace, Malvern WR14 2JE*

WILKINSON, Margaret Anne. b 46. Lon Univ MB, BS 70 MSc 74 MRCPsych 77. SAOMC 95. **d** 98 **p** 99. NSM Heston *Lon* 98–06; Chapl HM YOI Feltham 01–06; NSM Penge Lane H Trin *Roch* 07–13; NSM Beckenham St Geo 13–16; rtd 16; PtO *Roch* from 16. *27 River Grove Park, Beckenham BR3 1HX* T: (020) 8650 2312

WILKINSON, Marlene Sandra. *See* TURNBULL, Marlene Sandra

WILKINSON, Matthew John George. b 81. St Cuth Soc Dur BSc 02. St Mich Coll Llan BA 06. **d** 06 **p** 07. C Wrexham *St As* 06–11; PtO 11–12; C Minera w Coedpoeth and Bwlchgwyn 12–14; V Chirk 14–16; TV Offa Miss Area from 17. *The Vicarage, Trevor Road, Chirk, Wrexham LL14 5HD* T: (01691) 778519 E: vicarofchirk@hotmail.com

WILKINSON, Paul. b 69. **d** 11 **p** 12. OLM Ashill Fountain of Life *Nor* 11–19; Sen Min from 19. *10 Church Street, Ashill, Thetford IP25 7AW* T: (01760) 441443 E: paulwilkinson500@gmail.com

WILKINSON, Paul. b 51. Sarum & Wells Th Coll 75. **d** 78 **p** 79. C Allerton *Bradf* 78–80; C Baildon 80–83; V Hengoed w Gobowen *Lich* 83–90; V Potterne w Worton and Marston *Sarum* 90–03; Chapl Roundway Hosp Devizes 92–03; P-in-c Leckhampton St Pet *Glouc* 03–09; P-in-c Cheltenham Em w St Steph 08–09; TR S Cheltenham 10–15; rtd 15; PtO *Glouc* from 16. *41 Wheatway, Abbeydale, Gloucester GL4 5ET*

WILKINSON, Paul Martin. b 56. Brunel Univ BSc. Wycliffe Hall Ox 83. **d** 86 **p** 87. C Hinckley H Trin *Leic* 86–90; V Newbold on Avon *Cov* from 90. *The Vicarage, Main Street, Newbold, Rugby CV21 1HH* T: (01788) 543055 E: paulwilkinson54@btinternet.com

WILKINSON, Peter David Lloyd. b 67. Trin Coll Ox BA 89 MA 93. Ridley Hall Cam BA 94. **d** 95 **p** 96. C Brampton St Thos *Derby* 95–98; C Tunbridge Wells St Jo *Roch* 98–02; C Ox St Ebbe w H Trin and St Pet from 02. *10 Lincoln Road, Oxford OX1 4TB* T: (01865) 728885 E: peter.wilkinson@stebbes.org

WILKINSON, Rebecca Catherine. b 88. Homerton Coll Cam BA 10 Univ Coll Lon MA 11 Jes Coll Cam BTh 20. Westcott Ho Cam 18. **d** 21. C Hulme Ascension *Man* from 21. *St James's Vicarage, Vicarage Close, Salford M6 8EJ* E: rw354@cantab.ac.uk

WILKINSON, Robert. b 51. Univ of Wales (Ban) BSc 74 Nottm Univ PhD 79 Glynd r Univ 12. **d** 20 **p** 21. NSM Aberystwyth *St D* from 20. *Rhydyfiran Farm House, Dyffryn Paith, Aberystwyth SY23 4LU* T: (01970) 624202 E: robert@stmikes.net *or* robert.hannah-wilkinson@outlook.com

WILKINSON, Robert. *See* WILKINSON, Walter Edward Robert

WILKINSON, Robert Ian. b 43. MIMunE 73 MICE 84 CEng 73. Oak Hill NSM Course. **d** 88 **p** 89. NSM Hawkwell *Chelmsf* 88–89; NSM Thundersley 89–91; C New Thundersley 91–94; V Berechurch St Marg w St Mich 94–06; rtd 06; PtO *Bradf* 07–14; *Leeds* from 14. *140 Keighley Road, Skipton BD23 2QT* T: (01756) 799748

WILKINSON, Robert John. b 66. Birkbeck Coll Lon BA 98 Fitzw Coll Cam BA 00 ACIB 90. Westcott Ho Cam 98. **d** 01 **p** 02. C Southgate Ch Ch *Lon* 01–04; TV Wood Green St Mich w Bounds Green St Gabr etc 04–11; V Tottenham St Paul 11–18; C Friern Barnet All SS from 18. *4 Highlands, Oakleigh Road North, London N20 9HA* E: robert.wilkinson@london.anglican.org

WILKINSON, Robert Matthew. b 21. TCD BA 46. TCD Div Sch 47. **d** 47 **p** 48. C Limerick St Lawr w H Trin and St Jo

L & K 47–49; C Arm St Mark 49–51; I Mullavilly 51–55; I Derryloran 55–73; Can Arm Cathl 67–73; I Ballymore 73–87; Treas Arm Cathl 73–75; Chan Arm Cathl 75–83; Prec Arm Cathl 83–87; rtd 87. *60 Coleraine Road, Portrush BT56 8HN* T: (028) 7082 2758

WILKINSON, Robert Samuel. b 52. Wycliffe Hall Ox 92. **d** 94 **p** 95. C Boughton Monchelsea *Cant* 94–96; C Parkwood CD 95–96; C Plymouth St Andr and Stonehouse *Ex* 96–01; P-in-c Whimple, Talaton and Clyst St Lawr 01–11; TV Cullompton, Willand, Uffculme, Kentisbeare etc 11–14; rtd 14; PtO *Ex* from 17. *60 Heavitree Road, Exeter EX1 2LQ*

WILKINSON, Roy Geoffrey. b 42. Open Univ BSc 93 Linc Univ MSc 99. Sarum Th Coll 67. **d** 70 **p** 71. C Belsize Park *Lon* 70–73; C Heston 73–75; C Hythe *Cant* 75–79; V Croydon Woodside *S'wark* 79–86; Asst Mental Health Chapl Skegness and Winthorpe *Linc* 96–97; Asst Chapl Linc Distr Healthcare NHS Trust 96–97; Chapl Lincs Partnership NHS Trust 97–05; rtd 05. *287 Monks Road, Lincoln LN2 5JZ* T: (01522) 522671 M: 07745-755614 E: geoffreyandsarah@ntlworld.com

WILKINSON, Sharon Theresa. b 58. **d** 12 **p** 13. C Scotforth *Blackb* 12–16; V W Ardsley Leeds from 16. *The Vicarage, 1168 Dewsbury Road, Dewsbury WF12 7JL* E: fantine2001@aol.com

WILKINSON, Canon Simon Evelyn. b 49. Nottm Univ BA 74. Cuddesdon Coll 74. **d** 76 **p** 77. C Cheam *S'wark* 76–78; P-in-c Warlingham w Chelsham and Farleigh 78–83; Hd RS Radley Coll 83–89; R Bishop's Waltham and Upham *Portsm* 89–97; TR Shaston *Sarum* 97–03; P-in-c Amesbury 03–12; V 12–14; RD Stonehenge 03–10; Can and Preb Sarum Cathl 05–14; rtd 14; PtO *Sarum* 16–20. *5 Berkshire Road, Salisbury SP2 8NY*

WILKINSON, Stephen. b 69. Brighton Poly BEng 91. Ridley Hall Cam 08. **d** 10 **p** 11. C Gtr Corsham and Lacock *Bris* 10–14; P-in-c Brinkworth w Dauntsey 14–16; P-in-c Gt Somerford, Lt Somerford, Seagry, Corston etc 14–16; P-in-c Garsdon, Lea and Cleverton and Charlton 14–16; R Woodbridge from 16; AD N Wilts from 21. *The Rectory, Frog Lane, Great Somerford, Chippenham SN15 5JA* T: (01249) 723733 E: rector@woodbridgegroup.co.uk

WILKINSON, Mrs Susan Ann. b 62. SEITE 10. **d** 14. NSM Lewes St Anne and St Mich and St Thos etc *Chich* 14–17; NSM Willingdon from 17. *150 Macquarie Quay, Eastbourne BN23 5AW* T: (01323) 318510 M: 07713-097661 E: sueann_27@hotmail.com

WILKINSON, Walter Edward Robert. b 38. St Andr Univ MA 60. Lon Coll of Div BD 63 ALCD 63. **d** 63 **p** 64. C High Wycombe *Ox* 63–70; PV, Succ and Sacr Roch Cathl 70–73; P-in-c Asby w Ormside *Carl* 73–80; R Cherry Burton *York* 80–95; RD Beverley 88–94; P-in-c Grasmere *Carl* 95–03; rtd 03; PtO *Carl* from 03. *4 Heversham Gardens, Heversham, Milnthorpe LA7 7RA* T: (015395) 64044 E: bob@carliol.clara.co.uk

WILKS, Eric Percival. b 32. Wells Th Coll 67. **d** 68 **p** 69. C Fladbury w Throckmorton, Wyre Piddle and Moor *Worc* 68–70; PtO from 70. *4 Catherine Cottages, Droitwich Road, Hartlebury, Kidderminster DY10 4EL* T: (01299) 251580

WILLANS, Jonathan Michael Arthur. b 60. QUB BD. CITC 83. **d** 85 **p** 86. C Larne and Inver *Conn* 85–88; R Hawick *Edin* 88–91; P-in-c Brockham Green *S'wark* 91–16; P-in-c Leigh 91–16; V Brockham Green and Leigh from 17. *The Vicarage, Clayhill Road, Leigh, Reigate RH2 8PD* T/F: (01306) 611224 E: jmawilliams@gmail.com

WILLANS, William Richard Gore. b 48. Qu Coll Ox BA 70 MA 74 Ox Univ PGCE 71. CITC 77. **d** 79 **p** 80. C Bonne Bay Canada 79–80; P-in-c Bonne Bay N 80–82; R 82–87; R Thunder Bay St Thos 87–98; I Craigs w Dunaghy and Killagan *Conn* 98–18; rtd 18. *97 Hillmount Road, Cullybackey, Ballymena BT42 1NZ* T: (028) 2588 0428 M: 07880-992425 E: willans@btinternet.com

WILLARD, John Fordham. b 38. K Coll Lon BD 62 AKC 62. **d** 63 **p** 64. C Balham Hill Ascension *S'wark* 63–67; C Leigh Park *Portsm* 67–73; C-in-c Leigh Park St Clare CD 73–75; R Bishop's Waltham 75–87; P-in-c Upham 78–79; R 79–87; V Dalston H Trin w St Phil *Lon* 87–97; P-in-c Haggerston All SS 90–97; P-in-c Fairford *Glouc* 97–98; V Fairford and Kempsford w Whelford 98–04; rtd 04; PtO *Glouc* from 05. *15 Highwood Avenue, Cheltenham GL53 0JJ* T: (01242) 530051 E: john.willard2@btinternet.com

WILLCOCK, Canon Richard William. b 39. Hertf Coll Ox BA 62 MA 66. Ripon Hall Ox 62. **d** 64 **p** 65. C Ashton St Mich *Man* 64–68; Bp's Dom Chapl 68–72; V Charlestown 72–75; Chapl Casterton Sch Lancs 75–80; V Bamford *Man* 80–92; R Framlingham w Saxtead *St E* 92–04; RD Loes 95–97; Warden of Readers 98–03; Hon Can St E Cathl 00–04; rtd 04; PtO *Carl* from 05. *High Green Cottage, Sandford, Appleby-in-Westmorland CA16 6NR* T: (017683) 51021

WILLCOX, Canon Frederick John. b 29. Kelham Th Coll 49. **d** 54 **p** 55. C Tranmere St Paul *Ches* 54–56; LtO *S'well* 57–61; Miss P St Patr Miss Bloemfontein S Africa 62–65; Dir 65–70; P-in-c Derby St Andr w St Osmund 70–74; V 74–80; V Netherton St Andr *Worc* 80–94; Hon Can Worc Cathl 91–94; rtd 94; PtO *Worc* 94–10. *22 Capel Court, The Burgage, Prestbury, Cheltenham GL52 3EL* T: (01242) 256373

WILLCOX, Richard John Michael. b 39. Birm Univ BSc 62 PhD 67. Qu Coll Birm 78. **d** 80 **p** 81. C Boldmere *Birm* 80–83; V Edgbaston SS Mary and Ambrose 83–89; V Evercreech w Chesterblade and Milton Clevedon *B & W* 89–97; Dioc Development Rep 90–01; V Bridgwater H Trin 97–01; rtd 01; PtO *Heref* 05–13; *Bris* 14–19. *58 Forrester Green, Colerne, Chippenham SN14 8EA* E: rswillcox@waitrose.com

WILLESDEN, Area Bishop of. *Vacant*

WILLETT, Frank Edwin. b 45. Lichfield Th Coll 64. **d** 68 **p** 69. C Oswestry H Trin *Lich* 68–71; C Bilston St Leon 71–74; USPG Zambia 75–80; V Curbar and Stoney Middleton *Derby* 80–88; Area Sec USPG Derby and Leic 88–91; V Chesterfield SS Aug *Derby* 91–98; Chapl Walton Hosp 91–98; Ind Chapl Derby 98–03; P-in-c Brampton St Mark 03–09; Hon P-in-c Loundsley Green 03–09; rtd 10; Hon C Boldre w S Baddesley Win 09–13; PtO from 13. *57 Fawn Gardens, New Milton BH25 5GJ* E: frankfranceswillett@yahoo.com

WILLETT, Canon Geoffrey Thomas. b 38. Dur Univ BA 59 MA 82. Cranmer Hall Dur. **d** 62 **p** 63. C Widnes St Paul *Liv* 62–65; C Harborne Heath *Birm* 65–68; V Wakef St Andr and St Mary 68–75; V Hinckley H Trin *Leic* 75–89; TR 89; RD Sparkenhoe II 84–87; RD Sparkenhoe W 87–89; P-in-c Markfield 89–90; R 90–99; P-in-c Thornton, Bagworth and Stanton 96–99; R Markfield, Thornton, Bagworth and Stanton etc 99–04; RD Sparkenhoe E 91–99; Hon Can Leic Cathl 87–04; rtd 04; PtO *Derby* from 04; *Leic* 04–21; *Lich* 10–20. *22 Clifton Way, Burton-on-Trent DE15 9DW* T: (01283) 548868 E: carolynwillett79@googlemail.com

WILLETT, Canon John Ivon. b 40. Ch Ch Ox BA 63 MA 65. Chich Th Coll 61. **d** 63 **p** 64. C Leic St Andr 63–66; C Bordesley St Alb *Birm* 66–72; Min Can, Prec and Sacr Pet Cathl 72–82; R Uppingham w Ayston and Wardley w Belton 82–99; Can Pet Cathl 97–99; V Cantley *Sheff* 99–12; AD Doncaster 04–10; rtd 12; PtO *Sheff* from 12; *S'well* from 18. *16 Rosemary Close, Doncaster DN4 6BP* T: (01302) 370808

WILLETTS, Mrs Susan. b 60. EMMTC 05. **d** 08 **p** 09. C Burton All SS w Ch Ch *Lich* 08–11; TV Uttoxeter Area 11–16; V Loughb Gd Shep *Leic* from 16. *21 Parklands Drive, Loughborough LE11 2SZ* E: revsuewilletts@btinternet.com

WILLEY, Canon David Geoffrey. b 53. Imp Coll Lon BSc 74. Oak Hill Th Coll BA 86. **d** 86 **p** 87. C Cromer *Nor* 86–90; C High Halstow w All Hallows and Hoo St Mary *Roch* 90–94; R Gravesend St Geo 94–02; TR N Farnborough *Guildf* 02–17; V Farnborough St Pet 17–18; RD Aldershot 06–11; Hon Can Guildf Cathl 13–18; rtd 18; PtO *Chelmsf* from 18. *22 New Captains Road, West Mersea, Colchester CO5 8QP* E: david@willeyfamily.plus.com

WILLEY, Graham John. b 38. Moray Ord Course 91. **d** 93 **p** 94. NSM W Coast Jt Congregations *Mor* 93–99; NSM Stirling *St And* 99–03; rtd 03; Hon C Killin *St And* 04–13; Hon C Stirling from 13. *9 Victoria Terrace, Menstrie FK11 7EE* T: (01259) 761932

WILLIAMS, Alan Ronald Norman. b 60. RMN 85. Linc Th Coll 95. **d** 95 **p** 96. C Malvern Link w Cowleigh *Worc* 95–99; TV 03–08; V Risca *Mon* 99–03; P-in-c Amblecote *Worc* 08–17; V from 17. *The Vicarage, 4 The Holloway, Amblecote, Stourbridge DY8 4DL* T: (01384) 394057 E: fr.alan.williams@gmail.com

WILLIAMS, Canon Aled Wyn. b 47. Univ of Wales (Abth) BA 69. St Mich Coll Llan 69. **d** 71 **p** 72. C Llanelli *St D* 71–73; P-in-c Capel Colman w Llanfihangel Penbedw etc 73–74; V 74–81; V Llanddewi Brefi w Llanbadarn Odwyn 81–84; V Llanddewi Brefi w Llanbadarn Odwyn, Cellan etc 84–01; V Lampeter and Llanddewibrefi Gp 01–06; TR Bro Teifi Sarn Helen 06–11; AD Lampeter and Ultra-Aeron 96–11; Can St D Cathl 97–11; rtd 11; PtO *St D* from 11. *Cwmawel, Llanllwni, Pencader SA39 9DR* T: (01559) 395802 E: pedrbrefi@btopenworld.com

WILLIAMS, Alexandra Christine. b 66. Victoria Univ Man BSc 87. Ripon Coll Cuddesdon 15. **d** 17 **p** 18. C Edgehill Churches *Cov* 17–20; R W Kirby St Bridget *Ches* from 20. *St Bridget's Rectory, 40 Village Road, West Kirby, Wirral CH48 7HE* M: 07718-646863 E: alexcwilliams66@gmail.com

WILLIAMS, Miss Alison Lindsay. b 47. Univ of Wales (Abth) BA 69 PGCE 70. Wycliffe Hall Ox 00. **d** 00 **p** 01. C Stratton St Margaret w S Marston etc *Bris* 00–04; TV Cheadle Valley *Sarum* 04–12; rtd 12; PtO *Bris* from 13. *5 Cherry Orchard, Highworth, Swindon SN6 7AU* T: (01793) 979110 E: alisonlwilliams@talktalk.net

WILLIAMS, Mrs Alison Ruth. b 86. Win Univ BA 10. Cranmer Hall Dur BA 19. **d** 20 **p** 21. C Wheatley Hill, Thornley and Wingate w Hutton Henry *Dur* from 20. *8 Mulberry, Coxhoe, Durham DH6 4SN* E: alisonwilliams01@gmail.com

WILLIAMS, Andrew. b 68. **d** 19 **p** 20. NSM Woodbridge St Jo and Bredfield *St E* 19–20; C Bury St Edmunds St Mary from 20. *12 Constable Road, Bury St Edmunds IP33 3UQ*

WILLIAMS, Andrew Barrington. b 62. Ripon Coll Cuddesdon 96. **d** 98 **p** 99. C Oswaldtwistle Immanuel and All SS *Blackb* 98–01; C Whittle-le-Woods 01–02; P-in-c Hillock *Man* 02–08; P-in-c Unsworth 07–08; P-in-c Radcliffe St Andr 08–14; V Brinnington w Portwood *Ches* 14–18; TV Macclesfield Team from 18. *2 The Mallards, Chester Road, Macclesfield SK11 8PT* T: (01625) 432919 M: 07472-663279 E: revandywilliams@me.com *or* teamvicar.macc@gmail.com

WILLIAMS, Andrew David. b 67. Univ of Wales (Lamp) BA 91. Linc Th Coll 93. **d** 93 **p** 94. C Perry Street *Roch* 93–96; C Ealing St Pet Mt Park *Lon* 96–00; R Finchley St Mary 00–08; Warden of Readers Edmonton Area 05–08; R Applecross Australia 08–14; C Tottenham H Trin *Lon* 14–19; V Tottenham Hale St Fran from 20. *1 Eagle Heights, Waterside Way, London N17 9FU* E: perth08@googlemail.com

WILLIAMS, Andrew Gibson. b 31. Edin Univ MA 57. Edin Th Coll 56. **d** 59 **p** 60. C Todmorden *Wakef* 59–61; C Clitheroe St Mary *Blackb* 61–63; V Burnley St Jas 63–65; CF (TA) 64–65; CF 65–71; R Winterslow *Sarum* 71–84; P-in-c Condover *Heref* 84–88; P-in-c Acton Burnell w Pitchford 84–88; P-in-c Frodesley 84–88; R Condover w Frodesley, Acton Burnell etc 88–90; R Whimple, Talaton and Clyst St Lawr *Ex* 90–94; rtd 94; PtO *Ex* 94–08. *Flat 7, Manormead, Tilford Road, Hindhead GU26 6RA* T: (01428) 601507

WILLIAMS, Andrew John. b 64. Univ Coll Lon BSc 85 Keele Univ PGCE 87 Lon Univ MSc 91. STETS 08. **d** 11 **p** 12. NSM Twickenham All Hallows *Lon* 11–14; NSM Kingston *S'wark* 14–18; NSM Richmond St Mary w St Matthias and St Jo from 18. *51 Moor Mead Road, Twickenham TW1 1JS* M: 07824-310311 E: andrew.williams.london@gmail.com

WILLIAMS, Ann Joyce. *See* TEMPLEMAN, Ann Joyce

WILLIAMS, Ann Maureen Edith. b 46. ERMC 12. **d** 20 **p** 21. NSM St Neots *Ely* from 20. *15 Buckley Road, Eynesbury, St Neots PE19 2TR* T: (01480) 394709 M: 07722-127239 E: annmewilliams@ntlworld.com *or* annwilliams@stneots.org

WILLIAMS, Anthea Elizabeth. b 50. Trevelyan Coll Dur BA 71 Kent Univ MA 97 Middx Univ MSc 00 Univ of E Lon PhD 10. Linc Th Coll 72. **dss** 79 **d** 87 **p** 94. St Marylebone Ch Ch *Lon* 79–84; Maidstone St Martin *Cant* 84–91; Par Dn 87–91; Dn-in-c Rolvenden 91–94; P-in-c 94–04; P-in-c Sandhurst w Newenden 01–04; Chapl E Kent NHS and Soc Care Partnership Trust 91–04; Hon Chapl Kent Police *Cant* 95–20; PtO *Roch* 04–13; *Cant* from 04; *Chich* from 15. *2 Great Wigsell Cottages, Hastings Road, Bodiam, Robertsbridge TN32 5PU* T: (01580) 754948 E: chaplain2sk@btinternet.com

WILLIAMS, Anthony Clive. b 61. Ex Univ BA 83 Coll of SS Mark and Jo Plymouth MEd 04. SWMTC 09. **d** 11 **p** 12. NSM Elburton *Ex* 11–16; TV Plymouth Em w St Paul from 16. *22 Cranmere Road, Plymouth PL3 5JY* T: 03301-139088 E: tony.williams@emmanuelplymouth.co.uk *or* tonywilliams8643@gmail.com

WILLIAMS, Capt Anthony James. b 57. **d** 08 **p** 09. NSM Bream *Glouc* 08–13; P-in-c Forest of Dean Ch Ch w English Bicknor 13–14; R from 14; Chapl HM Pris *Glouc* 12–13; Chapl HM Pris Eastwood Park from 13. *HM Prison Eastwood Park, Falfield, Wotton-under-Edge GL12 8DB* T: (01454) 382100 E: revtonyw@hotmail.com *or* anthony.williams@justice.gov.uk

WILLIAMS, The Very Revd Arfon. b 58. Univ of Wales (Abth) BD 83 Univ of Wales (Ban) MA 84. Wycliffe Hall Ox 83. **d** 84 **p** 85. C Carmarthen St David *St D* 84–86; TV Aberystwyth 86–88; V Glanogwen *Ban* 88–94; C Ewhurst and Dir Oast Ho Retreat Cen *Chich* 95–98; Asst to RD Rye 95–98; Co-ord for Adult Educn (E Sussex Area) *Chich* 97–98; I Jordanstown *Conn* 98–02; Adn Meirionnydd *Ban* 02–04; R Dolgellau w Llanfachreth and Brithdir etc 02–04; Dean Elphin and Ardagh *K, E & A* from 04; I Sligo w Knocknarea and Rosses Pt from 04. *The Deanery, Strandhill Road, Sligo, Republic of Ireland* T: (00353) (71) 915 7993 E: arvonwilliams@eircom.net

WILLIAMS, Benjamin Gwyn. b 91. St Mellitus Coll 18. **d** 21. C Oadby *Leic* from 21. *11 Blackthorn Close, Lutterworth LE17 4UX*

WILLIAMS, Brian. b 48. WMMTC. **d** 83 **p** 84. NSM Lich St Chad 83–03; Asst Chapl Sandwell Health Care NHS Trust 98; Angl Chapl 98–99; Chapl Burton Hosps NHS Trust 99–03; Chapl R Bournemouth and Christchurch Hosps NHS Foundn Trust 03–14; rtd 14; PtO *Lich* 16–21. *82 Walsall Road, Lichfield WS13 8AF* T: (01543) 253120

WILLIAMS, Brian Frederick. b 55. Philippa Fawcett Coll CertEd 77 BEd 78. SEITE 98. **d** 01 **p** 02. NSM Folkestone St Mary and St Eanswythe *Cant* 01–10; NSM Folkestone St Mary, St Eanswythe and St Sav 09–11; PtO 11–12; C Alkham w Capel le Ferne and Hougham from 12. *The Vicarage, 20 Alexandra Road, Capel-le-Ferne, Folkestone CT18 7LD* T: (01303) 244119 E: capelvicarage@gmail.com

WILLIAMS, Canon Brian Luke. b 54. AKC 75. St Steph Ho Ox 76. **d** 77 **p** 78. C Kettering St Mary *Pet* 77–80; C Walsall St Gabr Fulbrook *Lich* 80–83; P-in-c Sneyd 83–85; V 85–20; RD Stoke N 94–99; Preb Lich Cathl 13–20; Can Ho Ghana from 14; rtd 20. *Flood Cottage, 215 Endon Road, Stoke-on-Trent ST6 8PA*

WILLIAMS, Ms Carol Jean Picknell. b 45. FCIPD 89. Ox NSM Course 86. **d** 89 **p** 94. NSM High Wycombe *Ox* 89–97; P-in-c Penn 97–01; rtd 01; PtO *Heref* 02–16; *Chich* from 16. *3 Gillham Wood Road, Bexhill-on-Sea TN39 3BN*

WILLIAMS, Carole. *See* GARNER, Carole

WILLIAMS, Mrs Catherine Anne. b 65. Selw Coll Cam BA 87 MA 91. SEITE 98. **d** 00 **p** 01. C Chatham St Steph *Roch* 00–02; C Bishop's Cleeve *Glouc* 03–06; Dioc Voc Officer 06–10; Asst Dioc Dir of Ords 08–10; Selection Sec Min Division 10–18; Nat Adv for Voc 11–15; Public Preacher *Glouc* from 11. *Abbey House, Church Street, Tewkesbury GL20 5SR* M: 07966-709577 E: revdcawilliams@gmail.com

WILLIAMS, Ms Catherine Lois. b 51. Swansea Coll of Educn CertEd 74 Univ of Wales (Swansea) BEd 80. St Mich Coll Llan. **d** 00 **p** 01. C Gorseinon *S & B* 00–02; C Cen Swansea 03; TV 03–11; rtd 11; PtO *S & B* from 12; *Llan* from 13; *St D* from 14. *41 Ffordd y Glowyr, Godrergraig, Swansea SA9 2BQ* T: (01639) 844814

WILLIAMS (née BRERETON), Mrs Catherine Louise. b 69. St Aid Coll Dur BSc 90 Cranfield Univ MSc 92 Lucy Cavendish Coll Cam BTh 00 Cliff Coll MA 13. Ridley Hall Cam 97. **d** 00 **p** 01. C S Bank *York* 00–03; V Middlesbrough St Chad 03–09; TV Woughton *Ox* 09–14; Miss and Evang Officer *Glouc* 14–20; Environmental Engagement Officer from 21. *Church House, College Green, Gloucester GL1 2LY* T: (01452) 410022

WILLIAMS, Canon Cecil Peter. b 41. TCD BA 63 MA 67 Lon Univ BD 67 PhD 86 Bris Univ MLitt 77. Clifton Th Coll 64. **d** 67 **p** 68. C Maghull *Liv* 67–70; LtO *Bris* 70–91; Tutor Clifton Th Coll 70–72; Tutor Trin Coll Bris 72–91; Lib 73–81; Course Ldr 81–85; Vice-Prin 85–91; V Ecclesall *Sheff* 91–06; Hon Can Sheff Cathl 01–06; rtd 06; V Jersey Gouray St Martin *Win* 06–12; PtO *Ox* from 13. *Shalom, 23 Sandmartin Close, Buckingham MK18 1SD* T: (01280) 308394 M: 07801-353786 E: peter.williams@shalom23.co.uk

WILLIAMS, Mrs Christine Mary. b 51. City Univ BSc 72 Middx Univ BA 05. NTMTC 02. **d** 05 **p** 06. NSM Pitsea w Nevendon *Chelmsf* 05–08; TV Grays Thurrock 08–19; rtd 19; PtO *Chelmsf* from 19. *2 Foxleigh, Billericay CM12 9NS* T: (01277) 654370 E: christine.mwilliams@btopenworld.com

WILLIAMS, Christopher David. b 62. Spurgeon's Coll BD 99. St Jo Coll Nottm MA 06. **d** 06 **p** 07. C Haslemere and Grayswood *Guildf* 06–08; C Godalming 08–09; R Liss *Portsm* from 09; AD Petersfield from 21. *The Rectory, 111 Station Road, Liss GU33 7AQ* M: 07506-517677 E: revchris007@gmail.com

WILLIAMS, Claire. b 71. St Hild Coll 15. **d** 18 **p** 19. NSM Grenoside *Sheff* from 18. *21 Heathercliff Way, Penistone, Sheffield S36 6FN* T: (01226) 762157 E: revclaire.williams@gmail.com

WILLIAMS, Preb Clive Gregory. b 45. Trin Coll Bris 83. **d** 85 **p** 86. C Bedhampton *Portsm* 85–88; V Highley w Billingsley, Glazeley etc *Heref* 88–12; P-in-c Stottesdon w Farlow, Cleeton St Mary etc 08–10; RD Bridgnorth 96–05; Preb Heref Cathl 99–12; rtd 12; PtO *Portsm* from 13. *120 Hazleton Way, Waterlooville PO8 9DW* T: (023) 9257 1745 E: cliveandsue2012@btinternet.com

WILLIAMS, Canon Colin Henry. b 52. Pemb Coll Ox BA 73 MA 78. St Steph Ho Ox BA 80. **d** 81 **p** 82. C Liv St Paul Stoneycroft 81–84; TV Walton St Mary 84–89; Chapl Walton Hosp *Liv* 86–89; Bp's Dom Chapl *Blackb* 89–94; Chapl Whalley Abbey 89–94; V Poulton-le-Fylde *Blackb* 94–99; Adn Lancaster 99–05; Gen Sec Conf of Eur Chs 05–10; Can Gib Cathl *Eur* 07–10; TR Ludlow *Heref* 10–15; Preb Heref Cathl 14–15; Adn Germany and N Eur 15–19; Adn E Adnry 15–19; rtd 19; PtO *Eur* from 19; *Blackb* 19–20. *Flat 1, 3 Ash Drive, Poulton-le-Fylde FY6 8DZ* E: colinw834@gmail.com

WILLIAMS, David. b 49. BTh. **d** 88 **p** 89. C Lurgan etc w Ballymachugh, Kildrumferton etc *K, E & A* 88–91; I Kinsale Union *C, C & R* 91–14; Miss to Seafarers 91–14; Can Cork and Cloyne Cathls *C, C & R* 95–97; Treas Cork Cathl 97–14; Preb Tymothan St Patr Cathl Dublin 97–14; rtd

14. *Kilbeg Upper, Clonbur, Co Galway, Republic of Ireland*
E: dhw@gofree.indigo.ie *or* dhwkilbeg@gmail.com

WILLIAMS, David. b 43. ACA 65 FCA. K Coll Lon AKC 69
BD 69. **d** 70 **p** 71. C Walkden Moor *Man* 70–72; C Deane
72–75; V Horwich St Cath 75–81; Hon C Chorley All SS
Blackb 84–86; P-in-c Weeton 86–87; V Singleton w Weeton
87–97; C Lancaster St Mary w St John and St Anne 98–00;
Chapl HM Pris Lanc Castle 98–00; rtd 00; PtO *Man* 02–08
and 10–18. *153 Crompton Way, Bolton BL2 2SQ* T: (01204)
373353 E: dw153jhw@gmail.com

WILLIAMS, David Frank. b 48. S Dios Minl Tr Scheme 91. **d** 94
p 95. NSM Romsey *Win* from 94. *24 Feltham Close, Romsey
SO51 8PB* T: (01794) 524050 E: revdfw@talk21.com

WILLIAMS, David Gareth. b 58. Lon Univ BD 81. Ripon Coll
Cuddesdon 82. **d** 84 **p** 85. C Chandler's Ford *Win* 84–88; C
Alton St Lawr 88–90; R Crawley and Littleton and Sparsholt
w Lainston 90–97; P-in-c Andover 97–09; TR Risborough
Ox from 09; AD Aylesbury from 17. *The Rectory, Church
Lane, Princes Risborough HP27 9AW* T: (01844) 344784
E: rector@stmarysrisborough.org.uk

WILLIAMS, Canon David Gordon. b 43. Selw Coll Cam
BA 65 MA 69. Oak Hill Th Coll 66. **d** 68 **p** 69. C Maidstone
St Luke *Cant* 68–71; C Rugby St Matt *Cov* 71–73;
P-in-c Budbrooke 73–74; V 74–81; V Lenton *S'well* 81–87;
TR Cheltenham St Mark *Glouc* 87–03; Hon Can Glouc
Cathl 96–03; R Toodyay w Goomalling Australia 03–08;
rtd 08; Miss Development P Avon Deanery 08–09; PtO
Derby 09–11; *Worc* 12–17; *Glouc* from 12. *28 Cleevemont,
Evesham Road, Cheltenham GL52 3JT* M: 07766-837571
E: canondwilliams@westnet.com.au

✠**WILLIAMS, The Rt Revd David Grant.** b 61. Bris Univ
BSocSc 83. Wycliffe Hall Ox 86. **d** 89 **p** 90 **c** 14. C
Ecclesall *Sheff* 89–92; V Dore 92–02; RD Ecclesall 97–02;
V Win Ch Ch 02–14; Hon Can Win Cathl 12–14; Suff
Bp Basingstoke from 14. *Bishop's Lodge, Colden Lane,
Old Alresford, Alresford SO24 9DY* M: 07889-547095
E: bishop.david@winchester.anglican.org

WILLIAMS, David Henry. b 33. Trin Coll Cam BA 56 MA 60
PhD 77. St D Coll Lamp 67. **d** 69 **p** 70. C Monmouth *Mon*
69–70; Chapl St Woolos Cathl 70–71; P-in-c Six Bells 71–76;
Libya 76–79; P-in-c Crumlin *Mon* 79–80; R Llanddewi Skirrid
w Llanvetherine etc 80–83; PtO 83–87; Guest Master Caldey
Abbey 83–87; V Buttington and Pool Quay *St As* 87–95;
Chapl Warsaw *Eur* 95–97; rtd 97; PtO *St D* from 14. *Flat
W16, The College of St Barnabas, Blackberry Lane, Lingfield
RH7 6NJ* T: (01342) 870260 E: dhw.1933@gmail.com

WILLIAMS, David Ivan Ross. b 47. Imp Coll Lon BSc 70
Leic Univ MSc 72 ARCS 70 FBIS. STETS 00. **d** 03 **p** 04.
NSM Havant *Portsm* 03–10; PtO *Ex* from 10. *11 Manor
Gardens, Exbourne, Okehampton EX20 3RW* T: (01837)
851710 M: 07866-772025 E: david@dirw.demon.co.uk *or*
davidivanross@gmail.com

WILLIAMS, David John. b 30. Open Univ BA 79. St D Coll
Lamp 64. **d** 66 **p** 67. C Mold *St As* 66–69; C Llanrhos
69–71; R Llangynhafal and Llanbedr Dyffryn Clwyd 71–86;
P-in-c Llanychan 77–85; P-in-c Llanbedr DC w Llangynhafal,
Llanychan etc 86; RD Dyffryn Clwyd 86–95; R Ruthin w
Llanrhydd 86–95; rtd 95; PtO *St As* from 09. *16 The Park,
Ruthin LL15 1PW* T: (01824) 705746

WILLIAMS, Canon David John. b 38. AKC 62. **d** 63 **p** 64. C
Benchill *Man* 63–66; C Heywood St Jas 66–69; V Leesfield
69–73; Chapl TS Arethusa 73–74; TV Southend St Jo w
St Mark, All SS w St Fran etc *Chelmsf* 74–80; V Horndon
on the Hill 80–93; RD Thurrock 83–92; P-in-c Rochford
93–02; RD 96–02; P-in-c Sutton w Shopland 98–02; Hon
Can Chelmsf Cathl 99–02; rtd 02; PtO *Ripon* 02–14; *Leeds*
from 14. *29 Stonebeck Avenue, Harrogate HG1 2BN* T: (01423)
522828

WILLIAMS, David John. b 43. Wadh Coll Ox BA 64. St Jo Coll
Nottm 73. **d** 75 **p** 76. C Newcastle w Butterton *Lich* 75–79;
P-in-c Oulton 79–89; P-in-c Stone Ch Ch 84–89; V Stone Ch Ch
and Oulton 89–96; P-in-c Ashley 96–04; P-in-c Mucklestone
96–04; R Ashley and Mucklestone 04–07; rtd 07; PtO *Heref*
from 08. *23 Gravel Hill, Ludlow SY8 1QR* T: (01584) 875884
E: williamsjandm@btinternet.com

WILLIAMS, David John. b 52. Liv Univ MTh 98. NOC 92. **d** 95
p 96. C Gt Crosby St Luke *Liv* 95–99; Acting Chapl Liv Hope
98–99; P-in-c W Derby St Jas *Liv* 99–04; Chapl R Liverpool
Children's NHS Trust 99–04; Present Spiritual Care Manager
and Lead Chapl Alder Hey Children's NHS Foundn Trust
from 04. *Alder Hey Children's Hospital, Eaton Road, Liverpool
L12 2AP* T: 0151-252 5465 E: revdw1999@hotmail.com *or*
david.j.williams@alderhey.nhs.uk

WILLIAMS, David Michael. b 50. JP 86. Ex Univ BA 71 Lon
Univ MA 77 FSA 81 FRSA 82. SEITE 05. **d** 08 **p** 09. NSM
Redhill St Jo *S'wark* 08–10; NSM Redhill St Matt 10–11;

P-in-c Gt Coxwell w Buscot, Coleshill etc *Ox* 11–14; V
14–19; AD Vale of White Horse 15–18; rtd 19; PtO *Ox*
from 19; *Guildf* from 20; *S'wark* from 20. *Pine Cottage,
Harrow Road West, Dorking RH4 3BE* T: (01306) 889754
E: davidwilliams24@btinternet.com

WILLIAMS, David Michael Rochfort. b 40. St Mich Coll
Llan 62. **d** 65 **p** 66. C Pembroke Dock *St D* 65–68; Chapl Miss
to Seamen and Ind Chapl 68–71; P-in-c Walwyn's Castle w
Robeston W 68–70; R 70–71; Ind Chapl *Mon* 71–74; Hon
Chapl St Woolos Cathl 71–74; V Blaenavon w Capel Newydd
74–77; Ind Chapl *St As* 77–88; V Whitford 81–87; V Ruabon
87–92; TR Cen Telford *Lich* 92–00; R Burton and Rosemarket
St D 00–02; Chapl Miss to Seafarers Milford Haven 00–02;
Southampton 02–05; rtd 05; PtO *Ox* 05–21. *13 Sturt Road,
Charlbury, Chipping Norton OX7 3SX* T: (01608) 811284
E: michael@michaelcara1965.plus.com

WILLIAMS, David Norman. b 54. Lanc Univ BSc 76 Leeds
Univ BA 83. Coll of Resurr Mirfield 81. **d** 84 **p** 85. C Ireland
Wood *Ripon* 84–87; C Beeston 87–91; V Cross Roads cum
Lees *Bradf* 91–99; V Skipton Ch Ch 99–07; P-in-c Carleton
and Lothersdale 03–07; V Skipton Ch Ch w Carleton 07–14;
Leeds 14–15; rtd 15. *Shorley Croft, 8 Penrith Road, Keswick
CA12 4HF* E: dngc@hotmail.co.uk

WILLIAMS, David Paul. *See* HOWELL, David Paul

WILLIAMS, Canon David Roger. b 49. Open Univ BA. St D Coll
Lamp. **d** 73 **p** 74. C Llansamlet *S & B* 73–76; C Oystermouth
76–79; V Aberedw w Llandeilo Graban and Llanbadarn etc
79–81; V Brynmawr 81–89; V Newport St Julian *Mon* 89–09;
R Penarth and Llandough *Llan* 09–15; Hon Can St Woolos
Cathl *Mon* 09–15; rtd 15; PtO *Mon* from 15; *Llan* from 16. *36
Priory Gardens, Usk NP15 1BB* E: fr.rogerwilliams@uwclub.net

WILLIAMS, Denise Laraine. b 50. Liv Univ TCert 71. NOC 00.
d 03 **p** 04. C Padgate *Liv* 03–08; P-in-c Cinnamon Brow
08–13; TR Warrington E 13–15; rtd 15; PtO *Ches* 15–16 and
from 20; PV Ches Cathl 16–19; Asst Dir of Ords from 20.
30 Rowcliffe Avenue, Chester CH4 7PW M: 07889-861869
E: denisewilliams50@btinternet.com

WILLIAMS, Derek Ivor. b 37. ACA 61 FCA 71. **d** 05 **p** 06. OLM
Chollerton w Birtley and Thockrington *Newc* 05–07; PtO
from 07. *Address temp unknown*

WILLIAMS, Derek Lawrence. b 45. Tyndale Hall Bris 65. **d** 69
p 70. C Cant St Mary Bredin 69–71; Gen Sec Inter-Coll Chr
Fellowship 71–75; LtO *St Alb* 78–84; LtO *Bris* 85–92; PtO *Pet*
92–02; Par and Miss Co-ord Northampton St Giles 93–97;
Dioc Millennium Officer 98–00; Dioc Communications
Officer 00–05; Dioc Communications Officer *Eur* 02–05;
Bp's Admin and Press Officer *Pet* 05–10; Hon C Brington w
Whilton and Norton etc 02–08; LtO from 08; rtd 11; Dioc
Media Adv *Pet* from 11; PtO from 12. *7 Montrose Close, Market
Harborough LE16 9LJ* T: (01858) 432709 M: 07770-981172

WILLIAMS, Diana Mary. b 36. Bris Univ CertEd 56 Leeds Univ
BSc 57. Oak Hill Th Coll 86. **d** 87 **p** 94. C S Mymms K Chas
St Alb 87–95; V 95–98; R Sandon, Wallington and Rushden
w Clothall 98–04; RD Buntingford 01–06; rtd 04; PtO *Ely*
05–13; *Sheff* from 14. *27 Newfield Crescent, Sheffield S17 3DE*
E: di.williams@btinternet.com

WILLIAMS, Diane Patricia. *See* BLAKEY WILLIAMS, Diane
Patricia

WILLIAMS, Canon Diane Ruth. b 52. Hull Univ BA 80 Nottm
Univ MA 94. Linc Th Coll 92. **d** 94 **p** 95. C Stokesley *York*
94–98; TV Louth *Linc* 98–06; Chapl Linc and Louth NHS
Trust 98–01; Chapl United Lincs Hosps NHS Trust 01–06;
P-in-c Needham Market w Badley *St E* 06–20; V from 20;
RD Bosmere 09–20; RD Stowmarket 17–20; RD Gipping
Valley from 20; Hon Can St E Cathl from 17. *10 Meadow
View, Needham Market, Ipswich IP6 8RH* T: (01449) 720316
E: diane.rev@btinternet.com

WILLIAMS, Doiran George. b 26. Barrister-at-Law (Gray's
Inn) 52. WMMTC 91. **d** 93 **p** 94. NSM Edvin Loach w
Tedstone Delamere etc *Heref* 93–98; PtO from 98. *Howberry,
Whitbourne, Worcester WR6 5RZ* T: (01886) 821189

WILLIAMS, Donna. b 67. UNISA BA 97 Witwatersrand
Univ HDipEd 89. St Mellitus Coll BA 18. **d** 18 **p** 19.
C Hounslow H Trin *Lon* 18–19; C St Margaret's-on-
Thames 19–21; V Hampton All SS from 21. *The Vicarage,
40 The Avenue, Hampton TW12 3RS* M: 07778-675164
E: vicar@allsaintshampton.co.uk

WILLIAMS, Canon Dylan John. b 72. Univ of Wales (Ban)
BTh 97. Ripon Coll Cuddesdon 97. **d** 99 **p** 00. C Holyhead
Ban 99–01; C Dolgellau w Llanfachreth and Brithdir etc
01–02; P-in-c Amlwch 02–03; R 03–10; P-in-c Porthmadog
and Ynyscynhaearn and Dolbenmaen 10–11; P-in-c Bro
Eifionydd 11–12; TR 12; V Bro'r Holl Saint 12–16; V Bro
Eifionydd 16–20; V and Min Area Ldr Bro Peblig from 20; AD
Llyn and Eifionydd 10–15; AD Synod Gogledd Meirionnydd
15–18; AD Synod Meirionydd 18–20; Asst Dir of Ords

11–15; Can Ban Cathl from 12. *The Rectory, Y Maes, Criccieth LL52 0AG* T: (01766) 523743 E: canondylan@gmail.com

WILLIAMS (*née* **WITHERS**), **Canon Eleanor Jane.** b 61. Univ of Wales Coll of Medicine MB, BCh 85 Anglia Ruskin Univ MA 07 MRCGP 89. ERMC 04. **d** 07 **p** 08. NSM Milton *Ely* 07–11; V Burwell w Reach from 11; Hon Can Ely Cathl from 20. *The Vicarage, 22 Isaacson Road, Burwell, Cambridge CB25 0AF* T: (01638) 741262 E: vicar@stmarysburwell.org.uk

WILLIAMS, Canon Emlyn Cadwaladr. b 64. St Jo Coll Nottm 02. **d** 04 **p** 05. C Glanogwen w St Ann's w Llanllechid *Ban* 04–07; R Llanfihangel Ysgeifiog w Llangristiolus etc 07–12; R Seintiau Braint a Chefni 12–14; V Bro Cadwaladr from 15; AD Malltraeth 13–15; AD Synod Ynys Mon from 15. *The Rectory, Holyhead Road, Gaerwen LL60 6HP* T: (01248) 421275

WILLIAMS (*née* **CALDERWOOD**), **Canon Emma Louise.** b 74. Derby Univ BSc 96 Univ of Wales (Cardiff) MTh 07. St Mich Coll Llan BTh 05. **d** 06 **p** 07. C Stanley w Stoneycroft St Paul *Liv* 06–11; V Stanley and Stoneycroft St Paul from 11; AD W Derby from 17; Hon Can Liv Cathl from 17. *The Vicarage, 28 Brookland Road, Liverpool L13 3BQ* T: 0151-228 2426 E: revdem1411@btinternet.com

WILLIAMS, Frederick Errol. b 41. MBIM 80. Sarum & Wells Th Coll 86. **d** 88 **p** 89. C Milton *Win* 88–91; P-in-c Chilbolton cum Wherwell 91–94; R 94–06; RD Andover 99–06; rtd 06; TV S Cotswolds *Glouc* 10–14; PtO *Sarum* from 15. *1A Central Street, Ludgershall, Andover SP11 9RA* T: (01264) 791487

WILLIAMS, Gareth Wynn. *See* RAYNER-WILLIAMS, Gareth Wynn

WILLIAMS, Gavin John. b 61. Down Coll Cam BA 84 Wycliffe Hall Ox BA 88 Barrister-at-Law 85. **d** 89 **p** 90. C Muswell Hill St Jas w St Matt *Lon* 89–92; Asst Chapl Shrewsbury Sch 92–95; Chapl 95–02; Chapl Westmr Sch 02–21; PV Westmr Abbey 05–21. *53 Port Hill Road, Shrewsbury SY3 8RN* T: (01743) 364393 E: revgav92@gmail.com

WILLIAMS, George Ola. b 55. Bradf Univ PhD 90 Waterloo Lutheran Univ MA 83. St Jo Coll Nottm MTh 95. **d** 96 **p** 97. C Enfield St Jas *Lon* 96–00; V Allerton *Bradf* 00–14; *Leeds* 14–21; rtd 21. *5 Hornbeam Close, Allerton, Bradford BD15 9LN* T: (01274) 011556 E: george.ola13@gmail.com

WILLIAMS, Canon Giles Peter. b 54. Lon Univ BA 77 MA 78. Trin Coll Bris 80. **d** 82 **p** 83. C Reading Greyfriars *Ox* 82–85; Rwanda Miss 85–90; Mid-Africa Min (CMS) 90–94; Can Kigali Cathl Rwanda from 90; V Woking St Jo *Guildf* 95–10; RD Woking 08–10; Chapl Cannes *Eur* from 10. *Résidence Kent, 4 avenue Général Ferrié, 06400 Cannes, France* T: (0033) 4 93 94 54 61 *or* 4 93 94 04 56 F: 4 93 94 04 43 E: mail@holytrinitycannes.org

WILLIAMS, Gillian Jean Richeldis. b 47. St Mich Coll Llan. **d** 99 **p** 02. C Llanishen *Llan* 99–05; P-in-c Rhondda Fach Uchaf 05; rtd 06; P-in-c Llanishen w Trellech Grange and Llanfihangel etc *Mon* 13–14; P-in-c Rockfield and Dingestow Gp 17–18. *Faith House, 82 Kings Fee, Monmouth NP25 5BQ* T: (01600) 716696 E: retired.rev@hotmail.com

WILLIAMS, Graham Parry. b 46. Bp Burgess Hall Lamp 67. **d** 70 **p** 71. C Ebbw Vale *Mon* 70–73; C Trevethin 73–74; V Nantyglo 74–76; Chapl RN 76–85; R Northlew w Ashbury *Ex* 85–87; R Bratton Clovelly w Germansweek 85–87; TV Pontypool *Mon* 88–90; C Skegness and Winthorpe *Linc* 90–91; V Sutton Bridge 91–94; P-in-c Witham Gp 94–97; P-in-c Ruskington 97–01; R 01–03; RD Lafford 02–03; P-in-c Ringstone in Aveland Gp 03–10; rtd 10; PtO *Linc* 17–20. *107 Churchfields Road, Folkingham, Sleaford NG34 0TY* T: (01529) 497545 E: frgraham@hotmail.co.uk

WILLIAMS, Harri Alan McClelland. b 85. Ball Coll Ox BA 07 MA 13 Univ of Wales PhD 18. St Mich Coll Llan BA 10. **d** 10 **p** 11. C Haverfordwest *St D* 10–13; V Milford Haven 13–18; P-in-c Walsingham, Houghton and Barsham *Nor* 18–21; V from 21. *The Vicarage, Church Street, Walsingham NR22 6BL* T: (01328) 821316 E: harri1985@gmail.com

WILLIAMS, Haydn Clifford. b 32. Univ of Wales (Abth) BA 54 DipEd 55. EMMTC 89. **d** 95 **p** 99. NSM Anstey *Leic* 95–01; NSM Broom Leys 01–03; rtd 03; PtO *Leic* 03–21. *9 Stamford Drive, Coalville LE67 4TA* T: (01530) 837889

WILLIAMS, Helen Clare. b 64. Somerville Coll Ox BA 86 Clare Coll Cam PhD 89. Sarum Th Coll 18. **d** 20 **p** 21. C Wareham *Sarum* from 20. *8 Wellstead Road, Wareham BH20 4EY* M: 07305-530815 E: drhelenw@hotmail.com

WILLIAMS, Helena Maria Alija. *See* CERMAKOVA, Helena Maria Alija

WILLIAMS, Hilary Susan. *See* PETTMAN, Hilary Susan

WILLIAMS, Howell Mark. b 56. Univ of Wales (Cardiff) BD 87. St Mich Coll Llan 84. **d** 87 **p** 88. C Swansea St Thos and Kilvey *S & B* 87–89; TV Aberystwyth *St D* 89–93; V Hirwaun *Llan* 93–99; V Swansea St Pet *S & B* 99–12; AD Penderi 05–12;

V Swansea St Jas from 12; AD Swansea 13–15. *The Vicarage, 1 Ffynone Drive, Swansea SA1 6DB* T: (01792) 470532 E: stjamesuplands1@googlemail.com

WILLIAMS, Canon Hugh Martin. b 45. AKC 73. St Aug Coll Cant 73. **d** 74 **p** 75. C Heston *Lon* 74–78; Chapl City Univ 78–84; PV Westmr Abbey 82–84; V Newquay *Truro* 84–93; V Christchurch *Win* 93–10; Hon Can Win Cathl 04–10; Preacher Charterhouse and Dep Master 10–14; V Cricket St Thomas *B & W* 14–21. *14 Church Street, Crewkerne TA18 7HU* T: (01460) 394814 M: 07904-186414 E: hugh.m.williams@ukgateway.net

WILLIAMS, Ian Withers. b 43. Linc Th Coll 68. **d** 69 **p** 70. C Burney Lane *Birm* 69–72; C Cleobury Mortimer w Hopton Wafers *Heref* 72–75; V Knowbury 75–79; P-in-c Coreley w Doddington 75–79; V Lich Ch Ch 79–06; rtd 06; PtO *Heref* from 07; *Worc* from 07. *23 The Oaklands, Tenbury Wells WR15 8FB* T: (01584) 810528 M: 07711-260521 E: ian@theoaklands.com

WILLIAMS, James Nicholas Owen. b 39. MBE . CEng. S'wark Ord Course. **d** 82 **p** 83. C Petersfield w Sheet *Portsm* 82–86; TV Droitwich Spa *Worc* 86–88; R Church Lench w Rous Lench and Abbots Morton 88–94; V Milton *B & W* 94–04; RD Locking 99–04; rtd 04; Dioc Ecum Officer *B & W* 04–08; Hon C Pill, Portbury and Easton-in-Gordano 04–09; PtO 09–21; *Bris* from 04. *151 Charlton Mead Drive, Brentry, Bristol BS10 6LP* T: 0117-950 4152 M: 07808-772908 E: jnowil64@gmail.com

WILLIAMS, Mrs Jane Lorette. b 66. Univ of Wales (Swansea) BSc 03 Dur Univ BA 16. **d** 16 **p** 17. C Wareham *Sarum* 16–19; R Bride Valley from 19. *The Rectory, Church Street, Burton Bradstock, Bridport DT6 4QS* T: (01308) 898799 E: bvrector@outlook.com

WILLIAMS, Janet Patricia. b 61. Univ Coll Ox BA 83 MSt 85 K Alfred's Coll Win PhD 98. WEMTC 06. **d** 09 **p** 10. NSM Cirencester *Glouc* 09–12; Tutor WEMTC 12–18; Dir Reader Tr 12–18; Hon Can Glouc Cathl 14–18; Vice Prin St Hild Coll from 18. *St Hild College, Stocks Bank Road, Mirfield WF14 0BW* M: 07989-707257 E: janet.williams@sthild.org

WILLIAMS, Janet Patricia. *See* FFRENCH, Janet Patricia

WILLIAMS, Jeffrey. b 52. Univ of Wales (Ban) BTh 06. Llan Ord Course 99. **d** 03 **p** 04. NSM Cardiff St Mary and St Steph w St Dyfrig etc *Llan* 03–07; Chapl Malta and Gozo *Eur* 07–13; P-in-c Chard Gd Shep Furnham *B & W* 13; V 13–20; rtd 20; PtO *B & W* 20. *36 Dinas Street, Cardiff CF11 6QZ* M: 07928-171187 E: fr.jeff@hotmail.com

WILLIAMS, Jeffrey. *See* WILLIAMS, Robert Jeffrey Hopkin

WILLIAMS, Jennifer Ruth. b 66. St Hugh's Coll Ox BA 88 PGCE 89 Man Univ MA 00 PhD 11. Wycliffe Hall Ox NOC 00. **d** 00 **p** 01. C Heatons *Man* 00–04; Hon C Burnage St Marg 04–05; Tutor Wycliffe Hall Ox 05–19; NSM Wootton *Ox* 11–19; R Ox St Matt from 19. *St Matthew's Vicarage, 65 Marlborough Road, Oxford OX1 4LW* T: (01865) 798587 M: 07784-304985 E: jenniwilliams0308@gmail.com

WILLIAMS, John. *See* WILLIAMS, David John

WILLIAMS, John Anthony. b 53. G&C Coll Cam BA 75 MA 79 St Jo Coll Dur BA 83 PhD 86. Cranmer Hall Dur 81. **d** 86 **p** 87. C Beverley Minster *York* 86–89; C Cloughton 89–90; P-in-c 90–93; Clergy Tr Officer E Riding 89–93; P-in-c Emley *Wakef* 93–98; Dioc Minl Tr Officer 93–02; Wakef Min Scheme Officer 97–06; Co-ord for Local Min *Wakef* 02–06; Dean Wakef Min Scheme 06–08; Hon Can Wakef Cathl 08; Sen Lect York St Jo Univ 08–17; rtd 17; PtO *York* 17–18. *75 Quarrydale Road, Sutton-in-Ashfield NG17 4DR* T: (01623) 550830 E: j.a.williams23@btinternet.com

WILLIAMS, John Barrie. b 38. Univ of Wales (Cardiff) MSc 77 DipEd 80 PhD 91. St Mich Coll Llan 89. **d** 87 **p** 88. NSM Newcastle *Llan* 87–89; C Port Talbot St Theodore 89; PtO from 89. *Shorncliffe, 11 Priory Oak, Bridgend CF31 2HY* T: (01656) 660369

WILLIAMS, John Beattie. b 42. Univ of Wales BA 66. Cuddesdon Coll 67. **d** 69 **p** 69. C St Helier *S'wark* 69–70; C Yeovil H Trin *B & W* 70–76; Chapl to the Deaf *Sarum* 76–78; P-in-c Ebbesbourne Wake w Fifield Bavant and Alvediston 76–78; Chapl to the Deaf *B & W* 78–83; TV Fareham H Trin *Portsm* 83–94; R W Wittering and Birdham w Itchenor *Chich* 94–11; rtd 11; PtO *Chich* from 12. *28 Harrow Drive, West Wittering, Chichester PO20 8EJ* T: (01243) 670843 E: witteringjohn@hotmail.com

WILLIAMS, John David Anthony. b 55. Open Univ BA 98. St Steph Ho Ox 85. **d** 87 **p** 88. C Paignton St Jo, St Andr and St Boniface *Ex* 87–90; C Heavitree w St Paul 90–91; TV 91–01; P-in-c Exminster and Kenn 01–15; R Exminster, Kenn, Kenton w Mamhead, and Powderham from 15. *The Rectory, Milbury Lane, Exminster, Exeter EX6 8AD* T: (01392) 824283 E: john_williams55@btinternet.com

WILLIAMS, John Francis Meyler. b 34. St Jo Coll Cam BA 56 MA 60. Sarum & Wells Th Coll 79. d 81 p 82. C Hadleigh w Layham and Shelley *St E* 81–84; P-in-c Campsey Ashe and Marlesford 84–87; P-in-c Parham w Hacheston 84–87; R Campsea Ashe w Marlesford, Parham and Hacheston 87–95; P-in-c Kedington 95–97; rtd 97; Chapl St Kath Convent Parmoor 97–98; PtO Ox 01–05. *2 Capel Court, The Burgage, Prestbury, Cheltenham GL52 3EL* T: (01242) 577764 E: denbygreen@gmail.com

WILLIAMS, John Gilbert. b 36. St Aid Birkenhead 64. d 67 p 68. C Bollington St Jo *Ches* 67–69; C Oxton 69–72; P-in-c Acton Beauchamp and Evesbatch w Stanford Bishop *Heref* 72–76; P-in-c Castle Frome 72–76; P-in-c Bishop's Frome 72–76; R Kingsland 76–83; P-in-c Eardisland 77–83; P-in-c Aymestrey and Leinthall Earles w Wigmore etc 82–83; R Cradley w Mathon and Storridge 83–94; R Norton St Philip w Hemington, Hardington etc B & W 94–01; rtd 01; PtO *St D* from 02; *S & B* from 14. *Bronydd, 69 St Davids Park, Llanfaes, Brecon LD3 8EQ* T: (01874) 938196 E: cynwyl@tiscali.co.uk

WILLIAMS, Canon John Keith. b 63. Ridley Hall Cam 95. d 97 p 98. C Potters Bar *St Alb* 97–99; C Bishop's Stortford St Mich 99–01; P-in-c Bishop's Stortford 01–08; TR Cheshunt 08–17; TR Hemel Hempstead from 17; Hon Can St Alb from 15. *The Rectory, High Street, Hemel Hempstead HP1 3AE* T: (01442) 265272 E: teamrector@hotmail.com

WILLIAMS, Prof John Mark Gruffydd. b 52. St Pet Coll Ox BA 73 MSc 76 MA 77 DPhil 79 Ox Univ DSc 98 FBA 08 FBPsS 84 FMedSci 04. EAMTC 86. d 89 p 90. NSM Girton *Ely* 89–91; PtO *Ban* 91–03; NSM Wheatley *Ox* 03–09; PtO 09–11; Hon Can Ch Ch 11–19; PtO from 19. *Holifield Cottage, 17 Bell Lane, Wheatley, Oxford OX33 1XY* T: (01865) 876288

WILLIAMS, Canon John Peter Philip. b 49. Open Univ BA 84. Chich Th Coll 71. d 72 p 73. C Abergele *St As* 72–77; R Henllan and Llannefydd 77–82; R Henllan and Llannefydd and Bylchau 82–11; AD Denbigh 98–09; Hon Can St As Cathl 01–11; rtd 11; PtO *St As* from 11. *72 Crud y Castell, Denbigh LL16 4PQ* T: (01745) 817319 E: jppwilliams@tiscali.co.uk

WILLIAMS, Canon John Richard. b 48. Rhodes Univ BA 68 K Coll Lon BD 72 AKC 72. d 73 p 74. C E London St Alb S Africa 73–74; C King William's Town 74–76; C Addington *Cant* 77–80; C Minster-in-Sheppey 80–86; R Temple Ewell w Lydden 86–90; V Hound *Win* 90–94; V Highcliffe w Hinton Admiral 94–03; RD Christchurch 98–03; Chapl Montreux w Gstaad *Eur* 03–06; Switzerland 04–06; rtd 08; PtO *Sarum* 14–22. *The Old Bakery, Gussage All Saints, Wimborne BH21 5ET* T: (01258) 841464

WILLIAMS, Canon John Roger. b 37. Westmr Coll Ox MTh 97. Lich Th Coll 60. d 63 p 64. C Wem *Lich* 63–66; C Wolverhampton St Pet 66–69; R Pudleston w Hatf *Heref* 69–74; P-in-c Stoke Prior and Ford w Humber 69–74; P-in-c Docklow 69–74; V Fenton *Lich* 74–81; R Shipston-on-Stour w Honington and Idlicote *Cov* 81–92; RD Shipston 83–90; Hon Can Cov Cathl 90–00; R Lighthorne 92–00; V Chesterton 92–00; V Newbold Pacey w Moreton Morrell 92–00; P-in-c Denstone w Ellastone and Stanton *Lich* 00–05; Master St Jo Hosp Lich 05–11; rtd 11; PtO *Lich* 11–21. *3 Curborough Road, Lichfield WS13 7NG* T: (01543) 419339

WILLIAMS, John Strettle. b 44. MBE 00. DipEd 73 BA 84. NOC 77. d 80 p 81. Chapl Cen Liv Coll of FE 80–85; Chapl City Coll Liv 85–09; NSM Liv St Paul Stoneycroft 80–83; NSM Liv Our Lady and St Nic 83–09; Chapl RNR 84–90; CF (VR) from 95; rtd 09. *3 Orchard Dene, Craven Road, Rainhill, Prescot L35 0LT* T: 0151-426 9598 M: 07736-629453

WILLIAMS, Jonathan Anthony. b 65. Wycliffe Hall Ox BTh 95. d 98 p 99. C Denton Ch Ch *Man* 98–02; R Burnage St Marg 02–05; Hon C Ox St Matt 09–11; P-in-c Wolvercote 11–18; V 18–19; Hon C Ox St Matt from 19. *St Matthew's Vicarage, 65 Marlborough Road, Oxford OX1 4LW*

WILLIAMS, Jonathan Lane. b 59. Dorset Inst of HE 85. STETS 96. d 99 p 00. NSM Moordown *Win* 96–16; NSM Winton, Moordown and Charminster from 16; Chapl Hants Hosps NHS Foundn Trust from 07. *28 Queen Mary Avenue, Moordown, Bournemouth BH9 1TS* T/F: (01202) 531630 M: 07977-444186 E: jonathan.williams7@ntlworld.com

WILLIAMS, The Ven Jonathan Simon. b 60. Univ of Wales (Cardiff) BSc 81. Coll of Resurr Mirfield 83. d 86 p 87. C Gelligaer *Llan* 86–89; C Cwmbran *Mon* 89–90; TV 90–97; V Marshfield and Peterstone Wentloog etc 97–00; TR Bassaleg 00–12; AD 99–12; Adn Newport from 12; Can St Woolos Cathl from 07; Prec from 14. *The Archdeaconry, 93 Stow Hill, Newport NP20 4EA* T: (01633) 215206 E: venjsw@gmail.com

WILLIAMS, Mrs Josephine. b 42. NOC 05. d 07 p 08. NSM Bootle Ch Ch *Liv* 07–16; PtO from 16. *1 Clayfield Close, Bootle L20 3QN* T: 0151-933 7729 F: 525 1995 E: josiewilliams1@aol.com

WILLIAMS, Ms Josephine Mary. b 47. Reading Univ BEd 78 Hatf Poly MEd 87. SAOMC 96. d 99 p 00. NSM Terriers *Ox* 99–02; Chapl HM YOI Aylesbury 02–09; rtd 09; PtO *Ox* 09–13; *Birm* from 13. *85 Newton Road, Knowle, Solihull B93 9HN* T: (01564) 898607 E: jo.williams58@gmail.com

WILLIAMS, Miss Josephine Sharne Emma. b 76. d 13 p 14. C Cen Wolverhampton *Lich* 13–16; V Reading St Mark and All SS *Ox* from 16. *Hamelsham, Downshire Square, Reading RT1 6NJ* M: 07977-142450 E: revdjowilliams@gmail.com

WILLIAMS, Joyce. *See* WILLIAMS, Kathleen Joyce

WILLIAMS, Julian Thomas. b 65. Clare Coll Cam BA 87. Wycliffe Hall Ox BA 90. d 91 p 92. Min Can St D Cathl 91–94; C St D Cathl 91–94; V Cil-y-Cwm and Ystrad-ffin w Rhandir-mwyn etc 94–00; R Nursling and Rownhams *Win* 00–19. *Flat 1, 27 Park Road, Southampton SO15 3AW* E: jtw1797@outlook.com

WILLIAMS, Miss Juliet Susan Joyce. b 83. K Coll Lon BA 04 Anglia Ruskin Univ MA 14. Ridley Hall Cam 09. d 11 p 12. C St Agnes and Mount Hawke w Mithian *Truro* 11–14; P-in-c Boscoppa from 14; P-in-c St Blazey from 16; P-in-c Luxulyan from 16. *St Luke's House, 5 Penhaligon Way, St Austell PL25 3AR* T: (01726) 76282 M: 07813-660961 E: revjules@btinternet.com

WILLIAMS, Karl André. b 61. All SS Cen for Miss & Min 10. d 16 p 17. C Gt Meols *Ches* 16–19; V Dukinfield St Mark from 19. *St Mark's Vicarage, 2 Church Square, Dukinfield SK16 4PX* T: 0161-330 2783 M: 07463-876753 E: rev.karl.williams@outlook.com

WILLIAMS, Mrs Kathleen Joyce. b 47. Dur Univ TCert 71. St Jo Coll Nottm 03. d 05 p 06. C Exning St Martin w Landwade *St E* 05–08; V 08–12; rtd 12; Hon C Bath St Sav w Swainswick and Woolley *B & W* 12–18; PtO *Ex* from 19. *9 Sunleigh, Livermead Hill, Torquay TQ2 6QP* E: joyfulwilliams2004@yahoo.co.uk

WILLIAMS, Keith. b 37. St Jo Coll Nottm 83. d 85 p 86. C Holbeck *Ripon* 85–88; R Swillington 88–95; V Batley All SS *Wakef* 95–01; P-in-c Purlwell 95–00; rtd 01; PtO *Ripon* 01–14; *Leeds* 14–19. *17 Kirkfield Drive, Colton, Leeds LS15 9DR* T: 0113-260 5852 M: 07709-027328

WILLIAMS, Keith Douglas. b 41. EMMTC 86. d 89 p 90. NSM Netherfield *S'well* 89–07; NSM Colwick 89–07; NSM Gedling 95–07; Chapl Notts Healthcare NHS Trust 93–03; rtd 07; PtO *S'well* from 07. *36 Bramble Court, Carnarvon Grove, Gedling, Nottingham NG4 3HX* T: 0115-961 4850 E: keiwil@ntlworld.com

WILLIAMS, Keith Graham. b 38. Reading Univ MSc 70 MRICS 62. Cranmer Hall Dur. d 77 p 78. C Almondbury *Wakef* 77–81; C Chapelthorpe 81–82; V Ryhill 82–88; V E Ardsley 88–99; RD Wakef 96–99; rtd 03; PtO *Chich* from 03. *The Granary, 52-54 Belle Hill, Bexhill-on-Sea TN40 2AP* T: (01424) 734093

WILLIAMS, Kelvin George John. b 36. ALCD 62. d 62 p 63. C Bath Abbey w St Jas *B & W* 62–65; CF (TA) 64–65 and 70–79; Chapl R Nat Hosp for Rheumatic Diseases Bath 64–65; CF 65–68; C Clevedon St Andr *B & W* 68–70; V Ston Easton w Farrington Gurney 70–74; P-in-c Bradford 74–75; R Bradford w Oake, Hillfarrance and Heathfield 75–76; NSM Puriton and Pawlett 89–91; V 92–02; NSM Bridgwater Deanery 91–92; rtd 02; PtO *B & W* 03–04 and from 07; P-in-c Weston Zoyland w Chedzoy 04–07. *Highlands, Knowleyards Road, Middlezoy, Bridgwater TA7 0NY* T: (01823) 698413 E: reverendwilliams@btinternet.com

WILLIAMS (née HANNAH), Mrs Kimberley Victoria. b 75. Bp Grosseteste Coll BSc 98. Ripon Coll Cuddesdon BTh 01. d 01 p 02. C Machynlleth w Llanwrin and Penegoes *Ban* 01–02; C Twrcelyn Deanery 02–10; P-in-c Porthmadoc and Ynyscynhaearn and Dolbenmaen 10–11; TV Bro Eifionydd 11–12; TV Bro'r Holl Saint 12–16; TV Bro Eifionydd 16–20; V from 20. *The Rectory, Y Maes, Criccieth LL52 0AG* T: (01766) 523743 E: revkimwilliams@gmail.com

WILLIAMS, Lea John. b 84. Wolv Univ BA 06 Aber Univ BA 10. Ripon Coll Cuddesdon MTh 16. d 16 p 17. C Gt Dunmow and Barnston *Chelmsf* 16–20; CMS from 21. *Church Mission Society, CMS House, Watlington Road, Cowley, Oxford OX4 6BZ* E: lea_williams@hotmail.com

WILLIAMS, Lee Lawrence. b 75. St Steph Ho Ox 98. d 01 p 02. C Cowbridge *Llan* 01–04. *34 Queens Drive, Llantwit Fadre, Pontypridd CF83 2NT*

WILLIAMS, Mrs Linda Leonie Paula. b 56. UEA BA 79. SEITE 04. d 07 p 08. NSM Kenley *S'wark* 07–10; C Harpenden St Nic *St Alb* 10–19; P-in-c Kimpton w Ayot St Lawrence from 19. *The Vicarage, 11 High Street, Kimpton, Hitchin SG4 8RA*

WILLIAMS, Lloyd. b 43. Oak Hill Th Coll 71. d 74 p 75. C Laisterdyke *Bradf* 74–77; C Hoole *Ches* 77–80; V Rawthorpe *Wakef* 80–84; Dep Chapl HM Pris Leeds 84–85; Chapl HM Pris Cardiff 85–88; Chapl HM Pris Aldington 88–95; R

Aldington w Bonnington and Bilsington *Cant* 88–95; RD N Lympne 94–95; P-in-c Tuen Mun Hong Kong 95–99; V Clayton *Bradf* 99–03; rtd 03; PtO *York* 04–07; *Wakef* 07–14; *Blackb* from 14. *18 Fosbrooke House, 8 Clifton Drive, Lytham St Annes FY8 5RQ* T: (01253) 667011 M: 07866-604345 E: revlloydwilliams@gmail.com

WILLIAMS, Lois. *See* WILLIAMS, Catherine Lois

WILLIAMS, Canon Louise Margaret. b 66. Lanc Univ BA 87. St Jo Coll Nottm 88. **d** 91 **p** 94. Par Dn W Ham *Chelmsf* 91–94; C Harold Hill St Geo 94–95; PtO 95–96; C Southend St Sav Westcliff 95–10; Chapl Asst Southend Health Care NHS Trust 97–10; R S Shoebury *Chelmsf* from 10; Hon Can Chelmsf Cathl from 17. *The Rectory, 42 Church Road, Shoeburyness, Southend-on-Sea SS3 9EU* T: (01702) 292778 E: revlwilliams@aol.com

WILLIAMS, Marion. b 56. St Mellitus Coll 13. **d** 14 **p** 15. NSM Romford St Andr *Chelmsf* 14–15; NSM Cranham 15–18; P-in-c 17–19; R from 19; Chapl St Clare Hospice 15–17. *1 Boyd Close, Upminster RM14 3BG* T: (01708) 228308 M: 07967-339079 E: marionbubbs@aol.com

WILLIAMS, Mark. b 64. St Mich Coll Llan BTh 94. **d** 97 **p** 98. C Mountain Ash *Llan* 97; C Mountain Ash and Miskin 97–99; C Neath w Llantwit 99–01; C Neath 01–02; V Skewen 02–12; V Port Talbot St Theodore 12–19; TR Littlehampton *Chich* 19–20; R from 20. *St Mary's Vicarage, 18 Church Street, Littlehampton BN17 5PX* T: (01903) 724410 E: markwilliams35@btinternet.com

WILLIAMS, Canon Mark. b 73. Pemb Coll Cam BA 94 MA 98 Ox Univ BA 98 MA 02. Ripon Coll Cuddesdon 95 Ven English Coll Rome 97. **d** 98 **p** 99. C Caerphilly *Llan* 98–00; V Walworth St Chris *S'wark* 00–10; Warden Pemb Coll Miss Walworth 00–10; V Kennington St Jo w St Jas from 10; Dioc Voc Adv from 02; Hon Can Asante Mampong Ghana from 15. *The Vicarage, 22 Vassall Road, London SW9 6JA* T: (020) 7735 9340 E: fr_mark@yahoo.com

WILLIAMS, Mark. *See* WILLIAMS, Howell Mark

WILLIAMS, Mark Andrew. b 71. STETS 11. **d** 14 **p** 15. C Portchester *Portsm* 14–17; P-in-c Gatten St Paul from 17; P-in-c Sandown Ch Ch from 17. *St Paul's Vicarage, 2 St Paul's Crescent, Shanklin PO37 7AW* M: 07873-406558 E: williams_mark1@sky.com *or* revwilliams71@gmail.com

WILLIAMS, Mark John. b 66. St Martin's Coll Lanc BA 88 PGCE 92 Heythrop Coll Lon MA 07 Man Univ MPhil 17. Cranmer Hall Dur 98. **d** 00 **p** 01. C Hockerill *St Alb* 00–03; TV Chipping Barnet 03–09; V Burnley St Matt w H Trin *Blackb* 09–17; TR Worsley *Man* 17–19; R Bowland Benefice *Blackb* from 19. *The Rectory, Sawley Road, Grindleton, Clitheroe BB7 4QS* T: (01200) 441152 E: rector.mark.john.williams@gmail.com

WILLIAMS, Mark Robert. b 62. Spurgeon's Coll Lon BA 83 Univ Coll of Swansea PGCE 84. Ripon Coll Cuddesdon 99. **d** 01 **p** 02. C Wellington and Distr *B & W* 01–05; V Belmont *S'wark* 05–19; Ecum Adv Croydon Area 13–19; V Deeping St James *Linc* from 19. *The Vicarage, 16 Church Street, Deeping St James, Peterborough PE6 8HD* T: (01778) 217366 E: revblots@outlook.com *or* vicar@dsj.org.uk

WILLIAMS, The Ven Martin Inffeld. b 37. SS Coll Cam BA 62 MA 92. Chich Th Coll 62. **d** 64 **p** 65. C Greenford H Cross *Lon* 64–70; Tutor Chich Th Coll 70–75; Vice-Prin 75–77; V Roath St German *Llan* 77–92; Adn Margam 92–01; Adn Morgannwg 02–04; Treas Llan Cathl 92–04; V Penydarren 92–04; rtd 04. *82 Walker Road, Splott, Cardiff CF24 2EN* T: (029) 2221 9392

WILLIAMS, Martin Jonathan. b 63. Birm Univ BA 84. Trin Coll Bris 96. **d** 98 **p** 99. C Bisley and W End *Guildf* 98–01; C Gerrards Cross and Fulmer *Ox* 01–09; R 09–18; Jt AD Amersham from 17. *Evenley House, Sly Corner, Lee Common, Great Missenden HP16 9LD* M: 07974-010703

WILLIAMS, Mary Edith. b 50. Darlington Tr Coll BEd 73. Cranmer Hall Dur 00. **d** 02 **p** 03. C Filey *York* 02–06; V 06–12; rtd 12; PtO *Ripon* 13–14; *Leeds* from 14. *The Mill House, Parkgate Lane, Brompton on Swale, Richmond DL10 7HA* T: (01748) 811241 E: wilbaric@hotmail.co.uk

WILLIAMS, Meurig Llwyd. b 61. Univ of Wales (Abth) BA 83 PGCE 84 Univ of Wales (Cardiff) BD 90. Westcott Ho Cam 90. **d** 92 **p** 93. C Holyhead w Rhoscolyn w Llanfair-yn-Neubwll *Ban* 92–95; P-in-c Denio w Abererch 95–96; V 96–99; V Cardiff Dewi Sant *Llan* 99–05; Adn Ban 05–11; TR Bangor 06–11; TV 11; Bp's Commissary and Chapl *Eur* 11–20; Adn France 16–20; Can Malta Cathl 11–20; I Mallow Union *C, C & R* from 21. *The Rectory, Bearforest Lower, Mallow, Co Cork, Republic of Ireland* E: mllwyd@aol.com

WILLIAMS, Michael. *See* WILLIAMS, David Michael Rochfort

WILLIAMS, Canon Michael Dermot Andrew. b 57. Ex Univ BA 86 Lon Univ MA 02. Ripon Coll Cuddesdon 90. **d** 92 **p** 93. NSM Christow, Ashton, Trusham and Bridford

Ex 92–97; NSM Marston w Elsfield *Ox* 97–99; Chief Exec Radcliffe Infirmary NHS Trust 97–99; V Shipton-under-Wychwood w Milton, Fifield etc *Ox* 99–02; RD Chipping Norton 01–02; Exec Dir Thames Valley HA 02–05; NSM Kennington *Ox* 04–05; Chief Exec Taunton and Somerset NHS Foundn Trust from 05; Hon C Topsham *Ex* 07–14; Hon C Wear 09–14; Hon C Topsham and Wear 14–17; Can Res Ex Cathl from 17; Treas from 18; PtO *Ex* from 21. *9 Cathedral Close, Exeter EX1 1EZ* T: (01392) 421832 E: williamsmda@btinternet.com

WILLIAMS, Canon Michael Joseph. b 42. St Jo Coll Dur BA 68. Bernard Gilpin Soc Dur 63 Cranmer Hall Dur 64. **d** 70 **p** 71. C Toxteth Park St Philemon *Liv* 70–75; TV Toxteth St Philemon w St Gabr 75–78; Dir Past Studies St Jo Coll Dur 78–88; Prin NOC 89–99; Hon Can Liv Cathl 92–99; P-in-c Bolton St Pet *Man* 99–04; V 04–07; P-in-c Bolton St Phil 04–07; Hon Can Man Cathl 00–07; AD Bolton 02–05; rtd 07; PtO *Man* from 08. *51 Cotswold Drive, Horwich, Bolton BL6 7DE* T: (01204) 667162 E: m.j.williams42@hotmail.co.uk

WILLIAMS, Michael Robert John. b 41. Cranmer Hall Dur 67. **d** 70 **p** 71. C Middleton *Man* 70–73; C-in-c Blackley White Moss St Mark CD 73–79; R Blackley St Mark White Moss 79–86; R Gorton Em 86–96; R Gorton Em w St Jas 96–06; rtd 06; PtO *Man* from 06. *26 Hawthorn Avenue, Bury BL8 1DU* T: 0161-761 4712

WILLIAMS, Nia Catrin. b 69. Univ of Wales (Cardiff) BTh 96. St As Minl Tr Course 97. **d** 98 **p** 99. C Llanrhos *St As* 98–02; C Colwyn Bay 02–06; P-in-c Towyn and St George 06–08; V Glanogwen and Llanllechid w St Ann's and Pentir *Ban* 08–12; AD Ogwen 10–12; Can Missr Ban Cathl 12–15; CMD Officer 12–15; Dir of Ords 12–14; Dir of Voc *St As* 15–16; CF from 16. *c/o MOD Chaplains (Army)* T: (01264) 383430 E: niacatrin13@gmail.com

WILLIAMS, Nicholas Jolyon. b 68. Univ of Wales (Swansea) BA 89. Wycliffe Hall Ox BTh 96. **d** 96 **p** 97. C Ditton *Roch* 96–99; C N Farnborough *Guildf* 99–05; P-in-c Tongham 05–11; V Guildf Ch Ch from 11; AD Guildf from 17. *Christ Church Vicarage, 25 Waterden Road, Guildford GU1 2AZ* T: (01483) 568870 E: nick@christchurchguildford.com

WILLIAMS, Nicholas Lindsey. b 62. Birkbeck Coll Lon BA 02 MA 18 Kent Univ BA 09. SEITE 06. **d** 09 **p** 10. NSM Dartford H Trin *Roch* 09–11; P-in-c Darenth 11–14; P-in-c Horton Kirby and Sutton-at-Hone 13–14; V Darent Valley 14–16; V E Malling, Wateringbury and Teston 16–19; V E Malling and Teston from 19; P-in-c Larkfield from 19. *The Vicarage, 2 The Grange, East Malling, West Malling ME19 6AH* T: (01732) 843282 E: father.nick@btinternet.com

WILLIAMS, Nick. *See* WILLIAMS, James Nicholas Owen

WILLIAMS, The Very Revd Nigel Howard. b 63. St Mich Coll Llan 93. **d** 95 **p** 96. C Denbigh and Nantglyn *St As* 95–97; P-in-c Llanrwst and Llanddoget and Capel Garmon 97–98; R 98–04; V Colwyn Bay 04–08; V Colwyn Bay w Brynymaen 08–11; AD Rhos 04–09; Dean and Lib St As Cathl from 11; TR St As from 11. *The Deanery, Upper Denbigh Road, St Asaph LL17 0RL* T: (01745) 583597 E: nigelwilliams@churchinwales.org.uk

WILLIAMS, Nigel Mark. b 89. Trin Coll Bris 17. **d** 19 **p** 20. C Keynsham *B & W* from 19. *37 Mayfields, Keynsham, Bristol BS31 1BW* E: nigelwilliams@keynshamparish.org.uk

WILLIAMS, Olivia Hazel. b 55. Dun Laoghaire Inst CertEd 98 TCD BTh 01. CITC 98. **d** 01 **p** 02. C Greystones *D & G* 01–05; Abp's Dom Chapl 03–05; I Carlow w Urglin and Staplestown *C, F & O* 05–16; rtd 16. *Tig an tSagairt, Slaney Rise, Ballymurphy Road, Tullow, Co Carlow, R93 FR90, Republic of Ireland* T: (00353) (59) 915 2780 M: 86-837 0794 E: williams.olivia2@gmail.com

WILLIAMS, Owen Leslie. b 80. Sussex Univ BSc 01 MSc Cam Univ BTh 13. Ridley Hall Cam 10. **d** 13 **p** 14. C Uppingham w Ayston and Belton w Wardley *Pet* 13–16; C Oakham, Ashwell, Braunston, Brooke, Egleton etc 16–17. *64A Nowton Road, Bury St Edmunds IP33 2BU* E: rev.o.l.williams@gmail.com

WILLIAMS, Canon Paul Andrew. b 62. Oak Hill Th Coll BA 91. **d** 91 **p** 92. C Ware Ch Ch *St Alb* 91–94; C Harold Wood *Chelmsf* 94–99; C Langham Place All So *Lon* 99–06; V Fulwood *Sheff* from 06; Hon Can Sheff Cathl from 11. *The Vicarage, 2 Chorley Drive, Sheffield S10 3RR* T: 0114-230 1911 E: paulwilliams@fulwoodchurch.co.uk

✠**WILLIAMS, The Rt Revd Paul Gavin.** b 68. Grey Coll Dur BA 89. Wycliffe Hall Ox 90. **d** 92 **p** 93 **c** 09. C Muswell Hill St Jas w St Matt *Lon* 92–96; C Clifton Ch Ch w Em *Bris* 96–99; R Gerrards Cross and Fulmer *Ox* 99–09; Hon Can Ch Ch 07–09; Area Bp Kensington *Lon* 09–15; Bp S'well and Nottm from 15. *Bishop's Manor, Bishop's Drive, Southwell NG25 0JR* T: (01636) 812112 E: bishop@southwell.anglican.org

WILLIAMS, Canon Paul Rhys. b 58. St Andr Univ MTheol 82. Westcott Ho Cam 83. **d** 86 **p** 87. Asst Chapl Selw Coll Cam 86–87; C Chatham St Steph *Roch* 87–90; V Gillingham St Aug 90–95; Bp's Dom Chapl 95–03; Hon Can Roch Cathl 01–03; V Tewkesbury w Walton Cardiff and Twyning *Glouc* from 03; AD Tewkesbury and Winchcombe 09–16; Hon Can Glouc Cathl from 06. *Abbey House, Church Street, Tewkesbury GL20 5SR* T: (01684) 293333 *or* 850959 F: 273113 E: vicar@tewkesburyabbey.org.uk

WILLIAMS, Mrs Pauline Mary. b 52. Univ of Wales (Cardiff) BD 96 Trin Coll Carmarthen PGCE 97. St Mich Coll Llan 00. **d** 02 **p** 03. C Coity w Nolton *Llan* 02–06; P-in-c Abercynon 06–11; V Baglan 11–13; Dioc Children's Officer 06–13; P-in-c Costa Almeria and Costa Calida *Eur* 13–16; PtO *Llan* from 16. *3 Ewenny Road, Wick, Cowbridge CF71 7QA* T: (01656) 890066 E: williamspm89@hotmail.com

WILLIAMS, Peter. *See* WILLIAMS, Cecil Peter

WILLIAMS, Peter Charles. b 50. SWMTC 98. **d** 01 **p** 02. OLM Landrake w St Erney and Botus Fleming *Truro* 01–15; rtd 15; PtO *B & W* from 15. *8 Parsons Close, Nether Stowey, Bridgwater TA5 1JS* E: peter.freda@btinternet.com

WILLIAMS, Canon Peter John. b 55. Southn Univ BTh 80. Chich Th Coll 76. **d** 80 **p** 81. C Chepstow *Mon* 80–84; C Morriston *S & B* 84–85; V Glantawe 85–88; R Reynoldston w Penrice and Llangennith 88–05; R Llangennith w Llanmadoc and Cheriton 05–14; Dioc Soc Resp Officer 88–14; Hon Can Brecon Cathl 04–11; Can Res Brecon Cathl 11–14; rtd 15; PtO *S & B* from 15. *10 Woodcote Green, Grovesend, Swansea SA4 8DR* T: (01792) 386391 E: canon.peter.williams@dreamorchid.co.uk

WILLIAMS, Philip Allan. b 48. Bris Univ BSc 69 CertEd 74. Trin Coll Bris 86. **d** 88 **p** 89. C Heref St Pet w St Owen and St Jas 88–93; R Peterchurch w Vowchurch, Turnastone and Dorstone 93–96; P-in-c Holmer w Huntington 96–01; V 01–13; rtd 13; PtO *Ches* from 14. *128 Rugby Drive, Macclesfield SK10 2JF* T: (01625) 432037 E: philtherev@gmail.com

WILLIAMS, The Ven Philip Andrew. b 64. Sheff Univ BA 86. Cranmer Hall Dur 88. **d** 90 **p** 91. C Hillsborough and Wadsley Bridge *Sheff* 90–94; C Lenton Abbey *S'well* 94–96; P-in-c 96–02; C Wollaton Park 94–96; V Porchester 02–17; AD Gedling 05–17; Assoc Adn Transition Min 17–19; Adn Nottingham *S'well* from 19; Hon Can S'well Minster from 11. *The Vicarage, 2 Cocker Beck, Lambley, Nottingham NG4 4QP* T: 0115-931 3874 E: archd-nottm@southwell.anglican.org

WILLIAMS, Philip James. b 52. St Chad's Coll Dur BA 73. Coll of Resurr Mirfield 74. **d** 76 **p** 77. C Stoke upon Trent *Lich* 76–80; TV 80; Chapl N Staffs Poly 80–84; TV Stoke-upon-Trent 80–84; R Shrewsbury St Giles w Sutton and Atcham 84–14; rtd 14. *6 Latchford Lane, Shrewsbury SY1 4YG* E: flyingvic@btinternet.com

WILLIAMS, Philip Robert. b 78. St Mellitus Coll. **d** 13 **p** 14. C Onslow Square and S Kensington St Aug *Lon* 13–14; C Spitalfields Ch Ch w All SS 14–16; R Shadwell St Paul w Ratcliffe St Jas from 16. *St Paul's Shadwell Rectory, 298 The Highway, London E1W 3DH* M: 07815-146350

WILLIAMS, Mrs Rachel Mary. b 65. All SS Cen for Miss & Min 12. **d** 15 **p** 16. NSM Bolsover *Derby* from 15; PtO *S'well* from 16. *Manor Farm, 25 Dawgates Lane, Sutton-in-Ashfield NG17 3DA* T: (01623) 513048 M: 07975-631066 E: revrwilliams25@gmail.com

WILLIAMS, Canon Richard Elwyn. b 57. Hull Univ BA 79. Coll of Resurr Mirfield 79. **d** 81 **p** 82. C Altrincham St Geo *Ches* 81–84; C Stockport St Thos 84–85; C Stockport St Thos w St Pet 86; R Withington St Crispin *Man* 86–95; V Alveston *Cov* 95–21; RD Fosse 99–07; Hon Can Cov Cathl from 06; rtd 21. *St Bridget's Rectory, 40 Village Road, West Kirby, Wirral CH48 7HE* E: rickthevic@googlemail.com

WILLIAMS, Canon Richard Henry Lowe. b 31. Liv Univ BA 52. K Coll (NS) BD 64 Ridley Hall Cam 54. **d** 56 **p** 57. C Drypool St Andr and St Pet *York* 56–59; Canada 59–64; V Kirkdale St Athanasius *Liv* 64–68; R Much Woolton 68–79; R Croft w Southworth 79–89; Dioc Communications Officer 79–97; Hon Can Liv Cathl 88–97; R Wavertree St Mary 89–97; rtd 97; PtO *Liv* from 97. *16 Childwall Crescent, Liverpool L16 7PQ* T: 0151-722 7962

WILLIAMS, Richard Huw. b 63. Bradf and Ilkley Coll BA 85. St Jo Coll Nottm 86. **d** 89 **p** 90. C Forest Gate St Edm *Chelmsf* 89–90; C Plaistow 90–92; C Canning Town St Matthias 92–96; V Southend St Sav Westcliff 96–10; RD Southend 05–10; PtO 10–13; Chapl Havens Hospices 12–13; TV Chalke Valley *Sarum* 13–17; Hon C Charfield and Kingswood w Wickwar etc *Glouc* from 17. *The Rectory, 36 Wotton Road, Charfield, Wotton-under-Edge GL12 8TG* T: (01454) 260476 M: 07833-940034 E: richard844williams@btinternet.com

WILLIAMS, Richard Lawrence. b 62. Warw Univ BSc 83 ACA 87. Wycliffe Hall Ox 95. **d** 97 **p** 98. C Wallington *S'wark* 97–00; V Addiscombe St Mary Magd w St Martin 00–09; P-in-c Cranbrook *Cant* 09–13; V 13–15; AD Weald 12–13; Finance Dir Roch DBF from 17; PtO *Cant* from 18. *Old Tannery Cottage, 3A Smallhythe Road, Tenterden TN30 7LH* T: (01634) 560009 M: 07947-010382

WILLIAMS, Robert Jeffrey Hopkin. b 62. Univ of Wales (Abth) BA 84 ALAM. Chich Th Coll BTh 90. **d** 90 **p** 91. C Eastbourne St Mary *Chich* 90–94; R Upper St Leonards St Jo 94–02; V Twickenham St Mary *Lon* from 02. *37 Arragon Road, Twickenham TW1 3NG* T: (020) 8892 2318

WILLIAMS, The Ven Robert John. b 51. Cartrefle Coll of Educn CertEd 72 Univ of Wales (Ban) BEd 73 MA 92. St Mich Coll Llan BD 76. **d** 76 **p** 77. C Swansea St Mary and H Trin *S & B* 76–78; Chapl Univ of Wales (Swansea) 78–84; Children's Adv 81–88; Asst Dir of Educn 81–88; Bp's Chapl for Th Educn 83–88; R Reynoldston w Penrice and Llangennith 84–88; R Denbigh and Nantglyn *St As* 88–94; V Sketty *S & B* 94–99; Dir of Ords 94–99; P-in-c Port Eynon w Rhosili and Llanddewi and Knelston 99–03; Can Brecon Cathl 95–00; Adn Gower 00–16; rtd 16; PtO *S & B* from 16; *Llan* from 18. *11 Raleigh Close, Sketty, Swansea SA2 8LE* T: (01792) 555501

WILLIAMS, Roger. *See* WILLIAMS, David Roger

WILLIAMS, Roger. *See* WILLIAMS, John Roger

WILLIAMS, Roger Anthony. b 54. Univ of Wales (Lamp) BA 76. Bp Burgess Hall Lamp 72 Qu Coll Birm 76. **d** 78 **p** 79. C Llanelli *St D* 78–82; V Monkton 82–86; Chapl to the Deaf *B & W* 86–90; Chapl amongst Deaf People *Ox* 90–16; rtd 16; PtO *Ox* from 16. *Denchworth House, Denchworth, Wantage OX12 0DX* T: (01235) 868248 E: roger@rawapt.org.uk

WILLIAMS, Roger Stewart. b 54. Qu Coll Cam BA 75 MA 79. Wycliffe Hall Ox BA 78 MA 82. **d** 79 **p** 80. C Hamstead St Paul *Birm* 79–82; C Barking St Marg w St Patr *Chelmsf* 82–85; V Mildmay Grove St Jude and St Paul *Lon* 85–95; P-in-c Charles w Plymouth St Matthias *Ex* 95–09; Chapl Plymouth Univ 95–09; TR Bloxwich *Lich* 09–19; rtd 19; PtO *Ex* from 20. *Lancarffe, Devon Tors Road, Yelverton PL20 6DN* T: (01822) 458040 E: williams.roger@gmail.com

WILLIAMS, Ronald Ernest Nathan. b 66. Univ of Sierra Leone BSc 95. St Jo Coll Nottm MTh 05. **d** 05 **p** 06. C Cowplain *Portsm* 05–09; V Rusthall *Roch* from 09. *The Vicarage, Bretland Road, Rusthall, Tunbridge Wells TN4 8PB* T: (01892) 521357 M: 07796-655225 E: ronnierenw@hotmail.com

WILLIAMS, Ronald Hywel. b 35. St D Coll Lamp BA 62. **d** 63 **p** 64. C Machynlleth and Llanwrin *Ban* 63–66; C Llanaber w Caerdeon 66–69; C Hawarden *St As* 69–73; R Llansantffraid Glan Conwy and Eglwysbach 73–77; V Rhosllannerchrugog 77–88; R Cilcain and Nannerch and Rhydymwyn 88–92; V Llanbadarn Fawr w Capel Bangor and Goginan *St D* 92–95; V Llanbadarn Fawr 95–00; RD Afon 94–00; rtd 00; PtO *St D* from 05. *15 Maes y Garn, Bow Street SY24 5DS* T: (01970) 820247

WILLIAMS, Rosamund Joy. b 80. Sheff Univ BA 03 St Martin's Coll Lanc PGCE 04 Middx Univ MA 17. St Mellitus Coll 19. **d** 21. C Cov St Mark Swanswell CD from 21. *23 Mary Herbert Street, Coventry CV3 5ER* M: 07921-771580 E: rosamundjoy@gmail.com

WILLIAMS (née TYDEMAN), Mrs Rosemary (Rose). b 47. Roehampton Inst TCert 69. SAOMC 97. **d** 00 **p** 01. NSM Walton H Trin *Ox* 00–03; NSM E and W Horndon w Lt Warley and Childerditch *Chelmsf* 03–12; rtd 12; PtO *Ox* from 12. *17 Wellington Avenue, Princes Risborough HP27 9HY* T: (01844) 274225 E: rosewilliamsgp@yahoo.co.uk

WILLIAMS, Canon Rowan Clare. b 67. K Coll Cam BA 90 MA 93 Jes Coll Cam BA 05 Clare Coll Cam PhD 14. Westcott Ho Cam 02. **d** 05 **p** 06. C Leic Resurr 05–08; Chapl Univ Hosps Leic NHS Trust 08–10; Chapl York Univ 10–18; Can Res and Prec *Pet* from 18. *Norman Hall, 15A Minster Precincts, Peterborough PE1 1XX* T: (01733) 355310 M: 07919-861912 E: canon.precentor@peterborough-cathedral.org.uk

WILLIAMS, Rowan Douglas. *See* WILLIAMS OF OYSTERMOUTH, Rowan Douglas

WILLIAMS, Mrs Sandra Elizabeth. b 60. STETS 06. **d** 09 **p** 10. C Wrockwardine Deanery *Lich* 09–13; C Appleshaw, Kimpton, Thruxton, Fyfield etc *Win* 13–17; P-in-c 17–19; C W Purbeck *Sarum* from 19. *The Vicarage, West Street, Bere Regis, Wareham BH20 7HQ* T: (01929) 792235 E: revsandrawestpurbeck@outlook.com

WILLIAMS (née CROSLAND), Mrs Sarah Rosita. b 50. St Mary's Coll Chelt CertEd 71 BEd 72. EAMTC 01. **d** 03 **p** 04. C Warmley, Syston and Bitton *Bris* 03–06; Asst Chapl Tervuren *Eur* 06–09; P-in-c Lydd *Cant* 09–13; R Brookland, Fairfield, Brenzett w Snargate etc 13–16; rtd 16; PtO *Cant* from 17. *Porfa Las, 15 Wheler Court, Faversham ME13 7NR* M: 07778-450357 E: revsarahwilliams@porfalas.plus.com

WILLIAMS, Canon Shamus Frank Charles. b 57. St Cath Coll Cam BA 79 MA 83. Ripon Coll Cuddesdon 81. **d** 84 **p** 85. C Swanage and Studland *Sarum* 84–87; C St Alb St Pet 87–90; TV Saffron Walden w Wendens Ambo and Littlebury *Chelmsf* 90–95; R Shingay Gp *Ely* from 95; RD Shingay 97–13; Hon Can Ely Cathl from 05. *18 High Street, Guilden Morden, Royston SG8 0JP* T: (01763) 853067 E: shamuswilliams@waitrose.com

WILLIAMS, Mrs Sheena Jane. b 72. Aber Univ LLB 95 Win Univ MA 11. STETS 07. **d** 10 **p** 11. C Swaythling *Win* 10–14; C Chandler's Ford 14–17; P-in-c N Stoneham and Bassett 17–20; R from 20; AD Southampton from 20. *The Rectory, 62 Glen Eyre Road, Southampton SO16 3NL* T: (023) 8076 8123 M: 07787-155321 E: rector@nsab.org.uk

WILLIAMS, Stephen Clark. b 47. Univ of Wales (Cardiff) BSc(Econ) 69 Warw Univ MSc 70. Wycliffe Hall Ox 91. **d** 93 **p** 94. C High Wycombe *Ox* 93–96; C Walton H Trin 96–97; TV 97–03; Acting TR 01–03; P-in-c E and W Horndon w Lt Warley and Childerditch *Chelmsf* 03–12; Ind Chapl 05–12; rtd 12; PtO *Ox* from 12. *17 Wellington Avenue, Princes Risborough HP27 9HY* T: (01844) 274225 E: stevecgs2003@yahoo.co.uk

WILLIAMS, Stephen Grant. b 51. K Coll Lon BD 73 AKC 73. **d** 75 **p** 76. C Paddington Ch Ch *Lon* 75–78; C Paddington St Jas 78–80; Chapl LSE 80–91; Chapl (Sen) Lon Univs 91–15; rtd 15. *4 Stanton Prior, 71 Darley Road, Eastbourne BN20 7UH* E: stephenwilliams6@gmail.com

WILLIAMS, Stephen James. b 52. Lon Univ BSc 73. Ridley Hall Cam 73. **d** 78 **p** 79. C Waltham Abbey *Chelmsf* 78–82; C Bedford St Paul *St Alb* 82–86; P-in-c Chalgrave 86–88; V Harlington 86–21; Chapl Luton Sixth Form Coll 08–09; Chapl Luton and Dunstable Univ Hosp NHS Foundn Trust 04–11; rtd 21. *Address temp unknown* M: 07530-783196

WILLIAMS, Canon Stephen Stuart. b 60. Magd Coll Ox BA 82 Dur Univ BA 88. Cranmer Hall Dur 86. **d** 89 **p** 90. C W Derby Gd Shep *Liv* 89–93; Relig Affairs Producer BBC Radio Merseyside 92–00; TV Liv Our Lady and St Nic w St Anne 93–01; P-in-c Prestwich St Gabr *Man* 01–19; V from 19; C Prestwich St Mary from 10; C Prestwich St Marg from 10; Bp's Dom Chapl 01–05; Interfaith Adv from 05; Hon Can Man Cathl from 10. *St Gabriel's Vicarage, 8 Bishops Road, Prestwich, Manchester M25 0HT* T: 0161-773 8839 M: 07757-411377 E: saintgabriel@talktalk.net

WILLIAMS, Susan. b 50. Swansea Coll of Educn CertEd 72. Ban Ord Course 94. **d** 97 **p** 98. NSM Criccieth w Treflys *Ban* 97–00; P-in-c 00–01; P-in-c Criccieth and Treflys w Llanystumdwy etc 01–02; R 02–10; rtd 11; PtO *Ban* from 11. *Taleifion, High Street, Criccieth LL52 0RN* T: (01766) 523222 or (01248) 354999 F: 523183

WILLIAMS, Ms Susan Jean. b 54. Ches Coll of HE MTh 00 Lanc Univ MA 02 PhD 09. NOC 95. **d** 98 **p** 99. C Prescot *Liv* 98–01; PtO *Blackb* 01–02; C Scotforth 02–05; P-in-c Chipping and Whitewell 05–09; Warden of Readers and Past Assts 09–13; Hon C Balderstone, Mellor and Samlesbury 11–13; V 13–16; Hon C Salesbury and Langho Billington 11–13; Vice-Prin LCTP 05–13; rtd 16; Hon C E Lonsdale *Blackb* 16–20; PtO from 20. *The New Vicarage, Church Lane, Tunstall, Carnforth LA6 2RQ* E: williams.ammasue@gmail.com

WILLIAMS, Mrs Susan Merrilyn Marsh. b 62. Univ of Wales (Ban) BTh 05. Ban Ord Course 00. **d** 03 **p** 04. C Botwnnog w Bryncroes w Llangwnnadl w Penllech *Ban* 03–08; P-in-c Nefyn w Tudweiliog w Llandudwen w Edern 08–11; V 11–12; TV Sidmouth, Woolbrook, Salcombe Regis, Sidbury etc *Ex* 12–18; R Chipstead *S'wark* from 18; Faith in the Countryside Officer from 21. *The Rectory, Starrock Lane, Chipstead, Coulsdon CR5 3QD* T: (01737) 552160 E: rector@smchipstead.org

WILLIAMS, Suzan. b 71. WEMTC. **d** 11 **p** 12. C Church Stretton *Heref* 11–16; TV Wrockwardine Deanery *Lich* 16–20; R Whittington and W Felton w Haughton from 20. *The Rectory, Castle Street, Whittington, Oswestry SY11 4DF* T: (01691) 238658 M: 07921-825532 E: revwilliams1991@icloud.com

WILLIAMS, Terence. b 36. Univ of Wales (Abth) BSc 57 Univ of Wales (Cardiff) MA 67 Aston Univ PhD 71. Glouc Sch of Min 78. **d** 81 **p** 81. NSM Deerhurst, Apperley w Forthampton and Chaceley *Glouc* 81–87; NSM Tarrington w Stoke Edith, Aylton, Pixley etc *Heref* 87–88; P-in-c Upper and Lower Slaughter w Eyford and Naunton *Glouc* 88–91; P-in-c Redmarley D'Abitot, Bromesberrow w Pauntley etc 91–95; R 95–99; RD Forest N 95–99; rtd 99; PtO *Glouc* 99–02; P-in-c Hasfield w Tirley and Ashleworth 02–05. *4 University Farm, Moreton-in-Marsh GL56 0DN*

WILLIAMS, Terence James. b 76. St Jo Coll Nottm BA 05. Cranmer Hall Dur 02. **d** 05 **p** 06. C Bolsover *Derby* 05–09; P-in-c Codnor 09–13; P-in-c Horsley and Denby and C Morley w Smalley and Horsley Woodhouse 11–13; P-in-c Loscoe 12–13; RD Heanor 11–13; PtO 13–16; Dioc

President Children's Soc from 14; C Burton All SS w Ch Ch *Lich* 15–16; C Branston 15–16; R Ashley and Mucklestone and Broughton and Croxton 16–19; PtO from 20. *Address withheld by request* E: wterry774@aol.com

WILLIAMS, Timothy John. b 54. BEd 83. Trin Coll Carmarthen. **d** 89 **p** 90. NSM Llansamlet *S & B* 89–97; P-in-c Bryngwyn and Newchurch and Llanbedr etc 97–01; V Aberedw w Llandeilo Graban and Llanbadarn etc 01–10; V Brecon St David w Llanspyddid and Llanilltyd 10–15; P-in-c Penderyn Mellte from 15; P-in-c Cefn Coed w Vaynor from 15. *The Rectory, 6 Lamb Road, Penderyn, Aberdare CF44 9JU* T: (01685) 811864 E: timothy.williams462@btinternet.com

WILLIAMS, Timothy John. b 64. Ch Ch Coll Cant BA 86. St Mich Coll Llan BD 89. **d** 89 **p** 90. C Killay *S & B* 89–91; C Llwynderw 91–94; Chapl Swansea NHS Trust 91–93; V Knighton and Norton *S & B* 94–00; Chapl Knighton Hosp 94–00; P-in-c Whitton and Pilleth and Cascob etc *S & B* 99–00; V Killay 00–15; Dioc Communications Officer 10–15; TR Kidderminster St Jo and H Innocents *Worc* from 15; RD Kidderminster 19–21; AD Kidderminster and Stourport from 21. *St John's Vicarage, 33 Lea Bank Avenue, Kidderminster DY11 6PA* T: (01562) 631856 M: 07901-502675 E: teamrector.kwtm@gmail.com

WILLIAMS, Mrs Tracey Lyn. b 62. Bris Univ BSc 83 MSc 85 PhD 88. Ripon Coll Cuddesdon 08. **d** 11 **p** 12. NSM Sunninghill and S Ascot *Ox* 11–18; PtO 18–21. *14 Devon Chase, Warfield, Bracknell RG42 3JN* M: 07979-897469 E: revdtraceywilliams@gmail.com

WILLIAMS, Tracy Grant. b 61. Sheff Univ BMus 84. ERMC 17. **d** 19 **p** 20. C Nor Heartsease St Fran from 19; C Thorpe St Matt 19–20. *31 Plumstead Road East, Norwich NR7 9NA* M: 07834-845623 E: thetracyisland@gmail.com

✠**WILLIAMS, The Rt Revd Trevor Russell.** b 48. TCD BA 71. St Jo Coll Nottm BA 73. **d** 74 **p** 75 **c** 08. C Maidenhead St Andr and St Mary *Ox* 74–77; Asst Chapl QUB 78–80; Relig Broadcasting Producer BBC 81–88; I Newcastle *D & D* 88–93; Ldr Corrymeela Community 93–03; I Belfast H Trin and St Silas *Conn* 03–08; Preb Rathmichael St Patr Cathl Dublin 02–08; Bp L & K 08–14; rtd 14. *50 Murlough View, Dundrum, Newcastle BT33 0WE* T: (028) 4375 1838 E: bishoptrevor.williams@gmail.com

WILLIAMS, Victoria Louise. See MORGAN, Victoria Louise

WILLIAMS, Mrs Virginia Grace. b 66. Man Univ BN 88 Brunel Univ MSc 01 RGN 88. ERMC 17. **d** 19 **p** 20. C Sancroft *St E* from 19. *4 Samuel Vince Road, Fressingfield, Eye IP21 5SP* M: 07572-872512 E: gini@godsearth.co.uk

WILLIAMS, Walter Haydn. b 31. Univ of Wales (Lamp) BA 53 Selw Coll Cam BA 55 MA 60. St Mich Coll Llan 55. **d** 56 **p** 57. C Denbigh *St As* 56–58; V Choral St As Cathl 58–61; C St As 58–61; R Llanfyllin 61–68; V Northop 68–73; V Mold 73–86; RD 79–86; Can St As Cathl 77–82; Prec 81–82; Preb and Chan 82–86; R Overton and Erbistock and Penley *St As* 86–94; Chmn Ch of Wales Liturg Cttee 86–94; rtd 94; PtO *St As* 09–14. *2 Park Lane, Craig y Don, Llandudno LL30 1PQ* T: (01492) 877294

WILLIAMS, Miss Wendy Irene. b 35. Univ of Wales (Ban) BA 57 MA 73 Man Univ BD 60. **d** 17 **p** 17. NSM Burscough Bridge *Liv* from 17; PtO *Blackb* from 17. *17 Middlecot Close, Orrell, Wigan WN5 8SQ* T: (01695) 623269 E: hughesedith@aol.com

WILLIAMS-HUNTER, Ian Roy. b 44. Trin Coll Bris 71. **d** 73 **p** 74. C Redhill H Trin *S'wark* 73–75; C Deane *Man* 76–80; R Hartshorne *Derby* 80–02; P-in-c Bretby w Newton Solney 01–02; R Hartshorne and Bretby 02–11; rtd 11; PtO *Derby* 11–18. *85 Hall Street, Church Gresley, Swadlincote DE11 9QT* T: (01283) 217866 or 224602

✠**WILLIAMS OF OYSTERMOUTH, The Rt Revd and Rt Hon Lord (Rowan Douglas).** b 50. PC 02. Ch Coll Cam BA 71 MA 75 Wadh Coll Ox DPhil 75 DD 89 Erlangen Hon DrTheol 99 FBA 90 Hon FGCM 00. Coll of Resurr Mirfield 75. **d** 77 **p** 78 **c** 92. Tutor Westcott Ho Cam 77–80; Hon C Chesterton St Geo *Ely* 80–83; Lect Div Cam Univ 80–86; Dean Clare Coll Cam 84–86; Can Th Leic Cathl 81–92; Lady Marg Prof Div Ox Univ 86–92; Can Res Ch Ch *Ox* 86–92; Bp Mon 92–02; Abp Wales 99–02; Abp Cant 02–12; Master Magd Coll Cam 13–20; Hon Asst Bp Ely 13–20; Hon Can Ely Cathl 14–20; rtd 20. *Address withheld by request* E: rw488@cam.ac.uk

WILLIAMS, Alister. See WILLIAMSON, Ivan Alister

WILLIAMSON, Andrew John. b 39. MRPharmS 62. St Alb Minl Tr Scheme 82. **d** 85 **p** 86. NSM Oxhey All SS *St Alb* 85–88; NSM Bricket Wood 88–97; NSM Campbeltown *Arg* 97–08; LtO 08–13; PtO *Win* from 13. *6 Julius Close, Chandlers Ford SO53 2AB* M: 07970-708191 E: andrew.ajgsw@gmail.com

WILLIAMSON, David Barry. b 56. St Jo Coll Nottm 80. **d** 83 **p** 84. C N Mymms *St Alb* 83–86; C Burley *Ripon* 86–92;

Project Worker CECS 92–96; Youth and Children's Adv *B & W* 96–04; Dir Time For God 04–11; P-in-c Shepton Mallet w Doulting *B & W* 11–14; PtO *Leeds* from 15; Chapl St Leon Hospice York 15–20. *12 Spencers Way, Harrogate HG1 3DN*

WILLIAMSON, Desmond Carl. b 63. QUB BSc 84 Westmr Coll Ox MTh 03. Trin Coll Bris 03. **d** 05 **p** 06. C Portishead *B & W* 05–10; V Tattenham Corner *Guildf* from 10; AD Epsom 15–20. *St Mark's Vicarage, St Mark's Road, Epsom KT18 5RD* T: (01737) 353011 E: minister@stmarkschurch.me.uk

WILLIAMSON, Gary. b 50. Surrey Univ BA 72 MA 92 MITI 01 MCIL 07. **d** 14 **p** 15. OLM Pirbright *Guildf* 14–18; PtO from 18. *Round Meadow, Aldershot Road, Pirbright, Woking GU24 0DQ* T: (01483) 236909 M: 07780-872897 E: revdgarywilliamson@yahoo.co.uk

WILLIAMSON, Ivan Alister. b 63. TCD BTh 90. CITC 87. **d** 90 **p** 91. C Lisburn St Paul *Conn* 90–95; C Roxbourne St Andr *Lon* 95–99; Lect QUB from 95; Bp's C Ematris w Rockcorry, Aghabog and Aughnamullan *Clogh* 99–01; I Errigle Keerogue w Ballygawley and Killeshil *Arm* 05–10. *Address temp unknown* M: 07502-185006 E: revdalisterwilliamson@yahoo.co.uk

WILLIAMSON, Mrs Jennifer Irene. b 44. Glas Univ MA 66 Sunderland Poly Dip Teaching 79. NEOC 89. **d** 92 **p** 94. NSM Easby w Brompton on Swale and Bolton on Swale *Ripon* 92–95; P-in-c Gilling and Kirkby Ravensworth 95–05; rtd 05; PtO *Leeds* from 17. *65 Whitefields Drive, Richmond DL10 7DL* T: (01748) 824365

WILLIAMSON, Kathleen Lindsay. b 50. Leeds Univ Medical Sch MB, ChB 74 Liv Univ BSc 87. NOC 00. **d** 03 **p** 04. NSM Stretton and Appleton Thorn *Ches* 03–06; NSM Frodsham 06–13; PtO from 13. *37 Waterside Drive, Frodsham WA6 7NF* T: 07899-664068 E: kath@kathwilliamson.org.uk

WILLIAMSON, Mrs Mary Christine. b 46. Bulmershe Coll of HE BEd 79. SWMTC 05. **d** 09 **p** 10. NSM Launceston *Truro* 09–16; rtd 16; NSM Abingdon *Ox* 16–19; PtO *Truro* from 19. *73 St John's Road, Launceston PL15 7DE* T: (01566) 779879

WILLIAMSON, Canon Michael John. b 39. ALCD 63. **d** 64 **p** 65. C Pennington *Man* 64–67; C Higher Openshaw 67–69; P-in-c Man St Jerome w Ardwick St Silas 69–72; C-in-c Holts CD 72–77; R Droylsden St Mary 77–04; Hon Can Man Cathl 97–04; rtd 04; PtO *Man* from 04. *49 Ennerdale Road, Astley, Tyldesley, Manchester M29 7AR* T: (01942) 870274

WILLIAMSON, Olwen Joan. b 43. **d** 03 **p** 04. OLM Mortlake w E Sheen *S'wark* 03–13; PtO from 13. *25 Christchurch Road, London SW14 7AB* T/F: (020) 8876 7183 E: olwenontour@hotmail.com

WILLIAMSON, Paul Stewart. b 48. K Coll Lon BD 71 AKC 71. **d** 72 **p** 73. C Deptford St Paul *S'wark* 72–75; Hon C Kennington St Jo 76–77; C Hoxton H Trin w St Mary *Lon* 78–83; C St Marylebone All SS 83–84; C Willesden St Mary 84–85; PtO 86–89; C Hanworth St Geo 89–92; P-in-c 92–19; rtd 19. *The Rectory, 7 Blakewood Close, Feltham TW13 7NL* T: (020) 8844 0457 E: 1stewart1@live.co.uk

WILLIAMSON, Philip Howard. b 59. Yorks Min Course. **d** 16 **p** 17. NSM Saddleworth *Man* from 16. *Thorn, Moorside Road, Slaithwaite, Huddersfield HD7 5UU* M: 07736-416126

WILLIAMSON, Ralph James. b 62. LSE BSc(Econ) 84 Ox Univ MSt 14. Ripon Coll Cuddesdon BA 89 MA 97 MTh 05. **d** 90 **p** 91. C Southgate St Andr *Lon* 90–93; TV Ross w Brampton Abbotts, Bridstow, Peterstow etc *Heref* 93–97; Chapl Ch Ch Ox 97–15; V Pimlico St Pet w Westmr Ch Ch *Lon* 15–21; R Stonesfield w Combe Longa *Ox* from 21. *The Rectory, Brook Lane, Stonesfield, Witney OX29 8PR* T: (01993) 891872 E: rector@scbenefice.org

WILLIAMSON, Robert Harvey (Robin). b 45. **d** 02 **p** 03. OLM Maidstone St Luke *Cant* 02–15; rtd 15; PtO *Cant* from 16. *Holly Bank, Bower Mount Road, Maidstone ME16 8AU* T: (01622) 682959

WILLIAMSON, Robert John. b 55. K Coll Lon BA 77. Coll of Resurr Mirfield 78. **d** 79 **p** 80. C Kirkby *Liv* 79–82; C Warrington St Elphin 82–84; P-in-c Burneside *Carl* 84–90; V Walney Is 90–00; V Darlington St Cuth *Dur* 00–16; V The Thorntons and The Otteringtons *York* 16–21; Chapl N Yorks Police 16–18; rtd 21; PtO *York* from 21. *Address temp unknown* E: revrobertwilliamson@gmail.com

WILLIAMSON, Robin. *See* WILLIAMSON, Robert Harvey

WILLIAMSON, Roger Brian. b 38. Imp Coll Lon BSc 59 MIET 61. St Steph Ho Ox 01. **d** 02 **p** 03. NSM Harting w Elsted and Treyford cum Didling *Chich* 02–05; P-in-c Stedham w Iping 05–15; rtd 15; PtO *Chich* from 16. *Hawthorn Cottage, North Lane, South Harting, Petersfield GU31 5PY* M: 07767-266031 E: rogerwilliamson1@btinternet.com

WILLIAMSON, Mrs Sheilagh Catherine. b 54. Dur Inst of Educn CertEd 76 St Martin's Coll Lanc MA 00. CBDTI 97. **d** 00 **p** 01. C Darlington St Hilda and St Columba *Dur*

00–03; P-in-c 03–18; P-in-c Darlington St Jo 13–18; rtd 18; PtO *York* from 18. *4 Endican Lane, Thornton le Moor, Northallerton DL7 9FB* T: (01609) 773758 E: sheilaghwilliamson@msn.com

WILLIAMSON, Canon Thomas George. b 33. AKC 57. **d** 58 **p** 59. C Winshill *Derby* 58–61; C Hykeham *Linc* 61–64; V Brauncewell w Dunsby 64–78; R S w N Leasingham 64–78; RD Lafford 78–87; V Cranwell 78–80; R Leasingham 78–80; V Billinghay 80–87; V Gosberton 87–97; V Gosberton, Gosberton Clough and Quadring 97–98; Can and Preb Linc Cathl 94–98; rtd 98; PtO *Linc* 98–01. *10 Newton Way, Woolsthorpe, Grantham NG33 5NR* T: (01476) 861749 E: thomaswilliamson99@btinternet.com

WILLIE, Canon Andrew Robert. b 43. Bris Univ BA 65 Fitzw Coll Cam BA 73 MA 77. Ridley Hall Cam 71. **d** 74 **p** 75. Chapl St Woolos Cathl *Mon* 74–79; Chapl St Woolos Hosp Newport 75–79; V Newbridge *Mon* 79–85; V Mathern and Mounton w St Pierre 85–98; Post-Ord Tr Officer 85–98; V Newport St Mark 98–13; Warden of Readers 91–13; Dioc Tr Officer Permanent Local Diaconate 99–06; Can St Woolos Cathl *Mon* 02–13; rtd 13; PtO *Mon* from 14. *6 Cordell Close, Llanfoist, Abergavenny NP7 9FE* T: (01873) 852063 E: andrew.robert.willie@gmail.com

WILLINGHAM (formerly TIMINGS), Mrs Julie Elizabeth. b 54. **d** 10 **p** 11. C Sleaford *Linc* 10–14; V Elloe Stone 14–16; PtO from 17. *Address temp unknown* M: 07931-387186

WILLIS, Andrew Lyn. b 48. Univ of Wales (Lamp) BA 73. **d** 74 **p** 75. C Swansea St Mary w H Trin and St Mark *S & B* 74–81; V Glasbury and Llowes 81–83; Chapl RAF 83–03; Chapl Moray Hosps from 04; Lic Min Mor 99. *Deanshaugh Croft, Mulben, Keith AB55 6YJ* T: (01542) 860240 E: andylwillis@hotmail.co.uk

WILLIS, Anthony Charles Sabine. b 53. Ex Coll Ox MA 82. ERMC 05. **d** 07 **p** 08. NSM Hatfield Hyde *St Alb* 07–10; PtO *Newc* 08–10. *Leazes House, Alston CA9 3NH* T: (01434) 382682 E: acswillis@gmail.com

WILLIS, Anthony David. b 40. Sarum & Wells Th Coll 87. **d** 89 **p** 90. C Ivybridge w Harford *Ex* 89–92; C Catherington and Clanfield *Portsm* 92–94; R Ellesborough, The Kimbles and Stoke Mandeville *Ox* 94–08; rtd 09; C Aylesbury *Ox* 09–12; PtO from 12. *12 Fairford Leys Way, Aylesbury HP19 7FQ* T: (01296) 431934 E: revwillis@btinternet.com

WILLIS, Canon Anthony John. b 38. MBE 00. Univ of Wales (Lamp) BA 62. Qu Coll Birm. **d** 64 **p** 65. C Kidderminster St Jo *Worc* 64–68; C Dunstable *St Alb* 68–72; V Rubery *Birm* 72–80; R Salwarpe and Hindlip w Martin Hussingtree *Worc* 80–92; Chapl to Agric and Rural Life 85–03; Hon Can Worc Cathl 99–03; rtd 03; PtO *Worc* 04–08. *1 Snowberry Avenue, Home Meadow, Worcester WR4 0JA* T: (01905) 723509 E: johnjosewillis@aol.com

WILLIS, David Anthony. b 81. Ripon Coll Cuddesdon BA 10. **d** 10 **p** 11. C Ifield *Chich* 10–13; V Midhurst from 13; R Woolbeding from 13. *The Vicarage, June Lane, Midhurst GU29 9EW* E: revdavewillis@live.co.uk

WILLIS, Geoffrey Stephen Murrell. b 58. Sussex Univ BA 80. Wycliffe Hall Ox 83. **d** 86 **p** 87. C Ashtead *Guildf* 86–89; Chapl Lee Abbey 89–94; R Dunsfold *Guildf* 94–01; R Dunsfold and Hascombe 01–06; PtO from 06. *The Barn, Stephens Orchard, Headley Road, Grayshott, Hindhead GU26 6DL* M: 07467-542958 E: willisgeoffrey@mac.com

WILLIS, Guy Robin Fraser. b 86. Jes Coll Cam BA 08 MA 11. St Steph Ho Ox 12. **d** 15 **p** 16. C Holborn St Alb w Saffron Hill St Pet *Lon* 15–18; C Old St Pancras 18–21; C St Andr Holborn 18–21; V Kentish Town from 21. *The Church House, Ospringe Road, London NW5 2JB* E: grfwillis@gmail.com

WILLIS, Hugh. b 39. Bris Univ BDS 63 MGDSRCSEng 82 FRSH 87. **d** 98 **p** 99. OLM Charminster and Stinsford *Sarum* 98–08; PtO from 09. *Glebe Farmhouse, West Hill, Charminster, Dorchester DT2 9RD* T/F: (01305) 262940 E: tournai@aol.com

WILLIS, Mrs Jane Elizabeth. b 59. Wycliffe Hall Ox 06. **d** 08 **p** 09. C Shrewsbury H Cross *Lich* 08–11; TV S Molton w Nymet St George, High Bray etc *Ex* 11–14; P-in-c Hurstpierpoint *Chich* 14–16; R from 16. *The Rectory, 21 Cuckfield Road, Hurstpierpoint, Hassocks BN6 9RP* T: (01273) 832203

WILLIS, Mrs Jennifer Anne. b 41. Bp Otter Coll TCert 63. **d** 11 **p** 12. OLM Wingerworth *Derby* from 11; Dioc Clergy Widows' and Widowers' Officer 16–21. *9 Pond Lane, Wingerworth, Chesterfield S42 6TW* T: (01246) 554430 E: jenn.willis@uwclub.net

WILLIS, John. *See* WILLIS, Anthony John

WILLIS, Joyce Muriel. b 42. Open Univ BA 86 CQSW 73. EAMTC 86. **d** 89 **p** 94. NSM Hadleigh *St E* 89–02; NSM Hadleigh, Layham and Shelley 02–07; rtd 07; PtO *St E* from

07. *26 Ramsey Road, Hadleigh, Ipswich IP7 6AN* T: (01473) 823165 E: willisjm@lineone.net

WILLIS, Maureen. d 15 **p** 16. NSM Branksome St Clem *Sarum* from 15. *9 White Close, Poole BH15 3PQ*

WILLIS, Mrs Patricia. b 50. RGN 85 Brunel Univ BSc 95 Ox Brookes Univ PGDE 98. SAOMC 96. **d** 99 **p** 00. C Warmley, Syston and Bitton *Bris* 99–03; V Hanham 03–10; rtd 10; PtO *Ox* from 10. *30 Tallis Lane, Reading RG30 3EB* M: 07731-331154 E: revpatwillis@yahoo.com

WILLIS, Peter Ambrose Duncan. b 34. Kelham Th Coll 55 Lich Th Coll 58. **d** 59 **p** 60. C Sevenoaks St Jo *Roch* 59–63; Trinidad and Tobago 63–68; P-in-c Diptford *Ex* 68–69; R 69–85; P-in-c N Huish 68–69; R 69–85; R Diptford, N Huish, Harberton and Harbertonford 85–96; rtd 99. *Sun Cottage, Church Street, Modbury, Ivybridge PL21 0QR* T: (01548) 830541

WILLIS, The Very Revd Robert Andrew. b 47. Warw Univ BA 68. Cuddesdon Coll 70. **d** 72 **p** 73. C Shrewsbury St Chad *Lich* 72–75; V Choral Sarum Cathl 75–78; TR Tisbury 78–87; RD Chalke 82–87; V Sherborne w Castleton and Lillington 87–92; Can and Preb Sarum Cathl 88–92; RD Sherborne 91–92; Chapl Cranborne Chase Sch 78–92; Dean Heref 92–01; P-in-c Heref St Jo 92–01; Dean Cant from 01. *The Deanery, The Precincts, Canterbury CT1 2EP* T: (01227) 865264 *or* 762862 E: dean@canterbury-cathedral.org

WILLMONT, Anthony Vernon. b 35. Lich Th Coll 62. **d** 63 **p** 64. C Yardley St Edburgha *Birm* 63–65; C Smethwick H Trin w St Alb 65–68; V Ropley w W Tisted *Win* 68–77; V Ipswich St Aug *St E* 77–84; R King's Worthy *Win* 84–90; R Headbourne Worthy 84–90; R Lapworth *Birm* 90–99; R Baddesley Clinton 90–99; P-in-c Thornton in Lonsdale w Burton in Lonsdale *Bradf* 99–02; rtd 02; PtO *Bradf* 02–14; *Leeds* from 14. *9 Lowcroft, Butts Lane, Bentham, Lancaster LA2 2FD* T: (01524) 261655

WILLMOT, Mrs Julie. b 66. St Mellitus Coll BA 16. **d** 16 **p** 17. NSM Maldon All SS w St Pet *Chelmsf* 16–19; P-in-c Purleigh from 19; NSM Woodham Mortimer w Hazeleigh 16–19; P-in-c from 19; NSM Woodham Walter 16–19; P-in-c from 19. *8 Mayflower Drive, Maldon CM9 6XX* M: 07413-416226 E: revjuliewillmot@gmail.com

WILLMOTT, Robert Owen Noel. b 41. Lich Th Coll 65. **d** 68 **p** 69. C Perry Hill St Geo *S'wark* 68–71; C Denham *Ox* 71–76; P-in-c Tingewick w Water Stratford 76–77; P-in-c Radclive 76–77; R Tingewick w Water Stratford, Radclive etc 77–89; R Wingrave w Rowsham, Aston Abbotts and Cublington 89–06; P-in-c Wing w Grove 04–06; rtd 06; PtO *Ox* from 10. *34 Portfield Way, Buckingham MK18 1BB* T: (01280) 813057

✠**WILLMOTT, The Rt Revd Trevor. b** 50. St Pet Coll Ox BA 71 MA 74. Westcott Ho Cam. **d** 74 **p** 75 **c** 02. C Norton *St Alb* 74–77; Asst Chapl Oslo w Bergen, Trondheim and Stavanger *Eur* 78–79; Chapl Naples w Sorrento, Capri and Bari 79–83; R Ecton *Pet* 83–89; Warden Ecton Ho 83–89; Dioc Dir of Ords and Dir Post-Ord Tr *Pet* 86–97; Can Res, Prec and Sacr Pet Cathl 89–97; Adn Dur and Can Res Dur Cathl 97–02; Suff Bp Basingstoke *Win* 02–09; Suff Bp Dover *Cant* 10–19; Asst Bp Sarum from 14; rtd 19; Hon Asst Bp Ox 18–20; Hon Asst Bp Win from 19; PtO *B & W* from 19; Hon Asst Bp B & W from 20. *Rose Cottage, 3 Compton Street, Butleigh, Glastonbury BA6 8SE* T: (01458) 850228

WILLOUGHBY, Diane Joyce. b 56. Ex Univ BTh 12. SWMTC 07. **d** 10 **p** 11. C St Agnes and Mount Hawke w Mithian *Truro* from 10; C St Clement 12–15; V from 15; C Perranzabuloe and Crantock w Cubert from 17. *The Vicarage, Mount Hawke, Truro TR4 8DE* M: 07776-152759 E: illogan@hotmail.co.uk

WILLOUGHBY, Canon Paul Moore. b 60. BA. **d** 86 **p** 87. C Dublin St Patr Cathl Gp *D & G* 86–90; C Glenageary 90–92; I Dublin Booterstown 92–94; I Kilmocomogue *C, C & R* from 94; Can Cork and Ross Cathls from 00; Can St Patr Cathl Dublin from 14. *The Rectory, Durrus, Bantry, Co Cork, Republic of Ireland* T: (00353) (27) 61011 F: 61608

WILLOWS, Michael John. b 35. Sarum & Wells Th Coll 70. **d** 72 **p** 73. C Pershore w Wick *Worc* 72–75; Ind Chapl 75–88; P-in-c Astley 75–81; P-in-c Hallow 81–85; V 85–88; V Wollaston 88–05; rtd 05; PtO *Worc* from 05; *Lich* 12–17. *39 Hyperion Road, Stourton, Stourbridge DY7 6SD* T: (01384) 379794 E: rev.willows@gmail.com

WILLOX, Peter. b 63. Sunderland Poly BSc 85. Cranmer Hall Dur 86. **d** 89 **p** 90. C Bradley *Wakef* 89–92; C Utley *Bradf* 92–95; TV Bingley All SS 95–02; Chapl St Martin's Coll and C Ambleside w Brathay *Carl* 02–07; P-in-c Ben Rhydding *Bradf* 07–12; V 12–14; *Leeds* from 14. *St John's Vicarage, 28 Wheatley Avenue, Ben Rhydding, Ilkley LS29 8PT* T: (01943) 607363 *or* 601430 E: peterwillox@yahoo.co.uk

WILLS, Canon Andrea Jennifer. CITC. **d** 09 **p** 10. NSM Killala w Dunfeeny, Crossmolina, Kilmoremoy etc *T, K & A*

09–13; P-in-c Straid from 13; Can Tuam Cathl from 16; Can Killala Cathl from 16. *Robin Hill, Foxford, Co Mayo, Republic of Ireland* T: (00353) (94) 925 6403 M: 86-261 7572 E: andreajwills@gmail.com

WILLS, David. b 58. Oak Hill Th Coll 92. **d** 94 **p** 95. C Chadwell *Chelmsf* 94–99; P-in-c Darlaston St Lawr *Lich* 99–09; R 09–10; C Darlaston All SS 99–10; TR Bilston 10–21; TV Tettenhall Regis from 21. *St Paul's Vicarage, 1 Talaton Close, Wolverhampton WV9 5LS*

WILLS, Preb David Stuart Ralph. b 36. Chich Th Coll 64. **d** 66 **p** 67. C Bodmin *Truro* 66–70; V Bude Haven 70–78; TV Banbury *Ox* 78–83; Accredited Cllr from 81; V Launceston St Steph w St Thos *Truro* 83–88; P-in-c Kenwyn St Geo 88–93; V Truro St Geo and St Jo 93–96; Preb St Endellion 95–01; rtd 96; Chapl Cornwall Partnership NHS Foundn Trust 99–06; PtO *Truro* from 16. *21 Park Kres, St Agnes TR5 0AL* T: (01872) 555822 M: 07773-402109 E: 8392dsrw@gmail.com

WILLS, Edward Richard. b 64. STETS 07. **d** 10 **p** 11. NSM Wedmore w Theale and Blackford *B & W* 10–13; Chapl RN from 13. *Royal Naval Chaplaincy Service Headquarters, Tanner Building, HMS Excellent, Whale Island, Portsmouth PO2 8ER* T: 0300-157　7544　M: 07971-511564 E: eddie@beonna.co.uk

WILLS, Canon Ian Leslie. b 49. Wycliffe Hall Ox 77. **d** 80 **p** 81. C Henbury *Bris* 80; C Gtr Corsham 80–83; C Whitchurch 83–86; Chapl HM Rem Cen Pucklechurch 86–96; P-in-c Pucklechurch and Abson w Dyrham *Bris* 86–87; V Pucklechurch and Abson 87–99; V Soundwell 99–15; Hon Can Bris Cathl 06–15; rtd 15; PtO *Bris* from 16. *39 The Laurels, Mangotsfield, Bristol BS16 9BT* M: 07860-584852 E: ianwills@icloud.com

WILLSON, Andrew William. b 64. Oriel Coll Ox BA 85 Nottm Univ BTh 90 MA 98. Linc Th Coll 87. **d** 90 **p** 91. C Northampton St Mary *Pet* 90–93; C Cov E 93–96; PtO 96–01; Chapl Solihull Sixth Form Coll 98–01; Assoc Chapl Imp Coll *Lon* 01–03; Co-ord Chapl Imp Coll Lon from 03; Assoc Chapl R Coll of Art 01–03; Co-ord Chapl from 03; Chapl (Sen) Lon Univs from 15. *1 Porchester Gardens, London W2 3LA* T: (020) 7229 6359 E: a.willson@imperial.ac.uk

WILLSON, Mrs Patricia Rosemary. b 45. Trin Coll Bris 12. **d** 13 **p** 14. OLM Horfield St Greg *Bris* 13–16; rtd 16; PtO *Linc* from 16. *100 Pinchbeck Road, Spalding PE11 1QL* T: (01775) 422815 M: 07976-986694 E: pat.willson@yahoo.co.uk

WILLSON, Stephen Geoffrey. b 63. St Jo Coll Nottm BTh 90. **d** 90 **p** 91. C Newport St Andr *Mon* 90–92; C Risca 92–94; TV Cyncoed 94–96; Dioc Youth Chapl 94–99; Lay Past Asst 96–98; TV Cyncoed *Mon* 98–01; TR 01–11; R Welshpool, Castle Caereinion and Pool Quay *St As* 11–14; R Welshpool and Castle Caereinion 14–17; Miss Area Ldr Pool Miss Area from 18; AD Pool from 15. *The Vicarage, Church Street, Welshpool SY21 7DP* T: (01938) 553164 E: revswillson@btinternet.com

WILMAN, Arthur Garth. b 37. EAMTC 84. **d** 87 **p** 88. NSM Swavesey *Ely* 87–90; NSM Fen Drayton w Conington 87–90; NSM Hardwick 90–98; NSM Toft w Caldecote and Childerley 90–98; PtO 98–19. *37 Prentice Close, Longstanton, Cambridge CB24 3DY* T: (01954) 781400

WILMAN, Mrs Dorothy Ann Jane. b 38. Reading Univ BSc 60. Westcott Ho Cam 89. **d** 90 **p** 94. NSM Toft w Caldecote and Childerley *Ely* 90–93; Dean's Asst Trin Hall Cam 92–98; Asst Chapl Cam St Edw *Ely* 93–98; P-in-c Hemingford Abbots 98–02; P-in-c Houghton w Wyton 98–02; rtd 02; PtO *Ely* 02–19. *37 Prentice Close, Longstanton, Cambridge CB24 3DY* T: (01954)　781400 E: dorothywilman@btinternet.com

WILMAN, Leslie Alan. b 37. Selw Coll Cam BA 61 MA 65. Ridley Hall Cam 61. **d** 63 **p** 64. C Skipton H Trin *Bradf* 63–67; C Guiseley 67–69; V Morton St Luke 69–79; R Swanton Morley w Worthing *Nor* 79–82; P-in-c E Bilney w Beetley 79–82; P-in-c Hoe 80–82; R Swanton Morley w Beetley w E Bilney and Hoe 82–89 and 89–00; RD Brisley and Elmham 87–93; rtd 00; PtO *Nor* from 00. *7 Wallers Lane, Foulsham, Dereham NR20 5TN* T: (01328) 684109 E: lesliewilman@btinternet.com

WILMOT, David Mark Baty. b 60. Liv Univ BA 82. Sarum & Wells Th Coll 84. **d** 87 **p** 88. C Penrith w Newton Reigny and Plumpton Wall *Carl* 87–91; C St Alb St Pet 91–93; Chapl City Coll St Alb 92–93; V Milton *Lich* 93–01; RD Leek 96–01; V Windermere St Mary and Troutbeck *Carl* 01–19; P-in-c Grasmere from 19; P-in-c Rydal from 19; Chapl Rydal Hall from 19; RD Windermere 16–20. *St Mary's Vicarage, Ambleside Road, Windermere LA23 1BA* M: 07305-777113 E: rev.grasmereryydal@hotmail.com

WILMOT, Canon Jonathan Anthony de Burgh. b 48. St Jo Coll Nottm BTh 74. **d** 74 **p** 75. C Cambridge St Martin *Ely* 74–77; Chapl Chantilly *Eur* 77–82; Asst Chapl Paris

St Mich 80–82; Chapl Versailles 82–87; V Blackheath St Jo *S'wark* 88–95; V Reading Greyfriars *Ox* 95–14; Hon Can Ch Ch 08–14; rtd 14. *7 Birkett Way, Chalfont St Giles HP8 4BH* E: jon.wilmot@gmail.com

WILMOT, Stuart Leslie. b 42. Oak Hill Th Coll 64. **d** 68 **p** 69. C Spitalfields Ch Ch w All SS *Lon* 68–71; C Islington St Mary 71–74; P-in-c Brixton St Paul *S'wark* 75–81; R Mursley w Swanbourne and Lt Horwood *Ox* 81–91; P-in-c Bermondsey St Jas w Ch Ch *S'wark* 91–96; V 96–99; V Bermondsey St Jas w Ch Ch and St Crispin 99–02; P-in-c Bermondsey St Anne 91–93; P-in-c Bermondsey St Anne and St Aug 93–96; V 96–02; RD Bermondsey 96–00; rtd 02. *Amberlea, College, East Chinnock, Yeovil BA22 9DY*

WILSHERE, Daile Marie. b 70. STETS 06. **d** 09 **p** 10. C Preston w Sutton Poyntz, Littlemoor etc *Sarum* 09–13; TV Savernake 13–15; R Saltford w Corston and Newton St Loe *B & W* from 15. *12 Beech Road, Saltford, Bristol BS31 3BE* T: (01225) 872275 M: 07810-551447 E: dailewilshere@live.co.uk

WILSHIRE, Rosanne Elizabeth. b 74. Herts Univ BSc 97. Westcott Ho Cam 14. **d** 16 **p** 17. C Heath Town *Lich* 16–20; P-in-c Willenhall St Steph from 20; C Willenhall St Giles from 20. *St Stephen's Vicarage, 27 Wolverhampton Street, Willenhall WV13 2PS* M: 07910-686171 E: revrosht@gmail.com

✠**WILSON, The Rt Revd Alan Thomas Lawrence.** b 55. St Jo Coll Cam BA 77 MA 81 Ball Coll Ox DPhil 89. Wycliffe Hall Ox 77. **d** 79 **p** 80 **c** 03. Hon C Eynsham *Ox* 79–81; C 81–82; C Caversham St Pet and Mapledurham etc 82–89; V Caversham St Jo 89–92; R Sandhurst 92–03; RD Sonning 98–03; Hon Can Ch Ch 02–03; Area Bp Buckingham from 03. *Sheridan, Grimms Hill, Great Missenden HP16 9BG* T: (01494) 862173 F: 890508 M: 07525-655756 E: bishopbucks@oxford.anglican.org

WILSON, Canon Andrew Alan. b 47. Nottm Univ BA 68. St Steph Ho Ox 68. **d** 71 **p** 72. C Streatham St Paul *S'wark* 71–75; TV Catford (Southend) and Downham 75–80; V Malden St Jas 80–89; Chapl Croydon Community Mental Health Unit 89–94; Chapl Bethlem and Maudsley NHS Trust Lon 94–99; Chapl S Lon and Maudsley NHS Foundn Trust 99–11; Mental Health Chapl (Croydon) 00–11; Hon Can S'wark Cathl 05–11; rtd 11; PtO *S'wark* from 11. *7 Roman Rise, London SE19 1JG* T: (020) 8761 0969 E: arwiljohn@btinternet.com

WILSON, Andrew Marcus William. b 69. Ex Coll Ox BA 91 CCC Cam BA 93 K Coll Lon MA 99. Westcott Ho Cam 91. **d** 94 **p** 95. C Forest Gate Em w Upton Cross *Chelmsf* 94–99; TV Poplar *Lon* 99–09; R S Hackney St Jo w Ch Ch from 09; AD Hackney from 20. *The Rectory, 9 Church Crescent, London E9 7DH* T: (020) 8985 5145 E: andrewmwwilson@tiscali.co.uk

WILSON, Andrew Martin. b 60. Bris Univ BSc 82 Univ Coll Chich BA 04. Trin Coll Bris 97. **d** 99 **p** 00. C Broadwater *Chich* 99–07; V Portsdown *Portsm* from 07; C Crookhorn from 13; C Purbrook 13–19; P-in-c from 19; Jt AD Havant 14–19. *St John's Vicarage, 9 Marrels Wood Gardens, Purbrook, Waterlooville PO7 5RS* E: vicar@christchurchportsdown.org

WILSON, Antony Charles. b 69. Em Coll Cam MA 92 PGCE 92. Wycliffe Hall Ox 01. **d** 03 **p** 04. C Bath Walcot *B & W* 03–08; V Ipswich St Jo *St E* 08–12; CF 12–16; P-in-c Dedham *Chelmsf* 16–17; C Ardleigh and The Bromleys 16–17; V Dedham and Ardleigh 17–21; Chapl Mill Hill Sch Lon from 21. *The Bungalow, The Ridgeway, London NW7 1QX*

WILSON, Arthur Neville. *See* RUSDELL-WILSON, Arthur Neville

WILSON, Ashley Peter. b 58. Edin Univ BSc 81 BVM&S 83 St Jo Coll Dur BA 99 PhD 08. Cranmer Hall Dur 97. **d** 00 **p** 01. C Nunthorpe *York* 00–03; P-in-c Rounton w Welbury 03–08; Chapl St Chad's Coll *Dur* 08–17; Vice Prin from 16; PtO from 17. *St Chad's College, 18 North Bailey, Durham DH1 3RH* T: 0191-334 3362 *or* 334 3358 E: ashley.wilson@durham.ac.uk

WILSON, Mrs Barbara Anne. b 38. Brighton Poly BEd 79. **d** 04. NSM Southwick *Chich* 04–11; NSM Kingston Buci 11–15; NSM Old Shoreham and Kingston Buci from 15. *10 Phoenix Crescent, Southwick, Brighton BN42 4HR* T: (01273) 269771 M: 07814-655121

WILSON, Mrs Barbara Joyce. b 51. CBDTI 98. **d** 01 **p** 02. OLM Leyland St Jo *Blackb* 01–07; NSM from 07. *43 Hall Lane, Leyland PR25 3YD* T: (01772) 435340 E: barbara.j.wilson@btinternet.com

WILSON, The Ven Barry Frank. b 58. Man Metrop Univ BA 89 MPhil 94 MTh 99 Liv Univ DMin 01 Univ of Wales (Trin St Dav) MBA 20 Keele Univ PGCE 90. NOC 94. **d** 97 **p** 98. C Stone St Mich w Aston St Sav *Lich* 97–99; Chapl Abbots Bromley Sch 00–04; V Madeley and Betley *Lich* 04–13; R Nantwich *Ches* 13–17; Can Res Ches Cathl 17–18; Adn Montgomery *St As* from 18. *The Rectory,*

Four Crosses, Llanymynech SY22 6RW T: (01691) 839667 E: archdeacon.montgomery@cinw.org.uk

WILSON, Barry Richard. b 46. WMMTC 88. **d** 91 **p** 92. NSM Leek and Meerbrook *Lich* 91–93; C Styvechale *Cov* 93–98; V Chesterton *Lich* 98–12; rtd 12; PtO *Lich* 13–21. *9 Westwood Park Avenue, Leek ST13 8LR* T: (01538) 384090

WILSON, Bernard Martin. b 40. St Jo Coll Cam BA 63 MA 68 Lon Univ CertEd 67. Ripon Hall Ox 72. **d** 73 **p** 74. C Bilton *Cov* 73–77; Dioc Development Officer *Birm* 78–83; Soc Resp Officer *Derby* 83–90; V Darley Abbey 83–90; Chapl Derbyshire R Infirmary 88–90; Educn Unit Dir Traidcraft Exchange 91; V Mickleover St Jo *Derby* 92–98; Adv to Bd of Miss and Soc Resp *Leic* 98–03; rtd 03; PtO *Leic* 03–06; *Lich* 06–21; *Heref* 14–20. *2 Dargate Close, Shrewsbury SY3 9QE* T: (01743) 236300

WILSON, Mrs Caroline Susan. b 62. St Cath Coll Cam BA 83 MA 87 ALCM 79. Ox Min Course 06. **d** 09 **p** 10. NSM Caversham St Andr *Ox* 09–11; PtO 11–12; St Alb 12–14; NSM St Alb St Sav 14–15; NSM Whittlesford *Ely* 15–18; NSM Pampisford 15–18; V Rushmere *St E* 18–19; PtO *St Alb* from 20. *27 Norfolk Road, Buntingford SG9 9AN* T: (01763) 274804 E: revd.carolinew@gmail.com

WILSON, Mrs Catherine Ann. b 61. Southn Univ BA 83 Leic Univ PGCE 84. SEITE 11. **d** 14 **p** 15. C Biddenden and Smarden *Cant* 14–18; V Bromham w Oakley and Stagsden *St Alb* from 18. *The Vicarage, 47 Stagsden Road, Bromham, Bedford MK43 8PY* T: (01234) 825665 M: 07511-625107 E: vicar@bromhambenefice.org

WILSON, Cecil Henry. b 40. CITC 67. **d** 69 **p** 70. C Lurgan St Jo *D & D* 69–72; Min Can Dromore Cathl 72–75; Youth Sec CMS Ireland 75–80; N Regional Sec 80–87; Gen Sec 87–07; Can Belf Cathl 00–07; rtd 07. *42A Magheraknock Road, Ballynahinch BT24 8TJ* T: (028) 9756 4300 E: cecilwilson@gmail.com

WILSON, Christella Helen. *See* HARRISON, Christella Helen

WILSON (*née* BRAVERY), The Very Revd Christine Louise. b 58. STETS 94. **d** 97 **p** 98. C Henfield w Shermanbury and Woodmancote *Chich* 97–02; TV Hove 02–08; P-in-c Goring-by-Sea 08–10; Adn Chesterfield *Derby* 10–16; Dean Linc from 16. *The Deanery, 11 Minster Yard, Lincoln LN2 1PJ* T: (01522) 561630 E: dean@lincolncathedral.com

WILSON, Christopher Harry. b 59. Man Univ MusB 80 Ox Univ MTh 01. Wycliffe Hall Ox 88. **d** 91 **p** 92. C S Lafford *Linc* 91–95; P-in-c Billingborough 95–96; P-in-c Sempringham w Pointon and Birthorpe 95–96; P-in-c Horbling 95–96; P-in-c Billingborough Gp 95–96; V 96–03; P-in-c Leamington Priors All SS *Cov* 03–15; V from 15; P-in-c Leamington Spa H Trin 03–15; V from 15. *Clive House, Kenilworth Road, Leamington Spa CV32 5TL* T: (01926) 424016 E: holy.trinity@btopenworld.com

WILSON, Mrs Claire Frances. b 43. Hull Univ BA 65. SWMTC 85. **d** 87 **p** 94. Par Dn Belsize Park *Lon* 87–94; C 94–97; C Chingford SS Pet and Paul *Chelmsf* 97–09; rtd 09; PtO *Lon* from 10. *Ground Floor Flat, 26 Frognal Lane, London NW3 7DT* T: (020) 7794 3801 E: revclairewilson@btinternet.com

WILSON, Mrs Claire Nicola. b 70. Univ of Wales (Abth) LLB 99. St Mellitus Coll 18. **d** 20 **p** 21. C Bunbury and Tilstone Fearnall *Ches* from 20. *9 Glastonbury Drive, Middlewich CW10 9HR* T: (01606) 737292 M: 07800-871790 E: revclairewilson70@hotmail.com

WILSON, Colin Edward. b 63. Ripon Coll Cuddesdon BTh 94. **d** 94 **p** 95. C High Wycombe *Ox* 94–98; P-in-c Broadwell, Evenlode, Oddington and Adlestrop *Glouc* 98–00; P-in-c Westcote w Icomb and Bledington 98–00; R Broadwell, Evenlode, Oddington, Adlestrop etc 00–03; PtO *Eur* 03–05; P-in-c Finchingfield and Cornish Hall End etc *Chelmsf* 05–19; R Gawsworth w North Rode *Ches* from 19. *The Rectory, Church Lane, Gawsworth, Macclesfield SK11 9RJ*

WILSON, Preb David Gordon. b 40. Man Univ BSc 61 Clare Coll Cam BA 63 MA 68. Ridley Hall Cam 63. **d** 65 **p** 66. C Clapham Common St Barn *S'wark* 65–69; C Onslow Square St Paul *Lon* 69–73; V Leic H Apostles 73–84; V Spring Grove St Mary *Lon* 84–05; P-in-c Isleworth St Fran 00–05; Chapl Brunel Univ 90–02; AD Hounslow 97–02; Preb St Paul's Cathl 02–05; rtd 05; PtO *Portsm* from 05. *8 Clover Close, Locks Heath, Southampton SO31 6SQ* T/F: (01489) 571426 E: david.gwilson20@ntlworld.com

WILSON, David Mark. b 53. Lon Univ BSc 75. Wycliffe Hall Ox BA 77 MA 82. **d** 78 **p** 79. C Romford Gd Shep *Chelmsf* 78–81; C Cheadle Hulme St Andr *Ches* 81–85; V Huntington and Chapl Bp's Blue Coat C of E High Sch 85–95; V Birkenhead Ch Ch *Ches* 95–04; V Over St Jo 04–10; P-in-c W Coker w Hardington Mandeville, E Chinnock etc *B & W* 10–13; R Coker Ridge 13–15; rtd 15; PtO *Sarum*

15–20. *6 Helston Close, Portesham, Weymouth DT3 4EY*
E: Revdavidwilson@gmail.com

WILSON, Delyth Anne. d 15 **p** 16. NSM Cynwyl Gaeo w Llansawel and Talley etc *St D* 15–20; P-in-c 18–20; P-in-c Bro Gwendraeth *St D* from 20. *14 Ffordd Werdd, Gorslas, Llanelli SA14 7NE* E: delythawilson@gmail.com

WILSON, Derick. b 33. Oak Hill Th Coll 69. **d** 71 **p** 72. C Lurgan Ch the Redeemer *D & D* 71–74; C Willowfield 74–75; I 83–88; I Knocknamuckley 75–83; I Tullylish 88–98; rtd 98. *Hollycroft, 6 Thornhill Crescent, Tandragee, Craigavon BT62 2NZ* T: (028) 3884 9900

WILSON, Mrs Dorothy Jean. b 35. St Mary's Coll Dur BA 57 DipEd 58 Newc Poly LLB 78. NEOC 86. **d** 88 **p** 96. NSM Dur St Giles 88–03; PtO *Newc* 88–96; Chapl Northumbria Univ 94–96; Chapl N Dur Healthcare NHS Trust 97–02; NSM Pittington, Shadforth and Sherburn *Dur* 03–05; rtd 05; PtO *Dur* 05–20. *86 Gilesgate, Durham DH1 1HY* T: 0191-386 5016 E: dorothy9.wilson@gmail.com

WILSON, Edith Yvonne. b 43. St Martin's Coll Lanc MA 98. CBDTI 97. **d** 97 **p** 98. NSM Skerton St Chad *Blackb* 97–05; PtO from 05. *28 Roedean Avenue, Morecambe LA4 6SB* T: (01524) 417097

WILSON, Miss Elizabeth Ann. b 76. Leic Univ BA 98 Southn Univ MA 01. St Jo Coll Nottm MTh 14. **d** 14 **p** 15. C Evington *Leic* 14–17; TV Oadby 17–19; V Leic St Anne, St Paul w St Aug from 19; Chapl Leic Gr Sch from 17. *St Anne's Vicarage, 76 Letchworth Road, Leicester LE3 6FH* M: 07510-797399 E: lizwilson738@gmail.com

WILSON, Jeffery. b 51. Lanc Univ BA 72. Trin Coll Bris 83. **d** 85 **p** 86. C Linthorpe *York* 85–89; V Hull St Martin w Transfiguration 89–98; AD W Hull 96–98; V Linthorpe 98–18; RD Middlesbrough 05–11; Can and Preb York Minster 05–18; rtd 18; PtO *York* 18–20 and from 21; P-in-c Hull St Jo Newland 20–21. *10 Dominican Walk, Eastgate, Beverley HU17 0HF* T: (01482) 867639 E: erik.wilson51@icloud.com

WILSON, Frances Mary. b 61. Leeds Univ BA 98 MPhil 06. Westcott Ho Cam. **d** 00 **p** 01. C Rothwell *Ripon* 00–04; V Catterick 04–11; Initial Reader Tr Officer 04–11; P-in-c Balkwell *Newc* 11–15; AD Tynemouth 15–18; Bp's Dir of Ords *Lich* 18–19; TR Canton Cardiff *Llan* from 19. *12 Thompson Avenue, Cardiff CF5 1EY* T: (029) 2056 2022 E: franceswilson59@gmail.com

WILSON, Geoffrey. b 42. **d** 97 **p** 98. OLM Gunton St Pet *Nor* 97–08; NSM Lowestoft St Marg 08–12; rtd 12; PtO *Nor* from 13. *7 Monet Square, Gunton, Lowestoft NR32 4LZ* T: (01502) 564064 E: g.wilson570@btinternet.com

WILSON, Geoffrey. *See* WILSON, Samuel Geoffrey

WILSON, Geoffrey Samuel Alan. b 46. TCD BA 69 QUB DipEd 70 TCD MA 72. CITC BTh 93. **d** 96 **p** 97. C Glendermott *D & R* 96–99; I Camus-juxta-Mourne 99–12; rtd 12. *42 Ferndale Park, Portstewart BT55 7JB* T: (028) 7083 3542 *or* 3834 2969 M: 07803-554386

WILSON, George Thomas. b 47. CBDTI 97. **d** 00 **p** 01. NSM Barrow St Paul *Carl* 00–06; P-in-c Bootle, Corney, Whicham and Whitbeck 06–10; NSM Cartmel Peninsula 10–19; rtd 19. *10 Fairfield, Flookburgh, Grange-over-Sands LA11 7NB* T: (01539) 559215 E: george860@btinternet.com

WILSON, Graham Whitelaw. b 46. Leeds Univ CertEd 77 Birm Univ MPhil 00 Derby Univ DMin 03. EMMTC. **d** 95 **p** 96. NSM Burbage w Aston Flamville *Leic* 95–97; C 97–01; C Fenn Lanes Gp 01–04; PtO from 04. *10 The Courtyard, Higham Lane, Stoke Golding, Nuneaton CV13 6EX* T: (01455) 213598

WILSON, Mrs Heather Clarissa. b 49. Hull Univ BA 71 Leic Univ PGCE 72 Anglia Poly Univ MA 05. EAMTC 01. **d** 03 **p** 04. NSM Duston *Pet* 03–15; TV 06–15; rtd 15; PtO *Pet* from 15. *12 Ardens Grove, Rothersthorpe, Northampton NN7 3JJ* T: (01604) 830714 M: 07702-033727 E: revdheather@aol.com

WILSON, Canon Ian Andrew. b 57. Nottm Univ BTh 89. Linc Th Coll 86. **d** 89 **p** 90. C Whitton and Thurleston w Akenham *St E* 89–93; P-in-c Elmsett w Aldham 93–02; R Elmsett w Aldham, Hintlesham, Chattisham etc 02; Chapl Woodbridge Sch 03–16; P-in-c Nacton and Levington w Bucklesham etc *St E* 16–20; P-in-c Waldringfield w Hemley and Newbourne 16–20; R Orwell and Deben from 20; Hon Can St E Cathl from 12. *The Rectory, Nacton, Ipswich IP10 0HY* T: (01473) 659875 E: reviwilson@yahoo.co.uk *or* revcanian@yahoo.com

WILSON, Mrs Irene Margaret. b 49. Leeds Univ BA 83 ALCM 69. Yorks Min Course 09. **d** 11 **p** 12. NSM Kingston upon Hull H Trin *York* from 11. *10 Westgate, North Cave, Brough HU15 2NJ* T: (01430) 470719 M: 07711-996519 E: irene@hullminster.org

WILSON, Canon James. b 65. St Steph Ho Ox. **d** 01 **p** 02. C Whitchurch *Bris* 01–03; C Horfield St Greg 03–05;

P-in-c 05–19; V from 19; Hon Can Bris Cathl from 13. *St Gregory's Vicarage, Filton Road, Horfield, Bristol BS7 0PD* T: 0117-969 2839 E: revjameswilson@aol.com

WILSON, James Lewis. b 39. TCD BA 62 HDipEd 63 MA 65 BD 71. TCD Div Sch Div Test 74. **d** 74 **p** 75. C Enniskillen *Clogh* 74–76; C Belfast St Matt *Conn* 76–79; I Killeshandra w Killegar *K, E & A* 79–81; I Derrylane 79–81; I Loughgilly w Clare *Arm* 81–10; rtd 10. *2 Tramway Drive, Bushmills BT57 8YS* T: (028) 2073 1353

WILSON, James Robert. b 36. CITC. **d** 66 **p** 67. C Ballywillan *Conn* 67–73; I Drummaul 73–79; I Drummaul w Duneane and Ballyscullion 79–01; Preb Conn Cathl 96; Treas Conn Cathl 96–98; Chan Conn Cathl 98–01; rtd 01. *90 Killycowan Road, Glarryford, Ballymena BT44 9HJ* T: (028) 2568 5737

WILSON, Canon Jane Jennifer. b 43. Ch Ch Coll Cant TCert 65 Open Univ BA 84. Wycliffe Hall Ox 89. **d** 91 **p** 94. Par Dn Northwood Em *Lon* 91–94; C 94–98; TV Blythburgh w Reydon *St E* 98; TV Sole Bay 98–02; TR 02–07; RD Halesworth 01–07; Hon Can St E Cathl 05–07; P-in-c Offwell, Northleigh, Farway, Cotleigh etc *Ex* 07–11; rtd 11; Bp's Adv for Women in Min *Ex* 11–15; PtO from 15. *Hawthorns, 17 Ashleigh Park, Bampton, Tiverton EX16 9LF* T: (01398) 332135 E: janeoffwell@aol.com

WILSON, Mrs Janet Mary. b 44. Bedf Coll of Educn TCert 66 SRN 74. **d** 03 **p** 04. OLM S Croydon Em *S'wark* 03–10; PtO from 11. *Elmwood, 2 Weybourne Place, Sanderstead CR2 0RZ* T: (020) 8657 2195 E: revjanwilson@blueyonder.co.uk

WILSON, Jeffery. b 59. **d** 06 **p** 07. OLM Kirton in Lindsey w Manton *Linc* from 06; OLM Grayingham from 06. *34 Richdale Avenue, Kirton Lindsey, Gainsborough DN21 4BL* T: (01652) 648687

WILSON, John Anthony. b 34. Linc Th Coll. **d** 83 **p** 84. C Nunthorpe *York* 83–85; V Whorlton w Carlton and Faceby 85–94; V E Coatham 94–99; rtd 99; PtO *York* 00–08; *Ripon* 00–03; P-in-c Lower Swale 03–08; PtO *Glouc* 08–19; *York* 10–15. *29 Letch Hill Drive, Bourton-on-the-Water, Cheltenham GL54 2DQ* T: (01451) 820571 E: johnjeanwilson58@gmail.com

WILSON, John Frederick. b 33. Qu Coll Birm 58. **d** 61 **p** 62. C Jarrow St Paul *Dur* 61–65; C Monkwearmouth All SS 65–68; Br Honduras 68–71; V Scunthorpe Resurr *Linc* 71–90; Chapl Divine Healing Miss Crowhurst 90–91; V Terrington St Clement *Ely* 91–99; rtd 99; PtO *Ely* from 99. *7 Oakleigh Crescent, Godmanchester, Huntingdon PE29 2JJ* T: (01480) 392791 E: alex.wilson2@ntlworld.com

WILSON, Canon John Hamilton. b 29. St Chad's Coll Dur BA 53. Sarum Th Coll 53. **d** 55 **p** 56. C W End *Win* 55–59; C Fishponds St Mary *Bris* 59–64; V Bedminster St Fran 64–73; RD Bedminster 68–73; R Horfield H Trin 73–96; Hon Can Bris Cathl 77–96; rtd 96; PtO *Bris* from 96. *2 West Croft, Bristol BS9 4PQ* T/F: 0117-962 9204 E: johnhollow72@hotmail.com

WILSON, Canon Judith Anne. b 48. Keele Univ BA 71 Leic Univ PGCE 72. S Dios Minl Tr Scheme 92. **d** 95 **p** 96. NSM Slaugham *Chich* 95–96; Sub Chapl HM Pris Wandsworth 95–96; Chapl HM Pris and YOI Hollesley Bay 96–01; Chapl HM Pris Nor 01–09; Chapl Gt Hosp Nor 09–15; P-in-c Nor St Helen 09–14; V 14–15; Bp's Adv for Women's Min 04–10; Hon Asst Dioc Dir of Ords 09–15; Hon Can Nor Cathl 07–15; rtd 15; PtO *Nor* from 15. *13 Hunter's Close, Blofield, Norwich NR13 4LS* T: (01603) 211509 E: revjudithwilson@gmail.com

WILSON, Julian. b 63. Plymouth Univ BSc 92. Ox Min Course 15. **d** 17 **p** 18. C Cirencester *Glouc* from 17. *The Parish Centre, Gosditch Street, Cirencester GL7 2AG* T: (01285) 659317

WILSON, Julian John. b 64. Collingwood Coll Dur BSc 85 Liv Univ BTh. NOC 01. **d** 04 **p** 05. C Uttoxeter Area *Lich* 04–07; Chapl Denstone Coll Uttoxeter 07–09; R Baschurch and Weston Lullingfield w Hordley *Lich* 09–15; World Development Officer (Salop) 11–15; RD Ellesmere 13–15; P-in-c Corfu *Eur* from 15. *Holy Trinity Corfu, 21 L.Mavili Street, Corfu 49100* E: julesjwilson@gmail.com

WILSON, Karen Amanda Francesca. b 67. St Mellitus Coll 15. **d** 18 **p** 19. C Okeford *Sarum* 18–20; C Iwerne Valley 20–21; P-in-c Devoran *Truro* 21; P-in-c Feock from 21; P-in-c St Stythians w Perranarworthal and Gwennap from 21. *10 The Hayes, Bodmin Road, Truro TR1 1FY* E: revdkarenwilson@outlook.com

WILSON, Mrs Kathleen. b 47. Bucks Coll of Educn BSc 90 Ox Brookes Univ MBA 93 RGN 69. **d** 03 **p** 04. OLM Iver Ox 03–10; P-in-c Colbury *Win* 10–13; Chapl Oakhaven Hospice Trust 12–17; rtd 17; PtO *Win* from 18. *16 Waverley Road, Fordingbridge SP6 1EX* T: (01425) 540669 M: 07770-944054 E: kate.wilson501@gmail.com

WILSON, Ms Lauretta Joy. b 64. Bath Univ BSc 87 CertEd 87. SAOMC 02. **d** 05 **p** 06. C Boxmoor St Jo *St Alb* 05–08; TV Langelei 08–15; TR Kegworth, Hathern, Long Whatton, Diseworth etc *Leic* from 15; AD Akeley E from 21. *The Rectory, 24 Nottingham Road, Kegworth, Derby DE74 2FH* M: 07840-753202 E: ljwilson33@btinternet.com

WILSON, Louis. *See* WILSON, Philip Louis

WILSON, Mark Anthony John. b 56. TCD BA 80. CITC 75. **d** 80 **p** 81. C Dublin Rathfarnham *D & G* 80–84; Bp's C Dublin Finglas 83–84; I Celbridge w Straffan and Newcastle-Lyons 85–88; CF 88–93; I Dundalk w Heynestown *Arm* 93–03; Chapl Adelaide and Meath Hosp Dublin 04–16; Chapl Algarve *Eur* 16–17; P-in-c Walbury Beacon *Ox* 17–20; rtd 20. *57 Ermin Street, Stockcross, Newbury RG20 8LJ* E: markajwilson1@gmail.com

WILSON, Mark Ashley John. b 87. Cranmer Hall Dur 12. **d** 15 **p** 16. C Kidsgrove *Lich* from 15; P-in-c W Bromwich St Jas and St Paul 18–21; V from 21. *90 Hall Green Road, West Bromwich B71 3LB* T: 0121-532 2865 E: vicar@sjpchurch.co.uk

WILSON, Martin. *See* WILSON, Bernard Martin

WILSON, Canon Mavis Kirby. b 42. Ex Univ BA 64 Cam Univ CertEd 71. S Dios Minl Tr Scheme 82. **dss** 84 **d** 87 **p** 94. Chessington *Guildf* 84–85; Epsom St Martin 85–86; Epsom Common Ch Ch 86–87; C 87–96; Dioc Adv in Miss, Evang, and Par Development 90–02; R Frimley 02–13; Hon Can Guildf Cathl 94–13; rtd 13; Hon PV Guildf Cathl from 21. *48 Byrefield Road, Guildford GU2 9UB* T: (01483) 808097 E: maviswilson2@gmail.com

WILSON, Mervyn Raynold Alwyn. b 33. Qu Coll Cam BA 57 MA 61. Ripon Hall Ox 57. **d** 59 **p** 60. C Rubery *Birm* 59–62; C Kings Norton 62–63; V Hamstead St Bernard 63–69; R Bermondsey St Mary w St Olave, St Jo etc *S'wark* 69–78; R Bulwick, Blatherwycke w Harringworth and Laxton *Pet* 78–03; rtd 03; PtO *B & W* from 04. *The Red Post House, Fivehead, Taunton TA3 6PX* T: (01460) 281558 E: margaretwilson426@gmail.com

WILSON, The Very Revd Mervyn Robert. b 22. Bris Univ BA 51 Lon Univ BD 58. Tyndale Hall Bris 52. **d** 52 **p** 53. C Ballymacarrett St Patr *D & D* 52–56; C Donaghcloney 56–59; C Newtownards 59–61; I Ballyphilip w Ardquin 61–70; I Newry St Patr 70–92; Preb Dromore Cathl 83–85; Can Belf Cathl 85–89; Dean Dromore *D & D* 90–92; rtd 92. *31 Manor Drive, Lisburn BT28 1JH* T: (028) 9266 6361

WILSON, Canon Michael. b 44. Liv Univ BA 66 Fitzw Coll Cam BA 68 MA 73 De Montfort Univ MBA 94. Westcott Ho Cam. **d** 69 **p** 70. C Worksop Priory *S'well* 69–71; C Gt Malvern St Mary *Worc* 71–75; V Leic St Anne 75–85; TR Leic Ascension 85–88; Hon Can Leic Cathl 85–88; Can Res and Treas Leic Cathl 88–09; rtd 09; PtO *Pet* from 09; *Leic* from 10. *8 Wensum Close, Oakham LE15 6FU* T: (01572) 720853 E: mwilson@keme.co.uk

WILSON, Neil. b 61. Newc Univ BA 83. Ripon Coll Cuddesdon 85. **d** 88 **p** 89. C Wallsend St Luke *Newc* 88–91; C Monkseaton St Pet 91–93; V Earsdon and Backworth 93–04; P-in-c Newc St Jo 04–11; V Haltwhistle and Greenhead 11–18; Chapl Northumbria Healthcare NHS Foundn Trust from 15. *25 Albany Mews, Montague Avenue, Newcastle upon Tyne NE3 4JW* E: neilwilson50@btinternet.com

WILSON, Paul David. b 64. Cranmer Hall Dur 96. **d** 98 **p** 99. C Bramley and Ravenfield w Hooton Roberts etc *Sheff* 98–01; V Hatfield 01–13; AD Snaith and Hatfield 11–13; Hon Can Sheff Cathl 12–13; R Warrington St Elphin *Liv* 13–19; AD Warrington 17–19; R Epworth Gp *Linc* from 19. *The Rectory, 16 Belton Road, Epworth, Doncaster DN9 1JL* E: revpdwilson@aol.com

WILSON, Peter Sheppard. b 39. TCD BA 61. CITC Div Test 62. **d** 62 **p** 63. C Killowen *D & R* 62–68; C Portadown St Columba *Arm* 68–70; I Convoy w Monellan and Donaghmore *D & R* 70–78; V Castletown *S & M* 78–83; R Kilmacolm and Bridge of Weir *Glas* 83–85; I Camus-juxta-Bann *D & R* 85–92; Bp's Dom Chapl 90–92; I Maguiresbridge w Derrybrusk *Clogh* 92–05; Chapl to Bp Clogh 98–00; Can Clogh Cathl 03–05; rtd 05. *25 Grogey Road, Fivemiletown BT75 0SQ* T: (028) 8952 1883

WILSON, Peter Stuart. b 45. Yorks Min Course 08. **d** 09 **p** 10. NSM Cross Roads cum Lees *Bradf* 09–14; Leeds 14–15; NSM Haworth *Bradf* 09–14; Leeds 14–15; rtd 15; PtO *Leeds* 17–21. *3 Epworth Place, Oakworth, Keighley BD22 7ST* M: 07870-134272 E: revdpeterwilson@gmail.com

WILSON, Philip Louis. b 68. Bris Univ LLB 91. Oak Hill Th Coll BA 09. **d** 09 **p** 10. NSM Broadwell, Evenlode, Oddington, Adlestrop etc *Glouc* 09–12; R Denton w S Heighton and Tarring Neville *Chich* from 12. *The Rectory, 6 Heighton Road, Newhaven BN9 0RB* T: (01273) 514319 E: landjwilson@btinternet.com

WILSON, Rachel Claire. b 68. **d** 12 **p** 13. C Dartford St Edm *Roch* 12–16; P-in-c Southborough St Thos 16–19; V from 19; Bp's Adv for Disability from 18. *St Thomas's Vicarage, 30 Pennington Road, Tunbridge Wells TN4 0SL* T: (01892) 525869 E: reverendrachelwilson@gmail.com

WILSON, Mrs Rachel Elizabeth. b 56. Keswick Hall Coll BEd 79. NOC 00. **d** 03 **p** 04. NSM Slaidburn and Long Preston w Tosside *Bradf* 03–10; NSM Lower Wharfedale *Leeds* 10–16; Min in Deaf Community 09–16; NSM Pocklington Wold *York* 16–17; NSM Londesborough Wold 16–17; rtd 17; PtO *Leeds* from 17. *25 Meagill Rise, Otley LS21 2EQ*

WILSON, Richard Graham. b 67. Bris Univ BSc 91 DipSW 93. Trin Coll Bris BA 01. **d** 01 **p** 02. C Wandsworth St Mich *S'wark* 01–05; TR Bath Twerton-on-Avon *B & W* 05–18; RD Bath 15–18; V Reigate St Mary *S'wark* from 18. *76 Church Street, Reigate RH2 0SP* T: (01225) 421438 M: 07792-693062 E: richard@stmichaelstwerton.com

WILSON, Canon Robert Malcolm (Robin). b 35. St Andr Univ MA 59. ALCD 62. **d** 62 **p** 63. C Wallington *S'wark* 62–66; C Dur St Nic 66–70; V Colchester St Pet *Chelmsf* 70–01; RD Colchester 93–98; Hon Can Chelmsf Cathl 94–01; rtd 01; PtO *St E* from 01; *Chelmsf* 01–10. *Hawthorns, Melton Road, Melton, Woodbridge IP12 1NH* T: (01394) 383514

WILSON, Robert Stoker. b 39. Dur Univ BSc 62. Oak Hill Th Coll 62. **d** 64 **p** 65. C High Elswick St Paul *Newc* 64–68; C Kirkheaton 68–70; Youth Chapl *Liv* 70–73; P-in-c S Shields St Steph *Dur* 73–78; R 78–83; Youth Chapl 73–77; P-in-c S Shields St Aid 81–83; V Greenside 83–94; P-in-c Fatfield 94–98; P-in-c Coniscliffe 98–04; Dioc Adv for IT 98–04; rtd 04; PtO *Dur* from 13. *9 Augusta Close, Darlington DL1 3HT* T: (01325) 350324 M: 07808-911928 E: stoker@stokerwilson.me.uk

WILSON, Mrs Rosamund Cynthia. b 54. Univ of Wales MSc 94 MCSP 75. Trin Coll Bris. **d** 01 **p** 02. NSM Stoke Bishop *Bris* 01–05; C Frenchay and Winterbourne Down 05–06; NSM Abbots Leigh w Leigh Woods 07–13; PtO 13–19. *10 Druid Stoke Avenue, Bristol BS9 1DD* T: 0117-968 7554 E: roswilson9@gmail.com

WILSON, Ross Robert. b 70. Bath Univ BSc 94. Trin Coll Bris MA 12. **d** 12 **p** 13. C Willowfield *D & D* 12–15; I Orangefield w Braniel from 15. *The Rectory, 397A Castlereagh Road, Belfast BT5 6AB* T: (028) 9070 4493 M: 07564-232344 E: ross.wilson@sent.com *or* ross@stjohnsorangefield.org

WILSON, Mrs Sally Jayne. b 57. Ripon Coll of Educn BA 79 PGCE 80 Teesside Univ MA(Ed) 99. **d** 19. NSM Danby w Castleton and Commondale *York* 19; NSM The Moorlands from 19. *17 Dale End, Danby, Whitby YO21 2JF* T: (01287) 660190 E: danbychurch@gmail.com

WILSON, The Very Revd Samuel Geoffrey. b 62. CITC BTh 04. **d** 04 **p** 05. C Swanlinbar w Tomregan, Kinawley, Drumlane etc *K, E & A* 04–07; I Kildallon and Swanlinbar 07–09; I Lurgan Ch the Redeemer *D & D* 09–16; Dean Dromore from 16; I Dromore Cathl from 16. *The Deanery, 28 Church Street, Dromore BT25 1AA* T: (028) 9269 3968 M: 07803-554386 E: revgeoffwilson@gmail.com

WILSON, Simon Anthony. b 67. Portsm Poly BA 88. Cranmer Hall Dur 96. **d** 99 **p** 00. NSM Barnham Broom *Nor* 99–00; NSM Barnham Broom and Upper Yare 00–02; NSM Hellesdon 02–03; Public Preacher 03–20; Chapl Norfolk Constabulary (Cen Area) 05–13; Chapl Norfolk Fire Service 05–13; Co-ord Dioc Forum for Soc and Community Concerns 06–13; Co Ecum Officer 10–13; NSM Heacham from 20. *The Vicarage, Church Lane, Heacham, King's Lynn PE31 7HJ* T: (01485) 570697 E: revsimonwilson@btinternet.com

WILSON, Stephen Charles. b 51. Newc Univ BA 73 Cam Univ BA 78 MA 82. Westcott Ho Cam. **d** 79 **p** 80. C Fulham All SS *Lon* 79–82; C W Hampstead St Jas 82–85; P-in-c Alexandra Park St Sav 85–93; V Preston next Faversham, Goodnestone and Graveney *Cant* 93–14; V Preston-next-Faversham 14–15; Hon Min Can Cant Cathl 98–15; Asst Dir of Ords 07–10; rtd 15; PtO *S'wark* from 16. *42 Mount Ash Road, London SE26 6LY* T: (020) 8699 8386 E: revdscwilson@gmail.com

WILSON, Stephen Graham. b 70. Ridley Hall Cam 09. **d** 11 **p** 12. C Overton w Laverstoke and Freefolk *Win* 11–15; CF from 15. *c/o MOD Chaplains (Army)* T: (01264) 383430 F: 381824 M: 07968-272116 E: revstephenwilson@btinternet.com

WILSON, Canon Stephen John. b 45. Bradf Univ BTech 69. Trin Coll Bris 90. **d** 92 **p** 93. C Marple All SS *Ches* 92–96; P-in-c Moulton 96–01; Chapl Mid Cheshire Hosps Trust 96–99; V Hyde St Geo *Ches* 01–10; RD Mottram 03–08; Hon Can Ches Cathl 06–10; rtd 10; PtO *Ches* from 11. *18 Green Park, Weaverham, Northwich CW8 3EH* T: (01606) 851294 E: stephen.wilson888@btinternet.com

WILSON, Stoker. *See* WILSON, Robert Stoker

WILSON, Stuart Arnold. b 47. SWMTC 94. **d** 97 **p** 98. NSM Okehampton w Inwardleigh, Bratton Clovelly etc *Ex* 97–02; TV 02–09; rtd 10; PtO *Ex* from 10. *Red Spider Cottage, Bratton Clovelly, Okehampton EX20 4JD* T: (01837) 871248 E: s.wilson45@btinternet.com

WILSON, Susan Annette. b 60. Bath Univ BPharm 81 PhD 86 MRPharmS 82. Westcott Ho Cam 98. **d** 00 **p** 01. C Newc St Geo 00–03; Chapl Dame Allan's Schs Newc 02–03; TV Willington *Newc* 03–07; V Newc St Gabr 07–13; rtd 13; PtO *Newc* from 13. *2 Amberdale Avenue, Newcastle upon Tyne NE6 4UF*

WILSON, Miss Susan Elizabeth. b 52. Lady Spencer Chu Coll of Educn BEd 75. WEMTC 96. **d** 99 **p** 00. NSM Saltford w Corston and Newton St Loe *B & W* 99–06; P-in-c Heversham and Milnthorpe *Carl* 06–16; rtd 16. *Penholme House, Charney Road, Grange-over-Sands LA11 6BP* E: revsuewilson@tiscali.co.uk

WILSON, Mrs Sylvia. b 57. Teesside Univ BA 96 Newc Univ MA 99. **d** 08 **p** 09. OLM Preston-on-Tees and Longnewton *Dur* 08–14; P-in-c Egglescliffe 14–21; rtd 21. *7 Daltry Close, Yarm TS15 9XQ* T: (01642) 892254 M: 07886-852154 E: sylviawilson50@yahoo.co.uk

WILSON, Thomas D. b 58. Univ of W Ontario BA 93 MDiv 99 Drew Univ New Jersey DMin 10. **d** 01 **p** 01. R Blyth and Brussels Canada 01–07; Hon C Nice w Vence *Eur* 07–08; Lic to Offic Huron Canada 08–11; P-in-c Cambridge St Luke 11–12; R Paisley H Trin and St Barn *Glas* 12–17; R Glas Gd Shep 16–17; Chapl St Raphaël *Eur* from 17. *91 rue Alphonse Daudet Le Périgord, Appt 5, 83600 Fréjus, France* T: (0033) 4 94 52 09 27 E: chaplain.straphael@gmail.com

WILSON, Thomas Kazimir. b 78. Ox Univ BA 01. Wycliffe Hall Ox BA 07. **d** 07 **p** 08. C Toxteth St Philemon w St Gabr and St Cleopas *Liv* 07–12; V Glouc St Jas and All SS and Ch Ch 12–15; Dir St Phil Cen *Leic* from 15. *St Philip's Centre, 2A Stoughton Drive North, Leicester LE5 5UB* T: 0116-273 3459 E: revtomwilson@gmail.com *or* director@stphilipscentre.co.uk

WILSON, Timothy Charles. b 62. Oak Hill Th Coll BA 90. **d** 90 **p** 91. C Highley *Heref* 90–94; C Margate H Trin *Cant* 94–98; P-in-c Margate St Phil 98–02; V 02–03; V Gt Chart 03–16; TV Ashford Town 16–18; AD Ashford 11–18; Hon Can Cant Cathl 11–18; P-in-c Wilden w Colmworth and Ravensden *St Alb* from 19; P-in-c Bolnhurst w Keysoe from 19. *The Vicarage, 47 Stagsden Road, Bromham, Bedford MK43 8PY* M: 07808-865716 E: revtimwilson@wcrchurches.org

WILSON, Timothy John. b 58. St Pet Coll Ox MA 80. Trin Coll Bris 81. **d** 83 **p** 84. C Gt Horton *Bradf* 83–86; C Handforth *Ches* 86–90; V Halifax All SS *Wakef* 90–07; TR S Crawley *Chich* from 07. *The Rectory, Forester Road, Crawley RH10 6EH* T: (01293) 523463 E: tim.wilson58@gmail.com

WILSON, William Adam. b 53. Sheff Univ BA 74 St Jo Coll Dur BA 84. Cranmer Hall Dur 82. **d** 85 **p** 86. C S Croydon Em *S'wark* 85–89; C Wandsworth All SS 89–93; Chapl Fontainebleau *Eur* 93–00; V S Lambeth St Steph *S'wark* 00–21; rtd 21. *35 Sandbourne Avenue, London SW19 3EW* M: 07905-046949

WILSON, William Gerard. b 42. St Chad's Coll Dur BA 65. **d** 67 **p** 68. C Hollinwood *Man* 67–71; V Oldham St Jas 71–79; R Birch w Fallowfield 79–93; V Paddington St Jas *Lon* 93–10; AD Westmr Paddington 97–06; rtd 10; PtO *Lon* from 10; Chich from 15. *20 Portland Street, Brighton BN1 1RN* M: 07976-363480 E: synaxis52@hotmail.com

WILSON, Yvonne. *See* WILSON, Edith Yvonne

WILSON-BARKER, Carol Amanda. *See* GREEN, Carol Amanda

WILTON, Mrs Carlyn Zena. b 54. R Holloway Coll Lon BA 75 Southn Univ PGCE 76. SWMTC 99. **d** 02 **p** 03. NSM Carbis Bay w Lelant Truro 02–20; rtd 20; PtO *Truro* from 21. *Venton Elwyn, 61 Queensway, Hayle TR27 4NL* T: (01736) 752863 E: ventonelwyn@aol.com

WILTON, Canon Christopher. b 52. Lon Univ LLB 75 Solicitor 79. NEOC 97. **d** 00 **p** 01. NSM Sherburn in Elmet w Saxton *York* from 00; P-in-c 03–09; V from 09; P-in-c Aberford w Micklefield from 12; RD Selby from 06; Hon Can Ho Ghana from 14; Can and Preb York Minster from 16. *The Vicarage, 2 Sir John's Lane, Sherburn in Elmet, Leeds LS25 6BJ* T: (01977) 682122 *or* 732222 M: 07968-268622 E: frwilton@aol.com

WILTON, Canon Gary Ian. b 60. Bath Univ BSc 83 Trin Coll Bris MA 93 Nottm Univ EdD 05. Wycliffe Hall Ox 85. **d** 88 **p** 89. C Clevedon St Andr and Ch Ch *B & W* 88–92; Lect UWE Bris 92–93; TV Bath Twerton-on-Avon *B & W* 93–97; Dir Studies and Lect Wilson Carlile Coll of Evang 98–04; Assoc Prin 04–05; Sen Lect York St Jo Univ 05–08; Hd Postgraduate Progr 06–08; C of E Rep Eur Union 08–11; Abp Cant's Rep 11–13; Can Brussels Cathl *Eur* 08–13; V Ecclesall *Sheff* 13–19; PtO *Eur* 18–19; Chapl Dinard 19–21; Hd of Tr

CA from 21. *Church Army, Wilson Carlile Centre, 50 Cavendish Street, Sheffield S3 7RZ* T: 0300-123 2113

WILTON (née ADAMS), Mrs Gillian Linda. b 57. SRN 79 SCM 81. Trin Coll Bris 82. **dss** 85 **d** 87 **p** 94. Easton H Trin w St Gabr and St Lawr and St Jude *Bris* 85–91; Par Dn 87–91; Regional Adv (SW) CMJ 91–97; PtO *B & W* 92–93; NSM Bath Twerton-on-Avon 93–97; Chapl Sheff Children's Hosp NHS Trust 98–06; Chapl Team Ldr Sheff Children's NHS Foundn Trust 06–10; PtO *Eur* 08–10; Asst Chapl Tervuren 10–13; P-in-c Leuven 10–11; PtO *Sheff* 13–14; Chapl St Luke's Hospice Sheff 14–19; Chapl Sheff Teaching Hosps NHS Foundn Trust 14–19; PtO *Eur* from 19. *Address temp unknown* E: gillian.wilton@hotmail.co.uk

WILTON, Glenn Warner Paul. b 33. Miami Univ Ohio BSc 55 Catholic Univ of America 69 Univ of Washington Seattle MSW 76. Pontifical Beda Coll Rome 66 Ch Div Sch of the Pacific (USA) 77. **d** 65 **p** 66. In RC Ch 65–72; NSM Seattle USA 77–81; Chapl Pastures Hosp Derby 82–88; Chapl St Martin's Hosp Cant 89–93; Chapl St Aug Hosp Cant 89–93; Chapl E Kent NHS and Soc Care Partnership Trust 93–03; rtd 03; PtO *Cant* from 03. *10 Lichfield Avenue, Canterbury CT1 3YA* T: (01227) 454230

WILTON-MORGAN, Taylor Benedict. b 93. St Andr Univ MA 15 MLitt 16 K Coll Cam BA 19. Westcott Ho Cam 17. **d** 20 **p** 21. C Thorpe St Andr *Nor* 20–21; C Ashmanhaugh, Barton Turf etc from 21. *36 Naseby Way, Norwich NR7 0TP* T: (01603) 387401 M: 07904-049173 E: twiltonmorgan@gmail.com *or* fr.taylor@outlook.com

WILTON-MORGAN, Timothy Edwin Francis Douglas. b 93. St Andr Univ MA 17 Em Coll Cam BTh 20. Westcott Ho Cam 18. **d** 21. C Nor Cathl from 21. *36 Naseby Way, Norwich NR7 0TP* T: (01603) 387401 M: 07872-987759 E: rev.edwin@outlook.com

WILTS, Archdeacon of. *See* GROOM, The Ven Susan Anne

WILTSHIRE, Mrs Jennifer Mary. b 42. Trin Coll Bris 09. **d** 11 **p** 12. OLM Soundwell *Bris* from 11; PtO *Portsm* from 17. *19 Yew Tree Drive, Bristol BS15 4UA* T: 0117-957 0435 E: jenny.wiltshire410@btinternet.com

WILTSHIRE, Robert Michael. b 50. WMMTC. **d** 89 **p** 90. NSM Droitwich Spa *Worc* 89–93; Asst Chapl HM Pris Wormwood Scrubs 93–94; Chapl HM Pris Standford Hill 94–97; Chapl HM Pris Whitemoor 97–99; Asst Chapl Gen of Pris 99–06; Chapl HM Pris Shrewsbury 06–13; C Edstaston, Fauls, Prees, Tilstock and Whixall *Lich* 13–14; rtd 14; Hon C Hodnet *Lich* 15–16; C Wrockwardine Deanery 16–17; RD Wrockwardine 16–17; PtO 17–19. *Whitehayes, Whitchurch Road, Prees SY13 3JZ* E: rm_wiltshire@btinternet.com

WIMSETT, Paul. b 58. Univ of Wales (Abth) BSc(Econ) 79 Hull Univ MA 86. St Jo Coll Nottm 82. **d** 85 **p** 86. C Nuneaton St Nic *Cov* 85–89; C Loughborough Em *Leic* 89–92; TV Totnes, Bridgetown and Berry Pomeroy etc *Ex* 92–99; V Chudleigh w Chudleigh Knighton and Trusham 99–20; RD Moreton 15–19; rtd 20; PtO *Ex* from 20. *Address temp unknown*

WINBOLT-LEWIS, Martin John. b 46. Fitzw Coll Cam BA 69 MA 72. St Jo Coll Nottm. **d** 75 **p** 76. C Highbury Ch Ch *Lon* 75–78; C Nottingham St Nic *S'well* 79–82; R Carlton Colville *Nor* 82–83; R Carlton Colville w Mutford and Rushmere 83–88; V Burley *Ripon* 88–96; Asst Chapl Pinderfields and Pontefract Hosps NHS Trust 96–99; Chapl 99–00; Lead Chapl 00–02; Lead Chapl Mid Yorks Hosps NHS Trust 02–05; Hd Chapl Services 05–10; rtd 11; PtO *Leeds* from 11. *12 Church Street, Boston Spa, Wetherby LS23 6DN* T: (01937) 919639 E: winboltlewis@btinternet.com

WINCHESTER, Paul. b 44. St Pet Coll Ox BA 66 MA 70 Weymouth Coll of Educn PGCE 73. Ridley Hall Cam 67. **d** 69 **p** 70. C Wednesfield Heath *Lich* 69–72; PtO *Sarum* 73–84; R Tushingham and Whitewell *Ches* 84–02; PtO *Ox* from 02. *12 The Pines, Faringdon SN7 8AU* T: (01367) 240725 E: p.winchester123@btinternet.com

WINCHESTER, Paul Marc. b 53. Univ of Wales (Lamp) BA 80. St Mich Coll Llan 82. **d** 84 **p** 85. C Bedwellty *Mon* 84–86; C Chepstow 86–89; V Cwmcarn 89–93; V Fleur-de-Lis 93–98; R Bedwas and Rudry 98–05; P-in-c Llantilio Pertholey w Bettws Chpl etc 05–10; V Brynmawr *S & B* 10–17; rtd 17; PtO *Mon* from 18. *12 Briardene, Llanfoist, Abergavenny NP7 9LJ* T: (01873) 598557 E: marcw1953@sky.com

WINCHESTER, Archdeacon of. *See* BRAND, The Ven Richard Harold Guthrie

WINCHESTER, Bishop of. *Vacant*

WINCHESTER, Dean of. *See* OGLE, The Very Revd Catherine

WINDEBANK, Clive Leonard. b 41. New Coll Ox BA 62 MA 85. Ox NSM Course 75. **d** 78 **p** 79. Asst Chapl Ahmadi Kuwait 78–83; NSM Brompton H Trin w Onslow Square St Paul *Lon* 83–84; NSM Basildon w Aldworth and Ashampstead *Ox* 85–88; NSM Streatley w Moulsford 88–00; NSM Wallingford

00–03; Chapl Abu Dhabi St Andr UAE 03–09; PtO *Ox* from 13. *The Coombe House, The Coombe, Streatley, Reading RG8 9QL* T: (01491) 872174

WINDER, Cynthia Frances. *See* CLEMOW, Cynthia Frances

WINDIATE, Mary Elizabeth. *See* WEST, Mary Elizabeth

WINDLE, Mrs Catharine Elizabeth. b 72. Hatf Coll Dur BA 95 Homerton Coll Cam PGCE 96. St Jo Coll Nottm MTh 02. **d** 03 **p** 04. C Hucknall Torkard *S'well* 03–05; Hon C Hullavington, Norton and Stanton St Quintin *Bris* 05–06; P-in-c Bath Widcombe *B & W* 06–08; Hon C Malmesbury w Westport and Brokenborough *Bris* 09–13; Chapl SS Helen and Kath Sch Abingdon 13–17; PtO *Ox* 15–18; Chapl *Sherborne Sch for Girls* from 18. *Sherborne School for Girls, Bradford Road, Sherborne DT9 3QN* T: (01935) 812245 E: royandkatie@gmail.com

WINDLE, Christopher Rodney. b 45. Univ of Wales (Lamp) BA 66. Qu Coll Birm. **d** 70 **p** 71. C Lache cum Saltney *Ches* 70–73; C Stockton Heath 73–76; P-in-c Bredbury St Barn 76–83; V 83–07; rtd 07; PtO *Ches* from 07. *6 Norbury Avenue, Marple, Stockport SK6 6NB* T: 0161-427 0375 E: kit.windle@gmail.com

WINDLEY, Caroline Judith. Trent Poly BA 84 Nottm Univ MA 97 CQSW 84. St Jo Coll Nottm MA 96. **d** 97 **p** 98. C Kidderminster St Geo *Worc* 97–01; P-in-c Quarry Bank 01–07; TV Brierley Hill 07–08; RD Kingswinford 04–08; Area Dir of Ord and Adv in Voc Development *Ox* 08–15; Dioc Dir of Ords 15–20; PtO *Heref* from 20. *Address withheld by request*

WINDON, Gary. b 62. N Staffs Poly BSc 85 Glynd r Univ MSc 12 Birm Univ BA 02. Qu Coll Birm 98. **d** 00 **p** 01. C Penn *Lich* 00–04; TV Radcliffe *Man* 04–08; Chapl Nightingale Ho Hospice from 08; LtO *St As* from 08; P-in-c Wrexham 08–13; Methodist Min 16–20; PtO *Ches* 16–21; Lich 17–20; P-in-c Adderley, Ash, Calverhall, Ightfield etc from 20. *The Rectory, Moreton Say, Market Drayton TF9 3RS* E: revgwindon@gmail.com

WINDRIDGE, Michael Harry. b 47. Sarum & Wells Th Coll 91. **d** 93 **p** 94. C Hempnall *Nor* 93–96; NSM Twickenham St Mary *Lon* 96–97; PtO *Nor* 98–20; C Cuckfield and Bolney *Chich* from 20. *The Vicarage, Cowfold Road, Bolney, Haywards Heath RH17 5QR*

WINDROSS, Preb Andrew. b 49. Univ of Wales (Ban) BA 71. Cuddesdon Coll 71. **d** 74 **p** 75. C Wakef St Jo 74–78; C Bromley All Hallows *Lon* 78–83; V De Beauvoir Town St Pet 83–02; AD Hackney 89–94; Bp's Officer for Ordained Min Stepney Area 02–11; Hon C S Hackney St Mich w Haggerston St Paul 02–11; Preb St Paul's Cathl 02–11; rtd 11; PtO *Nor* from 13. *Clare Cottage, Oulton, Norwich NR11 6NX* T: (01263) 587193 E: windrossandy@gmail.com

WINDROSS, Anthony Michael. b 50. CCC Cam BA 72 MA 75 Birm Univ PGCE 73. S Dios Minl Tr Scheme 90. **d** 93 **p** 94. NSM Eastbourne St Mary *Chich* 93–97; C E Grinstead St Swithun 97–99; V Sheringham *Nor* 99–08; V Hythe *Cant* 08–14; R Week St Mary Circle of Par *Truro* 14–18; RD Stratton 16–18; P-in-c Pevensey *Chich* 18–21; rtd 21; PtO *Chich* from 21. *15 Peppercombe Road, Eastbourne BN20 8JH* M: 07484-786035 E: amwindross@btinternet.com *or* anthonywindross@btinternet.com

WINDSLOW, Canon Kathryn Alison. b 62. Southn Univ BTh 83 K Coll Lon MPhil 01. Linc Th Coll 84. **dss** 86 **d** 87 **p** 94. Littlehampton and Wick *Chich* 86–89; Par Dn 87–89; Dn-in-c Scotton w Northorpe *Linc* 89–94; P-in-c 94–97; Asst Local Min Officer 89–97; Local Min Officer and Prin OLM Course 97–02; R Graffoe Gp 02–14; Can and Preb Linc Cathl 09–14; Bp's Adv in Women's Min 08–14; R Storrington *Chich* from 14; RD from 16; Can and Preb Chich Cathl from 19. *The Rectory, Rectory Road, Storrington, Pulborough RH20 4EF* T: (01903) 742888 E: kathryn.windslow@btinternet.com

WINDSOR, Joy Kathleen. b 66. Ox Min Course 15. **d** 17 **p** 18. NSM Alton *Win* 17–20; NSM Blendworth w Chalton w Idsworth *Portsm* from 20; NSM Rowlands Castle from 20. *6 Idsworth Close, Horndean, Waterlooville PO8 0DW* M: 07730-168291 E: revjoywindsor@gmail.com

WINDSOR, The Ven Julie Fiona. b 59. Ridley Hall Cam 98. **d** 00 **p** 01. C Chertsey *Guildf* 00–04; TV Papworth *Ely* 04–08; TR 08–14; Hon Can Ely Cathl 12–14; Adn Horsham *Chich* 14–20; rtd 20; Chapl to The Queen from 20; PtO *Ely* from 20; *Pet* from 21. *Middle Cottage, Main Street, Cotterstock, Peterborough PE8 5HD*

WINDSOR, Mark James. b 75. Bath Univ BSc 98. Wycliffe Hall Ox BTh 08. **d** 08 **p** 09. C Felsted and Lt Dunmow *Chelmsf* 08–12; Par Missr Harwich Peninsula 12–13; TV Vale of Pewsey *Sarum* from 13. *The Vicarage, Wilcot, Pewsey SN9 5NS* T: (01672) 564265 M: 07544-718191 E: markwindsor923@btinternet.com

WINDSOR, Dean of. *See* CONNER, The Rt Revd David John

WINFIELD, Alan Leslie. b 58. All SS Cen for Miss & Min 18. **d** 20 **p** 21. OLM Melbourne, Ticknall, Smisby and Stanton *Derby* from 20. *6 Irvine Close, Stenson Fields, Derby DE24 3HS* T: (01332) 765368 M: 07796-560814 E: winfieldalan28@yahoo.co.uk *or* curate@melbourneparishchurch.co.uk

WINFIELD, Canon Flora Jane Louise. b 64. Univ of Wales (Lamp) BA 85 Virginia Th Sem DD 10 FRSA 98. Ripon Coll Cuddesdon 87. **d** 89 **p** 94. Par Dn Stantonbury and Willen *Ox* 89–92; Co Ecum Officer *Glouc* 92–94; Chapl Mansf Coll Ox 94–97; Local Unity Sec Coun for Chr Unity 97–02; CF (VR) from 97; Can Res Win Cathl 02–05; Asst Sec Gen World Conf of Relig for Peace 05–06; Special Adv from 06; Sec Internat Affairs CTBI 06–09; Abp's Sec for Angl Relns *Cant* 07–14; P-in-c St Mary at Hill w St Andr Hubbard etc *Lon* 08–14; Angl Communion Rep UN Institutions Geneva 14–17; Abp's Special Rep to the Commonwealth from 17; Abp's Adv on Reconciliation from 19; PtO *Lon* from 15; *Leeds* 19–21. *Lambeth Palace, London SE1 7JU* T: (020) 7898 1697 E: flora.winfield@lambethpalace.org.uk

WINFIELD, Russell James. b 79. Sheff Hallam Univ BA 00 Down Coll Cam BTh 12. St Mellitus Coll MA 14. **d** 14 **p** 15. C Brentford *Lon* 14–17; Internat Development Manager St Mellitus Coll 17–20; Dean from 20; Public Preacher from 17. *St Mellitus College, 24 Collingham Road, London SW5 0LX* T: (020) 7052 0573 E: russjw@outlook.com *or* russell.winfield@stmellitus.ac.uk

WING, Mrs Julie. b 62. Teesside Univ BSc 99. NEOC 02. **d** 05 **p** 06. C Sunderland St Chad *Dur* 05–09; TV Gt Aycliffe 09–14; R Usworth from 14. *Usworth Rectory, 14 Prestwick Close, Washington NE37 2LP* M: 07812-589653

WING, Miss Myra Susan. b 45. Cranmer Hall Dur 92. **d** 94 **p** 95. C Appledore w Brookland, Fairfield, Brenzett etc *Cant* 94–98; Hon C Wittersham w Stone and Ebony 95–98; V Grayshott *Guildf* 98–08; rtd 08; PtO *Cant* from 09. *142 Minster Road, Westgate-on-Sea CT8 8DQ* T: (01843) 836430 E: susanwing14@gmail.com

WINGATE, Canon Andrew David Carlile. b 44. Worc Coll Ox BA 66 MA 71 MPhil 68 Birm Univ PhD 95. Linc Th Coll 70. **d** 72 **p** 73. C Halesowen *Worc* 72–75; Lect Tamilnadu Th Sem India 76–82; Prin WMMTC 82–90; Prin United Coll of Ascension Selly Oak 90–00; Hon Can Birm Cathl 97–00; Dir Min and Tr *Leic* 00–03; Dir Interfaith Relns and Co-ord Lay Tr 03–10; rtd 10; Can Th Leic Cathl from 00; Chapl to The Queen 07–14; PtO *Chich* from 16; *Leic* from 17; Assoc Dioc Interfaith Adv *Chich* from 18. *25 Prince Charles Road, Lewes BN7 2HY* T: (01273) 479012 M: 07808-586259 E: andrewwingate5@gmail.com

WINGFIELD, Christopher Laurence. b 57. Westmr Coll Ox BTh 99. Ripon Coll Cuddesdon 93. **d** 95 **p** 96. C Hadleigh *St E* 95–99; P-in-c Melton 99–00; R 00–01; R Sproughton w Burstall, Copdock w Washbrook etc 01–09; RD Samford 06–09; P-in-c Bromsgrove St Jo *Worc* 09–12; TR Bromsgrove 12–14; R Harton *York* from 14; RD S Ryedale from 18. *The Vicarage, Sand Hutton, York YO41 1LB* T: (01904) 468418 E: chris.wingfield@btinternet.com

WINGFIELD DIGBY, Canon Andrew Richard. b 50. Keble Coll Ox BA 72. Wycliffe Hall Ox 74. **d** 77 **p** 78. C Cockfosters Ch Ch CD *Lon* 77–80; C Hadley Wood St Paul Prop Chpl 80–84; Dir Chrs in Sport 84–02; V Ox St Andr 02–16; Six Preacher Cant Cathl 97–07; Hon Can Ch Ch *Ox* 13–16; rtd 16; PtO *Ox* from 17. *The Valley, Asthall Leigh, Witney OX29 9PX* T: (01993) 878243 M: 07768-611232 E: revandrew.wd@btinternet.com

WINKETT, Miss Lucy Clare. b 68. Selw Coll Cam BA 90 MA 94 ARCM 92. Qu Coll Birm BD 94. **d** 95 **p** 96. C Lt Ilford St Mich *Chelmsf* 95–97; Min Can and Chapl St Paul's Cathl *Lon* 97–03; Can Res and Prec 03–10; R Westmr St Jas from 10. *St James's Rectory, 197 Piccadilly, London W1 9LL* T: (020) 7734 4511 *or* 7292 4860 E: rector@sjp.org.uk

WINN, Alan John. b 42. FRSA 73. **d** 01 **p** 02. OLM Ringwould w Kingsdown *Cant* 01–04; OLM Ringwould w Kingsdown and Ripple etc 05–12; rtd 12; PtO *Cant* from 12. *Chilterns, Back Street, Ringwould, Deal CT14 8HL* T: (01304) 361030 E: revjohnwinn@aol.com

WINN, Paul William James. b 44. Liv Univ BSc 66. EMMTC 86. **d** 89 **p** 90. NSM Spalding St Paul *Linc* 89–98; PtO 98–00; P-in-c Cowbit 00–01; V 01–07; rtd 07; PtO *Linc* 17–20. *6 Hawthorn Chase, Moulton, Spalding PE12 6GA* T: (01406) 373662 E: paulwinn80@hotmail.com

WINN, Peter Anthony. b 60. Worc Coll Ox BA 82 MA 86. Wycliffe Hall Ox 83. **d** 86 **p** 87. C W Derby Gd Shep *Liv* 86–89; V Seaforth 89–02; P-in-c Anfield St Marg 02–09; V from 09. *St Margaret's Vicarage, Rocky Lane, Liverpool L6 4BA* T: 0151-263 3118

WINN, Simon Reynolds. b 66. Bris Univ BA 88. Trin Coll Bris BA 98. d 98 p 99. C Portswood Ch Ch *Win* 98–02; V Northolt St Jos *Lon* 02–10; Dir of Ords Willesden Area 07–10; V Hataitai-Kilbirnie NZ 10–15; Dir Ords Wellington 12–19; Can Wellington 15–19; C Gt Chesham *Ox* 19–21; V Greenwich St Alfege *S'wark* from 21. *St Alfege Church, Greenwich Church Street, London SE10 9BJ* T: (020) 8853 0687 M: 07951-029309 E: rev.simon.winn@gmail.com

WINN-SMITH, Mrs Joanna Elizabeth. b 78. Regent's Park Coll *Ox* MA 00 Kingston Coll BA 15 MBACP 15. Ripon Coll Cuddesdon MTh 19. d 19 p 20. NSM Thorpe *Guildf* from 19; Tutor Local Min Progr from 19. *Ambika, Woodham Park Way, Woodham, Addlestone KT15 3SG* T: (01932) 422847 M: 07962-780565 E: jowinnsmith@hotmail.com

WINNINGTON-INGRAM, David Robert. b 59. Hertf Coll Ox BA 82 MA 85 K Coll Cam BA 89. Westcott Ho Cam 87. d 90 p 91. C Bishop's Cleeve *Glouc* 90–94; TV Colyton, Southleigh, Offwell, Widworthy etc *Ex* 94–00; V S Brent and Rattery 00–17; rtd 17. *4 Wesley Place, Harberton, Totnes TQ9 7SW*

WINSBURY, Leigh Darren. b 67. St Jo Coll Nottm 13. d 15 p 16. C Bideford, Northam, Westward Ho!, Appledore etc *Ex* 15–17; C Bideford, Landcross, Littleham etc 17–19; TV Okehampton, Inwardleigh, Belstone, Sourton etc from 19. *The Rectory, Hatherleigh, Okehampton EX20 3JY* E: lwinsbury@googlemail.com

WINSLADE, Richard Clive. b 69. Aston Tr Scheme 91 Linc Th Coll BTh 93. d 96 p 97. C Waltham Cross *St Alb* 96–99; C Leavesden 99–03; R Maulden 03–13; V Gravenhurst, Shillington and Stondon from 13. *All Saints' Vicarage, Vicarage Close, Shillington, Hitchin SG5 3LS* T: (01462) 713797 E: richardrev@btinternet.com

WINSPER, Arthur William (Brother Benedict). b 46. Ox Brookes Univ BA 10. Glas NSM Course 89. d 91 p 92. SSF from 70; Min Eur Prov from 17; NSM Barrowfield *Glas* 91–96; P-in-c St Aug Miss Penhalonga Zimbabwe 96–98; PtO *Worc* 98–08; *Sheff* 09–12; *Chelmsf* 13–16; *Leeds* from 17; *Eur* from 14. *25 Karnac Road, Leeds LS8 5BL* T: 0113-226 0647 E: ministerssf@franciscans.org.uk *or* benedictssf@franciscans.org.uk

✠**WINSTANLEY, The Rt Revd Alan Leslie.** b 49. Nottm Univ BTh 72. St Jo Coll Nottm 68 ALCD 72. d 72 p 73 c 88. C Livesey *Blackb* 72–75; C Gt Sankey *Liv* 75–77; P-in-c Penketh 75–77; V 78–81; SAMS 81–93; Bp Bolivia and Peru 88–93; V Eastham *Ches* 94–03; Hon Asst Bp Ches 94–03; V Whittle-le-Woods *Blackb* 03–12; Hon Asst Bp Blackb 03–12; TV Shirwell, Loxhore, Kentisbury, Arlington, etc *Ex* 12–14; Hon Asst Bp Ex 12–14; rtd 14; Hon Asst Bp Ches from 15. *11 Thorneycroft Way, Crewe CW1 4FZ* M: 07774-314534 E: alanlwinstanley@gmail.com

WINSTANLEY, John Graham. b 47. K Coll Lon 67. d 71 p 72. C Wandsworth St Paul *S'wark* 71–74; Chapl Salford Univ *Man* 75–79; R Kersal Moor 79–87. *14 Lyndhurst Avenue, Prestwich, Manchester M25 0GF* T: 0161-740 2715 F: 720 6916

WINTER, Andrew Christopher. b 73. Dur Univ BSc 95 PGCE 96. d 03 p 04. C Mosman St Clem Australia 03–05; NSM Hinckley H Trin *Leic* 06–10; Chapl Ipswich Sch 10–15; Chapl Reed's Sch Cobham from 15. *Reed's School, Sandy Lane, Cobham KT11 2ES* T: (01932) 869044

WINTER, Anthony Cathcart. b 28. FCA. Ridley Hall Cam 54. d 56 p 57. C Childwall St Dav *Liv* 56–58; C Hackney St Jo *Lon* 58–63; V Newmarket All SS *St E* 63–73; LtO 74–81; PtO *Lon* 78–81 and 97–99; Hon C St Andr-by-the-Wardrobe w St Ann, Blackfriars 81–86; Hon C Smithfield St Bart Gt 86–95; Chapl S'wark Cathl from 99; PtO *Lon* from 08; *S'wark* from 99. *25 Bowater House, Golden Lane Estate, London EC1Y 0RJ* T: (020) 7490 5765 F: 7490 1064 E: a.c.winter@btinternet.com

WINTER, Christopher Louvain. b 74. SEITE BA 13 St Aug Coll of Th 17. d 20. NSM Burham and Wouldham *Roch* from 20. *23 St Margaret's Way, Rochester ME1 1TU* T: (01634) 408854 M: 07968-367392 E: chris@birinus.org

✠**WINTER, The Rt Revd Dagmar.** b 63. Heidelberg Univ DrTheol 96. Herborn Th Sem 93. d 96 p 97 c 19. C Bromley St Mark *Roch* 96–99; C Hexham *Newc* 99–06; P-in-c Kirkwhelpington, Kirkharle, Kirkheaton and Cambo 06–15; Dioc Officer for Rural Affairs 06–15; AD Morpeth 11–13; R Hexham 15–19; Bp's Adv for Women in Min 12–19; Hon Can Newc Cathl 11–19; Suff Bp Huntingdon *Ely* from 19. *14 Lynn Road, Ely CB6 1DA* T: (01353) 662137 E: bishop.huntingdon@elydiocese.org

WINTER, Canon David Brian. b 29. K Coll Lon BA 53 CertEd 54. Oak Hill NSM Course. d 87 p 88. NSM Finchley St Paul and St Luke *Lon* 87–89; Hd Relig Broadcasting BBC 87–89; Bp's Officer for Evang *Ox* 89–95; P-in-c Ducklington 89–95; Hon Can Ch Ch 95; rtd 95; Hon C Hermitage *Ox* 95–00; Hon C Dorchester 02–05; PtO 00–02 and 06–18.

51 Nideggen Close, Thatcham RG19 4HS T: (01635) 873639 E: david_winter1@btinternet.com

WINTER, Mrs Jane Marion. b 62. Avery Hill Coll BEd 84 York St Jo Coll MA 09. Ripon Coll Cuddesdon 12. d 14 p 15. C Orpington St Andr *Roch* 14–15; C Cray Valley from 15; Dioc Facilitator for Formation, Learning and Discipleship from 18. *39 Chelsfield Road, Orpington BR5 4DS* T: (01689) 872282 M: 07734-962140 E: revjanewinter@gmail.com *or* jane.winter@rochester.anglican.org

WINTER, Mrs Mary Elizabeth. b 56. Man Univ BEd 78 Leeds Univ AdDipEd 85. Yorks Min Course 08. d 11 p 12. C Skipton Ch Ch w Carleton *Bradf* 11–14; *Leeds* 14–15; C Skipton H Trin *Bradf* 11–14; *Leeds* 14–15; P-in-c Greengates 15–16; P-in-c Thorpe Edge 15–16; V Greengates and Thorpe Edge 16–20; C from 20. *Address temp unknown* M: 07813-687680 E: mary.winter@hotmail.co.uk

WINTER, Nichola Jane. b 58. Trevelyan Coll Dur BA 79. d 02 p 03. OLM Aldeburgh w Hazlewood *St E* 02–13; NSM 13–17; NSM Alde Sandlings from 17; Chapl Suffolk Coastal Primary Care Trust from 06. *Threeways, Donkey Lane, Friston, Saxmundham IP17 1PL* T: (01728) 688979 E: njwinter@clara.co.uk

WINTER, Rebecca Anne. *See* BEVAN, Rebecca Anne

WINTER, Stephen Christopher. b 55. Southn Univ BA 76. Trin Coll Bris 85. d 88 p 89. C Birm St Luke 88–92; TV Kings Norton 92–98; Ind Chapl *Worc* 98–04; Asst Dir Development (Discipleship) 04–11; C Finstall 04–11; rtd 11; PtO *Worc* 11–18; R Elmley Lovett w Hampton Lovett and Elmbridge w Rushock and Hartlebury and Ombersley w Doverdale from 18. *2 Canal Cottages, Hanbury Wharf, Hanbury Road, Droitwich WR9 7DU* E: mail@stephenwinter.net

WINTERBOTTOM, Canon Ian Edmund. b 42. St Andr Univ MA 66. Linc Th Coll 66. d 68 p 69. C Blackb St Steph 68–71; C Wingerworth *Derby* 71–73; P-in-c Brimington 73–77; R 77–89; RD Bolsover and Staveley 86–93; R Pleasley 89–94; P-in-c Shirebrook 92–94; TR E Scarsdale 94–00; Hon Can Derby Cathl 95–08; Prin Ind Chapl 00–08; rtd 08; PtO *Ely* from 17. *54 Wilkin Walk, Cottenham, Cambridge CB24 8TS* E: ianwinterbottom@aol.com

WINTERBURN, Derek Neil. b 60. Bris Univ BSc 82 Ox Univ BA 85. Wycliffe Hall Ox 83. d 86 p 87. C Mildmay Grove St Jude and St Paul *Lon* 86–89; C Hackney Marsh 89–91; V Hampton St Mary 96–16; V Hampton Hill from 16; AD Hampton 08–14. *The Vicarage, 46 St James's Road, Hampton Hill, Hampton TW12 1DQ* E: vicar@winterburn.me.uk

WINTGENS, Peter Brendon. b 47. Surrey Univ BSc 70 Cant Ch Ch Univ BA 12. SEITE 06. d 09 p 10. NSM Battersea St Mary *S'wark* 09–16; rtd 16; PtO *St E* from 17. *Priory Gate, 11 Seckford Street, Woodbridge IP12 4LY* T: (01394) 382097 E: wintgens@btinternet.com

WINTLE, Anthony Robert. b 44. K Coll Lon 64. St Mich Coll Llan. d 68 p 69. C Llandaff N *Llan* 68–70; C Baglan 70–75; V Treharris 75–85; V Treharris w Bedlinog 86–90; R St Fagans and Michaelston-super-Ely 90–13; rtd 13; PtO *St D* 13–16 and from 17; Hon C W Preseli Gp 17. *Porth y Castell, Market Street, Newport SA42 0PH* T: (01239) 820414 E: anthonywintle@btinternet.com

WINTLE, Graham. b 52. Bris Univ BSc 73. Oak Hill Th Coll BA 86. d 86 p 87. C Southgate *Chich* 86–89; C New Malden and Coombe *S'wark* 89–92; V Surbiton Hill Ch Ch 92–06; R Willoughby Australia 06–19; rtd 19. *23 Turner Street, Lambton NSW 2299, Australia* M: (0061) 41-462 3303 E: graham.wintle@gmail.com

WINTLE, Canon Ruth Elizabeth. b 31. Westf Coll Lon BA 53 St Hugh's Coll Ox BA 67 MA 74. St Mich Ho Ox 63. dss 72 d 87 p 94. Tutor St Jo Coll Dur 72–74; Selection Sec ACCM 74–83; St Jo in Bedwardine *Worc* 83–87; Par Dn 87–94; Dir of Ords 84–92; Hon Can Worc Cathl 87–97; rtd 95; Bp's Adv on Women's Min *Worc* 95–97; PtO from 98. *6 Coronation Avenue, Rushwick, Worcester WR2 5TF* T: (01905) 427109 E: ruth.wintle@btinternet.com

✠**WINTON, The Rt Revd Alan Peter.** b 58. Sheff Univ BA 83 PhD 87. Linc Th Coll 91. d 91 p 92 c 09. C Southgate Ch Ch *Lon* 91–95; P-in-c St Paul's Walden and Dioc CME Officer *St Alb* 95–99; R Welwyn w Ayot St Peter 99–05; TR Welwyn 05–09; Hon Can St Alb 07–09; Suff Bp Thetford *Nor* from 09. *Herfast House, 5 Vicar Street, Wymondham NR18 0PL* T: (01953) 528010 E: bishop.thetford@dioceseofnorwich.org

WINTOUR, Mrs Anne Elizabeth. b 52. d 03 p 04. OLM Melksham *Sarum* 03–12; OLM Atworth w Shaw and Whitley 07–12; OLM Broughton Gifford, Gt Chalfield and Holt 07–12; PtO from 12; Asst Dioc Dir of Ords 13–17; NSM Rowde and Bromham 14–17; NSM Melksham 14–17; rtd 17; PtO *Bris* from 21. *Weavers House, 264 Sandridge Lane, Bromham, Chippenham SN15 2JW* T: (01380) 850880 E: anniewintour@btinternet.com

WIPPELL, David Stanley. b 46. Univ of Qld BSc 67 Selw Coll Cam BA 77 MA. Westcott Ho Cam 76. **d** 78 **p** 79. C Wolvercote w Summertown *Ox* 78–80; Asst Chapl St Edw Sch Ox 78–00; Chapl 00–06; Housemaster 85–97; Chapl St Hugh's Coll Ox 80–85; NSM Ray Valley *Ox* 06–15; PtO from 15; *Eur* 99–19. *Rivermead, 1A Mill Street, Islip, Kidlington OX5 2SZ* T: (01865) 849497 M: 07970-024316 E: davidwippell1@gmail.com

WISDOM, Jeremy Paul. b 76. St Mellitus Coll 19. **d** 21. C Blackley St Andr *Man* from 21; C Blackley St Paul from 21; C Blackley St Pet from 21. *Holy Trinity Rectory, Goodman Street, Manchester M9 4BW* M: 07481-500477 E: jez@northmanccofe.org

WISE, Canon Pamela Margaret. b 51. CertEd 73 BA 79. Ripon Coll Cuddesdon 89. **d** 91 **p** 94. Par Dn Tokyngton St Mich *Lon* 91–94; C N Greenford All Hallows 94; C Bedford All SS *St Alb* 94–97; TV Hitchin 97–03; V Oxhey All SS from 03; Hon Can St Alb from 09; PtO *Lon* from 16. *All Saints' Vicarage, Gosforth Lane, Watford WD19 7AX* T: (020) 8421 5949 E: pamela.wise@gmail.com *or* revpamwise@hotmail.co.uk

WISE, Richard Edmund. b 67. Clare Coll Cam BA 88 MusB 88 LRAM 91. Cranmer Hall Dur 01. **d** 03 **p** 04. C Stanmore *Win* 03–07; P-in-c Bishopstoke 07–09; R from 09; AD Eastleigh from 20. *The Rectory, 10 Stoke Park Road, Eastleigh SO50 6DA* T: (023) 8061 2192 E: rwise@talktalk.net

WISE, Mrs Susan Jacqueline. b 57. Anglia Poly Univ BEd 92. St Mellitus Coll 14. **d** 15 **p** 16. NSM Wickford and Runwell *Chelmsf* from 15; TV from 20. *St Mary's Vicarage, Church End Lane, Runwell, Wickford SS11 7JQ* M: 07941-506156 E: sue.wise@sky.com

WISEMAN, Canon David John. b 51. Lon Univ BD 80 Derby Univ MA 99. Cranmer Hall Dur 77. **d** 80 **p** 81. C Bilston *Lich* 80–84; P-in-c W Bromwich St Phil 84–86; V 86–89; P-in-c Cheetham St Mark *Man* 89–94; Dioc Community Relns Officer 89–96; P-in-c Ashton N Trin 94–99; TR Ashton 00–03; Chapl Tameside Coll 94–03; Soc Resp Adv *Pet* 03–07; P-in-c Northampton Ch Ch 07–16; AD Gtr Northn 07–16; Can Pet Cathl 09–16; rtd 16; PtO *Heref* from 17. *Myndtown, Clun Road, Craven Arms SY7 9QS* T: (01588) 674738 E: davidwiseman50@gmail.com

WISEMAN, John. b 56. Sarum & Wells Th Coll 80. **d** 83 **p** 84. C Swinton St Pet *Man* 83–87; C Swinton and Pendlebury 87–88; TV Atherton 88–93; V Bedford Leigh 93–02; V Lt Lever from 02. *The Vicarage, Market Street, Little Lever, Bolton BL3 1HH* T: (01204) 700936

WISEMAN, The Revd Mother Julie. b 53. ERMC 05. **d** 08 **p** 09. NSM Roughton and Felbrigg, Metton, Sustead etc *Nor* 08–10; Public Preacher from 10. *32B Beeston Common, Sheringham NR26 8ES* T: (01263) 825623 E: juliessl@btinternet.com

WISHART, Michael Leslie. b 45. St Mich Coll Llan 70. **d** 73 **p** 74. C Llangyfelach *S & B* 73–76; Chapl RN 76–80 and 85–96; V Beguildy and Heyope *S & B* 80–84; V Gowerton 84–85; Chapl RNR 80–85; R Dowlais *Llan* 97–04; R Bishops Lydeard w Bagborough and Cothelstone *B & W* 04–11; P-in-c Lydeard St Lawrence and Combe Florey 10–11; rtd 11; PtO *Llan* from 11. *Hollands Cottage, Higher End, St Athan, Barry CF62 4LW* T: (01446) 751600 E: michael.wishart@btopenworld.com

WISKEN, Robert Daniel. b 40. ACT. **d** 60 **p** 60. C N Rockhampton St Barn Australia 60; V N Rockhampton St Matt 61–63; V Winton *Man* 63–65; R Luddington w Hemington and Thurning *Pet* 65–69; P-in-c Clopton *St E* 66–69; V Ipswich All SS 69–73; V Sompting *Chich* 74–78; Org Sec (SW England) CECS 78–80; R Edmundbyers w Muggleswick *Dur* 80–83; R Wexham *Ox* 83–86; Australia from 86; rtd 95. *11-64 Riverwalk Avenue, Robina QLD 4226, Australia* E: randjwisken@bigpond.com

WITCHELL, David William. b 47. St Jo Coll Nottm BTh 75. **d** 75 **p** 76. C Northampton St Mary *Pet* 75–78; C Oakham w Hambleton and Egleton 78–81; C Oakham, Hambleton, Egleton, Braunston and Brooke 81–82; V Weedon Bec w Everdon 82–90; V Wellingborough St Barn 90–00; RD Torbay 03–09; rtd 16; PtO *Ex* from 11. *1 Kintyre Close, Torquay, Paignton TQ2 7BQ* T: (01803) 316636

WITCHELL, Derek William Frederick. b 49. SAOMC 00. **d** 03 **p** 04. C Bloxham w Milcombe and S Newington *Ox* 03–06; P-in-c Wing w Grove 06–12; P-in-c Wingrave w Rowsham, Aston Abbotts and Cublington 06–12; P-in-c Cheddington w Mentmore 08–12; TV Cottesloe 12–13; rtd 13; PtO *Ox* from 13. *11 Hunt Road, Thame OX9 3LG* T: (01844) 215798 M: 07847-167507

WITCOMBE, The Very Revd John Julian. b 59. Cam Univ MA 84 Nottm Univ MPhil 91. St Jo Coll Nottm BA 83. **d** 84 **p** 85. C Birtley *Dur* 84–87; C Chilwell *S'well* 87–91; V Lodge

Moor St Luke *Sheff* 91–95; TR Uxbridge *Lon* 95–98; Dean St Jo Coll Nottm 98–05; Officer for Min *Glouc* 05–10; Hon Can Glouc Cathl 09–10; Can Res Glouc Cathl 10–13; Dir Discipleship and Min 10–13; Dean Cov from 13. *8 Priory Row, Coventry CV1 5EX* T: (024) 7652 1391

WITCOMBE, Michael David. b 53. Univ of Wales (Lamp) BA 76. Qu Coll Birm 76. **d** 78 **p** 79. C Neath w Llantwit *Llan* 78–80; C Whitchurch 80–83; V Newcastle 83–02; P-in-c Ewenny 84–86; V Llanishen 02–19; rtd 19. *Address temp unknown* E: fatherm@btinternet.com

WITCOMBE, Ricarda Jane. b 64. Ch Coll Cam BA 86 MA 90. St Jo Coll Nottm MA(TS) 99. **d** 01 **p** 02. C Wilford *S'well* 01–05; P-in-c Glouc St Paul 05–09; V Glouc St Paul and St Steph 09–13; PtO 13–14; Chapl Team Ldr Geo Eliot Hosp NHS Trust Nuneaton from 14. *The Chaplaincy, George Eliot Hospital, College Street, Nuneaton CV10 7DJ* T: (024) 7686 5281 E: ricarda.witcombe@geh.nhs.uk

WITCOMBE, Simon Christopher. b 61. Dundee Univ MA 83 PGCE 84 St Jo Coll Dur BA 90. Cranmer Hall Dur 88. **d** 91 **p** 92. C Earlham St Anne *Nor* 91–95; Assoc P Skegness and Winthorpe *Linc* 95–98; Gen Preacher 95–98; R Woodhall Spa Gp 98–07; V Codsall *Lich* 07–17; P-in-c Bilbrook and Coven 13–14; RD Penkridge 11–16; Sen Chapl Glos Univ *Glouc* from 17. *9 Loweswater Road, Cheltenham GL51 3AZ* M: 07715-041525 E: simonwitcombe50@gmail.com *or* switcombe@glos.ac.uk

WITHERIDGE, John Stephen. b 53. Kent Univ BA 76 Ch Coll Cam BA 78 MA 82 FRHistS. Ridley Hall Cam 78. **d** 79 **p** 80. C Luton St Mary *St Alb* 79–82; Asst Chapl Marlborough Coll 82–84; Abp's Chapl *Cant* 84–87; Conduct Eton Coll 87–96; Headmaster Charterhouse Sch Godalming 96–13; PtO *Guildf* 96–09; rtd 13; PtO *Ox* from 14; Hon Chapl Ch Ch from 14; Chapl to The Queen from 17. *Minster Cottage, Church Street, Charlbury, Chipping Norton OX7 3PR* T: (01608) 810383 E: john.witheridge@outlook.com

WITHERS, Eleanor Jane. *See* WILLIAMS, Eleanor Jane

WITHERS, Geoffrey Edward. b 68. QUB BSc 90 TCD BTh 93. CITC 90. **d** 93 **p** 94. C Ballymena w Ballyclug *Conn* 93–97; I Monkstown 97–01; Chapl RAF from 01. *Chaplaincy Services (RAF), HQ Air Command, RAF High Wycombe HP14 4UE* T: (01494) 496800 E: geoff.withers944@mod.gov.uk

WITHERS, Canon Gillian. b 58. Stranmillis Coll BEd 80. St Jo Coll Nottm 94. **d** 97 **p** 98. NSM Mossley *Conn* 97–03; C Bangor St Comgall *D & D* 03–05; V Knock 05–08; I Grey Abbey w Kircubbin from 08; Can Belf Cathl from 16. *4 Rectory Wood, Portaferry, Newtownards BT22 1LJ* T: (028) 4272 9307 E: vicarofdibley@hotmail.co.uk

WITHERS, John Geoffrey. b 39. St Jo Coll Dur BA 61 Birm Univ CertEd 63 CQSW 72. SWMTC 84. **d** 87 **p** 88. NSM Drewsteignton *Ex* 87–01; P-in-c 99–01; P-in-c Hittisleigh and Spreyton 99–01; P-in-c Chagford, Drewsteignton, Hittisleigh etc 01; C 01–07; Sub Chapl HM Pris *Ex* 96–07; PtO *Ex* from 07. *Lane's End, Broadwoodwidger, Lifton PL16 0JH* T: (01566) 780544

WITHEY, Michael John. b 45. Open Univ BA 80 Ox Univ MTh 98 SRN 66. Oak Hill Th Coll 71. **d** 74 **p** 75. C St Alb St Paul 74–76; C Luton St Mary 77; C Luton St Fran 77–80; V Woodside w E Hyde 80–87; CF (TA) 83–87; Dioc Stewardship Adv *Ox* 87–89; Chapl HM YOI Onley 89–91; V Hengoed w Gobowen *Lich* 91–95; Chapl Robert Jones and Agnes Hunt Orthopaedic Hosp 91–95; P-in-c Chasetown *Lich* 95–00; V 00–02; V Stroud H Trin *Glouc* 02–13; Chapl Cotswold and Vale Primary Care Trust 02–06; Chapl Glos Primary Care Trust 06–11; Chapl Glos Partnership Trust 02–11; rtd 13. *24 Cwrt Deri, Cwmann, Lampeter SA48 8EJ* E: meic.clydogau@media-maker.com

WITHINGTON, Canon Brian James. b 54. Leic Univ MSc 01 CQSW 76. EAMTC 94. **d** 97 **p** 98. NSM Pet St Jo 97–04; P-in-c Broughton w Loddington and Cransley etc 04–10; C 10–17; RD Kettering 07–17; R Aldwincle, Clopton, Pilton, Stoke Doyle etc 17–21; Bp's Adv for Pioneer Min 10–13; Can Pet Cathl 13–21; rtd 21; Asst Dir Ords *Pet* from 14. *16 Tennyson Road, Kettering NN16 0DD* E: canonbrian@uwclub.net

WITHINGTON, George Kenneth. b 37. Birm Univ BA 59. Wells Th Coll 59. **d** 61 **p** 62. C Hartcliffe St Andr CD *Bris* 61–65; V Swindon St Jo 65–73; V Cricklade w Latton 73–97; RD Cricklade 94–97; rtd 97; PtO *Heref* from 97; *Worc* 97–16. *19 Oak Drive, Colwall, Malvern WR13 6RA* T: (01684) 540590 E: kandjw@btinternet.com

WITHINGTON, Canon Keith. b 32. Univ of Wales (Lamp) BA 55. Qu Coll Birm 55. **d** 57 **p** 58. C Bournville *Birm* 57–61; V 61–00; RD Moseley 81–91; Hon Can Birm Cathl 83–00; rtd 00; PtO *Birm* from 00; *Worc* from 00. *44 Dugard Way, Droitwich WR9 8UX* T: (01905) 795847 E: keithkw1000@aol.com

WITHINGTON, Paul Martin. b 60. Kent Univ BSc 86. Trin Coll Bris 01. **d** 03 **p** 04. C Elworth and Warmingham *Ches* 03–06; TV Congleton 06–18; V Weaverham from 18. *St Mary's Vicarage, Church Street, Weaverham, Northwich CW8 3NJ* T: (01606) 851880 E: revpaul9@outlook.com

WITHNELL, Roderick David. b 55. EMMTC 86 Ridley Hall Cam 89. **d** 90 **p** 91. C Shenfield *Chelmsf* 90–94; C Woodleigh and Loddiswell *Ex* 94–95; TV Modbury, Bigbury, Ringmore w Kingston etc 95–00; Canada 00–01; TR Burrington, Chawleigh, Cheldon, Chulmleigh etc *Ex* 01–15; TR Teignmouth, Ideford w Luton, Ashcombe etc 15–20; rtd 20. *Address temp unknown* E: roderickwithnell@btinternet.com

WITT, Canon Bryan Douglas. b 52. St Mich Coll Llan BD 84. **d** 84 **p** 85. C Betws w Ammanford *St D* 84–87; V Llanllwni 87–91; V Llangennech and Hendy 91–04; V St Clears w Llangynin and Llanddowror etc 04–15; AD St Clears 13–14; P-in-c Llanarthne and Llanddarog 15–17; Hon Can St D Cathl 11–13; Can Cursal 13–17; PtO from 17. *Riverside, 20 Hillfield Villas, Kidwelly SA17 4UL* T: (01554) 891565 E: canonwitt@gmail.com

WITT, Caroline Elizabeth. *See* SACKLEY, Caroline Elizabeth

WITTER, Mrs Tania Judy Ingram. b 37. Girton Coll Cam BA 58 MA 63. Oak Hill Th Coll 94. **d** 95 **p** 96. NSM Highbury Ch Ch w St Jo and St Sav *Lon* 95–03 and from 14; PtO 03–13; *Eur* from 03. *26 Viewpoint Apartments, 30-32 Highbury Grove, London N5 2DL* T: (020) 7226 6908 E: tania.witter@btinternet.com

WITTS, Donald Roger. b 47. Cranmer Hall Dur 86. **d** 88 **p** 89. C Leyland St Ambrose *Blackb* 88–90; C Staines St Mary and St Pet *Lon* 90–93; Ind Missr *Man* 93–95; Dioc Communications Officer *Cant* 95–00; P-in-c Blean 95–01; V Birchington w Acol and Minnis Bay 01–17; rtd 17; Asst Chapl Costa Blanca *Eur* 18–19. *Calle Amsterdam 67, Bello Horizonte 2, 03530 La Nucia (Alicante), Spain* T: (0034) 966 896 426 *or* 611 242 476 M: 07749-201947 *or* (0034) 612 242 496 E: don.witts@btopenworld.com

WITTS, Preb Graham Robert. b 53. Newc Univ BEd Bris Univ MA 01. Linc Th Coll 79. **d** 82 **p** 83. C Horncastle w Low Toynton *Linc* 82–85; TV Gt Grimsby St Mary and St Jas 85–89; TR Yelverton, Meavy, Sheepstor and Walkhampton *Ex* 89–93; C Glastonbury w Meare *B & W* 93–03; RD Glastonbury 00–03; V Burnham from 03; Warden of Readers Wells Adnry from 10; Preb Wells Cathl from 18. *The Vicarage, Rectory Road, Burnham-on-Sea TA8 2BZ* T: (01278) 782991 E: thewittsonweb@hotmail.com

WIXON, Jack. b 44. Lich Th Coll 68. **d** 71 **p** 72. C Adlington *Blackb* 71–74; C St Annes St Thos 74–76; V Chorley St Jas 76–82; V Preston Em 82–94; V Ribby w Wrea 94–04; V Ribby cum Wrea and Weeton 04–08; rtd 08; Hon C Lytham St Jo *Blackb* 08–14; PtO *Leic* 15–18; Hon C Market Harborough and The Transfiguration etc from 18; PtO *Pet* 17–22. *14 Ryelands Close, Market Harborough LE16 7XE* T: (01858) 439974 E: j.wixon@btinternet.com

WOADDEN, Christopher Martyn. b 56. St Jo Coll Nottm LTh. **d** 87 **p** 88. C Mickleover All SS *Derby* 87–90; C Wirksworth w Alderwasley, Carsington etc 90–92; C Wirksworth 92; TV Gt and Lt Coates w Bradley *Linc* 92–98; V Holton-le-Clay and Tetney 98–07; V Holton-le-Clay, Tetney and N Cotes 07–20; rtd 20. *Address temp unknown*

WOAN, Susan Ann. b 52. Univ of Wales (Abth) BSc 72 Lon Univ PGCE 73 Ch Ch Coll Cant MA 91 Rob Coll Cam BA 95 Ex Univ PhD 08. Ridley Hall Cam 93. **d** 96 **p** 97. C Histon *Ely* 96–97; C Radipole and Melcombe Regis *Sarum* 97–00; Chapl Bournemouth and Poole Coll of FE *Win* 00–04; Hon C Bournemouth St Jo w St Mich 00–04; Vice-Prin Dioc Min Course *Nor* 04–06; Prin Dioc Min Course 07–13; Vice-Prin ERMC 07–10; rtd 13; PtO *Cant* from 14. *12 St Mildred's Avenue, Birchington CT7 9LD* T: (01843) 843336 M: 07710-869135 E: sue.woan1@gmail.com

WODEHOUSE, Carol Lylie. *See* KIMBERLEY, Countess of

WODEMAN, Cyril Peter Guy. b 28. Qu Coll Cam BA 50 MA 55 ARCO 54 LRAM 58 ARCM 58. Cranmer Hall Dur 72. **d** 73 **p** 74. C Penwortham St Mary *Blackb* 73–77; V Burnley St Steph 77–85; V Hornby w Claughton 85–93; rtd 93; PtO *Blackb* 93–20; *Carl* 93–20. *5 Harling Bank, Kirkby Lonsdale, Carnforth LA6 2DJ* T: (015242) 72474

WOFFENDEN (née HANCOCK), Mrs Dorothy Myfanwy. b 41. NOC 01. **d** 03 **p** 04. NSM Brinnington w Portwood *Ches* 03–05; C Waverton w Aldford and Bruera 05–09; PtO from 09. *8 Churchill Crescent, Marple, Stockport SK6 6HJ* T: 0161-427 6839 E: dwoffenden@talktalk.net

WOGAN, Adam Charles. b 87. Hull Univ BA 12. St Steph Ho Ox BTh 15. **d** 15 **p** 16. C Scarborough St Martin *York* 15–18; C Scarborough St Sav w All SS 15–18; V E Grinstead St Mary *Chich* from 18. *St Mary's Vicarage,*

Windmill Lane, East Grinstead RH19 2DS M: 07768-195363 E: adamwogan@hotmail.co.uk

WOLFE, Canon Michael Matheson. b 29. Pemb Coll Ox BA 49 MA 53. Cuddesdon Coll 51. **d** 53 **p** 54. C Moorfields *Bris* 53–57; P-in-c Fochabers *Mor* 57–58; Sub-Warden and Chapl Aberlour Orphanage 58–59; V Southport St Paul *Liv* 59–65; V Upholland 65–73; TR 73–82; RD Ormskirk 78–82; RD Ormskirk and Hon Can Liv Cathl 78–82; Can Res Liv Cathl 82–96; Merseyside Ecum Officer 82–89; AD Toxteth and Wavertree 89–96; rtd 96; PtO *Liv* 97–21; Hon Chapl Liv Cathl from 97; Hon Sen Fell Liv Hope Univ from 10. *23 Hunters Lane, Liverpool L15 8HL* T: 0151-733 1541 M: 07712-258027 E: mwolfe@hotmail.co.uk

WOLFENDEN, Peter Graham. b 40. St Pet Coll Ox BA 63 MA 66. Linc Th Coll 62. **d** 64 **p** 65. C Adlington *Blackb* 64–66; Asst Master Barton Peveril Gr Sch 66–69; Chapl Bp Wordsworth's Sch Salisbury 69–72; Hon C Bishopstoke *Win* 66–72; Hon C Ponteland *Newc* 72–02; Hd Master Richard Coates Middle Sch Ponteland 78–01; Chapl Malta and Gozo *Eur* 02–07; Chapl Málaga 07–10; P-in-c Ovingdean *Chich* 10–18. *St James Cottage, 17 Western Road, Shoreham-by-Sea BN43 5WD* E: pgwolfenden@gmail.com

WOLTON, Adrian Kevin. b 78. **d** 14 **p** 15. C Weston-super-Mare St Paul *B & W* 14–17; Chapl Ripley St Thos C of E High Sch Lanc 17–20; P-in-c Blackpool Ch Ch w All SS *Blackb* from 20. *Address temp unknown* E: adrian@beaconblackpool.co.uk

WOLTON, Andrew John. b 54. Cranfield Univ MDA 00. St Jo Coll Nottm BA 08. **d** 08 **p** 09. C Bures w Assington and Lt Cornard *St E* 08–11; R Saxmundham w Kelsale cum Carlton 11–20; rtd 20; PtO *St E* from 20. *95 Garrison Lane, Felixstowe IP11 7RG* T: (01394) 766928 M: 07769-946364 E: revandywolton@gmail.com

WOLVERHAMPTON, Area Bishop of. *See* GREGORY, The Rt Revd Clive Malcolm

WOLVERSON, Marc Ali Morad. b 68. Univ of Kansas BA 91. Ripon Coll Cuddesdon 93. **d** 96 **p** 97. C Nantwich *Ches* 96–99; C Baton Rouge St Luke USA 99–00; C Bramhall *Ches* 00–04; V High Lane 04–09; P-in-c Douglas All SS *S & M* 09–13; AD Douglas 12; P-in-c Leyland St Jas *Blackb* from 13; AD Leyland from 16. *St James's Vicarage, 201 Slater Lane, Leyland PR26 7SH* T: (01772) 421034

WOMACK, Michael John. b 62. Anglia Ruskin Univ MA 07. Westcott Ho Cam 08. **d** 10 **p** 11. C Framlingham w Saxtead *St E* 10–13; R Athelington, Denham, Horham, Hoxne etc 13–20; rtd 20; PtO *St E* from 20. *The Chalet, Wash Lane, Wacton, Norwich NR15 2UJ* E: retiredrector@gmail.com

WOMERSLEY, Sally Ann. b 61. Westcott Ho Cam 06. **d** 08 **p** 09. C Charing w Charing Heath and Lt Chart *Cant* 08–11; Chapl Cant Ch Ch Univ 11–14; TV N Hinckford *Chelmsf* 14–19; V Milton next Gravesend Ch Ch *Roch* 19–20; C Romsey *Win* from 20. *188 Rownhams Lane, North Baddesley, Southampton SO52 9LQ* E: sally.womersley@romseyabbey.org.uk

WONG (née RUNDLE), Hilary. b 65. St Hugh's Coll Ox BA 88 Cheltenham & Glouc Coll of HE PGCE 90. Trin Coll Bris 01. **d** 03 **p** 04. C Chipping Sodbury and Old Sodbury *Glouc* 03–07; P-in-c St Helier *S'wark* 07–11; V 11–17; R Wyoming Australia from 18. *72 Bourbon Street, Wyoming NSW 2250, Australia* E: hilary193wong@hotmail.co.uk

WOO, Arthur Cheumin. b 66. Qu Univ Kingston Ontario BSc 89 MEng 91. St Jo Coll Nottm MTh 08. **d** 08 **p** 09. C Highworth w Sevenhampton and Inglesham etc *Bris* 08–12; V Cheylesmore *Cov* from 12. *Christ Church Vicarage, 11 Frankpledge Road, Coventry CV3 5GT* T: (024) 7650 2770 E: arthur@2woos.co.uk

WOOD, Alastair Paul. b 59. Ox Min Course 06. **d** 09 **p** 10. C Headington Quarry *Ox* 09–13; V Hadley and Wellington Ch Ch *Lich* 13–18; V Studley *Sarum* from 18. *St John's Vicarage, 340 Frome Road, Trowbridge BA14 0ED* M: 07580-671890 E: vicar@stjohns-studley.org

WOOD, Alexander James. b 84. St Mellitus Coll. **d** 13 **p** 14. C Brighton St Pet *Chich* 13–16; P-in-c Portsea St Alb *Portsm* from 16; P-in-c Portsea St Geo from 18; TR Forton and Gosport from 21. *39 St Andrew's Road, Southsea PO5 1ER* M: 07731-465151 E: alex@harbourchurchportsmouth.org

WOOD, Mrs Alison Jaye (Alice). b 57. La Sainte Union Coll BEd 79. STETS 09. **d** 12 **p** 13. NSM Farlington *Portsm* 12–16; C Blackmoor and Whitehill from 16; C Greatham 16–18. *The Brackens, Drift Road, Whitehill, Borden GU35 9EA* T: (01420) 472656 M: 07808-276964 E: woodcrew@tiscali.co.uk

WOOD, Mrs Ann Rene. b 49. St Deiniol's Hawarden 87. **d** 90 **p** 94. Par Dn Bamber Bridge St Aid *Blackb* 90–93; C W Burnley All SS 93–95; V Marton Moss 95–00; Hon Can Blackb Cathl 98–00; R Whiston *Sheff* 00–07; V Kimberworth 07–11; AD Rotherham 04–08; P-in-c Kimberworth Park 10–11; C Rawmarsh w Parkgate 10–11; C Greasbrough 10–11; rtd 11; PtO *Blackb* 11–14 and from 20; AD Kirkham 14–15;

P-in-c Lytham St Jo 15–20. *10 Fosbrooke House, 8 Clifton Drive, Lytham St Annes FY8 5RQ* E: ann.wood6@btopenworld.com

WOOD (*née* **BLACKBURN**)**, Mrs Anne Dorothy.** b 54. Keele Univ BA 76 Bradf Univ MSc 90. NOC 95. **d** 98 **p** 99. NSM Batley St Thos *Wakef* 98–00; C Morley St Paul 01–02; C Bruntcliffe 01–02; C Morley 02–03; TV 03–07; TV Oakenshaw, Wyke and Low Moor *Bradf* 07–10; Chapl Wakefield Hospice 09–13; Tutor Leeds Dioc Sch Min from 13; PtO *Leeds* from 17. *24 Heaton Avenue, Earlsheaton, Dewsbury WF12 8AQ* T: (01924) 455343 M: 07929-452439 E: anne.d.wood@talk21.com

WOOD (*formerly* **SWINBANK**)**, Mrs Anne Jennifer.** b 52. SS Paul & Mary Coll Cheltenham BA 90. St Steph Ho Ox 08. **d** 09. NSM N Cheltenham *Glouc* from 09. *111 Sapphire Road, Bishop's Cleeve, Cheltenham GL52 7YT* T: (01242) 700128 E: jennifer.swinbank@northchelt.org.uk

WOOD, Preb Anthony James. b 38. Kelham Th Coll 58. **d** 63 **p** 64. C Shrewsbury St Alkmund *Lich* 63; C Harlescott 63–66; C Porthill 66–70; P-in-c Priorslee 70–76; Chapl Telford Town Cen 73–76; V Barton-under-Needwood *Lich* 76–97; V Barton under Needwood w Dunstall 97–09; V Barton under Needwood w Dunstall and Tatenhill 09–10; RD Tutbury 02–10; Preb Lich Cathl 08–09; rtd 10; PtO *Lich* 11–14 and 15–21; *Leic* 14–19. *2 Shipley Close, Branston, Burton-on-Trent DE14 3HB* T: (01283) 516772 E: tonywood@preb.co.uk

WOOD, Audrey Elizabeth. *See* COUPER, Audrey Elizabeth

WOOD, Barbara Ann. b 49. St Mich Coll Llan 00. **d** 02 **p** 03. C Glan Ely *Llan* 02–05; P-in-c Llanharan w Peterston-super-Montem 05–19; PtO from 19. *6 Caldicott Close, Beddau, Pontypridd CF38 2LE* M: 07960-638290 E: babswood01@hotmail.com

WOOD, Beresford Donald Richard. b 32. Leeds Univ BA 58. Cant Sch of Min 91. **d** 94 **p** 95. Chapl St Mary's Sch Westbrook 94–02; NSM Folkestone St Mary and St Eanswythe *Cant* 94–02; PtO 02–15. *St Katherine's Cottage, Pound Lane, Elham, Canterbury CT4 6TS* T: (01303) 840817

WOOD, Canon Beryl Jean. b 54. Linc Th Coll 85. **d** 87 **p** 94. C Gaywood, Bawsey and Mintlyn *Nor* 87–92; Asst Chapl Univ Hosp Nottm 93–95; R Shipdham w Bradenham *Nor* 95–06; RD Dereham in Mitford 00–04; Dep Warden Launde Abbey *Leic* 06–09; TR Gaywood *Nor* 10–15; Hon Can Nor Cathl 05–06 and 13–15; rtd 15; PtO *Nor* from 16. *51 Peckover Way, South Wootton, King's Lynn PE30 3UE* T: (01553) 676710 E: beryljwood@yahoo.com

WOOD, Mrs Brenda. b 46. Eliz Gaskell Coll Man TCert 67 Leeds Metrop Univ BEd 94 Leeds Univ MA 04. NOC 00. **d** 03 **p** 04. NSM Kirkstall *Ripon* 03–11; rtd 11. *18 Wentworth Crescent, Leeds LS17 7TW* T: 0113-226 7991 E: bwood@ntlworld.com

WOOD, Brian Richard. b 49. Sheff Univ BA 70 MCMI 78 RIBA 85 MRICS 00 FCIOB 00. Ox Min Course 04. **d** 07 **p** 08. NSM Blenheim *Ox* 07–12; NSM Akeman 12–19; rtd 19; PtO *Ox* 19; *Ex* from 19. *15B Arundel Crescent, Plymouth PL1 5DY* E: revbrianwood@gmail.com

WOOD, Mrs Bryony Ann. b 59. St Jo Coll Nottm BA 10. **d** 10 **p** 11. C Derby St Pet and Ch Ch w H Trin 10–11; C Ashbourne St Oswald w Mapleton 11–12; C Hadfield 12–14; V Whatton w Aslockton, Hawksworth, Scarrington etc *S'well* 14–17; TV Market Harborough and The Transfiguration etc *Leic* 17–20; rtd 20; PtO *S'well* from 21. *Cornerstones, Main Street, Clarborough, Retford DN22 9LN* M: 07967-113028 E: bryony.wood@yahoo.co.uk

WOOD, Sister Catherine Rosemary. b 54. Melbourne Coll of Div 82 St Jo Coll Auckland 83. **d** 83 **p** 84. C Howick NZ 83–87; C Auckland St Paul 88; P-in-c Mangere E 89–90; Co-ord Environmental Educn 90–95; N Fieldworker Chr World Service 96–01; Hon C Glen Eden 90–97; NSM Auckland Cathl 98–01; PtO *S'wark* 01–02; P-in-c Tatsfield 02–08; Min Limpsfield Chart St Andr CD 02–08; PtO 08–11; Chapl HM Pris Latchmere Ho 09–11; Chapl HM Pris Wormwood Scrubs 12–14; PtO *Lon* 13–17; *S'wark* 13–17; *Ox* from 17. *St Michael's Convent, Vicarage Way, Gerrards Cross SL9 8AT* M: 07960-088873 E: silentmiaow@yahoo.co.uk

WOOD, Christine Denise. b 48. EMMTC. **d** 05 **p** 06. NSM Clifton *S'well* 05–07; Asst Chapl Notts Healthcare NHS Trust 07–10; Lead Chapl St Andr Healthcare 10–13; NSM Morton and Stonebroom w Shirland *Derby* from 09. *The Old Post Office, 8 Main Road, Higham, Alfreton DE55 6EF* T: (01773) 833152 E: cdjoakwood8@btinternet.com

WOOD, Christopher David. b 60. Worc Coll Ox BA 83 Leeds Univ MA 06. Coll of Resurr Mirfield 04. **d** 06 **p** 07. C King's Lynn St Marg w St Nic *Nor* 06–09; R Hunstanton St Mary w Ringstead Parva etc *Nor* 09–14; R Nor St Jo w St Julian 14–19; Chapl Norfolk Constabulary 16–19; V Waddington *Blackb* from 19. *The Vicarage, Slaidburn Road, Waddington,*

Clitheroe BB7 3JQ E: christopherd1760@hotmail.co.uk *or* rector.timberhill@gmail.com

WOOD, Christopher William. b 44. Rhodes Univ BA 66 UNISA BTh 82. St Bede's Coll Umtata 79. **d** 80 **p** 82. S Africa 80–87; C Houghton Regis *St Alb* 87–00; C Milton *Portsm* 00–03; PtO *Lich* 04–21. *27 Penton Walk, Stoke-on-Trent ST3 3DG* T: (01782) 311779 E: candbwood@hotmail.co.uk

WOOD, The Ven Claire. b 63. SAOMC 03. **d** 06 **p** 07. C Buckingham *Ox* 06–09; R Olney 09–17; AD Newport 15–17; Adn Loughborough *Leic* from 17. *The Archdeaconry, 21 Church Road, Glenfield, Leicester LE3 8DP* M: 07772-718225 E: claire.wood@leccofe.org

WOOD, Clive Marcus. b 52. Bradf Univ BSc 75. SEITE BA 14. **d** 14 **p** 15. NSM Belvedere All SS *Roch* 14–18; V Sidcup TV Bexley from 19. *15 Denver Road, Dartford DA1 3LA* T: (01322) 270942 M: 07982-392809 E: clivemwood@yahoo.co.uk

WOOD, Canon Colin Arthur. b 41. S'wark Ord Course 86. **d** 89 **p** 90. C Tadworth *S'wark* 89–93; TV Morden 93–06; Hon Can S'wark Cathl 05–06; rtd 06; PtO *Chich* from 17. *44 Leonora Drive, Bognor Regis PO21 3NH* T: (01243) 264192 E: colinwood685@btinternet.com

WOOD, David Christopher. b 52. Oak Hill Th Coll 89. **d** 91 **p** 92. C Kendal St Thos *Carl* 91–95; P-in-c Asby, Bolton and Crosby Ravensworth 95–05; P-in-c Barton, Pooley Bridge and Martindale 05–13; V Barton, Pooley Bridge, Martindale etc 13–18; rtd 18. *Croft Hosue, Brookside, Warcop, Appleby-in-Westmorland CA16 6PF* E: revdavidcwood@hotmail.com

WOOD, David John. b 48. Newc Univ BSc 70 PGCE 71 Open Univ MA 91. **d** 01 **p** 02. OLM Bedlington *Newc* 01–07; OLM Shotley 07–15; NSM 15–17; rtd 17; PtO *Newc* from 17; Bp's Officer for Rtd Clergy from 18. *12 Wilding Place, Longhorsley, Morpeth NE65 8LB* E: davwd50@hotmail.com

WOOD, David Michael. b 39. Chich Th Coll. **d** 82 **p** 83. C Epping St Jo *Chelmsf* 82–85; C Totton *Win* 85–88; V Southway *Ex* 88–97; P-in-c Black Torrington, Bradford w Cookbury etc 97–01; R 01–04; rtd 04; PtO *Portsm* from 04. *5 Squires Court, Raleigh Mead, South Molton EX36 4FL*

WOOD, Dennis William. b 28. Qu Mary Coll Lon BSc 53 Glas Univ PhD 57. NEOC 82. **d** 85 **p** 85. NSM Stanhope *Dur* 85–86; NSM Stanhope w Frosterley 86–94; NSM Eastgate w Rookhope 86–94; NSM Melrose *Edin* from 94. *Gordonlee, Ormiston Terrace, Melrose TD6 9SP* T: (01896) 823835 E: d.wood835@btinternet.com

WOOD, Elaine Mary. *See* RICHARDSON, Elaine Mary

WOOD, Elizabeth Lucy. b 35. WMMTC 89. **d** 92 **p** 94. NSM Wellingborough St Mark *Pet* 92–95; P-in-c Stanwick w Hargrave 95–00; PtO 00–13; Chapl to Retired Clergy and Clergy Widows' Officer 08–12. *16 Stuart Court, High Street, Kibworth Beauchamp, Leicester LE8 0LR* T: 0116-429 8978

WOOD, Geoffrey James. b 47. NOC 88. **d** 91 **p** 92. C Stainton-in-Cleveland *York* 91–94; V Middlesbrough St Oswald 94–99; V Eskdaleside w Ugglebarnby and Sneaton 99–06; rtd 06; PtO *York* 06–21. *22 Hedley Street, Guisborough TS14 6EG* T: (01287) 619286 E: frgeoff@btinternet.com

WOOD, Heather Dawn. *See* ATKINSON, Heather Dawn

WOOD, Miss Helen Ruth. b 54. Bedf Coll Lon BA 75. Glouc Sch of Min 87. **d** 91 **p** 94. NSM Up Hatherley *Glouc* 91–94; NSM Cheltenham Em w St Steph 94–09; NSM S Cheltenham from 10; Asst Chapl Cheltenham Ladies' Coll from 91. *9 Southfield Manor Park, Sandy Lane, Charlton Kings, Cheltenham GL53 9DJ* T: (01242) 242793 E: woodh@cheltladiescollege.org

WOOD, Henry. b 70. SNWTP. **d** 13 **p** 14. NSM St Helens Town Cen *Liv* from 13. *12 Clipsley Crescent, Haydock, St Helens WA11 0UH* T: (01744) 454671 E: a1harry.wood@gmail.com

WOOD, Mrs Jane Lesley. b 60. Trent Poly BA 82. WEMTC 15. **d** 18 **p** 19. NSM Dursley, Uley, Owlpen etc *Glouc* from 18. *11 Spouthouse Lane, Cam, Dursley GL11 5JP* T: (01453) 544350 M: 07443-606582 E: jane_l_wood@yahoo.co.uk

WOOD, Jennifer. *See* WOOD, Anne Jennifer

WOOD, Mrs Jennifer Sarah. b 40. Sarum Dioc Tr Coll CertEd 60. Oak Hill Th Coll 92. **d** 94 **p** 95. C St Illogan *Truro* 94–98; R Heanton Punchardon w Marwood *Ex* 98–10; C Ilfracombe SS Phil and Jas w W Down 09–10; rtd 10; PtO *Ex* 11–21. *32 Stallards, Braunton EX33 1BP* T: (01271) 812730 E: revjswood@hotmail.co.uk

WOOD, Mrs Joanne. b 81. Derby Univ BA 03. Qu Foundn (Course) 14. **d** 17 **p** 18. NSM Peel Parishes *Lich* 17–19; C Brereton and Rugeley w Armitage 19–21; P-in-c Ormesby St Marg w Scratby, Ormesby St Mich etc *Nor* from 21. *The Rectory, Church View, Ormesby, Great Yarmouth NR29 3PZ* M: 07399-539139 E: revjoowood@hotmail.com

WOOD, John. b 37. LNSM course 75. **d** 77 **p** 79. NSM Haddington *Edin* from 77. *7 Herdmanflatt, Haddington EH41 3LN* T: (01620) 822838

WOOD, John Anthony Scriven. b 48. Leeds Univ BSc 70. St Jo Coll Nottm 76. d 79 p 80. C Colwich *Lich* 79–82; C W Bridgford *S'well* 82–90; V Gamston and Bridgford 90–95; Chapl Kings Mill Cen NHS Trust 95–01; Chapl Sherwood Forest Hosps NHS Foundn Trust 01–13; rtd 13; NSM Morton and Stonebroom w Shirland *Derby* 08–18; PtO from 18. *The Old Post Office, 8 Main Road, Higham, Alfreton DE55 6EF* T: (01773) 833152 E: john.wood1948@btinternet.com

WOOD, Preb John Maurice. b 58. MBE 14. Qu Coll Cam BA 80 MA 83. Wycliffe Hall Ox BA 87. d 87 p 88. C Northwood Em *Lon* 87–91; C Muswell Hill St Jas w St Matt 91–94; P-in-c S Tottenham St Ann 94–01; V 01–18; AD E Haringey 16–17; Preb St Paul's Cathl 17–18. *c/o Hope in Tottenham, The Trampery, 639 High Road, London N17 8AA* M: 07771-867359

WOOD, Canon John Samuel. b 47. Lanchester Poly Cov BSc 69 Sheff Univ DipEd. Westcott Ho Cam 72. d 81 p 82. NSM Haverhill *St E* 81–82; NSM Haverhill w Withersfield, the Wrattings etc 82–83; C Whitton and Thurleston w Akenham 83–86; P-in-c Walsham le Willows 86–88; P-in-c Finningham w Westhorpe 86–88; R Walsham le Willows and Finningham w Westhorpe 88–94; Min Can St E Cathl 89–94; TR Whitstable *Cant* 94–02; Chapl E Kent Community NHS Trust 94–02; Hon Min Can Cant Cathl 96–02; TR Swanage and Studland *Sarum* 02–16; PtO *Sarum* 16–22; Dioc Retirement Officer from 16. *16 Dunnabridge Street, Poundbury, Dorchester DT1 3TQ* T: (01305) 268749 E: john.s.wood@btinternet.com

WOOD, Josephine Helen. b 63. Southn Univ BA 86 Dur Univ PGCE 87 Anglia Poly Univ MA 00. Sarum Coll 18. d 21. NSM Stebbing and Lindsell w Gt and Lt Saling *Chelmsf* from 21; NSM Broxted w Chickney and Tilty etc from 21. *3 New Street, Dunmow CM6 1BH* T: (01371) 878219 M: 07880-937313 E: josephine.h.wood@btinternet.com

WOOD, Kathleen. b 46. EMMTC 04. d 06 p 07. NSM Newhall *Derby* 06–09; NSM Etwall w Egginton 09–10; P-in-c Stapenhill Immanuel 10–14; rtd 14; PtO *Derby* 14–16 and from 17; Hon C Newhall 16–17; PtO *Lich* 14–19. *28 Eastfield Road, Midway, Swadlincote DE11 0DG* T: (01283) 212490 M: 07401-292180

WOOD, Canon Keith Ernest. b 33. Qu Coll Ox BA 55 BCL 56 MA 70. Wycliffe Hall Ox 56. d 58 p 59. C Barking St Marg *Chelmsf* 58–61; Min Basildon St Andr ED 61–70; V Brampton Bierlow *Sheff* 70–82; R Grasmere *Carl* 82–94; RD Windermere 89–94; Hon Can Carl Cathl 91–94 and 98–01; Bp's Dom Chapl 94–01; rtd 01; PtO *Carl* from 01. *The Old Tower, Brackenburgh, Calthwaite CA11 9PW* T: (01768) 894273

WOOD, Lee David Paul. b 86. St Mellitus Coll 19. d 21. C Baguley *Man* from 21. *The Curatage, 39 Dalebrook Road, Sale M33 3LD* M: 07399-186230 E: fr.leewood@gmail.com

WOOD (née DROBIG), Mrs Marion. b 76. Hannover Univ MA 01 Pemb Coll Ox DPhil 05. ERMC 04. d 06 p 07. C Newmarket All SS *St E* 06–09; R Shaw cum Donnington *Ox* 09–20. *Address temp unknown* M: 07979-534948 E: mariondrobig@hotmail.com

WOOD, Mark Robert. b 68. Trin Coll Ox BA 89 ALCM 83 ARCO 89. STETS 02. d 05 p 06. C Mere w W Knoyle and Maiden Bradley *Sarum* 05–08; P-in-c Wilton w Netherhampton and Fugglestone 08–13; R from 13; RD Chalke 15–19. *The Rectory, 27A West Street, Wilton, Salisbury SP2 0DL* T: (01722) 742571 M: 07770-305990 E: rectorwilton@gmail.com

WOOD, Martin. *See* WOOD, Nicholas Martin

WOOD, Martin Robert. b 65. Birm Univ BSc 86. Trin Coll Bris 98. d 00 p 01. C Wells St Cuth w Wookey Hole *B & W* 00–03; C Shepton Mallet w Doulting 03–07; P-in-c Tedburn St Mary, Whitestone, Oldridge etc *Ex* 07–10; V Tedburn St Mary, Cheriton Bishop, Whitestone etc from 10; RD Kenn 11–19. *The Rectory, Church Lane, Cheriton Bishop, Exeter EX6 6HY* T: (01647) 24119 E: revwood163@gmail.com

WOOD, Matthew Laurence. b 76. Lanc Univ BA 18 Cant Ch Ch Univ PGCE 99 ATCL 97. Ripon Coll Cuddesdon 18. d 20 p 21. C Ranmoor *Sheff* from 20. *The Vicarage, 1 Barnfield Road, Sheffield S10 5TD* M: 07900-436762 E: matt.wood@stjohnsranmoor.org.uk

WOOD, Canon Michael Frank. b 55. Nottm Univ BCombStuds. Linc Th Coll. d 84 p 85. C Marton *Blackb* 84–88; TV Ribbleton 88–93; V Blackpool St Mary 93–00; P-in-c S Shore St Pet 98–00; RD Blackpool 96–00; TR Brighouse and Clifton *Wakef* 00–08; RD Brighouse and Elland 06–08; TR Castleford 08–14; *Leeds* 14–16; P-in-c Smawthorpe *Wakef* 11–12; Armley w New Wortley *Leeds* from 16; Hon Can Bradf Cathl from 19. *31 Hill End Crescent, Leeds LS12 3PW* M: 07974-274001 E: frmw@hotmail.co.uk

WOOD, Mrs Michaela. b 69. d 01 p 02. NSM Sunbury *Lon* 01–04; NSM Whitton St Aug 04–06; NSM Aylesbury *Ox* 06–13; NSM Salfords *S'wark* 13–19; PtO *Guildf* from 19. *The Vicarage, 1 Chestnut Avenue, Esher KT10 8JL* E: michaelawood@aol.com

WOOD, Canon Nicholas Martin. b 51. Univ of Wales (Lamp) MTh 09. AKC 74 St Aug Coll Cant 75. d 75 p 76. C E Ham w Upton Park and Forest Gate *Chelmsf* 75–78; C Leyton St Luke 78–81; V Rush Green 81–91; Chapl Barking Tech Coll 81–91; TR Elland *Wakef* 91–05; RD Brighouse and Elland 96–05; Hon Can Wakef Cathl 00–05; Par Development Adv (Bradwell Area) *Chelmsf* 05–12; Miss and Min Adv (Bradwell Area) 12–19; Chapl to Bp Bradwell 11–12; Hon C Basildon St Martin 11–19; Hon Can Chelmsf Cathl 08–19; rtd 19; PtO *Chelmsf* 19–20. *126 The Willows, Colchester CO2 8PZ* T: (01206) 562343 E: frmartinwood@gmail.com

WOOD, Mrs Patricia. d 18. NSM Upper Derwent *York* from 18. *The Nook, Dale End, Hutton Buscel, Scarborough YO13 9LR* T: (01723) 862227 E: patriciawoodthenook@btinternet.com

WOOD, The Ven Rachel Astrid. b 71. Birm Univ BA 92 MA 99. Qu Coll Birm BD 98. d 99 p 00. C Attercliffe, Darnall and Tinsley *Sheff* 99–01; C Roundhay St Edm *Ripon* 01–04; Local Min Development Officer *Newc* 12–17; V Monkseaton St Mary 17–21; Hon Can Newc Cathl 18–21; Adn Northd and Can Res Newc Cathl from 21. *16 Towers Avenue, Newcastle upon Tyne NE2 3QE* M: 07469-950198 E: northumberland@newcastle.anglican.org

WOOD, Raymond John Lee. b 28. ACII 55 ACIArb. Linc Th Coll 66. d 68 p 69. C Beaconsfield *Ox* 68–72; CF 70–72; V Wath-upon-Dearne w Adwick-upon-Dearne *Sheff* 72–77; R St Tudy w Michaelstow *Truro* 77–86; P-in-c St Mabyn 82–86; R St Tudy w St Mabyn and Michaelstow 86–95; Chapl Bodmin Fire Brigade 91–14; rtd 95; PtO *Truro* 96–14; *Chich* from 14. *11 Gannon Road, Worthing BN11 2DT* T: (01903) 232303 E: rjlwood@btinternet.com

WOOD, Richard. *See* WOOD, Beresford Donald Richard

WOOD, Richard James. b 71. Oak Hill Th Coll BA 07. d 08 p 09. C Dagenham *Chelmsf* 08–09; C Leyton Ch Ch 09–12; P-in-c Aberporth w Blaenporth w Betws Ifan *St D* 12–14; PtO *Ban* from 12; NSM Tranmere St Cath *Ches* 16–19; PtO from 19. *36 Halcyon Road, Birkenhead CH41 2UQ* M: 07947-137586 E: revdrjwood@gmail.com

WOOD, Richard Stanton. b 79. Univ of Wales (Abth) BSc 02 Univ of Wales (Cardiff) BA 08. d 08 p 09. C Henfynyw w Aberaeron and Llanddewi Aberarth etc *St D* 08–11; TV Llanelli 11–13; V Bro Madryn *Ban* 13–21; Min Area Ldr Bro Tysilio from 21. *The Vicarage, Mona Road, Menai Bridge LL59 5EA* T: (01248) 717073 M: 07572-776225 E: richardwood@churchinwales.org.uk

WOOD, Roger Graham. b 49. K Coll Lon BD. Chich Th Coll 74. d 76 p 77. C Skipton H Trin *Bradf* 76–79; Dioc Youth Chapl 79–87; V Queensbury 87–96; P-in-c Langcliffe w Stainforth and Horton 96–01; V 01–13; RD Bowland 08–14; R Bolton by Bowland w Grindleton 13–14; R Bolton by Bowland w Grindleton *Blackb* 14–19; rtd 19. *Address temp unknown* E: rgwood49@gmail.com

WOOD, Roger William. b 43. Leeds Univ BA 65 MA 67 Fitzw Coll Cam BA 69 MA 75. Westcott Ho Cam 67. d 70 p 71. C Bishop's Stortford St Mich *St Alb* 70–74; C Sundon w Streatley 75–79; V Streatley 80–09; rtd 09; PtO *St Alb* from 09. *8 Ramsey Road, Barton-le-Clay, Bedford MK45 4PE* T: (01582) 883277

WOOD, Ronald Ernest. b 49. Sarum & Wells Th Coll 79. d 81 p 82. C Weston-super-Mare Cen Par *B & W* 81–84; C Forest of Dean Ch Ch w English Bicknor *Glouc* 84–88; R Sixpenny Handley w Gussage St Andrew etc *Sarum* 88–05; P-in-c Seale, Puttenham and Wanborough *Guildf* 05–10; rtd 10; Hon C Camelot Par *B & W* 10–18; PtO from 18. *5 The Paddock, Galhampton, Yeovil BA22 7AR* T: (01963) 441192

WOOD, Sarah. *See* WOOD, Jennifer Sarah

WOOD, Shane Grant Lindsay. b 60. Southn Univ BTh 91. St Steph Ho Ox 95. d 97 p 98. C Parkstone St Pet w Branksea and St Osmund *Sarum* 97–00; V Teddington SS Pet and Paul and Fulwell *Lon* 00–06; TR Aylesbury *Ox* 06–13; V Salfords *S'wark* 13–19; Bp's Adv for Min Development 13–19; V Weston *Guildf* from 19. *The Vicarage, 1 Chestnut Avenue, Esher KT10 8JL* T: (020) 8398 1849 E: shaneglwood@aol.com *or* office@allsaintsweston.com

WOOD, Sorrel May. *See* SHAMEL-WOOD, Sorrel May

WOOD, Stella Margaret. b 70. Trin Coll Ox BA 91 MA DPhil 95. STETS 95. d 97 p 98. NSM Mere w W Knoyle and Maiden Bradley *Sarum* 97–08; Chapl Sherborne Sch for Girls 00–08; Teacher 08–14; Lic to RD Sarum 08–11; Co-ord for Learning and Discipleship *Sarum* 11–14; Chapl Godolphin Sch 14–21;

Chapl Bp Wordsworth's Sch Salisbury from 21; NSM Wilton w Netherhampton and Fugglestone *Sarum* from 14. *The Rectory, 27A West Street, Wilton, Salisbury SP2 0DL* T: (01722) 742571   E: woods@godolphin.wilts.sch.uk   *or* stella.wood70@gmail.com

WOOD, Steven Paul. b 54. Fitzw Coll Cam MA 75. ERMC. d 07 p 08. NSM Hitchin *St Alb* 07–10; P-in-c Streatley 10–15; V 15–19; P-in-c Burnham Gp of Par *Nor* from 19. *The Rectory, The Pound, Burnham Market, King's Lynn PE31 8UL* M: 07704-922984

WOOD, Susan Joyce. b 52. Sheff City Coll of Educn CertEd 74. d 09 p 10. OLM Ramsbottom and Edenfield *Man* 09–14 and from 16. *243 Whittingham Drive, Ramsbottom, Bury BL0 9NY* T: (01706) 825464 E: woodsuej@btinternet.com

WOOD, Susan Pauline. b 47. Maria Grey Coll Lon TCert 68. STETS 07. d 10 p 11. NSM Staines *Lon* 10–17; rtd 17; PtO *Lon* from 19. *60 St Nicholas Drive, Shepperton TW17 9LD* T: (01932) 228712

WOOD, Timothy Robert. b 55. d 02 p 03. OLM Maidstone St Paul *Cant* 02–06; NSM Hayling Is St Andr and N Hayling St Pet *Portsm* 08–12; NSM Purbrook 12–15; C Hayling Is St Andr 15–18; NSM Walbury Beacon *Ox* from 19. *St Laurence House, West Woodhay, Newbury RG20 0BL* T: (01488) 669261 E: revtimothywood@gmail.com

WOOD, Valerie Rosemary. *See* SMITH, Valerie Rosemary

WOOD-ROBINSON, David Michael. b 28. Glas Univ BSc 50 Lon Univ BD 54. d 57 p 57. C Erith St Jo *Roch* 57–58; CMS Japan 58–71; R Holton and Waterperry *Ox* 71–88; RD Aston and Cuddesdon 88–92; R Holton and Waterperry w Albury and Waterstock 88–94; Chapl Ox Brookes Univ 90–94; rtd 94; PtO *Heref* from 15. *16 Pound Meadow, Ledbury HR8 2EU* T: (01531) 632347

WOOD-ROE (née BRYANT), Mrs Sarah Elizabeth. b 82. Grey Coll Dur BA 05 Wolfs Coll Cam MPhil 07. Westcott Ho Cam 06. d 08 p 09. C Branksome St Aldhelm *Sarum* 08–11; Chapl St Jo Sch Leatherhead 11–15; C Clarendon *Sarum* 15–17; C Salisbury St Fran and Stratford sub Castle from 17. *9 Swaynes Close, Salisbury SP1 3AE*

WOODALL, Ms Bridget Ann. b 65. CQSW 92. St Jo Coll Nottm 11. d 13 p 14. C Brierley Hill *Worc* 13–17; TV Kidderminster Ismere 17–21; V N Ormesby *York* from 21. *The Vicarage, James Street, North Ormesby, Middlesbrough TS3 6LD* T: (01642) 286122 E: revbridget.woodall@gmail.com

WOODALL, David Paul. b 59. Ches Coll of HE BTh 03. NOC 00. d 03 p 04. C Darwen St Pet w Hoddlesden *Blackb* 03–06; TV Bacup and Stacksteads *Man* 06–12; P-in-c Norden w Ashworth 12–13; C Oakenrod and Bamford 12–13; V Norden w Ashworth and Bamford 13–15; Warden Foxhill Retreat and Conf Cen *Ches* 15–16; PtO *Man* 16–17; V E Crompton 17–21; rtd 21. *1 Owen Fold, Lees, Oldham OL4 3DT* M: 07940-721097 E: dpwoodall3@gmail.com

WOODALL, Ms Rosemary Helen. b 80. Newc Univ BSc 01. Ripon Coll Cuddesdon BA 09. d 10 p 11. C Glouc City and Hempsted 10–13; P-in-c Bisley, Chalford, France Lynch, and Oakridge 13–15; P-in-c Bussage 14–15; V Bisley, Chalford, France Lynch, and Oakridge etc 15–17; Bp's Chapl *Leic* 17–21; Bp's Chapl *Chelmsf* from 21. *Bishopscourt, Main Road, Margaretting, Ingatestone CM4 0HD* T: (01277) 352001 M: 07816-420788 E: rosiewoodall@hotmail.co.uk

WOODCOCK, Anne Caroline. *See* McMULLEN, Anne Caroline

WOODCOCK, Edward Marsden. b 47. Hull Univ MSc 01 Leeds Univ BA 03. Coll of Resurr Mirfield 01. d 03 p 04. C Wrenthorpe *Wakef* 03–06; C Alverthorpe 03–06; P-in-c Brotherton *Leeds* 06–15; V 15–17; P-in-c Ferrybridge 06–17; rtd 17. *11 Aldbury Close, Barnsley S71 2BW* E: edward@thewoodcocks.plus.com

WOODCOCK, Michael David. b 67. Avery Hill Coll BEd 91. Wycliffe Hall Ox BTh 96. d 96 p 97. C Orpington Ch Ch *Roch* 96–99; R Knockholt w Halstead 99–06; P-in-c Crosthwaite Kendal *Carl* 06–21; V from 21; P-in-c Cartmel Fell 06–21; V from 21; P-in-c Winster 06–21; V from 21; P-in-c Witherslack 06–21; V from 21; P-in-c Underbarrow w Helsington from 21. *The Vicarage, Crosthwaite, Kendal LA8 8HX* T: (015395) 68276 E: mich@elwoodcock.com

WOODCOCK, Mrs Michelle Lisa. b 74. Dartington Coll of Art BA 96 Cant Ch Ch Univ PGCE 98. LCTP 08. d 10 p 11. NSM Crosthwaite, Cartmel Fell, Winster and Witherslack *Carl* 10–15; TV Cartmel Peninsula 15–17; PtO 17–21; NSM Crosthwaite Kendal from 21; NSM Cartmel Fell from 21; NSM Winster from 21; NSM Witherslack from 21. *The Vicarage, Crosthwaite, Kendal LA8 8HX* T: (015395) 68276 E: michellewoodcock74@hotmail.com

WOODE, Mrs Elizabeth. b 43. d 06 p 07. NSM Middlewich w Byley *Ches* from 06. *6 The Grange, Hartford, Northwich CW8 1QH* T: (01606) 75030 E: tonylizwoode@hotmail.com

WOODERSON, Mrs Marguerite Ann. b 44. RGN SCM. Qu Coll Birm 86. d 89 p 94. Par Dn Stoneydelph St Martin CD *Lich* 89–90; Par Dn Glascote and Stonydelph 90–91; Par Dn Chasetown 91–94; C 94; C-in-c Chase Terrace St Jo Distr Ch 92–94; Chapl Naas Gen Hosp 94–98; I Celbridge w Straffan and Newcastle-Lyons *D & G* 98–06. *Lazena, Rosses Point, Co Sligo, Republic of Ireland* T: (00353) (71) 911 7852 E: annwooderson@gmail.com

WOODERSON, Michael George. b 39. Southn Univ BA 61. Lon Coll of Div BD 69. d 69 p 70. C Morden *S'wark* 69–73; C Aldridge *Lich* 73–81; V Chasetown and P-in-c Hammerwich 91–94; RD Lich 86–94; Preb Lich Cathl 89–94; I Naas w Kill and Rathmore *M & K* 94–06; rtd 06. *Lazena, Rosses Point, Co Sligo, Republic of Ireland* T: (00353) (71) 911 7852 M: 86-336 8503 E: michaelwooderson@icloud.com

WOODFIELD, Benjamin Robert. b 81. St Jo Coll Nottm. d 14 p 15. C Astley Bridge *Man* 14–18; LtO from 18. *24 Mackenzie Street, Bolton BL1 6QW* M: 07800-746918 E: revbenwoodfield@gmail.com

WOODGATE, Elizabeth Mary. *See* IZZARD, Elizabeth Mary

WOODGER, John McRae. b 36. Univ of Wales MTh 08. Tyndale Hall Bris 60. d 63 p 64. C Heref St Pet w St Owen 63–66; C Macclesfield St Mich *Ches* 66–69; V Llangarron w Llangrove *Heref* 69–74; P-in-c Garway 70–74; R Church Stretton 74–84; Preb Heref Cathl 82–84; V Watford *St Alb* 84–01; rtd 01; PtO *Heref* 01–16; *Chich* from 17. *22 Clock Tower Court, Park Avenue, Bexhill-on-Sea TN39 3HP* T: (01424) 552953 E: woodger@talktalk.net

WOODGER, Richard William. b 50. Sarum & Wells Th Coll 76. d 79 p 80. C Chessington *Guildf* 79–82; C Frimley and Frimley Green 82–85; V N Holmwood 85–90; TR Headley All SS 90–98; TR Penrith w Newton Reigny and Plumpton Wall *Carl* 98–05; P-in-c Northleach w Hampnett and Farmington etc *Glouc* 05–13; C Sherborne, Windrush, the Barringtons etc 08–13; AD Northleach 09–10; rtd 13; PtO *Lon* from 14. *6 Sylvia Avenue, Pinner HA5 4QE* E: dickwoodger@yahoo.co.uk

WOODHALL, Neil Baxter. b 53. Yorks Min Course 13. d 15 p 16. C Selby Abbey *York* from 15. *6 Priory Park Grove, Monk Fryston, Leeds LS25 5EU* T: (01977) 682091 E: nbwoodhall@btinternet.com

WOODHAM, Richard Medley Swift. b 43. Master Mariner 70. S'wark Ord Course 71. d 73 p 74. C Gravesend St Aid *Roch* 73–75; C Chessington *Guildf* 75–78; Warden Dioc Conf Ho Horstead *Nor* 78–87; R Horstead 78–87; Youth Chapl 78–88; V Nor St Mary Magd w St Jas 87–91; TR Norwich Over-the-Water 91–98; P-in-c Lakenham St Jo 98–99; V Nor Lakenham St Jo and All SS and Tuckswood 99–06; RD Nor E 02–06; rtd 06; PtO *Nor* from 06. *40 Anchor Street, Coltishall, Norwich NR12 7AQ* T: (01603) 736411 E: richardmwoodham@gmail.com

WOODHAMS, Raymond John. b 40. Garnett Coll Lon CertEd 68 IEng 68. STETS 98 Coll of Resurr Mirfield 01. d 01 p 02. NSM E Blatchington *Chich* 01–07; NSM Eastbourne St Sav and St Pet 07–10; PtO from 10. *23 Penlands Vale, Steyning BN44 3PL* T: (01903) 367163 E: raymondj.woodhams@googlemail.com

WOODHAMS, Canon Roy Owen. b 57. ARCM 76 GRSM 78 Lon Inst of Educn TCert 79. Ripon Coll Cuddesdon 91. d 93 p 94. C Deal St Leon and St Rich and Sholden *Cant* 93–97; P-in-c Cherbury *Ox* 97–02; P-in-c Gainfield 99–02; R Cherbury w Gainfield 02–04; AD Vale of White Horse 01–04; V Fleet *Guildf* 04–13; R Cranleigh from 13; AD from 19; Hon Can Guildf Cathl from 20. *The Rectory, 15 High Street, Cranleigh GU6 8AS* T: (01483) 800655 E: roy.woodhams@gmail.com

WOODHEAD, Miss Helen Mary. b 35. Bedf Coll Lon BA 57. Westcott Ho Cam 86. d 87 p 94. Par Dn Daventry *Pet* 87–90; Asst Dioc Dir of Ords *Guildf* 90–00; C Godalming 90–95; C Worplesdon 95–00; rtd 00; PtO *Lich* 00–13 and from 18. *48 Monks Close, Lichfield WS13 6QR* T: (01543) 307403

WOODHEAD, Canon Michael. b 51. St Jo Coll Nottm 88. d 90 p 91. C Stannington *Sheff* 90–93; V Deepcar 93–01; TV Crookes St Thos 01–05; TR 05–20; Hon Can Sheff Cathl 11–20; rtd 20. *Address temp unknown* E: mick.woodhead@sheffield.anglican.org

WOODHOUSE, Canon Alison Ruth. b 43. Bedf Coll of Educn CertEd 64. Dalton Ho Bris 68. dss 79 d 87 p 94. Bayston Hill *Lich* 79–81; W Derby St Luke *Liv* 81–86; Burscough Bridge 86–95; Par Dn 87–94; C 94–95; V Formby St Luke 95–07; AD Sefton 00–05; Hon Can Liv Cathl 02–07; rtd 07; Chapl to The Queen 06–13. *16 Fountains Way, Liverpool L37 4HE* T: (01704) 877423

WOODHOUSE, The Ven Charles David Stewart. b 34. Kelham Th Coll 55. d 59 p 60. C Leeds Halton St Wilfrid *Ripon* 59–63; Youth Chapl *Liv* 63–66; Bermuda 66–69; Asst Gen Sec CEMS 69–70; Gen Sec 70–76; Bp's Dom Chapl *Ex*

76–81; R Ideford, Luton and Ashcombe 76–81; V Hindley St Pet *Liv* 81–92; Hon Can Liv Cathl 83–01; rtd 01; PtO *Liv* from 03. *9 Rob Lane, Newton-le-Willows WA12 0DR*

WOODHOUSE, David Edwin. b 45. Lon Univ BSc 68. Cuddesdon Coll 68. **d** 71 **p** 72. C E Dulwich St Jo *S'wark* 71–74; LtO 74–77; PtO *Bris* 77–79; LtO 79–98; PtO *Sarum* 04–21; rtd 10; PtO *Bris* from 10. *34 Cambria Place, Swindon SN1 5DN* E: kingsburyhallcd@aol.com

WOODHOUSE, David Maurice. b 40. Lon Univ BA 62. Clifton Th Coll 63. **d** 65 **p** 66. C Wellington w Eyton *Lich* 65–68; C Meole Brace 68–71; V Colwich 71–82; P-in-c Gt Haywood 78–82; R Clitheroe St Jas *Blackb* 82–88; Ellel Grange Chr Healing Cen 88–91; V The Lye and Stambermill *Worc* 91–99; Chapl Acorn Chr Foundn 99–02; Dioc Healing Adv *Guildf* 00–02; rtd 02; PtO *Blackb* from 04. *1 Lilac Avenue, Penwortham, Preston PR1 9PB* T: (01772) 742088

WOODHOUSE, Canon Keith Ian. b 33. K Coll Lon 54. **d** 58 **p** 59. C Stockton St Chad CD *Dur* 58–61; C Man St Aid 61–64; V Peterlee *Dur* 64–99; AD Easington 72–98; Hon Can Dur Cathl 79–99; rtd 99; Dioc Pensions and Widows Officer *Dur* from 00; PtO from 04. *85 Baulkham Hills, Penshaw, Houghton le Spring DH4 7RZ* T/F: 0191-584　3977　E: keithianwoodhouse@excite.com　or keith.woodhouse@durham.anglican.org

WOODHOUSE, Canon Patrick Henry Forbes. b 47. Ch Ch Ox BA 69 MA 81. St Jo Coll Nottm 69 Lon Coll of Div ALCD 71 LTh 71. **d** 72 **p** 73. C Birm St Martin 72–74; C Whitchurch *Bris* 75–76; C Harpenden St Nic *St Alb* 76–80; Tanzania 80–81; Soc Resp Officer *Carl* 81–85; P-in-c Dean 81–85; Dir Soc Resp *Win* 85–90; V Chippenham St Andr w Tytherton Lucas *Bris* 90–00; Can Res and Prec Wells Cathl *B & W* 00–12; rtd 12; PtO *B & W* from 14. *Woodside, Rimpton, Yeovil BA22 8AF* T: (01935) 850915　M: 07812-395912 E: pwoodhouse09@gmail.com

WOODHOUSE, Canon Thomas Mark Bews. b 66. Chelt & Glouc Coll of HE BA 03 Glos Univ MA 05 FRSA 05. Aston Tr Scheme 90 Westcott Ho Cam 92. **d** 95 **p** 96. C Cainscross w Selsley *Glouc* 95–98; V Hardwicke and Elmore w Longney 98–05; P-in-c Wootton Bassett *Sarum* 05–10; V R Wootton Bassett 10–14; P-in-c Lyneham w Bradenstoke 11–14; NSM Woodhill 11–14; RD Calne 06–14; TR Dorchester and the Winterbournes 14–19; Can and Preb Sarum Cathl 09–19; Chapl to RVO and Qu Chpl of the Savoy from 19; Dep P in O from 19; Can Chpls R from 21; PtO *Lon* from 19; *S'wark* from 20. *The Queen's Chapel of the Savoy, Savoy Hill, London WC2R 0DA* T: (020) 7379 8088 E: twoodhouse@duchyoflancaster.co.uk

WOODING, Alison. b 67. Leeds Univ MA 11. Wilson Carlile Coll 03 Yorks Min Course 05. **d** 10 **p** 11. C Ranmoor *Sheff* 10–15; P-in-c Kimberworth and Kimberworth Park 15–17; C Rawmarsh w Parkgate 15–17; C Greasbrough 15–17; Asst Dean CA 17–21; TV Harden and Wilsden, Cullingworth and Denholme *Leeds* from 21. *The Vicarage, Halifax Road, Cullingworth, Bradford BD13 5DE* M: 07415-105965 E: revalisonwooding@gmail.com

WOODING JONES, The Ven Andrew David. b 61. Hull Univ MBA 01. Oak Hill Th Coll BA 91. **d** 91 **p** 92. C Welling *Roch* 91–95; TV Crookes St Thos *Sheff* 95–00; Resident Dir Ashburnham Trust 00–12; NSM Ashburnham w Penhurst *Chich* 01–12; Dir World Prayer Cen Birm 12–14; PtO *Roch* 14–18; *Chich* 15–18; Adn Roch from 18. *Lytlewood, Riding Lane, Hildenborough, Tonbridge TN11 9LR* M: 07843-358553 E: archdeacon.rochester@rochester.anglican.org

WOODLEY, David James. b 38. K Coll Lon BD 61 AKC 61 Open Univ BA 98. **d** 62 **p** 63. C Lancing St Jas *Chich* 62–64; C St Alb St Pet 64–67; Malaysia 67–70; LtO *Linc* 71–72; V Westoning w Tingrith *St Alb* 72–77; Asst Chapl HM Pris Wormwood Scrubs 77–78; Chapl HM Pris Cardiff 78–84; Chapl HM Rem Cen Risley 84–92; Chapl HM Pris Styal 92–98; rtd 98; PtO *Ches* 98–06; *B & W* 08–19. *18 Longcroft Road, Yeovil BA21 4RR* T: (01935) 474072

WOODLEY, Canon John Francis Chapman. b 33. Univ of Wales (Lamp) BA 58. Edin Th Coll 58. **d** 60 **p** 61. C Edin All SS 60–65; Chapl St Andr Cathl *Ab* 65–67; Prec 67–71; R Glas St Oswald 71–77; P-in-c Cumbernauld 77–93; Can St Mary's Cathl 82–99; CSG from 82; R Dalbeattie *Glas* 93–99; rtd 99; Hon Can St Mary's Cathl from 99; Dioc Supernumerary 99–03; LtO from 03. *McMillan House, 33 Buchanan Drive, Rutherglen, Glasgow G73 3PF* T: 0141-647 3118 E: jonfwoodley@icloud.com

WOODLEY, Priscilla Elizabeth. *See* SLUSAR, Priscilla Elizabeth

WOODLEY, Simon Andrew. b 66. Liv Univ BA 88 Univ of Cen England in Birm 96. Ridley Hall Cam BTh 00. **d** 00 **p** 01. C Birm St Martin w Bordesley St Andr 00–04; TR Bemerton *Sarum* 04–18; V Alderholt from 18. *The Vicarage, Daggons Road, Alderholt, Fordingbridge SP6 3DN* E: revwoodley@yahoo.co.uk

WOODMAN, Andrew Christopher. b 83. Ridley Hall Cam 15. **d** 17 **p** 18. C The Mitre Benefice *Nor* from 17; Chapl UEA from 21. *St Mary's Vicarage, Douglas Haig Road, Norwich NR5 8LD* M: 07834-189519 E: andy.woodman@stn.org.uk

WOODMAN, Oliver Nigel. b 47. FCIPD. Sarum Th Coll 67. **d** 70 **p** 82. C Stepney St Dunstan and All SS *Lon* 70–71; NSM Ovingdean w Rottingdean and Woodingdean *Chich* 81–87; NSM Eastbourne St Sav and St Pet 88–93; Asst to RD Eastbourne 93–98; NSM Eastbourne St Sav and St Pet 98–01; PtO *Win* 02–10; Hon Chapl Win and Eastleigh Healthcare NHS Trust 09–10; PtO *Lich* 10–16 and from 20. *25A Wissage Lane, Lichfield WS13 6DF* T: (01543) 256655 E: ojwoodman56@gmail.com

WOODMAN, The Ven Peter Wilfred. b 36. Univ of Wales (Lamp) BA 58. Wycliffe Hall Ox 58. **d** 60 **p** 61. C New Tredegar *Mon* 60–61; C Newport St Paul 61–64; C Llanfrechfa All SS 64–66; Abp of Wales's Messenger 66–67; V Llantilio Pertholey w Bettws Chpl etc *Mon* 67–74; V Bassaleg 74–90; Can St Woolos Cathl 84–01; V Caerwent w Dinham and Llanfair Discoed etc 90–96; Adn Mon 93–01; R Mamhilad and Llanfihangel Pontymoile 96–01; rtd 01. *Glaslyn, 40 Longhouse Barn, Penperlleni, Pontypool NP4 0BD* T: (01873) 881322 E: petglen@gmail.com

WOODMANSEY, Michael Balfour. b 55. Leic Univ BSc. Ridley Hall Cam. **d** 83 **p** 84. C St Paul's Cray St Barn *Roch* 83–89; C S Shoebury *Chelmsf* 89–93; R Stifford 93–01; TR Heworth H Trin *York* 01–07; R Heworth H Trin and St Wulstan 07–20; rtd 20. *Address temp unknown*

WOODMORE, Mrs Dilys Mary. b 44. SAOMC 98. **d** 01 **p** 02. NSM Dedworth *Ox* 01–04; NSM Burchetts Green 04–14; rtd 14; PtO *Ox* from 14. *59 Terrington Hill, Marlow SL7 2RE* T: (01628) 486274

WOODROW, Mark Jason. b 72. MInstLM 10 FRAS 18. Ripon Coll Cuddesdon 11. **d** 13 **p** 14. C Lavenham w Preston *St E* 13–16; P-in-c Stoke by Nayland w Leavenheath and Polstead 16–20; P-in-c Nayland w Wiston 16–20; R Stoke by Nayland w Leavenheath etc 20–21; RD Hadleigh 18–20; R Stour Valley from 21. *The Vicarage, 14 High Street, Clare, Sudbury CO10 8NY* T: (01787) 277515 E: revdmarkwoodrow@gmail.com

WOODRUFF, Mrs Celia Mary. b 52. **d** 14 **p** 15. NSM Vale and Cotswold Edge *Glouc* 14–17; P-in-c Burpham *Chich* from 17; P-in-c Poling from 17. *The Vicarage, Burpham, Arundel BN18 9RJ* E: ronaldandcelia@btinternet.com

WOODS, The Very Revd Alan Geoffrey. b 42. TD 93. ACCA 65 FCCA 80. Sarum Th Coll 67. **d** 70 **p** 71. C Bedminster St Fran *Bris* 70–73; Youth Chapl 73–76; Warden Legge Ho Res Youth Cen 73–76; P-in-c Neston *Bris* 76–79; TV Gtr Corsham 79–81; CF (TA) 80–94; P-in-c Charminster *Sarum* 81–83; V Charminster and Stinsford 83–90; RD Dorchester 85–90; Chapl Dorchester Hosps 86–87; V Calne and Blackland *Sarum* 90–96; RD Calne 90–96; Chapl St Mary's Sch Calne 90–96; Can and Preb Sarum Cathl 92–96; Sen Chapl Malta and Gozo *Eur* 96–03; Chan Malta Cathl 96–03; Dean Gib 03–08; V Gen to Bp Eur 03–05; Adn Gib 05–08; P-in-c Málaga 06–07; rtd 08; PtO *Sarum* from 08; *Eur* from 08; Dioc Retirement Officer *Sarum* 10–16. *6 Maumbury Square, Weymouth Avenue, Dorchester DT1 1TY* T: (01305) 264877 E: abwoods@tiscali.co.uk

WOODS, Andrea Ruth. b 68. ERMC 17. **d** 19 **p** 20. C Mattishall and the Tudd Valley *Nor* from 19. *The New Rectory, Rectory Road, Hockering, Dereham NR20 3HP* T: (01603) 928279　M: 07870-786212 E: andrea.woods@matvchurch.uk

WOODS, Christopher Guy Alistair. b 35. Dur Univ BA 60. Clifton Th Coll 60. **d** 62 **p** 63. C Rainham *Chelmsf* 62–65; C Edin St Thos 65–69; Sec Spanish and Portuguese Ch Aid Soc 69–79; C Willesborough w Hinxhill *Cant* 74–80; P-in-c Murston w Bapchild and Tonge 80–87; R 87–90; R Gt Horkesley *Chelmsf* 90–98; RD Dedham and Tey 91–98; rtd 98; P-in-c Tenerife Sur *Eur* 99–00; PtO *Chelmsf* from 00. *Bluebonnet, Mill Lane, Bradfield, Manningtree CO11 2UT* T: (01255) 870411

WOODS, Christopher Morrison. b 77. St Andr Univ MA 00 TCD BTh 04. CITC 01. **d** 04 **p** 05. C Dundela St Mark *D & D* 04–07; Chapl Ch Coll Cam 07–10; Sec C of E Liturg Commn and Nat Worship Development Officer Abps' Coun 11–13; Tutor Westcott Ho Cam 12–13; PV St Jo Coll Cam 12–13; P-in-c Hoxton St Anne w St Columba *Lon* 13–15; V 15–19; Educator in Adult Learning and Development Stepney Area 13–19; V Ox St Barn and St Paul w St Thos from 19. *St Barnabas' Vicarage, St Barnabas Street, Oxford OX2 6BG* T: (01865) 964041 E: revdchris@icloud.com

WOODS, David Benjamin. b 42. Linc Th Coll 88. **d** 90 **p** 91. C Louth *Linc* 90–93; P-in-c Ingoldmells w Addlethorpe 93–97;

R 97–01; P-in-c Sutton Bridge 01–08; rtd 08; Hon C Digby Gp *Linc* from 08. *10 Mayflower Drive, Heckington, Sleaford NG34 9UX* M: 07840-544384 E: woods_david4@sky.com

WOODS, Edward Christopher John. b 44. NUI BA 67. CITC 66. **d** 67 **p** 68. C Drumglass *Arm* 67–70; C Belfast St Mark *Conn* 70–73; I Kilcolman *L & K* 73–78; I Portarlington w Cloneyhurke and Lea *M & K* 78–84; Chan Kildare Cathl 81–84; I Killiney Ballybrack *D & G* 85–92; I Dublin Rathfarnham 93–14; Dir of Ords (Dub) 98–14; Internship Co-ord CITC 10–14; rtd 14; PtO *Liv* from 16. *St Peter's Vicarage, Cricket Path, Formby, Liverpool L37 7DP* T: (01704) 872824 E: tedwoods1607@gmail.com

WOODS, Canon Eric John. b 51. DL 12. Magd Coll Ox BA 72 MA 77 Trin Coll Cam BA 77 MA 83 FRSA 94. Westcott Ho Cam 75. **d** 78 **p** 79. C Bris St Mary Redcliffe w Temple etc 78–81; Hon C Clifton St Paul 81–83; Asst Chapl Bris Univ 81–83; V Wroughton 83–93; RD 88–93; V Sherborne w Castleton, Lillington and Longburton *Sarum* 93–16; TR 16–20; Chapl Sherborne Sch for Girls 93–99; RD Sherborne *Sarum* 96–04; Can and Preb Sarum Cathl 98–20; Chapl Dorset Community NHS Trust 93–00; Chapl SW Dorset Primary Care Trust 01–20; Chapl St Antony's Leweston Sch Sherborne 03–17; rtd 20; PtO *Sarum* from 21. *5 Hosey Road, Sturminster Newton DT10 1QP* M: 07900-682371 E: ejw1539@gmail.com

WOODS, Frederick James. b 45. Southn Univ BA 66 MPhil 74 Fitzw Coll Cam BA 76 MA 79. Ridley Hall Cam 74. **d** 77 **p** 78. C Stratford-on-Avon w Bishopton *Cov* 77–81; V Warminster Ch Ch *Sarum* 81–96; RD Heytesbury 95–96; TR Woodley *Ox* 96–01; V Colchester St Pet and St Botolph *Chelmsf* 01–11; rtd 11; PtO *St E* from 16. *36 Church Road, Otley, Ipswich IP6 9NP* T: (01473) 890786 E: fredjwoods@hotmail.com

WOODS, Geoffrey Edward. b 49. Lon Univ BD 70 K Coll Lon MA 94. Tyndale Hall Bris 67. **d** 73 **p** 74. C Gipsy Hill Ch Ch *S'wark* 73–76; C Uphill *B & W* 76–79; R Swainswick w Langridge and Woolley 79–84; PtO *Bris* 84–96; NSM Colerne w N Wraxall 96–12; NSM By Brook 06–11; NSM Box w Hazlebury and Ditteridge 11–12; rtd 14; PtO *Bris* from 12. *22 Watergates, Colerne, Chippenham SN14 8DR* T: (01225) 743675

WOODS, Michael. b 57. Ripon Coll Cuddesdon 99. **d** 01 **p** 02. C Bamber Bridge St Aid *Blackb* 01–06; P-in-c Rishton 06–11; V 11–15; AD Whalley 11–15; R Croston, Bretherton and Mawdesley w Bispham from 15. *The Rectory, 22 Out Lane, Croston, Leyland PR26 9HJ* T: (01772) 600548 E: revmwoods@gmail.com

WOODS, Canon Norman Harman. b 35. K Coll Lon BD 62 AKC 62. **d** 63 **p** 64. C Poplar All SS w St Frideswide *Lon* 63–68; C-in-c W Leigh CD *Portsm* 68–76; V Hythe *Cant* 76–01; RD Elham 83–89; Hon Can Cant Cathl 90–01; rtd 01; PtO *Cant* from 01. *36 Abbey Gardens, Canterbury CT2 7EU* T: (01227) 470957 E: normanwoods@talktalk.net

WOODS, Richard Thomas Evelyn Brownrigg. b 51. St Steph Ho Ox 83. **d** 85 **p** 86. C Southgate Ch Ch *Lon* 85–88; C Northampton All SS w St Kath *Pet* 88–89; V Maybridge *Chich* 89–99; V E Dean 99–05; R Singleton 99–05; V W Dean 99–05; R E Dean, Singleton, and W Dean 05–13; rtd 13; PtO *Cant* from 15. *12 Whittington Terrace, Cox Hill, Shepherdswell, Dover CT15 7NH* T: (01304) 268013 M: 07717-473774 E: rtebw@outlook.com

WOODS, Roger Andrew. b 60. Southn Univ BSc 81. Oak Hill Th Coll BA 01. **d** 98 **p** 99. C Audley *Lich* 98–02; TV Leek and Meerbrook 02–15; V Kings Heath *Pet* from 15; Dioc Urban Support Officer from 15. *The Vicarage, The Bartons Close, Northampton NN5 7HQ* T: (01604) 599902 E: rogerwoodsinbox@gmail.com

WOODS, Stephanie Ruth. b 64. Westhill Coll Birm BEd 92 TCD MTh 12. **d** 11 **p** 12. C Drung w Castleterra, Larah and Lavey etc *K, E & A* 12–15; I Lisbellaw *Clogh* from 15. *The Rectory, Drummeer Road, Faughard, Lisbellaw, Enniskillen BT94 5ES* T: (028) 6638 5894 M: 07759-949932 E: alldonkeysneedshelter@yahoo.ie *or* lisbellaw@clogher.anglican.org

WOODS, Timothy James. b 52. Poly Cen Lon BA 78 MSc 79 Ex Univ MA 96 ACIB 75. Qu Coll Birm 81. **d** 83 **p** 84. C Brierley Hill *Lich* 83–86; C Stoneydelph St Martin CD 86–88; World Development Officer 86–88; Chr Aid Area Sec (SE Lon) 88–91; V Estover *Ex* 91–97; TR Brixham w Churston Ferrers and Kingswear 97–00; Dir Bd of Ch and Soc *Sarum* 00–05; RD Salisbury 03–07; Advocacy and Middle E Desk Officer USPG 05–08; Regional Co-ord Wales and W of England 10; In Methodist Ch 08–09; LtO *Ex* 10–12; Miss Enabler Devonport St Aubyn and Plymouth Waterfront 13–17; rtd 17; PtO *B & W* from 18; *Ex* 18–19. *72 Parkhouse Road, Minehead TA24 8AF* T: (01643) 818665 E: timber.woods@yahoo.co.uk

WOODSFORD, Martyn Paul. b 64. Oak Hill Th Coll 01 Adelaide Coll of Div BMin 15. **d** 03 **p** 04. C Southover *Chich* 03–07; P-in-c S Malling 07–09; P-in-c Adelaide St Luke Australia 09–14; P-in-c Adelaide St Oswald 14–18; TR Halewood and Hunts Cross *Liv* from 18. *The Rectory, 3 Rectory Drive, Liverpool L26 6LJ* E: revwoody@me.com

WOODWARD, Andrew John. b 59. ACIB 85. SEITE 96. **d** 99 **p** 00. NSM Weybridge *Guildf* 99–03; NSM St Botolph Aldgate w H Trin Minories *Lon* 03–07; PtO *Guildf* 03–07; P-in-c Kemp Town St Mary *Chich* 07–19; V from 19; RD Brighton from 15. *10 Chesham Street, Brighton BN2 1NA* T: (01273) 698601 M: 07434-605749 E: ruraldeanbrighton@gmail.com

WOODWARD, Anthony John. b 50. Salford Univ BSc 78. St Jo Coll Nottm 79. **d** 81 **p** 82. C Deane *Man* 81–84; CF 84–87; R Norris Bank *Man* 87–90; V Lostock St Thos and St Jo 92–96; PtO 96–01; C Halliwell 01–02; TV 02–04; P-in-c Chard and Distr *B & W* 04–06; V Chard St Mary 06–09; P-in-c Combe St Nicholas w Wambrook and Whitestaunton 08–09; rtd 09; PtO *Man* from 14; C W Monkton w Kingston St Mary, Broomfield etc *B & W* 15–17. *58 Woodstock Drive, Bolton BL1 6BB* T: 07827-917209 E: tonyjohn1950@gmail.com

WOODWARD, Clive Ian. b 49. City of Lon Poly BSc 84 Win Univ MA 16. STETS 01. **d** 04 **p** 05. NSM Willingdon *Chich* 04–06 and 12–19; Chapl E Sussex Hosps NHS Trust 06–12; rtd 19; PtO *Chich* from 19. *61 Rowan Avenue, Eastbourne BN22 0RX* T: (01323) 509891 E: revd.clive@hotmail.com

WOODWARD, Dennis Andrew. b 82. Maastricht Hotel Management Sch BBA 06. Ridley Hall Cam 12. **d** 15 **p** 17. C Beckenham Ch Ch *Roch* 15–16; C Tonbridge St Steph 16–17; Chapl Rotterdam w Schiedam Miss to Seafarers *Eur* from 17. *Kweeper 10, 5251 TZ Vlijmen, The Netherlands* M: (0031) 61-377 2464 E: revdenniswoodward@gmail.com

WOODWARD, Canon Ian. b 44. OLM course 96. **d** 97 **p** 98. OLM Queen Thorne *Sarum* 97–99; Adv to Bd of Ch and Soc 97–00; NSM Wilton w Netherhampton and Fugglestone *Sarum* 00–02; R Bere Regis and Affpuddle w Turnerspuddle 02–14; Can and Preb Sarum Cathl 07–14; rtd 14; V of the Close Sarum Cathl 14–19; PtO from 19; *Portsm* from 21. *75 High Street, Portsmouth PO1 2HH* T: (023) 9273 0158 M: 07973-318866 E: revianw@btinternet.com

WOODWARD, Prof James Welford. b 61. K Coll Lon BD 82 AKC 82 Lambeth STh 85 Birm Univ MPhil 91 Open Univ PhD 99 FRSA 07. Westcott Ho Cam 83. **d** 85 **p** 86. C Consett *Dur* 85–87; Bp's Dom Chapl *Ox* 87–90; Chapl Qu Eliz Hosp Birm 90–96; Distr Chapl Co-ord S Birm HA 90–96; Chapl Manager Univ Hosp Birm NHS Trust 92–96; P-in-c Middleton *Birm* 96–98; P-in-c Wishaw 96–98; Bp's Adv on Health and Soc Care 96–09; V Temple Balsall 98–09; Master Foundn and Hosp of Lady Katherine Leveson 98–09; Dir Leveson Cen for the Study of Ageing, Spirituality and Soc Policy 00–09; Can Windsor 09–15; Prin Sarum Coll from 15; Visiting Prof Th Win Univ from 17; Can and Preb Sarum Cathl from 15. *Sarum College, 19 The Close, Salisbury SP1 2EE* T: (01722) 424801 E: jww@sarum.ac.uk

WOODWARD, Canon John Clive. b 35. Univ of Wales (Lamp) BA 56. St Jo Coll Dur 56. **d** 58 **p** 59. C Risca *Mon* 58–63; C Chepstow 63–66; V Ynysddu 66–74; V Newport Ch Ch 74–84; Can St Woolos Cathl 82–00; TR Cyncoed 84–00; rtd 00. *17 Carisbrooke Way, Cyncoed, Cardiff CF23 9HS* T: (029) 2048 4448

WOODWARD, Mrs Margaret Ruth. b 59. EMMTC 04. **d** 08 **p** 09. NSM Flintham *S'well* 08–14; NSM Car Colston w Screveton 08–14; NSM Hickling w Kinoulton and Broughton Sulney from 14. *The Rectory, 41 Main Street, Kinoulton, Nottingham NG12 3EN* T: (01949) 81183

WOODWARD, Mark Christian. b 73. Univ of Wales (Lamp) BA 95 Trin Coll Carmarthen PGCE 97. Trin Coll Bris MA 02. **d** 02 **p** 03. C Egham *Guildf* 02–06; R Stoke-next-Guildf from 06; Chapl Guildf Coll of FE and HE from 06. *8 Brockway Close, Guildford GU1 2LW* T: (01483) 535664 *or* 574562 M: 07949-630031 E: mark@stjohnstoke.com

WOODWARD, Matthew Thomas. b 75. Brunel Univ BA 97 K Coll Lon MA 99 Anglia Poly Univ MA 05. Westcott Ho Cam 99. **d** 01 **p** 02. C Hampstead St Jo *Lon* 01–05; P-in-c Pimlico St Sav 05–10; R San Mateo Transfiguration USA from 10. *3900 Alameda de las Pulgas, San Mateo CA 94403-4110, USA* T: (001) (650) 341 8206 E: matthewwoodward@mac.com

WOODWARD, Merriel Frances. b 55. Brighton Univ BA 08 RGN 81. Ripon Coll Cuddesdon 10. **d** 11 **p** 12. NSM Langney *Chich* 11–17; NSM Willingdon from 17. *61 Rowan Avenue, Eastbourne BN22 0RX* T: (01323) 509891 E: revd.merriel@hotmail.co.uk

WOODWARD (née HIGGINS), Natasha Caroline. b 76. Clare Coll Cam BA 98 MA 02. Westcott Ho Cam 03. **d** 06 **p** 07. C Crayford *Roch* 06–07; C Orpington All SS 08–10;

C Chingford SS Pet and Paul *Chelmsf* 10–13; V Kingsbury H Innocents *Lon* 13–20; C Brondesbury Ch Ch and St Laur from 20; Lic Lay Min Tr Officer Willesden Area from 15; Dean of Women's Min Willesden Area from 19. *49 Keslake Road, London NW6 6DH* E: natasha.c.woodward@gmail.com *or* natasha.woodward@london.anglican.org

WOODWARD, Canon Peter Cavell. b 36. St Cath Coll Cam BA 58 MA 62. Bps' Coll Cheshunt 58. **d** 60 **p** 61. C Chingford St Anne *Chelmsf* 60–63; Madagascar 63–75; V Weedon Bec *Pet* 75–76; P-in-c Everdon w Farthingstone 75–76; V Weedon Bec w Everdon 76–81; RD Daventry 79–81; Can Pet Cathl 81–02; V Brackley St Pet w St Jas 81–02; Chapl Brackley Cottage Hosp 81–02; RD Brackley *Pet* 82–88; rtd 02; PtO *Pet* from 02; Chapl to Retired Clergy and Clergy Widows' Officer from 08. *7 Glastonbury Road, Northampton NN4 8BB* T: (01604) 660679 E: peterandmary@oddbod.org.uk

WOODWARD, Roger David. b 38. WMMTC 87. **d** 90 **p** 91. C Castle Bromwich SS Mary and Marg *Birm* 90–93; C Kingstanding St Luke 93–04; C Kingstanding St Mark 93–04; rtd 04; Hon C Kingstanding St Mark *Birm* 04–07; PtO *Worc* from 10. *10 Baldwin Road, Bewdley DY12 2BP* T: (01827) 918037

WOODWARD-RUSSELL, Andrew Gregory. b 80. UEA BSc 02 St Edm Coll Cam BTh 05. Westcott Ho Cam 14. **d** 16 **p** 18. C E Greenwich *S'wark* 16–19; Chapl Methodist Homes for the Aged from 19; PtO *Cov* from 19; *Birm* from 20. *Herondale and Kingfisher House Care Home, 175 Yardley Green Road, Bordesley Green, Birmingham B9 5PU* M: 07952-856044 E: andrew.russell@gmx.com

WOODWELL, Sister Anita Marie. b 42. Nottm Univ BA 74 CertEd 80. St Deiniol's Hawarden 85. **dss** 86 **d** 87 **p** 05. Mottram in Longdendale w Woodhead *Ches* 86–89; Par Dn 87–89; Team Dn Birkenhead Priory 89; PtO *Ban* from 01; *St D* from 04; P-in-c Llanfrechfa and Llanddewi Fach w Llandegfeth *Mon* 05–09; Dioc Adv on Spirituality 09–13; PtO from 13. *1 White Houses, Pentwyn, Abersychan, Pontypool NP4 7SY* T: (01495) 753195 E: awoodwell@yahoo.com

WOOFF, Ms Erica Mielle. b 67. City Univ BSc 90 Lon Inst of Educn MA 95 Heythrop Coll Lon MA 05. SEITE 02. **d** 05 **p** 06. C Sydenham St Bart *S'wark* 05–08; P-in-c Charlton 08–09; R 09–16; P-in-c Stockwell St Andr and St Mich 16–19; V from 19. *St Michael's Vicarage, 78 Stockwell Park Road, London SW9 0DA* T: (020) 7274 6480

WOOKEY, Canon Frances Anne. b 52. ACII 73. WEMTC 94. **d** 97 **p** 98. C Glouc St Jas and All SS 97–01; V Hanley Castle, Hanley Swan and Welland *Worc* 01–15; P-in-c Upton-on-Severn, Ripple, Earls Croome etc 11–15; RD Upton 05–11; Hon Can Worc Cathl 07–15; rtd 15; PtO *Glouc* from 15; *Worc* from 15. *51 Marlstone Road, Norman Hill, Dursley GL11 5SA* T: (01453) 519099 E: fawookey@gmail.com

WOOKEY, Stephen Mark. b 54. Em Coll Cam BA 76 MA 80. Wycliffe Hall Ox 77. **d** 80 **p** 81. C Enfield Ch Ch Trent Park *Lon* 80–84; Asst Chapl Paris St Mich *Eur* 84–87; C Langham Place All So *Lon* 87–96; R Moreton-in-Marsh w Batsford, Todenham etc *Glouc* 96–20; RD Stow 99–04; rtd 20. *2 Little Preston Road, Ryde PO33 1DG* E: stevewookey@mac.com

WOOLCOCK, Christine Ann. See FROUDE, Christine Ann

WOOLCOCK, John. b 47. Open Univ BA 82 BA 86. Wm Temple Coll Rugby 69 Sarum & Wells Th Coll 70. **d** 72 **p** 73. C Kells Carl 72–76; C Barrow St Matt 76–78; R Distington 78–86; V Staveley w Kentmere 86–93; Soc Resp Officer 89–93; Hon Can Carl Cathl 91–93; TR Egremont and Haile 93–08; P-in-c Seascale and Drigg 08–13; RD Calder 07–12; rtd 13; PtO *Carl* from 13. *6 Highfields, Whitehaven CA28 6TS* T: (01946) 590685 E: john.woolcock@btinternet.com

WOOLCOCK, Mrs Olwen Sylvia. b 57. Birm Univ BA 78. WEMTC 02. **d** 05 **p** 06. C Claines St Jo *Worc* 05–08; TR Hugglescote w Donington, Ellistown and Snibston *Leic* 08–20; P-in-c Ketton and Tinwell *Pet* from 20. *4 Edmonds Drive, Ketton, Stamford PE9 3TH* E: olwen@woolcock.org

WOOLDRIDGE, Nicholas Lee. b 83. Aus Catholic Univ BEd 07. Wycliffe Hall Ox BTh 17. **d** 17 **p** 18. C Battersea Rise St Mark *S'wark* 17–20; NSM Wimbledon Em Ridgway Prop Chpl from 21. *226 Worple Road, London SW20 8RH* M: 07534-040554 E: nicklwooldridge@hotmail.com

WOOLF, Canon Elizabeth Louise. b 73. Qu Coll Cam BA 95 MA 99. Wycliffe Hall Ox BA 05. **d** 06 **p** 07. C Holborn St Geo w H Trin and St Bart *Lon* 06–08; C Hammersmith St Paul 08–09; C Leamington Priors St Paul *Cov* 09–17; TR Leeds St Geo from 17; Hon Can Bradf Cathl from 19. *208 Kirkstall Lane, Leeds LS5 2AB* E: lizzy.woolf@stgeorgesleeds.org.uk

WOOLFORD, Thomas Alan. b 85. Oak Hill Th Coll 13. **d** 17 **p** 18. C Bispham *Blackb* 17–20; V New Longton from 20; Tutor Em Th Coll from 21. *All Saints' Vicarage, 25A Station Road, New Longton, Preston PR4 4LN*

WOOLHOUSE, Kenneth. b 38. BNC Ox BA 61 MA 65. Cuddesdon Coll 61. **d** 64 **p** 65. C Old Brumby *Linc* 64–67; Pastor Michaelshoven Soc Work Village W Germany 67–68; Chapl Cov Cathl 68–75; C-in-c Hammersmith SS Mich and Geo White City Estate CD *Lon* 75–81; Dir Past Studies Chich Th Coll 81–86; P-in-c Birdham w W Itchenor *Chich* 81–86; Chapl W Sussex Inst of HE 86–95; TV N Lambeth *S'wark* 95–01; rtd 01; PtO *S'wark* from 01. *13 Tavistock Tower, Russell Place, London SE16 7PQ* T: (020) 7237 8147

WOOLLARD, Miss Bridget Marianne. b 56. K Coll Cam BA 77 MA 80 Sheff Univ PGCE 78 St Jo Coll Dur BA 81 Birm Univ MPhil 87. Cranmer Hall Dur 79. **dss** 82 **d** 87 **p** 94. Battersea St Pet and St Paul *S'wark* 82–84; Chapl Southn Univ *Win* 84–89; Tutor Past Th and Dir Past Studies Qu Coll Birm 89–92; LtO *Birm* 89–92; Telford Chr Coun Officer for Ind and Commerce *Lich* 92–97; PtO *Heref* 92–97; Lect in Past Th Trin Coll Melbourne Australia 97–98; Chapl Addenbrooke's NHS Trust 98–02; PtO *Lich* 98–08. *37 Hatters Court, Bedworth CV12 9AU*

WOOLLARD, David John. b 39. Leic Univ BSc 62. Trin Coll Bris 86. **d** 88 **p** 89. C Clifton *York* 88–91; C York St Luke 91–94; V Selby St Jas 94–07; V Wistow 94–96; rtd 07; PtO *York* from 07. *6 Town Street, Settrington, Malton YO17 8NR* T: (01944) 768665 E: dwoollard@yahoo.co.uk

WOOLLASTON, Brian. b 53. CertEd 76. St Paul's Coll Grahamstown 81. **d** 83 **p** 84. C Kington w Huntington, Old Radnor, Kinnerton etc *Heref* 88–89; C Tupsley 89–91; V Newbridge-on-Wye and Llanfihangel Brynpabuan etc *S & B* 91–98; CF 98–03; V Whiteshill and Randwick *Glouc* 03–14; TV Stroud Team 14–19; rtd 19. *The Vicarage, 98 Farmhill Lane, Stroud GL5 4DD*

WOOLLCOMBE (*née* DEARMER), Mrs Juliet. b 38. St Mary's Coll Dur BA 60 Hughes Hall Cam DipEd 61. Gilmore Course 74. **dss** 77 **d** 87 **p** 94. St Marylebone Ch Ch *Lon* 77–80; Dean of Women's Min (Lon Area) 87–89; Dn-in-c Upton Snodsbury and Broughton Hackett etc *Worc* 89–94; NSM Pershore w Pinvin, Wick and Birlingham 94–98; rtd 98; PtO *Worc* 98–10; *Cant* from 11. *36 Sturry Court Mews, Sturry Hill, Sturry, Canterbury CT2 0ND* T: (01227) 710346 E: juliet.woollcombe1238@btinternet.com

WOOLLEY, Justine Clare. See RICHARDS, Justine Clare

WOOLMER, Preb John Shirley Thursby. b 42. Wadh Coll Ox BA 63 MA 69. St Jo Coll Nottm 70. **d** 71 **p** 72. Asst Chapl Win Coll 72–75; C Ox St Aldate w H Trin 75–82; R Shepton Mallet w Doulting *B & W* 82–02; Chapl Bath and West Community NHS Trust 97–01; Preb Wells Cathl *B & W* 00–02; NSM Leic H Trin w St Jo 02–07; Par Evang 02–07; Springboard Missr 02–04; rtd 07; PtO *Leic* from 15. *Fig Tree Cottage, Roecliffe Road, Cropston, Leicester LE7 7HQ* T: 0116-235 5237 E: jstwoolmer@googlemail.com

WOOLMER, Kelvin Frederick. b 55. EAMTC 98. **d** 01 **p** 02. NSM Squirrels Heath *Chelmsf* 01–05; NSM Harold Hill St Paul 05–06; P-in-c Stratford New Town St Paul 06–12; Ind Chapl 06–12; TV Waltham H Cross 12–17; Chapl Lon City Airport 11–17; R Bedford St Pet w St Cuth *St Alb* from 17; PtO *Eur* from 18. *The Rectory, 36 De Parys Avenue, Bedford MK40 2TP* E: kelvin.fwoolmer@gmail.com

WOOLNOUGH, Murray Robert. Wycliffe Hall Ox 07. **d** 09 **p** 10. C Newbury *Ox* 09–11; P-in-c Woy Woy Australia 11–14; R Newcastle St Jo 14–18; Sen Chapl NSW Police from 18. *PO Box 7141, Watson ACT 2602, Australia* E: mrwoolnough@gmail.com

WOOLVEN, Mrs Catherine Merris. b 60. Trin Coll Bris 07. **d** 09 **p** 10. Chapl Lee Abbey 09–10; C Kilmington, Stockland, Dalwood, Yarcombe etc *Ex* 10–14; P-in-c Uplyme w Axmouth 14–15; R 15–19; PtO *Sarum* from 19. *2 Old Foundry Cottages, Salisbury Road, Coombe Bissett, Salisbury SP5 4JT* M: 07754-582395

WOOLWAY, Joanne. See GRENFELL, Joanne Woolway

WOOLWICH, Area Bishop of. See DORGU, The Rt Revd Woyin Karowei

WOON, Canon Edward Charles. b 43. SWMTC 94. **d** 96 **p** 97. OLM Tuckingmill *Truro* 96–02; P-in-c 02–11; TV Redruth w Lanner and Treleigh 04–13; Hon Can Truro Cathl 09–13; rtd 13; PtO *Truro* from 16. *31 Trevelthan Road, Redruth TR16 4DX* T: (01209) 212191 M: 07974-431863 E: eddie.woon@btopenworld.com

WOOSTER, Patrick Charles Francis. b 38. Qu Coll Birm 63. **d** 65 **p** 66. C Chippenham St Andr w Tytherton Lucas *Bris* 65–70; C Cockington *Ex* 70–72; V Stone w Woodford *Glouc* 72–73; P-in-c Hill 72–73; V Stone w Woodford and Hill 73–99; rtd 99; PtO *Worc* from 99. *20 Hylton Road, Hampton, Evesham WR11 2QB* T: (01386) 45907

WOOSTER, Mrs Ruth Mary. b 45. SAOMC 95. **d** 98 **p** 99. OLM High Wycombe *Ox* 98–16; PtO from 16. *2 Beechwood View, Wycombe Road, Saunderton, High Wycombe HP14 4HR* T: (01494) 566117 E: ruth.mikewooster@gmail.com

WOOTTON, Philip Charles. b 63. Hatf Coll Dur BA 85 Dur Inst of Educn PGCE 86. Cranmer Hall Dur 98. d 00 p 01. C Meopham w Nurstead *Roch* 00–04; TV S Chatham H Trin 04–12; TR Tettenhall Wood and Perton *Lich* from 12. *Tettenhall Wood Rectory, 7 Broxwood Park, Wolverhampton WV6 8LZ* T: (01902) 751116 E: philwootton@sky.com

WORCESTER, Archdeacon of. See JONES, The Ven Robert George

WORCESTER, Bishop of. See INGE, The Rt Revd John Geoffrey

WORCESTER, Dean of. See ATKINSON, The Very Revd Peter Gordon

WORDSWORTH, Paul. b 42. Birm Univ BA 64. Wells Th Coll 64. d 66 p 67. C Anlaby St Pet *York* 66–71; C Marfleet 71–74; TV 72–77; V Sowerby 77–90; P-in-c Sessay 77–90; V York St Thos w St Maurice 90–01; Local Community Miss Project Ldr 90–96; Abp's Miss Adv *York* 96–00; Miss Strategy Development Officer 01–07; Abp's Officer for Miss and Evang 01–07; rtd 07; PtO *York* from 07. *10 Burniston Grove, York YO10 3RP* T: (01904) 426891 M: 07711-371046 E: pandomw04@gmail.com

WORGAN, Maurice William. b 40. Ely Th Coll 62 Sarum Th Coll 64. d 65 p 66. C Cranbrook *Cant* 65–69; C Maidstone St Martin 69–72; R Lyminge w Paddlesworth 72–73; P-in-c Stanford w Postling and Radegund 72–73; R Lyminge w Paddlesworth, Stanford w Postling etc 73–88; V Cant St Dunstan w H Cross 88–09; rtd 09; PtO *Cant* 09–12. *Old Trees, 13 Weatherall Close, Dunkirk, Faversham ME13 9UL* T: (01227) 363339 E: maurice@maurice-worgan.co.uk

WORKMAN, Aileen Joan. b 55. Linc Sch of Th and Min 11. d 15 p 16. NSM Spalding St Paul *Linc* 15–17; NSM Spalding St Mary and St Nic 15–17; C from 17. *18 Maple Grove, Spalding PE11 2LE* T: (01775) 768944 M: 07980-436097 E: aileenworkman@hotmail.co.uk

WORKMAN, John Lewis. b 26. St Deiniol's Hawarden 82. d 83 p 84. C Brecon St Mary and Battle w Llanddew *S & B* 83–86; Min Can Brecon Cathl 83–86; P-in-c Swansea St Luke 86–87; V 87–95; rtd 95. *12 Grove House, Clyne Close, Mayals, Swansea SA3 5HL* T: (01792) 405674

WORLEDGE, Paul Robert. b 70. Hertf Coll Ox BA 91 Lon Inst of Educn PGCE 92. Oak Hill Th Coll BA 00. d 00 p 01. C Boscombe St Jo *Win* 00–04; V Ramsgate St Luke *Cant* from 04; P-in-c Westgate St Sav 13–16; P-in-c Ramsgate St Geo from 21; AD Thanet 09–15. *St Luke's Vicarage, St Luke's Avenue, Ramsgate CT11 7JX* T: (01843) 592562 E: vicar@stlukesramsgate.org

WORLEY, William. b 37. TD 89. Cranmer Hall Dur 69. d 72 p 73. C Consett *Dur* 72–76; V Seaton Carew 76–03; CF (VR) from 77; rtd 03; PtO Dur 03–20. *5 Peakston Close, Hartlepool TS26 0PN* T: (01429) 293494

WORMALD, Roy Henry. b 42. Chich Th Coll 64. d 67 p 68. C Walthamstow St Mich *Chelmsf* 67–69; C Cov St Thos 69–72; C Cov St Jo 69–72; C Wood Green St Mich *Lon* 72–77; P-in-c Hanwell St Mellitus 77–80; V Hanwell St Mellitus w St Mark 80–95; C Hillingdon St Jo 95–99; R Kirkley St Pet and St Jo *Nor* 99–09; rtd 09; PtO *Nor* from 09; St E 11–21. *12 Coppleston Close, Worlingham, Beccles NR34 7SF* T: (01502) 713331

WORMSLEY (née SAVAGE), Lucy Jane. b 90. Nottm Univ BA 11. St Jo Sch of Miss Nottm BA 16. d 16 p 17. C Ossett and Gawthorpe *Leeds* 16–19; V Wyke from 19. *The Vicarage, 6 Vicarage Close, Wyke, Bradford BD12 8QW* E: revdlucy16@hotmail.com

WORN, Nigel John. b 56. Sarum & Wells Th Coll. d 84 p 85. C Walworth St Jo *S'wark* 84–88; Succ S'wark Cathl 88–92; V Mitcham Ascension 92–01; RD Merton 97; V Kew 01–21; rtd 21. *Sunnyside, Tuckingmill, Tisbury, Salisbury SP3 6JF* T: (01747) 228610 E: nigel.worn@gmail.com

WORRALL, Suzanne. See SHERIFF, Suzanne

WORSDALE, Barry. b 46. d 10 p 11. NSM Elloughton and Brough w Brantingham *York* 10–13; P-in-c N Cave w Cliffe from 13; P-in-c Hotham from 13; Chapl HM Pris Wolds from 11. *The Vicarage, Church Lane, North Cave, Brough HU15 2GJ* T: (01430) 470716 E: bworsdale@hotmail.co.uk

WORSFOLD, Canon Caroline Jayne. b 61. St Steph Ho Ox. d 88 p 94. Chapl Asst Leic R Infirmary 88–90; C Sunderland Pennywell St Thos *Dur* 90–91; Sunderland HA Chapl 90–94; Chapl Priority Healthcare Wearside NHS Trust 94–06; Chapl Northumberland, Tyne and Wear NHS Foundn Trust from 06; Hon Can Dur Cathl from 15. *The Barton Centre, Cherry Knowle Hospital, Ryhope, Sunderland SR2 0NB* T: 0191-522 7347 *or* 565 6256 ext 43370

WORSFOLD, Mrs Natalie Kim. b 70. St Mellitus Coll BA 18. d 18 p 19. C High Wycombe *Ox* 18–21; C Reading Greyfriars from 21. *24 Wheatsheaf Close, Sindlesham, Wokingham RG41 5PT* M: 07867-537604 E: revnatalie@mail.com

WORSFOLD, The Ven Richard Vernon. b 64. Ex Univ LLB 86. Cranmer Hall Dur BA 94. d 95 p 96. C Countesthorpe w Foston *Leic* 95–99; TV Bradgate Team 99–01; TR 01–09; V Leic Martyrs 09–18; AD City of Leic 14–18; Adn Leic from 18. *46 Southernhay Road, Leicester LE2 3TJ* M: 07948-385097 E: rworsfold@virginmedia.com

WORSLEY, Christine Anne. b 52. Hull Univ BA 73 Bris Univ CertEd 74 Birm Univ MPhil 94. WMMTC 82. dss 84 d 87 p 94. Smethwick St Mary *Birm* 84–87; Par Dn Smethwick H Trin w St Alb 87–89; Par Dn Coventry Caludon *Cov* 89–91; Chapl Myton Hamlet Hospice 91–95; Tutor WMMTC 95–04; Minl and Adult Learning Officer *Ely* 05–13; Hon Can Ely Cathl 12–13; Kingdom People Development Officer *Worc* 13–15; NSM Bredon w Bredon's Norton 15–17; NSM Defford w Besford 15–17; NSM Eckington 15–17; NSM Elmley Castle w Bricklehampton and Combertons 15–17; NSM Overbury w Teddington, Alstone etc 15–17; rtd 17. *11 Oberon Way, Cottingley, Bingley BD16 1WH*

WORSLEY, Howard John. b 61. Man Univ BA 83 Leeds Univ PGCE 83 Birm Univ PhD 00. St Jo Coll Nottm MTh 93. d 93 p 94. C Huthwaite *S'well* 93–96; V Radford St Pet 96–01; Dir Studies St Jo Coll Nottm 02–04; Dir of Educn *S'well* 04–10; Dir of Educn *Lon* 10–11; Chapl Lon S Bank Univ *S'wark* 11–12; Sen Lect Cant Ch Ch Univ 12–15; Vice-Prin Trin Coll Bris from 13; PtO *S'wark* 12–13; *B & W* 15–17; NSM Banwell and Congresbury w Hewish, Puxton and W Wick from 17. *72 Bath Road, Wells BA5 3LJ* M: 07528-565600 E: h.worsley@trinitycollegebristol.ac.uk *or* hjworsley4@gmail.com

WORSLEY, Richard John. b 52. Qu Coll Cam BA 74 MA 78 Univ of Wales CertEd 76 Birm Univ MPhil 91 Warwick Univ MA 96. Qu Coll Birm 77. d 80 p 81. C Styvechale *Cov* 80–84; V Smethwick H Trin w St Alb *Birm* 84–89; TV Coventry Caludon *Cov* 89–96; Hon C Binley 96–05; PtO *Ely* 05–08; Hon C Soham and Wicken 08–13; P-in-c Overbury w Teddington, Alstone etc *Worc* 13–17; P-in-c Elmley Castle w Bricklehampton and Combertons 13–17; rtd 17. *11 Oberon Way, Cottingley, Bingley BD16 1WH* M: 07854-543218

✠**WORSLEY, The Rt Revd Ruth Elizabeth.** b 62. d 96 p 97 c 15. C Basford w Hyson Green *S'well* 96–98; C Hyson Green and Forest Fields 98–01; P-in-c 01–08; AD Nottm N 06–08; P-in-c Sneinton St Chris w St Phil 08–10; Dean of Women's Min 07–10; Hon Can S'well Minster 07–10; Par Development Officer Woolwich Area *S'wark* 10–13; Adn Wilts *Sarum* 13–15; Chapl to The Queen 09–15; Suff Bp Taunton *B & W* from 15. *The Palace, Wells BA5 2PD* T: 01749 672341 M: 07917-693285 E: bishop.taunton@bathwells.anglican.org

WORSLEY, Thomas Robert. b 54. Sunderland Univ CertEd 00. Lindisfarne Regional Tr Partnership 10. d 12 p 13. NSM Felling *Dur* from 12; P-in-c from 18. *28 Rectory Road East, Gateshead NE10 9DN* M: 07757-949836 E: tom.worsley@blueyonder.co.uk *or* trw@christchurchfelling.org

WORSSAM, Brother Nicholas Alan. b 65. Selw Coll Cam BA 87 MA 91. Qu Coll Birm MA 04. d 06 p 07. SSF from 99; PtO *Worc* from 15. *Glasshampton Monastery, Shrawley, Worcester WR6 6TQ* T: (01299) 896345 F: 896083 E: nicholasalanssf@btconnect.com

WORSSAM, Richard Mark. b 61. St Jo Coll Dur BA 83 Selw Coll Cam BA 92 Heythrop Coll Lon MA 06 K Coll Lon MSc 09. Ridley Hall Cam 90. d 93 p 94. C Green Street Green and Pratts Bottom *Roch* 93–97; R Fawkham and Hartley 97–08; V Otford 08–19; V Pembury from 19. *The Vicarage, Hastings Road, Pembury, Tunbridge Wells TN2 4PD* E: richard.worssam@tiscali.co.uk

WORT, Gavin. b 78. K Alfred's Coll Win BTh 99 St Jo Coll Dur MA 10. Westcott Ho Cam 00. d 02 p 03. C Eastleigh *Win* 02–06; Chapl Northumbria Univ *Newc* 06–11; V Newc H Cross 11–18; Co-ord Chapl Dur Univ from 18; Chapl Collingwood Coll Dur from 18; Chapl Grey Coll Dur from 18; Chapl Trev Coll Dur from 18; Chapl Van Mildert Coll Dur from 18. *Student Wellbeing Office, Durham University, Stockton Road, Durham DH1 3LE* T: 0191-334 4519 E: gavin.wort@durham.ac.uk

WORTELHOCK, Liza Alexandra. b 66. d 16 p 17. NSM Bath St Luke *B & W* 16–19; NSM Combe Down w Monkton Combe and S Stoke 19–20; NSM Bath Odd Down w Combe Hay from 20. *Newlands, 196 Old Frome Road, Bath BA2 5RH* E: mikeandlizaw@gmail.com *or* liza@stphilipstjames.org

WORTHEN, Canon Jeremy Frederick. b 65. Rob Coll Cam BA 86 MPhil 88 Toronto Univ PhD 92. Ripon Coll Cuddesdon 92. d 94 p 95. C Bromley SS Pet and Paul *Roch* 94–97; Tutor SEITE 97–05; Prin 05–13; Sec Ecum Relns and Th Coun for Chr Unity 14–20; TR Ashford Town *Cant* from 20; Jt AD Ashford from 21; Wiccamical Preb Chich Cathl from 09; Hon Can Cant Cathl from 11. *7 Augustine Drive,*

Finberry, Ashford TN25 7GH T: (01233) 556118 *or* 664820 E: jeremy.worthen@ashfordchurches.co.uk

WORTHINGTON, Mark. b 55. Leeds Poly BA 77 Solicitor 80. Cranmer Hall Dur 93. **d** 93 **p** 94. C Monkwearmouth St Andr *Dur* 93–96; C Chester le Street 96–00; V Harlow Green and Lamesley 00–21; rtd 21. *Address temp unknown* M: 07939-616159 E: markworthington55@me.com

WORTLEY, Lyn Sharon. b 59. Open Univ BA 94 Coll of Ripon & York St Jo MA 98. NOC 95. **d** 98 **p** 99. C Greasbrough *Sheff* 98–01; P-in-c Bramley and Ravenfield w Hooton Roberts etc 01–04; V Bramley 04–12; P-in-c Greasbrough 12–21; C Rawmarsh w Parkgate 12–17; P-in-c 17–21; C Kimberworth and Kimberworth Park 12–21; AD Rotherham 14–16 and 19–20; Hon Can Sheff Cathl 15–21; rtd 21. *2 Hatchell Drive, Doncaster DN4 6SH* E: lyn.wortley@gmail.com

WORTON, David Reginald *Paschal*. b 56. St Steph Ho Ox 88. **d** 90 **p** 90. SSF 77–11; NSM Anfield St Columba *Liv* 90–92; Asst P Harare Cathl Zimbabwe 92–93; Asst P St Aug Miss Penhalonga 93–94; LtO *Newc* 94–08; Guardian Alnmouth Friary 01–08; Asst P Shrine of Our Lady of Walsingham 08–11; TV Old St Pancras *Lon* from 12. *St Mary's House, Eversholt Street, London NW1 1BN* T: (020) 7387 7301 E: fr.paschal@posp.co.uk

WOSTENHOLM, David Kenneth. b 56. Edin Univ BSc 77 MB, ChB 80 Southn Univ BTh 88. Chich Th Coll 82. **d** 85 **p** 86. C Leytonstone St Marg w St Columba *Chelmsf* 85–90; V Brighton Annunciation *Chich* 90–01; TR Hove 01–07; RD 03–05; P-in-c Glas St Matt 07–15; R from 15. *104 Erradale Street, Glasgow G22 6PT* T: 0141-336 7480 *or* 347 1726 M: 07908-537085 E: stmatthews@btclick.com *or* david.wostenholm@hotmail.co.uk

WOTTON, David Ashley. b 44. Chich Th Coll 71. **d** 74 **p** 75. C Allington and Maidstone St Pet *Cant* 74–77; C Ham St Andr *S'wark* 78–79; Chapl HM Rem Cen Latchmere Ho 78–79; C Tattenham Corner and Burgh Heath *Guildf* 85–88; P-in-c E Molesey St Mary 88–93; R Headley w Box Hill 93–06; OCM 93–06; rtd 06; PtO *Chich* 12–17. *Lion House, 6 Copper Beeches, St Leonards-on-Sea TN37 7RR* T: (01424) 756122 E: dwottonatlion@tiscali.co.uk

WRAGG, Christopher William. b 60. SEITE 97. **d** 00 **p** 01. C Gt Warley Ch Ch *Chelmsf* 00–01; C Warley Ch Ch and Gt Warley St Mary 01–04; TV Buckhurst Hill 04–08; V Squirrels Heath from 08. *30 Wakerfield Close, Hornchurch RM11 2TH* T: (01708) 446571 M: 07714-507147 E: vicar@aschornchurch.org.uk

WRAGG, Peter Robert. b 46. Lon Univ BSc 68. Sarum & Wells Th Coll 71. **d** 74 **p** 75. C Feltham *Lon* 74–79; TV Hackney 79–85; P-in-c Isleworth St Mary 85–94; V Feltham 94–12; rtd 12; PtO *Chich* from 13. *3 Woodland Avenue, Eastbourne BN22 0HD* T: (01323) 507338

WRATTEN, Martyn Stephen. b 34. AKC 58 St Boniface Warminster 58. **d** 59 **p** 60. C Wandsworth Common St Mary *S'wark* 59–62; C Putney St Mary 62–65; C Pembury *Roch* 65–70; R Stone 70–76; Chapl Joyce Green Hosp Dartford 70–73; Stone Ho Hosp Kent 73–76; Hillcrest Hosp and Netherne Hosp Coulsdon 76–87; Hon C Netherne St Luke CD *S'wark* 76–87; V Gt Doddington *Pet* 87–88; V Gt Doddington and Wilby 88–95; Hon C N Petherton w Northmoor Green *B & W* 95–96; rtd 95; PtO *B & W* from 96. *1 Baymead Close, North Petherton, Bridgwater TA6 6QZ* T: (01278) 662873 E: martyn.wratten@btinternet.com

WRATTEN, Sonya Helen Jean. b 77. Liv Jo Moores Univ BA 00 Cardiff Univ BTh 12. St Mich Coll Llan 07. **d** 10 **p** 11. C Leic St Phil 10–14; P-in-c Bedford All SS *St Alb* 14–17; Chapl Univ Hosps Leic NHS Trust 17–21; V Reading St Mary the Virgin *Ox* from 21. *5 Mardy, Caversham, Reading RG4 7NY* M: 07948-714922 E: sonya.reverend@gmail.com

WRAY, Christopher. b 48. Hull Univ BA 70. Cuddesdon Coll 70. **d** 73 **p** 74. C Brighouse *Wakef* 73–76; C Almondbury 76–78; C Tong *Bradf* 78–80; V Ingleton w Chapel le Dale 80–86; R Brompton Regis w Upton and Skilgate *B & W* 86–91; V Yoxford and Peasenhall w Sibton *St E* 91–94; PtO *Carl* 94–97; R Brough w Stainmore, Musgrave and Warcop 97–02; R Walkingham Hill *Ripon* 02–07; V Ripponden and Barkisland w W Scammonden *Wakef* 07–13; rtd 13. *3 Stonelea, Barkisland, Halifax HX4 0HD* T: (01422) 825208

WRAY, Christopher Brownlow. b 46. Open Univ BA 91. Oak Hill Th Coll 86. **d** 88 **p** 89. C Quidenham *Nor* 88–91; TV Chippenham St Paul w Hardenhuish etc *Bris* 91–97; P-in-c Chipping Sodbury and Old Sodbury *Glouc* 97–09; P-in-c Horton and Lt Sodbury 04–09; rtd 09; Hon C Hardington Vale *B & W* 11–12; PtO *Sarum* 10–20. *52 Linden Park, Shaftesbury SP7 8RN* T: (01747) 851961

WRAY, Martin John. b 51. St Steph Ho Ox 86. **d** 88 **p** 89. C E Boldon *Dur* 88–90; C Seaham w Seaham Harbour 90–92; P-in-c Chopwell 92–95; V 95–97; C Shildon 98–00; C

Croxdale and Tudhoe 00–04; P-in-c 04–06; C Spennymoor, Whitworth and Merrington 04–06; V Horsley Hill St Lawr 06–11; rtd 11. *68 Bainbridge Avenue, South Shields NE34 9QY* E: m.wray@sky.com

WRAY, Michael. b 49. Univ of Wales (Cardiff) BSc(Econ) 77 Keele Univ PGCE 78 RGN 87. Ripon Coll Cuddesdon 80. **d** 82 **p** 83. C Blackpool St Steph *Blackb* 82–83; C Torrisholme 83–84; NSM Headington Quarry *Ox* 93–95; C Kennington *Cant* 95–99; CF (TA) 95–99; P-in-c Isham w Pytchley *Pet* 99–04; Chapl Rockingham Forest NHS Trust 99–01; Chapl Northants Healthcare NHS Trust 01–04; R Potterspury w Furtho and Yardley Gobion etc *Pet* 04–11; rtd 11. *19 Cosgrove Road, Old Stratford, Milton Keynes MK19 6AG* T: (01908) 566824 E: revwray@btinternet.com

WRAY-WEAR, Lucinda Jane. b 61. S Bank Univ MSc 03. Qu Foundn (Course) 15. **d** 18 **p** 19. NSM Uttoxeter Area *Lich* 18–19; NSM Lt Drayton from 19; NSM Woore and Norton in Hales from 21. *Address temp unknown* E: revlucindaww@gmail.com

WRAYFORD, Geoffrey John. b 38. Ex Coll Ox BA 61 MA 65. Linc Th Coll 61. **d** 63 **p** 64. C Cirencester *Glouc* 63–69; V 70–74; Chapl Chelmsf Cathl 69–74; V Canvey Is 74–76; TR 76–80; P-in-c Woodlands *B & W* 80–88; V 89–92; P-in-c Frome St Jo 80–88; P-in-c Frome Ch Ch 80–85; P-in-c Frome St Mary 85–88; V Frome St Jo and St Mary 89–92; V Minehead 92–03; Chapl Taunton and Somerset NHS Trust 92–03; rtd 03; PtO *Ex* from 03; *B & W* 07–15. *Little Garth, Longmeadow Road, Lympstone, Exmouth EX8 5LF* T: (01395) 267838 E: geoffjanw@gmail.com

WREFORD, Mark Paul. b 88. Nottm Univ BA 13 MA 14 PhD 19. St Mellitus Coll 19. **d** 21. C Linby w Papplewick *S'well* from 21; C Nottm Trin BMO from 21. *20 Frances Grove, Hucknall, Nottingham NG15 8DD* M: 07915-674211 E: mark.wreford@gmail.com

WREN, Ann. *See* WREN, Kathleen Ann

WREN, Christopher John. b 54. Dur Univ BEd 76 MA 85. St Steph Ho Ox 77. **d** 79 **p** 80. C Stockton St Pet *Dur* 79–82; C Newton Aycliffe 82–85; V Gateshead St Chad Bensham 85–91; TR Bensham 91–98; V Marton *Blackb* 98–16; rtd 16; LtO *Glas* from 17. *40 Park, Thornhill DG3 5JP* T: (01848) 332543 M: 07900-006795 E: parkhouse4012@gmail.com

WREN, Douglas Peter. b 59. Lanc Univ BA 82. Trin Coll Bris BA 88. **d** 88 **p** 89. C Nantwich *Ches* 88–91; C Chatham St Phil and St Jas *Roch* 91–94; R Kingsdown 94–02; R Speldhurst w Groombridge and Ashurst from 02; RD Tunbridge Wells from 18. *The Rectory, Southfields, Speldhurst, Tunbridge Wells TN3 0PD* T: (01892) 862821 E: douglas.wren12@gmail.com

WREN, Mrs Kathleen Ann. b 50. St Steph Ho Ox 83. dss 85 **d** 87. Gateshead St Cuth w St Paul *Dur* 85–86; Gateshead St Chad Bensham 86–91; Par Dn 87–91; Adv for Women's Min 90–98; Par Dn Bensham 91–94; C 94–98; Hon Can Dur Cathl 93–98; C Marton *Blackb* 98–16; rtd 16; LtO *Glas* from 17. *40 Park, Thornhill DG3 5JP* T: (01848) 332543 M: 07900-512062

WREN, Comdr Richard. b 35. S Dios Minl Tr Scheme 88. **d** 90 **p** 91. NSM Tisbury *Sarum* 90–01; TV 95–01; TV Nadder Valley *Sarum* 01–05; rtd 05; PtO *Sarum* 06–19. *Gaston House, Tisbury, Salisbury SP3 6LG* T: (01747) 870674 E: twowrens@cuffslane.plus.com

WRIGHT, Alan William. b 44. Hull Univ BA 66 Bris Univ PGCE 67 AMusTCL 61. **d** 95 **p** 96. OLM Barton upon Humber *Linc* from 95. *1 Birchdale, Barton-upon-Humber DN18 5ED* T: (01652) 632364 E: wrightherewrightnow@hotmail.com

WRIGHT, Canon Andrew David Gibson. b 58. St Andr Univ MTheol 81. Ridley Hall Cam. **d** 83 **p** 84. C W Derby Gd Shep *Liv* 83–86; C Carl H Trin and St Barn 86–88; V Wigan St Jas w St Thos *Liv* 88–91; Chapl St Edw Sch Ox 91–97 and 06–07; Ho Master 97–07; Miss Chapl R Nat Miss to Deep Sea Fishermen 07–13; Sec Gen Miss to Seafarers from 13; Asst Chapl St Mich Paternoster Royal *Lon* 14–21; PtO *Ox* 15–21; LtO from 21; Hon Can *Eur* from 16. *11 Davenant Road, Oxford OX2 8BT* T: (020) 7246 2934 M: 07876-824414 E: andrew.wright@missiontoseafarers.org

WRIGHT, Anne. *See* WRIGHT, Jacqueline Anne

WRIGHT, Anthony. *See* WRIGHT, Derek Anthony

WRIGHT, Canon Anthony John. b 47. Ex Univ MA 98 ACA 70 FCA 72. Ripon Coll Cuddesdon 86. **d** 88 **p** 89. C Kidderminster St Mary and All SS w Trimpley etc *Worc* 88–91; P-in-c Offenham and Bretforton 91–96; R Backwell w Chelvey and Brockley *B & W* 96–02; RD Portishead 01–02; P-in-c Tetbury w Beverston *Glouc* 02–03; R 03–06; R Tetbury, Beverston, Long Newnton etc 07–13; Hon Can Glouc Cathl 11–13; rtd 13; PtO *Worc* from 13; *Glouc* 16–18. *Fair Field House, 1 Bromwich Road, Worcester WR2 4AD* T: (01905) 339661 E: fairfieldwright@gmail.com

WRIGHT, Canon Anthony **Robert**. b 49. LVO 10. Lanchester Poly Cov BA 70. St Steph Ho Ox 70. **d** 73 **p** 74. C Amersham on the Hill *Ox* 73–76; C Reading St Giles 76–78; P-in-c Prestwood 78–84; P-in-c Wantage 84–87; V 87–92; RD 84–92; P-in-c W w E Hanney 88–91; V Portsea St Mary *Portsm* 92–98; Hon Can Portsm Cathl 96–98; R Westmr St Marg and Chapl to Speaker of Ho of Commons 98–10; Can Westmr Abbey 98–10; Sub Dean Westmr 05–10; Adn Westmr 09–10; rtd 10; PtO *Ox* 11–21. *23 Quarry High Street, Headington, Oxford OX3 8JU* T: (01865) 750656 E: priestpainter@googlemail.com

WRIGHT, Canon Barry Owen. b 38. S'wark Ord Course 66. **d** 69 **p** 70. C Plumstead Ascension *S'wark* 69–74; Hon C Welling 74–89; Hon Can S'wark Cathl 79–89; Sen Chapl W Midl Police *Birm* 89–93; Sen Chapl Metrop Police *Lon* 93–09; V Mill Hill St Mich 02–10; rtd 10; PtO *Roch* from 10; *S'wark* from 18. *54 Elmbourne Drive, Belvedere DA17 6JF* T: (01322) 463564 M: 07790-664115 E: barrywright769@gmail.com

WRIGHT, Catherine Jane Pryse. b 62. Bris Univ BA 84 MA 92 PhD 00 Selw Coll Cam BA 96. Ridley Hall Cam 94. **d** 97 **p** 98. C Highworth w Sevenhampton and Inglesham etc *Bris* 97–00; PtO *Ex* 00–01; NSM Stoke St Gregory w Burrowbridge and Lyng *B & W* 01–05; Dioc Voc Adv 02–10; Dir of Voc 10–14; Assoc Dir of Ords 02–14; Dean of Women Clergy and Preb Wells Cathl 05–14; Dir IME 4-7 10–14; Tutor Ridley Hall Cam 14–19; PtO *B & W* 15–19; NSM Hartford and Houghton w Wyton *Ely* from 19. *3 Rectory Lane, Wyton, Huntingdon PE28 2AQ* T: (01480) 461846 E: cjpwright28@gmail.com

WRIGHT, Charles **Kenneth**. b 38. CEng 73 MIMechE 73 MBIM 91. Sarum & Wells Th Coll 91. **d** 93 **p** 94. C Bridgwater St Mary, Chilton Trinity and Durleigh *B & W* 93–96; Chapl Workington *Carl* 96–03; C Camerton, Seaton and W Seaton 96–03; Chapl W Cumbria Health Care NHS Trust 96–01; Chapl N Cumbria Acute Hosps NHS Trust 01–03; rtd 03; PtO *Carl* from 03. *Naemair, 72 Ruskin Close, High Harrington, Workington CA14 4LS* T: (01946) 833536 E: kenwright@talktalk.net

WRIGHT, Canon Clifford Nelson. b 35. K Coll Lon BD 59 AKC 59. **d** 60 **p** 61. C Stevenage *St Alb* 60–67; V Camberwell St Luke *S'wark* 67–81; RD Camberwell 75–80; Hon Can S'wark Cathl 79–80; TR Basingstoke *Win* 81–93; RD 84–93; Hon Can Win Cathl 89–00; R Win St Matt 93–00; rtd 00; PtO *Win* from 01. *1 Valley Dene, Dibden Purlieu, Southampton SO45 4NG* T: (023) 8084 5898 E: cliffwright@waitrose.com

WRIGHT, Preb David William. b 63. Liv Univ LLB 85 Fitzw Coll Cam BA 92 Cam Univ MA 96 Univ of Wales (Cardiff) LLM 99 Barrister 86. Westcott Ho Cam 90. **d** 93 **p** 94. C Chorlton-cum-Hardy St Clem *Man* 93–97; P-in-c Donnington Wood *Lich* 97–99; V 99–09; TR Cen Wolverhampton from 09; AD Wolverhampton from 11; Preb Lich Cathl from 15. *The Rectory, 42 Park Road East, Wolverhampton WV1 4QA* M: 07500-780491 E: david.wright@lichfield.anglican.org

WRIGHT, Derek **Anthony**. b 35. ACP 66 Lon Univ CertEd 57. Cranmer Hall Dur 80. **d** 81 **p** 82. C Auckland St Andr and St Anne *Dur* 81–83; V Cornforth 83–87; P-in-c Thornley 87–88; R Gt and Lt Glemham, Blaxhall etc *St E* 88–90; V Evenwood *Dur* 90–93; P-in-c Satley and Tow Law 93–95; V 95–99; rtd 99; PtO *Dur* 00–16. *39 Hilltop Road, Bearpark, Durham DH7 7TA* E: tonywright39@btinternet.com

WRIGHT, Dominic Edwyn. b 76. Qu Coll Birm. **d** 13 **p** 14. C Birm St Martin w Bordesley St Andr 13–16; V Olton from 16. *The Vicarage, 5 Old Warwick Road, Solihull B92 7JU* M: 07871-814261 E: dominicwright1@gmail.com *or* vicarofolton@gmail.com

WRIGHT, Edward Maurice Alexanderson. b 54. Wycliffe Hall Ox. **d** 88 **p** 91. C Maidstone St Luke *Cant* 88–93; R Cliffe at Hoo w Cooling *Roch* 93–15; R Wrotham from 15. *The Rectory, Borough Green Road, Wrotham, Sevenoaks TN15 7RA* T: (01732) 882211 E: rector@wrothamchurch.org

WRIGHT, Edward **Michael**. b 37. St Cath Soc Ox BA 61 MA 65. Cuddesdon Coll. **d** 64 **p** 65. C Willesden St Andr *Lon* 64–68; Bahamas 68–71; V Lewisham St Steph and St Mark *S'wark* 72–80; V Ox St Barn and St Paul 80–07; rtd 07; PtO *Ox* 08–17. *F16, Marine Gate, Marine Drive, Brighton BN2 5TQ* M: 07973-952664 E: michael19371901@gmail.com

WRIGHT, Frank Albert. b 51. Portsm Univ MA 02. Sarum & Wells Th Coll 80. **d** 83 **p** 84. C Buckingham *Ox* 83–86; C Newport Pagnell w Lathbury and Moulsoe 86–89; TV W Slough 89–95; TR 95–99; TR Fareham H Trin *Portsm* 99–09; Dioc Interfaith Adv 01–06; R Westbourne *Chich* 09–16; rtd 16; PtO *B & W* from 17. *55 London Road, Milborne Port, Sherborne DT9 5DW*

WRIGHT, Frederic **Ian**. b 64. City Univ BSc 85. Wycliffe Hall Ox BTh 94. **d** 94 **p** 95. C Carl St Jo 94–98; C Bassenthwaite, Isel and Setmurthy 98–00; C Binsey 00–02; TV 02–07. *Aden*

House, The Square, Allonby, Maryport CA15 6QA T: (01900) 881095

WRIGHT, Graham John Aston. b 57. Moorlands Th Coll 77 Wycliffe Hall Ox 05. **d** 06 **p** 07. NSM Marston w Elsfield *Ox* 06–08; Asst Chapl St Edw Sch Ox 06–08; Chapl Queenswood Sch Herts 09–12; Chapl Qu Mary's Sch Baldersby Park 13–19; PtO *Guildf* 20–21; Chapl Gordon's Sch Woking from 21. *Gordon's School, Bagshot Road, West End, Woking GU24 9PT* E: gjawright@aol.com

WRIGHT, Gwynne Ann. b 49. Marymount Coll NY BA 71 Keller Graduate Sch of Management Illinois MA 98. Seabury-Western Th Sem MDiv 04. **d** 04 **p** 04. C Arlington Heights USA 04–06; P-in-c W Dundee 06–08; P-in-c Dekalb 08–10; R Northfield St Jas 10–14; PtO *York* from 14. *43 Rawcliffe Croft, York YO30 5US* T: (01904) 635095 M: 07710-496594 E: gwynne.wright@me.com

WRIGHT, Mrs Heather Margaret. b 47. EAMTC 93. **d** 96 **p** 97. NSM Heigham St Thos *Nor* 96–99; Hon Asst Dioc Chapl among deaf and deaf-blind people 99–03; Chapl from 03; NSM Sprowston w Beeston 03–16; PtO from 16. *133 Moore Avenue, Norwich NR6 7LQ* T/F: (01603) 301329 E: heatherwright404@btinternet.com

WRIGHT, Mrs Hilary. b 44. **d** 08. OLM Parkstone St Pet and St Osmund w Branksea *Sarum* 08–12; NSM 12–15; rtd 15; PtO *Sarum* from 15. *18 Springfield Crescent, Poole BH14 0LL* T: (01202) 747369 E: hilary@stpetersparkstone.org.uk *or* whilary18@gmail.com

WRIGHT, Canon Howard John Douglas. b 64. BA 85. Trin Coll Bris BA 94. **d** 96 **p** 97. C Ipswich St Matt *St E* 96–00; V Four Marks *Win* from 00; RD Alton 09–17; Hon Can Win Cathl from 16. *The Vicarage, 22 Lymington Bottom, Four Marks, Alton GU34 5AA* T: (01420) 563344 E: howardwright.cogs@gmail.com

WRIGHT, Canon Hugh Edward. b 57. BNC Ox BA 79 MA 87 Ex Univ CertEd 81. Sarum & Wells Th Coll 85. **d** 87 **p** 88. C Hobs Moat *Birm* 87–90; C W Drayton *Lon* 90–92; V Oakfield St Jo *Portsm* 92–13; RD E Wight 00–05; V Ventnor H Trin from 13; V Ventnor St Cath from 13; R Bonchurch from 13; Hon Can Portsm Cathl from 17. *The Vicarage, Maples Drive, Ventnor PO38 1NR* T: (01983) 853729 E: hugh.wright1957@btinternet.com

WRIGHT, Ian. b 65. Coll of Resurr Mirfield 97. **d** 99 **p** 00. C S Lafford *Linc* 99–01; C Hawley H Trin *Guildf* 01–03; Chapl Bonn w Cologne *Eur* 03–06; P-in-c Armley w New Wortley *Ripon* 06–14; *Leeds* 14–15; P-in-c Leeds Richmond Hill *Ripon* 12–14 and 14–15; V Eyres Monsell *Leic* 15–17. *c/o St Martin's House, 7 Peacock Lane, Leicester LE1 5PZ*

WRIGHT, Ian. *See* WRIGHT, Frederic Ian

WRIGHT, Miss Jacqueline **Anne**. b 39. Dalton Ho Bris 67. **dss** 76 **d** 87 **p** 94. BCMS Uganda 71–77; N Area Sec BCMS 78–88; Pudsey St Lawr and St Paul *Bradf* 82–88; Hon Par Dn 87–88; Par Dn Kingston upon Hull H Trin *York* 88–93; Hd of Min amongst Women CPAS 93–02; CPAS Consultant (W Midl) 96–02; Regional Consultant (Midl) 99–02; PtO *Cov* 93–04; *Birm* 96–02; *Worc* 96–02; *Leic* 99–02; rtd 02; PtO *York* from 04. *Oxenby, Whitby Road, Pickering YO18 7HL* T: (01751) 472689 E: jacqw@talktalk.net

WRIGHT, Jaime. b 90. Davis Coll (NY) BRE 14 Edin Univ MSc 15 PhD 20 Dur Univ BA 21. Scottish Episc Inst 18. **d** 21. C Edin Old St Paul from 21. *41 Jeffrey Street, Edinburgh EH1 1DH* M: 07778-398990 E: wrightjaimem@gmail.com

WRIGHT, Mrs Jane. b 62. LGSM 97. ERMC 12. **d** 15 **p** 16. NSM Monks Eleigh w Chelsworth and Brent Eleigh etc *St E* 15–18; R Westcote Barton w Steeple Barton, Duns Tew etc *Ox* from 18. *The Rectory, 29 Enstone Road, Westcote Barton, Chipping Norton OX7 7AA* T: (01869) 340510 M: 07432-240250 E: clergy.bartonbenefice@outlook.com *or* clergy.bartonbenefice@gmail.com

WRIGHT, Mrs Jean. b 41. Man Univ BA 63 CertEd 64. Carl Dioc Tr Inst 88. **d** 91 **p** 92. NSM Kirkby Stephen w Mallerstang etc *Carl* 91–13; PtO from 13. *Mains View, Crosby Garrett, Kirkby Stephen CA17 4PR* T: (017683) 71457 E: j.wright347@btinternet.com

WRIGHT, John. *See* WRIGHT, Anthony John

WRIGHT, Canon John Harold. b 36. Dur Univ BA 58 Ch Ch Coll Cant MA 96 ATCL. Ely Th Coll 58. **d** 61 **p** 62. C Boston *Linc* 61–64; C Willesborough w Hinxhill *Cant* 64–68; V Westwell 68–75; R Eastwell w Boughton Aluph 68–75; V Rolvenden 75–84; R Cheriton St Martin 84–01; Hon Can Cant Cathl 97–01; rtd 01; PtO *Cant* from 01. *1 Cliff Road, Hythe CT21 5XA* T: (01303) 265303

WRIGHT, Jonathan James Gerald. b 67. Oak Hill Th Coll. **d** 10 **p** 11. C Horncastle Gp *Linc* 10–14; R Hedon, Paull, Sproatley and Preston *York* 14–17; R Bingham *S'well* from 17. *The Rectory, East Street, Bingham, Nottingham NG13 8DR*

WRIGHT, Jonathon Stuart. b 84. Girton Coll Cam BA 06 MA 12 MPhil 07 Ox Univ DPhil 18. St Steph Ho Ox 12. **d** 15 **p** 16. C Whitchurch *Llan* 15–18; P-in-c Swansea St Pet *S & B* 18–20; V from 20. *235 Cockett Road, Cockett, Swansea SA2 0FH* T: (01792) 578700 E: priest@cockettparish.org.uk

WRIGHT, Judith Mary. b 44. Ex Univ MSc 98 BA 10 SRN 10 SCM 10. SWMTC 04. **d** 07 **p** 08. NSM Silverton, Butterleigh, Bickleigh and Cadeleigh *Ex* 07–11; C Bradninch and Clyst Hydon 11–16; C Broadhembury, Payhembury and Plymtree 11–16; rtd 16; PtO *Ex* from 16. *4 Hele Square, Hele, Exeter EX5 4PN* T: (01392) 882019 E: d.j.wright@btinternet.com

WRIGHT, Kenneth. See WRIGHT, Charles Kenneth

WRIGHT, Kevin John. b 54. Southn Univ BSc 75 PGCE 76. Ox Min Course 06. **d** 10 **p** 11. C Radley and Sunningwell *Ox* 10–13; C Kennington 10–13; R Woolavington w Cossington and Bawdrip *B & W* 13–19; P-in-c Three Saints 19–20; R from 20. *3 Ash Trees, East Brent, Highbridge TA9 4DQ* T: (01278) 760844 M: 07764-170463 E: revdkjwright@btinternet.com

WRIGHT, Mrs Kim Beatrice Elizabeth. b 66. STETS 07. **d** 10 **p** 11. NSM Walton-on-Thames *Guildf* 10–12; NSM Oxshott 12–14. *Address withheld by request* M: 07941-947866 E: kbewright@live.co.uk

WRIGHT, Lawrence Charles. b 57. Hull Univ MA 94. EMMTC 93. **d** 96 **p** 96. C Heathridge and Joondalup Australia 96–98; C Penzance St Jo *Truro* 98–02; TV Penzance St Mary w St Paul and St Jo 02–04; Chapl Yarlswood Immigration and Detention Cen 04–06; Chapl W Lon YMCA 06–07; SSF 07–09; R Birm St Geo 09–16; P-in-c Lozells St Paul and St Silas 14–16; TR Kings Norton from 16. *The Rectory, 273 Pershore Road South, Birmingham B30 3EX* E: stgeorge100@live.co.uk *or* parishoffice@kingsnorton.org.uk

WRIGHT, Mrs Louisa Mary (Lisa). b 33. S'wark Ord Course. **d** 87 **p** 94. NSM Streatham Hill St Marg *S'wark* 87–95; Hon C Streatham St Leon 95–02; rtd 02; PtO *S'wark* from 02. *19 Hillside Road, London SW2 3HL* T: (020) 8671 8037 E: lisaw@phonecoop.coop

WRIGHT, Mrs Marion Jane. b 47. Whitelands Coll Lon CertEd 69. Cranmer Hall Dur 73. **d** 00 **p** 02. NSM Scalby *York* 00–15; NSM Cloughton and Burniston 14–15; NSM Ravenscar and Staintondale 14–15; PtO from 15. *3 East Park Road, Scalby, Scarborough YO13 0PZ* T: (01723) 350208 E: marianne.forsyth@hotmail.co.uk

WRIGHT, Martin. b 48. Avery Hill Coll BEd 81 K Alfred's Coll Win CertEd 69 LRAM 76. SAOMC 95. **d** 98 **p** 99. NSM St Alb St Mary Marshalswick 98–01; C Gt Berkhamsted 02–05; V Reigate St Mark *S'wark* 05–13; rtd 13; PtO *Guildf* from 13. *18 Brocks Drive, Fairlands, Guildford GU3 3NE* M: 07774-923550

WRIGHT, Canon Martin Neave. b 37. AKC 61. St Boniface Warminster. **d** 62 **p** 63. C Corby St Columba *Pet* 62–65; Ind Chapl 65–71; Nigeria 71–75; P-in-c Honiley *Cov* 75–84; P-in-c Wroxall 75–84; Ind Chapl 75–84; Soc Resp Officer 84–96; Hon Can Cov Cathl 95–96; Bp's Chapl and Past Asst *B & W* 96–02; Preb Wells Cathl 96–02; Sub-Dean Wells Cathl 00–02; rtd 02; PtO *Cov* from 02. *2 Honiwell Close, Harbury, Leamington Spa CV33 9LY* T: (01926) 613699

WRIGHT, Michael. See WRIGHT, Edward Michael

WRIGHT, Michael Christopher. b 44. Leeds Univ BA 65 CertEd 67 *Sheff* 75 *Sheff* Univ PhD 02 FRSA 95. Wells Th Coll 65. **d** 67 **p** 68. C Dormanstown *York* 67–69; PtO *Linc* 69–88; *Sheff* 71–95; Hd Master Eastmoor High Sch Wakef 84–87; Hd Master Carleton High Sch Pontefract 87–95; C-in-c St Edm Anchorage Lane CD *Sheff* 95–96; Chapl Doncaster R Infirmary and Montagu Hosp NHS Trust 95–01; Research Fell *Sheff* Univ 01–03; Sen Research Fell Lanc Univ *Blackb* from 03; Hon C Gt Snaith *Sheff* 01–07; PtO *Wakef* 01–14; *Leeds* 14–16; *Eur* from 06; *Sheff* from 07. *Orchard End, Finkle Street, Hensall, Goole DN14 0QY* T: (01977) 661900 *or* (01524) 593152 E: mc.wright@btinternet.com

WRIGHT, Michael George. b 52. WEMTC 01. **d** 04 **p** 05. NSM Woodchester and Brimscombe *Glouc* 14–15. *The Trumpet, West End, Minchinhampton, Stroud GL6 9JA* T: (01453) 883027 M: 07974-303527

WRIGHT, Canon Nicholas Mark. b 59. Loughb Univ BSc 80. Qu Coll Birm 82. **d** 85 **p** 86. C Coney Hill *Glouc* 85–89; C Rotherham *Sheff* 89–91; TV Worc SE 91–98; R Inkberrow w Cookhill and Kington w Dormston 98–15; Hon Can Worc Cathl 11–15; rtd 15; NSM Bengeworth *Worc* 15–18; NSM Bengeworth and Hampton etc from 18. *6 St David's Drive, Evesham WR11 2AU* T: (01386) 443310 E: revnmwright@btinternet.com

✠**WRIGHT, The Rt Revd Prof Nicholas Thomas.** b 48. Ex Coll Ox BA 71 MA 75 DPhil 81 DD 00. Wycliffe Hall Ox BA 73. **d** 75 **p** 76 **c** 03. Fell Mert Coll Ox 75–78; Chapl 76–78; Chapl and Fell Down Coll Cam 78–81; Asst Prof NT Studies McGill Univ Montreal 81–86; Chapl and Fell Worc Coll Ox and Univ Lect Th 86–93; Dean Lich 93–99; Can Th Cov Cathl

92–99; Lector Theologiae and Can Westmr Abbey 00–03; Bp Dur 03–10; Research Prof NT and Early Christianity St Andr Univ *St And* 10–19; Sen Research Fell Wycliffe Hall Ox from 19; Hon Asst Bp Ox from 20. *Wycliffe Hall, 52-54 Banbury Road, Oxford OX2 6PW* E: ntw2@st-andrews.ac.uk

WRIGHT, Nigel Christopher James. b 67. Leeds Univ BA 07 MA 13 FCCA 99. NOC 04. **d** 07 **p** 08. NSM Utley *Bradf* 07–10; NSM Oxenhope 10–13; P-in-c 13–14; *Leeds* 14–16; V Roundhay St Edm from 16. *5A North Park Avenue, Leeds LS8 1DN* M: 07970-751670 E: nigel.wright@parishes.leeds.anglican.org *or* revnigelwright@gmail.com

WRIGHT, Miss Pamela Jean. b 38. ALA 63. NTMTC 02. **d** 03 **p** 04. NSM Harrow Trin St Mich *Lon* 03–05; NSM Harrow Weald St Mich 05–12; PtO from 12. *14 Broadlawns Court, Harrow HA3 7HN* T: (020) 8954 9821 E: pamela.jwright@btinternet.com

WRIGHT, Patricia. b 46. MBE 02. SRN 68. S'wark Ord Course 80. **dss** 85 **d** 89. Asst Chapl R Lon Hosp (Mile End) 83–85; Bethnal Green St Matt w St Jas the Gt *Lon* 85–88; Hon C St Botolph Aldgate w H Trin Minories 89–05; Cathl Dn and Dioc HIV/AIDS Co-ord Swaziland 00–04; Hon C St Geo-in-the-East St Mary *Lon* 06–14; PtO *Cant* from 15. *62 College Road, Deal CT14 6BS* T: (01304) 239031 E: patw@patthedeacon.com

WRIGHT, The Ven Paul. b 54. K Coll Lon BD 78 AKC 78 Heythrop Coll Lon MTh 90 Univ of Wales (Lamp) DMin 09. Ripon Coll Cuddesdon 78. **d** 79 **p** 80. C Beckenham St Geo *Roch* 79–83; Chapl Ch Sch Richmond 83–85; C Richmond St Mary w St Matthias and St Jo *S'wark* 83–85; V Gillingham St Aug *Roch* 85–90; R Crayford 90–99; RD Erith 93–97; V Sidcup St Jo 99–03; Adn Bromley and Bexley from 03; Bp's Adv for Inter-Faith Concerns 11–15; P-in-c Bromley Common St Luke 12–15; P-in-c Slade Green 16–19; Hon Can Roch Cathl from 98. *The Archdeaconry, The Glebe, Chislehurst BR7 5PX* T/F: (020) 8467 8743 M: 07985-902601 E: archdeacon.bromley@rochester.anglican.org

WRIGHT, Canon Paul Stephen. b 66. Cen Lancs Univ BA 88 Liv Univ MA 96 Univ of Wales (Cardiff) MTh 11. Westcott Ho Cam 90. **d** 93 **p** 94. C Upholland *Liv* 93–96; CF 96–08; Sen CF 08–14; Chapl Guards Chpl Lon 08–10; Chapl R Memorial Chpl Sandhurst 12–14; Sub-Dean HM Chpls R and Dep Clerk of the Closet from 15; Sub-Almoner and Dom Chapl to The Queen from 15; Can Chpls R from 15; G S Beckwith Gilbert Fell Princeton Univ USA from 16. *The Chapel Royal, St James's Palace, London SW1A 1BL* T: (020) 7024 5576 E: paul.wright@royal.uk

WRIGHT, Canon Peter. b 35. K Coll Lon AKC 61 Hull Univ MA 86. St Boniface Warminster 61. **d** 62 **p** 63. C Goole *Sheff* 62–67; V Norton Woodseats St Chad 67–80; R Aston cum Aughton 80–84; P-in-c Ulley 80–84; Chapl Rotherham Priority Health Services NHS Trust 80–84; R Aston cum Aughton and Ulley *Sheff* 84–93; TR Aston cum Aughton w Swallownest, Todwick etc 93–00; RD Laughton 85–93; Chapter Clerk and Hon Can Sheff Cathl 92–00; rtd 00; PtO *Sheff* from 01; Chapl to Rtd Clergy and Clergy Widows Officer from 09. *40 Chancet Wood Drive, Sheffield S8 7TR* T/F: 0114-274 7218 E: allsaints.pw@talk21.com

WRIGHT, Peter Geoffrey. b 60. Ex Univ BSc 81 FCIM 09. Ox Min Course 09. **d** 12 **p** 13. NSM Bicester w Bucknell, Caversfield and Launton *Ox* 12–18; TV from 18. *4 Orpine Close, Bicester OX26 3ZJ* T: (01869) 573177 M: 07966-531921 E: revpeterwright@gmail.com

WRIGHT, Philip John. b 69. Anglia Ruskin Univ MA 11. St Mellitus Coll BA 14. **d** 14 **p** 15. Chapl Barking, Havering and Redbridge Hosps NHS Trust from 08; NSM Cranham Park *Chelmsf* 14–17; PtO from 17. *57 Heron Way, Upminster RM14 1EW* M: 07976-378042 E: philwright69@gmail.com

WRIGHT, Robert. See WRIGHT, Anthony Robert

WRIGHT, Robert James. b 74. St Chad's Coll Dur BA 96 K Coll Lon MA 98. St Steph Ho Ox 00. **d** 02 **p** 04. C Ilfracombe, Lee, Woolacombe, Bittadon etc *Ex* 02–05; PtO *S'wark* 11–14; P-in-c Mitcham St Olave 14–18; TV N Cheltenham *Glouc* from 18. *8 Boulton Road, Cheltenham GL50 4RZ* M: 07909-043811 E: robwri99@gmail.com

WRIGHT, Robert John. b 47. St Jo Coll Dur BA 70. SEITE 00. **d** 03 **p** 04. NSM Notting Hill St Jo *Lon* 03–06; NSM Notting Hill St Pet 03–06; NSM N Hammersmith St Kath 06–08; NSM Cheddington w Mentmore *Ox* 08–12; TV Cottesloe 12–13; PtO from 14. *17 Clarence Court, Forest Close, Wendover, Aylesbury HP22 6AB* M: 07988-978419 E: robert@robert-wright.com

WRIGHT (née PRECIOUS), Sally Joanne. b 75. Hatf Coll Dur BA 97 Anglia Poly Univ MA 03. Westcott Ho Cam 00. **d** 02 **p** 03. C Chich St Paul and Westhampnett 02–05; PtO *S'wark* 05–06; Hon C Peckham St Jo w St Andr 06–09; Chapl Guildhall Sch of Music and Drama *Lon* 06–09; Hon

C Witney *Ox* from 09. *The Rectory, 13 Station Lane, Witney OX28 4BB* T: (01993) 704441 E: sjw0209@icloud.com

WRIGHT, Samuel. *See* WRIGHT, William Samuel

WRIGHT, Sarah Jane. b 64. Nottm Trent Univ BA 99. Ripon Coll Cuddesdon 99. **d** 01 **p** 02. C Clarendon Park St Jo w Knighton St Mich *Leic* 01–03; C Leic Martyrs 04–05; PtO 17–18; Chapl Univ Hosps Leic NHS Trust 18–21. *101 Waterworks Road, Coalville LE67 4JJ* T: (01530) 463692 M: 07908-757027 E: dragonfire.phoenixrising@outlook.com

WRIGHT, Simon Andrew. b 63. Clare Coll Cam BA 84 MA 88 Lon Univ MB, BS 87. SNWTP 10. **d** 12 **p** 13. OLM Davyhulme St Mary *Man* 12–19; C from 19. *12 Davyhulme Road, Urmston, Manchester M41 7DS* T: 0161-746 8758 M: 07759-814499 E: revdocwright@hotmail.com

WRIGHT, Canon Simon Christopher. b 44. AKC 67. **d** 68 **p** 69. C Bitterne Park *Win* 68–72; C Kirkby *Liv* 72–74; V Wigan St Anne 74–79; Abp's Dom Chapl and Dioc Dir of Ords *York* 79–84; V W Acklam 84–00; RD Middlesbrough 87–98; Can and Preb York Minster 94–00; V Dartmouth and Dittisham *Ex* 00–10; rtd 10; PtO *York* from 10. *48 Langton Road, Norton, Malton YO17 9AD* T: (01653) 698106 E: scwright44@btinternet.com

WRIGHT, Stephen Irwin. b 58. Ex Coll Ox BA 80 MA 84 Selw Coll Cam BA 85 MA 90 Lanc Univ MA 92 St Jo Coll Dur PhD 97 SFHEA 19. Ridley Hall Cam 83. **d** 86 **p** 87. C Newbarns w Hawcoat *Carl* 86–90; C Burton and Holme 90–94; NSM Esh *Dur* 94–97; NSM Hamsteels 94–97; C Consett 97–98; Dir Coll of Preachers 98–06; Tutor Spurgeon's Coll from 06; Vice Prin from 17; PtO *S'wark* from 99. *Spurgeon's College, 189 South Norwood Hill, London SE25 6DJ* T: (020) 8653 0850 ext 228 E: s.wright@spurgeons.ac.uk

WRIGHT, Canon Stephen Mark. b 60. Keele Univ BA 83. Trin Coll Bris BA 89. **d** 89 **p** 90. C Thorne *Sheff* 89–92; CMS 92–05; Dioc Missr Asaba Nigeria 93–98; Hon Can Asaba from 98; Chapl Ahmadi St Paul Kuwait 99–03; Chapl Dubai and Sharjah w N Emirates 03–14; P-in-c Quidenham Gp *Nor* from 15; RD Thetford and Rockland from 21; Bp's Interfaith Adv from 20. *The Rectory, Church Hill, Banham, Norwich NR16 2HN* T: (01953) 887183 M: 07952-813786 E: canonstevewright@gmail.com

WRIGHT, Stewart. *See* WRIGHT, William Charles Stewart

WRIGHT, Stuart Kendle. b 73. **d** 08 **p** 09. C Tollington *Lon* 08–14; P-in-c Hounslow H Trin w St Paul and St Mary 14–15; P-in-c Hounslow H Trin 15–19; V 19–21. *Address temp unknown* M: 07867-888999

WRIGHT, Susan Rachel. b 71. St Andr Univ MA 94. Ridley Hall Cam 19. **d** 21. C Herne Hill *S'wark* from 21. *20 Torrens Road, London SW2 5BT* M: 07706-755018 E: susan@hernehillparish.org.uk

WRIGHT, Thomas. *See* WRIGHT, Nicholas Thomas

WRIGHT, The Very Revd Timothy. b 63. NUU BSc 85 Univ of Wales (Cardiff) MTh 06. Cranmer Hall Dur 86. **d** 89 **p** 90. C Bramcote *S'well* 89–93; I Glenavy w Tunny w Crumlin *Conn* 93–98; Chapl RAF 98–18; Dep Chapl-in-Chief 13–18; Dean Kildare *M & K* from 18; I Kildare w Kilmeague and Curragh from 18; I Newbridge w Carnalway and Kilcullen from 18; QHC from 15; PtO *Eur* from 16. *The Deanery, Morristown Road, Newbridge, Co Kildare, Republic of Ireland* T: (00353) (45) 431352 M: 07470-998821 *or* 85-866 9357 E: dean@kildare.anglican.org

WRIGHT, Timothy John. b 41. K Coll Lon BD 63 AKC 63. **d** 64 **p** 65. C Highfield *Ox* 64–68; Asst Chapl Worksop Coll Notts 68–71; Chapl Malvern Coll 71–77; Master 77–86; Hd Master Jo Lyon Sch Harrow 86–01; rtd 01; PtO *Worc* from 09. *Beech House, Colwall Green, Malvern WR13 6DX* T: (01684) 541102

WRIGHT, Timothy Stanley. b 63. Derby Coll of Educn BEd 86. Cranmer Hall Dur 89. **d** 92 **p** 93. C Eccleshill *Bradf* 92–96; TV Southend *Chelmsf* 96–00; V Boulton *Derby* 00–13; Chapl HM YOI Glen Parva 13–15; PtO *Derby* 13–18; Chapl HM Pris Stocken from 15. *HM Prison Stocken, Stocken Hall Road, Stretton, Oakham LE15 7RD* T: (01780) 795100   E: timwright2005@talktalk.net   *or* timothy.wright@justice.gov.uk

WRIGHT, Canon Toby Christopher. b 75. New Coll Ox BA 98 MA 01 Leeds Univ MA 01. Coll of Resurr Mirfield 99. **d** 01 **p** 02. C Petersfield *Portsm* 01–04; P-in-c Peckham St Jo w St Andr *S'wark* 04–06; V 06–09; AD Camberwell 06–09; TR Witney *Ox* from 09; AD 13–19; Hon Can Ch Ch from 20. *The Rectory, 13 Station Lane, Witney OX28 4BB* T: (01993) 704441 E: rector@witneyparish.org.uk

WRIGHT, Mrs Vyvienne Mary. b 35. S Dios Minl Tr Scheme 80. **dss** 83 **d** 87 **p** 94. Martock w Ash *B & W* 83–00; Hon C 87–00; PtO 00–21. *36 Church Close, Martock TA12 6DS* T: (01935) 823292 M: 07931-686362

WRIGHT, William Charles Stewart. b 53. Ulster Poly BSc 81. CITC BTh 95. **d** 95 **p** 96. C Ballyholme *D & D* 95–98; I Conwal Union w Gartan *D & R* 98–16; Can Raphoe Cathl 10–16; rtd 16. *43 Mallory Park, Eglinton, Londonderry BT47 3XJ* T: (028) 7181 1222 E: stewartwright@live.ie

WRIGHT, The Very Revd William Samuel. b 59. TCD BTh 89 MA 90. **d** 87 **p** 88. C Belfast St Aid *Conn* 87–91; Sec Dioc Bd of Miss 90–91; I Cleenish w Mullaghdun *Clogh* 91–99; I Lisburn Ch Ch Cathl *Conn* from 99; Can and Preb Conn Cathl 01–16; Prec 12–16; Dean *Conn* from 16. *Cathedral Rectory, 11D Magheralave Road, Lisburn BT28 3BE* T: (028) 9209 0260 E: sam.wright@lisburncathedral.org

WRIGLEY, George Garnett. b 50. St Cath Coll Cam BA 71 Loughb Coll of Educn PGCE 72. NTMTC 02. **d** 04 **p** 05. NSM Hounslow H Trin w St Paul and St Mary *Lon* 04–08; P-in-c Langdale *Carl* 08–10; TV Loughrigg from 10. *Long Crag, Rydal Road, Ambleside LA22 9BA* E: georgewrig@hotmail.com

✠**WROE, The Rt Revd Mark.** b 69. Surrey Univ BA 92 Anglia Poly Univ MA 00. Ridley Hall Cam 94. **d** 96 **p** 97 **c** 21. C Chilvers Coton w Astley *Cov* 96–00; P-in-c Heworth St Alb *Dur* 00–03; V Windy Nook St Alb 03–07; V Jesmond H Trin *Newc* 07–19; P-in-c Newc St Barn and St Jude 07–17; AD Newc Cen 17–19; Adn Northd and Can Res Newc Cathl 19–21; Suff Bp Berwick from 21. *80 Moorside North, Newcastle upon Tyne NE4 9DU* T: 0191-270 4165 E: bishopofberwick@newcastle.anglican.org

WROE, Martin Daniel Edward. b 61. NTMTC. **d** 04 **p** 05. NSM Covent Garden St Paul *Lon* 04–07; NSM W Holloway St Luke from 07. *St Luke's Vicarage, Penn Road, London N7 9RE* T: (020) 7607 6086 E: martinwroe@mac.com

WUTSCHER, Christoph Johannes. b 79. Ban Univ MA 12. Westcott Ho Cam 10. **d** 13 **p** 14. C Wanstead St Mary w Ch Ch *Chelmsf* 13–16; R Stirling *St And* from 16. *The Rectory, 4 Bracken Lane, Stirling FK9 5AB* T: (01786) 359821 M: 07583-270533 E: christoph.wutscher@hotmail.com

WUYTS, Fabian René Marc. b 73. ISFSC BA 96. Tyndale Th Sem Amsterdam MA 99 Evang Th Faculty Leuven MTh 08. **d** 14 **p** 15. C Whitstable *Cant* 14–18; V Taunton St Jas *B & W* from 18. *69 Richmond Road, Taunton TA1 1EN* M: 07547-195760 E: fabian.wuyts@gmail.com

WYARD, Peter Joseph. b 54. Pemb Coll Cam MA 76 Sussex Univ MSc 80 Brunel Univ MSc 88 Anglia Ruskin Univ MA 07. EAMTC 99. **d** 02 **p** 03. C Framlingham w Saxtead *St E* 02–05; P-in-c Riverside *Ox* 05–08; V Colnbrook and Datchet 08–18; PtO from 18; Miss Partner CMS from 18; PtO *St E* 20–21. *Church Mission Society, Watlington Road, Cowley, Oxford OX4 6BZ* T: (01865) 787400 E: peter.wyard@btinternet.com

WYATT, Colin. b 27. Ex Coll Ox BA 54 MA 55 Lon Univ BD 62. Tyndale Hall Bris 60. **d** 63 **p** 64. C Radipole *Sarum* 63–66; C Southborough St Pet *Roch* 66–67; V Tetsworth *Ox* 67–72; Lect Bible Tr Inst Glas 72–74; R Hurworth *Dur* 74–79; P-in-c Dinsdale w Sockburn 74–76; R 76–79; R Sadberge 79–84; R Bacton w Wyverstone and Cotton *St E* 84–92; rtd 92; PtO *Ripon* 92–14; *Leeds* 14–16. *St Francis' Vicarage, 146 Tedder Road, South Croydon CR2 8AH* T: (020) 8657 7864

WYATT, David John. b 89. Heythrop Coll Lon BA 11. Ripon Coll Cuddesdon 17. **d** 19 **p** 20. C Canon Pyon w King's Pyon, Birley and Wellington *Heref* from 19. *Sunnybrook, Wellington, Hereford HR4 8AZ* E: revdavid.wyatt@outlook.com

WYATT, Canon David Stanley Chadwick. b 36. Fitzw Ho Cam BA 59 MA 71. Ely Th Coll 59. **d** 61 **p** 62. C Rochdale *Man* 61–63; Bp's Dom Chapl 63–68; R Salford St Paul w Ch Ch from 68; P-in-c Salford Ordsall St Clem 91–96; P-in-c Lower Broughton Ascension from 05; AD Salford 97; Hon Can Man Cathl from 82. *St Paul's Church House, Broadwalk, Salford M6 5FX* T: 0161-736 8868 E: salfordwyatts@yahoo.co.uk

WYATT, Peter Charles. b 62. Bris Univ BSc 85 CEng MIEE 92. St Jo Coll Nottm 05. **d** 07 **p** 08. C Becontree St Thos *Chelmsf* 07–11; Min Selsdon St Fran CD *S'wark* from 11. *St Francis' Vicarage, 146 Tedder Road, Croydon CR2 8AH* T: (020) 8657 7864 E: peter.michelle@gmail.com

WYATT, Peter John. b 38. Kelham Th Coll 58. **d** 64 **p** 65. C N Stoneham *Win* 64–68; C Brixham *Ex* 68–69; Dominica 69–75; Zambia 76–78; P-in-c Ettington *Cov* 78–79; V Butlers Marston and the Pillertons w Ettington 79–86; V Codnor and Loscoe *Derby* 86–91; Chapl for Deaf People 91–03; rtd 03; PtO *Heref* from 04; St As from 09. *16 Cae Melyn, Tregynon, Newtown SY16 3EF* T: (01686) 650368 E: pandpwyatt@btinternet.com

WYATT (née OWEN), Canon Susan Elizabeth. b 53. Bris Univ BSc 75 Anglia Poly Univ MA 03 Bath Univ PGCE 78. EAMTC 97. **d** 00 **p** 01. Asst Dioc Adv in Miss and Evang *Ely* 00–16; C Over 00–06; C Long Stanton w St Mich 02–06; Asst Dioc Adv in Miss and Evang 02–06; V Cherry Hinton St Jo 06–16; Hon Can Ely Cathl 10–16; rtd 16; PtO *Ely* from 16; RD Bourn 18–21. *5 Cottons Field,*

Dry Drayton, Cambridge CB23 8DG M: 07936-208989 E: sue.e.wyatt@btinternet.com

WYATT, Trevor. b 60. Keele Univ BSc 81 Heythrop Coll Lon MA 07. SEITE 97. **d** 00 **p** 01. NSM Wilmington *Roch* 00–14; V Bexleyheath Ch Ch from 14. *The Vicarage, 57 Townley Road, Bexleyheath DA6 7HY* M: 07860-306746 E: revtrevorwyatt@outlook.com

WYBER, Richard John. b 47. G&C Coll Cam BA 69 MA 72 FCA 73. SEITE 03. **d** 06 **p** 07. NSM Wanstead St Mary w Ch Ch *Chelmsf* from 06. *7 Mornington Close, Woodford Green IG8 0TT* T: (020) 8504 2447

WYBREW, Canon Hugh Malcolm. b 34. Qu Coll Ox BA 58 MA. Linc Th Coll 59. **d** 60 **p** 61. C E Dulwich St Jo *S'wark* 60–64; Tutor St Steph Ho Ox 65–71; Chapl Bucharest *Eur* 71–73; V Pinner *Lon* 73–83; Sec Fellowship of SS Alb and Sergius 84–86; Dean Jerusalem 86–89; Hon Can Gib Cathl *Eur* 89–04; V Ox St Mary Magd 89–04; Hon Can Ch Ch 01–04; rtd 04. *96 Warwick Street, Oxford OX4 1SY* T: (01865) 241355 E: hugh.wybrew@queens.ox.ac.uk

WYER, Mrs Janet Beatrice. b 58. UEA BA 00. ERMC 04. **d** 07 **p** 08. C Loddon, Sisland, Chedgrave, Hardley and Langley *Nor* 07–10; C Nor St Pet Mancroft w St Jo Maddermarket 10–15; R Kessingland, Gisleham and Rushmere 15–19; V Nor Heartsease St Fran from 19; C Thorpe St Matt from 19. *St Francis Vicarage, 100 Rider Haggard Road, Norwich NR7 9UQ* M: 07990-576118 E: revdjanetwyer@outlook.com

WYER, Keith George. b 45. St Paul's Coll Chelt CertEd 66 K Coll Lon BD 71 AKC 71. St Aug Coll Cant 71. **d** 72 **p** 73. C Moseley St Mary *Birm* 72–76; Chapl RNR 73–92; C Walsall *Lich* 76–77; Min Walsall St Martin 77–79; Chapl Colston's Sch Bris 79–86; Chapl Kelly Coll Tavistock 86–92; R Combe Martin and Berrynarbor *Ex* 92–95; TR Combe Martin, Berrynarbor, Lynton, Brendon etc 96–10; RD Shirwell 95–01; rtd 10; PtO *Ex* from 12. *Highlands, 6 Holland Park Avenue, Combe Martin, Ilfracombe EX34 0HL*

WYKES, Elaine Karen. b 74. Qu Foundn Birm 13. **d** 16 **p** 17. NSM Anstey and Thurcaston w Cropston *Leic* 16–19; Chapl HM Pris Drake Hall from 19. *HM Prison and Young Offender Institution, Drake Hall, Eccleshall, Stafford* T: (01785) 774100 E: elaine.wykes@justice.gov.uk

WYKES, Canon Peter. b 44. Lon Univ MB, BS 68. Ban & St As Minl Tr Course 97. **d** 00 **p** 01. NSM Trefnant w Tremeirchion *St As* 00–01; NSM Cefn w Trefnant w Tremeirchion 01–14; Hon Can St As Cathl 12–14; rtd 14; PtO *St As* from 14. *2 Llys y Tywysog, Tremeirchion, St Asaph LL17 0UL* T: (01745) 710363 E: peterwykes@gmail.com

WYLAM, John. b 43. AKC 66 FE TCert 75. **d** 67 **p** 68. C Derby St Bart 67–70; SSF 70–73; C Seaton Hirst *Newc* 74–77; V Byker St Silas 77–83; V Alwinton w Holystone and Alnham 83–98; V Chollerton w Birtley and Thockrington 98–09; rtd 09; PtO *Newc* from 09. *Nether House, Garleigh Road, Rothbury, Morpeth NE65 7RG* T: (01669) 622805 E: johnwylam@btopenworld.com

WYLD, Kevin Andrew. b 58. St Cath Coll Ox BA 79 MA 85 Univ Coll Dur MSc 83 Edin Univ BD 85. Edin Th Coll 82. **d** 85 **p** 86. C Winlaton *Dur* 85–87; C Houghton le Spring 87–90; V Medomsley 90–95; V High Spen and Rowlands Gill 95–00; R Winter Park St Rich USA 00–04. *15 Hullock Road, Newton Aycliffe DL5 4LT* E: kevinwyld@gmail.com

WYLD, Richard Michael. b 81. Surrey Univ BMus 04 St Jo Coll Dur BA 09 MA 10 PhD 14. Cranmer Hall Dur 06. **d** 13 **p** 14. C Sherborne w Castleton, Lillington and Longburton *Sarum* 13–17; Bp's Dom Chapl *Portsm* 17–20; Dir Portsm Pathway from 20; IME Officer 4-7 *Portsm* from 20. *Address temp unknown* M: 07971-876699 E: rickwyld4@hotmail.com

WYLD, Ruth Elizabeth. *See* CHAPMAN, Ruth Elizabeth

WYLES, Mrs Kate Elizabeth. b 66. Bournemouth Univ BA 89 Win Univ BA 11. STETS 07. **d** 11 **p** 12. C Godalming *Guildf* 11–13; C Stoke-next-Guildf 13–15; V Goldsworth Park 15–21. *Holly Cottage, 95 Hayes Lane, Wimborne BH21 2JD* E: kewyles@outlook.com

WYLIE, Alan. b 47. Is of Man Tr Inst 88. **d** 92 **p** 93. NSM Douglas St Geo *S & M* 92–97; NSM Challoch *Glas* 97–00; P-in-c Motherwell 00–16; P-in-c Wishaw 00–16; rtd 16; LtO *Glas* from 17. *8 Millard Avenue, Carfin, Motherwell ML1 4GA* T: (01669) 230869 E: alan.rev@hotmail.com

WYLIE, Clive George. b 64. QUB BSc 86 TCD BTh 90 MA 93. CITC 87. **d** 90 **p** 91. C Drumglass w Moygashel *Arm* 90–93; I Tynan, Aghavilly and Middletown 93–98; Hon V Choral Arm Cathl 93–98; Team P Glas E End 98–03; R 03–08; Miss 21 Co-ord 98–03; PtO *Nor* 09–12; R N and S Creake w Waterden, Syderstone etc from 12; RD Burnham and Walsingham from 20. *The Rectory, 18 Front Street, South Creake, Fakenham NR21 9PE* T: (01328) 823293 M: 07970-875052 E: clive.wylie@dioceseofnorwich.org

WYLIE, David Victor. b 61. ACA 86 LSE BSc(Econ) 82 Leeds Univ BA 91. Coll of Resurr Mirfield 89. **d** 92 **p** 93. C Kilburn St Aug w St Jo *Lon* 92–95; C Heston 95–98; Chapl RN 98–17; P-in-c Leigh-on-Sea St Marg *Chelmsf* from 17. *The Vicarage, 1465 London Road, Leigh-on-Sea SS9 2SB*

WYLIE, Mrs Emma Clare Anna. b 75. Kent Univ BA 96 MA 01. St Mellitus Coll 13. **d** 16 **p** 17. C Langdon Hills *Chelmsf* 16–19; P-in-c Boreham from 19. *The Vicarage, Church Road, Boreham, Chelmsford CM3 3EG* M: 07982-723539 E: revemswylie@gmail.com

WYLIE, Kenneth Andrew. b 66. St Mellitus Coll BA 14. **d** 14 **p** 15. C Hornchurch St Andr *Chelmsf* 14–20; V from 20; AD Havering from 21. *222 High Street, Hornchurch RM12 6QP* T: (01708) 441571 E: ken847@btinternet.com

WYMAN, Daniel Jonathan. b 91. Birm City Univ BMus 15. Coll of Resurr Mirfield BA 19. **d** 20 **p** 21. C Eltham H Trin *S'wark* from 20. *59A Southend Crescent, London SE9 2SD* M: 07800-568953 E: daniel.j.wyman@gmail.com

WYNBURNE, Canon John Paterson Barry. b 48. St Jo Coll Dur BA 70. Wycliffe Coll Toronto MDiv 72 Ridley Hall Cam 72. **d** 73 **p** 74. C Gt Stanmore *Lon* 73–76; Chapl Bucharest w Sofia *Eur* 76–77; C Dorking w Ranmore *Guildf* 77–80; V Send 80–88; V York Town St Mich 88–93; V Camberley St Mich Yorktown 93–95; TR Beaconsfield *Ox* 95–09; AD Amersham 04–09; V Long Crendon w Chearsley and Nether Winchendon 09–15; Hon Can Ch Ch 11–15; rtd 15; PtO *Ox* from 15. *66 Windmill Street, Brill, Aylesbury HP18 9TG* T: (01844) 238387 E: revwynburne@btinternet.com

WYNFORD-HARRIS, Robert William. b 61. Anglia Ruskin Univ BA 10 MA 14 LGSM 90. Ridley Hall Cam 06. **d** 08 **p** 09. C Sawbridgeworth *St Alb* 08–11; C Thorley 11–14; P-in-c St Helens *Portsm* 14–17; P-in-c Sea View 14–17; rtd 17; PtO *Ox* from 17. *Whiteoaks, Bucklebury Alley, Cold Ash, Thatcham RG18 9NN* M: 07722-068018 E: wynhar@hotmail.com

WYNN, Edward Laurence. b 65. MBE 11. Leeds Metrop Univ BSc 96 Leeds Univ MA 02 RGN 88. NOC 98. **d** 01 **p** 02. C Emley *Wakef* 01–04; C Flockton cum Denby Grange 01–04; Chapl RAF 04–12; Chapl Wolv Univ *Lich* 12–15; Chapl Birm Women's NHS Foundn Trust 12–15; Chapl RAuxAF 12–15; Chapl RAF from 15. *Chaplaincy Services (RAF), HQ Air Command, RAF High Wycombe HP14 4UE* T: (01494) 496800

WYNN (*née* ARMSTRONG), **Rosemary.** b 40. **d** 06. OLM Sturminster Newton, Hinton St Mary and Lydlinch *Sarum* 06–14; PtO 14–17. *2 Mounters Close, Marnhull, Sturminster Newton DT10 1NT* T: (01258) 820806

WYNNE, Preb Alan John. b 46. St Luke's Coll Ex CertEd 71. St Steph Ho Ox BA 71 MA 75. **d** 71 **p** 72. C Watford St Pet *St Alb* 71–74; Chapl Liddon Ho Lon 74–75; Chapl Abp Tenison's Sch Kennington 75–86; Hon C St Marylebone Annunciation Bryanston Street *Lon* 81–86; V Hoxton St Anne w St Columba 86–94; TR Poplar 94–14; Preb St Paul's Cathl 01–14; AD Tower Hamlets 01–06; rtd 14. *194 Long Lane, London SE1 4PZ* E: alanjwynne@tiscali.co.uk

WYNNE (*née* GORTON), **Mrs Angela Deborah.** b 60. Leeds Univ BSc 82 CSci 04. CBDTI 04. **d** 07 **p** 08. NSM Penwortham St Mary *Blackb* 07–11; NSM Charnock Richard 11–16; NSM Eccleston 13–16; TV Blackrod, Daisy Hill, Westhoughton and Wingates *Man* from 16. *St Katherine's Vicarage, Blackhorse Street, Blackrod, Bolton BL6 5EN* E: adwynne@yahoo.co.uk

WYNNE, The Very Revd Frederick John Gordon. b 44. Chu Coll Cam BA 66 MA 70. CITC 81. **d** 84 **p** 85. C Dublin St Patr Cathl Gp *D & G* 84–86; C Romsey *Win* 86–89; R Broughton, Bossington, Houghton and Mottisfont 89–97; I Dunleckney w Nurney, Lorum and Kiltennel *C, F & O* 97–08; I Leighlin w Grange Sylvae, Shankill etc 08–10; Chan Ossory Cathl 00–10; Chan Leighlin Cathl 00–04; Dean Leighlin 04–10; rtd 10; PtO *Win* from 13. *12 Avenue Road, Lymington SO41 9GJ* T: (01590) 672082

WYNNE, Ian Charles. b 53. Bris Univ MB, ChB 76 FRCGP 06. SNWTP 09. **d** 11 **p** 12. NSM Haydock St Jas *Liv* from 11. *123 Ashton Road, Newton-le-Willows WA12 0AH* M: 07885-823786 E: ian_cw@hotmail.com

WYNNE, Jago Robert Owen. b 76. Magd Coll Cam BA 98 MA 01. Wycliffe Hall Ox 08. **d** 10 **p** 11. C Onslow Square and S Kensington St Aug *Lon* 10–12; C Clapham H Trin *S'wark* 12–15; V from 15; P-in-c Clapham Park All SS from 16. *25 The Chase, London SW4 0NP* M: 07976-033602 E: jago.wynne@holytrinityclapham.org

WYNNE, Canon Teresa Anne Jane. b 58. Anglia Poly Univ BEd 94 Middx Univ BA 07. NTMTC 04. **d** 07 **p** 08. C Takeley w Lt Canfield *Chelmsf* 07–10; P-in-c Lexden 10–17; TV Cheshunt *St Alb* 17–21; TR from 21; Hon Can St Alb from 20. *The Vicarage, 5 Longlands Close, Cheshunt, Waltham Cross EN8 8LW* T: (01992) 640338 E: vicarccwc@gmail.com

WYNNE-GREEN, Roy Rowland. b 36. Chich Th Coll 67. **d** 70 **p** 71. C Fleetwood St Pet *Blackb* 70–73; C Cen Torquay *Ex* 73–75; Chapl SW Hosp Lon 75–85; Asst Chapl St Thos Hosp 75–85; Chapl R Surrey Co Hosp Guildf 85–94; Chapl R Surrey Co Hosp NHS Trust 94–01; Chapl Heathlands Mental Health Trust Surrey 94–98; Chapl Surrey Hants Borders NHS Trust 98–01; rtd 01; PtO *Guildf* 02–17. *St Benedict's House, 6 Lawn Road, Guildford GU2 5DE* T: (01483) 574582

WYNNE-JONES, Nicholas Winder. b 45. Jes Coll Ox BA 67 MA 72 Selw Coll Cam 71. Oak Hill Th Coll 69. **d** 72 **p** 73. C St Marylebone All So w SS Pet and Jo *Lon* 72–75; Chapl Stowe Sch 75–83; V Gt Clacton *Chelmsf* 83–95; V Beckenham Ch Ch *Roch* 95–13; RD Beckenham 00–05; rtd 13; Hon C Theale and Englefield *Ox* 13–18; V Englefield from 18. *St Mark's House, Englefield, Reading RG7 5EP* T: 0118-930 3595 E: nwwj@stmarksenglefield.org.uk

---

Y

YABBACOME, David Wallace. b 55. Bp Otter Coll BEd. Linc Th Coll. **d** 83 **p** 84. C Egham Hythe *Guildf* 83–86; C Cen Telford *Lich* 86–87; TV 87–92; R Cheadle w Freehay 92–00; V Linc St Nic w St Jo Newport 00–13; V E Trent *S'well* 13–15; rtd 15; PtO *Ely* from 16. *67 Primrose Avenue, Downham Market PE38 9GF* T: (01366) 386920 M: 07779-557541 E: revyabb@gmail.com

YABSLEY, Mrs Janet. b 42. St Alb Minl Tr Scheme 81. dss 84 **d** 87 **p** 94. Luton St Andr *St Alb* 84–87; NSM Luton St Aug Limbury 87–00; NSM Luton All SS w St Pet 00–06; PtO from 06. *11 Dale Road, Dunstable LU5 4PY* T: (01582) 661480

YACOMENI, Peter Frederick. b 34. Worc Coll Ox BA 58 MA 61. Wycliffe Hall Ox 58. **d** 60 **p** 61. C New Malden and Coombe *S'wark* 60–64; C Bethnal Green St Jas Less *Lon* 64–68; V Barton Hill St Luke w Ch Ch *Bris* 68–75; V Bishopsworth 75–86; RD Bedminster 84–86; P-in-c Wick w Doynton 86–87; V Wick w Doynton and Dyrham 87–98; RD Bitton 95–98; rtd 98; Chapl Wilts and Swindon Healthcare NHS Trust 98–08; Chapl Gt Western Hosps NHS Foundn Trust 08–10; PtO *Bris* from 98. *15 Orwell Close, Malmesbury SN16 9UB* T: (01666) 826628 E: peter.yacomeni@gmail.com

YACOMENI, Thomas Peter Bruce. b 71. Ex Univ BEng 94. Trin Coll Bris BA 09. **d** 09 **p** 10. C Weston-super-Mare St Paul *B & W* 09–13; Pioneer Min from 13; RD Locking from 18. *78 Bransby Way, Weston-super-Mare BS24 7BW* T: (01934) 517954 M: 07786-806640 E: tom.yacomeni@googlemail.com

YANDELL, Caroline Jane. b 63. St Hugh's Coll Ox BA 85 MA 92 Bris Univ MB, ChB 97 LSHTM MSc 05 Bris Univ PhD 07 Wolfs Coll Cam BTh 08 St Jo Coll Cam MPhil 09 MRCGP 01. Ridley Hall Cam 06. **d** 09 **p** 10. C Henleaze *Bris* 09–13; P-in-c Bassingbourn *Ely* 13–15; V 15–20; P-in-c Whaddon 13–15; V 15–20; PtO 20–21; NSM Bluntisham cum Earith w Colne and Holywell etc from 21. *171 Greenfields, Earith, Huntingdon PE28 3QZ* E: caroline.yandell@cantab.net

YAP, Thomas Fook Piau. b 75. Leeds Univ BA 98 MA 99. St Jo Coll Nottm MTh 02. **d** 03 **p** 04. C Starbeck *Ripon* 03–07; Chapl Essex Univ *Chelmsf* 07–12; Chapl S Lon and Maudsley NHS Foundn Trust 12–15; PtO *Lon* from 12; *S'wark* from 15. *5 Howerd Court, 20 Love Lane, London SE18 6GR* E: revthomas@hotmail.co.uk

YARRIEN (née FRYER), Cora Lynette. b 74. Man Univ BSc 95 Warwick Univ MSc 97 BA 01. Cranmer Hall Dur 12. **d** 14 **p** 15. C Epperstone, Gonalston, Oxton and Woodborough *S'well* 14–16; C Daybrook 16–18; P-in-c Retford Area 18–19; R The Idle and Sands 19–20; TV Dorchester and the Winterbournes *Sarum* from 21. *7 Capitol Close, Dorchester DT1 2QS* M: 07885-635374 E: cora.yarrien@icloud.com

YATES, Andrew Martin. b 55. St Chad's Coll Dur BA 77. Linc Th Coll 78. **d** 80 **p** 81. C Brightside St Thos and St Marg *Sheff* 80–83; TV Haverhill w Withersfield, the Wrattings etc *St E* 84–90; Ind Chapl 84–90; R Aylesham w Adisham *Cant* 90–96; P-in-c Dudley St Aug Holly Hall *Worc* 96–03; Chapl Merry Hill Shopping Cen 96–03; Dioc Soc Resp Officer *Truro* from 03; P-in-c Tresillian and Lamorran w Merther 03–12; P-in-c St Michael Penkevil 03–12; P-in-c Paul from 12; C Newlyn St Pet from 12; C Penzance St Mary w St Paul and St Jo from 12. *Hanover House, 6A Kings Road, Penzance TR18 4LG* T: (01736) 367863 E: andrew.yates@truro.anglican.org

YATES, Christopher David. b 80. Open Univ CSocSc 05. Ox Min Course 08. **d** 10 **p** 11. C Williamstown w Medowie and Mallabula Australia 10–12; R Raymond Terrace 12–16; Chapl NSW Police 11–16; V Eastbourne St Sav and St Pet *Chich* 16–17. *12 Gordon Avenue, Hamilton NSW 2303, Australia* M: (0061) 42-921 5917 E: chrsyates@yahoo.co.uk

YATES, Mrs Esther Christine. b 46. Moray Ho Coll of Educn DipEd 67 Cartrefle Coll of Educn BEd 80. St As Minl Tr Course 02. **d** 05 **p** 06. NSM Newtown w Llanllwchaiarn w Aberhafesp *St As* 05–07; NSM Llanllwchaiarn and Newtown w Aberhafesp 07–10; NSM Berriew 10–17; NSM Pool Miss Area 18–19; rtd 19; PtO *St As* from 19. *Gwawr-y-Grug, 7 Mill Fields, Milford, Newtown SY16 3JP* T: (01686) 625559 E: esther.yates@talktalk.net

YATES, Francis Edmund. b 49. Ox Univ BEd 72 Sheff Univ MEd 88. Linc Th Coll 95. **d** 95 **p** 96. C Chesterfield St Mary and All SS *Derby* 95–98; P-in-c Newlyn St Newlyn *Truro* 98–03; Dioc Adv for Schs and RE 98–03; P-in-c Tideswell *Derby* 03–11; V 11–12; C Wormhill, Peak Forest w Peak Dale and Dove Holes 07–11; rtd 12; PtO *Linc* 16–19. *Tanners, Alford Road, Bilsby, Alford LN13 9PY* T: (01507) 464890 E: frank298@btinternet.com

YATES, Herbert. See YATES, William Herbert

YATES, Jennifer Clare. See TOTNEY, Jennifer Clare

YATES, Miss Joanna Mary. b 49. St Anne's Coll Ox BA 71 MA 74 K Coll Lon PGCE 72. S'wark Ord Course 89. **d** 91 **p** 94. Promotions and Publications Officer Nat Soc 85–95; Chapl Ch Ho Westmr 91–95; C Regent's Park St Mark *Lon* 91–95; C Finchley St Mary 95–01; TV Leeds City *Ripon* 01–09; rtd 09; PtO *Lon* from 10. *8 Frith Court, London NW7 1JP* T: (020) 8349 1076 M: 07961-654430 E: revjoannayates325@btinternet.com

YATES, Lindsay Anne. b 69. Selw Coll Cam BA 91 MA 95 Univ of Wales (Lamp) MTh 10 Barrister 92. Ripon Coll Cuddesdon BTh 99. **d** 99 **p** 00. C Bampton w Clanfield *Ox* 99–02; Chapl Pemb Coll Cam 02–06; Chapl Westcott Ho Cam 07–14; NSM Winchmore Hill St Paul *Lon* 14–17; Tutor St Mellitus Coll 14–17; P-in-c Octagon *Chich* 17–18; R from 18. *The Vicarage, Compton, Chichester PO18 9HD* T: (023) 9263 1252 E: rector@theoctagonparish.org.uk

YATES, Margaret Helen. b 51. **d** 10 **p** 11. NSM Walbury Beacon *Ox* 10–14; NSM Newbury St Nic and Speen 15–18; PtO from 18. *5 Halfway Cottages, Bath Road, Newbury RG20 8NG* T: (01488) 658092

YATES, Michael Anthony. b 48. Oak Hill Th Coll. **d** 82 **p** 83. C Hebburn St Jo *Dur* 82–85; C Sheldon *Birm* 85–87; V Lea Hall 87–92; TV Old Brampton and Loundsley Green *Derby* 92–98; V Loundsley Green 98–01; V Riddings and Ironville 01–07; P-in-c Seale and Lullington w Coton in the Elms 07–11; R 11–17; C Walton-on-Trent w Croxall, Rosliston etc 13–17; rtd 17; PtO *York* from 18. *10 Park Avenue, Beverley HU17 7AT* E: mermaid23@hotmail.co.uk

YATES, Michael Peter. b 47. JP 91. Leeds Univ BA 69 MA 70 MPhil 85 Potchefstroom Univ PhD 03. Coll of Resurr Mirfield 69. **d** 71 **p** 72. C Crewe St Andr *Ches* 71–76; V Wheelock 76–79; Chapl Rainhill Hosp *Liv* 79–89; Chapl Barnsley Distr Gen Hosp 89–94; Chapl Barnsley Distr Gen Hosp NHS Trust 94–11; Chapl Barnsley Hosp NHS Foundn Trust 05–11; rtd 11; PtO *Leeds* from 17. *40 Rainton Grove, Barnsley S75 2QZ* E: mpyates@hotmail.com

YATES, Paul David. b 47. Sussex Univ BA 73 DPhil 80. Sarum & Wells Th Coll 88. **d** 91 **p** 92. NSM Lewes All SS, St Anne, St Mich and St Thos *Chich* 91–00; NSM Lewes St Mich and St Thos at Cliffe w All SS 00–10; NSM Lewes St Anne and St Mich and St Thos etc from 10. *17 St Swithun's Terrace, Lewes BN7 1UJ* T: (01273) 473463

YATES, Peter Francis. b 47. Sheff Univ BA 69. Kelham Th Coll 69 NW Ord Course 73. **d** 74 **p** 75. C Mexborough *Sheff* 74–78; C Sevenoaks St Jo *Roch* 78–81; CSWG from 81; LtO *Chich* from 85. *The Monastery, Crawley Down, Crawley RH10 4LH* T: (01342) 712074 E: father.peter@cswg.org.uk

YATES, Raymond Paul. b 55. Oak Hill Th Coll BA 88. **d** 88 **p** 89. C Bootle St Mary w St Paul *Liv* 88–91; C Drypool *York* 91–92; TV 92–97; C Orpington All SS *Roch* 97–00; R Beeford w Frodingham and Foston *York* 00–06; RD N Holderness 02–06; Chapl HM Pris Hull 01–02; P-in-c Quinton Road W St Boniface *Birm* 06–09; V 09–20; rtd 20. *Address temp unknown*

YATES, Ricky. *See* YATES, Warwick John

YATES, Canon Roger Alan. b 47. Trin Coll Cam BA 68 MA 72 MB, BChir 71 Bris Univ PhD 75 MRCP 77 FFPM 93. NOC 84. **d** 87 **p** 88. NSM Wilmslow *Ches* from 87; Bp's Officer for NSM 93–17; Hon Can Ches Cathl from 99; RD Knutsford 06–13. *3 Racecourse Park, Wilmslow SK9 5LU* T: (01625) 520246 E: raycandoc@yahoo.co.uk

YATES, Mrs Siân. b 57. Univ of Wales (Ban) Westmr Coll Ox MTh 91. Linc Th Coll 78. **d** 80 **p** 94. C Risca *Mon* 80–83; Chapl Ch Hosp Horsham 83–85; Team Dn Haverhill w Withersfield, the Wrattings etc *St E* 85–90; Dioc Youth Chapl *Cant* 90–93; Assoc Min Cant St Martin and St Paul 93–96; Educn Chapl *Worc* 96–03; P-in-c Dudley St Jas 96–03; P-in-c Dudley St Barn 01–02; P-in-c Tregony w St Cuby and Cornelly *Truro* 03–12; Dioc Adv in RE 03–10; TR Penzance St Mary w St Paul and St Jo from 12; C Newlyn St Pet from 12; C Paul from 12. *Hanover House, 6A Kings Road, Penzance TR18 4LG* T: (01736) 367863 E: yates252@btinternet.com *or* teamleader@penleecluster.org.uk

YATES, Stephen Richard. b 79. Univ of Wales (Ban) BSc 01. Trin Coll Bris 14. **d** 16. C Torquay St Matthias, St Mark and H Trin *Ex* 16–20; TR Brixham w Churston Ferrers and Kingswear from 20. *16 Holwell Road, Brixham TQ5 9NE* M: 07840-785426

YATES, Timothy John Sturgis. b 56. Bradf Univ BTech 83 Univ Coll Lon PhD 86. ERMC 05. **d** 07 **p** 08. NSM Gt Chesham *Ox* from 07. *16 Chapmans Crescent, Chesham HP5 2QU* T: (01494) 772914 M: 07802-155072 E: tim.yates3@btinternet.com

YATES, Warwick John (Ricky). b 52. Univ of Wales (Lamp) BA 78. Wycliffe Hall Ox 87. **d** 89 **p** 90. C Hoddesdon *St Alb* 89–93; R Finmere w Mixbury, Cottisford, Hardwick etc *Ox* 93–95; R Shelswell 95–08; P-in-c Prague *Eur* 08–17; rtd 17; PtO *Eur* from 17. *Stará Oleška 44, 405 02 Hunti̇́ ov, Czech Republic* M: (00420) 73-577 8426 E: ry@rickyyates.com

YATES, William Herbert. b 35. Man Univ BA 59. Chich Th Coll 60. **d** 61 **p** 62. C Blackpool St Steph *Blackb* 61–65; C Wednesbury St Jo *Lich* 65–69; V Porthill 69–78; R Norton in the Moors 78–84; R Church Aston 84–00; rtd 00; PtO *Lich* 01–21. *2 Red Lees, Telford TF1 5DE* T: (01952) 619218

YATES, Mrs Yvonne Louise. b 52. NEOC 01. **d** 04 **p** 05. NSM Kirkbymoorside w Gillamoor, Farndale etc *York* 04–07; Chapl Oakhill Secure Tr Cen 07–08; Co-ord Chapl HM Pris Kirklevington Grange 08–11; TV Combe Martin, Berrynarbor, Lynton, Brendon etc *Ex* 11–14; Chapl HM Pris Styal from 14. *HM Prison, Styal Road, Styal, Wilmslow SK9 4HR* T: (01625) 553000 E: yvonne.yates@justice.gov.uk

YAU, Timothy Sang. b 71. Ridley Hall Cam 06. **d** 08 **p** 09. C Farcet Hampton *Ely* 08–12; C Cringleford and Colney *Nor* from 17. *5 Poppy Close, Cringleford, Norwich NR4 7JZ* M: 07964-078330

YEADON, Ms Victoria Jane. b 69. Univ Coll Lon BSc 91 MSc 92 Anglia Ruskin Univ BA 09. Ridley Hall Cam 07. **d** 09 **p** 10. C Deptford St Nic and St Luke *S'wark* 09–12; TV Thamesmead 12–20; TV Waltham H Cross *Chelmsf* from 20. *The Vicarage, 15 Harrier Way, Waltham Abbey EN9 3JQ* T: (020) 8312 2566 E: janeyeadon@gmail.com

YEAGER, Robert Timothy. b 50. Univ of Iowa BA 72 JD 77. **d** 10 **p** 11. USA 10–14; TV E Greenwich *S'wark* 14–20; rtd 20. *89 Westcombe Park Road, London SE3 7RZ* T: (020) 8090 2036 M: 07804-614245 E: rtyeager@gmail.com

YEARWOOD, Jean Cornilia. b 43. Heythrop Coll Lon MA 05 RGN 74 RM 76. **d** 07 **p** 08. NSM Croydon Woodside *S'wark* 07–14; rtd 14; PtO *S'wark* from 14. *59 Bradley Road, London SE19 3NT* T: (020) 8771 7743 M: 07913-005545 E: j.yearwood@btopenworld.com

YEATES, James Paul. b 81. St Mellitus Coll. **d** 13 **p** 14. C Highgate St Mich *Lon* 13–16; C Telford Park *S'wark* 16–20; V Cricklewood St Gabr and St Mich *Lon* from 20. *St Gabriel's Vicarage, 156 Anson Road, London NW2 6BH* T: (020) 8830 6626 E: james.yeates@st-gabriels.org

YELDHAM, Anthony Paul Richard. *See* KYRIAKIDES-YELDHAM, Anthony Paul Richard

YELDHAM, Denise Linda. b 51. Leeds Univ BSc 72 MB, ChB 75 Univ of Wales (Lamp) MA 08 MRCPsych 80. Westcott Ho Cam 06. **d** 08 **p** 09. C Plymstock and Hooe *Ex* 08–11; PtO from 11; C Westmr St Steph w St Jo *Lon* 11–14; P-in-c Margate All SS *Cant* 14–17; P-in-c Margate St Jo 14–17; Chapl Eden Hall Marie Curie Hospice 18–19; NSM

Kilburn St Mary w All So and W Hampstead St Jas *Lon* from 19. *Flat 14, 19 Page Street, London SW1P 4JX* T: (020) 7932 0235 M: 07427-160204 E: denise.yeldham@gmail.com

YELLAND, Jeffrey Charles. b 46. CEng MIStructE 72. STETS 98. **d** 01 **p** 02. NSM Effingham w Lt Bookham *Guildf* 01–04; NSM Dorking St Paul 04–16; PtO from 16. *9 Mulberry Heights, Harrowlands Park, Dorking RH4 2RA* M: 07877-040770 E: jeff@stpaulsdorking.org.uk

YEMM, Ian Ira. b 70. Surrey Univ BA 93 Sarum Coll MA 12 LRAM 95. St Padarn's Inst 19. **d** 20 **p** 21. C Cowbridge *Llan* from 20. *3 Leoline Close, Cowbridge CF71 7BU* T: (01446) 311289 M: 07434-654312 E: ianyemm@cinw.org.uk

YENDALL, Canon John Edward Thomas. b 52. St Jo Coll Dur BA 88. Cranmer Hall Dur 84. **d** 88 **p** 89. C Bangor *Ban* 88–90; C Botwnnog 90–91; R Trefdraeth w Aberffraw etc 91–01; RD Malltraeth 97–01; V Llanwddyn and Llanfihangel-yng-Nghwynfa etc *St As* 01–07; V Llanrhaeadr ym Mochnant etc 07–11; P-in-c Llansantffraid Glyn Ceirog and Llanarmon etc 11–17; I Boyle and Elphin w Aghanagh, Kilbryan etc *K, E & A* from 17; Can Elphin Cathl from 17. *Tus Nua, Forest View, Boyle, Co Roscommon, Republic of Ireland* T: (00353) (71) 966 2639 E: edward.yendall2@btinternet.com

✠**YEOMAN, The Rt Revd David.** b 44. St Mich Coll Llan 66. **d** 70 **p** 71 **c** 04. C Cardiff St Jo *Llan* 70–72; C Caerphilly 72–76; V Ystrad Rhondda w Ynyscynon 76–81; V Mountain Ash 81–96; R Coity w Nolton 96–04; Can Llan Cathl 00–09; Asst Bp Llan 04–09; Adn Morgannwg 04–06; rtd 09; PtO *Llan* from 09. *4 Llety Gwyn, Bridgend CF31 1RG* T: (01656) 649919 M: 07971-926631

YEOMAN, Miss Ruth Jane. b 60. Sheff Univ BSc 82 MSc 85 Dur Univ PGCE 83. Ripon Coll Cuddesdon BA 90 MA 94. **d** 91 **p** 94. C Coleshill *Birm* 91–95; C Hodge Hill 95–01; Bp's Adv for Children's Work 95–01; L'Arche Lambeth Community 01–03; PtO *S'wark* 01–03; *Birm* 03; V Menston w Woodhead *Bradf* 03–14; *Leeds* 14–17; C Baildon from 17. *93 Hoyle Court Road, Baildon, Shipley BD17 6EL* M: 07752-912646 E: ruthjyeoman@hotmail.com

YEOMANS, Paul Dennis. b 46. **d** 12 **p** 12. C Waitaki N NZ 12; P 12–20; PtO *Nor* from 21. *1 The Bleach, Heath Road, Crostwight, North Walsham NR28 9PA* T: (01692) 773385 M: 07437-203535 E: paul@yeomans.info *or* paulyeomans65@gmail.com

YERBURGH, Canon David Savile. b 34. Magd Coll Cam BA 57 MA 61. Wells Th Coll 57. **d** 59 **p** 60. C Cirencester *Glouc* 59–63; C Bitterne Park *Win* 63–67; V Churchdown St Jo *Glouc* 67–74; RD Glouc N 73–74; V Charlton Kings St Mary 74–85; R Minchinhampton 85–95; Hon Can Glouc Cathl 86–95; rtd 95; PtO *Sarum* 95–21. *2 Mill Race Close, Mill Road, Salisbury SP2 7RX* T: (01722) 320064 E: d.yerburgh@btinternet.com

YERBURY, Gregory Howard. b 67. Trin Coll Bris BA 93. St Jo Coll Nottm 94. **d** 96 **p** 97. C Crofton *Portsm* 96–00; P-in-c Bolton St Jo *Man* 00–06; P-in-c Bolton Breightmet St Jas 05–06; TR Leverhulme 06–11; TR Penkridge *Lich* from 11; RD from 16. *The Rectory, New Road, Penkridge, Stafford ST19 5DN* T: (01785) 714344 E: rector@stmichaelspenkridge.co.uk

YETMAN, Miss Sarah Elizabeth. b 85. St Mary's Coll Dur BA 09 Cam Univ BTh 13. Ridley Hall Cam 10. **d** 13 **p** 14. C Yateley *Win* 13–17; P-in-c Bournemouth St Jo w St Mich 17–18; V from 18. *13 Durley Chine Road South, Bournemouth BH2 5JT* T: (01202) 241507 *or* 556645 E: revd.sarah.yetman@gmail.com

YILDIRIM, Engin. **d** 07 **p** 08. C Istanbul *Eur* 07–17; TV Wood Green St Mich w Bounds Green St Gabr etc *Lon* from 17. *27 Collings Close, London N22 8RL* M: 07908-335400 E: engnyldrm@icloud.com

YONG, Sok Han. b 61. Ox Brookes Univ MA 14. Malaysia Th Sem BTheol 86. **d** 10 **p** 11. NSM Ox St Aldate 10–11; NSM Abingdon 11–14; C St Andr Hong Kong 14–20; PtO *Ox* from 20. *St Helen's Church, St Helen's Court, Abingdon OX14 5BS*

YONGE, James Mohun (Brother Amos). b 47. Keele Univ BA 71. WMMTC 91. **d** 94 **p** 95. SSF from 76; PtO *Worc* 09–17. *Glasshampton Monastery, Shrawley, Worcester WR6 6TQ* T: (01299) 896345 F: 896083 E: amossf@franciscans.org.uk

YORK, Mrs Elizabeth Joy. b 70. Nottm Univ BA 94 Nottm Trent Univ PGCE 97 Ches Univ MTh 17. St Jo Coll Nottm 13. **d** 15 **p** 16. C Barrow upon Soar w Walton le Wolds *Leic* 15–17; C Wymeswold and Prestwold w Hoton 15–17; C Loughb Gd Shep 17–19; Chapl Loughborough Schs Foundn from 19. *Address withheld by request*

YORK, Canon Humphrey Bowmar. b 28. St Chad's Coll Dur BA 54 Univ of Wales (Lamp) MA 04. **d** 55 **p** 56. C Beamish *Dur* 55–57; C Tettenhall Regis *Lich* 57–62; P-in-c Lansallos w Pelynt *Truro* 62–63; R Lanreath 62–67; V Pelynt 63–67; P-in-c Lanlivery 67–74; P-in-c Luxulyan 67–74;

P-in-c Lanlivery w Luxulyan 74–83; RD Bodmin 76–82; R Antony w Sheviock 83–93; Hon Can Truro Cathl 90–93; rtd 93; PtO *Truro* 93–12; *Sarum* 93–17. *8 Huntingdon Street, Bradford-on-Avon BA15 1RF* E: canonhumphrey@tinyworld.co.uk

YORK, Mrs Paula. b 67. d 12 **p** 13. C Earls Barton *Pet* 12–15; R Yardley Hastings, Denton and Grendon etc 15–20; V Wellingborough All SS from 20; V Wellingborough All Hallows from 20. *The Vicarage, 154 Midland Road, Wellingborough NN8 1NF* E: revpaulayork@gmail.com

YORK, Archbishop of. *See* COTTRELL, The Most Revd Stephen Geoffrey

YORK, Archdeacon of. *See* RUSHTON, The Ven Samantha Jayne

YORK, Dean of. *See* FROST, The Rt Revd Jonathan Hugh

YORKE, John Andrew. b 47. Cranmer Hall Dur 70. d 73 **p** 74. C Spitalfields Ch Ch w All SS *Lon* 73–78; R Tuktoyaktuk Canada 78–88; R Fort McPherson 89–92; V Totland Bay *Portsm* 92–12; V Thorley 95–12; rtd 12; PtO *Portsm* from 12; *Sarum* from 15. *7 Broadmead, Trowbridge BA14 9BX* T: (01225) 680529 E: andyyorke.iow@tiscali.co.uk

YORKSTONE, Peter. b 48. Loughb Univ BTech 72. Oak Hill Th Coll 79. d 81 **p** 82. C Blackpool St Thos *Blackb* 81–85; V Copp 85–00; P-in-c Gigglesvick and Rathmell w Wigglesworth *Bradf* 00–07; V Kettlewell w Conistone, Hubberholme etc 07–14; rtd 14; PtO *Leic* from 16. *45 Hawthorne Avenue, Hathern, Loughborough LE12 5LP* E: peter@yorkstone.me.uk

YOUATT, Jennifer Alison. *See* MONTGOMERY, Jennifer Alison

YOUDE, Paul Crosland. b 47. Birm Univ LLB 68. WEMTC 93. d 96 **p** 97. NSM Cheltenham St Luke and St Jo *Glouc* 96–99; C Cirencester 99–03; P-in-c Lydney 03–09; P-in-c Woolaston w Alvington and Aylburton 07–09; rtd 09; Hon C Kemble, Poole Keynes, Somerford Keynes etc *Glouc* 09–13; PtO from 16. *107 Painswick Road, Cheltenham GL50 2EX* T: (01242) 463174 E: paul.youde@yahoo.co.uk

YOUELL, Mrs Deborah Mary. b 57. STETS 01. d 04 **p** 14. NSM Cowplain *Portsm* 04–08; NSM Crookhorn 08–20. *42 The Yews, Horndean, Waterlooville PO8 0BH* T: (023) 9279 9946 or 9225 6814 M: 07513-314441 E: debbie@cogs.org.uk

YOUENS, Edward. *See* MONTAGUE-YOUENS, Hubert Edward

YOUINGS, The Ven Adrian. b 65. Ex Univ BSc 86 Bath Univ PhD 90. Wycliffe Hall Ox 93. d 96 **p** 97. C Dorking St Paul *Guildf* 96–99; C S Croydon Em *S'wark* 99–03; R Trull w Angersleigh *B & W* 03–17; RD Taunton 15–17; Adn Bath and Preb Wells Cathl from 17. *56 Grange Road, Saltford, Bristol BS31 3AG* T: (01225) 873609 M: 07902-804569 E: adbath@bathwells.anglican.org

YOUNG, Andrew Charles. b 54. FIBMS 83. NOC 98. d 01 **p** 02. C Heywood *Man* 01–05; TV Eccles 05–16; AD 13–16; CMS Nepal from 16. *22 Southgate, Scarborough YO12 4NB* E: andrew.young66@ntlworld.com

YOUNG, Miss Anne Patricia. b 44. Cov Coll of Educn CertEd 66 Leeds Univ BEd 76 Sheff Univ MEd 82 Liv Univ BTh 05. NOC 01. d 05 **p** 06. NSM Middlestown *Wakef* 05–10; NSM Emley 11–14; NSM Flockton cum Denby Grange 11–14; PtO *Leeds* from 14. *58 The Crofts, Emley, Huddersfield HD8 9RU* T: (01924) 840738 M: 07478-696304 E: apyoung44@gmail.com

YOUNG, Arthur. b 65. Belf Bible Coll BTh 92. CITC 99. d 01 **p** 02. C Donaghadee *D & D* 01–04; I Tullylish 04–13; I Kill *D & G* 13–16; I Lisburn St Paul *Conn* from 16. *St Paul's Rectory, 3 Ballinderry Road, Lisburn BT28 1UD* E: youarthur@gmail.com

YOUNG, Mrs Carole Jane. b 58. Qu Foundn (Course) 16. d 18 **p** 19. NSM Kingsbury *Birm* from 18; NSM Baxterley w Hurley and Wood End and Merevale etc from 18. *84 Sycamore Road, Kingsbury, Tamworth B78 2JL* T: (01827) 874194 M: 07960-368524 E: rev.cj.young@gmail.com

YOUNG, Daniel George Harding. b 52. New Coll Ox BA 73 MA 83 Westmr Coll Ox PGCE 74. Cranmer Hall Dur 77. d 80 **p** 81. C Bushbury *Lich* 80–83; Chapl Dean Close Sch 83–99; Titus Trust 99–10; PtO *Win* 01–10; C Knutsford St Jo and Toft *Ches* 10–20; rtd 20. *35 Beggarmans Lane, Knutsford WA16 9BA* T: (01565) 228216 M: 07974-945651 E: youngdan52@talktalk.net

YOUNG, David Charles. b 54. Open Univ BA 95 PGCE 01 CQSW 82. SEITE 03. d 06 **p** 07. NSM Haywards Heath St Wilfrid *Chich* from 06. *4 Ashurst Place, Heath Road, Haywards Heath RH16 3EJ* T: (01444) 416074 M: 07921-144480

YOUNG, David John. b 43. Nottm Univ BA 64 MPhil 89 Lambeth STh 87 Birm Univ PhD 11. Coll of Resurr Mirfield 64. d 66 **p** 67. C Warsop *S'well* 66–68; C Harworth 68–71; P-in-c Hackenthorpe Ch Ch *Derby* 71–72; TV Frecheville and Hackenthorpe 73–75; V Chaddesden St Phil 75–83; R Narborough and Huncote *Leic* 83–89; RD Guthlaxton I 87–90; Chapl Leic Univ 90–95; V Eyres Monsell 95–98; PtO

98–99; rtd 03. *57 Castle Fields, Leicester LE4 1AN* T: 0116-220 3757 E: johnyoung58@virginmedia.com

YOUNG, David Lun Ming. b 81. Leeds Univ BA 02 St Jo Coll Dur BA 09 MA 12. Cranmer Hall Dur 07. d 10 **p** 11. C Upper Armley *Ripon* 10–14; TV Moor Allerton and Shadwell *Leeds* from 14; Asst Dir of Ords 15–20; Chapl Leeds Teaching Hosps NHS Trust from 20. *The Vicarage, 2 Church Farm Garth, Leeds LS17 8HD* M: 07736-678558 E: revdaveyoung@gmail.com

YOUNG, Derek John. b 42. St D Coll Lamp. d 73 **p** 74. C Griffithstown *Mon* 73–76; C Ebbw Vale 76–77; V Penmaen 77–81; V Penmaen and Crumlin 81–87; Chapl Oakdale Hosp Gwent 83–87; V New Tredegar *Mon* 87–99; V Llanfihangel Crucorney w Oldcastle etc 99–11; P-in-c from 12. *The Vicarage, Llanfihangel Crucorney, Abergavenny NP7 8DH* T: (01873) 890349

YOUNG, Mrs Diana Joan. b 56. St Hilda's Coll Ox BA 78 MA 82. Ripon Coll Cuddesdon 11. d 13 **p** 14. C Hampstead St Jo *Lon* 13–17; V Woburn Sands *St Alb* from 17. *30 Church Road, Woburn Sands, Milton Keynes MK17 8TA* E: revdianay@gmail.com

YOUNG, Emma. b 89. Trin Coll Ox BA 10 Aber Univ MTh 12. Ripon Coll Cuddesdon MTh 14. d 14 **p** 15. C Luton St Aug Limbury *St Alb* 14–17; V Darent Valley *Roch* from 17. *Darenth Vicarage, Green Street Green Road, Lane End, Dartford DA2 7JR* M: 07563-276794 E: revd.emma.young@hotmail.co.uk

YOUNG, George William. b 31. Lon Coll of Div ALCD 55. d 56 **p** 57. C Everton Em *Liv* 56–58; C Halliwell St Pet *Man* 58–61; V Newburn *Newc* 61–67; P-in-c Tyler's Green *Ox* 67–69; V 69–80; LtO 80–84; Area Sec (W England) SAMS 80–84; Hon C Purley Ch Ch *S'wark* 84–87; V Beckenham St Jo *Roch* 87–92; rtd 92; PtO *S'wark* 92–18. *9 Shortacres, High Street, Nutfield, Redhill RH1 4HJ* T: (01737) 822363 E: theyoungs88@yahoo.com

YOUNG, Graham Mark. b 83. UWE BSc 06 St Jo Coll Dur BA 17 Bath Univ QTS 07. Cranmer Hall Dur 16. d 17 **p** 18. C Sunderland St Mary and St Pet *Dur* 17–21; V Cleveleys *Blackb* from 21. *The Vicarage, Rough Lea Road, Thornton-Cleveleys FY5 1DP* T: (01253) 921266 E: revdgrahamyoung@outlook.com

YOUNG, Hyacinth Loretta. NTMTC 95. d 98 **p** 99. NSM Harlesden All So *Lon* 98–00; TV Wembley Park 00–12; V Tokyngton St Mich 12–19; rtd 19; PtO *Lon* from 20. *8 Nettleden Avenue, Wembley HA9 6DP* T: (020) 8900 1585 E: hyacinth513@hotmail.com

YOUNG, James Andrew. b 80. St Jo Coll Nottm. d 14 **p** 15. C Horsham *Chich* 14–18; C Crawley 18–21; V Penarth All SS *Llan* from 21. *2 Lower Cwrt-y-Vil Road, Penarth CF64 3HQ* M: 07903-813077 E: jimmy@christianjimmy.com

YOUNG, Jeremy Michael. b 54. Ch Coll Cam BA 76 MA 80 Lon Univ MTh 94. Coll of Resurr Mirfield 78. d 80 **p** 81. C Whitworth w Spennymoor *Dur* 80–83; C Boxmoor St Jo *St Alb* 83–86; V Croxley Green St Oswald 86–94; Dir Past Studies CITC 94–99; LtO *D & G* 99–03; PtO *B & W* from 06. *Westerley House, Tellisford, Bath BA2 7RL* T: (01373) 830920 E: jeremy_young@mac.com

YOUNG, John. *See* YOUNG, David John

YOUNG, Canon John David. b 37. Lon Univ BD 65 Sussex Univ MA 71. Clifton Th Coll 62. d 65 **p** 66. C Plymouth St Jude *Ex* 65–68; Hd of RE Northgate Sch Ipswich 68–71; Chapl and Sen Lect Bp Otter Coll Chich 71–81; Chapl and Sen Lect W Sussex Inst of HE 77–81; Chapl and Sen Lect York St Jo Coll 81–87; C York St Paul 87–88; Dioc Ev 88–02; Can and Preb York Minster 92–03; Miss Strategy Development Officer 00–02; rtd 02; LtO *York* 02–10; PtO from 10. *72 Middlethorpe Grove, York YO24 1JY* T: (01904) 704195 E: john.young@yorkcourses.co.uk

YOUNG, John Kenneth. Edin Th Coll 62. d 64 **p** 65. C Gosforth All SS *Newc* 64–67; C Newc St Gabr 67–69; R Bowers Gifford *Chelmsf* 69–72; R Bowers Gifford w N Benfleet 72–75; P-in-c Kirkwhelpington *Newc* 75–79; P-in-c Kirkharle 77–79; P-in-c Kirkheaton 75–79; P-in-c Cambo 77–79; V Kirkwhelpington, Kirkharle, Kirkheaton and Cambo 79–82; V Gosforth St Nic 82–92; V Healey and Slaley 92–97; rtd 97; PtO *Newc* from 97. *1 Raynes Close, Morpeth NE61 2XX* T: (01670) 515191

YOUNG, Canon Jonathan Priestland. b 44. AKC 68 Whitelands Coll Lon CertEd 74 Roehampton Univ Hon BEd 17. St Boniface Warminster 68. d 69 **p** 70. C Clapham H Trin *S'wark* 69–73; C Mitcham St Mark 73–74; V Godmanchester *Ely* 74–82; P-in-c Cambridge St Giles w St Pet 82; P-in-c Chesterton St Luke 82; TR Cambridge Ascension 82–01; Chapl St Jo Coll Sch Cam 88–93; P-in-c Ellington *Ely* 01–02; P-in-c Grafham 01–02; P-in-c Easton 01–02; P-in-c Spaldwick w Barham and Woolley

01–02; R E Leightonstone 02–14; P-in-c Alconbury cum Weston 04–11; P-in-c Buckworth 04–11; P-in-c Hamerton 09–11; P-in-c Winwick 09–11; P-in-c Gt w Lt Gidding and Steeple Gidding 09–11; RD Leightonstone 02–04; Hon Can Ely Cathl 01–14; rtd 14; PtO *Ely* from 14; Hon C Godmanchester and Hilton from 19. *Charis House, 15 Causeway, Godmanchester, Huntingdon PE29 2HA* T: (01480) 453350 E: jonathan.young@ely.anglican.org

YOUNG, Joshua Mark. b 87. Nottm Univ BA 10. Ripon Coll Cuddesdon MTh 13. **d** 13 **p** 14. C Welwyn Garden City *St Alb* 13–17; P-in-c Southfleet *Roch* 18–20. *Darenth Vicarage, Green Street Green Road, Lane End, Dartford DA2 7JR* M: 07957-978184 E: revdjoshyoung@hotmail.co.uk

YOUNG, Karen Georgina. b 58. Ox Poly BA 87 Dur Univ MA 14. Cranmer Hall Dur. **d** 13 **p** 14. C Chich St Paul and Westhampnett 13–16; V Heckmondwike w Norristhorpe and Liversedge *Leeds* from 16. *St James's Vicarage, 25 Church Street, Heckmondwike WF16 0AX* T: (01924) 405881 M: 07836-254320 E: karenyoung58@gmail.com

YOUNG, Karen Heather. b 66. Nottm Univ BA 01. Westcott Ho Cam 02. **d** 05 **p** 07. C Airedale w Fryston *Wakef* 05–06; Hon C Ravenshead *S'well* 07–09; Mental Health Chapl Notts Healthcare NHS Trust 08–09; NSM Shill Valley and Broadshire *Ox* 14–18; NSM Budleigh Salterton, E Budleigh w Bicton etc *Ex* 18–21. *Maranatha, Boucher Way, Budleigh Salterton EX9 6HQ* E: thereverendkarenyoung@gmail.com

YOUNG, Kathleen Margaret. *See* BROWN, Kathleen Margaret

YOUNG, Kenneth. *See* YOUNG, John Kenneth

YOUNG, Leonard Thomas. b 55. Ches Coll of HE BTh 04 Leeds Univ MA 06. Coll of Resurr Mirfield 04. **d** 06 **p** 07. C Failsworth H Family *Man* 06–09; P-in-c Man Clayton St Cross w St Paul 09–15; R 15–16; P-in-c Derby St Bart 16–17; P-in-c Derby St Luke 16–17; V Derby St Bart and St Luke from 17. *The Vicarage, 49 Addison Road, Derby DE24 8FH*

YOUNG, Mandy Elizabeth. b 58. Leeds Univ BA 91 PhD 94. SEITE 11. **d** 14 **p** 15. C Snodland All SS w Ch Ch *Roch* 14–19; C Dartford St Alb 19–20; P-in-c from 20; C Dartford St Edm 19–20; P-in-c from 20. *The Vicarage, St Edmund's Road, Dartford DA1 5ND* T: (01322) 280286 M: 07915-986393 E: mandyyoung612@outlook.com

YOUNG, Margaret Dorothy. *See* COOLING, Margaret Dorothy

YOUNG, Mrs Margaret Elizabeth. b 66. Open Univ BSc 00. All SS Cen for Miss & Min 07. **d** 10 **p** 11. C Wythenshawe *Man* 10–13; TV 13–15; V Easingwold w Raskelf *York* from 15; C Alne from 17; C Brafferton w Pilmoor, Myton-on-Swale etc from 17; C Coxwold and Husthwaite from 17; C Crayke w Brandsby and Yearsley from 17; C Skelton w Shipton and Newton on Ouse from 17; C Strensall from 17; C Forest of Galtres from 17. *The Vicarage, Church Hill, Easingwold, York YO61 3JT* T: (01347) 821394 E: margareteyoung@btopenworld.com

YOUNG, Mark Gilbert Campbell. b 60. Mert Coll Ox BA 88. Wycliffe Hall Ox 86. **d** 91 **p** 92. C Holborn St Geo w H Trin and St Bart *Lon* 91–95; C St Pancras w St Jas and Ch Ch 95–99; V W Hampstead Trin 99–06; P-in-c W Hampstead St Cuth 01–06; Hon C Smithfield St Bart Gt 09–15; Hon C St Bart Less 12–15; C St Andr Holborn from 15. *22A Huddleston Road, London N7 0AG* T: (020) 7583 7394 E: marky@standrewholborn.org.uk

YOUNG, Martin John. b 72. Univ Coll Lon BSc 93. Oak Hill Th Coll BA 01. **d** 01 **p** 02. C Heigham H Trin *Nor* 01–05; P-in-c Nor St Andr 05–16; V from 16; Chapl Nor Univ of the Arts from 16. *24 Carnoustie, Norwich NR4 6AY* T: (01603) 498821 E: martin@standrewsnorwich.org

YOUNG, Mrs Maureen. b 47. SEITE 02. **d** 04 **p** 12. NSM Roughey *Chich* 04–11; NSM Rusper w Colgate 11–13; NSM Bishop's Lydeard w Lydeard St Lawrence etc *B & W* 13–21. *1 Atlantic Villas, Watchet TA23 0JP* E: reverendmaureenyoung@gmail.com

YOUNG, Maurice. *See* YOUNG, William Maurice

YOUNG, Max Jonathan. b 44. **d** 06 **p** 07. NSM Filey *York* 06–10; rtd 10; PtO *Ox* from 10. *8 Eastfield Court, Church Street, Faringdon SN7 8SL* E: max1234@btinternet.com

YOUNG, Michael. b 47. STETS 08. **d** 11 **p** 12. NSM Wareham *Sarum* 11–19; PtO from 19. *5 Tuckers Mill Close, Wareham BH20 5BS* T: (01929) 552582 E: myng220@btopenworld.com

YOUNG, Norman Keith. b 35. EAMTC 85. **d** 87 **p** 88. C Burwell *Ely* 87–91; V Swaffham Bulbeck and Swaffham Prior w Reach 91–92; V Barnby Dun *Sheff* 92–05; Ind Chapl 92–05; AD Doncaster 98–04; rtd 05; P-in-c Aspull St Eliz *Liv* 05–06; Hon C Haigh and Aspull 06–12; PtO *Bradf* 12–14; *Leeds* 14–18; *Ely* from 19. *The Rectory, 3A Stocks Lane, Gamlingay, Sandy SG19 3JP*

YOUNG, Philip Anderson. b 53. St Jo Coll Dur BA 75 Fitzw Coll Cam BA 78 MA 89. Ridley Hall Cam 75. **d** 78

p 79. C Surbiton St Andr and St Mark *S'wark* 78–80; NSM Aylsham *Nor* 04–05; C Bressingham w N and S Lopham and Fersfield 05–07; C Roydon St Remigius 05–07; V Heigham St Thos 07–12; Dioc Environmental Officer 12–14; PtO from 14; *St E* from 16. *Cambridge House, South Hill, Felixstowe IP11 2AA* T: (01394) 809069 M: 07527-574982 E: philipyoung@btinternet.com

YOUNG, Phillip Andrew. b 82. Melbourne Univ BCom 04 Down Coll Cam BTh 19. Ridley Hall Cam 17. **d** 19 **p** 20. C Wootton *St Alb* from 19. *14 Folkes Road, Wootton, Bedford MK43 9BX* M: 07981-976179 E: payoung1982@gmail.com

YOUNG, Rachel Elizabeth. b 61. Man Univ MusB 82 Leeds Univ MA 09 Lon Inst of Educn PGCE 84. NOC 06. **d** 09 **p** 10. NSM Beverley Minster *York* 09–15; R Walkington, Bishop Burton, Rowley etc 15–17; Succ S'wark Cathl 17–20; C Rotherham *Sheff* from 20; C Masbrough from 20. *51 Hallam Road, Rotherham S60 3ED*

YOUNG, Richard Christian. b 65. Southn Univ LLB 87 Solicitor 91. St Jo Coll Nottm 02. **d** 04 **p** 05. C Alperton *Lon* 04–07; V Yiewsley from 07; AD Hillingdon from 18. *St Matthew's Vicarage, 93 High Street, Yiewsley, West Drayton UB7 7QH* T: (01895) 442093 M: 07886-782473 E: richard.youngsofyiewsley@gmail.com *or* vicar@stmatthewsyiewsley.org.uk

YOUNG, Richard Michael. b 63. **d** 96 **p** 97. NSM Brunswick *Man* 96–16; Lic Preacher 16–18; R Birch w Fallowfield from 18. *2 Birch Grove, Rusholme, Manchester M14 5JY* T: 0161-225 0884 M: 07939-585725 E: richardyoung09@gmail.com

YOUNG, Robert William. b 47. MRTPI 73. Cranmer Hall Dur 10. **d** 11 **p** 12. NSM Owlerton *Sheff* 11–12; P-in-c Wadsley 12–14; PtO 14–15; NSM Owlerton 15–17; NSM Tadley w Pamber Heath and Silchester *Win* 17–21; PtO from 21. *Hollyhock Cottage, Whistlers Lane, Silchester, Reading RG7 2NE* T: 0118-970 0884 E: robwyoung101@gmail.com

YOUNG, Ruth. *See* YOUNG, Vivienne Ruth

YOUNG, Simon Robert. b 72. Trevelyan Coll Dur BSc 94 Fitzw Coll Cam BA 98. Westcott Ho Cam BA 98 CTM 99. **d** 99 **p** 15. C Plaistow St Mary *Roch* 99–00; C Kingsnorth and Shadoxhurst *Cant* 14–15; C Faversham 15–17; C The Brents and Davington 15–17; C Faversham 17–19; C Milton Regis w Murston, Bapchild and Tonge from 19; Chapl Bapchild and Tonge C of E Primary Sch from 19. *The Rectory, 25 School Lane, Bapchild, Sittingbourne ME9 9NL* E: simonryoung@aol.com

YOUNG, Mrs Sophie Alexandra. b 81. St Aid Coll Dur BA 03 UWE MA 12. Ridley Hall Cam 17. **d** 19 **p** 20. C Cambridge St Paul *Ely* 19–20; C Cambridge St Phil from 20. *Bridge End Cottage, Sawston Road, Stapleford, Cambridge CB22 5DY* M: 07759-558011 E: sophie_young10@yahoo.co.uk

YOUNG, Stephen Edward. b 52. K Coll Lon BD 73 AKC 73 Open Univ PhD 04 Ch Ch Coll Cant CertEd 74. **d** 75 **p** 76. C Walton St Mary *Liv* 75–79; C Pimlico St Gabr *Lon* 83–85; Chapl Whitelands Coll of HE *S'wark* 85–88; Asst Chapl St Paul's Sch Barnes 88–91; Chapl 91–02; Chapl Dulwich Coll 02–11; Hon C Pimlico St Mary Bourne Street *Lon* 94–11; C Wilton Place St Paul 11–13; P-in-c Deal St Andr *Cant* 13–17; rtd 17; PtO *Cant* from 18; P in O 91–11; Dep P in O from 11. *28 St George's Road, Deal CT14 6BA* T: (01304) 268946 M: 07828-033399 E: stephenedwardyoung52@gmail.com

YOUNG, Steven Peter. b 81. Lon Inst BA 02 Leeds Univ BA 07 MA 08. Coll of Resurr Mirfield 05. **d** 08 **p** 09. C W Hendon St Jo *Lon* 08–11; P-in-c Mill Hill St Mich 11–17; V from 17; C Mill Hill Jo Keble Ch 11–15; Chapl N Lon Hospice from 19. *St Michael's Vicarage, 9 Flower Lane, London NW7 2JA* T: (020) 8343 8841 *or* 8959 1857 M: 07590-636912 E: steven_young81@hotmail.com *or* priest@smmh.org.uk

YOUNG, Stuart Kincaid. b 59. **d** 95 **p** 96. C Letchworth St Paul w Willian *St Alb* 95–00; V Pucklechurch and Abson *Bris* 00–21. *Address temp unknown* E: skypilot1@go-plus.net

YOUNG (née SMITH), Mrs Vivienne Ruth. b 57. St Jo Coll Dur BA 79. NOC 95. **d** 00 **p** 01. C Heckmondwike *Wakef* 00–03; TV Dewsbury 03–06; Community Miss Adv Livability from 06; PtO *Dur* from 15. *107 Lake Avenue, South Shields NE34 7AY* M: 07443-547906 E: ruth61157@gmail.com

YOUNG, William Maurice. b 32. St Jo Coll Nottm 80. **d** 81 **p** 82. C Harlescott *Lich* 81–84; V Hadley 84–94; rtd 94; PtO *Heref* 94–19. *Old Chapel School, Newport Street, Clun, Craven Arms SY7 8JZ* T: (01588) 640846

YOUNGER, Gillian Margaret. b 55. SNWTP 16. **d** 17 **p** 18. NSM Daresbury *Ches* from 17. *56 Norleane Crescent, Runcorn WA7 5ER* E: curate@daresburycofe.org.uk

YOUNGS, Denise. b 48. WMMTC. **d** 09 **p** 10. NSM Lich St Mich w St Mary and Wall from 09; PtO *Ely* from 19. *25 Rowan Close, Haddenham, Ely CB6 3QF*

YOUNGS-DUNNETT, Elizabeth Nigella. b 43. **d** 05 **p** 06. OLM Alde River *St E* 05–13; NSM 13; rtd 13; PtO *St E* from 14. *The Cottage, Ship Corner, Blaxhall, Woodbridge IP12 2DY* T: (01728) 688660 E: nigellaatblaxhall@btinternet.com

YOUNGSON, David Thoms. b 38. Cuddesdon Coll 71. **d** 73 **p** 74. C Norton St Mary *Dur* 73–76; C Hartlepool St Paul 76–79; P-in-c Stockton St Jo CD 79–84; V Stockton St Jo 84–86; V Owton Manor 86–90; rtd 90; PtO *Dur* 90–20. *35 Buxton Gardens, Billingham TS22 5AJ* E: david.youngson@ntlworld.com

YULE, John David. b 49. G&C Coll Cam BA 70 MA 74 PhD 76. Westcott Ho Cam 79. **d** 81 **p** 82. C Cherry Hinton St Andr *Ely* 81–84; C Almondbury w Farnley Tyas *Wakef* 84–87; V Swavesey *Ely* 87–95; V Fen Drayton w Conington 87–95; R Fen Drayton w Conington and Lolworth etc 95–15; rtd 15; PtO *Ely* 16–21. *46 Fen Road, Cambridge CB4 1TX* T: (01223) 561070 E: john.yule@gmail.com

Z

ZAIR, Canon Richard George. b 52. Newc Univ BSc 74. Trin Coll Bris 75 Cranmer Hall Dur 79. **d** 80 **p** 81. C Bishopsworth *Bris* 80–83; C New Malden and Coombe *S'wark* 83–91; Dir of Evang CPAS 91–99; Regional Dir 99–09; P-in-c Marcham w Garford *Ox* 09–14; P-in-c Shippon 11–14; AD Abingdon 13–16; V Marcham w Garford and Shippon 14–20; Hon Can Ch Ch 16–20; rtd 20. *41 North Street, Marcham, Abingdon OX13 6NQ* T: (01865) 391319 M: 07411-234710 E: r_zair@yahoo.co.uk

ZAMMIT, Mark Timothy Paul. b 60. Ox Brookes Univ MA 07. Aston Tr Scheme 90 Sarum & Wells Th Coll 94. **d** 94 **p** 95. C Bitterne Park *Win* 94–98; TV Shaston *Sarum* 98–03; TR 03–08; RD Blackmore Vale 01–08; Chapl Port Regis Sch 99–08; P-in-c Durrington *Sarum* 08–11; C Avon Valley 08–11; TR Avon River 11–15; RD Stonehenge 10–15; TR Almondbury w Farnley Tyas *Leeds* from 15; AD Almondbury 16–20; Jt AD Kirkburton 18–20; V Haxey *Linc* from 20; V Owston from 20. *The Vicarage, Church Street, Haxey, Doncaster DN9 2HY* T: (01427) 753004 M: 07733-077957 E: zammitparish@yahoo.co.uk

ZAPHIRIOU, Paul Victor. b 49. Hamilton Coll (NY) BA 73 INSEAD MBA 74. Wycliffe Hall Ox 00. **d** 02 **p** 03. C Brompton H Trin w Onslow Square St Paul *Lon* 02; C Holborn St Geo w H Trin and St Bart 02–06; V Hope Ch Islington from 06; Bp's Adv for Corporate Soc Resp from 05; AD Islington from 19. *108 Liverpool Road, London N1 0RE* T: (020) 7226 0854 M: 07899-796409 E: paul@hopechurchislington.org

ZAREK, Jennifer Hilary. b 51. Newnham Coll Cam BA 72 MA 76 Southn Univ MSc 73 PhD 78 Ox Univ BTh 98 Garnett Coll Lon CertEd 83. St Steph Ho Ox 95. **d** 97 **p** 98. C Caterham *S'wark* 97–00; V Hutton Cranswick w Skerne, Watton and Beswick *York* 00–05; rtd 05; PtO *York* from 06. *Horsedale House, Silver Street, Huggate, York YO42 1YB* T: (01377) 288525 E: jzarek@btinternet.com

ZASS-OGILVIE, Ian David. b 38. ARICS 72 FRICS 80 AKC 65. K Coll Lon 62 St Boniface Warminster 65. **d** 66 **p** 67. C Washington *Dur* 66–70; Bp's Soc and Ind Adv for N Dur 70–73; Hon C Newc St Jo 73–75; V Tynemouth St Jo 75–78; Hon C St Marylebone St Mary *Lon* 78–81; V Bromley St Jo *Roch* 81–84; R Keith *Mor* 84–88; R Huntly 84–88; R Aberchirder 84–88; R Edin St Pet 88–00; Dir Churches' Regional Commn in the NE Newc and *Dur* 00–05; PtO *Ab* from 05; *Dur* from 05; Research Fell and Tutor St Chad's Coll from 06. *12 St Giles Close, Gilesgate, Durham DH1 1XH* T: 0191-383 0887 E: ianzassogilvie@tiscali.co.uk

ZIHNI, Canon Andrew Stephen. b 77. Mert Coll Ox BA 99 MA 06. St Steph Ho Ox BA 01. **d** 02 **p** 03. C Goldthorpe w Hickleton *Sheff* 02–06; Min Can Windsor 06–14; Chapl St Geo Sch Windsor 06–14; Asst Dioc Dir of Ords *S'wark* 14–21; Asst Dir of Voc 18–21; Can Res and Prec S'wark Cathl from 21; PV Westmr Abbey from 18. *7 Temple West Mews, West Square, London SE11 4TJ* T: (020) 7367 6731 M: 07533-845181 E: andrew.zihni@southwark.anglican.org

ZIMMERMAN, Douglas Lee. b 69. Rhodes Coll Memphis BA 91. Virginia Th Sem MDiv 98. **d** 98 **p** 99. USA 98–14; TR Aylesbury *Ox* from 14. *St Mary's Vicarage, Parsons Fee, Aylesbury HP20 2QZ*

ZIPFEL, Marilyn Ellen. b 48. Open Univ BA 94 MA 98 Goldsmiths' Coll Lon TCert 70 LTCL 97. Dioc OLM tr scheme 01. **d** 03 **p** 04. OLM Oulton Broad *Nor* 03–18; Chapl Jas Paget Healthcare NHS Trust 11–15; PtO *Nor* from 18. *Rozel, Station Road, Lowestoft NR32 4QF* M: 07818-093133 E: marilynzipfel@outlook.com

ZIPPERLEN, John Marcus. b 71. **d** 13 **p** 14. C Haverfordwest St D 13–16; P-in-c Llangwm w Freystrop and Johnston 16–19; P-in-c Roose from 19. *The Rectory, The Kilns, Llangwm, Haverfordwest SA62 4NG* T: (01437) 899548 E: marcus@zipperlen.com *or* marcuszipperlen@cinw.org.uk

ZUCCA, Peter Rennie. b 43. **d** 96 **p** 97. NSM Spotland *Man* 96–99; NSM Bamford 99–05; NSM Rochdale St Geo w St Alb 99–05; NSM Oakenrod and Bamford 05–13; rtd 13. *19 Judith Street, Rochdale OL12 7HS* T: (01706) 675830 *or* 346003

ZUCKERT, Calum Bruno. b 91. SS Hild & Bede Coll Dur BA 12 K Coll Cam BA 16 MMus 17. St Mellitus Coll 18. **d** 19 **p** 20. C Winchmore Hill St Paul *Lon* 19–21; NSM from 21. *St Paul's Lodge, 58 Church Hill, London N21 1JA* T: (020) 3659 4543 M: 07986-301650 E: curate@spwh.org

ZUNDE-BAKER, Helga Elizabeth. b 70. Edin Univ MA 92. St Aug Coll Cant 18. **d** 21. NSM Hackbridge and Beddington Corner *S'wark* from 21. *Greenview, 1A Wrythe Lane, Carshalton SM5 2QU* E: revhelga@gmail.com

ZWALF, Canon Willem Anthony Louis (Wim). b 46. AKC 68. **d** 71 **p** 72. C Fulham St Etheldreda w St Clem *Lon* 71–74; Chapl City Univ 74–78; R Coalbrookdale, Iron-Bridge and Lt Wenlock *Heref* 78–90; V Wisbech SS Pet and Paul *Ely* 90–08; P-in-c Wisbech St Aug 03–04; C 04–08; RD Wisbech Lynn Marshland 02–08; Hon Can Ely Cathl 07–08; rtd 09; PtO *Pet* 12–18. *1 The Dell, Oakham LE15 6JG* T: (01572) 770082 E: wimzwalf@aol.com

ZYCH, Berkeley James. b 83. SS Coll Cam BA 05 MSci 05 MA 08 PhD 09 Fitzw Coll Cam BA 12. Westcott Ho Cam 10. **d** 13 **p** 14. C Grimshoe *Ely* 13–16; Prec and Min Can St Alb 16–19; V Harpenden St Jo 19–21. *4 Mount Road, Hertford SG14 2AH* E: b.j.zych.01@cantab.net

DEACONESSES

COOPER, Janet Pamela. b 46. Glos Coll of Educn TCert 67 Ox Poly CETD 79. Trin Coll Bris. **dss** 83. Patchway *Bris* 83–88; PtO *Glouc* 90–96. *Ephraim Cottage, Kington Mead Farm, Kington Road, Thornbury, Bristol BS35 1PQ* T: (01454) 415280 E: jan.ephraim@talktalk.net

GOUGH, Janet Ainley. b 46. SRN 67 RSCN 68 SCM 70. Dalton Ho Bris 70. **dss** 76. Leic H Apostles 73–80; Kansas City All SS USA 80–81; PtO *Leic* 81–96 and from 05. *1 Clarefield Road, Leicester LE3 6FB* E: jangough@hotmail.com

HINDE, Miss Mavis Mary. b 29. Lightfoot Ho Dur. **dss** 65. Hitchin St Mary *St Alb* 65–68; Ensbury *Sarum* 69–70; Portsea St Alb *Portsm* 70–76; Houghton Regis *St Alb* 77–85; Eaton Socon 85–94; rtd 94; PtO *Ely* 94–15. *8 Burnt Close, Eynesbury, St Neots PE19 2LZ* T: (01480) 218219 E: mmavishinde@gmail.com

HORNBY-NORTHCOTE, Mrs Vivien Sheena. b 42. Birkbeck Coll Lon BA 91 Warwick Univ MA 96. Gilmore Course 74. **dss** 79. Mitcham St Olave *S'wark* 79–81; St Dunstan in the West *Lon* 82–86; St Marg Lothbury and St Steph Coleman Street etc 86; rtd 98. *37 Carlton Mews, Wells BA5 1SG*

PIERSON, Mrs Valerie <u>Susan</u>. b 44. TCert 65. Trin Coll Bris 76. **dss** 79. Fulham St Matt *Lon* from 79. *48 Peterborough Road, London SW6 3EB* T: (020) 7731 6544 F: 7731 1858 E: sue@lancepierson.org

PRICE, Patricia Kate Lunn. *See* Patricia Kate Lunn SCHMIEGELOW

SCHMIEGELOW, Patricia Kate Lunn. b 37. St Mich Ho Ox IDC 65. **dss** 86. The Hague *Eur* 86–89; PtO *Glouc* from 90; Gen Sec ICS 92–97; rtd 97. *61 Coln St Aldwyns, Cirencester GL7 5AJ* T/F: (01285) 750218

DIOCESAN, AREA, SUFFRAGAN AND ASSISTANT BISHOPS AND PROVINCIAL EPISCOPAL VISITORS IN ENGLAND, WALES, SCOTLAND AND IRELAND

BATH AND WELLS
Bishop of Bath and Wells — *Vacant*
Honorary Assistant Bishops — A L J REDFERN
B C CASTLE
B ROGERSON
G H CASSIDY
J F PERRY
J M GOODALL
M A HILL
R D M MARTIN
R F SAINSBURY
T WILLMOTT
W M D PERSSON
W N STOCK
Suffragan Bishop of Taunton — R E WORSLEY

BIRMINGHAM
Bishop of Birmingham — D A URQUHART
Honorary Assistant Bishops — I K MOTTAHEDEH
J M GOODALL
M SANTER
M W SINCLAIR
R C H THOMAS
Suffragan Bishop of Aston — A E HOLLINGHURST

BLACKBURN
Bishop of Blackburn — J T HENDERSON
Honorary Assistant Bishops — A PORTER
C G ASHTON
Suffragan Bishop of Burnley — P J NORTH
Suffragan Bishop of Lancaster — J L C DUFF

BRISTOL
Bishop of Bristol — V F FAULL
Honorary Assistant Bishops — G H CASSIDY
J M GOODALL
P J FIRTH
R C H THOMAS
Suffragan Bishop of Swindon — L S RAYFIELD

CANTERBURY
Archbishop of Canterbury, Primate
of All England and Metropolitan — J P WELBY
Honorary Assistant Bishops — A M A TURNBULL
J R A LLEWELLIN
Suffragan Bishop of Dover — R J HUDSON-WILKIN
Suffragan Bishop of Ebbsfleet
(Provincial Episcopal Visitor) — *Vacant*
Suffragan Bishop of Maidstone — R C H THOMAS
Suffragan Bishop of Richborough
(Provincial Episcopal Visitor) — N BANKS

CARLISLE
Bishop of Carlisle — J W S NEWCOME
Honorary Assistant Bishops — G H THOMPSON
G L HACKER
J H RICHARDSON
N S MCCULLOCH
P S RAMSDEN
Suffragan Bishop of Penrith — *Vacant*

CHELMSFORD
Bishop of Chelmsford — G E FRANCIS-DEHQANI
Honorary Assistant Bishops — M T S MWAMBA
R C H THOMAS
Area Bishop of Barking — *Vacant*
Area Bishop of Bradwell — J PERUMBALATH
Area Bishop of Colchester — R A B MORRIS

CHESTER
Bishop of Chester — M S A TANNER
Honorary Assistant Bishops — A L WINSTANLEY
C F BAZLEY
G G DOW
G H WEBSTER
G S PEARSON
J D HAYDEN
R C H THOMAS
Suffragan Bishop of Birkenhead — J A CONALTY
Suffragan Bishop of Stockport — S J C CORLEY

CHICHESTER
Bishop of Chichester — M C WARNER
Honorary Assistant Bishops — A D CHESTERS
C H MORGAN
D P WILCOX
K L BARHAM
L A GREEN
M E ADIE
M E MARSHALL
M L LANGRISH
N S READE
Area Bishop of Horsham — R K F BUSHYAGER
Area Bishop of Lewes — W P G HAZLEWOOD

COVENTRY
Bishop of Coventry — C J COCKSWORTH
Honorary Assistant Bishops — D R J EVANS
J M GOODALL
Suffragan Bishop of Warwick — J R A STROYAN

DERBY
Bishop of Derby — E J H LANE
Honorary Assistant Bishops — J NICHOLLS
T W ELLIS
Suffragan Bishop of Repton — W M MACNAUGHTON

DURHAM
Bishop of Durham — P R BUTLER
Honorary Assistant Bishops — D S STANCLIFFE
G H WEBSTER
J L PRITCHARD
Suffragan Bishop of Jarrow — S E CLARK

ELY
Bishop of Ely — S D CONWAY
Honorary Assistant Bishops — G P KNOWLES
G R KINGS
M A SEELEY
N BANKS
P S DAWES
R C H THOMAS
Suffragan Bishop of Huntingdon — D WINTER

EXETER
Bishop of Exeter — R R ATWELL
Honorary Assistant Bishops — A M SHAW
G W E C ASHBY
J M GOODALL
M J RYLANDS
R C H THOMAS
Suffragan Bishop of Crediton — J A SEARLE
Suffragan Bishop of Plymouth — N H P MCKINNEL

GLOUCESTER

Bishop of Gloucester	R TREWEEK
Honorary Assistant Bishops	A M PRIDDIS
	C J HILL
	D W M JENNINGS
	J R G NEALE
	P J FIRTH
	R J S EVENS
Suffragan Bishop of Tewkesbury	R W SPRINGETT

GUILDFORD

Bishop of Guildford	A J WATSON
Honorary Assistant Bishops	C W HERBERT
	M A BAUGHEN
	N BANKS
Suffragan Bishop of Dorking	J C B WELLS

HEREFORD

Bishop of Hereford	R C JACKSON
Honorary Assistant Bishops	D THOMSON
	M G BOURKE
	M R WESTALL
Suffragan Bishop of Ludlow	Vacant

LEEDS

Bishop of Leeds	N BAINES
Honorary Assistant Bishops	C O BUCHANAN
	C P EDMONDSON
	D J L HAWKINS
	D M HOPE OF THORNES
	G C HANDFORD
	G H WEBSTER
	J L PRITCHARD
	J R FLACK
	M C R SOWERBY
	T F BUTLER
Suffragan Bishop of Bradford	T M HOWARTH
Suffragan Bishop of Huddersfield	J R GIBBS
Suffragan Bishop of Kirkstall	P J SLATER
Suffragan Bishop of Ripon	H M HARTLEY
Suffragan Bishop of Wakefield	A W ROBINSON

LEICESTER

Bishop of Leicester	M J SNOW
Honorary Assistant Bishops	P J FOX
	C J BOYLE
	R J FREEMAN
Suffragan Bishop of Loughborough	Vacant

LICHFIELD

Bishop of Lichfield	M G IPGRAVE
Honorary Assistant Bishops	A J MAGOWAN
	I K MOTTAHEDEH
	J E MCFARLANE
	J M GOODALL
	R C H THOMAS
Area Bishop of Shrewsbury	S R BULLOCK
Area Bishop of Stafford	M J PARKER
Area Bishop of Wolverhampton	C M GREGORY

LINCOLN

Bishop of Lincoln	Vacant
Honorary Assistant Bishops	A R GILLION
	D D J ROSSDALE
	D TUSTIN
	N BANKS
	N PEYTON
	T W ELLIS
Suffragan Bishop of Grantham	N A CHAMBERLAIN
Suffragan Bishop of Grimsby	D E COURT

LIVERPOOL

Bishop of Liverpool	P BAYES
Honorary Assistant Bishops	C G ASHTON
	G H WEBSTER
	S R LOWE
Suffragan Bishop of Warrington	B A MASON

LONDON

Bishop of London	S E MULLALLY
Honorary Assistant Bishops	A D POGGO
	E HOLLAND
	J A IDOWU-FEARON
	J A K MILLAR
	J M WHARTON
	M J COLCLOUGH
	P W WHEATLEY
	R C H THOMAS
	R D HARRIES OF PENTREGARTH
	R S LADDS
	S G PLATTEN
	T M THORNTON
	W P K MAKHULU
Area Bishop of Edmonton	R J WICKHAM
Area Bishop of Kensington	G S TOMLIN
Area Bishop of Stepney	J W GRENFELL
Area Bishop of Willesden	Vacant
Suffragan Bishop of Fulham	J M R BAKER
Suffragan Bishop of Islington	R C THORPE

MANCHESTER

Bishop of Manchester	D S WALKER
Honorary Assistant Bishops	F P SARGEANT
	G G DOW
	G H WEBSTER
	G K SINCLAIR
	J NICHOLLS
	R C H THOMAS
	R W N HOARE
Suffragan Bishop of Bolton	M D ASHCROFT
Suffragan Bishop of Hulme	Vacant
Suffragan Bishop of Middleton	M DAVIES

NEWCASTLE

Bishop of Newcastle	C E HARDMAN
Honorary Assistant Bishops	J H RICHARDSON
	J R PACKER
	M W BRYANT
	S G PLATTEN
Suffragan Bishop of Berwick	M WROE

NORWICH

Bishop of Norwich	G B USHER
Honorary Assistant Bishops	A C FOOTTIT
	D K GILLETT
	D LEAKE
	L G URWIN
	M J MENIN
	N BANKS
	P J FOX
	R C H THOMAS
	R GARRARD
Suffragan Bishop of Lynn	J E STEEN
Suffragan Bishop of Thetford	A P WINTON

OXFORD

Bishop of Oxford	S J L CROFT
Honorary Assistant Bishops	C W FLETCHER
	D W M JENNINGS
	H I J SOUTHERN
	H W SCRIVEN
	J M GOODALL
	J N JOHNSON
	N T WRIGHT
	R C H THOMAS
	T L WAMBUNYA
Area Bishop of Buckingham	A T L WILSON
Area Bishop of Dorchester	G A COLLINS
Area Bishop of Reading	O J GRAHAM

PETERBOROUGH

Bishop of Peterborough	D S ALLISTER
Honorary Assistant Bishop	A J PROUD
	E F CONDRY
Suffragan Bishop of Brixworth	J E HOLBROOK

PORTSMOUTH

Bishop of Portsmouth	*Vacant*
Honorary Assistant Bishops	I J BRACKLEY
	J W HIND
	K M GORHAM
	T J BAVIN
	T M THORNTON

ROCHESTER

Bishop of Rochester	*Vacant*
Honorary Assistant Bishops	A M A TURNBULL
	K S E OKEKE
	L A GREEN
	M J NAZIR-ALI
	R C H THOMAS
Suffragan Bishop of Tonbridge	S D BURTON-JONES

ST ALBANS

Bishop of St Albans	A G C SMITH
Honorary Assistant Bishops	N BANKS
	R J N SMITH
	S S VENNER
Suffragan Bishop of Bedford	R W B ATKINSON
Suffragan Bishop of Hertford	N M R BEASLEY

ST EDMUNDSBURY AND IPSWICH

Bishop of St Edmundsbury and Ipswich	M A SEELEY
Honorary Assistant Bishops	G D J WALSH
	G H REID
	G P KNOWLES
	J A K MILLAR
	N BANKS
	T J STEVENS
Suffragan Bishop of Dunwich	M R HARRISON

SALISBURY

Bishop of Salisbury	*Vacant*
Honorary Assistant Bishops	A L J REDFERN
	D M HALLATT
	R J C CHARTRES
	T WILLMOTT
Area Bishop of Ramsbury	A P RUMSEY
Area Bishop of Sherborne	K M GORHAM

SHEFFIELD

Bishop of Sheffield	P J WILCOX
Honorary Assistant Bishops	G H WEBSTER
	R C H THOMAS
	R F BLACKBURN
	T W ELLIS
Suffragan Bishop of Doncaster	S R JELLEY

SODOR AND MAN

Bishop of Sodor and Man	P A EAGLES
Assistant Bishop of Sodor and Man	P J FERGUSON

SOUTHWARK

Bishop of Southwark	C T J CHESSUN
Honorary Assistant Bishops	A D POGGO
	A R GILLION
	D J ATKINSON
	J A IDOWU-FEARON
	J M WHARTON
	M D DOE
	P S M SELBY
	P S OMUKU
	P W WHEATLEY
	R C H THOMAS
	R C THORPE
	R D HARRIES OF PENTREGARTH
	S G PLATTEN
	S J OLIVER
	T M THORNTON
	W N STOCK
Area Bishop of Croydon	J D CLARK
Area Bishop of Kingston-upon-Thames	R I CHEETHAM
Area Bishop of Woolwich	W K DORGU

SOUTHWELL AND NOTTINGHAM

Bishop of Southwell and Nottingham	P G WILLIAMS
Honorary Assistant Bishops	J T FINNEY
	M W JARRETT
	R J MILNER
Suffragan Bishop of Sherwood	A N EMERTON

TRURO

Bishop of Truro	P I MOUNSTEPHEN
Honorary Assistant Bishop	G R JAMES
	J M GOODALL
Suffragan Bishop of St Germans	H E NELSON

WINCHESTER

Bishop of Winchester	T J DAKIN
Honorary Assistant Bishops	G P ANNAS
	H W SCRIVEN
	T J BAVIN
	T WILLMOTT
Suffragan Bishop of Basingstoke	D G WILLIAMS
Suffragan Bishop of Southampton	D M SELLIN

WORCESTER

Bishop of Worcester	J G INGE
Honorary Assistant Bishops	A M PRIDDIS
	C J MAYFIELD
	J M GOODALL
	M SANTER
	M W HOOPER
	R M E PATERSON
Suffragan Bishop of Dudley	M C W GORICK

YORK

Archbishop of York, Primate of England and Metropolitan	S G COTTRELL
Honorary Assistant Bishops	D C JAMES
	D J SMITH
	D J WILBOURNE
	F WHITE
	G A CRAY
	G BATES
	J H FROST
	J S JONES
	M W WALLACE
	N BAINES
Suffragan Bishop of Beverley (Provincial Episcopal Visitor)	G H WEBSTER
Suffragan Bishop of Hull	A M WHITE
Suffragan Bishop of Selby	J B THOMSON
Suffragan Bishop of Whitby	P J FERGUSON

GIBRALTAR IN EUROPE

Bishop of Gibraltar in Europe	R N INNES
Honorary Assistant Bishops	A M A TURNBULL
	D J SMITH
	D S STANCLIFFE
	E HOLLAND
	F-R MULLER
	J M WHARTON
	J R FLACK
	M J COLCLOUGH
	M L LANGRISH
	N S READE
	P W WHALON
	R GARRARD
	LORD CHARTRES
	S S VENNER
Suffragan Bishop in Europe	D HAMID

CHURCH IN WALES

BANGOR
Bishop of Bangor A T G JOHN

LLANDAFF
Assistant Bishop E W M WALKER
Bishop of Llandaff J OSBORNE

MONMOUTH
Bishop of Monmouth C E VANN

ST ASAPH
Assistant Bishop *Vacant*
Bishop of St Asaph G K CAMERON

ST DAVIDS
Bishop of St Davids J S PENBERTHY

SWANSEA AND BRECON
Bishop of Swansea and Brecon *Vacant*
Honorary Assistant Bishops E W M WALKER
J K OLIVER

SCOTTISH EPISCOPAL CHURCH

ABERDEEN AND ORKNEY
Bishop of Aberdeen and Orkney A C DYER

ARGYLL AND THE ISLES
Bishop of Argyll and The Isles K G RIGLIN

BRECHIN
Bishop of Brechin A C SWIFT

EDINBURGH
Bishop of Edinburgh J A ARMES

Honorary Assistant Bishop *Vacant*

GLASGOW AND GALLOWAY
Bishop of Glasgow and Galloway K PEARSON
Honorary Assistant Bishop J M TAYLOR

MORAY, ROSS AND CAITHNESS
Bishop of Moray, Ross and Caithness M J STRANGE

ST ANDREWS, DUNKELD AND DUNBLANE
Bishop of St Andrews, Dunkeld and Dunblane I J PATON

CHURCH OF IRELAND

ARMAGH
Archbishop of Armagh and Primate
 of All Ireland and Metropolitan F J MCDOWELL

CASHEL, FERNS AND OSSORY
Bishop of Cashel, Ferns and Ossory M A J BURROWS

CLOGHER
Bishop of Clogher I W ELLIS

CONNOR
Bishop of Connor G T W DAVISON

CORK, CLOYNE AND ROSS
Bishop of Cork, Cloyne and Ross W P COLTON

DERRY AND RAPHOE
Bishop of Derry and Raphoe A J FORSTER

DOWN AND DROMORE
Bishop of Down and Dromore D A MCCLAY

DUBLIN AND GLENDALOUGH
Archbishop of Dublin, Bishop of
 Glendalough, Primate of Ireland
 and Metropolitan M G ST A JACKSON

KILMORE, ELPHIN AND ARDAGH
Bishop of Kilmore, Elphin and Ardagh S F GLENFIELD

LIMERICK AND KILLALOE
Bishop of Limerick and Killaloe *Vacant*

MEATH AND KILDARE
Bishop of Meath and Kildare P L STOREY

TUAM, KILLALA AND ACHONRY
Bishop of Tuam, Killala and Achonry *Vacant*

BISHOPS IN THE HOUSE OF LORDS

The Archbishops of Canterbury and York, and the Bishops of London, Durham and Winchester always have seats in the House of Lords. Twenty-one of the remaining Diocesan Bishops also sit in the Upper House. In general those places are filled on the basis of seniority in office as a Diocesan Bishop, any vacant place being filled by the Diocesan Bishop who has been longest in office without sitting in the House of Lords. However, for a transitional period of ten years from 2015, if there is a female Diocesan Bishop in office when a vacancy arises, she (or the most senior female Diocesan Bishop, if more than one are in office) will take up the place. Translation of a Bishop from one diocesan See to another does not affect his or her right to sit in the House of Lords.

The Bishop of Sodor and Man and the Bishop of Gibraltar in Europe are not eligible to sit in the House of Lords, but the former has a seat in the Upper House of the Tynwald, Isle of Man.

ARCHBISHOPS

	Enthroned	Introduced in the House of Lords
CANTERBURY	2013	2012
YORK	2020	2014

BISHOPS SITTING IN THE HOUSE OF LORDS
(as at 1 December 2021)

	Became Diocesan Bishop	Introduced in the House of Lords
LONDON	2018	2018
DURHAM	2009	2014
WINCHESTER	2011	2012
BIRMINGHAM	2006	2010
WORCESTER	2007	2012
COVENTRY	2008	2012
OXFORD	2009	2013
CARLISLE	2009	2013
ST ALBANS	2009	2013
PETERBOROUGH	2010	2014
ELY	2010	2014
SOUTHWARK	2011	2014
LEEDS	2011	2014
GLOUCESTER	2015	2015
LINCOLN	2011	2017
CHICHESTER	2012	2018
BRISTOL	2018	2018
DERBY	2019	2019
BLACKBURN	2013	2019
MANCHESTER	2013	2020
CHELMSFORD	2021	2021
EXETER	2014	2021
LIVERPOOL	2014	2021

BISHOPS AWAITING SEATS IN THE HOUSE OF LORDS
(in order of seniority)

	Became Diocesan Bishop
GUILDFORD	2014
ST EDMUNDSBURY & IPSWICH	2015
SOUTHWELL & NOTTINGHAM	2015
LEICESTER	2016
LICHFIELD	2016
SHEFFIELD	2017
TRURO	2018
NORWICH	2019
HEREFORD	2020
CHESTER	2020
BATH AND WELLS	*vacant*
PORTSMOUTH	*vacant*
SALISBURY	*vacant*
ROCHESTER	*vacant*
NEWCASTLE	*vacant*

HISTORICAL SUCCESSION OF ARCHBISHOPS AND BISHOPS

In a number of dioceses, especially for the mediaeval period, the dating of some episcopal appointments is not known for certain. For ease of reference, the date of consecration is given when known, or, in the case of more modern appointments, the date of confirmation of election. More information on the dates of individual bishops can be found in the Royal Historical Society's *Handbook of British Chronology*.

ENGLAND

PROVINCE OF CANTERBURY

Canterbury	

Description of arms. Azure, an archiepiscopal cross in pale or surmounted by a pall proper charged with four crosses patée fitchée sable.

597	Augustine
604	Laurentius
619	Mellitus
624	Justus
627	Honorius
655	Deusdedit
668	Theodorus
693	Berhtwald
731	Tatwine
735	Nothelm
740	Cuthbert
761	Bregowine
765	Jaenberht
793	Æthelheard
805	Wulfred
832	Feologild
833	Ceolnoth
870	Æthelred
890	Plegmund
914	Æthelhelm
923	Wulfhelm
942	Oda
959	Ælfsige
959	Byrhthelm
960	Dunstan
c.988	Athelgar
990	Sigeric Serio
995	Ælfric
1005	Ælfheah
1013	Lyfing [Ælfstan]
1020	Æthelnoth
1038	Eadsige
1051	Robert of Jumièges
1052	Stigand
1070	Lanfranc
1093	Anselm
1114	Ralph d'Escures
1123	William de Corbeil
1139	Theobald of Bec
1162	Thomas Becket
1174	Richard [of Dover]
1184	Baldwin
1193	Hubert Walter
1207	Stephen Langton

1229	Richard le Grant
1234	Edmund Rich
1245	Boniface of Savoy
1273	Robert Kilwardby
1279	John Pecham
1294	Robert Winchelsey
1313	Walter Reynolds
1328	Simon Mepham
1333	John Stratford
1349	Thomas Bradwardine
1349	Simon Islip
1366	Simon Langham
1368	William Whittlesey
1375	Simon Sudbury
1381	William Courtenay
1396	Thomas Arundel[1]
1398	Roger Walden
1414	Henry Chichele
1443	John Stafford
1452	John Kempe
1454	Thomas Bourgchier
1486	John Morton
1501	Henry Deane
1503	William Warham
1533	Thomas Cranmer
1556	Reginald Pole
1559	Matthew Parker
1576	Edmund Grindal
1583	John Whitgift
1604	Richard Bancroft
1611	George Abbot
1633	William Laud
1660	William Juxon
1663	Gilbert Sheldon
1678	William Sancroft
1691	John Tillotson
1695	Thomas Tenison
1716	William Wake
1737	John Potter
1747	Thomas Herring
1757	Matthew Hutton
1758	Thomas Secker
1768	Frederick Cornwallis
1783	John Moore
1805	Charles Manners Sutton
1828	William Howley
1848	John Bird Sumner
1862	Charles Thomas Longley
1868	Archibald Campbell Tait
1883	Edward White Benson
1896	Frederick Temple
1903	Randall Thomas Davidson
1928	Cosmo Gordon Lang
1942	William Temple
1945	Geoffrey Francis Fisher
1961	Arthur Michael Ramsey
1974	Frederick Donald Coggan
1980	Robert Alexander Kennedy Runcie
1991	George Leonard Carey
2002	Rowan Douglas Williams
2013	Justin Portal Welby

London	

Description of arms. Gules, two swords in saltire argent hilts and pommels or.

	Theanus
	Eluanus
	Cadar
	Obinus
	Conanus
	Palladius
	Stephanus
	Iltutus
	Theodwinus
	Theodredus
	Hilarius
314	Restitutus
	Guitelinus
	Fastidius
	Vodinus
	Theonus
c.604	Mellitus
664	Cedd[2]
666	Wini
675	Eorcenwald
693	Waldhere
716	Ingwald
745	Ecgwulf
772	Wigheah
782	Eadbeorht
789	Eadgar
793	Coenwalh
796	Eadbald
798	Heathoberht
803	Osmund
c.811	Æthelnoth
824	Ceolberht
862	Deorwulf
898	Swithwulf
898	Heahstan
900	Wulfsige
c.926	Æthelweard
926	Leofstan
926	Theodred
—	Wulfstan I
953	Brihthelm
959	Dunstan
964	Ælfstan
996	Wulfstan II
1004	Ælfhun
1014	Ælfwig

---

[1] On 19 October 1399 Boniface IX annulled Arundel's translation to St Andrews and confirmed him in the See of Canterbury.
[2] See vacant for a term of years.

1035	Ælfweard
1044	Robert of Jumièges
1051	William
1075	Hugh of Orival
1086	Maurice
1108	Richard de Belmeis
1128	Gilbert [the Universal]
1141	Robert de Sigillo
1152	Richard de Belmeis II
1163	Gilbert Foliot
1189	Richard Fitz Neal
1199	William of Ste-Mere-Eglise
1221	Eustace de Fauconberg
1229	Roger Niger
1244	Fulk Basset
1260	Henry Wingham
1263	Henry of Sandwich
1274	John Chishull
1280	Richard Gravesend
1306	Ralph Baldock
1313	Gilbert Segrave
1317	Richard Newport
1319	Stephen Gravesend
1338	Richard Bintworth
1340	Ralph Stratford
1355	Michael Northburgh
1362	Simon Sudbury
1375	William Courtenay
1382	Robert Braybrooke
1404	Roger Walden
1406	Nicholas Bubwith
1407	Richard Clifford
1421	John Kempe
1426	William Gray
1431	Robert Fitz-Hugh
1436	Robert Gilbert
1450	Thomas Kempe
1489	Richard Hill
1496	Thomas Savage
1502	William Warham
1504	William Barons [Barnes]
1506	Richard Fitz-James
1522	Cuthbert Tunstall [Tonstall]
1530	John Stokesley
1540	Edmund Bonner
1550	Nicholas Ridley
1553	Edmund Bonner (restored)
1559	Edmund Grindal
1570	Edwin Sandys
1577	John Aylmer
1595	Richard Fletcher
1597	Richard Bancroft
1604	Richard Vaughan
1607	Thomas Ravis
1610	George Abbot
1611	John King
1621	George Monteigne [Mountain]
1628	William Laud
1633	William Juxon
1660	Gilbert Sheldon
1663	Humfrey Henchman
1676	Henry Compton
1714	John Robinson
1723	Edmund Gibson
1748	Thomas Sherlock
1761	Thomas Hayter
1762	Richard Osbaldeston
1764	Richard Terrick
1778	Robert Lowth
1787	Beilby Porteus
1809	John Randolph
1813	William Howley
1828	Charles James Blomfield
1856	Archibald Campbell Tait
1869	John Jackson
1885	Frederick Temple
1897	Mandell Creighton
1901	Arthur Foley Winnington-Ingram
1939	Geoffrey Francis Fisher
1945	John William Charles Wand

1956	Henry Colville Montgomery Campbell
1961	Robert Wright Stopford
1973	Gerald Alexander Ellison
1981	Graham Douglas Leonard
1991	David Michael Hope
1995	Richard John Carew Chartres
2018	Sarah Elisabeth Mullally

Westminster[1]

1540	Thomas Thirlby

Winchester

Description of arms. Gules, two keys endorsed and conjoined at the bows in bend, the upper or, the lower argent, between which a sword in bend sinister of the third, hilt and pommel gold.

BISHOPS OF THE WEST SAXONS

634	Birinus
650	Ægilberht

BISHOPS OF WINCHESTER

660	Wine
670	Leutherius
676	Haedde
705	Daniel
744	Hunfrith
756	Cyneheard
778	Æthelheard
778	Ecbald
785	Dudd
c.785	Cyneberht
803	Eahlmund
814	Wigthegn
825	Herefrith[2]
838	Eadmund
c.838	Eadhun
839	Helmstan
852	Swithhun
867	Ealhferth
877	Tunberht
879	Denewulf
909	Frithestan
931	Byrnstan
934	Ælfheah I
951	Ælfsige I
960	Brihthelm
963	Æthelwold I
984	Ælfheah II
1006	Cenwulf
1006	Æthelwold II
c.1014	Ælfsige II
1032	Ælfwine
1043	Stigand Ælfsige III?
1070	Walkelin
1107	William Giffard
1129	Henry of Blois
1174	Richard of Ilchester (Toclyve)
1189	Godfrey de Lucy
1205	Peter des Roches
1244	Will. de Raleigh
1260	Aymer de Valance [of Lusignan]
1262	John Gervaise

1268	Nicholas of Ely
1282	John of Pontoise
1305	Henry Merewell [or Woodlock]
1316	John Sandale
1320	Rigaud of Assier
1323	John Stratford
1333	Adam Orleton
1346	William Edendon [Edington]
1367	William of Wykeham
1404	Henry Beaufort
1447	William of Waynflete
1487	Peter Courtenay
1493	Thomas Langton
1501	Richard Fox
1529	Thomas Wolsey
1531	Stephen Gardiner (deposed)
1551	John Ponet [Poynet]
1553	Stephen Gardiner (restored)
1556	John White (deposed)
1561	Robert Horne
1580	John Watson
1584	Thomas Cowper [Cooper]
1595	William Wickham [Wykeham]
1596	William Day
1597	Thomas Bilson
1616	James Montague
1619	Lancelot Andrewes
1628	Richard Neile
1632	Walter Curll
1660	Brian Duppa
1662	George Morley
1684	Peter Mews
1707	Jonathan Trelawney
1721	Charles Trimnell
1723	Richard Willis
1734	Benjamin Hoadly
1761	John Thomas
1781	Brownlow North
1820	George Pretyman Tomline
1827	Charles Richard Sumner
1869	Samuel Wilberforce
1873	Edward Harold Browne
1891	Anthony Wilson Thorold
1895	Randall Thomas Davidson
1903	Herbert Edward Ryle
1911	Edward Stuart Talbot
1923	Frank Theodore Woods
1932	Cyril Forster Garbett
1942	Mervyn George Haigh
1952	Alwyn Terrell Petre Williams
1961	Sherard Falkner Allison
1975	John Vernon Taylor
1985	Colin Clement Walter James
1995	Michael Charles Scott-Joynt
2011	Timothy John Dakin
2022	*vacant*

Bath and Wells

Description of arms. Azure, a saltire per saltire quarterly counterchanged or and argent.

BISHOPS OF WELLS

909	Athelm
925	Wulfhelm I
928	Ælfheah
938	Wulfhelm II
956	Byrhthelm

---

[1] Indicates a diocese no longer extant, or united with another diocese.
[2] Never signed without Wigthegn.

974	Cyneweard
979	Sigegar
997	Ælfwine
999	Lyfing
1013	Æthelwine (ejected)
1013	Beorhtwine (deposed)
	Æthelwine (restored)
	Beorhtwine (restored)
1024	Brihtwig [also Merehwit]
1033	Duduc
1061	Gisa
1088	John of Tours [de Villula]

BISHOPS OF BATH

1090	John of Tours [de Villula]
1123	Godfrey
1136	Robert
1174	Reg. Fitz Jocelin
1192	Savaric FitzGeldewin

BATH AND GLASTONBURY

1206	Jocelin of Wells

BATH AND WELLS

1244	Roger of Salisbury
1248	William Bitton I
1265	Walter Giffard
1267	William Bitton II
1275	Robert Burnell
1293	William of March
1302	Walter Hasleshaw
1309	John Droxford
1329	Ralph of Shrewsbury
1364	John Barnet
1367	John Harewell
1386	Walter Skirlaw
1388	Ralph Erghum
1401	Henry Bowet
1407	Nicholas Bubwith
1425	John Stafford
1443	Thomas Beckington
1466	Robert Stillington
1492	Richard Fox
1495	Oliver King
1504	Adriano de Castello [di Corneto]
1518	Thomas Wolsey
1523	John Clerk
1541	William Knight
1548	William Barlow
1554	Gilbert Bourne
1560	Gilbert Berkeley
1584	Thomas Godwin
1593	John Still
1608	James Montague
1616	Arthur Lake
1626	William Laud
1628	Leonard Mawe
1629	Walter Curll
1632	William Piers
1670	Robert Creighton
1673	Peter Mews
1685	Thomas Ken (deposed)
1691	Richard Kidder
1704	George Hooper
1727	John Wynne
1743	Edward Willes
1774	Charles Moss
1802	Richard Beadon
1824	George Henry Law
1845	Richard Bagot
1854	Robert John Eden, Lord Auckland
1869	Arthur Charles Hervey
1894	George Wyndham Kennion
1921	St John Basil Wynne Wilson
1937	Francis Underhill
1943	John William Charles Wand
1946	Harold William Bradfield
1960	Edward Barry Henderson
1975	John Monier Bickersteth
1987	George Leonard Carey
1991	James Lawton Thompson
2002	Peter Bryan Price
2014	Peter Hancock
2021	*vacant*

Birmingham

Description of arms. Per pale indented or and gules, five roundels, two, two, and one, and in chief two crosses patée all counterchanged.

1905	Charles Gore
1911	Henry Russell Wakefield
1924	Ernest William Barnes
1953	John Leonard Wilson
1969	Laurence Ambrose Brown
1978	Hugh William Montefiore
1987	Mark Santer
2002	John Mugabi Sentamu
2006	David Andrew Urquhart

Bristol

Description of arms. Sable, three ducal coronets in pale or.

1542	Paul Bush
1554	John Holyman
1562	Richard Cheyney
1581	John Bullingham (held Gloucester and Bristol 1586–9)
1589	Richard Fletcher
	[See vacant for ten years]
1603	John Thornborough
1617	Nicholas Felton
1619	Rowland Searchfield
1623	Robert Wright
1633	George Coke
1637	Robert Skinner
1642	Thomas Westfield
1644	Thomas Howell
1661	Gilbert Ironside
1672	Guy Carleton
1679	William Gulston
1684	John Lake
1685	Jonathan Trelawney
1689	Gilbert Ironside
1691	John Hall
1710	John Robinson
1714	George Smalridge
1719	Hugh Boulter
1724	William Bradshaw
1733	Charles Cecil
1735	Thomas Secker
1737	Thomas Gooch
1738	Joseph Butler
1750	John Conybeare
1756	John Hume
1758	Philip Yonge
1761	Thomas Newton
1782	Lewis Bagot
1783	Christopher Wilson
1792	Spencer Madan
1794	Henry Reginald Courtenay
1797	Ffolliott Herbert Walker Cornewall
1803	George Pelham

1807	John Luxmoore
1808	William Lort Mansel
1820	John Kaye
1827	Robert Gray
1834	Joseph Allen
[1836	to 1897 united with Gloucester]
1897	George Forrest Browne
1914	George Nickson
1933	Clifford Salisbury Woodward
1946	Frederick Arthur Cockin
1959	Oliver Stratford Tomkins
1976	Ernest John Tinsley
1985	Barry Rogerson
2003	Michael Arthur Hill
2018	Vivienne Frances Faull

Chelmsford

Description of arms. Or, on a saltire gules a pastoral staff of the first and a sword argent, hilt and pommel gold.

1914	John Edwin Watts-Ditchfield
1923	Frederic Sumpter Guy Warman
1929	Henry Albert Wilson
1951	Sherard Falkner Allison
1962	John Gerhard Tiarks
1971	Albert John Trillo
1986	John Waine
1996	John Freeman Perry
2003	John Warren Gladwin
2010	Stephen Geoffrey Cottrell
2021	Gulnar Eleanor Francis-Dehqani

Chichester

Description of arms. Azure, our blessed Lord in judgement seated in His throne, His dexter hand upraised or, His sinister hand holding an open book proper, and issuant from His mouth a two-edged sword point to the sinister gules.

BISHOPS OF SELSEY

681	Wilfrid
716	Eadberht
731	Eolla
733	Sigga [Sigeferth]
765	Aaluberht
c.765	Oswald [Osa]
780	Gislhere
786	Tota
c.789	Wihthun
c.811	Æthelwulf
824	Cynered
845	Guttheard
900	Wighelm
909	Beornheah

931	Wulfhun
943	Ælfred
955	Daniel
956	Brihthelm
963	Eadhelm
980	Æthelgar
990	Ordbriht
1009	Ælfmaer
1032	Æthelric I
1039	Grimketel
1047	Heca
1058	Æthelric II
1070	Stigand

BISHOPS OF CHICHESTER

1075	Stigand
1088	Godfrey
1091	Ralph Luffa
1125	Seffrid I [d'Escures Pelochin]
1147	Hilary
1174	John Greenford
1180	Seffrid II
1204	Simon FitzRobert
1215	Richard Poore
1218	Ranulf of Wareham
1224	Ralph Nevill
1245	Richard Wich
1254	John Climping
1262	Stephen Bersted [or Pagham]
1288	Gilbert de St Leofard
1305	John Langton
1337	Robert Stratford
1362	William Lenn
1369	William Reade
1386	Thomas Rushock
1390	Richard Mitford
1396	Robert Waldby
1397	Robert Reade
1417	Stephen Patrington
1418	Henry de la Ware
1421	John Kempe
1421	Thomas Polton
1426	John Rickingale
1431	Simon Sydenham
1438	Richard Praty
1446	Adam de Moleyns
1450	Reginald Pecock
1459	John Arundel
1478	Edward Story
1504	Richard Fitz-James
1508	Robert Sherburne
1536	Richard Sampson
1543	George Day (deposed)
1552	John Scory
1553	George Day (restored)
1557	John Christopherson
1559	William Barlow
1570	Richard Curtis
1586	Thomas Bickley
1596	Anthony Watson
1605	Lancelot Andrewes
1609	Samuel Harsnett
1619	George Carleton
1628	Richard Montague
1638	Brian Duppa
1642	Henry King
1670	Peter Gunning
1675	Ralph Brideoake
1679	Guy Carleton
1685	John Lake
1689	Simon Patrick
1691	Robert Grove
1696	John Williams
1709	Thomas Manningham
1722	Thomas Bowers
1724	Edward Waddington
1731	Francis Hare
1740	Matthias Mawson
1754	William Ashburnham
1798	John Buckner
1824	Robert James Carr
1831	Edward Maltby

1836	William Otter
1840	Philip Nicholas Shuttleworth
1842	Ashurst Turner Gilbert
1870	Richard Durnford
1896	Ernest Roland Wilberforce
1908	Charles John Ridgeway
1919	Winfrid Oldfield Burrows
1929	George Kennedy Allen Bell
1958	Roger Plumpton Wilson
1974	Eric Waldram Kemp
2001	John William Hind
2012	Martin Clive Warner

Coventry

Description of arms. Gules, within a bordure argent charged with eight torteaux, a cross potent quadrate of the second.

1918	Huyshe Wolcott Yeatman-Biggs
1922	Charles Lisle Carr
1931	Mervyn George Haigh
1943	Neville Vincent Gorton
1956	Cuthbert Killick Norman Bardsley
1976	John Gibbs
1985	Simon Barrington-Ward
1998	Colin James Bennetts
2008	Christopher John Cocksworth

Derby

Description of arms. Purpure, a cross of St Chad argent beneath three fountains in chief.

1927	Edmund Courtenay Pearce
1936	Alfred Edward John Rawlinson
1959	Geoffrey Francis Allen
1969	Cyril William Johnston Bowles
1988	Peter Spencer Dawes
1995	Jonathan Sansbury Bailey
2005	Alastair Llewellyn John Redfern
2019	Elizabeth Jane Holden Lane

Dorchester[1]

634	Birinus
650	Agilbert
c.660	Ætla
c.888	Ahlheard

Ely

Description of arms. Gules, three ducal coronets or.

1109	Hervey
1133	Nigel
1174	Geoffrey Ridel
1189	William Longchamp
1198	Eustace
1220	John of Fountains
1225	Geoffrey de Burgo
1229	Hugh of Northwold
1255	William of Kilkenny
1258	Hugh of Balsham
1286	John of Kirkby
1290	William of Louth
1299	Ralph Walpole
1303	Robert Orford
1310	John Ketton
1316	John Hotham
1337	Simon Montacute
1345	Thomas de Lisle
1362	Simon Langham
1367	John Barnet
1374	Thomas Arundel
1388	John Fordham
1426	Philip Morgan
1438	Lewis of Luxembourg
1444	Thomas Bourgchier
1454	William Grey
1479	John Morton
1486	John Alcock
1501	Richard Redman
1506	James Stanley
1515	Nicholas West
1534	Thomas Goodrich
1555	Thomas Thirlby
1559	Richard Cox
1600	Martin Heton
1609	Lancelot Andrewes
1619	Nicolas Felton
1628	John Buckeridge
1631	Francis White
1638	Matthew Wren
1667	Benjamin Laney
1675	Peter Gunning
1684	Francis Turner
1691	Simon Patrick
1707	John Moore
1714	William Fleetwood
1723	Thomas Greene
1738	Robert Butts
1748	Thomas Gooch
1754	Matthias Mawson
1771	Edmund Keene
1781	James Yorke
1808	Thomas Dampier
1812	Bowyer Edward Sparke
1836	Joseph Allen
1845	Thomas Turton
1864	Edward Harold Browne
1873	James Russell Woodford
1886	Alwyne Frederick Compton
1905	Frederick Henry Chase
1924	Leonard Jauncey White-Thomson
1934	Bernard Oliver Francis Heywood
1941	Harold Edward Wynn
1957	Noel Baring Hudson
1964	Edward James Keymer Roberts

---

[1] Originally a West Saxon, after Ahlheard's time a Mercian, bishopric. See transferred to Lincoln 1077.

1977	Peter Knight Walker
1990	Stephen Whitefield Sykes
2000	Anthony John Russell
2010	Stephen David Conway

Exeter

Description of arms. Gules, a sword erect in pale argent hilt or surmounted by two keys addorsed in saltire gold.

BISHOPS OF CORNWALL

870	Kenstec
893	Asser
931	Conan
950	Æthelge[ard]
c.955	Daniel
963	Wulfsige Comoere
990	Ealdred
1009	Æthelsige
1018	Buruhwold
1027	Lyfing, Bishop of Crediton, Cornwall and Worcester
1046	Leofric, Bishop of Crediton and Cornwall
	[See transferred to Exeter 1050]

BISHOPS OF CREDITON

909	Eadwulf
934	Æthelgar
953	Ælfwold I
973	Sideman
979	Ælfric
987	Ælfwold II
1008	Ælfwold III
1015	Eadnoth
1027	Lyfing
1046	Leofric[1]

BISHOPS OF EXETER

1050	Leofric
1072	Osbern Fitz-Osbern
1107	Will. Warelwast
1138	Robert Warelwast
1155	Robert II of Chichester
1161	Bartholomew
1186	John the Chanter
1194	Henry Marshall
1214	Simon of Apulia
1224	William Brewer
1245	Richard Blund
1258	Walter Bronescombe
1280	Peter Quinel [Wyvill]
1292	Thomas Bitton
1308	Walter Stapeldon
1327	James Berkeley
1328	John Grandisson
1370	Thomas Brantingham
1395	Edmund Stafford
1419	John Catterick
1420	Edmund Lacy
1458	George Nevill
1465	John Booth
1478	Peter Courtenay
1487	Richard Fox
1493	Oliver King

1496	Richard Redman
1502	John Arundel
1505	Hugh Oldham
1519	John Veysey (resigned)
1551	Miles Coverdale
1553	John Veysey (restored)
1555	James Turberville
1560	William Alley [or Allei]
1571	William Bradbridge
1579	John Woolton
1595	Gervase Babington
1598	William Cotton
1621	Valentine Carey
1627	Joseph Hall
1642	Ralph Brownrigg
1660	John Gauden
1662	Seth Ward
1667	Anthony Sparrow
1676	Thomas Lamplugh
1689	Jonathan Trelawney
1708	Offspring Blackall
1717	Lancelot Blackburn
1724	Stephen Weston
1742	Nicholas Claget
1747	George Lavington
1762	Frederick Keppel
1778	John Ross
1792	William Buller
1797	Henry Reginald Courtenay
1803	John Fisher
1807	George Pelham
1820	William Carey
1830	Christopher Bethell
1831	Henry Phillpotts
1869	Frederick Temple
1885	Edward Henry Bickersteth
1901	Herbert Edward Ryle
1903	Archibald Robertson
1916	Rupert Ernest William Gascoyne Cecil
1936	Charles Edward Curzon
1949	Robert Cecil Mortimer
1973	Eric Arthur John Mercer
1985	Geoffrey Hewlett Thompson
1999	Michael Laurence Langrish
2014	Robert Ronald Atwell

Gibraltar in Europe

Description of arms. Argent, in base rising out of the waves of the sea a rock proper, thereon a lion guardant or supporting a passion cross erect gules, on a chief engrailed of the last a crosier in bend dexter and a key in bend sinister or surmounted by a Maltese cross argent fimbriated gold.

BISHOPS OF GIBRALTAR

1842	George Tomlinson
1863	Walter John Trower
1868	Charles Amyand Harris
1874	Charles Waldegrave Sandford
1904	William Edward Collins
1911	Henry Joseph Corbett Knight
1921	John Harold Greig
1927	Frederick Cyril Nugent Hicks
1933	Harold Jocelyn Buxton

1947	Cecil Douglas Horsley
1953	Frederick William Thomas Craske
1960	Stanley Albert Hallam Eley
1970	John Richard Satterthwaite[2]

BISHOPS OF GIBRALTAR IN EUROPE

1980	John Richard Satterthwaite
1993	John William Hind
2001	Douglas Geoffrey Rowell
2014	Robert Neil Innes

Gloucester

Description of arms. zure, two keys addorsed in saltire the wards upwards or.

1541	John Wakeman *alias* Wiche
1551	John Hooper
1554	James Brooks
1562	Richard Cheyney[3]
1581	John Bullingham[4]
1598	Godfrey Goldsborough
1605	Thomas Ravis
1607	Henry Parry
1611	Giles Thompson
1612	Miles Smith
1625	Godfrey Goodman
1661	William Nicolson
1672	John Pritchett
1681	Robert Frampton
1691	Edward Fowler
1715	Richard Willis
1721	Joseph Wilcocks
1731	Elias Sydall
1735	Martin Benson
1752	James Johnson
1760	William Warburton
1779	James Yorke
1781	Samuel Hallifax
1789	Richard Beadon
1802	George Isaac Huntingford
1815	Henry Ryder
1824	Christopher Bethell
1830	James Henry Monk
[1836	to 1897, united with Bristol]

BISHOPS OF GLOUCESTER AND BRISTOL

1836	James Henry Monk
1856	Charles Baring
1861	William Thomson
1863	Charles John Ellicott[5]

BISHOPS OF GLOUCESTER

1897	Charles John Ellicott
1905	Edgar Charles Sumner Gibson
1923	Arthur Cayley Headlam
1946	Clifford Salisbury Woodward
1954	Wilfred Marcus Askwith
1962	Basil Tudor Guy
1975	John Yates
1992	Peter John Ball
1993	David Edward Bentley
2004	Michael Francis Perham
2015	Rachel Treweek

---

[1] Removed See from Crediton.   [2] Bishop of Fulham and Gibraltar from 1970 to 1980.   [3] Also Bishop of Bristol.
[4] Held Gloucester and Bristol 1581-9.   [5] Gloucester only from 1897.

Guildford

Description of arms. Gules, two keys conjoined wards outwards in bend, the uppermost or, the other argent, interposed between them in bend sinister a sword of the third, hilt and pommel gold, all within a bordure azure charged with ten wool-packs argent.

1927	John Harold Greig
1934	John Victor Macmillan
1949	Henry Colville Montgomery Campbell
1956	Ivor Stanley Watkins
1961	George Edmund Reindorp
1973	David Alan Brown
1983	Michael Edgar Adie
1994	John Warren Gladwin
2004	Christopher John Hill
2014	Andrew John Watson

Hereford

Description of arms. Gules, three leopards' faces jessant-de-lis reversed or.

676	Putta
688	Tyrhtel
710	Torhthere
*c.*731	Wahistod
736	Cuthberht
741	Podda
*c.*758	Acca
*c.*770	Headda
777	Aldberht
786	Esne
*c.*788	Ceolmund
*c.*798	Utel
801	Wulfheard
824	Beonna
*c.*832	Eadwulf
*c.*839	Cuthwulf
866	Mucel
*c.*866	Deorlaf
888	Cynemund
890	EadBar
*c.*931	Tidhelm
940	Wulfhelm
*c.*940	Ælfric
971	Æthelwulf
1016	Æthelstan
1056	Leofgar
1056	Ealdred, Bishop of Hereford and Worcester
1060	Walter
1079	Robert Losinga
1096	Gerard

1107	Reinhelm
1115	Geoffrey de Clive
1121	Richard de Capella
1131	Robert de Bethune
1148	Gilbert Foliot
1163	Robert of Melun
1174	Robert Foliot
1186	William de Vere
1200	Giles de Braose
1216	Hugh of Mapenore
1219	Hugh Foliot
1234	Ralph Maidstone
1240	Peter d'Aigueblanche
1269	John Breton
1275	Thomas Cantilupe
1283	Richard Swinfeld
1317	Adam Orleton
1327	Thomas Chariton
1344	John Trilleck
1361	Lewis Charleton
1370	William Courtenay
1375	John Gilbert
1389	John Trefnant
1404	Robert Mascall
1417	Edmund Lacy
1420	Thomas Polton
1422	Thomas Spofford
1449	Richard Beauchamp
1451	Reginald Boulers
1453	John Stanbury
1474	Thomas Milling
1492	Edmund Audley
1502	Adriano de Castello [di Corneto]
1504	Richard Mayeu
1516	Charles Booth
1535	Edward Fox
1539	John Skip
1553	John Harley
1554	Robert Parfew or Wharton
1559	John Scory
1586	Herbert Westfaling
1603	Robert Bennett
1617	Francis Godwin
1634	Augustine Lindsell
1635	Matthew Wren
1635	Theophilus Field
1636	George Coke
1661	Nicolas Monk
1662	Herbert Croft
1691	Gilbert Ironside
1701	Humphrey Humphries
1713	Philip Bisse
1721	Benjamin Hoadly
1724	Henry Egerton
1746	James Beauclerk
1787	John Harley
1788	John Butler
1803	Ffolliott Herbert Walker Cornewall
1808	John Luxmoore
1815	George Isaac Huntingford
1832	Edward Grey
1837	Thomas Musgrave
1848	Renn Dickson Hampden
1868	James Atlay
1895	John Percival
1918	Herbert Hensley Henson
1920	Martin Linton Smith
1931	Charles Lisle Carr
1941	Richard Godfrey Parsons
1949	Tom Longworth
1961	Mark Allin Hodson
1974	John Richard Gordon Eastaugh
1990	John Keith Oliver
2004	Anthony Martin Priddis
2014	Richard Michael Cokayne Frith
2020	Richard Charles Jackson

Leicester

see also under Lincoln

Description of arms. Gules, a pierced cinquefoil ermine, in chief a lion passant guardant grasping in the dexter forepaw a cross crosslet fitchée or.

NEW FOUNDATION

1927	Cyril Charles Bowman Bardsley
1940	Guy Vernon Smith
1953	Ronald Ralph Williams
1979	Cecil Richard Rutt
1991	Thomas Frederick Butler
1999	Timothy John Stevens
2016	Martyn James Snow

Lichfield

Description of arms. Per pale gules and argent, a cross potent quadrate in the centre per pale argent and or between four crosses patée those to the dexter argent and those to the sinister gold.

BISHOPS OF MERCIA

656	Diuma[1]
658	Ceollach
659	Trumhere
662	Jaruman

BISHOPS OF LICHFIELD

669	Chad[2]
672	Winfrith
676	Seaxwulf
691	Headda[3]
731	Aldwine
737	Hwita
757	Hemele
765	Cuthfrith
769	Berhthun
779	Hygeberht[4]
801	Aldwulf
816	Herewine
818	Æthelwald
830	Hunberht
836	Cyneferth
845	Tunberht
869	Eadberht
883	Wulfred
900	Wigmund or Wilferth
915	Ælfwine
941	Wulfgar
949	Cynesige
964	Wynsige

---

[1] Archbishop of the Mercians, the Lindisfari, and the Middle Angles. [2] Bishop of the Mercians and the Lindisfari.
[3] Bishop of Lichfield and Leicester. [4] Archbishop of Lichfield after 787.

975	Ælfheah
1004	Godwine
1020	Leofgar
1026	Brihtmaer
1039	Wulfsige
1053	Leofwine
1072	Peter

BISHOPS OF LICHFIELD, CHESTER AND COVENTRY[1]

1075	Peter
1086	Robert de Limesey
1121	Robert Peche
1129	Roger de Clinton
1149	Walter Durdent
1161	Richard Peche
1183	Gerard La Pucelle
1188	Hugh Nonant
1198	Geoffrey Muschamp
1215	William Cornhill
1224	Alex. Stavensby
1240	Hugh Pattishall
1246	Roger Weseham
1258	Roger Longespee
1296	Walter Langton
1322	Roger Northburgh
1360	Robert Stretton
1386	Walter Skirlaw
1386	Richard le Scrope
1398	John Burghill
1415	John Catterick
1420	William Heyworth
1447	William Booth
1452	Nicholas Close
1453	Reginald Boulers
1459	John Hales
1493	William Smith
1496	John Arundel
1503	Geoffrey Blyth
1534	Rowland Lee
1541	[Chester formed as a bishopric]
1543	Richard Sampson
1554	Ralph Baynes
1560	Thomas Bentham
1580	William Overton
1609	George Abbot
1610	Richard Neile
1614	John Overall
1619	Thomas Morton
1632	Robert Wright
1644	Accepted Frewen
1661	John Hackett
1671	Thomas Wood
1692	William Lloyd
1699	John Hough
1717	Edward Chandler
1731	Richard Smalbroke
1750	Fred. Cornwallis
1768	John Egerton
1771	Brownlow North
1775	Richard Hurd
1781	James Cornwallis [4th Earl Cornwallis]
1824	Henry Ryder
1836	[Coventry transferred to Worcester diocese]
1836	Samuel Butler
1840	James Bowstead
1843	John Lonsdale
1868	George Augustus Selwyn
1878	William Dalrymple Maclagan
1891	Augustus Legge
1913	John Augustine Kempthorne
1937	Edward Sydney Woods
1953	Arthur Stretton Reeve
1975	Kenneth John Fraser Skelton

1984	Keith Norman Sutton
2003	Jonathan Michael Gledhill
2016	Michael Geoffrey Ipgrave

Lincoln

Description of arms. Gules, two lions passant guardant or, on a chief azure, the Virgin ducally crowned sitting on a throne issuant from the chief, on her dexter arm the infant Jesus, and in her sinister hand a sceptre all gold.

BISHOPS OF LINDSEY

634	Birinus
650	Agilbert
660	Aetlai
678	Eadhaed
680	Æthelwine
693	(?)Edgar
731	(?)Cyneberht
733	Alwig
750	Aldwulf
767	Ceolwulf
796	Eadwulf
839	Beorhtred
869	Burgheard
933	Ælfred
953	Leofwine
996	Sigefrith

BISHOPS OF LEICESTER

664	Wilfrid, translated from York
679	Cuthwine
691	Headda[2] (founder of Lichfield Cathedral 705–37)
727	Aldwine
737	Torhthelm
764	Eadberht
785	Unwona
803	Wernberht
816	Raethhun
840	Ealdred
844	Ceolred
874	[See of Leicester removed to Dorchester]

BISHOPS OF DORCHESTER

(after	it became a Mercian See)
c.888	Ahlheard
900	Wigmund or Wilferth
909	Cenwulf
925	Wynsige
c.951	Osketel
953	Leofwine
975	Ælfnoth
979	Æscwig
1002	Ælfheln
1006	Eadnoth I
1016	Æthelric
1034	Eadnoth II
1049	Ulf
1053	Wulfwig
1067	Remigius

BISHOPS OF LINCOLN

1072	Remigius
1094	Robert Bloett
1123	Alexander
1148	Robert de Chesney
1183	Walter de Coutances
1186	Hugh of Avalon
1203	William of Blois
1209	Hugh of Wells
1235	Robert Grosseteste
1254	Henry Lexington [Sutton]
1258	Richard Gravesend
1280	Oliver Sutton [Lexington]
1300	John Dalderby
1320	Henry Burghersh
1342	Thomas Bek
1347	John Gynewell
1363	John Bokyngham [Buckingham]
1398	Henry Beaufort
1405	Philip Repingdon
1420	Richard Fleming
1431	William Gray
1436	William Alnwick
1450	Marmaduke Lumley
1452	John Chedworth
1472	Thomas Rotherham [Scott]
1480	John Russell
1495	William Smith
1514	Thomas Wolsey
1514	William Atwater
1521	John Longland
1547	Henry Holbeach [Rands]
1552	John Taylor
1554	John White
1557	Thomas Watson
1560	Nicholas Bullingham
1571	Thomas Cooper
1584	William Wickham
1595	William Chaderton
1608	William Barlow
1614	Richard Neile
1617	George Monteigne [Mountain]
1621	John Williams
1642	Thomas Winniffe
1660	Robt. Sanderson
1663	Benjamin Laney
1667	William Fuller
1675	Thomas Barlow
1692	Thomas Tenison
1695	James Gardiner
1705	William Wake
1716	Edmund Gibson
1723	Richard Reynolds
1744	John Thomas
1761	John Green
1779	Thomas Thurlow
1787	George Pretyman [Pretyman Tomline after June 1803]
1820	George Pelham
1827	John Kaye
1853	John Jackson
1869	Christopher Wordsworth
1885	Edward King
1910	Edward Lee Hicks
1920	William Shuckburgh Swayne
1933	Frederick Cyril Nugent Hicks
1942	Henry Aylmer Skelton
1946	Leslie Owen
1947	Maurice Henry Harland
1956	Kenneth Riches
1975	Simon Wilton Phipps
1987	Robert Maynard Hardy
2001	John Charles Saxbee
2011	Christopher Lowson
2021	*vacant*

---

[1] 1102 Robert de Limesey, Bishop of Lichfield, moved the See to Coventry. Succeeding bishops are usually termed *of Coventry* until 1228. Then *Coventry and Lichfield* was the habitual title until the Reformation. *Chester* was used by some 12th-century bishops, and popularly afterwards. After the Reformation *Lichfield and Coventry* was used until 1846.

[2] Bishop of Leicester and Lichfield.

Norwich

Description of arms. Azure, three labelled mitres or.

BISHOPS OF DUNWICH

631	Felix
648	Thomas
c.653	Berhtgils [Boniface]
c.670	Bisi
c.673	Æcce
693	Alric (?)
716	Eardred
731	Aldbeorht I
747	Æscwulf
747	Eardwulf
775	Cuthwine
775	Aldbeorht II
781	Ecglaf
781	Heardred
793	Ælfhun
798	Tidferth
824	Waermund[1]
825	Wilred
836	Husa
870	Æthelwold

BISHOPS OF ELMHAM

673	Beaduwine
706	Nothberht
c.731	Heathulac
736	Æthelfrith
758	Eanfrith
c.781	Æthelwulf
c.785	Alhheard
814	Sibba
824	Hunferth
824	Hunbeorht
836	Cunda[2]
c.933	Ælfred[3]
c.945	Æthelweald
956	Eadwulf
970	Ælfric I
974	Theodred I
982	Theodred II
997	Æthelstan
1001	Ælfgar
1021	Ælfwine
1038	Ælfric II
1039	Ælfric III
1043	Stigand[4]
1043	Grimketel[5]
1044	Stigand (restored)
1047	Æthelmaer

BISHOPS OF THETFORD

1070	Herfast
1086	William de Beaufai
1091	Herbert Losinga

BISHOPS OF NORWICH

1091	Herbert Losinga
1121	Everard of Montgomery
1146	William de Turbe
1175	John of Oxford
1200	John de Gray
1222	Pandulf Masca

1226	Thomas Blundeville
1239	William Raleigh
1245	Walter Suffield or Calthorp
1258	Simon Walton
1266	Roger Skerning
1278	William Middleton
1289	Ralph Walpole
1299	John Salmon
1325	[Robert de Baldock]
1325	William Ayermine
1337	Anthony Bek
1344	William of Norwich [Bateman]
1356	Thomas Percy
1370	Henry Spencer [Dispenser]
1407	Alexander Tottington
1413	Richard Courtenay
1416	John Wakeryng
1426	William Ainwick
1436	Thomas Brown
1446	Walter Lyhert [le Hart]
1472	James Goldwell
1499	Thomas Jane
1501	Richard Nykke
1536	William Reppes [Rugge]
1550	Thomas Thirlby
1554	John Hopton
1560	John Parkhurst
1575	Edmund Freke
1585	Edmund Scambler
1595	William Redman
1603	John Jegon
1618	John Overall
1619	Samuel Harsnett
1629	Francis White
1632	Richard Corbet
1635	Matthew Wren
1638	Richard Montagu
1641	Joseph Hall
1661	Edward Reynolds
1676	Antony Sparrow
1685	William Lloyd
1691	John Moore
1708	Charles Trimnell
1721	Thomas Green
1723	John Leng
1727	William Baker
1733	Robert Butts
1738	Thomas Gooch
1748	Samuel Lisle
1749	Thomas Hayter
1761	Philip Yonge
1783	Lewis Bagot
1790	George Horne
1792	Charles Manners Sutton
1805	Henry Bathurst
1837	Edward Stanley
1849	Samuel Hinds
1857	John Thomas Pelham
1893	John Sheepshanks
1910	Bertram Pollock
1942	Percy Mark Herbert
1959	William Launcelot Scott Fleming
1971	Maurice Arthur Ponsonby Wood
1985	Peter John Nott
1999	Graham Richard James
2019	Graham Barham Usher

Oxford

Description of arms. Sable, a fess argent, in chief three demi-ladies couped at the waist heads affrontée proper crowned or arrayed and veiled of the second, in base an ox of the last, horned and hoofed gold, passing a ford barry wavy of six azure and argent.

1542	Robert King[6]
1558	[Thomas Goldwell]
1567	Hugh Curen [Curwen]
1589	John Underhill
1604	John Bridges
1619	John Howson
1628	Richard Corbet
1632	John Bancroft
1641	Robert Skinner
1663	William Paul
1665	Walter Blandford
1671	Nathaniel Crewe [Lord Crewe]
1674	Henry Compton
1676	John Fell
1686	Samuel Parker
1688	Timothy Hall
1690	John Hough
1699	William Talbot
1715	John Potter
1737	Thomas Secker
1758	John Hume
1766	Robert Lowth
1777	John Butler
1788	Edward Smallwell
1799	John Randolph
1807	Charles Moss
1812	William Jackson
1816	Edward Legge
1827	Charles Lloyd
1829	Richard Bagot
1845	Samuel Wilberforce
1870	John Fielder Mackarness
1889	William Stubbs
1901	Francis Paget
1911	Charles Gore
1919	Hubert Murray Burge
1925	Thomas Banks Strong
1937	Kenneth Escott Kirk
1955	Harry James Carpenter
1971	Kenneth John Woollcombe
1978	Patrick Campbell Rodger
1987	Richard Douglas Harries
2007	John Lawrence Pritchard
2016	Steven John Lindsey Croft

[1] Bishop of Dunwich or Elmham.   [2] Bishop of Elmham or Dunwich.   [3] Bishop of Elmham or Lindsey.
[4] Deposed before consecration.   [5] Bishop of Selsey and Elmham.
[6] Bishop Rheon. *in partibus*. Of Oseney 1542-5. See transferred to Oxford 1545.

Peterborough

Description of arms. Gules, two keys in saltire the wards upwards between four cross crosslets fitchée or.

1541	John Chamber
1557	David Pole
1561	Edmund Scambler
1585	Richard Howland
1601	Thomas Dove
1630	William Piers
1633	Augustine Lindsell
1634	Francis Dee
1639	John Towers
1660	Benjamin Laney
1663	Joseph Henshaw
1679	William Lloyd
1685	Thomas White
1691	Richard Cumberland
1718	White Kennett
1729	Robert Clavering
1747	John Thomas
1757	Richard Terrick
1764	Robert Lambe
1769	John Hinchliffe
1794	Spencer Madan
1813	John Parsons
1819	Herbert Marsh
1839	George Davys
1864	Francis Jeune
1868	William Connor Magee
1891	Mandell Creighton
1897	Edward Carr Glyn
1916	Frank Theodore Woods
1924	Cyril Charles Bowman Bardsley
1927	Claude Martin Blagden
1949	Spencer Stottisbury Gwatkin Leeson
1956	Robert Wright Stopford
1961	Cyril Eastaugh
1972	Douglas Russell Feaver
1984	William John Westwood
1996	Ian Patrick Martyn Cundy
2010	Donald Spargo Allister

Portsmouth

Description of arms. Per fess or and gules, in chief upon waves of the sea proper a lymphad sable, and in base two keys conjoined wards outwards in bend, the uppermost or, the other argent, interposed between them in bend sinister a sword also argent, hilt and pommel gold.

1927	Ernest Neville Lovett
1936	Frank Partridge
1942	William Louis Anderson
1949	William Launcelot Scott Fleming

1960	John Henry Lawrence Phillips
1975	Archibald Ronald McDonald Gordon
1985	Timothy John Bavin
1995	Kenneth William Stevenson
2010	Christopher Richard James Foster
2021	*vacant*

Rochester

Description of arms. Argent, on a saltire gules an escallop or.

604	Justus
624	Romanus
633	Paulinus
644	Ithamar
664	Damianus
669	Putta
676	Cwichelm
678	Gebmund
716	Tobias
727	Aldwulf
741	Dunn
747	Eardwulf
772	Diora
785	Waermund I
805	Beornmod
844	Tatnoth
868	Badenoth
868	Waermund II
868	Cuthwulf
880	Swithwulf
900	Ceolmund
c.926	Cyneferth
c.934	Burhric
949	Beorhtsige
955	[Daniel?] Rochester or Selsey
964	Ælfstan
995	Godwine I
1046	Godwine II
1058	Siward
1076	Arnost
1077	Gundulf
1108	Ralph d'Escures
1115	Ernulf
1125	John
1137	John II
1142	Ascelin
1148	Walter
1182	Waleran
1185	Gilbert Glanvill
1215	Benedict of Sausetun [Sawston]
1227	Henry Sandford
1238	Richard Wendene
1251	Lawrence of St Martin
1274	Walter Merton
1278	John Bradfield
1283	Thomas Ingoldsthorpe
1292	Thomas of Wouldham
1319	Hamo Hethe
1353	John Sheppey
1362	William of Whittlesey
1364	Thomas Trilleck
1373	Thomas Brinton
1389	William Bottlesham [Bottisham]
1400	John Bottlesham
1404	Richard Young
1419	John Kempe
1422	John Langdon
1435	Thomas Brouns

1437	William Wells
1444	John Low
1468	Thomas Rotherham [otherwise Scott]
1472	John Alcock
1476	John Russell
1480	Edmund Audley
1493	Thomas Savage
1497	Richard Fitz-James
1504	John Fisher
1535	John Hilsey [Hildesleigh]
1540	Nicolas Heath
1544	Henry Holbeach
1547	Nicholas Ridley
1550	John Ponet [Poynet]
1551	John Scory
1554	Maurice Griffith
1560	Edmund Gheast [Guest]
1572	Edmund Freke
1576	John Piers
1578	John Young
1605	William Barlow
1608	Richard Neile
1611	John Buckeridge
1628	Walter Curil
1630	John Bowle
1638	John Warner
1666	John Dolben
1683	Francis Turner
1684	Thomas Sprat
1713	Francis Atterbury
1723	Samuel Bradford
1731	Joseph Wilcocks
1756	Zachary Pearce
1774	John Thomas
1793	Samuel Horsley
1802	Thomas Dampier
1809	Walker King
1827	Hugh Percy
1827	George Murray
1860	Joseph Cotton Wigram
1867	Thomas Legh Claughton
1877	Anthony Wilson Thorold
1891	Randall Thomas Davidson
1895	Edward Stuart Talbot
1905	John Reginald Harmer
1930	Martin Linton Smith
1940	Christopher Maude Chavasse
1961	Richard David Say
1988	Anthony Michael Arnold Turnbull
1994	Michael James Nazir-Ali
2010	James Henry Langstaff
2021	*vacant*

St Albans

Description of arms. Azure, a saltire or, overall a sword erect in pale proper, hilt and pommel gold, in chief a celestial crown of the same.

1877	Thomas Legh Claughton
1890	John Wogan Festing
1903	Edgar Jacob
1920	Michael Bolton Furse
1944	Philip Henry Loyd
1950	Edward Michael Gresford Jones
1970	Robert Alexander Kennedy Runcie
1980	John Bernard Taylor
1995	Christopher William Herbert
2009	Alan Gregory Clayton Smith

St Edmundsbury and Ipswich

Description of arms. Per pale gules and azure, between three ducal coronets a demi-lion passant guardant conjoined to the demi-hulk of an ancient ship or.

1914	Henry Bernard Hodgson
1921	Albert Augustus David
1923	Walter Godfrey Whittingham
1940	Richard Brook
1954	Arthur Harold Morris
1966	Leslie Wilfrid Brown
1978	John Waine
1986	John Dennis
1997	John Hubert Richard Lewis
2007	William Nigel Stock
2015	Martin Alan Seeley

Salisbury

Description of arms. Azure, our Lady crowned, holding in her dexter arm the infant Jesus, and in her sinister arm a sceptre all or, round both the heads circles of glory gold.

BISHOPS OF SHERBORNE

705	Ealdhelm
709	Forthhere
736	Herewald
774	Æthelmod
793	Denefrith
801	Wigberht
825	Ealhstan
868	Heahmund
877	Æthelheah
889	Wulfsige I
900	Asser
c.909	Æthelweard
c.909	Waerstan
925	Æthelbald
925	Sigehelm
934	Ælfred
943	Wulfsige II
958	Ælfwold I
979	Æthelsige I
992	Wulfsige III
1002	Æthelric
1012	Æthelsige II
1017	Brihtwine I
1017	Ælfmaer
1023	Brihtwine II
1045	Ælfwold II
1058	Hereman, Bishop of Ramsbury

BISHOPS OF RAMSBURY

909	Æthelstan
927	Oda
949	Ælfric I
951	Osulf
970	Ælfstan
981	Wulfgar
986	Sigeric
993	Ælfric II
1005	Brihtwold
1045	Hereman[1]

BISHOPS OF SALISBURY

1078	Osmund Osmer
1107	Roger
1142	Jocelin de Bohun
1189	Hubert Walter
1194	Herbert Poore
1217	Richard Poore
1229	Robert Bingham
1247	William of York
1257	Giles of Bridport
1263	Walter de la Wyle
1274	Robert Wickhampton
1284	Walter Scammel
1287	Henry Brandeston
1289	William de la Corner
1292	Nicholas Longespee
1297	Simon of Ghent
1315	Roger de Mortival
1330	Robert Wyville
1375	Ralph Erghum
1388	John Waltham
1395	Richard Mitford
1407	Nicholas Bubwith
1407	Robert Hallum
1417	John Chaundler
1427	Robert Nevill
1438	William Aiscough
1450	Richard Beauchamp
1482	Lionel Woodville
1485	Thomas Langton
1494	John Blythe
1500	Henry Deane
1502	Edmund Audley
1525	Lorenzo Campeggio
1535	Nicholas Shaxton
1539	John Salcot [Capon]
1560	John Jewell
1571	Edmund Gheast [Guest]
1577	John Piers
1591	John Coldwell
1598	Henry Cotton
1615	Robert Abbot
1618	Martin Fotherby
1620	Robert Townson [Toulson]
1621	John Davenant
1641	Brian Duppa
1660	Humfrey Henchman
1663	John Earle
1665	Alexander Hyde
1667	Seth Ward
1689	Gilbert Burnet
1715	William Talbot
1721	Richard Wilis
1723	Benjamin Hoadly
1734	Thomas Sherlock
1748	John Gilbert
1757	John Thomas
1761	Robert Hay Drummond
1761	John Thomas
1766	John Hume
1782	Shute Barrington
1791	John Douglas
1807	John Fisher
1825	Thomas Burgess
1837	Edward Denison
1854	Walter Kerr Hamilton
1869	George Moberly
1885	John Wordsworth

1911	Frederic Edward Ridgeway
1921	St Clair George Alfred Donaldson
1936	Ernest Neville Lovett
1946	Geoffrey Charles Lester Lunt
1949	William Louis Anderson
1963	Joseph Edward Fison
1973	George Edmund Reindorp
1982	John Austin Baker
1993	David Staffurth Stancliffe
2011	Nicholas Roderick Holtam
2021	*vacant*

Southwark

Description of arms. Argent, eleven fusils in cross conjoined, seven in pale fesswise, four in fess palewise, in the dexter chief a mitre all gules.

1905	Edward Stuart Talbot
1911	Hubert Murray Burge
1919	Cyril Forster Garbett
1932	Richard Godfrey Parsons
1942	Bertram Fitzgerald Simpson
1959	Arthur Mervyn Stockwood
1980	Ronald Oliver Bowlby
1991	Robert Kerr Williamson
1998	Thomas Frederick Butler
2011	Christopher Thomas James Chessun

Truro

Description of arms. Argent, on a saltire gules a sword and key or and in base a fleur-de-lis sable all within a bordure of the last charged with fifteen besants.

1877	Edward White Benson
1883	George Howard Wilkinson
1891	John Gott
1906	Charles William Stubbs
1912	Winfrid Oldfield Burrows
1919	Frederic Sumpter Guy Warman
1923	Walter Howard Frere
1935	Joseph Wellington Hunkin
1951	Edmund Robert Morgan
1960	John Maurice Key
1973	Graham Douglas Leonard
1981	Peter Mumford
1990	Michael Thomas Ball
1997	William Ind
2008	Timothy Martin Thornton
2018	Philip Ian Mounstephen

[1] Ramsbury was added to Sherbourne in 1058 when Hereman became Bishop of Sherbourne. The See was moved to Salisbury in 1078.

Worcester

Description of arms. Argent, ten
torteaux, four, three, two, and one.

680	Bosel
691	Oftfor
693	Ecgwine
718	Wilfrid I
745	Milred
775	Waermund
777	Tilhere
781	Heathured
798	Deneberht
822	Heahberht
845	Alhhun
873	Waerferth
915	Æthelhun
922	Wilferth II
929	Cenwald
957	Dunstan
961	Oswald
992	Ealdwulf
1002	Wulfstan I
1016	Leofsige
1027	Lyfing
1033	Brihtheah
1040	Æltric Puttoc, Bishop of York and Worcester
1041	Lyfing (restored)
1046	Ealdred Bishop of Hereford and Worcester 1056–60
1062	Wulfstan II
1096	Samson
1115	Theulf
1125	Simon

1151	John of Pagham
1158	Aldred
1164	Roger of Gloucester
1180	Baldwin
1186	William of Northolt
1191	Robert Fitz Ralph
1193	Henry de Sully
1196	John of Coutances
1200	Mauger
1214	Walter de Gray
1216	Silvester of Evesham
1218	William of Blois
1237	Walter Cantilupe
1266	Nicolas of Ely
1268	Godfrey Giffard
1302	William Gainsborough
1308	Walter Reynolds
1313	Walter Maidstone
1317	Thomas Cobham
1327	Adam Orleton
1334	Simon Montacute
1337	Thomas Hempnall
1339	Wulstan Bransford
1350	John Thoresby
1353	Reginald Brian
1362	John Barnet
1364	William of Whittlesey
1369	William Lenn
1375	Henry Wakefield
1396	Robert Tideman of Winchcomb
1401	Richard Clifford
1407	Thomas Peverel
1419	Philip Morgan
1426	Thomas Polton
1435	Thomas Bourgchier
1444	John Carpenter
1476	John Alcock
1487	Robert Morton
1497	Giovanni de' Gigli
1499	Silvestro de' Gigli
1521	Julius de Medici Guilio de Medici (administrator)
1523	Geronimo Ghinucci
1535	Hugh Latimer
1539	John Bell
1544	Nicholas Heath (deposed)

1552	John Hooper
1554	Nicholas Heath (restored)
1555	Richard Pates
1559	Edwin Sandys
1571	Nicholas Bullingham
1577	John Whitgift
1584	Edmund Freke
1593	Richard Fletcher
1596	Thomas Bilson
1597	Gervase Babington
1610	Henry Parry
1617	John Thornborough
1641	John Prideaux
1660	George Morley
1662	John Gauden
1662	John Earle
1663	Robert Skinner
1671	Walter Blandford
1675	James Fleetwood
1683	William Thomas
1689	Edward Stillingfleet
1699	William Lloyd
1717	John Hough
1743	Isaac Maddox
1759	James Johnson
1774	Brownlow North
1781	Richard Hurd
1808	Ffolliott Herbert Walker Cornewall
1831	Robert James Carr
1841	Henry Pepys
1861	Henry Philpott
1891	John James Stewart Perowne
1902	Charles Gore
1905	Huyshe Wolcott Yeatman-Biggs
1919	Ernest Harold Pearce
1931	Arthur William Thomson Perowne
1941	William Wilson Cash
1956	Lewis Mervyn Charles-Edwards
1971	Robert Wylmer Woods
1982	Philip Harold Ernest Goodrich
1997	Peter Stephen Maurice Selby
2007	John Geoffrey Inge

PROVINCE OF YORK

York

Description of arms. Gules, two keys in
saltire argent, in chief a regal crown
proper.

BISHOPS

314	Eborius
625	Paulinus [Vacancy 633–64]
664	Cedda
664	Wilfrid I
678	Bosa (retired)
686	Bosa (restored)
691	Wilfrith (restored)
706	John of Beverley
718	Wilfrid II

ARCHBISHOPS

734	Egberht
767	Æthelberht
780	Eanbald I
796	Eanbald II
808	Wulfsige
837	Wigmund
854	Wulfhere
900	Æthelbald
c.928	Hrothweard
931	Wulfstan I
956	Osketel
971	Oswald
971	Edwald
992	Ealdwulf[1]
1003	Wulfstan II
1023	Ælfric Puttoc
1041	Æthelric
1051	Cynesige
1061	Ealdred
1070	Thomas I of Bayeux
1100	Gerard
1109	Thomas II
1119	Thurstan
1143	William Fitzherbert
1147	Henry Murdac
1153	William Fitzherbert (restored)
1154	Roger of Pont l'Eveque

1191	Geoffrey Plantagenet
1215	Walter de Gray
1256	Sewal de Bovill
1258	Godfrey Ludham [Kineton]
1266	Walter Giffard
1279	William Wickwane
1286	John Romanus [le Romeyn]
1298	Henry Newark
1300	Thomas Corbridge
1306	William Greenfield
1317	William Melton
1342	William de la Zouche
1352	John Thoresby
1374	Alexander Neville
1388	Thomas Arundel
1396	Robert Waldby
1398	Richard le Scrope
1407	Henry Bowet
1426	John Kempe
1452	William Booth
1464	George Nevill
1476	Lawrence Booth
1480	Thomas Rotherham [Scott]
1501	Thomas Savage
1508	Christopher Bainbridge
1514	Thomas Wolsey
1531	Edward Lee
1545	Robert Holgate

---

[1] Ealdwulf and Wulfstan II held the Sees of York and Worcester together, Ælfric Puttoc held both 1040-41 and Ealdred 1060–61.

1555	Nicholas Heath	661	Colman	1217	Richard Marsh
1561	Thomas Young	664	Tuda [Complications	1228	Richard Poore
1570	Edmund Grindal		involving Wilfrid and	1241	Nicholas Farnham
1577	Edwin Sandys		Chad]	1249	Walter Kirkham
1589	John Piers	681	Eata	1261	Robert Stichill
1595	Matthew Hutton	685	Cuthberht [Vacancy during	1274	Robert of Holy Island
1606	Tobias Matthew		which Wilfrid administered	1284	Anthony Bek
1628	George Monteigne [Mountain]		the See]	1311	Richard Kellaw
1629	Samuel Harsnett	688	Eadberht	1318	Lewis de Beaumont
1632	Richard Neile	698	Eadfenh	1333	Richard of Bury
1641	John Williams	731	Æthelweald	1345	Thomas Hatfield
1660	Accepted Frewen	740	Cynewulf	1382	John Fordham
1664	Richard Sterne	781	Higbald	1388	Walter Skirlaw
1683	John Dolben	803	Ecgberht	1406	Thomas Langley
1688	Thomas Lamplugh	821	Heathwred	1438	Robert Nevill
1691	John Sharp	830	Ecgred	1457	Lawrence Booth
1714	William Dawes	845	Eanberht	1476	William Dudley
1724	Lancelot Blackburn	854	Eardwulf	1485	John Shirwood
1743	Thomas Herring			1494	Richard Fox
1747	Matthew Hutton	**BISHOPS OF HEXHAM**		1502	William Senhouse [Sever]
1757	John Gilben			1507	Christopher Bainbridge
1761	Roben Hay Drummond	664	Wilfrith	1509	Thomas Ruthall
1777	William Markham	678	Eata	1523	Thomas Wolsey
1808	Edward Venables Vernon	681	Tunberht	1530	Cuthbert Tunstall
	Harcourt	684	Cuthbert	1561	James Pilkington
1847	Thomas Musgrave	685	Eata (restored)	1577	Richard Barnes
1860	Charles Thomas Longley	687	John of Beverley	1589	Matthew Hutton
1863	William Thomson	709	Acca	1595	Tobias Matthew
1891	William Connor Magee	734	Frithoberht	1606	William James
1891	William Dalrymple Maclagan	767	Ahimund	1617	Richard Neile
1909	Cosmo Gordon Lang	781	Tilberht	1628	George Monteigne [Mountain]
1929	William Temple	789	Æthelberht	1628	John Howson
1942	Cyril Forster Garbett	797	Heardred	1632	Thomas Morton
1956	Arthur Michael Ramsey	800	Eanberht	1660	John Cosin
1961	Frederick Donald Coggan	813	Tidferth	1674	Nathaniel Crew [Lord Crew]
1975	Stuart Yarworth Blanch			1721	William Talbot
1983	John Stapylton Habgood	**BISHOPS OF CHESTER-LE-STREET**[2]		1730	Edward Chandler
1995	David Michael Hope			1750	Joseph Butler
2005	John Tucker Mugabi Sentamu	899	Eardwulf	1752	Richard Trevor
2020	Stephen Geoffrey Cottrell	899	Cutheard	1771	John Egerton
		915	Tilred	1787	Thomas Thurlow
		925	Wigred	1791	Shute Barrington
		944	Uhtred	1826	William Van Mildert

Durham

Description of arms. Azure, a cross or between four lions rampant argent.

		944	Seaxhelm	1836	Edward Maltby
		944	Ealdred	1856	Charles Thomas Longley
		968	Ælfsige	1860	Henry Montagu Villiers
		990	Aldhun	1861	Charles Baring
				1879	Joseph Barber Lightfoot
		BISHOPS OF DURHAM		1890	Brooke Foss Westcott
				1901	Handley Carr Glyn Moule
		990	Aldhun d. 1018 [See vacant	1920	Herbert Hensley Henson
			1018–1020]	1939	Alwyn Terrell Petre Williams
		1020	Edmund	1952	Arthur Michael Ramsey
		c.1040	Eadred	1956	Maurice Henry Harland
		1041	Æthelric	1966	Ian Thomas Ramsey
BISHOPS OF LINDISFARNE[1]		1056	Æthelwine	1973	John Stapylton Habgood
		1071	Walcher	1984	David Edward Jenkins
635	Aidan	1081	William of Saint Calais	1994	Anthony Michael Arnold
651	Finan	1099	Ralph [Ranulf] Flambard		Turnbull
		1133	Geoffrey Rufus	2003	Nicholas Thomas Wright
		1143	William of Sainte-Barbe	2011	Justin Portal Welby
		1153	Hugh of le Puiset	2014	Paul Roger Butler
		1197	Philip of Poitiers		

Blackburn

Description of arms. Per fess gules and or, in chief two keys in saltire wards downwards argent, in base a rose of the first barbed and seeded proper.

1926	Percy Mark Herbert
1942	Wilfred Marcus Askwith
1954	Walter Hubert Baddeley
1960	Charles Robert Claxton
1972	Robert Arnold Schürhoff Martineau
1982	David Stewart Cross
1989	Alan David Chesters
2004	Nicholas Stewart Reade
2013	Julian Tudor Henderson

Bradford

Description of arms. Azure, two keys in saltire or, in chief a woolpack proper corded gold.

1920	Arthur William Thomson Perowne
1931	Alfred Walter Frank Blunt
1956	Frederick Donald Coggan
1961	Clement George St Michael Parker
1972	Ross Sydney Hook
1981	Geoffrey John Paul
1984	Robert Kerr Williamson
1992	David James Smith
2002	David Charles James
2011	Nicholas Baines
2014	Dissolved upon the creation of the new Diocese of Leeds (q.v.)

Carlisle

Description of arms. Argent, on a cross sable a labelled mitre or.

1133	Æthelwulf
1203	Bernard
1219	Hugh of Beaulieu
1224	Walter Mauclerc
1247	Silvester Everdon
1255	Thomas Vipont
1258	Robert de Chause
1280	Ralph Ireton
1292	John of Halton
1325	John Ross
1332	John Kirkby
1353	Gilbert Welton
1363	Thomas Appleby
1396	Robert Reade
1397	Thomas Merks
1400	William Strickland
1420	Roger Whelpdale
1424	William Barrow
1430	Marmaduke Lumley
1450	Nicholas Close
1452	William Percy
1462	John Kingscote
1464	Richard le Scrope
1468	Edward Story
1478	Richard Bell
1496	William Senhouse [Sever]
1504	Roger Layburne
1508	John Penny
1521	John Kite
1537	Robert Aldrich
1556	Owen Oglethorpe
1561	John Best
1570	Richard Barnes
1577	John May
1598	Henry Robinson
1616	Robert Snowden
1621	Richard Milbourne
1624	Richard Senhouse
1626	Francis White
1629	Barnabas Potter
1642	James Ussher
1660	Richard Sterne
1664	Edward Rainbowe
1684	Thomas Smith
1702	William Nicolson
1718	Samuel Bradford
1723	John Waugh
1735	George Fleming
1747	Richard Osbaldeston
1762	Charles Lyttleton
1769	Edmund Law
1787	John Douglas
1791	Edward Venables Vernon [Harcourt]
1808	Samuel Goodenough
1827	Hugh Percy
1856	Henry Montagu Villiers
1860	Samuel Waldegrave
1869	Harvey Goodwin
1892	John Wareing Bardsley
1905	John William Diggle
1920	Henry Herbert Williams
1946	Thomas Bloomer
1966	Sydney Cyril Bulley
1972	Henry David Halsey
1989	Ian Harland
2000	Geoffrey Graham Dow
2009	James William Scobie Newcome

Chester

Description of arms. Gules, three labelled mitres or.

1541	John Bird
1554	George Cotes
1556	Cuthbert Scott
1561	William Downham
1579	William Chaderton
1595	Hugh Bellott
1597	Richard Vaughan
1604	George Lloyd
1616	Thomas Morton
1619	John Bridgeman
1660	Brian Walton
1662	Henry Ferne
1662	George Hall
1668	John Wilkins
1673	John Pearson
1686	Thomas Cartwright
1689	Nicolas Stratford
1708	William Dawes
1714	Francis Gastrell
1726	Samuel Peploe
1752	Edmund Keene
1771	William Markham
1777	Beilby Porteus
1788	William Cleaver
1800	Henry William Majendie
1810	Bowyer Edward Sparke
1812	George Henry Law
1824	Charles James Blomfield
1828	John Bird Sumner
1848	John Graham
1865	William Jacobson
1884	William Stubbs
1889	Francis John Jayne
1919	Henry Luke Paget
1932	Geoffrey Francis Fisher
1939	Douglas Henry Crick
1955	Gerald Alexander Ellison
1974	Hubert Victor Whitsey
1982	Michael Alfred Baughen
1996	Peter Robert Forster
2020	Mark Simon Austin Tanner

Leeds

Description of arms. Azure a cross formy throughout the limbs in pale taking the form of a Greek rho or, in the first quarter a rose argent barbed and seeded proper.

2014	Nicholas Baines

Liverpool

Description of arms. Argent, an eagle with wings expanded sable, holding in its dexter claw an ancient inkhorn proper, around its head a nimbus or, a chief paly azure and gules, the dexter charged with an open book or, inscribed with the words 'Thy Word is Truth', the sinister charged with a lymphad gold.

1880	John Charles Ryle
1900	Francis James Chavasse
1923	Albert Augustus David
1944	Clifford Arthur Martin
1966	Stuart Yarworth Blanch
1975	David Stuart Sheppard
1998	James Stuart Jones
2014	Paul Bayes
2022	*vacant*

Manchester

Description of arms. Or, on a pale engrailed gules three mitres of the first, on a canton of the second three bendlets enhanced gold.

1848	James Prince Lee
1870	James Fraser
1886	James Moorhouse
1903	Edmund Arbuthnott Knox
1921	William Temple
1929	Frederic Sumpter Guy Warman
1947	William Derrick Lindsay Greer
1970	Patrick Campbell Rodger
1979	Stanley Eric Francis Booth-Clibborn
1993	Christopher John Mayfield
2002	Nigel Simeon McCulloch
2013	David Stuart Walker

Newcastle

Description of arms. Gules, a cross between four lions rampant or, on a chief gold three triple-towered castles of the first.

1882	Ernest Roland Wilberforce
1896	Edgar Jacob
1903	Arthur Thomas Lloyd
1907	Norman Dumenil John Straton
1915	Herbert Louis Wild
1927	Harold Ernest Bilbrough
1941	Noel Baring Hudson
1957	Hugh Edward Ashdown
1973	Ronald Oliver Bowlby
1981	Andrew Alexander Kenny Graham
1997	John Martin Wharton
2015	Christine Elizabeth Hardman
2021	*vacant*

Ripon and Leeds (Ripon until 1999)

Description of arms. Argent, on a saltire gules two keys wards upwards or, on a chief of the second a Holy Lamb proper.

*c.*678	Eadheath
	NEW FOUNDATION
1836	Charles Thomas Longley
1857	Robert Bickersteth
1884	William Boyd Carpenter
1912	Thomas Wortley Drury
1920	Thomas Banks Strong
1926	Edward Arthur Burroughs
1935	Geoffrey Charles Lester Lunt
1946	George Armitage Chase
1959	John Richard Humpidge Moorman
1975	Stuart Hetley Price
1977	David Nigel de Lorentz Young
2000	John Richard Packer
2014	Dissolved upon the creation of the new Diocese of Leeds (q.v.)

Sheffield

Description of arms. Azure, a crosier in pale ensigned by a fleur-de-lis vert, between in fess a key surmounted by a sword in saltire to the dexter, and to the sinister eight arrows interlaced and banded saltirewise, all or.

1914	Leonard Hedley Burrows
1939	Leslie Stannard Hunter
1962	Francis John Taylor
1971	William Gordon Fallows
1980	David Ramsay Lunn
1997	John Nicholls
2009	Steven John Lindsey Croft
2017	Peter Jonathan Wilcox

Sodor and Man[1]

Description of arms. Argent, upon a pedestal between two coronetted pillars the Virgin Mary with arms extended, in her dexter hand a church proper and in base upon an escutcheon, surmounted by a mitre, the arms of Man – viz. gules, three legs in armour conjoined at the thigh and flexed at the knee.

447	Germanus
	Conindrius
	Romulus
	Machutus
	Conanus
	Contentus
	Baldus
	Malchus
	Torkinus
	Brendanus
	[Before 1080 Roolwer]
	William
	Hamond
1113	Wimund
1151	John
1160	Gamaliel
	Ragnald
	Christian of Argyle
	Michael
1203	Nicholas de Meaux
	Nicholas II
1217	Reginald
1226	John
1229	Simon of Argyle
1252	Richard
1275	Mark of Galloway
1305	Alan
1321	Gilbert Maclelan
1329	Bernard de Linton

---

[1] Included in the province of York by Act of Parliament 1542. Prior to Richard Oldham there is some uncertainty as to several names and dates. From 1425 to 1553 there was an English and Scottish succession. It is not easy to say which claimant was Bishop either *de jure* or *de facto*.

1334	Thomas
1348	William Russell
1387	John Donegan
1387	Michael
1392	John Sproten
1402	Conrad
1402	Theodore Bloc
1429	Richard Messing Andrew
1435	John Seyre
1455	Thomas Burton
1458	Thomas Kirklam
1472	Angus
1478	Richard Oldham
1487	Hugh Blackleach
1513	Hugh Hesketh
1523	John Howden
1546	Henry Man
1556	Thomas Stanley
1570	John Salisbury
1576	John Meyrick
1600	George Lloyd
1605	John Philips
1634	William Forster
1635	Richard Parr
1661	Samuel Rutter
1663	Isaac Barrow
1671	Henry Bridgman
1683	John Lake
1685	Baptist Levinz
1698	Thomas Wilson
1755	Mark Hildesley
1773	Richard Richmond
1780	George Mason
1784	Claudius Crigan
1814	George Murray
1828	William Ward
1838	James Bowstead
1840	Henry Pepys
1841	Thomas Vowler Short
1847	Walter Augustus Shirley
1847	Robert John Eden
1854	Horatio Powys
1877	Rowley Hill
1887	John Wareing Bardsley

1892	Norman Dumenil John Straton
1907	Thomas Wortley Drury
1912	James Denton Thompson
1925	Charles Leonard Thornton-Duesbery
1928	William Stanton Jones
1943	John Ralph Strickland Taylor
1954	Benjamin Pollard
1966	George Eric Gordon
1974	Vernon Sampson Nicholls
1983	Arthur Henry Attwell
1989	Noël Debroy Jones
2003	Graeme Paul Knowles
2008	Robert Mar Erskine Paterson
2017	Peter Andrew Eagles

Southwell and Nottingham (Southwell until 2005)

Description of arms. Sable, three fountains proper, on a chief or a pale azure, charged with a representation of the Virgin Mary seated bearing the Infant Christ or between a stag lodged proper and two staves raguly crossed vert.

1884	George Ridding
1904	Edwyn Hoskyns
1926	Bernard Oliver Francis Heywood

1928	Henry Mosley
1941	Frank Russell Barry
1964	Gordon David Savage
1970	John Denis Wakeling
1985	Michael Humphrey Dickens Whinney
1988	Patrick Burnet Harris
1999	George Henry Cassidy
2009	Paul Roger Butler
2015	Paul Gavin Williams

Wakefield

Description of arms. Or, a fleur-de-lis azure, on a chief of the last three celestial crowns gold.

1888	William Walsham How
1897	George Rodney Eden
1928	James Buchanan Seaton
1938	Campbell Richard Hone
1946	Henry McGowan
1949	Roger Plumpton Wilson
1958	John Alexander Ramsbotham
1968	Eric Treacy
1977	Colin Clement Walter James
1985	David Michael Hope
1992	Nigel Simeon McCulloch
2003	Stephen George Platten
2014	Dissolved upon the creation of the new Diocese of Leeds (q.v.)

BISHOPS SUFFRAGAN IN ENGLAND

Alnwick (Newcastle)

never filled

Aston (Birmingham)

1954	Clement George St Michael Parker
1962	David Brownfield Porter
1972	Mark Green
1982	Michael Humphrey Dickens Whinney
1985	Colin Ogilvie Buchanan
1989–92	*no appointment*
1992	John Michael Austin
2005–2008	*no appointment*
2008	Andrew John Watson
2015	Anne Elizabeth Hollinghurst

Aylesbury (Oxford)

never filled

Barking (Chelmsford)

[in St Albans diocese to 1914]

1901	Thomas Stevens
1919	James Theodore Inskip
1948	Hugh Rowlands Gough
1959	William Frank Percival Chadwick
1975	Albert James Adams
1983	James William Roxburgh
1991	Roger Frederick Sainsbury

2002	David John Leader Hawkins
2014	Peter Hill
2021	*vacant*

Barrow-in-Furness (Carlisle)

1889	Henry Ware
1909	Campbell West-Watson
1926	Henry Sidney Pelham
1944	*in abeyance*

Basingstoke (Winchester)

1973	Colin Clement Walter James
1977	Michael Richard John Manktelow
1994	Douglas Geoffrey Rowell
2002	Trevor Willmott
2010	Peter Hancock
2014	David Grant Williams

Bedford (St Albans)

1537	John Hodgkins[1]
1560–1879	*in abeyance*
1879	William Walsham How[2]
1888	Robert Claudius Billing[3]
1898–1935	*in abeyance*
1935	James Lumsden Barkway
1939	Aylmer Skelton
1948	Claude Thomas Thellusson Wood
1953	Angus Campbell MacInnes
1957	Basil Tudor Guy

1963	Albert John Trillo
1968	John Tyrrell Holmes Hare
1977	Andrew Alexander Kenny Graham
1981	David John Farmbrough
1994	John Henry Richardson
2003	Richard Neil Inwood
2012	Richard William Bryant Atkinson

Berwick (Newcastle)

[in Durham diocese to 2016]

1536	Thomas Sparke
1572–2016	*in abeyance*
2016	Mark Simon Austin Tanner
2021	Mark Wroe

Beverley (York)

1889	Robert Jarratt Crosthwaite
1923–94	*in abeyance*
1994	John Scott Gaisford
2000	Martyn William Jarrett
2013	Glyn Hamilton Webster
2022	*vacant*

Birkenhead (Chester)

1965	Eric Arthur John Mercer
1974	Ronald Brown
1993	Michael Laurence Langrish
2000	David Andrew Urquhart
2007	Gordon Keith Sinclair
2021	Julie Anne Conalty

[1] Appointed for the diocese of London.   [2] Appointed for the diocese of London.
[3] Appointed for the diocese of London, and retained title after resigning his suffragan duties in 1895.

Bishopwearmouth (Durham)

never filled

Bolton (Manchester)

1984	David George Galliford
1991	David Bonser
1999	David Keith Gillett
2008	Christopher Paul Edmondson
2016	Mark David Ashcroft

Boston (Lincoln)

never filled

Bradford (Leeds)

2014	Toby Matthew Howarth

Bradwell (Chelmsford)

1968	William Neville Welch
1973	John Gibbs
1976	Charles Derek Bond
1993	Laurence Alexander Green
2011	John Michael Wraw
2018	John Perumbalath

Bridgewater (Bath and Wells)

never filled

Bristol (Worcester)

1538	Henry Holbeach [Rands]
1542	*became diocesan see*

Brixworth (Peterborough)

1989	Paul Everard Barber
2002	Francis White
2011	John Edward Holbrook

Buckingham (Oxford)

1914	Edward Domett Shaw
1921	Philip Herbert Eliot
1944	Robert Milton Hay
1960	Gordon David Savage
1964	George Christopher Cutts Pepys
1974	Simon Hedley Burrows
1994	Colin James Bennetts
1998	Michael Arthur Hill
2003	Alan Thomas Lawrence Wilson

Burnley (Blackburn)

[in Manchester diocese to 1926]

1901	Edwyn Hoskyns
1905	Alfred Pearson
1909	Henry Henn
1931	Edgar Priestley Swain
1950	Charles Keith Kipling Prosser
1955	George Edward Holderness
1970	Richard Charles Challinor Watson
1988	Ronald James Milner
1994	Martyn William Jarrett
2000	John William Goddard
2015	Philip John North

Cambridge (Ely)

never filled

Chelsea (London)

never filled

Cirencester (Gloucester)

never filled

Colchester (Chelmsford)

[in London diocese to 1845
in Rochester diocese to 1877
in St Albans diocese 1877–1914]

1536	William More
1541–91	*in abeyance*
1592	John Sterne
1608–1882	*in abeyance*
1882	Alfred Blomfield
1894	Henry Frank Johnson
1909	Robert Henry Whitcombe
1922	Thomas Alfred Chapman
1933	Charles Henry Ridsdale
1946	Frederick Dudley Vaughan Narborough
1966	Roderic Norman Coote
1988	Michael Edwin Vickers
1995	Edward Holland
2001	Christopher Heudebourck Morgan
2014	Roger Anthony Brett Morris

Coventry (Worcester)

see also under Lichfield

1891	Henry Bond Bowlby
1894	Edmund Arbuthnott Knox
1903–18	*no appointment*
1918	*became diocesan see*

Crediton (Exeter)

1897	Robert Edward Trefusis
1930	William Frederick Surtees
1954	Wilfred Arthur Edmund Westall
1974	Philip John Pasterfield
1984	Peter Everard Coleman
1996	Richard Stephen Hawkins
2004	Robert John Scott Evens
2012	Nicholas Howard Paul McKinnel
2015	Sarah Elisabeth Mullally
2018	Jacqueline Ann Searle

Croydon (Southwark)

(in Canterbury diocese to 1985)

1904	Henry Horace Pereira
1924–30	*no appointment*
1930	Edward Sydney Woods
1937	William Louis Anderson
1942	Maurice Henry Harland
1947	Cuthbert Killick Norman Bardsley
1957	John Taylor Hughes
1977	Geoffrey Stuart Snell
1985	Wilfred Denniston Wood
2003	Nicholas Baines
2012	Jonathan Dunnett Clark

Derby (Southwell)

1889	Edward Ash Were
1909	Charles Thomas Abraham
1927	*became diocesan see*

Doncaster (Sheffield)

1972	Stuart Hetley Price
1976	David Stewart Cross
1982	William Michael Dermot Persson
1993	Michael Frederick Gear
2000	Cyril Guy Ashton
2012	Peter Burrows
2020	Sophie Rebecca Jelley

Dorchester (Oxford)

see also under Dorchester (*diocesan see*) *and* Lincoln

1939	Gerald Burton Allen
1952	Kenneth Riches
1957	David Goodwin Loveday

1972	Peter Knight Walker
1979	Conrad John Eustace Meyer
1988	Anthony John Russell
2000	Colin William Fletcher
2021	Gavin Andrew Collins

Dorking (Guildford)

[in Winchester diocese to 1927]

1905	Cecil Henry Boutflower
1909–68	*in abeyance*
1968	Kenneth Dawson Evans
1986	David Peter Wilcox
1996	Ian James Brackley
2016	Joanne Caladine Bailey Wells

Dover (Canterbury)

1537	Richard Yngworth
1545	Richard Thornden
1557–69	*no appointment*
1569	Richard Rogers
1597–1870	*in abeyance*
1870	Edward Parry
1890	George Rodney Eden
1898	William Walsh
1916	Harold Ernest Bilbrough
1927	John Victor Macmillan
1935	Alfred Careywollaston Rose
1957	Lewis Evan Meredith
1964	Anthony Paul Tremlett
1980	Richard Henry McPhail Third
1992	John Richard Allan Llewellin
1999	Stephen Squires Venner
2010	Trevor Willmott
2019	Rose Josephine Hudson-Wilkin

Dudley (Worcester)

1974	Michael Ashley Mann
1977	Anthony Charles Dumper
1993	Rupert William Noel Hoare
2000	David Stuart Walker
2014	Graham Barham Usher
2020	Martin Charles William Gorick

Dunwich (St Edmundsbury and Ipswich)

see also under Norwich

1934	Maxwell Homfray Maxwell-Gumbleton
1945	Clement Mallory Ricketts
1955	Thomas Herbert Cashmore
1967	David Rokeby Maddock
1977	William Johnston
1980	Eric Nash Devenport
1992	Jonathan Sansbury Bailey
1995	Timothy John Stevens
1999	Clive Young
2016	Michael Robert Harrison

Ebbsfleet (Canterbury)

1994	John Richards
1998	Michael Alan Houghton
2000	Andrew Burnham
2011	Jonathan Mark Richard Baker
2013	Jonathan Michael Goodall
2021	*vacant*

Edmonton (London)

1970	Alan Francis Bright Rogers
1975	William John Westwood
1985	Brian John Masters
1999	Peter William Wheatley
2015	Robert James Wickham

Europe (Europe)

1980	Ambrose Walter Marcus Weekes
1986	Edward Holland
1995	Henry William Scriven
2002	David Hamid

Fulham (London)[1]

1926	Basil Staunton Batty
1947	William Marshall Selwyn
1949	George Ernest Ingle
1955	Robert Wright Stopford
1957	Roderic Norman Coote
1966	Alan Francis Bright Rogers
1970	John Richard Satterthwaite[2]
1980–1982	no appointment
1982	Brian John Masters
1985	Charles John Klyberg
1996	John Charles Broadhurst
2013	Jonathan Mark Richard Baker

Grantham (Lincoln)

1905	Welbore MacCarthy
1920	John Edward Hine
1930	Ernest Morell Blackie
1935	Arthur Ivan Greaves
1937	Algernon Augustus Markham
1949	Anthony Otter
1965	Ross Sydney Hook
1972	Dennis Gascoyne Hawker
1987	William Ind
1997	Alastair Llewellyn John Redfern
2006	Timothy William Ellis
2015	Nicholas Alan Chamberlain

Grimsby (Lincoln)

1935	Ernest Morell Blackie
1937	Anhur Ivan Greaves
1958	Kenneth Healey
1966	Gerald Fitzmaurice Colin
1979	David Tustin
2000	David Douglas James Rossdale
2014	David Eric Court

Guildford (Winchester)

1874	John Sutton Utterton
1888	George Henry Sumner
1909	John Hugh Granville Randolph
1927	became diocesan see

Halifax (Leeds)

never filled

Hertford (St Albans)

1968	Albert John Trillo
1971	Hubert Victor Whitsey
1974	Peter Mumford
1982	Kenneth Harold Pillar
1990	Robin Jonathan Norman Smith
2001	Christopher Richard James Foster
2010	Paul Bayes
2015	Noel Michael Roy Beasley

Hexham (Newcastle)

never filled

Horsham (Chichester)

1968	Simon Wilton Phipps
1975	Ivor Colin Docker
1991	John William Hind
1993	Lindsay Goodall Urwin
2009	Mark Crispin Rake Sowerby
2020	Ruth Kathleen Frances Bushyager

Huddersfield (Leeds)

2014	Jonathan Robert Gibbs

Hull (York)

1538	Robert Sylvester (Pursglove)
1579–1891	in abeyance
1891	Richard Frederick Lefevre Blunt
1910	John Augustus Kempthome
1913	Francis Gurdon
1929–31	no appointment
1931	Bemard Oliver Francis Heywood
1934	Henry Townsend Vodden
1957	George Fredenck Townley
1965	Hubert Laurence Higgs
1977	Geoffrey John Paul
1981	Donald George Snelgrove
1994	James Stuart Jones
1998	Richard Michael Cockayne Frith
2015	Alison Mary White

Hulme (Manchester)

1924	John Charles Hill
1930	Thomas Sherwood Jones
1945	Hugh Leycester Homby
1953	Kenneth Venner Ramsey
1975	David George Galliford
1984	Colin John Fraser Scott
1999	Stephen Richard Lowe
2009	vacant

Huntingdon (Ely)

1966	Robert Arnold Schürhoff Martineau
1972	Eric St Quintin Wall
1980	William Gordon Roe
1997	John Robert Flack
2003	John Geoffrey Inge
2008	David Thomson
2019	Dagmar Winter

Ipswich (Norwich)

1536	Thomas Manning[3]
?–1899	in abeyance[4]
1899	George Carnac Fisher
1906	Henry Luke Paget
1909	no appointment
1914	became diocesan see with St Edmundsbury

Isle of Wight (Portsmouth)

never filled

Islington (London)

1898	Charles Henry Turner
1923–2015	in abeyance
2015	Richard Charles Thorpe

Jarrow (Durham)

1906	George Nickson
1914	John Nathaniel Quirk
1924	Samuel Kirshbaum Knight
1932	James Geoffrey Gordon
1939	Leslie Owen
1944	David Colin Dunlop
1950	John Alexander Ramsbotham
1958	Mervyn Armstrong
1965	Alexander Kenneth Hamilton
1980	Michael Thomas Ball
1990	Alan Smithson
2002	John Lawrence Pritchard
2007	Mark Watts Bryant
2019	Sarah Elizabeth Clark

Kendal (Carlisle)

never filled

Kensington (London)

1901	Frederic Edward Ridgeway
1911	John Primatt Maud
1932	Bertram Fitzgerald Simpson
1942	Henry Colville Montgomery Campbell
1949	Cyril Eastaugh
1962	Edward James Keymer Roberts
1964	Ronald Cedric Osbourne Goodchild
1981	Mark Santer
1987	John George Hughes
1994–96	no appointment
1996	Michael John Colclough
2009	Paul Gavin Williams
2015	Graham Stuart Tomlin

Kingston-upon-Thames (Southwark)

1905	Cecil Hook
1915	Samuel Mumford Taylor
1922	Percy Mark Herbert
1927	Frederick Ochterlony Taylor Hawkes
1952	William Percy Gilpin
1970	Hugh William Montefiore
1978	Keith Norman Sutton
1984	Peter Stephen Maurice Selby
1992	John Martin Wharton
1997	Peter Bryan Price
2002	Richard Ian Cheetham

Kirkstall (Leeds)

formerly Richmond
2015	Paul John Slater

Knaresborough (Ripon)

1905	Lucius Frederick Moses Bottomley Smith
1934	Paul Fulcrand Dalacour de Labilliere
1938	John Norman Bateman-Champain
1948	Henry Handley Vully de Candole
1965	John Howard Cruse
1972	Ralph Emmerson
1979	John Dennis
1986	Malcolm James Menin
1997	Frank Valentine Weston
2004	James Harold Bell
2014	renamed Ripon

Lancaster (Blackburn)

1936	Benjamin Pollard
1955	Anthony Leigh Egerton Hoskyns-Abrahall
1975	Dennis Fountain Page
1985	Ian Harland
1990	John Nicholls
1998	Geoffrey Stephen Pedley
2006	Geoffrey Seagrave Pearson
2018	Jillian Louise Calland Duff

Leicester (Peterborough)

see also under Lichfield and Lincoln
1888	Francis Henry Thicknesse
1903	Lewis Clayton
1913	Norman MacLeod Lang
1927	became diocesan see

Leominster (Hereford)

never filled

---

[1] From 1926 to 1980 exercised the Bishop of London's extra-diocesan jurisdiction over chaplaincies in Northern and Central Europe. Since 1996 has assisted the Diocesan Bishop in all matters not delegated to the Areas, and in pastoral care of parishes operating under the London Plan.
[2] Bishop of Fulham and Gibraltar.   [3] Manning does not appear to have acted as a suffragan bishop in the diocese of Norwich.
[4] The date of Manning's death is not known.

Lewes (Chichester)

1909	Leonard Hedley Burrows
1914	Herbert Edward Jones
1920	Henry Kemble Southwell
1926	Thomas William Cook
1929	William Champion Streatfield
1929	Hugh Maudsley Hordern
1946	Geoffrey Hodgson Warde
1959	James Herbert Lloyd Morrell
1977	Peter John Ball
1992	Ian Patrick Martyn Cundy
1997	Wallace Parke Benn
2014	Richard Charles Jackson
2020	William Peter Guy Hazlewood

Loughborough (Leicester)

2017	Gulnar Eleanor Francis-Dehqani
2021	*vacant*

Ludlow (Hereford)

1981	Stanley Mark Wood
1987	Ian Macdonald Griggs
1994	John Charles Saxbee
2002	Michael Wrenford Hooper
2009	Alistair James Magowan
2020	*dissolved*

Lynn (Norwich)

1963	William Somers Llewellyn
1972	William Aubrey Aitken
1986	David Edward Bentley
1994	David John Conner
1999	Anthony Charles Foottit
2004	James Henry Langstaff
2011	Cyril Jonathan Meyrick
2021	Jane Elizabeth Steen

Maidstone (Canterbury)

1944	Leslie Owen
1946–56	*no appointment*
1956	Stanley Woodley Betts
1966–69	*no appointment*
1969	Geoffrey Lewis Tiarks
1976	Richard Henry McPhail Third
1980	Robert Maynard Hardy
1987	David James Smith
1992	Gavin Hunter Reid
2001	Graham Alan Cray
2009–2015	*no appointment*
2015	Roderick Charles Howell Thomas

Malmesbury (Bristol)

1927	Ronald Erskine Ramsay
1946	Ivor Stanley Watkins
1956	Edward James Keymer Roberts
1962	Clifford Leofric Purdy Bishop
1973	Frederick Stephen Temple
1983	Peter James Firth
1994	*renamed* Swindon

Marlborough

1537	Thomas Morley (Bickley)[1]
c.1561–1888	*in abeyance*
1888	Alfred Earle[2]
1919	*in abeyance*

Middleton (Manchester)

1927	Richard Godfrey Parsons
1932	Cecil Wilfred Wilson
1938	Arthur Fawssett Alston
1943	Edward Worsfold Mowll
1952	Frank Woods
1958	Robert Nelson
1959	Edward Ralph Wickham

1982	Donald Alexander Tytler
1994	Stephen Squires Venner
1999	Michael Augustine Owen Lewis
2008	Mark Davies

Molton (Exeter)

never filled

Northampton (Peterborough)

never filled

Nottingham (Lincoln)

[in York diocese to 1837]

1567	Richard Barnes
1570–1870	*in abeyance*
1870	Henry Mackenzie
1877	Edward Trollope
1893	*in abeyance*

Oswestry (Lichfield)

never filled

Penrith (Carlisle)

see also under Richmond

1537	John Bird[3]
1539–1888	*in abeyance*
1888	John James Pulleine[4]
1939	Grandage Edwards Powell
1944	Herbert Victor Turner
1959	Sydney Cyril Bulley
1967	Reginald Foskett
1970	William Edward Augustus Pugh
1979	George Lanyon Hacker
1994	Richard Garrard
2002	James William Scobie Newcome
2011	Robert John Freeman
2019	Emma Gwynneth Ineson
2021	*vacant*

Plymouth (Exeter)

1923	John Howard Bertram Masterman
1934	Francis Whitfield Daukes
1950	Norman Harry Clarke
1962	Wilfred Guy Sanderson
1972	Richard Fox Cartwright
1982	Kenneth Albert Newing
1988	Richard Stephen Hawkins
1996	John Henry Garton
2005	John Frank Ford
2015	Nicholas Howard Paul McKinnel

Pontefract (Wakefield)

1931	Campbell Richard Hone
1939	Tom Longworth
1949	Arthur Harold Morris
1954	George William Clarkson
1961	Eric Treacy
1968	William Gordon Fallows
1971	Thomas Richard Hare
1993	John Thornley Finney
1998	David Charles James
2002	Anthony William Robinson
2014	*renamed* Wakefield

Ramsbury (Salisbury)

see also under Salisbury

1974	John Robert Geoffrey Neale
1989	Peter St George Vaughan
1999	Peter Fearnley Hullah
2006	Stephen David Conway
2012	Edward Francis Condry
2019	Andrew Paul Rumsey

Reading (Oxford)

1889	James Leslie Randall
1909–42	*in abeyance*
1942	Arthur Groom Parham
1954	Eric Henry Knell
1972	Eric Wild
1982	Ronald Graham Gregory Foley
1989	John Frank Ewan Bone
1997	Edward William Murray Walker
2004	Stephen Geoffrey Cottrell
2011	Andrew John Proud
2019	Olivia Josephine Graham

Repton (Derby)

1965	William Warren Hunt
1977	Stephen Edmund Verney
1986	Francis Henry Arthur Richmond
1999	David Christopher Hawtin
2007	Humphrey Ivo John Southern
2016	Janet Elizabeth McFarlane
2021	William Malcolm Macnaughton

Richborough (Canterbury)

1995	Edwin Ronald Barnes
2002	Keith Newton
2011	Norman Banks

Richmond (Leeds)

1889	John James Pulleine[5]
1913	Francis Charles Kilner
1921–2015	*in abeyance*
2015	Paul John Slater
2018	*renamed* Kirkstall

Ripon (Leeds)

formerly Knaresborough

2004	James Harold Bell
2018	Helen-Ann Macleod Hartley

Rochdale (Manchester)

never filled

St Germans (Truro)

1905	John Rundle Cornish
1918–74	*in abeyance*
1974	Cecil Richard Rutt
1979	Reginald Lindsay Fisher
1985	John Richard Allan Llewellin
1993	Graham Richard James
2000	Royden Screech
2013	Christopher David Goldsmith
2020	Hugh Edmund Nelson

Selby (York)

1939	Henry St John Stirling Woollcombe
1941	Carey Frederick Knyvett
1962	Douglas Noel Sargent
1972	Morris Henry St John Maddocks
1983	Clifford Conder Barker
1991	Humphrey Vincent Taylor
2003	Martin William Wallace
2014	John Bromilow Thomson

Shaftesbury (Salisbury)

[in Bristol diocese 1542–1836]

1539	John Bradley
?	*in abeyance*[6]

Sheffield (York)

1901	John Nathaniel Quirk
1914	*became diocesan see*

---

[1] Appointed for the diocese of London.   [2] Appointed for the diocese of London, but retained the title while Dean of Exeter 1900–18.
[3] Appointed for the diocese of Lichfield.   [4] Appointed for the diocese of Ripon.
[5] His suffragan title was changed from Penrith to Richmond by Royal Warrant.   [6] The date of Bradley's death is not known.

Sherborne (Salisbury)

1925	Robert Crowther Abbott
1928	Gerald Burton Allen
1936	Harold Nickinson Rodgers
1947	John Maurice Key
1960	Victor Joseph Pike
1976	John Dudley Galtrey Kirkham
2001	Timothy Martin Thornton
2009	Graham Ralph Kings
2016	Karen Marisa Gorham

Sherwood (Southwell)

1965	Kenneth George Thompson
1975	Harold Richard Darby
1989	Alan Wyndham Morgan
2006	Anthony Porter
2020	Andew Neil Emerton

Shrewsbury (Lichfield)

1537	Lewis Thomas[1]
1561–1888	*in abeyance*
1888	Sir Lovelace Tomlinson Stamer
1905–40	*in abeyance*
1940	Eric Knightley Chetwode Hamilton
1944	Robert Leighton Hodson
1959	William Alonzo Parker
1970	Francis William Cocks
1980	Leslie Lloyd Rees
1987	John Dudley Davies
1994	David Marrison Hallatt
2001	Alan Gregory Clayton Smith
2009	Mark James Rylands
2019	Sarah Ruth Bullock

Southampton (Winchester)

1895	William Awdry
1896	George Carnac Fisher
1898	The Hon Arthur Temple Lyttelton
1903	James Macarthur
1921	Cecil Henry Boutflower
1933	Arthur Baillie Lumsdaine Karney
1943	Edmund Robert Morgan
1951	Kenneth Edward Norman Lamplugh
1972	John Kingsmill Cavell
1984	Edward David Cartwright
1989	John Freeman Perry
1996	Jonathan Michael Gledhill
2004	Paul Roger Butler
2010	Jonathan Hugh Frost
2019	Deborah Mary Sellin

Southwark (Rochester)

1891	Huyshe Wolcott Yeatman-Biggs
1905	*became diocesan see*

Stafford (Lichfield)

1909	Edward Ash Were
1915	Lionel Payne Crawfurd
1934	Douglas Henry Crick
1938	Lemprière Durell Hammond
1958	Richard George Clitherow
1975	John Waine
1979	John Stevens Waller
1987	Michael Charles Scott-Joynt
1996	Christopher John Hill
2005	Alfred Gordon Mursell
2010	Geoffrey Peter Annas
2021	Matthew John Parker

Stepney (London)

1895	George Forrest Browne
1897	Arthur Foley Winnington-Ingram

Stockport (Chester)

1901	Cosmo Gordon Lang
1909	Henry Luke Paget
1919	Henry Mosley
1928	Charles Edward Curzon
1936	Robert Hamilton Moberly
1952	Joost de Blank
1957	Francis Evered Lunt
1968	Ernest Urban Trevor Huddleston
1978	James Lawton Thompson
1992	Richard John Carew Chartres
1996	John Mugabi Sentamu
2003	Stephen John Oliver
2011	Adrian Newman
2019	Joanne Woolway Grenfell

Stockport (Chester)

1949	Frank Jackson Okell
1951	David Henry Saunders Saunders-Davies
1965	Rupert Gordon Strutt
1984	Frank Pilkington Sargeant
1994	Geoffrey Martin Turner
2000	William Nigel Stock
2008	Robert Ronald Atwell
2015	Elizabeth Jane Holden Lane
2021	Samuel Jon Clint Corley

Swindon (Bristol)

formerly Malmesbury

1994	Michael David Doe
2005	Lee Stephen Rayfield

Taunton (Bath and Wells)

1538	William Finch
1559–1911	*in abeyance*
1911	Charles Fane de Salis
1931	George Arthur Hollis
1945	Harry Thomas
1955	Mark Allin Hodson
1962	Francis Horner West
1977	Peter John Nott
1986	Nigel Simeon McCulloch
1992	John Hubert Richard Lewis
1997	William Allen Stewart
1998	Andrew John Radford
2006	Peter David Maurice
2015	Ruth Elizabeth Worsley

Tewkesbury (Gloucester)

1938	Augustine John Hodson
1955	Edward Barry Henderson
1960	Forbes Trevor Horan
1973	Thomas Carlyle Joseph Robert Hamish Deakin
1986	Geoffrey David Jeremy Walsh
1996	John Stewart Went
2013	Martyn James Snow
2016	Robert Wilfred Springett

Thetford (Norwich)

see also under Norwich

1536	John Salisbury
1570–1894	*in abeyance*
1894	Arthur Thomas Lloyd
1903	John Philips Alcott Bowers
1926–45	*no appointment*
1945	John Walker Woodhouse
1953	Martin Patrick Grainge Leonard
1963	Eric William Bradley Cordingly
1977	Hugh Charles Blackburne
1981	Timothy Dudley-Smith
1992	Hugo Ferdinand de Waal
2001	David John Atkinson
2009	Alan Peter Winton

Tonbridge (Rochester)

1959	Russell Berridge White
1968	Henry David Halsey
1973	Philip Harold Ernest Goodrich
1982	David Henry Bartleet
1993	Brian Arthur Smith
2002	Brian Colin Castle
2018	Simon David Burton-Jones

Wakefield (Leeds)

formerly Pontefract

2014	Anthony William Robinson

Warrington (Liverpool)

1918	Martin Linton Smith
1920	Edwin Hone Kempson
1927	Herbert Gresford Jones
1946	Charles Robert Claxton
1960	Laurence Ambrose Brown
1970	John Monier Bickersteth
1976	Michael Henshall
1996	John Richard Packer
2000	David Wilfred Michael Jennings
2009	Richard Finn Blackburn
2018	Beverly Anne Mason

Warwick (Coventry)

1980	Keith Appleby Arnold
1990	Clive Handford
1996	Anthony Martin Priddis
2005	John Ronald Angus Stroyan

Whalley (Blackburn)

[in Manchester diocese to 1926]

1909	Atherton Gwillym Rawstorne
1936	*in abeyance*

Whitby (York)

1923	Harry St John Stirling Woollcombe
1939	Harold Evelyn Hubbard
1947	Walter Hubert Baddeley
1954	Philip William Wheeldon
1961	George D'Oyly Snow
1972	John Yates
1976	Clifford Conder Barker
1983	Gordon Bates
1999	Robert Sidney Ladds
2010	Martin Clive Warner
2014	Paul John Ferguson

Wigan (Liverpool)

never filled

Willesden (London)

1911	William Willcox Perrin
1929	Guy Vernon Smith
1940	Henry Colville Montgomery Campbell
1942	Edward Michael Gresford Jones
1950	Gerald Alexander Ellison
1955	George Ernest Ingle
1964	Graham Douglas Leonard
1974	Geoffrey Hewlett Thompson
1985	Thomas Frederick Butler
1992	Geoffrey Graham Dow
2001	Peter Alan Broadbent
2021	*vacant*

Wolverhampton (Lichfield)

1979	Barry Rogerson
1985	Christopher John Mayfield
1994	Michael Gay Bourke
2007	Clive Malcolm Gregory

[1] Not appointed for Lichfield, but probably for Llandaff.

Woolwich (Southwark)

1905	John Cox Leeke
1918	William Woodcock Hough
1932	Arthur Llewellyn Preston
1936	Leslie Hamilton Lang

1947	Robert William Stannard
1959	John Arthur Thomas Robinson
1969	David Stuart Sheppard
1975	Michael Eric Marshall
1984	Albert Peter Hall

1996	Colin Ogilvie Buchanan
2005	Christopher Thomas James Chessun
2012	Michael Geoffrey Ipgrave
2017	Woyin Karowei Dorgu

WALES

Archbishops of Wales

1920	Alfred George Edwards (St Asaph 1889–1934)
1934	Charles Alfred Howell Green (Bangor 1928–44)
1944	David Lewis Prosser (St Davids 1927–50)
1949	John Morgan (Llandaff 1939–57)
1957	Alfred Edwin Morris (Monmouth 1945–67)
1968	William Glyn Hughes Simon (Llandaff 1957–71)
1971	Gwilym Owen Williams (Bangor 1957–82)
1983	Derrick Greenslade Childs (Monmouth 1972–87)
1987	George Noakes (St Davids 1982–91)
1991	Alwyn Rice Jones (St Asaph 1982–99)
1999	Rowan Douglas Williams (Monmouth 1992–2002)
2003	Barry Cennydd Morgan (Llandaff 1999–2017)
2017	John David Edward Davies (Swansea and Brecon 2008–)
2021	*vacant*

Bangor[1]

Description of arms. Gules, a bend or guttée de poix between two mullets pierced argent.

c.550	Deiniol [Daniel]
c.775	Elfod [Elbodugen]
1092	Herve
	[Vacancy 1109–20]
1120	David the Scot
1140	Maurice (Meurig)
	[Vacancy 1161–77]
1177	Guy Rufus [Gwion Goch]
	[Vacancy c.1190–95]
1195	Alan [Alban]
1197	Robert of Shrewsbury
	[Vacancy 1212–15]
1215	Cadwgan
1237	Richard
1267	Anian [or Einion]
1307	Gruffydd ab Iowerth
1309	Anian [Einion] Sais
1328	Matthew de Englefield
1357	Thomas de Ringstead
1366	Gervase de Castro
1371	Hywel ap Gronwy
1372	John Gilbert

1376	John Swaffham
1400	Richard Young
	[Vacancy c.1404–8]
1408	Benedict Nicolls
1418	William Barrow
1425	John Cliderow
1436	Thomas Cheriton
1448	John Stanbury
1453	James Blakedon
1465	Richard Edenham
1495	Henry Dean
1500	Thomas Pigot
1505	Thomas Penny
1509	Thomas Skevington
1534	John Salcot [or Capon]
1539	John Bird
1542	Arthur Bulkeley
1555	William Glynn
1559	Rowland Meyrick
1566	Nicholas Robinson
1586	Hugh Bellot
1596	Richard Vaughan
1598	Henry Rowlands
1616	Lewis Bayly
1632	David Dolben
1634	Edmund Griffith
1637	William Roberts
1666	Robert Morgan
1673	Humphrey Lloyd
1689	Humphrey Humphreys
1702	John Evans
1716	Benjamin Hoadley
1721	Richard Reynolds
1723	William Baker
1728	Thomas Sherlock
1734	Charles Cecil
1738	Thomas Herring
1743	Matthew Hutton
1748	Zachary Pearce
1756	John Egerton
1769	John Ewer
1775	John Moore
1783	John Warren
1800	William Cleaver
1807	John Randolph
1809	Henry William Majendie
1830	Christopher Bethell
1859	James Colquhoun Campbell
1890	Daniel Lewis Lloyd
1899	Watkin Herbert Williams
1925	Daniel Davies
1928	Charles Alfred Howell Green (Archbishop of Wales 1934)
1944	David Edwardes Davies
1949	John Charles Jones
1957	Gwilym Owen Williams (Archbishop of Wales 1971)
1982	John Cledan Mears
1993	Barry Cennydd Morgan
1999	Francis James Saunders Davies
2004	Phillip Anthony Crockett
2008	Andrew Thomas Griffith John

Llandaff [2]

Description of arms. Sable, two pastoral staves endorsed in saltire, the dexter or, the sinister argent. On a chief azure three labelled mitres or.

c.550	Teiliau
c.872	Cyfeiliag
c.880	Libiau
c.940	Marchlwys
982	Gwyzan
c.995	Bledri
1027	Joseph
1056	Herewald
1107	Urban
	[Vacancy of six years]
1140	Uchtryd
1148	Nicolas ap Gwrgant
	[Vacancy of two years]
1186	William Saltmarsh
1193	Henry of Abergavenny
1219	William of Goldcliff
1230	Elias of Radnor
1245	William de Burgh
1254	John de Ware
1257	William of Radnor
1266	Willam de Breuse [or Brus]
1297	John of Monmouth
1323	John of Eaglescliffe
1344	John Paschal
1361	Roger Cradock
1383	Thomas Rushook
1386	William Bottesham
1389	Edmund Bromfield
1393	Tideman de Winchcomb
1395	Andrew Barret
1396	John Burghill
1398	Thomas Peverel
1408	John de la Zouch [Fulford]
1425	John Wells
1441	Nicholas Ashby
1458	John Hunden
1476	John Smith
1478	John Marshall
1496	John Ingleby
1500	Miles Salley
1517	George de Athequa
1537	Robert Holdgate [or Holgate]
1545	Anthony Kitchin
1567	Hugh Jones
1575	William Blethin
1591	Gervase Babington
1595	William Morgan
1601	Francis Godwin
1618	George Carleton
1619	Theophilus Field
1627	William Murray
1640	Morgan Owen

---

[1] Very few of the names of the Celtic bishops have been preserved.

[2] The traditional list of bishops of the Celtic Church has little historical foundation. But the names of the following, prior to Urban, may be regarded as fairly trustworthy, though the dates are very uncertain.

1660	Hugh Lloyd
1667	Francis Davies
1675	William Lloyd
1679	William Beaw
1706	John Tyler
1725	Robert Clavering
1729	John Harris
1739	Matthias Mawson
1740	John Gilbert
1749	Edward Cressett
1755	Richard Newcome
1761	John Ewer
1769	Jonathan Shipley
1769	Shute Barrington
1782	Richard Watson
1816	Herbert Marsh
1819	William Van Mildert
1826	Charles Richard Sumner
1828	Edward Copleston
1849	Alfred Ollivant
1883	Richard Lewis
1905	Joshua Pritchard Hughes
1931	Timothy Rees
1939	John Morgan (Archbishop of Wales 1949)
1957	William Glyn Hughes Simon (Archbishop of Wales 1968)
1971	Eryl Stephen Thomas
1975	John Richard Worthington Poole-Hughes
1985	Roy Thomas Davies
1999	Barry Cennydd Morgan (Archbishop of Wales 2003)
2017	June Osborne

Monmouth

Description of arms. Per pale azure and sable, two crosiers in satire or between in chief a besant charged with a lion passant guardant gules, in fess two fleurs-de-lis and in base a fleur-de-lis all of the third.

1921	Charles Alfred Howell Green
1928	Gilbert Cunningham Joyce
1940	Alfred Edwin Monahan
1945	Alfred Edwin Morris (Archbishop of Wales 1957)
1968	Eryl Stephen Thomas
1972	Derrick Greenslade Childs (Archbishop of Wales 1983)
1986	Royston Clifford Wright
1992	Rowan Douglas Williams (Archbishop of Wales 1999)
2003	Edward William Murray Walker
2013	Richard Edward Pain
2019	Cherry Elizabeth Vann

St Asaph[1]

Description of arms. Sable, two keys endorsed in saltire the wards upwards argent.

c.560	Kentigern
c.573	Asaph
1143	Gilbert
1152	Geoffrey of Monmouth
1154	Richard
1160	Godfrey
1175	Adam
1183	John I
1186	Reiner
1225	Abraham
1235	Hugh
1242	Hywel Ab Ednyfed
1249	Anian I [or Einion]
1267	John II
1268	Anian II
1293	Llywelyn de Bromfield
1315	Dafydd ap Bleddyn
1346	John Trevor I
1357	Llywelyn ap Madoc ab Ellis
1377	William de Spridlington
1382	Lawrence Child
1390	Alexander Bache
1395	John Trevor II
1411	Robert de Lancaster
1433	John Lowe
1444	Reginald Pecock
1451	Thomas Bird *alias* Knight
1471	Richard Redman
1496	Michael Deacon
1500	Dafydd ab Iorwerth
1504	Dafydd ab Owain
1513	Edmund Birkhead
1518	Henry Standish
1536	Robert Warton [or Parfew]
1555	Thomas Goldwell
1560	Richard Davies
1561	Thomas Davies
1573	William Hughes
1601	William Morgan
1604	Richard Parry
1624	John Hanmer
1629	John Owen
1660	George Griffith
1667	Henry Glemham
1670	Isaac Barrow
1680	William Lloyd
1692	Edward Jones
1703	George Hooper
1704	William Beveridge
1708	Will. Fleetwood
1715	John Wynne
1727	Francis Hare
1732	Thomas Tanner
1736	Isaac Maddox
1744	Samuel Lisle
1748	Robert Hay Drummond
1761	Richard Newcome
1769	Jonathan Shipley
1789	Samuel Hallifax
1790	Lewis Bagot
1802	Samuel Horsley
1806	William Cleaver
1815	John Luxmore
1830	William Carey
1846	Thomas Vowler Short

1870	Joshua Hughes
1889	Alfred George Edwards (Archbishop of Wales 1920)
1934	William Thomas Havard
1950	David Daniel Bartlett
1971	Harold John Charles
1982	Alwyn Rice Jones (Archbishop of Wales 1991)
1999	John Stewart Davies
2009	Gregory Kenneth Cameron

St Davids[2]

Description of arms. Sable, on a cross or five cinquefoils of the first.

c.601	David
c.606	Cynog
831	Sadyrnfyw
	Meurig
c.840	Novis
	?Idwal
c.906	Asser
	Llunwerth
944	Eneuris
c.961	Rhydderch
c.999	Morgeneu
1023	Morgeneu
1023	Erwyn
1039	Tramerin
1061	Joseph
1061	Bleddud
1072	Sulien
1078	Abraham
1080	Sulien
1085	Wilfrid
1115	Bernard
1148	David Fitz-Gerald
1176	Peter de Leia
1203	Geoffrey de Henlaw
1215	Gervase [Iorwerth]
1231	Anselm le Gras
1248	Thomas le Waleys
1256	Richard de Carew
1280	Thomas Bek
1296	David Martin
1328	Henry Gower
1347	John Thoresby
1350	Reginald Brian
1352	Thomas Fastolf
1362	Adam Houghton
1389	John Gilbert
1397	Guy de Mohne
1408	Henry Chichele
1414	John Catterick
1415	Stephen Patrington
1418	Benedict Nichols
1434	Thomas Rodburn [Rudborne]
1442	William Lindwood
1447	John Langton
1447	John de la Bere
1460	Robert Tully
1482	Richard Martin
1483	Thomas Langton
1485	Hugh Pavy
1496	John Morgan [Young]
1505	Robert Sherborn
1509	Edward Vaughan
1523	Richard Rawlins
1536	William Barlow

---

[1] Prior to the Norman period there is considerable uncertainty as to names and dates.
[2] The following names occur in early records though the dates given cannot always be reconciled.

1548 Robert Ferrar
1554 Henry Morgan
1560 Thomas Young
1561 Richard Davies
1582 Marmaduke Middleton
1594 Anthony Rudd
1615 Richard Milbourne
1621 William Laud
1627 Theophilus Field
1636 Roger Mainwaring
1660 William Lucy
1678 William Thomas
1683 Laurence Womock
1686 John Lloyd
1687 Thomas Watson
     [*Vacancy* 1699–1705]
1705 George Bull
1710 Philip Bisse
1713 Adam Ottley
1724 Richard Smallbrooke
1731 Elias Sydall
1732 Nicholas Claggett
1743 Edward Willes
1744 Richard Trevor
1753 Anthony Ellis
1761 Samuel Squire
1766 Robert Lowth
1766 Charles Moss
1774 James Yorke
1779 John Warren
1783 Edward Smallwell
1788 Samuel Horsley
1794 William Stewart
1801 George Murray
1803 Thomas Burgess

1825 John Banks Jenkinson
1840 Connop Thirlwall
1874 William Basil Tickell Jones
1897 John Owen
1927 David Lewis Prosser
     (Archbishop of Wales 1944)
1950 William Thomas Havard
1956 John Richards Richards
1971 Eric Matthias Roberts
1982 George Noakes (Archbishop of
     Wales 1987)
1991 John Ivor Rees
1996 David Huw Jones
2002 Carl Norman Cooper
2008 John Wyn Evans
2016 Joanna Susan Penberthy

Swansea and Brecon

Description of arms. Per fess azure and or, in chief surmounting a catherine wheel issuant an eagle rising regardant of the second and in base a fleur-de-lis of the first.

1923 Edward Latham Bevan
1934 John Morgan
1939 Edward William Williamson
1953 William Glyn Hughes Simon
1958 John James Absalom Thomas
1976 Benjamin Noel Young
     Vaughan
1988 Dewi Morris Bridges
1999 Anthony Edward Pierce
2008 John David Edward Davies
     (Archbishop of Wales 2017)
2021 *vacant*

Provincial Assistant Bishop

1996–2008 David Thomas

SCOTLAND

Sources: Bp Dowden's *The Bishops of Scotland* (Glasgow 1912), for all the sees up to the Reformation, and for Aberdeen and Moray to the present time.

For bishops after the Reformation (and for a few of the earliest ones before Queen Margaret) – Grub, *Ecclesiastical History of Scotland* (Edinburgh 1861, 4 Vols.) and Bp Keith and Bp Russel, *Scottish Bishops* (2nd ed. Edinburgh 1824).

Scottish episcopal elections became subject immediately to Roman confirmation in 1192. The subordination of the Scottish Church to York became less direct in 1165, and its independence was recognized in a bill of Celestine III in 1192. St Andrews was raised to metropolitan rank on 17 August 1472 and the Archbishop became primate of all Scotland with the same legative rights as the Archbishop of Canterbury on 27 March 1487.

The dates in the margin are those of the consecration or translation to the particular see of the bishops named; or in the case of bishops elect, who are not known to have been consecrated, they are those of the election; or in the case of titular bishops, of the date of their appointment.

The date of the death has been given where there was a long interregnum, or where there is dislocation (as at the Reformation and at the Revolution), or for some special reason to make the history intelligible.

The extra information in the list of College Bishops is given for the reason just stated.

St Andrews

St Andrews, Dunkeld and Dunblane

Description of arms. Quarterly, 1st azure, a saltire argent (for the See of St Andrews); 2nd per fess sable and vert, an open book proper in base, fore-edges and binding or, a dove argent, her wings displayed in chief perching thereon and holding in her beak a spray of olive of the second (for the See of Dunkeld); 3rd chevronny or and gules, a saltire engrailed azure, charged at the fess point with a crescent inverted argent (for the See of Dunblane); 4th azure, a saltire argent supported in front of and by St Andrew enhaloed or and vested pupure with mantle vert, and in base a crescent inverted of the second (for the See of St Andrews).

906	Cellach I
915(?)	Fothad I
955	Malisius I
963	Maelbridge
970	Cellach II
996(?)	Malasius II
(?)	Malmore
1025	Alwyn
1028	Maelduin
1055	Tuthald or Tuadal
1059	Fothad II
1077	Gregory (elect)
to	Catharas (elect)
1107	Edmarus (elect)
	Godricus (elect)
1109	Turgot
1120	Eadmer (elect)
1127	Robert
1159	Waldeve (elect)
1160	Ernald
1165	Richard
1178	Hugh
1180	John the Scot
1198	Roger de Beaumon
1202	William Malveisin
1238	Geoffrey (elect)
1240	David de Bernham
1253	Robert de Stuteville (elect)
1254	Abel de Golin
1255	Gamelin
1273	William Wischard

1280	William Fraser
1298	William de Lamberton
1328	James Bennet
1342	William de Laundels
1385	Stephen de Pay (elect)
1386(?)	Walter Trayl
1388	Alexander de Neville
1398	Thomas de Arundel
1401	Thomas Stewart (elect)
1402	Walter de Danielston (elect)
1403(?)	Gilbert Greenlaw
1403	Henry Wardlaw
1408	John Trevor
1440	James Kennedy

ARCHBISHOPS

1465	Patrick Graham
1478	William Scheves
1497	James Stewart (elect)
1504	Alexander Stewart (elect)
1513	John Hepburn (elect)
1513	Innocenzo Cibo (elect)
1514	Andrew Forman
1522	James Betoun
1538	David Betoun [coadjutor]
1547	John Hamilton
1551	Gavin Hamilton [coadjutor] died 1571
1572	John Douglas (titular)
1576	Patrick Adamson (titular) died 1592
1611	George Gladstanes
1615	John Spottiswoode, died 1639
1661	James Sharp
1679	Alexander Burnet
1684	Arthur Rose, died 1704

BISHOPS OF FIFE

[1704–26	See vacant]
1726	James Rose
1733	Robert Keith
1743	Robert White
1761	Henry Edgar

BISHOPS OF ST ANDREWS

1842	Patrick Torry
1853	Charles Wordsworth
1893	George Howard Wilkinson
1908	Charles Edward Plumb
1931	Edward Thomas Scott Reid
1938	James Lumsden Barkway
1949	Arnold Brian Burrowes
1955	John William Alexander Howe
1969	Michael Geoffrey Hare Duke
1995	Michael Harry George Henley
2005	David Robert Chillingworth
2018	Ian James Paton

†Dunkeld

849(?)	Tuathal
865(?)	Flaithbertach

1114	Cormac
1147	Gregory
1170	Richard I
1178	Walter de Bidun (elect)
1183(?)	John I, the Scot
1203	Richard II, de Prebenda
1212(?)	John II, de Leycester
1214(?)	Hugh de Sigillo
1229	Matthew Scot (elect)
1229	Gilbert
1236(?)	Geoffrey de Liberatione
1252	Richard III, of Inverkeithing
1273(?)	Robert de Stuteville
1283(?)	Hugh de Strivelin [Stirling] (elect)
1283	William
1288	Matthew de Crambeth
1309	John de Leek (elect)
1312	William Sinclair
1337	Malcolm de Innerpeffray (elect)
1344	Richard de Pilmor
1347	Robert de Den (elect)
1347(?)	Duncan de Strathearn
1355	John Luce
1370	John de Carrick (elect)
1371(?)	Michael de Monymusk
1377(?)	Andrew Umfray (elect)
1379	John de Peblys [? of Peebles]
1379	Robert de Derling
1390(?)	Nicholas Duffield
1391	Robert Sinclair
1398(?)	Robert de Cardeny
1430	William Gunwardby
1437	Donald MacNaughton (elect)
1438	James Kennedy
1440(?)	Thomas Livingston
1440	Alexander de Lawedre [Lauder] (elect)
1442	James de Brois [Brewhous]
1447	William Turnbull (elect)
1448	John Ralston
1452(?)	Thomas Lauder
1476	James Livingston
1483	Alexander Inglis (elect)
1484	George Brown
1515	Andrew Stewart (elect)
1516	Gavin Dougias
1524	Robert Cockburn
1526(?)	George Crichton
1546	John Hamilton
1552	Robert Crichton
1572	James Paton (titular)
1585	Peter Rollock (titular)
1607	James Nicolson (titular)
1611(?)	Alexander Lindsay (deposed 1638)
1662	George Haliburton
1665	Henry Guthrie
1677	William Lindsay
1679	Andrew Bruce
1686	John Hamilton
1717	Thomas Rattray
1743	John Alexander

† Indicates a diocese no longer extant, or united with another diocese.

1776(?) Charles Rose
1792 Jonathan Watson
1808 Patrick Torry
1842 Held with St Andrews

†Dunblane

1162 Laurence
c.1180 Symon
1196 W[illelmus]
1198 Jonathan
1215 Abraham
1225 Ralph (elect)
1227 Osbert
1233 Clement
1259 Robert de Prebenda
1284 William I
1296 Alpin
1301 Nicholas
1307 Nicholas de Balmyle
1318(?) Roger de Balnebrich (elect)
1322 Maurice
c.1347 William II
c.1361 Walter de Coventre
c.1372 Andrew
c.1380 Dougal
1403(?) Finlay or Dermoch
1419 William Stephen
1430 Michael Ochiltree
1447(?) Robert Lauder
1468 John Hepburn
1487 James Chisolm
1527 William Chisolm I
1561 William Chisolm II [coadjutor]
1575 Andrew Graham (titular)
1611 George Graham
1616 Adam Bellenden
1636 James Wedderburn
1661 Robert Leighton
1673 James Ramsay
1684 Robert Douglas
[1716–31   See vacant]
1731 John Gillan
1735 Robert White
1744 Thomas Ogilvie (elect)
1774 Charles Rose, died 1791
1776 Held with Dunkeld

Edinburgh

Description of arms. Azure, a saltire and, in chief, a labelled mitre argent.

1634 William Forbes
1634 David Lindsay
1662 George Wishart
1672 Alexander Young
1679 John Paterson
1687 Alexander Rose
1720 John Fullarton
1727 Arthur Millar
1727 Andrew Lumsden
1733 David Freebairn
[1739–76   See vacant]
1776 William Falconer
1787 William Abernethy
        Drummond
1806 Daniel Sandford
1830 James Walker
1841 Charles Hughes Terrot
1872 Henry Cotterill
1886 John Dowden

1910 George Henry Somerset
        Walpole
1929 Harry Seymour Reid
1939 Ernest Denny Logie Danson
1947 Kenneth Charles Harman
        Warner
1961 Kenneth Moir Carey
1975 Alastair Iain Macdonald
        Haggart
1986 Richard Frederick Holloway
2001 Brian Arthur Smith
2012 John Andrew Armes

Aberdeen

Aberdeen and Orkney

Description of arms. Azure, parted per pale: dexter, a chevron round embattled on its upper edge between a fleur-de-lis argent ensigned of an open crown or in dexter chief, and in base a bishop proper, attired of the second, mitred and holding in his sinister hand a pastoral staff of the third, his dexter hand raised in benediction over three children gules issuant from a cauldron of the third; sinister, an open boat or, an anchor argent pendant from its prow, issuant therefrom a saint proper, attired of the third, enhaloed and holding in his sinister hand a pastoral staff of the second; over all and issuant from the chief a sunburst or, the central ray projected along the palar line to the base.

BISHOPS AT MURTHLAC

(?)   Beyn [Beanus]
(?)   Donort
(?)   Cormac

BISHOPS AT ABERDEEN

1132 Nechtan
c.1150 Edward
c.1172 Matthew
c.1201 John
c.1208 Adam de Kalder
1228 Matthew Scot (elect)
1230 Gilbert de Strivelyn
1240 Radulf de Lamley
1247 Peter de Ramsey
1258 Richard de Pottun
1272 Hugh de Bennum
1282 Henry le Chene
1329 Walter Herok (elect)
1329 Alexander I, de Kyninmund
1344 William de Deyn
1351 John de Rate
1356 Alexander II, de Kyninmund
1380 Adam de Tynyngham
1391 Gilbert de Grenlaw
1422 Henry de Lychton [Leighton]
c.1441 Ingram de Lindsay
1458 Thomas Spens
1480 Robert Blackadder (elect)
1488 William Elphinstone
1515 Robert Forman (elect)
1516 Alexander Gordon
1519 Gavin Dunbar
1529 George Learmonth [coadjutor]
1533 William Stewart

1547 William Gordon
1577 David Cunningham (elect)
1611 Peter Blackburn
1616 Alexander Forbes
1618 Patrick Forbes of Corse
1635 Adam Bellenden [Bannatyne]
1662 David Mitchell
1663 Alexander Burnet
1664 Patrick Scougal
1682 George Halyburton
[1715–21   See vacant]
1721 Archibald Campbell
1724 James Gadderar
1733 William Dunbar
1746 Andrew Gerard
1768 Robert Kilgour
1786 John Skinner
1816 William Skinner
1857 Thomas George Spink Suther
1883 Arthur Gascoigne Douglas
1906 Rowland Ellis
1912 Anthony Mitchell
1917 Frederic Llewellyn Deane
1943 Herbert William Hall
1956 Edward Frederick Easson
1973 Ian Forbes Begg
1978 Frederick Charles Darwent
1992 Andrew Bruce Cameron
2007 Robert Arthur Gillies
2018 Anne Catherine Dyer

†Orkney

1035 Henry
1050 Turolf
1072 John I
1072 Adalbert
1073 Radulf
1102 William I, 'the Old'
1108 Roger
1114 Radulf Novell
1168(?) William II
1188(?) Bjarni
1224 Jofreyrr
1248 Henry I
1270 Peter
1286 Dolgfinn
1310 William III
c.1369 William IV
c.1384 Robert Sinclair
1384(?) John
1394 Henry II
1396(?) John Pak
1407 Alexander Vaus (elect)
1415 William Stephenson
1420 Thomas Tulloch
1461 William Tulloch
1477 Andrew Painter
1500 Edward Stewart
1524 John Benston [coadjutor]
1526(?) Robert Maxwell
1541 Robert Reid
1559 Adam Bothwell
1611 James Law
1615 George Graham
1639 Robert Barron (elect)
1661 Thomas Sydserf
1664 Andrew Honeyman
1677 Murdo Mackenzie
1688 Andrew Bruce, See afterwards
        administered with
        Caithness
1857 Held with Aberdeen

Brechin

Description of arms. Or, three piles in point purpure.

1153(?)	Samson
1178	Turpin
1202	Radulf
1215	Hugh
1218	Gregory
1246	Albin
1269(?)	William de Crachin (elect)
1275	William Comyn
1296	Nicholas
1298	John de Kyninmund
1328	Adam de Moravia
1350	Philip Wilde
1351	Patrick de Locrys [Leuchars]
1383	Stephen de Cellario
1411	Walter Forrester
1426	John de Crannach
1455	George Schoriswood
1464	Patrick Graham
1465	John Balfour
1489	William Meldrum
1523	John Hepburn
1557	Donald Campbell (elect)
1565(?)	John Sinclair (elect)
1566	Alexander Campbell (titular)
1610	Andrew Lamb
1619	David Lindsay
1634	Thomas Sydserf
1635	Walter Whitford
1662	David Strachan
1672	Robert Laurie
1678	George Haliburton
1682	Robert Douglas
1684	Alexander Cairncross
1684	James Drummond
1695–1709	Held with Edinburgh
1709	John Falconar
1724	Robert Norrie
1726	John Ochterlonie
1742	James Rait
1778	George Innes
1787	William Abernethy Drummond
1788	John Strachan
1810	George Gleig
1840	David Moir
1847	Alexander Penrose Forbes
1876	Hugh Willoughby Jermyn
1904	Walter John Forbes Robberds
1935	Kenneth Donald Mackenzie
1944	Eric Graham
1959	John Chappell Sprott
1975	Lawrence Edward Luscombe
1990	Robert Taylor Halliday
1997	Neville Chamberlain
2005	John Ambrose Cyril Mantle
2011	Nigel Peyton
2018	Andrew Christopher Swift

Moray

Moray, Ross and Caithness

Description of arms. Party per fess and in chief per pale: 1 or, two lions combatant gules, pulling at a cushion of the last issuant from a crescent azure, on a chief wavy of the third three mullets argent (for the See of Moray); 2 argent, a bishop standing in the sinister vested purpure, mitred and holding in his sinister hand a crosier or and pointing with the dexter hand to a saint affontée, his hands clasped on this breast proper, habited gules, above his head a halo of the third (for the See of Ross); 3 azure, issuant from an antique boat or, a demi-bishop proper vested argent, his mitre and pastoral staff in hand sinister of the second, accompanied by two demi-angels, one in the dexter and the other in the sinister chief holding open books proper, their wings addorsed, also of the second (for the See of Caithness).

1114	Gregory
1153(?)	William
1164	Felix
1172	Simon de Tonei
1187	Richard de Lincoln
1203	Brice de Douglas
1224(?)	Andrew de Moravia
1244(?)	Simon
1251	Radulf de Leycester (elect)
1253	Archibald
1299	David de Moravia
1326	John de Pilmor
1363	Alexander Bur
1397	William de Spyny
1407	John de Innes
1415	Henry Leighton
1422	Columba de Dunbar
1437	John de Winchester
1460(?)	James Stewart
1463	David Stewart
1477	William de Tulloch
1487	Andrew Stewart
1501(?)	Andrew Forman
1516(?)	James Hepburn
1525	Robert Shaw
1532(?)	Alexander Stewart
1538(?)	Patrick Hepburn
1574	George Douglas
1611	Alexander Douglas
1623	John Guthrie
1662	Murdo Mackenzie
1677	James Aitken
1680	Colin Falconer
1687	Alexander Rose
1688	William Hay
1707	Held with Edinburgh
1725	Held with Aberdeen
1727	William Dunbar
1737	George Hay (elect)
1742	William Falconar
1777	Arthur Petrie
1787	Andrew Macfarlane
1798	Alexander Jolly
1838	Held with Ross
1851	Robert Eden
1886	James Butler Knill Kelly
1904	Arthur John Maclean
1943	Piers Holt Wilson

1953	Duncan Macinnes
1970	George Minshull Sessford
1994	Gregor Macgregor
1999	John Michael Crook
2007	Mark Jeremy Strange

†Ross

1131(?)	Macbeth
1150(?)	Simon
1161	Gregory
1195	Reginald
1213	Andrew de Moravia (elect)
1215(?)	Robert I
1250	Robert II
1272	Matthew
1275(?)	Robert II de Fyvin
1295(?)	Adam de Derlingtun (elect)
1297(?)	Thomas de Dundee
1325	Roger
1351	Alexander Stewart
1372	Alexander de Kylwos
1398(?)	Alexander de Waghorn
1418	Thomas Lyell (elect)
	Griffin Yonge (elect)
1420	John Bulloch
1441(?)	Andrew de Munro (elect)
1441(?)	Thomas Tulloch
1464(?)	Henry Cockburn
1478	John Wodman
1481	William Elphinstone (elect)
1483	Thomas Hay
1492	John Guthrie
1498	John Frisel [Fraser]
c.1507	Robert Cockburn
1525	James Hay
c.1539	Robert Cairncross
1552	David Painter
1561(?)	Henry Sinclair
1566	John Lesley
1575	Alexander Hepburn
1611	David Lindsay
1613	Patrick Lindsay
1633	John Maxwell
1662	John Paterson
1679	Alexander Young
1684	James Ramsay
1696	See vacant or held with Caithness until 1727
1727	Held with Moray
1742	Held with Caithness
1762	Robert Forbes
1777	Held with Moray
1819	David Low
1851	Held with Moray

†Caithness

c.1146	Andrew
c.1187	John
1214	Adam
1223(?)	Gilbert de Moravia
1250(?)	William
1263	Walter de Baltrodin
1273(?)	Nicholas (elect)
1275	Archibald Herok
1278	Richard (elect)
1279(?)	Hervey de Dundee (elect)
1282	Alan de St Edmund
1295	John or James (elect)
1296	Adam de Derlingtun
1297	Andrew
1306	Fercard Belegaumbe
1328(?)	David
1341	Alan de Moravia
1343	Thomas de Fingask
1370	Malcolm de Dumbrek
1381	Alexander Man
1414	Alexander Vaus
1425	John de Crannach
1428	Robert Strabrok
1446	John Innes
1448	William Mudy
1478(?)	Prospero Camogli de Medici
1484(?)	John Sinclair (elect)

1502	Andrew Stewart I
1517(?)	Andrew Stewart II
1542	Robert Stewart (elect)
1600	George Gledstanes (elect)
1611	Alexander Forbes
1616	John Abernethy
1662	Patrick Forbes
1680	Andrew Wood
[1695	See vacant]
1731	Robert Keith
1741	Wm. Falconas
1762	Held with Ross
[1742	See Vacant]
1777	Held with Moray

Glasgow

Glasgow and Galloway

Description of arms. Party per pale: dexter, vert, a fess wavy argent charged with a bar wavy azure between a representation of St Mungo issuant from the fess proper, habited or, his dexter hand raised in benediction and in his sinister hand a Celtic cross of the same in chief, in nombril point a salmon proper and in base an annulet of the fourth; sinister, argent a representation of St Ninian standing full-faced proper, clothed in a pontifical robe purpure, on his head a mitre and in his dexter hand a crosier or.

550(?)	Kentigern or Mungo (no record of his successors)
1114(?)	(Michael)
1118(?)	John
1147	Herbert
1164	Ingram
1175	Jocelin
1199	Hugh de Roxburgh (elect)
1200	William Malveisin
1202	Florence (elect)
1208	Walter de St Albans
1233	William de Bondington
1259	Nicholas de Moffat (elect)
1259	John de Cheam
1268	Nicholas de Moffat (elect)
1271	William Wischard (elect)
1273	Robert Wischard
1317	Stephen de Donydouer (elect)
1318	John de Eglescliffe
1323	John de Lindsay
1337	John Wischard
1339	William Rae
1367	Walter Wardlaw
1388	Matthew de Glendonwyn
1391	John Framisden (titular)
1408	William Lauder
1427	John Cameron
1447	James de Brois [Brewhouse]
1448	William Turnbull
1456	Andrew de Durrisdeer
1475	John Laing
1483	George Carmichael (elect)

ARCHBISHOPS

1483	Robert Blackadder (Archbishop 9 Jan 1492)
1509	James Betoun I
1525	Gavin Dunbar
1551	Alexander Gordon
1552	James Betoun II (restored 1587)
1571	John Porterfield (titular)
1573	James Boyd (titular)
1581	Robert Montgomery (titular)
1585	William Erskine (titular)
1610	John Spottiswoode
1615	James Law
1633	Patrick Lindsay
1661	Andrew Fairfoul
1664	Alexander Burnet (restored 1674)
1671	Robert Leighton, died 1684 (resigned 1674)
1679	Arthur Rose
1684	Alexander Cairncross, died 1701
1687	John Paterson,[1] died 1708
[1708	Vacant]

BISHOPS

1731	Alexander Duncan, died 1733
[1733	Vacant]
1787	Held with Edinburgh
1805	William Abernethy Drummond
1809–37	Held with Edinburgh
1837	Michael Russell
1848	Walter John Trower
1859	William Scott Wilson
1888	William Thomas Harrison
1904	Archibald Ean Campbell
1921	Edward Thomas Scott Reid
1931	John Russell Darbyshire
1938	John Charles Halland How
1952	Francis Hamilton Moncreiff
1974	Frederick Goldie
1981	Derek Alec Rawcliffe
1991	John Mitchell Taylor
1998	Idris Jones
2010	Gregor Duthrie Duncan
2020	Kevin Pearson

†Galloway or Candida Casa or Whithorn[2]

	Ninian, died 432(?)
(?)	Octa
681	Trumwine
731	Penthelm, died 735(?)
735	Frithowald, died 764
763	Pehtwine, died 776
777	Ethelbert
791	Beadwulf
1140	Gilla-Aldan
1154	Christian
1189	John
1214	Walter
1235	Odo Ydonc (elect)
1235	Gilbert
1255	Henry
1294	Thomas de Kircudbright [de Daltoun]
1327	Simon de Wedale
1355	Michael Malconhalgh
1359(?)	Thomas Macdowell (elect)
1359	Thomas
1364	Adam de Lanark
(?)	David Douglas, died 1373
(?)	James Carron (resigned 1373)
1378	Ingram de Kethnis (elect)
1379	Oswald
1380	Thomas de Rossy
(?)	Francis Ramsay, died 1402

1406	Elisaeus Adougan
1414(?)	Gilbert Cavan (elect)
1415	Thomas de Butil
1422	Alexander Vaus
1451	Thomas Spens
1457(?)	Thomas Vaus (elect)
1459	Ninian Spot
1482(?)	George Vaus
1508(?)	James Betoun (elect)
1509(?)	David Arnot
1526	Henry Wemyss
1541(?)	Andrew Dury
1559(?)	Alexander Gordon
1610	Gavin Hamilton
1612(?)	William Couper
1619	Andrew Lamb
1635	Thomas Sydserf
1661	James Hamilton
1675	John Paterson
1679	Arthur Rose
1680	James Aitken
1688	John Gordon, died 1726
1697	Held with Edinburgh
1837	Held with Glasgow

Argyll or Lismore

Argyll and The Isles

Description of arms. Azure, two crosiers in saltire and in chief a mitre or.

1193	Harald
1240	William
1253	Alan
1268	Laurence de Erganis
1300	Andrew
1342	Angusde Ergadia (elect)
1344	Martinde Ergaill
1387	John Dugaldi
1397(?)	Bean Johannis
1420(?)	Finlay de Albany
1428	George Lauder
1476	Robert Colquhoun
1504	David Hamilton
1532	Robert Montgomery
1539(?)	William Cunningham (elect)
1553(?)	James Hamilton (elect)
1580	Neil Campbell (titular)
1611	John Campbell (titular)
1613	Andrew Boyd
1637	James Fairlie
1662	David Fletcher
1665	John Young (elect)
1666	William Scroggie
1675	Arthur Rose
1679	Colin Falconer
1680	Hector Maclean
1688	Alexander Monro (elect)
	Held with Ross
1847	Alexander Ewing
1874	George Mackarness
1883	James Robert Alexander Chinnery-Haldane
1907	Kenneth Mackenzie
1942	Thomas Hannay
1963	Richard Knyvet Wimbush
1977	George Kennedy Buchanan Henderson

[1] After the deposition of John Paterson at the Revolution the See ceased to be Archiepiscopal.

[2] The traditional founder of the See is St Ninian, but nothing authentic is known of the bishops prior to the accession of Gilla-Aldan between 1133 and 1140.

1993	Douglas MacLean Cameron
2004	Alexander Martin Shaw
2011	Kevin Pearson
2021	Keith Graham Riglin

†The Isles

900	Patrick
1080	Roolwer
1080	William
1095	Hamundr
1138	Wimund
1152	John I
1152(?)	Ragnald
1154	Gamaliel
1170	Christian
1194	Michael
1210	Nicholas I
1219	Nicholas II of Meaux
1226(?)	Reginald
1226	Simon
1249	Laurence (elect)
1253	Richard
1275	Gilbert (elect)
1275	Mark
1305	Alan
1324	Gilbert Maclelan
1328	Bernard de Linton
1331	Thomas de Rossy
1349	William Russell
1374	John Donkan
1387	Michael
1392	John Sproten (Man) (titular)
1402(?)	Conrad (Man) (titular)
1402(?)	Theodore Bloc (Man) (titular)
1410	Richard Messing (Man)
1422	Michael Anchire
1425(?)	John Burgherlinus (Man)
1428	Angus I
1441(?)	John Hectoris [McCachane] Macgilleon
1472	Angus II
1487	John Campbell
1511	George Hepburn
1514	John Campbell (elect)
1530(?)	Ferchar MacEachan (elect)
1550(?)	Roderick Maclean
1553(?)	Alexander Gordon
1567	John Carswell (titular)
1573	John Campbell
1605	Andrew Knox
1619	Thomas Knox
1628	John Leslie
1634	Neil Campbell
1662	Robert Wallace
1677	Andrew Wood

1680	Archibald Graham [or McIlvernock] Held with Orkney and Caithness
1819	Held with Argyll

College Bishops, Consecrated without Sees

1705	John Sage, died 1711
1705	John Fullarton (Edinburgh 1720), died 1727
1709	Henry Christie, died 1718
1709	John Falconar (Fife 1720), died 1723
1711	Archibald Campbell (Aberdeen 1721), died 1744
1712	James Gadderar (Aberdeen 1725, Moray 1725), died 1733
1718	Arthur Millar (Edinburgh 1727), died 1727
1718	William Irvine, died 1725
1722	Andrew Cant, died 1730
1722	David Freebairn (Edinburgh 1733)
1726	John Ochterlonie (Brechin 1731), died 1742
1726	James Ross (Fife 1731), died 1733
1727	John Gillan (Dunblane 1731), died 1735
1727	David Ranken, died 1728

Bishops who have held the Office of Primus

1704	Alexander Rose (Edinburgh 1704–20)
1720	John Fullarton (Edinburgh 1720–27)
1727	Arthur Millar (Edinburgh 1727)
1727	Andrew Lumsden (Edinburgh 1727–33)
1731	David Freebairn (Edinburgh 1733–39)
1738	Thomas Rattray (Dunkeld 1727–43)
1743	Robert Keith (Caithness 1731–41)
1757	Robert White (Dunblane 1735–43, St Andrews 1743–61)
1762	William Falconar (Orkney and Caithness 1741–62)

1782	Robert Kilgour (Aberdeen 1768–86)
1788	John Skinner (Aberdeen 1786–1816)
1816	George Gleig (Brechin 1810–40)
1837	James Walker (Edinburgh 1880–41)
1841	William Skinner (Aberdeen 1816–57)
1857	Charles Hughes Terrot (Edinburgh 1841–72)
1862	Robert Eden (Moray, Ross, and Caithness 1851–86)
1886	Hugh Willoughby Jermyn (Brechin 1875–1903)
1901	James Butler Knill Kelly (Moray, Ross, and Caithness 1886–1904)
1904	George Howard Wilkinson (St Andrews, Dunkeld, and Dunblane 1893–1907)
1908	Walter John Forbes Robberds (Brechin 1904–34)
1935	Arthur John Maclean (Moray, Ross, and Caithness 1904–43)
1943	Ernest Denny Logie Danson (Edinburgh 1939–46)
1946	John Charles Halland How (Glasgow and Galloway 1938–52)
1952	Thomas Hannay (Argyll and The Isles 1942–62)
1962	Francis Hamilton Moncreiff (Glasgow and Galloway 1952–74)
1974	Richard Knyvet Wimbush (Argyll and The Isles 1963–77)
1977	Alastair Iain Macdonald Haggart (Edinburgh 1975–85)
1985	Lawrence Edward Luscombe (Brechin 1975–90)
1990	George Kennedy Buchanan Henderson (Argyll and The Isles 1977–92)
1992	Richard Frederick Holloway (Edinburgh 1986–2000)
2000	Andrew Bruce Cameron (Aberdeen 1992–2006)
2006	Idris Jones (Glasgow and Galloway 1998–2009)
2009	David Robert Chillingworth (St Andrews, Dunkeld, and Dunblane 2005–17)
2017	Mark Jeremy Strange (Moray, Ross and Caithness 2007–)

IRELAND

PROVINCE OF ARMAGH

†Achonry

BISHOPS

c.558	Cathfuidh
1152	Mael Ruanaid ua Ruadain
1159	Gille na Naehm O Ruadain [Gelasius]
1208	Clemens O Sniadaig
1220	Connmach O Torpaig [Carus]
1226	Gilla Isu O Cleirig [Gelasius]
1237	Tomas O Ruadhan
1238	Oengus O Clumain [Elias]
1251	Tomas O Maicin

1266	Tomas O Miadachain [Dionysus]
1286	Benedict O Bracain
1312	David of Kilheny
1348	David II
1348	Nicol Alias Muircheartach O hEadhra
1374	William Andrew
1385	Simon
c.1390	Tomas mac Muirgheasa MacDonn-chadha
1401	Brian mac Seaain O hEadhra
1410	Maghnus O h Eadhra
1424	Donatus

1424	Richard Belmer
1436	Tadhg O Dalaigh
1442	James Blakedon
1449	Cornelius O Mochain
1463	Brian O hEasdhra [Benedictus]
1470	Nicholas Forden
1475	Robert Wellys
1484	Thomas fitzRichard
1484	Tomas O Conghalain
1489	John Bustamente
1492	Thomas Ford
1508	Eugenius O Flannagain
1522	Cormac O Snighe
1547	Thomas O Fihilly

† Indicates a diocese no longer extant, or united with another diocese.

1562 Eugene O'Harte
1613 Miler Magrath (with Cashel)
     United to Killala 1622

†Annadown

BISHOPS

1189 Conn ua Mellaig [Concors]
1202 Murchad ua Flaithbertaig
1242 Tomas O Mellaig
1251 Conchobar [Concors]
1283 John de Ufford
1308 Gilbert O Tigernaig
1323 Jacobus O Cethernaig
1326 Robert Petit
1328 Albertus
1329 Tomas O Mellaig
1359 Dionysius
1393 Johannes
1394 Henry Trillow
1402 John Bryt
1408 John Wynn
1421 John Boner [Camere]
1425 Seean Mac Braddaigh
1428 Seamus O Lonnghargain
1431 Donatus O Madagain
1446 Thomas Salscot
1450 Redmund Bermingham
1458 Thomas Barrett
1496 Francis Brunand
1540 John Moore
     United to Tuam c.1555

†Ardagh

454 Mel
c.670 Erard
874 Faelghus
     Cele 1048
1152 Mac Raith ua Morain
1172 Gilla Crist O hEothaig
     [Christianus]
     O'Tirlenain 1187
     ua hEislinnen
     Annud O Muiredaig 1216
1217 Robert
1224 M.
1228 Loseph mac Teichthechain
1229 Mac Raith Mac Serraig
1232 Gilla Isu mac in Scelaige O
     Tormaid [Gelasius]
1232 Iocelinus
1238 Brendan Mac Teichthechain
1256 Milo of Dunstable
1290 Matha O'h-Eothaig [Mattheus]
1323 Robert Wirsop (did not get
     possession)
1324 Mac Eoaighseoan
1347 Eoghan O Ferghail
     [Audovenus]
1368 William Mac Carmaic
1373 Cairbre O'Ferghail [Charles]
1373 John Aubrey
1392 Henry Nony (did not get
     possession)
1396 Comedinus Mac Bradaigh
     [Gilbert]
1400 Adam Leyns
1419 Conchobar O'Ferghail
     [Cornelius]
1425 Risdeard O'Ferghail
[1444 O'Murtry, not consecrated
     resigned]
1445 Cormac Mac Shamhradhain
1462 Seaan O'Ferghail
1467 Donatus O'Ferghail
1482 William O'Ferghail
1517 Ruaidri O'Maoileoin
1517 Rory O'Mallone [Roger O
     Melleine]
1541 Richard O'Ferrall
1553 Patrick MacMahon
[1572 John Garvey, not consecrated]
1583 Lysach O'Ferrall

1604 Robert Draper
1613 Thomas Moigne
1679 William Bedell
1633 John Richardson
1661 Robert Maxwell
1673 Francis Marsh
1682 William Sheridan
1692 Ulysses Burgh
1604–33, 1661–92 and 1692–1751 Held
     by the Bishops of Kilmore
1751–1839 Held by the Archbishops of
     Tuam
United to Kilmore 1839

Armagh

Description of arms. Azure, an
archiepiscopal staff in pale argent
ensigned with a cross pattée or,
surmounted by a pall argent fimbriated
and fringed or, charged with four
crosses pattées-fitchées sable.

BISHOPS

444 Patrick
     Benignus 467
     Jarlath 481
     Cormac 497
     Dubthach 513
     Ailill I 526
     Ailill II 536
     David O'Faranan 551
     Carlaen 588
     MacLaisre 623
–640 Thomian MacRonan
     Segeni 688
     Suibhne 730
–732 Congusa
     Affinth 794
–811 Nundha
–818 Artri
835 Forannan
     Mael Patraic I 862
     Fethgna 875
     Cathasach MacRobartach 883
     Mochta 893
900 Maelaithghin
     Cellach
     Mael Ciarain 915
     Joseph 936
     Mael Patraic II 936
     Cathasach MacDolgen 966
     Maelmiure 994
     Airindach 1000
     Maeltuile 1032
1032 Hugh O'Ferris
     Mael Patraic III 1096
1099 Caincomrac O'Boyle

ARCHBISHOPS

1105 Cellach mac Aeda meic Mael
     Isu [Celsus]
1132 Mael maedoc Ua Morgair
     [Malachais]
1137 Gilla Meic Liac mac Diarmata
     meic Ruaidri [Gelasius]
1174 Conchobar O Conchaille
     [Concors]
1175 Gille in Coimhedh O Caran
     [Gilbertus]
1180 Tomaltach O Conchobair
     [Thomas]

1184 Mael Isu Ua Cerbaill
     [Malachias]
1202 Echdonn mac Gilla Uidir
     [Eugenius]
1217 Lucas Neterville
1227 Donatus O Fidabra
1240 Albert Suebeer of Cologne
1247 Reginald
1258 Abraham O'Conallain
1261 Mael Patraic O Scannail
1270 Nicol Mac Mael Isu
1303 Michael MacLochlainn (not
     confirmed)
1304 Dionysius (not confirmed)
1306 John Taaffe
1307 Walter Jorz
1311 Roland Jorz
1324 Stephen Segrave
1334 David Mag Oireachtaigh
1347 Richard FitzRalph
1362 Milo Sweetman
1383 John Colton
1404 Nicholas Fleming
1418 John Swayne
1439 John Prene
1444 John Mey
1457 John Bole [Bull]
1471 John Foxhalls or Foxholes
1475 Edmund Connesburgh
1480 Ottaviano Spinelli [de Palatio]
1513 John Kite
1521 George Cromer
1543 George Dowdall
1552 Hugh Goodacre
1553 George Dowdall (again)
[1560 Donat MacTeague, not
     recognized by the Crown,
     1562]
1563 Adam Loftus
1568 Thomas Lancaster
1584 John Long
1589 John Garvey
1595 Henry Ussher
1613 Christopher Hampton
1625 James Ussher
     [Interregnum 1656–61]
1661 John Bramhall
1663 James Margetson
1679 Michael Boyle
1703 Narcissus Marsh
1714 Thomas Lindsay
1724 Hugh Boulter
1742 John Hoadly
1747 George Stone
1765 Richard Robinson [afterwards
     Baron Rokeby]
1795 William Newcome
1800 William Stuart
1822 John George Beresford
     United to Clogher 1850–86
1862 Marcus Gervais Beresford
1886 Robert Bentknox
1893 Robert Samuel Gregg
1896 William Alexander
1911 John Baptist Crozier
1920 Charles Frederick D'Arcy
1938 John Godfrey FitzMaurice Day
1939 John Allen Fitzgerald Gregg
1959 James McCann
1969 George Otto Simms
1980 John Ward Armstrong
1986 Robert Henry Alexander
     Eames
2007 Alan Edwin Thomas Harper
2012 Richard Lionel Clarke
2020 Francis John McDowell

Clogher

Description of arms. Azure, a bishop seated in full pontificals proper, in the act of benediction, and holding his pastoral staff in the left hand.

c.493	MacCarthinn or Ferdachrioch
	Ailill 869
1135	Cinaeth O Baigill
1135	Gilla Crist O Morgair
	[Christianus] (moved his
	see to Louth)

BISHOPS OF LOUTH

1135	Gilla Crist O Morgair
	[Christianus]
1138	Aed O Ceallaide [Edanus]
1178	Mael Isu O Cerbaill
	[Malachias]
1187	Gilla Crist O Mucaran
	[Christinus]
1194	Mael Isu Ua Mael Chiarain
1197	Gilla Tigernaig Mac Gilla
	Ronain [Thomas]

BISHOPS OF CLOGHER

1218	Donatus O Fidabra
1228	Nehemias
1245	David O Bracain
1268	Michael Mac an tSair
1287	Matthew Mac Cathasaigh I
–1310	Henricus
1316	Gelasius O Banain
1320	Nicholas Mac Cathasaigh
1356	Brian Mac Cathmaoil
	[Bernard]
1362	Matthew Mac Cathasaigh II
—	Aodh O hEothaigh [*alias* O Neill]
1373	John O Corcrain [Wurzburg]
1390	Art Mac Cathmhail
1433	Piaras Mag Uidhir [Petrus]
1450	Rossa mac Tomais Oig Mag Uidhir [Rogerius]
1475	Florence Woolley
[1484	Niall mac Seamuis Mac Mathghamna]
1484	John Edmund de Courci
1494	Seamus Mac Pilip Mac Mathghamna
1500	Andreas
1502	Nehemias O Cluainin
1504	Giolla Padraig O Conalaigh [Patrick]
1505	Eoghan Mac Cathmhail [Eugenius]
1517	Padraig O Cuilin
1535	Aodh O Cearbhalain [Odo]
1517	Patrick O'Cullen
1535	Hugh O'Carolan
1570	Miler Magrath
1605	George Montgomery
1621	James Spottiswood
1645	Henry Jones
1661	John Leslie
1671	Robert Leslie
1672	Roger Boyle
1691	Richard Tennison
1697	St George Ashe
1717	John Stearne
1745	Robert Clayton
1758	John Garnett
1782	John Hotham
1796	William Foster

1797	John Porter
1819	John George Beresford
1820	Percy Jocelyn
1822	Robert Ponsonby Tottenham Luftus
	United to Armagh 1850–86
1886	Charles Maurice Stack
1903	Charles Frederick D'Arcy
1908	Maurice Day
1923	James MacManaway
1944	Richard Tyner
1958	Alan Alexander Buchanan
1970	Richard Patrick Crosland Hanson
1973	Robert William Heavener
1980	Gordon McMullan
1986	Brian Desmond Anthony Hannon
2002	Michael Geoffrey St Aubyn Jackson
2011	Francis John McDowell
2021	Ian William Ellis

Connor

Description of arms. Azure, a lamb passant supporting with the dexter foreleg a staff proper flying therefrom a pennant argent charged with a saltire gules between three cross crosslets or; on a chief of the last two crosiers in saltire of the first.

506	Oengus MacNessa 514
	Lughadh 543
640	Dimma Dubh [the Black]
	Duchonna the Pious 725
	Cunnen or Cuinden 1038
	Flann O'Sculu 1117
1124	Mael Maedoc Ua Morgair [Malachias]
–1152	MaelPatraic O'Banain
1172	Nehemias
1178	Reginaldus
1226	Eustacius
1242	Adam
1245	Isaac de Newcastle-on-Tyne
1258	William de Portroyal
1261	William de Hay [or la Haye]
1263	Robert de Flanders
1275	Peter de Dunach
1293	Johannes
1320	Richard
1321	James de Couplith
1323	John de Eglecliff
1323	Robert Wirsop
1324	Jacabus O Cethernaig
1353	William Mercier
1374	Paulus
1389	Johannes
[1420	Seaan O Luachrain, not consecrated]
1423	Eoghan O'Domhnaill
1429	Domhnall O'Meraich
1431	John Fossade [Festade]
1459	Patricius
1459	Simon Elvington
	United to Down 1441
1945	Charles King Irwin
1956	Robert Cyril Hamilton Glover Elliott
1969	Arthur Hamilton Butler
1981	William John McCappin
1987	Samuel Greenfield Poyntz
1995	James Edward Moore

2002	Alan Edwin Thomas Harper
2007	Alan Francis Abernethy
2020	George Thomas William Davison

Derry

Derry and Raphoe

Description of arms. Party per pale: dexter gules, two swords in saltire proper, the hilts in base or, and on a chief azure a harp or stringed argent (for the See of Derry); sinister ermine, a chief per pale azure and or, the first charged with a sun in splendour of the last, the second with a cross pattée gules (for the See of Raphoe).

	Caencomhrac 927
–937	Finachta MacKellach
–949	Mael Finnen

BISHOPS OF MAGHERA

(Where the See was in the twelfth and the thirteenth centuries)

1107	Mael Coluim O Brolchain
—	Mael Brigte O Brolchain
1152	O Gormgaile Muiredach O Cobthaig [Mauricius]
1173	Amhlaim O Muirethaig
1185	Fogartach O Cerballain [Florentius]
c.1230	Gilla in Coimhded O Cerballain [Germanus]
c.1280	Fogartach O Cerballain II [Florentius]

BISHOPS OF DERRY

(Where the See was resettled)

1295	Enri Mac Airechtaig [O'Reghly] [of Ardagh]
1297	Gofraid MacLochlainn [Godfrey]
1316	Aed O Neill [Odo]
1319	Michael Mac Lochlainn [Maurice]
1349	Simon
1391	Johannes
1391	John Dongan
1394	Seoan O Mochain
1398	Aodh [Hugo]
1401	Seoan O Flannabhra
1415	Domhnall Mac Cathmhail
1419	Domhnall O Mearaich
1429	Eoghan O Domhnaill [Eugenius]
1433	John Oguguin
[1456	John Bole, appointment not completed, translated to Armagh]
1458	Bartholomew O Flannagain
c.1464	Johannes
1467	Nicholas Weston
1485	Domhnall O Fallamhain
1501	Seamus mac Pilip Mac Mathghamna [MacMahon]
1520	Ruaidhri O Domhnaill
1520	Rory O'Donnell
1554	Eugene O'Doherty
1568	F. [doubtful authority]
1569	Redmond O'Gallagher
[1603	Denis Campbell, not consecrated]

1605 George Montgomery
1610 Brutus Babington
[1611 Christopher Hampton, consecrated]
1613 John Tanner
1617 George Downham
1634 John Bramhall
1661 George Wild
1666 Robert Mossom
1680 Michael Ward
1681 Ezekiel Hopkins
1691 William King
1703 Charles Hickman
1714 John Hartstonge
1717 St George Ashe
1718 William Nicolson
1727 Henry Downes
1735 Thomas Rundle
1743 Carew Reynell
1745 George Stone
1747 William Barnard
1768 Frederick Augustus Hervey [afterwards Earl of Bristol]
1803 William Knox
1831 Richard Ponsonby
     Raphoe united to Derry from 1834
1853 William Higgin
1867 William Alexander
1896 George Alexander Chadwick (resigned)
1916 Joseph Irvine Peacocke
1945 Robert M'Neil Boyd
1958 Charles John Tyndall
1970 Cuthbert Irvine Peacocke
1975 Robert Henry Alexander Eames
1980 James Mehaffey
2002 Kenneth Raymond Good
2019 Andrew James Forster

Down

Down and Dromore

Description of arms. Quarterly, 1 and 4 azure, two keys endorsed in saltire the wards in chief or, surmounted in the fess point by a lamb passant proper (for the See of Down); 2 and 3 Argent, two keys endorsed in saltire the wards in chief gules, surmounted by an open book in fess proper between two crosses pattées-fitchées in pale sable (for the See of Dromore).

Fergus 584
Suibhne 825
Graithene 956
Finghin 964
Flaithbertach 1043
MaelKevin 1086
— Mael Muire 1117
Oengus Ua Gormain 1123
— [Anonymous]
c.1124 Mael Maedoc O Morgair [Malachias]
1152 Mael Isu mac in Chleirig Chuirr [Malachias]
1175 Gilla Domangairt Mac Cormaic
c.1176 Echmilid [Malachias]
c.1202 Radulfus
1224 Thomas

1251 Randulphus
1258 Reginaldus
1265 Thomas Lydel
1277 Nicholas le Blund
1305 Thomas Ketel
1314 Thomas Bright
1328 John of Baliconingham
1329 Ralph of Kilmessan
1353 Richard Calf I
1365 Robert of Aketon
1367 William White
1369 Richard Calf [II]
1386 John Ross
1394 John Dongan
1413 John Cely [or Sely]
1445 Ralph Alderle

BISHOPS OF DOWN AND CONNOR

1441 John Fossard
1447 Thomas Pollard
1451 Richard Wolsey
1456 Thomas Knight
1469 Tadh O Muirgheasa [Thaddaeus]
1489 Tiberio Ugolino
1520 Robert Blyth
1542 Eugene Magennis
1565 James MacCawell
1569 John Merriman
1572 Hugh Allen
1593 Edward Edgeworth
1596 John Charden
1602 Roben Humpston
1607 John Todd (resigned)
1612 James Dundas
1613 Robert Echlin
1635 Henry Leslie
1661 Jeremy Taylor
1667 Roger Boyle
1672 Thomas Hacket
1694 Samuel Foley
1695 Edward Walkington
1699 Edward Smyth
1721 Francis Hutchinson
1739 Carew Reynell
1743 John Ryder
1752 John Whitcombe
1752 Robert Downes
1753 Arthur Smyth
1765 James Traill
1784 William Dickson
1804 Nathaniel Alexander
1823 Richard Mant

BISHOPS OF DOWN, CONNOR AND DROMORE

1849 Robert Bent Knox
1886 William Reeves
1892 Thomas James Welland
1907 John Baptist Crozier
1911 Charles Frederick D'Arcy
1919 Charles Thornton Primrose Grierson
1934 John Frederick McNeice
1942 Charles King Irwin

BISHOPS OF DOWN AND DROMORE

1945 William Shaw Kerr
1955 Frederick Julian Mitchell
1970 George Alderson Quin
1980 Robert Henry Alexander Eames
1986 Gordon McMullan
1997 Harold Creeth Miller
2020 David Alexander McClay

†Dromore

Mael Brighde 974
Riagan 1101
1197 Ua Ruanada
1227 Geraldus
1245 Andreas
1284 Tigernach I

1290 Gervasius
— Tigernach II
1309 Florentius Mac Donnocain
1351 Anonymous
1366 Milo
1369 Christophorus Cornelius 1382
1382 John O'Lannoy
1398 Thomas Orwell
1400 John Waltham
1402 Roger Appleby
1408 Richard Payl
1410 Marcus
1411 John Chourles
1414 Seaan O Ruanadha
1419 Nicholas Wartre
1429 Thomas Rackelf
1431 William
1431 David Chirbury
1450 Thomas Scrope [Bradley]
1450 Thomas Radcliff
1456 Donatus O h-Anluain [Ohendua]
1457 Richard Messing
1463 William Egremond
— Aonghus [Aeneas] 1476
1476 Robert Kirke
1480 Yvo Guillen
1483 George Braua
1511 Tadhg O Raghallaigh [Thaddeus]
1536 Quintin O Quigley [Cogley]
1539 Roger McHugh
1540 Arthur Magennis
1607 John Todd
[1613 John Tanner, not consecrated]
1613 Theophilus Buckworth
1661 Robert Leslie
1661 Jeremy Taylor (administered the diocese)
1667 George Rust
1671 Essex Digby
1683 Capel Wiseman
1695 Tobias Pullein
1713 John Stearne
1717 Ralph Lambert
1727 Charles Cobbe
1732 Henry Maule
1744 Thomas Fletcher
1745 Jemmett Browne
1745 George Marlay
1763 John Oswald
1763 Edward Young
1765 Henry Maxwell
1766 William Newcome
1775 James Hawkins
1780 William de la Poer Beresford
1782 Thomas Percy
1811 George Hall
1812 John Leslie
1819 James Saurin
     United to Down since 1842

†Elphin

Domnall mac Flannacain Ua Dubhthaig 1136
Muiredach O Dubhthaig 1150
1152 Mael Isu O Connachtain
     Flannacan O Dubhthaig 1168
c.1177 Tomaltach mac Aeda Ua Conchobhair [Thomas]
c.1180 Florint Ua Riacain Ui Maelrvanaid
1206 Ardgar O Conchobhair
1226 Dionysius O Mordha
c.1230 Alanus
1231 Donnchad mac Fingein O Conchobhair [Dionysius Donatus]
1245 Eoin O Mugroin
1247 Tomaltach macToirrdelbaig O Conchobhair [Thomas]
1260 Mael Sechlainn O Conchobhair [Milo]

1262	Tomas mac Fergail mac Diarmata
1266	Muiris O Conchobhair
[1285	Amiaim O Tommaltaig, not consecrated]
1285	Gilla Isu mac in Liathana O Conchobhair
1297	Maelsechlainn mac Briain [Malachias]
1303	Donnchad O Flannacain, [Donatus]
1307	Cathal O Conchobhair
1310	Mael Sechlainn Mac Aedha
1313	Lurint O Lachtnain [Laurence]
1326	Sean O Finnachta
1355	Carolus
1357	Gregory O Mochain
1372	Thomas Barrett
1383	Seoan O Mochain
1407	Seaan O Grada
1405	Gerald Caneton
1412	Thomas Colby
1418	Robert Fosten
1421	Edmund Barrett
1427	Johannes
1429	Laurence O Beolain
1429	William O hEidighean
1448	Conchobhar O Maolalaidh
1458	Nicholas O Flanagan
1487	Hugo Arward
1492	Rlocard mac Briain O gCuanach
1499	George Brana
1501	Cornelius O Flannagain
1508	Christopher Fisher
1525	John Maxey
1539	William Maginn 1541(?)
1539	Gabriel de Sancto Serio
1541	Conach or Con O'Negall or O'Shyagall
1552	Roland Burke [de Burgo]
1582	Thomas Chester
1583	John Lynch
1611	Edward King
1639	Henry Tilson
1661	John Parker
1667	John Hodson
1691	Simon Digby
1720	Henry Downes
1724	Theophilus Bolton
1730	Robert Howard
1740	Edward Synge
1762	William Gore
1772	Jemmett Browne
1775	Charles Dodgson
1795	John Law
1810	Power le Poer Trench
1819	John Leslie 1854

United to Kilmore and Ardagh on the death of Bishop Beresford in 1841, when Bishop Leslie became Bishop of the united dioceses.

†Killala

Muiredach
Kellach
O Maolfogmair I 1137
O Maolfogmair II 1151
Imar O Ruaidhin 1176

1179	O Maolfogmair III
1199	Domnall Ua Becdha
1207	Cormac O'Tarpy
	O'Kelly 1214
1226	Aengus O Maolfogmair [Elias]
	Gille Cellaig O Ruaidhin
1253	Seoan O Laidlg
1281	Donnchad O Flaithbertaig [Donatus]
1307	John Tankard
	Sean O Flaithim 1343
1344	James Bermingham
1347	William O DusucBhda
1351	Robert Elyot

1381	Thomas Lodowys
1383	Conchobar O Coineoil [Cornelius]
1390	Thomas Horwell [Orwell]
1400	Thomas Barrett
1403	Muircheartach Cleirach mac Donnchadha O DusucBhda
	Connor O'Connell 1423
1427	Fergal Mac Martain
1431	Thaddaeus Mac Creagh
1432	Brian O Coneoil
1447	Robert Barrett
1452	Ruaidhri Bairead [Barrett]
1453	Thomas
1459	Richard Viel
	Miler O'Connell
1461	Donatus O Conchobhair
1470	Tomas Bairead [Barrett]
1487	John de Tuderto [Seaan O Caissin]
1500	Thomas Clerke
1508	Malachias O Clumhain
1513	Risdeard Bairead
1545	Redmond O'Gallagher
1570	Donat O'Gallagher
1580	John O'Casey
1592	Owen O'Conor
1613	Miler Magrath

Achonry united to Killala 1622

1623	Archibald Hamilton
1630	Archibald Adair (deposed, but subsequently restored)
164?	John Maxwell
1661	Henry Hall
1664	Thomas Bayly
1671	Thomas Otway
1680	John Smith
1681	William Smyth
1682	Richard Tennison
1691	William Lloyd
1717	Henry Downes
1720	Charles Cobbe
1727	Robert Howard
1730	Robert Clayton
173?	Mordecai Cary
175?	Richard Robinson [afterwards Baron Rokeby]
1759	Samuel Hutchinson
1781	William Cecil Pery
1784	William Preston
1787	John Law
1795	John Porter
1798	Joseph Stock
1810	James Verschoyle

United to Tuam since 1834

Kilmore

Kilmore, Elphin and Ardagh

Description of arms. Argent, on a cross azure a pastoral staff enfiling a mitre, all or (for the See of Kilmore). Sable, two pastoral staves in saltire or, in base a lamb couchant, argent (for the See of Elphin). Or, a cross gules between four trefoils slipped vert, on a chief sable, a key erect of the first (for the See of Ardagh).

—	Aed Ua Finn 1136
—	Muirchenach Ua Maelmoeherge 1149
1152	Tuathal Ua Connachtaig [Thadeus]

1202	Mi Ua Dobailen
—	Flann O Connachtaig [Florentius] 1231
1237	Congalach Mac Idneoil
1251	Simon O Ruairc
1286	Mauricius
—	Matha Mac Duibne 1314
1320	Padraig O Cridecain
—	Conchobhar Mac Conshnamha [Ford] 1355
1356	Richard O Raghilligh
1373	Johannes
1388	Thomas Rushook
1392	Sean O Raghilligh I [John]
1398	Nicol Mac Bradaigh
1401	Sean O'Raghilligh II
1407	John Stokes
1409	David O'Fairchellaigh
1422	Domhnall O Gabhann
1445	Aindrias Mac Bradaigh
1455	Fear Sithe Mag Dhuibhne
1465	Sean O Raghilligh II
1476	Cormac Mag Shamhradhain
1480	Tomas MacBradaigh
1512	Diarmaid O Raghilligh
1530	Edmund Nugent
1540	Sean Mac Bradaigh
1585	John Garvey
1604	Robert Draper
1613	Thomas Moigne
1629	William Bedell
1643	Robert Maxwell
1673	Francis Marsh
1682	William Sheridan
1693	William Smyth
1699	Edward Wetenhall
1715	Timothy Godwin
1727	Josiah Hott
1742	Joseph Story
1757	John Cradock
1772	Denison Cumberland
1775	George Lewis Jones
1790	William Foster
1796	Charles Broderick
1802	George de la Poer Beresford

Ardagh united to Kilmore 1839

Elphin united to Kilmore 1841

1841	John Leslie
1854	Marcus Gervais Beresford
1862	Hamilton Verschoyle
1870	Charles Leslie
1870	Thomas Carson
1874	John Richard Darley
1884	Samuel Shone
1897	Alfred George Elliott
1915	William Richard Moore
1930	Arthur William Barton
1939	Albert Edward Hughes
1950	Frederick Julian Mitchell
1956	Charles John Tyndall
1959	Edward Francis Butler Moore
1981	William Gilbert Wilson
1993	Michael Hugh Gunton Mayes
2001	Kenneth Harbert Clarke
2013	Samuel Ferran Glenfield

†Mayo

Gerald 732
Muiredach [or Murray]
Mcinracht 732
Aidan 773

1172	Gilla Isu Ua Mailin
	Cele O Dubhthaig 1210
1210	?Patricius
1428	William Prendergast
1430	Nicholas 'Wogmay'
1439	Odo O h-Uiginn
1432	Martin Campania
1457	Simon de Duren
1493	John Bel
1541	Eugenius Macan Brehon

United to Tuam 1559

†Raphoe

Sean O Gairedain
Donell O Garvan
Felemy O Syda
Oengus O'Lappin 959
1150 Muiredhach O'Cofley
1156 Gille in Coimhded Ua Carain
       [Gilbertus]
—   Anonymous
1204 Mael Isu Ua Doirig
—   Anonymous
1253 Mael Padraig O Scannail
       [Patricius]
1263 John de Alneto
1265 Cairpre O Scuapa
1275 Fergal O Firghil [Florentius]
1306 Enri Mac-in-Chrossain
       [Henricus]
1319 Tomas Mac Carmaic Ui
       Domhnaill
1363 Padraig Mac Maonghail
1367 Conchobar Mac Carmaic Ui
       Domhnaill [Cornelius]
1397 Seoan MacMenmain
1400 Eoin MacCarmaic [Johannes]
-1413 Anthony
-1414 Robert Rubire
1416 John McCormic
1420 Lochlainn O Gallchobhair I
       [Laurentius]
1440 Cornelius Mac Giolla Brighde
1443 Lochlainn O Gallchobhair II
       [Laurentius]
1479 John de Rogeriis
1482 Meanma Mac Carmail
       [Menclaus Mac Carmacain]
1514 Conn O Cathain [Cornelius]
1534 Eamonn O Gallchobhair
1547 Arthur o'Gallagher
1563 Donnell Magonigle [or
       McCongail]
[1603 Denis Campbell, not
       consecrated]
1605 George Montgomery
1611 Andrew Knox
1633 John Leslie
1661 Robert Leslie
1671 Ezekiel Hopkins
1682 William Smyth
1693 Alexander Cairncross
1701 Robert Huntington
1702 John Pooley
1713 Thomas Lindsay
1714 Edward Synge
1716 Nicholas Forster
1744 William Barnard
1747 Philip Twysden
1753 Robert Downes
1763 John Oswald
1780 James Hawkins

1807 John George Beresford
1819 William Magee
1822 William Bissett
       United to Derry since 1834

Tuam

Tuam, Killala and Achonry

Description of arms. Azure beneath a
triple architectural canopy three figures,
in the centre the Blessed Virgin Mary
holding in her arms the Holy Child,
between, on the dexter the figure of
a bishop (St Jarlath) in pontificalibus
and in the act of benediction, and, on
the sinister St John supporting with his
left arm a lamb argent, each in proper
vestments or, the hands, feet, and faces
proper.

BISHOPS

Murrough O'Nioc 1032
Hugh O'Hessian 1085
Cathusach Ua Conaill 1117
O Clerig 1137
Muiredach Ua Dubhthaig
       1150

ARCHBISHOPS

1152 Aed Ua h-Oisin [Edanus]
1167 Cadhla Ua Dubhthaig
       [Catholicus]
1202 Felix Ua Ruanada
1236 Mael Muire O Lachtain
       [Marianus]
1250 Flann Mac Flainn [Florentius]
[1256 James O'Laghtnan, not
       confirmed or consecrated]
1257 Walter de Salerno
1258 Tomaltach O Conchobair
       [Thomas]
1286 Stephen de Fulbourn
1289 William de Bermingham
1312 Mael Sechlainn Mac Aeda
1348 Tomas MacCerbhaill
       [MacCarwill]

1364 Eoin O Grada
1372 Gregory O Mochain I
1384 Gregory O Mochain II
1387 William O Cormacain
1393 Muirchertach mac Pilb O
       Cellaigh
1410 John Babingle
1411 Cornelius
1430 John Bermingham [Winfield]
1438 Tomas mac Muirchearthaigh
       O Cellaigh
1441 John de Burgo
1452 Donatus O Muiredaigh
1485 William Seoighe [Joyce]
1503 Philip Pinson
1506 Muiris O Fithcheallaigh
1514 Tomas O Maolalaidh
1537 Christopher Bodkin
1573 William O'Mullally [or Lealy]
       Annadown united to Tuam
       c.1555
       Mayo united to Tuam 1559
1595 Nehemiah Donnellan
1609 William O'Donnell [or Daniel]
1629 Randolph or Ralph Barlow
1638 Richard Boyle
1645 John Maxwell
1661 Samuel Pullen
1667 John Parker
1679 John Vesey
1716 Edward Synge
1742 Josiah Hort
1752 John Ryder
1775 Jemmett Browne
1782 Joseph Dean Bourke
       [afterwards Earl of Mayo]
1794 William Beresford [afterwards
       Baron Decies]
1819 Power le Poer Trench
       Killala united to Tuam from
       1834

BISHOPS

1839 Thomas Plunket [afterwards
       Baron Plunket]
1867 Charles Brodrick Bernard
1890 James O'Sullivan
1913 Benjamin John Plunket
1920 Arthur Edwin Ross
1923 John Ort
1928 John Mason Harden
1932 William Hardy Holmes
1939 John Winthrop Crozier
1958 Arthur Hamilton Butler
1970 John Coote Duggan
1986 John Robert Winder Neill
1998 Richard Crosbie Aitken
       Henderson
2011 Patrick William Rooke
2021 *vacant*

PROVINCE OF DUBLIN

†Ardfert

BISHOPS

Anmchad O h-Anmchada
       1117
1152 Mael Brenain Ua Ronain
Gilla Mac Aiblen
       O'Anmehadha 1166
Domnall O Connairche 1193
1200 David Ua Duibdithrib
Anonymous 1217
1218 John
1218 Gilbertus
1237 Brendan
1253 Christianus
1257 Philippus
1265 Johannes
1286 Nicolaus

1288 Nicol O Samradain
1336 Ailin O hEichthighirn
1331 Edmund of Caermaerthen
1348 John de Valle
1372 Cornelius O Tigernach
1380 William Bull
1411 Nicholas FitzMaurice
1404 Nicholas Ball
1405 Tomas O Ceallaigh
1409 John Attilburgh [Artilburch]
1450 Maurice Stack
1452 Maurice O Conchobhair
1461 John Stack
1461 John Pigge
1473 Philip Stack
1495 John FitzGerald
       [See vacant in 1534]
1536 James FitzMaurice
1588 Nicholas Kenan

1600 John Crosbie
1622 John Steere
1628 William Steere
1641 Thomas Fulwar
       United to Limerick 1661

†Ardmore

1153 Eugenius
       Incorporated with Lismore
       1192

Cashel

Cashel, Waterford, Lismore, Ossory, Ferns and Leighlin

Description of arms. Gules, two keys addorsed in saltire the wards in chief, or.

BISHOPS

Cormac MacCuillenan 908
Donnell O'Heney 1096 *or* 1098

ARCHBISHOPS

*c.*1111 Mael Ios Ua h-Ainmire
Mael Iosa Ua Fogludha [Mauricius] 1131
Domnall Ua Conaing 1137
Gilla Naomh O'Marty 1149
–1152 Donat O'Lonergan I
–*c.*1160 M.
1172 Domnall O h-Ualla-chain [Donatus]
1186 Muirghes O h-Enna [Matheus]
*c.*1208 Donnchad Ua Longargain I [Donatus]
1216 Donnchad Ua Longargain II [Donatus]
1224 Mairin O Briain [Marianus]
1238 David mac Ceallaig [O'Kelly]
1254 David Mac Cearbaill [Mac Carwill]
1290 Stiamna O Bracain
1303 Maurice Mac Cearbaill
1317 William FitzJohn
1327 Seoan Mac Cerbaill
1329 Walter le Rede
1332 Eoin O Grada
1346 Radulphus O Cellaigh [Kelly]
1362 George Roche [de Rupe]
1365 Tomas Mac Cearbhaill
1374 Philip of Torrington
1382 Michael
1384 Peter Hackett
1406 Richard O Hedian
1442 John Cantwell I
1452 John Cantwell II
1484 David Creagh
1504 Maurice FitzGerald
1525 Edmund Butler
1553 Roland Baron or FitzGerald
1567 James MacCawell
Emly united to Cashel 1569
1571 Miler Magrath (Bishop of Cashel and Waterford from 1582)
1623 Malcolm Hamilton
1630 Archibald Hamilton
1661 Thomas Fulwar
1667 Thomas Price
[See vacant 1685–91]
1691 Narcissus Marsh
1694 William Palliser
[1727 William Nicolson, not enthroned]
1727 Timothy Goodwin
1730 Theophilus Bolton
1744 Arthur Price
1752 John Whitcombe
1754 Michael Cox
1779 Charles Agar
1801 Charles Brodrick

1822 Richard Laurence
Waterford and Lismore united to Cashel from 1833; on the death of Abp Laurence in 1838 the province was united to Dublin and the see ceased to be an Archbishopric

BISHOPS

1839 Stephen Creagh Sandes
1843 Robert Daly
1872 Maurice FitzGerald Day
1900 Henry Stewart O'Hara
1919 Robert Miller
1931 John Frederick McNeice
1935 Thomas Arnold Harvey
1958 William Cecil De Pauley
1968 John Ward Armstrong
Ossory united to Cashel 1977
1980 Noel Vincent Willoughby
1997 John Robert Winder Neill
2003 Peter Francis Barrett
2006 Michael Andrew James Burrows

†Clonfert

Moena, or Moynean, or Moeinend 572
Cummin the Tall 662
Ceannfaeladh 807
Laithbheartach 822
Ruthnel or Ruthme 826
Cormac MacEdain 922
Ciaran O'Gabbla 953
Cathal 963
Eochu 1031
O'Corcoran 1095
Muiredach Ua h-Enlainge 1117
Gille Patraic Ua Ailcinned 1149
*c.*1152 Petrus Ua Mordha
1172 Mail Isu mac in Baird
1179 Celechair Ua h-Armedaig
Muirchertach Ua'Maeluidir 1187
Domnall Ua Finn 1195
Muirchertach Ua Carmacain 1204
1205 Mael Brigte Ua hErurain
1224 Cormac O Luimlin [Carus]
1248 Thomas
1259 Tomas mac Domnaill Moire O Cellaig
1266 Johannes de Alatre
1296 Robert
*c.*1302 John
1308 Gregorius O Brocaig
1320 Robert Le Petit
1322 Seoan O Leaain
1347 Tomas mac Gilbert O Cellaigh I
1378 Muircheartach mac Pilib O Cellaigh [Maurice]
1393 William O Cormacain
1398 David Corre
1398 Enri O Conmaigh
1405 Tomasi O Cellaigh II
1410 Cobhthach O Madagain
1438 Seaan O hEidin
1441 John White
1447 Conchobhar O Maolalaidh
1448 Cornelius O Cuinnlis
1463 Matthaeus Mag Raith
1508 David de Burgo
1509 Dionysius O'Mordha
1534 Roland de Burgo
1536 Richard Nangle
1580 Hugh
1582 Stephen Kirwan
1602 Roland Lynch
1627 Robert Dawson
1644 William Baily

1665 Edward Wolley
1691 William FitzGerald
1722 Theophilus Bolton
1724 Arthur Price
1730 Edward Synye
1732 Mordecai Cary
1716 John Whitcombe
1752 Arthur Smyth
1753 William Carmichael
1758 William Gote
1762 John Oswald
1763 Denison Cumberland
1772 Walter Cope
1782 John Law
1787 Richard Marlay
1795 Charles Broderick
1796 Hugh Hamilton
1798 Matthew Young
1801 George de la l'oer Beresford
1802 Nathaniel Alexander
1804 Christopher Butson
United to Killaloe since 1834

†Clonmacnoise

–663 Baitan O'Cormac
–839 Joseph [of Rossmore]
Maclodhar 890
Cairbre Crom 904
Loingsech 919
–940 Donough I
–953 Donough II
–966 Cormae O Cillin
Maenach 971
Conaing O'Cosgraigh 998
Male Poil 1001
Flaithbertach 1038
Celechar 1067
O'Mallaen 1093
Christian Aherne 1104
?1111 Domnall mac Flannacain Ua Dubthaig
1152 Muirchertach Ua Maeluidir
Cathal Ua Maeileoin 1207
*c.*1207 Muirchertach Ua Muiricen
1214 Aed O Maeileoin I
1227 Aed O Maeileoin II [Elias]
1236 Thomas Fitzpatrick
1252 Tomas O Cuinn
1280 Anonymous
1282 Gilbert (not consecrated)
1290 William O Dubhthaig
1298 William O Finnein
1303 Domnall O Braein
1324 Lughaid O Dalaigh
1337 Henricus
1349 Simon
1369 Richard [Braybroke]
1371 Hugo
1388 Philippus O Maoil
1389 Milo Corr
1397 O'Gallagher
1397 Philip Nangle
1423 David Prendergast
1426 Cormac Mac Cochlain [Cornelius]
1444 Sean O Dalaigh
1449 Thomas
1458 Robertus
1458 William
1459 John
1487 Walter Blake
1509 Tomas O Maolalaidh
1516 Quintin O h-Uiginn
1539 Richard O'Hogan
1539 Florence Kirwan
1556 Peter Wall [Wale]
United to Meath 1569

†Cloyne

Reachtaidh 887
1148 Gilla na Naem O Muirchertaig [Nehemias]
Ua Dubcroin 1159
Ua Flannacain 1167
1177 Matthaeus Ua Mongaig
1201 Laurence Ua Suilleabain
1205 C.
1281 Luke
c.1224 Florence
1226 Daniel
1237 David mac Cellaig [O'Kelly]
1240 Ailinn O Suilleabain
1247 Daniel
1265 Reginaldus
1275 Alan O Longain
1284 Nicholas of Effingham
1323 Maurice O Solchain
1333 John Brid
1351 John Whitekot
1363 John Swaffham
1376 Richard Wye
1394 Gerard Caneton
1413 Adam Payn
United to Cork 1418–1638
1638 George Synge
1661–78 Held by the Bishops of Cork
1679 Patrick Sheridan
1683 Edward Jones
1693 William Palliser
1694 Tobias Pullein
1695 St George Ashe
1697 John Pooley
1702 Charles Crow
1726 Henry Maule
1732 Edward Synge
1734 George Berkeley
1753 James Stopford
1759 Robert Johnson
1767 Frederick Augustus Hervery
1768 Charles Agar
1780 George Chinnery
1781 Richard Woodward
1794 William Bennett
1820 Charles Mongan Warburton
1826 John Brinkley
United to Cork on the death of Bp Brinkley in 1835

Cork

Cork, Cloyne and Ross

Description of arms. Argent, on a plain cross, the ends pattée, gules, a pastoral staff, surmounted on a mitre, or (for the See of Cork). Azure, a mitre proper labelled or, between three crosses pattées-fitchées argent (for the See of Cloyne). No arms are borne for the See of Ross.

Donnell 876
Soer Bhreatach 892
DusucBhdhurn O'Stefam 959
Cathmogh 969
Mugron O'Mutan 1057
1138 Gregory
? Ua Menngorain 1147
1148 Gilla Aedha Ua Maigin
1174 [Gregorius] O h-Aedha [O Hea]
c.1182 Reginaldus I

1187 Aicher
1192 Murchad Ua h-Aedha
Anonymous 1214
1215 Mairin Ua Briain [Marianus]
1225 Gilbertus
1248 Laurentius
1265 William of Jerpoint
1267 Reginaldus
1277 Robert Mac Donnchada
1302 Seoan Mac Cearbaill [Mac Carwill]
1321 Philip of Slane
1327 Walter le Rede
1330 John of Ballyconingham
1347 John Roche
1359 Gerald de Barri
1396 Roger Ellesmere
1406 Richard Kynmoure
1409 Patrick Fox
1409 Milo fitzJohn
1425 John Paston
1418 Adam Payn
1429 Jordan Purcell
1463 Gerald FitzGerald
1472 William Roche (Coadjutor)
1490 Tadhg Mac Carthaigh
1499 John FitzEdmund FitzGerald
1499 Patrick Cant
1523 John Benet
1536 Dominic Tyrre [Tirrey]
1562 Roger Skiddy
1570 Richard Dyxon
1572 Matthew Sheyn
Ross united to Cork 1583
1583 William Lyon
1618 John Boyle
1620 Richard Boyle
1638 William Chappell
1661 Michael Boyle
1663 Edward Synge
1679 Edward Wetenhall
1699 Dive Downes
1710 Peter Browne
1735 Robert Clayton
1745 Jemmett Browne
1772 Isaac Mann
1789 Euseby Cleaver
1789 William Foster
1790 William Bennet
1794 Thomas Stopford
1805 John George Beresford
1807 Thomas St Laurence
1831 Samuel Kyle
Cloyne united to Cork from 1835
1848 James Wilson
1857 William FitzGerald
1862 John Gregg
1878 Robert Samuel Gregg
1894 William Edward Meade
1912 Charles Benjamin Dowse
1933 William Edward Flewett
1938 Robert Thomas Hearn
1952 George Otto Sims
1957 Richard Gordon Perdue
1978 Samuel Greenfield Poyntz
1988 Robert Alexander Warke
1999 William Paul Colton

Dublin

Dublin and Glendalough

Description of arms. Azure, an episcopal staff argent, ensigned with a cross pattée or, surmounted by a pallium of the second edged and fringed or, charged with five crosses formée fitchée, sable.

BISHOPS

Sinhail 790
c.1028 Dunan [Donatus]
1074 Gilla Patraic
1085 Donngus
1096 Samuel Ua'h-Aingliu

ARCHBISHOPS

1121 Grene [Gregorius]
1162 Lorcan Ua'Tuathail [Laurentius]
1182 John Cumin
1213 Henry de Loundres
Glendalough united to Dublin
1230 Luke
125? Fulk de Sandford
1279 John de Derlington
1286 John de Sandford
1295 Thomas de Chadworth
1296 William de Hotham
1299 Richard de Ferings
[1307 Richard de Havering, not consecrated]
1311 John de Leche
1317 Alexander de Bicknor
1349 John de St Paul
1363 Thomas Minot
1376 Robert de Wikeford
1391 Robert Waldeby
1396 Richard Northalis
1397 Thomas Cranley
1418 Richard Talbot
1451 Michael Tregury
1472 John Walton
1484 Walter Fitzsimons
1512 William Rokeby
1521 Hugh Inge
1529 John Alan
1535 George Browne
1555 Hugh Curwin
1567 Adam Loftus
1605 Thomas Jones
1619 Lancelot Bulkeley
1661 James Margetson
1663 Michael Boyle
1679 John Parker
1682 Francis Marsh
1694 Narcissus Marsh
1703 William King
1730 John Hoadly
1743 Charles Cobbe
1765 William Carmichael
1766 Arthur Smyth
1772 John Cradock
1779 Robert Fowler
1801 Charles Agar [Earl of Normanton]
1809 Euseby Cleaver
1820 John George Beresford
1822 William Magee
1831 Richard Whately
Kildare united to Dublin 1846

1864	Richard Chenevix Trench (resigned)
1885	William Conyngham [Lord Plunket]
1897	Joseph Ferguson Peacocke
1915	John Henry Bernard
1919	Charles Frederick D'Arcy
1920	John Allen Fitzgerald Gregg
1939	Arthur William Barton
1956	George Otto Simms
1969	Alan Alexander Buchanan
1977	Henry Robert McAdoo
1985	Donald Arthur Richard Caird
1996	Walton Newcome Francis Empey
2002	John Robert Winder Neill
2011	Michael Geoffrey St Aubyn Jackson

†Emly

	Raidghil 881
	Ua Ruaich 953
	Faelan 980
	MaelFinan 1030
	Diarmait Ua Flainnchua 1114
1152	Gilla in Choimhded Ua h-Ardmhail Mael Isu Ua Laigenain 1163
1172	Ua Meic Stia
1177	Charles O'Buacalla
1177	Isaac O'Hamery
1192	Ragnall Ua Flainnchua
1205	M.
1209	William
1212	Henry
1227	John Collingham
1238	Daniel
1238	Christianus
1251	Gilbert O'Doverty
1266	Florence or Laurence O'hAirt
1272	Matthew MacGormain
1275	David O Cossaig
1286	William de Clifford
1306	Thomas Cantock [Quantock]
1309	William Roughead
1335	Richard le Walleys
1353	John Esmond
1363	David Penlyn [Foynlyn]
1363	William
1405	Nicholas Ball
1421	John Rishberry
1422	Robert Windell
1428	Thomas de Burgo
1428	Robert Portland
1445	Cornelius O Cuinnlis
1444	Robert
1448	Cornelius O Maolalaidh
1449	William O Hetigan
1476	Pilib O Cathail
1494	Donatus Mac Briain
1498	Cinneidigh Mac Briain
1507	Tomas O hUrthaille
1543	Angus O'Hernan
1551	Raymond de Burgo
	United to Cashel 1569
	Transferred to Limerick 1976

†Ferns

–598	Edan [or Maedoc or Hugh]
	Maeldogair 676
	Coman 678
	Diratus 693
	Cillenius 715
	Cairbre O'Kearney 1095
	Ceallach Ua Colmain 1117
	Mael Eoin Ua Dunacain 1125
	Ua Cattain 1135
1178	Loseph Ua h-Aeda
1186	Ailbe Ua Maelmuaid [Albinus]
1224	John of St John
1254	Geoffrey of St John
1258	Hugh of Lamport
1283	Richard of Northampton

1304	Simon of Evesham
1305	Robert Walrand
1312	Adam of Northampton
1347	Hugh de Saltu [of Leixlip]
1347	Geoffrey Grandfeld
1349	John Esmond
1350	William Charnells
1363	Thomas Dene
1400	Patrick Barret
1418	Robert Whittey
1453	Tadhg O Beirn
1457	John Purcell I
1479	Laurence Nevill
1505	Edmund Comerford
1510	Nicholas Comyn
1519	John Purcell II
1539	Alexander Devereux
1566	John Devereux
1582	Hugh Allen
	Leighlin united to Ferns 1597
1600	Robert Grave
1601	Nicholas Statford
1605	Thomas Ram
1635	George Andrews
1661	Robert Price
1667	Richard Boyle
1683	Narcissus Marsh
1691	Bartholomew Vigors
1722	Josiah Hort
1727	John Hoadly
1730	Arthur Price
1734	Edward Synge
1740	George Stone
1743	William Cottrell
1744	Robert Downes
1752	John Garnet
1758	William Carmichael
1758	Thomas Salmon
1759	Richard Robinson
1761	Charles Jackson
1765	Edward Young
1772	Joseph Deane Bourke
1782	Walter Cope
1787	William Preston
1789	Euseby Cleaver
1809	Percy Jocelyn
1820	Robert Ponsonby Tottenham Loftus
1822	Thomas Elrington
	United to Ossory 1835

†Glendalough

	Dairchell 678
	Eterscel 814
	Dungal 904
	Cormac 927
	Nuadha 920 [or Neva]
	Gilda Na Naomh c.1080
	Cormac O'Mail 1101
	Aed Ua Modain 1126
1140	Anonymous
1152	Gilla na Naem
1157	Cinaed O Ronain [Celestinus]
1176	Maelcallann Ua Cleirchen [Malchus]
1186	Macrobius
1192	William Piro
1214	Robert de Bedford
	United to Dublin
	After the union with Dublin some rival bishops appear.
c.1216	Bricheus
1468	John
1475	Michael
1481	Denis White John 1494
1494	Ivo Ruffi
1495	John
1500	Francis Fitzjohn of Corduba

†Iniscattery (Scattery Island)

861	Aidan
959	Cinaeda O'Chommind
973	Scandlam O'Lenz
	O'Bruil 1069
	O'Bruil II 1081
	Dermot O Lennain 1119
	Aed Ua Bechain I 1188
	Cearbhal Ua'h-Enna [Carolus] 1193
1360	Tomas Mac Mathghamhna
1392	John Donkan
1414	Richard Belmer
	Dionysius 1447
1447	John Grene
	Incorporated with Limerick

†Kells

	Mael Finnen 968
c.1152	Tuathal Ua Connachtarg
1185	Anonymous
1202	M. Ua Dobailen
	Incorporated with Meath

†Kildare

	Conlaedh 520
	Hugh [or Hed] the Black 639
	Maeldoborcon 709
	Eutigern 762
	Lomthiull 787
	Snedbran 787
	Tuatchar 834
	Orthanach 840
	Aedgene Britt 864
	Macnghal 870
	Lachtnan 875
	Suibhne 881
	Scannal 885
	Lergus 888
	Mael Findan 950
	Annchadh 981
	Murrough McFlan 986
1030	MaelMartain
	MaelBrighde 1042
	Finn 1085
	MaelBrighde O Brolchan 1097
	Hugh [Heremon] 1100
	Ferdomnach 1101
	Cormac O Cathassaig 1146
	Ua Duibhin 1148
1152	Finn mac Mael Muire Mac Cianain
	Fin mac Gussain Ua Gormain
1161	Malachias Ua Brain
1177	Nehemias
1206	Cornelius Mac Fealain
1223	Ralph of Bristol
1233	John of Taunton
1258	Simon of Kilkenny
1280	Nicholas Cusack
1300	Walter Calf [de Veel]
1333	Richard Houlot
1352	Thomas Giffard
1366	Robert of Aketon [Acton]
1404	John Madock
1431	William fitzEdward
1449	Geoffrey Hereford
1456	John Bole [Bull]
1464	Richard Lang
1474	David Cone
1475	James Wall
	William Barret
1480	Edward Lane
1526	Thomas Dillon
1529	Walter Wellesley
1540	William Miagh
1550	Thomas Lancaster
1555	Thomas Leverous
1560	Alexander Craik
1564	Robert Daly
1583	Daniel Neylan

1604	William Pilsworth
1636	Robert Ussher
1644	William Golborne
1661	Thomas Price
1667	Ambrose Jones
1679	Anthony Dopping
1682	William Moreton
1705	Welbore Ellis
1731	Charles Cobbe
1743	George Stone
1745	Thomas Fletcher
1761	Richard Robinson
1765	Charles Jackson
1790	George Lewis Jones
1804	Charles Lindsay
	United to Dublin after the death of Bp Lindsay in 1846
1976	Separated from Dublin and united to Meath

†Kilfenora

1172	Anonymous
1205	F.
1224	Johannes
1254	Christianus
	Anonymous 1264
1266	Mauricius
1273	Florentius O Tigernaig
1281	Congalach [O Lochlainn]
1291	G.
1299	Simon O Cuirrin
1303	Maurice O Briain
1323	Risdeard O Lochlainn
c.1355	Dionysius
1372	Henricus
	Cornelius
1390	Patricius
1421	Feidhlimidh mac Mathghamhna O Lochlainn [Florentius]
1433	Fearghal
1434	Dionysius O Connmhaigh
1447	John Greni
1476	[? Denis] O Tombaigh
1491	Muircheartach mac Murchadha O Briain [Mauricius]
1514	Maurice O'Kelly
1541	John O'Neylan
–1585	Daniel, bishop-elect
1606	Bernard Adams [with Limerick q.v.]
1617	John Steere
1622	William Murray
[1628	Richard Betts, not consecrated]
1630	James Heygate
1638	Robert Sibthorp
1661–1741	Held by the Archbishops of Tuam
1742–52	Held by the Bishop of Clonfert
	United to Killaloe 1752

†Killaloe

BISHOPS

	O'Gerruidher 1054
	Domnall Ua hEnna 1098
	Mael Muire O Dunain 1117
	Domnall Ua Conaing 1131
	Domnall Ua Longargain 1137
	Tadg Ua Longargain 1161
	Donnchad mac Diarmata Ua Briain 1164
1179	Constantin mac Toirrdelbaig Ua Briain
1194	Diarmait Ua Conaing
1201	Conchobhar Ua h-Enna [Cornelius]
1217	Robert Travers
1221	Domnall Ua h-Enna [Donatus]
1231	Domnall O Cenneitig [Donatus]

1253	Isoc O Cormacain [Isaac]
1268	Mathgamain O h-Ocain [O Hogan]
1281	Maurice O h-Ocain
1299	David Mac Mathghamna [Mac Mahon]
1317	Tomas O Cormacain I
1323	Brian O Cosgraig
1326	David Mac Briain [David of Emly]
?1326	Natus O Heime
1343	Tomas O h-Ogain
1355	Tomas O Cormacain II
1389	Mathghamain Mag Raith
1400	Donatus Mag Raith
1409	Robert Mulfield
1418	Eugenius O Faolain
1423	Thadeus Mag Raith I
1429	Seamus O Lonnghargain
1443	Donnchadh mac Toirdhealbhaigh O Briain
1460	Thadeus Mag Raith II
1463	Matthaeus O Griobhtha
1483	Toirdhealbhach mac Mathghamhna O Briain [Theodoricus]
1523	Thadeus
1526	Seamus O Cuirrin
1546	Cornelius O Dea
1554	Turlough [or Terence] O'Brien II
1570	Maurice [or Murtagh] O'Brien-Arra
1613	John Rider
1633	Lewis Jones
1647	Edward Parry
1661	Edward Worth
1669	Daniel Wytter
1675	John Roan
1693	Henry Ryder
1696	Thomas Lindsay
1713	Thomas Vesey
1714	Nicholas Forster
1716	Charles Carr
1740	Joseph Story
1742	John Ryder
1743	Jemmet Browne
1745	Richard Chenevix
1746	Nicholas Synge
	Kilfenora united to Killaloe 1752
1771	Robert Fowler
1779	George Chinnery
1780	Thomas Barnard
1794	William Knox
1803	Charles Dalrymple Lindsay
1804	Nathaniel Alexander
1804	Robert Ponsonby Tottenham Loftus
1820	Richard Mant
1823	Alexander Arbuthnot
1828	Richard Ponsonby
1831	Edmund Knox [with Clonfert]
	Clonfert united to Killaloe 1834
	Kilmacduagh united to Killaloe 1834
1834	Christopher Butson
1836	Stephen Crengh Sandes
1839	Ludlow Tonson [afterwards Baron Riversdale]
1862	William FitzGerald
1884	William Bennet Chester
1893	Frederick Richards Wynne
1897	Mervyn Archdall
1912	Charles Benjamin Dowse
1913	Thomas Sterling Berry (resigned)
1924	Henry Edmund Patton
1943	Robert M'Neil Boyd
1945	Hedley Webster
1953	Richard Gordon Perdue
1957	Henry Arthur Stanistreet
1972	Edwin Owen
1976	United to Limerick

†Kilmacduagh

?	Ua Cleirig 1137
	Imar Ua Ruaidin 1176
	Rugnad O'Rowan 1178
1179	Mac Gilla Cellaig Ua Ruaidin
1206	Ua Cellaig
	Mael Muire O Connmaig 1224
1227	Aed [Odo]
	Conchobhar O Muiredaig 1247
1248	Gilla Cellaig O Ruaidin [Gilbertus]
1249	David yFredrakern
1254	Mauricius O Leaain
1284	David O Setachain
1290	Luirint O Lachtnain [Laurentius]
1307	Lucas
1326	Johannes
1360	Nicol O Leaain
1394	Gregory O Leaain
1405	Enri O Connmhaigh
1409	Dionysius
1409	Eugene O Faolain
1418	Diarmaid O Donnchadha
1419	Nicol O Duibhghiolla
1419	Seaan O Connmhaigh
1441	Dionysius O Donnchadha
1479	Cornelius O Mullony
1503	Matthaeus O Briain
1533	Christopher Bodkin
1573	Stephen O'Kirwan
[1584	Thomas Burke, not consecrated]
1587	Roland Lynch
1627–1836	Held in commendam by the Bishops of Clonfert
	United to Killaloe since 1834

†Leighlin

–633	Laserian or Molaise
–865	Mainchin
–940	Conella McDonegan Daniel 969
	Cleitic O'Muinic 1050
c.1096	Ferdomnac
	Mael Eoin Ua Dunacain 1125
	Sluaigedach Ua Cathain 1145
1152	Dungal O Caellaide
1192	Johannes
1197	Johannes
1202	Herlewin
1217	Richard [Fleming]
1228	William le Chauniver
1252	Thomas
1275	Nicholas Chever
1309	Maurice de Blanchville
1321	Meiler le Poer
1344	Radulphus O Ceallaigh
1349	Thomas of Brakenberg
1360	Johannes
1362	William (not consecrated)
1363	John Young
1371	Philip FitzPeter
1385	John Griffin
1398	Thomas Peverell
1400	Richard Bocomb
1419	John Mulgan
1432	Thomas Fleming
—	Diarmaid 1464
1464	Milo Roche
1490	Nicholas Magwyr
1513	Thomas Halsey
1524	Mauricius O Deoradhain
1527	Matthew Sanders
1550	Robert Travers
1555	Thomas O'Fihelly
1567	Donnell or Daniel Cavanagh
1589	Richard Meredith
	United to Ferns since 1597 on the death of Bp Meredith

Limerick

Limerick, Ardfert, Aghadoe, Killaloe, Kilfenora, Clonfert, Kilmacduagh and Emly

Description of arms. Azure two keys addorsed in saltire the wards upwards; in the dexter chief a crosier paleways, in the sinister a mitre, all or.

–1106	Gilli alias Gilla Espaic
1140	Patricius
1150	Erolb [? = Harold]
1152	Torgesius
1179	Brictius
1203	Donnchad Ua'Briain [Donatus]
1207	Geoffrey
–1215	Edmund
1223	Hubert de Burgo
1252	Robert de Emly or Neil
1273	Gerald [or Miles] de Mareshall
1302	Robert de Dundonald
1312	Eustace de Aqua or de l'Eau
1336	Maurice de Rochfort
1354	Stephen Lawless
1360	Stephen Wall [de Valle]
1369	Peter Curragh
1399	Bernardus O Conchobhair
1400	Conchobhar O Deadhaidh
1426	John Mothel (resigned)
	Iniscattery incorporated with Limerick
1456	Thomas Leger
1458	William Russel, *alias* Creagh
1463	Thomas Arthur
[1486	Richard Stakpoll, not consecrated]
1486	John Dunowe
1489	John O'Phelan [Folan]
1524	Sean O Cuinn
1551	William Casey
1557	Hugh de Lacey or Lees (deposed)
1571	William Casey
1594	John Thornburgh
1604	Bernard Adams
1626	Francis Gough
1634	George Webb
1643	Robert Sibthorp
	Ardfert united to Limerick 1661
1661	Edward Synge
1664	William Fuller
1667	Francis Marsh
1673	John Vesey
1679	Simon Digby
1692	Nathaniel Wilson
1695	Thomas Smyth
1725	William Burscough
1755	James Leslie
1771	James Averill
1772	William Gore
1784	William Cecil Pery
1794	Thomas Barnard
1806	Charles Morgan Warburton
1820	Thomas Elrington
1823	John Jebb
1834	Edmund Knox
1849	William Higgin
1854	Henry Griffin
1866	Charles Graves
1899	Thomas Bunbury
1907	Raymond D'Audemra Orpen
1921	Harry Vere White
1934	Charles King Irwin
1942	Evelyn Charles Hodges
1961	Robert Wyse Jackson
1970	Donald Arthur Richard Caird
	Killaloe united to Limerick 1976
	Emly transferred to Limerick 1976
1976	Edwin Owen
1981	Walton Newcome Francis Empey
1985	Edward Flewett Darling
2000	Michael Hugh Gunton Mayes
2008	Trevor Russell Williams
2015	Kenneth Arthur Kearon
2021	*vacant*

†Lismore

	Ronan 764
	Cormac MacCuillenan 918
–999	Cinneda O'Chonmind
	Niall mac Meic Aedacain 1113
	Ua Daightig 1119
1121	Mael Isu Ua h-Ainmere
	Mael Muire Ua Loingsig 1150
1151	Gilla Crist Ua Connairche [Christianus]
1179	Felix
	Ardmore incorporated with Lismore 1192
1203	Malachias, O'Heda or O'Danus
1216	Thomas
1219	Robert of Bedford
1228	Griffin Christopher
1248	Ailinn O Suilleabain
1253	Thomas
1270	John Roche
1280	Richard Corre
1309	William Fleming
1310	R.
1322	John Leynagh
1356	Roger Cradock, provision annulled
1358	Thomas le Reve
	United to Waterford 1363

Meath

Meath and Kildare

Description of arms. Sable three mitres argent, two, and one.

BISHOPS OF THE SEE OF CLONARD

	Senach 588
–640	Colman 654
	DusucBhduin O'Phelan 718
	Tole 738
–778	Fulartach 779
	Clothcu 796
	Clemens 826
	Cormac MacSuibhne
	Cumsuth 858
	Suarlech 870
	Ruman MacCathasaid 922
	Colman MacAililid 926
	Tuathal O'Dubhamaigh 1028

BISHOPS OF MEATH

1096	Mael Muire Ua Dunain
1128	Eochaid O Cellaig
1151	Etru Ua Miadacain [Eleuzerius]
1177	Echtigern mac Mael Chiarain [Eugenius]
1192	Simon Rochfort
	(The See was transferred from Clonard to Newtown near Trim, 1202)
	Kells incorporated with Meath
1224	Donan De [Deodatus] (not consecrated)
1227	Ralph Petit
1231	Richard de la Corner
1253	Geoffrey Cusack
1255	Hugo de Taghmon
1283	Walter de Fulburn
1287	Thomas St Leger
1322	Seoan Mac Cerbaill [John MacCarwill]
1327	William de Paul
1350	William St Leger
1353	Nicholas [Allen]
1369	Stephen de Valle [Wall]
1380	William Andrew
1385	Alexander Petit [or de Balscot]
1401	Robert Montayne
1412	Edward Dantesey
[1430	Thomas Scurlog, apparently not consecrated]
1430	William Hadsor
1435	William Silk
1450	Edmund Ouldhall
1460	William Shirwood
1483	John Payne
1507	William Rokeby
1512	Hugh Inge
1523	Richard Wilson
1529	Edward Staples
1554	William Walsh
1563	Hugh Brady
	Clonmacnoise united to Meath 1569
1584	Thomas Jones
1605	Roger Dod
1612	George Montgomery
1621	James Usher
1625	Anthony Martin
	[Interregnum 1650–61]
1661	Henry Leslie
1661	Henry Jones
1682	Anthony Dopping
1697	Richard Tennison
1705	William Moreton
1716	John Evans
1724	Henry Downes
1727	Ralph Lambert
1732	Welbore Ellis
1734	Arthur Price
1744	Henry Maule
1758	William Carmichael
1765	Richard Pococke
1765	Arthur Smyth
1766	Henry Maxwell
1798	Thomas Lewis O'Beirne
1823	Nathaniel Alexander
1840	Charles Dickinson
1842	Edward Stopford
1850	Thomas Stewart Townsend
1852	James Henderson Singer
1866	Samuel Butcher
1876	William Conyngham [Lord Plunket]
1885	Charles Parsons Reichel
1894	Joseph Ferguson Peacocke
1897	James Bennett Keene
1919	Benjamin John Plunket
1926	Thomas Gibson George Collins
1927	John Orr
1938	William Hardy Holmes
1945	James McCann
1959	Robert Bonsall Pike
	Kildare united to Meath 1976
1976	Donald Arthur Richard Caird
1985	Walton Newcome Francis Empey
1996	Richard Lionel Clarke
2013	Patricia Louise Storey

†Ossory

	Dermot 973
1152	Domnall Ua Fogartaig
1180	Felix Ua Duib Slaine
1202	Hugo de Rous [Hugo Rufus]
1220	Peter Mauveisin
1231	William of Kilkenny
1233	Walter de Brackley
1245	Geoffrey de Turville
1251	Hugh de Mapilton
1260	Geoffrey St Leger
1287	Roger of Wexford
1289	Michael d'Exeter
1303	William FitzJohn
1317	Richard Ledred
1361	John de Tatenhale
1366	William
—	John of Oxford
1371	Alexander Petit [de Balscot]
1387	Richard Northalis
1396	Thomas Peverell
1399	John Waltham
1400	John Griffin
1400	John
1401	Roger Appleby
1402	John Waltham
1407	Thomas Snell
1417	Patrick Foxe
1421	Dionysius O Deadhaidh
1427	Thomas Barry
1460	David Hacket
1479	Seaan O hEidigheain
1487	Oliver Cantwell
1528	Milo Baron [or FitzGerald]
1553	John Bale
1554	John Tonory
1567	Christopher Gaffney
1577	Nicholas Walsh
1586	John Horsfall
1610	Richard Deane
1613	Jonas Wheeler
1641	Griffith Williams
1672	John Parry
1678	Benjamin Parry
1678	Michael Ward
1680	Thomas Otway
1693	John Hartstonge
1714	Thomas Vesey
1731	Edward Tennison
1736	Charles Este
1741	Anthony Dopping
1743	Michael Cox
1754	Edward Maurice
1755	Richard Pococke
1765	Charles Dodgson
1775	William Newcome
1779	John Hotham
1782	William Heresford
1795	Thomas Lewis O'Beirne
1799	Hugh Hamilton
1806	John Kearney
1813	Robert Fowler
	Ferns united to Ossory 1835
1842	James Thomas O'Brien
1874	Robert Samuel Gregg

1878	William Pakenham Walsh
1897	John Baptist Crozier
1907	Charles Frederick D'Arcy
1911	John Henry Bernard
1915	John Allen Fitzgerald Gregg
1920	John Godfrey FitzMaurice Day
1938	Ford Tichbourne
1940	John Percy Phair
1962	Henry Robert McAdoo
	United to Cashel 1977

†Ross

	Nechtan MacNechtain 1160
	Isaac O'Cowen 1161
	O'Carroll 1168
1177	Benedictus
1192	Mauricius
1198	Daniel
1224	Fineen O Clothna [Florentius]
c.1250	Malachy
1254	Mauricius
1269	Walter O Mithigein
1275	Peter O h-Uallachain [? Patrick]
1291	Laurentius
1310	Matthaeus O Finn
1331	Laurentius O h-Uallachain
1336	Dionysius
1379	Bernard O Conchobhair
1399	Peter Curragh
1400	Thadeus O Ceallaigh
1401	Mac Raith O hEidirsgeoil [Macrobius]
1402	Stephen Brown
1403	Matthew
1418	Walter Formay
1424	John Bloxworth
1426	Conchobhar Mac Fhaolchadha [Cornelius]
	Maurice Brown 1431
1431	Walter of Leicester
1434	Richard Clerk
1448	Domhnall O Donnobhain
	John 1460
1460	Robert Colynson
−1464	Thomas
1464	John Hornse *alias* Skipton
1473	Aodh O hEidirsgeoil [Odo]
1482	Tadhg Mac Carthaigh
1494	John Edmund Courci
1517	Seaan O Muirthile
1519	Tadgh O Raghallaigh [Thaddeus]
1523	Bonaventura
1526	Diarmaid Mac Carthaigh
1544	Dermot McDonnell
1551	John
1554	Maurice O'Fihelly
1559	Maurice O'Hea
1561	Thomas O'Herlihy
1582	William Lyon [with Cork and Cloyne after 1581]
	United to Cork 1583

†Waterford

1096	Mael lus Ua h-Ainmere
1152	Toistius
1175	Augustinus Ua Selbaig
	Anonymous 1199
1200	Robert I
1204	David the Welshman
1210	Robert II [Breathnach]
1223	William Wace
1227	Walter
1232	Stephen
1250	Henry
1252	Philip
1255	Walter de Southwell
1274	Stephen de Fulbourn
1286	Walter de Fulbourn
1308	Matthew
1323	Nicholas Welifed
1338	Richard Francis
1349	Robert Elyot
1350	Roger Cradock
	Lismore united to Waterford 1363
1363	Thomas le Reve
1394	Robert Read
1396	Thomas Sparklord
1397	John Deping
1400	Thomas Snell
1407	Roger of Appleby (*see under* Ossory)
1409	John Geese
1414	Thomas Colby
1421	John Geese
1426	Richard Cantwell
1446	Robert Poer
1473	Richard Martin
1475	John Bulcomb
1480	Nicol O hAonghusa
1483	Thomas Purcell
1519	Nicholas Comyn
1551	Patrick Walsh
1579	Marmaduke Middleton
1582	Miler Magrath (Bishop of Cashel and Waterford)
1589	Thomas Wetherhead [or Walley]
1592	Miler Magrath
1608	John Lancaster
1619	Michael Boyle
1636	John Atherton
1641	Archibald Adair
1661	George Baker
1666	Hugh Gore
1691	Nathaniel Foy
1708	Thomas Mills
1740	Charles Este
1746	Richard Chenevix
1779	William Newcome
1795	Richard Marlay
1802	Power le Poer Trench
1810	Joseph Stock
1813	Richard Bourke
	United to Cashel under Church Temporalities Act 1833

CATHEDRALS

CHURCH OF ENGLAND

(BATH AND) WELLS (St Andrew) Dean J H DAVIES
  Can Res THE VEN A E GELL, R W JA MES, N L JEPSON-BIDDLE, R M PAUL
BIRMINGHAM (St Philip) Dean M THOMPSON
  Can Res A M DELMEGE, J E M HOUGHTON
BLACKBURN (St Mary) Dean P HOWELL-JONES
  Can Res P J NORTH, G O'NEILL, R F PAILING
BRADFORD (St Peter) Dean *vacant* Can Res M R COUTTS, P D MAYBURY
BRISTOL (Holy Trinity) Dean A K FORD
  Can Res J M GAINSBOROUGH, J S PARKIN, N V STANLEY
CANTERBURY (Christ) Dean R A WILLIS Can Res A P DODD, T J N NAISH, E L PENNINGTON Prec M J KRAMER
CARLISLE (Holy Trinity) Dean M C BOYLING
  Can Res B H CARTER, M A MANLEY
CHELMSFORD (St Mary, St Peter and St Cedd)
  Dean N J HENSHALL Can Res A M KENNEDY, I R MOODY, I J NAY
CHESTER (Christ and Blessed Virgin Mary)
  Dean T R STRATFORD Can Res R J BROOKE, J N N C DUSSEK, S L FENBY
CHICHESTER (Holy Trinity) Dean S J WAINE
  Can Res N R DUNN, D D INMAN
COVENTRY (St Michael) Dean J J WITCOMBE
  Can Res K C FLEMING
DERBY (All Saints) Dean P J A ROBINSON
  Can Res R J ANDREWS, N J FENTON, Chapl A P DICKENS
DURHAM (Christ and Blessed Virgin Mary)
  Dean A TREMLETT Can Res C ALLEN, M J EVERITT, M H J HAMPEL, S A OLIVER
ELY (Holy Trinity) Dean M P J BONNEY
  Can Res J R GARRARD, J H MARTIN, J S REVELEY
EXETER (St Peter) Dean J D F GREENER
  Can Res C E EDMONDS, J E A MUSTARD, C J I PALMER
GLOUCESTER (St Peter and Holy Trinity) Dean S D LAKE
  Can Res N M ARTHY, A J BRADDOCK, THE VEN H J DAWSON, R J A MITCHELL, C S M THOMSON
GUILDFORD (Holy Spirit) Dean D L GWILLIAMS
  Can Res S A BEAKE, C P HOLLINGSHURST
HEREFORD (Blessed Virgin Mary and St Ethelbert)
  Dean S R D BROWN Can Res A PIPER, C PULLIN
  Chapl P A ROW
LEICESTER (St Martin) Dean D R M MONTEITH
  Can Res A M ADAMS, E L DAVIES, P D RATTIGAN, K S F ROOMS
LICHFIELD (Blessed Virgin Mary and St Chad)
  Dean A J DORBER Can Res THE RT REVD J E MCFARLANE, G A D PLATTEN, A M STEAD
LINCOLN (Blessed Virgin Mary) Dean C L WILSON
  Can Res N J W BROWN, P OVEREND, J A PATRICK
LIVERPOOL (Christ) Dean S H JONES
  Can Res P G ANDERSON, N D BARNES, M C KIRBY, E F LOUDON
LONDON (St Paul) Dean D J ISON Can Res J D BREWSTER, J H MILNE Min Can R L COUPLAND, R J MORTON
  Chapl P M HOLLINGSWORTH
MANCHESTER (St Mary, St Denys and St George)
  Dean R M GOVENDER Can Res D A HOLGATE, D J SHARPLES, M Z WALL Chapl P G BELLAMY-KNIGHTS, A M RHODES
NEWCASTLE (St Nicholas) Dean G V MILLER
  Can Res P D DOBSON, C MACLAREN, R J SANER-HAIGH

NORWICH (Holy Trinity) Dean J B HEDGES
  Can Res A W BRYANT, P M DOLL, K N JAMES, A S G PLATTEN
OXFORD (Christ Church) Dean M W PERCY
  Can Res N J BIGGAR, THE VEN J P M CHAFFEY, S R I FOOT, R C PEERS, G J WARD Succ P J WHITE Chapl C J Y HAYNS
PETERBOROUGH (St Peter, St Paul and St Andrew)
  Dean C C DALLISTON Can Res T M ALBAN JONES, S R D BROWN, R C WILLIAMS
PORTSMOUTH (St Thomas of Canterbury)
  Dean A W N S CANE Can Res K J PERCIVAL, N R RALPH, A C RUSTELL, J M M SPREADBURY
RIPON (St Peter and St Wilfrid) Dean J R DOBSON
  Can Res M A GISBOURNE, A B NEWBY, B J PYKE
ROCHESTER (Christ and Blessed Virgin Mary)
  Dean P J HESKETH Can Res S C BREWER, C D DENCH, G J GILES, M J RUSHTON
ST ALBANS (St Alban) Dean J KELLY-MOORE
  Can Res T M BULL, T M LOMAX, K A WALTON
  Min Can J J B LLOYD
ST EDMUNDSBURY (St James) Dean J P HAWES
  Can Res P C BANKS, S A GAZE, M J VERNON
SALISBURY (Blessed Virgin Mary) Dean N C PAPADOPULOS
  Can Res A MACHAM, E C PROBERT, R J TITLEY
  V of the Close N L DAVIES
SHEFFIELD (St Peter and St Paul) Dean A L THOMPSON
  Can Res K FARROW, P G HARBORD
SODOR AND MAN (St German) Dean N P GODFREY
  Can J P COLDWELL, J A T HEATON, J A WARD
SOUTHWARK (St Saviour and St Mary Overie)
  Dean A P NUNN Can Res J P COLWILL, M G RAWSON, L K ROBERTS, W S ROBINS, A S ZIHNI
SOUTHWELL (Blessed Virgin Mary) Dean N A SULLIVAN
  Can Res R J FRITH, A G MILBANK
TRURO (St Mary) Dean R C BUSH Can Res A G BASHFORTH, S M GRIFFITHS
WAKEFIELD (All Saints) Dean S C COWLING
  Can Res P J FARLEY-MOORE, L B VASEY-SAUNDERS, D WALMSLEY PV M R VASEY-SAUNDERS
WINCHESTER (Holy Trinity, St Peter, St Paul and St Swithun) Dean C OGLE Can Res R G A RIEM, A P C TRENIER C N P FENNEMORE
WORCESTER (Christ and Blessed Virgin Mary)
  Dean P G ATKINSON Can Res S M EDWARDS
  Min Can M R DORSETT
YORK (St Peter) Dean J H FROST Can Res M D SMITH, M A MCLEAN, V L JOHNSON Succ C M CUMMING

Collegiate Churches

WESTMINSTER ABBEY
ST GEORGE'S CHAPEL, WINDSOR
See Royal Peculiars, p. 933.

Diocese in Europe

GIBRALTAR (Holy Trinity) Dean I D TARRANT
MALTA Valletta (St Paul) Pro-Cathedral
  Chan S H M GODFREY
BRUSSELS (Holy Trinity) Pro-Cathedral Chan P D VROLIJK

CHURCH IN WALES

ST ASAPH (St Asaph) Dean N H WILLIAMS
BANGOR (St Deiniol) Dean *vacant*
ST DAVIDS (St David and St Andrew) Dean S C ROWLAND JONES

LLANDAFF (St Peter and St Paul) Dean G H CAPON
MONMOUTH Newport (St Woolos) Dean I C BLACK
(SWANSEA AND) BRECON (St John the Evangelist)
  Dean A P SHACKERLEY

SCOTTISH EPISCOPAL CHURCH

For the members of the chapter the *Scottish Episcopal Church Directory* should be consulted.

Aberdeen and Orkney
ABERDEEN (St Andrew) **Provost** I M POOBALAN

Argyll and The Isles
OBAN (St John) **Provost** M R CAMPBELL
CUMBRAE (Holy Spirit) Cathedral of The Isles **Provost** K G
RIGLIN *Bishop of Argyll and The Isles*

Brechin
DUNDEE (St Paul) **Provost** E J THOMSON

Edinburgh
EDINBURGH (St Mary) **Provost** J A CONWAY

Glasgow and Galloway
GLASGOW (St Mary) **Provost** K HOLDSWORTH

Moray, Ross and Caithness
INVERNESS (St Andrew) **Provost** S E MURRAY

St Andrews, Dunkeld and Dunblane
PERTH (St Ninian) **Provost** H B FARQUHARSON

CHURCH OF IRELAND

Most cathedrals are parish churches, and the dean is usually, but not always, the incumbent. For the members of the chapter the *Church of Ireland Directory* should be consulted.

NATIONAL CATHEDRAL OF ST PATRICK, Dublin **Dean** W W MORTON

CATHEDRAL OF ST ANNE, Belfast **Dean** S B FORDE
(St Anne's is a cathedral of the dioceses of Down and Dromore and of Connor)

Province of Armagh

Armagh
ARMAGH (St Patrick) T S FORSTER

Clogher
CLOGHER (St Macartan) K R J HALL
ENNISKILLEN (St Macartin) K R J HALL

Derry and Raphoe
DERRY (St Columb) R J STEWART
RAPHOE (St Eunan) *vacant*

Down and Dromore
DOWN (Holy and Undivided Trinity) T H HULL
DROMORE (Christ the Redeemer) S G WILSON

Connor
LISBURN (Christ) *(Dean of Connor)* W S WRIGHT

Kilmore, Elphin and Ardagh
KILMORE (St Fethlimidh) N N CROSSEY
SLIGO (St Mary and St John the Baptist) A WILLIAMS

Tuam, Killala and Achonry
TUAM (St Mary) L E A PEILOW
KILLALA (St Patrick) A J GRIMASON

Province of Dublin

Dublin and Glendalough
DUBLIN (Holy Trinity) Christ Church D P M DUNNE

Meath and Kildare
TRIM (St Patrick) P D BOGLE *Dean of Clonmacnoise*
KILDARE (St Brigid) T WRIGHT

Cashel and Ossory
CASHEL (St John the Baptist) G G FIELD
WATERFORD (Blessed Trinity) Christ Church M P JANSSON
LISMORE (St Carthage) P R DRAPER
KILKENNY (St Canice) D MACDONNELL *Dean of Ossory*
LEIGHLIN (St Laserian) T W GORDON
FERNS (St Edan) P G MOONEY

Cork, Cloyne and Ross
CORK (St Fin Barre) N K DUNNE
CLOYNE (St Colman) S D GREEN
ROSS (St Fachtna) C L PETERS

Limerick and Killaloe
LIMERICK (St Mary) N J SLOANE
KILLALOE (St Flannan) R L SMYTH

ROYAL PECULIARS, CLERGY OF THE QUEEN'S HOUSEHOLD, ETC

Royal Peculiars

Description of arms. Azure the reputed arms of Edward the Confessor, viz. a cross patonce between five martlets or, on a chief of the same, between two double roses of Lancaster and York, barbed and seeded proper, a pale charged with the Royal arms (*viz.* Quarterly of France and England).

Collegiate Church of St Peter in Westminster (Westminster Abbey)
Dean D M HOYLE
Can A J BALL, J D T HAWKEY, P D HILLAS, D J STANTON
Min Can M R BIRCH, R B N LATHAM
PV S E ARCHER, P A BAGOTT, A R BODDY, S R BUCKLEY, N J BUNKER, P A E CHESTER, C M CHIVERS, B D FENTON, R C GODSALL, A G GYLE, J IDOWU-FEARON, L J JØRGENSEN, G P KNOWLES, A P R KYRIAKIDES-YELDHAM, M D MACEY, P MCGEARY, A D P MOUGHTIN-MUMBY, J L OSBORNE, F L STEWART-DARLING, V A STOCK, C B STOLTZ, G D SWINTON, J M WHITE, A S ZIHNI

Description of arms. The arms of the Order of the Garter, viz. Argent, a St George's Cross gules. The shield is encircled by the blue Garter with its motto.

Queen's Free Chapel of St George Windsor Castle (St George's Chapel)
Dean THE RT REVD D J CONNER
Can H E FINLAY, M G POLL, M POWELL
Min Can J COORE

The Queen's Household

Royal Almonry
High Almoner THE RT REVD J G INGE (Bishop of Worcester)
Sub-Almoner P S WRIGHT

The College of Chaplains
Clerk of the Closet THE RT REVD J W S NEWCOME (Bishop of Carlisle)
Deputy Clerk of the Closet P S WRIGHT

Chaplains to The Queen

E ADEKUNLE	D C GLOVER	R M PRYCE
H W BEARN	S M GUNNER	G P RAVALDE
M E BIDE	P S HAWKINS	J B V RIVIERE
G A BYRNE	J D T HAWKEY	R B RUDDOCK
N J BUCK	E J LEWIS	A G STUDDERT-KENNEDY
R A CHARKHAM	T E MASON	J A TAYLOR
C CHIKE	L J MILLER	R C WHITE
I A DAVENPORT	D NICHOLSON	J F WINDSOR
A ELTRINGHAM	W A NOBLETT	J S WITHERIDGE
S E FIELD	G P POND	

Extra Chaplains to The Queen

J P ROBSON

Chapels Royal
Dean of the Chapels Royal THE BISHOP OF LONDON
Sub-Dean of the Chapels Royal P S WRIGHT
Priests in Ordinary R D E BOLTON, W A WHITCOMBE
Deputy Priests in Ordinary S F BLOXAM-ROSE, S D BROOKES, C L FRANSELLA, R J HALL, A G HOWE, M D OAKLEY, J L OSBORNE, T M B WOODHOUSE, S E YOUNG
Domestic Chaplain, Buckingham Palace P S WRIGHT
Domestic Chaplain, Windsor Castle THE DEAN OF WINDSOR
Domestic Chaplain, Sandringham J B V RIVIERE
Chaplain, Royal Chapel, Windsor Great Park M G POLL
Chaplain, Hampton Court Palace A G HOWE
Chaplain, HM Tower of London R J HALL

The Queen's Chapel of the Savoy

Chaplain T M B WOODHOUSE

Royal Foundation of St Katharine in Ratcliffe

Master R M H PREECE

DIOCESAN OFFICES

CHURCH OF ENGLAND

BATH AND WELLS
Diocesan Office, Flourish House, 2 Cathedral Avenue, Wells BA5 1FD
T: (01749) 670777   E: reception@bathwells.anglican.org
W: www.bathandwells.org.uk

BIRMINGHAM
Diocesan Office, 1 Colmore Row, Birmingham B3 2BJ
T: 0121-426 0400   W: www.cofebirmingham.com

BLACKBURN
Clayton House, Walker Industrial Estate, Walker Road, Guide, Blackburn BB1 2QE
T: (01254) 503070   E: diocese@blackburn.anglican.org
W: www.blackburn.anglican.org

BRISTOL
Hillside House, 1500 Bristol Parkway North, Newbrick Road, Stoke Gifford, Bristol BS34 8YU
T: 0117-906 0100
W: www.bristol.anglican.org

CANTERBURY
Diocesan House, Lady Wootton's Green, Canterbury CT1 1NQ
T: (01227) 459401   E: reception@diocant.org
W: www.canterburydiocese.org

CARLISLE
Church House, 19-24 Friargate, Penrith CA11 7XR
T: (01768) 807777   E: enquiries@carlislediocese.org.uk
W: www.carlislediocese.org.uk

CHELMSFORD
Diocesan Office, 53 New Street, Chelmsford CM1 1AT
T: (01245) 294400   F: 294477   E: reception@chelmsford.anglican.org
W: www.chelmsford.anglican.org

CHESTER
Church House, 5500 Daresbury Park, Daresbury, Warrington WA4 4GE
T: (01928) 718834   E: churchhouse@chester.anglican.org
W: www.chester.anglican.org

CHICHESTER
Diocesan Church House, 211 New Church Road, Hove BN3 4ED
T: (01273) 421021
W: www.chichester.anglican.org

COVENTRY
Cathedral and Diocesan Offices, 1 Hill Top, Coventry CV1 5AB
T: (024) 7652 1200
W: www.coventry.anglican.org

DERBY
Derby Church House, 1 Full Street, Derby DE1 3DR
T: (01332) 388650   E: enquiries@derby.anglican.org
W: www.derby.anglican.org

DURHAM
Cuthbert House, Stonebridge, Durham DH1 3RY
T: (01388) 604515   E: diocesan.office@durham.anglican.org
W: www.durhamdiocese.org

ELY
Diocesan Office, Bishop Woodford House, Barton Road, Ely CB7 4DX
T: (01353) 652701
W: www.elydiocese.org

EUROPE
Diocesan Office, 14 Tufton Street, London SW1P 3QZ
T: (020) 7898 1155   E: bron.panter@churchofengland.org
W: www.europe.anglican.org

EXETER
The Old Deanery, The Cloisters, Exeter EX1 1HS
T: (01392) 272686   E: admin@exeter.anglican.org
W: www.exeter.anglican.org

GLOUCESTER
Church House, College Green, Gloucester GL1 2LY
T: (01452) 410022   E: church.house@glosdioc.org.uk
W: www.gloucester.anglican.org

GUILDFORD
Church House, 20 Alan Turing Road, Surrey Research Park, Guildford GU2 7YF
T: (01483) 790300   E: info@cofeguildford.org.uk
W: www.cofeguildford.org.uk

HEREFORD
Diocesan Office, The Palace, Hereford HR4 9BL
T: (01432) 373300
W: www.hereford.anglican.org

LEEDS
Church House, 17-19 York Place, Leeds LS1 2EX
T: 0113-200 0540   E: enquiries@leeds.anglican.org
W: www.leeds.anglican.org

LEICESTER
St Martin's House, 7 Peacock Lane Leicester LE1 5PZ
T: 0116-261 5200   E: communications@leicestercofe.org
W: www.leicester.anglican.org

LICHFIELD
St Mary's House, The Close, Lichfield WS13 7LD
T: (01543) 306030
W: www.lichfield.anglican.org

DIOCESAN OFFICES

LINCOLN
Diocesan Office, Edward King House, Minster Yard, Lincoln LN2 1PU
T: (01522) 504050   E: reception@lincoln.anglican.org
W: www.lincoln.anglican.org

LIVERPOOL
St James's House, 20 St James Road, Liverpool L1 7BY
T: 0151-709 9722   E: centralservices@liverpool.anglican.org
W: www.liverpool.anglican.org

LONDON
Diocesan House, 36 Causton Street, London SW1P 4AU
T: (020) 7932 1100   F: 7932 1110   E: reception@london.anglican.org
W: www.london.anglican.org

MANCHESTER
Diocesan Office, Church House, 90 Deansgate, Manchester M3 2GH
T: 0161-828 1400   E: comms@manchester.anglican.org
W: www.manchester.anglican.org

NEWCASTLE
Church House, St John's Terrace, North Shields NE29 6HS
T: 0191-270 4100   E: info@newcastle.anglican.org
W: www.newcastle.anglican.org

NORWICH
Diocesan House, 109 Dereham Road, Easton, Norwich NR9 5ES
T: (01603) 880853   E: info@dioceseofnorwich.org
W: www.dioceseofnorwich.org

OXFORD
Church House Oxford, Langford Locks, Kidlington OX5 1GF
T: (01865) 208200
W: www.oxford.anglican.org

PETERBOROUGH
Diocesan Office, The Palace, Minster Precincts, Peterborough PE1 1YB
T: (01733) 887000   E: office@peterborough-diocese.org.uk
W: www.peterborough-diocese.org.uk

PORTSMOUTH
First Floor, Peninsular House, Wharf Road, Portsmouth PO2 8HB
T: (023) 9289 9650
W: www.portsmouth.anglican.org

ROCHESTER
St Nicholas Church, Boley Hill, Rochester ME1 1SL
T: (01634) 560000   E: enquiries@rochester.anglican.org
W: www.rochester.anglican.org

ST ALBANS
Holywell Lodge, 41 Holywell Hill, St Albans AL1 1HE
T: (01727) 854532
W: www.stalbans.anglican.org

ST EDMUNDSBURY AND IPSWICH
St Nicholas Centre, 4 Cutler Street, Ipswich IP1 1UQ
T: (01473) 298500   E: dbf@cofesuffolk.org
W: www.cofesuffolk.org

SALISBURY
Church House, Crane Street, Salisbury SP1 2QB
T: (01722) 411922   E: parishsupport@salisbury.anglican.org
W: www.salisbury.anglican.org

SHEFFIELD
Diocesan Church House, 95-99 Effingham Street, Rotherham S65 1BL
T: (01709) 309100   F: 512550   E: reception@sheffield.anglican.org
W: www.sheffield.anglican.org

SODOR AND MAN
Thie yn Aspick, 4 The Falls, Tromode Road, Cronkbourne, Isle of Man IM4 4PZ
T: (01624) 622108   E: secretary@sodorandman.im
W: www.sodorman.im

SOUTHWARK
Trinity House, 4 Chapel Court, Borough High Street, London SE1 1HW
T: (020) 7939 9400   F: 7939 9468   E: trinity@southwark.anglican.org
W: www.southwark.anglican.org

SOUTHWELL AND NOTTINGHAM
Jubilee House, 8 Westgate, Southwell NG25 0JH
T: (01636) 814331   E: reception@southwell.anglican.org
W: www.southwell.anglican.org

TRURO
Church House, Woodlands Court, Truro Business Park, Threemilestone, Truro TR4 9NH
T: (01872) 274351   E: info@truro.anglican.org
W: www.trurodiocese.org.uk

WINCHESTER
The Diocesan Office, Old Alresford Place, Old Alresford, Alresford SO24 9DH
T: (01962) 737300
W: www. winchester.anglican.org

WORCESTER
16 Lowesmoor Wharf, Lowesmoor, Worcester WR1 2RS
T: (01905) 20537
W: www.cofe-worcester.org.uk

YORK
The Diocese of York, Amy Johnson Way, York YO30 4XT
T: (01904) 699500   E: office@yorkdiocese.org
W: www.dioceseofyork.org.uk

CHURCH IN WALES

ST ASAPH	Diocesan Office, High Street, St Asaph LL17 0RD T: (01745) 582245 W: https://stasaph.churchinwales.org.uk
BANGOR	Diocesan Office, Cathedral Close, Bangor LL57 1RL T: (01248) 354999 E: bangor@churchinwales.org.uk W: https://bangor.eglwysyngnghymru.org.uk
ST DAVIDS	Diocesan Office, Abergwili, Carmarthen SA31 2JG T: (01267) 236145 W: https://stdavids.churchinwales.org.uk
LLANDAFF	Diocesan Office, The Court, Coychurch, Bridgend CF35 5EH T: (01656) 868868 W: https://llandaff.churchinwales.org.uk
MONMOUTH	Diocesan Office, 64 Caerau Road, Newport NP20 4HJ T: (01633) 267490 W: https://monmouth.churchinwales.org.uk
SWANSEA AND BRECON	Diocesan Centre, Cathedral Close, Brecon LD3 9DP T: (01874) 623716 W: https://swanseaandbrecon.churchinwales.org.uk

SCOTTISH EPISCOPAL CHURCH

ABERDEEN AND ORKNEY	Diocesan Office, Marischal College, Broad Street, Aberdeen AB10 1YS T: (01224) 662247 E: office@aberdeen.anglican.org W: https://aoepiscopal.scot
ARGYLL AND THE ISLES	St Moluag's Diocesan Centre, Croft Avenue, Oban PA34 5JJ T: (01631) 570870 E: office@argyll.anglican.org W: www.argyll.anglican.org
BRECHIN	Brechin Diocesan Office, 38 Langlands Street, Dundee DD4 6SZ T: 07444-161300 E: office@brechin.anglican.org W: www.thedioceseofbrechin.org
EDINBURGH	Diocesan Office, 21A Grosvenor Crescent, Edinburgh EH12 5EL T: 0131-538 7033 E: office@edinburgh.anglican.org W: https://edinburgh.anglican.org
GLASGOW AND GALLOWAY	Diocesan Centre, 5 St Vincent Place, Glasgow G1 2DH E: office@glasgow.anglican.org W: www.glasgow.anglican.org
MORAY, ROSS AND CAITHNESS	Diocesan Office, 9-11 Kenneth Street, Inverness IV3 5NR T: (01463) 237503 W: https://.morayepiscopalchurch.scot
ST ANDREWS, DUNKELD AND DUNBLANE	Perth Diocesan Centre, 28A Balhousie Street, Perth PH1 5HJ T: (01738) 443173 E: office@standrews.anglican.org W: https://standrews.anglican.org

CHURCH OF IRELAND

PROVINCE OF ARMAGH

ARMAGH	Church House, 46 Abbey Street, Armagh BT61 7DZ T: (028) 3752 2858 F: 3751 0596 E: office@armagh.anglican.org W: http://armagh.anglican.org
CLOGHER	Diocesan Office, St Macartin's Cathedral Hall, Hall's Lane, Enniskillen BT74 7DR T/F: (028) 6634 7879 E: secretary@clogher.anglican.org W: www.clogher.anglican.org
CONNOR	Diocesan Office, Church of Ireland House, 61-67 Donegall Street, Belfast BT1 2QH T: (028) 9082 8830 F: 9032 1635 E: office@connordiocese.org W: www.connor.anglican.org
DERRY AND RAPHOE	Diocesan Office, 24 London Street, Londonderry BT48 6RQ T: (028) 7137 7013 W: https://derryandraphoe.org
DOWN AND DROMORE	Diocesan Office, Church of Ireland House, 61-67 Donegall Street, Belfast BT1 2QH T: (028) 9082 8830 E: dco@downdromorediocese.org W: www.downanddromore.org
KILMORE	Kilmore Diocesan Office, The Rectory, Cootehill, Co Cavan, Republic of Ireland T: (00353) (49) 555 9954 E: office@kilmore.anglican.org W: http://www.dkea.ie
ELPHIN AND ARDAGH	69 Teemore Road, Garvary, Derrylin, Enniskillen BT92 9QB T: (00353) (89) 459 3219 E: diosecea@eirom.net W: http://www.dkea.ie/

TUAM, KILLALA AND ACHONRY	11 Ros Ard, Cappagh Road, Barna, Galway, Republic of Ireland T: (00353) (86) 833 6666 E: secretary@tuam.anglican.org W: www.tuam.anglican.org

PROVINCE OF DUBLIN

CASHEL AND OSSORY	Diocesan Office, The Palace Coach House, Church Lane, Kilkenny, Republic of Ireland T: (00353) (56) 776 1910 E: office@cashel.anglican.org W: www.cashel.anglican.org
CORK, CLOYNE AND ROSS	Diocesan Office, St Nicholas' House, 14 Cove Street, Cork, T12 RP40, Republic of Ireland T: (00353) (21) 500 5080 E: secretary@corkchurchofireland.com W: www.cork.anglican.org
DUBLIN AND GLENDALOUGH	Diocesan Office, Church of Ireland House, Church Avenue, Rathmines, Dublin 6, Republic of Ireland T: (00353) (1) 496 6981 E: admin@dublin.anglican.org W: www.dublin.anglican.org
LIMERICK AND KILLALOE	Kellysgrove, Ballinaslow, Galway, Republic of Ireland T: (00353) (87) 613 0063 E: diocesansecretary@limerick.anglican.org W: www.limerick.anglican.org
MEATH AND KILDARE	Meath and Kildare Diocesan Centre, Moyglare, Maynooth, Co Kildare, Republic of Ireland T: (00353) (1) 629 2163 E: secretary@meath.anglican.org W: www.meathandkildare.org

ARCHDEACONRIES, DEANERIES AND RURAL/AREA DEANS OF THE CHURCH OF ENGLAND AND THE CHURCH IN WALES

CHURCH OF ENGLAND

BATH AND WELLS

ARCHDEACONRY OF WELLS

1. AXBRIDGE   J M PHILPOTT
2. BRUTON AND CARY   K ROGERS
3. FROME   C H WALKER
4. GLASTONBURY JURISDICTION   D J L MACGEOCH
5. IVELCHESTER   B S FAULKNER
6. YEOVIL   *vacant*
7. SHEPTON MALLET   S DENYER

ARCHDEACONRY OF BATH

8. BATH   S P GIRLING
9. CHEW MAGNA   S A M'CAW
10. LOCKING   T P B YACOMENI
11. MIDSOMER NORTON   M G STREET
12. PORTISHEAD   J S TILLEY

ARCHDEACONRY OF TAUNTON

13. SEDGEMOOR   *vacant*
14. CREWKERNE   *vacant*
15. EXMOOR   C S RALPH
16. ILMINSTER   J ABBOTT
17. QUANTOCK   A J WATERS
18. TAUNTON   J D R COX
19. TONE   H L STAINER

BIRMINGHAM

ARCHDEACONRY OF BIRMINGHAM

1. HANDSWORTH AND CENTRAL   D T MACHIRIDZA
2. KINGS NORTON, MOSELEY AND SHIRLEY   P S O'HARE
3. WARLEY AND EDGBASTON   M J SERMON

ARCHDEACONRY OF ASTON

4. ASTON AND SUTTON COLDFIELD   A RICHARDSON
5. COLESHILL AND POLESWORTH   J L C SHAW
6. YARDLEY AND SOLIHULL   R N PARKER

BLACKBURN

ARCHDEACONRY OF BLACKBURN

1. ACCRINGTON   D A ARNOLD
2. BLACKBURN AND DARWEN   F E GREEN
3. BURNLEY   C N CASEY
4. CHORLEY   N G KELLEY
5. LEYLAND   M A M WOLVERSON
6. PENDLE   *vacant*
7. WHALLEY   R J CARMYLLIE

ARCHDEACONRY OF LANCASTER

8. BLACKPOOL   P A LILLICRAP
9. GARSTANG   A W WILKINSON
10. KIRKHAM   *vacant*
11. LANCASTER AND MORECAMBE   C J RIGNEY
12. POULTON   M P KEIGHLEY
13. PRESTON   *vacant*
14. TUNSTALL   *vacant*

BRISTOL

ARCHDEACONRY OF BRISTOL

1. BRISTOL SOUTH   R A WARING
2. BRISTOL WEST   C E SUTTON
3. CITY DEANERY   *vacant*

ARCHDEACONRY OF MALMESBURY

4. CHIPPENHAM   S A V WHEELER
5. KINGSWOOD AND SOUTH GLOUCESTERSHIRE   J C E ANDREW
6. NORTH WILTSHIRE   S WILKINSON
7. SWINDON   T A WIGLEY

CANTERBURY

ARCHDEACONRY OF CANTERBURY

1. EAST BRIDGE   S C THOMAS
2. WEST BRIDGE   R HOLY
3. CANTERBURY   M R GRIFFIN
4. RECULVER   C SMITH
5. THANET   A R BRADDY

ARCHDEACONRY OF ASHFORD

6. ASHFORD   C R T DENYER
7. DOVER   A J BAWTREE
8. ELHAM   J A WEEKS
9. SANDWICH   C G SPENCER
10. ROMNEY AND TENTERDEN   C T A HODGKINS

ARCHDEACONRY OF MAIDSTONE

11. WEALD   R G DREYER
12. MAIDSTONE   C P LAVENDER
13. NORTH DOWNS   J CORBYN
14. OSPRINGE   S H LILLICRAP
15. SITTINGBOURNE   J M STANIFORTH

CARLISLE

ARCHDEACONRY OF CARLISLE

1. APPLEBY   S J FYFE
2. BRAMPTON   E A JOHNSEN
3. CARLISLE   N D BEER
4. PENRITH   D G SARGENT

ARCHDEACONRY OF WEST CUMBERLAND

5. CALDER   T R LEE
6. DERWENT   C H HOPE
7. SOLWAY   T D HERBERT

ARCHDEACONRY OF WESTMORLAND AND FURNESS

8. BARROW   *vacant*
9. FURNESS   R J CROSSLEY
10. KENDAL   A E PETTIFOR
11. WINDERMERE   *vacant*

CHELMSFORD

ARCHDEACONRY OF BARKING (BISHOP OF BARKING)

1. BARKING AND DAGENHAM   M J COURT
2. HAVERING   K A WYLIE

ARCHDEACONRIES, DEANERIES AND RURAL/AREA DEANS

ARCHDEACONRY OF HARLOW (BISHOP OF BARKING)

3. EPPING FOREST AND ONGAR   L P BATSON
4. HARLOW   M J HARRIS

ARCHDEACONRY OF WEST HAM (BISHOP OF BARKING)

5. NEWHAM   D V CHESNEY
6. REDBRIDGE   M J HAWKES
7. WALTHAM FOREST   D R BRITTON

ARCHDEACONRY OF CHELMSFORD
(BISHOP OF BRADWELL)

8. BRENTWOOD   A G SMITH
9. CHELMSFORD   T W BALL
10. MALDON AND DENGIE   P E C BEGLEY

ARCHDEACONRY OF SOUTHEND
(BISHOP OF BRADWELL)

11. BASILDON   J S RICHARDS
12. HADLEIGH   D S C TUDOR
13. ROCHFORD   N E ROWAN
14. SOUTHEND-ON-SEA   *vacant*
15. THURROCK   D BARLOW

ARCHDEACONRY OF STANSTED
(BISHOP OF COLCHESTER)

16. BRAINTREE   R A M REID
17. DUNMOW AND STANSTED   M H PELLY
18. HINCKFORD   E G PAXTON
19. SAFFRON WALDEN   J C TREW

ARCHDEACONRY OF COLCHESTER
(BISHOP OF COLCHESTER)

20. COLCHESTER   P R NORRINGTON
21. HARWICH   *vacant*
22. ST OSYTH   L BOND
23. WITHAM   S F GARWOOD

CHESTER

ARCHDEACONRY OF CHESTER

1. BIRKENHEAD   J KENNEDY
2. CHESTER   H E A JOHNSTON
3. FRODSHAM   D W GUEST
4. GREAT BUDWORTH   J E PROUDFOOT
5. MALPAS   T D M HAYWARD
6. MIDDLEWICH   S M DREW
7. WALLASEY   A W WARD
8. WIRRAL NORTH   D A VESTERGAARD
9. WIRRAL SOUTH   E A GLOVER

ARCHDEACONRY OF MACCLESFIELD

10. BOWDON   G C JAQUISS
11. CONGLETON   S J CLAPHAM
12. KNUTSFORD   I BLAY
13. MACCLESFIELD   J E HARRIES
14. MOTTRAM   *vacant*
15. NANTWICH   A J FULFORD
16. CHADKIRK   L S CURRIE
17. CHEADLE   R S MUNRO
18. STOCKPORT   D T BREWSTER

CHICHESTER

ARCHDEACONRY OF CHICHESTER

1. ARUNDEL AND BOGNOR   M J STANDEN
2. CHICHESTER   M G WEATHERILL
3. MIDHURST   D B WELSMAN
4. PETWORTH   P M GILBERT
5. STORRINGTON   K A WINDSLOW
6. WESTBOURNE   M J LANE
7. WORTHING   H M BUQUÉ

ARCHDEACONRY OF HORSHAM

8. CUCKFIELD   M J MAINE
9. EAST GRINSTEAD   A R HAWKEN
10. HORSHAM   D M BEAL
11. HURST   P S J DOICK

ARCHDEACONRY OF HASTINGS

12. BATTLE AND BEXHILL   J J FRAIS
13. DALLINGTON   M A LLOYD
14. EASTBOURNE   D J KING
15. HASTINGS   D R HILL
16. ROTHERFIELD   *vacant*
17. RYE   C P IRVINE
18. UCKFIELD   P MACBAIN

ARCHDEACONRY OF BRIGHTON AND LEWES

19. BRIGHTON   A J WOODWARD
20. HOVE   D T HENDERSON
21. LEWES AND SEAFORD   J W HOLLINGSWORTH

COVENTRY

ARCHDEACONRY OF COVENTRY

1. COVENTRY EAST   E K FORBES STONE
2. COVENTRY NORTH   G I IRVINE
3. COVENTRY SOUTH   M T TAYLOR
4. KENILWORTH   S BAILEY
5. NUNEATON   D E POULTNEY
6. RUGBY   T D COCKELL

ARCHDEACONRY OF WARWICK

7. ALCESTER   C E MIER
8. FOSSE   *vacant*
9. SHIPSTON   S A EDMONDS
10. SOUTHAM   M C GREEN
11. WARWICK AND LEAMINGTON   R W S SUFFERN

DERBY

ARCHDEACONRY OF CHESTERFIELD

1. CARSINGTON   *vacant*
2. HARDWICK   I N L BLACK
3. NORTH EAST DERBYSHIRE   K E HAMBLIN
4. PEAK   A P KAUNHOVEN

ARCHDEACONRY OF DERBY

5. DERBY CITY   S J CARTWRIGHT
6. DOVE AND DERWENT   B J STOBER
7. MERCIA   M J FIRBANK
8. SOUTH EAST DERBYSHIRE   K PADLEY

DURHAM

ARCHDEACONRY OF DURHAM

1. DURHAM   H MURRAY
2. LANCHESTER   S CLARK

ARCHDEACONRY OF AUCKLAND

3. AUCKLAND   M P TARLING
4. BARNARD CASTLE   A J HARDING
5. DARLINGTON   M R EAST
6. HARTLEPOOL   J BURBURY
7. STANHOPE   D L SPOKES
8. STOCKTON   P S D NEVILLE

ARCHDEACONRY OF SUNDERLAND

9. CHESTER LE STREET AND HOUGHTON   J LINTERN
10. EASINGTON   F J GRIEVE
11. GATESHEAD   Y GREENER
12. GATESHEAD WEST   T I BRAZIER
13. JARROW   *vacant*
14. WEARMOUTH   D TOLHURST

ELY

ARCHDEACONRY OF CAMBRIDGE

1. BOURN   P E SLUSAR
2. CAMBRIDGE NORTH   A M DAFFERN
3. CAMBRIDGE SOUTH   R C ROSBOROUGH
4. FORDHAM AND QUY   D R CLEUGH
5. GRANTA   S J TALBOTT
6. NORTH STOWE   N J BLANDFORD-BAKER
7. SHINGAY   F A COUCH

ARCHDEACONRY OF HUNTINGDON AND WISBECH

8. ELY   R A DARMODY
9. FINCHAM AND FELTWELL   *vacant*
10. HUNTINGDON   I P BRENNAND
11. MARCH   A J SMITH
12. ST IVES   F J KILNER
13. ST NEOTS   L N BLAND
14. WISBECH LYNN MARSHLAND   N A WHITEHOUSE
15. YAXLEY   S C GOWER

EXETER

ARCHDEACONRY OF EXETER

1. AYLESBEARE   R SELLERS
2. CADBURY   M J TREGENZA
3. CHRISTIANITY   D J NIXON
4. HONITON   C E EDMONDS
5. KENN   D J AYLING
6. OTTERY   M WARD
7. TIVERTON AND CULLOMPTON   S G G TALBOT

ARCHDEACONRY OF TOTNES

8. NEWTON ABBOT   E P PARKES
9. OKEHAMPTON   P S SEATON-BURN
10. TORBAY   I N KIYAGA
11. TOTNES   D A PARSONS
12. WOODLEIGH   A B SHAW

ARCHDEACONRY OF BARNSTAPLE

13. BARNSTAPLE   *vacant*
14. HARTLAND   D J ARNOLD
15. HOLSWORTHY   R A FREEMAN
16. SHIRWELL   R E AUSTIN
17. SOUTH MOLTON   A M WELLS
18. TORRINGTON   T E DOYLE

ARCHDEACONRY OF PLYMOUTH

19. IVYBRIDGE   A J RYAN
20. PLYMOUTH CITY   J APPLEBY
21. TAVISTOCK   A J ATKINS

GLOUCESTER

ARCHDEACONRY OF GLOUCESTER

1. FOREST SOUTH   C W MACLAY
2. GLOUCESTER CITY   R P FITTER
3. SEVERN VALE   S I V MASON
4. STROUD   S J MURRAY
5. WOTTON   D J RUSSELL

ARCHDEACONRY OF CHELTENHAM

6. CHELTENHAM   G B GRADY
7. CIRENCESTER   V J HUGHES
8. NORTH COTSWOLD   K R SCOTT
9. TEWKESBURY AND WINCHCOMBE   S M M WALKER

GUILDFORD

ARCHDEACONRY OF SURREY

1. ALDERSHOT   M W HAYTON
2. CRANLEIGH   R O WOODHAMS
3. FARNHAM   J L WALKER
4. GODALMING   S D K TAYLOR
5. GUILDFORD   N J WILLIAMS
6. SURREY HEATH   J HILLMAN

ARCHDEACONRY OF DORKING

7. DORKING   P NEVINS
8. EMLY   A C COWIE
9. EPSOM   R A DONOVAN
10. LEATHERHEAD   R PITTARIDES
11. RUNNYMEDE   B H BEECROFT
12. WOKING   J M G THOMAS

HEREFORD

ARCHDEACONRY OF HEREFORD

1. ABBEYDORE   N G LOWTON
2. BROMYARD   C R EVANS
3. HEREFORD CITY   R C HULSE
4. KINGTON AND WEOBLEY   G A WILKINSON
5. LEDBURY   R WARD
6. LEOMINSTER   J A DAVIES
7. ROSS AND ARCHENFIELD   S A J SEMPLE

ARCHDEACONRY OF LUDLOW

8. BRIDGNORTH   M H DABORN
9. CLUN FOREST   S A C FOUNTAIN
10. CONDOVER   G D GARRETT
11. LUDLOW   W A BUCK
12. PONTESBURY   W K ROWELL
13. TELFORD SEVERN GORGE   C W PENN

LEICESTER

ARCHDEACONRY OF LEICESTER

1. CITY OF LEICESTER   A J LEES-SMITH
2. FRAMLAND (Melton)   M J A BARR
3. GARTREE   S A BAILEY
4. GOSCOTE   R M GLADSTONE
5. LAUNDE   A S W BOOKER

ARCHDEACONRY OF LOUGHBOROUGH

6. AKELEY EAST (Loughborough)   L J WILSON
7. GUTHLAXTON   A C RHOADES
8. NORTH WEST LEICESTERSHIRE   G PINNINGTON
9. SPARKENHOE EAST   R J TRETHEWEY
10. SPARKENHOE WEST   M S POSKITT

LICHFIELD

ARCHDEACONRY OF LICHFIELD

1. LICHFIELD   J L WATERFIELD
2. PENKRIDGE   G H YERBURY
3. RUGELEY   S C DAVIS
4. TAMWORTH   G D SIMMONS

ARCHDEACONRY OF STOKE-UPON-TRENT

5. ALSTONFIELD   J C BAINES
6. CHEADLE   M S FOLLIN
7. ECCLESHALL   D HEMING
8. LEEK   N R IRONS
9. NEWCASTLE   J A DAWSWELL
10. STAFFORD   *vacant*
11. STOKE-ON-TRENT   S A MORRIS
12. STONE   I R CARDINAL
13. TUTBURY   M R FREEMAN
14. UTTOXETER   B S P LEATHERS

ARCHDEACONRY OF SALOP

15. EDGMOND AND SHIFNAL   M W LEFROY
16. ELLESMERE   L J COX
17. HODNET   C SIMPSON
18. OSWESTRY   P T DARLINGTON
19. SHREWSBURY   P J CANSDALE
20. TELFORD   D J LOUGHRAN
21. WEM AND WHITCHURCH   A J B CLAYTON
22. WROCKWARDINE   D A ACKROYD

ARCHDEACONRY OF WALSALL

23. TRYSULL   J M CODY
24. WALSALL   R M MCINTYRE
25. WEDNESBURY   M M ENNIS
26. WEST BROMWICH   R A FARRELL
27. WOLVERHAMPTON   D W WRIGHT
28. WULFRUN   *vacant*

LINCOLN

ARCHDEACONRY OF STOW AND LINDSEY

1. ISLE OF AXHOLME   C KAY
2. CORRINGHAM   P WAIN
3. GRIMSBY AND CLEETHORPES   N D NAWROCKYI
4. HAVERSTOE   K BOHAN
5. LAWRES   R H CROSSLAND
6. MANLAKE   D J SWANNACK
7. WEST WOLD   C W HEWITT
8. YARBOROUGH   D P ROWETT

ARCHDEACONRY OF LINCOLN

9. BOLINGBROKE   P F COATES
10. CALCEWAITHE AND CANDLESHOE   R G HOLDEN
11. CHRISTIANITY   H W F JONES
12. GRAFFOE   *vacant*
13. HORNCASTLE   M N HOLDEN
14. LAFFORD   P A JOHNSON
15. LOUTHESK   J E ROBINSON

ARCHDEACONRY OF BOSTON

16. STAMFORD   M A N TAYLOR
17. BELTISLOE   S L BUCKMAN
18. ELLOE EAST   *vacant*
19. ELLOE WEST   M J HOWARD
20. GRANTHAM   S W CRADDUCK
21. HOLLAND   A J HIGGINSON
22. LOVEDEN   A I TUCKER

LIVERPOOL

ARCHDEACONRY OF LIVERPOOL

1. LIVERPOOL NORTH   W H ADDY
2. LIVERPOOL SOUTH-CHILDWALL   N C MILFORD
3. TOXTETH AND WAVERTREE   E JONES
4. WALTON   *vacant*
5. WEST DERBY   E L WILLIAMS

ARCHDEACONRY OF KNOWSLEY AND SEFTON

6. SEFTON SOUTH   A D STOTT
7. HUYTON   M K ROGERS
8. SEFTON NORTH   A E TAYLOR
9. NORTH MEOLS   S MCGANITY

ARCHDEACONRY OF ST HELENS AND WARRINGTON

10. ST HELENS   *vacant*
11. WARRINGTON   N G SHAW
12. WIDNES   R HARVEY
13. WINWICK   S B GREY

ARCHDEACONRY OF WIGAN AND WEST LANCASHIRE

14. ORMSKIRK   E HEANEY
15. WIGAN   S L NICHOLSON

LONDON

ARCHDEACONRY OF LONDON

1. THE CITY   K HEDDERLY

ARCHDEACONRY OF CHARING CROSS

2. WESTMINSTER PADDINGTON   P R THOMAS
3. WESTMINSTER ST MARGARET   P A E CHESTER
4. WESTMINSTER ST MARYLEBONE   C A E DOWDING

ARCHDEACONRY OF HACKNEY (STEPNEY AREA)

5. HACKNEY   A M W WILSON
6. ISLINGTON   P V ZAPHIRIOU
7. TOWER HAMLETS   J A C HODGES

ARCHDEACONRY OF MIDDLESEX (KENSINGTON AREA)

8. CHELSEA   J L WELSH
9. HAMMERSMITH AND FULHAM   C J COLLINGTON
10. HAMPTON   T M GARRETT
11. HOUNSLOW   *vacant*
12. KENSINGTON   J B HEARD
13. SPELTHORNE   J A D S FERNANDES

ARCHDEACONRY OF HAMPSTEAD (EDMONTON AREA)

14. BARNET   J A GITTOES
15. CAMDEN   J G F KESTER
16. ENFIELD   S GALLAGHER
17. HARINGEY   I G BOOTH

ARCHDEACONRY OF NORTHOLT (WILLESDEN AREA)

18. BRENT   A J TEATHER
19. EALING   D E NENO
20. HARROW   A L LYNES
21. HILLINGDON   R C YOUNG

MANCHESTER

ARCHDEACONRY OF MANCHESTER

1. MANCHESTER (NORTH AND EAST)   H T SCANLAN
2. MANCHESTER (SOUTH AND STRETFORD)   N E WATSON

ARCHDEACONRY OF BOLTON

3. BOLTON   S D J COOK
4. BURY AND ROSSENDALE   R MANN

ARCHDEACONRY OF ROCHDALE

5. OLDHAM AND ASHTON   A D RAMBLE
6. ROCHDALE   K L SMEETON

ARCHDEACONRY OF SALFORD

7. SALFORD AND LEIGH   C G PEARSON

NEWCASTLE

ARCHDEACONRY OF NORTHUMBERLAND

1. BEDLINGTON   *vacant*
2. NEWCASTLE CENTRAL   E J NATTRASS
3. NEWCASTLE EAST   R W LAWRANCE
4. NEWCASTLE WEST   C L BROWN
5. TYNEMOUTH   T J E MAYFIELD

ARCHDEACONRY OF LINDISFARNE

6. ALNWICK   A J HARDY
7. BAMBURGH AND GLENDALE   L M TAYLOR-KENYON
8. BELLINGHAM   S A LUNN
9. CORBRIDGE   D J KENNEDY
10. HEXHAM   A J PATTERSON
11. MORPETH   J C PARK
12. NORHAM   G R J KELSEY

NORWICH

ARCHDEACONRY OF NORWICH

1. NORWICH EAST   E J CARTER
2. NORWICH NORTH   S C STOKES
3. NORWICH SOUTH   P H RICHMOND

ARCHDEACONRY OF NORFOLK

4. BLOFIELD   M GREENLAND
5. DEPWADE   H Y WILCOX
6. GREAT YARMOUTH   S W J WARD
7. HUMBLEYARD   G P WILKINS
8. LODDON   D C OWEN
9. LOTHINGLAND   M J ASQUITH
10. REDENHALL   N O TUFFNELL
11. THETFORD AND ROCKLAND   S M WRIGHT
12. ST BENET AT WAXHAM AND TUNSTEAD   C H DOBSON

ARCHDEACONRY OF LYNN

13. BRECKLAND   S L THORP
14. BURNHAM AND WALSINGHAM   C G WYLIE
15. HEACHAM AND RISING   P R COOK
16. DEREHAM IN MITFORD   M A MCCAGHREY
17. HOLT   R H LAWRY
18. INGWORTH AND SPARHAM   K A F RENGERT
19. LYNN   J A NASH
20. REPPS   R H LAWRY

OXFORD

ARCHDEACONRY OF OXFORD

1. COWLEY   G B T BAYLISS
2. OXFORD   A G BUCKLEY

ARCHDEACONRY OF BERKSHIRE (BISHOP OF READING)

3. BRACKNELL   G S COLE
4. BRADFIELD   D J ARCHER
5. MAIDENHEAD AND WINDSOR   A L SWIFT
6. NEWBURY   D L R MCLEOD
7. READING   G FANCOURT
8. SONNING   R J LAMEY

ARCHDEACONRY OF BUCKINGHAM

9. AMERSHAM   M J WILLIAMS
10. AYLESBURY   D G WILLIAMS
11. BUCKINGHAM   R M ROBERTS
12. BURNHAM AND SLOUGH   *vacant*
13. CLAYDON   D J MEAKIN
14. MILTON KEYNES   T NORWOOD
15. MURSLEY   V I D F PLUMB
16. NEWPORT   G E ECCLESTONE
17. WENDOVER   D J O KEARLEY-HEYWOOD
18. WYCOMBE   D T BULL

ARCHDEACONRY OF DORCHESTER

19. ABINGDON   H G KENDRICK
20. ASTON AND CUDDESDON   S N CRONK
21. BICESTER AND ISLIP   J G MILLER
22. CHIPPING NORTON   D W SALTER
23. DEDDINGTON   S E SHARP
24. HENLEY   R S THEWSEY
25. VALE OF WHITE HORSE   J P ST JOHN NICOLLE
26. WALLINGFORD   D RICE
27. WANTAGE   W J N DURANT
28. WITNEY   T KUIN LAWTON
29. WOODSTOCK   J R AULD

PETERBOROUGH

ARCHDEACONRY OF NORTHAMPTON

1. BRACKLEY   C J M OLEY
2. BRIXWORTH   M J HAYES
3. DAVENTRY   S P BURROW
4. GREATER NORTHAMPTON   B J HOLLINS
5. TOWCESTER   R J ORMSTON
6. WELLINGBOROUGH   E G SMITH

ARCHDEACONRY OF OAKHAM

7. CORBY   I A PULLINGER
8. HIGHAM   C A YOUNGMAN
9. KETTERING   H M JEFFERY
10. OUNDLE   S J WEBSTER
11. PETERBOROUGH   M P J MOORE
12. RUTLAND   J E BAXTER

PORTSMOUTH

ARCHDEACONRY OF THE MEON

1. BISHOP'S WALTHAM   D T ISAAC
2. FAREHAM   I MEREDITH
3. GOSPORT   P M CHAMBERLAIN
4. PETERSFIELD   C D WILLIAMS

ARCHDEACONRY OF PORTSDOWN

5. HAVANT   I SNARES
6. PORTSMOUTH   R C WHITE

ARCHDEACONRY OF ISLE OF WIGHT

7. ISLE OF WIGHT   S J DAUGHTERY

ROCHESTER

ARCHDEACONRY OF ROCHESTER

1. COBHAM   A E DAVIE
2. DARTFORD   R J MORTIMER
3. GILLINGHAM   B S SENIOR
4. GRAVESEND   N I BOURNE
5. ROCHESTER   H M BURN
6. STROOD   S L COPESTAKE

ARCHDEACONRY OF TONBRIDGE

7. MALLING   W W NORTH
8. PADDOCK WOOD   A J AXON
9. SEVENOAKS   J A LE BAS
10. SHOREHAM   T R HATWELL
11. TONBRIDGE   M S A BARKER
12. TUNBRIDGE WELLS   D P WREN

ARCHDEACONRY OF BROMLEY AND BEXLEY

13. BECKENHAM   J A BLUNDEN
14. BROMLEY   V A PASK
15. ERITH   A J D FOOT
16. ORPINGTON   W J MUSSON
17. SIDCUP   M J JEMMETT

ST ALBANS

ARCHDEACONRY OF ST ALBANS

1. BERKHAMSTED   J A GORDON
2. HEMEL HEMPSTEAD   M D MACEY
3. HITCHIN   W T BRITT
4. RICKMANSWORTH   S G CUTMORE
5. ST ALBANS   K P J PADLEY
6. WATFORD   P M WADDELL
7. WHEATHAMPSTEAD   R M BANHAM

ARCHDEACONRY OF BEDFORD

8. AMPTHILL AND SHEFFORD   L KLIMAS
9. BEDFORD   G R CAPPLEMAN
10. BIGGLESWADE   G C BUCKLE
11. DUNSTABLE   N Y LENTHALL
12. LUTON   D W KESTERTON
13. SHARNBROOK   S J LILEY

ARCHDEACONRY OF HERTFORD

14. BARNET   L J HEWITT
15. BISHOP'S STORTFORD   *vacant*
16. BUNTINGFORD   R C PYKE
17. CHESHUNT   C E C HUDSON
18. WELWYN HATFIELD   J E FENNELL
19. HERTFORD AND WARE   M P DUNSTAN
20. STEVENAGE   A J THOMAS

ST EDMUNDSBURY AND IPSWICH

ARCHDEACONRY OF IPSWICH

1. IPSWICH   N S ATKINS

ARCHDEACONRY OF SUDBURY

2. CLARE   *vacant*
3. GIPPING VALLEY   D R WILLIAMS
4. HADLEIGH   J H DELFGOU
5. IXWORTH   K A VALENTINE
6. LAVENHAM   C M S ROBINSON
7. MILDENHALL   C CHILDS
8. SUDBURY   C J RAMSEY
9. THINGOE   M E OSBORNE

ARCHDEACONRY OF SUFFOLK

10. COLNEYS   A S DOTCHIN
11. HARTISMERE AND HOXNE   S A LOXTON
12. LOES   L SIU
13. SAMFORD   L OOSTERHOF
14. SAXMUNDHAM   S E HART
15. WAVENEY AND BLYTH   R HENDERSON
16. WOODBRIDGE   A J COOPER

ARCHDEACONRIES, DEANERIES AND RURAL/AREA DEANS

SALISBURY

ARCHDEACONRY OF SHERBORNE

1. DORCHESTER S C HILLMAN
2. LYME BAY D F B BALDWIN
3. SHERBORNE A J D GILBERT
4. WEYMOUTH AND PORTLAND N J CLARKE
5. BLACKMORE VALE *vacant*

ARCHDEACONRY OF DORSET

6. MILTON AND BLANDFORD J C E POTTINGER
7. POOLE AND NORTH BOURNEMOUTH L J HOLT
8. PURBECK S F EVERETT
9. WIMBORNE A J W ROWLAND

ARCHDEACONRY OF SARUM

10. ALDERBURY D G BACON
11. CHALKE G SOUTHGATE
12. HEYTESBURY P A REID
13. SALISBURY K J INGLIS
14. STONEHENGE E J RANCE

ARCHDEACONRY OF WILTS

15. BRADFORD A E EVANS
16. CALNE J D CURTIS
17. DEVIZES A J M SINCLAIR
18. MARLBOROUGH R R POWELL
19. PEWSEY G E R OSBORNE

SHEFFIELD

ARCHDEACONRY OF SHEFFIELD AND ROTHERHAM

1. ATTERCLIFFE P A KNOWLES
2. ECCLESALL M E BROWN
3. ECCLESFIELD P J SALMON
4. HALLAM M I RHODES
5. LAUGHTON V C CAMBER
6. ROTHERHAM P J BATCHFORD

ARCHDEACONRY OF DONCASTER

7. ADWICK-LE-STREET D N BERRY
8. DONCASTER R A HEARD
9. DONCASTER, WEST I SMITH
10. SNAITH AND HATFIELD J L SMITH
11. TANKERSLEY D J HOPKIN
12. WATH A R BREWERTON

SODOR AND MAN

ARCHDEACONRY OF SODOR AND MAN

Deaneries, deanery synods and the office of rural dean were abolished with effect from 1 January 2013 by the Mission and Pastoral Measure (Isle of Man) 2012 s.46, and deaneries were replaced by groupings of parishes known as "mission partnerships".

SOUTHWARK

ARCHDEACONRY OF LEWISHAM AND GREENWICH (BISHOP OF WOOLWICH)

1. CHARLTON *vacant*
2. DEPTFORD *vacant*
3. ELTHAM AND MOTTINGHAM C J SHELLEY
4. EAST LEWISHAM S P HALL
5. WEST LEWISHAM M BROOKS
6. PLUMSTEAD P ORGAN

ARCHDEACONRY OF SOUTHWARK (BISHOP OF WOOLWICH)

7. BERMONDSEY G J JENKINS
8. CAMBERWELL *vacant*
9. DULWICH S J HEIGHT
10. SOUTHWARK AND NEWINGTON J M W SEDGWICK

ARCHDEACONRY OF LAMBETH (BISHOP OF KINGSTON)

11. LAMBETH NORTH C A CLARKE
12. LAMBETH SOUTH J E CROUCHER
13. MERTON R S TAYLOR

ARCHDEACONRY OF WANDSWORTH (BISHOP OF KINGSTON)

14. BATTERSEA R G TAYLOR
15. KINGSTON R S STANIER
16. RICHMOND AND BARNES J A BARROW
17. TOOTING M T GIBBS
18. WANDSWORTH I S TATTUM

ARCHDEACONRY OF CROYDON

19. CROYDON ADDINGTON *vacant*
20. CROYDON CENTRAL S J D FOSTER
21. CROYDON NORTH *vacant*
22. CROYDON SOUTH P C ROBERTS

ARCHDEACONRY OF REIGATE (BISHOP OF CROYDON)

23. SUTTON A M A GBEBIKAN
24. REIGATE A C COLPUS
25. TANDRIDGE M K EDMONDS

SOUTHWELL AND NOTTINGHAM

ARCHDEACONRY OF NEWARK

1. BASSETLAW AND BAWTRY D R GOUGH
2. MANSFIELD *vacant*
3. NEWARK AND SOUTHWELL J R CHAMBERS
4. NEWSTEAD *vacant*

ARCHDEACONRY OF NOTTINGHAM

5. EAST BINGHAM S D HIPPISLEY-COX
6. WEST BINGHAM *vacant*
7. GEDLING *vacant*
8. NOTTINGHAM NORTH *vacant*
9. NOTTINGHAM SOUTH C D BOURNE

TRURO

ARCHDEACONRY OF CORNWALL

1. CARNMARTH NORTH C J B BUSH
2. CARNMARTH SOUTH G K BENNETT
3. KERRIER D G MILLER
4. PENWITH *vacant*
5. POWDER M C BAKER
6. PYDAR C C MCQUILLEN-WRIGHT

ARCHDEACONRY OF BODMIN

7. ST AUSTELL H M FLINT
8. STRATTON D K BARNES
9. TRIGG MAJOR P M KNIGHT
10. TRIGG MINOR AND BODMIN P R HOLLEY
11. EAST WIVELSHIRE C M PAINTER
12. WEST WIVELSHIRE S J MORGAN

WINCHESTER

ARCHDEACONRY OF WINCHESTER

1. ALRESFORD D M CHATTELL
2. ALTON B J PRITCHARD
3. ANDOVER T A LEWIS
4. BASINGSTOKE R J S C HARLOW
5. ODIHAM M E DE QUIDT
6. WHITCHURCH D M ROCHE
7. WINCHESTER K P KOUSSEFF

ARCHDEACONRY OF BOURNEMOUTH

8. BOURNEMOUTH J C NIGHTINGALE
9. CHRISTCHURCH G J PHILBRICK
10. EASTLEIGH R E WISE
11. LYNDHURST P B C SALISBURY
12. ROMSEY J M PITKIN
13. SOUTHAMPTON S J WILLIAMS

THE CHANNEL ISLANDS

14. GUERNSEY T R BARKER
15. JERSEY M R KEIRLE

WORCESTER

ARCHDEACONRY OF WORCESTER

1. KIDDERMINSTER AND STOURPORT   T J WILLIAMS
2. MALVERN AND UPTON   M BADGER
3. PERSHORE AND EVESHAM   S A DANGERFIELD
4. WORCESTER   D M COOKSEY

ARCHDEACONRY OF DUDLEY

5. GREATER DUDLEY   D J HOSKIN
6. REDDITCH AND BROMSGROVE   P LAWLOR

YORK

ARCHDEACONRY OF YORK (BISHOP OF SELBY)

1. NEW AINSTY   G R MUMFORD
2. DERWENT   N W R BIRD
3. EASINGWOLD   S WHITING
4. SELBY   C WILTON
5. SOUTH WOLD   C R PINCHBECK
6. SOUTHERN RYEDALE   C L WINGFIELD
7. CITY OF YORK   L D TILLETT

ARCHDEACONRY OF EAST RIDING (BISHOP OF HULL)

8. BEVERLEY   R F PARKINSON
9. BRIDLINGTON   M R POLLARD
10. HARTHILL   J A TONKIN
11. NORTH HOLDERNESS   S E HEBDEN
12. SOUTH HOLDERNESS   A M LAIRD
13. HOWDEN   M J PROCTOR
14. HULL   J C COWAN
15. SCARBOROUGH   S TAYLOR

ARCHDEACONRY OF CLEVELAND (BISHOP OF WHITBY)

16. GUISBOROUGH   D TEMBEY
17. MIDDLESBROUGH   G HOLLAND
18. MOWBRAY   F R MAYER-JONES

19. NORTHERN RYEDALE   G W ATHA
20. STOKESLEY   T STEPHENS
21. WHITBY   M G T GOBBETT

LEEDS

ARCHDEACONRY OF BRADFORD

1. AIRE AND WORTH   S R BENHAM
2. INNER BRADFORD   J E BAVINGTON
3. OUTER BRADFORD   *vacant*
4. SOUTH CRAVEN AND WHARFEDALE   *vacant*

ARCHDEACONRY OF HALIFAX

5. ALMONDBURY AND KIRKBURTON   J ANDERSON
6. BRIGHOUSE AND ELLAND   *vacant*
7. DEWSBURY AND BIRSTALL   *vacant*
8. HALIFAX AND CALDER VALLEY   K A SHOESMITH
9. HUDDERSFIELD   R N FIRTH

ARCHDEACONRY OF LEEDS

10. ALLERTON   K A FITZSIMONS
11. ARMLEY   L C PEARSON
12. HEADINGLEY   J R SEABOURNE
13. WHITKIRK   M PEAT

ARCHDEACONRY OF PONTEFRACT

14. BARNSLEY   S P RACE
15. PONTEFRACT   M GALLAGHER
16. WAKEFIELD   D I GERRARD

ARCHDEACONRY OF RICHMOND AND CRAVEN

17. BOWLAND AND EWECROSS   I F GREENHALGH
18. HARROGATE   J SMITH
19. RICHMOND   M FLETCHER
20. RIPON   *vacant*
21. SKIPTON   J W F THEODOSIUS
22. WENSLEY   P S YEADON

CHURCH IN WALES

ST ASAPH

ARCHDEACONRY OF ST ASAPH

1. ST ASAPH   *vacant*
2. DENBIGH   *vacant*
3. DYFFRYN CLWYD   *vacant*
4. HOLYWELL   *vacant*
5. LLANRWST AND RHOS   *vacant*

ARCHDEACONRY OF MONTGOMERY

6. CEDEWAIN   N W MORRIS
7. MATHRAFAL   *vacant*
8. PENEDEYRN   *vacant*
9. POOL   S G WILLSON
10. VALLE CRUCIS   *vacant*

ARCHDEACONRY OF WREXHAM

11. ALYN   P R-M DE G GOWER
12. DEE VALLEY   *vacant*
13. HAWARDEN   M J BATCHELOR
14. MOLD   *vacant*
15. WREXHAM   *vacant*

BANGOR

ARCHDEACONRY OF ANGLESEY

1. SYNOD YNYS MON   E C WILLIAMS

ARCHDEACONRY OF BANGOR

2. SYNOD BANGOR   *vacant*

ARCHDEACONRY OF MEIRIONNYDD

3. SYNOD MEIRIONYDD   *vacant*

ST DAVIDS

ARCHDEACONRY OF ST DAVIDS

1. DAUGLEDDAU   N HOOK
2. EAST LANDSKER   K G TAYLOR
3. GREATER DEWISLAND   M H ROWLANDS
4. NARBERTH AND TENBY   M L COX

ARCHDEACONRY OF CARDIGAN

5. CEMAIS AND SUB-AERON   *vacant*

ARCHDEACONRY OF ST DAVIDS

6. ROOSE   A M CHADWICK

ARCHDEACONRY OF CARDIGAN

7. EMLYN   *vacant*

ARCHDEACONRY OF ST DAVIDS

8. PEMBROKESHIRE, SOUTH WEST   P O JONES
9. CEMAES, WEST   C C BROWN

ARCHDEACONRY OF CARDIGAN

10. GLYN AERON   *vacant*
11. ABERYSTWYTH   M S ANSELL
12. LAMPETER AND ULTRA-AERON   *vacant*
13. BRO AERON MYDR   E DAVIES
14. LLANBADARN FAWR   *vacant*
15. BRO PADARN   A G LOAT

ARCHDEACONRY OF CARMARTHEN

16. CARMARTHEN   *vacant*

ARCHDEACONRY OF CARDIGAN

17. BRO TEIFI   J S BENNETT

ARCHDEACONRY OF CARMARTHEN

18. CYDWELI   *vacant*

ARCHDEACONRY OF CARDIGAN

19. BRO WYRE   J W SMITH

ARCHDEACONRY OF CARMARTHEN

20. DYFFRYN AMAN   *vacant*

ARCHDEACONRY OF CARDIGAN

21. DYFFRYN TEIFI   G M REID
22. GLYN AERON (Coastal)   J P LEWIS
23. LAMPETER   M A ROWLANDS

ARCHDEACONRY OF CARMARTHEN

24. ST CLEARS   *vacant*
25. BRO AMAN   S BALE
26. BRO CAERFYRDDIN   M A R HILL
27. BRO CYDWELI   T COPELAND
28. BRO DYFRI   V R SAYER
29. BRO LLIEDI   D H E MOSFORD
30. BRO SANCLER   E A HOWELLS
31. DINEFWR   S E JONES
32. LLANDEILO   *vacant*

LLANDAFF

ARCHDEACONRY OF LLANDAFF

1. CARDIFF   D C LLOYD
2. LLANDAFF   S M JOHN
3. MERTHYR TYDFIL AND CAERPHILLY   S P KIRK
4. PENARTH AND BARRY   A P JAMES
5. PONTYPRIDD   M D GABLE

ARCHDEACONRY OF MARGAM

6. BRIDGEND   I M HODGES
7. CYNON VALLEY   M K JONES
8. MARGAM   E JENKYNS
9. NEATH   C W COLES
10. RHONDDA   *vacant*
11. VALE OF GLAMORGAN   M J DAVIES

MONMOUTH

ARCHDEACONRY OF MONMOUTH

1. ABERGAVENNY   J F GRAY
2. MONMOUTH   *vacant*
3. NETHERWENT   J D HARRIS
4. RAGLAN-USK   T G CLEMENT

ARCHDEACONRY OF NEWPORT

5. BASSALEG   *vacant*
6. NEWPORT   *vacant*

ARCHDEACONRY OF THE GWENT VALLEYS

7. BEDWELLTY   M OWEN
8. PONTYPOOL   *vacant*

SWANSEA AND BRECON

ARCHDEACONRY OF BRECON

1. GREATER BRECON   R Y KHAN
2. RADNOR AND BUILTH   M T BEATON

ARCHDEACONRY OF GOWER

3. AFON TAWE (SWANSEA)   H M LERVY
4. GREATER GOWER   P BROOKS

ENGLISH BENEFICES AND CHURCHES

An index of benefices, conventional districts, local ecumenical projects, and proprietary chapels (shown in bold type), together with entries for churches and other licensed places of worship listed on the Parish Index of the Central Board of Finance. Where the church name is the same as that of the benefice (or as that of the place whose name forms the beginning of the benefice name), the church entry is omitted. Church dedications are indicated in brackets.

The benefice entry gives the full legal name, followed by the diocese, its deanery number (p. 938), the patron(s), and the name(s) and appointment(s) of clergy serving there. The following are the main abbreviations used; for others see the full list of abbreviations.

C	Curate	OLM	Ordained Local Minister
C-in-c	Curate-in-charge	P	Patron(s)
Dn-in-c	Deacon-in-charge	P-in-c	Priest-in-charge
Dss	Deaconess	Par Dn	Parish Deacon
Hon C	Honorary Curate	R	Rector
Hon Par Dn	Honorary Parish Deacon	TM	Team Minister
I	Incumbent (includes Rector or Vicar)	TR	Team Rector
Min	Minister	TV	Team Vicar
NSM	Non-stipendiary Minister	V	Vicar

Listed below are the elements in place names which are not normally treated as substantive in the index:

CENTRAL	HIGHER	MUCH	OVER
EAST	LITTLE	NETHER	SOUTH
GREAT	LOW	NEW	THE
GREATER	LOWER	NORTH	UPPER
HIGH	MIDDLE	OLD	WEST

Thus WEST WIMBLEDON (Christ Church) appears as **WIMBLEDON, WEST (Christ Church)** and CENTRAL TELFORD as **TELFORD, CENTRAL**. The only exception occurs where the second element of the place name is a common noun, thus NEW LANE remains as **NEW LANE**, and WEST TOWN as **WEST TOWN**.

4SAINTS TEAM (Huyton Deanery), comprising Huyton, Knowsley, Stockbridge Village, and West Derby *Liv 7* **P** *Patr Bd* **TV** J VAN DEN BERG-OWENS, N H LEA-WILSON **C** J W FORSTER

5FOLDS, comprising Long Stanton, Over, Swavesey, and Willingham *Ely 6* **P** *Patr Bd* **TR** S D GILL **TV** L E CLELAND **NSM** J TIPLADY

A453 churches of South Nottinghamshire, The, comprising Barton-in-Fabis, Gotham, Kingston-on-Soar, Ratcliffe-on-Soar, and Thrumpton *S'well 6* **P** *D&C, Bp and Ms M Seymour (1 turn), Ld Chan (1 turn)* **R** R I COLEMAN

AB KETTLEBY (St James) and Holwell w Asfordby *Leic 2* **P** *DBP, MMCET and V Rothley (jt)* **C** M CARROLL **NSM** P R TOWNS

ABBAS AND TEMPLECOMBE (Blessed Virgin Mary), Henstridge and Horsington *B & W 2* **P** *Bp and Ch Trust Fund Trust* **R** K ROGERS

ABBERLEY (St Mary) *see* Shrawley, Witley, Astley and Abberley *Worc*

ABBERLEY (St Michael) *as above*

ABBERTON (St Andrew) *see* Fingringhoe w E Donyland and Abberton etc *Chelmsf*

ABBERTON (St Edburga), The Flyfords, Naunton Beauchamp and Bishampton w Throckmorton *Worc 3* **P** *Bp and Croome Estate Trustees (1 turn), and Ld Chan (1 turn)* **C** E L GOLDBY, G R NOYES, S A DANGERFIELD

ABBESS RODING (St Edmund King and Martyr) *see* S Rodings *Chelmsf*

ABBEY CHAPEL (St Mary) *see* Annesley w Newstead and Kirkby Woodhouse *S'well*

ABBEY Group of Parishes, The, comprising East Halton, Habrough, Killingholme, Thornton Curtis, Ulceby, and Wootton *Linc 4* **P** *Ld Chan (1 turn), Bp and DBP (1 turn), Bp, DBP, Earl of Yarborough, J E Spilman Esq, and Trustees (1 turn)* **V** P J GREEN

ABBEY HULTON (St John) *see* Bucknall *Lich*

ABBEY WOOD (St Michael and All Angels) *S'wark 6* **P** *Bp* **V** D A SHERRATT

ABBEY WOOD (William Temple) *see* Thamesmead *S'wark*

ABBEYDALE *see* Sheff St Pet and St Oswald *Sheff*

ABBEYDALE (St John the Evangelist) and Millhouses *Sheff 2* **P** *Bp and Trustees (jt)* **NSM** A M LAUENER

ABBEYDORE (St Mary) *see* Ewyas Harold w Dulas, Kenderchurch etc *Heref*

ABBEYLANDS Team Ministry, comprising Hawksworth Wood w Moor Grange, Horsforth, and Kirkstall *Leeds 12* **P** *Patr Bd* **TR** N C SINCLAIR **TV** S M KAYE **C** R J FORD

ABBEYSTEAD (Christ Church) *see* Dolphinholme w Quernmore and Over Wyresdale *Blackb*

ABBOTS BICKINGTON (St James) *see* Bradworthy, Sutcombe, Putford etc *Ex*

ABBOTS BROMLEY (St Nicholas), Blithfield, Colton, Colwich and Great Haywood *Lich 3* **P** *Bp and D&C (jt)* **R** S C DAVIS **NSM** A V NOBLE, L J FARRINGTON, M A DAVYS

ABBOTS LANGLEY (St Lawrence) *St Alb 6* **P** *Bp* **P-in-c** P M WADDELL **C** M HOWARTH

ABBOTS LEIGH (Holy Trinity) w Leigh Woods *Bris 2* **P** *Bp* **V** S H E JONES

ABBOTS MORTON (St Peter) *see* Church Lench w Rous Lench and Abbots Morton etc *Worc*

ABBOTS RIPTON (St Andrew) *see* N Leightonstone *Ely*

ABBOTSBURY (St Mary) *see* Newton Abbot *Ex*

ABBOTSBURY (St Nicholas), Portesham and Langton Herring *Sarum 4* **P** *The Hon C A Townshend and Bp (alt)* **NSM** M PREUSS-HIGHAM

ABBOTSHAM (St Helen) *Ex 14* **P** *PCC* **C** R M ELKS

ABBOTSKERSWELL (The Blessed Virgin Mary) *see* Kingskerswell, Abbotskerswell and Coffinswell *Ex*

ABBOTSLEY (St Margaret) *see* Gt Gransden and Abbotsley and Lt Gransden etc *Ely*

ABBOTSWOOD (St Nicholas Family Centre) *see* Yate *Bris*

ABBOTTS ANN (St Mary) and Upper Clatford and Goodworth Clatford *Win 3* **P** *Exors T P de Paravicini Esq and Bp (jt)* **NSM** N J JUDD

ABDON (St Margaret) *see* Corvedale Benefice *Heref*

ABENHALL (St Michael) w Mitcheldean *Glouc 3* **P** *DBP* **R** D A GILL

ABERFORD (St Ricarius) w Micklefield *York 4* **P** *Abp and Oriel Coll Ox (jt)* **P-in-c** C WILTON **C** P G GRAYSON **NSM** C COMER-STONE

ABINGDON, NORTH (Christ Church) *Ox 19* **P** *Bp* **V** K O DUNNETT **C** K M COOKE, V J WATTS **NSM** P G COOKE

ABINGDON-ON-THAMES (St Helen) (St Michael and All Angels) (St Nicolas) *Ox 19* **P** *Patr Bd* **TR** E C MILLER **TV** P A SMITH **Hon C** P T C MASHEDER **NSM** J E BROWN

ABINGER (St James) and Coldharbour and Wotton and Holmbury St Mary *Guildf 7* **P** *Bp, Ch Patr Trust, and J P M H Evelyn Esq (jt)* **R** A N BERRY **NSM** J D GRUNDY

ABINGTON (St Peter and St Paul) *Pet 4* **P** *Bp* **R** B J KIM **C** R M HETHERINGTON

ABINGTON PIGOTTS (St Michael and All Angels) *see* Shingay Gp *Ely*

ABINGTON, GREAT (St Mary the Virgin) *see* Granta Vale Gp *Ely*

ABINGTON, LITTLE (St Mary) *as above*

ABRAM (St John)   *see* Wigan *Liv*

ABSON (St James the Great)   *see* Pucklechurch and Abson *Bris*

ABTHORPE (St John the Baptist)   *see* Silverstone and Abthorpe w Slapton etc *Pet*

ACASTER MALBIS (Holy Trinity) *York 1* **P** *R A G Raimes Esq* **V** *vacant*

ACASTER SELBY (St John)   *see* Appleton Roebuck w Acaster Selby *York*

ACCRINGTON (Christ Church) *Blackb 1* **P** *Bp and V S Shore H Trin (jt)* **V** P MCNALLY

ACCRINGTON (St Andrew) (St Mary Magdalen) (St Peter) and Church Kirk *Blackb 1* **P** *Bp and DBP (jt)* **R** D A ARNOLD **C** J D MCDERMOTT

ACCRINGTON (St James) (St Paul) *Blackb 1* **P** *Bp and DBP (jt)* **V** *vacant*

ACCRINGTON (St John) w Huncoat St Augustine *Blackb 1* **P** *Bp and V Accrington St Jas w St Paul (jt)* **P-in-c** H A SCRIVEN

ACKLAM (St John the Baptist)   *see* W Buckrose *York*

ACKLAM, WEST (St Mary) *York 17* **P** *Abp* **V** N R RAO

ACKLETON (Mission Room)   *see* Worfield *Heref*

ACKLINGTON (St John the Divine)   *see* Warkworth, Acklington and Shilbottle *Newc*

ACKWORTH (All Saints) (St Cuthbert) and Badsworth *Leeds 15* **P** *Duchy of Lancaster and BDP (alt)* **R** C SMITH **NSM** P A FOX

ACLE (St Edmund) and Bure to Yare *Nor 4* **P** *Bp, Ch Soc Trust, Personal Reps K M Mills Esq, and DBP (jt)* **R** M GREENLAND

ACOCKS GREEN (St Mary) *Birm 6* **P** *Trustees* **V** A T BULLOCK

ACOL (St Mildred)   *see* Birchington w Acol and Minnis Bay *Cant*

ACOMB (Holy Redeemer) *York 7* **P** *The Crown* **P-in-c** S C BIDDLESTONE

ACOMB (St Stephen and St Aidan) *York 7* **P** *Trustees* **V** P H VIVASH

ACOMB MOOR (James the Deacon) *York 7* **P** *Abp* **V** L D TILLETT

ACRISE (St Martin)   *see* Elham Valley *Cant*

ACTON (All Saints) w Great Waldingfield *St E 8* **P** *Bp* **V** F E M MARSDEN

ACTON (St Gabriel)   *see* N Acton St Gabr *Lon*

ACTON (St Martin)   *see* W Acton St Martin *Lon*

ACTON (St Mary) *Lon 19* **P** *Bp* **R** N G JONES **C** D M AYRES **NSM** M J SPREDBURY

ACTON (St Mary) and Worleston, Church Minshull and Wettenhall *Ches 15* **P** *Bp, V Over St Chad, and R C Roundell Esq (jt)* **V** S A LAWSON

ACTON BEAUCHAMP (St Giles)   *see* Frome Valley *Heref*

ACTON BURNELL (St Mary)   *see* Condover w Frodesley, Acton Burnell etc *Heref*

ACTON GREEN (St Peter) *Lon 11* **P** *Bp* **V** K J MORRIS **C** F PESCE

ACTON ROUND (St Mary)   *see* Bridgnorth and Morville Par *Heref*

ACTON SCOTT (St Margaret)   *see* Craven Arms *Heref*

ACTON TRUSSELL (St James)   *see* Penkridge *Lich*

ACTON TURVILLE (St Mary)   *see* Boxwell, Leighterton, Didmarton, Oldbury etc *Glouc*

ACTON, EAST (St Dunstan w St Thomas) *Lon 19* **P** *Bp* **V** J M WESTALL

ACTON, EAST (St Dunstan w St Thomas)   *see* E Acton St Dunstan w St Thos *Lon*

ACTON, NORTH (St Gabriel) *Lon 19* **P** *Bp* **V** T J N L'ESTRANGE

ACTON, SOUTH (All Saints)   *see* Acton St Mary *Lon*

ACTON, WEST (St Martin) *Lon 19* **P** *Bp* **V** J E PALMER **NSM** B D FRANKLIN

ADBASTON (St Michael and All Angels), High Offley, Knightley, Norbury, Woodseaves, Gnosall and Moreton *Lich 7* **P** *Bp* **R** *vacant*

ADDERBURY (St Mary) w Milton *Ox 23* **P** *New Coll Ox* **V** E A SIMPSON

ADDERLEY (St Peter), Ash, Calverhall, Ightfield and Moreton Say *Lich 17* **P** *C C Corbet Esq, Sir Algernon Heber-Percy KCVO, T C Heywood-Lonsdale Esq, and R Whitchurch (jt)* **P-in-c** G WINDON

ADDINGHAM (St Michael)   *see* Cross Fell Gp *Carl*

ADDINGHAM (St Peter) *Leeds 4* **P** *J R Thompson-Ashby Esq* **R** M H CANNON

ADDINGTON (St Margaret)   *see* Birling, Addington, Ryarsh and Trottiscliffe *Roch*

ADDINGTON (St Mary) *S'wark 19* **P** *Abp* **V** D J FORMAN **NSM** B C GENTILELLA

ADDINGTON (St Mary)   *see* Winslow w Gt Horwood and Addington *Ox*

ADDINGTON, GREAT (All Saints)   *see* Irthlingborough, Gt Addington, Lt Addington etc *Pet*

ADDINGTON, LITTLE (St Mary the Virgin)   *as above*

ADDINGTON, NEW (St Edward) *S'wark 19* **P** *Bp* **P-in-c** D C PREMRAJ **C** D D PREMRAJ

ADDISCOMBE (St Mary Magdalene) *S'wark 20* **P** *Trustees* **V** A S JOHNSON

ADDISCOMBE (St Mildred) *S'wark 20* **P** *Bp* **V** R C HAGON

ADDLESTONE (St Augustine) (St Paul) *Guildf 11* **P** *Bp* **V** B H BEECROFT **C** C M BEECROFT

ADDLETHORPE (St Nicholas)   *see* Skegness Gp *Linc*

ADEL (St John the Baptist) *Leeds 12* **P** *Brig R G Lewthwaite, D R Lewthwaite Esq, and J V Lewthwaite Esq (jt)* **R** A J BATTYE

ADEYFIELD (St Barnabas)   *see* Hemel Hempstead *St Alb*

ADFORTON (St Andrew)   *see* Wigmore Abbey *Heref*

ADISHAM (Holy Innocents)   *see* Barham Downs w Adisham *Cant*

ADLESTROP (St Mary Magdalene)   *see* Broadwell, Evenlode, Oddington, Adlestrop etc *Glouc*

ADLINGFLEET (All Saints)   *see* The Marshland *Sheff*

ADLINGTON (St John's Mission Church)   *see* Prestbury *Ches*

ADLINGTON (St Paul) *Blackb 4* **P** *Bp* **V** *vacant*

ADSTOCK (St Cecilia)   *see* Lenborough *Ox*

ADSTONE (All Saints)   *see* Lambfold *Pet*

ADSWOOD (St Gabriel's Mission Church)   *see* Stockport St Geo *Ches*

ADVENT (St Adwena)   *see* Camel-Allen *Truro*

ADWELL (St Mary)   *see* Thame *Ox*

ADWICK-LE-STREET (St Laurence) w Skelbrooke *Sheff 7* **P** *Mrs P N Fullerton and Bp (alt)* **NSM** J M GARDNER

ADWICK-UPON-DEARNE (St John the Baptist)   *see* Barnburgh w Melton on the Hill etc *Sheff*

AFFPUDDLE (St Laurence)   *see* W Purbeck *Sarum*

AIGBURTH (St Anne) *Liv 2* **P** *Trustees* **V** I R GREENWOOD **C** M G FERGUSON

AIKTON (St Andrew)   *see* Barony of Burgh *Carl*

AINDERBY STEEPLE (St Helen)   *see* Lower Swale *Leeds*

AINSDALE (St John) *Liv 9* **P** *R Walton, Bp, and Adn (jt)* **V** J E MORGAN

AINSTABLE (St Michael and All Angels)   *see* Inglewood Gp *Carl*

AINSTY, NORTH   *see* Marston Moor *York*

AINSTY, RURAL, comprising Bilton, Healaugh, Moor Monkton, and Wighill *York 1* **P** *Abp (3 turns), D&C (1 turn)* **C** L J BRENCHER, N J GARSIDE, R D BATTERSBY

AINSWORTH (Christ Church) *Man 4* **P** *Bp* **P-in-c** D F THOMSON **OLM** D J JOHNSTONE

AINTREE (St Giles) w St Peter *Liv 8* **P** *Bp* **V** N A THORPE **NSM** N J WEST

AIRE, UPPER, comprising Coniston Cold, Gargrave, and Kirkby-in-Malhamdale *Leeds 17* **P** *Bp and D&C Bradf (jt)* **V** A D STEER **NSM** S E MCWHINNEY

AIREDALE (Holy Cross) w Fryston *Leeds 15* **P** *Bp* **V** T A IBBOTSON **NSM** A L BROWNRIDGE

AIRMYN (St David), Hook and Rawcliffe *Sheff 10* **P** *Bp and Ch Soc Trust (jt)* **V** P J BALL

AISHOLT (All Saints), Enmore, Goathurst, Nether Stowey, Over Stowey and Spaxton w Charlynch *B & W 17* **P** *Bp, D&C Windsor, MMCET, and Ch Trust Fund Trust (jt)* **R** E O KING **C** N D BRADFORD **Hon C** K M SAX

AISLABY (St Margaret)   *see* Lower Esk *York*

AISTHORPE (St Peter)   *see* Springline *Linc*

AKELEY (St James)   *see* N Buckingham w Stowe *Ox*

AKEMAN, comprising Bletchingdon, Chesterton, Hampton Gay, Kirtlington, Middleton Stoney, Wendlebury, Weston-on-the-Green *Ox 21* **P** *New Coll and Ch Ch (1 turn), Qu Coll, St Jo Coll, and Period and Country Houses Ltd (1 turn)* **R** J G MILLER **Hon C** N KTORIDES

ALBERBURY (St Michael and All Angels)   *see* Ford, Gt Wollaston and Alberbury w Cardeston *Heref*

ALBOURNE (St Bartholomew) w Sayers Common and Twineham *Chich 11* **P** *Bp (2 turns), Ex Coll Ox (1 turn)* **R** *vacant*

ALBRIGHTON (St John the Baptist)   *see* Leaton and Albrighton w Battlefield *Lich*

ALBRIGHTON (St Mary Magdalene), Boningale and Donington *Lich 15* **P** *Haberdashers' Co and MMCET (jt)* **V** M R THOMAS **NSM** G A HARPER

ALBURGH (All Saints)   *see* Ditchingham, Hedenham, Broome, Earsham etc *Nor*

ALBURY (St Helen) w Tiddington, Holton, Waterperry, Waterstock and Wheatley *Ox 20* **P** *Bp and DBP (jt)* **V** N A R HAWKES **C** D C BENDOR-SAMUEL, M P DORMANDY

ALBURY (St Mary), Little Hadham and Much Hadham *St Alb 15* **P** *Bp Lon* **R** S D BATE

ALBURY (St Peter and St Paul) *see* Shere, Albury and Chilworth *Guildf*

ALBY (St Ethelbert) *see* Scarrowbeck *Nor*

ALCESTER MINSTER (St Nicholas) *Cov 7* **P** *Bp and Marquess of Hertford (jt)* **R** K L CROSS

ALCISTON (not known) *see* Arlington, Berwick, Selmeston w Alciston etc *Chich*

ALCOMBE (St Michael the Archangel) *B & W 15* **P** *Bp* **V** K J CROSS

ALCONBURY (St Peter and St Paul) *see* N Leightonstone *Ely*

ALDBOROUGH (St Andrew) w Boroughbridge and Roecliffe *Leeds 20* **P** *D&C York and Bp (alt)* **V** K J GARDINER

ALDBOROUGH (St Mary) *see* Aylsham and Distr *Nor*

ALDBOROUGH HATCH (St Peter) *Chelmsf 6* **P** *The Crown* **P-in-c** K P B LOVESEY

ALDBOURNE (St Michael) *see* Whitton *Sarum*

ALDBROUGH (St Bartholomew) and Mappleton w Goxhill and Withernwick *York 11* **P** *Ld Chan, Abp, and Adn E Riding (by turn)* **P-in-c** A M WHITE

ALDBROUGH (St Paul) *see* Forcett and Aldbrough and Melsonby *Leeds*

ALDBURY (St John the Baptist) *see* Tring *St Alb*

ALDE RIVER Benefice, The, comprising Benhall, Blaxhall, Farnham w Stratford St Andrew, Great Glemham, Little Glemham, Snape, and Sternfield *St E 14* **P** *Earl of Guilford, Major P W Hope-Cobbold, DBP, CPAS, Miss S F R Heycock-Hollond, and Exors Mrs A C V Wentworth (jt)* **R** R CORNISH **C** O H KEMSLEY **NSM** W D SOKOLIS

ALDE SANDLINGS, comprising Aldeburgh w Hazelwood, Aldringham w Thorpe, Friston, and Knodishall w Buxlow *St E 14* **P** *Mrs A C V Wentworth, Ch Patr Trust, and Ch Soc Trust (jt)* **C** J D MARSTON **NSM** J S MABEY, N J WINTER, S E HART

ALDE, UPPER, comprising Badingham, Bruisyard, Cransford, Dennington, Rendham, and Sweffling *St E 12* **P** R C Rous *Esq, DBP, and CPAS (jt)* **P-in-c** M E PERCIVAL

ALDEBURGH (St Peter and St Paul) *see* Alde Sandlings *St E*

ALDEBY (St Mary) *see* Waveney Marshlands *Nor*

ALDENHAM (St John the Baptist), Radlett and Shenley *St Alb 5* **P** *Patr Bd* **TV** O R BLEASE, R A FLETCHER

ALDERBROOK (St Richard) *see* Crowborough *Chich*

ALDERBURY (St Mary the Virgin) *see* Clarendon *Sarum*

ALDERCAR (St John) *see* Langley Mill and Aldercar *Derby*

ALDERFORD (St John the Baptist) *see* Reepham and Wensum Valley *Nor*

ALDERHOLT (St James) *Sarum 9* **P** *DBP* **V** S A WOODLEY

ALDERLEY (St Kenelm) *see* Tyndale *Glouc*

ALDERLEY (St Mary) w Birtles *Ches 12* **P** *Trustees and Bp (alt)* **R** A J HALE

ALDERLEY EDGE (St Philip) *Ches 12* **P** *Trustees* **V** R PYE **NSM** L C A ALEXANDER

ALDERMASTON (St Mary the Virgin) and Woolhampton *Ox 4* **P** *Bp, Keble Coll Ox, CPAS, Lady Dugdale, Worc Coll Ox, and DBP (jt)* **R** J E MANLEY

ALDERMINSTER (St Mary and Holy Cross) *see* Stourdene Gp *Cov*

ALDERNEY (St Anne) *Win 14* **P** *The Crown* **V** J K B FOWLER **C** A L FOWLER

ALDERSBROOK (St Gabriel) *Chelmsf 6* **P** *DBP* **V** M J HAWKES **NSM** C J SMALING, M A KENNY

ALDERSHOT (Holy Trinity) *Guildf 1* **P** *CPAS* **V** G P H NEWTON **C** D A PUSEY **NSM** C J B KELLAGHER

ALDERSHOT (St Augustine) *Guildf 1* **P** *Bp* **V** *vacant*

ALDERSHOT (St Michael the Archangel) (Ascension) *Guildf 1* **P** *Bp* **V** A A B PEREIRA

ALDERSLEY (Christ the King) *see* Tettenhall Regis *Lich*

ALDERTON (St Andrew) *see* Wilford Peninsula *St E*

ALDERTON (St Giles) *see* Gauzebrook *Bris*

ALDERTON (St Margaret of Antioch) *see* Winchcombe *Glouc*

ALDERTON (St Margaret) *see* Blisworth, Alderton, Grafton Regis etc *Pet*

ALDERWASLEY (All Saints) *see* Wirksworth *Derby*

ALDFIELD (St Lawrence) *see* Fountains Gp *Leeds*

ALDFORD (St John the Baptist) *see* Waverton w Aldford and Bruera *Ches*

ALDHAM (St Margaret and St Catherine) *see* Marks Tey and Aldham *Chelmsf*

ALDHAM (St Mary) *see* Elmsett w Aldham, Hintlesham, Chattisham etc *St E*

ALDINGBOURNE (St Mary the Virgin), Barnham and Eastergate *Chich 1* **P** *Bp and D&C (jt)* **NSM** A R BRANT, G REEVES, S M HIGGINS

ALDINGHAM (St Cuthbert) and Dendron and Rampside and Urswick *Carl 9* **P** *The Crown (1 turn), V Dalton-in-Furness and Resident Landowners of Urswick (1 turn)* **P-in-c** L A LUNN

ALDINGTON (St Martin) *see* Saxon Shoreline *Cant*

ALDRIDGE (St Mary the Virgin) (St Thomas) *Lich 24* **P** *MMCET* **R** P S DOEL **C** J A MIDDLETON, J E MORLEY **OLM** J E BAKEWELL

ALDRINGHAM (St Andrew) *see* Alde Sandlings *St E*

ALDRINGTON (St Leonard) *Chich 20* **P** *Bp* **V** *vacant*

ALDSWORTH (St Bartholomew) *see* Sherborne, Windrush, the Barringtons etc *Glouc*

ALDWARK (St Stephen) *see* Alne *York*

ALDWICK (St Richard) *Chich 1* **P** *Bp* **V** *vacant*

ALDWINCLE (St Peter), Clopton, Pilton, Stoke Doyle, Thorpe Achurch, Titchmarsh and Wadenhoe *Pet 10* **P** *G C Capron Esq, Wadenhoe Trust, Soc Merchant Venturers Bris, and DBP (jt)* **NSM** E A WALLER, H B BRANDON

ALDWORTH (St Mary the Virgin) *see* Basildon w Aldworth and Ashampstead *Ox*

ALEXANDRA PARK (St Andrew) *Lon 17* **P** *Bp* **P-in-c** I G BOOTH **C** A P R COATES

ALFINGTON (St James and St Anne) *see* Ottery St Mary, Alfington, W Hill, Tipton etc *Ex*

ALFOLD (St Nicholas) and Loxwood *Guildf 2* **P** *Bp and CPAS (jt)* **R** G D CUSHING **C** J A HANSON

ALFORD (All Saints) *see* Six Pilgrims *B & W*

ALFORD Group, The (St Wilfrid), including Beesby w Maltby, Bilsby, Farlesthorpe, Hannah cum Hagnaby w Markby, Saleby, Ulceby w Fordington, Well, and Willougby w Sloothby w Claxby *Linc 10* **P** *Bp, Ball Coll Ox, Baroness Willoughby de Eresby, Mrs A M Johnson, and DBP (jt)* **C** S V ANGUS **NSM** J M MORTON

ALFRED JEWEL, comprising Durston, North Newton, North Petherton, Northmoor Green, and Thurloxton *B & W 13* **P** *D&C Windsor (4 turns), Bp (2 turns), Sir Benjamin Slade Bt (1 turn)* **R** J HASLAM **C** S J TANCOCK **NSM** J W SUTTON, M H HASLAM

ALFRETON (St Martin) *Derby 2* **P** *Bp* **P-in-c** M J TAYLOR **C** I N L BLACK **NSM** J O K PENFOLD, K W G JOHNSON

ALFRICK (St Mary Magdalene) *see* Worcs W Rural *Worc*

ALFRISTON (St Andrew) w Lullington, Litlington, West Dean and Folkington *Chich 21* **P** *Ld Chan (3 turns), Duke of Devonshire, R A Brown Esq, and Mrs S J Harcourt-Smith (1 turn each)* **R** S STUCKES **Hon C** C E JAMES

ALGARKIRK (St Peter and St Paul) *see* Kirton in Holland w Algarkirk and Fosdyke *Linc*

ALHAM VALE, comprising Batcombe, Evercreech w Chesterblade, Lamyatt, Milton Clevedon, and Upton Noble *B & W 2* **P** *DBP* **V** H DREVER

ALHAMPTON (Mission Church) *see* Fosse Trinity *B & W*

ALKBOROUGH (St John the Baptist) *Linc 6* **P** *Bp* **V** *vacant*

ALKERTON (St Michael and All Angels) *see* Ironstone *Ox*

ALKHAM (St Anthony) w Capel le Ferne and Hougham *Cant 7* **P** *Abp* **C** B F WILLIAMS

ALKMONTON (St John) *see* S Dales *Derby*

ALL CANNINGS (All Saints) *see* Cannings and Redhorn *Sarum*

ALL SAINTS (All Saints) *see* Axminster, All Saints, Axmouth, Chardstock etc *Ex*

ALL SOULS, NORTH WARWICKSHIRE, comprising Austrey, Newton Regis, Seckington, Shuttington, and Warton *Birm 5* **P** *Ld Chan (1 turn), V Polesworth, Birm Dioc Trustees and Mrs E V G Inge-Innes Lillington (1 turn)* **R** J DYER

ALL STRETTON (St Michael and All Angels) *see* Church Stretton *Heref*

ALLENDALE (St Cuthbert) w Whitfield *Newc 10* **P** *Viscount Allendale and J C Blackett-Ord Esq (alt)* **R** *vacant*

ALLENSMORE (St Andrew) *see* Cagebrook *Heref*

ALLENTON (St Edmund) *see* Pride Park, Wilmorton, Allenton and Shelton Lock *Derby*

ALLER (St Andrew), High Ham w Low Ham and Huish Episcopi cum Langport *B & W 5* **P** *Adn Wells and Worc Coll Ox (jt)* **R** J PITMAN

ALLERSTON (St John) *see* Thornton Dale w Allerston, Ebberston *York*

ALLERTHORPE (St Botolph) *see* Barmby Moor Gp *York*

ALLERTON (All Hallows) *Liv 2* **P** *Sir Michael Bibby Bt* **R** N C MILFORD

ALLERTON (not known) *see* Isle of Wedmore *B & W*

ALLERTON (St Peter) (St Francis of Assisi) *Leeds 3* **P** *Bp* **C** W J GRANT

ALLERTON BYWATER (St Mary the Less), Kippax and Swillington *Leeds 13* **P** *Bp* **TR** R D BAILEY **TV** D M FLYNN

ALLESLEY (All Saints) *Cov 2* **P** *D R D Hamilton Esq*
R E A HOLLAND
ALLESLEY PARK (St Christopher) and Whoberley *Cov 3*
P *Bp* **V** A MARCH **C** C Y POWELL
ALLESTREE (St Edmund King and Martyr) and Darley
Abbey St Matthew *Derby 5* **P** *Bp and DBP (jt)*
V P BARHAM
ALLESTREE (St Nicholas) *Derby 5* **P** *Bp* **C** D M KNIGHT
ALLHALLOWS (All Saints) *see Binsey Carl*
ALLINGTON (St Nicholas) and Maidstone St Peter *Cant 12*
P *Abp* **P-in-c** C P LAVENDER
ALLINGTON (St Swithin) *see Bridport Sarum*
ALLINGTON, EAST (St Andrew) *see Stoke Fleming,*
Blackawton, Strete and E Allington Ex
ALLINGTON, WEST (Holy Trinity) *see Saxonwell Linc*
ALLITHWAITE (St Mary) *see Cartmel Peninsula Carl*
ALLONBY (Christ Church), Cross Canonby and Dearham
Carl 7 **P** *TR Solway Plain, D&C, and Bp (jt)* **V** M E DAY
ALMELEY (St Mary) *see Eardisley w Bollingham, Willersley,*
Brilley etc Heref
ALMER (St Mary) *see Red Post Sarum*
ALMONDBURY (St Michael and St Helen) (St Mary) (All
Hallows) w Farnley Tyas *Leeds 5* **P** *Bp Bd*
TR F G COWLING-GREEN **NSM** J L MALAY
ALMONDSBURY (St Mary the Virgin) *see S Severnside Bris*
ALNE (St Mary) *York 3* **P** *CPAS and MMCET (alt)*
P-in-c D M COYNE **C** M E YOUNG, M HARRISON, S WHITING
NSM C C CRANFIELD, C C GITTENS, C J TOASE, T M GANT
ALNE, GREAT (St Mary Magdalene) *see Alcester Minster Cov*
ALNHAM (St Michael and All Angels) *see Upper Coquetdale*
Newc
ALNMOUTH (St John the Baptist) *see Lesbury w Alnmouth*
Newc
ALNWICK (St Michael and St Paul) *Newc 6* **P** *Duke of*
Northumberland **V** P M SCOTT
ALPERTON (St James) *Lon 18* **P** *CPAS* **V** A I TAYLOR
C A S JACOB, S G TAYLOR
ALPHAMSTONE (not known) *see N Hinckford Chelmsf*
ALPHETON (St Peter and St Paul) *see Chadbrook St E*
ALPHINGTON (St Michael and All Angels), Shillingford
St George and Ide *Ex 3* **P** *DBP, D&C, and Mrs J M*
Michelmore (jt) **R** M J PARTRIDGE
ALRESFORD (St Andrew) *see Tenpenny Villages Chelmsf*
ALRESFORD, NEW (St John the Baptist) *see Arle Valley Win*
ALRESFORD, OLD (St Mary) *as above*
ALREWAS (All Saints) *Lich 1* **P** *Bp* **V** J W ALLAN
C A J HINES **NSM** E A WALL
ALSAGER (Christ Church) *Ches 11* **P** *Bp* **V** D WARD
NSM H S KEMBALL
ALSAGER (St Mary Magdalene) (St Patrick's Mission
Church) *Ches 11* **P** *Bp* **V** M S GOODRICH
C J A BRITCLIFFE
ALSAGERS BANK (St John), Audley and Talke *Lich 9* **P** *Patr*
Bd **R** S C R TOMKINS
ALSOP-EN-LE-DALE (St Michael and All Angels) *see Fenny*
Bentley, Thorpe, Tissington, Parwich etc Derby
ALSTON MOOR (St Augustine), including Garrigill,
Kirkhaugh, Knaresdale, Lambley, and Nenthead *Newc 10*
P *Bp* **R** M C V NASH-WILLIAMS
ALSTONE (St Margaret) *see Overbury w Teddington, Alstone*
etc Worc
ALSTONFIELD (St Peter), Ilam and Wetton *Lich 5* **P** *DBP,*
Bp, and Sir Andrew Walker-Okeover Bt (jt)
V J M AUSTERBERRY
ALTARNON (St Nonna) *see Moorland Gp Truro*
ALTCAR (St Michael and All Angels) *see Formby H Trin and*
Altcar Liv
ALTHAM (St James) w Clayton le Moors *Blackb 1* **P** *DBP*
and Trustees (alt) **V** T R WEBBER
ALTHORNE (St Andrew) and North Fambridge *Chelmsf 10*
P *Ld Chan* **V** *vacant*
ALTHORPE (St Oswald) *see Belton Gp Linc*
ALTOFTS (St Mary Magdalene) *Leeds 16* **P** *SMF*
V D C TEASDEL
ALTON (St Peter) w Bradley-le-Moors, Ellastone w Stanton,
and Mayfield *Lich 14* **P** *Earl of Shrewsbury and Waterford,*
DBP, Personal Reps Col Sir Walter Bromley-Davenport, Bp, and
Ch Soc Trust (jt) **V** B S P LEATHERS **C** M W SOAR
ALTON BARNES (St Mary the Virgin) *see Vale of Pewsey*
Sarum
ALTON PANCRAS (St Pancras) *see Piddle Valley, Hilton and*
Ansty, Cheselbourne etc Sarum
ALTON Resurrection (All Saints) (St Lawrence) *Win 2* **P** *Bp*
and D&C (jt) **V** A M MICKLEFIELD **C** G C RANDALL
NSM L D POWER, R C STURT, W J BURNHAMS
ALTRINCHAM (St George) *Ches 10* **P** *Bp* **NSM** D R LAW

ALVANLEY (St John the Evangelist) *Ches 3* **P** *Bp*
P-in-c R E IVESON
ALVASTON (St Michael and All Angels) *Derby 5* **P** *PCC*
V J C WHITNEY **NSM** I P MUNRO **OLM** S TILL
ALVECHURCH (St Lawrence) *Worc 6* **P** *Bp* **R** *vacant*
ALVEDISTON (St Mary) *see Chalke Valley Sarum*
ALVELEY (St Mary the Virgin) and Quatt *Heref 8* **P** J W H
Thompson Esq and Lady Labouchere (jt) **R** N S DUNLOP
ALVERDISCOTT (All Saints) *see Newton Tracey, Horwood,*
Alverdiscott etc Ex
ALVERSTOKE (St Faith) (St Francis) (St Mary) *Portsm 3*
P *Bp* **R** A P NORRIS **C** H O'SULLIVAN
ALVERTHORPE (St Paul) *see N Wakefield Leeds*
ALVESCOT (St Peter) *see Shill Valley and Broadshire Ox*
ALVESTON (St Helen) *see N Severnside Bris*
ALVESTON (St James) *Cov 8* **P** *R Hampton Lucy w Charlecote*
and Loxley **V** *vacant*
ALVINGHAM (St Adelwold) *see Mid Marsh Gp Linc*
ALVINGTON (St Andrew) *see Lydney, Woolaston, Alvington*
and Aylburton Glouc
ALVINGTON, WEST (All Saints) *see Kingsbridge, Dodbrooke,*
and W Alvington Ex
ALWALTON (St Andrew) and Chesterton *Ely 15* **P** *Bp and*
Sir Philip Naylor-Leyland Bt (jt) **P-in-c** S C GOWER
C A F G PODD
ALWINGTON (St Andrew) *see Parkham, Alwington,*
Buckland Brewer etc Ex
ALWINTON (St Michael and All Angels) *see Upper*
Coquetdale Newc
ALWOODLEY (St Barnabas) *see Moor Allerton and Shadwell*
Leeds
AMBERGATE (St Anne) and Heage *Derby 6* **P** *V Duffield and*
Exors M A T Johnson Esq **P-in-c** V M HART
AMBERLEY (Holy Trinity) *see Minchinhampton w Box and*
Amberley Glouc
AMBERLEY (no dedication) *see Maund Gp Heref*
AMBERLEY (St Michael) w North Stoke and Parham,
Wiggonholt and Greatham *Chich 5* **P** *Bp and Parham*
Estate Trustees (jt) **P-in-c** G M BURGESS
AMBLE (St Cuthbert) *Newc 6* **P** *Bp* **P-in-c** J A J MCDERMOTT
AMBLECOTE (Holy Trinity) *Worc 5* **P** *Bp* **V** A R N WILLIAMS
AMBLESIDE (St Mary) *see Loughrigg Carl*
AMBROSDEN (St Mary the Virgin) *see Ray Valley Ox*
AMCOTTS (St Mark) *see Belton Gp Linc*
AMERSHAM (St Mary the Virgin) *Ox 9* **P** *Capt F Tyrwhitt*
Drake **NSM** S M GILL **OLM** T J W BARNARD
AMERSHAM ON THE HILL (St Michael and All Angels) *Ox 9*
P *Bp* **V** D G OADES **NSM** P R BINNS
AMESBURY (St Mary and St Melor) *Sarum 14* **P** *D&C*
Windsor **P-in-c** D A'COURT
AMINGTON (St Editha) *Birm 5* **P** *Bp* **V** *vacant*
AMOTHERBY (St Helen) *see The Street Par York*
AMPFIELD (St Mark), Chilworth and N Baddesley *Win 12*
P *Mrs P M A T Chamberlayne-MacDonald* **V** V L ASHDOWN
NSM V J LAWRENCE
AMPLEFORTH (St Hilda) w Oswaldkirk, Gilling East and
Stonegrave *York 19* **P** *Abp and Trin Coll Cam (jt) and The*
Crown (by turn) **V** *vacant*
AMPNEY CRUCIS (Holy Rood) *see S Cotswolds Glouc*
AMPNEY ST MARY (St Mary) *as above*
AMPNEY ST PETER (St Peter) *as above*
AMPORT (St Mary) *see Portway and Danebury Win*
AMPTHILL (St Andrew) w Millbrook and Steppingley
St Alb 8 **P** *Ld Chan* **P-in-c** D J HOLROYD-THOMAS
AMPTON (St Peter) *see Blackbourne St E*
AMWELL, GREAT (St John the Baptist) w St Margaret's and
Stanstead Abbots *St Alb 19* **P** *Bp, Peache Trustees, and*
Haileybury Coll (jt) **P-in-c** S L FORREST
AMWELL, LITTLE (Holy Trinity) *see Hertford St Alb*
ANCASTER (St Martin) *see E Loveden Linc*
ANCHORSHOLME (All Saints) *Blackb 8* **P** *Bp, V Bispham,*
and Ch Soc Trust (jt) **V** A J BARNSHAW
ANCROFT (St Anne) *see Lowick and Kyloe w Ancroft Newc*
ANDERBY (St Andrew) *see Sutton, Huttoft and Anderby Linc*
ANDOVER (St Mary) *Win 3* **P** *St Mary's Coll Win*
V C J BRADISH **C** S O SCOTT **NSM** D G ROBERTS
ANDOVER (St Thomas) *see Pastrow Win*
ANDOVER, WEST (St Michael and All Angels) *see Portway*
and Danebury Win
ANDREAS (St Andrew) (St Jude), Ballaugh and Sulby *S & M*
P *The Crown* **R** I M SKIDMORE **C** W J MACKAY
ANERLEY (Christ Church) (St Paul) *Roch 13* **P** *Patr Bd*
TR M D FITTER
ANFIELD (St Columba) *Liv 4* **P** *Bp* **V** D T HOWARD
ANFIELD (St Margaret) *Liv 1* **P** *Bp* **V** P A WINN
NSM J E WINN

ANGELL TOWN (St John the Evangelist) *S'wark 11*   P *Bp*
V R S FAULKNER   **NSM** J N N ANAND

ANGERSLEIGH (St Michael) *see* Trull w Angersleigh *B & W*

ANGLESEY Group, The, comprising Bottisham, Lode w
Longmeadow, Swaffham Bulbeck, and Swaffham Prior *Ely 4*
P *Trin Coll Cam, D&C, and Bp (jt)* V S J GILES

ANGMERING (St Margaret) *Chich 1*   P C C F Somerset Esq
and Ch Patr Trust (jt)   R M J STANDEN   C B M R LUCAS
NSM P S GILES

ANLABY (St Peter) *York 14*   P *Abp and CPAS (jt)*
V S C F WILCOX

ANLABY COMMON (St Mark) *Hull* *York 14*   P *Abp*
V S C F WILCOX

ANMER (St Mary) *see* Dersingham, Anmer, Ingoldisthorpe
etc *Nor*

**ANNESLEY (Our Lady and All Saints) w Newstead and
Kirkby Woodhouse** *S'well 4*   P *Bp and Exors Major R P
Chaworth-Musters (jt)*   **P-in-c** H ROBINSON
NSM S D COTTERILL

ANNSCROFT (Christ Church) *see* Gt Hanwood and Longden
and Annscroft etc *Heref*

ANSFORD (St Andrew) *see* Castle Cary and Ansford *B & W*

ANSLEY (St Lawrence) and Arley *Cov 5*   P *Ch Patr Trust, N
W H Sylvester Esq, and A C D'O Ransom Esq (jt)*   R *vacant*

ANSLOW (Holy Trinity), Rolleston and Tutbury *Lich 13*
P *Duchy of Lancaster and MMCET (alt)*   R P M BAINBRIDGE

ANSTEY (St George) *see* Hormead, Wyddial, Anstey, Brent
Pelham etc *St Alb*

ANSTEY (St Mary) and Thurcaston w Cropston *Leic 9*   P *Bp
and Em Coll Cam (jt)*   R *vacant*

ANSTEY, EAST (St Michael) *see* Bishopsnympton, Charles, E
Anstey, High Bray etc *Ex*

ANSTEY, WEST (St Petrock) *as above*

ANSTON (St James) *Sheff 5*   P *Bp*   V J M HIDDEN
NSM B A CUSHING

ANSTY (St James) *see* Nadder Valley *Sarum*

ANSTY (St James) and Shilton *Cov 2*   P *Ld Chan*
P-in-c A D COLEMAN

ANTINGHAM (St Mary) *see* Poppyland *Nor*

ANTONY (St James the Great) *see* St Germans w Antony and
Sheviock *Truro*

ANTROBUS (St Mark) *Ches 4*   P *V Gt Budworth*
P-in-c A G BROWN

ANWICK (St Edith) *see* N Lafford Gp *Linc*

APEDALE Group, The, comprising Cardington, Eaton under
Heywood, Hope Bowdler, and Rushbury *Heref 10*   P *DBP,
Mrs R Bell, Bp Birm, and S Pennington Esq (by turn)*
R S A MANN   **NSM** S JELLEYMAN

APETHORPE (St Leonard) *see* Nassington, Apethorpe,
Thornhaugh etc *Pet*

APLEY (St Andrew) *see* Bardney *Linc*

APPERLEY (Holy Trinity) *see* Deerhurst and Apperley w
Forthampton etc *Glouc*

APPLEBY (St Bartholomew) *see* Winterton Gp *Linc*

APPLEBY (St Lawrence) *see* Heart of Eden *Carl*

APPLEBY MAGNA (St Michael and All Angels) *see* Woodfield
Leic

APPLEDORE (St Mary), Northam, and Westward Ho! *Ex 14*
P *Patr Bd*   **TR** D J ARNOLD   **TV** R M ELKS
C S DAVIES-FLETCHER

APPLEDORE (St Peter and St Paul) *see* Tenterden, Rother and
Oxney *Cant*

APPLEDRAM (St Mary the Virgin) *Chich 2*   P *D&C*
V *vacant*

APPLEFORD (St Peter and St Paul) *see* DAMASCUS *Ox*

**APPLESHAW (St Peter) Kimpton, Thruxton, Fyfield and
Shipton Bellinger** *Win 3*   P *Bp (1 turn), and Bp, D&C, and
R H Routh Esq (1 turn)*   R *vacant*

APPLETHWAITE (St Mary) *see* Windermere St Mary and
Troutbeck *Carl*

APPLETON (All Saints) *see* The Street Par *York*

APPLETON (St Laurence) *Ox 19*   P *Magd Coll Ox*
R P V PARKER

APPLETON (St Mary Magdalene) *see* Stockton Heath *Ches*

APPLETON ROEBUCK (All Saints) w Acaster Selby *York 1*
P *Abp*   V *vacant*

APPLETON THORN (St Cross) *see* Stretton and Appleton
Thorn *Ches*

APPLETON WISKE (St Mary) *see* Wiske Benefice *Leeds*

APPLETON-LE-MOORS (Christ Church) *see* Lastingham w
Appleton-le-Moors, Rosedale etc *York*

APPLETREEWICK (St John the Baptist) *see* Linton, Burnsall
and Rylstone *Leeds*

APPLEY BRIDGE (All Saints) and Parbold *Blackb 4*   P *Bp*
V S K TIMMINS   **NSM** M PLANT

APSLEY END (St Mary) *see* Langelei *St Alb*

ARBORFIELD (St Bartholomew) w Barkham *Ox 8*   P *DBP*
R E P BICKERSTETH   C J P BIDGOOD, M G HUDDLESTON

ARBORY (St Columba) and Castletown *S & M*   P *The Crown
and Bp (alt)*   V I C COWELL   **NSM** C L BARRY, J P BARWOOD

**ARDELEY (St Lawrence), Benington, Cottered w Throcking
and Walkern** *St Alb 16*   P *K Coll Cam, D&C St Paul's, and
Bp (jt)*   **P-in-c** M D BAILEY

ARDEN MARCHES, comprising Spernall, Morton Bagot and
Oldberrow, and Studley w Mappleborough Green *Cov 7*
P *Ld Chan, Mrs J M Pinney, and Bp (by turn)*   R C E MIER
C D J CORLETT

ARDEN VALLEY, comprising Bearley, Snitterfield, and
Wolverton w Norton Lindsey and Langley *Cov 7*   P *Bp and
V Wootton Wawen (jt)*   R R D MUTTER

ARDINGLY (St Peter) *Chich 8*   P *MMCET*   R J H CRUTCHLEY
NSM C D SUTTON

ARDINGTON (Holy Trinity) *see* Wantage Downs *Ox*

ARDLEIGH (St Mary the Virgin) *see* Dedham and Ardleigh
Chelmsf

ARDLEY (St Mary) *see* Cherwell Valley *Ox*

ARDSLEY (Christ Church) *Sheff 12*   P *R Darfield*
V F M KOUBLE   C C J M MOOREY

ARDSLEY, EAST (St Gabriel) (St Michael) *Leeds 11*   P E C S J
G Brudenell Esq   **P-in-c** M E WATSON

ARDSLEY, WEST (St Mary) *Leeds 11*   P E C S J G Brudenell Esq
V S T WILKINSON

ARELEY KINGS (St Bartholomew) *Worc 1*   P *R Martley*
R M TURNER   **NSM** J M CALAM

**ARICONIUM: Aston Ingham, Hope Mansel, Linton, The
Lea, Upton Bishop and Weston-under-Penyard** *Heref 7*
P *Bp (3 turns), St Jo Coll Ox (2 turns), Exors Preb H L Whatley
(1 turn)*   R D P HOWELL

ARKENDALE (St Bartholomew) *see* Walkingham Hill *Leeds*

ARKENGARTHDALE (St Mary) *see* Swaledale *Leeds*

ARKESDEN (St Mary the Virgin) *see* Clavering w Langley,
Arkesden etc *Chelmsf*

ARKHOLME (St John the Baptist) *see* Hornby w Claughton
and Whittington etc *Blackb*

ARKLEY (St Peter) *see* Chipping Barnet *St Alb*

ARKSEY (All Saints) *see* New Bentley w Arksey *Sheff*

ARLE VALLEY Benefice, The, comprising Bighton, New
Alresford, Old Alresford, and Ovington w Itchen Stoke
Win 1   P *Bp*   R *vacant*

ARLECDON (St Michael) *see* Crosslacon *Carl*

ARLESEY (St Andrew) (St Peter) w Astwick *St Alb 8*   P *DBP*
V G M BOULT

ARLEY (St Michael) *see* Ansley and Arley *Cov*

ARLEY (St Wilfred) *as above*

ARLEY, UPPER (St Peter) *see* Kidderminster Ismere *Worc*

ARLINGHAM (St Mary the Virgin) *see* Stroudwater *Glouc*

ARLINGTON (St James) *see* Shirwell, Loxhore, Kentisbury,
Arlington, etc *Ex*

**ARLINGTON (St Pancras), Berwick, Selmeston w Alciston
and Wilmington** *Chich 21*   P *Bp Lon, D&C, J Fitzherbert
Esq, and Mrs R Fitzherbert (jt)*   R P M BLEE

ARMATHWAITE (Christ and St Mary) *see* Inglewood Gp *Carl*

ARMINGHALL (St Mary) *see* Stoke H Cross w Dunston,
Arminghall etc *Nor*

ARMITAGE (St John the Baptist) *see* Brereton and Rugeley w
Armitage *Lich*

ARMITAGE BRIDGE (St Paul) *see* Newsome and Armitage
Bridge and S Crosland *Leeds*

ARMLEY (St Bartholomew) w New Wortley *Leeds 11*   P *Bp,
DBP, and Hyndman Trustees (jt)*   **P-in-c** M F WOOD

ARMLEY HEIGHTS (Church of the Ascension) *see* Upper
Armley *Leeds*

ARMLEY, UPPER (Christ Church) *Leeds 11*   P *Ch Patr Trust*
V P R ARNOLD   C D J ROSS, S J COCKBURN

ARMTHORPE (St Leonard and St Mary) *Sheff 8*   P *Bp*
R J M FODEN   **NSM** S J MAUGHAN

ARNCLIFFE (St Oswald) *see* Upper Wharfedale and
Littondale *Leeds*

ARNE (St Nicholas) *see* Wareham *Sarum*

ARNESBY (St Peter) *see* Hexagon *Leic*

ARNOLD (Emmanuel) *see* Bestwood Em and St Mark w Rise
Park *S'well*

ARNOLD (St Mary) *S'well 7*   P *Bp*   V M CAUNT

ARNSIDE (St James) *Carl 10*   P *Bp*   **P-in-c** A B NORMAN
NSM A MILLER

ARRETON (St George) *Portsm 7*   P *Bp*   **P-in-c** K F ABBOTT

ARRINGTON (St Nicholas) *see* Orwell Gp *Ely*

ARROW (Holy Trinity) *see* Alcester Minster *Cov*

ARROWVALE *see* Pembridge w Moor Court, Shobdon,
Staunton etc *Heref*

ARTHINGWORTH (St Andrew) and Harrington w Oxendon and East Farndon *Pet 2* **P** *St Jo Coll Ox (2 turns), Nugee Foundn (2 turns), and Bp (1 turn)* **C** J V J G WATSON

ARTHURET (St Michael and All Angels) w Kirkandrews-on-Esk and Nicholforest *Carl 2* **P** *Sir James Graham Bt (2 turns), Bp (1 turn)* **R** vacant

ARUNDEL (St Nicholas) w Tortington and South Stoke *Chich 1* **P** *Bp (2 turns), Duke of Norfolk (1 turn)* **V** D A TWINLEY **C** D A CHMIELEWSKI

ASBY (St Peter) *see Heart of Eden Carl*

ASCOT HEATH (All Saints) *Ox 3* **P** *Bp* **R** D D HANNAH **C** D J SAUNDERS

ASCOT, SOUTH (All Souls) *see Sunninghill and S Ascot Ox*

ASCOTT UNDER WYCHWOOD (Holy Trinity) *see Chase Ox*

ASFORDBY (All Saints) *see Ab Kettleby and Holwell w Asfordby Leic*

ASGARBY (St Andrew) *see Heckington and Helpringham Gp Linc*

ASH (Christ Church) *see Adderley, Ash, Calverhall, Ightfield etc Lich*

ASH (Holy Trinity) *see Martock w Kingsbury Episcopi and Ash B & W*

ASH (St Nicholas) *see Canonry Cant*

ASH (St Peter and St Paul) *Roch 1* **P** J R A B Scott Esq **R** H M REEVES **C** C J SHILLITO **NSM** E M ROBERTSON

ASH (St Peter) *Guildf 1* **P** *Win Coll* **R** K R M BRISTOW **NSM** C L MONK

ASH (Thomas Chapel) *see Sampford Peverell, Uplowman, Holcombe Rogus etc Ex*

ASH PRIORS (Holy Trinity) *see Milverton w Halse, Fitzhead and Ash Priors B & W*

ASH VALE (St Mary) *Guildf 1* **P** *Bp* **V** N J LAMBERT

ASHAMPSTEAD (St Clement) *see Basildon w Aldworth and Ashampstead Ox*

ASHBOCKING (All Saints) *see Carlford St E*

ASHBOURNE (St John the Baptist) *Derby 1* **P** *Wright Trustees* **P-in-c** D C J BALLARD **C** A J MARSHALL, C E MCDONALD

ASHBOURNE (St Oswald) w Mapleton *Derby 1* **P** *Bp* **P-in-c** D C J BALLARD **C** A J MARSHALL, C E MCDONALD

ASHBRITTLE (St John the Baptist) *see Wellington and Distr B & W*

ASHBURNHAM (St Peter) w Penhurst *Chich 12* **P** *Ashburnham Chr Trust* **NSM** J H SYKES

ASHBURTON (St Andrew), Bickington, Buckland in the Moor, Holne, Huccaby, Leusdon, Princetown, Postbridge, and Widecombe-in-the-Moor *Ex 8* **P** *Duchy of Cornwall (1 turn), Patr Bd (1 turn)* **P-in-c** M J RYLANDS **TV** G E C FENTON

ASHBURY (St Mary the Virgin) *see Shrivenham and Ashbury Ox*

ASHBY (St Mary) *see Somerleyton, Ashby, Fritton, Herringfleet etc Nor*

ASHBY (St Mary) *see Thurton w Ashby St Mary, Bergh Apton etc Nor*

ASHBY (St Paul) *see Bottesford w Ashby Linc*

ASHBY CUM FENBY (St Peter) *see Waltham Gp Linc*

ASHBY DE LA LAUNDE (St Hybald) *see Digby Gp Linc*

ASHBY FOLVILLE (St Mary) *see S Croxton Gp Leic*

ASHBY MAGNA (St Mary) *see Avon-Swift Leic*

ASHBY PARVA (St Peter) *see Upper Soar Leic*

ASHBY PUERORUM (St Andrew) *see Horncastle Gp Linc*

ASHBY ST LEDGERS (St Mary) *see Daventry Pet*

ASHBY, WEST (All Saints) *see Hemingby Gp Linc*

ASHBY-BY-PARTNEY (St Helen) *see Bolingbroke Deanery Linc*

ASHBY-DE-LA-ZOUCH (Holy Trinity) (St Helen) and Breedon on the Hill *Leic 8* **P** *Patr Bd* **TR** M E GREGORY **TV** T L PHILLIPS

ASHCHURCH (St Nicholas) and Kemerton *Glouc 9* **P** *DBP and K Storey Esq (jt)* **P-in-c** S GRINDROD

ASHCOMBE (St Nectan) *see Teignmouth, Ideford w Luton, Ashcombe etc Ex*

ASHCOTT (All Saints) *see Polden Wheel B & W*

ASHDON (All Saints) *see Saffron Walden and Villages Chelmsf*

ASHE (Holy Trinity and St Andrew) *see N Waltham and Steventon, Ashe and Deane Win*

ASHEN (St Augustine) *see Two Rivers Chelmsf*

ASHENDON (St Mary) *see Bernwode Ox*

ASHFIELD CUM THORPE (St Mary) *see Mid Loes St E*

ASHFIELD, GREAT (All Saints) *see Pakenham w Norton, Tostock etc St E*

ASHFORD (St Hilda) *Lon 13* **P** *Bp* **V** J A D S FERNANDES

ASHFORD (St Matthew) *Lon 13* **P** *Ld Chan* **P-in-c** S J KING **C** M W DOBSON

ASHFORD (St Peter) *see Pilton w Ashford Ex*

ASHFORD BOWDLER (St Andrew) *see The Ashfords Heref*

ASHFORD CARBONELL (St Mary) *as above*

ASHFORD HILL (St Paul) *see Kingsclere and Ashford Hill w Headley Win*

ASHFORD IN THE WATER (Holy Trinity) *see Bakewell, Ashford w Sheldon and Rowsley Derby*

ASHFORD TOWN (Christ Church) (St Francis) (St Mary the Virgin), including Great Chart, Kennington, Kingsnorth, Sevington, Shadoxhurst, Stubbs Cross, and Willesborough *Cant 6* **P** *Patr Bd* **TR** J F WORTHEN **TV** R W BELLAMY **C** A R J BROWN, B M WATSON, G M ABASOLO-MUNNERY **NSM** B APPLETON, C M ALDIS, D C STAMPER

ASHFORD, SOUTH (Christ Church) *see Ashford Town Cant*

ASHFORDS, The, including Ashford Bowdler, Ashford Carbonel, Caynham, Knowbury, Ludford, and Richards Castle *Heref 11* **P** *Bp* **R** L A MONEY **Hon C** N HELM

ASHILL (Blessed Virgin Mary) *see Isle Valley B & W*

ASHILL (Fountain of Life Network Church) *Nor 13* **C** A C POOLE **Min** P F WILKINSON

ASHILL (St Nicholas), Carbrooke, Ovington and Saham Toney *Nor 13* **P** *Bp, New Coll Ox, Cam Univ, and SMF (jt)* **V** vacant

ASHILL (St Stephen) *see Willand, Uffculme, Kentisbeare etc Ex*

ASHINGDON (St Andrew) w South Fambridge, Canewdon and Paglesham *Chelmsf 13* **P** *D&C Westmr, Hyndman Trustees, and CCC Cam (jt)* **P-in-c** E A GUEST **C** H ROGERS **OLM** G N EDWARDS

ASHINGTON (Holy Sepulchre) *Newc 11* **P** *Bp* **P-in-c** C J GROOCOCK

ASHINGTON (St Vincent) *see Chilton Cantelo, Ashington, Mudford, Rimpton etc B & W*

ASHLEWORTH (St Bartholomew), Corse, Hartpury, Hasfield, Maisemore, Staunton and Tirley *Glouc 3* **P** *Bp and W G F Meath-Baker Esq (1 turn), Ld Chan (1 turn), Bp (1 turn), and Bp and DBP (1 turn)* **R** J LONGUET-HIGGINS

ASHLEY (St Elizabeth) *see Hale and Ashley Ches*

ASHLEY (St James) *see Braydon Brook Bris*

ASHLEY (St John the Baptist) and Mucklestone and Broughton and Croxton *Lich 7* **P** *Bp, SMF, Mrs F F Friend, and T A J Hall Esq (jt)* **R** D J P ISIORHO **OLM** S A HUMPHRIES

ASHLEY (St Mary the Virgin) *see Stoke Albany w Wilbarston and Ashley etc Pet*

ASHLEY (St Mary) w Silverley *Ely 4* **P** *Bp and DBP (alt)* **P-in-c** N A WORMELL

ASHLEY (St Peter and St Paul) *see Somborne w Ashley Win*

ASHLEY (St Peter) *see Milton Win*

ASHLEY GREEN (St John the Evangelist) *see Gt Chesham Ox*

ASHMANHAUGH (St Swithin), Barton Turf, Beeston St Lawrence, Horning, Irstead and Neatishead *Nor 12* **P** *Bp and Sir Ronald Preston Bt (jt)* **R** D R SMITH **C** T B WILTON-MORGAN

ASHMANSWORTH (St James) *see NW Hants Win*

ASHMORE (St Nicholas) *see Iwerne Valley Sarum*

ASHMORE PARK (St Alban) *see Wednesfield Lich*

ASHOVER (All Saints) and Brackenfield w Wessington *Derby 2* **P** *Exors Revd J J C Nodder, Duke of Devonshire, V Crich and S Wingfield, and DBF (jt)* **R** vacant

ASHOW (Assumption of Our Lady) *see Stoneleigh w Ashow Cov*

ASHPERTON (St Bartholomew) *see Hop Churches Heref*

ASHPRINGTON (St David) *see Totnes w Bridgetown, Berry Pomeroy etc Ex*

ASHREIGNEY (St James) *Ex 18* **P** *DBP* **P-in-c** H S E BLAINE

ASHTEAD (St George) (St Giles) *Guildf 10* **P** *Bp* **R** J R JONES **C** N HILDING OHLSSON

ASHTON (Annunciation) *see W Kerrier Truro*

ASHTON (St Francis) *Bris 1* **P** *Bp* **R** A J DOARKS

ASHTON (St John the Baptist) *see Christow, Ashton, Bridford, Dunchideock etc Ex*

ASHTON (St Michael and All Angels) *see Salcey Pet*

ASHTON HAYES (St John the Evangelist) *Ches 2* **P** *Keble Coll Ox* **V** P R WESTON

ASHTON KEYNES (Holy Cross) *see Upper Thames Bris*

ASHTON UNDER HILL (St Barbara) *see Overbury w Teddington, Alstone etc Worc*

ASHTON, WEST (St John) *see Trowbridge St Thos and W Ashton Sarum*

ASHTON-IN-MAKERFIELD (Holy Trinity) *see Wigan Liv*

ASHTON-IN-MAKERFIELD (St Thomas) *as above*

ASHTON-ON-RIBBLE (St Andrew) *Blackb 13* **P** *Trustees* **V** J D G NASH

ASHTON-ON-RIBBLE (St Michael and All Angels) w Preston St Mark *Blackb 13* **P** *Trustees* **V** A EVANS

ASHTON-UNDER-LYNE (Christ Church) *Man 5*   **P** *Bp*
V D JACKS

**ASHTON-UNDER-LYNE Good Shepherd (Holy Trinity)
(St James) (St Michael and All Angels) (St Gabriel)
(St Peter)** *Man 5*   **P** *Patr Bd*   **TR** R FARNWORTH

ASHTON-UPON-MERSEY (St Martin) *Ches 10*   **P** *SMF*
R *vacant*

ASHTON-UPON-MERSEY (St Mary Magdalene) *Ches 10*
P *Trustees*   **V** S B RANKIN

ASHURST (St James) *Chich 5*   **P** *Bp*   **R** M D G HEATHER

ASHURST (St Martin of Tours) *see* Speldhurst w Groombridge
and Ashurst *Roch*

ASHURST WOOD (St Dunstan) *see* Forest Row *Chich*

**ASHWATER (St Peter ad Vincula), Halwill, Beaworthy,
Clawton, Tetcott w Luffincott, Black Torrington, and
Highampton** *Ex 15*   **P** *Bp, DBP, Revd Dr C A Friswell, and Sir
William Molesworth-St Aubyn (2 turns), Ld Chan (1 turn)*
R S J SKINNER

**ASHWELL (St Mary the Virgin) w Hinxworth and
Newnham** *St Alb 16*   **P** *Bp, N J A Farr Esq, and T D Smyth
Esq (jt) (1 turn), Bp (3 turns)*   **R** *vacant*

ASHWELL (St Mary) *see* Oakham, Ashwell, Braunston,
Brooke, Egleton etc *Pet*

ASHWELLTHORPE (All Saints) *see* Upper Tas Valley *Nor*

ASHWICK (St James) *see* Beacon Trinity *B & W*

**ASHWICKEN (All Saints) w Leziate, Bawsey and Mintlyn,
Congham, E Walton, Gayton, Gayton Thorpe, Gt
Massingham, Grimston, Harpley, Lt Massingham and
Roydon** *Nor 19*   **P** *Patr Bd*   **TV** J M POLLARD
NSM S M MARTIN

ASHWORTH (St James) *see* Norden w Ashworth and
Bamford *Man*

ASKAM (Church Centre) *see* Dalton-in-Furness and
Ireleth-with-Askam *Carl*

ASKAM (St Peter) *as above*

ASKERN (St Peter) *Sheff 7*   **P** *Bp*   **V** D J FRANKLIN

ASKHAM (St Nicholas) *see* The Rivers *S'well*

ASKHAM (St Peter) *see* N Westmorland *Carl*

ASKHAM BRYAN (St Nicholas) *York 1*   **P** *Abp*
V G R MUMFORD   **NSM** G M WEBB

ASKHAM RICHARD (St Mary) *see* Marston Moor *York*

ASKRIGG (St Oswald) *see* Upper Wensleydale *Leeds*

ASLACKBY (St James) *see* Billingborough Gp *Linc*

ASLACTON (St Michael) *see* Long Stratton and Pilgrim TM
Nor

ASLOCKTON (St Thomas) *see* Whatton w Aslockton,
Hawksworth, Scarrington etc *S'well*

ASPALL (St Mary of Grace) *see* Debenham and Helmingham
St E

ASPATRIA (St Kentigern) w Hayton and Gilcrux *Carl 7*
P *Bp*   **P-in-c** T D HERBERT   **Hon C** D R KING
NSM C J KENNEDY

ASPENDEN (St Mary), Buntingford and Westmill *St Alb 16*
P *CPAS, MCET, and K Coll Lon (jt)*   **R** *vacant*

ASPLEY (St Margaret) *S'well 8*   **P** *Trustees*   **V** R T K ATKINSON
C A R CLARKE, E A J C WALFORD, J SAVILL, J W J MORING,
P W SHAW   **NSM** D WATKINSON

**ASPLEY GUISE (St Botolph) w Husborne Crawley and
Ridgmont** *St Alb 8*   **P** *Ld Chan (1 turn), Trustees Bedf Estates
(1 turn), and Bp (2 turns)*   **R** *vacant*

ASPULL (St Elizabeth) *see* Wigan *Liv*

ASSINGTON (St Edmund) *see* Bures w Assington and Lt
Cornard *St E*

ASTBURY (St Mary) and Smallwood *Ches 11*   **P** *Sir Richard
Baker Wilbraham Bt*   **R** A NAYLOR

ASTERBY Group, The, comprising Benniworth, Biscathorpe,
Burgh-on-Bain, Donington-on-Bain, Gayton le Wold,
Goulceby, Ranby, Scamblesby, and Stenigot *Linc 13*   **P** *Bp,
DBP, C N A F Heneage Esq, and F Smith Esq (jt)*
P-in-c P E SMITH

ASTHALL (St Nicholas) *see* Burford w Fulbrook, Taynton,
Asthall etc *Ox*

ASTLEY (St Mary the Virgin) *see* Chilvers Coton w Astley *Cov*

ASTLEY (St Mary), Clive, Grinshill and Hadnall *Lich 21*   **P** *D
R B Thompson Esq*   **P-in-c** P H CAWTHORNE

ASTLEY (St Peter) *see* Shrawley, Witley, Astley and Abberley
Worc

ASTLEY (St Stephen), Tyldesley and Mosley Common
Man 7   **P** *DBP and V Leigh*   **TR** M B COX
TV J RUHUMULIZA   **C** C L ECCLES, D CLARKE

ASTLEY ABBOTTS (St Calixtus) *see* Bridgnorth and Morville
Par *Heref*

ASTLEY BRIDGE (St Paul) *Man 3*   **P** *The Crown*
V J J HARTLEY   **C** L M HIGSON

ASTON (St Giles) *see* Wigmore Abbey *Heref*

ASTON (St James) (St Peter and St Paul) and Nechells
Birm 4   **P** *Patr Bd*   **NSM** G S KAYLA

ASTON (St Mary) *see* Woore and Norton in Hales *Lich*

ASTON (St Peter) *see* Aston by Sutton, Lt Leigh and Lower
Whitley *Ches*

ASTON (St Saviour) *see* Stone St Mich and St Wulfad w
Aston St Sav *Lich*

ASTON ABBOTS (St James the Great) *see* Cottesloe *Ox*

ASTON BOTTERELL (St Michael and All Angels) *see* Ditton
Priors w Neenton, Burwarton etc *Heref*

**ASTON BY SUTTON (St Peter), Little Leigh and Lower
Whitley** *Ches 4*   **P** *Bp, V Gt Budworth, Lord Daresbury, and B
H Talbot Esq (jt)*   **V** C M Y JONES

**ASTON CANTLOW (St John the Baptist) and Wilmcote w
Billesley** *Cov 7*   **P** *SMF*   **P-in-c** D P BENSKIN
C A J HAMPTON   **NSM** J B HOLDEN

**ASTON CLINTON (St Michael and All Angels) w Buckland
and Drayton Beauchamp** *Ox 17*   **P** *Bp, A R Pegg Esq, and
Jes Coll Ox (jt)*   **R** S A BOTTOMER   **OLM** A J ROBERTS

**ASTON CUM AUGHTON (All Saints) w Swallownest and
Ulley** *Sheff 5*   **P** *Bp*   **TR** *vacant*

ASTON EYRE (not known) *see* Bridgnorth and Morville Par
Heref

ASTON FLAMVILLE (St Peter) *see* Burbage w Aston Flamville
Leic

ASTON INGHAM (St John the Baptist) *see* Ariconium *Heref*

**ASTON ON TRENT (All Saints), Elvaston, Weston on Trent
and Shardlow, Barrow upon Trent with Twyford and
Swarkestone** *Derby 7*   **P** *Bp, Earl of Harrington, and Repton
Sch (jt)*   **R** A LUKE   **NSM** P HYGATE

ASTON ROWANT (St Peter and St Paul) *see* Chinnor,
Sydenham, Aston Rowant and Crowell *Ox*

ASTON SANDFORD (St Michael and All Angels) *see* Wychert
Vale *Ox*

ASTON SOMERVILLE (St Mary) *see* Winchcombe *Glouc*

ASTON TIRROLD (St Michael) *see* The Churn *Ox*

ASTON UPTHORPE (All Saints) *as above*

ASTON, LITTLE (St Peter) *Lich 1*   **P** *Patr Bd*   **V** P S DANIEL

ASTON, NORTH (St Mary the Virgin) *see* Steeple Aston w N
Aston and Tackley *Ox*

**ASTON-LE-WALLS (St Leonard), Byfield, Boddington,
Eydon and Woodford Halse** *Pet 1*   **P** *Bp, CCC Ox, and Em
Coll Cam (2 turns), Ld Chan (1 turn)*   **R** P K TRATHEN

ASTON-SUB-EDGE (St Andrew) *see* Vale and Cotswold Edge
Glouc

ASTWELL Group of Parishes, The, comprising Helmdon w
Stuchbury and Radstone, Lois Weedon, Syresham,
Wappenham, and Whitfield *Pet 1*   **P** *Bp, Worc Coll Ox, Ox
Univ, Mert Coll Ox, DBP, and Jes Coll Ox (jt)*
R D C WHITTAKER

ASTWICK (St Guthlac) *see* Arlesey w Astwick *St Alb*

ASTWOOD BANK (St Matthias and St George) *see* Redditch
Ch the K *Worc*

ASUM GROUP *see* Bengeworth and Hampton etc *Worc*

ASWARBY (St Denys) *see* S Lafford *Linc*

ASWARDBY (St Helen) *see* Bolingbroke Deanery *Linc*

ATCHAM (St Eata) *see* Shrewsbury St Giles w Sutton and
Atcham *Lich*

**ATHELINGTON (St Peter), Denham, Horham, Hoxne,
Redlingfield, Syleham and Wingfield** *St E 11*   **P** *Bp, DBP,
Lt Comdr G C Marshall, and H F Soden Esq (jt)*
P-in-c E M GOODISON   **NSM** V J MCCRACKEN

ATHELNEY Benefice, The, comprising Burrowbridge, Lyng,
North Curry, and Stoke St Gregory *B & W 13*   **P** *D&C*
P-in-c S J BALE

ATHERINGTON (St Mary) *see* Newton Tracey, Horwood,
Alverdiscott etc *Ex*

ATHERSLEY (St Helen) and Carlton *Leeds 14*   **P** *DBP and Bp
(jt)*   **V** P D NEEDHAM

ATHERSTONE (St Mary) *Cov 5*   **P** *Ch Patr Trust*
V M J BRANDSMA

**ATHERTON (St John the Baptist) (St George) (St Philip)
and Hindsford w Howe Bridge** *Man 7*   **P** *DBP*
TV R W SINCLAIR, T A MARSHALL   **OLM** D N SIVILL

ATLOW (St Philip and St James) *see* Hulland, Atlow,
Kniveton, Bradley and Hognaston *Derby*

ATTENBOROUGH (St Mary the Virgin) *S'well 9*   **P** *CPAS*
V *vacant*

ATTERCLIFFE (St Alban) and Darnall *Sheff 1*   **P** *Bp, Dean
Sheff, and Sheff Ch Burgesses Trust (jt)*   **V** *vacant*

**ATTLEBOROUGH (Assumption of the Blessed Virgin Mary)
w Besthorpe** *Nor 11*   **P** *CR and Mrs N Bayntun (jt)*
R M C JACKSON   **C** R C WASHINGTON   **NSM** A K SLATER

ATTLEBOROUGH (Holy Trinity) *Cov 5*   **P** *V Nuneaton*
V A J EVANS

ATTLEBRIDGE (St Andrew)   *see* Reepham and Wensum Valley *Nor*

ATWICK (St Lawrence)   *see* Hornsea, Atwick and Skipsea *York*

ATWORTH (St Michael and All Angels) w Shaw and Whitley *Sarum 15*   **P** *D&C Bris and R Melksham (alt)* **V** J A PALMER   **C** A E EVANS

AUBOURN (St Peter)   *see* Withamside *Linc*

AUCKLAND (St Andrew)   *see* Bishop Auckland *Dur*

AUCKLAND (St Anne)   *as above*

AUCKLAND (St Helen) *Dur 3*   **P** *Bp*   **V** R I MCTEER **NSM** E J GUNN

AUCKLEY (St Saviour)   *see* Finningley w Auckley *Sheff*

AUDENSHAW (St Hilda) *Man 5*   **P** *Bp*   **V** *vacant*

AUDENSHAW (St Stephen) *Man 5*   **P** *Bp*   **C** M HOWARTH

AUDLEM (St James)   *see* Wybunbury and Audlem w Doddington *Ches*

AUDLEY (St James the Great)   *see* Alsagers Bank, Audley and Talke *Lich*

AUGHTON (All Saints)   *see* Bubwith w Skipwith *York*

AUGHTON (Christ Church) *Liv 14*   **P** *R Aughton St Mich* **V** S H O'DONOGHUE   **C** J M DAVIES   **NSM** G P RUTTER

AUGHTON (St Michael) and Bickerstaffe *Liv 14*   **P** *Bp and Earl of Derby (jt)*   **R** A A HOUSLEY

AUGHTON (St Saviour)   *see* Slyne w Hest and Halton w Aughton *Blackb*

AULT HUCKNALL (St John the Baptist) and Scarcliffe *Derby 2*   **P** *Bp and Duke of Devonshire (alt)* **V** J H HENDERSON SMITH

AUNSBY (St Thomas of Canterbury)   *see* S Lafford *Linc*

AUST (not known)   *see* N Severnside *Bris*

AUSTERFIELD (St Helen)   *see* Bawtry w Austerfield, Misson, Everton and Mattersey *S'well*

AUSTREY (St Nicholas)   *see* All So N Warks *Birm*

AUSTWICK (Epiphany)   *see* Clapham-with-Keasden and Austwick *Leeds*

AVEBURY (St James)   *see* Upper Kennet *Sarum*

AVELEY (St Michael)   *see* Mardyke *Chelmsf*

AVENHAM (St James)   *see* Preston Risen Lord *Blackb*

AVENING (Holy Cross) w Cherington *Glouc 7*   **P** E A Tarlton *Esq (1 turn), D&C (2 turns)*   **P-in-c** G P SOUTH

AVERHAM (St Michael and All Angels) w Kelham *S'well 3* **P** *DBP*   **C** G A L HADLEY

AVETON GIFFORD (St Andrew)   *see* Modbury, Bigbury, Ringmore etc *Ex*

AVINGTON (St Mary)   *see* Itchen Valley *Win*

AVON DASSETT w Farnborough and Fenny Compton *Cov 8* **P** G V L Holbech Esq and Mrs A D Seyfried (jt), CCC Ox, and *Bp (alt)*   **P-in-c** N M CHATTERTON

AVON RIVER Team, comprising Bulford, Durrington, Enford, Figheldean, Fittleton, Milston w Brigmerston, and Netheravon *Sarum 14*   **P** *Patr Bd*   **TR** P A BROMILEY **TV** G A HUNT   **C** H G BREAREY

AVON VALLEY PARTNERSHIP   *see* Fordingbridge and Hyde and Breamore etc *Win*

AVONMOUTH (St Andrew)   *see* Lawrence Weston and Avonmouth *Bris*

AVON-SWIFT Benefice, The, comprising Ashby Magna, Catthorpe, Gilmorton, Kimcote, Misterton, North Kilworth, Peatling Parva, Shawel, South Kilworth, Stanford, and Swinford *Leic 7*   **P** *Patr Bd (5 turns), Ld Chan (1 turn)* **NSM** R A HAY

AVONWICK (St James' Chapel)   *see* Diptford w N Huish, Ermington, Halwell etc *Ex*

AWBRIDGE (All Saints)   *see* Michelmersh and Awbridge and Braishfield etc *Win*

AWLISCOMBE (St Michael and All Angels)   *see* Honiton w Monkton, Awliscombe, Buckerell etc *Ex*

AWRE (St Andrew)   *see* Newnham w Awre and Blakeney *Glouc*

AWSWORTH (St Peter)   *see* Trowell, Awsworth and Cossall *S'well*

AXBRIDGE (St John the Baptist) w Shipham and Rowberrow *B & W 1*   **P** *Bp and D&C (alt)*   **R** *vacant*

AXE VALLEY   *see* Axminster, All Saints, Axmouth, Chardstock etc *Ex*

AXFORD (St Michael)   *see* Whitton *Sarum*

AXMINSTER (St Mary), All Saints, Axmouth, Chardstock, Combpyne w Rousdon, Membury and Uplyme *Ex 4* **P** *Patr Bd*   **TV** C M SEDGEWICK   **TV** N L DAVIES **Hon C** C E EDMONDS   **NSM** S GEORGE, T A VOYSEY

AXMOUTH (St Michael)   *see* Axminster, All Saints, Axmouth, Chardstock etc *Ex*

AYCLIFFE (Church Centre)   *see* Dover Town *Cant*

AYCLIFFE, GREAT (St Andrew) (St Clare) *Dur 3*   **P** *Patr Bd* **TR** A ANDERSON   **TV** J ANDERSON   **C** D J HUDSON

AYLBURTON (St Mary)   *see* Lydney, Woolaston, Alvington and Aylburton *Glouc*

AYLBURTON COMMON (Mission Church)   *as above*

AYLESBEARE (Blessed Virgin Mary), Clyst St George, Clyst St Mary, Farringdon, Woodbury w Exton, and Woodbury Salterton *Ex 1*   **P** *Bp, D&C, Lord Wraxall, and Mrs S Radcliffe (jt)*   **V** W H M LEMMEY

AYLESBURY (Holy Trinity)   *see* Walton H Trin *Ox*

AYLESBURY (St Mary the Virgin) *Ox 10*   **P** *Bp and Patr Bd (jt)* **TR** D L ZIMMERMAN   **TV** G E LANE, P J WHEELER **NSM** R H MADZORERA

AYLESBY (St Lawrence)   *see* Wolds Gateway Group *Linc*

AYLESFORD (St Peter and St Paul) *Roch 7*   **P** *D&C* **V** R M PEET

AYLESHAM (St Peter) *Cant 1*   **P** *Abp*   **P-in-c** S C THOMAS **C** N H B RATCLIFFE

AYLESTONE (St Andrew) w St James *Leic 1*   **P** *Bp* **R** R M BASS

AYLMERTON (St John the Baptist), Runton, Beeston Regis, Gresham *Nor 20*   **P** *Bp and Guild of All So (2 turns), Duchy of Lanc (1 turn)*   **P-in-c** J G SYKES

AYLSHAM (St Michael and All Angels) and District Team Ministry, The, including Aldborough and Thurgarton, Badersfield, Blickling, Brampton, Burgh-next-Aylsham, Buxton w Oxnead, Cawston, Haveringland, Heydon, Itteringham w Mannington, Lammas w Little Hautbois, Little Barningham, Marsham, Oulton w Imingland, and Wickmere w Wolterton *Nor 18*   **P** *Patr Bd*   **TV** A H LYNN, A P WHITEHEAD   **C** T J JESSOP   **NSM** S TOMLINSON

AYLTON (not known)   *see* Cider Churches *Heref*

AYMESTREY (St John the Baptist and St Alkmund)   *see* Kingsland w Eardisland, Aymestrey etc *Heref*

AYNHO (St Michael) and Croughton w Evenley and Farthinghoe and Hinton-in-the-Hedges w Steane *Pet 1* **P** *Bp (2 turns), Mrs E A J Cartwright-Hignett (1 turn), Magd Coll Ox (1 turn), and Ld Chan (1 turn)*   **R** S T COOPER

AYOT ST LAWRENCE (St Lawrence)   *see* Kimpton w Ayot St Lawrence *St Alb*

AYOT ST PETER (St Peter)   *see* Welwyn *St Alb*

AYSGARTH (St Andrew)   *see* Penhill *Leeds*

AYTHORPE RODING (St Mary)   *see* Gt Canfield w High Roding and Aythorpe Roding *Chelmsf*

AYTON, EAST (St John the Baptist)   *see* Seamer, E Ayton and Cayton *York*

AYTON, GREAT (All Saints) (Christ Church) w Easby and Newton under Roseberry *York 20*   **P** *Abp*   **V** P H PEVERELL **C** J ROBSON   **NSM** J C DEAN

BABBACOMBE (All Saints) *Ex 10*   **P** *V St Marychurch* **V** P E JONES

BABCARY (Holy Cross)   *see* Six Pilgrims *B & W*

BABRAHAM (St Peter) *Ely 5*   **P** H R T Adeane Esq **V** K J WAITE

BABWORTH (All Saints)   *see* The Idle and Sands *S'well*

BACKFORD (St Oswald) and Capenhurst *Ches 9*   **P** *Bp* **P-in-c** S M MANSFIELD

BACKWELL (St Andrew) w Chelvey and Brockley *B & W 12* **P** *DBP*   **R** C E GARNER

BACKWORTH (St John)   *see* Earsdon and Backworth *Newc*

BACONSTHORPE (St Mary)   *see* Matlaske *Nor*

BACTON (St Andrew), Happisburgh, Hempstead w Eccles and Lessingham, Ridlington, Sea Palling w Waxham, Walcott, and Witton *Nor 12*   **P** *Bp, Earl of Kimberley, K Coll Cam, and Sir Edward Evans-Lombe (jt)*   **R** C H DOBSON

BACTON (St Faith)   *see* Ewyas Harold w Dulas, Kenderchurch etc *Heref*

BACTON (St Mary the Virgin) w Wyverstone, Cotton and Old Newton, and Wickham Skeith *St E 3*   **P** *Patr Bd (2 turns), Ld Chan (1 turn)*   **R** C N MELVILLE

BACUP Christ Church and Stacksteads *Man 4*   **P** *Patr Bd* **TV** D ALLEN   **NSM** L M ALLEN   **OLM** D R J COOK

BADBY (St Mary) w Newnham and Charwelton w Fawsley and Preston Capes *Pet 3*   **P** *Bp*   **R** M J INGHAM

BADDESLEY CLINTON (St Michael) *Birm 2*   **P** T W *Ferrers-Walker Esq*   **R** P H GERARD

BADDESLEY ENSOR (St Nicholas) w Grendon *Birm 5*   **P** *Bp, V Polesworth, and PCC (jt)*   **V** *vacant*

BADDESLEY, NORTH (All Saints' Mission Church)   *see* Ampfield, Chilworth and N Baddesley *Win*

BADDESLEY, NORTH (St John the Baptist)   *as above*

BADDESLEY, SOUTH (St Mary the Virgin)   *see* Boldre w S Baddesley *Win*

BADDILEY (St Michael) and Wrenbury w Burleydam *Ches 15*   **P** *V Acton and Bp (alt)*   **P-in-c** A S G PIKE **NSM** D WOODS

BADDOW, GREAT (Meadgate Church Centre) (St Mary the Virgin) (St Paul) *Chelmsf 9*   **P** *Patr Bd*   **P-in-c** T W BALL

TV P J W SHELDRAKE   **C** O T O O A VAUGHAN
Hon C R C MATTHEWS   **NSM** S FINCH
BADDOW, LITTLE (St Mary the Virgin) *Chelmsf 9*   **P** *Bp*
   P-in-c J D JONES
BADGER (St Giles)   *see Beckbury, Badger, Kemberton, Ryton,*
   Stockton etc Lich
BADGEWORTH (Holy Trinity), Shurdington and Witcombe
   w Bentham *Glouc 3*   **P** *Bp and F D Hicks Beach Esq (jt)*
   R S P COOKE   **C** E R SPEAR
BADGWORTH (St Congar)   *see Crook Peak B & W*
BADINGHAM (St John the Baptist)   *see Upper Alde St E*
BADLESMERE (St Leonard)   *see Shepherds Lees Cant*
BADMINTON (St Michael and All Angels)   *see Boxwell,*
   Leighterton, Didmarton, Oldbury etc Glouc
BADMINTON, LITTLE (St Michael and All Angels) *as above*
BADSEY (St James)   *see E Vale and Avon Villages Worc*
BADSHOT LEA (St George) and Hale *Guildf 3*   **P** *Bp*
   R L J CRAWLEY   **NSM** A J CRAWLEY
BADSWORTH (St Mary the Virgin)   *see Ackworth and*
   Badsworth Leeds
BADWELL (St Mary) and Walsham, including Finningham,
   Langham, Walsham-le-Willows, Wattisfield, and Westhorpe
   St E 5   **P** *Bp, MMCET, DBP, R M Martineau Esq, and Ch Union*
   (jt)   **V** P J MERRY
BAG ENDERBY (St Margaret)   *see S Ormsby Gp Linc*
BAGBOROUGH (St Pancras)   *see Bishop's Lydeard w Lydeard*
   St Lawrence etc B & W
BAGBY (St Mary)   *see Thirkleby w Kilburn and Bagby York*
BAGENDON (St Margaret)   *see Churn Valley Glouc*
BAGINTON (St John the Baptist) w Bubbenhall and
   Ryton-on-Dunsmore *Cov 6*   **P** *D&C (2 turns), Bp (1 turn),*
   Lord Leigh and Bp (1 turn)   **V** D R WINTLE
BAGNALL (St Chad) w Endon *Lich 8*   **P** *R Leek and Meerbrook*
   and A D Owen Esq (jt)   **V** *vacant*
BAGSHOT (Good Shepherd)   *see Savernake Sarum*
BAGSHOT (St Anne) *Guildf 6*   **P** Ld Chan   **V** A SISTIG
   NSM J E TURTLE
BAGULEY (St John the Divine) Brooklands *Man 2*   **P** *Bp and*
   A W Hargreaves Esq (jt)   **V** R J SHERRATT   **C** L D P WOOD
BAILDON (St John the Evangelist) (St Hugh Mission
   Church) (St James) *Leeds 1*   **P** J P Baxter Esq
   V S R BENHAM   **C** R J YEOMAN
BAIN VALLEY Group, The, comprising Coningsby, Kirkby on
   Bain, Roughton, and Tattershall *Linc 13*   **P** *Baroness*
   Willoughby de Eresby, T J Spurrier Esq, and DBP (1 turn), Ld
   Chan (1 turn)   **R** S A ALLISON   **NSM** R E DONE
   OLM M DONE
BAINTON (St Andrew)   *see Woldsburn York*
BAINTON (St Mary)   *see Barnack w Ufford, Bainton,*
   Helpston and Wittering Pet
BAKEWELL (All Saints), Ashford in the Water w Sheldon
   and Rowsley *Derby 4*   **P** *Bp, D&C, and Duke of Rutland (jt)*
   V A P KAUNHOVEN   **NSM** B J JACKSON
BALBY (St John the Evangelist)   *see Wadworth w Loversall*
   and Balby Sheff
BALCOMBE (St Mary) *Chich 8*   **P** *W Gibson Esq*   **R** *vacant*
BALDERSBY (St James)   *see Topcliffe, Baldersby w Dishforth,*
   Dalton etc York
BALDERSTONE (St Leonard), Mellor and Samlesbury
   Blackb 7   **P** *V Blackb St Mary and St Paul*   **V** K J HERSCHELL
BALDERTON (St Giles), Barnby in the Willows and
   Coddington *S'well 3*   **P** *Ld Chan and Bp (alt)*
   V E L HOLLIDAY   **NSM** P R SMITH
BALDOCK (St Mary the Virgin) w Bygrave *St Alb 16*   **P** *Bp*
   and Marquess of Salisbury (jt)   **R** A P HOLFORD
BALDWIN (St Luke)   *see Marown, Foxdale and Baldwin S & M*
BALE (All Saints)   *see Stiffkey and Bale Nor*
BALHAM (St Mary and St John the Divine) *S'wark 17*   **P** *Bp*
   and Keble Coll Ox (jt)   **C** B Y C EXCELL
BALHAM (St Stephen)   *see Telford Park S'wark*
BALHAM (St Thomas) *as above*
BALHAM HILL (Ascension) *S'wark 17*   **P** *Bp*   **V** M T GIBBS
   C L STEVEN, T D COLLINS
BALKWELL (St Peter) *Newc 5*   **P** *Bp*   **P-in-c** L J CLEMINSON
BALLAM (St Matthew)   *see Ribby cum Wrea and Weeton*
   Blackb
BALLAUGH (St Mary Old Church)   *see Andreas, Ballaugh and*
   Sulby S & M
BALLAUGH (St Mary) *as above*
BALLINGER (St Mary Mission Hall)   *see Gt Missenden w*
   Ballinger and Lt Hampden Ox
BALSALL COMMON (St Peter) *Birm 6*   **P** *Bp*   **V** P W THOMAS
BALSALL HEATH (St Barnabas)   *see Sparkbrook St Agatha w*
   Balsall Heath St Barn Birm
BALSALL HEATH (St Paul) and Edgbaston *Birm 2*   **P** *Bp and*
   Sir Euan Anstruther-Gough-Calthorpe Bt (jt)   **V** *vacant*

BALSCOTE (St Mary Magdalene)   *see Ironstone Ox*
BALSHAM (Holy Trinity)   *see Granta Vale Gp Ely*
BALTERLEY (All Saints' Memorial Church)   *see Barthomley*
   Ches
BALTONSBOROUGH (St Dunstan) w Butleigh, West
   Bradley and West Pennard *B & W 4*   **P** *Bp*
   P-in-c C J HOPKINS
BAMBER BRIDGE (St Aidan) and Walton-le-Dale
   St Leonard *Blackb 5*   **P** *Bp and V Blackb St Mary and St Paul*
   (jt)   **V** S BALDWIN   **C** A K WALKER
BAMBER BRIDGE (St Saviour) *Blackb 5*   **P** *V Blackb*
   V *vacant*
BAMBURGH (St Aidan), Belford and Lucker *Newc 7*   **P** *Bp*
   V L M TAYLOR-KENYON   **NSM** P A CARRUTHERS
BAMFORD (St John the Baptist)   *see Hathersage w Bamford*
   and Derwent and Grindleford Derby
BAMFORD (St Michael)   *see Norden w Ashworth and*
   Bamford Man
BAMFURLONG (Good Shepherd)   *see Wigan Liv*
BAMPTON (Holy Trinity) (St James) (St Mary) w Clanfield
   Ox 28   **P** *Bp, DBP, St Jo Coll Ox, D&C Ex, and B Babington-*
   Smith Esq (jt)   **V** J M COLLIER   **C** M H J WELBORN,
   T KUIN LAWTON
BAMPTON (St Michael and All Angels), Morebath,
   Clayhanger, Petton and Huntsham *Ex 7*   **P** *Bp, DBP, and*
   D&C (jt)   **V** K D N CHANDRA
BAMPTON (St Patrick)   *see High Westmorland Carl*
BAMPTON ASTON (St James)   *see Bampton w Clanfield Ox*
BAMPTON LEW (Holy Trinity) *as above*
BAMPTON PROPER (St Mary) *as above*
BANBURY (St Francis) *Ox 23*   **P** *Bp*   **V** C T GAYNOR
BANBURY (St Hugh) *Ox 23*   **P** *Bp*   **V** A E SMITH
   NSM C G SMITH
BANBURY (St Leonard) *Ox 23*   **P** *Bp*   **V** E S BURCHELL
BANBURY (St Mary) *Ox 23*   **P** *Bp*   **R** S TAJIMA
   NSM H L ADEY HUISH, J J WEST, S M BOURNE
BANBURY (St Paul) *Ox 23*   **P** *Bp*   **V** D R H MCGOWAN
   C J H EGGERTSEN   **NSM** S J SHORT
BANHAM (St Mary)   *see Quidenham Gp Nor*
BANKFOOT (St Matthew) and Bowling St Stephen *Leeds 2*
   P *Bp and CPAS (jt)*   **V** J W HINTON   **C** H E RAITT
BANNINGHAM (St Botolph)   *see King's Beck Nor*
BANSFIELD, comprising Cowlinge, Denston, Lidgate,
   Ousden, Stansfield, Stradishall, and Wickhambrook *St E 2*
   P *DBP, Mrs G S M Slater, and Ld Chan (by turn)*   **R** E R BELL
BANSTEAD (All Saints) *Guildf 9*   **P** *Bp*   **V** P MAUDSLEY
BANWELL (St Andrew) and Congresbury w Hewish,
   Puxton and West Wick *B & W 10*   **P** *MMCET and D&C Bris*
   (jt)   **V** M J THOMSON   **NSM** H J WORSLEY
BAPCHILD (St Laurence)   *see Milton Regis w Murston,*
   Bapchild and Tonge Cant
BAR HILL (not known) *Ely 6*   **P** *Bp*   **V** *vacant*
BARBON (St Bartholomew)   *see Kirkby Lonsdale Carl*
BARBOURNE (St Stephen) *Worc 4*   **P** *Bp*   **P-in-c** A G TODD
   C L J COULTHARD   **NSM** G D MORPHY
BARBY (St Mary)   *see Daventry Pet*
BARCHESTON (St Martin)   *see S Warks Seven Gp Cov*
BARCOMBE (St Francis) (St Mary the Virgin) *Chich 21*
   P *Ld Chan*   **R** S N C CARTER
BARDFIELD SALING (St Peter and St Paul)   *see Stebbing*
   and Lindsell w Gt and Lt Saling Chelmsf
BARDFIELD, GREAT (St Mary the Virgin) and LITTLE
   (St Katherine) *Chelmsf 17*   **P** *Ch Union Trust*
   P-in-c R W F BEAKEN
BARDNEY (St Lawrence) *Linc 13*   **P** *DBP (1 turn), Bp (2*
   turns), and St Jo Coll Cam (1 turn)   **NSM** H E JEFFERY
BARDON HILL (St Peter)   *see Coalville w Bardon Hill and*
   Ravenstone Leic
BARDSEA (Holy Trinity)   *see Pennington and Lindal w Marton*
   and Bardsea Carl
BARDSEY (All Hallows) *Leeds 10*   **P** *G L Fox Esq*
   V A J HANNAFIN
BARDSLEY (Holy Trinity) *Man 5*   **P** *Wm Hulme Trustees*
   OLM E M LOWE
BARDWELL (St Peter and St Paul)   *see Blackbourne St E*
BARE (St Christopher) *Blackb 11*   **P** *Bp*   **V** D L HEAP
BARFORD (St Botolph)   *see Barnham Broom and Upper Yare*
   Nor
BARFORD (St John)   *see Deddington w Barford, Clifton and*
   Hempton Ox
BARFORD (St Martin)   *see Nadder Valley Sarum*
BARFORD (St Michael)   *see Deddington w Barford, Clifton*
   and Hempton Ox
BARFORD (St Peter) w Wasperton and Sherbourne *Cov 8*
   P *Major J M Mills, R Hampton Lucy, and Lady Jeryl*
   Smith-Ryland (jt)   **P-in-c** A B LARKIN

BARFORD, GREAT (All Saints)　*see* Riversmeet *St Alb*
BARFREYSTONE (St Nicholas)　*see* Bewsborough *Cant*
BARHAM (St Giles)　*see* S Leightonstone *Ely*
BARHAM (St John the Baptist)　*see* Barham Downs w
　Adisham *Cant*
BARHAM (St Mary)　*see* Claydon *St E*
BARHAM DOWNS w Adisham *Cant 1*　**P** *Abp*　**R** S C THOMAS
　C L A HARDY
BARHOLME (St Martin)　*see* Uffington Gp *Linc*
BARKBY (St Mary)　*see* Fosse Team *Leic*
BARKESTONE (St Peter and St Paul)　*see* Vale of Belvoir *Leic*
BARKHAM (St James)　*see* Arborfield w Barkham *Ox*
BARKING (Christ Church)　*see* Thames View *Chelmsf*
BARKING (St Erkenwald) *Chelmsf 1*　**P** *Bp*　**V** Y LEE
BARKING (St Margaret) *Chelmsf 1*　**P** *Patr Bd*　**NSM** E JOHN
BARKING (St Mary)　*see* S Bosmere *St E*
BARKING (St Patrick) *Chelmsf 1*　**P** *Bp*　**V** C D BOLSTER
BARKINGSIDE (Holy Trinity) *Chelmsf 6*　**P** *V Gt Ilford*
　C K A APPIAH　**NSM** R E POTTEN
BARKINGSIDE (St Cedd) *Chelmsf 6*　**P** *Bp*
　P-in-c P G HARCOURT
BARKINGSIDE (St Francis of Assisi) *Chelmsf 6*　**P** *Bp*
　NSM M L BRADLEY
BARKINGSIDE (St George) *Chelmsf 6*　**P** *Bp*　**V** B J WALLIS
BARKINGSIDE (St Laurence) *Chelmsf 6*　**P** *Bp*
　V C M BURROWS
BARKISLAND (Christ Church) w West Scammonden
　Leeds 6　**P** *V Halifax*　**P-in-c** S M SOUTHGATE
BARKSTON (St Nicholas)　*see* S Cliff Villages Gp *Linc*
BARKSTON ASH (Holy Trinity)　*see* Sherburn in Elmet w
　Saxton *York*
BARKWAY (St Mary Magdalene), Barley, Reed and
　Buckland *St Alb 16*　**P** *The Crown and DBP (alt)*　**R** R C PYKE
　NSM S R RICHARDSON
BARKWITH Group, The, comprising East Barkwith, Hainton,
　Sixhills, East Torrington, and South Willingham *Linc 7*
　P *D&C, C N A F Heneage Esq, K Coll Lon, and DBP (by turn)*
　P-in-c C W HEWITT
BARKWITH, EAST (St Mary)　*see* Barkwith Gp *Linc*
BARLASTON (St John the Baptist) *Lich 12*　**P** *Countess of*
　Sutherland　**V** S W JONES
BARLAVINGTON (St Mary), Burton w Coates and Sutton w
　Bignor *Chich 4*　**P** *Lord Egremont*　**P-in-c** J F H GREEN
BARLBOROUGH (St James) and Clowne *Derby 3*　**P** *Ld Chan*
　and Mrs A Hayward (alt)　**R** B R TAYLOR
　C M A FITZSIMMONS
BARLBY (All Saints)　*see* Riccall, Barlby and Hemingbrough
　York
BARLESTONE (St Giles)　*see* Newbold De Verdun, Barlestone,
　Kirkby Mallory and Peckleton *Leic*
BARLEY (St Margaret of Antioch)　*see* Barkway, Barley, Reed
　and Buckland *St Alb*
BARLEY HILL　*see* Thame *Ox*
BARLING MAGNA (All Saints)　*see* Roach Par *Chelmsf*
BARLINGS (St Edward) *Linc 5*　**P** *DBP*　**V** D P GREEN
　C J A BELLSHAW
BARLOW MOOR (Emmanuel)　*see* Didsbury St Jas and Em
　Man
BARLOW, GREAT (St Lawrence)　*see* Old Brampton and Gt
　Barlow *Derby*
BARMBY MOOR Group, The (St Catherine), including
　Allerthorpe, Fangfoss, Thornton and Melbourne, and
　Yapham-cum-Meltonby *York 5*　**P** *Abp (1 turn), Abp and*
　Trustees Duke of Norfolk's Settlement Everingham Fund (2
　turns)　**V** J F HARDY
BARMING (St Margaret of Antioch) w West Barming
　Roch 7　**P** *Ld Chan*　**R** W W NORTH
BARMING HEATH (St Andrew) *Cant 12*　**P** *Abp*
　P-in-c C P LAVENDER
BARMSTON (All Saints)　*see* Bridlington Em and Barmston w
　Fraisthorpe *York*
BARNACK (St John the Baptist) w Ufford, Bainton,
　Helpston and Wittering *Pet 11*　**P** *Bp, St Jo Coll Cam,*
　Burghley Ho Preservation Trust Ltd, and Sir Philip Naylor-
　Leyland Bt (jt)　**V** G ALDERSON
BARNACRE (All Saints)　*see* Scorton and Barnacre and Calder
　Vale *Blackb*
BARNARD CASTLE (St Mary) w Whorlton *Dur 4*　**P** *Trin Coll*
　Cam　**V** A J HARDING　**C** S J CLIFF
BARNARDISTON (All Saints)　*see* Stourhead *St E*
BARNBURGH (St Peter) w Melton on the Hill and
　Adwick-upon-Dearne *Sheff 12*　**P** *Ld Chan (2 turns), Bp (1*
　turn)　**P-in-c** K HERROD
BARNBY (St John the Baptist)　*see* Beccles w Worlingham, N
　Cove and Barnby *St E*

BARNBY DUN (St Peter and St Paul), Kirk Sandall and
　Edenthorpe United Benefice *Sheff 8*　**P** *Bp and Ld Chan*
　(alt)　**P-in-c** T A BROWN
BARNBY IN THE WILLOWS (All Saints)　*see* Balderton, Barnby
　in the Willows and Coddington *S'well*
BARNEHURST (St Martin) *Roch 15*　**P** *Bp*　**V** G J BOWEN
BARNES Team Ministry, The (St Mary) (Holy Trinity)
　(St Michael and All Angels) *S'wark 16*　**P** *Patr Bd*
　TR J B B HUTCHINGS　**TV** D M R COOKE, S F STAVROU
　NSM M N CALDERBANK
BARNET (Christ Church)　*see* S Mimms Ch Ch *Lon*
BARNET (St John the Baptist)　*see* Chipping Barnet *St Alb*
BARNET (St Stephen)　*as above*
BARNET VALE (St Mark)　*as above*
BARNET, EAST (St Mary the Virgin) *St Alb 14*　**P** *The Crown*
　R A S CORIO
BARNET, NEW (St James) *St Alb 14*　**P** *Ch Patr Trust*
　V L J HEWITT
BARNETBY LE WOLD (St Barnabas)　*see* Brocklesby Park,
　Croxton and North Wolds *Linc*
BARNEY (St Mary), Hindringham, Thursford, Great
　Snoring, Little Snoring and Kettlestone and Pensthorpe
　Nor 14　**P** *D&C (1 turn), DBP and Lord Hastings (1 turn), St Jo*
　Coll Cam (1 turn)　**R** J MUGGLETON
BARNHAM (St Gregory)　*see* Blackbourne *St E*
BARNHAM (St Mary)　*see* Aldingbourne, Barnham and
　Eastergate *Chich*
BARNHAM BROOM (St Peter and St Paul) and Upper Yare
　Nor 16　**P** *Bp, Mrs A C Briggs, the Revd J B Boston, Ch Soc*
　Trust, H Edwards Esq, MMCET, and the Earl of Kimberley (jt)
　R T A P WEATHERSTONE　**C** L PITTMAN
BARNINGHAM (St Andrew)　*see* Stanton *St E*
BARNINGHAM (St Michael and All Angels)　*see* Holmedale
　Leeds
BARNINGHAM WINTER (St Mary the Virgin)　*see* Matlaske
　Nor
BARNINGHAM, LITTLE (St Andrew)　*see* Aylsham and Distr
　Nor
BARNOLDBY LE BECK (St Helen)　*see* Waltham Gp *Linc*
BARNOLDSWICK (Holy Trinity) (St Mary le Gill) w
　Bracewell *Leeds 21*　**P** *Bp*　**V** S S MCMAIN　**C** C E HONESS
BARNSBURY (St Andrew) *Lon 6*　**P** *Patr Bd*　**TV** D E FELL
　C M FLETCHER
BARNSLEY (St Edward the Confessor)　*see* Cen Barnsley *Leeds*
BARNSLEY (St Mary)　*as above*
BARNSLEY (St Mary)　*see* S Cotswolds *Glouc*
BARNSLEY (St Paul) Old Town　*see* Cen Barnsley *Leeds*
BARNSLEY (St Peter and St John the Baptist) *Leeds 14*　**P** *Bp*
　P-in-c B W RADFORD
BARNSLEY, CENTRAL (St Edward the Confessor)
　(St George) (St Mary) (St Thomas) *Leeds 14*　**P** *Bp and V*
　Darton w Staincross and Mapplewell (jt)　**R** S P RACE
　C J L HEWITT, M SANCHEZ RODRIGUEZ, P J MARIES
　NSM S A OAKLEY
BARNSLEY, WEST, comprising Cawthorne, Dodworth,
　Hoylandswaine, and Silkstone *Leeds 14*　**P** *A J Fraser Esq and*
　Bp (jt)　**V** M L BROWELL
BARNSTAPLE (Holy Trinity) and Goodleigh *Ex 13*　**P** *Bp and*
　DBP (jt)　**V** P J TAYLOR　**NSM** S A PATERSON
BARNSTAPLE (St Peter and St Mary Magdalene) *Ex 13*
　P *Bp*　**V** D M FLETCHER
BARNSTON (Christ Church) *Ches 8*　**P** *Bp*　**C** C C MURPHY
BARNSTON (St Andrew)　*see* Gt Dunmow and Barnston
　Chelmsf
BARNSTONE (St Mary Mission Room)　*see* Wiverton in the
　Vale *S'well*
BARNT GREEN (St Andrew)　*see* Cofton Hackett w Barnt
　Green *Birm*
BARNTON (Christ Church) *Ches 4*　**P** *Bp*　**V** *vacant*
BARNWELL (All Saints) (St Andrew), Hemington,
　Luddington in the Brook, Lutton, Polebrook and
　Thurning *Pet 10*　**P** *Bp, MMCET, Em Coll Cam, DBP, and Sir*
　Philip Naylor-Leyland Bt (jt)　**R** C H BRAZIER
BARNWOOD (St Lawrence) *Glouc 2*　**P** *D&C*
　V R E CROFTON　**NSM** A D HAYMAN
BARONY OF BURGH, The (St Michael) *Carl 3*　**P** *Patr Bd*
　P-in-c T A BODDAM-WHETHAM
BARR, GREAT (St Margaret) *Lich 24*　**P** *M D S Farnham*
　V M C RUTTER
BARRINGTON (All Saints)　*see* Orwell Gp *Ely*
BARRINGTON (Blessed Virgin Mary)　*see* Winsmoor *B & W*
BARRINGTON, GREAT (St Mary)　*see* Sherborne, Windrush,
　the Barringtons etc *Glouc*
BARRINGTON, LITTLE (St Peter)　*as above*

BARROW (All Saints) *St E 9*   **P** *Ld Chan (1 turn), Mrs E C Gordon-Lennox, the Russell-Cooke Trust Co and Bp (1 turn), and St Jo Coll Cam (1 turn)*   **P-in-c** L A SEBBAGE
BARROW (Holy Trinity) and Goxhill *Linc 8*   **P** *Ld Chan*   **P-in-c** A E BROWN
BARROW (St Bartholomew) *Ches 2*   **P** *D Okell Esq*   **R** A J STINSON
BARROW (St Giles)   *see Broseley w Benthall, Jackfield, Linley etc Heref*
BARROW GURNEY (The Blessed Virgin Mary and St Edward King and Martyr)   *see Long Ashton w Barrow Gurney and Flax Bourton B & W*
BARROW HILL (St Andrew)   *see Staveley and Barrow Hill Derby*
BARROW IN FURNESS (St Paul) *Carl 8*   **P** *Simeon's Trustees*   **P-in-c** R P HAM   **C** S E D RICHARDSON   **NSM** E A BATES
BARROW UPON SOAR (Holy Trinity) w Walton le Wolds *Leic 6*   **P** *St Jo Coll Cam and DBP (jt)*   **P-in-c** C R WATTS   **NSM** F J M COTTON-BETTERIDGE
BARROW, NORTH (St Nicholas)   *see Six Pilgrims B & W*
BARROW, NORTH Team Ministry, The (St Francis)
St Matthew (St James the Great) *Carl 8*   **P** *Patr Bd*   **TR** J W KNILL-JONES   **C** A E LYNCH
BARROW, SOUTH (St Peter)   *see Six Pilgrims B & W*
BARROW, SOUTH Team Ministry, The (St Aidan)
(St George) *Carl 8*   **P** *Bp*   **P-in-c** C J HARDING   **TV** E LYNCH
BARROWBY (All Saints) and Great Gonerby *Linc 20*   **P** *R Grantham, and Duke of Devonshire (by turn)*   **R** *vacant*
BARROWDEN (St Peter) and Wakerley w South Luffenham and Morcott w Duddington and Tixover *Pet 12*   **P** *Burghley Ho Preservation Trust Ltd, P W Rowley Esq, and Bp (3 turns), Ball Coll Ox (1 turn)*   **P-in-c** C J ARMSTRONG
BARROWFORD (St Thomas) and Newchurch-in-Pendle *Blackb 6*   **P** *Ld Chan and trustees (alt)*   **V** J L SMITH   **NSM** D A HARGREAVES
BARROW-IN-FURNESS (St Aidan)   *see S Barrow Carl*
BARROW-IN-FURNESS (St George) *as above*
BARROW-IN-FURNESS (St James the Great)   *see N Barrow Carl*
BARROW-IN-FURNESS (St John the Evangelist) *Carl 8*   **P** *DBP*   **V** *vacant*
BARROW-IN-FURNESS (St Mark) *Carl 8*   **P** *Bp*   **P-in-c** A FORD
BARROW-IN-FURNESS (St Mary the Virgin)   *see Walney Is Carl*
BARROW-ON-HUMBER (Holy Trinity)   *see Barrow and Goxhill Linc*
BARROW-ON-TRENT (St Wilfrid)   *see Aston on Trent, Elvaston, Weston on Trent etc Derby*
BARSHAM (Holy Trinity)   *see Bungay St E*
BARSHAM, EAST (All Saints)   *see Walsingham, Houghton and Barsham Nor*
BARSHAM, NORTH (All Saints) *as above*
BARSHAM, WEST (The Assumption of the Blessed Virgin Mary) *as above*
BARSTON (St Swithin) *Birm 6*   **P** *MMCET*   **P-in-c** S C L DIMES
BARTESTREE CROSS Group of Parishes, comprising Dormington, Lugwardine w Bartestree, Weston Beggard, and Withington *Heref 5*   **P** *D&C (3 turns), Bp (1 turn), Personal Reps A T Foley (1 turn)*   **R** S J D TARLTON
BARTHOMLEY (St Bertoline) *Ches 11*   **P** *Lord O'Neill*   **P-in-c** P ENNION
BARTLEY GREEN (St Michael and All Angels) *Birm 3*   **P** *Bp*   **V** R I ATKINSON
BARTLOW (St Mary)   *see Linton Ely*
BARTON (St Cuthbert w St Mary)   *see E Dere Street Leeds*
BARTON (St Lawrence)   *see Fellside Team Blackb*
BARTON (St Mark's Chapel) w Peel Green and Winton *Man 7*   **P** *Bp, TR Eccles, and TR Worsley (jt)*   **V** I A HALL
BARTON (St Martin)   *see Torquay St Martin Barton Ex*
BARTON (St Michael), Pooley Bridge, Martindale and Watermillock *Carl 4*   **P** *Bp and Earl of Lonsdale (jt)*   **P-in-c** L S TOWNEND
BARTON (St Paul) *Portsm 7*   **P** *R Whippingham*   **P-in-c** D C MONEME
BARTON (St Peter)   *see Lordsbridge Ely*
BARTON BENDISH (St Andrew)   *see Wissey Valley Ely*
BARTON HARTSHORN (St James)   *see The Claydons and Swan Ox*
BARTON HILL (St Luke w Ch Ch) and Moorfields
St Matthew *Bris 3*   **P** *Bp, CPAS, and V Bris St Phil and St Jacob w Em (jt)*   **P-in-c** N J COLEMAN   **C** C M BUCKLAND   **OLM** W D GARDINER

BARTON IN FABIS (St George)   *see A453 churches of S Notts S'well*
BARTON MILLS (St Mary)   *see Forest Heath St E*
BARTON SEAGRAVE (St Botolph) w Warkton *Pet 9*   **P** *Ch Soc Trust (2 turns), Duke of Buccleuch (1 turn)*   **R** M W LUCAS   **C** A J CLARK
BARTON ST DAVID (St David)   *see Wheathill Priory Gp B & W*
BARTON STACEY (All Saints)   *see Lower Dever Win*
BARTON TURF (St Michael)   *see Ashmanhaugh, Barton Turf etc Nor*
BARTON UNDER NEEDWOOD (St James) w Dunstall and Tatenhill *Lich 13*   **P** *Bp and Sir Rupert Hardy Bt (jt)*   **V** A C SIMPSON
BARTON UPON HUMBER (St Mary) *Linc 8*   **P** *Bp*   **V** D P ROWETT   **NSM** R M JAGGS-FOWLER   **OLM** A W WRIGHT
BARTON, GREAT (Holy Innocents) and Thurston *St E 9*   **P** *Bp and Sir Michael Bunbury Bt (jt)*   **V** B J EDWARDS
BARTON-LE-CLEY (St Nicholas) w Higham Gobion and Hexton *St Alb 8*   **P** *The Crown (3 turns), Mrs F A A Cooper (1 turn)*   **R** A P JOHNSON
BARTON-LE-STREET (St Michael)   *see The Street Par York*
BARTON-ON-THE-HEATH (St Lawrence)   *see S Warks Seven Gp Cov*
BARWELL (St Mary) w Potters Marston and Stapleton *Leic 10*   **P** R J W Titley Esq   **R** P WATSON
BARWICK (St Mary Magdalene)   *see Yeovil H Trin w Barwick B & W*
BARWICK IN ELMET (All Saints)   *see Elmete Trin Leeds*
BASCHURCH (All Saints) and Weston Lullingfield w Hordley *Lich 16*   **P** *Ch Patr Trust and Bp (jt)*   **R** L J COX   **C** S ALSTON   **NSM** D M COATSWORTH
BASEGREEN (St Peter)   *see Gleadless Sheff*
BASFORD (St Leodegarius) (St Aidan) *S'well 8*   **P** *Bp*   **P-in-c** R T K ATKINSON   **C** L M M CORBETT   **NSM** D WATKINSON
BASFORD (St Mark) *Lich 9*   **P** *Bp*   **V** A M THOMAS   **C** P M GRIFFIN
BASHLEY (St John)   *see Milton Win*
BASILDON (St Andrew) (Holy Cross) *Chelmsf 11*   **P** *Bp*   **V** J S RICHARDS   **C** S M PEARCE   **NSM** K A WHITE
BASILDON (St Martin of Tours) *Chelmsf 11*   **P** *Bp*   **P-in-c** T J G BRAMPTON
BASILDON (St Stephen) w Aldworth and Ashampstead *Ox 4*   **P** *St Jo Coll Cam, Simeon's Trustees, and DBF (by turn)*   **V** G L FENSOME   **NSM** K WESTON
BASING, OLD (St Mary) and Lychpit *Win 4*   **P** *Magd Coll Ox*   **V** H S LEPPARD
BASINGSTOKE (All Saints) (St Michael) *Win 4*   **P** *Patr Bd*   **TR** J M STOKER   **NSM** P PALMER
BASINGSTOKE (St Gabriel)   *see Popley w Limes Park and Rooksdown Win*
BASINGSTOKE (St Mary)   *see Eastrop Win*
BASINGSTOKE Brighton Hill (Christ the King)   *see Basingstoke Win*
BASINGSTOKE Popley (Bethlehem Chapel) *as above*
BASINGSTOKE South Ham (St Peter) *as above*
BASLOW (St Anne) and Eyam *Derby 4*   **P** *Duke of Devonshire and Earl Temple (jt)*   **R** M V GILBERT   **NSM** M Z HARTLEY
BASSENTHWAITE (St Bega)   *see Binsey Carl*
BASSENTHWAITE (St John) *as above*
BASSETT (St Michael and All Angels)   *see N Stoneham and Bassett Win*
BASSINGBOURN (St Peter and St Paul) *Ely 7*   **P** *D&C Westmr*   **V** *vacant*
BASSINGHAM (St Michael and All Angels)   *see Withamside Linc*
BASSINGTHORPE (St Thomas à Becket)   *see Corby Glen Par Linc*
BASTON (St John the Baptist)   *see Ness Gp Linc*
BASWICH or Berkswich (Holy Trinity) *Lich 10*   **P** *Bp*   **V** G W ADAMSON   **NSM** D CLARK
BATCOMBE (Blessed Virgin Mary)   *see Alham Vale B & W*
BATCOMBE (St Mary)   *see Three Valleys Sarum*
BATH (Christ Church) Proprietary Chapel *B & W 10*   **P-in-c** K E J CHUMBLEY   **C** K R MAYLOR
BATH (St Barnabas) w Englishcombe *B & W 8*   **P** *Bp*   **V** *vacant*
BATH (St Bartholomew) *B & W 8*   **P** *Simeon's Trustees*   **V** I R LEWIS   **NSM** J R G HOVIL, T C LING
BATH (St Luke) *B & W 8*   **P** *Simeon's Trustees*   **V** M D H FRANKUM
BATH (St Mary Magdalene) Holloway, Extra-parochial Chapelry *B & W 10*   **Chapl** J J WISE
BATH (St Michael w St Paul) *B & W 8*   **P** *CPAS*   **R** R J DRIVER

BATH (St Saviour) w Swainswick and Woolley *B & W 8*
  P *Ch Patr Trust and Or Coll Ox (jt)* **R** R M DENSMORE
BATH (St Stephen) *see* Charlcombe w Bath St Steph *B & W*
BATH ABBEY (St Peter and St Paul) w St James *B & W 8*
  P *Simeon's Trustees* **R** G S BRIDGEWATER **C** C M MASON,
  S P GIRLING **NSM** C CANDISH, E M LEE-BARBER
BATH Bathwick (St John the Baptist) (Blessed Virgin Mary)
  B & W 8 **P** *Bp* **B** P R H EDWARDS
BATH Odd Down (St Philip and St James) w Combe Hay
  B & W 8 **P** *Simeon's Trustees* **V** P S FERGUSON
  NSM L A WORTELHOCK, M JOYCE
BATH Twerton-on-Avon (Ascension) (St Michael) *B & W 8*
  P *Patr Bd* **TR** R M WHITE **TV** R J PIMM
BATH Walcot (St Swithin) (St Swithin) *B & W 8* **P** *Simeon's*
  Trustees **R** T GLEGHORN **C** F A YOUINGS
BATH Weston (All Saints) w North Stoke and Langridge
  B & W 8 **P** *Ld Chan* **R** M R SEARLE
BATH Weston (St John the Evangelist) (Emmanuel) w
  Kelston *B & W 8* **P** *Ld Chan* **P-in-c** M T FARRIER
BATH Widcombe (St Matthew) (St Thomas à Becket)
  B & W 8 **P** *Simeon's Trustees* **V** T S BUCKLEY
BATHAMPTON (St Nicholas) w Claverton *B & W 8* **P** *D&C*
  Bris and the Revd C W D Skrine (jt) **R** J P FRITH
BATHEALTON (St Bartholomew) *see* Wellington and Distr
  B & W
BATHEASTON (St John the Baptist) (St Catherine) *B & W 8*
  P *Ch Ch Ox* **C** E M BENNETT
BATHFORD (St Swithun) *B & W 8* **P** *D&C Bris* **V** *vacant*
BATHWICK (Blessed Virgin Mary) *see* Bath Bathwick *B & W*
BATHWICK (St John the Baptist) *as above*
BATLEY (All Saints) (St Thomas) *Leeds 7* **P** *Bp, R E Brudenell*
  Esq, and R Dewsbury (jt) **V** M NAYLOR **C** M R UMPLEBY
BATLEY CARR (Holy Trinity) *see* Dewsbury *Leeds*
BATSFORD (St Mary) *see* Moreton-in-Marsh w Batsford,
  Todenham etc *Glouc*
BATTERSEA (Christ Church and St Stephen) *S'wark 14*
  P *Bp and V Battersea St Mary (alt)* **V** G N OWEN
BATTERSEA (St George) *see* Battersea Fields *S'wark*
BATTERSEA (St Luke) *S'wark 14* **P** *Bp*
  V M L FERNANDEZ-SMAL **C** Y KOH
BATTERSEA (St Mary) *S'wark 14* **P** *Earl Spencer* **V** S BUTLER
  C A J KENNEDY
BATTERSEA (St Michael) Wandsworth Common *S'wark 14*
  P *V Battersea St Mary* **V** T-A L EWINS
BATTERSEA (St Peter) (St Paul) *S'wark 14* **P** *V Battersea*
  St Mary **P-in-c** R P MALONE
BATTERSEA FIELDS (St Saviour) (All Saints) (St George)
  S'wark 14 **P** *Bp, CPAS, and Ch Patr Trust (jt)*
  P-in-c L W CARR **C** E BLATCHLEY, R C TURNER, S A A ANAND,
  V J ELSTON
BATTERSEA PARK (All Saints) *see* Battersea Fields *S'wark*
BATTERSEA PARK (St Saviour) *as above*
BATTERSEA RISE (St Mark) *S'wark 14* **P** *V Battersea St Mary*
  V M P LAYZELL **NSM** D G JOHNSON
BATTISFORD (St Mary) *see* S Bosmere *St E*
BATTLE (Church of the Ascension) (St Mary the Virgin)
  Chich 12 **P** *The Crown* **V** L C J DUCKETT **C** D P HAZELL
BATTLE HILL (Good Shepherd) *see* Willington *Newc*
BATTLESDEN (St Peter and All Saints) *see* Woburn w
  Eversholt, Milton Bryan, Battlesden etc *St Alb*
BATTYEFORD (Christ the King) *Leeds 7* **P** *V Mirfield*
  P-in-c E C PEETERS
BAUGHURST (St Stephen) and Ramsdell and Wolverton w
  Ewhurst and Hannington *Win 4* **P** *Ld Chan, Duke of*
  Wellington, and Bp (by turn) **R** *vacant*
BAULKING (St Nicholas) *see* Uffington, Shellingford,
  Woolstone and Baulking *Ox*
BAUMBER (St Swithin) *see* Hemingby Gp *Linc*
BAUNTON (St Mary Magdalene) *see* Churn Valley *Glouc*
BAVERSTOCK (St Editha) *see* Nadder Valley *Sarum*
BAWBURGH (St Mary and St Walstan) *see* Easton, Colton,
  Marlingford and Bawburgh *Nor*
BAWDESWELL (All Saints) *see* Heart of Norfolk *Nor*
BAWDRIP (St Michael and All Angels) *see* Woolavington w
  Cossington and Bawdrip *B & W*
BAWDSEY (St Mary) *see* Wilford Peninsula *St E*
BAWTRY (St Nicholas) w Austerfield, Misson, Everton and
  Mattersey *S'well 1* **P** *Bp and Ld Chan (alt)* **V** R J HANCOCK
BAXENDEN (St John) *Blackb 1* **P** *Bp* **V** *vacant*
BAXTERLEY (not known) w Hurley and Wood End and
  Merevale w Bentley *Birm 5* **P** *Ld Chan (1 turn), Bp and Sir*
  William Dugdale Bt (1 turn) **P-in-c** J C WHITE
  NSM C J YOUNG
BAYDON (St Nicholas) *see* Whitton *Sarum*
BAYFORD (Mission Room) *see* Charlton Musgrove,
  Cucklington and Stoke Trister *B & W*

BAYFORD (St Mary) *see* Lt Berkhamsted and Bayford,
  Essendon etc *St Alb*
BAYLHAM (St Peter) *see* Bramford w Lt Blakenham, Baylham
  and Nettlestead *St E*
BAYSTON HILL (Christ Church) *Lich 19* **P** *V Shrewsbury H*
  Trin w St Julian **V** P J HUBBARD **C** U F PENCAVEL
BAYSWATER (St Matthew) *Lon 2* **P** *Exors Dame Jewell*
  Magnus-Allcroft **V** W P H COLERIDGE **NSM** M J LEE
BAYTON (St Bartholomew) *see* Mamble w Bayton, Rock w
  Heightington etc *Worc*
BEACHAMPTON (Assumption of the Blessed Virgin Mary) *see*
  Blackthorn Chase *Ox*
BEACHAMWELL (St Mary) *see* Wissey Valley *Ely*
BEACON Parishes *see* Painswick, Sheepscombe, Cranham,
  The Edge etc *Glouc*
BEACON Team Ministry, The, comprising Burneside,
  Grayrigg, Kendal St George, Longsleddale, Selside, and
  Skelsmergh *Carl 10* **P** *Patr Bd* **P-in-c** P A ROGERS
  OLM J F RADLEY
BEACON TRINITY, comprising Ashwick, Binegar, and Oakhill
  B & W 7 **P** *Bp* **P-in-c** R A PRIESTLEY **C** M L PRIESTLEY,
  R J MILES
BEACON, The, comprising Burton Agnes, Harpham, and
  Lowthorpe *York 10* **P** *Ld Chan (2 turns), Sir Charles Legard*
  Bt (1 turn) **R** *vacant*
BEACONSFIELD (St Mary and All Saints) (St Michael and
  All Angels) *Ox 9* **P** *Patr Bd* **TR** J P BROOKS
  TV M R JOHNSON, S ROBERTS **NSM** M M SUTER
BEADLAM (St Hilda) *see* Kirkdale w Harome, Nunnington
  and Pockley *York*
BEADNELL (St Ebba), Ellingham and North Sunderland
  Newc 7 **P** *Bp and D&C Dur (1 turn), Newc Dioc Sec and Lord*
  Crewe's Trustees (1 turn) **V** A S MACPHERSON
BEAFORD (All Saints) *see* Newton Tracey, Horwood,
  Alverdiscott etc *Ex*
BEALINGS, GREAT (St Mary) *see* Woodbridge w Gt Bealings
  St E
BEALINGS, LITTLE (All Saints) *see* Kesgrave w Lt Bealings and
  Playford *St E*
BEAMINSTER AREA (St Mary of the Annunciation),
  including Broadwinsor w Burstock, Drimpton, Hooke,
  Melplash and Mapperton, Mosterton, Netherbury, Salway
  Ash, Seaborough, South Perrott and Chedington, Stoke
  Abbott, and Toller Porcorum *Sarum 2* **P** *Patr Bd*
  TR D F B BALDWIN **TV** J B NEARY **C** F J BEALE
BEAMISH (St Andrew) *see* Stanley and S Moor *Dur*
BEANE VALLEY Benefice, The, comprising Aston, Bramfield,
  Stapleford, Waterford and Watton at Stone *St Alb 19*
  P *Grocers' Co (1 turn), R M A Smith Esq (3 turns), Bp (1 turn)*
  R J GRAY **NSM** A LYNAS
BEARLEY (St Mary the Virgin) *see* Arden Valley *Cov*
BEARPARK (St Edmund) *see* Dur St Marg, Neville's Cross St Jo
  and Bearpark *Dur*
BEARSTED (Holy Cross) *see* N Downs *Cant*
BEARWOOD (St Catherine) *see* Winnersh *Ox*
BEARWOOD (St Mary the Virgin) *Birm 3* **P** *V Smethwick*
  V *vacant*
BEAUCHAMP RODING (St Botolph) *see* S Rodings *Chelmsf*
BEAUDESERT (St Nicholas) and Henley-in-Arden w
  Ullenhall *Cov 7* **P** *MMCET, Bp, and High Bailiff of*
  Henley-in-Arden (jt) **R** J F GANJAVI
BEAULIEU (Blessed Virgin and Holy Child) and Exbury and
  East Boldre *Win 11* **P** *Bp and Lord Montagu of Beaulieu (jt)*
  R J C WHITE
BEAUMONT CUM MOZE (St Leonard and St Mary) *see* Gt
  Oakley, Wix, Wrabness etc *Chelmsf*
BEAUMONT LEYS (Christ the King) *see* Stocking Farm and
  Beaumont Leys *Leic*
BEAUWORTH (St James) *see* Upper Itchen *Win*
BEAUXFIELD (St Peter) *see* Bewsborough *Cant*
BEAWORTHY (St Alban) *see* Ashwater, Halwill, Beaworthy,
  Clawton etc *Ex*
BEBINGTON (St Andrew) *Ches 8* **P** *M C Saunders-Griffiths*
  Esq **R** D A VESTERGAARD **C** A M RODGERS
BEBINGTON, HIGHER (Christ Church) *Ches 8* **P** *Bp*
  V M G LOACH **C** G L ROACH **NSM** E S BLACKMORE
BECCLES (St Michael) (St Luke's Church Centre) w
  Worlingham, North Cove and Barnby *St E 15* **P** *Simeon's*
  Trustees (2 turns) Ld Chan (1 turn) **R** R HENDERSON
  NSM M H BEE, P M CUDMORE
BECK ROW (St John) *see* Forest Heath *St E*
BECKBURY (St Milburga), Badger, Kemberton, Ryton,
  Stockton and Sutton Maddock *Lich 15* **P** *Lord Hamilton*
  of Dalzell, Or Coll Ox, and MMCET (2 turns), Ld Chan (1 turn)
  R K HODSON

BECKENHAM (Christ Church) *Roch 13* **P** *Ch Trust Fund Trust* **V** R M HINTON **C** N J G POOLE

BECKENHAM (Holy Trinity) *see Penge Lane H Trin Roch*

BECKENHAM (St George) (St Barnabas) *Roch 13* **P** *Bp and Keble Coll Ox (jt)* **R** J A BLUNDEN **C** T J HIDE **NSM** B M EJIMOFO

BECKENHAM (St James) (St Michael and All Angels) and St Augustine *Roch 13* **P** *Bp and SMF (jt)* **V** L C CARBERRY

BECKENHAM (St John the Baptist) Eden Park *Roch 13* **P** *Ch Trust Fund Trust, Bp and Adn Bromley (jt)* **V** D E JONES **C** S A SMITH, S J THOMAS **NSM** J W FOULGER

BECKENHAM, NEW (St Paul) *Roch 13* **P** *Bp* **V** S P M COUPER

BECKERMET (St Bridget Old Church) *see Seatallan Carl*

BECKERMET (St Bridget) *as above*

BECKERMET (St John) *as above*

BECKFORD (St John the Baptist) *see Overbury w Teddington, Alstone etc Worc*

BECKHAM, WEST (St Helen and All Saints) *see Weybourne Gp Nor*

BECKINGHAM (All Saints) *see Brant Broughton and Beckingham Linc*

BECKINGHAM (All Saints), Walkeringham, Misterton, West Stockwith, Clayworth and Gringley-on-the-Hill *S'well 1* **P** *D&C York (3 turns), Ld Chanc (1 turn), Bp (1 turn)* **V** *vacant*

BECKINGTON (St George) w Standerwick, Berkley, Rodden, Lullington and Orchardleigh *B & W 3* **P** *Bp (3 turns), Ch Soc Trust (1 turn), and Exors A Duckworth Esq* **P-in-c** S M J CROSSMAN

BECKLEY (All Saints) *see Brede w Udimore and Beckley and Peasmarsh Chich*

BECKLEY (Assumption of the Blessed Virgin Mary), Forest Hill, Horton-cum-Studley and Stanton St John *Ox 20* **P** *Linc Coll Ox and New Coll Ox (alt)* **V** A C BERESFORD

BECKTON (St Mark) *Chelmsf 5* **P** *Bp* **P-in-c** P M NGUGI

BECKWITHSHAW (St Michael and All Angels) *see Pannal w Beckwithshaw Leeds*

BECONTREE (St Cedd) *Chelmsf 1* **P** *Bp* **P-in-c** U A CHINDABATA **NSM** R A DOWLEY

BECONTREE (St Elisabeth) *Chelmsf 1* **P** *Bp* **P-in-c** C D BOLSTER **C** M J COURT

BECONTREE (St George) *Chelmsf 1* **P** *Bp* **P-in-c** S D BERRY

BECONTREE (St Mary) *Chelmsf 1* **P** *CPAS* **V** K R MILLER **C** T R H BROADBENT **NSM** C E MORKEH-YAMSON PELLIGRIN

BECONTREE (St Thomas) *Chelmsf 1* **P** *Bp* **P-in-c** G H E STOCK

BECONTREE SOUTH (St Alban) (St John the Divine) (St Martin) *Chelmsf 1* **P** *Patr Bd* **TR** F BAILEY **C** E G BROWN **OLM** R P C DESCOMBES

BEDALE (St Gregory) and Leeming and Thornton Watlass *Leeds 22* **P** *Bp, Sir Henry Beresford-Peirse Bt, R Kirklington w Burneston and Wath and Pickhill, and D S Dodsworth Esq (jt)* **R** S A MOOR

BEDDINGHAM (St Andrew) *see Glynde, W Firle and Beddingham Chich*

BEDDINGTON (St Mary) *S'wark 23* **P** *D&C* **R** A R FENBY

BEDDINGTON, SOUTH (St Michael and All Angels) and Roundshaw *S'wark 23* **P** *Bp* **V** A M A GBEBIKAN **C** P T FITZPATRICK

BEDFIELD (St Nicholas) *see Four Rivers St E*

BEDFONT, EAST (St Mary the Virgin) *Lon 11* **P** *Ld Chan* **V** P J SMITH

BEDFORD (All Saints) *St Alb 9* **P** *Bp* **P-in-c** P S DAVIES

BEDFORD (Christ Church) *St Alb 9* **P** *Bp* **V** R C HIBBERT **C** J G BELL

BEDFORD (St Andrew) *St Alb 9* **P** *Ld Chan* **V** L F DAVIS

BEDFORD (St John the Baptist) (St Leonard) *St Alb 9* **P** *MMCET* **R** V E BRYSON

BEDFORD (St Mark) *St Alb 9* **P** *Bp* **V** C ROYDEN **NSM** G R CAPPLEMAN

BEDFORD (St Martin) *St Alb 9* **P** *Bp* **V** P J NORWOOD

BEDFORD (St Michael and All Angels) *see Elstow St Alb*

BEDFORD (St Paul) *St Alb 9* **P** *Bp* **V** K I GOSS **C** L W LARNER

BEDFORD (St Peter de Merton) w St Cuthbert *St Alb 9* **P** *Ld Chan* **R** K F WOOLMER **NSM** R C SIMONS

BEDFORD LEIGH St Thomas (All Saints' Mission) *Man 7* **P** *V Leigh St Mary* **C** M B COX, R C ELOFF

BEDFORD PARK (St Michael and All Angels) *Lon 11* **P** *Bp* **V** K J MORRIS **C** F PESCE, T G I COUPER **NSM** G MORGAN

BEDGROVE (Holy Spirit) *Ox 10* **P** *DBP* **V** M G KUHRT

BEDHAMPTON (St Nicholas's Mission Church) (St Thomas) *Portsm 5* **P** *Bp* **R** M D CROSS

BEDINGFIELD (St Mary) *see Eye St E*

BEDINGHAM (St Andrew) *see Hempnall Nor*

BEDLINGTON (St Cuthbert), Cambois and Sleekburn *Newc 1* **P** *D&C Dur and D&C (alt)* **V** I J HENNEBRY

BEDMINSTER (St Paul) *see Bedminster and Southville Bris*

BEDMINSTER (St Aldhelm) and Southville St Paul *Bris 1* **P** *Bp* **C** J C KEAN, M L SOUTHCOMBE

BEDMINSTER (St Michael and All Angels) *Bris 1* **P** *Bp* **V** *vacant*

BEDMINSTER DOWN (St Oswald) *see Bishopsworth and Bedminster Down Bris*

BEDMOND (Ascension) *see Abbots Langley St Alb*

BEDNALL (All Saints) *see Penkridge Lich*

BEDSTONE (St Mary) *see Middle Marches Heref*

BEDWORTH (All Saints) *Cov 5* **P** *Patr Bd* **TR** D E POULTNEY **TV** A J POULTNEY **C** M BULL

BEDWYN, GREAT (St Mary) *see Savernake Sarum*

BEDWYN, LITTLE (St Michael) *as above*

BEECH (St Peter) *see Alton Win*

BEECH HILL (St Mary the Virgin) *see Loddon Reach Ox*

BEECH, HIGH (Holy Innocents) *see Waltham H Cross Chelmsf*

BEECHDALE ESTATE (St Chad) *see Blakenall Heath Lich*

BEECHINGSTOKE (St Stephen) *see Vale of Pewsey Sarum*

BEEDING (St Peter) and Bramber w Botolphs *Chich 5* **P** *Bp* **C** S H TUPPER

BEEDING, LOWER (Holy Trinity) (St John the Evangelist) and Cowfold *Chich 10* **P** *Bp and Bp Lon (jt)* **V** S J WHARTON **NSM** M MILLS

BEEDON (St Nicholas) *see E Downland Ox*

BEEFORD (St Leonard) w Frodingham and Foston *York 11* **P** *Abp and Ch Soc Trust (jt)* **R** J E GRAINGER-SMITH **NSM** S E HEBDEN

BEELEY (St Anne) and Edensor *Derby 4* **P** *Duke of Devonshire* **V** D PERKINS

BEELSBY (St Andrew) *see Wolds Gateway Group Linc*

BEENHAM VALENCE (St Mary) *see Aldermaston and Woolhampton Ox*

BEER (St Michael) *see Seaton and Beer Ex*

BEER HACKETT (St Michael) *see Three Valleys Sarum*

BEERCROCOMBE (St James) w Curry Mallet, Hatch Beauchamp, Orchard Portman, Staple Fitzpaine, Stoke St Mary w Thurlbear and West Hatch *B & W 16* **P** *Bp, Ch Trust Fund Trust, and D&C (4 turns), Duchy of Cornwall (1 turn)* **P-in-c** J K PORTER **Hon C** S R JONES

BEESANDS (St Andrew) *see Stokenham, Slapton, Charleton w Buckland etc Ex*

BEESBY (St Andrew) *see Alford Gp Linc*

BEESTON (St John the Baptist) *S'well 9* **P** *Duke of Devonshire* **V** W R PLIMMER **C** T F BYRNE **NSM** K D BUCHAN, R C W WIGGINS

BEESTON (St Lawrence) *see Ashmanhaugh, Barton Turf etc Nor*

BEESTON (St Mary the Virgin) *Leeds 11* **P** *Patr Bd* **TR** L C PEARSON

BEESTON NEXT MILEHAM (St Mary the Virgin) *see Launditch and the Upper Nar Nor*

BEESTON REGIS (All Saints) *see Aylmerton, Runton, Beeston Regis and Gresham Nor*

BEETHAM (St Michael and All Angels) *Carl 10* **P** *Bp* **P-in-c** A B NORMAN

BEETLEY (St Mary) *see Dereham and Distr Nor*

BEGBROKE (St Michael) *see Yarnton w Begbroke and Shipton-on-Cherwell Ox*

BEIGHTON (All Saints) *see Acle and Bure to Yare Nor*

BEIGHTON (St Mary the Virgin) *Sheff 1* **P** *Bp* **P-in-c** M H E HEALEY

BEKESBOURNE (St Peter) *see Bridge Cant*

BELAUGH (St Peter) *see Wroxham w Hoveton, Belaugh and Tunstead etc Nor*

BELBROUGHTON (Holy Trinity) w Fairfield and Clent *Worc 6* **P** *Ld Chan and St Jo Coll Ox (alt)* **Hon C** R J C NEWTON, V W BEYNON **NSM** K TOPHAM

BELCHALWELL (St Aldheim) *see Hazelbury Bryan and the Hillside Par Sarum*

BELCHAMP (St Paul and St Andrew) *see N Hinckford Chelmsf*

BELCHAMP OTTEN (St Ethelbert and All Saints) *as above*

BELCHAMP WALTER (St Mary the Virgin) *as above*

BELCHFORD (St Peter and St Paul) *see Hemingby Gp Linc*

BELFIELD (St Ann) *Man 6* **P** *Bp* **V** G BARNETT **C** E D O'BAKA-TORTO **NSM** S E WARD

BELFORD (St Mary) *see Bamburgh, Belford and Lucker Newc*

BELGRAVE (St Michael) *see Leic Resurr Leic*

BELGRAVE (St Peter) *as above*

BELHUS PARK (All Saints) *see Mardyke Chelmsf*

BELLE ABBEY (St Cairbre) *see Arbory and Castletown S & M*

BELLE GREEN (Mission) *see Wigan Liv*

BELLE ISLE (St John and St Barnabas) and Hunslet *Leeds 11* **P** *Bp and R Leeds City* **V** A C N BUCKLEY

BELLEAU (St John the Baptist) *see* Legbourne and Wold Marsh *Linc*

BELLERBY (St John) *see* Leyburn w Bellerby *Leeds*

BELLINGDON (St John the Evangelist) *see* Gt Chesham *Ox*

BELLINGHAM (St Cuthbert) *see* N Tyne and Redesdale *Newc*

BELLINGHAM (St Dunstan) *S'wark 4* P *Bp* P-in-c T B SINGH NSM D L RILEY

BELMONT (St Anselm) *Lon 20* P *Bp* V C M A ROBINSON

BELMONT (St John) *S'wark 23* P *R Cheam* V B L LEWIS

BELMONT (St Mary Magdalene) and Pittington *Dur 1* P *The Crown and D&C (alt)* V H MURRAY C E J HOLLIS

BELMONT (St Peter) *see* Turton Moorland *Man*

BELPER (Christ Church) w Turnditch *Derby 6* P *Bp* C R C BURDETT

BELPER (St Peter) *Derby 6* P V *Duffield* V A M STRATTON

BELSIZE PARK (St Peter) *Lon 15* P *D&C Westmr* P-in-c P S NICHOLSON

BELSTEAD (St Mary the Virgin) *see* Sproughton w Burstall, Copdock w Washbrook etc *St E*

BELSTONE (St Mary) *see* Okehampton, Inwardleigh, Belstone, Sourton etc *Ex*

BELTINGHAM (St Cuthbert) *see* Haydon Bridge and Beltingham w Henshaw *Newc*

BELTISLOE, NORTH Parishes, The, comprising Boothby Pagnell, Ingoldsby, Lenton, Old Somerby, Ropsley, and Sapperton w Braceby *Linc 17* P *Baroness Willoughby de Eresby, Ch Coll Cam, D&C, DBP, Sir Lyonel Tollemache Bt, Sir Richard Welby Bt, and Bp (jt)* V A K E SORENSEN

BELTON (All Saints) and Burgh Castle *Nor 6* P *Bp and Ld Chan (alt)* R R J BUNN OLM V E T RIDPATH

BELTON (St John the Baptist) *see* Kegworth, Hathern, Long Whatton, Diseworth etc *Leic*

BELTON (St Peter and St Paul) *see* S Cliff Villages Gp *Linc*

BELTON (St Peter) *see* Uppingham w Ayston and Belton w Wardley *Pet*

BELTON Group, The (All Saints), including Althorpe and Keadby, and Amcotts *Linc 1* P *Bp and The Crown (alt)* V C KAY

BELVEDERE (All Saints) *Roch 15* P *DBP* V S F ARCHER

BELVEDERE (St Augustine) *Roch 15* P *Bp* V C W JONES

BEMBRIDGE (Holy Trinity) (St Luke's Mission Church) *Portsm 7* P V *Brading* P-in-c S J DAUGHTERY

BEMERTON (St Andrew) (St John the Evangelist) (St Michael and All Angels) *Sarum 13* P *The Crown (2 turns) and Bp (1 turn)* TR K MARTIN

BEMPTON (St Michael) w Flamborough, Reighton w Speeton *York 9* P *Patr Bd* P-in-c S J PENN

BEN RHYDDING (St John the Evangelist) *Leeds 4* P V *Ilkey* V P WILLOX NSM J H COPSEY

BENCHILL (St Luke the Physician) *see* Wythenshawe *Man*

BENEFIELD (St Mary the Virgin) *see* Oundle w Ashton and Benefield w Glapthorn *Pet*

BENENDEN (St George and St Margaret) and Sandhurst *Cant 10* P *Abp* V D J COMMANDER NSM Y H B BLID-MACKENZIE

BENFIELDSIDE (St Cuthbert) *Dur 2* P *Bp* V M JACKSON NSM P A CARTER

BENFLEET, SOUTH (St Mary the Virgin) *Chelmsf 12* P *D&C Westmr* V vacant

BENGEO (Holy Trinity) *see* Hertford *St Alb*

BENGEO (St Leonard) *as above*

BENGEWORTH (St Peter) and Hampton w Sedgeberrow and Hinton-on-the-Green *Worc 3* P *Patr Bd* R M J G BINNEY C A K SMITH NSM N M WRIGHT

BENHALL (St Mary) *see* Alde River *St E*

BENHILTON (All Saints) *S'wark 23* P *Bp* V D E CHISLETT

BENINGTON (St Peter) *see* Ardeley, Benington, Cottered w Throcking etc *St Alb*

BENNETTS END (St Benedict) *see* Langelei *St Alb*

BENNIWORTH (St Julian) *see* Asterby Gp *Linc*

BENSHAM AND TEAMS (St Chad) *Dur 11* P *Bp* C A I G CRAWFORD, Y GREENER

BENSON (St Helen) w Ewelme *Ox 20* P *Merton Coll Ox, Ch Ch Ox, and Brigadier J N B Mogg (1 turn), The Crown (1 turn)* R P E GILDAY NSM S M COUSINS

BENTHAM (St John the Baptist), Burton-in-Lonsdale, Chapel-le-Dale, Ingleton and Thornton-in-Lonsdale *Leeds 17* P *Bp* TR A RUSSELL TV D S TATE, W N D TRENHOLME

BENTILEE (St Stephen) *see* Bucknall *Lich*

BENTLEY (Emmanuel) and Willenhall Holy Trinity *Lich 28* P *Patr Bd* TV H L DUCKETT

BENTLEY (St Mary) *see* Sproughton w Burstall, Copdock w Washbrook etc *St E*

BENTLEY (St Mary), Binsted and Froyle *Win 2* P *D&C, Adn Surrey, and Guild of All So (jt)* R Y DUBREUIL NSM C W OGILVIE THOMPSON

BENTLEY (St Peter) *Sheff 7* P *Bp* V D N BERRY

BENTLEY COMMON (St Paul), Kelvedon Hatch and Navestock *Chelmsf 8* P *Bp* P-in-c J A HARDY OLM J W BIDDULPH

BENTLEY HEATH (St James) *see* Dorridge *Birm*

BENTLEY, GREAT (St Mary the Virgin) *see* St Osyth and Great Bentley *Chelmsf*

BENTLEY, LITTLE (St Mary) *see* Lawford, Lt Bentley and The Bromleys *Chelmsf*

BENTLEY, LOWER (St Mary) *see* Tardebigge *Worc*

BENTLEY, NEW (St Philip and St James) w Arksey *Sheff 7* P *Bp and DBP (jt)* V S P DICKINSON

BENTWORTH (St Mary), Lasham, Medstead and Shalden *Win 2* P *J L Jervoise Esq and Ld Chan (alt)* R vacant

BENWELL (St James) (St John) (Venerable Bede) and Scotswood Team, The *Newc 4* P *Bp* TR A D KIRKWOOD TV D J COAD C C D MINCHIN

BEOLEY (St Leonard) *see* Redditch H Trin *Worc*

BEOLEY Church Hill (St Andrew's Church Centre) *as above*

BEPTON (St Mary) *see* Cocking w W Lavington, Bepton and Heyshott *Chich*

BERDEN (St Nicholas) *see* Clavering w Langley, Arkesden etc *Chelmsf*

BERE ALSTON (Holy Trinity) *see* Bere Ferrers *Ex*

BERE FERRERS (St Andrew) *Ex 21* P *DBP* R N C LAW C D OAKLEY

BERE REGIS (St John the Baptist) *see* W Purbeck *Sarum*

BERGH APTON (St Peter and St Paul) *see* Thurton w Ashby St Mary, Bergh Apton etc *Nor*

BERGHOLT, EAST (St Mary the Virgin) and Brantham *St E 13* P *Em Coll Cam* R S VAN DER TOORN

BERGHOLT, WEST (St Mary the Virgin) and Great Horkesley *Chelmsf 20* P *Bp and Ball Coll Ox (alt)* C H GREENLAND, H R COOPER, R G GIBBS, S L HAYWARD NSM P W MANN OLM A L MASON

BERINSFIELD (St Mary and St Berin) *see* Dorchester *Ox*

BERKELEY (St Mary the Virgin) w Wick, Breadstone, Newport, Stone, Woodford and Hill *Glouc 5* P *Bp, Berkeley Will Trustees, and Mrs J D Jenner-Fust (jt)* P-in-c S P GODSELL

BERKHAMSTED, GREAT (All Saints) (St Peter), Great Gaddesden, Little Gaddesden, Nettleden and Potten End *St Alb 1* P *Patr Bd* TR J B RUSSELL TV J S ROBERTS, S J OWEN NSM L GEOGHEGAN

BERKHAMSTED, LITTLE (St Andrew) and Bayford, Essendon and Ponsbourne *St Alb 19* P *Marquess of Salisbury (2 turns), CPAS (1 turn), and Bp (1 turn)* R T T MUSIWACHO

BERKHAMSYTCH (St Mary and St John) *see* Butterton, Ipstones-w-Berkhamsytch etc *Lich*

BERKLEY (Blessed Virgin Mary) *see* Beckington w Standerwick, Berkley, Rodden etc *B & W*

BERKSWELL (St John the Baptist) *Cov 4* P *Trustees Col C J H Wheatley* R M Q BRATTON

BERMONDSEY (St Hugh) Charterhouse Mission Conventional District *S'wark 10* Min M G RAWSON

BERMONDSEY (St James w Christ Church) (St Anne) *S'wark 7* P *Bp, R Bermondsey St Mary, and F W Smith Esq (3 turns), The Crown (1 turn)* V G J JENKINS C J L C MERCER NSM S O LEWIS

BERMONDSEY (St Katharine) w St Bartholomew *S'wark 7* P *Bp and R Rotherhithe St Mary w All SS (jt)* V E J F GBONDA

BERMONDSEY (St Mary Magdalen w St Olave, St John and St Luke) *S'wark 7* P *Ch Patr Soc (2 turns), Ld Chan (1 turn), and Bp (1 turn)* R C D MOORE

BERNWODE, comprising Ashendon, Boarstall, Brill, Chilton, Dorton, Ludgershall, and Wotton Underwood *Ox 10* P *Bp, CPAS, Earl Temple of Stowe, and Sir Henry Aubrey-Fletcher Bt (jt)* R G L BEESLEY C J EDMANS

BERRICK SALOME (St Helen) *see* Chalgrove w Berrick Salome *Ox*

BERRINGTON (All Saints) *see* Wenlock *Heref*

BERROW (Blessed Virgin Mary) and Breane *B & W 1* P *Adn Wells* R J M PHILPOTT C J M A HEALEY

BERROW (St Faith) w Pendock, Eldersfield, Hollybush and Birtsmorton *Worc 2* P *Bp, D&C, and Exors Sir Berwick Lechmere Bt (jt)* R J M JAMES A E L ELSTON

BERRY POMEROY (St Mary) *see* Totnes w Bridgetown, Berry Pomeroy etc *Ex*

BERRY, GREAT (St John) *see* Langdon Hills *Chelmsf*

BERRYNARBOR (St Peter) *see* Ilfracombe SS Phil and Jas, Combe Martin and Berrynarbor *Ex*

BERSTED, NORTH (Holy Cross) *Chich 1* P *Abp* V J C KING

BERSTED, SOUTH (St Mary Magdalene) w NORTH *Chich 1*
  P *Abp* **V** T M CROOK
BERWICK (Holy Trinity) (St Mary) *Newc 12* **P** *Bp (2 turns),*
  D&C Dur (1 turn) **V** D F HANDLEY **C** T I SAMPLE, T L USHER
BERWICK (St John) *see* Chalke Valley *Sarum*
BERWICK (St Michael and All Angels) *see* Arlington, Berwick,
  Selmeston w Alciston etc *Chich*
BERWICK ST JAMES (St James) *see* Wylye and Till Valley
  Sarum
BERWICK, LITTLE (not known) Shrewsbury *Lich 19*
  I *vacant*
BESFORD (St Peter's Chapelry) *see* Defford w Besford *Worc*
BESSACARR, WEST (St Francis of Assisi) *Sheff 8* **P** *Bp*
  V R A HEARD **C** S S MCHUGH
BESSELSLEIGH (St Lawrence) *Ox 19* **P** *Ox Ch Trust*
  R P V PARKER
BESSINGBY (St Magnus) *see* Bridlington Ch Ch w Bessingby
  and Ulrome *York*
BESSINGBY (St Mark) *as above*
BESSINGHAM (St Mary) *see* Roughton and Felbrigg, Metton,
  Sustead etc *Nor*
BESTHORPE (All Saints) *see* Attleborough w Besthorpe *Nor*
BESTHORPE (Holy Trinity) *see* E Trent *S'well*
BESTWOOD (Emmanuel) (St Mark) w Rise Park *S'well 8*
  P *Bp and Ch Patr Trust (jt)* **V** N J BATES **C** C LITTLE
BESTWOOD (St Matthew on the Hill) (St Philip) *S'well 8*
  P *Bp and Ch Patr Trust (jt)* **V** *vacant*
BESTWOOD PARK (no dedication) *S'well 8* **P** *Bp and Ch*
  Patr Trust (jt) **V** *vacant*
BESWICK (St Margaret) *see* Hutton Cranswick w Skerne,
  Watton and Beswick *York*
BETCHWORTH (St Michael and All Angels) and Buckland
  S'wark 24 **P** *D&C Windsor and All So Coll Ox (jt)*
  R A MOORE
BETHERSDEN (St Margaret) w High Halden and
  Woodchurch *Cant 10* **P** *Abp* **R** S E ROSE
BETHESDA (Shared Church) *see* Hallwood Ecum Par *Ches*
BETHNAL GREEN (St Barnabas) *Lon 7* **P** *D&C Cant*
  V B C RALPH **NSM** S M LEE
BETHNAL GREEN (St James the Less) *Lon 7* **P** *CPAS*
  V C D NEWMAN-DAY
BETHNAL GREEN (St John) *see* St Jo on Bethnal Green *Lon*
BETHNAL GREEN (St Matthew w St James the Great) *Lon 7*
  P *Bp* **R** E M CLARK **NSM** J E BLACKBURN
BETHNAL GREEN (St Peter) (St Thomas) *Lon 7* **P** *City Corp*
  V H M A ATKINSON **NSM** A J MULROY
BETLEY (St Margaret) *Lich 9* **P** *DBP* **V** T J WATSON
  C J J BESWICK PALLISTER **NSM** G A BAILEY
BETTISCOMBE (St Stephen) *see* Golden Cap Team *Sarum*
BETTON STRANGE (St Margaret) *see* Wenlock *Heref*
BETTWS-Y-CRWYN (St Mary) *see* Clun Valley *Heref*
BEVENDEAN (Holy Nativity) *see* Moulsecoomb w Bevendean
  and Coldean *Chich*
BEVERLEY (St John and St Martin) w Routh All Saints *York 8*
  P *Patr Bd* **R** J W BAKER **C** T P KELLY, W A WALE
BEVERLEY (St Mary) *York 8* **P** *Abp* **V** R A LUMLEY
BEVERLEY (St Nicholas) *York 8* **P** *Abp* **V** M R PEATMAN
BEVERLEY MINSTER (St John and St Martin) *see* Beverley
  St Jo and St Martin w Routh All SS *York*
BEVERSTON (St Mary the Virgin) *see* Tetbury, Beverston,
  Long Newnton etc *Glouc*
BEWBUSH (St Mary Magdalene) *see* Gossops Green and
  Bewbush *Chich*
BEWCASTLE (St Cuthbert), Stapleton and Kirklinton w
  Hethersgill *Carl 2* **P** *Bp, D&C, and DBP (jt)*
  P-in-c R P C BROWN
BEWDLEY (St Anne) *see* Ribbesford w Bewdley and Dowles
  and Wribbenhall *Worc*
BEWERLEY GRANGE (Chapel) *see* Upper Nidderdale *Leeds*
BEWHOLME (St John the Baptist) *see* Sigglesthorne w
  Nunkeeling and Bewholme *York*
BEWICK, OLD (Holy Trinity) *see* Chatton w Chillingham,
  Eglingham and S Charlton and Ingram *Newc*
BEWSBOROUGH, comprising Barfreystone, Coldred,
  Eythorne, Sibertswold, and Whitfield *Cant 7* **P** *Abp, D&C,*
  St Jo Coll Ox, and Earl of Guilford (jt) **P-in-c** S A SHEFFIELD
BEXHILL (All Saints) *see* Sidley *Chich*
BEXHILL (St Augustine) *Chich 12* **P** *Bp* **V** R COATES
BEXHILL (St Barnabas) *Chich 12* **P** *Bp* **V** *vacant*
BEXHILL (St Mark) *Chich 12* **P** *Bp* **R** J J FRAIS
BEXHILL (St Peter) (St Michael) (Good Shepherd)
  (St Andrew) *Chich 12* **P** *Bp* **TR** *vacant*
BEXHILL (St Stephen) *Chich 12* **P** *Bp* **P-in-c** K J ROBINSON
BEXLEY Team Ministry (St John the Evangelist) (St Mary)
  Roch 17 **P** *The Crown and Patr Bd (alt)* **TR** R E L HARDING

TV C M WOOD, E R BARLOW **C** M J HODDER
  NSM S E TWYNAM
BEXLEYHEATH (Christ Church) *Roch 15* **P** *Bp* **V** T WYATT
BEXLEYHEATH (St Peter) *Roch 15* **P** *Bp* **V** J R CHARLES
BEXWELL (St Mary) *see* Denver and Ryston w Roxham etc
  Ely
BEYTON (All Saints) *see* Rougham, Beyton w Hessett and
  Rushbrooke *St E*
BIBURY (St Mary) *see* S Cotswolds *Glouc*
BICESTER (St Edburg) w Bucknell, Caversfield and
  Launton *Ox 21* **P** *Patr Bd* **TR** V BREED **TV** I R BISCOE,
  P G WRIGHT **C** C S HUNT, E J BISCOE **NSM** C HILL
BICKENHILL (St Peter) *see* Hampton-in-Arden w Bickenhill
  Birm
BICKER (St Swithin) *see* Haven Gp *Linc*
BICKERSHAW (St James and St Elizabeth) *see* Wigan *Liv*
BICKERSTAFFE (Holy Trinity) *see* Aughton St Mich and
  Bickerstaffe *Liv*
BICKERTON (Holy Trinity) *see* Malpas and Threapwood and
  Bickerton *Ches*
BICKINGTON (St Andrew) *see* Fremington, Instow and
  Westleigh *Ex*
BICKINGTON (St Mary the Virgin) *see* Ashburton,
  Bickington, Buckland in the Moor etc *Ex*
BICKINGTON, HIGH (St Mary) *see* Newton Tracey, Horwood,
  Alverdiscott etc *Ex*
BICKLEIGH (St Mary) *see* Silverton, Butterleigh, Bickleigh
  and Cadeleigh *Ex*
BICKLEIGH Roborough (St Mary the Virgin) and Shaugh
  Prior *Ex 20* **P** *Patr Bd* **P-in-c** S P RUNDELL
BICKLEY (St George) *Roch 14* **P** *SMF* **V** *vacant*
BICKLEY (St Wenefrede) *Ches 5* **P** *Marquess of Cholmondeley*
  P-in-c R J DIGGLE
BICKNACRE (St Andrew) *see* Woodham Ferrers and
  Bicknacre *Chelmsf*
BICKNOLLER (St George) *see* Quantock Towers *B & W*
BICKNOR (St James) *see* Tunstall and Bredgar *Cant*
BICTON (Holy Trinity), Montford w Shrawardine and Fitz
  Lich 19 **P** *Earl of Powis, N E E Stephens Esq, and J G O*
  Wingfield Esq (jt) **P-in-c** H M LINS **C** P G ALLAN
BICTON (St Mary) *see* Budleigh Salterton, E Budleigh w
  Bicton etc *Ex*
BIDBOROUGH (St Lawrence) and Southborough St Peter
  Roch 12 **P** *CPAS Patr Trust* **R** S A HILLS **C** D M BUBB
BIDDENDEN (All Saints) and Smarden *Cant 10* **P** *Abp*
  R *vacant*
BIDDENHAM (St James) *St Alb 9* **P** *Bp* **V** E J LOMAX
BIDDESTONE (St Nicholas) *see* By Brook *Bris*
BIDDISHAM (St John the Baptist) *see* Crook Peak *B & W*
BIDDLESDEN (St Margaret) *see* W Buckingham *Ox*
BIDDULPH (St Lawrence) *Lich 8* **P** *MMCET* **V** *vacant*
BIDDULPH MOOR (Christ Church) and Knypersley *Lich 8*
  P *Ch Patr Trust and MMCET (jt)* **R** D A FRASER
BIDEFORD (St Mary), Landcross, Littleham, Monkleigh,
  and Weare Gifford *Ex 14* **P** *Patr Bd*
  TR C P ROSE-CASEMORE **TV** M COCKFIELD
  C C J HUTCHINS, S R PIRRIE **NSM** A GLOVER, K L C BEER
BIDFORD-ON-AVON (St Laurence) *see* Heart of England *Cov*
BIDSTON (St Oswald) *Ches 1* **P** *Bp* **P-in-c** J P SMITH
BIELBY (St Giles) *see* Holme and Seaton Ross *Gp York*
BIERLEY (St John the Evangelist) *Leeds 3* **P** *DBP*
  V P A WHEELHOUSE
BIERLEY, EAST (St Luke) *see* Birkenshaw w Hunsworth *Leeds*
BIERTON (St James the Great) and Hulcott *Ox 10* **P** *Bp and*
  D&C Linc (jt) **P-in-c** D E BEESLEY
BIGBURY (St Lawrence) *see* Modbury, Bigbury, Ringmore etc
  Ex
BIGBY (All Saints) *see* Brocklesby Park, Croxton and North
  Wolds *Linc*
BIGGIN (St Thomas) *see* Taddington, Chelmorton and
  Monyash etc *Derby*
BIGGIN HILL (St Mark) *Roch 16* **P** *Bp* **V** A M NEWMAN
  C R L ARCHER
BIGGLESWADE (St Andrew) *St Alb 10* **P** *Bp*
  V E J OGLESBY-ELONG
BIGHTON (All Saints) *see* Arle Valley *Win*
BIGNOR (Holy Cross) *see* Barlavington, Burton w Coates,
  Sutton and Bignor *Chich*
BIGRIGG (St John) *see* Egremont and Haile *Carl*
BILBOROUGH (St John) (St Martin) and Strelley *S'well 8*
  P *SMF and Bp (jt)* **P-in-c** R T K ATKINSON **C** J SAVILL,
  P W SHAW **NSM** D WATKINSON
BILBROOK (Holy Cross) *see* Tettenhall Regis *Lich*
BILBROUGH (St James) *see* Marston Moor *York*
BILDESTON (St Mary Magdalene) w Wattisham and
  Lindsey, Whatfield w Semer, Nedging and Naughton

St E 4 **P** *Abp, Bp, CPAS, Jes Coll Cam, and Reformation Ch Trust (jt)* **R** E B E CATTERMOLE

BILHAM, comprising Brodsworth, Frickley, Hooton Pagnell, and Marr *Sheff 12* **P** *Bp, Major W Warde-Aldam, W G A Warde-Norbury Esq, and Mrs S Grant-Dalton (jt)* **P-in-c** K HERROD

BILLERICAY (Christ Church) (Emmanuel) (St John the Divine) (St Mary Magdalen) and Little Burstead *Chelmsf 11* **P** *Bp* **TR** P A CARR **TV** R C A HANKEY **NSM** M J FOWLER

BILLESDON (St John the Baptist) *see Coplow Leic*

BILLESLEY COMMON (Holy Cross) *Birm 2* **P** *Bp* **V** D M COLLINS **NSM** C L CHALMERS

BILLING, GREAT (St Andrew) w LITTLE (All Saints) *Pet 4* **P** *BNC Ox and Bp (alt)* **R** R J BURBIDGE **Hon C** D LUNN

BILLINGBOROUGH Group, The (St Andrew), including Aslackby, Dowsby, Horbling, and Sempringham w Pointon *Linc 14* **P** *The Crown (2 turns), Bp and St Jo Coll Dur (1 turn)* **OLM** J G SPREADBURY

BILLINGE (St Aidan) *see Wigan Liv*

BILLINGFORD (St Leonard) *see Redenhall w Scole Nor*

BILLINGFORD (St Peter) *see Heart of Norfolk Nor*

BILLINGHAM (St Aidan) (St Cuthbert) (St John) (St Mary Magdalene) (St Peter) *Dur 8* **P** *Patr Bd* **TV** R B RADLEY **NSM** P J JOHNSON

BILLINGHAY (St Michael) *see Carr Dyke Gp Linc*

BILLINGSHURST (St Mary) *Chich 10* **P** *Bp* **V** D M BEAL

BILLINGSLEY (St Mary) *see Highley w Billingsley, Glazeley etc Heref*

BILLINGTON (St Michael and All Angels) *see Ouzel Valley St Alb*

BILLOCKBY (All Saints) *see S Trin Broads Nor*

BILLY MILL (St Aidan) *Newc 5* **P** *Bp* **V** vacant

BILNEY, EAST (St Mary) *see Dereham and Distr Nor*

BILSBORROW (St Hilda) *see Fellside Team Blackb*

BILSBY (Holy Trinity) *see Alford Gp Linc*

BILSDALE MIDCABLE (St John) *see Upper Ryedale York*

BILSDALE PRIORY (St Hilda) *see Ingleby Greenhow, Bilsdale Priory etc York*

BILSINGTON (St Peter and St Paul) *see Saxon Shoreline Cant*

BILSON (Mission Church) *see Cinderford w Littledean Glouc*

BILSTHORPE (St Margaret) *S'well 3* **P** *DBP* **P-in-c** Z BURTON **NSM** M A GROVES

BILSTON (St Leonard) (St Chad) (St Mary the Virgin) *Lich 27* **P** *Patr Bd* **TV** S P SKIDMORE

BILTON (St John the Evangelist) and St Luke *Leeds 18* **P** *Bp* **TR** S P DOWSON **TV** A PATRICK **C** L M MARTIN

BILTON (St Mark) *Cov 6* **P** N M Assheton Esq **R** T D COCKELL **C** J E SMITH **NSM** G F LOWDE

BILTON IN HOLDERNESS (St Peter) *York 12* **P** *Abp* **V** W J BRADLEY

BILTON, NEW (St Matthew and St Oswald) *see Rugby W Cov*

BILTON-IN-AINSTY (St Helen) *see Rural Ainsty York*

BINBROOK Group, The (St Mary), including Kelstern, Ludford Magna, Swinhope, Thorganby, and Wold Newton *Linc 15* **P** *Ld Chan, DBP and G F Sleight Esq (alt)* **R** P J MCEUNE

BINCOMBE (Holy Trinity) *see Weymouth Ridgeway Sarum*

BINEGAR (Holy Trinity) *see Beacon Trinity B & W*

BINFIELD (All Saints) (St Mark) *Ox 3* **P** *Ld Chan* **R** L A J TAYLOR **NSM** S A MORTIMER

BINGFIELD (St Mary) *see St Oswald in Lee w Bingfield Newc*

BINGHAM (St Mary and All Saints) *S'well 5* **P** *The Crown* **R** J J G WRIGHT

BINGLEY (All Saints) *Leeds 1* **P** *Bp* **V** M G WEAVER **C** R H DOWSON

BINGLEY (Holy Trinity) *Leeds 1* **P** *Bp* **V** A J CLARKE

BINHAM (St Mary) *see Stiffkey and Bale Nor*

BINLEY (St Bartholomew) *Cov 1* **P** *Bp* **V** J P TAYLOR **NSM** R W BROMLEY

BINSEY (St Margaret) *see Osney Ox*

BINSEY Team Ministry, comprising Allhallows, Bassenthwaite, Bolton All Saints, Ireby, Isel, Plumbland, Setmurthy, Torpenhow, Uldale, and Wythop *Carl 6* **P** *Patr Bd* **TR** S J BANKS **TV** P W GILROY **NSM** C C FRYER-SPEDDING

BINSTEAD (Holy Cross) *Portsm 7* **P** *Bp* **R** vacant

BINSTED (Holy Cross) *see Bentley, Binsted and Froyle Win*

BINSTED (St Mary) *see Walberton w Binsted Chich*

BINTON (St Peter) *see Heart of England Cov*

BINTREE (St Swithin) *see Heart of Norfolk Nor*

BIRCH (St James) w Fallowfield *Man 2* **P** *Bp* **R** R M YOUNG **NSM** J WALKER

BIRCH (St Mary) *see Langley Man*

BIRCHAM NEWTON (All Saints) *see Docking, The Birchams, Fring etc Nor*

BIRCHAM, GREAT (St Mary the Virgin) *as above*

BIRCHANGER (St Mary the Virgin) *see Stansted Mountfitchet w Birchanger and Farnham Chelmsf*

BIRCHENCLIFFE (St Philip the Apostle) *see Birkby and Birchencliffe Leeds*

BIRCHES HEAD (St Matthew) *see Hanley H Ev Lich*

BIRCHFIELD (Holy Trinity) *Birm 1* **P** *Bp* **V** E I PITTS

BIRCHILLS, THE (St Andrew) *see Walsall St Andr Lich*

BIRCHIN COPPICE (St Peter) *see Kidderminster St Jo and H Innocents Worc*

BIRCHINGTON (All Saints) w Acol and Minnis Bay *Cant 5* **P** *Abp* **P-in-c** M P HAM

BIRCH-IN-RUSHOLME (St Agnes) w Longsight St John w St Cyprian *Man 1* **P** *The Crown and Bp (alt)* **R** vacant

BIRCHMOOR (St John) *see Polesworth Birm*

BIRCHOVER (St Michael) *see Youlgreave, Middleton, Stanton-in-Peak etc Derby*

BIRCHWOOD (Mission Church) *see Blackdown B & W*

BIRCHWOOD (St Luke) *Linc 11* **P** *Bp* **V** L M HARRIS

BIRCHWOOD (Transfiguration) *see Warrington E Liv*

BIRCLE (St John the Baptist) *Man 4* **P** *R Middleton St Leon* **V** H T NICOL

BIRDBROOK (St Augustine) *see Two Rivers Chelmsf*

BIRDHAM (St James) *see W Wittering and Birdham w Itchenor Chich*

BIRDINGBURY (St Leonards) *see Draycote Gp Cov*

BIRDLIP (St Mary in Hamlet) *see Brimpsfield w Birdlip, Syde, Daglingworth etc Glouc*

BIRDSALL (St Mary) *see W Buckrose York*

BIRKBY (St Cuthbert) Huddersfield and Birchencliffe *Leeds 9* **P** *V Lindley and Bp (jt)* **V** J P HUSTWICK **C** R E FORT

BIRKBY (St John the Evangelist) Huddersfield and Woodhouse *Leeds 9* **P** *Bp and DBP (jt)* **P-in-c** C P TYLER

BIRKBY (St Peter) *see Wiske Benefice Leeds*

BIRKDALE (St James) *Liv 9* **P** *Trustees* **C** B J DYER

BIRKDALE (St John) *Liv 9* **P** *Trustees* **V** vacant

BIRKDALE (St Peter) *Liv 9* **P** *Trustees* **C** B J DYER

BIRKENHEAD (Christ Church) *Ches 1* **P** *Bp* **P-in-c** G V TETZLAFF **NSM** A W GOODE

BIRKENHEAD (St James) w St Bede *Ches 1* **P** *Trustees* **V** K P ADDENBROOKE

BIRKENHEAD PRIORY (Christ the King) *Ches 1* **P** *Patr Bd* **R** P N BENTLEY **C** D M WILKINSON

BIRKENSHAW (St Paul) w Hunsworth *Leeds 7* **P** *V Birstall* **P-in-c** K NICHOLL **OLM** R DAVIDSON

BIRKIN (St Mary) *see Haddlesey w Hambleton and Birkin York*

BIRLEY (St Peter) *see Canon Pyon w King's Pyon, Birley and Wellington Heref*

BIRLING (All Saints), Addington, Ryarsh and Trottiscliffe *Roch 7* **P** *Bp* **R** vacant

BIRLING, LOWER (Christ Church) *see Snodland All SS w Ch Ch Roch*

BIRLINGHAM (St James the Great) *see Pershore w Pinvin, Wick and Birlingham Worc*

BIRMINGHAM (Bishop Latimer w All Saints) *Birm 1* **P** *St Martin's Trustees* **R** vacant

BIRMINGHAM (St George w St Michael) *see Edgbaston St Geo Birm*

BIRMINGHAM (St George) *see Lozells and Newtown Birm*

BIRMINGHAM (St John the Evangelist) *see Ladywood St Jo and St Pet Birm*

BIRMINGHAM (St Luke) *Birm 1* **P** *Trustees* **P-in-c** T D L HUGHES **C** A E HERBERT, K V H STOCK, N J DRAKE, T W BATEMAN

BIRMINGHAM (St Martin-in-the-Bull-Ring) w Bordesley St Andrew *Birm 1* **P** *St Martin's Trustees* **R** J R ALLCOCK **C** I D E LEWIS, M CHURCHOUSE **NSM** E BLAIR-CHAPPELL

BIRMINGHAM (St Paul) *Birm 1* **P** *St Martin's Trustees* **V** D R TOMLINSON **NSM** C M M CHITHAM-MOSLEY

BIRSTALL (St James the Great) and Wanlip *Leic 4* **P** *Bp and C A Palmer-Tomkinson Esq (jt)* **R** A H DIGMAN

BIRSTALL (St Peter) *Leeds 7* **P** *Bp* **P-in-c** J H DAVIS

BIRSTWITH (St James) *see Hampsthwaite and Killinghall and Birstwith Leeds*

BIRTLES (St Catherine) *see Alderley w Birtles Ches*

BIRTLEY (St Giles) *see Chollerton w Birtley and Thockrington Newc*

BIRTLEY (St John the Evangelist) *Dur 9* **P** *R Chester le Street* **V** E G LLOYD

BIRTSMORTON (St Peter and St Paul) *see Berrow w Pendock, Eldersfield, Hollybush etc Worc*

BISBROOKE (St John the Baptist) *see Lyddington, Bisbrooke, Caldecott, Glaston etc Pet*

BISCATHORPE (St Helen) *see Asterby Gp Linc*

BISCOT (Holy Trinity) *St Alb 12*   **P** *Bp*   **V** T B SINGH

BISHAM (All Saints) *see* Gt Marlow w Marlow Bottom, Lt Marlow and Bisham *Ox*

BISHAMPTON (St James) *see* Abberton, The Flyfords, Naunton Beauchamp etc *Worc*

BISHOP AUCKLAND (St Andrew) (St Anne) *Dur 3*   **P** *The Crown and Bp (alt)*   **V** M P KEDDILTY   **C** S A PRICE

BISHOP BURTON (All Saints) *see* Walkington, Bishop Burton, Rowley etc *York*

BISHOP CAUNDLE (not known) *see* Three Valleys *Sarum*

BISHOP MIDDLEHAM (St Michael) *see* Upper Skerne *Dur*

BISHOP MONKTON (St John the Baptist) *see* Ripon Cathl Benefice *Leeds*

BISHOP NORTON (St Peter), Waddingham and Snitterby *Linc 8*   **P** *Bp and The Crown (alt)*   **R** K E COLWELL   **NSM** P J DICKINSON

BISHOP SUTTON (Holy Trinity) *see* Clutton w Cameley, Bishop Sutton and Stowey *B & W*

BISHOP THORNTON (St John the Evangelist), Burnt Yates, Markington, Ripley and South Stainley *Leeds 20*   **P** *Sir Thomas Ingilby Bt*   **R** P R HARFORD   **NSM** L M C BOON

BISHOP WILTON (St Edith) *see* Garrowby Hill *York*

BISHOPHILL JUNIOR (St Mary) *see* York St Clem w St Mary Bishophill *York*

BISHOPHILL SENIOR (St Clement w St Mary) *as above*

BISHOP'S CANNINGS (St Mary the Virgin) *see* Cannings and Redhorn *Sarum*

BISHOP'S CASTLE (St John the Baptist) w Mainstone, Lydbury North and Edgton *Heref 9*   **P** *Earl of Powis (3 turns), Ld Chan (1 turn), and Mrs R E Bell (1 turn)*   **P-in-c** S A C FOUNTAIN   **NSM** J W DANIELS

BISHOP'S CLEEVE (St Michael and All Angels) and Woolstone w Gotherington and Oxenton *Glouc 9*   **P** *Patr Bd*   **TR** M ALLEN

BISHOP'S FROME (St Mary the Virgin) *see* Frome Valley *Heref*

BISHOP'S HATFIELD (St Etheldreda) (St Luke) (St John) (St Michael and All Angels), Lemsford and North Mymms *St Alb 18*   **P** *Patr Bd*   **TR** D V COLLINS   **TV** A N GARDNER, R BARR   **C** K ALFORD, L A COLLINGRIDGE   **Hon C** R CHAPMAN   **NSM** F C SOUTER, P J THOMSON, S M STILWELL

BISHOP'S HULL (St John the Evangelist) *see* Taunton St Mary and St Jo *B & W*

BISHOP'S HULL (St Peter and St Paul) *B & W 18*   **P** *Adn Taunton*   **V** P J HUGHES

BISHOP'S ITCHINGTON (St Michael) *Cov 10*   **P** *Bp*   **P-in-c** M C GREEN

BISHOP'S LAVINGTON (All Saints) *see* The Lavingtons, Cheverells, and Easterton *Sarum*

BISHOP'S LYDEARD (Blessed Virgin Mary) w Lydeard St Lawrence, Bagborough, Combe Florey and Cothelstone *B & W 19*   **P** *Bp, D&C, W H J Hancock Esq, and Mrs P M G Mitford (jt)*   **P-in-c** M T HURLEY

BISHOP'S STORTFORD (Holy Trinity) *St Alb 15*   **P** *Bp*   **NSM** R P MOATE

BISHOP'S STORTFORD (St Michael) *St Alb 15*   **P** *Bp*   **V** D G WILLIAMS

BISHOP'S SUTTON (St Nicholas) and Ropley and West Tisted *Win 1*   **P** *Peache Trustees*   **P-in-c** C WELHAM

BISHOP'S TACHBROOK (St Chad) *Cov 11*   **P** *Bp*   **V** *vacant*

BISHOPS TAWTON (St John the Baptist) *see* Newport and Bishops Tawton *Ex*

BISHOP'S WALTHAM (St Peter) *Portsm 1*   **P** *Bp*   **R** J C HUNT   **NSM** J BELOE, K F WICKERT

BISHOPS WOOD (St John the Evangelist) *Lich 2*   **P** *V Brewood*   **V** P MOON

BISHOP'S WOOD (St Mary) *see* Elmley Lovett w Hampton Lovett and Elmbridge w Rushock and Hartlebury and Ombersley w Doverdale *Worc*

BISHOPSBOURNE (St Mary) *see* Barham Downs w Adisham *Cant*

BISHOPSNYMPTON (St Mary the Virgin), Charles, East Anstey, High Bray, Knowstone, Mariansleigh, Molland, North Molton w Twitchen, Rose Ash, and West Anstey *Ex 17*   **P** *Patr Bd*   **TR** D P BAKER   **TV** A G FORMAN   **NSM** P A LAWSON   **OLM** A J ROGERS

BISHOPSTEIGNTON (St John the Baptist) *see* Teignmouth, Ideford w Luton, Ashcombe etc *Ex*

BISHOPSTOKE (St Mary) (St Paul) *Win 10*   **P** *Bp*   **R** R E WISE

BISHOPSTON (Church of the Good Shepherd) *see* Bishopston and St Andrews *Bris*

BISHOPSTON (St Michael and All Angels) *as above*

BISHOPSTON (St Michael and All Angels) (Church of the Good Shepherd) and St Andrews *Bris 3*   **P** *Patr Bd*   **P-in-c** J C W STEVENSON   **TV** W P MASSEY   **NSM** B J PULLAN

BISHOPSTONE (St Lawrence) *see* Magnis Gp *Heref*

BISHOPSTONE (St Mary the Virgin) *see* Lyddington and Wanborough and Bishopstone etc *Bris*

BISHOPSTONE (St Andrew) *see* E Blatchington and Bishopstone *Chich*

BISHOPSTONE (St John the Baptist) *see* Chalke Valley *Sarum*

BISHOPSTROW (St Aldhelm) *see* River Were *Sarum*

BISHOPSWOOD (All Saints) *see* Wye Reaches Gp *Heref*

BISHOPSWORTH (St Peter) and Bedminster Down *Bris 1*   **P** *Bp*   **TR** T R J GODDEN

BISHOPTHORPE (St Andrew) *York 1*   **P** *Abp*   **P-in-c** S L BRAY   **C** J K DAY

BISHOPTON (St Peter) *see* Stockton Country Par *Dur*

BISHOPWEARMOUTH (Good Shepherd) *Dur 14*   **P** *Bp*   **P-in-c** B SKELTON

BISHOPWEARMOUTH (St Gabriel) *Dur 14*   **P** *V Sunderland*   **V** *vacant*

BISHOPWEARMOUTH (St Luke Pallion) *see* Millfield St Mark and Pallion St Luke *Dur*

BISHOPWEARMOUTH (St Mary) *see* Millfield St Mary *Dur*

BISHOPWEARMOUTH (St Nicholas) (Christ Church) *Dur 14*   **P** *Bp*   **V** *vacant*

BISLEY (All Saints), Chalford, France Lynch, and Oakridge and Bussage w Eastcombe *Glouc 4*   **P** *Ld Chan (1 turn), Bp and Adn (1 turn)*   **V** S J MURRAY

BISLEY (St John the Baptist) and West End (Holy Trinity) *Guildf 6*   **P** *Bp*   **R** F E SIMON

BISPHAM (All Hallows) *Blackb 8*   **P** *Ch Soc Trust*   **R** J W S LEE   **C** J R H CRAWFORD

BISTERNE (St Paul) *see* Ringwood w Ellingham and Harbridge etc *Win*

BITCHFIELD (St Mary Magdalene) *see* Corby Glen Par *Linc*

BITTADON (St Peter) *see* Ilfracombe, Lee, Woolacombe, Bittadon etc *Ex*

BITTERING PARVA (St Peter and St Paul) *see* Launditch and the Upper Nar *Nor*

BITTERLEY (St Mary) *see* Bromfield *Heref*

BITTERNE (Holy Saviour) *Win 13*   **P** *Bp*   **V** A P S PALMER

BITTERNE PARK (All Hallows) (Ascension) *Win 13*   **P** *Bp*   **V** S J ROBERTSON   **C** M J ALLEZ, P N GOODALL

BITTESWELL (St Mary) *see* Lutterworth w Cotesbach and Bitteswell *Leic*

BITTON (St Mary) *see* Warmley, Syston and Bitton *Bris*

BIX (St James) *see* Nettlebed w Bix, Highmoor, Pishill etc *Ox*

BIXLEY (St Wandregesilus) *see* Poringland *Nor*

BLABY (All Saints) *Leic 7*   **P** *Bp*   **P-in-c** J C MICKLETHWAITE

BLACK BOURTON (St Mary the Virgin) *Ox 28*   **P** *Ch Ch Ox*   **V** T KUIN LAWTON

BLACK COMBE, Drigg, Eskdale, Irton, Muncaster and Waberthwaite *Carl 5*   **P** *Bp, Adn W Cumberland, Mrs I Frost-Pennington, the Hon J N Lowther, P Stanley Esq, and DBP (jt)*   **C** A M OVERTON-BENGE

BLACK MOUNTAINS Group, The, comprising Craswall, Clodock, Llanveynoe, Longtown, Michaelchurch Escley, Newton, and St Margaret's *Heref 1*   **P** *DBP (2 turns), MMCET (1 turn)*   **V** N G LOWTON

BLACK NOTLEY (St Peter and St Paul), Great Notley and Rayne *Chelmsf 16*   **P** *St Jo Coll Cam and DBP (jt)*   **V** R E M PRIOR   **OLM** R H KUKIEWICZ

BLACK TORRINGTON (St Mary) *see* Ashwater, Halwill, Beaworthy, Clawton etc *Ex*

BLACKAWTON (St Michael) *see* Stoke Fleming, Blackawton, Strete and E Allington *Ex*

BLACKBIRD LEYS (Holy Family) *Ox 1*   **P** *Bp*   **V** H R CARTER

BLACKBOURNE, comprising Ampton, Bardwell, Barnham, Euston, Fakenham Magna, Great Livermere, Honington, Ingham, Ixworth, Ixworth Thorpe, and Troston *St E 5*   **P** *Patr Bd*   **TR** K BURTON   **NSM** L J NORBURN

BLACKBROOK (St Paul) *see* Parr *Liv*

BLACKBURN (Christ Church w St Matthew) *Blackb 2*   **P** *Bp*   **V** A RAYNES

BLACKBURN (Holy Trinity Worship Centre) *see* N and E Blackb *Blackb*

BLACKBURN (St Aidan) (St Luke) St Mark and St Philip *Blackb 2*   **P** *Bp and V Blackb (jt)*   **V** C E BROOKS   **C** J M GARDNER   **NSM** B D PECK

BLACKBURN (St Barnabas) *Blackb 2*   **P** *Bp*   **V** *vacant*

BLACKBURN (St Gabriel) *Blackb 2*   **P** *Bp*   **V** S P CORBETT

BLACKBURN (St Jude) *see* N and E Blackb *Blackb*

BLACKBURN (St Luke) *see* Blackb St Aid, St Luke, St Mark and St Phil *Blackb*

BLACKBURN (St Michael and All Angels) *see* N and E Blackb *Blackb*

BLACKBURN (St Silas) *Blackb 2*   **P** *Trustees*   **P-in-c** S M ASTON

BLACKBURN (St Stephen) (St James) *Blackb 2* **P** *Bp, DBP, and Exors the Ven C W D Carroll (jt)* **V** S S GILL
NSM J C MACHOLC
BLACKBURN The Redeemer (St Bartholomew) (The Saviour) *Blackb 2* **P** *Bp and CPAS (jt)* **V** C D ANDERTON
BLACKBURN, NORTH and EAST (St Jude) (St Michael and All Angels) (Holy Trinity Worship Centre) *Blackb 2* **P** *V Blackb, J Whittaker Esq, and Mrs V Edge (jt)* **P-in-c** N J HEALE
BLACKDOWN (Holy Trinity) *see* Beaminster Area *Sarum*
BLACKDOWN Benefice, The, comprising Buckland St Mary, Churchstanton, Corfe, Otterford, and Pitminster *B & W 16* **P** *DBP (4 turns), Pitminster PCC and Corfe PCC (1 turn)* **R** J A FALLON **C** N D JERRETT
BLACKFEN (Good Shepherd) *see* Lamorbey H Redeemer *Roch*
BLACKFORD (Holy Trinity) *see* Isle of Wedmore *B & W*
BLACKFORD (St John the Baptist) *see* Rockcliffe and Blackford *Carl*
BLACKFORD (St Michael) *see* Camelot Par *B & W*
BLACKFORDBY (St Margaret) and Woodville *Leic 8* **P** *Bp* **V** *vacant*
BLACKHALL (St Andrew), Castle Eden and Monkhesleden *Dur 10* **P** *Bp* **P-in-c** K G MCNEIL
BLACKHAM (All Saints) *see* Withyham St Mich *Chich*
BLACKHEATH (All Saints) *S'wark 4* **P** *V Lewisham St Mary* **V** N W S CRANFIELD **Hon C** T W CHATTERTON
BLACKHEATH (Ascension) *see* Deptford St Jo w H Trin and Ascension *S'wark*
BLACKHEATH (St John the Evangelist) *S'wark 1* **P** *CPAS* **V** E F A L SCRASE-FIELD **C** C W A HANNING
NSM A M BESWETHERICK
BLACKHEATH (St Martin) *see* Wonersh w Blackheath *Guildf*
BLACKHEATH (St Paul) *Birm 3* **P** *Bp* **C** A ANEES
BLACKHEATH PARK (St Michael and All Saints) *S'wark 1* **P** *Bp* **V** A R CHRISTIE **C** T T AJAYI
BLACKLAND (St Peter) *see* Marden Vale *Sarum*
BLACKLANDS Hastings (Christchurch and St Andrew) *Chich 15* **P** *Ch Patr Trust* **P-in-c** C M HILL
BLACKLEY (Holy Trinity) *Man 1* **P** *Bp* **R** P HUTCHINS
BLACKLEY (St Andrew) *Man 1* **P** *Bp* **P-in-c** E M ROBERTS
C J P WISDOM **NSM** A D SMITH, C NIGHTINGALE
OLM J M REYNOLDS, P SMITH
BLACKLEY (St Paul) *Man 1* **P** *Bp* **P-in-c** E M ROBERTS
C J P WISDOM **NSM** A D SMITH, H TOMLINSON
OLM J M REYNOLDS, P SMITH
BLACKLEY (St Peter) *Man 1* **P** *D&C* **P-in-c** E M ROBERTS
C J P WISDOM **NSM** A D SMITH **OLM** J M REYNOLDS, P SMITH
BLACKMOOR (St Matthew) and Whitehill *Portsm 4* **P** *Bp* **V** D J CLARKE **C** A J WOOD
BLACKMORE (St Laurence) and Stondon Massey *Chelmsf 3* **P** *Bp* **V** S E BRAZIER-GIBBS
BLACKPOOL (Christ Church w All Saints) (St Andrew) *Blackb 8* **P** *Bp and Trustees (jt)* **P-in-c** A K WOLTON
BLACKPOOL (Holy Cross) South Shore *Blackb 8* **P** *Bp* **V** M FISH
BLACKPOOL (Holy Trinity) *see* S Shore H Trin *Blackb*
BLACKPOOL (St Christopher) *see* Hawes Side and Marton Moss *Blackb*
BLACKPOOL (St John) *Blackb 8* **P** *Trustees* **V** *vacant*
BLACKPOOL (St Mark) *see* Layton and Staining *Blackb*
BLACKPOOL (St Mary) South Shore *Blackb 8* **P** *Bp* **P-in-c** L H A PEARSON
BLACKPOOL (St Michael and All Angels) *see* Layton and Staining *Blackb*
BLACKPOOL (St Nicholas) *see* Hawes Side and Marton Moss *Blackb*
BLACKPOOL (St Paul's Worship Centre) *Blackb 8* **P** *Trustees* **P-in-c** D A PREST **NSM** J L PARKER
BLACKPOOL (St Peter) *see* S Shore St Pet *Blackb*
BLACKPOOL (St Stephen on the Cliffs) *Blackb 8* **P** *Bp, R Bispham All Hallows, and Ch Wardens (jt)* **V** A G SAGE
BLACKPOOL (St Thomas) *Blackb 8* **P** *CPAS* **V** D O'BRIEN **C** E J SWARBRICK
BLACKPOOL (St Wilfrid) Mereside *Blackb 8* **P** *Bp* **P-in-c** L M TOMKINSON
BLACKROD (St Katharine), Daisy Hill, Westhoughton and Wingates *Man 3* **P** *Patr Bd* **TR** C H PHARAOH
TV A D WYNNE **C** A L JONES, M J WEARING
BLACKTHORN CHASE, comprising Beachampton, Thorn w Nash, Thornborough, and Whaddon *Ox 11* **P** *Adn Buckingham, G&C Coll Cam, and Ms E Railson (jt)* **R** J M DOVE **NSM** J F KING
BLACKTOFT (Holy Trinity) *see* Howden *York*
BLACKWATER, NORTH, comprising Salcott Virley, Tollesbury, Tolleshunt d'Arcy, and Tolleshunt Major *Chelmsf 23* **P** *Patr*

Bd **P-in-c** T L CASWELL **C** S C J CLARE
NSM S M GODSMARK
BLACKWELL (All Saints) and Salutation *Dur 5* **P** *Bp* **V** J S CROFT **C** K C LONG **NSM** S C JAY
BLACKWELL (St Catherine) *see* The Lickey *Birm*
BLACKWELL (St Werburgh) w Tibshelf *Derby 2* **P** *Bp and MMCET (jt)* **V** G MANLEY **NSM** S L MASON
OLM D HESKETH
BLADON (St Martin) *see* Woodstock and Bladon *Ox*
BLAGDON (St Andrew) w Compton Martin and Ubley *B & W 7* **P** *Bp and Sir John Wills Bt (jt)* **R** S W LEWIS
BLAGREAVES (St Andrew) *Derby 5* **P** *Bp, Churchwardens, and CPAS (jt)* **P-in-c** A C M DRING **C** R BROOKS
BLAISDON (St Michael and All Angels) *see* Westbury-on-Severn w Flaxley, Blaisdon etc *Glouc*
BLAKEDOWN (St James the Great) *see* Churchill-in-Halfshire w Blakedown and Broome *Worc*
BLAKEMERE (St Leonard) *see* Cusop w Blakemere, Bredwardine w Brobury etc *Heref*
BLAKENALL HEATH (Christ Church) *Lich 24* **P** *Patr Bd* **TR** *vacant*
BLAKENEY (All Saints) *see* Newnham w Awre and Blakeney *Glouc*
BLAKENEY (St Nicholas w St Mary and St Thomas) w Cley, Wiveton, Glandford and Letheringsett *Nor 17* **P** *Bp and Keble Coll Ox (jt)* **R** R H SAVAGE
BLAKENHAM, GREAT (St Mary) *see* Claydon *St E*
BLAKENHAM, LITTLE (St Mary) *see* Bramford w Lt Blakenham, Baylham and Nettlestead *St E*
BLAKESLEY (St Mary) *see* Lambfold *Pet*
BLANCHLAND (St Mary's Abbey) w Hunstanworth and Edmundbyers and Muggleswick *Newc 9* **P** *D E Scott-Harden Esq, Lord Crewe's Trustees and D&C (alt)* **R** H SAVAGE
BLANDFORD ST MARY (St Mary) *see* Spetisbury w Charlton Marshall etc *Sarum*
BLANKNEY (St Oswald) *see* Metheringham w Blankney and Dunston *Linc*
BLASTON (St Giles) *see* Six Saints circa Holt *Leic*
BLATCHINGTON, EAST (St John the Evangelist) (St Peter) and Bishopstone *Chich 21* **P** *Bp and Bp Lon (alt)* **R** A M C FOLKES **C** J M PADFIELD **Hon C** T C SMYTH
BLATCHINGTON, WEST (St Peter) *Chich 20* **P** *Bp* **R** T A J GAGE **NSM** J H BUTTER
BLAXHALL (St Peter) *see* Alde River *St E*
BLAYDON (St Cuthbert) *Dur 12* **P** *Bp* **P-in-c** D T H RYAN **NSM** L O GARDNER
BLEADON (St Peter and St Paul) and Bournville *B & W 10* **P** *Bp and Guild of All So (jt)* **R** T J ERRIDGE **C** P J WEBB
BLEAN (St Cosmus and St Damian) *Cant 3* **P** *Master of Eastbridge Hosp* **V** S C E LAIRD
BLEASBY (St Mary) *see* W Trent *S'well*
BLEASDALE (St Eadmor) *see* Fellside Team *Blackb*
BLEATARN (Chapel of Ease) *see* Heart of Eden *Carl*
BLECHINGLEY *see* Bletchingley and Nutfield *S'wark*
BLEDINGTON (St Leonard) *see* Broadwell, Evenlode, Oddington, Adlestrop etc *Glouc*
BLEDLOW (Holy Trinity) *see* Risborough *Ox*
BLEDLOW RIDGE (St Paul) *see* W Wycombe w Bledlow Ridge, Bradenham and Radnage *Ox*
BLENDON (St James the Great) *Roch 17* **P** *The Crown* **V** I SMITH **NSM** P A PERCIVAL
BLENDWORTH (Holy Trinity) w Chalton w Idsworth *Portsm 5* **P** *Bp* **P-in-c** V L MORGAN **NSM** J K WINDSOR
BLETCHINGDON (St Giles) *see* Akeman *Ox*
BLETCHINGLEY (St Mary) and Nutfield *S'wark 25* **P** *Em Coll Cam and Jes Coll Ox (jt)* **R** P K PAMPHILON-GREEN
NSM P J SHERRINGTON
BLETCHLEY (St Mary) St John's District Church *Ox 14* **P** *DBP* **R** D R MCDOUGALL **C** B M THORPE, P C PAVLOU, P G LANDRY, R M M CIAMPOLI **NSM** H M AKIBO-BETTS
BLETSOE (St Mary) *see* Riseley w Bletsoe *St Alb*
BLEWBURY (St Michael and All Angels) *see* The Churn *Ox*
BLICKLING (St Andrew) *see* Aylsham and Distr *Nor*
BLIDWORTH (St Mary of the Purification) w Rainworth *S'well 2* **P** *DBP and Ld Chan (alt)* **P-in-c** Z BURTON
BLIDWORTH, NEW (St Andrew) *see* Blidworth w Rainworth *S'well*
BLINDLEY HEATH (St John the Evangelist) *see* Godstone and Blindley Heath *S'wark*
BLISLAND (St Protus and St Hyacinth) *see* Camelside *Truro*
BLISWORTH (St John the Baptist), Alderton, Grafton Regis, Milton Malsor and Stoke Bruerne w Shutlanger *Pet 5* **P** *Bp, MMCET and Hyndman Trustees (2 turns), Ld Chan (1 turn)* **R** R B STAINER

BLITHFIELD (St Leonard)   *see* Abbots Bromley, Blithfield, Colton, Colwich etc *Lich*

BLO' NORTON (St Andrew)   *see* Guiltcross *Nor*

BLOCKLEY (St Peter and St Paul)   *see* Vale and Cotswold Edge *Glouc*

BLOFIELD (St Andrew and St Peter) *Nor 4*   **P** *G&C Coll Cam and Ch Soc Trust (jt)*   **R** K M BILLSON

BLOOMSBURY (St George) w Woburn Square (Christ Church) *Lon 15*   **P** *Ld Chan*   **R** D T PEEBLES   **C** J HOGAN

BLORE RAY (St Bartholomew)   *see* Calton, Cauldon, Grindon, Waterfall etc *Lich*

BLOXHAM (Our Lady of Bloxham) w Milcombe and South Newington *Ox 23*   **P** *Ex Coll Ox and Eton Coll (jt)*   **V** D R GINGRICH

BLOXHOLME (St Mary)   *see* Digby Gp *Linc*

BLOXWICH (All Saints) (Holy Ascension) *Lich 24*   **P** *Patr Bd*   **TV** C E DAVIES   **OLM** P A NESBITT

BLOXWORTH (St Andrew)   *see* Red Post *Sarum*

BLUBBERHOUSES (St Andrew)   *see* Washburn and Mid-Wharfe *Leeds*

BLUE BELL HILL (St Alban)   *see* S Chatham H Trin *Roch*

BLUNDELLSANDS (St Michael) *Liv 8*   **P** *Trustees*   **V** N R SHORT

BLUNDELLSANDS (St Nicholas) *Liv 8*   **P** *Trustees*   **V** E A ANDERSON   **NSM** K R THORNBOROUGH

BLUNDESTON (St Mary)   *see* Somerleyton, Ashby, Fritton, Herringfleet etc *Nor*

BLUNHAM (St Edmund King and Martyr and St James)   *see* Riversmeet *St Alb*

BLUNSDON (St Andrew)   *see* N Swindon St Andr *Bris*

BLUNTISHAM (St Mary) cum Earith w Colne and Holywell cum Needingworth *Ely 12*   **P** *Ch Ch Ox and Bp (jt)*   **V** S M ANTHONY   **NSM** C J YANDELL

BLURTON (St Alban)   *see* Blurton and Dresden *Lich*

BLURTON (St Bartholomew) (St Alban) and Dresden *Lich 11*   **P** *Bp*   **V** A E BRYAN

BLYBOROUGH (St Alkmund)   *see* Trentcliffe Gp *Linc*

BLYFORD (All Saints)   *see* Blyth Valley *St E*

BLYMHILL (St Mary)   *see* Watershed *Lich*

BLYTH (St Cuthbert) *Newc 1*   **P** *Bp*   **V** A A TOOBY

BLYTH (St Mary and St Martin) and Scrooby w Ranskill *S'well 1*   **P** *Bp and Trin Coll Cam (jt)*   **V** *vacant*

BLYTH (St Mary) *Newc 1*   **P** *Bp*   **V** C A MACPHERSON

BLYTH VALLEY Team Ministry, The, comprising Blyford, Bramfield, Chediston, Halesworth, Holton, Linstead Parva, Spexhall, Thorington, Walpole, Wenhaston, and Wissett *St E 15*   **P** *Patr Bd*   **TR** D J A DOBLE   **NSM** A K R ALDER, C J HELD, L M BERRY

BLYTHBURGH (Holy Trinity)   *see* Sole Bay *St E*

BLYTON (St Martin)   *see* Trentcliffe Gp *Linc*

BOARHUNT (St Nicholas)   *see* Southwick w Boarhunt *Portsm*

BOARSTALL (St James)   *see* Bernwode *Ox*

BOBBING (St Bartholomew)   *see* Sittingbourne w Bobbing *Cant*

BOBBINGTON (Holy Cross)   *see* Smestow Vale *Lich*

BOBBINGWORTH (St Germain)   *see* Fyfield, Moreton w Bobbingworth etc *Chelmsf*

BOCKING (St Mary) and Panfield *Chelmsf 16*   **P** *Abp Cant and Bp (jt)*   **P-in-c** R A M REID   **C** C M TOWNER

BOCKING (St Peter) *Chelmsf 16*   **P** *Abp Cant*   **P-in-c** T BARNES

BOCONNOC (not known)   *see* Lostwithiel Parishes *Truro*

BODDINGTON (St John the Baptist)   *see* Aston-le-Walls, Byfield, Boddington, Eydon etc *Pet*

BODDINGTON (St Mary Magdalene)   *see* Twigworth, Down Hatherley, Norton, The Leigh etc *Glouc*

BODENHAM (St Michael and All Angels)   *see* Maund Gp *Heref*

BODHAM (All Saints)   *see* Weybourne Gp *Nor*

BODIAM (St Giles) *Chich 17*   **P** *All So Coll Ox*   **P-in-c** C P IRVINE

BODICOTE (St John the Baptist) *Ox 23*   **P** *New Coll Ox*   **V** S E SHARP   **C** H N FIELDEN

BODINNICK (St John)   *see* Trelawny *Truro*

BODLE STREET GREEN (St John the Evangelist)   *see* Warbleton, Bodle Street Green and Dallington *Chich*

BODMIN (St Petroc) Team Benefice, The, including Cardynham, Lanhydrock, and Lanivet *Truro 10*   **P** *Patr Bd*   **TR** P R HOLLEY   **C** C R JONES   **NSM** C F CLEMOW, E J MUNDAY

BODNEY (St Mary)   *see* Hilborough w Bodney *Nor*

BOGNOR (St Wilfrid) *Chich 1*   **P** *Abp*   **V** J J MENNIE

BOLAM (St Andrew)   *see* Heighington and Darlington St Matt and St Luke *Dur*

BOLAM (St Andrew) w Whalton and Hartburn w Meldon *Newc 11*   **P** *Ld Chan (2 turns), J I K Walker Esq (1 turn), and D&C Dur (1 turn)*   **P-in-c** F J SAMPLE

BOLAS MAGNA (St John the Baptist)   *see* Tibberton w Bolas Magna and Waters Upton *Lich*

BOLDMERE (St Michael) *Birm 4*   **P** *Birm Dioc Trustees*   **V** R G BIRCHALL   **NSM** S R COCKS

BOLDON, The (St George) (St Nicholas) *Dur 13*   **P** *Bp (2 turns), The Crown (1 turn)*   **P-in-c** P BARKER

BOLDRE (St John the Baptist) w South Baddesley *Win 11*   **P** *Bp and Lord Teynham (jt)*   **V** S F E NEWHAM   **Hon C** A D I NEAUM   **NSM** R D C ELLIOTT

BOLDRE, EAST (St Paul)   *see* Beaulieu and Exbury and E Boldre *Win*

BOLE (St Martin)   *see* The Clays *S'well*

BOLINGBROKE (St Peter and St Paul)   *see* Bolingbroke Deanery *Linc*

BOLINGBROKE DEANERY, comprising Ashby-by-Partney, Aswardby, Bolingbroke, Candlesby, Dalby, East Keal, Eastville, Firsby, Great Steeping, Hagnaby, Halton Holgate, Hareby, Hundleby, Langton-by-Partney, Little Steeping, Lusby, Mavis Enderby, Miningsby w East Kirkby, Partney, Raithby, Sausthorpe, Scremby, Skendleby, Spilsby, Stickford, Stickney, Toynton, and West Keal *Linc 9*   **P** *Patr Bd*   **TR** P F COATES   **TV** F A JEFFRIES, T M I M MCLAUGHLIN   **NSM** J A SIMONS   **OLM** J COATES

BOLINGBROKE, NEW (St Peter)   *see* Sibsey w Frithville *Linc*

BOLLINGTON (Holy Trinity)   *see* Rostherne w Bollington *Ches*

BOLLINGTON (St Oswald) (Holy Trinity) *Ches 13*   **P** *V Prestbury*   **V** N E GOODRICH

BOLNEY (St Mary Magdalene)   *see* Cuckfield and Bolney *Chich*

BOLNHURST (St Dunstan) w Keysoe *St Alb 13*   **P** *Bp*   **P-in-c** T C WILSON

BOLSOVER (St Mary and St Laurence) *Derby 2*   **P** *Bp*   **V** R C GOULDTHORPE   **NSM** R M WILLIAMS

BOLSTERSTONE (St Mary)   *see* Cornerstone *Sheff*

BOLTBY (Holy Trinity)   *see* Felixkirk w Boltby *York*

BOLTON (All Saints)   *see* Binsey *Carl*

BOLTON (All Saints)   *see* N Westmorland *Carl*

BOLTON (Christ Church)   *see* Heaton Ch Ch w Halliwell St Marg *Man*

BOLTON (Emmanuel)   *see* W Bolton *Man*

BOLTON (St Chad)   *see* Leverhulme *Man*

BOLTON (St James w St Chrysostom) *Leeds 3*   **P** *Bp*   **Hon C** P B STOODLEY

BOLTON (St Matthew w St Barnabas)   *see* W Bolton *Man*

BOLTON (St Thomas the Apostle)   *as above*

BOLTON ABBEY (St Mary and St Cuthbert) *Leeds 21*   **P** *Duke of Devonshire*   **R** N J MERCER

BOLTON Breightmet (St James)   *see* Leverhulme *Man*

BOLTON BY BOWLAND (St Peter and St Paul)   *see* Bowland Benefice *Blackb*

BOLTON Chapel (unknown)   *see* Whittingham and Edlingham w Bolton Chapel *Newc*

BOLTON LE MOORS (St Bede) *Man 3*   **P** *Bp*   **V** V C WHITWORTH   **C** B A BRADY

BOLTON ON SWALE (St Mary)   *see* Easby w Skeeby and Brompton on Swale etc *Leeds*

BOLTON PERCY (All Saints) *York 1*   **P** *Abp*   **R** G R MUMFORD   **NSM** G M WEBB

BOLTON Top o' th' Moss (St John the Evangelist)   *see* Leverhulme *Man*

BOLTON, WEST (Emmanuel) (St Luke) (St Matthew w St Barnabas) (St Paul) (St Thomas the Apostle) *Man 3*   **P** *Patr Bd*   **TR** S TRANTER   **TV** D R PETCH, F ADMAN   **C** J O'NEILL, L A MASIH

BOLTON-LE-MOORS (St Peter) (St Philip) *Man 3*   **P** *Bp*   **V** C A BRACEGIRDLE   **C** G E HART, S D J COOK   **NSM** B S GASKELL, I M G HEPBURN, K G C NEWPORT

BOLTON-LE-SANDS (Holy Trinity) *Blackb 14*   **P** *Bp*   **V** *vacant*

BOLTONS, THE   *see* W Brompton St Mary w St Peter and St Jude *Lon*

BOLTON-UPON-DEARNE (St Andrew the Apostle) *Sheff 12*   **P** *SMF*   **P-in-c** C R SCHAEFER

BOLVENTOR (Holy Trinity)   *see* Moorland Gp *Truro*

BOMERE HEATH (Mission Room)   *see* Leaton and Albrighton w Battlefield *Lich*

BONBY (St Andrew) *Linc 8*   **P** *DBP*   **V** *vacant*

BONCHURCH (St Boniface) (St Boniface Old Church) *Portsm 7*   **P** *Ch Patr Trust*   **R** H E WRIGHT   **C** A C LAWRENCE

BONDLEIGH (St James the Apostle)   *see* Chagford, Gidleigh, Throwleigh etc *Ex*

BONINGALE (St Chad)   *see* Albrighton, Boningale and Donington *Lich*

BONNINGTON (St Rumwold)   *see* Saxon Shoreline *Cant*

BONSALL (St James the Apostle)   *see* Wirksworth *Derby*

BOOKER (Christ the Servant King)   *see* High Wycombe *Ox*

BOOKHAM, GREAT (St Nicolas) *Guildf 10* **P** *Bp*
R A D JENKINS C J K HEINE **OLM** R J MCDONALD
BOOKHAM, LITTLE (All Saints) *see* Effingham w Lt Bookham
Guildf
BOOSBECK (St Aidan) and Lingdale *York 16* **P** *Abp*
V V E M-B HAYNES
BOOTHBY GRAFFOE (St Andrew) *see* Graffoe Gp *Linc*
BOOTHBY PAGNELL (St Andrew) *see* N Beltisloe Par *Linc*
BOOTHSTOWN (St Andrew's Church Institute) *see* Worsley
Man
BOOTLE (Christ Church) *Liv 6* **P** *Bp* **V** *vacant*
BOOTLE (St Matthew w St Mary) (St Leonard) *Liv 6* **P** *Patr*
Bd C H J GOLDSMITH, P R A BRIDSON
BOOTLE (St Michael) *see* Black Combe, Drigg, Eskdale etc
Carl
BORASTON (not known) *see* Tenbury *Heref*
BORDEN (St Peter and St Paul) *Cant 15* **P** *SMF*
P-in-c R D LANE
BORDER Group of Parishes *see* Llanyblodwel,
Llanymynech, Morton and Trefonen *Lich*
BORDESLEY (St Alban the Martyr and St Patrick) *see*
Highgate *Birm*
BORDESLEY (St Benedict) *Birm 6* **P** *Keble Coll Ox* **V** *vacant*
BORDESLEY GREEN (St Paul) *see* Ward End w Bordesley
Green *Birm*
BORDON (St Mark) *Guildf 3* **P** *Bp* **V** *vacant*
BOREHAM (St Andrew) *Chelmsf 9* **P** *Bp* **P-in-c** E C A WYLIE
C D C PIERCE, J S PEARSON
BOREHAM (St John the Evangelist) *see* River Were *Sarum*
BOREHAMWOOD (All Saints) *see* Elstree and Borehamwood
St Alb
BOREHAMWOOD (Holy Cross) *as above*
BOREHAMWOOD (St Michael and All Angels) *as above*
BORLEY (not known) *see* N Hinckford *Chelmsf*
BOROUGH GREEN (Good Shepherd) *Roch 10* **P** *Bp*
P-in-c C M TURNER
BOROUGHBRIDGE (St James) *see* Aldborough w
Boroughbridge and Roecliffe *Leeds*
BORROWASH (St Stephen's Chapel) *see* Ockbrook *Derby*
BORROWDALE (St Andrew) *see* Keswick St Jo w Borrowdale
Carl
BORSTAL (St Matthew) *Roch 5* **P** *V Rochester St Marg*
P-in-c J A LOVE C B A A LAWAL
BORWICK (St Mary) *see* Warton St Oswald w Yealand
Conyers *Blackb*
BOSBURY (Holy Trinity) *see* Hop Churches *Heref*
BOSCASTLE Group of Churches, comprising Forrabury and
Minster, Jacobstow w Warbstow and Treneglos, Otterham,
St Juliot and Lesnewth, St Gennys, Tintagel, and Trevalga
Truro 8 **P** *Bp, DBP, D&C Windsor, and Earl of St Germans (jt)*
R H J ASTON
BOSCOMBE (St Andrew) *Win 8* **P** *Bp* **P-in-c** N J HOULTON
BOSCOMBE (St Andrew) *see* Bourne Valley *Sarum*
BOSCOMBE (St Clement) *see* Bournemouth St Clem *Win*
BOSCOMBE (St John the Evangelist) *Win 8* **P** *Peache*
Trustees **V** R P KHAKHRIA
BOSCOPPA (St Luke) *Truro 7* **P** *The Crown*
P-in-c J S J WILLIAMS
BOSHAM (Holy Trinity) *Chich 6* **P** *Bp* **V** M J LANE
C L SULLIVAN
BOSLEY (St Mary the Virgin) *see* Sutton, Wincle,
Wildboarclough and Bosley *Ches*
BOSMERE, NORTH, comprising Coddenham, Creeting
St Mary, Creeting St Peter, Crowfield, Earl Stonham w
Stonham Parva, Gosbeck, Hemingstone, and Stonham
Aspal and Mickfield *St E 3* **P** *Bp, Pemb Coll Cam, and DBP*
(jt) R P J PAYNE **NSM** H NORRIS
BOSMERE, SOUTH, comprising Barking w Darmsden,
Battisford, Flowton, Great Bricett, Offton, Ringshall,
Somersham, and Willisham *St E 3* **P** *Bp, MMCET, Dr I de la*
Bere, and Ch Patr Trust (jt) R D D HARRISON
BOSSALL (St Botolph) *see* Harton *York*
BOSSINGTON (St James) *see* Mid Test *Win*
BOSTALL HEATH (St Andrew) *Roch 15* **P** *DBP*
V S SHAHZAD
BOSTON (St Botolph) (St Christopher) (St Thomas) *Linc 21*
P *Bp* **TR** A C BUXTON **TV** J E ROBERTSON C S A CLIFTON
BOSTON SPA (St Mary) *see* Bramham *York*
BOSWORTH (St Peter), including Cadeby, Carlton,
Congerstone, Nailstone, Shackerston, and Sutton Cheney
Leic 10 **P** *S J Warner Esq and DBP (3 turns), Ld Chan (2*
turns) R M S POSKITT **NSM** A E HALL
BOTCHERBY (St Andrew) *see* Carl St Aid and Ch Ch *Carl*
BOTESDALE (St Botolph) *see* Redgrave cum Botesdale w
Rickinghall *St E*

BOTHAL (St Andrew) and Pegswood w Longhirst *Newc 11*
P *Bp* R J PARK
BOTHAMSALL (Our Lady and St Peter) *see* The Idle and
Sands *S'well*
BOTHENHAMPTON (Holy Trinity) *see* Bridport *Sarum*
BOTLEY (All Saints) *Portsm 1* **P** *Bp* R G R MENSINGH
NSM R J WHARTON
BOTLEY (St Peter and St Paul) *see* Osney *Ox*
BOTLEYS AND LYNE (Holy Trinity) *see* Chertsey, Lyne and
Longcross *Guildf*
BOTTESFORD (St Mary the Virgin) *see* Vale of Belvoir *Leic*
BOTTESFORD (St Peter) w Ashby *Linc 6* **P** *Patr Bd*
TR K R DYKE C S C DEAN **NSM** M STONIER
BOTTISHAM (Holy Trinity) *see* Anglesey Gp *Ely*
BOTUS FLEMING (St Mary) *see* Landrake w St Erney and
Botus Fleming *Truro*
BOUGHTON (All Saints) *see* Wissey Valley *Ely*
BOUGHTON (St John the Baptist) *see* Pitsford w Boughton
Pet
BOUGHTON (St Matthew) *see* Ollerton w Boughton *S'well*
BOUGHTON ALUPH (All Saints) *see* Wye *Cant*
BOUGHTON ALUPH (St Christopher) *as above*
BOUGHTON MALHERBE (St Nicholas) *see* Len Valley *Cant*
BOUGHTON MONCHELSEA (St Augustine) (St Peter)
Cant 13 **P** *Abp* **V** P J F GOODEY
BOUGHTON-UNDER-BLEAN (St Barnabas) (St Peter and
St Paul) w Dunkirk, Goodnestone w Graveney, and
Hernhill *Cant 14* **P** *Abp* **V** *vacant*
BOULGE (St Michael) *see* Carlford *St E*
BOULTHAM (Holy Cross) (St Helen) *Linc 11* **P** *DBP*
R D J OSBOURNE **NSM** A J BORMAN
BOULTON (St Mary the Virgin) *Derby 5* **P** *Bp* **V** *vacant*
BOURN (St Helena and St Mary) *see* Papworth *Ely*
BOURNE (St Peter and St Paul) *Linc 17* **P** *DBP*
V C J ATKINSON
BOURNE END (St John) *see* Sunnyside w Bourne End *St Alb*
BOURNE END (St Mark) *see* Hedsor and Bourne End *Ox*
BOURNE VALLEY, comprising Allington w Boscombe,
Cholderton, Idmiston w Porton and Gomeldon, Newton
Tony, Winterbourne Earls and Dauntsey, and Winterbourne
Gunner *Sarum 10* **P** *Oriel Coll Ox and Bp (jt)*
R P A OSTLI-EAST
BOURNE, LOWER (St Martin) *see* The Bourne and Tilford
Guildf
BOURNE, The (St Thomas) and Tilford *Guildf 3* **P** *Bp and*
Adn Surrey (alt) **V** J O MORRIS C S L CLARKE
Hon C N FAIRLAMB **NSM** E M LANE
BOURNEMOUTH (Holy Epiphany) *Win 8* **P** *Bp* **V** *vacant*
BOURNEMOUTH (St Alban) *see* Winton, Moordown and
Charminster *Win*
BOURNEMOUTH (St Ambrose) *Win 8* **P** *Bp*
P-in-c A F PEARCE
BOURNEMOUTH (St Andrew) Bennett Road *Win 8*
P *Trustees* **V** *vacant*
BOURNEMOUTH (St Barnabas) Queen's Park *see*
Holdenhurst and Iford *Win*
BOURNEMOUTH (St Christopher) *see* Southbourne St Chris
Win
BOURNEMOUTH (St Clement) (St Swithun) *Win 8* **P** *DBP*
P-in-c T J MATTHEWS C C T MUIR, J RADVAN,
T M HODKINSON **NSM** M T A VILLAR
BOURNEMOUTH (St Francis) *Win 8* **P** *CR*
P-in-c J C NIGHTINGALE
BOURNEMOUTH (St John the Baptist) *see* Winton,
Moordown and Charminster *Win*
BOURNEMOUTH (St John) (St Michael and All Angels)
Win 8 **P** *Bp and S R Willcox Esq (jt)* **V** S E YETMAN
C L M CHESHIRE
BOURNEMOUTH (St Luke) *see* Winton, Moordown and
Charminster *Win*
BOURNEMOUTH Town Centre (St Augustin) (St Peter)
(St Stephen) w St Swithun and Holy Trinity *Win 8* **P** *Patr*
Bd **TR** I A TERRY
BOURNVILLE (St Andrew) *see* Bleadon and Bournville *B & W*
BOURNVILLE (St Francis) *Birm 2* **P** *Bp* C G ROGERS
BOURTON (Holy Trinity) *see* Wenlock *Heref*
BOURTON (St George) *see* Upper Stour *Sarum*
BOURTON (St James) *see* Shrivenham and Ashbury *Ox*
BOURTON (St Peter) *see* Draycote Gp *Cov*
BOURTON ON THE HILL (St Lawrence) *see* Vale and
Cotswold Edge *Glouc*
BOURTON, GREAT (All Saints) *see* Shires' Edge *Ox*
BOURTON-ON-THE-WATER (St Lawrence) w Clapton and
The Rissingtons *Glouc 8* **P** *Wadh Coll Ox, DBP and C T R*
Wingfield Esq, and Ld Chan (by turn) R R N KING
NSM N M J SUMMERFIELD

BOVEY TRACEY (St John the Evangelist) w Heathfield *Ex 8*
P *Guild of All So*   **P-in-c** N J DEBNEY
**BOVEY TRACEY (St Peter and St Paul and St Thomas of
Canterbury) w Hennock** *Ex 8*   **P** *The Crown (2 turns),
MMCET (1 turn)*   **V** W G HAMILTON
BOVEY, NORTH (St John the Baptist) *see* Moretonhampstead,
Manaton, N Bovey and Lustleigh *Ex*
BOVINGDON (St Lawrence) *St Alb 4*   **P** *Ch Soc Trust*
V C E BURCH
BOW (All Hallows) *see* Bromley by Bow All Hallows *Lon*
BOW (St Bartholomew) w Broad Nymet *Ex 2*   **P** *DBP*
R *vacant*
BOW (St Mary) and Holy Trinity w Bromley St Leonard
Lon 7   **P** *Bp and Grocers' Co (jt)*   **R** T G MAY   **C** A RIDER
BOW BRICKHILL (All Saints) *see* Brickhills and Stoke
Hammond *Ox*
BOW COMMON (St Paul) *Lon 7*   **P** *Bp*   **V** B G HEGARTY
**BOWBROOK, comprising Crowle w Bredicot, Hadzor w
Oddingly and Tibberton, Hanbury, and Himbleton w
Huddington** *Worc 3*   **P** *Patr Bd*   **V** A D MORRIS
BOWBURN (Christ the King) and Tudhoe Grange
St Andrew *Dur 3*   **P** *Bp*   **V** J LIVESLEY
BOWDEN HILL (St Anne) *see* Gtr Corsham and Lacock *Bris*
BOWDEN, GREAT (St Peter and St Paul) *see* Market
Harborough and The Transfiguration etc *Leic*
BOWDEN, LITTLE (St Hugh) *as above*
BOWDEN, LITTLE (St Nicholas) *as above*
BOWDON (St Luke) (St Mary the Virgin) *Ches 10*   **P** *Bp*
V I M RUMSEY
BOWERCHALKE (Holy Trinity) *see* Chalke Valley *Sarum*
**BOWERS GIFFORD (St John) (St Margaret) w North
Benfleet** *Chelmsf 11*   **P** *Em Coll Cam and J R F Bryers Esq
(alt)*   **P-in-c** D A O IBIAYO   **NSM** M A POWER
BOWES (St Giles) *see* Lower Teesdale *Leeds*
BOWES PARK (St Michael-at-Bowes) *see* Wood Green St Mich
w Bounds Green St Gabr etc *Lon*
BOWLAND and The Flyfords *see* Abberton, The Flyfords,
Naunton Beauchamp etc *Worc*
BOWLAND Benefice, The, comprising Bolton by Bowland,
Gisburn and Grindleton *Blackb 7*   **P** *Bp and V Hurst Green
and Mitton (jt)*   **R** M J WILLIAMS
BOWLEE (St Thomas) *see* Langley *Man*
BOWLING (St John) *Leeds 2*   **P** *V Bradford*
P-in-c T C R THOMAS
BOWLING (St Stephen) *see* Bankfoot and Bowling St Steph
Leeds
BOWNESS ON SOLWAY (St Michael) *see* Barony of Burgh
Carl
**BOWNESS-ON-SOLWAY (St Michael), Kirkbride and
Newton Arlosh** *Carl 3*   **P** *Earl of Lonsdale (2 turns), V Holme
Cultram (1 turn)*   **R** *vacant*
BOWTHORPE (St Michael) *Nor 3*   **P** *Bp and CPAS (jt)*
V *vacant*
BOX (St Barnabas) *see* Minchinhampton w Box and
Amberley *Glouc*
BOX (St Thomas à Becket) w Hazlebury and Ditteridge
Bris 4   **P** *Bp*   **P-in-c** J M ANDERSON-MACKENZIE
OLM C M SOUTHGATE
BOX HILL (St Andrew) *see* Headley and Box Hill w Walton
on the Hill *Guildf*
BOX RIVER *see* Boxford, Edwardstone, Groton etc *St E*
BOXFORD (St Andrew) *see* E Downland *Ox*
**BOXFORD (St Mary), Edwardstone, Groton, Little
Waldingfield and Newton** *St E 8*   **P** *DBP and The Hon
Thomas Lindsay (1 turn), Ld Chan (2 turns), Peterho Cam (1
turn)*   **R** R T PARKER-MCGEE   **NSM** J S RIDGE
BOXGROVE (St Mary and St Blaise) *Chich 2*   **P** *Duke of
Richmond and Gordon*   **V** I M FORRESTER
BOXLEY (St Mary the Virgin and All Saints) *see* N Downs
Cant
BOXMOOR (St John the Evangelist) *St Alb 2*   **P** *Bp*
V M D MACEY
BOXTED (Holy Trinity) *see* Glemsford, Hartest w Boxted,
Somerton etc *St E*
BOXTED (St Peter) *see* Langham w Boxted *Chelmsf*
**BOXWELL (St Mary the Virgin), Leighterton, Didmarton,
Oldbury-on-the-Hill, Sopworth, Badminton w Little
Badminton, Acton Turville, Hawkesbury, Westonbirt
and Lasborough** *Glouc 5*   **P** *Duke of Beaufort, J A Huntley
Esq, and Westonbirt Sch (jt)*   **P-in-c** R W B THOMSON
BOXWORTH (St Peter) *see* Papworth *Ely*
BOYATT WOOD (St Peter) *Win 10*   **P** *Bp*   **V** *vacant*
**BOYLESTONE (St John the Baptist), Church Broughton,
Dalbury, Longford, Long Lane, Radbourne, Sutton on
the Hill and Trusley** *Derby 6*   **P** *Patr Bd*   **C** P F WALLEY,
S J GREENWOOD

BOYNE HILL (All Saints) *Ox 5*   **P** *Bp*   **V** J M HARRIS
BOYNTON (St Andrew) *see* Rudston, Boynton, Carnaby etc
York
BOYTHORPE (St Francis) *see* Chesterfield SS Aug *Derby*
**BOYTON (Holy Name), North Tamerton, Werrington,
St Giles-in-the-Heath and Virginstow** *Truro 9*   **P** *Duchy of
Cornwall, MMCET, Ld Chan, and R Williams Esq (by turn)*
P-in-c P M KNIGHT   **NSM** H DAVIES
BOYTON (St Andrew) *see* Wilford Peninsula *St E*
BOYTON (St Mary the Virgin) *see* Upper Wylye Valley *Sarum*
BOZEAT (St Mary) *see* Wollaston w Strixton and Bozeat etc
Pet
BRABOURNE (St Mary the Blessed Virgin) *see* Stour Downs
Cant
BRACEBOROUGH (St Margaret) *see* Uffington Gp *Linc*
BRACEBRIDGE (All Saints) *Linc 11*   **P** *Mrs B M Ellison-
Lendrum*   **V** A J JACKSON-PARR
BRACEBRIDGE HEATH (St John the Evangelist) *Linc 11*
P *Bp*   **V** J A BELL
BRACEBY (St Margaret) *see* N Beltisloe Par *Linc*
BRACEWELL (St Michael) *see* Barnoldswick w Bracewell *Leeds*
BRACKENFIELD (Holy Trinity) *see* Ashover and Brackenfield
w Wessington *Derby*
BRACKLEY (St Peter w St James) *Pet 1*   **P** *Bp*
V R W DUNCAN
BRACKNELL (Church at the Pines) *see* Easthampstead *Ox*
BRACKNELL (Holy Trinity) *Ox 3*   **P** *Bp*   **C** M M CHALMERS
BRACKNELL (St Francis and St Clare) *see* Easthampstead
Ox
BRACON ASH (St Nicholas) *see* Mulbarton w Bracon Ash,
Hethel and Flordon *Nor*
BRADBOURNE (All Saints) *see* Wirksworth *Derby*
BRADDAN (St Brendan) *S & M*   **P** *Bp*   **V** D M H RICHARDS
BRADDEN (St Michael) *see* Towcester w Caldecote and
Easton Neston etc *Pet*
**BRADELEY (St Mary and All Saints), Church Eaton,
Derrington and Haughton** *Lich 10*   **P** *Bp and Mrs M N
Nutt (jt)*   **R** C BRUMFITT
BRADENHAM (St Botolph) *see* W Wycombe w Bledlow
Ridge, Bradenham and Radnage *Ox*
BRADENHAM, WEST (St Andrew) *see* Dereham and Distr *Nor*
BRADENSTOKE (St Mary) *see* Lyneham and Woodhill *Sarum*
BRADFIELD (St Giles) *see* Trunch Group *Nor*
BRADFIELD (St Lawrence) *see* Mistley w Manningtree and
Bradfield *Chelmsf*
BRADFIELD (St Nicholas) *Sheff 3*   **P** *V Ecclesfield*
R A T ISAACSON
BRADFIELD and Stanford Dingley *Ox 4*   **P** *Ch Soc Trust*
NSM L E BLISS
BRADFIELD COMBUST (All Saints) *see* St Edm Way *St E*
**BRADFIELD ST CLARE (St Clare), Bradfield St George w
Little Whelnetham, Cockfield, Felsham and Gedding**
St E 6   **P** *St Jo Coll Cam (1 turn), Bp and Lt Col J G Aldous (1
turn)*   **R** S J POTTER   **NSM** H L GROVER, R L STAINER
BRADFIELD ST GEORGE (St George) *see* Bradfield St Clare,
Bradfield St George etc *St E*
BRADFORD (All Saints) *see* Bradworthy, Sutcombe, Putford
etc *Ex*
BRADFORD (St Augustine) (St Clement) *Leeds 2*   **P** *Bp and
V Bradf*   **V** R A FAIRHURST
BRADFORD (St Columba w St Andrew) *see* Gt Horton and
Lidget Green *Leeds*
BRADFORD (St Martin) *see* Girlington, Heaton and
Manningham *Leeds*
BRADFORD (St Oswald) *see* Lt Horton *Leeds*
BRADFORD (St Saviour) *see* Fairweather Green *Leeds*
BRADFORD (St Stephen) *see* Bankfoot and Bowling St Steph
Leeds
BRADFORD (St Wilfrid) *see* Gt Horton and Lidget Green
Leeds
BRADFORD ABBAS (St Mary the Virgin) *see* Three Valleys
Sarum
BRADFORD City Centre Resource Church *Leeds 2*
C P W GUNSTONE   **Min** L J MASLEN
**BRADFORD ON AVON (Holy Trinity), Westwood and
Wingfield** *Sarum 15*   **P** *Bp, D&C Sarum, D&C Bris, and CPAS
(jt)*   **R** J M ABECASSIS   **NSM** A M GREEN, S D JACKSON
**BRADFORD ON AVON, NORTH (Christ Church) and
Villages, including** Monkton Farleigh, South Wraxall, and
Winsley *Sarum 15*   **P** *D&C Bris (2 turns), Bp (1 turn), V Bradf
H Trin (1 turn)*   **R** A B KEATING   **C** T G MANN
BRADFORD ON TONE (St Giles) *see* Wellington and Distr
B & W
BRADFORD PEVERELL (Church of the Assumption) *see*
Charminster, Stinsford and the Chalk Stream villages *Sarum*
BRADFORD, WEST (St Catherine) *see* Waddington *Blackb*

BRADING (St Mary the Virgin)   *see* Seaview, St Helens, Brading and Yaverland *Portsm*

BRADLEY (All Saints)   *see* Farleigh, Candover and Wield *Win*

BRADLEY (All Saints)   *see* Hulland, Atlow, Kniveton, Bradley and Hognaston *Derby*

BRADLEY (St George)   *see* Gt and Lt Coates w Bradley *Linc*

BRADLEY (St John the Baptist)   *see* Wychebrook *Worc*

BRADLEY (St Martin) *Lich 27*   **P** *Baldwin Pugh Trustees*   **V** C D WATSON

BRADLEY (St Mary)   *see* Kildwick, Cononley and Bradley *Leeds*

BRADLEY (St Thomas) *Leeds 9*   **P** *Bp*   **P-in-c** I D JAMIESON

BRADLEY STOKE (Christ the King) (Holy Trinity) *Bris 5*   **P** *Bp and Bris Ch Trustees (jt)*   **P-in-c** R P SYMMONS

BRADLEY, GREAT (St Mary the Virgin)   *see* Stourhead *St E*

BRADLEY, LITTLE (All Saints) *as above*

BRADLEY, NORTH (St Nicholas), Southwick, Heywood and Steeple Ashton *Sarum 15*   **P** *Win Coll and Magd Coll Cam (jt)*   **V** O J LEARMONT

BRADLEY, WEST (not known)   *see* Baltonsborough w Butleigh, W Bradley etc *B & W*

BRADLEY-LE-MOORS (St Leonard)   *see* Alton w Bradley-le-Moors, Ellastone w Stanton, and Mayfield *Lich*

BRADMORE (Mission Room)   *see* Keyworth and Stanton-on-the-Wolds and Bunny etc *S'well*

BRADNINCH (St Disen) *Ex 7*   **P** *D&C Windsor*   **P-in-c** O H J MEARS

BRADNOP (Mission Church)   *see* Butterton, Ipstones-w-Berkhamsytch etc *Lich*

BRADOC (Blessed Virgin Mary)   *see* Lostwithiel Parishes *Truro*

BRADPOLE (Holy Trinity)   *see* Bridport *Sarum*

BRADSHAW (St John the Evangelist) and Holmfield *Leeds 8*   **P** *Bp*   **V** K A SHOESMITH   **C** J A CLARKE   **NSM** S M HEPTINSTALL

BRADSHAW (St Maxentius)   *see* Turton Moorland *Man*

BRADWELL (Holy Trinity)   *see* Coggeshall, Markshall, Cressing etc *Chelmsf*

BRADWELL (St Barnabas)   *see* Hope, Castleton and Bradwell *Derby*

BRADWELL (St Barnabas) and Porthill *Lich 9*   **P** *Bp*   **V** C S B ROUTLEDGE

BRADWELL (St Lawrence and Methodist United)   *see* Stantonbury and Willen *Ox*

BRADWELL (St Nicholas) *Nor 6*   **P** *Bp*   **R** S C DEALL   **NSM** C M UPTON, S D UPTON

BRADWELL ON SEA (St Thomas) (St Peter-on-the-Wall) and St Lawrence *Chelmsf 10*   **P** *Bp*   **P-in-c** S K POSS

BRADWELL, NEW (St James)   *see* Stantonbury and Willen *Ox*

BRADWORTHY (St John the Baptist), Sutcombe, Putford, Abbots Bickington, Bulkworthy, Milton Damerel, Bradford w Cookbury and Thornbury *Ex 15*   **P** *The Crown (1 turn), Bp and DBP (2 turns)*   **R** R A FREEMAN

BRAFFERTON (St Peter) w Pilmoor, Myton-on-Swale and Thormanby *York 3*   **P** *Abp and Prof Sir Anthony Milnes Coates Bt (jt)*   **P-in-c** D M COYNE   **C** M E YOUNG, M HARRISON, S WHITING   **NSM** C C CRANFIELD, C C GITTENS, C J TOASE, T M GANT

BRAFIELD ON THE GREEN (St Laurence)   *see* Cogenhoe and Gt and Lt Houghton w Brafield *Pet*

BRAILES (St George) *Cov 9*   **P** *D&C*   **V** G HEIGHTON   **Hon C** H C W PARBURY   **NSM** J W ROLFE

BRAILSFORD (All Saints) w Shirley, Osmaston w Edlaston and Yeaveley *Derby 1*   **P** *Bp, Earl Ferrers, and Sir Peter Walker-Okeover Bt (by turn)*   **R** P M TAYLOR   **NSM** F M GRANT

BRAINTREE (St Michael) *Chelmsf 16*   **P** *Ch Trust Fund Trust*   **P-in-c** N C ADAMS

BRAINTREE (St Paul) *Chelmsf 16*   **P** *Ch Trust Fund Trust*   **P-in-c** R W CHAND

BRAISHFIELD (All Saints)   *see* Michelmersh and Awbridge and Braishfield etc *Win*

BRAITHWAITE (St Herbert)   *see* Upper Derwent *Carl*

BRAITHWELL (St James)   *see* Ravenfield, Hooton Roberts and Braithwell *Sheff*

BRAMBER (St Nicholas)   *see* Beeding and Bramber w Botolphs *Chich*

BRAMBLETON (not known)   *see* The Bourne and Tilford *Guildf*

BRAMCOTE (St Michael and All Angels) *S'well 9*   **P** CPAS   **V** P F REYNOLDS

BRAMDEAN (St Simon and St Jude)   *see* Upper Itchen *Win*

BRAMDEAN COMMON (Church in the Wood) *as above*

BRAMERTON (St Peter)   *see* Rockland St Mary w Hellington, Bramerton etc *Nor*

BRAMFIELD (St Andrew)   *see* Beane Valley *St Alb*

BRAMFIELD (St Andrew)   *see* Blyth Valley *St E*

BRAMFORD (St Mary the Virgin) w Little Blakenham, Baylham and Nettlestead *St E 3*   **P** *MMCET, Bp and D&C Cant (jt)*   **P-in-c** E FALLA

BRAMHALL (St Michael and All Angels) (Hall Chapel) *Ches 17*   **P** *Bp*   **V** C L PIPER

BRAMHAM (All Saints), including Boston Spa, Thorp Arch, and Walton *York 1*   **P** *Ch Ch Ox, G F Lane Fox Esq, and Lady Elizabeth Hastings Estate Charity (jt)*   **P-in-c** N J MORGAN   **NSM** P M ANSLOW

BRAMHOPE (St Giles) *Leeds 12*   **P** *Trustees*   **V** *vacant*

BRAMLEY (Holy Trinity) and Grafham *Guildf 2*   **P** *Ld Chan*   **P-in-c** A G DAVIS, C E Z WHITE

BRAMLEY (St Francis) *Sheff 6*   **P** *Bp and Sir Philip Naylor-Leyland Bt (jt)*   **V** *vacant*

BRAMLEY (St James)   *see* Sherfield-on-Loddon and Stratfield Saye etc *Win*

BRAMLEY (St Peter) *Leeds 11*   **P** *V Leeds City*   **R** P A CRABB

BRAMPFORD SPEKE (St Peter), Cadbury, Newton St Cyres, Rewe, Stoke Canon, Thorverton and Upton Pyne *Ex 2*   **P** *Bp, Earl of Iddlesleigh, DBP, D&C (1 turn), Ld Chan (1 turn)*   **NSM** J A DALLEN, J L C HOCKING

BRAMPTON (St Mark) *Derby 3*   **P** *Bp*   **P-in-c** K E HAMBLIN   **C** J D LOMAS   **NSM** H J MOORE

BRAMPTON (St Martin)   *see* Eden, Gelt and Irthing *Carl*

BRAMPTON (St Mary Magdalene)   *see* E Leightonstone *Ely*

BRAMPTON (St Peter)   *see* Aylsham and Distr *Nor*

BRAMPTON (St Thomas the Martyr) *Derby 3*   **P** *Bp*   **C** M R BROOMHEAD   **NSM** H J MOORE

BRAMPTON ASH (St Mary)   *see* Desborough, Brampton Ash, Dingley and Braybrooke *Pet*

BRAMPTON BIERLOW (Christ Church) *Sheff 12*   **P** *V Wath-upon-Dearne*   **V** *vacant*

BRAMPTON BRYAN (St Barnabas)   *see* Wigmore Abbey *Heref*

BRAMPTON, OLD (St Peter and St Paul) (Cutthorpe Institute) and Great Barlow *Derby 3*   **P** *Bp and TR Staveley and Barrow Hill (jt)*   **R** S M COLVER

BRAMSHALL (St Laurence)   *see* Uttoxeter Area *Lich*

BRAMSHAW (St Peter)   *see* Forest and Avon *Sarum*

BRAMSHILL (Mission Church)   *see* Darby Green and Eversley *Win*

BRAMSHOTT (St Mary the Virgin) and Liphook *Portsm 4*   **P** *Qu Coll Ox*   **P-in-c** V W INGLIS-JONES

BRANCASTER (St Mary the Virgin)   *see* Hunstanton and Saxon Shore *Nor*

BRANCEPETH (St Brandon) *Dur 1*   **P** *Bp*   **P-in-c** A L BROOKER   **NSM** A C HOBBS

BRANDESBURTON (St Mary) and Leven *York 11*   **P** *St Jo Coll Cam and Simeon's Trustees (jt)*   **V** J E GRAINGER-SMITH

BRANDESTON (All Saints)   *see* Orebeck *St E*

BRANDLESHOLME (St Francis House Chapel)   *see* Kirklees Valley *Man*

BRANDON (Chapel)   *see* S Cliff Villages Gp *Linc*

BRANDON (St John the Evangelist) and Ushaw Moor *Dur 1*   **P** *R Brancepeth*   **P-in-c** C R PETERS

BRANDON (St Peter) *St E 7*   **P** *M A F Carter Esq*   **V** S D COBURN   **NSM** D A COBURN, K PALMER

BRANDON PARVA (All Saints)   *see* Barnham Broom and Upper Yare *Nor*

BRANDSBY (All Saints)   *see* Crayke w Brandsby and Yearsley *York*

BRANDWOOD (St Bede) *Birm 2*   **P** *Bp*   **OLM** C FARRELL

BRANKSEA ISLAND (St Mary)   *see* Parkstone St Pet and St Osmund w Branksea *Sarum*

BRANKSOME (St Aldhelm) (St Francis) *Sarum 7*   **P** *Bp*   **V** P J MARTIN   **NSM** S J FLATT

BRANKSOME (St Clement) (St Barnabas) *Sarum 7*   **P** *MMCET*   **C** L J BOWERMAN   **NSM** M WILLIS

BRANKSOME PARK (All Saints) *Sarum 7*   **P** *MMCET*   **V** C R BOYLE

BRANSCOMBE (St Winifred)   *see* Colyton, Branscombe, Musbury, Northleigh and Southleigh *Ex*

BRANSDALE (St Nicholas)   *see* Kirkbymoorside w Gillamoor, Farndale etc *York*

BRANSFORD (St John the Baptist)   *see* Worcs W Rural *Worc*

BRANSGORE (St Mary the Virgin) and Hinton Admiral *Win 9*   **P** *Sir George Meyrick Bt and Exors P W Jesson (jt)*   **P-in-c** B C SARGENT

BRANSHOLME (St John the Evangelist) *York 14*   **P** *Abp*   **V** A SILLEY

BRANSTON (All Saints) w Nocton and Potterhanworth *Linc 12*   **P** *Stowe Sch (2 turns), Ld Chan (1 turn), and Nocton Ltd (1 turn)*   **R** L D BRABIN-SMITH

BRANSTON (St Saviour) and Burton All Saints w Christ Church *Lich 13*   **P** *CPAS, Ch Soc Trust, and Simeon's Trustees (jt)*   **V** D L COLLIER

BRANSTON BY BELVOIR (St Guthlac) see High Framland Par Leic

BRANT BROUGHTON (St Helen) and Beckingham Linc 22 **P** Bp and Sir Richard Sutton Bt (alt) **R** C A GOLDSMITH

BRANT ROAD (Church Centre) see Bracebridge Linc

BRANTHAM (St Michael and All Angels) see E Bergholt and Brantham St E

BRANTINGHAM (All Saints) see Elloughton and Brough w Brantingham York

BRANXTON (St Paul) Newc 12 **P** Abp **P-in-c** G R J KELSEY **NSM** M N M SENTAMU

BRASSINGTON (St James) see Wirksworth Derby

BRASTED (St Martin) Roch 9 **P** Abp **R** vacant

BRATHAY (Holy Trinity) see Loughrigg Carl

BRATOFT (St Peter and St Paul) see Burgh Gp Linc

BRATTLEBY (St Cuthbert) see Springline Linc

BRATTON (St James the Great) (Oratory), Edington and Imber, Erlestoke and Coulston Sarum 17 **P** Bp and V Westbury (jt) **R** A J M SINCLAIR

BRATTON CLOVELLY (St Mary the Virgin) see Okehampton, Inwardleigh, Belstone, Sourton etc Ex

BRATTON FLEMING (St Peter) see Shirwell, Loxhore, Kentisbury, Arlington, etc Ex

BRATTON ST MAUR (St Nicholas) see Camelot Par B & W

BRAUGHING (St Mary the Virgin), Furneux Pelham and Stocking Pelham St Alb 15 **P** Bp and the Hon R P Hamilton (jt) **R** J A GAWTHROPE

BRAUNSTON (All Saints) see Daventry Pet

BRAUNSTON (All Saints) see Oakham, Ashwell, Braunston, Brooke, Egleton etc Pet

BRAUNSTONE PARK (St Peter) Leic 1 **P** Bp **NSM** N J ROOMS

BRAUNSTONE TOWN (St Crispin) w Thorpe Astley Leic 9 **P** Bp **P-in-c** D J HOVER

BRAUNTON (St Brannock) Ex 13 **P** Bp **V** vacant

BRAXTED, GREAT (All Saints) see Thurstable and Winstree Chelmsf

BRAXTED, LITTLE (St Nicholas) see Wickham Bishops w Lt Braxted Chelmsf

BRAY (St Michael) and Braywood Ox 5 **P** Bp **V** A L SWIFT **C** K P COLYER

BRAY, HIGH (All Saints) see Bishopsnympton, Charles, E Anstey, High Bray etc Ex

BRAYBROOKE (All Saints) see Desborough, Brampton Ash, Dingley and Braybrooke Pet

BRAYDESTON (St Michael) see Yare Valley Nor

BRAYDON BROOK, comprising Ashley, Charlton, Crudwell, Hankerton, Minety, and Oaksey Bris 6 **P** Duchy of Lancaster (1 turn), Bp and Ch Soc Trust (3 turns) **R** T NIXON **OLM** S J WYMAN

BRAYTON (St Wilfrid) York 4 **P** Abp **R** P D WATSON **C** R P SUEKARRAN

BREADSALL (All Saints) Derby 5 **P** Miss A I M Harpur-Crewe **P-in-c** K J PLANT

BREAGE (St Breaca) see W Kerrier Truro

BREAM (St James) Glouc 1 **P** Bp **V** C W MACLAY

BREAMORE (St Mary) see Fordingbridge and Hyde and Breamore etc Win

BREAN (St Bridget) see Berrow and Breane B & W

BREARTON (St John the Baptist) see Knaresborough, Goldsborough, Nidd and Brearton Leeds

BREASTON (St Michael) see Wilne and Draycott w Breaston Derby

BRECKLES (St Margaret) see Caston, Griston, Merton, Thompson etc Nor

BREDBURY (St Barnabas) Ches 16 **P** V Bredbury St Mark **P-in-c** S E W SHRINE

BREDBURY (St Mark) Ches 16 **P** Bp **V** A D BULL **C** M S MAKIN

BREDE (St George) see Brede w Udimore and Beckley and Peasmarsh Chich

BREDE (St George) w Udimore and Beckley and Peasmarsh Chich 17 **P** Bp, SS Coll Cam, Univ Coll Ox, and Dr P M J Crook (jt) **R** O D EDWARDS **Hon C** J D JELLEY

BREDENBURY (St Andrew) Heref 2 **P** DBP, V Bromyard, and J H Barneby Esq (jt) **R** E S SIDWELL

BREDFIELD (St Andrew) see Woodbridge St Jo and Bredfield St E

BREDGAR (St John the Baptist) see Tunstall and Bredgar Cant

BREDHURST (St Peter) see S Gillingham Roch

BREDICOT (St James the Less) see Bowbrook Worc

BREDON (St Giles) w Bredon's Norton Worc 3 **P** Bp **P-in-c** A C DAVIES **C** M K LECLÉZIO

BREDON'S NORTON (not known) see Bredon w Bredon's Norton Worc

BREDWARDINE (St Andrew) see Cusop w Blakemere, Bredwardine w Brobury etc Heref

BREDY, LITTLE (St Michael and All Angels) see Bride Valley Sarum

BREEDON ON THE HILL (St Mary and St Hardulph) see Ashby-de-la-Zouch and Breedon on the Hill Leic

BREIGHTMET (St James) see Leverhulme Man

BREIGHTMET Top o' th' Moss (St John the Evangelist) as above

BREINTON (St Michael) see W Heref Heref

BREMHILL (St Martin) see Marden Vale Sarum

BRENCHLEY (All Saints) Roch 8 **P** D&C Cant **V** R C PAGET

BRENDON (St Brendon) see Lynton, Brendon, Countisbury etc Ex

BRENT ELEIGH (St Mary) see Monks Eleigh w Chelsworth and Brent Eleigh etc St E

BRENT KNOLL (St Michael) see Three Saints B & W

BRENT PELHAM (St Mary the Virgin) see Hormead, Wyddial, Anstey, Brent Pelham etc St Alb

BRENT TOR (Christ Church) see Tavistock, Gulworthy and Brent Tor Ex

BRENT TOR (St Michael) as above

BRENT, EAST (The Blessed Virgin Mary) see Three Saints B & W

BRENT, SOUTH (St Petroc) see Buckfastleigh, Dean Prior, Littlehempston etc Ex

BRENTFORD (St Paul w St Lawrence and St George) (St Faith) Lon 11 **P** Bp **P-in-c** S H GUINNESS **C** C J CURRY, O D PENNANT

BRENTWOOD (St George the Martyr) Chelmsf 8 **P** DBP **P-in-c** J BRADBURY

BRENTWOOD (St Thomas) Chelmsf 8 **P** DBP **V** M R NORTH **C** M R G AUSTEN

BRENZETT (St Eanswith) see Romney Marsh Cant

BRERETON (St Michael) and Rugeley w Armitage Lich 3 **P** Patr Bd **TR** D M A EVANS **TV** P O HART **OLM** B D TABERNOR

BRERETON (St Oswald) Ches 11 **P** DBP **V** A C FISHER

BRESSINGHAM (St John the Baptist) see Diss Nor

BRETBY (St Wystan) see Winshill and Bretby Derby

BRETFORTON (St Leonard) see E Vale and Avon Villages Worc

BRETHERTON (St John the Baptist) see Croston, Bretherton and Mawdesley w Bispham Blackb

BRETTENHAM (St Andrew) see E w W Harling, Bridgham w Roudham, Larling etc Nor

BRETTENHAM (St Mary) see Rattlesden w Thorpe Morieux, Brettenham etc St E

BRETTON (Holy Spirit) see Pet H Spirit Bretton Pet

BREWHAM, SOUTH (St John the Baptist) see Bruton, Brewham, Pitcombe and Shepton Montague B & W

BREWOOD (St Mary and St Chad) Lich 2 **P** Bp **V** P MOON

BRICETT, GREAT (St Mary and St Lawrence) see S Bosmere St E

BRICKENDON (Holy Cross and St Alban) see Lt Berkhamsted and Bayford, Essendon etc St Alb

BRICKET WOOD (St Luke) St Alb 5 **P** CPAS **V** K A HODGINS

BRICKHILL, GREAT (St Mary the Virgin) see Brickhills and Stoke Hammond Ox

BRICKHILL, LITTLE (St Mary Magdalene) as above

BRICKHILL, NORTH (St Mark) see Bedf St Mark St Alb

BRICKHILLS and Stoke Hammond, The Ox 15 **P** Bp, Major Sir Philip Duncefort-Duncombe Bt, St Edw Sch Ox, and Cam Univ (jt) **R** J WALLER

BRICKLEHAMPTON (St Michael) see Elmley Castle w Bricklehampton and Combertons Worc

BRIDE (St Bridget), Lezayre and North Ramsey S & M **P** The Crown **R** B G EVANS-SMITH

BRIDE VALLEY, comprising Burton Bradstock and Chilcombe, Little Bredy, Litton Cheney, Long Bredy, Puncknowle, Shipton Gorge, and Swyre Sarum 2 **P** Sir Robert Williams Bt and G A L-F Pitt-Rivers Esq (jt) **R** J L WILLIAMS **C** E M HOWLETT

BRIDEKIRK (St Bridget) see Cockermouth Area Carl

BRIDESTOWE (St Bridget) see Okehampton, Inwardleigh, Belstone, Sourton etc Ex

BRIDFORD (St Thomas à Becket) see Christow, Ashton, Bridford, Dunchideock etc Ex

BRIDGE (St Peter) Cant 1 **P** Abp and St Jo Coll Ox (jt) **P-in-c** E R LAST **C** M J BIER HINKSMAN

BRIDGE Benefice, Coventry, comprising Canley and Westwood Cov 3 **P** Bp **V** D G HAMMOND **C** E A PEACHEY, S E ASHELBY

BRIDGE Parishes, The, comprising Kingston Lacy, Shapwick, and Sturminster Marshall Sarum 6 **P** Eton Coll and Nat Trust (alt) **V** vacant

BRIDGE SOLLARS (St Andrew) see Magnis Gp Heref

BRIDGE, The *see Meon Bridge Portsm*

BRIDGEMARY (St Matthew), Elson and Rowner *Portsm 3*
P *Patr Bd* **TR** R A ENGLAND **TV** J C GREENFIELD,
S T MARTELL

BRIDGERULE (St Bridget) *see Holsworthy, Hollacombe,*
Pyworthy etc *Ex*

BRIDGFORD, EAST (St Peter) and Kneeton *S'well 5* **P** *Magd*
Coll Ox (2 turns), C G Neale Esq (1 turn) **P-in-c** R M COLBY

BRIDGFORD, WEST (St Giles) *S'well 6* **P** *Waddington Trustees*
R L J PROUDLOVE

BRIDGHAM (St Mary) *see E w W Harling, Bridgham w*
Roudham, Larling etc *Nor*

BRIDGNORTH (St Mary Magdalene) (St Leonard)
(St James) and Morville Parishes Team Ministry,
including Acton Round, Astley Abbotts, Aston Eyre,
Monkhopton w Upton Cressett, Morville, Oldbury,
Quatford, and Tasley *Heref 8* **P** *Ld Chan (1 turn), DBP (3*
turns) **TR** S H CAWDELL **TV** S H L CAWDELL **C** T B KING

BRIDGWATER (Holy Trinity) and Durleigh St Hugh
B & W 13 **P** *Bp (2 turns) and Ld Chan (1 turn)*
V W H H LANE

BRIDGWATER (St Francis of Assisi) *B & W 13* **P** *Bp*
P-in-c C R CARLYON

BRIDGWATER (St John the Baptist) *B & W 13* **P** *Bp*
V E J SPARROW **C** J E SCOTT

BRIDGWATER (St Mary) and Chilton Trinity *B & W 13* **P** *Ld*
Chan **V** S J OSMOND

BRIDLINGTON (Christ Church) w Bessingby and Ulrome
York 9 **P** *Abp, R Bridlington Priory, and R J Wright Esq (jt)*
V M J CAREY **C** M G THURLOW, O R PRESTON

BRIDLINGTON (Emmanuel) and Barmston w Fraisthorpe
York 9 **P** *Abp* **V** R W HARE **C** R J TOWNEND
NSM B F BANCROFT

BRIDLINGTON (Holy Trinity) and Sewerby w Marton *York 9*
P *Abp* **V** D J MATHER

BRIDLINGTON (St Mary's Priory Church) *York 9* **P** *Simeon's*
Trustees **R** M R POLLARD **NSM** C A STRAND, J E FOWLER,
M D WALLER

BRIDPORT (St Mary) *Sarum 2* **P** *Patr Bd (2 turns) and Ld*
Chan (1 turn) **TR** D J SMITH **TV** P J M STONE
C H L CROUD **NSM** L D JOHNSON

BRIDSTOW (St Bridget) *see StowCaple Heref*

BRIERCLIFFE (St James) *Blackb 3* **P** *Hulme Trustees*
V S S GREENSMITH

BRIERFIELD (St Luke) *Blackb 6* **P** *Bp* **V** M DIN

BRIERLEY HILL (St Michael) (St Paul) *Worc 5* **P** *Ld Chan (2*
turns), Patr Bd (1 turn) **TR** D J HOSKIN **NSM** B I PRITCHETT,
C N WESTON

BRIGG (St John the Evangelist), Wrawby and Cadney cum
Howsham *Linc 8* **P** *Bp* **V** *vacant*

BRIGHAM (St Bridget), Clifton, Dean and Mosser *Carl 6*
P *Patr Bd* **R** *vacant*

BRIGHOUSE (St Chad) *see Lightcliffe and Hove Edge Leeds*

BRIGHOUSE (St Martin) and Clifton *Leeds 6* **P** *Bp*
V J P WEBB

BRIGHSTONE (St Mary the Virgin) *see W Wight Portsm*

BRIGHTLING (St Thomas of Canterbury), Mountfield and
Netherfield *Chich 13* **P** *Bp, Adn Lewes and Hastings, H C*
Grissell Esq, Mrs A Egerton, and Mrs L A Fraser (jt)
P-in-c A CROSSE

BRIGHTLINGSEA (All Saints) (St James) *Chelmsf 22* **P** *Ld*
Chan **V** C E BECKETT

BRIGHTON (Annunciation) *Chich 19* **P** *Wagner Trustees*
V A J R MURLEY

BRIGHTON (Chapel Royal) *Chich 19* **P** *Bp* **V** D J BIGGS

BRIGHTON (Good Shepherd) Preston *Chich 19* **P** *Bp*
V F P A MASCARENHAS **NSM** M PHILIP

BRIGHTON (St Bartholomew) *Chich 19* **P** *Wagner Trustees*
V B M EADON

BRIGHTON (St Cuthman) *see Whitehawk Chich*

BRIGHTON (St George w St Anne and St Mark) *Chich 19*
P *Bp and V Brighton (jt)* **V** A H MANSON-BRAILSFORD

BRIGHTON (St John) *see Preston St Jo w Brighton St Aug and*
St Sav *Chich*

BRIGHTON (St Luke) Queen's Park *Chich 19* **P** *Bp*
Dn-in-c J NEWSON

BRIGHTON (St Martin) w St Wilfrid and St Alban *Chich 19*
P *SMF* **V** T G BUXTON

BRIGHTON (St Mary the Virgin) *see Kemp Town St Mary*
Chich

BRIGHTON (St Matthias) *Chich 19* **P** *V Preston*
P-in-c T J HOLBIRD **C** J A C HARLEY

BRIGHTON (St Michael and All Angels) (St Paul) *Chich 19*
P *SMF* **NSM** K L HUMPHRYS

BRIGHTON (St Nicholas of Myra) *Chich 19* **P** *Bp*
V D KEECH **C** J A J C REID

BRIGHTON (St Peter) *Chich 19* **P** *Bp and V Brompton H Trin*
(jt) **V** R M COATES **C** A J MARSHALL, H K MILNE,
H L F GARRATT, J A BAILEY, J P GUMBEL, T J HOLBIRD
NSM R C AMESS

BRIGHTON, NEW (St James) (Emmanuel) *Ches 7* **P** *Bp*
V H D ATKINSON

BRIGHTSIDE (St Thomas and St Margaret) w Wincobank
Sheff 3 **P** *The Crown and Sheff Ch Burgesses (alt)*
V P N WARMAN

BRIGHTWALTON (All Saints) *see W Downland Ox*

BRIGHTWELL (St Agatha) *see Wallingford Ox*

BRIGHTWELL (St John the Baptist) *see Martlesham w*
Brightwell *St E*

BRIGHTWELL BALDWIN (St Bartholomew) *see Benson w*
Ewelme *Ox*

BRIGNALL (St Mary) *see Lower Teesdale Leeds*

BRIGSLEY (St Helen) *see Waltham Gp Linc*

BRIGSTOCK (St Andrew) w Stanion and Lowick and
Sudborough *Pet 7* **P** *Bp (2 turns), L G Stopford Sackville Esq*
(1 turn) **R** H J LOWE

BRILL (All Saints) *see Bernwode Ox*

BRILLEY (St Mary) *see Eardisley w Bollingham, Willersley,*
Brilley etc *Heref*

BRIMFIELD (St Michael) *see Leominster Heref*

BRIMINGTON (St Michael) *Derby 3* **P** *V Chesterfield*
R D B COOKE **OLM** M PYATT

BRIMPSFIELD (St Michael) w Birdlip, Syde, Daglingworth,
The Duntisbournes, Winstone, Miserden and
Edgeworth *Glouc 7* **P** *Ld Chan (1 turn), Bp, DBP, Major M N*
T H Wills and CCC Ox (1 turn) **R** V J THORNE

BRIMPTON (St Peter) *see Aldermaston and Woolhampton*
Ox

BRIMSCOMBE (Holy Trinity) *see Rodborough, Woodchester*
and Brimscombe *Glouc*

BRINDLE (St James) *Blackb 4* **P** *Trustees* **R** D G WARD

BRINGHURST (St Nicholas) *see Six Saints circa Holt Leic*

BRINGTON (All Saints) *see W Leightonstone Ely*

BRINGTON (St Mary w St John) w Whilton and Norton
and Church Brampton w Chapel Brampton and
Harlestone and East Haddon and Holdenby *Pet 2* **P** *Patr*
Bd (5 turns), The Crown (1 turn) **R** A L WATKINS
C K R EVANS

BRININGHAM (St Maurice) *see Brinton, Briningham,*
Hunworth, Stody etc *Nor*

BRINKBURN (St Peter and St Paul) *see Longframlington w*
Brinkburn *Newc*

BRINKHILL (St Philip) *see S Ormsby Gp Linc*

BRINKLEY (St Mary) *see Raddesley Gp Ely*

BRINKLOW (St John the Baptist) *see Revel Gp Cov*

BRINKWORTH (St Michael and All Angels) *see Woodbridge*
Bris

BRINNINGTON (St Luke) *see Stockport and Brinnington*
Ches

BRINSCALL (St Luke) *see Heapey and Withnell Blackb*

BRINSLEY (St James the Great) w Underwood *S'well 4*
P *Bp* **P-in-c** D A STEVENSON

BRINSOP (St George) *see Magnis Gp Heref*

BRINSWORTH (St Andrew) *see Rivers Team Sheff*

BRINTON (St Andrew), Briningham, Hunworth, Stody,
Swanton Novers and Thornage *Nor 17* **P** *J S Howlett Esq,*
Lord Hastings, and DBP (by turn) **R** *vacant*

BRISLEY (St Bartholomew) *see Upper Wensum Village Gp*
Nor

BRISLINGTON (St Anne) *Bris 1* **P** *Bp* **P-in-c** I L GARRETT

BRISLINGTON (St Christopher) *Bris 1* **P** *Simeon's Trustees*
P-in-c A W E SCHUMAN

BRISLINGTON (St Cuthbert) *Bris 1* **P** *Bp*
P-in-c I L GARRETT

BRISLINGTON (St Luke) *Bris 1* **P** *Bp* **V** *vacant*

BRISTOL (Christ Church w Emmanuel) *see Clifton Ch Ch w*
Em *Bris*

BRISTOL (Christ Church) w St Ewen, All SS and St George
Bris 3 **P** *J E Heal Esq* **R** *vacant*

BRISTOL (Christ the Servant) Stockwood *Bris 1* **P** *Bp*
V D G OWEN

BRISTOL (St Aidan) w St George, Fishponds St John the
Divine, and Two Mile Hill St Michael The Archangel
Bris 3 **P** *The Crown (1 turn), Bp and SMF (2 turns)*
V R J LING **C** M HOTCHKISS **NSM** M M CRITCHLOW
OLM N G CALLEN

BRISTOL (St Andrew w St Bartholomew) *see Bishopston and*
St Andrews *Bris*

BRISTOL (St Andrew) Hartcliffe *Bris 1* **P** *Bp*
P-in-c D A J MADDOX **C** J L BRADSHAW

BRISTOL (St Anne w St Mark and St Thomas) *see Eastville*
St Anne w St Mark and St Thos *Bris*

BRISTOL (St Mary the Virgin) Redcliffe w Temple and Bedminster St John the Baptist *Bris 1* P *Bp* V D F TYNDALL   C A K Y PALAIRET, K M CAMPION-SPALL, S C GOODMAN   NSM A D EVERITT

BRISTOL (St Matthew and St Nathanael) (St Katharine) *Bris 3* P *Bp and CPAS (jt)* V I J TOMKINS   C G DOHERTY   NSM R N PENDLEBURY

BRISTOL (St Nicholas) *Bris 3* C-in-c T J B FLINT   C J L BRADSHAW

BRISTOL (St Philip and St Jacob w Emmanuel) *Bris 3* P *Trustees* V T J SILK

BRISTOL (St Stephen) w St James and St John the Baptist w St Michael and St George *Bris 3* P *Ld Chan (1 turn), Bp, Bris Ch Trustees, and D&C (2 turns)* NSM F M HOUGHTON, R G CROFT

BRISTOL Lockleaze (St Mary Magdalene w St Francis) *Bris 3* P *Bp* C R S J SMITH

BRISTOL St Paul's (St Agnes) *Bris 3* P *Bp and Bris Ch Trustees (1 turn), Ld Chan (1 turn)* P-in-c M OTTO

BRISTOL, EAST (St Aidan) *see* Bris St Aid w St Geo, Fishponds St Jo, and Two Mile Hill *Bris*

BRISTOL, EAST (St Ambrose) (St Leonard) *Bris 3* P *Bp* P-in-c N J COLEMAN   C C M BUCKLAND

BRISTON (All Saints), Burgh Parva, Hindolveston and Melton Constable *Nor 17* P *Bp, Lord Hastings, and D&C (jt)* R *vacant*

BRITFORD (St Peter) *see* Chalke Valley *Sarum*

BRITWELL (St George) *Ox 12* P *Eton Coll* V N MCCATHIE

BRITWELL SALOME (St Nicholas) *see* Icknield *Ox*

BRIXHAM (St Mary) (All Saints) w Churston Ferrers and Kingswear *Ex 10* P *The Crown* TR S R YATES   TV J C N GAY

BRIXTON (St John the Evangelist) *see* Angell Town St Jo *S'wark*

BRIXTON (St Mary), Newton Ferrers, Revelstoke, Wembury and Yealmpton *Ex 19* P *Patr Bd* TR A J RYAN   TV K R LOVELL

BRIXTON (St Matthew) (St Jude) *S'wark 11* P *Abp and Ch Soc Trust (jt)* V S M SICHEL   NSM A HOLE

BRIXTON (St Paul) (St Saviour) *S'wark 11* P *Ch Soc Trust* V S J WHITTINGTON

BRIXTON DEVERILL (St Michael) *see* Cley Hill Villages *Sarum*

BRIXTON ROAD (Christ Church) *S'wark 11* P *CPAS* V *vacant*

BRIXTON, NORTH (Christ Church) *see* Brixton Road Ch Ch *S'wark*

BRIXWORTH (All Saints) w Holcot *Pet 2* P *Bp* R D R REITH

BRIZE NORTON (St Britius) and Carterton *Ox 28* P *Patr Bd* TR A C M TWEEDY   TV I B HOWARD

BROAD BLUNSDON (St Leonard) *Bris 7* P *Bp* P-in-c G D SOWDEN

BROAD CAMPDEN (St Michael and All Angels) *see* Vale and Cotswold Edge *Glouc*

BROAD HINTON (St Peter ad Vincula) *see* Upper Kennet *Sarum*

BROAD OAK (St George) *see* Heathfield *Chich*

BROAD TOWN (Christ Church) *see* Lyneham and Woodhill *Sarum*

BROADBOTTOM (St Mary Magdalene) *see* Mottram in Longdendale *Ches*

BROADBRIDGE HEATH (St John) *Chich 10* P *Bp* V M H LAVENDER

BROADCHALKE (All Saints) *see* Chalke Valley *Sarum*

BROADCLYST (St John the Baptist), Clyst Honiton, Clyst Hydon, Clyst St Lawrence, Rockbeare, Sowton, Talaton and Whimple *Ex 6* P *Patr Bd* TR M R KERSLAKE   TV B C LANE

BROADFIELD (Christ the Lord) *see* S Crawley *Chich*

BROADHEATH (Christ Church) *see* Hallow and Grimley w Holt etc *Worc*

BROADHEATH (St Alban) *Ches 10* P *Bp* V D GILL   NSM L REDFERN

BROADHEMBURY (St Andrew the Apostle and Martyr), Dunkeswell, Luppitt, Plymtree, Sheldon, and Upottery *Ex 4* P *Bp, D&C, MMCET, Oriel Coll Ox, and M Corfield Esq (jt)* R G J S HAYHOE   NSM J R PENN

BROADHEMPSTON (St Peter and St Paul) *see* Ipplepen w Torbryan, Denbury, Broadhempston and Woodland *Ex*

BROADMAYNE (St Martin) *see* Watercombe *Sarum*

BROADOAK (St Paul) *see* Eggardon and Colmers *Sarum*

BROADSIDE, comprising Ranworth, South Walsham, Upton and Fishley, and Woodbastwick *Nor 4* P *Bp, Qu Coll Cam, and J Cator Esq (jt)* C K M BILLSON

BROADSTAIRS (Holy Trinity) *Cant 5* P *V St Peter-in-Thanet* R B D FENTON   C J K WALTERS

BROADSTAIRS (St Andrew) *see* Reading Street *Cant*

BROADSTONE (not known) *see* Corvedale Benefice *Heref*

BROADSTONE (St John the Baptist) *Sarum 7* P *Bp* V H M BAILEY   C L J S WEBB

BROADWAS (St Mary Magdalene) *see* Worcs W Rural *Worc*

BROADWATER (Queen Street Church Centre) *see* Broadwater *Chich*

BROADWATER (St Mary) (St Stephen) (Queen Street Church Centre) *Chich 7* P *Patr Bd* TR G J DALY   TV G R NEAL

BROADWATER DOWN *see* Tunbridge Wells St Mark *Roch*

BROADWATERS (St Oswald) *see* Kidderminster Ismere *Worc*

BROADWAY (St Aldhem and St Eadburga) *see* Isle Valley *B & W*

BROADWAY (St Eadburgha) (St Michael and All Angels) w Wickhamford *Worc 3* P *Peache Trustees and Ch Ch Ox (jt)* P-in-c M E WARD   NSM J M WILLIAMSON

BROADWELL (Good Shepherd) *see* Coleford, Staunton, Newland, Redbrook etc *Glouc*

BROADWELL (St Paul), Evenlode, Oddington, Adlestrop and Westcote w Icomb and Bledington *Glouc 8* P *Bp, Ch Soc Trust, Lord Leigh and DBP (1 turn), and Ch Ch Ox and D&C Worc (1 turn)* P-in-c O J STRANGE   NSM S BLAKE

BROADWELL (St Peter and St Paul) *see* Shill Valley and Broadshire *Ox*

BROADWEY (St Nicholas) *see* Weymouth Ridgeway *Sarum*

BROADWINDSOR (St John the Baptist) *see* Beaminster Area *Sarum*

BROADWOODKELLY (All Saints) *Ex 18* P *DBP* P-in-c H S E BLAINE

BROADWOODWIDGER (St Nicholas) *see* Lifton, Broadwoodwidger, Stowford etc *Ex*

BROCKDISH (St Peter and St Paul) *see* Redenhall w Scole *Nor*

BROCKENHURST (St Nicholas) (St Saviour) *Win 11* P E J F Morant Esq V S F E NEWHAM

BROCKHALL (St Peter and St Paul) *see* Heyford w Stowe Nine Churches and Flore etc *Pet*

BROCKHAM GREEN (Christ Church) and Leigh *S'wark 24* P *The Hon R P Hamilton and J N Charrington Esq (jt)* V J M A WILLANS

BROCKHAMPTON (All Saints) *see* Fownhope w Mordiford, Brockhampton etc *Heref*

BROCKHAMPTON (Chapel) *see* Bromyard and Stoke Lacy *Heref*

BROCKHOLES (St George) *see* Honley *Leeds*

BROCKLESBY PARK (All Saints), Croxton and North Wolds *Linc 8* P *Earl of Yarborough (3 turns), Ld Chan (1 turn), Bp, D&C and DBP (1 turn)* R L GABEL

BROCKLEY (St Andrew) *see* Horringer *St E*

BROCKLEY (St Peter) *S'wark 2* P *Bp* P-in-c B M JONES   C C GAUL

BROCKLEY HILL (St Saviour) *S'wark 5* P *V Forest Hill Ch Ch* P-in-c M D VYVYAN

BROCKMOOR (St John) *see* Brierley Hill *Worc*

BROCKWORTH (St George) *Glouc 3* P *DBP* V M D SMITH

BROCTON (All Saints) *see* Baswich *Lich*

BRODSWORTH (St Michael and All Angels) *see* Bilham *Sheff*

BROKENBOROUGH (St John the Baptist) *see* Malmesbury and Upper Avon *Bris*

BROKERS WOOD (All Saints) *see* White Horse *Sarum*

BROMBOROUGH (St Barnabas) *Ches 9* P *D&C* R J S GILLIES

BROME (St Mary) *see* N Hartismere *St E*

BROMESWELL (St Edmund) *see* Wilford Peninsula *St E*

BROMFIELD (St Mary the Virgin), including Bitterley w Middleton, Bromfield, Clee St Margaret and Cold Weston, Onibury, Stanton Lacy, and Stoke St Milborough w The Heath and Hopton Cangeford *Heref 11* P *Bp, Earl of Plymouth, Mrs O T M Rogers-Coltman, Exors Miss M F Rouse-Boughton, DBP and Walcot Trustees (by turn)* R J T PARKER

BROMFIELD (St Mungo) *see* Solway Plain *Carl*

BROMFORD FIRS (not known) *see* Hodge Hill *Birm*

BROMHAM (St Nicholas) *see* Rowde and Bromham *Sarum*

BROMHAM (St Owen) w Oakley and Stagsden *St Alb 13* P *Bp* V C A WILSON

BROMLEY (Christ Church) *Roch 14* P *CPAS* V I J BROOMFIELD   C D M LLOYD   Hon C V G WILKINS

BROMLEY (St Andrew) *Roch 14* P *Bp* V J E BOWEN   NSM E J DAVIS

BROMLEY (St John the Evangelist) *Roch 14* P *Bp* V A D MCCLELLAN   C D R WHIFFIN

BROMLEY (St Mark) *Roch 14* P *V Bromley SS Pet & Paul* V V A PASK   NSM E R LONGHURST

BROMLEY (St Mary) *see* Plaistow St Mary *Roch*

BROMLEY (St Peter and St Paul) *Roch 14* P *Bp* V J M HARRATT   NSM S L SUTHERLAND

BROMLEY BY BOW (All Hallows) *Lon 7* **P** *Bp and Grocers' Co (jt)* **R** C I ROGERS **NSM** R M ROGERS

BROMLEY COMMON (Holy Trinity) *Roch 14* **P** *The Crown* **V** R BRISTOW

BROMLEY COMMON (St Augustine) (St Luke) *Roch 14* **P** *Bp* **V** S R SPENCER **C** R M WINN

BROMLEY CROSS (St Andrew's Mission Church) *see* Turton Moorland *Man*

BROMLEY, GREAT (St George) *see* Lawford, Lt Bentley and The Bromleys *Chelmsf*

BROMLEY, LITTLE (St Mary the Virgin) *as above*

BROMPTON (Holy Trinity) *see* Onslow Square and S Kensington St Aug *Lon*

BROMPTON (St Thomas) w Deighton *York 18* **P** *D&C Dur* **V** J M E COOPER

BROMPTON ON SWALE (St Paul) *see* Easby w Skeeby and Brompton on Swale etc *Leeds*

BROMPTON RALPH (The Blessed Virgin Mary) *see* Wiveliscombe and the Hills *B & W*

BROMPTON REGIS (Blessed Virgin Mary) *see* Dulverton w Brushford, Brompton Regis etc *B & W*

BROMPTON, NEW (St Luke) *Roch 3* **P** *Bp* **P-in-c** G F JENKINS

BROMPTON, WEST (St Jude) (St Mary) St Peter *Lon 8* **P** *Bp and Sir Laurence Magnus Bt (jt)* **V** J L WELSH

BROMPTON-BY-SAWDON (All Saints) *see* Upper Derwent *York*

BROMSBERROW (St Mary the Virgin) *see* Redmarley D'Abitot, Bromesberrow, Pauntley etc *Glouc*

BROMSGROVE (All Saints) (St John the Baptist), including Catshill, Charford, Finstall, and Marlbrook *Worc 6* **P** *Patr Bd* **TR** D S FORD **TV** B A ROBERTSON, R A KHAN **C** R J M SANDLAND **NSM** J A HATTON

BROMWICH, WEST (All Saints) (St Mary Magdalene) (St Philip) *Lich 26* **P** *Bp* **V** J E M DICKER **C** D JARRATT, L J MITCHELL

BROMWICH, WEST (Good Shepherd w St John) *Lich 26* **P** *Bp* **V** vacant

BROMWICH, WEST (Holy Trinity) *Lich 26* **P** *Peache Trustees* **V** J N ROBBIE

BROMWICH, WEST (St Andrew) (Christ Church) *Lich 26* **P** *Bp and V W Bromwich All SS (jt)* **V** vacant

BROMWICH, WEST (St Francis of Assisi) *Lich 26* **P** *Bp* **V** R A FARRELL

BROMWICH, WEST (St James) (St Paul) *Lich 26* **P** *Bp and V Tipton St Martin and St Paul* **V** M A J WILSON

BROMWICH, WEST (St Peter) *Lich 26* **P** *Bp* **V** vacant

BROMYARD (St Peter) and Stoke Lacy *Heref 2* **P** *Bp (4 turns), Exors P H G Morgan Esq (1 turn)* **V** C R EVANS **C** K P N ROBERTSHAW

BRONDESBURY (Christ Church) (St Laurence) *Lon 18* **P** *Ld Chan* **C** N C WOODWARD

BRONDESBURY St Anne w Kilburn (Holy Trinity) *Lon 18* **P** *Bp and Ch Patr Soc (alt)* **V** C E CARGILL

BROOKE (St Mary the Virgin) *see* W Wight *Portsm*

BROOKE (St Peter) *see* Oakham, Ashwell, Braunston, Brooke, Egleton etc *Pet*

BROOKE (St Peter), Kirstead, Mundham w Seething and Thwaite *Nor 5* **P** *G&C Coll Cam, Gt Hosp and Countess Ferrers, and Ld Chan (by turn)* **P-in-c** L M CHAPMAN

BROOKFIELD (St Anne), Highgate Rise *Lon 15* **P** *Bp* **V** A J B MELDRUM **NSM** S P WALSH

BROOKFIELD (St Margaret) *York 20* **P** *Abp* **V** C D TODD

BROOKFIELD (St Mary) *Lon 15* **P** *Bp* **V** D D R MASON

BROOKHOUSE (St Paul) *see* Caton w Littledale *Blackb*

BROOKLAND (St Augustine) *see* Romney Marsh *Cant*

BROOKSBY (St Michael and All Angels) *see* Upper Wreake *Leic*

BROOKSIDE (Pastoral Centre) *see* Cen Telford *Lich*

BROOKWOOD (St Saviour) *see* Knaphill w Brookwood *Guildf*

BROOM (St Matthew) *see* Heart of England *Cov*

BROOM LEYS (St David) *Leic 8* **P** *Bp* **V** B A MURPHY

BROOME (St Michael) *see* Ditchingham, Hedenham, Broome, Earsham etc *Nor*

BROOME (St Peter) *see* Churchill-in-Halfshire w Blakedown and Broome *Worc*

BROOMFIELD (St Margaret) *see* N Downs *Cant*

BROOMFIELD (St Mary and All Saints) *see* S Quantock *B & W*

BROOMFIELD (St Mary w St Leonard) *Chelmsf 9* **P** *Bp* **V** C A TIBBOTT **C** D C PIERCE, D M BUTCHER **OLM** D M GARFIELD

BROOMFLEET (St Mary) *see* S Cave and Ellerker w Broomfleet *York*

BROOMHILL (St Mark) *see* Sheff St Mark Broomhill *Sheff*

BROSELEY (All Saints) w Benthall, Jackfield, Linley, Willey and Barrow *Heref 13* **P** *Patr Bd* **R** C W PENN **C** L C BEYNON

BROTHERTOFT Group, The (St Gilbert of Sempringham), including Holland Fen, Kirton Holme, Langrick, and Thornton Le Fen *Linc 21* **P** *Bp (2 turns), V Algarkirk (1 turn)* **V** C TODD

BROTHERTON (St Edward the Confessor) *Leeds 15* **P** *D&C York* **P-in-c** S L BROWN **NSM** S HULME

BROTTON PARVA (St Margaret) *York 16* **P** *Abp* **R** J P RHODES

BROUGH (All Saints) *see* Elloughton and Brough w Brantingham *York*

BROUGH (St Michael) *see* Upper Eden *Carl*

BROUGHAM (St Wilfrid Chapel) *see* N Westmorland *Carl*

BROUGHTON (All Saints) *see* Warboys w Broughton and Bury w Wistow *Ely*

BROUGHTON (All Saints), Marton and Thornton *Leeds 21* **P** *Ch Ch Ox and Exors Dame Harriet Nelson (jt)* **R** R C FINDLOW **NSM** A J LADDS

BROUGHTON (Ascension) *see* Lower Broughton Ascension *Man*

BROUGHTON (no church) *Ox 10* **P** *Ch Patr Trust* **V** P C WHITE **C** J E TALBOT **NSM** S P Z SMITH

BROUGHTON (St Andrew) w Cransley and Mawsley *Pet 9* **P** *Bp* **R** N HOBBS

BROUGHTON (St James) (St Clement and St Matthias) St John the Evangelist *Man 7* **P** *Patr Bd* **P-in-c** C E THRELFALL **C** M F ROBERTS

BROUGHTON (St John the Baptist) *Blackb 13* **P** *Trustees* **OLM** P F TAYLOR

BROUGHTON (St Mary Magdalene) (Holy Innocents) and Duddon *Carl 9* **P** *V Millom, Lt Col D A S Pennefather, and Ch Patr Trust (by turn)* **P-in-c** S W TUDWAY

BROUGHTON (St Mary the Virgin) *see* Wykeham *Ox*

BROUGHTON (St Mary) *Linc 8* **P** *MMCET* **P-in-c** D J EAMES

BROUGHTON (St Mary) *see* Mid Test *Win*

BROUGHTON (St Mary) *see* Myddle and Broughton, Loppington and Newtown *Lich*

BROUGHTON (St Peter) *see* Ashley and Mucklestone and Broughton and Croxton *Lich*

BROUGHTON ASTLEY (St Mary) and Croft w Stoney Stanton *Leic 7* **P** *Bp and A I Steele Esq (jt)* **R** S J CONSTABLE **C** L M JACKSON

BROUGHTON GIFFORD (St Mary the Virgin), Great Chalfield and Holt St Katharine *Sarum 15* **P** *D&C Bris (3 turns), Ld Chan (2 turns), and R C Floyd Esq (1 turn)* **R** A E EVANS **C** C L JACKSON, K JACKSON **NSM** R MECREDY

BROUGHTON HACKETT (St Leonard) *see* Peopleton and White Ladies Aston w Churchill etc *Worc*

BROUGHTON IN FURNESS (St Mary Magdalene) *see* Broughton and Duddon *Carl*

BROUGHTON MILLS (Holy Innocents) *as above*

BROUGHTON MOOR (St Columba) *see* Maryport, Netherton, Flimby and Broughton Moor *Carl*

BROUGHTON POGGS (St Peter) *see* Shill Valley and Broadshire *Ox*

BROUGHTON, GREAT (Christ Church) *see* Cockermouth Area *Carl*

BROUGHTON, LOWER (Ascension) *Man 7* **P** *Trustees* **P-in-c** D S C WYATT **C** F SHER, R C ELOFF

BROUGHTON, NETHER (St Mary the Virgin) *see* Old Dalby, Nether Broughton, Saxelbye etc *Leic*

BROUGHTON, UPPER (St Luke) *see* Hickling w Kinoulton and Broughton Sulney *S'well*

BROWN CANDOVER (St Peter) *see* Farleigh, Candover and Wield *Win*

BROWN CLEE *see* Ditton Priors w Neenton, Burwarton etc *Heref*

BROWNHILL (St Saviour) *Leeds 7* **P** *V Batley* **V** L A MATTACKS **C** M A GREEN

BROWNSOVER (Christ Church) *see* Clifton w Newton and Brownsover *Cov*

BROWNSWOOD PARK (St John the Evangelist) *Lon 5* **P** *City Corp* **V** A E SMITH

BROXBOURNE (St Augustine) w Wormley *St Alb 17* **P** *Bp and Peache Trustees (jt)* **R** C E C HUDSON **C** A DAVID

BROXTED (St Mary the Virgin) w Chickney and Tilty and Great and Little Easton *Chelmsf 17* **P** *Bp (2 turns), DBP (1 turn), and MMCET (1 turn)* **P-in-c** S E HURLEY **NSM** J E PARKER, J H WOOD

BROXTOWE (St Martha) *S'well 8* **P** *Bp* **C** P A HUXTABLE **NSM** D WATKINSON

BRUERA (St Mary) *see* Waverton w Aldford and Bruera *Ches*

BRUISYARD (St Peter) *see* Upper Alde *St E*

BRUMBY (St Hugh) (All Saints) *Linc 6*   **P** *Bp*
TR C A B MARTIN   **NSM** J A CLARK
BRUNDALL (St Lawrence) *see Yare Valley Nor*
BRUNDISH (St Lawrence) *see Four Rivers St E*
BRUNSTEAD (St Peter) *see Stalham, E Ruston, Brunstead,
Sutton and Ingham Nor*
BRUNSWICK (Christ Church) *Man 2*   **P** *Ch Soc Trust*
R S J T GATENBY   **C** K SHAHBAZ
BRUNSWICK (St Cuthbert) *see Ch the King Newc*
BRUNTCLIFFE (St Andrew) *see Morley Leeds*
BRUNTINGTHORPE (St Mary) *see Hexagon Leic*
BRUNTON PARK (St Aidan) *see Ch the King Newc*
BRUSHFORD (St Mary the Virgin) *Ex 18*   **P** *D&C*
P-in-c H S E BLAINE
BRUSHFORD (St Nicholas) *see Dulverton w Brushford,
Brompton Regis etc B & W*
**BRUTON (St Mary the Virgin), Brewham, Pitcombe and
Shepton Montague** *B & W 2*   **P** *Bp*   **R** J E EVANS
**BRYANSTON SQUARE (St Mary) w St Marylebone
(St Mark)** *Lon 4*   **P** *The Crown*   **R** J P T PETERS
C M R COOMBS   **NSM** B J KISSELL
BRYANSTON STREET (Annunciation)   *see St Marylebone
Annunciation Bryanston Street Lon*
BRYHER (All Saints) *see Is of Scilly Truro*
BRYMPTON (St Andrew) *B & W 6*   **P** C E B Clive-Ponsonby-
Fane Esq   **R** *vacant*
BUBBENHALL (St Giles) *see Baginton w Bubbenhall and
Ryton-on-Dunsmore Cov*
BUBWITH (All Saints) w Skipwith *York 2*   **P** *Abp and D&C,
and Ld Chan (alt)*   **NSM** D A ROGERS
BUCKDEN (St Mary) w the Offords *Ely 13*   **P** *Bp and Ld
Chan (alt)*   **P-in-c** D O SHEPPARD
BUCKENHAM, NEW (St Martin) *see Quidenham Gp Nor*
BUCKENHAM, OLD (All Saints) *as above*
BUCKERELL (St Mary and St Giles) *see Honiton w Monkton,
Awliscombe, Buckerell etc Ex*
BUCKFAST SANCTUARY (not known) *see Buckfastleigh,
Dean Prior, Littlehempston etc Ex*
**BUCKFASTLEIGH (Holy Trinity) (St Luke), Dean Prior,
Littlehempston, Rattery, South Brent and Staverton w
Landscove** *Ex 11*   **P** *Patr Bd*   **TV** G M RADFORD
C F WIMSETT, L E MCADAM
BUCKHORN WESTON (St John the Baptist) *see Stour Vale
Sarum*
**BUCKHURST HILL (St Elisabeth) (St John the Baptist)
(St Stephen)** *Chelmsf 3*   **P** *Patr Bd*   **TR** I D FARLEY
NSM T L PAYNE
BUCKINGHAM (St Peter and Paul), including Radclive cum
Chackmore *Ox 11*   **P** *Bp and New Coll Ox (jt)*
R W O C PEARSON-GEE   **C** K L E PELLEREAU
BUCKINGHAM, NORTH w Stowe, including Akeley,
Leckhampstead, Lillingstone Dayrell, Lillingstone Lovell, and
Maids Moreton *Ox 11*   **P** *Ch Soc Trust, O A J Robarts Esq,
and Stowe Sch (jt)*   **R** J A TALING   **C** C E PEARCE
BUCKINGHAM, WEST, comprising Biddlesden, Shalstone,
Tingewick, Turweston, Water Stratford, and Westbury *Ox 11*
P *Bp, D&C Westmr, G Purefoy Esq, and R L Randall Esq (1
turn), New Coll Ox (1 turn), and DBP (1 turn)*   **R** P SMITH
BUCKLAND (All Saints) *see Aston Clinton w Buckland and
Drayton Beauchamp Ox*
BUCKLAND (St Mary the Virgin) *see Betchworth and
Buckland S'wark*
BUCKLAND (St Mary the Virgin) *see Cherbury w Gainfield
Ox*
BUCKLAND (St Michael) *see Winchcombe Glouc*
BUCKLAND BREWER (St Mary and St Benedict) *see Parkham,
Alwington, Buckland Brewer etc Ex*
BUCKLAND DINHAM (St Michael and All Angels) *see Mells w
Buckland Dinham, Elm, Whatley etc B & W*
BUCKLAND FILLEIGH (St Mary and Holy Trinity) *see
Shebbear, Buckland Filleigh, Sheepwash etc Ex*
BUCKLAND IN THE MOOR (St Peter) *see Ashburton,
Bickington, Buckland in the Moor etc Ex*
BUCKLAND MONACHORUM (St Andrew) *Ex 21*   **P** *Bp*
V A J BOWDEN   **C** A FARMER
**BUCKLAND NEWTON (Holy Rood), Cerne Abbas,
Godmanstone and Minterne Magna** *Sarum 1*   **P** *Adn
Sherborne, Lord Digby, D H C Batten Esq, H E Gallia Esq, and
Col J L Yeatman (jt)*   **V** J T L STILL
BUCKLAND RIPERS (St Nicholas) *see Weymouth Ridgeway
Sarum*
BUCKLAND ST MARY (Blessed Virgin Mary) *see Blackdown
B & W*
BUCKLAND TOUT SAINTS (St Peter) *see Stokenham,
Slapton, Charleton w Buckland etc Ex*
BUCKLAND VALLEY (St Nicholas) *see Dover Town Cant*

BUCKLAND, EAST (St Michael) *see Swimbridge, W Buckland,
Landkey, and E Buckland Ex*
BUCKLAND, WEST (Blessed Virgin Mary) *see Wellington and
Distr B & W*
BUCKLAND, WEST (St Peter) *see Swimbridge, W Buckland,
Landkey, and E Buckland Ex*
BUCKLAND-IN-DOVER (St Andrew) *see Dover Town Cant*
BUCKLEBURY (St Mary) w Marlston *Ox 4*   **P** *C J Pratt Esq*
P-in-c J T D M GADSBY   **NSM** L E BLISS
BUCKLEBURY, UPPER (All Saints) *see Bucklebury w Marlston
Ox*
BUCKLERS HARD (St Mary) *see Beaulieu and Exbury and E
Boldre Win*
BUCKLESHAM (St Mary) *see Orwell and Deben St E*
BUCKMINSTER (St John the Baptist) *see S Framland Leic*
BUCKNALL (St Margaret) *see Woodhall Spa Gp Linc*
BUCKNALL Team Ministry, The (St Mary the Virgin),
including Abbey Hulton and Bentilee *Lich 11*   **P** *Patr Bd*
TR D STREET   **C** M G R MYCOCK   **NSM** R N GODDARD
OLM J MARSHALL
BUCKNELL (St Mary) *see Middle Marches Heref*
BUCKNELL (St Peter) *see Bicester w Bucknell, Caversfield
and Launton Ox*
BUCKROSE CARRS, comprising Rillington, Scampston w
Wintringham, Sherburn, Thorpe Bassett, and West
Heslerton *York 6*   **P** *The Crown, H J N Cholmley Esq, Sir Philip
Naylor-Leyland Bt, and D&C (by turn)*   **R** *vacant*
BUCKROSE, WEST, comprising Acklam, Birdsall, Burythorpe,
Langton, Leavening, North Grimston, Settrington, and
Westow *York 6*   **P** *Ld Chan (1 turn), Lord Middleton and Abp
(3 turns)*   **R** S P WALKER   **NSM** P M HALL
BUCKS MILLS (St Anne) *see Parkham, Alwington, Buckland
Brewer etc Ex*
BUCKSHAW VILLAGE CHURCH (Conventional District)
Blackb 5   **Min** J J GWYN-THOMAS
BUCKWORTH (All Saints) *see N Leightonstone Ely*
BUDBROOKE (St Michael) *Cov 11*   **P** *MMCET*   **V** D A BROWN
NSM R M DAVIES
BUDE Coast and Country Benefice, comprising Bude Haven,
Marhamchurch, Poundstock, St Mary Week, and Whitstone
Truro 8   **P** *Bp, Bude Haven PCC, Walsingham Coll, SS Coll
Cam, and Guild of All So (jt)*   **R** D K BARNES
BUDE HAVEN (St Michael and All Angels) *see Bude Coast and
Country Truro*
**BUDLEIGH SALTERTON (St Peter), East Budleigh w Bicton,
and Otterton** *Ex 1*   **P** *Lord Clinton*   **V** M JACQUES
BUDLEIGH, EAST (All Saints) *see Budleigh Salterton, E
Budleigh w Bicton etc Ex*
BUDOCK (St Budock) *Truro 2*   **P** *Bp*   **V** G K BENNETT
C B R MORGAN LUNDIE
BUDWORTH, GREAT (St Mary and All Saints) *Ches 4*   **P** *Ch
Ch Ox*   **V** A G BROWN   **NSM** C K B WESTWELL, J S MCKAY
BUDWORTH, LITTLE (St Peter) *see Whitegate w Lt Budworth
Ches*
**BUGBROOKE (St Michael and All Angels), Harpole,
Kislingbury and Rothersthorpe** *Pet 3*   **P** *Bp, Exors E W
Harrison, DBP, and Sir Philip Naylor-Leyland Bt (jt)*
R S R J FRENCH
BUGLAWTON (St John the Evangelist) *see Congleton Ches*
BUGTHORPE (St Andrew) *see Garrowby Hill York*
BUILDWAS (Holy Trinity) *see Wrockwardine Deanery Lich*
BULCOTE (Holy Trinity) *see Burton Joyce, Bulcote and Stoke
Bardolph etc S'well*
BULFORD (St Leonard) *see Avon River Sarum*
BULKINGTON (Christ Church) *see Wellsprings Sarum*
BULKINGTON (St James) *Cov 5*   **P** *Ld Chan*   **V** C C HIGGINS
BULKWORTHY (St Michael) *see Bradworthy, Sutcombe,
Putford etc Ex*
BULLEY (St Michael and All Angels) *see Huntley and
Longhope, Churcham and Bulley Glouc*
BULLINGHOPE, UPPER (St Peter) *see Heref S Wye Heref*
BULLINGTON (St Michael and All Angels) *see Lower Dever
Win*
BULMER (St Andrew) *see N Hinckford Chelmsf*
BULMER (St Martin) *see Howardian Gp York*
BULPHAN (St Mary the Virgin) *see Orsett and Bulphan and
Horndon on the Hill Chelmsf*
BULWELL (St John the Divine) *S'well 8*   **P** *Bp*   **V** *vacant*
BULWELL (St Mary the Virgin and All Souls) *S'well 8*   **P** *Bp*
R A J FISHER
BULWICK (St Nicholas) *see King's Cliffe, Bulwick and
Blatherwycke, Collyweston etc Pet*
BUNBURY (St Boniface) and Tilstone Fearnall *Ches 5*
P *Haberdashers' Co*   **V** T D M HAYWARD   **C** C N WILSON
BUNCTON (All Saints) *see Chanctonbury Chich*

BUNGAY (Holy Trinity) *St E 15*　**P** *DBP, Mrs B I T Suckling, and CPAS (jt)*　**P-in-c** J J BAILEY

BUNNY (St Mary the Virgin)　*see* Keyworth and Stanton-on-the-Wolds and Bunny etc *S'well*

BUNTINGFORD (St Peter)　*see* Aspenden, Buntingford and Westmill *St Alb*

BUNWELL (St Michael and All Angels)　*see* Long Stratton and Pilgrim TM *Nor*

BURBAGE (All Saints)　*see* Savernake *Sarum*

BURBAGE (Christ Church)　*see* Buxton w Burbage and King Sterndale *Derby*

BURBAGE (St Catherine) w Aston Flamville *Leic 10*　**P** *Ball Coll Ox*　**R** A D HALL　**C** R E HARPER

BURCHETTS GREEN, comprising Hurley, Littlewick, and Stubbings *Ox 5*　**P** *DBP and Bp (jt)*　**NSM** J F AINSLIE, T M MOLYNEUX

BURES (St Mary the Virgin) w Assington and Lt Cornard *St E 8*　**P** *DBP and Bp (jt)*　**NSM** M J CANTACUZENE, S J WHITE

BURFORD (St John the Baptist) w Fulbrook, Taynton, Asthall, Swinbrook and Widford *Ox 28*　**P** *Bp and Capt D Mackinnon (jt)*　**V** T D PUTT　**NSM** R J D WAINWRIGHT

BURFORD (St Mary)　*see* Tenbury *Heref*

BURGATE (St Mary)　*see* N Hartismere *St E*

BURGESS HILL (St Andrew) *Chich 11*　**P** *Bp*　**V** A R ANGEL

BURGESS HILL (St Edward) *Chich 11*　**P** *Bp Chich, Bp Horsham, and R Clayton w Keymer (jt)*　**V** *vacant*

BURGESS HILL (St John the Evangelist) *Chich 11*　**P** *Bp Chich, Bp Horsham, and R Clayton w Keymer (jt)*　**V** *vacant*

BURGH (St Botolph)　*see* Carlford *St E*

BURGH (St Margaret and St Mary)　*see* S Trin Broads *Nor*

BURGH (St Peter)　*see* Waveney Marshlands *Nor*

BURGH CASTLE (St Peter and St Paul)　*see* Belton and Burgh Castle *Nor*

BURGH Group, The, comprising Bratoft, Burgh le Marsh, Gunby, Irby-in-the-Marsh, Orby, Welton le Marsh *Linc 10*　**P** *Bp (2 turns), L J Montgomery-Massingberd Esq and Miss H F Montgomery-Massingberd (1 turn), SMF (1 turn)*　**R** T STEELE

BURGH HEATH (St Mary the Virgin)　*see* Nork w Burgh Heath *Guildf*

BURGH LE MARSH (St Peter and St Paul)　*see* Burgh Gp *Linc*

BURGH PARVA (St Mary)　*see* Briston, Burgh Parva, Hindolveston etc *Nor*

BURGH-BY-SANDS (St Michael)　*see* Barony of Burgh *Carl*

BURGHCLERE (Ascension) (All Saints) w Newtown and Ecchinswell w Sydmonton *Win 6*　**P** *Earl of Carnarvon*　**P-in-c** A J SMITH

BURGHFIELD (St Mary the Virgin) *Ox 4*　**P** *Earl of Shrewsbury*　**R** G V LAUTENBACH　**NSM** L D COLAM

BURGHILL (St Mary the Virgin) Group of Parishes, including Pipe-cum-Lyde, Moreton-on-Lugg and Stretton Sugwas *Heref 6*　**P** *DBP (2 turns), Bp, Ch Union Trust, and D&C (1 turn)*　**R** P J BROWN

BURGH-NEXT-AYLSHAM (St Mary)　*see* Aylsham and Distr *Nor*

BURGH-ON-BAIN (St Helen)　*see* Asterby Gp *Linc*

BURGHWALLIS (St Helen) and Campsall *Sheff 7*　**P** *Bp (2 turns), Mrs E H I Ellison-Anne (1 turn)*　**NSM** C HERBERT

BURHAM and Wouldham *Roch 7*　**P** *Bp and Ld Chan (alt)*　**R** M J HAYES　**NSM** C L WINTER

BURITON (St Mary the Virgin) *Portsm 4*　**P** *Bp*　**R** W P M HUGHES　**C** A M WATERHOUSE　**NSM** J M BEE

BURLESCOMBE (St Mary)　*see* Sampford Peverell, Uplowman, Holcombe Rogus etc *Ex*

BURLEY (St Matthias) *Leeds 12*　**P** *G M Bedford Esq, J C Yeadon Esq, E Beety Esq, Mrs M E Dunham, and Mrs L M Rawse (jt)*　**P-in-c** J A M BARNETT　**C** N W LATTIMER

BURLEY IN WHARFEDALE (St Mary the Virgin) *Leeds 4*　**P** *Bp*　**V** A J KIRK

BURLEY VILLE (St John the Baptist) *Win 9*　**P** *V Ringwood*　**V** *vacant*

BURLEYDAM (St Mary and St Michael)　*see* Baddiley and Wrenbury w Burleydam *Ches*

BURLINGHAM (St Andrew)　*see* Blofield *Nor*

BURLINGHAM (St Edmund King and Martyr) w Lingwood, Strumpshaw w Hassingham and Buckenham *Nor 4*　**P** *Ch Soc Trust, MMCET, and Bp (jt)*　**R** D K WAKEFIELD

BURLTON (St Anne)　*see* Myddle and Broughton, Loppington and Newtown *Lich*

BURMANTOFTS (St Agnes) and Harehills, Leeds *Leeds 10*　**P** *Ch Trust Fund Trust and Bp (jt)*　**V** A S KASIBANTE

BURMARSH (All Saints)　*see* Romney Marsh *Cant*

BURMINGTON (St Nicholas and St Barnabas)　*see* S Warks Seven Gp *Cov*

BURNAGE (St Margaret) *Man 1*　**P** *Bp*　**R** M R M CALLADINE

BURNAGE (St Nicholas) *Man 2*　**P** *Trustees*　**C** M R HEWERDINE　**NSM** A J SIMPSON

BURNBY (St Giles)　*see* Pocklington Wold *York*

BURNESIDE (St Oswald)　*see* Beacon TM *Carl*

BURNESTON (St Lambert)　*see* Kirklington w Burneston and Wath and Pickhill *Leeds*

BURNETT (St Michael)　*see* Keynsham *B & W*

BURNEY LANE (Christ Church)　*see* Ward End w Bordesley Green *Birm*

BURNHAM (St Andrew) *B & W 1*　**P** *D&C*　**V** G R WITTS　**NSM** M H I HAYWARD, S A ELDERGILL

BURNHAM (St Mary the Virgin) *Chelmsf 10*　**P** *N D Beckett Esq and Walsingham Coll Trust (jt)*　**V** *vacant*

BURNHAM (St Peter) *Ox 12*　**P** *Eton Coll*　**V** J M MINKKINEN　**C** S KUPONIYI

BURNHAM DEEPDALE (St Mary)　*see* Hunstanton and Saxon Shore *Nor*

BURNHAM NORTON (St Margaret)　*see* Burnham Gp of Par *Nor*

BURNHAM OVERY (St Clement) *as above*

BURNHAM THORPE (All Saints) *as above*

BURNHAM ULPH (All Saints) *as above*

BURNHAM WESTGATE (St Mary), Burnham Norton, Burnham Overy, Burnham Thorpe, and Burnham Sutton w Ulph (The Burnham Group of Parishes) *Nor 14*　**P** *Ch Coll Cam (1 turn), Ld Chan (2 turns), and DBP (1 turn)*　**P-in-c** S P WOOD

BURNHAM-ON-CROUCH (St Mary the Virgin)　*see* Burnham *Chelmsf*

BURNHAM-ON-SEA (St Andrew) *as above*

BURNLEY (St Andrew) w St Margaret and Burnley St James *Blackb 3*　**P** *The Crown and R Burnley St Pet (alt)*　**V** A J A EDWARDS　**C** P J BENFIELD

BURNLEY (St Catherine) (St Alban) and St Paul *Blackb 3*　**P** *R Burnley*　**V** R T D PARKER

BURNLEY (St Cuthbert) *Blackb 3*　**P** *R Burnley*　**V** M DIN

BURNLEY (St Mark) *Blackb 3*　**P** *Bp*　**C** P J BENFIELD

BURNLEY (St Matthew the Apostle) Habergham Eaves w Holy Trinity *Blackb 3*　**P** *R Burnley*　**V** A D J FROST　**C** K F M GREGORY-WITHAM

BURNLEY (St Peter) (St Stephen) *Blackb 3*　**P** *Bp and DBP (jt)*　**Hon C** P J PAYTON

BURNLEY, WEST (All Saints) *Blackb 3*　**P** *Bp and R Burnley (jt)*　**V** C W HILL

BURNMOOR (St Barnabas) *Dur 9*　**P** *Lord Lambton*　**R** *vacant*

BURNOPFIELD (St James)　*see* Tanfield w Burnopfield and Dipton *Dur*

BURNSALL (St Wilfrid)　*see* Linton, Burnsall and Rylstone *Leeds*

BURNT OAK (St Alphage)　*see* Hendon St Alphage *Lon*

BURNT YATES (St Andrew)　*see* Bishop Thornton, Burnt Yates, Markington etc *Leeds*

BURNTWOOD (Christ Church), Chase Terrace, Chasetown and Hammerwich *Lich 1*　**P** *Patr Bd*　**TV** M WALLACE, R A WESTWOOD　**C** R J EDMONDS　**NSM** S R D MORGAN

BURPHAM (Holy Spirit) (St Luke) Guildford *Guildf 5*　**P** *Bp*　**V** J A LEVASIER　**C** D MCCARLEY, J M LEVASIER

BURPHAM (St Mary the Virgin) *Chich 1*　**P** *D&C*　**P-in-c** C M WOODRUFF

BURRADON (Good Shepherd)　*see* Weetslade *Newc*

BURRILL (Mission Church)　*see* Bedale and Leeming and Thornton Watlass *Leeds*

BURRINGTON (Holy Trinity)　*see* Wrington w Butcombe and Burrington *B & W*

BURRINGTON (Holy Trinity), Chawleigh, Cheldon, Chulmleigh, Meshaw, Thelbridge, Wembworthy w Eggesford, Witheridge w Creacombe and Romansleigh, East Worlington and West Worlington *Ex 17*　**P** *Patr Bd*　**TR** A N ROCKEY　**TV** A M WELLS　**C** J M MAY

BURRINGTON (St George)　*see* Wigmore Abbey *Heref*

BURROUGH GREEN (St Augustine of Canterbury)　*see* Raddesley Gp *Ely*

BURROUGH HILL Parishes, The: Burrough on the Hill, Great Dalby, Little Dalby, Pickwell and Somerby *Leic 2*　**P** *Bp, DBP, and Mrs M Burdett Fisher (jt)*　**P-in-c** N STOTHERS　**NSM** J E WALKER

BURROUGH ON THE HILL (St Mary the Virgin)　*see* Burrough Hill Pars *Leic*

BURROWBRIDGE (St Michael)　*see* Athelney *B & W*

BURRSVILLE (St Mark)　*see* Gt Clacton *Chelmsf*

BURSCOUGH BRIDGE (St John) (St Andrew) (St Cyprian) *Liv 14*　**P** *V Ormskirk*　**V** D P BANBURY　**C** C J NEILSON, E J IRETON　**NSM** W I WILLIAMS

BURSDON MOOR (St Martin)　*see* Parkham, Alwington, Buckland Brewer etc *Ex*

BURSEA (Chapel)　*see* Holme and Seaton Ross Gp *York*

BURSLEDON (St Leonard) *Win 10* **P** *Bp* **P-in-c** J PAWSON
C J E KELLS
BURSLEDON Pilands Wood (St Paul) *see* Bursledon *Win*
BURSLEM (St John the Baptist) (St Paul) *Lich 11* **P** *Bp and MMCET (jt)* **P-in-c** S L PENDUCK
BURSLEM (St Werburgh) *see* N Potteries *Lich*
BURSTALL (St Mary the Virgin) *see* Sproughton w Burstall, Copdock w Washbrook etc *St E*
BURSTEAD, GREAT (St Mary Magdalene) w Ramsden Crays *Chelmsf 11* **P** *Bp* **P-in-c** M A HALL
BURSTEAD, LITTLE (St Mary) *see* Billericay and Lt Burstead *Chelmsf*
BURSTOCK (St Andrew) *see* Beaminster Area *Sarum*
BURSTON (St Mary) *see* Diss *Nor*
BURSTON (St Rufin) *see* Mid Trent *Lich*
BURSTOW (St Bartholomew) *see* The Windmill *S'wark*
BURSTWICK (All Saints), Burton Pidsea, Humbleton w Elsternwick, Halsham, and Thorngumbald *York 12*
P *Abp (2 turns), Ld Chan (1 turn), D&C (1 turn)*
Hon C P W WEST
BURTLE (St Philip and St James) *see* Polden Wheel *B & W*
BURTON (St Aidan) (St Paul) *Lich 13* **P** *Bp and Lord Burton (jt)* **OLM** R F TROTTER
BURTON (St James) and Holme *Carl 10* **P** *Simeon's Trustees*
V G J BURROWS
BURTON (St Luke) and Sopley *Win 9* **P** *Bp and D&C Cant (alt)* **V** vacant
BURTON (St Nicholas) and Shotwick *Ches 9* **P** *D&C (1 turn) and St Jo Hosp Lich (2 turns)* **V** C M HELM
BURTON (St Richard) *see* Barlavington, Burton w Coates, Sutton and Bignor *Chich*
BURTON AGNES (St Martin) *see* The Beacon *York*
BURTON BRADSTOCK (St Mary) *see* Bride Valley *Sarum*
BURTON BY LINCOLN (St Vincent) *see* Springline *Linc*
BURTON COGGLES (St Thomas à Becket) *see* Corby Glen Par *Linc*
BURTON DASSETT (All Saints) *Cov 8* **P** *Bp*
P-in-c N M CHATTERTON
BURTON FLEMING (St Cuthbert) *see* Rudston, Boynton, Carnaby etc *York*
BURTON GREEN (Chapel of Ease) *see* Kenilworth St Nic *Cov*
BURTON HASTINGS (St Botolph) *Cov 5* **P** *Bp*
V C C HIGGINS
BURTON JOYCE (St Helen), Bulcote and Stoke Bardolph w Lowdham, Caythorpe and Gunthorpe *S'well 7* **P** *MMCET and Bp (jt)* **V** A K ALLS **C** S N JONES
BURTON LATIMER (St Mary the Virgin) *Pet 9* **P** *Bp*
R J SAFFORD
BURTON LAZARS (St James) *see* Melton Mowbray *Leic*
BURTON LEONARD (St Leonard) *see* Ripon Cathl Benefice *Leeds*
BURTON OVERY (St Andrew) *see* Oadby *Leic*
BURTON PEDWARDINE (St Andrew and the Blessed Virgin Mary and St Nicholas) *see* Heckington and Helpringham Gp *Linc*
BURTON PIDSEA (St Peter) *see* Burstwick, Burton Pidsea etc *York*
BURTON UPON STATHER (St Andrew) *see* Flixborough w Burton upon Stather *Linc*
BURTON w COATES (St Agatha) *see* Barlavington, Burton w Coates, Sutton and Bignor *Chich*
BURTON-IN-LONSDALE (All Saints) *see* Bentham, Burton-in-Lonsdale, Chapel-le-Dale etc *Leeds*
BURTON-ON-TRENT (All Saints) *see* Branston and Burton All SS w Ch Ch *Lich*
BURTON-ON-TRENT (St Aidan) *see* Burton St Aid and St Paul *Lich*
BURTON-ON-TRENT (St Chad) *Lich 13* **P** *Bp*
V G J CROSSLEY **C** B L CARE, H R P DAVIS
BURTON-ON-TRENT (St Modwen) *see* Burton St Modwen *Lich*
BURTON-ON-TRENT (St Paul) *see* Burton St Aid and St Paul *Lich*
BURTON-UPON-TRENT (St Modwen) *Lich 13* **P** *Bp*
OLM R F TROTTER
BURTONWOOD (St Michael) *Liv 13* **P** *R Warrington*
NSM V M HANCOCK
BURWARDSLEY (St John) *see* Tattenhall w Burwardsley and Handley *Ches*
BURWASH (St Bartholomew), Burwash Weald and Etchingham *Chich 13* **P** *Bp and BNC Ox (jt)* **C** G R LEWIS
BURWASH WEALD (St Philip) *see* Burwash, Burwash Weald and Etchingham *Chich*
BURWELL (St Andrew) (St Mary) w Reach *Ely 4* **P** *DBP*
V E J WILLIAMS **NSM** P SPALDING
BURY (All Saints) *see* Kirklees Valley *Man*

BURY (Christ Church) *see* Walmersley Road, Bury *Man*
BURY (Christ the King) *see* Bury, Roch Valley *Man*
BURY (Holy Cross) *see* Warboys w Broughton and Bury w Wistow *Ely*
BURY (St John the Evangelist), Coldwaltham, Hardham and Houghton *Chich 4* **P** *Pemb Coll Ox, D&C, and Col Sir Brian Barttelot Bt (jt)* **V** P A MALLINSON
BURY (St John w St Mark) *see* Walmersley Road, Bury *Man*
BURY (St Mary the Virgin) *Man 4* **P** *Earl of Derby*
R J R HEATON **C** R E JONES, R MANN, S L ECCLESTON
OLM S R BEATTIE
BURY (St Peter) *see* Bury, Roch Valley *Man*
BURY ST EDMUNDS (All Saints) *see* Lark Valley and N Bury *St E*
BURY ST EDMUNDS (Cathedral of St James) District *St E 9*
C S J GEILESKEY
BURY ST EDMUNDS (Christ Church) Moreton Hall *St E 9*
P *Bp, V Bury St Edm St Jas, and V Bury St Edm St Mary (jt)*
V J L ALDERTON-FORD
BURY ST EDMUNDS (St George) *see* Lark Valley and N Bury *St E*
BURY ST EDMUNDS (St John the Evangelist) *as above*
BURY ST EDMUNDS (St Mary) (St Peter) *St E 9* **P** *Hyndman Trustees* **V** S J HARVEY **C** A WILLIAMS, L E H POPE
BURY St Paul *Man 4* **P** *Trustees* **V** J R HEATON **C** R E JONES, S L ECCLESTON **OLM** S R BEATTIE
BURY, NEW (St Catherine) (St George) (St James) w Great Lever *Man 3* **P** *Bp* **TR** M A COWLING
BURY, ROCH VALLEY (Christ the King) (St Peter) *Man 4*
P *Patr Bd* **V** H T NICOL **NSM** J L LYSSEJKO
BURYTHORPE (All Saints) *see* W Buckrose *York*
BUSBRIDGE (St John the Baptist) and Hambledon *Guildf 4*
P *Patr Bd* **R** S D K TAYLOR **C** P S SAMUELS, S P WILLETTS
NSM C A SOH, M P W SPENCER **OLM** A SPENCER, D W JENKINS
BUSCOT (St Mary) *see* Gt Coxwell w Buscot, Coleshill etc *Ox*
BUSH END (St John the Evangelist) *see* Hatfield Broad Oak and Bush End *Chelmsf*
BUSH HILL PARK (St Mark) *Lon 16* **P** *Bp*
P-in-c A O CHRISTIAN-IWUAGWU **NSM** J M FOOT
BUSH HILL PARK (St Stephen) *Lon 16* **P** *V Edmonton All SS*
NSM J M FOOT
BUSHBURY (St Mary) *Lich 28* **P** *Patr Bd* **TR** I R M POOLE
TV G R SMITH **C** R P CLAY
BUSHEY (Holy Trinity) (St James) (St Paul) *St Alb 6* **P** *Bp*
R J G EDWARDS **C** A G BURGESS, T H VICKERS
BUSHEY HEATH (St Peter) *St Alb 6* **P** *Bp* **V** A J BURTON
BUSHLEY (St Peter) *see* Longdon, Castlemorton, Bushley, Queenhill etc *Worc*
BUSHMEAD (Christ Church) *St Alb 12* **P** *Bp*
V T P MADELEY
BUSSAGE (St Michael and All Angels) *see* Bisley, Chalford, France Lynch, and Oakridge etc *Glouc*
BUTCOMBE (St Michael and All Angels) *see* Wrington w Butcombe and Burrington *B & W*
BUTLEIGH (St Leonard) *see* Baltonsborough w Butleigh, W Bradley etc *B & W*
BUTLERS MARSTON (St Peter and St Paul) *see* Stourdene Gp *Cov*
BUTLEY (St John the Baptist) *see* Wilford Peninsula *St E*
BUTTERCRAMBE (St John the Evangelist) *see* Harton *York*
BUTTERLEIGH (St Matthew) *see* Silverton, Butterleigh, Bickleigh and Cadeleigh *Ex*
BUTTERMERE (St James the Great) *see* Savernake *Sarum*
BUTTERMERE (St James) *see* Lorton and Loweswater w Buttermere *Carl*
BUTTERSHAW (St Aidan) *see* Shelf w Buttershaw St Aid *Leeds*
BUTTERTON (St Bartholomew), Ipstones-w-Berkhamsytch and Onecote-w-Bradnop *Lich 5* **P** *Bp, R Leek and Meerbrook, and V Alton etc (jt)* **V** vacant
BUTTERTON (St Thomas) *see* Newcastle w Butterton *Lich*
BUTTERWICK (St Andrew) *see* Freiston, Butterwick w Bennington, and Leverton *Linc*
BUTTERWICK (St Nicholas) *see* Langtoft w Foxholes, Butterwick, Cottam etc *York*
BUTTERWICK, EAST (St Andrew) *see* Messingham w E Butterwick, Scotter w E Ferry and Scotton w Northorpe *Linc*
BUTTERWICK, WEST (St Mary the Virgin) *see* Epworth Gp *Linc*
BUTTSBURY (St Mary) *see* Margaretting w Mountnessing and Buttsbury *Chelmsf*
BUXHALL (St Mary) *see* Combs and Finborough *St E*
BUXTED (St Margaret the Queen) (St Mary) and Hadlow Down *Chich 18* **P** *Abp, Bp, and Wagner Trustees (jt)*
R P L MOLLOY
BUXTON (St Andrew) *see* Aylsham and Distr *Nor*

BUXTON (St Anne) (St John the Baptist) (St Mary the Virgin) w Burbage and King Sterndale *Derby 4*　**P** *Patr Bd*　**TR** E A ENGLAND　**C** C M HUBBARD, D E BARNSLEY　**NSM** M M SLYFIELD

BUXTON (Trinity Chapel) Proprietary Chapel *Derby 4*　**C-in-c** R MARSDEN

BUXWORTH (St James)　*see* Hayfield and Chinley w Buxworth *Derby*

BY BROOK, comprising Biddestone, Castle Combe, Grittleton and Leigh Delamere, Littleton Drew, Nettleton, Slaughterford, West Kington, and Yatton Keynell *Bris 4*　**P** *Patr Bd*　**TR** M D TERRY　**C** A M KANAGARATNAM　**NSM** G E PARKIN

BYERS GREEN (St Peter) *Dur 3*　**P** *Bp*　**P-in-c** B A HILTON　**NSM** D J HODGE

BYFIELD (Holy Cross)　*see* Aston-le-Walls, Byfield, Boddington, Eydon etc *Pet*

BYFLEET (St Mary) *Guildf 12*　**P** *Ld Chan*　**R** J H MCCABE　**Hon C** P M S ROSS-MCCABE

BYFLEET, WEST (St John) *Guildf 12*　**P** *Bp*　**P-in-c** K A ELFORD

BYFORD (St John the Baptist)　*see* Letton w Staunton, Byford, Mansel Gamage etc *Heref*

BYGRAVE (St Margaret of Antioch)　*see* Baldock w Bygrave *St Alb*

BYKER (St Anthony) *Newc 3*　**P** *Bp*　**V** *vacant*

BYKER (St Martin) Newcastle upon Tyne *Newc 3*　**P** *Bp*　**NSM** H M LUNN

BYKER (St Michael w St Lawrence) *Newc 3*　**P** *Bp*　**P-in-c** H B GILL

BYKER (St Silas) *Newc 3*　**P** *Bp*　**V** H B GILL　**NSM** A F TAYLOR

BYKER St Mark and Walkergate (St Oswald) *Newc 3*　**P** *Bp and Ch Trust Fund Trust (jt)*　**V** *vacant*

BYLAND, OLD (All Saints)　*see* Upper Ryedale *York*

BYLAUGH (St Mary)　*see* Reepham and Wensum Valley *Nor*

BYLEY CUM LEES (St John the Evangelist)　*see* Middlewich w Byley *Ches*

BYRNESS (St Francis)　*see* N Tyne and Redesdale *Newc*

BYTHAM Parishes, The, including Careby w Holywell and Aunby, Castle Bytham, Creeton, Little Bytham, North Witham, and South Witham *Linc 17*　**P** *D&C (1 turn), Bp (1 turn), Ld Chan (1 turn), DBP (1 turn), Bp and Sir Lyonel Tollemache Bt (1 turn)*　**V** *vacant*

BYTHAM, LITTLE (St Medardus)　*see* Bytham Par *Linc*

BYTHORN (St Lawrence)　*see* W Leightonstone *Ely*

BYTON (St Mary)　*see* Pembridge w Moor Court, Shobdon, Staunton etc *Heref*

BYWELL (St Peter) and Mickley *Newc 9*　**P** *Bp and Adn Lindisfarne (jt)*　**P-in-c** P M MORAN

BYWORTH (St Francis)　*see* Farnham *Guildf*

CABLE STREET (St Mary)　*see* St Geo-in-the-East St Mary *Lon*

CABOURNE (St Nicholas)　*see* Caistor *Linc*

CADBURY (St Michael and All Angels)　*see* Brampford Speke, Cadbury, Newton St Cyres etc *Ex*

CADBURY, NORTH (St Michael the Archangel)　*see* Camelot Par *B & W*

CADBURY, SOUTH (St Thomas à Becket) *as above*

CADDINGTON (All Saints) *St Alb 12*　**P** *D&C St Paul's*　**V** R P O'NEILL　**C** S J CURTIS　**NSM** L MOSS

CADEBY (All Saints)　*see* Bosworth *Leic*

CADELEIGH (St Bartholomew)　*see* Silverton, Butterleigh, Bickleigh and Cadeleigh *Ex*

CADGWITH (St Mary)　*see* St Keverne, St Ruan w St Grade and Landewednack *Truro*

CADISHEAD (St Mary the Virgin) *Man 7*　**P** *Bp*　**V** *vacant*

CADMORE END (St Mary le Moor)　*see* S Chilterns *Ox*

CADNEY (All Saints)　*see* Brigg, Wrawby and Cadney cum Howsham *Linc*

CADOGAN SQUARE (St Simon Zelotes)　*see* Upper Chelsea St Simon *Lon*

CAERHAYS (St Michael)　*see* St Goran w Caerhays *Truro*

CAGE GREEN (St Philip)　*see* Tonbridge SS Pet and Paul *Roch*

CAGEBROOK Parishes, comprising Allensmore, Clehonger, Eaton Bishop, Kingstone, and Thruxton *Heref 1*　**P** *Bp (2 turns), The Crown (1 turn)*　**NSM** E A HITCHINER

CAINSCROSS (St Matthew)　*see* Stroud Team *Glouc*

CAISTER NEXT YARMOUTH (Holy Trinity) (St Edmund) *Nor 6*　**P** SMF　**R** D WELLS

CAISTOR (St Peter and St Paul), including Cabourn, Clixby, Cuxwold, Grasby, Rothwell, Searby w Owmby, and Swallow *Linc 7*　**P** *Bp and D&C (3 turns), Earl of Yarborough and J R Thorold Esq (1 turn)*　**V** I ROBINSON　**Hon C** S W ANDREW　**NSM** C J WYLIE, J MCMANN

CAISTOR ST EDMUNDS (St Edmund)　*see* Stoke H Cross w Dunston, Arminghall etc *Nor*

CALBOURNE (All Saints)　*see* W Wight *Portsm*

CALCOT (St Birinus)　*see* Tilehurst St Cath and Calcot *Ox*

CALDBECK (St Mungo) (Fellside), Castle Sowerby and Sebergham *Carl 3*　**P** *Bp and D&C (alt)*　**P-in-c** E REID　**NSM** R T CORRIE

CALDECOTE (All Saints), Northill and Old Warden *St Alb 10*　**P** *Grocers' Co (2 turns), R O Shuttleworth Remembrance Trust (1 turn)*　**V** F COLEMAN

CALDECOTE (St Michael and All Angels)　*see* Lordsbridge *Ely*

CALDECOTT (St John the Evangelist)　*see* Lyddington, Bisbrooke, Caldecott, Glaston etc *Pet*

CALDER VALE (Mission)　*see* Scorton and Barnacre and Calder Vale *Blackb*

CALDER VALE (St John the Evangelist) *as above*

CALDERBROOK (St James the Great)　*see* Littleborough *Man*

CALDWELL (Chapel)　*see* Forcett and Aldbrough and Melsonby *Leeds*

CALDWELL (St Giles)　*see* Stapenhill w Cauldwell *Derby*

CALDY (Church of the Resurrection and All Saints)　*see* W Kirby St Bridget *Ches*

CALEDONIAN ROAD (All Saints Hall)　*see* Barnsbury *Lon*

CALEHILL w Westwell, comprising Charing, Charing Heath, Egerton, Hothfield, Little Chart, Pluckley, and Westwell *Cant 6*　**P** *Abp, D&C, and Lord Hothfield (jt)*　**R** E A MARSH

CALIFORNIA (St Mary and St John)　*see* Finchampstead and California *Ox*

CALLINGTON (St Mary)　*see* Callington Cluster *Truro*

CALLINGTON Cluster, The, including Linkinhorne, South Hill, and Stoke Climsland *Truro 11*　**P** *Duchy of Cornwall (1 turn), Bp, DBP, PCC South Hill, and PCC Callington (1 turn)*　**R** J LANNON

CALLOW END (St James)　*see* Powick and Guarlford and Madresfield w Newland *Worc*

CALMORE (St Anne) and Eling *Win 11*　**P** *Bp*　**V** *vacant*

CALNE (Holy Trinity)　*see* Marden Vale *Sarum*

CALNE (St Mary the Virgin) *as above*

CALOW (St Peter) and Sutton cum Duckmanton *Derby 3*　**P** *Bp and V Chesterfield (jt)*　**R** *vacant*

CALSHOT (St George)　*see* Fawley *Win*

CALSTOCK (St Andrew)　*see* Tamar Valley *Truro*

CALSTONE WELLINGTON (St Mary the Virgin)　*see* Oldbury *Sarum*

CALTHORPE (Our Lady w St Margaret)　*see* Scarrowbeck *Nor*

CALTHWAITE (All Saints)　*see* Inglewood Gp *Carl*

CALTON (St Mary the Virgin), Cauldon, Grindon, Waterfall and Blore Ray w Okeover *Lich 5*　**P** *Bp and Sir Peter Walker-Okeover Bt (jt)*　**R** A BEAHAN

CALUDON (Holy Cross) Coventry *Cov 1*　**P** *Ld Chan and Bp (alt)*　**OLM** E A HARRIS

CALVELEY CHURCH (not known)　*see* Bunbury and Tilstone Fearnall *Ches*

CALVERHALL or CORRA (Holy Trinity)　*see* Adderley, Ash, Calverhall, Ightfield etc *Lich*

CALVERLEIGH (St Mary the Virgin)　*see* Washfield, Stoodleigh, Withleigh etc *Ex*

CALVERLEY (St Wilfrid) *Leeds 11*　**P** *Bp*　**V** *vacant*

CALVERTON (All Saints)　*see* Stony Stratford w Calverton *Ox*

CALVERTON (St Wilfrid) *S'well 7*　**P** *Bp*　**V** S J HUSTWAYTE

CAM (St George) w Stinchcombe *Glouc 5*　**P** *Bp*　**V** F J CROCKER　**NSM** A N L HILL, S C A ACLAND

CAM VALE, comprising Corton Denham, Queen Camel, Sparkford, Sutton Montis, West Camel, and Weston Bampfylde *B & W 2*　**P** *Bp and DBP (2 turns), CPAS, MMCET and Revd G Bennett (1 turn)*　**R** K M HAWKSLEY

CAM, LOWER (St Bartholomew) w Coaley *Glouc 5*　**P** *Bp*　**NSM** P T FEWINGS

CAMBER (St Thomas)　*see* Rye *Chich*

CAMBERLEY (St Martin) Old Dean *Guildf 6*　**P** *Bp*　**V** C E RICHARDSON　**OLM** K M MURRAY

CAMBERLEY (St Mary) *Guildf 6*　**P** *Bp*　**V** A J KNOWLES　**C** S A DUPLOCK

CAMBERLEY (St Michael) Yorktown *Guildf 6*　**P** *Bp*　**V** P FORD　**NSM** A MITCHELL

CAMBERLEY (St Paul) *Guildf 6*　**P** *Bp*　**V** T J DARWENT　**C** S R LOVESMITH

CAMBERLEY HEATHERSIDE (Community Centre) *Guildf 6*　**P** *Bp*　**P-in-c** L J W BAIN

CAMBERWELL (Christ Church) *S'wark 8*　**P** MMCET　**V** H R BALFOUR

CAMBERWELL (St George) *S'wark 8*　**P** *Bp and Trin Coll Cam (jt)*　**V** S DAWSON

CAMBERWELL (St Giles) (St Matthew) *S'wark 8*　**P** *Bp*　**V** N P GEORGE

CAMBERWELL (St Luke) *S'wark 8*　**P** *Bp*　**V** S V SCHLOSS　**NSM** C DURUEKE

CAMBERWELL (St Matthew) Conventional District *S'wark 8*　**Min** S NJOKA

CAMBERWELL (St Michael and All Angels w All Souls w Emmanuel) *S'wark* 10   **P** *DBP*   **V** J G A ROBERTS

CAMBERWELL (St Philip) and St Mark *S'wark* 7   **P** *The Crown*   **P-in-c** H HARKNETT

CAMBO (Holy Trinity) *see* Kirkwhelpington, Kirkharle, Kirkheaton and Cambo *Newc*

CAMBOIS (St Andrew's Mission Church) *see* Bedlington, Cambois and Sleekburn *Newc*

CAMBORNE (St Martin and St Meriadoc), Tuckingmill and Penponds *Truro* 1   **P** *The Crown and Patr Bd (alt)* **P-in-c** R E BROWNING   **C** G J ADAMSON   **NSM** N J POTTER

CAMBOURNE (no dedication) *Ely* 1   **P** *Bp*   **V** *vacant*

CAMBRIDGE (Christ Church) *see* Cambridge St Andr Less *Ely*

CAMBRIDGE (Good Shepherd) *see* Chesterton Gd Shep *Ely*

CAMBRIDGE (Holy Cross) *Ely* 2   **P** *Bp*   **V** *vacant*

CAMBRIDGE (Holy Sepulchre) (St Andrew the Great) *Ely* 2   **P** *PCC*   **V** A D M PAINE   **C** R J STRACHAN

CAMBRIDGE (Holy Trinity) *Ely* 3   **P** *D&C and Peache Trustees (jt)*   **P-in-c** S J BROWNING   **C** O W Y BENYON

CAMBRIDGE (St Andrew the Great) *see* Cambridge H Sepulchre *Ely*

CAMBRIDGE (St Andrew the Less) (Christ Church) *Ely* 2   **P** *Ch Trust Fund Trust*   **V** S N MIDGLEY   **C** D A TODD, M J W NICHOLSON, R A H EVANS

CAMBRIDGE (St Augustine of Canterbury) *see* Cambridge Ascension *Ely*

CAMBRIDGE (St Barnabas) *Ely* 3   **P** *V Cam St Paul*   **V** A F MACLAURIN   **C** D J DRIVER, T S SMITH

CAMBRIDGE (St Benedict) *Ely* 3   **P** *CCC Cam*   **V** A R MATTHEWS   **NSM** O FABRIKANT-BURKE

CAMBRIDGE (St Botolph) *Ely* 3   **P** *Qu Coll Cam*   **R** *vacant*

CAMBRIDGE (St Clement) *Ely* 2   **P** *Jes Coll Cam* **P-in-c** N I MOIR

CAMBRIDGE (St Edward King and Martyr) Proprietary Chapel *Ely* 3   **C-in-c** M SCARLATA   **C** M GREBE

CAMBRIDGE (St Giles) *see* Cambridge Ascension *Ely*

CAMBRIDGE (St James) *Ely* 3   **P** *Bp*   **V** S ROTHWELL   **C** A E STRAUSS   **NSM** D P FORD, R HEWITT

CAMBRIDGE (St Luke the Evangelist) *see* Cambridge Ascension *Ely*

CAMBRIDGE (St Mark) *Ely* 3   **P** *DBP*   **V** R C ROSBOROUGH   **NSM** A R HURST

CAMBRIDGE (St Martin) (St Thomas) *Ely* 3   **P** *V Cam St Paul*   **V** J ROTH   **NSM** C A COLE

CAMBRIDGE (St Mary the Great) w St Michael *Ely* 2   **P** *Trin Coll Cam*   **V** A M DAFFERN   **C** D C G BAGNALL, D S MCLACHLAN, H M ORR, J SANDERS   **NSM** A C DAY, S S HOLDER

CAMBRIDGE (St Mary the Less) *Ely* 3   **P** *Peterho Cam*   **V** R M MACKLEY   **NSM** M A BISHOP

CAMBRIDGE (St Matthew) *Ely* 2   **P** *V Cam St Andr the Less*   **V** F L PRICE   **C** T W N SIMPSON

CAMBRIDGE (St Paul) *Ely* 3   **P** *Ch Trust Fund Trust*   **NSM** C J ROSE

CAMBRIDGE (St Philip) (St Stephen) *Ely* 3   **P** *Ch Trust Fund Trust*   **C** S A YOUNG   **Hon C** C R IEVINS

CAMBRIDGE (St Thomas) *see* Cambridge St Martin *Ely*

CAMBRIDGE Ascension (St Giles) (St Luke the Evangelist) (St Augustine of Canterbury) (All Souls Chapel) *Ely* 2   **P** *Bp*   **TR** P A KING   **TV** J C BUNKER   **Hon C** T AMBROSE

CAMDEN SQUARE (St Paul) *see* Old St Pancras *Lon*

CAMDEN TOWN (St Michael) *see* Old St Pancras *Lon*

CAMEL, WEST (All Saints) *see* Cam Vale *B & W*

CAMEL-ALLEN Benefice, The, comprising Advent, Lanteglos-by-Camelford, and St Teath *Truro* 10   **P** *Duchy of Cornwall and Bp (by turn)*   **R** A J COOPER   **NSM** R J TERRY

CAMELFORD (St Julitta) *see* Camel-Allen *Truro*

CAMELFORD (St Thomas of Canterbury) *as above*

CAMELOT Parishes, The, comprising Blackford, Bratton St Maur, Compton Pauncefoot, Holton, Maperton, North Cadbury, North Cheriton, South Cadbury, and Yarlington *B & W* 2   **P** *Patr Bd*   **R** T G RAE SMITH   **C** A C CREEDON   **NSM** A L PARRIS

CAMELSDALE (St Paul) *see* Fernhurst, Lynchmere and Camelsdale *Chich*

CAMELSIDE Benefice, The, comprising Blisland, Helland, St Berward, St Mabyn, and St Tudy w Michaelstow *Truro* 10   **P** *Duchy of Cornwall (1 turn), D&C, Ch Ox, SMF, MMCET, and Viscount Falmouth (1 turn)*   **R** D R R SEYMOUR   **C** R J THWAITES   **NSM** S E WILLIAMS

CAMERTON (St Peter) *see* Timsbury w Priston, Camerton and Dunkerton *B & W*

CAMERTON (St Peter), Seaton and West Seaton *Carl* 7   **P** *D&C and Ch Trust Fund Trust (jt)*   **V** I GRAINGER   **NSM** I FEARON

CAMMERINGHAM (St Michael) *see* Springline *Linc*

CAMP HILL (St Mary and St John) *Cov* 5   **P** *Bp*   **V** *vacant*

CAMPDEN HILL (St George) *see* Holland Park *Lon*

CAMPSALL (St Mary Magdalene) *see* Burghwallis and Campsall *Sheff*

CAMPSEA ASHE (St John the Baptist) *see* Orebeck *St E*

CAMPTON (All Saints), Clophill and Haynes *St Alb* 8   **P** *Bp and Ball Coll Ox (alt)*   **R** *vacant*

CANALSIDE Benefice, The, comprising Hilperton w Whaddon, Semington, and Staverton w Hilperton Marsh *Sarum* 15   **P** *Magd Coll Cam and R Trowbridge St Jas and Keevil (alt)*   **R** J N REES   **NSM** J E ALBONE

CANDLESBY (St Benedict) *see* Bolingbroke Deanery *Linc*

CANEWDON (St Nicholas) *see* Ashingdon w S Fambridge, Canewdon and Paglesham *Chelmsf*

CANFIELD, GREAT (St Mary) w High Roding and Aythorpe Roding *Chelmsf* 17   **P** *A Sainthill Esq, Ch Soc Trust, and Bp (by turn)*   **P-in-c** R D STONE   **C** G A FLEMING   **NSM** T E GOODBODY

CANFIELD, LITTLE (All Saints) *see* Takeley w Lt Canfield *Chelmsf*

CANFORD CLIFFS (Transfiguration) and Sandbanks *Sarum* 7   **P** *Bp*   **V** A D O'BRIEN   **C** T J PELHAM

CANFORD HEATH (St Paul) *Sarum* 7   **P** *Bp*   **V** M D WILLIAMS

CANFORD MAGNA (no dedication) (Bearwood) (The Lantern) *Sarum* 9   **P** *Patr Bd*   **TR** M TUFNELL   **TV** C M TEBBUTT   **C** K A FRANKLIN, P J NESBITT   **NSM** S E TEBBUTT

CANLEY (St Stephen) *see* The Bridge, Cov *Cov*

CANNING TOWN (St Matthias) *Chelmsf* 5   **P** *Bp*   **V** *vacant*

CANNINGS AND REDHORN, The, comprising All Cannings, Bishop's Cannings and Etchilhampton, Chirton and Patney, Marden, Urchfont w Stert, and Wilsford *Sarum* 17   **P** *Patr Bd*   **TR** L R CURTIS

CANNINGTON (Blessed Virgin Mary), Otterhampton, Combwich and Stockland *B & W* 17   **P** *Bp*   **R** A J WATERS   **NSM** J M CHURCH

CANNOCK (St Luke) and Huntington *Lich* 3   **P** *Bp and D&C (jt)*   **V** V R FLEMING   **C** M T M MEREDITH   **OLM** G M JOYNSON

CANON FROME (St James) *see* Hop Churches *Heref*

CANON PYON (St Lawrence) w King's Pyon, Birley and Wellington *Heref* 6   **P** *Bp, Ch Union, and D&C (jt)*   **V** J A DAVIES   **C** D J WYATT

CANONBURY (St Stephen) *Lon* 6   **P** *V Islington St Mary*   **V** *vacant*

CANONRY Benefice, The, comprising Ash w Westmarsh, Chillenden w Knowlton, Elmstone w Preston and Stourmouth, Goodnestone, Nonington, and Wingham *Cant* 1   **P** *Abp, D&C, and Lord Fitzwalter (jt)*   **V** D I MOULDEN

CANTERBURY (All Saints) *Cant* 3   **P** *Abp*   **P-in-c** P GREIG   **C** L FYFE-JAMIESON

CANTERBURY (St Dunstan w Holy Cross) (St Mildred) (St Peter w St Alphege) *Cant* 3   **P** *Abp, Ld Chan, and D&C (by turn)*   **R** J S RICHARDS   **C** J E B WALPOLE

CANTERBURY (St Martin) (St Paul) *Cant* 3   **P** *Abp*   **R** M R GRIFFIN   **C** H N THOMSON

CANTERBURY (St Mary Bredin) *Cant* 3   **P** *Simeon's Trustees*   **V** B J D L T DE BERRY   **C** C F MUIR, S L CARTER

CANTERBURY (St Stephen) *see* Hackington *Cant*

CANTLEY (St Margaret) *see* Acle and Bure to Yare *Nor*

CANTLEY (St Wilfrid) *Sheff* 8   **P** *Guild of All So*   **V** A HOWARD

CANTLEY, NEW (St Hugh of Lincoln) (Holy Trinity) *Sheff* 8   **P** *Guild of All So and SMF (jt)*   **V** W J STOKOE

CANVEY ISLAND (St Anne) (St Katherine's Worship Centre) (St Nicholas) *Chelmsf* 12   **P** *Bp and Patr Bd (jt)*   **TR** D S C TUDOR   **TV** M G WALFORD   **NSM** L A MCGLYNN   **OLM** T F BROWN

CANWICK (All Saints) *see* Washingborough w Heighington and Canwick *Linc*

CAPEL (St John the Baptist) *see* Surrey Weald *Guildf*

CAPEL (St Thomas à Becket) United Benefice, including Tudeley and Five Oak Green *Roch* 8   **P** *Bp*   **V** J G A IVE   **C** P F IVE

CAPEL LE FERNE (St Radigund) *see* Alkham w Capel le Ferne and Hougham *Cant*

CAPEL ST MARY (St Mary) w Little Wenham and Great Wenham *St E* 13   **P** *Bp and SMF (jt)*   **C** S J LETMAN

CAPENHURST (Holy Trinity) *see* Backford and Capenhurst *Ches*

CAPESTHORNE (Holy Trinity) *see* Marton, Siddington w Capesthorne etc *Ches*

CAR COLSTON (St Mary) w Screveton *S'well* 5   **P** *H S Blagg Esq*   **P-in-c** R M COLBY

CARBIS BAY (St Anta and All Saints) w Lelant (St Uny) *Truro* 4   **P** *Bp*   **P-in-c** E VAN BLERK

CARBROOKE (St Peter and St Paul) *see* Watton *Nor*

CARDESTON (St Michael) *see* Ford, Gt Wollaston and Alberbury w Cardeston *Heref*

CARDINGTON (St James) *see* Apedale Gp *Heref*

CARDINGTON (St Mary) *see* Elstow *St Alb*

CARDYNHAM (St Meubred) *see* Bodmin *Truro*

CAREBY (St Stephen) *see* Bytham Par *Linc*

CARHAM (St Cuthbert) *see* Cornhill w Carham *Newc*

CARHAMPTON (St John the Baptist) *see* Dunster, Carhampton, Withycombe w Rodhuish etc *B & W*

CARHARRACK (St Piran's Mission Church) *see* Chacewater w St Day and Carharrack *Truro*

CARISBROOKE (St Mary the Virgin) *see* Newport and Carisbrooke *Portsm*

CARLBY (St Stephen) *see* Ryhall w Essendine and Carlby *Pet*

CARLETON (St Chad) *see* Poulton Carleton and Singleton *Blackb*

CARLETON (St Mary the Virgin) *see* Skipton Ch Ch w Carleton *Leeds*

CARLETON (St Michael) and E Hardwick *Leeds* 15 **P** *V Pontefract and Cawood Trustees (jt)* **V** S A STACEY **NSM** K REYNOLDS

CARLETON (St Peter) *see* Rockland St Mary w Hellington, Bramerton etc *Nor*

CARLETON IN CRAVEN *see* Skipton Ch Ch w Carleton *Leeds*

CARLETON RODE (All Saints) *see* Long Stratton and Pilgrim TM *Nor*

CARLETON, EAST (St Mary) *see* Swardeston w E Carleton, Intwood, Keswick etc *Nor*

CARLFORD, comprising Ashbocking, Boulge, Burgh, Clopton, Culpho, Grundisburgh, Hasketon, Otley, and Swilland *St E* 16 **P** *Bp (1 turn), DBP (2 turns), Ld Chan (1 turn)* **R** K M DYKES **NSM** M C S CRESSWELL

CARLIN HOW (St Helen) *see* Loftus and Carlin How w Skinningrove *York*

CARLINGHOW (St John the Evangelist) *see* Staincliffe and Carlinghow *Leeds*

CARLISLE (Holy Trinity) (St Barnabas) *Carl* 3 **P** *Patr Bd* **P-in-c** M A MARTINSON

CARLISLE (St Aidan) and Christ Church *Carl* 3 **P** *Bp* **P-in-c** K TEASDALE

CARLISLE (St Cuthbert) *Carl* 3 **P** *D&C* **V** K TEASDALE

CARLISLE (St Elisabeth) Harraby *see* Harraby *Carl*

CARLISLE (St Herbert) w St Stephen *Carl* 3 **P** *Bp* **V** A JONES

CARLISLE (St James) *see* Denton Holme *Carl*

CARLISLE (St John the Evangelist) *Carl* 3 **P** *CPAS* **V** S DONALD

CARLISLE (St Luke) Morton *Carl* 3 **P** *Bp* **P-in-c** M A MARTINSON

CARLISLE (St Michael) *see* Stanwix *Carl*

CARLISLE Belah (St Mark) *as above*

CARLTON (St Aidan) *see* Helmsley *York*

CARLTON (St Andrew) *see* Bosworth *Leic*

CARLTON (St Botolph) *see* Whorlton Gp *York*

CARLTON (St John the Baptist) *S'well* 7 **P** *Bp* **C** D E MOYO

CARLTON (St John the Evangelist) *see* Athersley and Carlton *Leeds*

CARLTON (St Mary) *see* Chellington *St Alb*

CARLTON (St Peter) *see* Raddesley Gp *Ely*

CARLTON (St Peter) *see* Saxmundham w Kelsale cum Carlton *St E*

CARLTON BY SNAITH (St Mary) and Drax *York* 4 **P** *Abp and Ch Trust Fund Trust (jt)* **P-in-c** A V BURR **C** R J ALLRIGHT

CARLTON COLVILLE (St Peter) and Mutford *Nor* 9 **P** *Simeon's Trustees and G&C Coll Cam (jt)* **P-in-c** S E QUANTRILL

CARLTON CURLIEU (St Mary the Virgin) *see* Oadby *Leic*

CARLTON FOREHOE (St Mary) *see* Barnham Broom and Upper Yare *Nor*

CARLTON HUSTHWAITE (St Mary) *see* Coxwold and Husthwaite *York*

CARLTON MINIOTT (St Lawrence) *see* Thirsk *York*

CARLTON SCROOP (St Nicholas) *see* S Cliff Villages Gp *Linc*

CARLTON, EAST (St Peter) *see* Gretton w Rockingham and Cottingham w E Carlton *Pet*

CARLTON, GREAT (St John the Baptist) *see* Mid Marsh Gp *Linc*

CARLTON, NORTH (St Luke) *see* Springline *Linc*

CARLTON, SOUTH (St John the Baptist) *as above*

CARLTON-IN-LINDRICK (St John the Evangelist) and Langold w Oldcotes *S'well* 1 **P** *Bp and Ld Chan (alt)* **R** M ORR

CARLTON-IN-THE-WILLOWS (St Paul) *S'well* 7 **P** *MMCET* **NSM** W S MURPHY

CARLTON-LE-MOORLAND (St Mary) *see* Withamside *Linc*

CARLTON-ON-TRENT (St Mary) *see* Norwell w Ossington, Cromwell etc *S'well*

CARNABY (St John the Baptist) *see* Rudston, Boynton, Carnaby etc *York*

CARNFORTH (Christ Church) *Blackb* 14 **P** *Bp* **V** S L JONES

CARNFORTH (Holy Trinity) *see* Bolton-le-Sands *Blackb*

CARR CLOUGH (St Andrew) *see* Kersal Moor *Man*

CARR DYKE GROUP, The, comprising Billinghay, Martin, North Kyme, South Kyme, Timberland, and Walcott *Linc* 14 **P** *Sir Philip Naylor-Leyland Bt and Ld Chan (alt)* **V** S R HOLT **NSM** H M EKE **OLM** D E WESTON

CARR MILL (St David) *Liv* 10 **P** *V St Helens St Mark and Bp (jt)* **V** S L DAVIES

CARRINGTON (St John the Evangelist) *S'well* 9 **P** *Bp* **V** *vacant*

CARRINGTON (St Paul) *see* Sibsey w Frithville *Linc*

CARSHALTON (All Saints) *S'wark* 23 **P** *Bp* **R** D S FISHER **C** D J BURTON

CARSHALTON BEECHES (Good Shepherd) *S'wark* 23 **P** *Bp* **V** K J LEWIS **C** H GORDON

CARSINGTON (St Margaret) *see* Wirksworth *Derby*

CARTERTON (St John the Evangelist) *see* Brize Norton and Carterton *Ox*

CARTMEL FELL (St Anthony) *Carl* 10 **P** *Bp* **V** M D WOODCOCK **Hon C** S C HOWARD **NSM** M L WOODCOCK

CARTMEL PENINSULA Team Ministry, The (St Mary and St Michael), including Allithwaite, Field Broughton, Finsthwaite, Flookburgh, Grange-over-Sands, Haverthwaite, Lindale, and Staveley-in-Cartmel *Carl* 11 **P** *Patr Bd* **TV** N E DEVENISH, R L STAVERT

CASSINGTON (St Peter) *see* Eynsham and Cassington *Ox*

CASTERTON (Holy Trinity) *see* Kirkby Lonsdale *Carl*

CASTERTON, GREAT (St Peter and St Paul) and Tickencote and Little Casterton w Pickworth *Pet* 12 **P** *Burghley Ho Preservation Trust Ltd (2 turns), Lord Chesham (1 turn), and Bp (1 turn)* **P-in-c** J J S MCGARRIGLE

CASTERTON, LITTLE (All Saints) *see* Gt Casterton and Tickencote and Lt Casterton w Pickworth *Pet*

CASTLE ACRE (St James) *see* Nar Valley *Nor*

CASTLE ASHBY (St Mary Magdalene) *see* Yardley Hastings, Denton and Grendon etc *Pet*

CASTLE BOLTON (St Oswald) *see* Penhill *Leeds*

CASTLE BROMWICH (St Clement) *Birm* 5 **P** *Bp* **V** *vacant*

CASTLE BROMWICH (St Mary and St Margaret) *Birm* 5 **P** *Earl of Bradf* **R** M J HOPKINS

CASTLE BYTHAM (St James) *see* Bytham Par *Linc*

CASTLE CAMPS (All Saints) *see* Linton *Ely*

CASTLE CARROCK (St Peter) *see* Eden, Gelt and Irthing *Carl*

CASTLE CARY (All Saints) and Ansford *B & W* 2 **P** *Bp* **P-in-c** E ISTED

CASTLE CHURCH (St Mary) *Lich* 10 **P** *Bp* **V** P J SOWERBUTTS **C** I A LINGWOOD **NSM** C V SYKES

CASTLE COMBE (St Andrew) *see* By Brook *Bris*

CASTLE DONINGTON (St Edward the King and Martyr) and Lockington cum Hemington *Leic* 6 **P** *Lady Gretton and C H C Coaker Esq (jt)* **V** A J RACE

CASTLE EATON (St Mary the Virgin) *see* S Cotswolds *Glouc*

CASTLE FROME (St Michael) *see* Frome Valley *Heref*

CASTLE HEDINGHAM (St Nicholas) *see* The Hedinghams and Upper Colne *Chelmsf*

CASTLE NORTHWICH (Holy Trinity) *see* Northwich H Trin *Ches*

CASTLE RISING (St Lawrence) *Nor* 15 **P** *G Howard Esq* **R** J B V RIVIERE

CASTLE SOWERBY (St Kentigern) *see* Caldbeck, Castle Sowerby and Sebergham *Carl*

CASTLE VALE (St Cuthbert of Lindisfarne) w Minworth *Birm* 4 **P** *Bp* **V** J B A COPE

CASTLE VIEW ESTATE (St Francis) *see* Langley Marish *Ox*

CASTLECROFT (The Good Shepherd) *see* Tettenhall Wood and Perton *Lich*

CASTLEFIELDS (All Saints and St Michael) *see* Shrewsbury All SS w St Mich *Lich*

CASTLEFORD Team Parish (All Saints) (St Michael and All Angels), including Glasshoughton, Hightown, and Whitwood *Leeds* 15 **P** *Duchy of Lanc and Bp (alt)* **TR** K I FREEMAN **TV** G K RUSZCZYNSKI

CASTLEMORTON (St Gregory) *see* Longdon, Castlemorton, Bushley, Queenhill etc *Worc*

CASTLESIDE (St John the Evangelist) *Dur* 2 **P** *Bp* **P-in-c** M JACKSON **NSM** P A CARTER

CASTLETHORPE (St Simon and St Jude) *see* Hanslope w Castlethorpe *Ox*

CASTLETON (St Edmund) *see* Hope, Castleton and Bradwell *Derby*

CASTLETON (St Mary Magdalene)   *see* Sherborne w Castleton, Lillington and Longburton *Sarum*

CASTLETON (St Michael and St George)   *see* The Moorlands *York*

CASTLETON MOOR (St Martin) *Man 6*   **P** *Bp*   **V** F C GUITE   **NSM** S SHEPHERD

CASTON (St Cross), Griston, Merton, Thompson, Stow Bedon, Breckles and Great Hockham *Nor 13*   **P** *Bp and DBP (jt)*   **R** *vacant*

CASTOR (St Kyneburgha) w Upton and Stibbington and Water Newton, Marholm and Sutton *Pet 11*   **P** *Mrs V S V Gunnery, Sir Philip Naylor-Leyland Bt, and Keble Coll Ox (jt)*   **R** D RIDGEWAY

CATCLIFFE (St Mary)   *see* Rivers Team *Sheff*

CATCOTT (St Peter)   *see* Polden Wheel *B & W*

CATERHAM (St Mary the Virgin) (St Laurence) (St Paul) (St John the Evangelist) *S'wark 25*   **P** *Bp*
P-in-c T A MAPSTONE   **TV** C L DOWLAND-PILLINGER, H J BURNETT, J GARTON, P A KURK   **NSM** A-M GARTON, F M LONG

CATESBY (St Mary)   *see* Daventry *Pet*

CATFIELD (All Saints)   *see* Ludham, Potter Heigham, Hickling and Catfield *Nor*

CATFORD (St Andrew) *S'wark 4*   **P** *Bp*   **V** L T F MCKENNA

CATFORD (St John) Southend and Downham *S'wark 4*   **P** *Bp*   **TV** N S WALSH, S D LECK

CATFORD (St Laurence) *S'wark 4*   **P** *Bp*   **V** C F PICKSTONE
P-in-c R F HUTCHINS   **NSM** A M GOTHARD

CATHERINGTON (All Saints) and Clanfield *Portsm 5*   **P** *Bp*

CATHERINGTON LEWESTON (St Mary)   *see* Golden Cap Team *Sarum*

CATON (St Paul) w Littledale *Blackb 14*   **P** *V Lanc*
V P R BOULTER

CATSFIELD (St Laurence) and Crowhurst *Chich 12*   **P** *Bp and J P Papillon (alt)*   **R** *vacant*

CATSHILL (Christ Church)   *see* Bromsgrove *Worc*

CATTERICK (St Anne) *Leeds 19*   **P** *Bp*   **V** L M SOUTHERN

CATTHORPE (St Thomas)   *see* Avon-Swift *Leic*

CATTISTOCK (St Peter and St Paul)   *see* Melbury *Sarum*

CATTON (All Saints)   *see* Stamford Bridge Gp *York*

CATTON (St Nicholas and the Blessed Virgin Mary)   *see* Walton-on-Trent w Croxall, Rosliston etc *Derby*

CATTON, NEW (Christ Church) *Nor 2*   **P** *Bp*
P-in-c S C STOKES   **C** D M DORAN-SMITH

CATTON, NEW (St Luke) w St Augustine *Nor 2*   **P** *Bp, D&C, and CPAS (jt)*   **V** *vacant*

CATTON, OLD (St Margaret) *Nor 2*   **P** *D&C*
V D E HAGAN-PALMER

CATWICK (St Michael)   *see* Skirlaugh, Catwick, Long Riston, Rise, Swine w Ellerby *York*

CATWORTH, GREAT (St Leonard)   *see* W Leightonstone *Ely*

CAULDON (St Mary and St Laurence)   *see* Calton, Cauldon, Grindon, Waterfall etc *Lich*

CAUNDLE MARSH (St Peter and St Paul)   *see* Three Valleys *Sarum*

CAUNTON (St Andrew)   *see* Norwell w Ossington, Cromwell etc *S'well*

CAUSEWAY HEAD (St Paul)   *see* Solway Plain *Carl*

CAUTLEY (St Mark)   *see* Western Dales *Carl*

CAVENDISH (St Mary)   *see* Stour Valley *St E*

CAVENHAM (St Andrew)   *see* Forest Heath *St E*

CAVERSFIELD (St Laurence)   *see* Bicester w Bucknell, Caversfield and Launton *Ox*

CAVERSHAM (Park Church)   *see* Emmer Green w Caversham Park *Ox*

CAVERSHAM (St Andrew) *Ox 7*   **P** *Bp*   **V** N D JONES

CAVERSHAM (St John the Baptist)   *see* Caversham Thameside and Mapledurham *Ox*

CAVERSHAM (St Peter)   *as above*

CAVERSHAM HEIGHTS (St Andrew)   *see* Caversham St Andr *Ox*

CAVERSHAM THAMESIDE (St Peter) (St John the Baptist) and Mapledurham *Ox 7*   **P** *Ch Ch Ox, Eton Coll, and Bp (jt)*
R M K J SMITH   **C** P J CUTHBERT   **NSM** A J STORCH, R A ROSS

CAVERSWALL (St Peter) and Weston Coyney w Dilhorne *Lich 6*   **P** *D&C*   **V** *vacant*

CAWOOD (All Saints) w Ryther and Wistow *York 4*   **P** *Abp and Ld Chan (alt)*   **R** *vacant*

CAWSAND (St Andrew's Mission Church)   *see* Maker w Rame, Millbrook, St John and Torpoint *Truro*

CAWSTON (St Agnes)   *see* Aylsham and Distr *Nor*

CAWTHORNE (All Saints)   *see* W Barnsley *Leeds*

CAXTON (St Andrew)   *see* Papworth *Ely*

CAYNHAM (St Mary)   *see* The Ashfords *Heref*

CAYTHORPE (St Aidan)   *see* Burton Joyce, Bulcote and Stoke Bardolph etc *S'well*

CAYTHORPE (St Vincent)   *see* S Cliff Villages Gp *Linc*

CAYTON (St John the Baptist)   *see* Seamer, E Ayton and Cayton *York*

CENTRAL   *see under substantive place name*

CERNE ABBAS (St Mary)   *see* Buckland Newton, Cerne Abbas, Godmanstone etc *Sarum*

CERNEY WICK (Holy Trinity)   *see* S Cerney w Cerney Wick, Siddington and Preston *Glouc*

CERNEY, NORTH (All Saints)   *see* Churn Valley *Glouc*

CERNEY, SOUTH (All Hallows) w Cerney Wick, Siddington and Preston *Glouc 7*   **P** *Bp and Mrs P Chester-Master (1 turn), Ld Chan (1 turn)*   **V** J M MCKENZIE

CHACELEY (St John the Baptist)   *see* Deerhurst and Apperley w Forthampton etc *Glouc*

CHACEWATER (St Paul) w St Day and Carharrack *Truro 1*   **P** *D&C and R Kenwyn w St Allen (jt)*   **C** R D WALLIS   **NSM** J ROWE

CHACOMBE (St Peter and St Paul)   *see* Chenderit *Pet*

CHADBROOK, comprising Alpheton, Shimplingthorne, and Long Melford *St E 8*   **P** *Bp and DBP (jt)*   **R** M C O LAWSON   **NSM** J A OFFORD

CHADDERTON (Christ Church) (St Saviour) *Man 5*   **P** *Ch Soc Trust*   **V** *vacant*

CHADDERTON (St Mark) and Middleton Junction *Man 5*   **P** *The Crown and Bp (alt)*   **V** S SMITH

CHADDERTON (St Matthew) St Luke *Man 5*   **P** *Bp and The Crown (alt)*   **V** D R PENNY

CHADDERTON Emmanuel (St George) *Man 5*   **P** *Trustees*   **V** E D H LEAF

CHADDESDEN (St Mary) *Derby 5*   **P** MMCET   **V** J D WARD

CHADDESDEN (St Philip) w Derby St Mark *Derby 5*   **P** *Bp*
P-in-c J F HOLLYWELL   **C** S L WATSON   **Hon C** M R FUTERS

CHADDESLEY CORBETT (St Cassian)   *see* Kidderminster E *Worc*

CHADDLEWORTH (St Andrew)   *see* W Downland *Ox*

CHADLINGTON (St Nicholas)   *see* Chase *Ox*

CHADSMOOR (St Aidan) (St Chad) *Lich 3*   **P** *Bp and D&C (jt)*   **V** N UPSON-SMITH

CHADWELL (Emmanuel) (St Mary) *Chelmsf 15*   **P** *Ch Soc Trust*   **R** *vacant*

CHADWELL HEATH (St Chad) *Chelmsf 1*   **P** *Vs Dagenham and Ilford (alt)*   **V** M J COURT   **C** C F NDUKU   **NSM** C J HARDING

CHAFFCOMBE (St Michael and All Angels), Cricket Malherbie w Knowle St Giles, Tatworth, Thorncombe and Winsham *B & W 16*   **P** *Bp and C G S Eyre Esq (jt)*
V P I C BUTCHER   **NSM** J ABBOTT

CHAFFORD HUNDRED (All Saints)   *see* Grays Thurrock *Chelmsf*

CHAGFORD (St Michael), Gidleigh, Throwleigh, Drewsteignton, South Tawton, Spreyton, Hittisleigh, North Tawton, Bondleigh, Honeychurch and Sampford Courtenay *Ex 9*   **P** *Patr Bd*   **TR** P S SEATON-BURN   **TV** N P WELDON   **C** M A NEAVE   **NSM** H M EVERY

CHAILEY (St Peter) *Chich 18*   **P** *J P B Tillard Esq*
P-in-c P K MUNDY

CHALBURY (All Saints)   *see* Wimborne Minster and Villages *Sarum*

CHALDON (St Peter and St Paul)   *see* Caterham *S'wark*

CHALDON HERRING (St Nicholas)   *see* W Purbeck *Sarum*

CHALE (St Andrew) *Portsm 7*   **P** *Keble Coll Ox*   **R** *vacant*

CHALFIELD, GREAT (All Saints)   *see* Broughton Gifford, Gt Chalfield and Holt *Sarum*

CHALFONT ST GILES (St Giles), Seer Green and Jordans *Ox 9*   **P** *Bp*   **NSM** J M TEBBOTH, M T BLEAKLEY, P E HENDERSON

CHALFONT ST PETER (St Peter) *Ox 9*   **P** *St Jo Coll Ox*
R J P GOODMAN

CHALFONT, LITTLE (St George)   *see* Chenies and Lt Chalfont, Latimer and Flaunden *Ox*

CHALFORD (Christ Church)   *see* Bisley, Chalford, France Lynch, and Oakridge etc *Glouc*

CHALGRAVE (All Saints)   *see* Toddington and Chalgrave *St Alb*

CHALGROVE (St Mary) w Berrick Salome *Ox 20*   **P** *Ch Ch Ox*   **V** M J LAKEY   **NSM** S H MORGAN

CHALK (St Mary) *Roch 4*   **P** *CPAS and Bp (jt)*   **V** N I BOURNE

CHALK FARM (St Saviour) *Lon 15*   **P** *V Hampstead St Jo*
P-in-c P S NICHOLSON

CHALKE VALLEY (Team Ministry), comprising Berwick St John, Bishopstone and Stratford Tony, Bowerchalke, Britford, Broadchalke, Charlton-All-Saints, Coombe Bissett w Homington, Ebbesbourne Wake w Fifield Bavant and Alvediston, and Odstock w Nunton and Bodenham *Sarum 11*   **P** *Bp, DBP, and K Coll Cam (by turn)*
TR C BLUNDELL   **TV** J A TAYLOR   **NSM** R N S LEAKE

CHALLACOMBE (Holy Trinity) *see* Shirwell, Loxhore, Kentisbury, Arlington, etc *Ex*

CHALLOCK (St Cosmas and St Damian) *see* King's Wood *Cant*

CHALLOW, EAST (St Nicolas) *see* Vale *Ox*

CHALLOW, WEST (St Laurence) *see* Ridgeway *Ox*

CHALTON (St Michael and All Angels) *see* Blendworth w Chalton w Idsworth *Portsm*

CHALVEY (St Peter) *see* Upton cum Chalvey *Ox*

CHALVINGTON (St Bartholomew) *see* Laughton w Ripe and Chalvington *Chich*

CHANCTONBURY, comprising Ashington, Washington and Wiston w Buncton *Chich 5* **P** *Bp and R H Goring Esq (alt)* **R** J A DI CASTIGLIONE **C** J W B WADDELL, P J DONOVAN **NSM** P H T PEARSON-MILES

CHANDLER'S FORD (St Boniface) (St Martin in the Wood) *Win 10* **P** *Bp* **V** I N BIRD **NSM** H J RICHENS, P A THATCHER

CHANTRY (Holy Trinity) *see* Mells w Buckland Dinham, Elm, Whatley etc *B & W*

CHAPEL ALLERTON (St Matthew) *Leeds 10* **P** *V Leeds St Pet* **NSM** S RUSHOLME

CHAPEL CHORLTON (St Laurence), Maer and Whitmore *Lich 7* **P** *Bp and G Cavenagh-Mainwaring Esq (jt)* **R** N A CLEMAS

CHAPEL GREEN (St Oswald) *see* Lt Horton *Leeds*

CHAPEL HOUSE (Holy Nativity) *Newc 4* **P** *Bp* **V** *vacant*

CHAPEL LAWN (St Mary) *see* Middle Marches *Heref*

CHAPEL PLAISTER (not known) *see* Box w Hazlebury and Ditteridge *Bris*

CHAPEL ST LEONARDS (St Leonard) and Hogsthorpe and Mumby and Cumberworth *Linc 10* **P** *Bp, Ball Coll Ox, and Baroness Willoughby de Eresby (jt)* **V** *vacant*

CHAPEL-EN-LE-FRITH (St Thomas Becket) *Derby 4* **P** *PCC* **V** *vacant*

CHAPEL-LE-DALE (St Leonard) *see* Bentham, Burton-in-Lonsdale, Chapel-le-Dale etc *Leeds*

CHAPELTHORPE (St James) *Leeds 16* **P** *V Sandal* **V** K A N GREAVES **C** K J A GOLDSMITH

CHAPELTOWN (St John the Baptist) *Sheff 3* **P** *Bp* **V** R A STORDY **C** J G M CROSSLEY **NSM** A D WHITEHEAD

CHAPMANSLADE (St Philip and St James) *see* Cley Hill Villages *Sarum*

CHAPPEL (St Barnabas) *see* Gt and Lt Tey w Wakes Colne and Chappel *Chelmsf*

CHARD (Blessed Virgin Mary) w Combe St Nicholas, Wambrook and Whitestaunton *B & W 16* **P** *Bp and T V D Eames Esq (jt)* **R** A E KEMBER **C** G A VYE **NSM** J G ROLLINGS

CHARD (Good Shepherd) Furnham *B & W 14* **P** *Bp* **V** *vacant*

CHARDSTOCK (All Saints) *see* Axminster, All Saints, Axmouth, Chardstock etc *Ex*

CHARDSTOCK (St Andrew) *as above*

CHARFIELD (St John) and Kingswood w Wickwar, Rangeworthy and Hillesley *Glouc 5* **P** *Bp, DBP, R W Neeld Esq, and Earl of Ducie (jt)* **R** D J RUSSELL **Hon C** R H WILLIAMS

CHARFORD (St Andrew) *see* Bromsgrove *Worc*

CHARING (St Peter and St Paul) *see* Calehill w Westwell *Cant*

CHARING HEATH (Holy Trinity) *as above*

CHARLBURY (St Mary the Virgin) w Shorthampton *Ox 22* **P** *St Jo Coll Ox* **V** S A WELCH **NSM** J W FIELDEN, P M BIRD

CHARLCOMBE (Blessed Virgin Mary) w Bath (St Stephen) *B & W 8* **P** *DBP and Simeon's Trustees (jt)* **R** P A HAWTHORN **C** A R AVRAMENKO **NSM** D J POW

CHARLECOTE (St Leonard) *see* Hampton Lucy w Charlecote and Loxley *Cov*

CHARLES (St John the Baptist) *see* Bishopsnympton, Charles, E Anstey, High Bray etc *Ex*

CHARLES w Plymouth St Matthias *Ex 20* **P** *Ch Patr Trust* **P-in-c** O H D RYDER **C** M A KNIGHT, R V CROSSLEY

CHARLESTOWN (St George) *see* Salford All SS *Man*

CHARLESTOWN (St Thomas the Apostle) *see* Southowram *Leeds*

CHARLESWORTH (St John the Evangelist) and Gamesley *Derby 4* **P** *The Crown* **V** F A WALTERS

CHARLETON (St Mary) *see* Stokenham, Slapton, Charleton w Buckland etc *Ex*

CHARLTON (Holy Trinity) *see* Wantage *Ox*

CHARLTON (St John the Baptist) *see* Braydon Brook *Bris*

CHARLTON (St John the Baptist) *see* St Bartholomew *Sarum*

CHARLTON (St John) *see* Fladbury, Hill and Moor, Wyre Piddle etc *Worc*

CHARLTON (St Luke w Holy Trinity) (St Richard) (St Thomas) *S'wark 1* **P** *Bp and Viscount Gough (jt)* **R** E A NEWMAN **C** A DAVIES **NSM** J P LEE

CHARLTON (St Peter and St Paul) *see* Dover Town *Cant*

CHARLTON (St Peter) *see* Vale of Pewsey *Sarum*

CHARLTON ABBOTS (St Martin) *see* Sevenhampton w Charlton Abbots, Hawling etc *Glouc*

CHARLTON ADAM (St Peter and St Paul) *see* Somerton w The Charltons and Kingsdon *B & W*

CHARLTON HORETHORNE (St Peter and St Paul) *see* Milborne Port w Goathill etc *B & W*

CHARLTON KINGS (Holy Apostles) *Glouc 6* **P** *R Cheltenham* **V** A S COLLISHAW **C** R BEERE

CHARLTON KINGS (St Mary) *Glouc 6* **P** *Bp* **V** G P BOWKETT **C** A M BEERE

CHARLTON MACKRELL (St Mary the Virgin) *see* Somerton w The Charltons and Kingsdon *B & W*

CHARLTON MARSHALL (St Mary the Virgin) *see* Spetisbury w Charlton Marshall etc *Sarum*

CHARLTON MUSGROVE (St John) (St Stephen), Cucklington and Stoke Trister *B & W 2* **P** *Bp* **R** R C ASHLEY

CHARLTON ON OTMOOR (St Mary) *see* Ray Valley *Ox*

CHARLTON, SOUTH (St James) *see* Chatton w Chillingham, Eglingham and S Charlton and Ingram *Newc*

CHARLTON-ALL-SAINTS (All Saints) *see* Chalke Valley *Sarum*

CHARLWOOD (St Nicholas) *S'wark 24* **P** *DBP* **R** *vacant*

CHARMINSTER (St Mary the Virgin), Stinsford and the Chalk Stream villages *Sarum 1* **P** *Bp, the Hon C Townshend, and Win Coll (jt)* **R** M S PHILLIPS **C** L I N MATHER **NSM** P A C KENNEDY

CHARMOUTH (St Andrew) *see* Golden Cap Team *Sarum*

CHARNEY BASSETT (St Peter) *see* Cherbury w Gainfield *Ox*

CHARNOCK RICHARD (Christ Church) *see* Eccleston and Charnock Richard *Blackb*

CHARSFIELD W DEBACH (St Peter) *see* Mid Loes *St E*

CHART SUTTON (St Michael) *see* Headcorn and The Suttons *Cant*

CHART, GREAT (St Mary) *see* Ashford Town *Cant*

CHART, LITTLE (St Mary) *see* Calehill w Westwell *Cant*

CHARTERHOUSE-ON-MENDIP (St Hugh) *see* Blagdon w Compton Martin and Ubley *B & W*

CHARTHAM (St Mary) and Upper Hardres w Stelling *Cant 2* **P** *Abp and Trustees Lord Tomlin (jt)* **P-in-c** L C VINCER

CHARWELTON (Holy Trinity) *see* Badby w Newham and Charwelton w Fawsley etc *Pet*

CHASE, comprising Ascott-under-Wychwood, Chadlington, Enstone, and Spelsbury *Ox 22* **P** *Bp and D&C Ch Ch (jt)* **R** M E J ABREY **NSM** I C CHEYNE

CHASE, comprising Chettle, Farnham, Gussage All Saints, Gussage St Michael, Tarrant Gunville, Tarrant Hinton, Tarrant Keynston w Tarrant Crawford, Tarrant Monkton w Tarrant Launceston, and Tollard Royal *Sarum 6* **P** *Bp, Adn Dorset, Ch Soc Trust, Pemb Coll Cam, Univ Coll Ox, T Sweet-Escott Esq (4 turns), Ld Chan (1 turn)* **R** *vacant*

CHASETOWN (St Anne) *see* Burntwood, Chase Terrace etc *Lich*

CHASETOWN (St John) *as above*

CHASTLETON (St Mary the Virgin) *see* Chipping Norton *Ox*

CHATBURN (Christ Church) *see* Clitheroe St Mary and St Paul, Chatburn and Downham *Blackb*

CHATHAM (St David) *see* S Chatham H Trin *Roch*

CHATHAM (St Mary and St John) *Roch 5* **P** *D&C* **P-in-c** C J A MORGAN

CHATHAM (St Paul w All Saints) *Roch 5* **P** *Bp* **NSM** J M WARRINGTON

CHATHAM (St Philip and St James) *Roch 5* **P** *Ch Soc Trust* **V** M L J SAUNDERS **C** A K VAUGHAN, L N BACON **NSM** S C SPENCER

CHATHAM (St Stephen) *Roch 5* **P** *Bp* **V** B J LINNEY

CHATHAM, SOUTH Holy Trinity (St William) (St Alban) (St David) *Roch 5* **P** *Bp* **TR** E CRANMER **TV** D A KICHENSIDE **NSM** P A ROBINSON

CHATTERIS (St Peter and St Paul) *Ely 11* **P** *G&C Coll Cam* **V** W L THOMSON

CHATTISHAM (All Saints and St Margaret) *see* Elmsett w Aldham, Hintlesham, Chattisham etc *St E*

CHATTON (Holy Cross) w Chillingham, Eglingham and South Charlton and Ingram *Newc 7* **P** *Bp and Duke of Northumberland (1 turn), Ld Chan (1 turn)* **V** *vacant*

CHAVEY DOWN (St Martin) *see* Winkfield and Cranbourne *Ox*

CHAWLEIGH (St James) *see* Burrington, Chawleigh, Cheldon, Chulmleigh etc *Ex*

CHAWTON (St Nicholas) *see* Northanger *Win*

CHEADLE (All Hallows) (St Philip's Mission Church)
Ches 17   **P** *R Cheadle*   **V** P J CUMMING   **C** C J JOHNSON
NSM G H HALL
CHEADLE (St Cuthbert) (St Mary) *Ches 17*   **P** *Ch Soc Trust*
R R S MUNRO   **C** I L CHIDLOW, J E M NEWMAN,
S J E TOMALIN
CHEADLE (St Giles) w Freehay *Lich 6*   **P** *DBP*   **R** N J F GREY
C F A BRIDGEWATER
CHEADLE HULME (All Saints) *Ches 17*   **P** *Bp*   **V** S HANCOCK
CHEADLE HULME (St Andrew) *Ches 17*   **P** *R Cheadle*
V C J P HOBBS   **NSM** P L SELBY
CHEAM (St Dunstan) (St Alban the Martyr) (St Oswald)
S'wark 23   **P** *Patr Bd*   **TR** N J PEACOCK   **TV** B L LEWIS
C S A NADARAJAH   **NSM** F A NORRIS, F J A PERLMAN
CHEARSLEY (St Nicholas) *see* Long Crendon w Chearsley
and Nether Winchendon *Ox*
**CHEBSEY (All Saints), Creswell, Ellenhall, Ranton and
Seighford** *Lich 7*   **P** *D&C, Qu Eliz Grant Trustees, Trustees
Earl of Lich, and J Eld Esq (jt)*   **P-in-c** D HEMING
CHECKENDON (St Peter and St Paul) *see* Langtree *Ox*
CHECKLEY (Mission Room) *see* Fownhope w Mordiford,
Brockhampton etc *Heref*
CHECKLEY (St Mary and All Saints) *see* Uttoxeter Area *Lich*
CHEDBURGH (All Saints) *see* Chevington w Hargrave,
Chedburgh w Depden etc *St E*
CHEDDAR (St Andrew), Draycott and Rodney Stoke
B & W 1   **P** *Bp and D&C (jt)*   **R** S S BURNS
NSM D L OLIVER, R C MOTION
CHEDDINGTON (St Giles) *see* Cottesloe *Ox*
**CHEDDLETON (St Edward the Confessor), Horton,
Longsdon and Rushton Spencer** *Lich 8*   **P** *Bp and R Leek
and Meerbrook (jt)*   **V** vacant
CHEDDON FITZPAINE (The Blessed Virgin Mary) *see* S
Quantock *B & W*
CHEDGRAVE (All Saints) *see* Loddon, Sisland, Chedgrave,
Hardley and Langley *Nor*
CHEDISTON (St Mary) *see* Blyth Valley *St E*
**CHEDWORTH (St Andrew), Yanworth and Stowell, Coln
Rogers and Coln St Denys** *Glouc 8*   **P** *Ld Chan (2 turns), Qu
Coll Ox (1 turn)*   **R** S J GOUNDREY-SMITH
CHEDZOY (The Blessed Virgin Mary) *see* Weston Zoyland w
Chedzoy *B & W*
CHEETHAM (St Mark) and Lower Crumpsall *Man 1*   **P** *Patr
Bd*   **V** S L FLETCHER
CHELBOROUGH, EAST (St James) *see* Melbury *Sarum*
CHELBOROUGH, WEST (St Andrew) *as above*
CHELDON (St Mary) *see* Burrington, Chawleigh, Cheldon,
Chulmleigh etc *Ex*
**CHELFORD (St John the Evangelist) and Lower Withington
w Marthall** *Ches 12*   **P** *DBP*   **P-in-c** F H A ROBINSON
CHELL (St Michael) *Lich 11*   **P** *Ch Patr Trust and V Newchapel
St Jas (jt)*   **V** C J COUPE   **NSM** P A LUCKING
CHELL HEATH (Saviour) *see* Chell *Lich*
CHELLASTON (St Peter) *Derby 5*   **P** *Bp*   **V** J FACEY
CHELLINGTON Team Benefice, The, comprising Carlton w
Chellington, Harrold, Odell, Podington w Farndish,
Stevington, Turvey, and Wymington *St Alb 13*   **P** *Patr Bd*
TR J E CURTIS   **TV** P F TURNBULL   **C** L K SANDLE
CHELLS (St Hugh and St John) *see* Stevenage St Hugh and
St Jo *St Alb*
CHELMARSH (St Peter) *see* Highley w Billingsley, Glazeley
etc *Heref*
CHELMONDISTON (St Andrew) *see* Shoreline *St E*
CHELMORTON AND FLAGG (St John the Baptist) *see*
Taddington, Chelmorton and Monyash etc *Derby*
CHELMSFORD (Ascension w All Saints) *Chelmsf 9*   **P** *Bp*
V T W PAGE   **C** J LACEY   **NSM** T S EMMANUEL
CHELMSFORD (St Andrew) *Chelmsf 9*   **P** *Bp*   **C** S D PEARCE
OLM A MERCHANT
CHELMSLEY WOOD (St Andrew) *Birm 5*   **P** *Bp*
C A B THOMAS   **NSM** H HORAN
CHELSEA (All Saints) (Old Church) *Lon 8*   **P** *R Chelsea
St Luke and Earl Cadogan (jt)*   **V** vacant
CHELSEA (St John w St Andrew) (St John) *Lon 8*   **P** *CPAS
and Lon Coll of Div (jt)*   **V** P R DAWSON
C E J G LEES-MILLAIS   **NSM** A MASON
CHELSEA (St Luke) (Christ Church) *Lon 8*   **P** *Earl Cadogan*
R B LEATHARD   **C** S G A RYLANDS, S R HOLE
CHELSEA, UPPER (Holy Trinity) (St Saviour) *Lon 8*   **P** *Earl
Cadogan*   **R** N P WHEELER   **Hon C** N NASSAR
NSM F B BUTLER GALLIE
CHELSEA, UPPER (St Simon Zelotes) *Lon 8*   **P** *Hyndman's
Trustees*   **V** M R J NEVILLE   **NSM** P J STEWART
**CHELSFIELD (St Martin of Tours) w Green Street Green
and Pratts Bottom** *Roch 16*   **P** *Bp and All So Coll Ox (jt)*
R S F ATKINSON-JONES   **C** M J GENTRY

CHELSHAM (St Christopher) *see* Warlingham w Chelsham
and Farleigh *S'wark*
CHELSHAM (St Leonard) *as above*
CHELSTON (St Peter) *see* Cockington *Ex*
CHELSWORTH (All Saints) *see* Monks Eleigh w Chelsworth
and Brent Eleigh etc *St E*
CHELTENHAM (All Saints) *see* N Cheltenham *Glouc*
CHELTENHAM (Christ Church) *Glouc 6*   **P** *Simeon's Trustees*
V S A HERON   **C** E J CARMICHAEL
CHELTENHAM (Emmanuel) *see* S Cheltenham *Glouc*
CHELTENHAM (Holy Apostles) *see* Charlton Kings H
Apostles *Glouc*
CHELTENHAM (Holy Trinity) (St Paul) *Glouc 6*   **P** *Patr Bd*
TR A K E BLYTH   **TV** R J WIDDECOMBE, T R GREW
CHELTENHAM (St Luke) (St Mary) (St Matthew) *Glouc 6*
P *Simeon's Trustees*   **R** R M COOMBS   **C** P E WHEATON
NSM C L DYSON
CHELTENHAM (St Michael) *Glouc 6*   **P** *Bp*
P-in-c A S COLLISHAW   **C** J H WHITE
CHELTENHAM (St Stephen) *see* S Cheltenham *Glouc*
CHELTENHAM, NORTH, comprising Pittville, Elmstone
Hardwicke, Prestbury, and Swindon *Glouc 6*   **P** *Patr Bd*
TR N R BROMFIELD   **TV** G S DAVIS, R J WRIGHT   **C** T A COOK
NSM A J WOOD
CHELTENHAM, SOUTH (Emmanuel) (St Stephen),
including Leckhampton *Glouc 6*   **P** *Patr Bd*   **TR** N D DAVIES
TV G B GRADY   **C** J R HENSON, S J M HAMILTON
NSM H R WOOD
**CHELTENHAM, WEST (St Mark) (St Barnabas) (St Aidan)
(Emmanuel)** *Glouc 6*   **P** *MMCET*   **R** R J PATERSON
C S A WALKER   **NSM** A P HOLDERNESS
CHELVESTON (St John the Baptist) *see* Higham Ferrers w
Chelveston *Pet*
CHELVEY (St Bridget) *see* Backwell w Chelvey and Brockley
B & W
CHELWOOD (St Leonard) *see* Publow w Pensford, Compton
Dando and Chelwood *B & W*
CHELWOOD GATE (not known) *see* Danehill *Chich*
CHENDERIT, comprising Chacombe, Greatworth, Marston
St Lawrence, Middleton Cheney, Thenford, and Warkworth
Pet 1   **P** *Bp and BNC Ox (2 turns), Ld Chan (1 turn)*
R N W M LEGGETT   **Hon C** C J M OLEY
**CHENIES (St Michael) and Little Chalfont, Latimer and
Flaunden** *Ox 9*   **P** *Bedford Estates Trustees and Lord Chesham
(jt)*   **P-in-c** D WHALE   **NSM** B P LUDLOW, M M LUDLOW,
R F BOUGHTON
CHEQUERFIELD (St Mary) *see* Pontefract *Leeds*
CHERBURY w Gainfield, including Buckland, Charney
Bassett, Hinton Waldrist, Littleworth, Longworth, Lyford,
and Pusey *Ox 25*   **P** *Bp, DBP, Jes Coll, Oriel Coll, and Worc
Coll Ox (jt)*   **R** T I A T MACLEOD   **Hon C** J B MYNORS
CHERHILL (St James the Great) *see* Oldbury *Sarum*
CHERINGTON (St John the Baptist) *see* S Warks Seven Gp
Cov
CHERINGTON (St Nicholas) *see* Avening w Cherington
Glouc
CHERITON (St Martin) w Newington Benefice, The *Cant 8*
P *Abp*   **P-in-c** J A ROBERTSON, S A CROFTS
CHERITON (St Michael and All Angels) *see* Upper Itchen *Win*
CHERITON BISHOP (St Mary) *see* Tedburn St Mary, Cheriton
Bishop, Whitestone etc *Ex*
CHERITON FITZPAINE (St Matthew) *see* N Creedy *Ex*
CHERITON STREET (All Souls) *see* Cheriton w Newington
Cant
CHERITON, NORTH (St John the Baptist) *see* Camelot Par
B & W
CHERRY BURTON (St Michael) *York 8*   **P** *E D F Burton*
R R F PARKINSON
CHERRY HINTON (St Andrew) *Ely 3*   **P** *Peterho Cam*
V K L VOTH HARMAN   **C** R M BARRY   **NSM** P V IEVINS
CHERRY HINTON (St John the Evangelist) *Ely 3*   **P** *Bp*
V J D G SHAKESPEARE   **C** C E CAMPBELL   **Hon C** P S HESLAM
NSM C J PAYNE, M SWAMY
CHERRY WILLINGHAM (St Peter and St Paul) *see* S Lawres Gp
Linc
CHERTSEY (St Peter w All Saints), Lyne and Longcross
Guildf 11   **P** *Bp and Haberdashers' Co (jt)*   **V** T J HILLIER
C A L NORTON, L W GAMLEN, M P WHITE
CHERWELL VALLEY, comprising Ardley w Fewcott, Fritwell,
Lower Heyford, Somerton, Souldern, and Upper Heyford
Ox 21   **P** *Patr Bd*   **TR** H C BARNES   **TV** J D A PARSONS
C A E BRADLEY-STOW
CHESELBOURNE (St Martin) *see* Piddle Valley, Hilton and
Ansty, Cheselbourne etc *Sarum*
CHESHAM BOIS (St Leonard) *Ox 9*   **P** *Peache Trustees*
R L S CLOW   **NSM** C CLARE

CHESHAM, GREAT (Christ Church) (Emmanuel) (St Mary the Virgin) *Ox 9* P *Patr Bd* TR E M C BOWES-SMITH C C J GERCKE **NSM** J M MOODEY, T J S YATES

CHESHUNT (St Mary the Virgin) *St Alb 17* P *Patr Bd* TR T A J WYNNE **TV** E E HANSHAW, H A BRYAN C V V I HADLEY-SPENCER

CHESSINGTON (St Mary the Virgin) *Guildf 9* P *Mert Coll Ox* V S EDWARDS

CHESTER (Christ Church) *Ches 2* P *Bp and Simeon's Trustees (jt)* C A L LEYDEN **NSM** G JONES, R J KEMP

CHESTER (Holy Trinity without the Walls) *Ches 2* P *Bp* R C P UPTON C C P BURKETT

CHESTER (St John the Baptist) *Ches 2* P *Duke of Westminster* V D N CHESTERS

CHESTER (St Mary-without-the-Walls) *Ches 2* P *Duke of Westmr* R R P WHAITE **NSM** L C RHODES

CHESTER (St Peter) *Ches 2* P *Bp* V J R PHILLIPS **NSM** G D THOMAS, M J LEYDEN

CHESTER GREEN (St Paul) *see* Derby St Paul *Derby*

CHESTER LE STREET (St Mary and St Cuthbert) *Dur 9* P *St Jo Coll Dur* C M HARRISON

CHESTER SQUARE (St Michael) (St Philip) *Lon 3* P *CPAS* V R A CHARKHAM C S T BANNER

CHESTER St Oswald (St Thomas of Canterbury) *Ches 2* P *D&C* **P-in-c** S A SHERIDAN

CHESTER St Paul (St Luke) *Ches 2* P R *Ches* V C J S BLUNT

CHESTERFIELD (Holy Trinity) (Christ Church) *Derby 3* P *CPAS* **P-in-c** J C HANCOCK C K E HAMBLIN, M R BROOMHEAD

CHESTERFIELD (St Augustine of Hippo and St Augustine of Canterbury) *Derby 3* P *Bp* C K E HAMBLIN, S BEECHAM **NSM** H J MOORE

CHESTERFIELD (St Mary and All Saints) *Derby 3* P *Bp* V P F COLEMAN C J C MILWAIN, K E HAMBLIN, M R BROOMHEAD **NSM** H J MOORE

CHESTERFORD, GREAT (All Saints) *see* Saffron Walden and Villages *Chelmsf*

CHESTERFORD, LITTLE (St Mary the Virgin) *as above*

CHESTERTON (Good Shepherd) *Ely 2* P *Bp* V D J MAHER C C A LOWE **NSM** E M WESTRIP, J D TORRANCE

CHESTERTON (Holy Trinity) (St Chad) *Lich 9* P *The Crown* V *vacant*

CHESTERTON (St Andrew) *Ely 2* P *Trin Coll Cam* V N I MOIR **NSM** A J COLES, D H PEYTON JONES

CHESTERTON (St George) *Ely 2* P *Bp* C A ATKINS **NSM** D N ANDREW, J A RIGLIN

CHESTERTON (St Giles) *Cov 8* P *Lady Willoughby de Broke* **P-in-c** L J LILLEY

CHESTERTON (St Lawrence) *see* Cirencester *Glouc*

CHESTERTON (St Michael) *see* Alwalton and Chesterton *Ely*

CHESTERTON, GREAT (St Mary) *see* Akeman *Ox*

CHESWARDINE (St Swithun), Childs Ercall, Hales, Hinstock, Sambrook and Stoke on Tern *Lich 17* P *Patr Bd* TR R M RICHARDS **NSM** C SIMPSON

CHET VALLEY, The *see* Loddon, Sisland, Chedgrave, Hardley and Langley *Nor*

CHETNOLE (St Peter) *see* Three Valleys *Sarum*

CHETTISHAM (St Michael and All Angels) *see* Ely *Ely*

CHETTLE (St Mary) *see* Chase *Sarum*

CHETTON (St Giles) *see* Ditton Priors w Neenton, Burwarton etc *Heref*

CHETWODE (St Mary and St Nicholas) *see* The Claydons and Swan *Ox*

CHETWYND (St Michael and All Angels) *see* Newport w Longford, and Chetwynd *Lich*

CHEVELEY (St Mary) *Ely 4* P *DBP and Mrs D A Bowlby (alt)* **P-in-c** N A WORMELL

CHEVENING (St Botolph) *Roch 9* P *Abp* R H E ADAMS

CHEVERELL, GREAT (St Peter) *see* The Lavingtons, Cheverells, and Easterton *Sarum*

CHEVERELL, LITTLE (St Peter) *as above*

CHEVINGTON (All Saints) w Hargrave, Chedburgh w Depden, Rede and Hawkedon *St E 2* P *Guild of All So (1 turn), Ld Chan (2 turns), Bp and DBP (1 turn)* R *vacant*

CHEVINGTON (St John the Divine) *Newc 6* P *Bp* V *vacant*

CHEVITHORNE (St Thomas) *see* Tiverton St Pet and Chevithorne w Cove *Ex*

CHEW MAGNA (St Andrew) w Dundry, Norton Malreward and Stanton Drew *B & W 9* P *Bp and Adn (jt)* R R Q GREATREX

CHEW STOKE (St Andrew) w Nempnett Thrubwell *B & W 9* P *Bp and SMF (jt)* **P-in-c** I K MILLS

CHEW VALLEY EAST *see* Chew Magna w Dundry, Norton Malreward etc *B & W*

CHEW VALLEY WEST *see* Chew Stoke w Nempnett Thrubwell *B & W*

CHEWTON (Mission Church) *see* Keynsham *B & W*

CHEWTON MENDIP (St Mary Magdalene) w Ston Easton, Litton and Emborough *B & W 7* P *Earl Waldegrave (2 turns), Bp (1 turn)* **P-in-c** C L TOWNS **NSM** H J LATTY

CHEYLESMORE (Christ Church) *Cov 3* P *Ch Trust Fund Trust* V A C WOO

CHICHELEY (St Laurence) *see* Sherington w Chicheley, N Crawley, Astwood etc *Ox*

CHICHESTER (Immanuel) Bishop's Mission Order *Chich 2* **Min** J A NICKOLS, P M COLLINS

CHICHESTER (St Pancras and St John) *Chich 2* P *Simeon's Trustees (2 turns), St Jo Chpl Trustees (1 turn)* R M J T PAYNE C M D MILMINE

CHICHESTER (St Paul) and Westhampnett St Peter *Chich 2* P *Bp and D&C (jt)* R S P HOLLAND **NSM** B M COUZENS, R HAWES

CHICHESTER (St Wilfrid) *Chich 2* P *Bp* **P-in-c** S P MILLS

CHICKERELL (St Mary) w Fleet *Sarum 4* P *Bp* R *vacant*

CHICKLADE (All Saints) *see* Nadder Valley *Sarum*

CHIDDINGFOLD (St Mary) *Guildf 4* P *Ld Chan* R R E GREENE

CHIDDINGLY (not known) w East Hoathly *Chich 18* P *Bp* R P A HODGINS

CHIDDINGSTONE (St Mary) *see* Penshurst, Fordcombe and the Chiddingstone Chs *Roch*

CHIDDINGSTONE CAUSEWAY (St Luke) *as above*

CHIDEOCK (St Giles) *see* Golden Cap Team *Sarum*

CHIDHAM (St Mary) *Chich 6* P *Bp* **P-in-c** A G J BIRKS

CHIEVELEY (St Mary the Virgin) *see* E Downland *Ox*

CHIGNAL SMEALEY (St Nicholas) *see* The Chignals w Mashbury *Chelmsf*

CHIGNALS w Mashbury, The *Chelmsf 9* P *CPAS (2 turns), Bp (1 turn)* C D C PIERCE **NSM** S SYKES **OLM** D M GARFIELD

CHIGWELL (St Mary) *see* Vale of Roding *Chelmsf*

CHIGWELL (St Winifred) *as above*

CHIGWELL ROW (All Saints) *as above*

CHILBOLTON (St Mary) *see* The Downs *Win*

CHILCOMB (St Andrew) *see* E Win *Win*

CHILCOMBE (not known) *see* Bride Valley *Sarum*

CHILCOMPTON (St John the Baptist) w Downside and Stratton on the Fosse *B & W 11* P *Bp, MMCET, and V Midsomer Norton (jt)* R E SMITH C S D MILES

CHILCOTE (St Matthew's Chapel) *see* Mease Valley *Lich*

CHILDE OKEFORD (St Nicholas) *see* Okeford *Sarum*

CHILDERDITCH (All Saints and St Faith) *see* E and W Horndon w Lt Warley and Childerditch *Chelmsf*

CHILDREY (St Mary the Virgin) *see* Ridgeway *Ox*

CHILDS ERCALL (St Michael and All Angels) *see* Cheswardine, Childs Ercall, Hales, Hinstock etc *Lich*

CHILDS HILL (All Saints) *see* Hendon All SS Childs Hill *Lon*

CHILDSWYCKHAM (St Mary the Virgin) *see* Winchcombe *Glouc*

CHILDWALL (All Saints) *Liv 2* P *Bp* V A J COLMER C H DEEGAN **OLM** S J GILLIES

CHILDWALL (St David) *Liv 5* P *Bp* V *vacant*

CHILDWALL VALLEY (St Mark) *see* Gateacre *Liv*

CHILDWICK (St Mary) *see* St Alb St Mich *St Alb*

CHILFROME (Holy Trinity) *see* Melbury *Sarum*

CHILHAM (St Mary) *see* King's Wood *Cant*

CHILLENDEN (All Saints) *see* Canonry *Cant*

CHILLESFORD (St Peter) *see* Wilford Peninsula *St E*

CHILLINGHAM (St Peter) *see* Chatton w Chillingham, Eglingham and S Charlton and Ingram *Newc*

CHILLINGTON (St James) *see* Winsmoor *B & W*

CHILMARK (St Margaret of Antioch) *see* Nadder Valley *Sarum*

CHILTERNS, SOUTH, comprising Cadmore End, Ibstone, Lane End, and Stokenchurch *Ox 18* P *Patr Bd* TR C M ACKFORD **TV** P D SMITH

CHILTHORNE DOMER (Blessed Virgin Mary) *see* Tintinhull w Chilthorne Domer, Yeovil Marsh etc *B & W*

CHILTINGTON, EAST (not known) *see* Plumpton w E Chiltington cum Novington *Chich*

CHILTINGTON, WEST (St Mary) *Chich 5* P *Bp* R S R MERRIMAN

CHILTON (All Saints) *see* Harwell w Chilton *Ox*

CHILTON (St Aidan) *Dur 1* P *Bp* V *vacant*

CHILTON (St Mary) *see* Bernwode *Ox*

CHILTON CANTELO (St James) w Ashington, Mudford, Rimpton and Marston Magna *B & W 6* P *DBP and D&C, D&C Bris, and Bp Lon (by turn)* R *vacant*

CHILTON FOLIAT (St Mary) *see* Whitton *Sarum*

CHILTON MOOR (St Andrew) *Dur 9* P *Bp* **P-in-c** J W ESTALL **NSM** C E BRITCLIFFE, T HOLDEN

CHILTON POLDEN (St Edward) *see* Polden Wheel *B & W*

CHILTON TRINITY (Holy Trinity) *see* Bridgwater St Mary and Chilton Trinity *B & W*

CHILVERS COTON (All Saints) w Astley *Cov 5*   P *Viscount Daventry*   V F P SELDON   NSM D WATERTON, J L FRYER
OLM R ALLEN
CHILWELL (Christ Church) *S'well 9*   P *CPAS*
V A S G TUFNELL   C L P B O'BOYLE, M S FORSYTH
CHILWORTH (St Denys)   *see* Ampfield, Chilworth and N Baddesley *Win*
CHILWORTH (St Thomas)   *see* Shere, Albury and Chilworth *Guildf*
CHINEHAM (Christ Church) *Win 4*   P *Bp*   V J G CLARK
CHINESE CONGREGATION   *see* St Martin-in-the-Fields *Lon*
CHINGFORD (All Saints) (St Peter and St Paul) *Chelmsf 7*
P *Bp*   R J G LEWIS-ANTHONY   NSM H MUSKER
OLM K R WARD, M P CLAYDON
CHINGFORD (St Anne) *Chelmsf 7*   P *Bp*   V J R BULLOCK
OLM M L SCOTCHMER
CHINGFORD (St Edmund) *Chelmsf 7*   P *Bp*
V L A GOLDSMITH   C J B GILDER
CHINLEY (St Mary)   *see* Hayfield and Chinley w Buxworth *Derby*
CHINNOCK, EAST (Blessed Virgin Mary)   *see* Coker Ridge *B & W*
CHINNOCK, MIDDLE (St Margaret)   *see* Ham Hill Villages *B & W*
CHINNOCK, WEST (Blessed Virgin Mary) *as above*
CHINNOR (St Andrew), Sydenham, Aston Rowant and Crowell *Ox 20*   P *Bp, DBP, and Peache Trustees (jt)*
R J A BARR
CHIPPENHAM (St Andrew) w Tytherton Lucas *Bris 4*   P *Ch Ch Ox*   V R C H KEY   C A P CAMPBELL
CHIPPENHAM (St Margaret)   *see* Three Rivers Gp *Ely*
CHIPPENHAM (St Paul) w Hardenhuish and Langley Burrell *Bris 4*   P *Patr Bd*   P-in-c S D DUNN
C S P S WILLIAMS, T M HUNTON
CHIPPENHAM (St Peter) *Bris 4*   P *Bp*   P-in-c A M GUBBINS
CHIPPERFIELD (St Paul)   *see* Sarratt and Chipperfield *St Alb*
CHIPPING (St Bartholomew) *Blackb 7*   P *Bp*   V *vacant*
CHIPPING BARNET (St John the Baptist) (St Mark) (St Stephen) (St Peter) *St Alb 14*   P *The Crown (2 turns) and Bp (1 turn)*   TR T D CHAPMAN   NSM N C WHEELER
CHIPPING CAMPDEN (St James)   *see* Vale and Cotswold Edge *Glouc*
CHIPPING NORTON (St Mary the Virgin) *Ox 22*   P *Patr Bd*
TR J E KENNEDY   TV D W SALTER   C T L ARTIS
OLM J E MARSHALL
CHIPPING ONGAR (St Martin) w Shelley, Greensted juxta Ongar and Stanford Rivers *Chelmsf 3*   P *Duchy of Lancaster (1 turn), Keble Coll Ox, Guild of All So, and Bp Lon (2 turns)*   R N R TAYLOR   C J QUINTON   NSM N A TAYLOR
CHIPPING SODBURY (St John the Baptist)   *see* Sodbury Vale *Glouc*
CHIPPING WARDEN (St Peter and St Paul)   *see* Culworth w Sulgrave and Thorpe Mandeville etc *Pet*
CHIPSTABLE (All Saints)   *see* Wiveliscombe and the Hills *B & W*
CHIPSTEAD (Good Shepherd)   *see* Chevening *Roch*
CHIPSTEAD (St Margaret of Antioch) *S'wark 24*   P *Abp*
R S M M WILLIAMS
CHIRBURY (St Michael), Marton, Middleton and Trelystan w Leighton *Heref 12*   P *Bp (3 turns), N E E Stephens Esq (1 turn)*   V W K ROWELL
CHIRTON (St John the Baptist)   *see* Cannings and Redhorn *Sarum*
CHISELBOROUGH (St Peter and St Paul)   *see* Ham Hill Villages *B & W*
CHISHILL, GREAT (St Swithun)   *see* Icknield Way Villages *Chelmsf*
CHISHILL, LITTLE (St Nicholas) *as above*
CHISLEDON (Holy Cross)   *see* Ridgeway *Sarum*
CHISLEHURST (Annunciation) *Roch 14*   P *Keble Coll*
V P A FARTHING
CHISLEHURST (Christ Church) *Roch 14*   P *CPAS*
V D G S JOHNSTON
CHISLEHURST (St Nicholas) *Roch 14*   P *Bp*   R J N BAUER
NSM J B HURN
CHISLET (St Mary the Virgin)   *see* Wantsum Gp *Cant*
CHISWICK (St Michael and All Angels)   *see* Bedford Park *Lon*
CHISWICK (St Michael) *Lon 11*   P *V St Martin-in-the-Fields*
V M A OBORNE
CHISWICK (St Nicholas w St Mary Magdalene) *Lon 11*
P *D&C St Paul's*   V S F BRANDES   C A N TRIGLE
CHISWICK (St Paul) Grove Park *Lon 11*   P *V Chiswick*
V M C RILEY
CHITHURST (St Mary)   *see* Rogate w Terwick and Trotton w Chithurst *Chich*

CHITTERNE (All Saints and St Mary)   *see* Salisbury Plain *Sarum*
CHITTLEHAMHOLT (St John)   *see* S Molton w Nymet St George, Chittlehamholt etc *Ex*
CHITTLEHAMPTON (St Hieritha) *as above*
CHITTS HILL (St Cuthbert) *Lon 17*   P *CPAS*
P-in-c M JONES PARRY
CHIVELSTONE (St Sylvester)   *see* Stokenham, Slapton, Charleton w Buckland etc *Ex*
CHOBHAM (St Lawrence) w Valley End *Guildf 6*   P *Bp and Brig R W Acworth (alt)*   V D J STORK BANKS
CHOLDERTON (St Nicholas)   *see* Bourne Valley *Sarum*
CHOLESBURY (St Lawrence)   *see* Hawridge w Cholesbury and St Leonard *Ox*
CHOLLERTON (St Giles) w Birtley and Thockrington *Newc 8*   P *Mrs P I Enderby (2 turns), Newc Dioc Soc (1 turn)*
P-in-c S A LUNN
CHOLSEY (St Mary) and Moulsford *Ox 26*   P *Ld Chan and Bp (alt)*   V A M PETIT   OLM V M L GIBBONS
CHOPPARDS (Mission Room)   *see* Upper Holme Valley *Leeds*
CHOPPINGTON (St Paul the Apostle) *Newc 1*   P *D&C*
V T MOAT
CHOPWELL (St John the Evangelist) *Dur 12*   P *Bp*   V *vacant*
CHORLEY (All Saints) *Blackb 4*   P *Bp*   V E N STRASZAK
CHORLEY (St George) *Blackb 4*   P *R Chorley*   V M G PRINT
CHORLEY (St James) *Blackb 4*   P *R Chorley*   V D K PHILLIPS
CHORLEY (St Laurence) *Blackb 4*   P *Bp*   R N G KELLEY
C M T BALDWIN   Hon C T H STOKES
CHORLEY (St Peter) *Blackb 4*   P *R Chorley*   V *vacant*
CHORLEY (St Philip)   *see* Alderley Edge *Ches*
CHORLEYWOOD (Christ Church) *St Alb 4*   P *CPAS*
V D M HALL   C N Y WOLF   NSM T W RUSSOFF
CHORLEYWOOD (St Andrew) *St Alb 4*   P *Bp*
V T E HORLOCK   C J A O RIGBY
CHORLTON-CUM-HARDY (St Clement) (St Barnabas) *Man 2*   P *D&C*   R K FLOOD   OLM L M WINDLE
CHORLTON-CUM-HARDY (St Werburgh) *Man 2*   P *Bp*
R J F C NEAL   C A BIRD
CHRISHALL (Holy Trinity)   *see* Icknield Way Villages *Chelmsf*
CHRIST THE KING in the Diocese of Newcastle, comprising Brunswick, Brunton Park, Dinnington, and North Gosforth *Newc 2*   P *Patr Bd*   TR P H PEARSON   P-in-c G K B RUNDELL
TV M A EDWARDS   NSM R E HEWETT
CHRISTCHURCH (Holy Trinity) *Win 9*   P *Bp*   V C STEWART
C R B PARTRIDGE
CHRISTCHURCH Stourvale (St George)   *see* Christchurch *Win*
CHRISTIAN MALFORD (All Saints)   *see* Draycot Bris
CHRISTLETON (St James) *Ches 2*   P *Bp*   R S J COLLIER
NSM R F CROFT
CHRISTON (Blessed Virgin Mary)   *see* Crook Peak *B & W*
CHRISTOW (St James), Ashton, Bridford, Dunchideock, Dunsford and Doddiscombsleigh *Ex 5*   P *Bp, MMCET, SMF, Mrs J M Michelmore, Viscount Exmouth, and F C Fulford Esq (jt)*   V R FRAMPTON
CHUDLEIGH (St Mary and St Martin) w Chudleigh Knighton and Trusham *Ex 8*   P *Patr Bd*
NSM M J FLETCHER
CHUDLEIGH KNIGHTON (St Paul)   *see* Chudleigh w Chudleigh Knighton and Trusham *Ex*
CHULMLEIGH (St Mary Magdalene)   *see* Burrington, Chawleigh, Cheldon, Chulmleigh etc *Ex*
CHURCH AROUND THE CLIFFE, comprising Ruyton XI Towns, Great Ness and Little Ness *Lich 16*   P *Bp and Guild of All So (jt) and Ld Chan (alt)*   P-in-c L R BURNS
CHURCH ASTON (St Andrew) *Lich 15*   P *R Edgmond*
P-in-c Z N HEMING
CHURCH BRAMPTON (St Botolph)   *see* Brington w Whilton and Norton etc *Pet*
CHURCH BROUGHTON (St Michael)   *see* Boylestone, Church Broughton, Dalbury, etc *Derby*
CHURCH EATON (St Editha)   *see* Bradeley, Church Eaton, Derrington and Haughton *Lich*
CHURCH GRESLEY (St George and St Mary)   *see* Gresley *Derby*
CHURCH HONEYBOURNE (St Ecgwyn)   *see* Vale and Cotswold Edge *Glouc*
CHURCH HULME (St Luke) *Ches 11*   P *V Sandbach*
V R I MCLAREN
CHURCH IN THE WOOTTONS, The *Nor 19*   P *Ld Chan and G Howard Esq (alt)*   R J A NASH   C D M R TANSEY, J D SWINTON
OLM L ASHBY
CHURCH KNOWLE (St Peter)   *see* St Aldhelm *Sarum*
CHURCH LANGLEY (Church and Community Centre) *Chelmsf 4*   P *V Harlow*   V *vacant*
CHURCH LANGTON (St Peter)   *see* The Langtons and Shangton *Leic*

CHURCH LAWFORD (St Peter)   *see* Wolston and Church
Lawford *Cov*
CHURCH LAWTON (All Saints) *Ches 11*   **P** *J Lawton Esq*
R S J CLAPHAM
**CHURCH LENCH (All Saints) w Rous Lench and Abbots
Morton and Harvington** *Worc 3*   **P** *Bp and D&C (jt)*
R R J G THORNILEY   **NSM** C P SHEEHAN
CHURCH MINSHULL (St Bartholomew)   *see* Acton and
Worleston, Church Minshull etc *Ches*
CHURCH OAKLEY (St Leonard)   *see* Oakley w Wootton
St Lawrence *Win*
CHURCH ON THE HEATH (Northampton)   *see* Kings Heath
Pet
CHURCH PREEN (St John the Baptist)   *see* Wenlock *Heref*
CHURCH STRETTON (St Laurence) *Heref 10*   **P** *Ch Patr Trust*
R S G JOHNSON   **C** D J ANDREWS   **NSM** C M K HARGRAVES
CHURCHAM (St Andrew)   *see* Huntley and Longhope,
Churcham and Bulley *Glouc*
CHURCHDOWN (St Andrew) (St Bartholomew) *Glouc 3*
P *D&C*   **V** *vacant*
CHURCHDOWN (St John the Evangelist) and Innsworth
Glouc 3   **P** *Bp*   **V** J D HYDE   **NSM** J E SCHOLES
CHURCHILL (All Saints)   *see* Chipping Norton *Ox*
CHURCHILL (St John the Baptist) and Langford *B & W 10*
P *D&C Bris*   **V** *vacant*
**CHURCHILL-IN-HALFSHIRE (St James) w Blakedown and
Broome** *Worc 6*   **P** *Exors Viscount Cobham and N A Bourne
Esq (alt)*   **P-in-c** V W BEYNON
CHURCHOVER (Holy Trinity)   *see* Revel Gp *Cov*
CHURCHSTANTON   (St Peter and St Paul)   *see* Blackdown
B & W
CHURCHSTOKE (St Nicholas) w Hyssington and Sarn
Heref 9   **P** *The Crown (1 turn), Earl of Powis (2 turns)*
P-in-c S A C FOUNTAIN   **C** C J WHITTOCK
CHURCHSTOW (St Mary)   *see* Thurlestone, S Milton,
Churchstow etc *Ex*
CHURCHTOWN (St Helen)   *see* Garstang St Helen and
St Michaels-on-Wyre *Blackb*
CHURN VALLEY Benefice, The, comprising Bagendon,
Baunton, Coberley, Colesbourne, Cowley, Elkstone, North
Cerney, Rendcomb, and Stratton *Glouc 7*   **P** *Jes Coll Ox,
Univ Coll Ox, Mrs P Chester-Master, Sir H Elwes, Mrs S Pearce,
Major M Wills (2 turns), Ld Chan (1 turn)*   **R** D A MINNS
**CHURN, THE (Aston Tirrold w Aston Upthorpe, Blewbury,
Hagbourne, North Moreton, South Moreton, and
Upton)** *Ox 26*   **P** *Bp and Magd Coll Ox (1 turn), Adn Berks
and Hertf Coll Ox (1 turn)*   **R** J P ST JOHN NICOLLE
OLM L G N BUTLER
CHURNSIDE   *see* S Cerney w Cerney Wick, Siddington and
Preston *Glouc*
CHURSTON FERRERS (St Mary the Virgin)   *see* Brixham w
Churston Ferrers and Kingswear *Ex*
CHURT (St John the Evangelist) and Hindhead *Guildf 3*
P *Adn Surrey*   **V** R T BODLE   **C** D J HOLBIRD, D L SMITH
NSM W A SUTTON   **OLM** R J MANLEY-COOPER
CHURWELL (All Saints)   *see* Morley *Leeds*
CHUTE (St Nicholas)   *see* Savernake *Sarum*
CIDER CHURCHES Benefice, The, comprising Aylton, Little
Marcle, Much Marcle w Yatton, Pixley, Putley, and
Wellington Heath *Heref 5*   **P** *Bp (3 turns), D&C (1 turn), J F S
Hervey-Bathhurst Esq (1 turn), C E Money-Kyrle Esq (1 turn)*
V V J TAIT
**CINDERFORD (St John the Evangelist) (St Stephen) w
Littledean** *Glouc 1*   **P** *The Crown and Ch Patr Trust (alt)*
V M J BARNSLEY   **OLM** R W BLAGG
CINDERHILL (Christ Church) *S'well 8*   **P** *Bp*
NSM D WATKINSON
CINNAMON BROW (Resurrection)   *see* Warrington E *Liv*
CIPPENHAM (St Andrew) *Ox 12*   **P** *Eton Coll*   **V** *vacant*
CIRENCESTER (St John the Baptist), including Chesterton
and Watermoor *Glouc 7*   **P** *Bp*   **V** G E MORRIS   **C** A J LOVE,
J C MOTTRAM, J WILSON   **Hon C** M J BETTIS
CLACTON, GREAT (St John the Baptist) *Chelmsf 22*   **P** *Ch
Patr Trust*   **V** T M MULRYNE   **C** T A L CHASE
CLACTON, LITTLE (St James)   *see* Weeley and Lt Clacton
Chelmsf
CLACTON-ON-SEA (St Christopher) (St James) *Chelmsf 22*
P *Bp*   **V** J F HUTCHERSON   **C** L E OLIVER   **NSM** M L OLIVER
CLACTON-ON-SEA (St Paul) *Chelmsf 22*   **P** *Ch Patr Trust*
V D J LOWER
CLAINES (St George w St Mary Magdalene)   *see* Worc St Geo
w St Mary Magd *Worc*
CLAINES (St John the Baptist) *Worc 4*   **P** *Bp*
P-in-c J C MUSSON   **NSM** D P DAVIES, S E POLLARD

**CLANDON, EAST (St Thomas of Canterbury) and WEST
(St Peter and St Paul)** *Guildf 5*   **P** *Earl of Onslow and Bp
(alt)*   **R** B C R PERKINS
CLANFIELD (St James)   *see* Catherington and Clanfield
Portsm
CLANFIELD (St Stephen)   *see* Bampton w Clanfield *Ox*
CLANNABOROUGH (St Petrock)   *see* N Creedy *Ex*
CLAPHAM (Christ Church) (St John the Evangelist)
S'wark 11   **P** *Bp*   **V** P J ROSE-CASEMORE
CLAPHAM (Holy Spirit) *S'wark 11*   **P** *Bp*
V R A BURGE-THOMAS
CLAPHAM (Holy Trinity) *S'wark 11*   **P** *DBP*   **V** J R O WYNNE
C J E J MULVANEY, T G JONES
CLAPHAM (St James) *S'wark 12*   **P** *CPAS*   **V** N K GUNASEKERA
Hon C J MARSHALL
CLAPHAM (St Mary the Virgin)   *see* Findon w Clapham and
Patching *Chich*
CLAPHAM (St Paul) *S'wark 11*   **P** *Bp*   **V** J T BOARDMAN
C D J POVALL
CLAPHAM (St Peter) *S'wark 11*   **P** *Bp*   **P-in-c** J T BOARDMAN
CLAPHAM (St Thomas of Canterbury) *St Alb 13*   **P** *MMCET*
V S J LILEY
CLAPHAM COMMON (St Barnabas) *S'wark 14*   **P** *Ch Trust
Fund Trust*   **V** R G TAYLOR   **C** I N LUKE-MACAULEY
CLAPHAM PARK (All Saints) *S'wark 12*   **P** *CPAS*
P-in-c J R O WYNNE
CLAPHAM PARK (St Stephen)   *see* Telford Park *S'wark*
CLAPHAM PARK (St Thomas)   *see* Telford Park *S'wark*
CLAPHAM-WITH-KEASDEN (St James) and Austwick
Leeds 17   **P** *Bp*   **V** J DAVIES
CLAPTON (St James) *Lon 5*   **P** *Bp*   **V** R BROWN
CLAPTON (St James)   *see* Bourton-on-the-Water w Clapton
etc *Glouc*
CLAPTON PARK (The Risen Christ)   *see* Homerton *Lon*
CLAPTON, UPPER (St Matthew) *Lon 5*   **P** *D&C Cant*
P-in-c A O BADEJO, W G CAMPBELL-TAYLOR
CLAPTON, UPPER (St Thomas)   *see* Stamford Hill St Thos
Lon
CLARBOROUGH (St John the Baptist)   *see* The Clays *S'well*
CLARE (St Peter and St Paul)   *see* Stour Valley *St E*
CLARENCE GATE GARDENS (St Cyprian)   *see* St Marylebone
St Cypr *Lon*
CLARENDON (Team Ministry), comprising Alderbury, Farley
w Pitton, West Dean w East Grimstead, West Grimstead,
Whiteparish, and Winterslow *Sarum 10*   **P** *Patr Bd*
TR S P CHAMBERS   **TV** F J DUNLOP   **NSM** D PERRY,
L M RODRIGUES
CLARENDON PARK (St John the Baptist)   *see* Emmaus Par
Team *Leic*
CLARKSFIELD (St Barnabas) and Waterhead *Man 5*   **P** *The
Crown*   **V** P M S MONK   **C** D OWEN   **NSM** J HYDE
CLATFORD, UPPER (All Saints)   *see* Abbotts Ann and Upper
Clatford and Goodworth Clatford *Win*
CLATWORTHY (St Mary Magdalene)   *see* Wiveliscombe and
the Hills *B & W*
CLAUGHTON VILLAGE (St Bede)   *see* Birkenhead St Jas w
St Bede *Ches*
CLAVERDON (St Michael and All Angels) w Preston Bagot
Cov 7   **P** *Bp*   **P-in-c** A J HAMPTON   **NSM** J B HOLDEN
CLAVERHAM (St Barnabas)   *see* Yatton Moor *B & W*
**CLAVERING (St Mary and St Clement) w Langley,
Arkesden, Wicken Bonhunt, Manuden and Berden**
Chelmsf 20   **P** *Ch Hosp and Keble Coll Ox (jt)*   **V** M A DAVIS
CLAVERLEY (All Saints) w Tuckhill *Heref 8*   **P** *Bp and E M A
Thompson Esq (jt)*   **V** G W WARD
CLAVERTON (Blessed Virgin Mary)   *see* Bathampton w
Claverton *B & W*
CLAWTON (St Leonard)   *see* Ashwater, Halwill, Beaworthy,
Clawton etc *Ex*
CLAXBY (St Mary)   *see* Walesby Gp *Linc*
CLAXTON (St Andrew)   *see* Rockland St Mary w Hellington,
Bramerton etc *Nor*
CLAY CROSS (St Bartholomew)   *see* N Wingfield, Clay Cross
and Pilsley *Derby*
CLAY HILL (St John the Baptist) (St Luke) *Lon 16*   **P** *V
Enfield St Andr and Bp (jt)*   **V** *vacant*
CLAYBROOKE (St Peter)   *see* Upper Soar *Leic*
CLAYDON (no church), including Barham, Great Blakenham,
and Henley *St E 3*   **P** *Bp, DBP, MMCET and Mrs M Rusinow
(jt)*   **P-in-c** M N HAWORTH   **NSM** C B AUSTIN
CLAYDON (St James the Great)   *see* Shires' Edge *Ox*
**CLAYDONS, The (St Mary) (All Saints) (St Michael) and
Swan** *Ox 13*   **P** *Patr Bd*   **TR** D A HISCOCK   **TV** A MANN,
L G SIMPSON-GRAY

CLAYGATE (Holy Trinity) *Guildf 8* **P** *Ch Patr Trust*
V P J BATEMAN   **C** K M WILLIS, R E RUGG, S P SADLER, T HILL
NSM M R HARLE

CLAYHANGER (Holy Trinity Worship Centre) *see* Ogley Hay
Lich

CLAYHANGER (St Peter) *see* Bampton, Morebath,
Clayhanger, Petton etc *Ex*

CLAYHIDON (St Andrew) *see* Hemyock w Culm Davy,
Clayhidon and Culmstock *Ex*

CLAYPOLE (St Peter) *Linc 22* **P** *DBP (2 turns), J R Thorold Esq*
(1 turn) **R** A I TUCKER

CLAYS, The, Retford, comprising Bole, Clarborough,
Habblesthorpe, Hayton, Littleborough, North and South
Leverton, North Wheatley, Saundby, and Sturton *S'well 1*
P *Bp, Lord Middleton, and G M T Foljambe Esq (jt)*
R M J CANTRILL

CLAYTON (St Cross w St Paul) *see* Man Clayton St Cross w
St Paul *Man*

CLAYTON (St James the Great) *Lich 9* **P** *Bp* **V** J B BABB
NSM G SHILKOFF

CLAYTON (St John the Baptist) *Leeds 3* **P** *V Bradf*
V V POLLARD   **C** W J GRANT

CLAYTON (St John the Baptist) w Keymer *Chich 11* **P** *BNC*
Ox **R** A BAXTER   **C** S J EARNSHAW

CLAYTON BROOK (Community Church) *see* Whittle-le-
Woods *Blackb*

CLAYTON LE MOORS (All Saints) *see* Altham w Clayton le
Moors *Blackb*

CLAYTON LE MOORS (St James) *as above*

CLAYTON WEST w HIGH HOYLAND (All Saints) *see* High
Hoyland, Scissett and Clayton W *Leeds*

CLAYWORTH (St Peter) *see* Beckingham, Walkeringham,
Misterton, etc *S'well*

CLEADON (All Saints) *Dur 13* **P** *R Whitburn*
P-in-c V J CUTHBERT

CLEADON PARK (St Mark and St Cuthbert) *Dur 13* **P** *Bp*
P-in-c K L BOARDMAN

CLEARWELL (St Peter) *see* Coleford, Staunton, Newland,
Redbrook etc *Glouc*

CLEASBY (St Peter) *see* E Dere Street *Leeds*

CLEATOR (St Leonard) *see* Crosslacon *Carl*

CLECKHEATON (St John the Evangelist) *see* Cleckheaton
Leeds

CLECKHEATON (St Luke) *as above*

CLECKHEATON (St Luke) (St John the Evangelist)
(Whitechapel) *Leeds 7* **P** *Bp and V Birstall (jt)*
V B H G JAMES   **NSM** R M CAVE

CLECKHEATON (Whitechapel) *see* Cleckheaton *Leeds*

CLEDFORD (Mission Room) *see* Middlewich w Byley *Ches*

CLEE HILL (St Peter) *see* Tenbury *Heref*

CLEE HILL (St Peter's Mission Room) *see* Wigmore Abbey
Heref

CLEE ST MARGARET (St Margaret) *see* Bromfield *Heref*

CLEE, NEW (St John the Evangelist) (St Stephen) *Linc 3*
P *Bp* **P-in-c** K S JONES   **NSM** A P TAPPIN

CLEE, OLD (Holy Trinity and St Mary the Virgin) *Linc 3*
P *Bp* **V** N D NAWROCKYI   **NSM** L M SMITH

CLEETHORPE (Christ Church) *see* Clee *Linc*

CLEETHORPES (St Aidan) *Linc 3* **P** *Bp* **V** N D NAWROCKYI
NSM L M SMITH

CLEETHORPES (St Francis) Conventional District *Linc 3*
NSM L M SMITH   **Min** N D NAWROCKYI

CLEETHORPES (St Peter) *Linc 3* **P** *Bp* **R** P HUNTER
NSM D H WEBSTER

CLEETON (St Mary) *see* Stottesdon w Farlow, Cleeton
St Mary etc *Heref*

CLEEVE (Holy Trinity) *see* Yatton Moor *B & W*

CLEEVE PRIOR (St Andrew) *see* E Vale and Avon Villages
Worc

CLEEVE, OLD (St Andrew), Leighland and Treborough
B & W 15 **P** *Selw Coll Cam (2 turns), Personal Reps G R
Wolseley Esq (1 turn)* **R** R E HIGGINS

CLEHONGER (All Saints) *see* Cagebrook *Heref*

CLENCHWARTON (St Margaret) *Ely 14* **P** *DBP*
R B L BURTON

CLENT (St Leonard) *see* Belbroughton w Fairfield and Clent
Worc

**CLEOBURY MORTIMER (St Mary the Virgin) w Hopton
Wafers, Neen Sollars and Milson, Neen Savage w Kinlet
and Doddington** *Heref 11* **P** *Patr Bd (2 turns), Ld Chan (1
turn)* **R** W A BUCK   **C** J R SIMONS   **NSM** S L BARRETT

CLEOBURY NORTH (St Peter and St Paul) *see* Ditton Priors w
Neenton, Burwarton etc *Heref*

CLERKENWELL (Our Most Holy Redeemer) *Lon 6*
P *Trustees* **V** C P TRUNDLE   **C** A D BARTLETT
NSM A S MCGREGOR

CLERKENWELL (St James and St John) (St Peter) *Lon 6*
P *Ch Patr Trust and PCC (jt)* **P-in-c** P J NICHOLAS
C M B JACKSON

CLERKENWELL (St Mark) *Lon 6* **P** *City Corp* **V** C P TRUNDLE
C A D BARTLETT, J G HOBSON

CLEVEDON (Christchurch) *B & W 12* **P** *Simeon's Trustees*
V C J JENNINGS   **C** S KIRKHAM

CLEVEDON (St Andrew) (St Peter) *B & W 12* **P** *Ld Chan*
V T R CRANSHAW

CLEVEDON (St John the Evangelist) *B & W 12* **P** *SMF*
P-in-c B D CLOVER

**CLEVEDON, EAST (All Saints) w Clapton in Gordano,
Walton Clevedon, Walton in Gordano and Weston in
Gordano** *B & W 12* **P** *Bp and SMF (jt)* **R** N A HECTOR
Hon C C E SACKLEY

CLEVELEYS (St Andrew) *Blackb 12* **P** *Trustees* **V** G M YOUNG

CLEWER (St Andrew) *Ox 5* **P** *Eton Coll* **R** R WEBB

CLEWER (St Stephen and St Agnes) *see* New Windsor *Ox*

CLEY (St Margaret) *see* Blakeney w Cley, Wiveton,
Glandford etc *Nor*

CLEY HILL Villages, The, comprising Corsley and
Chadmanslade, and the Deverills and Horningsham
Sarum 12 **P** *Bp and DBP (jt)* **R** P A REID   **C** G C MAYNARD

CLIBURN (St Cuthbert) *see* N Westmorland *Carl*

CLIDDESDEN (St Leonard) *see* Farleigh, Candover and Wield
Win

CLIFF VILLAGES Group, The SOUTH, comprising Barkston,
Belton, Carlton Scroop w Normanton, Caythorpe, Fulbeck,
Honington, Hough-on-the-Hill, Hougham, Marston, and
Syston *Linc 22* **P** *Sir Anthony Thorold Bt (1 turn), J R Thorold
Esq (1 turn), Lord Brownlow (1 turn), Sir Lyonel Tollemache Bt
(1 turn), J F Fane Esq, Exors S J Packe-Drury-Lowe Esq, and Bp
(1 turn)* **R** S J HADLEY   **C** L E M HALL

CLIFFE (St Andrew) *see* Riccall, Barlby and Hemingbrough
York

CLIFFE AT HOO (St Helen) w Cooling *Roch 6* **P** *D&C*
P-in-c A D HOBBS

CLIFFE, SOUTH (St John) *see* N Cave w Cliffe *York*

CLIFFORD (St Luke) *York 1* **P** *G Lane-Fox Esq*
P-in-c K F A GABBADON

CLIFFORD (St Mary the Virgin) *see* Cusop w Blakemere,
Bredwardine w Brobury etc *Heref*

CLIFFORD CHAMBERS (St Helen) *see* Stratford-upon-Avon,
Luddington etc *Cov*

CLIFFORDS MESNE (St Peter) *see* Newent and Gorsley w
Cliffords Mesne *Glouc*

CLIFFSEND (St Mary the Virgin) *see* St Laur in Thanet *Cant*

CLIFTON (All Saints w St John) *Bris 2* **P** *Bp* **V** C E SUTTON
C W E BRAY   **NSM** J CANNAN

CLIFTON (All Saints) and Southill *St Alb 8* **P** *Bp and C E S
Whitbread Esq (jt)* **R** C T TOPLEY   **NSM** C W STEER

CLIFTON (Christ Church w Emmanuel) *Bris 2* **P** *Simeon's
Trustees* **V** P J LANGHAM   **C** C S BROWN, J N WALFORD
NSM E C BEBB, R M LILLINGTON   **OLM** J LEE

CLIFTON (Holy Trinity) *Derby 1* **P** *Mrs M F Stanton, T W
Clowes Esq, and V Ashbourne (by turn)* **P-in-c** D C J BALLARD
C A J MARSHALL, C E MCDONALD

CLIFTON (Holy Trinity) (St Francis) (St Mary the Virgin)
S'well 2 **P** *DBP* **TR** L CARTWRIGHT   **C** E HUTCHINSON,
R H DAVEY   **NSM** G M HALL

CLIFTON (Holy Trinity, St Andrew the Less and St Peter)
Bris 3 **P** *Simeon's Trustees* **NSM** F M HOUGHTON,
R G CROFT

CLIFTON (Mission Church) *see* Conisbrough *Sheff*

CLIFTON (St Anne) (St Thomas) *Man 7* **P** *Bp* **V** *vacant*

CLIFTON (St Cuthbert) *see* N Westmorland *Carl*

CLIFTON (St George) *see* E Trent *S'well*

CLIFTON (St James) *Sheff 6* **P** *Bp* **P-in-c** T F GIBBONS
C K R SKIDMORE

CLIFTON (St John the Evangelist) *see* Brighouse and Clifton
Leeds

CLIFTON (St John the Evangelist) *see* Lund *Blackb*

CLIFTON (St Luke) *see* Brigham, Clifton, Dean and Mosser
Carl

CLIFTON (St Paul) *see* Cotham St Sav w St Mary and Clifton
St Paul *Bris*

CLIFTON (St Philip and St James) *York 7* **P** *Trustees*
V A J GREADY   **C** J M HOYLAND, K A DENNETT

CLIFTON CAMPVILLE (St Andrew) *see* Mease Valley *Lich*

CLIFTON HAMPDEN (St Michael and All Angels) *see*
Dorchester *Ox*

CLIFTON REYNES (St Mary the Virgin) *see* Lavendon w Cold
Brayfield, Clifton Reynes etc *Ox*

**CLIFTON UPON DUNSMORE (St Mary) w Newton and
Brownsover** *Cov 6* **P** *Bp and H A F W Boughton-Leigh Esq
(jt)* **P-in-c** P J G BONE

CLIFTON-ON-TEME (St Kenelm) *see* Worcs W Rural *Worc*
CLIFTONVILLE (St Paul) *Cant 5*   **P** *Ch Patr Trust*
    V P L S ELLISDON   **C** P M DULLEY
CLIPPESBY (St Peter) *see* Martham and Repps w Bastwick,
    Thurne etc *Nor*
CLIPSHAM (St Mary) *see* Cottesmore and Burley, Clipsham,
    Exton etc *Pet*
CLIPSTON (All Saints), Haselbech, Kelmarsh, Marston
    Trussell, Naseby, Sibbertoft and Welford *Pet 2*   **P** *Bp,*
    Kelmarsh Trust, Ch Coll Cam, and DBP (4 turns), Bp (1 turn)
    R M J HAYES   **C** K R SEWARD
CLIPSTONE (All Saints) *S'well 2*   **P** *Bp*   **V** *vacant*
CLITHEROE (St James) *Blackb 7*   **P** *Trustees*
    R M W L PICKETT   **C** I SARGINSON
CLITHEROE (St Mary Magdalene) (St Paul), Chatburn and
    Downham *Blackb 7*   **P** *Bp and Lord Clitheroe (jt)*
    V A W FROUD   **C** C A HALE-HEIGHWAY
CLIVE (All Saints) *see* Astley, Clive, Grinshill and Hadnall
    Lich
CLOFORD (St Mary) *see* Nunney and Witham Friary,
    Marston Bigot etc *B & W*
CLOPHILL (St Mary the Virgin) *see* Campton, Clophill and
    Haynes *St Alb*
CLOPTON (St Mary) *see* Carlford *St E*
CLOPTON (St Peter) *see* Aldwincle, Clopton, Pilton, Stoke
    Doyle etc *Pet*
CLOSWORTH (All Saints) *see* Coker Ridge *B & W*
CLOUGHTON (St Mary) and Burniston *York 15*   **P** *Abp*
    P-in-c C STAZIKER
CLOVELLY (All Saints) *see* Parkham, Alwington, Buckland
    Brewer etc *Ex*
CLOVELLY (St Peter) *as above*
CLOWNE (St John the Baptist) *see* Barlborough and Clowne
    Derby
CLOWS TOP (Mission Room) *see* Mamble w Bayton, Rock w
    Heightington etc *Worc*
CLUBMOOR (St Andrew) *Liv 5*   **P** *Bp*   **V** J E M GREEN
    C T J GRIFFITHS
CLUMBER PARK (St Mary the Virgin) *see* Worksop Priory
    S'well
CLUN (St George) *see* Clun Valley *Heref*
CLUN VALLEY Benefice, The, comprising Bettwys-y-Crwyn,
    Clun, Clunbury w Clunton, Hopesay, and Newcastle *Heref 9*
    P *Earl of Powis (5 turns), Earl of Powis and Mrs R E Bell (1*
    turn)   **V** *vacant*
CLUNBURY (St Swithin) *see* Clun Valley *Heref*
CLUNGUNFORD (St Cuthbert) *see* Middle Marches *Heref*
CLUNTON (St Mary) *see* Clun Valley *Heref*
CLUTTON (St Augustine of Hippo) w Cameley, Bishop
    Sutton and Stowey *B & W 9*   **P** *Bp, DBP, and Exors J P*
    Hippisley Esq (jt)   **R** M CREGAN
CLYFFE PYPARD (St Peter) *see* Lyneham and Woodhill *Sarum*
CLYMPING (St Mary the Virgin) and Yapton w Ford *Chich 1*
    P *Bp (2 turns), Ld Chan (1 turn)*   **R** R H HAYES
CLYST HEATH *see* Ex H Trin *Ex*
CLYST HONITON (St Michael and All Angels) *see* Broadclyst,
    Clyst Honiton, Clyst Hydon etc *Ex*
CLYST HYDON (St Andrew) *as above*
CLYST ST GEORGE (St George) *see* Aylesbeare, Clyst
    St George, Clyst St Mary etc *Ex*
CLYST ST LAWRENCE (St Lawrence) *see* Broadclyst, Clyst
    Honiton, Clyst Hydon etc *Ex*
CLYST ST MARY (St Mary) *see* Aylesbeare, Clyst St George,
    Clyst St Mary etc *Ex*
COALBROOKDALE (Holy Trinity), Iron-Bridge and Little
    Wenlock *Heref 13*   **P** *Bp, Lord Forester, V Madeley, and V*
    Much Wenlock (jt)   **R** *vacant*
COALEY (St Bartholomew) *see* Lower Cam w Coaley *Glouc*
COALPIT HEATH (St Saviour) *Bris 5*   **P** *Bp*   **V** *vacant*
COALVILLE (Christ Church) w Bardon Hill and Ravenstone
    Leic 8   **P** *Simeon's Trustees and R Hugglescote (2 turns), Ld*
    Chan (1 turn)   **V** G PINNINGTON   **C** R L O'ROURKE
COASTAL Group, The *see* Bacton, Happisburgh, Hempstead
    w Eccles etc *Nor*
COATES (Holy Trinity) *see* Whittlesey, Pondersbridge and
    Coates *Ely*
COATES (St Edith) *see* Stow Gp *Linc*
COATES (St Matthew) *see* Kemble, Poole Keynes, Somerford
    Keynes etc *Glouc*
COATES, GREAT (St Nicholas) and LITTLE (Bishop Edward
    King Church) (St Michael) w Bradley *Linc 3*   **P** *Patr Bd*
    TR D M MCCORMICK   **TV** A I MCCORMICK   **C** J CAMM
COATES, NORTH (St Nicholas) *see* Holton-le-Clay, Tetney
    and N Cotes *Linc*
COATHAM (Christ Church) and Dormanstown *York 16*
    P *Abp*   **V** R M HAUGHTY

COBBOLD ROAD (St Saviour) w St Mary *Lon 9*   **P** *Bp*
    V C J B LEE
COBERLEY (St Giles) *see* Churn Valley *Glouc*
COBHAM (St Andrew) (St John the Divine) *Guildf 10*   **P** *D*
    C H Combe Esq   **V** M P BRANSCOMBE   **NSM** C HOLLINGTON
    OLM M BABATUNDE
COBHAM (St Mary Magdalene) w Luddesdowne and
    Dode *Roch 1*   **P** *Earl of Darnley and CPAS (alt)*
    P-in-c A J WALKER
COBHAM Sole Street (St Mary's Church Room) *see* Cobham
    w Luddesdowne and Dode *Roch*
COBRIDGE (Christ Church) *see* Hanley H Ev *Lich*
COCKAYNE HATLEY (St John the Baptist) *see* Potton w
    Sutton and Cockayne Hatley *St Alb*
COCKERHAM (St Michael) w Winmarleigh St Luke and
    Glasson Christ Church *Blackb 11*   **P** *Bp (2 turns), Trustees (1*
    turn)   **V** G LEWIS   **NSM** O A J HAINES
COCKERINGTON, SOUTH (St Leonard) *see* Mid Marsh Gp
    Linc
COCKERMOUTH AREA Team, The (All Saints) (Christ
    Church), including Bridekirk and Great Broughton *Carl 6*
    P *Patr Bd*   **TR** J E E CHARMAN   **TV** A D THOMPSON
    C D J HODDINOTT   **NSM** G DAVIDSON
COCKERNHOE (St Hugh) *see* Luton St Fran *St Alb*
COCKERTON (St Mary) *Dur 5*   **P** *Bp*   **V** D J BAGE
    C C P ABERNETHY
COCKFIELD (St Mary) *Dur 4*   **P** *Bp*   **P-in-c** B WHITLEY
    C L R EVANS
COCKFIELD (St Peter) *see* Bradfield St Clare, Bradfield
    St George etc *St E*
COCKFOSTERS (Christ Church) Trent Park *see* Enfield Ch Ch
    Trent Park *Lon*
COCKING (not known) w West Lavington, Bepton and
    Heyshott *Chich 3*   **P** *Ld Chan and Bp (alt)*   **R** J JONG
COCKINGTON (St George and St Mary) (St Matthew)
    Ex 10   **P** *Bp*   **P-in-c** D GEORGE   **NSM** P D EVANS
COCKLEY CLEY (All Saints) w Gooderstone *Nor 13*   **P** *Bp*
    R *vacant*
COCKSHUTT (St Simon and St Jude) *see* Petton w
    Cockshutt, Welshampton and Lyneal etc *Lich*
COCKYARD (Church Hall) *see* Chapel-en-le-Frith *Derby*
CODDENHAM (St Mary) *see* N Bosmere *St E*
CODDINGTON (All Saints) *see* Balderton, Barnby in the
    Willows and Coddington *S'well*
CODDINGTON (All Saints) *see* Colwall w Upper Colwall and
    Coddington *Heref*
CODDINGTON (St Mary) *see* Farndon and Coddington *Ches*
CODFORD (St Mary) *see* Upper Wylye Valley *Sarum*
CODFORD (St Peter) *as above*
CODICOTE (St Giles) *see* Welwyn *St Alb*
CODNOR (St James) *see* Denby Gp *Derby*
CODSALL (St Nicholas) *Lich 2*   **P** *Bp and Lady Wrottesley (jt)*
    V M M MATTOCKS
CODSALL WOOD (St Peter) *see* Codsall *Lich*
COFFINSWELL (St Bartholomew) *see* Kingskerswell,
    Abbotskerswell and Coffinswell *Ex*
COFTON (St Mary) *see* Dawlish w Holcombe, Cofton and
    Starcross *Ex*
COFTON HACKETT (St Michael) w Barnt Green *Birm 2*
    P *Bp*   **V** *vacant*
COGENHOE (St Peter) and Great Houghton and Little
    Houghton w Brafield on the Green *Pet 6*   **P** C G V
    Davidge Esq, Mrs A C Usher, Magd Coll Ox, and DBP (jt)
    R E G SMITH   **NSM** I P M COBLEY
COGGES (St Mary) and South Leigh *Ox 28*   **P** *Bp and Ch*
    Patr Trust (jt)   **V** S T KIRBY   **C** A S MCCULLOCH, D R SPENCE
COGGESHALL (St Peter ad Vincula), Markshall, Cressing,
    Stisted, Bradwell-juxta-Coggeshall and Pattiswick
    Chelmsf 16   **P** *Bp, SMF, Exors Mrs D E G Keen and Abp Cant*
    (jt)   **R** H PRENTICE   **NSM** K M KING
COGGESHALL, LITTLE (St Nicholas) *see* Coggeshall,
    Markshall, Cressing etc *Chelmsf*
COKER RIDGE, The, comprising Closworth, East Chinnock,
    East Coker, Hardington Mandeville, Pendomer, Sutton
    Bingham, and West Coker *B & W 6*   **P** *D&C Ex, MMCET, Ox*
    Chs Trust, and DBP (jt)   **R** C G SIMPSON
COKER, EAST (St Michael and All Angels) *see* Coker Ridge
    B & W
COKER, WEST (St Martin of Tours) *as above*
COLATON RALEIGH (St John the Baptist) *see* Ottery St Mary,
    Alfington, W Hill, Tipton etc *Ex*
COLBURN (St Cuthbert) *see* Hipswell *Leeds*
COLBURY (Christ Church) *Win 11*   **P** *Bp*   **P-in-c** G K MAYER
COLBY (St Giles) *see* King's Beck *Nor*
COLCHESTER (Christ Church w St Mary at the Walls)
    Chelmsf 20   **P** *Bp*   **R** P R NORRINGTON

COLCHESTER (St Andrew) *see* Greenstead w Colchester St Anne *Chelmsf*

COLCHESTER (St Anne) *as above*

COLCHESTER (St Barnabas) Old Heath *Chelmsf 20* **P** *Bp*
V R E TILLBROOK

COLCHESTER (St James) and St Paul w All Saints, St Nicholas and St Runwald *Chelmsf 20* **P** *Bp*
R J T MCCLUSKEY

COLCHESTER (St John the Evangelist) *Chelmsf 20* **P** *Adn Colchester* **P-in-c** A J SACHS

COLCHESTER (St Luke) *Chelmsf 20* **P** *Adn Colchester*
P-in-c H R COOPER **C** C J SMITH, H GREENLAND,
L R S CLARKE-MOISLEY, R G GIBBS, S L HAYWARD
NSM P W MANN **OLM** A L MASON

COLCHESTER (St Matthew) *see* Greenstead w Colchester St Anne *Chelmsf*

COLCHESTER (St Michael) Myland *Chelmsf 20* **P** *Ball Coll Ox* **P-in-c** R G GIBBS **C** H GREENLAND, H R COOPER,
S L HAYWARD **NSM** P W MANN

COLCHESTER (St Peter) (St Botolph) *Chelmsf 20* **P** *Bp and Simeon's Trustees (jt)* **P-in-c** M D WALLACE

COLCHESTER (St Stephen) *see* Colchester, New Town and The Hythe *Chelmsf*

COLCHESTER, New Town and The Hythe (St Stephen, St Mary Magdalen and St Leonard) *Chelmsf 20*
R L G BADGER-WATTS **C** D P CANT, S L BATTS-NEALE

COLD ASH (St Mark) *see* Hermitage *Ox*

COLD ASHBY (St Denys) *see* Guilsborough and Hollowell and Cold Ashby etc *Pet*

COLD ASHTON (Holy Trinity) *see* Marshfield w Cold Ashton and Tormarton etc *Bris*

COLD ASTON (St Andrew) *see* Northleach w Hampnett and Farmington etc *Glouc*

COLD BRAYFIELD (St Mary) *see* Lavendon w Cold Brayfield, Clifton Reynes etc *Ox*

COLD HIGHAM (St Luke) *see* Pattishall w Cold Higham and Gayton w Tiffield *Pet*

COLD KIRBY (St Michael) *see* Upper Ryedale *York*

COLD NORTON (St Stephen) w Stow Maries *Chelmsf 10*
P *Bp and Charterhouse (jt)* **V** *vacant*

COLD OVERTON (St John the Baptist) *see* Whatborough Gp *Leic*

COLD SALPERTON (All Saints) *see* Sevenhampton w Charlton Abbots, Hawling etc *Glouc*

COLDEAN (St Mary Magdalene) *see* Moulsecoomb w Bevendean and Coldean *Chich*

COLDEN COMMON (Holy Trinity) *see* S Downs Gateway Churches *Win*

COLDHARBOUR (Christ Church) *see* Abinger and Coldharbour and Wotton and Holmbury St Mary *Guildf*

COLDHARBOUR (St Alban Mission Church) *see* Mottingham St Andr w St Alban *S'wark*

COLDHURST (Holy Trinity) and Oldham St Stephen and All Martyrs *Man 5* **P** *Patr Bd* **V** D S J AUSTIN

COLDRED (St Pancras) *see* Bewsborough *Cant*

COLDRIDGE (St Matthew) *see* N Creedy *Ex*

COLDWALTHAM (St Giles) *see* Bury, Coldwaltham, Hardham and Houghton *Chich*

COLEBROOKE (St Andrew) *Ex 2* **P** *D&C* **V** *vacant*

COLEBY (All Saints) *see* Graffoe Gp *Linc*

COLEFORD (Holy Trinity) w Holcombe *B & W 11* **P** *Bp and V Kilmersdon (jt)* **P-in-c** C R D CRIDLAND

COLEFORD (St John the Evangelist), Staunton, Newland, Redbrook and Clearwell *Glouc 1* **P** *Bp* **V** S BICK
C B M ERSKINE

COLEGATE (St George) *see* Nor Colegate and Tombland *Nor*

COLEHILL (St Michael and All Angels) *Sarum 9* **P** *Governors of Wimborne Minster* **V** S M PATTLE **OLM** L L MCGREGOR

COLEMAN'S HATCH (Holy Trinity) *see* Hartfield w Coleman's Hatch *Chich*

COLEORTON (St Mary the Virgin) *see* Ashby-de-la-Zouch and Breedon on the Hill *Leic*

COLERNE (St John the Baptist) w North Wraxall *Bris 4*
P *New Coll and Oriel Coll Ox (alt)*
C J M ANDERSON-MACKENZIE **NSM** G E PARKIN
OLM C M SOUTHGATE

COLESBOURNE (St James) *see* Churn Valley *Glouc*

COLESHILL (All Saints) *see* Amersham *Ox*

COLESHILL (All Saints) *see* Gt Coxwell w Buscot, Coleshill etc *Ox*

COLESHILL (St Peter and St Paul) *Birm 5* **P** J K Wingfield Digby Esq **V** *vacant*

COLEY (St John the Baptist) *Leeds 6* **P** *V Halifax*
P-in-c J T ALLISON **C** L J FOX

COLGATE (St Saviour) and Roffey *Chich 10* **P** *Bp and P H Calvert Esq (alt)* **V** R J STAGG **NSM** D J HOWLAND

COLINDALE (St Matthias) *Lon 14* **P** *Bp*
P-in-c M R DUCKETT **NSM** S J ATKINSON

COLKIRK (St Mary) *see* Upper Wensum Village Gp *Nor*

COLLATON (St Mary the Virgin) *see* Goodrington and Collaton St Mary *Ex*

COLLIER ROW (Ascension) *see* Romford Ascension Collier Row *Chelmsf*

COLLIER ROW (Good Shepherd) *see* Romford Gd Shep *Chelmsf*

COLLIER ROW (St James) and Havering-atte-Bower *Chelmsf 2* **P** *CPAS and Bp (jt)* **V** D E ANDERTON
NSM G D CLARKE

COLLIER STREET (St Margaret) *see* Yalding w Collier Street *Roch*

COLLIERLEY (St Thomas) *see* Harelaw and Annfield Plain *Dur*

COLLIERS END (St Mary) *see* High Cross *St Alb*

COLLIERS WOOD (Christ Church) *see* Merton Priory *S'wark*

COLLINGBOURNE DUCIS (St Andrew) *see* Savernake *Sarum*

COLLINGBOURNE KINGSTON (St Mary) *as above*

COLLINGHAM (All Saints) *see* E Trent *S'well*

COLLINGHAM (St John the Baptist) *as above*

COLLINGHAM (St Oswald) w Harewood *Leeds 18* **P** *Earl of Harewood and Trustees Lady Elizabeth Hastings Charity (jt)*
V *vacant*

COLLINGTON (St Mary) *see* Bredenbury *Heref*

COLLINGTREE (St Columba) *see* Salcey *Pet*

COLLYHURST (The Saviour) *Man 1* **P** *Bp and Trustees (jt)*
P-in-c N R ELLIOTT **OLM** M B ROGERS, S PAGE

COLLYWESTON (St Andrew) *see* King's Cliffe, Bulwick and Blatherwycke, Collyweston etc *Pet*

COLMWORTH (St Denys) *see* Wilden w Colmworth and Ravensden *St Alb*

COLN RIVER GROUP, The *see* Sevenhampton w Charlton Abbots, Hawling etc *Glouc*

COLN ROGERS (St Andrew) *see* Chedworth, Yanworth and Stowell, Coln Rogers etc *Glouc*

COLN ST ALDWYN (St John the Baptist) *see* S Cotswolds *Glouc*

COLN ST DENYS (St James the Great) *see* Chedworth, Yanworth and Stowell, Coln Rogers etc *Glouc*

COLNBROOK (St Thomas) and Datchet *Ox 12* **P** *Bp and D&C Windsor (jt)* **V** J D F M CHESTERFIELD-TERRY

COLNE (Christ Church) *see* Foulridge, Laneshawbridge and Trawden *Blackb*

COLNE (Holy Trinity) (St Bartholomew) *Blackb 6* **P** *Bp and DBP* **R** A J OEHRING

COLNE (St Helen) *see* Bluntisham cum Earith w Colne and Holywell etc *Ely*

COLNE ENGAINE (St Andrew) *see* Halstead Area *Chelmsf*

COLNEY (St Andrew) *see* Cringleford and Colney *Nor*

COLNEY (St Peter) *see* London Colney *St Alb*

COLNEY HEATH (St Mark) *St Alb 5* **P** *Trustees*
V C L KEIGHTLEY **NSM** J SUTTIE

COLSTERWORTH Parishes, The (St John the Baptist), including Great Ponton, Gunby, Little Ponton, North and South Stoke w Easton, Skillington, and Stainby *Linc 17*
P *Bp Linc (2 turns), J R Thorold Esq and N E McCorquodale Esq (1 turn), Bp and Sir Lyonel Tollemache Bt (1 turn)*
V N T GRIFFITHS

COLSTON BASSETT (St John the Divine) *see* Wiverton in the Vale *S'well*

COLTISHALL (St John the Baptist) w Great Hautbois, Frettenham, Hainford, Horstead and Stratton Strawless *Nor 18* **P** *D&C, Bp, K Coll Cam, and Ch Soc Trust (jt)*
R C J ENGELSEN **OLM** K A DIGNUM

COLTON (Holy Trinity) *see* Coniston and the Crake Valley *Carl*

COLTON (St Andrew) *see* Easton, Colton, Marlingford and Bawburgh *Nor*

COLTON (St Mary the Virgin) *see* Abbots Bromley, Blithfield, Colton, Colwich etc *Lich*

COLTON (St Paul) *see* Bolton Percy *York*

COLWALL (St Crispin's Chapel) (St James the Great) w Upper Colwall (Good Shepherd) and Coddington *Heref 5*
P *Bp* **R** M J HORTON

COLWICH (St Michael and All Angels) *see* Abbots Bromley, Blithfield, Colton, Colwich etc *Lich*

COLWICK (St John the Baptist) *S'well 7* **P** *DBP*
C D E MOYO

COLYFORD (St Michael) *see* Colyton, Branscombe, Musbury, Northleigh and Southleigh *Ex*

COLYTON (St Andrew), Branscombe, Musbury, Northleigh and Southleigh *Ex 4* **P** *D&C* **R** S E MARTIN
NSM V F CHESTER

COMBE (St Swithin) *see* Walbury Beacon *Ox*
**COMBE DOWN (Holy Trinity) (St Andrew) w Monkton
Combe and South Stoke** *B & W 8* **P** *R Bath, Ox Chs Trust,
and Comdr H R Salmer (jt)* **V** s d swinney
C k j partridge, t m p lewis **NSM** c j absolon
COMBE FLOREY (St Peter and St Paul) *see* Bishop's Lydeard
w Lydeard St Lawrence etc *B & W*
COMBE HAY (not known) *see* Bath Odd Down w Combe
Hay *B & W*
COMBE LONGA (St Laurence) *see* Stonesfield w Combe
Longa *Ox*
COMBE MARTIN (St Peter ad Vincula) *see* Ilfracombe SS Phil
and Jas, Combe Martin and Berrynarbor *Ex*
COMBE PYNE (St Mary the Virgin) *see* Axminster, All Saints,
Axmouth, Chardstock etc *Ex*
COMBE RALEIGH (St Nicholas) *see* Honiton w Monkton,
Awliscombe, Buckerell etc *Ex*
COMBE ST NICHOLAS (St Nicholas) *see* Chard St Mary w
Combe St Nicholas, Wambrook etc *B & W*
COMBEINTEIGNHEAD (All Saints) *see* Shaldon,
Stokeinteignhead, Combeinteignhead etc *Ex*
COMBERFORD (St Mary and St George) *see* Wigginton *Lich*
COMBERTON (St Mary) *see* Lordsbridge *Ely*
COMBERTON, GREAT (St Michael) *see* Elmley Castle w
Bricklehampton and Combertons *Worc*
COMBERTON, LITTLE (St Peter) *as above*
COMBROOK (St Mary and St Margaret) *see* Edgehill
Churches *Cov*
COMBS (St Mary) and Finborough, including Buxhall,
Harleston, Onehouse, and Shelland *St E 3* **P** *Bp (2 turns),
Pemb Coll Ox (1 turn)* **Hon C** p m higham
COMBWICH (St Peter) *see* Cannington, Otterhampton,
Combwich and Stockland *B & W*
COMER GARDENS (St David) *see* Worc City W *Worc*
COMMONDALE (St Peter) *see* The Moorlands *York*
COMPTON (All Saints), Hursley, and Otterbourne *Win 7*
P *Bp, Mrs P M A T Chamberlayne-Macdonald, and the Hon J T
W Hewitt (jt)* **R** w a prescott
COMPTON (St Mary and St Nicholas) *see* Hermitage *Ox*
COMPTON (St Mary) *see* Octagon *Chich*
COMPTON (St Nicholas) *Guildf 4* **P** *M More-Molyneux Esq*
R j r h hubbard
COMPTON ABBAS (St Mary the Virgin) *see* Shaftesbury
Sarum
COMPTON ABDALE (St Oswald) *see* Northleach w
Hampnett and Farmington etc *Glouc*
COMPTON BASSETT (St Swithin) *see* Oldbury *Sarum*
COMPTON BEAUCHAMP (St Swithun) *see* Shrivenham and
Ashbury *Ox*
COMPTON BISHOP (St Andrew) *see* Crook Peak *B & W*
COMPTON CHAMBERLAYNE (St Michael) *see* Nadder Valley
Sarum
COMPTON DANDO (Blessed Virgin Mary) *see* Publow w
Pensford, Compton Dando and Chelwood *B & W*
COMPTON DUNDON (St Andrew) *see* Street w Walton and
Compton Dundon *B & W*
COMPTON GREENFIELD (All Saints) *see* S Severnside *Bris*
COMPTON MARTIN (St Michael) *see* Blagdon w Compton
Martin and Ubley *B & W*
COMPTON PAUNCEFOOT (Blessed Virgin Mary) *see*
Camelot Par *B & W*
COMPTON VALENCE (St Thomas à Beckett) *see* Dorchester
and the Winterbournes *Sarum*
COMPTON, LITTLE (St Denys) *see* Chipping Norton *Ox*
COMPTON, NETHER (St Nicholas) *see* Queen Thorne *Sarum*
COMPTON, OVER (St Michael) *as above*
CONDICOTE (St Nicholas) *see* Stow on the Wold, Condicote
and The Swells *Glouc*
**CONDOVER (St Andrew and St Mary) w Frodesley, Acton
Burnell and Pitchford** *Heref 10* **P** *Bp, Revd E W Serjeantson,
and Mrs C R Colthurst (jt)* **R** g d garrett
CONEY HILL (St Oswald) *Glouc 2* **P** *The Crown*
V j p faragher **C** s t newton
CONEY WESTON (St Mary) *see* Stanton *St E*
CONEYSTHORPE (Chapel) *see* The Street Par *York*
CONGERSTONE (St Mary the Virgin) *see* Bosworth *Leic*
CONGHAM (St Andrew) *see* Ashwicken w Leziate, Bawsey
etc *Nor*
CONGLETON (St James) *Ches 11* **P** *Bp* **V** c j sanderson
**CONGLETON (St John the Evangelist) (St Peter)
(St Stephen)** *Ches 11* **P** *Patr Bd* **R** i p enticott
CONGRESBURY (St Andrew) *see* Banwell and Congresbury
w Hewish, Puxton and W Wick *B & W*
CONINGSBY (St Michael) *see* Bain Valley Gp *Linc*
CONISBROUGH (St Peter) *Sheff 9* **P** *Bp* **P-in-c** m mugge

CONISCLIFFE (St Edwin) *Dur 5* **P** *Bp* **V** j s croft
NSM d v robinson
CONISHOLME (St Peter) *see* Marshchapel, Somercotes and
Grainthorpe w Conisholme *Linc*
CONISTON (St Andrew) and the Crake Valley *Carl 9* **P** *Bp,
MMCET, Peache Trustees, Trustees, patron landowners of
Colton, and A C I Naylor Esq (jt)* **R** b t streeter
CONISTON COLD (St Peter) *see* Upper Aire *Leeds*
CONISTONE (St Mary) *see* Upper Wharfedale and Littondale
Leeds
CONONLEY (St John the Evangelist) *see* Kildwick, Cononley
and Bradley *Leeds*
CONSETT (Christ Church) *Dur 2* **P** *Bp* **P-in-c** s grundy
CONSTABLE LEE (St Paul) *see* Rawtenstall and Constable Lee
Man
CONSTANTINE (St Constantine) *Truro 3* **P** *D&C*
P-in-c s g turner **NSM** t r a ebbens
COOKBURY (St John the Baptist and the Seven Maccabees)
see Bradworthy, Sutcombe, Putford etc *Ex*
COOKHAMS, The (Holy Trinity) (St John the Baptist) *Ox 5*
P *Mrs E U Rogers* **V** n plant **C** h chamberlain
NSM d joynes
COOKHILL (St Paul) *see* Inkberrow w Cookhill and Kington
w Dormston *Worc*
COOKLEY (St Michael and All Angels) *see* Heveningham *St E*
COOKLEY (St Peter) *see* Kidderminster Ismere *Worc*
COOKRIDGE (Holy Trinity) *Leeds 12* **P** *R Adel*
V p w atkinson
COOMBE (Christ Church) *see* New Malden and Coombe
S'wark
COOMBE BISSETT (St Michael and All Angels) *see* Chalke
Valley *Sarum*
COOMBES (not known) *see* Lancing w Coombes *Chich*
COOPERSALE (St Alban) *see* Epping Distr *Chelmsf*
COPDOCK (St Peter) *see* Sproughton w Burstall, Copdock w
Washbrook etc *St E*
COPFORD (St Michael and All Angels) *see* Thurstable and
Winstree *Chelmsf*
COPGROVE (St Michael) *see* Walkingham Hill *Leeds*
COPLE (All Saints), Moggerhanger and Willington
St Alb 10 **P** *Bp (2 turns), Ch Ch Ox (1 turn)* **C** k e franks
COPLOW Benefice, The, comprising Billesdon cum Goadby
and Rolleston, Hungarton, and Skeffington *Leic 5* **P** *Bp*
V a s w booker
COPMANTHORPE (St Giles) *York 1* **P** *R York St Clement w
St Mary Bishophill* **V** g r mumford **NSM** g m webb
COPNOR (St Alban) *see* Portsea St Alb *Portsm*
COPNOR (St Cuthbert) *see* Portsea St Cuth *Portsm*
COPP (St Anne) w Inskip *Blackb 9* **P** *V Garstang St Helen and
St Michaels-on-Wyre* **V** p g hunter
COPPENHALL (All Saints and St Paul) *see* Crewe All SS and
St Paul w St Pet *Ches*
COPPENHALL (St Laurence) *see* Penkridge *Lich*
COPPENHALL (St Michael) *Ches 15* **P** *Bp* **R** j x leal
COPPULL (not known) *see* Coppull *Blackb*
COPPULL (St John the Divine) *Blackb 4* **P** *R Standish*
R m hornby
COPSTON MAGNA (St John) *see* Wolvey, Copston Magna
and Withybrook *Cov*
COPT HEWICK (Holy Innocents) *see* Ripon Cathl Benefice
Leeds
COPT OAK (St Peter) *see* Markfield, Thornton, Bagworth
and Stanton etc *Leic*
COPTHORNE (St John the Evangelist) *Chich 9* **P** *Bp*
V w j mauritz **NSM** a j wheeler
COPYTHORNE (St Mary) and Netley Marsh *Win 11* **P** *Bp*
R j r reeve
COQUETDALE, UPPER, comprising Alnham, Alwinton,
Hepple, Holystone, Rothbury, and Thropton *Newc 6*
P *Duchy of Lanc (2 turns), Ld Chan (1 turn), and Duke of
Northumberland (1 turn)* **R** j r sinclair **NSM** j r storey,
s d joyner
CORBRIDGE (St Andrew) w Halton and Newton Hall
Newc 9 **P** *D&C Carl* **V** d j kennedy **C** l f caudwell,
s g lochead
CORBY (St Columba and the Northern Saints) *Pet 7* **P** *Bp*
V i a pullinger **C** k f m montgomery
CORBY (St John the Baptist) (Epiphany) *Pet 7* **P** *E Brudenell
Esq* **R** p w frost
CORBY (St Peter and St Andrew) (Kingswood Church)
Pet 7 **P** *Bp* **P-in-c** a m searle
CORBY GLEN Parishes, The (St John the Evangelist),
including Bassingthorpe w Westby, Bitchfield, Burton le
Goggles, Irnham, and Swayfield *Linc 17* **P** *Ld Chan (2
turns), Margaret Lady Benton Jones (1 turn), Baroness
Willoughby de Eresby, Ch Coll Cam, D&C, DBP, Sir Lyonel*

Tollemache Bt, Sir Richard Welby Bt and Bp (1 turn)
V S L BUCKMAN   **C** A W F DONALDSON
CORELEY (St Peter)   *see Tenbury Heref*
CORFE (St Nicholas)   *see Blackdown B & W*
CORFE CASTLE (St Edward the Martyr)   *see St Aldhelm Sarum*
CORFE MULLEN (St Hubert) *Sarum 9*   **P** *Bp*   **R** J E BURGESS
C M G SMITH   **Hon C** C A R BURGESS
CORHAMPTON (not known)   *see Meon Bridge Portsm*
CORLEY (not known)   *see Fillongley and Corley Cov*
CORNARD, GREAT (St Andrew) *St E 8*   **P** *Bp*   **V** C J RAMSEY
NSM J M RIDLEY, R BAREHAM
CORNARD, LITTLE (All Saints)   *see Bures w Assington and Lt Cornard St E*
CORNELLY (St Cornelius)   *see Tregony w St Cuby and Cornelly Truro*
CORNERSTONE Benefice, The, comprising Bolsterstone, Deepcar, and Stocksbridge *Sheff 3*   **P** *Bp (2 turns), R B Rimington Wilson Esq (1 turn)*   **V** H R ISAACSON
Hon C S T PENDLEBURY   **NSM** K J CROOKES
CORNERSTONE TEAM, The, comprising Houghton on the Hill and Thurnby *Leic 3*   **P** *Patr Bd*   **TR** R A MILES
TV S E RANSLEY   **C** M J CREBER-DAVIES, S P SWEET, T C DEVAS
NSM H M BENCE
CORNEY (St John the Baptist)   *see Black Combe, Drigg, Eskdale etc Carl*
CORNFORTH (Holy Trinity) and Ferryhill *Dur 1*   **P** *D&C (2 turns), Bp (1 turn)*   **V** G NORMAN   **NSM** P G E TYLER
CORNHILL (St Helen) w Carham *Newc 12*   **P** *Abp (2 turns), E M Straker-Smith Esq (1 turn)*   **P-in-c** G R J KELSEY
NSM M N M SENTAMU
CORNHOLME (St Michael and All Angels)   *see Todmorden w Cornholme and Walsden Leeds*
CORNISH HALL END (St John the Evangelist)   *see Finchingfield and Cornish Hall End etc Chelmsf*
CORNWELL (St Peter)   *see Chipping Norton Ox*
CORNWOOD (St Michael and All Angels)   *see Ivybridge, Cornwood, Harford and Sparkwell Ex*
CORNWORTHY (St Peter)   *see Totnes w Bridgetown, Berry Pomeroy etc Ex*
CORONATION SQUARE (St Aidan)   *see W Cheltenham Glouc*
CORRINGHAM (St John the Evangelist) (St Mary the Virgin) and Fobbing *Chelmsf 15*   **P** *Bp and SMF (jt)*
R D ROLLINS   **C** J M NODDINGS   **OLM** W S MOTT
CORRINGHAM (St Lawrence)   *see Lea Gp Linc*
CORSCOMBE (St Mary the Virgin)   *see Melbury Sarum*
CORSE (St Margaret)   *see Ashleworth, Corse, Hartpury, Hasfield etc Glouc*
CORSENSIDE (All Saints)   *see N Tyne and Redesdale Newc*
CORSENSIDE (St Cuthbert)   *as above*
CORSHAM, GREATER (St Bartholomew) and Lacock *Bris 4*
P *Patr Bd*   **P-in-c** A R JOHNSON   **TV** M V GUBBINS
Hon C V J HOWLETT
CORSLEY (St Margaret of Antioch)   *see Cley Hill Villages Sarum*
CORSLEY (St Mary the Virgin)   *as above*
CORSTON (All Saints)   *see Malmesbury and Upper Avon Bris*
CORSTON (All Saints)   *see Saltford w Corston and Newton St Loe B & W*
CORTON (St Bartholomew)   *see Abbotsbury, Portesham and Langton Herring Sarum*
CORTON (St Bartholomew)   *see Hopton, Corton and Gunton Nor*
CORTON DENHAM (St Andrew)   *see Cam Vale B & W*
CORVEDALE Benefice, The, comprising Culmington, Diddlebury, Holdgate, Munslow, and Tugford *Heref 11*
P *Bp (3 turns), D&C (1 turn), Bp Lich (1 turn), Mrs O T M Togers-Coltman (1 turn)*   **R** J S BEESLEY
CORYTON (St Andrew)   *see Milton Abbot, Dunterton, Lamerton etc Ex*
COSBY (St Michael and All Angels) and Whetstone *Leic 7*
P *Bp*   **C** S D BETTS
COSELEY (Christ Church) (St Cuthbert) *Worc 5*   **P** *Bp*
V E J STANFORD
COSELEY (St Chad) *Worc 5*   **P** *Bp*   **P-in-c** G HARTILL
COSGROVE (St Peter and St Paul)   *see Potterspury w Furtho and Yardley Gobion etc Pet*
COSHAM (St Philip) *Portsm 6*   **P** *Bp*   **V** A L WEBB
C D K JOHNSTON
COSSALL (St Catherine)   *see Trowell, Awsworth and Cossall S'well*
COSSINGTON (All Saints)   *see Sileby, Cossington and Seagrave Leic*
COSSINGTON (Blessed Virgin Mary)   *see Woolavington w Cossington and Bawdrip B & W*
COSTESSEY (St Edmund) *Nor 3*   **P** *Gt Hosp Nor*
P-in-c E C LAND   **C** M T LUSCOMBE

COSTESSEY, NEW (St Helen)   *see Costessey Nor*
COSTOCK (St Giles)   *see E and W Leake, Stanford-on-Soar, Rempstone etc S'well*
COSTON (St Andrew)   *see S Framland Leic*
COTEBROOKE (St John and Holy Cross)   *see Tarporley Ches*
COTEHELE HOUSE (Chapel)   *see Tamar Valley Truro*
COTEHILL (St John the Evangelist)   *see Scotby and Cotehill w Cumwhinton Carl*
COTES HEATH (St James) and Standon and Swynnerton and Tittensor *Lich 12*   **P** *Bp, V Eccleshall, and Simeon's Trustees (jt)*   **R** *vacant*
COTESBACH (St Mary)   *see Lutterworth w Cotesbach and Bitteswell Leic*
COTGRAVE (All Saints) *S'well 5*   **P** *DBP*   **R** P D S MASSEY
COTHAM (St Saviour w St Mary) and Clifton St Paul *Bris 3*
P *Bp*   **V** D J STEPHENSON   **C** P J WHITE   **NSM** V H ROYSTON
COTHELSTONE (St Thomas of Canterbury)   *see Bishop's Lydeard w Lydeard St Lawrence etc B & W*
COTHERIDGE (St Leonard)   *see Worcs W Rural Worc*
COTHERSTONE (St Cuthbert)   *see Lower Teesdale Leeds*
COTLEIGH (St Michael and All Angels)   *see Honiton w Monkton, Awliscombe, Buckerell etc Ex*
COTMANHAY (Christ Church) *Derby 8*   **P** *Bp*   **V** *vacant*
COTON (St Peter)   *see Lordsbridge Ely*
COTON-IN-THE-ELMS (St Mary)   *see Seale and Lullington w Coton in the Elms Derby*
COTSWOLDS, SOUTH Team Ministry, comprising Ampney Crucis, Ampney St Peter w Ampney St Mary, Barnsley, Bibury and Winston, Castle Easton, Coln St Aldwyn, Down Ampney, Driffield, Eastleach, Fairford, Kempsford w Whelford, Lechlade, Meysey Hampton w Marston Meysey, Poulton, and Southrop *Glouc 7*   **P** *Patr Bd*   **TR** J J SWANTON
TV A V CINNAMOND, C J SYMCOX, K BROWN
C G W GRIFFITH   **NSM** D HYDE, H CAINE, S F L BRIGNALL, T M HASTIE-SMITH
COTTENHAM (All Saints) w Rampton *Ely 6*   **P** *Bp*
R L DAVIES   **NSM** M P A LUCCHETTA-REDMOND
COTTERED (St John the Baptist)   *see Ardeley, Benington, Cottered w Throcking etc St Alb*
COTTERIDGE (St Agnes) *Birm 2*   **P** *R Kings Norton*
P-in-c M J CLARIDGE   **NSM** R R COLLINS
COTTERSTOCK (St Andrew)   *see Warmington, Tansor and Cotterstock etc Pet*
COTTESBROOKE (All Saints)   *see Guilsborough and Hollowell and Cold Ashby etc Pet*
COTTESLOE, comprising Aston Abbots, Cheddington w Mentmore, Cublington, Soulbury, Stewkley, Wing w Grove, and Wingrave *Ox 15*   **P** *Patr Bd*   **TR** J H ROBSON
TV A J KRAUSS   **Hon C** P LYMBERY
COTTESMORE (St Nicholas) and Burley, Clipsham, Exton, Greetham, Stretton and Thistleton *Pet 12*   **P** *Bp, DBP, E R Hanbury Esq, and Sir David Davenport-Handley (jt)*
V A ORAM
COTTIMORE (St John)   *see Walton-on-Thames Guildf*
COTTINGHAM (St Mary Magdalene)   *see Gretton w Rockingham and Cottingham w E Carlton Pet*
COTTINGHAM (St Mary) *York 14*   **P** *Abp*   **R** N J BOWN
COTTINGLEY (St Michael and All Angels) *Leeds 1*   **P** *Bp*
V M G HENDRY
COTTINGWITH, EAST (St Mary)   *see Derwent Ings York*
COTTISFORD (St Mary the Virgin)   *see Shelswell Ox*
COTTON (St Andrew)   *see Bacton w Wyverstone, Cotton and Old Newton etc St E*
COTTON (St John the Baptist)   *see Kingsley and Foxt-w-Whiston and Oakamoor etc Lich*
COTTON MILL (St Julian)   *see St Alb St Steph St Alb*
COTTONSTONES (St Mary)   *see Ryburn Leeds*
COUGHTON (St Peter)   *see Alcester Minster Cov*
COULSDON (St Andrew) *S'wark 22*   **P** *Bp*   **V** E R FOSS
COULSDON (St John) *S'wark 22*   **P** *Abp*   **R** P C ROBERTS
NSM S L THOMAS
COULSTON, EAST (St Thomas of Canterbury)   *see Bratton, Edington and Imber, Erlestoke etc Sarum*
COUND (St Peter)   *see Wenlock Heref*
COUNDON (St George)   *see Cov St Geo Cov*
COUNDON (St James) and Eldon *Dur 3*   **P** *Bp and The Crown (alt)*   **P-in-c** G NICHOLSON   **C** C HARRIS
COUNTESS WEAR (St Luke)   *see Topsham and Wear Ex*
COUNTESTHORPE (St Andrew)   *see Four Saints Leic*
COUNTISBURY (St John the Evangelist)   *see Lynton, Brendon, Countisbury etc Ex*
COURTEENHALL (St Peter and St Paul)   *see Salcey Pet*
COVE (St John the Baptist) (St Christopher) *Guildf 1*   **P** *Bp*
R G M H FOSTER   **C** A C RICHARDSON, P D RICHARDSON
COVEHITHE (St Andrew)   *see Wrentham, Covehithe w Benacre etc St E*

COVEN (St Paul) *Lich 2* **P** *Bp* **V** *vacant*

COVENEY (St Peter ad Vincula) *Ely 8* **P** *Bp* **R** *vacant*

COVENHAM (Annunciation of the Blessed Virgin Mary) *see* Fotherby, N Thoresby and Grainsby w Waithe *Linc*

COVENT GARDEN (St Paul) *Lon 3* **P** *Bp* **R** S J GRIGG **NSM** J L MEADER

COVENTRY (Holy Trinity) *Cov 2* **P** *Ld Chan* **V** *vacant*

COVENTRY (St Alban) *Cov 1* **P** *Bp* **R** Z L PIMENTEL **C** B PIMENTEL

COVENTRY (St Francis of Assisi) North Radford *Cov 2* **P** *Bp* **V** *vacant*

COVENTRY (St George) *Cov 2* **P** *Bp* **V** J R WICKHAM

COVENTRY (St John the Baptist) *Cov 2* **P** *Trustees* **R** D L BRACEY

COVENTRY (St Laurence) *see* Foleshill St Laur *Cov*

COVENTRY (St Mark) Swanswell (Conventional District) *Cov 1* **C** M D FORD, R J WILLIAMS **Min** P J ATKINSON

COVENTRY (St Mary Magdalen) *Cov 3* **P** *Bp* **V** E L LE BRUN POWELL

COVENTRY (St Michael) Stoke *see* Stoke St Mich, Coventry *Cov*

COVENTRY (St Nicholas) *see* Radford *Cov*

COVENTRY (St Peter) *Cov 1* **P** *Bp* **C** A CLASPER

COVENTRY ALL SAINTS (St Anne and All Saints) (St Margaret) *Cov 1* **P** *Bp* **R** *vacant*

COVENTRY Holbrooks (St Luke) *see* Holbrooks *Cov*

COVERACK (St Peter) *see* St Keverne, St Ruan w St Grade and Landewednack *Truro*

COVERDALE (St Botolph) *see* Middleham w Coverdale and E Witton etc *Leeds*

COVINGHAM (St Paul) *see* Swindon Dorcan *Bris*

COVINGTON (All Saints) *see* S Leightonstone *Ely*

COWARNE, LITTLE (not known) *see* Bredenbury *Heref*

COWARNE, MUCH (St Mary the Virgin) *see* Frome Valley *Heref*

COWBIT (St Mary) *Linc 19* **P** *Ld Chan and DBP (alt)* **V** *vacant*

COWCLIFFE (St Hilda) *see* Fixby and Cowcliffe *Leeds*

COWDEN (St Mary Magdalene) *Chich 9* **P** *Ch Soc Trust* **R** *vacant*

COWES (Holy Trinity) (St Mary the Virgin) *Portsm 7* **P** *CPAS and R Newport and Carisbrooke (jt)* **V** A N POPPE

COWES, EAST (St James) *see* Whippingham w E Cowes *Portsm*

COWESBY (St Michael) *York 18* **P** *Abp* **P-in-c** D E GAMBLE **NSM** K M BROWN, W A DEWING

COWFOLD (St Peter) *see* Lower Beeding and Cowfold *Chich*

COWGATE (St Peter) *Newc 4* **P** *Bp* **V** A M PATERSON **C** O J DEMPSEY, W H M NION

COWGILL (St John the Evangelist) *see* Western Dales *Carl*

COWICK (Holy Trinity) *see* Gt Snaith *Sheff*

COWLAM (St Mary) *see* Waggoners *York*

COWLEIGH (St Peter) *see* Malvern Link w Cowleigh *Worc*

COWLEY (St James) (St Francis) *Ox 1* **P** *Patr Bd* **TR** G B T BAYLISS **NSM** M M DÍAZ BUTRÓN, M OXBROW

COWLEY (St John) (St Alban) (St Bartholomew) (St Mary and St John) *Ox 1* **P** *St Steph Ho Ox* **V** P S J RITCHIE **C** C A L BROWES

COWLEY (St Laurence) *Lon 21* **P** *Bp* **P-in-c** J A HUGHMAN

COWLEY (St Mary) *see* Churn Valley *Glouc*

COWLING (Holy Trinity) *see* Sutton w Cowling and Lothersdale *Leeds*

COWLINGE (St Margaret) *see* Bansfield *St E*

COWPEN (St Benedict) *Newc 1* **P** *Bp* **P-in-c** I H FLINTOFT

COWPLAIN (St Wilfrid) *Portsm 5* **P** *Bp* **V** I SNARES **C** J L JACKSON

COWTON, EAST (All Saints) *see* Wiske Benefice *Leeds*

COX GREEN (Good Shepherd) *Ox 5* **P** *Bp* **V** J R HICKS

COXFORD Group, The *see* E w W Rudham, Helhoughton etc *Nor*

COXHEATH (Holy Trinity), East Farleigh, Hunton, Linton and West Farleigh *Roch 7* **P** *Ld Chan (1 turn), Abp, Lord Cornwallis, and D&C (1 turn)* **C** L C FAULKNER

COXHOE (St Mary) *see* Kelloe and Coxhoe *Dur*

COXLEY (Christ Church) w Godney, Henton and Wookey *B & W 7* **P** *Bp* **P-in-c** J E SHELLARD-JAMES **C** G E MARTIN-SCOTT

COXWELL, GREAT (St Giles) w Buscot, Coleshill and Eaton Hastings *Ox 25* **P** *Bp and Lord Faringdon (jt)* **V** M TURNER

COXWELL, LITTLE (St Mary) *see* Gt Faringdon w Lt Coxwell *Ox*

COXWOLD (St Michael) and Husthwaite *York 3* **P** *Abp* **C** D M COYNE, M E YOUNG, M HARRISON, S WHITING **NSM** C C CRANFIELD, C C GITTENS, C J TOASE, T M GANT

CRABBS CROSS (St Peter) *see* Redditch Ch the K *Worc*

CRADLEY (St James) w Mathon and Storridge *Heref 5* **P** *Bp and D&C Westmr (jt)* **R** R WARD

CRADLEY (St Peter) *see* Halas *Worc*

CRADLEY HEATH (St Luke) *see* Dudley Wood and Cradley Heath *Worc*

CRAGG VALE (St John the Baptist in the Wilderness) *see* Erringden *Leeds*

CRAKEHALL (St Gregory) *see* Lower Wensleydale *Leeds*

CRAMBE (St Michael) *see* Harton *York*

CRAMLINGTON (St Nicholas) *Newc 1* **P** *Bp* **TR** W S H DOCHERTY **TV** D M GRAY

CRAMPMOOR (St Swithun) *see* Romsey *Win*

CRANBORNE (St Mary and St Bartholomew) w Boveridge, Edmondsham, Wimborne St Giles and Woodlands *Sarum 9* **P** *Viscount Cranborne, Earl of Shaftesbury, and Mrs J E Smith (jt)* **R** R D SIMPSON

CRANBOURNE (St Peter) *see* Winkfield and Cranbourne *Ox*

CRANBROOK (St Dunstan) *Cant 11* **P** *Abp* **V** A E J POLLINGTON

CRANFIELD (St Peter and St Paul) and Hulcote w Salford *St Alb 9* **P** *MMCET* **P-in-c** I T PAIN

CRANFORD (Holy Angels) (St Dunstan) *Lon 11* **P** *R J G Berkeley Esq and W Cardale Esq (jt)* **R** M J GILL

CRANFORD (St John the Baptist) w Grafton Underwood and Twywell *Pet 9* **P** *Boughton Estates, DBP, and Sir John Robinson Bt (by turn)* **R** *vacant*

CRANHAM (All Saints) *Chelmsf 2* **P** *St Jo Coll Ox* **R** M WILLIAMS **NSM** P A BROOKS

CRANHAM (St James the Great) *see* Painswick, Sheepscombe, Cranham, The Edge etc *Glouc*

CRANHAM PARK (St Luke) *Chelmsf 2* **P** *Bp* **V** M VICKERS **C** K P BARNARD, N BARRETT **NSM** J A HEININK, K R PERKINS

CRANHAM PARK Moor Lane (not known) *see* Cranham Park *Chelmsf*

CRANLEIGH (St Nicolas) *Guildf 2* **P** *Bp* **R** R O WOODHAMS **C** T J CLIFFORD HILL **NSM** R B VICCAJEE

CRANMORE, WEST (St Bartholomew) *see* Shepton Mallet w Doulting *B & W*

CRANOE (St Michael) *see* Welham, Glooston and Cranoe and Stonton Wyville *Leic*

CRANSFORD (St Peter) *see* Upper Alde *St E*

CRANSLEY (St Andrew) *see* Broughton w Cransley and Mawsley *Pet*

CRANTOCK (St Carantoc) *see* Perranzabuloe and Crantock w Cubert *Truro*

CRANWELL (St Andrew) *see* N Lafford Gp *Linc*

CRANWICH (St Mary) *Nor 13* **P** *CPAS* **R** *vacant*

CRANWORTH (St Mary the Virgin) *see* Barnham Broom and Upper Yare *Nor*

CRASSWALL (St Mary) *see* Black Mountains Gp *Heref*

CRASTER (Mission Church) *see* Embleton w Rennington and Rock *Newc*

CRATFIELD (St Mary) *see* Four Rivers *St E*

CRATHORNE (All Saints) *see* Whorlton Gp *York*

CRAVEN ARMS, comprising Acton Scott, Halford w Sibdon Carwood, Stokesay, and Wistanstow *Heref 10* **P** *Bp (2 turns), Personal Reps T P D La Touche, (1 turn), Hubert J R Holden Esq (1 turn), and DBP (1 turn)* **Hon C** H C SANDERS, M SANDERS **NSM** M G WILLIAMS

CRAWCROOK (Church of the Holy Spirit) *see* Greenside *Dur*

CRAWLEY (St John the Baptist) (St Elizabeth) *Chich 9* **P** *Bp* **V** S BURSTON **C** M J WALKER, S R BUCK

CRAWLEY (St Mary) *see* The Downs *Win*

CRAWLEY (St Peter) *see* W Green *Chich*

CRAWLEY (St Richard) *see* Three Bridges *Chich*

CRAWLEY DOWN (All Saints) *Chich 9* **P** *R Worth* **V** C E KEYTE **NSM** S J BALE

CRAWLEY, NORTH (St Firmin) *see* Sherington w Chicheley, N Crawley, Astwood etc *Ox*

CRAWLEY, SOUTH (St Mary) *Chich 9* **P** *Patr Bd* **TR** T J WILSON **TV** H W SCHNAAR **NSM** G D M RICHARDS, J A E ALDERTON

CRAY (St Barnabas) *see* St Paul's Cray St Barn *Roch*

CRAY VALLEY (St Mary and St Paulinus) (St Andrew) *Roch 16* **P** *Bp* **V** J J E DANIELS-WHITE **C** J M WINTER

CRAY, NORTH (St James) *see* Bexley *Roch*

CRAYFORD (St Paulinus) *Roch 15* **P** *Bp* **R** P F PRENTICE **C** A J SPENCE

CRAYKE (St Cuthbert) w Brandsby and Yearsley *York 3* **P** *The Crown and Abp (alt)* **C** D M COYNE, M E YOUNG, M HARRISON, S WHITING **NSM** C C CRANFIELD, C C GITTENS, C J TOASE, T M GANT

CRAZIES HILL (Mission Room) *see* Wargrave w Knowl Hill *Ox*

CREAKE, NORTH (St Mary) and SOUTH (St Mary) w Waterden, Syderstone w Barmer and Sculthorpe *Nor 14*

989

P *Bp, Earl Spencer, Earl of Leicester, Guild of All So, J Labouchere Esq, Mrs M E Russell, and DBP (jt)* **R** C G WYLIE

CREATON, GREAT (St Michael and All Angels) *see* Guilsborough and Hollowell and Cold Ashby etc *Pet*

CREDITON (Holy Cross) (St Lawrence) Shobrooke and Sandford w Upton Hellions *Ex 2* **P** *12 Govs of Crediton Ch* **R** M J TREGENZA **C** L S EDEN

CREECH ST MICHAEL (St Michael) and Ruishton w Thornfalcon *B & W 18* **P** *Bp, MMCET, and Dr W R C Batten (jt)* **V** L R MULLEN

CREED (St Crida) *see* Probus, Ladock and Grampound w Creed and St Erme *Truro*

CREEDY, NORTH: Cheriton Fitzpaine, Woolfardisworthy, Kennerley, Washford Pyne, Puddington, Poughill, Stockleigh English, Morchard Bishop, Stockleigh Pomeroy, Down St Mary, Clannaborough, Lapford, Nymet Rowland, and Coldridge *Ex 2* **P** *Ld Chan (1 turn), Patr Bd (5 turns)* **C** R J GORDON

CREEKMOOR (Christ Church) *Sarum 7* **P** *Bp* **V** J E AUDIBERT **NSM** J R A AUDIBERT

CREEKSEA (All Saints) *Chelmsf 10* **P** *Bp* **P-in-c** V M WADMAN

CREETING (St Mary) *see* N Bosmere *St E*

CREETING (St Peter) *as above*

CREETON (St Peter) *see* Bytham Par *Linc*

CREGNEISH (St Peter) *see* Rushen *S & M*

CRESSAGE (Christ Church) *see* Wenlock *Heref*

CRESSBROOK (St John the Evangelist) *see* Tideswell *Derby*

CRESSING (All Saints) *see* Coggeshall, Markshall, Cressing etc *Chelmsf*

CRESSINGHAM, GREAT (St Michael) and LITTLE (St Andrew), w Threxton *Nor 13* **P** *Bp and Sec of State for Defence* **R** *vacant*

CRESSWELL (St Bartholomew) and Lynemouth *Newc 11* **P** *Bp* **P-in-c** A W MUNNS **NSM** D M BAKER

CRESWELL (St Mary Magdalene) *see* Elmton w Creswell and Whitwell w Steetley *Derby*

CRETINGHAM (St Peter) *see* Mid Loes *St E*

CREWE (All Saints and St Paul) (St Peter) *Ches 15* **P** *Bp* **P-in-c** O C IGWE **C** A S EDDLESTON, P BENNETT

CREWE (St Andrew w St John the Baptist) *Ches 15* **P** *Bp* **P-in-c** O C IGWE **C** A S EDDLESTON, P BENNETT

CREWE (St Barnabas) *Ches 15* **P** *Bp* **V** R D POWELL

CREWE GREEN (St Michael and All Angels) *see* Haslington w Crewe Green and Wheelock *Ches*

CREWKERNE (St Bartholomew) *see* Wulfric Benefice *B & W*

CRICH (St Mary) and South Wingfield *Derby 2* **P** *Ch Trust Fund Trust and Duke of Devonshire (jt)* **P-in-c** I R WHITEHEAD

CRICK (St Margaret) and Yelvertoft w Clay Coton and Lilbourne *Pet 2* **P** *MMCET and St Jo Coll Ox (jt)* **R** G E ANDERSON

CRICKET MALHERBIE (St Mary Magdalene) *see* Chaffcombe, Cricket Malherbie etc *B & W*

CRICKET ST THOMAS (St Thomas) *B & W 16* **P** *Bp* **V** *vacant*

CRICKLADE (St Sampson) *see* Upper Thames *Bris*

CRICKLEWOOD (St Gabriel) and St Michael *Lon 18* **P** *Bp* **V** J P YEATES

CRIFTINS (St Matthew) w Dudleston and Welsh Frankton *Lich 16* **P** *Bp and V Ellesmere (jt)* **C** A D CRANSTON

CRIMPLESHAM (St Mary) *see* Denver and Ryston w Roxham etc *Ely*

CRINGLEFORD (St Peter) and Colney *Nor 7* **P** *Exors E H Barclay Esq and Gt Hosp Nor (alt)* **R** G P WILKINS **C** T S YAU

CROCKENHILL (All Souls) *Roch 2* **P** *Bp* **V** J E PETERSEN

CROCKHAM HILL (Holy Trinity) *Roch 11* **P** *J St A Warde Esq* **P-in-c** A B COOPER

CROFT (All Saints) *see* The Wainfleet Gp *Linc*

CROFT (Christ Church) *see* Newchurch Culcheth w Croft *Liv*

CROFT (St Michael and All Angels) *see* Broughton Astley and Croft w Stoney Stanton *Leic*

CROFT (St Peter) *see* E Dere Street *Leeds*

CROFTON (All Saints) *Leeds 16* **P** *Duchy of Lanc* **R** L TINNISWOOD **NSM** H WALKER **OLM** A JORDAN

CROFTON (Holy Rood) (St Edmund) *Portsm 2* **P** *Bp* **V** R A ENGLAND **C** D J GREENFIELD **NSM** C R PRESTIDGE

CROFTON (St Paul) *Roch 16* **P** *V Orpington* **V** B A ABAYOMI-COLE

CROFTON PARK (St Hilda w St Cyprian) *S'wark 5* **P** *V Lewisham St Mary* **V** S G BATES

CROMER (St Peter and St Paul) *Nor 20* **P** *CPAS* **V** W J WARREN **C** B J ROGERS **OLM** J M HODGKINSON

CROMFORD (St Mary) *see* Matlock Bath and Cromford *Derby*

CROMHALL (St Andrew), Tortworth, Tytherington, Falfield and Rockhampton *Glouc 5* **P** *Bp, R Thornbury and Oldbury etc, Adn, and J Leigh Esq (1 turn), Earl of Ducie, Oriel Coll Ox, and MMCET (1 turn)* **Hon C** S P PHILLIPSON-MASTERS

CROMPTON FOLD (St Saviour) *see* E Crompton *Man*

CROMPTON, EAST (St James) *Man 5* **P** *Bp* **OLM** W H MOSTON

CROMPTON, HIGH (St Mary) and Thornham *Man 5* **P** *Bp* **V** K H CUNLIFFE **C** P D PRITCHARD **NSM** M C SANDERSON **OLM** D MORRIS

CROMWELL (St Giles) *see* Norwell w Ossington, Cromwell etc *S'well*

CRONDALL (All Saints) and Ewshot *Guildf 3* **P** *Bp* **V** T C L HELLINGS **C** L J ROOSE **NSM** S M R CUMMING-LATTEY

CROOK (St Catherine) *Carl 10* **P** *CPAS* **P-in-c** G W BRIGGS

CROOK (St Catherine) *Dur 7* **P** *R Brancepeth* **P-in-c** L LINDSAY

CROOK PEAK, comprising Badgworth, Biddisham, Christon, Compton Bishop, Loxton, and Weare *B & W 1* **P** *R M Dodd Esq (1 turn), Ld Chan (2 turns), Bp Lon (1 turn)* **R** *vacant*

CROOKES (St Thomas) *Sheff 4* **P** *Patr Bd* **TR** T J FINNEMORE **NSM** C A STRINE

CROOKES (St Timothy) *Sheff 4* **P** *Sheff Ch Burgesses* **C** A M S HOLE

CROOKHAM (Christ Church) *Guildf 1* **P** *V Crondall and Ewshot* **V** S A FRANKLIN

CROOKHORN (Good Shepherd) *Portsm 5* **P** *Simeon's Trustees* **V** J E SMITH **C** A M WILSON

CROPREDY (St Mary the Virgin) *see* Shires' Edge *Ox*

CROPTHORNE (St Michael) *see* Fladbury, Hill and Moor, Wyre Piddle etc *Worc*

CROPTON (St Gregory) *see* Lastingham w Appleton-le-Moors, Rosedale etc *York*

CROPWELL BISHOP (St Giles) *see* Wiverton in the Vale *S'well*

CROSBY (St George) (St Michael) *Linc 6* **P** *Sir Reginald Sheffield Bt* **V** J A WEARING

CROSBY GARRETT (St Andrew) *see* Upper Eden *Carl*

CROSBY RAVENSWORTH (St Lawrence) *see* N Westmorland *Carl*

CROSBY, GREAT (All Saints) *see* Thornton and Crosby *Liv*

CROSBY, GREAT (St Faith) and Waterloo Park St Mary the Virgin *Liv 6* **P** *St Chad's Coll Dur and Trustees (jt)* **P-in-c** J W REED **Hon C** D A SMITH

CROSBY, GREAT (St Luke) *Liv 8* **P** *Bp* **V** A J BRUCE **C** L J N PARRY **NSM** D A LOWRIE

CROSBY-ON-EDEN (St John the Evangelist) *see* Eden, Gelt and Irthing *Carl*

CROSCOMBE (Blessed Virgin Mary) *see* Pilton w Croscombe, N Wootton and Dinder *B & W*

CROSLAND MOOR (St Barnabas) and Linthwaite *Leeds 9* **P** *Bp and R Almondbury (jt)* **P-in-c** P M WITTS

CROSLAND, SOUTH (Holy Trinity) *see* Newsome and Armitage Bridge and S Crosland *Leeds*

CROSS CANONBY (St John the Evangelist) *see* Allonby, Cross Canonby and Dearham *Carl*

CROSS COUNTRY PARISHES *see* Acton and Worleston, Church Minshull etc *Ches*

CROSS FELL Group, The, comprising Addingham, Culgaith, Edenhall, Kirkland, Langwathby, Melmerby, Ousby, and Skirwith *Carl 4* **P** *D&C (2 turns) and DBP (1 turn)* **R** A S PYE **C** K M BUTTERFIELD

CROSS GREEN (St Hilda) (St Saviour) and Richmond Hill *Leeds 13* **P** *Bp and Keble Coll Ox (jt)* **V** D J PERCIVAL

CROSS HEATH (St Michael and All Angels) *Lich 9* **P** *Bp* **V** S C MADDISON

CROSS IN HAND (St Bartholomew) *see* Waldron *Chich*

CROSS ROADS CUM LEES (St James) *see* Haworth and Cross Roads cum Lees *Leeds*

CROSS TOWN (St Cross) *see* Knutsford St Cross *Ches*

CROSSCRAKE (St Thomas) *Carl 10* **P** *V Heversham and Milnthorpe* **NSM** L A FOSTER

CROSSENS (St John) *see* N Meols *Liv*

CROSSFLATTS (St Aidan) *see* Bingley All SS *Leeds*

CROSSLACON Team Ministry, comprising Arlecdon, Cleator, Cleator Moor, and Frizington *Carl 5* **P** *Patr Bd* **P-in-c** N G PENNINGTON

CROSSPOOL (St Columba) *Sheff 4* **P** *Bp* **NSM** L A YAULL

CROSTHWAITE (St Kentigern) Keswick *Carl 6* **P** *Bp* **P-in-c** A G MURPHIE

CROSTHWAITE (St Mary) Kendal *Carl 10* **P** *DBP* **V** M D WOODCOCK **Hon C** S C HOWARD **NSM** M L WOODCOCK

CROSTON (St Michael and All Angels), Bretherton and Mawdesley w Bispham *Blackb 4*   **P** *M G Rawstorne Esq and Patr Bd (jt)*   **R** M WOODS   **NSM** J H TAYLOR
CROSTWICK (St Peter)   *see* Horsham St Faith, Spixworth and Crostwick *Nor*
CROSTWIGHT (All Saints)   *see* Smallburgh w Dilham w Honing and Crostwight *Nor*
CROUCH END HILL (Christ Church)   *see* Hornsey Ch Ch *Lon*
CROUGHTON (All Saints)   *see* Aynho and Croughton w Evenley etc *Pet*
CROWAN (St Crewenna) and Treslothan *Truro 1*   **P** D L C *Roberts Esq and Mrs W A Pendarves (jt)*
P-in-c R E BROWNING   **C** G J ADAMSON
CROWBOROUGH (All Saints) *Chich 16*   **P** *Ld Chan*
V S P REES   **C** B R THORNDIKE, M S ASHWORTH
NSM J A HOBBS, R P DILLINGHAM
CROWBOROUGH (St John the Evangelist) *Chich 16*
P *Guild of All So*   **P-in-c** R E M DOWLER
CROWCOMBE (Holy Ghost)   *see* Quantock Towers *B & W*
CROWELL (Nativity of the Blessed Virgin Mary)   *see* Chinnor, Sydenham, Aston Rowant and Crowell *Ox*
CROWFIELD (All Saints)   *see* N Bosmere *St E*
CROWHURST (St George)   *see* Catsfield and Crowhurst *Chich*
CROWHURST (St George)   *see* Oxted *S'wark*
CROWLAND (St Mary and St Bartholomew and St Guthlac) *Linc 19*   **P** *Earl of Normanton*
P-in-c C H BROWN   **NSM** J A M BILLSON
CROWLE (St John the Baptist)   *see* Bowbrook *Worc*
CROWLE Group, The (St Oswald), including Garthorpe and Luddington *Linc 1*   **P** *Bp (2 turns), The Crown (1 turn)*
V G M LINES
CROWMARSH GIFFORD (St Mary Magdalene)   *see* Wallingford *Ox*
CROWN EAST AND RUSHWICK (St Thomas)   *see* Worcs W Rural *Worc*
CROWNHILL (Ascension)   *see* Plymouth Crownhill Ascension *Ex*
CROWTHORNE (St John the Baptist) *Ox 8*   **P** *Bp*
V L M CORNWELL
CROWTON (Christ Church)   *see* Norley, Crowton and Kingsley *Ches*
CROXALL-CUM-OAKLEY (St John the Baptist)   *see* Seale and Lullington w Coton in the Elms *Derby*
CROXBY (All Saints)   *see* Walesby Gp *Linc*
CROXDALE (St Bartholomew) and Tudhoe *Dur 3*   **P** *D&C*
P-in-c B A HILTON   **NSM** D J HODGE
CROXDEN (St Giles)   *see* Rocester, Denstone and Croxden w Hollington *Lich*
CROXLEY GREEN (All Saints) *St Alb 4*   **P** *V Rickmansworth*
V M R MUGAN   **NSM** P PALMER
CROXLEY GREEN (St Oswald) *St Alb 4*   **P** *Bp*
V R J RILEY-BRALEY
CROXTETH (St Paul) *Liv 5*   **P** *R W Derby and Bp (jt)*   **V** *vacant*
CROXTETH PARK (St Cuthbert) *Liv 5*   **P** *Bp*
V L L LEATHERBARROW
CROXTON (All Saints)   *see* Thetford *Nor*
CROXTON (St James)   *see* Papworth *Ely*
CROXTON (St John the Baptist)   *see* S Croxton Gp *Leic*
CROXTON (St John the Evangelist)   *see* Brocklesby Park, Croxton and North Wolds *Linc*
CROXTON (St Paul)   *see* Ashley and Mucklestone and Broughton and Croxton *Lich*
CROXTON Group, The SOUTH (St John the Baptist), including Ashby Folville, Beeby, Gaddesby, Thorpe Satchville, and Twyford *Leic 2*   **P** *DBP, Ch Soc Trust, and MMCET (jt)*   **P-in-c** N STOTHERS
CROXTON KERRIAL (St Botolph and St John the Baptist)   *see* High Framland Par *Leic*
CROYDE (St Mary Magdalene)   *see* Georgeham *Ex*
CROYDON (Christ Church) Broad Green *S'wark 20*
P *Simeon's Trustees*   **V** L P P JESUDASON
CROYDON (Emmanuel)   *see* S Croydon Em *S'wark*
CROYDON (Holy Saviour) *S'wark 21*   **P** *Bp*   **V** *vacant*
CROYDON (St Andrew) *S'wark 20*   **P** *Trustees*
P-in-c O O MAKANJUOLA   **NSM** C MBANUDE
CROYDON (St Augustine)   *see* S Croydon St Pet and St Aug *S'wark*
CROYDON (St John the Baptist) *S'wark 20*   **P** *Abp*
P-in-c A S BISHOP   **C** D W D ADAMSON-HILL, F A BAYES, O O MAKANJUOLA   **NSM** G S A I GERMAIN-POWELL
CROYDON (St Luke)   *see* Croydon Woodside *S'wark*
CROYDON (St Mary Magdalene)   *see* Addiscombe St Mary Magd w St Martin *S'wark*
CROYDON (St Matthew) *S'wark 20*   **P** *V Croydon*
V S J D FOSTER   **NSM** L M FOX

CROYDON (St Michael and All Angels w St James)
S'wark 20   **P** *Trustees*   **V** T D PIKE   **C** L DEMETRI
CROYDON (St Peter)   *see* S Croydon St Pet and St Aug *S'wark*
CROYDON MINSTER   *see* Croydon St Jo *S'wark*
CROYDON Woodside (St Luke) *S'wark 21*   **P** *Bp*
V S J DENNIS   **C** C DAWSON
CROYDON, SOUTH (Emmanuel) *S'wark 20*   **P** *Ch Trust Fund Trust*   **V** J F ADAMS
CROYDON, SOUTH (St Peter) (St Augustine) *S'wark 20*
P *V Croydon and Bp (jt)*   **V** G J W DUMBRECK
NSM A ONYEKWELU
CRUDGINGTON (St Mary Mission Church)   *see* Wrockwardine Deanery *Lich*
CRUDWELL (All Saints)   *see* Braydon Brook *Bris*
CRUMPSALL (St Matthew w St Mary) *Man 1*   **P** *Bp*
P-in-c D J VALENTINE
CRUMPSALL, LOWER (St Thomas)   *see* Cheetham and Lower Crumpsall *Man*
CRUNDALE (St Mary the Blessed Virgin)   *see* King's Wood *Cant*
CRUWYS MORCHARD (Holy Cross)   *see* Washfield, Stoodleigh, Withleigh etc *Ex*
CRUX EASTON (St Michael and All Angels)   *see* NW Hants *Win*
CUBBINGTON (St Mary) *Cov 11*   **P** *Bp*   **V** G R COLES
CUBERT (St Cubert)   *see* Perranzabuloe and Crantock w Cubert *Truro*
CUBLEY (St Andrew)   *see* S Dales *Derby*
CUBLINGTON (St Nicholas)   *see* Cottesloe *Ox*
CUCKFIELD (Holy Trinty) and Bolney *Chich 8*   **P** *K Coll Lon and Bp (jt)*   **V** M J MAINE   **C** M H WINDRIDGE
NSM M MILLS
CUCKLINGTON (St Lawrence)   *see* Charlton Musgrove, Cucklington and Stoke Trister *B & W*
CUDDESDON (All Saints)   *see* Garsington, Cuddesdon and Horspath *Ox*
CUDDINGTON (St Mary) *Guildf 9*   **P** *Bp*
P-in-c T L RICKETTS
CUDDINGTON (St Nicholas)   *see* Wychert Vale *Ox*
CUDHAM (St Peter and St Paul) and Downe *Roch 16*   **P** *Ch Soc Trust and Bp (jt)*   **V** W J MUSSON
CUDWORTH (St John) *Leeds 14*   **P** *Bp*   **V** D NICHOLSON
CUDWORTH (St Michael)   *see* Winsmoor *B & W*
CUFFLEY (St Andrew)   *see* Northaw and Cuffley *St Alb*
CULBONE (St Beuno)   *see* Oare w Culbone *B & W*
CULFORD (St Mary)   *see* Lark Valley and N Bury *St E*
CULGAITH (All Saints)   *see* Cross Fell Gp *Carl*
CULHAM (St Paul)   *see* Dorchester *Ox*
CULLERCOATS (St George) *Newc 5*   **P** *Duke of Northumberland*   **V** A J HUGHES
CULLERCOATS (St Paul)   *see* Tynemouth Cullercoats St Paul *Newc*
CULLINGWORTH (St John the Evangelist)   *see* Harden and Wilsden, Cullingworth and Denholme *Leeds*
CULLOMPTON (St Andrew) (Langford Chapel) *Ex 7*
P *CPAS*   **R** E Q HOBBS   **C** M A SANDERS, O H J MEARS
CULM DAVY (St Mary's Chapel)   *see* Hemyock w Culm Davy, Clayhidon and Culmstock *Ex*
CULMINGTON (All Saints)   *see* Corvedale Benefice *Heref*
CULMSTOCK (All Saints)   *see* Hemyock w Culm Davy, Clayhidon and Culmstock *Ex*
CULPHO (St Botolph)   *see* Carlford *St E*
CULWORTH (St Mary the Virgin) w Sulgrave and Thorpe Mandeville and Chipping Warden w Edgcote and Moreton Pinkney *Pet 1*   **P** T M Sergison-Brooke Esq, DBP, D L P Humfrey Esq, Ch Patr Trust, and Oriel Coll Ox (jt)
P-in-c M CHESHER   **C** N W M LEGGETT
CUMBERWORTH (St Nicholas), Denby, Denby Dale and Shepley *Leeds 5*   **P** *V Kirkburton, V Penistone, and Bp (jt)*
P-in-c S L HUNTER   **Hon C** S C CLARKE
CUMDIVOCK (St John)   *see* Dalston w Cumdivock, Raughton Head and Wreay *Carl*
CUMMERSDALE (St James)   *see* Denton Holme *Carl*
CUMNOR (St Michael) *Ox 19*   **P** *St Pet Coll Ox*
V J M WIDDESS   **NSM** H A AZER
CUMREW (St Mary the Virgin)   *see* Eden, Gelt and Irthing *Carl*
CUMWHINTON (St John's Hall)   *see* Scotby and Cotehill w Cumwhinton *Carl*
CUMWHITTON (St Mary the Virgin)   *see* Eden, Gelt and Irthing *Carl*
CUNDALL (St Mary and All Saints)   *see* Kirby-on-the-Moor, Cundall w Norton-le-Clay etc *Leeds*
CURBAR (All Saints)   *see* Longstone, Curbar and Stony Middleton *Derby*
CURBRIDGE (St John the Baptist)   *see* Witney *Ox*

CURDRIDGE (St Peter) *Portsm 1*   **P** *D&C Win*
V G R MENSINGH   **NSM** R J WHARTON
CURDWORTH (St Nicholas and St Peter ad Vincula)
(St George), Middleton and Wishaw *Birm 4*   **P** *Bp*
R N W PHILLIPS
CURRY MALLET (All Saints)   *see* Beercrocombe w Curry
Mallet, Hatch Beauchamp etc *B & W*
CURRY RIVEL (St Andrew) w Fivehead and Swell *B & W 5*
  P *D&C Bris (1 turn), P G H Speke Esq (2 turns)*
R S R PATTERSON
CURRY, NORTH (St Peter and St Paul)   *see* Athelney *B & W*
CURY (St Corentine)   *see* Mullion and Cury w Gunwalloe
Truro
CUSOP (St Mary) w Blakemere, Bredwardine w Brobury,
Clifford, Dorstone, Hardwicke, Moccas and Preston-on-
Wye *Heref 1*   **P** *Bp, D&C, CPAS, MMCET, P M I S Trumper
Esq, S Penoyre Esq, and F Chester-Master Esq (jt)*
R L J MORRISS   **NSM** C J LISVANE
CUTCOMBE (St John the Evangelist)   *see* Exmoor *B & W*
CUTSDEAN (St James)   *see* The Guitings, Cutsdean, Farmcote
etc *Glouc*
CUXHAM (Holy Rood)   *see* Benson w Ewelme *Ox*
CUXTON (St Michael and All Angels) and Halling *Roch 6*
  P *Bp and D&C (jt)*   **R** R I KNIGHT
CUXWOLD (St Nicholas)   *see* Caistor *Linc*
DACRE (Holy Trinity) w Hartwith and Darley w
Thornthwaite *Leeds 20*   **P** *Bp, D&C Ripon, V Masham and
Healey, and Mrs K A Dunbar (jt)*   **V** A J FERNELEY
  NSM A J COLLINS
DACRE (St Andrew) *Carl 4*   **P** *Trustees*   **V** *vacant*
DADLINGTON (St James)   *see* Fenn Lanes Gp *Leic*
DAGENHAM (St Cedd)   *see* Becontree St Cedd *Chelmsf*
DAGENHAM (St Martin)   *see* Becontree S *Chelmsf*
DAGENHAM (St Peter and St Paul) *Chelmsf 1*   **P** *Ch Soc Trust*
  V J K EDWARDS
DAGLINGWORTH (Holy Rood)   *see* Brimpsfield w Birdlip,
Syde, Daglingworth etc *Glouc*
DAISY HILL (St James)   *see* Blackrod, Daisy Hill,
Westhoughton and Wingates *Man*
DALBURY (All Saints)   *see* Boylestone, Church Broughton,
Dalbury, etc *Derby*
DALBY (St James)   *see* W Coast *S & M*
DALBY (St Lawrence and Blessed Edward King)   *see*
Bolingbroke Deanery *Linc*
DALBY (St Peter)   *see* Howardian Gp *York*
DALBY, GREAT (St Swithun)   *see* Burrough Hill Pars *Leic*
DALBY, LITTLE (St James) *as above*
DALBY, OLD (St John the Baptist), Nether Broughton,
Saxelbye w Shoby, Grimston and Wartnaby *Leic 2*   **P** *Bp,
MMCET, V Rothley, and Personal Reps K J M Madocks-Wright
Esq (jt)*   **P-in-c** J H MACKAY   **NSM** P R TOWNS
DALE ABBEY (All Saints)   *see* Stanton-by-Dale w Dale Abbey
and Risley *Derby*
DALE HEAD (St James)   *see* Slaidburn w Tosside *Leeds*
DALHAM (St Mary)   *see* Forest Heath *St E*
DALLAM (St Mark) *Liv 11*   **P** *R Warrington and Bp (jt)*
  V *vacant*
DALLINGHOO (St Mary)   *see* Mid Loes *St E*
DALLINGTON (St Giles)   *see* Warbleton, Bodle Street Green
and Dallington *Chich*
DALLINGTON (St Mary the Virgin) and St James *Pet 4*
  P *Bp and Earl Spencer (jt)*   **V** S A FAULKNER
DALSTON (Holy Trinity) w St Philip and Haggerston All
Saints *Lon 5*   **P** *Ld Chan and Bp (alt)*   **V** L J LUZ
DALSTON (St Barnabas) Bishop's Mission Order *Lon 5*
  Min N J CHARLES
DALSTON (St Mark w St Bartholomew) *Lon 5*   **P** *Ch Patr
Trust*   **V** J ZVIMBA
DALSTON (St Michael) w Cumdivock, Raughton Head and
Wreay *Carl 3*   **P** *Bp, DBP, and D&C (jt)*   **P-in-c** B G PHILLIPS
DALTON (Holy Trinity) *Sheff 6*   **P** *Bp*   **V** *vacant*
DALTON (St James)   *see* Holmedale *Leeds*
DALTON (St John the Evangelist)   *see* Topcliffe, Baldersby w
Dishforth, Dalton etc *York*
DALTON (St Michael Parbold)   *see* Up Holland and Dalton
Liv
DALTON HOLME (St Mary)   *see* Etton w Dalton Holme *York*
DALTON LE DALE (St Andrew) *Dur 10*   **P** *D&C*   **V** *vacant*
DALTON, NORTH (All Saints)   *see* Woldsburn *York*
DALTON-IN-FURNESS (St Mary) and Ireleth-with-Askam
Carl 9   **P** *Bp*   **V** R J CROSSLEY
DALWOOD (St Peter)   *see* Kilmington, Stockland, Dalwood,
Yarcombe etc *Ex*
DAMASCUS, comprising Appleford, Drayton, Milton,
Steventon, and Sutton Courtenay *Ox 19*   **P** *Bp, Ch Ch Ox,*

D&C Westmr, and D&C Windsor (jt)   **R** H G KENDRICK
  C P F SUTTON   **NSM** M A HEYWOOD, R BRUCE
DAMERHAM (St George)   *see* W Downland *Sarum*
DANBURY (St John the Baptist) *Chelmsf 9*   **P** *Lord Fitzwalter*
  P-in-c J D JONES
DANBY (St Hilda)   *see* The Moorlands *York*
DANBY WISKE (not known)   *see* Wiske Benefice *Leeds*
DANE BANK (St George)   *see* Denton Ch Ch *Man*
DANEHILL (All Saints) *Chich 18*   **P** *Ch Soc Trust*
  V P MACBAIN
DANESMOOR (St Barnabas)   *see* N Wingfield, Clay Cross and
Pilsley *Derby*
DARBY END (St Peter) and Netherton *Worc 5*   **P** *Bp*
  P-in-c R A HACKETT
DARBY GREEN (St Barnabas) and Eversley *Win 5*   **P** *Bp*
  P-in-c L W CAMPBELL   **NSM** R F HARTLAND
DARENT VALLEY (St Margaret), comprising Darenth, Horton
Kirby and Sutton-at-Hone *Roch 2*   **P** *Bp and D&C (jt)*
  V E J YOUNG
DARENTH (St Margaret)   *see* Darent Valley *Roch*
DARESBURY (All Saints) *Ches 4*   **P** *D G Greenhall Esq*
  NSM G M YOUNGER
DARFIELD (All Saints) *Sheff 12*   **P** *MMCET*   **R** *vacant*
DARLASTON (All Saints) (St Lawrence) and Moxley *Lich 25*
  P *Patr Bd (2 turns), The Crown (1 turn)*   **TR** J C E SYLVESTER
  TV G DAVID   **OLM** A J DUCKWORTH
DARLEY (Christ Church)   *see* Dacre w Hartwith and Darley w
Thornthwaite *Leeds*
DARLEY (St Helen), South Darley and Winster *Derby 1*
  P *Bp*   **R** S D MONK
DARLEY ABBEY (St Matthew)   *see* Allestree St Edm and Darley
Abbey *Derby*
DARLEY, SOUTH (St Mary the Virgin)   *see* Darley, S Darley
and Winster *Derby*
DARLINGSCOTT (St George)   *see* Tredington and
Darlingscott *Cov*
DARLINGTON (All Saints)   *see* Blackwell All SS and Salutation
Dur
DARLINGTON (Holy Trinity) *Dur 5*   **P** *Adn Dur*
  P-in-c T J HARVEY
DARLINGTON (St Cuthbert) *Dur 5*   **P** *Lord Barnard*
  P-in-c T J HARVEY
DARLINGTON (St Herbert) *Dur 5*   **P** *The Crown*   **V** *vacant*
DARLINGTON (St James) *Dur 5*   **P** *The Crown*
  P-in-c M D WAY
DARLINGTON (St John) *Dur 5*   **P** *The Crown*
  P-in-c A ROACHE   **C** L J BROWN
DARLINGTON (St Mark) w St Paul *Dur 5*   **P** *Bp and St Jo Coll
Dur*   **V** P A BAKER
DARLINGTON (St Matthew)   *see* Heighington and
Darlington St Matt and St Luke *Dur*
DARLINGTON St Hilda and (St Columba) *Dur 5*   **P** *Bp*
  P-in-c A ROACHE   **C** L J BROWN
DARNALL (Church of Christ)   *see* Attercliffe and Darnall *Sheff*
DARRINGTON (St Luke and All Saints)   *see* Went Valley *Leeds*
DARSHAM (All Saints)   *see* Yoxmere *St E*
DARTFORD (Christ Church) *Roch 2*   **P** *V Dartford H Trin*
  V R J MORTIMER
DARTFORD (Holy Trinity) *Roch 2*   **P** *Bp*   **V** M J HENWOOD
DARTFORD (St Alban) *Roch 2*   **P** *V Dartford H Trin*
  P-in-c M E YOUNG   **C** K A NELSON   **NSM** E R BEVAN
DARTFORD (St Edmund the King and Martyr) *Roch 2*   **P** *Bp*
  P-in-c M E YOUNG   **C** K A NELSON   **NSM** E R BEVAN
DARTINGTON (St Mary)   *see* Totnes w Bridgetown, Berry
Pomeroy etc *Ex*
DARTMOUTH (St Petrox) (St Saviour) and Dittisham *Ex 11*
  P *Sir John Seale Bt, DBP, and Bp (jt)*   **V** A P LANGLEY
DARTON (All Saints) w Staincross and Mapplewell *Leeds 14*
  P *Bp*   **V** T D STEVENS
DARWEN (St Barnabas) *Blackb 2*   **P** *Bp*   **V** D J BACON
DARWEN (St Cuthbert) w Tockholes St Stephen *Blackb 2*
  P *Bp*   **P-in-c** N E DAVIS
DARWEN (St Peter) *Blackb 2*   **P** *Bp and V Blackburn (jt)*
  V F E GREEN
DARWEN, LOWER (St James) *Blackb 2*   **P** *V Blackb*
  V R H ROBERTS   **C** A A J COLE
DARWEN, OVER (St James) and Hoddlesden *Blackb 2*   **P** *Bp
and V Blackb (jt)*   **P-in-c** R H ROBERTS   **C** A A J COLE
DATCHET (St Mary the Virgin)   *see* Colnbrook and Datchet
Ox
DATCHWORTH (All Saints)   *see* Welwyn *St Alb*
DAUBHILL (St George the Martyr)   *see* W Bolton *Man*
DAUNTSEY (St James Great)   *see* Woodbridge *Bris*
DAVENHAM (St Wilfrid) *Ches 6*   **P** *Bp*   **R** R G IVESON
  NSM V G GERAERTS

DAVENTRY (Holy Cross) *Pet 3* **P** *Patr Bd* **P-in-c** D A STOKES
TV D J BATTISON, N E FRY, N J WHITE
DAVIDSTOW (St David) *see* Moorland Gp *Truro*
DAVINGTON (St Mary Magdalene) *see* Faversham *Cant*
DAVYHULME (Christ Church) and Urmston *Man 2* **P** *Bp*
C J A D SPENCE **OLM** C A BAILEY
DAVYHULME (St Mary) *Man 2* **P** *Bp* **V** C S FORD
C J M BEAUMONT, S A WRIGHT
DAWLEY (Holy Trinity) *see* Cen Telford *Lich*
DAWLEY (St Jerome) *see* W Hayes *Lon*
DAWLISH (St Gregory) w Holcombe, Cofton and Starcross
Ex 5 **P** *D&C Ex, D&C Sarum, and Earl of Devon (jt)*
R D J AYLING **C** T P COLLINS
DAWLISH WARREN (Church Hall) *see* Dawlish w Holcombe,
Cofton and Starcross *Ex*
DAYBROOK (St Paul) *S'well 7* **P** *Bp* **V** *vacant*
DAYLESFORD (St Peter) *see* Chipping Norton *Ox*
DE BEAUVOIR TOWN (St Peter) *Lon 5* **P** *Bp* **V** *vacant*
DEAL (St Andrew) *Cant 9* **P** *Abp* **R** P F BLANCH
DEAL (St George the Martyr) *Cant 9* **P** *Abp* **V** C G SPENCER
C B J FORBES
DEAL (St Leonard) (St Richard) and Sholden w Great
Mongeham *Cant 9* **P** *Abp* **P-in-c** M E CAMERON
NSM P T KAVANAGH
DEAN (All Hallows) *see* The Stodden Churches *St Alb*
DEAN (St Oswald) *see* Brigham, Clifton, Dean and Mosser
Carl
DEAN COURT (St Andrew) *see* Cumnor *Ox*
DEAN FOREST (Christ Church) *see* Forest of Dean Ch Ch w
English Bicknor *Glouc*
DEAN FOREST (St Paul) *see* Parkend and Viney Hill *Glouc*
DEAN PRIOR (St George the Martyr) *see* Buckfastleigh, Dean
Prior, Littlehempston etc *Ex*
DEANE (All Saints) *see* N Waltham and Steventon, Ashe and
Deane *Win*
DEANE (St Mary the Virgin) *Man 3* **P** *Patr Bd*
TR T P CLARK **TV** V C WHITWORTH **C** B A BRADY,
B M WILKINSON
DEANE VALE Benefice, The, comprising Heathfield w
Cotford St Luke, Hillfarrance, and Oake *B & W 19* **P** *Bp and*
PCCs Heathfield, Hillfarrance, and Oake (jt)
P-in-c C SHAW NOTICE
DEANSHANGER (Holy Trinity) *see* Passenham *Pet*
DEARHAM (St Mungo) *see* Allonby, Cross Canonby and
Dearham *Carl*
DEARNLEY (St Andrew), Wardle and Smallbridge *Man 6*
P *Bp* **V** R D BATTERSHELL
DEBDEN (St Mary the Virgin) *see* Saffron Walden and
Villages *Chelmsf*
DEBENHAM (St Mary Magdalene) and Helmingham *St E 12*
P *Ld Chan, Lord Henniker, MMCET, Bp, and Lord Tollemache*
(by turn) **R** S R BATES **C** T L JAMES
DEDDINGTON (St Peter and St Paul) Barford, Clifton and
Hempton *Ox 23* **P** *D&C Windsor and Bp (jt)*
V A L GOLDTHORP
DEDHAM (St Mary the Virgin) and Ardleigh *Chelmsf 21*
P *Duchy of Lanc, Lectureship Trustees, and Ld Chan (by turn)*
V *vacant*
DEDWORTH (All Saints) *Ox 5* **P** *Bp* **V** P C WALKER
DEEPCAR (St John the Evangelist) *see* Cornerstone *Sheff*
DEEPING ST JAMES (St James) *Linc 19* **P** *Burghley Ho*
Preservation Trust Ltd **V** M R WILLIAMS
NSM S M C MARSHALL
DEEPING ST NICHOLAS (St Nicholas) *Linc 19* **P** *Bp*
V *vacant*
DEEPING, WEST (St Andrew) *see* Uffington Gp *Linc*
DEEPLISH (St Luke) and Newbold *Man 6* **P** *Bp*
V A E GILBERT **C** D QUINLAN **NSM** R K GRAY
DEERHURST (St Mary) and Apperley w Forthampton,
Chaceley, Tredington, Stoke Orchard and Hardwicke
Glouc 9 **P** *Bp, V Longdon, and J S Yorke Esq (jt)*
P-in-c I FERWERDA **C** K MUNDY
DEFFORD (St James) w Besford *Worc 3* **P** *D&C Westmr*
V A C DAVIES
DEIGHTON (All Saints) *see* Brompton w Deighton *York*
DELABOLE (St John the Evangelist) *see* Camel-Allen *Truro*
DELAMERE (St Peter) *Ches 6* **P** *The Crown* **R** A C ASKWITH
DELAVAL (Our Lady) *Newc 1* **P** *Lord Hastings* **V** *vacant*
DEMBLEBY (St Lucia) *see* S Lafford *Linc*
DENABY MAIN (All Saints) *Sheff 7* **P** *Bp* **V** *vacant*
DENBURY (St Mary the Virgin) *see* Ipplepen w Torbryan,
Denbury, Broadhempston and Woodland *Ex*
DENBY (St John the Evangelist) *see* Cumberworth, Denby,
Denby Dale etc *Leeds*
DENBY DALE (Holy Trinity) *as above*

DENBY Group, The (St Mary the Virgin), comprising
Codnor, Denby, Horsley, Horsley Woodhouse, and Loscoe
Derby 8 **P** *The Crown (1 turn), Bp (1 turn), Mrs L B Palmer*
and Bp (1 turn) **OLM** C C HOLDEN
DENCHWORTH (St James) *see* Vale *Ox*
DENDRON (St Matthew) *see* Aldingham, Dendron,
Rampside and Urswick *Carl*
DENESIDE (All Saints) *see* Seaham and Dawdon *Dur*
DENFORD (Holy Trinity) *see* Thrapston, Denford and Islip
Pet
DENGIE (St James) w Asheldham *Chelmsf 10* **P** *Bp*
P-in-c S K POSS
DENHAM (St John the Baptist) *see* Athelington, Denham,
Horham, Hoxne etc *St E*
DENHAM (St Mark) (St Mary the Virgin) *Ox 9* **P** *L J Way*
Esq **R** C W LINDNER **Hon C** I M JENNINGS
NSM N R MADUKA
DENHAM (St Mary) *see* Barrow *St E*
DENHAM, NEW (St Francis) *see* Denham *Ox*
DENMEAD (All Saints) *Portsm 5* **P** *Ld Chan*
V E J RACKLYEFT **C** J S WILLIAMS **NSM** A C L JOHNSON
DENNINGTON (St Mary) *see* Upper Alde *St E*
DENSHAW (Christ Church) *see* Saddleworth *Man*
DENSTON (St Nicholas) *see* Bansfield *St E*
DENSTONE (All Saints) *see* Rocester, Denstone and Croxden
w Hollington *Lich*
DENT (St Andrew) *see* Western Dales *Carl*
DENTON (Christ Church) (St George) *Man 5* **P** *Bp*
P-in-c M HOWARTH
DENTON (Holy Spirit) *Newc 4* **P** *Bp* **P-in-c** N HESLOP
DENTON (St Andrew) *see* Harlaxton Gp *Linc*
DENTON (St Helen) *see* Washburn and Mid-Wharfe *Leeds*
DENTON (St Lawrence) *Man 5* **P** *Earl of Wilton*
P-in-c K J MAMBU **C** M HOWARTH
DENTON (St Leonard) w South Heighton and Tarring
Neville *Chich 21* **P** *MMCET and Bp (alt)* **R** P L WILSON
C J H LOWRIES
DENTON (St Margaret) *see* Yardley Hastings, Denton and
Grendon etc *Pet*
DENTON (St Mary Magdalene) *see* Elham Valley *Cant*
DENTON (St Mary) *see* Ditchingham, Hedenham, Broome,
Earsham etc *Nor*
DENTON HOLME (St James) *Carl 3* **P** *Trustees*
V S C BICKERSTETH **C** N M ORCHARD
DENTON, NETHER (St Cuthbert) *see* Lanercost, Walton,
Gilsland and Nether Denton *Carl*
DENVER (St Mary) and Ryston w Roxham and Bexwell and
Crimplesham *Ely 9* **P** *Bp and G&C Coll Cam (jt)* **R** *vacant*
DEOPHAM (St Andrew) *see* High Oak, Hingham and
Scoulton w Wood Rising *Nor*
DEPDEN (St Mary the Virgin) *see* Chevington w Hargrave,
Chedburgh w Depden etc *St E*
DEPTFORD (St John) (Holy Trinity) (Ascension) *S'wark 2*
P *Patr Bd* **TV** A Y BENNETT **C** L MASEKO
DEPTFORD (St Nicholas) (St Luke) *S'wark 2* **P** *MMCET,*
Peache Trustees, and CPAS (jt)
V L A J CODRINGTON-MARSHALL
DEPTFORD (St Paul) *S'wark 2* **P** *Bp* **R** P D BUTLER
DEPTFORD Brockley (St Peter) *see* Brockley St Pet *S'wark*
DERBY (St Alkmund) (St Werburgh) *Derby 5* **P** *Simeon's*
Trustees **C** A J D BOND, J GOLDING, J M DURRANT,
J M NEWMAN, P D MANN, S R CURTIS
DERBY (St Andrew w St Osmund) *see* Pride Park, Wilmorton,
Allenton and Shelton Lock *Derby*
DERBY (St Anne) *Derby 5* **P** *Bp* **P-in-c** G A C ORTON
DERBY (St Augustine) *see* Walbrook Epiphany *Derby*
DERBY (St Barnabas) *Derby 5* **P** *Bp* **V** D G HONOUR
NSM J R FERGUSON
DERBY (St Bartholomew) (St Luke) *Derby 5* **P** *Bp*
V L T YOUNG
DERBY (St John the Evangelist) *Derby 5* **P** *Bp* **C** E J JONES
DERBY (St Mark) *see* Chaddesden St Phil w Derby St Mark
Derby
DERBY (St Paul) *Derby 5* **P** *Bp* **P-in-c** J M DURRANT
DERBY (St Peter and Christ Church w Holy Trinity) *Derby 5*
P *CPAS* **C** A K MATTHEWS **NSM** N J PARISH
DERBY (St Thomas) *see* Walbrook Epiphany *Derby*
DERBY, WEST (Good Shepherd) *Liv 5* **P** *Bp and R W Derby*
(jt) **C** E P THORPE
DERBY, WEST (St John the Baptist) *Liv 5* **P** *Trustees*
V N R JOHNSON
DERBY, WEST (St Luke) *see* 4Saints Team *Liv*
DERBY, WEST (St Mary) St James *Liv 5* **P** *Bp and Adn Liv (jt)*
V S W BOYD
DERBYSHIRE HILL (St Philip) *see* Parr *Liv*

DERE STREET, EAST, comprising Barton, Cleasby w Stapleton, Croft, Eryholme, Manfield, and Middleton Tyas w Moulton *Leeds 19* **P** *The Crown (1 turn), Bp, R Forcett and Aldbrough and Melsonby, V Gilling and Kirkby Ravensworth, and D&C Ripon (1 turn)* **R** *vacant*

DEREHAM (St Nicholas) and District *Nor 16* **P** *Ld Chan (2 turns), Patr Bd (1 turn)* **TR** P CUBITT **TV** J R ROSIE **OLM** J L NURSEY

DEREHAM, WEST (St Andrew) *see Wissey Valley Ely*

DERRINGHAM BANK (Ascension) (St Thomas) *York 14* **P** *Abp* **V** S J WHALEY

DERRINGTON (St Matthew) *see Bradeley, Church Eaton, Derrington and Haughton Lich*

DERRY HILL (Christ Church) *see Marden Vale Sarum*

DERSINGHAM (St Nicholas), Anmer, Ingoldisthorpe and Shernborne *Nor 15* **P** *HM The Queen and Bp (alt)* **R** M A CAPRON **C** D J COSSEY **Hon C** A F AUBREY-JONES

DERWENT INGS, comprising Elvington, Sutton-on-Derwent, Thorganby, and Wheldrake *York 2* **P** *Abp, Lt Col J Darlington, and Lady Caroline Dunnington-Jefferson (jt)* **P-in-c** J M DOYLE-BRETT

DERWENT, UPPER, comprising Borrowdale, Newlands, and Thornthwaite *Carl 6* **P** *V Keswick St Jo (1 turn), V Crosthwaite (2 turns)* **P-in-c** A G MURPHIE

DERWENT, UPPER, comprising Brompton-by-Sawdon, Hutton Buscell, Snainton, and Wykeham *York 19* **P** *Viscountess Downe (1 turn), Sir Philip Naylor-Leyland Bt (1 turn), Abp (2 turns)* **P-in-c** J T KINSELLA **NSM** P WOOD, S E GOUGH

DESBOROUGH (St Giles), Brampton Ash, Dingley and Braybrooke *Pet 9* **P** *Bp, Earl Spencer, and DBP (by turn)* **R** H M JEFFERY **C** S V COWAN **NSM** N M CLARKE

DESFORD (St Martin) and Kirby Muxloe *Leic 9* **P** *Bp and Ld Chan (alt)* **R** G K HUTCHINSON **NSM** R C MARSH

DETHICK (St John the Baptist) *see Matlock, Dethick, Lea and Holloway Derby*

DETLING (St Martin) *see N Downs Cant*

DEVER, LOWER, comprising Barton Stacey, Bullington, and South Wonston *Win 7* **P** *Bp and D&C (jt)* **R** *vacant*

DEVER, UPPER, comprising East Stratton, Micheldever, Stoke Charity w Hunton, Wonston, and Woodmancote w Popham *Win 7* **P** *Lord Northbrook (3 turns), Bp (2 turns)* **P-in-c** J A RENNIE **NSM** R D REES

DEVIZES (St John) (St Mary) *Sarum 17* **P** *Ld Chan* **C** G J LYNCH

DEVIZES (St Peter) *Sarum 17* **P** *Bp* **V** *vacant*

DEVONPORT (St Bartholomew) and Ford St Mark *Ex 20* **P** *Bp and Trustees (jt)* **V** R T SILK **C** J R DEVEREUX

DEVONPORT (St Boniface) (St Philip) *Ex 20* **P** *Bp* **V** M C DOYLE

DEVONPORT (St Budeaux) *Ex 20* **P** *CPAS* **V** S J BEACH **C** A J PRICE

DEVONPORT (St Michael) (St Barnabas) (St Aubyn) *Ex 20* **P** *Bp* **V** T J BUCKLEY **NSM** S M NICHOLAS

DEVONPORT (St Thomas) *see Plymouth St Pet and H Apostles Ex*

DEVORAN (St John the Evangelist and St Petroc) *Truro 5* **P** *Bp* **P-in-c** K A F WILSON **C** R D WALLIS **NSM** J ROWE

DEWCHURCH, LITTLE (St David) *see S Wye Rural Par Heref*

DEWCHURCH, MUCH (St David) *see Wormelow Hundred Heref*

DEWLISH (All Saints) *see Puddletown, Tolpuddle and Milborne w Dewlish Sarum*

DEWSALL (St Michael) *see Wormelow Hundred Heref*

DEWSBURY (All Saints) (St Mark) (St Matthew and St John the Baptist) *Leeds 7* **P** *Bp, Adn Pontefract, RD Dewsbury, and Lay Chmn Dewsbury Deanery Syn (jt)* **TR** S A CASH **C** D BERTSCHMANN, N D WALPOLE

DEWSBURY MOOR (St John the Evangelist) *see Dewsbury Leeds*

DHOON (Christ Church) *see Maughold and S Ramsey S & M*

DIBDEN (All Saints) *Win 11* **P** *MMCET* **R** P S STARK TOLLER

DIBDEN PURLIEU (St Andrew) *see Dibden Win*

DICKER, UPPER (Holy Trinity) *see Hellingly and Upper Dicker Chich*

DICKLEBURGH (All Saints) and The Pulhams *Nor 10* **P** *Ld Chan (1 turn), Patr Bd (2 turns), The Crown (1 turn)* **R** S E WALSH **OLM** D J ADLAM, P D SCHWIER

DIDBROOK (St George) *see Winchcombe Glouc*

DIDCOT (All Saints) *Ox 26* **P** *BNC Ox* **P-in-c** A M LORD **C** B M BODEKER, H R BOORMAN, S L REEVES

DIDCOT (St Peter) *Ox 26* **P** *Bp* **P-in-c** H C REYNOLDS **NSM** K O HEBDEN **OLM** F M CHILDS

DIDCOT Ladygrove *see Didcot All SS Ox*

DIDDINGTON (St Laurence) *see The Paxtons w Diddington and Southoe Ely*

DIDLINGTON (St Michael) *Nor 13* **P** *CPAS* **V** *vacant*

DIDMARTON (St Lawrence) *see Boxwell, Leighterton, Didmarton, Oldbury etc Glouc*

DIDSBURY (St James) (Emmanuel) *Man 2* **P** *Patr Bd* **TR** N J BUNDOCK **TV** L K BATTYE **C** K A TANNER-IHM

DIDSBURY, WEST (Christ Church) and Withington St Christopher *Man 2* **P** *Trustees and The Crown (alt)* **R** A PILKINGTON **C** T L STUDMAN, T W PHIPPS

DIGBY GROUP, The (St Thomas of Canterbury), including Ashby-de-la-Launde, Bloxholme, Dorrington, Kirkby Green, Rowston, and Scopwick *Linc 14* **P** *Mrs H E Gillatt, Ld Chan, and DBP (by turn)* **P-in-c** M P D KENNARD **Hon C** D B WOODS

DIGMOOR (Christ the Servant) *see Up Holland and Dalton Liv*

DIGSWELL (Christ the King) (St John the Evangelist) *St Alb 18* **P** *SMF* **R** R P MARSHALL **NSM** S A EVANS

DILHAM (St Nicholas) *see Smallburgh w Dilham w Honing and Crostwight Nor*

DILHORNE (All Saints) *see Caverswall and Weston Coyney w Dilhorne Lich*

DILTON MARSH (Holy Trinity) *see White Horse Sarum*

DILTON or LEIGH (Holy Saviour) *as above*

DILWYN AND STRETFORD (St Mary the Virgin) *see Leominster Heref*

DINDER (St Michael and All Angels) *see Pilton w Croscombe, N Wootton and Dinder B & W*

DINEDOR (St Andrew) *see S Wye Rural Par Heref*

DINES GREEN (St Michael) *see Worc City W Worc*

DINGLE (St Gabriel) (St Cleopas) *Liv 3* **P** *Simeon's Trustees* **V** S GASSON

DINGLEY (All Saints) *see Desborough, Brampton Ash, Dingley and Braybrooke Pet*

DINNINGTON (St Leonard) *Sheff 5* **P** S B V Weston Esq **R** *vacant*

DINNINGTON (St Matthew) *see Ch the King Newc*

DINNINGTON (St Nicholas) *see Merriott w Hinton, Dinnington and Lopen B & W*

DINSDALE (St John the Baptist) w Sockburn *Dur 5* **P** *D&C and Sherburn Hosp (alt)* **R** *vacant*

DINTING VALE (Holy Trinity) *Derby 4* **P** *Bp* **P-in-c** N P GURNEY

DINTON (St Mary) *see Nadder Valley Sarum*

DINTON (St Peter and St Paul) *see Wychert Vale Ox*

DIPTFORD (St Mary the Virgin) w North Huish, Ermington, Halwell, Harberton, Harbertonford, Moreleigh and Ugborough *Ex 11* **P** *The Crown (1 turn), Bp, D&C and Grocers' Co (3 turns)* **R** P D SAYLE

DISCOED (St Michael) *see Presteigne w Discoed, Kinsham, Lingen and Knill Heref*

DISEWORTH (St Michael and All Angels) *see Kegworth, Hathern, Long Whatton, Diseworth etc Leic*

DISHLEY (All Saints) *see Thorpe Acre w Dishley Leic*

DISLEY (St Mary the Virgin) *Ches 16* **P** *Lord Newton* **V** A S CORNES

DISS Team Ministry, The (St Mary), including Bressingham, Burston, Fersfield, Gissing, North and South Lopham, Roydon, Shelfanger, Tivetshall and Winfarthing *Nor 10* **P** *Ld Chan (1 turn), Patr Bd (5 turns)* **TR** A C BILLETT **TV** J J CRUSE **C** S S THORP

DISTINGTON (Holy Spirit) *see Harrington and Distington Carl*

DITCHEAT (St Mary Magdalene) *see Fosse Trinity B & W*

DITCHINGHAM (St Mary), Hedenham, Broome, Earsham, Alburgh and Denton *Nor 10* **P** *Abp, Bp, Countess Ferrers, J M Meade Esq, and St Jo Coll Cam (jt)* **R** C HUTTON **OLM** R A KIRKPATRICK, S L CRAMP

DITCHLING (St Margaret), Streat and Westmeston *Chich 11* **P** *Bp* **R** D P WALLIS

DITTERIDGE (St Christopher) *see Box w Hazlebury and Ditteridge Bris*

DITTISHAM (St George) *see Dartmouth and Dittisham Ex*

DITTON (St Basil and All Saints) *see Hough Green St Basil and All SS Liv*

DITTON (St Michael) (St Thomas) *Liv 12* **P** *Bp* **V** L RILEY-DAWKIN **OLM** L MOSS

DITTON (St Peter ad Vincula) *Roch 7* **P** *Ch Trust Fund Trust* **R** J R TERRANOVA

DITTON PRIORS (St John the Baptist) w Neenton, Burwarton, Cleobury North, Aston Botterell, Wheathill and Loughton and Chetton *Heref 8* **P** *Bp, Princess Josephine zu Loewenstein, and Exors Viscount Boyne (jt)* **R** *vacant*

DIXTON NEWTON (St Peter) *see Wye Reaches Gp Heref*

DOBCROSS (Holy Trinity) *see Saddleworth Man*

DOCCOMBE (Chapel) *see* Moretonhampstead, Manaton, N Bovey and Lustleigh *Ex*
DOCK (Mission Church) *see* Immingham *Linc*
DOCKENFIELD (Church of the Good Shepherd) *see* Frensham *Guildf*
DOCKING (St Mary), The Birchams, Fring, Stanhoe and Sedgeford *Nor 15* **P** *Bp, D&C, and Mrs A J Ralli (3 turns), HM The Queen (1 turn)* **R** P R COOK **NSM** R J M COLLIER
DOCKLOW (St Bartholomew) *see* Leominster *Heref*
DODBROOKE (St Thomas à Beckett) *see* Kingsbridge, Dodbrooke, and W Alvington *Ex*
DODDERHILL (St Augustine) *see* Droitwich, and Salwarpe and Hindlip w Martin Hussingtree *Worc*
DODDINGHURST (All Saints) *Chelmsf 8* **P** *Bp*
P-in-c A V COLEMAN **OLM** J W BIDDULPH
DODDINGTON (St John the Baptist) *see* Cleobury Mortimer w Hopton Wafers etc *Heref*
DODDINGTON (St John the Baptist) *see* Kingsdown, Creekside and High Downs *Cant*
DODDINGTON (St John) *see* Wybunbury and Audlem w Doddington *Ches*
DODDINGTON (St Mary and St Michael), Ilderton, Kirknewton and Wooler *Newc 7* **P** *Bp and Duke of Northumberland (1 turn), Ld Chan (1 turn)* **V** S COOKE **NSM** E J DOBSON
DODDINGTON (St Mary) *see* Six Fen Churches *Ely*
DODDINGTON (St Peter) *see* Skellingthorpe w Doddington *Linc*
DODDINGTON, GREAT (St Nicholas) and Wilby and Ecton *Pet 6* **P** *Ld Chan, Exors Lt Col H C M Stockdale, and The Crown (by turn)* **R** J R BUCK
DODDISCOMBSLEIGH (St Michael) *see* Christow, Ashton, Bridford, Dunchideock etc *Ex*
DODFORD (Holy Trinity and St Mary) *Worc 6* **P** *Bp*
V D S FORD **C** R J M SANDLAND
DODFORD (St Mary the Virgin) *see* Weedon Bec w Everdon and Dodford *Pet*
DODLESTON (St Mary) *Ches 2* **P** *D&C* **R** E H CLARKE
DODWORTH (St John the Baptist) *see* W Barnsley *Leeds*
DOGMERSFIELD (All Saints) *see* Hartley Wintney, Elvetham, Winchfield etc *Win*
DOGSTHORPE (Christ the Carpenter) *see* Pet Ch Carpenter *Pet*
DOLPHINHOLME (St Mark) w Quernmore and Over Wyresdale *Blackb 11* **P** *Bp and V Lanc (jt)* **V** C J RIGNEY **NSM** C I WALKER
DOLTON (St Edmund King and Martyr), Dowland, Iddesleigh, and Monkokehampton *Ex 18* **P** *Bp and Ch Soc Trust (jt)* **R** S Y OLDHAM
DONCASTER (Holy Trinity) *see* New Cantley *Sheff*
DONCASTER (St George) *Sheff 8* **P** *Bp* **V** D L STEVENS **C** D J PARKINSON
DONCASTER (St Hugh of Lincoln) *see* New Cantley *Sheff*
DONCASTER (St James) *Sheff 8* **P** *Hyndman's Trustees* **P-in-c** C J MCCARTHY **NSM** M G PARNELL
DONCASTER (St Jude) *see* Edlington and Hexthorpe *Sheff*
DONCASTER (St Leonard and St Jude) *Sheff 7* **P** *The Crown* **P-in-c** D P D'SILVA
DONCASTER (St Mary) (St Paul) *Sheff 8* **P** *Hyndman's Trustees and Bp (jt)* **P-in-c** A R THOMAS **C** A J PRIESTLEY
DONHEAD ST ANDREW (St Andrew) *see* St Bartholomew *Sarum*
DONHEAD ST MARY (St Mary the Virgin) *as above*
DONINGTON (St Cuthbert) *see* Albrighton, Boningale and Donington *Lich*
DONINGTON (St Mary and the Holy Rood) *see* Haven Gp *Linc*
DONINGTON-ON-BAIN (St Andrew) *see* Asterby Gp *Linc*
DONISTHORPE (St John) *see* Woodfield *Leic*
DONNINGTON (St George) *Chich 2* **P** *Bp* **V** J P COOPER
DONNINGTON (St Mary) *see* Redmarley D'Abitot, Bromesberrow, Pauntley etc *Glouc*
DONNINGTON WOOD (St Matthew) *Lich 20* **P** *Bp*
P-in-c P M SMITH
DONYATT (Blessed Virgin Mary) *see* Isle Valley *B & W*
DONYLAND, EAST (St Lawrence) *see* Fingringhoe w E Donyland and Abberton etc *Chelmsf*
DORCHESTER (St George) (St Mary the Virgin) (St Peter, Holy Trinity and All Saints) and the Winterbournes *Sarum 1* **P** *Ld Chan (1 turn), Patr Bd (4 turns)* **TR** R K R MAGEE **TV** C L YARRIEN, J HOLDEN **NSM** J LACY-SMITH, J M CULLIFORD, J SADDINGTON, R RAJ-SINGH
DORCHESTER (St Peter and St Paul) *Ox 20* **P** *Patr Bd* **TR** S E BOOYS **TV** C N KING, P G WIGNALL, T M STEWART-SYKES **C** C L SCHNEIDER, S M SHAMEL-WOOD **NSM** J P MORTON, R C CARNEGIE

DORDON (St Leonard) *Birm 5* **P** *V Polesworth* **V** *vacant*
DORE (Christ Church) *Sheff 2* **P** *Sir Philip Naylor-Leyland Bt* **V** *vacant*
DORKING (St Martin) w Ranmore *Guildf 7* **P** *Bp* **V** D J TIGHE
DORKING (St Paul) *Guildf 7* **P** *Ch Patr Trust* **V** A X CACOURIS **C** R HEATH-TAYLOR **OLM** J A FIRTH
DORMANSLAND (St John) *see* Lingfield and Dormansland *S'wark*
DORMANSTOWN (All Saints) *see* Coatham and Dormanstown *York*
DORMINGTON (St Peter) *see* Bartestree Cross *Heref*
DORMSTON (St Nicholas) *see* Inkberrow w Cookhill and Kington w Dormston *Worc*
DORNEY (St James the Less) *see* Eton w Eton Wick, Boveney and Dorney *Ox*
DORRIDGE (St Philip) *Birm 2* **P** *Bp* **V** T D HILL-BROWN **Hon C** R J HILL-BROWN
DORRINGTON (St Edward) w Leebotwood, Longnor, Stapleton, Smethcote and Woolstaston *Heref 10* **P** *DBP and J J C Coldwell Esq (jt)* **R** L M HNATIUK
DORRINGTON (St James) *see* Digby w Dorrington *Linc*
DORSINGTON (St Peter) *see* Vale and Cotswold Edge *Glouc*
DORSTONE (St Faith) *see* Cusop w Blakemere, Bredwardine w Brobury etc *Heref*
DORTON (St John the Baptist) *see* Bernwode *Ox*
DOSTHILL (St Paul) *Birm 5* **P** *Bp* **V** J L C SHAW **C** M A WATERSTREET
DOTTERY (St Saviour) *see* Eggardon and Colmers *Sarum*
DOUGLAS (St George) (All Saints) *S & M* **P** *Bp* **NSM** A R BROWN
DOUGLAS (St Ninian) *S & M* **P** *CPAS* **V** J P COLDWELL **NSM** J E GUILFORD
DOUGLAS (St Thomas the Apostle) *S & M* **P** *Bp* **V** I BRADY **NSM** L BRADY
DOUGLAS-IN-PARBOLD (Christ Church) *see* Appley Bridge and Parbold *Blackb*
DOULTING (St Aldhelm) *see* Shepton Mallet w Doulting *B & W*
DOVE HOLES (St Paul) *see* Fairfield, Peak Forest and Dove Holes *Derby*
DOVECOT (Holy Spirit) *Liv 5* **P** *Bp* **V** P F SMYTH
DOVER (St Martin) *see* Dover Town *Cant*
DOVER TOWN (St Mary the Virgin) *Cant 7* **P** *Patr Bd* **P-in-c** C J TUCKER **TV** M J CARTER **C** J P DE SOUZA **NSM** A M STUPPLE
DOVERCOURT (All Saints) *see* Harwich Peninsula *Chelmsf*
DOVERDALE (St Mary) *see* Elmley Lovett w Hampton Lovett and Elmbridge w Rushock and Hartlebury and Ombersley w Doverdale *Worc*
DOVERIDGE (St Cuthbert) *see* S Dales *Derby*
DOWDESWELL (St Michael) *see* Sevenhampton w Charlton Abbots, Hawling etc *Glouc*
DOWLAND (St Peter) *see* Dolton, Dowland, Iddesleigh etc *Ex*
DOWLES Button Oak (St Andrew) *see* Ribbesford w Bewdley and Dowles and Wribbenhall *Worc*
DOWLISHWAKE (St Andrew) *see* Winsmoor *B & W*
DOWN AMPNEY (All Saints) *see* S Cotswolds *Glouc*
DOWN HATHERLEY (St Mary and Corpus Christi) *see* Twigworth, Down Hatherley, Norton, The Leigh etc *Glouc*
DOWN ST MARY (St Mary the Virgin) *see* N Creedy *Ex*
DOWN STREET (Christ Church) *Mayfair* *Lon 3* **P** *Bp* **V** M J FULLER **C** N G ASHTON, S R FUREY, J O ROACH **NSM** P ALLCOCK
DOWN, East (St John the Baptist) *see* Shirwell, Loxhore, Kentisbury, Arlington, etc *Ex*
DOWNDERRY (St Nicholas) *see* St Germans w Antony and Sheviock *Truro*
DOWNE (St Mary Magdalene) *see* Cudham and Downe *Roch*
DOWNEND (Christ Church) (Church Centre) *Bris 5* **P** *Peache Trustees* **C** A P L WATSON, P J PETERSON **Hon C** C J DOBSON
DOWNHAM (St Barnabas) *see* Catford (Southend) and Downham *S'wark*
DOWNHAM (St Leonard) *see* Clitheroe St Mary and St Paul, Chatburn and Downham *Blackb*
DOWNHAM (St Leonard) *see* Ely *Ely*
DOWNHAM (St Luke) *see* Catford (Southend) and Downham *S'wark*
DOWNHAM (St Margaret) w S Hanningfield and Ramsden Bellhouse *Chelmsf 9* **P** *Bp and Reformation Ch Trust (jt)* **Hon C** B R HOBSON **NSM** J ANDREWS
DOWNHAM MARKET (St Edmund) and Stradsett *Ely 9* **P** *Bp* **R** J W MATHER **Hon C** D J ADDINGTON
DOWNHAM, NORTH (St Mark) *see* Catford (Southend) and Downham *S'wark*

DOWNHEAD (All Saints)   *see* Leigh upon Mendip w Stoke St Michael *B & W*

DOWNHOLME (St Michael and All Angels)   *see* Richmond w Hudswell and Downholme and Marske *Leeds*

DOWNLEY (St James the Great)   *see* High Wycombe *Ox*

DOWNS BARN and NEAT HILL (Community Church)   *see* Stantonbury and Willen *Ox*

DOWNS Benefice, The, comprising Chilbolton, Crawley, Littleton, Sparsholt w Lainston, and Wherwell *Win 3*   **P** *Ld Chan (1 turn), Bp and Marquess Camden (1 turn)* **R** J J MACHIN

DOWNSIDE (St Michael's Chapel)   *see* Ockham w Hatchford and Downside *Guildf*

DOWNSWAY (All Souls Worship Centre)   *see* Southwick *Chich*

DOWNTON (St Giles)   *see* Wigmore Abbey *Heref*

DOWNTON (St Laurence)   *see* Forest and Avon *Sarum*

DOWSBY (St Andrew)   *see* Billingborough Gp *Linc*

DOXEY (St Thomas and St Andrew)   *see* Stafford St Paul and St Thos *Lich*

DOYNTON (Holy Trinity)   *see* Wick w Doynton and Dyrham *Bris*

DRAKES BROUGHTON (St Barnabas)   *see* Stoulton w Drake's Broughton and Pirton etc *Worc*

DRAUGHTON (St Augustine)   *see* Skipton H Trin *Leeds*

DRAUGHTON (St Catherine)   *see* Maidwell w Draughton, Lamport w Faxton *Pet*

DRAX (St Peter and St Paul)   *see* Carlton and Drax *York*

DRAYCOT, comprising Christian Malford, Kington Langley and Draycot Cerne, Seagry, Sutton Benger, and Tytherton Kellaways *Bris 6*   **P** *Bp, M Neeld Esq, D&C Sarum, and MMCET (jt)* **C** M SIDDALL

DRAYCOTE Group, The, comprising Birdingbury, Bourton, Frankton, and Stretton-on-Dunsmore *Cov 6*   **P** *Bp (2 turns), Simeon's Trustees (1 turn), and Mrs J H Shaw-Fox (1 turn)* **R** *vacant*

DRAYCOTT (St Mary)   *see* Wilne and Draycott w Breaston *Derby*

DRAYCOTT (St Peter)   *see* Cheddar, Draycott and Rodney Stoke *B & W*

DRAYCOTT IN THE CLAY (St Augustine)   *see* Hanbury, Newborough and Rangemoor *Lich*

DRAYCOTT-LE-MOORS (St Margaret) w Forsbrook *Lich 6*   **P** *Bp*   **R** J P H ROBERTS   **C** S T CROSSLEY

DRAYTON (St Catherine)   *see* Levels Arc *B & W*

DRAYTON (St Margaret) *Nor 2*   **P** *Bp*   **P-in-c** M R PALMER

DRAYTON (St Peter)   *see* DAMASCUS *Ox*

DRAYTON (St Peter) Banbury   *see* Ironstone *Ox*

DRAYTON BASSETT (St Peter)   *see* Peel Parishes *Lich*

DRAYTON IN HALES (St Mary) *Lich 17*   **P** C C *Corbet Esq* **V** C S MCBRIDE   **NSM** N I MACFARLANE

DRAYTON PARSLOW (Holy Trinity)   *see* Newton Longville, Mursley, Swanbourne etc *Ox*

DRAYTON ST LEONARD (St Leonard and St Catherine)   *see* Dorchester *Ox*

DRAYTON, EAST (St Peter)   *see* The Rivers *S'well*

DRAYTON, LITTLE (Christ Church) *Lich 17*   **P** *V Drayton in Hales*   **P-in-c** J A MORRIS   **NSM** L J WRAY-WEAR

DRAYTON, WEST (St Martin) *Lon 21*   **P** *Bp*   **V** R J BARRIE

DRAYTON, WEST (St Paul)   *see* The Idle and Sands *S'well*

DRAYTON-BEAUCHAMP (St Mary the Virgin)   *see* Aston Clinton w Buckland and Drayton Beauchamp *Ox*

DRESDEN (Resurrection)   *see* Blurton and Dresden *Lich*

DREWSTEIGNTON (Holy Trinity)   *see* Chagford, Gidleigh, Throwleigh etc *Ex*

DRIFFIELD (St Mary)   *see* S Cotswolds *Glouc*

DRIFFIELD, GREAT (All Saints) and LITTLE (St Peter) *York 10*   **P** *Abp*   **V** S P GRANT

DRIGG (St Peter)   *see* Black Combe, Drigg, Eskdale etc *Carl*

DRIGHLINGTON (St Paul) and Gildersome *Leeds 11*   **P** *Bp and V Batley (jt)*   **C** P N A SENIOR   **NSM** B DUXBURY

DRIMPTON (St Mary)   *see* Beaminster Area *Sarum*

DRINGHOUSES (St Edward the Confessor) *York 7*   **P** *Abp* **V** R C CAREW   **NSM** A J MORRISON

DRINKSTONE (All Saints)   *see* Woolpit w Drinkstone *St E*

DROITWICH (St Andrew w St Mary de Witton) (St Nicholas) (St Peter), and Salwarpe and Hindlip w Martin Hussingtree *Worc 4*   **P** *Patr Bd*   **TR** N G BYARD **TV** L J HANDY

DRONFIELD (St John the Baptist) w Holmesfield *Derby 3*   **P** *Ld Chan*   **TR** P E BOLD   **TV** I WEBB, P D MELLARS   **C** J T BIRD   **NSM** D J WALKER, I A PRICE

DROPMORE (St Anne)   *see* Taplow and Dropmore *Ox*

DROXFORD (St Mary and All Saints)   *see* Meon Bridge *Portsm*

DROYLSDEN (St Andrew) (St Martin) *Man 5*   **P** *Bp* **R** J H FARNWORTH   **C** E C ROWLES

DROYLSDEN (St Mary) (St John) *Man 5*   **P** *Bp* **OLM** N ALEXANDER, S BALL

DRY DODDINGTON (St James)   *see* Claypole *Linc*

DRY DRAYTON (St Peter and St Paul)   *see* Lordsbridge *Ely*

DRY SANDFORD (St Helen) *Ox 19*   **P** *Ox Churches Trust* **V** *vacant*

DRYBROOK (Holy Trinity), Lydbrook and Ruardean *Glouc 1* **P** *The Crown and Bp (alt)*   **R** D C EDWARDS

DRYPOOL (St Columba) (St John) *York 14*   **P** *Patr Bd* **TR** D L GRIFFITH-JONES   **TV** M J WESTBY

DUCKLINGTON (St Bartholomew) *Ox 28*   **P** *DBP*   **R** *vacant*

DUCKMANTON (St Peter and St Paul)   *see* Calow and Sutton cum Duckmanton *Derby*

DUDDENHOE END (The Hamlet Church)   *see* Icknield Way Villages *Chelmsf*

DUDDESTON (St Matthew)   *see* Aston and Nechells *Birm*

DUDDINGTON (St Mary)   *see* Barrowden and Wakerley w S Luffenham etc *Pet*

DUDDON (St Peter)   *see* Tarvin *Ches*

DUDLESTON (St Mary)   *see* Criftins w Dudleston and Welsh Frankton *Lich*

DUDLEY (St Andrew)   *see* Darby End and Netherton *Worc*

DUDLEY (St Augustine) (St Barnabas) (St Francis) (St James) (St Thomas and St Luke) *Worc 5*   **P** *Patr Bd* **TR** H A BURTON   **TV** R L AKERS   **C** C J BURKE, F O A ENWEREM, J TREASURE, S R BARDELL   **NSM** S M HALE

DUDLEY (St John) Kate's Hill *Worc 5*   **P** *Bp*   **V** *vacant*

DUDLEY (St Paul)   *see* Weetslade *Newc*

DUDLEY (Top Church)   *see* Dudley *Worc*

DUDLEY WOOD (St John) and Cradley Heath *Worc 5*   **P** *The Crown and V Darby End and Netherton (alt)*   **V** *vacant*

DUFFIELD (St Alkmund) and Little Eaton *Derby 6*   **P** *Patr Bd* **V** J T HUGHES

DUFTON (St Cuthbert)   *see* Heart of Eden *Carl*

DUKINFIELD (St John) (St Alban Mission Church) *Ches 14* **P** *R Stockport St Mary*   **V** T J HAYES   **C** C W VINEY

DUKINFIELD (St Luke) *Ches 14*   **P** *Bp*   **V** *vacant*

DUKINFIELD (St Mark) *Ches 14*   **P** *Bp*   **V** K A WILLIAMS **NSM** J M DUNLOP

DULLINGHAM (St Mary)   *see* Raddesley Gp *Ely*

DULOE (St Cuby) and Herodsfoot *Truro 12*   **P** *Ch Soc Trust and Ball Coll Ox (jt)*   **R** *vacant*

DULVERTON (All Saints) w Brushford, Brompton Regis, Upton and Skilgate *B & W 15*   **P** *Bp, D&C, Em Coll Cam, and Keble Coll Ox (jt)*   **R** D P CONNING **NSM** R M V COLLETT

DULWICH (Grace Church) Bishop's Mission Order *S'wark 12*   **Min** S M C DOWDY

DULWICH (St Barnabas) *S'wark 9*   **P** *Bp*   **V** J C WATSON **C** E A BARNETT, R E GLEDHILL   **NSM** E A LANDER, T BUCKLER

DULWICH (St Clement) St Peter *S'wark 9*   **P** *Bp* **V** C SCHNYDER

DULWICH, EAST (St John the Evangelist) *S'wark 9*   **P** *Ripon Coll Cuddesdon*   **V** G O'NEILL   **NSM** G K P L BIRT **OLM** A CLARKE

DULWICH, NORTH (St Faith) *S'wark 9*   **P** *Bp*   **V** S J HEIGHT

DULWICH, SOUTH (St Stephen) *S'wark 9*   **P** *Dulwich Coll* **V** B G SCHÜNEMANN   **C** T L REED

DULWICH, WEST (All Saints) *S'wark 12*   **P** *Bp* **V** A N EVERETT   **Hon C** C WILES

DULWICH, WEST (Emmanuel) *S'wark 12*   **P** *Bp* **V** K G A ANSAH   **P-in-c** J E CROUCHER

DUMBLETON (St Peter)   *see* Winchcombe *Glouc*

DUMMER (All Saints)   *see* Farleigh, Candover and Wield *Win*

DUNCHIDEOCK (St Michael and All Angels)   *see* Christow, Ashton, Bridford, Dunchideock etc *Ex*

DUNCHURCH (St Peter) *Cov 6*   **P** *Bp*   **V** P O TOWNSHEND

DUNCTON (Holy Trinity) *Chich 4*   **P** *Lord Egremont* **P-in-c** D R CROOK

DUNDRY (St Michael)   *see* Chew Magna w Dundry, Norton Malreward etc *B & W*

DUNHAM MASSEY (St Margaret) (St Mark) (All Saints) *Ches 10*   **P** J G *Turnbull Esq*   **P-in-c** A N SEAGO

DUNHAM, GREAT (St Andrew)   *see* Launditch and the Upper Nar *Nor*

DUNHAM, LITTLE (St Margaret)   *as above*

DUNHAM-ON-THE-HILL (St Luke)   *see* Helsby and Dunham-on-the-Hill *Ches*

DUNHOLME (St Chad)   *see* Welton and Dunholme w Scothern *Linc*

DUNKERTON (All Saints)   *see* Timsbury w Priston, Camerton and Dunkerton *B & W*

DUNKESWELL AND DUNKESWELL ABBEY (St Nicholas)   *see* Broadhembury, Dunkeswell, Luppitt, Plymtree, Sheldon, and Upottery *Ex*

DUNMOW, GREAT (St Mary the Virgin) and Barnston
Chelmsf 17 **P** *Ld Chan (2 turns), CPAS (1 turn)*
P-in-c T Z WARMINGTON   **NSM** E J M BOUFFLER
DUNMOW, LITTLE (St Mary the Virgin) *see* Felsted and Lt
Dunmow *Chelmsf*
DUNNINGTON (not known) *see* Heart of England *Cov*
DUNNINGTON (St Nicholas) *see* Beeford w Frodingham and
Foston *York*
DUNNINGTON (St Nicholas) *see* Rural E York *York*
DUNS TEW (St Mary Magdalene) *see* Westcote Barton w
Steeple Barton, Duns Tew etc *Ox*
DUNSBY (All Saints) *see* Ringstone in Aveland Gp *Linc*
DUNSCROFT (St Edwin) *Sheff 10* **P** *Bp* **V** *vacant*
DUNSDEN (All Saints) *see* Shiplake w Dunsden and
Harpsden *Ox*
DUNSFOLD (St Mary and All Saints) and Hascombe
Guildf 2 **P** *Bp and SMF (jt)* **P-in-c** I MASLIN
DUNSFORD (St Mary) *see* Christow, Ashton, Bridford,
Dunchideock etc *Ex*
DUNSFORTH (St Mary) *see* Aldborough w Boroughbridge
and Roecliffe *Leeds*
DUNSMORE (Chapel of the Resurrection) *see* Ellesborough,
The Kimbles and Stoke Mandeville *Ox*
DUNSOP BRIDGE (St George) *see* Slaidburn w Tosside *Leeds*
DUNSTABLE (St Augustine of Canterbury) (St Fremund
the Martyr) *St Alb 11* **P** *Bp* **TR** R S PHILLIPS
TV R R TURNER, T A DAVIS   **C** J D DEARDEN
DUNSTALL (St Mary) *see* Barton under Needwood w
Dunstall and Tatenhill *Lich*
DUNSTER (St George), Carhampton, Withycombe w
Rodhuish, Timberscombe and Wootton Courtenay
B & W 15 **P** *Bp* **R** C S RALPH   **Hon C** G A WILKINSON
DUNSTON (Church House) *see* Newbold w Dunston *Derby*
DUNSTON (St Leonard) *see* Penkridge *Lich*
DUNSTON (St Nicholas) w (Christ Church) *Dur 12* **P** *Bp*
V D ATKINSON
DUNSTON (St Peter) *see* Metheringham w Blankney and
Dunston *Linc*
DUNSTON (St Remigius) *see* Stoke H Cross w Dunston,
Arminghall etc *Nor*
DUNSWELL (St Faith's Mission Church) *see* Hull St Jo
Newland *York*
DUNTERTON (All Saints) *see* Milton Abbot, Dunterton,
Lamerton etc *Ex*
DUNTISBOURNE ABBOTS (St Peter) *see* Brimpsfield w
Birdlip, Syde, Daglingworth etc *Glouc*
DUNTISBOURNE ROUS (St Michael and All Angels) *as above*
DUNTON (St Martin) *see* Schorne *Ox*
DUNTON (St Mary Magdalene) w Wrestlingworth and
Eyeworth *St Alb 10* **P** *Ld Chan and DBP (alt)*
P-in-c M P PHILLIPS
DUNTON BASSETT (All Saints) *see* Upper Soar *Leic*
DUNWICH (St James) *see* Yoxmere *St E*
DURHAM (St Giles), Shadforth and Sherburn *Dur 1*
P *D&C* **NSM** A P HUGHES, R A M THOMAS
DURHAM (St Margaret of Antioch), Neville's Cross St John
and Bearpark St Edmund *Dur 1* **P** *D&C* **R** B T HUISH
NSM N C CHATER
DURHAM (St Nicholas) *Dur 1* **P** *CPAS* **V** A ARORA
C C S ELWOOD   **NSM** M C M SHERLOCK, R S BRIGGS
DURHAM (St Oswald King and Martyr) and Shincliffe
Dur 1 **P** *D&C* **P-in-c** P Z KASHOURIS
DURHAM NORTH (St Cuthbert), including Esh and
Hamsteels, Kimblesworth, Langley Park, Newton Hall, and
Witton Gilbert and Sacriston *Dur 1* **P** *The Crown (1 turn),*
Patr Bd (2 turns) **TR** C A DICK **TV** M J PEERS
C M B WACHEPA
DURLEIGH (St Hugh) *see* Bridgwater H Trin and Durleigh
B & W
DURLEY (Holy Cross) *Portsm 1* **P** *Ld Chan* **R** G R MENSINGH
NSM R J WHARTON
DURNFORD (St Andrew) *see* Woodford Valley w Archers
Gate *Sarum*
DURRINGTON (All Saints) *see* Avon River *Sarum*
DURRINGTON (St Symphorian) *Chich 7* **P** *Bp*
V R J NORBURY   **C** I H EDGAR
DURSLEY (St James the Great), Uley, Owlpen and
Nympsfield (The Ewelme Benefice) *Glouc 5* **P** *Ld Chan*
and Bp (alt) **R** M G COZENS **NSM** I N GARDNER, J L WOOD
DURSTON (St John the Baptist) *see* Alfred Jewel *B & W*
DURWESTON (St Nicholas) *see* Pimperne, Stourpaine,
Durweston and Bryanston *Sarum*
DUSTON (St Francis) (St Luke) and Upton *Pet 4* **P** *Bp*
TR A J MARRIOTT **TV** R J KELLOW **C** L J HOLLAND
DUXFORD (St Peter) w St John *Ely 5* **P** *Bp* **P-in-c** L J SMITH
DYMCHURCH (St Peter and St Paul) *see* Romney Marsh *Cant*

DYMOCK (St Mary the Virgin) *see* Redmarley D'Abitot,
Bromesberrow, Pauntley etc *Glouc*
DYRHAM (St Peter) *see* Wick w Doynton and Dyrham *Bris*
EAGLE (All Saints) *see* Swinderby *Linc*
EAKRING (St Andrew) *S'well 3* **P** *DBP* **P-in-c** Z BURTON
NSM M A GROVES
EALING (All Saints) *Lon 19* **P** *Bp* **V** R E MARSZALEK
EALING (Ascension) *see* Hanger Hill Ascension and W
Twyford St Mary *Lon*
EALING (Christ the Saviour) *Lon 19* **P** *Bp* **V** R A COLLINS
EALING (St Barnabas) *Lon 19* **P** *Bp* **V** J D C DODD
C F M JACK
EALING (St Mary) *Lon 19* **P** *Bp* **V** S D PAYNTER
NSM A VOLOSSEVICH, W M CHOW
EALING (St Paul) *Lon 19* **P** *Bp* **V** M P MELLUISH
C B M STRAIN, C FOX, S P PLUMB, T S RADCLIFFE
NSM C S BURRELL
EALING (St Peter) Mount Park *Lon 19* **P** *Bp* **V** D E NENO
C A A DOBRZYNSKI **NSM** J O A CHOUFAR
EALING (St Stephen) Castle Hill *Lon 19* **P** *D&C St Paul's*
V S M NEWBOLD **NSM** C S NEWBOLD
EALING COMMON (St Matthew) *Lon 19* **P** *Bp*
V M C C BARTER
EALING, WEST (St John) w St James *Lon 19* **P** *Bp*
P-in-c M P MELLUISH **C** S SANYA **Hon C** J E MORRIS
EARBY (All Saints) w Kelbrook *Leeds 21* **P** *Bp* **V** H FIELDEN
EARDISLAND (St Mary the Virgin) *see* Kingsland w
Eardisland, Aymestrey etc *Heref*
EARDISLEY (St Mary Magdalene) w Bollingham,
Willersley, Brilley, Michaelchurch, Whitney, Winforton,
Almeley and Kinnersley *Heref 4* **P** *Patr Bd* **R** M J SMALL
NSM G A WILKINSON
EARL SHILTON (St Simon and St Jude) w Elmesthorpe
Leic 10 **P** *Bp* **P-in-c** M R CASTLE **NSM** P D CUMMINS
EARL SOHAM (St Mary) *see* Mid Loes *St E*
EARL STERNDALE (St Michael and All Angels) *see*
Taddington, Chelmorton and Monyash etc *Derby*
EARL STONHAM (St Mary) *see* N Bosmere *St E*
EARLESTOWN (St John the Baptist) *see* Newton *Liv*
EARLEY (St Bartholomew) *see* Reading St Luke w St Bart *Ox*
EARLEY (St Nicolas) *Ox 7* **P** *DBP* **V** A C BECKERLEG
EARLEY (St Peter) *Ox 7* **P** *DBP* **V** P P HOBDAY
C H E HOBDAY
EARLEY (Trinity Church) *Ox 7* **P** *DBP* **V** J SALMON
EARLHAM (St Anne) (St Elizabeth) (St Mary) *Nor 3* **P** *Bp*
and Trustees (jt) **R** D M ROWLANDSON
NSM C S PRITCHARD, T J WATTS
EARLS BARTON (All Saints) *Pet 6* **P** *DBP* **V** J R INGRAM
EARLS COLNE (St Andrew) *see* Halstead Area *Chelmsf*
EARL'S COURT (St Cuthbert) (St Matthias) *Lon 8*
P *Trustees* **P-in-c** P A BAGOTT **C** J P CHEGWIDDEN
EARLS COURT (St Luke) *see* S Kensington St Luke *Lon*
EARL'S COURT ROAD (St Philip) *Lon 12* **P** *Bp*
V P A TURNER **NSM** L A PERRY, M F A AYO
EARLS CROOME (St Nicholas) *see* Upton-on-Severn, Ripple,
Earls Croome etc *Worc*
EARL'S HEATON *see* Dewsbury *Leeds*
EARLSDON (St Barbara) *Cov 3* **P** *Bp* **V** T D RAISTRICK
EARLSFIELD (St Andrew) *S'wark 18* **P** *Bp* **V** J BROWN
NSM J P B SERTIN
EARLSFIELD (St John the Divine) *S'wark 18* **P** *Bp*
P-in-c H J WHITTAKER, J KIDDLE
EARNLEY (not known) and East Wittering *Chich 2* **P** *Bp (2*
turns), Bp Lon (1 turn) **R** S J DAVIES
EARNSHAW BRIDGE (St John) *see* Leyland St Jo *Blackb*
EARSDON (St Alban) and Backworth *Newc 5* **P** *Bp*
V T J E MAYFIELD
EARSHAM (All Saints) *see* Ditchingham, Hedenham, Broome,
Earsham etc *Nor*
EARSWICK, NEW (St Andrew) *see* Huntington *York*
EARTHAM (St Margaret) *see* Slindon, Eartham and
Madehurst *Chich*
EASBY (St Agatha) w Skeeby and Brompton on Swale and
Bolton on Swale *Leeds 19* **P** *Bp* **V** Y S CALLAGHAN
EASEBOURNE (St Mary) *see* Easebourne, Lodsworth and
Selham *Chich*
EASEBOURNE (St Mary), Lodsworth and Selham *Chich 3*
P *Bp* **V** D B WELSMAN **NSM** A M HALLIWELL
EASINGTON (All Saints) w Liverton *York 16* **P** *Ld Chan*
P-in-c A D WALKER
EASINGTON (All Saints) w Skeffling, Keyingham,
Ottringham, Patrington, Welwick and Winestead *York 12*
P *Abp and CPAS (1 turn), Ld Chan (1 turn)* **V** A M LAIRD
Hon C J A SHARP, P W WEST
EASINGTON (St Hugh) *see* Banbury St Hugh *Ox*

EASINGTON (St Mary) and Easington Colliery *Dur 10*   **P** *Bp*
R L M MOSS

EASINGTON (St Peter)   *see* Benson w Ewelme *Ox*

EASINGTON COLLIERY (The Ascension)   *see* Easington and Easington Colliery *Dur*

EASINGWOLD (St John the Baptist and All Saints) w Raskelf *York 3*   **P** *Abp*   **V** M E YOUNG   **C** D M COYNE, M HARRISON, S WHITING   **NSM** C C CRANFIELD, C C GITTENS, C J TOASE, T M GANT

EAST   *see also under substantive place name*

EAST DEAN (All Saints), Singleton, and West Dean *Chich 6*   **P** *Bp (2 turns), D&C (1 turn)*   **R** S J MANOUCH

EAST DEAN (St Simon and St Jude) w Friston and Jevington *Chich 14*   **P** *Duke of Devonshire (1 turn), D&C (2 turns)*   **R** D A BAKER   **Hon C** A J M SPEAR

EAST DEAN (St Winifred)   *see* Thorngate *Win*

EAST DOWNLAND, comprising Beedon, Boxford, Chieveley w Winterbourne and Oare, Farnborough, Peasemore, Stockcross, and West Ilsley *Ox 6*   **P** *Bp and Adn (jt)*   **R** J P TOOGOOD   **NSM** D J DALES, W MCDOWELL

EAST HAM (St George and St Ethelbert) *Chelmsf 5*   **P** *Bp*   **V** D T HAOKIP

EAST HAM (St Paul) *Chelmsf 5*   **P** *Ch Patr Trust*   **V** M L PLAYLE   **C** O E CHIKE

EAST HAM Holy Trinity (St Mary Magdalene) (St Bartholomew) (St Alban) (St Edmund King and Martyr) *Chelmsf 5*   **P** *Patr Bd*   **TR** S J LUCAS   **TV** Q B D PEPPIATT   **C** M G FILIPE LOPES   **NSM** A R EASTER   **OLM** J R KING

EAST LANE (St Mary)   *see* W Horsley *Guildf*

EAST MARSHLAND, comprising Terrington St John, Tilney All Saints, Tilney St Lawrence, Wiggenhall St Germans w St Mary the Virgin, and Wiggenhall St Mary Magdalene *Ely 14*   **P** *Bp and MMCET (1 turn), Pemb Coll Cam (2 turns, The Crown (1 turn), and Ld Chan (1 turn)*   **V** M N DALE

EAST TRENT Group of Parishes, The, comprising Collingham, Harby w Swinethorpe, Holme, Langford, North and South Clifton, South Scarle w Besthorpe, Girton and Spalford, Thorney w Wigsley, and Winthorpe *S'well 3*   **P** *Bp, Ld Chan, D&C Pet, and Keble Coll Ox (by turn)*   **V** A J CARTWRIGHT

EAST VALE AND AVON VILLAGES, comprising Badsey w Aldington, Bretforton, Cleeve Prior, North and Middle Littleton, Offenham, and South Littleton *Worc 3*   **P** *Patr Bd*   **V** P J MORTON

EAST WINCH (All Saints)   *see* Middlewinch *Nor*

EASTBOURNE (All Saints) *Chich 14*   **P** *Trustees*   **V** J R KNOWLES   **C** J P HAINES

EASTBOURNE (All Souls) *Chich 14*   **P** *Ch Soc Trust*   **V** M D REDHOUSE

EASTBOURNE (Christ Church) (St Philip) *Chich 14*   **P** *Bp and V Eastbourne (jt)*   **V** D G CHARLES

EASTBOURNE (Holy Trinity) *Chich 14*   **P** *Ch Soc Trust*   **V** P J COEKIN

EASTBOURNE (St Andrew) *Chich 14*   **P** *Bp*   **V** D J KING

EASTBOURNE (St Elisabeth) *Chich 14*   **P** *Bp*   **V** *vacant*

EASTBOURNE (St John) Meads *Chich 14*   **P** *Trustees*   **V** G M G CARPENTER   **C** B L SLEEP   **NSM** J A PREECE

EASTBOURNE (St Mary) *Chich 14*   **P** *Bp*   **V** T O MENDEL

EASTBOURNE (St Michael and All Angels) Ocklynge *Chich 14*   **P** *V Eastbourne*   **P-in-c** G M G CARPENTER   **C** B L SLEEP

EASTBOURNE (St Saviour and St Peter) *Chich 14*   **P** *Keble Coll Ox*   **V** M J S MCAULAY   **C** T P V CROWLEY

EASTBURY (St James the Great)   *see* Lambourn Valley *Ox*

EASTCHURCH (All Saints) w Leysdown and Harty *Cant 15*   **P** *Abp and Keble Coll Ox (jt)*   **R** *vacant*

EASTCOMBE (St Augustine)   *see* Bisley, Chalford, France Lynch, and Oakridge etc *Glouc*

EASTCOTE (St Lawrence) *Lon 21*   **P** *Bp*   **C** J SEYMOUR   **NSM** J M BEVIS-KNOWLES

EASTER, HIGH (St Mary the Virgin) and Good Easter w Margaret Roding *Chelmsf 17*   **P** *Bp Lon, CPAS, and D&C St Paul's (by turn)*   **P-in-c** R D STONE   **C** G A FLEMING   **NSM** T E GOODBODY

EASTERGATE (St George)   *see* Aldingbourne, Barnham and Eastergate *Chich*

EASTERN GREEN (St Andrew) *Cov 3*   **P** *R Allesley*   **V** *vacant*

EASTERTON (St Barnabas)   *see* The Lavingtons, Cheverells, and Easterton *Sarum*

EASTFIELD (Holy Nativity) *York 15*   **P** *Abp*   **V** S TAYLOR   **C** J C PARKER

EASTGATE (All Saints)   *see* Upper Weardale *Dur*

EASTHAM (St Mary the Blessed Virgin) (St Peter's Chapel) (Chapel of the Holy Spirit) *Ches 9*   **P** *D&C*   **V** E A GLOVER   **NSM** M R J TURNER

EASTHAM (St Peter and St Paul)   *see* Teme Valley S *Worc*

EASTHAMPSTEAD (St Michael and St Mary Magdalene) (St Francis and St Clare) (Church at the Pines) *Ox 3*   **P** *Ch Ch Ox*   **R** G S COLE   **C** C A DUNK

EASTHOPE (St Peter)   *see* Wenlock *Heref*

EASTHORPE (St Mary the Virgin)   *see* Thurstable and Winstree *Chelmsf*

EASTINGTON (St Michael and All Angels)   *see* Stroudwater *Glouc*

EASTLANDS   *see* Manchester Gd Shep and St Barn *Man*

EASTLEACH (St Andrew)   *see* S Cotswolds *Glouc*

EASTLEIGH (All Saints) *Win 10*   **P** *Bp*   **V** I P FLETCHER

EASTLEIGH Nightingale Avenue (St Francis)   *see* Eastleigh *Win*

EASTLING (St Mary)   *see* Kingsdown, Creekside and High Downs *Cant*

EASTMOORS (St Mary Magdalene)   *see* Helmsley *York*

EASTNEY (St Margaret)   *see* Southsea *Portsm*

EASTNOR (St John the Baptist)   *see* Ledbury w Eastnor *Heref*

EASTOFT (St Bartholomew)   *see* The Marshland *Sheff*

EASTOKE (St Andrew)   *see* Hayling Is St Andr *Portsm*

EASTON (All Hallows) *Bris 3*   **P** *Guild of All So*   **V** J C MUTEMWAKWENDA

EASTON (All Saints)   *see* Orebeck *St E*

EASTON (Holy Trinity w St Gabriel and St Lawrence and St Jude) *Bris 3*   **P** *Trustees*   **P-in-c** D J P MOORE   **C** S M MATTHEWS

EASTON (St Mary)   *see* Itchen Valley *Win*

EASTON (St Paul)   *see* Westbury sub Mendip w Easton *B & W*

EASTON (St Peter)   *see* S Leightonstone *Ely*

EASTON (St Peter), Colton, Marlingford and Bawburgh *Nor 16*   **P** *Bp, D&C, Adn, and Sir Edward Evans-Lombe (jt)*   **V** L A MONTGOMERY   **NSM** P J GOODMAN

EASTON GREY (not known)   *see* Gauzebrook *Bris*

EASTON IN GORDANO (St George)   *see* Pill, Portbury and Easton-in-Gordano *B & W*

EASTON MAUDIT (St Peter and St Paul)   *see* Wollaston w Strixton and Bozeat etc *Pet*

EASTON NESTON (St Mary)   *see* Towcester w Caldecote and Easton Neston etc *Pet*

EASTON ON THE HILL (All Saints)   *see* King's Cliffe, Bulwick and Blatherwycke, Collyweston etc *Pet*

EASTON ROYAL (Holy Trinity)   *see* Vale of Pewsey *Sarum*

EASTON, GREAT (St Andrew)   *see* Six Saints circa Holt *Leic*

EASTON, GREAT (St John and St Giles)   *see* Broxted w Chickney and Tilty etc *Chelmsf*

EASTON, LITTLE (St Mary the Virgin) *as above*

EASTRINGTON (St Michael)   *see* Howden *York*

EASTROP (St Mary) *Win 4*   **P** CPAS   **R** R G PHILLIPS   **NSM** C E WEST

EASTRY (St Mary Blessed Virgin) and Woodnesborough *Cant 9*   **P** *Abp and Lord Northbourne (jt)*   **NSM** R STEVENSON

EASTTHORPE (St Paul)   *see* Mirfield *Leeds*

EASTVILLE (St Anne w St Mark and St Thomas) *Bris 3*   **P** *Bp*   **P-in-c** M OTTO   **Hon C** J S F HADLEY

EASTWELL (St Michael)   *see* Ironstone Villages *Leic*

EASTWICK (St Botolph)   *see* High Wych and Gilston w Eastwick *St Alb*

EASTWOOD (St David) *Chelmsf 12*   **P** *Bp*   **V** *vacant*

EASTWOOD (St Laurence and All Saints) *Chelmsf 12*   **P** *Ld Chan*   **P-in-c** K N AKWASI-YEBOAH

EASTWOOD (St Mary) *S'well 4*   **P** J N Plumptre Esq   **P-in-c** D A STEVENSON

EATON (All Saints)   *see* The Idle and Sands *S'well*

EATON (Christ Church) *Nor 3*   **P** *D&C*   **V** P H RICHMOND

EATON (Christ Church)   *see* Marton, Siddington w Capesthorne etc *Ches*

EATON (St Andrew) *Nor 3*   **P** *D&C*   **V** P R RODD   **C** J D COOK

EATON (St Denys)   *see* Ironstone Villages *Leic*

EATON (St Thomas)   *see* Tarporley *Ches*

EATON BISHOP (St Michael and All Angels)   *see* Cagebrook *Heref*

EATON BRAY (St Mary the Virgin) w Edlesborough *St Alb 11*   **P** *DBP*   **V** J E COUSANS   **NSM** S R BURGE

EATON HASTINGS (St Michael and All Angels)   *see* Gt Coxwell w Buscot, Coleshill etc *Ox*

EATON SOCON (St Mary) *St Alb 10*   **P** E W Harper Esq   **V** T S ROBB

EATON, LITTLE (St Paul)   *see* Duffield and Lt Eaton *Derby*

EATON-UNDER-HEYWOOD (St Edith)   *see* Apedale Gp *Heref*

EBBERSTON (St Mary)   *see* Thornton Dale w Allerston, Ebberston etc *York*

EBBESBOURNE WAKE (St John the Baptist)   *see* Chalke Valley *Sarum*

EBCHESTER (St Ebba) *Dur 2*   **P** *Bp*   **P-in-c** J FISHER
   NSM I W WAUGH
EBERNOE (Holy Trinity)   *see* N Chapel w Ebernoe *Chich*
EBONY (St Mary the Virgin)   *see* Tenterden, Rother and
   Oxney *Cant*
EBRINGTON (St Eadburgha)   *see* Vale and Cotswold Edge
   Glouc
ECCHINSWELL (St Lawrence)   *see* Burghclere w Newtown
   and Ecchinswell w Sydmonton *Win*
ECCLES (St Mary the Virgin)   *see* Quidenham Gp *Nor*
ECCLES (St Mary the Virgin) (St Andrew) *Man 7*   **P** *Patr Bd*
   and Ld Chan (alt)   **TR** A R GARNER   **TV** A HARPER
   OLM J J LEWIS
ECCLESALL (St Gabriel)   *see* Greystones *Sheff*
ECCLESALL BIERLOW (All Saints) *Sheff 2*   **P** *Dean*
   P-in-c M E BROWN   **C** D C CHRISTIAN
ECCLESFIELD (St Mary the Virgin) *Sheff 3*   **P** *DBF*
   V T C GILL
ECCLESHALL (Holy Trinity) *Lich 7*   **P** *Bp*   **V** *vacant*
ECCLESHILL (St Luke) *Leeds 3*   **P** V *Bradf*   **V** J P HARTLEY
ECCLESTON (Christ Church) (St Luke) (St James), including
   Ravenshead and Thatto Heath *Liv 10*   **P** *Patr Bd*
   TR H T COFFEY   **TV** G R BANTON, S J DORAGH   **C** G STEWART
   NSM A G FATH
ECCLESTON (St Mary the Virgin) and Charnock Richard
   Christ Church *Blackb 4*   **P** *DBP*   **R** A J BROWN
ECCLESTON (St Mary the Virgin) and Pulford *Ches 2*
   P *Duke of Westmr*   **R** *vacant*
ECCLESTON (St Thomas)   *see* St Helens Town Cen *Liv*
ECCLESTON PARK (St James)   *see* Eccleston *Liv*
ECCLESTON, GREAT   *see* Copp w Inskip *Blackb*
ECKINGTON (Holy Trinity) *Worc 3*   **P** *D&C Westmr*
   V A C DAVIES
ECKINGTON (St Peter and St Paul) and Ridgeway *Derby 3*
   P *The Crown and Patr Bd (alt)*   **R** A D WALKER
ECKINGTON, UPPER (St Luke)   *see* Eckington and Ridgeway
   Derby
ECTON (St Mary Magdalene)   *see* Gt Doddington and Wilby
   and Ecton *Pet*
EDALE (Holy and Undivided Trinity) *Derby 4*   **P** *Rep*
   Landowners   **P-in-c** S H COCKSEDGE
EDBURTON (St Andrew)   *see* Poynings w Edburton,
   Newtimber and Pyecombe *Chich*
EDEN PARK (St John the Baptist)   *see* Beckenham St Jo *Roch*
EDEN, Gelt and Irthing Team Ministry, The, comprising
   Brampton, Castle Carrock, Crosby-on-Eden, Cumrew,
   Cumwhitton, Farlam, Hayton, Irthington, Scaleby, and
   Talkin *Carl 2*   **P** *Patr Bd*   **TR** S A ROBERTSON
   TV E A JOHNSEN
EDEN, UPPER (St Peter and St Paul), comprising Brough w Stainmore, and Kirkby
   Stephen w Mallerstang and Crosby Garrett w Soulby *Carl 1*
   P *Bp, Lord Hothfield, and the Hon J N Lowther (jt)*   **R** *vacant*
EDENBRIDGE (St Peter and St Paul) *Roch 11*   **P** *Bp*
   V S A J MITCHELL
EDENFIELD (not known)   *see* Ramsbottom and Edenfield *Man*
EDENHALL (St Cuthbert)   *see* Cross Fell Gp *Carl*
EDENHAM (St Michael) w Witham on the Hill and
   Swinstead *Linc 17*   **P** *Baroness Willoughby de Eresby, Ld*
   Chan, and Bp (by turn)   **V** E J R MARTIN   **NSM** I K WILLIAMS
   OLM P W R LISTER
EDENSOR (St Paul)   *see* Longton Hall *Lich*
EDENSOR (St Peter)   *see* Beeley and Edensor *Derby*
EDGBASTON (St Augustine) *Birm 3*   **P** *Bp*
   V M R E TOMLINSON
EDGBASTON (St Bartholomew) *Birm 3*   **P** *Sir Euan*
   Anstruther-Gough-Calthorpe Bt   **V** N J C TUCKER
   C C H BUTLER
EDGBASTON (St George w St Michael) (St Michael's Hall)
   Birm 3   **P** *Sir Euan Anstruther-Gough-Calthorpe Bt*
   V S J GIBSON
EDGBASTON (St Germain) *Birm 3*   **P** *Trustees*   **V** S C HAYES
   C S L SIEBER   **NSM** O A OLADUNJOYE
EDGBASTON (St Mary and St Ambrose)   *see* Balsall Heath
   and Edgbaston SS Mary and Ambrose *Birm*
EDGCOTE (St James)   *see* Culworth w Sulgrave and Thorpe
   Mandeville etc *Pet*
EDGCOTT (St Michael)   *see* The Claydons and Swan *Ox*
EDGE HILL (St Dunstan)   *see* St Luke in the City *Liv*
EDGE HILL (St Mary)   *see* Liv All SS *Liv*
EDGE, THE (St John the Baptist)   *see* Painswick,
   Sheepscombe, Cranham, The Edge etc *Glouc*
EDGEFIELD (St Peter and St Paul)   *see* Matlaske *Nor*
EDGEHILL CHURCHES, comprising Combroke, Kineton,
   Radway, Ratley, Shotteswell, and Warmington *Cov 8*   **P** *Bp*
   and Lord Willoughby de Broke (jt)   **R** B J JACKSON
   C R J COOKE   **Hon C** B I D L T HARTLESS

EDGELEY (St Mark) (St Matthew) and Cheadle Heath
   Ches 18   **P** *Bp*   **V** D T BREWSTER
EDGESIDE (St Anne) *Man 4*   **P** *CPAS*   **V** R BEVAN
EDGEWORTH (St Mary)   *see* Brimpsfield w Birdlip, Syde,
   Daglingworth etc *Glouc*
EDGMOND (St Peter) w Kynnersley and Preston
   Wealdmoors *Lich 15*   **P** *Bp, Adn Salop, Chan Lich, MMCET,*
   and Preston Trust Homes Trustees (jt)   **R** H M MORBY
EDGTON (St Michael the Archangel)   *see* Bishop's Castle w
   Mainstone, Lydbury N etc *Heref*
EDGWARE (St Alphage)   *see* Hendon St Alphage *Lon*
EDGWARE (St Andrew) (St Margaret) (St Peter) *Lon 14*
   P *MMCET*   **TR** F ADU-BOACHIE   **C** S W J REA
   NSM K CHRISTODOULOU
EDINGALE (Holy Trinity)   *see* Mease Valley *Lich*
EDINGLEY (St Giles) w Halam *S'well 3*   **P** *Bp*   **V** *vacant*
EDINGTHORPE (All Saints)   *see* N Walsham, Edingthorpe,
   Worstead and Westwick *Nor*
EDINGTON (St George)   *see* Polden Wheel *B & W*
EDINGTON (St Mary, St Katharine and All Saints)   *see*
   Bratton, Edington and Imber, Erlestoke etc *Sarum*
EDITH WESTON (St Mary)   *see* Empingham, Edith Weston,
   Lyndon, Manton etc *Pet*
EDLASTON (St James)   *see* Brailsford w Shirley, Osmaston w
   Edlaston etc *Derby*
EDLINGHAM (St John the Baptist w Bolton Chapel)   *see*
   Whittingham and Edlingham w Bolton Chapel *Newc*
EDLINGTON (St Helen)   *see* Hemingby Gp *Linc*
EDLINGTON (St John the Baptist) and Hexthorpe *Sheff 9*
   P *Bp*   **V** *vacant*
EDMONDSHAM (St Nicholas)   *see* Cranborne w Boveridge,
   Edmondsham etc *Sarum*
EDMONTON (All Saints) (St Michael) *Lon 16*   **P** *D&C*
   St Paul's   **NSM** A C PHILLIPS
EDMONTON (St Aldhelm) *Lon 16*   **P** *V Edmonton All SS*
   V A STUTTARD   **NSM** P J BROWN
EDMONTON (St Alphege) *Lon 16*   **P** *Bp*   **P-in-c** S G BROWN
EDMONTON (St Mary w St John) (St Mary's Centre) *Lon 16*
   P *D&C St Paul's*   **V** N H ASBRIDGE
EDMONTON (St Peter w St Martin) *Lon 16*   **P** *Bp*
   V T J KELSEY
EDMUNDBYERS (St Edmund)   *see* Blanchland w
   Hunstanworth and Edmundbyers etc *Newc*
EDSTASTON (St Mary the Virgin)   *see* Prees, Edstaston and
   Whixall *Lich*
EDSTONE (St Michael)   *see* Kirkbymoorside w Gillamoor,
   Farndale etc *York*
EDVIN LOACH (St Mary) w Tedstone Delamere, Tedstone
   Wafer, Upper Sapey, Wolferlow and Whitbourne *Heref 2*
   P *Bp, BNC Ox, Sir Francis Winnington Bt, and D P Barneby Esq*
   (jt)   **NSM** D B HYETT
EDWALTON (Holy Rood) *S'well 6*   **P** *Exors Major R P*
   Chaworth-Musters   **P-in-c** M A FRASER   **C** A D PERHAM
EDWARDSTONE (St Mary the Virgin)   *see* Boxford,
   Edwardstone, Groton etc *St E*
EDWINSTOWE (St Mary) *S'well 2*   **P** *Earl Manvers' Trustees*
   V *vacant*
EDWYN RALPH (St Michael)   *see* Bredenbury *Heref*
EFFINGHAM (St Lawrence) w Little Bookham *Guildf 10*
   P *Keble Coll Ox*   **V** A S MACVEAN
EFFORD (St Paul)   *see* Plymouth Em w St Paul *Ex*
EGDEAN (St Bartholomew) *Chich 4*   **P** *Bp*   **R** P M GILBERT
EGERTON (St James)   *see* Calehill w Westwell *Cant*
EGGARDON and Colmers, comprising Askerswell, Loders,
   Powerstock, and Symondsbury *Sarum 2*   **P** *Bp, D&C, and*
   Lady Laskey (3 turns), Ld Chan (1 turn)   **R** C K GRASSKE
EGGBUCKLAND (St Edward) w Estover *Ex 20*   **P** *Ld Chan*
   and Bp (alt)   **V** C J ROUTLEDGE   **C** K A MURPHY
   NSM A E HOSKING
EGGESFORD (All Saints)   *see* Burrington, Chawleigh,
   Cheldon, Chulmleigh etc *Ex*
EGGINGTON (St Michael)   *see* Ouzel Valley *St Alb*
EGGINTON (St Wilfrid)   *see* Etwall w Egginton *Derby*
EGGLESCLIFFE (St John the Baptist) *Dur 8*   **P** *Bp*   **R** *vacant*
EGGLESTON (Holy Trinity) *Dur 4*   **P** *The Crown*
   P-in-c J BARKER   **NSM** A P WALLBANK
EGHAM (St John the Baptist) *Guildf 11*   **P** *Ch Soc Trust*
   V E T PRIOR   **C** J R ELLIN, S B L FRASER
   NSM M J CALLAGHAN, M T PRIOR, W C BISSETT
EGHAM HYTHE (St Paul) *Guildf 11*   **P** *Bp*   **V** R C HOAD
   OLM J FRANCK
EGLETON (St Edmund)   *see* Oakham, Ashwell, Braunston,
   Brooke, Egleton etc *Pet*
EGLINGHAM (St Maurice)   *see* Chatton w Chillingham,
   Eglingham and S Charlton and Ingram *Newc*
EGLOSHAYLE (St Petroc)   *see* St Breoke and Egloshayle *Truro*

EGLOSKERRY (St Petrock and St Keri), North Petherwin, Tremaine, Tresmere and Trewen *Truro 9* **P** *Duchy of Cornwall and Bp (alt)* **P-in-c** A J HARDY **C** N FARR

EGMANTON (Our Lady of Egmanton) *S'well 3* **P** SMF **P-in-c** Z BURTON **NSM** M A GROVES

EGREMONT (St Mary and St Michael) and Haile *Carl 5* **P** *Patr Bd* **TR** M J APPLEBY **NSM** D JACKSON, T R TAYLOR

EGTON (St Hilda) *see* Middle Esk Moor *York*

EGTON-CUM-NEWLAND (St Mary the Virgin) *see* Coniston and the Crake Valley *Carl*

EIGHT ASH GREEN (All Saints) *see* Fordham *Chelmsf*

EIGHTON BANKS (St Thomas) *Dur 11* **P** *Bp* **P-in-c** N CLEE

ELBERTON (St John) *see* N Severnside *Bris*

ELBURTON (St Matthew) *Ex 20* **P** CPAS **V** J C W CROUCHER **C** T J BRASSIL

ELDENE (not known) *see* Swindon Dorcan *Bris*

ELDERSFIELD (St John the Baptist) *see* Berrow w Pendock, Eldersfield, Hollybush etc *Worc*

ELDON (St Mark) *see* Coundon and Eldon *Dur*

ELDWICK (St Lawrence) *see* Bingley All SS *Leeds*

ELFORD (St Peter) *see* Mease Valley *Lich*

ELHAM (St Mary the Virgin) Valley Group, The, including Acrise, Denton, Lyminge, Paddlesworth, Postling, Radegund, Stanford, Swingfield and Wootton *Cant 8* **P** *Abp and Mert Coll Ox (jt)* **R** J A WEEKS **C** D L SCOBLE **OLM** S G DOUGAL

ELING (St Mary) *see* Calmore and Eling *Win*

ELING, NORTH (St Mary) *see* Copythorne and Netley Marsh *Win*

ELKESLEY (St Giles) *see* The Idle and Sands *S'well*

ELKINGTON, SOUTH (All Saints) *see* Louth *Linc*

ELKSTONE (St John the Baptist) *see* Longnor, Quarnford, Sheen etc *Lich*

ELKSTONE (St John the Evangelist) *see* Churn Valley *Glouc*

ELLAND (All Saints) (St Mary the Virgin) *Leeds 6* **P** *V Halifax* **R** D BURROWS **C** R A CHAPMAN **OLM** P E CHADWICK

ELLASTONE (St Peter) *see* Alton w Bradley-le-Moors, Ellastone w Stanton, and Mayfield *Lich*

ELLEL (St John the Evangelist) *Blackb 11* **P** *V Cockerham w Winmarleigh and Glasson* **V** C A ABBOTT **C** I J MCGRATH

ELLENBROOK (St Mary's Chapel) *see* Worsley *Man*

ELLENHALL (St Mary) *see* Chebsey, Creswell, Ellenhall, Ranton etc *Lich*

ELLERBURN (St Hilda) *see* Thornton Dale w Allerston, Ebberston etc *York*

ELLERBY (St James) *see* Skirlaugh, Catwick, Long Riston, Rise, Swine w Ellerby *York*

ELLERKER (not known) *see* S Cave and Ellerker w Broomfleet *York*

ELLESBOROUGH (St Peter and St Paul), The Kimbles and Stoke Mandeville *Ox 17* **P** *Chequers Trustees, The Hon I Hope-Morley, and D&C Linc (by turn)* **P-in-c** J M WALES

ELLESMERE (St Mary) *Lich 16* **P** *Bp* **V** P S HAWKINS

ELLESMERE (St Peter) *Sheff 3* **P** *Bp* **C** P J SALMON

ELLESMERE PORT, comprising Stoak and Whitby *Ches 9* **P** *Bp* **R** G B MCGUINNESS **C** G S FOSTER **NSM** G J WELCH

ELLINGHAM (St Mary and All Saints) *see* Ringwood w Ellingham and Harbridge etc *Win*

ELLINGHAM (St Mary) *see* Waveney Marshlands *Nor*

ELLINGHAM (St Maurice) *see* Beadnell, Ellingham and N Sunderland *Newc*

ELLINGHAM, GREAT (St James), LITTLE (St Peter), Rockland All Saints, Rockland St Peter and Shropham w Snetterton *Nor 11* **P** *Bp, Major E H C Garnier, and CCC Cam (jt)* **P-in-c** C M MASON **Hon C** S STRUTT

ELLINGTON (All Saints) *see* E Leightonstone *Ely*

ELLISFIELD (St Martin) *see* Farleigh, Candover and Wield *Win*

ELLISTOWN (St Christopher) *see* Hugglescote w Donington, Ellistown and Snibston *Leic*

ELLOE FEN Group, The, comprising Gedney Hill, Sutton St Edmund, Sutton St James, and Whaplode Drove *Linc 18* **P** *Bp, Feoffees, and V Long Sutton w Lutton etc (jt)* **V** M G ONGYERTH **C** J BAREHAM-SIVERS

ELLOE STONE Parishes, The, comprising Moulton, Holbeach Fen, and Whaplode *Linc 18* **P** *Bp and DBP (1 turn), Ld Chan (1 turn)* **OLM** B A HUTCHINSON

ELLOE, MID *see* Mid Elloe Gp *Linc*

ELLOUGHTON (St Mary) and Brough w Brantingham *York 13* **P** *Abp and D&C Dur (jt)* **V** M A FRYER

ELM (All Saints) *see* Fen Orchards *Ely*

ELM (St Mary Magdalene) *see* Mells w Buckland Dinham, Elm, Whatley etc *B & W*

ELM PARK (St Nicholas) Hornchurch *Chelmsf 2* **P** *Bp* **V** A J KEIGHLEY **NSM** D M PERRY, T C KEIGHLEY

ELMBRIDGE (St Mary) *see* Elmley Lovett w Hampton Lovett and Elmbridge w Rushock and Hartlebury and Ombersley w Doverdale *Worc*

ELMDON (St Nicholas) *see* Icknield Way Villages *Chelmsf*

ELMDON (St Nicholas) (St Stephen's Church Centre) (Valley Church Centre) *Birm 6* **P** *Ch Trust Fund Trust* **R** *vacant*

ELMERS END (St James) *see* Beckenham St Jas w St Mich and St Aug *Roch*

ELMESTHORPE (St Mary) *see* Earl Shilton w Elmesthorpe *Leic*

ELMETE TRINITY, comprising Barwick, Scholes, and Thorner *Leeds 13* **P** *Duchy of Lanc and Earl of Mexborough (alt)* **NSM** A B HAIGH

ELMHAM, NORTH (St Mary) *see* Heart of Norfolk *Nor*

ELMHURST (Mission Room) *see* Lich St Chad *Lich*

ELMLEY *see* Lepton, Emley and Flockton w Denby Grange *Leeds*

ELMLEY CASTLE (St Mary) w Bricklehampton and the Combertons *Worc 3* **P** *Bp* **P-in-c** M K LECLÉZIO **C** A C DAVIES

ELMLEY LOVETT (St Michael) w Hampton Lovett and Elmbridge w Rushock and Hartlebury and Ombersley w Doverdale *Worc 1* **P** *Patr Bd* **R** S C WINTER

ELMORE (St John the Baptist) *see* Hardwicke and Elmore w Longney *Glouc*

ELMSALL, NORTH (St Margaret) *see* S and N Elmsall *Leeds*

ELMSALL, SOUTH and NORTH (St Mary the Virgin) *Leeds 15* **P** *Bp* **V** M GALLAGHER **C** G V FLEURY

ELMSETT (St Peter) w Aldham, Hintlesham, Chattisham and Kersey *St E 4* **P** *Bp, MMCET, and St Chad's Coll Dur (jt)* **P-in-c** S J CROMPTON-BATTERSBY **NSM** A W J WALLER

ELMSTEAD (St Anne and St Laurence) *see* Tenpenny Villages *Chelmsf*

ELMSTONE (not known) *see* Canonry *Cant*

ELMSTONE HARDWICKE (St Mary Magdalene) *see* N Cheltenham *Glouc*

ELMSWELL (St John the Divine) *St E 6* **P** MMCET **R** P W GOODRIDGE **C** I E OKEKE

ELMTON (St Peter) w Creswell and Whitwell w Steetley *Derby 3* **P** *Bp* **R** K COCKING

ELSDON (St Cuthbert) *see* N Tyne and Redesdale *Newc*

ELSECAR (Holy Trinity) *see* Worsbrough w Elsecar *Sheff*

ELSENHAM (St Mary the Virgin) *see* Henham and Elsenham w Ugley *Chelmsf*

ELSFIELD (St Thomas of Canterbury) *see* Marston w Elsfield *Ox*

ELSHAM (All Saints) *see* Brocklesby Park, Croxton and North Wolds *Linc*

ELSING (St Mary) *see* Reepham and Wensum Valley *Nor*

ELSON (St Thomas) *see* Bridgemary, Elson and Rowner *Portsm*

ELSTEAD (St James) *Guildf 4* **P** *Adn Surrey* **R** H T MOORE **NSM** D J ORME

ELSTED (St Paul) *see* Harting w Elsted and Treyford cum Didling *Chich*

ELSTERNWICK (St Laurence) *see* Burstwick, Burton Pidsea etc *York*

ELSTON (All Saints) w Elston Chapelry *S'well 3* **P** J C S Darwin *Esq* **P-in-c** E I MURRAY

ELSTOW (St Mary and St Helena) *St Alb 9* **P** *Patr Bd* **P-in-c** P J MESSAM **TV** S T SMITH

ELSTREE (St Nicholas) and Borehamwood *St Alb 14* **P** *Patr Bd (3 turns), Ld Chan (1 turn)* **TR** T G WARR **TV** L R COLLINS

ELSWICK (St Stephen) (St Paul) *Newc 4* **P** *Ch Soc Trust and Trustees (jt)* **V** G R CURRY

ELSWICK, HIGH (St Philip) *see* Newc St Phil and St Aug and St Matt w St Mary *Newc*

ELSWORTH (Holy Trinity) *see* Papworth *Ely*

ELTHAM (Holy Trinity) *S'wark 3* **P** *Bp* **V** B E WARD **C** D J WYMAN

ELTHAM (St Barnabas) *S'wark 3* **P** *Bp* **V** S COOK

ELTHAM (St John the Baptist) *S'wark 3* **P** DBP **V** C L RISDON

ELTHAM (St Saviour) *S'wark 3* **P** *Bp* **V** *vacant*

ELTHAM PARK (St Luke) *S'wark 3* **P** *Bp* **V** *vacant*

ELTHAM, NEW (All Saints) *S'wark 3* **P** *Bp* **V** A S ROSE

ELTISLEY (St Pandionia and St John the Baptist) *see* Papworth *Ely*

ELTON (All Saints) *Ely 15* **P** *Sir William Proby Bt* **V** R J GIBBS **C** M W PYBUS

ELTON (All Saints) *see* Kirklees Valley *Man*

ELTON (St John) *Dur 8* **P** *St Chad Coll Dur* **V** W E BRAVINER **C** P MURRAY **NSM** D T ACKERLEY

ELTON (St Mary the Virgin) *see* Wigmore Abbey *Heref*

ELTON (St Stephen) *Man 4*   **P** *V Elton All SS*
   P-in-c P SANDERSON
ELTON-ON-THE-HILL (St Michael) *see* Wiverton in the Vale
   S'well
ELVASTON (St Bartholomew) *see* Aston on Trent, Elvaston,
   Weston on Trent etc *Derby*
ELVEDEN (St Andrew and St Patrick) *see* Lakenheath, Santon
   Downham and Elveden *St E*
ELVINGTON (Holy Trinity) *see* Derwent Ings *York*
ELWICK HALL (St Peter) *see* Hart w Elwick Hall *Dur*
ELWORTH (St Peter) *Ches 11*   **P** *V Sandbach*   **V** D J PAGE
   NSM A P RIGBY
ELY (Holy Trinity w St Mary), including Chettisham,
   Downham, Little Thetford, Prickwillow, Stretham, and
   Stuntney *Ely 8*   **P** *Patr Bd*   **TR** C M HILL   **TV** P E MARSH
   C D R HOLMES   **NSM** J R HICKISH
ELY (St Peter) Proprietary Chapel *Ely 8*   **Min** P D ANDREWS
EMBERTON (All Saints) *see* Lamp *Ox*
EMBLETON (Holy Trinity) w Rennington and Rock *Newc 6*
   P *Mert Coll Ox*   **P-in-c** A J HARDY   **NSM** B K COOPER,
   I P CHADWICK
EMBLETON (St Cuthbert) *see* Binsey *Carl*
EMBROOK (Community of St Nicholas) *see* Wokingham
   St Paul *Ox*
EMBSAY (St Mary the Virgin) w Eastby *Leeds 21*   **P** *R Skipton*
   H Trin   **V** M E RUSSELL   **NSM** T CALOW
EMERY DOWN (Christ Church) *see* Lyndhurst and Emery
   Down and Minstead *Win*
EMLEY (St Michael the Archangel) *see* Lepton, Emley and
   Flockton w Denby Grange *Leeds*
EMMAUS Parish Team, The *Leic 1*   **P** *Bp*   **P-in-c** J LINDSEY
   C A K SIMPSON-SMITH, C S BEAUMONT   **NSM** I BENNETT
EMMER GREEN (St Barnabas) w Caversham Park *Ox 7*
   P *Bp and Ch Ch Ox (jt)*   **R** *vacant*
EMNETH (St Edmund) *see* Fen Orchards *Ely*
EMPINGHAM (St Peter), Edith Weston, Lyndon, Manton,
   North Luffenham, Pilton, Preston, Ridlington, Whitwell
   and Wing *Pet 12*   **P** *Bp, Baroness Willoughby de Eresby, Sir*
   John Conant Bt, Em Coll Cam, and DBP (jt)   **R** P J MADGWICK
   C J W SALT   **NSM** J L DUFFY
EMPSHOTT (Holy Rood) *see* Greatham, Empshott and
   Hawkley w Priors Dean *Portsm*
EMSCOTE (All Saints) *see* Warwick *Cov*
EMSWORTH (St James) *see* Warblington w Emsworth *Portsm*
ENBORNE (St Michael and All Angels) *see* Walbury Beacon
   Ox
ENDCLIFFE (St Augustine) *Sheff 2*   **P** *Ch Burgesses*
   P-in-c C L DAWSON   **C** B M TANNER   **NSM** L M N HALL
ENDERBY (St John the Baptist) w Lubbesthorpe and
   Thurlaston *Leic 7*   **P** *Bp and F B Drummond Esq*
   V J C TAYLOR   **C** R I BALMER
ENDON (St Luke) *see* Bagnall w Endon *Lich*
ENFIELD (Christ Church) Trent Park *Lon 16*   **P** *CPAS Patr*
   Trust   **V** J D TUCKWELL   **C** C D EDWARDS,
   J M FEATHERSTONE
ENFIELD (Jesus Church) *see* Forty Hill Jes Ch *Lon*
ENFIELD (St Andrew) *Lon 16*   **P** *Trin Coll Cam*
   V S M GRIFFITHS
ENFIELD (St George) *Lon 16*   **P** *Bp*   **V** A T OH
   NSM V T P SHEEHAN
ENFIELD (St James) (St Barnabas) *Lon 16*   **P** *V Enfield*
   V I M GALLAGHER   **NSM** H R GEORGE, K C ONWUKA
ENFIELD (St John the Baptist) *see* Clay Hill St Jo and St Luke
   Lon
ENFIELD (St Luke) *as above*
ENFIELD (St Mark) *see* Bush Hill Park St Mark *Lon*
ENFIELD (St Matthew) *see* Ponders End St Matt *Lon*
ENFIELD (St Michael and All Angels) *Lon 16*   **P** *V Enfield*
   V S M TAYLOR
ENFIELD (St Peter and St Paul) *Lon 16*   **P** *Bp*
   V S GALLAGHER   **C** S I A JONES
ENFIELD (St Stephen) *see* Bush Hill Park St Steph *Lon*
ENFIELD CHASE (St Mary Magdalene) *Lon 16*   **P** *Bp*
   V J B LAWSON
ENFORD (All Saints) *see* Avon River *Sarum*
ENGLEFIELD (St Mark) *Ox 4*   **P** *Englefield Estate Trust*
   V N W WYNNE-JONES
ENGLEFIELD GREEN (St Jude) *Guildf 11*   **P** *Bp*
   V J M ALLFORD
ENGLISH BICKNOR (St Mary) *see* Forest of Dean Ch Ch w
   English Bicknor *Glouc*
ENGLISHCOMBE (St Peter) *see* Bath St Barn w Englishcombe
   B & W
ENHAM ALAMEIN (St George) *see* Pastrow *Win*
ENMORE (St Michael) *see* Aisholt, Enmore, Goathurst,
   Nether Stowey etc *B & W*

ENMORE GREEN (St John the Evangelist) *see* Shaftesbury
   Sarum
ENNERDALE (St Mary) *see* Lamplugh w Ennerdale *Carl*
ENSBURY PARK (St Thomas) *Sarum 7*   **P** *Bp*   **V** S A EVANS
ENSTONE (St Kenelm) *see* Chase *Ox*
ENVILLE (St Mary the Virgin) *see* Kinver and Enville *Lich*
EPPERSTONE (Holy Cross), Gonalston, Oxton and
   Woodborough *S'well 7*   **P** *Bp, Ld Chan, and C P L Francklin*
   Esq (by turn)   **R** A R GILES   **NSM** L M RAYNOR
EPPING District (All Saints) (St John the Baptist) *Chelmsf 3*
   P *Patr Bd*   **TR** L P BATSON   **TV** O C MAXFIELD-COOTE
   C A L SUMMERS   **NSM** J M BOSTOCK
EPSOM (St Barnabas) *Guildf 9*   **P** *Bp*   **V** *vacant*
EPSOM (St Martin) (St Stephen on the Downs) *Guildf 9*
   P *Bp*   **V** N A PARISH   **C** D J CANDLIN
EPSOM COMMON (Christ Church) *Guildf 9*   **P** *Bp*
   V R A DONOVAN
EPWELL (St Anne) *see* Wykeham *Ox*
EPWORTH Group, The (St Andrew), including West
   Butterwick and Wroot *Linc 1*   **P** *The Crown (2 turns), Ld*
   Chan (1 turn)   **R** P D WILSON
ERCALL, HIGH (St Michael and All Angels) *see* Wrockwardine
   Deanery *Lich*
ERDINGTON (St Barnabas) *Birm 4*   **P** *Bp and Aston Patr Trust*
   (jt)   **V** E C M SYKES   **C** S M PEARSON
ERDINGTON (St Chad) *Birm 4*   **P** *Bp and Aston Patr Trust (jt)*
   V *vacant*
ERDINGTON Christ the King *Birm 4*   **P** *Bp*   **V** R R SOUTER
ERIDGE GREEN (Holy Trinity) *see* Frant w Eridge *Chich*
ERISWELL (St Laurence and St Peter) *see* Forest Heath *St E*
ERITH (Christ Church) *Roch 15*   **P** *Bp*   **V** *vacant*
ERITH (St John the Baptist) *Roch 15*   **P** *Bp*
   P-in-c A J D FOOT   **NSM** N J BUNKER
ERITH (St Paul) Northumberland Heath *Roch 15*   **P** *CPAS*
   V C BEAZLEY-LONG
ERLESTOKE (Holy Saviour) *see* Bratton, Edington and Imber,
   Erlestoke etc *Sarum*
ERMINGTON (St Peter and St Paul) *see* Diptford w N Huish,
   Ermington, Halwell etc *Ex*
ERNESETTLE (St Aidan), Whitleigh and Honicknowle *Ex 20*
   P *Ld Chan and Bp (alt)*   **V** D R BAILEY   **NSM** D WATSON
ERPINGHAM (St Mary) *see* Scarrowbeck *Nor*
ERRINGDEN, comprising Cragg Vale and Mytholmroyd
   Leeds 8   **P** *Bp and V Halifax (jt)*   **V** C B REARDON
   C D J MILES   **NSM** M D BULL
ERWARTON (St Mary the Virgin) *see* Shoreline *St E*
ERYHOLME (St Mary) *see* E Dere Street *Leeds*
ESCOMB (Saxon Church) and Witton Park *Dur 3*   **P** *Bp*
   V *vacant*
ESCOT (St Philip and St James) *see* Ottery St Mary,
   Alfington, W Hill, Tipton etc *Ex*
ESCRICK (St Helen) and Stillingfleet w Naburn *York 2*
   P *Abp, D&C, and C D Forbes Adam Esq (jt)*
   NSM D A ROGERS
ESH (St Michael and All Angels) *see* Dur N *Dur*
ESHER (Christ Church) (St George) *Guildf 8*   **P** *Wadh Coll*
   Ox   **R** D M MCCALLIG
ESHOLT (St Paul) *see* Guiseley w Esholt *Leeds*
ESK PARISHES *see* Arthuret w Kirkandrews-on-Esk and
   Nicholforest *Carl*
ESK, LOWER, comprising Aislaby, Eskdaleside, and Sneaton
   York 21   **P** *Abp*   **V** *vacant*
ESKDALE (St Bega's Mission) *see* Black Combe, Drigg,
   Eskdale etc *Carl*
ESKDALE (St Catherine) *as above*
ESSENDINE (St Mary the Virgin) *see* Ryhall w Essendine and
   Carlby *Pet*
ESSENDON (St Mary the Virgin) *see* Lt Berkhamsted and
   Bayford, Essendon etc *St Alb*
ESSINGTON (St John the Evangelist), Featherstone and
   Shareshill *Lich 2*   **P** *Simeon's Trustees, Bp, and R Bushbury*
   (jt)   **V** *vacant*
ESTON (Christ Church) w Normanby *York 17*   **P** *Abp*
   TR G A J POTTER
ESTOVER (Christ Church) *see* Eggbuckland w Estover *Ex*
ETAL (St Mary the Virgin) *see* Ford and Etal *Newc*
ETCHILHAMPTON (St Andrew) *see* Cannings and Redhorn
   Sarum
ETCHING HILL (The Holy Spirit) *see* Brereton and Rugeley w
   Armitage *Lich*
ETCHINGHAM (The Assumption and St Nicholas) *see*
   Burwash, Burwash Weald and Etchingham *Chich*
ETHERLEY (St Cuthbert) *Dur 3*   **P** *Bp*   **R** *vacant*
ETON (St John the Evangelist) w Eton Wick, Boveney and
   Dorney *Ox 12*   **P** *Eton Coll and Mrs J M Palmer (jt)*
   V R R LA STACEY   **NSM** C J GOODING

ETON WICK (St John the Baptist) *see* Eton w Eton Wick, Boveney and Dorney *Ox*

ETTINGSHALL (Holy Trinity) *Lich 27*   **P** *Bp*   **V** D P A FEENEY   **C** R T BROOKS   **NSM** A P M EDWARDS

ETTINGTON (Holy Trinity and St Thomas of Canterbury) *see* Stourdene Gp *Cov*

ETTON (St Stephen) *see* Glinton, Etton, Maxey, Peakirk and Northborough *Pet*

ETTON (St Mary) w Dalton Holme *York 8*   **P** Lord Hotham   **P-in-c** R F PARKINSON

ETWALL (St Helen) w Egginton *Derby 6*   **P** *Bp*, Sir Henry Every Bt, Major J W Chandos-Pole, and DBP (by turn)   **P-in-c** S J GREENWOOD

EUSTON (St Genevieve) *see* Blackbourne *St E*

EUXTON (not known) *Blackb 4*   **P** *Bp*   **V** J S SMITH   **C** A BLAND

EVE HILL (St James the Great) *see* Dudley *Worc*

EVEDON (St Mary) *see* N Lafford Gp *Linc*

EVENLEY (St George) *see* Aynho and Croughton w Evenley etc *Pet*

EVENLODE (St Edward King and Martyr) *see* Broadwell, Evenlode, Oddington, Adlestrop etc *Glouc*

EVENWOOD (St Paul) *Dur 4*   **P** *Bp*   **P-in-c** B WHITLEY   **C** L R EVANS

EVERDON (St Mary) *see* Weedon Bec w Everdon and Dodford *Pet*

EVERINGHAM (St Everilda) *see* Holme and Seaton Ross Gp *York*

EVERSDEN, GREAT (St Mary) *see* Lordsbridge *Ely*

EVERSDEN, LITTLE (St Helen) *as above*

EVERSHOLT (St John the Baptist) *see* Woburn w Eversholt, Milton Bryan, Battlesden etc *St Alb*

EVERSHOT (St Osmund) *see* Melbury *Sarum*

EVERSLEY (St Mary) *see* Darby Green and Eversley *Win*

EVERTON (Holy Trinity) *see* Bawtry w Austerfield, Misson, Everton and Mattersey *S'well*

EVERTON (St George) *Liv 1*   **P** *Bp*   **V** A R MAYNARD

EVERTON (St Mary) *see* Gamlingay and Everton *Ely*

EVERTON (St Mary) *see* Milford *Win*

EVERTON (St Peter) (St John Chrysostom) (Emmanuel) *Liv 1*   **P** Patr Bd   **R** H CORBETT

EVESBATCH (St Andrew) *see* Frome Valley *Heref*

EVESHAM (All Saints w St Lawrence) w Norton and Lenchwick *Worc 3*   **P** *Bp* and *D&C (jt)*   **V** A SPURR

EVINGTON (St Denys) *Leic 1*   **P** *Bp*   **V** A J LEES-SMITH   **C** N ROSTOCK

EVINGTON, NORTH (St Stephen) *Leic 1*   **P** *Bp*   **P-in-c** I ST C RICHARDS

EWELL (St Francis of Assisi) Ruxley Lane *Guildf 9*   **P** *Bp*   **P-in-c** F M ELLINGHAM

EWELL (St Mary the Virgin) *Guildf 9*   **P** *Bp*   **V** vacant

EWELL, WEST (All Saints) *Guildf 9*   **P** *Bp*   **V** J W MARROW

EWELME *see* Dursley, Uley, Owlpen etc *Glouc*

EWELME (St Mary the Virgin) *see* Benson w Ewelme *Ox*

EWERBY (St Andrew) *see* Kirkby Laythorpe *Linc*

EWHURST (St James the Great) *Chich 17*   **P** K Coll Cam   **P-in-c** C P IRVINE

EWHURST (St Peter and St Paul) w Okewood and Forest Green *Guildf 2*   **P** Ld Chan (1 turn), Bp and J P M H Evelyn Esq (1 turn)   **R** C F SHEPHERD   **NSM** J MARSH

EWOOD (St Bartholomew) *see* Blackb Redeemer *Blackb*

EWSHOT (St Mary the Virgin) *see* Crondall and Ewshot *Guildf*

EWYAS HAROLD (St Michael and All Angels) w Dulas, Kenderchurch, Abbeydore, Bacton, Kentchurch, Llangua, Rowlestone, Llancillo, Walterstone, Kilpeck, St Devereux and Wormbridge *Heref 1*   **P** *Bp*, E Harley Esq, Mrs B Sexton, J Lucas-Scudamore Esq, Mrs M Barneby, G Clive Esq, and D&C (2 turns), Ld Chan (1 turn)   **R** M R GODSON

EXBOURNE (St Mary the Virgin) *see* Okehampton, Inwardleigh, Belstone, Sourton etc *Ex*

EXBURY (St Katherine) *see* Beaulieu and Exbury and E Boldre *Win*

EXE, WEST (St Paul) *see* Tiverton St Geo and St Paul *Ex*

EXETER (St David) (St Michael and All Angels) *Ex 3*   **P** D&C   **V** N GUTHRIE   **C** A J LEIGHTON PLOM   **Hon C** P A LEE   **NSM** A B SPEED-ANDREWS

EXETER (St James) *Ex 3*   **P** D&C   **R** H H D PRYSE   **NSM** S R TURNER

EXETER (St Leonard w Holy Trinity) *Ex 3*   **P** CPAS   **R** S N AUSTEN   **C** C J KEANE, P D SUTTON

EXETER (St Mark) *Ex 3*   **P** *Bp*   **R** T HOCKLEY-STILL   **NSM** T WILSON

EXETER (St Mary Steps) *see* Heavitree and St Mary Steps *Ex*

EXETER (St Matthew) (St Sidwell) *Ex 3*   **P** D&C   **P-in-c** E R J HODGES   **C** M A CLAYTON, V PESTRIDGE

EXETER (St Thomas the Apostle) (Emmanuel) (St Andrew) (St Philip) *Ex 3*   **P** *Bp*   **TR** D J NIXON   **NSM** S P CUMMING

EXETER Holy Trinity *Ex 3*   **P** *Bp* and Ch Soc Trust (jt)   **V** J P A ELVIN   **C** O P OSBORN, P L BROKENSHIRE

EXETER, CENTRAL (St Martin) (St Mary Arches) (St Olave) (St Pancras) (St Petrock) (St Stephen) *Ex 3*   **P** Patr Bd   **P-in-c** S R SWARBRICK

EXFORD (St Mary Magdalene) *see* Exmoor *B & W*

EXHALL (St Giles) *see* Heart of England *Cov*

EXHALL (St Giles) *Cov 5*   **P** *Bp*   **V** G A PHILLIP   **C** J C PARKER

EXMINSTER (St Martin), Kenn, Kenton w Mamhead, and Powderham *Ex 5*   **P** 12 Govs of Crediton Ch, D&C Sarum, SMF, Mrs M P L Bate, and Earl of Devon (jt)   **R** J D A WILLIAMS

EXMOOR (St Luke) *B & W 15*   **P** Ld Chan (1 turn), Bp, Em Coll Cam, Peterho Cam, G A Warren Esq, and D M Warren Esq (2 turns)   **R** D A WEIR   **NSM** N M BUTT

EXMOUTH (All Saints) *see* Withycombe Raleigh *Ex*

EXMOUTH (Holy Trinity) *see* Littleham-cum-Exmouth w Lympstone *Ex*

EXMOUTH (St John in the Wilderness) *see* Withycombe Raleigh *Ex*

EXMOUTH (St John the Evangelist) *as above*

EXNING (St Agnes) *see* Newmarket St Mary w Exning St Agnes *St E*

EXNING (St Martin) (St Philip) w Landwade *St E 7*   **P** D&C Cant   **P-in-c** J C HARDY

EXTON (St Andrew) *see* Aylesbeare, Clyst St George, Clyst St Mary etc *Ex*

EXTON (St Peter and St Paul) *see* Cottesmore and Burley, Clipsham, Exton etc *Pet*

EXTON (St Peter and St Paul) *see* Meon Bridge *Portsm*

EXTON (St Peter) *see* Exmoor *B & W*

EXWICK (St Andrew) *Ex 3*   **P** Lord Wraxall   **V** J P BIRD

EYAM (St Lawrence) *see* Baslow and Eyam *Derby*

EYDON (St Nicholas) *see* Aston-le-Walls, Byfield, Boddington, Eydon etc *Pet*

EYE (St Matthew), Newborough and Thorney *Pet 11*   **P** *Bp* and The Crown (alt)   **V** C HURST

EYE (St Peter and St Paul) *St E 11*   **P** *Bp*, SMF, and Lt Comdr G C Marshall (jt)   **R** G SUMPTER

EYEWORTH (All Saints) *see* Dunton w Wrestlingworth and Eyeworth *St Alb*

EYKE (All Saints) *see* Wilford Peninsula *St E*

EYNESBURY (St Mary) *see* St Neots *Ely*

EYNSFORD (St Martin) w Farningham and Lullingstone *Roch 10*   **P** D&C   **R** M D MCGARVEY

EYNSHAM (St Leonard) and Cassington *Ox 29*   **P** Wycliffe Hall Ox and Ch Ch Ox (alt)   **V** D P FRASER   **NSM** A C ATHERSTONE   **OLM** R ASTON

EYPE (St Peter) *see* Eggardon and Colmers *Sarum*

EYRES MONSELL (St Hugh) *Leic 1*   **P** *Bp*   **P-in-c** S Y LEE

EYTHORNE (St Peter and St Paul) *see* Bewsborough *Cant*

EYTON (All Saints) *see* Leominster *Heref*

EYTON (St Catherine) *see* Wellington All SS w Eyton *Lich*

FACCOMBE (St Barnabas) *see* Pastrow *Win*

FACEBY (St Mary Magdalene) *see* Whorlton Gp *York*

FACIT (St John the Evangelist) *see* Whitworth w Facit *Man*

FAILAND (St Bartholomew) *see* Wraxall *B & W*

FAILSWORTH (Holy Family) *Man 5*   **P** The Crown and Bp (alt)   **R** P HUTCHINS

FAILSWORTH (St John) (St John the Evangelist) *Man 5*   **P** *Bp*   **R** vacant

FAIR OAK (St Thomas) *Win 10*   **P** *Bp*   **NSM** R G NICHOLLS

FAIRBURN (St James) *see* Ledsham w Fairburn *York*

FAIRFIELD (St Mark) *see* Belbroughton w Fairfield and Clent *Worc*

FAIRFIELD (St Peter), Peak Forest and Dove Holes *Derby 4*   **P** Patr Bd   **V** C F EDWARDS   **OLM** M WASHBROOK

FAIRFIELD (St Thomas à Becket) *see* Romney Marsh *Cant*

FAIRFORD (St Mary the Virgin) *see* S Cotswolds *Glouc*

FAIRHAVEN (St Paul) *Blackb 10*   **P** J C Hilton Esq   **V** P A BYE   **C** K J MULHOLLAND

FAIRLIGHT (St Andrew) (St Peter) and Pett *Chich 17*   **P** Patr Bd   **Hon C** H E PATTEN

FAIRSEAT (Holy Innocents) *see* Stansted w Fairseat and Vigo *Roch*

FAIRSTEAD (St Mary) *see* Witham and Villages *Chelmsf*

FAIRWARP (Christ Church) *Chich 18*   **P** *Bp*   **P-in-c** J P CAPERON

FAIRWEATHER GREEN (St Saviour) *Leeds 3*   **P** *Bp*   **P-in-c** V POLLARD   **C** W J GRANT

FAKENHAM MAGNA (St Peter) *see* Blackbourne *St E*

FALCONWOOD (Bishop Ridley Church) *Roch 15*   **P** *Bp*   **V** M TARIQ

FALDINGWORTH (All Saints) *see* Middle Rasen Gp *Linc*

FALFIELD (St George) *see* Cromhall, Tortworth,
  Tytherington, Falfield etc *Glouc*
FALKENHAM (St Ethelbert) *see* Orwell and Deben *St E*
FALLOWFIELD (Holy Innocents) *see* Birch w Fallowfield *Man*
FALLOWFIELD (St Crispin) *see* Withington St Crispin *Man*
FALMER (St Laurence) *see* Stanmer w Falmer *Chich*
FALMOUTH (All Saints) *Truro 2* **P** *Bp*
  P-in-c W R STUART-WHITE **C** D BAYLOR, H B BAYLOR,
  S CHATTEN
FALMOUTH (King Charles the Martyr) *Truro 2* **P** *Bp*
  P-in-c W R STUART-WHITE **C** D BAYLOR, H B BAYLOR
FALSTONE (St Peter) *see* N Tyne and Redesdale *Newc*
FAMBRIDGE, NORTH (Holy Trinity) *see* Althorne and N
  Fambridge *Chelmsf*
FAMBRIDGE, SOUTH (All Saints) *see* Ashingdon w S
  Fambridge, Canewdon and Paglesham *Chelmsf*
FANGFOSS (St Martin) *see* Barmby Moor Gp *York*
FAR FOREST (Holy Trinity) *see* Mamble w Bayton, Rock w
  Heightington etc *Worc*
FARCET (St Mary) *see* Stanground and Farcet *Ely*
FAREHAM (Holy Trinity) (St Columba) *Portsm 2* **P** *Bp*
  C G K BAKKER, W M JACOBS
FAREHAM (St John the Evangelist) *Portsm 2* **P** *CPAS*
  V B G DEANS
FAREHAM (St Peter and St Paul) *Portsm 2* **P** *Bp*
  P-in-c R JACKSON
FAREWELL (St Bartholomew) and Gentleshaw *Lich 1*
  P *MMCET* **V** L M MCKEON
FARFORTH (St Peter) *see* S Ormsby Gp *Linc*
FARINGDON, GREAT (All Saints) w Little Coxwell *Ox 25*
  P *Simeon's Trustees* **V** J S BELLAMY
FARINGDON, LITTLE (St Margaret of England) *see* Shill
  Valley and Broadshire *Ox*
FARLAM (St Thomas à Becket) *see* Eden, Gelt and Irthing
  Carl
FARLEIGH (St Andrew), Candover and Wield, including
  Bradley, and Northington w Swarraton *Win 1* **P** *Ld Chan (1*
  turn), Bp, D&C, Earl of Portsmouth, and Lord Ashburton (1
  turn) **R** D M CHATTELL **C** S P E MOURANT
FARLEIGH (St Mary) *see* Warlingham w Chelsham and
  Farleigh *S'wark*
FARLEIGH HUNGERFORD (St Leonard) *see* Hardington Vale
  B & W
FARLEIGH WALLOP (St Andrew) *see* Farleigh, Candover and
  Wield *Win*
FARLEIGH, EAST (not known) *see* Coxheath, E Farleigh,
  Hunton, Linton etc *Roch*
FARLEIGH, WEST (All Saints) *as above*
FARLESTHORPE (St Andrew) *see* Alford Gp *Linc*
FARLEY (All Saints) *see* Clarendon *Sarum*
FARLEY CHAMBERLAYNE (St John) *see* Michelmersh and
  Awbridge and Braishfield etc *Win*
FARLEY GREEN (St Michael) *see* Shere, Albury and Chilworth
  Guildf
FARLEY HILL (St John the Baptist) *St Alb 12* **P** *Bp*
  V R P O'NEILL **C** S J CURTIS
FARLEY HILL (St John the Evangelist) *see* Loddon Reach *Ox*
FARLINGTON (St Andrew) (Church of the Resurrection)
  Portsm 6 **P** *Mrs S J Wynter-Bee and Nugee Foundn (jt)*
  R P D GULLY **C** P L GOOD
FARLINGTON (St Leonard) *see* Forest of Galtres *York*
FARLOW (St Giles) *see* Stottesdon w Farlow, Cleeton St Mary
  etc *Heref*
FARMBOROUGH (All Saints) and Marksbury and Stanton
  Prior *B & W 9* **P** *MMCET (3 turns), Duchy of Cornwall (1*
  turn), and DBF (1 turn) **R** *vacant*
FARMCOTE (St Faith) *see* The Guitings, Cutsdean, Farmcote
  etc *Glouc*
FARMINGTON (St Peter) *see* Northleach w Hampnett and
  Farmington etc *Glouc*
FARMOOR (St Mary) *see* Cumnor *Ox*
FARNBOROUGH (All Saints) *see* E Downland *Ox*
FARNBOROUGH (Good Shepherd) *Guildf 1* **P** *CPAS Patr*
  Trust **V** R M SMART
FARNBOROUGH (St Botolph) *see* Avon Dassett w
  Farnborough and Fenny Compton *Cov*
FARNBOROUGH (St Giles) (St Nicholas) *Roch 16* **P** *Em Coll*
  Cam **R** M J HUGHES **C** S K BROADIE
FARNBOROUGH (St Peter) *Guildf 1* **P** *CPAS Patr Trust*
  V E A ETHERINGTON **C** B J PERKINS, G R M DICKS,
  S J NORBRON **NSM** R N COBBOLD
FARNBOROUGH, SOUTH (St Mark) *Guildf 1* **P** *Bp* **V** *vacant*
FARNCOMBE (St John the Evangelist) *Guildf 4* **P** *Bp*
  R J RATTUE
FARNDALE (St Mary) *see* Kirkbymoorside w Gillamoor,
  Farndale etc *York*

FARNDON (St Chad) and Coddington *Ches 5* **P** *Duke of*
  Westmr and D&C (jt) **V** D SCURR
FARNDON (St Peter) w Thorpe, Hawton and Cotham
  S'well 3 **P** *Ld Chan* **P-in-c** E I MURRAY
FARNDON, EAST (St John the Baptist) *see* Arthingworth,
  Harrington w Oxendon and E Farndon *Pet*
FARNHAM (St Andrew) (St Francis) *Guildf 3* **P** *Bp*
  R H D UFFINDELL
FARNHAM (St Laurence) *see* Chase *Sarum*
FARNHAM (St Mary the Virgin) *see* Stansted Mountfitchet w
  Birchanger and Farnham *Chelmsf*
FARNHAM (St Mary) *see* Alde River *St E*
FARNHAM (St Oswald) *see* Walkingham Hill *Leeds*
FARNHAM COMMON (St John the Evangelist) *see* Farnham
  Royal w Hedgerley *Ox*
FARNHAM ROYAL (St Mary the Virgin) w Hedgerley *Ox 12*
  P *Bp and Eton Coll (jt)* **R** C A M THOMAS
FARNHAM ROYAL SOUTH (St Michael) *see* Manor Park and
  Whitby Road *Ox*
FARNINGHAM (St Peter and St Paul) *see* Eynsford w
  Farningham and Lullingstone *Roch*
FARNLEY (All Saints) *see* Washburn and Mid-Wharfe *Leeds*
FARNLEY TYAS (St Lucias) *see* Almondbury w Farnley Tyas
  Leeds
FARNLEY, NEW (St James) *see* Wortley and Farnley *Leeds*
FARNSFIELD (St Michael) *S'well 3* **P** *Bp* **P-in-c** C G PEARSE
FARNWORTH (All Saints) (St John), Kearsley and
  Stoneclough *Man 3* **P** *Ld Chan and Patr Bd (alt)*
  TR S C NOLAN
FARNWORTH (Cronton Mission) *see* E Widnes *Liv*
FARNWORTH (St George) *see* New Bury w Gt Lever *Man*
FARNWORTH (St Luke) *see* E Widnes *Liv*
FARRINGDON (All Saints) *see* Northanger *Win*
FARRINGDON (St Petrock and St Barnabas) *see* Aylesbeare,
  Clyst St George, Clyst St Mary etc *Ex*
FARRINGTON GURNEY (St John the Baptist) *see* Paulton w
  Farrington Gurney and High Littleton *B & W*
FARSLEY (St John the Evangelist) *Leeds 11* **P** *V Calverley*
  P-in-c G H HOWLES **NSM** L M STEVENSON TATE
FARTHINGHOE (St Michael and All Angels) *see* Aynho and
  Croughton w Evenley etc *Pet*
FARTHINGSTONE (St Mary the Virgin) *see* Lambfold *Pet*
FARWAY (St Michael and All Angels) *see* Offwell, Farway and
  Widworthy *Ex*
FATFIELD (St George) *Dur 9* **P** *Lord Lambton*
  V N J BARR-HAMILTON
FAULKBOURNE (St Germanus) *see* Witham and Villages
  Chelmsf
FAULS (Holy Immanuel), Tilstock and Whitchurch *Lich 21*
  P *Bp* **R** J M HUNT **C** S M JOHNSON
FAVELL, WEST (Emmanuel) *see* Northampton Em *Pet*
FAVERSHAM (St Mary of Charity), including Ospringe,
  Preston-next-Faversham, and The Brents and Davington
  Cant 14 **P** *D&C, St Jo Coll Cam, and Abp (jt)*
  V S D ROWLANDS **C** D C CORCORAN
FAWDON (St Mary the Virgin) *Newc 2* **P** *Bp*
  OLM M A ATKINSON
FAWKHAM (St Mary) and Hartley *Roch 1* **P** *Bp and D&C (jt)*
  P-in-c A BARKER **C** C J SHILLITO
FAWLEY (All Saints) *Win 11* **P** *Bp* **P-in-c** A BENNETT
FAWLEY (St Mary the Virgin) *see* Hambleden Valley *Ox*
FAWLEY (St Mary) *see* W Downland *Ox*
FAWSLEY (St Mary the Virgin) *see* Badby w Newham and
  Charwelton w Fawsley etc *Pet*
FAZAKERLEY (Emmanuel) (St Paul) (St George) *Liv 4*
  P *Patr Bd* **TR** A J BROWN **TV** M A HINDLEY
FAZAKERLEY (St Nathanael) *see* Walton-on-the-Hill *Liv*
FAZELEY (St Paul) *see* Peel Parishes *Lich*
FAZELEY Mile Oak (St Barnabas) *as above*
FEATHERSTONE (All Saints) (St Thomas) *Leeds 15* **P** *Ch Ch*
  Ox and Bp (jt) **V** I GROSU **NSM** P J CLAPHAM
FECKENHAM (St John the Baptist) *see* Wychebrook *Worc*
FEERING (All Saints) *see* Kelvedon and Feering *Chelmsf*
FELBRIDGE (St John) *S'wark 25* **P** *DBP* **V** M S FRANCIS
FELBRIGG (St Margaret) *see* Roughton and Felbrigg, Metton,
  Sustead etc *Nor*
FELIXKIRK (St Felix) w Boltby *York 18* **P** *Abp*
  P-in-c D E GAMBLE **NSM** K M BROWN, W A DEWING
FELIXSTOWE (Christ Church) *St E 10* **P** *Ch Patr Trust*
  V M A MAK **NSM** E B LIVEY, P G LIVEY
FELIXSTOWE (St John the Baptist) (St Edmund) *St E 10*
  P *Bp* **V** A S DOTCHIN **NSM** P H BRINKLEY
FELIXSTOWE (St Peter and St Paul) (St Andrew)
  (St Nicholas) *St E 10* **P** *Ch Trust Fund Trust* **V** C A HOOD
  C E E HAGGAR **NSM** D P WHITE
FELKIRK (St Peter) *see* Royston and Felkirk *Leeds*

FELLING (Christ Church) *Dur 11*   **P** *CPAS*
NSM T R WORSLEY
FELLISCLIFFE (Mission Church) *see* Hampsthwaite and
Killinghall and Birstwith *Leeds*
FELLSIDE TEAM, The, comprising Barton, Bilsborrow,
Bleasdale, Goosnargh, and Whitechapel *Blackb 9*   **P** *Patr Bd*
TR S P C COOPER   **TV** G WHITTAKER   **C** S SALT
FELMERSHAM (St Mary) *see* Sharnbrook, Felmersham and
Knotting w Souldrop *St Alb*
FELMINGHAM (St Andrew) *see* King's Beck *Nor*
FELPHAM (St Mary the Virgin) *Chich 1*   **P** *D&C*
R J W A CHALLIS
FELSHAM (St Peter) *see* Bradfield St Clare, Bradfield
St George etc *St E*
FELSTED (Holy Cross) and Little Dunmow *Chelmsf 17*
P *CPAS*   **V** C J TAYLOR
FELTHAM (St Dunstan) *Lon 11*   **P** *Bp*   **V** A M E DOLLERY
FELTHORPE (St Margaret) *see* Horsford, Felthorpe and
Hevingham *Nor*
FELTON (St Katharine and the Noble Army of Martyrs) *see*
Winford w Felton Common Hill *B & W*
FELTON (St Michael and All Angels) *Newc 6*   **P** *Bp*
NSM C M A HEPPER
FELTON (St Michael the Archangel) *see* Maund Gp *Heref*
FELTON, WEST (St Michael) *see* Whittington and W Felton
w Haughton *Lich*
FELTWELL (St Mary) *see* Grimshoe *Ely*
FEN AND HILL Group, The, comprising Hameringham,
Mareham le Fen, Mareham on the Hill, and Scrivelsby
Linc 13   **P** *Bp, DBP, G J R Wiggins-Davies Esq, and Lt Col J L
M Dymoke (jt)*   **R** A J ROBERTS   **OLM** K A BUSH
FEN DITTON (St Mary the Virgin) *Ely 2*   **P** *Bp*   **R** *vacant*
FEN DRAYTON (St Mary the Virgin) w Fenstanton *Ely 10*
P *Ch Coll Cam and Bp (jt)*   **R** R TALLOWIN
FEN ORCHARDS, The, comprising Elm, Emneth, and Friday
Bridge w Coldham *Ely 14*   **P** *Bp*   **V** *vacant*
FENCE-IN-PENDLE (St Anne) and Higham *Blackb 6*   **P** *Bp
and Ld Chan (alt)*   **V** L HINCHCLIFFE
FENHAM (Holy Cross) *see* Newc H Cross *Newc*
FENHAM (St James and St Basil) *Newc 4*   **P** *Bp*
V J MCGOWAN
FENISCLIFFE (St Francis) *Blackb 2*   **P** *Bp*   **P-in-c** D J ROSCOE
FENISCOWLES (Immanuel) *Blackb 2*   **P** *V Blackb*
P-in-c D J ROSCOE
FENITON (St Andrew) *see* Ottery St Mary, Alfington, W Hill,
Tipton etc *Ex*
FENN LANES Group, The, comprising Fenny Drayton,
Higham-on-the-Hill, Stoke Golding, and Witherley *Leic 10*
P *Bp, D&C, and Lord O'Neill (jt)*   **R** *vacant*
**FENNY BENTLEY (St Edmund King and Martyr), Thorpe,
Tissington, Parwich and Alsop-en-le-Dale** *Derby 1*   **P** *Bp,
D A G Shields Esq, and Sir Richard FitzHerbert Bt (jt)*
P-in-c E MCDONALD
FENNY COMPTON (St Peter and St Clare) *see* Avon Dassett
w Farnborough and Fenny Compton *Cov*
FENNY DRAYTON (St Michael and All Angels) *see* Fenn
Lanes Gp *Leic*
FENNY STRATFORD (St Martin) *Ox 14*   **P** *Bp*
V J A BULLOCK   **NSM** I W THOMAS
FENSTANTON (St Peter and St Paul) *see* Fen Drayton w
Fenstanton *Ely*
FENTON (Christ Church) *see* Stoke-upon-Trent and Fenton
Lich
FEOCK (St Feock) *Truro 5*   **P** *Bp*   **P-in-c** K A F WILSON
C R D WALLIS   **NSM** J ROWE
FERNDOWN (St Mary) *see* Hampreston *Sarum*
FERNHAM (St John the Evangelist) *see* Shrivenham and
Ashbury *Ox*
FERNHURST (St Margaret), Lynchmere and Camelsdale
Chich 3   **P** *The Crown and Bp (alt)*   **V** N P HAIGH
FERNILEE (Holy Trinity) *see* Whaley Bridge *Ches*
FERRIBY, NORTH (All Saints) *York 14*   **P** *CPAS*
V M C BRAILSFORD   **NSM** A C YOUNG
FERRIBY, SOUTH (St Nicholas) *Linc 8*   **P** *Bp*   **R** D P ROWETT
FERRING (St Andrew) *Chich 7*   **P** *D&C*   **V** G S INGRAM
FERRYBRIDGE (St Andrew) *Leeds 15*   **P** *D&C York*
P-in-c S L BROWN   **NSM** S HULME
FERRYHILL (St Luke) *see* Cornforth and Ferryhill *Dur*
FERSFIELD (St Andrew) *see* Diss *Nor*
FETCHAM (St Mary) *Guildf 10*   **P** *Bp*   **R** P HEIDARI
C J K PARTRIDGE
FEWSTON (St Michael and St Lawrence) *see* Washburn and
Mid-Wharfe *Leeds*
FIDDINGTON (St Martin) *see* Quantock Coast *B & W*
FIELD BROUGHTON (St Peter) *see* Cartmel Peninsula *Carl*
FIELD DALLING (St Andrew) *see* Stiffkey and Bale *Nor*

FIFEHEAD MAGDALEN (St Mary Magdalene) *see* Stour Vale
Sarum
FIFEHEAD NEVILLE (All Saints) *see* Hazelbury Bryan and the
Hillside Par *Sarum*
FIFIELD (St John the Baptist) *see* Wychwood *Ox*
FIFIELD BAVANT (St Martin) *see* Chalke Valley *Sarum*
FIGHELDEAN (St Michael and All Angels) *see* Avon River
Sarum
FILBY (All Saints) *see* S Trin Broads *Nor*
FILEY (St John) (St Oswald) *York 15*   **P** *PCC*
V N L CHAPMAN   **NSM** J R H WARING
FILKINS (St Peter) *see* Shill Valley and Broadshire *Ox*
FILLEIGH (St Paul) *see* S Molton w Nymet St George,
Chittlehamholt etc *Ex*
FILLINGHAM (St Andrew) *see* Springline *Linc*
FILLONGLEY (St Mary and All Saints) and Corley *Cov 5*
P *Bp and Ch Soc Trust (jt)*   **V** A J MASSEY
FILTON (St Gregory) *see* Horfield St Greg *Bris*
FILTON (St Peter) *Bris 5*   **P** *Bp*   **R** E L A GREGORY
FILWOOD PARK (St Barnabas) *Bris 1*   **P** *Bp and Bris Ch
Trustees (jt)*   **V** C L GARDINER
FIMBER (St Mary) *see* Waggoners *York*
FINBOROUGH, GREAT (St Andrew) *see* Combs and
Finborough *St E*
FINBOROUGH, LITTLE (St Mary) *as above*
FINCHAM (St Martin) *see* W Norfolk Priory Gp *Ely*
FINCHAMPSTEAD (St James) and California *Ox 8*   **P** *DBP*
R L C ONUGHA   **C** A ELLIOTT, J W MCALLEN
**FINCHINGFIELD (St John the Baptist) and Cornish Hall End
and Wethersfield w Shalford** *Chelmsf 16*   **P** *CPAS and Bp
(alt)*   **P-in-c** A D J SHANNON
FINCHLEY (Christ Church) *Lon 14*   **P** *Ch Patr Trust*
V D A WALKER
FINCHLEY (Holy Trinity) *Lon 15*   **P** *Bp*   **P-in-c** M MIRT
FINCHLEY (St Barnabas) *see* Woodside Park St Barn *Lon*
FINCHLEY (St Mary) *Lon 14*   **P** *Bp*   **R** P A DAVISON
C R D MAGRATH
FINCHLEY (St Paul) (St Luke) *Lon 14*   **P** *Simeon Trustees and
Ch Patr Trust (jt)*   **V** N R PYE
FINCHLEY, EAST (All Saints) *Lon 14*   **P** *Bp*   **V** I N CHANDLER
FINDERN (All Saints) *Derby 7*   **P** *Bp*   **V** *vacant*
FINDON (St John the Baptist) w Clapham and Patching
Chich 7   **P** *Abp, Bp, and C C F Somerset Esq (jt)*
V H M BUQUÉ   **NSM** C J COX
FINDON VALLEY (All Saints) *Chich 7*   **P** *Bp*   **V** *vacant*
FINEDON (St Mary the Virgin) *Pet 8*   **P** *Bp*   **V** R K R COLES
FINGEST (St Bartholomew) *see* Hambleden Valley *Ox*
FINGHALL (St Andrew) *see* Lower Wensleydale *Leeds*
**FINGRINGHOE (St Andrew) w East Donyland and
Abberton w Langenhoe** *Chelmsf 23*   **P** *Bp (3 turns), Ld
Chan (1 turn)*   **R** *vacant*
FINHAM (St Martin in the Fields) *Cov 3*   **P** *Bp*
V M T TAYLOR   **C** A L RHODES
FINMERE (St Michael) *see* Shelswell *Ox*
FINNINGHAM (St Bartholomew) *see* Badwell and Walsham
St E
FINNINGLEY (Holy Trinity and St Oswald) w Auckley *Sheff 9*
P *Bp*   **R** N M REDEYOFF   **C** C J LEE
FINSBURY (St Clement) (St Barnabas) (St Matthew) *Lon 6*
P *D&C St Paul's*   **V** D E ALLEN   **NSM** V E DAVIES
FINSBURY PARK (St Saviour) *see* Hanley Road *Lon*
FINSBURY PARK (St Thomas) *Lon 6*   **P** *Abp*   **V** *vacant*
FINSTALL (St Godwald) *see* Bromsgrove *Worc*
FINSTHWAITE (St Peter) *see* Cartmel Peninsula *Carl*
FINSTOCK (Holy Trinity) *see* Forest Edge *Ox*
FIR VALE (St Cuthbert) *see* Sheff St Cuth *Sheff*
FIRBANK (St John the Evangelist) *see* Western Dales *Carl*
FIRBECK (St Martin) w Letwell *Sheff 5*   **P** *Bp*   **R** *vacant*
FIRLE, WEST (St Peter) *see* Glynde, W Firle and Beddingham
Chich
FIRSBY (St Andrew) *see* Bolingbroke Deanery *Linc*
FIRSWOOD (St Hilda) and Gorse Hill *Man 2*   **P** *The Crown*
R T R MALKIN   **C** J JARRETT
FISHBOURNE, NEW (St Peter and St Mary) *Chich 2*   **P** *Ld
Chan*   **R** *vacant*
FISHBURN (St Catherine) *see* Upper Skerne *Dur*
FISHERMEAD (Trinity Church) *see* Woughton *Ox*
FISHERTON ANGER (St Paul) *Sarum 13*   **P** *Ch Patr Trust*
R C J RYALLS   **NSM** A ETHERIDGE
**FISHLAKE (St Cuthbert) w Sykehouse and Kirk Bramwith
w Fenwick and Moss** *Sheff 10*   **P** *Duchy of Lanc (1 turn),
D&C Dur (2 turns), and Bp (1 turn)*   **P-in-c** J M S JONES
FISHLEY (St Mary) *see* Broadside *Nor*
FISHPOND (St John the Baptist) *see* Golden Cap Team *Sarum*
FISHPONDS (St John) *see* Bris St Aid w St Geo, Fishponds
St Jo, and Two Mile Hill *Bris*

FISHPONDS (All Saints) (St Mary) *Bris 3* **P** *Bp*
  V E A KESTEVEN **C** D M SIMMS, J A S HILLER
FISHTOFT (St Guthlac) *Linc 21* **P** *DBP* **R** M A R COOPER
FISKERTON (St Clement) *see* S Lawres Gp *Linc*
FITTLETON (All Saints) *see* Avon River *Sarum*
FITTLEWORTH (St Mary the Virgin) *see* Stopham and
  Fittleworth *Chich*
FITTON HILL (St Cuthbert) *see* Bardsley *Man*
FITZ (St Peter and St Paul) *see* Bicton, Montford w
  Shrawardine and Fitz *Lich*
FITZHEAD (St James) *see* Milverton w Halse, Fitzhead and
  Ash Priors *B & W*
FIVE ALIVE *see* Fladbury, Hill and Moor, Wyre Piddle etc
  Worc
FIVE ASHES (Church of the Good Shepherd) *see* Mayfield
  Chich
FIVE OAK GREEN (St Luke) *see* Capel United Ben *Roch*
FIVEFOLDS *see* 5folds *Ely*
FIVEHEAD (St Martin) *see* Curry Rivel w Fivehead and Swell
  B & W
FIXBY (St Francis) and Cowcliffe, Huddersfield *Leeds 9*
  P *DBP* **P-in-c** I D JAMIESON
FLACKWELL HEATH (Christ Church) *Ox 18* **P** *DBP*
  C I J KNIGHT **OLM** M H COURTNEY
**FLADBURY (St John the Baptist), Hill and Moor, Wyre
  Piddle, Cropthorne and Charlton** *Worc 3* **P** *Bp and D&C*
  (jt) **P-in-c** S A DANGERFIELD **C** E L GOLDBY, G R NOYES
FLAMBOROUGH (St Oswald) *see* Bempton w Flamborough,
  Reighton w Speeton *York*
FLAMSTEAD (St Leonard) and Markyate Street *St Alb 7*
  P *Bp and Univ Coll Ox (jt)* **V** vacant
FLAUNDEN (St Mary Magdalene) *see* Chenies and Lt
  Chalfont, Latimer and Flaunden *Ox*
FLAX BOURTON (St Michael and All Angels) *see* Long
  Ashton w Barrow Gurney and Flax Bourton *B & W*
FLAXLEY (St Mary the Virgin) *see* Westbury-on-Severn w
  Flaxley, Blaisdon etc *Glouc*
FLAXTON (St Lawrence) *see* Harton *York*
FLECKNEY (St Nicholas) *see* Wistow *Leic*
FLECKNOE (St Mark) *see* Leam Valley *Cov*
FLEET (All Saints) (St Philip and St James) *Guildf 1* **P** *Bp*
  V M W HAYTON **C** C M L BURCH
FLEET (Holy Trinity) *see* Chickerell w Fleet *Sarum*
FLEET (St Mary Magdalene) *see* Mid Elloe Gp *Linc*
FLEETWOOD (St Nicholas) *Blackb 12* **P** *Bp and SMF (jt)*
  V C A LEITCH
FLEETWOOD (St Peter) (St David's Church Centre)
  Blackb 12 **P** *SMF* **V** J M HALL
**FLEGG COASTAL Benefice, The: Hemsby, Winterton, East
  and West Somerton and Horsey** *Nor 6* **P** *Bp, D&C, SMF,
  and Major R A Ferrier (jt)* **P-in-c** J S BLOOMFIELD
FLEGG GROUP (Martham) *see* Martham and Repps w
  Bastwick, Thurne etc *Nor*
FLEGG GROUP (Ormesby) *see* Ormesby St Marg w Scratby,
  Ormesby St Mich etc *Nor*
FLEGG GROUP (South Trinity Broads) *see* S Trin Broads
  Nor
FLEGGBURGH *as above*
FLEMPTON (St Catherine of Alexandria) *see* Lark Valley and
  N Bury *St E*
FLETCHAMSTEAD (St James) *Cov 3* **P** *Bp* **V** S R BURCH
FLETCHING (St Mary and St Andrew) *Chich 18* **P** *Abp*
  V D A KNIGHT
FLETTON (St Margaret) *Ely 15* **P** *Sir Philip Naylor-Leyland Bt*
  R vacant
FLIMBY (St Nicholas) *see* Maryport, Netherton, Flimby and
  Broughton Moor *Carl*
FLIMWELL (St Augustine of Canterbury) *see* Ticehurst and
  Flimwell *Chich*
FLINTHAM (St Augustine of Canterbury) *S'well 5* **P** *R H T
  Hildyard Esq* **P-in-c** R M COLBY
FLITCHAM (St Mary the Virgin) *see* Sandringham w W
  Newton and Appleton etc *Nor*
FLITTON (St John the Baptist) *see* Silsoe, Pulloxhill and
  Flitton *St Alb*
FLITWICK (St Andrew) (St Peter and St Paul) *St Alb 8*
  P *DBP* **V** vacant
FLIXBOROUGH (All Saints) w Burton upon Stather *Linc 6*
  P *Sir Reginald Sheffield Bt* **V** vacant
FLIXTON (St John) *Man 2* **P** *Bp* **P-in-c** D J BLAIR
  C N E WATSON **OLM** R W GREEN
FLIXTON (St Mary) *see* The Saints *St E*
FLIXTON (St Michael) *Man 2* **P** *Bp* **P-in-c** H D THOMAS
  OLM F A JENKINSON
FLOCKTON (St James the Great) *see* Lepton, Emley and
  Flockton w Denby Grange *Leeds*

FLOOKBURGH (St John the Baptist) *see* Cartmel Peninsula
  Carl
FLORDON (St Michael) *see* Mulbarton w Bracon Ash, Hethel
  and Flordon *Nor*
FLORE (All Saints) *see* Heyford w Stowe Nine Churches and
  Flore etc *Pet*
FLOWTON (St Mary) *see* S Bosmere *St E*
FLUSHING (St Peter) *see* Mylor w Flushing *Truro*
FLYFORD FLAVELL (St Peter) *see* Abberton, The Flyfords,
  Naunton Beauchamp etc *Worc*
FOBBING (St Michael) *see* Corringham and Fobbing *Chelmsf*
FOLESHILL (St Laurence) Coventry *Cov 2* **P** *Ld Chan*
  V G I IRVINE **C** J S SAMUEL **NSM** J A IRVINE
FOLESHILL (St Paul) Coventry *Cov 2* **P** *Ld Chan*
  V A HOGGER-GADSBY
FOLEY PARK (Holy Innocents) *see* Kidderminster St Jo and H
  Innocents *Worc*
FOLKE (St Lawrence) *see* Three Valleys *Sarum*
**FOLKESTONE (St Augustine) (St Mary and St Eanswythe)
  St Saviour** *Cant 8* **P** *Abp* **P-in-c** J A P WALKER
FOLKESTONE (St John the Baptist) *Cant 8* **P** *CPAS*
  V A S DENLEY
FOLKESTONE (St Peter) *Cant 8* **P** *Trustees*
  P-in-c M V HALDON-JONES
**FOLKESTONE Trinity Benefice, The (Holy Trinity w Christ
  Church) (St George) (St Paul)** *Cant 8* **P** *Abp and Ld Chan
  (alt)* **V** R P WELDON **NSM** R O SMITH
FOLKESWORTH (St Helen) *see* Stilton w Denton and
  Caldecote etc *Ely*
FOLKINGHAM (St Andrew) *see* S Lafford *Linc*
FOLKINGTON (St Peter ad Vincula) *see* Alfriston w
  Lullington, Litlington, W Dean and Folkington *Chich*
FOLKTON (St John) *see* Hertford *York*
FOLLIFOOT (St Joseph and St James) *see* Spofforth w Kirk
  Deighton *Leeds*
FONTHILL BISHOP (All Saints) *see* Nadder Valley *Sarum*
FONTHILL GIFFORD (Holy Trinity) *as above*
FONTMELL MAGNA (St Andrew) *see* Iwerne Valley *Sarum*
FOOLOW (St Hugh) *see* Baslow and Eyam *Derby*
FOORD (St John the Baptist) *see* Folkestone St Jo *Cant*
FOOTSCRAY (All Saints) *see* Sidcup St Jo w Footscray *Roch*
FORCETT (St Cuthbert) and Aldbrough and Melsonby
  Leeds 19 **P** *DBP and Univ Coll Ox (alt)*
  R C A CAMPLING-DENTON
FORD (St Andrew) *see* Clymping and Yapton w Ford *Chich*
FORD (St John of Jerusalem) *see* Leominster *Heref*
FORD (St Mark) *see* Devonport St Bart and Ford St Mark *Ex*
FORD (St Michael and All Angels) and Etal *Newc 12* **P** *Lord
  Joicey* **P-in-c** C E OSBORN
**FORD (St Michael), Gt Wollaston and Alberbury w
  Cardeston** *Heref 12* **P** *Bp (3 turns), Sir Michael Leighton Bt
  (1 turn)* **R** G S ROBERTS **OLM** M E NEAL
FORD END (St John the Evangelist) *see* Gt Waltham w Ford
  End *Chelmsf*
FORDCOMBE (St Peter) *see* Penshurst, Fordcombe and the
  Chiddingstone Chs *Roch*
FORDHAM (All Saints) *Chelmsf 20* **P** *Reformation Ch Trust,
  Ball Coll Ox (alt)* **R** F C BLIGHT
FORDHAM (St Peter and St Mary Magdalene) *see* Three
  Rivers Gp *Ely*
FORDHOUSES (St James) *see* Bushbury *Lich*
**FORDINGBRIDGE (St Mary) and Hyde and Breamore and
  Hale with Woodgreen** *Win 9* **P** *K Coll Cam, Keble Coll Ox,
  Sir Edward Hulse Bt, and Mrs C R d'O Hickman (jt)*
  R G J PHILBRICK **C** T BURDEN
FORDON (St James) *see* Rudston, Boynton, Carnaby etc *York*
FOREMARK (St Saviour) and Repton w Newton Solney
  Derby 7 **P** *Bp and DBP (jt)* **V** M J FLOWERDEW
  OLM J C SCOTT
FOREST (St Stephen) *see* Rainow w Saltersford and Forest
  Ches
**FOREST AND AVON, comprising Bramshaw, Downton,
  Landford, Morgan's Vale, Plaitford, and Redlynch** *Sarum 10*
  P *Patr Bd* **TV** D G BACON **NSM** V BATCHELOR
FOREST EDGE *see* Huntley and Longhope, Churcham and
  Bulley *Glouc*
**FOREST EDGE, comprising Finstock w Fawler, Leafield w
  Wychwood, Ramsden, and Wilcote** *Ox 22* **P** *Bp, V
  Charlbury, and Sir Mark Norman Bt (jt)* **V** P J MANSELL
FOREST GATE (All Saints) *Chelmsf 5* **P** *Bp* **P-in-c** J S FRASER
  C M G P BENNETT **NSM** F ASHFORD-OKAI
FOREST GATE (Emmanuel w St Peter) Upton Cross
  Chelmsf 5 **P** *Bp* **V** C CHIKE **OLM** A SUBARAN
FOREST GATE (St Edmund) *see* E Ham H Trin *Chelmsf*
FOREST GATE (St James) *see* Stratford St Jo w Ch Ch *Chelmsf*

FOREST GATE (St Mark) *Chelmsf 5*   **P** *Ch Patr Trust*
   V B W KING

FOREST GATE (St Saviour) (St James) *Chelmsf 5*   **P** *CPAS*
   V C A HENRY   **NSM** J A BRAITHWAITE

FOREST GREEN (Holy Trinity) *see* Ewhurst w Okewood and
   Forest Green *Guildf*

FOREST HEATH Team Ministry, The, comprising Barton
   Mills, Beck Row w Kenny Hill, Dalham, Eriswell,
   Freckenham, Gazeley, Higham Green, Icklingham, Kentford,
   Mildenhall, Moulton, Tuddenham w Cavenham,
   Herringswell and Red Lodge, West Row and Worlington
   St E 7   **P** *Patr Bd*   **TV** C CHILDS, D A BUTCHER, D J EVERETT,
   S M LEATHLEY   **C** R MOLTON   **NSM** C BUTCHER

FOREST HILL (Christ Church) (St George) w Lower
   Sydenham St Michael and All Angels *S'wark 5*   **P** *Patr Bd*
   P-in-c R P LANE   **TV** I E C CHUKUKA

FOREST HILL (St Nicholas) *see* Beckley, Forest Hill,
   Horton-cum-Studley and Stanton St John *Ox*

FOREST OF DEAN (Christ Church) w English Bicknor
   Glouc 1   **P** *The Crown (3 turns), SMF (1 turn)*
   R A J WILLIAMS

FOREST OF DEAN (Holy Trinity) *see* Drybrook, Lydbrook and
   Ruardean *Glouc*

FOREST OF GALTRES (Farlington, Marton w Moxby, Sheriff
   Hutton, and Sutton-on-the-Forest) *York 3*   **P** *Abp (2*
   turns), Ld Chan (1 turn)   **P-in-c** S WHITING   **C** D M COYNE,
   M E YOUNG, M HARRISON   **NSM** C C CRANFIELD,
   C C GITTENS, C J TOASE, T M GANT

FOREST ROW (Holy Trinity) *Chich 9*   **P** V E Grinstead
   V A F MARTIN

FOREST TOWN (St Alban) *S'well 2*   **P** *Bp*   **P-in-c** P J STEAD

FOREST-IN-TEESDALE (St Mary the Virgin) *see* Middleton-in-
   Teesdale w Forest and Frith *Dur*

FORESTSIDE (Christ Church) *see* Octagon *Chich*

FORMBY (Holy Trinity) and Altcar *Liv 8*   **P** *Bp and Trustees*
   (jt)   **V** M R STANFORD   **NSM** D C M TAYLOR

FORMBY (St Luke) *Liv 8*   **P** *Bp*   **V** M W DAVIS

FORMBY (St Peter) *Liv 8*   **P** R Walton   **V** A E TAYLOR
   C S M J MACAULAY

FORNCETT (St Mary) *see* Upper Tas Valley *Nor*

FORNCETT (St Peter) *as above*

FORNCETT END (St Edmund) *as above*

FORNHAM ALL SAINTS (All Saints) *see* Lark Valley and N
   Bury *St E*

FORNHAM ST MARTIN (St Martin) *as above*

FORRABURY (St Symphorian) *see* Boscastle Gp *Truro*

FORSBROOK (St Peter) *see* Draycott-le-Moors w Forsbrook
   Lich

FORTHAMPTON (St Mary) *see* Deerhurst and Apperley w
   Forthampton etc *Glouc*

FORTON (All Saints) *Lich 15*   **P** *Bp*   **P-in-c** P W THOMAS
   Hon C W E WARD

FORTON (St James) *see* Shireshead *Blackb*

FORTON (St John the Evangelist), Gosport Christ Church
   and Gosport Holy Trinity *Portsm 3*   **P** *Patr Bd*
   TR A J WOOD   **TV** G CHIGUMIRA, R D C DRISCOLL

FORTY HILL (Jesus Church) *Lon 16*   **P** V Enfield
   V I H CROFTS

FOSDYKE (All Saints) *see* Kirton in Holland w Algarkirk and
   Fosdyke *Linc*

FOSSE Team, The, comprising Barkby, East Goscote,
   Queniborough, Rearsby, Syston, Thrussington w Ratcliffe on
   the Wreake, and Thurmaston *Leic 4*   **P** *Patr Bd*
   TV M C A'HERNE-SMITH, T R DAY   **Hon C** C T DOLBY
   NSM B F SAUNDERS, I M HILL

FOSSE TRINITY, comprising Ditcheat, East Pennard, and Pylle
   B & W 7   **P** *Bp and Canon D S Salter (jt)*   **R** *vacant*

FOSTON (All Saints) *see* Harton *York*

FOSTON (St Bartholomew) *see* Four Saints *Leic*

FOSTON (St Peter) *see* Saxonwell *Linc*

FOSTON-ON-THE-WOLDS (St Andrew) *see* Beeford w
   Frodingham and Foston *York*

FOTHERBY (St Mary), North Thoresby and Grainsby w
   Waithe *Linc 15*   **P** *Ld Chan (2 turns), R H C Haigh Esq,*
   Trustees, and Adn Linc (1 turn), DBP, G F Sleight Esq, MMCET,
   and Bp (2 turns), R H C Haigh Esq, Trustees and Exors Mrs M F
   Davis (1 turn)   **V** *vacant*

FOTHERINGHAY (St Mary and All Saints) *see* Warmington,
   Tansor and Cotterstock etc *Pet*

FOULDEN (All Saints) *see* Oxborough w Foulden and
   Caldecote *Nor*

FOULRIDGE (St Michael and All Angels), Laneshawbridge
   and Trawden *Blackb 6*   **P** *Bp and DBP*   **R** J W KNOTT

FOULSHAM (Holy Innocents) *see* Heart of Norfolk *Nor*

FOUNTAINS Group, The, comprising Aldfield, Dallowgill,
   Grewelthorpe, Kirkby Malzeard, Mickley, Sawley, and

Winksley *Leeds 20*   **P** *D&C Ripon*   **P-in-c** I B KITCHEN
   NSM K COUCHMAN

FOUR ELMS (St Paul) *see* Hever, Four Elms and Mark Beech
   Roch

FOUR MARKS (Good Shepherd) *Win 2*   **P** *Bp*
   V H J D WRIGHT   **C** J V ROOKE

FOUR OAKS (All Saints) *Birm 4*   **P** *Bp*   **V** D A LEAHY

FOUR RIVERS, comprising Bedfield, Brundish, Cratfield,
   Laxfield, Monk Soham, Tannington, Wilby, and
   Worlingworth w Southolt *St E 11*   **P** *Bp, Dr F H C Marriott,*
   Simeon's Trustees, R C Rouse, and DBP (jt)   **R** D P BURRELL
   NSM C M SMART, D J MULRENAN, R J ARTISS

FOUR SAINTS Benefice, The, comprising Countesthorpe,
   Foston, Peatling Magna, and Willoughby Waterleys *Leic 7*
   P *Bp and DBP (jt)*   **R** R F REAKES   **C** J S HOVER

FOUR SAINTS Team, The *see* 4Saints Team *Liv*

FOUR VILLAGES *see* Bideford, Landcross, Littleham etc *Ex*

FOURSTONES (St Aidan) *see* Warden w Newbrough *Newc*

FOVANT (St George), Sutton Mandeville and Teffont Evias
   w Teffont Magna and Compton Chamberlayne *Sarum 11*
   P *Reformation Ch Trust, Bp, and Ch Soc Trust (jt)*   **R** *vacant*

FOWEY (St Fimbarrus) *Truro 7*   **P** *Ch Soc Trust*   **V** *vacant*

FOWLMERE (St Mary), Foxton, Shepreth and Thriplow
   Ely 7   **P** *Bp*   **R** A E MELANIPHY   **C** D J LEE

FOWNHOPE (St Mary) w Mordiford, Brockhampton and
   Woolhope *Heref 5*   **P** *D&C (4 turns), and J N Hereford Esq (1*
   turn)   **R** C K W MOORE

FOXCOTE (St James the Less) *see* Peasedown St John w
   Wellow and Foxcote etc *B & W*

FOXDALE (St Paul) *see* Marown, Foxdale and Baldwin *S & M*

FOXEARTH (St Peter and St Paul) *see* N Hinckford *Chelmsf*

FOXHAM (St John the Baptist) *see* Marden Vale *Sarum*

FOXHILL (Chapel) *see* Frodsham *Ches*

FOXHOLE (St Boniface) *see* Paignton St Jo, St Andr and
   St Boniface *Ex*

FOXLEY (not known) *see* Gauzebrook *Bris*

FOXLEY (St Thomas) *see* Heart of Norfolk *Nor*

FOXT (St Mark the Evangelist) *see* Kingsley and Foxt-w-
   Whiston and Oakamoor etc *Lich*

FOXTON (St Andrew) w Gumley and Laughton *Leic 3*   **P** *Bp*
   Leic and D&C Linc (alt)   **P-in-c** P J OXLEY

FOXTON (St Laurence) *see* Fowlmere, Foxton, Shepreth and
   Thriplow *Ely*

FOY (St Mary) *see* StowCaple *Heref*

FRADLEY (St Stephen) *see* Alrewas *Lich*

FRADSWELL (St James the Less) *see* Mid Trent *Lich*

FRAMFIELD (St Thomas à Becket) *Chich 18*   **P** *Mrs E R Wix*
   V C D LAWRENCE

FRAMILODE (St Peter) *see* Stroudwater *Glouc*

FRAMINGHAM EARL (St Andrew) *see* Poringland *Nor*

FRAMINGHAM PIGOT (St Andrew) *see* Thurton w Ashby
   St Mary, Bergh Apton etc *Nor*

FRAMLAND Parishes, The HIGH, comprising Branston-by-
   Belvoir, Croxton Kerrial, Harston, Knipton, Saltby, and
   Sproxton *Leic 2*   **P** *Duke of Rutland and Sir Lyonel Tollemache*
   Bt (jt)   **P-in-c** D J COWIE

FRAMLAND, SOUTH, comprising Buckminster, Coston, Saxby
   w Stapleford and Wyfordby, and Wymondham *Leic 2*   **P** *Ld*
   Chan, Duke of Rutland, Lady Gretton, and Sir Lyonel
   Tollemache Bt (by turn)   **P-in-c** D J COWIE

FRAMLINGHAM (St Michael) w Saxtead *St E 12*   **P** *Pemb*
   Coll Cam   **P-in-c** C M DAVEY

FRAMPTON (St Mary) *see* Charminster, Stinsford and the
   Chalk Stream villages *Sarum*

FRAMPTON (St Mary) (St Michael) *Linc 21*   **P** *Trustees*
   V S SARVANANTHAN

FRAMPTON COTTERELL (St Peter) *see* Fromeside *Bris*

FRAMPTON MANSELL (St Luke) *see* Kemble, Poole Keynes,
   Somerford Keynes etc *Glouc*

FRAMPTON ON SEVERN (St Mary) *see* Stroudwater *Glouc*

FRAMSDEN (St Mary) *see* Debenham and Helmingham *St E*

FRAMWELLGATE MOOR (St Aidan) *see* Dur N *Dur*

FRANCE LYNCH (St John the Baptist) *see* Bisley, Chalford,
   France Lynch, and Oakridge etc *Glouc*

FRANCHE (St Barnabas) *see* Kidderminster Ismere *Worc*

FRANKBY (St John the Divine) w Greasby St Nicholas
   Ches 8   **P** *D&C*   **V** K P OWEN   **C** J D SEDANO

FRANKLEY (St Leonard) *Birm 2*   **P** *Bp*   **P-in-c** J M PLATT

FRANKTON (St Nicholas) *see* Draycote Gp *Cov*

FRANSHAM, GREAT (All Saints) *see* Launditch and the Upper
   Nar *Nor*

FRANSHAM, LITTLE (St Mary) *as above*

FRANT (St Alban) w Eridge *Chich 16*   **P** *Bp and Marquess of*
   Abergavenny (jt)   **R** B J MARTIN   **NSM** I A J TRASK

FREASLEY (St Mary) *see* Dordon *Birm*

FRECHEVILLE (St Cyprian) *Sheff 1*   **P** *Bp*   **R** *vacant*

FRECKENHAM (St Andrew) *see* Forest Heath *St E*
FRECKLETON (Holy Trinity) and Warton St Paul *Blackb 10*
  P *Bp and Ch Ch Ox (jt)* **V** J GREENHALGH **NSM** F E HAINES
FREEBY (St Mary) *see* Melton Mowbray *Leic*
FREEHAY (St Chad) *see* Cheadle w Freehay *Lich*
FREELAND (St Mary the Virgin) *see* Hanborough and
  Freeland *Ox*
FREEMANTLE (Christ Church) *Win 13* **P** *Bp* **R** *vacant*
FREETHORPE (All Saints) *see* Acle and Bure to Yare *Nor*
**FREISTON (St Peter), Butterwick w Bennington, and
  Leverton** *Linc 21* **P** *Ld Chan and Bp (alt)*
  P-in-c A J HIGGINSON
FREMINGTON (St Peter), Instow and Westleigh *Ex 13*
  P *D&C, Christie Trustees, and MMCET (jt)* **R** S J SPANKIE
FRENCHAY (St John the Baptist) and Stapleton *Bris 5* **P** *Bp*
  and St Jo Coll Ox (jt) **R** C E SUGDEN **C** R M HARDING
  NSM J M LEE
FRENSHAM (St Mary the Virgin) *Guildf 3* **P** *Ld Chan*
  V J L WALKER
**FRESHFORD (St Peter) w Limpley Stoke and Hinton
  Charterhouse** *B & W 8* **P** *Simeon's Trustees and V Norton
  St Phil (jt)* **P-in-c** M S TAYLOR
FRESHWATER (All Saints) *see* W Wight *Portsm*
FRESHWATER BAY (St Agnes) *as above*
FRESSINGFIELD (St Peter and St Paul) *see* Sancroft *St E*
FRESTON (St Peter) *see* Holbrook, Stutton, Freston,
  Woolverstone etc *St E*
FRETHERNE (St Mary the Virgin) *see* Stroudwater *Glouc*
FRETTENHAM (St Swithin) *see* Coltishall w Gt Hautbois,
  Frettenham etc *Nor*
FRIAR PARK (St Francis of Assisi) *see* W Bromwich St Fran
  Lich
FRIARMERE (St Thomas) *see* Saddleworth *Man*
FRICKLEY (All Saints) *see* Bilham *Sheff*
FRIDAY BRIDGE (St Mark) *see* Fen Orchards *Ely*
FRIDAYTHORPE (St Mary) *see* Waggoners *York*
FRIERN BARNET (All Saints) *Lon 14* **P** *Bp*
  P-in-c K QUAK-WINSLOW **C** R J WILKINSON
  NSM D J BOOKER, H LAMB
**FRIERN BARNET (St James the Great) (St John the
  Evangelist)** *Lon 14* **P** *D&C St Paul's* **R** D L V WILKINSON
FRIERN BARNET (St Peter le Poer) *Lon 14* **P** *D&C St Paul's*
  P-in-c P H SUDELL **NSM** H C HENDRY
FRIESTHORPE (St Peter) *see* Middle Rasen Gp *Linc*
FRIETH (St John the Baptist) *see* Hambleden Valley *Ox*
FRIEZLAND (Christ Church) *see* Saddleworth *Man*
FRILSHAM (St Frideswide) *see* Hermitage *Ox*
FRIMLEY (St Francis) (St Peter) *Guildf 6* **P** *R Ash*
  R S G THOMAS **OLM** G E C SHORTLAND
FRIMLEY GREEN (St Andrew) and Mytchett *Guildf 6* **P** *Bp*
  V S V MENON
FRINDSBURY (All Saints) w Upnor and Chattenden *Roch 6*
  P *Bp* **V** N J COOPER **C** S F VALLENTE-KERR
FRING (All Saints) *see* Docking, The Birchams, Fring etc *Nor*
FRINGFORD (St Michael) *see* Shelswell *Ox*
FRINSTED (St Dunstan) *see* Tunstall and Bredgar *Cant*
**FRINTON (St Mary Magdalene) (St Mary the Virgin Old
  Church)** *Chelmsf 22* **P** *CPAS* **R** D E SMITH **Hon C** L BOND
FRISBY-ON-THE-WREAKE (St Thomas of Canterbury) *see*
  Upper Wreake *Leic*
FRISKNEY (All Saints) *Linc 21* **P** *Bp* **V** *vacant*
FRISTON (St Mary Magdalene) *see* Alde Sandlings *St E*
FRISTON (St Mary the Virgin) *see* E Dean w Friston and
  Jevington *Chich*
FRITHELSTOCK (St Mary and St Gregory) *see* Gt and Lt
  Torrington and Frithelstock *Ex*
FRITHVILLE (St Peter) *see* Sibsey w Frithville *Linc*
FRITTENDEN (St Mary) *see* Sissinghurst w Frittenden *Cant*
FRITTON (St Catherine) *see* Hempnall *Nor*
FRITTON (St Edmund) *see* Somerleyton, Ashby, Fritton,
  Herringfleet etc *Nor*
FRITWELL (St Olave) *see* Cherwell Valley *Ox*
FRIZINGHALL (St Margaret) *Leeds 2* **P** *Bp* **V** *vacant*
FRIZINGTON (St Paul) *see* Crosslacon *Carl*
FROCESTER (St Andrew) *see* Stroudwater *Glouc*
FRODESLEY (St Mark) *see* Condover w Frodesley, Acton
  Burnell etc *Heref*
FRODINGHAM (St Lawrence) and New Brumby *Linc 6*
  P *Lord St Oswald* **V** P BRENT **C** J MILES, L A E COCKRAM,
  S TIERNEY
FRODINGHAM, NORTH (St Elgin) *see* Beeford w Frodingham
  and Foston *York*
FRODSHAM (St Lawrence) *Ches 3* **P** *Ch Ch Ox* **V** E ATACK
FROGMORE (Holy Trinity) *St Alb 5* **P** *CPAS* **V** N J WEIR
  NSM N A WARD
FROLESWORTH (St Nicholas) *see* Upper Soar *Leic*

FROME (Christ Church) (St Mary) *B & W 3* **P** *Bp*
  V E A DUDLEY
FROME (Holy Trinity) *B & W 3* **P** *Bp* **V** *vacant*
FROME (St John the Baptist) *B & W 3* **P** *DBP* **V** C ALSBURY
FROME ST QUINTON (St Mary) *see* Melbury *Sarum*
FROME VALLEY Group of Parishes, The, comprising Acton
  Beauchamp, Bishops Frome, Castle Frome, Evesbatch,
  Fromes Hill, Much Cowarne, Ocle Pychard, and Stanford
  Bishop *Heref 2* **P** *Bp (6 turns), MMCET (2 turns), D&C (1
  turn)* **V** S BAGGS **C** R J ALLAWAY
FROME VAUCHURCH (St Mary) *see* Melbury *Sarum*
FROMES HILL (St Matthew) *see* Frome Valley *Heref*
FROMESIDE, comprising Frampton Cotterell, Iron Acton,
  Winterbourne, and Winterbourne Down *Bris 5* **P** *SMF, Ch
  Ch Ox, and St Jo Coll Ox (jt)* **R** M STRANGE **C** D G JONES,
  W K MORRIS **NSM** H V SMITH **OLM** J C CHARD,
  J L HODGE, R CONWAY
FROSTENDEN (All Saints) *see* Wrentham, Covehithe w
  Benacre etc *St E*
FROXFIELD (All Saints) *see* Whitton *Sarum*
FROXFIELD (St Peter on the Green) *see* Steep and Froxfield w
  Privett *Portsm*
FROXFIELD (St Peter) *as above*
FROYLE (Assumption of the Blessed Virgin Mary) *see* Bentley,
  Binsted and Froyle *Win*
FRYERNING (St Mary the Virgin) *see* Ingatestone w Fryerning
  Chelmsf
FUGGLESTONE (St Peter) *see* Wilton w Netherhampton and
  Fugglestone *Sarum*
FULBECK (St Nicholas) *see* S Cliff Villages Gp *Linc*
FULBOURN (St Vigor w All Saints) *Ely 4* **P** *St Jo Coll Cam*
  R A A GOODMAN
FULBROOK (St James the Great) *see* Burford w Fulbrook,
  Taynton, Asthall etc *Ox*
FULFORD (St Oswald) *York 7* **P** *Abp* **P-in-c** S SHERIFF
FULFORD-IN-STONE (St Nicholas) w Hilderstone *Lich 12*
  P *D&C* **V** *vacant*
FULHAM (All Saints) *Lon 9* **P** *Bp* **V** P A SEABROOK
  C C G C MEYRICK, J N A MACNEANEY **NSM** A O ADELAJA
FULHAM (Christ Church) *Lon 9* **P** *CPAS* **V** S C R LEES
FULHAM (St Alban) (St Augustine) *Lon 9* **P** *Bp and City
  Corp (jt)* **V** *vacant*
FULHAM (St Andrew) Fulham Fields *Lon 9* **P** *Bp*
  V L A BILINDA **NSM** J A COWLEY
FULHAM (St Dionis) Parson's Green *Lon 9* **P** *Bp*
  V T J STILWELL **C** W R VAN DER HART **NSM** C GIBBS,
  L D M VAN DER HART
FULHAM (St Etheldreda) (St Clement) *Lon 9* **P** *Bp*
  V R GUNDERSON
FULHAM (St Mary) North End *Lon 9* **P** *Ch Soc Trust*
  P-in-c S G DOWNHAM
FULHAM (St Matthew) *Lon 9* **P** *Ch Patr Trust* **V** W J ROGERS
  C K MILLER **Dss** V S PIERSON
FULHAM (St Peter) *Lon 9* **P** *Bp* **V** R B C STANDRING
  C S DICKSON
FULKING (Good Shepherd) *see* Poynings w Edburton,
  Newtimber and Pyecombe *Chich*
FULL SUTTON (St Mary) *see* Garrowby Hill *York*
FULLBROOK (St Gabriel) *see* Walsall St Gabr Fulbrook *Lich*
FULLETBY (St Andrew) *see* Hemingby Gp *Linc*
FULMER (St James) *see* Gerrards Cross and Fulmer *Ox*
FULMODESTON (Christ Church) w Croxton *Nor 14* **P** *CCC
  Cam* **R** *vacant*
FULSHAW (St Anne) *see* Wilmslow *Ches*
FULSTOW (St Laurence) *see* Fotherby, N Thoresby and
  Grainsby w Waithe *Linc*
FULWELL (St Michael and St George) *Lon 10* **P** *Bp*
  V E J KENDALL **C** S D PEDLEY
FULWOOD (Christ Church) *Blackb 13* **P** *V Lanc*
  P-in-c C P BOLAND **C** E M MCLEAN
FULWOOD (Christ Church) *Sheff 4* **P** *CPAS*
  V P A WILLIAMS **C** A A FEARNLEY, M J LAWES, P F SCAMMAN,
  S G RAE
FULWOOD (St Cuthbert) *see* Preston St Cuth *Blackb*
FULWOOD Lodge Moor (St Luke) *see* Lodge Moor St Luke
  Sheff
FUNDENHALL (St Nicholas) *see* Upper Tas Valley *Nor*
FUNTINGTON (St Mary) and West Stoke w Sennicotts
  Chich 6 **P** *Bp* **P-in-c** A G J BIRKS
FUNTLEY (St Francis) *see* Fareham SS Pet and Paul *Portsm*
FURNACE GREEN (St Andrew) *Chich 9* **P** *CPAS*
  V R E POOLE
FURNESS VALE (St John) *see* Disley *Ches*
FURNEUX PELHAM (St Mary the Virgin) *see* Braughing,
  Furneux Pelham and Stocking Pelham *St Alb*

FURNHAM (Good Shepherd)   *see* Chard Gd Shep Furnham
B & W
FURZE PLATT (St Peter) *Ox 5*   **P** *Bp*   **V** D K SHORT
C C COOPER   **NSM** J E ELLINGTON
FURZEBANK (Worship Centre)   *see* Bentley Em and
Willenhall H Trin *Lich*
FURZEDOWN (St Paul) *S'wark 17*   **P** *Patr Bd*   **TR** R J POWELL
TV M S RICHEUX   **Hon C** G M VEVERS
FURZTON (not known)   *see* Watling Valley *Ox*
FYFIELD (St Nicholas)   *see* Appleshaw, Kimpton, Thruxton,
Fyfield etc *Win*
FYFIELD (St Nicholas)   *see* Upper Kennet *Sarum*
FYFIELD (St Nicholas) w Tubney and Kingston Bagpuize
Ox 19   **P** *St Jo Coll Ox*   **V** D A A PICKERING
FYFIELD (St Nicholas), Moreton w Bobbingworth and
Willingale w Shellow and Berners Roding *Chelmsf 3*
P *Ld Chan, St Jo Coll Cam, MMCET, and Major G N*
Capel-Cure (by turn)   **P-in-c** C A HAWKINS
FYLINGDALES (St Stephen) and Hawsker cum Stainsacre
York 21   **P** *Abp*   **V** S J SMALE
GADDESBY (St Luke)   *see* S Croxton Gp *Leic*
GADDESDEN, GREAT (St John the Baptist)   *see* Gt
Berkhamsted, Gt and Lt Gaddesden etc *St Alb*
GADDESDEN, LITTLE (St Peter and St Paul)   *as above*
GAINFORD (St Mary) *Dur 4*   **P** *Trin Coll Cam*
P-in-c E K G HARROP
GAINSBOROUGH (All Saints) (St George) and Morton
Linc 2   **P** *Bp*   **TR** S W JOHNSON   **C** E A JOHNSON
GALLEY COMMON (St Peter)   *see* Hartshill and Galley
Common *Cov*
GALLEYWOOD (Junior School Worship Centre)   *see*
Galleywood Common *Chelmsf*
GALLEYWOOD COMMON (St Michael and All Angels)
Chelmsf 9   **P** *CPAS*   **V** D J CATTLE   **C** G E FRASER,
S R GILLINGHAM
GALMINGTON (St Michael) *B & W 18*   **P** *Bp*
V J C RICHARDS   **C** T L POTTAGE
GALMPTON (Chapel of The Good Shepherd)   *see* Brixham w
Churston Ferrers and Kingswear *Ex*
GAMESLEY (Bishop Geoffrey Allen Church and County
Centre)   *see* Charlesworth and Gamesley *Derby*
GAMLINGAY (St Mary the Virgin) and Everton *Ely 13*
P *Bp, Clare Coll Cam, and Down Coll Cam (by turn)*
P-in-c H A F YOUNG
GAMSTON (St Luke) and Bridgford *S'well 6*   **P** *DBP*
V M A FRASER   **C** A D PERHAM, E CHARKHAM, J R MOLE
GANAREW (St Swithin)   *see* Wye Reaches Gp *Heref*
GANTON (St Nicholas)   *see* Hertford *York*
GARBOLDISHAM (St John the Baptist)   *see* Guiltcross *Nor*
GARFORD (St Luke)   *see* Marcham w Garford and Shippon
Ox
GARFORTH (St Mary the Virgin) *Leeds 13*   **P** *DBP*
R J C D BROWN   **C** D J BRENNAN
GARGRAVE (St Andrew)   *see* Upper Aire *Leeds*
GARRETTS GREEN (St Thomas) and Lea Hall *Birm 5*   **P** *Bp*
V P M BRACHER   **NSM** S J LARKIN, W H MARTIN
GARRIGILL (St John)   *see* Alston Moor *Newc*
GARROWBY HILL, comprising Bishop Wilton, Bugthorpe, Full
Sutton, Kirby Underdale, and Skirpenbeck *York 5*   **P** *Ld*
Chan (1 turn), Abp, D&C, and Earl of Halifax (3 turns)
R L C MUNT   **NSM** M L KAVANAGH
GARSDALE (St John the Baptist)   *see* Western Dales *Carl*
GARSDON (All Saints)   *see* Woodbridge *Bris*
GARSINGTON (St Mary), Cuddesdon and Horspath *Ox 20*
P *Ripon Coll Cuddesdon, Trin Coll Ox, and DBP (jt)*
V K CHARMAN   **NSM** M D CHAPMAN
GARSTANG (St Helen) Churchtown and St Michaels-on-
Wyre *Blackb 9*   **P** *Dr I R H Jackson and R P Hornby Esq (jt)*
V A W WILKINSON
GARSTANG (St Thomas) *Blackb 9*   **P** *V Churchtown St Helen*
V *vacant*
GARSTON (St Michael) *Liv 2*   **P** *Trustees*   **V** A M TUNSTALL
GARSTON, EAST (All Saints)   *see* Lambourn Valley *Ox*
GARSWOOD (St Andrew)   *see* Wigan *Liv*
GARTHORPE (St Mary)   *see* Crowle Gp *Linc*
GARTON IN HOLDERNESS (St Michael)   *see* S Holderness
Coast *York*
GARTON ON THE WOLDS (St Michael and All Angels)   *see*
Woldsburn *York*
GARVESTON (St Margaret)   *see* Barnham Broom and Upper
Yare *Nor*
GARWAY (St Michael)   *see* St Weonards *Heref*
GASTARD (St John the Baptist)   *see* Gtr Corsham and Lacock
Bris
GATCOMBE (St Olave) *Portsm 7*   **P** *Qu Coll Ox*
C E COOKSEY, S A SUTCLIFFE

GATE BURTON (St Helen)   *see* Lea Gp *Linc*
GATE HELMSLEY (St Mary)   *see* Harton *York*
GATEACRE (St Stephen) *Liv 2*   **P** *Bp*   **TR** P H JANVIER
TV S P DOORE   **NSM** K A CANTY
GATELEY (St Helen)   *see* Upper Wensum Village Gp *Nor*
GATESHEAD (St Chad)   *see* Bensham and Teams *Dur*
GATESHEAD (St Edmund's Chapel w Holy Trinity)
(Venerable Bede) *Dur 11*   **P** *Bp and The Crown (alt)*
P-in-c M MACKAY   **NSM** A PHILLIPS
GATESHEAD (St George) *Dur 11*   **P** *Trustees*   **P-in-c** R GRANT
C A R I JONES, S L M JONES
GATESHEAD (St Helen) *Dur 11*   **P** *Bp*   **P-in-c** Y GREENER
C A I G CRAWFORD
GATESHEAD (St Ninian) Harlow Green   *see* Harlow Green and
Lamesley *Dur*
GATESHEAD FELL (St John) *Dur 11*   **P** *Bp*
P-in-c D M LINDLEY   **C** D M HUDSON   **NSM** K COULSON
GATESHEAD Lobley Hill (All Saints)   *see* Hillside *Dur*
GATLEY (St James) *Ches 17*   **P** *R Stockport St Thos*
V M D CARLISLE
GATTEN (St Paul) *Portsm 7*   **P** *CPAS*   **P-in-c** M A WILLIAMS
GATTON (St Andrew)   *see* Merstham, S Merstham and
Gatton *S'wark*
GAULBY (St Peter) *Leic 5*   **P** *Ch Soc Trust*   **V** *vacant*
GAUTBY (All Saints)   *see* Bardney *Linc*
GAUZEBROOK, comprising Alderton, Easton Grey, Foxley w
Bremilham, Hullavington, Luckington, Norton, Sherston
Magna, and Stanton St Quintin *Bris 6*   **P** *Bp, D&C, Eton*
Coll, and M Neeld Esq (jt)   **R** A J BEAUMONT
OLM S E HARVEY
GAWBER (St Thomas)   *see* Cen Barnsley *Leeds*
GAWCOTT (Holy Trinity)   *see* Lenborough *Ox*
GAWSWORTH (St James) w North Rode *Ches 13*   **P** *T R R*
Richards Esq and Bp (jt)   **R** C E WILSON
GAYDON (St Giles) w Chadshunt *Cov 8*   **P** *Bp*
P-in-c N M CHATTERTON
GAYHURST (St Peter) w Ravenstone, Stoke Goldington
and Weston Underwood *Ox 16*   **P** *Bp and Lord Hesketh (jt)*
R C E PUMFREY
GAYTON (St Mary)   *see* Pattishall w Cold Higham and
Gayton w Tiffield *Pet*
GAYTON (St Nicholas)   *see* Ashwicken w Leziate, Bawsey etc
Nor
GAYTON (St Peter)   *see* Mid Trent *Lich*
GAYTON LE WOLD (St Peter)   *see* Asterby Gp *Linc*
GAYTON THORPE (St Mary)   *see* Ashwicken w Leziate,
Bawsey etc *Nor*
GAYWOOD (St Faith) King's Lynn *Nor 19*   **P** *Patr Bd*
TV K T K KERR   **C** L L PURNELL
GAZELEY (All Saints)   *see* Forest Heath *St E*
GEDDING (St Mary the Virgin)   *see* Bradfield St Clare,
Bradfield St George etc *St E*
GEDDINGTON (St Mary Magdalene) w Weekley *Pet 9*
P *Boughton Estates*   **P-in-c** G F GAMBLE
GEDLING (All Hallows) *S'well 7*   **P** *DBP*   **R** M D JOHNSON
C J E LAMB
GEDNEY (St Mary Magdalene)   *see* Mid Elloe Gp *Linc*
GEDNEY Drove End (Christ Church)   *see* Long Sutton w
Lutton etc *Linc*
GEDNEY HILL (Holy Trinity)   *see* Elloe Fen Gp *Linc*
GEDNEY HILL (St Polycarp)   *as above*
GEE CROSS (Holy Trinity) (St Philip's Mission Room)
Ches 14   **P** *V Werneth*   **P-in-c** H SCARISBRICK   **C** K L WADE
GELDESTON (St Michael)   *see* Waveney Marshlands *Nor*
GENTLESHAW (Christ Church)   *see* Farewell and Gentleshaw
Lich
GEORGEHAM (St George) *Ex 13*   **P** *MMCET*
R M C NEWBON
GERMAN (St John the Baptist) The Royal Chapel   *see* W Coast
S & M
GERMANSWEEK (St German)   *see* Okehampton, Inwardleigh,
Belstone, Sourton etc *Ex*
GERMOE (St Germoe)   *see* W Kerrier *Truro*
GERRANS (St Gerran) w St Anthony-in-Roseland and
Philleigh *Truro 5*   **P** *Bp and MMCET (jt)*   **R** *vacant*
GERRARDS CROSS (St James) and Fulmer *Ox 9*   **P** *Bp and*
Simeon's Trustees (jt)   **R** M D BEEBY   **C** B M CLARKE,
J R W FORWARD, R A MUNGAVIN   **NSM** J M ROTH,
M R L BEEBEE
GESTINGTHORPE (St Mary)   *see* Halstead Area *Chelmsf*
GIDDING, GREAT (St Michael)   *see* N Leightonstone *Ely*
GIDDING, LITTLE (St John)   *as above*
GIDEA PARK (St Michael) *Chelmsf 2*   **P** *Bp*   **V** D J P KIRK
GIDLEIGH (Holy Trinity)   *see* Chagford, Gidleigh, Throwleigh
etc *Ex*

GIGGETTY LANE (The Venerable Bede)   *see* Smestow Vale *Lich*
GIGGLESWICK (St Alkelda) and Rathmell w Wigglesworth *Leeds 17*   **P** *Bp and Ch Trust Fund Trust (jt)*
P-in-c J M CLARKSON   **C** S C DAWSON
GILCRUX (St Mary)   *see* Aspatria w Hayton and Gilcrux *Carl*
GILDERSOME (St Peter)   *see* Drighlington and Gildersome *Leeds*
GILLAMOOR (St Aidan)   *see* Kirkbymoorside w Gillamoor, Farndale etc *York*
GILLING (St Agatha)   *see* Holmedale *Leeds*
GILLING EAST (Holy Cross)   *see* Ampleforth w Oswaldkirk, Gilling E etc *York*
GILLINGHAM (Holy Trinity) *Roch 3*   **P** *Bp*   **V** M A K NELSON   **NSM** S A TAYLOR
GILLINGHAM (St Augustine) *Roch 3*   **P** *Bp*
P-in-c A J MASKELL   **NSM** N J P RAWLINS
GILLINGHAM (St Barnabas) *Roch 3*   **P** *Bp*   **P-in-c** E A COX
GILLINGHAM (St Luke)   *see* New Brompton St Luke *Roch*
GILLINGHAM (St Mark) *Roch 3*   **P** *Hyndman Trustees*
V V M L MUTHALALY
GILLINGHAM (St Mary Magdalene) *Roch 3*   **P** *DBP*
P-in-c E A COX
GILLINGHAM (St Mary the Virgin), Milton-on-Stour and Silton *Sarum 5*   **P** *Bp and DBP (jt)*   **R** J P GREENWOOD
C E C PEGLER   **NSM** T F HEATON
GILLINGHAM (St Mary)   *see* Waveney Marshlands *Nor*
GILLINGHAM, SOUTH (St Matthew) *Roch 3*   **P** *Patr Bd*
TR R B SENIOR   **TV** P M LENTON DE DICKIN   **C** W A S DAVIE
NSM P M ALEXANDER
GILMORTON (All Saints)   *see* Avon-Swift *Leic*
GILSLAND (St Mary Magdalene)   *see* Lanercost, Walton, Gilsland and Nether Denton *Carl*
GILSTEAD (St Wilfrid)   *see* Bingley H Trin *Leeds*
GILSTON (St Mary)   *see* High Wych and Gilston w Eastwick *St Alb*
GIMINGHAM (All Saints)   *see* Trunch Group *Nor*
GIPPING (Chapel of St Nicholas)   *see* Bacton w Wyverstone, Cotton and Old Newton etc *St E*
GIPSY HILL (Christ Church) *S'wark 12*   **P** *CPAS*
V J E CROUCHER   **C** E P LOWTH, L M WHITEMAN
GIPTON (Church of the Epiphany) and Oakwood *Leeds 10*
P *Bp and DBF (jt)*   **V** K A FITZSIMONS   **C** D NOUWEN
GIRLINGTON (St Philip), Heaton and Manningham *Leeds 2*
P *Patr Bd*   **R** C J W CHORLTON
GIRTON (St Andrew) *Ely 6*   **P** *Ld Chan*   **R** M D BIGG
GIRTON (St Cecilia)   *see* E Trent *S'well*
GISBURN (St Mary the Virgin)   *see* Bowland Benefice *Blackb*
GISLEHAM (Holy Trinity)   *see* Kessingland, Gisleham and Rushmere *Nor*
GISLINGHAM (St Mary)   *see* S Hartismere *St E*
GISSING (St Mary the Virgin)   *see* Diss *Nor*
GITTISHAM (St Michael)   *see* Honiton w Monkton, Awliscombe, Buckerell etc *Ex*
GIVENDALE, GREAT (St Ethelburga)   *see* Pocklington Wold *York*
GLAISDALE (St Thomas)   *see* Middle Esk Moor *York*
GLANDFORD (St Martin)   *see* Blakeney w Cley, Wiveton, Glandford etc *Nor*
GLANVILLES WOOTTON (St Mary the Virgin)   *see* Three Valleys *Sarum*
GLAPTHORN (St Leonard)   *see* Oundle w Ashton and Benefield w Glapthorn *Pet*
GLAPWELL (St Andrew)   *see* Ault Hucknall and Scarcliffe *Derby*
GLASCOTE (St George) and Stonydelph *Lich 4*   **P** *Patr Bd*
TR G D SIMMONS   **C** S G BENNETT   **OLM** P D FAULTLESS
GLASCOTE HEATH (St Peter)   *see* Glascote and Stonydelph *Lich*
GLASSHOUGHTON (St Paul)   *see* Castleford *Leeds*
GLASSON (Christ Church)   *see* Cockerham w Winmarleigh and Glasson *Blackb*
GLASTON (St Andrew)   *see* Lyddington, Bisbrooke, Caldecott, Glaston etc *Pet*
GLASTONBURY (St John the Baptist) (St Benedict) w Meare *B & W 4*   **P** *Bp*   **V** D J L MACGEOCH
C D M GREENFIELD   **NSM** M C KITTO
GLATTON (St Nicholas)   *see* Sawtry, Glatton and Holme w Conington *Ely*
GLAVEN VALLEY Group   *see* Blakeney w Cley, Wiveton, Glandford etc *Nor*
GLAZEBURY (All Saints) w Hollinfare *Liv 13*   **P** *Bp and R Warrington (jt)*   **Hon C** A COOPER   **NSM** J HARNEY
GLAZELEY (St Bartholomew)   *see* Highley w Billingsley, Glazeley etc *Heref*

GLEADLESS (Christ Church) *Sheff 1*   **P** *DBP*
P-in-c P R ALLEN   **NSM** A RHODES, C D I REES, K A GREEN
GLEADLESS VALLEY (Holy Cross) *Sheff 1*   **P** *DBP*
V D J MIDDLETON   **C** S C DEERING
GLEM VALLEY   *see* Glemsford, Hartest w Boxted, Somerton etc *St E*
GLEMHAM, GREAT (All Saints)   *see* Alde River *St E*
GLEMHAM, LITTLE (St Andrew)   *as above*
GLEMSFORD (St Mary the Virgin), Hartest w Boxted, Somerton and Stanstead (Glem Valley United Benefice) *St E 8*   **P** *Bp, The Crown, and Ch Soc Trust (by turn)*
R P J PRIGG   **NSM** J S PERKINS
GLEN AULDYN (St Fingan)   *see* Bride, Lezayre and N Ramsey *S & M*
GLEN GROUP, The, comprising Pinchbeck, Surfleet, and West Pinchbeck *Linc 19*   **P** *Bp*   **V** D C SWEETING
GLENEAGLES *Pet 6*   **P** *Bp*   **V** D J AIREY
GLENFIELD (St Peter) and Newtown Linford *Leic 9*   **P** *Bp*
R R J TRETHEWEY   **NSM** S E ANDREWS
GLENHOLT (St Anne)   *see* Bickleigh and Shaugh Prior *Ex*
GLENTHAM (St Peter)   *see* Owmby Gp *Linc*
GLENTWORTH (St Michael)   *see* Trentcliffe Gp *Linc*
GLINTON (St Benedict), Etton, Maxey, Peakirk and Northborough *Pet 11*   **P** *D&C and Sir Philip Naylor-Leyland Bt (jt)*   **V** M-A B TISDALE
GLODWICK (St Mark w Christ Church) *Man 5*   **P** *Bp*
V *vacant*
GLOOSTON (St John the Baptist)   *see* Welham, Glooston and Cranoe and Stonton Wyville *Leic*
GLOSSOP (All Saints) *Derby 4*   **P** *Patr Bd*   **P-in-c** D H MUNDY
NSM C MITCHELL   **OLM** N W SHAW
GLOUCESTER (St Aldate)   *see* Coney Hill *Glouc*
GLOUCESTER (St Catharine) *Glouc 2*   **P** *Bp*   **V** J F PESTELL
C L B E FALVEY
GLOUCESTER (St George) w Whaddon *Glouc 2*   **P** *Bp*
V R G BECK
GLOUCESTER (St James and All Saints) (Christ Church) *Glouc 2*   **P** *Bp*   **V** J H JENSEN   **C** H M MCGEOCH
NSM J M HOWARD, S E OSUNSANMI
GLOUCESTER (St Paul) and St Stephen *Glouc 2*   **P** *Bp*
V R P FITTER   **C** H L DE GRUYTHER
GLOUCESTER CITY St Mark (St Mary de Crypt) (St John the Baptist) (St Mary de Lode) (St Nicholas) and Hempsted *Glouc 2*   **P** *D&C (1 turn), Bp (3 turns), Ld Chan (1 turn)*   **R** N M ARTHY
GLOUCESTER DOCKS Mariners' Church Proprietary Chapel *Glouc 2*   **C-in-c** K C DOUGLASS
GLOUCESTER ROAD (St Stephen)   *see* S Kensington St Steph *Lon*
GLYMPTON (St Mary)   *see* Wootton w Glympton and Kiddington *Ox*
GLYNDE (St Mary), West Firle and Beddingham *Chich 21*
P *Bp and D&C Windsor (alt)*   **V** P C OWEN-JONES
GNOSALL (St Lawrence)   *see* Adbaston, High Offley, Knightley, Norbury etc *Lich*
GOADBY (St John the Baptist)   *see* Coplow *Leic*
GOADBY MARWOOD (St Denys)   *see* Ironstone Villages *Leic*
GOATHILL (St Peter)   *see* Milborne Port w Goathill etc *B & W*
GOATHLAND (St Mary)   *see* Middle Esk Moor *York*
GOATHURST (St Edward the King and Martyr)   *see* Aisholt, Enmore, Goathurst, Nether Stowey etc *B & W*
GOBOWEN (All Saints)   *see* Selattyn and Hengoed w Gobowen *Lich*
GODALMING (St Peter and St Paul) *Guildf 4*   **P** *Bp*
P-in-c J P HARKIN   **C** S T SAMUELS
GODINGTON (Holy Trinity)   *see* Shelswell *Ox*
GODMANCHESTER (St Mary) and Hilton *Ely 10*   **P** *D&C Westmr and Bp (jt)*   **V** D W BUSK   **Hon C** J P YOUNG
GODMANSTONE (Holy Trinity)   *see* Buckland Newton, Cerne Abbas, Godmanstone etc *Sarum*
GODMERSHAM (St Lawrence the Martyr)   *see* King's Wood *Cant*
GODREVY, comprising Gwinear, Hayle, Phillack, and St Erth *Truro 4*   **P** *Patr Bd*   **TR** S CLIFTON   **NSM** P M MURLEY, S A CHALCRAFT
GODSHILL (All Saints) *Portsm 7*   **P** *Guild of All So*
C C A SMITH
GODSHILL (St Giles)   *see* Fordingbridge and Hyde and Breamore etc *Win*
GODSTONE (St Nicholas) and Blindley Heath *S'wark 25*
P *Bp and Ms C Goad (jt)*   **R** P D O'CONNELL
GOFF'S OAK (St James)   *see* Cheshunt *St Alb*
GOLBORNE (St Thomas)   *see* Lowton and Golborne *Liv*
GOLCAR (St John the Evangelist) and Longwood *Leeds 9*
P V *Huddersfield*   **V** S C CROOK   **NSM** J SARGENT

GOLDEN CAP TEAM (Team Ministry), comprising Bettiscombe and Pilsdon, Catherston Leweston, Charmouth, Chideock, Hawkchurch, Lyme Regis, Marshwood, Monkton Wyld, Whitchurch Canonicorum w Stanton St Gabriel and Fishpond, and Wootton Fitzpaine *Sarum 2* **P** *Patr Bd* **TR** C E MARTIN **TV** S J GODFREY, V LUCKETT

GOLDENHILL St John the Evangelist and Tunstall *Lich 11* **P** *Bp* **V** T W J STATHER

GOLDERS GREEN (St Alban the Martyr and St Michael) *Lon 14* **P** *Bp* **V** K BHATTI

GOLDHANGER (St Peter) *see* Gt Totham and Lt Totham w Goldhanger *Chelmsf*

GOLDINGTON (St Mary the Virgin) *St Alb 9* **P** *Bp* **V** S P DOMMETT **C** M OTTAVIANI

GOLDS HILL (St Paul) *see* W Bromwich St Jas and St Paul *Lich*

GOLDSBOROUGH (St Mary) *see* Knaresborough, Goldsborough, Nidd and Brearton *Leeds*

GOLDSWORTH PARK (St Andrew) *Guildf 12* **P** *Bp* **NSM** J A M VICKERS

GOLDTHORPE (St John the Evangelist and St Mary Magdalene) w Hickleton *Sheff 12* **P** *CR (2 turns), Earl of Halifax (1 turn)* **V** C R SCHAEFER **Hon C** A BRISCOE

GOMERSAL (St Mary) *Leeds 7* **P** *Bp* **V** K NICHOLL

GONALSTON (St Laurence) *see* Epperstone, Gonalston, Oxton and Woodborough *S'well*

GONERBY, GREAT (St Sebastian) *see* Barrowby and Gt Gonerby *Linc*

GOOD EASTER (St Andrew) *see* High Easter and Good Easter w Margaret Roding *Chelmsf*

GOODERSTONE (St George) *see* Cockley Cley w Gooderstone *Nor*

GOODLEIGH (St Gregory) *see* Barnstaple H Trin and Goodleigh *Ex*

GOODMANHAM (All Saints) *York 5* **P** *Abp* **R** C R PINCHBECK **C** J A KENNY

GOODMAYES (All Saints) *Chelmsf 6* **P** *Hyndman Trustees* **V** A W ELEYAE

GOODMAYES (St Paul) *Chelmsf 6* **P** *Bp* **V** J E F BUCHAN

GOODNESTONE (Holy Cross) *see* Canonry *Cant*

GOODRINGTON (St George) and Collaton St Mary *Ex 10* **P** *Bp* **V** G DEIGHTON **C** G M J VAN OMMEREN

GOODSHAW (St Mary and All Saints) and Crawshawbooth *Man 4* **P** *Bp and Wm Hulme Trustees (jt)* **V** vacant

GOODWORTH CLATFORD (St Peter) *see* Abbotts Ann and Upper Clatford and Goodworth Clatford *Win*

GOOLE (St John the Evangelist) (St Mary) (Mariners' Club and Chapel) *Sheff 10* **P** *Bp* **P-in-c** H PATTON **C** G P DOWLING, J H J BLUNT

GOOSE GREEN (St Paul) *see* Wigan *Liv*

GOOSEY (All Saints) *see* Stanford in the Vale w Goosey and Hatford *Ox*

GOOSNARGH (St Mary the Virgin) *see* Fellside Team *Blackb*

GOOSTREY (St Luke) *Ches 11* **P** *V Sandbach* **V** H E BUCKLEY

GORAN HAVEN (St Just) *see* St Goran w Caerhays *Truro*

GOREFIELD (St Paul) *see* Wisbech St Mary and Guyhirn w Ring's End etc *Ely*

GORING (St Thomas of Canterbury) and Streatley with South Stoke *Ox 24* **P** *Ch Ch Ox and Bp (jt)* **V** B L M PHILLIPS **C** J E ALLEN **NSM** E J DOWDING, W J MIDDLETON

GORING-BY-SEA (St Mary) (St Laurence) *Chich 7* **P** *Bp* **V** K D LITTLEJOHN **C** N D STANNARD

GORLESTON (St Andrew) *Nor 6* **P** *Ch Trust Fund Trust* **V** B HALL

GORLESTON (St Mary Magdalene) *Nor 6* **P** *Bp and Ch Trust Fund Trust (jt)* **V** M J PRICE

GORNAL (St Peter) and Sedgley *Worc 5* **P** *Patr Bd* **TR** G E HEWLETT **TV** C A MITCHELL

GORNAL, LOWER (St James the Great) *Worc 5* **P** *Bp* **V** J W MOTT

GORSLEY (Christ Church) *see* Newent and Gorsley w Cliffords Mesne *Glouc*

GORTON (Emmanuel) (St James) (St Philip) and Abbey Hey *Man 1* **P** *Patr Bd and Prime-Min (alt)* **TR** C P SMITH **TV** C MASTERS **C** C A HEWISON

GOSBECK (St Mary) *see* N Bosmere *St E*

GOSBERTON (St Peter and St Paul), Gosberton Clough and Quadring *Linc 19* **P** *Bp and D&C (jt)* **V** I R WALTERS

GOSBERTON CLOUGH (St Gilbert and St Hugh) *see* Gosberton, Gosberton Clough and Quadring *Linc*

GOSCOTE, EAST (St Hilda) *see* Fosse Team *Leic*

GOSFIELD (St Catherine) *see* Halstead Area *Chelmsf*

GOSFORTH (All Saints) *Newc 2* **P** *Bp* **V** A J SHIPTON **C** B A DAVIES

GOSFORTH (St Hugh) *Newc 2* **P** *Bp* **P-in-c** A J SHIPTON **C** B A DAVIES

GOSFORTH (St Mary) *see* Seatallan *Carl*

GOSFORTH (St Nicholas) *Newc 2* **P** *Bp* **V** E J NATTRASS

GOSFORTH VALLEY (St Andrew) *see* Dronfield w Holmesfield *Derby*

GOSFORTH, NORTH (St Columba) *see* Ch the King *Newc*

GOSPEL LANE (St Michael) *see* Hall Green St Mich *Birm*

GOSPORT (Christ Church) *see* Forton and Gosport *Portsm*

GOSPORT (Holy Trinity) *as above*

GOSPORT NORTH *see* Bridgemary, Elson and Rowner *Portsm*

GOSPORT SOUTH *see* Forton and Gosport *Portsm*

GOSSOPS GREEN (St Alban) and Bewbush *Chich 9* **P** *Bp* **V** A M ALEXANDER **C** E A GREEN

GOTHAM (St Lawrence) *see* A453 churches of S Notts *S'well*

GOUDHURST (St Mary the Virgin) w Kilndown *Cant 11* **P** *Abp and The Crown (alt)* **V** R H ROBERTSON

GOULCEBY (All Saints) *see* Asterby Gp *Linc*

GOXHILL (All Saints) *see* Barrow and Goxhill *Linc*

GOXHILL (St Giles) *see* Aldbrough, Mappleton w Goxhill and Withernwick *York*

GRADE (St Grada and the Holy Cross) *see* St Keverne, St Ruan w St Grade and Landewednack *Truro*

GRAFFHAM (St Giles) w Woolavington *Chich 4* **P** *Bp* **P-in-c** V A E TURNER

GRAFFOE Group, comprising Boothby Graffoe, Coleby, Harmston, Navenby, Temple Bruer, and Wellingore *Linc 12* **P** *Ch Coll Cam, D&C and Bp (jt), Oriel Coll Ox, and Mrs P N Fullerton (by turn)* **R** M J GODBOLD **NSM** S G WILLIAMS, S J DAVIES

GRAFHAM (All Saints) *see* E Leightonstone *Ely*

GRAFHAM (St Andrew) *see* Bramley and Grafham *Guildf*

GRAFTON FLYFORD (St John the Baptist) *see* Abberton, The Flyfords, Naunton Beauchamp etc *Worc*

GRAFTON REGIS (St Mary) *see* Blisworth, Alderton, Grafton Regis etc *Pet*

GRAFTON UNDERWOOD (St James the Apostle) *see* Cranford w Grafton Underwood and Twywell *Pet*

GRAFTON, EAST (St Nicholas) *see* Savernake *Sarum*

GRAHAME PARK (St Augustine) Conventional District *Lon 14* **Min** B J GABOR

GRAIN (St James) w Stoke *Roch 6* **P** *DBP* **V** vacant

GRAINSBY (St Nicholas) *see* Fotherby, N Thoresby and Grainsby w Waithe *Linc*

GRAINTHORPE (St Clement) *see* Marshchapel, Somercotes and Grainthorpe w Conisholme *Linc*

GRAMPOUND (St Nun) *see* Probus, Ladock and Grampound w Creed and St Erme *Truro*

GRANBOROUGH (St John the Baptist) *see* Schorne *Ox*

GRANBY (All Saints) *see* Wiverton in the Vale *S'well*

GRAND UNION Benefice *see* Blisworth, Alderton, Grafton Regis etc *Pet*

GRANDBOROUGH (St Peter) *see* Leam Valley *Cov*

GRANGE (Holy Trinity) *see* Keswick St Jo w Borrowdale *Carl*

GRANGE (St Andrew) *Ches 3* **P** *Bp* **V** E L SPEAKE **C** D A DALBY

GRANGE FELL (not known) *see* Cartmel Peninsula *Carl*

GRANGE MOOR (St Bartholomew) *see* Kirkheaton *Leeds*

GRANGE PARK (St Peter) *Lon 16* **P** *Bp* **V** S P L COLEMAN **C** J R BELL

GRANGE-OVER-SANDS (St Paul) *see* Cartmel Peninsula *Carl*

GRANGETOWN (St Aidan) *Dur 14* **P** *V Ryhope* **V** D RAINE

GRANGETOWN (St Hilda of Whitby) *York 17* **P** *Abp* **V** E L MATHIAS-JONES

GRANSDEN, GREAT (St Bartholomew) and Abbotsley and Lt Gransden and Waresley *Ely 13* **P** *Pemb Coll Cam (1 turn), Clare Coll Cam (2 turns), and Ball Coll Ox (1 turn)* **R** R E BLANCHFLOWER

GRANSDEN, LITTLE (St Peter and St Paul) *see* Gt Gransden and Abbotsley and Lt Gransden etc *Ely*

GRANTA VALE Group, The, comprising Balsham, Great and Little Abington, Hildersham, West Wickham, West Wratting, and Weston Colville *Ely 5* **P** *Patr Bd* **R** I G MCCOLL **NSM** K R BISHOP

GRANTCHESTER (St Andrew and St Mary) *Ely 3* **P** *CCC Cam* **V** R C ROSBOROUGH **NSM** A R HURST

GRANTHAM (St Anne) *see* S Grantham *Linc*

GRANTHAM (St John the Evangelist) *see* Grantham, Manthorpe *Linc*

GRANTHAM (St Wulfram) *Linc 20* **P** *Bp* **R** S W CRADDUCK **C** J C ROUNDTREE, J G TITLEY **NSM** J M ROWLAND, J T FARLEY

GRANTHAM (The Ascension) *see* Grantham, Harrowby w Londonthorpe *Linc*

GRANTHAM (The Epiphany) Earlesfield *see* S Grantham *Linc*

GRANTHAM Harrowby (The Ascension) w Londonthorpe
Linc 20　**P** *Bp*　**V** S J PARSONS　**OLM** B A D MANTERFIELD,
L BATTY
GRANTHAM Manthorpe (St John the Evangelist) *Linc* 20
P *Bp*　**P-in-c** S W CRADDUCK　**C** J G TITLEY
**GRANTHAM, SOUTH The Trinity (St Anne) (St John the
Evangelist)** *Linc* 20　**P** *Bp and R Grantham (jt)*
V D SHENTON　**C** J S PARKIN
GRAPPENHALL (St Wilfrid) *Ches* 4　**P** *P G Greenall Esq*
R J E PROUDFOOT
GRASBY (All Saints) *see* Caistor *Linc*
GRASMERE (St Oswald) *Carl* 11　**P** *Qu Coll Ox*
P-in-c D M B WILMOT
GRASSENDALE (St Mary) *Liv* 2　**P** *Trustees*　**V** P ELLIS
GRATELEY (St Leonard) *see* Portway and Danebury *Win*
GRATWICH (St Mary the Virgin) *see* Uttoxeter Area *Lich*
GRAVELEY (St Botolph) *see* Papworth *Ely*
GRAVELEY (St Mary) *see* Stevenage St Nic and Graveley
St Alb
GRAVELLY HILL (All Saints) *Birm* 4　**P** *Bp*　**V** vacant
GRAVENEY (All Saints) *see* Boughton-under-Blean w Dunkirk
etc *Cant*
GRAVENHURST (no church), Shillington and Stondon
St Alb 8　**P** *Bp*　**V** R C WINSLADE
GRAVESEND (Holy Family) w Ifield *Roch* 4　**P** *Bp and Mrs S
Edmeades-Stearns (jt)*　**P-in-c** E HURST
GRAVESEND (St Aidan) *Roch* 4　**P** *Bp*　**V** M J PAYNE
NSM J P LITTLEWOOD
GRAVESEND (St George) *Roch* 4　**P** *Bp*　**R** J A FLETCHER
C M J EDWARDS
GRAVESEND (St Mary) *Roch* 4　**P** *R Gravesend*　**V** T OLIVER
GRAYINGHAM (St Radegunda) *Linc* 8　**P** *Bp*　**R** K E COLWELL
NSM P J DICKINSON　**OLM** J WILSON
GRAYRIGG (St John) *see* Beacon TM *Carl*
GRAYS NORTH (St John the Evangelist) *Chelmsf* 15　**P** *Bp*
V C P RUSSELL
**GRAYS THURROCK (St Peter and St Paul), including Little
Thurrock, West Thurrock, and Chafford Hundred** *Chelmsf* 15
P *DBP*　**TR** D BARLOW　**TV** D N N PETERSON　**C** S E FRYER
NSM C A COCKCROFT　**OLM** C L HASLER
GRAYSHOTT (St Luke) *Guildf* 3　**P** *Bp*　**V** J W D HASWELL
Hon C G E KNIFTON
GRAYSWOOD (All Saints) *see* Haslemere and Grayswood
Guildf
GRAYTHWAITE (Mission Room) *see* Hawkshead and Low
Wray w Sawrey and Rusland etc *Carl*
GREASBROUGH (St Mary) *Sheff* 6　**P** *Sir Philip Naylor-Leyland
Bt*　**NSM** D ETCHELL, N ELSOM
GREASBY (St Nicholas) *see* Frankby w Greasby *Ches*
GREASLEY (St Mary) *S'well* 4　**P** *Bp*　**V** vacant
GREAT *see also under substantive place name*
**GREAT CAMBRIDGE ROAD (St John the Baptist and
St James)** *Lon* 17　**P** *D&C St Paul's*　**V** vacant
GREAT GLEN (St Cuthbert) *see* Oadby *Leic*
GREAT MOOR (St Saviour) *see* Stockport St Sav *Ches*
GREATER *see under substantive place name*
GREATFORD (St Thomas à Becket) *see* Uffington Gp *Linc*
GREATHAM (not known) *see* Amberley w N Stoke and
Parham, Wiggonholt etc *Chich*
GREATHAM (St John the Baptist) *Dur* 6　**P** *Trustees*
P-in-c P M BULLOCK
**GREATHAM (St John the Baptist), Empshott and Hawkley
w Priors Dean** *Portsm* 4　**P** *Bp and DBP (jt)*　**V** P A SUTTON
C K LLOYD JONES
GREATSTONE (St Peter) *see* Romney Marsh *Cant*
GREATWORTH (St Peter) *see* Chenderit *Pet*
GREEN HAMMERTON (St Thomas) *see* Gt and Lt Ouseburn
w Marton cum Grafton etc *Leeds*
GREEN HEATH (St Saviour) *see* Hednesford *Lich*
GREEN STREET GREEN (St Mary) *see* Chelsfield w Green
Street Green and Pratts Bottom *Roch*
GREEN VALE (Holy Trinity) *see* Stockton H Trin w St Mark
Dur
GREENFIELD (St Mary) *see* Saddleworth *Man*
GREENFIELDS (United Church) *see* Shrewsbury St Geo w
Greenfields *Lich*
GREENFORD (Holy Cross) (St Edward the Confessor)
Lon 19　**P** *K Coll Cam*　**R** G W MILLER
GREENFORD, NORTH (All Hallows) *Lon* 19　**P** *Bp*
P-in-c K M GREENIDGE-SILCOTT
GREENGATES (St John the Evangelist) and Thorpe Edge
Leeds 3　**P** *D&C Bradf and Vs Bradf, Calverley and Idle (jt)*
C C R C BAXFIELD, M E WINTER　**NSM** S O NUTTALL
GREENHAM (St Mary the Virgin) *Ox* 6　**P** *Bp*
V D L R MCLEOD　**NSM** B R JONES, J BRAMHALL
GREENHAM (St Peter) *see* Wellington and Distr *B & W*

GREENHEAD (St Cuthbert) *see* Haltwhistle and Greenhead
Newc
GREENHILL (St John the Baptist) *Lon* 20　**P** *Bp, Adn, and V
Harrow St Mary (jt)*　**V** B D HINGSTON　**C** A Y MORE
Hon C D P BYRNE
GREENHILL (St Peter) *Sheff* 2　**P** *Bp*　**V** E J LUNN
C P M BROWN, T K HOLE
GREENHITHE (St Mary) *Roch* 4　**P** *Ch Soc Trust and Personal
Reps Canon T L Livermore (jt)*　**P-in-c** C L LLOYD-EVANS
GREENHOW HILL (St Mary) *see* Upper Nidderdale *Leeds*
GREENLANDS (St Anne) *Blackb* 8　**P** *Bp and V Blackpool
St Steph (jt)*　**P-in-c** D A PREST　**NSM** J L PARKER
GREENLANDS (St John the Evangelist) *see* Ipsley *Worc*
GREEN'S NORTON (St Bartholomew) *see* Towcester w
Caldecote and Easton Neston etc *Pet*
GREENSIDE (St John) *Dur* 12　**P** *R Ryton w Hedgefield*
V T I BRAZIER　**NSM** R HENDRY
**GREENSTEAD (St Andrew) (St Edmund's Church Hall)
(St Matthew) w Colchester St Anne** *Chelmsf* 20　**P** *Patr Bd
and Ld Chan (alt)*　**TV** S E HOWLETT　**C** S L BATTS-NEALE
NSM P J HOWLETT
GREENSTEAD GREEN (St James Apostle) *see* Halstead Area
Chelmsf
GREENSTED-JUXTA-ONGAR (St Andrew) *see* Chipping
Ongar w Shelley etc *Chelmsf*
GREENWICH (St Alfege) *S'wark* 1　**P** *The Crown*　**V** S R WINN
C P A MANN　**NSM** F G WAKELING, S K NSHIMYE
**GREENWICH, EAST (Christ Church) (St Andrew w
St Michael) (St George)** *S'wark* 1　**P** *Patr Bd*　**TR** M CAVE
TV J M PETRIE, L J FATUROTI　**NSM** J N PHILPOTT-HOWARD
GREETE (St James) *see* Tenbury *Heref*
GREETHAM (All Saints) *see* Horncastle Gp *Linc*
GREETHAM (St Mary the Virgin) *see* Cottesmore and Burley,
Clipsham, Exton etc *Pet*
GREETLAND (St Thomas) and West Vale *Leeds* 6　**P** *V
Halifax*　**P-in-c** I SPARKS
GREETWELL (All Saints) *see* S Lawres Gp *Linc*
GREINTON (St Michael and All Angels) *see* Middlezoy w
Othery, Moorlinch and Greinton *B & W*
GRENDON (All Saints) *see* Baddesley Ensor w Grendon *Birm*
GRENDON (St Mary) *see* Yardley Hastings, Denton and
Grendon etc *Pet*
GRENDON BISHOP (St John the Baptist) *see* Bredenbury
Heref
GRENDON UNDERWOOD (St Leonard) *see* The Claydons
and Swan *Ox*
GRENOSIDE (St Mark) *Sheff* 3　**P** *Bp and V Ecclesfield (jt)*
NSM C WILLIAMS
GRESHAM (All Saints) *see* Aylmerton, Runton, Beeston Regis
and Gresham *Nor*
GRESLEY (St George and St Mary) *Derby* 7　**P** *Simeon's
Trustees*　**V** M J FIRBANK　**C** R Z ALLPRESS
GRESSENHALL (Assumption of the Blessed Virgin Mary) *see*
Launditch and the Upper Nar Valley *Nor*
GRESSINGHAM (St John the Evangelist) *see* Hornby w
Claughton and Whittington etc *Blackb*
GRETTON (Christ Church) *see* Winchcombe *Glouc*
**GRETTON (St James the Great) w Rockingham and
Cottingham w East Carlton** *Pet* 7　**P** *Bp, Comdr L M M
Saunders Watson, Sir Geoffrey Palmer Bt, and BNC Ox (jt)*
P-in-c P W FROST　**C** A J OLIVER
GREWELTHORPE (St James) *see* Fountains Gp *Leeds*
GREYSTOKE (St Andrew) *see* Greystoke w Penruddock,
Mungrisdale etc *Carl*
**GREYSTOKE (St Andrew) w Penruddock, Mungrisdale and
Matterdale** *Carl* 4　**P** *Patr Bd*　**R** vacant
GREYSTONES (St Gabriel) *Sheff* 2　**P** *Dean*
P-in-c A P STEVENSON
GREYWELL (St Mary) *see* N Hants Downs *Win*
GRIMEHILLS (St Mary) *see* Darwen St Barn *Blackb*
GRIMETHORPE (St Luke) w Brierley *Leeds* 14　**P** *SMF*
P-in-c P CARTWRIGHT　**C** J E FLEURY,
T H R S J BATES-BOURNE　**NSM** M SCHOLEY
GRIMLEY (St Bartholomew) *see* Hallow and Grimley w Holt
etc *Worc*
GRIMOLDBY (St Edith) *see* Mid Marsh Gp *Linc*
GRIMSARGH (St Michael) *Blackb* 13　**P** *R Preston*　**V** N SALT
GRIMSBURY (St Leonard) *see* Banbury St Leon *Ox*
GRIMSBY (St Augustine of Hippo) *Linc* 3　**P** *TR Gt Grimsby
SS Mary and Jas*　**V** vacant
GRIMSBY, GREAT (St Andrew w St Luke and All Saints)
Linc 3　**P** *Bp*　**V** vacant
**GRIMSBY, GREAT (St Mary and St James) (St Hugh)
(St Mark) (St Martin)** *Linc* 3　**P** *Bp*　**TV** K L A FARRELL
NSM J M VASEY, P M BARLOW

GRIMSBY, LITTLE (St Edith)   *see* Fotherby, N Thoresby and Grainsby w Waithe *Linc*

GRIMSHOE, comprising Feltwell, Hockwold w Wilton, Northwold, Southery, and Weeting *Ely 9*   **P** *Bp, G&C Coll Cam, Guild of All So (by turn)*   **R** J A HORAN   **NSM** J M HAWTHORNE

GRIMSTEAD, EAST (Holy Trinity)   *see* Clarendon *Sarum*

GRIMSTEAD, WEST (St John) *as above*

GRIMSTON (St Botolph)   *see* Ashwicken w Leziate, Bawsey etc *Nor*

GRIMSTON (St John the Baptist)   *see* Old Dalby, Nether Broughton, Saxelbye etc *Leic*

GRIMSTON, NORTH (St Nicholas)   *see* W Buckrose *York*

GRINDALE (St Nicholas)   *see* Rudston, Boynton, Carnaby etc *York*

GRINDLETON (St Ambrose)   *see* Bowland Benefice *Blackb*

GRINDON (All Saints)   *see* Calton, Cauldon, Grindon, Waterfall etc *Lich*

GRINDON (St James)   *see* Stockton Country Par *Dur*

GRINDON (St Oswald)   *see* Sunderland St Mary, St Thos and St Oswald *Dur*

GRINGLEY-ON-THE-HILL (St Peter and St Paul)   *see* Beckingham, Walkeringham, Misterton, etc *S'well*

GRINSHILL (All Saints)   *see* Astley, Clive, Grinshill and Hadnall *Lich*

GRINSTEAD, EAST (St Mary the Virgin) *Chich 9*   **P** *Bp*   V A C WOGAN   **NSM** D W HADFIELD, J GAYFORD

GRINSTEAD, EAST (St Swithun) *Chich 9*   **P** *Bp*   V A R HAWKEN   **NSM** J K PEATY, K E HIGGS

GRINSTEAD, WEST (St George) *Chich 10*   **P** *Bp*   **P-in-c** A C LETSCHKA   **NSM** S MITCHELL

GRINTON (St Andrew)   *see* Swaledale *Leeds*

GRISTHORPE (St Thomas)   *see* Filey *York*

GRISTON (St Peter and St Paul)   *see* Caston, Griston, Merton, Thompson etc *Nor*

GRITTLETON (St Mary the Virgin)   *see* By Brook *Bris*

GROBY (St Philip and St James) and Ratby *Leic 9*   **P** *Bp and Baroness Mowbray, Segrave and Stourton (jt)*   R E T W BAMPTON   **NSM** L N COLLEY

GROOMBRIDGE (St John the Evangelist)   *see* Speldhurst w Groombridge and Ashurst *Roch*

GROOMBRIDGE, NEW (St Thomas) *Chich 16*   **P** *R Withyham*   **NSM** T K HARRISON

GROSMONT (St Matthew)   *see* Middle Esk Moor *York*

GROSVENOR CHAPEL (no dedication) Chapel of Ease in the parish of Hanover Square St George w St Mark *Lon 3*   **P-in-c** R M FERMER   **Hon C** S D DEWEY   **NSM** A R L PIGGOT

GROTON (St Bartholomew)   *see* Boxford, Edwardstone, Groton etc *St E*

GROVE (St Helen)   *see* The Rivers *S'well*

GROVE (St John the Baptist)   *see* Vale *Ox*

GROVE PARK (St Augustine)   *see* Lee St Aug *S'wark*

GROVEHILL (Resurrection)   *see* Hemel Hempstead *St Alb*

GRUNDISBURGH (St Mary the Virgin)   *see* Carlford *St E*

GUARLFORD (St Mary)   *see* Powick and Guarlford and Madresfield w Newland *Worc*

GUERNSEY (Holy Trinity) *Win 14*   **P** *Trustees*   V J P HONOUR

GUERNSEY (St André de la Pommeraye) *Win 14*   **P** *The Crown*   R T R BARKER   **NSM** J E C ROBILLIARD

GUERNSEY (St John the Evangelist) *Win 14*   **P** *Trustees*   V M E J BARRETT   **C** P A GRAYSMITH

GUERNSEY (St Marguerite de la Foret) *Win 14*   **P** *The Crown*   R C M CLAXTON

GUERNSEY (St Martin) *Win 14*   **P** *The Crown*   R D J FOOT

GUERNSEY (St Matthew) Cobo *Win 14*   **P** *R Ste Marie du Castel*   V S I LAMB   **NSM** B J HERVÉ

GUERNSEY (St Michel du Valle) *Win 14*   **P** *The Crown*   R S K TANSWELL

GUERNSEY (St Peter Port) *Win 14*   **P** *The Crown*   R M E J BARRETT   **C** P A GRAYSMITH

GUERNSEY (St Philippe de Torteval) *Win 14*   **P** *The Crown*   R M R CHARMLEY   **NSM** T B CHARMLEY

GUERNSEY (St Pierre du Bois) *Win 14*   **P** *The Crown*   R A DATTA

GUERNSEY (St Sampson) *Win 14*   **P** *The Crown*   R *vacant*

GUERNSEY (St Saviour) (Chapel of St Apolline) *Win 14*   **P** *The Crown*   R M R CHARMLEY   **NSM** T B CHARMLEY

GUERNSEY (St Stephen) *Win 14*   **P** *R St Peter Port*   V *vacant*

GUERNSEY (Ste Marie du Castel) *Win 14*   **P** *The Crown*   R S I LAMB   **NSM** B J HERVÉ

GUERNSEY L'Islet (St Mary)   *see* Guernsey St Sampson *Win*

GUESTLING (St Laurence)   *see* Westfield and Guestling *Chich*

GUESTWICK (St Peter)   *see* Heart of Norfolk *Nor*

GUILDEN MORDEN (St Mary)   *see* Shingay Gp *Ely*

GUILDEN SUTTON (St John the Baptist)   *see* Plemstall w Guilden Sutton *Ches*

GUILDFORD (All Saints) *Guildf 5*   **P** *Bp*   V B A WATSON

GUILDFORD (Christ Church) *Guildf 5*   **P** *Simeon's Trustees*   V N J WILLIAMS   **C** J C TRICKEY   **NSM** B G MCNAIR SCOTT

GUILDFORD (Holy Spirit)   *see* Burpham *Guildf*

GUILDFORD (Holy Trinity) (St Mary the Virgin) (St Michael) *Guildf 5*   **P** *Bp*   R R L COTTON   C T G E POTE   **NSM** B CAHILL-NICHOLLS   **OLM** J J HEDGECOCK, R M PIERCE

GUILDFORD (St Luke)   *see* Burpham *Guildf*

GUILDFORD (St Nicolas) *Guildf 5*   **P** *Bp*   R N C ROBERTS

GUILDFORD (St Saviour) *Guildf 5*   **P** *Simeon's Trustees*   R M C L NORRIS   C K MORRIS, L M WEBB   **NSM** J T MANKEL, P A FENNER

GUILSBOROUGH (St Ethelreda) and Hollowell and Cold Ashby and Cottesbrooke w Great Creaton and Thornby and Ravensthorpe and Spratton *Pet 2*   **P** *Bp, DBP, A R MacDonald-Buchanan Esq, and J S McCall Esq (jt)*   R A TWIGG   C J H CRAIG PECK   **NSM** C MOSS, C N BURNETT

GUILTCROSS, comprising Blo' Norton, Garboldisham, Kenninghall, and Riddlesworth *Nor 11*   **P** *Bp, Mrs C Noel, Exors C P B Goldson, and DBP (jt)*   R *vacant*

GUISBOROUGH (St Nicholas) *York 16*   **P** *Abp*   R A PHILLIPSON

GUISELEY (St Oswald King and Martyr) w Esholt *Leeds 12*   **P** *Bp, Trin Coll Cam, and Mrs N A Gottlieb (jt)*   R D PICKETT   **NSM** J T RICHARDSON

GUIST (St Andrew)   *see* Heart of Norfolk *Nor*

GUITING POWER (St Michael)   *see* The Guitings, Cutsdean, Farmcote etc *Glouc*

GUITINGS, Cutsdean, Farmcote, Upper and Lower Slaughter w Eyford and Naunton, The *Glouc 8*   **P** *Bp, Ch Ch Ox, Guiting Manor Amenity Trust, and F E B Witts Esq (jt)*   R K R SCOTT   C C A COWIE   **OLM** S B PESTELL

GULDEFORD, EAST (St Mary)   *see* Rye *Chich*

GULVAL (St Gulval) and Madron *Truro 4*   **P** *Ld Chan and Bp (jt)*   **NSM** J S THOMAS, P G BUTTERFIELD

GULWORTHY (St Paul)   *see* Tavistock, Gulworthy and Brent Tor *Ex*

GUMLEY (St Helen)   *see* Foxton w Gumley and Laughton *Leic*

GUNBY (St Nicholas)   *see* Colsterworth Par *Linc*

GUNBY (St Peter)   *see* Burgh Gp *Linc*

GUNHOUSE (St Barnabas)   *see* Trentside E *Linc*

GUNN CHAPEL (Holy Name)   *see* Swimbridge, W Buckland, Landkey, and E Buckland *Ex*

GUNNERTON (St Christopher)   *see* Chollerton w Birtley and Thockrington *Newc*

GUNNESS (St Barnabas)   *see* Trentside E *Linc*

GUNNISLAKE (St Anne)   *see* Tamar Valley *Truro*

GUNTHORPE (St John the Baptist)   *see* Burton Joyce, Bulcote and Stoke Bardolph etc *S'well*

GUNTHORPE (St Mary)   *see* Stiffkey and Bale *Nor*

GUNTON (St Benedict)   *see* Hopton, Corton and Gunton *Nor*

GUNTON (St Peter) *as above*

GUNWALLOE (St Winwalloe)   *see* Mullion and Cury w Gunwalloe *Truro*

GURNARD (All Saints) w Cowes St Faith *Portsm 7*   **P** *Bp*   V A COLLINSON   **NSM** D M NETHERWAY

GUSSAGE (St Andrew)   *see* Sixpenny Handley w Gussage St Andrew etc *Sarum*

GUSSAGE ALL SAINTS (All Saints)   *see* Chase *Sarum*

GUSSAGE ST MICHAEL (St Michael) *as above*

GUSTARD WOOD (St Peter)   *see* Wheathampstead *St Alb*

GUSTON (St Martin of Tours)   *see* Dover Town *Cant*

GWEEK (Mission Church)   *see* Constantine *Truro*

GWENNAP (St Weneppa)   *see* St Stythians w Perranarworthal and Gwennap *Truro*

GWINEAR (St Winnear)   *see* Godrevy *Truro*

GWITHIAN (St Gwithian) *as above*

HABBERLEY (St Mary)   *see* Minsterley, Habberley and Hope w Shelve *Heref*

HABERGHAM (All Saints)   *see* W Burnley All SS *Blackb*

HABERGHAM EAVES (St Matthew the Apostle)   *see* Burnley St Matt w H Trin *Blackb*

HABROUGH (St Margaret)   *see* Abbey Gp *Linc*

HABTON, GREAT (St Chad)   *see* Kirby Misperton w Normanby and Salton *York*

HACCOMBE (St Blaise)   *see* Shaldon, Stokeinteignhead, Combeinteignhead etc *Ex*

HACCONBY (St Andrew)   *see* Ringstone in Aveland Gp *Linc*

HACHESTON (St Andrew)   *see* Orebeck *St E*

HACKBRIDGE and Beddington Corner (All Saints) *S'wark 23*   **P** *Bp*   V S L BILLIN   **NSM** H E ZUNDE-BAKER

HACKENTHORPE (Christ Church) *Sheff 1*   **P** *Bp*   **P-in-c** P R ALLEN   **NSM** C D I REES, K A GREEN

HACKFORD (St Mary the Virgin)   *see* High Oak, Hingham and Scoulton w Wood Rising *Nor*

HACKINGTON (St Stephen) *Cant 3* **P** *Adn Cant*
R K MADDY **Hon C** S C E LAIRD
HACKNESS (St Peter) w Harwood Dale *York 15* **P** *Lord*
Derwent **P-in-c** M A HAND
HACKNEY (All Souls) *see* Homerton *Lon*
HACKNEY (St James) *see* Clapton St Jas *Lon*
HACKNEY (St John) (St Luke) *Lon 5* **P** *Bp, Adn, Lord*
Amherst, and St Olave Hart Street Trustees (jt) **R** A S GORDON
C C C BRODIE-LEVINSOHN, M D NELSON, N A MAXWELL
HACKNEY (St Luke) Homerton Terrace *see* Hackney *Lon*
HACKNEY (St Michael and All Angels) *see* S Hackney St Mich
w Haggerston St Paul *Lon*
HACKNEY (St Thomas) *see* Stamford Hill St Thos *Lon*
HACKNEY Mount Pleasant Lane (St Matthew) *see* Upper
Clapton St Matt *Lon*
HACKNEY WICK (St Mary of Eton) *Lon 5* **P** *Eton Coll*
V S MAKIN **NSM** D C GRAY
HACKNEY, OVER (Mission Room) *see* Darley, S Darley and
Winster *Derby*
HACKNEY, SOUTH (St John of Jerusalem) *see* S Hackney St Jo
w Ch Ch *Lon*
HACKNEY, SOUTH (St John of Jerusalem) w Christ Church
Lon 5 **P** *Lord Amherst* **R** A M W WILSON **C** S A MALONEY
**HACKNEY, SOUTH (St Michael and All Angels) London
Fields w Haggerston St Paul** *Lon 5* **P** R S Hackney St Jo w
Ch Ch **V** D GERRANS
HACKNEY, WEST (St Paul) *Lon 5* **P** *Bp* **R** W D N WEIR
NSM J C GAU
HACKTHORN (St Michael and All Angels) *see* Owmby Gp
Linc
HACONBY (St Andrew) *see* Ringstone in Aveland Gp *Linc*
HADDENHAM (Holy Trinity) *Ely 8* **P** *Adn Ely*
NSM J STIMPSON
HADDENHAM (St Mary the Virgin) *see* Wychert Vale *Ox*
HADDISCOE (St Mary) *see* Waveney Marshlands *Nor*
HADDLESEY (St John the Baptist) w Hambleton and Birkin
York 4 **P** *Abp and Simeon's Trustees (jt)* **P-in-c** A V BURR
Ely
HADDON (St Mary) *see* Stilton w Denton and Caldecote etc
Ely
HADDON, EAST (St Mary the Virgin) *see* Brington w
Whilton and Norton etc *Pet*
HADDON, OVER (St Anne) *see* Bakewell, Ashford w Sheldon
and Rowsley *Derby*
HADDON, WEST (All Saints) *see* Long Buckby w Watford and
W Haddon w Winwick *Pet*
HADFIELD (St Andrew) *Derby 4* **P** *Bp* **V** F A WALTERS
HADHAM, LITTLE (St Cecilia) *see* Albury, Lt Hadham and
Much Hadham *St Alb*
HADHAM, MUCH (St Andrew) *as above*
HADLEIGH (St Barnabas) *Chelmsf 12* **P** *Bp*
P-in-c R CARTWRIGHT **NSM** J E TURNER
HADLEIGH (St James the Less) *Chelmsf 12* **P** *Dr P W M*
Copeman and A R C Copeman Esq (jt) **P-in-c** R CARTWRIGHT
NSM J E TURNER
HADLEIGH (St Mary), Layham and Shelley *St E 4* **P** *St Jo*
Coll Cam and Abp (alt) **V** J H DELFGOU
HADLEY (Holy Trinity) and Wellington Christ Church
Lich 20 **P** *Bp, Adn Salop, and V Wellington All SS w Eyton*
V S J HOWES
HADLEY WOOD (St Paul) Proprietary Chapel *Lon 16*
Min R MACKAY
HADLOW (St Mary) *Roch 8* **P** *Exors Miss I N King*
V P J WHITE
HADLOW DOWN (St Mark) *see* Buxted and Hadlow Down
Chich
HADNALL (St Mary Magdalene) *see* Astley, Clive, Grinshill
and Hadnall *Lich*
HADSTOCK (St Botolph) *see* Saffron Walden and Villages
Chelmsf
HADZOR w Oddingley (St James) *see* Bowbrook *Worc*
HAGBOURNE (St Andrew) *see* The Churn *Ox*
HAGGERSTON (St Chad) *Lon 5* **P** *The Crown*
V J J WESTCOTT
HAGLEY (St John the Baptist) *Worc 5* **P** *Exors Viscount*
Cobham **R** R J C NEWTON **NSM** K TOPHAM
HAGLEY, WEST (St Saviour) *see* Hagley *Worc*
HAGNABY (St Andrew) *see* Bolingbroke Deanery *Linc*
HAGWORTHINGHAM (Holy Trinity) *as above*
HAIGH (St David) *see* Wigan *Liv*
HAIL WESTON (St Nicholas) *see* The Staughtons w Hail
Weston *Ely*
HAILE (not known) *see* Egremont and Haile *Carl*
HAILES (Chapel) *see* Winchcombe *Glouc*
HAILEY (St John the Evangelist) *see* Witney *Ox*
HAILSHAM (St Mary) (Emmanuel) *Chich 13* **P** *Ch Soc Trust*
V D J BOURNE **C** D P GRIFFIN, R M GRAHAM

HAINAULT (St Paul) *Chelmsf 6* **P** *Bp* **V** K ASHTON
NSM S A CLARKE-MOISLEY
HAINFORD (All Saints) *see* Coltishall w Gt Hautbois,
Frettenham etc *Nor*
HAINTON (St Mary) *see* Barkwith Gp *Linc*
HALA (St Paul's Centre) *see* Scotforth *Blackb*
HALAM (St Michael) *see* Edingley w Halam *S'well*
**HALAS, comprising Cradley, Halesowen, Hasbury, Lapal, and
Romsley** *Worc 5* **P** *Patr Bd* **TR** R S HALL **TV** D MELVILLE,
H CHARLTON **C** M J BEYNON
HALBERTON (St Andrew) *see* Sampford Peverell, Uplowman,
Holcombe Rogus etc *Ex*
HALDEN, HIGH (St Mary the Virgin) *see* Bethersden w High
Halden and Woodchurch *Cant*
HALDENS (Christ the King) *see* Digswell *St Alb*
HALDON *see* Teignmouth, Ideford w Luton, Ashcombe etc
Ex
HALE (St David) *see* Timperley *Ches*
HALE (St John the Evangelist) *see* Badshot Lea and Hale
Guildf
HALE (St Mary) *see* Fordingbridge and Hyde and Breamore
etc *Win*
HALE (St Mary) *see* S Widnes *Liv*
HALE (St Peter) and Ashley *Ches 10* **P** *V Bowdon*
V K J STANTON **NSM** A G RUSTED
HALE BARNS (All Saints) w Ringway *Ches 10* **P** *Bp*
V G C JAQUISS
HALE, GREAT (St John the Baptist) *see* Heckington and
Helpringham Gp *Linc*
HALE, UPPER (St Mark) *see* Badshot Lea and Hale *Guildf*
HALES (St Mary) *see* Cheswardine, Childs Ercall, Hales,
Hinstock etc *Lich*
HALESOWEN (St John the Baptist) *see* Halas *Worc*
HALESWORTH (St Mary) *see* Blyth Valley *St E*
**HALEWOOD (St Nicholas) (St Mary) and Hunts Cross
Team, The** *Liv 2* **P** *Patr Bd* **TR** M P WOODSFORD
TV A J RADFORD
HALEY HILL (All Souls) *see* Halifax w Siddal *Leeds*
HALFORD (Our Blessed Lady) *see* Stourdene Gp *Cov*
HALFORD (St Thomas) *see* Craven Arms *Heref*
HALFWAY (St Peter) *see* W Sheppey *Cant*
HALIFAX (St Hilda) *see* Warley and Halifax St Hilda *Leeds*
HALIFAX (All Saints) *Leeds 8* **P** *Ch Trust Fund Trust* **V** *vacant*
HALIFAX (Christ Church) *see* Halifax St Aug and Mount
Pellon *Leeds*
HALIFAX (Holy Trinity) (St Jude) *Leeds 8* **P** *Bp, V Halifax,
and trustees (jt)* **V** S M STOBART
HALIFAX (St Anne-in-the-Grove) *see* Southowram *Leeds*
HALIFAX (St John the Baptist) (All Souls) w Siddal *Leeds 8*
P *The Crown and Ch Trust Fund Trust (alt)* **V** H J BARBER
C J L FINN **Hon C** D J CARPENTER
HALIFAX MINSTER *see* Halifax w Siddal *Leeds*
HALIFAX St Augustine (School Hall) and Mount Pellon
Leeds 8 **P** *Bp, Simeon's Trustees, and local trustees (jt)*
V *vacant*
HALL GREEN (Church of the Ascension) *Birm 2* **P** *Bp, V
Yardley, and Vice-Chmn of PCC (jt)* **V** N BOUMENJEL
HALL GREEN (St Michael) *Birm 2* **P** *Bp*
P-in-c M W STEPHENSON **C** J N BROWN
OLM I D CROCKFORD
HALL GREEN (St Peter) *Birm 2* **P** *Bp* **V** M W STEPHENSON
C J N BROWN
HALL STREET (St Andrew) *see* Stockport and Brinnington
Ches
HALLAM, WEST (St Wilfrid) and Mapperley w Stanley
Derby 8 **P** *Bp* **R** G R TURNER-CALLIS
OLM J V HUTCHINSON
**HALLATON (St Michael and All Angels) and Allexton, w
Horninghold, Tugby, and East Norton, and Slawston**
Leic 5 **P** *Bp, DBP, and E Brudenell Esq (jt)* **R** *vacant*
HALLING (St John the Baptist) *see* Cuxton and Halling *Roch*
**HALLINGBURY, GREAT (St Giles) (St Andrew) and LITTLE
(St Mary the Virgin)** *Chelmsf 4* **P** *Bp and Charterhouse (jt)*
P-in-c D W HERRICK **C** D JEWSON, R L CHALLIS
HALLIWELL (St Luke) *see* W Bolton *Man*
HALLIWELL (St Margaret) *see* Heaton Ch Ch w Halliwell
St Marg *Man*
**HALLIWELL (St Peter) (Barrow Bridge Mission)
(St Andrew's Mission Church)** *Man 3* **P** *Trustees*
C D BRAE
HALLOUGHTON (St James) *see* W Trent *S'well*
**HALLOW (St Philip and St James) and Grimley w Holt and
Lower Broadheath** *Worc 4* **P** *Bp* **R** K K BREWIS
HALLWOOD Ecumenical Parish (St Mark) *Ches 3* **P** *DBP*
V L J MACINNES

HALSALL (St Cuthbert), Lydiate and Downholland *Liv 14*
  P *Bp and Brig D H Blundell-Hollinshead-Blundell (jt)*
  NSM A D L BAKER, G L GARDNER

HALSE (Mission Church) *see* Brackley St Pet w St Jas *Pet*

HALSE (St James the Less) *see* Milverton w Halse, Fitzhead
  and Ash Priors *B & W*

HALSETOWN (St John's in the Fields) *see* St Ives and
  Halsetown *Truro*

HALSHAM (All Saints) *see* Burstwick, Burton Pidsea etc *York*

HALSTEAD (St Margaret) *see* Knockholt w Halstead *Roch*

HALSTEAD AREA (St Andrew), including Colne Engaine,
  Earls Colne, Gestingthorpe, Gosfield, Great Maplestead,
  Greenstead Green, Little Maplestead, Pebmarsh, and White
  Colne *Chelmsf 18* **P** *Patr Bd* **P-in-c** K E DE BOURCIER
  TV B VINCENT, M D PAYNE **C** J J PARROTT, R F BRAISBY
  NSM S D QUILTER

HALSTOCK (St Mary) *see* Melbury *Sarum*

HALSTOW, HIGH (St Margaret) (All Hallows) and Hoo
  St Mary *Roch 6* **P** *MMCET and Ch Soc Trust (jt)*
  R S G GWILT

HALSTOW, LOWER (St Margaret) *see* The Six *Cant*

HALTER DEVIL (Mission Room) *see* Mugginton and Kedleston
  Derby

HALTON (St Mary) *Ches 3* **P** *Bp* **V** A MITCHELL

HALTON (St Michael and All Angels) *see* Wendover and
  Halton *Ox*

HALTON (St Oswald and St Cuthbert and King Alfwald) *see*
  Corbridge w Halton and Newton Hall *Newc*

HALTON (St Wilfred) *see* Slyne w Hest and Halton w
  Aughton *Blackb*

HALTON (St Wilfrid) and Osmondthorpe St Philip *Leeds 13*
  P *Bp* **V** H J SMITH **C** R G DENTON

HALTON HOLGATE (St Andrew) *see* Bolingbroke Deanery
  Linc

HALTON QUAY (St Indract's Chapel) *see* Tamar Valley *Truro*

HALTON WEST (Mission Church) *see* Hellifield and Long
  Preston *Leeds*

HALTON, EAST (St Peter) *see* Abbey Gp *Linc*

HALTON, WEST (St Etheldreda) *see* Alkborough *Linc*

HALTWHISTLE (Holy Cross) and Greenhead *Newc 10* **P** *Bp*
  V *vacant*

HALVERGATE (St Peter and St Paul) *see* Acle and Bure to Yare
  Nor

HALWELL (St Leonard) *see* Diptford w N Huish, Ermington,
  Halwell etc *Ex*

HALWILL (St Peter and St James) *see* Ashwater, Halwill,
  Beaworthy, Clawton etc *Ex*

HAM (All Saints) *see* Savernake *Sarum*

HAM (St Andrew) *S'wark 15* **P** *K Coll Cam* **V** A H L PETTIT

HAM (St Barnabas Mission Church) *see* Chard St Mary w
  Combe St Nicholas, Wambrook etc *B & W*

HAM (St James the Less) *see* Plymouth St Pet and H Apostles
  Ex

HAM (St Richard) *S'wark 16* **P** *Bp* **V** S C COUPLAND
  NSM S E ATKINS

HAM HILL VILLAGES, comprising Chiselborough, Middle
  Chinnock, Montacute, Norton-sub-Hamdon, Odcombe,
  Stoke sub Hamdon, and West Chinnock *B & W 5* **P** *Bp, Ch
  Patr Trust, and Ch Ch Ox (jt)* **P-in-c** N J CLARKE
  C M A GURNER **NSM** G J W EDMUNDS

HAMBLE LE RICE (St Andrew) *Win 10* **P** *St Mary's Coll Win*
  V G J WHITING

HAMBLEDEN (St Mary the Virgin) *see* Hambleden Valley *Ox*

HAMBLEDEN VALLEY, comprising Fawley, Fingest,
  Hambleden w Frieth, Medmenham, and Turville *Ox 18*
  P *Bp, Viscount Hambleden, and Miss M Mackenzie (jt)*
  P-in-c S E LEPP **NSM** S A MORTON

HAMBLEDON (St Peter and St Paul) *see* Soberton, Newtown
  and Hambledon *Portsm*

HAMBLEDON (St Peter) *see* Busbridge and Hambledon
  Guildf

HAMBLETON (St Andrew) *see* Oakham, Ashwell, Braunston,
  Brooke, Egleton etc *Pet*

HAMBLETON (St Mary) *see* Haddlesey w Hambleton and
  Birkin *York*

HAMBLETON (The Blessed Virgin Mary) *see* Over Wyre
  Blackb

HAMBRIDGE (St James the Less) *see* Isle Valley *B & W*

HAMER (All Saints) and Healey *Man 6* **P** *Bp*
  P-in-c G BARNETT **C** E D O'BAKA-TORTO

HAMERINGHAM (All Saints) *see* Fen and Hill Gp *Linc*

HAMERTON (All Saints) *see* N Leightonstone *Ely*

HAMILTON Conventional District *Leic 1* **Min** E W DOWN

HAMILTON TERRACE (St Mark) *see* St Marylebone St Mark
  Hamilton Terrace *Lon*

HAMMER (St Michael) *see* Fernhurst, Lynchmere and
  Camelsdale *Chich*

HAMMERFIELD (St Francis of Assisi) *see* Boxmoor St Jo *St Alb*

HAMMERSMITH (Holy Innocents) (St John the Evangelist)
  Lon 9 **P** *Bp* **P-in-c** D W G MATTHEWS
  NSM P P Y MULLINGS

HAMMERSMITH (St Luke) *Lon 9* **P** *Bp* **V** R M BASTABLE
  C W M HAMILTON-BOX

HAMMERSMITH (St Matthew) *Lon 9* **P** *Trustees* **V** *vacant*

HAMMERSMITH (St Michael and St George) *see* White City
  Lon

HAMMERSMITH (St Paul) *Lon 9* **P** *Bp* **V** S G DOWNHAM
  C M F J RUOFF, P J P WYNTER **NSM** V I THOMAS

HAMMERSMITH (St Peter) *Lon 9* **P** *Bp* **V** C C CLAPHAM

HAMMERSMITH (St Saviour) *see* Cobbold Road St Sav w
  St Mary *Lon*

HAMMERSMITH (St Simon) *Lon 9* **P** *Simeon's Trustees*
  V C J COLLINGTON

HAMMERSMITH, NORTH (St Katherine) *Lon 9* **P** *Bp*
  P-in-c J TATE **NSM** L C TATE

HAMMERWICH (St John the Baptist) *see* Burntwood, Chase
  Terrace etc *Lich*

HAMMOON (St Paul) *see* Okeford *Sarum*

HAMNISH (St Dubricius and All Saints) *see* Leominster *Heref*

HAMPDEN PARK (St Mary) and The Hydneye *Chich 14*
  P *Bp* **P-in-c** A J RANSOM **NSM** J MANN

HAMPDEN, GREAT (St Mary Magdalene) *see* Prestwood and
  Gt Hampden *Ox*

HAMPDEN, LITTLE (not known) *see* Gt Missenden w
  Ballinger and Lt Hampden *Ox*

HAMPNETT (St George) *see* Northleach w Hampnett and
  Farmington etc *Glouc*

HAMPRESTON (All Saints) *Sarum 9* **P** *Patr Bd* **TR** S A L PIX
  TV P CHABALA **C** O S G FRICKER

HAMPSTEAD (Christ Church) *Lon 15* **P** *SMF*
  V P D CONRAD

HAMPSTEAD (Emmanuel) West End *Lon 15* **P** *Bp*
  V J G F KESTER **C** H J J SIMS-WILLIAMS **NSM** A ARNELL,
  A FRITZE-SHANKS

HAMPSTEAD (St Cuthbert) *see* W Hampstead St Cuth *Lon*

HAMPSTEAD (St James) *see* Kilburn St Mary w All So and W
  Hampstead St Jas *Lon*

HAMPSTEAD (St John) *Lon 15* **P** *DBP* **V** J J FLETCHER
  C G S DUNN

HAMPSTEAD (St John) Downshire Hill Proprietary Chapel
  Lon 15 **C** C J BRIXTON **Min** T A WATTS

HAMPSTEAD (St Jude on the Hill) *see* Hampstead Garden
  Suburb *Lon*

HAMPSTEAD (St Luke) *see* W Hampstead St Luke *Lon*

HAMPSTEAD (St Saviour) *see* Chalk Farm *Lon*

HAMPSTEAD (St Stephen w All Hallows) *Lon 15* **P** *DBP and
  D&C Cant (jt)* **V** D N C HOULDING

HAMPSTEAD Belsize Park (St Peter) *see* Belsize Park *Lon*

HAMPSTEAD GARDEN SUBURB (St Jude on the Hill) *Lon 14*
  P *Bp* **V** A R G WALKER

HAMPSTEAD NORREYS (St Mary) *see* Hermitage *Ox*

HAMPSTEAD, WEST (Holy Trinity) *Lon 15* **P** *MMCET*
  V A K KEIGHLEY **C** K L BREUSS

HAMPSTEAD, WEST (St Cuthbert) *Lon 15* **P** *Ch Trust Fund
  Trust* **P-in-c** J G F KESTER **NSM** H V THOMAS

HAMPSTEAD, WEST (St Luke) *Lon 15* **P** *CPAS*
  V A C TRESIDDER

**HAMPSTHWAITE (St Thomas à Becket) and Killinghall and
  Birstwith** *Leeds 18* **P** *Mrs S J Finn, Sir James Aykroyd Bt, Sir
  Thomas Ingilby Bt, and Bp (jt)* **V** S MCCARTER

HAMPTON (All Saints) *Lon 10* **P** *Ld Chan* **V** D WILLIAMS

HAMPTON (no dedication) *Ely 15* **P** *Bp* **V** S P KINDER
  C J G WICKS, R H HILDITCH

HAMPTON (St Andrew) *see* Herne Bay Ch Ch *Cant*

HAMPTON (St Mary the Virgin) *Lon 10* **P** *Ld Chan*
  V B R LOVELL **NSM** C F LOVELL, C I G M E O GISLESKOG

HAMPTON BISHOP (St Andrew) *see* Tupsley w Hampton
  Bishop *Heref*

HAMPTON GAY (St Giles) *see* Akeman *Ox*

HAMPTON HILL (St James) *Lon 10* **P** *V Hampton St Mary*
  V D N WINTERBURN **NSM** J A CAMMIDGE

HAMPTON LOVETT (St Mary and All Saints) *see* Elmley
  Lovett w Hampton Lovett and Elmbridge w Rushock and
  Hartlebury and Ombersley w Doverdale *Worc*

**HAMPTON LUCY (St Peter ad Vincula) w Charlecote and
  Loxley** *Cov 8* **P** *Sir Edmund Fairfax-Lucy Bt (3 turns), Col A
  M H Gregory-Hood (1 turn)* **P-in-c** A B LARKIN

HAMPTON POYLE (St Mary the Virgin) *see* Kidlington w
  Hampton Poyle *Ox*

HAMPTON WICK (St John the Baptist) *Lon 10* **P** *Bp*
  V J M FIELD **C** A R EVANS, T J T SIMPSON

HAMPTON, GREAT AND LITTLE (St Andrew) *see* Bengeworth and Hampton etc *Worc*
HAMPTON-IN-ARDEN (St Mary and St Bartholomew) w Bickenhill St Peter *Birm 6* **P** *Birm Dioc Trustees and Guild of All So (jt)* **R** S C L DIMES **C** C C M DEAN
HAMSEY (St Peter) *Chich 21* **P** *Bp* **P-in-c** A C DUNLOP
HAMSTALL RIDWARE (St Michael and All Angels) *see* Kings Bromley, The Ridwares and Yoxall *Lich*
HAMSTEAD (St Bernard) *Birm 1* **P** *Bp* **V** *vacant*
HAMSTEAD (St Paul) *Birm 1* **P** *Bp* **V** S C BRIDGE
HAMSTEAD MARSHALL (St Mary) *see* Walbury Beacon *Ox*
HAMSTERLEY (St James) and Witton-le-Wear *Dur 3* **P** *Bp and The Crown (alt)* **P-in-c** J FISHER
HAMWORTHY (St Gabriel) (St Michael) *Sarum 7* **P** *MMCET* **R** T J NISBET **C** A D ROSS **NSM** S TAYLOR
HANBOROUGH (St Peter and St Paul) and Freeland *Ox 29* **P** *St Jo Coll Ox* **R** S J STEWART **NSM** M J MADDEN
HANBURY (St Mary the Virgin) *see* Bowbrook *Worc*
HANBURY (St Werburgh), Newborough and Rangemore *Lich 13* **P** *DBP and Personal Reps Lord Burton (jt)* **V** *vacant*
HANDBRIDGE (St Mary without the Walls) *see* Ches St Mary *Ches*
HANDCROSS (All Saints) *see* Slaugham and Staplefield Common *Chich*
HANDFORTH (St Chad) *Ches 17* **P** *R Cheadle* **V** S J BURMESTER
HANDLEY (All Saints) *see* Tattenhall w Burwardsley and Handley *Ches*
HANDLEY (St Mark) *see* N Wingfield, Clay Cross and Pilsley *Derby*
HANDSWORTH (Good News Asian Church) Proprietary Chapel *Birm 1* **NSM** J M CHAUDHARY
HANDSWORTH (St Andrew) *Birm 1* **P** *Bp* **V** *vacant*
HANDSWORTH (St James) *Birm 1* **P** *Bp* **NSM** W HAMILTON
HANDSWORTH (St Mary) *Sheff 1* **P** *DBP* **R** K H JOHNSON
HANDSWORTH (St Mary) Epiphany *Birm 1* **P** *Bp* **R** R STEPHEN
HANDSWORTH (St Michael) (St Peter) *Birm 1* **P** *Bp* **NSM** J M CHAUDHARY
HANDSWORTH WOODHOUSE (St James) *see* Woodhouse St Jas *Sheff*
HANFORD (St Matthias) *Lich 12* **P** *Bp* **V** S A MORRIS **OLM** D J AITKEN
HANGER HILL (Ascension) and West Twyford *Lon 19* **P** *Bp and DBP (jt)* **V** S J REED **NSM** P D HARRIS
HANGER LANE (St Ann) *see* S Tottenham St Ann *Lon*
HANGING HEATON (St Paul) *see* Batley *Leeds*
HANGLETON (St Helen) (St Richard) *Chich 20* **P** *Bp* **V** *vacant*
HANHAM (Christ Church) (St George) *Bris 5* **P** *Bp* **P-in-c** B M CHARLES **C** S J DYSON **NSM** C E EVANS
HANKERTON (Holy Cross) *see* Braydon Brook *Bris*
HANLEY (All Saints) *see* Stoke-upon-Trent and Fenton *Lich*
HANLEY CASTLE (St Mary), Hanley Swan and Welland *Worc 2* **P** *Ld Chan and Exors Sir Berwick Lechmere Bt (alt)* **P-in-c** B UNWIN **NSM** S M E ADENEY
HANLEY CHILD (St Michael and All Angels) *see* Teme Valley S *Worc*
HANLEY Holy Evangelists (St Luke) *Lich 11* **P** *Bp* **TR** P E JONES **TV** S A SMITH **C** P D SWAN **NSM** J BIRKIN
HANLEY ROAD (St Saviour) *Lon 6* **P** *CPAS Patr Trust* **V** P HUGHES **C** M R TINSLEY, M W M SEYMOUR **NSM** R E DAYNES
HANLEY SWAN (St Gabriel) *see* Hanley Castle, Hanley Swan and Welland *Worc*
HANLEY WILLIAM (All Saints) *see* Teme Valley S *Worc*
HANNAH (St Andrew) cum Hagnaby *see* Alford Gp *Linc*
HANNEY, WEST (St James the Great) *see* Vale *Ox*
HANNINGFIELD, EAST (All Saints) *Chelmsf 9* **P** *CPAS* **P-in-c** T G A BROWN **NSM** S S EDMUNDSON
HANNINGFIELD, SOUTH (St Peter) *see* Downham w S Hanningfield and Ramsden Bellhouse *Chelmsf*
HANNINGFIELD, WEST (St Mary and St Edward) *Chelmsf 9* **P** *DBP* **P-in-c** S W NEED **NSM** M K SEAMAN
HANNINGTON (All Saints) *see* Baughurst, Ramsdell, Wolverton w Ewhurst etc *Win*
HANNINGTON (St John the Baptist) *see* Highworth w Sevenhampton and Inglesham etc *Bris*
HANNINGTON (St Peter and St Paul) *see* Walgrave w Hannington and Wold and Scaldwell *Pet*
HANOVER SQUARE (St George) *Lon 3* **P** *Bp* **R** R N S LEECE **NSM** A R L PIGGOT, A W MCCORMACK
HANSLOPE (St James the Great) w Castlethorpe *Ox 16* **P** *Bp* **V** G E ECCLESTONE **C** A H BURNHAM
HANWELL (St Christopher) *Lon 19* **P** *Bp* **R** S VERNON-YORKE

HANWELL (St Mary) *Lon 19* **P** *Bp* **V** A J DAND **NSM** S E DAND
HANWELL (St Mellitus w St Mark) *Lon 19* **P** *Bp* **P-in-c** M P MELLUISH **C** S P PLUMB **NSM** J R G HYDE
HANWELL (St Peter) *see* Ironstone *Ox*
HANWELL (St Thomas) *Lon 19* **P** *The Crown* **V** R B CHAPMAN
HANWOOD, GREAT (St Thomas) and Longden and Annscroft w Pulverbatch *Heref 12* **P** *J A de Grey-Warter Esq, Bp, and MMCET (jt)* **R** G D PHILLIPS
HANWORTH (All Saints) *Lon 11* **P** *Bp* **P-in-c** S DIDUK
HANWORTH (Church at the Pines) *see* Easthampstead *Ox*
HANWORTH (St Bartholomew) *see* Roughton and Felbrigg, Metton, Sustead etc *Nor*
HANWORTH (St George) *Lon 11* **P** *Bp* **P-in-c** M W DOBSON
HANWORTH (St Richard of Chichester) *Lon 11* **P** *Bp* **V** D WIGNALL
HAPPISBURGH (St Mary) *see* Bacton, Happisburgh, Hempstead w Eccles etc *Nor*
HAPTON (St Margaret) *see* Padiham w Hapton and Padiham Green *Blackb*
HAPTON (St Margaret) *see* Upper Tas Valley *Nor*
HARBERTON (St Andrew) *see* Diptford w N Huish, Ermington, Halwell etc *Ex*
HARBERTONFORD (St Peter) *as above*
HARBLEDOWN (St Michael and All Angels) *Cant 3* **P** *Abp* **R** P J HARNDEN
HARBORNE (St Faith and St Laurence) *Birm 3* **P** *Bp* **V** P A WHITE
HARBORNE (St Peter) *Birm 3* **P** *Bp* **P-in-c** K E STOWE **C** C L GIBSON
HARBORNE HEATH (St John the Baptist) *Birm 3* **P** *Ch Soc Trust* **V** L J BROWNE **C** F J R GREGSON, J M TATTERSALL
HARBOROUGH MAGNA (All Saints) *see* Revel Gp *Cov*
HARBRIDGE (All Saints) *see* Ringwood w Ellingham and Harbridge etc *Win*
HARBURY (All Saints) and Ladbroke *Cov 10* **P** *Bp* **P-in-c** A G BATCHELOR
HARBY (All Saints) *see* E Trent *S'well*
HARBY (St Mary the Virgin) *see* Vale of Belvoir *Leic*
HARDEN (St Saviour) and Wilsden, Cullingworth and Denholme *Leeds 1* **P** *Patr Bd* **TR** E C R BURGE **TV** A WOODING **C** A L LUMB **NSM** E MOY
HARDENHUISH (St Nicholas) *see* Chippenham St Paul w Hardenhuish etc *Bris*
HARDHAM (St Botolph) *see* Bury, Coldwaltham, Hardham and Houghton *Chich*
HARDINGHAM (St George) *see* Barnham Broom and Upper Yare *Nor*
HARDINGSTONE (St Edmund), Piddington w Horton and Quinton and Preston Deanery *Pet 4* **P** *Bp* **V** *vacant*
HARDINGTON MANDEVILLE (Blessed Virgin Mary) *see* Coker Ridge *B & W*
HARDINGTON VALE, comprising Farleigh Hungerford, Hemington, Laverton, Norton St Philip, Rode, and Tellisford *B & W 3* **P** *Bp and the Revd P J Owen-Jones (jt)* **R** C H WALKER **C** J S ROBINSON
HARDLEY (St Margaret) *see* Loddon, Sisland, Chedgrave, Hardley and Langley *Nor*
HARDRAW (St Mary and St John) *see* Upper Wensleydale *Leeds*
HARDRES, LOWER (St Mary) *see* Bridge *Cant*
HARDRES, UPPER (St Peter and St Paul) *see* Chartham and Upper Hardres w Stelling *Cant*
HARDWICK (St Leonard) *see* Mears Ashby and Hardwick and Sywell etc *Pet*
HARDWICK (St Margaret) *see* Hempnall *Nor*
HARDWICK (St Mary) *see* Lordsbridge *Ely*
HARDWICK, EAST (St Stephen) *see* Carleton and E Hardwick *Leeds*
HARDWICK-CUM-TUSMORE (St Mary) *see* Shelswell *Ox*
HARDWICKE (Holy Trinity) *see* Cusop w Blakemere, Bredwardine w Brobury etc *Heref*
HARDWICKE (St Mary the Virgin) *see* Schorne *Ox*
HARDWICKE (St Nicholas) and Elmore w Longney *Glouc 2* **P** *Adn Glouc and Ld Chan (alt)* **P-in-c** R A MARTIN **NSM** G R W PARFITT
HAREBY (St Peter and St Paul) *see* Bolingbroke Deanery *Linc*
HAREFIELD (St Mary the Virgin) *Lon 21* **P** *The Hon J E F Newdegate* **V** W M DAVIES
HAREHILLS (St Aidan) *see* Leeds St Aid *Leeds*
HAREHILLS (St Cyprian and St James) *see* Burmantofts and Harehills *Leeds*
HAREHILLS (St Wilfrid) *see* Leeds St Wilfrid *Leeds*
HARELAW (St Thomas) and Annfield Plain *Dur 2* **P** *Bp and The Crown (alt)* **P-in-c** L A SUTHERLAND **C** S M MARTIN

HARESCOMBE (St John the Baptist)   *see* Painswick,
Sheepscombe, Cranham, The Edge etc *Glouc*
HARESFIELD (St Peter)   *see* Stroudwater *Glouc*
HAREWOOD (Methodist Chapel)   *see* Collingham w
Harewood *Leeds*
HARFORD (St Petroc)   *see* Ivybridge, Cornwood, Harford and
Sparkwell *Ex*
HARGRAVE (All Saints)   *see* Raunds, Hargrave, Ringstead and
Stanwick *Pet*
HARGRAVE (St Edmund King and Martyr)   *see* Chevington w
Hargrave, Chedburgh w Depden etc *St E*
HARGRAVE (St Peter) *Ches 5*   **P** *Bp*   **V** *vacant*
HARKSTEAD (St Mary)   *see* Shoreline *St E*
HARLASTON (St Matthew)   *see* Mease Valley *Lich*
HARLAXTON Group, The (St Mary and St Peter), including
Denton, Stroxton, Woolsthorpe, and Wyville *Linc 20*   **P** *Bp,*
DBP, Sir Richard Welby Bt, D&C, and Duke of Rutland (jt)
R *vacant*
HARLESCOTT (Holy Spirit) (Emmanuel) *Lich 19*   **P** *Bp*
C M J HEATH   **NSM** G W SMALL
HARLESDEN (All Souls) *Lon 18*   **P** *The Crown*   **V** *vacant*
HARLESDEN (St Mark)   *see* Kensal Rise St Mark *Lon*
HARLESTON (St Augustine)   *see* Combs and Finborough *St E*
HARLESTON (St John the Baptist)   *see* Redenhall w Scole *Nor*
HARLESTONE (St Andrew)   *see* Brington w Whilton and
Norton etc *Pet*
HARLEY (St Mary)   *see* Wenlock *Heref*
HARLING, EAST (St Peter and St Paul) w West, Bridgham
w Roudham, Larling, Brettenham and Rushford *Nor 11*
P *Ld Chan (1 turn), DBP, Sir Robin Nugent Bt, C D F Musker*
Esq, Major E H C Garnier, and Exors Sir John Musker (3 turns)
R *vacant*
HARLINGTON (Christ Church)   *see* W Hayes *Lon*
HARLINGTON (St Mary the Virgin), Tingrith and
Westoning *St Alb 8*   **P** *Ld Chan and Bp (alt)*
V N L WASHINGTON   **C** L J WASHINGTON
HARLINGTON (St Peter and St Paul) *Lon 21*   **P** *Bp*
P-in-c D M TALBOT
HARLOW (St Mary and St Hugh w St John the Baptist)
Chelmsf 4   **P** *Simeon's Trustees and Bp (alt)*   **V** S J SWIFT
HARLOW (St Mary Magdalene) *Chelmsf 4*   **P** *V Harlow*
St Mary and St Hugh etc   **V** J W E RODLEY   **NSM** G R NEAVE
HARLOW GREEN (St Ninian) and Lamesley *Dur 11*   **P** *Bp*
NSM G J LACKENBY
HARLOW Town Centre (St Paul) w Little Parndon *Chelmsf 4*
P *Patr Bd*   **TR** M J HARRIS   **TV** J G M POYNTZ
C N J JOSS-POTHEN   **NSM** A T KEEBLE
HARLSEY (St Oswald)   *see* Osmotherley w Harlsey and
Ingleby Arncliffe *York*
HARLTON (Assumption of the Blessed Virgin Mary)   *see*
Lordsbridge *Ely*
HARMANSWATER (St Paul)   *see* Bracknell *Ox*
HARMONDSWORTH (St Mary the Virgin) *Lon 21*   **P** *DBP*
P-in-c D M TALBOT   **NSM** C K OKPALA, T B I OLISA
HARMSTON (All Saints)   *see* Graffoe Gp *Linc*
HARNHAM (St George) (All Saints) *Sarum 13*   **P** *Bp (1 turn),*
V Britford (2 turns)   **V** R M ROBERTS   **NSM** J G POPPLETON,
M BADGER
HARNHILL (St Michael and All Angels)   *see* S Cotswolds *Glouc*
HAROLD HILL (St George) *Chelmsf 2*   **P** *Bp*   **V** *vacant*
HAROLD HILL (St Paul) *Chelmsf 2*   **P** *Bp*   **V** *vacant*
HAROLD WOOD (St Peter) *Chelmsf 2*   **P** *New Coll Ox*
V R A HUDSON   **C** A D BELLIS, R V J POWER
HAROME (St Saviour)   *see* Kirkdale w Harome, Nunnington
and Pockley *York*
HARPENDEN (St John the Baptist) *St Alb 7*   **P** *DBP*
V *vacant*
HARPENDEN (St Nicholas) (All Saints) *St Alb 7*   **P** *Ld Chan*
R D L STAMPS   **C** J C BROWN, S L GOODSON
HARPFORD (St Gregory the Great)   *see* Ottery St Mary,
Alfington, W Hill, Tipton etc *Ex*
HARPHAM (St John of Beverley)   *see* The Beacon *York*
HARPLEY (St Lawrence)   *see* Ashwicken w Leziate, Bawsey etc
Nor
HARPOLE (All Saints)   *see* Bugbrooke, Harpole, Kislingbury
etc *Pet*
HARPSDEN (St Margaret)   *see* Shiplake w Dunsden and
Harpsden *Ox*
HARPSWELL (St Chad)   *see* Trentcliffe Gp *Linc*
HARPTREE, EAST (St Laurence) w WEST (Blessed Virgin
Mary) and Hinton Blewett *B & W 9*   **P** *Duchy of Cornwall*
R *vacant*
HARPUR HILL (St James)   *see* Buxton w Burbage and King
Sterndale *Derby*
HARPURHEY (Christ Church) *Man 1*   **P** *Bp and Trustees (jt)*
P-in-c N R ELLIOTT

HARPURHEY (St Stephen)   *see* Harpurhey *Man*
HARRABY (St Elisabeth) *Carl 3*   **P** *Bp*
P-in-c R O GOODFELLOW   **Hon C** E M SMITH
HARRIETSHAM (St John the Baptist)   *see* Len Valley *Cant*
HARRINGAY (St Paul) *Lon 17*   **P** *Bp*   **P-in-c** P R SNOW
C P J HENDERSON
HARRINGTON (St Mary)   *see* S Ormsby Gp *Linc*
HARRINGTON (St Mary) and Distington *Carl 7*   **P** *The Hon J*
N Lowther and Mrs E H S Thornely (jt)   **R** J H POWLEY
HARRINGTON (St Peter and St Paul)   *see* Arthingworth,
Harrington w Oxendon and E Farndon *Pet*
HARRINGWORTH (St John the Baptist)   *see* Lyddington,
Bisbrooke, Caldecott, Glaston etc *Pet*
HARROGATE (St Luke's Church Centre)   *see* Bilton *Leeds*
HARROGATE (St Mark) *Leeds 18*   **P** *Peache Trustees*
V M J RESCH   **C** D J WATTS, J A DUFF, K S MASON
NSM J W HANDLEY
HARROGATE (St Wilfrid) *Leeds 18*   **P** *Bp*
TR G R WADDINGTON   **NSM** T J BUCKINGHAM
HARROGATE, HIGH (Christ Church) *Leeds 18*   **P** *Bp*
V M S EVANS
HARROGATE, HIGH (St Peter) *Leeds 18*   **P** *Ch Patr Trust*
V A J P GARROW   **C** C C CLAYTON   **Hon C** T J HURREN
NSM R T NOLAN
HARROLD (St Peter and All Saints)   *see* Chellington *St Alb*
HARROW (All Saints)   *see* Harrow Weald All SS *Lon*
HARROW (Christ Church)   *see* Roxeth *Lon*
HARROW (Holy Trinity)   *see* Wealdstone H Trin *Lon*
HARROW (St Alban)   *see* N Harrow St Alb *Lon*
HARROW (St Mary)   *see* Harrow St Mary *Lon*
HARROW (St Michael and All Angels)   *see* Harrow Weald
St Mich *Lon*
HARROW (St Paul)   *see* S Harrow St Paul *Lon*
HARROW (St Peter)   *see* W Harrow St Pet *Lon*
HARROW GREEN (Holy Trinity and St Augustine of Hippo)
see Leytonstone H Trin and St Aug Harrow Green *Chelmsf*
HARROW ON THE HILL (St Mary) *Lon 20*   **P** *Bp, Adn, and Hd*
Master Harrow Sch (jt)   **V** J E POWER   **Hon C** A J CHRISTIAN
NSM G W DALE
HARROW ROAD (Emmanuel)   *see* W Kilburn St Luke and
Harrow Road Em *Lon*
HARROW WEALD (All Saints) *Lon 20*   **P** *Bp, Adn, V Harrow*
St Mary, and R Bushey (jt)   **V** J W BARKER
HARROW WEALD (St Michael and All Angels) *Lon 20*   **P** *Bp*
V J STOWELL
HARROW, NORTH (St Alban) *Lon 20*   **P** *Bp*   **V** S E ARCHER
HARROW, SOUTH (St Paul) *Lon 20*   **P** *R St Bride Fleet Street w*
Bridewell and Trin Gough Square   **V** I P DOWSETT
C M S SEEVARATNAM, S B JOHNSON
HARROW, WEST (St Peter) *Lon 20*   **P** *Bp and Ch Patr Trust*
(jt)   **C** R E CAMPBELL
HARROWBARROW (All Saints)   *see* Tamar Valley *Truro*
HARROWBY (The Ascension)   *see* Grantham, Harrowby w
Londonthorpe *Linc*
HARROWDEN, GREAT (All Saints) w LITTLE (St Mary the
Virgin) and Orlingbury and Isham w Pytchley *Pet 6*
P *Bp and Sir Philip Naylor-Leyland Bt (jt)*   **R** D C MAUD
HARSTON (All Saints) w Hauxton and Newton *Ely 5*   **P** *Bp*
(2 turns), D&C (1 turn)   **V** S J TALBOTT
C S M BOWDEN-PICKSTOCK
HARSTON (St Michael and All Angels)   *see* High Framland
Par *Leic*
HARSWELL (St Peter)   *see* Holme and Seaton Ross Gp *York*
HART (St Mary Magdalene) w Elwick Hall *Dur 6*   **P** *Bp and*
DBP (alt)   **P-in-c** J BURBURY
HART PLAIN   *see* Hartplain *Portsm*
HARTBURN (All Saints)   *see* Stockton St Pet *Dur*
HARTBURN (St Andrew)   *see* Bolam w Whalton and Hartburn
w Meldon *Newc*
HARTCLIFFE (St Andrew)   *see* Bris St Andr Hartcliffe *Bris*
HARTEST (All Saints)   *see* Glemsford, Hartest w Boxted,
Somerton etc *St E*
HARTFIELD (St Mary) w Coleman's Hatch *Chich 16*   **P** *Bp*
and Earl De la Warr (jt)   **R** J A C SEAR
HARTFORD (All Saints) and Houghton w Wyton *Ely 10*
P *Bp*   **R** G J BOUCHER   **NSM** A O'NEILL, C J P WRIGHT,
E J G STRICKLAND
HARTFORD (St John the Baptist) *Ches 6*   **P** *Ch Soc Trust*
V M I A SMITH   **C** D ALLDRIDGE, J M TEASDALE
NSM G AGAR, J E ROBSON
HARTHILL (All Hallows) and Thorpe Salvin *Sheff 5*   **P** *Bp*
P-in-c G SCHOFIELD
HARTING (St Mary and St Gabriel) w Elsted and Treyford
cum Didling *Chich 3*   **P** *Bp*   **R** H A NEALE-STEVENS
HARTINGTON (St Giles)   *see* Taddington, Chelmorton and
Monyash etc *Derby*

HARTISMERE, NORTH, comprising Brome, Burgate, Palgrave, Stuston, Thrandeston, and Wortham *St E 11* **P** *MMCET, K Coll Cam, Bp, and DBP (jt)* **R** A R WATKINS

HARTISMERE, SOUTH, comprising Gislingham, Mellis, Stoke Ash w Thwaite, Thorndon w Rishangles, Thornham Magna, Thornham Parva, Wetheringsett, and Yaxley *St E 11* **P** *Bp, Comdr F P Brooke-Popham, MMCET, Ch Soc Trust, SMF, and Lord Henniker (jt)* **R** J C LALL **NSM** L M MOORE

HARTLAND (St Nectan) *see* Parkham, Alwington, Buckland Brewer etc *Ex*

HARTLAND COAST *see* Parkham, Alwington, Buckland Brewer etc *Ex*

HARTLEBURY (St James) *see* Elmley Lovett w Hampton Lovett and Elmbridge w Rushock and Hartlebury and Ombersley w Doverdale *Worc*

HARTLEPOOL (Holy Trinity) (St Mark's Centre) *Dur 6* **P** *Bp* **V** R HALL

HARTLEPOOL (St Aidan) (St Columba) *Dur 6* **P** *Bp* **V** *vacant*

HARTLEPOOL (St Hilda) *Dur 6* **P** *Bp* **P-in-c** V J BROWN **NSM** S P EDGE

HARTLEPOOL (St Luke) *Dur 6* **P** *Bp* **P-in-c** N R SHAVE

HARTLEPOOL (St Oswald) *Dur 6* **P** *Bp* **V** G BUTTERY

HARTLEPOOL (St Paul) *Dur 6* **P** *Bp* **V** R E MASSHEDAR

HARTLEY (All Saints) *see* Fawkham and Hartley *Roch*

HARTLEY BROOK (Mission Hall) *see* Becontree St Mary *Chelmsf*

HARTLEY MAUDITT (St Leonard) *see* Northanger *Win*

HARTLEY WESPALL (St Mary) *see* Sherfield-on-Loddon and Stratfield Saye etc *Win*

HARTLEY WINTNEY (St John the Evangelist), Elvetham, Winchfield and Dogmersfield *Win 5* **P** *Bp and Sir Euan Anstruther-Gough-Calthorpe Bt (jt)* **V** A SMITH **C** M R BIANCHI, S J CHANDLER

HARTLEY, NEW (St Michael and All Angels) *see* Delaval *Newc*

HARTLIP (St Michael and All Angels) *see* The Six *Cant*

HARTON (St Peter) (St Lawrence) *Dur 13* **P** *D&C* **P-in-c** K L BOARDMAN

HARTON, comprising Bossal, Crambe, Flaxton, Foston, Gate Helmsley, Sand Hutton, Upper Helmsley, and Whitwell *York 6* **P** *Abp and D&C Dur (1 turn) Abp (1 turn)* **R** C L WINGFIELD

HARTPLAIN (not known) *Portsm 5* **P** *DBP* **Dn-in-c** K A MACFARLANE

HARTPURY (St Mary the Virgin) *see* Ashleworth, Corse, Hartpury, Hasfield etc *Glouc*

HARTSHEAD (St Peter), Hightown, Roberttown and Scholes *Leeds 7* **P** V Birstall, TR Dewsbury, and Bp (alt) **V** S WALLACE-JONES **NSM** S P ROCHELL **OLM** J C LEE

HARTSHILL (Holy Trinity) and Galley Common *Cov 5* **P** *Ch Patr Trust and Bp (jt)* **V** H D BARNES **NSM** S L CROFTS

HARTSHILL (Holy Trinity), Penkhull and Trent Vale *Lich 11* **P** *Bp and R Stoke-upon-Trent (jt)* **R** C J RUSHTON

HARTSHORNE (St Peter) *see* Swadlincote and Hartshorne *Derby*

HARTWELL (St John the Baptist) *see* Salcey *Pet*

HARTWITH (St Jude) *see* Dacre w Hartwith and Darley w Thornthwaite *Leeds*

HARTY (St Thomas Apostle) *see* Eastchurch w Leysdown and Harty *Cant*

HARVINGTON (St James) *see* Church Lench w Rous Lench and Abbots Morton etc *Worc*

HARWELL (St Matthew) w Chilton *Ox 26* **P** *DBP and CPAS (jt)* **R** J L MOBEY **OLM** P M ROLLS

HARWICH PENINSULA, The (St Nicholas), including Dovercourt, Parkeston, and Ramsey *Chelmsf 21* **P** *Patr Bd* **TR** M A SHAW

HARWOOD (Christ Church) *Man 3* **P** *DBP* **V** W L OLIVER **OLM** A E MORGAN, H MOLLOY, J K GORDON

HARWOOD DALE (St Margaret) *see* Hackness w Harwood Dale *York*

HARWOOD, GREAT (St Bartholomew) St John *Blackb 7* **P** *Patr Bd* **V** G J BIRCH

HARWORTH (All Saints) *S'well 1* **P** *Sir John Whitaker Bt* **P-in-c** N R SKIPWORTH

HASBURY (St Margaret) *see* Halas *Worc*

HASCOMBE (St Peter) *see* Dunsfold and Hascombe *Guildf*

HASELBECH (St Michael) *see* Clipston, Haselbech, Kelmarsh, Marston Trussell etc *Pet*

HASELBURY PLUCKNETT (St Michael and All Angels) *see* Wulfric Benefice *B & W*

HASELEY (St Mary) *see* Hatton w Haseley, Rowington w Lowsonford etc *Cov*

HASELEY, GREAT (St Peter) *see* Gt w Lt Milton and Gt Haseley *Ox*

HASELOR (St Mary and All Saints) *see* Alcester Minster *Cov*

HASELTON (St Andrew) *see* Northleach w Hampnett and Farmington etc *Glouc*

HASFIELD (St Mary) *see* Ashleworth, Corse, Hartpury, Hasfield etc *Glouc*

HASKETON (St Andrew) *see* Carlford *St E*

HASLAND (St Paul) *Derby 3* **P** V *Chesterfield* **R** G N BORROWDALE

HASLEMERE (St Bartholomew) (St Christopher) and Grayswood *Guildf 4* **P** *Ld Chan* **R** C D BESSANT **NSM** E J COLLINS, F J GWYNN **OLM** R J MANLEY-COOPER

HASLINGDEN (St James) w Grane and Stonefold *Blackb 1* **P** *Bp and Hulme Trustees (jt)* **V** D STEPHENSON **C** A D HOLMES

HASLINGDEN (St Peter) *see* Laneside *Blackb*

HASLINGDEN (St Thomas) *see* Musbury *Blackb*

HASLINGFIELD (All Saints) *see* Lordsbridge *Ely*

HASLINGTON (St Matthew) w Crewe Green and Wheelock *Ches 15* **P** *Bp and V Sandbach (jt)* **P-in-c** P J LLOYD

HASSALL GREEN (St Philip) *see* Sandbach Heath w Hassall Green *Ches*

HASSINGHAM (St Mary) *see* Burlingham St Edmund w Lingwood, Strumpshaw etc *Nor*

HASTINGS (Christ Church and St Andrew) *see* Blacklands Hastings Ch Ch and St Andr *Chich*

HASTINGS (Emmanuel and St Mary in the Castle) *Chich 15* **P** *MMCET and Hyndman Trustees (alt)* **V** M G LANE **NSM** R BROWNING

HASTINGS (Holy Trinity) *Chich 15* **P** *Bp* **V** S G D LARKIN **C** T J LANCASTER

HASTINGS (St Clement) (All Saints) *Chich 15* **P** *Bp* **P-in-c** P M HUNT

HASTINGS (St Peter and St Paul) *see* Hollington St Jo *Chich*

HASWELL (St Paul) and Shotton *Dur 10* **P** *Bp* **V** F J GRIEVE **NSM** M PETERS

HATCH BEAUCHAMP (St John the Baptist) *see* Beercrocombe w Curry Mallet, Hatch Beauchamp etc *B & W*

HATCH END (St Anselm) *Lon 20* **P** *Bp* **V** D M GREEN

HATCH WARREN AND BEGGARWOOD (Immanuel) *Win 4* **P** *Bp* **V** *vacant*

HATCH, WEST (St Andrew) *see* Beercrocombe w Curry Mallet, Hatch Beauchamp etc *B & W*

HATCHAM (St Catherine) *S'wark 2* **P** *Haberdashers' Co* **V** S A JAMES **NSM** E B KORMI, J ELLIOTT

HATCHAM (St James) (St George) (St Michael) *S'wark 2* **P** *Ch Patr Soc* **V** *vacant*

HATCHAM PARK (All Saints) *S'wark 2* **P** *Hyndman Trustees (2 turns), Haberdashers' Co (1 turn)* **V** G W V BOLTON-DEBBAGE **OLM** J FRANCIS

HATCLIFFE (St Mary) *see* Wolds Gateway Group *Linc*

HATFIELD *see* Bishop's Hatfield, Lemsford and N Mymms *St Alb*

HATFIELD (St Lawrence) *Sheff 10* **P** *Bp* **V** E A TURNER-LOISEL **NSM** G SALTER

HATFIELD (St Leonard) *see* Leominster *Heref*

HATFIELD BROAD OAK (St Mary the Virgin) and Bush End *Chelmsf 4* **P** *Bp* **P-in-c** D JEWSON **C** D W HERRICK, R L CHALLIS

HATFIELD HEATH (Holy Trinity) and Sheering *Chelmsf 4* **P** *Ch Ch Ox and V Hatfield Broad Oak (alt)* **P-in-c** D JEWSON **C** D W HERRICK, R L CHALLIS

HATFIELD HYDE (St Mary Magdalene) *St Alb 18* **P** *Marquess of Salisbury* **P-in-c** E K HOPEGOOD JONES

HATFIELD PEVEREL (St Andrew) w Ulting *Chelmsf 23* **P** *Bp* **V** S R NORTHFIELD **NSM** D R CLARK-MAYERS

HATFIELD REGIS *see* Hatfield Broad Oak and Bush End *Chelmsf*

HATHERDEN (Christ Church) *see* Pastrow *Win*

HATHERLEIGH (St John the Baptist) *see* Okehampton, Inwardleigh, Belstone, Sourton etc *Ex*

HATHERN (St Peter and St Paul) *see* Kegworth, Hathern, Long Whatton, Diseworth etc *Leic*

HATHEROP (St Nicholas) *see* S Cotswolds *Glouc*

HATHERSAGE (St Michael and All Angels) w Bamford and Derwent, and Grindleford *Derby 4* **P** *Duke of Devonshire, Earl Temple, and A C H Barnes Esq (jt)* **P-in-c** P H MOORE **C** C L V WALLINGTON

HATHERTON (St Saviour) *Lich 3* **P** *A R W Littleton Esq* **V** V R FLEMING **C** M T M MEREDITH **OLM** G M JOYNSON

HATLEY ST GEORGE (St George) *see* Gamlingay and Everton *Ely*

HATTERS LANE (St Andrew) *see* High Wycombe *Ox*

HATTERSLEY (St Barnabas) *Ches 14* **P** *Bp* **V** D A HAYES

HATTON (All Saints) *Derby 6* **P** *Bp and N J M Spurrier Esq (jt)* **V** *vacant*

HATTON (Holy Trinity) w Haseley, Rowington w Lowsonford and Honiley and Wroxall *Cov 4*　**P** *Bp*　**R** *vacant*
HATTON (St Stephen)　*see Hemingby Gp Linc*
HAUGH (St Leonard)　*see* S Ormsby Gp *Linc*
HAUGHLEY (St Mary the Virgin) w Wetherden and Stowupland *St E 3*　**P** *Ld Chan, Bp, and DBP (by turn)*　**P-in-c** D B SINGLETON
HAUGHTON (St Anne) *Man 5*　**P** *DBP*　**P-in-c** K J MAMBU　**C** M HOWARTH
HAUGHTON (St Chad)　*see* Whittington and W Felton w Haughton *Lich*
HAUGHTON (St Giles)　*see* Bradeley, Church Eaton, Derrington and Haughton *Lich*
HAUGHTON (St Mary the Virgin) *Man 5*　**P** *Bp*　**R** M R GLEW　**NSM** R D BREWIS
HAUGHTON LE SKERNE (St Andrew) *Dur 5*　**P** *Bp*　**R** M R EAST　**NSM** J J BLACKBURN, S CHEW
HAUTBOIS, GREAT (Holy Trinity)　*see* Coltishall w Gt Hautbois, Frettenham etc *Nor*
HAUXTON (St Edmund)　*see* Harston w Hauxton and Newton *Ely*
HAUXWELL (St Oswald)　*see* Lower Wensleydale *Leeds*
HAVANT (St Faith) *Portsm 5*　**P** *Bp*　**R** T P KENNAR
HAVEN Group, The, comprising Bicker, Donington, Sutterton, Swineshead, and Wigtoft *Linc 21*　**P** *Bp, D&C, Simeon's Trustees, and DBP (2 turns), The Crown (1 turn)*　**V** C P ROBERTSON　**NSM** S L HENTLEY
HAVENSTREET (St Peter) *Portsm 7*　**P** *SMF*　**V** *vacant*
HAVERHILL (St Mary the Virgin) w Withersfield *St E 2*　**P** *Bp*　**P-in-c** M L D DRINKWATER　**C** C D EYDEN, F W NORRIS
HAVERIGG (St Luke)　*see* Millom *Carl*
HAVERING-ATTE-BOWER (St John)　*see* Collier Row St Jas and Havering-atte-Bower *Chelmsf*
HAVERINGLAND (St Peter)　*see* Aylsham and Distr *Nor*
HAVERSHAM (St Mary)　*see* Lamp *Ox*
HAVERSTOCK HILL (Holy Trinity)　*see* Kentish Town St Silas and H Trin w St Barn *Lon*
HAVERTHWAITE (St Anne)　*see* Cartmel Peninsula *Carl*
HAWBUSH (St Paul)　*see* Brierley Hill *Worc*
HAWES (St Margaret)　*see* Upper Wensleydale *Leeds*
HAWES SIDE (St Christopher) and Marton Moss St Nicholas *Blackb 8*　**P** *Bp*　**V** L M DANIELS
HAWKCHURCH (St John the Baptist)　*see* Golden Cap Team *Sarum*
HAWKEDON (St Mary)　*see* Chevington w Hargrave, Chedburgh w Depden etc *St E*
HAWKESBURY (St Mary)　*see* Boxwell, Leighterton, Didmarton, Oldbury etc *Glouc*
HAWKHURST (St Laurance) *Cant 11*　**P** *Ch Ch Ox*　**V** R G DREYER
HAWKINGE (St Luke) *Cant 8*　**P** *Abp*　**P-in-c** R P GRINSELL
HAWKLEY (St Peter and St Paul)　*see* Greatham, Empshott and Hawkley w Priors Dean *Portsm*
HAWKRIDGE (St Giles)　*see* Exmoor *B & W*
HAWKSHAW (St Mary)　*see* Holcombe and Hawkshaw *Man*
HAWKSHEAD (St Michael and All Angels) and Low Wray w Sawrey and Rusland and Satterthwaite *Carl 11*　**P** *Bp*　**V** J S DIXON　**NSM** N F HALLAM
HAWKSWOOD (Emmanuel)　*see* Hailsham *Chich*
HAWKSWORTH (St Mary and All Saints)　*see* Whatton w Aslockton, Hawksworth, Scarrington etc *S'well*
HAWKSWORTH WOOD (St Mary)　*see* Abbeylands *Leeds*
HAWKWELL (Emmanuel) (St Mary the Virgin) *Chelmsf 13*　**P** *CPAS*　**R** N E ROWAN　**C** S J FINCH
HAWLEY (Holy Trinity) *Guildf 1*　**P** *Keble Coll Ox*　**V** W F P PERRY
HAWLEY, SOUTH (All Saints)　*see* Hawley H Trin *Guildf*
HAWLING (St Edward)　*see* Sevenhampton w Charlton Abbots, Hawling etc *Glouc*
HAWNBY (All Saints)　*see* Upper Ryedale *York*
HAWORTH (St Michael and All Angels) and Cross Roads cum Lees *Leeds 1*　**P** *Bp, V Bradf, and Haworth Ch Lands Trust (jt)*　**R** P M MULLINS　**C** A R BENNETT　**NSM** J ROBERTS
HAWRIDGE (St Mary) w Cholesbury and St Leonard *Ox 17*　**P** *Bp, Chpl Trust, and Neale's Charity (jt)*　**R** C J HAYWOOD
HAWSKER (All Saints)　*see* Fylingdales and Hawsker cum Stainsacre *York*
HAWSTEAD (All Saints)　*see* St Edm Way *St E*
HAWTHORN (St Michael and All Angels) *Dur 10*　**P** *Exors I Pemberton Esq*　**V** L M MOSS　**NSM** P P PATERSON
HAWTON (All Saints)　*see* Farndon w Thorpe, Hawton and Cotham *S'well*
HAXBY (St Mary) and Wigginton *York 7*　**P** *Abp and Ld Chan (alt)*　**R** K D JACKSON　**NSM** N A S BENSON
HAXEY (St Nicholas) *Linc 1*　**P** *Ld Chan*　**V** M T P ZAMMIT

HAY MILL (St Cyprian)　*see* Yardley St Cypr Hay Mill *Birm*
HAYDOCK (St James) *Liv 13*　**P** *R Ashton-in-Makerfield*　**NSM** I C WYNNE
HAYDOCK (St Mark) *Liv 10*　**P** *MMCET*　**V** D B LEATHERS　**C** J A WALLACE　**NSM** A J CARSON
HAYDON BRIDGE (St Cuthbert) and Beltingham w Henshaw *Newc 10*　**P** *Bp and V Haltwhistle and Greenhead (jt)*　**NSM** G ALEXANDER
HAYDON WICK (St John) *Bris 7*　**P** *CPAS*　**V** R W ADAMS
HAYES (Christ Church)　*see* W Hayes *Lon*
HAYES (St Anselm) *Lon 21*　**P** *Bp*　**P-in-c** M J CASHMORE
HAYES (St Edmund of Canterbury) *Lon 21*　**P** *Bp*　**V** P S MACKENZIE　**NSM** V THORNBOROUGH
HAYES (St Jerome)　*see* W Hayes *Lon*
HAYES (St Mary the Virgin) *Roch 14*　**P** *D&C*　**R** *vacant*
HAYES (St Mary) *Lon 21*　**P** *Keble Coll Ox*　**R** N G T WHEELER
HAYES, NORTH (St Nicholas) *Lon 21*　**P** *Bp and Keble Coll Ox (jt)*　**V** J A EVANS
HAYES, WEST (Christ Church) (St Jerome) *Lon 21*　**P** *Bp and Hyndman Trustees (jt)*　**V** I W JONES
HAYFIELD (St Matthew) and Chinley w Buxworth *Derby 4*　**P** *Bp and Resident Freeholders (jt)*　**V** J F HUDGHTON
HAYLE (St Elwyn)　*see* Godrevy *Truro*
HAYLING ISLAND (St Andrew) Eastoke *Portsm 5*　**P** *DBP*　**P-in-c** J C GAFFIN　**C** D A CURRAM
HAYLING, NORTH (St Peter) *Portsm 5*　**P** *DBP*　**P-in-c** J C GAFFIN
HAYLING, SOUTH (St Mary) *Portsm 5*　**P** *DBP*　**P-in-c** J C GAFFIN
HAYNES (Mission Room)　*see* Campton, Clophill and Haynes *St Alb*
HAYNES (St Mary) *as above*
HAYTON (St James)　*see* Aspatria w Hayton and Gilcrux *Carl*
HAYTON (St Martin)　*see* Pocklington Wold *York*
HAYTON (St Mary Magdalene)　*see* Eden, Gelt and Irthing *Carl*
HAYTON (St Peter)　*see* The Clays *S'well*
HAYWARDS HEATH (Church of the Ascension) *Chich 8*　**P** *Bp*　**V** M P JONES
HAYWARDS HEATH (Church of the Presentation)　*see* Haywards Heath St Wilfrid *Chich*
HAYWARDS HEATH (St Richard) *Chich 8*　**P** *Bp*　**V** C BRADING　**Hon C** L D POODHUN
HAYWARDS HEATH (St Wilfrid) (Church of the Presentation) *Chich 8*　**P** *Bp*　**V** E R PRITCHETT　**NSM** D C YOUNG, J M ELLIOTT
HAYWOOD, GREAT (St Stephen)　*see* Abbots Bromley, Blithfield, Colton, Colwich etc *Lich*
HAZELBURY BRYAN (St Mary and St James) and the Hillside Parishes *Sarum 5*　**P** *Duke of Northumberland (2 turns), DBP, G A L-F Pitt-Rivers Esq, Exors F N Kent Esq, and Bp (1 turn each)*　**NSM** D GREENWOOD
HAZELWELL (St Mary Magdalen) *Birm 2*　**P** *Bp*　**V** M R FORBES
HAZELWOOD (St John the Evangelist), Holbrook and Milford *Derby 6*　**P** *Bp and DBP (jt)*　**P-in-c** J M PAGE
HAZLEMERE (Holy Trinity) *Ox 18*　**P** *Peache Trustees*　**V** M J MEARDON　**C** C L GERARD, D W E MEERING
HEACHAM (St Mary) *Nor 15*　**P** *Bp*　**R** V M WILSON　**NSM** S A WILSON
HEADBOURNE WORTHY (St Swithun) *Win 7*　**P** *Univ Coll Ox and Lord Northbrook (alt)*　**R** P E BRADISH　**NSM** J C LEWIS
HEADCORN (St Peter and St Paul) and The Suttons *Cant 11*　**P** *Abp*　**V** F A HASKETT
HEADINGLEY (St Michael and All Angels) (St Chad) and All Hallows *Leeds 12*　**P** *Patr Bd*　**TR** H F LIEVESLEY　**TV** A E BIRKIN, H GROENEWALD　**C** J C D PECKETT
HEADINGTON (St Andrew) *Ox 1*　**P** *Keble Coll Ox*　**V** D W MCFARLAND　**C** L NORMAN　**NSM** J R STRAWBRIDGE
HEADINGTON (St Mary) *Ox 1*　**P** *Bp*　**V** E P BOSSWARD　**C** B A BAKER
HEADINGTON QUARRY (Holy Trinity) *Ox 1*　**P** *Bp*　**V** L R BIRON-SCOTT　**NSM** R J C GILBERT
HEADLESS CROSS (St Luke)　*see* Redditch Ch the K *Worc*
HEADLEY (All Saints) *Guildf 3*　**P** *Qu Coll Ox*　**R** *vacant*
HEADLEY (St Mary the Virgin) and Box Hill w Walton on the Hill *Guildf 9*　**P** *Bp*　**R** H N L LATHAM　**C** L M BATES　**NSM** C M J HANCOCK
HEADLEY (St Peter)　*see* Kingsclere and Ashford Hill w Headley *Win*
HEADON (St Peter)　*see* The Rivers *S'well*
HEADSTONE (St George) *Lon 20*　**P** *Bp*　**V** S R KEEBLE
HEAGE (St Luke)　*see* Ambergate and Heage *Derby*
HEALAUGH (St John the Baptist)　*see* Rural Ainsty *York*

HEALD GREEN (St Catherine) *Ches 17* **P** *Bp*
  V J DEVADASON **NSM** J DEVADASON, P M DOOLEY
HEALEY (Christ Church) *see* Hamer and Healey *Man*
HEALEY (St John) *see* Slaley, Healey and Whittonstall *Newc*
HEALEY (St Paul) *see* Masham and Healey *Leeds*
HEALING (St Peter and St Paul) *see* Wolds Gateway Group *Linc*
HEAMOOR (St Thomas) *see* Gulval and Madron *Truro*
HEANOR (St Lawrence) *Derby 8* **P** *Wright Trustees*
  P-in-c K PADLEY **C** L SHEMILT
HEANTON PUNCHARDON (St Augustine), Marwood and West Down *Ex 13* **P** *Bp, CPAS, and St Jo Coll Cam (jt)*
  P-in-c S N PAINTING **C** C J RABY
HEAP BRIDGE (St Thomas and St George) *see* Heywood St Marg and Heap Bridge *Man*
HEAPEY (St Barnabas) and Withnell *Blackb 4* **P** *V Leyland*
  V A F HOGARTH **NSM** G K BULLOCK
HEAPHAM (All Saints) *see* Lea Gp *Linc*
HEART OF EDEN, The, comprising Appleby, Asby, Dufton, Kirkby Thore, Long Marton, Milburn, Newbiggin, Ormside, Temple Sowerby, and Warcop w Musgrave *Carl 1* **P** *Bp, Adn Carl, D&C, Lord Hothfield, and Major and Mrs Sawrey-Cookson (jt)* **R** C A HICKS **C** P J BOYLES, S J FYFE **NSM** D J PATTIMORE, K PATTIMORE
HEART OF ENGLAND, The, comprising Bidford-on-Avon, Binton, Exhall w Wixford, Salford Priors, and Temple Grafton *Cov 7* **P** *Bp, Peache Trustees, and Dioc Trustees (jt)*
  R P A WALKER **C** S M BRIDGE
HEART OF NORFOLK Team Ministry, The, comprising Bawdeswell, Billingford, Bintree, Foulsham, Foxley, Guestwick, Guist, North Elmham, Stibbard, Themelthorpe, Twyford, Wood Norton, and Worthing *Nor 18* **P** *Patr Bd*
  TR S E KIMMIS **TV** C J DAVIES, W M CARTWRIGHT
HEATH (All Saints) *Derby 2* **P** *Duke of Devonshire and Simeon's Trustees (jt)* **P-in-c** A E MANN
HEATH (Mission Church) *see* Uttoxeter Area *Lich*
HEATH AND REACH (St Leonard) *see* Ouzel Valley *St Alb*
HEATH HAYES (St John) *Lich 3* **P** *Bp and D&C (jt)* **V** *vacant*
HEATH TOWN (Holy Trinity) *Lich 27* **P** *CPAS*
  V R C MERRICK **C** K E TINGLE **Hon C** P E V GOLDRING
HEATH, LITTLE (Christ Church) *see* Lt Heath *St Alb*
HEATH, THE (not known) *see* Bromfield *Heref*
HEATHCOTE *Cov 11* **P** *Bp and Ld Chan (alt)* **V** R J BUDD
HEATHER (St John the Baptist) *see* Ibstock w Heather *Leic*
HEATHERLANDS (St John the Evangelist) *Sarum 7*
  P *MMCET* **V** D G M PRICE **C** P D HOMDEN
HEATHERYCLEUGH (St Thomas) *see* Upper Weardale *Dur*
HEATHFIELD (All Saints) (St Richard) *Chich 13* **P** *Bp*
  V C S MITCHELL **C** T H FIKSEAUNET
HEATHFIELD (St Catherine) *see* Bovey Tracey St Jo w Heathfield *Ex*
HEATHFIELD (St John the Baptist) *see* Deane Vale *B & W*
HEATON (Christ Church) w Halliwell St Margaret *Man 3*
  P *Patr Bd* **Hon C** P H BURMAN
HEATON (St Barnabas) *see* Girlington, Heaton and Manningham *Leeds*
HEATON (St Gabriel) *see* Newc St Gabr *Newc*
HEATON (St Martin) *see* Girlington, Heaton and Manningham *Leeds*
HEATON CHAPEL (St Thomas) *see* Heatons *Man*
HEATON MERSEY (St John the Baptist) *as above*
HEATON MOOR (St Paul) *as above*
HEATON NORRIS (Christ w All Saints) *as above*
HEATON REDDISH (St Mary) *Man 1* **P** *Trustees* **R** *vacant*
HEATON, HIGH (St Francis) *see* Newc St Fran *Newc*
HEATONS, comprising Heaton Mersey, Heaton Moor, Heaton Norris, and Norris Bank *Man 1* **P** *Patr Bd (4 turns), The Crown (1 turn)* **TV** D BROWNHILL **C** C F ALLISON, F YASINI, W E RUBIE **NSM** O MOLUDY
HEAVITREE (St Michael and All Angels) (St Lawrence) and St Mary Steps *Ex 3* **P** *Patr Bd* **TV** J F SEWARD **C** A HOBBS **NSM** A P JOHNSON
HEBBURN (St Cuthbert) (St Oswald) *Dur 13* **P** *The Crown and TR Jarrow (alt)* **V** *vacant*
HEBBURN (St John) *Dur 13* **P** *Bp* **P-in-c** I M SOMASUNDRAM **NSM** E GRAY
HEBDEN (St Peter) *see* Linton, Burnsall and Rylstone *Leeds*
HEBDEN BRIDGE (St James) and Heptonstall *Leeds 8* **P** *V Halifax* **P-in-c** K L MARSHALL
HEBRON (St Cuthbert) *see* Mitford and Hebron *Newc*
HECK (St John the Baptist) *see* Gt Snaith *Sheff*
HECKFIELD (St Michael) *see* Whitewater *Win*
HECKINGTON (St Andrew) and Helpringham Group of Parishes, The, including Asgarby, Burton Pedwardine, Great Hale and Little Hale, Scredington, and Swaton *Linc 14*

P *Bp, D&C, DBP, and the Rt Revd A C Foottit (1 turn), Ld Chan (1 turn)* **R** C R HARRINGTON
HECKMONDWIKE (All Souls) (St James) w Norristhorpe and Liversedge *Leeds 7* **P** *V Birstall* **V** K G YOUNG
HEDDINGTON (St Andrew) *see* Oldbury *Sarum*
HEDDON-ON-THE-WALL (St Andrew) *Newc 9* **P** *Ld Chan*
  P-in-c R L S SCHEFFER **C** T D K BIRCH
HEDENHAM (St Peter) *see* Ditchingham, Hedenham, Broome, Earsham etc *Nor*
HEDGE END (St John the Evangelist) *Win 10* **P** *Bp*
  V C M ROWBERRY **NSM** K ROWBERRY
HEDGE END (St Luke) *Win 10* **P** *Bp* **V** B M O JONES
  NSM E V WILLIAMS
HEDGERLEY (St Mary the Virgin) *see* Farnham Royal w Hedgerley *Ox*
HEDINGHAMS and Upper Colne, The, comprising Castle Hedingham, Gt Yeldham, Lt Yeldham, Sible Hedingham, Stambourne, Tilbury juxta Clare, and Toppesfield *Chelmsf 18* **P** *Duchy of Lanc (1 turn), The Crown (1 turn), Bp, J Lindsay Esq and Trustees (1 turn), Ld Chan (1 turn)*
  R E G PAXTON **C** A BROWN, J M TOMKINS
  NSM M H M BURSELL
HEDNESFORD (St Peter) *Lich 3* **P** *Bp* **V** P KELLY
  C A C T KELLY
HEDON (St Augustine), Paull, Sproatley and Preston in Holderness *York 12* **P** *Abp* **R** S H PULKO
  Hon C P W WEST
HEDSOR (St Nicholas) and Bourne End *Ox 18* **P** *Bp*
  R J V BINNS
HEDWORTH (St Nicholas) *see* The Boldons *Dur*
HEELEY (Christ Church) w Arbourthorne and Norfolk Park *Sheff 1* **P** *The Crown (1 turn), Bp and V Sheffield (1 turn)*
  V S R EVANS
HEENE (St Botolph) *Chich 7* **P** *D&C* **P-in-c** P D C KANE
HEIGHAM (Holy Trinity) *Nor 3* **P** *Ch Trust Fund Trust*
  R R D JAMES **C** J N PINTO
HEIGHAM (St Barnabas) *see* The Mitre Benefice *Nor*
HEIGHAM (St Thomas) *as above*
HEIGHINGTON (St Michael) and Darlington St Matthew and St Luke *Dur 5* **P** *D&C and Bp (alt)* **V** L M SCOTT **C** D J LUCAS
HEIGHTINGTON (St Giles) *see* Mamble w Bayton, Rock w Heightington etc *Worc*
HELHOUGHTON (All Saints) *see* E w W Rudham, Helhoughton etc *Nor*
HELIONS BUMPSTEAD (St Andrew) *see* Two Rivers *Chelmsf*
HELLAND (St Helena) *see* Camelside *Truro*
HELLESDON (St Mary) (St Paul and St Michael) *Nor 2* **P** *Bp*
  V A ALDER
HELLIDON (St John the Baptist) *see* Daventry *Pet*
HELLIFIELD (St Aidan) and Long Preston *Leeds 17* **P** *Ch Ch Ox* **V** *vacant*
HELLINGLY (St Peter and St Paul) and Upper Dicker *Chich 13* **P** *Abp and Bp (jt)* **V** J J N SYKES
HELMDON (St Mary Magdalene) *see* Astwell Gp *Pet*
HELME (Christ Church) *see* Meltham *Leeds*
HELMINGHAM (St Mary) *see* Debenham and Helmingham *St E*
HELMSLEY (All Saints) *York 19* **P** *The Hon Jake Duncombe*
  NSM H RAWLINGS
HELMSLEY, UPPER (St Peter) *see* Harton *York*
HELPERTHORPE (St Peter) *see* Weaverthorpe w Helperthorpe, Luttons Ambo etc *York*
HELPRINGHAM (St Andrew) *see* Heckington and Helpringham Gp *Linc*
HELPSTON (St Botolph) *see* Barnack w Ufford, Bainton, Helpston and Wittering *Pet*
HELSBY (St Paul) and Dunham-on-the-Hill *Ches 3* **P** *Bp*
  V *vacant*
HELSINGTON (St John) *see* Underbarrow w Helsington *Carl*
HELSTON (St Michael) and Wendron *Truro 3* **P** *Patr Bd*
  TR D G MILLER **C** C SCHMAUS, K RICHARDS
  NSM T R A EBBENS
HEMBLINGTON (All Saints) *see* Blofield *Nor*
HEMEL HEMPSTEAD (Holy Trinity) Leverstock Green *see* Langelei *St Alb*
HEMEL HEMPSTEAD (St Alban) (St Barnabas) (St Mary) (St Paul) (Resurrection) *St Alb 2* **P** *Ld Chan*
  TR J K WILLIAMS **TV** A S JANES, P J STEVENSON, R W GRAHAM **NSM** L GEOGHEGAN, T J BARTON
HEMEL HEMPSTEAD (St Benedict) Bennetts End *see* Langelei *St Alb*
HEMEL HEMPSTEAD (St Mary) Apsley End *as above*
HEMINGBROUGH (St Mary the Virgin) *see* Riccall, Barlby and Hemingbrough *York*

HEMINGBY Group, The (St Margaret), including West Ashby, Baumber, Belchford, Edlington, Fulletby, Hatton, and Great Sturton *Linc 13* **P** *Bp, DBP, and Keble Coll Ox (2 turns), Ld Chan (1 turn)* **R** *vacant*
HEMINGFORD ABBOTS (St Margaret of Antioch) *Ely 10* **P** *Lord Hemingford* **P-in-c** P H CUNLIFFE   C E B ATLING
HEMINGFORD GREY (St James) *Ely 10* **P** *CPAS*
V P H CUNLIFFE   C E B ATLING   **NSM** J M SMITH
HEMINGSTONE (St Gregory) *see* N Bosmere *St E*
HEMINGTON (St Peter and St Paul) *see* Barnwell, Hemington, Luddington in the Brook etc *Pet*
HEMLEY (All Saints) *see* Orwell and Deben *St E*
HEMPNALL (St Margaret) *Nor 5* **P** *Ld Chan (1 turn), Patr Bd (5 turns)* **TV** E N BILLETT
HEMPSTEAD (All Saints) *see* Matlaske *Nor*
HEMPSTEAD (All Saints) *see* S Gillingham *Roch*
HEMPSTEAD (St Andrew) *see* Bacton, Happisburgh, Hempstead w Eccles etc *Nor*
HEMPSTEAD (St Andrew) *see* Thaxted, The Sampfords, Radwinter and Hempstead *Chelmsf*
HEMPSTED (St Swithun) *see* Glouc City and Hempsted *Glouc*
HEMPTON (Holy Trinity) and Pudding Norton *Nor 14* **P** *The Crown* **V** *vacant*
HEMPTON (St John the Evangelist) *see* Deddington w Barford, Clifton and Hempton *Ox*
HEMSBY (St Mary) *see* Flegg Coastal Benefice *Nor*
HEMSWELL (All Saints) *see* Trentcliffe Gp *Linc*
HEMSWORTH (St Helen) *Leeds 15* **P** *Bp* **R** R W HART
HEMYOCK (St Mary) w Culm Davy, Clayhidon and Culmstock *Ex 7* **P** *DBP, SMF, and D&C (jt)* **R** R H TOTTERDELL
HENBURY (St Mary the Virgin) *Bris 2* **P** *Lord Middleton (1 turn), Bp (3 turns)* **V** D P LLOYD
HENBURY (St Thomas) *see* Macclesfield St Jo w Henbury *Ches*
HENDFORD (Holy Trinity) *see* Yeovil H Trin w Barwick *B & W*
HENDON (All Saints) Childs Hill *Lon 14* **P** *Bp* **P-in-c** R J A SIMS-WILLIAMS
HENDON (St Alphage) *Lon 14* **P** *Bp* **V** H D MOORE
HENDON (St Ignatius) *Dur 14* **P** *Bp* **R** A C JONES
HENDON (St Mary) (Christ Church) *Lon 14* **P** *Bp* **V** J A GITTOES   **C** M A KWAPONG   **NSM** M P RINSLER
HENDON (St Paul) Mill Hill *Lon 14* **P** *Bp* **V** J E JAMES
C J E LOWE, R M VENN-DUNN
HENDON, WEST (St John) and Cricklewood St Peter *Lon 14* **P** *Bp* **V** R W HUTCHINSON
HENDRED, EAST (St Augustine of Canterbury) *see* Wantage Downs *Ox*
HENDRED, WEST (Holy Trinity) *as above*
HENFIELD (St Peter) w Shermanbury and Woodmancote *Chich 11* **P** *Bp* **R** P S J DOICK   **C** H J WILKIN
HENGROVE (Christ Church) *Bris 1* **P** *Bp and Simeon's Trustees (alt)* **P-in-c** S SHEPPARD
HENHAM (St Mary the Virgin) and Elsenham w Ugley *Chelmsf 19* **P** *Ch Hosp, Ch Soc Trust, and Bp (jt)* **V** *vacant*
HENLEAZE (St Peter) *Bris 2* **P** *Bp* **V** C M PILGRIM
C K F DOUGLAS
HENLEY (St Peter) *see* Claydon *St E*
HENLEY IN ARDEN (St John the Baptist) *see* Beaudesert and Henley-in-Arden w Ullenhall *Cov*
HENLEY-ON-THAMES (Holy Trinity) *Ox 24* **P** *R Rotherfield Greys St Nich* **V** D R B CARTER   **C** S P W BREWSTER
HENLEY-ON-THAMES (St Mary the Virgin) w Remenham *Ox 24* **P** *Bp and Jes Coll Ox (jt)* **R** J C TAYLER
NSM R E POSTON
HENLOW (St Mary the Virgin) and Langford *St Alb 8* **P** *Ld Chan* **V** S L SPELLER
HENNOCK (St Mary) *see* Bovey Tracey SS Pet, Paul and Thos w Hennock *Ex*
HENNY, GREAT (St Mary) *see* N Hinckford *Chelmsf*
HENSALL (St Paul) *see* Gt Snaith *Sheff*
HENSHAW (All Hallows) *see* Haydon Bridge and Beltingham w Henshaw *Newc*
HENSINGHAM (St John) (Keekle Mission) *Carl 5* **P** *Trustees* **V** F T PEARSON   **C** S G N WALKER
HENSTEAD (St Mary) *see* Wrentham, Covehithe w Benacre etc *St E*
HENSTRIDGE (St Nicholas) *see* Abbas and Templecombe, Henstridge and Horsington *B & W*
HENTLAND (St Dubricius) *see* St Weonards *Heref*
HENTON (Christ Church) *see* Coxley w Godney, Henton and Wookey *B & W*
HEPPLE (Christ Church) *see* Upper Coquetdale *Newc*
HEPTONSTALL (St Thomas à Becket and St Thomas the Apostle) *see* Hebden Bridge and Heptonstall *Leeds*

HEPWORTH (Holy Trinity) *see* Upper Holme Valley *Leeds*
HEPWORTH (St Peter) *see* Stanton *St E*
HEREFORD (St Francis) *see* Heref S Wye *Heref*
HEREFORD (St Martin) *as above*
HEREFORD (St Paul) *see* Tupsley w Hampton Bishop *Heref*
HEREFORD (St Peter w St Owen) (St James) *Heref 3* **P** *Simeon's Trustees* **V** A P MORGAN   **C** A J DODWELL, E S T SWATTRIDGE   **NSM** L J AYLEN
HEREFORD SOUTH WYE (St Francis) (St Martin) *Heref 3* **P** *Bp* **TR** A M DOWDESWELL   **C** L C N BELL
HEREFORD, LITTLE (St Mary Magdalene) *see* Tenbury *Heref*
HEREFORD, WEST Team Ministry (All Saints) (Holy Trinity) (St Michael) (St Nicholas) *Heref 3* **P** *Patr Bd (3 turns) Ld Chan (1 turn)* **TR** R C HULSE   **C** J M BURDEN
HERMITAGE (Holy Trinity) *Ox 6* **P** *Patr Bd* **TR** E W LAUTENBACH   **TV** S M WEBSTER
HERMITAGE (St Mary) *see* Three Valleys *Sarum*
HERNE (St Martin) *Cant 4* **P** *Abp* **V** C SMITH   **C** C DARKINS
NSM S E RAND
HERNE BAY (Christ Church) (St Andrew's Church and Centre) *Cant 4* **P** *Simeon's Trustees* **V** A W EVERETT
HERNE BAY (St Bartholomew) *see* Reculver and Herne Bay St Bart and Hoath *Cant*
HERNE HILL (St Paul) (St Saviour) *S'wark 9* **P** *Bp and Simeon's Trustees (jt)* **V** B GOODYEAR   **C** S R WRIGHT
NSM B J HUGHES, G S TAYLEUR
HERNER (Chapel) *see* Newport and Bishops Tawton *Ex*
HERNHILL (St Michael) *see* Boughton-under-Blean w Dunkirk etc *Cant*
HERODSFOOT (All Saints) *see* Duloe and Herodsfoot *Truro*
HERONSGATE (St John the Evangelist) *see* Mill End and Heronsgate w W Hyde *St Alb*
HERRIARD (St Mary) *see* N Hants Downs *Win*
HERRINGFLEET (St Margaret) *see* Somerleyton, Ashby, Fritton, Herringfleet etc *Nor*
HERRINGSWELL (St Ethelbert) *see* Forest Heath *St E*
HERRINGTHORPE (St Cuthbert) *Sheff 6* **P** *Bp* **V** K R SKIDMORE   **C** T F GIBBONS
HERRINGTON (St Aidan), Penshaw and Shiney Row *Dur 9* **P** *Bp and The Crown (alt)* **R** *vacant*
HERSHAM (St Peter) *Guildf 8* **P** *Bp* **V** J A RICHARDSON
C K T JENKINS
HERSTMONCEUX (All Saints) and Wartling *Chich 13* **P** *Bp* **P-in-c** R J STEVEN
HERSTON (St Mark) *see* Swanage and Studland *Sarum*
HERTFORD (All Saints) (St Andrew) *St Alb 19* **P** *Ld Chan (1 turn), Duchy of Lanc (2 turns), Patr Bd (1 turn)* **TR** J M H LOVERIDGE   **TV** H A STEWART, R C THOMPSON, S J DRYDEN
HERTFORD HEATH (Holy Trinity) *see* Hertford *St Alb*
HERTFORD, comprising Folkton, Ganton, Hunmanby, Muston, and Willerby *York 15* **P** *MMCET (1 turn), Abp, N H T Wrigley Esq, and MMCET (1 turn)* **R** T P PARKER
HERTINGFORDBURY (St Mary) *see* Hertford *St Alb*
HESKETH (All Saints) w Becconsall *Blackb 5* **P** *Trustees* **R** D C DICKINSON
HESKET-IN-THE-FOREST (St Mary the Virgin) *see* Inglewood Gp *Carl*
HESLERTON, WEST (All Saints) *see* Buckrose Carrs *York*
HESLINGTON (St Paul) *York 2* **P** *Abp* **P-in-c** J A ROMANIS
HESSAY (St John the Baptist) *see* Rural Ainsty *York*
HESSENFORD (St Anne) *see* St Germans w Antony and Sheviock *Truro*
HESSETT (St Ethelbert) *see* Rougham, Beyton w Hessett and Rushbrooke *St E*
HESSLE (All Saints) *York 14* **P** *Ld Chan* **V** G D TURNER
NSM C R TETLEY
HESTER WAY LANE (St Silas) *see* W Cheltenham *Glouc*
HESTON (All Saints) (St Leonard) *Lon 11* **P** *Bp* **NSM** D SOLANKI
HESWALL (Church of the Good Shepherd) (St Peter) *Ches 8* **P** *W A B Davenport Esq* **R** M S J CANNAM   **C** D M HARRIS, J A CARLSON
HETHE (St Edmund King and Martyr and St George) *see* Shelswell *Ox*
HETHEL (All Saints) *see* Mulbarton w Bracon Ash, Hethel and Flordon *Nor*
HETHERSETT (St Remigius) w Canteloff w Little Melton and Great Melton *Nor 7* **P** *G&C Coll Cam, E C Evans-Lombe Esq, and Em Coll Cam (by turn)* **R** D A MCCLEAN
HETHERSGILL (St Mary) *see* Bewcastle, Stapleton and Kirklinton etc *Carl*
HETTON, SOUTH (Holy Trinity) *see* Murton and S Hetton *Dur*

HETTON-LYONS (St Michael and St Nicholas) w Eppleton *Dur 9* **P** *Bp (1 turn), The Crown (2 turns)* **P-in-c** T WALL **NSM** H AVENT

HEVENINGHAM (St Margaret) w Ubbeston, Huntingfield and Cookley *St E 15* **P** *Capt the Revd J S Peel* **P-in-c** D J A DOBLE

HEVER (St Peter), Four Elms and Mark Beech *Roch 11* **P** *Bp and C Talbot Esq (jt)* **P-in-c** S BRAID

HEVERSHAM (St Peter) and Milnthorpe *Carl 10* **P** *Trin Coll Cam* **P-in-c** B T KERR

HEVINGHAM (St Mary the Virgin and St Botolph) *see* Horsford, Felthorpe and Hevingham *Nor*

HEWELSFIELD (St Mary Magdalene) *see* St Briavels w Hewelsfield and Brockweir *Glouc*

HEWISH (Good Shepherd) *see* Wulfric Benefice *B & W*

HEWORTH (Christ Church) *York 7* **P** *Ch Trust Fund Trust* **V** P E DEO

HEWORTH (Holy Trinity) (St Wulstan) *York 7* **P** *Ch Trust Fund Trust* **R** *vacant*

HEWORTH (St Alban) *see* Windy Nook St Alb *Dur*

HEWORTH (St Mary) *Dur 11* **P** *Bp* **V** *vacant*

HEWORTH (St Wulstan) Conventional District *York 7* **P-in-c** A J RYCROFT, S SHERIFF

HEXAGON, The: Arnesby w Shearsby, Bruntingthorpe, Husbands Bosworth, Mowsley and Knaptoft, and Theddingworth *Leic 7* **P** *Bp and DBP (jt)* **R** A E A BICKLEY **C** S J MARCH

HEXHAM (St Andrew) *Newc 10* **P** *Mercers' Co and Viscount Allendale (alt)* **R** D C GLOVER **C** H J HOPE **NSM** E L RYDER

HEXTABLE (St Peter) *see* Swanley St Paul *Roch*

HEXTHORPE (St Jude) *see* Edlington and Hexthorpe *Sheff*

HEXTON (St Faith) *see* Barton-le-Cley w Higham Gobion and Hexton *St Alb*

HEY (St John the Baptist) *Man 5* **P** *R Ashton-under-Lyne Gd Shep* **V** L E M WOODALL **C** A SHERIDAN **NSM** C S STEEL

HEYBRIDGE (St Andrew) (St George) w Langford *Chelmsf 10* **P** *D&C St Paul's and Lord Byron (alt)* **P-in-c** A J HUMPHREYS

HEYDON (Holy Trinity) *see* Icknield Way Villages *Chelmsf*

HEYDON (St Peter and St Paul) *see* Aylsham and Distr *Nor*

HEYDOUR (St Michael and All Angels) *see* E Loveden *Linc*

HEYFORD (St Peter and St Paul) w Stowe Nine Churches and Flore w Brockhall *Pet 3* **P** *The Revd S Hope, Ch Ch Ox, DBP and Bp (by turn)* **R** S P BURROW

HEYFORD PARK Chapel *see* Cherwell Valley *Ox*

HEYFORD, LOWER (St Mary) *as above*

HEYFORD, UPPER (St Mary) *as above*

HEYHOUSES (St Nicholas) *see* W Pendleside *Blackb*

HEYHOUSES ON SEA (St Anne) *see* St Annes St Anne *Blackb*

HEYSHAM (St Peter) (St Andrew) (St James) *Blackb 11* **P** *C E C Royds Esq* **R** A T OSBORN

HEYSHOTT (St James) *see* Cocking w W Lavington, Bepton and Heyshott *Chich*

HEYSIDE (St Mark) and Royton *Man 5* **P** *Bp and Trustees (jt)* **V** E J DEVALL

HEYTESBURY (St Peter and St Paul) *see* Upper Wylye Valley *Sarum*

HEYTHROP (St Nicholas) *see* Gt w Lt Tew and Heythrop *Ox*

HEYWOOD (St James) *Man 6* **P** *Bp* **C** S ROBINSON

HEYWOOD (St John) (St Luke) *Man 6* **P** *Patr Bd* **V** K H SCREETON

HEYWOOD (St Margaret) and Heap Bridge *Man 6* **P** *Patr Bd* **C** S ROBINSON

HIBALDSTOW (St Hybald) *see* Scawby, Redbourne and Hibaldstow *Linc*

HICKLETON (St Wilfrid) *see* Goldthorpe w Hickleton *Sheff*

HICKLING (St Luke) w Kinoulton and Broughton Sulney (Upper Broughton) *S'well 5* **P** *The Crown, Qu Coll Cam, and Bp (by turn)* **P-in-c** P D S MASSEY **NSM** M R WOODWARD

HICKLING (St Mary) *see* Ludham, Potter Heigham, Hickling and Catfield *Nor*

HIGH *see also under substantive place name*

HIGH BROOMS (St Matthew) *Roch 12* **P** *CPAS Patr Trust* **V** C B WICKS

HIGH CROSS (St John the Evangelist) *St Alb 19* **P** *DBP* **V** A J DUNCAN

HIGH GREEN (St Saviour) *see* Mortomley St Sav High Green *Sheff*

HIGH HAM (St Andrew) *see* Aller, High w Low Ham and Huish Episcopi cum Langport *B & W*

HIGH LANE (St Thomas) *Ches 16* **P** *R Stockport* **V** H E HUPFIELD

HIGH LEGH (St John) *Ches 12* **P** *R H Cornwall-Legh Esq* **P-in-c** P J ROBINSON **NSM** P M COPE, P M ROBINSON

HIGH OAK, Hingham and Scoulton w Wood Rising, including Deopham, Hackford, Morley St Botolph, Morley St Peter, and Wicklewood *Nor 7* **P** *Bp, Adn Humbleyard, D&C, D&C Cant, Earl of Kimberley, Earl of Verulam, Sir A E H Heber-Percy, and Trustees* **P** *vacant*

HIGHAM (St John the Evangelist) *see* Fence-in-Pendle and Higham *Blackb*

HIGHAM (St John the Evangelist) and Merston *Roch 6* **P** *St Jo Coll Cam* **V** *vacant*

HIGHAM (St Mary), Holton St Mary, Raydon and Stratford St Mary *St E 4* **P** *Duchy of Lanc, Reformation Ch Trust, and Mrs S E F Holden* **P-in-c** M A CROSSMAN **NSM** M R CARR, N J TINDALL

HIGHAM FERRERS (St Mary the Virgin) w Chelveston *Pet 8* **P** *Bp* **V** M A C DALLISTON

HIGHAM GOBION (St Margaret) *see* Barton-le-Cley w Higham Gobion and Hexton *St Alb*

HIGHAM GREEN (St Stephen) *see* Forest Heath *St E*

HIGHAM-ON-THE-HILL (St Peter) *see* Fenn Lanes Gp *Leic*

HIGHAMPTON (Holy Cross) *see* Ashwater, Halwill, Beaworthy, Clawton etc *Ex*

HIGHAMS PARK (All Saints) Hale End *Chelmsf 7* **P** *Bp* **V** M D PORTER

HIGHBRIDGE (St John the Evangelist) *B & W 1* **P** *Bp* **P-in-c** B M LITTLE **C** D D CROUCH

HIGHBROOK (All Saints) and West Hoathly *Chich 8* **P** *Ld Chan* **P-in-c** N W KINRADE

HIGHBURY (Christ Church) (St John) (St Saviour) *Lon 6* **P** *CPAS* **V** A J CHRICH **C** R M RIMMER **NSM** T J I WITTER

HIGHBURY NEW PARK (St Augustine) *Lon 6* **P** *CPAS* **V** G A M ANSTIS

HIGHCLERE (St Michael and All Angels) *see* NW Hants *Win*

HIGHCLIFFE (St Mark) *Win 9* **P** *Bp* **V** V M BROWN

HIGHER *see under substantive place name*

HIGHERTOWN (All Saints) and Baldhu *Truro 5* **P** *Bp and Viscount Falmouth (alt)* **P-in-c** J J PUTNAM **C** P A GILBERT **NSM** H A PRESTON, J C MULLETT

HIGHFIELD (All Saints) *Ox 1* **P** *Bp* **P-in-c** L P CATALLO

HIGHFIELD (Christ Church) *see* Portswood Ch Ch *Win*

HIGHFIELD (St Catherine) *see* New Bury w Gt Lever *Man*

HIGHFIELD (St Mary) *see* Sheff St Mary Bramall Lane *Sheff*

HIGHFIELD (St Matthew) *see* Wigan *Liv*

HIGHFIELD (St Paul) *see* Hemel Hempstead *St Alb*

HIGHFIELD (St Peter) and Leicester St Philip *Leic 1* **P** *Bp and Trustees (jt)* **R** J M SURRIDGE **NSM** C R BROWN

HIGHGATE (All Saints) *Lon 17* **P** *Bp* **P-in-c** T I MILLER **NSM** A J M MCKAY, J H ROGERS

HIGHGATE (St Alban the Martyr and St Patrick) *Birm 1* **P** *Keble Coll Ox* **V** G A SYKES

HIGHGATE (St Augustine) *Lon 17* **P** *Bp* **P-in-c** T I MILLER **Hon C** W A WHITCOMBE

HIGHGATE (St Michael) *Lon 17* **P** *Bp* **V** O AYODEJI **NSM** J H ROGERS

HIGHLEY (St Mary) w Billingsley, Glazeley and Deuxhill and Chelmarsh *Heref 8* **P** *MMCET* **V** M A HARRIS **NSM** D R POYNER, V R SMITH

HIGHNAM (Holy Innocents), Tibberton w Rudford and Taynton *Glouc 3* **P** *D&C, T J Fenton Esq, and A E Woolley (jt)* **R** *vacant*

HIGHTERS HEATH (Immanuel) *Birm 2* **P** *Bp* **P-in-c** D M COLLINS **OLM** S LANGSTON

HIGHTOWN (All Saints) *see* Castleford *Leeds*

HIGHTOWN (St Matthew) Luton *see* Luton St Mary and St Matt *St Alb*

HIGHTOWN (St Stephen) *Liv 8* **P** *Bp* **V** J H H ASHTON

HIGHWEEK (All Saints) *see* Newton Abbot *Ex*

HIGHWORTH (St Michael) w Sevenhampton and Inglesham and Hannington *Bris 7* **P** *Bp (4 turns), Mrs M G Hussey-Freke (1 turn)* **V** G D SOWDEN **C** E R M SWINERD

HILBOROUGH (All Saints) w Bodney *Nor 13* **P** *DBP* **Hon C** L M LUBBE

HILDENBOROUGH (St John the Evangelist) *Roch 11* **P** *V Tonbridge* **V** T R SAIET

HILDERSHAM (Holy Trinity) *see* Granta Vale Gp *Ely*

HILDERSTONE (Christ Church) *see* Fulford w Hilderstone *Lich*

HILFIELD (St Nicholas) *see* Three Valleys *Sarum*

HILGAY (All Saints) *Ely 9* **P** *Hertf Coll Ox* **R** *vacant*

HILL (St James) *Birm 4* **P** *Bp* **NSM** J A RAMBLE

HILL (St Michael) *see* Berkeley w Wick, Breadstone, Newport, Stone etc *Glouc*

HILL CROOME (St Mary) *see* Upton-on-Severn, Ripple, Earls Croome etc *Worc*

HILL TOP (St James) *see* W Bromwich St Jas and St Paul *Lich*

HILLESDEN (All Saints) *see* Lenborough *Ox*

HILLESLEY (St Giles)   *see* Charfield and Kingswood w Wickwar etc *Glouc*
HILLFARRANCE (Holy Cross)   *see* Deane Vale *B & W*
HILLINGDON (All Saints) *Lon 21*   P *Bp*   V D P BANISTER NSM D CICILY ANTONY
HILLINGDON (St John the Baptist) *Lon 21*   P *Bp* V A BRADFORD
HILLINGTON (St Mary the Virgin) *Nor 15*   P *E W Dawnay Esq*   R J B V RIVIERE
HILLMORTON (St John the Baptist) *Cov 6*   P *Bp* P-in-c S E GOLD   C A MARSH   Hon C M I SIMMONS
HILLOCK (St Andrew) and Unsworth *Man 4*   P *Bp, R Stand All SS, and R Prestwich St Mary (jt)*   V D A WILLIAMS C S MAWHINNEY   NSM A M WHITTLEWORTH   OLM M RYAN
HILLSBOROUGH and Wadsley Bridge (Christ Church) *Sheff 4*   P *Ch Patr Trust*   P-in-c P J GOODACRE   C H E TERRY NSM R R OTIENO
HILLSIDE Lobley Hill and Marley Hill *Dur 12*   P *Bp and The Crown (alt)*   V G MACKNIGHT   C R J BALFOUR
HILMARTON (St Lawrence)   *see* Lyneham and Woodhill *Sarum*
HILPERTON (St Michael and All Angels)   *see* Canalside Benefice *Sarum*
HILPERTON MARSH (St Mary Magdalen) *as above*
HILSTON (St Margaret)   *see* S Holderness Coast *York*
HILTON (All Saints)   *see* Piddle Valley, Hilton and Ansty, Cheselbourne etc *Sarum*
HILTON (St Mary Magdalene)   *see* Godmanchester and Hilton *Ely*
HILTON (St Peter)   *see* Stainton w Hemlington and Hilton *York*
HILTON w Marston-on-Dove *Derby 6*   P *N J M Spurrier Esq* V *vacant*
HIMBLETON (St Mary Magdalene)   *see* Bowbrook *Worc*
HIMLEY (St Michael and All Angels)   *see* Smestow Vale *Lich*
HINCASTER (Mission Room)   *see* Heversham and Milnthorpe *Carl*
HINCHLEY WOOD (St Christopher) *Guildf 8*   P *Bp* V P D JENNER   NSM C A MULLINS
HINCKFORD, NORTH, comprising Alphamstone, Belchamp, Belchamp Otten, Belchamp Walter, Bulmer, Foxearth, Great and Little Henny, Lamarsh, Liston and Borley, Middleton, Ovington, Pentlow, Twinstead, and Wickham *Chelmsf 18* P *Patr Bd (4 turns), Ld Chan (1 turn)*   TR G M MORGAN NSM K M SALE
HINCKLEY (Assumption of St Mary the Virgin) (St Francis) (St Paul) *Leic 10*   P *Bp*   V I R HILL
HINCKLEY (Holy Trinity) *Leic 10*   P *DBP*   R S J WEARN C M G A COOPER
HINCKLEY (St John the Evangelist) *Leic 10*   P *DBP* V G J WESTON   C D R MATTHEW, J M BERRY
HINDERCLAY (St Mary)   *see* Stanton *St E*
HINDERWELL (St Hilda), Roxby and Staithes w Lythe, Ugthorpe and Sandsend *York 21*   P *Abp*   R M JACKSON
HINDHEAD (St Alban)   *see* Churt and Hindhead *Guildf*
HINDLEY (All Saints)   *see* Wigan *Liv*
HINDLEY (St Peter) *as above*
HINDLEY GREEN (St John) *as above*
HINDOLVESTON (St George)   *see* Briston, Burgh Parva, Hindolveston etc *Nor*
HINDON (St John the Baptist)   *see* Nadder Valley *Sarum*
HINDRINGHAM (St Martin)   *see* Barney, Hindringham, Thursford, Great Snoring, Little Snoring and Kettlestone and Pensthorpe *Nor*
HINGHAM (St Andrew)   *see* High Oak, Hingham and Scoulton w Wood Rising *Nor*
HINKSEY, NEW (St John the Evangelist)   *see* S Hinksey *Ox*
HINKSEY, NORTH (St Lawrence)   *see* Osney *Ox*
HINKSEY, SOUTH (St Laurence) *Ox 2*   P *Bp*   V *vacant*
HINSTOCK (St Oswald)   *see* Cheswardine, Childs Ercall, Hales, Hinstock etc *Lich*
HINTLESHAM (St Nicholas)   *see* Elmsett w Aldham, Hintlesham, Chattisham etc *St E*
HINTON ADMIRAL (St Michael and All Angels)   *see* Bransgore and Hinton Admiral *Win*
HINTON AMPNER (All Saints)   *see* Upper Itchen *Win*
HINTON BLEWETT (St Margaret)   *see* E w W Harptree and Hinton Blewett *B & W*
HINTON CHARTERHOUSE (St John the Baptist)   *see* Freshford, Limpley Stoke and Hinton Charterhouse *B & W*
HINTON MARTEL (St John the Evangelist)   *see* Wimborne Minster and Villages *Sarum*
HINTON PARVA (St Swithun)   *see* Lyddington and Wanborough and Bishopstone etc *Bris*
HINTON ST GEORGE (St George)   *see* Merriott w Hinton, Dinnington and Lopen *B & W*

HINTON ST MARY (St Mary)   *see* Sturminster Newton, Hinton St Mary and Lydlinch *Sarum*
HINTON WALDRIST (St Margaret)   *see* Cherbury w Gainfield *Ox*
HINTON-IN-THE-HEDGES (Holy Trinity)   *see* Aynho and Croughton w Evenley etc *Pet*
HINTON-ON-THE-GREEN (St Peter)   *see* Bengeworth and Hampton etc *Worc*
HINTS (St Bartholomew) *Lich 1*   P *Personal Reps A E Jones Esq*   V *vacant*
HINXHILL (St Mary)   *see* Wye *Cant*
HINXTON (St Mary and St John) *Ely 5*   P *Jes Coll Cam* P-in-c L J SMITH
HINXWORTH (St Nicholas)   *see* Ashwell w Hinxworth and Newnham *St Alb*
HIPSWELL (St John the Evangelist) *Leeds 19*   P *Bp* V A R M CROMARTY
HISTON (St Andrew) *Ely 6*   P *MMCET* V N J BLANDFORD-BAKER   C R M CHAMBERLAIN
HITCHAM (All Saints)   *see* Rattlesden w Thorpe Morieux, Brettenham etc *St E*
HITCHAM (St Mary) *Ox 12*   P *Eton Coll*   V S A SAMPSON
HITCHIN (Holy Saviour) (St Faith) (St Mark) (St Mary) and St Paul's Walden *St Alb 3*   P *Patr Bd*   TR C E BUNCE TV I C TODD, M CROWLEY, N W SMITH, S L FIELDING C M J INCH   NSM F S E GIBBS
HITHER GREEN (St Swithun)   *see* Lewisham St Swithun *S'wark*
HITTISLEIGH (St Andrew)   *see* Chagford, Gidleigh, Throwleigh etc *Ex*
HIXON (St Peter)   *see* Mid Trent *Lich*
HOAR CROSS (Holy Angels) w Newchurch *Lich 13*   P *Bp and Meynell Ch Trust*   P-in-c G P BOTT
HOARWITHY (St Catherine)   *see* St Weonards *Heref*
HOATH (Holy Cross)   *see* Reculver and Herne Bay St Bart and Hoath *Cant*
HOATHLY, EAST (not known)   *see* Chiddingly w E Hoathly *Chich*
HOATHLY, WEST (St Margaret)   *see* Highbrook and W Hoathly *Chich*
HOBS MOAT (St Mary) *Birm 6*   P *Bp*   P-in-c L GRANNER
HOBY (All Saints)   *see* Upper Wreake *Leic*
HOCKERILL (All Saints) *St Alb 15*   P *Bp Lon* V S D MANSFIELD
HOCKERING (St Michael)   *see* Mattishall and the Tudd Valley *Nor*
HOCKHAM, GREAT (Holy Trinity)   *see* Caston, Griston, Merton, Thompson etc *Nor*
HOCKLEY (St Matthew)   *see* Wilnecote *Lich*
HOCKLEY (St Peter and St Paul) *Chelmsf 13*   P *Wadh Coll Ox*   Hon C S S STROEBEL
HOCKLIFFE (St Nicholas)   *see* Ouzel Valley *St Alb*
HOCKWOLD w WILTON (St James)   *see* Grimshoe *Ely*
HOCKWORTHY (St Simon and St Jude)   *see* Sampford Peverell, Uplowman, Holcombe Rogus etc *Ex*
HODDESDON (St Catherine and St Paul) *St Alb 17* P *Peache Trustees*   V R E B PENNANT   C K E CARTER
HODDLESDEN (St Paul)   *see* Over Darwen St Jas and Hoddlesden *Blackb*
HODGE HILL (St Philip and St James) *Birm 5*   P *Bp* TR A D BARRETT   NSM G D SMITH, S A NASH
HODNET (St Luke) *Lich 17*   P *Sir Algernon Heber-Percy KCVO* P-in-c E QUIREY
HOE (St Andrew)   *see* Dereham and Distr *Nor*
HOGGESTON (Holy Cross)   *see* Schorne *Ox*
HOGHTON (Holy Trinity) *Blackb 5*   P *V Leyland* V H R BOYD   C B G NAYLOR
HOGNASTON (St Bartholomew)   *see* Hulland, Atlow, Kniveton, Bradley and Hognaston *Derby*
HOGSTHORPE (St Mary)   *see* Chapel St Leonards and Hogsthorpe *Linc*
HOLBEACH (All Saints) *Linc 18*   P *Bp*   V *vacant*
HOLBEACH FEN (St John)   *see* Elloe Stone *Linc*
HOLBEACH HURN (St Luke)   *see* Mid Elloe Gp *Linc*
HOLBEACH MARSH (St Mark) *as above*
HOLBECK (St Luke the Evangelist) *Leeds 11*   P *Bp, V Leeds St Pet, and Meynell Ch Trust (jt)*   C J PÉCHER, P R MASON
HOLBETON (All Saints) *Ex 19*   P *The Crown*   P-in-c A J RYAN C K R LOVELL
HOLBORN (St Alban the Martyr) w Saffron Hill St Peter *Lon 15*   P *D&C St Paul's*   V C M SMITH   NSM R G CORP
HOLBORN (St George the Martyr) Queen Square (Holy Trinity) (St Bartholomew) Grays Inn Road *Lon 15*   P *Ch Soc Trust*   C J R HAITH   NSM P B HOWARTH
HOLBORN (St Giles-in-the-Fields)   *see* St Giles-in-the-Fields *Lon*

HOLBROOK (All Saints), Stutton, Freston, Woolverstone and Wherstead *St E 13*   **P** *Patr Bd*   **R** J M SEGGAR   **NSM** D C W MYATT

HOLBROOK (St Mark) *Chich 10*   **P** *Abp Cant, Bp, and Bp Horsham (jt)*   **V** R S COLDICOTT   **NSM** E JINKS

HOLBROOK (St Michael)   *see* Hazelwood, Holbrook and Milford *Derby*

HOLBROOK ROAD (St Swithin)   *see* Belper *Derby*

HOLBROOKS (St Luke) *Cov 2*   **P** *Bp*   **V** S P OAKES

HOLBURY (Good Shepherd)   *see* Fawley *Win*

HOLCOMBE (Emmanuel) (Canon Lewis Hall) and Hawkshaw *Man 4*   **P** *R Bury St Mary and CPAS (jt)*   **R** P H SUMSION   **C** I J FLEMING   **OLM** R W AIREY, V J D FLETCHER

HOLCOMBE (St Andrew)   *see* Coleford w Holcombe *B & W*

HOLCOMBE (St George)   *see* Dawlish w Holcombe, Cofton and Starcross *Ex*

HOLCOMBE BURNELL (St John the Baptist)   *see* Tedburn St Mary, Cheriton Bishop, Whitestone etc *Ex*

HOLCOMBE ROGUS (All Saints)   *see* Sampford Peverell, Uplowman, Holcombe Rogus etc *Ex*

HOLCOT (St Mary and All Saints)   *see* Brixworth w Holcot *Pet*

HOLDENHURST (St John the Evangelist) and Iford *Win 8*   **P** *Bp*   **V** A L MCPHERSON   **C** J M SEARE

HOLDERNESS COAST, SOUTH, comprising Garton-in-Holderness w Grimston, Hilston, Hollym, Holmpton, Owthorne, Roos, Tunstall and Withernsea *York 12*   **P** *Abp, SMF, and Ld Chan (by turn)*   **V** M T FAULKNER   **Hon C** P W WEST   **NSM** D J BERRY

HOLDGATE (Holy Trinity)   *see* Corvedale Benefice *Heref*

HOLFORD (St Mary the Virgin)   *see* Quantock Coast *B & W*

HOLKHAM (St Withiburga) w Egmere w Warham, Wells-next-the-Sea and Wighton *Nor 14*   **P** *Viscount Coke (2 turns), M J Beddard Esq (2 turns), and D&C (1 turn)*   **R** B A STEWART

HOLLACOMBE (St Petroc)   *see* Holsworthy, Hollacombe, Pyworthy etc *Ex*

HOLLAND FEN (All Saints)   *see* Brothertoft Gp *Linc*

HOLLAND PARK (St George the Martyr) (St John the Baptist) *Lon 12*   **P** *Trustees and Bp (jt)*   **V** J B HEARD   **C** N O TRAYNOR   **NSM** D L ENGLISH, P WOLTON

HOLLAND, GREAT (All Saints)   *see* Kirby-le-Soken w Gt Holland *Chelmsf*

HOLLAND, NEW (Christ Church)   *see* Barrow and Goxhill *Linc*

HOLLAND-ON-SEA (St Bartholomew) *Chelmsf 22*   **P** *Ch Patr Trust*   **C** D J LOWER   **OLM** S E WIGGINS

HOLLESLEY (All Saints)   *see* Wilford Peninsula *St E*

HOLLINFARE (St Helen)   *see* Glazebury w Hollinfare *Liv*

HOLLINGBOURNE (All Saints)   *see* N Downs *Cant*

HOLLINGTON (St John the Evangelist)   *see* Rocester, Denstone and Croxden w Hollington *Lich*

HOLLINGTON (St John the Evangelist) (St Peter and St Paul) *Chich 15*   **P** *Ch Patr Trust*   **V** L J W DEAN   **NSM** M HINKLEY

HOLLINGTON (St Leonard) (St Anne) *Chich 15*   **P** *CPAS*   **R** R M M CREIGHTON

HOLLINGWORTH (St Hilda)   *see* Milnrow and New Hey *Man*

HOLLINGWORTH (St Mary) w Tintwistle *Ches 14*   **P** *Patr Bd*   **V** B A PERRIN

HOLLINWOOD (St Margaret) and Limeside *Man 5*   **P** *Bp and V Prestwich (jt)*   **V** T H DAVIS

HOLLOWAY (Emmanuel)   *see* Hornsey Road *Lon*

HOLLOWAY (St Saviour) Hanley Road   *see* Hanley Road *Lon*

HOLLOWAY, UPPER (St John the Evangelist) *Lon 6*   **P** *Ch Patr Trust*   **V** A COMFORT

HOLLOWAY, WEST (St Luke) *Lon 6*   **P** *CPAS*   **V** J C N MACKENZIE   **C** E R CAMPBELL   **NSM** M D E WROE

HOLLOWELL (St James)   *see* Guilsborough and Hollowell and Cold Ashby etc *Pet*

HOLLY HALL (St Augustine)   *see* Dudley *Worc*

HOLLY HILL (Church Centre)   *see* Frankley *Birm*

HOLLYBUSH (All Saints)   *see* Berrow w Pendock, Eldersfield, Hollybush etc *Worc*

HOLLYM (St Nicholas)   *see* S Holderness Coast *York*

HOLMBRIDGE (St David)   *see* Upper Holme Valley *Leeds*

HOLMBURY ST MARY (St Mary the Virgin)   *see* Abinger and Coldharbour and Wotton and Holmbury St Mary *Guildf*

HOLME (All Saints) and Seaton Ross Group, The, including Everingham and Harswell *York 5*   **P** *St Jo Coll Cam and Ld Chan (alt)*   **R** S V COPE

HOLME (Holy Trinity)   *see* Burton and Holme *Carl*

HOLME (St Giles)   *see* E Trent *S'well*

HOLME (St Giles)   *see* Sawtry, Glatton and Holme w Conington *Ely*

HOLME CULTRAM (St Cuthbert)   *see* Solway Plain *Carl*

HOLME CULTRAM (St Mary) *as above*

HOLME EDEN (St Paul) and Wetheral w Warwick *Carl 2*   **P** *D&C and DBP (jt)*   **P-in-c** G J SKINNER   **C** P G DIXON, S J JONES

HOLME HALE (St Andrew)   *see* Necton, Holme Hale w N and S Pickenham *Nor*

HOLME PIERREPONT (St Edmund King and Martyr)   *see* Lady Bay w Holme Pierrepont and Adbolton *S'well*

HOLME VALLEY, The UPPER, comprising Hepworth, Holmbridge, Holmfirth, Netherthong, New Mill, Thurstonland, and Upperthong *Leeds 5*   **P** *Patr Bd*   **TR** J S ROBERTSHAW   **TV** K GRIFFIN, M D ELLERTON, N M HEATON   **NSM** A R BROOKE, S W DIXON

HOLME WOOD (St Christopher)   *see* Tong and Laisterdyke *Leeds*

HOLME, EAST (St John the Evangelist)   *see* Wareham *Sarum*

HOLMEDALE, comprising Barningham, Gilling, Hutton Magna, Kirkby Ravensworth, and Wycliffe *Leeds 19*   **P** *Bp and A C P Wharton Esq (jt)*   **R** A P KIRBY

HOLME-IN-CLIVIGER (St John) w Worsthorne *Blackb 3*   **P** *Patr Bd*   **V** C N CASEY

HOLME-NEXT-THE-SEA (St Mary)   *see* Hunstanton and Saxon Shore *Nor*

HOLME-ON-SPALDING-MOOR (All Saints)   *see* Holme and Seaton Ross Gp *York*

HOLME-ON-SPALDING-MOOR (Old School Mission Room) *as above*

HOLMER (St Bartholomew) (St Mary) w Huntington *Heref 3*   **P** *D&C*   **V** S M LEE   **C** E BUTLER, R J ORAM

HOLMER GREEN (Christ Church)   *see* Penn Street *Ox*

HOLMES CHAPEL (St Luke)   *see* Church Hulme *Ches*

HOLMESDALE (St Philip)   *see* Dronfield w Holmesfield *Derby*

HOLMESFIELD (St Swithin) *as above*

HOLMEWOOD (St Alban Mission)   *see* Heath *Derby*

HOLMFIRTH (Holy Trinity)   *see* Upper Holme Valley *Leeds*

HOLMPTON (St Nicholas)   *see* S Holderness Coast *York*

HOLMSIDE (St John the Evangelist)   *see* Lanchester and Burnhope *Dur*

HOLMWOOD (St Mary Magdalene)   *see* Surrey Weald *Guildf*

HOLMWOOD, NORTH (St John the Evangelist) *Guildf 7*   **P** *Bp*   **P-in-c** P NEVINS   **OLM** C LAZENBY, J E SCHOFIELD

HOLNE (St Mary the Virgin)   *see* Ashburton, Bickington, Buckland in the Moor etc *Ex*

HOLNEST (Church of the Assumption)   *see* Three Valleys *Sarum*

HOLSWORTHY (St Peter and St Paul), Hollacombe, Pyworthy, Pancrasweek and Bridgerule *Ex 15*   **P** *DBP*   **R** E M A BURKE

HOLT (St Andrew) w High Kelling *Nor 17*   **P** *St Jo Coll Cam*   **R** H C STOKER   **NSM** G D GOULD

HOLT (St Katharine)   *see* Broughton Gifford, Gt Chalfield and Holt *Sarum*

HOLT (St Martin)   *see* Hallow and Grimley w Holt etc *Worc*

HOLTBY (Holy Trinity)   *see* Rural E York *York*

HOLTON (St Bartholomew)   *see* Albury w Tiddington etc *Ox*

HOLTON (St Nicholas)   *see* Camelot Par *B & W*

HOLTON (St Peter)   *see* Blyth Valley *St E*

HOLTON ST MARY (St Mary)   *see* Higham, Holton St Mary, Raydon and Stratford *St E*

HOLTON-CUM-BECKERING (All Saints)   *see* Wragby Gp *Linc*

HOLTON-LE-CLAY (St Peter), Tetney and North Cotes *Linc 4*   **P** *Ld Chan, Bp, and Duchy of Lancaster (by turn)*   **NSM** J WEST

HOLTON-LE-MOOR (St Luke)   *see* Woldmoor Gp *Linc*

HOLTS (St Hugh)   *see* Leesfield *Man*

HOLTSPUR (St Thomas)   *see* Beaconsfield *Ox*

HOLWELL (St Laurence)   *see* Three Valleys *Sarum*

HOLWELL (St Leonard)   *see* Ab Kettleby and Holwell w Asfordby *Leic*

HOLWELL (St Mary the Virgin)   *see* Shill Valley and Broadshire *Ox*

HOLWELL (St Peter), Ickleford and Pirton *St Alb 3*   **P** *DBP and D&C Ely (jt)*   **R** M FANE DE SALIS   **NSM** M S HOLFORD

HOLWORTH (St Catherine by the Sea)   *see* Watercombe *Sarum*

HOLY ISLAND (St Mary the Virgin) *Newc 12*   **P** *Bp*   **V** S A ST L HILLS   **NSM** S J QUILTY

HOLYBOURNE (Holy Rood)   *see* Alton *Win*

HOLYMOORSIDE (St Peter)   *see* Brampton St Thos *Derby*

HOLYSTONE (St Mary the Virgin)   *see* Upper Coquetdale *Newc*

HOLYWELL (St John the Baptist)   *see* Bluntisham cum Earith w Colne and Holywell etc *Ely*

HOLYWELL (St Mary)   *see* Seghill *Newc*

HOMERSFIELD (St Mary)   *see* The Saints *St E*

HOMERTON (St Barnabas) (Christ Church on the Mead) (The Risen Christ) *Lon 5* **P** *Bp, Grocers' Co, and Trustees (jt)* **R** C T MAIN **NSM** S P PLUMB

HOMINGTON (St Mary the Virgin) *see* Chalke Valley *Sarum*

HONEYCHURCH (St Mary) *see* Chagford, Gidleigh, Throwleigh etc *Ex*

HONICKNOWLE (St Francis) *see* Ernesettle, Whitleigh and Honicknowle *Ex*

HONILEY (St John the Baptist) *see* Hatton w Haseley, Rowington w Lowsonford etc *Cov*

HONING (St Peter and St Paul) *see* Smallburgh w Dilham w Honing and Crostwight *Nor*

HONINGHAM (St Andrew) *Nor 16* **P** *DBP* **V** *vacant*

HONINGTON (All Saints) *see* Blackbourne *St E*

HONINGTON (All Saints) *see* Shipston-on-Stour w Honington and Idlicote *Cov*

HONINGTON (St Wilfred) *see* S Cliff Villages Gp *Linc*

HONITON (St Paul) w Monkton, Awliscombe, Buckerell, Combe Raleigh, Cotleigh and Gittisham *Ex 4* **P** *Patr Bd* **TR** S E ROBERTS

HONLEY (St Mary) *Leeds 5* **P** *R Almondbury* **V** M R SHORT

HONOR OAK PARK (St Augustine of Canterbury) *S'wark 5* **P** *Bp* **P-in-c** C J L BOSWELL **NSM** M BROOKS

HOO (All Hallows) *see* High Halstow w All Hallows and Hoo St Mary *Roch*

HOO (St Andrew and St Eustachius) *see* Mid Loes *St E*

HOO (St Werburgh) *Roch 6* **P** *D&C* **P-in-c** M L BORLEY

HOOBROOK (St Cecilia) *see* Kidderminster E *Worc*

HOOE (St John the Evangelist) *see* Plymstock and Hooe *Ex*

HOOE (St Oswald) *Chich 12* **P** *Bp* **P-in-c** P A FROSTICK

HOOK (St John the Evangelist) *see* Whitewater *Win*

HOOK (St Mary the Virgin) *see* Airmyn, Hook and Rawcliffe *Sheff*

HOOK (St Mary) w Warsash *Portsm 2* **P** *Bp* **P-in-c** J M TERRY, N S TERRY

HOOK (St Paul) *see* Tolworth, Hook and Surbiton *S'wark*

HOOK COMMON (Good Shepherd) *see* Upton-on-Severn, Ripple, Earls Croome etc *Worc*

HOOK NORTON (St Peter) w Great Rollright, Swerford and Wigginton *Ox 22* **P** *Bp, DBP, BNC Ox, and Jes Coll Ox (jt)* **R** J D FAULL

HOOKE (St Giles) *see* Beaminster Area *Sarum*

HOOLE (All Saints) *Ches 2* **P** *Simeon's Trustees* **C** S DURDANT-HOLLAMBY

HOOLE (St Michael) *Blackb 5* **P** *Reps of Mrs E A Dunne and Mrs D Downes (jt)* **R** A J TEMPLEMAN

HOOTON (St Paul) *Ches 9* **P** *Trustees* **V** K HOWARD

HOOTON PAGNELL (All Saints) *see* Bilham *Sheff*

HOOTON ROBERTS (St John) *see* Ravenfield, Hooton Roberts and Braithwell *Sheff*

HOP CHURCHES Benefice, The, comprising Bosbury, Canon Frome, Munsley, Stoke Edith, Stretton Grandison w Ashperton, Tarrington, and Yarkhill *Heref 5* **P** *Bp (4 turns), D&C (2 turns), Exors A T Foley Esq (2 turns), R Hopton Esq (1 turn), H W Wiggin Esq (1 turn)* **V** A J WILLIAMS **NSM** E N SEABRIGHT

HOPE (Holy Trinity) *see* Minsterley, Habberley and Hope w Shelve *Heref*

HOPE (St James) and Pendlebury St John *Man 7* **P** *Trustees* **V** G M THOMAS **C** L NIKROO **OLM** P M MANLEY

HOPE (St Peter), Castleton and Bradwell *Derby 4* **P** *Bp and D&C Lich (jt)* **P-in-c** L A M PETHERAM **OLM** J E BARNES

HOPE BAGOT (St John the Baptist) *see* Tenbury *Heref*

HOPE BOWDLER (St Andrew) *see* Apedale Gp *Heref*

HOPE CHURCH ISLINGTON (St Mary Magdalene) (St David) *Lon 6* **P** *Bp and V Islington St Mary (jt)* **V** P V ZAPHIRIOU **C** M P WAY

HOPE COVE (St Clements) *see* Malborough, Salcombe and S Huish *Ex*

HOPE MANSEL (St Michael) *see* Ariconium *Heref*

HOPESAY (St Mary the Virgin) *see* Clun Valley *Heref*

HOPE-UNDER-DINMORE (St Mary the Virgin) *see* Leominster *Heref*

HOPTON (All Saints) *see* Stanton *St E*

HOPTON (St Margaret), Corton and Gunton *Nor 9* **P** *D&C and CPAS Patr Trust (2 turns), Ld Chan (1 turn)* **R** N J LACEY

HOPTON (St Peter) *see* Mid Trent *Lich*

HOPTON CASTLE (St Edward) *see* Middle Marches *Heref*

HOPTON WAFERS (St Michael and All Angels) *see* Cleobury Mortimer w Hopton Wafers etc *Heref*

HOPTON, UPPER (St John the Evangelist) *see* Mirfield *Leeds*

HOPWAS (St Chad) *see* Tamworth *Lich*

HOPWOOD (St John) *see* Heywood St Jo and St Luke *Man*

HORAM (Christ Church) (St James) *Chich 13* **P** *Bp* **V** P-J GUY

HORBLING (St Andrew) *see* Billingborough Gp *Linc*

HORBURY (St Peter and St Leonard) w Horbury Bridge (St John) *Leeds 16* **P** *Dean* **V** C N JOHNSON

HORBURY JUNCTION (St Mary) *Leeds 16* **P** *DBP* **NSM** D M WALKER

HORDEN (St Mary) *Dur 10* **P** *Bp* **P-in-c** K G MCNEIL

HORDLE (All Saints) *Win 11* **P** *Bp* **NSM** E A ELLIOTT

HORDLEY (St Mary the Virgin) *see* Baschurch and Weston Lullingfield w Hordley *Lich*

HORFIELD (Holy Trinity) *Bris 3* **P** *Bp* **R** D J MCGLADDERY

HORFIELD (St Gregory) *Bris 3* **P** *Bp* **V** J WILSON

HORHAM (St Mary) *see* Athelington, Denham, Horham, Hoxne etc *St E*

HORKESLEY, GREAT (All Saints) *see* W Bergholt and Gt Horkesley *Chelmsf*

HORKESLEY, GREAT (St John) *as above*

HORKESLEY, LITTLE (St Peter and St Paul) *see* Wormingford, Mt Bures and Lt Horkesley *Chelmsf*

HORKSTOW (St Maurice) *Linc 8* **P** *DBP* **V** D P ROWETT

HORLEY (St Bartholomew) (St Francis) (St Wilfrid) *S'wark 24* **P** *Patr Bd* **TR** L J WELLS **TV** N NGURURI **C** S BOSLEY

HORLEY (St Etheldreda) *see* Ironstone *Ox*

HORLEY ROW (St Wilfrid) *see* Horley *S'wark*

HORMEAD (St Nicholas), Wyddial, Anstey, Brent Pelham and Meesden *St Alb 16* **P** *St Jo Coll Cam, Ch Coll Cam, and Bp (by turn)* **R** J T L SAWYER

HORN HILL (St Paul) *see* Chalfont St Peter *Ox*

HORNBLOTTON (St Peter) *see* Six Pilgrims *B & W*

HORNBY (St Margaret) w Claughton and Whittington w Arkholme and Gressingham *Blackb 14* **P** *Patr Bd* **V** M J HAMPSON

HORNBY (St Mary) *see* Lower Wensleydale *Leeds*

HORNCASTLE Group, The (St Mary the Virgin), including Ashby Puerorum, Greetham, High Toynton, Martin, Thimbleby, and Thornton *Linc 13* **P** *Bp, Baroness Willoughby de Eresby and D&C (jt)* **R** P C PATRICK **C** L HAWKINS **NSM** J F PARKIN

HORNCHURCH (Holy Cross) *Chelmsf 2* **P** *Bp and New Coll Ox (alt)* **P-in-c** J F PATCHING

HORNCHURCH (St Andrew) (St George) (St Matthew) *Chelmsf 2* **P** *New Coll Ox* **V** K A WYLIE **NSM** M R HAYWARD

HORNCHURCH (St Nicholas) Elm Park *see* Elm Park St Nic Hornchurch *Chelmsf*

HORNCHURCH, SOUTH (St John and St Matthew) *Chelmsf 2* **P** *MMCET* **V** K J BROWNING

HORNDALE (St Francis) *see* Gt Aycliffe *Dur*

HORNDON EAST (St Francis) and West Horndon w Little Warley and Childerditch *Chelmsf 8* **P** *Sir Antony Browne's Sch, Bp and MMCET (jt)* **V** *vacant*

HORNDON ON THE HILL (St Peter and St Paul) *see* Orsett and Bulphan and Horndon on the Hill *Chelmsf*

HORNE (St Mary) *see* The Windmill *S'wark*

HORNING (St Benedict) *see* Ashmanhaugh, Barton Turf etc *Nor*

HORNINGHOLD (St Peter) *see* Hallaton and Allexton, w Horninghold, Tugby etc *Leic*

HORNINGLOW (St John the Divine) *Lich 13* **P** *Trustees* **V** M R FREEMAN **C** D B GORWOOD

HORNINGSEA (St Peter) *Ely 2* **P** *St Jo Coll Cam* **V** *vacant*

HORNINGSHAM (St John the Baptist) *see* Cley Hill Villages *Sarum*

HORNINGTOFT (St Edmund) *see* Upper Wensum Village Gp *Nor*

HORNSEA (St Nicholas), Atwick and Skipsea *York 11* **P** *Ld Chan and Abp (alt)* **V** C N MINETT STEVENS

HORNSEY (Christ Church) *Lon 17* **P** *Bp* **V** A O J PYMBLE **C** J O L ARMSTRONG

HORNSEY (Holy Innocents) *Lon 17* **P** *Bp* **V** B KERRIDGE **C** P J HENDERSON

HORNSEY (St Mary) (St George) *Lon 17* **P** *Bp* **R** B BATSTONE **C** M JAMES

HORNSEY RISE (St Mary) *Lon 6* **P** *Ch Patr Trust* **V** T L R MERCHANT **NSM** R I MERCHANT

HORNSEY ROAD (Emmanuel) *Lon 6* **P** *CPAS Patr Trust* **V** E L CLUTTERBUCK

HORNTON (St John the Baptist) *see* Ironstone *Ox*

HORRABRIDGE (St John the Baptist) *see* Yelverton, Meavy, Sheepstor, Walkhampton, Sampford Spiney and Horrabridge *Ex*

HORRINGER (St Leonard), including Brockley, Westley, and Whepstead *St E 9* **P** *Bp and DBP (jt)* **R** M E OSBORNE

HORSEHEATH (All Saints) *see* Linton *Ely*

HORSELL (St Mary the Virgin) *Guildf 12* **P** *Bp* **V** D LUTSENKO

HORSENDON (St Michael and All Angels) *see* Risborough *Ox*

　　　　　　　　　　　　　　　　　　　　　　　　　　　　HUCKNALL

HORSEY (All Saints)　*see* Flegg Coastal Benefice *Nor*

HORSFORD (All Saints), Felthorpe and Hevingham *Nor 2*
P *Sir Thomas Agnew Beevor Bt and Bp (jt)*　**R** M T M MCPHEE

HORSFORTH (St Margaret)　*see* Abbeylands *Leeds*

**HORSHAM (Holy Trinity) (St Leonard) (St Mary the Virgin)
(St Mark)** *Chich 10*　**P** *Patr Bd*　**TR** L H BARNETT
TV D W BOUSKILL　**C** R J TUCK　**NSM** B P NEW

HORSHAM (St Mark)　*see* Holbrook *Chich*

**HORSHAM ST FAITH (St Andrew and St Mary), Spixworth
and Crostwick** *Nor 2*　**P** *Bp and DBP (jt)*
P-in-c R H MASKELL

HORSINGTON (All Saints)　*see* Woodhall Spa Gp *Linc*

HORSINGTON (St John the Baptist)　*see* Abbas and
Templecombe, Henstridge and Horsington *B & W*

HORSLEY (Holy Trinity)　*see* N Tyne and Redesdale *Newc*

HORSLEY (St Clement)　*see* Denby Gp *Derby*

HORSLEY (St Martin)　*see* Nailsworth w Shortwood, Horsley
etc *Glouc*

HORSLEY HILL (St Lawrence the Martyr) South Shields
Dur 13　**P** *D&C*　**P-in-c** P W D CHILD

HORSLEY WOODHOUSE (St Susanna)　*see* Denby Gp *Derby*

HORSLEY, EAST (St Martin) *Guildf 10*　**P** *D&C Cant*
R R PITTARIDES　**C** S A MANGAR　**NSM** R DURWARD

HORSLEY, WEST (St Mary) *Guildf 10*　**P** *Col A R N Weston*
R P HERRINGTON　**C** S G GREEN

HORSMONDEN (St Margaret) *Roch 8*　**P** *Bp*　**R** T E FFRENCH
C J P FFRENCH

HORSPATH (St Giles)　*see* Garsington, Cuddesdon and
Horspath *Ox*

HORSTEAD (All Saints)　*see* Coltishall w Gt Hautbois,
Frettenham etc *Nor*

HORSTED KEYNES (St Giles) *Chich 8*　**P** *Bp*
P-in-c D J MURDOCH

HORSTED PARVA (St Michael and All Angels)　*see* Lt Horsted
Chich

HORSTED, LITTLE (St Michael and All Angels) *Chich 18*
P *The Rt Revd P J Ball*　**R** J C WALL　**NSM** M T Z MUTIKANI

HORTON (St James the Elder)　*see* Sodbury Vale *Glouc*

HORTON (St Mary the Virgin)　*see* Newsham and Horton
Newc

HORTON (St Michael and All Angels) and Wraysbury *Ox 12*
P *Major J M Halford and D&C Windsor (jt)*　**V** C T GIBSON

HORTON (St Michael)　*see* Cheddleton, Horton, Longsdon
and Rushton Spencer *Lich*

HORTON (St Peter)　*see* Isle Valley *B & W*

HORTON (St Wolfrida)　*see* Wimborne Minster and Villages
Sarum

HORTON KIRBY (St Mary)　*see* Darent Valley *Roch*

**HORTON, GREAT (St John the Evangelist) and Lidget
Green** *Leeds 2*　**P** *Bp and V Bradf St Pet (jt)*
V J E BAVINGTON　**C** A A DICKSON

HORTON, LITTLE (All Saints) (St Oswald) *Leeds 2*　**P** *Bp and
J F Bardsley Esq (jt)*　**P-in-c** D A JONES　**C** J W HINTON

HORTON-CUM-STUDLEY (St Barnabas)　*see* Beckley, Forest
Hill, Horton-cum-Studley and Stanton St John *Ox*

HORTON-IN-RIBBLESDALE (St Oswald)　*see* Langcliffe w
Stainforth and Horton *Leeds*

**HORWICH (Holy Trinity) (St Catherine) (St Elizabeth) and
Rivington** *Man 3*　**P** *Patr Bd*　**TV** M C BEHREND
C N J BUTTERWORTH, N J GILLARD　**OLM** C P TRACEY,
G M SMART, P D HARLEY

HORWOOD (St Michael)　*see* Newton Tracey, Horwood,
Alverdiscott etc *Ex*

HORWOOD, GREAT (St James)　*see* Winslow w Gt Horwood
and Addington *Ox*

HORWOOD, LITTLE (St Nicholas)　*see* Newton Longville,
Mursley, Swanbourne etc *Ox*

HOSE (St Michael)　*see* Vale of Belvoir *Leic*

HOTHAM (St Oswald) *York 13*　**P** *Ld Chan*
P-in-c B WORSDALE

HOTHFIELD (St Margaret)　*see* Calehill w Westwell *Cant*

HOUGH GREEN (St Basil and All Saints) *Liv 12*　**P** *Bp*
V P W DAWKIN

HOUGHAM (All Saints)　*see* S Cliff Villages Gp *Linc*

HOUGHAM (St Laurence)　*see* Alkham w Capel le Ferne and
Hougham *Cant*

HOUGH-ON-THE-HILL (All Saints)　*see* S Cliff Villages Gp *Linc*

HOUGHTON (All Saints)　*see* Mid Test *Win*

HOUGHTON (St Giles)　*see* Walsingham, Houghton and
Barsham *Nor*

HOUGHTON (St John the Evangelist) (St Peter) *Carl 3*
P *Trustees*　**V** A P J TOWNER　**C** G A TUBBS

HOUGHTON (St Martin)　*see* E w W Rudham, Helhoughton
etc *Nor*

HOUGHTON (St Nicholas)　*see* Bury, Coldwaltham, Hardham
and Houghton *Chich*

HOUGHTON CONQUEST (All Saints)　*see* Wilshamstead and
Houghton Conquest *St Alb*

HOUGHTON LE SPRING (St Michael and All Angels) *Dur 9*
P *Bp*　**P-in-c** J W BARRON　**C** J M D'SILVA

HOUGHTON REGIS (All Saints) (St Thomas) *St Alb 11*
P *DBP*　**P-in-c** D GALANZINO

HOUGHTON w WYTON (St Mary)　*see* Hartford and
Houghton w Wyton *Ely*

HOUGHTON, GREAT (St Mary)　*see* Cogenhoe and Gt and Lt
Houghton w Brafield *Pet*

HOUGHTON, LITTLE (St Mary the Blessed Virgin) *as above*

HOUGHTON, NEW (Christ Church)　*see* E Scarsdale *Derby*

HOUGHTON-ON-THE-HILL (St Catharine)　*see* Cornerstone
Team *Leic*

HOUND (St Edward the Confessor) (St Mary the Virgin)
Win 10　**P** *St Mary's Coll Win*　**V** vacant

HOUNSLOW (Holy Trinity) *Lon 11*　**P** *Bp*　**V** S BAILY
C D R ROBERTS, I CHRISTIAN

HOUNSLOW (St Paul) (Good Shepherd) *Lon 11*　**P** *Bp*
V C M A CLARKE　**C** D J THOMAS

HOUNSLOW (St Stephen) *Lon 11*　**P** *Bp*　**P-in-c** D M CLOAKE
C C C HENLEY

HOVE (All Saints) *Chich 20*　**P** *Bp*　**V** R A GREEN
C A D I REID

**HOVE (Bishop Hannington Memorial Church) (Holy
Cross)** *Chich 20*　**P** *Trustees*　**V** P R MOON　**C** B G MARTIN,
D A HOWARTH

HOVE (St Andrew Old Church) *Chich 20*　**P** *Bp*
V D T HENDERSON

HOVE (St Barnabas) and St Agnes *Chich 20*　**P** *Bp and V
Hove (alt)*　**V** J K T ELDRIDGE

HOVE (St John the Baptist) *Chich 20*　**P** *Bp*　**V** E M COLLINS
NSM J F GREENFIELD

HOVE (St Philip) *Chich 20*　**P** *Bp*　**V** J K T ELDRIDGE

HOVE EDGE (St Chad)　*see* Lightcliffe and Hove Edge *Leeds*

HOVERINGHAM (St Michael)　*see* W Trent *S'well*

HOVETON (St John)　*see* Wroxham w Hoveton, Belaugh and
Tunstead etc *Nor*

HOVETON (St Peter) *as above*

HOVINGHAM (All Saints)　*see* The Street Par *York*

HOW CAPLE (St Andrew and St Mary)　*see* StowCaple *Heref*

HOWARDIAN GROUP, The, comprising Bulmer, Dalby w
Whenby, Huttons Ambo, Terrington, and Welburn *York 6*
P *Abp*　**R** vacant

HOWDEN Team Ministry, The (St Peter), comprising
Blacktoft, Eastrington, Howden w Barmby on the Marsh,
Laxton, Newport, and Wressle *York 13*　**P** *Abp (4 turns), Ld
Chan (1 turn)*　**TR** J H LITTLE　**TV** L A KENNY

HOWE (St Mary the Virgin)　*see* Poringland *Nor*

HOWE BRIDGE (St Michael and All Angels)　*see* Atherton and
Hindsford w Howe Bridge *Man*

HOWELL HILL (St Paul) *Guildf 9*　**P** *Bp*　**C** H M LAMAISON,
P DEVER　**NSM** D N SENIOR, S THOMAS

HOWGILL (Holy Trinity)　*see* Western Dales *Carl*

HOWICK (St Michael and All Angels)　*see* Longhoughton w
Howick *Newc*

HOWLE HILL (St John the Evangelist)　*see* Ross w Walford and
Brampton Abbotts *Heref*

HOWSHAM (St John)　*see* Harton *York*

HOXNE (St Peter and St Paul)　*see* Athelington, Denham,
Horham, Hoxne etc *St E*

HOXTON (Holy Trinity) (St Mary) *Lon 5*　**P** *Bp*　**V** vacant

HOXTON (St Anne) (St Columba) *Lon 5*　**P** *The Crown*
V B L BELL　**C** A JONES

HOXTON (St John the Baptist) w Christ Church *Lon 5*
P *Haberdashers' Co and Adn (jt)*　**V** G HUNTER
C R M J GREAVES-BROWN

HOYLAKE (Holy Trinity and St Hildeburgh) *Ches 8*　**P** *Bp*
V P A ROSSITER　**NSM** J C HARRISON, R L SKINNER

HOYLAND (St Peter) (St Andrew) *Sheff 11*　**P** *Bp and Sir
Philip Naylor-Leyland Bt (jt)*　**V** R B PARKER

HOYLAND, HIGH (All Saints), Scissett and Clayton West
Leeds 5　**P** *Bp*　**R** S L FARRIMOND　**NSM** E BARROW,
J R JONES, K B CURRIE

HOYLANDSWAINE (St John the Evangelist)　*see* W Barnsley
Leeds

HUBBERHOLME (St Michael and All Angels)　*see* Upper
Wharfedale and Littondale *Leeds*

HUCCABY (St Raphael)　*see* Ashburton, Bickington, Buckland
in the Moor etc *Ex*

HUCCLECOTE (St Philip and St James) *Glouc 2*　**P** *Bp*
P-in-c M W CLOSE　**C** D S HUTCHISON　**OLM** M R B DAVIS

HUCKING (St Margaret)　*see* N Downs *Cant*

**HUCKNALL (St Mary Magdalene) (St Peter and St Paul)
(St John's Mission Church)** *S'well 4*　**P** *Bp*　**R** H F CHANTRY

HUCKNALL (St Peter and St Paul)　*see* W Hucknall *S'well*

HUCKNALL, WEST (St Peter and St Paul) S'well 4   **P** Bp
  V vacant

HUDDERSFIELD (Holy Trinity) Leeds 9   **P** Simeon's Trustees
  V M R WILKINS   **C** S T D WALTERS

HUDDERSFIELD (St Francis) Fixby   see Fixby and Cowcliffe
  Leeds

HUDDERSFIELD (St Hilda) Cowcliffe as above

HUDDERSFIELD (St John the Evangelist)   see Birkby and
  Woodhouse Leeds

HUDDERSFIELD (St Peter) Leeds 9   **P** DBP   **V** R N FIRTH
  C A J OGILVIE-BERRY   **C** A HAWKINS

HUDDERSFIELD All Saints (St Thomas) Leeds 9   **P** DBP
  V L A PINFIELD

HUDDERSFIELD Emmanuel   see Newsome and Armitage
  Bridge and S Crosland Leeds

HUDDERSFIELD, NORTH (St Cuthbert)   see Birkby and
  Birchencliffe Leeds

HUDDINGTON (St James)   see Bowbrook Worc

HUGGATE (St Mary)   see Pocklington Wold York

HUGGLESCOTE (St John the Baptist) w Donington,
  Ellistown and Snibston Leic 8   **P** Bp   **NSM** S D O'ROURKE

HUGHENDEN (St Michael and All Angels) Ox 18   **P** DBP
  V K M JOHNSON   **NSM** H E PETERS, T A JONES

HUGHLEY (St John the Baptist)   see Wenlock Heref

HUISH (St James the Less)   see Shebbear, Buckland Filleigh,
  Sheepwash etc Ex

HUISH (St Nicholas)   see Vale of Pewsey Sarum

HUISH CHAMPFLOWER (St Peter)   see Wiveliscombe and the
  Hills B & W

HUISH EPISCOPI (Blessed Virgin Mary)   see Aller, High w Low
  Ham and Huish Episcopi cum Langport B & W

HUISH, SOUTH (Holy Trinity)   see Malborough, Salcombe and
  S Huish Ex

HULCOTE (St Nicholas)   see Cranfield and Hulcote w Salford
  St Alb

HULCOTT (All Saints)   see Bierton and Hulcott Ox

HULL (Ascension)   see Derringham Bank York

HULL (Holy Apostles)   see Kingston upon Hull H Trin York

HULL (Most Holy and Undivided Trinity) as above

HULL (St Aidan) Southcoates   see Kingston upon Hull St Aid
  Southcoates York

HULL (St Alban)   see Kingston upon Hull St Alb York

HULL (St Cuthbert) York 14   **P** Abp   **V** J C COWAN
  NSM M L MEESAM

HULL (St John the Baptist)   see Newington w Hull St Andr
  York

HULL (St John) Newland York 14   **P** Abp   **P-in-c** R S WHITE

HULL (St Martin) w The Transfiguration York 14   **P** Abp
  V J C HILL   **C** L M WHITE

HULL (St Mary the Virgin) Lowgate   see Kingston upon Hull
  St Mary York

HULL (St Mary) Sculcoates York 14   **P** V Sculcoates
  V P LAMB

HULL (St Nicholas)   see Kingston upon Hull St Nic York

HULL (St Paul)   see Sculcoates York

HULL (St Thomas)   see Derringham Bank York

HULL MINSTER   see Kingston upon Hull H Trin York

HULL, NORTH (St Michael and All Angels) York 14   **P** Abp
  V D A WALKER

HULLAND (Christ Church), Atlow, Kniveton, Bradley and
  Hognaston Derby 1   **P** Patr Bd   **R** P L MICHELL

HULLAVINGTON (St Mary Magdalene)   see Gauzebrook Bris

HULLBRIDGE (St Thomas of Canterbury)   see Rettendon and
  Hullbridge Chelmsf

HULME (Ascension) Man 2   **P** Trustees
  R A D A FRANCE-WILLIAMS   **C** R C WILKINSON
  NSM P J HIBBERT

HULME WALFIELD (St Michael)   see Marton, Siddington w
  Capesthorne etc Ches

HULTON, LITTLE (St John the Baptist)   see Walkden and Lt
  Hulton Man

HULTON, OVER (St Andrew)   see Deane Man

HUMBER (St Mary the Virgin)   see Leominster Heref

HUMBERSTON (St Peter) Linc 4   **P** Bp   **OLM** P R SALMON

HUMBERSTONE (St Mary)   see Humberstone and Thurnby
  Lodge Leic

HUMBERSTONE (St Mary) (St Barnabas) and Thurnby
  Lodge Leic 1   **P** DBP   **P-in-c** P A SAVAGE
  NSM P G EMBERTON

HUMBLE, WEST (St Michael)   see Leatherhead and
  Mickleham Guildf

HUMBLETON (St Peter)   see Burstwick, Burton Pidsea etc York

HUMPHREY PARK (St Clement)   see Davyhulme Ch Ch and
  Urmston Man

HUMSHAUGH (St Peter) w Simonburn and Wark Newc 8
  P Bp   **NSM** C E ROBSON

HUNCOAT (St Augustine)   see Accrington St Jo w Huncoat
  Blackb

HUNCOTE (St James the Greater)   see Narborough and
  Huncote Leic

HUNDLEBY (St Mary)   see Bolingbroke Deanery Linc

HUNDON (All Saints)   see Stour Valley St E

HUNDRED RIVER and Wainford, comprising Brampton,
  Ellough and Weston, Ilketshall St Andrew, Redisham,
  Ringsfield, Shadingfield, Sotterley w Willingham, Stoven,
  and Westhall St E 15   **P** DBP, Shadingfield Property Ltd, Bp, F
  D L Barnes Esq, Miss to Seafarers, Magd Coll Cam, and Ch Soc
  Trust (jt)   **R** P H O MILLER   **NSM** C E KIDDY

HUNGARTON (St John the Baptist)   see Coplow Leic

HUNGERFORD (St Lawrence) and Denford Ox 6   **P** D&C
  Windsor   **V** M W SAUNDERS   **NSM** T R SHARPLES

HUNMANBY (All Saints)   see Hertford York

HUNNINGHAM (St Margaret)   see Offchurch Gp Cov

HUNSDON (St Dunstan) (St Francis) w Widford and
  Wareside St Alb 19   **P** DBP   **R** M P DUNSTAN

HUNSINGORE (St John the Baptist)   see Lower Nidderdale
  Leeds

HUNSTANTON (St Edmund) (St Mary) and Saxon Shore
  Nor 15   **P** Patr Bd   **TR** R I E DINES   **TV** K E ALLAN
  NSM A J MONRO

HUNSTANWORTH (St James)   see Blanchland w
  Hunstanworth and Edmundbyers etc Newc

HUNSTON (St Leodegar)   see N Mundham w Hunston and
  Merston Chich

HUNSTON (St Michael)   see Pakenham w Norton, Tostock
  etc St E

HUNTINGDON (All Saints) (St Barnabas) (St Mary) Ely 10
  P Bp (2 turns), Ld Chan (1 turn)   **R** J A RANDALL
  C J C D NEWCOMBE, L M DAVIS   **Hon C** M P M BOOKER
  NSM E L DAVIS

HUNTINGFIELD (St Mary)   see Heveningham St E

HUNTINGTON (All Saints) York 7   **P** D&C
  R I G BIRKINSHAW   **C** C J PARK   **NSM** J I LINDSEY

HUNTINGTON (St Luke)   see Ches St Paul w St Luke Ches

HUNTINGTON (St Mary Magdalene)   see Holmer w
  Huntington Heref

HUNTINGTON (St Thomas à Becket)   see Kington w
  Huntington, Old Radnor, Kinnerton etc Heref

HUNTINGTON (St Thomas)   see Cannock and Huntington
  Lich

HUNTLEY (St John the Baptist) and Longhope, Churcham
  and Bulley Glouc 3   **P** Bp and D&C (jt)   **P-in-c** L S BLOOM

HUNTON (St James)   see Upper Dever Win

HUNTON (St Mary)   see Coxheath, E Farleigh, Hunton,
  Linton etc Roch

HUNTS CROSS (St Hilda)   see Halewood and Hunts Cross Liv

HUNTSHAM (All Saints)   see Bampton, Morebath,
  Clayhanger, Petton etc Ex

HUNTSHAW (St Mary Magdalene)   see Newton Tracey,
  Horwood, Alverdiscott etc Ex

HUNTSPILLS, The (All Saints) (St Peter and All Hallows)
  and Mark B & W 1   **P** Bp and Ball Coll Ox (jt)
  P-in-c C A JUDSON

HUNWICK (St Paul)   see Hunwick and Willington Dur

HUNWICK (St Paul) and Willington Dur 7   **P** V Bp Auckland
  and R Brancepeth (alt)   **V** D L SPOKES   **NSM** G P COPLEY

HUNWORTH (St Lawrence)   see Brinton, Briningham,
  Hunworth, Stody etc Nor

HURDSFIELD (Holy Trinity) Ches 13   **P** Hyndman Trustees
  V J C R GIBSON   **C** J A FROST

HURLEY (Resurrection)   see Baxterley w Hurley and Wood
  End and Merevale etc Birm

HURLEY (St Mary the Virgin)   see Burchetts Green Ox

HURSLEY (All Saints)   see Compton, Hursley, and Otterbourne
  Win

HURST (St John the Evangelist) Man 5   **P** The Crown
  V vacant

HURST (St Nicholas)   see Ruscombe and Twyford w Hurst Ox

HURST GREEN (Holy Trinity)   see Salehurst, Hurst Green and
  Robertsbridge Chich

HURST GREEN (St John the Evangelist)   see Oxted S'wark

HURST GREEN (St John the Evangelist) and Mitton Blackb 7
  P Bp and J E R Aspinall Esq (jt)   **P-in-c** B R MCCONKEY

HURSTBOURNE PRIORS (St Andrew), Longparish, St Mary
  Bourne and Woodcott Win 6   **P** Bp and J C Woodcock Esq
  (jt)   **P-in-c** H O'SULLIVAN   **NSM** D M MARSDEN,
  R J SUTCLIFFE

HURSTBOURNE TARRANT (St Peter)   see Pastrow Win

HURSTPIERPOINT (Holy Trinity) (St George) Chich 11
  P Hurstpierpoint Coll   **R** J E WILLIS   **C** J D NAUDÉ
  NSM D M BEER

HURSTWOOD, HIGH (Holy Trinity) *Chich 18* **P** *Abp*
P-in-c M S ASHWORTH
HURWORTH (All Saints) *Dur 5* **P** *Ch Soc Trust* **R** *vacant*
HUSBANDS BOSWORTH (All Saints) *see* Hexagon *Leic*
HUSBORNE CRAWLEY (St Mary Magdalene or St James) *see* Aspley Guise w Husborne Crawley and Ridgmont *St Alb*
HUSTHWAITE (St Nicholas) *see* Coxwold and Husthwaite *York*
HUTHWAITE (All Saints) *S'well 4* **P** *V* Sutton-in-Ashfield
V C A K MAIDEN
HUTTOFT (St Margaret) *see* Sutton, Huttoft and Anderby *Linc*
HUTTON (All Saints) (St Peter) *Chelmsf 8* **P** *D&C St Paul's*
R A G SMITH **NSM** A BAXTER, L J WHYMARK
HUTTON (Blessed Virgin Mary) and Locking *B & W 10*
P *DBP and MMCET (jt)* **R** A L WILKINS **C** F E MAYNE
HUTTON BUSCEL (St Matthew) *see* Upper Derwent *York*
HUTTON CRANSWICK (St Peter) w Skerne, Watton and Beswick *York 10* **P** *Abp* **V** S R J ELLIOTT
HUTTON HENRY (St Francis) *see* Wheatley Hill, Thornley and Wingate w Hutton Henry *Dur*
HUTTON MAGNA (St Mary) *see* Holmedale *Leeds*
HUTTON ROOF (St John the Divine) *see* Kirkby Lonsdale *Carl*
HUTTON, OLD (St John the Baptist) and New Hutton (St Stephen) *Carl 10* **P** *V* Kendal **P-in-c** A WHITTAKER
C C A BENTLEY **NSM** L A FOSTER, M MASHITER
HUTTON-IN-THE-FOREST (St James) *see* Inglewood Gp *Carl*
HUTTON-LE-HOLE (St Chad) *see* Lastingham w Appleton-le-Moors, Rosedale etc *York*
HUTTONS AMBO (St Margaret) *see* Howardian Gp *York*
HUXHAM (St Mary the Virgin) *see* Brampford Speke, Cadbury, Newton St Cyres etc *Ex*
HUXLEY (St Andrew) *see* Hargrave *Ches*
HUYTON (St George) *see* 4Saints Team *Liv*
HUYTON (St Michael) *Liv 7* **P** *Earl of Derby* **V** M J RAFFAY
HUYTON QUARRY (St Gabriel) *Liv 7* **P** *V* Huyton St Mich
V M K ROGERS **NSM** L CONNOLLY
HYDE (Holy Ascension) *see* Fordingbridge and Hyde and Breamore etc *Win*
HYDE (St George) (St Thomas) *Ches 14* **P** *Bp, R Cheadle, and R Stockport (jt)* **V** J D BENTLIFF **C** C BOOTHROYD
HYDE HEATH (Mission Church) *see* Lt Missenden *Ox*
HYDE PARK (St John) *see* Paddington St Jo w St Mich *Lon*
HYDE, WEST (St Thomas of Canterbury) *see* Mill End and Heronsgate w W Hyde *St Alb*
HYDNEYE (St Peter) *see* Hampden Park and The Hydneye *Chich*
HYKEHAM (All Saints) (St Hugh) (St Michael and All Angels) *Linc 12* **P** *Ld Chan and Bp (alt)* **R** P G COLLINS
NSM G F REID
HYSON GREEN (St Stephen) and Forest Fields *S'well 9*
P *CPAS* **V** C R BURROWS **C** N BAHADUR
HYSSINGTON (St Etheldreda) *see* Churchstoke w Hyssington and Sarn *Heref*
HYTHE (St John the Baptist) *Win 11* **P** *Bp* **V** *vacant*
HYTHE (St Leonard) (Holy Cross) *Cant 8* **P** *R* Saltwood
V *vacant*
HYTHE Butts Ash (St Anne) *see* Hythe *Win*
IBBERTON (St Eustace) *see* Hazelbury Bryan and the Hillside Par *Sarum*
IBSTOCK (St Denys) w Heather *Leic 8* **P** *Bp and MMCET (jt)*
R A J HARTROPP
IBSTONE (St Nicholas) *see* S Chilterns *Ox*
ICKBURGH (St Peter) w Langford *Nor 13* **P** *Bp* **R** *vacant*
ICKENHAM (St Giles) *Lon 21* **P** *Eton Coll* **R** F A DAVIES
NSM N W THOMPSON
ICKFORD (St Nicholas) *see* Worminghall w Ickford, Oakley and Shabbington *Ox*
ICKHAM (St John the Evangelist) *see* Lt Stour *Cant*
ICKLEFORD (St Katherine) *see* Holwell, Ickleford and Pirton *St Alb*
ICKLESHAM (St Nicolas) *see* Winchelsea and Icklesham *Chich*
ICKLETON (St Mary Magdalene) *Ely 5* **P** *Ld Chan*
P-in-c L J SMITH
ICKLINGHAM (All Saints w St James) *see* Forest Heath *St E*
ICKNIELD WAY VILLAGES, comprising Great Chishill, Little Chishill, Chrishall, Duddenhoe End, Elmdon, Heydon, and Strethall *Chelmsf 19* **P** *Patr Bd* **R** D A R SODADASI
ICKNIELD, comprising Britwell Salome, Pyrton and Shirburn, Swyncombe, and Watlington *Ox 20* **P** *Ld Chan (1 turn), Ch Ch Ox (1 turn), Bp and Earl of Macclesfield (1 turn)*
R D E J THOMPSON **C** D BENSKIN **NSM** A M PATERSON
ICOMB (St Mary) *see* Broadwell, Evenlode, Oddington, Adlestrop etc *Glouc*

IDBURY (St Nicholas) *see* Wychwood *Ox*
IDDESLEIGH (St James) *see* Dolton, Dowland, Iddesleigh etc *Ex*
IDE (St Ida) *see* Alphington, Shillingford St George and Ide *Ex*
IDE HILL (St Mary the Virgin) *see* Sundridge w Ide Hill and Toys Hill *Roch*
IDEFORD (St Mary the Virgin) *see* Teignmouth, Ideford w Luton, Ashcombe etc *Ex*
IDEN (All Saints) *see* Rye *Chich*
IDLE (Holy Trinity) *Leeds 3* **P** *V* Calverley **V** N J TAYLOR
C C R C BAXFIELD, L J THOMPSON
IDLE, The, and Sands Retford, comprising Babworth, Bothamsall, Eaton, Elkesley, Osberton, Ranby, Scofton, Sutton-cum-Lound, and West Drayton *S'well 1* **P** *Sir John Whitaker Bt, G M T Foljambe Esq, Bp, SMF, and D&C York (jt)*
R *vacant*
IDLICOTE (St James the Great) *see* Shipston-on-Stour w Honington and Idlicote *Cov*
IDRIDGEHAY (St James) *see* Wirksworth *Derby*
IDSWORTH (St Hubert) *see* Blendworth w Chalton w Idsworth *Portsm*
IFFLEY (St Mary the Virgin) *Ox 1* **P** *Ch Ch Ox*
V A R MCKEARNEY **C** N CHRISTENSEN
IFIELD (St Margaret) *Chich 9* **P** *Bp* **R** C P SPENCER
C J GATER
IFIELD (St Margaret) *see* Gravesend H Family w Ifield *Roch*
IFORD (St Nicholas) w Kingston and Rodmell and Southease *Chich 21* **P** *Bp and Gorham Trustees (jt)*
V G M DAW
IFORD (St Saviour) *see* Holdenhurst and Iford *Win*
IGHTFIELD (St John the Baptist) *see* Adderley, Ash, Calverhall, Ightfield etc *Lich*
IGHTHAM (St Peter) *Roch 10* **P** *Mrs L K Ford*
R T R HATWELL
IKEN (St Botolph) *see* Wilford Peninsula *St E*
ILAM (Holy Cross) *see* Alstonfield, Ilam and Wetton *Lich*
ILCHESTER (St Mary Major) w Northover, Limington, Yeovilton and Podimore *B & W 5* **P** *Bp Lon (7 turns), Bp (1 turn), and Wadh Coll Ox (1 turn)* **R** B S FAULKNER
ILDERTON (St Michael) *see* Doddington, Ilderton, Kirknewton and Wooler *Newc*
ILFORD, GREAT (St Alban) *Chelmsf 6* **P** *Bp* **V** *vacant*
ILFORD, GREAT (St Andrew) *Chelmsf 6* **P** *Bp* **V** M SEGAL
OLM H J MORRIS
ILFORD, GREAT (St John the Evangelist) *Chelmsf 6* **P** *Bp*
P-in-c K P B LOVESEY
ILFORD, GREAT (St Luke) *Chelmsf 6* **P** *Bp* **V** J BROWN
NSM B D DEUCHAR DE MELLO
ILFORD, GREAT (St Margaret of Antioch) (St Clement)
Chelmsf 6 **P** *Patr Bd* **V** S G PUGH
ILFORD, GREAT (St Mary the Virgin) *Chelmsf 6* **P** *V Gt Ilford* **V** G E J P JONES
ILFORD, LITTLE (St Barnabas) *Chelmsf 5* **P** *Bp*
P-in-c R L RYAN
ILFORD, LITTLE (St Michael and All Angels) *Chelmsf 5*
P *Hertf Coll Ox* **P-in-c** B L TAYLOR
ILFRACOMBE (Holy Trinity) (St Peter), Lee, Woolacombe, Bittadon and Mortehoe *Ex 16* **P** *Patr Bd* **TR** J W ROLES
TV G A B KING-SMITH **C** A E LEWIS **NSM** L WALTERS
ILFRACOMBE (St Philip and St James), Combe Martin and Berrynarbor *Ex 16* **P** *Bp and Ch Trust Fund Trust (jt)*
R *vacant*
ILKESTON (Holy Trinity) *Derby 8* **P** *Bp*
P-in-c D L LAWRENCE-MARCH
ILKESTON (St John the Evangelist) *Derby 8* **P** *V* Ilkeston St Mary **P-in-c** A J BAGULEY **C** C FRENCH, O J ANOZIE
ILKESTON (St Mary the Virgin) *Derby 8* **P** *Bp*
P-in-c A J BAGULEY **C** O J ANOZIE
ILKETSHALL ST ANDREW (St Andrew) *see* Hundred River and Wainford *St E*
ILKETSHALL ST JOHN (St John the Baptist) *see* The Saints *St E*
ILKETSHALL ST LAWRENCE (St Lawrence) *as above*
ILKETSHALL ST MARGARET (St Margaret) *as above*
ILKLEY (All Saints) *Leeds 4* **P** *Hyndman Trustees* **V** M S COE
C A J ROEBUCK **Hon C** D M REES-JONES **NSM** R F WATSON
ILKLEY (St Margaret) *Leeds 4* **P** *CR* **V** *vacant*
ILLOGAN (St Illogan) *see* St Illogan *Truro*
ILLSTON (St Michael and All Angels) *see* Gaulby *Leic*
ILMER (St Peter) *see* Risborough *Ox*
ILMINGTON (St Mary) and Stretton-on-Fosse and Ditchford w Preston-on-Stour w Whitchurch and Atherstone-on-Stour *Cov 9* **P** *Bp, MMCET, and Ms C A Alston-Roberts-West (jt)* **R** *vacant*
ILMINSTER (Blessed Virgin Mary) and Whitelackington
B & W 16 **P** *Bp* **V** J E STOBART **C** J M SWAN

ILSINGTON (St Michael) *Ex 8* **P** *D&C Windsor* **V** *vacant*

ILSLEY, EAST (St Mary) *see* Hermitage *Ox*

ILSLEY, WEST (All Saints) *see* E Downland *Ox*

ILTON (St Peter) *see* Isle Valley *B & W*

IMMINGHAM (St Andrew) *Linc 4* **P** *Bp and DBP (jt)*
V J DONN   **OLM** J M GLOSSOP

IMPINGTON (St Andrew) *Ely 6* **P** *Adn Cam*
V N J BLANDFORD-BAKER   **C** R M CHAMBERLAIN

INCE (St James) *see* Thornton-le-Moors w Ince and Elton
Ches

INCE IN MAKERFIELD (Christ Church) *see* Wigan *Liv*

INCE IN MAKERFIELD (St Mary) *as above*

INDIAN QUEEN (St Francis) *see* St Enoder *Truro*

INGATESTONE (St Edmund and St Mary) w Fryerning
Chelmsf 8 **P** *Bp and Wadh Coll Ox (jt)* **C** S A CROFT

INGESTRE (St Mary the Virgin) *see* Stafford St Jo and Tixall w
Ingestre *Lich*

INGHAM (All Saints) *see* Springline *Linc*

INGHAM (Holy Trinity) *see* Stalham, E Ruston, Brunstead,
Sutton and Ingham *Nor*

INGHAM (St Bartholomew) *see* Blackbourne *St E*

INGLEBOROUGH *see* Bentham, Burton-in-Lonsdale,
Chapel-le-Dale etc *Leeds*

INGLEBY ARNCLIFFE (All Saints) *see* Osmotherley w Harlsey
and Ingleby Arncliffe *York*

INGLEBY BARWICK (St Francis) *York 20* **P** *Abp*
C N J B STEVENSON

**INGLEBY GREENHOW (St Andrew), Bilsdale Priory and
Kildale w Kirkby-in-Cleveland** *York 20* **P** *Abp, Adn
Cleveland, Bp Whitby, Viscount De L'Isle, R G Beckett Esq, and
A H W Sutcliffe Esq (jt)* **V** M A HEADING

INGLETON (St John the Evangelist) *Dur 5* **P** *Lord Barnard*
V *vacant*

INGLETON (St Mary the Virgin) *see* Bentham, Burton-in-
Lonsdale, Chapel-le-Dale etc *Leeds*

INGLEWOOD Group, The, comprising Ainstable,
Armathwaite, Calthwaite, Hesket-in-the-Forest, Hutton-in-
the-Forest, Ivegill, and Skelton *Carl 4* **P** *Bp, D&C, CCC Ox,
and E P Ecroyd Esq (jt)* **P-in-c** M R HOUSTON
C B G PHILLIPS

INGOL (St Margaret) *Blackb 13* **P** *Bp* **P-in-c** C P WALKER

INGOLDISTHORPE (St Michael) *see* Dersingham, Anmer,
Ingoldisthorpe etc *Nor*

INGOLDMELLS (St Peter and St Paul) *see* Skegness Gp *Linc*

INGOLDSBY (St Bartholomew) *see* N Beltisloe Par *Linc*

INGRAM (St Michael) *see* Chatton w Chillingham,
Eglingham and S Charlton and Ingram *Newc*

INGRAVE (St Nicholas) (St Stephen) *Chelmsf 8* **P** *Bp and Ch
Patr Trust (jt)* **V** P S HAMILTON

INGRAVE (St Stephen) Conventional District *Chelmsf 8*
NSM J A SEDANO

INGROW (St John the Evangelist) with Hainworth *Leeds 1*
P *Bp* **P-in-c** T A RAISTRICK **NSM** J M INESON

INGS (St Anne) *see* Staveley, Ings and Kentmere *Carl*

INGWORTH (St Lawrence) *see* Scarrowbeck *Nor*

INHAM NOOK (St Barnabas) *see* Chilwell *S'well*

INKBERROW (St Peter) *see* Inkberrow w Cookhill and
Kington w Dormston *Worc*

**INKBERROW (St Peter) w Cookhill and Kington w
Dormston** *Worc 3* **P** *Bp* **R** B E RIENSTRA
NSM D HAYWARD-WRIGHT

INKERSALL (St Columba) *see* Staveley and Barrow Hill *Derby*

INKPEN (St Michael) *see* Walbury Beacon *Ox*

INNS COURT (Holy Cross) *see* Filwood Park *Bris*

INSKIP (St Peter) *see* Copp w Inskip *Blackb*

INSTOW (All Saints Chapel) *see* Fremington, Instow and
Westleigh *Ex*

INSTOW (St John the Baptist) *as above*

INTWOOD (All Saints) *see* Swardeston w E Carleton,
Intwood, Keswick etc *Nor*

INWARDLEIGH (St Petroc) *see* Okehampton, Inwardleigh,
Belstone, Sourton etc *Ex*

INWORTH (All Saints) *see* Thurstable and Winstree *Chelmsf*

IPING (St Mary) *see* Linch w Iping Marsh, Milland and Rake
etc *Chich*

**IPPLEPEN (St Andrew) w Torbryan, Denbury,
Broadhempston and Woodland** *Ex 8* **P** *The Crown (1
turn), D&C Windsor and SMF (jt)* **R** A S DOWN

IPSDEN (St Mary the Virgin) *see* Langtree *Ox*

IPSLEY (St Peter) *Worc 6* **P** *Patr Bd* **TR** G E P NATHANIEL
TV I D EVANS

IPSWICH (All Hallows) *St E 1* **P** *Bp* **P-in-c** C MANSELL
C K P LOTAY

IPSWICH (All Saints) *see* Triangle, St Matt and All SS *St E*

IPSWICH (St Augustine of Hippo) *St E 1* **P** *Bp*
V A A METCALFE **C** A KEY, M T KEY **NSM** I G DANIELS

IPSWICH (St Bartholomew) *St E 1* **P** *Bp* **V** P J CARTER

**IPSWICH (St Francis) (St Clare's Church Centre), Chantry
and Pinewood** *St E 1* **P** *Bp* **V** *vacant*

IPSWICH (St Helen) (Holy Trinity) (St Clement w St Luke)
St E 1 **P** *Ch Patr Trust* **R** *vacant*

IPSWICH (St John the Baptist) (St Andrew) *St E 1*
P *Simeon's Trustees and Bp (jt)* **V** M N PRENTICE
NSM J BACHU

IPSWICH (St Margaret) *St E 1* **P** *Simeon's Trustees*
V D CUTTS

IPSWICH (St Mary at the Elms) *St E 1* **P** *Guild of All So*
P-in-c J A THACKRAY

IPSWICH (St Mary) Stoke *St E 1* **P** *Bp* **NSM** K PALMER

IPSWICH (St Mary-le-Tower) (St Nicholas) *St E 1* **P** *Bp (3
turns), Ch Patr Trust (1 turn)* **P-in-c** T J MUMFORD

IPSWICH (St Matthew) *see* Triangle, St Matt and All SS *St E*

IPSWICH (St Peter) Stoke Park *St E 1* **P** *Bpq* **NSM** M J DYE

IPSWICH (St Thomas) *St E 1* **P** *Bp* **P-in-c** R J REVELY
C C H V CONNOLLY **NSM** J H IRWIN

IPSWICH Triangle (Community Centre) *see* Triangle,
St Matt and All SS *St E*

IPSWICH Waterfront Churches *see* Ipswich St Helen, H
Trin, and St Luke *St E*

IRBY (St Chad's Mission Church) *see* Thurstaston *Ches*

IRBY ON HUMBER (St Andrew) *see* Wolds Gateway Group
Linc

IRBY-IN-THE-MARSH (All Saints) *see* Burgh Gp *Linc*

IRCHESTER (St Katharine) w Stanton Cross *Pet 6* **P** *Bp*
V C M LOMAS

IREBY (St James) *see* Binsey *Carl*

IRELAND WOOD (St Paul) *Leeds 12* **P** *R Adel*
V M J HARLOW **C** M D BROUGHTON

IRLAM (St John the Baptist) *Man 7* **P** *Trustees*
V J E WARHURST

IRNHAM (St Andrew) *see* Corby Glen Par *Linc*

IRON ACTON (St James the Less) *see* Fromeside *Bris*

IRONBRIDGE (St Luke) *see* Coalbrookdale, Iron-Bridge and
Lt Wenlock *Heref*

IRONSTONE VILLAGES Family of Churches, The, comprising
Eastwell, Eaton, Goadby Marwood, Scalford, Stonesby, and
Waltham-on-the-Wolds *Leic 2* **P** *Lady Gretton, Ld Chan,
Duke of Rutland, Bp, and Sir Lyonel Tollemache Bt (by turn)*
R M J A BARR

**IRONSTONE: Drayton, Hanwell, Horley, Hornton,
Shenington w Alkerton, and Wroxton w Balscote** *Ox 23*
P *Ld Chan (1 turn), Bp, Earl De la Warr, and DBP (1 turn)*
R A M BAKER

IRONVILLE (Christ Church) *see* Riddings and Ironville *Derby*

IRSTEAD (St Michael) *see* Ashmanhaugh, Barton Turf etc *Nor*

IRTHINGTON (St Kentigern) *see* Eden, Gelt and Irthing *Carl*

**IRTHLINGBOROUGH (St Peter), Great Addington, Little
Addington and Woodford** *Pet 8* **P** *Bp, Sir Philip
Naylor-Leyland Bt, and DBP (jt)* **R** J T P HALL **C** M FROST

IRTON (St Paul) *see* Black Combe, Drigg, Eskdale etc *Carl*

ISEL (St Michael) *see* Binsey *Carl*

ISFIELD (St Margaret) *Chich 18* **P** *Abp* **R** J C WALL
NSM M T Z MUTIKANI

ISHAM (St Peter) *see* Gt w Lt Harrowden and Orlingbury
and Isham etc *Pet*

ISLE ABBOTTS (Blessed Virgin Mary) *see* Isle Valley *B & W*

ISLE BREWERS (All Saints) *as above*

ISLE OF DOGS (Christ Church and St John) (St Luke) *Lon 7*
P *Bp* **V** T F PYKE **C** E J DIX, T B BROWNE

ISLE VALLEY, comprising Ashill, Broadway, Donyatt,
Hambridge w Earnshill, Horton, Ilton, Isle Abbotts, and Isle
Brewers *B & W 16* **P** *Bp, D&C Bris, and Dr W P Palmer (jt)*
V P DENISON **NSM** P P ALBROW

ISLEHAM (St Andrew) *see* Three Rivers Gp *Ely*

**ISLES OF SCILLY: St Mary's, St Agnes, St Martin's, Bryher
and Tresco** *Truro 5* **P** *Duchy of Cornwall* **Chapl** P R GAY

ISLEWORTH (All Saints) *Lon 11* **P** *D&C Windsor*
V A C WALTON

ISLEWORTH (St Francis of Assisi) *Lon 11* **P** *Bp*
V P VANNOZZI

ISLEWORTH (St John the Baptist) (St Mary the Virgin)
Lon 11 **P** *Bp and V Isleworth All SS (jt)* **V** D S MACLURE
C O A DOUGLAS-PENNANT

ISLEWORTH (St Luke) *see* Spring Grove St Mary *Lon*

ISLEWORTH (St Mary) Osterley Road *as above*

ISLEY WALTON (All Saints) *see* Ashby-de-la-Zouch and
Breedon on the Hill *Leic*

ISLINGTON (St James the Apostle) (St Peter) *Lon 6* **P** *Bp*
V A J BURNISTON

ISLINGTON (St Jude and St Paul) *see* Mildmay Grove St Jude
and St Paul *Lon*

ISLINGTON (St Mark) *see* Clerkenwell St Mark *Lon*

ISLINGTON (St Mary Magdalene)   *see* Hope Ch Islington *Lon*
ISLINGTON (St Mary) *Lon 6*   P *CPAS*   V J C HUGHESDON
ISLINGTON Hope Church   *see* Hope Ch Islington *Lon*
ISLIP (St Nicholas)   *see* Ray Valley *Ox*
ISLIP (St Nicholas)   *see* Thrapston, Denford and Islip *Pet*
ISTEAD RISE (St Barnabas) *Roch 1*   P *Bp*   V *vacant*
ITCHEN ABBAS (St John the Baptist)   *see* Itchen Valley *Win*
ITCHEN VALLEY, The, comprising Avington, Easton, Itchen
   Abbas, and Martyr Worthy *Win 1*   P *Ld Chan*   R *vacant*
ITCHEN, UPPER, comprising Beauworth, Bramdean,
   Cheriton, Hinton Ampner, Kilmeston, and Tichborne *Win 1*
   P *The Crown (2 turns), D&C (1 turn)*   R C W DURRANT
   C J L BROOKSHAW
ITCHENOR, WEST (St Nicholas)   *see* W Wittering and
   Birdham w Itchenor *Chich*
ITCHINGFIELD (St Nicolas) w Slinfold *Chich 9*   P *Bp*
   R S J HALL   NSM R A CATTELL
ITTERINGHAM   *see* Aylsham and Distr *Nor*
IVEGILL (Christ Church)   *see* Inglewood Gp *Carl*
IVER (St Peter) *Ox 12*   P *Trustees*   V R H GOODING
   NSM S E SMITH
IVER HEATH (St Margaret) *Ox 12*   P *Trustees*
   R A S MONTGOMERIE
IVINGHOE (St Mary the Virgin) w Pitstone and Slapton
   and Marsworth *Ox 15*   P *Bp and Ch Ch Ox (jt)*   V *vacant*
IVINGTON (St John)   *see* Leominster *Heref*
IVYBRIDGE (St John the Evangelist), Cornwood, Harford
   and Sparkwell *Ex 19*   P *Bp and D&C Windsor (jt)*
   V P F HINCKLEY
IVYCHURCH (St George)   *see* Romney Marsh *Cant*
IWADE (All Saints)   *see* The Six *Cant*
IWERNE COURTNEY (St Mary)   *see* Iwerne Valley *Sarum*
IWERNE MINSTER (St Mary) *as above*
IWERNE VALLEY, comprising Ashmore, Fontmell Magna,
   Iwerne Courtney and Iwerne Steepleton, Iwerne Minster,
   and Sutton Waldron *Sarum 7*   P *D&C Windsor, DBP, G A L F
   Pitt-Rivers Esq, and Mrs P Kelway-Bamber (jt)*   V D W JOHN
IXWORTH (St Mary)   *see* Blackbourne *St E*
IXWORTH THORPE (All Saints) *as above*
JACKFIELD (St Mary)   *see* Broseley w Benthall, Jackfield,
   Linley etc *Heref*
JACOBSTOW (St James)   *see* Boscastle Gp *Truro*
JACOBSTOWE (St James)   *see* Okehampton, Inwardleigh,
   Belstone, Sourton etc *Ex*
JARROW (St John the Baptist) (St Paul) (St Peter) and
   Simonside *Dur 13*   P *The Crown and Bp (alt)*   R L M JONES
   C S G HILL
JARROW GRANGE (Christ Church) *Dur 13*   P *Lord
   Northbourne*   P-in-c I M SOMASUNDRAM   NSM E GRAY
JARVIS BROOK (St Michael and All Angels) *Chich 16*   P *Bp*
   V A W WEAVER
JAYWICK (St Christopher)   *see* Clacton St Jas *Chelmsf*
JENNETTS PARK (St Francis and St Clare)   *see* Easthampstead
   Ox
JERSEY (All Saints) *Win 15*   P *R St Helier, Bp, and The Crown
   (by turn)*   V D G GRANTHAM
JERSEY (Holy Trinity) *Win 15*   P *The Crown*
   R G J HOUGHTON
JERSEY (St Andrew) *Win 15*   P *Dean of Jersey*
   V M H BARRETT
JERSEY (St Brelade) (Communicare Chapel) (St Aubin)
   Win 15   P *The Crown*   R M F W BOND
JERSEY (St Clement) *Win 15*   P *The Crown*   R D M SHAW
   NSM M J DRYDEN, T L C BROMLEY
JERSEY (St Helier) *Win 15*   P *The Crown*   R M R KEIRLE
   C J R PORTER   NSM A D WILLIAMS
JERSEY (St John) *Win 15*   P *The Crown*   R B L SPROATS
JERSEY (St Lawrence) *Win 15*   P *The Crown*   R P J WARREN
JERSEY (St Luke) w St James *Win 15*   P *Bp and The Crown
   (alt)*   V N B P BARRY
JERSEY (St Mark) *Win 15*   P *Bp*   V *vacant*
JERSEY (St Martin) *Win 15*   P *The Crown*   R J A SCOTT,
   J R WATTLEY
JERSEY (St Mary) *Win 15*   P *The Crown*   R T J NEILL
JERSEY (St Ouen) (St George) *Win 15*   P *The Crown*
   R I PALLENT
JERSEY (St Paul) Proprietary Chapel *Win 15*
   Min P J BROOKS
JERSEY (St Peter) *Win 15*   P *The Crown*   R M J PHILLIPS
JERSEY (St Saviour) *Win 15*   P *The Crown*   R *vacant*
JERSEY (St Simon) *Win 15*   P *R St Helier, Bp, and The Crown
   (by turn)*   V D G GRANTHAM
JERSEY DE GROUVILLE (St Martin) (St Peter la Roque)
   Win 15   P *The Crown*   P-in-c H L GUNTON
JERSEY Gouray (St Martin) *Win 15*   P *Bp and The Crown (alt)*
   V *vacant*

JERSEY Greve d'Azette (St Nicholas)   *see* Jersey St Clem *Win*
JERSEY Millbrook (St Matthew) *Win 15*   P *The Crown*
   V P J WARREN
JESMOND (Clayton Memorial Church) *Newc 2*   P *Trustees*
   V D R J HOLLOWAY   C J J S PRYKE   Hon C A F MUNDEN
JESMOND (Holy Trinity) *Newc 2*   P *Patr Bd*   V T SANDERSON
   C A C MCCARTHY
JESMOND (St George)   *see* Newc St Geo and St Hilda *Newc*
JESMOND (St Hilda) *as above*
JEVINGTON (St Andrew)   *see* E Dean w Friston and Jevington
   Chich
JOYDENS WOOD (St Barnabas)   *see* Bexley *Roch*
KAIROS (Network Church) Bishop's Mission Order *Leeds 18*
   C J V BRADLEY   Min B P ASKEW
KATE'S HILL (St John)   *see* Dudley St Jo *Worc*
KEA (All Hallows) (Old Church) *Truro 5*   P *V St Clement*
   V M C BAKER   C W F HARWOOD
KEAL, EAST (St Helen)   *see* Bolingbroke Deanery *Linc*
KEAL, WEST (St Helen) *as above*
KEARSLEY (St Stephen)   *see* Farnworth, Kearsley and
   Stoneclough *Man*
KEASDEN (St Matthew)   *see* Clapham-with-Keasden and
   Austwick *Leeds*
KEDINGTON (St Peter and St Paul)   *see* Stourhead *St E*
KEEDWELL HILL (Ascension)   *see* Long Ashton w Barrow
   Gurney and Flax Bourton *B & W*
KEELBY (St Bartholomew)   *see* Wolds Gateway Group *Linc*
KEELE (St John the Baptist) *Lich 9*   P T H G Howard-Sneyd
   Esq   V P C JONES
KEEVIL (St Leonard)   *see* Trowbridge St Jas and Keevil *Sarum*
KEGWORTH (St Andrew), Hathern, Long Whatton,
   Diseworth, Belton and Osgathorpe *Leic 6*   P *Patr Bd*
   TR L J WILSON   TV L D CORKE
KEIGHLEY (All Saints) (St Andrew) *Leeds 1*   P *Patr Bd*
   TR M C CANSDALE   C N C THOMAS, T A RAISTRICK
   Hon C M S FOY   NSM J LONG, J M INESON
KEINTON MANDEVILLE (St Mary Magdalene)   *see* Wheathill
   Priory Gp *B & W*
KELBROOK (St Mary)   *see* Earby w Kelbrook *Leeds*
KELBY (St Andrew)   *see* E Loveden *Linc*
KELHAM (St Wilfrid)   *see* Averham w Kelham *S'well*
KELLET, NETHER (St Mark)   *see* Bolton-le-Sands *Blackb*
KELLET, OVER (St Cuthbert) *Blackb 14*   P *Reformation Ch
   Trust*   V *vacant*
KELLING (St Mary)   *see* Weybourne Gp *Nor*
KELLINGTON (St Edmund)   *see* Knottingley and Kellington
   w Whitley *Leeds*
KELLOE (St Helen) and Coxhoe *Dur 1*   P *Bp*   V *vacant*
KELLS (St Peter) *Carl 5*   P *Bp*   V *vacant*
KELLY (St Mary the Virgin)   *see* Lifton, Broadwoodwidger,
   Stowford etc *Ex*
KELMARSH (St Denys)   *see* Clipston, Haselbech, Kelmarsh,
   Marston Trussell etc *Pet*
KELMSCOTT (St George)   *see* Shill Valley and Broadshire *Ox*
KELSALE (St Peter)   *see* Saxmundham w Kelsale cum Carlton
   St E
KELSALL (St Philip) *Ches 2*   P *V Tarvin*   P-in-c S J BANKS
KELSEY, NORTH (All Hallows)   *see* Woldmoor Gp *Linc*
KELSEY, SOUTH (St Mary) *as above*
KELSHALL (St Faith)   *see* Therfield w Kelshall *St Alb*
KELSTERN (St Faith)   *see* Binbrook Gp *Linc*
KELSTON (St Nicholas)   *see* Bath Weston St Jo w Kelston
   B & W
KELVEDON (St Mary the Virgin) and Feering *Chelmsf 23*
   P *Bp*   P-in-c S F GARWOOD
KELVEDON HATCH (St Nicholas)   *see* Bentley Common,
   Kelvedon Hatch and Navestock *Chelmsf*
KEMBERTON (St Andrew)   *see* Beckbury, Badger, Kemberton,
   Ryton, Stockton etc *Lich*
KEMBLE (All Saints), Poole Keynes, Somerford Keynes w
   Sharncote, Coates, Rodmarton and Sapperton w
   Frampton Mansell *Glouc 7*   P *Bp, Lord Bathurst, Mrs L R
   Rank, Guild of All So, and DBP (2 turns), Duchy of Lanc (1
   turn)*   R T G KEMP   NSM A M AUSTIN
KEMERTON (St Nicholas)   *see* Ashchurch and Kemerton
   Glouc
KEMP TOWN (St Mary) *Chich 19*   P *Bp, Mrs R A Hinton, A C
   R Elliott Esq, T J Elliott Esq, and the Revd Canon D H
   McKittrick (jt)*   V A J WOODWARD   NSM H M BENNETT,
   S J VAN DEN DRIESSCHE
KEMPLEY (St Edward)   *see* Redmarley D'Abitot,
   Bromesberrow, Pauntley etc *Glouc*
KEMPSEY (St Mary the Virgin) and Severn Stoke w
   Croome d'Abitot *Worc 2*   P *D&C and Croome Estate
   Trustees (alt)*   R M BADGER
KEMPSFORD (St Mary)   *see* S Cotswolds *Glouc*

KEMPSHOTT (St Mark) *Win 4*   **P** *Bp*   **V** N J SUCH
C K P ROBINS
KEMPSTON (All Saints) *St Alb 9*   **P** *Bp*   **V** E J LOMAX
KEMPSTON (Transfiguration) *St Alb 9*   **P** *Bp*   **V** A J MAFFEI
KEMSING (St Mary the Virgin) and Woodlands *Roch 10*
  P *DBP*   **V** *vacant*
KENARDINGTON (St Mary)   *see Saxon Shoreline Cant*
KENCHESTER (St Michael)   *see Magnis Gp Heref*
KENCOT (St George)   *see Shill Valley and Broadshire Ox*
KENDAL (Holy Trinity) (All Hallows Chapel) *Carl 10*   **P** *Trin*
  Coll Cam   **C** A F UNDERWOOD   **NSM** G SKILLING,
  L A FOSTER, P A HENDERSON
KENDAL (St George)   *see Beacon TM Carl*
KENDAL (St Thomas) *Carl 10*   **P** *CPAS*   **P-in-c** G W BRIGGS
  C V A SEKASI
KENDAL (St Thomas)   *see Beacon TM Carl*
KENDRAY (St Andrew) *Sheff 12*   **P** *V Ardsley*
  V P C W JACKSON
KENILWORTH (St John) *Cov 4*   **P** *Simeon's Trustees*
  V A M ATTWOOD
KENILWORTH (St Nicholas) (St Barnabas) *Cov 4*   **P** *Ld Chan*
  V S BAILEY   **C** A G BAXTER, R B R MOORE
KENLEY (All Saints) *S'wark 22*   **P** *Abp*   **P-in-c** J MIDDLEMISS
  NSM E J GOODRIDGE
KENLEY (St John the Baptist)   *see Wenlock Heref*
KENN (St Andrew)   *see Exminster, Kenn, Kenton w*
  Mamhead, and Powderham *Ex*
KENN (St John the Evangelist)   *see Yatton Moor B & W*
KENNERLEIGH (St John the Baptist)   *see N Creedy Ex*
KENNET, EAST (Christ Church)   *see Upper Kennet Sarum*
KENNETT (St Nicholas)   *see Three Rivers Gp Ely*
KENNINGHALL (St Mary)   *see Guiltcross Nor*
KENNINGTON (St John the Divine w St James the Apostle)
  S'wark 11   **P** *Ripon Coll Cuddesdon and Bp (jt)*
  V M WILLIAMS   **C** N J QUANRUD   **NSM** C J M BELL,
  S D T HARRIES, S LABRAN
KENNINGTON (St Mark) *S'wark 11*   **P** *Abp*   **V** S H COULSON
KENNINGTON (St Mary)   *see Ashford Town Cant*
KENNINGTON (St Swithun)   *see Radley, Sunningwell and*
  Kennington *Ox*
KENNINGTON CROSS (St Anselm)   *see N Lambeth S'wark*
KENNINGTON PARK (St Agnes) *S'wark 10*   **P** *SMF*
  V P G ENSOR
KENSAL GREEN (St John) *Lon 2*   **P** *Bp*   **V** D M ACKERMAN
KENSAL RISE (St Mark) *Lon 18*   **P** *Bp and Trustees (jt)*
  V W P G LEAF   **C** A M CARMICHAEL
KENSAL RISE (St Martin) *Lon 18*   **P** *Bp and Trustees (jt)*
  V G P NOYCE   **C** S R HOWARD-JONES   **Hon C** E J BARRATT
KENSAL TOWN (St Thomas) (St Andrew) (St Philip) *Lon 12*
  P *Hyndman Trustees*   **V** S J MCNALLY-CROSS
KENSINGTON (Christ Church) *Lon 12*   **P** *Bp*   **C** A FENTON,
  M HARRIS, R G POWELL
KENSINGTON (Holy Trinity w All Saints)   *see S Kensington H*
  Trin w All SS *Lon*
KENSINGTON (St Barnabas) *Lon 12*   **P** *V Kensington St Mary*
  Abbots w St Geo and Ch Ch   **V** A J H BUCKLER   **C** J J SERGENT
KENSINGTON (St Clement)   *see Notting Dale St Clem w*
  St Mark and St Jas *Lon*
KENSINGTON (St George)   *see Holland Park Lon*
KENSINGTON (St Helen) w Holy Trinity *Lon 12*   **P** *Bp*
  V S R DIVALL
KENSINGTON (St James)   *see Notting Dale St Clem w*
  St Mark and St Jas *Lon*
KENSINGTON (St Luke)   *see S Kensington St Luke Lon*
KENSINGTON (St Mary Abbots) *Lon 12*   **P** *Bp*
  V E R DINWIDDY SMITH   **C** A E ORMONDROYD, C T A ROGERS
KENSINGTON (St Stephen)   *see S Kensington St Steph Lon*
KENSINGTON All Saints   *see Liv All SS Liv*
KENSINGTON, SOUTH (Holy Trinity w All Saints) *Lon 3*
  P *D&C Westmr*   **V** *vacant*
KENSINGTON, SOUTH (St Luke) *Lon 8*   **P** *Ch Patr Trust*
  V N G P GUMBEL   **C** D J MATTHEWS
KENSINGTON, SOUTH (St Stephen) *Lon 12*   **P** *Guild of All*
  So   **P-in-c** P R BARNES   **C** A H RIMMER
KENSINGTON, WEST (St Andrew)   *see Fulham St Andr Lon*
KENSINGTON, WEST (St Mary)   *see Fulham St Mary N End*
  Lon
KENSINGTON, WEST (St Mary) The Boltons   *see W*
  Brompton St Mary w St Peter and St Jude *Lon*
KENSWORTH (St Mary the Virgin), Studham and
  Whipsnade *St Alb 11*   **P** *Ld Chan and D&C St Paul's (alt)*
  V N Y LENTHALL
KENTCHURCH (St Mary)   *see Ewyas Harold w Dulas,*
  Kenderchurch etc *Heref*
KENTFORD (St Mary)   *see Forest Heath St E*

KENTISBEARE (St Mary)   *see Willand, Uffculme, Kentisbeare*
  etc *Ex*
KENTISBURY (St Thomas)   *see Shirwell, Loxhore, Kentisbury,*
  Arlington, etc *Ex*
KENTISH TOWN (St Benet and All Saints) *Lon 15*   **P** *The*
  Crown and D&C St Paul's (alt)   **V** G R F WILLIS
KENTISH TOWN (St Luke)   *see Oseney Crescent St Luke Lon*
KENTISH TOWN (St Martin) (St Andrew) *Lon 15*   **P** *Exors*
  Dame Jewell Magnus-Allcroft   **V** C M BARRETT FORD
KENTISH TOWN (St Silas) and (Holy Trinity) w St Barnabas
  Lon 15   **P** *Bp and D&C St Paul's (jt)*   **V** G C ROWLANDS
KENTMERE (St Cuthbert)   *see Staveley, Ings and Kentmere*
  Carl
KENTON (All Saints)   *see Debenham and Helmingham St E*
KENTON (All Saints)   *see Exminster, Kenn, Kenton w*
  Mamhead, and Powderham *Ex*
KENTON (Ascension) *Newc 2*   **P** *Bp*   **V** *vacant*
KENTON (St Mary the Virgin) *Lon 20*   **P** *Bp*   **V** E J LEWIS
  NSM M J STILL
KENTON, SOUTH (Annunciation) *Lon 18*   **P** *Bp*
  P-in-c T P GODDARD
KENWYN (St Keyne) w St Allen *Truro 5*   **P** *Bp*
  R C P PARSONS   **OLM** R W HUMPHRIES
KERESLEY (St Thomas) and Coundon *Cov 2*   **P** *Bp*
  V M NORRIS
KERESLEY END (Church of the Ascension)   *see Keresley and*
  Coundon *Cov*
KERRIDGE (Holy Trinity)   *see Bollington Ches*
KERRIER, WEST, comprising Breage w Godolphin and
  Ashton, Porthleven, Sithney, and St Germoe *Truro 3*   **P** *Bp*
  and The Crown (alt)   **P-in-c** D G MILLER   **C** K RICHARDS
KERSAL MOOR (St Paul) *Man 7*   **P** *Trustees*   **R** L P LONGDEN
  OLM H A SHEDLOCK, M J DYSON
KERSAL, LOWER (St Aidan)   *see Salford All SS Man*
KERSEY (St Mary)   *see Elmsett w Aldham, Hintlesham,*
  Chattisham etc *St E*
KERSWELL GREEN (St John the Baptist)   *see Kempsey and*
  Severn Stoke w Croome d'Abitot *Worc*
KESGRAVE (All Saints) w Little Bealings and Playford
  St E 10   **P** *Bp*   **V** R SPITTLE   **NSM** G JONES
KESSINGLAND (St Edmund), Gisleham and Rushmere
  Nor 9   **P** *Ld Chan (1 turns) and Bp (2 turns)*   **R** M L BISHOP
KESTON (not known) (St Audrey) *Roch 16*   **P** *D&C*
  R C F MORRISON
KESWICK (All Saints)   *see Swardeston w E Carleton, Intwood,*
  Keswick etc *Nor*
KESWICK (St John) w Borrowdale *Carl 6*   **P** *Trustees*
  V C H HOPE   **C** L D BASHAM
KESWICK, EAST (St Mary Magdalene)   *see Bardsey Leeds*
KETLEY (St Mary the Virgin)   *see Cen Telford Lich*
KETTERING (All Saints) *Pet 9*   **P** *SMF*   **P-in-c** D C WALSH
  C A L J WATSON, C GLOVER, C R WALSH   **NSM** J E BURNS
KETTERING (Christ the King) *Pet 9*   **P** *R Barton Seagrave w*
  Warkton   **V** R J BEWLEY   **C** E R JEANS, P J KELLEHER
KETTERING (St Andrew) *Pet 9*   **P** *Bp*   **V** T M HOUSTON
KETTERING (St Mary the Virgin) (St John the Evangelist)
  Pet 9   **P** *SMF*   **P-in-c** J E MOWBRAY
KETTERING (St Peter and St Paul) (St Michael and All
  Angels) *Pet 9*   **P** *Comdr L M M Saunders Watson*
  R D C WALSH   **C** A L J WATSON, C GLOVER, C R WALSH
  NSM J E BURNS
KETTERINGHAM (St Peter)   *see Swardeston w E Carleton,*
  Intwood, Keswick etc *Nor*
KETTLEBASTON (St Mary)   *see Monks Eleigh w Chelsworth*
  and Brent Eleigh etc *St E*
KETTLEBROOK (St Andrew)   *see Tamworth Lich*
KETTLEBURGH (St Andrew)   *see Orebeck St E*
KETTLESTONE (All Saints)   *see Barney, Hindringham,*
  Thursford, Great Snoring, Little Snoring and Kettlestone
  and Pensthorpe *Nor*
KETTLETHORPE (St Peter and St Paul)   *see Saxilby Gp Linc*
KETTLEWELL (St Mary)   *see Upper Wharfedale and Littondale*
  Leeds
KETTON (St Mary the Virgin) and Tinwell *Pet 12*   **P** *Bp and*
  Burghley Ho Preservation Trust Ltd (jt)   **P-in-c** O S WOOLCOCK
KEW (St Anne) *S'wark 16*   **P** *The Crown*   **V** *vacant*
KEW (St Francis of Assisi) *Liv 9*   **P** *Bp, Adn Warrington, and V*
  Southport All SS and All So (jt)   **V** A P J GALBRAITH
KEW (St Philip and All Saints) (St Luke) *S'wark 16*   **P** *Bp*
  V M L HARRINGTON
KEWSTOKE (St Paul)   *see Milton and Kewstoke B & W*
KEYHAM, NORTH (St Thomas)   *see Plymouth St Pet and H*
  Apostles *Ex*
KEYINGHAM (St Nicholas)   *see Easington w Skeffling,*
  Keyingham, Ottringham etc *York*

KEYMER (St Cosmas and St Damian) *see* Clayton w Keymer *Chich*

KEYMER (St Francis of Assisi) *as above*

KEYNSHAM (St Francis) (St John the Baptist) *B & W 9*
  P *Patr Bd* **TR** S A M'CAW **TV** A GARDINER, M R BURKE
  C N M WILLIAMS

KEYSOE (St Mary the Virgin) *see* Bolnhurst w Keysoe *St Alb*

KEYSTON (St John the Baptist) *see* W Leightonstone *Ely*

KEYWORTH (St Mary Magdalene) and Stanton-on-the-Wolds and Bunny w Bradmore *S'well 5* **P** *Bp and Ld Chan (alt)* **R** T H C MEYRICK

KIBWORTH (St Wilfrid) and Smeeton Westerby and Saddington *Leic 3* **P** *Mert Coll Ox and Bp (jt)*
  R L FREMMER

KIDBROOKE (St James) *S'wark 1* **P** *Patr Bd* **R** K W HITCH

KIDBROOKE (St Nicholas) *S'wark 1* **P** *Bp and Simeon's Trustees (jt)* **V** T M LINKENS

KIDDERMINSTER (St John the Baptist) (Holy Innocents) *Worc 1* **P** *Patr Bd* **TR** T J WILLIAMS **TV** L C BETSON
  C C L HENSON **NSM** A VACCARO, C J BETSON

KIDDERMINSTER (St Mary and All Saints) Ismere *Worc 1*
  P *Patr Bd* **TR** N R TAYLOR **TV** S A ARCHER
  C S P ARMSTRONG

KIDDERMINSTER EAST (St George) (St Chad) (St Cecilia), including Chaddesley Corbett and Stone *Worc 1* **P** *Ld Chan (1 turn), Patr Bd (2 turns)* **TR** D HILDRED **TV** R J LEGGE

KIDDERMINSTER WEST *see* Kidderminster St Jo and H Innocents *Worc*

KIDDINGTON (St Nicholas) *see* Wootton w Glympton and Kiddington *Ox*

KIDLINGTON (St Mary the Virgin) w Hampton Poyle *Ox 2*
  P *Patr Bd* **TR** F M SCROGGIE **TV** M J DAVIS **C** S BROUARD

KIDLINGTON, SOUTH (St John the Baptist) *see* Kidlington w Hampton Poyle *Ox*

KIDMORE END (St John the Baptist) *see* Rotherfield Peppard and Kidmore End etc *Ox*

KIDSGROVE (St Thomas) *Lich 9* **P** *MMCET* **V** I BAKER

KILBURN (Mission Room) *see* Denby Gp *Derby*

KILBURN (St Augustine) (St John) *Lon 2* **P** *SMF*
  V C J AMOS

KILBURN (St Mary) *see* Thirkleby w Kilburn and Bagby *York*

KILBURN Priory Road (St Mary) w All Souls and W Hampstead St James *Lon 15* **P** *Bp, Ch Patr Trust, and trustees (jt)* **V** R G THOMPSON **C** C N RINK
  NSM D L YELDHAM, R HUTCHISON

KILBURN, WEST (St Luke) and Harrow Road Emmanuel *Lon 2* **P** *CPAS and Simeon's Trustees (jt)* **V** A G THOM
  C J F BARRY

KILBY (St Mary Magdalene) *see* Wistow *Leic*

KILDALE (St Cuthbert) *see* Ingleby Greenhow, Bilsdale Priory etc *York*

KILDWICK (St Andrew), Cononley and Bradley *Leeds 4*
  P *Bp and Ch Ch Ox (jt)* **V** *vacant*

KILHAM (All Saints) *see* Rudston, Boynton, Carnaby etc *York*

KILKHAMPTON (St James the Great) *see* N Kernow *Truro*

KILLAMARSH (St Giles) and Renishaw *Derby 3* **P** *The Crown*
  R H GUEST

KILLERTON (Holy Evangelist) *see* Broadclyst, Clyst Honiton, Clyst Hydon etc *Ex*

KILLINGHALL (St Thomas the Apostle) *see* Hampsthwaite and Killinghall and Birstwith *Leeds*

KILLINGHOLME, NORTH (St Denys) *see* Abbey Gp *Linc*

KILLINGTON (All Saints) *see* Western Dales *Carl*

KILLINGWORTH (St John) *Newc 1* **P** *V Longbenton St Bart*
  NSM A H MEIGHEN

KILMERSDON (St Peter and St Paul) w Babington *B & W 11*
  P *Lord Hylton* **R** *vacant*

KILMESTON (St Andrew) *see* Upper Itchen *Win*

KILMINGTON (St Giles), Stockland, Dalwood, Yarcombe and Shute *Ex 4* **P** *Bp and D&C (2 turns), The Crown (1 turn)*
  V *vacant*

KILMINGTON (St Mary the Virgin) *see* Upper Stour *Sarum*

KILNDOWN (Christ Church) *see* Goudhurst w Kilndown *Cant*

KILNGREEN (Diggle Mission Church) *see* Saddleworth *Man*

KILNHURST (St Thomas) *Sheff 12* **P** *Ld Chan*
  V A R BREWERTON **C** B C SHIRES

KILNWICK (All Saints) *see* Woldsburn *York*

KILPECK (St Mary and St David) *see* Ewyas Harold w Dulas, Kenderchurch etc *Heref*

KILSBY (St Faith) *see* Daventry *Pet*

KILVE (Blessed Virgin Mary) *see* Quantock Coast *B & W*

KILVERSTONE (St Andrew) *see* Thetford *Nor*

KILVINGTON (St Mary) *S'well 3* **P** *E G Staunton Esq*
  P-in-c E I MURRAY

KILVINGTON, SOUTH (St Wilfrid) *see* Thirsk *York*

KILWORTH, NORTH (St Andrew) *see* Avon-Swift *Leic*

KILWORTH, SOUTH (St Nicholas) *as above*

KIMBERLEY (Holy Trinity) and Nuthall *S'well 8* **P** *Bp*
  R B M HOLBROOK

KIMBERLEY (St Peter) *see* Barnham Broom and Upper Yare *Nor*

KIMBERWORTH (St Thomas) (St Mark) and Kimberworth Park *Sheff 6* **P** *Bp* **P-in-c** L BROADHEAD

KIMBERWORTH PARK (St John) *see* Kimberworth and Kimberworth Park *Sheff*

KIMBLE, GREAT (St Nicholas) *see* Ellesborough, The Kimbles and Stoke Mandeville *Ox*

KIMBLE, LITTLE (All Saints) *as above*

KIMBLESWORTH (St Philip and St James) *see* Dur N *Dur*

KIMBOLTON (St Andrew) *see* S Leightonstone *Ely*

KIMBOLTON (St James the Great) *see* Leominster *Heref*

KIMCOTE (All Saints) *see* Avon-Swift *Leic*

KIMMERIDGE (St Nicholas of Myra) *see* St Aldhelm *Sarum*

KIMPTON (St Peter and St Paul) *see* Appleshaw, Kimpton, Thruxton, Fyfield etc *Win*

KIMPTON (St Peter and St Paul) w Ayot St Lawrence *St Alb 7* **P** *Bp* **P-in-c** L L P WILLIAMS

KINETON (St Peter) *see* Edgehill Churches *Cov*

KING CROSS (St Paul) *Leeds 8* **P** *Bp* **V** *vacant*

KING STERNDALE (Christ Church) *see* Buxton w Burbage and King Sterndale *Derby*

KINGHAM (St Andrew) *see* Chipping Norton *Ox*

KINGMOOR (St Peter) *see* Houghton *Carl*

KING'S BECK, comprising Banningham, Colby, Felmingham, Skeyton, Sloley, Suffield, Swanton Abbot, and Tuttington *Nor 12* **P** *Bp, D&C, P H C Barber Esq, S D Shaw Esq, and DBP (jt)* **R** *vacant*

KINGS BROMLEY (All Saints), The Ridwares and Yoxall *Lich 1* **P** *Bp, D&C, and Personal Reps Lord Leigh (jt)*
  R J C BRADING

KING'S CAPLE (St John the Baptist) *see* StowCaple *Heref*

KING'S CLIFFE (All Saints), Bulwick and Blatherwycke, Collyweston, Easton-on-the-Hill and Laxton *Pet 10* **P** *Bp, Exors G T G Conant, F&A George Ltd, and Burghley Ho Preservation Trust Ltd (2 turns), Ld Chan (1 turn)*
  V P J DAVIES **C** K T M DOW

KINGS HEATH (All Saints) *Birm 2* **P** *V Moseley St Mary*
  V Q D WARBRICK **C** T J MATSVERU

KINGS HEATH (Church on the Heath) *Pet 4* **P** *Bp*
  V R A WOODS

KINGS LANGLEY (All Saints) *see* Langelei *St Alb*

KING'S LYNN (All Saints) *see* S and W Lynn *Nor*

KING'S LYNN (St John the Evangelist) *Nor 19* **P** *Bp*
  V R J ROGERS **C** J M PRICE

KING'S LYNN (St Margaret) w St Nicholas *Nor 19* **P** *D&C*
  TR M J DIMOND **TV** R J ROGERS **C** A C RAYNER

KING'S NORTON (St John the Baptist) *see* Gaulby *Leic*

KINGS NORTON (St Nicolas) *Birm 2* **P** *Patr Bd*
  TR L C WRIGHT **C** C E MATLOCK **NSM** E C IKECHUKWU

KING'S NYMPTON (St James) *see* S Molton w Nymet St George, Chittlehamholt etc *Ex*

KING'S PYON (St Mary the Virgin) *see* Canon Pyon w King's Pyon, Birley and Wellington *Heref*

KINGS RIPTON (St Peter) *see* N Leightonstone *Ely*

KING'S STANLEY (St George) *see* Stroudwater *Glouc*

KING'S SUTTON (St Peter and St Paul) and Newbottle and Charlton *Pet 1* **P** *SMF and Lady Townsend (jt)*
  V M J ROBINSON

KING'S WALDEN (St Mary) and Offley w Lilley *St Alb 3*
  P *Sir Thomas Pilkington Bt (2 turns), St Jo Coll Cam (1 turn), D K C Salusbury-Hughes Esq and Mrs P A L McGrath (2 turns)*
  V T J BELL

KING'S WOOD, comprising Challock and Molash, Chilham, Crundale, and Godmersham *Cant 2* **P** *Abp and J S Wheeler Esq (jt)* **P-in-c** C M SIGRIST **NSM** K BURGESS

KING'S WORTHY (St Mary) (St Mary's Chapel) *Win 7*
  P *Univ Coll Ox and Lord Northbrook (alt)* **R** P E BRADISH
  NSM J C LEWIS

KINGSBRIDGE (St Edmund the King and Martyr), Dodbrooke, and West Alvington *Ex 12* **P** *Bp Ex and D&C Sarum (jt)* **R** J M TAYLOR **C** M R GORTON

KINGSBURY (Holy Innocents) *Lon 18* **P** *D&C St Paul's*
  V S V SCHUIL-BREWER **NSM** S HAMEEM

KINGSBURY (St Andrew) *Lon 18* **P** *The Crown* **V** J RENDELL

KINGSBURY (St Peter and St Paul) *Birm 5* **P** *Bp*
  P-in-c J C WHITE **NSM** C J YOUNG

KINGSBURY EPISCOPI (St Martin) *see* Martock w Kingsbury Episcopi and Ash *B & W*

KINGSCLERE (St Mary) and Ashford Hill w Headley *Win 6*
  P *Bp* **V** B S READ

KINGSCLERE WOODLANDS (St Paul) *see* Kingsclere and Ashford Hill w Headley *Win*

KINGSCOTE (St John the Baptist) *see* Nailsworth w Shortwood, Horsley etc *Glouc*

KINGSDON (All Saints) *see* Somerton w The Charltons and Kingsdon *B & W*

KINGSDOWN (St Edmund the King and Martyr) *Roch 10* **P** *D&C* **R** S CORRY **C** A J CLAMPIN

KINGSDOWN (St John the Evangelist) *see* Walmer and Cornilo *Cant*

KINGSDOWN, Creekside and High Downs *Cant 14* **P** *Ld Chan (1 turn), Abp, Adn Cant, D&C, Exors Sir Frederick Croft, and MMCET (1 turn)* **V** S H LILLICRAP **C** C M TURVEY, J T PYE

KINGSEY (St Nicholas) *see* Wychert Vale *Ox*

KINGSHURST (St Barnabas) *Birm 5* **P** *Bp* **V** F J JOHNSON

KINGSKERSWELL (St Mary), Abbotskerswell and Coffinswell *Ex 8* **P** *Ld Chan* **V** M J D WILKIE

KINGSLAND (St Michael and All Angels) w Eardisland, Aymestrey and Leinthall Earles *Heref 6* **P** *DBP (2 turns), Ld Chan (1 turn)* **P-in-c** J M READ **NSM** K M SMITH

KINGSLEY (All Saints) *see* Northanger *Win*

KINGSLEY (St John the Evangelist) *see* Norley, Crowton and Kingsley *Ches*

KINGSLEY (St Werburgh) and Foxt-w-Whiston and Oakamoor w Cotton *Lich 6* **P** *R Cheadle w Freehay and Mrs N A Faulkner (jt)* **R** S M SYMONS **NSM** C A SIEGERTSZ

KINGSNORTH (St Michael and All Angels) *see* Ashford Town *Cant*

KINGSNYMPTON *see* S Molton w Nymet St George, Chittlehamholt etc *Ex*

KINGSTAG (not known) *see* Spire Hill *Sarum*

KINGSTANDING (St Luke) *Birm 1* **P** *Bp* **V** B A I SMART

KINGSTANDING (St Mark) *Birm 1* **P** *Bp* **V** P CALVERT

KINGSTEIGNTON (St Michael) and Teigngrace *Ex 8* **P** *Bp* **V** M P SMITH **NSM** S J GILL

KINGSTHORPE (St John the Baptist) (St David) (St Mark) *Pet 4* **P** *Patr Bd* **TR** L J BUTLER **C** S L LEE **NSM** J J W LEE

KINGSTON (All Saints and St Andrew) *see* Papworth *Ely*

KINGSTON (All Saints) (St John the Evangelist) (St John the Baptist) *S'wark 15* **P** *Patr Bd* **TR** J P WILKES **TV** A R BECK, M A STAFFORD **NSM** D BELL

KINGSTON (St Giles) *see* Barham Downs w Adisham *Cant*

KINGSTON (St James) *see* Modbury, Bigbury, Ringmore etc *Ex*

KINGSTON (St James) *see* St Aldhelm *Sarum*

KINGSTON (St James) *see* W Wight *Portsm*

KINGSTON (St Pancras) *see* Iford w Kingston and Rodmell and Southease *Chich*

KINGSTON BAGPUIZE (St John the Baptist) w Southmoor *see* Fyfield w Tubney and Kingston Bagpuize *Ox*

KINGSTON BUCI (St Giles) *see* Old Shoreham and Kingston Buci *Chich*

KINGSTON BUCI (St Julian) *as above*

KINGSTON DEVERILL (St Mary) *see* Cley Hill Villages *Sarum*

KINGSTON HILL (St Paul) *S'wark 15* **P** *DBP* **V** A G RYLETT **C** C MADANAT **NSM** F M M DE QUIDT

KINGSTON LACY (St Stephen) *see* Bridge Par *Sarum*

KINGSTON LISLE (St John the Baptist) *see* Ridgeway *Ox*

KINGSTON PARK (not known) *Newc 2* **P** *Bp* **P-in-c** A GRAY

KINGSTON SEYMOUR (All Saints) *see* Yatton Moor *B & W*

KINGSTON ST MARY (The Blessed Virgin Mary) *see* S Quantock *B & W*

KINGSTON UPON HULL (Most Holy and Undivided Trinity) *York 14* **P** *CPAS* **V** D P BLACK **Hon C** I R S WALKER **NSM** I M WILSON

KINGSTON UPON HULL (St Aidan) Southcoates *York 14* **P** *Simeon's Trustees* **V** R P PHILLIPS

KINGSTON UPON HULL (St Alban) *York 14* **P** *Abp* **V** G P THORNALLEY **NSM** L A GILLARD

KINGSTON UPON HULL (St Cuthbert) *see* Hull St Cuth *York*

KINGSTON UPON HULL (St John the Baptist) *see* Newington w Hull St Andr *York*

KINGSTON UPON HULL (St Martin) *see* Hull St Martin w Transfiguration *York*

KINGSTON UPON HULL (St Mary the Virgin) *York 14* **P** *Abp* **P-in-c** I R S WALKER

KINGSTON UPON HULL (St Matthew) *see* Newington w Hull St Andr *York*

KINGSTON UPON HULL (St Nicholas) *York 14* **P** *Abp* **V** P COPLEY **C** J R FOREMAN

KINGSTON UPON HULL (St Paul) *see* Sculcoates *York*

KINGSTON UPON HULL (St Stephen) *as above*

KINGSTON UPON THAMES (All Saints) *see* Kingston *S'wark*

KINGSTON UPON THAMES (St John the Evangelist) *as above*

KINGSTON UPON THAMES (St Luke) *S'wark 15* **P** *Bp* **V** M G HISLOP

KINGSTON VALE (St John the Baptist) *see* Kingston *S'wark*

KINGSTONE (St John and All Saints) *see* Winsmoor *B & W*

KINGSTONE (St John the Baptist) *see* Uttoxeter Area *Lich*

KINGSTONE (St Michael and All Angels) *see* Cagebrook *Heref*

KINGSTON-ON-SOAR (St Winifred) *see* A453 churches of S Notts *S'well*

KINGSWEAR (St Thomas of Canterbury) *see* Brixham w Churston Ferrers and Kingswear *Ex*

KINGSWINFORD (St Mary) *Worc 5* **P** *Bp* **P-in-c** A R HADLEY

KINGSWOOD (Church of the Ascension) (Holy Trinity) *Bris 5* **P** *Patr Bd* **P-in-c** B M CHARLES **C** S J DYSON **NSM** C E EVANS

KINGSWOOD (Conventional District) Hull *York 14* **C-in-c** B J NORTON

KINGSWOOD (St Andrew) *S'wark 24* **P** *Bp and R&S Ch Trust (jt)* **P-in-c** C A COLTON

KINGSWOOD (St Mary the Virgin) *see* Charfield and Kingswood w Wickwar etc *Glouc*

KINGSWOOD Benefice, The, comprising Clothall, Rushden, Sandon, Wallington and Weston *St Alb 16* **P** *Duchy of Lanc (1 turn), Bp, Marquess of Salisbury, and J A Cherry (4 turns)* **R** F K WHEATLEY

KINGSWOOD, LOWER (Wisdom of God) *see* Kingswood *S'wark*

KINGTON (St James) *see* Inkberrow w Cookhill and Kington w Dormston *Worc*

KINGTON (St Mary) w Huntington, Old Radnor, Kinnerton and Titley *Heref 4* **P** *Patr Bd* **R** B L T GRIFFITH **C** L K MACDERMOTT **NSM** P J BUCKINGHAM

KINGTON LANGLEY (St Peter) *see* Draycot *Bris*

KINGTON MAGNA (All Saints) *see* Stour Vale *Sarum*

KINGTON ST MICHAEL (St Michael) *Bris 4* **P** *Patr Bd* **V** *vacant*

KINGTON, WEST (St Mary the Virgin) *see* By Brook *Bris*

KINGWESTON (All Saints) *see* Wheathill Priory Gp *B & W*

KINLET (St John the Baptist) *see* Cleobury Mortimer w Hopton Wafers etc *Heref*

KINNERLEY (St Mary) w Melverley, Knockin w Maesbrook and Maesbury *Lich 18* **P** *Bp and Trustees (jt)* **R** C PRECIOUS **OLM** P L WEST

KINNERSLEY (St James) *see* Eardisley w Bollingham, Willersley, Brilley etc *Heref*

KINNERTON (St Mary the Virgin) *see* Kington w Huntington, Old Radnor, Kinnerton etc *Heref*

KINNERTON, HIGHER (All Saints) *see* Dodleston *Ches*

KINNINVIE (Mission Room) *see* Barnard Castle w Whorlton *Dur*

KINOULTON (St Luke) *see* Hickling w Kinoulton and Broughton Sulney *S'well*

KINSBOURNE GREEN (St Mary) *see* Harpenden St Nic *St Alb*

KINSHAM (All Saints) *see* Presteigne w Discoed, Kinsham, Lingen and Knill *Heref*

KINSLEY (Resurrection) w Wragby *Leeds 15* **P** *Bp and Lord St Oswald (jt)* **V** J HADJIOANNOU

KINSON (St Andrew) (St Philip) and West Howe *Sarum 7* **P** *Patr Bd* **TR** L SHIRVILL **TV** C A BROOKS **C** D D DALTON

KINTBURY (St Mary the Virgin) *see* Walbury Beacon *Ox*

KINVER (St Peter) and Enville *Lich 23* **P** *Bp, Mrs A D Williams, and DBP (jt)* **R** R A CLARKSON **OLM** N M CAINES

KINWARTON (St Mary the Virgin) *see* Alcester Minster *Cov*

KIPPAX (St Mary the Virgin) *see* Allerton Bywater, Kippax and Swillington *Leeds*

KIPPINGTON (St Mary) *see* W Sevenoaks *Roch*

KIRBY BEDON (St Andrew) *see* Rockland St Mary w Hellington, Bramerton etc *Nor*

KIRBY BELLARS (St Peter) *see* Upper Wreake *Leic*

KIRBY CANE (All Saints) *see* Waveney Marshlands *Nor*

KIRBY GRINDALYTHE (St Andrew) *see* Weaverthorpe w Helperthorpe, Luttons Ambo etc *York*

KIRBY MISPERTON (St Laurence) w Normanby and Salton *York 19* **P** *Lady Clarissa Collin, Abp, and St Jo Coll Cam (by turn)* **V** R G BARKER **C** M BROSNAN

KIRBY MUXLOE (St Bartholomew) *see* Desford and Kirby Muxloe *Leic*

KIRBY SIGSTON (St Lawrence) *see* Northallerton w Kirby Sigston *York*

KIRBY UNDERDALE (All Saints) *see* Garrowby Hill *York*

KIRBY WISKE (St John the Baptist) *see* Lower Swale *Leeds*

KIRBY, WEST (St Andrew) *Ches 8* **P** *D&C* **V** *vacant*

KIRBY, WEST (St Bridget) *Ches 8* **P** *D&C* **R** A C WILLIAMS **NSM** D K CHESTER

KIRBY, WEST (St Michael and All Angels) *see* Newton *Ches*

KIRBY-LE-SOKEN (St Michael) w Great Holland *Chelmsf 22* **P** *Bp and CPAS (jt)* **R** M D J HOLDAWAY

KIRBY-ON-THE-MOOR (All Saints), Cundall w Norton-le-Clay and Skelton-cum-Newby *Leeds* 20 **P** *Bp, Sir Arthur Collins, and R E J Compton Esq (jt)* **V** *vacant*
KIRDFORD (St John the Baptist) *Chich* 4 **P** *Lord Egremont* **P-in-c** C R JENKINS
KIRK ANDREAS (St Andrew) *see* Andreas, Ballaugh and Sulby *S & M*
KIRK BRAMWITH (St Mary) *see* Fishlake w Sykehouse and Kirk Bramwith etc *Sheff*
KIRK CHRIST RUSHEN (Holy Trinity) *see* Rushen *S & M*
KIRK DEIGHTON (All Saints) *see* Spofforth w Kirk Deighton *Leeds*
KIRK ELLA (St Andrew) and Willerby *York* 14 **P** *D&C* R A S B CARTER C J A TELFORD
KIRK FENTON (St Mary) *see* Tadcaster *York*
KIRK HALLAM (All Saints) *Derby* 8 **P** *Bp* **P-in-c** C FRENCH
KIRK HAMMERTON (St John the Baptist) *see* Lower Nidderdale *Leeds*
KIRK IRETON (Holy Trinity) *see* Wirksworth *Derby*
KIRK LANGLEY (St Michael) *Derby* 6 **P** *G Meynell Esq and J M Clark-Maxwell Esq (alt)* **P-in-c** B J STOBER
KIRK MAROWN (St Runius) *see* Marown, Foxdale and Baldwin *S & M*
KIRK MAUGHOLD (St Maughold) *see* Maughold and S Ramsey *S & M*
KIRK ONCHAN (St Peter) *see* Onchan, Lonan and Laxey *S & M*
KIRK PATRICK (Holy Trinity) *see* W Coast *S & M*
KIRK SANDALL and Edenthorpe (Good Shepherd) *see* Barnby Dun, Kirk Sandall and Edenthorpe *Sheff*
KIRK SMEATON (St Peter) *see* Went Valley *Leeds*
KIRKANDREWS ON EDEN (St Mary) *see* Barony of Burgh *Carl*
KIRKANDREWS ON ESK (St Andrew) *see* Arthuret w Kirkandrews-on-Esk and Nicholforest *Carl*
KIRKBAMPTON (St Peter) *see* Barony of Burgh *Carl*
KIRKBRIDE (St Bride) *see* Solway Plain *Carl*
KIRKBRIDE (St Bridget) *see* Bride, Lezayre and N Ramsey *S & M*
KIRKBURN (St Mary) *see* Woldsburn *York*
KIRKBURTON (All Hallows) and Shelley *Leeds* 5 **P** *Bp* **P-in-c** S L HUNTER C A R A GRANT **Hon C** S C CLARKE **OLM** J M CRAVEN
KIRKBY (St Andrew) *see* Woldmoor Gp *Linc*
KIRKBY (St Chad) (St Mark) (St Martin) (St Andrew) *Liv* 7 **P** *Patr Bd* **TR** J D FAGAN **TV** A L LAWLOR, P C LEA
KIRKBY FLEETHAM (St Mary) *see* Lower Swale *Leeds*
KIRKBY GREEN (Holy Cross) *see* Digby Gp *Linc*
KIRKBY IN ASHFIELD (St Thomas) *S'well* 4 **P** *Bp* **NSM** K CHARLES
KIRKBY IN ASHFIELD (St Wilfrid) *S'well* 4 **P** *Bp* **R** *vacant*
KIRKBY IRELETH (St Cuthbert) *Carl* 9 **P** *D&C York* **P-in-c** S W TUDWAY
KIRKBY KNOWLE (St Wilfrid) *York* 18 **P** *Abp* **P-in-c** D E GAMBLE **NSM** K M BROWN, W A DEWING
KIRKBY KNOWLE (St Wilfrid) *see* Kirkby Knowle *York*
KIRKBY LAYTHORPE (St Denys) *Linc* 14 **P** *Bp and DBP (alt)* **OLM** V GREENE
KIRKBY LONSDALE (St Mary the Virgin) Team Ministry, including Barbon, Casterton, Hutton Roof, Lupton, Mansergh, Middleton, and Preston Patrick *Carl* 10 **P** *Patr Bd* **TR** J J SNOW **TV** A E PETTIFOR **NSM** S M O'LOUGHLIN
KIRKBY MALHAM (St Michael the Archangel) *see* Upper Aire *Leeds*
KIRKBY MALLORY (All Saints) *see* Newbold De Verdun, Barlestone, Kirkby Mallory and Peckleton *Leic*
KIRKBY MALZEARD (St Andrew) *see* Fountains Gp *Leeds*
KIRKBY OVERBLOW (All Saints) *see* Lower Wharfedale *Leeds*
KIRKBY RAVENSWORTH (St Peter and St Felix) *see* Holmedale *Leeds*
KIRKBY STEPHEN (not known) *see* Upper Eden *Carl*
KIRKBY THORE (St Michael) *see* Heart of Eden *Carl*
KIRKBY UNDERWOOD (St Mary and All Saints) *see* Ringstone in Aveland Gp *Linc*
KIRKBY WHARFE (St John the Baptist) *see* Tadcaster *York*
KIRKBY WOODHOUSE (St John the Evangelist) *see* Annesley w Newstead and Kirkby Woodhouse *S'well*
KIRKBY, SOUTH (All Saints) *Leeds* 15 **P** *Guild of All So* **P-in-c** P CARTWRIGHT C J E FLEURY, T H R S J BATES-BOURNE **NSM** M J BURNS, M SCHOLEY
KIRKBY-IN-CLEVELAND (St Augustine) *see* Ingleby Greenhow, Bilsdale Priory etc *York*
KIRKBYMOORSIDE (All Saints) w Gillamoor, Farndale, Bransdale and Edstone *York* 19 **P** *Lady Clarissa Collin and Abp (jt)* **V** M BROSNAN **NSM** B J GILLESPIE
KIRKBY-ON-BAIN (St Mary) *see* Bain Valley Gp *Linc*

KIRKDALE (St Athanaseus with St Mary) *Liv* 1 **P** *Simeon's Trustees* **V** *vacant*
KIRKDALE (St Gregory) w Harome, Nunnington and Pockley *York* 19 **P** *Abp, Adn Cleveland, and Lady Clarissa Collin (2 turns), Ox Univ (1 turn)* **V** S J BINKS C M BURNSIDE
KIRKDALE (St Lawrence) *Liv* 1 **P** *CPAS* **V** M J GRIFFIN **NSM** G HOY
KIRKDALE (St Paul) *see* Kirkdale St Lawr *Liv*
KIRKHAM (St Michael) *Blackb* 10 **P** *Ch Ch Ox* **V** *vacant*
KIRKHARLE (St Wilfrid) *see* Kirkwhelpington, Kirkharle, Kirkheaton and Cambo *Newc*
KIRKHAUGH (Holy Paraclete) *see* Alston Moor *Newc*
KIRKHEATON (St Bartholomew) *see* Kirkwhelpington, Kirkharle, Kirkheaton and Cambo *Newc*
KIRKHEATON (St John the Baptist) *Leeds* 5 **P** *Ch Trust Fund Trust* **R** I R JONES C E E WALTERS
KIRKHOLT (St Thomas) *Man* 6 **P** *Bp* **V** *vacant*
KIRKLAND (Mission Church) *see* Lamplugh w Ennerdale *Carl*
KIRKLAND (St Lawrence) *see* Cross Fell Gp *Carl*
KIRKLEATHAM (St Cuthbert) (St Hilda) *York* 16 **P** *Abp* **V** M D STRAND C P KING
KIRKLEES VALLEY, comprising Brandlesholme, Elton, and Woolfold *Man* 4 **P** *R Bury St Mary* **V** *vacant*
KIRKLEVINGTON (St Martin and St Hilary) *see* Yarm w Kirklevington, Picton and Worsall *York*
KIRKLEY (St Peter and St John) *Nor* 9 **P** *Bp and DBP (jt)* **R** H CHANDLER
KIRKLINGTON (St Michael) w Burneston and Wath and Pickhill *Leeds* 22 **P** *Ch Soc Trust, Mrs M St B Anderson, G W Prior-Wandesforde Esq, and DBP (jt)* **R** *vacant*
KIRKLINGTON (St Swithin) w Hockerton *S'well* 3 **P** *Bp* **P-in-c** C G PENNOCK **NSM** M A GROVES
KIRKLINTON (St Cuthbert) *see* Bewcastle, Stapleton and Kirklinton etc *Carl*
KIRKNEWTON (St Gregory) *see* Doddington, Ilderton, Kirknewton and Wooler *Newc*
KIRKOSWALD (St Oswald), Renwick w Croglin, Great Salkeld and Lazonby *Carl* 4 **P** *Bp* **R** K M BUTTERFIELD **NSM** A BURRELL
KIRKSTALL (St Stephen) *see* Abbeylands *Leeds*
KIRKSTEAD (St Leonard) *see* Woodhall Spa Gp *Linc*
KIRKTHORPE (St Peter) *see* Warmfield *Leeds*
KIRKWHELPINGTON (St Bartholomew) w Kirkharle and Kirkheaton, and Cambo *Newc* 11 **P** *Ld Chan (2 turns), J P P Anderson Esq (1 turn), and Bp (1 turn)* **V** *vacant*
KIRMINGTON (St Helen) *see* Brocklesby Park, Croxton and North Wolds *Linc*
KIRMOND-LE-MIRE (St Martin) *see* Walesby Gp *Linc*
KIRSTEAD (St Margaret) *see* Brooke, Kirstead, Mundham w Seething and Thwaite *Nor*
KIRTLING (All Saints) *Ely* 4 **P** *Mrs D A Bowlby and Countess Ellesmere (alt)* **P-in-c** N A WORMELL
KIRTLINGTON (St Mary the Virgin) *see* Akeman *Ox*
KIRTON (Holy Trinity) *S'well* 3 **P** *SMF* **P-in-c** Z BURTON **NSM** M A GROVES
KIRTON (St Mary and St Martin) *see* Orwell and Deben *St E*
KIRTON HOLME (Christ Church) *see* Brothertoft Gp *Linc*
KIRTON IN HOLLAND (St Peter and St Paul) w Algarkirk and Fosdyke *Linc* 21 **P** *Bp and Mercers' Co (1 turn), The Crown (1 turn)* **V** *vacant*
KIRTON IN LINDSEY (St Andrew) w Manton *Linc* 8 **P** *Bp* **R** K E COLWELL C K M DARBY **NSM** P J DICKINSON **OLM** J WILSON
KISLINGBURY (St Luke) *see* Bugbrooke, Harpole, Kislingbury etc *Pet*
KITT GREEN (St Francis of Assisi) *see* Wigan *Liv*
KITTISFORD (St Nicholas) *see* Wellington and Distr *B & W*
KNAITH (St Mary) *see* Lea Gp *Linc*
KNAPHILL (Holy Trinity) w Brookwood *Guildf* 12 **P** *CPAS* **V** N J HOPKINS **OLM** J LEVETT
KNAPTON (St Peter) *see* Trunch Group *Nor*
KNAPWELL (All Saints) *see* Papworth *Ely*
KNARESBOROUGH (Holy Trinity) (St John the Baptist), Goldsborough, Nidd and Brearton *Leeds* 18 **P** *Patr Bd* **TR** G A F HINCHCLIFFE **TV** S G MCDERMOTT
KNARESDALE (St Jude) *see* Alston Moor *Newc*
KNEBWORTH (St Martin) (St Mary the Virgin and St Thomas of Canterbury) *St Alb* 20 **P** *Hon D A Fromanteel* **R** *vacant*
KNEESALL (St Bartholomew) w Laxton and Wellow *S'well* 3 **P** *DBP and Bp (jt)* **P-in-c** Z BURTON **NSM** M A GROVES
KNEETON (St Helen) *see* E Bridgford and Kneeton *S'well*
KNIGHTLEY (Christ Church) *see* Adbaston, High Offley, Knightley, Norbury etc *Lich*

KNIGHTLEY PARISHES   *see* Badby w Newham and Charwelton w Fawsley etc *Pet*

KNIGHTON (St Guthlac)   *see* Knighton *Leic*

KNIGHTON (St Mary Magdalene) *Leic 1*   **P** *Bp*
V M A R JONES   C M J C GOUGH

KNIGHTON, WEST (St Peter)   *see* Watercombe *Sarum*

KNIGHTON-ON-TEME (St Michael and All Angels)   *see* Teme Valley N *Worc*

KNIGHT'S ENHAM (St Michael and All Angels) (St Paul's Church Centre) *Win 3*   **P** *Bp*   **V** *vacant*

KNIGHTSBRIDGE (St Paul) Wilton Place   *see* Wilton Place St Paul *Lon*

KNILL (St Michael and All Angels)   *see* Presteigne w Discoed, Kinsham, Lingen and Knill *Heref*

KNIPTON (All Saints)   *see* High Framland Par *Leic*

KNIVETON (St Michael and All Angels)   *see* Hulland, Atlow, Kniveton, Bradley and Hognaston *Derby*

KNOCKHOLT (St Katharine) w Halstead *Roch 9*   **P** *D&C*
R T M EDWARDS

KNOCKIN (St Mary)   *see* Kinnerley w Melverley, Knockin w Maesbrook and Maesbury *Lich*

KNODISHALL (St Lawrence)   *see* Alde Sandlings *St E*

KNOOK (St Margaret)   *see* Upper Wylye Valley *Sarum*

KNOSSINGTON (St Peter)   *see* Whatborough Gp *Leic*

KNOTTINGLEY (St Botolph) and Kellington w Whitley *Leeds 15*   **P** *Patr Bd*   **TR** C A FLATTERS

KNOTTY ASH (St John) *Liv 5*   **P** R W *Derby*   **V** J M JESSON

KNOWBURY (St Paul)   *see* The Ashfords *Heref*

KNOWL HILL (St Peter)   *see* Wargrave w Knowl Hill *Ox*

KNOWLE (Holy Nativity) *Bris 1*   **P** *Bp*   **V** *vacant*

KNOWLE (St Barnabas)   *see* Filwood Park *Bris*

KNOWLE (St John the Baptist, St Lawrence and St Anne) *Birm 6*   **P** *Bp*   **V** G P LANHAM   **C** E J SPENCER, S A JOHNSON

KNOWLE (St John)   *see* Budleigh Salterton, E Budleigh w Bicton etc *Ex*

KNOWLE (St Martin) *Bris 1*   **P** *Bp*   **V** R A WARING
C L J VERRALL-KELLY

KNOWLE, WEST (Holy Cross)   *see* Filwood Park *Bris*

KNOWSLEY (St Mary)   *see* 4Saints Team *Liv*

KNOWSTONE (St Peter)   *see* Bishopsnympton, Charles, E Anstey, High Bray etc *Ex*

KNOYLE, EAST (St Mary the Virgin)   *see* St Bartholomew *Sarum*

KNOYLE, WEST (St Mary the Virgin)   *see* Mere w W Knoyle and Maiden Bradley *Sarum*

KNUTSFORD (St Cross) Cross Town *Ches 12*   **P** Mrs J Singer
V P D DEAKIN

KNUTSFORD (St John the Baptist) and Toft *Ches 12*   **P** *Bp* (3 turns), Mrs L M Anderson (1 turn)   **V** N T ATKINSON
C T R HOLLINGSBEE   **NSM** H E ECCLES, M J LACY

KNUTTON (St Mary) *Lich 9*   **P** Sir Beville Stanier Bt and T H G Howard-Sneyd Esq (alt)   **V** J WATKINS
NSM S M SIDEBOTTOM

KNUZDEN (St Oswald) *Blackb 2*   **P** *Bp*   **V** M A MORRIS

KNYPERSLEY (St John the Evangelist)   *see* Biddulph Moor and Knypersley *Lich*

KYME, NORTH (St Luke)   *see* Carr Dyke Gp *Linc*

KYME, SOUTH (St Mary and All Saints)   *as above*

KYNNERSLEY (St Chad)   *see* Edgmond w Kynnersley and Preston Wealdmoors *Lich*

KYRE WYARD (St Mary)   *see* Teme Valley S *Worc*

LACEBY (St Margaret)   *see* Wolds Gateway Group *Linc*

LACEY GREEN (Church Hall)   *see* Wilmslow *Ches*

LACEY GREEN (St John the Evangelist)   *see* Risborough *Ox*

LACH DENNIS (All Saints)   *see* Lostock Gralam *Ches*

LACHE CUM SALTNEY (St Mark) *Ches 2*   **P** *Bp*
V H E A JOHNSTON   C A J THOMAS, H HELVADJIAN,
S CHESTERS

LACKFORD (St Lawrence)   *see* Lark Valley and N Bury *St E*

LACOCK (St Cyriac)   *see* Gtr Corsham and Lacock *Bris*

LADBROKE (All Saints)   *see* Harbury and Ladbroke *Cov*

LADBROKE GROVE (St Michael and All Angels)   *see* Notting Hill St Mich and Ch Ch *Lon*

LADDINGFORD (St Mary)   *see* Yalding w Collier Street *Roch*

LADOCK (St Ladoca)   *see* Probus, Ladock and Grampound w Creed and St Erme *Truro*

LADY BAY (All Hallows) w Holme Pierrepont and Adbolton *S'well 6*   **P** *Bp and DBP* (jt)   **V** *vacant*

LADYBARN (St Chad) *Man 2*   **P** *Bp*   **R** M R HEWERDINE
NSM A J SIMPSON

LADYBROOK (St Mary the Virgin)   *see* Mansfield St Jo w St Mary *S'well*

LADYWOOD (St John the Evangelist) (St Peter) *Birm 1*
P Trustees   **V** I HARPER

LAFFORD Group, The NORTH, comprising Anwick, Cranwell, Evedon, Leasingham, and Ruskington *Linc 14*   **P** *Bp and*

DBP (jt)   **P-in-c** D A JENKINS   **NSM** L M HUNTER,
N R PANTING

LAFFORD, SOUTH, comprising Aswarby, Aunsby, Dembleby, Folkingham, Newton, Osbournby, Pickworth, Scott Willoughby, Swarby, Threekingham, and Walcot *Linc 14*
P G Heathcote Esq, Bp, J Wilson Esq, D&C, DBP, N Playne Esq, Sir Bruno Welby Bt, and Lady Willoughby de Eresby (by turn)
R *vacant*

LAINDON (St Nicholas) w Dunton *Chelmsf 11*   **P** *Bp*
P-in-c A A PETRINE

LAIRA (St Augustine)   *see* Plymouth Em w St Paul *Ex*

LAIRA (St Mary the Virgin)   *see* Sutton-on-Plym, Plymouth St Simon and St Mary *Ex*

LAISTERDYKE (St Mary)   *see* Tong and Laisterdyke *Leeds*

LAITHKIRK (not known)   *see* Lower Teesdale *Leeds*

LAKE (Good Shepherd) *Portsm 7*   **P** *Bp*   **C** C A SMITH

LAKENHAM (St Alban)   *see* The Mitre Benefice *Nor*

LAKENHAM (St John the Baptist and All Saints)   *see* Nor Lakenham St Jo and All SS and Tuckswood *Nor*

LAKENHAM (St Mark)   *see* Nor Lakenham St Mark *Nor*

LAKENHEATH (St Mary), Santon Downham and Elveden *St E 7*   **P** *Bp, Earl of Iveagh, and D&C Ely* (1 turn), *Ld Chan* (1 turn)   **NSM** P W TAMS

LALEHAM (All Saints) *Lon 13*   **P** Earl of Lucan   **V** A SAVILLE
C J M LAWES   **NSM** E J A SAVILLE

LAMARSH (Holy Innocents)   *see* N Hinckford *Chelmsf*

LAMBERHURST (St Mary) and Matfield *Roch 8*   **P** *D&C and V Brenchley* (jt)   **V** A J AXON   **NSM** A J CAMERON

LAMBETH (St John the Evangelist)   *see* Waterloo St Jo w St Andr *S'wark*

LAMBETH, NORTH (St Anselm) (St Peter) *S'wark 11*   **P** *The Crown* (1 turn), *Patr Bd* (2 turns)   **TR** A R AAGAARD
TV D L GIBBS   **C** M I JOHN   **Hon C** S MOUGHTIN
NSM M A K HILBORN, S E DAVIDSON

LAMBETH, SOUTH (St Anne and All Saints) *S'wark 11*
P Abp and Bp   **V** F C DYER   **C** L M ENGEHAM, V J ELSTON

LAMBETH, SOUTH (St Margaret the Queen)   *see* Streatham Hill St Marg *S'wark*

LAMBETH, SOUTH (St Stephen) *S'wark 11*   **P** *CPAS*
V *vacant*

LAMBFOLD Benefice, The, comprising Adstone, Blakesley, Farthingstone, Lichborough, and Maidford *Pet 5*   **P** *Bp, Hertf Coll Ox, Sons of Clergy Corp, and S R de C Grant-Rennick Esq* (alt)   **R** S D M STANLEY

LAMBLEY (Holy Trinity) *S'well 7*   **P** Revd W J Gull
P-in-c M D JOHNSON

LAMBLEY (St Mary and St Patrick)   *see* Alston Moor *Newc*

LAMBOURN VALLEY, The (St Michael and All Angels) *Ox 6*
P *Bp and Ch Ch Ox* (jt)   **V** J M MINTERN

LAMBOURNE (St Mary and All Saints)   *see* Vale of Roding *Chelmsf*

LAMBROOK, EAST (St James)   *see* S Petherton w The Seavingtons and The Lambrooks *B & W*

LAMERTON (St Peter)   *see* Milton Abbot, Dunterton, Lamerton etc *Ex*

LAMESLEY (St Andrew)   *see* Harlow Green and Lamesley *Dur*

LAMMAS (St Andrew)   *see* Aylsham and Distr *Nor*

LAMORBEY (Holy Redeemer) *Roch 17*   **P** *Bp*   **V** M J JEMMETT

LAMORBEY (Holy Trinity) *Roch 17*   **P** Mrs H K L Whittow
V M F J BLAKELY   **NSM** R L C TULLOH

LAMORRAN (St Moran)   *see* Tresillian and Lamorran w Merther *Truro*

LAMP, comprising Emberton, Haversham w Little Linford, and Tyringham w Filgrave *Ox 16*   **P** *CPAS*
OLM H J LOWNDES

LAMPLUGH (St Michael) w Ennerdale *Carl 5*   **P** Trustees
R *vacant*

LAMPORT (All Saints)   *see* Maidwell w Draughton, Lamport w Faxton *Pet*

LAMYATT (St Mary and St John)   *see* Alham Vale *B & W*

LANCASTER (Christ Church) *Blackb 11*   **P** V Lanc and Trustees (alt)   **V** C L BACKHOUSE

LANCASTER (St Chad)   *see* Skerton St Chad *Blackb*

LANCASTER (St Mary) w St John and St Anne *Blackb 11*
P Trustees   **V** L B VASEY-SAUNDERS

LANCASTER (St Paul)   *see* Scotforth *Blackb*

LANCASTER (St Thomas) *Blackb 11*   **P** *CPAS*
V J L SCAMMAN   **C** C COOKE, H C SCAMMAN,
M W A GUILDER   **OLM** A M LETCHFORD

LANCHESTER (All Saints) and Burnhope *Dur 2*   **P** Ld Chan (2 turns), The Crown (1 turn)   **P-in-c** L A SUTHERLAND
C S M MARTIN

LANCING (St James the Less) w Coombes *Chich 7*   **P** *Bp*
Lon   **R** *vacant*

LANCING (St Michael and All Angels) *Chich 7*   **P** *Bp*
V F A J SMITH   **C** T K FINK-JENSEN

LANDBEACH (All Saints) *Ely 6* **P** *CCC Cam*
P-in-c D J CHAMBERLIN　**C** P H BUTLER　**NSM** S BRADFORD
LANDCROSS (Holy Trinity) *see* Bideford, Landcross,
Littleham etc *Ex*
LANDEWEDNACK (St Wynwallow) *see* St Keverne, St Ruan w
St Grade and Landewednack *Truro*
LANDFORD (St Andrew) *see* Forest and Avon *Sarum*
LANDKEY (St Paul) *see* Swimbridge, W Buckland, Landkey,
and E Buckland *Ex*
LANDRAKE (St Michael) w St Erney and Botus Fleming
Truro 11 **P** *Bp and MMCET (jt)* **V** *vacant*
LANDSCOVE (St Matthew) *see* Buckfastleigh, Dean Prior,
Littlehempston etc *Ex*
LANDULPH (St Leonard and St Dilpe) *see* Tamar Valley *Truro*
LANDYWOOD (St Andrew) *see* Gt Wyrley *Lich*
LANE END (Holy Trinity) *see* S Chilterns *Ox*
LANEAST (St Sidwell and St Gulvat) *see* Moorland Gp *Truro*
LANEHAM (St Peter) *see* The Rivers *S'well*
LANERCOST (St Mary Magdalene), Walton, Gilsland and
Nether Denton *Carl 2* **P** *Bp, Adn, and the Hon P C W*
Howard (jt) **P-in-c** A M HUGHES
LANESIDE (St Peter) *Blackb 1* **P** *V Haslingden St Jas*
V S C BROWN
LANGAR (St Andrew) *see* Wiverton in the Vale *S'well*
LANGCLIFFE (St John the Evangelist) w Stainforth and
Horton-in-Ribblesdale *Leeds 17* **P** *Bp, Adn Craven, W R G*
Bell Esq, N Caton Esq, and Churchwardens of Horton-in-
Ribblesdale (jt) **P-in-c** S C DAWSON
LANGDALE (Holy Trinity) *see* Loughrigg *Carl*
LANGDALE END (St Peter) *see* Upper Derwent *York*
LANGDALE, LITTLE (Mission Chapel) *see* Loughrigg *Carl*
LANGDON HILLS (St Mary and All Saints) *Chelmsf 11*
P *D&C St Paul's* **R** *vacant*
LANGDON, EAST (St Augustine) *see* St Margarets-at-Cliffe w
Westcliffe etc *Cant*
LANGDON, WEST (St Mary the Virgin) *as above*
LANGELEI, comprising Apsley End, Bennetts End, King's
Langley, and Leverstock Green *St Alb 2* **P** *Patr Bd*
TR E M HOOD　**TV** J A MCDONALD, R L HOWLETT
NSM J C PERRIS
LANGFORD (Blessed Virgin Mary) *see* Churchill and
Langford *B & W*
LANGFORD (St Andrew) *see* Henlow and Langford *St Alb*
LANGFORD (St Bartholomew) *see* E Trent *S'well*
LANGFORD (St Giles) *see* Heybridge w Langford *Chelmsf*
LANGFORD (St Matthew) *see* Shill Valley and Broadshire *Ox*
LANGFORD BUDVILLE (St Peter) *see* Wellington and Distr
B & W
LANGFORD, LITTLE (St Nicholas of Mira) *see* Wylye and Till
Valley *Sarum*
LANGHAM (St George) *see* Gillingham, Milton-on-Stour
and Silton *Sarum*
LANGHAM (St Mary the Virgin) *see* Badwell and Walsham
St E
LANGHAM (St Mary the Virgin) w Boxted *Chelmsf 20* **P** *Bp*
and Duchy of Lanc (alt) **C** H GREENLAND, H R COOPER,
R G GIBBS, S L HAYWARD　**NSM** P W MANN
OLM A L MASON
LANGHAM (St Peter and St Paul) *see* Oakham, Ashwell,
Braunston, Brooke, Egleton etc *Pet*
LANGHAM EPISCOPI (St Andrew and St Mary) *see* Stiffkey
and Bale *Nor*
LANGHAM PLACE (All Souls) *Lon 4* **P** *The Crown*
R C W D SKRINE　**C** L A IJAZ, M B JACKSON, P J NICHOLAS,
P KEEN, R I TICE　**Hon C** M J H MEYNELL
LANGHO BILLINGTON (St Leonard) *Blackb 7* **P** *V Blackb*
V T J SWINDELLS
LANGLEY (All Saints and Martyrs) *Man 6* **P** *Patr Bd*
V P H MILLER　**NSM** A M CLISSOLD, N R WHITAKER,
S D MORGAN
LANGLEY (St Francis) *see* Fawley *Win*
LANGLEY (St John the Evangelist) *see* Clavering w Langley,
Arkesden etc *Chelmsf*
LANGLEY (St John) *see* Oldbury, Langley and Londonderry
Birm
LANGLEY (St Mary the Virgin) *see* Arden Valley *Cov*
LANGLEY (St Mary) *see* N Downs *Cant*
LANGLEY (St Michael) *see* Loddon, Sisland, Chedgrave,
Hardley and Langley *Nor*
LANGLEY BURRELL (St Peter) *see* Chippenham St Paul w
Hardenhuish etc *Bris*
LANGLEY GREEN (St Leonard) *see* Ifield *Chich*
LANGLEY MARISH (St Mary the Virgin) *Ox 12* **P** *Patr Bd*
TV O I AOKO
LANGLEY MARSH (St Luke's Mission Church) *see*
Wiveliscombe and the Hills *B & W*

LANGLEY MILL (St Andrew) and Aldercar *Derby 8* **P** *V*
Heanor **P-in-c** K PADLEY　**C** L SHEMILT, P M HALLSWORTH
LANGLEY PARK (All Saints) *see* Dur N *Dur*
LANGLEYBURY (St Paul) *St Alb 6* **P** *D W A Loyd Esq*
V R J C WEBSTER
LANGNEY (St Richard of Chichester) *Chich 14* **P** *Bp*
V *vacant*
LANGOLD (St Luke) *see* Carlton-in-Lindrick and Langold w
Oldcotes *S'well*
LANGRICK (St Margaret of Scotland) *see* Brothertoft Gp *Linc*
LANGRIDGE (St Mary Magdalene) *see* Bath Weston All SS w
N Stoke and Langridge *B & W*
LANGRISH (St John the Evangelist) *Portsm 4* **P** *Bp*
Hon C M P JEPP
LANGSETT (St Bartholomew) *see* Sheffield Vine *Sheff*
LANGSTONE (St Nicholas) *see* Havant *Portsm*
LANGTOFT (St Michael) *see* Ness Gp *Linc*
LANGTOFT (St Peter) w Foxholes, Butterwick, Cottam and
Thwing *York 10* **P** *Abp and Keble Coll Ox (2 turns), Ld Chan*
(1 turn) **V** S P GRANT
LANGTON (St Andrew) *see* W Buckrose *York*
LANGTON (St Margaret) *see* Woodhall Spa Gp *Linc*
LANGTON (St Peter) *as above*
LANGTON BY PARTNEY (St Peter and St Paul) *see*
Bolingbroke Deanery *Linc*
LANGTON GREEN (All Saints) *Roch 12* **P** *R Speldhurst*
V L J TRAINOR　**C** C M A MILLS
LANGTON HERRING (St Peter) *see* Abbotsbury, Portesham
and Langton Herring *Sarum*
LANGTON LONG (All Saints) *see* Blandford Forum and
Langton Long *Sarum*
LANGTON MATRAVERS (St George) *see* St Aldhelm *Sarum*
LANGTON ON SWALE (St Wilfrid) *see* Lower Swale *Leeds*
LANGTON, GREAT (St Wilfrid) *as above*
LANGTON-BY-WRAGBY (St Giles) *see* Wragby Gp *Linc*
LANGTONS and Shangton, The, comprising Church
Langton w Tur Langton, Shangton, and Thorpe Langton
Leic 5 **P** *Bp, E Brudenell Esq, and MMCET (jt)* **V** *vacant*
LANGTREE (All Saints) *see* Shebbear, Buckland Filleigh,
Sheepwash etc *Ex*
LANGTREE, comprising Checkendon, Ipsden, North Stoke,
Stoke Row, Whitchurch, and Woodcote *Ox 24* **P** *Patr Bd*
TR K G DAVIES　**TV** J R LEACH, J W BLAIR, L J SMITH
NSM A M LINTON
LANGWATHBY (St Peter) *see* Cross Fell Gp *Carl*
LANGWITH, UPPER (Holy Cross) *see* E Scarsdale *Derby*
LANGWORTH (St Hugh) *see* Barlings *Linc*
LANHYDROCK (St Hydrock) *see* Bodmin *Truro*
LANIVET (not known) *as above*
LANLIVERY (St Brevita) *see* Lostwithiel Parishes *Truro*
LANLIVERY (St Brevita) *Truro 10* **P** *Bp (1 turn), Adn Bodmin*
(1 turn), and DBP (2 turns) **V** *vacant*
LANN PYDAR Benefice, The, comprising St Columb Major,
St Ervan, St Eval, and St Mawgan-in-Pydar *Truro 6* **P** *Bp and*
D&C (jt) **R** H C BABER　**C** T L LOWE
LANNER (Christ Church) *see* Redruth w Lanner and Treleigh
Truro
LANREATH (St Marnarch) *see* Trelawny *Truro*
LANSALLOS (St Ildierna) *as above*
LANSDOWN (St Stephen) *see* Charlcombe w Bath St Steph
B & W
LANTEGLOS BY FOWEY (St Wyllow) *see* Trelawny *Truro*
LAPAL (St Peter) *see* Halas *Worc*
LAPFORD (St Thomas of Canterbury) *see* N Creedy *Ex*
LAPLEY (All Saints) *see* Watershed *Lich*
LAPWORTH (St Mary the Virgin) *Birm 2* **P** *Mert Coll Ox*
R P H GERARD
LARK VALLEY and North Bury, comprising Bury St Edmunds
All Saints, St George and St John, Culford, Flempton,
Fornham, Lackford, Timworth, and West Stow and
Wordwell *St E 9* **P** *Patr Bd* **TR** A P MILLER　**TV** A MILLER,
V E GAGEN　**NSM** J C MANN, M M WEBB
LARKFIELD (Holy Trinity) *Roch 7* **P** *DBP*
P-in-c N L WILLIAMS
LARLING (St Ethelbert) *see* E w W Harling, Bridgham w
Roudham, Larling etc *Nor*
LASBOROUGH (St Mary) *see* Boxwell, Leighterton,
Didmarton, Oldbury etc *Glouc*
LASHAM (St Mary) *see* Bentworth, Lasham, Medstead and
Shalden *Win*
LASHBROOK (Mission Room) *see* Shiplake w Dunsden and
Harpsden *Ox*
LASTINGHAM (St Mary) w Appleton-le-Moors, Rosedale
and Cropton *York 19* **P** *Abp (2 turns), Ld Chan (1 turn)*
NSM D HADDON-REECE

LATCHFORD (Christ Church) *Ches 4*   **P** *R Grappenhall*
C R J ICKE
LATCHFORD (St James) (St Hilda) *Ches 4*   **P** *R Grappenhall*
P-in-c M L RIDLEY   **C** R J ICKE
LATCHINGDON (Christ Church)   *see* Mayland and
Latchingdon *Chelmsf*
LATHBURY (All Saints)   *see* Newport Pagnell w Lathbury and
Moulsoe *Ox*
LATHOM PARK (St John)   *see* Ormskirk *Liv*
LATIMER (St Mary Magdalene)   *see* Chenies and Lt Chalfont,
Latimer and Flaunden *Ox*
LATTON (St John the Baptist)   *see* Upper Thames *Bris*
LATTON (St Mary the Virgin)   *see* St Mary-at-Latton *Chelmsf*
LAUGHTON (All Saints)   *see* Trentcliffe Gp *Linc*
LAUGHTON (All Saints) w Ripe and Chalvington *Chich 21*
P *Bp (2 turns), Hertf Coll Ox (1 turn)*   **R** G R SMITH
LAUGHTON (St Luke)   *see* Foxton w Gumley and Laughton
Leic
LAUGHTON-EN-LE-MORTHEN (All Saints) and Throapham
Sheff 5   **P** *Bp*   **P-in-c** M RAJKOVIC
LAUNCELLS (St Andrew and St Swithin)   *see* N Kernow *Truro*
LAUNCESTON (St Mary Magdalene) (St Thomas the
Apostle) (St Stephen) *Truro 9*   **P** *Patr Bd*
P-in-c P M KNIGHT   **TV** A J HARDY, S P CLANCY   **C** N FARR
NSM H DAVIES
LAUNDITCH AND THE UPPER NAR, comprising Beeston-
next-Mileham, Bittering Parva, East Lexham, Great
Dunham, Great and Little Fransham, Gressenhall, Litcham
w Kempston, Little Dunham, Longham, Mileham,
Rougham, Stanfield, Tittleshall w Godwick, Weasenham,
Wellingham, Wendling, and West Lexham *Nor 16*   **P** *Ld*
Chan (1 turn), Patr Bd (2 turns)   **C** M A FIFE
NSM H B DE LYON, J HEMP, K D BLOGG
LAUNTON (Assumption of the Blessed Virgin Mary)   *see*
Bicester w Bucknell, Caversfield and Launton *Ox*
LAVANT (St Mary) (St Nicholas) *Chich 2*   **P** *Duke of*
Richmond and Gordon   **P-in-c** M G WEATHERILL
LAVENDER HILL (The Ascension) and Battersea St Philip w
St Bartholomew *S'wark 14*   **P** *Bp and Keble Coll Ox (jt)*
V P R J KENNEDY
LAVENDON (St Michael) w Cold Brayfield, Clifton Reynes
and Newton Blossomville *Ox 16*   **P** *T V Sutthery Esq, The*
Revd S F Hamill-Stewart, Exors M E Farrer Esq, and Bp (jt)
R C E PUMFREY
LAVENHAM (St Peter and St Paul) w Preston *St E 6*   **P** *G&C*
Coll Cam, and Em Coll Cam (by turn)   **R** S G F EARL
C G D NAYLOR
LAVER, HIGH (All Saints) w Magdalen Laver and Little
Laver and Matching *Chelmsf 3*   **P** *Bp*   **P-in-c** C A HAWKINS
LAVER, LITTLE (St Mary the Virgin)   *see* High Laver w
Magdalen Laver and Lt Laver etc *Chelmsf*
LAVERSTOCK (St Andrew)   *see* Salisbury St Mark and
Laverstock *Sarum*
LAVERSTOKE (St Mary)   *see* Overton w Laverstoke and
Freefolk *Win*
LAVERTON (Blessed Virgin Mary)   *see* Hardington Vale *B & W*
LAVINGTONS, Cheverells, and Easterton, The *Sarum 17*
P *Bp and Ch Ch Ox (jt)*   **R** M J HARRISON
LAWFORD (St Mary), Little Bentley and The Bromleys
Chelmsf 21   **P** *St Jo Coll Cam, Community of the Resurr*
Mirfield, and Em Coll Cam (jt)   **NSM** S J MORRIS
LAWHITTON (St Michael)   *see* Three Rivers *Truro*
LAWLEY (St John the Evangelist)   *see* Cen Telford *Lich*
LAWRENCE WESTON (St Peter) and Avonmouth *Bris 2*
P *Bp*   **P-in-c** A J MURRAY   **C** E C KING, M J GRIFFITHS
NSM F E BREALEY
LAWRES Group, The SOUTH, comprising Cherry Willingham,
Fiskerton, and Reepham *Linc 5*   **P** *D&C Linc, D&C Pet, and*
Mercers' Co (jt)   **R** D P GREEN   **C** J A BELLSHAW
OLM C BASON
LAWSHALL (All Saints)   *see* St Edm Way *St E*
LAWTON (All Saints)   *see* Church Lawton *Ches*
LAWTON MOOR (St Michael and All Angels) *Man 2*   **P** *Bp*
V C D HEWITT
LAXEY (Christ Church)   *see* Onchan, Lonan and Laxey *S & M*
LAXFIELD (All Saints)   *see* Four Rivers *St E*
LAXTON (All Saints)   *see* King's Cliffe, Bulwick and
Blatherwycke, Collyweston etc *Pet*
LAXTON (St Michael)   *see* Kneesall w Laxton and Wellow
S'well
LAXTON (St Peter)   *see* Howden *York*
LAYER BRETON (St Mary the Virgin)   *see* Thurstable and
Winstree *Chelmsf*
LAYER MARNEY (St Mary the Virgin) *as above*
LAYER-DE-LA-HAYE (St John the Baptist) *as above*
LAYHAM (St Andrew)   *see* Hadleigh, Layham and Shelley *St E*

LAYSTON   *see* Aspenden, Buntingford and Westmill *St Alb*
LAYTON (St Mark) and Staining St Luke *Blackb 8*   **P** *CPAS*
V P A LILLICRAP   **C** M J ROBINSON
LAYTON, EAST (Christ Church)   *see* Forcett and Aldbrough
and Melsonby *Leeds*
LAZONBY (St Nicholas)   *see* Kirkoswald, Renwick w Croglin,
Gt Salkeld etc *Carl*
LEA (St Christopher) (St Barnabas) *Blackb 13*   **P** *Bp*
V P G HAMBORG   **NSM** M R CLAYTON
LEA (St Giles)   *see* Woodbridge *Bris*
LEA CROSS (St Anne)   *see* Pontesbury I and II *Heref*
LEA Group, The (St Helen), including Corringham, Gate
Burton, Heapham, Knaith, Marton, Pilham, Springthorpe,
and Upton w Kexby *Linc 2*   **P** *DBP, Bp, and Exors Lt Col J E*
W G Sandars (1 turn), Ld Chan (1 turn)   **R** P WAIN
OLM D J COTTON
LEA HALL (St Richard)   *see* Garretts Green and Lea Hall *Birm*
LEA MARSTON (St John the Baptist)   *see* The Whitacres, Lea
Marston, and Shustoke *Birm*
LEA, THE (St John the Baptist)   *see* Ariconium *Heref*
LEADEN RODING (St Michael)   *see* S Rodings *Chelmsf*
LEADENHAM (St Swithin) *Linc 22*   **P** *P R Reeve Esq*
R C A GOLDSMITH
LEADGATE (St Ives) *Dur 2*   **P** *Bp*   **P-in-c** J FISHER
LEADON VALE   *see* Redmarley D'Abitot, Bromesberrow,
Pauntley etc *Glouc*
LEAFIELD (St Michael and All Angels)   *see* Forest Edge *Ox*
LEAGRAVE (St Luke) *St Alb 12*   **P** *Bp*
V G K N SENTAMU BAVERSTOCK
LEAKE (St Mary) w Over and Nether Silton and Kepwick
York 18   **P** *Abp*   **P-in-c** D E GAMBLE   **NSM** K M BROWN,
W A DEWING
LEAKE, EAST (St Mary), WEST (St Helena), Stanford-on-
Soar, Rempstone and Costock *S'well 6*   **P** *Bp, DBP, Lord*
Belper, and SS Coll Cam (jt)   **P-in-c** T J PARKER
C M W M ALLEN
LEAKE, OLD (St Mary) w Wrangle *Linc 21*   **P** *Bp and DBP*
(alt)   **V** *vacant*
LEALHOLM (St James's Chapel)   *see* Middle Esk Moor *York*
LEAM LANE (St Andrew) *Dur 11*   **P** *Bp*   **V** *vacant*
LEAM VALLEY, comprising Flecknoe, Grandborough,
Leamington Hastings, and Willoughby *Cov 6*   **P** *Bp (2 turns),*
Mrs H M O Lodder (1 turn)   **Hon C** B C CLUTTON
LEAMINGTON HASTINGS (All Saints)   *see* Leam Valley *Cov*
LEAMINGTON PRIORS (All Saints) *Cov 11*   **P** *Bp*
V C H WILSON
LEAMINGTON PRIORS (St Mary) *Cov 11*   **P** *Ch Patr Trust*
V R A JONES
LEAMINGTON PRIORS (St Paul) *Cov 11*   **P** *Ch Patr Trust*
V J N JEE   **C** A D RUFFHEAD   **Hon C** G L PRINGLE
LEAMINGTON SPA (Holy Trinity) *Cov 11*   **P** *Bp and M*
Heber-Percy Esq (jt)   **V** C H WILSON   **C** E L PEERS
NSM F A SMITH
LEAMINGTON SPA (St Mark)   *see* New Milverton *Cov*
LEAMINGTON, SOUTH (St John the Baptist) *Cov 11*   **P** *Bp*
V S PARKER
LEAMORE (St Aidan)   *see* Blakenall Heath *Lich*
LEASINGHAM (St Andrew)   *see* N Lafford Gp *Linc*
LEASOWE (St Chad) *Ches 7*   **P** *Bp*   **P-in-c** D S MARSHALL
LEATHERHEAD (All Saints) (St Mary and St Nicholas) and
Mickleham *Guildf 10*   **P** *Bp Guildf and D&C Roch (jt)*
R G D OSBORNE
LEATHLEY (St Oswald)   *see* Washburn and Mid-Wharfe *Leeds*
LEATON (Holy Trinity) and Albrighton w Battlefield *Lich 19*
P *Mrs J M Jagger*   **P-in-c** H M LINS
LEAVELAND (St Laurence)   *see* Shepherds Lees *Cant*
LEAVENHEATH (St Matthew)   *see* Stoke by Nayland w
Leavenheath etc *St E*
LEAVENING (not known)   *see* W Buckrose *York*
LEAVESDEN (All Saints) *St Alb 6*   **P** *Bp*   **V** E B GREEN
C P L MADDOX
LECHLADE (St Lawrence)   *see* S Cotswolds *Glouc*
LECK (St Peter)   *see* E Lonsdale *Blackb*
LECKFORD (St Nicholas)   *see* Mid Test *Win*
LECKHAMPSTEAD (Assumption of the Blessed Virgin Mary)
see N Buckingham w Stowe *Ox*
LECKHAMPSTEAD (St James)   *see* W Downland *Ox*
LECKHAMPTON (St Christopher)   *see* S Cheltenham *Glouc*
LECKHAMPTON (St Peter) *as above*
LECKHAMPTON (St Philip and St James) *as above*
LECONFIELD (St Catherine)   *see* Lockington and Lund and
Scorborough w Leconfield *York*
LEDBURY (St Michael and All Angels) w Eastnor *Heref 5*
P *Bp (2 turns), J F S Hervey-Bathhurst Esq (1 turn)*
V K G M HILTON-TURVEY   **NSM** W F SIMMONDS

LEDGEMOOR (Mission Room) *see* Canon Pyon w King's Pyon, Birley and Wellington *Heref*
LEDSHAM (All Saints) w Fairburn *York 4* **P** *Lady Elizabeth Hastings Estate Charity* **V** *vacant*
LEDSTON LUCK (Mission Church) *see* Ledsham w Fairburn *York*
LEE (Good Shepherd) (St Peter) *S'wark 4* **P** *R Lee St Marg* **V** B C SHEPHERD **C** P J ADLINGTON **NSM** T NDEGWA
LEE (St Augustine) Grove Park *S'wark 4* **P** *Bp* **V** G A BERRIMAN
LEE (St John the Baptist) *see* The Lee *Ox*
LEE (St Margaret) *S'wark 4* **P** *Ld Chan* **R** T GOODE **C** D A WALKER
LEE (St Matthew) *see* Ilfracombe, Lee, Woolacombe, Bittadon etc *Ex*
LEE (St Mildred) Burnt Ash Hill *S'wark 4* **P** *Bp* **V** T W C LAKE **NSM** D S CLIFTON, M BARBER
LEE (St Oswald) *see* St Oswald in Lee w Bingfield *Newc*
LEE BROCKHURST (St Peter) *see* Wem, Lee Brockhurst etc *Lich*
LEE, The (St John the Baptist) *Ox 17* **P** *Bp* **V** C J HAYWOOD
LEEBOTWOOD (St Mary) *see* Dorrington w Leebotwood, Longnor, Stapleton etc *Heref*
LEEDS (All Hallows) *see* Headingley and All Hallows *Leeds*
LEEDS (All Souls) *see* Potternewton w Lt London *Leeds*
LEEDS (Parish Church) *see* Leeds City *Leeds*
LEEDS (St Aidan) *Leeds 10* **P** *R Leeds City* **V** A M HOFBAUER **C** S J OSBORN
LEEDS (St Cyprian and St James) *see* Burmantofts and Harehills *Leeds*
LEEDS (St Edmund King and Martyr) *see* Roundhay St Edm *Leeds*
LEEDS (St George) *Leeds 12* **P** *Simeon's Trustees* **TR** E L WOOLF **TV** A W C SMITH, J L COCKAYNE, J R SEABOURNE, J SWALES **C** E R RIDGEWAY, J WILKINS **Hon C** J H WALKER **NSM** C R SEABOURNE
LEEDS (St Nicholas) *see* N Downs *Cant*
LEEDS (St Paul) *see* Ireland Wood *Leeds*
LEEDS (St Saviour) *see* Cross Green and Richmond Hill *Leeds*
LEEDS (St Wilfrid) *Leeds 10* **P** *Bp* **V** *vacant*
LEEDS (St Wilfrid) Halton *see* Halton and Osmondthorpe *Leeds*
LEEDS Belle Isle (St John and St Barnabas) and Hunslet *see* Belle Isle and Hunslet *Leeds*
LEEDS CITY (St Peter) (Holy Trinity) *Leeds 10* **P** *DBP* **C** J A CLARK **NSM** S J ROBINSON
LEEDS Gipton (Church of the Epiphany) *see* Gipton and Oakwood *Leeds*
LEEDSTOWN (St James's Mission Church) *see* Crowan and Treslothan *Truro*
LEEK (All Saints) (St Edward the Confessor) (St John the Evangelist) (St Luke) (St Paul) and Meerbrook *Lich 8* **P** *Patr Bd* **TR** N R IRONS **TV** M J MALINS
LEEK WOOTTON (All Saints) *Cov 4* **P** *Lord Leigh* **V** J E PERRYMAN
LEEMING (St John the Baptist) *see* Bedale and Leeming and Thornton Watlass *Leeds*
LEEMING BAR (St Augustine) *as above*
LEE-ON-THE-SOLENT (St Faith) *Portsm 3* **P** *Bp* **V** P M CHAMBERLAIN **NSM** B T WILLIAMS, S E DENT
LEES HILL (Mission Hall) *see* Lanercost, Walton, Gilsland and Nether Denton *Carl*
LEESFIELD (St Thomas) *Man 5* **P** *Bp* **V** L E M WOODALL **C** A D RAMBLE, A SHERIDAN **NSM** C S STEEL
LEESFIELD Knoll's Lane (St Agnes) *see* Leesfield *Man*
LEGBOURNE (All Saints) and Wold Marsh *Linc 15* **P** *Ld Chan (1 turn), Bp, Exors Viscountess Chaplin, Ch Trust Fund Trust, D&C, and DBP (1 turn), Duchy of Lanc (1 turn)* **V** J E ROBINSON
LEGSBY (St Thomas) *Linc 7* **P** *Bp* **V** C V WALKER
LEICESTER (All Saints) *see* Scraptoft *Leic*
LEICESTER (Church of the Nativity) *see* Emmaus Par Team *Leic*
LEICESTER (Holy Apostles) (St Oswald) *Leic 1* **P** *DBP and Ridley Hall Cam (jt)* **P-in-c** J K RIDGE **C** K SZEJNMANN **NSM** A R LEIGHTON
LEICESTER (Holy Spirit) (St Andrew) (St Nicholas) *Leic 1* **P** *Bp* **TV** H F FADRIQUELA **C** J ARENS
LEICESTER (Holy Trinity w St John the Divine) *Leic 1* **P** *Peache Trustees* **V** E A SUTHERLAND **C** C W SZEJNMANN, J A A NORRIS, J K PATEL, L P DOBSON
LEICESTER (Martyrs) *Leic 1* **P** *Bp* **V** O B HERMO
LEICESTER (St Aidan) *Leic 1* **P** *Bp* **V** *vacant*
LEICESTER (St Alban) *see* Leic Resurr *Leic*
LEICESTER (St Anne) (St Paul) w St Augustine *Leic 1* **P** *Bp* **V** E A WILSON

LEICESTER (St Chad) *Leic 1* **P** *Bp* **P-in-c** M J COURT **C** C M KING
LEICESTER (St Christopher) *Leic 1* **P** *MMCET* **V** C P COLLINS **C** C R NDIGIRWA
LEICESTER (St James the Greater) *Leic 1* **P** *Bp* **V** A QUIGLEY **NSM** J M SHARP
LEICESTER (St John the Baptist) *see* Emmaus Par Team *Leic*
LEICESTER (St Margaret and All Saints) *see* The Abbey *Leic Leic*
LEICESTER (St Mary de Castro) *Leic 1* **P** *Bp* **NSM** S P WARD
LEICESTER (St Peter) *see* Highfield St Pet and Leic St Phil *Leic*
LEICESTER (St Philip) *as above*
LEICESTER (St Stephen) *see* N Evington *Leic*
LEICESTER (St Theodore of Canterbury) *Leic 1* **P** *Bp* **P-in-c** S LEIGHTON
LEICESTER Emmaus *see* Emmaus Par Team *Leic*
LEICESTER FOREST EAST (St Andrew) *Leic 9* **P** *Bp* **P-in-c** D J HOVER
LEICESTER Resurrection (St Alban) (All Saints) (St Peter) *Leic 1* **P** *Bp* **P-in-c** P CLEMENT **C** S GEORGE
LEICESTER, The Abbey (St Margaret and All Saints) *Leic 1* **P** *Bp* **TR** *vacant*
LEIGH (All Saints' Mission) *see* Bedford Leigh *Man*
LEIGH (All Saints) *see* Upper Thames *Bris*
LEIGH (All Saints) *see* Uttoxeter Area *Lich*
LEIGH (Holy Saviour) *see* White Horse *Sarum*
LEIGH (St Andrew) *see* Three Valleys *Sarum*
LEIGH (St Bartholomew) *see* Brockham Green and Leigh *S'wark*
LEIGH (St Catherine) *see* Twigworth, Down Hatherley, Norton, The Leigh etc *Glouc*
LEIGH (St Clement) *Chelmsf 12* **P** *Bp* **P-in-c** C R HILLMAN **NSM** C E SANDOVER
LEIGH (St Edburga) *see* Worcs W Rural *Worc*
LEIGH (St Mary the Virgin) *Man 7* **P** *Bp* **V** K D CRINKS **NSM** K E SLAYEN
LEIGH (St Mary) *Roch 11* **P** *Ch Trust Fund Trust* **V** L W G KEVIS
LEIGH PARK (St Francis) *Portsm 5* **P** *Bp* **V** J G P JEFFERY
LEIGH UPON MENDIP (St Giles) w Stoke St Michael *B & W 3* **P** *DBP and V Doulting (jt)* **P-in-c** A E DICKSON
LEIGH WOODS (St Mary the Virgin) *see* Abbots Leigh w Leigh Woods *Bris*
LEIGH, LITTLE (St Michael and All Angels) *see* Aston by Sutton, Lt Leigh and Lower Whitley *Ches*
LEIGH, NORTH (St Mary) *Ox 28* **P** *Ld Chan* **V** M I G DIXON
LEIGH, SOUTH (St James the Great) *see* Cogges and S Leigh *Ox*
LEIGH, WEST (St Alban) *Portsm 5* **P** *Bp* **P-in-c** K B GREEN
LEIGHLAND (St Giles) *see* Old Cleeve, Leighland and Treborough *B & W*
LEIGH-ON-SEA (St Aidan) the Fairway *Chelmsf 12* **P** *Bp* **V** G M TARRY
LEIGH-ON-SEA (St James) *Chelmsf 12* **P** *Bp* **V** W G BULLOCH
LEIGH-ON-SEA (St Margaret of Antioch) *Chelmsf 12* **P** *Bp* **P-in-c** D V WYLIE
LEIGHS, GREAT (St Mary the Virgin) and LITTLE (St John) and Little Waltham *Chelmsf 9* **P** *Linc Coll Ox, Reformation Ch Trust, and Ex Coll Ox (jt)* **C** D C PIERCE **NSM** S SYKES
LEIGHTERTON (St Andrew) *see* Boxwell, Leighterton, Didmarton, Oldbury etc *Glouc*
LEIGHTON (St Mary) *see* Wrockwardine Deanery *Lich*
LEIGHTON BROMSWOLD (St Mary) *see* W Leightonstone *Ely*
LEIGHTON BUZZARD (All Saints) *see* Ouzel Valley *St Alb*
LEIGHTON-CUM-MINSHULL VERNON (St Peter) and Warmingham *Ches 15* **P** *Bp and J C Crewe Esq (jt)* **V** C G CLEGHORN
LEIGHTONSTONE, EAST, comprising Brampton, Ellington, and Grafham *Ely 10* **P** *Bp and Peterho Cam (jt)* **P-in-c** D R GOLDTHORPE
LEIGHTONSTONE, NORTH, comprising Abbots Ripton, Alconbury, Buckworth, Great Gidding, Great and Little Stukeley, Hamerton, Kings Ripton, Upton, Winwick and Wood Walton *Ely 10* **P** *Patr Bd* **R** M C FLAHERTY **C** F E G BRAMPTON
LEIGHTONSTONE, SOUTH, comprising Barham and Woolley, Covington, Easton, Kimbolton, Spaldwick, Stow Longa, and Tilbrook *Ely 10* **P** *Patr Bd* **V** P M HOWSON
LEIGHTONSTONE, WEST, comprising Brington, Catworth, Keyston, Leighton Bromswold, Molesworth, and Old Weston *Ely 10* **P** *Bp and Sir Philip Naylor-Leyland Bt (jt)* **R** C M BRENNAND
LEINTHALL EARLES (St Andrew) *see* Kingsland w Eardisland, Aymestrey etc *Heref*

LEINTHALL STARKES (St Mary Magdalene) *see* Wigmore Abbey *Heref*

LEINTWARDINE (St Mary Magdalene) *as above*

LEIRE (St Peter) *see* Upper Soar *Leic*

LEISTON (St Margaret) *St E 14* **P** *Ch Hosp* **P-in-c** R W FINCH **NSM** M A H FINCH

LELANT (St Uny) *see* Carbis Bay w Lelant *Truro*

LEMINGTON, LOWER (St Leonard) *see* Moreton-in-Marsh w Batsford, Todenham etc *Glouc*

LEMSFORD (St John the Evangelist) *see* Bishop's Hatfield, Lemsford and N Mymms *St Alb*

LEN VALLEY, The, comprising Boughton Malherbe, Harrietsham, Lenham, and Ulcombe *Cant 13* **P** *Abp, All So Coll Ox, Viscount Chilston, and Lord Cornwallis (jt)* **P-in-c** J P HUGGINS **NSM** C L COLES

LENBOROUGH, comprising Adstock, Gawcott, Hillesden, and Padbury *Ox 11* **P** *Ch Ch Ox, Cam Univ, and New Coll Ox (2 turns), Ld Chan (1 turn)* **V** R M ROBERTS

LENHAM (St Mary) *see* Len Valley *Cant*

LENTON (Holy Trinity) (Priory Church of St Anthony) *S'well 9* **P** *CPAS* **NSM** M E HAMPSON

LENTON (St Peter) *see* N Beltisloe Par *Linc*

LENTON ABBEY (St Barnabas) *S'well 9* **P** *CPAS* C G T WHITE, J R LEES-ROBINSON, L P B O'BOYLE

LENWADE (All Saints) *see* Reepham and Wensum Valley *Nor*

LEOMINSTER (St Peter and St Paul) *Heref 6* **P** *Patr Bd* **TV** M BURNS, R W NOY **NSM** W DUMMERT **OLM** P SMITH

LEONARD STANLEY (St Swithun) *see* Stroudwater *Glouc*

LEPTON (St John the Evangelist), Emley and Flockton w Denby Grange *Leeds 5* **P** *Lord Savile, R Carter's Trustees, and R Kirkheaton (jt)* **R** V KEATING

LESBURY (St Mary) w Alnmouth *Newc 6* **P** *Dioc Soc* **NSM** B K COOPER

LESNEWTH (St Michael and All Angels) *see* Boscastle Gp *Truro*

LESSINGHAM (All Saints) *see* Bacton, Happisburgh, Hempstead w Eccles etc *Nor*

LETCHWORTH (St Mary the Virgin) (St Michael) *St Alb 3* **P** *Guild of All So* **P-in-c** R J KOZAK

LETCHWORTH (St Paul) w Willian *St Alb 3* **P** *Bp* **V** J C MCQUAID **C** R E SNOW **NSM** A J FERRIS

LETCOMBE BASSETT (St Michael and All Angels) *see* Ridgeway *Ox*

LETCOMBE REGIS (St Andrew) *as above*

LETHERINGHAM (St Mary) *see* Mid Loes *St E*

LETHERINGSETT (St Andrew) *see* Blakeney w Cley, Wiveton, Glandford etc *Nor*

LETTON (St John the Baptist) w Staunton, Byford, Mansel Gamage and Monnington *Heref 4* **P** *Sir John Cotterell Bt (2 turns), Exors Mrs Dew (1 turn), Ch Ch Ox (3 turns), and DBP (1 turn)* **R** P I HARVEY

LETWELL (St Peter) *see* Firbeck w Letwell *Sheff*

LEUSDON (St John the Baptist) *see* Ashburton, Bickington, Buckland in the Moor etc *Ex*

LEVEDALE (Mission Church) *see* Penkridge *Lich*

LEVELS ARC Benefice, The, comprising Drayton, Long Sutton and Long Load, Muchelney, and Pitney *B & W 5* **P** *Bp, Adn Wells, D&C, D&C Bris, and V Martock (jt)* **V** *vacant*

LEVEN (Holy Trinity) *see* Brandesburton and Leven *York*

LEVENS (St John the Evangelist) *Carl 10* **P** *Trustees* **P-in-c** B T KERR

LEVENSHULME (St Andrew) (St Mark) (St Peter) *Man 1* **P** *Bp and Trustees (jt)* **R** G E C REEVES

LEVER BRIDGE (St Stephen and All Martyrs) *see* Leverhulme *Man*

LEVER, GREAT (St Michael w St Bartholomew) *see* New Bury w Gt Lever *Man*

LEVER, LITTLE (St Matthew) *Man 3* **P** *V Bolton-le-Moors St Pet* **V** J WISEMAN **NSM** I C ANTHONY

LEVERHULME, comprising Breightmet, Lever Bridge, Tonge Fold, and Top o' th' Moss *Man 3* **P** *The Crown* **P-in-c** J I MOORES **TV** V C MASTERS

LEVERINGTON (St Leonard), Newton and Tydd St Giles *Ely 14* **P** *Bp* **R** S K GARDNER

LEVERSTOCK GREEN (Holy Trinity) *see* Langelei *St Alb*

LEVERTON (St Helena) *see* Freiston, Butterwick w Bennington, and Leverton *Linc*

LEVERTON, NORTH (St Martin) *see* The Clays *S'well*

LEVERTON, SOUTH (All Saints) *as above*

LEVINGTON (St Peter) *see* Orwell and Deben *St E*

LEVISHAM (St John the Baptist) *see* Pickering w Lockton and Levisham *York*

LEWANNICK (St Martin) *see* Three Rivers *Truro*

LEWES (St Anne) (St Michael) (St Thomas at Cliffe) w All Saints *Chich 21* **P** *Bp and SMF (1 turn), Ld Chan (1 turn)* **R** B B M BROWN **C** D N A BROAD **NSM** J A EGAR, P D YATES

LEWES (St John sub Castro) *see* Trin in Lewes *Chich*

LEWES (St John sub Castro) and South Malling *Chich 21* **P** *Bp and MMCET (jt)* **R** *vacant*

LEWES (St Mary) *see* Lewes St Anne and St Mich and St Thos etc *Chich*

LEWISHAM (St Mary) *S'wark 4* **P** *Earl of Dartmouth* **V** S P HALL **C** M J MARSH

LEWISHAM (St Stephen) and St Mark *S'wark 4* **P** *Keble Coll Ox* **V** M J BAILEY **NSM** P J HUDSON

LEWISHAM (St Swithun) Hither Green *S'wark 4* **P** *V Lewisham St Mary* **P-in-c** J A EVANS

LEWKNOR (St Margaret) *see* Thame *Ox*

LEWSEY (St Hugh) *see* Luton Lewsey St Hugh *St Alb*

LEWTRENCHARD (St Peter) *see* Lifton, Broadwoodwidger, Stowford etc *Ex*

LEXDEN (St Leonard) *Chelmsf 20* **P** *Bp* **P-in-c** M J SIMPKINS **OLM** J V MESSINGER, M F T WHITEMAN, V E MENDHAM

LEXHAM, EAST (St Andrew) *see* Launditch and the Upper Nar *Nor*

LEXHAM, WEST (St Nicholas) *as above*

LEYBOURNE (St Peter and St Paul) *Roch 7* **P** *Major Sir David Hawley Bt* **R** *vacant*

LEYBURN (St Matthew) w Bellerby *Leeds 22* **P** *Lord Bolton and Mrs M E Scragg (alt)* **V** S J HANSCOMBE

LEYFIELDS (St Francis) *see* Tamworth *Lich*

LEYLAND (St Ambrose) *Blackb 5* **P** *V Leyland* **NSM** C D F CROMBIE

LEYLAND (St Andrew) *Blackb 5* **P** *CPAS* **V** D G WHITEHOUSE **C** D J BELL, M B COOK

LEYLAND (St James) *Blackb 5* **P** *Sir Henry Farington Bt* **P-in-c** M A M WOLVERSON

LEYLAND (St John) *Blackb 5* **P** *V Leyland St Andr and CPAS (jt)* **V** A S MEESON **C** M WOODING **NSM** B J WILSON

LEYTON (All Saints) *Chelmsf 7* **P** *V St Mary's Leyton* **V** *vacant*

LEYTON (Christ Church) *Chelmsf 7* **P** *CPAS* **C** P B BRENTFORD

LEYTON (Emmanuel) *Chelmsf 7* **P** *Bp* **V** A ADEMOLA **NSM** E C ROSE

LEYTON (St Catherine) (St Paul) *Chelmsf 7* **P** *V Leyton St Mary w St Edw* **V** W N DONOGHUE

LEYTON (St Mary w St Edward) and St Luke *Chelmsf 7* **P** *Simeon's Trustees* **P-in-c** A S GORDON **C** M D NELSON, S P OPIE

LEYTONSTONE (Holy Trinity and St Augustine of Hippo) Harrow Green *Chelmsf 7* **P** *Bp* **C** P R KERSYS-HULL

LEYTONSTONE (St Andrew) *Chelmsf 7* **P** *Bp* **V** J P KENNINGTON

LEYTONSTONE (St John the Baptist) *Chelmsf 7* **P** *Bp* **V** D R BRITTON **C** E H BLACKHAM, P R KERSYS-HULL **NSM** P A KHAN

LEYTONSTONE (St Margaret w St Columba) *Chelmsf 7* **P** *Bp* **V** N WALSH

LEZANT (St Briochus) *see* Three Rivers *Truro*

LEZAYRE (Holy Trinity) *see* Bride, Lezayre and N Ramsey *S & M*

LICHBOROUGH (St Martin) *see* Lambfold *Pet*

LICHFIELD (Christ Church) and Longdon *Lich 1* **P** *Bp* **V** J L WATERFIELD

LICHFIELD (St Chad) *Lich 1* **P** *D&C* **R** P R CLARK **NSM** S FOSTER

LICHFIELD (St John's Hospital) Proprietary Chapel *Lich 1* **P** *Bp* **Master** *vacant*

LICHFIELD (St Michael) (St Mary) and Wall St John *Lich 1* **P** *D&C* **NSM** D YOUNGS, R L C BULL

LICKEY, The (Holy Trinity) *Birm 2* **P** *V Bromsgrove* **V** S L GIDNEY

LIDEN (St Timothy) *see* Swindon Dorcan *Bris*

LIDGATE (St Mary) *see* Bansfield *St E*

LIDGET GREEN (St Wilfrid) *see* Gt Horton and Lidget Green *Leeds*

LIFTON (St Mary), Broadwoodwidger, Stowford, Lewtrenchard, Thrushelton and Kelly w Bradstone *Ex 21* **P** *Bp, Mrs A M Baring-Gould Almond, W F Kelly Esq, and J B Wollocombe Esq (jt)* **P-in-c** P J CONWAY

LIGHTBOWNE (St Luke) *Man 1* **P** *D&C* **R** P HUTCHINS

LIGHTCLIFFE (St Matthew) and Hove Edge *Leeds 6* **P** *Bp and V Halifax (jt)* **V** K M BUCK

LIGHTHORNE (St Laurence) *Cov 8* **P** *Lady Willoughby de Broke* **P-in-c** L J LILLEY

LIGHTHOUSE LONDON *see* W Hampstead Trin *Lon*

LIGHTWATER (All Saints) *Guildf 6* **P** *Ld Chan and Bp (alt)* **V** D SIGSWORTH **OLM** R KIDD

LILBOURNE (All Saints) *see* Crick and Yelvertoft w Clay Coton and Lilbourne *Pet*

LILLESHALL (St Michael and All Angels) and Muxton *Lich 15* **P** *Bp* **V** M W LEFROY **C** V E DAY **OLM** J EVANS

LILLEY (St Peter) *see* King's Walden and Offley w Lilley *St Alb*

LILLINGSTONE DAYRELL (St Nicholas) *see* N Buckingham w Stowe *Ox*

LILLINGSTONE LOVELL (Assumption of the Blessed Virgin Mary) *as above*

LILLINGTON (St Martin) *see* Sherborne w Castleton, Lillington and Longburton *Sarum*

LILLINGTON (St Mary Magdalene) and Old Milverton *Cov 11* **P** *Bp* **V** W M SMITH **NSM** R C PANTLING, S M FAIRHURST

LILLIPUT (Holy Angels) *Sarum 7* **P** *Bp* **V** E L ELLIS **NSM** A J SMITH

LIMBER, GREAT (St Peter) *see* Brocklesby Park, Croxton and North Wolds *Linc*

LIMEHOUSE (St Anne) (St Peter) *Lon 7* **P** *BNC Ox* **R** R A BRAY **C** C T ELWOOD, M C C NODDER

LIMESIDE (St Chad) *see* Hollinwood and Limeside *Man*

LIMINGTON (The Blessed Virgin Mary) *see* Ilchester w Northover, Limington, Yeovilton etc *B & W*

LIMPENHOE (St Botolph) *see* Acle and Bure to Yare *Nor*

LIMPLEY STOKE (St Mary) *see* Freshford, Limpley Stoke and Hinton Charterhouse *B & W*

LIMPSFIELD (St Peter) (St Andrew) and Tatsfield *S'wark 25* **P** *Bp* **TR** H J COOK **TV** P J S PERKIN, V C SHORT

LINBY (St Michael) w Papplewick *S'well 4* **P** T W A Cundy *Esq* **P-in-c** T H RAAFF **C** M P WREFORD

LINCH (St Luke) w Iping Marsh, Milland and Rake and Stedham w Iping *Chich 3* **P** *Bp* **R** P A BANCROFT

LINCHMERE (St Peter) *see* Fernhurst, Lynchmere and Camelsdale *Chich*

LINCOLN (All Saints) *Linc 11* **P** *Bp* **V** P V NOBLE **C** R S COPLEY

LINCOLN (St Faith) (St Martin) (St Peter-at-Arches) *Linc 11* **P** *Bp* **P-in-c** J A PRESTWOOD **C** B E BRADY

LINCOLN (St George) Swallowbeck *Linc 11* **P** *Bp and V Skellingthorpe (jt)* **C** K P PICKERING

LINCOLN (St Giles) *Linc 11* **P** *Bp* **V** N J BUCK **C** M D WEBB

LINCOLN (St John the Baptist) (St John the Evangelist) *Linc 11* **P** *Bp* **V** R HESKINS

LINCOLN (St Mary Magdalene w St Paul in the Bail) (St Michael on the Mount) *Linc 11* **P** *Bp, D&C, and Adn Linc (jt)* **P-in-c** H W F JONES **NSM** J M HEPBURN

LINCOLN (St Mary-le-Wigford) (St Benedict) (St Mark) *Linc 11* **P** *Bp* **P-in-c** J S CULLIMORE **Hon C** N BURGESS

LINCOLN (St Nicholas) (St John) Newport *Linc 11* **P** *Bp and D&C (alt)* **V** H W F JONES **C** A E JOLLEY

LINCOLN (St Peter in Eastgate) *Linc 11* **P** *Bp* **NSM** S R ASTON

LINCOLN (St Peter-at-Gowts) w St Andrew and St Botolph *Linc 11* **P** *Bp* **V** J S CULLIMORE **Hon C** N BURGESS

LINCOLN (St Swithin) *Linc 11* **P** *Bp* **V** J A PRESTWOOD **C** B E BRADY, M RODGERS **Hon C** N BURGESS

LINCOLN St Peter in Carlton *Linc 11* **P** *Bp* **V** vacant

LINDAL AND MARTON (St Peter) *see* Pennington and Lindal w Marton and Bardsea *Carl*

LINDFIELD (All Saints) *Chich 8* **P** *Ch Soc Trust* **V** S R C NICHOLS **C** H E BOURNE, S C SILK

LINDLEY (St Stephen) *Leeds 9* **P** *V Huddersfield* **V** A L PALMER

LINDOW (St John) *Ches 12* **P** *Bp* **V** S R GALES

LINDRIDGE (St Lawrence) *see* Teme Valley N *Worc*

LINDSELL (St Mary the Virgin) *see* Stebbing and Lindsell w Gt and Lt Saling *Chelmsf*

LINDSEY (St Peter) *see* Bildeston w Wattisham and Lindsey etc *St E*

LINFORD (St Francis) *see* E and W Tilbury and Linford *Chelmsf*

LINFORD, GREAT (St Andrew) *see* Stantonbury and Willen *Ox*

LINFORD, LITTLE (St Leonard) *see* Lamp *Ox*

LINGDALE (Mission Room) *see* Boosbeck and Lingdale *York*

LINGEN (St Michael and All Angels) *see* Presteigne w Discoed, Kinsham, Lingen and Knill *Heref*

LINGFIELD (St Peter and St Paul) and Dormansland *S'wark 25* **P** *Bp* **P-in-c** I P WHITLEY **NSM** N K HINTON

LINGWOOD (St Peter) *see* Burlingham St Edmund w Lingwood, Strumpshaw etc *Nor*

LINKENHOLT (St Peter) *see* Pastrow *Win*

LINKINHORNE (St Mellor) *see* Callington Cluster *Truro*

LINSLADE (St Barnabas) *see* Ouzel Valley *St Alb*

LINSLADE (St Mary) *as above*

LINSTEAD PARVA (St Margaret) *see* Blyth Valley *St E*

LINTHORPE (St Barnabas) *York 17* **P** *Abp* **V** D J GOODHEW **C** M N WALLEY **Hon C** L J E GOODHEW

LINTHWAITE (Christ Church) *see* Crosland Moor and Linthwaite *Leeds*

LINTON (Christ Church) *see* Walton-on-Trent w Croxall, Rosliston etc *Derby*

LINTON (St Mary the Virgin) *see* Ariconium *Heref*

LINTON (St Mary) *Ely 5* **P** *Patr Bd* **TV** I ST J FISHER **C** M L WILCOCKSON

LINTON (St Michael), Burnsall and Rylstone *Leeds 21* **P** *CPAS Patr Trust, DBP and D&C Ripon (jt)* **R** D MACHA

LINTON (St Nicholas) *see* Coxheath, E Farleigh, Hunton, Linton etc *Roch*

LINWOOD (St Cornelius) *Linc 7* **P** *MMCET* **R** C V WALKER

LIPHOOK (Church Centre) *see* Bramshott and Liphook *Portsm*

LISCARD (St Thomas) *Ches 7* **P** *Bp* **Hon C** R T NELSON

LISCARD Resurrection (St Mary w St Columba) *Ches 7* **P** *Bp* **P-in-c** P T COOPER **C** E WHITE **NSM** C M TURNER

LISKEARD (St Martin) and St Keyne *Truro 12* **P** *Simeon's Trustees* **V** S J MORGAN **C** P T AINDOW

LISS (St Mary) (St Peter) (St Saviour) *Portsm 4* **P** *Bp* **R** C D WILLIAMS

LISSET (St James of Compostella) *see* Beeford w Frodingham and Foston *York*

LISSINGTON (St John the Baptist) *Linc 7* **P** *D&C York* **V** C V WALKER

LISSINGTON (St John the Baptist) *see* Lissington *Linc*

LISTON (not known) *see* N Hinckford *Chelmsf*

LITCHAM (All Saints) *see* Launditch and the Upper Nar *Nor*

LITCHFIELD (St James the Less) *see* Whitchurch w Tufton and Litchfield *Win*

LITHERLAND (St John and St James) (St Paul) (St Philip) and Orrell Hey Team Ministry *Liv 6* **P** *Patr Bd* **TR** A D STOTT **TV** R S SANGRA **NSM** A J FINCH, G M CARTER

LITLINGTON (St Catherine) *see* Shingay Gp *Ely*

LITLINGTON (St Michael the Archangel) *see* Alfriston w Lullington, Litlington, W Dean and Folkington *Chich*

LITTLE *see also under substantive place name*

LITTLE BIRCH (St Mary) *see* Wormelow Hundred *Heref*

LITTLE DART Team Ministry *see* Burrington, Chawleigh, Cheldon, Chulmleigh etc *Ex*

LITTLE HEATH (Christ Church) *St Alb 14* **P** *Ch Patr Trust* **V** T M MALONEY

LITTLE VENICE (St Mary) (St Saviour) *Lon 2* **P** *Bp* **V** G S BRADLEY **C** A D NORWOOD

LITTLEBOROUGH (Holy Trinity) (St James) (St Barnabas) *Man 6* **P** *Bp, TR Rochdale, and D&C (jt)* **V** I BULLOCK **NSM** C D BINNS, D NEWTON **Dss** K J OLIVER

LITTLEBURY (Holy Trinity) *see* Saffron Walden and Villages *Chelmsf*

LITTLEBURY GREEN (St Peter) *as above*

LITTLEDEAN (St Ethelbert) *see* Cinderford w Littledean *Glouc*

LITTLEHAM (St Margaret) w Lympstone *Ex 1* **P** *Patr Bd* **TR** S C JONES **TV** B H CAMBRIDGE **C** J M REYNOLDS

LITTLEHAM (St Swithin) *see* Bideford, Landcross, Littleham etc *Ex*

LITTLEHAMPTON (St James) (St Mary) *Chich 1* **P** *Bp* **R** M WILLIAMS **NSM** P P SEDLMAYR

LITTLEHEMPSTON (St John the Baptist) *see* Buckfastleigh, Dean Prior, Littlehempston etc *Ex*

LITTLEMOOR (St Francis of Assisi) *see* Weymouth Ridgeway *Sarum*

LITTLEMORE (St Mary the Virgin and St Nicholas) w Sandford-on-Thames *Ox 1* **P** *Bp and Oriel Coll Ox (jt)* **V** M C M ARMITSTEAD **C** H R CARTWRIGHT **NSM** R C MORGAN, T J MORGAN

LITTLEOVER (St Peter) *Derby 5* **P** *PCC* **V** A C M DRING **C** R BROOKS

LITTLEPORT (St George) *Ely 8* **P** *Bp* **P-in-c** M R ALBERT

LITTLETON (St Catherine of Alexandria) *see* The Downs *Win*

LITTLETON (St Mary Magdalene) *Lon 13* **P** *C W L Barratt Esq* **V** T M ROSE

LITTLETON DREW (All Saints) *see* By Brook *Bris*

LITTLETON, HIGH (Holy Trinity) *see* Paulton w Farrington Gurney and High Littleton *B & W*

LITTLETON, NORTH (St Nicholas) *see* E Vale and Avon Villages *Worc*

LITTLETON, SOUTH (St Michael the Archangel) *as above*

LITTLETON, WEST (St James) *see* Marshfield w Cold Ashton and Tormarton etc *Bris*

LITTLETON-ON-SEVERN (St Mary of Malmesbury) *see* N Severnside *Bris*

LITTLEWICK (St John the Evangelist) *see* Burchetts Green *Ox*

LITTLEWORTH (Holy Ascension) *see* Cherbury w Gainfield *Ox*

LITTON (Christ Church) *see* Tideswell *Derby*

LITTON (St Mary the Virgin) *see* Chewton Mendip w Ston Easton, Litton etc *B & W*

LITTON CHENEY (St Mary) *see* Bride Valley *Sarum*

LIVERMERE, GREAT (St Peter) *see* Blackbourne *St E*

LIVERPOOL (All Souls) Springwood *Liv 2* **P** *The Crown*
V P ELLIS

LIVERPOOL (Christ Church) Norris Green *Liv 5* **P** *Bp*
V H A EDWARDS **C** T R LANGDON-SMITH

LIVERPOOL (Our Lady and St Nicholas) *Liv 1* **P** *Sir Charles Gladstone Bt* **R** C A PAILING **C** T G PRABHAKARA RAO **NSM** J A BRADY, M A MONTROSE, W H ADDY

LIVERPOOL (St Anne) *see* Stanley and Stoneycroft St Paul *Liv*

LIVERPOOL (St Christopher) Norris Green *Liv 5* **P** *Bp*
NSM B A SMITH

LIVERPOOL (St James in the City) *Liv 3* **P** *Bp* **V** J PADFIELD **C** J HARDY, M A GOODWIN

LIVERPOOL (St Luke in the City) (St Bride w St Saviour) (St Michael in the City) (St Stephen w St Catherine) *Liv 3* **P** *Patr Bd* **TR** M THRELFALL-HOLMES **TV** L S FERGUSON **C** L J JOHNSON **NSM** S DOYLE

LIVERPOOL (St Philip w St David) *see* Liv All SS *Liv*

LIVERPOOL All Saints (St Mary) (St Philip w St David) St John the Divine *Liv 1* **P** *Patr Bd* **V** M D COATES **C** H E PURCELL, R KISA **NSM** I D CASSIDY

LIVERSEDGE (Christ Church) *see* Heckmondwike (w Norristhorpe) and Liversedge *Leeds*

LIVERTON (St Michael) *see* Easington w Liverton *York*

LIVERTON MINES (St Hilda) *as above*

LIVESEY (St Andrew) *Blackb 2* **P** *Trustees* **V** *vacant*

LIVING BROOK Benefice, The *see* Hardingstone, Piddington w Horton and Quinton and Preston Deanery *Pet*

LLANDINABO (St Junabius) *see* Wormelow Hundred *Heref*

LLANFAIR WATERDINE (St Mary) *see* Middle Marches *Heref*

LLANGARRON (St Deinst) *see* Wye Brooks Benefice *Heref*

LLANGROVE (Christ Church) *as above*

LLANGUA (St James) *see* Ewyas Harold w Dulas, Kenderchurch etc *Heref*

LLANVEYNOE (St Beuno and St Peter) *see* Black Mountains Gp *Heref*

LLANWARNE (Christ Church) *see* Wormelow Hundred *Heref*

LLANYBLODWEL (St Michael), Llanymynech, Morton and Trefonen *Lich 18* **P** *Ld Chan (1 turn), Bp and Earl of Powis (2 turns)* **R** K R TRIMBY

LLANYMYNECH (St Agatha) *see* Llanyblodwel, Llanymynech, Morton and Trefonen *Lich*

LOBLEY HILL (All Saints) *see* Hillside *Dur*

LOCKERLEY (St John) *see* Thorngate *Win*

LOCKING (St Augustine) *see* Hutton and Locking *B & W*

LOCKINGE (All Saints) *see* Wantage Downs *Ox*

LOCKINGE, WEST (All Souls) *as above*

LOCKINGTON (St Mary) and Lund and Scorborough w Leconfield *York 8* **P** *Abp* **R** C FISHER-BAILEY

LOCKINGTON (St Nicholas) *see* Castle Donington and Lockington cum Hemington *Leic*

LOCKS HEATH (St John the Baptist) *Portsm 2* **P** *Bp* **C** M A P MORITZ

LOCKTON (St Giles) *see* Pickering w Lockton and Levisham *York*

LODDINGTON (St Leonard) *see* Rothwell w Orton and Rushton w Glendon etc *Pet*

LODDINGTON (St Michael and All Angels) *Leic 5* **P** *Bp* **P-in-c** A M MYERS

LODDISWELL (St Michael and All Angels) *see* Thurlestone, S Milton, Churchstow etc *Ex*

LODDON (Holy Trinity), Sisland, Chedgrave, Hardley and Langley *Nor 8* **P** *Bp, E G Gilbert Esq, Gt Hosp, and Sir Christopher Beauchamp Bt (jt)* **V** D C OWEN **OLM** A M BALL, J C HAYLOCK

LODDON REACH, comprising Beech Hill, Shinfield, Spencers Wood and Grazeley, and Swallowfield *Ox 7* **P** *Patr Bd* **TV** D J LITTLE **NSM** C A SPENCE

LODE (St James) *see* Anglesey Gp *Ely*

LODERS (St Mary Magdalene) *see* Eggardon and Colmers *Sarum*

LODGE MOOR (St Luke) *Sheff 4* **P** *CPAS*
NSM G J SMALLMAN, T MORRIS

LODGE, The (St John) *see* St Martins and Weston Rhyn *Lich*

LODSWORTH (St Peter) *see* Easebourne, Lodsworth and Selham *Chich*

LOFTHOUSE (Christ Church) *see* Rothwell, Lofthouse, Methley etc *Leeds*

LOFTUS-IN-CLEVELAND (St Leonard) and Carlin How w Skinningrove *York 16* **P** *Ld Chan (2 turns), Abp (1 turn)* **R** A GAUNT

LONAN (All Saints) *see* Onchan, Lonan and Laxey *S & M*

LONDESBOROUGH (All Saints) *see* Weighton Wold *York*

LONDON (St Bartholomew the Less) Smithfield Gate *see* Smithfield Gt St Bart *Lon*

LONDON (St Martin Ludgate) *see* St Andr-by-the-Wardrobe w St Ann, Blackfriars and St Martin Ludgate *Lon*

LONDON CITY CHURCHES:

All Hallows Berkynchirche-by-the-Tower w St Dunstan-in-the-East *Lon 1* **P** *Abp* **V** K HEDDERLY **NSM** S C A ACLAND

Great St Bartholomew, Smithfield *Lon 1* **P** *D&C Westmr* **R** M A WALKER **C** P E MCWILLIAMS

St Andrew-by-the-Wardrobe w St Ann, Blackfriars and St Martin Ludgate *Lon 1* **P** *PCC, Mercers' Co, and D&C St Paul's (jt)* **R** L J MILLER **C** C D FISHLOCK, T C W WRIGHT **Hon C** J L OSBORNE

St Botolph Aldgate w Holy Trinity Minories *Lon 1* **P** *Bp* **V** L J JØRGENSEN **C** J A ROBINSON-BROWN

St Botolph without Bishopgate *Lon 1* **P** *D&C St Paul's* **R** D T ARMSTRONG

St Bride Fleet Street w Bridewell and Trinity Gough Square *Lon 1* **P** *D&C Westmr* **R** A J JOYCE **NSM** J R LAKE

St Edmund-the-King and St Mary Woolnoth w St Nicholas Acons, All Hallows Lombard Street, St Benet Gracechurch, St Leonard Eastcheap, St Dionis Backchurch and St Mary Woolchurch Haw and St Clement Eastcheap w St Martin Orgar *Lon 1* **P** *Patr Bd* **R** R C THORPE **C** A AGBAJE, A J BAUGHEN

St Giles Cripplegate w St Bartholomew Moor Lane and St Alphage London Wall and St Luke Old Street w St Mary Charterhouse and St Paul Clerkenwell *Lon 1* **P** *D&C St Paul's* **C** J HOGAN **NSM** A F NORRIS

St Helen, Bishopsgate w St Andrew Undershaft and St Ethelburga, Bishopsgate and St Martin Outwich and St Mary Axe *Lon 1* **P** *Merchant Taylors' Co* **R** W T TAYLOR **C** A GLYN, A P BALCH, E J UNDERHILL, H EATOCK-TAYLOR, J J CHILD, L CORNELIUS, P O HUDSON **NSM** J H HOUGHTON

St James Garlickhythe w St Michael Queenhithe and Holy Trinity-the-Less *Lon 1* **P** *D&C St Paul's* **R** T J HANDLEY **NSM** D C WHITE

St Magnus the Martyr w St Margaret New Fish Street and St Michael Crooked Lane *Lon 1* **P** *DBP* **R** J P WARNER

St Margaret Lothbury and St Stephen Coleman Street w St Christopher-le-Stocks, St Bartholomew-by-the-Exchange, St Olave Old Jewry, St Martin Pomeroy, St Mildred Poultry and St Mary Colechurch *Lon 1* **P** *Simeon's Trustees* **R** W J H CROSSLEY

St Mary at Hill w St Andrew Hubbard, St George Botolph Lane and St Botolph by Billingsgate *Lon 1* **P** *Ball Coll Ox (2 turns), PCC (1 turn), and Abp (1 turn)* **R** *vacant*

St Mary le Bow w St Pancras Soper Lane, All Hallows Honey Lane, All Hallows Bread Street, St John the Evangelist Watling Street, St Augustine w St Faith under St Paul's and St Mildred Bread Street w St Margaret Moyses *Lon 1* **P** *Grocers' Co (1 turn), Abp (2 turns)* **R** G R BUSH

St Michael Cornhill w St Peter le Poer and St Benet Fink *Lon 1* **P** *Drapers' Co* **C** H EATOCK-TAYLOR

St Olave Hart Street w All Hallows Staining and St Catherine Coleman *Lon 1* **P** *Trustees* **R** A SEN **NSM** N J L MOTTERSHEAD

St Peter Cornhill *Lon 1* **P** *City Corp* **R** W T TAYLOR **C** L CORNELIUS **NSM** J H HOUGHTON

St Sepulchre w Christ Church Greyfriars and St Leonard Foster Lane *Lon 1* **P** *St Jo Coll Ox* **P-in-c** N J L MOTTERSHEAD **C** T M BOSWORTH

St Stephen Walbrook and St Swithun London Stone w St Benet Sherehog and St Mary Bothaw w St Laurence Pountney *Lon 1* **P** *Grocers' Co and Magd Coll Cam (alt)* **P-in-c** S R BAXTER

St Vedast w St Michael-le-Querne, St Matthew Friday Street, St Peter Cheap, St Alban Wood Street, St Olave Silver Street, St Michael Wood Street, St Mary Staining, St Anne and St Agnes and St John

Zachary Gresham Street *Lon 1* **P** *D&C St Paul's*
R P A KENNEDY
LONDON COLNEY (St Peter) *St Alb 5* **P** *Bp* **V** P A JONES
NSM P S GREEN
LONDON DOCKS (St Peter) w Wapping St John *Lon 7*
P *Bp* **R** J W BESWICK **Hon C** R S LADDS
LONDON GUILD CHURCHES:
All Hallows London Wall *Lon 1* **P** *Ld Chan* **V** *vacant*
St Andrew Holborn *Lon 1* **P** *Bp* **C** M G C YOUNG **St Benet**
Paul's Wharf *Lon 1* **P** *Bp* **P-in-c** A GLYN
St Botolph without Aldersgate *Lon 1* **P** *Bp* **C** P C MARTIN
St Dunstan in the West *Lon 1* **P** *Abp* **P-in-c** J D WILKINSON
St Katharine Cree *Lon 1* **P** *Bp* **NSM** N J L MOTTERSHEAD
St Lawrence Jewry *Lon 1* **P** *City Corp* **V** D W PARROTT
St Margaret Pattens *Lon 1* **P** *Ld Chan* **NSM** A J KEEP
St Mary Abchurch *Lon 1* **P** *CCC Cam* **V** *vacant*
St Mary Aldermary *Lon 1* **P** *The Crown and Ld Chan (alt)*
P-in-c P A KENNEDY
St Michael Paternoster Royal *Lon 1* **P** *Bp* **V** *vacant*
LONDONDERRY (St Mark) *see* Oldbury, Langley and
Londonderry *Birm*
LONDONTHORPE (St John the Baptist) *see* Grantham,
Harrowby w Londonthorpe *Linc*
**LONG ASHTON (All Saints) w Barrow Gurney and Flax
Bourton** *B & W 12* **P** *Bp and Lady Virginia Gibbs (jt)*
R J D HARRIS
LONG BENNINGTON (St Swithin) *see* Saxonwell *Linc*
LONG BENTON (St Bartholomew) *Newc 3* **P** *Ball Coll Ox*
NSM F G CHARLTON
LONG BENTON (St Mary Magdalene) *Newc 3* **P** *Ball Coll*
Ox **NSM** N J TERRY
LONG BREDY (St Peter) *see* Bride Valley *Sarum*
**LONG BUCKBY (St Lawrence) w Watford and West
Haddon w Winwick** *Pet 2* **P** *Bp and DBP (1 turn), Ld Chan*
(1 turn) **V** G I COLLINGRIDGE
LONG CLAWSON (St Remigius) *see* Vale of Belvoir *Leic*
LONG COMPTON (St Peter and St Paul) *see* S Warks Seven
Gp *Cov*
**LONG CRENDON (St Mary the Virgin) w Chearsley and
Nether Winchendon** *Ox 10* **P** *Bp and R V Spencer-Bernard*
Esq (jt) **V** R M PHILLIPS
LONG DITTON (St Mary) *Guildf 8* **P** *Bp S'wark*
C A M BAVERSTOCK, K SATKUNANAYAGAM
LONG EATON (St John) *Derby 8* **P** *Bp* **V** S J TREDWELL
LONG EATON (St Laurence) *Derby 8* **P** *Bp*
V D L LAWRENCE-MARCH
LONG HANBOROUGH (Christ Church) *see* Hanborough and
Freeland *Ox*
LONG ITCHINGTON (Holy Trinity) and Marton *Cov 10*
P *Bp* **V** *vacant*
LONG LANE (Christ Church) *see* Boylestone, Church
Broughton, Dalbury, etc *Derby*
LONG MARSTON (All Saints) *see* Marston Moor *York*
LONG MARTON (St Margaret and St James) *see* Heart of
Eden *Carl*
LONG MELFORD (Holy Trinity) *see* Chadbrook *St E*
LONG MELFORD (St Catherine) *as above*
LONG NEWNTON (Holy Trinity) *see* Tetbury, Beverston,
Long Newnton etc *Glouc*
LONG PRESTON (St Mary the Virgin) *see* Hellifield and Long
Preston *Leeds*
LONG RISTON (St Margaret) *see* Skirlaugh, Catwick, Long
Riston, Rise, Swine w Ellerby *York*
LONG STANTON (All Saints) *see* 5folds *Ely*
LONG STANTON (St Michael and All Angels) *see* Wenlock
Heref
LONG STRATTON and Pilgrim Team Ministry, The,
comprising Aslacton, Bunwell, Carleton Rode, Great
Moulton, Stratton St Mary, Stratton St Michael, Tibenham,
and Wacton *Nor 5* **P** *Patr Bd* **TR** H Y WILCOX
TV J Y MADINDA **OLM** G M OSBORNE
LONG SUTTON (All Saints) *see* N Hants Downs *Win*
LONG SUTTON (Holy Trinity) *see* Levels Arc *B & W*
**LONG SUTTON (St Mary) w Lutton and Gedney Drove
End, Dawsmere** *Linc 18* **P** *The Crown, Bp, and Ld Chan (by*
turn) **V** J P E SIBLEY **OLM** H M DEAN
LONG WHATTON (All Saints) *see* Kegworth, Hathern, Long
Whatton, Diseworth etc *Leic*
LONG WITTENHAM (St Mary the Virgin) *see* Dorchester
Ox
LONGBOROUGH (St James) *see* Moreton-in-Marsh w
Batsford, Todenham etc *Glouc*
LONGBRIDGE (St John the Baptist) *Birm 2* **P** *Bp*
V C J CORKE
LONGBRIDGE DEVERILL (St Peter and St Paul) *see* Cley Hill
Villages *Sarum*

LONGBURTON (St James) *see* Sherborne w Castleton,
Lillington and Longburton *Sarum*
LONGCOT (St Mary the Virgin) *see* Shrivenham and
Ashbury *Ox*
LONGDEN (St Ruthen) *see* Gt Hanwood and Longden and
Annscroft etc *Heref*
LONGDON (St James) *see* Lichfield and Longdon *Lich*
**LONGDON (St Mary), Castlemorton, Bushley, Queenhill w
Holdfast** *Worc 2* **P** *Bp, D&C Westmr, and Soc of the Faith (jt)*
V C A MOSS
LONGDON-UPON-TERN (St Bartholomew) *see*
Wrockwardine Deanery *Lich*
LONGFIELD (Mission Room) (St Mary Magdalene) *Roch 1*
P *Ld Chan* **P-in-c** A BARKER **C** C J SHILLITO
LONGFLEET (St Mary) *Sarum 7* **P** *MMCET* **V** A N PERRY
C M A HAY
LONGFORD (St Chad) *see* Boylestone, Church Broughton,
Dalbury, etc *Derby*
LONGFORD (St Thomas) *Cov 2* **P** *Bp* **P-in-c** R F T MURPHY
LONGFRAMLINGTON (St Mary the Virgin) w Brinkburn
Newc 6 **P** *Bp* **NSM** C M A HEPPER
LONGHAM (St Andrew and St Peter) *see* Launditch and the
Upper Nar *Nor*
LONGHILL (St Margaret) *see* Sutton St Mich *York*
LONGHIRST (St John the Evangelist) *see* Bothal and
Pegswood w Longhirst *Newc*
LONGHOPE (All Saints) *see* Huntley and Longhope,
Churcham and Bulley *Glouc*
LONGHORSLEY (St Helen) *Newc 11* **P** *Ld Chan*
P-in-c A D MCCARTAN
**LONGHOUGHTON (St Peter and St Paul) (including
Boulmer) w Howick** *Newc 6* **P** *Duke of Northumberland and*
Bp (alt) **NSM** B K COOPER
LONGLEVENS (Holy Trinity) *see* Wotton St Mary *Glouc*
LONGNEWTON (St Mary) *see* Preston-on-Tees and
Longnewton *Dur*
LONGNEY (St Lawrence) *see* Hardwicke and Elmore w
Longney *Glouc*
**LONGNOR (St Bartholomew), Quarnford, Sheen and
Warslow w Elkstone** *Lich 5* **P** *Bp, V Alstonfield, and DBP*
(jt) **V** J C BAINES **C** D M GREEN
LONGNOR (St Mary) *see* Dorrington w Leebotwood,
Longnor, Stapleton etc *Heref*
LONGPARISH (St Nicholas) *see* Hurstbourne Priors,
Longparish etc *Win*
LONGRIDGE (St Lawrence) (St Paul) *Blackb 13* **P** *Trustees*
V M J BARTON **C** S J KING
LONGSDON (St Chad) *see* Cheddleton, Horton, Longsdon
and Rushton Spencer *Lich*
LONGSIGHT (St Agnes) *see* Birch-in-Rusholme St Agnes w
Longsight St Jo etc *Man*
LONGSIGHT (St Luke) *Man 1* **P** *D&C and Trustees (jt)*
R *vacant*
LONGSLEDDALE (St Mary) *see* Beacon TM *Carl*
LONGSOLE (Mission Room) *see* Barming *Roch*
LONGSTOCK (St Mary) *see* Mid Test *Win*
LONGSTONE (St Giles), Curbar and Stony Middleton
Derby 4 **P** *V Bakewell etc and R Hathersage etc (jt)*
V J S CROFT
LONGSTOWE (St Mary) *see* Papworth *Ely*
LONGTHORPE (St Botolph) *Pet 11* **P** *Sir Philip Naylor-*
Leyland Bt **V** J BULLEN
LONGTON (St Andrew) *Blackb 5* **P** *A F Rawstorne Esq*
V *vacant*
LONGTON (St James and St John) and Meir *Lich 11* **P** *Bp*
R P W BENNETT
LONGTON (St Mary and St Chad) *Lich 11* **P** *Bp*
V K A PALMER
LONGTON HALL (St Paul) *Lich 11* **P** *The Crown* **V** J ALESSI
LONGTON, NEW (All Saints) *Blackb 5* **P** *Bp*
V T A WOOLFORD
LONGWELL GREEN (All Saints) *Bris 5* **P** *Bp*
P-in-c B W GOODWIN **C** M Y Y S NAM **OLM** S P BRITTON
LONGWORTH (St Mary) *see* Cherbury w Gainfield *Ox*
**LONSDALE, EAST, comprising Tatham, Tatham Fells, Tunstall
w Melling and Leck, and Wray** *Blackb 14* **P** *Patr Bd*
V *vacant*
LOOE (St Nicholas) and Morval *Truro 12* **P** *Ld Chan (1*
turn), Bp and D&C (1 turn) **R** *vacant*
LOOSE (All Saints) *Cant 12* **P** *Abp* **V** S A PRICE
LOPEN (All Saints) *see* Merriott w Hinton, Dinnington and
Lopen *B & W*
LOPHAM NORTH (St Nicholas) *see* Diss *Nor*
LOPHAM SOUTH (St Andrew) *as above*
LOPPINGTON (St Michael and All Angels) *see* Myddle and
Broughton, Loppington and Newtown *Lich*

LORD'S HILL *see* Southampton Lord's Hill and Lord's Wood *Win*

LORDSBRIDGE Team, The, comprising Barton, Caldecote, Comberton, Coton, Dry Drayton, Great Eversden, Hardwick, Harlton, Haslingfield, Little Eversden, and Toft *Ely 1* **P** *Ld Chan (1 turn), Patr Bd (2 turns)* **TV** C M ROBERTSON, M D NEWTON **C** C M REDSELL, P O GARNELL **NSM** C I A FRASER, C WESTGARTH, M J REISS

LORTON (St Cuthbert) and Loweswater w Buttermere *Carl 6* **P** *Bp and Earl of Lonsdale (alt)* **V** *vacant*

LOSCOE (St Luke) *see* Denby Gp *Derby*

LOSTOCK (St Thomas and St John) *Man 3* **P** *Bp and TR Deane St Mary the Virgin (jt)* **V** T P CLARK **C** B M WILKINSON

LOSTOCK GRALAM (St John the Evangelist) *Ches 6* **P** *V Witton* **P-in-c** A R RIDLEY

LOSTOCK HALL (St James) and Farington Moss *Blackb 5* **P** *Bp and V Penwortham (jt)* **V** M P MCMURRAY

LOSTWITHIEL (St Bartholomew) Parishes *Truro 10* **P** *D&C, DBP, and A D G Fortescue Esq (jt)* **P-in-c** P J BEYNON **NSM** S I BAWDEN

LOTHERSDALE (Christ Church) *see* Sutton w Cowling and Lothersdale *Leeds*

LOTHERTON (St James) *see* Aberford w Micklefield *York*

LOTTISHAM (The Blessed Virgin Mary) *see* Baltonsborough w Butleigh, W Bradley etc *B & W*

LOUDWATER (St Peter) *Ox 10* **P** MMCET **V** D C RODGERS

LOUGHBOROUGH (All Saints) w Holy Trinity *Leic 6* **P** *Bp and Em Coll Cam (jt)* **R** W M DALRYMPLE **C** E J SHARMAN, E PIKI

LOUGHBOROUGH (Emmanuel) *Leic 6* **P** *Bp and Em Coll Cam (jt)* **P-in-c** M J BROADLEY

LOUGHBOROUGH (Good Shepherd) *Leic 6* **P** *Bp* **V** B J GARDNER, S WILLETTS

LOUGHRIGG Team Ministry, The, comprising Ambleside, Brathay, and Langdale *Carl 11* **P** *Patr Bd* **TR** B LOCK **NSM** G G WRIGLEY, J M L NATTRASS, N F HALLAM

LOUGHTON (All Saints) *see* Watling Valley *Ox*

LOUGHTON (not known) *see* Ditton Priors w Neenton, Burwarton etc *Heref*

LOUGHTON (St John the Baptist) (St Gabriel) (St Nicholas) *Chelmsf 3* **P** W W Maitland Esq **R** C M DAVIES **C** S B S PETERS, S R H MAGINNIS **NSM** B A READ

LOUGHTON (St Mary the Virgin) *Chelmsf 3* **P** *Bp* **V** M C MACDONALD

LOUGHTON (St Michael and All Angels) *Chelmsf 3* **P** *Bp* **V** L A PETITT **NSM** E A PRICE, M P PETITT

LOUND (St John the Baptist) *see* Somerleyton, Ashby, Fritton, Herringfleet etc *Nor*

LOUNDSLEY GREEN (Church of the Ascension) *Derby 3* **P** *Bp* **P-in-c** S M COLVER

LOUTH (Holy Trinity Church Centre) (St James) (St Michael) *Linc 15* **P** *Patr Bd* **P-in-c** J C WATT **C** A M M ROBINSON **OLM** R W MANSFIELD

LOVEDEN, EAST, comprising Ancaster, Greylees, Heydour, Kelby, Rauceby, Welby, and Wilsford *Linc 22* **P** *Bp (2 turns), DBP (1 turn), and Mrs G V Hoare (1 turn)* **R** G MACHELL

LOVERSALL (St Katherine) *see* Wadworth w Loversall and Balby *Sheff*

LOVINGTON (St Thomas à Becket) *see* Six Pilgrims *B & W*

LOW FELL (St Helen) *see* Gateshead St Helen *Dur*

LOW HILL (Good Shepherd) *see* Bushbury *Lich*

LOW MOOR (Holy Trinity) and Oakenshaw *Leeds 3* **P** *Bp and V Bradf (jt)* **V** I R JENNINGS

LOWDHAM (St Mary the Virgin) *see* Burton Joyce, Bulcote and Stoke Bardolph etc *S'well*

LOWER *see also under substantive place name*

LOWER MOOR (St Stephen and All Martyrs) *see* Coldhurst and Oldham St Steph *Man*

LOWESBY (All Saints) *see* Whatborough Gp *Leic*

LOWESTOFT (Christ Church) *Nor 9* **P** CPAS **P-in-c** J M CARTER

LOWESTOFT (Good Shepherd) *see* Lowestoft St Marg *Nor*

LOWESTOFT (St Andrew) *Nor 9* **P** *Ch Patr Tr* **V** D ROGERS

LOWESTOFT (St Margaret) *Nor 9* **P** *Bp, Adn Norfolk, and DBP (jt)* **R** M J ASQUITH

LOWESWATER (St Bartholomew) *see* Lorton and Loweswater w Buttermere *Carl*

LOWICK (St John the Baptist) and Kyloe w Ancroft *Newc 12* **P** *D&C Dur (2 turns), Bp (1 turn)* **P-in-c** C E OSBORN

LOWICK (St Luke) *see* Coniston and the Crake Valley *Carl*

LOWICK (St Peter) *see* Brigstock w Stanion and Lowick and Sudborough *Pet*

LOWSONFORD (St Luke) *see* Hatton w Haseley, Rowington w Lowsonford etc *Cov*

LOWTHER (St Michael) *see* N Westmorland *Carl*

LOWTHORPE (St Martin) *see* The Beacon *York*

LOWTON (St Luke) (St Mary) and Golborne *Liv 13* **P** *Patr Bd* **TR** J R STOTT **TV** T HODSON

LOXBEARE (St Michael and All Angels) *see* Washfield, Stoodleigh, Withleigh etc *Ex*

LOXHORE (St Michael and All Angels) *see* Shirwell, Loxhore, Kentisbury, Arlington, etc *Ex*

LOXLEY (St Nicholas) *see* Hampton Lucy w Charlecote and Loxley *Cov*

LOXTON (St Andrew) *see* Crook Peak *B & W*

LOXWOOD (St John the Baptist) *see* Alfold and Loxwood *Guildf*

LOZELLS (St Paul and St Silas) and Newtown *Birm 1* **P** *St Martin's Trust* **P-in-c** A J COZENS

LUBENHAM (All Saints) *see* Market Harborough and The Transfiguration etc *Leic*

LUCCOMBE (The Blessed Virgin Mary) *see* Porlock and Porlock Weir w Stoke Pero etc *B & W*

LUCKER (St Hilda) *see* Bamburgh, Belford and Lucker *Newc*

LUCKINGTON (St Mary) *see* Gauzebrook *Bris*

LUDBOROUGH (St Mary) *see* Fotherby, N Thoresby and Grainsby w Waithe *Linc*

LUDDENDEN (St Mary) w Luddenden Foot *Leeds 8* **P** *Bp and V Halifax (alt)* **P-in-c** I SPARKS

LUDDESDOWN (St Peter and St Paul) *see* Cobham w Luddesdowne and Dode *Roch*

LUDDINGTON (All Saints) *see* Stratford-upon-Avon, Luddington etc *Cov*

LUDDINGTON (St Margaret) *see* Barnwell, Hemington, Luddington in the Brook etc *Pet*

LUDDINGTON (St Oswald) *see* Crowle Gp *Linc*

LUDFORD (St Giles) *see* The Ashfords *Heref*

LUDFORD MAGNA (St Mary) *see* Binbrook Gp *Linc*

LUDGERSHALL (St Mary the Virgin) *see* Bernwode *Ox*

LUDGERSHALL (St James) and Tidworth *Sarum 14* **P** *Ld Chan and DBP (alt)* **V** T J LAUNDON

LUDGVAN (St Ludgvan and St Paul), Marazion, St Hilary and Perranuthnoe *Truro 4* **P** *D&C, Lord St Levan, and H M Parker Esq (jt)* **R** N G MARNS **C** J E RISBRIDGER, S M V TROCZYNSKA **NSM** L P GARTHWAITE

LUDHAM (St Catherine), Potter Heigham, Hickling and Catfield *Nor 12* **P** *Bp and G M H Mills Esq (jt)* **V** *vacant*

LUDLOW (St John) (St Laurence) *Heref 11* **P** *Bp and Earl of Plymouth (jt)* **R** K I PRICE **C** L B GITTINS, W M DAVIES

LUFFENHAM, NORTH (St John the Baptist) *see* Empingham, Edith Weston, Lyndon, Manton etc *Pet*

LUFFENHAM, SOUTH (St Mary the Virgin) *see* Barrowden and Wakerley w S Luffenham etc *Pet*

LUFTON (St Peter and St Paul) *see* Tintinhull w Chilthorne Domer, Yeovil Marsh etc *B & W*

LUGWARDINE (St Peter) *see* Bartestree Cross *Heref*

LULLINGSTONE (St Botolph) *see* Eynsford w Farningham and Lullingstone *Roch*

LULLINGTON (All Saints) *see* Beckington w Standerwick, Berkley, Rodden etc *B & W*

LULLINGTON (All Saints) *see* Seale and Lullington w Coton in the Elms *Derby*

LULLINGTON (Good Shepherd) *see* Alfriston w Lullington, Litlington, W Dean and Folkington *Chich*

LULWORTH, EAST (St Andrew) *see* W Purbeck *Sarum*

LULWORTH, WEST (Holy Trinity) *as above*

LUMLEY (Christ Church) *Dur 9* **P** *Bp* **P-in-c** J W ESTALL **NSM** C E BRITCLIFFE, T HOLDEN

LUND (All Saints) *see* Lockington and Lund and Scorborough w Leconfield *York*

LUND (St John the Evangelist) *Blackb 10* **P** *Ch Ch Ox* **V** *vacant*

LUNDWOOD (St Mary Magdalene) *Leeds 14* **P** *Bp* **P-in-c** B W RADFORD

LUNDY ISLAND (St Helen) *see* Parkham, Alwington, Buckland Brewer etc *Ex*

LUPPITT (St Mary) *see* Broadhembury, Dunkeswell, Luppitt, Plymtree, Sheldon, and Upottery *Ex*

LUPSET (St George) *Leeds 16* **P** *Bp* **P-in-c** M C CRABTREE **C** D N KOMOROWSKI

LUPTON (All Saints) *see* Kirkby Lonsdale *Carl*

LURGASHALL (St Lawrence) *Chich 4* **P** *Lord Egremont* **P-in-c** K A BAILEY

LUSBY (St Peter) *see* Bolingbroke Deanery *Linc*

LUSTLEIGH (St John the Baptist) *see* Moretonhampstead, Manaton, N Bovey and Lustleigh *Ex*

LUTON (All Saints) (St Peter) *St Alb 12* **P** *Bp* **V** D W KESTERTON **NSM** J M BURKE

LUTON (Christ Church) *Roch 5* **P** R Chatham **P-in-c** A S LEONARD

LUTON (Christ Church) *see* Bushmead *St Alb*

LUTON (Holy Cross) *see* Marsh Farm *St Alb*

LUTON (St Andrew) *St Alb 12* **P** *Bp* **V** G A FINLAYSON

LUTON (St Anne) (St Christopher) Round Green *St Alb 12*
P *Bp, V Luton St Mary, and Peache Trustees* **V** A D CROSBY

LUTON (St Francis) *St Alb 12* **P** *Peache Trustees, Bp, and V
Luton (jt)* **V** *vacant*

LUTON (St John) *see* Teignmouth, Ideford w Luton,
Ashcombe etc *Ex*

LUTON (St Mary) (St Matthew) *St Alb 12* **P** *Trustees Peache
Advowson Trust (CPAS)* **V** M C JONES **C** N K MWANDIA
NSM C A MOSS

LUTON (St Paul) *St Alb 12* **P** *Peache Trustees*
P-in-c K J LOMAX

LUTON (St Saviour) *St Alb 12* **P** *Bp* **P-in-c** Y M SMEJKAL

LUTON Lewsey (St Hugh) *St Alb 12* **P** *Bp* **V** J PIENAAR,
M P L SHEA

LUTON Limbury (St Augustine of Canterbury) *St Alb 12*
P *Bp* **V** J O NYAONGO

LUTTERWORTH (St Mary) w Cotesbach and Bitteswell
Leic 7 **P** *The Crown (3 turns), Ld Chan (1 turn), and Ch Hosp
(1 turn)* **R** C A M STYLES **C** T E BROWN

LUTTON (St Nicholas) *see* Long Sutton w Lutton etc *Linc*

LUTTON (St Peter) *see* Barnwell, Hemington, Luddington in
the Brook etc *Pet*

LUTTONS AMBO (St Mary) *see* Weaverthorpe w
Helperthorpe, Luttons Ambo etc *York*

LUXBOROUGH (Blessed Virgin Mary) *see* Exmoor *B & W*

LUXULYAN (St Cyrus and St Julietta) *Truro 7* **P** *Bp (1 turn),
Adn Cornwall (1 turn), and DBP (2 turns)*
P-in-c J S J WILLIAMS

LYDBROOK (Holy Jesus) *see* Drybrook, Lydbrook and
Ruardean *Glouc*

LYDBURY NORTH (St Michael and All Angels) *see* Bishop's
Castle w Mainstone, Lydbury N etc *Heref*

LYDD (All Saints) *see* Romney Marsh *Cant*

LYDDEN (St Mary the Virgin) *see* Temple Ewell w Lydden
Cant

**LYDDINGTON (All Saints) and Wanborough and
Bishopstone w Hinton Parva** *Bris 7* **P** *Bp and Ld Chan (alt)*
V *vacant*

**LYDDINGTON (St Andrew), Bisbrooke, Caldecott, Glaston,
Harringworth, Seaton and Stoke Dry** *Pet 12* **P** *Bp, G T G
Conant Esq, Exors R E M Elborne Esq, Burghley Ho Preservation
Trust Ltd, and Peterho Cam (jt)* **V** J E BAXTER

LYDEARD ST LAWRENCE (St Lawrence) *see* Bishop's Lydeard
w Lydeard St Lawrence etc *B & W*

LYDFORD (St Petrock) *see* Okehampton, Inwardleigh,
Belstone, Sourton etc *Ex*

LYDFORD ON FOSSE (St Peter) *see* Wheathill Priory Gp
B & W

LYDGATE (St Anne) *see* Saddleworth *Man*

LYDHAM (Holy Trinity) *see* Wentnor w Ratlinghope,
Myndtown, Norbury etc *Heref*

LYDIARD MILLICENT (All Saints) *see* NW Swindon and
Lydiard Millicent *Bris*

LYDIARD TREGOZE (St Mary) *see* W Swindon and Lydiard
Tregoze *Bris*

LYDIATE (St Thomas) *see* Halsall, Lydiate and Downholland
Liv

LYDLINCH (St Thomas à Beckett) *see* Sturminster Newton,
Hinton St Mary and Lydlinch *Sarum*

**LYDNEY (St Mary the Virgin), Woolaston, Alvington and
Aylburton** *Glouc 1* **P** *Ld Chan (2 turns), DBP (1 turn)*
R D A GARDINER

LYE, THE (Christchurch) and Stambermill *Worc 5* **P** *Bp and
CPAS (alt)* **V** S M FALSHAW **C** J M EVANS **NSM** C A KENT

LYFORD (St Mary) *see* Cherbury w Gainfield *Ox*

LYME REGIS (St Michael the Archangel) *see* Golden Cap
Team *Sarum*

LYMINGE (St Mary and St Ethelburga) *see* Elham Valley *Cant*

LYMINGTON (St Thomas the Apostle) (All Saints) *Win 11*
P *Bp* **V** P B C SALISBURY

LYMINSTER (St Mary Magdalene) and Wick *Chich 1* **P** *Bp
and Eton Coll on nomination of BNC Ox (jt)* **V** T I ROBSON
C M D RODGER, V L BARON

LYMM (St Mary the Virgin) *Ches 4* **P** *Bp* **R** B J JAMESON
C J F ELSTON

LYMPNE (St Stephen) and Saltwood *Cant 8* **P** *Abp*
R B J F KNOTT **NSM** P F HILL

LYMPSHAM (St Christopher) *see* Three Saints *B & W*

LYMPSTONE (Nativity of the Blessed Virgin Mary) *see*
Littleham-cum-Exmouth w Lympstone *Ex*

LYNDHURST (St Michael) and Emery Down and Minstead
Win 11 **P** *Bp and P J P Green Esq (jt)* **P-in-c** D S POTTERTON

LYNDON (St Martin) *see* Empingham, Edith Weston,
Lyndon, Manton etc *Pet*

LYNEAL (St John the Evangelist) *see* Petton w Cockshutt,
Welshampton and Lyneal etc *Lich*

LYNEHAM (St Michael) and Woodhill, including
Bradenstoke, Broad Town, Clyffe Pypard, Hilmarton, and
Tockenham *Sarum 16* **P** *The Crown (2 turns), DBP (1 turn),
Ld Chan (1 turn)* **R** E R H ABBOTT

LYNESACK (St John the Evangelist) *Dur 4* **P** *Bp*
P-in-c B WHITLEY **C** L R EVANS

LYNG (St Bartholomew) *see* Athelney *B & W*

LYNG (St Margaret) *see* Reepham and Wensum Valley *Nor*

LYNGFORD (St Peter) *see* Taunton Lyngford *B & W*

LYNMOUTH (St John the Baptist) *see* Lynton, Brendon,
Countisbury etc *Ex*

LYNN, SOUTH and WEST (All Saints) *Nor 19* **P** *Bp*
R A R LING **C** J R E BELL

LYNN, WEST (St Peter) *see* S and W Lynn *Nor*

LYNSTED (St Peter and St Paul) *see* Kingsdown, Creekside
and High Downs *Cant*

**LYNTON (St Mary the Virgin), Brendon, Countisbury,
Parracombe, Martinhoe and Trentishoe** *Ex 16* **P** *Bp*
R S M STAYTE

LYONS (St Michael and All Angels) *see* Hetton-Lyons w
Eppleton *Dur*

LYONSDOWN (Holy Trinity) *St Alb 14* **P** *Ch Patr Trust*
V *vacant*

LYONSHALL (St Michael and All Angels) *see* Pembridge w
Moor Court, Shobdon, Staunton etc *Heref*

**LYTCHETTS, The (not known) (St Mary the Virgin) and
Upton** *Sarum 7* **P** *Patr Bd* **TR** M J SIMPSON
TV S H PARTRIDGE **OLM** H D PAGE-CLARK

LYTHAM (St Cuthbert) *Blackb 10* **P** *DBP* **V** N A WELLS

LYTHAM (St John the Divine) *Blackb 10* **P** J C Hilton Esq
P-in-c N A WELLS

LYTHAM ST ANNE (St Margaret of Antioch) *see* St Annes
St Marg *Blackb*

LYTHAM ST ANNE (St Thomas) *see* St Annes St Thos *Blackb*

LYTHAM ST ANNES (St Paul) *see* Fairhaven *Blackb*

LYTHE (St Oswald) *see* Hinderwell, Roxby and Staithes etc
York

MABE (St Laudus) *Truro 2* **P** *Bp* **V** *vacant*

MABLETHORPE (St Mary) w Trusthorpe *Linc 10* **P** *Bp Lon
(2 turns), Bp Linc (1 turn)* **R** P J LILEY **Hon C** C H LILLEY
OLM J TOMPKINS

MACCLESFIELD (Holy Trinity) *see* Hurdsfield *Ches*

MACCLESFIELD (St John the Evangelist) w Henbury
Ches 13 **P** *Bp* **V** *vacant*

MACCLESFIELD (St Paul) *Ches 13* **P** *Bp* **V** *vacant*

**MACCLESFIELD Team Parish, The (All Saints) (Christ
Church) (St Michael and All Angels) (St Peter)
(St Barnabas)** *Ches 13* **P** *Patr Bd* **TR** M N STEPHENS
TV A B WILLIAMS **NSM** A M MARSHALL, R WARDLE

MACKWORTH (All Saints) *Derby 6* **P** J M Clark-Maxwell Esq
P-in-c B J STOBER

MACKWORTH (St Francis) *Derby 5* **P** *Bp* **P-in-c** P D MANN
C A J D BOND

MADEHURST (St Mary Magdalene) *see* Slindon, Eartham
and Madehurst *Chich*

MADELEY (All Saints) *Lich 9* **P** J C Crewe Esq **V** T J WATSON
C J J BESWICK PALLISTER **NSM** G A BAILEY

MADELEY (St Michael) *Heref 13* **P** *CPAS Patr Trust*
V A H WALDEN **C** I R MCINTYRE

MADINGLEY (St Mary Magdalene) *Ely 6* **P** *Bp* **V** M D BIGG

**MADLEY (Nativity of the Blessed Virgin Mary) w Tyberton,
Peterchurch, Vowchurch and Turnastone** *Heref 1* **P** *Bp
and D&C (jt)* **R** S D LOCKETT

MADRESFIELD (St Mary) *see* Powick and Guarlford and
Madresfield w Newland *Worc*

MADRON (St Maddern) *see* Gulval and Madron *Truro*

MAER (St Peter) *see* Chapel Chorlton, Maer and Whitmore
Lich

MAESBROOK (St John) *see* Kinnerley w Melverley, Knockin
w Maesbrook and Maesbury *Lich*

MAESBURY (St John the Baptist) *as above*

MAGDALEN LAVER (St Mary Magdalen) *see* High Laver w
Magdalen Laver and Lt Laver etc *Chelmsf*

MAGHULL (St Andrew) (St James) (St Peter) and Melling
Liv 8 **P** *Patr Bd* **TV** D HAMLETT, S M ELLIOTT
C G I MACLEOD **NSM** G ARDERN

MAGNIS Group Benefice, The, comprising Bishopstone,
Bridge Sollars, Brinsop w Wormsley, Credenhill, Kenchester,
and Mansel Lacy w Yazor *Heref 3* **P** R M Ecroyd Esq, Major D
J C Davenport and Bp (3 turns), Ld Chan (1 turn)
P-in-c R R D DAVIES-JAMES **NSM** A C DEANE

MAIDA VALE (St Peter)   *see* Paddington St Mary Magd and St Pet *Lon*

MAIDA VALE (St Saviour)   *see* Lt Venice *Lon*

MAIDEN BRADLEY (All Saints)   *see* Mere w W Knoyle and Maiden Bradley *Sarum*

MAIDEN NEWTON (St Mary)   *see* Melbury *Sarum*

MAIDENHEAD (St Andrew and St Mary Magdalene) *Ox 5*
P *Peache Trustees*   **V** W M C STILEMAN   **C** D A ATALLAH, I D D MILLER, J C DRAKE, N WATKINSON

MAIDENHEAD (St Luke) *Ox 5*   **P** *Bp*   **V** S M LYNCH
NSM P SOPP

MAIDENHEAD (St Mark's Hospital Church)   *see* Furze Platt *Ox*

MAIDENHEAD (St Peter)   *see* Furze Platt *Ox*

MAIDFORD (St Peter and St Paul)   *see* Lambfold *Pet*

MAIDS MORETON (St Edmund)   *see* N Buckingham w Stowe *Ox*

MAIDSTONE (All Saints) (St Philip) w St Stephen Tovil *Cant 12*   **P** *Abp*   **V** *vacant*

MAIDSTONE (St Faith) *Cant 12*   **P** *Abp*   **P-in-c** A J HOUSTON

MAIDSTONE (St Luke the Evangelist) *Cant 12*   **P** *Abp and CPAS*   **V** G L DICKINSON

MAIDSTONE (St Martin) *Cant 12*   **P** *Abp*
P-in-c J H ADDISON   **C** A J EDWARDS

MAIDSTONE (St Michael and All Angels) *Cant 12*   **P** *Abp*
V N D BRYSON

MAIDSTONE (St Paul) *Cant 12*   **P** *Abp*   **P-in-c** C P LAVENDER
NSM A J MITCHELL

MAIDSTONE Barming Heath (St Andrew)   *see* Barming Heath *Cant*

MAIDWELL (St Mary) w Draughton and Lamport w Faxton *Pet 2*   **P** *Bp (3 turns), Sir Ian Isham Bt (1 turn)*
C J V J G WATSON

MAINSTONE (St John the Baptist)   *see* Bishop's Castle w Mainstone, Lydbury N etc *Heref*

MAISEMORE (St Giles)   *see* Ashleworth, Corse, Hartpury, Hasfield etc *Glouc*

MAKER (St Mary and St Julian) w Rame, Millbrook, St John and Torpoint *Truro 11*   **P** *The Crown (1 turn), Bp, Earl of Mount Edgcumbe, and Sir John Carew Pole Bt (1 turn)*
R M B BROWN   **NSM** A I KING

MALDEN (St James) *S'wark 15*   **P** *Bp*   **V** K J THOMAS

MALDEN (St John) *S'wark 15*   **P** *Mert Coll Ox*
V M D A ROPER

MALDEN, NEW (Christ Church) (St John the Divine) and Coombe *S'wark 15*   **P** *CPAS*   **V** S J KUHRT   **C** E K OSGOOD

MALDON (All Saints w St Peter) *Chelmsf 10*   **P** *Bp*
P-in-c A J HUMPHREYS

MALDON (St Mary) w Mundon *Chelmsf 10*   **P** *D&C Westmr*
P-in-c J F DICKENS   **NSM** R J WIGGS

MALEW (St Lupus) (St Mark) and Santan *S & M*   **P** *The Crown*   **V** R M RADCLIFFE

MALIN BRIDGE (St Polycarp) *Sheff 4*   **P** *Bp*   **V** *vacant*

MALINSLEE (St Leonard)   *see* Cen Telford *Lich*

MALLERSTANG (St Mary)   *see* Upper Eden *Carl*

MALLING, EAST (St James) and Teston *Roch 7*   **P** *Peache Trustees and D&C (jt)*   **V** N L WILLIAMS

MALLING, SOUTH (St Michael the Archangel)   *see* Trin in Lewes *Chich*

MALLING, WEST (St Mary) w Offham *Roch 7*   **P** *Ld Chan and DBP (alt)*   **V** D R J GREEN   **C** M MONTGOMERY

MALMESBURY (St Peter and St Paul) and Upper Avon *Bris 6*   **P** *Ch Trust Fund Trust (2 turns), Ld Chan (1 turn)*
V O C M ROSS

MALPAS (St Andrew)   *see* St Clement *Truro*

MALPAS (St Oswald) and Threapwood and Bickerton *Ches 5*   **P** *Patr Bd*   **R** *vacant*

MALTBY (St Bartholomew) *Sheff 5*   **P** *Bp*   **TR** M RAJKOVIC

MALTON (St Michael) and Old Malton *York 6*   **P** *Sir Philip Naylor-Leyland Bt*   **V** G W DIGGINS

MALTON, OLD (St Mary the Virgin)   *see* Malton and Old Malton *York*

MALVERN (Holy Trinity) (St James) *Worc 2*   **P** *Bp and D&C Westmr (jt)*   **V** R C ELLIOTT

MALVERN (St Andrew)   *see* Malvern Chase *Worc*

MALVERN CHASE (St Andrew), including Pickersleigh and Wyche *Worc 2*   **P** *Patr Bd*   **TR** D C BRUCE   **TV** L SPARKES
C P J L MYRES

MALVERN LINK (Church of the Ascension) (St Matthias) w Cowleigh *Worc 2*   **P** *Trustees of late Else Countess Beauchamp*
V P T JOHNSON

MALVERN, GREAT (Christchurch) *Worc 2*   **P** *Bp*
C J GORDON

MALVERN, GREAT (St Mary and St Michael) *Worc 2*   **P** *Bp*
V R G CORKE

MALVERN, LITTLE (St Giles) *Worc 2*   **P** *Exors T M Berington Esq*   **V** S SEALY

MALVERN, WEST (St James)   *see* Malvern H Trin and St Jas *Worc*

MAMBLE (St John the Baptist) w Bayton, Rock w Heightington w Far Forest *Worc 1*   **P** *Ld Chan and R Ribbesford w Bewdley etc (alt)*   **P-in-c** S E BUTCHER
NSM J M A QUINN

MAMHEAD (St Thomas the Apostle)   *see* Exminster, Kenn, Kenton w Mamhead, and Powderham *Ex*

MANACCAN (St Manaccus and St Dunstan)   *see* Meneage *Truro*

MANATON (St Winifred)   *see* Moretonhampstead, Manaton, N Bovey and Lustleigh *Ex*

MANBY (St Mary)   *see* Mid Marsh Gp *Linc*

MANCETTER (St Peter) *Cov 5*   **P** *Ch Patr Trust*   **V** L A MUDD

MANCHESTER (Apostles) w Miles Platting *Man 1*   **P** *DBP*
P-in-c E L TRIMBLE   **NSM** P M SCOTT

MANCHESTER (Church of the Resurrection)   *see* Manchester Gd Shep and St Barn *Man*

MANCHESTER (St Ann) *Man 2*   **P** *Bp*   **R** J N ASHWORTH
C P R HORLOCK, S N ISAAC

MANCHESTER (St John Chrysostom) Victoria Park *Man 1*
P *Bp*   **R** I D GOMERSALL   **C** A O CHIMHOWU
Hon C K A C WASEY   **OLM** C N HARTLEY

MANCHESTER Clayton (St Cross w St Paul) *Man 1*   **P** *Bp*
R C J MOORE

MANCHESTER Good Shepherd (St Barnabas) (Church of the Resurrection) *Man 1*   **P** *The Crown and Trustees (alt)*
C A J ROBERTSON

MANEA (St Nicholas)   *see* Six Fen Churches *Ely*

MANEY (St Peter) *Birm 4*   **P** *Bp*   **V** R L STEPHENS
C E S ROBOTTOM-SCOTT

MANFIELD (All Saints)   *see* E Dere Street *Leeds*

MANGOTSFIELD (St James) *Bris 5*   **P** *Peache Trustees*
V T M TAYLOR   **Hon C** P G HUZZEY

MANLEY (St John the Evangelist)   *see* Alvanley *Ches*

MANNINGFORD BRUCE (St Peter)   *see* Vale of Pewsey *Sarum*

MANNINGTON (St Paul and St Jude)   *see* Girlington, Heaton and Manningham *Leeds*

MANNINGS HEATH (Church of the Good Shepherd)   *see* Nuthurst and Mannings Heath *Chich*

MANOR PARK (St Barnabas)   *see* Lt Ilford St Barn *Chelmsf*

MANOR PARK (St John the Baptist) and Whitby Road *Ox 12*   **P** *Eton Coll*   **V** *vacant*

MANOR PARK (St Mary the Virgin)   *see* Lt Ilford St Mich *Chelmsf*

MANOR PARK (St Michael and All Angels) *as above*

MANOR PARK (William Temple)   *see* Sheff Manor *Sheff*

MANSEL LACY (St Michael)   *see* Magnis Gp *Heref*

MANSERGH (St Peter)   *see* Kirkby Lonsdale *Carl*

MANSFIELD (St Augustine) and Pleasley Hill St Barnabas *S'well 2*   **P** *Bp*   **V** *vacant*

MANSFIELD (St John the Evangelist) (St Mary) *S'well 2*
P *Bp*   **V** C M LEE

MANSFIELD (St Lawrence) *S'well 2*   **P** *Bp*   **V** *vacant*

MANSFIELD (St Mark) *S'well 2*   **P** *Bp*   **V** C J PHILLIPS
C J S CURRY, P A SCOTT

MANSFIELD (St Peter and St Paul) *S'well 2*   **P** *Bp*
V C J PHILLIPS   **C** J S CURRY, P A SCOTT

MANSFIELD Oak Tree Lane *S'well 2*   **P** *DBP*   **P-in-c** P J STEAD

MANSFIELD WOODHOUSE (St Edmund King and Martyr) *S'well 2*   **P** *Bp*   **V** *vacant*

MANSTON (St Catherine)   *see* St Laur in Thanet *Cant*

MANSTON (St James) *Leeds 13*   **P** *R Barwick in Elmet*
V C A JAMES

MANSTON (St Nicholas)   *see* Okeford *Sarum*

MANTHORPE (St John the Evangelist)   *see* Grantham, Manthorpe *Linc*

MANTON (St Mary the Virgin)   *see* Empingham, Edith Weston, Lyndon, Manton etc *Pet*

MANTON (St Paul)   *see* Worksop St Paul *S'well*

MANUDEN (St Mary the Virgin)   *see* Clavering w Langley, Arkesden etc *Chelmsf*

MAPERTON (St Peter and St Paul)   *see* Camelot Par *B & W*

MAPLEBECK (St Radegund) *S'well 3*   **P** *Sir Philip Naylor-Leyland Bt*   **P-in-c** C G PEARSE   **NSM** M A GROVES

MAPLEDURHAM (St Margaret)   *see* Caversham Thameside and Mapledurham *Ox*

MAPLEDURWELL (St Mary)   *see* N Hants Downs *Win*

MAPLESTEAD, GREAT (St Giles)   *see* Halstead Area *Chelmsf*

MAPLESTEAD, LITTLE (St John) *as above*

MAPPERLEY (Holy Trinity)   *see* W Hallam and Mapperley w Stanley *Derby*

MAPPERLEY (St Jude)   *see* Nottingham St Jude *S'well*

MAPPLEBOROUGH GREEN (Holy Ascension)   *see* Arden Marches *Cov*

MAPPLETON (All Saints) *see* Aldbrough, Mappleton w Goxhill and Withernwick *York*

MAPPOWDER (St Peter and St Paul) *see* Hazelbury Bryan and the Hillside Par *Sarum*

MARAZION (All Saints) *see* Ludgvan, Marazion, St Hilary and Perranuthnoe *Truro*

MARBURY (St Michael) w Tushingham and Whitewell *Ches 5* **P** *MMCET and Bp (jt)* **P-in-c** V G GREEN

MARCH (St John) (St Mary) (St Peter) (St Wendreda) *Ely 11* **P** *Patr Bd* **TR** A J SMITH **NSM** J E REES

MARCHAM (All Saints) w Garford and Shippon *Ox 19* **P** *Bp and Ch Ch Ox (jt)* **NSM** R C SIEBERT

MARCHINGTON (St Peter) *see* Uttoxeter Area *Lich*

MARCHINGTON WOODLANDS (St John) *as above*

MARCHWOOD (St John) *Win 11* **P** *Bp* **P-in-c** S A HONES

MARCLE, LITTLE (St Michael and All Angels) *see* Cider Churches *Heref*

MARCLE, MUCH (St Bartholomew) *as above*

MARDEN (All Saints) *see* Cannings and Redhorn *Sarum*

MARDEN (St Hilda) w Preston Grange *Newc 5* **P** *Bp* **V** *vacant*

MARDEN (St Mary the Virgin) *see* Maund Gp *Heref*

MARDEN (St Michael and All Angels) *Cant 11* **P** *Abp* **V** N J HARVEY

MARDEN ASH (St James) *see* High Ongar w Norton Mandeville *Chelmsf*

MARDEN VALE, comprising Bremhill, Calne and Blackland, Derry Hill, and Foxham *Sarum 16* **P** *The Crown and Patr Bd* (alt) **TR** R A KENWAY **TV** L S CARTER, T M MICHAUX

MARDEN, EAST (St Peter) *see* Octagon *Chich*

MARDEN, NORTH (St Mary) *as above*

MARDYKE Team, The, comprising Aveley, Belhus Park, Purfleet, and South Ockendon *Chelmsf 15* **P** *Patr Bd* **TR** A T FRANKLAND **TV** M J DRUMMOND

MAREHAM ON THE HILL (All Saints) *see* Fen and Hill Gp *Linc*

MAREHAM-LE-FEN (St Helen) *as above*

MARESFIELD (St Bartholomew) *Chich 18* **P** *Ch Trust Fund Trust* **R** B W SEAR **NSM** P C INGRAM

MARFLEET (St Giles) (St George) (St Hilda) (St Philip) *York 14* **P** *Patr Bd* **TV** A J MACPHERSON

MARGARET MARSH (St Margaret) *see* Shaftesbury *Sarum*

MARGARET RODING (St Margaret) *see* High Easter and Good Easter w Margaret Roding *Chelmsf*

MARGARET STREET (All Saints) *see* St Marylebone All SS *Lon*

MARGATE (All Saints) *Cant 5* **P** *Abp* **P-in-c** D L WATSON

MARGATE (Holy Trinity) *Cant 5* **P** *Ch Patr Trust* **V** C B STOCKING **C** J P HUFFMAN

MARGATE (St John the Baptist in Thanet) *Cant 5* **P** *Abp* **P-in-c** D L WATSON

MARGATE (St Paul) *see* Cliftonville *Cant*

MARGATE (St Philip) Northdown Park *Cant 5* **P** *Ch Patr Trust* **V** S GAY

MARHAM (Holy Trinity) *see* W Norfolk Priory Gp *Ely*

MARHAMCHURCH (St Marwenne) *see* Bude Coast and Country *Truro*

MARHOLM (St Mary the Virgin) *see* Castor w Upton and Stibbington etc *Pet*

MARIANSLEIGH (St Mary) *see* Bishopsnympton, Charles, E Anstey, High Bray etc *Ex*

MARISHES, THE (St Francis) *see* Pickering w Lockton and Levisham *York*

MARK (Holy Cross) *see* The Huntspills and Mark *B & W*

MARK BEECH (Holy Trinity) *see* Hever, Four Elms and Mark Beech *Roch*

MARK CROSS (St Mark) *see* Rotherfield w Mark Cross *Chich*

MARKBY (St Peter) *see* Alford Gp *Linc*

MARKET BOSWORTH (St Peter) *see* Bosworth *Leic*

MARKET DEEPING (St Guthlac) *Linc 19* **P** *Ld Chan* **R** G L HOLDING

MARKET DRAYTON (St Mary) *see* Drayton in Hales *Lich*

MARKET HARBOROUGH (St Dionysius) (The Transfiguration) - Little Bowden w Lubenham and Great Bowden *Leic 3* **P** *Patr Bd* **TR** B L HILL **TV** A J ILIFFE, H M CORCORAN **C** A W GILES, J R PICKERSGILL, R P LEVERITT, S J HILL, T A G GRANT **Hon C** A T HELM, J WIXON, P T MACKENZIE **NSM** D G PALMER, S M COOPER

MARKET LAVINGTON (St Mary of the Assumption) *see* The Lavingtons, Cheverells, and Easterton *Sarum*

MARKET OVERTON (St Peter and St Paul) *see* Oakham, Ashwell, Braunston, Brooke, Egleton etc *Pet*

MARKET RASEN (St Thomas the Apostle) *Linc 7* **P** *Ld Chan* **V** C V WALKER

MARKET WEIGHTON (All Saints) *York 5* **P** *Abp* **V** *vacant*

MARKET WEIGHTON (All Saints) *see* Weighton Wold *York*

MARKET WESTON (St Mary) *see* Stanton *St E*

MARKFIELD (St Michael), Thornton, Bagworth and Stanton under Bardon, and Copt Oak *Leic 9* **P** *MMCET* **R** A SMITH **NSM** P ASHBY

MARKHAM CLINTON (All Saints) *see* Tuxford w Weston, Markham Clinton etc *S'well*

MARKHAM, EAST (St John the Baptist) *see* The Rivers *S'well*

MARKINGTON (St Michael) *see* Bishop Thornton, Burnt Yates, Markington etc *Leeds*

MARKS GATE (St Mark) Chadwell Heath *Chelmsf 1* **P** *Bp* **P-in-c** A J GUEST

MARKS TEY (St Andrew) and Aldham *Chelmsf 20* **P** *CPAS and MMCET (jt)* **P-in-c** I M SCOTT-THOMPSON

MARKSBURY (St Peter) *see* Farmborough, Marksbury and Stanton Prior *B & W*

MARKYATE STREET (St John the Baptist) *see* Flamstead and Markyate Street *St Alb*

MARLBOROUGH (All Saints), Salcombe and South Huish *Ex 12* **P** *Keble Coll Ox and D&C Sarum (jt)* **V** D A FRENCH **C** C D J HILL

MARLBOROUGH (St Mary the Virgin) *Sarum 18* **P** *Patr Bd* **TR** C J SMITH **TV** P D SAINSBURY

MARLBROOK (St Luke) *see* Bromsgrove *Worc*

MARLBROOK Team Ministry, The *see* Bath Twerton-on-Avon *B & W*

MARLDON (St John the Baptist) *see* Totnes w Bridgetown, Berry Pomeroy etc *Ex*

MARLESFORD (St Andrew) *see* Orebeck *St E*

MARLEY HILL (St Cuthbert) *see* Hillside *Dur*

MARLINGFORD (Assumption of the Blessed Virgin Mary) *see* Easton, Colton, Marlingford and Bawburgh *Nor*

MARLOW BOTTOM (St Mary the Virgin) *see* Gt Marlow w Marlow Bottom, Lt Marlow and Bisham *Ox*

MARLOW, GREAT (All Saints) w Marlow Bottom, Little Marlow and Bisham *Ox 18* **P** *Patr Bd* **TR** D T BULL **TV** G H L WATTS, S A L WATTS, S FITZGERALD **C** M F GOULD, R G SLADE, S R EDEN-JONES **NSM** J R SMITH

MARLOW, LITTLE (St John the Baptist) *see* Gt Marlow w Marlow Bottom, Lt Marlow and Bisham *Ox*

MARLPIT HILL (St Paulinus) *see* Edenbridge *Roch*

MARLPOOL (All Saints) *Derby 8* **P** V *Heanor* **V** K PADLEY **C** L SHEMILT

MARLSTON (St Mary) *see* Bucklebury w Marlston *Ox*

MARNHULL (St Gregory) *Sarum 5* **P** *DBF* **P-in-c** P M SARGENT **C** G M HOCKEY

MAROWN (Old Parish Church) (St Runius), Foxdale and Baldwin *S & M* **P** *The Crown* **V** J A WARD **NSM** S J HERRON

MARPLE (All Saints) *Ches 16* **P** *R Stockport St Mary* **V** D R CURRIE **C** J S BEATTY, L S CURRIE

MARPLE, LOW (St Martin) *Ches 16* **P** *Keble Coll Ox* **V** T HUPFIELD

MARR (St Helen) *see* Bilham *Sheff*

MARSDEN (St Bartholomew) and Slaithwaite w East Scammonden *Leeds 9* **P** R *Almondbury w Farnley Tyas and* V *Huddersfield (jt)* **V** G R HOLDSWORTH **NSM** J N BAXTER FIELDING

MARSDEN, GREAT (St John's Church Centre) w Nelson St Philip *Blackb 6* **P** *The Crown and Bp (alt)* **V** L A HILLIARD **C** V SOHAIL

MARSDEN, LITTLE (St Paul) w Nelson St Mary and Nelson St Bede *Blackb 6* **P** *Bp* **V** G S JAMIESON **C** S C LLOYD

MARSH (St George) *see* Lancaster St Mary w St John and St Anne *Blackb*

MARSH BALDON (St Peter) *see* Dorchester *Ox*

MARSH FARM (Holy Cross) *St Alb 12* **P** *Bp* **P-in-c** R A H BROWN

MARSH GIBBON (St Mary the Virgin) *see* The Claydons and Swan *Ox*

MARSHALSWICK (St Mary) *see* St Alb St Mary Marshalswick *St Alb*

MARSHAM (All Saints) *see* Aylsham and Distr *Nor*

MARSHCHAPEL (St Mary the Virgin), Somercotes and Grainthorpe w Conisholme *Linc 15* **P** *Duchy of Lancaster (4 turns), Bp and Magd Coll Cam (2 turns), R H C Haigh Esq, Trustees, and Adn Linc (1 turn), R H C Haigh Esq, Trustees, and Exors Mrs M F Davis (1 turn)* **V** *vacant*

MARSHFIELD (St Mary the Virgin) w Cold Ashton and Tormarton w West Littleton *Bris 4* **P** *New Coll Ox and Bp (alt)* **V** S A V WHEELER **NSM** A M E KEMP **OLM** C L GODFREY

MARSHLAND, The, comprising Adlingfleet, Eastoft, Swinefleet, and Whitgift *Sheff 10* **P** *Ld Chan and Bp (alt)* **P-in-c** J L SMITH **C** A TEASDALE

MARSHWOOD (St Mary) *see* Golden Cap Team *Sarum*

MARSKE (St Edmund King and Martyr) *see* Richmond w Hudswell and Downholme and Marske *Leeds*

MARSKE IN CLEVELAND (St Mark) *York 16* P *Abp*
 V D TEMBEY
MARSKE, NEW (St Thomas) *York 16* P *Abp* V A M F REED
MARSTON (St Leonard) *see* Stafford St Mary and Marston
 Lich
MARSTON (St Mary) *see* S Cliff Villages Gp *Linc*
MARSTON (St Nicholas) w Elsfield *Ox 1* P *Bp and D&C (jt)*
 V E K DENNO **NSM** A G G GOSLER
MARSTON BIGOT (St Leonard) *see* Nunney and Witham
 Friary, Marston Bigot etc *B & W*
MARSTON GREEN (St Leonard) *Birm 5* P *Birm Dioc Trustees*
 V *vacant*
MARSTON MAGNA (Blessed Virgin Mary) *see* Chilton
 Cantelo, Ashington, Mudford, Rimpton etc *B & W*
MARSTON MEYSEY (St James) *see* S Cotswolds *Glouc*
MARSTON MONTGOMERY (St Giles) *see* S Dales *Derby*
MARSTON MOOR, comprising Askham Richard, Bilbrough,
 Long Marston, Rufforth, and Tockwith *York 1* P *MMCET, C*
 York Esq, Abp, and N W Wailes-Fairbairn Esq (jt)
 V M J OTTER
MARSTON MORTEYNE (St Mary the Virgin) w Lidlington
 St Alb 9 P *Bp and St Jo Coll Cam (alt)* R *vacant*
MARSTON ON DOVE (St Mary) *see* Hilton w Marston-on-
 Dove *Derby*
MARSTON SICCA (St James the Great) *see* Quinton,
 Welford, Weston and Marston Sicca *Glouc*
MARSTON ST LAWRENCE (St Lawrence) *see* Chenderit *Pet*
MARSTON TRUSSELL (St Nicholas) *see* Clipston, Haselbech,
 Kelmarsh, Marston Trussell etc *Pet*
MARSTON, NEW (St Michael and All Angels) *Ox 1* P *Bp*
 V E B BARDWELL
MARSTON, NORTH (Assumption of the Blessed Virgin Mary)
 see Schorne *Ox*
MARSTON, SOUTH (St Mary Magdalene) *see* Stratton
 St Margaret w S Marston etc *Bris*
MARSTOW (St Matthew) *see* Wye Brooks Benefice *Heref*
MARSWORTH (All Saints) *see* Ivinghoe w Pitstone and
 Slapton and Marsworth *Ox*
**MARTHAM (St Mary) and Repps w Bastwick, Thurne and
 Clippesby** *Nor 6* P *Bp, D&C, DBP and K Edw VI Gr Sch (jt)*
 P-in-c S R SIVYER
MARTIN (All Saints) *see* W Downland *Sarum*
MARTIN (Holy Trinity) *see* Carr Dyke Gp *Linc*
MARTIN (St Michael) *see* Horncastle Gp *Linc*
MARTIN HUSSINGTREE (St Michael) *see* Droitwich, and
 Salwarpe and Hindlip w Martin Hussingtree *Worc*
MARTINDALE (Old Church) *see* Barton, Pooley Bridge,
 Martindale etc *Carl*
MARTINDALE (St Peter) *as above*
MARTINHOE (St Martin) *see* Lynton, Brendon, Countisbury
 etc *Ex*
MARTLESHAM (St Mary the Virgin) w Brightwell *St E 10*
 P *Bp* R T J TATE **NSM** C A PINDER, M RITTMAN
MARTLESHAM HEATH (St Michael and All Angels) *see*
 Martlesham w Brightwell *St E*
MARTLEY (St Peter) *see* Worcs W Rural *Worc*
MARTOCK (All Saints) w Kingsbury Episcopi and Ash
 B & W 5 P *Bp and D&C (jt)* V P L FILLERY
MARTON (Room) *see* Middleton, Newton and Sinnington
 York
MARTON (St Esprit) *see* Long Itchington and Marton *Cov*
**MARTON (St James), Siddington w Capesthorne, and
 Eaton w Hulme Walfield and Swettenham** *Ches 11* P *Bp,*
 MMCET, and Sir W A B Davenport (jt) V I M ARCH
MARTON (St Margaret of Antioch) *see* Lea Gp *Linc*
MARTON (St Mary) *see* Forest of Galtres *York*
MARTON (St Paul) *Blackb 8* P *V Poulton-le-Fylde*
 V L A ATKINS
MARTON CUM GRAFTON (Christ Church) *see* Gt and Lt
 Ouseburn w Marton cum Grafton etc *Leeds*
MARTON IN CRAVEN (St Peter) *see* Broughton, Marton and
 Thornton *Leeds*
MARTON-IN-CHIRBURY (St Mark) *see* Chirbury, Marton,
 Middleton and Trelystan etc *Heref*
MARTON-IN-CLEVELAND (St Cuthbert) w Easterside
 York 17 P *Abp* V C M TAYLOR C S M TYNDALL
MARTYR WORTHY (St Swithun) *see* Itchen Valley *Win*
MARWOOD (St Michael and All Angels) *see* Heanton
 Punchardon, Marwood and W Down *Ex*
MARY TAVY (St Mary) *see* Peter Tavy and Mary Tavy *Ex*
MARYFIELD (St Philip and St James) *see* Maker w Rame,
 Millbrook, St John and Torpoint *Truro*
MARYLEBONE ROAD (St Marylebone) *see* St Marylebone w
 H Trin *Lon*
**MARYPORT (St Mary) (Christ Church), Netherton, Flimby
 and Broughton Moor** *Carl 7* P *Patr Bd* **TR** *vacant*

MARYSTOWE (St Mary the Virgin) *see* Milton Abbot,
 Dunterton, Lamerton etc *Ex*
MASBROUGH (St Paul) *Sheff 6* P *Bp and Ld Chan (alt)*
 P-in-c P J BATCHFORD C A J MIDDLETON, R E YOUNG
 NSM S C ARMSTRONG
MASHAM (St Mary the Virgin) and Healey *Leeds 20* P *Trin*
 Coll Cam C S L LAWTON
MASSINGHAM, GREAT (St Mary) *see* Ashwicken w Leziate,
 Bawsey etc *Nor*
MASSINGHAM, LITTLE (St Andrew) *as above*
MATCHBOROUGH (Christ Church) *see* Ipsley *Worc*
MATCHING (St Mary) *see* High Laver w Magdalen Laver and
 Lt Laver etc *Chelmsf*
MATCHING GREEN (St Edmund) *as above*
MATFEN (Holy Trinity) *see* Stamfordham w Matfen *Newc*
MATFIELD (St Luke) *see* Lamberhurst and Matfield *Roch*
MATHON (St John the Baptist) *see* Cradley w Mathon and
 Storridge *Heref*
MATLASKE (St Peter), including Baconsthorpe, Barningham,
 Edgefield, Hempstead, Plumstead, and Saxthorpe w
 Corpusty *Nor 17* P *Duchy of Lanc (1 turn), CPAS, D&C, T J R*
 Courtauld Esq, SMF, and Pemb Coll Cam (2 turns)
 R D J H LONGE
**MATLOCK (St Giles) (St John the Baptist), Dethick, Lea
 and Holloway** *Derby 1* P *Bp and DBF (jt)*
 R B M CROWTHER-ALWYN
MATLOCK BANK (All Saints) and Tansley *Derby 1* P *Bp*
 V R B READE
MATLOCK BATH (Holy Trinity) and Cromford *Derby 1*
 P *Ch Trust Fund Trust* V *vacant*
MATSON (St Katharine) *Glouc 2* P *D&C* **P-in-c** S J TODD
MATTERDALE (not known) *see* Greystoke w Penruddock,
 Mungrisdale etc *Carl*
MATTERSEY (All Saints) *see* Bawtry w Austerfield, Misson,
 Everton and Mattersey *S'well*
MATTINGLEY (not known) *see* Whitewater *Win*
MATTISHALL (All Saints) and the Tudd Valley *Nor 16* P *Bp,*
 G&C Coll Cam, DBP, and J V Berney Esq (jt)
 R M A MCCAGHREY C A R WOODS **NSM** S E THURGILL
MATTISHALL BURGH (St Peter) *see* Mattishall and the Tudd
 Valley *Nor*
MAULDEN (St Mary) *St Alb 8* P *Bp* R L KLIMAS
MAUNBY (St Michael) *see* Lower Swale *Leeds*
MAUND Group of Parishes, comprising Bodenham, Felton
 and Preston Wynne, Marden w Amberley and Wisteston,
 and Sutton St Nicholas and Sutton St Michael *Heref 6* P *Bp*
 (2 turns), D&C (1 turn) R P M ROBERTS C N A JENNINGS
MAUTBY (St Peter and St Paul) *see* S Trin Broads *Nor*
MAVESYN RIDWARE (St Nicholas) *see* Kings Bromley, The
 Ridwares and Yoxall *Lich*
MAVIS ENDERBY (St Michael) *see* Bolingbroke Deanery *Linc*
MAWDESLEY (St Peter) *see* Croston, Bretherton and
 Mawdesley w Bispham *Blackb*
MAWNAN (St Mawnan) (St Michael) *Truro 2* P *Bp*
 P-in-c J H CLARE
MAXEY (St Peter) *see* Glinton, Etton, Maxey, Peakirk and
 Northborough *Pet*
MAXSTOKE (St Michael and All Angels) *Birm 5* P *Lord*
 Leigh V *vacant*
MAY HILL (All Saints) *see* Huntley and Longhope, Churcham
 and Bulley *Glouc*
MAYBRIDGE (St Richard) and West Tarring *Chich 7* P *Abp*
 Cant and Bp (jt) R M J LYON C I H EDGAR
 NSM G T SPENCER
MAYBUSH (St Peter) and Southampton St Jude *Win 13*
 P *Bp* **P-in-c** J J BAKKER **NSM** J C ATTENBOROUGH
MAYBUSH Redbridge (All Saints) *see* Maybush and
 Southampton St Jude *Win*
MAYFAIR (Christ Church) *see* Down Street Ch Ch *Lon*
MAYFIELD (St Dunstan) *Chich 16* P *Keble Coll Ox* V *vacant*
MAYFIELD (St John the Baptist) *see* Alton w Bradley-le-
 Moors, Ellastone w Stanton, and Mayfield *Lich*
MAYFORD (Emmanuel) *see* Woking St Jo *Guildf*
**MAYLAND (St Barnabas) (St Barnabas Family Centre) and
 Latchingdon** *Chelmsf 10* P *Bp and Abp (jt)* V *vacant*
MEANWOOD (Holy Trinity) *Leeds 12* P *Bp* V J ROGERS
 NSM M J BRADLEY
MEARE (Blessed Virgin Mary and All Saints) *see* Glastonbury
 w Meare *B & W*
**MEARS ASHBY (All Saints) and Hardwick and Sywell w
 Overstone** *Pet 6* P *Duchy of Cornwall (2 turns), Bracegirdle*
 Trustees (1 turn), and Mrs C K Edmiston (1 turn)
 R K M HUTCHINS **NSM** L S TOMALIN
MEASE VALLEY, comprising Clifton Campville, Edingale,
 Elford, and Harlaston *Lich 4* P *Bp, Exors Major F C*

Pipe-Wolferstan, and Mrs E V G Inge-Innes-Lillingston (jt)
R J W R GRICE **OLM** N J BUSBY

MEASHAM (St Laurence) *see* Woodfield *Leic*

MEAVY (St Peter) *see* Yelverton, Meavy, Sheepstor, Walkhampton, Sampford Spiney and Horrabridge *Ex*

MEDBOURNE (St Giles) *see* Six Saints circa Holt *Leic*

MEDMENHAM (St Peter and St Paul) *see* Hambleden Valley *Ox*

MEDOMSLEY (St Mary Magdalene) *Dur 2* **P** *Bp*
P-in-c J FISHER **NSM** I W WAUGH

MEDSTEAD (St Andrew) *see* Bentworth, Lasham, Medstead and Shalden *Win*

MEERBROOK (St Matthew) *see* Leek and Meerbrook *Lich*

MEESDEN (St Mary) *see* Hormead, Wyddial, Anstey, Brent Pelham etc *St Alb*

MEETH (St Michael and All Angels) *see* Okehampton, Inwardleigh, Belstone, Sourton etc *Ex*

MEIR (Holy Trinity) *see* Longton and Meir *Lich*

MEIR HEATH (St Francis of Assisi) and Normacot *Lich 11*
P *Bp and DBP (jt)* **V** D W MCHARDY

MEIR PARK (St Clare) *see* Meir Heath and Normacot *Lich*

MELBECKS (Holy Trinity) *see* Swaledale *Leeds*

MELBOURN (All Saints) *Ely 7* **P** *D&C*
P-in-c E A MURGATROYD-SHIPP **NSM** M L PRICE

MELBOURNE (St Michael), Ticknall, Smisby and Stanton by Bridge *Derby 7* **P** *Bp* **V** S T SHORT **OLM** A L WINFIELD

MELBURY *Sarum 3* **P** *Patr Bd* **TR** T J GREENSLADE
TV D E INGLES

MELBURY ABBAS (St Thomas) *see* Shaftesbury *Sarum*

MELBURY BUBB (St Mary the Virgin) *see* Melbury *Sarum*

MELBURY OSMUND (St Osmund) *as above*

MELCHBOURNE (St Mary Magdalene) *see* The Stodden Churches *St Alb*

MELCOMBE HORSEY (St Andrew) *see* Piddle Valley, Hilton and Ansty, Cheselbourne etc *Sarum*

MELDON (St John the Evangelist) *see* Bolam w Whalton and Hartburn w Meldon *Newc*

MELDRETH (Holy Trinity) *Ely 7* **P** *D&C*
P-in-c E A MURGATROYD-SHIPP **NSM** M L PRICE

MELKSHAM (St Barnabas) (St Michael and All Angels)
Sarum 15 **P** *DBP* **TR** C H THOMSON **TV** A SOWTON
NSM H BEGLEY

MELKSHAM FOREST (St Andrew) *see* Melksham *Sarum*

MELLING (St Thomas) *see* Maghull and Melling *Liv*

MELLING (St Wilfrid) *see* E Lonsdale *Blackb*

MELLIS (St Mary the Virgin) *see* S Hartismere *St E*

MELLOR (St Mary) *see* Balderstone, Mellor and Samlesbury *Blackb*

MELLOR (St Thomas) *Ches 16* **P** *Bp* **V** T WARD

MELLS (St Andrew) w Buckland Dinham, Elm, Whatley, Vobster and Chantry *B & W 3* **P** *DBP (2 turns), Bp (1 turn)*
R C A FAIRCLOUGH

MELMERBY (St John the Baptist) *see* Cross Fell Gp *Carl*

MELPLASH (Christ Church) *see* Beaminster Area *Sarum*

MELSONBY (St James the Great) *see* Forcett and Aldbrough and Melsonby *Leeds*

MELTHAM (St Bartholomew) *see* Meltham *Leeds*

MELTHAM Christ the King (St Bartholomew) (St James)
Leeds 5 **P** *Simeon's Trustees, R Almondbury w Farnley Tyas, and Bp (jt)* **V** J S DRACUP **NSM** D SHIELDS, P ROLLS
OLM J F RADCLIFFE

MELTHAM MILLS (St James) *see* Meltham *Leeds*

MELTON (St Andrew) and Ufford *St E 16* **P** *D&C Ely (3 turns), and T R E Blois-Brooke Esq (1 turn)* **R** P G HAMBLING

MELTON CONSTABLE (St Peter) *see* Briston, Burgh Parva, Hindolveston etc *Nor*

MELTON MOWBRAY (St Mary) *Leic 2* **P** *Patr Bd*
TR K P ASHBY **TV** M E BARR

MELTON ROSS (Ascension) *see* Brocklesby Park, Croxton and North Wolds *Linc*

MELTON, GREAT (All Saints) *see* Hethersett w Canteloff w Lt and Gt Melton *Nor*

MELTON, HIGH (St James) *see* Barnburgh w Melton on the Hill etc *Sheff*

MELTON, LITTLE (All Saints) *see* Hethersett w Canteloff w Lt and Gt Melton *Nor*

MELVERLEY (St Peter) *see* Kinnerley w Melverley, Knockin w Maesbrook and Maesbury *Lich*

MEMBURY (St John the Baptist) *see* Axminster, All Saints, Axmouth, Chardstock etc *Ex*

MENDHAM (All Saints) *see* Sancroft *St E*

MENDLESHAM (St Mary) *St E 3* **P** *SMF* **V** P T GRAY

MENEAGE (St Anthony) (St Martin) (St Mawgan) (St Manaccus and St Dunstan) *Truro 3* **P** *Ld Chan and Bp (alt)* **R** *vacant*

MENHENIOT (St Lalluwy and St Antoninus) *Truro 12* **P** *Ex Coll Ox* **P-in-c** R M BELL **C** L J SELMAN

MENSTON (St John the Divine) w Woodhead *Leeds 4* **P** *Bp*
V S PROUDLOVE **NSM** A J HOWORTH

MENTMORE (St Mary the Virgin) *see* Cottesloe *Ox*

MEOLE BRACE (Holy Trinity) *Lich 19* **P** *J K Bather Esq*
V P J CANSDALE **C** F M H IDDON **NSM** C RUXTON, V PITT

MEOLS, GREAT (St John the Baptist) *Ches 8* **P** *Bp*
V G A ROSSITER **NSM** F SKINNER

MEOLS, NORTH Team Ministry, The (St Cuthbert), including Banks and Crossens *Liv 9* **P** *Patr Bd*
TR K J R CLARKE **C** C P GREGORY, S MCTAGGART

MEON BRIDGE, comprising Droxford, Exton, and Meonstoke w Corhampton *Portsm 1* **P** *Bp* **R** A W FORREST
C D B MORGAN

MEON, EAST (All Saints) *Portsm 4* **P** *Ld Chan*
Hon C M P JEPP

MEON, WEST (St John the Evangelist) and Warnford
Portsm 4 **P** *Bp and DBP (alt)* **Hon C** M P JEPP

MEONSTOKE (St Andrew) *see* Meon Bridge *Portsm*

MEOPHAM (St John the Baptist) w Nurstead *Roch 1*
P *D&C and Mrs S Edmeades-Stearns (jt)* **R** A E DAVIE

MEPAL (St Mary) *see* Witcham w Mepal *Ely*

MEPPERSHALL (St Mary the Virgin) and Shefford *St Alb 8*
P *Bp and St Jo Coll Cam (alt)* **V** V M GOODMAN

MERE (St Michael the Archangel) w West Knoyle and Maiden Bradley *Sarum 12* **P** *Bp* **V** *vacant*

MERES AND MEADOWS *see* Petton w Cockshutt, Welshampton and Lyneal etc *Lich*

MERESIDE (St Wilfrid) *see* Blackpool St Wilfrid *Blackb*

MEREVALE (St Mary the Virgin) *see* Baxterley w Hurley and Wood End and Merevale etc *Birm*

MEREWORTH (St Lawrence), Wateringbury and West Peckham *Roch 7* **P** *D&C and Viscount Falmouth (jt)*
R G TOWNSEND

MERIDEN (St Laurence) *Cov 4* **P** *Chapter Cov Cathl*
R *vacant*

MERRINGTON (St John the Evangelist) *Dur 3* **P** *D&C*
P-in-c B A HILTON **NSM** D J HODGE

MERRIOTT (All Saints) w Hinton, Dinnington and Lopen
B & W 14 **P** *D&C Bris (2 turns), Bp (1 turn)* **R** J R HICKS
C R B HICKS

MERROW (St John the Evangelist) *Guildf 5* **P** *Earl of Onslow*
R R STUART-BOURNE

MERRY HILL (St Joseph of Arimathea) *see* Penn Fields *Lich*

MERRYMEET (St Mary) *see* Menheniot *Truro*

MERSEA, WEST (St Peter and St Paul) w East (St Edmund), Peldon, Great and Little Wigborough *Chelmsf 23* **P** *The Crown (1 turn), Patr Bd (2 turns)* **P-in-c** J A BEVAN
C T E WALKER

MERSHAM (St John the Baptist) *see* Stour Downs *Cant*

MERSTHAM (St Katharine), South Merstham and Gatton
S'wark 24 **P** *Patr Bd* **TR** P M PULLINGER

MERSTHAM, SOUTH (All Saints) *see* Merstham, S Merstham and Gatton *S'wark*

MERTON (All Saints) *see* Shebbear, Buckland Filleigh, Sheepwash etc *Ex*

MERTON (St James) *S'wark 13* **P** *Bp and V Merton St Mary (jt)*
NSM A M BUDDEN

MERTON (St John the Divine) *see* Merton Priory *S'wark*

MERTON (St Mary) *S'wark 13* **P** *Bp* **V** J A HAYWARD
NSM J A BERSWEDEN

MERTON (St Peter) *see* Caston, Griston, Merton, Thompson etc *Nor*

MERTON (St Swithun) *see* Ray Valley *Ox*

MERTON PRIORY *S'wark 13* **P** *Patr Bd* **TR** M F EMINSON
TV A G JUDGE **C** S A ASQUITH **Hon C** D J SWAN
NSM B S ALAGOA

MESHAW (St John) *see* Burrington, Chawleigh, Cheldon, Chulmleigh etc *Ex*

MESSING (All Saints) *see* Thurstable and Winstree *Chelmsf*

MESSINGHAM (Holy Trinity) w East Butterwick, Scotter w East Ferry and Scotton w Northorpe *Linc 6* **P** *Bp (2 turns), Ld Chan (1 turn)* **R** D J SWANNACK
OLM D L LANGFORD, W KEAST

MESTY CROFT (St Luke) *see* Wednesbury St Paul Wood Green *Lich*

METFIELD (St John the Baptist) *see* Sancroft *St E*

METHERINGHAM (St Wilfred) w Blankney and Dunston
Linc 12 **P** *Bp (2 turns), DBP (1 turn)* **V** *vacant*

METHLEY (St Oswald) *see* Rothwell, Lofthouse, Methley etc *Leeds*

METHWOLD (St George) *see* Wissey Valley *Ely*

METTINGHAM (All Saints) *see* Bungay *St E*

METTON (St Andrew) *see* Roughton and Felbrigg, Metton, Sustead etc *Nor*

MEVAGISSEY (St Peter)   *see* St Mewan w Mevagissey and
St Ewe *Truro*
MEXBOROUGH (St John the Baptist) *Sheff 12*   **P** *Adn York*
P-in-c E J S MORRISON
MEYSEY HAMPTON (St Mary)   *see* S Cotswolds *Glouc*
MICHAEL (St Michael and All Angels)   *see* W Coast *S & M*
MICHAELCHURCH ESCLEY (St Michael)   *see* Black Mountains
Gp *Heref*
MICHAELSTOW (St Michael)   *see* Camelside *Truro*
MICHELDEVER (St Mary)   *see* Upper Dever *Win*
**MICHELMERSH (Our Lady) and Awbridge and Braishfield
and Farley Chamberlayne and Timsbury** *Win 12*   **P** *Bp*
R T H F BENSON   **NSM** J E C THOMPSON
MICKLEFIELD (St Mary the Virgin)   *see* Aberford w Micklefield
York
MICKLEGATE (Holy Trinity)   *see* York H Trin Micklegate *York*
MICKLEHAM (St Michael)   *see* Leatherhead and Mickleham
Guildf
MICKLEOVER (All Saints) (St John the Evangelist) *Derby 5*
P *Bp and MMCET (jt)*   **V** P F WALLIS   **NSM** M P STAUNTON
OLM I D GODLINGTON, P M PRITCHARD
MICKLETON (St Lawrence)   *see* Vale and Cotswold Edge
Glouc
MICKLEY (St George)   *see* Bywell and Mickley *Newc*
MICKLEY (St John the Evangelist)   *see* Fountains Gp *Leeds*
MID CHURNET   *see* Kingsley and Foxt-w-Whiston and
Oakamoor etc *Lich*
MID ELLOE Group, The, comprising Holbeach Hurn,
Holbeach Marsh, Fleet, and Gedney *Linc 18*   **P** *V Holbeach
and DBP (1 turn), The Crown (1 turn)*   **NSM** E D CRUST
MID LOES, comprising Ashfield-cum-Thorpe, Charsfield w
Debach, Cretingham, Dallinghoo, Earl Soham, Hoo,
Letheringham, and Monewden *St E 12*   **P** *Ld Chan (1 turn),
MMCET, CPAS, Bp, and Wadh Coll Ox (1 turn)*
C K L B MARTIN
MID MARSH Group, The, comprising Alvingham, Great
Carlton, Grimoldby, Manby, and South Cockerington
Linc 15   **P** *A M D Hall Esq, Bp, D&C, and Lady Mowbray (by
turn)*   **OLM** J R SELFE
MID TEST, The, comprising Broughton w Bossington,
Houghton, Leckford, Longstock, Mottisfont, and
Stockbridge *Win 12*   **P** *Ld Chan (1 turn), C M Brendish Esq
(1 turn), Bp and St Jo Coll Ox (1 turn)*   **R** P W BOWDEN
MID TRENT, comprising Fradswell, Gayton, Hixon, Milwich,
Salt, Sandon, Stowe-by-Chartley, and Weston-upon-Trent
Lich 10   **P** *Patr Bd*   **TR** J P B B PHILLIPS
TV M G CADWALLADER   **OLM** C V STARKIE
MIDDLE   *see also under substantive place name*
MIDDLE ESK MOOR, comprising Egton, Glaisdale,
Goathland, and Grosmont *York 21*   **P** *Abp*   **V** *vacant*
MIDDLE MARCHES Benefice, The, comprising Bedstone,
Bucknell, Chapel Lawn, Clungunford, Hopton Castle,
Llanfair Waterdine, and Stowe *Heref 9*   **P** *Earl of Powis, J
Coltman-Rogers Esq, Grocers' Co (1 turn), Mrs E B Rocke, Sir
Huw Ripley Bt, P J H Barnes Esq (1 turn)*   **P-in-c** M S QUAYLE
MIDDLE RASEN Group, The, comprising Faldingworth w
Buslingthorpe, Friesthorpe w Snarford, Middle Rasen Drax,
Newton and Toft, and West Rasen *Linc 7*   **P** *Bp,
Charterhouse, and DBP (jt)*   **R** B S DIXON
MIDDLE WOODFORD   *see* Woodford Valley w Archers Gate
Sarum
**MIDDLEHAM (St Mary and St Alkelda) w Coverdale and
East Witton and Thornton Steward** *Leeds 22*   **P** *Bp, R
Craven-Smith-Milnes Esq, and W R Burdon Esq (jt)*
R J M PAYNE   **C** E J MOODY
MIDDLESBROUGH (All Saints) *York 17*   **P** *Abp*
V G HOLLAND
MIDDLESBROUGH (Ascension) *York 17*   **P** *Abp*
P-in-c E NAZIR MASIH
MIDDLESBROUGH (St Columba w St Paul) *York 17*   **P** *Abp*
V S COOPER   **NSM** P M KRONBERGS
MIDDLESBROUGH (St John the Evangelist) *York 17*   **P** *Abp*
V S COOPER
MIDDLESBROUGH (St Martin of Tours) (St Cuthbert)
York 17   **P** *Abp*   **V** T BURGESS
MIDDLESBROUGH (St Mary)   *see* W Acklam *York*
MIDDLESBROUGH (St Oswald) (St Chad) *York 17*   **P** *Abp*
V S RICHARDSON   **C** V C KIRBY   **NSM** K A DEAN
MIDDLESBROUGH (St Thomas) *York 17*   **P** *Abp*
V T M LEATHLEY
MIDDLESMOOR (St Chad)   *see* Upper Nidderdale *Leeds*
MIDDLESTOWN (St Luke) *Leeds 16*   **P** *R Thornhill*
P-in-c J M GEARY
MIDDLETON (All Saints)   *see* N Hinckford *Chelmsf*
MIDDLETON (Holy Ghost)   *see* Kirkby Lonsdale *Carl*
MIDDLETON (Holy Trinity)   *see* Bromfield *Heref*

MIDDLETON (Holy Trinity)   *see* Yoxmere *St E*
MIDDLETON (St Andrew), Newton and Sinnington *York 19*
P *Abp (2 turns), Simeon's Trustees (1 turn)*   **R** R G BARKER
MIDDLETON (St John the Baptist)   *see* Curdworth, Middleton
and Wishaw *Birm*
MIDDLETON (St Leonard) (St Margaret) and Thornham
Man 6   **P** *Bp*   **R** A M BAILIE   **C** H A BRIDLE
OLM D E BROOKS, K HAMNETT, P J DEMAIN, S L SPENCER
MIDDLETON (St Mary the Virgin) (St Cross) *Leeds 11*   **P** *V
Rothwell and DBP (jt)*   **V** *vacant*
MIDDLETON (St Mary)   *see* Middlewinch *Nor*
MIDDLETON (St Michael and All Angels)   *see* Youlgreave,
Middleton, Stanton-in-Peak etc *Derby*
MIDDLETON (St Nicholas) *Chich 1*   **P** *D&C*   **V** *vacant*
MIDDLETON CHENEY (All Saints)   *see* Chenderit *Pet*
MIDDLETON JUNCTION (St Gabriel)   *see* Chadderton
St Mark *Man*
MIDDLETON ON LEVEN (St Cuthbert)   *see* Whorlton Gp *York*
MIDDLETON ON THE WOLDS (St Andrew)   *see* Woldsburn
York
MIDDLETON SCRIVEN (St John the Baptist)   *see* Stottesdon w
Farlow, Cleeton St Mary etc *Heref*
MIDDLETON ST GEORGE (St George) (St Laurence) *Dur 5*
P *Bp*   **R** *vacant*
MIDDLETON STONEY (All Saints)   *see* Akeman *Ox*
MIDDLETON TYAS (St Michael and All Angels)   *see* E Dere
Street *Leeds*
MIDDLETON-BY-WIRKSWORTH (Holy Trinity)   *see*
Wirksworth *Derby*
MIDDLETON-IN-CHIRBY (Holy Trinity)   *see* Chirbury, Marton,
Middleton and Trelystan etc *Heref*
**MIDDLETON-IN-TEESDALE (St Mary the Virgin) w Forest
and Frith** *Dur 4*   **P** *Lord Barnard and The Crown (alt)*
P-in-c J BARKER   **NSM** A P WALLBANK
MIDDLEWICH (St Michael and All Angels) w Byley *Ches 6*
P *Bp*   **V** S M DREW   **NSM** A P BOULTON, C M HUGHES,
E WOODE, L V REED
MIDDLEWINCH, comprising East Winch w West Bilney,
Middleton, North Runcton, and West Winch *Nor 19*   **P** *Ld
Chan (2 turns), Bp and W O Lancaster Esq (1 turn), Ms E J C
Bostock and Ms C M Mackay (1 turn)*   **R** R MUBARAK
**MIDDLEZOY (Holy Cross) w Othery, Moorlinch and
Greinton** *B & W 4*   **P** *Bp*   **C** A L HARWOOD
MIDGHAM (St Matthew)   *see* Aldermaston and
Woolhampton *Ox*
MIDHURST (St Mary Magdalene and St Denis) *Chich 3*
P *Bp*   **V** D A WILLIS   **NSM** J E ROBERTS
MIDSOMER NORTON (St John the Baptist) w Clandown
B & W 11   **P** *Ch Ch Ox*   **V** G C SCOTT   **NSM** P J HOPPER
MID-WYEDEAN CHURCHES   *see* Coleford, Staunton,
Newland, Redbrook etc *Glouc*
MILBER (St Luke)   *see* Newton Abbot *Ex*
MILBORNE (St Andrew)   *see* Puddletown, Tolpuddle and
Milborne w Dewlish *Sarum*
**MILBORNE PORT (St John the Evangelist) w Goathill and
Charlton Horethorne w Stowell** *B & W 2*   **P** *Bp and J K
Wingfield Digby Esq (jt)*   **V** *vacant*
MILBORNE WICK (Mission Church)   *see* Milborne Port w
Goathill etc *B & W*
MILBOURNE (Holy Saviour)   *see* Ponteland *Newc*
MILBURN (St Cuthbert)   *see* Heart of Eden *Carl*
MILCOMBE (St Laurence)   *see* Bloxham w Milcombe and S
Newington *Ox*
MILDEN (St Peter)   *see* Monks Eleigh w Chelsworth and
Brent Eleigh etc *St E*
MILDENHALL (St John the Baptist)   *see* Marlborough *Sarum*
MILDENHALL (St Mary)   *see* Forest Heath *St E*
MILDMAY GROVE (St Jude and St Paul) *Lon 6*   **P** *CPAS*
P-in-c J A S HILL
MILE CROSS (St Catherine) *Nor 2*   **P** *Dr J P English, Canon G
F Bridger, the Revd K W Habershon, and the Revd H Palmer (jt)*
V M J E HARTLEY   **OLM** R E LAMBERT
MILE OAK (The Good Shepherd)   *see* Portslade St Nic and
St Andr and Mile Oak *Chich*
MILEHAM (St John the Baptist)   *see* Launditch and the Upper
Nar *Nor*
MILES PLATTING (St Cuthbert)   *see* Man Apostles w Miles
Platting *Man*
MILFORD (St John the Evangelist) *Guildf 4*   **P** *V Witley*
V C G POTTER
MILFORD, SOUTH (St Mary the Virgin)   *see* Monk Fryston
and S Milford *York*
MILFORD-ON-SEA (All Saints) *Win 11*   **P** *Bp*
P-in-c N S ANDERSON
MILL END (St Peter) and Heronsgate w West Hyde *St Alb 4*
P *Bp and V Rickmansworth*   **V** S G CUTMORE

MILL HILL (John Keble Church) *Lon 14* **P** *Bp*
P-in-c S M ROWBORY

MILL HILL (St Michael and All Angels) *Lon 14* **P** *Bp*
V S P YOUNG **NSM** H BETTS

MILL HILL (St Paul) *see* Hendon St Paul Mill Hill *Lon*

MILLAND (St Luke) *see* Linch w Iping Marsh, Milland and
Rake etc *Chich*

MILLBROOK (All Saints) *see* Maker w Rame, Millbrook,
St John and Torpoint *Truro*

MILLBROOK (Christ the King) *see* Kettering Ch the King *Pet*

MILLBROOK (Holy Trinity) *Win 13* **P** *Bp* **R** *vacant*

MILLBROOK (St James) *Ches 14* **P** *Bp,* V Stalybridge St Paul,
and Mrs E Bissill (jt) **P-in-c** T J HAYES **C** C W VINEY

MILLBROOK (St Michael and All Angels) *see* Ampthill w
Millbrook and Steppingley *St Alb*

MILLERS DALE (St Anne) *see* Tideswell *Derby*

MILLFIELD (St Mark) and Pallion St Luke *Dur 14* **P** *Bp*
NSM H WALLACE

MILLFIELD (St Mary) *Dur 14* **P** *The Crown* **V** B SKELTON

MILLHOUSES (Holy Trinity) *see* Abbeydale and Millhouses
Sheff

MILLHOUSES (St Oswald) *see* Sheff St Pet and St Oswald
Sheff

MILLINGTON (St Margaret) *see* Pocklington Wold *York*

MILLOM (Holy Trinity) (St George) *Carl 9* **P** *Bp and Trustees*
(jt) **C** C CARTER

MILNROW (St James) and New Hey *Man 6* **P** *Bp and R*
Rochdale **V** J E PITMAN **NSM** S E WARD

MILNSHAW (St Mary Magdalen) *see* Accrington St Andr,
St Mary and St Pet and Church Kirk *Blackb*

MILNTHORPE (St Thomas) *see* Heversham and Milnthorpe
Carl

MILSON (St George) *see* Cleobury Mortimer w Hopton
Wafers etc *Heref*

MILSTEAD (St Mary and the Holy Cross) *see* Tunstall and
Bredgar *Cant*

MILSTON (St Mary) *see* Avon River *Sarum*

MILTON (All Saints) *Ely 6* **P** *K Coll Cam* **R** D J CHAMBERLIN
NSM J C METCALFE, S BRADFORD

MILTON (St Blaise) *see* DAMASCUS *Ox*

**MILTON (St James) (St Andrew's Church Centre)
(St Patrick)** *Portsm 6* **P** *V Portsea St Mary*
P-in-c P R ARMSTEAD **C** H C DEADMAN

MILTON (St John the Evangelist) *see* Adderbury w Milton *Ox*

MILTON (St Mary Magdalene) *Win 9* **P** *V Milford*
R A H BAILEY

MILTON (St Peter) w St Jude and Kewstoke *B & W 10* **P** *Ld*
Chan **P-in-c** C S A DEAKIN, G L THOMAS

MILTON (St Philip and St James) and Norton *Lich 8* **P** *Bp*
and Walsingham Coll Trust Assn (jt) **P-in-c** K E PETHERICK

MILTON (St Simon and St Jude) *see* Gillingham,
Milton-on-Stour and Silton *Sarum*

MILTON ABBAS (St James the Great) *see* Winterborne Valley
and Milton Abbas *Sarum*

**MILTON ABBOT (St Constantine), Dunterton, Lamerton,
Sydenham Damerel, Marystowe and Coryton** *Ex 21*
P *Bp, Bedford Estates,* J W Tremayne Esq, Mrs E J Bullock, P T L
Newman Esq (jt) **V** A J ATKINS

MILTON BRYAN (St Peter) *see* Woburn w Eversholt, Milton
Bryan, Battlesden etc *St Alb*

MILTON CLEVEDON (St James) *see* Alham Vale *B & W*

MILTON COMBE (Holy Spirit) *see* Buckland Monachorum *Ex*

MILTON DAMEREL (Holy Trinity) *see* Bradworthy, Sutcombe,
Putford etc *Ex*

MILTON ERNEST (All Saints), Pavenham and Thurleigh
St Alb 13 **P** *Bp (2 turns), Lord Luke (1 turn)* **P-in-c** P R KAY

MILTON KEYNES (Christ the Cornerstone) *Ox 14* **P** *Bp*
V E LOZADA-UZURIAGA **C** T NORWOOD
NSM K STRAUGHAN, P OXLEY

MILTON KEYNES VILLAGE (All Saints) *see* Walton Milton
Keynes *Ox*

MILTON LILBOURNE (St Peter) *see* Vale of Pewsey *Sarum*

MILTON MALSOR (Holy Cross) *see* Blisworth, Alderton,
Grafton Regis etc *Pet*

MILTON NEXT GRAVESEND (Christ Church) *Roch 4* **P** *Bp*
V A P DAVEY **NSM** J P LITTLEWOOD

**MILTON NEXT GRAVESEND (St Peter and St Paul) w
Denton** *Roch 4* **P** *Bp* **R** G V HERBERT

**MILTON REGIS (Holy Trinity) w Murston, Bapchild and
Tonge** *Cant 15* **P** *Abp, D&C, and St Jo Coll Cam (jt)*
C S R YOUNG

MILTON REGIS (St Mary) *see* Sittingbourne w Bobbing *Cant*

**MILTON, GREAT (St Mary the Virgin) w Little (St James)
and Great Haseley** *Ox 20* **P** *Bp and D&C Windsor (jt)*
R S N CRONK

MILTON, SOUTH (All Saints) *see* Thurlestone, S Milton,
Churchstow etc *Ex*

MILTON-UNDER-WYCHWOOD (St Simon and St Jude) *see*
Wychwood *Ox*

MILVERTON (St Michael) w Halse, Fitzhead and Ash Priors
B & W 19 **P** *Bp, Adn, R Wiveliscombe and the Hills, and
MMCET (jt)* **R** H L STAINER **C** E J KENDALL

MILVERTON, NEW (St Mark) *Cov 11* **P** *CPAS* **V** J C PARKER
C H J ELSON, R M SMITH

MILVERTON, OLD (St James) *see* Lillington and Old
Milverton *Cov*

MILWICH (All Saints) *see* Mid Trent *Lich*

MIMMS *see also* MYMMS

MIMMS, SOUTH (Christ Church) *Lon 14* **P** *Ch Patr Trust*
V A M RIMMER

MINCHINHAMPTON (Holy Trinity) w Box and Amberley
Glouc 4 **P** *Bp and DBP (jt)* **R** H N GILBERT **C** C E FRANCIS
NSM P J SPIERS

MINEHEAD (St Andrew) (St Michael) (St Peter) *B & W 15*
P *Lt Col G W F Luttrell and Bp (jt)* **V** S J ROBINSON

MINETY (St Leonard) *see* Braydon Brook *Bris*

MININGSBY WITH EAST KIRKBY (St Nicholas) *see*
Bolingbroke Deanery *Linc*

MINLEY (St Andrew) *Guildf 1* **P** *Bp* **V** W F P PERRY

MINNIS BAY (St Thomas) *see* Birchington w Acol and
Minnis Bay *Cant*

MINSKIP (Mission Room) *see* Aldborough w Boroughbridge
and Roecliffe *Leeds*

MINSTEAD (All Saints) *see* Lyndhurst and Emery Down and
Minstead *Win*

MINSTER (St Mary the Virgin) *see* Wantsum Gp *Cant*

MINSTER (St Merteriana) *see* Boscastle Gp *Truro*

MINSTER IN SHEPPEY (St Mary and St Sexburga) *see* W
Sheppey *Cant*

MINSTER LOVELL (St Kenelm) *see* Witney *Ox*

MINSTERLEY (Holy Trinity), Habberley and Hope w Shelve
Heref 12 **P** *Bp (3 turns), DBP (3 turns), New Coll Ox (2 turns),
J J C Coldwell Esq (1 turn)* **R** G P SMITH

MINSTERWORTH (St Peter) *see* Westbury-on-Severn w
Flaxley, Blaisdon etc *Glouc*

MINTERNE MAGNA (St Andrew) *see* Buckland Newton,
Cerne Abbas, Godmanstone etc *Sarum*

MINTING (St Andrew) *see* Bardney *Linc*

MIREHOUSE (St Andrew) *Carl 5* **P** *Bp* **C** F T PEARSON,
P M KERRY

MIRFIELD (St Mary) *Leeds 7* **P** *Bp* **V** H C BAKER
NSM C H S SHEARD, H C BUTLER

MISERDEN (St Andrew) *see* Brimpsfield w Birdlip, Syde,
Daglingworth etc *Glouc*

**MISSENDEN, GREAT (St Peter and St Paul) w Ballinger and
Little Hampden** *Ox 17* **P** *Bp* **V** *vacant*

MISSENDEN, LITTLE (St John the Baptist) *Ox 17* **P** *Earl
Howe* **P-in-c** J V SIMPSON

MISSON (St John the Baptist) *see* Bawtry w Austerfield,
Misson, Everton and Mattersey *S'well*

MISTERTON (All Saints) *see* Beckingham, Walkeringham,
Misterton, etc *S'well*

MISTERTON (St Leonard) *see* Avon-Swift *Leic*

MISTERTON (St Leonard) *see* Wulfric Benefice *B & W*

**MISTLEY (St Mary and St Michael) w Manningtree and
Bradfield** *Chelmsf 21* **P** *DBP and Bp (jt)* **R** D TURNER
NSM J R BRIEN **OLM** C F SCARGILL

MITCHAM (Ascension) Pollards Hill *S'wark 13* **P** *Bp*
V J M THOMAS

MITCHAM (Christ Church) *see* Merton Priory *S'wark*

MITCHAM (St Barnabas) *S'wark 13* **P** *Bp* **V** J G CAVALCANTI

MITCHAM (St Mark) *S'wark 13* **P** *Bp* **V** N J STONE

MITCHAM (St Olave) *S'wark 13* **P** *The Crown*
P-in-c G PIPER

MITCHAM (St Peter and St Paul) *S'wark 13* **P** *Keble Coll Ox*
V D M B PENNELLS **NSM** M J COCKFIELD

MITCHELDEAN (St Michael and All Angels) *see* Abenhall w
Mitcheldean *Glouc*

MITFORD (St Mary Magdalene) and Hebron *Newc 11* **P** *Ld
Chan and the Revd B W J Mitford (alt)* **V** *vacant*

MITRE, The, comprising Heigham St Barnabas w
St Bartholomew, Heigham St Thomas, and Lakenham
St Alban *Nor 3* **P** *Bp and D&C (jt)* **P-in-c** T R EAGLES
C A C WOODMAN, D C HENDRA, D M ROWLANDSON,
D Z LLOYD, E C LAND, J N PAYNE, P J BROMBLEY
NSM M C A HUTTON

MITTON (All Hallows) *see* Hurst Green and Mitton *Blackb*

MIXBURY (All Saints) *see* Shelswell *Ox*

MIXENDEN (Holy Nativity) and Illingworth *Leeds 8* **P** *Bp
and V Halifax (jt)* **V** R SUTHERLAND **NSM** Y J K HAGAN

MOBBERLEY (St Wilfrid) *Ches 12* **P** *Bp* **R** I BLAY

MOCCAS (St Michael and All Angels) *see* Cusop w
Blakemere, Bredwardine w Brobury etc *Heref*
**MODBURY (St George), Bigbury, Ringmore, Kingston, and
Aveton Gifford** *Ex 12* **P** *Bp Ex, D&C Ex, DBP, MMCET, and
P K M Ramm Esq* **R** M J ROWLAND
MODDERSHALL (All Saints) *see* Stone Ch Ch and Oulton
Lich
MOGGERHANGER (St John the Evangelist) *see* Cople,
Moggerhanger and Willington *St Alb*
MOLASH (St Peter) *see* King's Wood *Cant*
MOLDGREEN (Christ Church) and Rawthorpe St James
Leeds 5 **P** R Kirkheaton and DBP (jt) **P-in-c** C A CHESHIRE
MOLESCROFT (St Leonard) *see* Beverley St Jo and St Martin
w Routh All SS *York*
MOLESEY, EAST (St Mary) *Guildf 8* **P** *Bp* **V** N W KURZ
MOLESEY, EAST (St Paul) *Guildf 8* **P** *Bp* **V** A L FARMER
MOLESEY, WEST (St Peter) *Guildf 8* **P** *The Revd S Trott*
V A I MUNRO
MOLESWORTH (St Peter) *see* W Leightonstone *Ely*
MOLLAND (St Mary) *see* Bishopsnympton, Charles, E
Anstey, High Bray etc *Ex*
MOLLINGTON (All Saints) *see* Shires' Edge *Ox*
MOLTON, NORTH (All Saints) *see* Bishopsnympton, Charles,
E Anstey, High Bray etc *Ex*
**MOLTON, SOUTH (St Mary Magdalene) w Nymet
St George, Chittlehamholt, Chittlehampton w
Umberleigh, Filleigh, Kingsnympton, and Warkleigh w
Satterleigh** *Ex 17* **P** *Patr Bd* **TR** F M GRANDEY
TV D K COLEMAN **C** B J SANDERS **NSM** C M G POUNCEY
MONEWDEN (St Mary) *see* Mid Loes *St E*
MONGEHAM, GREAT (St Martin) *see* Deal St Leon w St Rich
and Sholden etc *Cant*
MONK BRETTON (St Paul) *Leeds 14* **P** V Royston
V B T B BELL
MONK FRYSTON (St Wilfrid of Ripon) and South Milford
York 4 **P** Ld Chan and Abp (alt) **R** P F ROBERTS
MONK SHERBORNE (All Saints) *see* The Sherbornes w
Pamber *Win*
MONK SOHAM (St Peter) *see* Four Rivers *St E*
MONKEN HADLEY (St Mary the Virgin) *Lon 14* **P** *Bp*
R T RENZ
MONKHOPTON (St Peter) *see* Bridgnorth and Morville Par
Heref
MONKLAND (All Saints) *see* Leominster *Heref*
MONKLEIGH (St George) *see* Bideford, Landcross, Littleham
etc *Ex*
MONKMOOR (St Peter) *see* Shrewsbury H Cross *Lich*
MONKOKEHAMPTON (All Saints) *see* Dolton, Dowland,
Iddesleigh etc *Ex*
**MONKS ELEIGH (St Peter) w Chelsworth and Brent Eleigh
w Milden and Kettlebaston** *St E 6* **P** *Bp, Guild of All So, Ld
Chan (2 turns), and M J Hawkins Esq* **P-in-c** H M BIRT
MONKS HORTON (St Peter) *see* Stour Downs *Cant*
MONKS KIRBY (St Edith) *see* Revel Gp *Cov*
MONKS RISBOROUGH (St Dunstan) *see* Risborough *Ox*
MONKSEATON (St Mary) *Newc 5* **P** *Bp* **C** B J F JARVIS
NSM M C CONNORS
MONKSEATON (St Peter) *Newc 5* **P** *Bp* **V** vacant
MONKSILVER (All Saints) *see* Quantock Towers *B & W*
MONKTON (St Mary Magdalene) *see* Wantsum Gp *Cant*
MONKTON COMBE (St Michael) *see* Combe Down w
Monkton Combe and S Stoke *B & W*
MONKTON FARLEIGH (St Peter) *see* N Bradford on Avon
and Villages *Sarum*
MONKTON WYLD (St Andrew) *see* Golden Cap Team *Sarum*
MONKTON, WEST (St Augustine) *see* S Quantock *B & W*
MONKWEARMOUTH (All Saints) (St Andrew) (St Peter)
Dur 14 **P** *Bp* **TR** R G E BRADSHAW **TV** A M WATSON
C T P MAY
MONKWOOD (Mission Church) *see* Bishop's Sutton and
Ropley and W Tisted *Win*
MONNINGTON-ON-WYE (St Mary) *see* Letton w Staunton,
Byford, Mansel Gamage etc *Heref*
MONTACUTE (St Catherine of Alexandria) *see* Ham Hill
Villages *B & W*
MONTFORD (St Chad) *see* Bicton, Montford w Shrawardine
and Fitz *Lich*
MONTON (St Paul) *see* Eccles *Man*
MONXTON (St Mary) *see* Portway and Danebury *Win*
MONYASH (St Leonard) *see* Taddington, Chelmorton and
Monyash etc *Derby*
MOOR (St Thomas) *see* Fladbury, Hill and Moor, Wyre
Piddle etc *Worc*
**MOOR ALLERTON (St John the Evangelist) (St Stephen)
and Shadwell Team Ministry,** including Alwoodley and

Moortown *Leeds 10* **P** *Patr Bd* **TV** D L M YOUNG, S V KAYE
C L H JONES
MOOR COURT (St Mary) *see* Pembridge w Moor Court,
Shobdon, Staunton etc *Heref*
MOOR GRANGE (St Andrew) *see* Abbeylands *Leeds*
MOOR MONKTON (All Saints) *see* Rural Ainsty *York*
MOORCOURT (St Mary) *see* Pembridge w Moor Court,
Shobdon, Staunton etc *Heref*
MOORE MILNER (Church Institute) *see* Daresbury *Ches*
MOORENDS (St Wilfrith) *Sheff 10* **P** *Bp* **V** vacant
MOORHOUSE (Chantry Chapel) *see* Kneesall w Laxton and
Wellow *S'well*
MOORHOUSES (St Lawrence) *see* Fen and Hill Gp *Linc*
MOORLAND Group, The, comprising Altarnon, Davidstow,
Laneast, and St Clether *Truro 9* **P** Duchy of Cornwall (1
turn), Bp, D&C, and SMF (1 turn) **P-in-c** A J HARDY
C N FARR, S P CLANCY
MOORLAND TEAM *see* Ashburton, Bickington, Buckland in
the Moor etc *Ex*
MOORLANDS, The, comprising Castleton, Commondale,
Danby, Moorsholm, and Westerdale *York 21* **P** Abp and
Viscountess Downe (jt) **NSM** S J WILSON
MOORLINCH (Blessed Virgin Mary) *see* Middlezoy w Othery,
Moorlinch and Greinton *B & W*
MOORSHOLM (St Mary) *see* The Moorlands *York*
MOORSIDE (St Thomas) *see* Oldham Moorside *Man*
MOORTOWN (St Stephen) *see* Moor Allerton and Shadwell
Leeds
MORBORNE (All Saints) *see* Stilton w Denton and Caldecote
etc *Ely*
MORCHARD BISHOP (St Mary) *see* N Creedy *Ex*
MORCOTT (St Mary the Virgin) *see* Barrowden and Wakerley
w S Luffenham etc *Pet*
**MORDEN (St Lawrence) (St George) (St Martin)
(Emmanuel Church Hall)** *S'wark 13* **P** *Patr Bd*
TR D R HEATH-WHYTE **TV** A D WENHAM, D M RUDDICK,
M S H DAVEY **Hon C** P S OMUKU
MORDEN (St Mary) *see* Red Post *Sarum*
MORDIFORD (Holy Rood) *see* Fownhope w Mordiford,
Brockhampton etc *Heref*
MORE (St Peter) *see* Wentnor w Ratlinghope, Myndtown,
Norbury etc *Heref*
MOREBATH (St George) *see* Bampton, Morebath,
Clayhanger, Petton etc *Ex*
MORECAMBE (Holy Trinity) *see* Poulton-le-Sands w
Morecambe St Laur *Blackb*
MORECAMBE (St Barnabas) *Blackb 11* **P** R Poulton-le-Sands
V M T CHILDS
MORECAMBE (St Christopher) *see* Bare *Blackb*
MORECAMBE (St James) *see* Heysham *Blackb*
MORECAMBE (St John) *see* Sandylands *Blackb*
MORECAMBE (St Peter) *see* Heysham *Blackb*
MORECAMBE (The Ascension) *see* Torrisholme *Blackb*
MORELEIGH (All Saints) *see* Diptford w N Huish, Ermington,
Halwell etc *Ex*
MORESBY (St Bridget) *Carl 5* **P** Earl of Lonsdale
P-in-c P M KERRY
MORESBY PARKS (Mission Church) *see* Moresby *Carl*
MORESTEAD (not known) *see* S Downs Gateway Churches
Win
MORETON (Christ Church) *Ches 8* **P** Simeon's Trustees
R G J COUSINS **NSM** B A TURNER, D A STOTT
MORETON (St Mary) *see* Adbaston, High Offley, Knightley,
Norbury etc *Lich*
MORETON (St Mary) *see* Fyfield, Moreton w Bobbingworth
etc *Chelmsf*
**MORETON (St Nicholas), Woodsford and Crossways w
Tincleton** *Sarum 1* **P** R Frampton-Hobb Esq
R G L DONNELL
MORETON CORBET (St Bartholomew) *Lich 21* **P** C C Corbet
Esq **R** R J CRESSWELL
MORETON HALL (Christ Church) *see* Bury St Edmunds Ch
Ch *St E*
MORETON MORRELL (Holy Cross) *see* Newbold Pacey w
Moreton Morrell *Cov*
MORETON PINKNEY (St Mary the Virgin) *see* Culworth w
Sulgrave and Thorpe Mandeville etc *Pet*
MORETON SAY (St Margaret of Antioch) *see* Adderley, Ash,
Calverhall, Ightfield etc *Lich*
MORETON VALENCE (St Stephen) *see* Stroudwater *Glouc*
MORETON, NORTH (All Saints) *see* The Churn *Ox*
MORETON, SOUTH (St John the Baptist) *as above*
**MORETONHAMPSTEAD (St Andrew), Manaton, North
Bovey and Lustleigh** *Ex 9* **P** Bp and DBP (jt)
C S SHEPPARD

MORETON-IN-MARSH (St David) w Batsford, Todenham, Lower Lemington and Longborough w Sezincote *Glouc 8*
P *Bp and Lord Dulverton (1 turn), and Bp, Lord Dulverton, Lord Leigh, and Mrs S Peake (1 turn)* **P-in-c** J H CURRAN
NSM B J P THOMPSON

MORETON-ON-LUGG (St Andrew)   *see Burghill Gp Heref*
MORGAN'S VALE (St Birinus)   *see Forest and Avon Sarum*
MORLAND (St Lawrence)   *see N Westmorland Carl*
MORLEY (St Matthew) and Smalley *Derby 8*   **P** *Bp*
P-in-c K J PLANT

MORLEY (St Peter) (St Paul) *Leeds 11*   **P** *Patr Bd*
TV O OGUNYINKA, P N HARRIS, S M FORREST-REDFERN
C E TIDBALL   **OLM** K M DAVIS

MORLEY ST BOTOLPH (St Botolph)   *see High Oak, Hingham and Scoulton w Wood Rising Nor*
MORLEY ST PETER (St Peter)   *as above*
MORNINGTHORPE (St John the Baptist)   *see Hempnall Nor*
MORPETH (St Aidan) (St James) (St Mary the Virgin)
Newc 11   **P** *Bp*   **R** S J H WHITE   **NSM** E A M G BROWN, P W RUSBY   **OLM** J L J COOPER
MORRIS GREEN (St Bede)   *see Bolton St Bede Man*
MORSTON (All Saints)   *see Stiffkey and Bale Nor*
MORTEHOE (St Mary Magdalene)   *see Ilfracombe, Lee, Woolacombe, Bittadon etc Ex*
MORTIMER COMMON (St John)   *see Stratfield Mortimer and Mortimer W End etc Ox*
MORTIMER WEST END (St Saviour)   *as above*
MORTLAKE (St Mary) w East Sheen *S'wark 16*   **P** *Patr Bd*
TR A L NICKSON   **TV** C R GRIFFITHS, J A BARROW
NSM S COLLINS-MAYO
MORTOMLEY (St Saviour) High Green *Sheff 3*   **P** *Bp*
V *vacant*
MORTON (Holy Cross) and Stonebroom w Shirland
Derby 2   **P** *Bp, St Jo Coll Cam, Adn Chesterfield, and trustees (by turn)*   **NSM** C D WOOD, J A EPTON
MORTON (St Denis)   *see W Trent S'well*
MORTON (St John the Baptist)   *see Ringstone in Aveland Gp Linc*
MORTON (St Luke) and Riddlesden *Leeds 1*   **P** *Bp*
V A C ST J WALKER
MORTON (St Paul)   *see Gainsborough and Morton Linc*
MORTON (St Philip and St James)   *see Llanyblodwel, Llanymynech, Morton and Trefonen Lich*
MORTON BAGOT (Holy Trinity)   *see Arden Marches Cov*
MORTON, EAST   *see Morton and Riddlesden Leeds*
MORVAH (St Bridget of Sweden)   *see Pendeen w Morvah Truro*
MORVAL (St Wenna)   *see Looe and Morval Truro*
MORVILLE (St Gregory)   *see Bridgnorth and Morville Par Heref*
MORWENSTOW (St John the Baptist)   *see N Kernow Truro*
MOSBOROUGH (St Mark) *Sheff 1*   **P** *Bp*   **V** S T STEWART
NSM L S CASTLE
MOSELEY (St Agnes) *Birm 2*   **P** *V Moseley St Mary*
V P H ANSELL
MOSELEY (St Anne) (St Mary) *Birm 2*   **P** *Bp*   **V** D J STRATHIE
C M M SMITH, S E MOORE
MOSLEY COMMON (St John)   *see Astley, Tyldesley and Mosley Common Man*
MOSS BANK (Mission Church)   *see Carr Mill Liv*
MOSS SIDE (Christ Church) *Man 2*   **P** *Trustees*
R S D A KILLWICK
MOSS SIDE (St James w St Clement)   *see Whalley Range St Edm and Moss Side etc Man*
MOSSER (St Michael's Chapel)   *see Brigham, Clifton, Dean and Mosser Carl*
MOSSER (St Philip)   *as above*
MOSSLEY (Holy Trinity)   *see Congleton Ches*
MOSSLEY (St George) *Man 5*   **P** *Bp and R Ashton-under-Lyne (jt)*   **V** D WARNER   **NSM** I C BROCKLEHURST
OLM D BRADWELL
MOSSLEY ESTATE (St Thomas Church)   *see Bloxwich Lich*
MOSSLEY HILL (St Matthew and St James) *Liv 2*   **P** *Trustees*
R A KENNEDY   **NSM** S-A MASON
MOSSWOOD (St Barnabas)   *see Cannock and Huntington Lich*
MOSTERTON (St Mary)   *see Beaminster Area Sarum*
MOSTON (St Luke)   *see Lightbowne Man*
MOSTON (St Mary) *Man 1*   **P** *D&C*   **R** *vacant*
MOTCOMBE (St Mary)   *see Shaftesbury Sarum*
MOTSPUR PARK (Holy Cross) *S'wark 13*   **P** *Bp*   **V** R S TAYLOR
NSM A F P COCKING
MOTTINGHAM (St Andrew) (St Alban Mission Church)
S'wark 3   **P** *Bp*   **R** I M WELCH
MOTTINGHAM (St Edward the Confessor) *S'wark 3*   **P** *Bp*
V C J SHELLEY   **C** K J KELLY

MOTTISFONT (St Andrew)   *see Mid Test Win*
MOTTISTONE (St Peter and St Paul)   *see W Wight Portsm*
MOTTRAM IN LONGDENDALE (St Michael) *Ches 14*   **P** *Bp*
V C J WALKER
MOULSECOOMB (St Andrew) w Bevendean and Coldean
Chich 19   **P** *Bp*   **TV** B GRAY-HAMMOND
NSM J W M COLLINS
MOULSFORD (St John the Baptist)   *see Cholsey and Moulsford Ox*
MOULSHAM (St John the Evangelist) *Chelmsf 9*   **P** *Dean*
P-in-c G E FRASER   **C** D J CATTLE, S R GILLINGHAM
NSM E S MCALLISTER
MOULSHAM (St Luke) *Chelmsf 9*   **P** *Bp*   **P-in-c** G E FRASER
C D J CATTLE, S R GILLINGHAM
MOULSOE (The Assumption of the Blessed Virgin Mary)   *see Newport Pagnell w Lathbury and Moulsoe Ox*
MOULTON (All Saints)   *see Elloe Stone Linc*
MOULTON (Mission Church)   *see E Dere Street Leeds*
MOULTON (St James)   *see Elloe Stone Linc*
MOULTON (St Peter and St Paul) *Pet 4*   **P** *Ch Soc Trust*
C J J DEJA, N E ALEXANDER, N J EDWARDS
MOULTON (St Peter)   *see Forest Heath St E*
MOULTON (St Stephen the Martyr) *Ches 6*   **P** *R Davenham*
P-in-c M R GREEN
MOULTON, GREAT (St Michael)   *see Long Stratton and Pilgrim TM Nor*
MOUNT BURES (St John)   *see Wormingford, Mt Bures and Lt Horkesley Chelmsf*
MOUNT GOULD (St Simon)   *see Sutton-on-Plym, Plymouth St Simon and St Mary Ex*
MOUNT HAWKE (St John the Baptist)   *see St Agnes and Mount Hawke w Mithian Truro*
MOUNT PELLON (Christ Church)   *see Halifax St Aug and Mount Pellon Leeds*
MOUNTFIELD (All Saints)   *see Brightling, Mountfield and Netherfield Chich*
MOUNTNESSING (St Giles)   *see Margaretting w Mountnessing and Buttsbury Chelmsf*
MOUNTSORREL (Christ Church) (St Peter) *Leic 6*   **P** *CPAS and Bp*   **P-in-c** C E RESCH
MOW COP (St Luke's Mission Church)   *see Odd Rode Ches*
MOW COP (St Thomas) *Lich 11*   **P** *The Crown*
NSM P A JACKSON
MOWSLEY (St Nicholas)   *see Hexagon Leic*
MOXLEY (All Saints)   *see Darlaston and Moxley Lich*
MUCH   *see also under substantive place name*
MUCH BIRCH (St Mary and St Thomas à Becket)   *see Wormelow Hundred Heref*
MUCHELNEY (St Peter and St Paul)   *see Levels Arc B & W*
MUCKLESTONE (St Mary)   *see Ashley and Mucklestone and Broughton and Croxton Lich*
MUDEFORD (All Saints) *Win 9*   **P** *Bp*   **V** *vacant*
MUDFORD (Blessed Virgin Mary)   *see Chilton Cantelo, Ashington, Mudford, Rimpton etc B & W*
MUGGINTON (All Saints) and Kedleston *Derby 6*   **P** *Major J W Chandos-Pole*   **P-in-c** B J STOBER
MUGGLESWICK (All Saints)   *see Blanchland w Hunstanworth and Edmundbyers etc Newc*
MUKER (St Mary)   *see Swaledale Leeds*
MULBARTON (St Mary Magdalene) w Bracon Ash, Hethel and Flordon *Nor 7*   **P** *R T Berney Esq (1 turn), Mrs R M Watkinson (2 turns), DBP (1 turn), and Ld Chan (1 turn)*
R A D MILLER
MULLION (St Mellanus) and Cury w Gunwalloe *Truro 3*
P *Bp*   **V** S O GRIFFITHS
MUMBY (St Thomas of Canterbury)   *see Chapel St Leonards and Hogsthorpe etc Linc*
MUNCASTER (St Michael)   *see Black Combe, Drigg, Eskdale etc Carl*
MUNDEN, LITTLE (All Saints)   *see Standon and The Mundens w Sacombe St Alb*
MUNDESLEY (All Saints)   *see Trunch Group Nor*
MUNDFORD (St Leonard) w Lynford *Nor 13*   **P** *Ch Patr Trust*
Hon C L M LUBBE
MUNDHAM (St Peter)   *see Brooke, Kirstead, Mundham w Seething and Thwaite Nor*
MUNDHAM, NORTH (St Stephen) w Hunston and Merston
Chich 2   **P** *St Jo Coll Cam*   **R** M W BARKER
NSM S R EVERARD
MUNGRISDALE (St Kentigern)   *see Greystoke w Penruddock, Mungrisdale etc Carl*
MUNSLEY (St Bartholomew)   *see Hop Churches Heref*
MUNSLOW (St Michael)   *see Corvedale Benefice Heref*
MUNSTER SQUARE (Christ Church) (St Mary Magdalene)
Lon 15   **P** *Bp*   **P-in-c** S J JONES
MURCOTT (Mission Room)   *see Ray Valley Ox*

MURROW (Corpus Christi) *see* Wisbech St Mary and Guyhirn w Ring's End etc *Ely*

MURSLEY (St Mary the Virgin) *see* Newton Longville, Mursley, Swanbourne etc *Ox*

MURSTON (All Saints) *see* Milton Regis w Murston, Bapchild and Tonge *Cant*

MURTON (Holy Trinity) and South Hetton *Dur 10* **P** *Bp* **R** *vacant*

MURTON (St James) *see* Osbaldwick w Murton *York*

MURTON (St John the Baptist) *see* Heart of Eden *Carl*

MUSBURY (St Michael) *see* Colyton, Branscombe, Musbury, Northleigh and Southleigh *Ex*

MUSBURY (St Thomas) *Blackb 1* **P** *The Crown* **V** D STEPHENSON **C** A D HOLMES **NSM** J A BALKWELL

MUSGRAVE (St Theobald) *see* Heart of Eden *Carl*

MUSKHAM, NORTH (St Wilfrid) and SOUTH (St Wilfrid) *S'well 3* **P** *Ld Chan* **C** G A L HADLEY

MUSTON (All Saints) *see* Hertford *York*

MUSTON (St John the Baptist) *see* Vale of Belvoir *Leic*

MUSWELL HILL (St James) (St Matthew) *Lon 17* **P** *Bp and CPAS (jt)* **V** C M GREEN **C** M A MURTHEN, P J MULLINS **NSM** H C HENDRY

MUTFORD (St Andrew) *see* Carlton Colville and Mutford *Nor*

MUXTON (St John the Evangelist) *see* Lilleshall and Muxton *Lich*

MYDDELTON SQUARE (St Mark) *see* Clerkenwell St Mark *Lon*

MYDDLE (St Peter) and Broughton, Loppington and Newtown *Lich 21* **P** *Bp, D R B Thompson Esq, and R Wem etc (jt)* **R** A J B CLAYTON

MYLAND (St Michael) *see* Colchester St Mich Myland *Chelmsf*

MYLOR (St Mylor) w Flushing *Truro 2* **P** *Bp* **P-in-c** A J EVANS **A** J STEVENSON

MYLOR BRIDGE (All Saints) *see* Mylor w Flushing *Truro*

MYMMS *see also* MIMMS

MYMMS, NORTH (St Mary) *see* Bishop's Hatfield, Lemsford and N Mymms *St Alb*

MYMMS, SOUTH (King Charles the Martyr) *see* Potters Bar K Chas *St Alb*

MYMMS, SOUTH (St Giles) and Ridge *St Alb 14* **P** *DBP* **V** *vacant*

MYNDTOWN (St John the Baptist) *see* Wentnor w Ratlinghope, Myndtown, Norbury etc *Heref*

MYTHOLMROYD (St Michael) *see* Erringden *Leeds*

MYTON ON SWALE (St Mary) *see* Brafferton w Pilmoor, Myton-on-Swale etc *York*

NABURN (St Matthew) *see* Escrick and Stillingfleet w Naburn *York*

NACKINGTON (St Mary) *see* Bridge *Cant*

NACTON (St Martin) *see* Orwell and Deben *St E*

NADDER VALLEY, comprising Ansty, Barford St Martin and Burcombe, Baverstock, Chilmark, Compton Chamberlayne, Dinton, Fonthill Bishop w Berick St Leonard, Fonthill Gifford, Fovant, Hindon w Chicklade and Pertwood, Sutton Mandeville, Swallowcliffe, Teffont Evias w Teffont Magna, and Tisbury *Sarum 11* **P** *Patr Bd (4 turns), Ld Chan (1 turn)* **TR** G SOUTHGATE **TV** E BRIGHTWELL, J M HULME **C** M H G HAYTER **NSM** J M NAISH, T FOX **Dss** A R SYMES

NAFFERTON (All Saints) w Wansford *York 10* **P** *Abp* **V** S R J ELLIOTT

NAILSEA (Christ Church) w Tickenham *B & W 12* **P** *CPAS (3 turns), Ld Chan (1 turn)* **R** J C HARRIS

NAILSEA (Holy Trinity) *B & W 12* **P** *MMCET* **R** J M PACKMAN **C** J S TILLEY **NSM** T S DEAN

NAILSTONE (All Saints) *see* Bosworth *Leic*

NAILSWORTH (St George) w Shortwood, Horsley and Newington Bapath w Kingscote *Glouc 4* **P** *Bp* **V** C A BLAND

NANPANTAN (St Mary in Charnwood) *Leic 6* **P** *Bp and Em Coll Cam (jt)* **V** A E ADSHEAD

NANPEAN (St George) *see* St Stephen in Brannel *Truro*

NANSTALLON (St Stephen's Mission Room) *see* Bodmin *Truro*

NANTWICH (St Mary) *Ches 15* **P** *Q H Crewe Esq and J C Crewe Esq (jt)* **R** M HART **C** P K WHEELER **NSM** V D LAYFIELD

NAPTON-ON-THE-HILL (St Lawrence), Lower Shuckburgh and Stockton *Cov 10* **P** *Ld Chan (1 turn), Sir Rupert Shuckburgh Bt (1 turn), and New Coll Ox (2 turns)* **P-in-c** G S ROBERTS

NAR VALLEY, The, comprising Castle Acre, Narborough, Newton-by-Castle Acre, Pentney, South Acre, and West Acre *Nor 13* **P** *Bp (1 turn), Earl of Leicester, H C Birkbeck Esq, and Bp (1 turn)* **R** S R NAIRN **NSM** R G HOWELLS

NARBOROUGH (All Saints) *see* Nar Valley *Nor*

NARBOROUGH (All Saints) and Huncote *Leic 7* **P** *SMF* **P-in-c** S Y LEE

NARFORD (St Mary) *see* Nar Valley *Nor*

NASEBY (All Saints) *see* Clipston, Haselbech, Kelmarsh, Marston Trussell etc *Pet*

NASH (All Saints) *see* Blackthorn Chase *Ox*

NASH (St John the Baptist) *see* Tenbury *Heref*

NASSINGTON (St Mary the Virgin and All Saints), Apethorpe, Thornhaugh and Wansford, Woodnewton and Yarwell (The Watersmete Benefice) *Pet 10* **P** *Bp and Personal Reps Lord Brassey of Apethorpe (jt)* **V** J D TAILBY

NATELY SCURES (St Swithun) *see* N Hants Downs *Win*

NATLAND (St Mark) *Carl 10* **P** *V Kendal H Trin* **P-in-c** A WHITTAKER **C** C A BENTLEY **NSM** L A FOSTER, M MASHITER

NAUGHTON (St Mary) *see* Bildeston w Wattisham and Lindsey etc *St E*

NAUNTON (St Andrew) *see* The Guitings, Cutsdean, Farmcote etc *Glouc*

NAUNTON BEAUCHAMP (St Bartholomew) *see* Abberton, The Flyfords, Naunton Beauchamp etc *Worc*

NAVENBY (St Peter) *see* Graffoe Gp *Linc*

NAVESTOCK (St Thomas) *see* Bentley Common, Kelvedon Hatch and Navestock *Chelmsf*

NAWTON (St Hilda) *see* Kirkdale w Harome, Nunnington and Pockley *York*

NAYLAND (St James) *see* Stoke by Nayland w Leavenheath etc *St E*

NAZEING (All Saints) (St Giles) *Chelmsf 4* **P** *Ld Chan* **V** *vacant*

NEASDEN (St Catherine w St Paul) *Lon 18* **P** *Bp and D&C St Paul's (jt)* **V** R W HARRISON

NEATISHEAD (St Peter) *see* Ashmanhaugh, Barton Turf etc *Nor*

NECHELLS (St Matthew) *see* Aston and Nechells *Birm*

NECTON (All Saints), Holme Hale w Pickenham, North and South *Nor 13* **P** *Major-Gen R S Broke, Ch Soc Trust, MMCET and S Pickenham Estate Co Ltd (jt)* **R** S L THORP

NEDGING (St Mary) *see* Bildeston w Wattisham and Lindsey etc *St E*

NEEDHAM (St Peter) *see* Redenhall w Scole *Nor*

NEEDHAM MARKET (St John the Baptist) w Badley *St E 3* **P** *PCC* **V** D R WILLIAMS **C** S E HOUSSEMAYNE DU BOULAY

NEEN SAVAGE (St Mary) *see* Cleobury Mortimer w Hopton Wafers etc *Heref*

NEEN SOLLARS (All Saints) *as above*

NEENTON (All Saints) *see* Ditton Priors w Neenton, Burwarton etc *Heref*

NEITHROP (St Paul) *see* Banbury St Paul *Ox*

NELSON (St John the Evangelist) *see* Gt Marsden w Nelson St Phil *Blackb*

NELSON (St Mary) *see* Lt Marsden w Nelson St Mary and Nelson St Bede *Blackb*

NELSON (St Paul) *as above*

NEMPNETT THRUBWELL (Blessed Virgin Mary) *see* Chew Stoke w Nempnett Thrubwell *B & W*

NENE CROSSINGS *see* Irthlingborough, Gt Addington, Lt Addington etc *Pet*

NENTHEAD (St John) *see* Alston Moor *Newc*

NESS Group, The, comprising Baston, Langtoft, and Thurlby *Linc 19* **P** *Ld Chan (1 turn), Bp and DBP (2 turns)* **V** C BAILEY **OLM** M J HOWARD

NESS, GREAT (St Andrew) *see* Ch around the Cliffe *Lich*

NESS, LITTLE (St Martin) *as above*

NESTON (St Mary and St Helen) *Ches 9* **P** *D&C* **V** A D H DAWSON **NSM** J CALVERT

NESTON (St Phillip and St James) *see* Gtr Corsham and Lacock *Bris*

NESTON, LITTLE (St Michael and All Angels) *see* Neston *Ches*

NETHER *see under substantive place name*

NETHERAVON (All Saints) *see* Avon River *Sarum*

NETHERBURY (St Mary) *see* Beaminster Area *Sarum*

NETHEREXE (St John the Baptist) *see* Brampford Speke, Cadbury, Newton St Cyres etc *Ex*

NETHERFIELD (St George) *S'well 7* **P** *DBP* **R** *vacant*

NETHERFIELD (St John the Baptist) *see* Brightling, Mountfield and Netherfield *Chich*

NETHERHAMPTON (St Katherine) *see* Wilton w Netherhampton and Fugglestone *Sarum*

NETHERLEY (Christ Church) *see* Gateacre *Liv*

NETHERSEAL (St Peter) *see* Seale and Lullington w Coton in the Elms *Derby*

NETHERTHONG (All Saints) *see* Upper Holme Valley *Leeds*

NETHERTHORPE (St Stephen) *see* Sheffield Vine *Sheff*

NETHERTON (All Souls) *see* Maryport, Netherton, Flimby and Broughton Moor *Carl*

NETHERTON (St Andrew) *see* Darby End and Netherton *Worc*

NETHERTON (St Andrew) *see* Middlestown *Leeds*

NETHERTON (St Oswald) and Sefton *Liv 6* **P** *Patr Bd* **TR** D H STATTER

NETHERWITTON (St Giles) *see* Nether Witton *Newc*

NETLEY MARSH (St Matthew) *see* Copythorne and Netley Marsh *Win*

NETTLEBED (St Bartholomew) w Bix, Highmoor, Pishill and Rotherfield Greys *Ox 24* **P** *DBP, Earl of Macclesfield, Ch Patr Trust, and Trin Coll Ox (jt)* **P-in-c** M J AINSWORTH

NETTLECOMBE (Blessed Virgin Mary) *see* Quantock Towers *B & W*

NETTLEDEN (St Lawrence) *see* Gt Berkhamsted, Gt and Lt Gaddesden etc *St Alb*

NETTLEHAM (All Saints) *Linc 5* **P** *Bp* **V** R H CROSSLAND **C** T J TWELVES **NSM** C A ZOTOV, J A SHAW

NETTLESTEAD (St Mary the Virgin) *see* E Peckham and Nettlestead *Roch*

NETTLESTEAD (St Mary) *see* Bramford w Lt Blakenham, Baylham and Nettlestead *St E*

NETTLETON (St John the Baptist) *see* Woldmoor Gp *Linc*

NETTLETON (St Mary) *see* By Brook *Bris*

NEVENDON (St Peter) *see* Pitsea w Nevendon *Chelmsf*

NEVILLE'S CROSS (St John) *see* Dur St Marg, Neville's Cross St Jo and Bearpark *Dur*

NEW *see also under substantive place name*

NEW BOROUGH and Leigh (St John the Evangelist) *Sarum 9* **P** *Ch Soc Trust* **V** P H BRECKWOLDT **C** M T LEE

NEW BUILDINGS (Beacon Church) *see* Crediton, Shobrooke and Sandford etc *Ex*

NEW FERRY (St Mark) *Ches 8* **P** *R Bebington* **V** A Q GREENHOUGH

NEW HAW (All Saints) *Guildf 11* **P** *Bp* **V** A K REID **C** P A BARLOW

NEW HEY (St Thomas) *see* Milnrow and New Hey *Man*

NEW MILL (Christ Church) *see* Upper Holme Valley *Leeds*

NEW MILLS (St George) *Derby 4* **P** *V Glossop* **V** G O MITCHELL

NEW PARKS (St Aidan) *see* Leic St Aid *Leic*

NEWARK-ON-TRENT (Christ Church) *S'well 3* **P** *The Crown* **V** P S FRANKLIN

NEWARK-ON-TRENT (St Mary Magdalene) (St Leonard) *S'well 3* **P** *The Crown* **P-in-c** D C PICKERSGILL

NEWBALD (St Nicholas) *York 13* **P** *Abp* **P-in-c** M R BUSHBY

NEWBARNS (St Paul) *see* Barrow St Paul *Carl*

NEWBIGGIN (St Edmund) *see* Heart of Eden *Carl*

NEWBIGGIN HALL (St Wilfrid) *Newc 4* **P** *Bp* **P-in-c** A M PATERSON **C** O J DEMPSEY, W H M NION

NEWBIGGIN-BY-THE-SEA (St Bartholomew) *see* Woodhorn w Newbiggin *Newc*

NEWBOLD (St John the Evangelist) w Dunston *Derby 3* **P** *R Chesterfield* **C** C R BLACKWELL **NSM** G M BALL

NEWBOLD (St Peter) *see* Deeplish and Newbold *Man*

NEWBOLD DE VERDUN (St James), Barlestone, Kirkby Mallory and Peckleton *Leic 10* **P** *Bp and Trin Coll Ox (1 turn), Ld Chan (1 turn)* **C** H M AUCKEN **NSM** J A DOWNS

NEWBOLD ON AVON (St Botolph) *Cov 6* **P** H A F W *Boughton Leigh Esq* **V** P M WILKINSON **NSM** D J BUSSEY

NEWBOLD ON STOUR (St David) *see* Stourdene Gp *Cov*

NEWBOLD PACEY (St George) w Moreton Morrell *Cov 8* **P** *Qu Coll Ox and Lt Col J E Little (alt)* **P-in-c** L J LILLEY

NEWBOROUGH (All Saints) *see* Hanbury, Newborough and Rangemoor *Lich*

NEWBOROUGH (St Bartholomew) *see* Eye, Newborough and Thorney *Pet*

NEWBOTTLE (St James) *see* King's Sutton and Newbottle and Charlton *Pet*

NEWBOTTLE (St Matthew) *Dur 9* **P** *Bp* **V** E WILKINSON

NEWBOURNE (St Mary) *see* Orwell and Deben *St E*

NEWBROUGH (St Peter) *see* Warden w Newbrough *Newc*

NEWBURGH (Christ Church) w Westhead *Liv 14* **P** *Bp and V Ormskirk (jt)* **OLM** C DRAPER, J SEPHTON

NEWBURN (St Michael and All Angels) *Newc 4* **P** *MMCET* **V** A J HARDING **C** M A JONES

NEWBURY (St George) (St John the Evangelist) *Ox 6* **P** *Bp* **V** R A BEVAN **C** G S COLLINS, J A HOWELL **NSM** T WINROW

NEWBURY (St Nicolas and St Mary Speenhamland) *Ox 6* **P** *Bp* **R** W D HUNTER SMART **C** J FOUNTAIN, J M MAWDESLEY **NSM** J M MACDONALD

NEWBY (St Mark) *York 15* **P** *Abp* **C** S A MORAY

NEWCASTLE (St John the Evangelist) *see* Clun Valley *Heref*

NEWCASTLE UNDER LYME (St George) *Lich 9* **P** *R Newcastle w Butterton* **V** M F BALL

NEWCASTLE UNDER LYME (St Giles) w Butterton *Lich 9* **P** *Simeon's Trustees* **R** J P J PENDUCK **NSM** P NISBECK **OLM** J WALKER

NEWCASTLE UNDER LYME (St Paul) *Lich 9* **P** *Trustees* **V** S C MADDISON

NEWCASTLE UPON TYNE (Christ Church) (St Ann) *Newc 2* **P** *Bp* **V** A W MARKS

NEWCASTLE UPON TYNE (Holy Cross) *Newc 4* **P** *Bp* **V** *vacant*

NEWCASTLE UPON TYNE (St Andrew) *Newc 2* **P** *Bp and V Newc St Nic (jt)* **V** M J HILLS

NEWCASTLE UPON TYNE (St Francis) High Heaton *Newc 3* **P** *Bp* **V** R W LAWRANCE **C** K WATSON, Y C DANIEL

NEWCASTLE UPON TYNE (St Gabriel) Heaton *Newc 3* **P** *Bp* **V** J H LAWSON **NSM** A R WHITE

NEWCASTLE UPON TYNE (St George) (St Hilda) *Newc 2* **P** *Bp* **V** B C HURST **C** S L KEATES **NSM** D A AVERY

NEWCASTLE UPON TYNE (St John the Baptist) *Newc 2* **P** *V Newc* **P-in-c** K I CRAWFORD

NEWCASTLE UPON TYNE (St Luke) *Newc 2* **P** *Bp and V Newcastle (jt)* **P-in-c** A B WARD

NEWCASTLE UPON TYNE (St Oswald) *see* Byker St Mark and Walkergate St Oswald *Newc*

NEWCASTLE UPON TYNE (St Paul) *see* Elswick *Newc*

NEWCASTLE UPON TYNE (St Philip) and St Augustine and (St Matthew w St Mary) *Newc 4* **P** *Bp* **V** R G S DEADMAN

NEWCASTLE UPON TYNE (St Thomas) Proprietary Chapel *Newc 2* **C** A J SMITH **NSM** B DOOLAN

NEWCASTLE UPON TYNE Christ the King *see* Ch the King *Newc*

NEWCHAPEL (St James the Apostle) *Lich 11* **P** *CPAS* **V** J R ARNOLD

NEWCHURCH (All Saints) *Portsm 7* **P** *Bp* **P-in-c** K F ABBOTT

NEWCHURCH (not known) Culcheth w Croft *Liv 13* **P** *Bp* **R** *vacant*

NEWCHURCH (St Nicholas w St John) *Man 4* **P** *Bp* **C** S G RICHARDSON **NSM** A J WHYTE

NEWCHURCH (St Peter and St Paul) *see* Romney Marsh *Cant*

NEWDIGATE (St Peter) *see* Surrey Weald *Guildf*

NEWENDEN (St Peter) *see* Tenterden, Rother and Oxney *Cant*

NEWENT (St Mary the Virgin) and Gorsley w Cliffords Mesne *Glouc 3* **P** *Bp* **R** S I V MASON **NSM** R G CHIVERS

NEWHALL (St John) *Derby 7* **P** *Bp* **P-in-c** P J DOUGLAS **C** R Z ALLPRESS

NEWHAVEN (St Michael) *Chich 21* **P** *Ch Patr Trust* **R** M M MILLER

NEWHEY (St Thomas) *see* Milnrow and New Hey *Man*

NEWICK (St Mary) *Chich 18* **P** *V Eastbourne St Mary* **R** P K MUNDY

NEWINGTON (St Christopher) *see* St Laur in Thanet *Cant*

NEWINGTON (St Giles) *see* Dorchester *Ox*

NEWINGTON (St John the Baptist) w Hull St Andrew *York 14* **P** *Abp and V Hull H Trin (jt)* **V** T A COTSON

NEWINGTON (St Martin) *see* Hull St Martin w Transfiguration *York*

NEWINGTON (St Mary the Virgin) *see* The Six *Cant*

NEWINGTON (St Mary) *S'wark 10* **P** *Bp* **R** G A FRASER *Hon* **C** M E TODD

NEWINGTON (St Nicholas) *see* Cheriton w Newington *Cant*

NEWINGTON (St Paul) *S'wark 10* **P** *Bp* **V** J A CARRUTHERS

NEWINGTON, SOUTH (St Peter ad Vincula) *see* Bloxham w Milcombe and S Newington *Ox*

NEWLAND (All Saints) *see* Coleford, Staunton, Newland, Redbrook etc *Glouc*

NEWLAND (St John) *see* Hull St Jo Newland *York*

NEWLAND (St Lawrence) *see* Bradwell on Sea and St Lawrence *Chelmsf*

NEWLANDS (not known) *see* Upper Derwent *Carl*

NEWLAY LANE (St Margaret's Church Hall) *see* Bramley *Leeds*

NEWLYN (St Newlyn) *Truro 4* **P** *Bp* **V** *vacant*

NEWLYN (St Peter) *Truro 4* **P** *Bp* **P-in-c** K R OWEN **C** A M YATES, S YATES

NEWMARKET (All Saints) *St E 7* **P** *Bp* **C** S M ALLISON **NSM** S P SHAW

NEWMARKET (St Mary the Virgin) w Exning St Agnes *St E 7* **P** *Bp and DBP (alt)* **R** J C HARDY **NSM** C P BELDING, J R LIND

NEWNHAM (St Mark) *see* Cambridge St Mark *Ely*

NEWNHAM (St Michael and All Angels) *see* Badby w Newnham and Charwelton w Fawsley etc *Pet*

NEWNHAM (St Nicholas) *see* N Hants Downs *Win*

NEWNHAM (St Peter and St Paul) *see* Kingsdown, Creekside and High Downs *Cant*

NEWNHAM (St Peter) w Awre and Blakeney *Glouc 1*
P *Haberdashers' Co and Bp (alt)* **P-in-c** R E SAUM
C J D KNIGHT **OLM** B D BROBYN
NEWNHAM (St Vincent) *see* Ashwell w Hinxworth and
Newnham *St Alb*
NEWNTON, NORTH (St James) *see* Vale of Pewsey *Sarum*
NEWPORT (St John the Baptist) and Bishops Tawton *Ex 13*
P *Bp* **NSM** C R SCOFFIELD
NEWPORT (St Mary the Virgin) w Widdington, Quendon
and Rickling *Chelmsf 20* **P** *Bp and DBP (jt)* **V** *vacant*
NEWPORT (St Nicholas) w Longford, and Chetwynd
Lich 15 **P** *Bp* **R** M A SMITH
NEWPORT (St Stephen) *see* Howden *York*
NEWPORT (St Thomas à Becket and St Thomas the
Apostle) (St John the Baptist) and Carisbrooke *Portsm 7*
P *Patr Bd* **TR** P P LEONARD **TV** E COOKSEY, S A SUTCLIFFE
C H F BARRACLOUGH
NEWPORT MINSTER *see* Newport and Carisbrooke *Portsm*
NEWPORT PAGNELL (St Luke) w Lathbury and Moulsoe
Ox 16 **P** *Bp, Ch Ch Ox, and Lord Carrington (jt)*
R N A P EVANS
NEWQUAY (St Michael) *Truro 6* **P** *Bp* **P-in-c** J S THOROLD
C L M G CHANTLER **NSM** P J KNEEBONE
NEWSHAM (St Bede) and Horton *Newc 1* **P** *Bp and V*
Woodhorn w Newbiggin (jt) **V** I H FLINTOFT
C S A M HUGHES CAREW
NEWSHOLME (St John) *see* Oakworth *Leeds*
NEWSOME (St John the Evangelist) and Armitage Bridge
and South Crosland *Leeds 5* **P** *DBP, TR Almondbury w*
Farnley Tyas, and R Kirkheaton (jt) **R** J ANDERSON
NSM D KENT **OLM** C A SYKES
NEWSTEAD (St Mary the Virgin) *see* Annesley w Newstead
and Kirkby Woodhouse *S'well*
NEWTIMBER (St John the Evangelist) *see* Poynings w
Edburton, Newtimber and Pyecombe *Chich*
NEWTON (Good Shepherd) *see* Clifton w Newton and
Brownsover *Cov*
NEWTON (Mission Church) *see* Embleton w Rennington
and Rock *Newc*
NEWTON (St Botolph) *see* S Lafford *Linc*
NEWTON (St John the Baptist) *see* Black Mountains Gp *Heref*
NEWTON (St Luke) *see* Bishop's Hatfield, Lemsford and N
Mymms *St Alb*
NEWTON (St Margaret) *see* Harston w Hauxton and Newton
Ely
NEWTON (St Mary) w Flowery Field *Ches 14* **P** *V Mottram*
P-in-c S M O'FLAHERTY
NEWTON (St Michael and All Angels) *Ches 8* **P** *R W Kirby*
St Bridget **V** C J COVERLEY **NSM** A C WHORTON
NEWTON (St Oswald) *see* Gt Ayton w Easby and Newton
under Roseberry *York*
NEWTON (St Petrock) *see* Shebbear, Buckland Filleigh,
Sheepwash etc *Ex*
NEWTON ABBOT (All Saints) (St Mary) (St Paul) *Ex 8*
P *Patr Bd* **TR** E P PARKES **TV** G D REGAN, N J DEBNEY
C B L MAYNARD
NEWTON ARLOSH (St John the Evangelist) *see* Solway Plain
Carl
NEWTON AYCLIFFE (St Clare) *see* Gt Aycliffe *Dur*
NEWTON BLOSSOMVILLE (St Nicolas) *see* Lavendon w Cold
Brayfield, Clifton Reynes etc *Ox*
NEWTON BROMSWOLD (St Peter) *see* Rushden St Mary w
Newton Bromswold *Pet*
NEWTON BY TOFT (St Michael) *see* Middle Rasen Gp *Linc*
NEWTON FERRERS (Holy Cross) *see* Brixton, Newton Ferrers,
Revelstoke etc *Ex*
NEWTON FLOTMAN (St Mary the Virgin), Swainsthorpe,
Tasburgh, Tharston, Saxlingham Nethergate and
Shotesham *Nor 5* **P** *Patr Bd* **TR** D M DAVIDSON
TV A C UZOIGWE **C** C H STANFORTH
NEWTON GREEN (All Saints) *see* Boxford, Edwardstone,
Groton etc *St E*
NEWTON HALL (All Saints) *see* Dur N *Dur*
NEWTON HARCOURT (St Luke) *see* Wistow *Leic*
NEWTON HEATH (All Saints) *Man 1* **P** *The Crown and D&C*
(alt) **R** A P WICKENS
NEWTON IN MAKERFIELD (Emmanuel) *see* Newton *Liv*
NEWTON IN MAKERFIELD (St Peter) *as above*
NEWTON IN THE ISLE (St James) *see* Leverington, Newton
and Tydd St Giles *Ely*
NEWTON KYME (St Andrew) *see* Tadcaster *York*
NEWTON LONGVILLE (St Faith), Mursley, Swanbourne,
Little Horwood and Drayton Parslow *Ox 15* **P** *New Coll*
Ox, Ch Soc Trust, Lord Cottesloe, Ch Patr Trust, and MMCET
(jt) **V** S G FAULKS **NSM** D TALKS **OLM** J K BROWN

NEWTON ON OUSE (All Saints) *see* Skelton w Shipton and
Newton on Ouse *York*
NEWTON POPPLEFORD (St Luke) *see* Ottery St Mary,
Alfington, W Hill, Tipton etc *Ex*
NEWTON PURCELL (St Michael) *see* Shelswell *Ox*
NEWTON REGIS (St Mary) *see* All So N Warks *Birm*
NEWTON REIGNY (St John) *see* Penrith w Newton Reigny
and Plumpton Wall *Carl*
NEWTON SOLNEY (St Mary the Virgin) *see* Foremark and
Repton w Newton Solney *Derby*
NEWTON ST CYRES (St Cyr and St Julitta) *see* Brampford
Speke, Cadbury, Newton St Cyres etc *Ex*
NEWTON ST LOE (Holy Trinity) *see* Saltford w Corston and
Newton St Loe *B & W*
NEWTON Team, The (All Saints) (Emmanuel) (St John the
Baptist) (St Peter) *Liv 13* **P** *Patr Bd* **TR** C J STAFFORD
TV S B GREY **NSM** C A CLOSE
NEWTON TONY (St Andrew) *see* Bourne Valley *Sarum*
NEWTON TRACEY (St Thomas à Becket), Horwood,
Alverdiscott, Huntshaw, Yarnscombe, Tawstock,
Atherington, High Bickington, Roborough, St Giles in
the Wood and Beaford *Ex 18* **P** *Ld Chan (1 turn), Patr Bd*
(3 turns) **TR** G J OWEN **NSM** T E DOYLE
NEWTON VALENCE (St Mary) *see* Northanger *Win*
NEWTON, NORTH (St Peter) *see* Alfred Jewel *B & W*
NEWTON, OLD (St Mary) *see* Bacton w Wyverstone, Cotton
and Old Newton etc *St E*
NEWTON, SOUTH (St Andrew) *see* Wylye and Till Valley
Sarum
NEWTON, WEST (St Matthew) *see* Solway Plain *Carl*
NEWTON, WEST (St Peter and St Paul) *see* Sandringham w
W Newton and Appleton etc *Nor*
NEWTON-BY-CASTLE-ACRE (All Saints) *see* Nar Valley *Nor*
NEWTON-IN-WIRRAL (St Michael and All Angels) *see*
Newton *Ches*
NEWTON-LE-WILLOWS (All Saints) *as above*
NEWTON-ON-RAWCLIFFE (St John) *see* Middleton, Newton
and Sinnington *York*
NEWTON-ON-TRENT (St Peter) *see* Saxilby Gp *Linc*
NEWTOWN (Holy Spirit) *see* W Wight *Portsm*
NEWTOWN (Holy Trinity) *see* Soberton, Newtown and
Hambledon *Portsm*
NEWTOWN (King Charles the Martyr) *see* Myddle and
Broughton, Loppington and Newtown *Lich*
NEWTOWN (St George) *see* Lozells and Newtown *Birm*
NEWTOWN (St Mary the Virgin and St John the Baptist) *see*
Burghclere w Newtown and Ecchinswell w Sydmonton *Win*
NEWTOWN (St Paul) *see* Longnor, Quarnford, Sheen etc
Lich
NEWTOWN LINFORD (All Saints) *see* Glenfield and
Newtown Linford *Leic*
NIBLEY, NORTH (St Martin) *see* Tyndale *Glouc*
NICHOLFOREST (St Nicholas) *see* Arthuret w Kirkandrews-
on-Esk and Nicholforest *Carl*
NIDD (St Paul and St Margaret) *see* Knaresborough,
Goldsborough, Nidd and Brearton *Leeds*
NIDDERDALE, LOWER, comprising Hunsingore, Kirk
Hammerton, and Nun Monkton *Leeds 20* **P** *Trustees K Bell*
Esq, DBP, and C J Dent Esq (jt) **R** M P SPURGEON
NIDDERDALE, UPPER, comprising Bewerley Grange,
Greenhow Hill, Middlesmoor, Pateley Bridge, Ramsgill, and
Wilsill *Leeds 20* **P** *D&C Ripon and V Masham and Healey (jt)*
V D C HALL
NINEBANKS (St Mark) *see* Allendale w Whitfield *Newc*
NINEFIELDS (St Lawrence School Worship Centre) *see*
Waltham H Cross *Chelmsf*
NINFIELD (St Mary the Virgin) *Chich 12* **P** *D&C Cant*
P-in-c P A FROSTICK
NITON (St John the Baptist) *Portsm 7* **P** *Qu Coll Ox*
R *vacant*
NOAK HILL (St Thomas) *Chelmsf 2* **P** *Bp*
P-in-c D E ANDERTON
NOCTON (All Saints) *see* Branston w Nocton and
Potterhanworth *Linc*
NOEL PARK (St Mark) *Lon 17* **P** *Bp* **V** S P J CLARK
NOKE (St Giles) *see* Ray Valley *Ox*
NONINGTON (St Mary the Virgin) *see* Canonry *Cant*
NORBITON (St Peter) *S'wark 15* **P** *V Kingston All SS*
V H C A FOXWOOD
NORBURY (All Saints) *see* Wentnor w Ratlinghope,
Myndtown, Norbury etc *Heref*
NORBURY (St Mary and St Barlok) w Snelston *Derby 1*
P *Mrs M F Stanton, L A Clowes Esq, and V Ashbourne (by turn)*
P-in-c D C J BALLARD **C** A J MARSHALL, C E MCDONALD
NORBURY (St Oswald) *S'wark 21* **P** *Bp* **V** A BRUNT
C A M FORSTER

NORBURY (St Peter) *see* Adbaston, High Offley, Knightley, Norbury etc *Lich*
NORBURY (St Philip) *S'wark 21* **P** *Bp* **V** vacant
NORBURY (St Stephen) and Thornton Heath *S'wark 21* **P** *Bp* **V** G P THOMPSON **OLM** J B FORBES
NORBURY (St Thomas) *Ches 16* **P** *Lord Newton* **V** J C ASKWITH **NSM** V G HINDMARSH
NORDEN (St Paul) w Ashworth and Bamford *Man 6* **P** *Bp* **V** J C POWELL **C** K L SMEETON
NORFOLK PARK (St Leonard) *see* Heeley w Arbourthorne and Norfolk Park *Sheff*
NORFOLK, WEST *see* W Norfolk Priory Gp *Ely*
NORHAM (St Cuthbert) and Duddo *Newc 12* **P** *D&C (1 turn), D&C Dur (2 turns)* **V** G R J KELSEY **NSM** M N M SENTAMU
NORK (St Paul) w Burgh Heath *Guildf 9* **P** *The Crown and Bp (alt)* **V** A L WILLIAMS
NORLAND (St Luke) *see* Ryburn *Leeds*
NORLANDS (St James) *see* Notting Dale St Clem w St Mark and St Jas *Lon*
NORLEY (St John the Evangelist), Crowton and Kingsley *Ches 3* **P** *Bp, V Frodsham, and V Weaverham (jt)* **V** R E IVESON **NSM** H MERRINGTON
NORMACOT (Holy Evangelists) *see* Meir Heath and Normacot *Lich*
NORMANBY (St Andrew) *see* Kirby Misperton w Normanby and Salton *York*
NORMANBY (St George) *see* Eston w Normanby *York*
NORMANBY-LE-WOLD (St Peter) *see* Walesby Gp *Linc*
NORMANTON (All Saints) *Leeds 16* **P** *Trin Coll Cam* **V** A MURRAY
NORMANTON (St Giles) *Derby 5* **P** *CPAS* **V** N A A BARBER **C** S J BOSWELL, W A ELEY
NORMANTON, SOUTH (St Michael) *Derby 2* **P** *MMCET* **R** S M POTTER
NORMANTON-LE-HEATH (Holy Trinity) *see* Woodfield *Leic*
NORMANTON-ON-SOAR (St James) *see* Sutton Bonington w Normanton-on-Soar *S'well*
NORMANTON-ON-TRENT (St Matthew) *see* Tuxford w Weston, Markham Clinton etc *S'well*
NORRIS BANK (St Martin) *see* Heatons *Man*
NORRIS GREEN (St Christopher) *see* Liv St Chris Norris Green *Liv*
NORRISTHORPE (All Souls) *see* Heckmondwike (w Norristhorpe) and Liversedge *Leeds*
NORTH *see also under substantive place name*
NORTH CAVE (All Saints) w Cliffe *York 13* **P** *C H J Carver Esq* **P-in-c** B WORSDALE
NORTH CHAPEL (St Michael) w Ebernoe *Chich 4* **P** *Lord Egremont* **P-in-c** K A BAILEY
NORTH CORNWALL Cluster of Churches, comprising Port Isaac, St Endellion, St Kew, and St Minver w St Enodoc and St Michael Rock *Truro 10* **P** *Bp and DBP (jt)* **R** E J WILD **C** R H JONES **NSM** G ASHTON
NORTH COVE (St Botolph) *see* Beccles w Worlingham, N Cove and Barnby *St E*
NORTH DOWNS, comprising Bearsted, Boxley, Detling, Hollingbourne, Hucking, Leeds and Broomfield, Otham w Langley, and Thurnham *Cant 13* **P** *Patr Bd* **TR** J CORBYN **TV** M A PAVEY, R J TUGWELL **C** F C NGANGIRA
NORTH END (Ascension) *see* Portsea Ascension *Portsm*
NORTH END (Chapel of Ease) *see* Burton Dassett *Cov*
NORTH END (St Francis) *see* Portsea N End St Mark *Portsm*
NORTH END (St Mark) *as above*
NORTH END (St Nicholas) *as above*
NORTH HAMPSHIRE DOWNS Benefice, The, comprising Herriard w Winslade, Long Sutton, Newnham w Nately Scures w Mapledurwell w Up Nately w Greywell, Odiham, South Warnborough, Tunworth, Upton Grey, and Weston Patrick *Win 5* **P** *Bp, Qu Coll Ox, St Jo Coll Ox, N McNair Scott Esq, and J L Jervoise Esq (jt)* **R** S R BUTLER **C** A R D L P BERESFORD **NSM** C P DUDGEON
NORTH KERNOW, comprising Kilkhampton, Launcells, Morwenstow, Poughill, and Stratton *Truro 8* **P** *Duchy of Cornwall (1 turn), Bp, DBP, Ch Soc Trust and CPAS Patr Trust (1 turn)* **R** T L FOLLAND
NORTH SHIELDS (St Augustin) (Christ Church) *Newc 5* **P** *Patr Bd* **TR** G EVANS **C** M HALL **NSM** D A ROBINSON
NORTH WARWICKSHIRE *see* All So N Warks *Birm*
NORTH WEALD BASSETT (St Andrew) *Chelmsf 3* **P** *Bp* **P-in-c** L P BATSON
NORTH WEST HAMPSHIRE Benefice, The, comprising Ashmansworth, Crux Easton, East Woodhay, Highclere, and Woolton Hill *Win 6* **P** *Bp and Earl of Carnarvon (jt)* **R** C DALE **Hon C** M J BAMFORTH

NORTHALLERTON (All Saints) w Kirby Sigston *York 18* **P** *D&C Dur* **V** F R MAYER-JONES **C** C L SODERMAN, D JOHNSON
NORTHAM (St Margaret) *see* Appledore, Northam and Westward Ho! *Ex*
NORTHAMPTON (All Saints w St Katharine) (St Peter) *Pet 4* **P** *Bp and R Foundn of St Kath (jt)* **R** O J COSS
NORTHAMPTON (Christ Church) *Pet 4* **P** *Bp* **V** A CUTHBERTSON **NSM** A M MARCH
NORTHAMPTON (Church on the Heath) *see* Kings Heath *Pet*
NORTHAMPTON (Emmanuel) *Pet 4* **P** *DBP* **TR** H DU G SPENCELEY **C** Y DESROCHES **Hon C** C J PEARSON **NSM** D SPENCELEY
NORTHAMPTON (Holy Sepulchre w St Andrew and St Lawrence) *Pet 4* **P** *Bp* **V** M W J HILLS **NSM** A M MARCH
NORTHAMPTON (Holy Trinity) (St Paul) *Pet 4* **P** *Bp* **V** A C MCGOWAN **NSM** A M MARCH
NORTHAMPTON (St Alban the Martyr) *Pet 4* **P** *Bp* **V** J A EVANS **C** C M E T TREMTHTHANMOR **NSM** P H HEFFRON
NORTHAMPTON (St Benedict) *Pet 4* **P** *Bp* **V** J A GRIFFITHS
NORTHAMPTON (St David) *see* Kingsthorpe *Pet*
NORTHAMPTON (St Giles) *Pet 4* **P** *Simeon's Trustees* **V** S A KELLY **C** A J WAGNER
NORTHAMPTON (St James) *see* Dallington and St James *Pet*
NORTHAMPTON (St Mary the Virgin) *Pet 4* **P** *Bp* **Hon C** S M COLES
NORTHAMPTON (St Matthew) *Pet 4* **P** *DBP* **V** N M SETTERFIELD
NORTHAMPTON (St Michael and All Angels w St Edmund) *Pet 4* **P** *Bp* **V** M W J HILLS **NSM** A M MARCH, P D MUNCH
NORTHANGER Benefice, The, comprising Chawton, East Tisted w Colemore, East Worldham, Farringdon, Hartley Mauditt w West Worldham, Kingsley w Oakhanger, Newton Valence, and Selborne *Win 2* **P** *Bp (1 turn), D&C (1 turn), Bp and Sir James Scott Bt (1 turn)* **R** A J PEARS **NSM** C E WALSHAW, L A LEON
NORTHAW (St Thomas of Canterbury) and Cuffley *St Alb 17* **P** *Mrs S Peasley* **V** C R H KILGOUR
NORTHBOROUGH (St Andrew) *see* Glinton, Etton, Maxey, Peakirk and Northborough *Pet*
NORTHBOURNE (St Augustine) *see* Eastry and Woodnesborough *Cant*
NORTHCHURCH (St Mary) and Wigginton *St Alb 1* **P** *Duchy of Cornwall and Bp (alt)* **R** J A GORDON **NSM** M D SELDON, M J EGGLETON
NORTHDOWN PARK (St Philip) *see* Margate St Phil *Cant*
NORTHEN PLAIN, The *see* Andreas, Ballaugh and Sulby *S & M*
NORTHENDEN (St Wilfrid) *Man 2* **P** *Bp* **P-in-c** A R BRADLEY
NORTHFIELD (St Laurence) *Birm 2* **P** *Keble Coll Ox* **R** J E CHAPMAN **C** T C MORTON **NSM** D PYCOCK
NORTHFLEET (All Saints) *see* Perry Street *Roch*
NORTHFLEET (St Botolph) and Rosherville *Roch 4* **P** *Patr Bd and The Crown (alt)* **P-in-c** C R S SHOWERS
NORTHGATE (St Elizabeth) *see* Three Bridges *Chich*
NORTHIAM (St Mary) *Chich 17* **P** *MMCET* **R** R H WHITE
NORTHILL (St Mary the Virgin) *see* Caldecote, Northill and Old Warden *St Alb*
NORTHINGTON (St John the Evangelist) *see* Farleigh, Candover and Wield *Win*
NORTHLEACH (St Peter and St Paul) w Hampnett and Farmington, Cold Aston w Notgrove and Turkdean, and Compton Abdale w Haselton *Glouc 8* **P** *Bp (2 turns), Ld Chan (1 turn)* **P-in-c** V A M TIMMIS
NORTHLEIGH (St Giles) *see* Colyton, Branscombe, Musbury, Northleigh and Southleigh *Ex*
NORTHLEW (St Thomas of Canterbury) *see* Okehampton, Inwardleigh, Belstone, Sourton etc *Ex*
NORTHMOOR *see* Okehampton, Inwardleigh, Belstone, Sourton etc *Ex*
NORTHMOOR (St Denys) *see* Lower Windrush *Ox*
NORTHMOOR GREEN (St Peter and St John) *see* Alfred Jewel *B & W*
NORTHOLT (St Joseph the Worker) (St Hugh) West End *Lon 19* **P** *DBP* **V** A PIMENTA **C** S F METRY
NORTHOLT (St Mary) (St Richard) *Lon 19* **P** *BNC Ox* **NSM** A A DIAS
NORTHOLT PARK (St Barnabas) *Lon 19* **P** *Bp* **V** E A J CARGILL THOMPSON **NSM** P M A LINDERS
NORTHORPE (St John the Baptist) *see* Messingham w E Butterwick, Scotter w E Ferry and Scotton w Northorpe *Linc*

NORTHOWRAM (St Matthew) *Leeds 6* P *Bp*
P-in-c J T ALLISON C L J FOX
NORTHREPPS (St Mary) *see* Poppyland *Nor*
NORTHUMBERLAND HEATH (St Paul) *see* Erith St Paul *Roch*
NORTHWICH (Holy Trinity) *Ches 6* P *Bp*
P-in-c C S SEDDON
NORTHWICH (St Helen) *see* Witton *Ches*
NORTHWICH (St Luke) *Ches 6* P *Bp* V *vacant*
NORTHWOLD (St Andrew) *see* Grimshoe *Ely*
NORTHWOOD (Emmanuel) *Lon 20* P *CPAS Patr Trust*
V T J MEATHREL C C L BRITTON, N K ÓSKARSDÓTTIR,
T D SCOTT
NORTHWOOD (Holy Trinity) *Lon 20* P *Trustees*
V A L LYNES C A M RICHARDSON, R J RICHARDSON
NSM J M BRIDGES
NORTHWOOD (Holy Trinity) *see* Hanley H Ev *Lich*
NORTHWOOD (St John the Baptist) *Portsm 7* P *Bp*
R A COLLINSON NSM D M NETHERWAY
NORTHWOOD GREEN (Mission Church) *see* Westbury-on-
Severn w Flaxley, Blaisdon etc *Glouc*
NORTHWOOD HILLS (St Edmund the King) *Lon 20* P *Bp*
V M A MILLER NSM H HUTCHINS
NORTHWOOD Pinner Road (St Edmund the King) *see*
Northwood Hills St Edm *Lon*
NORTON (All Saints) *see* Brington w Whilton and Norton
etc *Pet*
NORTON (All Saints) *see* Gauzebrook *Bris*
NORTON (St Andrew) *see* Pakenham w Norton, Tostock etc
St E
NORTON (St Berteline and St Christopher) *Ches 3* P *DBP*
V *vacant*
NORTON (St Egwin) *see* Evesham w Norton and Lenchwick
Worc
NORTON (St George) (St Nicholas) *St Alb 3* P *Bp*
V T A SHARP C C L HARALD
NORTON (St James) *Sheff 2* P *CCC Cam* P-in-c T K HOLE
C E J LUNN, P M BROWN
NORTON (St James) *see* Stoulton w Drake's Broughton and
Pirton etc *Worc*
NORTON (St Mary the Virgin) *Dur 8* P *Bp*
P-in-c M E ANDERSON NSM C WALTON, J L EASTERBY
NORTON (St Mary) *see* Kingsdown, Creekside and High
Downs *Cant*
NORTON (St Mary) *see* Twigworth, Down Hatherley,
Norton, The Leigh etc *Glouc*
NORTON (St Michael and All Angels) *Dur 8* P V *Norton
St Mary* P-in-c M E ANDERSON NSM C WALTON,
J L EASTERBY
NORTON (St Michael and All Angels) and Wollaston
Worc 5 P *Bp* Hon C D M FARMER
NORTON (St Peter) *see* Norton juxta Malton *York*
NORTON BAVANT (All Saints) *see* Upper Wylye Valley *Sarum*
NORTON BRIDGE (St Luke) *see* Chebsey, Creswell, Ellenhall,
Ranton etc *Lich*
NORTON CANES (St James) *Lich 3* P *Bp* R N L HIBBINS
NORTON CANON (St Nicholas) *see* Weobley w Sarnesfield
and Norton Canon *Heref*
NORTON CUCKNEY (St Mary) *S'well 1* P *Lady Alexandra
Cavendish Bentinck* P-in-c D R GOUGH C R J HANFORD
NORTON DISNEY (St Peter) *see* Withamside *Linc*
NORTON FITZWARREN (All Saints) *see* Staplegrove w Norton
Fitzwarren *B & W*
NORTON IN HALES (St Chad) *see* Woore and Norton in
Hales *Lich*
NORTON IN THE MOORS (St Bartholomew) *see* Milton and
Norton *Lich*
NORTON JUXTA MALTON (St Peter) *York 6* P *Abp* V *vacant*
NORTON JUXTA TWYCROSS (Holy Trinity) *see* Woodfield
Leic
NORTON LEES (St Paul) *Sheff 2* P R *Norton* V P M BROWN
C E A LANGNER, E J LUNN, T K HOLE
NORTON LINDSEY (Holy Trinity) *see* Arden Valley *Cov*
NORTON MALREWARD (Holy Trinity) *see* Chew Magna w
Dundry, Norton Malreward etc *B & W*
NORTON MANDEVILLE (All Saints) *see* High Ongar w
Norton Mandeville *Chelmsf*
NORTON ST PHILIP (St Philip and St James) *see* Hardington
Vale *B & W*
NORTON SUB HAMDON (The Blessed Virgin Mary) *see* Ham
Hill Villages *B & W*
NORTON SUBCOURSE (St Mary) *see* Waveney Marshlands
Nor
NORTON WOODSEATS (St Chad) *see* Woodseats St Chad
Sheff
NORTON, EAST (All Saints) *see* Hallaton and Allexton, w
Horninghold, Tugby etc *Leic*

NORTON, OVER (St James) *see* Chipping Norton *Ox*
NORWELL (St Laurence) w Ossington, Cromwell, Caunton,
and Sutton w Carlton on Trent *S'well 3* P *Bp and SMF (jt)*
V *vacant*
NORWICH (Christ Church) *see* Eaton Ch Ch *Nor*
NORWICH (Christ Church) *see* New Catton Ch Ch *Nor*
NORWICH (Holy Trinity) *see* Heigham H Trin *Nor*
NORWICH (St Andrew) *Nor 1* P *PCC* V M J YOUNG
C M HAYDEN
NORWICH (St Andrew) *see* Eaton St Andr *Nor*
NORWICH (St Anne) *see* Earlham *Nor*
NORWICH (St Barnabas) *see* The Mitre Benefice *Nor*
NORWICH (St Catherine) *see* Mile Cross *Nor*
NORWICH (St Elizabeth) *see* Earlham *Nor*
NORWICH (St Francis) *see* Nor Heartsease St Fran *Nor*
NORWICH (St Giles) *Nor 1* P *Ld Chan and Bp (alt)* V *vacant*
NORWICH (St Helen) *Nor 1* P *Gt Hosp Nor* V E S LANGAN
NORWICH (St John the Baptist) Timberhill w Norwich
St Julian *Nor 1* P *Bp, Guild of All So, and D&C (jt)*
P-in-c R O STANTON
NORWICH (St Julian) *see* Nor St Jo w St Julian *Nor*
NORWICH (St Luke) *see* New Catton St Luke w St Aug *Nor*
NORWICH (St Mary Magdalene) w St James *Nor 2* P *D&C*
P-in-c L S TILLETT
NORWICH (St Mary) *see* Earlham *Nor*
NORWICH (St Matthew) *see* Thorpe St Matt *Nor*
NORWICH (St Michael) *see* Bowthorpe *Nor*
NORWICH (St Peter Mancroft) (St John Maddermarket)
Nor 1 P *PCC* R E J CARTER C F H HAWORTH
NSM L G ALLIES
NORWICH (St Stephen) *Nor 1* P *D&C* V M M LIGHT
C I FIFIELD
NORWICH (St Thomas) *see* The Mitre Benefice *Nor*
NORWICH Colegate and Tombland (St George) *Nor 1*
P *Bp and D&C* V A M E LEWIS NSM F A BLYTH
NORWICH Heartsease (St Francis) *Nor 1* P *Bp* V J B WYER
C P G JORDAN, T G WILLIAMS
NORWICH Lakenham (St Mark) *Nor 1* P *D&C*
V S E WEST-LINDELL
NORWICH, Lakenham (St John the Baptist and All Saints)
and Tuckswood St Paul *Nor 1* P *Bp and D&C (jt)*
P-in-c P G RIDER
NORWOOD (All Saints) *see* Upper Norwood All SS *S'wark*
NORWOOD (Holy Innocents) *see* S Norwood H Innocents
and St Mark *S'wark*
NORWOOD (St Alban the Martyr) *see* S Norwood St Alb
S'wark
NORWOOD (St John) *see* Upper Norwood St Jo *S'wark*
NORWOOD (St Leonard) *see* Sheff St Leon Norwood *Sheff*
NORWOOD (St Luke) *see* W Norwood St Luke *S'wark*
NORWOOD (St Mark) *see* S Norwood H Innocents and
St Mark *S'wark*
NORWOOD (St Mary the Virgin) *Lon 19* P *SMF*
P-in-c D J C BOOKLESS C A K BOOKLESS
NORWOOD, SOUTH (Holy Innocents) (St Mark) *S'wark 21*
P *Bp* V R F EVERSLEY
NORWOOD, SOUTH (St Alban the Martyr) *S'wark 21* P *Bp*
V S W GILBERT
NORWOOD, UPPER (All Saints) *S'wark 21* P V *Croydon*
V *vacant*
NORWOOD, UPPER (St John) *S'wark 21* P *Bp*
V J A PRITCHARD
NORWOOD, WEST (St Luke) *S'wark 12* P *Abp* V D R DAVIS
NOTGROVE (St Bartholomew) *see* Northleach w Hampnett
and Farmington etc *Glouc*
NOTTING DALE (St Clement) (St Mark) and Norlands
St James *Lon 12* P *Bp* V G K WARDELL NSM N H MORRIS
NOTTING HILL (All Saints) (St Columb) *Lon 12* P *SMF*
V P P CORBETT NSM B MAHILUM, J BLACKBURNE
NOTTING HILL (St John) *Lon 12* P *Bp* V W H TAYLOR
C L R GALON
NOTTING HILL (St Michael and All Angels) (Christ Church)
(St Francis) *Lon 12* P *Trustees* P-in-c P P CORBETT
NSM B MAHILUM, J BLACKBURNE
NOTTING HILL (St Peter) *Lon 12* P *Bp* V P ALLERTON
NSM A MAY
NOTTINGHAM (St Andrew) *S'well 9* P *Peache Trustees*
V *vacant*
NOTTINGHAM (St Ann w Emmanuel) *S'well 9* P *Trustees*
V A M COLLINS C N J HILL
NOTTINGHAM (St George w St John the Baptist) *S'well 9*
P *Bp* V I D MCCORMACK C J A FRANKLIN
NOTTINGHAM (St Jude) *S'well 7* P *CPAS* V J C ALLISTER
NOTTINGHAM (St Mary the Virgin) the Lace Market
S'well 9 P *Bp* V T A GILLUM C G R WALTON

NOTTINGHAM (St Nicholas) *S'well 9* **P** *CPAS*
R S D SILVESTER **C** F A FINN, G E A FRANK, L J BLAKELEY
NSM I B PAUL
NOTTINGHAM (St Peter and St James) (All Saints) *S'well 9*
P *Bp* **R** C D HARRISON **C** R H DAVEY
NOTTINGHAM (St Saviour) *S'well 9* **P** *CPAS* **V** H L HALL
NOTTINGHAM (St Stephen) *see* Hyson Green and Forest
Fields *S'well*
NOTTINGHAM (Trinity Church) Bishop's Mission Order
S'well 9 **C** A C L HUGHES, B BRUMLEY, J W L HUGHES,
M P WREFORD
NOWTON (St Peter) *see* St Edm Way *St E*
NUFFIELD (Holy Trinity) *Ox 24* **P** *MMCET* **R** *vacant*
NUN MONKTON (St Mary) *see* Lower Nidderdale *Leeds*
NUNBURNHOLME (St James) *see* Pocklington Wold *York*
NUNEATON (St Mary) *Cov 5* **P** *V Nuneaton* **V** *vacant*
NUNEATON (St Nicolas) *Cov 5* **P** *The Crown* **V** *vacant*
NUNHEAD (St Antony) (St Silas) *S'wark 8* **P** *Bp*
V D J OGUNYEMI **Hon C** M N A TORRY
NUNNEY (All Saints) and Witham Friary, Marston Bigot,
Wanstrow and Cloford *B & W 3* **P** *Bp, SMF, and C N*
Clarke Esq and Duke of Somerset (jt) **P-in-c** A E DICKSON
NUNNINGTON (All Saints) *see* Kirkdale w Harome,
Nunnington and Pockley *York*
NUNTHORPE (St Mary the Virgin) (St Mary's Church Hall)
York 20 **P** *Abp* **V** T STEPHENS **C** L R WILD
NSM L M OPALA
NUNTON (St Andrew) *see* Chalke Valley *Sarum*
NURSLING (St Boniface) and Rownhams *Win 12* **P** *Bp*
R G DIXON
NURSTEAD (St Mildred) *see* Meopham w Nurstead *Roch*
NUTBOURNE (St Wilfrid) *see* Chidham *Chich*
NUTFIELD (St Peter and St Paul) *see* Bletchingley and
Nutfield *S'wark*
NUTFIELD, SOUTH (Christ Church) *S'wark 25* **P** *Ch Patr*
Trust **P-in-c** L J ABRAMS
NUTHALL (St Patrick) *see* Kimberley and Nuthall *S'well*
NUTHURST (St Andrew) and Mannings Heath *Chich 10*
P *Bp Lon* **R** *vacant*
NUTHURST (St Thomas) *see* Packwood w Hockley Heath
Birm
NUTLEY (St James the Less) *Chich 18* **P** *R Maresfield*
V B W SEAR **NSM** P C INGRAM
NYMET (St George) *see* S Molton w Nymet St George,
Chittlehamholt etc *Ex*
NYMET ROWLAND (St Bartholomew) *see* N Creedy *Ex*
NYMPSFIELD (St Bartholomew) *see* Dursley, Uley, Owlpen
etc *Glouc*
NYNEHEAD (All Saints) *see* Wellington and Distr *B & W*
OADBY (St Paul) (St Peter) Great Glen, including Burton
Overy, Carlton Curlieu, and Glen Magna *Leic 3* **P** *Patr Bd*
TR S A BAILEY **TV** J LINDSEY, K K FORD **C** B G WILLIAMS,
J P TEARNE, M E JUKES, S J COLLINS
OAK HILL Parishes *see* Winchcombe *Glouc*
OAKAMOOR (Holy Trinity) *see* Kingsley and Foxt-w-Whiston
and Oakamoor etc *Lich*
OAKDALE (St George) *Sarum 7* **P** *Bp* **V** P M DRAPER
OAKE (St Bartholomew) *see* Deane Vale *B & W*
OAKENGATES (Holy Trinity), Priors Lee and Wrockwardine
Wood *Lich 20* **P** *Bp and V Shifnal (jt)* **R** D J LOUGHRAN
C G INGHAM, L R HARPER
OAKENSHAW CUM WOODLANDS (St Andrew) *see* Low
Moor and Oakenshaw *Leeds*
OAKFORD (St Peter) *see* Washfield, Stoodleigh, Withleigh
etc *Ex*
OAKHAM (All Saints), Ashwell, Braunston, Brooke,
Egleton, Hambleton, Langham, Market Overton, Teigh
and Whissendine *Pet 12* **P** *Patr Bd* **TR** S R GRIFFITHS
TV C J RATTENBERRY, D L MARSH **C** R M THOMPSON,
S E B NURMAHI, S J ALEY
OAKHANGER (St Luke's Mission Church) *see* Alsager Ch Ch
Ches
OAKHANGER (St Mary Magdalene) *see* Northanger *Win*
OAKHILL (All Saints) *see* Beacon Trinity *B & W*
OAKINGTON (St Andrew) *Ely 6* **P** *Qu Coll Cam*
V J C ALEXANDER
OAKLEY (St Leonard) w Wootton St Lawrence *Win 4* **P** *Qu*
Coll Ox and D&C (alt) **R** B A KAUTZER **NSM** S E COLMAN
OAKLEY (St Mary) *see* Bromham w Oakley and Stagsden
St Alb
OAKLEY (St Mary) *see* Worminghall w Ickford, Oakley and
Shabbington *Ox*
OAKLEY (St Nicholas) *see* N Hartismere *St E*
OAKLEY (St Peter) *see* Henham and Elsenham w Ugley
Chelmsf
OAKLEY SQUARE (St Matthew) *see* Old St Pancras *Lon*

OAKLEY, GREAT (All Saints), Wix, Wrabness, Tendring and
Beaumont-cum-Moze *Chelmsf 21* **P** *Ld Chan (1 turn), Ch*
Patr Trust, St Jo Coll Cam, DBP, and Ball Coll Ox (2 turns)
C K D EMERSON **NSM** L F GARNHAM
OAKLEY, GREAT (St Michael) and LITTLE (St Peter) *Pet 7*
P *H W G de Capell Brooke Esq and Boughton Estates Ltd (alt)*
P-in-c A M SEARLE
OAKRIDGE (St Bartholomew) *see* Bisley, Chalford, France
Lynch, and Oakridge etc *Glouc*
OAKS IN CHARNWOOD (St James the Greater) *see* Shepshed
and Oaks in Charnwood *Leic*
OAKSEY (All Saints) *see* Braydon Brook *Bris*
OAKWOOD (no dedication) *Derby 5* **P** *Bp and MMCET (jt)*
V *vacant*
OAKWOOD (St Thomas) *Lon 16* **P** *Bp* **V** R J L ALLDRITT
OAKWORTH (Christ Church) *Leeds 1* **P** *Bp*
NSM B G PARTRIDGE
OARE (Blessed Virgin Mary) w Culbone *B & W 15* **P** *Bp*
R *vacant*
OARE (Holy Trinity) *see* Vale of Pewsey *Sarum*
OARE (St Bartholomew) *see* E Downland *Ox*
OARE (St Peter) *see* Kingsdown, Creekside and High Downs
Cant
OATLANDS (St Mary) *Guildf 8* **P** *Bp* **V** F O OLOKOSE
OBORNE (St Cuthbert) *see* Queen Thorne *Sarum*
OCCOLD (St Michael) *see* Eye *St E*
OCKBROOK (All Saints) *Derby 8* **P** *Lt Col T H Pares*
V T M SUMPTER **NSM** B G JOHNSON
OCKENDON, NORTH (St Mary Magdalene) *Chelmsf 2* **P** *Bp*
R *vacant*
OCKENDON, SOUTH (St Nicholas) *see* Mardyke *Chelmsf*
OCKER HILL (St Mark) *Lich 25* **P** *Bp* **V** M LIDDELL
OCKFORD RIDGE (St Mark) *see* Godalming *Guildf*
OCKHAM (All Saints) w Hatchford and Downside *Guildf 10*
P *Bp* **R** *vacant*
OCKLEY (St Margaret) *see* Surrey Weald *Guildf*
OCLE PYCHARD (St James the Great) *see* Frome Valley *Heref*
OCTAGON, comprising Compton, East Marden, Forestside,
North Marden, Racton, and Stoughton *Chich 6* **P** *Bp, Bp*
Lon,and Stansted Park Foundation (jt) **R** L A YATES
ODCOMBE (St Peter and St Paul) *see* Ham Hill Villages
B & W
ODD RODE (All Saints) *Ches 11* **P** *R Astbury*
R P S ATKINSON
ODDINGTON (Holy Ascension) *see* Broadwell, Evenlode,
Oddington, Adlestrop etc *Glouc*
ODDINGTON (St Andrew) *see* Ray Valley *Ox*
ODDINGTON (St Nicholas) *see* Broadwell, Evenlode,
Oddington, Adlestrop etc *Glouc*
ODELL (All Saints) *see* Chellington *St Alb*
ODIHAM (All Saints) *see* N Hants Downs *Win*
ODSTOCK (St Mary) *see* Chalke Valley *Sarum*
OFFCHURCH Group, The (St Gregory), including
Hunningham, Wappenbury, and Weston under Wetherley
Cov 10 **P** *Ld Chan (1 turn), Bp (3 turns)* **V** H PRIESTNER
OFFENHAM (St Mary and St Milburgh) *see* E Vale and Avon
Villages *Worc*
OFFERTON (St Alban) (St John) *Ches 18* **P** *Bp*
P-in-c C M RABLEN
OFFHAM (Old St Peter) *see* Hamsey *Chich*
OFFHAM (St Michael) *see* W Malling w Offham *Roch*
OFFLEY (St Mary Magdalene) *see* King's Walden and Offley
w Lilley *St Alb*
OFFLEY, HIGH (St Mary the Virgin) *see* Adbaston, High
Offley, Knightley, Norbury etc *Lich*
OFFORD D'ARCY w OFFORD CLUNY (All Saints) *see* Buckden
w the Offords *Ely*
OFFTON (St Mary) *see* S Bosmere *St E*
OFFWELL (St Mary the Virgin), Farway and Widworthy
Ex 4 **P** *Bp and R J T Marker Esq (jt)* **V** *vacant*
OGBOURNE ST ANDREW (St Andrew) *see* Ridgeway *Sarum*
OGBOURNE ST GEORGE (St George) *as above*
OGLEY HAY (St James) *Lich 1* **P** *Bp* **V** G K GREENWAY
OGWELL (St Bartholomew) *see* Newton Abbot *Ex*
OKEFORD Benefice, The, comprising Childe Okeford,
Hammoon, Manston, Okeford Fitzpaine, and Shillingstone
Sarum 5 **P** *G A L-F Pitt-Rivers Esq and DBP (alt)* **R** *vacant*
OKEFORD FITZPAINE (St Andrew) *see* Okeford *Sarum*
OKEHAMPTON (All Saints) (St James), Inwardleigh,
Belstone, Sourton, Bridestowe, Bratton Clovelly,
Germansweek, Lydford, Hatherleigh, Northlew w
Ashbury, Exbourne, Meeth and Jacobstow *Ex 9* **P** *Patr*
Bd (5 turns), Duchy of Cornwall (1 turn) **TR** S W COOK
TV A J BROOK, L D WINSBURY **C** R A F BACHE
OKEWOOD (St John the Baptist) *see* Ewhurst w Okewood
and Forest Green *Guildf*

OLD   *see also under substantive place name*
OLD FORD (St Paul) (St Mark) *Lon 7*   **P** *Hyndman Trustees and CPAS (jt)*   **V** D O WEITHERS   **C** D S PILKINGTON
NSM A I KEECH, W A O'REILLY
OLD HEATH (St Barnabas)   *see* Colchester St Barn *Chelmsf*
OLD HILL (Holy Trinity) *Worc 5*   **P** *Ch Soc Trust*
V N S GOWERS
OLD KIRK BRADDAN (St Brendan)   *see* Braddan *S & M*
OLD LANE (Mission Church)   *see* Bloxwich *Lich*
OLDBERROW (St Mary)   *see* Arden Marches *Cov*
OLDBURY (Christ Church), Langley, and Londonderry
Birm 3   **P** *The Crown (1 turn), Bp (3 turns)*   **V** *vacant*
OLDBURY (St Nicholas)   *see* Bridgnorth and Morville Par
Heref
OLDBURY, comprising Calstone Wellington, Cherhill, Compton Bassett, Heddington, and Yatesbury *Sarum 16*
P *Bp, CPAS, Marquess of Lansdowne, and C E R Money-Kyrle Esq (jt)*   **R** M C EARWICKER
OLDBURY-ON-SEVERN (St Arilda)   *see* Thornbury and
Oldbury-on-Severn w Shepperdine *Glouc*
OLDCOTES (St Mark's Mission Church)   *see* Carlton-in-
Lindrick and Langold w Oldcotes *S'well*
OLDHAM (St Barnabas)   *see* Clarksfield and Waterhead *Man*
OLDHAM (St Chad)   *see* Hollinwood and Limeside *Man*
OLDHAM (St James) (St Ambrose) *Man 5*   **P** *Bp and R Prestwich (jt)*   **V** *vacant*
OLDHAM (St Mary w St Peter) *Man 5*   **P** *Patr Bd*
V D J PALMER   **NSM** J M HURLSTON
OLDHAM (St Paul) and Werneth *Man 5*   **P** *Bp*
V N J ANDREWES   **Hon C** D J QUARMBY
OLDHAM (St Stephen and All Martyrs)   *see* Coldhurst and
Oldham St Steph *Man*
OLDHAM Moorside (St Thomas) *Man 5*   **P** *Trustees*
V D OWEN   **C** R A DASHWOOD
OLDHURST (St Peter)   *see* Somersham w Pidley and Oldhurst
and Woodhurst *Ely*
OLDLAND (St Anne) *Bris 5*   **P** *Bp*   **V** B W GOODWIN
C M Y Y S NAM
OLDRIDGE (St Thomas)   *see* Tedburn St Mary, Cheriton
Bishop, Whitestone etc *Ex*
OLDSWINFORD (St Mary)   *see* Old Swinford Stourbridge
Worc
OLIVER'S BATTERY (St Mark)   *see* Stanmore *Win*
OLLERTON (St Giles) (St Paulinus) w Boughton *S'well 3*
P *Ld Chan and Bp (alt)*   **P-in-c** Z BURTON   **NSM** M A GROVES
OLNEY (St Peter and St Paul) *Ox 16*   **P** *Bp*
R A J D PRITCHARD-KEENS
OLTON (St Margaret) *Birm 6*   **P** *Bp and V Bickenhill (jt)*
V D E WRIGHT   **C** T E TEAROE
OLVESTON (St Mary the Virgin)   *see* N Severnside *Bris*
OMBERSLEY (St Andrew)   *see* Elmley Lovett w Hampton
Lovett and Elmbridge w Rushock and Hartlebury and
Ombersley w Doverdale *Worc*
ONCHAN (St Peter), Lonan and Laxey *S & M*   **P** *The Crown*
TR A M DI CHIARA   **TV** J DUDLEY
ONECOTE (St Luke)   *see* Butterton, Ipstones-w-Berkhamsytch
etc *Lich*
ONEHOUSE (St John the Baptist)   *see* Combs and Finborough
St E
ONGAR, HIGH (St Mary the Virgin) w Norton Mandeville
Chelmsf 3   **P** *Ch Soc Trust*   **P-in-c** S H GIBBS
ONIBURY (St Michael and All Angels)   *see* Bromfield *Heref*
ONNY CAMLAD   *see* Wentnor w Ratlinghope, Myndtown,
Norbury etc *Heref*
ONSLOW SQUARE (Holy Trinity) (St Paul) and South
Kensington St Augustine *Lon 8*   **P** *Bp, MMCET, and Keble Coll Ox (jt)*   **V** N G P GUMBEL   **C** A AGBAJE, A C WEBB,
A J WOOLDRIDGE, B J WILLIS, B M BRYANT, D M SIMPSON,
F CARRILLO, G A WATKINSON, G B CUTLER, J A O'SULLIVAN,
J A POWELL, J A STANDLEY, J D BAINES, J HALEY, J M LEES,
J S SIMPSON, J S WILLIS, K K Y CHOW, L P DEAN, M R TATTON,
N E AINSWORTH, N K LEE, P W COWLEY, R J BARSTOW,
R RODRIGUES, R S L WOOLDRIDGE, S J FOLLETT, W L PERRY
Hon C J A K MILLAR   **NSM** A J MORLEY, J A C RAY,
M D ROPER, S C M JACKSON, T C JACKSON
OPENSHAW (St Barnabas)   *see* Manchester Gd Shep and
St Barn *Man*
OPENSHAW, HIGHER (St Clement) *Man 1*   **P** *Trustees*
P-in-c P G JUMP   **C** D R J MULLANEY
OPENWOODGATE (St Mark)   *see* Belper *Derby*
ORBY (All Saints)   *see* Burgh Gp *Linc*
ORCHARD (Community Centre)   *see* Egglescliffe *Dur*
ORCHARD PORTMAN (St Michael)   *see* Beercrocombe w
Curry Mallet, Hatch Beauchamp etc *B & W*
ORCHARD WAY (St Barnabas)   *see* W Cheltenham *Glouc*

ORCHARDLEIGH (Blessed Virgin Mary)   *see* Beckington w
Standerwick, Berkley, Rodden etc *B & W*
ORCHESTON (St Mary)   *see* Salisbury Plain *Sarum*
ORCOP (St John the Baptist)   *see* St Weonards *Heref*
ORDSALL (All Hallows)   *see* Ordsall and Retford St Mich *S'well*
ORDSALL (All Hallows) and Retford St Michael *S'well 1*
P *SMF and Bp (jt)*   **NSM** D A BEAN
ORDSALL (St Clement) and Salford Quays *Man 7*   **P** *Bp*
R *vacant*
ORE (Christ Church) *Chich 15*   **P** *Simeon's Trustees*
P-in-c T L BELL   **C** K A PENFOLD
ORE (St Helen) (St Barnabas) *Chich 15*   **P** *Simeon's Trustees*
P-in-c T L BELL   **C** K A PENFOLD
OREBECK *St E 12*   **P** *The Crown (1 turn), MMCET, J Austin Esq,
Capt J L Round-Turner, Ch Soc Trust, and Lord Marlesford (1
turn)*   **P-in-c** G HEDGER
ORESTON (Church of the Good Shepherd)   *see* Plymstock
and Hooe *Ex*
ORFORD (St Andrew) *Liv 11*   **P** *Bp*   **P-in-c** G F HITCHEN
ORFORD (St Bartholomew)   *see* Wilford Peninsula *St E*
ORFORD (St Margaret) *Liv 11*   **P** *Bp*   **V** *vacant*
ORLESTONE (St Mary)   *see* Saxon Shoreline *Cant*
ORLETON (St George)   *see* Leominster *Heref*
ORLINGBURY (St Mary)   *see* Gt w Lt Harrowden and
Orlingbury and Isham etc *Pet*
ORMESBY (St Cuthbert) *York 17*   **P** *Abp*   **NSM** J E CALDWELL
**ORMESBY ST MARGARET (St Margaret) w Scratby,
Ormesby St Michael and Rollesby** *Nor 6*   **P** *Bp, D&C, DBP
and R J H Tacon Esq (jt)*   **P-in-c** J WOOD
ORMESBY ST MICHAEL (St Michael)   *see* Ormesby St Marg w
Scratby, Ormesby St Mich etc *Nor*
ORMESBY, NORTH (Holy Trinity) *York 17*   **P** *Abp*
V B A WOODALL
**ORMSBY Group, The South (St Leonard), including Bag
Enderby, Brinkhill, Harrington, Haugh, Ruckland w Farforth,
Maidenwell and Oxcombe, Somersby, and Tetford** *Linc 9*
P *Mrs A Price, Sir Thomas Ingilby Bt, Mert Coll Ox, Bp, DBP,
and Personal Reps J Measures (jt)*   **R** *vacant*
ORMSGILL (St Francis)   *see* N Barrow *Carl*
ORMSIDE (St James)   *see* Heart of Eden *Carl*
ORMSKIRK (St Peter and St Paul) *Liv 14*   **P** *Earl of Derby*
P-in-c P A BICKNELL   **NSM** S E HAYNES
ORPINGTON (All Saints) *Roch 16*   **P** *D&C*   **V** G M A ROGERS
ORPINGTON (Christ Church) *Roch 16*   **P** *Ch Trust Fund
Trust, Bp, and V Orpington (jt)*   **V** S SMITH   **C** H E MUSSON
ORRELL (St Luke)   *see* Wigan *Liv*
ORRELL HEY (St John and St James)   *see* Litherland and Orrell
Hey *Liv*
**ORSETT (St Giles and All Saints) and Bulphan and
Horndon on the Hill** *Chelmsf 15*   **P** *Bp and D&C St Paul's
(jt)*   **R** S M MANN   **NSM** M A JAIYESIMI, S R BLAKE
ORSTON (St Mary)   *see* Whatton w Aslockton, Hawksworth,
Scarrington etc *S'well*
ORTON (All Saints)   *see* High Westmorland *Carl*
**ORTON GOLDHAY (Christ Church) Local Ecumenical
Projecgt** *Ely 13*   **Min** S C GOWER
ORTON GOLDHAY (St John)   *see* The Ortons *Ely*
ORTON LONGUEVILLE (Holy Trinity) *as above*
ORTON MALBORNE (not known) *as above*
ORTON WATERVILLE (St Mary) *as above*
ORTON, GREAT (St Giles)   *see* Barony of Burgh *Carl*
ORTON-ON-THE-HILL (St Edith of Polesworth)   *see* Sheepy
Leic
ORTONS, The (Holy Trinity) (St Mary) (St John) *Ely 15*
P *Bp and Pemb Coll Cam (jt)*   **P-in-c** I R FALVEY
C A F G PODD
**ORWELL and Deben Rural Benefice, The, comprising
Bucklesham and Foxhall, Falkenham, Hemley, Kirton,
Levington, Nacton, Newbourne, and Waldringfield** *St E 10*
P *DBP, Mrs S E F Holden, and A Waller Esq (1 turn), Ld Chan
(1 turn)*   **R** I A WILSON   **C** S J JENKINS
**ORWELL Group, The (St Andrew), including Arrington,
Barrington, Croydon, and Wimpole** *Ely 7*   **P** *Bp, DBP, and
Trin Coll Cam (jt)*   **R** F A COUCH   **C** J M NORRIS
OSBALDWICK (St Thomas) w Murton *York 2*   **P** *Abp*
P-in-c J NOBEL
OSBOURNBY (St Peter and St Paul)   *see* S Lafford *Linc*
OSENEY CRESCENT (St Luke) *Lon 15*   **P** *Bp*   **V** J MARCH
C C S BROOKES, E R OSBORNE, L A EDWARDS, N S BECKLES
OSGATHORPE (St Mary the Virgin)   *see* Kegworth, Hathern,
Long Whatton, Diseworth etc *Leic*
OSMASTON (St Martin)   *see* Brailsford w Shirley, Osmaston
w Edlaston etc *Derby*
OSMINGTON (St Osmond)   *see* Weymouth Ridgeway *Sarum*
OSMONDTHORPE (St Philip)   *see* Halton and Osmondthorpe
Leeds

OSMOTHERLEY (St Peter) w Harlsey and Ingleby Arncliffe
York 18 **P** *J N Barnard Esq (1 turn), Ld Chan (2 turns)*
P-in-c D E GAMBLE **NSM** K M BROWN, W A DEWING
OSMOTHERLY (St John) *see Ulverston St Mary w H Trin Carl*
OSNEY (St Frideswide) *Ox 2* **P** *Bp and Ch Ch Ox (jt)*
R C M SYKES
OSPRINGE (St Peter and St Paul) *see Faversham Cant*
OSSETT (Holy and Undivided Trinity) and Gawthorpe
Leeds 16 **P** *Bp and R Dewsbury (jt)* **P-in-c** S M HARVEY
C A N GRIFFIN **OLM** A SHACKLETON
OSSETT, SOUTH (Christ Church) *Leeds 16* **P** *Bp*
P-in-c S M HARVEY **C** A N GRIFFIN
OSSINGTON (Holy Rood) *see Norwell w Ossington,*
Cromwell etc S'well
OSWALDKIRK (St Oswald) *see Ampleforth w Oswaldkirk,*
Gilling E etc York
OSWALDTWISTLE (Immanuel) (All Saints) (St Paul)
Blackb 1 **P** *Bp, DBP, R Church Kirk, The Ven C W D Carroll,*
G F Garnett Esq, and PCCs (jt) **V** M J T JOSS
NSM C GARNER
OSWESTRY (Holy Trinity) *Lich 18* **P** *Bp* **V** P T DARLINGTON
C J WEAVER
OSWESTRY (St Oswald) *Lich 18* **P** *Earl of Powis*
V H L GIBBONS
OTFORD (St Bartholomew) *Roch 10* **P** *D&C Westmr*
V D A GUEST
OTHAM (St Nicholas) *see N Downs Cant*
OTHERY (St Michael) *see Middlezoy w Othery, Moorlinch*
and Greinton B & W
OTLEY (All Saints) *Leeds 12* **P** *Bp* **V** G C BUTTANSHAW
OTLEY (St Mary) *see Carlford St E*
OTTER VALE *see Ottery St Mary, Alfington, W Hill, Tipton*
etc Ex
OTTERBOURNE (St Matthew) *see Compton, Hursley, and*
Otterbourne Win
OTTERBURN (St John the Evangelist) *see N Tyne and*
Redesdale Newc
OTTERFORD (St Leonard) *see Blackdown B & W*
OTTERHAM (St Denis) *see Boscastle Gp Truro*
OTTERINGTON, NORTH (St Michael and All Angels) *see The*
Thorntons and The Otteringtons York
OTTERINGTON, SOUTH (St Andrew) *as above*
OTTERSHAW (Christ Church) *Guildf 11* **P** *Bp*
V S C FACCINI
OTTERTON (St Michael) *see Budleigh Salterton, E Budleigh*
w Bicton etc Ex
OTTERY ST MARY (St Mary the Virgin), Alfington, West
Hill, Tipton St John, Venn Ottery, Newton Poppleford,
Harpford, Colaton Raleigh, Payhembury, Feniton and
Escot *Ex 6* **P** *Patr Bd* **TR** L M S COOK
TV D J CARRINGTON, M WARD **Hon C** A E H TURNER,
J G PANGBOURNE
OTTRINGHAM (St Wilfrid) *see Easington w Skeffling,*
Keyingham, Ottringham etc York
OUGHTIBRIDGE (Ascension) *Sheff 3* **P** *Ch Patr Trust*
P-in-c C E D TUFNELL
OUGHTRINGTON (St Peter) and Warburton *Ches 10* **P** *Bp*
and Viscount Ashbrook (jt) **R** E M BURGESS
OULTON (St John the Evangelist) *see Stone Ch Ch and*
Oulton Lich
OULTON (St John) *see Rothwell, Lofthouse, Methley etc*
Leeds
OULTON (St Michael) *see Oulton Broad Nor*
OULTON (St Peter and St Paul) *see Aylsham and Distr Nor*
OULTON BROAD (St Mark) (St Luke) (St Michael) *Nor 9*
P *Patr Bd* **TR** H L JARY **C** A S BUNTER **OLM** M A BARNES
OUNDLE (St Peter) w Ashton and Benefield w Glapthorn
Pet 10 **P** *Bp and Mrs G S Watts-Russell (jt)* **R** S J WEBSTER
C A S M COPELAND, J G JACKSON
OUSBY (St Luke) *see Cross Fell Gp Carl*
OUSDEN (St Peter) *see Bansfield St E*
OUSEBURN, GREAT (St Mary) and LITTLE (Holy Trinity) w
Marton cum Grafton and Whixley w Green Hammerton
Leeds 20 **P** *Bp, R Knaresborough and DBP (3 turns), St Jo Coll*
Cam (1 turn) **V** S C FEASTER
OUT RAWCLIFFE (St John the Evangelist) *see Over Wyre*
Blackb
OUTLANE (St Mary Magdalene) *see Stainland and Outlane*
Leeds
OUTWELL (St Clement) *Ely 14* **P** *Bp*
P-in-c N A WHITEHOUSE **NSM** D A CALVERT
OUTWOOD (St John the Baptist) *see The Windmill S'wark*
OUTWOOD (St Mary Magdalene) *see N Wakefield Leeds*
OUTWOOD COMMON (St John the Divine) *see Billericay*
and Lt Burstead Chelmsf

OUZEL VALLEY, The, comprising Billington, Egginton, Heath
and Reach, Hockliffe, Leighton Buzzard, and Linslade
St Alb 11 **P** *Patr Bd* **TR** C F IRVINE **TV** B J MINTON,
N MCGEENEY, S P MARSH **C** K L BORTHWICK **OLM** W JONES
OVAL WAY (All Saints) *see Chalfont St Peter Ox*
OVENDEN (St George) *Leeds 8* **P** *V Halifax*
P-in-c A MAXWELL **NSM** G ROPER
OVENDEN (St John the Evangelist) *see Bradshaw and*
Holmfield Leeds
OVER *see also under substantive place name*
OVER (St Chad) *Ches 6* **P** *Bp* **V** vacant
OVER (St John the Evangelist) *Ches 6* **P** *Lord Delamere and*
W R Cullimore Esq (jt) **V** G T CROWDER
OVER (St Mary) *see Sfolds Ely*
OVER WALLOP (St Peter) *see Portway and Danebury Win*
OVERBURY (St Faith) w Teddington, Alstone and Little
Washbourne w Beckford and Ashton under Hill *Worc 3*
P *D&C and MMCET (jt)* **P-in-c** M K LECLÉZIO **C** A C DAVIES
OVERSEAL (St Matthew) *see Seale and Lullington w Coton*
in the Elms Derby
OVERSTONE (St Nicholas) *see Mears Ashby and Hardwick*
and Sywell etc Pet
OVERSTRAND (St Martin) *see Poppyland Nor*
OVERTON (St Helen) *Blackb 11* **P** *V Lanc* **V** L S MOFFATT
OVERTON (St Mary) w Laverstoke and Freefolk *Win 6*
P *Bp* **R** J A TOMKINS-RUSSELL **C** A ROCHE
OVERTON (St Michael and All Angels) *see Upper Kennet*
Sarum
OVING (All Saints) *see Schorne Ox*
OVING (St Andrew) *see Tangmere and Oving Chich*
OVINGDEAN (St Wulfran) *Chich 19* **P** *SMF*
R R J BUTCHER-TUSET
OVINGHAM (St Mary the Virgin) and Wylam *Newc 9* **P** *Bp*
V T D K BIRCH **NSM** L DEAN
OVINGTON (St John the Evangelist) *see Watton Nor*
OVINGTON (St Mary) *see N Hinckford Chelmsf*
OVINGTON (St Peter) *see Arle Valley Win*
OWERMOIGNE (St Michael) *see Watercombe Sarum*
OWERSBY, NORTH (St Martin) *see Woldmoor Gp Linc*
OWLERTON (St John the Baptist) *Sheff 4* **P** *Ch Patr Trust*
P-in-c J E FRENCH
OWLPEN (Holy Cross) *see Dursley, Uley, Owlpen etc Glouc*
OWLSMOOR (St George) *Ox 8* **P** *Bp* **V** C M VAUGHAN
OWLSWICK (Chapel) *see Risborough Ox*
OWMBY Group, The (St Peter and St Paul), including
Glentham w Caenby, Hackthorn, Saxby, and Spridlington
Linc 5 **P** *Duchy of Lanc, Bp and D&C, Bp and Mrs S Hutton,*
and C W A Cracroft-Eley (by turn) **R** S E TURNBULL
OLM S DEACON
OWSLEBURY (St Andrew) *see S Downs Gateway Churches*
Win
OWSTON (All Saints) *Sheff 7* **P** *DBP* **P-in-c** S J GARDNER
OWSTON (St Andrew) *see Whatborough Gp Leic*
OWSTON (St Martin) *Linc 1* **P** *The Crown* **V** M T P ZAMMIT
OWTHORNE (St Matthew) *see S Holderness Coast York*
OWTHORPE (St Margaret) *S'well 5* **P** *Trustees Sir Rupert*
Bromley Bt **P-in-c** P D S MASSEY
OWTON MANOR (St James) *Dur 6* **P** *Bp* **V** S J LOCKE
OXBOROUGH (St John the Evangelist) w Foulden and
Caldecote *Nor 13* **P** *G&C Coll Cam* **Hon C** L M LUBBE
OXCLOSE (not known) *Dur 9* **P** *R Washington, TR Usworth,*
and V Fatfield (jt) **P-in-c** G M RUSHTON
OXENDON (St Helen) *see Arthingworth, Harrington w*
Oxendon and E Farndon Pet
OXENHALL (St Anne) *see Redmarley D'Abitot,*
Bromesberrow, Pauntley etc Glouc
OXENHOPE (St Mary the Virgin) *Leeds 1* **P** *Bp*
V C M THATCHER **C** E CANSDALE **NSM** J ROBERTS
OXENTON (St John the Baptist) *see Bishop's Cleeve and*
Woolstone w Gotherington etc Glouc
OXFORD (St Aldate) *Ox 2* **P** *Simeon's Trustees* **R** S FOSTER
C S C R PONSONBY, W J STUART-LEE **NSM** D L HAMES,
L G HARRIS, M BRICKMAN
OXFORD (St Andrew) *Ox 2* **P** *Trustees* **V** D J HEYWARD
C J R DWYER, P M WHITE, T C MURRAY **NSM** E J PITKETHLY,
J HARVEY, T W HOWELL
OXFORD (St Barnabas and St Paul) (St Thomas the
Martyr) *Ox 2* **P** *Keble Coll Ox and Ch Ch Ox (jt)*
V C M WOODS **C** S GILLINGHAM **NSM** M R C SALISBURY
OXFORD (St Clement) *Ox 1* **P** *Ox Ch Trust* **R** R E GIBSON
C J TARASSENKO
OXFORD (St Ebbe w Holy Trinity and St Peter-le-Bailey)
Ox 2 **P** *Ox Ch Trust* **R** V E ROBERTS **C** B C G VANE,
G B NESBITT, J M KNIGHT, P D L WILKINSON, P E BOLTON,
T C DOSSOR **NSM** A M HORN, J C POOLE
OXFORD (St Frideswide) *see Osney Ox*

OXFORD (St Giles) St Philip and St James (St Margaret)
Ox 2 **P** *St Jo Coll Ox* **C** D G T WALTERS **NSM** A C HOLMES
OXFORD (St Luke) Canning Crescent *see* Ox St Matt *Ox*
OXFORD (St Mary Magdalen) *Ox 2* **P** *Ch Ch Ox*
V P J GROVES **C** E D BRAZIL
**OXFORD (St Mary the Virgin) (St Cross or Holywell)
(St Peter in the East)** *Ox 2* **P** *Or Coll Ox and Mert Coll Ox
(jt)* **V** W R S LAMB **NSM** A E RAMSEY,
C B M BANNISTER-PARKER
OXFORD (St Matthew) (St Luke) *Ox 2* **P** *Ox Ch Trust*
R J R WILLIAMS **Hon C** J A WILLIAMS **NSM** J LEES,
M J RAYNER
**OXFORD (St Michael at the North Gate w St Martin and
All Saints)** *Ox 2* **P** *Linc Coll Ox* **V** A G BUCKLEY
OXHEY (All Saints) *St Alb 6* **P** *Bp* **V** P M WISE **C** E J GUEST
OXHEY (St Matthew) *St Alb 6* **P** *DBP* **V** S F FRAMPTON
OXHILL (St Lawrence) *see* Tysoe w Oxhill and Whatcote *Cov*
OXLEY (Epiphany) and Wednesfield St Gregory *Lich 28*
P *Bp* **C** A E MARTIN
OXNEAD (St Michael & all Angels) *see* Aylsham and Distr
Nor
OXSHOTT (St Andrew) *Guildf 10* **P** *Bp* **V** F A TRICKEY
C P J L DAVIES **Hon C** C J TRICKEY
OXTED (St Mary) *S'wark 25* **P** *Bp* **TR** A ELTRINGHAM
TV J P ASHTON **C** L FARODOYE, M S ANDERSON
OXTON (St Peter and St Paul) *see* Epperstone, Gonalston,
Oxton and Woodborough *S'well*
OXTON (St Saviour) *Ches 1* **P** *DBP* **V** J KENNEDY
C H G TORR **NSM** T A DIXON
PACKINGTON (Holy Rood) *see* Woodfield *Leic*
PACKWOOD (St Giles) w Hockley Heath *Birm 2* **P** *Bp and
M R Parkes Esq (alt)* **V** M CATLEY
PADBURY (St Mary the Virgin) *see* Lenborough *Ox*
PADDINGTON (St James) *Lon 2* **P** *Bp* **V** P R THOMAS
C O J DOBSON
**PADDINGTON (St John the Evangelist) (St Michael and All
Angels)** *Lon 2* **P** *DBP* **V** S D MASON **C** G F ELSEY
PADDINGTON (St Mary Magdalene) (St Peter) *Lon 2*
P *Keble Coll Ox and Ch Patr Trust* **V** R H EVERETT
PADDINGTON (St Mary) *see* Lt Venice *Lon*
PADDINGTON (St Saviour) *as above*
PADDINGTON (St Stephen w St Luke) *Lon 2* **P** *Bp*
V R J DRYER **NSM** M J LEE
PADDINGTON GREEN (St Mary) *see* Lt Venice *Lon*
PADDLESWORTH (St Oswald) *see* Elham Valley *Cant*
PADDOCK WOOD (St Andrew) *Roch 8* **P** *D&C Cant*
V B T KNAPP
PADGATE (Christ Church) *see* Warrington E *Liv*
PADIHAM (St Leonard) w Hapton and Padiham Green
Blackb 3 **P** *Bp* **V** M A JONES **NSM** C S J WALKER
**PADSTOW (St Petroc), St Merryn and St Issey w St Petroc
Minor** *Truro 6* **P** *Bp, Keble Coll Ox, and P J N Prideaux-Brune
Esq (jt)* **R** I R GULLAND **NSM** F GIORLA
PADWORTH (St John the Baptist) *see* Stratfield Mortimer and
Mortimer W End etc *Ox*
PAGANHILL (Holy Spirit) *see* Stroud Team *Glouc*
PAGHAM (St Thomas à Becket) *Chich 1* **P** *Abp* **V** *vacant*
PAGLESHAM (St Peter) *see* Ashingdon w S Fambridge,
Canewdon and Paglesham *Chelmsf*
PAIGNTON (Christ Church) and Preston St Paul *Ex 10*
P *Bp and Peache Trustees (jt)* **V** J R POUT
PAIGNTON (St John the Baptist) (St Andrew) (St Boniface)
Ex 10 **P** *DBP* **V** N A KNOX
PAILTON (St Denis) *see* Revel Gp *Cov*
**PAINSWICK (St Mary the Virgin), Sheepscombe, Cranham,
The Edge, Pitchcombe, Harescombe and Brookthorpe**
Glouc 4 **P** *Bp, D&C, Mrs N Owen (1 turn), and Ld Chan (1
turn)* **V** J E TURVILLE **NSM** A J P LEACH
OLM D W NEWELL
PAKEFIELD (All Saints and St Margaret) *Nor 9* **P** *Ch Patr
Trust* **R** S R LORD **C** R E BENSUSAN
**PAKENHAM (St Mary) w Norton, Tostock, Great Ashfield,
Hunston and Stowlangtoft** *St E 5* **P** *Bp, Peterho Coll Cam,
and DBP (jt)* **R** K A VALENTINE **NSM** J S G PRICE
PALGRAVE (St Peter) *see* N Hartismere *St E*
PALLION (St Luke) *see* Millfield St Mark and Pallion St Luke
Dur
PALMARSH (Holy Cross) *see* Hythe *Cant*
PALMERS GREEN (St John the Evangelist) *Lon 16*
P *V Southgate Ch Ch* **V** J V COLEMAN
PALTERTON (St Luke's Mission Room) *see* Ault Hucknall and
Scarcliffe *Derby*
PAMBER (St Mary and St John the Baptist) *see* The
Sherbornes w Pamber *Win*
PAMPISFORD (St John the Baptist) *Ely 5* **P** *Mrs B A
Killander* **V** *vacant*

PANCRASWEEK (St Pancras) *see* Holsworthy, Hollacombe,
Pyworthy etc *Ex*
PANFIELD (St Mary the Virgin) *see* Bocking St Mary and
Panfield *Chelmsf*
**PANGBOURNE (St James the Less) w Tidmarsh and
Sulham** *Ox 4* **P** *Bp, Ch Soc Trust, and Mrs I E Moon (jt)*
R *vacant*
PANNAL (St Robert of Knaresborough) w Beckwithshaw
Leeds 18 **P** *Bp and Peache Trustees (jt)* **V** J SMITH
C N P MURRAY
PANSHANGER (United Church) *St Alb 18* **P** *Bp*
V P E SEYMOUR
PAPPLEWICK (St James) *see* Linby w Papplewick *S'well*
PAPWORTH (St Peter) *Ely 1* **P** *Patr Bd*
TR N A DI CASTIGLIONE **TV** S M DAY **NSM** G J DODGSON
PAR (St Mary the Virgin) (Good Shepherd) *Truro 7* **P** *The
Crown* **V** *vacant*
PARHAM (St Mary the Virgin) *see* Orebeck *St E*
PARHAM (St Peter) *see* Amberley w N Stoke and Parham,
Wiggonholt etc *Chich*
PARK (St John the Evangelist) *see* Sheff St Jo *Sheff*
PARK BARN (St Clare) *see* Westborough *Guildf*
PARKEND (St Paul) and Viney Hill *Glouc 1* **P** *Bp and Univ
Coll Ox (jt)* **V** S C NORTON
PARKGATE (St Thomas) *see* Neston *Ches*
**PARKHAM (St James), Alwington, Buckland Brewer,
Hartland, Welcombe, Clovelly, Woolfardisworthy West,
Bucks Mills and Lundy** *Ex 14* **P** *Patr Bd (4 turns), The
Crown (1 turn)* **TR** J M SKINNER **TV** M M E BRAY
NSM J HAYES
PARKSTONE (Good Shepherd) *see* Heatherlands *St Jo
Sarum*
PARKSTONE (St John the Evangelist) *as above*
PARKSTONE (St Luke) *Sarum 7* **P** *Ch Trust Fund Trust*
V C M STRAIN
PARKSTONE (St Peter) and St Osmund w Branksea St Mary
Sarum 7 **P** *Patr Bd* **R** M E TROTMAN **C** S BEDBOROUGH
OLM P E SOUTHGATE
PARKWOOD (St Paul) *see* S Gillingham *Roch*
PARLAUNT ROAD (Christ the Worker) *see* Langley Marish
Ox
PARLEY, WEST (All Saints) (St Mark) *Sarum 9* **P** *P E E
Prideaux-Brune Esq* **R** E C BOOTH
PARNDON, GREAT (St Mary) *Chelmsf 4* **P** *Bp*
P-in-c R J ATTEW
PARNDON, LITTLE (St Mary) *see* Harlow Town Cen w Lt
Parndon *Chelmsf*
PARR (St Peter) (St Paul) (St Philip) *Liv 10* **P** *Patr Bd*
TR C DORAN **OLM** M E TAYLOR
PARR MOUNT (Holy Trinity) *Liv 10* **P** *R St Helens Town Cen*
C T M COATES
PARRACOMBE (Christ Church) *see* Lynton, Brendon,
Countisbury etc *Ex*
PARSON'S GREEN (St Dionis) *see* Fulham St Dionis *Lon*
PARTINGTON (St Mary) and Carrington *Ches 10* **P** *Bp and
V Bowdon (alt)* **P-in-c** A W KNIGHT **C** L A M BREWSTER
PARTNEY (St Nicholas) *see* Bolingbroke Deanery *Linc*
PARTRIDGE GREEN (St Michael and All Angels) *see* W
Grinstead *Chich*
PARWICH (St Peter) *see* Fenny Bentley, Thorpe, Tissington,
Parwich etc *Derby*
PASSENHAM (St Guthlac) *Pet 5* **P** *MMCET*
R J E PENNINGTON
PASTON (All Saints) *Pet 11* **P** *Bp* **R** P N WHITELEY
PASTON (St Margaret) *see* Trunch Group *Nor*
**PASTROW, comprising Charlton w Foxcotte, Faccombe,
Hatherden w Tangley, Hurstbourne Tarrant, Penton
Mewsey, Smannell w Enham Alamein, Vernham Dean and
Linkenholt, and Weyhill** *Win 3* **P** *Qu Coll Ox, St Mary's Coll
Win, and Bp (jt)* **V** A P RANDLE-BISSELL **C** T A LEWIS,
T C ETHERTON
PATCHAM (All Saints) *Chich 19* **P** *MMCET*
V A L FLOWERDAY **C** C M DUNK
PATCHING (St John the Divine) *see* Findon w Clapham and
Patching *Chich*
PATCHWAY (St Chad) *Bris 5* **P** *Trustees* **P-in-c** H K JAMESON
PATELEY BRIDGE (St Cuthbert) *see* Upper Nidderdale *Leeds*
PATRICK BROMPTON (St Patrick) *see* Lower Wensleydale
Leeds
PATRICROFT (Christ Church) *see* Eccles *Man*
PATRINGTON (St Patrick) *see* Easington w Skeffling,
Keyingham, Ottringham etc *York*
PATRIXBOURNE (St Mary) *see* Bridge *Cant*
PATTERDALE (St Patrick) *Carl 4* **P** *Bp and the Hon J N
Lowther (jt)* **P-in-c** M RODHAM
PATTERN CHURCH *see* Swindon St Aug *Bris*

PATTINGHAM (St Chad) w Patshull *Lich 23* **P** *Bp and M Kwiatkowska Esq (jt)* **V** *vacant*

PATTISHALL (Holy Cross) w Cold Higham and Gayton w Tiffield *Pet 5* **P** *Bp, SS Coll Cam, and SMF (jt)* R K A I JONGMAN

PAUL (St Pol de Lion) *Truro 4* **P** *Ld Chan* **P-in-c** A M YATES C K R OWEN, S YATES

PAULERSPURY (St James the Apostle) *see* Silverstone and Abthorpe w Slapton etc *Pet*

PAULL (St Andrew and St Mary) *see* Hedon, Paull, Sproatley and Preston *York*

PAULSGROVE (St Michael and All Angels) *Portsm 6* **P** *Bp* **V** *vacant*

PAULTON (Holy Trinity) w Farrington Gurney and High Littleton *B & W 11* **P** *Bp and Hyndman Trustees (jt)* **P-in-c** A S PITT

PAUNTLEY (St John the Evangelist) *see* Redmarley D'Abitot, Bromesberrow, Pauntley etc *Glouc*

PAVENHAM (St Peter) *see* Milton Ernest, Pavenham and Thurleigh *St Alb*

PAWLETT (St John the Baptist) *see* Puriton and Pawlett *B & W*

PAXFORD (Mission Church) *see* Vale and Cotswold Edge *Glouc*

PAXTONS, The (Holy Trinity) (St James) w Diddington and Southoe *Ely 13* **P** *D&C Linc (2 turns), E G W Thornhill Esq and Mert Coll Ox (1 turn each)* **V** A S REED

PAYHEMBURY (St Mary the Virgin) *see* Ottery St Mary, Alfington, W Hill, Tipton etc *Ex*

PEACEHAVEN (Ascension) and Telscombe Cliffs w Piddinghoe and Telscombe Village *Chich 21* **P** *Bp and Gorham Trustees (jt)* **V** T J MILLS **C** D M HAKE

PEAK DALE (Holy Trinity) *see* Tideswell *Derby*

PEAK FOREST (Charles the King and Martyr) *see* Fairfield, Peak Forest and Dove Holes *Derby*

PEAKIRK (St Pega) *see* Glinton, Etton, Maxey, Peakirk and Northborough *Pet*

PEAR TREE (Jesus Chapel) *see* Southampton St Mary Extra *Win*

PEASEDOWN ST JOHN (St John the Baptist) w Wellow and Foxcote w Shoscombe *B & W 11* **P** *Bp* **V** M G STREET C S REILLY

PEASEMORE (St Barnabas) *see* E Downland *Ox*

PEASENHALL (St Michael) *see* Yoxmere *St E*

PEASLAKE (St Mark) *see* Shere, Albury and Chilworth *Guildf*

PEASMARSH (St Michael) *see* Shalford *Guildf*

PEASMARSH (St Peter and St Paul) *see* Brede w Udimore, Beckley and Peasmarsh *Chich*

PEATLING MAGNA (All Saints) *see* Four Saints *Leic*

PEATLING PARVA (St Andrew) *see* Avon-Swift *Leic*

PEBMARSH (St John the Baptist) *see* Halstead Area *Chelmsf*

PEBWORTH (St Peter) *see* Vale and Cotswold Edge *Glouc*

PECKHAM (All Saints) Blenheim Grove *S'wark 8* **P** *CPAS* **V** J M MORTIMER **C** J C DAWKINS

PECKHAM (Christ Church) *see* Camberwell Ch Ch *S'wark*

PECKHAM (St John w St Andrew) *S'wark 8* **P** *Bp* **V** E O K ADELOYE

PECKHAM (St Luke) *see* Camberwell St Luke *S'wark*

PECKHAM (St Mary Magdalene) (St Paul) *S'wark 8* **P** *Ch Patr Soc* **V** O A ADAMS

PECKHAM (St Saviour) *S'wark 9* **P** *Bp* **V** P E COLLIER

PECKHAM, EAST (Holy Trinity) and Nettlestead *Roch 8* **P** *St Pet Coll Ox and D&C Cant (jt)* **R** A H CARR **NSM** S M MORRELL

PECKHAM, WEST (St Dunstan) *see* Mereworth, Wateringbury and W Peckham *Roch*

PECKLETON (St Mary Magdalene) *see* Newbold De Verdun, Barlestone, Kirkby Mallory and Peckleton *Leic*

PEDMORE (St Peter) and Wollescote *Worc 5* **P** *Patr Bd* **R** W D NICHOL

PEEL (St German's Cathedral) *see* W Coast *S & M*

PEEL (St Paul) *see* Walkden and Lt Hulton *Man*

PEEL GREEN (St Michael and All Angels) *see* Barton w Peel Green and Winton *Man*

PEEL Parishes, The *Lich 4* **P** *Bp* **R** J R IDDON **NSM** R G DAVIES

PEGSWOOD (St Margaret) *see* Bothal and Pegswood w Longhirst *Newc*

PELDON (St Mary) *see* W w E Mersea, Peldon, Gt and Lt Wigborough *Chelmsf*

PELSALL (St Michael and All Angels) *Lich 24* **P** *Bp* **NSM** A M MORRIS

PELTON (Holy Trinity) and West Pelton *Dur 9* **P** *Bp* **V** J LINTERN

PELTON, WEST (St Paul) *see* Pelton and W Pelton *Dur*

PELYNT (St Nun) *see* Trelawny *Truro*

PEMBERTON (St John) *see* Wigan *Liv*

PEMBRIDGE (St Mary the Virgin) w Moor Court, Shobdon, Staunton-on-Arrow, Byton and Lyonshall *Heref 4* **P** *Ld Chan (1 turn), Patr Bd (4 turns)* **R** A L BRANSTON

PEMBURY (St Peter) *Roch 8* **P** *Ch Ch Ox* **V** R M WORSSAM

PEN SELWOOD (St Michael) *B & W 2* **P** *Bp* **R** A J WAY

PENCOMBE (St John) *see* Bredenbury *Heref*

PENCOYD (St Denys) *see* St Weonards *Heref*

PENCOYS (St Andrew) *see* Redruth w Lanner and Treleigh *Truro*

PENDEEN (St John the Baptist) w Morvah *Truro 4* **P** R A H Aitken Esq and C W M Aitken Esq (jt) **P-in-c** K E WEDGEWOOD

PENDEFORD (St Paul) *see* Tettenhall Regis *Lich*

PENDLEBURY (St Augustine) *see* Swinton and Pendlebury *Man*

PENDLESIDE, WEST, comprising Heyhouses, Pendleton, and Whalley *Blackb 7* **P** *Bp and J E R Aspinall (jt)* **V** R J CARMYLLIE **C** J LEE

PENDLETON (All Saints) *see* W Pendleside *Blackb*

PENDLETON (St Thomas) *see* Salford All SS *Man*

PENDLETON Claremont (Holy Angels) *as above*

PENDOCK CROSS (Holy Redeemer) *see* Berrow w Pendock, Eldersfield, Hollybush etc *Worc*

PENDOMER (St Roch) *see* Coker Ridge *B & W*

PENGE (Christ Church w Holy Trinity) *see* Anerley *Roch*

PENGE (Holy Trinity) (St John the Evangelist) *Roch 13* **P** *Bp and Simeon's Trustees* **V** J C SMITH

PENGE (St Paul) *see* Anerley *Roch*

PENGE LANE (Holy Trinity) *Roch 13* **P** *Bp* **V** *vacant*

PENHILL (St Peter) *Bris 7* **P** *Bp* **V** *vacant*

PENHILL, comprising Aysgarth, Bolton cum Redmire, Preston-under-Scar cum Wensley, and West Witton *Leeds 22* **P** *Trin Coll Cam and Lord Bolton (jt)* **R** T L RINGLAND **NSM** P S YEADON

PENHURST (St Michael the Archangel) *see* Ashburnham w Penhurst *Chich*

PENISTONE (St John the Baptist) and Thurlstone *Sheff 11* **P** *Bp* **TR** D J HOPKIN **C** J M TWIGG

PENKETH (St Paul) *see* Warrington W *Liv*

PENKEVIL (St Michael) *see* St Michael Penkevil *Truro*

PENKHULL (St Thomas) *see* Hartshill, Penkhull and Trent Vale *Lich*

PENKRIDGE Team, The (St Michael and All Angels), including Acton Trussell and Dunston *Lich 2* **P** *Patr Bd* **TR** G H YERBURY **TV** S MAYO **C** A M ARTHUR

PENN (Holy Trinity) and Tylers Green *Ox 9* **P** *Earl Howe* **V** M D BISSET **NSM** G SUMMERS

PENN (St Bartholomew) (St Anne) *Lich 23* **P** *Bp* **V** B N WHITMORE **NSM** A STORER

PENN FIELDS St Philip (St Aidan) *Lich 23* **P** *Ch Trust Fund Trust* **V** P H SMITH **C** T M LARKIN, T W EADY **NSM** J DALE

PENN STREET (Holy Trinity) *Ox 9* **P** *Earl Howe* **P-in-c** R A ATKINSON

PENNARD, EAST (All Saints) *see* Fosse Trinity *B & W*

PENNARD, WEST (St Nicholas) *see* Baltonsborough w Butleigh, W Bradley etc *B & W*

PENNINGTON (Christ Church) *Man 7* **P** *Trustees* **V** A W SAUNDERS

PENNINGTON (St Mark) *Win 11* **P** *V Milford* **P-in-c** R N NOEL

PENNINGTON (St Michael and the Holy Angels) and Lindal w Marton and Bardsea *Carl 9* **P** *Bp and DBP (jt)* **V** *vacant*

PENNY LANE (St Barnabas) *Liv 2* **P** *Bp* **P-in-c** A L RAYMENT **C** K J WHITE

PENNYCROSS (St Pancras) *Ex 20* **P** *CPAS* **V** L BRASCHI **C** D HOLLANDS, S J SHARLAND

PENNYWELL (St Thomas) *see* Sunderland St Mary, St Thos and St Oswald *Dur*

PENPONDS (Holy Trinity) *see* Camborne, Tuckingmill and Penponds *Truro*

PENRITH (Christ Church) (St Andrew) w Newton Reigny and Plumpton Wall *Carl 4* **P** *Bp* **TR** D G SARGENT **TV** G M CREGEEN **C** A L JONES, M G EDWARDS, M R HOUSTON

PENRUDDOCK (All Saints) *see* Greystoke w Penruddock, Mungrisdale etc *Carl*

PENSAX (St James the Great) *see* Teme Valley N *Worc*

PENSBY (St Michael and All Angels) *see* Barnston *Ches*

PENSHAW (All Saints) *see* Herrington, Penshaw and Shiney Row *Dur*

PENSHURST (St John the Baptist), Fordcombe and the Chiddingstone Churches *Roch 11* **P** *Abp Cant, Bp, and Viscount De Lisle (jt)* **R** L C CORNELL

PENSILVA (St John) *see* St Ive and Pensilva w Quethiock *Truro*

PENSNETT (St Mark) *Worc 5*   **P** *Bp*   **V** V J TOBIN

PENTEWAN (All Saints) *see* St Austell *Truro*

PENTLOW (St George and St Gregory) *see* N Hinckford *Chelmsf*

PENTNEY (St Mary Magdalene) *see* Nar Valley *Nor*

PENTON MEWSEY (Holy Trinity) *see* Pastrow *Win*

PENTONVILLE (St Silas w All Saints) (St James) *Lon 6*   **P** *Bp*   **V** R A WAKELING   **C** A L MASON

PENTRICH (St Matthew) *see* Swanwick and Pentrich *Derby*

PENTRIDGE (St Rumbold) *see* Sixpenny Handley w Gussage St Andrew etc *Sarum*

PENWERRIS (St Michael and All Angels) (Holy Spirit) *Truro 2*   **P** *V St Gluvias*   **V** *vacant*

PENWORTHAM (St Leonard) *Blackb 5*   **P** *Bp*   **V** J N MANSFIELD

PENWORTHAM (St Mary) *Blackb 5*   **P** *Miss A M Rawstorne*   **V** C J NELSON

PENZANCE (St Mary) (St Paul) (St John the Baptist) *Truro 4*   **P** *Bp*   **TR** S YATES   **C** A M YATES, K R OWEN

PEOPLETON (St Nicholas) and White Ladies Aston w Churchill and Spetchley and Upton Snodsbury and Broughton Hackett *Worc 3*   **P** *Bp, Croom Estate Trustees, and Major R J G Berkley (1 turn), and Ld Chan (1 turn)*   **R** G R NOYES   **C** E L GOLDBY, S A DANGERFIELD   **NSM** C BILLINGTON

PEOVER, OVER (St Lawrence) w Lower Peover (St Oswald) *Ches 12*   **P** *DBP and Man Univ (jt)*   **V** M A L ALDRIDGE-COLLINS

PEPER HAROW (St Nicholas) *see* Shackleford and Peper Harow *Guildf*

PEPLOW (The Epiphany) *see* Hodnet *Lich*

PERIVALE (St Nicholas) *Lon 19*   **P** *Trustees*   **P-in-c** A P JOHNSON

PERLETHORPE (St John the Evangelist) *S'well 2*   **P** *Earl Manvers' Trustees*   **V** *vacant*

PERRANARWORTHAL (St Piran) *see* St Stythians w Perranarworthal and Gwennap *Truro*

PERRANPORTH (St Michael's Mission Church) *see* Perranzabuloe and Crantock w Cubert *Truro*

PERRANUTHNOE (St Michael and St Piran) *see* Ludgvan, Marazion, St Hilary and Perranuthnoe *Truro*

PERRANZABULOE (St Piran) and Crantock w Cubert *Truro 6*   **P** *Patr Bd*   **P-in-c** A E BROWN   **C** D J WILLOUGHBY   **NSM** R J MONIE

PERROTT, NORTH (St Martin) *see* Wulfric Benefice *B & W*

PERROTT, SOUTH (St Mary) *see* Beaminster Area *Sarum*

PERRY BARR (St John the Evangelist) *Birm 1*   **P** *Bp and trustees (jt)*   **V** B SCOTT   **C** L L WARD

PERRY BEECHES (St Matthew) *Birm 1*   **P** *St Martin's Trustees*   **V** *vacant*

PERRY COMMON (St Martin) *see* Erdington Ch the K *Birm*

PERRY GREEN (St Thomas) *see* Albury, Lt Hadham and Much Hadham *St Alb*

PERRY HILL (St George) *see* Forest Hill w Lower Sydenham *S'wark*

PERRY STREET (All Saints) *Roch 4*   **P** *Bp*   **P-in-c** J F SOUTHWARD   **NSM** S J WALKER

PERSHORE (Holy Cross) w Pinvin, Wick and Birlingham *Worc 3*   **P** *Patr Bd*   **P-in-c** C A LORDING   **C** S DUNTON

PERTENHALL (St Peter) *see* The Stodden Churches *St Alb*

PETER TAVY (St Peter) and Mary Tavy *Ex 21*   **P** *Guild of All So*   **R** *vacant*

PETERBOROUGH (All Saints) *Pet 11*   **P** *Bp*   **V** *vacant*

PETERBOROUGH (Christ the Carpenter) *Pet 11*   **P** *Bp*   **V** S K KAYE

PETERBOROUGH (Holy Spirit) Bretton *Pet 11*   **P** *Bp*   **V** H M E DEL PINO

PETERBOROUGH (St John the Baptist) (Mission Church) *Pet 11*   **P** *Bp*   **V** *vacant*

PETERBOROUGH (St Jude) *Pet 11*   **P** *Bp*   **V** *vacant*

PETERBOROUGH (St Mark) *Pet 11*   **P** *Bp*   **V** A C HOLDSTOCK Hon **C** N J COLE

PETERBOROUGH (St Mary) Boongate *Pet 11*   **P** *D&C*   **V** M P J MOORE   **C** K A MORROW

PETERBOROUGH (St Paul) *Pet 11*   **P** *Bp*   **V** R F WATKINSON

PETERCHURCH (St Peter) *see* Madley w Tyberton, Peterchurch, Vowchurch etc *Heref*

PETERLEE (St Cuthbert) *Dur 10*   **P** *Bp*   **V** E E JONES   **C** H M RICHARDSON

PETERSFIELD (St Peter) *Portsm 4*   **P** *Bp*   **V** W P M HUGHES   **C** A M WATERHOUSE   **NSM** H M MITCHELL, J M BEE

PETERSHAM (All Saints) (St Peter) *S'wark 16*   **P** *Bp*   **V** *vacant*

PETERSMARLAND (St Peter) *see* Shebbear, Buckland Filleigh, Sheepwash etc *Ex*

PETERSTOW (St Peter) *see* StowCaple *Heref*

PETHAM (All Saints) *see* Wye *Cant*

PETHERTON, NORTH (St Mary the Virgin) *see* Alfred Jewel *B & W*

PETHERTON, SOUTH (St Peter and St Paul) w The Seavingtons and The Lambrooks *B & W 14*   **P** *Bp and D&C (jt)*   **R** *vacant*

PETHERWIN, NORTH (St Paternus) *see* Egloskerry, N Petherwin, Tremaine, Tresmere etc *Truro*

PETHERWIN, SOUTH (St Paternus) *see* Three Rivers *Truro*

PETROCKSTOWE (St Petrock) *see* Shebbear, Buckland Filleigh, Sheepwash etc *Ex*

PETT (St Mary and St Peter) *see* Fairlight and Pett *Chich*

PETT LEVEL (St Nicholas) *as above*

PETTAUGH (St Catherine) *see* Debenham and Helmingham *St E*

PETTISTREE (St Peter and St Paul) *see* Wickham Market w Pettistree *St E*

PETTON (not known) w Cockshutt, Welshampton and Lyneal w Colemere *Lich 16*   **P** *Bp and R K Mainwaring Esq (jt)*   **P-in-c** M E READ   **NSM** D BARNETT

PETTON (St Petrock) *see* Bampton, Morebath, Clayhanger, Petton etc *Ex*

PETTS WOOD (St Francis) *Roch 16*   **P** *Bp*   **V** S A NIECHCIAL

PETWORTH (St Mary) *Chich 4*   **P** *Lord Egremont*   **R** P M GILBERT

PEVENSEY (St Nicolas) (St Wilfrid) *Chich 14*   **P** *Bp*   **V** *vacant*

PEWSEY (St John the Baptist) *see* Vale of Pewsey *Sarum*

PHEASEY (St Chad) *Lich 24*   **P** *DBP*   **V** *vacant*

PHILADELPHIA (St Thomas) Extra-Parochial Place *Sheff 4*   **C** L H SABLAN, M J RUTTER

PHILLACK (St Felicitas) *see* Godrevy *Truro*

PHILLEIGH (St Philleigh) *see* Gerrans w St Anthony-in-Roseland and Philleigh *Truro*

PICCADILLY (St James) *see* Westmr St Jas *Lon*

PICKENHAM, NORTH (St Andrew) *see* Necton, Holme Hale w N and S Pickenham *Nor*

PICKENHAM, SOUTH (All Saints) *as above*

PICKERING (St Peter and St Paul) w Lockton and Levisham *York 19*   **P** *Abp*   **V** G W ATHA

PICKHILL (All Saints) *see* Kirklington w Burneston and Wath and Pickhill *Leeds*

PICKWELL (All Saints) *see* Burrough Hill Pars *Leic*

PICKWORTH (All Saints) *see* Gt Casterton and Tickencote and Lt Casterton w Pickworth *Pet*

PICKWORTH (St Andrew) *see* S Lafford *Linc*

PIDDINGHOE (St John) *see* Peacehaven and Telscombe Cliffs w Piddinghoe etc *Chich*

PIDDINGTON (St John the Baptist) *see* Hardingstone, Piddington w Horton and Quinton and Preston Deanery *Pet*

PIDDINGTON (St Nicholas) *see* Ray Valley *Ox*

PIDDLE VALLEY, Hilton and Ansty, Cheselbourne and Melcombe Horsey, The *Sarum 1*   **P** *Bp, Eton Coll, G A L-F Pitt-Rivers Esq, D&C Sarum, and D&C Win (by turn)*   **V** R J BUTCHER

PIDDLE, NORTH (St Michael) *see* Abberton, The Flyfords, Naunton Beauchamp etc *Worc*

PIDDLEHINTON (St Mary the Virgin) *see* Piddle Valley, Hilton and Ansty, Cheselbourne etc *Sarum*

PIDDLETRENTHIDE (All Saints) *as above*

PIDLEY CUM FENTON (All Saints) *see* Somersham w Pidley and Oldhurst and Woodhurst *Ely*

PIERCEBRIDGE (St Mary) *see* Coniscliffe *Dur*

PILHAM (All Saints) *see* Lea Gp *Linc*

PILL (Christ Church), Portbury and Easton-in-Gordano *B & W 12*   **P** *Bp*   **V** A L TIESEMA-SAMSOM

PILLATON (St Modwen) *see* Penkridge *Lich*

PILLATON (St Odulph) *see* Tamar Valley *Truro*

PILLERTON HERSEY (St Mary) *see* Stourdene Gp *Cov*

PILLEY (Mission Church) *see* Tankersley, Thurgoland and Wortley *Sheff*

PILLEY (St Nicholas) *see* Boldre w S Baddesley *Win*

PILLING (St John the Baptist) *see* Over Wyre *Blackb*

PILNING (St Peter) *see* S Severnside *Bris*

PILSLEY (St Mary the Virgin) *see* N Wingfield, Clay Cross and Pilsley *Derby*

PILTON (All Saints) *see* Aldwincle, Clopton, Pilton, Stoke Doyle etc *Pet*

PILTON (St John the Baptist) w Croscombe, North Wootton and Dinder *B & W 7*   **P** *Bp and Peache Trustees (jt)*   **R** C J BUTLER

PILTON (St Mary the Virgin) w Ashford *Ex 13*   **P** *Ld Chan*   **NSM** M SANDERS

PILTON (St Nicholas)   *see* Empingham, Edith Weston, Lyndon, Manton etc *Pet*
PIMLICO (St Barnabas) *Lon 3*   **P** *Bp*
P-in-c J M PEARSON-HICKS
PIMLICO (St Gabriel) *Lon 3*   **P** *Bp*   **V** O C G HIGGS
PIMLICO (St James the Less)   *see* Westminster St Jas the Less *Lon*
PIMLICO (St Mary) Bourne Street *Lon 3*   **P** *Trustees*
V A S WALKER   **C** S C KORN
PIMLICO (St Peter) w Westminster Christ Church *Lon 3*
P *Bp*   **C** J M KHOVACS   **NSM** J A MILLER
PIMLICO (St Saviour) *Lon 3*   **P** *Bp*   **V** M J CATTERICK
PIMLICO Bourne Street (St Mary)   *see* Pimlico St Mary Bourne Street *Lon*
PIMPERNE (St Peter), Stourpaine, Durweston and Bryanston *Sarum 6*   **P** *DBP (2 turns), D&C (1 turn)*
P-in-c B-J MARFLITT
PINCHBECK (St Mary)   *see* Glen Gp *Linc*
PINCHBECK, WEST (St Bartholomew) *as above*
PINHOE (Hall)   *see* Pinhoe w Poltimore *Ex*
PINHOE (St Michael and All Angels) w Poltimore *Ex 3*
P *D&C*   **R** E M SLATER   **NSM** A M HOUGH
PINNER (St Anselm)   *see* Hatch End St Anselm *Lon*
PINNER (St John the Baptist) *Lon 20*   **P** *V Harrow*
V P C HULLYER   **C** E K WEBBER   **NSM** M J ARNOLD
PINNER VIEW (St George)   *see* Headstone St Geo *Lon*
PINVIN (St Nicholas)   *see* Pershore w Pinvin, Wick and Birlingham *Worc*
PINXTON (St Helen) (Church Hall) *Derby 2*   **P** *Bp*   **R** *vacant*
PIPE-CUM-LYDE (St Peter)   *see* Burghill Gp *Heref*
PIRBRIGHT (St Michael and All Angels) *Guildf 12*   **P** *Ld Chan*   **V** *vacant*
PIRTON (St Mary)   *see* Holwell, Ickleford and Pirton *St Alb*
PIRTON (St Peter)   *see* Stoulton w Drake's Broughton and Pirton etc *Worc*
PISHILL (not known)   *see* Nettlebed w Bix, Highmoor, Pishill etc *Ox*
PITCHCOMBE (St John the Baptist)   *see* Painswick, Sheepscombe, Cranham, The Edge etc *Glouc*
PITCHFORD (St Michael and All Angels)   *see* Condover w Frodesley, Acton Burnell etc *Heref*
PITCOMBE (St Leonard)   *see* Bruton, Brewham, Pitcombe and Shepton Montague *B & W*
PITMINSTER (St Mary and St Andrew)   *see* Blackdown *B & W*
PITNEY (St John the Baptist)   *see* Levels Arc *B & W*
PITSEA (St Gabriel) w Nevendon *Chelmsf 11*   **P** *Bp*
R S A LAW
PITSFORD (All Saints) w Boughton *Pet 2*   **P** *Bp*   **R** S TROTT
PITSMOOR (Christ Church) *Sheff 3*   **P** *Ch Patr Trust*
P-in-c P J SALMON   **NSM** S A GOODMAN, W H THOMAS
PITTINGTON (St Laurence)   *see* Belmont and Pittington *Dur*
PITTON (St Peter)   *see* Clarendon *Sarum*
PITTVILLE (All Saints)   *see* N Cheltenham *Glouc*
PIXHAM (St Mary the Virgin)   *see* Dorking w Ranmore *Guildf*
PIXLEY (St Andrew)   *see* Cider Churches *Heref*
PLAISTOW (Holy Trinity)   *see* Kirdford *Chich*
PLAISTOW (St Martin) *Chelmsf 5*   **P** *Bp*   **V** J V MEADWAY
C M G FILIPE LOPES   **NSM** C T OLADUJI
PLAISTOW (St Mary) *Roch 14*   **P** *Bp*   **V** A KEELER
PLAISTOW (St Philip and St James) (St Mary) *Chelmsf 5*
P *Bp*   **V** D A HOYTE   **NSM** C T OLADUJI
PLAITFORD (St Peter)   *see* Forest and Avon *Sarum*
PLAS NEWTON (St Michael) *Ches 2*   **P** *Simeon's Trustees*
V P RUGEN   **NSM** C J JONES
PLATT (Holy Trinity)   *see* Rusholme H Trin *Man*
PLATT (St Mary the Virgin) *Roch 10*   **P** *Bp*   **V** L E TURNER
PLATT BRIDGE (St Nathaniel)   *see* Wigan *Liv*
PLAXTOL (not known)   *see* Shipbourne w Plaxtol *Roch*
PLAYDEN (St Michael)   *see* Rye *Chich*
PLAYFORD (St Mary)   *see* Kesgrave w Lt Bealings and Playford *St E*
PLEASLEY (St Michael)   *see* E Scarsdale *Derby*
PLEASLEY HILL (St Barnabas)   *see* Mansfield St Aug and Pleasley Hill *S'well*
PLEASLEY VALE (St Chad)   *see* Mansfield Woodhouse *S'well*
PLEMSTALL (St Peter) w Guilden Sutton *Ches 2*   **P** *Capt P Egerton Warburton*   **V** H S CARTY
PLESHEY (Holy Trinity) *Chelmsf 9*   **P** *Bp*   **P-in-c** M J ASTON
C D C PIERCE
PLUCKLEY (St Nicholas)   *see* Calehill w Westwell *Cant*
PLUMBLAND (St Cuthbert)   *see* Binsey *Carl*
PLUMPTON (All Saints) (St Michael and All Angels) w East Chiltington cum Novington *Chich 21*   **P** *Ld Chan*
P-in-c A C DUNLOP
PLUMPTON WALL (St John the Evangelist)   *see* Penrith w Newton Reigny and Plumpton Wall *Carl*

PLUMSTEAD (All Saints) Shooters Hill *S'wark 6*   **P** *CPAS*
V H O APARANGA
PLUMSTEAD (Ascension)   *see* Plumstead Common *S'wark*
PLUMSTEAD (St John the Baptist) w St James and St Paul *S'wark 6*   **P** *Simeon's Trustees and CPAS (alt)*   **V** *vacant*
PLUMSTEAD (St Mark and St Margaret)   *see* Plumstead Common *S'wark*
PLUMSTEAD (St Michael)   *see* Matlaske *Nor*
PLUMSTEAD (St Nicholas) *S'wark 6*   **P** *V Plumstead St Mark w St Marg*   **V** A G STEVENS
PLUMSTEAD COMMON (St Mark and St Margaret) (Ascension) *S'wark 6*   **P** *Bp and DBP (jt)*   **V** C R WELHAM
C B T ASMELASH
PLUMSTEAD, GREAT (St Mary) and LITTLE (St Gervase and Protase), Rackheath w Salhouse and Witton *Nor 4*   **P** *Bp and D&C (jt)*   **R** D J PLATTIN
PLUMTREE (St Mary) *S'well 5*   **P** *DBP*   **R** T H KIRKMAN
PLUNGAR (St Helen)   *see* Vale of Belvoir *Leic*
PLYMOUTH (Emmanuel) w St Paul *Ex 20*   **P** *Patr Bd*
TR K F FREEMAN   **TV** A C WILLIAMS   **NSM** B J CREE, D L CREE, R H BROWN
PLYMOUTH (St Andrew) and St Paul Stonehouse *Ex 20*
P *Patr Bd*   **TR** J M DENT   **TV** L P T SIM   **C** P CAIRNS, T D PARTRIDGE
PLYMOUTH (St Bartholomew)   *see* Devonport St Bart and Ford St Mark *Ex*
PLYMOUTH (St Gabriel) Peverell *Ex 20*   **P** *Bp*
P-in-c R T SILK
PLYMOUTH (St John the Evangelist)   *see* Sutton-on-Plym, Plymouth St Simon and St Mary *Ex*
PLYMOUTH (St Jude) *Ex 20*   **P** *CPAS Patr Trust*
P-in-c T SMITH
PLYMOUTH (St Mark)   *see* Devonport St Bart and Ford St Mark *Ex*
PLYMOUTH (St Mary the Virgin)   *see* Plymouth Em w St Paul *Ex*
PLYMOUTH (St Mary the Virgin)   *see* Sutton-on-Plym, Plymouth St Simon and St Mary *Ex*
PLYMOUTH (St Matthias)   *see* Charles w Plymouth St Matthias *Ex*
PLYMOUTH (St Pancras)   *see* Pennycross *Ex*
PLYMOUTH (St Peter) and the Holy Apostles *Ex 20*   **P** *Bp and Keble Coll Ox (jt)*   **P-in-c** D C WAY
PLYMOUTH (St Simon)   *see* Sutton-on-Plym, Plymouth St Simon and St Mary *Ex*
PLYMOUTH Crownhill (Ascension) *Ex 20*   **P** *Bp*
P-in-c T THORP   **C** R H WAKERELL
PLYMPTON (St Mary the Blessed Virgin) (St Maurice) *Ex 20*   **P** *Patr Bd*   **TR** R D HARRIS
PLYMSTOCK (St Mary and All Saints) and Hooe *Ex 20*
P *Patr Bd*   **TR** J APPLEBY   **TV** C J BUDDEN
PLYMTREE (St John the Baptist)   *see* Broadhembury, Dunkeswell, Luppitt, Plymtree, Sheldon, and Upottery *Ex*
POCKLEY (St John the Baptist)   *see* Kirkdale w Harome, Nunnington and Pockley *York*
POCKLINGTON (All Saints)   *see* Pocklington Wold *York*
POCKLINGTON WOLD (All Saints), including Burnby, Great Givendale, Hayton, Huggate, Kilnwick Percy, Millington, and Nunburnholme *York 5*   **P** *Abp*   **R** J J BELDER
NSM D B BROADHURST
PODIMORE (St Peter)   *see* Ilchester w Northover, Limington, Yeovilton etc *B & W*
PODINGTON (St Mary the Virgin)   *see* Chellington *St Alb*
POINT CLEAR (Mission)   *see* St Osyth and Great Bentley *Chelmsf*
POINTON (Christ Church)   *see* Billingborough Gp *Linc*
POKESDOWN (All Saints) *Win 8*   **P** *V Christchurch*
V M R POWIS
POKESDOWN (St James) *Win 8*   **P** *Bp*   **V** *vacant*
POLDEN WHEEL, The, comprising Ashcott, Burtle, Catcott, Chilton Polden, Edington, and Shapwick *B & W 4*   **P** *Bp*
V R W TWEEDY
POLEBROOK (All Saints)   *see* Barnwell, Hemington, Luddington in the Brook etc *Pet*
POLEGATE (St John) (St Wilfrid) *Chich 14*   **P** *Bp*
V C G SPINKS   **C** C J STYLES   **NSM** R A HERKES
POLESWORTH (St Editha) *Birm 5*   **P** *Ld Chan*   **V** P A WELLS
POLING (St Nicholas) *Chich 1*   **P** *Bp*   **P-in-c** C M WOODRUFF
POLLARDS HILL (The Ascension)   *see* Mitcham Ascension *S'wark*
POLLINGTON (St John the Baptist)   *see* Gt Snaith *Sheff*
POLPERRO (St John the Baptist)   *see* Trelawny *Truro*
POLRUAN (St Saviour) *as above*
POLSTEAD (St Mary)   *see* Stoke by Nayland w Leavenheath etc *St E*
POLTIMORE (St Mary the Virgin)   *see* Pinhoe w Poltimore *Ex*

PONDERS END (St Matthew) *Lon 16* **P** *V Enfield* **V** *vacant*
PONDERSBRIDGE (St Thomas) *see* Whittlesey, Pondersbridge and Coates *Ely*
PONSANOOTH (St Michael and All Angels) *see* Mabe *Truro*
PONSBOURNE (St Mary) *see* Lt Berkhamsted and Bayford, Essendon etc *St Alb*
PONSONBY (not known) *see* Seatallan *Carl*
PONTEFRACT (All Saints) (St Giles) *Leeds 15* **P** *Bp*
V J M LAWSON **C** C M WATKINS, S J FLETCHER
NSM K B WARRENER, R G WALKER, W D PHILLIPS
PONTELAND (St Mary the Virgin) *Newc 4* **P** *Mert Coll Ox*
V P T ALLINSON **NSM** C L BROWN, R E HARRISON
PONTESBURY First and Second Portions (St George)
Heref 12 **P** *St Chad's Coll Dur* **R** G P SMITH
PONTON, GREAT (Holy Cross) *see* Colsterworth Par *Linc*
PONTON, LITTLE (St Guthlac) *as above*
POOL (St Wilfrid) *see* Lower Wharfedale *Leeds*
POOLBROOK (St Andrew) *see* Malvern Chase *Worc*
POOLE (St James w St Paul) *Sarum 7* **P** *Ch Soc Trust*
R L J HOLT **Hon C** A C OEHRING
POOLE KEYNES (St Michael and All Angels) *see* Kemble, Poole Keynes, Somerford Keynes etc *Glouc*
POOLEY BRIDGE (St Paul) *see* Barton, Pooley Bridge, Martindale etc *Carl*
POORTON, NORTH (St Mary Magdalene) *see* Eggardon and Colmers *Sarum*
POPLAR (All Saints) *Lon 7* **P** *Patr Bd* **TR** J A C HODGES
TV M W WALL **NSM** J C SHELDON
POPLEY w Limes Park and Rooksdown (St Gabriel) *Win 4*
P *Bp* **V** A BOTHAM
POPPLETON, NETHER (St Everilda) w Upper (All Saints)
York 1 **P** *Abp* **P-in-c** S C BIDDLESTONE
POPPYLAND, comprising Antingham, Northrepps, Overstrand, Sidestrand, Southrepps, Thorpe Market, and Trimingham *Nor 20* **P** *Duchy of Lancaster (2 turns), DBP, MMCET, and Bp (4 turns)* **R** S J M READING
PORCHESTER (St James) *S'well 7* **P** *Bp* **V** *vacant*
PORINGLAND (All Saints) *Nor 8* **P** *Bp, BNC Ox, J D Alston Esq, and G H Hastings Esq (3 turns) and DBP (1 turn)*
R R H PARSONAGE **OLM** R M FOSTER
PORKELLIS (St Christopher) *see* Helston and Wendron *Truro*
PORLOCK (St Dubricius) and Porlock Weir w Stoke Pero, Selworthy and Luccombe *B & W 15* **P** *Ld Chan*
R A M GIBBS **NSM** S R B HUMPHREYS
PORLOCK WEIR (St Nicholas) *see* Porlock and Porlock Weir w Stoke Pero etc *B & W*
PORT ERIN (St Catherine) *see* Rushen *S & M*
PORT ISAAC (St Peter) *see* N Cornwall Cluster *Truro*
PORT ST MARY (St Mary) *see* Rushen *S & M*
PORTBURY (Blessed Virgin Mary) *see* Pill, Portbury and Easton-in-Gordano *B & W*
PORTCHESTER (St Mary) *Portsm 2* **P** *J R Thistlethwaite Esq*
V I MEREDITH
PORTESHAM (St Peter) *see* Abbotsbury, Portesham and Langton Herring *Sarum*
PORTHILL (St Andrew) *see* Bradwell and Porthill *Lich*
PORTHLEVEN (St Bartholomew) *see* W Kerrier *Truro*
PORTHPEAN (St Levan) *see* St Austell *Truro*
PORTISHEAD (St Peter) *B & W 12* **P** *Patr Bd*
TR R M E DEWING **TV** M J T FULLER **C** L E DOWNS
PORTLAND Team Minstry (All Saints) (St Andrew)
(St John) *Sarum 4* **P** *Patr Bd* **TR** T F GOMM
PORTLEMOUTH, EAST (St Winwaloe Onocaus) *see* Stokenham, Slapton, Charleton w Buckland etc *Ex*
PORTLOE (All Saints) *see* Veryan w Ruan Lanihorne *Truro*
PORTMAN SQUARE (St Paul) *see* Langham Place All So *Lon*
PORTON (St Nicholas) *see* Bourne Valley *Sarum*
PORTREATH (St Mary) *see* St Illogan *Truro*
PORTSDOWN (Christ Church) *Portsm 5* **P** *Simeon's Trustees*
V A M WILSON **C** J E SMITH, M R GROVE
NSM L B CAMERON
PORTSEA (All Saints) *Portsm 6* **P** *V Portsea St Mary and Bp (jt)* **P-in-c** A D HARGREAVES
PORTSEA (St Alban) *Portsm 6* **P** *Bp* **P-in-c** A J WOOD
PORTSEA (St Cuthbert) *Portsm 6* **P** *Bp* **V** A KERR
C R D SIDHU **NSM** C G GULLY, K E MARLOW
PORTSEA (St George) *Portsm 6* **P** *Bp* **P-in-c** A J WOOD
PORTSEA (St Luke) *see* Southsea St Luke and St Pet *Portsm*
PORTSEA (St Mary) (St Faith and St Barnabas) (St Wilfrid)
Portsm 6 **P** *Win Coll* **V** R C WHITE **C** M C COLLIE,
S A CULLEN **NSM** S K WHITELOCK
PORTSEA (St Saviour) *Portsm 6* **P** *Bp*
P-in-c B E A WEITZMANN
PORTSEA (The Ascension) *Portsm 6* **P** *Bp*
P-in-c B E A WEITZMANN **C** B M HACKETT

PORTSEA North End (St Mark) *Portsm 6* **P** *DBP*
P-in-c B M HACKETT **TV** B E A WEITZMANN, S J DUDDLES
NSM R E WEEKS
PORTSLADE (St Nicolas) (St Andrew) and Mile Oak
Chich 20 **P** *Bp* **P-in-c** D M SWYER **NSM** P G PANNETT
PORTSWOOD (Christ Church) *Win 13* **P** *Bp*
P-in-c M J ARCHER **C** N J LOBO **NSM** E J ROBERTS
PORTSWOOD (St Denys) *Win 13* **P** *Bp* **P-in-c** M J ARCHER
C S V RUMBLE
PORTWAY AND DANEBURY Benefice, The, comprising Amport, Grateley, Monxton, Nether Wallop, Over Wallop, Quarley, and West Andover *Win 3* **P** *Patr Bd*
Hon C M R GRAYSHON
POSBURY (St Francis Proprietary Chapel) *see* Crediton, Shobrooke and Sandford etc *Ex*
POSLINGFORD (St Mary) *see* Stour Valley *St E*
POSTBRIDGE (St Gabriel) *see* Ashburton, Bickington, Buckland in the Moor etc *Ex*
POSTLING (St Mary and St Radegund) *see* Elham Valley *Cant*
POSTWICK (All Saints) *see* Yare Valley *Nor*
POTT SHRIGLEY (St Christopher) *Ches 13* **P** *MMCET*
P-in-c D J SWALES
POTTEN END (Holy Trinity) *see* Gt Berkhamsted, Gt and Lt Gaddesden etc *St Alb*
POTTER HEIGHAM (St Nicholas) *see* Ludham, Potter Heigham, Hickling and Catfield *Nor*
POTTERHANWORTH (St Andrew) *see* Branston w Nocton and Potterhanworth *Linc*
POTTERIES, NORTH, comprising Burslem St Werburgh, Smallthorn, and Sneyd *Lich 11* **P** *Patr Bd* **TR** A C SWIFT
C G R THOMAS
POTTERNE (St Mary the Virgin) *see* Wellsprings *Sarum*
POTTERNEWTON (St Martin) w Little London *Leeds 10*
P *Simeon's Trustees, R Leeds City, DBP, and Trustees (jt)*
V N LO POLITO **C** E T MAPFUMO **NSM** G W W TURNBULL,
H BANKS, S J DE GAY
POTTERS BAR (King Charles the Martyr) *St Alb 14* **P** *Bp*
Lon **V** A C GAINES
POTTERS BAR (St Mary and All Saints) *St Alb 14* **P** *Bp Lon*
V S CHRYSOSTOMOU
POTTERS GREEN (St Philip Deacon) *Cov 1* **P** *Ld Chan*
V M L EAMAN
POTTERS MARSTON (St Mary) *see* Barwell w Potters Marston and Stapleton *Leic*
POTTERSPURY (St Nicholas) w Furtho and Yardley Gobion
w Cosgrove and Wicken *Pet 5* **P** *D&C, Jes Coll Ox, and Soc Merchant Venturers Bris (jt)* **R** *vacant*
POTTO (St Mary) *see* Whorlton Gp *York*
POTTON (St Mary the Virgin) w Sutton and Cockayne Hatley *St Alb 10* **P** *The Crown (3 turns), St Jo Coll Ox (1 turn)*
R A WHEATLEY
POUGHILL (St Michael and All Angels) *see* N Creedy *Ex*
POUGHILL (St Olaf King and Martyr) *see* N Kernow *Truro*
POULNER (St John) *see* Ringwood w Ellingham and Harbridge etc *Win*
POULSHOT (St Peter) *see* Wellsprings *Sarum*
POULTON (St Michael and All Angels) *see* S Cotswolds *Glouc*
POULTON CARLETON (St Chad) and Singleton *Blackb 12*
P *DBP and Exors R Dumbreck Esq (jt)* **V** M P KEIGHLEY
C L G WARD
POULTON LANCELYN (Holy Trinity) *Ches 8* **P** *R Bebington*
V R K WILES **NSM** P LEWIS
POULTON-LE-FYLDE (St Chad) *see* Poulton Carleton and Singleton *Blackb*
POULTON-LE-SANDS (Holy Trinity) w Morecambe St Laurence *Blackb 11* **P** *V Lanc* **R** C J M KRAWIEC
C C L HAYDON
POUND HILL (St Barnabas) *see* Worth, Pound Hill and Maidenbower *Chich*
POUNDSBRIDGE (Chapel) *see* Penshurst, Fordcombe and the Chiddingstone Chs *Roch*
POUNDSTOCK (St Winwaloe) *see* Bude Coast and Country *Truro*
POWDERHAM (St Clement Bishop and Martyr) *see* Exminster, Kenn, Kenton w Mamhead, and Powderham *Ex*
POWERSTOCK (St Mary the Virgin) *see* Eggardon and Colmers *Sarum*
POWICK (St Peter) and Guarlford and Madresfield w Newland *Worc 2* **P** *Bp, Lady Rosalind Morrison, and Croome Estate Trustees (jt)* **R** G P CRELLIN
POYNINGS (Holy Trinity) w Edburton, Newtimber and Pyecombe *Chich 11* **P** *Ld Chan (1 turn), Bp and Abp (1 turn)* **R** T W HARFORD
POYNTINGTON (All Saints) *see* Queen Thorne *Sarum*

POYNTON (St George) *Ches 17* **P** *Bp*
V M SWIRES-HENNESSY **NSM** C J BUCKLEY
POYNTON, HIGHER (St Martin) *see Poynton Ches*
PRATTS BOTTOM (All Souls) *see Chelsfield w Green Street*
Green and Pratts Bottom *Roch*
PREES (St Chad), Edstaston and Whixall *Lich 21* **P** *Bp and*
R Wem, Lee Brockhurst and Weston under Redcastle (jt)
V D R WALTON
PREESALL (St Oswald) *see Over Wyre Blackb*
PRENTON (St Stephen) *Ches 1* **P** *Bp* **V** M J GRAHAM
PRENTON DELL (St Alban) *see Prenton Ches*
PRESCOT (St Mary) (St Paul) *Liv 7* **P** *K Coll Cam*
C K MANNINGS
PRESHUTE (St George) *see Marlborough Sarum*
PRESTBURY (St Mary) *see N Cheltenham Glouc*
PRESTBURY (St Nicolas) *as above*
PRESTBURY (St Peter) *Ches 13* **P** *Ms C J C B Legh*
V P J M ANGIER **NSM** S C J MURPHY
PRESTEIGNE (St Andrew) w Discoed, Kinsham, Lingen and
Knill *Heref 4* **P** *Patr Bd* **R** S HOLLINGHURST
NSM D VENABLES
PRESTON (All Saints) *see Hedon, Paull, Sproatley and*
Preston *York*
PRESTON (All Saints) *Blackb 13* **P** *Trustees* **V** N J BUTTERY
C S H GRIFFITHS
PRESTON (All Saints) *see S Cerney w Cerney Wick,*
Siddington and Preston *Glouc*
PRESTON (Church of the Ascension) *Lon 18* **P** *Bp*
V J SHALLOE
PRESTON (Emmanuel) *Blackb 13* **P** *R Preston*
V P G HAMBORG
PRESTON (Good Shepherd) *see Brighton Gd Shep Preston*
Chich
PRESTON (St Andrew) *see Weymouth Ridgeway Sarum*
PRESTON (St Cuthbert) *Blackb 13* **P** *Bp* **V** M J BRADFORD
C M T HUTCHINSON **NSM** F E GETHIN
PRESTON (St John the Baptist) *see Redmarley D'Abitot,*
Bromesberrow, Pauntley etc *Glouc*
PRESTON (St John) (St George the Martyr) (Christ the
King Chapel) *Blackb 13* **P** *DBP* **R** S E HAIGH
C A J DYKES, D A CRAVEN, D M OWENS, T F ROBERTS
PRESTON (St John) w Brighton St Augustine and
St Saviour *Chich 19* **P** *Bp* **V** A V BOWMAN
PRESTON (St Martin) *see Hitchin and St Paul's Walden St Alb*
PRESTON (St Mary the Virgin) *see Lavenham w Preston St E*
PRESTON (St Matthias) *see Brighton St Matthias Chich*
PRESTON (St Mildred) *see Canonry Cant*
PRESTON (St Paul) *see Paignton Ch Ch and Preston St Paul*
Ex
PRESTON (St Peter and St Paul) *see Empingham, Edith*
Weston, Lyndon, Manton etc *Pet*
PRESTON (St Stephen) *Blackb 13* **P** *Bp* **V** D J HANSON
C B J HOUGHTON
PRESTON Acregate Lane (Mission) *see Preston Risen Lord*
Blackb
PRESTON BAGOT (All Saints) *see Claverdon w Preston Bagot*
Cov
PRESTON BISSET (St John the Baptist) *see The Claydons and*
Swan *Ox*
PRESTON CANDOVER (St Mary the Virgin) *see Farleigh,*
Candover and Wield *Win*
PRESTON CAPES (St Peter and St Paul) *see Badby w Newham*
and Charwelton w Fawsley etc *Pet*
PRESTON NEXT FAVERSHAM (St Catherine) *see Faversham*
Cant
PRESTON ON STOUR (St Mary) *see Ilmington w*
Stretton-on-Fosse etc *Cov*
PRESTON PATRICK (St Patrick) *see Kirkby Lonsdale Carl*
PRESTON PLUCKNETT (St James the Great) (St Peter)
B & W 6 **P** *Bp (2 turns), Mrs S W Rawlins (1 turn)*
V D M KEEN **C** R E CHAPMAN
PRESTON The Risen Lord (St Matthew) (St Hilda)
(St James) *Blackb 13* **P** *Patr Bd* **R** A MCHAFFIE
C D J FREEMAN
PRESTON UNDER SCARR (St Margaret) *see Penhill Leeds*
PRESTON WEALDMOORS (St Lawrence) *see Edgmond w*
Kynnersley and Preston Wealdmoors *Lich*
PRESTON WYNNE (Holy Trinity) *see Maund Gp Heref*
PRESTON, EAST (St Mary) w Kingston *Chich 1* **P** *D&C*
V A J PERRY **C** E L HAM-RICHE
PRESTON-ON-TEES (All Saints) and Longnewton *Dur 8*
P *Bp* **P-in-c** M J LEVINSOHN
PRESTON-ON-WYE (St Lawrence) *see Cusop w Blakemere,*
Bredwardine w Brobury etc *Heref*
PRESTONVILLE (St Luke) *Chich 19* **P** *CPAS* **V** M B POOLE

PRESTWICH (St Gabriel) *Man 4* **P** *Bp* **V** S S WILLIAMS
NSM M TRIVASSE
PRESTWICH (St Hilda) *Man 4* **P** *Trustees* **V** *vacant*
PRESTWICH (St Margaret) (St George) *Man 4* **P** *R*
Prestwich St Mary **V** D S A SANDERCOCK-PICKLES
C S S WILLIAMS **NSM** S A WALKER
PRESTWICH (St Mary the Virgin) *Man 4* **P** *Trustees*
P-in-c S CONLON **C** S S WILLIAMS **OLM** C A BARNET,
K A MCKIE
PRESTWOLD (St Andrew) *see Wymeswold and Prestwold w*
Hoton *Leic*
PRESTWOOD (Holy Trinity) and Great Hampden *Ox 17*
P *Bp and Hon I H Hope-Morley (jt)*
R D J O KEARLEY-HEYWOOD **C** K J LOVELL, N C O SPOOR
PRIDDY (St Lawrence) *B & W 1* **P** *Bp* **V** A J HOLMES
PRIDE PARK, Wilmorton, Allenton and Shelton Lock
Derby 5 **P** *Bp* **C** C A M HOLLYWELL, J F HOLLYWELL,
S L WATSON
PRIESTWOOD (St Andrew) *see Bracknell Ox*
PRIMROSE HILL (Holy Trinity) *see Lydney, Woolaston,*
Alvington and Aylburton *Glouc*
PRIMROSE HILL (St Mary the Virgin) w Avenue Road
(St Paul) *Lon 15* **P** *Trustees* **V** M J BROWN
C E A KOLLTVEIT **NSM** M J WAKEFIELD, R T JONES
PRINCE'S PARK (Christ the King) *Roch 5* **P** *Bp*
V P J FILMER
PRINCES RISBOROUGH (St Mary) *see Risborough Ox*
PRIOR'S DEAN (not known) *see Greatham, Empshott and*
Hawkley w Priors Dean *Portsm*
PRIORS HARDWICK (St Mary the Virgin) w Priors Marston
and Wormleighton *Cov 10* **P** *Earl Spencer*
P-in-c G S ROBERTS
PRIORS LEE (St Peter) *see Oakengates, Priors Lee and*
Wrockwardine Wood *Lich*
PRIORS MARSTON (St Leonard) *see Priors Hardwick, Priors*
Marston and Wormleighton *Cov*
PRISTON (St Luke) *see Timsbury w Priston, Camerton and*
Dunkerton *B & W*
PRITTLEWELL (St Luke) *Chelmsf 14* **P** *Bp* **P-in-c** B G DRURY
PRITTLEWELL (St Mary the Virgin) *Chelmsf 14* **P** *Bp*
V P D MACKAY **OLM** J LINDOE
PRITTLEWELL (St Peter) w Westcliff St Cedd and the Saints
of Essex *Chelmsf 14* **P** *Bp* **P-in-c** C S BALDWIN
C B NOGHIU
PRITTLEWELL (St Stephen) *Chelmsf 14* **P** *Bp*
P-in-c S BALDWIN **C** B NOGHIU
PROBUS (St Probus and St Grace), Ladock and
Grampound w Creed and St Erme *Truro 5* **P** *DBP*
TR J P W FOOT **C** P W SALAMAN **Hon C** M E RICHARDS
NSM L C WHETTER
PRUDHOE (St Mary Magdalene) *Newc 9* **P** *Dioc Soc*
V D J FREYHAN
PSALTER LANE (St Andrew) *Sheff 2* **P** *Trustees* **V** *vacant*
PUBLOW (All Saints) w Pensford, Compton Dando and
Chelwood *B & W 9* **P** *Bp* **P-in-c** D M CALVERLEY
PUCKINGTON (St Andrew) *see Winsmoor B & W*
PUCKLECHURCH (St Thomas à Becket) and Abson *Bris 5*
P *D&C* **V** *vacant*
PUDDINGTON (St Thomas à Becket) *see N Creedy Ex*
PUDDLETOWN (St Mary the Virgin), Tolpuddle and
Milborne w Dewlish *Sarum 1* **P** *Bp, Ch Ch Ox, Viscount*
Rothermere, and trustees (jt) **R** S C HILLMAN
PUDLESTON (St Peter) *see Leominster Heref*
PUDSEY (St James the Great) *see Thornbury, Woodhall and*
Waterloo *Leeds*
PUDSEY (St Lawrence and St Paul) *Leeds 11* **P** *Bp and V*
Calverley (jt) **V** R J DIMERY **C** S M HARRISON
PULBOROUGH (St Mary) *Chich 5* **P** *Lord Egremont*
R P R SEAMAN
PULFORD (St Mary the Virgin) *see Eccleston and Pulford*
Ches
PULHAM (St Thomas à Beckett) *see Three Valleys Sarum*
PULHAM MARKET (St Mary Magdalene) *see Dickleburgh and*
The Pulhams *Nor*
PULHAM ST MARY (St Mary the Virgin) *as above*
PULLOXHILL (St James the Apostle) *see Silsoe, Pulloxhill and*
Flitton *St Alb*
PULVERBATCH (St Edith) *see Gt Hanwood and Longden and*
Annscroft etc *Heref*
PUNCKNOWLE (St Mary the Blessed Virgin) *see Bride Valley*
Sarum
PURBECK, WEST, comprising Affpuddle w Turnerspuddle,
Bere Regis, The Lulworths, Winfrith Newburgh and
Chaldon, and Wool and East Stoke *Sarum 8* **P** *Ball Coll Ox,*
Keble Coll Ox, J Weld Esq, and Bp (by turn) **C** J M ALIDINA,
S E WILLIAMS

PURBROOK (St John the Baptist) *Portsm 5*　**P** *Bp*
　P-in-c A M WILSON　C J E SMITH, M R GROVE
　NSM L B CAMERON
PUREWELL (St John)　*see Christchurch Win*
PURFLEET (St Stephen)　*see Mardyke Chelmsf*
PURITON (St Michael and All Angels) and Pawlett
　B & W 13　**P** *Ld Chan (1 turn), D&C Windsor (2 turns)*
　V *vacant*
PURLEIGH (All Saints) *Chelmsf 10*　**P** *Oriel Coll Ox*
　P-in-c J WILLMOT
PURLEY (Christ Church) *S'wark 22*　**P** *Bp*　**V** D J L MCHARDIE
　C L L FAIRMAN-BROWN　**Hon C** S P STOCKS
　OLM S P BISHOP
PURLEY (St Barnabas) *S'wark 22*　**P** *Bp*　P-in-c J MIDDLEMISS
　NSM E J GOODRIDGE
PURLEY (St Mark) (St Swithun) *S'wark 22*　**P** *Bp*
　V F M WEAVER
PURLEY (St Mary the Virgin) *Ox 4*　**P** *Ld Chan*
　R D J ARCHER　C A D JONES, B J BAILEY
PURLWELL (St Andrew)　*see Batley Leeds*
PURSE CAUNDLE (St Peter)　*see Spire Hill Sarum*
PURTON (St John)　*see Sharpness, Purton, Brookend and Slimbridge Glouc*
PURTON (St Mary) *Bris 7*　**P** *Bp*　**V** I D TWEEDIE-SMITH
　OLM J M WELLS
PUSEY (All Saints)　*see Cherbury w Gainfield Ox*
PUTFORD (St Stephen)　*see Bradworthy, Sutcombe, Putford etc Ex*
PUTLEY (not known)　*see Cider Churches Heref*
PUTNEY (St Margaret) *S'wark 18*　**P** *Bp*　**V** B Z GREEN
PUTNEY (St Mary) (All Saints) *S'wark 18*　**P** *Patr Bd*
　TR J WHITTAKER　**TV** D M TROTT　C J K W HAYNES,
　M J ANDREWS
PUTNEY, EAST (St Stephen)　*see Wandsworth St Mich w St Steph S'wark*
PUTTENHAM (St John the Baptist)　*see Seale, Puttenham and Wanborough Guildf*
PYECOMBE (Transfiguration)　*see Poynings w Edburton, Newtimber and Pyecombe Chich*
PYLLE (St Thomas à Becket)　*see Fosse Trinity B & W*
PYPE HAYES (Church of the Holy Family) *Birm 4*　**P** *Bp and Aston Patr Trust (jt)*　**V** T J MEARDON
PYRFORD (Church of the Good Shepherd)　*see Wisley w Pyrford Guildf*
PYRFORD (St Nicholas) *as above*
PYRTON (St Mary)　*see Icknield Ox*
PYTCHLEY (All Saints)　*see Gt w Lt Harrowden and Orlingbury and Isham etc Pet*
PYWORTHY (St Swithun)　*see Holsworthy, Hollacombe, Pyworthy etc Ex*
QUADRING (St Margaret)　*see Gosberton, Gosberton Clough and Quadring Linc*
QUAINTON (Holy Cross and St Mary)　*see Schorne Ox*
QUANTOCK COAST Benefice, The, comprising Dodington, East Quantoxhead, Fiddington, Holford w Dodington, Kilve w Kilton and Lilstock, Stogursey, and Stringston *B & W 17*
　P *Bp, DBP, Eton Coll, and Lady Gass (jt)*　**R** N MORGAN
QUANTOCK TOWERS, The, comprising Bicknoller, Crowcombe, Monksilver, Nettlecombe, Sampford Brett, and Stogumber *B & W 17*　**P** *Bp, D&C Windsor, and D&C Wells (jt)*　**R** A V I BERNERS-WILSON
QUANTOCK, SOUTH Benefice, The, comprising Broomfield, Cheddon Fitzpaine, Kingston St Mary, and West Monkton *B & W 18*　**P** *Bp and D&C (jt)*　**R** M E STYLES　C J D R COX,
　T A HALLETT
QUANTOXHEAD, EAST (Blessed Virgin Mary)　*see Quantock Coast B & W*
QUANTOXHEAD, WEST (St Ethelreda) *as above*
QUARLEY (St Michael and All Angels)　*see Portway and Danebury Win*
QUARNDON (St Paul) *Derby 5*　**P** *Exors Viscount Scarsdale*
　C D M KNIGHT
QUARNFORD (St Paul)　*see Longnor, Quarnford, Sheen etc Lich*
QUARRENDON ESTATE (St Peter)　*see Aylesbury Ox*
QUARRINGTON (St Botolph) w Old Sleaford *Linc 14*　**P** *Bp*
　R M S THOMSON　C R M ROCK
QUARRY BANK (Christ Church)　*see Brierley Hill Worc*
QUATFORD (St Mary Magdalene)　*see Bridgnorth and Morville Par Heref*
QUATT (St Andrew)　*see Alveley and Quatt Heref*
QUEDGELEY (St James) *Glouc 2*　**P** *Bp*　**V** *vacant*
QUEEN CAMEL (St Barnabas)　*see Cam Vale B & W*
QUEEN CHARLTON (St Margaret)　*see Keynsham B & W*
QUEEN THORNE, comprising Oborne, Over Compton and Nether Compton, Poyntington, Sandford Orcas, and Trent

Sarum 3　**P** *Bp, The Revd J M P Goodden, K E Wingfield Digby Esq, and MMCET (jt)*　**R** D H T BOND
QUEENBOROUGH (Holy Trinity)　*see W Sheppey Cant*
QUEENHILL (St Nicholas)　*see Longdon, Castlemorton, Bushley, Queenhill etc Worc*
QUEEN'S GATE (St Augustine)　*see Onslow Square and S Kensington St Aug Lon*
QUEEN'S PARK (St Barnabas)　*see Holdenhurst and Iford Win*
QUEEN'S PARK (St Luke)　*see Brighton St Luke Queen's Park Chich*
QUEENSBURY (All Saints) *Lon 20*　**P** *The Crown*
　V K N BLAKE
QUEENSBURY (Holy Trinity) *Leeds 3*　**P** *Bp*　**V** S GOTT
QUENDON (St Simon and St Jude)　*see Newport w Widdington, Quendon and Rickling Chelmsf*
QUENIBOROUGH (St Mary)　*see Fosse Team Leic*
QUENINGTON (St Swithun)　*see S Cotswolds Glouc*
QUERNMORE (St Peter)　*see Dolphinholme w Quernmore and Over Wyresdale Blackb*
QUETHIOCK (St Hugh)　*see St Ive and Pensilva w Quethiock Truro*
QUIDENHAM Group, The (St Andrew), including Banham, Eccles, New Buckenham, Old Buckenham, and Wilby *Nor 11*
　P *Ld Chan (1 turn), Bp, Sir Thomas Beevor Bt, Major E H C Garnier, Trustees, and New Buckenham PCC (3 turns)*
　P-in-c S M WRIGHT
QUINTET GROUP　*see Aylmerton, Runton, Beeston Regis and Gresham Nor*
QUINTON (St Swithun), Welford, Weston and Marston Sicca *Glouc 8*　**P** *Bp, D&C Worc, and DBP (jt)*
　V R GREENHALGH　C J C K EDIE　NSM A Y GRUNDY
QUINTON and PRESTON DEANERY (St John the Baptist)　*see Hardingstone, Piddington w Horton and Quinton and Preston Deanery Pet*
QUINTON ROAD WEST (St Boniface) *Birm 3*　**P** *Bp*
　V *vacant*
QUINTON, The (Christ Church) *Birm 3*　**P** *Bp*
　P-in-c R J HEATHFIELD　NSM A P WELLS
QUORN (St Bartholomew)　*see Quorndon Leic*
QUORNDON (St Bartholomew) *Leic 6*　**P** *Bp*　**V** *vacant*
QUY (St Mary)　*see Anglesey Gp Ely*
RACKENFORD (All Saints)　*see Washfield, Stoodleigh, Withleigh etc Ex*
RACKHEATH (Holy Trinity)　*see Gt and Lt Plumstead, Rackheath w Salhouse and Witton Nor*
RACTON (St Peter)　*see Octagon Chich*
RADBOURNE (St Andrew)　*see Boylestone, Church Broughton, Dalbury, etc Derby*
RADCLIFFE (St Andrew) Black Lane *Man 4*　**P** *R Radcliffe St Mary*　**V** J E MCKEE
RADCLIFFE (St Mary) (St Thomas and St John) (St Philip Mission Church) *Man 4*　**P** *Patr Bd*　P-in-c J D CLAWSON
RADCLIFFE-ON-TRENT (St Mary) and Shelford *S'well 5*
　P *DBP and Ld Chan (alt)*　**V** M S TANNER　**C** B R EVANS
RADCLIVE (St John the Evangelist)　*see Buckingham Ox*
RADDESLEY Group of Parishes, The, comprising Brinkley, Burrough Green, Carlton, Dullingham, Stetchworth, and Westley Waterless *Ely 4*　**P** *R J H Vestey Esq, Mrs B O Killander, S F B Taylor Esq, Duke of Sutherland, Exors C Thomas (5 turns), St Jo Coll Cam (1 turn)*　**R** *vacant*
RADDINGTON (St Michael)　*see Wiveliscombe and the Hills B & W*
RADDON　*see Brampford Speke, Cadbury, Newton St Cyres etc Ex*
RADFORD (All Souls) (St Peter) *S'well 9*　**P** *Bp*　**V** *vacant*
RADFORD (St Nicholas) *Cov 2*　**P** *Bp*　P-in-c A D COLEMAN
RADFORD SEMELE (St Nicholas) *Cov 10*　**P** *Bp*
　P-in-c M C GREEN
RADFORD, NORTH (St Francis of Assisi)　*see Cov St Fran N Radford Cov*
RADIPOLE (Emmanuel) (St Adhelm) (St Ann) and Melcombe Regis *Sarum 4*　**P** *Patr Bd*　**TR** N J CLARKE
　TV J E HAINE, T P COOPEY　**C** M J C RENYARD
　NSM G A HEBBERN
RADLETT (Christ Church)　*see Aldenham, Radlett and Shenley St Alb*
RADLETT (St John) *as above*
RADLEY (St James the Great), Sunningwell and Kennington *Ox 19*　**P** *Bp, DBP, and Radley Coll (jt)*
　R R M GLENNY　C A K MATHEW　OLM G J BECKETT
RADNAGE (St Mary)　*see W Wycombe w Bledlow Ridge, Bradenham and Radnage Ox*
RADNOR, OLD (St Stephen)　*see Kington w Huntington, Old Radnor, Kinnerton etc Heref*

RADSTOCK (St Nicholas) w Writhlington *B & W 11* **P** *Bp*
  R *vacant*
RADSTONE (St Lawrence) *see* Astwell Gp *Pet*
RADWAY (St Peter) *see* Edgehill Churches *Cov*
RADWELL (All Saints) *see* Stotfold and Radwell *St Alb*
RADWINTER (St Mary the Virgin) *see* Thaxted, The
  Sampfords, Radwinter and Hempstead *Chelmsf*
RAGDALE (All Saints) *see* Upper Wreake *Leic*
RAINBOW HILL (St Barnabas) *see* Worc St Barn w Ch Ch
  Worc
RAINFORD (All Saints) *Liv 14* **P** *V Prescot* **V** J E HEIGHTON
  C E N MCGARRIGLE
RAINHAM (St Helen and St Giles) w Wennington *Chelmsf 2*
  P *MMCET* **R** E M PETERSON **NSM** D J STAINER
RAINHAM (St Margaret) *Roch 3* **P** *Bp* **V** N J WARD
  C J P JENNINGS **NSM** C A ALLEN
RAINHILL (St Ann) *Liv 10* **P** *Trustees* **V** A R CONANT
  C D P HALLIWELL
RAINOW (Holy Trinity) w Saltersford and Forest *Ches 13*
  P *Bp* **V** S D L GOWLER
RAINTON (not known) *see* Topcliffe, Baldersby w Dishforth,
  Dalton etc *York*
RAINTON, EAST (St Cuthbert) *Dur 9* **P** *D&C*
  P-in-c J W ESTALL **NSM** C E BRITCLIFFE, T HOLDEN
RAINTON, WEST (St Mary) *Dur 9* **P** *Bp* **P-in-c** J W ESTALL
  NSM C E BRITCLIFFE, T HOLDEN
RAINWORTH (St Simon and St Jude) *see* Blidworth w
  Rainworth *S'well*
RAITHBY (Holy Trinity) *see* Bolingbroke Deanery *Linc*
RAITHBY (St Peter) *see* Legbourne and Wold Marsh *Linc*
RAME (St Germanus) *see* Maker w Rame, Millbrook, St John
  and Torpoint *Truro*
RAMPISHAM (St Michael and All Angels) *see* Melbury *Sarum*
RAMPSIDE (St Michael) *see* Aldingham, Dendron, Rampside
  and Urswick *Carl*
RAMPTON (All Saints) *see* Cottenham w Rampton *Ely*
RAMPTON (All Saints) *see* The Rivers *S'well*
RAMSBOTTOM (St Andrew) (St John) (St Paul) and
  Edenfield *Man 4* **P** *Patr Bd (3 turns), The Crown (1 turn)*
  TR A J LINDOP **OLM** L HALLAM, S J WOOD
RAMSBURY (Holy Cross) *see* Whitton *Sarum*
RAMSDELL (Christ Church) *see* Baughurst, Ramsdell,
  Wolverton w Ewhurst etc *Win*
RAMSDEN (St James) *see* Forest Edge *Ox*
RAMSDEN BELLHOUSE (St Mary the Virgin) *see* Downham w
  S Hanningfield and Ramsden Bellhouse *Chelmsf*
RAMSDEN HEATH (St John) *as above*
RAMSEY (St Michael) *see* Harwich Peninsula *Chelmsf*
RAMSEY (St Thomas à Becket) *see* The Ramseys and Upwood
  Ely
RAMSEY ST MARY'S (St Mary) *as above*
RAMSEY, NORTH (St Olave) *see* Bride, Lezayre and N Ramsey
  S & M
RAMSEY, SOUTH (St Paul) *see* Maughold and S Ramsey
  S & M
RAMSEYS (St Thomas à Becket) (St Mary) and Upwood,
  The *Ely 12* **P** *Lord De Ramsey and Bp (jt)* **R** I G OSBORNE
RAMSGATE (St Mark) *see* St Laur in Thanet *Cant*
RAMSGATE (Christ Church) *Cant 5* **P** *Ch Patr Trust*
  V *vacant*
RAMSGATE (Holy Trinity) *Cant 5* **P** *Abp* **R** P F BLANCH
RAMSGATE (St George) *Cant 5* **P** *Abp*
  P-in-c P R WORLEDGE
RAMSGATE (St Luke) *Cant 5* **P** *CPAS* **V** P R WORLEDGE
  C C L COLEMAN
RAMSGILL (St Mary) *see* Upper Nidderdale *Leeds*
RAMSHOLT (All Saints) *see* Wilford Peninsula *St E*
RANBY (St German) *see* Asterby Gp *Linc*
RANBY (St Martin) *see* The Idle and Sands *S'well*
RAND (St Oswald) *see* Wragby Gp *Linc*
RANDWICK (St John the Baptist) *see* Stroud Team *Glouc*
RANGEMORE (All Saints) *see* Hanbury, Newborough and
  Rangemoor *Lich*
RANGEWORTHY (Holy Trinity) *see* Charfield and Kingswood
  w Wickwar etc *Glouc*
RANMOOR (St John the Evangelist) *Sheff 4* **P** *Trustees*
  V M I RHODES **C** M L WOOD
RANMORE (St Barnabas) *see* Dorking w Ranmore *Guildf*
RANSKILL (St Barnabas) *see* Blyth and Scrooby w Ranskill
  S'well
RANTON (All Saints) *see* Chebsey, Creswell, Ellenhall,
  Ranton etc *Lich*
RANWORTH (St Helen) *see* Broadside *Nor*
RASEN DRAX, MIDDLE (St Peter and St Paul) *see* Middle
  Rasen Gp *Linc*
RASEN, WEST (All Saints) *as above*

RASKELF (St Mary) *see* Easingwold w Raskelf *York*
RASTRICK (St John the Divine) (St Matthew) *Leeds 6* **P** *Bp*
  and V Halifax (jt) **V** M D PETCH **NSM** R S HANNAM
RATBY (St Philip and St James) *see* Groby and Ratby *Leic*
RATCLIFFE CULEY (All Saints) *see* Sheepy *Leic*
RATCLIFFE ON THE WREAKE (St Botolph) *see* Fosse Team *Leic*
RATCLIFFE-ON-SOAR (Holy Trinity) *see* A453 churches of S
  Notts *S'well*
RATHMELL (Holy Trinity) *see* Giggleswick and Rathmell w
  Wigglesworth *Leeds*
RATLEY (St Peter ad Vincula) *see* Edgehill Churches *Cov*
RATLINGHOPE (St Margaret) *see* Wentnor w Ratlinghope,
  Myndtown, Norbury etc *Heref*
RATTERY (Blessed Virgin Mary) *see* Buckfastleigh, Dean Prior,
  Littlehempston etc *Ex*
RATTLESDEN (St Nicholas) w Thorpe Morieux, Brettenham
  and Hitcham *St E 6* **P** *Bp (3 turns), Ld Chan (1 turn)*
  R C M S ROBINSON
RAUCEBY (St Peter) *see* E Loveden *Linc*
RAUGHTON HEAD (All Saints) *see* Dalston w Cumdivock,
  Raughton Head and Wreay *Carl*
RAUNDS (St Peter), Hargrave, Ringstead and Stanwick
  Pet 8 **P** *Ld Chan (1 turn), Bp and L G Stopford-Sackville Esq (2*
  turns) **R** J F ALDWINCKLE
RAVENDALE, EAST (St Martin) *see* Waltham Gp *Linc*
RAVENFIELD (St James), Hooton Roberts and Braithwell
  Sheff 6 **P** *Bp and Sir Philip Naylor-Leyland Bt (jt)*
  P-in-c P J HUGHES
RAVENGLASS (Mission Room) *see* Black Combe, Drigg,
  Eskdale etc *Carl*
RAVENHEAD (St John the Evangelist) *see* Eccleston *Liv*
RAVENINGHAM (St Andrew) *see* Waveney Marshlands *Nor*
RAVENSBOURNE *see* Deptford St Jo w H Trin and Ascension
  S'wark
RAVENSCAR (St Hilda) and Staintondale *York 15* **P** *Abp*
  P-in-c C STAZIKER
RAVENSDEN (All Saints) *see* Wilden w Colmworth and
  Ravensden *St Alb*
RAVENSHEAD (St Peter) *S'well 4* **P** *Bp* **V** C M BYROM
  C C L MELLESS
RAVENSTHORPE (St Denys) *see* Guilsborough and Hollowell
  and Cold Ashby etc *Pet*
RAVENSTHORPE (St Saviour) and Thornhill Lees w Savile
  Town *Leeds 7* **P** *Bp and V Mirfield (jt)* **P-in-c** G SPENCER
RAVENSTONE (All Saints) *see* Gayhurst w Ravenstone, Stoke
  Goldington etc *Ox*
RAVENSTONE (St Michael and All Angels) *see* Coalville w
  Bardon Hill and Ravenstone *Leic*
RAVENSTONEDALE (St Oswald) *see* High Westmorland *Carl*
RAWCLIFFE (St James) *see* Airmyn, Hook and Rawcliffe *Sheff*
RAWCLIFFE (St Mark) *see* Clifton *York*
RAWDON (St Peter) *Leeds 12* **P** *Trustees* **V** M G R D SMITH
RAWMARSH (St Mary the Virgin) w Parkgate *Sheff 6* **P** *Ld
  Chan* **R** *vacant*
RAWMARSH (St Nicolas) *see* Ryecroft St Nic *Sheff*
RAWNSLEY (St Michael) *see* Hednesford *Lich*
RAWRETH (St Nicholas) *Chelmsf 13* **P** *Pemb Coll Cam*
  P-in-c R W JORDAN **Hon C** B C WALLACE, E A JORDAN
RAWTENSTALL (St Mary) and Constable Lee *Man 4*
  P *CPAS* **NSM** J A BARRATT
RAWTHORPE (St James) *see* Moldgreen and Rawthorpe *Leeds*
RAY VALLEY, The, comprising Ambrosden, Charlton-on-
  Otmoor, Islip, Merton, Noke, Oddington, Piddington, and
  Woodeaton *Ox 21* **P** *Canon E G A W Page-Turner, Ex Coll
  Ox, and Piddington PCC (1 Turn), D&C Westmr, Qu Coll Ox,
  and Walsingham Coll (1 turn)* **R** S A HAYES
  Hon C L R THIRTLE **NSM** L C HOLMES
RAYDON (St Mary) *see* Higham, Holton St Mary, Raydon
  and Stratford *St E*
RAYLEIGH (Holy Trinity) (St Michael) *Chelmsf 13* **P** *Patr Bd*
  NSM T J NUTTER
RAYNE (All Saints) *see* Black Notley, Gt Notley and Rayne
  Chelmsf
RAYNES PARK (St Saviour) *S'wark 13* **P** *Bp*
  P-in-c P J KELLEY
RAYNHAM, EAST (St Mary) *see* E w W Rudham,
  Helhoughton etc *Nor*
RAYNHAM, SOUTH (St Martin) *as above*
REACH (St Etheldreda and the Holy Trinity) *see* Burwell w
  Reach *Ely*
READ (St John the Evangelist) and Simonstone St Peter
  Blackb 7 **P** *V Whalley* **V** *vacant*
READ IN WHALLEY (St John the Evangelist) *see* Read and
  Simonstone *Blackb*
READING (Christ Church) *Ox 7* **P** *Bp* **V** P A DAY
READING (Holy Trinity) *Ox 7* **P** *SMF* **P-in-c** R J SIMMONDS

READING (St Agnes w St Paul) (St Barnabas) *Ox 7* **P** *Bp*
P-in-c K DOLPHIN **C** S J CADY
READING (St Giles w St Saviour) *Ox 7* **P** *Bp* **R** D A HARRIS
C K T KREJCI
READING (St John the Evangelist and St Stephen) *Ox 7*
P *Simeon's Trustees* **V** C L ALCOCK
READING (St Laurence) *Ox 7* **P** *Bp* **C** C R JONES
READING (St Luke) (St Bartholomew) *Ox 7* **P** *Bp and V*
Reading St Giles (alt) **V** R A MEIKLE **NSM** C F BLACKMAN
READING (St Mark) (All Saints) *Ox 7* **P** *Bp*
V J S E WILLIAMS **NSM** J R LEWIS
READING (St Mary the Virgin) *Ox 7* **P** *Bp* **V** S H J WRATTEN
C G FANCOURT **NSM** A M COGLE, A T BOND
OLM J E SUMNER
READING (St Matthew) *Ox 7* **P** *Bp* **V** M P DOLPHIN
READING Greyfriars *Ox 7* **P** *Ch Trust Fund Trust*
V D G WALKER **C** A CAVENDER, J N FREEMAN, N J HILL,
N K WORSFOLD
READING STREET (St Andrew) *Cant 5* **P** *Abp* **V** P MUSINDI
REAPSMOOR (St John) *see* Longnor, Quarnford, Sheen etc
Lich
REARSBY (St Michael and All Angels) *see* Fosse Team *Leic*
RECULVER (St Mary the Virgin), St Bartholomew Herne
Bay and Holy Cross Hoath *Cant 4* **P** *Abp*
P-in-c S J MARTIN **NSM** S PARRETT
RED HOUSE (St Cuthbert) *see* N Wearside *Dur*
RED LODGE (St Christopher) LEP *see* Forest Heath *St E*
RED POST, comprising Almer and Charborough, Bloxworth,
Morden, Winterbourne Kingston, and Winterbourne
Zelstone w Thomson and Anderson *Sarum 6* **P** *Mrs V M*
Chattey, R G Plunkett-Ernle-Erle-Drax Esq, and Bp (by turn)
V J C E POTTINGER **NSM** C M CHICHESTER
REDBOURN (St Mary) *St Alb 7* **P** *Earl of Verulam*
V W J M GIBBS
REDBROOK (St Saviour) *see* Coleford, Staunton, Newland,
Redbrook etc *Glouc*
REDCAR (St Peter) *York 16* **P** *Abp* **V** *vacant*
REDCLIFFE BAY (St Nicholas) *see* Portishead *B & W*
REDCLIFFE WAY (St Mary the Virgin) *see* Bris St Mary
Redcliffe w Temple etc *Bris*
REDDISH (St Elisabeth) *Man 1* **P** *Bp* **R** A M STANTON
NSM A J MITCHELL
REDDISH (St Mary) *see* Heaton Reddish *Man*
REDDISH, NORTH (St Agnes) *Man 1* **P** *The Crown*
C H T SCANLAN
REDDITCH (St Stephen) *see* Redditch H Trin *Worc*
REDDITCH Christ the King, comprising Astwood Bank,
Crabbs Cross, and Headless Cross *Worc 6* **P** *Patr Bd*
TV G T READING **C** V L G BARLOW
REDDITCH Holy Trinity (St Stephen), including Beoley and
Webheath *Worc 6* **P** *Patr Bd* **TR** R M CLARK **TV** P LAWLOR
C F D MOLONEY
REDE (All Saints) *see* Chevington w Hargrave, Chedburgh w
Depden etc *St E*
REDENHALL (Assumption of the Blessed Virgin Mary) w
Scole *Nor 10* **P** *Bp, Ex Coll Ox, MMCET, Adn Norfolk, and Sir*
Rupert Mann (jt) **R** N O TUFFNELL
REDGRAVE (St Mary) cum Botesdale St Mary w Rickinghall
St E 11 **P** *P J H Wilson Esq* **R** C R NORBURN
REDHILL (Christ Church) *see* Wrington w Butcombe and
Burrington *B & W*
REDHILL (Holy Trinity) *S'wark 24* **P** *Simeon's Trustees*
V M J HOUGH **C** S L ALEXANDER
REDHILL (St John the Evangelist) (Meadvale Hall) *S'wark 24*
P *Bp* **V** J S KRONENBERG
REDHILL (St Matthew) *S'wark 24* **P** *Bp* **V** A T CUNNINGTON
C J A BROOKS
REDISHAM (St Peter) *see* Hundred River and Wainford *St E*
REDLAND (not known) *Bris 3* **P** *Ch Trust Fund Trust*
V W J FAIRBAIRN **C** S P FAUX **NSM** N S CRAWLEY,
S A TRUSCOTT
REDLANDS (St Luke) *see* Reading St Luke w St Bart *Ox*
REDLINGFIELD (St Andrew) *see* Athelington, Denham,
Horham, Hoxne etc *St E*
REDLYNCH (St Mary) *see* Forest and Avon *Sarum*
REDLYNCH (St Peter) *see* Bruton, Brewham, Pitcombe and
Shepton Montague *B & W*
REDMARLEY D'ABITOT (St Bartholomew), Bromesberrow,
Pauntley, Upleadon, Oxenhall, Dymock, Donnington,
Kempley and Preston *Glouc 3* **P** *Pemb Coll Ox, Bp, R D*
Marcon Esq, and Miss C Daniel (jt) **P-in-c** K M MEPHAM
NSM J M BOND
REDMARSHALL (St Cuthbert) *see* Stockton Country Par *Dur*
REDMILE (St Peter) *see* Vale of Belvoir *Leic*
REDMIRE (St Mary) *see* Penhill *Leeds*

REDNAL (St Stephen the Martyr) *Birm 2* **P** *Bp*
V T B A SOTONWA **NSM** S J JONES
REDRUTH (St Andrew) (St Euny) w Lanner and Treleigh
Truro 1 **P** *DBP* **TR** C J B BUSH
REED (St Mary) *see* Barkway, Barley, Reed and Buckland
St Alb
REEDHAM (St John the Baptist) *see* Acle and Bure to Yare *Nor*
REEPHAM (St Mary) and Wensum Valley Team Ministry,
The, including Alderford w Attlebridge, Bylaugh, Elsing,
Great w Little Witchingham, Lyng, Reepham and Hackford
w Whitwell and Kerdiston, Salle, Sparham, Swannington,
Thurning, Wood Dalling, and Weston Longville w
Morton-on-the-Hill *Nor 18* **P** *Patr Bd* **TR** H C RENGERT
TV K A F RENGERT **C** R A TURK **Hon C** J SWEETMAN
REEPHAM (St Peter and St Paul) *see* S Lawres Gp *Linc*
REGENT'S PARK (St Mark) *Lon 15* **P** *D&C St Paul's*
V W D F GULLIFORD
REGIL (St James Mission Church) *see* Winford w Felton
Common Hill *B & W*
REIGATE (St Luke) *S'wark 24* **P** *Bp* **V** A C COLPUS
NSM A J ELSON
REIGATE (St Mark) *S'wark 24* **P** *Bp* **V** M P COLTON
NSM R GRANT
REIGATE (St Mary Magdalene) *S'wark 24* **P** *Trustees*
V R G WILSON **C** E V GILMOUR, K F CAPPER, N T GRIFFITHS
NSM H J FRASER
REIGATE (St Philip) *S'wark 24* **P** *Bp* **V** J A PENN
REIGATE HEATH (not known) *see* Reigate St Mary *S'wark*
REIGHTON (St Peter) *see* Bempton w Flamborough,
Reighton w Speeton *York*
REKENDYKE (St Jude) *Dur 13* **P** *The Crown and D&C*
V *vacant*
REMENHAM (St Nicholas) *see* Henley w Remenham *Ox*
REMPSTONE (All Saints) *see* E and W Leake, Stanford-on-
Soar, Rempstone etc *S'well*
RENDCOMB (St Peter) *see* Churn Valley *Glouc*
RENDHAM (St Michael) *see* Upper Alde *St E*
RENDLESHAM (St Gregory the Great) *see* Wilford Peninsula
St E
RENHOLD (All Saints) *St Alb 9* **P** *MMCET* **P-in-c** I M SMITH
RENISHAW (St Matthew) *see* Killamarsh and Renishaw *Derby*
RENNINGTON (All Saints) *see* Embleton w Rennington and
Rock *Newc*
RENWICK (All Saints) *see* Kirkoswald, Renwick w Croglin, Gt
Salkeld etc *Carl*
REPPS (St Peter) *see* Martham and Repps w Bastwick, Thurne
etc *Nor*
REPTON (St Wystan) *see* Foremark and Repton w Newton
Solney *Derby*
RESTON, NORTH (St Edith) *see* Legbourne and Wold Marsh
Linc
RETFORD (St Saviour) *S'well 1* **P** *Simeon's Trustees*
R B T CLAYTON **C** B C MARSTON **NSM** K BOTTLEY
RETFORD (St Swithun) *S'well 1* **P** *Bp* **R** *vacant*
RETFORD The Clays *see* The Clays *S'well*
RETFORD The Idle and Sands *see* The Idle and Sands *S'well*
RETFORD The Rivers *see* The Rivers *S'well*
RETFORD, WEST (St Michael the Archangel) *see* Ordsall and
Retford St Mich *S'well*
RETTENDON (All Saints) and Hullbridge *Chelmsf 13* **P** *Ld*
Chan and Bp (alt) **P-in-c** R W JORDAN
Hon C B C WALLACE, E A JORDAN
REVEL GROUP, The, comprising Brinklow, Churchover,
Harborough Magna, Monks Kirkby, and Willey *Cov 6* **P** *Bp,*
Trin Coll Cam, and H A F W Boughton-Leigh Esq (2 turns), Ld
Chan (1 turn) **R** *vacant*
REVELSTOKE (St Peter) *see* Brixton, Newton Ferrers,
Revelstoke etc *Ex*
REVESBY (St Lawrence) *see* Fen and Hill Gp *Linc*
REWE (St Mary the Virgin) *see* Brampford Speke, Cadbury,
Newton St Cyres etc *Ex*
REYDON (St Margaret) *see* Sole Bay *St E*
REYMERSTON (St Peter) *see* Barnham Broom and Upper
Yare *Nor*
RHODES (All Saints) *see* Tonge, Rhodes and Alkrington *Man*
RHODES (All Saints) (St Thomas) *Man 6* **P** *R Middleton*
V *vacant*
RHYDYCROESAU (Christ Church) *Lich 18* **P** *Bp*
R H L GIBBONS
RIBBESFORD (St Leonard) w Bewdley and Dowles and
Wribbenhall *Worc 1* **P** *E J Winnington-Ingram Esq and R*
Kidderminster (alt) **R** M C GIBBINS
RIBBLETON (St Mary Magdalene) (Ascension) *Blackb 13*
P *Bp, DBP, K Simpson Esq, D V Johnson Esq, and the Ven K*
Gibbons (jt) **R** K J FENTON

RIBBY CUM WREA (St Nicholas) and Weeton St Michael
Blackb 10   **P** *V Kirkham*   **V** P V F CHEW
RIBCHESTER (St Wilfrid) w Stydd *Blackb 7*   **P** *Bp*
R B R MCCONKEY
RIBSTON, LITTLE (St Helen)   *see* Spofforth w Kirk Deighton
Leeds
RIBY (St Edmund)   *see* Wolds Gateway Group *Linc*
RICCALL (St Mary), Barlby and Hemingbrough *York 2*
P *Abp*   **V** G HORNER   **NSM** D A LAMBETH
RICHARDS CASTLE (All Saints)   *see* The Ashfords *Heref*
RICHINGS PARK (St Leonard)   *see* Iver *Ox*
RICHMOND (Holy Trinity and Christ Church) *S'wark 16*
P *CPAS*   **V** D M WELLS
RICHMOND (St Luke)   *see* Kew St Phil and All SS w St Luke
S'wark
**RICHMOND (St Mary Magdalene) (St Matthias) (St John
the Divine)** *S'wark 16*   **P** *K Coll Cam*   **TR** W ROEST
TV A E CRAWFORD, N T SUMMERS   **C** C E SMITH
NSM A J WILLIAMS
**RICHMOND (St Mary w Holy Trinity) w Hudswell and
Downholme and Marske** *Leeds 19*   **P** *Bp*   **R** M FLETCHER
C P J SUNDERLAND
RICHMOND HILL (St Saviour) Leeds   *see* Cross Green and
Richmond Hill *Leeds*
RICKERSCOTE (St Peter) *Lich 10*   **P** *Bp and V Stafford St Paul
(jt)*   **V** Y KHUSHI
RICKLING (All Saints)   *see* Newport w Widdington, Quendon
and Rickling *Chelmsf*
RICKMANSWORTH (St Mary the Virgin) *St Alb 4*   **P** *Bp*
V D J SNOWBALL   **NSM** S M TALBOTT
RIDDINGS (Holy Spirit)   *see* Bottesford w Ashby *Linc*
RIDDINGS (St James) and Ironville *Derby 2*   **P** *Wright
Trustees and V Alfreton (jt)*   **P-in-c** M J TAYLOR
NSM J O K PENFOLD, K W G JOHNSON
RIDDLESDEN (St Mary the Virgin)   *see* Morton and
Riddlesden *Leeds*
RIDDLESDOWN (St James) *S'wark 22*   **P** *Bp*
P-in-c G G COHEN
RIDDLESWORTH (St Peter)   *see* Guiltcross *Nor*
RIDGE (St Margaret)   *see* S Mymms and Ridge *St Alb*
RIDGE, The   *see* Redditch H Trin *Worc*
RIDGEWAY (St John the Evangelist)   *see* Eckington and
Ridgeway *Derby*
RIDGEWAY Churches, The   *see* Bishop's Castle w Mainstone,
Lydbury N etc *Heref*
RIDGEWAY, comprising Childrey w West Challow, Letcombe
Bassett, Letcombe Regis, and Sparsholt w Kingston Lisle
Ox 27   **P** *DBP, CCC Ox, and Qu Coll Ox (jt)*   **R** L A HILL
C A D COLBROOK
RIDGEWAY, comprising Chiseldon w Draycot Folliat,
Ogbourne St Andrew, and Ogbourne St George *Sarum 18*
P *D&C Windsor and O H Langton Esq (jt)*   **R** R R POWELL
RIDGEWELL (St Laurence)   *see* Two Rivers *Chelmsf*
RIDGMONT (All Saints)   *see* Aspley Guise w Husborne
Crawley and Ridgmont *St Alb*
RIDING MILL (St James) *Newc 9*   **P** *Viscount Allendale*
P-in-c D JOHNSON
RIDLEY (St Peter) *Roch 1*   **P** *J R A B Scott Esq*   **R** H M REEVES
C C J SHILLITO   **NSM** E M ROBERTSON
RIDLINGTON (St Mary Magdalene and St Andrew)   *see*
Empingham, Edith Weston, Lyndon, Manton etc *Pet*
RIDLINGTON (St Peter)   *see* Bacton, Happisburgh,
Hempstead w Eccles etc *Nor*
RIEVAULX (St Mary)   *see* Helmsley *York*
RIGSBY (St James)   *see* Alford Gp *Linc*
RIGTON, NORTH (St John)   *see* Lower Wharfedale *Leeds*
RILLINGTON (St Andrew)   *see* Buckrose Carrs *York*
RIMPTON (Blessed Virgin Mary)   *see* Chilton Cantelo,
Ashington, Mudford, Rimpton etc *B & W*
RINGLAND (St Peter)   *see* Taverham w Ringland *Nor*
RINGMER (St Mary the Virgin) *Chich 21*   **P** *Abp*   **V** *vacant*
RINGMORE (All Hallows)   *see* Modbury, Bigbury, Ringmore
etc *Ex*
RINGSFIELD (All Saints)   *see* Hundred River and Wainford *St E*
RINGSHALL (St Catherine)   *see* S Bosmere *St E*
RINGSTEAD (Nativity of the Blessed Virgin Mary)   *see* Raunds,
Hargrave, Ringstead and Stanwick *Pet*
RINGSTEAD (St Andrew)   *see* Hunstanton and Saxon Shore
Nor
RINGSTONE IN AVELAND Group, The, comprising Dunsby,
Haconby, Kirkby Underwood, Morton, and Rippingale
Linc 17   **P** *Bp (2 turns), Baroness Willoughby de Eresby and
Charterhouse (1 turn)*   **R** N G O BULLEN
RINGWAY Hale Barns (All Saints)   *see* Hale Barns w Ringway
Ches

**RINGWOOD (St Peter and St Paul) w Ellingham and
Harbridge and St Leonards and St Ives** *Win 9*   **P** *K Coll
Cam, Earl of Normanton, and Bp (jt)*   **V** M J H TRICK
C K M PEAD   **NSM** S D MATTHEWS
RINGWOULD (St Nicholas)   *see* Walmer and Cornilo *Cant*
RIPE (St John the Baptist)   *see* Laughton w Ripe and
Chalvington *Chich*
RIPLEY (All Saints) *Derby 8*   **P** *Wright Trustees*
V J M WIGRAM   **OLM** M BROOKES
RIPLEY (All Saints)   *see* Bishop Thornton, Burnt Yates,
Markington etc *Leeds*
RIPLEY (St Mary) *Guildf 12*   **P** *Bp*   **V** C J ELSON
RIPON (Holy Trinity) *Leeds 20*   **P** *Simeon's Trustees*
V C BUTLER   **C** M Y LEPINE
**RIPON CATHEDRAL BENEFICE (St Peter and St Wilfrid),
including** Bishop Monkton, Burton Leonard, and Sharow w
Copt Hewick and Marton-le-Moor *Leeds 20*   **P** *The Crown*
V J R DOBSON   **C** R E NEWTON   **NSM** R N WAINWRIGHT
RIPPINGALE (St Andrew)   *see* Ringstone in Aveland Gp *Linc*
RIPPLE (St Mary the Virgin)   *see* Walmer and Cornilo *Cant*
RIPPLE (St Mary)   *see* Upton-on-Severn, Ripple, Earls Croome
etc *Worc*
RIPPONDEN (St Bartholomew) *Leeds 6*   **P** *Bp and V Halifax
(jt)*   **P-in-c** S M SOUTHGATE
RISBOROUGH, comprising Bledlow w Saunderton and
Horsenden, Lacey Green, Monks Risborough, and Princes
Risborough w Ilmer *Ox 10*   **P** *Ld Chan (2 turns), Patr Bd (1
turn)*   **TR** D G WILLIAMS   **TV** A F BUNDOCK, P J H GODDEN
C P K KERR   **NSM** M D HUNT, N CHUMU MUTUKU
RISBY (St Giles)   *see* Barrow *St E*
RISE (All Saints)   *see* Skirlaugh, Catwick, Long Riston, Rise,
Swine w Ellerby *York*
RISE PARK   *see* Bestwood Em and St Mark w Rise Park *S'well*
RISEHOLME (St Mary)   *see* Nettleham *Linc*
RISELEY (All Saints) w Bletsoe *St Alb 13*   **P** *MMCET*
V J A ISAACS
RISHTON (St Peter and St Paul) *Blackb 7*   **P** *Trustees*
V E W C CARR
RISHWORTH (St John)   *see* Ripponden *Leeds*
RISLEY (All Saints)   *see* Stanton-by-Dale w Dale Abbey and
Risley *Derby*
RISSINGTON, GREAT (St John the Baptist)   *see* Bourton-on-
the-Water w Clapton etc *Glouc*
RISSINGTON, LITTLE (St Peter) *as above*
RIVENHALL (St Mary the Virgin and All Saints)   *see* Witham
and Villages *Chelmsf*
RIVER (St Peter and St Paul) *Cant 7*   **P** *Abp*
P-in-c A J BAWTREE
RIVER WERE Benefice, The, comprising Bishopstrow and
Boreham, Warminster St Denys, and Upton Scudamore
Sarum 12   **P** *Bp, Qu Coll Ox, and DBP (jt)*   **C** S C HART
NSM M R COLLINS
RIVERHEAD (St Mary)   *see* W Sevenoaks *Roch*
RIVERS Team Ministry, The, comprising Brinsworth,
Catcliffe, Tinsley, and Treeton *Sheff 6*   **P** *Patr Bd*
NSM P L BARRINGER
RIVERS, The, Retford, comprising Askham, East Drayton, East
Markham, Grove, Headon, Laneham, Rampton, Stokeham,
and Treswell and Cottam *S'well 1*   **P** *SMF, Grove Estate
Trustees, Bp, and D&C York (jt)*   **R** E B GAMBLE
RIVERSMEET Benefice, The, comprising Blunham, Great
Barford, Roxton, and Tempsford w Little Barford *St Alb 10*
P *The Crown, Trin Coll Cam (2 turns), and Ball Coll Ox (by
turn)*   **P-in-c** G C BUCKLE
RIVINGTON (not known)   *see* Horwich and Rivington *Man*
ROACH Parishes, comprising Barling Magna, Foulness, Little
and Great Wakering, Rochford and Sutton w Shopland
Chelmsf 13   **P** *Patr Bd*   **TR** K A LEPLEY   **TV** S M GUEST
ROADE (St Mary the Virgin)   *see* Salcey *Pet*
ROADWATER (St Luke)   *see* Old Cleeve, Leighland and
Treborough *B & W*
ROBERTSBRIDGE (Mission Room)   *see* Salehurst, Hurst Green
and Robertsbridge *Chich*
ROBERTTOWN (All Saints)   *see* Hartshead, Hightown,
Roberttown and Scholes *Leeds*
ROBOROUGH   *see* Bickleigh and Shaugh Prior *Ex*
ROBOROUGH (St Peter)   *see* Newton Tracey, Horwood,
Alverdiscott etc *Ex*
ROBY (St Bartholomew) *Liv 7*   **P** *Bp*   **V** K E WHARTON
C C M ALDRIDGE
**ROCESTER (St Michael), Denstone and Croxden w
Hollington** *Lich 14*   **P** *Bp and Trustees (jt)*   **V** E J JONES
C G R HIGGS
ROCHDALE (St Aidan)   *see* Sudden and Heywood All So *Man*

ROCHDALE (St Chad) St Edmund (St John the Divine)
(St Mary) *Man 6* **P** *Bp* **R** A E GILBERT **C** D QUINLAN
NSM R K GRAY
ROCHE (St Gomonda of the Rock) *Truro 7* **P** *Bp and DBP*
(jt) **P-in-c** K P ARTHUR
ROCHESTER (St Justus) *Roch 5* **P** *Bp* **V** H M BURN
C A L J PYRKE
ROCHESTER (St Peter) (St Margaret) *Roch 5* **P** *Bp and D&C*
(jt) **V** J A LOVE **C** B A A LAWAL
ROCHFORD (St Andrew) *see Roach Par Chelmsf*
ROCHFORD (St Michael) *see Teme Valley S Worc*
ROCK (St Peter and St Paul) *see Mamble w Bayton, Rock w*
Heightington etc *Worc*
ROCK (St Philip and St James) *see Embleton w Rennington*
and Rock *Newc*
ROCK FERRY (St Peter) *Ches 1* **P** *Bp* **V** C R SLATER
ROCKBEARE (St Mary w St Andrew) *see Broadclyst, Clyst*
Honiton, Clyst Hydon etc *Ex*
ROCKBOURNE (St Andrew) *see W Downland Sarum*
ROCKCLIFFE (St Mary the Virgin) and Blackford *Carl 2*
P *D&C* **P-in-c** I JOHNSTON
ROCKHAMPTON (St Oswald) *see Cromhall, Tortworth,*
Tytherington, Falfield etc *Glouc*
ROCKINGHAM (St Leonard) *see Gretton w Rockingham and*
Cottingham w E Carlton *Pet*
ROCKLAND (All Saints) *see Gt and Lt Ellingham, Rockland*
and Shropham etc *Nor*
ROCKLAND (St Peter) *as above*
ROCKLAND ST MARY (St Mary) with Hellington,
Bramerton, Surlingham, Claxton, Carleton St Peter and
Kirby Bedon w Whitlingham *Nor 8* **P** *Bp, Adn Nor,*
MMCET, and BNC Ox (jt) **P-in-c** N J H GARRARD
C C A TURNER **NSM** E H GARRARD **OLM** M ANSELL
RODBOROUGH (St Mary Magdalene), Woodchester and
Brimscombe *Glouc 4* **P** *Simeon's Trustees and Bp (jt)*
R P A FRANCIS **C** S K HASLAM
RODBOURNE (Holy Rood) *see Malmesbury and Upper Avon*
Bris
RODBOURNE CHENEY (St Mary) *Bris 7* **P** *CPAS*
R N D J LINES
RODDEN (All Saints) *see Beckington w Standerwick, Berkley,*
Rodden etc *B & W*
RODE (St Lawrence) *see Hardington Vale B & W*
RODE HEATH (Good Shepherd) *see Odd Rode Ches*
RODE, NORTH (St Michael) *see Gawsworth w North Rode*
Ches
RODHUISH (St Bartholomew) *see Dunster, Carhampton,*
Withycombe w Rodhuish etc *B & W*
RODING, HIGH (All Saints) *see Gt Canfield w High Roding*
and Aythorpe Roding *Chelmsf*
RODINGS, SOUTH, comprising Abbess Roding, Beauchamp
Roding, Leaden Roding, and White Roding *Chelmsf 17*
P *Ld Chan, Bp, and Viscount Gough (by turn)*
P-in-c R D STONE **C** G A FLEMING **NSM** T E GOODBODY
RODINGTON (St George) *see Wrockwardine Deanery Lich*
RODLEY (Ecumenical Centre) *see Farsley Leeds*
RODLEY (Mission Church) *see Westbury-on-Severn w Flaxley,*
Blaisdon etc *Glouc*
RODMELL (St Peter) *see Iford w Kingston and Rodmell and*
Southease *Chich*
RODMERSHAM (St Nicholas) *see Tunstall and Bredgar Cant*
RODNEY STOKE (St Leonard) *see Cheddar, Draycott and*
Rodney Stoke *B & W*
ROEHAMPTON (Holy Trinity) *S'wark 18* **P** *Bp* **V** J B REY
ROFFEY (All Saints) *see Colgate and Roffey Chich*
ROGATE (St Bartholomew) w Terwick and Trotton w
Chithurst *Chich 3* **P** *Ld Chan* **R** E M DOYLE
ROGERS LANE (St Andrew's Chapel) *see Stoke Poges Ox*
ROLLESTON (St George) *see Ormesby St Marg w Scratby,*
Ormesby St Mich etc *Nor*
ROLLESTON (Holy Trinity) *see W Trent S'well*
ROLLESTON (St John the Baptist) *see Coplow Leic*
ROLLESTON (St Mary) *see Anslow, Rolleston and Tutbury*
Lich
ROLLRIGHT, GREAT (St Andrew) *see Hook Norton w Gt*
Rollright, Swerford etc *Ox*
ROLLRIGHT, LITTLE (St Phillip) *see Chipping Norton Ox*
ROLVENDEN (St Mary the Virgin) *see Tenterden, Rother and*
Oxney *Cant*
ROMALDKIRK (St Romald) *see Lower Teesdale Leeds*
ROMANBY (St James) *see Northallerton w Kirby Sigston York*
ROMANSLEIGH (St Rumon) *see Burrington, Chawleigh,*
Cheldon, Chulmleigh etc *Ex*
ROMFORD (Ascension) Collier Row *Chelmsf 2* **P** *Trustees*
P-in-c A J GUEST

ROMFORD (Good Shepherd) Collier Row *Chelmsf 2*
P *CPAS* **V** D H HAGUE **C** D M HARRIGAN
Hon C K S TURNER
ROMFORD (St Alban) *Chelmsf 2* **P** *Bp* **V** R S P HINGLEY
ROMFORD (St Andrew) (St Agnes) *Chelmsf 2* **P** *New Coll*
Ox **P-in-c** L E DOSE
ROMFORD (St Augustine) Rush Green *see Rush Green*
Chelmsf
ROMFORD (St Edward the Confessor) *Chelmsf 2* **P** *New*
Coll Ox **V** D J SIMPSON
ROMILEY (St Chad) *Ches 16* **P** *R Stockport St Mary*
V R L PENNYSTAN **C** W DRAIN
ROMNEY MARSH Benefice, The, comprising Brenzett,
Brookland, Burmarsh, Dymchurch, Fairfield, Ivychurch,
Lydd, New Romney, Old Romney, Romney St Mary-in-the-
Marsh, St Mary's Bay, and Snargate *Cant 10* **P** *Patr Bd*
TR C T A HODGKINS **TV** C G MACLEAN **C** J S RICHARDSON
NSM J DARLING, S J BODY
ROMNEY, NEW (St Nicholas) *see Romney Marsh Cant*
ROMNEY, OLD (St Clement) *as above*
ROMSEY (St Mary and St Ethelflaeda) *Win 12* **P** *Bp*
V T G WHARTON **C** L A THOMPSON, S A WOMERSLEY
NSM D F WILLIAMS, F M JENVEY,
M D S ERLEWYN-LAJEUNESSE, P HOLLINGWORTH
ROMSLEY (Mission Room) *see Halas Worc*
ROMSLEY (St Kenelm) *as above*
ROOKERY, THE (St Saviour) *see Mow Cop Lich*
ROOS (All Saints) *see S Holderness Coast York*
ROOSE (St Perran) *see S Barrow Carl*
ROPLEY (St Peter) *see Bishop's Sutton and Ropley and W*
Tisted *Win*
ROPSLEY (St Peter) *see N Beltisloe Par Linc*
ROSE ASH (St Peter) *see Bishopsnympton, Charles, E Anstey,*
High Bray etc *Ex*
ROSEDALE (St Lawrence) *see Lastingham w Appleton-le-*
Moors, Rosedale etc *York*
ROSHERVILLE (St Mark) *see Northfleet and Rosherville Roch*
ROSLEY (Holy Trinity) *see Westward, Rosley-w-Woodside and*
Welton *Carl*
ROSLISTON (St Mary) *see Seale and Lullington w Coton in*
the Elms *Derby*
ROSS (St Mary the Virgin) w Walford and Brampton
Abbotts *Heref 7* **P** *Bp (4 turns), Ld Chan (1 turn)*
R S A J SEMPLE **C** T M JACKSON **Hon C** C J BLANCHARD
NSM C E A PASCOE
ROSSINGTON (St Michael) *Sheff 9* **P** *Bp* **R** *vacant*
ROSSINGTON, NEW (St Luke) *Sheff 9* **P** *Bp* **V** *vacant*
ROSTHERNE (St Mary) w Bollington *Ches 12* **P** C L S
Cornwall-Legh Esq **V** P J ROBINSON **NSM** P M COPE,
P M ROBINSON
ROTHBURY (All Saints) *see Upper Coquetdale Newc*
ROTHERBY (All Saints) *see Upper Wreake Leic*
ROTHERFIELD (St Denys) w Mark Cross *Chich 16* **P** *Bp, Adn*
Lewes and Hastings, and Ch Patr Trust (jt) **R** N F MASON
C S R WICKENS
ROTHERFIELD GREYS (Holy Trinity) *see Henley H Trin Ox*
ROTHERFIELD GREYS (St Nicholas) *see Nettlebed w Bix,*
Highmoor, Pishill etc *Ox*
ROTHERFIELD PEPPARD (All Saints) and Kidmore End and
Sonning Common *Ox 24* **P** *Bp and Jes Coll Ox (jt)*
R J E DE G STICKINGS **NSM** S WALKER
ROTHERHAM (All Saints) *Sheff 6* **P** *Bp* **V** P J BATCHFORD
C A J MIDDLETON, R E YOUNG **NSM** S C ARMSTRONG
ROTHERHITHE (Holy Trinity) *S'wark 7* **P** *R Rotherhithe*
St Mary **V** A M DOYLE
ROTHERHITHE (St Katharine) *see Bermondsey St Kath w*
St Bart *S'wark*
ROTHERHITHE (St Mary) w All Saints *S'wark 7* **P** *Clare Coll*
Cam **R** M R NICHOLLS
ROTHERSTHORPE (St Peter and St Paul) *see Bugbrooke,*
Harpole, Kislingbury etc *Pet*
ROTHERWICK (not known) *see Whitewater Win*
ROTHLEY (St Mary the Virgin and St John the Baptist)
Leic 4 **P** MMCET **V** R M GLADSTONE
ROTHWELL (Holy Trinity) w Orton and Rushton w
Glendon and Pipewell and Loddington and Thorpe
Malsor *Pet 9* **P** *Bp, J N Hipwell Esq, Mert Coll Ox, Hosp of*
Jes, and Keble Coll Ox (3 turns), Ld Chan (1 turn)
R J R WESTWOOD
ROTHWELL (Holy Trinity), Lofthouse, Methley w
Mickletown and Oulton w Woodlesford Team Ministry,
The *Leeds 13* **P** *Duchy of Lancaster (1 turn), Patr Bd (3 turns)*
TR A A JOHN **TV** A L RHODES, S A HANCOX
ROTHWELL (St Mary the Virgin) *see Caistor Linc*
ROTTINGDEAN (St Margaret) *Chich 19* **P** *Bp*
V A M MOORE

ROUGH CLOSE (St Matthew)   *see* Meir Heath and Normacot *Lich*

ROUGH COMMON (St Gabriel)   *see* Harbledown *Cant*

ROUGH HAY (St Christopher)   *see* Darlaston and Moxley *Lich*

ROUGHAM (St Mary)   *see* Launditch and the Upper Nar *Nor*

ROUGHAM (St Mary), Beyton w Hessett and Rushbrooke *St E 6*   **P** *Bp, MMCET (2 turns), and Ld Chan*   **R** N CUTLER

ROUGHTON (St Margaret)   *see* Bain Valley Gp *Linc*

ROUGHTON (St Mary) and Felbrigg, Metton, Sustead, Bessingham and Gunton w Hanworth *Nor 20*   **P** *Bp and Exors G Whately Esq (jt)*   **R** *vacant*

ROUGHTOWN (St John the Baptist) *Man 5*   **P** *Bp* **NSM** I C BROCKLEHURST

ROUGHTOWN (St John the Baptist)   *see* Mossley *Man*

ROUNDHAY (St Edmund King and Martyr) *Leeds 10*   **P** *Bp* **V** N C J WRIGHT   **C** J R M GLENWRIGHT

ROUNDS GREEN (St James) *Birm 3*   **P** *V Langley* **OLM** J M MACDONALD

ROUNDSHAW (St Paul)   *see* S Beddington and Roundshaw *S'wark*

ROUNTON, WEST (St Oswald) and East (St Laurence) w Welbury *York 18*   **P** *Ld Chan*   **R** J M E COOPER

ROUS LENCH (St Peter)   *see* Church Lench w Rous Lench and Abbots Morton etc *Worc*

ROUSHAM (St Leonard and St James) *Ox 21*   **P** *C Cottrell-Dormer Esq*   **P-in-c** R C SMAIL

ROUTH (All Saints)   *see* Beverley St Jo and St Martin w Routh All SS *York*

ROWBERROW (St Michael and All Angels)   *see* Axbridge w Shipham and Rowberrow *B & W*

ROWDE (St Matthew) and Bromham *Sarum 17*   **P** *DBP and J A L Spicer Esq (jt)*   **R** R E SCHOFIELD   **C** H F SMITH

ROWINGTON (St Laurence)   *see* Hatton w Haseley, Rowington w Lowsonford etc *Cov*

ROWLAND LUBBOCK (Memorial Hall)   *see* E Horsley *Guildf*

ROWLANDS CASTLE (St John the Baptist) *Portsm 5*   **P** *Bp* **P-in-c** V L MORGAN   **NSM** J K WINDSOR

ROWLANDS GILL (St Barnabas)   *see* High Spen and Rowlands Gill *Dur*

ROWLEDGE (St James) *Guildf 3*   **P** *Adn Surrey*   **V** R W GANT **Hon C** S J CRABTREE   **NSM** R E PARKER

ROWLESTONE (St Peter)   *see* Ewyas Harold w Dulas, Kenderchurch etc *Heref*

ROWLEY (St Peter)   *see* Walkington, Bishop Burton, Rowley etc *York*

ROWLEY REGIS (St Giles) *Birm 3*   **P** *Ld Chan*   **V** J J BRIDGE

ROWNER (St Mary the Virgin)   *see* Bridgemary, Elson and Rowner *Portsm*

ROWNEY GREEN (Mission Chapel)   *see* Alvechurch *Worc*

ROWNHAMS (St John the Evangelist)   *see* Nursling and Rownhams *Win*

ROWSLEY (St Katherine)   *see* Bakewell, Ashford w Sheldon and Rowsley *Derby*

ROWSTON (St Clement)   *see* Digby Gp *Linc*

ROWTON (All Hallows)   *see* Wrockwardine Deanery *Lich*

ROXBOURNE (St Andrew) *Lon 20*   **P** *Bp*   **V** L P NORTH

ROXBY (St Mary)   *see* Winterton Gp *Linc*

ROXBY (St Nicholas)   *see* Hinderwell, Roxby and Staithes etc *York*

ROXETH (Christ Church) *Lon 20*   **P** *Bp and Ch Patr Trust (jt)* **V** S J DURRANT   **NSM** E WEAVER, M MOTT

ROXHOLME   *see* N Lafford Gp *Linc*

ROXTON (St Mary Magdalene)   *see* Riversmeet *St Alb*

ROXWELL (St Michael and All Angels) *Chelmsf 9*   **P** *New Coll Ox*   **P-in-c** A D CANT

ROYAL WOOTTON BASSETT (St Bartholomew and All Saints) *Sarum 16*   **P** *DBP*   **V** J D CURTIS

ROYDON (All Saints)   *see* Ashwicken w Leziate, Bawsey etc *Nor*

ROYDON (St Peter) *Chelmsf 4*   **P** *Earl Cowley* **P-in-c** R J ATTEW

ROYDON (St Remigius)   *see* Diss *Nor*

ROYSTON (St John the Baptist) *St Alb 16*   **P** *Bp* **V** H A HUNTLEY   **NSM** J H FIDLER

ROYSTON (St John the Baptist) and Felkirk *Leeds 14*   **P** *Bp* **V** M C TOMLINSON

ROYTON (St Paul) *Man 5*   **P** *R Prestwich St Mary* **V** G HOLLOWOOD   **C** N R JOHNSON

ROYTON Longsight (St Anne)   *see* Heyside and Royton *Man*

RUAN LANIHORNE (St Rumon)   *see* Veryan w Ruan Lanihorne *Truro*

RUAN MINOR (St Rumon)   *see* St Keverne, St Ruan w St Grade and Landewednack *Truro*

RUARDEAN (St John the Baptist)   *see* Drybrook, Lydbrook and Ruardean *Glouc*

RUBERY (St Chad) *Birm 2*   **P** *The Crown*   **V** C E TURNER

RUCKINGE (St Mary Magdalene)   *see* Saxon Shoreline *Cant*

RUCKLAND (St Olave)   *see* S Ormsby Gp *Linc*

RUDBY IN CLEVELAND (All Saints)   *see* Whorlton Gp *York*

RUDDINGTON (St Peter) *S'well 6*   **P** *Simeon's Trustees* **V** A D BUCHANAN

RUDFORD (St Mary the Virgin)   *see* Highnam, Tibberton w Rudford etc *Glouc*

RUDGWICK (Holy Trinity) *Chich 10*   **P** *Ld Chan* **V** M P J KING

RUDHAM, EAST and WEST (St Mary), Helhoughton, Houghton-next-Harpley, The Raynhams, Tatterford, and Tattersett *Nor 14*   **P** *Bp, The Most Revd G D Hand, Marquess of Cholmondeley, and Marquess Townshend (jt)* **R** E L BUNDOCK

RUDHEATH (Licensed Room)   *see* Witton *Ches*

RUDSTON (All Saints), Boynton, Carnaby, Kilham, Burton Fleming w Fordon, Grindale and Wold Newton *York 9* **P** *Abp (1 turn), Abp and MMCET (2 turns), Ld Chan (1 turn)* **V** G J OWEN   **NSM** A P LEACH, B E HODGSON

RUFFORD (St Mary the Virgin) and Tarleton *Blackb 5*   **P** *Bp and St Pet Coll Ox (jt)*   **R** M SOADY

RUFFORTH (All Saints)   *see* Marston Moor *York*

RUGBY (St Andrew) *Cov 6*   **P** *Bp*   **R** J NEWEY

RUGBY (St George) *Cov 6*   **P** *Bp*   **V** *vacant*

RUGBY (St Peter and St John) *Cov 6*   **P** *Bp*   **V** S M BRIDGE

RUGBY WEST (St Matthew and St Oswald) *Cov 6*   **P** *Dioc Trustees and Ch Trust Fund Trust (jt)*   **V** A J HULME **NSM** J I HULME

RUGELEY (St Augustine)   *see* Brereton and Rugeley w Armitage *Lich*

RUGELEY (The Good Shepherd)   *as above*

RUISHTON (St George)   *see* Creech St Michael and Ruishton w Thornfalcon *B & W*

RUISLIP (St Martin) *Lon 21*   **P** *D&C Windsor*   **C** Y S WALKER **NSM** J R WHITE

RUISLIP (St Mary) *Lon 21*   **P** *Bp*   **V** E J LOBSINGER **NSM** A J BEATTIE

RUISLIP MANOR (St Paul) *Lon 21*   **P** *Bp*   **V** M E SELBY **NSM** A CLARRIDGE

RUMBURGH (St Michael and All Angels and St Felix)   *see* The Saints *St E*

RUNCORN (All Saints) (Holy Trinity) *Ches 3*   **P** *Bp and Ch Ch Ox (jt)*   **V** D W GUEST

RUNCORN (St Andrew)   *see* Grange St Andr *Ches*

RUNCORN (St John the Evangelist) Weston *Ches 3*   **P** *Bp* **V** V B GISBY

RUNCORN (St Michael and All Angels) *Ches 3*   **P** *Bp* **V** K BRADY   **NSM** H BROWNE

RUNCTON HOLME (St James)   *see* W Norfolk Priory Gp *Ely*

RUNCTON, NORTH (All Saints)   *see* Middlewinch *Nor*

RUNCTON, SOUTH (St Andrew)   *see* W Norfolk Priory Gp *Ely*

RUNHALL (All Saints)   *see* Barnham Broom and Upper Yare *Nor*

RUNHAM (St Peter and St Paul)   *see* S Trin Broads *Nor*

RUNNINGTON (St Peter and St Paul)   *see* Wellington and Distr *B & W*

RUNTON (Holy Trinity)   *see* Aylmerton, Runton, Beeston Regis and Gresham *Nor*

RUNTON, EAST (St Andrew)   *as above*

RUNWELL (St Mary)   *see* Wickford and Runwell *Chelmsf*

RURAL EAST YORK, comprising Dunnington, Holtby, Stockton-on-Forest, and Warthill- *York 2*   **P** *Abp* **R** N W R BIRD   **C** M POOLE

RUSCOMBE (St James the Great) and Twyford w Hurst *Ox 8*   **P** *Bp*   **V** A C HARWOOD   **Hon C** G F THEOBALD

RUSH GREEN (St Augustine) Romford *Chelmsf 2*   **P** *Bp* **V** M D HOWSE

RUSHALL (Christ the King) (St Michael the Archangel) *Lich 24*   **P** *Sir Andrew Buchanan Bt and H C S Buchanan Esq (jt)*   **V** C R SUCH

RUSHALL (St Mary)   *see* Dickleburgh and The Pulhams *Nor*

RUSHALL (St Matthew)   *see* Vale of Pewsey *Sarum*

RUSHBROOKE (St Nicholas)   *see* Rougham, Beyton w Hessett and Rushbrooke *St E*

RUSHBURY (St Peter)   *see* Apedale Gp *Heref*

RUSHDEN (St Mary)   *see* Kingswood *St Alb*

RUSHDEN (St Mary) w Newton Bromswold *Pet 8*   **P** *CPAS* **R** S K PRIOR   **C** P J NIGHTINGALE

RUSHDEN (St Peter) *Pet 8*   **P** *CPAS*   **V** R A HAWKINS **C** J ALLEN

RUSHDEN Whitefriars   *see* Whitefriars Rushden *Pet*

RUSHEN Christ Church (Holy Trinity) *S & M*   **P** *The Crown* **V** J A T HEATON   **NSM** E S C HULL

RUSHEY MEAD (St Theodore of Canterbury)   *see* Leic St Theodore *Leic*

RUSHFORD (St John the Evangelist)   *see* E w W Harling,
  Bridgham w Roudham, Larling etc *Nor*
RUSHLAKE GREEN (Little St Mary)   *see* Warbleton, Bodle
  Street Green and Dallington *Chich*
RUSHMERE (St Andrew) *St E 1*   **P** *Bp*   **V** S D FOSTER
  NSM M J WALKER
RUSHMERE (St Michael)   *see* Kessingland, Gisleham and
  Rushmere *Nor*
RUSHOCK (St Michael)   *see* Elmley Lovett w Hampton Lovett
  and Elmbridge w Rushock and Hartlebury and Ombersley
  w Doverdale *Worc*
RUSHOLME (Holy Trinity) *Man 2*   **P** *CPAS*   **R** P M MATHOLE
  C R B CRIDDLE, S R FOULDS, T J WICKHAM, W J MARSH
  NSM P J GASKELL
RUSHTON (All Saints)   *see* Rothwell w Orton and Rushton w
  Glendon etc *Pet*
RUSHTON SPENCER (St Lawrence)   *see* Cheddleton, Horton,
  Longsdon and Rushton Spencer *Lich*
RUSKIN PARK (St Saviour)   *see* Herne Hill *S'wark*
RUSKINGTON (All Saints)   *see* N Lafford Gp *Linc*
RUSLAND (St Paul)   *see* Hawkshead and Low Wray w Sawrey
  and Rusland etc *Carl*
RUSPER (St Mary Magdalene) *Chich 10*   **P** *Bp*   **R** N A FLINT
RUSTHALL (St Paul) (St Paul's Mission Church) *Roch 12*
  P *R Speldhurst*   **V** R E N WILLIAMS
RUSTINGTON (St Peter and St Paul) *Chich 1*   **P** *Bp*
  V N L LOVELESS   **C** L E DARRALL
RUSTON PARVA (St Nicholas)   *see* The Beacon *York*
RUTLAND WATER   *see* Empingham, Edith Weston, Lyndon,
  Manton etc *Pet*
RUXLEY (St Francis of Assisi)   *see* Ewell St Fran *Guildf*
RYAL (All Saints)   *see* Stamfordham w Matfen *Newc*
RYARSH (St Martin)   *see* Birling, Addington, Ryarsh and
  Trottiscliffe *Roch*
RYBURGH, GREAT (St Andrew)   *see* Upper Wensum Village
  Gp *Nor*
**RYBURN Benefice, The (Cottonstones, Norland and
  Sowerby)** *Leeds 8*   **P** *Bp and DBP (jt)*   **V** J ROBERTS
  C I SPARKS
RYDAL (St Mary) *Carl 11*   **P** *Bp*   **P-in-c** D M B WILMOT
RYDE (All Saints) *Portsm 7*   **P** *Bp*   **C** H J MONAGHAN
RYDE (St James) Proprietary Chapel *Portsm 7*
  C-in-c J H A LEGGETT
RYDE (St John the Baptist) Oakfield and Holy Trinity
  Portsm 7   **P** *Bp and V St Helens (jt)*   **P-in-c** S A THEOBALD
  NSM D K MABEY
RYE (St Mary the Virgin) *Chich 17*   **P** *Patr Bd*   **TR** *vacant*
RYE HARBOUR (Holy Spirit)   *see* Rye *Chich*
RYE PARK (St Cuthbert) *St Alb 17*   **P** *DBP*   **V** N L SHARP
RYECROFT (St Nicolas) Rawmarsh *Sheff 6*   **P** *Bp*   **V** *vacant*
RYEDALE, UPPER, comprising Bilsdale Midcable, Old Byland,
  Cold Kirby, Hawnby, and Scawton *York 19*   **P** *Abp and the
  Hon Jake Duncombe (jt)*   **NSM** H RAWLINGS
RYHALL (St John the Evangelist) w Essendine and Carlby
  Pet 12   **P** *Burghley Ho Preservation Trust Ltd*
  P-in-c J M SAUNDERS
RYHILL (St James) *Leeds 16*   **P** *Bp*   **P-in-c** P CARTWRIGHT
  C J E FLEURY, T H R S J BATES-BOURNE   **NSM** M J BURNS,
  M SCHOLEY
RYHOPE (St Paul) *Dur 14*   **P** *Bp*   **V** D E CHADWICK
RYLSTONE (St Peter)   *see* Linton, Burnsall and Rylstone *Leeds*
RYME INTRINSECA (St Hypolytus)   *see* Three Valleys *Sarum*
RYSTON (St Michael)   *see* Denver and Ryston w Roxham etc
  Ely
RYTHER (All Saints)   *see* Cawood w Ryther and Wistow *York*
RYTON (Holy Cross) *Dur 12*   **P** *Bp*
  P-in-c A M STEWART SMITH
RYTON (Mission Chapel)   *see* Condover w Frodesley, Acton
  Burnell etc *Heref*
RYTON (St Andrew)   *see* Beckbury, Badger, Kemberton,
  Ryton, Stockton etc *Lich*
RYTON ON DUNSMORE (St Leonard)   *see* Baginton w
  Bubbenhall and Ryton-on-Dunsmore *Cov*
SACOMBE (St Catherine)   *see* Standon and The Mundens w
  Sacombe *St Alb*
SACRED HEART MISSION COMMUNITY   *see* Sutton-on-
  Plym, Plymouth St Simon and St Mary *Ex*
SADBERGE (St Andrew) *Dur 5*   **P** *Bp*   **R** M R EAST
  NSM J J BLACKBURN, S CHEW
SADDINGTON (St Helen)   *see* Kibworth and Smeeton
  Westerby and Saddington *Leic*
SADDLEWORTH (St Chad) *Man 5*   **P** *Patr Bd*   **TR** S A JONES
  TV J R ROSEDALE   **C** A A JACKMAN   **Hon C** H A EDGERTON
  NSM M C DONMALL, P H WILLIAMSON, R J LAMBERT
  OLM B CHRISTOPHER, P J GILLIAN

SAFFRON WALDEN (St Mary) and Villages, including
  Ashdon, Debden, Great Chesterford, Hadstock, Little
  Chesterford, Littlebury, Wendens Ambo, and Wimbish w
  Thunderley *Chelmsf 19*   **P** *Ld Chan (1 turn), Patr Bd (2 turns)*
  TR J C TREW   **TV** A JEEWAN, C M CURRER, J SAXON
SAHAM TONEY (St George)   *see* Ashill, Carbrooke, Ovington
  and Saham Toney *Nor*
ST AGNES (St Agnes)   *see* Is of Scilly *Truro*
ST AGNES (St Agnes) and Mount Hawke w Mithian *Truro 5*
  P *Bp and D&C (alt)*   **P-in-c** A E BROWN   **C** D J WILLOUGHBY
  NSM R J MONIE
ST ALBANS (Christ Church) *St Alb 5*   **P** *Trustees*
  V J M FOLLETT
ST ALBANS (St Luke) *St Alb 5*   **P** *DBP*   **V** M A SLATER
  NSM D M HALSEY
ST ALBANS (St Mary) Marshalswick *St Alb 5*   **P** *Bp*
  V G W HOLMES, K E PEARSON
ST ALBANS (St Michael) *St Alb 5*   **P** *Earl of Verulam*
  V K P J PADLEY   **C** C E B KING
ST ALBANS (St Paul) *St Alb 5*   **P** *V St Alb St Pet*
  V J E TREGALE   **C** D R TREGALE   **NSM** A R PIKE, A RADMALL,
  P G CRUMPLER
ST ALBANS (St Peter) *St Alb 5*   **P** *The Crown*
  V M C DEARNLEY   **C** A J HUZZEY
ST ALBANS (St Saviour) *St Alb 5*   **P** *Bp*   **V** R F WATSON
  C C QUAK-WINSLOW   **NSM** A N FERRAR, T J HALTON
ST ALBANS (St Stephen) *St Alb 5*   **P** *J N W Dudley Esq*
  V R M LEACH   **C** K A WAINWRIGHT   **NSM** P J MORIARTY
ST ALDHELM, comprising Church Knowle, Corfe Castle,
  Kimmeridge, Kingston, Langton Matravers, Steeple w
  Tyneham, and Worth Matravers *Sarum 8*   **P** *Major M J A
  Bond, Nat Trust, Exors D E Scott Esq, Bp, and R Swanage and
  Studland (jt)*   **R** I JACKSON   **C** J J MERCER, N J WEBB
ST ALLEN (St Alleyne)   *see* Kenwyn w St Allen *Truro*
ST ANNES-ON-THE-SEA (St Anne) Heyhouses *Blackb 10*   **P** *J
  C Hilton Esq*   **V** *vacant*
ST ANNES-ON-THE-SEA (St Margaret of Antioch) *Blackb 10*
  P *Bp*   **V** A HODGSON
ST ANNES-ON-THE-SEA (St Thomas) *Blackb 10*   **P** *J C Hilton
  Esq*   **V** C M SCARGILL
ST ANTHONY-IN-MENEAGE (St Anthony)   *see* Meneage *Truro*
ST AUSTELL (Holy Trinity) *Truro 7*   **P** *The Crown*
  V H M FLINT   **C** M C MOLANO   **NSM** C EDLESTON
ST BARTHOLOMEW, comprising Donhead St Andrew,
  Donhead St Mary, East Knoyle, Sedgehill, and Semley
  Sarum 11   **P** *Ch Ox, New Coll Ox, and DBP (by turn)*
  R C MCFARLANE
ST BEES (St Mary and St Bega) *Carl 5*   **P** *Trustees*
  P-in-c R A GIBBS
ST BENEDICT, UNITED BENEFICE OF   *see* Ashmanhaugh,
  Barton Turf etc *Nor*
ST BLAZEY (St Blaise) *Truro 7*   **P** *Bp*   **P-in-c** J S J WILLIAMS
ST BREOKE (St Breoke) and Egloshayle in Wadebridge
  Truro 10   **P** *Bp and DBP (jt)*   **P-in-c** S M PAYNE
ST BREWARD (St Breward)   *see* Camelside *Truro*
**ST BRIAVELS (St Mary the Virgin) w Hewelsfield and
  Brockweir** *Glouc 1*   **P** *D&C Heref*   **P-in-c** D O TREHARNE
  C N J BULLIVANT   **OLM** D M REES
ST BURYAN (St Buriana), St Levan and Sennen *Truro 4*
  P *Duchy of Cornwall*   **R** *vacant*
ST CLEER (St Clarus) *Truro 12*   **P** *Ld Chan*   **P-in-c** R M BELL
  C L J SELMAN
ST CLEMENT (St Clement) *Truro 5*   **P** *Bp*
  V D J WILLOUGHBY
ST CLETHER (St Clederus)   *see* Moorland Gp *Truro*
ST COLAN (St Colan)   *see* St Columb Minor and St Colan
  Truro
ST COLUMB MAJOR (St Columba)   *see* Lann Pydar *Truro*
ST COLUMB MINOR (St Columba) and St Colan *Truro 6*
  P *Bp*   **P-in-c** C C MCQUILLEN-WRIGHT   **C** J S THOROLD,
  L M G CHANTLER
ST CROSS SOUTH ELMHAM (St George)   *see* The Saints *St E*
ST DECUMANS   *see* Watchet and Williton *B & W*
ST DENNIS (St Denys) *Truro 7*   **P** *Bp*   **P-in-c** K P ARTHUR
ST DEVEREUX (St Dubricius)   *see* Ewyas Harold w Dulas,
  Kenderchurch etc *Heref*
ST DOMINIC (St Dominica)   *see* Tamar Valley *Truro*
ST EDMUND WAY, comprising Bradfield Combust, Great
  Whelnetham, Hawstead, Lawshall, Nowton, and
  Stanningfield *St E 6*   **P** *Bp, Mrs J Oakes, and Lord de Saumarez*
  NSM M HINDE
ST ENDELLION (St Endelienta)   *see* N Cornwall Cluster *Truro*
ST ENODER (St Enoder) *Truro 6*   **P** *Bp*   **R** *vacant*
ST ENODOC (St Enodoc)   *see* N Cornwall Cluster *Truro*
ST ERME (St Hermes)   *see* Probus, Ladock and Grampound w
  Creed and St Erme *Truro*

ST ERNEY (St Erney)　*see* Landrake w St Erney and Botus Fleming *Truro*
ST ERTH (St Erth)　*see* Godrevy *Truro*
ST ERVAN (St Ervan)　*see* Lann Pydar *Truro*
ST EVAL (St Uvelas)　*as above*
ST EWE (All Saints)　*see* St Mewan w Mevagissey and St Ewe *Truro*
ST GENNYS (St Gennys)　*see* Boscastle Gp *Truro*
ST GEORGE-IN-THE-EAST (St Mary) *Lon 7*　**P** *Bp*
V P MCGEARY
ST GEORGE-IN-THE-EAST w St Paul *Lon 7*　**P** *Bp*
R R K SPRINGER　**C** A J HARRIS, V J E MCCARTHY
Hon C T CLAPTON　**NSM** A W M RITCHIE, J L HARRIS
ST GEORGES' (St George) *Lich 20*　**P** *Bp*　**C** K S EVANS
ST GERMANS (St Germans of Auxerre) w Antony and Sheviock *Truro 11*　**P** *Bp, Sir John Carew Pole Bt, and D&C Windsor (jt)*　**V** L PARKER　**C** L M BUSHELL HAWKE
ST GILES IN THE WOOD (St Giles)　*see* Newton Tracey, Horwood, Alverdiscott etc *Ex*
ST GILES-IN-THE-FIELDS *Lon 3*　**P** *Bp*　**R** T W SANDER
ST GILES-IN-THE-HEATH (St Giles)　*see* Boyton, N Tamerton, Werrington etc *Truro*
ST GLUVIAS (St Gluvias) *Truro 2*　**P** *Bp*　**P-in-c** A J EVANS
ST GORAN (St Goranus) w Caerhays *Truro 7*　**P** *Bp*
P-in-c B A MCQUILLEN
ST HELENS (St Catherine by the Green)　*see* Seaview, St Helens, Brading and Yaverland *Portsm*
ST HELENS (St Helen)　*as above*
ST HELENS Town Centre (St Helen) (Barton Street Mission) (St Andrew) (St Mark) (St Thomas) *Liv 10*
P *Patr Bd*　**TR** C J DANIEL　**TV** R SHUTTLEWORTH
C D M DAVIES, N J WHITE　**NSM** H WOOD, S BRIDGE
ST HELIER (St Peter) (Bishop Andrewes Church) *S'wark 23*
P *Bp*　**V** T M MARLOW　**NSM** A E DOERR
ST HILARY (St Hilary)　*see* Ludgvan, Marazion, St Hilary and Perranuthnoe *Truro*
ST ILLOGAN (St Illogan) *Truro 1*　**P** *Ch Soc Trust*
R S P ROBINSON　**C** A M SHARP
ST IPPOLYTS (St Ippolyts) w Great and Little Wymondley *St Alb 3*　**P** *Bp and MMCET (jt)*　**R** V A DEAR
ST ISSEY (St Issey)　*see* Padstow, St Merryn and St Issey w St Petroc Minor *Truro*
ST IVE (St Ive) and Pensilva w Quethiock *Truro 12*　**P** *Bp (1 turn), The Crown (2 turns)*　**P-in-c** R M BELL　**C** L J SELMAN
ST IVES (All Saints) *Ely 12*　**P** *Guild of All So*　**V** J M AMEY
C S PEREZ CRIADO
ST IVES (St Ia the Virgin) *Truro 4*　**P** *D&C and V Carbis Bay w Lelant (jt)*　**V** N J WIDDOWS　**NSM** K E MARWOOD
ST JAMES (St James)　*see* Shaftesbury *Sarum*
ST JOHN (St John the Baptist)　*see* Maker w Rame, Millbrook, St John and Torpoint *Truro*
ST JOHN IN BEDWARDINE (St John in Bedwardine)　*see* Worc City W *Worc*
ST JOHN IN WEARDALE (St John the Baptist)　*see* Upper Weardale *Dur*
ST JOHN LEE (St John of Beverley) *Newc 10*　**P** *Viscount Allendale*　**R** J J T THOMPSON
ST JOHN ON BETHNAL GREEN *Lon 7*　**P** *Patr Bd*
TR A J E GREEN　**NSM** C B HALL
ST JOHN'S WOOD (St John) *Lon 4*　**P** *Bp*　**V** A K BERGQUIST
C K T ANDRÉASSON
ST JOHN'S-IN-THE-VALE (St John), St Mary's Threlkeld and Wythburn *Carl 6*　**P** *Bp, Adn, V Crosthwaite, and Earl of Lonsdale (jt)*　**P-in-c** C H HOPE
ST JULIOT (St Julitta)　*see* Boscastle Gp *Truro*
ST JUST IN PENWITH (St Just) *Truro 4*　**P** *Ld Chan*
P-in-c K E WEDGEWOOD
ST JUST-IN-ROSELAND (St Just) and St Mawes *Truro 5*　**P** *A M J Galsworthy Esq*　**P-in-c** E L A DUROSE
ST KEVERNE (St Keverne), St Ruan w St Grade and Landewednack *Truro 3*　**P** *CPAS and P J Vyvyan-Robinson Esq (jt)*　**R** vacant
ST KEW (St James the Great)　*see* N Cornwall Cluster *Truro*
ST KEYNE (St Keyna)　*see* Liskeard and St Keyne *Truro*
ST LAURENCE in the Isle of Thanet (St Laurence) *Cant 5*
P *Patr Bd*　**TR** I A JACOBSON　**NSM** K I R COX
ST LAWRENCE (Old Church) (St Lawrence) *Portsm 7*　**P** *Bp*
R vacant
ST LAWRENCE (St Lawrence)　*see* Bradwell on Sea and St Lawrence *Chelmsf*
ST LEONARD (St Leonard)　*see* Hawridge w Cholesbury and St Leonard *Ox*
ST LEONARDS (Christ Church and St Mary Magdalen) St Peter and St Paul *Chich 15*　**P** *Bp and SMF (jt)*
P-in-c P W WHEATLEY　**C** N W ARCHER　**NSM** R G RALPH

ST LEONARDS AND ST IVES (All Saints)　*see* Ringwood w Ellingham and Harbridge etc *Win*
ST LEONARDS, UPPER (St John the Evangelist) *Chich 15*
P *Trustees*　**R** D R HILL　**NSM** J N HARTMAN, M P TURNBULL
ST LEONARDS-ON-SEA (St Matthew)　*see* Silverhill St Matt *Chich*
ST LEONARDS-ON-SEA St Leonard (St Ethelburga) *Chich 15*
P *Hyndman Trustees*　**P-in-c** M J FOY　**Hon C** E V WHEELER
ST LEVAN (St Levan)　*see* St Buryan, St Levan and Sennen *Truro*
ST MABYN (St Mabena)　*see* Camelside *Truro*
ST MARGARET'S (St Margaret)　*see* Black Mountains Gp *Heref*
ST MARGARETS-AT-CLIFFE (St Margaret of Antioch) w Westcliffe and East Langdon w West Langdon *Cant 7*
P *Abp*　**P-in-c** K S REEVES
ST MARGARET'S-ON-THAMES (All Souls) *Lon 11*　**P** *Bp*
V J M C SELLERS
ST MARTHA-ON-THE-HILL (St Martha)　*see* Shere, Albury and Chilworth *Guildf*
ST MARTIN (St Martin)　*see* Looe and Morval *Truro*
ST MARTIN-IN-MENEAGE (St Martin)　*see* Meneage *Truro*
ST MARTIN-IN-THE-FIELDS *Lon 3*　**P** *Bp*　**V** S M B WELLS
C C V DUCE, H L CHING, J A H EVENS, R A CARTER,
S A HITCHINER
ST MARTIN'S (St Martin)　*see* Is of Scilly *Truro*
ST MARTINS (St Martin) and Weston Rhyn *Lich 18*　**P** *Bp (2 turns), Bp and Lord Trevor (1 turn)*　**V** S J JERMY
ST MARY ABBOTS　*see* Kensington St Mary Abbots *Lon*
ST MARY BOURNE (St Peter)　*see* Hurstbourne Priors, Longparish etc *Win*
ST MARY LE STRAND w St Clement Danes *Lon 3*　**P** *Ld Chan and Burghley Ho Preservation Trust Ltd (alt)*
P-in-c P G BABINGTON　**NSM** C E BRADLEY, J O M CRAIG,
P L HANAWAY, S E LENTON
ST MARY-AT-LATTON Harlow (St Mary the Virgin)
Chelmsf 4　**P** J L H Arkwright Esq　**V** L S HURRY
C B D K JOSS-POTHEN　**NSM** M C R GREEN
ST MARYCHURCH (St Mary the Virgin) *Ex 10*　**P** *D&C*
P-in-c R J CARLTON
ST MARY-IN-THE-MARSH (St Mary the Virgin)　*see* Romney Marsh *Cant*
ST MARYLEBONE (All Saints) *Lon 4*　**P** *Bp*　**V** P B ANTHONY
C M N R BOWIE　**NSM** J BROWNING
ST MARYLEBONE (All Souls)　*see* Langham Place All So *Lon*
ST MARYLEBONE (Annunciation) Bryanston Street *Lon 4*
P *Bp*　**V** L HARVEY
ST MARYLEBONE (St Cyprian) *Lon 4*　**P** *Bp*
Hon C M G FULLER
ST MARYLEBONE (St Mark w St Luke)　*see* Bryanston Square St Mary w St Marylebone St Mark *Lon*
ST MARYLEBONE (St Mark) Hamilton Terrace *Lon 4*　**P** *The Crown*　**V** K M HARRISON
ST MARYLEBONE (St Marylebone) (Holy Trinity) *Lon 4*
P *The Crown*　**R** S J EVANS　**C** J M NOBLE,
K L HACKER HUGHES
ST MARYLEBONE (St Paul) *Lon 4*　**P** *The Crown*
R C A E DOWDING　**C** D L MCDOWELL
ST MARYLEBONE (St Peter)　*see* Langham Place All So *Lon*
ST MARY'S (St Mary)　*see* Is of Scilly *Truro*
ST MARY'S BAY (All Saints)　*see* Romney Marsh *Cant*
ST MAWES (St Mawes)　*see* St Just-in-Roseland and St Mawes *Truro*
ST MAWGAN (St Mawgan)　*see* Lann Pydar *Truro*
ST MAWGAN-IN-MENEAGE (St Mawgan)　*see* Meneage *Truro*
ST MELLION (St Melanus)　*see* Tamar Valley *Truro*
ST MERRYN (St Merryn)　*see* Padstow, St Merryn and St Issey w St Petroc Minor *Truro*
ST MEWAN (St Mewan) w Mevagissey and St Ewe *Truro 7*
P *Bp, DBP, Penrice Ho (St Austell) Ltd, and A M J Galsworthy Esq (jt)*　**R** M L BARRETT
ST MICHAEL PENKEVIL (St Michael) *Truro 5*　**P** *Viscount Falmouth*　**R** vacant
ST MICHAEL ROCK (St Michael)　*see* N Cornwall Cluster *Truro*
ST MICHAELCHURCH (St Michael)　*see* Alfred Jewel *B & W*
ST MICHAELS-ON-WYRE (St Michael)　*see* Garstang St Helen and St Michaels-on-Wyre *Blackb*
ST MINVER (St Menefreda)　*see* N Cornwall Cluster *Truro*
ST NECTAN (St Nectan)　*see* Lostwithiel Parishes *Truro*
ST NEOT (St Neot) and Warleggan *Truro 12*　**P** R G Grylls Esq (2 turns), DBP (1 turn)　**Hon C** P J BIGGS
ST NEOTS (St Mary) Team Ministry *Ely 13*　**P** *Patr Bd*
TR A P HUTCHINSON　**C** H L TAME, W J A H LYON TUPMAN
NSM A M E WILLIAMS
ST NEWLYN EAST (St Newlina)　*see* Newlyn St Newlyn *Truro*

ST NICHOLAS (St Nicholas) *see* Shaldon, Stokeinteignhead, Combeinteignhead etc *Ex*

ST NICHOLAS AT WADE (St Nicholas) *see* Wantsum Gp *Cant*

ST OSWALD IN LEE w Bingfield (St Mary) *Newc 8*   **P** *Bp*
P-in-c S A LUNN

ST OSYTH (St Peter and St Paul) and Great Bentley *Chelmsf 22*   **P** *Bp*   **V** S E A MILES

ST PANCRAS (Holy Cross) (St Jude) (St Peter) *Lon 15*   **P** *Bp*
V C W CAWRSE

ST PANCRAS (Holy Trinity) *see* Kentish Town St Silas and H Trin w St Barn *Lon*

ST PANCRAS (Old Church) *Lon 15*   **P** *Patr Bd*   **TR** J I ELSTON
TV D R P WORTON, M R D THOMAS

ST PANCRAS (St Pancras) (St James) (Christ Church) *Lon 15*   **P** *D&C St Paul's*   **V** A H STEVENS

ST PAUL'S CRAY (St Barnabas) *Roch 16*   **P** *CPAS*
V N G COLEMAN   **Hon C** J E RAWLING

ST PETER in the Isle of Thanet (St Peter the Apostle) *Cant 5*   **P** *Abp*   **V** J DURRANS   **NSM** A B J BATES

ST PETROC MINOR (St Petroc) *see* Padstow, St Merryn and St Issey w St Petroc Minor *Truro*

ST SAMPSON (St Sampson) *Truro 7*   **P** *Bp*   **R** *vacant*

ST STEPHEN IN BRANNEL (not known) *Truro 7*   **P** *Capt J D G Fortescue*   **P-in-c** E J WESTERMANN-CHILDS

ST STEPHENS (St Stephen) *see* Saltash *Truro*

ST STYTHIANS (St Stythian) w Perranarworthal and Gwennap *Truro 1*   **P** *Viscount Falmouth (2 turns), D&C (1 turn)*   **P-in-c** K A F WILSON   **C** R D WALLIS   **NSM** J ROWE

ST TEATH (St Teatha) *see* Camel-Allen *Truro*

ST TUDY (St Tudy) *see* Camelside *Truro*

ST VEEP (St Cyricius) *see* Lostwithiel Parishes *Truro*

ST WENN (St Wenna) and Withiel *Truro 6*   **P** *Bp and DBP*
V *vacant*

ST WEONARDS (St Weonard) *Heref 7*   **P** *Bp, D&C, and MMCET (jt)*   **NSM** F J PHILLIPS

ST WINNOW (St Winnow) *see* Lostwithiel Parishes *Truro*

SAINTS, The, comprising South Elmham and Ilketshall *St E 15*   **P** *Bp (3 turns), Ld Chan (1 turn), and Duke of Norfolk (1 turn)*
P-in-c L J COLLYER

SALCEY Benefice, The, comprising Ashton, Collingtree, Courteenhall, Hartwell, and Roade *Pet 5*   **P** *Ld Chan and Bp (1 turn), N C Phipps Walker Esq and H C Wake Esq (1 turn)*
P-in-c N M DONNELLY

SALCOMBE (Holy Trinity) *see* Malborough, Salcombe and S Huish *Ex*

SALCOMBE REGIS (St Mary and St Peter) *see* Sidmouth, Woolbrook, Salcombe Regis, Sidbury etc *Ex*

SALCOTT VIRLEY (St Mary the Virgin) *see* N Blackwater *Chelmsf*

SALE (St Anne) (St Francis's Church Hall) *Ches 10*   **P** *DBP*
V A C COX   **NSM** D MURRAY

SALE (St Paul) *Ches 10*   **P** *Trustees*   **V** R C MATHEW

SALEBY (St Margaret) *see* Alford Gp *Linc*

SALEHURST (St Mary), Hurst Green and Robertsbridge *Chich 13*   **P** *Bp*   **V** A M HAWKINS

SALESBURY (St Peter) *Blackb 7*   **P** *V Blackb*
NSM S G CHEESMAN

SALFORD (Sacred Trinity) *Man 7*   **P** *Sir Josslyn Gore-Booth Bt*
V A I SALMON   **NSM** R C CRAVEN

SALFORD (St Clement) Ordsall *see* Ordsall and Salford Quays *Man*

SALFORD (St Mary) *see* Chipping Norton *Ox*

SALFORD (St Mary) *see* Cranfield and Hulcote w Salford *St Alb*

SALFORD (St Paul w Christ Church) *Man 7*   **P** *The Crown and Trustees (alt)*   **R** D S C WYATT

SALFORD (St Philip w St Stephen) *Man 7*   **P** *Bp and D&C (jt)*
V G J ROBINSON   **C** C T SAYBURN, H E J STODDART, M J BRINICOMBE, S T WATKINSON

SALFORD All Saints, comprising Lower Kersal, Pendleton and Claremont, and Weaste, Seedley and Langworthy *Man 7*
P *Patr Bd*   **TR** D J A BURTON   **TV** I C J GORTON
C C P HAMILTON

SALFORD PRIORS (St Matthew) *see* Heart of England *Cov*

SALFORDS (Christ the King) *S'wark 24*   **P** *Bp*
P-in-c J M ROSENTHAL   **NSM** D ROSS

SALHOUSE (All Saints) *see* Gt and Lt Plumstead, Rackheath w Salhouse and Witton *Nor*

SALING, GREAT (St James) *see* Stebbing and Lindsell w Gt and Lt Saling *Chelmsf*

SALING, LITTLE (St Peter and St Paul) *as above*

SALISBURY (St Francis) and St Lawrence Stratford sub Castle *Sarum 13*   **P** *Bp (3 turns), D&C (1 turn)*
V J H T DE GARIS   **C** S E WOOD-ROE   **NSM** J M TERRY

SALISBURY (St Mark) and Laverstock *Sarum 13*   **P** *D&C and Bp (alt)*   **V** A M BOUSFIELD

SALISBURY (St Martin) *Sarum 13*   **P** *Bp*   **V** D B FISHER

SALISBURY (St Thomas and St Edmund) *Sarum 13*   **P** *Bp and D&C (alt)*   **R** K J INGLIS   **C** A ALEXANDER
Hon C S F DEACON

SALISBURY PLAIN, comprising Chitterne, Orcheston, Shrewton, and Tilshead *Sarum 14*   **P** *Ld Chan (1 turn), Bp (2 turns), D&C (1 turn)*   **V** E J RANCE   **C** S J M JAVELLE

SALKELD, GREAT (St Cuthbert) *see* Kirkoswald, Renwick w Croglin, Gt Salkeld etc *Carl*

SALLE (St Peter and St Paul) *see* Reepham and Wensum Valley *Nor*

SALT (St James the Great) *see* Mid Trent *Lich*

SALTASH (St Nicholas and St Faith) *Truro 11*   **P** *Patr Bd*
NSM P M SELLIX

SALTBURN-BY-THE-SEA (Emmanuel) *York 16*   **P** *Abp*
V A M F REED

SALTBY (St Peter) *see* High Framland Par *Leic*

SALTDEAN (St Nicholas) *Chich 19*   **P** *Bp*   **V** S J HORTON
NSM K E LAWSON

SALTER STREET (St Patrick) *Birm 2*   **P** *Bp and V Tamworth (jt)*
V D G JONES

SALTERHEBBLE (All Saints) *see* Halifax All SS *Leeds*

SALTERSFORD (St John the Baptist) *see* Rainow w Saltersford and Forest *Ches*

SALTFLEETBY (St Peter) *Linc 15*   **P** *Or Coll Ox, Bp, and MMCET (jt)*   **V** *vacant*

SALTFORD (Blessed Virgin Mary) w Corston and Newton St Loe *B & W 9*   **P** *DBP (2 turns), Duchy of Cornwall (1 turn)*
R D M WILSHERE

SALTHOUSE (St Nicholas) *see* Weybourne Gp *Nor*

SALTLEY (St Saviour) and Washwood Heath *Birm 6*   **P** *Bp and Trustees (jt)*   **V** A THOMPSON

SALTNEY (St Mark) *see* Lache cum Saltney *Ches*

SALTNEY FERRY (St Matthew) *see* Lache cum Saltney *Ches*

SALTON (St John of Beverley) *see* Kirby Misperton w Normanby and Salton *York*

SALTWAY Team, The *see* Droitwich, and Salwarpe and Hindlip w Martin Hussingtree *Worc*

SALTWOOD (St Peter and St Paul) *see* Lympne and Saltwood *Cant*

SALVINGTON (St Peter) *see* Findon Valley *Chich*

SALWARPE (St Michael) *see* Droitwich, and Salwarpe and Hindlip w Martin Hussingtree *Worc*

SALWAY ASH (Holy Trinity) *see* Beaminster Area *Sarum*

SAMBOURNE (Mission Church) *see* Alcester Minster *Cov*

SAMBROOK (St Luke) *see* Cheswardine, Childs Ercall, Hales, Hinstock etc *Lich*

SAMFORD, NORTH *see* Sproughton w Burstall, Copdock w Washbrook etc *St E*

SAMLESBURY (St Leonard the Less) *see* Balderstone, Mellor and Samlesbury *Blackb*

SAMPFORD ARUNDEL (Holy Cross) *see* Wellington and Distr *B & W*

SAMPFORD BRETT (St George) *see* Quantock Towers *B & W*

SAMPFORD COURTENAY (St Andrew) *see* Chagford, Gidleigh, Throwleigh etc *Ex*

SAMPFORD PEVERELL (St John the Baptist), Uplowman, Holcombe Rogus, Hockworthy, Burlescombe and Halberton w Ash Thomas *Ex 7*   **P** *Patr Bd*
TR G H B LEWRY

SAMPFORD SPINEY (St Mary) *see* Yelverton, Meavy, Sheepstor, Walkhampton, Sampford Spiney and Horrabridge *Ex*

SAMPFORD, GREAT (St Michael) *see* Thaxted, The Sampfords, Radwinter and Hempstead *Chelmsf*

SAMPFORD, LITTLE (St Mary) *as above*

SANCREED (St Creden) *Truro 4*   **P** *D&C*   **V** *vacant*

SANCROFT, comprising Fressingfield, Mendham, Metfield, Stradbroke, Weybread, and Withersdale *St E 11*   **P** *Bp, Ch Soc Trust, Em Coll Cam, and SMF (jt)*   **R** S A LOXTON
C V G WILLIAMS   **NSM** D E EKINS-POWELL, P A SCHWIER

SANCTON (All Saints) *York 5*   **P** *Abp*   **V** C R PINCHBECK
C J A KENNY

SAND HILL (Church of the Good Shepherd) *see* Farnborough Gd Shep *Guildf*

SAND HUTTON (St Mary) *see* Harton *York*

SANDAL (St Catherine) *see* Wakefield St Andr and St Mary and Belle Vue *Leeds*

SANDAL MAGNA (St Helen) *Leeds 16*   **P** *Peache Trustees*
V *vacant*

SANDBACH (St Mary) *Ches 11*   **P** *DBP*   **V** B A BOYDE

SANDBACH HEATH (St John the Evangelist) w Hassall Green *Ches 11*   **P** *V Sandbach*   **V** B J SWORD

SANDBANKS (St Nicolas) *see* Canford Cliffs and Sandbanks *Sarum*

SANDCROFT (St Cross) *see* The Saints *St E*

SANDCROFT (St George) *as above*
SANDERSTEAD (All Saints) (St Antony) (St Edmund the King and Martyr) *S'wark 22* **P** *Bp* **P-in-c** M R GREENFIELD **NSM** J C GROOMBRIDGE
SANDERSTEAD (St Mary) *S'wark 22* **P** *Bp* **V** G G COHEN **Hon C** R J WHITELEY
SANDFORD (All Saints) *see* Winscombe and Sandford *B & W*
SANDFORD (St Martin) *see* Wareham *Sarum*
SANDFORD (St Swithin) *see* Crediton, Shobrooke and Sandford etc *Ex*
SANDFORD ORCAS (St Nicholas) *see* Queen Thorne *Sarum*
SANDFORD ST MARTIN (St Martin) *see* Westcote Barton w Steeple Barton, Duns Tew etc *Ox*
SANDFORD-ON-THAMES (St Andrew) *see* Littlemore w Sandford-on-Thames *Ox*
SANDGATE (St Paul) *see* Folkestone Trin *Cant*
SANDHURST (Mission Church) *see* Benenden and Sandhurst *Cant*
SANDHURST (St Lawrence) *see* Twigworth, Down Hatherley, Norton, The Leigh etc *Glouc*
SANDHURST (St Michael and All Angels) *Ox 8* **P** *Bp* **R** J A CASTLE
SANDHURST (St Nicholas) *see* Benenden and Sandhurst *Cant*
SANDHURST, LOWER (St Mary) *see* Sandhurst *Ox*
SANDHUTTON (St Leonard) *see* Thirsk *York*
SANDIACRE (St Giles) *Derby 8* **P** *Ld Chan* **R** O TRELENBERG
SANDIWAY (St John the Evangelist) *Ches 6* **P** *Bp* **V** R E MOCK
SANDLEHEATH (St Aldhelm) *see* Fordingbridge and Hyde and Breamore etc *Win*
SANDON (All Saints) *see* Kingswood *St Alb*
SANDON (All Saints) *see* Mid Trent *Lich*
SANDON (St Andrew) *Chelmsf 9* **P** *Qu Coll Cam* **R** T G A BROWN
SANDOWN (Christ Church) *Portsm 7* **P** *CPAS* **P-in-c** M A WILLIAMS **NSM** T B RICHARDS
SANDOWN, LOWER (St John the Evangelist) *Portsm 7* **P** *Bp* **P-in-c** J HALL **NSM** T B RICHARDS
SANDRIDGE (St Leonard) *St Alb 7* **P** *Earl Spencer* **V** W SELLERS
SANDRINGHAM (St Mary Magdalene) w West Newton and Appleton, Wolferton w Babingley and Flitcham *Nor 15* **P** *The Crown* **R** J B V RIVIERE
SANDS (Church of the Good Shepherd) *see* Seale, Puttenham and Wanborough *Guildf*
SANDS (St Mary and St George) *see* High Wycombe *Ox*
SANDSEND (St Mary) *see* Hinderwell, Roxby and Staithes etc *York*
SANDWELL (St Philip) *see* W Bromwich All SS w St Mary and St Phil *Lich*
SANDWICH (St Clement) and Worth *Cant 9* **P** *Abp and Adn Cant (jt)* **R** J M A ROBERTS **NSM** R A BENDALL
SANDY (St Swithun) *St Alb 10* **P** *Lord Pym* **R** P H DAVIES **C** P R MACAULAY
SANDY LANE (St Mary and St Nicholas) *see* Rowde and Bromham *Sarum*
SANDYLANDS (St John) *Blackb 11* **P** *Bp* **V** L MACLUSKIE
SANKEY, GREAT (St Mary) *see* Warrington W *Liv*
SANTON DOWNHAM (St Mary the Virgin) *see* Lakenheath, Santon Downham and Elveden *St E*
SAPCOTE (All Saints) and Sharnford w Wigston Parva *Leic 10* **P** *Ld Chan and DBP (alt)* **R** *vacant*
SAPEY, LOWER (St Bartholomew) *see* Worcs W Rural *Worc*
SAPEY, UPPER (St Michael) *see* Edvin Loach w Tedstone Delamere etc *Heref*
SAPPERTON (St Kenelm) *see* Kemble, Poole Keynes, Somerford Keynes etc *Glouc*
SAPPERTON (St Nicholas) *see* N Beltisloe Par *Linc*
SARISBURY (St Paul) *Portsm 2* **P** *V Titchfield* **V** A J MATHESON
SARK (St Peter) *Win 14* **P** *Le Seigneur de Sercq* **P-in-c** T R BARKER
SARN (Holy Trinity) *see* Churchstoke w Hyssington and Sarn *Heref*
SARNESFIELD (St Mary) *see* Weobley w Sarnesfield and Norton Canon *Heref*
SARRATT (Holy Cross) and Chipperfield *St Alb 4* **P** *Churchwardens and DBP (jt)* **R** M M DU SAIRE
SATLEY (St Cuthbert), Stanley and Tow Law *Dur 7* **P** *Bp, Ld Chan, and R Brancepeth (by turn)* **P-in-c** J P L WHALLEY
SATTERTHWAITE (All Saints) *see* Hawkshead and Low Wray w Sawrey and Rusland etc *Carl*
SAUGHALL, GREAT (All Saints) *Ches 9* **P** *Bp* **P-in-c** S M MANSFIELD
SAUL (St James the Great) *see* Stroudwater *Glouc*

SAUNDERTON (St Mary and St Nicholas) *see* Risborough *Ox*
SAUNTON (St Anne) *see* Braunton *Ex*
SAUSTHORPE (St Andrew) *see* Bolingbroke Deanery *Linc*
SAVERNAKE FOREST (St Katharine) *see* Savernake *Sarum*
SAVERNAKE, comprising Burbage, Chute w Chute Forest, Collingbourne Ducis and Everleigh, Collingbourne Kingston, East Grafton, Great Bedwyn, Ham, Little Bedwyn, Savernake Forest, Shalbourne, and Tidcombe and Fosbury *Sarum 19* **P** *Patr Bd* **TR** M T MCHUGH **TV** C M HEBER-PERCY, J REID
SAW MILLS (St Mary) *see* Ambergate and Heage *Derby*
SAWBRIDGEWORTH (Great St Mary) *St Alb 15* **P** *Bp* **V** S J VIVIAN **NSM** D HORE
SAWLEY (All Saints) (St Mary) *Derby 8* **P** *D&C Lich* **R** A J STREET **C** E JONES **NSM** S J DENNIS
SAWLEY (St Michael) *see* Fountains Gp *Leeds*
SAWREY (St Peter) *see* Hawkshead and Low Wray w Sawrey and Rusland etc *Carl*
SAWSTON (St Mary) *Ely 5* **P** *SMF* **V** K J WAITE
SAWTRY (All Saints) and Glatton *Ely 15* **P** *Duke of Devonshire* **R** *vacant*
SAWTRY (All Saints), Glatton and Holme w Conington *Ely 15* **P** *Ld Chan (1 turn), Bp and Miss T Belcher (1 turn)* **V** R M DYBALL **C** D L KUTAR
SAXBY (St Helen) *see* Owmby Gp *Linc*
SAXBY ALL SAINTS (All Saints) *Linc 8* **P** *F C H H Barton Esq* **R** D P ROWETT
SAXELBYE (St Peter) *see* Old Dalby, Nether Broughton, Saxelbye etc *Leic*
SAXHAM, GREAT (St Andrew) *see* Barrow *St E*
SAXHAM, LITTLE (St Nicholas) *as above*
SAXILBY Group, The (St Botolph), including Kettlethorpe and Newton-on-Trent *Linc 2* **P** *Bp and DBP (jt)* **OLM** G STEVENS, J A VICKERS
SAXLINGHAM (St Margaret) *see* Stiffkey and Bale *Nor*
SAXLINGHAM NETHERGATE (St Mary) *see* Newton Flotman, Swainsthorpe, Tasburgh, etc *Nor*
SAXMUNDHAM (St John the Baptist) w Kelsale cum Carlton *St E 14* **P** *Patr Bd* **P-in-c** D N PREECE **NSM** N J STUCHFIELD
SAXON SHORE *see* Hunstanton and Saxon Shore *Nor*
SAXON SHORELINE, The, comprising Aldington, Bilsington, Bonnington, Kenardington, Orlestone w Snave, Ruckinge, and Warehorne *Cant 10* **P** *Abp and Ld Chan (alt)* **R** G HALSALL
SAXONWELL, comprising Foston, Long Bennington, Sedgebrook, and West Allington *Linc 22* **P** *Duchy of Lanc (2 turns), Ld Chan (1 turn)* **R** *vacant*
SAXTEAD (All Saints) *see* Framlingham w Saxtead *St E*
SAXTHORPE (St Andrew) *see* Matlaske *Nor*
SAXTON (All Saints) *see* Sherburn in Elmet w Saxton *York*
SAYERS COMMON (Christ Church) *see* Albourne w Sayers Common and Twineham *Chich*
SCACKLETON (St George the Martyr) *see* The Street Par *York*
SCALBY (St Laurence) *York 15* **P** *Abp* **P-in-c** M A HAND
SCALDWELL (St Peter and St Paul) *see* Walgrave w Hannington and Wold and Scaldwell *Pet*
SCALEBY (All Saints) *see* Eden, Gelt and Irthing *Carl*
SCALFORD (St Egelwin) *see* Ironstone Villages *Leic*
SCAMBLESBY (St Martin) *see* Asterby Gp *Linc*
SCAMMONDEN, WEST (St Bartholomew) *see* Barkisland w W Scammonden *Leeds*
SCAMPSTON (St Martin) *see* Buckrose Carrs *York*
SCAMPTON (St John the Baptist) *see* Springline *Linc*
SCARBOROUGH (St Columba) (St James w Holy Trinity) *York 15* **P** *Abp and CPAS (1 turn), Abp (1 turn)* **V** D J BELL **C** F E HILL
SCARBOROUGH (St Luke) *York 15* **P** *Abp* **V** *vacant*
SCARBOROUGH (St Martin) *York 15* **P** *Trustees* **V** D M DIXON
SCARBOROUGH (St Mary) w Christ Church and (Holy Apostles) *York 15* **P** *Abp* **V** R J WALKER **C** H A MADIN, J L MADIN **NSM** A M INGHAM, J C WELLS
SCARBOROUGH (St Saviour w All Saints) *York 15* **P** *Abp* **V** D M DIXON
SCARCLIFFE (St Leonard) *see* Ault Hucknall and Scarcliffe *Derby*
SCARISBRICK (St Mark) (Good Shepherd) *Liv 14* **P** *V Ormskirk* **V** E HEANEY
SCARLE, NORTH (All Saints) *see* Swinderby *Linc*
SCARLE, SOUTH (St Helena) *see* E Trent *S'well*
SCARNING (St Peter and St Paul) *see* Dereham and Distr *Nor*
SCARRINGTON (St John of Beverley) *see* Whatton w Aslockton, Hawksworth, Scarrington etc *S'well*

SCARROWBECK, comprising Alby, Calthorpe, Erpingham, Ingworth, and Thwaite *Nor* 18　**P** *Bp, Lord Walpole, Gt Hosp Nor, and DBP (jt)*　**P-in-c** H D BUTCHER

SCARSDALE, EAST, comprising Pleasley, Shirebrook, Upper Langwith, and Whaley Thorns *Derby* 2　**P** *Patr Bd*　**TR** J E DRAYCOTT　**TV** K T BRADLEY　**C** E LAUNDERS-BROWN　**OLM** J A PALMER

SCARTHO (St Giles) St Matthew *Linc* 3　**P** *Jes Coll Ox*　**R** S F CLEATON

SCAWBY (St Hybald), Redbourne and Hibaldstow *Linc* 8　**P** T M S Nelthorpe Esq (2 turns), Bp (1 turn), and Duke of St Alb (1 turn)　**P-in-c** D J EAMES

SCAWTHORPE (St Luke) *see* Doncaster St Leon and St Jude *Sheff*

SCAWTON (St Mary) *see* Upper Ryedale *York*

SCAYNES HILL (St Augustine) *Chich* 8　**P** *Bp*　**V** B A MILES

SCHOLES (St Philip and St James) *see* Hartshead, Hightown, Robertstown and Scholes *Leeds*

SCHOLES (St Philip) *see* Elmete Trin *Leeds*

SCHORNE, comprising Dunton, Granborough, Hardwick, Hoggeston, North Marston, Oving w Pitchcott, Quainton, Waddesdon, Westcott, Over Winchendon and Fleet Marston, and Whitchurch w Creslow *Ox* 13　**P** *Patr Bd (2 turns), Ld Chan (1 turn)*　**TR** D J MEAKIN　**TV** C S E WAINMAN, P ELSMORE　**NSM** S T FLASHMAN

SCISSETT (St Augustine) *see* High Hoyland, Scissett and Clayton W *Leeds*

SCOFTON (St John the Evangelist) *see* The Idle and Sands *S'well*

SCOLE (St Andrew) *see* Redenhall w Scole *Nor*

SCOPWICK (Holy Cross) *see* Digby Gp *Linc*

SCORBOROUGH (St Leonard) *see* Lockington and Lund and Scorborough w Leconfield *York*

SCORTON (St Peter) and Barnacre All Saints and Calder Vale St John the Evangelist *Blackb* 9　**P** *Bp, V Lanc St Mary w St Jo and St Anne, and Mrs V O Shepherd-Cross (jt)*　**V** A M MÜLLER

SCOTBY (All Saints) and Cotehill w Cumwhinton *Carl* 2　**P** *Trustees (2 turns), The Crown (1 turn)*　**V** I S LAWRENCE

SCOTFORTH (St Paul) *Blackb* 11　**P** *The Rt Revd J Nicholls*　**V** R B AECHTNER

SCOTHERN (St Germain) *see* Welton and Dunholme w Scothern *Linc*

SCOTSWOOD (St Margaret) *see* Benwell and Scotswood *Newc*

SCOTT WILLOUGHBY (St Andrew) *see* S Lafford *Linc*

SCOTTER (St Peter) *see* Messingham w E Butterwick, Scotter w E Ferry and Scotton w Northorpe *Linc*

SCOTTON (St Genewys) *as above*

SCOTTON (St Thomas) *see* Walkingham Hill *Leeds*

SCOTTOW (All Saints) *Nor* 18　**P** *Bp*　**V** *vacant*

SCOULTON (Holy Trinity) *see* High Oak, Hingham and Scoulton w Wood Rising *Nor*

SCRAPTOFT (All Saints) *Leic* 1　**P** *Bp, Dr M J A Sharp, and DBP (jt)*　**V** M J COURT

SCRAYINGHAM (St Peter and St Paul) *see* Stamford Bridge Gp *York*

SCREDINGTON (St Andrew) *see* Heckington and Helpringham Gp *Linc*

SCREMBY (St Peter and St Paul) *see* Bolingbroke Deanery *Linc*

SCREMERSTON (St Peter), Spittal and Tweedmouth *Newc* 12　**P** *Bp, Mercers' Co and D&C Dur (jt)*　**V** E R A HUDSON

SCREVETON (St Wilfrid) *see* Car Colston w Screveton *S'well*

SCRIVELSBY (St Benedict) *see* Fen and Hill Gp *Linc*

SCROOBY (St Wilfrid) *see* Blyth and Scrooby w Ranskill *S'well*

SCROPTON (St Paul) *see* S Dales *Derby*

SCRUTON (St Radegund) *see* Lower Swale *Leeds*

SCULCOATES (St Mary) *see* Hull St Mary Sculcoates *York*

SCULCOATES (St Paul) (St Stephen) *York* 14　**P** *Abp and V Hull H Trin (1 turn), Ld Chan (1 turn)*　**V** P LAMB

SCULTHORPE (St Mary and All Saints) *see* N and S Creake w Waterden, Syderstone etc *Nor*

SCUNTHORPE (All Saints) *see* Brumby *Linc*

SCUNTHORPE (The Resurrection) *see* Trentside E *Linc*

SEA MILLS (St Edyth) *Bris* 2　**P** *Bp*　**V** J E MONAGHAN

SEA PALLING (St Margaret) *see* Bacton, Happisburgh, Hempstead w Eccles etc *Nor*

SEABOROUGH (St John) *see* Beaminster Area *Sarum*

SEABROOK (Mission Hall) *see* Cheriton w Newington *Cant*

SEACOMBE (St Paul) w Poulton *Ches* 7　**P** *Bp and trustees (jt)*　**V** P T COOPER　**C** E WHITE　**NSM** C M TURNER

SEACROFT (St James) (Church of the Ascension) (St Richard) (St Luke) (St Paul) *Leeds* 13　**P** *DBF*　**TV** D J MUGHAL

SEAFORD (St Leonard) w Sutton *Chich* 21　**P** *Ld Chan*　**V** J W HOLLINGSWORTH　**C** D A J LEE-PHILPOT

SEAGRAVE (All Saints) *see* Sileby, Cossington and Seagrave *Leic*

SEAGRY (St Mary the Virgin) *see* Draycot Bris

SEAHAM (St Mary the Virgin) and Dawdon *Dur* 10　**P** *Bp*　**V** P J A KENNEDY

SEAHAM HARBOUR (St John) *see* Seaham and Dawdon *Dur*

SEAHAM, NEW (Christ Church) *Dur* 10　**P** *Bp*　**V** P T HARRISON

SEAL (St Peter and St Paul) *Roch* 9　**P** *DBP*　**V** J A LE BAS

SEAL CHART (St Lawrence) w Underriver *Roch* 9　**P** *Bp*　**V** S L WILLOUGHBY

SEALE (St Lawrence), Puttenham and Wanborough *Guildf* 4　**P** *Adn Surrey, C R I Perkins Esq, and Ld Chan (by turn)*　**R** S B THATCHER　**C** P E ROCHE

SEALE (St Peter) (St Matthew) and Lullington w Coton in the Elms *Derby* 7　**P** *Bp, R D Nielson Esq, and C W Worthington Esq (jt)*　**OLM** C A BUCKLEY

SEAMER (St Martin), East Ayton and Cayton *York* 15　**P** *Abp*　**V** A J MORELAND　**NSM** J A DEAN

SEAMER IN CLEVELAND (St Martin) *see* Stokesley w Seamer *York*

SEARBY (St Nicholas) *see* Caistor *Linc*

SEASALTER (St Alphege) *see* Whitstable *Cant*

SEASCALE (St Cuthbert) *see* Seatallan *Carl*

SEATALLAN, comprising Beckermet St John, Beckermet w Ponsonby, Gosforth and Wasdale, and Seascale *Carl* 5　**P** *Bp, Adn W Cumberland, the Hon J N Lowther, P Stanley Esq, V St Bees, and DBP (jt)*　**R** J G RILEY, P J DORLING

SEATHWAITE (Holy Trinity) *see* Broughton and Duddon *Carl*

SEATON (All Hallows) *see* Lyddington, Bisbrooke, Caldecott, Glaston etc *Pet*

SEATON (St Gregory) and Beer *Ex* 4　**P** *Lord Clinton and D&C (jt)*　**NSM** A FINCH, S J HITCHCOCK

SEATON (St Paul) *see* Camerton, Seaton and W Seaton *Carl*

SEATON CAREW (Holy Trinity) *Dur* 6　**P** *Bp*　**P-in-c** P M BULLOCK

SEATON HIRST (St John) (St Andrew) *Newc* 11　**P** *Bp*　**P-in-c** D J B TWOMEY　**C** J R SWINHOE

SEATON ROSS (St Edmund) *see* Holme and Seaton Ross Gp *York*

SEATON SLUICE (St Paul) *see* Delaval *Newc*

SEATON, WEST (Holy Trinity) *see* Camerton, Seaton and W Seaton *Carl*

SEAVIEW (St Peter), St Helens, Brading and Yaverland *Portsm* 7　**P** *Bp and Trin Coll Cam (jt)*　**R** A R MORLEY

SEAVINGTON (St Michael and St Mary) *see* S Petherton w The Seavingtons and The Lambrooks *B & W*

SEBERGHAM (St Mary) *see* Caldbeck, Castle Sowerby and Sebergham *Carl*

SECKINGTON (All Saints) *see* All So N Warks *Birm*

SEDBERGH (St Andrew) *see* Western Dales *Carl*

SEDGEBERROW (St Mary the Virgin) *see* Bengeworth and Hampton etc *Worc*

SEDGEBROOK (St Lawrence) *see* Saxonwell *Linc*

SEDGEFIELD (St Edmund) *see* Upper Skerne *Dur*

SEDGEFORD (St Mary) *see* Docking, The Birchams, Fring etc *Nor*

SEDGEHILL (St Katherine) *see* St Bartholomew *Sarum*

SEDGLEY (All Saints) *see* Gornal and Sedgley *Worc*

SEDGLEY (St Mary the Virgin) *Worc* 5　**P** *Bp and V Sedgley All SS (jt)*　**V** E J STANFORD　**NSM** T WESTWOOD

SEDLESCOMBE (St John the Baptist) w Whatlington *Chich* 12　**P** *Ld Chan and Bp (alt)*　**P-in-c** K A MEPHAM

SEEND (Holy Cross) *see* Wellsprings *Sarum*

SEER GREEN (Holy Trinity) *see* Chalfont St Giles, Seer Green and Jordans *Ox*

SEETHING (St Margaret) *see* Brooke, Kirstead, Mundham w Seething and Thwaite *Nor*

SEFTON PARK (Christ Church) *see* Toxteth Park Ch Ch and St Mich w St Andr *Liv*

SEGHILL (Holy Trinity) *Newc* 1　**P** *The Crown*　**C** D M BELL

SEIGHFORD (St Chad) *see* Chebsey, Creswell, Ellenhall, Ranton etc *Lich*

SELATTYN (St Mary) and Hengoed w Gobowen *Lich* 18　**P** *Bp and Mrs A F Hamilton-Hill (jt)*　**V** S J NICHOLSON

SELBORNE (St Mary) *see* Northanger *Win*

SELBY (St James the Apostle) *York* 4　**P** *Simeon's Trustees*　**V** C J REID　**Hon C** D M REID

SELBY ABBEY (St Mary and St Germain) (St Richard) *York* 4　**P** *Abp*　**V** J C WEETMAN　**C** D J THOMAS　**NSM** J S WATSON, N B WOODHALL

SELHAM (St James) *see* Easebourne, Lodsworth and Selham *Chich*

SELLACK (St Tysilio) *see* StowCaple *Heref*

SELLINDGE (St Mary the Virgin) *see* Stour Downs *Cant*

SELLING (St Mary the Virgin) *see* Shepherds Lees *Cant*

SELLY OAK (St Mary) *Birm 3* **P** *Bp* **V** H S WHITE **NSM** D J PARKER, J M ADAMS

SELLY PARK (Christ Church) *Birm 2* **P** *Trustees* **P-in-c** B C GREEN

SELLY PARK (St Stephen) (St Wulstan) *Birm 2* **P** *Trustees* **V** C B HOBBS **C** A P MARTIN, B T WILLIAMS

SELMESTON (St Mary) *see* Arlington, Berwick, Selmeston w Alciston etc *Chich*

SELSDON (St Francis) Conventional District *S'wark 19* **Min** P C WYATT

SELSDON (St John) (St Francis) *S'wark 19* **P** *Bp* **R** Y FRANCIS

SELSEY (St Peter) *Chich 2* **P** *Bp* **R** A E WILKES

SELSIDE (St Thomas) *see* Beacon TM *Carl*

SELSLEY (All Saints) *see* Stroudwater *Glouc*

SELSTON (St Helen) *S'well 4* **P** *Wright Trustees* **V** M F SHOULER **C** L V GORDON **NSM** A DEMPSTER

SELWORTHY (All Saints) *see* Porlock and Porlock Weir w Stoke Pero etc *B & W*

SELWORTHY (Lynch Chapel) *as above*

SEMER (All Saints) *see* Bildeston w Wattisham and Lindsey etc *St E*

SEMINGTON (St George) *see* Canalside Benefice *Sarum*

SEMLEY (St Leonard) *see* St Bartholomew *Sarum*

SEMPRINGHAM (St Andrew) *see* Billingborough Gp *Linc*

SEND (St Mary the Virgin) *Guildf 12* **P** *Bp* **P-in-c** A J SHUTT

SENNEN (St Sennen) *see* St Buryan, St Levan and Sennen *Truro*

SENNICOTTS (St Mary) *see* Funtington and W Stoke w Sennicotts *Chich*

SESSAY (St Cuthbert) *York 18* **P** *Viscountess Downe* **P-in-c** D J BIGGS **NSM** P PERCY

SETCHEY (St Mary) *see* Middlewinch *Nor*

SETMURTHY (St Barnabas) *see* Binsey *Carl*

SETTLE (Holy Ascension) *Leeds 17* **P** *Trustees* **P-in-c** J M CLARKSON **C** S C DAWSON

SETTRINGTON (All Saints) *see* W Buckrose *York*

SEVEN SAINTS *see* New Bury w Gt Lever *Man*

SEVEN SOWERS *see* Beercrocombe w Curry Mallet, Hatch Beauchamp etc *B & W*

SEVEN TOWERS *see* Twigworth, Down Hatherley, Norton, The Leigh etc *Glouc*

SEVENHAMPTON (St Andrew) w Charlton Abbots, Hawling and Whittington, Dowdeswell and Andoversford w The Shiptons and Cold Salperton, and Withington *Glouc 8* **P** *Bp, MMCET, T W Bailey Esq, E M Bailey Esq, and Mrs J A Stringer (1 turn); Bp, MMCET, and Mrs L E Evans (1 turn)* **R** C A RANDALL

SEVENHAMPTON (St James) *see* Highworth w Sevenhampton and Inglesham etc *Bris*

SEVENOAKS (St John the Baptist) *Roch 9* **P** *Guild of All So* **V** R D E JONES

SEVENOAKS (St Luke) *see* W Sevenoaks *Roch*

SEVENOAKS (St Nicholas) *Roch 9* **P** *Trustees* **R** A M MACLEAY **C** J R READ, M A TAYLOR, N E ROSS **Hon C** N N HENSHAW

SEVENOAKS WEALD (St George) *Roch 9* **P** R *Sevenoaks* **V** A H CARR

SEVENOAKS, WEST Team Ministry, The, including Kippington and Riverhead w Dunton Green *Roch 9* **P** *Patr Bd* **TR** M S BRIDGEN **TV** A C BOURNE, A D FINN **NSM** L LEITHEAD, S OSEI-MENSAH

SEVERN STOKE (St Dennis) *see* Kempsey and Severn Stoke w Croome d'Abitot *Worc*

SEVERNSIDE, NORTH, comprising Alveston, Elberton, Littleton-on-Severn, and Olveston w Aust *Bris 2* **P** *Bp and D&C (jt)* **V** D S MOSS **Hon C** S J ORAM **NSM** D H BONE **OLM** A LLOYD

SEVERNSIDE, SOUTH, comprising Almondsbury, Compton Greenfield, and Pilning *Bris 2* **P** *Bp and D&C (jt)* **V** P W ROWE **Hon C** P A VAN ROSSUM **NSM** D H BONE **OLM** A LLOYD

SEVINGTON (St Mary) *see* Ashford Town *Cant*

SEWARDS END (St James) *see* Saffron Walden and Villages *Chelmsf*

SEWERBY (St John) *see* Bridlington H Trin and Sewerby w Marton *York*

SEWSTERN (Holy Trinity) *see* S Framland *Leic*

SHABBINGTON (St Mary Magdalene) *see* Worminghall w Ickford, Oakley and Shabbington *Ox*

SHACKERSTONE (St Peter) *see* Bosworth *Leic*

SHACKLEFORD (St Nicholas) and Peper Harow *Guildf 4* **P** *Bp* **R** H T MOORE **NSM** D J ORME

SHADFORTH (St Cuthbert) *see* Dur St Giles, Shadforth and Sherburn *Dur*

SHADINGFIELD (St John the Baptist) *see* Hundred River and Wainford *St E*

SHADOXHURST (St Peter and St Paul) *see* Ashford Town *Cant*

SHADWELL (St Paul) *see* Moor Allerton and Shadwell *Leeds*

SHADWELL (St Paul) w Ratcliffe St James *Lon 7* **P** *Bp* **R** P R WILLIAMS **C** C I ROGERS, P COOK

SHAFTESBURY (St James) (St Peter) *Sarum 5* **P** *Patr Bd* **TV** P R RINK

SHALBOURNE (St Michael and All Angels) *see* Savernake *Sarum*

SHALDEN (St Peter and St Paul) *see* Bentworth, Lasham, Medstead and Shalden *Win*

SHALDON (St Nicholas) (St Peter), Stokeinteignhead, Combeinteignhead and Haccombe *Ex 8* **P** *SMF and Col G P Arnold (jt)* **R** vacant

SHALFLEET (St Michael the Archangel) *see* W Wight *Portsm*

SHALFORD (St Andrew) *see* Finchingfield and Cornish Hall End etc *Chelmsf*

SHALFORD (St Mary the Virgin) *Guildf 5* **P** *Ld Chan* **V** S J LLOYD

SHALSTONE (St Edward the Confessor) *see* W Buckingham *Ox*

SHAMLEY GREEN (Christ Church) *Guildf 2* **P** *Bp* **V** S J DAVIES

SHANGTON (St Nicholas) *see* The Langtons and Shangton *Leic*

SHANKLIN (St Blasius) *Portsm 7* **P** *Bp* **P-in-c** J HALL

SHANKLIN (St Paul) *see* Gatten St Paul *Portsm*

SHANKLIN (St Saviour on the Cliff) *Portsm 7* **P** *Bp* **V** vacant

SHAP (St Michael) *see* High Westmorland *Carl*

SHAPWICK (St Bartholomew) *see* Bridge Par *Sarum*

SHAPWICK (The Blessed Virgin Mary) *see* Polden Wheel *B & W*

SHARD END (All Saints) *Birm 5* **P** *Keble Coll Ox* **V** A J CLUCAS

SHARDLOW (St James) *see* Aston on Trent, Elvaston, Weston on Trent etc *Derby*

SHARESHILL (St Luke and St Mary the Virgin) *see* Essington, Featherstone and Shareshill *Lich*

SHARLSTON (St Luke) *Leeds 16* **P** *Bp* **V** D C TEASDEL

SHARNBROOK (St Peter), Felmersham and Knotting w Souldrop *St Alb 13* **P** *Bp* **R** P DI LEO

SHARNFORD (St Helen) *see* Sapcote and Sharnford w Wigston Parva *Leic*

SHAROW (St John the Evangelist) *see* Ripon Cathl Benefice *Leeds*

SHARPNESS (St Andrew), Purton, Brookend and Slimbridge *Glouc 5* **P** *Magd Coll Ox and Bp (alt)* **R** W J BOON **NSM** G M TUCKER

SHARRINGTON (All Saints) *see* Stiffkey and Bale *Nor*

SHAUGH PRIOR (St Edward) *see* Bickleigh and Shaugh Prior *Ex*

SHAVINGTON (St Mark) *see* Weston *Ches*

SHAW (Christchurch) *see* Atworth w Shaw and Whitley *Sarum*

SHAW (Holy Trinity) *Man 5* **P** *R Prestwich St Mary* **V** K H CUNLIFFE **C** D MORRIS, P D PRITCHARD **NSM** M C SANDERSON

SHAW (Holy Trinity) *see* W Swindon and Lydiard Tregoze *Bris*

SHAW (St Mary) cum Donnington *Ox 6* **P** *DBP* **R** vacant

SHAWBURY (St Mary the Virgin) *Lich 21* **P** *C C Corbet Esq* **V** R J CRESSWELL

SHAWELL (All Saints) *see* Avon-Swift *Leic*

SHEARSBY (St Mary Magdalene) *see* Hexagon *Leic*

SHEBBEAR (St Michael), Buckland Filleigh, Sheepwash, Langtree, Newton St Petrock, Petrockstowe, Petersmarland, Merton and Huish *Ex 18* **P** *Ld Chan (1 turn), Patr Bd (2 turns)* **TR** M J WARREN **TV** S E METZ

SHEDFIELD (St John the Baptist) and Wickham *Portsm 1* **P** *DBP and Sir Richard Rashleigh Bt (jt)* **R** P J ISAAC **C** R M HOWLETT-SHIPLEY **Hon C** J MONTAGUE

SHEEN (St Luke) *see* Longnor, Quarnford, Sheen etc *Lich*

SHEEN, EAST (All Saints) *see* Mortlake w E Sheen *S'wark*

SHEEN, EAST (Christ Church) *as above*

SHEEPSTOR (St Leonard) *see* Yelverton, Meavy, Sheepstor, Walkhampton, Sampford Spiney and Horrabridge *Ex*

SHEEPWASH (St Lawrence) *see* Shebbear, Buckland Filleigh, Sheepwash etc *Ex*

SHEEPY (All Saints), including including Orton-on-the-Hill, Ratcliffe Culey, Shenton, Sibson, and Twycross *Leic 10* **P** *Ld*

Chan, Pemb Coll Ox, and MMCET (by turn)
R J G HARGREAVES
SHEERING (St Mary the Virgin)   *see* Hatfield Heath and
Sheering *Chelmsf*
SHEERNESS (Holy Trinity w St Paul)   *see* W Sheppey *Cant*
SHEERWATER (St Michael and All Angels)   *see* Woodham
Guildf
SHEET (St Mary Magdalen) *Portsm 4*   **P** *Bp*
NSM A J MARSH, P W MICKLETHWAITE
SHEFFIELD (St Aidan w St Luke)   *see* Sheff Manor *Sheff*
SHEFFIELD (St Andrew)   *see* Psalter Lane St Andr *Sheff*
SHEFFIELD (St Bartholomew)   *see* Sheffield Vine *Sheff*
SHEFFIELD (St Catherine of Siena) Richmond Road *Sheff 1*
P *The Crown*   **V** P A KNOWLES
SHEFFIELD (St Cuthbert) *Sheff 3*   **P** *Ch Burgesses*
C P J SALMON
SHEFFIELD (St John the Evangelist) *Sheff 1*   **P** *Ch Burgesses*
P-in-c D D EASTWOOD
SHEFFIELD (St Leonard) Norwood *Sheff 3*   **P** *Bp*
P-in-c K RYDER-WEST   **C** A T POULTNEY   **NSM** J H DALEY
SHEFFIELD (St Mark) Broomhill *Sheff 4*   **P** *Ch Burgesses*
V S HAMMERSLEY   **C** C E THOMSON, E G KEITH
NSM S E RUSH
SHEFFIELD (St Mary) Bramall Lane *Sheff 2*   **P** *Ch Burgesses*
and Dean (alt)   **V** C L DAWSON   **NSM** K E CRIBB, L M N HALL
SHEFFIELD (St Matthew) Carver Street *Sheff 2*   **P** *Bp and*
Sheff Ch Burgess Trust (jt)   **V** G L NAYLOR   **Hon C** A WATSON
SHEFFIELD (St Oswald) St Peter *Sheff 2*   **P** *Ch Burgesses*
V A NASCIMENTO DE JESUS COOK
SHEFFIELD (St Paul) Wordsworth Avenue *Sheff 3*   **P** *DBP*
P-in-c A T POULTNEY   **C** C E WELCH
SHEFFIELD MANOR (St Aidan w St Luke) (St Swithun)
(William Temple) *Sheff 1*   **P** *Patr Bd*   **NSM** K COLLEY,
S BATTEN
SHEFFIELD PARK (St John the Evangelist)   *see* Sheff St Jo *Sheff*
SHEFFIELD St Cecilia Parson Cross *Sheff 3*   **P** *Bp*
V K RYDER-WEST   **C** A T POULTNEY
SHEFFIELD The Vine, comprising Netherthorpe and Langsett
Sheff 4   **P** *Ch Burgesses and Ch Patr Trust (jt)*   **V** W J BRIGGS
C A M S HOLE
SHEFFORD (St Michael)   *see* Meppershall and Shefford *St Alb*
SHEFFORD, GREAT (St Mary)   *see* W Downland *Ox*
SHEINTON (St Peter and St Paul)   *see* Wenlock *Heref*
SHELDON (St Giles) and Tile Cross *Birm 5*   **P** *Bp and K E*
Wingfield Digby Esq (jt)   **V** A E LAVIN   **C** M J HARRIS
SHELDON (St James the Greater)   *see* Broadhembury,
Dunkeswell, Luppitt, Plymtree, Sheldon, and Upottery *Ex*
SHELDON (St John)   *see* Shirley St Jo *S'wark*
SHELDON (St Michael and All Angels)   *see* Bakewell, Ashford
w Sheldon and Rowsley *Derby*
SHELDWICH (St James)   *see* Shepherds Lees *Cant*
SHELF (St Michael and All Angels) w Buttershaw St Aidan
Leeds 3   **P** *Bp*   **TV** A J GREIFF   **C** J L TRENHOLME
SHELFANGER (All Saints)   *see* Diss *Nor*
SHELFIELD (St Mark) and High Heath *Lich 24*   **P** *R Walsall*
V *vacant*
SHELFORD (St Peter and St Paul)   *see* Radcliffe-on-Trent and
Shelford *S'well*
SHELFORD, GREAT (St Mary) *Ely 5*   **P** *Bp*   **V** S J TALBOTT
SHELFORD, LITTLE (All Saints) *Ely 5*   **P** *Bp*   **R** S J SCOTT
C E J G KEENE
SHELLAND (King Charles the Martyr)   *see* Combs and
Finborough *St E*
SHELLEY (All Saints)   *see* Hadleigh, Layham and Shelley *St E*
SHELLEY (Emmanuel)   *see* Kirkburton and Shelley *Leeds*
SHELLEY (St Peter)   *see* Chipping Ongar w Shelley etc
Chelmsf
SHELLINGFORD (St Faith)   *see* Uffington, Shellingford,
Woolstone and Baulking *Ox*
SHELROCK   *see* Gt and Lt Ellingham, Rockland and
Shropham etc *Nor*
SHELSLEY BEAUCHAMP (All Saints)   *see* Worcs W Rural *Worc*
SHELSLEY WALSH (St Andrew)   *as above*
SHELSWELL, comprising Cottisford and Hardwick-cum-
Tusmore, Finmere, Fringford, Hethe, Mixbury, Newton
Purcell w Shelswell, Stoke Lyne, and Stratton Audley and
Godington *Ox 21*   **P** *Ld Chan (1 turn) and Ch Ch Ox, CCC*
Ox, Baroness von Maltzahn, and R J Vallings Esq (1 turn)
R A E GOODALL   **C** Y B MULLINS
SHELTON (Christ Church) and Oxon *Lich 19*   **P** *V*
Shrewsbury St Chad w St Mary   **V** C GOMPERTZ
SHELTON (St Mark)   *see* Hanley H Ev *Lich*
SHELTON (St Mary and All Saints) *S'well 3*   **P** *Bp*
P-in-c E I MURRAY
SHELTON (St Mary)   *see* Hempnall *Nor*
SHELTON (St Mary)   *see* The Stodden Churches *St Alb*

SHELVE (All Saints)   *see* Minsterley, Habberley and Hope w
Shelve *Heref*
SHENFIELD (St Mary the Virgin) *Chelmsf 8*   **P** *Personal Reps*
R H Courage   **P-in-c** C J MANN
SHENINGTON (Holy Trinity)   *see* Ironstone *Ox*
SHENLEY (St Mary)   *see* Watling Valley *Ox*
SHENLEY GREEN (St David) *Birm 2*   **P** *Bp*   **V** *vacant*
SHENSTONE (St John the Baptist) and Stonnall *Lich 1*
P *MMCET*   **V** E A CHAMBERLAIN   **C** G M WIGLEY
SHENTON (St John the Evangelist)   *see* Sheepy *Leic*
SHEPHERD'S BUSH (St Luke) Uxbridge Road   *see*
Hammersmith St Luke *Lon*
SHEPHERD'S BUSH (St Stephen) (St Thomas) *Lon 9*   **P** *Bp*
V D ADIDE   **C** P J HOYLE   **NSM** C S FREEMAN
SHEPHERDS LEES, comprising Badlesmere w Leaveland,
Selling, and Sheldwich *Cant 14*   **P** *Abp and D&C (jt)*
P-in-c P J NEWELL
SHEPLEY (St Paul)   *see* Cumberworth, Denby, Denby Dale etc
Leeds
SHEPPERDINE (Chapel)   *see* Thornbury and Oldbury-on-
Severn w Shepperdine *Glouc*
SHEPPERTON (St Nicholas) *Lon 13*   **P** *Bp*   **R** C GEORGE
SHEPPEY, WEST, comprising Halfway, Minster in Sheppey,
Queenborough, and Sheerness *Cant 15*   **P** *Abp and Ch Patr*
Trust (jt)   **P-in-c** P A KITE   **C** J M MCLAREN, P A RUSH
SHEPRETH (All Saints)   *see* Fowlmere, Foxton, Shepreth and
Thriplow *Ely*
SHEPSHED (St Botolph) and Oaks in Charnwood *Leic 6*
P *DBP and Lord Crawshaw (jt)*   **V** L A HUMPHREYS
NSM J A BIRD
SHEPTON BEAUCHAMP (St Michael)   *see* Winsmoor *B & W*
SHEPTON MALLET (St Peter and St Paul) w Doulting
B & W 7   **P** *Duchy of Cornwall and Bp (alt)*
R J HUNTER DUNN
SHEPTON MONTAGUE (St Peter)   *see* Bruton, Brewham,
Pitcombe and Shepton Montague *B & W*
SHERBORNE (Abbey Church of St Mary) (All Souls)
(St Paul) w Castleton, Lillington and Longburton
Sarum 3   **P** *Patr Bd*   **TR** M P LEE   **TV** J M CRAW,
L A MCCREADIE   **C** R C J R MARTIN
SHERBORNE (St Mary Magdalene), Windrush, the
Barringtons and Aldsworth *Glouc 8*   **P** *C T R Wingfield*
Esq, Ch Ch Ox, and DBP (by turn)   **P-in-c** G G MOATE
SHERBORNES (St Andrew) (Vyne Chapel) w Pamber, The
Win 4   **P** *Bp and Qu Coll Ox (jt)*   **R** D R NEWMAN
SHERBOURNE (All Saints)   *see* Barford w Wasperton and
Sherbourne *Cov*
SHERBURN (St Hilda)   *see* Buckrose Carrs *York*
SHERBURN (St Mary)   *see* Dur St Giles, Shadforth and
Sherburn *Dur*
SHERBURN IN ELMET (All Saints) w Saxton *York 4*   **P** *Abp*
V C WILTON   **C** P G GRAYSON   **NSM** C COMER-STONE,
W L J PLANT
SHERE (St James), Albury and Chilworth *Guildf 2*   **P** *Bp,*
Mrs H Bray, Duke of Northumberland, W F P Hugonin Esq, and
the Hon M W Ridley (jt)   **R** T D HEANEY   **C** A M PEARSON,
M L CURRIER   **NSM** S F HUTTON   **OLM** D I OAKDEN
SHEREFORD (St Nicholas)   *see* Upper Wensum Village Gp *Nor*
SHERFIELD ENGLISH (St Leonard)   *see* E w W Wellow and
Sherfield English *Win*
SHERFIELD-ON-LODDON (St Leonard) and Stratfield Saye
w Hartley Wespall w Stratfield Turgis and Bramley *Win 5*
P *Bp, Duke of Wellington, D&C Windsor, and Qu Coll Ox (jt)*
NSM K WEST
SHERFORD (St Martin)   *see* Stokenham, Slapton, Charleton w
Buckland etc *Ex*
SHERIFF HUTTON (St Helen and the Holy Cross)   *see* Forest of
Galtres *York*
SHERIFFHALES (St Mary)   *see* Shifnal, Sheriffhales and Tong
Lich
SHERINGHAM (St Peter) *Nor 20*   **P** *Bp*   **V** C J HEYCOCKS
SHERINGHAM, UPPER (All Saints)   *see* Weybourne Gp *Nor*
SHERINGTON (St Laud) w Chicheley, North Crawley,
Astwood and Hardmead *Ox 16*   **P** *Bp (2 turns), MMCET (1*
turn), and Major J G B Chester (1 turn)   **P-in-c** C P MANSFIELD
SHERMANBURY (St Giles)   *see* Henfield w Shermanbury and
Woodmancote *Chich*
SHERNBOURNE (St Peter and St Paul)   *see* Dersingham,
Anmer, Ingoldisthorpe etc *Nor*
SHERRARDS GREEN (St Mary the Virgin)   *see* Malvern Chase
Worc
SHERRINGTON (St Cosmo and St Damian)   *see* Upper Wylye
Valley *Sarum*
SHERSTON MAGNA (Holy Cross)   *see* Gauzebrook *Bris*
SHERWOOD (St Martin) *S'well 8*   **P** *Bp*   **V** B I BAGULEY
C S M PENDENQUE   **NSM** D M BAGULEY

SHERWOOD PARK (St Philip) *see* Tunbridge Wells St Phil *Roch*

SHEVINGTON (St Anne) *Blackb 4* **P** *R Standish* **V** A BROWN **C** J BROWN

SHEVIOCK (Blessed Virgin Mary) *see* St Germans w Antony and Sheviock *Truro*

SHIELDS, SOUTH (St Simon) *see* Jarrow and Simonside *Dur*

SHIFFORD (St Mary) *see* Bampton w Clanfield *Ox*

SHIFNAL (St Andrew), Sheriffhales and Tong *Lich 15* **P** R I *Legge Esq and Bp (jt)* **V** C D C THORPE **OLM** M W SHAW

SHILBOTTLE (St James) *see* Warkworth, Acklington and Shilbottle *Newc*

SHILDON (St John) *Dur 3* **P** *Bp* **P-in-c** C HARRIS **Hon C** P ROBSON **NSM** F COOPER

SHILL VALLEY and Broadshire, comprising Alvescot, Black Bourton, Broadwell w Kelmscott, Broughton Poggs w Filkins, Holwell, Kencot, Langford, Little Faringdon, Shilton, and Westwell *Ox 28* **P** *J Heyworth Esq, Mrs P Allen, and Ch Ch Ox (1 turn), Ch Soc Tr, F R Goodenough Esq, and D F Goodenough Esq (1 turn)* **R** H C MACINNES **C** M R HODSON

SHILLING OKEFORD (Holy Rood) *see* Okeford *Sarum*

SHILLINGFORD (St George) *see* Alphington, Shillingford St George and Ide *Ex*

SHILLINGSTONE (Holy Rood) *see* Okeford *Sarum*

SHILLINGTON (All Saints) *see* Gravenhurst, Shillington and Stondon *St Alb*

SHILTON (Holy Rood) *see* Shill Valley and Broadshire *Ox*

SHILTON (St Andrew) *see* Ansty and Shilton *Cov*

SHIMPLINGTHORNE (St George) *see* Chadbrook *St E*

SHINCLIFFE (St Mary the Virgin) *see* Dur St Oswald and Shincliffe *Dur*

SHINEY ROW (St Oswald) *see* Herrington, Penshaw and Shiney Row *Dur*

SHINFIELD (St Mary) *see* Loddon Reach *Ox*

SHINGAY Group of Parishes, The, comprising Abington Pigotts, Guilden Morden, Litlington, Steeple Morden, Tadlow, and Wendy w Shingay *Ely 7* **P** *Bp, Mrs E E Sclater, Ch Patr Trust, Down Coll Cam, New Coll Ox, and Jes Coll Cam (jt)* **R** S F C WILLIAMS **NSM** A K R BOL

SHIPBOURNE (St Giles) w Plaxtol *Roch 10* **P** *Bp and F Read Esq (jt)* **R** P J HAYLER **NSM** M H PACKER

SHIPDHAM (All Saints) *see* Dereham and Distr *Nor*

SHIPHAM (St Leonard) *see* Axbridge w Shipham and Rowberrow *B & W*

SHIPHAY COLLATON (St John the Baptist) *Ex 10* **P** *Bp* **P-in-c** P IRETON

SHIPLAKE (St Peter and St Paul) w Dunsden and Harpsden *Ox 24* **P** *All So Coll Ox, D&C Windsor, and DBP (jt)* **R** R S THEWSEY **C** S J NESBITT

SHIPLEY (St Mary the Virgin) *Chich 10* **P** *Sir Charles Burrell Bt* **P-in-c** C D ALLEN

SHIPLEY (St Paul) *Leeds 1* **P** *Simeon's Trustees* **NSM** J F BUTLER

SHIPLEY (St Peter) *Leeds 1* **P** *V Shipley St Paul* **V** J C RAINER

SHIPPON (St Mary Magdalene) *see* Marcham w Garford and Shippon *Ox*

SHIPSTON-ON-STOUR (St Edmund) w Honington and Idlicote *Cov 9* **P** *Jes Coll Ox, D&C Worc, Bp (jt)* **R** S A EDMONDS **C** H J GREGORY **NSM** J TUCKER

SHIPTON (Holy Evangelist) *see* Skelton w Shipton and Newton on Ouse *York*

SHIPTON (St James) *see* Wenlock *Heref*

SHIPTON BELLINGER (St Peter) *see* Appleshaw, Kimpton, Thruxton, Fyfield etc *Win*

SHIPTON GORGE (St Martin) *see* Bride Valley *Sarum*

SHIPTON MOYNE (St John the Baptist) *see* Tetbury, Beverston, Long Newnton etc *Glouc*

SHIPTON OLIFFE (St Oswald) *see* Sevenhampton w Charlton Abbots, Hawling etc *Glouc*

SHIPTON ON CHERWELL (Holy Cross) *see* Yarnton w Begbroke and Shipton-on-Cherwell *Ox*

SHIPTONTHORPE (All Saints) *see* Weighton Wold *York*

SHIPTON-UNDER-WYCHWOOD (St Mary) *see* Wychwood *Ox*

SHIREBROOK (Holy Trinity) *see* E Scarsdale *Derby*

SHIREGREEN (St James and St Christopher) *Sheff 3* **P** *Bp and Dean (alt)* **P-in-c** D F DEAN-REVILL

SHIREHAMPTON (St Mary) *Bris 2* **P** *Bp* **C** S A LEIGHTON

SHIREMOOR (St Mark) *Newc 5* **P** *Bp* **P-in-c** R S CARO

SHIREOAKS (St Luke) *see* Worksop Ch Ch and Shireoaks *S'well*

SHIRES' EDGE, Claydon, Cropredy, Great Bourton, Mollington, and Wardington *Ox 23* **P** *Bp* **V** H A CAMPBELL

SHIRESHEAD (St James) *Blackb 11* **P** *V Cockerham w Winmarleigh and Glasson* **P-in-c** P J BALLARD

SHIRLAND (St Leonard) *see* Morton and Stonebroom w Shirland *Derby*

SHIRLEY (St George) *S'wark 19* **P** *Bp* **V** B HENGIST **Hon C** H A FIFE

SHIRLEY (St James the Great) *Birm 2* **P** *Patr Bd* **V** P G DAY

SHIRLEY (St James) (St John) *Win 13* **P** *Ch Patr Trust* **P-in-c** D A CLARK **C** G A CONDELL **NSM** L PHILLIPS

SHIRLEY (St John the Divine) *see* Shirley *Birm*

SHIRLEY (St John) *S'wark 19* **P** *Bp* **V** L C GALE

SHIRLEY (St Michael) *see* Brailsford w Shirley, Osmaston w Edlaston etc *Derby*

SHIRWELL (St Peter), Loxhore, Kentisbury, Arlington, East Down, Bratton Fleming, Challacombe and Stoke Rivers *Ex 16* **P** *Patr Bd* **TR** R E AUSTIN **C** M C TYRRELL

SHOBDON (St John the Evangelist) *see* Pembridge w Moor Court, Shobdon, Staunton etc *Heref*

SHOBROOKE (St Swithin) *see* Crediton, Shobrooke and Sandford etc *Ex*

SHOCKLACH (St Edith) *see* Tilston and Shocklach *Ches*

SHOEBURY, NORTH (St Mary the Virgin) *Chelmsf 14* **P** *Ld Chan* **V** vacant

SHOEBURY, SOUTH (St Andrew) (St Peter) *Chelmsf 14* **P** *Hyndman Trustees* **R** L M WILLIAMS **C** H R ROBINSON

SHOLDEN (St Nicholas) *see* Deal St Leon w St Rich and Sholden etc *Cant*

SHOLING (St Francis of Assisi) (St Mary) *Win 13* **P** *Bp* **V** G P ROBERTS

SHOOTERS HILL (All Saints) *see* Plumstead All SS *S'wark*

SHOOTERS HILL (Christ Church) *S'wark 6* **P** *Bp* **V** A R M VAN DEN HOF

SHORE (St Barnabas) *see* Littleborough *Man*

SHOREDITCH (All Saints) Haggerston Road *see* Dalston H Trin w St Phil and Haggerston All SS *Lon*

SHOREDITCH (St Anne) Hoxton Street *see* Hoxton St Anne w St Columba *Lon*

SHOREDITCH (St Leonard) w St Michael *Lon 5* **P** *Bp and Adn (jt)* **V** A S GORDON

SHOREHAM (St Peter and St Paul) *Roch 10* **P** *D&C Westmr* **V** D E REES

SHOREHAM, NEW (St Mary de Haura) and Shoreham Beach (Good Shepherd) *Chich 20* **P** *Bp* **V** A E WAIZENEKER **C** J L BARTLETT, S J EMERSON **NSM** J-J S AIDLEY

SHOREHAM, OLD (St Nicolas) and Kingston Buci *Chich 20* **P** *Bp and Lord Egremont (jt)* **R** J N GRANT **NSM** B A WILSON

SHORELINE Benefice, The, comprising Chelmondiston, Erwarton, Harkstead, and Shotley *St E 13* **P** *Ld Chan (1 turn), Bp (3 turns)* **R** L OOSTERHOF

SHORNE (St Peter and St Paul) *Roch 4* **P** *D&C* **V** E HURST

SHORT HEATH (Holy Trinity) *see* Bentley Em and Willenhall H Trin *Lich*

SHORT HEATH (St Margaret) *see* Erdington Ch the K *Birm*

SHORTHAMPTON (All Saints) *see* Charlbury w Shorthampton *Ox*

SHORTLANDS (St Mary) *Roch 13* **P** *Bp* **V** G J BEST **NSM** J E PETERS

SHORWELL (St Peter) *see* W Wight *Portsm*

SHOSCOMBE (St Julian) *see* Peasedown St John w Wellow and Foxcote etc *B & W*

SHOTESHAM (All Saints w St Mary) *see* Newton Flotman, Swainsthorpe, Tasburgh, etc *Nor*

SHOTLEY (St John) *Newc 9* **P** *Lord Crewe's Trustees* **P-in-c** G PURCELL SMITH

SHOTLEY (St Mary) *see* Shoreline *St E*

SHOTTERMILL (St Stephen) *Guildf 4* **P** *Adn Surrey* **V** J J RIDDLESTONE **NSM** H R MITCHELL

SHOTTERY (St Andrew) *Cov 8* **P** *Bp* **V** C R GROOCOCK **C** M J STEWART **NSM** P EDMONDSON

SHOTTESBROOKE (St John the Baptist) *see* Waltham St Lawrence and Shottesbrooke *Ox*

SHOTTESWELL (St Lawrence) *see* Edgehill Churches *Cov*

SHOTTISHAM (St Margaret) *see* Wilford Peninsula *St E*

SHOTTLE (St Lawrence) *see* Hazelwood, Holbrook and Milford *Derby*

SHOTTON (St Saviour) *see* Haswell and Shotton *Dur*

SHOTWICK (St Michael) *see* Burton and Shotwick *Ches*

SHOULDHAM (All Saints) *see* W Norfolk Priory Gp *Ely*

SHOULDHAM THORPE (St Mary) *as above*

SHRAWARDINE (St Mary) *see* Bicton, Montford w Shrawardine and Fitz *Lich*

SHRAWLEY (St Mary), Witley, Astley and Abberley *Worc 1* **P** *Bp and Guild of All So (jt)* **P-in-c** E G WHITTAKER **C** M TURNER

SHRED (Mission Church) *see* Marsden and Slaithwaite w E Scammonden *Leeds*

SHREWSBURY (All Saints and St Michael) *Lich 19* **P** *Bp*
V S B SAYER **C** J D WALTON
SHREWSBURY (Christ Church) *see* Shelton and Oxon *Lich*
SHREWSBURY (Holy Cross) (St Peter) *Lich 19* **P** *Bp*
V T D ATFIELD **C** K S HEWETT
SHREWSBURY (Holy Trinity) (St Julian) *Lich 19* **P** *Bp and*
Ch Patr Trust (jt) **V** *vacant*
SHREWSBURY (St Chad) St Mary (St Alkmund) *Lich 19*
P *Bp* **V** Y S PETERS
SHREWSBURY (St George of Cappadocia) w Greenfields
United Church *Lich 19* **P** *V Shrewsbury St Chad*
V T R VASBY-BURNIE
SHREWSBURY (St Giles) w Sutton and Atcham *Lich 19*
P *Bp and R L Burton Esq (jt)* **R** A R KNIGHT
SHREWTON (St Mary) *see* Salisbury Plain *Sarum*
SHRIVENHAM (St Andrew) and Ashbury *Ox 25* **P** *Ld Chan*
V N FERGUSSON **Hon C** P RICHARDSON
SHROPHAM (St Peter) *see* Gt and Lt Ellingham, Rockland
and Shropham etc *Nor*
SHROTON (St Mary) *see* Iwerne Valley *Sarum*
SHRUB END (All Saints) (St Cedd) *Chelmsf 20* **P** *Bp*
V *vacant*
SHUCKBURGH, LOWER (St John the Baptist) *see* Napton-on-
the-Hill, Lower Shuckburgh etc *Cov*
SHUDY CAMPS (St Mary) *see* Linton *Ely*
SHURDINGTON (St Paul) *see* Badgeworth, Shurdington and
Witcombe w Bentham *Glouc*
SHUSTOKE (St Cuthbert) *see* The Whitacres, Lea Marston,
and Shustoke *Birm*
SHUTE (St Michael) *see* Kilmington, Stockland, Dalwood,
Yarcombe etc *Ex*
SHUTFORD (St Martin) *see* Wykeham *Ox*
SHUTTINGTON (St Matthew) *see* All So N Warks *Birm*
SIBBERTOFT (St Helen) *see* Clipston, Haselbech, Kelmarsh,
Marston Trussell etc *Pet*
SIBERTSWOLD (St Andrew) *see* Bewsborough *Cant*
SIBFORD (Holy Trinity) *see* Wykeham *Ox*
SIBLE HEDINGHAM (St Peter) *see* The Hedinghams and
Upper Colne *Chelmsf*
SIBSEY (St Margaret) w Frithville *Linc 21* **P** *Ld Chan*
V C TODD
SIBSON (St Botolph) *see* Sheepy *Leic*
SIBTHORPE (St Peter) *S'well 3* **P** *Bp* **P-in-c** E I MURRAY
SIBTON (St Peter) *see* Yoxmere *St E*
SICKLINGHALL (St Peter) *see* Lower Wharfedale *Leeds*
SID VALLEY *see* Sidmouth, Woolbrook, Salcombe Regis,
Sidbury etc *Ex*
SIDBURY (St Giles and St Peter) *see* Sidmouth, Woolbrook,
Salcombe Regis, Sidbury etc *Ex*
SIDCUP (Christ Church) Longland *Roch 17* **P** *Ch Trust Fund*
Trust **V** T J PARSONS **C** A J CURTIS
SIDCUP (St Andrew) *Roch 17* **P** *Bp* **V** *vacant*
SIDCUP (St John the Evangelist) w Footscray *Roch 17* **P** *Ld*
Chan and D&C (alt) **V** C M KNIGHT-SCOTT **C** E I ASIEGBU
NSM A S J HEALY
SIDDAL (St Mark) *see* Halifax w Siddal *Leeds*
SIDDINGTON (All Saints) *see* Marton, Siddington w
Capesthorne etc *Ches*
SIDDINGTON (St Peter) *see* S Cerney w Cerney Wick,
Siddington and Preston *Glouc*
SIDESTRAND (St Michael) *see* Poppyland *Nor*
SIDFORD (St Peter) *see* Sidmouth, Woolbrook, Salcombe
Regis, Sidbury etc *Ex*
SIDLESHAM (St Mary Our Lady) *Chich 2* **P** *Bp* **V** *vacant*
SIDLEY (All Saints) *Chich 12* **P** *R Bexhill* **V** *vacant*
SIDLOW BRIDGE (Emmanuel) *S'wark 24* **P** *DBP* **R** *vacant*
SIDMOUTH (St Nicholas w St Giles), Woolbrook, Salcombe
Regis, Sidbury w Sidford, and All Saints Sidmouth *Ex 6*
P *Patr Bd* **TR** D R CAPORN **TV** K D MATHERS, L M SELMAN,
M R SELMAN **C** N V CANDELENT
SIGGLESTHORNE (St Lawrence) w Nunkeeling and
Bewholme *York 11* **P** *The Crown* **R** *vacant*
SILCHESTER (St Mary) *see* Tadley w Pamber Heath and
Silchester *Win*
SILCHESTER COMMON (Mission Church) *as above*
SILEBY (St Mary), Cossington and Seagrave *Leic 4* **P** *Patr*
Bd **R** D C BEET
SILK WILLOUGHBY (St Denis) *Linc 14* **P** *Sir Lyonel*
Tollemache Bt **R** *vacant*
SILKSTONE (All Saints) *see* W Barnsley *Leeds*
SILKSTONE COMMON (Mission Room) *as above*
SILKSWORTH (St Matthew) *see* Sunderland St Matt and
St Wilfrid *Dur*
SILLOTH (Christ Church) *see* Solway Plain *Carl*
SILSDEN (St James) *Leeds 4* **P** *Bp, Adn Craven, and Trustees*
(jt) **V** D J GRIFFITHS **C** S A GRIFFITHS

SILSOE (St James), Pulloxhill and Flitton *St Alb 8* **P** *Ball*
Coll Ox and Bp (alt) **P-in-c** D C PAYNE
SILTON (St Nicholas) *see* Gillingham, Milton-on-Stour and
Silton *Sarum*
SILTON, NETHER (All Saints) *see* Leake w Over and Nether
Silton and Kepwick *York*
SILTON, OVER (St Mary) *as above*
SILVER END (St Francis) *see* Witham and Villages *Chelmsf*
SILVERDALE (St John) *Blackb 14* **P** *V Warton*
P-in-c M I ASHTON
SILVERDALE (St Luke) *Lich 9* **P** *T H G Howard-Sneyd Esq*
V P C JONES
SILVERHILL (St Matthew) *Chich 15* **P** *Simeon's Trustees*
P-in-c M J FOY
SILVERSTONE (St Michael) and Abthorpe w Slapton and
Whittlebury and Paulerspury *Pet 5* **P** *T L Langton-Lockton*
Esq, Leeson's Trustees, and New Coll Ox (3 turns), The Crown
(2 turns) **R** P D MCLEOD **C** G I FROST
SILVERTON (St Mary), Butterleigh, Bickleigh and
Cadeleigh *Ex 7* **P** *Bp and Sir Rivers Carew Bt*
R P A KINGDOM **NSM** C JENKINS
SILVINGTON (St Michael) *see* Stottesdon w Farlow, Cleeton
St Mary etc *Heref*
SIMONBURN (St Mungo) *see* Humshaugh w Simonburn and
Wark *Newc*
SIMONSTONE (St Peter) *see* Read and Simonstone *Blackb*
SIMPSON (St Thomas) *see* Woughton *Ox*
SINFIN (St Stephen) *Derby 5* **P** *CPAS* **V** *vacant*
SINFIN MOOR (not known) *Derby 5* **P** *Bp*
P-in-c P DESBOROUGH
SINGLETON (Blessed Virgin Mary) *see* E Dean, Singleton,
and W Dean *Chich*
SINGLETON (St Anne) *see* Poulton Carleton and Singleton
Blackb
SINNINGTON (All Saints) *see* Middleton, Newton and
Sinnington *York*
SISLAND (St Mary) *see* Loddon, Sisland, Chedgrave, Hardley
and Langley *Nor*
SISSINGHURST (Holy Trinity) w Frittenden *Cant 11*
P *CPAS* **R** P DEAVES
SITHNEY (St Sithney) *see* W Kerrier *Truro*
SITTINGBOURNE (Holy Trinity) (St Mary) (St Michael) w
Bobbing *Cant 15* **P** *Patr Bd* **TV** D G RIDLEY
C C J PENFOLD **OLM** S M SAMSON
SIX FEN Churches, comprising Christchurch, Doddington w
Benwick, Manea, Welney, and Wimblington *Ely 11* **P** *Bp,*
St Jo Coll Dur, R Raynar Esq, and R T Townley Esq (jt)
R I BRADY **C** L BRADY
SIX HILLS (Mission) *see* Old Dalby, Nether Broughton,
Saxelbye etc *Leic*
SIX MILE BOTTOM (St George) *see* Lt Wilbraham *Ely*
SIX PILGRIMS, The, comprising Alford, Babcary, Hornblotton,
Lovington, North Barrow, and South Barrow *B & W 2* **P** *Ch*
Soc Trust, D&C, DBF, and Bp (by turn) **R** *vacant*
SIX SAINTS circa Holt, comprising Blaston, Bringhurst, Great
Easton, Medbourne cum Holt, and Stockerston *Leic 5*
P *D&C Pet and Adn Leic (2 turns), St Jo Coll Cam (1 turn)*
R S J BISHOP
SIX, The, comprising Hartlip, Iwade, Lower Halstow,
Newington, Stockbury, and Upchurch *Cant 15* **P** *Abp,*
D&C, and Adn Maidstone (jt) **V** J M STANIFORTH
C S Z B NEVELL **NSM** A M LANE, N A CARPENTER
SIXHILLS (All Saints) *see* Barkwith Gp *Linc*
SIXPENNY HANDLEY (St Mary) w Gussage St Andrew and
Pentridge *Sarum 6* **P** *D&C Windsor and DBP (alt)*
P-in-c R M A HANCOCK
SKEEBY (St Agatha's District Church) *see* Easby w Skeeby and
Brompton on Swale etc *Leeds*
SKEFFINGTON (St Thomas à Beckett) *see* Coplow *Leic*
SKEGBY (St Andrew) w Teversal *S'well 4* **P** *DBP and Ld*
Chan (alt) **R** P T CHANTRY
SKEGNESS Group, The (St Clement) (St Matthew),
including Addlethorpe and Ingoldmells *Linc 10* **P** *Bp and*
DBP (2 turns), and Ld Chan (1 turn) **R** R G HOLDEN
OLM C ANDERSON
SKELBROOKE (St Michael and All Angels) *see* Adwick-le-
Street w Skelbrooke *Sheff*
SKELLINGTHORPE (St Lawrence) w Doddington *Linc 12*
P *MMCET* **R** S J DURANT **OLM** F CLARKE
SKELLOW (St Michael and All Angels) *see* Owston *Sheff*
SKELMANTHORPE (St Aidan) *Leeds 5* **P** *Bp*
P-in-c K B CURRIE **NSM** E BARROW, J R JONES
SKELMERSDALE (St Paul) *Liv 14* **P** *V Ormskirk*
P-in-c C B SPITTLE **NSM** A KAZICH **OLM** C JACKSON
SKELSMERGH (St John the Baptist) *see* Beacon TM *Carl*

SKELTON (All Saints) w Upleatham *York 16*   P *Abp*
R V E M-B HAYNES

SKELTON (St Giles) w Shipton and Newton on Ouse *York 3*
  P *Abp*   C D M COYNE, M E YOUNG, M HARRISON, S WHITING
NSM C C CRANFIELD, C C GITTENS, C J TOASE, T M GANT

SKELTON (St Michael)   *see* Inglewood Gp *Carl*

SKELTON-CUM-NEWBY (St Helen's Old Church)   *see*
Kirby-on-the-Moor, Cundall w Norton-le-Clay etc *Leeds*

SKENDLEBY (St Peter and St Paul)   *see* Bolingbroke Deanery
Linc

SKERNE (St Leonard)   *see* Hutton Cranswick w Skerne,
Watton and Beswick *York*

SKERNE, UPPER, comprising Bishop Middleham, Fishburn,
Sedgefield, Trimdon, and Trimdon Grange *Dur 8*   P *Ld
Chan (1 turn), Patr Bd (2 turns)*   TV E A BLAND

SKERTON (St Chad) *Blackb 11*   P *Bp*
V C L CARMICHAEL-DAVIS

SKERTON (St Luke) *Blackb 11*   P *Trustees*
V C L CARMICHAEL-DAVIS

SKEYTON (All Saints)   *see* King's Beck *Nor*

SKIDBY (St Michael)   *see* Walkington, Bishop Burton, Rowley
etc *York*

SKILGATE (St John the Baptist)   *see* Dulverton w Brushford,
Brompton Regis etc *B & W*

SKILLINGTON (St James)   *see* Colsterworth Par *Linc*

SKIPSEA (All Saints)   *see* Hornsea, Atwick and Skipsea *York*

SKIPTON (Christ Church) w Carleton St Mary *Leeds 21*
  P *Ch Ch Ox and R Skipton H Trin (jt)*   V *vacant*

SKIPTON (Holy Trinity) *Leeds 21*   P *Ch Ch Ox*
R J W F THEODOSIUS   C R A MITCHELL

SKIPTON ON SWALE (St John)   *see* Topcliffe, Baldersby w
Dishforth, Dalton etc *York*

SKIPWITH (St Helen)   *see* Bubwith w Skipwith *York*

SKIRBECK (Holy Trinity) *Linc 21*   P *Trustees*   V E WARD
C I S WARD, J P SPEIRS-DAVIES

SKIRBECK (St Nicholas) *Linc 21*   P *DBP*   R J S L UNDERHILL

SKIRBECK QUARTER (St Thomas)   *see* Boston *Linc*

SKIRLAUGH (St Augustine), Catwick, Long Riston, Rise,
Swine w Ellerby *York 11*   P *Abp, Abp and Baroness de
Stempel, and Ld Chan (by turn)*   V *vacant*

SKIRPENBECK (St Mary)   *see* Garrowby Hill *York*

SKIRWITH (St John the Evangelist)   *see* Cross Fell Gp *Carl*

SLAD (Holy Trinity)   *see* Stroud Team *Glouc*

SLADE GREEN (St Augustine) *Roch 15*   P *Bp*   V J D BENNETT
NSM E M ROY-JOHNSON

SLAIDBURN (St Andrew) w Tosside *Leeds 17*   P *Bp and Ch
Soc Trust (jt)*   R *vacant*

SLAITHWAITE (St James)   *see* Marsden and Slaithwaite w E
Scammonden *Leeds*

SLALEY (St Mary the Virgin), Healey and Whittonstall
Newc 9   P *Bp, V Bywell St Pet, and D&C (jt)*   V H SAVAGE

SLAPTON (Holy Cross)   *see* Ivinghoe w Pitstone and Slapton
and Marsworth *Ox*

SLAPTON (St Botolph)   *see* Silverstone and Abthorpe w
Slapton etc *Pet*

SLAPTON (St James the Great)   *see* Stokenham, Slapton,
Charleton w Buckland etc *Ex*

SLAUGHAM (St Mary) and Staplefield Common *Chich 8*
  P *Mrs D M Irwin-Clark*   R C A SMITH
Hon C K W HABERSHON

SLAUGHTER, LOWER (St Mary)   *see* The Guitings, Cutsdean,
Farmcote etc *Glouc*

SLAUGHTER, UPPER (St Peter)   *as above*

SLAUGHTERFORD (St Nicholas)   *see* By Brook *Bris*

SLAWSTON (All Saints)   *see* Hallaton and Allexton, w
Horninghold, Tugby etc *Leic*

SLEAFORD (St Denys) *Linc 14*   P *Bp*   V P A JOHNSON

SLEDMERE (St Mary)   *see* Waggoners *York*

SLEEKBURN (St John)   *see* Bedlington, Cambois and
Sleekburn *Newc*

SLEIGHTS (St John)   *see* Lower Esk *York*

SLIMBRIDGE (St John the Evangelist)   *see* Sharpness, Purton,
Brookend and Slimbridge *Glouc*

SLINDON (St Chad)   *see* Eccleshall *Lich*

SLINDON (St Mary), Eartham and Madehurst *Chich 1*
  P *Bp, D&C, and Mrs J Izard (jt)*   R *vacant*

SLINFOLD (St Peter)   *see* Itchingfield w Slinfold *Chich*

SLINGSBY (All Saints)   *see* The Street Par *York*

SLIPTON (St John the Baptist) *Pet 9*   P *L G Stopford Sackville
Esq*   V *vacant*

SLITTING MILL (St John the Baptist)   *see* Brereton and
Rugeley w Armitage *Lich*

SLOANE STREET (Holy Trinity)   *see* Upper Chelsea H Trin and
St Sav *Lon*

SLOLEY (St Bartholomew)   *see* King's Beck *Nor*

SLOUGH (St Paul) (Christ Church) *Ox 12*   P *Trustees*
V T L WAMBUNYA

SLYNE WITH HEST (St Luke) and Halton St Wilfrid w
Aughton St Saviour *Blackb 14*   P *Bp and Exors R T
Sanderson (jt)*   R S M SEED

SMALL HEATH (All Saints) *Birm 6*   P *Patr Bd*
V J R A SAMPSON

SMALLBURGH (St Peter) w Dilham w Honing and
Crostwight *Nor 12*   P *Bp, T R Cubitt Esq, and J C Wickman
Esq (jt)*   OLM A P BEVAN

SMALLEY (St John the Baptist)   *see* Morley and Smalley *Derby*

SMALLFIELD (Church Room)   *see* The Windmill *S'wark*

SMALLHYTHE (St John the Baptist)   *see* Tenterden, Rother
and Oxney *Cant*

SMALLTHORNE (St Saviour)   *see* N Potteries *Lich*

SMALLWOOD (St John the Baptist)   *see* Astbury and
Smallwood *Ches*

SMANNELL (Christ Church)   *see* Pastrow *Win*

SMARDEN (St Michael)   *see* Biddenden and Smarden *Cant*

SMEATON, GREAT (St Eloy)   *see* Wiske Benefice *Leeds*

SMEETH (St Mary)   *see* Stour Downs *Cant*

SMEETON WESTERBY (Christ Church)   *see* Kibworth and
Smeeton Westerby and Saddington *Leic*

SMESTOW VALE TEAM, comprising Bobbington, Himley,
Swindon, Trysull, and Wombourne *Lich 23*   P *Patr Bd*
TR A P BROWN   TV R J FISHER   C S J WATSON

SMETHCOTT (St Michael)   *see* Dorrington w Leebotwood,
Longnor, Stapleton etc *Heref*

SMETHWICK (Old Church) *Birm 3*   P *Dorothy Parkes Trustees*
V D BUCKLEY   C C C SHEKERIE

SMETHWICK (Resurrection) (St Stephen and St Michael)
Birm 3   P *Bp*   V D R GOULD   NSM N M ROSS

SMETHWICK (St Matthew w St Chad) *Birm 3*   P *Bp and V
Smethwick (alt)*   P-in-c L M ARLIDGE   NSM B M HAMILTON

SMISBY (St James)   *see* Melbourne, Ticknall, Smisby and
Stanton *Derby*

SMITHILLS HALL (Chapel)   *see* Halliwell St Pet *Man*

SMORRALL LANE (St Andrew)   *see* Bedworth *Cov*

SNAILWELL (St Peter)   *see* Three Rivers Gp *Ely*

SNAINTON (St Stephen)   *see* Upper Derwent *York*

SNAITH (St Laurence Priory)   *see* Gt Snaith *Sheff*

SNAITH, GREAT (Holy Trinity) (St John the Baptist)
(St Paul) *Sheff 10*   P *Bp*   TR E E M ROBERTSHAW
NSM P W HIBBS

SNAPE (St John the Baptist)   *see* Alde River *St E*

SNAPE CASTLE (Chapel of St Mary)   *see* W Tanfield and Well
w Snape and N Stainley *Leeds*

SNARESTONE (St Bartholomew)   *see* Woodfield *Leic*

SNARGATE (St Dunstan)   *see* Romney Marsh *Cant*

SNEAD (St Mary the Virgin)   *see* Wentnor w Ratlinghope,
Myndtown, Norbury etc *Heref*

SNEATON (St Hilda)   *see* Lower Esk *York*

SNEINTON (St Christopher) w St Philip *S'well 9*   P *CPAS
and Trustees (alt)*   P-in-c N J HILL

SNEINTON (St Cyprian) *S'well 9*   P *Bp*   V *vacant*

SNEINTON (St Stephen) w St Matthias *S'well 9*   P *Bp and
SMF (jt)*   P-in-c J M BLAKELEY   C L J BLAKELEY

SNELLAND (All Saints)   *see* Wragby Gp *Linc*

SNELSTON (St Peter)   *see* Norbury w Snelston *Derby*

SNETTISHAM (St Mary) *Nor 15*   P *CPAS Patr Trust*
P-in-c P R COOK   C R C ALEXANDER

SNEYD (Holy Trinity)   *see* N Potteries *Lich*

SNEYD GREEN (St Andrew) *Lich 11*   P *Bp*   V J N GANDON
C T R OWEN

SNIBSTON (St Mary)   *see* Hugglescote w Donington,
Ellistown and Snibston *Leic*

SNITTERBY (St Nicholas)   *see* Bishop Norton, Waddingham
and Snitterby *Linc*

SNITTERFIELD (St James the Great)   *see* Arden Valley *Cov*

SNODLAND (All Saints) (Christ Church) *Roch 7*   P *Bp and
CPAS (jt)*   R D A PEARSON-SMITH

SNORING, GREAT (St Mary)   *see* Barney, Hindringham,
Thursford, Great Snoring, Little Snoring and Kettlestone
and Pensthorpe *Nor*

SNORING, LITTLE (St Andrew)   *as above*

SNOWSHILL (St Barnabas)   *see* Winchcombe *Glouc*

SOBERTON (St Peter), Newtown and Hambledon *Portsm 1*
  P *Ld Chan and Bp (jt)*   V D B MORGAN   C A W FORREST

SOCKBURN (All Saints)   *see* Dinsdale w Sockburn *Dur*

SODBURY VALE Benefice, The, comprising Chipping
Sodbury, Horton, Little Sodbury, and Old Sodbury *Glouc 5*
  P *D&C Worc, Duke of Beaufort, and CPAS (jt)*   R D BOWERS
C J M JONES-WILLIAMS

SODBURY, LITTLE (St Adeline)   *see* Sodbury Vale *Glouc*

SODBURY, OLD (St John the Baptist)   *as above*

SOHAM (St Andrew) *Ely 8* **P** *Pemb Coll Cam*
R E J WHALLEY **C** H M RICHARDSON
SOHO (St Anne) (St Thomas) (St Peter) *Lon 3* **P** *R Westmr*
St Jas **P-in-c** R S F BUCKLEY **C** P A GURNHAM
SOLE BAY, comprising Blythburgh, Reydon, Sotherton, South
Cove, Southwold, Uggeshall, Walberswick, and Wangford
St E 15 **P** *Patr Bd* **TR** S J PITCHER **TV** A D PERRY
NSM J E A MILLER
SOLIHULL (Catherine de Barnes) (St Alphege) (St Helen)
(St Michael) *Birm 6* **P** *Patr Bd* **TV** H T GREENHAM,
S H MARSHALL **NSM** S M CHANDLER
SOLLERS HOPE (St Michael) *see* StowCaple *Heref*
SOLWAY PLAIN, comprising Bromfield, Holme Cultram,
Silloth, Waverton, and West Newton *Carl 7* **P** *Patr Bd*
R B ROTHWELL **NSM** A D CALLAWAY
SOMBORNE (St Peter and St Paul) w Ashley *Win 12* **P** *Bp*
P-in-c C T H F BENSON **Hon C** R A BURNINGHAM
SOMERBY (All Saints) *see* Burrough Hill Pars *Leic*
SOMERBY (St Margaret) *see* Brocklesby Park, Croxton and
North Wolds *Linc*
SOMERBY, NEW (St Anne) *see* S Grantham *Linc*
SOMERBY, OLD (St Mary Magdalene) *see* N Beltisloe Par *Linc*
SOMERCOTES (St Thomas) *Derby 2* **P** *Bp*
P-in-c I N L BLACK **C** M J TAYLOR **NSM** J O K PENFOLD,
K W G JOHNSON
SOMERCOTES, NORTH (St Mary) *see* Marshchapel,
Somercotes and Grainthorpe w Conisholme *Linc*
SOMERFORD (All Saints) *see* Astbury and Smallwood *Ches*
SOMERFORD KEYNES (All Saints) *see* Kemble, Poole Keynes,
Somerford Keynes etc *Glouc*
SOMERFORD, GREAT (St Peter and St Paul) *see* Woodbridge
Bris
SOMERFORD, LITTLE (St John the Baptist) *as above*
SOMERLEYTON (St Mary), Ashby, Fritton, Herringfleet,
Blundeston and Lound *Nor 9* **P** *Lord Somerleyton and SMF*
(jt) **R** G BROOKS
SOMERS TOWN (St Mary the Virgin) *see* Old St Pancras *Lon*
SOMERSAL HERBERT (St Peter) *see* S Dales *Derby*
SOMERSBY (St Margaret) *see* S Ormsby Gp *Linc*
SOMERSHAM (St John the Baptist) w Pidley and Oldhurst
and Wooodhurst *Ely 12* **P** *Bp* **V** S F SIMPSON
NSM S G EVANS
SOMERSHAM (St Mary) *see* S Bosmere *St E*
SOMERTON (St James) *see* Cherwell Valley *Ox*
SOMERTON (St Margaret) *see* Glemsford, Hartest w Boxted,
Somerton etc *St E*
SOMERTON (St Michael and All Angels) w The Charltons
and Kingsdon *B & W 5* **P** *Bp (2 turns), DBP (1 turn)*
P-in-c A J SYMONDS
SOMERTON, WEST (St Mary) *see* Flegg Coastal Benefice *Nor*
SOMPTING (St Mary the Virgin) (St Peter) *Chich 7* **P** *OStJ*
V *vacant*
SONNING (St Andrew) (St Patrick) *Ox 8* **P** *Bp*
V J A F TAYLOR **NSM** K L WAKEMAN-TOOGOOD
SONNING COMMON (Christ the King) *see* Rotherfield
Peppard and Kidmore End etc *Ox*
SOOKHOLME (St Augustine) *see* Warsop *S'well*
SOPLEY (St Michael and All Angels) *see* Burton and Sopley
Win
SOPWORTH (St Mary the Virgin) *see* Boxwell, Leighterton,
Didmarton, Oldbury etc *Glouc*
SOTHERTON (St Andrew) *see* Sole Bay *St E*
SOTWELL (St James) *see* Wallingford *Ox*
SOUDLEY (St Michael) *see* Cinderford w Littledean *Glouc*
SOULBURY (All Saints) *see* Cottesloe *Ox*
SOULDERN (Annunciation of the Blessed Virgin Mary) *see*
Cherwell Valley *Ox*
SOULDROP (All Saints) *see* Sharnbrook, Felmersham and
Knotting w Souldrop *St Alb*
SOUNDWELL (St Stephen) *Bris 5* **P** *Bp* **P-in-c** L J WIGMORE
NSM A J G COOPER **OLM** J M WILTSHIRE
SOURTON (St Thomas of Canterbury) *see* Okehampton,
Inwardleigh, Belstone, Sourton etc *Ex*
SOUTH *see also under substantive place name*
SOUTH ACRE (St George) *see* Nar Valley *Nor*
SOUTH BANK (St John) *York 17* **P** *Abp* **V** T M LEATHLEY
NSM J EMSON
SOUTH CAVE (All Saints) and Ellerker w Broomfleet *York 13*
P *CPAS and D&C Dur (jt)* **V** M J PROCTOR
NSM P R DRAPER
SOUTH COVE (St Lawrence) *see* Sole Bay *St E*
SOUTH DALES, The, comprising Alkmonton, Cubley,
Doveridge, Marston Montgomery, Scropton, Somersal
Herbert, and Sudbury *Derby 6* **P** *Bp and Duke of Devonshire*
(jt) **R** J J VICKERSTAFF **NSM** J M LEGH, P R JONES

SOUTH DOWNS GATEWAY Churches, comprising Colden
Common, Morestead, Owslebury, and Twyford *Win 7* **P** *Bp*
and Em Coll Cam (jt) **V** D A DRAISEY
SOUTH HILL (St Sampson) *see* Callington Cluster *Truro*
SOUTH MOOR (St George) *see* Stanley and S Moor *Dur*
SOUTH PARK (St Luke) *see* Reigate St Luke *S'wark*
SOUTH POOL (St Nicholas and St Cyriac) *see* Stokenham,
Slapton, Charleton w Buckland etc *Ex*
SOUTH SHIELDS (All Saints) (St Mary w St Martin) *Dur 13*
P *Patr Bd* **TR** M P THOMPSON
SOUTH SHIELDS (St Hilda) w St Thomas *Dur 13* **P** *D&C*
P-in-c A M MAWHINNEY
SOUTH SHIELDS (St Lawrence the Martyr) *see* Horsley Hill
St Lawr *Dur*
SOUTH SHIELDS St Aidan (St Stephen) The Lawe *Dur 13*
P *Bp and D&C* **R** *vacant*
SOUTH SHORE (Holy Trinity) *Blackb 8* **P** *J C Hilton Esq*
V T CHARNOCK
SOUTH SHORE (St Mary) *see* Blackpool St Mary *Blackb*
SOUTH SHORE (St Peter) *Blackb 8* **P** *Bp* **V** T CHARNOCK
SOUTH TRINITY BROADS, The, comprising Billockby, Burgh
St Margaret (Fleggburgh), Filby, Mautby, Runham,
Stokesby, and Thrigby *Nor 6* **P** *Bp, Adn Nor, DBP, Mrs Z K
Cognetti, R T Daniel Esq, and I F M Lucas Esq (jt)*
P-in-c S M HEMSLEY HALLS
SOUTH WARWICKSHIRE SEVEN Group, The, comprising
Barcheston, Barton-on-the-Heath, Burmington, Cherington,
Long Compton, Whichford, and Wolford *Cov 9* **P** *Bp, Mert
Coll Ox, Ch Ch Ox, and Trin Coll Ox (jt)* **C** B H DYSON
SOUTH WYE *see* Heref S Wye *Heref*
SOUTHALL (Christ the Redeemer) *Lon 19* **P** *Bp*
V W MASIH
SOUTHALL (Emmanuel) *Lon 19* **P** *Bp and Ch Patr Trust (jt)*
V W E GILL
SOUTHALL (Holy Trinity) *Lon 19* **P** *Ch Patr Trust*
V M F BOLLEY
SOUTHALL (St George) *Lon 19* **P** *D&C St Paul's*
V C RAMSAY
SOUTHALL GREEN (St John) *Lon 19* **P** *Ch Patr Trust*
V A L POULSON **C** I M DUNMORE
SOUTHAM (Ascension) *see* Bishop's Cleeve and Woolstone w
Gotherington etc *Glouc*
SOUTHAM (St James) *Cov 10* **P** *The Crown* **R** *vacant*
SOUTHAMPTON (Christ Church) Portswood *see* Portswood
Ch Ch *Win*
SOUTHAMPTON (St Alban the Martyr) *see* Swaythling *Win*
SOUTHAMPTON (St Barnabas) *Win 13* **P** *Bp* **V** *vacant*
SOUTHAMPTON (St Denys) Portswood *see* Portswood
St Denys *Win*
SOUTHAMPTON (St Jude) *see* Maybush and Southampton
St Jude *Win*
SOUTHAMPTON (St Mark) *Win 13* **P** *Ch Patr Trust*
V K E HICKEN
SOUTHAMPTON (St Mary Extra) *Win 13* **P** *Bp*
P-in-c M J A NEWTON
SOUTHAMPTON (St Mary) *Win 13* **P** *Bp* **P-in-c** J M FINCH
C J GOODCHILD **NSM** N D LEIGH
SOUTHAMPTON (St Michael the Archangel) *Win 13* **P** *Bp*
NSM P R HAND
SOUTHAMPTON Lord's Hill and Lord's Wood *Win 13* **P** *Bp*
V C H KNIGHTS
SOUTHAMPTON Thornhill (St Christopher) *Win 13* **P** *Bp*
V D W JENNINGS **NSM** M D J RENSHAW
SOUTHBERGH (St Andrew) *see* Barnham Broom and Upper
Yare *Nor*
SOUTHBOROUGH (Christ Church) *Roch 12* **P** *CPAS Patr
Trust* **R** N S CORNELL **C** D M BUBB
SOUTHBOROUGH (St Matthew) *see* High Brooms *Roch*
SOUTHBOROUGH (St Peter) *see* Bidborough St Lawr and
Southborough St Pet *Roch*
SOUTHBOROUGH (St Thomas) *Roch 12* **P** *Bp*
V R C WILSON **C** D J DE MATTOS
SOUTHBOURNE (All Saints) *see* Pokesdown All SS *Win*
SOUTHBOURNE (St Christopher) *Win 8* **P** *Bp*
P-in-c A L MCPHERSON
SOUTHBOURNE (St John the Evangelist) w West Thorney
Chich 6 **P** *MMCET* **V** M J LUFF
SOUTHBOURNE (St Katharine) (St Nicholas) *Win 8* **P** *Bp*
NSM D J TALBOT
SOUTHBROOM (St James) *Sarum 17* **P** *D&C* **V** K J BRINDLE
C R J SAINT **NSM** S A IBBETSON
SOUTHCHURCH (Christ Church) *Chelmsf 14* **P** *Bp*
V S N ROSCOE
SOUTHCHURCH (Holy Trinity) *Chelmsf 14* **P** *Abp Cant*
P-in-c R T HUMBLE **NSM** T A ARNOLD

SOUTHCOURT (Good Shepherd) *Ox 10*   P *Ch Patr Trust*
V C R HARTLEY
SOUTHEA (Emmanuel)   *see* Wisbech St Mary and Guyhirn w
Ring's End etc *Ely*
SOUTHEASE (St Peter)   *see* Iford w Kingston and Rodmell
and Southease *Chich*
SOUTHEND (All Saints) *Chelmsf 14*   P *Bp*   V W N PAXTON
NSM P E OWEN
SOUTHEND (St Alban)   *see* Westcliff St Alban and Southend
St Mark *Chelmsf*
SOUTHEND (St John the Baptist) *Chelmsf 14*   P *Bp*
P-in-c T LOH   C M M WALKER, S P COLLIER
Hon C M A BALLARD
SOUTHEND (St Peter)   *see* Bradfield and Stanford Dingley *Ox*
SOUTHEND-ON-SEA (St Mark)   *see* Westcliff St Alban and
Southend St Mark *Chelmsf*
SOUTHEND-ON-SEA (St Saviour) Westcliff *Chelmsf 14*
P *Bp, Adn Southend, and Churchwardens (jt)*
NSM J F WILKINSON
SOUTHERY (St Mary)   *see* Grimshoe *Ely*
SOUTHFIELDS (St Barnabas) *S'wark 18*   P *Bp*   V I S TATTUM
SOUTHFIELDS (St Michael and All Angels)   *see* Wandsworth
St Mich w St Steph *S'wark*
SOUTHFLEET (St Nicholas) *Roch 1*   P *CPAS*   R *vacant*
SOUTHGATE (Christ Church) *Lon 16*   P V *Edmonton All SS*
V C LIMBERT
SOUTHGATE (St Andrew) *Lon 16*   P *Bp*   V E N TURNER
SOUTHGATE, NEW (St Paul) *Lon 14*   P V *Southgate Ch Ch*
V M M HARBAGE
SOUTHILL (All Saints)   *see* Clifton and Southill *St Alb*
SOUTHLAKE (St James) *Ox 7*   P *DBP*   V L R SMITH
SOUTHLEIGH (St Lawrence)   *see* Colyton, Branscombe,
Musbury, Northleigh and Southleigh *Ex*
SOUTHMEAD (St Stephen) *Bris 2*   P *Bp*   V J C ROBERTS
SOUTHMINSTER (St Leonard) and Steeple *Chelmsf 10*
P *Govs Charterhouse and Lord Fitzwalter (jt)*   V P E C BEGLEY
C J M KING
SOUTHOE (St Leonard)   *see* The Paxtons w Diddington and
Southoe *Ely*
SOUTHOVER (St John the Baptist)   *see* Trin in Lewes *Chich*
SOUTHOWRAM (St Anne-in-the-Grove) *Leeds 8*   P V
Halifax   NSM E S KILPATRICK
SOUTHPORT (All Saints) *Liv 9*   P *Trustees*
P-in-c T D L CARPENTER   C S T MARSHALL
SOUTHPORT (Christ Church) *Liv 9*   P *Trustees*
V S MCGANITY   C R HILL   NSM R MILTON
SOUTHPORT (Emmanuel) *Liv 9*   P *PCC*
P-in-c S MCTAGGART
SOUTHPORT (Holy Trinity) *Liv 9*   P *Trustees*
V T D L CARPENTER   C N P BRUNSKILL
SOUTHPORT (St James)   *see* Birkdale St Jas *Liv*
SOUTHPORT (St Luke) *Liv 9*   P V *Southport H Trin*
P-in-c T D L CARPENTER   C N P BRUNSKILL
SOUTHPORT (St Peter)   *see* Birkdale St Pet *Liv*
SOUTHPORT (St Philip and St Paul) *Liv 9*   P V *Southport Ch
Ch and Trustees (jt)*   P-in-c S MCGANITY   NSM R E BRAY
SOUTHPORT (St Simon and St Jude) All Souls *Liv 9*
P *Trustees*   V A D LIGGINS
SOUTHPORT, KEW (St Francis of Assisi)   *see* Kew *Liv*
SOUTHREPPS (St James)   *see* Poppyland *Nor*
SOUTHREY (St John the Divine)   *see* Bardney *Linc*
SOUTHROP (St Peter)   *see* S Cotswolds *Glouc*
SOUTHSEA (Holy Spirit) *Portsm 6*   P *Bp*   P-in-c R T LAWSON
C P R ARMSTEAD
SOUTHSEA (St Jude) *Portsm 6*   P *Trustees*   V A M TAMS
C N R SMART
SOUTHSEA (St Luke) (St Peter) *Portsm 6*   P *Bp and CPAS (jt)*
V A-M MCCABE   C J A TWINE   NSM B W R STEPHENSON
SOUTHSEA (St Margaret of Scotland) *Portsm 6*   P *Bp*
V *vacant*
SOUTHSEA (St Simon) *Portsm 6*   P *CPAS*   V *vacant*
SOUTHTOWN (St Mary)   *see* Gt Yarmouth *Nor*
SOUTHWARK (Christ Church) *S'wark 10*   P *Marshall's
Charity*   R I J MOBSBY   C J W HENRY
SOUTHWARK (Holy Trinity w St Matthew) *S'wark 10*   P *Bp*
R H F ADÁN FERNÁNDEZ   C A GARCIA FUERTE
SOUTHWARK (St George the Martyr) (St Alphege)
(St Jude) *S'wark 10*   P *Lon Corp (1 turn), Ld Chan (4 turns),
Walsingham Coll Trust Assn (1 turn)*   R J M W SEDGWICK
C R A SLATER-CARR   Hon C F Y-C HUNG   OLM D PAPE
SOUTHWATER (Holy Innocents) *Chich 10*   P V *Horsham*
V G F KESARI
SOUTHWAY (The Holy Spirit)   *see* Tamerton Foliot and
Southway *Ex*
SOUTHWELL (Holy Trinity) *S'well 3*   P *CPAS*   V A W PORTER
SOUTHWELL (St Andrew)   *see* Portland *Sarum*

SOUTHWICK (Holy Trinity)   *see* N Wearside *Dur*
SOUTHWICK (St James) w Boarhunt *Portsm 1*   P *R
Thistlewayte Esq*   P-in-c S BROCKLEHURST
SOUTHWICK (St Mary the Virgin)   *see* Warmington, Tansor
and Cotterstock etc *Pet*
SOUTHWICK (St Michael and All Angels) (St Peter)
Chich 20   P *Bp and Ld Chan (alt)*   R J D S FRENCH
SOUTHWICK (St Thomas)   *see* N Bradley, Southwick,
Heywood and Steeple Ashton *Sarum*
SOUTHWOLD (St Edmund King and Martyr)   *see* Sole Bay
St E
SOWERBY (St Mary)   *see* Ryburn *Leeds*
SOWERBY (St Oswald) *York 18*   P *Abp*   P-in-c D J BIGGS
NSM P PERCY
SOWERBY (St Peter)   *see* Ryburn *Leeds*
SOWERBY BRIDGE (Christ Church) *Leeds 8*   P V *Halifax*
V A DICK
SOWTON (St Michael and All Angels)   *see* Broadclyst, Clyst
Honiton, Clyst Hydon etc *Ex*
SPALDING (St John the Baptist) *Linc 19*   P *Bp*
P-in-c G S BANNISTER
SPALDING (St Mary and St Nicolas) *Linc 19*   P *Feoffees*
V J D BENNETT   C A J WORKMAN
SPALDWICK (St James)   *see* S Leightonstone *Ely*
SPARHAM (St Mary)   *see* Reepham and Wensum Valley *Nor*
SPARKBROOK (Christ Church) *Birm 6*   P *Aston Trustees*
P-in-c T N CROWE
SPARKBROOK (St Agatha) w Balsall Heath St Barnabas
Birm 1   P *Bp*   V *vacant*
SPARKFORD (St Mary Magdalene)   *see* Cam Vale *B & W*
SPARKHILL (St John the Evangelist) *Birm 6*   P *Dioc Trustees
and Aston Trustees (alt)*   P-in-c T N CROWE
SPARKWELL (All Saints)   *see* Ivybridge, Cornwood, Harford
and Sparkwell *Ex*
SPARROW HALL (St George)   *see* Fazakerley Em *Liv*
SPARSHOLT (Holy Cross)   *see* Ridgeway *Ox*
SPARSHOLT (St Stephen)   *see* The Downs *Win*
SPAXTON (St Margaret)   *see* Aisholt, Enmore, Goathurst,
Nether Stowey etc *B & W*
SPEEN (St Mary the Virgin)   *see* Newbury St Nic and Speen
Ox
SPEETON (St Leonard)   *see* Bempton w Flamborough,
Reighton w Speeton *York*
SPEKE (St Aidan) (All Saints) *Liv 2*   P *Bp*   R P SALTMARSH
C G J L MORGAN
SPELDHURST (St Mary the Virgin) w Groombridge and
Ashurst *Roch 12*   P *DBP*   R D P WREN
SPELSBURY (All Saints)   *see* Chase *Ox*
SPEN, HIGH (St Patrick) and Rowlands Gill *Dur 12*   P *Bp*
P-in-c D T H RYAN   NSM L O GARDNER
SPENCER Benefice   *see* Brington w Whilton and Norton etc
Pet
SPENCERS WOOD (St Michael and All Angels)   *see* Loddon
Reach *Ox*
SPENNITHORNE (St Michael)   *see* Lower Wensleydale *Leeds*
SPENNYMOOR (St Paul) and Whitworth *Dur 3*   P *D&C*
V M P TARLING   C A J SMITH
SPETISBURY (St John the Baptist) w Charlton Marshall and
Blandford St Mary *Sarum 6*   P *Worc Coll Ox (1 turn), Bp (2
turns)*   P-in-c C M COUZENS   NSM S J ATKINS
SPEXHALL (St Peter)   *see* Blyth Valley *St E*
SPILSBY (St James)   *see* Bolingbroke Deanery *Linc*
SPIRE HILL, comprising Purse Caundle, Stalbridge, Stock
Gaylard, and Stourton Caundle *Sarum 5*   P *Bp, CCC Cam,
and Mrs J C M Langmead (jt)*   R *vacant*
SPITAL (St Agnes)   *see* Clewer St Andr *Ox*
SPITAL (St Leonard's Mission Room)   *see* Chesterfield St Mary
and All SS *Derby*
SPITALFIELDS (Christ Church w All Saints) *Lon 7*
P *MMCET*   R D J WOLF
SPITALGATE (St John the Evangelist)   *see* S Grantham *Linc*
SPITTAL (St John)   *see* Scremerston, Spittal and Tweedmouth
Newc
SPIXWORTH (St Peter)   *see* Horsham St Faith, Spixworth and
Crostwick *Nor*
SPOFFORTH (All Saints) w Kirk Deighton *Leeds 18*   P *Bp*
NSM B RYAN
SPONDON (St Werburgh) *Derby 5*   P *Mrs L B Palmer*
V J F HOLLYWELL   C W P WATERS   NSM L K SMEDLEY
SPOTLAND (St Clement) and Oakenrod *Man 6*   P *Bp*
NSM S BARRON
SPRATTON (St Andrew)   *see* Guilsborough and Hollowell and
Cold Ashby etc *Pet*
SPREYTON (St Michael)   *see* Chagford, Gidleigh, Throwleigh
etc *Ex*
SPRIDLINGTON (St Hilary)   *see* Owmby Gp *Linc*

SPRING GROVE (St Mary) *Lon 11* **P** *Ch Patr Trust*
V E A MATTHEWS
SPRING PARK (All Saints) *S'wark 19* **P** *Bp* **V** Y V CLARKE
SPRINGFIELD (All Saints) *Chelmsf 9* **P** *Air Cdre N S Paynter*
P-in-c S M M ISKANDER **C** D C PIERCE
SPRINGFIELD (Holy Trinity) *Chelmsf 9* **P** *Simeon's Trustees*
V K A RODDY **OLM** I D FULLER
SPRINGFIELD (St Christopher) *Birm 6* **P** *Trustees*
V T THOMAS
SPRINGFIELD, EAST (Church of Our Saviour) (not known)
Chelmsf 9 **P** *Bp* **C** A P GREAVES-BROWN
NSM M C HEWSON
SPRINGFIELD, NORTH (St Augustine of Canterbury)
Chelmsf 9 **P** *Bp* **P-in-c** C J BROWN **C** D C PIERCE
SPRINGFIELDS (St Stephen) *see* Wolverhampton St Martin
and St Steph *Lich*
SPRINGLINE, comprising Aisthorpe, Brattleby, Burton by
Lincoln, Cammeringham, North Carlton, South Carlton,
Fillingham, Ingham, and Scampton *Linc 5* **P** *Lady Monson,*
Ball Coll Ox, J M Wright Esq, Bp, and DBP (jt)
R S T MATTAPALLY **OLM** S DEACON
SPRINGTHORPE (St George and St Laurence) *see* Lea Gp *Linc*
SPRINGWELL (St Mary the Virgin) *see* Sunderland St Mary
and St Pet *Dur*
SPRINGWOOD (All Souls) *see* Liv All So Springwood *Liv*
SPROATLEY (St Swithin) *see* Hedon, Paull, Sproatley and
Preston *York*
SPROTBROUGH (St Mary the Virgin) *Sheff 7* **P** *Bp*
R B A J BARRACLOUGH **NSM** R A HEATON
SPROUGHTON (All Saints) w Burstall, Copdock w
Washbrook and Belstead and Bentley w Tattingstone
St E 13 **P** *Patr Bd* **R** A D SHANNON
SPROWSTON (St Cuthbert) (St Mary and St Margaret) w
Beeston *Nor 2* **P** *D&C* **R** S C STOKES **C** B CHISANU,
B CHISHANU, D AKRILL, D M DORAN-SMITH,
G V KIRK-SPRIGGS **NSM** M A HIDER
SPROXTON (St Bartholomew) *see* High Framland Par *Leic*
SPROXTON (St Chad) *see* Helmsley Gp *York*
SQUIRRELS HEATH (All Saints) *Chelmsf 2* **P** *Bp*
V C W WRAGG
STADHAMPTON (St John the Baptist) *see* Dorchester *Ox*
STAFFHURST WOOD (St Silvan) *see* Limpsfield and Tatsfield
S'wark
STAFFORD (St Bertelin) and Whitgreave St John *Lich 10*
P *Bp and Earl of Harrowby (jt)* **V** J E EVANS
STAFFORD (St Chad) *Lich 10* **P** *Bp* **V** R J S GRIGSON
C D D J PAYNE
STAFFORD (St John the Baptist) and Tixall w Ingestre
Lich 10 **P** *Bp and Earl of Shrewsbury and Talbot (jt)*
R C N RUDD **C** D D J PAYNE
STAFFORD (St Mary) and Marston *Lich 10* **P** *Bp and Earl of*
Harrowby (jt) **V** R J S GRIGSON **C** D D J PAYNE
STAFFORD (St Paul) (St Thomas and St Andrew) *Lich 10*
P *V Castle Ch and Hyndman Trustees (jt)* **V** M G STRANG
C I C T PERRY
STAFFORD, WEST (St Andrew) *see* Dorchester and the
Winterbournes *Sarum*
STAGSDEN (St Leonard) *see* Bromham w Oakley and
Stagsden *St Alb*
STAGSHAW CHAPEL (St Aidan) *see* St John Lee *Newc*
STAINBY (St Peter) *see* Colsterworth Par *Linc*
STAINCLIFFE (Christ Church) and Carlinghow *Leeds 7* **P** V
Brownhill and V Batley (jt) **V** G NEWTON
Hon C M G INMAN
STAINCROSS (St John the Evangelist) *see* Darton w
Staincross and Mapplewell *Leeds*
STAINDROP (St Mary) *Dur 4* **P** *Lord Barnard* **V** *vacant*
STAINES (Christ Church) *Lon 13* **P** *Bp* **V** M BURLEY
STAINES (St Mary) (St Peter) *Lon 13* **P** *Ld Chan*
V J A SAMADI
STAINFIELD (St Andrew) *see* Bardney *Linc*
STAINFORTH (St Mary) *Sheff 10* **P** *Bp* **P-in-c** J M S JONES
STAINFORTH (St Peter) *see* Langcliffe w Stainforth and
Horton *Leeds*
STAINING (St Luke Mission Church) *see* Layton and Staining
Blackb
STAINLAND (St Andrew) and Outlane *Leeds 6* **P** V *Halifax*
V R A CHAPMAN
STAINLEY, NORTH (St Mary the Virgin) *see* W Tanfield and
Well w Snape and N Stainley *Leeds*
STAINLEY, SOUTH (St Wilfrid) *see* Bishop Thornton, Burnt
Yates, Markington etc *Leeds*
STAINMORE (St Stephen) *see* Upper Eden *Carl*
STAINTON (St Peter and St Paul) w Hemlington and Hilton
York 20 **P** *Abp* **V** C D TODD
STAINTON (St Winifred) *see* Tickhill w Stainton *Sheff*

STAINTON BY LANGWORTH (St John the Baptist) *see*
Barlings *Linc*
STAINTON LE VALE (St Andrew) *see* Walesby Gp *Linc*
STAINTON, GREAT (All Saints) *see* Stockton Country Par *Dur*
STAINTONDALE (St John the Baptist) *see* Ravenscar and
Staintondale *York*
STAITHES (St Peter) *see* Hinderwell, Roxby and Staithes etc
York
STAKEFORD (Holy Family) *see* Choppington *Newc*
STALBRIDGE (St Mary) *see* Spire Hill *Sarum*
STALHAM (St Mary), East Ruston, Brunstead, Sutton and
Ingham *Nor 12* **P** *Bp, DBP and Mrs S F Baker (jt)*
OLM A P BEVAN
STALISFIELD (St Mary) *see* Kingsdown, Creekside and High
Downs *Cant*
STALLING BUSK (St Matthew) *see* Upper Wensleydale *Leeds*
STALLINGBOROUGH (St Peter and St Paul) *see* Wolds
Gateway Group *Linc*
STALMINE (St James) *see* Over Wyre *Blackb*
STALYBRIDGE (Holy Trinity and Christ Church) *Ches 14*
P *Trustees* **V** G KENNAUGH **C** S P STRIDE
STALYBRIDGE (St George) *Man 5* **P** *Lord Deramore and R*
Ashton-under-Lyne St Mich (jt) **V** P A WARNER
STALYBRIDGE (St Paul) *Ches 14* **P** *Trustees* **V** K E HANDLEY
STAMBOURNE (St Peter and St Thomas Becket) *see* The
Hedinghams and Upper Colne *Chelmsf*
STAMBRIDGE (St Mary and All Saints) *Chelmsf 13* **P** *Ld*
Chan (1 turn), Charterhouse (3 turns) **R** *vacant*
STAMFORD (All Saints) w St John the Baptist *Linc 16* **P** *Ld*
Chan and Burghley Ho Preservation Trust Ltd (alt) **R** N J SHAW
Hon C D M BOND
STAMFORD (Christ Church) *Linc 16* **P** *Bp* **V** A O LAOTAN
STAMFORD (St George) (St Paul) *Linc 16* **P** *Burghley Ho*
Preservation Trust Ltd **R** M A N TAYLOR **C** A D ACHESON,
B M TOPHAM, G S BANNISTER, S R SIMCOX
STAMFORD (St Mary) (St Martin) *Linc 16* **P** *Burghley Ho*
Preservation Trust Ltd **R** *vacant*
STAMFORD BRIDGE Group of Parishes, The (St John the
Baptist), including Catton and Scrayingham *York 5* **P** *Lord*
Egremont (2 turns), The Crown (1 turn) **R** S G PRITCHARD
STAMFORD HILL (St Bartholomew) *Lon 5* **P** *The Crown*
V C L CARD-REYNOLDS
STAMFORD HILL (St Thomas) *Lon 5* **P** *R Hackney*
V W G CAMPBELL-TAYLOR **NSM** M F E STEWART, S C EJIAKU
STAMFORDHAM (St Mary the Virgin) w Matfen *Newc 9*
P *Ld Chan* **P-in-c** R L S SCHEFFER
STANBRIDGE (St John the Baptist) *see* Totternhoe,
Stanbridge and Tilsworth *St Alb*
STANBURY (Mission Church) *see* Haworth and Cross Roads
cum Lees *Leeds*
STAND (All Saints) *Man 4* **P** *Earl of Wilton* **C** D A WILLIAMS
NSM A M WHITTLEWORTH
STANDISH (St Nicholas) *see* Stroudwater *Glouc*
STANDISH (St Wilfrid) *Blackb 4* **P** *Bp* **R** A HOLLIDAY
C R A M FEENEY **NSM** C L GABRIEL
STANDLAKE (St Giles) *see* Lower Windrush *Ox*
STANDON (All Saints) *see* Cotes Heath and Standon and
Swynnerton etc *Lich*
STANDON (St Mary) and The Mundens w Sacombe
St Alb 15 **P** *Ch Trust Fund Trust, K Coll Cam, and R*
Abel-Smith Esq (1 turn), Ch Trust Fund Trust (1 turn)
R E J CHITHAM **NSM** A C HUDSON, C HUDSON
STANFIELD (St Margaret) *see* Launditch and the Upper Nar
Nor
STANFORD (All Saints) *Nor 13* **P** *Bp* **V** *vacant*
STANFORD (All Saints) *see* Elham Valley *Cant*
STANFORD (St Nicholas) *see* Avon-Swift *Leic*
STANFORD BISHOP (St James) *see* Frome Valley *Heref*
STANFORD DINGLEY (St Denys) *see* Bradfield and Stanford
Dingley *Ox*
STANFORD IN THE VALE (St Denys) w Goosey and Hatford
Ox 25 **P** *D&C Westmr (3 turns), Simeon's Trustees (2 turns)*
V P A EDDY
STANFORD RIVERS (St Margaret) *see* Chipping Ongar w
Shelley etc *Chelmsf*
STANFORD-LE-HOPE (St Margaret) w Mucking *Chelmsf 15*
P MMCET **P-in-c** T ROUT
STANFORD-ON-AVON (St Nicholas) *see* Avon-Swift *Leic*
STANFORD-ON-SOAR (St John the Baptist) *see* E and W
Leake, Stanford-on-Soar, Rempstone etc *S'well*
STANFORD-ON-TEME (St Mary) *see* Teme Valley S *Worc*
STANGROUND (St John the Baptist) (St Michael and All
Angels) and Farcet *Ely 15* **P** *Em Coll Cam*
P-in-c A J AVERY **C** C R AVERY
STANHOE (All Saints) *see* Docking, The Birchams, Fring etc
Nor

STANHOPE (St Thomas) *see* Upper Weardale *Dur*

STANION (St Peter) *see* Brigstock w Stanion and Lowick and Sudborough *Pet*

STANLEY (All Saints) *see* W Hallam and Mapperley w Stanley *Derby*

STANLEY (St Andrew) *as above*

STANLEY (St Andrew) and South Moor *Dur 2* **P** *Bp (3 turns) and The Crown (1 turn)* **V** S CLARK **C** T J DAGLISH

STANLEY (St Anne) and Stoneycroft St Paul *Liv 5* **P** V W *Derby St Mary and St Chad's Coll Dur (jt)* **V** E L WILLIAMS **C** G HUGHES **Hon C** C WARRILOW **NSM** T P DUNSBY

STANLEY (St Thomas) *see* Satley, Stanley and Tow Law *Dur*

STANLEY PONTLARGE (Chapel) *see* Winchcombe *Glouc*

STANMER w Falmer *Chich 19* **P** *Bp* **V** *vacant*

STANMORE (St Luke) *Win 7* **P** *Bp* **P-in-c** E P A DINES **C** M S FOSTER

STANMORE, GREAT (St John the Evangelist) *Lon 20* **P** R O *Bernays Esq* **R** I M STONE **C** J D RAPSON

STANMORE, LITTLE (St Lawrence) *Lon 20* **P** *Bp* **R** P M REECE

STANNINGFIELD (St Nicholas) *see* St Edm Way *St E*

STANNINGLEY (St Thomas) *Leeds 11* **P** V *Leeds St Pet* **R** R I M COUTTS

STANNINGTON (Christ Church) *Sheff 4* **P** *Bp* **NSM** A M COOK

STANNINGTON (St Mary the Virgin) *Newc 11* **P** *Bp* **V** *vacant*

STANSFIELD (All Saints) *see* Bansfield *St E*

STANSTEAD (St James) *see* Glemsford, Hartest w Boxted, Somerton etc *St E*

STANSTEAD ABBOTS (St Andrew) *see* Gt Amwell w St Margaret's and Stanstead Abbots *St Alb*

STANSTEAD ST MARGARET (St Mary the Virgin) *as above*

STANSTED (St Mary) w Fairseat and Vigo *Roch 10* **P** *Bp* **R** C J L NOBLE

STANSTED MOUNTFITCHET (St John) w Birchanger and Farnham *Chelmsf 17* **P** *Bp, New Coll Ox, and Mrs L A Murphy (jt)* **P-in-c** C M FAIRWEATHER **NSM** H M FLACK

STANTON (All Saints) United Benefice, including Barningham, Coney Weston, Hepworth, Hinderclay, Hopton, Market Weston, and Thelnetham *St E 5* **P** K Coll Cam, MMCET, Exors S Holt-Wilson, and Bp (1 turn), The Crown (1 turn), Ld Chan (1 turn)* **R** C R BLADEN **NSM** A J BARCLAY

STANTON (St Gabriel) *see* Golden Cap Team *Sarum*

STANTON (St Mary and All Saints) *see* Markfield, Thornton, Bagworth and Stanton etc *Leic*

STANTON (St Mary) *see* Alton w Bradley-le-Moors, Ellastone w Stanton, and Mayfield *Lich*

STANTON (St Michael and All Angels) *see* Winchcombe *Glouc*

STANTON BY BRIDGE (St Michael) *see* Melbourne, Ticknall, Smisby and Stanton *Derby*

STANTON DREW (St Mary the Virgin) *see* Chew Magna w Dundry, Norton Malreward etc *B & W*

STANTON FITZWARREN (St Leonard) *see* Stratton St Margaret w S Marston etc *Bris*

STANTON HARCOURT (St Michael) *see* Lower Windrush *Ox*

STANTON HILL (All Saints) *see* Skegby w Teversal *S'well*

STANTON LACY (St Peter) *see* Bromfield *Heref*

STANTON ON HINE HEATH (St Andrew) *Lich 21* **P** *Sir Beville Stanier Bt* **V** R J CRESSWELL

STANTON PRIOR (St Lawrence) *see* Farmborough, Marksbury and Stanton Prior *B & W*

STANTON ST BERNARD (All Saints) *see* Vale of Pewsey *Sarum*

STANTON ST JOHN (St John the Baptist) *see* Beckley, Forest Hill, Horton-cum-Studley and Stanton St John *Ox*

STANTON ST QUINTIN (St Giles) *see* Gauzebrook *Bris*

STANTONBURY (Christ Church) and Willen *Ox 14* **P** *Patr Bd* **TR** P A SMITH **TV** N A POPHAM **NSM** C O IWUAGWU **OLM** S R MUTHUVELOE

STANTON-BY-DALE (St Michael and All Angels) w Dale Abbey and Risley *Derby 8* **P** *Bp* **R** P J SELBY **C** J A LEE

STANTON-IN-PEAK (Holy Trinity) *see* Youlgreave, Middleton, Stanton-in-Peak etc *Derby*

STANTON-ON-THE-WOLDS (All Saints) *see* Keyworth and Stanton-on-the-Wolds and Bunny etc *S'well*

STANWAY (St Albright) (St Andrew) *Chelmsf 20* **P** *Magd Coll Ox* **P-in-c** A C BUSHELL **C** A L DAVIS **NSM** C D WILLIS, W J PAGDEN

STANWAY (St Peter) *see* Winchcombe *Glouc*

STANWELL (St Mary the Virgin) *Lon 13* **P** *Ld Chan* **P-in-c** S J KING **C** M W DOBSON

STANWICK (St Laurence) *see* Raunds, Hargrave, Ringstead and Stanwick *Pet*

STANWIX (St Michael) *Carl 3* **P** *Bp* **V** N D BEER **NSM** A QUINN, J R LIBBY

STAPEHILL (All Saints) *see* Hampreston *Sarum*

STAPENHILL (Immanuel) *Derby 7* **P** *Ch Soc Trust* **OLM** C A BUCKLEY

STAPENHILL (St Peter) w Cauldwell *Derby 7* **P** *Ch Soc Trust* **V** M ANDREYEV

STAPLE (St James) *see* Eastry and Woodnesborough *Cant*

STAPLE FITZPAINE (St Peter) *see* Beercrocombe w Curry Mallet, Hatch Beauchamp etc *B & W*

STAPLE TYE (St James) *Chelmsf 4* **P** *Bp* **P-in-c** C C OKEKE

STAPLECROSS (St Mark) *see* Ewhurst *Chich*

STAPLEFIELD COMMON (St Mark) *see* Slaugham and Staplefield Common *Chich*

STAPLEFORD (All Saints) *see* Withamside *Linc*

STAPLEFORD (St Andrew) *Ely 5* **P** *D&C* **V** S J TALBOTT **C** C L G COATES **NSM** S W TAYLOR

STAPLEFORD (St Helen) (St Luke) *S'well 8* **P** *CPAS* **NSM** K A HANFORD

STAPLEFORD (St Mary) *see* Beane Valley *St Alb*

STAPLEFORD (St Mary) *see* Wylye and Till Valley *Sarum*

STAPLEFORD ABBOTTS (St Mary) *see* Vale of Roding *Chelmsf*

STAPLEFORD TAWNEY (St Mary the Virgin) *see* Theydon Par *Chelmsf*

STAPLEGROVE (St John the Evangelist) w Norton Fitzwarren *B & W 18* **P** *Bp and MMCET (jt)* **R** P J IRVING

STAPLEHURST (All Saints) *Cant 11* **P** *St Jo Coll Cam* **R** S TETZLAFF

STAPLETON (Holy Trinity) *see* Frenchay and Stapleton *Bris*

STAPLETON (St John) *see* Dorrington w Leebotwood, Longnor, Stapleton etc *Heref*

STAPLETON (St Martin) *see* Barwell w Potters Marston and Stapleton *Leic*

STAPLETON (St Mary) *see* Bewcastle, Stapleton and Kirklinton etc *Carl*

STARBECK (St Andrew) *Leeds 18* **P** V *Harrogate Ch Ch* **V** P G CARMAN **C** S A PICKERING

STARCROSS (St Paul) *see* Dawlish w Holcombe, Cofton and Starcross *Ex*

STARSTON (St Margaret) *see* Dickleburgh and The Pulhams *Nor*

START BAY *see* Stokenham, Slapton, Charleton w Buckland etc *Ex*

STARTFORTH (Holy Trinity) *see* Lower Teesdale *Leeds*

STATFOLD (St Matthew) *see* Mease Valley *Lich*

STATHERN (St Guthlac) *see* Vale of Belvoir *Leic*

STAUGHTONS, The (St Andrew) (All Saints) w Hail Weston *Ely 13* **P** *Mert Coll Ox, St Jo Coll Ox, and CCC Ox (by turn)* **V** L N BLAND

STAUNTON (All Saints) *see* Coleford, Staunton, Newland, Redbrook etc *Glouc*

STAUNTON (St James) *see* Ashleworth, Corse, Hartpury, Hasfield etc *Glouc*

STAUNTON (St Mary) w Flawborough *S'well 3* **P** E G *Staunton Esq* **P-in-c** E I MURRAY

STAUNTON-ON-ARROW (St Peter) *see* Pembridge w Moor Court, Shobdon, Staunton etc *Heref*

STAUNTON-ON-WYE (St Mary the Virgin) *see* Letton w Staunton, Byford, Mansel Gamage etc *Heref*

STAVELEY (All Saints) *see* Walkingham Hill *Leeds*

STAVELEY (St James), Ings and Kentmere *Carl 11* **P** V *Kendal H Trin* **P-in-c** S H P THOMPSON **C** J J RICHARDS

STAVELEY (St John the Baptist) and Barrow Hill *Derby 3* **P** *Bp, Adn Chesterfield, and Duke of Devonshire (jt)* **TR** S F JONES **TV** A P ARNOLD

STAVELEY IN CARTMEL (St Mary) *see* Cartmel Peninsula *Carl*

STAVERTON (St Catherine) *see* Twigworth, Down Hatherley, Norton, The Leigh etc *Glouc*

STAVERTON (St Mary the Virgin) *see* Daventry *Pet*

STAVERTON (St Paul de Leon) *see* Buckfastleigh, Dean Prior, Littlehempston etc *Ex*

STAWELL (St Francis) *see* Middlezoy w Othery, Moorlinch and Greinton *B & W*

STAWLEY (St Michael and All Angels) *see* Wellington and Distr *B & W*

STEANE (St Peter) *see* Aynho and Croughton w Evenley etc *Pet*

STEART BAY (St Andrew) *see* Cannington, Otterhampton, Combwich and Stockland *B & W*

STEBBING (St Mary the Virgin) and Lindsell w Great and Little (Bardfield) Saling *Chelmsf 17* **P** *Bp* **P-in-c** S E HURLEY **NSM** I P ELLIOTT, J H WOOD **OLM** M H PELLY

STECHFORD (All Saints) (St Andrew) *Birm 6* **P** *St Pet Coll Ox* **V** *vacant*

STEDHAM (St James) *see* Linch w Iping Marsh, Milland and Rake etc *Chich*
STEEP (All Saints) and Froxfield w Privett *Portsm 4* **P** *Ld Chan and Magd Coll Cam (alt)* **V** J E OWEN **NSM** S R COLLINGRIDGE
STEEPING, GREAT (All Saints) *see* Bolingbroke Deanery *Linc*
STEEPING, LITTLE (St Andrew) *as above*
STEEPLE (St Lawrence and All Saints) *see* Southminster and Steeple *Chelmsf*
STEEPLE (St Michael and All Angels) *see* St Aldhelm *Sarum*
STEEPLE ASHTON (St Mary the Virgin) *see* N Bradley, Southwick, Heywood and Steeple Ashton *Sarum*
STEEPLE ASTON (St Peter and St Paul) w North Aston and Tackley *Ox 29* **P** *BNC Ox, St Jo Coll Ox, and J D Taylor Esq (jt)* **R** E M GREEN
STEEPLE BARTON (St Mary) *see* Westcote Barton w Steeple Barton, Duns Tew etc *Ox*
STEEPLE BUMPSTEAD (St Mary) *see* Two Rivers *Chelmsf*
STEEPLE CLAYDON (St Michael) *see* The Claydons and Swan *Ox*
STEEPLE LANGFORD (All Saints) *see* Wylye and Till Valley *Sarum*
STEEPLE MORDEN (St Peter and St Paul) *see* Shingay Gp *Ely*
STEETLEY (All Saints) *see* Elmton w Creswell and Whitwell w Steetley *Derby*
STEETON (St Stephen) *Leeds 1* **P** *V Kildwick* **V** D COLEMAN
STELLA (St Cuthbert) *see* Blaydon *Dur*
STELLING (St Mary) *see* Chartham and Upper Hardres w Stelling *Cant*
STENIGOT (St Nicholas) *see* Asterby Gp *Linc*
STEPNEY (St Dunstan and All Saints) *Lon 7* **P** *Bp* **R** T F CRITCHLOW
STEPPINGLEY (St Lawrence) *see* Ampthill w Millbrook and Steppingley *St Alb*
STERNFIELD (St Mary Magdalene) *see* Alde River *St E*
STERT (St James) *see* Cannings and Redhorn *Sarum*
STETCHWORTH (St Peter) *see* Raddesley Gp *Ely*
STEVENAGE (All Saints) Pin Green *St Alb 20* **P** *Bp* **V** P J ORTON
STEVENAGE (Holy Trinity) (Christ the King) *St Alb 20* **P** *Bp* **V** R E CARROLL **NSM** A J THOMAS
STEVENAGE (Oak Church) Bishop's Mission Order *St Alb 20* **Min** A P PRIOR
STEVENAGE (St Andrew and St George) *St Alb 20* **P** *Bp* **R** K I MITCHELL
STEVENAGE (St Hugh) (St John) Chells *St Alb 20* **P** *Bp* **V** C K PERERA **NSM** C E A DOUGLAS
STEVENAGE (St Mary) Shephall *St Alb 20* **P** *Bp* **V** V A HATHAWAY
STEVENAGE (St Nicholas) and Graveley *St Alb 20* **P** *Bp* **V** D M BROWN
STEVENAGE (St Peter) Broadwater *St Alb 20* **P** *Bp* **V** C R SHARPLES **C** P FOSTER
STEVENTON (St Michael and All Angels) *see* DAMASCUS *Ox*
STEVENTON (St Nicholas) *see* N Waltham and Steventon, Ashe and Deane *Win*
STEVINGTON (Church Room) *see* Chellington *St Alb*
STEVINGTON (St Mary the Virgin) *as above*
STEWKLEY (St Michael and All Angels) *see* Cottesloe *Ox*
STEWTON (St Andrew) *see* Louth *Linc*
STEYNING (St Andrew and St Cuthman) *Chich 5* **P** *Bp* **V** M D G HEATHER
STIBBARD (All Saints) *see* Heart of Norfolk *Nor*
STIBBINGTON (St John the Baptist) *see* Castor w Upton and Stibbington etc *Pet*
STICKER (St Mark's Mission Church) *see* St Mewan w Mevagissey and St Ewe *Truro*
STICKFORD (St Helen) *see* Bolingbroke Deanery *Linc*
STICKLEPATH (St Mary) *see* Okehampton, Inwardleigh, Belstone, Sourton etc *Ex*
STICKLEPATH (St Paul) w Roundswell *Ex 13* **P** *Bp* **V** G CHAVE-COX
STICKNEY (St Luke) *see* Bolingbroke Deanery *Linc*
STIFFKEY (St John and St Mary) and Bale *Nor 17* **P** *MMCET, Bp, DBP, Keble Coll Ox, and Sir Euan Hamilton Anstruther-Gough-Calthorpe Bt (jt)* **R** I C WHITTLE
STIFFORD (St Cedd) (St Mary) *Chelmsf 15* **P** *Bp* **R** A R B HIGGS
STILLINGFLEET (St Helen) *see* Escrick and Stillingfleet w Naburn *York*
STILLINGTON (St John) *see* Stockton Country Par *Dur*
STILLINGTON (St Nicholas) *see* Forest of Galtres *York*
STILTON (St Mary Magdalene) w Denton and Caldecote and Folkesworth w Morborne and Haddon *Ely 15* **P** *MMCET and Bp, Ld Chan (alt)* **R** R J GIBBS **C** M W PYBUS

STINCHCOMBE (St Cyr) *see* Cam w Stinchcombe *Glouc*
STINSFORD (St Michael) *see* Charminster, Stinsford and the Chalk Stream villages *Sarum*
STIPERSTONES *see* Minsterley, Habberley and Hope w Shelve *Heref*
STIRCHLEY (All Saints) *see* Cen Telford *Lich*
STIRCHLEY (Ascension) *Birm 2* **P** *R Kings Norton* **V** C A GRYLLS
STISTED (All Saints) *see* Coggeshall, Markshall, Cressing etc *Chelmsf*
STITHIANS (St Stythian) *see* St Stythians w Perranarworthal and Gwennap *Truro*
STIXWOULD (St Peter) *see* Woodhall Spa Gp *Linc*
STOAK (St Lawrence) *see* Ellesmere Port *Ches*
STOCK (St Barnabas) *see* Spire Hill *Sarum*
STOCK HARVARD (All Saints) *Chelmsf 9* **P** *Guild of All So* **R** S W NEED **NSM** M K SEAMAN
STOCKBRIDGE (Old St Peter) *see* Mid Test *Win*
STOCKBRIDGE (St Peter) *as above*
STOCKBRIDGE VILLAGE (St Jude) *see* 4Saints Team *Liv*
STOCKBURY (St Mary Magdalene) *see* The Six *Cant*
STOCKCROSS (St John) *see* E Downland *Ox*
STOCKERSTON (St Peter) *see* Six Saints circa Holt *Leic*
STOCKING FARM (St Luke) and Beaumont Leys *Leic 1* **P** *Bp* **V** R C HINSLEY
STOCKING PELHAM (St Mary) *see* Braughing, Furneux Pelham and Stocking Pelham *St Alb*
STOCKINGFORD (St Paul) *Cov 5* **P** *V Nuneaton* **V** K I MASSEY **C** J L JOYCE
STOCKLAND (St Mary Magdalene) *see* Cannington, Otterhampton, Combwich and Stockland *B & W*
STOCKLAND (St Michael and All Angels) *see* Kilmington, Stockland, Dalwood, Yarcombe etc *Ex*
STOCKLAND GREEN (St Mark) *Birm 4* **P** *The Crown* **V** *vacant*
STOCKLEIGH ENGLISH (St Mary the Virgin) *see* N Creedy *Ex*
STOCKLEIGH POMEROY (St Mary the Virgin) *as above*
STOCKLINCH (St Mary Magdalene) *see* Winsmoor *B & W*
STOCKPORT (St George) *Ches 18* **P** *Trustees* **V** E C HALL **C** J B ARNOTT
STOCKPORT (St Mark) *see* Edgeley and Cheadle Heath *Ches*
STOCKPORT (St Martin) *see* Heatons *Man*
STOCKPORT (St Mary) (St Thomas) (St Andrew) and Brinnington *Ches 18* **P** *Bp and G&C Coll Cam (jt)* **R** L S CULLENS **C** J A PIPER, M L FLINT
STOCKPORT (St Matthew) *see* Edgeley and Cheadle Heath *Ches*
STOCKPORT (St Peter) *Ches 18* **P** *Ch Union* **R** *vacant*
STOCKPORT (St Saviour) *Ches 18* **P** *Trustees* **V** D V COOKSON
STOCKSFIELD (St John) *see* Bywell and Mickley *Newc*
STOCKTON (St Andrew) *see* Teme Valley N *Worc*
STOCKTON (St Chad) *see* Beckbury, Badger, Kemberton, Ryton, Stockton etc *Lich*
STOCKTON (St John the Baptist) *see* Wylye and Till Valley *Sarum*
STOCKTON (St Michael and All Angels) *see* Napton-on-the-Hill, Lower Shuckburgh etc *Cov*
STOCKTON (St Michael and All Angels) *see* Waveney Marshlands *Nor*
STOCKTON CHRISTCHURCH (St Chad) (St James) (St John the Baptist) *Dur 8* **P** *Bp* **P-in-c** J L SHARPE
STOCKTON Country Parish, comprising Bishopton, Great Stainton, Grindon, Redmarshall, Stillington, and Wynyard Park *Dur 8* **P** *Bp, Ld Chan, The Crown, and D&C (by turn)* **P-in-c** C A GIBBS
STOCKTON HEATH (St Thomas) *Ches 4* **P** *P G Greenall Esq* **V** M L RIDLEY **C** R J ICKE
STOCKTON ON TEES (Holy Trinity) (St Mark) *Dur 8* **P** *Bp* **P-in-c** P S D NEVILLE
STOCKTON Parish Church (no dedication) *Dur 8* **P** *Bp* **P-in-c** M G MILLER **C** J C BELL
STOCKTON-ON-TEES (St Paul) *Dur 8* **P** *The Crown* **P-in-c** P A ARNOLD
STOCKTON-ON-TEES (St Peter) *Dur 8* **P** *Bp* **V** W E BRAVINER **C** P MURRAY **NSM** D T ACKERLEY
STOCKTON-ON-TEES (St Thomas) *see* Stockton Par Ch *Dur*
STOCKTON-ON-THE-FOREST (Holy Trinity) *see* Rural E York *York*
STOCKWELL (St Andrew) (St Michael) *S'wark 11* **P** *Bp* **V** E M WOOFF
STOCKWITH, EAST (St Peter) *see* Trentcliffe Gp *Linc*
STOCKWITH, WEST (St Mary the Virgin) *see* Beckingham, Walkeringham, Misterton, etc *S'well*

STOCKWOOD (Christ the Servant) *see* Bris Ch the Servant Stockwood *Bris*

STODDEN Churches, The, comprising Dean, Melchbourne, Pertenhall, Shelton, Swineshead, and Yelden *St Alb 13* **P** *MMCET and DBP (alt)* **R** S C HOLROYD

STODMARSH (St Mary) *see* Lt Stour *Cant*

STODY (St Mary) *see* Brinton, Briningham, Hunworth, Stody etc *Nor*

STOGUMBER (Blessed Virgin Mary) *see* Quantock Towers *B & W*

STOGURSEY (St Andrew) *see* Quantock Coast *B & W*

STOKE (St Mary and St Andrew) *see* Colsterworth Par *Linc*

STOKE (St Michael) Coventry *Cov 1* **P** *Bp and Ld Chan (alt)* **R** C MCARTHUR **C** D S BENNETT **NSM** J S WATKINS-WOLLNER

STOKE (St Peter and St Paul) *see* Grain w Stoke *Roch*

STOKE ABBOTT (St Mary) *see* Beaminster Area *Sarum*

STOKE ALBANY (St Botolph) w Wilbarston and Ashley w Weston-by-Welland and Sutton Bassett *Pet 7* **P** *Comdr L M M Saunders-Watson (2 turns), Bp (1 turn), DBP (1 turn)* **P-in-c** A J OLIVER

STOKE ALDERMOOR (St Catherine) and New Century Park *Cov 1* **P** *Ld Chan and Bp (alt)* **V** E K FORBES STONE

STOKE ASH (All Saints) *see* S Hartismere *St E*

STOKE BARDOLPH (St Luke) *see* Burton Joyce, Bulcote and Stoke Bardolph etc *S'well*

STOKE BISHOP (St Mary Magdalene) *Bris 2* **P** *Bp* **V** J M BALL **C** J D WHITE, J MORRIS, S J POTTER **NSM** A K CATTELL, H J TRAPNELL, M J HALL

STOKE BLISS (St Peter) *see* Teme Valley S *Worc*

STOKE BRUERNE (St Mary the Virgin) *see* Blisworth, Alderton, Grafton Regis etc *Pet*

STOKE BY CLARE (St John the Baptist) *see* Stour Valley *St E*

STOKE BY NAYLAND (St Mary) w Leavenheath and Polstead, and Nayland w Wissington *St E 4* **P** *DBP, Mrs S E F Holden, and St John's Coll Ox (1 turn), Ld Chan (1 turn)* **R** *vacant*

STOKE CANON (St Mary Magdalene) *see* Brampford Speke, Cadbury, Newton St Cyres etc *Ex*

STOKE CHARITY (St Mary and St Michael) *see* Upper Dever *Win*

STOKE CLIMSLAND (not known) *see* Callington Cluster *Truro*

STOKE D'ABERNON (St Mary the Virgin) *Guildf 10* **P** *K Coll Cam* **R** *vacant*

STOKE DAMEREL (St Andrew w St Luke) *Ex 20* **P** *The Crown* **R** K A ROBUS

STOKE DOYLE (St Rumbold) *see* Aldwincle, Clopton, Pilton, Stoke Doyle etc *Pet*

STOKE DRY (St Andrew) *see* Lyddington, Bisbrooke, Caldecott, Glaston etc *Pet*

STOKE EDITH (St Mary) *see* Hop Churches *Heref*

STOKE FLEMING (St Peter), Blackawton, Strete and East Allington *Ex 12* **P** *Bp and DBP (jt)* **V** A B SHAW

STOKE GABRIEL (St Gabriel) *see* Totnes w Bridgetown, Berry Pomeroy etc *Ex*

STOKE GIFFORD (St Michael) *Bris 5* **P** *Bp* **R** S JONES **C** T Y BENYON, V L WICKS **NSM** J C BRADLEY

STOKE GOLDING (St Margaret) *see* Fenn Lanes Gp *Leic*

STOKE GOLDINGTON (St Peter) *see* Gayhurst w Ravenstone, Stoke Goldington etc *Ox*

STOKE HAMMOND (St Luke) *see* Brickhills and Stoke Hammond *Ox*

STOKE HEATH (St Alban) *see* Cov St Alb *Cov*

STOKE HILL (St Peter) *Guildf 5* **P** *Bp* **V** K L ROSSLYN-SMITH

STOKE HOLY CROSS (Holy Cross) w Dunston, Arminghall and Caistor St Edmunds w Markshall *Nor 8* **P** *D&C and Mrs D Pott (jt)* **R** R J BAKER **NSM** L MARSH

STOKE LACY (St Peter and St Paul) *see* Bromyard and Stoke Lacy *Heref*

STOKE LYNE (St Peter) *see* Shelswell *Ox*

STOKE MANDEVILLE (St Mary the Virgin) *see* Ellesborough, The Kimbles and Stoke Mandeville *Ox*

STOKE NEWINGTON (St Andrew) *Lon 5* **P** *Bp* **P-in-c** C A ENGA

STOKE NEWINGTON (St John the Evangelist) *see* Brownswood Park *Lon*

STOKE NEWINGTON (St Mary) (Old Parish Church) *Lon 5* **P** *Bp* **R** H M BAKER **C** R H LIDDELL **NSM** A SHEERAN

STOKE NEWINGTON (St Olave) *Lon 5* **P** *Ld Chan* **V** V A ROBERTS

STOKE NEWINGTON COMMON (St Michael and All Angels) *Lon 5* **P** *Bp* **V** S A GAYLE **Hon C** W G CAMPBELL-TAYLOR

STOKE NEWINGTON St Faith (St Matthias) and All Saints *Lon 5* **P** *City Corp* **V** D J LAMBERT

STOKE ORCHARD (St James the Great) *see* Deerhurst and Apperley w Forthampton etc *Glouc*

STOKE PARK (St Peter) *see* Ipswich St Pet Stoke Park *St E*

STOKE PERO (not known) *see* Porlock and Porlock Weir w Stoke Pero etc *B & W*

STOKE POGES (St Giles) *Ox 12* **P** *Ch Ch Ox* **V** N D BRADY

STOKE PRIOR (St Michael) *see* Wychebrook *Worc*

STOKE PRIOR (St Luke) *see* Leominster *Heref*

STOKE RIVERS (St Bartholomew) *see* Shirwell, Loxhore, Kentisbury, Arlington, etc *Ex*

STOKE ROW (St John the Evangelist) *see* Langtree *Ox*

STOKE ST GREGORY (St Gregory) *see* Athelney *B & W*

STOKE ST MARY (St Mary) *see* Beercrocombe w Curry Mallet, Hatch Beauchamp etc *B & W*

STOKE ST MICHAEL (St Michael) *see* Leigh upon Mendip w Stoke St Michael *B & W*

STOKE ST MILBOROUGH (St Milburgha) *see* Bromfield *Heref*

STOKE SUB HAMDON (The Blessed Virgin Mary) *see* Ham Hill Villages *B & W*

STOKE TALMAGE (St Mary Magdalene) *see* Thame *Ox*

STOKE TRISTER (St Andrew) *see* Charlton Musgrove, Cucklington and Stoke Trister *B & W*

STOKE UPON TERN (St Peter) *see* Cheswardine, Childs Ercall, Hales, Hinstock etc *Lich*

STOKE, EAST (St Oswald) w Syerston *S'well 3* **P** *Bp* **P-in-c** E I MURRAY

STOKE, NORTH (St Martin) *see* Bath Weston All SS w N Stoke and Langridge *B & W*

STOKE, NORTH (St Mary the Virgin) *see* Langtree *Ox*

STOKE, SOUTH (St Andrew) *see* Goring and Streatley w S Stoke *Ox*

STOKE, SOUTH (St James the Great) *see* Combe Down w Monkton Combe and S Stoke *B & W*

STOKE, SOUTH (St Leonard) *see* Arundel w Tortington and S Stoke *Chich*

STOKE, WEST (St Andrew) *see* Funtington and W Stoke w Sennicotts *Chich*

STOKEHAM (St Peter) *see* The Rivers *S'well*

STOKEINTEIGNHEAD (St Andrew) *see* Shaldon, Stokeinteignhead, Combeinteignhead etc *Ex*

STOKENCHURCH (St Peter and St Paul) *see* S Chilterns *Ox*

STOKE-NEXT-GUILDFORD (St John the Evangelist) *Guildf 5* **P** *Simeon's Trustees* **R** M C WOODWARD **C** J LAMBERTH **OLM** N S SHARPE

STOKENHAM (St Michael and All Angels), Slapton, Charleton w Buckland-Tout-Saints, East Portlemouth, South Pool, and Chivelstone *Ex 12* **P** *The Crown (1 turn), Bp, DBP, Sir Neil Jephcott Bt, and Ms S Tyler (1 turn), and Ld Chan (1 turn)* **NSM** M V BERRETT

STOKESAY (St John the Baptist) *see* Craven Arms *Heref*

STOKESBY (St Andrew) *see* S Trin Broads *Nor*

STOKESLEY (St Peter and St Paul) w Seamer *York 20* **P** *Abp* **P-in-c** B L W GUNTER

STOKE-UPON-TRENT (St Peter-ad-Vincula) (St Paul) and Fenton *Lich 11* **P** *Bp* **TR** A S L J WICKENS **TV** G E EZE, T P MERRY **C** V L FLANAGAN **NSM** G HARRISON **OLM** H W DUROSE

STOLFORD (St Peter) *see* Quantock Coast *B & W*

STON EASTON (Blessed Virgin Mary) *see* Chewton Mendip w Ston Easton, Litton etc *B & W*

STONDON (All Saints) *see* Gravenhurst, Shillington and Stondon *St Alb*

STONDON MASSEY (St Peter and St Paul) *see* Blackmore and Stondon Massey *Chelmsf*

STONE (All Saints) *see* Berkeley w Wick, Breadstone, Newport, Stone etc *Glouc*

STONE (Christ Church) and Oulton-with-Moddershall *Lich 12* **P** *Simeon's Trustees* **V** P H C KINGMAN

STONE (St John the Baptist) *see* Wychert Vale *Ox*

STONE (St Mary the Virgin) *see* Kidderminster E *Worc*

STONE (St Michael and St Wulfad) w Aston (St Saviour) *Lich 12* **P** *Bp* **R** I R CARDINAL **C** A M HUDSON **NSM** J G COTTERILL, J P CARTLIDGE

STONE CROSS (St Luke) w Langney, North *Chich 14* **P** *Bp* **V** J D VINE **C** D L PEGG

STONE near Dartford (St Mary) *Roch 2* **P** *Bp* **R** K W CLARK **NSM** A B S HARRIS-FAULKNER

STONE QUARRY (St Luke) *see* E Grinstead St Swithun *Chich*

STONEBRIDGE (St Michael and All Angels) *Lon 18* **P** *Bp* **V** S J LIEBERT

STONEBROOM (St Peter) *see* Morton and Stonebroom w Shirland *Derby*

STONEGATE (St Peter) *see* Wadhurst, Tidebrook and Stonegate *Chich*

STONEGRAVE (Holy Trinity) *see* Ampleforth w Oswaldkirk, Gilling E etc *York*

STONEHAM, NORTH (St Nicholas) (All Saints) and Bassett
Win 10   **P** *R H W Fleming Esq*   **R** S J WILLIAMS
C J B HARVEY, S J ARCHER   **Hon C** N BOAKES
NSM R PRIETO-DURAN

STONEHAM, SOUTH (St Mary)   *see* Swaythling *Win*

STONEHOUSE (St Paul)   *see* Plymouth St Andr and
Stonehouse *Ex*

STONE-IN-OXNEY (St Mary the Virgin)   *see* Tenterden,
Rother and Oxney *Cant*

STONELEIGH (St John the Baptist) *Guildf 9*   **P** *Bp*
C D G ANDREW

STONELEIGH (St Mary the Virgin) w Ashow *Cov 4*   **P** *Lord
Leigh and Bp (jt)*   **R** *vacant*

STONESBY (St Peter)   *see* Ironstone Villages *Leic*

STONESFIELD (St James the Great) w Combe Longa *Ox 29*
  P *Duke of Marlborough*   **R** R J WILLIAMSON

STONEY MIDDLETON (St Martin)   *see* Longstone, Curbar and
Stony Middleton *Derby*

STONEY STANTON (St Michael)   *see* Broughton Astley and
Croft w Stoney Stanton *Leic*

STONEYCROFT (All Saints) *Liv 5*   **P** *Bp*
V A J H LEATHERBARROW   **NSM** D JEYARAJ

STONEYCROFT (St Paul)   *see* Stanley and Stoneycroft St Paul
Liv

STONHAM ASPAL (St Mary and St Lambert)   *see* N Bosmere
St E

STONNALL (St Peter)   *see* Shenstone and Stonnall *Lich*

STONTON WYVILLE (St Denys)   *see* Welham, Glooston and
Cranoe and Stonton Wyville *Leic*

STONY MIDDLETON (St Martin)   *see* Longstone, Curbar
and Stony Middleton *Derby*

STONY STRATFORD (St Mary and St Giles) w Calverton
Ox 14   **P** *Bp and DBP (jt)*   **R** R NORTHING

STONYDELPH (St Martin in the Delph)   *see* Glascote and
Stonydelph *Lich*

STOODLEIGH (St Margaret)   *see* Washfield, Stoodleigh,
Withleigh etc *Ex*

STOPHAM (St Mary the Virgin) and Fittleworth *Chich 4*
  P *D&C and Col Sir Brian Barttelot Bt (jt)*   **P-in-c** D R CROOK

STOPSLEY (St Thomas) *St Alb 12*   **P** *Bp*   **V** D G ALEXANDER

STORRIDGE (St John the Baptist)   *see* Cradley w Mathon and
Storridge *Heref*

STORRINGTON (St Mary) *Chich 5*   **P** *Keble Coll Ox*
R K A WINDSLOW   **Hon C** C A HADLEY   **NSM** A R ROSS,
R W TOOVEY

STOTFOLD (St Mary the Virgin) and Radwell *St Alb 3*   **P** *Bp*
V W T BRITT   **NSM** G J CLARK

**STOTTESDON (St Mary) w Farlow, Cleeton St Mary,
Silvington, Sidbury and Middleton Scriven** *Heref 8*   **P** *Bp*
R M H DABORN

STOUGHTON (Emmanuel) *Guildf 5*   **P** *Simeon's Trustees*
V F SCAMMELL   **OLM** R P F MASTERS

STOUGHTON (St Mary)   *see* Octagon *Chich*

**STOULTON (St Edmund) w Drake's Broughton and Pirton
and Norton** *Worc 3*   **P** *Croome Estate Trustees, D&C, and Bp
(jt)*   **C** E L GOLDBY, G R NOYES, S A DANGERFIELD

STOUR DOWNS Benefice, The, comprising Brabourne,
Mersham, Monks Horton, Sellindge, Smeeth, and Stowting
Cant 6   **P** *Abp*   **V** C R T DENYER   **NSM** S J MANNERS

STOUR PROVOST (St Michael and All Angels)   *see* Stour Vale
Sarum

STOUR VALE, comprising Buckhorn Weston, East Stour,
Fifehead Magdalen, Kington Magna, Stour Provost, Stour
Row, Todber, and West Stour *Sarum 5*   **P** *Bp*   **V** R P PRIEST

STOUR VALLEY, The, comprising Cavendish, Clare w
Poslingford, Hundon, Stoke-by-Clare, and Wixoe *St E 2*
  P *DBP, Jes Coll Cam, Lady Loch, and Duchy of Lanc (by turn)*
R M J WOODROW

STOUR, EAST (Christ Church)   *see* Stour Vale *Sarum*

STOUR, LITTLE Benefice, The, comprising Ickham,
Littlebourne, Stodmarsh, Wickhambreaux and Wingham
Cant 1   **P** *Abp, D&C, Ch Trust Fund Trust, and Adn Cant (jt)*
R *vacant*

STOUR, LOWER   *see* Spetisbury w Charlton Marshall etc
Sarum

STOUR, UPPER, comprising Bourton, Kilmington, Stourton,
and Zeals *Sarum 12*   **P** *H C Hoare Esq (1 turn), Bp (2 turns),
and Bourton Chpl Trustees (1 turn)*
P-in-c B O RUNDELL-EVANS   **NSM** M I MACCORMACK

STOUR, WEST (St Mary)   *see* Stour Vale *Sarum*

STOURBRIDGE (St Thomas) *Worc 5*   **P** *Bp*   **V** A K SILLIS

STOURDENE Group, The, comprising Alderminster, Butler's
Marston, Ettington, Halford, Newbold-on-Stour, and
Pillerton Hersey w Pillerton Priors *Cov 9*   **P** *SMF, Bp, Major
and Mrs J E Shirley, Miss M L P Shirley, P E Shirley Esq, Ch Ch
Ox, Jes Coll Ox, and Mr and Mrs G Howell*   **R** S L GOBLE

STOURHEAD, comprising Barnardiston, Great Bradley, Great
Thurlow, Great Wratting, Kedington, Little Bradley, Little
Thurlow, and Little Wratting *St E 2*   **P** *E H Vestey Esq,
St Chad's Coll Dur, Ridley Hall Cam, and Walsingham Coll
Trust (jt)*   **R** C J GILES

STOURPAINE (Holy Trinity)   *see* Pimperne, Stourpaine,
Durweston and Bryanston *Sarum*

**STOURPORT-ON-SEVERN (St Michael and All Angels) and
Wilden** *Worc 1*   **P** *Earl Baldwin of Bewdley and V
Kidderminster St Mary and All SS (jt)*   **V** C J SALEH

STOURTON (St Peter)   *see* Upper Stour *Sarum*

STOURTON CAUNDLE (St Peter)   *see* Spire Hill *Sarum*

STOVEN (St Margaret)   *see* Hundred River and Wainford *St E*

STOW BARDOLPH (Holy Trinity)   *see* W Norfolk Priory Gp *Ely*

STOW BEDON (St Botolph)   *see* Caston, Griston, Merton,
Thompson etc *Nor*

STOW BRIDGE Mission (St Peter)   *see* W Norfolk Priory Gp
Ely

STOW Group, The (St Mary the Virgin), including Coates,
Torksey, and Willingham-by-Stow *Linc 2*   **P** *Bp and DBP (jt)*
OLM J A VICKERS

STOW LONGA (St Botolph)   *see* S Leightonstone *Ely*

STOW MARIES (St Mary and St Margaret)   *see* Cold Norton w
Stow Maries *Chelmsf*

**STOW ON THE WOLD (St Edward), Condicote and The
Swells** *Glouc 8*   **P** *DBP and Ch Ch Ox (jt)*   **R** *vacant*

STOW, WEST (St Mary)   *see* Lark Valley and N Bury *St E* ·

STOWCAPLE *Heref 7*   **P** *Bp (7 turns), D&C (2 turns), Exors Brig
A F L Clive (1 turn)*   **R** C M R PEMBERTON

STOWE (Assumption of St Mary the Virgin)   *see* N
Buckingham w Stowe *Ox*

STOWE (St Michael and All Angels)   *see* Middle Marches *Heref*

STOWE BY CHARTLEY (St John the Baptist)   *see* Mid Trent
Lich

STOWE NINE CHURCHES (St Michael)   *see* Heyford w Stowe
Nine Churches and Flore etc *Pet*

STOWE, UPPER (St James) *as above*

STOWELL (St Leonard)   *see* Chedworth, Yanworth and
Stowell, Coln Rogers etc *Glouc*

STOWELL (St Mary Magdalene)   *see* Milborne Port w
Goathill etc *B & W*

STOWEY (St Nicholas and Blessed Virgin Mary)   *see* Clutton
w Cameley, Bishop Sutton and Stowey *B & W*

STOWEY, NETHER (Blessed Virgin Mary)   *see* Aisholt, Enmore,
Goathurst, Nether Stowey etc *B & W*

STOWEY, OVER (St Peter and St Paul) *as above*

STOWFORD (St John the Baptist)   *see* Lifton,
Broadwoodwidger, Stowford etc *Ex*

STOWLANGTOFT (St George)   *see* Pakenham w Norton,
Tostock etc *St E*

STOWMARKET (St Peter and St Mary) *St E 3*   **P** *Ch Patr
Trust*   **V** M W EDEN   **NSM** R M STRETCH

STOWTING (St Mary the Virgin)   *see* Stour Downs *Cant*

STOWUPLAND (Holy Trinity)   *see* Haughley w Wetherden
and Stowupland *St E*

STRADBROKE (All Saints)   *see* Sancroft *St E*

STRADISHALL (St Margaret)   *see* Bansfield *St E*

STRADSETT (St Mary)   *see* Downham Market and Stradsett
Ely

STRAGGLETHORPE (St Michael)   *see* Brant Broughton and
Beckingham *Linc*

STRAITS, The (St Andrew)   *see* Gornal and Sedgley *Worc*

STRAMSHALL (St Michael and All Angels)   *see* Uttoxeter Area
Lich

STRANTON (All Saints) *Dur 6*   **P** *St Jo Coll Dur*   **V** N R SHAVE
C M M DELVES   **NSM** C R HALL

**STRATFIELD MORTIMER (St Mary) and Mortimer West End
w Padworth** *Ox 4*   **P** *Eton Coll, Ld Chan, and Englefield
Estate Trust Corp (by turn)*   **V** P CHAPLIN

STRATFIELD SAYE (St Mary)   *see* Sherfield-on-Loddon and
Stratfield Saye etc *Win*

STRATFORD (St John the Evangelist w Christ Church)
Chelmsf 5   **P** *V W Ham*   **C** C C ASINUGO, D M SCOTT,
R S OTULE

STRATFORD (St Paul) and St James *Chelmsf 5*   **P** *Ch Patr
Trust*   **V** I B ANDERSON   **C** R S G MOREIRA, S M RYAN

STRATFORD ST MARY (St Mary)   *see* Higham, Holton
St Mary, Raydon and Stratford *St E*

STRATFORD SUB CASTLE (St Lawrence)   *see* Salisbury St Fran
and Stratford sub Castle *Sarum*

**STRATFORD-UPON-AVON (Holy Trinity), Luddington and
Clifford Chambers** *Cov 8*   **P** *Bp*   **R** P J TAYLOR
C S R JARVIS   **NSM** K DYER

STRATTON (St Andrew)   *see* N Kernow *Truro*

STRATTON (St Mary the Virgin)   *see* Charminster, Stinsford
and the Chalk Stream villages *Sarum*

STRATTON (St Peter)   *see* Churn Valley *Glouc*
STRATTON AUDLEY (St Mary and St Edburga)   *see* Shelswell *Ox*
STRATTON ON THE FOSSE (St Vigor)   *see* Chilcompton w Downside and Stratton on the Fosse *B & W*
STRATTON ST MARGARET (St Margaret) w South Marston and Stanton Fitzwarren *Bris 7*   **P** *Bp and Mert Coll Ox (jt)*   **P-in-c** E MEAD   **NSM** M J TIDEY
STRATTON ST MARY (St Mary)   *see* Long Stratton and Pilgrim TM *Nor*
STRATTON ST MICHAEL (St Michael) *as above*
STRATTON STRAWLESS (St Margaret)   *see* Coltishall w Gt Hautbois, Frettenham etc *Nor*
STRATTON, EAST (All Saints)   *see* Upper Dever *Win*
STRATTON, UPPER (St Philip) *Bris 7*   **P** *Bp*   **V** *vacant*
STREAT (not known)   *see* Ditchling, Streat and Westmeston *Chich*
STREATHAM (Christ Church) *S'wark 12*   **P** *Bp and R Streatham St Leon (jt)*   **V** A R GILLION   **NSM** T R BRUNT
STREATHAM (Immanuel) (St Andrew) *S'wark 12*   **P** *Bp, Hyndman Trustees, and R Streatham St Leon (jt)*   **V** S J SIMPSON
STREATHAM (St Leonard) *S'wark 12*   **P** *Bp*   **R** A E NORMAN-WALKER   **C** H N ARGLES-GRANT
STREATHAM (St Peter) *S'wark 12*   **P** *St Steph Ho Ox*   **V** S I M MATHIAS
STREATHAM (St Stephen)   *see* Telford Park *S'wark*
STREATHAM (St Thomas) *as above*
STREATHAM HILL (St Margaret the Queen) *S'wark 12*   **P** *Bp*   **P-in-c** G S A I GERMAIN-POWELL
STREATHAM PARK (St Alban)   *see* Furzedown *S'wark*
STREATHAM VALE (Holy Redeemer) *S'wark 12*   **P** *CPAS*   **V** I H GILMOUR
STREATHAM, WEST (St James)   *see* Furzedown *S'wark*
STREATLEY (St Margaret) *St Alb 12*   **P** *Bp*   **V** N C RICHARDS
STREATLEY (St Mary)   *see* Goring and Streatley w S Stoke *Ox*
STREET (Holy Trinity) (Mission Church) w Walton and Compton Dundon *B & W 4*   **P** *DBP and Bp Lon (jt)*   **R** A J LAWRENCE   **C** D M GREENFIELD
STREET Parishes, The, comprising Amotherby, Barton-le-Street, Hovingham, and Slingsby *York 6*   **P** *Abp, SMF, Sir William Worsley Bt, and Mrs C Roberts (jt)*   **R** *vacant*
STREETLY (All Saints) *Lich 24*   **P** *Bp*   **V** A F WALKER
STRELLEY (All Saints)   *see* Bilborough and Strelley *S'well*
STRENSALL (St Mary the Virgin) *York 3*   **P** *Abp*   **V** M HARRISON   **C** D M COYNE, K A MCBRIDE, M E YOUNG, S WHITING   **NSM** C C CRANFIELD, C C GITTENS, C J TOASE, D V HICKS, T M GANT
STRETE (St Michael)   *see* Stoke Fleming, Blackawton, Strete and E Allington *Ex*
STRETFORD (All Saints) *Man 2*   **P** *Bp*   **R** L K MAGUIRE   **C** A M K BENNISON   **OLM** M K HOUGH
STRETFORD (St Bride)   *see* Old Trafford St Bride *Man*
STRETFORD (St Matthew) *Man 2*   **P** *D&C*   **R** K L BURGESS   **NSM** S W SCHOFIELD
STRETHALL (St Mary the Virgin)   *see* Icknield Way Villages *Chelmsf*
STRETHAM (St James)   *see* Ely *Ely*
STRETTON (St John)   *see* Penkridge *Lich*
STRETTON (St Mary) w Claymills *Lich 13*   **P** *Baroness Gretton*   **P-in-c** G J CROSSLEY   **C** B L CARE, H R P DAVIS
STRETTON (St Matthew) and Appleton Thorn *Ches 4*   **P** *Mrs P F du Bois Grantham and Dr S P L du Bois Davidson (jt)*   **V** A D J JEWELL
STRETTON (St Nicholas)   *see* Cottesmore and Burley, Clipsham, Exton etc *Pet*
STRETTON GRANDISON (St Lawrence)   *see* Hop Churches *Heref*
STRETTON ON DUNSMORE (All Saints)   *see* Draycote Gp *Cov*
STRETTON ON DUNSMORE (Mission Church) *as above*
STRETTON ON FOSSE (St Peter)   *see* Ilmington w Stretton-on-Fosse etc *Cov*
STRETTON PARVA (St John the Baptist)   *see* Gaulby *Leic*
STRETTON SUGWAS (St Mary Magdalene)   *see* Burghill Gp *Heref*
STRETTON, LITTLE (All Saints)   *see* Church Stretton *Heref*
STRICKLAND, GREAT (St Barnabas)   *see* N Westmorland *Carl*
STRINES (St Paul)   *see* Marple All SS *Ches*
STRINGSTON (St Mary the Virgin)   *see* Quantock Coast *B & W*
STRIXTON (St Romwald)   *see* Wollaston w Strixton and Bozeat etc *Pet*
STROOD (St Francis) *Roch 6*   **P** *Bp*   **V** S L COPESTAKE   **C** S F VALLENTE-KERR
STROOD (St Nicholas) w St Mary *Roch 6*   **P** *Bp and D&C (jt)*   **V** D W GREEN   **C** S F VALLENTE-KERR

STROUD (Holy Trinity)   *see* Stroud Team *Glouc*
STROUD (Mission Church)   *see* Steep and Froxfield w Privett *Portsm*
STROUD (St Alban Mission Church)   *see* Stroud Team *Glouc*
STROUD GREEN (Holy Trinity) *Lon 17*   **P** *Bp*   **V** P J HENDERSON
STROUD Team Ministry, The (St Laurence) (Holy Trinity) (St Alban Mission Church), including Cainscross, Randwick, Uplands, and Whiteshill *Glouc 4*   **P** *Patr Bd*   **TR** K E STACEY   **TV** S G HOWELL   **C** H L HILL   **NSM** M J PAGE
STROUDWATER Team, The, comprising Arlingham, Eastington, Framilode, Frampton-on-Severn, Fretherne, Frocester, Haresfield, Kings Stanley, Leonard Stanley, Moreton Valence, Saul, Selsley, Standish, Stonehouse, and Whitminster *Glouc 4*   **P** *Patr Bd*   **TR** S G HARRISON   **TV** D BISHOP, E PALIN   **C** J R THOMPSON
STROXTON (All Saints)   *see* Harlaxton Gp *Linc*
STRUBBY (St Oswald)   *see* Legbourne and Wold Marsh *Linc*
STRUMPSHAW (St Peter)   *see* Burlingham St Edmund w Lingwood, Strumpshaw etc *Nor*
STUBBINGS (St James the Less)   *see* Burchetts Green *Ox*
STUBBINS (St Philip)   *see* Ramsbottom and Edenfield *Man*
STUBBS CROSS (St Francis)   *see* Ashford Town *Cant*
STUBSHAW CROSS (St Luke)   *see* Wigan *Liv*
STUBTON (St Martin)   *see* Claypole *Linc*
STUDHAM (St Mary the Virgin)   *see* Kensworth, Studham and Whipsnade *St Alb*
STUDLAND (St Nicholas)   *see* Swanage and Studland *Sarum*
STUDLEY (Nativity of the Blessed Virgin Mary)   *see* Arden Marches *Cov*
STUDLEY (St John the Evangelist) *Sarum 15*   **P** *R Trowbridge St Jas*   **V** A P WOOD
STUKELEY, GREAT (St Bartholomew)   *see* N Leightonstone *Ely*
STUKELEY, LITTLE (St Martin) *as above*
STUNTNEY (Holy Cross)   *see* Ely *Ely*
STURMER (St Mary)   *see* Two Rivers *Chelmsf*
STURMINSTER MARSHALL (St Mary)   *see* Bridge Par *Sarum*
STURMINSTER NEWTON (St Mary), Hinton St Mary and Lydlinch *Sarum 5*   **P** *Col J L Yeatman (1 turn), G A L-F Pitt-Rivers Esq (3 turns), V Iwerne Valley (1 turn)*   **V** P M SARGENT
STURRY (St Nicholas) w Fordwich and Westbere w Hersden *Cant 3*   **P** *Abp, Ld Chan, and St Aug Foundn Cant (by turn)*   **R** *vacant*
STURTON (St Hugh)   *see* Stow Gp *Linc*
STURTON, GREAT (All Saints)   *see* Hemingby Gp *Linc*
STURTON-LE-STEEPLE (St Peter and St Paul)   *see* The Clays *S'well*
STUSTON (All Saints)   *see* N Hartismere *St E*
STUTTON (St Aidan)   *see* Tadcaster *York*
STUTTON (St Peter)   *see* Holbrook, Stutton, Freston, Woolverstone etc *St E*
STYDD (St Saviour)   *see* Ribchester w Stydd *Blackb*
STYVECHALE (St James) *Cov 3*   **P** *Col A M H Gregory-Hood*   **V** J M MAYNARD
SUCKLEY (St John the Baptist)   *see* Worcs W Rural *Worc*
SUDBOROUGH (All Saints)   *see* Brigstock w Stanion and Lowick and Sudborough *Pet*
SUDBOURNE (All Saints)   *see* Wilford Peninsula *St E*
SUDBROOKE (St Edward)   *see* Barlings *Linc*
SUDBURY (All Saints)   *see* S Dales *Derby*
SUDBURY (All Saints) w Ballingdon and Brundon *St E 8*   **P** *Simeon's Trustees*   **P-in-c** C A COLLINS   **C** C J RAMSEY   **NSM** J M RIDLEY
SUDBURY (St Andrew) *Lon 18*   **P** *Bp*   **V** G S THOMAS
SUDBURY (St Gregory) St Peter and Chilton *St E 8*   **P** *Bp (3 turns), Ch Soc Trust (1 turn)*   **R** C A COLLINS   **NSM** J M RIDLEY
SUDDEN (St Aidan) and Heywood All Souls *Man 6*   **P** *Patr Bd*   **V** M A READ
SUDELEY MANOR (St Mary)   *see* Winchcombe *Glouc*
SUFFIELD (St Margaret)   *see* King's Beck *Nor*
SUFFIELD PARK (St Martin)   *see* Cromer *Nor*
SUFFOLK HEIGHTS   *see* Chevington w Hargrave, Chedburgh w Depden etc *St E*
SUGLEY (Holy Saviour) *Newc 4*   **P** *Bp*   **P-in-c** N HESLOP
SULBY (St Stephen's Chapel)   *see* Andreas, Ballaugh and Sulby *S & M*
SULGRAVE (St James the Less)   *see* Culworth w Sulgrave and Thorpe Mandeville etc *Pet*
SULHAM (St Nicholas)   *see* Pangbourne w Tidmarsh and Sulham *Ox*
SULHAMSTEAD ABBOTS (St Mary) and Bannister w Ufton Nervet *Ox 4*   **P** *Qu Coll Ox and Or Coll Ox (alt)*   **P-in-c** J W S PATON

SULLINGTON (St Mary) and Thakeham w Warminghurst
Chich 5   **P** *Bp and DBP (alt)*   **P-in-c** S STEVENS
NSM J SIMPSON
SUMMERFIELD (Christ Church) (Cavendish Road Hall)
Birm 3   **P** R *Birm St Martin w Bordesley*   **V** *vacant*
SUMMERSDALE (St Michael) *see* Chich St Paul and
Westhampnett *Chich*
SUMMERSTOWN (St Mary) *S'wark* 17   **P** *Ch Soc Trust*
V J J G FLETCHER
SUMMERTOWN (St Michael and All Angels) *Ox* 2   **P** *St Jo*
Coll Ox   **V** G R KNIGHT   **NSM** C E LEAL, S J S CROSS,
W L A PRYOR
SUNBURY, UPPER (St Saviour) *Lon* 13   **P** *V Sunbury*
V A C BOWER   **C** S L RAESIDE
SUNBURY-ON-THAMES (St Mary) *Lon* 13   **P** *D&C St Paul's*
V A V J DOWNES
SUNDERLAND (St Bede) Town End Farm   *see* N Wearside *Dur*
SUNDERLAND (St Chad) *Dur* 14   **P** *Bp*   **V** *vacant*
SUNDERLAND (St Cuthbert) Red House   *see* N Wearside *Dur*
SUNDERLAND (St Ignatius)   *see* Hendon *Dur*
SUNDERLAND (St Mary the Virgin) (St Peter) *Dur* 14   **P** *Bp*
P-in-c K J BAGNALL   **C** S SWEETING   **NSM** R PENMAN
SUNDERLAND (St Matthew) (St Wilfrid) *Dur* 14   **P** *Bp*
V D TOLHURST   **C** W KUIPER
SUNDERLAND MINSTER (St Michael and All Angels and
St Benedict Biscop) *Dur* 14   **P** *Bp*   **C** A C DOWSETT
Hon C C S HOWSON   **NSM** C I WATSON, J TYSON
SUNDERLAND POINT (Mission Church)   *see* Overton *Blackb*
SUNDERLAND St Mary (St Thomas) (St Oswald) *Dur* 14
P *Bp*   **V** *vacant*
SUNDERLAND, NORTH (St Paul)   *see* Beadnell, Ellingham
and N Sunderland *Newc*
SUNDON (St Mary) *St Alb* 12   **P** *Bp*   **P-in-c** Y M SMEJKAL
SUNDRIDGE (St Mary) w Ide Hill and Toys Hill *Roch* 9
P *Abp*   **R** P E DAVIES
SUNNINGDALE (Holy Trinity) *Ox* 3   **P** *Bp*
V J G HUTCHINSON   **NSM** T E WARD-HALL
SUNNINGHILL (St Michael and All Angels) and South
Ascot *Ox* 3   **P** *St Jo Coll Cam*   **C** S E MORTIMER
NSM V A MABUZA
SUNNINGWELL (St Leonard)   *see* Radley, Sunningwell and
Kennington *Ox*
SUNNYSIDE (St Barnabas)   *see* E Grinstead St Swithun *Chich*
SUNNYSIDE (St Michael and All Angels) w Bourne End
St Alb 1   **P** *CPAS*   **V** R S FARDELL   **C** R E M HAMILTON
NSM H A KEMP
SURBITON (St Andrew) (St Mark) *S'wark* 15   **P** *Bp*
V R S STANIER   **C** M J JOHNS-PERRING   **NSM** J A PRICE
SURBITON (St Matthew)   *see* Tolworth, Hook and Surbiton
S'wark
SURBITON HILL (Christ Church) *S'wark* 15   **P** *Ch Soc Trust*
and Trustees (jt)   **V** J M SHEPHERD   **C** A N APPADOO,
J B ERLEBACH   **NSM** E O BAIKIE
SURFLEET (St Laurence)   *see* Glen Gp *Linc*
SURLINGHAM (St Mary)   *see* Rockland St Mary w Hellington,
Bramerton etc *Nor*
SURREY WEALD, comprising Capel, Holmwood, Newdigate
and Ockley *Guildf* 7   **P** *Patr Bd (1 turn), Ld Chan (2 turns)*
TR A D J COE   **TV** E R RICHARDSON   **NSM** N E COE
SUSTEAD (St Peter and St Paul)   *see* Roughton and Felbrigg,
Metton, Sustead etc *Nor*
SUTCOMBE (St Andrew)   *see* Bradworthy, Sutcombe, Putford
etc *Ex*
SUTTERTON (St Mary)   *see* Haven Gp *Linc*
SUTTON (All Saints)   *see* Potton w Sutton and Cockayne
Hatley *St Alb*
SUTTON (All Saints)   *see* Wilford Peninsula *St E*
SUTTON (Christ Church) (St Barnabas) (St Nicholas)
S'wark 23   **P** *Patr Bd*   **P-in-c** F M ARNOLD   **TV** P BROOKS
NSM B FRASER, D R BILLIN
SUTTON (St Andrew) *Ely* 8   **P** *D&C*   **V** M HANCOCK
SUTTON (St Barnabas' Mission Church)   *see* Macclesfield
Team *Ches*
SUTTON (St Clement), Huttoft and Anderby *Linc* 10   **P** *Bp*
(2 turns), Magd Coll Cam (1 turn)   **R** P J LILEY
Hon C C H LILLEY   **OLM** J TOMPKINS
SUTTON (St James) *York* 14   **P** *Abp*   **V** G NAYLOR
SUTTON (St James), Wincle, Wildboarclough and Bosley
Ches 13   **P** *Patr Bd*   **V** J E HARRIES   **C** A M CERVAL-PENA
NSM S R MORRIS
SUTTON (St John the Baptist)   *see* Barlavington, Burton w
Coates, Sutton and Bignor *Chich*
SUTTON (St Mary)   *see* Calow and Sutton cum Duckmanton
Derby
SUTTON (St Michael and All Angels)   *see* Castor w Upton
and Stibbington etc *Pet*

SUTTON (St Michael)   *see* Stalham, E Ruston, Brunstead,
Sutton and Ingham *Nor*
SUTTON (St Nicholas) (All Saints) (St Michael and All
Angels) *Liv* 10   **P** *Patr Bd*   **TR** M L MOORE
TV L M JACKSON   **C** S Q MOORE
SUTTON (St Thomas) w Cowling and Lothersdale *Leeds* 4
P *Ch Ch Ox and Bp (jt)*   **V** H M COLLINGS   **C** B J GREENFIELD
SUTTON BASSETT (All Saints)   *see* Stoke Albany w Wilbarston
and Ashley etc *Pet*
SUTTON BENGER (All Saints)   *see* Draycot *Bris*
SUTTON BINGHAM (All Saints)   *see* Coker Ridge *B & W*
SUTTON BRIDGE (St Matthew) and Tydd St Mary *Linc* 18
P *Bp and Ld Chan (alt)*   **P-in-c** P J CAREY-SLATER
SUTTON BY DOVER (St Peter and St Paul)   *see* Walmer and
Cornilo *Cant*
SUTTON CHENEY (St James)   *see* Bosworth *Leic*
SUTTON COLDFIELD (Holy Trinity) *Birm* 4   **P** *Bp*
R W J ROUTH   **C** L CARR
SUTTON COLDFIELD (St Chad) *Birm* 4   **P** *Bp*   **V** J NICHOLAS
SUTTON COLDFIELD (St Columba) *Birm* 4   **P** *Bp*
V R S ALLEN
SUTTON COURTENAY (All Saints)   *see* DAMASCUS *Ox*
SUTTON GREEN (All Souls)   *see* Woking St Pet *Guildf*
SUTTON HILL (Pastoral Centre) and Woodside *Heref* 13
P *CPAS Patr Trust*   **V** D A TAFFINDER
SUTTON IN ASHFIELD (St Mary Magdalene) *S'well* 4   **P** *Bp*
V *vacant*
SUTTON IN ASHFIELD St Michael and All Angels *S'well* 4
P *Bp*   **C** J E COTTERILL
SUTTON IN HOLDERNESS (St Michael and All Angels)
York 14   **P** *Abp*   **V** W J BRADLEY
SUTTON LE MARSH (St Clement)   *see* Sutton, Huttoft and
Anderby *Linc*
SUTTON MADDOCK (St Mary)   *see* Beckbury, Badger,
Kemberton, Ryton, Stockton etc *Lich*
SUTTON MANDEVILLE (All Saints)   *see* Nadder Valley *Sarum*
SUTTON MONTIS (Holy Trinity)   *see* Cam Vale *B & W*
SUTTON ON DERWENT (St Michael)   *see* Derwent Ings *York*
SUTTON ON THE FOREST (All Hallows)   *see* Forest of Galtres
York
SUTTON ON THE HILL (St Michael)   *see* Boylestone, Church
Broughton, Dalbury, etc *Derby*
SUTTON PARK (St Andrew) and Wawne *York* 14   **P** *Abp*
V C J VAN STRAATEN   **C** E S CONNOLLY   **NSM** F ROBINSON
SUTTON ST EDMUND (St Edmund King and Martyr)   *see*
Elloe Fen Gp *Linc*
SUTTON ST JAMES (St James) *as above*
SUTTON ST MICHAEL (St Michael)   *see* Maund Gp *Heref*
SUTTON ST NICHOLAS   *see* Long Sutton w Lutton etc *Linc*
SUTTON ST NICHOLAS (St Nicholas)   *see* Maund Gp *Heref*
SUTTON UNDER BRAILES (St Thomas à Becket) *Cov* 9   **P** *Bp*
R G HEIGHTON   **Hon C** H C W PARBURY   **NSM** J W ROLFE
SUTTON VALENCE (St Mary the Virgin)   *see* Headcorn and
The Suttons *Cant*
SUTTON VENY (St John the Evangelist)   *see* Upper Wylye
Valley *Sarum*
SUTTON WALDRON (St Bartholomew)   *see* Iwerne Valley
Sarum
SUTTON, EAST (St Peter and St Paul)   *see* Headcorn and The
Suttons *Cant*
SUTTON, GREAT (St John the Evangelist) *Ches* 9   **P** *V*
Eastham   **V** A J DUTTON   **NSM** R A MONTGOMERY
SUTTON, NORTH   *see* Plymouth Em w St Paul *Ex*
SUTTON-AT-HONE (St John the Baptist)   *see* Darent Valley
Roch
SUTTON-CUM-LOUND (St Bartholomew)   *see* The Idle and
Sands *S'well*
SUTTON-ON-PLYM (St John the Evangelist), Plymouth
St Simon and St Mary Laira *Ex* 20   **P** *Bp, St Simon Trustees,*
and Keble Coll Ox (jt)   **V** *vacant*
SUTTON-ON-SEA (St Clement)   *see* Sutton, Huttoft and
Anderby *Linc*
SUTTON-ON-TRENT (All Saints)   *see* Norwell w Ossington,
Cromwell etc *S'well*
SWABY (St Nicholas)   *see* Legbourne and Wold Marsh *Linc*
SWADLINCOTE (Emmanuel) and Hartshorne *Derby* 7
P *V Gresley and MMCET (jt)*   **C** A J REDSHAW, P J DOUGLAS,
R Z ALLPRESS   **OLM** C A BUCKLEY
SWAFFHAM (St Peter and St Paul) and Sporle *Nor* 13   **P** *Bp*
(2 turns), DBP (1 turn)   **V** J R ALLAN
C V A VENMORE-ROWLAND
SWAFFHAM BULBECK (St Mary)   *see* Anglesey Gp *Ely*
SWAFFHAM PRIOR (St Mary) *as above*
SWAFIELD (St Nicholas)   *see* Trunch Group *Nor*
SWAINSTHORPE (St Peter)   *see* Newton Flotman,
Swainsthorpe, Tasburgh, etc *Nor*

SWAINSWICK (Blessed Virgin Mary)   *see* Bath St Sav w Swainswick and Woolley *B & W*

SWALCLIFFE (St Peter and St Paul)   *see* Wykeham *Ox*

SWALE, LOWER, comprising Ainderby Steeple w Yafforth and Kirby Wiske w Maunby, and Kirkby Fleetham w Langton on Swale and Scruton *Leeds 22*   **P** *D&C York, Duke of Northumberland, and Bp (jt)*   **R** J M LANE

SWALECLIFFE (St John the Baptist)   *see* Whitstable *Cant*

SWALEDALE, comprising Arkengarthdale, Grinton, Melbecks, and Muker *Leeds 19*   **P** *Bp*   **V** C J HEWLETT   **C** L M C BLUNDELL

SWALLOW (Holy Trinity)   *see* Caistor *Linc*

SWALLOWBECK (St George)   *see* Linc St Geo Swallowbeck *Linc*

SWALLOWCLIFFE (St Peter)   *see* Nadder Valley *Sarum*

SWALLOWFIELD (All Saints)   *see* Loddon Reach *Ox*

SWALWELL (Holy Trinity) *Dur 12*   **P** *Bp*   **V** B J ABBOTT

SWALWELL (Holy Trinity)   *see* Swalwell *Dur*

SWANAGE (All Saints) (St Mary the Virgin) and Studland *Sarum 8*   **P** *Patr Bd*   **TR** J O MANN   **C** S S L SONET

SWANBOURNE (St Swithun)   *see* Newton Longville, Mursley, Swanbourne etc *Ox*

SWANLAND (St Barnabas) *York 14*   **P** *CPAS*   **V** F R SCOTT

SWANLEY (St Mary) *Roch 2*   **P** *Guild of All So*   **V** D C BATLEY-GLADDEN

SWANLEY (St Paul) *Roch 2*   **P** *Merchant Taylors' Co*   **V** J W D DOUGLAS

SWANMORE (St Barnabas) *Portsm 1*   **P** *DBP*   **V** *vacant*

SWANMORE (St Michael and All Angels) *Portsm 7*   **P** *SMF*   **C** H J MONAGHAN

SWANNINGTON (St George)   *see* Whitwick, Thringstone and Swannington *Leic*

SWANNINGTON (St Margaret)   *see* Reepham and Wensum Valley *Nor*

SWANSCOMBE (St Peter and St Paul) *Roch 4*   **P** *DBP*   **P-in-c** C L LLOYD-EVANS

SWANTON ABBOT (St Michael)   *see* King's Beck *Nor*

SWANTON MORLEY (All Saints)   *see* Dereham and Distr *Nor*

SWANTON NOVERS (St Edmund)   *see* Brinton, Briningham, Hunworth, Stody etc *Nor*

SWANWICK (St Andrew) and Pentrich *Derby 8*   **P** *Wright Trustees and Duke of Devonshire (alt)*   **V** A B SIMPSON

SWARBY (St Mary and All Saints)   *see* S Lafford *Linc*

SWARCLIFFE (St Luke)   *see* Seacroft *Leeds*

SWARDESTON (St Mary the Virgin) w East Carleton, Intwood, Keswick and Ketteringham *Nor 7*   **P** *Bp, DBP, and Miss M B Unthank (jt)*   **R** P D BURR

SWARKESTONE (St James)   *see* Aston on Trent, Elvaston, Weston on Trent etc *Derby*

SWATON (St Michael)   *see* Heckington and Helpringham Gp *Linc*

SWAVESEY (St Andrew)   *see* 5folds *Ely*

SWAY (St Luke) *Win 11*   **P** *Bp*   **V** E J MITCHELL   **NSM** K S SMITH

SWAYFIELD (St Nicholas)   *see* Corby Glen Par *Linc*

SWAYTHLING (St Mary) (St Alban the Martyr) *Win 13*   **P** *Bp and TR Southn City Cen (jt)*   **V** P M DOCKREE   **NSM** D EISENTRAEGER

SWEFFLING (St Mary)   *see* Upper Alde *St E*

SWELL (St Catherine)   *see* Curry Rivel w Fivehead and Swell *B & W*

SWELL, LOWER (St Mary)   *see* Stow on the Wold, Condicote and The Swells *Glouc*

SWELL, UPPER (St Mary)   *as above*

SWEPSTONE (St Peter)   *see* Woodfield *Leic*

SWERFORD (St Mary)   *see* Hook Norton w Gt Rollright, Swerford etc *Ox*

SWETTENHAM (St Peter)   *see* Marton, Siddington w Capesthorne etc *Ches*

SWILLAND (St Mary)   *see* Carlford *St E*

SWILLINGTON (St Mary)   *see* Allerton Bywater, Kippax and Swillington *Leeds*

SWIMBRIDGE (St James the Apostle), West Buckland, Landkey, and East Buckland *Ex 16*   **P** *Bp and Trustees Earl Fortescue (jt)*   **P-in-c** S O'ROURKE

SWINBROOK (St Mary)   *see* Burford w Fulbrook, Taynton, Asthall etc *Ox*

SWINDERBY (All Saints) *Linc 12*   **P** *Bp, Ld Chan, E M K Kirk Esq, and D&C (by turn)*   **P-in-c** A C J VAUGHAN   **NSM** J T ROOKE   **OLM** P W WALKER

SWINDON (All Saints) (St Barnabas) *Bris 7*   **P** *Bp*   **V** C C M OKORONKWO   **OLM** B A SHEPPARD

SWINDON (Christ Church) (St Mary) *Bris 7*   **P** *Ld Chan*   **V** S M STEVENETTE   **NSM** D A HARDWICK

SWINDON (St Andrew) (St John the Baptist) *Bris 7*   **P** *Ld Chan*   **NSM** L M MOREY

SWINDON (St Augustine) (Pattern Church) *Bris 7*   **P** *Bp*   **P-in-c** J P SALES   **C** K E SMITH, P W FREELAND, T R MORGAN

SWINDON (St John the Evangelist)   *see* Smestow Vale *Lich*

SWINDON (St Lawrence)   *see* N Cheltenham *Glouc*

SWINDON (St Peter)   *see* Penhill *Bris*

SWINDON Dorcan, comprising Covingham, Eldene, and Liden *Bris 7*   **P** *Bp*   **R** T A WIGLEY   **OLM** S F FISHER

SWINDON New Town (St Mark) (St Adhelm) (St Luke) (St Saviour) *Bris 7*   **P** *Bp*   **P-in-c** T J BOUTLE

SWINDON, NORTH (St Andrew) *Bris 7*   **P** *Bp*   **P-in-c** S A ROBERTSON   **NSM** P C ASHBY

SWINDON, NORTH WEST and Lydiard Millicent *Bris 7*   **P** *Bp*   **V** T V ROBERTS   **NSM** P F ROBERTS

SWINDON, WEST and Lydiard Tregoze *Bris 7*   **P** *Bp*   **V** C D DEVERELL   **NSM** P C ASHBY, T L TOWNSEND, T M DAY

SWINE (St Mary)   *see* Skirlaugh, Catwick, Long Riston, Rise, Swine w Ellerby *York*

SWINEFLEET (St Margaret)   *see* The Marshland *Sheff*

SWINESHEAD (St Mary)   *see* Haven Gp *Linc*

SWINESHEAD (St Nicholas)   *see* The Stodden Churches *St Alb*

SWINFORD (All Saints)   *see* Avon-Swift *Leic*

SWINFORD, OLD Stourbridge (St Mary) *Worc 5*   **P** *Bp*   **R** J F FLITCROFT

SWINHOPE (St Helen)   *see* Binbrook Gp *Linc*

SWINNOW (Christ the Saviour)   *see* Stanningley St Thos *Leeds*

SWINSTEAD (St Mary)   *see* Edenham w Witham on the Hill and Swinstead *Linc*

SWINTON (Holy Rood) *Man 7*   **P** *TR Swinton and Pendlebury*   **V** A C WHITTLE   **C** C G PEARSON

SWINTON (St Margaret) *Sheff 12*   **P** *Sir Philip Naylor-Leyland Bt*   **V** C J BARLEY

SWINTON (St Peter) and Pendlebury *Man 7*   **P** *Patr Bd*   **TR** J P SHEEHY

SWISS COTTAGE (Holy Trinity)   *see* W Hampstead Trin *Lon*

SWITHLAND (St Leonard)   *see* Woodhouse, Woodhouse Eaves and Swithland *Leic*

SWYNCOMBE (St Botolph)   *see* Icknield *Ox*

SWYNNERTON (St Mary)   *see* Cotes Heath and Standon and Swynnerton etc *Lich*

SWYRE (Holy Trinity)   *see* Bride Valley *Sarum*

SYDE (St Mary)   *see* Brimpsfield w Birdlip, Syde, Daglingworth etc *Glouc*

SYDENHAM (All Saints) *S'wark 5*   **P** *V Sydenham St Bart*   **P-in-c** P H SMITH

SYDENHAM (Holy Trinity) and Forest Hill *S'wark 5*   **P** *Simeon's Trustees*   **V** *vacant*

SYDENHAM (St Bartholomew) *S'wark 5*   **P** *Earl of Dartmouth*   **V** J M PERRY

SYDENHAM (St Mary)   *see* Chinnor, Sydenham, Aston Rowant and Crowell *Ox*

SYDENHAM (St Philip) *S'wark 5*   **P** *V Sydenham St Bart*   **V** P W TIERNAN

SYDENHAM DAMEREL (St Mary)   *see* Milton Abbot, Dunterton, Lamerton etc *Ex*

SYDENHAM, LOWER (St Michael and All Angels)   *see* Forest Hill w Lower Sydenham *S'wark*

SYDERSTONE (St Mary)   *see* N and S Creake w Waterden, Syderstone etc *Nor*

SYDLING ST NICHOLAS (St Nicholas)   *see* Charminster, Stinsford and the Chalk Stream villages *Sarum*

SYERSTON (All Saints)   *see* E Stoke w Syerston *S'well*

SYKEHOUSE (Holy Trinity)   *see* Fishlake w Sykehouse and Kirk Bramwith etc *Sheff*

SYLEHAM (St Mary)   *see* Athelington, Denham, Horham, Hoxne etc *St E*

SYMONDS GREEN (Christ the King)   *see* Stevenage H Trin *St Alb*

SYMONDSBURY (St John the Baptist)   *see* Eggardon and Colmers *Sarum*

SYRESHAM (St James)   *see* Astwell Gp *Pet*

SYSONBY (St Leonard)   *see* Melton Mowbray *Leic*

SYSTON (St Anne)   *see* Warmley, Syston and Bitton *Bris*

SYSTON (St Mary)   *see* S Cliff Villages Gp *Linc*

SYSTON (St Peter and St Paul)   *see* Fosse Team *Leic*

SYWELL (St Peter and St Paul)   *see* Mears Ashby and Hardwick and Sywell etc *Pet*

TABLEY, OVER (St Paul) *Ches 12*   **P** *Bp*   **P-in-c** P J ROBINSON   **NSM** P M COPE, P M ROBINSON

TACKLEY (St Nicholas)   *see* Steeple Aston w N Aston and Tackley *Ox*

TACOLNESTON (All Saints)   *see* Upper Tas Valley *Nor*

TADCASTER (St Mary the Virgin) *York 1*   **P** *Abp, J Fielden Esq, and T E Fielden Esq (1 turn), Abp (1 turn)*   **C** L J BRENCHER

TADDINGTON (St Michael), Chelmorton and Monyash, Hartington, Biggin and Earl Sterndale *Derby 4* **P** *Duke of Devonshire and V Bakewell (jt)* **V** *vacant*

TADDIPORT (St Mary Magdalene) *see* Gt and Lt Torrington and Frithelstock *Ex*

TADLEY (St Mary) (St Peter) (St Paul) w Pamber Heath and Silchester *Win 4* **P** *Bp and Duke of Wellington (jt)* **R** R J S C HARLOW **C** J HUDSON, S A MCKAY

TADLEY (St Paul) *see* Tadley w Pamber Heath and Silchester *Win*

TADLEY (St Peter) *as above*

TADLEY, NORTH (St Mary) *as above*

TADLOW (St Giles) *see* Shingay Gp *Ely*

TADMARTON (St Nicholas) *see* Wykeham *Ox*

TADWORTH (Good Shepherd) *S'wark 24* **P** *V Kingswood St Andr* **V** T R ASTIN

TAKELEY (Holy Trinity) w Little Canfield *Chelmsf 17* **P** *Bp and Ch Coll Cam* **P-in-c** C M FAIRWEATHER

TALATON (St James the Apostle) *see* Broadclyst, Clyst Honiton, Clyst Hydon etc *Ex*

TALBOT VILLAGE (St Mark) *Sarum 7* **P** *Trustees* **V** R A HIGGINS

TALKE O' THE HILL (St Martin) *see* Alsagers Bank, Audley and Talke *Lich*

TALKIN (not known) *see* Eden, Gelt and Irthing *Carl*

TALLAND (St Tallan) *see* Trelawny *Truro*

TALLINGTON (St Lawrence) *see* Uffington Gp *Linc*

TAMAR VALLEY Benefice, The, comprising Calstock, Landulph, St Dominick, and St Mellion w Pillaton *Truro 11* **P** *Duchy of Cornwall (1 turn), SMF, D&C, and Trustees Major J Coryton (1 turn)* **R** C M PAINTER

TAMERTON FOLIOT (St Mary) and Southway *Ex 20* **P** *Ld Chan* **TR** D B M GILL **TV** I M ROBERTSON

TAMERTON, NORTH (St Denis) *see* Boyton, N Tamerton, Werrington etc *Truro*

TAMWORTH (St Editha) *Lich 4* **P** *Bp* **C** V M C VAN DEN BERGH **NSM** B ROSTILL

TANDRIDGE (St Peter) *see* Oxted *S'wark*

TANFIELD (St Margaret of Antioch) w Burnopfield and Dipton *Dur 2* **P** *Bp* **V** *vacant*

TANFIELD, WEST (St Nicholas) and Well w Snape and North Stainley *Leeds 20* **P** *Bp (1 turn), C Bourne-Arton Esq and J Bourne-Arton Esq (1 turn)* **C** S L LAWTON

TANGLEY (St Thomas of Canterbury) *see* Pastrow *Win*

TANGMERE (St Andrew) and Oving *Chich 2* **P** *Bp and Duke of Richmond and Gordon (jt)* **P-in-c** T MARSHALL

TANKERSLEY (St Peter), Thurgoland and Wortley *Sheff 11* **P** *Dowager Countess of Wharncliffe, Sir Philip Naylor-Leyland Bt, and V Silkstone (jt)* **R** K J E HALE

TANNINGTON (St Ethelbert) *see* Four Rivers *St E*

TANSLEY (Holy Trinity) *see* Matlock Bank and Tansley *Derby*

TANSOR (St Mary) *see* Warmington, Tansor and Cotterstock etc *Pet*

TANWORTH (St Mary Magdalene) *Birm 2* **P** *F D Muntz Esq* **V** *vacant*

TAPLOW (St Nicolas) and Dropmore *Ox 12* **P** *Eton Coll and DBP (jt)* **V** J S CRESSWELL **NSM** S J JOHNSON

TARDEBIGGE (St Bartholomew) *Worc 6* **P** *Earl of Plymouth* **V** R M CLARK

TARLETON (Holy Trinity) *see* Rufford and Tarleton *Blackb*

TARPORLEY (St Helen) *Ches 5* **P** *Bp (4 turns), D&C (1 turn), and Sir John Grey Regerton Bt (1 turn)* **R** J W BRIDGMAN **NSM** J M OSBORNE

TARRANT GUNVILLE (St Mary) *see* Chase *Sarum*

TARRANT HINTON (St Mary) *as above*

TARRANT KEYNSTON (All Saints) *as above*

TARRANT MONKTON (All Saints) *as above*

TARRANT RUSHTON (St Mary) *as above*

TARRING NEVILLE (St Mary) *see* Denton w S Heighton and Tarring Neville *Chich*

TARRING, WEST (St Andrew) *see* Maybridge and W Tarring *Chich*

TARRINGTON (St Philip and St James) *see* Hop Churches *Heref*

TARVIN (St Andrew) *Ches 2* **P** *Bp* **V** A L D FRIEND **NSM** B A KING

TAS VALLEY *see* Newton Flotman, Swainsthorpe, Tasburgh, etc *Nor*

TAS VALLEY, UPPER *see* Upper Tas Valley *Nor*

TASBURGH (St Mary) *see* Newton Flotman, Swainsthorpe, Tasburgh, etc *Nor*

TASLEY (St Peter and St Paul) *see* Bridgnorth and Morville Par *Heref*

TATENHILL (St Michael and All Angels) *see* Barton under Needwood w Dunstall and Tatenhill *Lich*

TATHAM (St James the Less) *see* E Lonsdale *Blackb*

TATHAM FELLS (Good Shepherd) *as above*

TATHWELL (St Vedast) *see* Legbourne and Wold Marsh *Linc*

TATSFIELD (St Mary) *see* Limpsfield and Tatsfield *S'wark*

TATTENHALL (St Alban) w Burwardsley and Handley *Ches 5* **P** *Bp, Miss N C Barbour, and D&C (jt)* **R** L MUTETE

TATTENHAM CORNER (St Mark) *Guildf 9* **P** *Bp* **V** D C WILLIAMSON

TATTENHOE (St Giles) *see* Watling Valley *Ox*

TATTERFORD (St Margaret) *see* E w W Rudham, Helhoughton etc *Nor*

TATTERSETT (All Saints and St Andrew) *as above*

TATTERSHALL (Holy Trinity) *see* Bain Valley Gp *Linc*

TATTINGSTONE (St Mary) *see* Sproughton w Burstall, Copdock w Washbrook etc *St E*

TATWORTH (St John the Evangelist) *see* Chaffcombe, Cricket Malherbie etc *B & W*

TAUNTON (All Saints) *B & W 18* **P** *Bp* **V** E M SHEARCROFT

TAUNTON (Holy Trinity) *B & W 18* **P** *Bp* **V** J B V LAURENCE

TAUNTON (St Andrew) *B & W 18* **P** *Bp* **V** R P LODGE **C** K M GOUGH

TAUNTON (St James) *B & W 18* **P** *Simeon's Trustees* **V** F R M WUYTS **C** D R WILKIE

TAUNTON (St Mary Magdalene) (St John the Evangelist) *B & W 18* **P** *Bp and Ch Patr Trust (jt)* **V** T C OSMOND **Hon C** J R EASTELL **NSM** J M FRENCH, L A BALE

TAUNTON (St Peter) Lyngford *B & W 18* **P** *Bp* **V** D TURLEY

TAVERHAM (St Edmund) w Ringland *Nor 2* **P** *Bp* **R** P SEABROOK **C** V J HOOKER **NSM** P CHARLESWORTH

TAVISTOCK (St Eustachius), Gulworthy and Brent Tor *Ex 21* **P** *Bp* **C** E R ILLINGWORTH, J A BLOWEY **NSM** H J BUTLAND

TAW and Torridge Estuary *see* Fremington, Instow and Westleigh *Ex*

TAWSTOCK (St Peter) *see* Newton Tracey, Horwood, Alverdiscott etc *Ex*

TAWTON, NORTH (St Peter) *see* Chagford, Gidleigh, Throwleigh etc *Ex*

TAWTON, SOUTH (St Andrew) *as above*

TAXAL (St James) *see* Whaley Bridge *Ches*

TAYNTON (St John the Evangelist) *see* Burford w Fulbrook, Taynton, Asthall etc *Ox*

TAYNTON (St Laurence) *see* Highnam, Tibberton w Rudford etc *Glouc*

TEALBY (All Saints) *see* Walesby Gp *Linc*

TEAN, UPPER (Christ Church) *see* Uttoxeter Area *Lich*

TEBAY (St James) *see* High Westmorland *Carl*

TEDBURN ST MARY (St Mary), Cheriton Bishop, Whitestone w Oldridge and Holcombe Burnell *Ex 5* **P** *Bp, DBP, and Em Coll Cam (jt)* **V** M R WOOD **C** P W JAMES

TEDDINGTON (St Mark) *Lon 11* **P** *Bp* **V** K A WELLMAN

TEDDINGTON (St Mary) (St Alban the Martyr) *Lon 10* **P** *Bp* **V** J B MOFFATT **C** C E HALMSHAW **NSM** M E HAWES

TEDDINGTON (St Nicholas) *see* Overbury w Teddington, Alstone etc *Worc*

TEDDINGTON (St Peter and St Paul) *Lon 10* **P** *Bp* **P-in-c** J B MOFFATT

TEDSTONE DELAMERE (St James) *see* Edvin Loach w Tedstone Delamere etc *Heref*

TEESDALE, LOWER, comprising Bowes, Laithkirk, Romaldkirk w Cotherstone, and Startforth and Rokeby w Brignall *Leeds 19* **P** *Ld Chan (1 turn), Earl of Strathmore and Kinghorne (1 turn), Bp, Lords of the Manor of Bowes, and DBP (1 turn)* **R** J BARKER **NSM** A P WALLBANK

TEFFONT EVIAS (St Michael) *see* Nadder Valley *Sarum*

TEFFONT MAGNA (St Edward) *as above*

TEIGH (Holy Trinity) *see* Oakham, Ashwell, Braunston, Brooke, Egleton etc *Pet*

TEIGN VALLEY and Haldon Hill *see* Christow, Ashton, Bridford, Dunchideock etc *Ex*

TEIGNGRACE (St Peter and St Paul) *see* Kingsteignton and Teigngrace *Ex*

TEIGNMOUTH (St James) (St Michael the Archangel), Ideford w Luton, Ashcombe and Bishopsteignton *Ex 5* **P** *Patr Bd* **P-in-c** C A GREEN **TV** J H FROST **NSM** S ASTBURY

TELFORD PARK (St Stephen) (St Thomas) *S'wark 12* **P** *V Streatham and CPAS (jt)* **P-in-c** S M COOKE

TELFORD, CENTRAL (Christ the King): Dawley, Lawley, Malinslee, Stirchley, Brookside and Hollinswood *Lich 20* **P** *Patr Bd (3 turns), The Crown (1 turn)* **C** A M ROBERTS, J G CASTILLO-BURLEY, L S LENANDER, S H WARRELL

TELFORD, EAST *see* Oakengates, Priors Lee and Wrockwardine Wood *Lich*

TELLISFORD (All Saints) *see* Hardington Vale *B & W*

TELSCOMBE (St Laurence) *see* Peacehaven and Telscombe Cliffs w Piddinghoe etc *Chich*

TEME VALLEY NORTH: Knighton-on-Teme, Lindridge, Pensax, Menith Wood, and Stockton *Worc 1* **P** *Bp and D&C (alt)* **P-in-c** E G WHITTAKER

TEME VALLEY SOUTH: Eastham, Rochford, Stoke Bliss, Hanley Child, Hanley William, Kyre Wyard and Stanford-on-Teme *Worc 1* **P** *Ld Chan, Bp, and Mrs M M Miles (by turn)* **P-in-c** J CURTIS

TEME VALLEY, LOWER *see* Worcs W Rural *Worc*

TEMPLE (St Catherine) *see* Camelside *Truro*

TEMPLE BALSALL (St Mary) *Birm 6* **P** *Lady Leveson Hosp* **V** K A M LLOYD ROBERTS

TEMPLE BRUER (St John the Baptist) *see* Graffoe Gp *Linc*

TEMPLE CLOUD (St Barnabas) *see* Clutton w Cameley, Bishop Sutton and Stowey *B & W*

TEMPLE EWELL (St Peter and St Paul) w Lydden *Cant 7* **P** *Abp* **P-in-c** I R PARRISH

TEMPLE GRAFTON (St Andrew) *see* Heart of England *Cov*

TEMPLE GUITING (St Mary) *see* The Guitings, Cutsdean, Farmcote etc *Glouc*

TEMPLE HIRST (St John the Baptist) *see* Haddlesey w Hambleton and Birkin *York*

TEMPLE NORMANTON (St James the Apostle) *Derby 3* **P** *Bp* **V** G N BORROWDALE

TEMPLE SOWERBY (St James) *see* Heart of Eden *Carl*

TEMPLECOMBE (Blessed Virgin Mary) *see* Abbas and Templecombe, Henstridge and Horsington *B & W*

TEMPLETON (St Margaret) *see* Washfield, Stoodleigh, Withleigh etc *Ex*

TEMPSFORD (St Peter) *see* Riversmeet *St Alb*

TEN LAMPS *see* Timsbury w Priston, Camerton and Dunkerton *B & W*

TEN MILE BANK (St Mark) *see* Hilgay *Ely*

TENBURY Team Minstry, The (St Mary) (St Michael and All Angels), including Boraston, Burford, Clee Hill, Coreley, Greete, Hope Bagot, Little Hereford, Nash, and Whitton *Heref 11* **P** *Patr Bd* **TR** S E HARRIS **TV** M J INGLIS **NSM** E R WOMACK, S FOSTER

TENDRING (St Edmund King and Martyr) *see* Gt Oakley, Wix, Wrabness etc *Chelmsf*

TENPENNY VILLAGES, The, comprising Alresford, Elmstead, and Frating w Thorrington *Chelmsf 22* **P** *Bp, Jes Coll Cam, and St Jo Coll Cam (jt)* **V** A I FORDYCE **C** T M SOLOSY **NSM** P J HART

TENTERDEN (St Mildred) (St Michael and All Angels), Rother and Oxney *Cant 10* **P** *Patr Bd* **TR** L J HAMMOND **C** J T KENNETT

TERLING (All Saints) *see* Witham and Villages *Chelmsf*

TERRIERS (St Francis) *see* High Wycombe *Ox*

TERRINGTON (All Saints) *see* Howardian Gp *York*

TERRINGTON ST CLEMENT (St Clement) *Ely 14* **P** *The Crown* **V** R J SLIPPER

TERRINGTON ST JOHN (St John) *see* E Marshland *Ely*

TERWICK (St Peter) *see* Rogate w Terwick and Trotton w Chithurst *Chich*

TESTON (St Peter and St Paul) *see* E Malling and Teston *Roch*

TESTWOOD (St Winfrid) *see* Totton *Win*

TETBURY (St Mary the Virgin and St Mary Magdalen), Beverston, Long Newnton and Shipton Moyne *Glouc 7* **P** *DBP, R Boggis-Rolfe Esq, and Mrs J C B Joynson (4 turns), The Crown (1 turn)* **R** V J HUGHES **C** P J SETTERFIELD

TETCOTT (Holy Cross) *see* Ashwater, Halwill, Beaworthy, Clawton etc *Ex*

TETFORD (St Mary) *see* S Ormsby Gp *Linc*

TETNEY (St Peter and St Paul) *see* Holton-le-Clay, Tetney and N Cotes *Linc*

TETSWORTH (St Giles) *see* Thame *Ox*

TETTENHALL REGIS (St Michael and All Angels) *Lich 23* **P** *Patr Bd* **TR** R M REEVE **TV** D WILLS, S A DOUGLAS **C** C M A LEIGHTON

TETTENHALL WOOD (Christ Church) and Perton *Lich 23* **P** *Patr Bd* **TR** P C WOOTTON **TV** J M CODY **NSM** L M VAWER

TEVERSAL (St Katherine) *see* Skegby w Teversal *S'well*

TEVERSHAM (All Saints) *Ely 2* **P** *Bp* **R** *vacant*

TEW, GREAT (St Michael and All Angels) w Little (St John the Evangelist) and Heythrop *Ox 22* **P** *Bp and J M Johnston Esq (jt)* **V** W S D BURKE

TEWIN (St Peter) *see* Welwyn *St Alb*

TEWKESBURY (Holy Trinity) *Glouc 9* **P** *Ch Soc Trust* **V** S M M WALKER

TEWKESBURY (St Mary the Virgin) w Walton Cardiff and Twyning *Glouc 9* **P** *Ld Chan (2 turns) and Ch Ch Ox (1 turn)* **V** P R WILLIAMS **C** E P SAUVEN, W A RUFFLE **Hon C** R D HESKETH

TEY, GREAT (St Barnabas) and LITTLE (St James the Less) w Wakes Colne and Chappel *Chelmsf 18* **P** *Bp, DBP, PCC Chappel and Ch Patr Trust (jt)* **R** *vacant*

TEYNHAM (Primary School Worship Centre) *see* Kingsdown, Creekside and High Downs *Cant*

TEYNHAM (St Mary) *as above*

THAKEHAM (St Mary) *see* Sullington and Thakeham w Warminghurst *Chich*

THAME (St Mary the Virgin) (Barley Hill Church) *Ox 20* **P** *Patr Bd* **TR** M D READING **TV** R B CROSS **NSM** G C CHOLDCROFT, G P WATERSON

THAMES DITTON (St Nicholas) *Guildf 8* **P** *K Coll Cam* **V** A C COWIE

THAMES VIEW (Christ Church) *Chelmsf 1* **P** *Bp* **V** U A CHINDABATA

THAMESHEAD *see* Kemble, Poole Keynes, Somerford Keynes etc *Glouc*

THAMESMEAD (Church of the Cross) (St Paul's Ecumenical Centre) (William Temple) *S'wark 6* **P** *Bp* **TR** H P EGGLESTON **TV** J E G MACY **C** E O AKANO-ADESOYE **NSM** H O B AKINGBEMISILU

THANET (St Andrew) *see* Reading Street *Cant*

THANET (St Peter the Apostle) *see* St Peter-in-Thanet *Cant*

THANINGTON (St Nicholas) (St Faith's Mission Church) *Cant 3* **P** *Abp* **V** *vacant*

THARSTON (St Mary) *see* Newton Flotman, Swainsthorpe, Tasburgh, etc *Nor*

THATCHAM (St Mary) *Ox 6* **P** *Patr Bd* **TR** M D BENNET **TV** N A HULKS **C** A H BRENNAN **NSM** B HARLAND **OLM** M E FONTAINE

THATTO HEATH (St Matthew) *see* Eccleston *Liv*

THAXTED (St John the Baptist, Our Lady and St Laurence), The Sampfords, Radwinter and Hempstead *Chelmsf 19* **P** *Bp, Guild of All So, New Coll Ox, and Keble Coll Ox (jt)* **OLM** S M LACON

THE *see under substantive place name*

THEALE (Christ Church) *see* Isle of Wedmore *B & W*

THEALE (Holy Trinity) *Ox 4* **P** *Magd Coll Ox* **V** M E DAVY

THEBERTON (St Peter) *see* Yoxmere *St E*

THEDDINGWORTH (All Saints) *see* Hexagon *Leic*

THEDDLETHORPE (St Helen) *Linc 15* **P** *Baroness Willoughby de Eresby (2 turns), Bp (1 turn)* **R** *vacant*

THELBRIDGE (St David) *see* Burrington, Chawleigh, Cheldon, Chulmleigh etc *Ex*

THELNETHAM (St Nicholas) *see* Stanton *St E*

THELVETON (St Andrew) *see* Dickleburgh and The Pulhams *Nor*

THELWALL (All Saints) *Ches 4* **P** *Keble Coll Ox* **V** D J BLACK

THEMELTHORPE (St Andrew) *see* Heart of Norfolk *Nor*

THENFORD (St Mary the Virgin) *see* Chenderit *Pet*

THERFIELD (St Mary the Virgin) w Kelshall *St Alb 16* **P** *Ld Chan and D&C St Paul's (alt)* **R** E H STEELE

THETFORD (St Cuthbert) St Peter *Nor 11* **P** *Patr Bd* **TR** P D HERBERT **TV** M W HOUGHTON, R A HEYWOOD

THETFORD, LITTLE (St George) *see* Ely *Ely*

THEYDON BOIS (St Mary) *see* Theydon Par *Chelmsf*

THEYDON GARNON (All Saints) *as above*

THEYDON MOUNT (St Michael) *as above*

THEYDON Parishes, The, including Stapleford Tawney w Theydon Mount, Theydon Bois, and Theydon Garnon *Chelmsf 3* **P** *Bp and DBP (jt)* **V** J E FRY **NSM** C A NEWNHAM

THIMBLEBY (St Margaret) *see* Horncastle Gp *Linc*

THIRKLEBY (All Saints) w Kilburn and Bagby *York 18* **P** *Abp* **P-in-c** D J BIGGS **NSM** P PERCY

THIRSK (St Mary) *York 18* **P** *Abp* **R** D J SIMPSON **C** M ROLLS **NSM** J M GILLANDERS, R W SIDGWICK

THISTLETON (St Nicholas) *see* Cottesmore and Burley, Clipsham, Exton etc *Pet*

THIXENDALE (St Mary) *see* Waggoners *York*

THOCKRINGTON (St Aidan) *see* Chollerton w Birtley and Thockrington *Newc*

THOMPSON (St Martin) *see* Caston, Griston, Merton, Thompson etc *Nor*

THORESBY, NORTH (St Helen) *see* Fotherby, N Thoresby and Grainsby w Waithe *Linc*

THORESBY, SOUTH (St Andrew) *see* Legbourne and Wold Marsh *Linc*

THORESWAY (St Mary) *see* Walesby Gp *Linc*

THORGANBY (All Saints) *see* Binbrook Gp *Linc*

THORGANBY (St Helen) *see* Derwent Ings *York*

THORINGTON (St Peter) *see* Blyth Valley *St E*

THORLEY (St James the Great) *St Alb 15* **P** *Bp* **R** G P TRACEY

THORLEY (St Swithun) *see* W Wight *Portsm*

THORMANBY (St Mary Magdalene) *see* Brafferton w Pilmoor, Myton-on-Swale etc *York*

THORNABY, NORTH (St Luke) (St Paul) *York 17* **P** *Abp* **V** C H RAZZALL

THORNABY, SOUTH (St Mark) (St Peter ad Vincula) *York 17* **P** *Abp* **V** R A DESICS

THORNAGE (All Saints) *see* Brinton, Briningham, Hunworth, Stody etc *Nor*

THORNBOROUGH (St Mary) *see* Blackthorn Chase *Ox*

THORNBURY (St Anna) *see* Bredenbury *Heref*

THORNBURY (St Margaret), Woodhall and Waterloo *Leeds 2* **P** *Bp* **V** N CLEWS **NSM** R A JOHNSON

THORNBURY (St Mary) (St Paul) and Oldbury-on-Severn w Shepperdine *Glouc 5* **P** *Ch Ch Ox* **P-in-c** J E LUDLOW

THORNBURY (St Peter) *see* Bradworthy, Sutcombe, Putford etc *Ex*

THORNBY (St Helen) *see* Guilsborough and Hollowell and Cold Ashby etc *Pet*

THORNCOMBE (The Blessed Virgin Mary) *see* Chaffcombe, Cricket Malherbie etc *B & W*

THORNDON (All Saints) *see* S Hartismere *St E*

THORNE (St Nicholas) *Sheff 10* **P** *Bp* **V** *vacant*

THORNE COFFIN (St Andrew) *see* Tintinhull w Chilthorne Domer, Yeovil Marsh etc *B & W*

THORNE ST MARGARET (St Margaret) *see* Wellington and Distr *B & W*

THORNER (St Peter) *see* Elmete Trin *Leeds*

THORNES (St James) w Christ Church *Leeds 16* **P** *DBP* **P-in-c** M C CRABTREE **C** D N KOMOROWSKI

THORNEY (St Helen) *see* E Trent *S'well*

THORNEY HILL (All Saints) *see* Bransgore and Hinton Admiral *Win*

THORNEY, WEST (St Nicholas) *see* Southbourne w W Thorney *Chich*

THORNEYBURN (St Aidan) *see* N Tyne and Redesdale *Newc*

THORNFALCON (Holy Cross) *see* Creech St Michael and Ruishton w Thornfalcon *B & W*

THORNFORD (St Mary Magdalene) *see* Three Valleys *Sarum*

THORNGATE, comprising East Dean, East and West Tytherley, and Lockerley *Win 12* **P** *DBP (1 turn), H B G Dalgety Esq (2 turns)* **V** J M PITKIN

THORNGUMBALD (St Mary) *see* Burstwick, Burton Pidsea etc *York*

THORNHAM (All Saints) *see* Hunstanton and Saxon Shore *Nor*

THORNHAM (St James) *see* High Crompton and Thornham *Man*

THORNHAM (St John) *see* Middleton and Thornham *Man*

THORNHAM MAGNA (St Mary Magdalene) *see* S Hartismere *St E*

THORNHAM PARVA (St Mary) *as above*

THORNHAUGH (St Andrew) *see* Nassington, Apethorpe, Thornhaugh etc *Pet*

THORNHILL (Mission Church) *see* Seatallan *Carl*

THORNHILL (St Christopher) *see* Southampton Thornhill St Chris *Win*

THORNHILL (St Michael and All Angels) and Whitley Lower *Leeds 7* **P** *Lord Savile* **R** D NASH

THORNLEY (St Bartholomew) *see* Wolsingham and Thornley *Dur*

THORNTHWAITE (St Mary the Virgin) *see* Upper Derwent *Carl*

THORNTHWAITE (St Saviour) *see* Dacre w Hartwith and Darley w Thornthwaite *Leeds*

THORNTON (St Frideswyde) and Crosby All Saints *Liv 8* **P** *Bp, CPAS, and V Gt Crosby St Luke (jt)* **V** *vacant*

THORNTON (St James) *Leeds 3* **P** *V Bradf* **V** C H GWINNETT **NSM** G HARDISTY

THORNTON (St Michael) *see* Barmby Moor Gp *York*

THORNTON (St Peter) *see* Markfield, Thornton, Bagworth and Stanton etc *Leic*

THORNTON (St Wilfrid) *see* Horncastle Gp *Linc*

THORNTON CURTIS (St Lawrence) *see* Abbey Gp *Linc*

THORNTON DALE (All Saints) w Allerston, Ebberston, Ellerburn and Wilton *York 19* **P** *Abp* **P-in-c** J T KINSELLA **NSM** S E GOUGH

THORNTON HEATH (St Jude w St Aidan) *S'wark 21* **P** *Bp* **P-in-c** J M NJUE

THORNTON HEATH (St Paul) *S'wark 21* **P** *The Crown* **V** D L THOMPSON

THORNTON HOUGH (All Saints) *Ches 9* **P** *Simeon's Trustees* **V** V L BARRETT

THORNTON IN CRAVEN (St Mary) *see* Broughton, Marton and Thornton *Leeds*

THORNTON LE FEN (St Peter) *see* Brothertoft Gp *Linc*

THORNTON LE STREET (St Leonard) *see* The Thorntons and The Otteringtons *York*

THORNTON RUST (Mission Room) *see* Penhill *Leeds*

THORNTON STEWARD (St Oswald) *see* Middleham w Coverdale and E Witton etc *Leeds*

THORNTON WATLASS (St Mary the Virgin) *see* Bedale and Leeming and Thornton Watlass *Leeds*

THORNTON, LITTLE (St John) *Blackb 12* **P** *Bp* **V** J L ATKINSON

THORNTON-IN-LONSDALE (St Oswald) *see* Bentham, Burton-in-Lonsdale, Chapel-le-Dale etc *Leeds*

THORNTON-LE-FYLDE (Christ Church) *Blackb 12* **P** *Trustees* **V** D E PLATT

THORNTON-LE-MOOR (All Saints) *see* Woldmoor Gp *Linc*

THORNTON-LE-MOORS St Mary w Ince and Elton *Ches 3* **P** *Bp* **V** J HELLEWELL **NSM** J E PILLING

THORNTONS, The (St Leonard) and The Otteringtons *York 18* **P** *Ch Ch Ox, Linc Coll Ox, and Abp (by turn)* **V** A S TREASURE

THOROTON (St Helena) *see* Whatton w Aslockton, Hawksworth, Scarrington etc *S'well*

THORP ARCH (All Saints) *see* Bramham *York*

THORPE (St Andrew) (Good Shepherd) *Nor 1* **P** *Trustees W J Birkbeck Esq* **R** J W STEWART

THORPE (St Laurence) *see* Farndon w Thorpe, Hawton and Cotham *S'well*

THORPE (St Leonard) *see* Fenny Bentley, Thorpe, Tissington, Parwich etc *Derby*

THORPE (St Mary) *Guildf 11* **P** *Keble Coll Ox* **V** D S HARRISON-MILES **NSM** G H MEE, J E WINN-SMITH

THORPE (St Matthew) *Nor 1* **P** *R Thorpe St Andr* **V** P G JORDAN **C** J B WYER

THORPE (St Peter) *see* The Wainfleet Gp *Linc*

THORPE ABBOTS (All Saints) *see* Redenhall w Scole *Nor*

THORPE ACHURCH (St John the Baptist) *see* Aldwincle, Clopton, Pilton, Stoke Doyle etc *Pet*

THORPE ACRE w Dishley (All Saints) *Leic 6* **P** *Bp* **V** *vacant*

THORPE ARNOLD (St Mary the Virgin) *see* Melton Mowbray *Leic*

THORPE AUDIN (Mission Room) *see* Woolley *Leeds*

THORPE BASSETT (All Saints) *see* Buckrose Carrs *York*

THORPE BAY (St Augustine) *Chelmsf 14* **P** *The Crown* **V** *vacant*

THORPE CONSTANTINE (St Constantine) *see* Mease Valley *Lich*

THORPE EDGE (St John the Divine) *see* Greengates and Thorpe Edge *Leeds*

THORPE END (St David) *Nor 1* **P** *Bp* **V** T C DAWSON

THORPE EPISCOPI (St Andrew) *see* Thorpe St Andr *Nor*

THORPE HESLEY (Holy Trinity) *Sheff 6* **P** *Sir Philip Naylor-Leyland Bt* **V** L BROADHEAD

THORPE LANGTON (St Leonard) *see* The Langtons and Shangton *Leic*

THORPE MALSOR (All Saints) *see* Rothwell w Orton and Rushton w Glendon etc *Pet*

THORPE MANDEVILLE (St John the Baptist) *see* Culworth w Sulgrave and Thorpe Mandeville etc *Pet*

THORPE MARKET (St Margaret) *see* Poppyland *Nor*

THORPE MORIEUX (St Mary the Virgin) *see* Rattlesden w Thorpe Morieux, Brettenham etc *St E*

THORPE SALVIN (St Peter) *see* Harthill and Thorpe Salvin *Sheff*

THORPE SATCHVILLE (St Michael and All Angels) *see* S Croxton Gp *Leic*

THORPE WILLOUGHBY (St Francis of Assisi) *see* Brayton *York*

THORPE-LE-SOKEN (St Michael) *Chelmsf 22* **P** *Bp* **V** *vacant*

THORPE-NEXT-HADDISCOE (St Matthias) *see* Waveney Marshlands *Nor*

THORPE-ON-THE-HILL (St Michael) *see* Swinderby *Linc*

THORRINGTON (St Mary Magdalene) *see* Tenpenny Villages *Chelmsf*

THORVERTON (St Thomas of Canterbury) *see* Brampford Speke, Cadbury, Newton St Cyres etc *Ex*

THRANDESTON (St Margaret) *see* N Hartismere *St E*

THRAPSTON (St James), Denford and Islip *Pet 10* **P** *Ld Chan (2 turns), L G Stopford-Sackville Esq (1 turn)* **R** N D R ROBSON

THREAPWOOD (St John) *see* Malpas and Threapwood and Bickerton *Ches*

THRECKINGHAM (St Peter) *see* S Lafford *Linc*

THREE BRIDGES (St Richard) *Chich 9* **P** *Bp* **V** *vacant*

THREE LEGGED CROSS (All Saints) *see* Verwood *Sarum*

THREE RIVERS Group, The, comprising Chippenham, Fordham, Isleham, Kennett, and Snailwell *Ely 4* **P** *Jes Coll Cam and Mrs D A Crawley (2 turns), Ld Chan (1 turn)* **R** D R CLEUGH **C** A H JONES

THREE RIVERS, The, comprising Lawhitton, Lewannick, Lezant, North Hill, and South Petherwin *Truro 9* **P** *Ld Chan (1 turn), Ox Univ, Bp, and DBP (1 turn)* **P-in-c** S P CLANCY

THREE SAINTS, comprising Brent Knoll, East Brent and Lympsham *B & W 1* **P** *Adn Wells (1 turn), Bp (2 turns)* **R** K J WRIGHT **NSM** N BIDDISCOMBE

THREE VALLEYS, The, comprising Batcombe, Beer Hackett, Bishop's Caundle, Bradford Abbas w Clifton Maybank, Caundle Marsh, Chetnole, Folke, Glanvilles Wootton, Hermitage, Holnest, Holwell, Leigh, Pulham, Ryme Intrinseca, Thornford, and Yetminster and Hilfield *Sarum 3* **P** *Patr Bd* **TR** A J D GILBERT **TV** G R MOODY, J R F KIRLEW **C** L J FRY **NSM** J L NELSON

THREEKINGHAM (St Peter) *see* S Lafford *Linc*

THRELKELD (St Mary) *see* St John's-in-the-Vale, Threlkeld and Wythburn *Carl*

THREXTON (All Saints) *see* Gt and Lt Cressingham w Threxton *Nor*

THRIGBY (St Mary) *see* S Trin Broads *Nor*

THRIMBY (St Mary) *see* N Westmorland *Carl*

THRINGSTONE (St Andrew) *see* Whitwick, Thringstone and Swannington *Leic*

THRIPLOW (St George) *see* Fowlmere, Foxton, Shepreth and Thriplow *Ely*

THROCKING (Holy Trinity) *see* Ardeley, Benington, Cottered w Throcking etc *St Alb*

THROCKLEY (St Mary the Virgin) *see* Newburn *Newc*

THROCKMORTON (Chapelry) *see* Abberton, The Flyfords, Naunton Beauchamp etc *Worc*

THROOP (St Paul) *Win 8* **P** *Ch Soc Trust* **P-in-c** J FINDLAY

THROPTON (St Andrew) *see* Upper Coquetdale *Newc*

THROWLEIGH (St Mary the Virgin) *see* Chagford, Gidleigh, Throwleigh etc *Ex*

THROWLEY (St Michael and All Angels) *see* Kingsdown, Creekside and High Downs *Cant*

THRUMPTON (All Saints) *see* A453 churches of S Notts *S'well*

THRUSHELTON (St George) *see* Lifton, Broadwoodwidger, Stowford etc *Ex*

THRUSSINGTON (Holy Trinity) *see* Fosse Team *Leic*

THRUXTON (St Bartholomew) *see* Cagebrook *Heref*

THRUXTON (St Peter and St Paul) *see* Appleshaw, Kimpton, Thruxton, Fyfield etc *Win*

THRYBERGH (St Leonard) *Sheff 6* **P** *Mrs P N Fullerton* **R** *vacant*

THUNDERSLEY (St Michael and All Angels) (St Peter) *Chelmsf 12* **P** *Bp* **P-in-c** A J HUDSON

THUNDERSLEY, NEW (St George) *Chelmsf 12* **P** *Bp* **C** P HILLMAN

THUNDRIDGE (St Mary) *St Alb 19* **P** *Bp* **V** A J DUNCAN

THURCASTON (All Saints) *see* Anstey and Thurcaston w Cropston *Leic*

THURCROFT (St Simon and St Jude) *Sheff 5* **P** *Bp* **V** *vacant*

THURGARTON (St Peter) *see* W Trent *S'well*

THURGOLAND (Holy Trinity) *see* Tankersley, Thurgoland and Wortley *Sheff*

THURLASTON (All Saints) *see* Enderby w Lubbesthorpe and Thurlaston *Leic*

THURLASTON (St Edmund) *see* Dunchurch *Cov*

THURLBY (St Firmin) *see* Ness Gp *Linc*

THURLBY (St Germain) *see* Withamside *Linc*

THURLEIGH (St Peter) *see* Milton Ernest, Pavenham and Thurleigh *St Alb*

THURLESTONE (All Saints), South Milton, Churchstow, Woodleigh and Loddiswell *Ex 12* **P** *Bp Ex, D&C Ex, D&C Sarum, and MMCET (jt)* **R** D G HARTLEY

THURLOW, GREAT (All Saints) *see* Stourhead *St E*

THURLOW, LITTLE (St Peter) *as above*

THURLOXTON (St Giles) *see* Alfred Jewel *B & W*

THURLSTONE (St Saviour) *see* Penistone and Thurlstone *Sheff*

THURLTON (All Saints) *see* Waveney Marshlands *Nor*

THURMASTON (St Michael and All Angels) *see* Fosse Team *Leic*

THURNBY (St Luke) *see* Cornerstone Team *Leic*

THURNBY LODGE (Christ Church) *see* Humberstone and Thurnby Lodge *Leic*

THURNE (St Edmund) *see* Martham and Repps w Bastwick, Thurne etc *Nor*

THURNHAM (St Mary the Virgin) *see* N Downs *Cant*

THURNING (St Andrew) *see* Reepham and Wensum Valley *Nor*

THURNING (St James the Great) *see* Barnwell, Hemington, Luddington in the Brook etc *Pet*

THURNSCOE (St Helen) (St Hilda) *Sheff 12* **P** *Bp and Sir Philip Naylor-Leyland Bt (jt)* **R** *vacant*

THURROCK, LITTLE (St John the Evangelist) *see* Grays North *Chelmsf*

THURROCK, LITTLE (St Mary the Virgin) *see* Grays Thurrock *Chelmsf*

THURROCK, WEST (Church Centre) *as above*

THURSBY (St Andrew) *Carl 7* **P** *D&C* **P-in-c** G P RAVALDE

THURSFORD (St Andrew) *see* Barney, Hindringham, Thursford, Great Snoring, Little Snoring and Kettlestone and Pensthorpe *Nor*

THURSLEY (St Michael and All Angels) *Guildf 4* **P** *V Witley* **V** H T MOORE **NSM** D J ORME

THURSTABLE and Winstree, comprising Birch w Layer Breton, Copford, Easthorpe, Great Braxted, Inworth, Layer de la Haye, Layer Marney, Messing, and Tolleshunt Knights w Tiptree *Chelmsf 23* **P** *Duchy of Lanc (1 turn), Ld Chan (1 turn), Patr Bd (3 turns)* **TR** A-M L RENSHAW

THURSTASTON (St Bartholomew) *Ches 8* **P** *D&C* **R** E J TURNER

THURSTON (St Peter) *see* Gt Barton and Thurston *St E*

THURSTONLAND (St Thomas) *see* Upper Holme Valley *Leeds*

THURTON (St Ethelbert) w Ashby St Mary, Bergh Apton w Yelverton and Framingham Pigot *Nor 8* **P** *Bp and Major J H Thursby, Bp and MMCET, and Ld Chan (by turn)* **R** C D ELLIS

THUXTON (St Paul) *see* Barnham Broom and Upper Yare *Nor*

THWAITE (All Saints) *see* Scarrowbeck *Nor*

THWAITE (St Mary) *see* Brooke, Kirstead, Mundham w Seething and Thwaite *Nor*

THWAITES (St Anne) *see* Millom *Carl*

THWAITES BROW (St Barnabas) *see* Keighley *Leeds*

THWING (All Saints) *see* Langtoft w Foxholes, Butterwick, Cottam etc *York*

TIBBERTON (All Saints) w Bolas Magna and Waters Upton *Lich 15* **P** *R Edgmond w Kynnersley etc, MMCET, and A B Davies Esq (jt)* **R** H M MORBY

TIBBERTON (Holy Trinity) *see* Highnam, Tibberton w Rudford etc *Glouc*

TIBBERTON (St Peter ad Vincula) *see* Bowbrook *Worc*

TIBENHAM (All Saints) *see* Long Stratton and Pilgrim TM *Nor*

TIBSHELF (St John the Baptist) *see* Blackwell w Tibshelf *Derby*

TICEHURST (St Mary) and Flimwell *Chich 16* **P** *Bp, Mrs A Sellick, and J Pilcher Esq (jt)* **V** A F EVANS

TICHBORNE (St Andrew) *see* Upper Itchen *Win*

TICHMARSH (St Mary the Virgin) *see* Aldwincle, Clopton, Pilton, Stoke Doyle etc *Pet*

TICKENHAM (St Quiricus and St Julietta) *see* Nailsea Ch Ch w Tickenham *B & W*

TICKHILL (St Mary) w Stainton *Sheff 9* **P** *Bp* **V** *vacant*

TICKNALL (St George) *see* Melbourne, Ticknall, Smisby and Stanton *Derby*

TICKTON (St Paul) *see* Beverley St Jo and St Martin w Routh All SS *York*

TIDCOMBE (St Michael) *see* Savernake *Sarum*

TIDDINGTON *see* Albury w Tiddington etc *Ox*

TIDDINGTON (St Peter) *see* Alveston *Cov*

TIDEBROOK (St John the Baptist) *see* Wadhurst, Tidebrook and Stonegate *Chich*

TIDEFORD (St Luke) *see* St Germans w Antony and Sheviock *Truro*

TIDENHAM (St Mary) w Beachley and Lancaut *Glouc 1* **P** *Bp* **V** D O TREHARNE **C** N J BULLIVANT **OLM** D M REES

TIDENHAM CHASE (St Michael and All Angels) *see* Tidenham w Beachley and Lancaut *Glouc*

TIDESWELL (St John the Baptist) *Derby 4* **P** *D&C Lich* **V** S I D WHITE **C** N M MCNALLY **NSM** G M WHITE

TIDMARSH (St Laurence) *see* Pangbourne w Tidmarsh and Sulham *Ox*

TIDMINGTON (not known) *see* Shipston-on-Stour w Honington and Idlicote *Cov*

TIDWORTH (Holy Trinity) *see* Ludgershall and Tidworth *Sarum*

TIFFIELD (St John the Baptist) *see* Pattishall w Cold Higham and Gayton w Tiffield *Pet*

TILBROOK (All Saints) *see* S Leightonstone *Ely*

TILBURY DOCKS (St John the Baptist) *Chelmsf 15* **P** *Bp* **V** T M CODLING

TILBURY, EAST (St Katherine) and West Tilbury and Linford *Chelmsf 15* **P** *Ld Chan* **P-in-c** M J MARSHALL

TILBURY-JUXTA-CLARE (St Margaret) *see* The Hedinghams and Upper Colne *Chelmsf*

TILE CROSS (St Peter) *see* Sheldon and Tile Cross *Birm*

TILE HILL (St Oswald) *Cov 3* **P** *Bp* **P-in-c** E G BACKHOUSE

TILEHURST (St Catherine of Siena) and Calcot *Ox 7* **P** *Magd Coll Ox* **V** G M ROWELL **C** P H PRICE

TILEHURST (St George) (St Mary Magdalen) *Ox 7* **P** *Bp* **V** A J CARLILL **NSM** P E FALCONER

TILEHURST (St Michael) *Ox 7* **P** *Magd Coll Ox*
R E C RATCLIFFE **NSM** T J WATKINS
TILFORD (All Saints) *see* The Bourne and Tilford *Guildf*
TILGATE (Holy Trinity) *see* S Crawley *Chich*
TILLINGHAM (St Nicholas) *Chelmsf 10* **P** *D&C St Paul's*
P-in-c S K POSS
TILLINGTON (All Hallows) *Chich 4* **P** *Lord Egremont*
P-in-c D R CROOK
TILMANSTONE (St Andrew) *see* Eastry and
Woodnesborough *Cant*
TILNEY ALL SAINTS (All Saints) *see* E Marshland *Ely*
TILNEY ST LAWRENCE (St Lawrence) *as above*
TILSHEAD (St Thomas à Becket) *see* Salisbury Plain *Sarum*
TILSTOCK (Christ Church) *see* Fauls, Tilstock and
Whitchurch *Lich*
TILSTON (St Mary) and Shocklach *Ches 5* **P** *Bp*
R T ROBINSON **NSM** N G ROBINSON
TILSTONE FEARNALL (St Jude) *see* Bunbury and Tilstone
Fearnall *Ches*
TILSWORTH (All Saints) *see* Totternhoe, Stanbridge and
Tilsworth *St Alb*
TILTON ON THE HILL (St Peter) *see* Whatborough Gp *Leic*
TILTY (St Mary the Virgin) *see* Broxted w Chickney and Tilty
etc *Chelmsf*
TIMBERHILL (St John the Baptist) *see* Nor St Jo w St Julian
Nor
TIMBERLAND (St Andrew) *see* Carr Dyke Gp *Linc*
TIMBERSCOMBE (St Petroc) *see* Dunster, Carhampton,
Withycombe w Rodhuish etc *B & W*
TIMPERLEY (Christ Church) (Holy Cross) *Ches 10*
P *Trustees* **V** *vacant*
**TIMSBURY (Blessed Virgin Mary) w Priston, Camerton and
Dunkerton** *B & W 11* **P** *Bp, Ball Coll Ox, and R W Lovegrove
Esq (jt)* **R** M A BLEWETT **C** J P DAVIES **NSM** A R G ROAKE
TIMSBURY (St Andrew) *see* Michelmersh and Awbridge and
Braishfield etc *Win*
TIMWORTH (St Andrew) *see* Lark Valley and N Bury *St E*
TINCLETON (St John the Evangelist) *see* Moreton,
Woodsford and Crossways w Tincleton *Sarum*
TINGEWICK (St Mary Magdalene) *see* W Buckingham *Ox*
TINGRITH (St Nicholas) *see* Harlington, Tingrith and
Westoning *St Alb*
TINSLEY (St Lawrence) *see* Rivers Team *Sheff*
TINTAGEL (St Materiana) *see* Boscastle Gp *Truro*
**TINTINHULL (St Margaret) w Chilthorne Domer w Yeovil
Marsh and Thorne Coffin and Lufton** *B & W 6* **P** *Guild of
All So* **P-in-c** P M DOWN
TINTWISTLE (Christ Church) *see* Hollingworth w Tintwistle
Ches
TINWELL (All Saints) *see* Ketton and Tinwell *Pet*
TIPTOE (St Andrew) *see* Hordle *Win*
TIPTON (St John the Evangelist) *Lich 25* **P** V W Bromwich
St Jas **V** *vacant*
TIPTON (St John) *see* Ottery St Mary, Alfington, W Hill,
Tipton etc *Ex*
TIPTON (St Mark) *see* Ocker Hill *Lich*
TIPTON (St Matthew) St Martin and St Paul *Lich 25*
P *MMCET, and Simeon's Trustees (jt)* **V** *vacant*
TIPTREE (St Luke) *see* Thurstable and Winstree *Chelmsf*
TIRLEY (St Michael) *see* Ashleworth, Corse, Hartpury,
Hasfield etc *Glouc*
TISBURY (St John the Baptist) *see* Nadder Valley *Sarum*
TISMANS COMMON (St John the Baptist) *see* Rudgwick
Chich
TISSINGTON (St Mary) *see* Fenny Bentley, Thorpe,
Tissington, Parwich etc *Derby*
TISTED, EAST w Colemore (St James) *see* Northanger *Win*
TISTED, WEST (St Mary Magdalene) *see* Bishop's Sutton and
Ropley and W Tisted *Win*
TITCHFIELD (St Peter) *Portsm 2* **P** *D&C Win*
NSM J A TREVITHICK
TITCHWELL (St Mary) *see* Hunstanton and Saxon Shore *Nor*
TITLEY (St Peter) *see* Kington w Huntington, Old Radnor,
Kinnerton etc *Heref*
TITTENSOR (St Luke) *see* Cotes Heath and Standon and
Swynnerton etc *Lich*
TITTLESHALL (St Mary) *see* Launditch and the Upper Nar
Nor
TIVERTON (St Andrew) *Ex 7* **P** *Bp* **C** R L MAUDSLEY
TIVERTON (St George) (St Paul) *Ex 7* **P** *MMCET and Peache
Trustees (jt)* **P-in-c** A J HUMM **C** J M MONTAGUE
TIVERTON (St Peter) and Chevithorne w Cove *Ex 7*
P *Peache Trustees (3 turns), Ld Chan (1 turn)* **R** *vacant*
TIVETSHALL (St Mary and St Margaret) *see* Diss *Nor*
**TIVIDALE (St Michael the Archangel) (Holy Cross)
(St Augustine)** *Lich 25* **P** *Bp* **V** M M ENNIS

TIVINGTON (St Leonard) *see* Porlock and Porlock Weir w
Stoke Pero etc *B & W*
TIXALL (St John the Baptist) *see* Stafford St Jo and Tixall w
Ingestre *Lich*
TIXOVER (St Luke) *see* Barrowden and Wakerley w S
Luffenham etc *Pet*
TOCKENHAM (St Giles) *see* Lyneham and Woodhill *Sarum*
TOCKHOLES (St Stephen) *see* Darwen St Cuth w Tockholes
St Steph *Blackb*
TOCKWITH (Epiphany) *see* Marston Moor *York*
TODBER (St Andrew) *see* Stour Vale *Sarum*
TODDINGTON (St Andrew) *see* Winchcombe *Glouc*
TODDINGTON (St George of England) and Chalgrave
St Alb 11 **P** *Bp and DBP (jt)* **P-in-c** L J WASHINGTON
TODENHAM (St Thomas of Canterbury) *see* Moreton-in-
Marsh w Batsford, Todenham etc *Glouc*
**TODMORDEN (St Mary) (Christ Church) w Cornholme
and Walsden** *Leeds 8* **P** *DBP and Bp (jt)* **V** J C JUKES
NSM J L FLOOD, N K WHITE
TODWICK (St Peter and St Paul) *Sheff 5* **P** *Bp*
P-in-c V C CAMBER
TOFT (St Andrew) *see* Lordsbridge *Ely*
TOFT (St John the Evangelist) *see* Knutsford St Jo and Toft
Ches
TOFT MONKS (St Margaret) *see* Waveney Marshlands *Nor*
TOFTREES (All Saints) *Nor 14* **P** *Marquess Townshend*
V *vacant*
TOFTS, WEST and Buckenham Parva *Nor 13* **P** *Guild of All
So* **R** *vacant*
TOKYNGTON (St Michael) *Lon 18* **P** *Bp*
P-in-c S F MELCHOR
TOLLADINE (Christ Church) *see* Worc St Barn w Ch Ch *Worc*
TOLLAND (St John the Baptist) *see* Wiveliscombe and the
Hills *B & W*
TOLLARD ROYAL (St Peter ad Vincula) *see* Chase *Sarum*
TOLLER FRATRUM (St Basil) *see* Melbury *Sarum*
TOLLER LANE (St Chad) *Leeds 2* **P** *Keble Coll Ox*
P-in-c L P BEADLE
TOLLER PORCORUM (St Andrew) *see* Beaminster Area *Sarum*
TOLLERTON (St Michael) *see* Alne *York*
TOLLERTON (St Peter) *S'well 5* **P** *Ld Chan* **R** *vacant*
TOLLESBURY (St Mary) *see* N Blackwater *Chelmsf*
TOLLESHUNT D'ARCY (St Nicholas) *as above*
TOLLESHUNT MAJOR (St Nicholas) *as above*
TOLLINGTON PARK (St Mark) *Lon 6* **P** *CPAS Patr Trust*
V T GOLDING
TOLPUDDLE (St John the Evangelist) *see* Puddletown,
Tolpuddle and Milborne w Dewlish *Sarum*
TOLWORTH (Emmanuel) *see* Surbiton Hill Ch Ch *S'wark*
TOLWORTH (St George), Hook and Surbiton *S'wark 15*
P *The Crown (1 turn), Patr Bd (2 turns)* **TR** H M HANCOCK
TV L I WICKINGS **C** N K LEBEY **NSM** C G LUCAS
TOMBLAND (St George) *see* Nor Colegate and Tombland
Nor
**TONBRIDGE (St Peter and St Paul) (St Andrew) (St Philip)
(St Saviour)** *Roch 11* **P** *CPAS* **C** W D CARR
TONBRIDGE (St Stephen) (St Eanswythe Mission Church)
Roch 11 **P** *CPAS* **V** M BARKER **C** M S A BARKER
TONG (St Bartholomew) *see* Shifnal, Sheriffhales and Tong
Lich
TONG (St James) and Laisterdyke *Leeds 3* **P** *Simeon's
Trustees and CR (jt)* **R** G S HODGSON **C** H M HODGSON,
P J SLINGSBY
TONGE (St Giles) *see* Milton Regis w Murston, Bapchild and
Tonge *Cant*
TONGE (St Michael), Rhodes and Alkrington *Man 6* **P** *Patr
Bd* **V** *vacant*
TONGE FOLD (St Chad) *see* Leverhulme *Man*
TONGE MOOR (St Augustine) (St Aidan) *Man 3* **P** *Keble
Coll Ox* **V** D A DAVIES
TONGHAM (St Paul) *Guildf 1* **P** *Adn Surrey* **V** C F HOLT
TOOT BALDON (St Lawrence) *see* Dorchester *Ox*
TOOTING (All Saints) *S'wark 17* **P** *Bp* **V** M E CHRISTIE
NSM S A WHITEHOUSE **OLM** G R WALLER
TOOTING GRAVENEY (St Nicholas) *S'wark 17* **P** *MMCET*
R C J DAVIS
TOOTING, UPPER (Holy Trinity) (St Augustine) *S'wark 17*
P *Bp and R Streatham St Leon (jt)* **C** D NYIRONGO
TOP VALLEY (St Philip) *see* Bestwood St Matt w St Phil *S'well*
**TOPCLIFFE (St Columba), Baldersby w Dishforth, Dalton
and Skipton on Swale** *York 18* **P** *Abp, Viscountess Downe,
and D&C (jt)*
TOPCROFT (St Margaret) *see* Hempnall *Nor*
TOPPESFIELD (St Margaret) *see* The Hedinghams and Upper
Colne *Chelmsf*

TOPSHAM (St Margaret) and Wear *Ex 3* **P** *D&C*
V L S GRACE **NSM** J J HORWOOD
TORBAY (Bay Church) Bishop's Mission Order *Ex 10*
C G E M HARPER **Min** M R J BRAY
TORBRYAN (Holy Trinity) *see* Ipplepen w Torbryan, Denbury,
Broadhempston and Woodland *Ex*
TORKSEY (St Peter) *see* Stow Gp *Linc*
TORMARTON (St Mary Magdalene) *see* Marshfield w Cold
Ashton and Tormarton etc *Bris*
TORPENHOW (St Michael and all Angels) *see* Binsey *Carl*
TORPOINT (St James) *see* Maker w Rame, Millbrook, St John
and Torpoint *Truro*
TORQUAY (St John) *see* Torre and Torquay St Jo *Ex*
TORQUAY (St Luke) *Ex 10* **P** *D&C* **V** P J MARCH
C P JACKSON
TORQUAY (St Martin) Barton *Ex 10* **P** *V St Marychurch*
V *vacant*
TORQUAY (St Matthias) (St Mark) (Holy Trinity) *Ex 10*
P *Ch Patr Trust, Bp and Torwood Trustees (jt)* **R** J A BECKETT
C P J NORRIS **NSM** P M B BARTON
TORRE (All Saints) and Torquay St John *Ex 10* **P** *Bp*
V P J MARCH **C** P JACKSON **NSM** S J BALL
TORRIDGE *see* Shebbear, Buckland Filleigh, Sheepwash etc
Ex
TORRINGTON, EAST (St Michael) *see* Barkwith Gp *Linc*
**TORRINGTON, GREAT (St Michael), Little Torrington and
Frithelstock** *Ex 18* **P** *Ch Ch Ox (8 turns), Lord Clinton (1
turn), Prayer Book Soc (1 turn)* **V** *vacant*
TORRINGTON, LITTLE (St Giles) *see* Gt and Lt Torrington
and Frithelstock *Ex*
TORRISHOLME (Ascension) *Blackb 11* **P** *Bp* **V** D M PORTER
C M A ZAMBON
TORTWORTH (St Leonard) *see* Cromhall, Tortworth,
Tytherington, Falfield etc *Glouc*
TORVER (St Luke) *see* Coniston and the Crake Valley *Carl*
TOSELAND (St Michael) *see* Papworth *Ely*
TOSSIDE (St Bartholomew) *see* Slaidburn w Tosside *Leeds*
TOSTOCK (St Andrew) *see* Pakenham w Norton, Tostock etc
St E
**TOTHAM, GREAT (St Peter) and Little Totham w
Goldhanger** *Chelmsf 23* **P** *Bp and Ld Chan (alt)*
P-in-c T L CASWELL **C** S C J CLARE **NSM** S M GODSMARK
TOTHAM, LITTLE (All Saints) *see* Gt Totham and Lt Totham
w Goldhanger *Chelmsf*
TOTLAND BAY (Christ Church) *see* W Wight *Portsm*
TOTLEY (All Saints) *Sheff 2* **P** *Bp* **NSM** A F CREASEY
**TOTNES (St Mary) w Bridgetown, Berry Pomeroy,
Dartington, Marldon, Ashprington, Cornworthy and
Stoke Gabriel** *Ex 11* **P** *Patr Bd* **TR** J D BARLOW
TV D A PARSONS **C** C E HARRIS, G STILL **NSM** A D SUMNER
TOTON (St Peter) *S'well 9* **P** *CPAS* **V** *vacant*
TOTTENHAM (All Hallows) *Lon 17* **P** *D&C St Paul's*
V R B PEARSON
TOTTENHAM (Holy Trinity) *Lon 17* **P** *Bp* **V** O A FAGBEMI
TOTTENHAM (St Bartholomew) *see* Stamford Hill St Bart *Lon*
TOTTENHAM (St Benet Fink) *Lon 17* **P** *D&C St Paul's*
V J A H HILL **NSM** M G BURRIDGE
TOTTENHAM (St Cuthbert) *see* Chitts Hill St Cuth *Lon*
TOTTENHAM (St Mary the Virgin) *Lon 17* **P** *Bp*
V S J MORRIS
TOTTENHAM (St Paul) *Lon 17* **P** *V Tottenham All Hallows*
V S A DAWKINS
TOTTENHAM (St Philip the Apostle) *Lon 17* **P** *Bp*
P-in-c L R CLARK **NSM** M G BURRIDGE
TOTTENHAM HALE (St Francis at the Engine Room) *Lon 17*
P *Bp* **V** A D WILLIAMS
TOTTENHAM, SOUTH (St Ann) *Lon 17* **P** *D&C St Paul's*
V J S SWIFT
TOTTENHILL (St Botolph) *see* W Norfolk Priory Gp *Ely*
TOTTERIDGE (St Andrew) *St Alb 14* **P** *R Hatfield*
V T P SEAGO
TOTTERNHOE (St Giles), Stanbridge and Tilsworth
St Alb 11 **P** *Bp* **V** K DAVID
TOTTINGTON (St Ann) *Man 4* **P** *R Bury St Mary*
V H W BEARN **OLM** R B MOFFAT
TOTTON (St Winifrid) *Win 11* **P** *Bp* **R** A E HILL
TOVE *see* Towcester w Caldecote and Easton Neston etc *Pet*
TOW LAW (St Philip and St James) *see* Satley, Stanley and
Tow Law *Dur*
**TOWCESTER (St Lawrence) w Caldecote and Easton
Neston and Greens Norton and Bradden (The Tove
Benefice)** *Pet 5* **P** *The Crown (1 turn), Bp, Lord Hesketh, and
J E Grant-Ives Esq (1 turn)* **V** P E CHALLEN **C** E W PELLY
NSM A HAMMETT
TOWEDNACK (St Tewinock) *Truro 4* **P** *Bp*
P-in-c E V A FOOT

TOWER CHAPEL (St Nicholas) *see* Whitehaven *Carl*
TOWERSEY (St Catherine) *see* Thame *Ox*
TOWN END FARM (St Bede) *see* N Wearside *Dur*
TOWNEND (St Paul) *see* Morley *Leeds*
TOWNSTAL (St Clement) *see* Dartmouth and Dittisham *Ex*
TOXTETH (St Bede) (St Clement) *Liv 3* **P** *Simeon's Trustees*
V E JONES
TOXTETH (St Gabriel) *see* Dingle *Liv*
TOXTETH (St Margaret) *Liv 3* **P** *St Chad's Coll Dur*
P-in-c R G LEWIS **NSM** J STEPHENSON
TOXTETH (St Philemon) *Liv 3* **P** *CPAS* **R** B R ELFICK
C A J SIMMONS
**TOXTETH PARK (Christ Church) (St Michael-in-the-
Hamlet) (St Andrew)** *Liv 3* **P** *Simeon's Trustees and Trustees
(jt)* **V** K J HITCHMAN
TOXTETH PARK (St Agnes and St Pancras) *Liv 3* **P** *St Chad's
Coll Dur* **V** *vacant*
TOXTETH PARK (St Cleopas) *see* Dingle *Liv*
TOYNTON ALL SAINTS (All Saints) *see* Bolingbroke Deanery
Linc
TOYNTON ST PETER (St Peter) *as above*
TOYNTON, HIGH (St John the Baptist) *see* Horncastle Gp
Linc
TOYS HILL (Hall) *see* Hever, Four Elms and Mark Beech *Roch*
TRAFALGAR SQUARE (St Martin-in-the-Fields) *see*
St Martin-in-the-Fields *Lon*
TRAFFORD, OLD (St Bride) *Man 2* **P** *Trustees*
R P J MATTHEWS **OLM** O H SAMUEL
TRAFFORD, OLD (St Hilda) *see* Firswood and Gorse Hill *Man*
TRAFFORD, OLD (St John the Evangelist) *Man 2* **P** *The
Crown* **R** J D HUGHES **OLM** C J ASPINALL
TRANMERE (St Catherine) *Ches 1* **P** *R Bebington*
V J R TERRY
TRANMERE (St Paul w St Luke) *Ches 1* **P** *Bp*
P-in-c M G LOACH
TRAWDEN (St Mary the Virgin) *see* Foulridge,
Laneshawbridge and Trawden *Blackb*
TREALES (Christ Church) *Blackb 10* **P** *V Kirkham*
NSM C M MORTON
TREBOROUGH (St Peter) *see* Old Cleeve, Leighland and
Treborough *B & W*
TREDINGTON (St Gregory) and Darlingscott *Cov 9* **P** *Jes
Coll Ox* **R** *vacant*
TREDINGTON (St John the Baptist) *see* Deerhurst and
Apperley w Forthampton etc *Glouc*
TREETON (St Helen) *see* Rivers Team *Sheff*
TREFONEN (All Saints) *see* Llanyblodwel, Llanymynech,
Morton and Trefonen *Lich*
TREGADILLET (St Mary's Mission) *see* Launceston *Truro*
TREGONY (not known) w St Cuby and Cornelly *Truro 5*
P *Bp* **R** *vacant*
TREKNOW (Holy Family) *see* Boscastle Gp *Truro*
**TRELAWNY, comprising Lanreath, Lansallos, Lanteglos by
Fowey, Pelynt, and Talland** *Truro 12* **P** *DBP, D&C, W G
Mills Esq, J B Kitson Esq, and H M Parker Esq (jt)* **R** J ALLEN
TRELEIGH (St Stephen) *see* Redruth w Lanner and Treleigh
Truro
TRELYSTAN (St Mary the Virgin) *see* Chirbury, Marton,
Middleton and Trelystan etc *Heref*
TREMAINE (St Winwalo) *see* Egloskerry, N Petherwin,
Tremaine, Tresmere etc *Truro*
TRENDLEWOOD (Conventional District) *B & W 12*
C M D TAYLOR **Min** J S TILLEY
TRENEGLOS (St Gregory) *see* Boscastle Gp *Truro*
TRENT (St Andrew) *see* Queen Thorne *Sarum*
TRENT VALE (St John the Evangelist) *see* Hartshill, Penkhull
and Trent Vale *Lich*
**TRENT, WEST, comprising Bleasby, Halloughton,
Hoveringham, Morton, Rolleston, Thurgarton, and Upton**
S'well 3 **P** *Trin Coll Cam (1 turn), Ld Chan (2 turns)*
V P W WHITE
**TRENTCLIFFE Group, The, comprising Blyborough, Blyton,
East Stockwith, Glentworth, Harpswell, Hemswell,
Laughton, and Willoughton** *Linc 2* **P** *Bp, Ch Soc Trust,
MMCET, and SMF (1 turn), Ld Chan (1 turn)* **V** M BRISCOE
NSM C A SULLY
TRENTHAM (St Mary and All Saints) *Lich 12* **P** *CPAS*
V A G STONE **NSM** D PAMMENT
TRENTISHOE (St Peter) *see* Lynton, Brendon, Countisbury
etc *Ex*
**TRENTSIDE EAST, comprising Gunness and Scunthorpe the
Resurrection** *Linc 6* **P** *Bp Linc (2 turns), Bp Lon (1 turn)*
R *vacant*
TRESCO (St Nicholas) *see* Is of Scilly *Truro*
TRESHAM (not known) *see* Tyndale *Glouc*

TRESILLIAN (Holy Trinity) and Lamorran w Merther *Truro 5*
  P *Viscount Falmouth* **R** *vacant*
TRESLOTHAN (St John the Evangelist) *see* Crowan and
  Treslothan *Truro*
TRESWELL (St John the Baptist) *see* The Rivers *S'well*
TRETHEVY (St Piran) *see* Boscastle Gp *Truro*
TRETIRE (St Mary) *see* St Weonards *Heref*
TREVALGA (St Petroc) *see* Boscastle Gp *Truro*
TREVENSON (St Illogan) *see* St Illogan *Truro*
TREVERBYN (St Peter) *Truro 7* **P** *The Crown*
  P-in-c K P ARTHUR
TREVONE (St Saviour) *see* Padstow, St Merryn and St Issey w
  St Petroc Minor *Truro*
TREWEN (St Michael) *see* Egloskerry, N Petherwin, Tremaine,
  Tresmere etc *Truro*
TREYFORD CUM DIDLING (St Andrew) *see* Harting w Elsted
  and Treyford cum Didling *Chich*
TRIANGLE (All Saints) (St Matthew) (Community Centre)
  Ipswich *St E 1* **P** *Bp and Ld Chan (alt)* **R** N S ATKINS
  C D F MORRISON, D J A H THEULINGS **NSM** L A CAREY,
  L PEPPER, R H BEST
TRIGG MAJOR Conventional District *Truro 9*
  P-in-c P M KNIGHT
TRIMDON (St Mary Magdalene) *see* Upper Skerne *Dur*
TRIMDON GRANGE (St Alban) *as above*
TRIMINGHAM (St John the Baptist) *see* Poppyland *Nor*
TRIMLEY (St Martin) *see* Walton and Trimley *St E*
TRIMPLEY (Holy Trinity) *see* Kidderminster Ismere *Worc*
TRING (St Martha) (St Peter and St Paul) (St Mary) *St Alb 1*
  P *Bp* **TR** H BELLIS **TV** J C BANISTER, M E GRACE
  C S MARSHALL
TRINITY IN LEWES, including Lewes St John sub Castro,
  South Malling, and Southover *Chich 21* **P** *CPAS Patr Trust*
  C J J R MIDDLETON **NSM** J J BAMBER
TROSTON (St Mary the Virgin) *see* Blackbourne *St E*
TROTTISCLIFFE (St Peter and St Paul) *see* Birling, Addington,
  Ryarsh and Trottiscliffe *Roch*
TROTTON (St George) *see* Rogate w Terwick and Trotton w
  Chithurst *Chich*
TROUTBECK (Jesus Church) *see* Windermere St Mary and
  Troutbeck *Carl*
TROWBRIDGE (Holy Trinity) *see* Trowbridge St Thos and W
  Ashton *Sarum*
TROWBRIDGE (St James) and Keevil *Sarum 15* **P** *Ch Patr*
  Trust and D&C (jt) **R** *vacant*
TROWBRIDGE (St Thomas) and West Ashton *Sarum 15*
  P *CPAS* **V** J A COUTTS
TROWELL (St Helen) *see* Trowell, Awsworth and Cossall
  S'well
TROWELL (St Helen), Awsworth and Cossall *S'well 8* **P** *Bp*
  and Lord Middleton (jt) **NSM** P C WHITEHEAD
TROWSE (St Andrew) *Nor 1* **P** *D&C* **P-in-c** R R BRABY
TRULL (All Saints) w Angersleigh *B & W 18* **P** *DBP and M V*
  Spurway Esq (jt) **R** A J WADSWORTH **C** I K BALL, J P BALL
TRUMPINGTON (St Mary and St Michael) *Ely 3* **P** *Trin Coll*
  Cam **V** M J MAXWELL **C** S R DOVE **NSM** S M HARRIS
TRUNCH GROUP, The (St Botolph), comprising Gimingham,
  Knapton, Mundesley, Paston, and Trunch w Swafield and
  Bradfield *Nor 20* **P** *Duchy of Lancaster (3 turns), Bp, Adn,*
  DBP, and Peterho Cam (1 turn) **R** A E JONES
  C J M HAYWOOD
TRURO (St Mary's Cathedral and Parish Church) *Truro 5*
  P *The Crown* **Hon C** A G BASHFORTH
TRURO St Paul (St George the Martyr) (St John the
  Evangelist) *Truro 5* **P** *The Crown (1 turn), Bp and V Kenwyn*
  St Cuby (1 turn) **V** *vacant*
TRUSHAM (St Michael and All Angels) *see* Chudleigh w
  Chudleigh Knighton and Trusham *Ex*
TRUSLEY (All Saints) *see* Boylestone, Church Broughton,
  Dalbury, etc *Derby*
TRUSTHORPE (St Peter) *see* Mablethorpe w Trusthorpe *Linc*
TRYSULL (All Saints) *see* Smestow Vale *Lich*
TUBNEY (St Lawrence) *see* Fyfield w Tubney and Kingston
  Bagpuize *Ox*
TUCKHILL (Holy Innocents) *see* Claverley w Tuckhill *Heref*
TUCKINGMILL (All Saints) *see* Camborne, Tuckingmill and
  Penponds *Truro*
TUCKSWOOD (St Paul) *see* Nor Lakenham St Jo and All SS
  and Tuckswood *Nor*
TUDDENHAM (St Martin) *see* Westerfield and Tuddenham w
  Witnesham *St E*
TUDDENHAM (St Mary) *see* Forest Heath *St E*
TUDDENHAM, EAST (All Saints) *see* Mattishall and the Tudd
  Valley *Nor*
TUDDENHAM, NORTH (St Mary the Virgin) *as above*
TUDELEY (All Saints) *see* Capel United Ben *Roch*

TUDHOE (St David) *see* Croxdale and Tudhoe *Dur*
TUDHOE GRANGE (St Andrew) *see* Bowburn and Tudhoe
  Grange *Dur*
TUEBROOK (St John the Baptist) *see* W Derby St Jo *Liv*
TUFFLEY (St Barnabas) *Glouc 2* **P** *Bp* **V** S J TODD
TUFNELL PARK (St George and All Saints) *Lon 6* **P** *Trustees*
  and CPAS (jt) **P-in-c** A M LILLEY **NSM** D ONYEKWULUJE
TUFTON (St Mary) *see* Whitchurch w Tufton and Litchfield
  Win
TUGBY (St Thomas à Becket) *see* Hallaton and Allexton, w
  Horninghold, Tugby etc *Leic*
TUGFORD (St Catherine) *see* Corvedale Benefice *Heref*
TULSE HILL (Holy Trinity and St Matthias) *S'wark 12*
  P *Simeon's Trustees and Peache Trustees (jt)* **V** R P DORMANDY
  NSM W W SHARPE
TUNBRIDGE WELLS (Christ Church) *Roch 12* **P** *Mabledon*
  Trust and CPAS (jt) **V** T M HUMPHREY **C** G E J TAYLOR
TUNBRIDGE WELLS (King Charles the Martyr) *Roch 12*
  P *Trustees* **V** L J POWELL **NSM** C L ALLWOOD,
  S M PARTRIDGE
TUNBRIDGE WELLS (St Barnabas) *Roch 12* **P** *Guild of All So*
  V J F CASTER
TUNBRIDGE WELLS (St James) *Roch 12* **P** *CPAS Patr Trust*
  V J P STEWART **C** J A HAMMILL
TUNBRIDGE WELLS (St John) *Roch 12* **P** *CPAS and V*
  Tunbridge Wells H Trin (jt) **V** T J NASH
TUNBRIDGE WELLS (St Luke) *Roch 12* **P** *Five Trustees*
  V C M GLASS
TUNBRIDGE WELLS (St Mark) Broadwater Down *Roch 12*
  P *Bp* **P-in-c** L J POWELL **NSM** C L ALLWOOD
TUNBRIDGE WELLS (St Peter) Windmill Fields *Roch 12*
  P *Trustees and CPAS (jt)* **V** M P WARREN
TUNBRIDGE WELLS (St Philip) *Roch 12* **P** *CPAS*
  V R N THOMAS
TUNSTALL (All Saints) *see* S Holderness Coast *York*
TUNSTALL (Christ Church) *see* Goldenhill and Tunstall *Lich*
TUNSTALL (Holy Trinity) *see* Catterick *Leeds*
TUNSTALL (St John the Baptist) *see* E Lonsdale *Blackb*
TUNSTALL (St John the Baptist) and Bredgar *Cant 15*
  P *Abp, D&C, O P Doubleday Esq, S G McCandlish Esq, Lady*
  Kingsdown, and J Nightingale Esq (jt) **R** A E PINNEGAR
  NSM P K JARDINE-ROSE
TUNSTALL (St Michael and All Angels) *see* Wilford Peninsula
  St E
TUNSTEAD (St Mary) *see* Wroxham w Hoveton, Belaugh
  and Tunstead etc *Nor*
TUNSTEAD (Holy Trinity) *see* Bacup and Stacksteads *Man*
TUNWORTH (All Saints) *see* N Hants Downs *Win*
TUPSLEY (St Paul) w Hampton Bishop *Heref 3* **P** *Bp*
  V N P ARMSTRONG **C** S M E CHIPPER
TUPTON (St John) *see* N Wingfield, Clay Cross and Pilsley
  Derby
TUR LANGTON (St Andrew) *see* The Langtons and Shangton
  Leic
TURKDEAN (All Saints) *see* Northleach w Hampnett and
  Farmington etc *Glouc*
TURNASTONE (St Mary Magdalene) *see* Madley w Tyberton,
  Peterchurch, Vowchurch etc *Heref*
TURNDITCH (All Saints) *see* Belper Ch Ch w Turnditch *Derby*
TURNERS HILL (St Leonard) *Chich 9* **P** *Bp*
  P-in-c D A TICKNER
TURNFORD (St Clement) *see* Cheshunt *St Alb*
TURNHAM GREEN (Christ Church) *Lon 11* **P** *Bp*
  V N L MOY **C** J M HOLDER, L J HOLDER **NSM** R J MOY
TURNWORTH (St Mary) *see* Winterborne Valley and Milton
  Abbas *Sarum*
TURTON MOORLAND MINISTRY (St Anne) (St James)
  Man 3 **P** *Patr Bd* **TR** P H REISS **TV** C T HAYDEN
  C H K LANE **OLM** A M BULCOCK, C D JAMIESON
TURVEY (All Saints) *see* Chellington *St Alb*
TURVILLE (St Mary) *see* Hambleden Valley *Ox*
TURWESTON (Assumption of the Blessed Virgin Mary) *see* W
  Buckingham *Ox*
TUSHINGHAM (St Chad) *see* Marbury w Tushingham and
  Whitewell *Ches*
TUTBURY (St Mary the Virgin) *see* Anslow, Rolleston and
  Tutbury *Lich*
TUTSHILL (St Luke) *see* Tidenham w Beachley and Lancaut
  Glouc
TUTTINGTON (St Peter and St Paul) *see* King's Beck *Nor*
TUXFORD (St Nicholas) w Weston, Markham Clinton,
  Normanton upon Trent and Marnham *S'well 3* **P** *Bp and*
  Ld Chan (alt) **V** G P PRICE
TWEEDMOUTH (St Bartholomew) *see* Scremerston, Spittal
  and Tweedmouth *Newc*
TWERTON-ON-AVON *see* Bath Twerton-on-Avon *B & W*

TWICKENHAM (All Hallows) *Lon 10* **P** *D&C St Paul's*
V K D BELL

TWICKENHAM (All Saints) *Lon 10* **P** *Bp* **V** A J LANE

TWICKENHAM (St Augustine of Canterbury) *see* Whitton
St Aug *Lon*

TWICKENHAM (St Mary the Virgin) *Lon 10* **P** *D&C Windsor*
V R J H WILLIAMS

TWICKENHAM COMMON (Holy Trinity) *Lon 10* **P** *Bp*
V T M GARRETT **C** C L KEAR **Hon C** N R GARRETT

TWICKENHAM, EAST (St Stephen) (St Paul) *Lon 10* **P** *CPAS*
V J P B BARNES **C** D A COKAYNE, R J BEDFORD

**TWIGWORTH, Down Hatherley, Norton, The Leigh,
Evington, Sandhurst and Staverton w Boddington**
Glouc 3 **P** *Ld Chan (1 turn), Bp Glouc and D&C Bris (1 turn)*
NSM P J DONALD

TWINEHAM (St Peter) *see* Albourne w Sayers Common and
Twineham *Chich*

TWINSTEAD (St John the Evangelist) *see* N Hinckford
Chelmsf

TWITCHEN (St Peter) *see* Bishopsnympton, Charles, E
Anstey, High Bray etc *Ex*

TWO GATES (St Peter) *see* Wilnecote *Lich*

TWO MILE ASH (not known) *see* Watling Valley *Ox*

TWO MILE HILL (St Michael the Archangel) *see* Bris St Aid w
St Geo, Fishponds St Jo, and Two Mile Hill *Bris*

TWO RIVERS *see* Holbrook, Stutton, Freston, Woolverstone
etc *St E*

TWO RIVERS *see* Newton Tracey, Horwood, Alverdiscott etc
Ex

TWO RIVERS, The, comprising Ashen, Birdbrook, Helions
Bumpstead, Ridgewell, Steeple Bumpstead, and Sturmer
Chelmsf 18 **P** *Duchy of Lancaster (1 turn), Bp and DBP (1
turn), Ld Chan (1 turn)* **R** J D LOWE **Hon C** S E CRUSE
NSM T C LOWE

TWO SHIRES *see* Chaffcombe, Cricket Malherbie etc *B & W*

TWYCROSS (St James) *see* Sheepy *Leic*

TWYFORD (Assumption of the Blessed Virgin Mary) *see* The
Claydons and Swan *Ox*

TWYFORD (St Andrew) *see* Aston on Trent, Elvaston, Weston
on Trent etc *Derby*

TWYFORD (St Andrew) *see* S Croxton Gp *Leic*

TWYFORD (St Mary the Virgin) *see* Ruscombe and Twyford
w Hurst *Ox*

TWYFORD (St Nicholas) *see* Heart of Norfolk *Nor*

TWYNING (St Mary Magdalene) *see* Tewkesbury w Walton
Cardiff and Twyning *Glouc*

TWYWELL (St Nicholas) *see* Cranford w Grafton Underwood
and Twywell *Pet*

TYBERTON (St Mary) *see* Madley w Tyberton, Peterchurch,
Vowchurch etc *Heref*

TYDD ST GILES (St Giles) *see* Leverington, Newton and Tydd
St Giles *Ely*

TYDD ST MARY (St Mary) *see* Sutton Bridge and Tydd
St Mary *Linc*

TYE GREEN (St Barnabas) *see* Coggeshall, Markshall,
Cressing etc *Chelmsf*

TYE GREEN (St Stephen) w St Andrew Netteswell *Chelmsf 4*
P J L H Arkwright Esq **P-in-c** D L MCINDOE **C** S H WELLER
Hon C C C OKEKE

TYLDESLEY (St George) *see* Astley, Tyldesley and Mosley
Common *Man*

TYLERS GREEN (St Margaret) *see* Penn and Tylers Green *Ox*

TYLER'S HILL (St George) *see* Gt Chesham *Ox*

TYNDALE, comprising Alderley, North Nibley, and
Wotton-under-Edge w Ozleworth *Glouc 5* **P** *Ch Ch Ox and
Bp (jt)* **V** R E COOK **NSM** M E LANGLEY, P C E MARSH

TYNE, NORTH and Redesdale Team, comprising
Bellingham, Corsenside, Elsdon, Falstone w Greystead and
Thorneyburn, Horsley w Byrness, and Otterburn *Newc 8*
P *Patr Bd* **TR** *vacant*

TYNEMOUTH (St John Percy) *Newc 5* **P** *Dioc Soc*
P-in-c L J CLEMINSON

TYNEMOUTH Balkwell (St Peter) *see* Balkwell *Newc*

TYNEMOUTH Cullercoats (St Paul) *Newc 5* **P** *Dioc Soc*
V J VILASECA-BRUCH

TYNEMOUTH PRIORY (Holy Saviour) *Newc 5* **P** *Dioc Soc*
V S DIXON **NSM** M RAILTON

TYNINGS LANE (St Mary's Mission Church) *see* Aldridge *Lich*

TYRINGHAM (St Peter) *see* Lamp *Ox*

TYRLEY (Mission Room) *see* Drayton in Hales *Lich*

TYSELEY (St Edmund) *Birm 6* **P** *The Crown*
OLM A E KNIGHT

**TYSOE (Assumption of the Blessed Virgin Mary) w Oxhill
and Whatcote** *Cov 9* **P** *Marquess of Northampton and DBP
(jt)* **P-in-c** G HEIGHTON **Hon C** H C W PARBURY

TYTHBY (Holy Trinity) *see* Wiverton in the Vale *S'well*

TYTHERINGTON (St James) *see* Cromhall, Tortworth,
Tytherington, Falfield etc *Glouc*

TYTHERINGTON (St James) *see* Upper Wylye Valley *Sarum*

TYTHERLEY, EAST (St Peter) *see* Thorngate *Win*

TYTHERLEY, WEST (St Peter) *as above*

TYTHERTON KELLAWAYS (St Giles) *see* Draycot *Bris*

TYTHERTON LUCAS (St Nicholas) *see* Chippenham St Andr
w Tytherton Lucas *Bris*

TYWARDREATH (St Andrew) w Tregaminion *Truro 7*
P *DBP* **V** *vacant*

UBLEY (St Bartholomew) *see* Blagdon w Compton Martin
and Ubley *B & W*

UCKFIELD (Holy Cross) (St Saviour) *Chich 18* **P** *Abp*
R J C WALL **NSM** M T Z MUTIKANI

UDIMORE (St Mary) *see* Brede w Udimore and Beckley and
Peasmarsh *Chich*

UFFCULME (St Mary the Virgin) *see* Willand, Uffculme,
Kentisbeare etc *Ex*

UFFINGTON (Holy Trinity) *see* Wrockwardine Deanery *Lich*

**UFFINGTON (St Mary), Shellingford, Woolstone and
Baulking** *Ox 25* **P** *Bp (2 turns), J J Twynam Esq (1 turn)*
R J H GOULSTON

UFFINGTON Group, The (St Michael and All Angels),
including Barholme, Braceborough, Greatford, Tallington,
West Deeping, and Wilsthorpe *Linc 16* **P** *Ld Chan (2 turns),
Bp (2 turns), D&C (1 turn)* **R** A P BEESLEY

UFFORD (Assumption of the Blessed Virgin Mary) *see* Melton
and Ufford *St E*

UFTON (St Michael and All Angels) *Cov 10* **P** *Bp*
P-in-c A G BATCHELOR

UGBOROUGH (St Peter) *see* Diptford w N Huish, Ermington,
Halwell etc *Ex*

UGGESHALL (St Mary) *see* Sole Bay *St E*

UGGLEBARNBY (All Saints) *see* Lower Esk *York*

UGLEY (St Peter) *see* Henham and Elsenham w Ugley
Chelmsf

UGTHORPE (Christ Church) *see* Hinderwell, Roxby and
Staithes etc *York*

UKELEY (St Peter) *see* Henham and Elsenham w Ugley
Chelmsf

ULCEBY (All Saints) *see* Alford Gp *Linc*

ULCEBY (St Nicholas) *see* Abbey Gp *Linc*

ULCOMBE (All Saints) *see* Len Valley *Cant*

ULDALE (St James) *see* Binsey *Carl*

ULEY (St Giles) *see* Dursley, Uley, Owlpen etc *Glouc*

ULGHAM (St John the Baptist) *Newc 11* **P** *Bp* **V** *vacant*

ULLENHALL (St Mary the Virgin) *see* Beaudesert and
Henley-in-Arden w Ullenhall *Cov*

ULLESKELFE (St Saviour) *see* Tadcaster *York*

ULLEY (Holy Trinity) *see* Aston cum Aughton w Swallownest
and Ulley *Sheff*

ULLINGSWICK (St Luke) *see* Bredenbury *Heref*

ULPHA (St John) *see* Broughton and Duddon *Carl*

ULROME (St Andrew) *see* Bridlington Ch Ch w Bessingby
and Ulrome *York*

ULTING (All Saints) *see* Hatfield Peverel w Ulting *Chelmsf*

ULVERSTON (St Mary w Holy Trinity) (St Jude) *Carl 9*
P *Peache Trustees* **R** A C BING **C** M B SIMPSON

UMBERLEIGH (Church of the Good Shepherd) *see* S Molton
w Nymet St George, Chittlehamholt etc *Ex*

UNDERBARROW (All Saints) w Helsington *Carl 10* **P** *V
Kendal H Trin* **P-in-c** M D WOODCOCK

UNDERRIVER (St Margaret) *see* Seal Chart w Underriver *Roch*

UNDERSKIDDAW (Parish Room) *see* Crosthwaite Keswick
Carl

UNDERWOOD (St Michael and All Angels) *see* Brinsley w
Underwood *S'well*

UNITED BENEFICE OF ST BENEDICT *see* Ashmanhaugh,
Barton Turf etc *Nor*

UNSTONE (St Mary) *see* Dronfield w Holmesfield *Derby*

UNSWORTH (St Andrew) *see* Hillock and Unsworth *Man*

UNSWORTH (St George) *see* Hillock and Unsworth *Man*

UP HATHERLEY (St Philip and St James) *Glouc 6* **P** *Ch
Union* **V** M L CATHERALL

UP HOLLAND (St Thomas the Martyr) and Dalton *Liv 14*
P *Bp, Adn Wigan, and Lay Chair Ormskirk Deanery Synod (jt)*
R P A LOCK **C** J E B SHEPHERD **NSM** C J DUNBAR

UP MARDEN (St Michael) *see* Octagon *Chich*

UP NATELY (St Stephen) *see* N Hants Downs *Win*

UP WALTHAM *see* Upwaltham *Chich*

UPAVON (St Mary the Virgin) *see* Vale of Pewsey *Sarum*

UPCHURCH (St Mary the Virgin) *see* The Six *Cant*

UPHAM (All Saints) (Blessed Mary of Upham) *Portsm 1*
P *Ld Chan* **R** J C HUNT **NSM** J BELOE, K F WICKERT

UPHILL (St Barnabas Mission Church) *see* Weston-super-Mare
St Nic w St Barn *B & W*

UPHILL (St Nicholas) *as above*

UPLANDS (All Saints) *see* Stroud Team *Glouc*

UPLANDS GROUP *see* Guilsborough and Hollowell and Cold Ashby etc *Pet*

UPLEADON (St Mary the Virgin) *see* Redmarley D'Abitot, Bromesberrow, Pauntley etc *Glouc*

UPLOWMAN (St Peter) *see* Sampford Peverell, Uplowman, Holcombe Rogus etc *Ex*

UPLYME (St Peter and St Paul) *see* Axminster, All Saints, Axmouth, Chardstock etc *Ex*

UPMINSTER (St Laurence) *Chelmsf 2*   P *W R Holden Esq*   R S M BRASIER   NSM R J MURRAY

UPNOR (St Philip and St James) *see* Frindsbury w Upnor and Chattenden *Roch*

UPOTTERY (St Mary the Virgin) *see* Broadhembury, Dunkeswell, Luppitt, Plymtree, Sheldon, and Upottery *Ex*

UPPER *see also under substantive place name*

UPPER KENNET, comprising Avebury, Broad Hinton, Overton and Fyfield w East Kennett, Winterbourne Bassett, and Winterbourne Monkton w Berwick Bassett *Sarum 18*   P *Bp*   R M T SHEPHERDSON

UPPER SOAR, comprising Ashby Parva, Claybrooke, Dunton Bassett, Frolesworth, and Leire *Leic 7*   P *The Crown (1 turn)*, *Mrs A M Finn, Adn Loughb, and Ball Coll Ox (1 turn)*   R E A HEATON

UPPER TAS VALLEY, comprising Ashwellthorpe, Forncett End, Forncett St Mary, Forncett St Peter, Fundenhall, Hapton, Tacolneston, and Wreningham *Nor 7*   P *Bp, Keble Coll Ox, Ch Coll Cam, and MMCET (by turn)*   P-in-c L D A AVERY

UPPER THAMES, comprising Ashton Keynes, Cricklade, Latton, and Leigh *Bris 6*   P *Bp, D&C, and Hon P N Eliot (jt)*   P-in-c D M DEWES   NSM S E DANBY

UPPERBY (St John the Baptist) *Carl 3*   P *D&C*   P-in-c R O GOODFELLOW

UPPERBY (St John the Baptist) *see* Upperby *Carl*

UPPERTHONG (St John the Evangelist) *see* Upper Holme Valley *Leeds*

UPPINGHAM (St Peter and St Paul) w Ayston and Belton w Wardley *Pet 12*   P *Bp*   R R D WATTS   C D J SMITH-WILDS

UPPINGTON (Holy Trinity) *see* Wrockwardine Deanery *Lich*

UPSHIRE (St Thomas) *see* Waltham H Cross *Chelmsf*

UPTON (All Saints) *see* Lea Gp *Linc*

UPTON (Holy Ascension) *Ches 2*   P *Duke of Westmr*   V P NEWMAN   NSM D O'BRIEN

UPTON (St Dunstan) *see* The Lytchetts and Upton *Sarum*

UPTON (St James) *see* Dulverton w Brushford, Brompton Regis etc *B & W*

UPTON (St John the Baptist) *see* Castor w Upton and Stibbington etc *Pet*

UPTON (St Laurence) *see* Upton cum Chalvey *Ox*

UPTON (St Margaret) *see* Broadside *Nor*

UPTON (St Margaret) *see* N Leightonstone *Ely*

UPTON (St Mary Magdalene) *Ex 10*   P *Simeon's Trustees and Ch Patr Trust (alt)*   R S M LEACH   C E L DORNAN   NSM I N KIYAGA, J H GARNER

UPTON (St Mary the Virgin) *see* The Churn *Ox*

UPTON (St Mary) *Ches 8*   P *Simeon's Trustees*   V N J EASTWOOD   C A G HAM

UPTON (St Peter and St Paul) *see* W Trent *S'well*

UPTON BISHOP (St John the Baptist) *see* Ariconium *Heref*

UPTON CROSS (St Paul) *see* Callington Cluster *Truro*

UPTON CUM CHALVEY (St Mary) *Ox 12*   P *Bp*   TV A C STEWART   NSM L R HILLIER

UPTON GREY (St Mary) *see* N Hants Downs *Win*

UPTON HELLIONS (St Mary the Virgin) *see* Crediton, Shobrooke and Sandford etc *Ex*

UPTON LOVELL (St Augustine of Canterbury) *see* Upper Wylye Valley *Sarum*

UPTON MAGNA (St Lucia) *see* Wrockwardine Deanery *Lich*

UPTON NOBLE (St Mary Magdalene) *see* Alham Vale *B & W*

UPTON PARK (St Alban) *see* E Ham H Trin *Chelmsf*

UPTON PRIORY (Church of the Resurrection) *Ches 13*   P *Bp*   NSM A S RAVENSCROFT

UPTON PYNE (Our Lady) *see* Brampford Speke, Cadbury, Newton St Cyres etc *Ex*

UPTON SCUDAMORE (St Mary the Virgin) *see* River Were *Sarum*

UPTON SNODSBURY (St Kenelm) *see* Peopleton and White Ladies Aston w Churchill etc *Worc*

UPTON ST LEONARDS (St Leonard) *Glouc 2*   P *Bp*   C J R TURK

UPTON WARREN (St Michael) *see* Wychebrook *Worc*

UPTON-ON-SEVERN (St Peter and St Paul), Ripple, Earls Croome w Hill Croome and Strensham *Worc 2*   P *Bp (2 turns), Mrs A J Hyde-Smith and Mrs A L Wynne (1 turn)*   P-in-c B UNWIN   NSM G R MOORE, S M E ADENEY

UPWALTHAM (St Mary the Virgin) *Chich 4*   P *Lord Egremont*   P-in-c D R CROOK

UPWELL (St Peter) *Ely 14*   P *R T Townley Esq*   P-in-c N A WHITEHOUSE   NSM D A CALVERT

UPWELL CHRISTCHURCH (Christ Church) *see* Six Fen Churches *Ely*

UPWEY (St Laurence) *see* Weymouth Ridgeway *Sarum*

UPWOOD (St Peter) *see* The Ramseys and Upwood *Ely*

URCHFONT (St Michael and All Angels) *see* Cannings and Redhorn *Sarum*

URMSTON (St Clement) *see* Davyhulme Ch Ch and Urmston *Man*

URSWICK (St Mary the Virgin and St Michael) *see* Aldingham, Dendron, Rampside and Urswick *Carl*

USHAW MOOR (St Luke) *see* Brandon and Ushaw Moor *Dur*

USSELBY (St Margaret) *see* Woldmoor Gp *Linc*

USWORTH (Holy Trinity) (St Michael and All Angels) *Dur 9*   P *Bp*   R J WING

UTKINTON (St Paul) *see* Tarporley *Ches*

UTLEY (St Mark) *see* Keighley *Leeds*

UTTERBY (St Andrew) *see* Fotherby, N Thoresby and Grainsby w Waithe *Linc*

UTTOXETER AREA (St Mary the Virgin) (Heath Mission Church), including Bramshall, Checkley, Gratwich, Kingstone, Leigh, Marchington, Marchington Woodlands, Stramshall, and Upper Tean *Lich 14*   P *Patr Bd*   TR M J SHERWIN   TV J C CANT, J L WALKER   OLM C H BROWN, C W DALE, J S LANDER

UXBRIDGE (St Andrew) (St Margaret) (St Peter) *Lon 21*   P *Bp*   TR A G STUDDERT-KENNEDY   TV A D THOMPSON   C E J WILDING   Hon C T D ATKINS   NSM J JENKINS, T A RAPSON

UXBRIDGE ROAD (St Luke) *see* Hammersmith St Luke *Lon*

VALE AND COTSWOLD EDGE, comprising Blockley, Bourton-on-the-Hill, Chipping Campden, Church Honeybourne, Dorsington, Ebrington, Mickleton, Pebworth, Weston-sub-Edge w Aston-sub-Edge, and Willersey w Saintbury *Glouc 8*   P *Patr Bd (3 turns) and Ld Chan (1 turn)*   TR S C BISHOP   TV D L DELAP, S A WATTS   C J R J NIBLETT   NSM K S GRUMBALL

VALE OF BELVOIR Parishes, comprising Barkestone, Bottesford, Harby, Hose, Long Clawson, Muston, Plungar, Redmile, and Stathern *Leic 2*   P *Patr Bd (2 turns), Ld Chan (1 turn)*   C J H MACKAY

VALE OF PEWSEY, comprising Alton Barnes w Alton Priors, Beechingstoke, Charlton, Easton Royal, Huish and Oare, Manningford Bruce and Manningford Abbots, Milton Lilbourne, North Newnton, Pewsey, Rushall, Stanton St Bernard, Upavon, Wilcot, and Woodborough w Manningford Bohune *Sarum 19*   P *Patr Bd*   TR D F LARKEY   TV M J WINDSOR   OLM G E R OSBORNE

VALE OF RODING, comprising Chigwell, Chigwell Row, Lambourne w Abridge, and Stapleford Abbots *Chelmsf 3*   P *The Crown (1 turn), Ld Chan (1 turn), Patr Bd (2 turns)*   TR C A KOSLA   TV P A PRESTON   NSM A L KOSLA, L A SMART

VALE, comprising Challow, Denchworth, Grove, and Hanney *Ox 27*   P *Bp, D&C Windsor, and Worc Coll Ox (jt)*   V W J N DURANT   C A J GILL, C M ASHTON   NSM P D B GOODING

VALLEY END (St Saviour) *see* Chobham w Valley End *Guildf*

VALLEY PARK (St Francis) *Win 10*   P *Bp*   P-in-c S P MCCLELLAND   C J SWEETNAM

VANGE (St Chad) *Chelmsf 11*   P *MMCET*   R D A O IBIAYO

VAUXHALL (St Peter) *see* N Lambeth *S'wark*

VENN OTTERY (St Gregory) *see* Ottery St Mary, Alfington, W Hill, Tipton etc *Ex*

VENTA GROUP *see* Belton and Burgh Castle *Nor*

VENTNOR (Holy Trinity) *Portsm 7*   P *Bp*   V H E WRIGHT   C A C LAWRENCE

VENTNOR (St Alban) *see* Godshill *Portsm*

VENTNOR (St Catherine) *Portsm 7*   P *CPAS*   V H E WRIGHT   C A C LAWRENCE

VERNHAM DEAN (St Mary the Virgin) *see* Pastrow *Win*

VERWOOD (St Michael and All Angels) *Sarum 9*   P *Bp*   V D L MATTHEWS

VERYAN (St Symphorian) w Ruan Lanihorne *Truro 5*   P *D&C and DBP (jt)*   R *vacant*

VICTORIA DOCKS (Ascension) *Chelmsf 5*   P *Bp*   V D V CHESNEY

VICTORIA DOCKS (St Luke) *Chelmsf 5*   P *Ld Chan*   V A E STOTT

VICTORIA PARK (St Chrysostom) *see* Man Victoria Park *Man*

VICTORIA PARK (St Mark) *see* Old Ford St Paul and St Mark *Lon*

VIGO (Village Hall) *see* Stansted w Fairseat and Vigo *Roch*

VINEY HILL (All Saints) *see* Parkend and Viney Hill *Glouc*
VIRGINIA WATER (Christ Church) *Guildf 11* **P** *Simeon's Trustees* **V** S D N VIBERT **C** V F MURPHY **NSM** S R BEAK
VIRGINSTOW (St Bridget) *see* Boyton, N Tamerton, Werrington etc *Truro*
VOWCHURCH (St Bartholomew) *see* Madley w Tyberton, Peterchurch, Vowchurch etc *Heref*
WABERTHWAITE (St John) *see* Black Combe, Drigg, Eskdale etc *Carl*
WACTON (All Saints) *see* Long Stratton and Pilgrim TM *Nor*
WADDESDON (St Michael and All Angels) *see* Schorne *Ox*
WADDINGHAM (St Mary and St Peter) *see* Bishop Norton, Waddingham and Snitterby *Linc*
WADDINGTON (St Helen) *Blackb 7* **P** E C Parker Esq
V C D WOOD
WADDINGTON (St Michael) *Linc 12* **P** *Linc Coll Ox*
R *vacant*
WADDON (St George) *see* Croydon St Jo *S'wark*
WADEBRIDGE *see* St Breoke and Egloshayle *Truro*
WADENHOE (St Michael and All Angels) *see* Aldwincle, Clopton, Pilton, Stoke Doyle etc *Pet*
WADHURST (St Peter and St Paul), Tidebrook and Stonegate *Chich 16* **P** *Patr Bd* **V** P R RATCLIFF
WADSLEY (no dedication) *Sheff 4* **P** *Ch Patr Trust*
P-in-c D J BROWN **C** J A M BETTS
WADWORTH (St John the Baptist) *see* Wadworth w Loversall and Balby *Sheff*
WADWORTH (St John the Baptist) w Loversall and Balby *Sheff 9* **P** *Bp (2 turns), V Doncaster (1 turn), DBP (1 turn)*
V A PRICE **NSM** E G STRAFFORD
WAGGONERS, comprising Cowlam, Fimber, Fridaythorpe, Sledmere, Thixendale, and Wetwang *York 10* **P** *Abp and Sir Tatton Sykes Bt, and Ld Chan (alt)* **P-in-c** J A TONKIN
WAINCLIFFE (St David) *see* Beeston *Leeds*
WAINFLEET Group, The (All Saints) (St Mary) (St Michael), including Croft and Thorpe *Linc 10* **P** *Ld Chan, Bp and T E Pitts Esq (alt)* **R** G MORGAN
WAITHE (St Martin) *see* Fotherby, N Thoresby and Grainsby w Waithe *Linc*
WAKEFIELD (St Andrew) St Mary (St Swithun's Centre) and Belle Vue St Catherine *Leeds 16* **P** *Peache Trustees and V Sandal Magna (jt)* **V** D I GERRARD **C** K ROBERTSON
NSM D DODGSON
WAKEFIELD (St John the Baptist) *Leeds 16* **P** *Dean*
V S J BUCHANAN **C** R J HARPER **NSM** P ELLIS
WAKEFIELD (St Michael the Archangel) *see* Westgate Common *Leeds*
WAKEFIELD CATHEDRAL BENEFICE (All Saints) (St Mary's Chantry) *Leeds 16* **V** S C COWLING **C** T W CARROLL
WAKEFIELD, NORTH, comprising Alverthorpe, Outwood, Stanley, and Wrenthorpe *Leeds 16* **P** *Bp and Dean Wakefield (jt)* **V** G COGGINS **C** J J P BISH, J KERSHAW **NSM** D TEECE
WAKERING, GREAT (St Nicholas) *see* Roach Par *Chelmsf*
WAKERING, LITTLE (St Mary the Virgin) *as above*
WAKES COLNE (All Saints) *see* Gt and Lt Tey w Wakes Colne and Chappel *Chelmsf*
WALBERSWICK (St Andrew) *see* Sole Bay *St E*
WALBERTON (St Mary) w Binsted *Chich 1* **P** *Bp*
V T J C WARD
WALBROOK Epiphany (St Augustine) (St Thomas) *Derby 5*
P *Patr Bd* **TR** A J WARD **TV** S J CARTWRIGHT
C R L E REEVE **NSM** A R TILL
WALBURY BEACON Benefice, The, comprising Combe, Enborne, Hamstead Marshall, Inkpen, Kintbury, and West Woodhay *Ox 6* **P** *Bp, D&C Windsor, DBP, and H M Henderson Esq (jt)* **NSM** T R WOOD
WALCOT (St Nicholas) *see* S Lafford *Linc*
WALCOTT (All Saints) *see* Bacton, Happisburgh, Hempstead w Eccles etc *Nor*
WALCOTT (St Oswald) *see* Carr Dyke Gp *Linc*
WALDEN, LITTLE (St John) *see* Saffron Walden and Villages *Chelmsf*
WALDERSLADE (St William) *see* S Chatham H Trin *Roch*
WALDINGFIELD, GREAT (St Lawrence) *see* Acton w Gt Waldingfield *St E*
WALDINGFIELD, LITTLE (St Lawrence) *see* Boxford, Edwardstone, Groton etc *St E*
WALDITCH (St Mary) *see* Bridport *Sarum*
WALDRINGFIELD (All Saints) *see* Orwell and Deben *St E*
WALDRON (All Saints) *Chich 13* **P** *Ex Coll Ox*
P-in-c G M PITCHER
WALES (St John the Baptist) *Sheff 5* **P** *Bp* **V** G SCHOFIELD
WALESBY (St Edmund) *S'well 3* **P** *DBP* **P-in-c** Z BURTON
NSM M A GROVES
WALESBY Group, The (St Mary and All Saints), including Brookenby, Claxby, Croxby, Kirmond-le-Mire, Normanby le

Wold, North Willingham, Stainton-le-Vale, Tealby, and Thoresway *Linc 7* **P** C Drakes Esq, DBP, and Bp (jt)
V C W HEWITT **OLM** E TURNER
WALFORD (St Michael and All Angels) *see* Ross w Walford and Brampton Abbotts *Heref*
WALGRAVE (St Peter) w Hannington and Wold and Scaldwell *Pet 2* **P** *Bp (2 turns), BNC Ox (1 turn)*
R D M BENT **C** H M BENT
WALHAM GREEN (St John) (St James) *Lon 9* **P** *Bp*
V C B RANKINE
WALKDEN (St Paul) and Little Hulton *Man 7* **P** *Patr Bd*
TR D P COOPER **OLM** E HARTIGAN
WALKER (Christ Church) *Newc 3* **P** *Bp* **P-in-c** P J A MEDLEY
WALKERGATE (St Oswald) *see* Byker St Mark and Walkergate St Oswald *Newc*
WALKERINGHAM (St Mary Magdalene) *see* Beckingham, Walkeringham, Misterton, etc *S'well*
WALKERN (St Mary the Virgin) *see* Ardeley, Benington, Cottered w Throcking etc *St Alb*
WALKHAMPTON (St Mary the Virgin) *see* Yelverton, Meavy, Sheepstor, Walkhampton, Sampford Spiney and Horrabridge *Ex*
WALKINGHAM HILL, comprising Arkendale, Copgrove, Farnham, Scotton, and Staveley *Leeds 18* **P** *Bp, DBP, R Knaresborough, MMCET, and Major Sir Arthur Collins (jt)*
R C L RENSHAW
WALKINGTON (All Hallows), Bishop Burton, Rowley and Skidby *York 8* **P** *Abp and N A C Hildyard Esq (1 turn), Abp (1 turn)* **R** D H MESSER
WALKLEY (St Mary) *Sheff 4* **P** *Bp* **P-in-c** S HAMMERSLEY
C M I RHODES
WALL (St George) *see* St Oswald in Lee w Bingfield *Newc*
WALL (St John the Baptist) *see* Lich St Mich w St Mary and Wall *Lich*
WALL HEATH (Ascension) *see* Kingswinford St Mary *Worc*
WALLASEY (St Hilary) *Ches 7* **P** *Bp* **R** A W WARD
NSM R H AVERY
WALLASEY (St Nicholas) All Saints *Ches 7* **P** *Bp and DBP (jt)* **V** J J STAPLES
WALLINGFORD (St Mary le More w All Hallows) (St Leonard) *Ox 26* **P** *Bp* **TR** D RICE **TV** K V BEER
WALLINGTON (Holy Trinity) *S'wark 23* **P** *Ch Soc Trust*
V J L HILLS **C** H R FROST
WALLINGTON (Springfield Church) Extra-Parochial Place *S'wark 23* **C** D S ATKINSON **Min** J M LINDSAY-SCOTT
WALLINGTON (St Mary) *see* Kingswood *St Alb*
WALLINGTON (St Michael and All Angels) *see* S Beddington and Roundshaw *S'wark*
WALLINGTON (St Patrick) *S'wark 23* **P** *Ch Soc Trust*
V D M KING
WALLISDOWN (St Saviour) *see* Talbot Village *Sarum*
WALLOP, NETHER (St Andrew) *see* Portway and Danebury *Win*
WALLSEND (St John the Evangelist) *Newc 5* **P** *Bp*
P-in-c E C DUFF
WALLSEND (St Peter) (St Luke) *Newc 5* **P** *Bp* **R** *vacant*
WALMER (St Mary) (St Saviour) (Blessed Virgin Mary) and Cornilo *Cant 9* **P** *Abp, Ch Patr Trust, and S Toynbee Esq (jt)*
R S W COOPER **C** C M T WOOD, S J O'CONNOR
WALMERSLEY ROAD (Christ Church) (St John w St Mark) *Man 4* **P** R Bury St Mary and trustees (jt) **V** D J THOMPSON
WALMGATE (St Denys) *see* York St Denys *York*
WALMLEY (St John the Evangelist) *Birm 4* **P** *Trustees*
V A J EVANS **C** B W COOK, C L REID
WALMSLEY (Christ Church) *see* Turton Moorland *Man*
WALNEY ISLAND (St Mary the Virgin) *Carl 8* **P** V Dalton-in-Furness **V** *vacant*
WALPOLE (St Mary the Virgin) *see* Blyth Valley *St E*
WALPOLE ST PETER (St Peter and St Paul) w Walpole St Andrew *Ely 14* **P** *The Crown and DBP (alt)*
R B L BURTON
WALSALL (Annunciation of Our Lady) *see* Walsall St Gabr Fulbrook *Lich*
WALSALL (St Andrew) *Lich 24* **P** *Bp* **V** I M TEMPLETON
WALSALL (St Gabriel) Fulbrook *Lich 24* **P** *Bp*
V R M MCINTYRE **C** R F HUME
WALSALL (St Luke) *Lich 24* **P** *Bp* **V** *vacant*
WALSALL (St Martin) *Lich 24* **P** *Bp* **V** J E MAYO-LYTHALL
WALSALL (St Matthew) *Lich 24* **P** *Patr Bd* **R** J W TROOD
C J L SMITH
WALSALL (St Paul) *Lich 24* **P** R Walsall **V** *vacant*
WALSALL (St Peter) *Lich 24* **P** R Walsall **V** A G BURNAGE
C C P LANE
WALSALL THE PLECK (St John) and Bescot *Lich 24* **P** V Walsall **V** E J REYNOLDS

WALSALL WOOD (St John) *Lich 24* **P** R *Walsall*
  P-in-c D P S BABBINGTON
WALSDEN (St Peter) *see* Todmorden w Cornholme and
  Walsden *Leeds*
WALSGRAVE ON SOWE (St Mary) *Cov 1* **P** *Ld Chan*
  V M TYLER
WALSHAM LE WILLOWS (St Mary) *see* Badwell and Walsham
  St E
WALSHAM, NORTH (St Nicholas), Edingthorpe, Worstead
  and Westwick *Nor 12* **P** *Duchy of Lancaster (1 turn), Bp and*
  D&C (2 turns) **OLM** N J M PATERSON
WALSHAM, SOUTH (St Mary) *see* Broadside *Nor*
WALSHAW (Christ Church) *Man 4* **P** *Simeon's Trustees*
  V S P OPENSHAW
WALSINGHAM (St Mary and All Saints) (St Peter),
  Houghton and Barsham *Nor 14* **P** *J Gurney Esq and Capt J*
  D A Keith (jt) **V** H A M MILLMAN
WALSOKEN (All Saints) *Ely 14* **P** *DBP* **R** A R LANDALL
WALTERSTONE (St Mary) *see* Ewyas Harold w Dulas,
  Kenderchurch etc *Heref*
WALTHAM (Holy Cross) *Chelmsf 3* **P** *Patr Bd* **TR** P H SMITH
  TV V J YEADON **NSM** J M SMITH, S A J BEGLEY, T I SCOTT
WALTHAM CROSS (Christ Church) *see* Cheshunt *St Alb*
WALTHAM Group, The (All Saints) (St Matthew), including
  Ashby, Barnoldby le Beck, Brigsley, and Ravendale *Linc 4*
  P *Parkinson Settled Estates and Bp (1 turn), The Crown (1 turn),*
  Ld Chan (1 turn) **R** K BOHAN **NSM** A HUNDLEBY,
  R M FOWLER
WALTHAM ON THE WOLDS (St Mary Magdalene) *see*
  Ironstone Villages *Leic*
WALTHAM ST LAWRENCE (St Lawrence) and
  Shottesbrooke *Ox 5* **P** *Lord Braybrooke and B E E Smith Esq*
  (jt) **V** C O MASON
WALTHAM, GREAT (St Mary and St Lawrence) w Ford End
  Chelmsf 9 **P** *Trin Coll Ox* **C** C A TIBBOTT, D C PIERCE
  NSM S SYKES
WALTHAM, LITTLE (St Martin) *see* Gt and Lt Leighs and Lt
  Waltham *Chelmsf*
WALTHAM, NEW (St Matthew) *see* Waltham Gp *Linc*
WALTHAM, NORTH (St Michael) and Steventon, Ashe and
  Deane *Win 6* **P** *DBP* **P-in-c** J A TOMKINS-RUSSELL
WALTHAMSTOW (St Andrew) *Chelmsf 7* **P** *Bp*
  P-in-c S G O O OLUKANMI **NSM** H GILBERT
WALTHAMSTOW (St Barnabas and St James the Great)
  Chelmsf 7 **P** *Bp* **P-in-c** S R S TELEN
WALTHAMSTOW (St Gabriel) St Luke (St Mary)
  (St Stephen) *Chelmsf 7* **P** *Patr Bd* **TR** V C CONANT
  TV A T STEWART **C** A C MOSS, A R CHILDS,
  D P T EDMONDSON, J V MOWBRAY
WALTHAMSTOW (St John) *Chelmsf 7* **P** *TR Walthamstow*
  V K J C BUSH
WALTHAMSTOW (St Michael and All Angels) *Chelmsf 7*
  P *Bp* **V** vacant
WALTHAMSTOW (St Peter-in-the-Forest) *Chelmsf 7* **P** *Bp*
  C A W M SUMMERS **NSM** S E DIPLOCK
WALTHAMSTOW (St Saviour) *Chelmsf 7* **P** *Bp*
  V S R S TELEN
WALTON (Holy Trinity) *Ox 10* **P** *Ch Patr Trust*
  V C R TREFUSIS
WALTON (Holy Trinity) *see* Street w Walton and Compton
  Dundon *B & W*
WALTON (not known) *see* Avon-Swift *Leic*
WALTON (St John the Evangelist) *Ches 4* **P** P G Greenall Esq
  V A J RAGGETT
WALTON (St John) *Derby 3* **P** *Bp* **V** N GREEN **C** S BEECHAM
  NSM H J MOORE, R SMITH
WALTON (St Mary) *see* Lanercost, Walton, Gilsland and
  Nether Denton *Carl*
WALTON (St Mary) (St Philip) and Trimley *St E 10* **P** *Ld*
  Chan (1 turn) Ch Trust Fund Trust and Bp (1 turn)
  R P I CLARKE **NSM** W P SMITH
WALTON (St Paul) *see* Sandal St Helen *Leeds*
WALTON (St Peter) *see* Bramham *York*
WALTON (St Thomas) *see* Baswich *Lich*
WALTON BRECK (Christ Church) (Holy Trinity) *Liv 1*
  P *Simeon's Trustees* **V** D G GAVIN
WALTON CLEVEDON (St Mary) *see* E Clevedon w Clapton in
  Gordano etc *B & W*
WALTON D'EIVILLE (St James) *Cov 8* **P** *Sir Richard Hamilton*
  Bt **R** G J BARTLEM **NSM** B COLEMAN, S W HOOD
WALTON IN GORDANO (St Paul) *see* E Clevedon w Clapton
  in Gordano etc *B & W*
WALTON LE SOKEN (All Saints) *Chelmsf 22* **P** *Bp*
  P-in-c P D EDWARDS
WALTON LE WOLDS (St Mary) *see* Barrow upon Soar w
  Walton le Wolds *Leic*

WALTON Milton Keynes, comprising Milton Keynes Village
  and Wavendon *Ox 14* **P** *DBP* **R** M J TRENDALL
WALTON ON THE HILL (St John) *Liv 4* **P** *Bp, Adn, and R*
  Walton (jt) **V** F E MYATT
WALTON ON THE HILL (St Luke) *Liv 4* **P** *Bp* **V** F R CAIN
WALTON STREET (St Saviour) *see* Upper Chelsea H Trin and
  St Sav *Lon*
WALTON, EAST (St Mary) *see* Ashwicken w Leziate, Bawsey
  etc *Nor*
WALTON, HIGHER (All Saints) *Blackb 5* **P** V *Blackb*
  V H R BOYD **C** B G NAYLOR
WALTON, WEST (St Mary) *Ely 14* **P** *Ld Chan* **R** B L BURTON
WALTON-LE-DALE (St Leonard) *see* Bamber Bridge St Aid
  and Walton-le-Dale St Leon *Blackb*
WALTON-ON-THAMES (St Mary) *Guildf 8* **P** *Bp*
  V C J BLAIR, J L BLAIR **C** C J MERRICK **NSM** V RAKIN
WALTON-ON-THE-HILL (St Mary) (St Aidan) (St Nathanael)
  Liv 8 **P** *Bp* **C** F C PENNIE
WALTON-ON-THE-HILL (St Peter) *see* Headley and Box Hill
  w Walton on the Hill *Guildf*
WALTON-ON-TRENT (St Lawrence) w Croxall, Rosliston w
  Linton and Castle Gresley *Derby 7* **P** *Bp and R D Nielson*
  Esq (jt) **OLM** C A BUCKLEY
WALWORTH (St Christopher) *S'wark 10* **P** *Bp and Pemb Coll*
  Miss **P-in-c** E L EAMES **C** J A MOORE
WALWORTH (St John w the Lady Margaret) *S'wark 10* **P** *Bp*
  V J F WALKER **Hon C** G S ASKEY
WALWORTH (St Peter) *S'wark 10* **P** *Bp*
  R A D P MOUGHTIN-MUMBY **C** D E GREEN
WAMBROOK (Blessed Virgin Mary) *see* Chard St Mary w
  Combe St Nicholas, Wambrook etc *B & W*
WANBOROUGH (St Andrew) *see* Lyddington and
  Wanborough and Bishopstone etc *Bris*
WANBOROUGH (St Bartholomew) *see* Seale, Puttenham and
  Wanborough *Guildf*
WANDSWORTH (All Saints) (Holy Trinity) *S'wark 18* **P** *Ch*
  Soc Trust **V** G S PRIOR **C** J O'GRADY
WANDSWORTH (St Anne) (St Faith) *S'wark 18* **P** *Bp*
  V vacant
WANDSWORTH (St Michael and All Angels) (St Stephen)
  S'wark 18 **P** *CPAS and Ch Soc Trust (jt)* **V** S MELLUISH
  C L D DAVIES, R BOOTHROYD, T S ARMSTRONG
  NSM P M TAYLOR
WANDSWORTH (St Paul) Wimbledon Park *S'wark 18* **P** *Bp*
  V S M BOLEN **NSM** N A VON FRAUNHOFER
WANDSWORTH COMMON (St Mary Magdalene) *S'wark 17*
  P *Bp* **V** P J BOARDMAN **C** S V SHODEINDE
WANDSWORTH COMMON (St Michael) *see* Battersea
  St Mich *S'wark*
WANGFORD (St Peter) *see* Sole Bay *St E*
WANLIP (Our Lady and St Nicholas) *see* Birstall and Wanlip
  Leic
WANSFORD (St Mary the Virgin) *see* Nassington, Apethorpe,
  Thornhaugh etc *Pet*
WANSFORD (St Mary) *see* Nafferton w Wansford *York*
WANSTEAD (Holy Trinity) Hermon Hill *Chelmsf 6* **P** *Bp*
  P-in-c A J TODD **C** J E HUFF **Hon C** P J MOSSOP
WANSTEAD (St Mary) (Christ Church) *Chelmsf 6* **P** *Bp*
  P-in-c M J HAWKES **C** T A BRITT **Hon C** C V TAYLOR
  NSM O E THURSBY, R J WYBER
WANSTROW (Blessed Virgin Mary) *see* Nunney and Witham
  Friary, Marston Bigot etc *B & W*
WANTAGE (St Peter and St Paul) *Ox 27* **P** *D&C Windsor*
  V P A WELLS **C** B D S TYLER
WANTAGE DOWNS, comprising Ardington w Lockinge, East
  Hendred, and West Hendred *Ox 27* **P** *Bp, CCC Ox, and C L*
  Loyd Esq (jt) **R** O CAMAIONI
WANTISDEN (St John the Baptist) *see* Wilford Peninsula *St E*
WANTSUM Group, The, comprising Chislet, Minster,
  Monkton, and St Nicholas-at-Wade *Cant 5* **P** *Abp*
  V A R BRADDY **C** M D W DARKINS
WAPLEY (St Peter) *see* Yate *Bris*
WAPPENBURY (St John the Baptist) *see* Offchurch Gp *Cov*
WAPPENHAM (St Mary the Virgin) *see* Astwell Gp *Pet*
WARBLETON (St Mary), Bodle Street Green and
  Dallington *Chich 13* **P** *Bp and The Revd E S Haviland (jt)*
  R M A LLOYD
WARBLINGTON (St Thomas à Becket) w Emsworth
  Portsm 5 **P** *Bp and J H Norris Esq (alt)* **R** A F SHEARD
  C J E NORTHEY **NSM** J E PRICE
WARBOROUGH (St Lawrence) *Ox 20* **P** *CCC Ox*
  V S E BOOYS
WARBOYS (St Mary Magdelene) w Broughton and Bury w
  Wistow *Ely 12* **P** *Bp and Ch Soc Trust (jt)*
  R G A DAWSON-JONES **NSM** M A DEAN
WARBSTOW (St Werburgh) *see* Boscastle Gp *Truro*

WARBURTON (St Werburgh)   *see* Oughtrington and Warburton *Ches*

WARCOP (St Columba)   *see* Heart of Eden *Carl*

WARD END (Christ Church)   *see* Ward End w Bordesley Green *Birm*

WARD END Holy Trinity (St Margaret) w Bordesley Green *Birm 6*   **P** *The Crown (1 turn), Bp and Aston Patr Trust (1 turn)*   **V** R K DONEGAN-CROSS

WARDEN (St Michael and All Angels) w Newbrough *Newc 10*   **P** *Bp*   **V** J J T THOMPSON

WARDEN, OLD (St Leonard)   *see* Caldecote, Northill and Old Warden *St Alb*

WARDINGTON (St Mary Magdalene)   *see* Shires' Edge *Ox*

WARDLEWORTH (St Mary w St James)   *see* Rochdale *Man*

WARDLEY (All Saints)   *see* Swinton and Pendlebury *Man*

WARDLOW (Good Shepherd)   *see* Longstone, Curbar and Stony Middleton *Derby*

WARE (Christ Church) *St Alb 19*   **P** *CPAS*   **V** J L W HOOKWAY

WARE (St Mary the Virgin) *St Alb 19*   **P** *Trin Coll Cam*   **V** Y R PENTELOW

WAREHAM (Lady St Mary) (St Martin) *Sarum 8*   **P** *Patr Bd*   **TR** R S F EVERETT   **TV** S J COCKSEDGE   **C** H C WILLIAMS   **NSM** H R BOND

WAREHORNE (St Matthew)   *see* Saxon Shoreline *Cant*

WARESIDE (Holy Trinity)   *see* Hunsdon w Widford and Wareside *St Alb*

WARESLEY (St James)   *see* Gt Gransden and Abbotsley and Lt Gransden etc *Ely*

WARFIELD (St Michael the Archangel) (All Saints) (St Peter) *Ox 3*   **P** *DBP*   **V** C M MABUZA   **C** D G BROWN, M L PORTER-BABBAGE   **NSM** D W CHISLETT

WARGRAVE (St Mary the Virgin) w Knowl Hill *Ox 8*   **P** *Lord Remnant*   **V** J R M COOK   **C** H N BARNE, R M S EVES   **NSM** S W TURVILLE

WARHAM (All Saints)   *see* Holkham w Egmere w Warham etc *Nor*

WARK (St Michael)   *see* Humshaugh w Simonburn and Wark *Newc*

WARKLEIGH (St John)   *see* S Molton w Nymet St George, Chittlehamholt etc *Ex*

WARKTON (St Edmund King and Martyr)   *see* Barton Seagrave w Warkton *Pet*

WARKWORTH (St Lawrence), Acklington and Shilbottle *Newc 6*   **P** *Bp, Duke of Northumberland and Dioc Soc (jt)*   **V** H L O'SULLIVAN   **NSM** C A SHIELD

WARKWORTH (St Mary the Virgin)   *see* Chenderit *Pet*

WARLEGGAN (St Bartholomew)   *see* St Neot and Warleggan *Truro*

WARLEY (Christ Church) and Gt Warley St Mary *Chelmsf 8*   **P** *Bp and Hon G C D Jeffreys (jt)*   **P-in-c** S J HULL   **C** A W MCCONNAUGHIE

WARLEY (St John the Evangelist) and Halifax St Hilda *Leeds 8*   **P** *V Halifax and Bp*   **V** C E GREENWOOD

WARLEY WOODS (St Hilda) *Birm 3*   **P** *Bp*   **V** J R CREWES

WARLEY, GREAT (St Mary the Virgin)   *see* Warley Ch Ch and Gt Warley St Mary *Chelmsf*

WARLEY, LITTLE (St Peter)   *see* E and W Horndon w Lt Warley and Childerditch *Chelmsf*

WARLINGHAM (All Saints) w Chelsham and Farleigh *S'wark 25*   **P** *Patr Bd*   **TR** M K EDMONDS   **TV** L E FLETCHER   **C** R E CHAPMAN

WARMFIELD (St Peter) *Leeds 16*   **P** *Oley Trustees Clare Coll Cam*   **V** L TINNISWOOD

WARMINGHAM (St Leonard)   *see* Leighton-cum-Minshull Vernon and Warmingham *Ches*

WARMINGTON (St Mary the Blessed Virgin), Tansor and Cotterstock and Fotheringhay and Southwick *Pet 10*   **P** *Bp and D&C Linc (alt)*   **V** D C R MCFADYEN   **Hon C** C M FURLONG

WARMINGTON (St Michael)   *see* Edgehill Churches *Cov*

WARMINSTER (Christ Church) *Sarum 12*   **P** *R Warminster St Denys etc*   **V** L S DOBBINS   **C** C J SPINDLOW   **NSM** A J EDWARDS

WARMINSTER (St Denys)   *see* River Were *Sarum*

WARMLEY (St Barnabas), Syston and Bitton *Bris 5*   **P** *Bp*   **R** J C E ANDREW   **OLM** R A HUMPHREY

WARMSWORTH (St Peter) *Sheff 9*   **P** *Bp*   **R** I SMITH   **C** C B BISHOP

WARMWELL (Holy Trinity)   *see* Watercombe *Sarum*

WARNBOROUGH, SOUTH (St Andrew)   *see* N Hants Downs *Win*

WARNDON (St Nicholas) *Worc 4*   **P** *Bp*   **C** D M COOKSEY   **NSM** R E J MOSS

WARNDON (St Wulstan)   *see* Worc St Wulstan *Worc*

WARNERS END (St Alban)   *see* Hemel Hempstead *St Alb*

WARNFORD (Our Lady)   *see* W Meon and Warnford *Portsm*

WARNHAM (St Margaret) *Chich 10*   **P** *J C Lucas Esq*   **V** *vacant*

WARREN PARK (St Clare) *Portsm 5*   **P** *Bp*   **V** J G P JEFFERY

WARREN ROW (St Paul)   *see* Wargrave w Knowl Hill *Ox*

WARRINGTON (Holy Trinity) (St Ann) *Liv 11*   **P** *R Warrington and Simeon's Trustees (jt)*   **V** S COWAN   **C** J L WHEATLEY   **OLM** C E BATEY, P LOVATT

WARRINGTON (St Barnabas) Bank Quay *Liv 11*   **P** *R Warrington and Bp (jt)*   **V** K L F TIMMIS

WARRINGTON (St Elphin) (St John) *Liv 11*   **P** *Lord Lilford*   **R** J L STEVENTON   **C** D A LOVATT

WARRINGTON EAST (Christ Church) (Transfiguration) (Resurrection) (Ascension) *Liv 11*   **P** *Patr Bd*   **TR** N G SHAW   **TV** T MCLOUGHLIN   **C** H HADDOW, S J RENISON

WARRINGTON WEST, comprising Great Sankey, Penketh, and Westbrook *Liv 11*   **P** *Patr Bd*   **TR** J C TEAR   **TV** M X THORPE, S F PEPPIATT

WARSLOW (St Lawrence)   *see* Longnor, Quarnford, Sheen etc *Lich*

WARSOP (St Peter and St Paul) *S'well 2*   **P** *Trustees*   **R** A FLETCHER

WARTHILL (St Mary)   *see* Rural E York *York*

WARTLING (St Mary Magdalene)   *see* Herstmonceux and Wartling *Chich*

WARTNABY (St Michael)   *see* Old Dalby, Nether Broughton, Saxelbye etc *Leic*

WARTON (Holy Trinity)   *see* All So N Warks *Birm*

WARTON (St Oswald or Holy Trinity) w Yealand Conyers *Blackb 14*   **P** *Bp*   **V** R A R FIGG

WARTON (St Paul)   *see* Freckleton and Warton St Paul *Blackb*

WARWICK SQUARE (St Gabriel)   *see* Pimlico St Gabr *Lon*

WARWICK Team, The New (St Mary) (St Nicholas) (St Paul) *Cov 11*   **P** *Ld Chan and Patr Bd (alt)*   **TR** V S ROBERTS   **TV** D THOMPSON, J HEARN, L J DUCKERS   **C** E J HALE, J M AYTON, S L CUSHING   **NSM** A N C MORGAN

WARWICKSHIRE, SOUTH   *see* S Warks Seven Gp *Cov*

WASDALE HEAD (St Olaf)   *see* Seatallan *Carl*

WASDALE, NETHER (St Michael) *as above*

WASH COMMON (St George)   *see* Newbury St Geo and St Jo *Ox*

WASHBOURNE, GREAT (St Mary)   *see* Winchcombe *Glouc*

WASHBURN and Mid-Wharfe, comprising Blubberhouses, Denton, Farnley, Fewston, Leathley, and Weston *Leeds 18*   **P** *Bp, G N le G Horton-Fawkes Esq, Lt Col H V Dawson and C Wyvill Esq (jt)*   **R** S T J MCCAULAY

WASHFIELD (St Mary the Virgin), Stoodleigh, Withleigh, Calverleigh, Oakford, Templeton, Loxbeare, Rackenford, and Cruwys Morchard *Ex 7*   **P** *Patr Bd*   **TR** S K GORDON-JEFFS

WASHFORD (St Mary)   *see* Old Cleeve, Leighland and Treborough *B & W*

WASHFORD PYNE (St Peter)   *see* N Creedy *Ex*

WASHINGBOROUGH (St John) w Heighington and Canwick *Linc 12*   **P** *DBP and Mercers' Co (jt)*   **R** G C GOALBY

WASHINGTON (Holy Trinity) *Dur 9*   **P** *Bp*   **P-in-c** P J LOCKLEY   **NSM** B R FORRESTER

WASHINGTON (St Mary)   *see* Chanctonbury *Chich*

WASHWOOD HEATH (St Mark)   *see* Saltley and Washwood Heath *Birm*

WASING (St Nicholas)   *see* Aldermaston and Woolhampton *Ox*

WASKERLEY (St Andrew)   *see* Blanchland w Hunstanworth and Edmundbyers etc *Newc*

WASPERTON (St John the Baptist)   *see* Barford w Wasperton and Sherbourne *Cov*

WASS (St Thomas)   *see* Coxwold and Husthwaite *York*

WATCHET (St Decuman) (Holy Cross Chapel) and Williton *B & W 17*   **P** *Bp*   **V** *vacant*

WATCHFIELD (St Thomas's Chapel)   *see* Shrivenham and Ashbury *Ox*

WATER EATON (St Frideswide) *Ox 14*   **P** *Bp*   **P-in-c** C BUTT   **C** A O I A AUDU, S J HALLETT

WATER NEWTON (St Remigius)   *see* Castor w Upton and Stibbington etc *Pet*

WATER ORTON (St Peter and St Paul) *Birm 5*   **P** *Patr Bd*   **V** P B TULLETT

WATER STRATFORD (St Giles)   *see* W Buckingham *Ox*

WATERBEACH (St John) *Ely 6*   **P** *Bp*   **P-in-c** D J CHAMBERLIN   **C** P H BUTLER   **NSM** S BRADFORD

WATERCOMBE, comprising Broadmayne, Owermoigne, Warmwell, and West Knighton *Sarum 1*   **P** *M Cree Esq (1 turn), MMCET (2 turns), and Sir Robert Williams Bt (1 turn)*   **R** *vacant*

WATERDEN (All Saints)   *see* N and S Creake w Waterden, Syderstone etc *Nor*

WATERFALL (St James and St Bartholomew) *see* Calton, Cauldon, Grindon, Waterfall etc *Lich*

WATERFORD (St Michael and All Angels) *see* Beane Valley *St Alb*

WATERHEAD (Holy Trinity) *see* Clarksfield and Waterhead *Man*

WATERHOUSES (St Paul) *Dur 1* **P** *R Brancepeth Esq* **V** *vacant*

WATERINGBURY (St John the Baptist) *see* Mereworth, Wateringbury and W Peckham *Roch*

WATERLOO (Christ Church) St John *Liv 6* **P** *Trustees and Simeon's Trustees (jt)* **V** G J CUFF

WATERLOO (St John the Evangelist) (St Andrew) *S'wark 11* **P** *Abp and CPAS (jt)* **V** G W GODDARD **Hon C** R M LAMPARD **NSM** G S N KAZIRO, L M BEWICK **OLM** D PAPE

WATERLOOVILLE (St George the Martyr) *Portsm 5* **P** *Bp* **V** C R LAWLOR

WATERMILLOCK (All Saints) *see* Barton, Pooley Bridge, Martindale etc *Carl*

WATERMOOR (Holy Trinity) *see* Cirencester *Glouc*

WATERPERRY (St Mary the Virgin) *see* Albury w Tiddington etc *Ox*

WATERS UPTON (St Michael) *see* Tibberton w Bolas Magna and Waters Upton *Lich*

WATERSHED, comprising Blymhill, Lapley, and Weston-under-Lizard *Lich 2* **P** *Keble Coll Ox and Earl of Bradford Trustees (jt)* **R** R E DALE

WATERSIDE GROUP *see* Ludham, Potter Heigham, Hickling and Catfield *Nor*

WATERSTOCK (St Leonard) *see* Albury w Tiddington etc *Ox*

WATERTHORPE (Emmanuel) *see* Beighton *Sheff*

WATFORD (Christ Church) (St Mark) *St Alb 6* **P** *Bp, V Watford, and Churchwardens (jt)* **V** J D CAMPBELL

WATFORD (St Andrew) *St Alb 6* **P** *Bp and Churchwardens (jt)* **V** I C PANKHURST

WATFORD (St John) *St Alb 6* **P** *Bp* **V** D E STEVENSON

WATFORD (St Luke) *St Alb 6* **P** *Bp, Adn St Alb, V Watford, and Ch Trust Fund Trust (jt)* **V** M J NORMAN

WATFORD (St Mary) *St Alb 6* **P** *Ch Trust Fund Trust* **V** A W RINDL **C** J P BROCKLESBY

WATFORD (St Michael and All Angels) *St Alb 6* **P** *Bp* **V** G R CALVERT

WATFORD (St Peter and St Paul) *see* Long Buckby w Watford and W Haddon w Winwick *Pet*

WATFORD (St Peter) *St Alb 6* **P** *Bp* **P-in-c** V J KERSWILL **NSM** M PILAVACHI

WATH (St Mary) *see* Kirklington w Burneston and Wath and Pickhill *Leeds*

WATH-UPON-DEARNE (All Saints) *Sheff 12* **P** *Ch Ch Ox* **V** J D PARKER **C** C E BURTON

WATLING VALLEY, Milton Keynes (not known) *Ox 14* **P** *Patr Bd* **TR** M J MORRIS **TV** S C GRENHAM-THOMPSON **C** R V HARLEY **NSM** A L ADEBIYI

WATLINGTON (St Leonard) *see* Icknield *Ox*

WATLINGTON (St Peter and St Paul) *see* W Norfolk Priory Gp *Ely*

WATTISFIELD (St Margaret) *see* Badwell and Walsham *St E*

WATTON (St Mary) *Nor 13* **P** *Ld Chan* **C** M A SØRENSEN

WATTON (St Mary) *see* Hutton Cranswick w Skerne, Watton and Beswick *York*

WATTON AT STONE (St Mary and St Andrew) *see* Beane Valley *St Alb*

WAVENDON (Assumption of the Blessed Virgin Mary) *see* Walton Milton Keynes *Ox*

WAVENEY MARSHLANDS, comprising Aldeby, Burgh St Peter, Ellingham, Geldeston, Gillingham, Haddiscoe, Kirby Cane, Norton Subcourse, Raveningham, Stockton, Thorpe-next-Haddiscoe, Thurlton, Toft Monks, and Wheatacre *Nor 8* **P** *Bp, Sir Nicholas Bacon Bt, D&C, K Coll Cam, DBP, Ms C L H Mikkelsen, MMCET, and Ch Trust Fund Trust (1 turn), Ld Chan (1 turn)* **R** D R SMITH **Hon C** A M R HOUSMAN

WAVERTON (Christ Church) *see* Solway Plain *Carl*

WAVERTON (St Peter) w Aldford and Bruera *Ches 5* **P** *Bp, D&C, and Duke of Westmr (jt)* **R** J T P BEAUCHAMP **NSM** K R B JONES

WAVERTREE (Holy Trinity) *Liv 3* **P** *Bp* **R** R J E CLACK **NSM** J GRIFFITHS

WAVERTREE (St Bridget) (St Thomas) *Liv 3* **P** *Simeon's Trustees and R Wavertree H Trin (jt)* **C** E JONES, R A GARLAND **NSM** E A ROBERTS

WAVERTREE (St Mary) *Liv 3* **P** *Bp* **R** J P ASQUITH

WAWNE (St Peter) *see* Sutton Park and Wawne *York*

WAXHAM, GREAT (St John) *see* Bacton, Happisburgh, Hempstead w Eccles etc *Nor*

WAYFORD (St Michael and All Angels) *see* Wulfric Benefice *B & W*

WAYLAND Group, The *see* Caston, Griston, Merton, Thompson etc *Nor*

WEALD (St George) *see* Sevenoaks Weald *Roch*

WEALD, SOUTH (St Peter) *Chelmsf 8* **P** *Bp* **V** J BRADBURY

WEALDSTONE (Holy Trinity) *Lon 20* **P** *Bp* **V** *vacant*

WEARDALE, UPPER, comprising Eastgate, Frosterley, Heatherycleugh, St John's Chapel, Stanhope and Rookhope, and Westgate *Dur 7* **P** *Bp (5 turns), Duchy of Lancaster (1 turn), and Ld Chan (1 turn)* **P-in-c** C L MCCLELLAND **NSM** H ROSS

WEARE (St Gregory) *see* Crook Peak *B & W*

WEARE GIFFARD (Holy Trinity) *see* Bideford, Landcross, Littleham etc *Ex*

WEARSIDE, NORTH, comprising Red House, Southwick, and Town End Farm *Dur 14* **P** *Patr Bd* **TV** C M NOPPEN, J A BRADSHAW

WEASENHAM (All Saints) *see* Launditch and the Upper Nar *Nor*

WEASENHAM (St Peter) *as above*

WEASTE (St Luke w All Saints) *see* Salford All SS *Man*

WEAVERHAM (St Mary the Virgin) *Ches 6* **P** *Bp* **V** P M WITHINGTON **C** P W BISHOP

WEAVERTHORPE (St Andrew) w Helperthorpe, Luttons Ambo and Kirby Grindalythe w Wharram *York 6* **P** *Abp and D&C (jt)* **V** A D BOWDEN

WEBHEATH (St Philip) *see* Redditch H Trin *Worc*

WEDDINGTON (St James) and Caldecote *Cov 5* **P** *Bp* **C** A M GUTHRIE

WEDMORE, The Isle of (St Mary), including Allerton, Blackford and Theale *B & W 1* **P** *Bp and D&C (jt)* **V** R W NEILL **C** S R HEALEY

WEDNESBURY (St Bartholomew) (St James) St John *Lich 25* **P** *Bp and Trustees (jt)* **R** M J DANKS

WEDNESBURY (St Paul) Wood Green *Lich 25* **P** *Bp* **V** D C NJUGUNA

WEDNESFIELD (St Gregory) *see* Oxley and Wednesfield St Greg *Lich*

WEDNESFIELD (St Thomas) (St Augustine and St Chad) (St Alban) *Lich 28* **P** *Patr Bd* **TV** T R H FISH

WEEDON (School Chapel) *see* Schorne *Ox*

WEEDON BEC (St Peter and St Paul) w Everdon and Dodford *Pet 3* **P** *Bp* **P-in-c** B J GALLAGHER

WEEDON LOIS (St Mary and St Peter) *see* Astwell Gp *Pet*

WEEFORD (St Mary the Virgin) *see* Whittington w Weeford *Lich*

WEEK (St Barnabas) *see* Win St Barn *Win*

WEEK ST MARY (St Mary the Virgin) *see* Bude Coast and Country *Truro*

WEEKLEY (St Mary the Virgin) *see* Geddington w Weekley *Pet*

WEELEY (St Andrew) and Little Clacton *Chelmsf 22* **P** *Bp and BNC Ox (alt)* **R** *vacant*

WEETHLEY (St James) *see* Alcester Minster *Cov*

WEETING (St Mary) *see* Grimshoe *Ely*

WEETON (St Barnabas) *see* Lower Wharfedale *Leeds*

WEETON (St Michael) *see* Ribby cum Wrea and Weeton *Blackb*

WEETSLADE (St Paul) *Newc 1* **P** *Bp* **V** A MAUGHAN **NSM** S RENDALL

WEIGHTON WOLD, comprising Londesborough, Market Weighton, and Shiptonthorpe *York 5* **P** *Abp (1 turn), Abp and Mrs P R Rowlands (1 turn)* **R** C R PINCHBECK **C** J A KENNY

WELBORNE (All Saints) *see* Mattishall and the Tudd Valley *Nor*

WELBOURN (St Chad) *Linc 22* **P** *Simeon's Trustees* **R** C A GOLDSMITH

WELBURN (St John the Evangelist) *see* Howardian Gp *York*

WELBURY (St Leonard) *see* Rounton w Welbury *York*

WELBY (St Bartholemew) *see* E Loveden *Linc*

WELBY (St Bartholomew) *see* Melton Mowbray *Leic*

WELCOMBE (St Nectan) *see* Parkham, Alwington, Buckland Brewer etc *Ex*

WELDON (St Mary the Virgin) w Deene *Pet 7* **P** *DBP and E Brudenell Esq (jt)* **R** K M TAYLOR **NSM** F M ILIFFE

WELFORD (St Gregory) *see* W Downland *Ox*

WELFORD (St Peter) *see* Quinton, Welford, Weston and Marston Sicca *Glouc*

WELHAM (St Andrew), Glooston and Cranoe and Stonton Wyville *Leic 5* **P** *Bp, E Brudenell Esq, and MMCET (jt)* **R** *vacant*

WELL (St Margaret) *see* Alford Gp *Linc*

WELL (St Michael) *see* W Tanfield and Well w Snape and N Stainley *Leeds*

WELL HILL (Mission)　see Chelsfield w Green Street Green and Pratts Bottom *Roch*

WELLAND (St James)　see Hanley Castle, Hanley Swan and Welland *Worc*

WELLESBOURNE (St Peter) *Cov 8*　**P** *Ld Chan*
V G J BARTLEM　**NSM** B COLEMAN, S W HOOD, W E BIDDINGTON

WELLING (St John the Evangelist) *Roch 15*　**P** *Bp*
V A J D FOOT　**C** G R MACBEAN

WELLING (St Mary the Virgin) *S'wark 6*　**P** *Bp*
P-in-c N D R NICHOLLS

WELLINGBOROUGH (All Hallows) *Pet 6*　**P** *Exors Major E C S Byng-Maddick* **V** P YORK　**Hon C** C A OSTLER, M A H JOHNSON

WELLINGBOROUGH (All Saints) *Pet 6*　**P** *V Wellingborough*
V P YORK　**Hon C** C A OSTLER, M A H JOHNSON

WELLINGBOROUGH (St Andrew) (St Barnabas) *Pet 6*　**P** *Bp*
V M S COTTON　**Hon C** M A H JOHNSON　**NSM** R RAILTON

WELLINGBOROUGH (St Mark) *Pet 6*　**P** *Bp*　**V** B W D LEWIS

WELLINGBOROUGH (St Mary the Virgin) *Pet 6*　**P** *Guild of All So*　**V** R J T FARMER

WELLINGHAM (St Andrew)　see Launditch and the Upper Nar *Nor*

WELLINGORE (All Saints)　see Graffoe Gp *Linc*

WELLINGTON (All Saints) (St John the Baptist) and District *B & W 16*　**P** *Patr Bd*　**P-in-c** M L KIRKBRIDE
TV A G ELLACOTT　**C** R P KELLEY　**Hon C** S M BEAUMONT

WELLINGTON (All Saints) w Eyton (St Catherine) *Lich 20*
P *Ch Trust Fund Trust*　**V** T S CARTER　**C** D J SIMS

WELLINGTON (Christ Church)　see Hadley and Wellington Ch Ch *Lich*

WELLINGTON (St Margaret of Antioch)　see Canon Pyon w King's Pyon, Birley and Wellington *Heref*

WELLINGTON HEATH (Christ Church)　see Cider Churches *Heref*

WELLOW (St Julian the Hospitaller)　see Peasedown St John w Wellow and Foxcote etc *B & W*

WELLOW (St Swithin)　see Kneesall w Laxton and Wellow *S'well*

WELLOW, EAST w WEST (St Margaret) and Sherfield English *Win 12*　**P** *Bp and CPAS (jt)*　**V** *vacant*

WELLS (St Cuthbert) w Wookey Hole *B & W 7*　**P** *D&C*
V S DENYER　**C** L C T JORDAN

WELLS (St Thomas) w Horrington *B & W 7*　**P** *D&C*
P-in-c C L TOWNS　**NSM** N T FRIDD

WELLS-NEXT-THE-SEA (St Nicholas)　see Holkham w Egmere w Warham etc *Nor*

WELLSPRINGS Benefice, The, comprising Bulkington, Potterne, Poulshot, Seend, and Worton and Marston *Sarum 17*　**P** *Bp and D&C (jt)*　**R** A C BRIDEWELL
C A P BURHOLT

WELNEY (St Mary)　see Six Fen Churches *Ely*

WELSH FRANKTON (St Andrew)　see Criftins w Dudleston and Welsh Frankton *Lich*

WELSH NEWTON (St Mary the Virgin)　see Wye Brooks Benefice *Heref*

WELSHAMPTON (St Michael)　see Petton w Cockshutt, Welshampton and Lyneal etc *Lich*

WELTON (St Helen) w Melton *York 14*　**P** *DBP*　**V** E E BIELBY

WELTON (St James)　see Westward, Rosley-w-Woodside and Welton *Carl*

WELTON (St Martin)　see Daventry *Pet*

WELTON (St Mary) and Dunholme w Scothern *Linc 5*　**P** *Bp and DBP (jt)*　**V** A S WATSON　**C** J E FOSTER-SMITH
NSM P D MAPLE, P J IEVINS　**OLM** C A JONES

WELTON-LE-MARSH (St Martin)　see Burgh Gp *Linc*

WELTON-LE-WOLD (St Martin)　see Louth *Linc*

WELWICK (St Mary)　see Easington w Skeffling, Keyingham, Ottringham etc *York*

WELWYN GARDEN CITY (St Francis of Assisi) *St Alb 18*
P *Bp*　**V** J E FENNELL　**C** R C WAKEFIELD
NSM E M N LAVELLE

WELWYN Team Ministry (St Mary the Virgin) (St Michael), including Ayot St Peter, Codicote, Datchworth, and Tewin *St Alb 18*　**P** *Patr Bd*　**TR** D L MUNCHIN　**TV** P T WALLER, S L UNDERWOOD　**NSM** S V BECK

WEM (St Peter and St Paul), Lee Brockhurst and Weston under Redcastle *Lich 21*　**P** *Lord Barnard and Sir Algernon Heber-Percy KCVO (jt)*　**R** N P HERON

WEMBDON (St George) *B & W 13*　**P** *Ch Soc Trust*
V C D E MOLL　**NSM** S P TAYLOR

WEMBLEY (Annunciation)　see S Kenton *Lon*

WEMBLEY (Church of the Ascension)　see Preston *Lon*

WEMBLEY (St Augustine)　see Wembley Park *Lon*

WEMBLEY (St John the Evangelist) *Lon 18*　**P** *Ch Patr Trust*
P-in-c C N NJOKU

WEMBLEY PARK (St Augustine) *Lon 18*　**P** *Bp*
V H M ASKWITH

WEMBLEY, NORTH (St Cuthbert) *Lon 18*　**P** *Bp*
C T P GODDARD

WEMBURY (St Werburgh)　see Brixton, Newton Ferrers, Revelstoke etc *Ex*

WEMBWORTHY (St Michael)　see Burrington, Chawleigh, Cheldon, Chulmleigh etc *Ex*

WENDENS AMBO (St Mary the Virgin)　see Saffron Walden and Villages *Chelmsf*

WENDLEBURY (St Giles)　see Akeman *Ox*

WENDLING (St Peter and St Paul)　see Launditch and the Upper Nar *Nor*

WENDOVER (St Mary) (St Agnes's Chapel) and Halton *Ox 17*　**P** *Ld Chan*　**R** S M MORING　**C** N J ROSE
NSM S E PRENDERGAST

WENDRON (St Wendron)　see Helston and Wendron *Truro*

WENDY (All Saints)　see Shingay Gp *Ely*

WENHAM, GREAT (St John)　see Capel St Mary w Lt and Gt Wenham *St E*

WENHASTON (St Peter)　see Blyth Valley *St E*

WENLOCK, comprising Berrington w Betton Strange, Church Preen, Cound, Cressage, Easthope, Harley, Hughley, Kenley, Much Wenlock w Bourton, Sheinton, Shipton, and Stanton Long *Heref 10*　**P** *Patr Bd*　**TR** M C STAFFORD
C A M WALKER

WENLOCK, LITTLE (St Lawrence)　see Coalbrookdale, Iron-Bridge and Lt Wenlock *Heref*

WENLOCK, MUCH (Holy Trinity)　see Wenlock *Heref*

WENNINGTON (St Mary and St Peter)　see Rainham w Wennington *Chelmsf*

WENSLEYDALE, LOWER, comprising Crakehall, Finghall, Hauxwell, Hornby, Patrick Brompton w Hunton, and Spennithorne *Leeds 22*　**P** *Bp (1 turn), D&C York (1 turn), Sir Henry Beresford-Peirse Bt (1 turn), R J Dalton Esq and M C A Wyvill Esq (1 turn)*　**R** R D C LAWTON

WENSLEYDALE, UPPER, comprising Askrigg, Hardraw, Hawes, and Stalling Busk *Leeds 22*　**P** *Bp, R Penhill, G L Metcalfe, and E A Cherniavsky (jt)*　**V** D J CLARK

WENSUM Village Group, UPPER, comprising Brisley, Colkirk w Oxwick w Pattesley, Gateley, Great Ryburgh, Horningtoft, Shereford w Dunton, and Whissonsett *Nor 14*　**P** *Marquess Townshend, the Revd C S P Douglas Lane, Ch Coll Cam, and DBP (jt)*　**R** R D STAPLEFORD

WENT VALLEY, comprising Darrington, Kirk Smeaton, and Wentbridge *Leeds 15*　**P** *Bp, Earl of Rosse, and Sir Philip Naylor-Leyland Bt (jt)*　**V** A T JUDD

WENTBRIDGE (St John)　see Went Valley *Leeds*

WENTNOR (St Michael and All Angels) w Ratlinghope, Myndtown, Norbury, More, Lydham and Snead *Heref 9*
P *Ch Ch Ox (4 turns) and J J C Coldwell Esq (1 turn)*
P-in-c V G HATTON

WENTWORTH (Harley Mission Church) (Holy Trinity) *Sheff 12*　**P** *Sir Philip Naylor-Leyland Bt*　**V** *vacant*

WENTWORTH (St Peter)　see Witchford w Wentworth *Ely*

WEOBLEY (St Peter and St Paul) w Sarnesfield and Norton Canon *Heref 4*　**P** *Bp (2 turns), R A Marshall Esq (1 turn)*
V P I HARVEY

WEOLEY CASTLE (St Gabriel) *Birm 3*　**P** *Bp*
V F J HARRISON-SMITH

WEREHAM (St Margaret)　see Wissey Valley *Ely*

WERNETH (St Paul) *Ches 16*　**P** *DBP*　**V** L BOYLE
NSM W S ATKINSON

WERRINGTON (St John the Baptist w Emmanuel) *Pet 11*
P *Bp*　**C** S J FEAR　**NSM** K C FEAR

WERRINGTON (St Martin of Tours)　see Boyton, N Tamerton, Werrington etc *Truro*

WERRINGTON (St Philip) and Wetley Rocks *Lich 6*　**P** *Bp and V Caverswall and Weston Coyney w Dilhorne (jt)*
V M S FOLLIN　**OLM** I T COPELAND, S J PARKER

WESHAM (Christ Church) *Blackb 10*　**P** *V Kirkham*
V A R BEVERLEY

WESSINGTON (Christ Church)　see Ashover and Brackenfield w Wessington *Derby*

WEST　see also under substantive place name

WEST ACRE (All Saints)　see Nar Valley *Nor*

WEST BAY (St John)　see Bridport *Sarum*

WEST COAST, comprising Dalby, German, Kirk Patrick, and Michael *S & M*　**V** N P GODFREY　**C** R K WALKER
NSM J E HAMER

WEST DEAN (All Saints)　see Alfriston w Lullington, Litlington, W Dean and Folkington *Chich*

WEST DEAN (St Andrew)　see E Dean, Singleton, and W Dean *Chich*

WEST DEAN (St Mary)　see Clarendon *Sarum*

WEST DOWN (St Calixtus) *see* Heanton Punchardon, Marwood and W Down *Ex*

WEST DOWNLAND, comprising Brightwalton w Catmore, Chaddleworth, Fawley, Great Shefford, Leckhampstead, and Welford w Wickham *Ox 6* **P** *Bp, Sir Philip Wroughton, and D&C Westmr (jt)* **R** M F KEEN

WEST END *see* Northolt St Jos *Lon*

WEST END (Holy Trinity) *see* Bisley and W End *Guildf*

WEST END (St George) *see* Esher *Guildf*

WEST END (St James) *Win 10* **P** *Bp* **V** V A MAUNDER **NSM** L S GALVIN

WEST GREEN (Christ Church w St Peter) *Lon 17* **P** *Bp* **NSM** G D BOND

WEST GREEN (St Peter) *Chich 9* **P** *Bp* **C** J M BALDWIN

WEST HAM (All Saints) *Chelmsf 5* **P** *The Crown* **C** A S GORDON, S R NICHOLLS **NSM** D P WADE

WEST HAM (St Matthew) *Chelmsf 5* **P** *CPAS* **V** C C ASINUGO **NSM** S M ELDRIDGE

WEST HEATH (St Anne) *Birm 2* **P** *Bp* **P-in-c** P H-S CHO

WEST HILL (St Michael the Archangel) *see* Ottery St Mary, Alfington, W Hill, Tipton etc *Ex*

WEST MOORS (St Mary the Virgin) *Sarum 9* **P** *Bp* **V** A P MUCKLE **NSM** L MORRIS

WEST NORFOLK Priory Group, The, comprising Fincham, Marham, Nordelph, Shouldham, Shouldham Thorpe, South Runcton, Stow Bardolph and Stow Bridge, Tottenhill, Watlington, Wimbotsham, and Wormegay *Ely 9* **P** *Bp, St Jo Coll Cam, and R T Townley Esq (jt)* **R** D KAROON **C** N P MOAT

WEST OF SEVERN *see* Ashleworth, Corse, Hartpury, Hasfield etc *Glouc*

WEST ORCHARD (St Luke) *see* Shaftesbury *Sarum*

WEST ROW (St Peter) *see* Forest Heath *St E*

WEST WIGHT, comprising Brighstone, Brook, Calbourne, Freshwater, Mottistone, Newtown, Shalfleet, Shorwell w Kingston, Thorley, Totland Bay, and Yarmouth *Portsm 7* **P** *Patr Bd* **TR** J MAW **TV** L C POTTER

WESTBERE (All Saints) *see* Sturry w Fordwich and Westbere w Hersden *Cant*

WESTBOROUGH (All Saints) *see* Claypole *Linc*

WESTBOROUGH (St Clare) (St Francis) *Guildf 5* **P** *Bp* **TR** S M HODGES **TV** S POWNALL

WESTBOURNE (Christ Church) Chapel *Win 8* **Min** N R T HISCOCKS

WESTBOURNE (St John the Baptist) *Chich 6* **P** *Bp* **R** A P C DOYE

WESTBROOK (All Saints) *see* Margate All SS *Cant*

WESTBROOK (St James) *see* Warrington W *Liv*

WESTBROOK (St Philip) *as above*

WESTBURY (All Saints) *see* White Horse *Sarum*

WESTBURY (St Augustine) *see* W Buckingham *Ox*

WESTBURY (St Mary), Worthen and Yockleton *Heref 12* **P** *Bp (2 turns), New Coll Ox (1 turn)* **R** D MOSS **OLM** R M LEIGH

WESTBURY PARK (St Alban) *see* Westbury-on-Trym St Alb *Bris*

WESTBURY SUB MENDIP (St Lawrence) w Easton *B & W 1* **P** *Bp* **V** A J HOLMES

WESTBURY-ON-SEVERN (St Peter and St Paul) w Flaxley, Blaisdon and Minsterworth *Glouc 3* **P** *Bp, D&C Heref, and Sir Thomas Crawley-Boevey Bt (jt)* **V** *vacant*

WESTBURY-ON-TRYM (Holy Trinity) *Bris 2* **P** *SMF* **V** A H HART **C** C HAWKINS

WESTBURY-ON-TRYM (St Alban) *Bris 2* **P** *Bp* **V** E L LANGLEY **Hon C** M H JAMES **OLM** J M DOYLE

WESTCLIFF (Church of Reconciliation) *see* Brumby *Linc*

WESTCLIFF (St Alban) and Southend St Mark *Chelmsf 14* **P** *Bp* **V** N M DALLEY **C** C M ABRAHAM **NSM** C E SANDOVER, P E OWEN

WESTCLIFF (St Andrew) *Chelmsf 14* **P** *Bp* **P-in-c** P A GAMBLING **OLM** C LUCAS

WESTCLIFF (St Cedd and the Saints of Essex) *see* Prittlewell St Pet w Westcliff St Cedd *Chelmsf*

WESTCLIFF (St Michael and All Angels) *Chelmsf 14* **P** *Bp* **P-in-c** T LOH **C** N J PUCENOT **OLM** C LUCAS

WESTCLIFF (St Peter) *see* Prittlewell St Pet w Westcliff St Cedd *Chelmsf*

WESTCLIFF (St Saviour) *see* Southend St Sav Westcliff *Chelmsf*

WESTCLIFFE (St Peter) *see* St Margarets-at-Cliffe w Westcliffe etc *Cant*

WESTCOMBE PARK (St George) *see* E Greenwich *S'wark*

WESTCOTE (St Mary the Virgin) *see* Broadwell, Evenlode, Oddington, Adlestrop etc *Glouc*

WESTCOTE BARTON (St Edward the Confessor) w Steeple Barton, Duns Tew and Sandford St Martin and Over w

Nether Worton *Ox 29* **P** *Bp, DBP, Duke of Marlborough, Exors Mrs S C Rittson-Thomas, P J Schuster, and D C C Webb Esq (jt)* **R** J WRIGHT

WESTCOTT (Holy Trinity) *Guildf 7* **P** *Bp* **V** *vacant*

WESTCOTT (St Mary) *see* Schorne *Ox*

WESTDENE (The Ascension) *see* Patcham *Chich*

WESTERDALE (Christ Church) *see* The Moorlands *York*

WESTERFIELD (St Mary Magdalene) and Tuddenham w Witnesham *St E 1* **P** *Bp, Peterho Cam, and DBP (alt)* **P-in-c** C A COOK

WESTERHAM (St Mary the Virgin) *Roch 9* **P** *J St A Warde Esq* **P-in-c** D F FOX-BRANCH

WESTERLEIGH (St James the Great) *see* Yate *Bris*

WESTERN DALES, comprising Cautley, Cowgill, Dent, Firbank, Garsdale, Howgill, Killington, and Sedbergh *Carl 10* **P** *Patr Bd* **C** R GILBERT

WESTERN DOWNLAND, comprising Damerham, Martin, Rockbourne, and Whitsbury *Sarum 11* **P** *Hyndman Trustees, A N Hanbury Esq, and W J Purvis Esq (jt)* **R** L M PLAYER

WESTFIELD (St Andrew) *see* Barnham Broom and Upper Yare *Nor*

WESTFIELD (St John the Baptist) and Guestling *Chich 17* **P** *Bp and DBP (jt)* **P-in-c** J C COLLINS

WESTFIELD (St Mark) *see* Woking St Pet *Guildf*

WESTFIELD (St Mary) *Carl 7* **P** *Bp* **V** S G AXTELL

WESTFIELD (St Peter) *B & W 11* **P** *Bp* **P-in-c** I D ROUSELL

WESTGATE (St Andrew) *see* Upper Weardale *Dur*

WESTGATE (St James) *Cant 5* **P** *Abp* **V** *vacant*

WESTGATE (St Martin of Tours) *see* Torrisholme *Blackb*

WESTGATE COMMON (St Michael the Archangel) *Leeds 16* **P** *V Alverthorpe* **P-in-c** V IWANUSCHAK

WESTGATE-ON-SEA (St Saviour) *Cant 5* **P** *Abp* **P-in-c** K A GOODING

WESTHALL (St Andrew) *see* Hundred River and Wainford *St E*

WESTHAM (St Mary the Virgin) *Chich 14* **P** *Duke of Devonshire* **P-in-c** D J GILLARD

WESTHAMPNETT (St Peter) *see* Chich St Paul and Westhampnett *Chich*

WESTHEAD (St James) *see* Newburgh w Westhead *Liv*

WESTHIDE (St Bartholomew) *see* Bartestree Cross *Heref*

WESTHOPE (Mission Room) *see* Canon Pyon w King's Pyon, Birley and Wellington *Heref*

WESTHORPE (St Margaret) *see* Badwell and Walsham *St E*

WESTHOUGHTON (St Bartholomew) *see* Blackrod, Daisy Hill, Westhoughton and Wingates *Man*

WESTLANDS (St Andrew) *Lich 9* **P** *Simeon's Trustees* **V** J A DAWSWELL

WESTLEIGH (St Peter) *see* Fremington, Instow and Westleigh *Ex*

WESTLEIGH (St Peter) (St Paul) *Man 7* **P** *Bp, V Leigh St Mary, and Dioc Chan (jt)* **NSM** J AITKEN, K E SLAYEN

WESTLETON (St Peter) *see* Yoxmere *St E*

WESTLEY (St Mary) *see* Horringer *St E*

WESTLEY WATERLESS (St Mary the less) *see* Raddesley Gp *Ely*

WESTMESTON (St Martin) *see* Ditchling, Streat and Westmeston *Chich*

WESTMILL (St Mary the Virgin) *see* Aspenden, Buntingford and Westmill *St Alb*

WESTMINSTER (St James the Less) *Lon 3* **P** *D&C Westmr* **V** E A GODDARD **C** M O IFODE-BLEASE **Hon C** A J GODDARD **NSM** F M LAU

WESTMINSTER (St James) Piccadilly *Lon 3* **P** *Bp (2 turns), Ld Chan (1 turn)* **R** L C WINKETT **C** J L RUSSELL **NSM** D R NORRIS, I P KHOVACS

WESTMINSTER (St Mary le Strand) *see* St Mary le Strand w St Clem Danes *Lon*

WESTMINSTER (St Matthew) *Lon 3* **P** *D&C Westmr* **V** P A E CHESTER **NSM** J W P AITKEN, P L HANAWAY, S E LENTON

WESTMINSTER (St Michael) *see* Ches Square St Mich w St Phil *Lon*

WESTMINSTER (St Saviour) *see* Pimlico St Sav *Lon*

WESTMINSTER (St Stephen) w St John *Lon 3* **P** *The Crown* **V** G M BUCKLE **C** H J BICKLEY-PERCIVAL **NSM** J J CAVANAGH

WESTMINSTER Hanover Square (St George) *see* Hanover Square St Geo *Lon*

WESTMORLAND, HIGH, comprising Bampton, Orton w Tebay, Ravenstonedale, and Shap w Swindale *Carl 1* **P** *Bp, Adn Carl, Mrs A Browning, M Metcalfe-Gibson Esq, the Hon J N Lowther, and Resident Landowners (jt)* **NSM** F A PARKINSON

WESTMORLAND, NORTH comprising Askham and Lowther, Bolton, Cliburn, Clifton and Brougham, Crosby Ravensworth, Great Strickland, Morland, and

Thrimby *Carl 1* **P** D&C, Lord Hothfield, DBP, and the Hon J N Lowther *(jt)* **R** S J FYFE **NSM** S P CLARK, S R PEARL

WESTOE, SOUTH (St Michael and All Angels) *Dur 13* **P** *Bp* **P-in-c** A M MAWHINNEY

WESTON (All Saints) *Ches 15* **P** *Bp* **V** R J GRIFFITHS

WESTON (All Saints) *Guildf 8* **P** *Bp* **V** S G L WOOD

WESTON (All Saints) *see* Bath Weston All SS w N Stoke and Langridge *B & W*

WESTON (All Saints) *see* Quinton, Welford, Weston and Marston Sicca *Glouc*

WESTON (All Saints) *see* Tuxford w Weston, Markham Clinton etc *S'well*

WESTON (All Saints) *see* Washburn and Mid-Wharfe *Leeds*

WESTON (Emmanuel) *see* Bath Weston St Jo w Kelston *B & W*

WESTON (Holy Trinity) *Win 13* **P** *Bp* **P-in-c** D MEDWAY

WESTON (Holy Trinity) *see* Kingswood *St Alb*

WESTON (St John the Evangelist) *see* Bath Weston St Jo w Kelston *B & W*

WESTON (St John the Evangelist) *see* Runcorn St Jo Weston *Ches*

WESTON (St Mary) *see* Cowbit *Linc*

WESTON (St Peter) *see* Hundred River and Wainford *St E*

WESTON BAMPFYLDE (Holy Cross) *see* Cam Vale *B & W*

WESTON BEGGARD (St John the Baptist) *see* Bartestree Cross *Heref*

WESTON BY WELLAND (St Mary) *see* Stoke Albany w Wilbarston and Ashley etc *Pet*

WESTON COLVILLE (St Mary) *see* Granta Vale Gp *Ely*

WESTON COYNEY (St Andrew) *see* Caverswall and Weston Coyney w Dilhorne *Lich*

WESTON FAVELL (St Peter) *Pet 4* **P** *DBP* **R** B J HOLLINS **C** M SMITH **Hon C** M C W WEBBER

WESTON GREEN (All Saints) *see* Weston *Guildf*

WESTON HILLS (St John the Evangelist) *see* Cowbit *Linc*

WESTON IN GORDANO (St Peter and St Paul) *see* E Clevedon w Clapton in Gordano etc *B & W*

WESTON LONGVILLE (All Saints) *see* Reepham and Wensum Valley *Nor*

WESTON LULLINGFIELD (Holy Trinity) *see* Baschurch and Weston Lullingfield w Hordley *Lich*

WESTON MILL (St Philip) *see* Devonport St Boniface and St Philip *Ex*

WESTON ON TRENT (St Mary the Virgin) *see* Aston on Trent, Elvaston, Weston on Trent etc *Derby*

WESTON PATRICK (St Lawrence) *see* N Hants Downs *Win*

WESTON RHYN (St John) *see* St Martins and Weston Rhyn *Lich*

WESTON SUPER MARE (All Saints) and St Saviour *B & W 10* **P** *Bp* **P-in-c** A K W HUGHES

WESTON SUPER MARE (Christ Church) (Emmanuel) *B & W 10* **P** *Trustees* **V** T G E WEBBER **C** L M T TRUST **NSM** J A BIRKETT

WESTON SUPER MARE (St John the Baptist) *B & W 10* **P** *Bp and Trustees (jt)* **R** P M ASHMAN

WESTON TURVILLE (St Mary the Virgin) *Ox 17* **P** All So Coll *Ox* **R** D N WALES **NSM** S E FELLOWS

WESTON UNDER REDCASTLE (St Luke) *see* Wem, Lee Brockhurst etc *Lich*

WESTON UNDER WETHERLEY (St Michael) *see* Offchurch Gp *Cov*

WESTON UNDERWOOD (St Laurence) *see* Gayhurst w Ravenstone, Stoke Goldington etc *Ox*

WESTON UPON TRENT (St Andrew) *see* Mid Trent *Lich*

WESTON ZOYLAND (Blessed Virgin Mary) w Chedzoy *B & W 13* **P** *Bp* **V** C D KEYS

WESTON, OLD (St Swithun) *see* W Leightonstone *Ely*

WESTON, SOUTH (St Mary) *see* Thame *Ox*

WESTONING (St Mary Magdalene) *see* Harlington, Tingrith and Westoning *St Alb*

WESTON-ON-THE-GREEN (St Mary) *see* Akeman *Ox*

WESTON-SUB-EDGE (St Lawrence) *see* Vale and Cotswold Edge *Glouc*

WESTON-SUPER-MARE (St Nicholas) (St Barnabas) *B & W 10* **P** *Patr Bd* **R** M K MADELEY

WESTON-SUPER-MARE (St Paul) *B & W 10* **P** *Bp* **C** C P SINCLAIR

WESTON-SUPER-MARE (St Peter) *see* Milton and Kewstoke *B & W*

WESTON-UNDER-LIZARD (St Andrew) *see* Watershed *Lich*

WESTON-UNDER-PENYARD (St Lawrence) *see* Ariconium *Heref*

WESTOW (St Mary) *see* W Buckrose *York*

WESTWARD (St Hilda), Rosley-with-Woodside and Welton *Carl 3* **P** *D&C* **P-in-c** E REID **NSM** R T CORRIE

WESTWARD HO! (Holy Trinity) *see* Appledore, Northam and Westward Ho! *Ex*

WESTWAY (St Katherine) *see* N Hammersmith St Kath *Lon*

WESTWELL (St Mary) *see* Calehill w Westwell *Cant*

WESTWELL (St Mary) *see* Shill Valley and Broadshire *Ox*

WESTWICK (St Botolph) *see* N Walsham, Edingthorpe, Worstead and Westwick *Nor*

WESTWOOD (St John the Baptist) *see* The Bridge, Cov *Cov*

WESTWOOD (St Mary the Virgin) *see* Bradford on Avon H Trin, Westwood and Wingfield *Sarum*

WESTWOOD (St Mary) Jacksdale *see* Selston *S'well*

WESTWOOD, LOW (Christ Church) *see* Ebchester *Dur*

WETHERAL (Holy Trinity and St Constantine) *see* Holme Eden and Wetheral w Warwick *Carl*

WETHERBY (St James) *Leeds 18* **P** *Bp* **P-in-c** B A GIBLIN

WETHERDEN (St Mary the Virgin) *see* Haughley w Wetherden and Stowupland *St E*

WETHERINGSETT (All Saints) *see* S Hartismere *St E*

WETHERSFIELD (St Mary Magdalene) *see* Finchingfield and Cornish Hall End etc *Chelmsf*

WETLEY ROCKS (St John the Baptist) *see* Werrington and Wetley Rocks *Lich*

WETTENHALL (St David) *see* Acton and Worleston, Church Minshull etc *Ches*

WETTON (St Margaret) *see* Alstonfield, Ilam and Wetton *Lich*

WETWANG (St Nicholas) *see* Waggoners *York*

WEXHAM (St Mary) *Ox 12* **P** *Ld Chan* **R** A M PARRY

WEYBOURNE (All Saints), Upper Sheringham, Kelling, Salthouse, Bodham and East and West Beckham (The Weybourne Group) *Nor 17* **P** *Bp (2 turns), Sir Thomas Mott-Radclyffe (1 turn), D&C (1 turn), and Lord Walpole (1 turn)* **P-in-c** I H DYBLE

WEYBREAD (St Andrew) *see* Sancroft *St E*

WEYBRIDGE (St James) *Guildf 8* **P** *Ld Chan* **R** B D PROTHERO **C** L S BISHOP

WEYHILL (St Michael and All Angels) *see* Pastrow *Win*

WEYMOUTH (Holy Trinity) (St Nicholas) *Sarum 4* **P** *Bp* **V** A S GOUGH

WEYMOUTH (St Edmund) *see* Wyke Regis *Sarum*

WEYMOUTH (St John) *see* Radipole and Melcombe Regis *Sarum*

WEYMOUTH (St Mary) *as above*

WEYMOUTH (St Paul) *Sarum 4* **P** *Bp* **V** A LIPOVSKY

WEYMOUTH RIDGEWAY, comprising Bincombe and Broadwey, Buckland Ripers, Littlemoor, Osmington w Poxwell, Preston w Sutton Poyntz, and Upwey *Sarum 4* **P** *Patr Bd* **TR** J K MENZIES **TV** P ELLIOTT

WHADDON (St Margaret) *see* Glouc St Geo w Whaddon *Glouc*

WHADDON (St Mary the Virgin) *see* Canalside Benefice *Sarum*

WHADDON (St Mary) *Ely 7* **P** *D&C Windsor* **V** *vacant*

WHADDON (St Mary) *see* Blackthorn Chase *Ox*

WHADDON (St Mary) *see* Clarendon *Sarum*

WHADDON (St Michael) *see* Cheltenham St Mich *Glouc*

WHALEY BRIDGE (St James) *Ches 16* **P** *Bp and Bp Derby (alt)* **R** F M ECCLESTON

WHALEY THORNS (St Luke) *see* E Scarsdale *Derby*

WHALLEY (St Mary and All Saints) *see* W Pendleside *Blackb*

WHALLEY RANGE (St Edmund) and Moss Side St James w St Clement *Man 2* **P** *Bp and Simeon's Trustees (jt)* **R** A W HARDY **C** G R E THOMAS **OLM** S AWALE

WHALLEY RANGE (St Margaret) *Man 2* **P** *Trustees* **R** *vacant*

WHALTON (St Mary Magdalene) *see* Bolam w Whalton and Hartburn w Meldon *Newc*

WHAPLODE (St Mary) *see* Elloe Stone *Linc*

WHAPLODE DROVE (St John the Baptist) *see* Elloe Fen Gp *Linc*

WHARFEDALE, LOWER, comprising Kirkby Overblow w Sicklinghall, Pool and Arthington, and Weeton w North Rigton and Stainburn *Leeds 18* **P** *Bp, V Otley, and W G C Sheepshanks Esq (jt)* **R** C L MARSHALL **Hon C** D J WHEELER **NSM** R HUDSPETH

WHARFEDALE, UPPER and Littondale, comprising Arncliffe w Halton Gill, Hubberholme, and Kettlewell w Conistone *Leeds 21* **P** *Bp, Mrs J E Wright, and W R G Bell Esq (jt)* **V** T P LUSTY

WHARRAM (St Mary) *see* Weaverthorpe w Helperthorpe, Luttons Ambo etc *York*

WHARTON (Christ Church) *Ches 6* **P** R Davenham **V** T D HANSON

WHATBOROUGH Group of Parishes, The, comprising Cold Overton, Knossington, Lowesby, Owston and Withcote, and Tilton-on-the-Hill *Leic 5* **P** *Bp* **P-in-c** J L LEWIS

WHATCOTE (St Peter) *see* Tysoe w Oxhill and Whatcote *Cov*

WHATFIELD (St Margaret) *see* Bildeston w Wattisham and Lindsey etc *St E*

WHATLEY (St George) *see* Mells w Buckland Dinham, Elm, Whatley etc *B & W*

WHATLINGTON (St Mary Magdalene) *see* Sedlescombe w Whatlington *Chich*

WHATTON (St John of Beverley) w Aslockton, Hawksworth, Scarrington, Orston and Thoroton *S'well 5* **P** *Trustees* **V** T J E CHAMBERS

WHEATACRE (All Saints) *see* Waveney Marshlands *Nor*

WHEATCROFT (St Michael and All Angels) *see* Scarborough St Martin *York*

WHEATFIELD (St Andrew) *see* Thame *Ox*

WHEATHAMPSTEAD (St Helen) *St Alb 7* **P** *Bp* **R** R M BANHAM

WHEATHILL (Holy Trinity) *see* Ditton Priors w Neenton, Burwarton etc *Heref*

WHEATHILL PRIORY Group of Parishes, The, comprising Barton St David, Keinton Mandeville w Kingweston, and Lydford on Fosse *B & W 2* **P** *Ch Soc Trust and J H Cordle Esq (1 turn), A J Whitehead Esq (2 turns), Bp (1 turn), and Mrs E J Burden (1 turn)* **P-in-c** E J DURHAM

WHEATLEY (St Mary the Virgin) *see* Albury w Tiddington etc *Ox*

WHEATLEY (St Mary) *see* Doncaster St Mary and St Paul *Sheff*

WHEATLEY HILL (All Saints), Thornley and Wingate w Hutton Henry *Dur 10* **P** *Bp* **V** F J GRIEVE **C** A R WILLIAMS

WHEATLEY HILLS (St Aidan) w Intake *Sheff 8* **P** *Bp* **V** *vacant*

WHEATLEY PARK (St Paul) *see* Doncaster St Mary and St Paul *Sheff*

WHEATLEY, NORTH (St Peter and St Paul) *see* The Clays *S'well*

WHEATON ASTON (St Mary) *see* Watershed *Lich*

WHEELOCK (Christ Church) *see* Haslington w Crewe Green and Wheelock *Ches*

WHELDRAKE (St Helen) *see* Derwent Ings *York*

WHELFORD (St Anne) *see* S Cotswolds *Glouc*

WHELLEY (St Stephen) *see* Wigan *Liv*

WHELNETHAM, GREAT (St Thomas à Becket) *see* St Edm Way *St E*

WHELNETHAM, LITTLE (St Mary) *see* Bradfield St Clare, Bradfield St George etc *St E*

WHEPSTEAD (St Petronilla) *see* Horringer *St E*

WHERSTEAD (St Mary) *see* Holbrook, Stutton, Freston, Woolverstone etc *St E*

WHERWELL (St Peter and Holy Cross) *see* The Downs *Win*

WHETSTONE (St John the Apostle) *Lon 14* **P** *Bp* **P-in-c** K QUAK-WINSLOW

WHETSTONE (St Peter) *see* Cosby and Whetstone *Leic*

WHICHAM (St Mary) *see* Black Combe, Drigg, Eskdale etc *Carl*

WHICHFORD (St Michael) *see* S Warks Seven Gp *Cov*

WHICKHAM (St Mary the Virgin) *Dur 12* **P** *Ld Chan* **R** B J ABBOTT

WHIDDON Team Ministry, The *see* Chagford, Gidleigh, Throwleigh etc *Ex*

WHILTON (St Andrew) *see* Brington w Whilton and Norton etc *Pet*

WHIMPLE (St Mary) *see* Broadclyst, Clyst Honiton, Clyst Hydon etc *Ex*

WHINBURGH (St Mary) *see* Barnham Broom and Upper Yare *Nor*

WHINMOOR (St Paul) *see* Seacroft *Leeds*

WHINNEY HILL (St Peter) *see* Thrybergh *Sheff*

WHIPPINGHAM (St Mildred) w East Cowes *Portsm 7* **P** *Ld Chan* **R** S A PATERSON

WHIPSNADE (St Mary Magdalene) *see* Kensworth, Studham and Whipsnade *St Alb*

WHIPTON (St Boniface) *Ex 3* **P** *Bp* **P-in-c** C A ROBINSON

WHISSENDINE (St Andrew) *see* Oakham, Ashwell, Braunston, Brooke, Egleton etc *Pet*

WHISSONSETT (St Mary) *see* Upper Wensum Village Gp *Nor*

WHISTON (St Mary Magdalene) *Sheff 6* **P** *Bp* **P-in-c** K R SKIDMORE **C** T F GIBBONS

WHISTON (St Mary the Virgin) *see* Yardley Hastings, Denton and Grendon etc *Pet*

WHISTON (St Mildred) *see* Kingsley and Foxt-w-Whiston and Oakamoor etc *Lich*

WHISTON (St Nicholas) *Liv 7* **P** *V Prescot* **V** A J TELFER

WHITACRE, NETHER (St Giles) *see* The Whitacres, Lea Marston, and Shustoke *Birm*

WHITACRE, OVER (St Leonard) *as above*

WHITACRES, Lea Marston, and Shustoke, The *Birm 5* **P** K E Wingfield Digby Esq (1 turn), Bp (2 turns), and Ld Chan (1 turn) **C** M A WATERSTREET

WHITBECK (St Mary) *see* Black Combe, Drigg, Eskdale etc *Carl*

WHITBOURNE (St John the Baptist) *see* Edvin Loach w Tedstone Delamere etc *Heref*

WHITBURN (no dedication) *Dur 14* **P** *Bp* **P-in-c** V J CUTHBERT

WHITBY (St Hilda) (St John) (St Mary) w Ruswarp *York 21* **P** *Abp* **TR** M G T GOBBETT **C** P C BURNETT, W D ELLIS

WHITBY (St Thomas) *see* Ellesmere Port *Ches*

WHITCHURCH (All Hallows) w Tufton and Litchfield *Win 6* **P** *Bp* **P-in-c** D M ROCHE **C** N SMALLWOOD **Hon C** M R CHRISTIAN

WHITCHURCH (St Alkmund) *see* Fauls, Tilstock and Whitchurch *Lich*

WHITCHURCH (St Andrew) *Ex 21* **P** *Bp* **P-in-c** S A BRASSIL **NSM** M L DONNE

WHITCHURCH (St Augustine) *Bris 1* **P** *Bp* **C** J C KEAN, M L SOUTHCOMBE

WHITCHURCH (St Dubricius) *see* Wye Reaches Gp *Heref*

WHITCHURCH (St John the Evangelist) *see* Schorne *Ox*

WHITCHURCH (St Mary the Virgin) *see* Ilmington w Stretton-on-Fosse etc *Cov*

WHITCHURCH (St Mary the Virgin) *see* Langtree *Ox*

WHITCHURCH (St Nicholas) *Bris 1* **P** *Bp* **V** *vacant*

WHITCHURCH CANONICORUM (St Candida and Holy Cross) *see* Golden Cap Team *Sarum*

WHITCHURCH HILL (St John the Baptist) *see* Langtree *Ox*

WHITE CITY (St Michael and St George) *Lon 9* **P** *Bp* **V** B P HUMPHRIES **NSM** A J ROONEY

WHITE COLNE (St Andrew) *see* Halstead Area *Chelmsf*

WHITE HORSE, The, comprising Dilton Marsh and Westbury *Sarum 12* **P** *Bp* **TR** R S HARRIS **TV** C E HUSBAND **C** H J NEWTON

WHITE LADIES ASTON (St John) *see* Peopleton and White Ladies Aston w Churchill etc *Worc*

WHITE NOTLEY (St Etheldreda) *see* Witham and Villages *Chelmsf*

WHITE RODING (St Martin) *see* S Rodings *Chelmsf*

WHITE WALTHAM (St Mary the Virgin) *Ox 5* **P** *Sir John Smith* **P-in-c** D A ATALLAH **C** W M C STILEMAN

WHITECHAPEL (St James) *see* Fellside Team *Blackb*

WHITEFIELD (St Andrew) *see* Hillock and Unsworth *Man*

WHITEFRIARS (no dedication) *Rushden Pet 8* **P** CPAS **V** C A YOUNGMAN **C** J D THORNE

WHITEGATE (St Mary) w Little Budworth *Ches 6* **P** *Bp, Lord Delamere and W R Cullimore Esq (alt)* **V** P C O DAWSON **NSM** J T STOPFORD, S J MILLINCHIP

WHITEHALL (St Ambrose) *see* E Bris St Ambrose and St Leon *Bris*

WHITEHALL PARK (St Andrew) *Lon 6* **P** *Ch Patr Trust* **V** S R CLARKE

WHITEHAVEN (St James) *Carl 5* **P** *Patr Bd* **P-in-c** R JACKSON

WHITEHAWK (St Cuthman) *Chich 19* **P** *Bp* **P-in-c** R M COATES **C** B A ATKINS, R B MERRICK

WHITEHILLS (St Mark) *see* Kingsthorpe *Pet*

WHITELACKINGTON (Blessed Virgin Mary) *see* Ilminster and Whitelackington *B & W*

WHITELEAS (St Mary w St Martin) *see* S Shields All SS *Dur*

WHITELEY (Community Centre) *Portsm 2* **P** *Bp* **V** P J MILLS **C** A V ADENIRAN

WHITEPARISH (All Saints) *see* Clarendon *Sarum*

WHITESHILL (St Paul) *see* Stroud Team *Glouc*

WHITESTAUNTON (St Andrew) *see* Chard St Mary w Combe St Nicholas, Wambrook etc *B & W*

WHITESTONE (St Catherine) *see* Tedburn St Mary, Cheriton Bishop, Whitestone etc *Ex*

WHITESTONE (St John the Evangelist) *as above*

WHITEWATER Benefice, The, comprising Heckfield w Mattingley and Rotherwick, and Hook *Win 5* **P** *Bp and New Coll Ox (alt)* **R** M E DE QUIDT **NSM** S M HOAD

WHITEWELL (St Mary) *see* Marbury w Tushingham and Whitewell *Ches*

WHITEWELL (St Michael) *Blackb 7* **P** *Bp* **V** *vacant*

WHITFIELD (Holy Trinity) *see* Allendale w Whitfield *Newc*

WHITFIELD (St James) (St Luke) *Derby 4* **P** *Bp* **V** T S MAY **NSM** C M NOWAK

WHITFIELD (St John the Evangelist) *see* Astwell Gp *Pet*

WHITFIELD (St John) *see* Allendale w Whitfield *Newc*

WHITFIELD (St Peter) *see* Bewsborough *Cant*

WHITFORD (St Mary at the Cross) *see* Kilmington, Stockland, Dalwood, Yarcombe etc *Ex*

WHITGIFT (St Mary Magdalene) *see* The Marshland *Sheff*

WHITGREAVE (St John the Evangelist) *see* Stafford St Bertelin and Whitgreave St Jo *Lich*
WHITKIRK (St Mary) *Leeds 13* **P** *Meynell Ch Trust* **V** M PEAT
WHITLEIGH (St Chad) *see* Ernesettle, Whitleigh and Honicknowle *Ex*
WHITLEY (Christ Church) *see* Reading Ch Ch *Ox*
WHITLEY (St Helen) *Newc 10* **P** *Bp* **V** A J PATTERSON
WHITLEY (St James) *Cov 1* **P** *Bp* **P-in-c** A M RICHARDS
WHITLEY LOWER (St Mary and St Michael) *see* Thornhill and Whitley Lower *Leeds*
WHITLEY, LOWER or NETHER (St Luke) *see* Aston by Sutton, Lt Leigh and Lower Whitley *Ches*
WHITLINGHAM (St Andrew) *see* Rockland St Mary w Hellington, Bramerton etc *Nor*
WHITMINSTER (St Andrew) *see* Stroudwater *Glouc*
WHITMORE (St Mary and All Saints) *see* Chapel Chorlton, Maer and Whitmore *Lich*
WHITNASH (St Margaret) *Cov 11* **P** *Lord Leigh*
R R W S SUFFERN
WHITNEY (St Peter and St Paul) *see* Eardisley w Bollingham, Willersley, Brilley etc *Heref*
WHITSBURY (St Leonard) *see* W Downland *Sarum*
WHITSTABLE (All Saints) (St Alphage) (St Andrew) (St Peter) *Cant 4* **P** *DBP* **TR** R C WEBBLEY
TV P J STUBBINGS, S C TILLOTSON **C** J R GREENHALF
WHITSTONE (St Anne) *see* Bude Coast and Country *Truro*
WHITTINGHAM (St Bartholomew) and Edlingham w Bolton Chapel *Newc 6* **P** *D&C Carl and D&C Dur (alt)*
V *vacant*
WHITTINGTON (Christ Church) *see* Wissey Valley *Ely*
WHITTINGTON (St Bartholomew) *Derby 3* **P** *Bp*
R J E MORRIS **OLM** J QUICK
WHITTINGTON (St Bartholomew) *see* Sevenhampton w Charlton Abbots, Hawling etc *Glouc*
WHITTINGTON (St Giles) w Weeford *Lich 1* **P** *Bp* **V** *vacant*
WHITTINGTON (St John the Baptist) and West Felton w Haughton *Lich 18* **P** *Bp and Mrs A F Hamilton-Hill (jt)*
R S WILLIAMS
WHITTINGTON (St Michael the Archangel) *see* Hornby w Claughton and Whittington etc *Blackb*
WHITTINGTON (St Philip and St James) *see* Worc SE *Worc*
WHITTINGTON, NEW (St Barnabas) *see* Whittington *Derby*
WHITTLEBURY (St Mary) *see* Silverstone and Abthorpe w Slapton etc *Pet*
WHITTLE-LE-WOODS (St John the Evangelist) *Blackb 4* **P** *V Leyland* **V** P R M VENABLES **C** P T DAVIES
WHITTLESEY (St Andrew) (St Mary), Pondersbridge and Coates *Ely 11* **P** *Ld Chan (2 turns), Patr Bd (1 turn)*
TR *vacant*
WHITTLESFORD (St Mary and St Andrew) *Ely 5* **P** *Jes Coll Cam* **NSM** O M K COLES
WHITTLEWOOD *see* Silverstone and Abthorpe w Slapton etc *Pet*
WHITTON (St Augustine of Canterbury) *Lon 10* **P** *Bp*
V J K KAOMA
WHITTON (St John the Baptist) *see* Alkborough *Linc*
WHITTON (St Mary and St Botolph) and Thurleston w Akenham *St E 1* **P** *Bp (2 turns), Exors G K Drury Esq (1 turn)*
P-in-c M N C SOKANOVIC **NSM** M A BONSALL
WHITTON (St Mary) *see* Tenbury *Heref*
WHITTON (St Philip and St James) *Lon 10* **P** *V Twickenham St Mary* **V** D M CLOAKE
WHITTON, comprising Aldbourne, Axford, Baydon, Chilton Foliat, Froxfield, and Ramsbury *Sarum 18* **P** *Patr Bd*
TR S E HUTTON **TV** R C FLOATE, S E RODD **C** K M RIZZELLO
WHITTONSTALL (St Philip and St James) *see* Slaley, Healey and Whittonstall *Newc*
WHITWELL (St John the Evangelist) *see* Harton *York*
WHITWELL (St Lawrence) *see* Elmton w Creswell and Whitwell w Steetley *Derby*
WHITWELL (St Mary and St Rhadegunde) *Portsm 7* **P** *Bp*
V *vacant*
WHITWELL (St Michael and All Angels) *see* Empingham, Edith Weston, Lyndon, Manton etc *Pet*
WHITWELL (St Michael and All Angels) *see* Reepham and Wensum Valley *Nor*
WHITWICK (St John the Baptist), Thringstone and Swannington *Leic 8* **P** *Duchy of Lanc (2 turns), Bp (1 turn)*
R D B WALKER
WHITWOOD (All Saints) *see* Castleford *Leeds*
WHITWORTH (not known) *see* Spennymoor and Whitworth *Dur*
WHITWORTH (St Bartholomew) w Facit *Man 4* **P** *Bp and Keble Coll Ox (jt)* **NSM** J M WATSON
WHIXALL (St Mary) *see* Prees, Edstaston and Whixall *Lich*

WHIXLEY (Ascension) *see* Gt and Lt Ouseburn w Marton cum Grafton etc *Leeds*
WHORLTON (St John the Evangelist) *Newc 4* **P** *Bp*
P-in-c M G HUNTER
WHORLTON (St Mary) *see* Barnard Castle w Whorlton *Dur*
WHORLTON Group, The, comprising Carlton in Cleveland, Crathorne, Faceby, Middleton-upon-Leven, Rudby-in-Cleveland, and Whorlton *York 20* **P** *Abp, Lord Dugdale, and Mrs A P F Kynge (jt)* **R** R OPALA **NSM** D J SUDRON
WHYKE (St George) w Rumboldswhyke St Mary and Portfield All Saints *Chich 2* **P** *Bp* **R** *vacant*
WHYTELEAFE (St Luke) *see* Caterham *S'wark*
WIBSEY (St Paul) *Leeds 3* **P** *Bp* **V** T J-L GUILLEMIN
C J L TRENHOLME
WIBTOFT (Assumption of Our Lady) *see* Upper Soar *Leic*
WICHENFORD (St Lawrence) *see* Worcs W Rural *Worc*
WICK (All Saints) *see* Lyminster and Wick *Chich*
WICK (St Bartholomew) w Doynton and Dyrham *Bris 5*
P *Simeon's Trustees, Ld Chan, and M H W Blaythwayt Esq (by turn)* **P-in-c** T J K BELL **C** R J STEWART
WICK (St Mary) *see* Pershore w Pinvin, Wick and Birlingham *Worc*
WICK ST LAWRENCE (St Lawrence) *see* Worle *B & W*
WICKEN (St John the Evangelist) *see* Potterspury w Furtho and Yardley Gobion etc *Pet*
WICKEN (St Laurence) *Ely 4* **P** *Ch Patr Trust* **R** *vacant*
WICKEN BONHUNT (St Margaret) *see* Clavering w Langley, Arkesden etc *Chelmsf*
WICKENBY (St Peter and St Lawrence) *see* Wragby Gp *Linc*
WICKERSLEY (St Alban) *Sheff 6* **P** *DBP* **R** P J HUGHES
WICKFORD (St Andrew) (St Catherine) and Runwell *Chelmsf 11* **P** *Patr Bd* **TV** S J WISE **OLM** S J LISSENDEN
WICKHAM (St Nicholas) *see* Shedfield and Wickham *Portsm*
WICKHAM (St Swithun) *see* W Downland *Ox*
WICKHAM BISHOPS (St Bartholomew) w Little Braxted *Chelmsf 23* **P** *Bp (3 turns), CCC Cam (1 turn)*
P-in-c J H LE SÈVE **NSM** D R CLARK-MAYERS
WICKHAM MARKET (All Saints) w Pettistree *St E 12* **P** *Ch Trust Fund Trust and Ld Chan (alt)* **V** L SIU
NSM J A CATCHPOLE
WICKHAM SKEITH (St Andrew) *see* Bacton w Wyverstone, Cotton and Old Newton etc *St E*
WICKHAM ST PAUL (St Paul and All Saints) *see* N Hinckford *Chelmsf*
WICKHAM, EAST (St Michael the Archangel) *S'wark 6*
P *D&C* **V** P ORGAN **C** T M C BATES **NSM** M W SMITH
WICKHAM, WEST (St Francis) (St Mary of Nazareth) *S'wark 19* **P** *Bp* **V** H M O'SULLIVAN
WICKHAM, WEST (St John) *S'wark 19* **P** *Bp* **V** J J H WARD
WICKHAM, WEST (St Mary) *see* Granta Vale Gp *Ely*
WICKHAMBREAUX (St Andrew) *see* Lt Stour *Cant*
WICKHAMBROOK (All Saints) *see* Bansfield *St E*
WICKHAMFORD (St John the Baptist) *see* Broadway w Wickhamford *Worc*
WICKHAMPTON (St Andrew) *see* Acle and Bure to Yare *Nor*
WICKLEWOOD (All Saints) *see* High Oak, Hingham and Scoulton w Wood Rising *Nor*
WICKMERE (St Andrew) *see* Aylsham and Distr *Nor*
WICKWAR (Holy Trinity) *see* Charfield and Kingswood w Wickwar etc *Glouc*
WIDDINGTON (St Mary) *see* Newport w Widdington, Quendon and Rickling *Chelmsf*
WIDDRINGTON (Holy Trinity) *Newc 11* **P** *Bp* **V** *vacant*
WIDECOMBE-IN-THE-MOOR (St Pancras) *see* Ashburton, Bickington, Buckland in the Moor etc *Ex*
WIDEMOUTH BAY (Our Lady and St Anne) *see* Bude Coast and Country *Truro*
WIDFORD (St John the Baptist) *see* Hunsdon w Widford and Wareside *St Alb*
WIDFORD (St Mary) (Holy Spirit) *Chelmsf 9* **P** *CPAS*
R S R GILLINGHAM **C** D J CATTLE, G E FRASER
WIDFORD (St Oswald) *see* Burford w Fulbrook, Taynton, Asthall etc *Ox*
WIDMER END (Good Shepherd) *see* Hazlemere *Ox*
WIDMERPOOL (St Peter) *see* Willoughby-on-the-Wolds w Wysall and Widmerpool *S'well*
WIDNES (St John) (St Paul) *Liv 12* **P** *Bp* **V** G S SHARPLES
C B G NOBLE, C S GAUDION, P J STRADLING
WIDNES, EAST (St Ambrose) (St Luke) (Cronton Mission) *Liv 12* **P** *Patr Bd* **P-in-c** R L PEARSON **TV** L C MCIVER
WIDNES, SOUTH (St Mary) *Liv 12* **P** *Bp* **R** R HARVEY
WIDWORTHY (St Cuthbert) *see* Offwell, Farway and Widworthy *Ex*
WIELD (St James) *see* Farleigh, Candover and Wield *Win*
WIGAN (All Saints) (St Andrew) (St Anne) (St Catharine) (St George) (St James) (St John the Baptist) (St Michael

and All Angels) (St Stephen) (St Thomas), including
Ashton-in-Makerfield, Billinge, Bryn, Goose Green,
Highfield, Kitt Green, Marsh Green, Newtown, Orrell, and
Pemberton *Liv 15*   **P** *Patr Bd*   **TR** N J COOK
TV C O NICHOLSON, D G GOSLING, D M BROOKE,
J F SHOESMITH, J P THOMAS, M J WADE, R M SHEEHAN,
S A BECK, S HIGGINSON, S L NICHOLSON, S Y FULFORD,
W J GIBBONS   **C** C J COSSLETT, F M HUMPHRY, J M MAGILL,
J R TAYLOR, P G WHITTINGTON, S JONES   **NSM** A PARKINSON,
S D CLARKE, S M A THOMAS   **OLM** M JENNINGS, M L PERRIN
WIGAN (St James) *see Wigan Liv*
WIGBOROUGH, GREAT (St Stephen) *see W w E Mersea,*
Peldon, Gt and Lt Wigborough *Chelmsf*
WIGBOROUGH, LITTLE (St Nicholas) *as above*
WIGGATON (St Edward the Confessor) *see Ottery St Mary,*
Alfington, W Hill, Tipton etc *Ex*
WIGGENHALL ST GERMANS (St Mary the Virgin) *see E*
Marshland *Ely*
WIGGENHALL ST MARY (St Mary Magdalene) *as above*
WIGGINTON (St Bartholomew) *see Northchurch and*
Wigginton *St Alb*
WIGGINTON (St Giles) *see Hook Norton w Gt Rollright,*
Swerford etc *Ox*
WIGGINTON (St Leonard) (St James) *Lich 4*   **P** *V Tamworth*
V D A DYSON   **NSM** R DAVIES
WIGGINTON (St Nicholas) *see Haxby and Wigginton York*
WIGGONHOLT (not known) *see Amberley w N Stoke and*
Parham, Wiggonholt etc *Chich*
WIGHILL (All Saints) *see Rural Ainsty York*
WIGHTON (All Saints) *see Holkham w Egmere w Warham*
etc *Nor*
WIGMORE (St James the Apostle) *see Wigmore Abbey Heref*
WIGMORE ABBEY, comprising Adforton, Aston, Brampton
Bryan, Burrington, Downton, Elton, Leinthall Starkes,
Leintwardine, and Wigmore *Heref 6*   **P** *Trustees*
R M D CATLING
WIGSLEY *see E Trent S'well*
WIGSTON (All Saints) (St Wistan) (St Thomas) *Leic 3*
P *Haberdashers' Co*   **V** T THURSTON-SMITH   **C** C J JOHNSON,
N G BAKER, P L BETTS
WIGSTON (St Wistan) *see Wigston Leic*
WIGSTON MAGNA (All Saints) *as above*
WIGSTON PARVA (St Mary the Virgin) *see Sapcote and*
Sharnford w Wigston Parva *Leic*
WIGSTON, SOUTH (St Thomas) *see Wigston Leic*
WIGTOFT (St Peter and St Paul) *see Haven Gp Linc*
WIGTON (St Mary) *Carl 7*   **P** *Bp*   **V** G P RAVALDE
WILBARSTON (All Saints) *see Stoke Albany w Wilbarston and*
Ashley etc *Pet*
WILBERFOSS (St John the Baptist) w Kexby *York 5*
P *Viscount de Vesci and Lord Egremont (alt)*
P-in-c S G PRITCHARD
WILBRAHAM, GREAT (St Nicholas) *Ely 4*   **P** *DBP*
V A A GOODMAN
WILBRAHAM, LITTLE (St John) *Ely 4*   **P** *CCC Cam*
R A A GOODMAN
WILBURTON (St Peter) *Ely 8*   **P** *Adn Ely*   **NSM** J STIMPSON
WILBURY (St Thomas) *St Alb 3*   **P** *Bp*   **V** J J MCLAREN
WILBY (All Saints) *see Quidenham Gp Nor*
WILBY (St Mary the Virgin) *see Gt Doddington and Wilby*
and Ecton *Pet*
WILBY (St Mary) *see Four Rivers St E*
WILCOT (Holy Cross) *see Vale of Pewsey Sarum*
WILCOTE (St Peter) *see Forest Edge Ox*
WILDBOARCLOUGH (St Saviour) *see Sutton, Wincle,*
Wildboarclough and Bosley *Ches*
WILDEN (All Saints) *see Stourport and Wilden Worc*
WILDEN (St Nicholas) w Colmworth and Ravensden
St Alb 13   **P** *Ld Chan, Bp, and DBP (by turn)*
P-in-c T C WILSON
WILFORD (St Wilfrid) *S'well 6*   **P** *Lt Col Peter Clifton*
R *vacant*
WILFORD HILL (St Paul) *S'well 6*   **P** *DBP*   **V** T P FOX
WILFORD PENINSULA, The, comprising Alderton, Bawdsey,
Boyton, Bromeswell, Butley, Chillesford, Eyke, Hollesley,
Iken, Orford, Ramsholt, Rendlesham, Shottisham,
Sudbourne, Sutton, Tunstall, and Wantisden *St E 16*   **P** *Patr*
Bd   **TR** G D TULK   **TV** M E REYNOLDS
WILKSBY (All Saints) *see Fen and Hill Gp Linc*
WILLAND (St Mary the Virgin), Uffculme, Kentisbeare and
Blackborough *Ex 7*   **P** *Bp, CPAS, and H Chandler Esq (jt)*
P-in-c S G G TALBOT   **C** G M THOMAS, M E PARTON
WILLASTON (Christ Church) *Ches 9*   **P** *DBF*
NSM L R BANNON
WILLASTON (St Luke) *see Wistaston Ches*

WILLEN (St Mary Magdalene) *see Stantonbury and Willen*
Ox
WILLENHALL (Holy Trinity) *see Bentley Em and Willenhall*
H Trin *Lich*
WILLENHALL (St Anne) *Lich 28*   **P** *Mrs L Grant-Wilson*
P-in-c S BOYCE   **C** R E WILSHIRE
WILLENHALL (St Giles) *Lich 28*   **P** *Trustees*   **P-in-c** S BOYCE
C R E WILSHIRE
WILLENHALL (St John the Divine) *Cov 1*   **P** *V Cov H Trin*
V P I A HOWELL   **C** C L JACKSON
WILLENHALL (St Stephen) *Lich 28*   **P** *Bp*
P-in-c R E WILSHIRE   **C** S BOYCE   **OLM** M P BATCHELOR
WILLERBY (St Luke) *see Kirk Ella and Willerby York*
WILLERBY (St Peter) *see Hertford York*
WILLERSEY (St Peter) *see Vale and Cotswold Edge Glouc*
WILLESBOROUGH (St Mary the Virgin) *see Ashford Town*
Cant
WILLESDEN (St Mark) *see Kensal Rise St Mark Lon*
WILLESDEN (St Martin) *see Kensal Rise St Martin Lon*
WILLESDEN (St Mary) *Lon 18*   **P** *D&C St Paul's*
V C P PHILLIPS
WILLESDEN (St Matthew) *Lon 18*   **P** *Bp*   **V** A J TEATHER
WILLESDEN GREEN (St Andrew) (St Francis of Assisi)
Lon 18   **P** *Bp*   **V** C P M PATTERSON
WILLEY (St Leonard) *see Revel Gp Cov*
WILLIAN (All Saints) *see Letchworth St Paul w Willian St Alb*
WILLINGALE (St Christopher) *see Fyfield, Moreton w*
Bobbingworth etc *Chelmsf*
WILLINGDON (St Mary the Virgin) *Chich 14*   **P** *D&C*
NSM M F WOODWARD, S A WILKINSON
WILLINGHAM (St Mary and All Saints) *see 5folds Ely*
WILLINGHAM BY STOW (St Helen) *see Stow Gp Linc*
WILLINGHAM, NORTH (St Thomas) *see Walesby Gp Linc*
WILLINGHAM, SOUTH (St Martin) *see Barkwith Gp Linc*
WILLINGTON (St Lawrence) *see Cople, Moggerhanger and*
Willington *St Alb*
WILLINGTON (St Michael) *Derby 7*   **P** *CPAS*   **V** *vacant*
WILLINGTON (St Stephen) *see Hunwick and Willington Dur*
WILLINGTON QUAY (St Paul) *see Willington Newc*
WILLINGTON Team, The (Good Shepherd) (St Mary the
Virgin) (St Paul) *Newc 5*   **P** *The Crown*   **TR** S MCCORMACK
TV J MOONEY   **NSM** E M K WATSON, K WEARS
WILLISHAM (St Mary) *see S Bosmere St E*
WILLITON (St Peter) *see Watchet and Williton B & W*
WILLOUGHBY (St Helen) *see Alford Gp Linc*
WILLOUGHBY (St Nicholas) *see Leam Valley Cov*
WILLOUGHBY WATERLEYS (St Mary) *see Four Saints Leic*
WILLOUGHBY-ON-THE-WOLDS (St Mary and All Saints) w
Wysall and Widmerpool *S'well 5*   **P** *MMCET*
R S D HIPPISLEY-COX
WILLOUGHTON (St Andrew) *see Trentcliffe Gp Linc*
WILMCOTE (St Andrew) *see Aston Cantlow and Wilmcote w*
Billesley *Cov*
WILMINGTON (St Mary and St Peter) *see Arlington,*
Berwick, Selmeston w Alciston etc *Chich*
WILMINGTON (St Michael) *Roch 2*   **P** *D&C*
V C M CHAMBERS
WILMSLOW (St Bartholomew) *Ches 12*   **P** *Bp*
R C E THROUP   **C** J R PRINCE   **NSM** R A YATES
WILNE (St Chad) and Draycott w Breaston *Derby 8*   **P** *Bp*
R C J SMEDLEY   **NSM** G W DUNDAS
WILNECOTE (Holy Trinity) *Lich 4*   **P** *V Tamworth*
V O HARRISON
WILSDEN (St Matthew) *see Harden and Wilsden,*
Cullingworth and Denholme *Leeds*
WILSFORD (St Mary) *see E Loveden Linc*
WILSFORD (St Michael) *see Woodford Valley w Archers Gate*
Sarum
WILSFORD (St Nicholas) *see Cannings and Redhorn Sarum*
WILSHAMSTEAD (All Saints) and Houghton Conquest
St Alb 9   **P** *St Jo Coll Cam and Bp (alt)*   **V** *vacant*
WILSHAW (St Mary) *see Meltham Leeds*
WILSILL (St Michael and All Angels) *see Upper Nidderdale*
Leeds
WILSTHORPE (St Faith) *see Uffington Gp Linc*
WILSTONE (St Cross) *see Tring St Alb*
WILTON (St Cuthbert) *York 16*   **P** *Abp*   **V** *vacant*
WILTON (St George) *B & W 18*   **P** *Mrs E C Cutbush*
V N P GRIFFIN
WILTON (St George) *see Thornton Dale w Allerston,*
Ebberston etc *York*
WILTON (St Mary and St Nicholas) w Netherhampton and
Fugglestone *Sarum 11*   **P** *Earl of Pembroke*   **R** M R WOOD
NSM S C TITLEY, S M WOOD
WILTON PLACE (St Paul) *Lon 3*   **P** *Bp*   **V** A G GYLE
Hon C N S MERCER   **NSM** L GIOIA

WIMBISH (All Saints)　see Saffron Walden and Villages *Chelmsf*

WIMBLEDON (Emmanuel) Ridgway Proprietary Chapel *S'wark 13*　**C** J SKIDMORE　**NSM** N L WOOLDRIDGE **Min** R A R WEEKES

WIMBLEDON (St Luke)　see Wimbledon Park St Luke *S'wark*

WIMBLEDON (St Mary) (St Matthew) (St Mark) (St John the Baptist) *S'wark 13*　**P** Patr Bd　**TR** A J HODGSON **TV** C B GARDNER, H C ORCHARD, S P A EDMONDS **C** A J M NEWMAN　**Hon C** N H S BERSWEDEN

WIMBLEDON PARK (St Luke) *S'wark 13*　**P** Simeon's Trustees **V** R J R PAICE

WIMBLEDON PARK (St Paul)　see Wandsworth St Paul *S'wark*

WIMBLEDON, SOUTH (All Saints) *S'wark 13*　**P** Bp **P-in-c** C W NOKE

WIMBLEDON, SOUTH (Holy Trinity and St Peter)　see Merton Priory *S'wark*

WIMBLEDON, SOUTH (St Andrew) *S'wark 13*　**P** Bp **P-in-c** C J D LAMONT　**C** B W RICKARDS, S THOMAS

WIMBLEDON, WEST (Christ Church) *S'wark 13*　**P** TR *Wimbledon*　**V** M J BURNS

WIMBLINGTON (St Peter)　see Six Fen Churches *Ely*

WIMBORNE (St John the Evangelist)　see New Borough and Leigh *Sarum*

WIMBORNE MINSTER (St Cuthberga) and Wimborne Villages, including Hinton Martel, Holt, Horton and Chalbury, and Witchampton, Stanbridge and Long Crichel w More Crichel *Sarum 9*　**P** Governors of Wimborne Minster (3 turns), DBP (1 turn)　**R** A J W ROWLAND　**C** N WELLS, S C ALLEN　**NSM** H WALDSAX, S BOYLE

WIMBORNE ST GILES (St Giles)　see Cranborne w Boveridge, Edmondsham etc *Sarum*

WIMBOTSHAM (St Mary)　see W Norfolk Priory Gp *Ely*

WIMPOLE (St Andrew)　see Orwell Gp *Ely*

WINCANTON (St Peter and St Paul) *B & W 2*　**P** D&C **R** A J WAY

WINCH, WEST (St Mary)　see Middlewinch *Nor*

WINCHCOMBE (St Peter) *Glouc 9*　**P** Patr Bd **P-in-c** J P HOSKINS　**TV** J A HOOK, J A NEWCOMBE **C** R E MURRAY

WINCHELSEA (St Thomas) (St Richard) and Icklesham *Chich 17*　**P** Bp and Guild of All So (jt)　**R** J P MEYER

WINCHENDON, NETHER (St Nicholas)　see Long Crendon w Chearsley and Nether Winchendon *Ox*

WINCHENDON, OVER (St Mary Magdalene)　see Schorne *Ox*

WINCHESTER (All Saints)　see E Win *Win*

WINCHESTER (Christ Church) *Win 7*　**P** Simeon's Trustees **V** S J L CANSDALE　**C** A J DENNISS, C CARSON, C E PHILBRICK, J P WHYMARK, M S FOSTER　**NSM** B R WAKELIN

WINCHESTER (Holy Trinity) *Win 7*　**P** Bp　**R** *vacant*

WINCHESTER (St Barnabas) *Win 7*　**P** Bp　**V** E P A DINES **NSM** T N PEPPIATT

WINCHESTER (St Bartholomew) (St Lawrence) (St Swithun-upon-Kingsgate) *Win 7*　**P** Ld Chan **R** K P KOUSSEFF　**C** E C PHIPPS　**NSM** A GOULDING

WINCHESTER (St John the Baptist w St Martin Winnall)　see E Win *Win*

WINCHESTER (St Luke)　see Stanmore *Win*

WINCHESTER (St Matthew) (St Paul's Mission Church) *Win 7*　**P** Bp　**NSM** E B STUART

WINCHESTER St Faith (St Cross Hospital) *Win 7*　**P** Bp **R** P L KRINKS　**NSM** H L HEALEY

WINCHESTER, EAST (All Saints) (St John the Baptist w St Martin Winnall), including Chilcomb *Win 7*　**P** Bp and Ld Chan (alt)　**R** M J GRIFFITHS　**C** J E HOLDER **NSM** C M SMITH

WINCHFIELD (St Mary the Virgin)　see Hartley Wintney, Elvetham, Winchfield etc *Win*

WINCHMORE HILL (Holy Trinity) *Lon 16*　**P** V Winchmore Hill St Paul　**P-in-c** R D E BOLTON

WINCHMORE HILL (St Paul) *Lon 16*　**P** V Edmonton **V** D P SANDHAM　**NSM** C B ZUCKERT

WINCLE (St Michael)　see Sutton, Wincle, Wildboarclough and Bosley *Ches*

WINCOBANK (St Thomas)　see Brightside w Wincobank *Sheff*

WINDERMERE (St Martin) *Carl 11*　**P** Bp and Trustees (jt) **R** J J RICHARDS　**C** S H P THOMPSON

WINDERMERE (St Mary) Applethwaite and Troutbeck *Carl 11*　**P** Bp　**C** J J RICHARDS, S H P THOMPSON

WINDHILL (Christ Church) *Leeds 1*　**P** Bp　**V** *vacant*

WINDLESHAM (St John the Baptist) *Guildf 6*　**P** Ld Chan **R** J HILLMAN　**C** S D BEAGLEY

WINDMILL, The, comprising Burstow, Horne, and Outwood *S'wark 25*　**P** Ld Chan (1 turn), Bp (2 turns)　**R** N J CALVER **NSM** C E SARGENT

WINDRUSH (St Peter)　see Sherborne, Windrush, the Barringtons etc *Glouc*

WINDRUSH, LOWER, comprising Northmoor, Standlake, Stanton Harcourt, and Yelford *Ox 28*　**P** Bp, DBP, St Jo Coll Ox, D&C Ex, and B Babington-Smith Esq (jt)　**R** J HURST

WINDSOR, NEW (Holy Trinity) (St John the Baptist w All Saints) *Ox 5*　**P** Ld Chan　**TR** S N LODGE

WINDSOR, OLD (St Peter and St Andrew) (St Luke's Mission Room) *Ox 5*　**P** Ld Chan　**V** A S M SHOKRALLA

WINDY NOOK (St Alban) *Dur 11*　**P** V Heworth St Mary **P-in-c** D M LINDLEY　**C** D M HUDSON　**NSM** K COULSON

WINESTEAD (St German)　see Easington w Skeffling, Keyingham, Ottringham etc *York*

WINFARTHING (St Mary)　see Diss *Nor*

WINFORD (Blessed Virgin Mary and St Peter) w Felton Common Hill *B & W 9*　**P** Worc Coll Ox and N R Pullman Esq (jt)　**P-in-c** I K MILLS

WINFORTON (St Michael and All Angels)　see Eardisley w Bollingham, Willersley, Brilley etc *Heref*

WINFRITH NEWBURGH (St Christopher)　see W Purbeck *Sarum*

WING (St Peter and St Paul)　see Empingham, Edith Weston, Lyndon, Manton etc *Pet*

WING w Grove (All Saints)　see Cottesloe *Ox*

WINGATE GRANGE (Holy Trinity)　see Wheatley Hill, Thornley and Wingate w Hutton Henry *Dur*

WINGATES (St John the Evangelist)　see Blackrod, Daisy Hill, Westhoughton and Wingates *Man*

WINGERWORTH (All Saints) *Derby 3*　**P** Bp　**R** J D POSTON **OLM** J A WILLIS

WINGFIELD (St Andrew)　see Athelington, Denham, Horham, Hoxne etc *St E*

WINGFIELD (St Mary)　see Bradford on Avon H Trin, Westwood and Wingfield *Sarum*

WINGFIELD, NORTH (St Lawrence), Clay Cross and Pilsley *Derby 2*　**P** Bp　**TV** L C HAYLER　**C** A B ALLISON

WINGFIELD, SOUTH (All Saints)　see Crich and S Wingfield *Derby*

WINGHAM (St Mary the Virgin)　see Canonry *Cant*

WINGRAVE (St Peter and St Paul)　see Cottesloe *Ox*

WINKBURN (St John of Jerusalem) *S'well 3*　**P** Bp **P-in-c** C G PEARSE　**NSM** M A GROVES

WINKFIELD (St Mary the Virgin) and Cranbourne *Ox 3* **P** Bp　**V** *vacant*

WINKLEBURY (Good Shepherd) and Worting *Win 4* **P** MMCET　**R** J A K WIGMORE　**C** T W DENNIS

WINKLEIGH (All Saints) *Ex 18*　**P** D&C　**P-in-c** H S E BLAINE

WINKSLEY (St Cuthbert and St Oswald)　see Fountains Gp *Leeds*

WINLATON (St Paul) *Dur 12*　**P** Bp **P-in-c** A M STEWART SMITH

WINMARLEIGH (St Luke)　see Cockerham w Winmarleigh and Glasson *Blackb*

WINNERSH (St Mary the Virgin) *Ox 8*　**P** Bp　**R** *vacant*

WINNINGTON (St Luke)　see Northwich St Luke *Ches*

WINSCOMBE (St James) and Sandford *B & W 10*　**P** D&C **P-in-c** A J HISCOX

WINSFORD (St Mary Magdalene)　see Exmoor *B & W*

WINSHAM (St Stephen)　see Chaffcombe, Cricket Malherbie etc *B & W*

WINSHILL (St Mark) and Bretby *Derby 7*　**P** Bp, Baroness Gretton, and Mrs E M Meynell (jt)　**V** P R BOSHER **NSM** F D STARTIN

WINSLEY (St Nicholas)　see N Bradford on Avon and Villages *Sarum*

WINSLOW (St Laurence) w Great Horwood and Addington *Ox 13*　**P** Ld Chan (3 turns), New Coll Ox (2 turns), and DBP (1 turn)　**R** R A LIGHTBOWN　**C** M NELSON **NSM** D F JAQUET

WINSMOOR, comprising Barrington, Chillington, Cudworth, Dowlishwake, Kingstone, Puckington, Shepton Beauchamp, and Stocklinch *B & W 14*　**P** Bp, D&C, CR, and P G H Speke Esq (jt)　**V** G A WADE

WINSON (St Michael)　see S Cotswolds *Glouc*

WINSTER (Holy Trinity) *Carl 10*　**P** V Kendal H Trin **V** M D WOODCOCK　**Hon C** S C HOWARD **NSM** M L WOODCOCK

WINSTER (St John the Baptist)　see Darley, S Darley and Winster *Derby*

WINSTON (St Andrew) *Dur 4*　**P** Bp　**P-in-c** E K G HARROP

WINSTON (St Andrew)　see Debenham and Helmingham *St E*

WINSTONE (St Bartholomew)　see Brimpsfield w Birdlip, Syde, Daglingworth etc *Glouc*

WINTERBORNE CLENSTON (St Nicholas)　see Winterborne Valley and Milton Abbas *Sarum*

WINTERBORNE HOUGHTON (St Andrew)　as above

WINTERBORNE KINGSTON (St Nicholas) *see* Red Post *Sarum*

WINTERBORNE STICKLAND (St Mary) *see* Winterborne Valley and Milton Abbas *Sarum*

WINTERBORNE VALLEY and Milton Abbas, The *Sarum 6* **P** *Bp (3 turns) and P D H Chichester Esq (1 turn)* **V** L N PEARSON

WINTERBORNE WHITECHURCH (St Mary) *see* Winterborne Valley and Milton Abbas *Sarum*

WINTERBOURNE (St James) *see* E Downland *Ox*

WINTERBOURNE (St Michael the Archangel) *see* Fromeside *Bris*

WINTERBOURNE ABBAS (St Mary) *see* Dorchester and the Winterbournes *Sarum*

WINTERBOURNE BASSETT (St Katharine) *see* Upper Kennet *Sarum*

WINTERBOURNE DOWN (All Saints) *see* Fromeside *Bris*

WINTERBOURNE EARLS (St Michael and All Angels) *see* Bourne Valley *Sarum*

WINTERBOURNE GUNNER (St Mary) *as above*

WINTERBOURNE MONKTON (St Mary Magdalene) *see* Upper Kennet *Sarum*

WINTERBOURNE MONKTON (St Simon and St Jude) *see* Dorchester and the Winterbournes *Sarum*

WINTERBOURNE ST MARTIN (St Martin) *as above*

WINTERBOURNE STEEPLETON (St Michael) *as above*

WINTERBOURNE STOKE (St Peter) *see* Wylye and Till Valley *Sarum*

WINTERBOURNE ZELSTONE (St Mary) *see* Red Post *Sarum*

WINTERINGHAM (All Saints) *see* Winterton Gp *Linc*

WINTERSLOW (All Saints) *see* Clarendon *Sarum*

WINTERSLOW (St John) *as above*

WINTERTON (Holy Trinity and All Saints) *see* Flegg Coastal Benefice *Nor*

WINTERTON Group, The (All Saints), including Appleby, Roxby, and Winteringham *Linc 6* **P** *Bp, Lord St Oswald, Exors Capt J G G P Elwes, and Em Coll Cam (jt)* **V** A C NUNN **NSM** P A COOKE **OLM** J J WHITEHEAD

WINTHORPE (All Saints) *see* E Trent *S'well*

WINTHORPE (St Mary) *see* Skegness Gp *Linc*

WINTON (St Alban), Moordown and Charminster *Win 8* **P** *Bp* **V** M E SMITH **C** J M SHARP **NSM** J L WILLIAMS

WINTON (St Mary Magdalene) *see* Barton w Peel Green and Winton *Man*

WINWICK (All Saints) *see* N Leightonstone *Ely*

WINWICK (St Michael and All Angels) *see* Long Buckby w Watford and W Haddon w Winwick *Pet*

WINWICK (St Oswald) *Liv 13* **P** *Bp* **NSM** V M HANCOCK

WIRKSWORTH (St Mary), including Bonsall, Bradbourne, Brassington, Carsington, Elton, Idridgehay, Kirk Ireton, Middleton, and Wirksworth *Derby 1* **P** *Bp* **TR** D C TRUBY **TV** C A T L VICENCIO PRIOR **NSM** R H PRINCE **OLM** J E SPREADBOROUGH

WISBECH (St Augustine) *Ely 14* **P** *Bp* **V** M L BRADBURY **NSM** S SQUIRES-DUTTON

WISBECH (St Peter and St Paul) *Ely 14* **P** *Bp* **V** M L BRADBURY **C** C J WILKINSON **NSM** S SQUIRES-DUTTON

WISBECH ST MARY (St Mary) and Guyhirn w Ring's End and Gorefield and Southea w Murrow and Parson Drove *Ely 14* **P** *Bp* **V** *vacant*

WISBOROUGH GREEN (St Peter ad Vincula) *Chich 4* **P** *Bp Lon* **V** C R JENKINS

WISHAW (St Chad) *see* Curdworth, Middleton and Wishaw *Birm*

WISHFORD, GREAT (St Giles) *see* Wylye and Till Valley *Sarum*

WISKE Benefice, The, comprising Birkby, Danby Wiske w Hutton Bonville, Great Smeaton w Appleton Wiske, and the Cowtons *Leeds 19* **P** *MMCET and Bp (jt)* **P-in-c** D W BARTLETT **Hon C** S J GOLDING

WISLEY (not known) w Pyrford *Guildf 12* **P** *Bp* **R** N J AIKEN **C** D DAVIDSON, M R A POTTER

WISSETT (St Andrew) *see* Blyth Valley *St E*

WISSEY VALLEY Benefice, The, comprising Barton Bendish, Beachamwell w Shingham, Boughton, Methwold, Wereham, West Dereham, Whittington, and Wretton w Stoke Ferry *Ely 9* **P** *Ld Chan (1 turn), Bp, DBP and Ch Patr Trust (2 turns)* **C** C A NICHOLAS-LETCH **NSM** I J MACK, R M BURMAN

WISSINGTON (St Mary the Virgin) *see* Stoke by Nayland w Leavenheath etc *St E*

WISTANSTOW (Holy Trinity) *see* Craven Arms *Heref*

WISTASTON (St Mary) *Ches 15* **P** *Trustees* **R** M F TURNBULL **C** P A NORTH

WISTOW (All Saints) *see* Cawood w Ryther and Wistow *York*

WISTOW (St John the Baptist) *see* Warboys w Broughton and Bury w Wistow *Ely*

WISTOW (St Wistan) *Leic 3* **P** *Bp and The Hon Ann Brooks (jt)* **V** P J O'REILLY **C** S D MATTHEWS

WITCHAM (St Martin) w Mepal *Ely 8* **P** *D&C* **R** M HANCOCK

WITCHAMPTON (St Mary and St Cuthberga and All Saints) *see* Wimborne Minster and Villages *Sarum*

WITCHFORD (St Andrew) w Wentworth *Ely 8* **P** *D&C* **NSM** J STIMPSON

WITCHINGHAM GREAT (St Mary) *see* Reepham and Wensum Valley *Nor*

WITCOMBE, GREAT (St Mary) *see* Badgeworth, Shurdington and Witcombe w Bentham *Glouc*

WITHAM (St Nicolas) and Villages, including Fairstead, Faulkbourne, Rivenhall and Silver End, Terling, and White Notley *Chelmsf 23* **P** *Patr Bd* **TR** J L PRITCHARD **TV** P E WATKIN **C** C A NEWMARCH, W J ABBOTT **NSM** S M MALAM

WITHAM FRIARY (Blessed Virgin Mary and St John the Baptist and All Saints) *see* Nunney and Witham Friary, Marston Bigot etc *B & W*

WITHAM, NORTH (St Mary) *see* Bytham Par *Linc*

WITHAM, SOUTH (St John the Baptist) *as above*

WITHAM-ON-THE-HILL (St Andrew) *see* Edenham w Witham on the Hill and Swinstead *Linc*

WITHAMSIDE, comprising Aubourn, Bassingham, Carlton-le-Moorland, Norton Disney, Stapleford, and Thurlby *Linc 12* **P** *Lady Jean Nevile, CCC Ox, Lord Middleton, Bp, and W R S Brown Esq (jt)* **R** D L FREEMAN

WITHCALL (St Martin) *see* Legbourne and Wold Marsh *Linc*

WITHERIDGE (St John the Baptist) *see* Burrington, Chawleigh, Cheldon, Chulmleigh etc *Ex*

WITHERLEY (St Peter) *see* Fenn Lanes Gp *Leic*

WITHERNWICK (St Alban) *see* Aldbrough, Mappleton w Goxhill and Withernwick *York*

WITHERSDALE (St Mary Magdalene) *see* Sancroft *St E*

WITHERSFIELD (St Mary the Virgin) *see* Haverhill w Withersfield *St E*

WITHERSLACK (St Paul) *Carl 10* **P** *DBP* **V** M D WOODCOCK **Hon C** S C HOWARD **NSM** M L WOODCOCK

WITHIEL (St Clement) *see* St Wenn and Withiel *Truro*

WITHIEL FLOREY (St Mary Magdalene) *see* Dulverton w Brushford, Brompton Regis etc *B & W*

WITHINGTON (St Christopher) *see* W Didsbury and Withington St Chris *Man*

WITHINGTON (St Crispin) *Man 2* **P** *Bp* **R** P C S DAVIES

WITHINGTON (St John the Baptist) *see* Wrockwardine Deanery *Lich*

WITHINGTON (St Michael and All Angels) *see* Sevenhampton w Charlton Abbots, Hawling etc *Glouc*

WITHINGTON (St Paul) *Man 2* **P** *Trustees* **R** *vacant*

WITHINGTON (St Peter) *see* Bartestree Cross *Heref*

WITHINGTON, LOWER (St Peter) *see* Chelford and Lower Withington w Marthall *Ches*

WITHLEIGH (St Catherine) *see* Washfield, Stoodleigh, Withleigh etc *Ex*

WITHNELL (St Paul) *see* Heapey and Withnell *Blackb*

WITHYBROOK (All Saints) *see* Wolvey, Copston Magna and Withybrook *Cov*

WITHYCOMBE (St Nicholas) *see* Dunster, Carhampton, Withycombe w Rodhuish etc *B & W*

WITHYCOMBE RALEIGH (St John the Evangelist) (St John in the Wilderness) (All Saints) *Ex 1* **P** *Patr Bd* **TR** R SELLERS **TV** S J HOYLE

WITHYHAM (St John the Evangelist) *see* Crowborough St Jo *Chich*

WITHYHAM (St Michael and All Angels) *Chich 16* **P** *Earl De la Warr* **R** J M CAMPBELL

WITHYPOOL (St Andrew) *see* Exmoor *B & W*

WITHYWOOD (shared church) *Bris 1* **P** *Bp* **P-in-c** D A J MADDOX **C** J L BRADSHAW **NSM** P A HUNTER

WITLEY (All Saints) *Guildf 4* **P** *Bp* **V** J O MCKERAN

WITLEY, GREAT (St Michael) *see* Shrawley, Witley, Astley and Abberley *Worc*

WITLEY, LITTLE (St Michael) *as above*

WITNESHAM (St Mary) *see* Westerfield and Tuddenham w Witnesham *St E*

WITNEY (St Mary the Virgin) (Holy Trinity) *Ox 28* **P** *Patr Bd* **TR** T C WRIGHT **TV** V J BRUNNER-ELLIS **C** H R B WHITE **Hon C** M W THOMAS, S J WRIGHT **NSM** J R COLLICUTT MCGRATH

WITTENHAM, LITTLE (St Peter) *see* Dorchester *Ox*

WITTERING (All Saints) *see* Barnack w Ufford, Bainton, Helpston and Wittering *Pet*

WITTERING, EAST (St Anne) *see* Earnley and E Wittering *Chich*

WITTERING, WEST (St Peter and St Paul) and Birdham w Itchenor *Chich 2* **P** *Bp* **R** J R SWINDELLS **NSM** B F HOLBEN, C A A GODDARD, J M MOULD

WITTERSHAM (St John the Baptist) *see* Tenterden, Rother and Oxney *Cant*

WITTON (St Helen) *Ches 6* **P** *Bp* **V** A R RIDLEY

WITTON (St Margaret) *see* Bacton, Happisburgh, Hempstead w Eccles etc *Nor*

WITTON (St Margaret) *see* Gt and Lt Plumstead, Rackheath w Salhouse and Witton *Nor*

WITTON GILBERT (St Michael and All Angels) *see* Dur N *Dur*

WITTON LE WEAR (St Philip and St James) *see* Hamsterley and Witton-le-Wear *Dur*

WITTON, EAST (St John the Evangelist) *see* Middleham w Coverdale and E Witton etc *Leeds*

WITTON, NETHER (St Giles) *Newc 11* **P** *Ld Chan* **P-in-c** F J SAMPLE

WITTON, WEST (St Bartholomew) *see* Penhill *Leeds*

WIVELISCOMBE (St Andrew) and the Hills *B & W 19* **P** *Bp and A H Trollope-Bellew Esq (4 turns), Ld Chan (1 turn)* **R** M J WALKER **NSM** J M GOSLING-BROWN

WIVELSFIELD (St Peter and St John the Baptist) *Chich 8* **P** *DBP* **V** C J POWELL **C** S D J SHOREY

WIVENHOE (St Mary) *Chelmsf 20* **P** *Bp* **R** E B E LAMMENS **C** E RING, S L BATTS-NEALE

WIVERTON IN THE VALE *S'well 5* **P** *CPAS and Bp, Ld Chan (alt)* **R** R E MITCHELL

WIVETON (St Mary) *see* Blakeney w Cley, Wiveton, Glandford etc *Nor*

WIX (St Mary the Virgin) *see* Gt Oakley, Wix, Wrabness etc *Chelmsf*

WIXFORD (St Milburga) *see* Heart of England *Cov*

WIXOE (St Leonard) *see* Stour Valley *St E*

WOBURN (St Mary) w Eversholt, Milton Bryan, Battlesden and Pottesgrove *St Alb 8* **P** *Bedf Estates Trustees* **V** S W NUTH

WOBURN SANDS (St Michael) *St Alb 8* **P** *Bp* **V** D J YOUNG

WOKING (Christ Church) *Guildf 12* **P** *Ridley Hall Cam* **V** A N BEAVIS **C** D V EDWARDS **NSM** M S SMITH, P A SIMPSON

WOKING (St John the Baptist) *Guildf 12* **P** *V Woking St Pet* **V** G A LUCAS **C** P J CHAMBERLIN

WOKING (St Mary of Bethany) *Guildf 12* **P** *V Woking Ch Ch* **V** M G WALLACE **C** R A CLARK, S A TAPP

WOKING (St Paul) *Guildf 12* **P** *Ridley Hall Cam* **V** N P HUTCHINSON **C** S E WATSON

WOKING (St Peter) *Guildf 12* **P** *Patr Bd* **P-in-c** J M G THOMAS **C** S WAAKO

WOKINGHAM (All Saints) *Ox 8* **P** *Bp* **R** D P HODGSON **C** H V HIGGINSON, R MEDLICOTT

WOKINGHAM (St Paul) *Ox 8* **P** *DBP* **R** J LAMEY **C** C L J SMART **NSM** J H A HATTAWAY

WOKINGHAM (St Sebastian) *Ox 8* **P** *Bp* **V** A P MARSDEN

WOLBOROUGH (St Mary) *see* Newton Abbot *Ex*

WOLD (St Andrew) *see* Walgrave w Hannington and Wold and Scaldwell *Pet*

WOLD NEWTON (All Saints) *see* Binbrook Gp *Linc*

WOLD NEWTON (All Saints) *see* Rudston, Boynton, Carnaby etc *York*

WOLDINGHAM (St Agatha) *see* Caterham *S'wark*

WOLDINGHAM (St Paul) *as above*

WOLDMOOR Group of Parishes, The, comprising Holton le Moor, Kirkby w Kingerby, Nettleton, North and South Kelsey, North Owersby, Thornton le Moor, and Usselby *Linc 7* **P** *Bp (3 turns), J M B Young Esq and S B Young Esq (1 turn)* **V** M E C TOYNE

WOLDS GATEWAY Group, The, Aylesby, Beelsby, Hatcliffe, Healing, Irby on Humber, Keelby, Laceby, Riby, and Stallingborough *Linc 4* **P** *DBP, Bp, Earl of Yarborough, J E Spilman Esq and Ridley Hall Cam (jt)* **C** M A HUTSON, P L REEVES

WOLDSBURN, comprising Bainton, Garton on the Wolds, Kilnwick, Kirkburn, Middleton on the Wolds, and North Dalton *York 10* **P** *Abp, St Jo Coll Ox, and A J Page Esq (1 turn), and Ld Chan (1 turn)* **R** J V ANDERSON

WOLFERTON (St Peter) *see* Sandringham w W Newton and Appleton etc *Nor*

WOLFORD (St Michael) *see* S Warks Seven Gp *Cov*

WOLLASTON (St James) *see* Norton and Wollaston *Worc*

WOLLASTON (St Mary) w Strixton and Bozeat and Easton Maudit *Pet 6* **P** *Bp and Marquess of Northn (jt)* **V** A I MORTON

WOLLASTON, GREAT (All Saints) *see* Ford, Gt Wollaston and Alberbury w Cardeston *Heref*

WOLLASTON, GREAT (St John the Baptist) *as above*

WOLLATON (St Leonard) *S'well 8* **P** *Lord Middleton* **R** T J PULLEN

WOLLATON PARK (St Mary) *S'well 9* **P** *CPAS* **V** *vacant*

WOLLESCOTE (St Andrew) *see* Pedmore and Wollescote *Worc*

WOLSINGHAM (St Mary and St Stephen) and Thornley *Dur 7* **P** *Bp* **P-in-c** J P L WHALLEY

WOLSTANTON (St Margaret) *Lich 9* **P** *Bp* **P-in-c** A M THOMAS **C** P M GRIFFIN

WOLSTON (St Margaret) and Church Lawford *Cov 6* **P** *DBP (2 turns), Bp (1 turn)* **V** K J FLANAGAN **Hon C** P A H SIMMONDS

WOLVERCOTE (St Peter) and Wytham *Ox 2* **P** *Ch Ch Ox and Mert Coll Ox (jt)* **V** K A TUCKETT **NSM** S A CROWTHER, W H WHYTE

WOLVERHAMPTON (All Saints) *see* Cen Wolverhampton *Lich*

WOLVERHAMPTON (St Andrew) *Lich 27* **P** *Bp* **V** C L THOMAS

WOLVERHAMPTON (St Chad and St Mark) *see* Cen Wolverhampton *Lich*

WOLVERHAMPTON (St John) *as above*

WOLVERHAMPTON (St Jude) *Lich 27* **P** *CPAS* **V** P S ROBERTSON

WOLVERHAMPTON (St Luke) Blakenhall *Lich 27* **P** *Trustees* **V** R J ESPIN-BRADLEY

WOLVERHAMPTON (St Martin) (St Stephen) *Lich 27* **P** *Bp* **C** R T BROOKS

WOLVERHAMPTON (St Matthew) *Lich 27* **P** *Baldwin Pugh Trustees* **V** M HIRD

WOLVERHAMPTON (St Peter) *see* Cen Wolverhampton *Lich*

WOLVERHAMPTON Pond Lane (Mission Hall) *see* Wolverhampton St Luke *Lich*

WOLVERHAMPTON, CENTRAL (All Saints) (St Chad and St Mark) (St John in the Square) (St Peter) *Lich 27* **P** *Patr Bd* **TR** D W WRIGHT **TV** R G GASTON **C** A K WALSH, H BABIY **NSM** M S HATHORNE, V FAIRCLOUGH

WOLVERLEY (St John the Baptist) *see* Kidderminster Ismere *Worc*

WOLVERTON (Holy Trinity) (St George the Martyr) *Ox 14* **P** *Bp* **R** G S BARROW-JONES

WOLVERTON (St Catherine) *see* Baughurst, Ramsdell, Wolverton w Ewhurst etc *Win*

WOLVERTON (St Mary the Virgin) *see* Arden Valley *Cov*

WOLVEY (St John the Baptist), Copston Magna and Withybrook *Cov 5* **P** *Bp* **V** J M VAUGHAN

WOLVISTON (St Peter) *see* Billingham *Dur*

WOMBOURNE (St Benedict) *see* Smestow Vale *Lich*

WOMBRIDGE (St Mary and St Leonard) *Lich 20* **P** *W J Charlton Meyrick Esq* **P-in-c** K S EVANS

WOMBWELL (St Mary) (St George) *Sheff 12* **P** *Trin Coll Cam* **R** J G ARMSTRONG

WOMERSLEY (St Martin) *Leeds 15* **P** *Earl of Rosse* **V** *vacant*

WONERSH (St John the Baptist) w Blackheath *Guildf 2* **P** *Selw Coll Cam* **V** D PETERS **NSM** K L PAKENHAM

WONSTON (Holy Trinity) *see* Upper Dever *Win*

WONSTON, SOUTH (St Margaret) *see* Lower Dever *Win*

WOOBURN (St Paul) (St Mary) *Ox 18* **P** *Bp* **V** P E F CUDBY

WOOD DALLING (St Andrew) *see* Reepham and Wensum Valley *Nor*

WOOD DITTON (St Mary) w Saxon Street *Ely 4* **P** *Duke of Sutherland* **P-in-c** N A WORMELL

WOOD END (St Chad) *Cov 1* **P** *Ld Chan* **V** B J NASH

WOOD END (St Michael and All Angels) *see* Baxterley w Hurley and Wood End and Merevale etc *Birm*

WOOD GREEN (St Michael) w Bounds Green (St Gabriel) (St Michael-at-Bowes) *Lon 17* **P** *Patr Bd* **TR** I G BOOTH **TV** E YILDIRIM **C** T R SMITH

WOOD GREEN (St Paul) *see* Wednesbury St Paul Wood Green *Lich*

WOOD NORTON (All Saints) *see* Heart of Norfolk *Nor*

WOOD STREET (St Alban) *see* Worplesdon *Guildf*

WOODBASTWICK (St Fabian and St Sebastian) *see* Broadside *Nor*

WOODBOROUGH (St Mary Magdalene) *see* Vale of Pewsey *Sarum*

WOODBOROUGH (St Swithun) *see* Epperstone, Gonalston, Oxton and Woodborough *S'well*

WOODBRIDGE (St John the Evangelist) and Bredfield *St E 16* **P** *Ch Patr Trust (3 turns), and Ld Chan (1 turn)* **NSM** M M E ROBERTS, W HERBERT

WOODBRIDGE (St Mary the Virgin) w Great Bealings *St E 16* **P** *Bp* **R** N J PRIOR

WOODBRIDGE, comprising Brinkworth, Dauntsey, Garsdon, Great Somerford, Lea and Cleverton, and Little Somerford

Bris 6   **P** *Bp, Ch Soc Trust, and Ex Coll Ox (jt)*
R S WILKINSON   **C** M D STONE   **OLM** M J GRAHAM
WOODBURY (Holy Cross)   *see* Axminster, All Saints,
  Axmouth, Chardstock etc *Ex*
WOODBURY (St Swithun)   *see* Aylesbeare, Clyst St George,
  Clyst St Mary etc *Ex*
WOODBURY SALTERTON (Holy Trinity) *as above*
WOODCHESTER (St Mary)   *see* Rodborough, Woodchester
  and Brimscombe *Glouc*
WOODCHURCH (All Saints)   *see* Bethersden w High Halden
  and Woodchurch *Cant*
WOODCHURCH (Holy Cross) *Ches 1*   **P** *DBP*   **R** C J BROAD
  NSM J TUPLIN
WOODCOTE (St Leonard)   *see* Langtree *Ox*
WOODCOTE (St Mark)   *see* Purley St Mark and St Swithun
  S'wark
WOODCOTT (St James)   *see* Hurstbourne Priors, Longparish
  etc *Win*
WOODDITTON (St Mary)   *see* Wood Ditton w Saxon Street
  Ely
WOODEATON (Holy Rood)   *see* Ray Valley *Ox*
WOODFIELD Team Benefice, The, comprising Appleby
  Magna and Swepstone w Snarestone and Norton-juxta-
  Twycross, Donisthorpe, Measham, Normanton le Heath,
  and Packington *Leic 8*   **P** *Patr Bd (6 turns), The Crown (1*
  turn), Ld Chan (1 turn)   **TV** R C TETT   **NSM** W T COLLEY
WOODFORD (All Saints)   *see* Woodford Valley w Archers
  Gate *Sarum*
WOODFORD (Christ Church) *Ches 17*   **P** *W A B Davenport*
  Esq   **V** D J T RUSSELL
WOODFORD (St Barnabas) *Chelmsf 6*   **P** *Bp*   **V** W OBEDOZA
WOODFORD (St Mary the Virgin)   *see* Irthlingborough, Gt
  Addington, Lt Addington etc *Pet*
WOODFORD (St Mary w St Philip and St James) *Chelmsf 6*
  P *Bp*   **R** E M LOWSON
WOODFORD BRIDGE (St Paul) *Chelmsf 6*   **P** *R Woodford*
  V O FRANKLIN
WOODFORD HALSE (St Mary the Virgin)   *see* Aston-le-Walls,
  Byfield, Boddington, Eydon etc *Pet*
WOODFORD VALLEY w Archers Gate, including the
  Durnfords and Wilsford cum Lake *Sarum 14*   **P** *Bp*
  V M J M PERRY
WOODFORD WELLS (All Saints) (St Andrew) *Chelmsf 6*
  P *Trustees*   **V** P G HARCOURT   **C** D D BAKER, G L WILSON,
  M P CASTLETON, T P JEE   **NSM** D J BLACKLEDGE, M D PORTER
WOODFORD, SOUTH (Holy Trinity)   *see* Wanstead H Trin
  Hermon Hill *Chelmsf*
WOODGATE VALLEY (St Francis)   *see* Bartley Green *Birm*
WOODGREEN (St Boniface)   *see* Fordingbridge and Hyde and
  Breamore etc *Win*
WOODHALL SPA Group, including Bucknall, Horsington,
  Kirkstead, Langton in Old Woodhall, and Stixwould *Linc 13*
  P *Bp and DBP (jt)*   **R** J D G SNELLING
WOODHAM (All Saints) *Guildf 12*   **P** *Bp*   **V** I W FORBES
WOODHAM (St Elizabeth of Hungary)   *see* Gt Aycliffe *Dur*
WOODHAM FERRERS (St Mary) and Bicknacre *Chelmsf 9*
  P *Lord Fitzwalter*   **P-in-c** C M BALL
WOODHAM FERRERS, SOUTH (Holy Trinity) (St Mary)
  Chelmsf 9   **P** *Bp*   **V** C M BALL
WOODHAM MORTIMER (St Margaret) w Hazeleigh
  Chelmsf 10   **P** *Bp*   **P-in-c** J WILLMOT
WOODHAM WALTER (St Michael) *Chelmsf 10*   **P** *Ch Soc*
  Trust   **P-in-c** J WILLMOT
WOODHAY, EAST (St Martin)   *see* NW Hants *Win*
WOODHAY, WEST (St Laurence)   *see* Walbury Beacon *Ox*
WOODHORN (no church) w Newbiggin *Newc 11*   **P** *Bp*
  V A D O'GRADY
WOODHOUSE (Christ Church)   *see* Birkby and Woodhouse
  Leeds
WOODHOUSE (St James) *Sheff 1*   **P** *Bp*   **P-in-c** P R ALLEN
  NSM C D I REES, J K FOX, K A GREEN
WOODHOUSE (St Mary in the Elms), Woodhouse Eaves
  and Swithland *Leic 6*   **P** *Ld Chan and DBP (alt)*
  R L C TEMPERLEY-BARNES
WOODHOUSE EAVES (St Paul)   *see* Woodhouse, Woodhouse
  Eaves and Swithland *Leic*
WOODHOUSE PARK (Wm Temple Church)   *see*
  Wythenshawe *Man*
WOODHOUSE St Mark and Wrangthorn *Leeds 12*   **P** *DBP*
  P-in-c A W C SMITH
WOODHOUSES (not known)   *see* Bardsley *Man*
WOODHURST (St John the Baptist)   *see* Somersham w Pidley
  and Oldhurst and Woodhurst *Ely*
WOODINGDEAN (Holy Cross) *Chich 19*   **P** *Bp*   **V** H A ROSE
  NSM A BOUCH
WOODKIRK (St Mary)   *see* W Ardsley *Leeds*

WOODLAND (St John the Baptist)   *see* Ipplepen w Torbryan,
  Denbury, Broadhempston and Woodland *Ex*
WOODLAND (St John the Evangelist)   *see* Broughton and
  Duddon *Carl*
WOODLAND (St Mary)   *see* Lynesack *Dur*
WOODLANDS (All Saints) *Sheff 7*   **P** *Bp*   **V** S J GARDNER
WOODLANDS (Ascension)   *see* Cranborne w Boveridge,
  Edmondsham etc *Sarum*
WOODLANDS (St Katherine) *B & W 3*   **P** *DBP*   **V** C ALSBURY
WOODLANDS (St Mary)   *see* Kemsing and Woodlands *Roch*
WOODLEIGH (St Mary the Virgin)   *see* Thurlestone, S Milton,
  Churchstow etc *Ex*
WOODLEY (Emmanuel) *Ox 7*   **P** *DBP*   **V** S C RIORDAN
WOODLEY (St James)   *see* Southlake *Ox*
WOODLEY (St John the Evangelist) *Ox 7*   **P** *DBP*
  V E MÁRQUEZ-PICÓN, L R SMITH   **C** S P M TEMPLETON
WOODMANCOTE (Mission Church)   *see* Westbourne *Chich*
WOODMANCOTE (St James)   *see* Upper Dever *Win*
WOODMANCOTE (St Mark)   *see* Dursley, Uley, Owlpen etc
  Glouc
WOODMANCOTE (St Peter)   *see* Henfield w Shermanbury
  and Woodmancote *Chich*
WOODMANSEY (St Peter)   *see* Beverley St Jo and St Martin w
  Routh All SS *York*
WOODMANSTERNE (St Peter) *S'wark 24*   **P** *Ld Chan*
  R J M ITUMU
WOODNESBOROUGH (St Mary the Blessed Virgin)   *see*
  Eastry and Woodnesborough *Cant*
WOODNEWTON (St Mary)   *see* Nassington, Apethorpe,
  Thornhaugh etc *Pet*
WOODPLUMPTON (St Anne) *Blackb 9*   **P** *V St Michael's-on-*
  Wyre   **V** *vacant*
WOODRISING (St Nicholas)   *see* High Oak, Hingham and
  Scoulton w Wood Rising *Nor*
WOODSEATS (St Chad) *Sheff 2*   **P** *Bp*   **V** T K HOLE
  C E J LUNN, P M BROWN
WOODSETTS (St George) *Sheff 5*   **P** *Bp*   **V** *vacant*
WOODSFORD (St John the Baptist)   *see* Moreton, Woodsford
  and Crossways w Tincleton *Sarum*
WOODSIDE (St Andrew) *St Alb 12*   **P** *D&C St Paul's*
  P-in-c N K MWANDIA
WOODSIDE (St James) *Leeds 12*   **P** *Bp*   **V** J M F CAIN
WOODSIDE (St Luke)   *see* Croydon Woodside *S'wark*
WOODSIDE GREEN (St Andrew)   *see* Gt Hallingbury and Lt
  Hallingbury *Chelmsf*
WOODSIDE PARK (St Barnabas) *Lon 14*   **P** *Ch Patr Trust*
  V H D KENDAL   **C** A J GLIDDON, A M CLARKE, H L SHANNON,
  M PAVLOU
WOODSTOCK (St Mary Magdalene) and Bladon *Ox 29*
  P *Duke of Marlborough and Bp (jt)*   **R** J R AULD
  NSM A L WADE, S C HENSON
WOODSTON (St Augustine of Canterbury) (Mission
  Church) *Ely 15*   **P** *Bp*   **R** *vacant*
WOODTHORPE (St Mark) *S'well 7*   **P** *Bp*   **V** M H ROBERTS
  C J A BULL
WOODTON (All Saints)   *see* Hempnall *Nor*
WOODVILLE (St Stephen)   *see* Blackfordby and Woodville
  Leic
WOOKEY (St Matthew)   *see* Coxley w Godney, Henton and
  Wookey *B & W*
WOOKEY HOLE (St Mary Magdalene)   *see* Wells St Cuth w
  Wookey Hole *B & W*
WOOL (Holy Rood)   *see* W Purbeck *Sarum*
WOOLACOMBE (St Sabinus)   *see* Ilfracombe, Lee,
  Woolacombe, Bittadon etc *Ex*
WOOLASTON (St Andrew)   *see* Lydney, Woolaston,
  Alvington and Aylburton *Glouc*
WOOLAVINGTON (Blessed Virgin Mary) w Cossington
  and Bawdrip *B & W 13*   **P** *D&C Windsor and J A Church Esq*
  (alt)   **P-in-c** K J WELLS
WOOLBEDING (All Hallows) *Chich 3*   **P** *Bp*   **R** D A WILLIS
WOOLBROOK (St Francis of Assisi)   *see* Sidmouth,
  Woolbrook, Salcombe Regis, Sidbury etc *Ex*
WOOLER (St Mary)   *see* Doddington, Ilderton, Kirknewton
  and Wooler *Newc*
WOOLFARDISWORTHY (Holy Trinity)   *see* Parkham,
  Alwington, Buckland Brewer etc *Ex*
WOOLFARDISWORTHY EAST (St Mary)   *see* N Creedy *Ex*
WOOLFOLD (St James)   *see* Kirklees Valley *Man*
WOOLHAMPTON (St Peter)   *see* Aldermaston and
  Woolhampton *Ox*
WOOLHOPE (St George)   *see* Fownhope w Mordiford,
  Brockhampton etc *Heref*
WOOLLAND (not known)   *see* Hazelbury Bryan and the
  Hillside Par *Sarum*

WOOLLEY (All Saints) *see* Bath St Sav w Swainswick and Woolley *B & W*

WOOLLEY (St Peter) *Leeds 16* P *Bp* P-in-c K A N GREAVES C K J A GOLDSMITH

WOOLPIT (Blessed Virgin Mary) w Drinkstone *St E 6* P *Bp and A Harvie-Clark Esq (alt)* R M R FARRELL

WOOLSTASTON (St Michael and All Angels) *see* Dorrington w Leebotwood, Longnor, Stapleton etc *Heref*

WOOLSTHORPE (St James) *see* Harlaxton Gp *Linc*

WOOLSTON (Church of the Ascension) *see* Warrington E *Liv*

WOOLSTON (St Mark) *Win 13* P *Bp* V M J A NEWTON

WOOLSTONE (All Saints) *see* Uffington, Shellingford, Woolstone and Baulking *Ox*

WOOLSTONE (Holy Trinity) *see* Woughton *Ox*

WOOLSTONE (St Martin) *see* Bishop's Cleeve and Woolstone w Gotherington etc *Glouc*

WOOLTON HILL (St Thomas) *see* NW Hants *Win*

WOOLTON, MUCH (St Peter) *Liv 2* P *Bp* R C J CROOKS C J E PRATT

WOOLVERSTONE (St Michael) *see* Holbrook, Stutton, Freston, Woolverstone etc *St E*

WOOLWICH (St Mary Magdalene and St Andrew) (St Michael and All Angels) *S'wark 1* P *Bp and Keble Coll Ox (jt)* R J VAN DER VALK

WOOLWICH (St Thomas) *see* Charlton *S'wark*

WOOLWICH, NORTH (St John) w Silvertown *Chelmsf 5* P *Bp and Lon Corp (alt)* V J S FRASER NSM P E EJINKONYE

WOORE (St Leonard) and Norton in Hales *Lich 17* P *Bp and CPAS (jt)* C J A MORRIS NSM L J WRAY-WEAR

WOOSEHILL (Community Church) *see* Wokingham St Paul *Ox*

WOOTTON (St Andrew) *see* Abbey Gp *Linc*

WOOTTON (St Edmund) *Portsm 7* P *DBP* R *vacant*

WOOTTON (St George the Martyr) *Pet 4* P *Ex Coll Ox* V L A JEFFREYS

WOOTTON (St Martin) *see* Elham Valley *Cant*

WOOTTON (St Mary the Virgin) *St Alb 9* P *MMCET* V P M ACKROYD C P A YOUNG Hon C A S ATKINS

WOOTTON (St Mary) w Glympton and Kiddington *Ox 29* P *New Coll Ox (2 turns), Bp (1 turn), and Exors E W Towler Esq (1 turn)* R E E S JONES

WOOTTON (St Peter) *Ox 19* P *Bp* V *vacant*

WOOTTON BASSETT (St Bartholomew and All Saints) *see* R Wootton Bassett *Sarum*

WOOTTON BRIDGE (St Mark) *see* Wootton *Portsm*

WOOTTON COURTENAY (All Saints) *see* Dunster, Carhampton, Withycombe w Rodhuish etc *B & W*

WOOTTON FITZPAINE (not known) *see* Golden Cap Team *Sarum*

WOOTTON RIVERS (St Andrew) *see* Vale of Pewsey *Sarum*

WOOTTON ST LAWRENCE (St Lawrence) *see* Oakley w Wootton St Lawrence *Win*

WOOTTON WAWEN (St Peter) *Cov 7* P *K Coll Cam* P-in-c A J HAMPTON NSM J B HOLDEN

WOOTTON, NORTH (All Saints) *see* The Ch in the Woottons *Nor*

WOOTTON, NORTH (St Peter) *see* Pilton w Croscombe, N Wootton and Dinder *B & W*

WOOTTON, SOUTH (St Mary) *see* The Ch in the Woottons *Nor*

WORCESTER (All Saints) *see* Worc St Nic and All SS w St Helen *Worc*

WORCESTER (St Barnabas) (Christ Church) *Worc 4* P *Bp* TR J A WATSON

WORCESTER (St George w St Mary Magdalene) *Worc 4* P *Bp and V Claines (alt)* P-in-c J C MUSSON NSM D P DAVIES, S E POLLARD

WORCESTER (St Helen) *see* Worc St Nic and All SS w St Helen *Worc*

WORCESTER (St Martin in the Cornmarket) w St Swithun and St Paul *Worc 4* P *Patr Bd* V C S BUTLER NSM T J CLARKE

WORCESTER (St Nicholas) *see* Warndon St Nic *Worc*

WORCESTER (St Stephen) *see* Barbourne *Worc*

WORCESTER (St Wulstan) *Worc 4* P *Bp* V S E NORTHALL

WORCESTER CITY WEST (St Clement) (St Michael) (St John in Bedwardine) *Worc 4* P *Patr Bd* TR P J BRADFORD TV S L COTTRILL

WORCESTER PARK (Christ Church w St Philip) *S'wark 23* P *R Cheam* V *vacant*

WORCESTER SOUTH EAST (St Martin w St Peter) (St Mark in the Cherry Orchard) (Holy Trinity w St Matthew) (St Philip and St James) *Worc 4* P *Patr Bd* TR P W HART TV A G STAND, R J FARMER NSM R A PARRY

WORCESTER St Nicholas (All Saints) (St Helen) *Worc 4* P *Patr Bd* V R W JOHNSON C F J OATES, J K FELLOWS, O T GALLACHER

WORCESTERSHIRE WEST RURAL Team Ministry, The, comprising Alfrick and Lulsley, Broadwas, Clifton-upon-Teme, Cotheridge, Crown East, Leigh and Bransford, Lower Sapey, Martley, Rushwick, Shelsley Beauchamp, Shelsley Walsh, Suckley, and Wichenford *Worc 4* P *Patr Bd (2 turns), The Crown (1 turn)* TR D R SHERWIN TV A M POTTER NSM J DENNISTON

WORDSLEY (Holy Trinity) *Worc 5* P *Patr Bd* TR C S JONES C R L ROWSON

WORFIELD (St Peter) *Heref 8* P *Trustees of the late J R S Greenshields Esq* V J H STOKES

WORKINGTON (St John) *Carl 7* P R *Workington* P-in-c F E F WARD

WORKINGTON (St Michael) *Carl 7* P *Mrs E H S Thornely* P-in-c F E F WARD C P J POWELL

WORKSOP (Christ Church) and Shireoaks *S'well 1* P *Bp and CPAS (jt)* V L H DE ANDRADE LIMA C A A T SHIELLS

WORKSOP (St Anne) *S'well 1* P *Bp* V D R GOUGH C R J HANFORD

WORKSOP (St John the Evangelist) *S'well 1* P *CPAS* P-in-c T C STANFORD

WORKSOP (St Paul) *S'well 1* P *Bp* P-in-c N SPICER C J E COOPER

WORKSOP PRIORY (St Mary and St Cuthbert) *S'well 1* P *St Steph Ho Ox* V N SPICER C J E COOPER, J M O VYSE

WORLABY (St Clement) *Linc 8* P *DBP* V *vacant*

WORLDHAM, EAST (St Mary the Virgin) *see* Northanger *Win*

WORLDHAM, WEST (St Nicholas) *as above*

WORLE (St Martin) (St Mark's Church Centre) *B & W 10* P *Ld Chan* TV C G ELMS NSM G C BUNCE

WORLESTON (St Oswald) *see* Acton and Worleston, Church Minshull etc *Ches*

WORLINGHAM (All Saints) *see* Beccles w Worlingham, N Cove and Barnby *St E*

WORLINGTON (All Saints) *see* Forest Heath *St E*

WORLINGTON, EAST (St Mary) *see* Burrington, Chawleigh, Cheldon, Chulmleigh etc *Ex*

WORLINGTON, WEST (St Mary) *as above*

WORLINGWORTH (St Mary) *see* Four Rivers *St E*

WORMBRIDGE (St Peter) *see* Ewyas Harold w Dulas, Kenderchurch etc *Heref*

WORMEGAY (St Michael and All Angels and Holy Cross) *see* W Norfolk Priory Gp *Ely*

WORMELOW HUNDRED, comprising Dewsall w Callow, Little Birch, Llandinabo, Llanwarne, Much Birch, and Much Dewchurch *Heref 7* P *A W Twiston-Davies Esq (1 turn), Bp (3 turns), and Ld Chan (1 turn)* R M JOHNSON

WORMHILL (St Margaret) *see* Tideswell *Derby*

WORMINGFORD (St Andrew), Mount Bures and Little Horkesley *Chelmsf 20* P *Exors J J Tufnell Esq and Keble Coll Ox (jt)* C H GREENLAND, H R COOPER, R G GIBBS, S L HAYWARD NSM P W MANN

WORMINGHALL (St Peter and St Paul) w Ickford, Oakley and Shabbington *Ox 10* P *Bp and Guild of All So (jt)* R D R KABOLEH

WORMINGTON (St Katharine) *see* Winchcombe *Glouc*

WORMLEIGHTON (St Peter) *see* Priors Hardwick, Priors Marston and Wormleighton *Cov*

WORMLEY (Church Room) *see* Broxbourne w Wormley *St Alb*

WORMLEY (St Laurence) *as above*

WORMSHILL (St Giles) *see* Tunstall and Bredgar *Cant*

WORPLESDON (St Mary the Virgin) *Guildf 5* P *Eton Coll* R A B RUSSELL C B J HANSON NSM T J WEIL

WORSALL, HIGH AND LOW (All Saints) *see* Yarm w Kirklevington, Picton and Worsall *York*

WORSBROUGH (St Mary) w Elsecar *Sheff 11* P *DBP and Sir Philip Naylor-Leyland Bt (alt)* V S G CHAPMAN

WORSBROUGH (St Thomas) *see* Worsbrough Common w Worsbrough St Thos *Sheff*

WORSBROUGH COMMON (St Luke) w Worsbrough St Thomas and St James *Sheff 11* P *Bp (2 turns), The Crown (1 turn)* V A BATEMAN

WORSLEY (St Mark) *Man 7* P *Bp* TR A C WHITTLE TV K HOPWOOD OWEN

WORSLEY MESNES (not known) *see* Wigan *Liv*

WORSTEAD (St Mary) *see* N Walsham, Edingthorpe, Worstead and Westwick *Nor*

WORSTHORNE (St John the Evangelist) *see* Holme-in-Cliviger w Worsthorne *Blackb*

WORTH (St Nicholas), Pound Hill and Maidenbower *Chich 9* P *DBP* R M J BOAG C S L UPCHURCH NSM G J SAWYER, G M W PARRY

WORTH (St Peter and St Paul)   *see* Sandwich and Worth *Cant*
WORTH MATRAVERS (St Aldhelm)   *see* St Aldhelm *Sarum*
WORTH MATRAVERS (St Nicholas) *as above*
WORTHAM (St Mary the Virgin)   *see* N Hartismere *St E*
WORTHEN (All Saints)   *see* Westbury, Worthen and Yockleton *Heref*
WORTHING (Christ Church) *Chich 7*   **P** *R Broadwater, Bp and Bp Horsham, Ch Soc Trust, and CPAS (jt)*   **V** D W RENSHAW
WORTHING (St Andrew) *Chich 7*   **P** *Keble Coll Ox*   **P-in-c** T L PESKETT   **C** W J J DELIA
WORTHING (St George) (Emmanuel) *Chich 7*   **P** *Ch Soc Trust*   **V** J B P BROOK
WORTHING (St Margaret)   *see* Heart of Norfolk *Nor*
WORTHING (St Matthew) *Chich 7*   **P** *R Broadwater, Bp and Bp Horsham, Ch Soc Trust, and CPAS (jt)*   **V** P F D TAYLOR
WORTHING, WEST (St John the Divine) *Chich 7*   **P** *Bp*   **V** T L PESKETT   **C** W J J DELIA
WORTHINGTON (St Matthew)   *see* Ashby-de-la-Zouch and Breedon on the Hill *Leic*
WORTH (St Thomas of Canterbury)   *see* Winklebury and Worting *Win*
WORTLEY (St John the Evangelist) and Farnley *Leeds 11*   **P** *Bp and Trustees (jt)*   **P-in-c** C M CORLEY   **C** C M N BALDING
WORTLEY (St Leonard)   *see* Tankersley, Thurgoland and Wortley *Sheff*
WORTON (Christ Church)   *see* Wellsprings *Sarum*
WORTON, NETHER (St James)   *see* Westcote Barton w Steeple Barton, Duns Tew etc *Ox*
WORTON, OVER (Holy Trinity) *as above*
WOTTON (St John the Evangelist)   *see* Abinger and Coldharbour and Wotton and Holmbury St Mary *Guildf*
WOTTON ST MARY WITHOUT (Holy Trinity) *Glouc 2*   **P** *Bp*   **V** *vacant*
WOTTON UNDERWOOD (All Saints)   *see* Bernwode *Ox*
WOTTON-UNDER-EDGE (St Mary the Virgin)   *see* Tyndale *Glouc*
WOUGHTON, comprising Fishermead, Simpson, Woolstone, and Woughton-on-the-Green *Ox 14*   **P** *Bp*   **R** I C HERBERT   **OLM** P NORRIS
WOUGHTON-ON-THE-GREEN (St Mary)   *see* Woughton *Ox*
WOULDHAM (All Saints)   *see* Burham and Wouldham *Roch*
WRABNESS (All Saints)   *see* Gt Oakley, Wix, Wrabness etc *Chelmsf*
WRAGBY (St Michael and Our Lady)   *see* Kinsley w Wragby *Leeds*
WRAGBY Group, The (All Saints), including Holton cum Beckering, Langton by Wragby, Rand, Snelland, and Wickenby *Linc 13*   **P** *Bp, MMCET, and DBP (jt)*   **R** M N HOLDEN
WRAMPLINGHAM (St Peter and St Paul)   *see* Barnham Broom and Upper Yare *Nor*
WRANGLE (St Mary and St Nicholas)   *see* Old Leake w Wrangle *Linc*
WRANGTHORN (St Augustine of Hippo)   *see* Woodhouse and Wrangthorn *Leeds*
WRATTING, GREAT (St Mary)   *see* Stourhead *St E*
WRATTING, LITTLE (St Mary) *as above*
WRATTING, WEST (St Andrew)   *see* Granta Vale Gp *Ely*
WRAWBY (St Mary the Virgin)   *see* Brigg, Wrawby and Cadney cum Howsham *Linc*
WRAXALL (All Saints) *B & W 12*   **P** *Trustees*   **R** *vacant*
WRAXALL (St Mary)   *see* Melbury *Sarum*
WRAXALL, NORTH (St James)   *see* Colerne w N Wraxall *Bris*
WRAXALL, SOUTH (St James)   *see* N Bradford on Avon and Villages *Sarum*
WRAY (Holy Trinity)   *see* E Lonsdale *Blackb*
WRAYSBURY (St Andrew)   *see* Horton and Wraysbury *Ox*
WREAKE, UPPER, comprising Brooksby, Frisby-on-the-Wreake, Hoby, Kirby Bellars, Ragdale, and Rotherby *Leic 2*   **P** *Bp and DBP (jt)*   **P-in-c** D P HARKNETT   **C** C MCALLISTER
WREAY (St Mary)   *see* Dalston w Cumdivock, Raughton Head and Wreay *Carl*
WRECCLESHAM (St Peter) *Guildf 3*   **P** *Bp*   **V** J A DRAKE-SMITH
WRENBURY (St Margaret)   *see* Baddiley and Wrenbury w Burleydam *Ches*
WRENINGHAM (All Saints)   *see* Upper Tas Valley *Nor*
WRENTHAM (St Nicholas), Covehithe w Benacre, Henstead w Hulver and Frostenden *St E 15*   **P** *Susan Lady Gooch*   **V** J M LOFTUS
WRENTHORPE (St Anne)   *see* N Wakefield *Leeds*
WRESSLE (St John of Beverly)   *see* Howden *York*
WRESTLINGWORTH (St Peter)   *see* Dunton w Wrestlingworth and Eyeworth *St Alb*
WRETHAM (St Ethelbert)   *see* Thetford *Nor*

WRETTON (All Saints)   *see* Wissey Valley *Ely*
WRIBBENHALL (All Saints)   *see* Ribbesford w Bewdley and Dowles and Wribbenhall *Worc*
WRIGHTINGTON (St James the Great) *Blackb 4*   **P** *Bp*   **V** S M DNISTRIANSKYJ
WRINGTON (All Saints) w Butcombe and Burrington *B & W 10*   **P** *Patr Bd*   **R** D R GENT   **NSM** A M HEMMING, S HOSKINS
WRITTLE (All Saints) w Highwood *Chelmsf 9*   **P** *New Coll Ox*   **P-in-c** A D CANT
WROCKWARDINE WOOD (Holy Trinity)   *see* Oakengates, Priors Lee and Wrockwardine Wood *Lich*
WROCKWARDINE, The Deanery of (St Peter) *Lich 22*   **P** *Patr Bd*   **TR** D A ACKROYD   **TV** I S NAYLOR   **C** L A KNIGHT   **NSM** C V TOUGH
WROOT (St Pancras)   *see* Epworth Gp *Linc*
WROSE (St Cuthbert) *Leeds 3*   **P** *The Crown*   **C** C R C BAXFIELD   **Hon C** P B STOODLEY
WROTHAM (St George) *Roch 10*   **P** *D&C*   **R** E M A WRIGHT
WROUGHTON (St John the Baptist and St Helen) and Wichelstowe *Bris 7*   **P** *Bp*   **V** P R N HARRISON   **C** C P HUNTER   **OLM** B M ABREY
WROXALL (St John the Evangelist) *Portsm 7*   **P** *Bp*   **P-in-c** K F ABBOTT
WROXETER (St Mary)   *see* Wrockwardine Deanery *Lich*
WROXHAM (St Mary) w Hoveton St John w Hoveton St Peter, Belaugh and Tunstead w Sco' Ruston *Nor 12*   **P** *Bp*   **R** E A JUMP
WROXTON (All Saints)   *see* Ironstone *Ox*
WULFRIC Benefice, The, comprising Crewkerne, Haselbury Plucknett, Misterton, North Perrott, and Wayford *B & W 14*   **P** *Ld Chan (4 turns), Bp and H W F Hoskyns Esq (1 turn)*   **C** J R MORRIS
WYBERTON (St Leodegar) *Linc 21*   **P** *DBP*   **R** S SARVANANTHAN
WYBUNBURY (St Chad) and Audlem w Doddington *Ches 15*   **P** *Bp and Lady Rona Delves Broughton (jt)*   **V** A J FULFORD
WYCH, HIGH (St James) and Gilston w Eastwick *St Alb 15*   **P** *V Sawbridgeworth (2 turns), P T S Bowlby Esq (1 turn)*   **NSM** S A TARRAN
WYCHBOLD (St Mary de Wyche)   *see* Wychebrook *Worc*
WYCHE (All Saints)   *see* Malvern Chase *Worc*
WYCHEBROOK, comprising Feckenham, Stock and Bradley, Stoke Prior, Upton Warren and Wychbold *Worc 6*   **P** *Patr Bd*   **NSM** P HONNIBALL
WYCHERT VALE, comprising Aston Sandford, Cuddington, Haddenham, Kingsey, and Stone w Dinton and Hartwell *Ox 10*   **P** *Bp, D&C Roch, and Grocers' Co (jt)*   **R** C M MESSERVY   **C** P N GROVES   **NSM** J D HAWKINS, P M MANDER   **OLM** N H FEATHERSTON
WYCHLING (St Margaret)   *see* Kingsdown, Creekside and High Downs *Cant*
WYCHNOR (St Leonard) *Lich 1*   **P** *Personal Reps W H Harrison Esq*   **V** J W ALLAN   **C** A J HINES   **NSM** E A WALL
WYCHWOOD, comprising Fifield w Idbury, Milton-under-Wychwood, and Shipton-under-Wychwood *Ox 22*   **P** *Bp*   **V** G P CLEMENT
WYCK RISSINGTON (St Laurence)   *see* Bourton-on-the-Water w Clapton etc *Glouc*
WYCLIFFE (St Mary)   *see* Holmedale *Leeds*
WYCOMBE AND CHADWELL (St Mary)   *see* Ironstone Villages *Leic*
WYCOMBE LANE (St Mary)   *see* Wooburn *Ox*
WYCOMBE MARSH (St Anne and St Peter)   *see* High Wycombe *Ox*
WYCOMBE, HIGH (All Saints) (St Andrew) (St Anne and St Peter) (Christ the Servant King) (St James) (St Mary and St George) *Ox 18*   **P** *Patr Bd*   **TR** H W ELLIS   **TV** C D OWEN, H K GRAHAM, J-S S GALLANT, S P DUST, W J BULL   **C** A J DIXON, G L MORLEY, S RUSSELL   **NSM** E S CARR, P VINEY   **OLM** J LOCK
WYCOMBE, WEST (St Laurence) (St Paul) w Bledlow Ridge, Bradenham and Radnage *Ox 18*   **P** *Bp, DBP, Peache Trustees, and Sir Francis Dashwood Bt (jt)*   **NSM** J S ELLIS, L J RICHARDSON, V J BEAUMONT
WYDDIAL (St Giles)   *see* Hormead, Wyddial, Anstey, Brent Pelham etc *St Alb*
WYE (St Gregory and St Martin) *Cant 2*   **P** *Abp*   **V** R HOLY   **C** L M LAWRENCE   **OLM** L A CROSS
WYE BROOKS Benefice, The, comprising Goodrich, Llangarron, Llangrove, Marstow, Welsh Bicknor, and Welsh Newton w Llanrothal *Heref 7*   **P** *Bp (2 turns), D&C and DBP (2 turns)*   **V** P J BENTHAM   **NSM** R C B JONES
WYE DORE   *see* Madley w Tyberton, Peterchurch, Vowchurch etc *Heref*

WYE REACHES Group, The, comprising Bishopswood, Dixton Newton, Ganarew, and Whitchurch *Heref 7* **P** *Bp (5 turns)*, *Ld Chan (1 turn)* **P-in-c** T G J STARLING **NSM** P A POWDRILL

WYE, SOUTH Rural Parishes, including Ballingham, Dinedor, Holme Lacy, and Little Dewchurch *Heref 7* **P** *Bp (1 turn)*, *D&C (1 turn)*, *Worc Coll Ox (1 turn)* **V** *vacant*

WYESHAM (St James) *see Wye Reaches Gp Heref*

WYFORDBY (St Mary) *see S Framland Leic*

WYKE (Holy Trinity) *see Bruton, Brewham, Pitcombe and Shepton Montague B & W*

WYKE (St Barnabas) *see Win St Barn Win*

WYKE (St Mark) *Guildf 5* **P** *Bp* **V** A R M CRAVEN

WYKE (St Mary the Virgin) *Leeds 3* **P** *Bp* **V** L J WORMSLEY **Hon C** M R M LYONS

WYKE REGIS (All Saints) (St Edmund) *Sarum 4* **P** *D&C* **R** A S KAY

WYKEHAM (All Saints) *see Upper Derwent York*

WYKEHAM: Broughton w North Newington, Epwell w Sibford, Shutford, Swalcliffe, and Tadmarton *Ox 23* **P** *New Coll, Worc Coll, and Lord Saye and Sele (jt)* **R** N BOWLER **NSM** J H TATTERSALL

WYKEN (Holy Cross) *see Caludon H Cross Cov Cov*

WYKEN (St Mary Magdalene) (Church of the Risen Christ) *Cov 1* **P** *Ld Chan and Bp (alt)* **OLM** E A HARRIS

WYLAM (St Oswin) *see Ovingham and Wylam Newc*

WYLDE GREEN (Emmanuel) *Birm 4* **P** *Bp* **V** *vacant*

WYLYE (St Mary the Virgin) *see Wylye and Till Valley Sarum*

WYLYE AND TILL VALLEY, comprising Berwick St James, Great Wishford, Little Langford, South Newton, Stapleford, Steeple Langford, Stockton, Winterbourne Stoke, and Wylye *Sarum 14* **P** *D&C Windsor, Bp, D&C, and DBP (jt)* **P-in-c** J PLOWS **NSM** M V METCALFE

WYLYE VALLEY TEAM, UPPER, comprising Boyton, Codford St Mary, Codford St Peter, Heytesbury w Tytherington and Knook, Norton Bavant, Sherrington, Sutton Veny, and Upton Lovell *Sarum 12* **P** *Patr Bd (5 turns), Ld Chan (1 turn)* **TR** T HOBSON **TV** C G STRIDE **C** J R J HISCOX

WYMERING (St Peter and St Paul) *Portsm 6* **P** *Nugee Foundn* **V** A L WEBB **C** D K JOHNSTON

WYMESWOLD (St Mary) and Prestwold w Hoton *Leic 6* **P** S J Packe-Drury-Lowe Esq and Bp (by turn) **P-in-c** C R WATTS **NSM** F J M COTTON-BETTERIDGE

WYMINGTON (St Lawrence) *see Chellington St Alb*

WYMONDHAM (St Mary and St Thomas) *Nor 7* **P** *Bp* **V** C P RELF-PENNINGTON

WYMONDHAM (St Peter) *see S Framland Leic*

WYMONDLEY, GREAT (St Mary the Virgin) *see St Ippolyts w Gt and Lt Wymondley St Alb*

WYMONDLEY, LITTLE (St Mary the Virgin) *as above*

WYMYNSWOLD (St Margaret) *see Barham Downs w Adisham Cant*

WYNYARD PARK (Chapel) *see Stockton Country Par Dur*

WYRE PIDDLE (St Anne) *see Fladbury, Hill and Moor, Wyre Piddle etc Worc*

WYRE, OVER, comprising Hambleton, Out Rawcliffe, Pilling, Preesall, and Stalmine *Blackb 9* **P** *Bp, V Kirkham, V Garstang St Helen etc, V Lancaster St Mary etc, and H D H Elleston Esq (jt)* **V** A J SHAW **C** N H S BARRACLOUGH **OLM** J M KIRKHAM

WYRESDALE, OVER (Christ Church) *see Dolphinholme w Quernmore and Over Wyresdale Blackb*

WYRLEY, GREAT (St Mark) *Lich 3* **P** R Cannock **V** M JUDSON

WYSALL (Holy Trinity) *see Willoughby-on-the-Wolds w Wysall and Widmerpool S'well*

WYTHALL (St Mary) *Birm 2* **P** R Kings Norton **V** A J FEATHERSTONE

WYTHAM (All Saints) *see Wolvercote and Wytham Ox*

WYTHBURN (not known) *see St John's-in-the-Vale, Threlkeld and Wythburn Carl*

WYTHENSHAWE (St Francis of Assisi) (St Luke) (St Martin) (St Richard of Chichester) (William Temple Church) *Man 2* **P** *Patr Bd* **TR** I C FELLOWS **TV** C D HEWITT **C** C A SCHOFIELD **OLM** G R MILLER

WYTHENSHAWE Lawton Moor (St Michael and All Angels) *see Lawton Moor Man*

WYTHER (Venerable Bede) *Leeds 11* **P** *Bp* **P-in-c** A J PEARSON

WYTHOP (St Margaret) *see Binsey Carl*

WYVERSTONE (St George) *see Bacton w Wyverstone, Cotton and Old Newton etc St E*

WYVILLE (St Catherine) *see Harlaxton Gp Linc*

YAFFORTH (All Saints) *see Lower Swale Leeds*

YALDING (St Peter and St Paul) w Collier Street *Roch 8* **P** *Ld Chan* **V** P A KISH

YANWORTH (St Michael) *see Chedworth, Yanworth and Stowell, Coln Rogers etc Glouc*

YAPHAM (St Martin) *see Barmby Moor Gp York*

YAPTON (St Mary) *see Clymping and Yapton w Ford Chich*

YARCOMBE (St John the Baptist) *see Kilmington, Stockland, Dalwood, Yarcombe etc Ex*

YARDLEY (St Cyprian) Hay Mill *Birm 6* **P** *Bp* **P-in-c** A J W FRENCH

YARDLEY (St Edburgha) *Birm 6* **P** *St Pet Coll Ox* **V** W J SANDS

YARDLEY (St Lawrence) *see Ardeley, Benington, Cottered w Throcking etc St Alb*

YARDLEY GOBION (St Leonard) *see Potterspury w Furtho and Yardley Gobion etc Pet*

YARDLEY HASTINGS (St Andrew), Denton and Grendon w Castle Ashby and Whiston *Pet 6* **P** *Marquess of Northampton and Bp (alt)* **R** M M H SIMPSON **Hon C** J E TEBBY

YARDLEY WOOD (Christ Church) *Birm 2* **P** *Bp* **V** L M GASTON

YARDLEY, SOUTH (St Michael and All Angels) *Birm 6* **P** *Bp* **P-in-c** A J W FRENCH

YARE VALLEY Churches, The, comprising Braydeston, Brundall, and Postwick *Nor 4* **P** *Bp and MMCET (jt)* **R** P-J B LEECH **C** M T LUSCOMBE

YARKHILL (St John the Baptist) *see Hop Churches Heref*

YARLINGTON (Blessed Virgin Mary) *see Camelot Par B & W*

YARM (St Mary Magdalene) w Kirklevington, Picton and Worsall *York 20* **P** *Abp* **R** D R MOORE

YARMOUTH (St James) *see W Wight Portsm*

YARMOUTH, GREAT (St Nicholas) (St Paul) (St Mary) *Nor 6* **P** *Patr Bd* **TR** S W J WARD **TV** J J SANDER-HEYS **C** H LYNCH **NSM** F W CLIFF **OLM** S R ANDREWS

YARNFIELD (Mission Room St Barnabas) *see Cotes Heath and Standon and Swynnerton etc Lich*

YARNSCOMBE (St Andrew) *see Newton Tracey, Horwood, Alverdiscott etc Ex*

YARNTON (St Batholomew) w Begbroke and Shipton-on-Cherwell *Ox 29* **P** *Duke of Marlborough, Bp, and Brasenose Coll Ox (jt)* **R** O R H PETTER

YARWELL (St Mary Magdalene) *see Nassington, Apethorpe, Thornhaugh etc Pet*

YATE (St Mary) *Bris 5* **P** *Bp* **TR** I M WALLACE **TV** I P MACFARLANE **C** H G SNOOK, W K MORRIS **OLM** J L HODGE

YATELEY (St Peter) *Win 5* **P** *Bp* **R** T STOREY **C** F M BAILEY

YATESBURY (All Saints) *see Oldbury Sarum*

YATTENDON (St Peter and St Paul) *see Hermitage Ox*

YATTON (All Saints) *see Cider Churches Heref*

YATTON KEYNELL (St Margaret) *see By Brook Bris*

YATTON MOOR (St Mary the Virgin), including Claverham, Cleeve, Kenn, and Kingston Seymour *B & W 12* **P** *DBF* **TR** T C N SCOTT **TV** N B THOMAS **Hon C** F M BINDING

YAVERLAND (St John the Baptist) *see Seaview, St Helens, Brading and Yaverland Portsm*

YAXHAM (St Peter) *see Mattishall and the Tudd Valley Nor*

YAXLEY (St Mary the Virgin) *see S Hartismere St E*

YAXLEY (St Peter) *Ely 15* **P** *Ld Chan* **V** S L HARE

YEADON (St John the Evangelist) *Leeds 12* **P** *Bp and R Guiseley w Esholt (jt)* **V** R M WALKER **C** C J BROWN

YEALAND CONYERS (St John the Evangelist) *see Warton St Oswald w Yealand Conyers Blackb*

YEALM and Erme *see Brixton, Newton Ferrers, Revelstoke etc Ex*

YEALMPTON (St Bartholomew) *see Brixton, Newton Ferrers, Revelstoke etc Ex*

YEARSLEY (Holy Trinity) *see Crayke w Brandsby and Yearsley York*

YEAVELEY (Holy Trinity) *see Brailsford w Shirley, Osmaston w Edlaston etc Derby*

YEDINGHAM (St John the Baptist) *see Buckrose Carrs York*

YELDEN (St Mary) *see The Stodden Churches St Alb*

YELDHAM, GREAT (St Andrew) *see The Hedinghams and Upper Colne Chelmsf*

YELDHAM, LITTLE (St John the Baptist) *as above*

YELFORD (St Nicholas and St Swithin) *see Lower Windrush Ox*

YELLING (Holy Cross) *see Papworth Ely*

YELVERTOFT (All Saints) *see Crick and Yelvertoft w Clay Coton and Lilbourne Pet*

YELVERTON (St Mary) *see Thurton w Ashby St Mary, Bergh Apton etc Nor*

YELVERTON (St Paul), Meavy, Sheepstor, Walkhampton, Sampford Spiney and Horrabridge *Ex 21* **P** *Bp, D&C*

Windsor and Lord Roborough (1 turn), Duchy of Cornwall (1 turn), Ld Chan (1 turn)   **R** A N THOMAS   **C** P M BELLOWS
YEOFORD CHAPEL (Holy Trinity)   see Crediton, Shobrooke and Sandford etc Ex
YEOVIL (St Andrew) (St John the Baptist) w Kingston Pitney B & W 6   **P** DBP   **R** J DUDLEY-SMITH   **C** B R GRAHAM   **NSM** G C BEVERLY
YEOVIL (St James the Great)   see Preston Plucknett B & W
YEOVIL (St Michael and All Angels) B & W 6   **P** Bp   **V** D R ANDERSON
YEOVIL (St Peter)   see Preston Plucknett B & W
YEOVIL MARSH (All Saints)   see Tintinhull w Chilthorne Domer, Yeovil Marsh etc B & W
YETMINSTER (St Andrew)   see Three Valleys Sarum
YIEWSLEY (St Matthew) Lon 21   **P** V Hillingdon   **V** R C YOUNG   **C** A V BASTIDAS, U KURKALANG
YOCKLETON (Holy Trinity)   see Westbury, Worthen and Yockleton Heref
YORK (All Saints) North Street York 7   **P** D&C   **NSM** J M HANKS
YORK (All Saints) Pavement w St Crux and St Michael Spurriergate York 7   **P** Abp   **P-in-c** E C HASSALL   **NSM** D C E SIMPSON, D J HOBMAN, K G BOULTON, N D M GLADSTONE
YORK (Christ Church)   see Heworth Ch Ch York
YORK (Holy Redeemer)   see Acomb H Redeemer York
YORK (Holy Trinity) Micklegate York 7   **P** D&C   **NSM** D J HOBMAN
YORK (James the Deacon)   see Acomb Moor York
YORK (St Barnabas) York 7   **P** CPAS   **P-in-c** J M A LEE, P R MILLARD   **C** M R WOODCOCK
YORK (St Chad) York 7   **P** Abp   **P-in-c** S L BRAY   **C** J K DAY
YORK (St Clement w St Mary) Bishophill York 7   **P** Abp and D&C (jt)   **C** J K DAY, S L BRAY   **NSM** G J PETERS

YORK (St Denys) York 7   **P** Abp   **P-in-c** E C HASSALL   **NSM** D C E SIMPSON, D J HOBMAN, K G BOULTON, N D M GLADSTONE
YORK (St Helen) Stonegate w (St Martin) Coney Street York 7   **P** Abp   **P-in-c** E C HASSALL   **NSM** D C E SIMPSON, D J HOBMAN, K G BOULTON, N D M GLADSTONE
YORK (St Hilda) York 7   **P** Abp   **V** vacant
YORK (St Lawrence w St Nicholas) York 7   **P** D&C   **P-in-c** A J A ROMANIS   **NSM** D J HOBMAN
YORK (St Luke) York 7   **P** Abp   **NSM** N F SYKES
YORK (St Michael-le-Belfrey) (St Cuthbert) York 7   **P** Abp   **V** M J PORTER   **C** A J BAKER, M J PERKINS, V J EARLL   **NSM** M G SWAFFIELD, W J ROBERTS
YORK (St Olave w St Giles) York 7   **P** Abp   **P-in-c** E C HASSALL   **NSM** D C E SIMPSON, D J HOBMAN, K G BOULTON, N D M GLADSTONE
YORK (St Paul) Holgate Road York 7   **P** CPAS   **R** P R MILLARD   **C** M R WOODCOCK
YORK (St Stephen)   see Acomb St Steph and St Aid York
YORK (St Thomas w St Maurice) York 7   **P** Abp   **P-in-c** A J RYCROFT
YORK Acomb (St Aidan)   see Acomb St Steph and St Aid York
YORK, Rural East   see Rural E York York
YOULGREAVE (All Saints), Middleton, Stanton-in-Peak and Birchover Derby 4   **P** Duke of Devonshire and N B B Davie-Thornhill Esq (jt)   **V** vacant
YOXALL (St Peter)   see Kings Bromley, The Ridwares and Yoxall Lich
YOXFORD (St Peter)   see Yoxmere St E
YOXMERE Benefice, The, comprising Darsham, Dunwich, Middleton cum Fordley, Peasenhall, Sibton, Theberton w Eastbridge, Westleton, and Yoxford St E 14   **P** The Crown (1 turn), Ch Patr Trust, Lady Penelope Gilbey, Shadingfield Property, J K A Brooke Esq, CPAS, and Bp (2 turns)   **V** T H ROGERS   **NSM** B E R JOLLEY
ZEAL MONACHORUM (St Peter) Ex 2   **P** DBP   **R** vacant
ZEALS (St Martin)   see Upper Stour Sarum
ZENNOR (St Senera) Truro 4   **P** Bp   **P-in-c** E V A FOOT

WELSH BENEFICES AND CHURCHES

An index of benefices of the Church in Wales (shown in bold type), together with entries for churches and other licensed places of worship. Where the church name is the same as the benefice (or the first place name in the benefice), the church entry is omitted. Church dedications are indicated in brackets.

The benefice entry gives the full legal name, followed by the diocese, its deanery number (p. 945), and the name(s) and appointment(s) of the clergy serving there. The following are the main abbreviations used; for others see the full list of abbreviations.

C	Curate	**P-in-c**	Priest-in-charge
C-in-c	Curate-in-charge	**Par Dn**	Parish Deacon
Hon C	Honorary Curate	**R**	Rector
Hon Par Dn	Honorary Parish Deacon	**TR**	Team Rector
I	Incumbent	**TV**	Team Vicar
NSM	Non-stipendiary Minister	**V**	Vicar

ABBEY CWMHIR (St Mary the Virgin) *see* Ithon Valley *S & B*
ABERAERON (Holy Trinity) *see* Glyn Aeron (Coastal) *St D*
ABERAMAN (St Margaret) and Cwmaman *Llan 7*
 P-in-c M GIBBON
ABERAVON (St Mary) (Holy Trinity), including Port Talbot
 Llan 8 **TR** N CAHILL **TV** B ANDREWS, M T PATEMAN
ABERBARGOED (St Peter) *see* Upper Islwyn *Mon*
ABERCANAID (St Peter) *see* Merthyr Tydfil St Dav and
 Abercanaid *Llan*
ABERCONWY Mission Area, comprising Bryn Pydew,
 Craigydon, Deganwy, Eglwysbach, Glan Conwy,
 Llanddoget, Llandudno Junction, Llangystenin, Llanrhos,
 Llanrwst, and Penrhyn Bay *St As 5* **I** S B ERLANDSON
 TV S F HILDRETH **C** B LINES, E PARRY, J FRASER
 Hon C V A BURTON
ABERCRAF (St David) *see* Cwmtawe Uchaf *S & B*
ABERCYNON (St Donat) (St Gwynno) *Llan 7* **V** P A LEWIS
ABERDARE (St Fagan) *Llan 7* **V** R A GREEN
ABERDARE (St John the Baptist) (St Elvan) (St Matthew)
 (St John the Evangelist) *Llan 7* **V** R E DAVIES
ABERDARON (St Hywyn) *see* Bro Enlli *Ban*
ABERDYFI (St Peter) *see* Bro Ystumanner *Ban*
ABEREDW (St Cewydd) *see* Erwood Gp w Painscastle Gp
 S & B
ABERERCH (St Cawrdaf) *see* Bro Eifionydd *Ban*
ABERFFRAW (St Beuno) *see* Bro Cadwaladr *Ban*
ABERGAVENNY (Holy Trinity) (Christ Church) *Mon 1*
 V J R CONNELL **C** J A PEARSE
ABERGAVENNY (St Mary) (Christchurch) w Llanwenarth
 Citra *Mon 1* **V** J R CONNELL **C** J A PEARSE
ABERGELE (St Michael) *see* Aled Miss Area *St As*
ABERGORLECH (St David) *see* Bro Dyfri *St D*
ABERGWILI (St David) *see* Bro Caerfyrddin *St D*
ABERGWYNGREGYN (St Bodfan) *see* Dwylan *Ban*
ABERGYNOLWYN *see* Bro Ystumanner *Ban*
ABERHAFESP (St Gwynog) *see* Cedewain Miss Area *St As*
ABERKENFIG (St John) *see* Llansantffraid, Bettws and
 Aberkenfig *Llan*
ABERMEURIG (St Gartheli) *see* Lampeter *St D*
ABER-MORFA Mission Area, comprising Bodelwyddan,
 Rhuddlan, Rhyl, Rhyl St Ann, and Towyn *St As 1*
 I G R MANSFIELD **C** C M LAWTON, C S SPENCER, J COXALL,
 J CRANE
ABERNANT (St Lucia) *see* Bro Sancler *St D*
ABERNANT (St Matthew) *see* Aberdare *Llan*
ABERPERGWM (St Cadoc) *see* Vale of Neath *Llan*
ABER-PORTH (St Cynwyl) *see* Bro Teifi *St D*
ABERTILLERY (St Michael) w Cwmtillery w Llanhilleth w
 Six Bells *Mon 8* **V** *vacant*
ABERTYSSWG (St Paul) *see* Rhymney *Mon*
ABERYSKIR (St Mary and St Cynidr) *see* Dan yr
 Eppynt *S & B*
ABERYSTWYTH (Holy Trinity) (St Anne) (St Mary)
 (St Michael) Local Ministry Area *St D 8* **P-in-c** C J REES,
 E M REES, M S ANSELL **C** R R D EVANS **NSM** R WILKINSON
AFAN VALE *see* Glyncorrwg and the Upper Afan Valley etc
 Llan
ALED Mission Area, comprising Abergele, Betws-yn-Rhos w
 Trofarth, Brynymaen, Colwyn, Colwyn Bay, Llanddulas,
 Llandrillo-yn-Rhos, Llanelian, Llysfaen, Petryal, and
 St George *St As 5* **P-in-c** G COOPER, J E BROWN,
 P N BARRATT **TV** C R OWEN, K A JOHNSON
 NSM C A THOMAS, J SEARL, S STOREY
ALLTMAWR (St Mauritius) *see* Buallt *S & B*

ALLTWEN (St John the Baptist) *see* Cilybebyll *Llan*
ALYN Mission Area, comprising Broughton w Berse, Brymbo,
 Bwlchgwyn, Gresford, Gwersyllt, Holt, Isycoed, Llay, Minera
 w Coedpoeth, Rossett, and Southsea *St As 11*
 I P R-M DE G GOWER **TV** H BUTLER, J P HARRIS, J T HUGHES,
 W R MARSHALL **C** G BEARWOOD **NSM** S PIERCY, Y PRYCE
AMBLESTON (St Mary) *see* Spittal w Trefgarn and Ambleston
 w St Dogwells *St D*
AMLWCH (St Eleth) *see* Bro Eleth *Ban*
AMMANFORD (All Saints) *see* Bro Aman *St D*
AMMANFORD (St Michael) *as above*
AMROTH (St Elidyr) *see* Narberth and Tenby *St D*
ANGLE (St Mary) *see* S W Pembrokeshire *St D*
ARTHOG (St Catherine) *see* Bro Cymer *Ban*
BAGILLT (St Mary and St Peter) *see* Estuary and Mountain
 Miss Area *St As*
BAGLAN (St Catherine) (St Baglan) *Llan 8*
 P-in-c S JENKYNS **C** E JENKYNS
BALA (Christ Church) *see* Penedeyrn Miss Area *St As*
BANGOR (Eglwys y Groes) *see* Bro Deiniol *Ban*
BANGOR (St David) *as above*
BANGOR (St Mary) *as above*
BANGOR (St Peter) *as above*
BANGOR MONACHORUM (St Dunawd) *see* Maelor Miss
 Area *St As*
BANGOR TEIFI (St David) *see* Dyffryn Teifi *St D*
BARGOED (St Gwladys) and Deri w Brithdir *Llan 3*
 P-in-c R A D LINDSAY
BARMOUTH *see* Bro Ardudwy *Ban*
BARRY (All Saints) (St Cadoc) (St Dyfan and St Teilo)
 (St Mary) *Llan 4* **TR** Z E KING **TV** D S BARNES-DAVIES,
 R C PARRISH **C** C C SEATON
BASSALEG (St Basil) *Mon 5* **TR** C M L STONE
 TV P A GOLLEDGE
BEACON HILL *S & B 2* **V** *vacant*
BEACONS, THE *S & B 1* **P-in-c** K RICHARDS **C** A N JEVONS
 OLM E BRAMLEY
BEAUFORT (St David) *see* Upper Ebbw Valleys *Mon*
BEAUMARIS (St Catherine) *see* Bro Seiriol *Ban*
BEAUMARIS (St Cawrdaf) *as above*
BEAUMARIS (St Mary and St Nicholas) *as above*
BEAUMARIS (St Michael) *as above*
BEAUMARIS (St Seiriol) *as above*
BEDDGELERT (St Mary) *see* Bro Eifionydd *Ban*
BEDWAS (St Barrwg) w Machen w Michaelston-y-Fedw w
 Rudry *Mon 5* **R** D A ROBERTS **NSM** A B PARKES,
 R P MULCAHY
BEDWELLTY (St Sannan) *see* Upper Islwyn *Mon*
BEGELLY (St Mary) *see* Narberth and Tenby *St D*
BERRIEW (St Beuno) *see* Pool Miss Area *St As*
BERSHAM (St Mary) *see* Wrexham *St As*
BETTISFIELD (St John the Baptist) *see* Maelor Miss Area *St As*
BETTWS *see* Dan yr Eppynt *S & B*
BETTWS (St David) *Mon 6* **P-in-c** H J DAVIES
BETTWS (St David) *see* Llansantffraid, Bettws and Aberkenfig
 Llan
BETTWS CHAPEL *see* Llantilio Pertholey w Bettws Chpl etc
 Mon
BETTWS DISSERTH (St Mary) *see* Colwyn *S & B*
BETTWS NEWYDD (not known) *see* Raglan Gp *Mon*
BETWS (Holy Trinity) *see* Glasbury and Llowes w Clyro and
 Betws *S & B*
BETWS (St David) *see* Bro Aman *St D*
BETWS CEDEWAIN (St Beuno) *see* Cedewain Miss Area *St As*

BETWS GARMON (St Garmon) *see* Bro Peblig *Ban*
BETWS LEUCU (St Lucia) *see* Lampeter *St D*
BETWS-Y-COED (St Mary) *see* Bro Gwydyr *Ban*
BETWS-YN-RHOS (St Michael) *see* Aled Miss Area *St As*
BEULAH *see* Blaenau Irfon *S & B*
BIRCHGROVE (St John) *see* Llansamlet *S & B*
BISHOPSTON (St Teilo) *see* Three Cliffs *S & B*
BISHTON (St Cadwaladr) *see* Magor *Mon*
BISTRE (All Saints) *see* Borderlands Miss Area *St As*
BISTRE (Emmanuel) *as above*
BISTRE (St Cecilia) *as above*
BLACKWOOD (St Margaret) *see* Upper Islwyn *Mon*
BLAENAU FFESTINIOG (St David) *see* Bro Moelwyn
  Ban
BLAENAU IRFON *S & B 2* **P-in-c** P M E B BERESFORD-WEBB
BLAENAVON (St Peter) w Capel Newydd *Mon 8*
  P-in-c C R WALTERS
BLAENGWRACH (St Mary) *see* Vale of Neath *Llan*
BLAENPENNAL (St David) *see* Lampeter *St D*
BLAENPORTH (St David) *see* Bro Teifi *St D*
BLAENWYSG *S & B 1* **V** M P WILDING
BLAINA (St Peter) *see* Upper Ebbw Valleys *Mon*
BLEDDFA (St Mary Magdalene) *see* Beacon Hill *S & B*
BLETHERSTON (St Mary) *see* Daugleddau *St D*
BODEDERN (St Edern) *see* Bro Cwyfan *Ban*
BODELWYDDAN (St Margaret) *see* Aber-Morfa Miss Area
  St As
BODEWRYD (St Mary) *see* Bro Padrig *Ban*
BODFARI (St Stephen) *see* Denbigh Miss Area *St As*
BODWROG (St Twrog) *see* Bro Cyngar *Ban*
BONTDDU *see* Bro Ardudwy *Ban*
BONVILSTON (St Mary) *see* E Vale *Llan*
BONYMAEN (St Margaret) *see* Glantawe *S & B*
BORDERLANDS Mission Area, comprising Bistre, Broughton,
  Buckley, Connah's Quay, Ewloe, Hawarden, Hope,
  Llanfynydd, Pentrobin, Sandycroft, Sealand, and Shotton
  St As 13 **I** M J BATCHELOR **P-in-c** A O MAYES, P POWELL
  TV A R PAWLEY, A S JONES, D B EVANS, N A KELLY, S D GREEN
  C G K STANNING, G L ERLANDSON, H DAWSON
  NSM A CRONIN, G WOODWARD, S BAIRD
BOSHERSTON (St Michael) *see* S W Pembrokeshire *St D*
BOTWNNOG (St Beuno) *see* Bro Madryn *Ban*
BOUGHROOD (St Cynog) *see* Llandefalle and Llyswen w
  Boughrood etc *S & B*
BRACKLA (St Mary) *see* Coity, Nolton and Brackla w
  Coychurch *Llan*
BRAWDY (St David) *see* Gtr Dewisland *St D*
BRECHFA (St Teilo) *see* Bro Dinefwr *St D*
BRECON (Cathedral of St John the Evangelist) *S & B 1*
  V vacant
BRECON (St David) w Llanspyddid and Llanilltyd *S & B 1*
  V vacant
BRECON (St Mary) *S & B 1* **P-in-c** S E GRIFFITH
  C A BESSANT **NSM** J M DAY **OLM** G TODD
BRIDELL (St David) *see* Bro Teifi *St D*
BRIDGEND (St Illtud) *see* Newcastle *Llan*
BRIDGEND (St Mary) *see* Coity, Nolton and Brackla w
  Coychurch *Llan*
BRIGHTON, NEW (St James) *see* Mold Miss Area
  St As
BRITHDIR (St David) *see* Bargoed and Deri w Brithdir
  Llan
BRITHDIR (St Mary) *see* Tanat-Vyrnwy *St As*
BRO AERON MYDR *St D 9* **P-in-c** E DAVIES, R W MASKELL
BRO AMAN, comprising Ammanford, Betws, Brynaman,
  Cwm-Coch, Cwmaman, Cwmgors, Cwmllynfell, Llandybie,
  Llandyfan, and Pontaman *St D 16* **P-in-c** A TEALE,
  C E JONES, S BALE **NSM** D L REES, P N BARROCCU
BRO ARDUDWY, including Caerdeon, Harlech, Llanaber,
  Llanddwywe, Llandecwyn, Llanfair-juxta-Harlech, and
  Llanfihangel-y-Traethau *Ban 3* **V** W A HODGES **C** P ODAM
  NSM L R BAILY
BRO ARWYSTLI, including Llangurig, Llanidloes, Trefeglwys,
  and Camo *Ban 3* **V** A C GWALCHMAI **C** J PRICE
BRO CADWALADR *Ban 1* **V** E C WILLIAMS **NSM** A HUGHES,
  E R ROBERTS, N WEBB
BRO CAERFYRDDIN, comprising Abergwili, Bronwydd Arms,
  Carmarthen, Cynwyl Elfed, Cwmduad, Llangunnor,
  Llanpumsaint, Newchurch, and Pontarsais *St D 17*
  P-in-c D A RICHARDS, G L JONES-HIGGS, M A R HILL
  C M J WEBSTER **NSM** J M BRITTON, K M GODDEN-GRIFFITHS,
  R M MOORE
BRO CELYNNIN *Ban 2* **V** D A PARRY **C** E PARRY
BRO CWYFAN *Ban 1* **R** V S MORRIS
BRO CYBI *Ban 1* **V** A F HERRICK **C** J R BAILEY, N A RIDINGS

BRO CYDWELI, comprising Cwmffrwd, Ferryside, Kidwelly,
  Llanarthne, Llandyfaelog, Llangyndeyrn, Mynyddygarreg,
  and St Ishmaels *St D 18* **P-in-c** D J L ROBERTS,
  H DE GRUCHY, T COPELAND, W J LAMBERT
  NSM E J VOYLE-WILLIAMS
BRO CYFEILIOG and Mawddwy, including Machynlleth and
  Mallwyd *Ban 3* **V** M J BEECROFT **NSM** J M EVANS,
  P N WARD
BRO CYMER, including Arthog, Brithdir, Bryncoedifor,
  Dolgellau, Fairbourne, Llanelltud, Llanfachreth,
  Llangelynnin, and Rhoslefain *Ban 3* **R** T R WEBB
  NSM R L FORD
BRO CYNGAR *Ban 1* **R** S R LEYLAND
BRO DEINIOL, including Conwy and Caerhun *Ban 2*
  TR K L JONES **C** C V JOHN, T J JONES
BRO DINEFWR, comprising Carmel, Cwrt-Henri, Felin-gwm,
  Golden Grove, Llanfihangel Rhos-y-Corn, Llanfihangel-
  Uwch-Gwili, Llanfynydd, Llangathen, Llangwad
  Nantgaredig, and Pontargothi *St D 23* **V** R J PATTINSON
  P-in-c S E JONES **NSM** R NOCK, V A HOPE-BELL
BRO DWYNWEN *Ban 1* **V** R L MOULES-JONES
BRO DYFRI, comprising Abergorlech, Capel Dewi Sant,
  Cilycwm, Cynghordy, Cynwyl Gaeo, Llandovery, Llanfair,
  Llansadwrn, Llansawel, Llanwrda, Manordeilo, Myddfai,
  Rhandirmwyn, Talley, and Ystrad-ffin *St D 19*
  P-in-c E A MCKNIGHT, V R SAYER **C** P J PRITCHARD
  NSM D J THOMAS, P C A MANSEL LEWIS, T B NELSON
BRO EIFIONYDD, including Abererch, Beddgelert, Criccieth,
  Dolbenmaen, Llanarmon, Llangybi, Llanystymdwy,
  Porthmadog, and Treflys *Ban 3* **V** K V WILLIAMS
  NSM N GOLDING
BRO ELETH *Ban 1* **R** K S ELLIS **NSM** P E JONES
BRO ENLLI, including Aberdaron, Llanbedrog, Llanfaerlrhys,
  Llanengan, Llanglan, Llannor, and Pwllheli *Ban 3* **V** A JONES
  C J FLETCHER, M R LEWIS
BRO ERYRI, including Llanberis, Penisarwaun, and Deiniolen
  Ban 2 **C** R W TOWNSEND **NSM** A F C WILCOX
BRO GWENDRAETH, comprising Burry Port, Cross Hands,
  Gorslas, Llandyry, Llanedi, Llannon, Pembrey, Pontyberem,
  Pwll, Saron, Tumble, and Tycroes *St D 11*
  P-in-c D A WILSON, D G DAVIES, N P JONES **C** L F MORGAN
  NSM B RIGG, C MILLS, J B JONES
BRO GWYDYR *Ban 2* **P-in-c** S ELLIOTT
BRO LLIEDI, comprising Dafen, Felin-Foel, Hendy, Llanelli,
  Llangennech, and Llwynhendy *St D 21*
  P-in-c A W COLEMAN, D H E MOSFORD, J FLANAGAN
  NSM G PAYNE, H NICHOLLS, R C LOWE
BRO MADRYN, including Botwnnog, Bryncroes, Edern,
  Llandudwen, Llangwnnadl, Llaniestyn, Nefyn, Pistyll, and
  Tudweiliog *Ban 3* **C** S L ROBERTS
BRO MOELWYN, including Blaenau Ffestiniog, Ffestiniog,
  Maentwrog, Penrhyndeudraeth, and Trawsfynydd *Ban 3*
  V R P BARNES
BRO OGWEN (Christ Church) *Ban 2* **V** J G MATTHEWS
  NSM C E MCCREA
BRO PADARN, comprising Bontgoch, Borth, Capel Bangor,
  Eglwysfach, Llandre, Llanafan, Llanfihangel y Creuddyn,
  Llangorwen, Llantrisant, Penrhyncoch, Ysbyty Cynfyn and
  Ysbyty Ystwyth *St D 10* **P-in-c** A G LOAT **C** L L DAFIS
  NSM F CROXON-HALL, H R EVANS, R G MORRIS
BRO PADRIG *Ban 1* **R** N E STARKEY
BRO PEBLIG, including Bettws Garmon, Caernarfon and
  Griffith's Crossing *Ban 2* **V** D J WILLIAMS
BRO SANCLER, comprising Abernant, Llanfihangel,
  Llangynin, Llangynog, Llanllwch, Llansteffan, Laugharne,
  St Clears, and Trelech a'r Betws *St D 22*
  P-in-c C R LEWIS-JENKINS, E A HOWELLS **C** L J BRADLEY
  NSM C A COURT, H A F BRUCE
BRO SEIRIOL *Ban 1* **V** vacant
BRO TEIFI, comprising Aberporth, Blaenporth, Bridell,
  Brongest, Capel Colman, Cardigan, Cilgerran,
  Llandygwydd, Llanfair Nant-Gwyn, Llangoedmor, Llechryd,
  Manordeifi, Monington, Nevern, St Dogmaels, Y Ferwig,
  and Y Mwnt *St D 11* **P-in-c** C D FROST, J S BENNETT,
  P G B RATCLIFFE **NSM** A G KENT, A M BEMAN, E A ROWE
BRO TYSILIO, including Menai Bridge, Pentraeth, and
  Benllech *Ban 1* **V** R S WOOD **NSM** H JONES, L J RENDLE,
  T AP SION
BRO WYRE, comprising Llanddeiniol, Llanfihangel Lledrod,
  Llangwyryfon, Llanilar, Llanrhystyd, Llansantffraed, Nebo,
  and Tynygraig *St D 12* **P-in-c** A J EVANS, J W SMITH
  NSM T L DAVIS
BRO YSTUMANNER, including Aberdyfi, Bryn-Cruf,
  Llanegryn, Llanfihangel-y-Pennant, Tal-y-Llyn, and Tywyn
  Ban 3 **V** R P HANSFORD **C** G WILLIAMS
  NSM C C TEN WOLDE, S J ROLLINS

BRONINGTON (Holy Trinity) *see* Maelor Miss Area *St As*
BRONLLYS (St Mary) *see* Talgarth w Bronllys w Llanfilo *S & B*
BRONWYDD (St Celynnin) *see* Bro Caerfyrddin *St D*
BROUGHTON (St Mary) *see* Borderlands Miss Area *St As*
BROUGHTON (St Paul) *see* Alyn Miss Area *St As*
BRYMBO (St Mary) *as above*
BRYN (St Tydfil) *see* Llangynwyd w Maesteg *Llan*
BRYN A MOR Mission Area, comprising Cwm, Dyserth,
Ffynnongroyw, Gwaenysgor, Llanasa, Meliden, Prestatyn,
and Trelawnyd *St As 1* **I** D T B LEWIS **P-in-c** D N ASH,
J C HARVEY, T W LIPSCOMB **C** G LACHLANN-WADDELL
BRYN PYDEW (St Katherine) *see* Aberconwy Miss Area
St As
BRYNAMAN (St Catherine) *see* Bro Aman *St D*
BRYNCETHIN *see* Llansantffraid, Bettws and Aberkenfig
Llan
BRYNCOEDIFOR (St Paul) *see* Bro Cymer *Ban*
BRYNCROES (St Mary) *see* Bro Madryn *Ban*
BRYNEGLWYS (St Tysilio) *see* Valle Crucis Miss Area *St As*
BRYNFORD (St Michael) *see* Estuary and Mountain Miss
Area *St As*
BRYNGLAS (All Saints) *see* Newport All SS *Mon*
BRYNGWRAN *see* Bro Cwyfan *Ban*
BRYNGWYN (St Michael) *see* Erwood Gp w Painscastle Gp
S & B
BRYNGWYN (St Peter) *see* Raglan Gp *Mon*
BRYNMAWR (St Mary the Virgin) *S & B 1* **V** *vacant*
BRYNNA *see* Llantrisant *Llan*
BRYNYMAEN (Christ Church) *see* Aled Miss Area *St As*
BUALLT (St Mary) *S & B 2* **OLM** J DAY
BUCKHOLT (St John the Baptist) *see* Rockfield w Monmouth
w Overmonnow etc *Mon*
BUCKLEY (Good Shepherd) *see* Borderlands Miss Area
St As
BUCKLEY (St Matthew) *as above*
BUILTH WELLS (St Mary) *see* Buallt *S & B*
BULWARK (St Christopher) *see* Chepstow *Mon*
BURRY PORT (St Mary) *see* Bro Gwendraeth *St D*
BURTON (St Mary) *see* Roose *St D*
BUTE TOWN (St Aidan) *see* Pontlottyn and Fochriw *Llan*
BUTTINGTON (All Saints) *see* Pool Miss Area *St As*
BWLCH (All Saints) *see* Llyn Safaddan *S & B*
BWLCHGWYN (Christ Church) *see* Alyn Miss Area *St As*
BWLCHYCIBAU (Christ Church) *see* Tanat-Vyrnwy *St As*
BYLCHAU (St Thomas) *see* Denbigh Miss Area *St As*
CADOXTON-JUXTA-BARRY (St Cadoc) *see* Barry *Llan*
CADOXTON-JUXTA-BARRY (St Mary) *as above*
CADOXTON-JUXTA-NEATH (St Catwg) and Tonna *Llan 9*
P-in-c A J M MEREDITH
CAERAU (St Cynfelin) *see* Glyncorrwg and the Upper Afan
Valley etc *Llan*
CAERAU w Ely (St David) (St Timothy) *Llan 2* **V** J L SMITH
CAERDEON (St Philip) *see* Bro Ardudwy *Ban*
CAEREINION Mission Area, comprising Garthbeibio,
Llanerfyl, Llanfair Caereinion, Llangadfan, Llangynyw,
Llanllugan, Manafon, Meifod, Pont Dolanog, and Pont
Robert *St As 7* **I** J E JAMES **NSM** E G JONES
CAEREITHIN (St Teilo) *S & B 3* **V** *vacant*
CAERFALLWCH (St Paul) *see* Estuary and Mountain Miss
Area *St As*
CAERGEILIOG *see* Bro Cwyfan *Ban*
CAERGYBI *see* Bro Cybi *Ban*
CAERHUN (St Mary) *see* Bro Celynnin *Ban*
CAERLEON (St Cadoc) and Llanfrechfa Group, The *Mon 6*
V S A PRATTEN **C** W C TAYLER
CAERNARFON (Feed My Lambs) *see* Bro Peblig *Ban*
CAERNARFON (St Mary) *as above*
CAERPHILLY (St Andrew) *see* Eglwysilan and Caerphilly *Llan*
CAERPHILLY (St Catherine) *as above*
CAERPHILLY (St Martin) *as above*
CAERWENT (St Stephen and St Tathan) *see* Wentwood
Mon
CAERWYS (St Michael) *see* Denbigh Miss Area *St As*
CALDICOT (St Mary) *Mon 3* **TR** D C FRETT, R M REARDON
TV G C HUBBARD
CALLWEN (St John the Baptist) *see* Cwmtawe Uchaf *S & B*
CAMROSE (St Ishmael) *see* Daugleddau *St D*
CANTON (St Catherine) *Llan 1* **V** *vacant*
CANTON (St John) *Llan 1* **R** *vacant*
CANTON Cardiff (St Luke) *Llan 1* **TR** F M WILSON
TV E L REES-KENNY **C** B YATES **NSM** J R JENKINS
CANTREF (St Mary) *see* The Beacons *S & B*
CAPEL (Dewi Sant) *see* Bro Dyfri *St D*
CAPEL COELBREN (Capel Coelbren) *see* Cwmtawe Uchaf
S & B
CAPEL COLMAN (St Colman) *see* Bro Teifi *St D*

CAPEL CYNON (St Cynon) *see* Bro Aeron Mydr *St D*
CAPEL DEWI (St David) *see* Dyffryn Teifi *St D*
CAPEL IFAN (St John the Baptist) *see* Gwendraeth Fawr *St D*
CAPEL LLANILLTERNE (St Ellteyrn) *see* Pentyrch and Capel
Llanillterne *Llan*
CAPEL MAIR *see* Dyffryn Teifi *St D*
CAPEL NEWYDD (St Paul) *see* Blaenavon w Capel Newydd
Mon
CAPEL-Y-FFIN (St Mary) *see* Hay w Llanigon and Capel-y-Ffin
S & B
CARDIFF (Christ Church) Roath Park *Llan 1*
P-in-c T O HUGHES **NSM** J HILLEBERT, S BRYNACH
CARDIFF (Citizen Church) *Llan 1* **P-in-c** R J FOREY
CARDIFF (Dewi Sant) *Llan 1* **V** D C LLOYD
NSM R W LINECAR
CARDIFF (St Andrew and St Teilo) *see* Cardiff Citizen Ch
Llan
CARDIFF (St German) *see* Roath St German *Llan*
CARDIFF (St Luke) *see* Canton Cardiff *Llan*
CARDIFF (St Mary) *Llan 1* **P-in-c** D J ATKINS
CARDIFF (St Michael and All Angels) *see* Cathays *Llan*
CARDIFF (St Saviour) *see* Roath St Sav *Llan*
CARDIFF City Parish (St John the Baptist) *Llan 1*
P-in-c S J JONES **C** L M HANNEY **NSM** R W LINECAR
CARDIGAN (St Mary) *see* Bro Teifi *St D*
CAREW (St Mary) *see* S W Pembrokeshire *St D*
CARMARTHEN (Christ Church) *see* Bro Caerfyrddin *St D*
CARMARTHEN (St John the Evangelist) *as above*
CARMARTHEN (St Peter) *as above*
CARMEL (Eglwys Fair) *see* Bro Dinefwr *St D*
CARNO (St John) *see* Bro Arwystli *Ban*
CARROG (St Ffraid) *see* Valle Crucis Miss Area *St As*
CASCOB (St Michael) *see* E Radnor *S & B*
CASLLWCHWR and Gorseinon *S & B 4* **V** A MORGAN
CASTELLAN *see* Bro Teifi *St D*
CASTLE BYTHE *see* W Cemaes *St D*
CASTLE CAEREINION (St Garmon) *see* Pool Miss Area *St As*
CATHAYS (St Michael and All Angels) *Llan 1*
P-in-c C R DOWNS
CATHEDINE (St Michael) *see* Llyn Safaddan *S & B*
CEDEWAIN Mission Area, comprising Aberhafesp, Betws
Cedewain, Dolfor, Kerry, Llanllwchaiarn and Newtown,
Llanmerewig, Llanwyddelan, Mochdre, and Tregynon
St As 6 **I** N W MORRIS **P-in-c** J M WILKES
CEFN (St Mary) *see* Denbigh Miss Area *St As*
CEFN COED (St John the Baptist) w Vaynor *S & B 1*
P-in-c T J WILLIAMS
CEFN FOREST (St Thomas) *see* Upper Islwyn *Mon*
CEFNLLYS (St Michael) *see* Glan Ithon *S & B*
CELLAN (All Saints) *see* Lampeter *St D*
CEMAES *see* Bro Padrig *Ban*
CEMAES, WEST, comprising Clarbeston Road, Dinas Cross,
Fishguard, Henry's Moat, Letterston, Little Newcastle,
Llanchaer, Llangolman, Llanwnda, Maenclochog,
Manorowen, New Moat, Newport, Pontfaen, Puncheston,
and Trecwn *St D 7* **P-in-c** A T FURSE, C C BROWN,
N A LLEWELLYN **C** J J L SPENCER **NSM** J M ANNIS,
R DAVIES, S BARNETT
CEMAIS (St Tydecho) *see* Bro Cyfeiliog and Mawddwy *Ban*
CENARTH (St Llawddog) *see* Dyffryn Teifi *St D*
CERRIGYDRUDION (St Mary Magdalene) *see* Penedeyrn Miss
Area *St As*
CHEPSTOW (St Mary) *Mon 3* **V** P R AVERAY **C** L RYDER
CHERITON (St Cadoc) *see* N Gower *S & B*
CHIRK (St Mary) *see* Offa Miss Area *St As*
CILCAIN (St Mary) *see* Mold Miss Area *St As*
CILCENNIN (Holy Trinity) *see* Bro Aeron Mydr *St D*
CILFYNYDD (St Luke) *see* Pontypridd *Llan*
CILGERRAN (St Llawddog) *see* Bro Teifi *St D*
CILIAU AERON (St Michael) *see* Bro Aeron Mydr *St D*
CILYBEBYLL (St John the Evangelist) *Llan 9* **P-in-c** J SHAW
CILYCWM (St Michael) *see* Bro Dyfri *St D*
CLOCAENOG (St Foddhyd) *see* Dyffryn Clwyd Miss Area
St As
CLUNDERWEN (St David) *see* E Landsker *St D*
CLYDACH (St Mary) (St Michael) *S & B 3*
C-in-c D T MARTIN
CLYDACH VALE (St Thomas) *see* Tonypandy w Clydach Vale
w Williamstown *Llan*
CLYDAU (St Clydai) *see* E Landsker *St D*
CLYNNOG FAWR (St Beuno) *see* Uwch Gwyrfai Beuno Sant
Ban
CLYRO (St Michael and All Angels) *see* Glasbury and Llowes
w Clyro and Betws *S & B*
CLYTHA *see* Llanarth w Clytha and Llansantffraed etc *Mon*
COCKETT (St Peter) *see* Swansea St Pet *S & B*

COEDKERNEW   *see* Marshfield w St Bride's Wentloog *Mon*

COEDYPAEN (Christchurch)   *see* Usk Min Area *Mon*

COETMOR (Christ Church)   *see* Bro Ogwen *Ban*

COITY (St Mary), Nolton and Brackla w Coychurch *Llan 6*   **R** M KOMOR, M R C THORNE   **C** C HOLLOWAY

COLVA (St David)   *see* New Radnor and Llanfihangel Nantmelan etc *S & B*

COLWINSTON (St Michael), Llandow and Llysworney *Llan 11*   **P-in-c** A M KETTLE

COLWYN *S & B 2*   **C** L M WATSON

COLWYN (St John the Baptist)   *see* Aled Miss Area *St As*

COLWYN BAY (St David) *as above*

COLWYN BAY (St Paul) *as above*

CONNAH'S QUAY (St David's Mission Church)   *see* Borderlands Miss Area *St As*

CONNAH'S QUAY (St Mark) *as above*

CONWY (St Mary and All Saints)   *see* Bro Celynnin *Ban*

CORRIS (Holy Trinity)   *see* Bro Cyfeiliog and Mawddwy *Ban*

CORWEN (St Mael and St Sulien)   *see* Valle Crucis Miss Area *St As*

COSHESTON (St Michael)   *see* S W Pembrokeshire *St D*

COWBRIDGE (Holy Cross) *Llan 11*   **TR** S P ADAMS   **TV** V L ASHLEY   **C** I I YEMM   **NSM** J D PETERS

COYCHURCH (St Crallo)   *see* Coity, Nolton and Brackla w Coychurch *Llan*

CRAI (St Ilid)   *see* Blaenwysg *S & B*

CRAIGYDON (St Paul)   *see* Aberconwy Miss Area *St As*

CREGRINA (St David)   *see* Colwyn *S & B*

CRIBYN (St Silin)   *see* Bro Aeron Mydr *St D*

CRICCIETH (St Catherine)   *see* Bro Eifionydd *Ban*

CRICKADARN (St Mary)   *see* Erwood Gp w Painscastle Gp *S & B*

CRICKHOWELL (St Edmund) w Cwmdu and Tretower *S & B 1*   **V** R Y KHAN

CRIGGION (St Michael)   *see* Pool Miss Area *St As*

CRINDAU (All Saints)   *see* Newport All SS *Mon*

CROESCEILIOG (St Mary)   *see* Cwmbran *Mon*

CROSS HANDS (St Anne)   *see* Bro Gwendraeth *St D*

CROSS INN (Holy Trinity)   *see* Glyn Aeron (Coastal) *St D*

CROSSGATES   *see* Ithon Valley *S & B*

CRUGYBYDDAR (St Peter)   *see* Beacon Hill *S & B*

CRYNANT (St Margaret)   *see* Dulais Valley *Llan*

CWM (St Mael and St Sulien)   *see* Bryn a Mor Miss Area *St As*

CWM (St Paul)   *see* Upper Ebbw Valleys *Mon*

CWMAFAN (St Michael) *Llan 8*   **P-in-c** E JENKYNS   **C** S JENKYNS

CWMAMAN (Christ Church)   *see* Bro Aman *St D*

CWMAMAN (St Joseph)   *see* Aberaman and Cwmaman *Llan*

CWMANN (St James)   *see* Lampeter *St D*

CWMAVON (St Michael)   *see* Cwmafan *Llan*

CWMBACH (St Mary Magdalene) *Llan 7*   **V** *vacant*

CWMBACH LLECHRYD (St John the Divine)   *see* Upper Wye *S & B*

CWMBRAN (St Gabriel) *Mon 8*   **V** N C PERRY   **TV** E E KERL   **C** B SUMMERS   **NSM** F M A EVANS, H D THOMAS, K PARDOE, S M HOBBS

CWMCARVAN (St Clement)   *see* St Maughen's w Llangattock-vibon-Avel w Llanfihangel-ystern-Llewern etc *Mon*

CWM-COCH (St Mark)   *see* Bro Aman *St D*

CWMDARE (St Luke)   *see* Aberdare St Fagan *Llan*

CWMDDAUDDWR (St Bride)   *see* Gwastedyn *S & B*

CWMDDAUDDWR (St Winifred) *as above*

CWMDU (St Michael the Archangel)   *see* Crickhowell w Cwmdu and Tretower *S & B*

CWMDUAD (St Alban)   *see* Bro Caerfyrddin *St D*

CWMFFRWD (St Anne)   *see* Bro Cydweli *St D*

CWMLLYNFELL (St Margaret)   *see* Bro Aman *St D*

CWMPARC (St George)   *see* Pen Rhondda Fawr *Llan*

CWMTAWE UCHAF *S & B 3*   **V** *vacant*

CWMTILLERY (St Paul)   *see* Abertillery w Cwmtillery w Llanhilleth etc *Mon*

CWMYOY (St Martin)   *see* Llanfihangel Crucorney w Oldcastle etc *Mon*

CWRT-HENRI (St Mary)   *see* Bro Dinefwr *St D*

CYFFIG (St Cyffig)   *see* E Landsker *St D*

CYMAU (All Saints)   *see* Borderlands Miss Area *St As*

CYMMER (St John the Evangelist)   *see* Porth Newydd *Llan*

CYNCOED (All Saints) (St Edeyrn) *Mon 5*   **TR** J A HENLEY   **C** J THORNE   **NSM** B A SMITH

CYNIN ELFED (St Cynwyl)   *see* Bro Caerfyrddin *St D*

CYNWYD (St John the Evangelist)   *see* Valle Crucis Miss Area *St As*

CYNWYL GAEO (St Cynwyl)   *see* Bro Dyfri *St D*

DAFEN (St Michael and All Angels)   *see* Bro Lliedi *St D*

DALE (St James)   *see* Roose *St D*

DAN YR EPPYNT *S & B 1*   **P-in-c** M BAILEY

DAROWEN (St Tudur)   *see* Bro Cyfeiliog and Mawddwy *Ban*

DAUGLEDDAU Local Ministry Area *St D 1*   **P-in-c** D R REES, M L OSBORNE, N HOOK   **NSM** H CALE

DEFYNNOG (St Cynog)   *see* Blaenwysg *S & B*

DEGANWY (All Saints)   *see* Aberconwy Miss Area *St As*

DENBIGH (St Marcella)   *see* Denbigh Miss Area *St As*

DENBIGH (St Mary) *as above*

DENBIGH Mission Area, comprising Bodfari, Bylchau, Caerwys, Cefn, Henllan, Llandyrnog, Llangwyfan, Llannefydd, Llanrhaeadr-yng-Nghinmeirch, Nantglyn, Sinan, Trefnant, and Tremeirchion *St As 2*   **I** R SPAREY-TAYLOR   **P-in-c** M D PRITCHARD   **TV** V C ROWLANDS

DENIO (St Peter)   *see* Bro Eifionydd *Ban*

DERI (St Peter)   *see* Bargoed and Deri w Brithdir *Llan*

DEVAUDEN (St James)   *see* Itton and St Arvans w Penterry and Kilgwrrwg w Devauden *Mon*

DEWISLAND, GREATER, comprising Brawdy, Grandston, Hayscastle, Jordanston, Llanhywel, Llanrhian, Mathry, Nolton Haven, Roch, St Nicholas, Upper Solva, Whitchurch, and Wolfscastle *St D 3*   **P-in-c** D C HOARE, M H ROWLANDS   **NSM** D BOLTON, M I PLANT

DIHEWYD (St Vitalis)   *see* Bro Aeron Mydr *St D*

DINAS (Misson) w Penygraig *Llan 10*   **P-in-c** J M THOMAS

DINAS (St Brynach)   *see* W Cemaes *St D*

DINGESTOW (St Dingad)   *see* St Maughen's w Llangattock-vibon-Avel w Llanfihangel-ystern-Llewern etc *Mon*

DINHAM   *see* Wentwood *Mon*

DINMAEL (St Catherine)   *see* Penedeyrn Miss Area *St As*

DISERTH (St Cewydd)   *see* Glan Ithon *S & B*

DOLBENMAEN (St Mary)   *see* Bro Eifionydd *Ban*

DOLFOR (St Paul)   *see* Cedewain Miss Area *St As*

DOLGARROG (St Mary)   *see* Bro Celynnin *Ban*

DOLGELLAU (St Mary)   *see* Bro Cymer *Ban*

DOLWYDDELAN (St Gwyddelan)   *see* Bro Gwydyr *Ban*

DOWLAIS (All Saints) (Christ Church) and Penydarren *Llan 3*   **P-in-c** C A OWEN

DULAIS VALLEY *Llan 9*   **C** E STREET

DWYGYFYLCHI (St David)   *see* Dwylan *Ban*

DWYGYFYLCHI (St Gwynin) *as above*

DWYGYFYLCHI (St Seiriol) *as above*

DWYLAN *Ban 2*   **V** T SAUNDERS

DYFFRYN   *see* Bro Ardudwy *Ban*

DYFFRYN (St Matthew) *Llan 9*   **V** S J BODYCOMBE

DYFFRYN CLWYD Mission Area, comprising Clocaenog, Derwen, Efenechtyd, Gyffylliog, Llanarmon yn Ial, Llanbedr Dyffryn Clwyd, Llanelidan, Llanfair Dyffryn Clwyd, Llanfwrog, Llangynhafal, and Llanychan w Llanynys *St As 3*   **R** H A BRYANT   **TV** J S EVANS, R W CARTER   **C** N QUINN-THOMAS

DYFFRYN HONDDU (St Cynog)   *see* Dan yr Eppynt *S & B*

DYFFRYN TEIFI, comprising Bangor Teifi, Capel Dewi, Cenarth, Cilrhedyn, Llanfihangel-ar-arth, Llandyfriog, Llandysul, Llangeler, Llangynllo, Newcastle Emlyn, and Pen-boyr *St D 13*   **P-in-c** B D TIMOTHY, G M REID, J E PARKER

DYSERTH (St Bridget)   *see* Bryn a Mor Miss Area *St As*

DYSERTH (St Mael and St Sulien) *as above*

DYSERTH (St Michael) *as above*

EAST VALE, The, comprising Bonvilston, Llancarfan, Llantrithyd, Pendoylan, Peterson-super-Ely, St Bride's-super-Ely, St Nicholas, and Welsh St Donats *Llan 11*   **TR** M J DAVIES   **TV** D T MORRIS   **NSM** A COOPER

EBBW VALE (Christchurch)   *see* Upper Ebbw Valleys *Mon*

EDERN (St Edern)   *see* Bro Madryn *Ban*

EFENECHTYD (St Michael)   *see* Dyffryn Clwyd Miss Area *St As*

EGLWYS GYMYN (St Margaret)   *see* E Landsker *St D*

EGLWYS OEN DUW   *see* Blaenau Irfon *S & B*

EGLWYSILAN (St Ilan) and Caerphilly *Llan 3*   **TR** M GREENAWAY-ROBBINS   **TV** P P SMITH   **NSM** M LEWIS

EGLWYSRHOS (St Eleri and St Mary)   *see* Aberconwy Miss Area *St As*

EGLWYSWRW (St Cristiolus)   *see* Bro Teifi *St D*

ELY (St David)   *see* Caerau w Ely *Llan*

ELY (St Timothy) *as above*

ERBISTOCK (St Hilary)   *see* Maelor Miss Area *St As*

ERWOOD Group w The Painscastle Group, The *S & B 2*   **P-in-c** P G KEOWN

ESCLUSHAM (Holy Trinity)   *see* Wrexham *St As*

ESGAIRGEILIOG   *see* Bro Cyfeiliog and Mawddwy *Ban*

ESTUARY AND MOUNTAIN Mission Area, comprising Bagillt, Brynford, Caerfallwch, Flint, Gorsedd, Halkyn, Holywell, Mostyn, Rhescyae, Whitford, and Ysgeifiog *St As 4*   **P-in-c** D A CAWDELL, K L EVANS   **TV** B HARVEY, H N BURGESS   **C** R BATEMAN   **NSM** A HOOPER

EVANCOYD (St Peter)   *see* New Radnor and Llanfihangel Nantmelan etc *S & B*
EWENNY (St Michael)   *see* Glamorgan Heritage Coast *Llan*
EWLOE (Holy Spirit)   *see* Borderlands Miss Area *St As*
EYTON (St Deiniol)   *see* Maelor Miss Area *St As*
FAIRBOURNE (St Cynon)   *see* Bro Cymer *Ban*
FAIRWATER (St Peter) *Llan 2*   **V** C P SUTTON
FAWR   *see* Llandeilo Fawr and Taliaris *St D*
FELINDRE (St Barnabas)   *see* Dyffryn Teifi *St D*
FELIN-FOEL (Holy Trinity)   *see* Bro Lliedi *St D*
FELIN-GWM (St John)   *see* Bro Dinefwr *St D*
FERNDALE (St Dunstan)   *see* Rhondda Fach Uchaf *Llan*
FERRYSIDE (St Thomas)   *see* Bro Cydweli *St D*
FFESTINIOG (St Michael)   *see* Bro Moelwyn *Ban*
FFYNNONGROYW (All Saints)   *see* Bryn a Mor Miss Area *St As*
FISHGUARD (St Mary)   *see* W Cemaes *St D*
FLEMINGSTON (St Michael)   *see* Cowbridge *Llan*
FLEUR-DE-LIS (St David)   *see* Upper Islwyn *Mon*
FLINT (St Mary and St David)   *see* Estuary and Mountain Miss Area *St As*
FLINT (St Thomas)   *as above*
FOCHRIW (St Mary and St Andrew)   *see* Pontlottyn and Fochriw *Llan*
FORDEN (St Michael)   *see* Pool Miss Area *St As*
FREYSTROP (St Justinian)   *see* Roose *St D*
FRONCYSYLLTE (St David)   *see* Offa Miss Area *St As*
GABALFA (St Mark) and Tremorfa *Llan 1*   **V** M J R NELSON
GAERWEN   *see* Bro Cadwaladr *Ban*
GARTHBEIBIO (St Tydecho)   *see* Caereinion *St As*
GARTHMYL (St John's Mission Church)   *see* Pool Miss Area *St As*
GELLIGAER (St Catwg) (St Margaret) *Llan 3*   **P-in-c** G C POWELL
GILESTON (St Giles)   *see* Glamorgan Heritage Coast *Llan*
GILFACH GOCH (St Barnabas)   *see* Tonyrefail w Gilfach Goch *Llan*
GILVACH (St Margaret)   *see* Gelligaer *Llan*
GLADWESTRY (St Mary)   *see* New Radnor and Llanfihangel Nantmelan etc *S & B*
GLAIS (St Paul)   *see* Llansamlet *S & B*
GLAMORGAN Heritage Coast, comprising Ewenny, Gileston, Llanmihangel, Llantwit Major, Marcross, Monknash, St Athan, St Brides Major, St Donats, and Southerndown *Llan 11*   **TR** E C R COUNSELL
   TV C A VAUGHAN, K R PRIME
GLAN ELY (Resurrection) *Llan 2*   **P-in-c** J GOULD
GLAN ITHON *S & B 2*   **R** A PERRIN   **C** B E CURNOW, L MORGAN, P LETSON
GLANGRWYNEY (Mission Church)   *see* Vale of Gwrynne *S & B*
GLANOGWEN (Christ Church)   *see* Bro Ogwen *Ban*
GLANTAWE (St Margaret) (St Peter) *S & B 3*   **V** vacant
GLASBURY (St Peter) (All Saints) and Llowes w Clyro and Betws *S & B 1*   **V** D E THOMAS
GLASCOED (St Michael)   *see* Mamhilad w Monkswood and Glascoed Chapel *Mon*
GLASCOMBE (St David)   *see* Colwyn *S & B*
GLYN   *see* Brecon St David w Llanspyddid and Llanilltyd *S & B*
GLYN AERON (Coastal), comprising Aberaeron, Aberarth, Cross Inn, Henfynyw, Llanina, Llanbadarn Trefeglwys, Llandysiliogogo, Llangranog, Newquay, and Penbryn *St D 14*   **P-in-c** J P LEWIS, M F BAYNHAM   **C** H A EVANS   **NSM** J A MORTON
GLYNCORRWG (St John the Baptist) and the Upper Afan Valley w Caerau St Cynfelyn *Llan 8*   **P-in-c** B J REANEY
GLYNDYFRDWY (St Thomas)   *see* Valle Crucis Miss Area *St As*
GLYNTAFF (St Mary)   *see* Pontypridd *Llan*
GOETRE (St Peter) w Llanover *Mon 4*   **R** J A COLLIER
GOLDCLIFFE (St Mary Magdalen)   *see* Magor *Mon*
GOLDEN GROVE (St Michael)   *see* Bro Dinefwr *St D*
GORSEDD (St Paul)   *see* Estuary and Mountain Miss Area *St As*
GORSEINON (St Catherine)   *see* Casllwchwr and Gorseinon *S & B*
GORS-LAS (St Lleian)   *see* Bro Gwendraeth *St D*
GOVILON (Christchurch) w Llanfoist w Llanellen *Mon 1*   **P-in-c** J R CONNELL
GOWER, NORTH, comprising Cheriton, Gwernffrwd, Llangennith, Llanmadoc, Llanrhidian, Llanyrnewydd, and Penclawdd *S & B 4*   **V** N P DOYLE, T D P ARDOUIN
GOWER, SOUTH WEST *S & B 4*   **R** N P DOYLE   **C** J W DAVIES
GOWERTON (St John the Evangelist)   *see* Pont Gors Fawr *S & B*
GRAIG (St John)   *see* Pontypridd *Llan*
GRANDSTON (St Catherine)   *see* Gtr Dewisland *St D*

GRANGETOWN (St Paul) w Cardiff St Dyfrig and St Samson *Llan 1*   **V** E F OWEN
GRESFORD (All Saints)   *see* Alyn Miss Area *St As*
GRIFFITHSTOWN (St Hilda)   *see* Mid Torfaen *Mon*
GROESWEN (St David)   *see* Pentyrch and Capel Llanilllterne *Llan*
GROSMONT (St Nicholas) and Skenfrith and Llangattock Lingoed and Llanfair Chapel *Mon 1*   **P-in-c** G E BURRETT   **C** M MOORE
GUILSFIELD (St Aelhaiarn)   *see* Pool Miss Area *St As*
GUMFRESTON (St Lawrence)   *see* Narberth and Tenby *St D*
GWAENYSGOR   *see* Bryn a Mor Miss Area *St As*
GWASTEDYN *S & B 2*   **P-in-c** L R SHARPE   **NSM** E RONICLE
GWEHELOG   *see* Usk Min Area *Mon*
GWENDDWR (St Dubricius)   *see* Erwood Gp w Painscastle Gp *S & B*
GWENDRAETH FAWR *St D 11*   **P-in-c** M C CHARLES
GWENLLI (St Mark)   *see* Bro Aeron Mydr *St D*
GWERNAFFIELD (Holy Trinity)   *see* Mold Miss Area *St As*
GWERNFFRWD (St David)   *see* N Gower *S & B*
GWERSYLLT (Holy Trinity)   *see* Alyn Miss Area *St As*
GWRYNNE   *see* Vale of Gwrynne *S & B*
GWYDDELWERN (St Beuno)   *see* Valle Crucis Miss Area *St As*
GWYNFE (All Saints)   *see* Bro Dyfri *St D*
GYFFIN (St Benedict)   *see* Bro Celynnin *Ban*
GYFFYLLIOG (St Mary)   *see* Dyffryn Clwyd Miss Area *St As*
HAFOD (St John)   *see* Cen Swansea *S & B*
HAKIN (St Mary)   *see* Roose *St D*
HALKYN (St Mary the Virgin)   *see* Estuary and Mountain Miss Area *St As*
HANMER (St Chad)   *see* Maelor Miss Area *St As*
HARLECH (St Tanwg)   *see* Bro Ardudwy *Ban*
HAROLDSTON ST ISSELLS (St Issell)   *see* Narberth *St D*
HAROLDSTON WEST (St Madog)   *see* Roose *St D*
HAVERFORDWEST (St Martin)   *see* Daugleddau *St D*
HAVERFORDWEST (St Mary)   *as above*
HAWARDEN (St Deiniol)   *see* Borderlands Miss Area *St As*
HAY (St Mary) (St John) w Llanigon and Capel-y-Ffin *S & B 1*   **V** R D WILLIAMS
HAYSCASTLE (St Mary)   *see* Gtr Dewisland *St D*
HENDY (St David)   *see* Bro Lliedi *St D*
HENEGLWYS (St Llwydian)   *see* Bro Cyngar *Ban*
HENFYNYW (St David)   *see* Glyn Aeron (Coastal) *St D*
HENLLAN (St Sadwrn)   *see* Denbigh Miss Area *St As*
HENLLYS (St Peter)   *see* Cwmbran *Mon*
HENRYD (St Celynin Old Parish Church)   *see* Bro Celynnin *Ban*
HENRY'S MOAT (St Bernard)   *see* W Cemaes *St D*
HEOL-Y-CYW (St Paul)   *see* Llanilid w Pencoed *Llan*
HERBRANDSTON (St Mary)   *see* Roose *St D*
HEYOPE (St David)   *see* Beacon Hill *S & B*
HIGH CROSS (St Anne)   *see* Bassaleg *Mon*
HIRWAUN (St Lleurwg) (St Winifred) *Llan 7*   **P-in-c** P GODSALL
HOLT (St Chad)   *see* Alyn Miss Area *St As*
HOLY ISLAND   *see* Bro Cybi *Ban*
HOLYHEAD (Morawelon)   *see* Bro Cybi *Ban*
HOLYHEAD (St Cybi)   *as above*
HOLYHEAD (St Ffraid)   *as above*
HOLYHEAD (St Gwenfaen)   *as above*
HOLYWELL (Holy Trinity)   *see* Estuary and Mountain Miss Area *St As*
HOLYWELL (St James)   *as above*
HOLYWELL (St Peter)   *as above*
HOPE (St Cynfarch)   *see* Borderlands Miss Area *St As*
HOWEY (St David)   *see* Glan Ithon *S & B*
HUBBERSTON (Holy Spirit)   *see* Roose *St D*
HUBBERSTON (St David)   *as above*
HUNDLETON (St David)   *see* S W Pembrokeshire *St D*
ILSTON (St Illtyd)   *see* Three Cliffs *S & B*
IRFON VALLEY *S & B 2*   **P-in-c** P M E B BERESFORD-WEBB   **NSM** C JONES
ISLWYN, LOWER Ministry Area, comprising Abercarn, Newbridge and Risca *Mon 7*   **V** N GILL   **Hon C** M J JEFFORD   **NSM** M REDWOOD, S T SMITH
ISLWYN, UPPER, comprising Aberbargoed, Bedwellty, Blackwood, Cefn Fforest, Fleur-de-Lis, Mynyddislwyn, New Tredegar, Penmaen, Pontllanfraith and Ynysddu *Mon 7*   **TR** M OWEN   **TV** N S ADAMS, V J BUTLER   **C** L TAYLOR   **Hon C** T MORGAN   **NSM** A NELMES, B JONES, H L REES
ISYCOED (St Paul)   *see* Alyn Miss Area *St As*

ITHON VALLEY, The *S & B 2*　C L MORGAN, L MCKEOWN, R STORER

ITTON (St Deiniol) and St Arvans w Penterry and Kilgwrrwg w Devauden *Mon 3*　V M J GOLLOP NSM M E ZORAB

JEFFREYSTON (St Jeffrey)　*see* Narberth and Tenby *St D*

JOHNSTON (St Peter)　*see* Roose *St D*

JORDANSTON (St Cawrda)　*see* Gtr Dewisland *St D*

KEMEYS COMMANDER (All Saints)　*see* Raglan Gp *Mon*

KENFIG　*see* Pyle w Kenfig *Llan*

KENFIG HILL (St Theodore) *Llan 8*　P-in-c J R H DURLEY

KERRY (St Michael)　*see* Cedewain Miss Area *St As*

KIDWELLY (St Mary)　*see* Bro Cydweli *St D*

KILGWRRWG (Holy Cross)　*see* Itton and St Arvans w Penterry and Kilgwrrwg w Devauden *Mon*

KILLAY (St Hilary) (St Martin) *S & B 4*　V P J GWYNN

KILVEY (All Saints)　*see* Swansea St Thos and Kilvey *S & B*

KNELSTON　*see* SW Gower *S & B*

KNIGHTON (St Edward)　*see* E Radnor *S & B*

LALESTON (St David) and Merthyr Mawr w Penyfai *Llan 6* P-in-c A M BEER

LAMPETER (St Bledrws) (St Peter), including Abermeurig, Blaenpenal, Betws Leucu, Cellan, Cwmann, Llanfair Clydogau, Llancrwys, Llandewi Brefi, Llangeitho, Llanllwni, Llanybydder, Pencarreg, Strata Florida, and Ystrad Meurig *St D 15*　P-in-c M A ROWLANDS　C C HAMILTON, N J A BEE NSM A W LEWIS, T A HACKETT

LAMPETER VELFREY (St Peter)　*see* E Landsker *St D*

LAMPHEY (St Faith and St Tyfei)　*see* S W Pembrokeshire *St D*

LANDORE and Treboeth *S & B 3*　V D JONES

LANDSKER, EAST *St D 2*　P-in-c K G TAYLOR, P H DAVIES

LANGSTONE (not known)　*see* Magor *Mon*

LAUGHARNE (St Martin)　*see* Bro Sancler *St D*

LAWRENNY (St Caradog)　*see* Narberth and Tenby *St D*

LECKWITH　*see* Penarth and Llandough *Llan*

LETTERSTON (St Giles)　*see* W Cemaes *St D*

LISVANE (St Denys) *Llan 1*　V J B GRIFFITHS

LITTLE NEWCASTLE (St Peter)　*see* W Cemaes *St D*

LLANABER (St David)　*see* Bro Ardudwy *Ban*

LLANABER (St John) *as above*

LLANABER (St Mary) *as above*

LLANAELHAEARN (St Aelhaiarn)　*see* Uwch Gwyrfai Beuno Sant *Ban*

LLANAFAN FAWR (St Afan)　*see* Upper Wye *S & B*

LLANALLGO (St Gallo)　*see* Bro Eleth *Ban*

LLANANNO (St Anno)　*see* Ithon Valley *S & B*

LLANARMON (St Garmon)　*see* Bro Eifionydd *Ban*

LLANARMON DYFFRYN CEIRIOG (St Garmon)　*see* Valle Crucis Miss Area *St As*

LLANARMON MYNYD (St Garmon)　*see* Tanat-Vyrnwy *St As*

LLANARMON YN IAL (St Garmon)　*see* Dyffryn Clwyd Miss Area *St As*

LLANARTH (St David)　*see* Bro Aeron Mydr *St D*

LLANARTH (St Teilo) *as above*

LLANARTH w Clytha and Llansantffraed St Bride w Llanddewi Rhyderch and Llangattock-juxta-Usk *Mon 1* P-in-c J HUMPHRIES

LLANARTHNE (St David)　*see* Bro Cydweli *St D*

LLANASA (St Asaph and St Cyndeyrn)　*see* Bryn a Mor Miss Area *St As*

LLANBABO (St Pabo)　*see* Bro Cwyfan *Ban*

LLANBADARN FAWR (St Padarn)　*see* Ithon Valley *S & B*

LLANBADARN FYNYDD (St Padarn) *as above*

LLANBADARN TREFEGLWYS (St Padarn)　*see* Glyn Aeron (Coastal) *St D*

LLANBADARN-Y-GARREG (St Padarn)　*see* Erwood Gp w Painscastle Gp *S & B*

LLANBADOC (St Madog)　*see* Usk Min Area *Mon*

LLANBADRIG (St Padrig)　*see* Bro Padrig *Ban*

LLANBEBLIG (St Peblig)　*see* Bro Peblig *Ban*

LLANBEDR (St Peter)　*see* Bro Ardudwy *Ban*

LLANBEDR DYFFRYN CLWYD (St Peter)　*see* Dyffryn Clwyd Miss Area *St As*

LLANBEDR PAINSCASTLE (St Peter)　*see* Erwood Gp w Painscastle Gp *S & B*

LLANBEDR YSTRAD YW (St Peter)　*see* Vale of Gwrynne *S & B*

LLANBEDR, UPPER (St Peter)　*see* Bro Gwydyr *Ban*

LLANBEDRGOCH (St Peter)　*see* Bro Tysilio *Ban*

LLANBEDROG (St Pedrog)　*see* Bro Enlli *Ban*

LLANBERIS (St Padarn)　*see* Bro Eryri *Ban*

LLANBERIS (St Peris) *as above*

LLANBISTER (St Cynllo)　*see* Ithon Valley *S & B*

LLANBLETHIAN (St Blethian)　*see* Cowbridge *Llan*

LLANBOIDY (St Brynach)　*see* Meidrim and Llanboidy and Merthyr *St D*

LLANBRYN-MAIR (St Mary)　*see* Bro Cyfeiliog and Mawddwy *Ban*

LLANCARFAN (St Cadoc)　*see* E Vale *Llan*

LLANDAFF (Cathedral of St Peter and St Paul w St Dyfrig, St Teilo and St Euddogwy) *Llan 2*　V G H CAPON

LLANDAFF NORTH (All Saints)　*see* Whitchurch *Llan*

LLANDANWG　*see* Bro Ardudwy *Ban*

LLANDAVENNY　*see* Wentwood *Mon*

LLANDDAROG (St Twrog)　*see* Bro Cydweli *St D*

LLANDDEINIOL (St Deiniol)　*see* Bro Wyre *St D*

LLANDDEINIOLEN (St Deiniol)　*see* Bro Eryri *Ban*

LLANDDERFEL (St Derfel)　*see* Penedeyrn Miss Area *St As*

LLANDDEW (St David) *S & B 1*　OLM G TODD

LLANDDEWI　*see* Blaenau Irfon *S & B*

LLANDDEWI (St David)　*see* SW Gower *S & B*

LLANDDEWI ABERARTH (St David)　*see* Glyn Aeron (Coastal) *St D*

LLANDDEWI BREFI (St David)　*see* Lampeter *St D*

LLANDDEWI FACH (St David)　*see* Erwood Gp w Painscastle Gp *S & B*

LLANDDEWI RHONDDA (St David)　*see* Pontypridd *Llan*

LLANDDEWI RHYDDERCH (St David)　*see* Llanarth w Clytha and Llansantffraed etc *Mon*

LLANDDEWI VELFREY (St David)　*see* E Landsker *St D*

LLANDDEWI YSTRADENNI (St David)　*see* Ithon Valley *S & B*

LLANDDEWI'R CWM (St David)　*see* Buallt *S & B*

LLANDDOGET (St Doged)　*see* Aberconwy Miss Area *St As*

LLANDDONA (St Dona)　*see* Bro Seiriol *Ban*

LLANDDOWROR (St Teilo)　*see* Bro Sancler *St D*

LLANDDULAS (St Cynfryd)　*see* Aled Miss Area *St As*

LLANDDWYWE (St Ddwywe)　*see* Bro Ardudwy *Ban*

LLANDECWYN (St Tecwyn) *as above*

LLANDEFAELOG-FACH (St Maelog)　*see* Dan yr Eppynt *S & B*

LLANDEFALLE (St Matthew) and Llyswen w Boughrood and Llanstephen w Talachddu *S & B 1*　R vacant

LLANDEGFAN (St Tegfan)　*see* Bro Tysilio *Ban*

LLANDEGLA (St Tecla)　*see* Valle Crucis Miss Area *St As*

LLANDEGLEY (St Tecla)　*see* Ithon Valley *S & B*

LLANDEGVETH (St Tegfeth)　*see* Caerleon and Llanfrechfa *Mon*

LLANDEILO FAWR (St Teilo) and Taliaris *St D 24* V M S SADLER

LLANDEILO GRABAN (St Teilo)　*see* Erwood Gp w Painscastle Gp *S & B*

LLANDEILO TAL-Y-BONT (St Teilo) (St Michael) *S & B 4* V J N GILLIBRAND

LLANDENNY (St John the Apostle)　*see* Raglan Gp *Mon*

LLANDEUSSANT (St Simon and St Jude)　*see* Bro Dyfri *St D*

LLANDEVAUD (St Peter)　*see* Wentwood *Mon*

LLANDEWI FACH　*see* Caerleon and Llanfrechfa *Mon*

LLANDEWI SKIRRID (St David)　*see* Llantilio Pertholey w Bettws Chpl etc *Mon*

LLANDILO'R FAN (St Teilo)　*see* Blaenwysg *S & B*

LLANDINAM (St Llonio)　*see* Bro Arwystli *Ban*

LLANDINGAT (St Dingad)　*see* Bro Dyfri *St D*

LLANDINORWIG (Christ Church)　*see* Bro Eryri *Ban*

LLANDOGO (St Oudoceus) w Whitebrook Chapel and Tintern Parva *Mon 2*　P-in-c N P JUCKES　OLM J F AVERY, R A DAGGER

LLANDOUGH (St Dochdwy)　*see* Cowbridge *Llan*

LLANDOUGH (St Dochdwy)　*see* Penarth and Llandough *Llan*

LLANDOW (Holy Trinity)　*see* Colwinston, Llandow and Llysworney *Llan*

LLANDRILLO (St Trilio)　*see* Penedeyrn Miss Area *St As*

LLANDRILLO-YN-RHOS (St George)　*see* Aled Miss Area *St As*

LLANDRILLO-YN-RHOS (St Trillo) *as above*

LLANDRINDOD (Holy Trinity)　*see* Glan Ithon *S & B*

LLANDRINDOD (Old Parish Church) *as above*

LLANDRINIO (St Trinio, St Peter and St Paul)　*see* Pool Miss Area *St As*

LLANDRYGARN (St Trygarn)　*see* Bro Cyngar *Ban*

LLANDUDNO (St Tudno) (Holy Trinity) *Ban 2*　V A C SULLY C M K R STALLARD　NSM S RHYS EVANS

LLANDUDNO JUNCTION (St Michael)　*see* Aberconwy Miss Area *St As*

LLANDUDWEN (St Tudwen)　*see* Bro Madryn *Ban*

LLANDULAIS IN TIR ABAD (St David)　*see* Blaenau Irfon *S & B*

LLANDWROG (St Twrog)　*see* Uwch Gwyrfai Beuno Sant *Ban*

LLANDYBIE (St Tybie)　*see* Bro Aman *St D*

LLANDYFAELOG (St Maelog)　*see* Bro Cydweli *St D*

LLANDYFAN (Church)　*see* Bro Aman *St D*

LLANDYFODWG (St Tyfodwg) and Cwm Ogwr *Llan 6* P-in-c J J JENKINS

LLANDYFRIOG (St Tyfriog) *see* Dyffryn Teifi *St D*
LLANDYFRYDOG (St Tyfrydog) *see* Bro Eleth *Ban*
LLANDYGAI (St Ann) *see* Bro Ogwen *Ban*
LLANDYGAI (St Tegai) *as above*
LLANDYGWYDD (St Tygwydd) *see* Bro Teifi *St D*
LLANDYRNOG (St Cwyfan) *see* Denbigh Miss Area *St As*
LLANDYRNOG (St Tyrnog) *as above*
LLANDYRY (Church) *see* Bro Gwendraeth *St D*
LLANDYSILIO (St Mary) *see* Pool Miss Area *St As*
LLANDYSILIO (St Tysilio) *see* Bro Tysilio *Ban*
LLANDYSILIO (St Tysilio) *see* E Landsker *St D*
LLANDYSILIO (St Tysilio) *see* Pool Miss Area *St As*
LLANDYSILIOGOGO (St Tysilio) *see* Glyn Aeron (Coastal)
  St D
LLANDYSSIL (St Tyssil) *see* Pool Miss Area *St As*
LLANDYSUL (St Tysul) *see* Dyffryn Teifi *St D*
LLANEDEYRN (All Saints) *see* Cyncoed *Mon*
LLANEDI (St Edith) *see* Bro Gwendraeth *St D*
LLANEDI (St Edith) w Tycroes and Saron *St D 12*
  P-in-c V K JONES
LLANEDWEN (St Edwen) *see* Bro Dwynwen *Ban*
LLANEGRYN (St Mary and St Egryn) *see* Bro Ystumanner *Ban*
LLANEGWAD (St Egwad) *see* Bro Dinefwr *St D*
LLANEILIAN (St Eilian) *see* Bro Eleth *Ban*
LLANELEN (St Helen) *see* Govilon w Llanfoist w Llanellen
  Mon
LLANELIAN (St Elian) *see* Aled Miss Area *St As*
LLANELIDAN (St Elidan) *see* Dyffryn Clwyd Miss Area *St As*
LLANELLI (St Elli) *S & B 1* **P-in-c** C J BEVAN
LLANELLI (St Elli) *see* Bro Lliedi *St D*
LLANELLI (St Peter) *as above*
LLANELLTUD (St Illtyd) *see* Bro Cymer *Ban*
LLANELWEDD (St Matthew) *see* Colwyn *S & B*
LLANENDDWYN (St Enddwyn) *see* Bro Ardudwy *Ban*
LLANENGAN (St Engan) *see* Bro Enlli *Ban*
LLANERCH AERON (St Non) *see* Bro Aeron Mydr *St D*
LLANERCH-Y-MEDD (St Mair) *see* Bro Eleth *Ban*
LLANERFYL (St Erfyl) *see* Caereinion *St As*
LLANEUGRAD (St Eugrad) *see* Bro Eleth *Ban*
LLANFABON (St Mabon) *see* Treharris, Trelewis, Bedlinog
  and Llanfabon *Llan*
LLANFACHRAETH (St Machraeth) *see* Bro Cwyfan *Ban*
LLANFACHRETH (St Machreth) *see* Bro Cymer *Ban*
LLANFAELOG (St Maelog) *see* Bro Cwyfan *Ban*
LLANFAELRHYS (St Maelrhys) *see* Bro Enlli *Ban*
LLANFAES *see* Brecon St David w Llanspyddid and Llanilltyd
  S & B
LLANFAETHLU (St Maethlu) *see* Bro Padrig *Ban*
LLANFAIR (St Mary) *see* Bro Dyfi *St D*
LLANFAIR (St Mary) *see* Grosmont and Skenfrith and
  Llangattock etc *Mon*
LLANFAIR CAEREINION (St Mary) *see* Caereinion *St As*
LLANFAIR CLYDOGAU (St Mary) *see* Lampeter *St D*
LLANFAIR DISCOED (St Mary) *see* Wentwood *Mon*
LLANFAIR DYFFRYN CLWYD (St Cynfarch and St Mary) *see*
  Dyffryn Clwyd Miss Area *St As*
LLANFAIR KILGEDDIN *see* Raglan Gp *Mon*
LLANFAIR MATHAFARN EITHAF (St Mary) *see* Bro Tysilio *Ban*
LLANFAIR NANT-GWYN (St Mary) *see* Bro Teifi *St D*
LLANFAIR NANT-Y-GOF (St Mary) *see* W Cemaes *St D*
LLANFAIR TALHAEARN (St Mary) *see* Aled Miss Area *St As*
LLANFAIR-AR-Y-BRYN (St Mary) *see* Bro Dyfri *St D*
LLANFAIRFECHAN (Christ Church) *see* Dwylan *Ban*
LLANFAIR-IS-GAER (Old Parish Church) Griffith's Crossing *see*
  Bro Peblig *Ban*
LLANFAIR-IS-GAER (St Mary) *as above*
LLANFAIR-JUXTA-HARLECH (St Mary) *see* Bro Ardudwy *Ban*
LLANFAIRPWLLGWYNGYLLGOGERYCHWYRNDROBW
  LL-LLANTISILIOGOGOGOCH (St Mary) *see* Bro Dwynwen
  Ban
LLANFAIR-YNG-NGHORNWY (St Mary) *see* Bro Padrig *Ban*
LLANFAIR-YN-NEUBWLL (St Mary) *see* Bro Cwyfan *Ban*
LLANFAIR-YN-Y-CWMMWD (St Mary) *see* Bro Dwynwen *Ban*
LLANFALLTEG w Castell Dwyran *St D 15* **V** *vacant*
LLANFAREDD (St Mary) *see* Colwyn *S & B*
LLANFECHAIN (St Garmon) *see* Tanat-Vyrnwy *St As*
LLANFECHAN (St Afan) *see* Irfon Valley *S & B*
LLANFECHELL (St Mechell) *see* Bro Padrig *Ban*
LLANFERRES (St Berres) *see* Mold Miss Area *St As*
LLANFEUGAN (St Meugan) *see* The Beacons *S & B*
LLANFFINNAN (St Ffinan) *see* Bro Cadwaladr *Ban*
LLANFFLEWIN (St Fflewin) *see* Bro Padrig *Ban*
LLANFIHANGEL ABERCYWYN (St Michael) *see* Bro Sancler
  St D
LLANFIHANGEL ABERGWESSIN *see* Blaenau Irfon *S & B*

LLANFIHANGEL ABERYTHYCH (St Michael) *see* Bro Dinefwr
  St D
LLANFIHANGEL BRYNPABUAN (St Michael and All Angels)
  see Upper Wye *S & B*
**LLANFIHANGEL CRUCORNEY (St Michael) w Oldcastle and
  Cwmyoy and Llanthony** *Mon 1* **P-in-c** D J YOUNG
LLANFIHANGEL FECHAN (St Michael) *see* Dan yr Eppynt
  S & B
LLANFIHANGEL GLYN MYFYR (St Michael) *see* Penedeyrn
  Miss Area *St As*
LLANFIHANGEL GOBION (St Michael) *see* Raglan Gp *Mon*
LLANFIHANGEL HELYGEN (St Michael) *see* Glan Ithon *S & B*
LLANFIHANGEL LLEDROD (St Michael) *see* Bro Wyre *St D*
LLANFIHANGEL NANTBRAN (St Michael) *see* Dan yr Eppynt
  S & B
LLANFIHANGEL NANTMELAN (St Michael) *see* New Radnor
  and Llanfihangel Nantmelan etc *S & B*
LLANFIHANGEL PENBEDW (St Michael) *see* Bro Teifi *St D*
LLANFIHANGEL PONTYMOILE (St Michael) *see* Mid Torfaen
  Mon
LLANFIHANGEL RHOS-Y-CORN (St Michael) *see* Bro Dinefwr
  St D
LLANFIHANGEL RHYDITHON (St Michael) *see* Ithon Valley
  S & B
LLANFIHANGEL ROGIET *see* Caldicot *Mon*
LLANFIHANGEL TALYLLYN (St Michael) *see* Llyn Safaddan
  S & B
LLANFIHANGEL TRE'R BEIRDD (St Mihangel) *see* Bro Eleth
  Ban
LLANFIHANGEL YSGEIFIOG (St Michael) *see* Bro Cadwaladr
  Ban
LLANFIHANGEL YSTRAD (St Michael) *see* Bro Aeron Mydr
  St D
LLANFIHANGEL-AR-ARTH (St Michael) *see* Dyffryn Teifi *St D*
LLANFIHANGEL-TOR-Y-MYNYDD (St Michael) *see* Llanishen
  w Trellech Grange and Llanfihangel etc *Mon*
LLANFIHANGEL-UWCH-GWILI (St Michael) *see* Bro Dinefwr
  St D
LLANFIHANGEL-YN-NHYWYN *see* Bro Cwyfan *Ban*
LLANFIHANGEL-Y-PENNANT (St Michael) *see* Bro
  Ystumanner *Ban*
LLANFIHANGEL-YSTERN-LLEWERN (St Michael) *see*
  St Maughen's w Llangattock-vibon-Avel w Llanfihangel-
  ystern-Llewern etc *Mon*
LLANFIHANGEL-Y-TRAETHAU (St Michael) *see* Bro Ardudwy
  Ban
LLANFILO (St Bilo) *see* Talgarth w Bronllys w Llanfilo *S & B*
LLANFOIST (St Ffwyst) *see* Govilon w Llanfoist w Llanellen
  Mon
LLANFRECHFA (All Saints) *see* Caerleon and Llanfrechfa *Mon*
LLANFRYNACH (St Brynach) *see* Cowbridge *Llan*
LLANFRYNACH (St Brynach) *see* The Beacons *S & B*
LLANFWROG (St Mwrog and St Mary) *see* Dyffryn Clwyd
  Miss Area *St As*
LLANFYLLIN (St Myllin) *see* Tanat-Vyrnwy *St As*
LLANFYNYDD (St Egwad) *see* Bro Dinefwr *St D*
LLANFYNYDD (St Michael) *see* Borderlands Miss Area *St As*
LLANFYRNACH (St Brynach) *see* E Landsker *St D*
LLANGADFAN (St Cadfan) *see* Caereinion *St As*
LLANGADOG (St Cadog) *see* Bro Dyfri *St D*
LLANGADWALADR (St Cadwaladr) *see* Bro Cadwaladr *Ban*
LLANGADWALADR (St Cadwaladr) *see* Tanat-Vyrnwy *St As*
LLANGAFFO (St Caffo) *see* Bro Cadwaladr *Ban*
LLANGAMMARCH (St Cadmarch) *see* Irfon Valley *S & B*
LLANGAN (St Canna) *see* Cowbridge *Llan*
LLANGANTEN (St Cannen) *see* Irfon Valley *S & B*
LLANGASTY TALYLLYN (St Gastyn) *see* Llyn Safaddan *S & B*
LLANGATHEN (St Cathen) *see* Bro Dinefwr *St D*
LLANGATTOCK (St Cattwg) and Llangynidr *S & B 1*
  R *vacant*
LLANGATTOCK LINGOED (St Cadoc) *see* Grosmont and
  Skenfrith and Llangattock etc *Mon*
LLANGATTOCK-JUXTA-USK (St Cadoc) *see* Llanarth w
  Clytha and Llansantffraed etc *Mon*
LLANGATTOCK-VIBON-AVEL (St Cadoc) *see* St Maughen's w
  Llangattock-vibon-Avel w Llanfihangel-ystern-Llewern etc
  Mon
LLANGEDWYN (St Cedwyn) *see* Tanat-Vyrnwy *St As*
LLANGEFNI (St Cyngar) *see* Bro Cyngar *Ban*
LLANGEINOR (St Ceinor) and the Garw Valley *Llan 6*
  P-in-c R T PITMAN
LLANGEINWEN (St Ceinwen) *see* Bro Dwynwen *Ban*
LLANGEITHO (St Ceitho) *see* Lampeter *St D*
LLANGELER (St Celer) *see* Dyffryn Teifi *St D*
LLANGELYNNIN (St Celynin) *see* Bro Cymer *Ban*
LLANGENNECH (St Gwynog) *see* Bro Lliedi *St D*

LLANGENNI (St Cenau) *see* Vale of Gwrynne *S & B*
LLANGENNITH (St Cenydd) *see* N Gower *S & B*
LLANGERNYW (St Digain) *see* Aled Miss Area *St As*
LLANGIAN (St Gian) *see* Bro Enlli *Ban*
LLANGIWG *S & B 3* **V** G H GREEN **C** D T MARTIN
NSM S NORTHCOTT
LLANGLYDWEN (St Cledwyn) *see* E Landsker *St D*
LLANGOEDMOR (St Cynllo) *see* Bro Teifi *St D*
LLANGOLLEN (St Collen) *see* Valle Crucis Miss Area *St As*
LLANGOLLEN (St John) *as above*
LLANGOLMAN (St Colman) *see* W Cemaes *St D*
LLANGORSE (St Paulinus) *see* Llyn Safaddan *S & B*
LLANGRANNOG (St Carannog) *see* Glyn Aeron (Coastal)
St D
LLANGRISTIOLUS (St Cristiolus) *see* Bro Cadwaladr *Ban*
LLANGUNNOG *see* Llanishen w Trellech Grange and
Llanfihangel etc *Mon*
LLANGURIG (St Curig) *see* Bro Arwystli *Ban*
LLANGWLLONG (St Anau) *see* Bro Cyngar *Ban*
LLANGWM (St Catherine) *see* Penedeyrn Miss Area *St As*
LLANGWM (St Jerome) *see* Roose *St D*
LLANGWM ISAF (St John) *see* Usk Min Area *Mon*
LLANGWNNADL (St Gwynhoedl) *see* Bro Madryn *Ban*
LLANGWYFAN *see* Denbigh Miss Area *St As*
LLANGWYFAN (St Cwyfan Old Church) *see* Bro Cwyfan *Ban*
LLANGWYFAN (St Cwyfan) *as above*
LLANGWYLLOG (St Cwyllog) *see* Bro Cyngar *Ban*
LLANGWYRYFON (St Ursula) *see* Bro Wyre *St D*
LLANGYBI (St Cybi) *see* Bro Eifionydd *Ban*
LLANGYBI (St Cybi) *see* Lampeter *St D*
LLANGYBI (St Cybi) *see* Usk Min Area *Mon*
**LLANGYFELACH (St David and St Cyfelach) (St Teilo-on-
the-Clase)** *S & B 3* **C** A D PORTER
LLANGYNDEYRN (St Cyndeyrn) *see* Bro Cydweli *St D*
LLANGYNDIR (St Cynidr and St Mary) *see* Llangattock and
Llangyndir *S & B*
LLANGYNHAFAL (St Cynhafal) *see* Dyffryn Clwyd Miss Area
St As
LLANGYNIN (St Cynin) *see* Bro Sancler *St D*
LLANGYNLLO (St Cynllo) *see* Beacon Hill *S & B*
LLANGYNLLO (St Cynllo) *see* Dyffryn Teifi *St D*
LLANGYNNWR (St Ceinwr) *see* Bro Caerfyrddin *St D*
LLANGYNOG *see* Buallt *S & B*
LLANGYNOG (St Cynog) *see* Bro Sancler *St D*
LLANGYNOG (St Cynog) *see* Tanat-Vyrnwy *St As*
LLANGYNWYD (St Cynwyd) (St Tydfil) w Maesteg *Llan 6*
V M H EVANS **C** W G JOHN
LLANGYNYW (St Cynyw) *see* Caereinion *St As*
LLANGYSTENNIN (St Cystenin) *see* Aberconwy Miss Area
St As
LLANHAMLACH (St Peter and St Illtyd) *see* The Beacons
S & B
LLANHARAN (St Julius and St Aaron) *see* Llantrisant *Llan*
LLANHARRY (St Illtud) *as above*
LLANHENNOCK (St John) *see* Caerleon and Llanfrechfa *Mon*
LLANHILLETH (St Mark) *see* Abertillery w Cwmtillery w
Llanhilleth etc *Mon*
LLANHYWEL (St Hywel) *see* Gtr Dewisland *St D*
LLANIDAN (St Nidan) *see* Bro Dwynwen *Ban*
LLANIDLOES (St Idloes) *see* Bro Arwystli *Ban*
LLANIESTYN (St Iestyn) *see* Bro Madryn *Ban*
LLANIESTYN (St Iestyn) *see* Bro Seiriol *Ban*
LLANIGON (St Eigon) *see* Hay w Llanigon and Capel-y-Ffin
S & B
LLANILAR (St Hilary) *see* Bro Wyre *St D*
LLANILID (St Illid and St Curig) w Pencoed *Llan 6*
R I M HODGES **NSM** G OGLESBEE
LLANINA (St Ina) *see* Glyn Aeron (Coastal) *St D*
LLANISHEN (Christ Church) *see* Cardiff Ch Ch Roath Park
Llan
**LLANISHEN (St Dennis) w Trellech Grange and
Llanfihangel Tor-y-Mynydd w Llangunnog and Llansoy**
Mon 2 **V** vacant
LLANISHEN (St Isan) (St Faith) *Llan 1* **V** C B W SMITH
LLANLLAWDDOG (St Llawddog) *see* Bro Caerfyrddin *St D*
LLANLLAWER *see* W Cemaes *St D*
LLANLLECHID (St Cross) *see* Bro Ogwen *Ban*
LLANLLEONFEL (Parish Church) *see* Irfon Valley *S & B*
LLANLLOWELL (St Llywel) *see* Usk Min Area *Mon*
LLANLLUGAN (St Mary) *see* Caereinion *St As*
LLAN-LLWCH (St Mary) *see* Bro Sancler *St D*
LLANLLWCHAIARN (All Saints) *see* Cedewain Miss Area *St As*
LLANLLWCHAIARN (St Llwchaiarn) *as above*
LLANLLWNI (St Luke or St Llonio) *see* Lampeter *St D*
LLANLLYFNI (Christ Church) *see* Uwch Gwyrfai Beuno Sant
Ban

LLANLLYFNI (St John) *as above*
LLANLLYFNI (St Rhedyw) *as above*
LLANLLYR-YN-RHOS (St Llyr) *see* Glan Ithon *S & B*
LLANMADOC (St Madoc) *see* N Gower *S & B*
LLANMAES (St Catwg) *see* Glamorgan Heritage Coast *Llan*
LLANMARTIN (St Martin) *see* Magor *Mon*
LLANMEREWIG (St Llwchaiarn) *see* Cedewain Miss Area
St As
LLANMIHANGEL (St Michael) *see* Glamorgan Heritage Coast
Llan
LLANNEFYDD (St Nefydd and St Mary) *see* Denbigh Miss
Area *St As*
LLAN-NON (St Non) *see* Bro Gwendraeth *St D*
LLANNOR (Holy Cross) *see* Bro Enlli *Ban*
LLANOVER (St Bartholomew) *see* Goetre w Llanover *Mon*
LLANPUMSAINT (Five Saints) *see* Bro Caerfyrddin *St D*
LLANRHAEADR-YM-MOCHNANT (St Dogfan) *see*
Tanat-Vyrnwy *St As*
LLANRHAEADR-YNG-NGHINMEIRCH (St Dyfnog) *see*
Denbigh Miss Area *St As*
LLANRHIAN (St Rhian) *see* Gtr Dewisland *St D*
LLANRHIDIAN (St Rhidian and St Illtyd) *see* N Gower
S & B
LLANRHUDDLAD (St Rhuddlad) *see* Bro Padrig *Ban*
LLANRHWYDRUS *as above*
LLANRHYCHWYN (St Rhychwyn) *see* Bro Gwydyr *Ban*
LLANRHYDD (St Meugan) *see* Dyffryn Clwyd Miss Area
St As
LLANRHYSTUD (St Restitutis) *see* Bro Wyre *St D*
LLANRUG (St Michael) *see* Bro Eryri *Ban*
LLANRUMNEY (St Dyfrig) *Mon 5* **P-in-c** M I R DOWSETT
NSM A J JENKINS
LLANRWST (St Grwst) *see* Aberconwy Miss Area *St As*
LLANSADWRN (St Sadwrn) *see* Bro Tysilio *Ban*
LLANSADWRNEN (St Sadwrnen) *see* Bro Dyfri *St D*
LLAN-SAINT (All Saints) *see* Bro Cydweli *St D*
LLANSAMLET (St Samlet) (St John) (St Paul) *S & B 3*
V G D WATHAN **C** J PAGE
LLANSANNAN (St Sannan) *see* Aled Miss Area *St As*
LLANSANNOR (St Senwyr) *see* Cowbridge *Llan*
LLANSANTFFRAED (St Bridget) *see* Bro Wyre *St D*
LLANSANTFFRAED (St Bridget) *see* Llanarth w Clytha and
Llansantffraed etc *Mon*
LLANSANTFFRAED-IN-ELWELL (St Bridget) *see* Colwyn
S & B
LLANSANTFFRAED-JUXTA-USK (St Bride) *see* The Beacons
S & B
LLANSANTFFRAID GLAN CONWAY (St Ffraid) *see* Aberconwy
Miss Area *St As*
LLANSANTFFRAID GLYN CEIRIOG (St Ffraid) *see* Valle Crucis
Miss Area *St As*
LLANSANTFFRAID, Bettws and Aberkenfig *Llan 6*
V S BRUMWELL
LLANSANTFFRAID-YN-MECHAIN (St Ffraid) *see* Tanat-
Vyrnwy *St As*
LLANSANTFFRAID GLYN DYFRDWY (St Ffraid) *see* Valle Crucis
Miss Area *St As*
LLANSAWEL (St Mary), Briton Ferry *Llan 9* **V** S BIRDSALL
LLANSAWEL (St Sawyl) *see* Bro Dyfri *St D*
LLANSILIN (St Silin) *see* Tanat-Vyrnwy *St As*
LLANSOY (St Tysoi) *see* Llanishen w Trellech Grange and
Llanfihangel etc *Mon*
LLANSPYDDID (St Cattwg) *see* Brecon St David w
Llanspyddid and Llanilltyd *S & B*
LLANSTADWEL (St Tudwal) *see* Roose *St D*
LLANSTEFFAN (St Ystyffan) *see* Bro Sancler *St D*
LLANSTEPHEN (St Steffan) *see* Llandefalle and Llyswen w
Boughrood etc *S & B*
LLANTARNAM (St Michael) *see* Cwmbran *Mon*
LLANTHETTY (St Tetti) *see* The Beacons *S & B*
LLANTHONY (St David) *see* Llanfihangel Crucorney w
Oldcastle etc *Mon*
**LLANTILIO CROSSENNY (St Teilo) and Penrhos w
Llanvetherine and Llanvapley** *Mon 1* **P-in-c** C H A PRINCE
NSM A DAWSON
**LLANTILIO PERTHOLEY (St Teilo) w Bettws Chapel and
Llanddewi Skirrid** *Mon 1* **P-in-c** J F GRAY
Hon C P VOWLES **NSM** J L HUGHES
LLANTRISANT (St Afran, St Ieuan and St Sanan) *see* Bro
Cwyfan *Ban*
**LLANTRISANT (St Illtyd, St Gwynno and St Dyfodwg)
(St Michael) (St David),** including Beddau, Brynna,
Llanharan, Llanharry, Llantwit Fardre, Miskin, Pontyclun,
and Talygarn *Llan 5* **TR** S T A FREEMAN, V L GARDNER
TV P M N GULLIDGE, R HILL **C** D G JONES, R J GRATTON

LLANTRISANT (St Peter, St Paul and St John)   *see* Usk Min Area *Mon*

LLANTRITHYD (St Illtyd)   *see* E Vale *Llan*

LLANTWIT FARDRE (St Illtyd)   *see* Llantrisant *Llan*

LLANTWIT MAJOR (St Illtud)   *see* Glamorgan Heritage Coast *Llan*

LLANTYSILIO (St Tysilio)   *see* Valle Crucis Miss Area *St As*

LLANULID (St Ilid)   *see* Blaenwysg *S & B*

LLANVACHES (St Dyfrig)   *see* Wentwood *Mon*

LLANVAPLEY (St Mable)   *see* Llantilio Crossenny w Penrhos, Llanvetherine etc *Mon*

LLANVETHERINE (St James the Elder)   *as above*

LLANWDDYN (St Wyddyn)   *see* Tanat-Vyrnwy *St As*

LLANWELLWYFO (St Gwenllwyfo)   *see* Bro Eleth *Ban*

LLANWENARTH CITRA (St Peter)   *see* Abergavenny St Mary w Llanwenarth Citra *Mon*

LLANWENOG (St Gwenog)   *see* Lampeter *St D*

LLANWERN (St Mary)   *see* Magor *Mon*

LLANWINIO (St Gwynio)   *see* E Landsker *St D*

LLANWNDA (St Gwyndaf)   *see* Uwch Gwyrfai Beuno Sant *Ban*

LLANWNDA (St Gwyndaf)   *see* W Cemaes *St D*

LLANWNNEN (St Lucia)   *see* Lampeter *St D*

LLANWNNOG (St Gwynog)   *see* Bro Arwystli *Ban*

LLANWNNWS (St Gwnnws)   *see* Bro Wyre *St D*

LLANWRDA (St Cwrdaf)   *see* Bro Dyfri *St D*

LLANWRIN (St Ust and St Dyfrig)   *see* Bro Cyfeiliog and Mawddwy *Ban*

LLANWRTHWL (St Gwrthwl)   *see* Gwastedyn *S & B*

LLANWRTYD (St David)   *see* Blaenau Irfon *S & B*

LLANWRTYD WELLS (St James)   *as above*

LLANWYDDELAN (St Gwyddelan)   *see* Cedewain Miss Area *St As*

LLANWYNNO (Christ Church)   *see* Pontypridd *Llan*

LLANWYNNO (St Gwynno)   *as above*

LLANYBYDDER (St Peter)   *see* Lampeter *St D*

LLANYCHAEARN (St Llwchaiarn)   *see* Aberystwyth *St D*

LLANYCHAN (St Hychan)   *see* Dyffryn Clwyd Miss Area *St As*

LLANYCHAR (St David)   *see* W Cemaes *St D*

LLANYCHLWYDOG   *as above*

LLANYCRWYS (St David)   *see* Lampeter *St D*

LLANYNGHENEDL VALLEY (St Michael)   *see* Bro Cwyfan *Ban*

LLANYNYS   *see* Buallt *S & B*

LLANYNYS (St Saeran)   *see* Dyffryn Clwyd Miss Area *St As*

LLANYRE   *see* Glan Ithon *S & B*

LLANYRNEWYDD (St Gwynour)   *see* N Gower *S & B*

LLANYSTYMDWY (St John the Baptist)   *see* Bro Eifionydd *Ban*

LLANYWERN (St Mary the Virgin)   *see* Llyn Safaddan *S & B*

LLAWHADEN (St Aidan) w Bletherston and Uzmaston *St D 1*   **V** *vacant*

LLAWRYBETWS (St James)   *see* Penedeyrn Miss Area *St As*

LLAY (St Martin)   *see* Alyn Miss Area *St As*

LLECHRYD (St Tydfil)   *see* Bro Teifi *St D*

LLECHYLCHED (Holy Trinity)   *see* Bro Cwyfan *Ban*

LLISWERRY   *see* Newport Maindee and Lliswerry *Mon*

LLOWES (St Meilig)   *see* Glasbury and Llowes w Clyro and Betws *S & B*

LLWYDCOED (St James)   *see* Aberdare St Fagan *Llan*

LLWYDIARTH (St Mary)   *see* Tanat-Vyrnwy *St As*

LLWYNDERW (Holy Cross) (Clyne Chapel) *S & B 4*   **V** J B DAVIES   **C** H D GRIFFITHS   **OLM** B WIGLEY

LLWYNGWRIL   *see* Bro Cymer *Ban*

LLWYNHENDY (St David)   *see* Bro Lliedi *St D*

LLWYNYPIA   *see* Pont Rhondda *Llan*

LLYN SAFADDAN *S & B 1*   **P-in-c** K RICHARDS   **C** A N JEVONS, P LODGE   **OLM** E BRAMLEY

LLYSFAEN (St Cynfran)   *see* Aled Miss Area *St As*

LLYSWEN (St Gwendoline)   *see* Llandefalle and Llyswen w Boughrood etc *S & B*

LLYSWORNEY (St Tydfil)   *see* Colwinston, Llandow and Llysworney *Llan*

LLYS-Y-FRAN (St Meilyr)   *see* W Cemaes *St D*

LLYWEL (St David)   *see* Blaenwysg *S & B*

LOUGHOR (St David)   *see* Casllwchwr and Gorseinon *S & B*

LOVESTON (St Leonard)   *see* Narberth and Tenby *St D*

LUDCHURCH (St Elidyr)   *as above*

MACHEN (St John the Baptist)   *see* Bedwas w Machen w Michaelston-y-Fedw w Rudry *Mon*

MACHEN (St Michael)   *as above*

MACHYNLLETH (St Peter)   *see* Bro Cyfeiliog and Mawddwy *Ban*

MAELOR Mission Area, comprising Bangor Monachorum, Bettisfield, Bronington, Erbistock, Hanmer and Tallarn Green, Marchwiel, Overton, Penley, and Worthenbury

---

St As 12   **I** S M HUYTON   **P-in-c** P J MACKRIELL   **TV** C HUGHES   **NSM** M WINWOOD

MAENCLOCHOG (St Mary)   *see* W Cemaes *St D*

MAENTWROG (St Twrog)   *see* Bro Moelwyn *Ban*

MAESGLAS (St Thomas)   *see* Bassaleg *Mon*

MAESMYNIS AND LLANYNYS (St David)   *see* Buallt *S & B*

MAESTEG (St David)   *see* Llangynwyd w Maesteg *Llan*

MAESTEG (St Michael)   *as above*

MAESTEILO (St John)   *see* Llandeilo Fawr and Taliaris *St D*

MAESTIR (St Mary)   *see* Lampeter *St D*

MAGOR (St Mary) *Mon 3*   **TR** J D HARRIS   **TV** C L JONES   **C** S PATTERSON   **NSM** A R DAVIES, H I PREST, M EAST

MAINDEE NEWPORT   *see* Newport Maindee and Lliswerry *Mon*

MALLWYD (St Tydecho)   *see* Bro Cyfeiliog and Mawddwy *Ban*

MALPAS (St Mary) *Mon 6*   **P-in-c** R C STEVENS   **C** M SELLERS   **NSM** J A SIMS

MAMHILAD (St Illtud) w Monkswood and Glascoed Chapel *Mon 4*   **R** J A COLLIER

MANAFON (St Michael)   *see* Caereinion *St As*

MANORBIER (St James)   *see* Narberth and Tenby *St D*

MANORDEIFI (St David)   *see* Bro Teifi *St D*

MANORDEILO (St Paul)   *see* Bro Dyfri *St D*

MANOROWEN (St Mary)   *see* W Cemaes *St D*

MANSELTON (St Michael and All Angels) and Cwmbwrla *S & B 3*   **P-in-c** I DREW-JONES

MARCHWIEL (St Marcella)   *see* Maelor Miss Area *St As*

MARCROSS (Holy Trinity)   *see* Glamorgan Heritage Coast *Llan*

MARGAM (St Mary) (St David) *Llan 8*   **V** *vacant*

MARLOES (St Peter)   *see* Roose *St D*

MARSHFIELD (St Mary) w St Bride's Wentloog *Mon 5*   **P-in-c** D E COLLINGBOURNE, S L COLLINGBOURNE

MATHERN (St Tewdric) *Mon 3*   **V** J E L WHITE   **NSM** R HAYES

MATHRY (Holy Martyrs)   *see* Gtr Dewisland *St D*

MATTHEWSTOWN (All Saints)   *see* Penrhiwceiber, Matthewstown and Ynysboeth *Llan*

MAUDLAM (St Mary Magdalene)   *see* Pyle w Kenfig *Llan*

MEIDRIM (St David) and Llanboidy and Merthyr *St D 10*   **V** *vacant*

MEIFOD (St Tysilio and St Mary)   *see* Caereinion *St As*

MELIDEN (St Mary Magdalene)   *see* Bryn a Mor Miss Area *St As*

MELIDEN (St Melyd)   *as above*

MENAI BRIDGE (St Mary)   *see* Bro Tysilio *Ban*

MERTHYR (St Martin)   *see* Meidrim and Llanboidy and Merthyr *St D*

MERTHYR CYNOG (St Cynog)   *see* Dan yr Eppynt *S & B*

MERTHYR DYFAN (St Dyfan and St Teilo)   *see* Barry *Llan*

MERTHYR MAWR (St Teilo)   *see* Laleston and Merthyr Mawr w Penyfai *Llan*

MERTHYR TYDFIL (Christ Church) (St Luke) *Llan 3*   **V** M WALFORD

MERTHYR TYDFIL (St David) (St Tydfil's Well) and Abercanaid *Llan 3*   **P-in-c** M N PREVETT

MERTHYR VALE (St Mary and Holy Innocents)   *see* Troedyrhiw w Merthyr Vale *Llan*

MICHAELSTON-LE-PIT (St Michael and All Angels)   *see* St Andrews Major w Michaelston-le-Pit *Llan*

MICHAELSTON-SUPER-AVON   *see* Cwmafan *Llan*

MICHAELSTON-Y-FEDW (St Michael)   *see* Bedwas w Machen w Michaelston-y-Fedw w Rudry *Mon*

MICHEL TROY (St Michael)   *see* Rockfield w Monmouth w Overmonnow etc *Mon*

MILFORD HAVEN (St Katherine)   *see* Roose *St D*

MILFORD HAVEN (St Peter)   *as above*

MINERA (St Mary)   *see* Alyn Miss Area *St As*

MINERA (St Tudfil)   *as above*

MINWEAR (St Womar)   *see* Narberth and Tenby LMA *St D*

MOCHDRE (All Saints)   *see* Cedewain Miss Area *St As*

MOLD (St Mary) Mission Area, comprising Cilcain, Gwernaffield, Llanferres, Mold, Nannerch, Nercwys, Northop, Pontblyddyn, Rhyd-y-mwyn, and Treuddyn *St As 14*   **I** C M POOLMAN   **P-in-c** K S STEWART   **TV** D J S STROUD, K G HORSWELL   **NSM** A JOHNSON, J WILLIAMS

MONINGTON (St Nicholas)   *see* Bro Teifi *St D*

MONKNASH (St Mary)   *see* Glamorgan Heritage Coast *Llan*

MONKSWOOD (St Matthew)   *see* Mamhilad w Monkswood and Glascoed Chapel *Mon*

MONKTON (St Nicholas and St John)   *see* S W Pembrokeshire *St D*

MONMOUTH (St Mary the Virgin)   *see* Rockfield w Monmouth w Overmonnow etc *Mon*

MONTGOMERY (St Nicholas)   *see* Pool Miss Area *St As*

MORFIL *see* W Cemaes *St D*
MORRISTON (St David) *S & B 3* **V** H M LERVY
MOSTYN (Christ Church) *see* Estuary and Mountain Miss
Area *St As*
MOUNTAIN ASH (St Margaret) and Miskin *Llan 7*
V M K JONES
MOUNTON (St Andoenus) *see* Mathern *Mon*
MWNT (Holy Cross) *see* Bro Teifi *St D*
MYDDFAI (St Michael) *see* Bro Dyfri *St D*
MYDROILYN (Holy Trinity) *see* Bro Aeron Mydr *St D*
MYNACHLOGDDU (St Dogmael) *see* E Landsker *St D*
MYNDDYGARREG (St Teilo) *see* Bro Cydweli *St D*
MYNYDD ISA *see* Borderlands Miss Area *St As*
MYNYDDISLWYN (St Tudor) *see* Upper Islwyn *Mon*
NANNERCH (St Michael) *see* Mold Miss Area *St As*
NANTGLYN (St James) *see* Denbigh Miss Area *St As*
NANTMEL (St Cynllo) *see* Gwastedyn *S & B*
NANTYGLO (Holy Trinity and St Anne) *see* Upper Ebbw
Valleys *Mon*
NARBERTH (St Andrew) and Tenby Local Ministry Area
St D 4 **P-in-c** A J GRACE, M L COX, S A BRETT
C S A HARGRAVE, S MURPHY **NSM** B H ROBERTS,
J W MORGAN
NARBERTH (St Catherine) Princes Gate *see* E Landsker *St D*
NASH (St Mary) *see* Magor *Mon*
NASH (St Mary) *see* S W Pembrokeshire *St D*
NEATH (St Thomas) (St David) (St Catherine) (St Peter
and St Paul) *Llan 9* **TR** L E NEWMAN **TV** R G AP ROBERT
C S GHEZZI
NEBO (Dewi Sant) *see* Bro Wyre *St D*
NEFYN (St David) *see* Bro Madryn *Ban*
NELSON (St John the Baptist) *see* Treharris, Trelewis,
Bedlinog and Llanfabon *Llan*
NERCWYS (St Mary) *see* Mold Miss Area *St As*
NEVERN (St Brynach) *see* Bro Teifi *St D*
NEW HEDGES (St Anne) *see* Narberth and Tenby *St D*
NEW MOAT (St Nicholas) *see* W Cemaes *St D*
NEW RADNOR (St Mary) and Llanfihangel Nantmelan and
Evancoyd w Gladwestry and Colva *S & B 2* **R** M T BEATON
NEW TREDEGAR (St Dingat) *see* Upper Islwyn *Mon*
NEWBOROUGH (St Peter) *see* Bro Dwynwen *Ban*
NEWBRIDGE (St Paul) *see* Lower Islwyn Min Area *Mon*
NEWBRIDGE (St Peter) *as above*
NEWBRIDGE-ON-WYE (All Saints) *see* Upper Wye *S & B*
NEWCASTLE (St Illtud) *Llan 6* **V** D E C LLOYD
NEWCASTLE EMLYN (Holy Trinity) *see* Bro Teifi *St D*
NEWCHURCH (St Mary) *see* Erwood Gp w Painscastle Gp
S & B
NEWCHURCH (St Michael) *see* Bro Caerfyrddin *St D*
NEWCHURCH (St Peter) *see* Wentwood *Mon*
NEWPORT (All Saints) *Mon 6* **P-in-c** C WATKINS
NSM E F JONES
NEWPORT (Cathedral of St Woolos) (St Martin) (St Mark)
Mon 6 **V** *vacant*
NEWPORT (St John Baptist) *Mon 6* **V** *vacant*
NEWPORT (St Mark) *see* Newport St Woolos w St Mark *Mon*
NEWPORT (St Mary) *see* W Cemaes *St D*
NEWPORT Christ Church *Mon 6* **NSM** S BLEWETT
NEWPORT Maesglas (St Paul) (St Stephen) and Holy
Trinity (St Thomas) *Mon 6* **P-in-c** J S J GROVES
NEWPORT Maindee and Lliswerry (St Andrew) (St John
the Evangelist) (St Mary) (St Philip) *Mon 6*
V W C INGLE-GILLIS **NSM** L BATT
NEWPORT St Julian (St Julius and St Aaron) (St Teilo)
Mon 6 **P-in-c** D C MATTHEWS **NSM** S J HELKVIST
NEWQUAY (St Llwchaiarn) *see* Glyn Aeron (Coastal) *St D*
NEWTON (St Peter) *S & B 4* **V** C M DARVILL
NEWTON NOTTAGE (St John the Baptist) (All Saints)
(St David) *Llan 8* **R** P R MASSON **C** M P BROADWAY
NSM G LUNN
NEYLAND (St Clement) *see* Roose *St D*
NICHOLASTON (St Nicholas) *see* Three Cliffs *S & B*
NOLTON (St Madog) *see* Gtr Dewisland *St D*
NOLTON (St Mary) *see* Coity, Nolton and Brackla w
Coychurch *Llan*
NORTHOP (St Eurgain and St Peter) *see* Mold Miss Area *St As*
NORTHOP (St Mary) *as above*
NORTON (Mission Church) *see* Oystermouth *S & B*
NORTON (St Andrew) *see* E Radnor *S & B*
NOTTAGE (St David) *see* Newton Nottage *Llan*
OFFA Mission Area, comprising Chirk, Penycae,
Rhosllanerchrugog, Ruabon, and Rhosymedre *St As 12*
TV M J G WILKINSON, P K BETTINSON
NSM H M E SHOTTON, P M OWENS
OGMORE VALE (St David) *see* Llandyfodwg and Cwm Ogwr
Llan

OVERMONNOW (St Thomas) *see* Rockfield w Monmouth w
Overmonnow etc *Mon*
OVERTON (St Mary the Virgin) *see* Maelor Miss Area
St As
OXWICH (St Illtyd) *see* SW Gower *S & B*
OYSTERMOUTH (All Saints) *S & B 4* **V** K EVANS
PAINSCASTLE (St Peter) *see* Erwood Gp w Painscastle Gp
S & B
PANTEG (St Mary) *see* Mid Torfaen *Mon*
PANTYFFRID (Mission Church) *see* Pool Miss Area *St As*
PATRICIO (St Issui the Martyr) *see* Vale of Gwrynne *S & B*
PEMBREY (St Illtud) *see* Bro Gwendraeth *St D*
PEMBROKE (St Mary) *see* S W Pembrokeshire *St D*
PEMBROKE DOCK (St John) *as above*
PEMBROKE DOCK (St Patrick) *as above*
PEMBROKE DOCK (St Teilo) *as above*
PEMBROKESHIRE, SOUTH WEST *St D 6* **P-in-c** A GRACE,
J A C R BARDER, J P MAYNARD, P O JONES **NSM** M A EVANS,
S J ALLEN
PEN RHONDDA FAWR *Llan 10* **P-in-c** P A LEYSHON
PENALLT (Old Church) *see* St Maughen's w Llangattock-
vibon-Avel w Llanfihangel-ystern-Llewern etc *Mon*
PENALLY (St Nicholas and St Teilo) *see* Narberth and Tenby
LMA *St D*
PENARTH (All Saints) (St Peter) *Llan 4* **V** J A YOUNG
C A REEVES
PENARTH (St Augustine) (Holy Nativity) and Llandough
Llan 4 **P-in-c** M JONES **NSM** R M GRIFFITHS
PEN-BOYR (St Llawddog) *see* Dyffryn Teifi *St D*
PENBRYN (St Michael) *see* Glyn Aeron (Coastal) *St D*
PENCADER (St Mary) *see* Dyffryn Teifi *St D*
PENCARREG (St Patrick) *see* Lampeter *St D*
PENCLAWDD (St Gwynour) *see* N Gower *S & B*
PENCOED (St David) *see* Llanilid w Pencoed *Llan*
PENCOED (St Paul) *as above*
PENDERYN MELLTE (St Cynog) *S & B 1* **P-in-c** T J WILLIAMS
PENDINE (St Margaret) *see* E Landsker *St D*
PENDOLYAN (St Cadoc) *see* E Vale *Llan*
PENEDEYRN Mission Area, comprising Bala, Cerrigydrudion,
Cynwyd, Llandderfel, Llandrillo-yn-Edeirnion, Llanfihangel
Glyn Myfyr, and Llangwm *St As 8* **TV** S J ROBERTS
PENEGOES (St Cadfarch) *see* Bro Cyfeiliog and Mawddwy
Ban
PENHOW (St John the Baptist) *see* Wentwood *Mon*
PENISARWAEN (St Helen) *see* Bro Eryri *Ban*
PENLEY (St Mary Magdalene) *see* Maelor Miss Area *St As*
PENLLECH *see* Bro Madryn *Ban*
PENLLERGAER (St David) *S & B 4* **V** *vacant*
PENLLYN (St John the Evangelist) *see* Cowbridge *Llan*
PENMACHNO (St Tudclud) *see* Bro Gwydyr *Ban*
PENMAEN (St David) *see* Upper Islwyn *Mon*
PENMAEN (St John the Baptist) *see* Three Cliffs *S & B*
PENMAENMAWR *see* Dwylan *Ban*
PENMARK (St Mary) *see* Porthkerry, Rhoose and Penmark
Llan
PENNANT MELANGELL (St Melangel) *see* Tanat-Vyrnwy
St As
PENNARD (St Mary) *see* Three Cliffs *S & B*
PENPONT (no dedication) *see* Dan yr Eppynt *S & B*
PENRHIWCEIBER (St Winifred), Matthewstown and
Ynysboeth *Llan 7* **P-in-c** B T RABJOHNS
PENRHOS (Holy Trinity) *see* Pool Miss Area *St As*
PENRHOS (St Cadoc) *see* Llantilio Crossenny w Penrhos,
Llanvetherine etc *Mon*
PENRHOSLLUGWY (St Michael) *see* Bro Eleth *Ban*
PENRHYNDEUDRAETH (Holy Trinity) *see* Bro Moelwyn
Ban
PENRHYNSIDE BAY (St David) *see* Aberconwy Miss Area
St As
PENRHYS (no dedication) *see* Rhondda Fach Uchaf *Llan*
PENRICE (St Andrew) *see* SW Gower *S & B*
PENSARN (St David) *see* Aled Miss Area *St As*
PENSTROWED (St Gwrhai) *see* Bro Arwystli *Ban*
PENTERRY (St Mary) *see* Itton and St Arvans w Penterry and
Kilgwrrwg w Devauden *Mon*
PENTIR (St Cedol) *see* Bro Ogwen *Ban*
PENTRAETH (St Mary) *see* Bro Tysilio *Ban*
PENTRE (St Peter) *see* Ystradyfodwg *Llan*
PENTRECHWYTH (St Peter) *see* Glantawe *S & B*
PENTROBIN (St John) *see* Borderlands Miss Area *St As*
PENTWYN (St David) *see* Cyncoed *Mon*
PENTYRCH (St Cadwg) and Capel Llanillterne *Llan 2*
V S M JOHN
PENYBONTFAWR (St Thomas) *see* Tanat-Vyrnwy *St As*
PENYCAE (St Thomas) *see* Offa Miss Area *St As*

PENYCLAWDD (St Martin) *see* St Maughen's w Llangattock-vibon-Avel w Llanfihangel-ystern-Llewern etc *Mon*
PENYFAI (All Saints) *see* Laleston and Merthyr Mawr w Penyfai *Llan*
PENYFFORDD (Emmanuel) *see* Borderlands Miss Area *St As*
PENYGRAIG (St Barnabas) *see* Dinas w Penygraig *Llan*
PENYWAUN (St Winifred) *see* Hirwaun *Llan*
PETERSTON-SUPER-ELY (St Peter) *see* E Vale *Llan*
PETERSTON-SUPER-MONTEM (St Peter) *see* Llantrisant *Llan*
PILLETH (Our Lady of Pilleth) *see* E Radnor *S & B*
PISTYLL (St Beuno) *see* Bro Madryn *Ban*
PONT AMAN (St Thomas) *see* Bro Aman *St D*
PONT DOLANOG (St John the Evangelist) *see* Caereinion *St As*
PONT GORS FAWR, comprising Gowerton and Waunarlwydd *S & B 4*   **V** A F PYE   **C** S RUMBELOW
PONT RHONDDA *Llan 10*   **V** P S GALE
PONT ROBERT (St John the Evangelist) *see* Caereinion *St As*
PONTARDAWE (St Peter) *see* Llangiwg *S & B*
PONTARDDULAIS *see* Llandeilo Tal-y-bont *S & B*
PONTARGOTHI (Holy Trinity) *see* Bro Dinefwr *St D*
PONTBLYDDYN (Christ Church) *see* Mold Miss Area *St As*
PONTFADOG (St John) *see* Valle Crucis Miss Area *St As*
PONTFAEN (St Brynach) *see* W Cemaes *St D*
PONT-IETS (St Mary) *see* Bro Gwendraeth *St D*
PONTLLANFRAITH (St Augustine) *see* Upper Islwyn *Mon*
PONTLLIW (St Anne) *see* Penllergaer *S & B*
PONTLOTTYN (St Tyfaelog) (St Aidan) and Fochriw *Llan 3* **P-in-c** R A D LINDSAY
PONTNEATHVAUGHAN (St John) *see* Penderyn Mellte *S & B*
PONTNEWYDD (Holy Trinity) *see* Cwmbran *Mon*
PONTPRENNAU (no dedication) *see* Cyncoed *Mon*
PONTSIAN (St John) *see* Dyffryn Teifi *St D*
PONTYATES (St Mary) *see* Gwendraeth Fawr *St D*
PONTYBEREM (St John) *see* Bro Gwendraeth *St D*
PONTYCLUN (St Paul) *see* Llantrisant *Llan*
PONTYCYMMER (St David) *see* Llangeinor and the Garw Valley *Llan*
PONTYPOOL (St Matthew) *see* Mid Torfaen *Mon*
PONTYPRIDD *Llan 5*   **TR** C L RUSHTON   **TV** M D GABLE **NSM** P B WATSON
PONTYPRIDD (St Catherine) *see* Pontypridd *Llan*
POOL Mission Area, comprising Berriew, Buttington, Castle Caereinion, Criggion, Forden, Guilsfield, Llandrinio, Llandysilio, Llandyssil, Montgomery, Penrhos, Pool Quay, and Welshpool *St As 9*   **I** S G WILLSON   **P-in-c** A E J SMITH, C L RHODES, J S THOMPSON   **C** T JONES
POOL QUAY (St John the Evangelist) *see* Pool Miss Area *St As*
PORT EYNON (St Cattwg) *see* SW Gower *S & B*
PORT TALBOT (St Agnes) *see* Aberavon *Llan*
PORT TALBOT (St David) *see* Margam *Llan*
PORT TALBOT (St Theodore) *see* Aberavon *Llan*
PORTH NEWYDD *Llan 10*   **P-in-c** J M THOMAS
PORTHCAWL (All Saints) *see* Newton Nottage *Llan*
PORTHKERRY (St Curig), Rhoose and Penmark *Llan 4* **P-in-c** M A PRINCE
PORTHMADOG (St John) *see* Bro Eifionydd *Ban*
PORTMADOC (St Cyngar) *as above*
PORTSKEWETT (St Mary) *see* Caldicot *Mon*
PRENDERGAST (St David) *see* Daugleddau *St D*
PRESELI, WEST *St D 1*   **V** vacant
PRESTATYN (Christ Church) *see* Bryn a Mor Miss Area *St As*
PRESTATYN (Church of Holy Spirit) *as above*
PUNCHESTON (St Mary) *see* W Cemaes *St D*
PWLL (Holy Trinity) *see* Bro Gwendraeth *St D*
PWLLHELI (St Peter) *see* Bro Enlli *Ban*
PYLE (St James) (St Mary Magdalene) w Kenfig *Llan 8* **V** D A WALKER
QUAR, THE (St Tydfil's Well) *see* Merthyr Tydfil St Dav and Abercanaid *Llan*
QUEENSFERRY (St Andrew) *see* Borderlands Miss Area *St As*
RADNOR (St Mary) *see* New Radnor and Llanfihangel Nantmelan etc *S & B*
RADNOR, EAST *S & B 2*   **V** vacant
RADNOR, WEST *see* Ithon Valley *S & B*
RADYR (St John the Baptist) (Christ Church) *Llan 2* **P-in-c** V E BURROWS   **C** B HUXTABLE-GOY
RAGLAN GROUP (St Cadoc) *Mon 4*   **R** K J HASLER, T G CLEMENT
REDBERTH (Church) *see* S W Pembrokeshire *St D*
REDWICK (St Thomas) *see* Magor *Mon*
RESOLVEN (St David) *see* Vale of Neath *Llan*
REYNOLDSTON (St George) *see* SW Gower *S & B*
REYNOLDSTON (St James) *see* Narberth and Tenby *St D*

RHANDIRMWYN (St Barnabas) *see* Bro Dyfri *St D*
RHAYADER (St Clement) *see* Gwastedyn *S & B*
RHESYCAE (Christ Church) *see* Estuary and Mountain Miss Area *St As*
RHEWL (Church) *see* Dyffryn Clwyd Miss Area *St As*
RHONDDA FACH UCHAF *Llan 10*   **P-in-c** D M JONES
RHOOSE (St Peter) *see* Porthkerry, Rhoose and Penmark *Llan*
RHOS (St James) *see* Dyffryn Teifi *St D*
RHOSBEIRIO *see* Bro Padrig *Ban*
RHOSCOLYN *see* Bro Cybi *Ban*
RHOSDDU *see* Wrexham *St As*
RHOSESEMOR *see* Estuary and Mountain Miss Area *St As*
RHOSILI (St Mary the Virgin) *see* SW Gower *S & B*
RHOSLLANNERCHRUGOG (St David) *see* Offa Miss Area *St As*
RHOSLLANNERCHRUGOG (St Mary) *as above*
RHOSTIE *see* Bro Wyre *St D*
RHOSYMEDRE (St John the Evangelist) *see* Offa Miss Area *St As*
RHUDDLAN (St Mary) *see* Aber-Morfa Miss Area *St As*
RHULEN (St David) *see* Colwyn *S & B*
RHYDYBRIW (Capel Rhydybriw) *see* Blaenwysg *S & B*
RHYDYFELIN (St Luke) *see* Pontypridd *Llan*
RHYD-Y-MWYN (St John the Evangelist) *see* Mold Miss Area *St As*
RHYL *see* Aber-Morfa Miss Area *St As*
RHYMNEY (St David) *Mon 7*   **V** vacant
RISCA (St Margaret) *see* Lower Islwyn Min Area *Mon*
RISCA (St Mary) *as above*
ROATH (St Edward) (St Margaret) *Llan 1*   **V** S LISK **NSM** R COOMBS
ROATH (St German) *Llan 1*   **V** vacant
ROATH (St Martin) *Llan 1*   **V** I D HAMER
ROATH (St Saviour) *Llan 1*   **NSM** C J LEE
ROATH PARK (Christ Church) *see* Cardiff Ch Ch Roath Park *Llan*
ROBESTON WATHEN (Church) *see* Narberth and Tenby *St D*
ROBESTON WEST (St Andrew) *see* Roose *St D*
ROCH (St Mary) *see* Gtr Dewisland *St D*
ROCKFIELD (St Cenedlon) w Monmouth w Overmonnow w Wonastow w Michel Troy *Mon 2*   **P-in-c** T W DACK **C** C M HAYNES
ROGERSTONE (St John the Baptist) *see* Bassaleg *Mon*
ROGIET (St Mary) *see* Caldicot *Mon*
ROOSE, comprising Burton, Dale, Hakin, Herbrandston, Hubberston, Johnston, Little Haven, Llangwm, Llanstadwell, Marloes, Milford Haven, Neyland, Robeston West, St Brides, St Ishmael's, Steynton, and Walwyn's Castle *St D 5*   **V** A P BOOKLESS   **P-in-c** A M CHADWICK, A P JOHNSON, J M ZIPPERLEN, J R CECIL, R M M JOHNSON   **C** H KARPATY **NSM** G FORD, J L HANCOCK, S M BESSANT
ROSEMARKET (St Ishmael) *see* Roose *St D*
ROSSETT (Christ Church) *see* Alyn Miss Area *St As*
RUABON (All Saints) *see* Offa Miss Area *St As*
RUABON (St Mary) *as above*
RUDBAXTON (St Michael) *see* Daugleddau *St D*
RUDRY (St James) *see* Bedwas w Machen w Michaelston-y-Fedw w Rudry *Mon*
RUMNEY (St Augustine) *Mon 5*   **V** vacant
RUTHIN (St Peter) *see* Dyffryn Clwyd Miss Area *St As*
ST ANDREWS MAJOR (St Andrew) (St Peter) w Michaelston-le-Pit *Llan 4*   **P-in-c** A P JAMES **C** J R ORMROD
ST ASAPH (Cathedral of St Asaph and St Cyndeyrn) *St As 1* **TR** N H WILLIAMS   **C** S E HARPER
ST ATHAN (St Tathan) *see* Glamorgan Heritage Coast *Llan*
ST BRIDES (St Bridget) *see* Roose *St D*
ST BRIDES MAJOR (St Bridget) *see* Glamorgan Heritage Coast *Llan*
ST BRIDES MINOR (St Bride) *see* Llansantffraid, Bettws and Aberkenfig *Llan*
ST BRIDES NETHERWENT (St Bridget) *see* Wentwood *Mon*
ST BRIDE'S WENTLOOG *see* Marshfield w St Bride's Wentloog *Mon*
ST BRIDES-SUPER-ELY (St Bride) *see* E Vale *Llan*
ST CLEARS (St Mary Magdalene) *see* Bro Sancler *St D*
ST DAVIDS (Cathedral of St David and St Andrew) *St D 7* **C** S WHITMARSH   **NSM** G BUTCHER
ST DOGMAEL'S (St Thomas) *see* Bro Teifi *St D*
ST DOGWELLS (St Dogfael) *see* Daugleddau *St D*
ST DONATS (St Donat) *see* Glamorgan Heritage Coast *Llan*
ST FAGANS (St Mary) and Michaelston-super-Ely *Llan 2* **R** V E BURROWS

ST FLORENCE (St Florentius) *see* Narberth and Tenby *St D*

ST GEORGE (St George) *see* Aled Miss Area *St As*

ST HARMON (St Garmon) *see* Gwastedyn *S & B*

ST HILARY (St Hilary) *see* Cowbridge *Llan*

ST ISHMAEL'S (St Ishmael) *see* Bro Cydweli *St D*

ST ISHMAEL'S (St Ishmael) *see* Roose *St D*

ST ISSELL'S (St Issell) *see* Narberth and Tenby *St D*

ST LYTHANS (St Bleiddian) *see* Wenvoe and St Lythans *Llan*

ST MARY CHURCH (St Mary) *see* Cowbridge *Llan*

ST MARY HILL (St Mary) *as above*

ST MAUGHEN'S (St Meugan) *see* St Maughen's w Llangattock-vibon-Avel w Llanfihangel-ystern-Llewern etc *Mon*

ST MAUGHEN'S (St Meugan) w Llangattock-vibon-Avel w Llanfihangel-ystern-Llewern w Dingestow w Llangovan and Penyclawdd w Tregaer w Cwmcarvan w Trellech and Penallt *Mon 2* **P-in-c** K A DACK

ST MELLONS (St Mellon) (Resurrection) *Mon 5* **V** D KELLEN

ST NICHOLAS (St Nicholas) *see* E Vale *Llan*

ST NICHOLAS (St Nicholas) *see* Gtr Dewisland *St D*

ST PIERRE (St Peter) *see* Mathern *Mon*

ST THOMAS *see* Haverfordwest *St D*

ST TWYNNELLS (St Gwynog) *see* S W Pembrokeshire *St D*

SANDFIELDS *see* Aberavon *Llan*

SANDYCROFT (St Francis) *see* Borderlands Miss Area *St As*

SARON (St David) *see* Bro Gwendraeth *St D*

SEALAND (St Bartholomew) *see* Borderlands Miss Area *St As*

SEBASTOPOL (St Oswald) *see* Mid Torfaen *Mon*

SENGHENYDD (St Peter) *see* Eglwysilan and Caerphilly *Llan*

SEVEN SISTERS (St David) *see* Dulais Valley *Llan*

SEVEN SISTERS (St Mary) *as above*

SHIRENEWTON (St Thomas à Becket) *see* Mathern *Mon*

SHOTTON (St Ethelwold) *see* Borderlands Miss Area *St As*

SINAN (All Saints) *see* Denbigh Miss Area *St As*

SIX BELLS (St John) *see* Abertillery w Cwmtillery w Llanhilleth etc *Mon*

SKENFRITH (St Bride) *see* Grosmont and Skenfrith and Llangattock etc *Mon*

SKETTY (St Paul) (Holy Trinity) *S & B 4* **V** R J DAVIES-HANNEN **OLM** M THOMAS

SKEWEN (St John) (St Mary) *Llan 9* **P-in-c** C W COLES

SOLVA (St Aidan) *see* Gtr Dewisland *St D*

SOUTHERNDOWN (All Saints) *see* Glamorgan Heritage Coast *Llan*

SOUTHSEA (All Saints) *see* Alyn Miss Area *St As*

SPITTAL (St Mary) *see* Daugleddau LMA *St D*

STACKPOLE ELIDOR (St James and St Elidyr) *see* S W Pembrokeshire *St D*

STEYNTON (St Cewydd and St Peter) *see* Roose *St D*

STRATA FLORIDA (St Mary) *see* Lampeter *St D*

SULLY (St John the Baptist) *Llan 4* **P-in-c** J R ORMROD **NSM** K BARRY

SWANSEA (Christ Church) *see* Cen Swansea *S & B*

SWANSEA (Holy Trinity) *as above*

SWANSEA (St Barnabas) *S & B 3* **P-in-c** D M GRIFFITHS

SWANSEA (St Gabriel) *S & B 3* **V** D M GRIFFITHS

SWANSEA (St James) *S & B 3* **V** H M WILLIAMS

SWANSEA (St Luke) *see* Manselton and Cwmbwrla *S & B*

SWANSEA (St Mary) *see* Cen Swansea *S & B*

SWANSEA (St Nicholas-on-the-Hill) and St Jude *S & B 3* **V** vacant

SWANSEA (St Peter) *S & B 3* **V** J S WRIGHT

SWANSEA (St Thomas) (St Stephen) and Kilvey *S & B 3* **V** S L BUNTING **C** M G THOMAS

SWANSEA, CENTRAL (Christ Church) (St John) (St Mary and Holy Trinity) *S & B 3* **C** I M FOLKS, S ALDRED, S HARRIS **NSM** J T ANTHONY

TAI'RGWAITH (St David) *see* Bro Aman *St D*

TALACHDDU (St Mary) *see* Llandefalle and Llyswen w Boughrood etc *S & B*

TALBENNY (St Mary) *see* Roose *St D*

TALGARREG (St David) *see* Bro Aeron Mydr *St D*

TALGARTH (St Gwendoline) w Bronllys w Llanfilo *S & B 1* **V** R T EDWARDS

TALIARIS (Holy Trinity) *see* Llandeilo Fawr and Taliaris *St D*

TALLEY (St Michael) *see* Bro Dyfri *St D*

TALYBONT (St Cross) *see* Bro Ogwen *Ban*

TALYGARN (St Anne) *see* Llantrisant *Llan*

TAL-Y-LLYN (St David) *see* Bro Ystumanner *Ban*

TANAT-VYRNWY Mission Area, comprising Bwlchycibau, Llanfechain, Llanfyllin w Llanwddyn, Llangadwaladr, Llangedwyn, Llangynog, Llansantffraid-ym-Mechain, Llansilin, Llwydiarth, Pennant Melangell, and Penybontfawr *St As 7* **R** R P BURTON **P-in-c** H J MORRIS, S E BURTON **TV** N F M MORRIS **Hon C** C M BROWNE **NSM** P W HEANEY, S HAYES

TEMPLETON (St John) *see* Narberth and Tenby *St D*

TENBY (St Julian's Chapel) *as above*

TENBY (St Mary) *as above*

THREE CLIFFS, comprising Bishopston, Ilston, Nicholaston, Penmaen, and Pennard *S & B 4* **V** N P DOYLE, P BROOKS **NSM** N E KING, S WAITE

TINTERN (St Michael) *see* Llandogo w Whitebrook Chpl and Tintern Parva *Mon*

TON PENTRE *see* Ystradyfodwg *Llan*

TONDU (St John) *see* Llansantffraid, Bettws and Aberkenfig *Llan*

TONGWYNLAIS (St Michael) (St James) *Llan 2* **V** vacant

TONMAWR (St Teilo) *see* Neath *Llan*

TONNA (St Anne) *see* Cadoxton-juxta-Neath and Tonna *Llan*

TONYPANDY (St Andrew) w Clydach Vale w Williamstown *Llan 10* **P-in-c** T J COX **C** J M THOMAS

TONYREFAIL (St David) (St Alban) w Gilfach Goch *Llan 10* **V** vacant

TON-YR-YWEN (School) *see* Llanishen *Llan*

TORFAEN, MID, including Pontypool, Sebastopol and Trevethin *Mon 8* **V** K O'SULLIVAN **C** P W GODSELL **NSM** A S LITTLER

TOWNHILL *see* Swansea St Nic and St Jude *S & B*

TOWYN (St Mary) *see* Aber-Morfa Miss Area *St As*

TRAEAN-GLAS (St Mary) *see* Blaenwysg *S & B*

TRALLWNG (St David) *see* Dan yr Eppynt *S & B*

TRAWSFYNYDD (St Madryn) *see* Bro Moelwyn *Ban*

TREALAW (All Saints) *see* Pont Rhondda *Llan*

TREBANOS (St Michael) *see* Clydach *S & B*

TREBOETH (St Alban) *see* Landore and Treboeth *S & B*

TREDEGAR (St George) (St James) *Mon 7* **V** M P DAVIS **NSM** E JONES

TREDUNNOC (St Andrew) *see* Usk Min Area *Mon*

TREFDRAETH (Eglwys Crist y Brenin) *see* Bro Cadwaladr *Ban*

TREFDRAETH (St Beuno) *as above*

TREFEGLWYS (St Michael) *see* Bro Arwystli *Ban*

TREFGARN (St Michael) *see* Daugleddau *St D*

TREFILAN (St Hilary) *see* Bro Aeron Mydr *St D*

TREFLYS (St Michael) *see* Bro Eifionydd *Ban*

TREFNANT (Holy Trinity) *see* Denbigh Miss Area *St As*

TREFRIW (St Mary) *see* Bro Gwydyr *Ban*

TREGAEAN (St Caian) *see* Bro Cyngar *Ban*

TREGAER (St Mary) *see* St Maughen's w Llangattock-vibon-Avel w Llanfihangel-ystern-Llewern etc *Mon*

TREGARON (St Caron) *see* Lampeter *St D*

TREGARTH (St Mair) *see* Bro Ogwen *Ban*

TRE-GROES (St Ffraid) *see* Dyffryn Teifi *St D*

TREGYNON (St Cynon) *see* Cedewain Miss Area *St As*

TREHARRIS (St Matthias), Trelewis, Bedlinog and Llanfabon *Llan 3* **P-in-c** G J COOMBES

TREHERBERT (St Mary Communion Centre) *see* Pen Rhondda Fawr *Llan*

TRELAWNYD (St Michael) *see* Bryn a Mor Miss Area *St As*

TRE-LECH A'R BETWS (St Teilo) *see* Bro Sancler *St D*

TRELLECH (St Nicholas) *see* St Maughen's w Llangattock-vibon-Avel w Llanfihangel-ystern-Llewern etc *Mon*

TRELLECH GRANGE (not known) *see* Llanishen w Trellech Grange and Llanfihangel etc *Mon*

TREMEIRCHION (Corpus Christi) *see* Denbigh Miss Area *St As*

TREMORFA (St Philip) *see* Gabalfa and Tremorfa *Llan*

TREORCHY (St Matthew) *see* Pen Rhondda Fawr *Llan*

TRETHOMAS (St Thomas) *see* Bedwas w Machen w Michaelston-y-Fedw w Rudry *Mon*

TRETOWER (St John the Evangelist) *see* Crickhowell w Cwmdu and Tretower *S & B*

TREUDDYN (St Mary) *see* Mold Miss Area *St As*

TREVETHIN (St Cadoc) *see* Mid Torfaen *Mon*

TREVETHIN (St John the Divine) *as above*

TREVOR (Church) *see* Valle Crucis Miss Area *St As*

TREWALCHMAI (St Morhaiarn) *see* Bro Cyngar *Ban*

TROEDRHIWGARTH (St Mary the Virgin) *Llan 6* **V** C T REANEY

TROED-YR-AUR (St Michael) *see* Dyffryn Teifi *St D*

TROEDYRHIW (St John) w Merthyr Vale *Llan 3* **V** S J BARNES

TROSTEY (St David) *see* Raglan Gp *Mon*

TROWBRIDGE MAWR (St Hilary) *see* Rumney *Mon*

TUDWEILIOG (St Cwyfan) *see* Bro Madryn *Ban*

TUMBLE (Dewi Sant) *see* Bro Gwendraeth *St D*
TYCOCH (All Souls) *S & B 4* **V** P J GWYNN
TYCROES (St Edmund) *see* Bro Gwendraeth *St D*
TYLORSTOWN (Holy Trinity) *see* Rhondda Fach Uchaf *Llan*
TYWYN (St Cadfan) *see* Bro Ystumanner *Ban*
UNDY (St Mary) *see* Magor *Mon*
UPPER EBBW VALLEYS *Mon 8* **NSM** C I LEWIS, P V GRIFFITHS
URBAN CROFTERS Conventional District *Llan 1*
P-in-c W E L SOUTER
USK (St Mary) Ministry Area *Mon 4* **V** S INGLE-GILLIS
Hon C G W OPPERMAN **NSM** P E LOVE, R J W GREENLAND
UWCH GWYRFAI Beuno Sant *Ban 2* **V** *vacant*
UZMASTON (St Ismael) *see* Daugleddau *St D*
VALE OF GWRYNNE, The *S & B 1* **P-in-c** C P BOWLER
C A ELLETSON
VALE OF NEATH *Llan 9* **V** A J DAVIES **C** E STREET
VALLE CRUCIS Mission Area, comprising Bryneglwys,
Corwen, Glyndyfrdwy, Gwyddelwern, Llanarmon Dyffryn
Ceiriog, Llandegla, Llangollen and Trevor, Llantysilio,
Llansantffraid Glyn Ceiriog, Llansantffraid Glyn Dyfrdwy,
and Portfadog *St As 10* **P-in-c** L A TAYLOR, P J CAREY
C H E-A GHEORGHIU GOULD **NSM** D M P EVANS
VALLEY (St Michael) *see* Bro Cwyfan *Ban*
VAYNOR (St Gwynno) *see* Cefn Coed w Vaynor *S & B*
WALTON EAST (St Mary) *see* Daugleddau *St D*
WALTON WEST (All Saints) *see* Roose *St D*
WALWYN'S CASTLE (St James the Great) *as above*
WAUNARLLWYDD (St Barnabas) *see* Pont Gors Fawr *S & B*
WAUNFELIN (St John the Divine) *see* Mid Torfaen *Mon*
WELSH ST DONATS (St Donat) *see* E Vale *Llan*
WELSHPOOL (St Mary) *see* Pool Miss Area *St As*
WENTWOOD *Mon 3* **C** K DENLY **NSM** J S WATERS
WENVOE (St Mary) and St Lythans *Llan 4*
P-in-c J R ORMROD **NSM** K BARRY
WHITCHURCH (St David) *see* Gtr Dewisland *St D*
WHITCHURCH (St Mary) (St Thomas) (All Saints) *Llan 2*
TR J G DAVIS **TV** P A MORTIMER **Hon C** H G LEWIS
NSM A D C HIGHWAY
WHITFORD (St Mary and St Beuno) *see* Estuary and
Mountain Miss Area *St As*
WHITLAND (St Mary) *see* E Landsker *St D*
WHITTON (St David) *see* E Radnor *S & B*

WICK (St James) *see* Glamorgan Heritage Coast *Llan*
WILCRICK (St Mary) *see* Magor *Mon*
WILLIAMSTON, EAST (Church) *see* Narberth and Tenby *St D*
WILLIAMSTOWN (St Illtud) *see* Tonypandy w Clydach Vale
w Williamstown *Llan*
WISTON (St Mary Magdalene) *see* Daugleddau *St D*
WOLFSCASTLE (St Lawrence) *see* Gtr Dewisland *St D*
WOLVESNEWTON (St Thomas à Becket) *see* Usk Min Area
Mon
WONASTOW (St Wonnow) *see* Rockfield w Monmouth w
Overmonnow etc *Mon*
WORTHENBURY (St Deiniol) *see* Maelor Miss Area *St As*
WREXHAM (St Giles's Parish Church) (St Mark) (St Mary)
(All Saints) (St Margaret) (St James) (St John) *St As 15*
P-in-c D C PARRY JONES **TV** J P SMITH, J S BRAY,
S ERRINGTON **C** A J KITCHEN, L BRISTOWE, R J KITCHEN
NSM J M MACKRIELL, J TOUT
WYE, UPPER *S & B 2* **P-in-c** P M E B BERESFORD-WEBB
WYNDHAM (St David) *see* Llandyfodwg and Cwm Ogwr
Llan
Y FERWIG (St Pedrog) *see* Bro Teifi *St D*
YNYSBOETH *see* Penrhiwceiber, Matthewstown and
Ynysboeth *Llan*
YNYSCYNON (St Cynon) *see* Pont Rhondda *Llan*
YNYSDDU (St Theodore) *see* Upper Islwyn *Mon*
YNYSHIR (St Anne) *Llan 10* **V** *vacant*
YSFA (St Mark) *see* Gwastedyn *S & B*
YSGEIFIOG (St Mary) *see* Estuary and Mountain Miss Area
St As
YSTALYFERA (St David) *S & B 3* **V** T J HEWITT
YSTRAD MEURIG (St John the Baptist) *see* Lampeter *St D*
YSTRAD MYNACH (Holy Trinity) w Llanbradach *Llan 3*
V S P KIRK
YSTRAD RHONDDA (St Stephen) *see* Pont Rhondda *Llan*
YSTRAD ROAD (St Illtyd) *see* Swansea St Pet *S & B*
YSTRADFELLTE (St Mary) *see* Penderyn Mellte *S & B*
YSTRAD-FFIN (St Paulinus) *see* Bro Dyfri *St D*
YSTRADGYNLAIS (St Cynog) *S & B 3* **R** D ROBERTS
NSM J C HOWARD **OLM** D OWEN
YSTRADOWEN (St Owain) *see* Cowbridge *Llan*
YSTRADYFODWG (St John the Baptist) *Llan 10*
V H H ENGLAND-SIMON

SCOTTISH INCUMBENCIES

An index of incumbencies of the Scottish Episcopal Church. The incumbency entry gives the full legal name, followed by the diocese and the name(s) and appointment(s) of the clergy serving there. Church dedications are indicated in brackets. The following are the main abbreviations used; for others see the full list of abbreviations.

C	Curate	NSM	Non-stipendiary Minister
Dss	Deaconess	P-in-c	Priest-in-charge
Hon C	Honorary Curate	R	Rector

ABERCHIRDER (St Marnan) *Mor* P-in-c M L E LAST
ABERDEEN (Cathedral of St Andrew) *Ab* R I M POOBALAN
ABERDEEN (St Clement) R *vacant*
ABERDEEN (St Devenick) *see* Bieldside *Ab*
ABERDEEN (St James) *Ab* P-in-c R GREEN C J SOUTER
 NSM R B EDWARDS
ABERDEEN (St John the Evangelist) *Ab* C J HOLDEN
 Hon C C S GIBSON
ABERDEEN (St Margaret of Scotland) *Ab* R A E NIMMO
 Hon C D H WRIGHT
ABERDEEN (St Mary) *Ab* R T TAGGART C J M HOBBS
ABERDEEN (St Ninian) *Ab* P-in-c J B LYON
 NSM J J TSUKADA
ABERDOUR (St Columba) - All Souls Fife *St And*
 P-in-c D L NORBY NSM C LATIMER
ABERFOYLE (St Mary) *St And* R J CONNELL
ABERLOUR (St Margaret of Scotland) R *vacant*
ABOYNE (St Peter) *Ab* R V R HANCOCK
AIRDRIE (St Paul and St John the Evangelist) R *vacant*
ALEXANDRIA (St Mungo) R *vacant*
ALFORD (St Andrew) *Ab* C M BLAKE
ALL SOULS FIFE - See ABERDOUR; BURNTISLAND; and
 INVERKEITHING TR *vacant*
ALLOA (St John the Evangelist) R *vacant*
ALYTH (St Ninian) *St And* R K E LAFFERTY
 NSM D A CAMERON
ANNAN (St John the Evangelist) *Glas*
 P-in-c M P CALLAGHAN
APPIN *see* W Highland Region *Arg*
ARBROATH (St Mary) *Bre* R P T MEAD C S CLINK
ARDBRECKNISH (St James) *Arg* R M R CAMPBELL
ARDROSSAN (St Andrew) R *vacant*
ARPAFEELIE (St John the Evangelist) *Mor* R M O LANGILLE
ARRAN, ISLE OF *Arg* P-in-c S P M MACKENZIE
AUCHENBLAE *see* Drumtochty *Bre*
AUCHINDOIR (St Mary) *Ab* NSM D ATKINSON
AUCHMITHIE (St Peter) *Bre* R P T MEAD C S CLINK
AUCHTERARDER (St Kessog) *St And* P-in-c T A DOWLING
AYR (Holy Trinity) *Glas* R M A TREMBATH
BAILLIESTON (St John) *see* Glas E End *Glas*
BALERNO (St Mungo) *Edin* R M J H ROUND C O CLEGG
BALLACHULISH (St John) R *vacant*
BALLATER (St Kentigern) *Ab* R V R HANCOCK
BANCHORY (St Ternan) *Ab* R L M DOWNS
BANFF (St Andrew) *Ab* P-in-c J M PAISEY
BARROWFIELD (St John the Baptist) R *vacant*
BATHGATE (St Columba) *Edin* R C A BARCLAY
 C P WOODIFIELD
BEARSDEN (All Saints) *Glas* R K H FREEMAN
BIELDSIDE (St Devenick) *Ab* R G BOWYER
 Dss J E MACCORMACK
BIRNAM *see* Dunkeld *St And*
BISHOPBRIGGS (St James-the-Less) *Glas* R P R WATSON
 C H OXLEY
BLAIR ATHOLL *see* Kilmaveonaig *St And*
BLAIRGOWRIE (St Catherine) *St And* R K E LAFFERTY
 NSM D A CAMERON
BO'NESS (St Catharine) *Edin* R W J SHAW C S WARD
BRAEMAR (St Margaret) R *vacant*
BRECHIN (St Andrew) *Bre* R J T SKINNER
BRIDGE OF ALLAN (St Saviour) *St And* R E F J MULLINER
BRIDGE OF WEIR (St Mary) *Glas* C L CURTICE
BRIDGEND *see* Islay *Arg*
BRORA (St Columba) *Mor* P-in-c J E P CURRALL
 C D GRANT NSM S L SCOTT
BROUGHTY FERRY (St Mary) *Bre* R F W BRIDGER
 C H R BRIDGER
BUCKIE (All Saints) *Ab* P-in-c J M PAISEY
BUCKSBURN (St Machar) *Ab* P-in-c D HEDDLE
BUCKSTONE (St Fillan) *see* Edin St Fillan *Edin*
BURNSIDE *see* Moffat *Glas*

BURNTISLAND (St Serf) - All Souls Fife *St And*
 P-in-c D L NORBY NSM C LATIMER
BURRAVOE (St Colman) *Ab* P-in-c N A BRICE
 NSM E H MCNAB, G R BOOTH
CALLANDER (St Andrew) *St And* R J CONNELL
CAMBUSLANG (St Cuthbert) R *vacant*
CAMPBELTOWN (St Kiaran) R *vacant*
CARNOUSTIE (Holy Rood) *Bre* P-in-c M E ALLWOOD
CASTLE DOUGLAS (St Ninian) *Glas* R C G KETLEY
CATHEDRAL OF THE ISLES *see* Cumbrae (or Millport) *Arg*
CATTERLINE (St Philip) R *vacant*
CHALLOCH (All Saints) R *vacant*
CHAPELHILL *see* Cruden Bay *Ab*
CHOIR Chapl St Ninian's Cathl Perth I *vacant*
CLARKSTON (St Aidan) *Glas* R N H TAYLOR
CLERMISTON *see* Edin Clermiston Em *Edin*
CLYDEBANK (St Columba) R *vacant*
COATBRIDGE (St John the Evangelist) R *vacant*
COLDSTREAM (St Mary and All Souls) *Edin* R J B SMITH
 P-in-c C I JONES
COLINTON *see* Edin St Cuth *Edin*
COMRIE (St Serf) *St And* R G S EVANS
COUPAR ANGUS (St Anne) *St And* R K E LAFFERTY
 NSM D A CAMERON
COURTHILL Chapel *see* Kishorn *Mor*
COVE BAY (St Mary) R *vacant*
CRAIGHALL *see* Ellon *Ab*
CRIEFF (St Columba) *St And* R G S EVANS
CROACHY *see* Strathnairn St Paul *Mor*
CROMARTY (St Regulus) *Mor* R M O LANGILLE
CRUDEN BAY (St James the Less) *Ab* R D B A BERK
 NSM G P WHALLEY
CULLODEN (St Mary-in-the-Fields) R *vacant*
CUMBERNAULD (Holy Name) R *vacant*
CUMBRAE (Cathedral of The Isles and Collegiate Church
 of the Holy Spirit) R *vacant*
CUMINESTOWN (St Luke) R *vacant*
CUPAR (St James the Great) *St And* R R ANETTS
 Hon C J B BLACK
DALBEATTIE (Christ Church) *Glas* R C G KETLEY
DALKEITH (St Mary) *Edin* R P S HARRIS C J DU ROCHER
 NSM E S JONES, J O GODFREY, M E JONES
DALMAHOY (St Mary) *Edin* R C DOWNEY
DALRY (St Peter) R *vacant*
DENNISTOUN (St Kentigern) *see* Glas E End *Glas*
DINGWALL (St James the Great) *Mor* P-in-c J BOOTHBY
 NSM V C SAUNDERS
Dioc Chapl I *vacant*
DIOCESAN AIDS Officer I *vacant* R C I LOWDON
DOLLAR (St James the Great) *St And* P-in-c J E P CURRALL
DORNOCH (St Finnbarr) *Mor* R A M PEDEN
DOUNE (St Modoc) *St And* R A M PEDEN
DOWNFIELD (St Luke) *see* Dundee St Luke *Bre*
DRUMLITHIE (St John the Baptist) *Bre* R M J R TURNER
DRUMTOCHTY (St Palladius) *Bre* R M J R TURNER
DUFFTOWN (St Michael and All Angels) *Mor*
 P-in-c M L E LAST
DUMBARTON (St Augustine) *Glas* R H GONZALEZ PENA
DUMFRIES (St John the Evangelist) *Glas* R J H AITON
 Hon C A M SHUKMAN, G J SIMMONS, G M WARWICK,
 S P BALLARD NSM J M G CLARK MAXWELL
DUNBAR (St Anne) *Edin* R D M HALL
DUNBLANE (St Mary) *St And* R N A BROWN
DUNDEE (Cathedral of St Paul) *Bre* R M J R TURNER
DUNDEE (St John the Baptist) *Bre* C H R BRIDGER
DUNDEE (St Luke) *Bre* P-in-c K J DIXON
DUNDEE (St Margaret) R *vacant*
DUNDEE (St Martin) *Bre* P-in-c F W BRIDGER
 C H R BRIDGER
DUNDEE (St Mary Magdalene) *Bre* P-in-c K G G GIBSON
 C R E CAMPBELL

DUNDEE (St Ninian) *Bre* **P-in-c** E M LAMONT
DUNDEE (St Salvador) *Bre* **P-in-c** D J GORDON
DUNFERMLINE (Holy Trinity) *St And* **R** K W RATHBAND
DUNKELD (St Mary) w Birnam *St And* **P-in-c** L CRADDOCK
DUNOON (Holy Trinity) *Arg* **R** D J RAILTON
DUNS (Christ Church) *Edin* **P-in-c** C I JONES
DUROR (St Adamnan) *see* W Highland Region *Arg*
EAST END *see* Glas E End *Glas*
EAST KILBRIDE (St Mark) *Glas* **R** P G M FLETCHER
EASTGATE (St Peter) *see* Peebles *Edin*
EASTRIGGS (St John the Evangelist) *Glas*
  P-in-c M P CALLAGHAN
EDINBURGH (Cathedral of St Mary) *Edin* **R** J A CONWAY
  NSM G P FOSTER **Chapl** A PHILIP
EDINBURGH (Christ Church) *Edin* **R** L DAVIDSON
  C J A GREEN, J A WRIGHT, L G GRAHAM
EDINBURGH (Emmanuel) **R** *vacant*
EDINBURGH (Good Shepherd) *Edin* **R** D J B FOSTEKEW
  C R DUNCAN
EDINBURGH (Holy Cross) *Edin* **R** S M HOLMES
EDINBURGH (Old St Paul) *Edin* **R** J M MCLUCKIE
  C J WRIGHT
EDINBURGH (St Barnabas) *Edin* **P-in-c** P D DIXON
  NSM A C ANDERSON
EDINBURGH (St Columba) *Edin* **R** D G PATON-WILLIAMS
  TV R O GOULD **C** A C W WAGSTAFF
EDINBURGH (St Cuthbert) *Edin* **R** N MCNELLY
EDINBURGH (St David of Scotland) *Edin* **P-in-c** A J BAIN
EDINBURGH (St Fillan) *Edin* **R** R INNES
EDINBURGH (St James the Less) *Edin* **R** I N C LOTHIAN
  NSM J P MITCHELL
EDINBURGH (St John the Evangelist) *Edin* **R** M DÜNZKOFER
  C D COOPER, R A ADDIS **NSM** C A HUME, P J BRAND,
  S KILBEY
EDINBURGH (St Margaret of Scotland) *Edin*
  P-in-c R J CORNFIELD
EDINBURGH (St Mark) *Edin* **R** S B MARRIAGE **C** D TODD
EDINBURGH (St Martin of Tours) **R** *vacant*
EDINBURGH (St Michael and All Saints) *Edin*
  R M D ROBSON **C** J B PENMAN
EDINBURGH (St Ninian) *Edin* **R** F S BURBERRY
EDINBURGH (St Paul and St George) *Edin* **R** D G RICHARDS
  C E L TALBOT, J S TWIGG
EDINBURGH (St Peter) *Edin* **R** N R WILLS
EDINBURGH (St Philip and St James) *Edin*
  P-in-c J L MACLAREN
EDINBURGH (St Salvador) *Edin* **P-in-c** A J BAIN
  C M WOJCIECHOWSKI
EDINBURGH (St Thomas) Private Chapel *Edin*
  I D W MCCARTHY
EDINBURGH (St Vincent) *Edin* **C** W L F MOUNSEY
ELGIN (Holy Trinity) w Lossiemouth (St Margaret) *Mor*
  R T N RONGONG **NSM** J SCLATER
ELIE AND EARLSFERRY (St Michael and All Angels) *St And*
  P-in-c S I BUTLER
ELLON (St Mary on the Rock) *Ab* **R** D B A BERK
  NSM C A FOX, G P WHALLEY, R SPENCER, S SPENCER
EOROPAIDH (St Moluag) *Arg* **P-in-c** P J MOGER
  NSM C P A LOCKHART
ERSKINE *see* Renfrew *Glas*
EYEMOUTH (St Ebba) *Edin* **P-in-c** C I JONES
FALKIRK (Christ Church) *Edin* **R** S L K SHAW
FASQUE (St Andrew) *Bre* **R** M J R TURNER
FETTERCAIRN *see* Fasque *Bre*
FOCHABERS Gordon Chapel *Mor* **P-in-c** M L E LAST
FORFAR (St John the Evangelist) *St And* **R** E C GARMAN
FORRES (St John the Evangelist) *Mor* **P-in-c** H INBADAS
FORT WILLIAM (St Andrew) *Arg* **R** G A GUINNESS
FORTROSE (St Andrew) *Mor* **R** M O LANGILLE
FRASERBURGH (St Peter) **R** *vacant*
FYVIE (All Saints) *Ab* **P-in-c** A R MACDONALD
GALASHIELS (St Peter) *Edin* **C** S C E CAKE
GALLOWGATE *see* Aberdeen St Marg *Ab*
GARTCOSH (St Andrew) **R** *vacant*
GATEHOUSE OF FLEET (St Mary) *Glas* **R** S D HAZLETT
GLASGOW (All Saints) *Glas* **P-in-c** S M P MAITLAND
GLASGOW (Cathedral of St Mary the Virgin) *Glas*
  R K HOLDSWORTH
GLASGOW (Good Shepherd) *Glas* **R** D K M DAVISON
GLASGOW (St Bride) *Glas* **R** K FRANCIS
GLASGOW (St George) **R** *vacant*
GLASGOW (St Margaret) *Glas* **R** G B FYFE, S ROBERTSON
GLASGOW (St Matthew) *Glas* **R** D K WOSTENHOLM
GLASGOW (St Ninian) **R** *vacant*
GLASGOW (St Oswald) **R** *vacant*

GLASGOW (St Silas) Private Chapel *Glas* **R** M J AYERS
  C J D LAPPING
GLASGOW East End (St John) (St Kentigern) (St Serf) *Glas*
  P-in-c M J W BENTON-EVANS **NSM** L A IRELAND
GLENCARSE (All Saints) **R** *vacant*
GLENCOE (St Mary) **R** *vacant*
GLENROTHES (St Luke the Evangelist) - Central Fife Team
  Ministry *St And* **C** G F DILLON
GLENURQUHART (St Ninian) **R** *vacant*
GOUROCK (St Bartholomew) **R** *vacant*
GRANGEMOUTH (St Mary) *Edin* **R** W J SHAW **C** S WARD
GRANTOWN-ON-SPEY (St Columba) *Mor*
  Hon C A G SPARHAM, R J GILLINGS
GREENOCK (St John the Evangelist) *Glas* **R** W NESBITT
GRETNA (All Saints) *Glas* **P-in-c** M P CALLAGHAN
GREYFRIARS *see* Kirkcudbright *Glas*
GRULINE (St Columba) *see* W Highland Region *Arg*
GULLANE (St Adrian) *Edin* **R** S D METZNER **C** J EDWARDS
HADDINGTON (Holy Trinity) *Edin* **R** E A O'RYAN
  NSM J WOOD
HAMILTON (St Mary the Virgin) *Glas* **R** M LITTLE
  NSM D JASPER
HARRIS, ISLE OF (Christ Church) *Arg* **P-in-c** J D L DAVIES
HAWICK (St Cuthbert) *Edin* **C** S C E CAKE
HELENSBURGH (St Michael and All Angels) *Glas*
  R D M IND
HILLINGTON (Good Shepherd) *see* Glas Gd Shep *Glas*
HUNTLY (Christ Church) *Mor* **P-in-c** M L E LAST
HYNDLAND (St Bride) *see* Glas St Bride *Glas*
INNERLEITHEN (St Andrew) *Edin* **R** A TAYLOR-COOK
  NSM C B AITCHISON, C CHAPLIN
INSCH (St Drostan) *Ab* **P-in-c** A R MACDONALD
INVERARAY (All Saints) *Arg* **P-in-c** S P M MACKENZIE
INVERBERVIE (St David of Scotland) **R** *vacant*
INVERGORDON (St Ninian) *Mor* **P-in-c** J BOOTHBY
INVERGOWRIE (All Souls) *Bre* **P-in-c** D J GORDON
INVERKEITHING (St Peter) - All Souls Fife *St And*
  P-in-c D L NORBY **NSM** C LATIMER
INVERNESS (Cathedral of St Andrew) *Mor* **C** K O'NEILL,
  N A J HIGGOTT
INVERNESS (St John the Evangelist) **R** *vacant*
INVERNESS (St Michael and All Angels) *Mor*
  P-in-c I MACRITCHIE **Hon C** G H STRANRAER-MULL
INVERURIE (St Mary) *Ab* **NSM** D ATKINSON
IONA (St Columba) **R** *vacant*
ISLAY (St Columba) **R** *vacant*
ISLE OF HARRIS *see* Harris Ch Ch *Arg*
JEDBURGH (St John the Evangelist) **R** *vacant*
JOHNSTONE (St John) *Glas* **R** R J PRESTON
JORDANHILL (All Saints) *see* Glas All SS *Glas*
KEITH (Holy Trinity) *Mor* **P-in-c** M L E LAST
KELSO (St Andrew) *Edin* **R** R D KING **C** G REDPATH
  Hon C I D L CLARK
KEMNAY (St Anne) *Ab* **NSM** D ATKINSON
KENTALLEN (St Moluag) *see* W Highland Region *Arg*
KESSOCK-TORE *see* Arpafeelie *Mor*
KILLIN (St Fillan) *St And* **R** G S EVANS
KILMACOLM (St Fillan) *Glas* **C** L CURTICE
KILMARNOCK (Holy Trinity) **R** *vacant*
KILMARTIN (St Columba) *Arg* **P-in-c** S P M MACKENZIE
KILMAVEONAIG (St Adamnan) *St And* **R** E M J M BAKER
KINCARDINE O'NEIL (Christ Church) **R** *vacant*
KINGHORN (St Mary and St Leonard) *St And* **R** C N FRASER
KINLOCH RANNOCH (All Saints) *St And* **R** E M J M BAKER
KINLOCHLEVEN (St Paul) *see* W Highland Region *Arg*
KINLOCHMOIDART (St Finian) **R** *vacant*
KINROSS (St Paul) *St And* **R** D G MACKENZIE MILLS
KIRKCALDY (St Peter) *St And* **R** C N FRASER **C** S GRAY
KIRKCUDBRIGHT (St Francis of Assisi) *Glas* **R** S D HAZLETT
KIRKWALL (St Olaf) *Ab* **R** D DAWSON
KIRRIEMUIR (St Mary) *St And* **P-in-c** R P HARLEY
KISHORN Chapel **R** *vacant*
LADYBANK (St Mary) *St And* **R** R ANETTS
LADYCROFT *see* Balerno *Edin*
LANARK (Christ Church) w Douglas *Glas* **R** A R SHERIDAN
  C L JOHNSTON
LANGHOLM (All Saints) **R** *vacant*
LARGS (St Columba) **R** *vacant*
LASSWADE (St Leonard) *Edin* **R** P S HARRIS
  C J DU ROCHER **NSM** E S JONES, J O GODFREY, M E JONES
LAURENCEKIRK (St Laurence) *Bre* **R** M J R TURNER
LEITH (St James the Less) *see* Edin St Jas *Edin*
LENZIE (St Cyprian) *Glas* **R** L S IRELAND
LERWICK (St Magnus) *Ab* **R** N A BRICE **NSM** E H MCNAB,
  G R BOOTH

LEVEN (St Margaret) - Central Fife Team Ministry *St And*
  P-in-c B J EVANS-HILLS
LEWIS, ISLE OF *see* Stornoway *Arg*
LINLITHGOW (St Peter) *Edin* **R** C A BARCLAY
  C P WOODIFIELD
LOCHALSH (St Donnan) **R** *vacant*
LOCHEARNHEAD (St Angus) *St And* **R** G S EVANS
LOCHEE (St Margaret) *see* Dundee St Marg *Bre*
LOCHGELLY (St Finnian) - Central Fife Team Ministry
  St And **NSM** M A DINELEY
LOCHGILPHEAD (Christ Church) *Arg*
  P-in-c S P M MACKENZIE
LOCHINVER (St Gilbert) *Mor* **P-in-c** C Y CALEY
LOCKERBIE (All Saints) *Glas* **R** PS JOB RETNASELVAM
  P-in-c M P CALLAGHAN
LONGSIDE (St John) *Ab* **R** R N O'SULLIVAN
LOSSIEMOUTH (St Margaret) *see* Elgin w Lossiemouth *Mor*
LUNAN HEAD (St Margaret) *St And* **R** E C GARMAN
MARYGATE *see* Pittenweem *St And*
MASTRICK (St Clement) *see* Aberdeen St Clem *Ab*
MAYBOLE (St Oswald) *Glas* **P-in-c** J W GEEN, **C** E CRUMLISH
MELROSE (Holy Trinity) *Edin* **R** P V P BLACKLEDGE
  C M PEDERSEN **NSM** D W WOOD
MILLPORT *see* Cumbrae (or Millport) *Arg*
MILNGAVIE (St Andrew) *Glas* **R** A HAGENBUCH
MOFFAT (St John the Evangelist) *Glas*
  R PS JOB RETNASELVAM **P-in-c** M P CALLAGHAN
MONIFIETH (Holy Trinity) *Bre* **P-in-c** M E ALLWOOD
  NSM W J MCAUSLAND
MONKLANDS *see* Airdrie *Glas*
MONKSTOWN *see* Ladybank *St And*
MONTROSE (St Mary and St Peter) **R** *vacant*
MORNINGSIDE (Christ Church) *see* Edin Ch Ch *Edin*
MOTHERWELL (Holy Trinity) *Glas* **R** R E KILGOUR
MUCHALLS (St Ternan) **R** *vacant*
MULL, ISLE OF *see* W Highland Region *Arg*
MURRAYFIELD (Good Shepherd) *see* Edin Gd Shep *Edin*
MUSSELBURGH (St Peter) *Edin* **R** A J REID
MUTHILL (St James) *St And* **P-in-c** T A DOWLING
NAIRN (St Columba) *Mor* **R** A J SIMPSON **C** K SANDERSON
NETHER LOCHABER (St Bride) **R** *vacant*
NEW GALLOWAY (St Margaret of Scotland) *Glas*
  P-in-c P J SWIFT
NEW PITSLIGO (St John the Evangelist) **R** *vacant*
NEWBURGH (St Katherine) **R** *vacant*
NEWLANDS (St Margaret) *see* Glas St Marg *Glas*
NEWPORT-ON-TAY (St Mary) **R** *vacant*
NEWTON STEWART *see* Challoch *Glas*
NORTH BALLACHULISH *see* Onich *Arg*
NORTH BERWICK (St Baldred) *Edin* **R** S D METZNER
  C J EDWARDS
NORTH MEARNS *see* Stonehaven *Bre*
OBAN (Cathedral of St John) *Arg* **C** R CANSDALE
  Hon C I E WALTER
OLD DEER (St Drostan) *Ab* **R** R N O'SULLIVAN
OLDMELDRUM (St Matthew) *Ab* **P-in-c** R SPENCER
ONICH (St Bride) **R** *vacant*
PAISLEY (Holy Trinity and St Barnabas) *Glas*
  R D A W DAVISON
PEEBLES (St Peter) *Edin* **R** A TAYLOR-COOK
  NSM C B AITCHISON, C CHAPLIN
PENICUIK (St James the Less) *Edin* **R** N J BOWRY
  NSM N F SUTTLE
PERTH (Cathedral of St Ninian) *St And*
  R H B FARQUHARSON
PERTH (St John the Baptist) *St And* **R** G S TAYLOR
  C A HUGHES
PETERHEAD (St Peter) *Ab* **R** R N O'SULLIVAN

PILTON (St David) *see* Edin St Dav *Edin*
PITLOCHRY (Holy Trinity) *St And* **R** E M J M BAKER
PITTENWEEM (St John the Evangelist) *St And*
  P-in-c S I BUTLER
POLLOCKSHIELDS (St Ninian) *see* Glas St Ninian
  Glas
POLTALLOCH *see* Kilmartin *Arg*
POOLEWE (St Maelrubha) **R** *vacant*
PORT GLASGOW (St Mary the Virgin) *Glas* **C** L CURTICE
PORTNACROIS (Holy Cross) *see* W Highland Region *Arg*
PORTPATRICK (St Ninian) **R** *vacant*
PORTREE (St Columba) *Arg* **Hon C** R F BUNGARD
POSSILPARK (St Matthew) *see* Glas St Matt *Glas*
PRESTONPANS (St Andrew) **R** *vacant*
PRESTWICK (St Ninian) *Glas* **R** H J ROSS
RENFREW (St Margaret) *Glas* **R** R J PRESTON
ROSLIN (Collegiate Church of St Matthew) *Edin*
  P-in-c J E ROULSTON
ROTHESAY (St Paul) *Arg* **R** D J RAILTON
ROTHIEMURCHUS (St John the Baptist) *Mor*
  Hon C A G SPARHAM, R J GILLINGS **NSM** J M JONES
ST ANDREWS (All Saints) *St And* **R** A C COLES
  Hon C D W DAY, G J M SAUNDERS, M C ALDCROFT
  NSM I M MICHAEL
ST ANDREWS (St Andrew) *St And* **R** T A HART
  NSM R T EVANS
ST FILLANS (Church of the Holy Spirit) **R** *vacant*
SANDYLOAN *see* Gullane *Edin*
SELKIRK (St John the Evangelist) *Edin* **C** S C E CAKE
  Hon C D D SCEATS
SHETTLESTON (St Serf) *see* Glas E End *Glas*
SKYE, ISLE OF *see* Portree *Arg*
SOUTH QUEENSFERRY (Priory Church St Mary of Mount
  Carmel) *Edin* **P-in-c** T J HARKIN **NSM** I MACROBERT
STANLEY (St Columba) **R** *vacant*
STIRLING (Holy Trinity) *St And* **R** C J WUTSCHER
  Hon C G J WILLEY
STONEHAVEN (St James) **R** *vacant*
STORNOWAY (St Peter) *Arg* **P-in-c** P J MOGER
STRANRAER (St John the Evangelist) **R** *vacant*
STRATHNAIRN (St Paul) *Mor* **P-in-c** K B COLLINS
STRATHPEFFER (St Anne) *Mor* **P-in-c** J BOOTHBY
  NSM V C SAUNDERS
STRATHTAY (St Andrew) *St And* **R** E M J M BAKER
STRICHEN (All Saints) **R** *vacant*
STROMNESS (St Mary) *Ab* **P-in-c** T P MILLER
STRONTIAN **R** *vacant*
TAIN (St Andrew) *Mor* **P-in-c** J E P CURRALL
  NSM S L SCOTT
TARFSIDE (St Drostan) *Bre* **P-in-c** J NELSON
TAYPORT (St Margaret of Scotland) **R** *vacant*
TEINDHILLGREEN *see* Duns *Edin*
THURSO (St Peter and Holy Rood) *Mor* **C** E CHARMAN
TOFTS *see* Dalry *Glas*
TROON (St Ninian) *Glas* **R** K D THOMASSON
TURRIFF (St Congan) **R** *vacant*
UDDINGSTON (St Andrew) *Glas* **R** M LITTLE
ULLAPOOL (St Mary the Virgin) *Mor* **P-in-c** C Y CALEY
WEST HIGHLAND Region *Arg* **P-in-c** A A C FAIRCLOUGH
WEST LINTON (St Mungo) *Edin* **R** N J BOWRY
WESTGATE *see* Dunbar *Edin*
WESTHILL Community Church *Ab* **R** I J FERGUSON
WHITERASHES (All Saints) **R** *vacant*
WHITING BAY *see* Is of Arran *Arg*
WICK (St John the Evangelist) *Mor* **C** E CHARMAN
WISHAW (St Andrew) *Glas* **R** R E KILGOUR
WOODHEAD OF FETTERLETTER *see* Fyvie *Ab*
YELL *see* Burravoe *Ab*

IRISH BENEFICES AND CHURCHES

An index of benefices of the Church of Ireland (shown in bold type), together with entries for churches and other licensed places of worship. Where the church name is the same as that of the benefice (or the first place name in the benefice), the church entry is omitted. Church dedications are indicated in brackets.

The benefice entry gives the full legal name, together with the diocese and the name(s) and appointment(s) of clergy serving there. The following are the main abbreviations used; for others see the full list of abbreviations.

Bp's C	Bishop's Curate	I	Incumbent (includes Rector or Vicar)
C	Curate	NSM	Non-stipendiary Minister
C-in-c	Curate-in-charge	P-in-c	Priest-in-charge
Hon C	Honorary Curate		

AASLEAGH (St John the Baptist) *see* Tuam w Cong and Aasleagh *T, K & A*
ABBEYLEIX (St Michael and All Angels) w Ballyroan, Ballinakill, Killermogh, Aughmacart, Durrow and Attanagh *C, F & O* **I** P A HARVEY
ABBEYSTREWRY (no dedication) w Creagh, Tullagh, Castlehaven and Caheragh *C, C & R* **I** J K ARDIS
ABINGTON (St John and St Ailbe) *see* Limerick City *L & K*
ACHILL (Holy Trinity) *see* Aughaval w Achill, Knappagh, Dugort etc *T, K & A*
ACTON (no dedication) and Drumbanagher *Arm* **I** G B SPENCE **Bp's C** D W R DUNN
ADARE (St Nicholas) and Kilmallock w Kilpeacon, Croom, Kilflynn, Kilfinane, Knockaney, Bruff and Caherconlish *L & K* **I** E P BEASLEY
AGHABOG (no dedication) *see* Ematris w Rockcorry, Aghabog and Aughnamullan *Clogh*
AGHADE (All Saints) *see* Fenagh w Myshall, Aghade and Ardoyne *C, F & O*
AGHADERG (St Mellan) w Donaghmore and Scarva *D & D* **I** R R MAGENNIS
AGHADOE *see* Killarney w Aghadoe and Muckross *L & K*
AGHADOWEY (St Guaire) *D & R* **I** L D A CRAWFORD-MCCAFFERTY
AGHADOWN (Church Cross) *see* Ballydehob w Aghadown *C, C & R*
AGHADOWN (St Matthew) *as above*
AGHADRUMSEE (no dedication) w Clogh and Drumsnatt *Clogh* **I** *vacant*
AGHALEE (Holy Trinity) *D & D* **I** G P MCADAM
AGHALURCHER, comprising Colebrook (no dedication) w Tattykeeran, Cooneen and Mullaghfad *Clogh* **I** J M MCCLENAGHAN
AGHANAGH (no dedication) *see* Boyle and Elphin w Aghanagh, Kilbryan etc *K, E & A*
AGHANCON (no dedication) *see* Shinrone w Aghancon etc *L & K*
AGHANLOO (St Lugha) *see* Tamlaghtard w Aghanloo *D & R*
AGHAVEA (no dedication) *Clogh* **I** J R MCLOUGHLIN
AGHAVILLY (St Mary) *see* Tynan w Middletown and Aghavilly *Arm*
AGHAVOE (no dedication) *see* Rathdowney w Castlefleming, Donaghmore etc *C, F & O*
AGHER (no dedication) *see* Dunboyne and Rathmolyon *M & K*
AGHERTON (St John the Baptist) *Conn* **I** M R K FERRY
AGHOLD (no dedication) *see* Tullow w Shillelagh, Aghold and Mullinacuff *C, F & O*
AGHOUR (St Lachtan) *see* Kilkenny w Aghour and Kilmanagh *C, F & O*
AHASCRAGH *see* Aughrim w Ballinasloe etc *L & K*
AHERLA *see* Moviddy Union *C, C & R*
AHOGHILL (St Colmanell) w Portglenone *Conn* **I** D C CHRISTIE
ALDERGROVE *see* Killead w Gartree *Conn*
ALMORITIA (St Nicholas) *see* Mullingar, Portnashangan, Moyliscar, Kilbixy etc *M & K*
ALTEDESERT (no dedication) *see* Kildress w Altedesert *Arm*
ANNACLONE (Christ Church) *see* Magherally w Annaclone *D & D*
ANNADUFF (St Ann) *see* Kiltoghart w Drumshambo, Annaduff and Kilronan *K, E & A*
ANNAGH (St Andrew) w Drumaloor, Cloverhill and Drumlane *K, E & A* **I** T J WOODS
ANNAGHMORE (St Francis) *Arm* **I** D S MCVEIGH
ANNAHILT (Ascension) w Magherahamlet *D & D* **I** J R HOWARD

ANNALONG (no dedication) *D & D* **I** G HAMILTON
ANNESTOWN *see* Waterford w Killea, Drumcannon and Dunhill *C, F & O*
ANTRIM (All Saints) *Conn* **I** S R MCBRIDE **C** P S BLAKE
ANTRIM (St Patrick) *see* Connor w Antrim St Patr *Conn*
ARBOE (no dedication) *see* Ballinderry, Tamlaght and Arboe *Arm*
ARDAGH (St Patrick) w Tashinny, Shrule and Kilcommick *K, E & A* **I** *vacant*
ARDAMINE (St John the Evangelist) w Kiltennel, Glascarrig, Kilnamanagh, Kilmuckridge and Monamolin *C, F & O* **I** R J GRAY
ARDARA (St Connall) w Glencolumbkille, Inniskeel, Glenties and Lettermacaward *D & R* **C** R WRAY
ARDCARNE (no dedication) *see* Boyle and Elphin w Aghanagh, Kilbryan etc *K, E & A*
ARDCLINIS (St Mary) and Tickmacrevan w Layde and Cushendun *Conn* **I** *vacant*
ARDCOLM (no dedication) *see* Wexford and Kilscoran Union *C, F & O*
ARDEE (St Mary) *see* Drogheda w Ardee, Collon and Termonfeckin *Arm*
ARDGLASS (St Nicholas) *see* Lecale Gp *D & D*
ARDKEEN (Christ Church) *see* Ballyhalbert w Ardkeen *D & D*
ARDMORE (no dedication) w Craigavon *D & D* **Bp's C** T J CADDEN
ARDMORE (St Paul) *see* Youghal Union *C, C & R*
ARDNAGEEHY (no dedication) *see* Fermoy Union *C, C & R*
ARDOYNE (Holy Trinity) *see* Fenagh w Myshall, Aghade and Ardoyne *C, F & O*
ARDOYNE (Immanuel) *see* Belfast H Trin and St Silas *Conn*
ARDQUIN (no dedication) *see* Ballyphilip w Ardquin *D & D*
ARDRAHAN *see* Aughrim w Ballinasloe etc *L & K*
ARDSTRAW (St Eugene) w Baronscourt, Badoney Lower and Badoney Upper and Greenan *D & R* **I** E DINSMORE
ARDTREA (St Andrew) w Desertcreat *Arm* **I** D J BELL
ARKLOW (St Saviour) w Inch and Kilbride *D & G* **I** K A L BARRETT, N J W SHERWOOD
ARMAGH (St Mark) *Arm* **I** M T KINGSTON
ARMAGHBREAGUE (no dedication) *see* Keady, Armaghbreague, Derrynoose and Newtownhamilton *Arm*
ARMOY (St Patrick) w Loughguile and Drumtullagh *Conn* **I** C R A EASTON **NSM** D J STEELE
ARVAGH (no dedication) w Carrigallen, Gowna and Columbkille *K, E & A* **P-in-c** H R HICKS
ASHFIELD (no dedication) *see* Drumgoon *K, E & A*
ASKEATON (St Mary) *see* Rathkeale w Askeaton, Kilcornan and Kilnaughtin *L & K*
ATHBOY (St James) *see* Trim and Athboy Gp *M & K*
ATHLONE (St Mary) w Benown, Kiltoom and Forgney *M & K* **I** W L STEACY
ATHY (St Michael) w Kilberry, Fontstown and Kilkea *D & G* **I** O M R DONOHOE
AUGHANUNSHIN *see* Conwal Union w Gartan *D & R*
AUGHAVAL (no dedication) w Achill, Knappagh, Dugort, Castlebar and Turlough *T, K & A* **I** J K MCWHIRTER **OLM** M M O'HERLIHY
AUGHAVAS (no dedication) *see* Mohill w Farnaught, Aughavas, Oughteragh etc *K, E & A*
AUGHER (no dedication) w Newtownsaville and Eskrahoole *Clogh* **I** *vacant*
AUGHMACART (St Tighernagh) *see* Abbeyleix w Ballyroan etc *C, F & O*
AUGHNACLIFFE *see* Arvagh w Carrigallen, Gowna and Columbkille *K, E & A*
AUGHNACLOY *see* Carnteel and Crilly *Arm*

AUGHNAMULLAN (Christ Church) *see* Ematris w Rockcorry, Aghabog and Aughnamullan *Clogh*
AUGHRIM (Holy Trinity) w Ballinasloe, Clontuskert, Ahascragh, Woodlawn, Kilmacduagh and Ardrahan *L & K* I J M GODFREY
AUGHRIM (St John the Evangelist) *see* Castlemacadam w Ballinaclash, Aughrim etc *D & G*
BADONEY LOWER (St Patrick) *see* Ardstraw w Baronscourt, Badoney Lower etc *D & R*
BADONEY UPPER (St Aichen) *as above*
BAGENALSTOWN *see* Dunleckney w Nurney, Lorum and Kiltennel *C, F & O*
BAILIEBOROUGH (no dedication) w Knockbride, Shercock and Mullagh *K, E & A* I I HORNER
BALBRIGGAN (St George) *see* Holmpatrick w Balbriggan and Kenure *D & G*
BALGRIFFIN (St Doulagh) *see* Malahide w Balgriffin *D & G*
BALLAGHTOBIN (no dedication) *see* Kells Gp *C, F & O*
BALLEE (no dedication) *see* Bright w Ballee and Killough *D & D*
BALLIGAN *see* Ballywalter w Inishargie *D & D*
BALLINA *see* Killala w Dunfeeny, Crossmolina, Kilmoremoy etc *T, K & A*
BALLINACLASH (no dedication) *see* Castlemacadam w Ballinaclash, Aughrim etc *D & G*
BALLINADEE (no dedication) *see* Bandon Union *C, C & R*
BALLINAFAD *see* Boyle and Elphin w Aghanagh, Kilbryan etc *K, E & A*
BALLINAKILL (All Saints) *see* Abbeyleix w Ballyroan etc *C, F & O*
BALLINALEA *see* Mostrim w Granard, Clonbroney, Killoe etc *K, E & A*
BALLINALECK *see* Cleenish w Mullaghdun *Clogh*
BALLINAMALLARD *see* Magheracross *Clogh*
BALLINAMORE *see* Mohill w Farnaught, Aughavas, Oughteragh etc *K, E & A*
BALLINASLOE (St John the Evangelist) *see* Aughrim w Ballinasloe etc *L & K*
BALLINATONE *see* Castlemacadam w Ballinaclash, Aughrim etc *D & G*
BALLINDERRY (no dedication) *Conn* I T CLELAND
BALLINDERRY (St John), Tamlaght and Arboe *Arm* I W B PAINE
BALLINEEN *see* Kinneigh Union *C, C & R*
BALLINGARRY (no dedication) *see* Cloughjordan w Borrisokane etc *L & K*
BALLINLOUGH *see* Roscommon Gp *K, E & A*
BALLINROBE (St Mary) *see* Tuam w Cong and Aasleagh *T, K & A*
BALLINTEMPLE (no dedication) *see* Kilmore w Ballintemple *K, E & A*
BALLINTEMPLE (St Mary) *see* Cashel w Magorban, Tipperary, Clonbeg etc *C, F & O*
BALLINTOGHER *see* Taunagh w Kilmactranny, Ballysumaghan etc *K, E & A*
BALLINTOY (no dedication) w Rathlin and Dunseverick *Conn* I P M BARTON
BALLINTUBBERT (St Brigid) *see* Stradbally w Ballintubbert, Coraclone etc *C, F & O*
BALLISODARE (Holy Trinity) w Collooney and Emlaghfad *T, K & A* I A P ISON
BALLIVOR *see* Trim and Athboy Gp *M & K*
BALLNACARGY *see* Mullingar, Portnashangan, Moyliscar, Kilbixy etc *M & K*
BALLYBAY (Christ Church) w Mucknoe and Clontibret *Clogh* I E DUNNE
BALLYBEEN (St Mary) *D & D* I J W CHESHIRE NSM N GORDON
BALLYBRACK (St Matthias) *see* Killiney Ballybrack *D & G*
BALLYBUNNION *see* Tralee w Kilmoyley, Ballymacelligott etc *L & K*
BALLYCANEW (no dedication) *see* Gorey w Kilnahue, Leskinfere and Ballycanew *C, F & O*
BALLYCARNEY (no dedication) *see* Ferns w Kilbride, Toombe, Kilcormack etc *C, F & O*
BALLYCARRY *see* Kilroot and Templecorran *Conn*
BALLYCASTLE (Holy Trinity) *see* Ramoan w Ballycastle and Culfeightrin *Conn*
BALLYCLARE *see* Ballynure and Ballyeaston *Conn*
BALLYCLOG (St Patrick) *see* Brackaville w Donaghendry and Ballyclog *Arm*
BALLYCLUG (St Patrick) *see* Ballymena w Ballyclug *Conn*
BALLYCOMMON *see* Geashill w Killeigh and Ballycommon *M & K*
BALLYCONNELL *see* Swanlinbar Gp *K, E & A*
BALLYCOTTON *see* Youghal Union *C, C & R*

BALLYCULTER (Christ Church) *see* Lecale Gp *D & D*
BALLYDEHOB (St Matthias) w Aghadown *C, C & R* I S T MCCANN
BALLYEASTON (St John the Evangelist) *see* Ballynure and Ballyeaston *Conn*
BALLYEGLISH (St Matthias) *see* Desertlyn w Ballyeglish *Arm*
BALLYFIN (no dedication) *see* Maryborough w Dysart Enos and Ballyfin *C, F & O*
BALLYGAWLEY (no dedication) *see* Errigle Keerogue w Ballygawley and Killeshil *Arm*
BALLYHAISE *see* Drung w Castleterra, Larah and Lavey etc *K, E & A*
BALLYHALBERT (St Andrew) w Ardkeen *D & D* I *vacant*
BALLYHOLME (St Columbanus) *D & D* I S E DOOGAN C J STEVENSON
BALLYHOOLEY (no dedication) *see* Fermoy Union *C, C & R*
BALLYJAMESDUFF (no dedication) *see* Kildrumferton w Ballymachugh and Ballyjamesduff *K, E & A*
BALLYKELLY *see* Tamlaghtfinlagan w Myroe *D & R*
BALLYLESSON *see* Drumbo *D & D*
BALLYMACARRETT (St Patrick) (St Christopher) (St Martin) *D & D* I J J CUNNINGHAM
BALLYMACASH (St Mark) *Conn* I L M GIBSON C W K JEFFREY
BALLYMACELLIGOTT (no dedication) *see* Tralee w Kilmoyley, Ballymacelligott etc *L & K*
BALLYMACHUGH (St Paul) *see* Kildrumferton w Ballymachugh and Ballyjamesduff *K, E & A*
BALLYMACKEY (St Michael) *see* Nenagh *L & K*
BALLYMACORMACK (no dedication) *see* Templemichael w Clongish, Clooncumber etc *K, E & A*
BALLYMAGLASSON *see* Dunboyne and Rathmolyon *M & K*
BALLYMAHON *see* Ardagh w Tashinny, Shrule and Kilcommick *K, E & A*
BALLYMARTLE (no dedication) *see* Kinsale Union *C, C & R*
BALLYMASCANLAN (St Mary) w Creggan and Rathcor *Arm* NSM R W R MOORE
BALLYMENA (St Patrick) w Ballyclug *Conn* I R M MCCONNELL C E M CARSON
BALLYMONEY *see* Kinneigh Union *C, C & R*
BALLYMONEY (St Patrick) w Finvoy and Rasharkin *Conn* I A J SWEENEY NSM B M HOWE, S A REID
BALLYMORE *see* Clondehorkey w Cashel *D & R*
BALLYMORE (St Mark) *Arm* I T S FORSTER
BALLYMORE EUSTACE (St John) *see* Blessington w Kilbride, Ballymore Eustace etc *D & G*
BALLYMOTE *see* Ballisodare w Collooney and Emlaghfad *T, K & A*
BALLYMOYER (St Luke) *see* Camlough, Mullaglass and Ballymoyer *Arm*
BALLYNAFEIGH (St Jude) *D & D* I P C BOURKE
BALLYNAHINCH *see* Magheradroll *D & D*
BALLYNAKILL (St Thomas) *see* Omey w Ballynakill, Errislannan and Roundstone *T, K & A*
BALLYNASCREEN *see* Kilcronaghan w Draperstown and Sixtowns *D & R*
BALLYNURE (Ascension) *see* Baltinglass w Ballynure etc *C, F & O*
BALLYNURE (Christ Church) and Ballyeaston *Conn* I J D CAMPBELL-SMYTH
BALLYPHILIP (no dedication) w Ardquin *D & D* I *vacant*
BALLYRASHANE (St John the Baptist) w Kildollagh *Conn* I A E ADAMS
BALLYROAN (no dedication) *see* Abbeyleix w Ballyroan etc *C, F & O*
BALLYSALLY (St Andrew) *see* Coleraine *Conn*
BALLYSCULLION (no dedication) *see* Drummaul w Duneane and Ballyscullion *Conn*
BALLYSCULLION (St Tida) *D & R* P-in-c B J HASSAN
BALLYSEEDY (no dedication) *see* Tralee w Kilmoyley, Ballymacelligott etc *L & K*
BALLYSHANNON *see* Kilbarron w Rossnowlagh and Drumholm *D & R*
BALLYSILLAN *see* Belfast St Mark *Conn*
BALLYSUMAGHAN (no dedication) *see* Taunagh w Kilmactranny, Ballysumaghan etc *K, E & A*
BALLYWALTER (Holy Trinity) w Inishargie *D & D* I S C BELL
BALLYWARD *see* Drumgath w Drumgooland and Clonduff *D & D*
BALLYWILLAN (Holy Trinity) *Conn* I P K MCDOWELL
BALRATHBOYNE *see* Kells Union *M & K*
BALTEAGH (St Canice) w Carrick *D & R* I R JONES
BALTIMORE *see* Abbeystrewry Union *C, C & R*

BALTINGLASS (St Mary) w Ballynure, Stratford-on-Slaney and Rathvilly *C, F & O* **I** M J HANLEY
BANAGHER (St Moresuis) *see* Cumber Lower w Banagher *D & R*
BANAGHER (St Paul) *see* Clonfert Gp *L & K*
BANBRIDGE *see* Seapatrick *D & D*
BANDON (St Peter) w Rathclaren, Innishannon, Ballinadee and Brinny *C, C & R* **I** D F A MACCARTHY **NSM** E C M FERGUSON **OLM** P CULLETON
BANGOR (St Columbanus) *see* Ballyholme *D & D*
BANGOR (St Comgall) *D & D* **I** N H PARKER
BANGOR ABBEY (Bangor Abbey) *D & D* **I** R NESBITT
BANGOR Primacy (Christ Church) *D & D* **I** *vacant*
BANNOW (no dedication) *see* Taghmon w Horetown and Bannow *C, F & O*
BANTRY *see* Kilmocomogue *C, C & R*
BARONSCOURT (no dedication) *see* Ardstraw w Baronscourt, Badoney Lower etc *D & R*
BARR (no dedication) *see* Donacavey w Barr *Clogh*
BEARA (St Peter) *see* Kilmocomogue *C, C & R*
BECTIVE *see* Trim and Athboy Gp *M & K*
BELFAST (All Saints) *Conn* **I** T S JOHNSTON **C** P BLAIR
BELFAST (Cathedral of St Anne) *Conn* **NSM** J M ELSDON
BELFAST (Christ Church) *Conn* **I** *vacant*
BELFAST (Holy Trinity) (St Silas) *Conn* **I** *vacant*
BELFAST (St Aidan) *Conn* **I** *vacant*
BELFAST (St Andrew) *Conn* **OLM** W F A BELL
BELFAST (St Bartholomew) *Conn* **I** T K D GRAHAM
BELFAST (St Brendan) *D & D* **C** J HARRIS
BELFAST (St Christopher) *see* Ballymacarrett *D & D*
BELFAST (St Clement) *D & D* **OLM** C BIRNIE
BELFAST (St Donard) *D & D* **I** K HIGGINS
BELFAST (St George) *Conn* **I** B STEWART **NSM** I M FRAZER
BELFAST (St Jude) *see* Ballynafeigh St Jude *D & D*
BELFAST (St Katharine) *Conn* **I** W J TAGGART
BELFAST (St Mark) *Conn* **I** R H MOORE
BELFAST (St Martin) *see* Ballymacarrett *D & D*
BELFAST (St Mary Magdalene) *Conn* **NSM** R E COTTER
BELFAST (St Mary) (Holy Redeemer) *Conn* **P-in-c** R H MOORE
BELFAST (St Matthew) *Conn* **I** T MCROBERTS
BELFAST (St Michael) *Conn* **I** *vacant*
BELFAST (St Nicholas) *Conn* **P-in-c** T S JOHNSTON **C** P BLAIR
BELFAST (St Ninian) *Conn* **I** *vacant*
BELFAST (St Patrick) *see* Ballymacarrett *D & D*
BELFAST (St Paul) (St Barnabas) *Conn* **C** I HAWTHORNE-STEELE
BELFAST (St Peter) (St James) *Conn* **I** C B LACEY
BELFAST (St Simon) (St Philip) *Conn* **P-in-c** R MOORE
BELFAST (St Stephen) (St Luke) *Conn* **P-in-c** J I CARSON **OLM** J SPENCE
BELFAST (St Thomas) *Conn* **I** P JACK
BELFAST Malone (St John) *Conn* **I** S A FIELDING
BELFAST Titanic Quarter *D & D* **I** *vacant*
BELFAST Upper Falls (St John the Baptist) *Conn* **NSM** M A REID
BELFAST Upper Malone (Epiphany) *Conn* **I** *vacant*
BELFAST Whiterock (St Columba) *Conn* **OLM** W F A BELL
BELLAGHY *see* Ballyscullion *D & R*
BELLEEK (no dedication) *see* Garrison w Slavin and Belleek *Clogh*
BELLEEK (St Luke) *see* Camlough, Mullaglass and Ballymoyer *Arm*
BELLERENA *see* Tamlaghtard w Aghanloo *D & R*
BELMONT (St Peter) *see* Londonderry Ch Ch, Culmore, Muff and Belmont *D & R*
BELTURBET *see* Annagh w Drumaloor, Cloverhill and Drumlane *K, E & A*
BELVOIR (Transfiguration) *D & D* **I** A A MCCARTNEY **C** C I BENNETT
BENOWN (no dedication) *see* Athlone w Benown, Kiltoom and Forgney *M & K*
BILBOA (no dedication) *see* Castlecomer w Colliery Ch, Mothel and Bilboa *C, F & O*
BILLIS (no dedication) *see* Lurgan w Billis, Killinkere and Munterconnaught *K, E & A*
BILLY (no dedication) w Derrykeighan *Conn* **I** *vacant*
BIRR (St Brendan) w Eglish, Lorrha, Dorrha and Lockeen *L & K* **NSM** R M GILL
BLACKLION *see* Killinagh w Kiltyclogher and Innismagrath *K, E & A*
BLACKROCK (All Saints) *see* Stillorgan w Blackrock *D & G*
BLACKROCK (St Michael) *see* Douglas Union w Frankfield *C, C & R*
BLARNEY *see* Carrigrohane Union *C, C & R*

BLESSINGTON (St Mary) w Kilbride, Ballymore Eustace and Holywood *D & G* **I** L W RUDDOCK
BLOOMFIELD (St Donard) *see* Belfast St Donard *D & D*
BOHO (no dedication) *see* Devenish w Boho *Clogh*
BOOTERSTOWN (St Philip and St James) *see* Dublin Booterstown *D & G*
BORNACOOLA *see* Templemichael w Clongish, Clooncumber etc *K, E & A*
BORRIS Clonagoose *see* Leighlin w Grange Sylvae, Shankill etc *C, F & O*
BORRIS Littleton *see* Kilcooley w Littleon, Crohane and Fertagh *C, F & O*
BORRIS-IN-OSSORY (no dedication) *see* Clonenagh w Offerlane, Borris-in-Ossory etc *C, F & O*
BORRISNAFARNEY (no dedication) *see* Cloughjordan w Borrisokane etc *L & K*
BORRISOKANE (no dedication) *as above*
BOURNEY (St Burchin) *see* Roscrea w Kyle, Bourney and Corbally *L & K*
BOVEVAGH (St Eugenius) *see* Dungiven w Bovevagh *D & R*
BOYLE (no dedication) and Elphin w Aghanagh, Kilbryan, Ardcarne and Croghan *K, E & A* **I** J E T YENDALL
BRACKAVILLE (Holy Trinity) w Donaghendry and Ballyclog *Arm* **I** A RAWDING
BRANIEL (St Brigid's Hall) *see* Orangefield w Braniel *D & D*
BRANTRY (Holy Trinity) *see* Killylea, Caledon, and Brantry *Arm*
BRAY (Christ Church) *D & G* **I** B T STANLEY
BRIGHT (no dedication) w Ballee and Killough *D & D* **I** *vacant*
BRIGOWN (St George) *see* Fermoy Union *C, C & R*
BRINNY (no dedication) *see* Bandon Union *C, C & R*
BROOKEBOROUGH *see* Aghavea *Clogh*
BROOMHEDGE (St Matthew) *Conn* **I** P J GALBRAITH
BROUGHSHANE *see* Skerry w Rathcavan and Newtowncrommelin *Conn*
BRYANSFORD *see* Castlewellan w Kilcoo *D & D*
BUNBEG *see* Gweedore, Carrickfin and Templecrone *D & R*
BUNCLODY (St Mary) w Kildavin, Clonegal and Kilrush *C, F & O* **I** T H SARGENT
BUNCRANA *see* Fahan Lower and Upper *D & R*
BUNDORAN *see* Cloonclare w Killasnett, Lurganboy and Drumlease *K, E & A*
BUSH *see* Ballymascanlan w Creggan and Rathcor *Arm*
BUSHMILLS *see* Dunluce *Conn*
CAHERAGH (St Mary) *see* Abbeystrewry Union *C, C & R*
CAHERCONLISH (St Ailbe) *see* Adare and Kilmallock w Kilpeacon, Croom etc *L & K*
CAHIR (St Paul) *see* Clonmel w Innislounagh, Tullaghmelan etc *C, F & O*
CAIRNCASTLE (St Patrick) *see* Kilwaughter and Cairncastle w Craigy Hill *Conn*
CALARY (no dedication) *see* Newcastle w Newtownmountkennedy and Calary *D & G*
CALEDON (St John) *see* Killylea, Caledon, and Brantry *Arm*
CALRY (no dedication) *K, E & A* **I** P H BAMBER
CAMLOUGH (Christ the Redeemer), Mullaglass and Ballymoyer *Arm* **I** A P S SYNNOTT **C** W J MCCRACKEN
CAMP *see* Dingle w Killiney and Kilgobbin *L & K*
CAMUS-JUXTA-BANN (St Mary) *D & R* **I** P LYONS
CAMUS-JUXTA-MOURNE (Christ Church) *D & R* **I** J M WHITE
CAPPAGH (St Eugene) w Lislimnaghan *D & R* **I** D J QUINN
CAPPOQUIN (St Anne) *see* Lismore w Cappoquin, Kilwatermoy, Dungarvan etc *C, F & O*
CARBURY (no dedication) *see* Clonsast w Rathangan, Thomastown etc *M & K*
CARLOW (St Mary) w Urglin and Staplestown *C, F & O* **I** D P J WHITE
CARNALEA (St Gall) *D & D* **I** M A PARKER
CARNALWAY (St Patrick) *see* Newbridge w Carnalway and Kilcullen *M & K*
CARNDONAGH *see* Moville w Greencastle, Donagh, Cloncha etc *D & R*
CARNEW (All Saints) *see* Crosspatrick Gp *C, F & O*
CARNLOUGH *see* Ardclinis and Tickmacrevan w Layde and Cushendun *Conn*
CARNMONEY (Holy Evangelists) *Conn* **I** A J HEBER **NSM** C R HARVEY
CARNTEEL (St James) and Crilly *Arm* **I** E R G WEST
CARRICK (no dedication) *see* Balteagh w Carrick *D & R*
CARRICKFERGUS (St Nicholas) *Conn* **I** C G ST JOHN **C** H A COOKE
CARRICKFIN (St Andrew) *see* Gweedore, Carrickfin and Templecrone *D & R*

CARRICKMACROSS (St Fin Barre) w Magheracloone *Clogh*
  I C A MCCONAGHIE
CARRICK-ON-SHANNON *see* Kiltoghart w Drumshambo,
  Annaduff and Kilronan *K, E & A*
CARRIGALINE (St Mary) w Killanully and Monkstown
  C, C & R I E M E MURRAY NSM A M MURPHY,
  H E A MINION
CARRIGALLEN (no dedication) *see* Arvagh w Carrigallen,
  Gowna and Columbkille *K, E & A*
CARRIGANS *see* Taughboyne, Craigadooish,
  Newtowncunningham etc *D & R*
CARRIGART *see* Mevagh w Glenalla *D & R*
CARRIGROHANE (St Peter) w Garrycloyne, Inniscarra and
  Magourney *C, C & R* C R J FERRIS
CARROWDORE (Christ Church) w Millisle *D & D*
  I C A J DAVIS
CARRYDUFF (St Ignatius) *see* Killaney w Carryduff *D & D*
CASHEL (Cathedral of St John the Baptist) w Magorban,
  Tipperary, Clonbeg and Ballintemple *C, F & O*
  I G G FIELD
CASHEL (no dedication) *see* Clondehorkey w Cashel *D & R*
CASTLEARCHDALE (St Patrick) *see* Derryvullen N w
  Castlearchdale *Clogh*
CASTLEBAR (Christ Church) *see* Aughaval w Achill,
  Knappagh, Dugort etc *T, K & A*
CASTLEBLAYNEY *see* Ballybay w Mucknoe and Clontibret
  Clogh
CASTLECOMER (St Mary) w the Colliery Church, Mothel
  and Bilboa *C, F & O* I E C WAKELY
CASTLECONNELL *see* Killaloe w Stradbally *L & K*
CASTLECONNOR (no dedication) *see* Killala w Dunfeeny,
  Crossmolina, Kilmoremoy etc *T, K & A*
CASTLEDAWSON (Christ Church) *D & R* I C R J WELSH
CASTLEDERG *see* Derg w Termonamongan *D & R*
CASTLEDERMOT (St James) *see* Narraghmore and Timolin w
  Castledermot etc *D & G*
CASTLEFLEMING (no dedication) *see* Rathdowney w
  Castlefleming, Donaghmore etc *C, F & O*
CASTLEGREGORY *see* Dingle w Killiney and Kilgobbin *L & K*
CASTLEHAVEN (no dedication) *see* Abbeystrewry Union
  C, C & R
CASTLEKNOCK (St Brigid) and Mulhuddart w Clonsilla
  D & G I W P HOUSTON
CASTLELOST *see* Mullingar, Portnashangan, Moyliscar,
  Kilbixy etc *M & K*
CASTLEMACADAM (Holy Trinity) w Ballinaclash, Aughrim
  and Macreddin *D & G* P-in-c S S HARRIS
CASTLEMAINE *see* Kilcolman w Kiltallagh, Killorglin,
  Knockane etc *L & K*
CASTLEMARTYR (St Anne) *see* Youghal Union *C, C & R*
CASTLEPOLLARD (St Michael) and Oldcastle w
  Loughcrew, Mount Nugent, Mayne and Drumcree *M & K*
  I D G O'CATHAIN
CASTLEREA *see* Roscommon Gp *K, E & A*
CASTLERICKARD *see* Dunboyne and Rathmolyon *M & K*
CASTLEROCK (Christ Church) w Dunboe and Fermoyle
  D & R I C MAC BRUITHIN NSM A QUIGLEY
CASTLETERRA (no dedication) *see* Drung w Castleterra,
  Larah and Lavey etc *K, E & A*
CASTLETOWN *see* Kells Union *M & K*
CASTLETOWN *see* Killeshin w Cloydagh and Killabban
  C, F & O
CASTLETOWN *see* Rathkeale w Askeaton, Kilcornan and
  Kilnaughtin *L & K*
CASTLETOWNBERE (St Peter) *see* Kilmocomogue *C, C & R*
CASTLETOWNROCHE (no dedication) *see* Mallow Union
  C, C & R
CASTLETOWNSEND *see* Abbeystrewry Union *C, C & R*
CASTLEVENTRY (no dedication) *see* Ross Union *C, C & R*
CASTLEWELLAN (St Paul) w Kilcoo *D & D* I vacant
CAVAN *see* Urney w Denn and Derryheen *K, E & A*
CELBRIDGE (Christ Church) w Straffan and Newcastle-
  Lyons *D & G* I S M NEILL
CHAPELIZOD (St Laurence) *see* Dublin Crumlin w
  Chapelizod *D & G*
CHARLEMONT (no dedication) *see* Moy w Charlemont *Arm*
CLABBY (St Margaret) *see* Tempo and Clabby *Clogh*
CLANABOGAN (no dedication) *see* Edenderry w Clanabogan
  D & R
CLANE (St Michael and All Angels) w Donadea and
  Coolcarrigan *M & K* C R J O'KELLY OLM J REID
CLARA (St Brigid) w Liss, Moate and Clonmacnoise *M & K*
  I vacant
CLARE (no dedication) *see* Loughgilly w Clare *Arm*
CLAUDY *see* Cumber Upper w Learmount *D & R*

CLEENISH (no dedication) w Mullaghdun *Clogh*
  I G P BRIDLE
CLIFDEN *see* Omey w Ballynakill, Errislannan and
  Roundstone *T, K & A*
CLOGH (Holy Trinity) *see* Aghadrumsee w Clogh and
  Drumsnatt *Clogh*
CLOGHER (Cathedral of St Macartan) w Errigal Portclare
  Clogh I O M G DOWNEY
CLOGHERNY (St Patrick) w Seskinore and Drumnakilly
  Arm NSM A MCWILLIAMS
CLONAGOOSE (St Moling) *see* Leighlin w Grange Sylvae,
  Shankill etc *C, F & O*
CLONAKILTY *see* Kilgariffe Union *C, C & R*
CLONALLON (no dedication) and Warrenpoint w
  Kilbroney *D & D* I D J MCCARTNEY
CLONARD *see* Mullingar, Portnashangan, Moyliscar, Kilbixy
  etc *M & K*
CLONASLEE *see* Mountmellick w Coolbanagher, Rosenallis
  etc *M & K*
CLONBEG (St Sedna) *see* Cashel w Magorban, Tipperary,
  Clonbeg etc *C, F & O*
CLONBRONEY (St John) *see* Mostrim w Granard,
  Clonbroney, Killoe etc *K, E & A*
CLONBULLOGUE *see* Clonsast w Rathangan, Thomastown
  etc *M & K*
CLONCHA (no dedication) *see* Moville w Greencastle,
  Donagh, Cloncha etc *D & R*
CLONDALKIN (St John) w Rathcoole *D & G* I A J RUFLI
  NSM A A SHINE
CLONDEHORKEY (St John) w Cashel *D & R* I vacant
CLONDEVADDOCK (Christ the Redeemer) w Portsalon
  and Leatbeg *D & R* I vacant
CLONDUFF (St John) *see* Drumgath w Drumgooland and
  Clonduff *D & D*
CLONE (St Paul) *see* Enniscorthy w Clone, Clonmore,
  Monart etc *C, F & O*
CLONEGAL (no dedication) *see* Bunclody w Kildavin,
  Clonegal and Kilrush *C, F & O*
CLONEGAM (Holy Trinity) *see* Fiddown w Clonegam,
  Guilcagh and Kilmeaden *C, F & O*
CLONENAGH (no dedication) w Offerlane, Borris-in-
  Ossory, Seirkieran and Roskelton *C, F & O*
  I V R A FITZPATRICK
CLONES (St Tighernach) w Killeevan *Clogh* I R TAYLOR
CLONEYHURKE (no dedication) *see* Portarlington w
  Cloneyhurke, Lea etc *M & K*
CLONFADFORAN *see* Tullamore w Durrow,
  Newtownfertullagh, Rahan etc *M & K*
CLONFEACLE (St Patrick), Derrygortreavy and Eglish *Arm*
  I S J COUSINS
CLONFERT (Cathedral of St Brendan) w Donanaughta,
  Banagher and Lickmolassy *L & K* I vacant
CLONGISH (St Paul) *see* Templemichael w Clongish,
  Clooncumber etc *K, E & A*
CLONLARA *see* Killaloe w Stradbally *L & K*
CLONLEIGH (St Lugadius) *see* Raphoe w Raymochy and
  Clonleigh *D & R*
CLONMACNOISE (St Kieran) *see* Clara w Liss, Moate and
  Clonmacnoise *M & K*
CLONMEL (St Mary) w Innislounagh, Tullaghmelan,
  Fethard, Kilvemnon and Cahir *C, F & O* I B Y FRYDAY
CLONMELLON *see* Trim and Athboy Gp *M & K*
CLONMORE (St John) *see* Enniscorthy w Clone, Clonmore,
  Monart etc *C, F & O*
CLONMORE (St John) *see* Kiltegan w Hacketstown,
  Clonmore and Moyne *C, F & O*
CLONOE (St Michael) *see* Tullaniskin w Clonoe *Arm*
CLONSAST (no dedication) w Rathangan, Thomastown,
  Monasteroris, Carbury and Rahan *M & K* I S L MARRY
  OLM A MELBOURNE
CLONSILLA (St Mary) *see* Castleknock and Mulhuddart w
  Clonsilla *D & G*
CLONTARF *see* Dublin Clontarf *D & G*
CLONTIBRET (St Colman) *see* Ballybay w Mucknoe and
  Clontibret *Clogh*
CLONTUSKERT (St Matthew) *see* Aughrim w Ballinasloe etc
  L & K
CLOONCLARE (no dedication) w Killasnett, Lurganboy
  and Drumlease *K, E & A* P-in-c B M MCCARTHY
  C R A BEADLE OLM A DAWSON
CLOONCUMBER (no dedication) *see* Templemichael w
  Clongish, Clooncumber etc *K, E & A*
CLOONEY (All Saints) w Strathfoyle *D & R* I D R MCBETH
  NSM M T E PEOPLES
CLOUGH *see* Craigs w Dunaghy and Killagan *Conn*
CLOUGHFERN (Ascension) *Conn* C A E STEWART

CLOUGHJORDAN (St Kieran) w Borrisokane, Ballingary, Borrisnafarney and Templeharry *L & K* **I** T I MITCHELL
CLOUGHMILLS *see* Craigs w Dunaghy and Killagan *Conn*
CLOVERHILL (St John) *see* Annagh w Drumaloor, Cloverhill and Drumlane *K, E & A*
CLOYDAGH (no dedication) *see* Killeshin w Cloydagh and Killabban *C, F & O*
CLOYNE (Cathedral of St Colman) w Inch, Corkbeg, Midleton and Gurranekennefeake *C, C & R* **I** S D GREEN
COACHFORD *see* Carrigrohane Union *C, C & R*
COALISLAND *see* Brackaville w Donaghendry and Ballyclog *Arm*
COLAGHTY *see* Lack *Clogh*
COLEBROOK *see* Aghalurcher w Tattykeeran, Cooneen etc *Clogh*
COLERAINE *see* Killowen *D & R*
COLERAINE (St Patrick) *Conn* **I** R COOKE
COLIN (St Andrew) *see* Derriaghy w Colin *Conn*
COLLIERY CHURCH, THE *see* Castlecomer w Colliery Ch, Mothel and Bilboa *C, F & O*
COLLON (no dedication) *see* Drogheda w Ardee, Collon and Termonfeckin *Arm*
COLLOONEY (St Paul) *see* Ballisodare w Collooney and Emlaghfad *T, K & A*
COLPE (St Columba) *see* Julianstown and Colpe w Drogheda and Duleek *M & K*
COLUMBKILLE (St Thomas) *see* Arvagh w Carrigallen, Gowna and Columbkille *K, E & A*
COMBER (St Mary) *D & D* **P-in-c** S H JOHNSTON
COMERAGH *see* Lismore w Cappoquin, Kilwatermoy, Dungarvan etc *C, F & O*
CONARY (St Bartholomew) *see* Dunganstown w Redcross and Conary *D & G*
CONG (St Mary) *see* Tuam w Cong and Aasleagh *T, K & A*
CONNOR (St Saviour) w Antrim St Patrick *Conn*
I I W MAGOWAN
CONVOY (St Ninian) w Monellan and Donaghmore *D & R*
I *vacant*
CONWAL (no dedication) w Aughanunshin and Gartan *D & R* **I** D A HOULTON
COOKSTOWN *see* Derryloran *Arm*
COOLBANAGHER (St John) *see* Mountmellick w Coolbanagher, Rosenallis etc *M & K*
COOLCARRIGAN (no dedication) *see* Clane w Donadea and Coolcarrigan *M & K*
COOLKELLURE (St Edmund) *see* Fanlobbus Union *C, C & R*
COOLOCK (St John) *see* Raheny w Coolock *D & G*
COONEEN (no dedication) *see* Aghalurcher w Tattykeeran, Cooneen etc *Clogh*
COOTEHILL *see* Drumgoon *K, E & A*
CORACLONE (St Peter) *see* Stradbally w Ballintubbert, Coraclone etc *C, F & O*
CORBALLY (Christ Church) *see* Roscrea w Kyle, Bourney and Corbally *L & K*
CORK (Cathedral of St Fin Barre) (St Nicholas) *C, C & R*
I N K DUNNE
CORK (St Ann) Shandon w St Mary *C, C & R*
P-in-c P L ROBINSON
CORKBEG (St Michael and All Angels) *see* Cloyne Union *C, C & R*
CORRAWALLEN (no dedication) *see* Kildallon Gp *K, E & A*
COURTMACSHERRY (St John the Evangelist) *see* Kilgariffe Union *C, C & R*
CRAIGADOOISH (no dedication) *see* Taughboyne, Craigadooish, Newtowncunningham etc *D & R*
CRAIGAVAD *see* Glencraig *D & D*
CRAIGAVON (St Saviour) *see* Ardmore w Craigavon *D & D*
CRAIGS (no dedication) w Dunaghy and Killagan *Conn*
NSM A R HALLIGAN, T S KELLY
CRAIGY HILL (All Saints) *see* Kilwaughter and Cairncastle w Craigy Hill *Conn*
CREAGH *see* Abbeystrewry Union *C, C & R*
CREAGH *see* Aughrim w Ballinasloe etc *L & K*
CRECORA *see* Adare and Kilmallock w Kilpeacon, Croom etc *L & K*
CREGAGH (St Finnian) *D & D* **I** J D M PIERCE
CREGGAN (no dedication) *see* Ballymascanlan w Creggan and Rathcor *Arm*
CRILLY (St George) *see* Carnteel and Crilly *Arm*
CRINKEN (St James) *D & G* **I** W J STEVENSON
CROGHAN (Holy Trinity) *see* Boyle and Elphin w Aghanagh, Kilbryan etc *K, E & A*
CROHANE (no dedication) *see* Kilcooley w Littleon, Crohane and Fertagh *C, F & O*
CROM (Holy Trinity) *see* Kinawley w H Trin *K, E & A*
CROOKHAVEN (St Brendan) *see* Kilmoe Union *C, C & R*

CROOM (no dedication) *see* Adare and Kilmallock w Kilpeacon, Croom etc *L & K*
CROSSGAR *see* Kilmore and Inch *D & D*
CROSSHAVEN *see* Templebreedy w Tracton and Nohoval *C, C & R*
CROSSMOLINA (no dedication) *see* Killala w Dunfeeny, Crossmolina, Kilmoremoy etc *T, K & A*
CROSSPATRICK Group (no dedication) w Kilcommon, Kilpipe, Preban and Carnew, The *C, F & O* **I** R K ELMES
CRUMLIN *see* Dublin Crumlin w Chapelizod *D & G*
CRUMLIN (St John) *see* Glenavy w Tunny and Crumlin *Conn*
CRUMLIN ROAD *see* Belfast St Mary w H Redeemer *Conn*
CULDAFF (no dedication) *see* Moville w Greencastle, Donagh, Cloncha etc *D & R*
CULFEIGHTRIN (no dedication) *see* Ramoan w Ballycastle and Culfeightrin *Conn*
CULLYBACKEY *see* Craigs w Dunaghy and Killagan *Conn*
CULMORE (Holy Trinity) *see* Londonderry Ch Ch, Culmore, Muff and Belmont *D & R*
CUMBER LOWER (Holy Trinity) w Banagher *D & R* **I** *vacant*
CUMBER UPPER (no dedication) w Learmount *D & R*
I J R D SLATER
CURRAGH (Garrison Church of St Paul) *see* Kildare w Kilmeague and Curragh *M & K*
CURRIN (St Andrew) w Drum and Newbliss *Clogh* **I** *vacant*
CUSHENDALL *see* Ardclinis and Tickmacrevan w Layde and Cushendun *Conn*
CUSHENDUN (no dedication) *as above*
DALKEY (St Patrick) *D & G* **I** B J HAYES **NSM** K P CONROY
DARTREY *see* Ematris w Rockcorry, Aghabog and Aughnamullan *Clogh*
DELGANY (Christ Church) *D & G* **I** N J W WAUGH
NSM H E A LEW
DENN (no dedication) *see* Urney w Denn and Derryheen *K, E & A*
DERG (no dedication) w Termonamongan *D & R*
I P A FERGUSON
DERNAKESH (Chapel of Ease) *see* Drumgoon *K, E & A*
DERRALOSSARY *see* Rathdrum w Glenealy, Derralossary and Laragh *D & G*
DERRIAGHY (Christ Church) w Colin *Conn*
I A D G MCALISTER
DERRYBRUSK (St Michael) *see* Maguiresbridge w Derrybrusk *Clogh*
DERRYGONNELLY *see* Inishmacsaint *Clogh*
DERRYGORTREAVY (St Columba) *see* Clonfeacle, Derrygortreavy and Eglish *Arm*
DERRYHEEN (no dedication) *see* Urney w Denn and Derryheen *K, E & A*
DERRYKIGHAN (St Colman) *see* Billy w Derrykeighan *Conn*
DERRYLANE (no dedication) *see* Killeshandra w Killegar and Derrylane *K, E & A*
DERRYLIN *see* Kinawley w H Trin *K, E & A*
DERRYLORAN (St Luran) *Arm* **I** R J N PORTEUS
NSM W J A DAWSON
DERRYNOOSE (St John) *see* Keady, Armaghbreague, Derrynoose and Newtownhamilton *Arm*
DERRYVOLGIE (St Columba) *Conn* **I** W J BOYD
DERRYVULLEN NORTH (St Tighernach) w Castlearchdale *Clogh* **I** P THOMPSON
DERRYVULLEN SOUTH (St Tighernach) w Garvary *Clogh*
NSM E G M THOMPSON
DERVOCK *see* Billy w Derrykeighan *Conn*
DESERTCREAT (no dedication) *see* Ardtrea w Desertcreat *Arm*
DESERTLYN (St John) w Ballyeglish *Arm* **I** A N STRINGER
DESERTMARTIN (St Conghall) w Termoneeny *D & R*
I *vacant*
DESERTOGHILL (no dedication) *see* Errigal w Garvagh *D & R*
DESERTSERGES (no dedication) *see* Kinneigh Union *C, C & R*
DEVENISH (St Molaise) w Boho *Clogh* **Bp's** C S C AJUKA
DIAMOND (St Paul) *see* Tartaraghan w Diamond *Arm*
DINGLE (St James) w Killiney and Kilgobbin *L & K* **I** *vacant*
DOAGH *see* Kilbride *Conn*
DOLLINGSTOWN (St Saviour) *see* Magheralin w Dollingstown *D & D*
DONABATE (St Patrick) *see* Swords w Donabate and Kilsallaghan *D & G*
DONACAVEY (no dedication) w Barr *Clogh* **I** J J WOODS
DONADEA (St Peter) *see* Clane w Donadea and Coolcarrigan *M & K*
DONAGH (no dedication) *see* Moville w Greencastle, Donagh, Cloncha etc *D & R*
DONAGH (St Salvator) w Tyholland and Errigal Truagh *Clogh* **C** L A CAPPER
DONAGHADEE (no dedication) *D & D* **R** I R GAMBLE

DONAGHCLONEY (St Patrick) w Waringstown *D & D*
I *vacant*
DONAGHEADY (St James) *D & R* I *vacant*
DONAGHENDRY (St Patrick) *see* Brackaville w Donaghendry
and Ballyclog *Arm*
DONAGHMORE (no dedication) *see* Rathdowney w
Castlefleming, Donaghmore etc *C, F & O*
DONAGHMORE (St Bartholomew) *see* Aghaderg w
Donaghmore and Scarva *D & D*
DONAGHMORE (St Michael) w Donaghmore Upper *Arm*
I P A THOMPSON
DONAGHMORE (St Patrick) *see* Convoy w Monellan and
Donaghmore *D & R*
DONAGHMORE, UPPER (St Patrick) *see* Donaghmore w
Donaghmore Upper *Arm*
DONAGHPATRICK (St Patrick) *see* Kells Union *M & K*
DONANON (no dedication) *see* Roscommon Gp *K, E & A*
DONANAUGHTA (St John the Baptist) *see* Clonfert Gp *L & K*
DONARD (no dedication) *see* Donoughmore and Donard w
Dunlavin *D & G*
**DONEGAL (no dedication) w Killymard, Lough Eske and
Laghey** *D & R* I D I HUSS
DONEGORE (St John) *see* Templepatrick w Donegore *Conn*
DONEMANA *see* Donagheady *D & R*
DONERAILE (St Mary) *see* Mallow Union *C, C & R*
DONNYBROOK (St Mary) *see* Dublin Irishtown w
Donnybrook *D & G*
DONOUGHMORE (no dedication) and Donard w Dunlavin
D & G I N J O'RAW
DORRHA (no dedication) *see* Birr w Lorrha, Dorrha and
Lockeen *L & K*
**DOUGLAS (St Luke) w Blackrock, Frankfield and
Marmullane** *C, C & R* I A M WILKINSON
DOWN (Cathedral of the Holy and Undivided Trinity)
D & D I *vacant*
DOWN (St Margaret) w Hollymount *D & D* I *vacant*
DOWNPATRICK *see* Down Cathl *D & D*
DOWNPATRICK *see* Down w Hollymount *D & D*
DRAPERSTOWN (St Columb) *see* Kilcronaghan w
Draperstown and Sixtowns *D & R*
DREW MEMORIAL *see* Belfast St Simon w St Phil *Conn*
DRIMOLEAGUE (St Matthew) *see* Fanlobbus Union *C, C & R*
DRINAGH (Christ Church) *as above*
DROGHEDA (St Mary) *see* Julianstown and Colpe w
Drogheda and Duleek *M & K*
DROGHEDA (St Peter) w Ardee, Collon and Termonfeckin
Arm I I B JAMIESON NSM J MOORE
DROMAHAIR *see* Cloonclare w Killasnett, Lurganboy and
Drumlease *K, E & A*
DROMARA (St John) w Garvaghy *D & D* I C TAYLOR
DROMARD (Christ Church) *see* Skreen w Kilmacshalgan and
Dromard *T, K & A*
DROMOD (St Michael and All Angels) *see* Kenmare w
Sneem, Waterville etc *L & K*
DROMORE (Cathedral of Christ the Redeemer) *D & D*
I S G WILSON NSM T J MCKEOWN
DROMORE (Holy Trinity) *Clogh* I A T E QUILL
DRUM (no dedication) *see* Currin w Drum and Newbliss
Clogh
DRUMACHOSE (Christ Church) *D & R* I *vacant*
DRUMALOOR (St Andrew) *see* Annagh w Drumaloor,
Cloverhill and Drumlane *K, E & A*
DRUMANY (Christ Church) *see* Kinawley w H Trin *K, E & A*
DRUMBANAGHER (St Mary) *see* Acton and Drumbanagher
Arm
DRUMBEG (St Patrick) *D & D* I W S NIXON
DRUMBO (Holy Trinity) *D & D* I W M N JAMISON
DRUMCANNON (Christ Church) *see* Waterford w Killea,
Drumcannon and Dunhill *C, F & O*
DRUMCAR *see* Kilsaran w Drumcar, Dunleer and Dunany
Arm
**DRUMCLAMPH (no dedication) w Lower Langfield and
Upper Langfield** *D & R* I R G KEOGH
**DRUMCLIFFE (St Columba) w Kilrush, Kilfenora, Kilfarboy,
Kilnasoolagh, Shannon and Kilferagh** *L & K*
I K M O'BRIEN NSM P E MCKEE HANNA
DRUMCLIFFE (St Columba) w Lissadell and Munninane
K, E & A I I J HANNA OLM M YOUNG
DRUMCONDRA *see* Dublin Drumcondra w N Strand *D & G*
DRUMCONRATH (St Peter) *see* Kingscourt w Syddan *M & K*
DRUMCREE (Ascension) *Arm* I G F GALWAY
DRUMCREE (St John) *see* Castlepollard and Oldcastle w
Loughcrew etc *M & K*
DRUMGATH (St John) w Drumgooland and Clonduff
D & D I B I LINTON

DRUMGLASS (St Anne) w Moygashel *Arm* I B R MARTIN
C G HARE NSM M E M STEVENSON
DRUMGOOLAND (no dedication) *see* Drumgath w
Drumgooland and Clonduff *D & D*
**DRUMGOON (All Saints) w Ashfield, Killesherdoney and
Dernakesh** *K, E & A* I *vacant*
DRUMHOLM (no dedication) *see* Kilbarron w Rossnowlagh
and Drumholm *D & R*
DRUMINISKILL (Chapel of Ease) *see* Killesher *K, E & A*
DRUMKEERAN *see* Killinagh w Kiltyclogher and
Innismagrath *K, E & A*
**DRUMKEERAN (no dedication) w Templecarne and
Muckross** *Clogh* NSM C G EAMES
DRUMLANE (no dedication) *see* Annagh w Drumaloor,
Cloverhill and Drumlane *K, E & A*
DRUMLEASE (no dedication) *see* Cloonclare w Killasnett,
Lurganboy and Drumlease *K, E & A*
DRUMMAUL (St Brigid) w Duneane and Ballyscullion *Conn*
I D P KERR
DRUMMULLY (no dedication) *see* Galloon w Drummully
and Sallaghy *Clogh*
DRUMNAKILLY (Holy Trinity) *see* Clogherny w Seskinore and
Drumnakilly *Arm*
DRUMQUIN *see* Drumclamph w Lower and Upper Langfield
D & R
DRUMRAGH (St Columba) w Mountfield *D & R* I *vacant*
DRUMREILLY (no dedication) *see* Mohill w Farnaught,
Aughavas, Oughteragh etc *K, E & A*
DRUMSHAMBO (St John) *see* Kiltoghart w Drumshambo,
Annaduff and Kilronan *K, E & A*
DRUMSNATT (St Molua) *see* Aghadrumsee w Clogh and
Drumsnatt *Clogh*
DRUMTALLAGH (no dedication) *see* Armoy w Loughguile
and Drumtullagh *Conn*
**DRUNG (no dedication) w Castleterra, Larah and Lavey
and Killoughter** *K, E & A* I N T JONES
**DUBLIN (Christ Church Cathedral) Group: (St Andrew)
(St Werburgh) (St Michan) and Grangegorman** *D & G*
V D A PIERPOINT
DUBLIN (Irish Church Missions) and St Thomas *D & G*
I *vacant*
DUBLIN (St Ann) (St Stephen) *D & G* I D I GILLESPIE
NSM M J O'CONNOR, Y A GANNELLY
DUBLIN (St Bartholomew) w Leeson Park *D & G*
I A MCCROSKERY
DUBLIN (St Catherine and St James) (St Audoen) *D & G*
I M D GARDNER C E HEASLIP NSM C E BAKER,
M M WALLER
DUBLIN (St George and St Thomas) *D & G* I *vacant*
DUBLIN (Zion Church) *D & G* I S A FARRELL
DUBLIN Booterstown (St Philip and St James) *D & G*
I G V WHARTON
DUBLIN Clontarf (St John the Baptist) *D & G*
I E C L ROBINSON NSM A E LODGE
DUBLIN Crumlin (St Mary) w Chapelizod *D & G*
I R E JACKSON
DUBLIN Drumcondra (St John the Baptist) w North Strand
D & G I E G BUNTING
DUBLIN Irishtown (St Matthew) w Donnybrook *D & G*
I *vacant*
DUBLIN Mount Merrion (St Thomas) *D & G*
I G V WHARTON
DUBLIN Rathfarnham (no dedication) *D & G* I A GALLIGAN
DUBLIN Rathmines (Holy Trinity) w Harold's Cross *D & G*
I R D JONES
DUBLIN Sandford (no dedication) w Milltown *D & G*
I S GYLES NSM A M O'FARRELL
DUBLIN Sandymount (St John the Evangelist) *D & G*
P-in-c P A BARLOW
DUBLIN Santry (St Pappan) w Glasnevin and Finglas *D & G*
I D W OXLEY
DUBLIN Whitechurch (no dedication) *D & G*
I A H N MCKINLEY
DUGORT (St Thomas) *see* Aughaval w Achill, Knappagh,
Dugort etc *T, K & A*
DULEEK *see* Julianstown and Colpe w Drogheda and Duleek
M & K
DUN LAOGHAIRE (Christ Church) *D & G*
I Á B ÓLAFSDÓTTIR O'HANLON
DUNAGHY (St James) *see* Craigs w Dunaghy and Killagan
Conn
DUNANY *see* Kilsaran w Drumcar, Dunleer and Dunany *Arm*
DUNBOE (St Paul) *see* Castlerock w Dunboe and Fermoyle
D & R

DUNBOYNE (St Peter and St Paul) w Rathmolyon, Dunshaughlin, Maynooth, Agher and Rathcore *M & K*
I E T GRIFFIN   C A E G IRVINE

DUNDALK (St Nicholas) w Heynestown *Arm*
NSM R W R MOORE

DUNDELA (St Mark) *D & D*   I H STEED

DUNDONALD (St Elizabeth) *D & D*   I T G ANDERSON

DUNDRUM   *see* Cashel w Magorban, Tipperary, Clonbeg etc *C, F & O*

DUNDRUM (St Donard)   *see* Kilmegan w Maghera *D & D*

DUNEANE (no dedication)   *see* Drummaul w Duneane and Ballyscullion *Conn*

DUNFANAGHY (Holy Trinity), Raymunterdoney and Tullaghbegley *D & R*   I D SKUCE

DUNFEENY (no dedication)   *see* Killala w Dunfeeny, Crossmolina, Kilmoremoy etc *T, K & A*

DUNGANNON   *see* Drumglass w Moygashel *Arm*

DUNGANSTOWN (St Kevin) w Redcross and Conary *D & G*
I J R HEANEY

DUNGARVAN (St Mary)   *see* Lismore w Cappoquin, Kilwatermoy, Dungarvan etc *C, F & O*

DUNGIVEN (no dedication) w Bovevagh *D & R*
I M W J LONEY

DUNGLOE   *see* Gweedore, Carrickfin and Templecrone *D & R*

DUNHILL (St John the Baptist)   *see* Waterford w Killea, Drumcannon and Dunhill *C, F & O*

DUNKERRIN (no dedication)   *see* Shinrone w Aghancon etc *L & K*

DUNLAVIN (St Nicholas)   *see* Donoughmore and Donard w Dunlavin *D & G*

DUNLECKNEY (St Mary) w Nurney, Lorum and Kiltennel *C, F & O*   I K M RONNÉ

DUNLEER (no dedication)   *see* Kilsaran w Drumcar, Dunleer and Dunany *Arm*

DUNLUCE (St John the Baptist) *Conn*   I G E GRAHAM

DUNMANWAY   *see* Fanlobbus Union *C, C & R*

DUNMORE EAST   *see* Waterford w Killea, Drumcannon and Dunhill *C, F & O*

DUNMURRY (St Colman) *Conn*   I A R MCLAUGHLIN

DUNNALONG (St John)   *see* Leckpatrick w Dunnalong *D & R*

DUNSEVERICK (no dedication)   *see* Ballintoy w Rathlin and Dunseverick *Conn*

DUNSFORD (St Mary)   *see* Lecale Gp *D & D*

DUNSHAUGHLIN (St Seachnal)   *see* Dunboyne and Rathmolyon *M & K*

DURROW (St Columba)   *see* Tullamore w Durrow, Newtownfertullagh, Rahan etc *M & K*

DURROW (St Fintan)   *see* Abbeyleix w Ballyroan etc *C, F & O*

DURRUS (St James the Apostle)   *see* Kilmocomogue *C, C & R*

DYSART ENOS (Holy Trinity)   *see* Maryborough w Dysart Enos and Ballyfin *C, F & O*

EASKEY (St Anne)   *see* Killala w Dunfeeny, Crossmolina, Kilmoremoy etc *T, K & A*

EDENDERRY   *see* Clonsast w Rathangan, Thomastown etc *M & K*

EDENDERRY (no dedication) w Clanabogan *D & R*
I R W CLARKE

EDGEWORTHSTOWN   *see* Mostrim w Granard, Clonbroney, Killoe etc *K, E & A*

EGLANTINE (All Saints) *Conn*   I J W KERNOHAN

EGLINTON   *see* Faughanvale *D & R*

EGLISH (Holy Trinity)   *see* Clonfeacle, Derrygortreavy and Eglish *Arm*

ELPHIN (no dedication)   *see* Boyle and Elphin w Aghanagh, Kilbryan etc *K, E & A*

EMATRIS (St John the Evangelist) w Rockcorry, Aghabog and Aughnamullan *Clogh*   NSM M B PRINGLE

EMLAGHFAD (no dedication)   *see* Ballisodare w Collooney and Emlaghfad *T, K & A*

ENNIS   *see* Drumcliffe w Kilnasoolagh *L & K*

ENNISCORTHY (St Mary) w Clone, Clonmore, Monart and Templescobin *C, F & O*   I N J HALFORD

ENNISKEEN   *see* Kingscourt w Syddan *M & K*

ENNISKERRY   *see* Powerscourt w Kilbride *D & G*

ENNISKILLEN   *see* Rossorry *Clogh*

ENNISKILLEN (Cathedral of St Macartin) *Clogh*   I K R J HALL

ENNISNAG (St Peter)   *see* Kells Gp *C, F & O*

ERRIGAL (St Paul) w Garvagh *D & R*   I C M HAYES

ERRIGAL PORTCLARE (no dedication)   *see* Clogh w Errigal Portclare *Clogh*

ERRIGAL TRUAGH (St Muadhan)   *see* Donagh w Tyholland and Errigal Truagh *Clogh*

ERRIGLE KEEROGUE (no dedication) w Ballygawley and Killeshil *Arm*   I N C QUINN

ERRISLANNAN (no dedication)   *see* Omey w Ballynakill, Errislannan and Roundstone *T, K & A*

ESKRAHOOLE (no dedication)   *see* Augher w Newtownsaville and Eskrahoole *Clogh*

EYRECOURT   *see* Clonfert Gp *L & K*

FAHAN LOWER (Christ Church) and UPPER (St Mura)
D & R   I J H MCGAFFIN

FALLS, LOWER (St Luke)   *see* Belfast St Steph w St Luke *Conn*

FALLS, UPPER   *see* Belfast Upper Falls *Conn*

FANLOBBUS (St Mary) w Drimoleague, Drinagh and Coolkellure *C, C & R*   I C P JEFFERS

FARNAUGHT (no dedication)   *see* Mohill w Farnaught, Aughavas, Oughteragh etc *K, E & A*

FAUGHANVALE (St Canice) *D & R*   I D P HOEY

FENAGH (All Saints) w Myshall, Aghade and Ardoyne
C, F & O   I L D D SCOTT

FERMOY (Christ Church) w Ballyhooley, Knockmourne, Ardnageehy and Brigown *C, C & R*   I G A PAULSEN
NSM W H HILL

FERMOYLE (no dedication)   *see* Castlerock w Dunboe and Fermoyle *D & R*

FERNS (Cathedral of St Edan) w Kilbride, Toombe, Kilcormack and Ballycarney *C, F & O*   I P G MOONEY

FERRY, EAST   *see* Cloyne Union *C, C & R*

FERTAGH (no dedication)   *see* Kilcooley w Littleon, Crohane and Fertagh *C, F & O*

FETHARD (Holy Trinity)   *see* Clonmel w Innislounagh, Tullaghmelan etc *C, F & O*

FETHARD (St Mogue)   *see* New w Old Ross, Whitechurch, Fethard etc *C, F & O*

FIDDOWN (no dedication) w Clonegam, Guilcagh and Kilmeaden *C, F & O*   P-in-c V M LYNCH

FINAGHY (St Polycarp) *Conn*   I A L STEWART

FINGLAS (St Canice)   *see* Dublin Santry w Glasnevin and Finglas *D & G*

FINNER (Christ Church)   *see* Killinagh w Kiltyclogher and Innismagrath *K, E & A*

FINTONA   *see* Donacavey w Barr *Clogh*

FINVOY (no dedication)   *see* Ballymoney w Finvoy and Rasharkin *Conn*

FIVEMILETOWN (St John) *Clogh*   I T K HANLON

FLORENCECOURT   *see* Killesher *K, E & A*

FONTSTOWN (St John the Evangelist)   *see* Athy w Kilberry, Fontstown and Kilkea *D & G*

FORGNEY (St Munis)   *see* Athlone w Benown, Kiltoom and Forgney *M & K*

FOUNTAINS   *see* Lismore w Cappoquin, Kilwatermoy, Dungarvan etc *C, F & O*

FOXFORD   *see* Straid *T, K & A*

FOYNES   *see* Rathkeale w Askeaton, Kilcornan and Kilnaughtin *L & K*

FRANKFIELD (Holy Trinity)   *see* Douglas Union w Frankfield *C, C & R*

FRENCH CHURCH   *see* Portarlington w Cloneyhurke, Lea etc *M & K*

FRENCHPARK   *see* Roscommon Gp *K, E & A*

GALLOON (St Comgall) w Drummully and Sallaghy *Clogh*
I *vacant*

GALWAY (St Nicholas) w Kilcummin *T, K & A*
I L E A PEILOW   OLM C REYNOLDS

GARRISON (no dedication) w Slavin and Belleek *Clogh*
I *vacant*

GARRYCLOYNE (no dedication)   *see* Carrigrohane Union *C, C & R*

GARTAN (St Columba)   *see* Conwal Union w Gartan *D & R*

GARTREE (no dedication)   *see* Killead w Gartree *Conn*

GARVAGH   *see* Errigal w Garvagh *D & R*

GARVAGHY (no dedication)   *see* Dromara w Garvaghy *D & D*

GARVARY (Holy Trinity)   *see* Derryvullen S w Garvary *Clogh*

GEASHILL (St Mary) w Killeigh and Ballycommon *M & K*
P-in-c F M GRASHAM

GILFORD   *see* Tullylish *D & D*

GILFORD (St Paul) *D & D*   I D I CADDOO

GILNAHIRK (St Dorothea) *D & D*   NSM M S WALSHE

GLANDORE   *see* Ross Union *C, C & R*

GLASCARRIG (no dedication)   *see* Ardamine w Kiltennel, Glascarrig etc *C, F & O*

GLASLOUGH   *see* Donagh w Tyholland and Errigal Truagh *Clogh*

GLASNEVIN (St Mobhi)   *see* Dublin Santry w Glasnevin and Finglas *D & G*

GLENAGEARY (St Paul) *D & G*   I G G DOWD

GLENALLA (St Columbkille)   *see* Mevagh w Glenalla *D & R*

GLENARM   *see* Ardclinis and Tickmacrevan w Layde and Cushendun *Conn*

GLENAVY (St Aidan) w Tunny and Crumlin *Conn*
I L N CRONIN

GLENBEIGH (St John) *see* Kilcolman w Kiltallagh, Killorglin, Knockane etc *L & K*

GLENCAIRN *see* Belfast St Andr *Conn*

GLENCAR *see* Cloonclare w Killasnett, Lurganboy and Drumlease *K, E & A*

GLENCOLUMBKILLE (St Columba) *see* Ardara w Glencolumbkille, Inniskeel etc *D & R*

GLENCRAIG (Holy Trinity) *D & D* I C J SIMPSON

GLENDERMOTT (no dedication) *D & R* I S R T BOYD C N J CAIRNS, W I MCALEAVEY **NSM** W A BURNS

GLENEALY (no dedication) *see* Rathdrum w Glenealy, Derralossary and Laragh *D & G*

GLENOE *see* Glynn w Raloo *Conn*

GLENTIES (no dedication) *see* Ardara w Glencolumbkille, Inniskeel etc *D & R*

GLENVILLE *see* Fermoy Union *C, C & R*

GLYNN (St John) w Raloo *Conn* I D LOCKHART

GORESBRIDGE *see* Leighlin w Grange Sylvae, Shankill etc *C, F & O*

GOREY (Christ Church) w Kilnahue, Leskinfere and Ballycanew *C, F & O* I M J J HAYDEN **NSM** C CASSERLEY-FARRAR

GORTIN *see* Ardstraw w Baronscourt, Badoney Lower etc *D & R*

GOWNA (no dedication) *see* Arvagh w Carrigallen, Gowna and Columbkille *K, E & A*

GRACEFIELD (no dedication) *see* Woodschapel w Gracefield *Arm*

GRANARD (St Patrick) *see* Mostrim w Granard, Clonbroney, Killoe etc *K, E & A*

GRANGE (St Aidan) *see* Loughgall w Grange *Arm*

GRANGE SYLVAE (St George) *see* Leighlin w Grange Sylvae, Shankill etc *C, F & O*

GRANGEGORMAN (All Saints) *see* Dublin Ch Ch Cathl Gp *D & G*

GREENAN (no dedication) *see* Ardstraw w Baronscourt, Badoney Lower etc *D & R*

GREENCASTLE (St Finian) *see* Moville w Greencastle, Donagh, Cloncha etc *D & R*

GREENISLAND (Holy Name) *Conn* **P-in-c** J MOULD

GREY ABBEY (St Saviour) w Kircubbin *D & D* I G WITHERS

GREYSTONES (St Patrick) *D & G* I D S MUNGAVIN **NSM** R G GUILDEA

GROOMSPORT (no dedication) *D & D* I D J M POLLOCK

GUILCAGH (St John the Evangelist) *see* Fiddown w Clonegam, Guilcagh and Kilmeaden *C, F & O*

GURRANEKENNEFEAKE (no dedication) *see* Cloyne Union *C, C & R*

GWEEDORE (St Patrick), Carrickfin and Templecrone *D & R* **P-in-c** T D ALLEN C E A FITZGERALD

HACKETSTOWN (St John the Baptist) *see* Kiltegan w Hacketstown, Clonmore and Moyne *C, F & O*

HAROLD'S CROSS (no dedication) *see* Dublin Rathmines w Harold's Cross *D & G*

HELEN'S BAY (St John the Baptist) *D & D* I T C KINAHAN

HEYNESTOWN (St Paul) *see* Dundalk w Heynestown *Arm*

HIGHFIELD *see* Belfast Whiterock *Conn*

HILLSBOROUGH (St Malachi) *D & D* I B A FOLLIS C J BROWN

HILLTOWN *see* Drumgath w Drumgooland and Clonduff *D & D*

HOLLYFORT *see* Gorey w Kilnahue, Leskinfere and Ballycanew *C, F & O*

HOLLYMOUNT (no dedication) *see* Down H Trin w Hollymount *D & D*

HOLMPATRICK (St Patrick) w Balbriggan and Kenure *D & G* I A KELLY **NSM** T A O'BRIEN

HOLYCROSS *see* Templemore w Thurles and Kilfithmone *C, F & O*

HOLYWOOD (St Kevin) *see* Blessington w Kilbride, Ballymore Eustace etc *D & G*

HOLYWOOD (St Philip and St James) *D & D* I G A HARRON C K D MCGRATH

HORETOWN (St James) *see* Taghmon w Horetown and Bannow *C, F & O*

HORSELEAP *see* Clara w Liss, Moate and Clonmacnoise *M & K*

HOWTH (St Mary) *D & G* I W K M BREW

INCH *see* Cloyne Union *C, C & R*

INCH (no dedication) *see* Arklow w Inch and Kilbride *D & G*

INCH (no dedication) *see* Kilmore and Inch *D & D*

INISHARGIE (St Andrew) *see* Ballywalter w Inishargie *D & D*

INISHMACSAINT (St Ninnidh) *Clogh* I vacant

INISTIOGE (St Mary) *see* Kells Gp *C, F & O*

INNISCALTRA (St Caimin) *see* Killaloe w Stradbally *L & K*

INNISCARRA (no dedication) *see* Carrigrohane Union *C, C & R*

INNISHANNON (Christ Church) *see* Bandon Union *C, C & R*

INNISKEEL (no dedication) *see* Ardara w Glencolumbkille, Inniskeel etc *D & R*

INNISLOUNAGH (St Patrick) *see* Clonmel w Innislounagh, Tullaghmelan etc *C, F & O*

INNISMAGRATH (no dedication) *see* Killinagh w Kiltyclogher and Innismagrath *K, E & A*

INVER *see* Larne and Inver *Conn*

INVER (St John the Evangelist) w Mountcharles, Killaghtee and Killybegs *D & R* **Bp's** C L E FARRELL

IRISHTOWN *see* Dublin Irishtown w Donnybrook *D & G*

IRVINESTOWN *see* Derryvullen N w Castlearchdale *Clogh*

ISLANDMAGEE (St John) *see* Whitehead and Islandmagee *Conn*

JOANMOUNT *see* Belfast H Trin and St Silas *Conn*

JOHNSTOWN *see* Kilcooley w Littleon, Crohane and Fertagh *C, F & O*

JORDANSTOWN (St Patrick) *Conn* I N P BAYLOR **OLM** B O'LOAN

JULIANSTOWN (St Mary) and Colpe w Drogheda and Duleek *M & K* I K M POULTON

KEADY (St Matthew), Armaghbreague, Derrynoose and Newtownhamilton *Arm* I D T MOSES

KELLS (St Columba) w Balrathboyne, Moynalty, Donaghpatrick and Castletown *M & K* I W A SEALE

KELLS (St Mary) w Ballaghtobin, Kilmoganny, Ennisnag, Inistioge and Kilfane *C, F & O* **P-in-c** J G MULHALL

KENAGH *see* Ardagh w Tashinny, Shrule and Kilcommick *K, E & A*

KENMARE (St Patrick) w Sneem, Dromod and Valentia *L & K* **P-in-c** M R CAVANAGH

KENTSTOWN (St Mary) *see* Navan w Kentstown, Tara, Slane, Painestown etc *M & K*

KENURE (no dedication) *see* Holmpatrick w Balbriggan and Kenure *D & G*

KESH *see* Magheraculmoney *Clogh*

KILBARRON (St Anne) w Rossnowlagh and Drumholm *D & R* I B R RUSSELL

KILBERRY (no dedication) *see* Athy w Kilberry, Fontstown and Kilkea *D & G*

KILBIXY (St Bigseach) *see* Mullingar, Portnashangan, Moyliscar, Kilbixy etc *M & K*

KILBONANE (St Mark) *see* Moviddy Union *C, C & R*

KILBRIDE (Holy Trinity) *see* Ferns w Kilbride, Toombe, Kilcormack etc *C, F & O*

KILBRIDE (no dedication) *see* Blessington w Kilbride, Ballymore Eustace etc *D & G*

KILBRIDE (St Bride) *Conn* I W D HUMPHRIES

KILBRIDE (St Brigid) *see* Arklow w Inch and Kilbride *D & G*

KILBRIDE BRAY (no dedication) *see* Powerscourt w Kilbride *D & G*

KILBRONEY (no dedication) *see* Clonallon and Warrenpoint w Kilbroney *D & D*

KILBRYAN (no dedication) *see* Boyle and Elphin w Aghanagh, Kilbryan etc *K, E & A*

KILCLEAGH *see* Clara w Liss, Moate and Clonmacnoise *M & K*

KILCLIEF (no dedication) *see* Lecale Gp *D & D*

KILCLUNEY (St John) *see* Mullabrack w Markethill and Kilcluney *Arm*

KILCOCK *see* Dunboyne and Rathmolyon *M & K*

KILCOLMAN (no dedication) w Kiltallagh, Killorglin, Knockane and Glenbeigh *L & K* **P-in-c** F A KEEGAN C A-M L STUART

KILCOMMICK (no dedication) *see* Ardagh w Tashinny, Shrule and Kilcommick *K, E & A*

KILCOMMON (no dedication) *see* Crosspatrick Gp *C, F & O*

KILCOO (no dedication) *see* Castlewellan w Kilcoo *D & D*

KILCOOLEY (no dedication) w Littleton, Crohane and Fertagh *C, F & O* I G A C P SAWYER

KILCOOLEY (St Columba) *see* Bangor Abbey *D & D*

KILCORMACK (St Cormac) *see* Ferns w Kilbride, Toombe, Kilcormack etc *C, F & O*

KILCORNAN (no dedication) *see* Rathkeale w Askeaton, Kilcornan and Kilnaughtin *L & K*

KILCROHANE *see* Kenmare w Sneem, Waterville etc *L & K*

KILCRONAGHAN (no dedication) w Draperstown and Sixtowns *D & R* I R G DIFFIN

KILCULLEN (St John) *see* Newbridge w Carnalway and Kilcullen *M & K*

KILCUMMIN (no dedication) *see* Galway w Kilcummin *T, K & A*

KILDALLON (no dedication) Group of Parishes, including Newtowngore and Corrawallen *K, E & A* I R L WALLER

KILDARE (Cathedral of St Brigid) w Kilmeague and Curragh Garrison Church *M & K* I T WRIGHT
KILDARTON (no dedication) *see* Lisnadill w Kildarton *Arm*
KILDAVIN (St Paul) *see* Bunclody w Kildavin, Clonegal and Kilrush *C, F & O*
KILDOLLAGH (St Paul) *see* Ballyrashane w Kildollagh *Conn*
KILDRESS (St Patrick) w Altedesert *Arm* I D M MATCHETT
KILDRUMFERTON (St Patrick) w Ballymachugh and Ballyjamesduff *K, E & A* **Bp's C** M A SMITH
KILFANE (no dedication) *see* Kells Gp *C, F & O*
KILFARBOY (Christ Church) *see* Drumcliffe w Kilnasoolagh *L & K*
KILFAUGHNABEG (Christ Church) *see* Ross Union *C, C & R*
KILFENORA (Cathedral of St Fachan) *see* Drumcliffe w Kilnasoolagh *L & K*
KILFERAGH (no dedication) *as above*
KILFINANE (St Andrew) *see* Adare and Kilmallock w Kilpeacon, Croom etc *L & K*
KILFITHMONE (no dedication) *see* Templemore w Thurles and Kilfithmone *C, F & O*
KILFLYNN (no dedication) *see* Adare and Kilmallock w Kilpeacon, Croom etc *L & K*
KILGARIFFE (no dedication) w Kilmalooda, Kilnagross, Timoleague and Courtmacsherry *C, C & R* I K E SUTTON
KILGLASS (no dedication) *see* Killala w Dunfeeny, Crossmolina, Kilmoremoy etc *T, K & A*
KILGLASS (St Anne) *see* Mostrim w Granard, Clonbroney, Killoe etc *K, E & A*
KILGOBBIN (no dedication) *see* Dingle w Killiney and Kilgobbin *L & K*
KILHORNE *see* Annalong *D & D*
KILKEA (no dedication) *see* Athy w Kilberry, Fontstown and Kilkea *D & G*
KILKEE *see* Drumcliffe w Kilnasoolagh *L & K*
KILKEEL (Christ Church) *D & D* I A N CALVIN
KILKEEVIN (Holy Trinity) *see* Roscommon Gp *K, E & A*
KILKENNY (Cathedral of St Canice) (St John), Aghour and Kilmanagh *C, F & O* I D MACDONNELL C D COMPTON
KILKENNY WEST *see* Athlone w Benown, Kiltoom and Forgney *M & K*
KILL (no dedication) *D & G* I A T BREEN
KILL (St John) *see* Naas w Kill and Rathmore *M & K*
KILL O' THE GRANGE *see* Kill *D & G*
KILLABBAN (no dedication) *see* Killeshin w Cloydagh and Killabban *C, F & O*
KILLADEAS (Priory Church) *see* Trory w Killadeas *Clogh*
KILLAGAN (no dedication) *see* Craigs w Dunaghy and Killagan *Conn*
KILLAGHTEE (St Peter) *see* Inver w Mountcharles, Killaghtee and Killybegs *D & R*
KILLALA (Cathedral of St Patrick) w Dunfeeny, Crossmolina, Kilmoremoy, Castleconnor, Easkey and Kilglass *T, K & A* I S J MCWHIRTER **OLM** C MOORE, C MORROW, K G DUIGNAN
KILLALLON (St John) *see* Trim and Athboy Gp *M & K*
KILLALOE (Cathedral of St Flannan) w Stradbally, Clonlara, Mountshannon and Tuomgraney *L & K* **NSM** I J GREEN
KILLANEY (St Andrew) w Carryduff *D & D* I S H LOWRY
KILLANLEY *see* Killala w Dunfeeny, Crossmolina, Kilmoremoy etc *T, K & A*
KILLANNE (St Anne) w Killegney, Rossdroit and Templeshanbo *C, F & O* I I M CRUICKSHANK
KILLANULLY *see* Carrigaline Union *C, C & R*
KILLARGUE (no dedication) *see* Killinagh w Kiltyclogher and Innismagrath *K, E & A*
KILLARNEY (St Mary) w Aghadoe and Muckross *L & K* **P-in-c** S J LUMBY
KILLASHEE (St Paul) *see* Templemichael w Clongish, Clooncumber etc *K, E & A*
KILLASNETT (no dedication) *see* Cloonclare w Killasnett, Lurganboy and Drumlease *K, E & A*
KILLCONNELL *see* Aughrim w Ballinasloe etc *L & K*
KILLEA (St Andrew) *see* Waterford w Killea, Drumcannon and Dunhill *C, F & O*
KILLEA (St Fiach) *see* Taughboyne, Craigadooish, Newtowncunningham etc *D & R*
KILLEAD (St Catherine) w Gartree *Conn* I *vacant*
KILLEDMOND *see* Dunleckney w Nurney, Lorum and Kiltennel *C, F & O*
KILLEEVAN (no dedication) *see* Clones w Killeevan *Clogh*
KILLEGAR (no dedication) *see* Killeshandra w Killegar and Derrylane *K, E & A*
KILLEGNEY (no dedication) *see* Killanne w Killegney, Rossdroit and Templeshanbo *C, F & O*

KILLEIGH (no dedication) *see* Geashill w Killeigh and Ballycommon *M & K*
KILLELAGH (no dedication) *see* Maghera w Killelagh *D & R*
KILLENAULE (no dedication) *see* Kilcooley w Littleon, Crohane and Fertagh *C, F & O*
KILLERMOGH (no dedication) *see* Abbeyleix w Ballyroan etc *C, F & O*
KILLERY *see* Taunagh w Kilmactranny, Ballysumaghan etc *K, E & A*
KILLESHANDRA (no dedication) w Killegar and Derrylane *K, E & A* I *vacant*
KILLESHER (St John) *K, E & A* I R J WEST
KILLESHERDONEY (St Mark) *see* Drumgoon *K, E & A*
KILLESHIL (St Paul) *see* Errigle Keerogue w Ballygawley and Killeshil *Arm*
KILLESHIN (no dedication) w Cloydagh and Killabban *C, F & O* **P-in-c** R J STOTESBURY
KILLESK (All Saints) *see* New w Old Ross, Whitechurch, Fethard etc *C, F & O*
KILLETER *see* Derg w Termonamongan *D & R*
KILLINAGH (no dedication) w Kiltyclogher and Innismagrath *K, E & A* I *vacant*
KILLINCHY (no dedication) w Kilmood and Tullynakill *D & D* I S T R GAMBLE
KILLINEY (Holy Trinity) *D & G* I G L HASTINGS
KILLINEY (St Brendan) *see* Dingle w Killiney and Kilgobbin *L & K*
KILLINEY Ballybrack (St Matthias) *D & G* I W P OLHAUSEN
KILLINICK (no dedication) *see* Wexford and Kilscoran Union *C, F & O*
KILLINKERE (no dedication) *see* Lurgan w Billis, Killinkere and Munterconnaught *K, E & A*
KILLISKEY (no dedication) *see* Wicklow w Killiskey *D & G*
KILLODIERNAN (no dedication) *see* Nenagh *L & K*
KILLOE (St Catherine) *see* Mostrim w Granard, Clonbroney, Killoe etc *K, E & A*
KILLORAN (no dedication) *see* Tubbercurry w Killoran *T, K & A*
KILLORGLIN (no dedication) *see* Kilcolman w Kiltallagh, Killorglin, Knockane etc *L & K*
KILLOUGH (St Anne) *see* Bright w Ballee and Killough *D & D*
KILLOUGHTER (no dedication) *see* Drung w Castleterra, Larah and Lavey etc *K, E & A*
KILLOUGHY *see* Tullamore w Durrow, Newtownfertullagh, Rahan etc *M & K*
KILLOWEN *see* Kinneigh Union *C, C & R*
KILLOWEN (St John) *D & R* I D M COLLINS **NSM** W J HOLMES
KILLSALLAGHAN (St David) *see* Swords w Donabate and Kilsallaghan *D & G*
KILLUCAN (St Etchen) *see* Mullingar, Portnashangan, Moyliscar, Kilbixy etc *M & K*
KILLURIN (no dedication) *see* Wexford and Kilscoran Union *C, F & O*
KILLYBEGS (no dedication) *see* Inver w Mountcharles, Killaghtee and Killybegs *D & R*
KILLYGARVAN (St Columb) *see* Tullyaughnish w Kilmacrennan and Killygarvan *D & R*
KILLYLEA (St Mark), Caledon, and Brantry *Arm* I F W ATKINS
KILLYLEAGH (St John the Evangelist) *D & D* I C P DARLING
KILLYMAN (St Andrew) *Arm* I M R W LENNOX
KILLYMARD (no dedication) *see* Donegal w Killymard, Lough Eske and Laghey *D & R*
KILMACABEA (no dedication) *see* Ross Union *C, C & R*
KILMACDUAGH (no dedication) *see* Aughrim w Ballinasloe etc *L & K*
KILMACRENNAN (St Finnian and St Mark) *see* Tullyaughnish w Kilmacrennan and Killygarvan *D & R*
KILMACSHALGAN (St Mary) *see* Skreen w Kilmacshalgan and Dromard *T, K & A*
KILMACTHOMAS (no dedication) *see* Lismore w Cappoquin, Kilwatermoy, Dungarvan etc *C, F & O*
KILMACTRANNY (no dedication) *see* Taunagh w Kilmactranny, Ballysumaghan etc *K, E & A*
KILMAINHAMWOOD *see* Kingscourt w Syddan *M & K*
KILMAKEE (St Hilda) *Conn* I D H BOYLAND
KILMALLOCK (St Peter and St Paul) *see* Adare and Kilmallock w Kilpeacon, Croom etc *L & K*
KILMALOODA (All Saints) *see* Kilgariffe Union *C, C & R*
KILMANAGH (St Mary) *see* Kilkenny w Aghour and Kilmanagh *C, F & O*
KILMEADEN (St Mary) *see* Fiddown w Clonegam, Guilcagh and Kilmeaden *C, F & O*
KILMEAGUE (no dedication) *see* Kildare w Kilmeague and Curragh *M & K*

KILMEEN (Christ Church) *see* Kinneigh Union *C, C & R*
KILMEGAN (no dedication) w Maghera *D & D*
  I C J CARSON
KILMOCOMOGUE (St Brendan the Navigator) w
  Castletownbere and Durrus *C, C & R* **I** P M WILLOUGHBY
KILMOE, comprising Teampol-na-mbocht, Schull and
  Crookhaven *C, C & R* **I** *vacant*
KILMOGANNY (St Matthew) *see* Kells Gp *C, F & O*
KILMOOD (St Mary) *see* Killinchy w Kilmood and
  Tullynakill *D & D*
KILMORE (Cathedral of St Fethlimidh) w Ballintemple
  K, E & A **I** N N CROSSEY
KILMORE (Christ Church) and Inch *D & D* **I** W R S SMYTH
KILMORE (no dedication) *see* Kiltoghart w Drumshambo,
  Annaduff and Kilronan *K, E & A*
KILMORE (no dedication) *see* Monaghan w Tydavnet and
  Kilmore *Clogh*
KILMORE (St Aidan) (St Saviour) *Arm* **I** C E BAXTER
KILMOREMOY (St Michael) *see* Killala w Dunfeeny,
  Crossmolina, Kilmoremoy etc *T, K & A*
KILMOYLEY *see* Tralee w Kilmoyley, Ballymacelligott etc
  L & K
KILMUCKRIDGE (no dedication) *see* Ardamine w Kiltennel,
  Glascarrig etc *C, F & O*
KILMURRY (St Andrew) *see* Moviddy Union *C, C & R*
KILNAGROSS (no dedication) *see* Kilgariffe Union *C, C & R*
KILNAHUE (St John the Evangelist) *see* Gorey w Kilnahue,
  Leskinfere and Ballycanew *C, F & O*
KILNALECK *see* Kildrumferton w Ballymachugh and
  Ballyjamesduff *K, E & A*
KILNAMANAGH (St John) *see* Ardamine w Kiltennel,
  Glascarrig etc *C, F & O*
KILNASOOLAGH (no dedication) *see* Drumcliffe w
  Kilnasoolagh *L & K*
KILNAUGHTIN (St Brendan) *see* Rathkeale w Askeaton,
  Kilcornan and Kilnaughtin *L & K*
KILPEACON (St Beacon) *see* Adare and Kilmallock w
  Kilpeacon, Croom etc *L & K*
KILPIPE (no dedication) *see* Crosspatrick Gp *C, F & O*
KILREA (St Patrick), Tamlaght O'Crilly Upper and Lower
  D & R **I** G MILLAR
KILRONAN (St Thomas) *see* Kiltoghart w Drumshambo,
  Annaduff and Kilronan *K, E & A*
KILROOT (St Colman) and Templecorran *Conn*
  I N D J KIRKPATRICK
KILROSSANTY (no dedication) *see* Lismore w Cappoquin,
  Kilwatermoy, Dungarvan etc *C, F & O*
KILRUSH *see* Drumcliffe w Kilnasoolagh *L & K*
KILRUSH (St Brigid) *see* Bunclody w Kildavin, Clonegal and
  Kilrush *C, F & O*
KILSARAN (St Mary) w Drumcar, Dunleer and Dunany *Arm*
  I *vacant*
KILSCORAN (no dedication) *see* Wexford and Kilscoran
  Union *C, F & O*
KILSKEERY (no dedication) w Trillick *Clogh* **I** P J BRYSON
KILTALLAGH (St Carthage) *see* Kilcolman w Kiltallagh,
  Killorglin, Knockane etc *L & K*
KILTEEVOGUE (St John) *see* Stranorlar w Meenglas and
  Kilteevogue *D & R*
KILTEGAN (St Peter) w Hacketstown, Clonmore and
  Moyne *C, F & O* **I** R W JONES
KILTENNEL (no dedication) *see* Ardamine w Kiltennel,
  Glascarrig etc *C, F & O*
KILTENNEL (St Peter) *see* Dunleckney w Nurney, Lorum and
  Kiltennel *C, F & O*
KILTERNAN (St Kiernan) *D & G* **I** R W CLEMENTS
KILTINANLEA (no dedication) *see* Killaloe w Stradbally *L & K*
KILTOGHART (St George) w Drumshambo, Anaduff and
  Kilronan *K, E & A* **I** *vacant*
KILTOOM *see* Athlone w Benown, Kiltoom and Forgney
  M & K
KILTUBRIDE (St Brigid) *see* Mohill w Farnaught, Aughavas,
  Oughteragh etc *K, E & A*
KILTULLAGH (no dedication) *see* Roscommon Gp *K, E & A*
KILTYCLOGHER (no dedication) *see* Killinagh w Kiltyclogher
  and Innismagrath *K, E & A*
KILVEMNON (St Hugh) *see* Clonmel w Innislounagh,
  Tullaghmelan etc *C, F & O*
KILWARLIN UPPER (St John) w LOWER (St James) *D & D*
  P-in-c R R SATHYARAJ
KILWATERMOY (St Mary) *see* Lismore w Cappoquin,
  Kilwatermoy, Dungarvan etc *C, F & O*
KILWAUGHTER (no dedication) w Cairncastle and Craigy
  Hill *Conn* **P-in-c** P R BENSON
KINAWLEY (no dedication) w Holy Trinity *K, E & A*
  I A P DONALDSON

KINAWLEY (St Paul) *see* Swanlinbar Gp *K, E & A*
KINGSCOURT (St Ernan) w Drumconrath, Syddan and
  Moybologue *M & K* **I** M O'KELLY
KINLOUGH *see* Killinagh w Kiltyclogher and Innismagrath
  K, E & A
KINNEAGH (no dedication) *see* Narraghmore and Timolin w
  Castledermot etc *D & G*
KINNEIGH (St Bartholomew) w Ballymoney, Kilmeen,
  Desertserges, Killowen and Murragh *C, C & R*
  I I J RUITERS
KINNITTY (St Trinnian) *see* Shinrone w Aghancon etc *L & K*
KINSALE (St Multose) w Runcurran, Ballymartle and
  Templetrine *C, C & R* **I** P M RUTHERFORD
KIRCONRIOLA *see* Ballymena w Ballyclug *Conn*
KIRCUBBIN (Holy Trinity) *see* Grey Abbey w Kircubbin *D & D*
KNAPPAGH (St Thomas) *see* Aughaval w Achill, Knappagh,
  Dugort etc *T, K & A*
KNOCK (St Columba) *D & D* **I** J R AUCHMUTY
KNOCKANE (no dedication) *see* Kilcolman w Kiltallagh,
  Killorglin, Knockane etc *L & K*
KNOCKANEY (St John) *see* Adare and Kilmallock w
  Kilpeacon, Croom etc *L & K*
KNOCKBREDA (no dedication) *D & D* **I** W J PRESS
KNOCKBRIDE (no dedication) *see* Bailieborough w
  Knockbride, Shercock and Mullagh *K, E & A*
KNOCKLOUGHRIM *see* Desertmartin w Termoneeny *D & R*
KNOCKMOURNE (no dedication) *see* Fermoy Union
  C, C & R
KNOCKNAGONEY (Annunciation) *D & D* **I** *vacant*
KNOCKNAMUCKLEY (St Matthias) *D & D* **I** G N HAUGH
KNOCKNAREA (St Anne) *see* Sligo w Knocknarea and Rosses
  Pt *K, E & A*
KYLE (no dedication) *see* Roscrea w Kyle, Bourney and
  Corbally *L & K*
LACK (no dedication) *Clogh* **I** A D IRWIN
LAGHEY (no dedication) *see* Donegal w Killymard, Lough
  Eske and Laghey *D & R*
LAMBEG (no dedication) *Conn* **I** E J COULTER
LANESBOROUGH *see* Roscommon Gp *K, E & A*
LANGFIELD, LOWER (no dedication) *see* Drumclamph w
  Lower and Upper Langfield *D & R*
LANGFIELD, UPPER (no dedication) *as above*
LARAGH (St John) *see* Rathdrum w Glenealy, Derralossary
  and Laragh *D & G*
LARAH AND LAVEY (no dedication) *see* Drung w Castleterra,
  Larah and Lavey etc *K, E & A*
LARNE AND INVER (St Cedma) *Conn* **I** D LOCKHART
LAVEY *see* Drung w Castleterra, Larah and Lavey etc *K, E & A*
LAYDE (no dedication) *see* Ardclinis and Tickmacrevan w
  Layde and Cushendun *Conn*
LEA (no dedication) *see* Portarlington w Cloneyhurke, Lea
  etc *M & K*
LEAP *see* Ross Union *C, C & R*
LEARMOUNT (no dedication) *see* Cumber Upper w
  Learmount *D & R*
LEATBEG (no dedication) *see* Clondevaddock w Portsalon
  and Leatbeg *D & R*
**LECALE Group: Saul, Ardglass, Dunsford, Ballyculter and
  Kilclief** *D & D* **I** T H HULL **TV** A T W DORRIAN **C** J BELL
LECKPATRICK (St Patrick) w Dunnalong *D & R*
  I K P WHITTAKER
LEESON PARK (Christ Church) *see* Dublin St Bart w Leeson
  Park *D & G*
LEIGHLIN (Cathedral of St Laserian) w Grange Sylvae,
  Shankill, Clonagoose and Gowran *C, F & O*
  I T W GORDON
LEITRIM, SOUTH *see* Mohill w Farnaught, Aughavas,
  Oughteragh etc *K, E & A*
LEIXLIP (St Mary) *see* Lucan w Leixlip *D & G*
LESKINFERE (no dedication) *see* Gorey w Kilnahue,
  Leskinfere and Ballycanew *C, F & O*
LETTERKENNY *see* Conwal Union w Gartan *D & R*
LETTERMACAWARD (no dedication) *see* Ardara w
  Glencolumbkille, Inniskeel etc *D & R*
LICKMOLASSY *see* Clonfert Gp *L & K*
LIFFORD *see* Raphoe w Raymochy and Clonleigh *D & R*
LIMAVADY *see* Drumachose *D & R*
LIMAVADY *see* Tamlaghtfinlagan w Myroe *D & R*
LIMERICK CITY (Cathedral of St Mary) (St Michael) *L & K*
  I N J SLOANE
LISBELLAW (no dedication) *Clogh* **I** S R WOODS
  OLM C D BROWNSMITH
LISBURN (Christ Church Cathedral) *Conn* **I** W S WRIGHT
  TV D S MCCULLAGH
LISBURN (Christ Church) *Conn* **I** E P DUNDAS
  C D C HARRINGTON

LISBURN (St Paul) *Conn* I A YOUNG
LISLIMNAGHAN (Holy Trinity) *see* Cappagh w Lislimnaghan *D & R*
LISMORE (Cathedral of St Carthage) w Cappoquin, Kilwatermoy, Dungarvan, Kilrossanty, Stradbally and Kilmacthomas *C, F & O* I P R DRAPER
LISNADILL (St John) w Kildarton *Arm* **P-in-c** G CLUNIE **Bp's C** J D MCCOMB
LISNASKEA (Holy Trinity) *Clogh* I W A CAPPER
LISS (no dedication) *see* Clara w Liss, Moate and Clonmacnoise *M & K*
LISSADELL (no dedication) *see* Drumcliffe w Lissadell and Munninane *K, E & A*
LISSAN (no dedication) *Arm* I T A CROSS
LISTOWEL *see* Tralee w Kilmoyley, Ballymacelligott etc *L & K*
LITTLETON (no dedication) *see* Kilcooley w Littleon, Crohane and Fertagh *C, F & O*
LOCKEEN (no dedication) *see* Birr w Lorrha, Dorrha and Lockeen *L & K*
LONDONDERRY *see* Templemore *D & R*
LONDONDERRY (Christ Church), Culmore, Muff and Belmont *D & R* I R S MILLER **NSM** K M MCATEER
LONDONDERRY (St Augustine) *D & R* I *vacant*
LONGFORD *see* Templemichael w Clongish, Clooncumber etc *K, E & A*
LORRHA (St Ruadhan) *see* Birr w Lorrha, Dorrha and Lockeen *L & K*
LORUM (no dedication) *see* Dunleckney w Nurney, Lorum and Kiltennel *C, F & O*
LOUGH ESKE (Christ Church) *see* Donegal w Killymard, Lough Eske and Laghey *D & R*
LOUGHBRICKLAND *see* Aghaderg w Donaghmore and Scarva *D & D*
LOUGHCREW *see* Castlepollard and Oldcastle w Loughcrew etc *M & K*
LOUGHGALL (St Luke) w Grange *Arm* I P R SMITH
LOUGHGILLY (St Patrick) w Clare *Arm* I *vacant*
LOUGHGUILE (All Saints) *see* Armoy w Loughguile and Drumtullagh *Conn*
LOUGHINISLAND (no dedication) *D & D* I *vacant*
LUCAN (St Andrew) w Leixlip *D & G* I J S PEOPLES
LUGGACURREN (Resurrection) *see* Stradbally w Ballintubbert, Coraclone etc *C, F & O*
LURGAN (Christ the Redeemer) (St Andrew) *D & D* I J M HARVEY **C** G GIMPEL
LURGAN (no dedication) w Billis, Killinkere and Munterconnaught *K, E & A* I C W L MCCAULEY
LURGAN (St John the Evangelist) *D & D* I R J C KETTYLE
LURGANBOY (Chapel of Ease) *see* Cloonclare w Killasnett, Lurganboy and Drumlease *K, E & A*
MACOSQUIN *see* Camus-juxta-Bann *D & R*
MACREDDIN *see* Castlemacadam w Ballinaclash, Aughrim etc *D & G*
MACROOM *see* Moviddy Union *C, C & R*
MAGHABERRY (Methodist church) *D & D* **P-in-c** C P E KAKURU
MAGHERA (no dedication) *see* Kilmegan w Maghera *D & D*
MAGHERA (St Lurach) w Killelagh *D & R* I T P KERR
MAGHERACLOONE (St Molua) *see* Carrickmacross w Magheracloone *Clogh*
MAGHERACROSS (no dedication) *Clogh* I B J HARPER
MAGHERACULMONEY (St Mary) *Clogh* I F G RUTLEDGE
MAGHERADROLL (no dedication) *D & D* I W W RUSSELL
MAGHERAFELT (St Swithin) *Arm* I T SCOTT
MAGHERAGALL (no dedication) *Conn* I N J DARK
MAGHERAHAMLET (no dedication) *see* Annahilt w Magherahamlet *D & D*
MAGHERALIN (Holy and Undivided Trinity) w Dollingstown *D & D* I S A GENOE
MAGHERALLY (St John the Evangelist) w Annaclone *D & D* I *vacant*
MAGORBAN (no dedication) *see* Cashel w Magorban, Tipperary, Clonbeg etc *C, F & O*
MAGOURNEY *see* Carrigrohane Union *C, C & R*
MAGUIRESBRIDGE (Christ Church) w Derrybrusk *Clogh* **OLM** A G T STOREY
MALAHIDE (St Andrew) w Balgriffin *D & G* I *vacant*
MALIN *see* Moville w Greencastle, Donagh, Cloncha etc *D & R*
MALLOW (St James) w Doneraile and Castletownroche *C, C & R* I M L WILLIAMS
MALLUSK (St Brigid) *Conn* I W A BOYCE
MALONE *see* Belfast Malone St Jo *Conn*
MALONE, UPPER *see* Belfast Upper Malone (Epiphany) *Conn*
MANORCUNNINGHAM *see* Raphoe w Raymochy and Clonleigh *D & R*

MANORHAMILTON *see* Cloonclare w Killasnett, Lurganboy and Drumlease *K, E & A*
MARKETHILL (no dedication) *see* Mullabrack w Markethill and Kilcluney *Arm*
MARMULLANE (St Mary) *see* Douglas Union w Frankfield *C, C & R*
MARYBOROUGH (St Peter) w Dysart Enos and Ballyfin *C, F & O* **P-in-c** P TARLETON **OLM** J FINLAY
MAYNE *see* Castlepollard and Oldcastle w Loughcrew etc *M & K*
MAYNOOTH (St Mary) *see* Dunboyne and Rathmolyon *M & K*
MAYO (no dedication) *see* Killeshin w Cloydagh and Killabban *C, F & O*
MEALIFFE *see* Templemore w Thurles and Kilfithmone *C, F & O*
MEENGLASS (Ascension) *see* Stranorlar w Meenglas and Kilteevogue *D & R*
MEVAGH (Holy Trinity) w Glenalla *D & R* I *vacant*
MIDDLE CHURCH (no dedication) *see* Ballinderry *Conn*
MIDDLETOWN (St John) *see* Tynan w Middletown and Aghavilly *Arm*
MIDLETON (St John the Baptist) *see* Cloyne Union *C, C & R*
MILLISLE (St Patrick) *see* Carrowdore w Millisle *D & D*
MILLTOWN *see* Kilcolman w Kiltallagh, Killorglin, Knockane etc *L & K*
MILLTOWN (St Andrew) *Arm* I G G WALMSLEY
MILLTOWN (St Philip) *see* Dublin Sandford w Milltown *D & G*
MILLTOWN MALBAY *see* Drumcliffe w Kilnasoolagh *L & K*
MITCHELSTOWN *see* Fermoy Union *C, C & R*
MOATE (St Mary) *see* Clara w Liss, Moate and Clonmacnoise *M & K*
MOHILL (St Mary) w Farnaught, Aughavas, Oughteragh, Kiltubride and Drumreilly *K, E & A* I L M FROST **OLM** S FROST
MOIRA (St John) *D & D* I J M MEGARRELL
MONAGHAN (St Patrick) w Tydavnet and Kilmore *Clogh* I I T H BERRY
MONAMOLIN (St Molig) *see* Ardamine w Kiltennel, Glascarrig etc *C, F & O*
MONART (St Peter) *see* Enniscorthy w Clone, Clonmore, Monart etc *C, F & O*
MONASTEREVAN (St John the Evangelist) *see* Portarlington w Cloneyhurke, Lea etc *M & K*
MONASTERORIS (no dedication) *see* Clonsast w Rathangan, Thomastown etc *M & K*
MONELLAN (St Anne) *see* Convoy w Monellan and Donaghmore *D & R*
MONEYMORE *see* Desertlyn w Ballyeglish *Arm*
MONEYREAGH (no dedication) *D & D* I *vacant*
MONKSTOWN (Good Shepherd) *Conn* I *vacant*
MONKSTOWN (no dedication) *D & G* I R H BYRNE
MONKSTOWN (St John) *see* Carrigaline Union *C, C & R*
MOSSLEY (Holy Spirit) *Conn* I P B JONES **OLM** E L BOWES
MOSTRIM (St John) w Granard, Clonbroney, Killoe, Rathaspeck and Streete *K, E & A* **P-in-c** C S SNELL
MOTHEL (no dedication) *see* Castlecomer w Colliery Ch, Mothel and Bilboa *C, F & O*
MOUNT MERRION (Pentecost) *D & D* I *vacant*
MOUNT MERRION (St Thomas) *see* Dublin Mt Merrion *D & G*
MOUNT NUGENT (St Bride) *see* Castlepollard and Oldcastle w Loughcrew etc *M & K*
MOUNTCHARLES (Christ Church) *see* Inver w Mountcharles, Killaghtee and Killybegs *D & R*
MOUNTFIELD (no dedication) *see* Drumragh w Mountfield *D & R*
MOUNTMELLICK (St Paul) w Coolbanagher, Rosenallis and Clonaslee *M & K* I S T IRVINE
MOUNTRATH *see* Clonenagh w Offerlane, Borris-in-Ossory etc *C, F & O*
MOUNTSHANNON *see* Killaloe w Stradbally *L & K*
MOVIDDY (no dedication), Kilbonane, Kilmurry, Templemartin and Macroom *C, C & R* **P-in-c** D G D BOWLES
MOVILLA (no dedication) *D & D* I A N PEEK
MOVILLE (St Columb) w Greencastle, Donagh, Cloncha and Culdaff *D & R* I *vacant*
MOY (St James) w Charlemont *Arm* I A W A MAYES
MOYBOLOGUE *see* Kingscourt w Syddan *M & K*
MOYDOW (no dedication) *see* Ardagh w Tashinny, Shrule and Kilcommick *K, E & A*
MOYGASHEL (no dedication) *see* Drumglass w Moygashel *Arm*

MOYGLARE (All Saints) *see* Dunboyne and Rathmolyon *M & K*

MOYLISCAR *see* Mullingar, Portnashangan, Moyliscar, Kilbixy etc *M & K*

MOYNALTY (St Mary) *see* Kells Union *M & K*

MOYNE (St John) *see* Kiltegan w Hacketstown, Clonmore and Moyne *C, F & O*

MOYNTAGHS *see* Ardmore w Craigavon *D & D*

MOYRUS *see* Omey w Ballynakill, Errislannan and Roundstone *T, K & A*

MUCKAMORE (St Jude) (St Matthias) *Conn* I J MCCLURE

MUCKNOE (St Maeldoid) *see* Ballybay w Mucknoe and Clontibret *Clogh*

MUCKROSS (Holy Trinity) *see* Killarney w Aghadoe and Muckross *L & K*

MUCKROSS (St John) *see* Drumkeeran w Templecarne and Muckross *Clogh*

MUFF (no dedication) *see* Londonderry Ch Ch, Culmore, Muff and Belmont *D & R*

MULHUDDART (St Thomas) *see* Castleknock and Mulhuddart w Clonsilla *D & G*

MULLABRACK (no dedication) w Markethill and Kilcluney *Arm* I P D MUNCE

MULLAGH (no dedication) *see* Bailieborough w Knockbride, Shercock and Mullagh *K, E & A*

MULLAGHDUN (no dedication) *see* Cleenish w Mullaghdun *Clogh*

MULLAGHFAD (All Saints) *see* Aghalurcher w Tattykeeran, Cooneen etc *Clogh*

MULLAGLASS (St Luke) *see* Camlough, Mullaglass and Ballymoyer *Arm*

MULLAVILLY (no dedication) *Arm* I D E CAIRNS

MULLINACUFF (no dedication) *see* Tullow w Shillelagh, Aghold and Mullinacuff *C, F & O*

MULLINGAR (All Saints) w Portnashangan, Moyliscar, Kilbixy, Almoritia, Killucan, Clonard and Castlelost *M & K* I M A GRAHAM   **NSM** H M SCULLY, T N HOLMES

MULRANKIN (St David) *see* Wexford and Kilscoran Union *C, F & O*

MUNNINANE (St Kevin) *see* Drumcliffe w Lissadell and Munninane *K, E & A*

MUNTERCONNAUGHT (no dedication) *see* Lurgan w Billis, Killinkere and Munterconnaught *K, E & A*

MURRAGH (no dedication) *see* Kinneigh Union *C, C & R*

MYROE (St John) *see* Tamlaghtfinlagan w Myroe *D & R*

MYROSS *see* Ross Union *C, C & R*

MYSHALL (Christ the Redeemer) *see* Fenagh w Myshall, Aghade and Ardoyne *C, F & O*

NAAS (St David) w Kill and Rathmore *M & K* I P G HEAK   **OLM** C J HENNESSY

NARRAGHMORE (Holy Saviour) and Timolin w Castledermot and Kinneagh *D & G* **NSM** N R STRATFORD

NAVAN (St Mary) w Kentstown, Tara, Slane, Painestown and Stackallen *M & K* I J D M CLARKE   **NSM** A V STEWART, E ARMSTRONG

NENAGH (St Mary) w Ballymackey, Templederry and Killodiernan *L & K* I R L SMYTH   **NSM** P E MCKEE HANNA

NEWBLISS (no dedication) *see* Currin w Drum and Newbliss *Clogh*

NEWBRIDGE (St Patrick) w Carnalway and Kilcullen *M & K* I T WRIGHT

NEWCASTLE (no dedication) w Newtownmountkennedy and Calary *D & G* I R STYLES

NEWCASTLE (St John) *D & D* I vacant

NEWCASTLE-LYONS (no dedication) *see* Celbridge w Straffan and Newcastle-Lyons *D & G*

NEWCESTOWN *see* Kinneigh Union *C, C & R*

NEWMARKET-ON-FERGUS *see* Drumcliffe w Kilnasoolagh *L & K*

NEWRY (St Mary) (St Patrick) *D & D* I S J MCDONALD

NEWTOWNARDS (St Mark) *D & D* I C J MATCHETT   **C** P HILTON   **OLM** S DOHERTY

NEWTOWNBARRY *see* Bunclody w Kildavin, Clonegal and Kilrush *C, F & O*

NEWTOWNBUTLER *see* Galloon w Drummully and Sallaghy *Clogh*

NEWTOWNCROMMELIN (no dedication) *see* Skerry w Rathcavan and Newtowncrommelin *Conn*

NEWTOWNCUNNINGHAM (All Saints) *see* Taughboyne, Craigadooish, Newtowncunningham etc *D & R*

NEWTOWNFERTULLAGH *see* Tullamore w Durrow, Newtownfertullagh, Rahan etc *M & K*

NEWTOWNFORBES *see* Templemichael w Clongish, Clooncumber etc *K, E & A*

NEWTOWNGORE (no dedication) *see* Kildallon Gp *K, E & A*

NEWTOWNHAMILTON (St John) *see* Keady, Armaghbreague, Derrynoose and Newtownhamilton *Arm*

NEWTOWNMOUNTKENNEDY (St Matthew) *see* Newcastle w Newtownmountkennedy and Calary *D & G*

NEWTOWNSAVILLE (no dedication) *see* Augher w Newtownsaville and Eskrahoole *Clogh*

NEWTOWNSTEWART *see* Ardstraw w Baronscourt, Badoney Lower etc *D & R*

NOHOVAL (no dedication) *see* Templebreedy w Tracton and Nohoval *C, C & R*

NURNEY (no dedication) *see* Portarlington w Cloneyhurke, Lea etc *M & K*

NURNEY (St John) *see* Dunleckney w Nurney, Lorum and Kiltennel *C, F & O*

OFFERLANE (no dedication) *see* Clonenagh w Offerlane, Borris-in-Ossory etc *C, F & O*

OLD LEIGHLIN *see* Leighlin w Grange Sylvae, Shankill etc *C, F & O*

OLDCASTLE (St Bride) *see* Castlepollard and Oldcastle w Loughcrew etc *M & K*

OMAGH *see* Drumragh w Mountfield *D & R*

OMEY (Christ Church) w Ballynakill, Errislannan and Roundstone *T, K & A* I vacant

ORANGEFIELD (St John the Evangelist) w Braniel *D & D* I R R WILSON   **OLM** R BLAKE-KNOX

OSSORY *see* Kilcooley w Littleon, Crohane and Fertagh *C, F & O*

OUGHTERAGH (no dedication) *see* Mohill w Farnaught, Aughavas, Oughteragh etc *K, E & A*

OUGHTERARD *see* Galway w Kilcummin *T, K & A*

PACKANE *see* Nenagh *L & K*

PAINESTOWN *see* Navan w Kentstown, Tara, Slane, Painestown etc *M & K*

PALLASKENRY *see* Rathkeale w Askeaton, Kilcornan and Kilnaughtin *L & K*

PASSAGE WEST *see* Douglas Union w Frankfield *C, C & R*

PAULSTOWN *see* Leighlin w Grange Sylvae, Shankill etc *C, F & O*

PETTIGO *see* Drumkeeran w Templecarne and Muckross *Clogh*

PILTOWN *see* Fiddown w Clonegam, Guilcagh and Kilmeaden *C, F & O*

POMEROY (no dedication) *Arm* I vacant

PORT LAOIS *see* Maryborough w Dysart Enos and Ballyfin *C, F & O*

PORTADOWN (St Columba) *Arm* I W M ADAIR

PORTADOWN (St Gobhan) *see* Seagoe *D & D*

PORTADOWN (St Mark) *Arm* I W J C ORR   **C** K W MARSHALL, L A M BURDEN

PORTAFERRY *see* Ballyphilip w Ardquin *D & D*

PORTARLINGTON (St Paul) w Cloneyhurke, Lea, Monasterevin, Nurney and Rathdaire *M & K* I L T C STEVENSON   **OLM** A ROBINSON

PORTGLENONE (no dedication) *see* Ahoghill w Portglenone *Conn*

PORTLAOISE *see* Maryborough w Dysart Enos and Ballyfin *C, F & O*

PORTLAW *see* Fiddown w Clonegam, Guilcagh and Kilmeaden *C, F & O*

PORTNASHANGAN *see* Mullingar, Portnashangan, Moyliscar, Kilbixy etc *M & K*

PORTRUSH *see* Ballywillan *Conn*

PORTSALON (All Saints) *see* Clondevaddock w Portsalon and Leatbeg *D & R*

PORTSTEWART *see* Agherton *Conn*

PORTUMNA (Christ Church) *see* Clonfert Gp *L & K*

POWERSCOURT (St Patrick) w Kilbride *D & G* I C J HALLISSEY   **NSM** R I T LILBURN

PREBAN (St John) *see* Crosspatrick Gp *C, F & O*

RAHAN *see* Clonsast w Rathangan, Thomastown etc *M & K*

RAHAN (St Carthach) *see* Tullamore w Durrow, Newtownfertullagh, Rahan etc *M & K*

RAHENY (All Saints) w Coolock *D & G* I N MCCAUSLAND

RALOO (no dedication) *see* Glynn w Raloo *Conn*

RAMELTON *see* Tullyaughnish w Kilmacrennan and Killygarvan *D & R*

RAMOAN (St James) w Ballycastle and Culfeightrin *Conn* I D E FERGUSON

RANDALSTOWN *see* Drummaul w Duneane and Ballyscullion *Conn*

RAPHOE (Cathedral of St Eunan) w Raymochy and Clonleigh *D & R* I vacant

RASHARKIN (St Andrew) *see* Ballymoney w Finvoy and Rasharkin *Conn*

RATHANGAN (no dedication) *see* Clonsast w Rathangan, Thomastown etc *M & K*

RATHASPECK (St Thomas) *see* Mostrim w Granard, Clonbroney, Killoe etc *K, E & A*

RATHBARRON *see* Tubbercurry w Killoran *T, K & A*

RATHCAVAN (no dedication) *see* Skerry w Rathcavan and Newtowncrommelin *Conn*

RATHCLAREN (Holy Trinity) *see* Bandon Union *C, C & R*

RATHCLINE (no dedication) *see* Roscommon Gp *K, E & A*

RATHCOOLE (no dedication) *see* Clondalkin w Rathcoole *D & G*

RATHCOOLE (St Comgall) *Conn* **P-in-c** A MOORE

RATHCOR (no dedication) *see* Ballymascanlan w Creggan and Rathcor *Arm*

RATHCORE (St Ultan) *see* Dunboyne and Rathmolyon *M & K*

RATHDAIRE (Ascension) *see* Portarlington w Cloneyhurke, Lea etc *M & K*

RATHDOWNEY (no dedication) w Castlefleming, Donaghmore, Rathsaran and Aghavoe *C, F & O* I R D SEYMOUR-WHITELEY

RATHDRUM (St Saviour) w Glenealy, Derralossary and Laragh *D & G* I B M O'REILLY

RATHFARNHAM *see* Dublin Rathfarnham *D & G*

RATHFRILAND *see* Drumgath w Drumgooland and Clonduff *D & D*

RATHGAR *see* Dublin Zion Ch *D & G*

RATHKEALE (Holy Trinity) w Askeaton, Foynes, Kilcornan and Kilnaughtin *L & K* **P-in-c** P COMERFORD

RATHLIN (St Thomas) *see* Ballintoy w Rathlin and Dunseverick *Conn*

RATHMICHAEL (no dedication) *D & G* I S J K HANILY

RATHMINES *see* Dublin Rathmines w Harold's Cross *D & G*

RATHMOLYON (St Michael and All Angels) *see* Dunboyne and Rathmolyon *M & K*

RATHMORE (St Columbkille) *see* Naas w Kill and Rathmore *M & K*

RATHMULLAN *see* Tullyaughnish w Kilmacrennan and Killygarvan *D & R*

RATHMULLAN (no dedication) w Tyrella *D & D* I *vacant*

RATHOWEN *see* Mostrim w Granard, Clonbroney, Killoe etc *K, E & A*

RATHSARAN (no dedication) *see* Rathdowney w Castlefleming, Donaghmore etc *C, F & O*

RATHVILLY (St Mary) *see* Baltinglass w Ballynure etc *C, F & O*

RAYMOCHY (no dedication) *see* Raphoe w Raymochy and Clonleigh *D & R*

RAYMUNTERDONEY (St Paul) *see* Dunfanaghy, Raymunterdoney and Tullaghbegley *D & R*

REDCROSS (Holy Trinity) *see* Dunganstown w Redcross and Conary *D & G*

REDHILLS *see* Drung w Castleterra, Larah and Lavey etc *K, E & A*

RICHHILL (St Matthew) *Arm* I G MCMURRAY

RIVERSTOWN *see* Taunagh w Kilmactranny, Ballysumaghan etc *K, E & A*

ROCHFORT BRIDGE *see* Mullingar, Portnashangan, Moyliscar, Kilbixy etc *M & K*

ROCKCORRY (no dedication) *see* Ematris w Rockcorry, Aghabog and Aughnamullan *Clogh*

ROSCOMMON (St Colman) w Donamon, Rathcline, Kilkeevin, Kiltullagh and Tybohine *K, E & A* **OLM** E SMYTH

ROSCREA (St Cronan) w Kyle, Bourney and Corbally *L & K* I J A GALBRAITH

ROSENALLIS (St Brigid) *see* Mountmellick w Coolbanagher, Rosenallis etc *M & K*

ROSKELTON (no dedication) *see* Clonenagh w Offerlane, Borris-in-Ossory etc *C, F & O*

ROSS (Cathedral of St Fachtna) w Kilmacabea, Myross, Kilfaughnabeg and Castleventry *C, C & R* I C L PETERS

ROSS, NEW (St Mary) w OLD (St Mary), Whitechurch, Fethard, Killesk and Tintern *C, F & O* I *vacant*

ROSSCARBERY *see* Ross Union *C, C & R*

ROSSDROIT (St Peter) *see* Killanne w Killegney, Rossdroit and Templeshanbo *C, F & O*

ROSSES POINT (no dedication) *see* Sligo w Knocknarea and Rosses Pt *K, E & A*

ROSSINVER (no dedication) *see* Killinagh w Kiltyclogher and Innismagrath *K, E & A*

ROSSMIRE *see* Lismore w Cappoquin, Kilwatermoy, Dungarvan etc *C, F & O*

ROSSNAKILL *see* Clondevaddock w Portsalon and Leatbeg *D & R*

ROSSNOWLAGH (St John) *see* Kilbarron w Rossnowlagh and Drumholm *D & R*

ROSSORRY (no dedication) *Clogh* **NSM** F I NIXON

ROSTREVOR *see* Clonallon and Warrenpoint w Kilbroney *D & D*

ROUNDSTONE (no dedication) *see* Omey w Ballynakill, Errislannan and Roundstone *T, K & A*

RUNCURRAN *see* Kinsale Union *C, C & R*

RUTLAND *see* Carlow w Urglin and Staplestown *C, F & O*

RYNAGH *see* Clonfert Gp *L & K*

SAINTFIELD (no dedication) *D & D* I C J POLLOCK

SALLAGHY (no dedication) *see* Galloon w Drummully and Sallaghy *Clogh*

SANDFORD *see* Dublin Sandford w Milltown *D & G*

SANDHILL *see* Sligo w Knocknarea and Rosses Pt *K, E & A*

SANDYMOUNT *see* Dublin Sandymount *D & G*

SANTRY *see* Dublin Santry w Glasnevin and Finglas *D & G*

SAUL (St Patrick) *see* Lecale Gp *D & D*

SCARVA (St Matthew) *see* Aghaderg w Donaghmore and Scarva *D & D*

SCHULL (Holy Trinity) *see* Kilmoe Union *C, C & R*

SCOTSHOUSE *see* Currin w Drum and Newbliss *Clogh*

SEAFORDE *see* Lecale Gp *D & D*

SEAGOE (St Gobhan) *D & D* I T J CADDEN C S W MOLES OLM J FLEMING

SEAPATRICK (Holy Trinity) (St Patrick) *D & D* I T R WEST C A T R IRWIN **NSM** J R CORBETT

SEIRKIERAN (St Kieran) *see* Clonenagh w Offerlane, Borris-in-Ossory etc *C, F & O*

SESKINORE (no dedication) *see* Clogherny w Seskinore and Drumnakilly *Arm*

SEYMOUR HILL *see* Kilmakee *Conn*

SHANDON (St Ann) *see* Cork St Ann's Union *C, C & R*

SHANKILL *see* Belfast St Matt *Conn*

SHANKILL *see* Lurgan Ch the Redeemer *D & D*

SHANKILL (St John) *see* Leighlin w Grange Sylvae, Shankill etc *C, F & O*

SHANNON (Christ Church) *see* Drumcliffe w Kilnasoolagh *L & K*

SHERCOCK (no dedication) *see* Bailieborough w Knockbride, Shercock and Mullagh *K, E & A*

SHILLELAGH (no dedication) *see* Tullow w Shillelagh, Aghold and Mullinacuff *C, F & O*

SHINRONE (St Mary) w Aghancon, Dunkerrin and Kinnitty *L & K* **P-in-c** R C MCCARTNEY

SHRULE (no dedication) *see* Ardagh w Tashinny, Shrule and Kilcommick *K, E & A*

SION MILLS (Good Shepherd) *see* Urney w Sion Mills *D & R*

SIXMILECROSS (St Michael) w Termonmaguirke *Arm* I A BARR

SIXTOWNS (St Anne) *see* Kilcronaghan w Draperstown and Sixtowns *D & R*

SKERRIES *see* Holmpatrick w Balbriggan and Kenure *D & G*

SKERRY (St Patrick) w Rathcavan and Newtowncrommelin *Conn* I A P CAMPBELL

SKIBBEREEN *see* Abbeystrewry Union *C, C & R*

SKREEN (no dedication) w Kilmacshalgan and Dromard *T, K & A* **P-in-c** N H L REGAN

SLANE (St Patrick) *see* Navan w Kentstown, Tara, Slane, Painestown etc *M & K*

SLAVIN (no dedication) *see* Garrison w Slavin and Belleek *Clogh*

SLIGO (Cathedral of St Mary and St John the Baptist) w Knocknarea and Rosses Point *K, E & A* I A WILLIAMS

SNEEM (Transfiguration) *see* Kenmare w Sneem, Waterville etc *L & K*

SPANISH POINT *see* Drumcliffe w Kilnasoolagh *L & K*

STACKALLEN *see* Navan w Kentstown, Tara, Slane, Painestown etc *M & K*

STAPLESTOWN (no dedication) *see* Carlow w Urglin and Staplestown *C, F & O*

STEWARTSTOWN *see* Brackaville w Donaghendry and Ballyclog *Arm*

STILLORGAN (St Brigid) w Blackrock *D & G* I I GALLAGHER **NSM** R D MARSHALL

STONEYFORD (St John) *Conn* **P-in-c** W J FARR

STORMONT (St Molua) *D & D* I E C RUTHERFORD

STRABANE *see* Camus-juxta-Mourne *D & R*

STRADBALLY (All Saints) *see* Killaloe w Stradbally *L & K*

STRADBALLY (St James) *see* Lismore w Cappoquin, Kilwatermoy, Dungarvan etc *C, F & O*

STRADBALLY (St Patrick) w Ballintubbert, Coraclone, Timogue and Luggacurren *C, F & O* **P-in-c** A PURSER

STRAFFAN (no dedication) *see* Celbridge w Straffan and Newcastle-Lyons *D & G*

STRAID (no dedication) *T, K & A* **P-in-c** A J WILLS

STRAND, NORTH (no dedication) *see* Dublin Drumcondra w N Strand *D & G*

STRANGFORD *see* Lecale Gp *D & D*

STRANMILLIS (St Bartholomew) *see* Belfast St Bart *Conn*
STRANORLAR (no dedication) w Meenglas and
  Kilteevogue *D & R* I A W PULLEN
STRATFORD-ON-SLANEY (St John the Baptist) *see* Baltinglass
  w Ballynure etc *C, F & O*
STRATHFOYLE (no dedication) *see* Clooney w Strathfoyle
  D & R
STREETE (no dedication) *see* Mostrim w Granard,
  Clonbroney, Killoe etc *K, E & A*
SUMMER COVE *see* Kinsale Union *C, C & R*
SWANLINBAR (St Augustine) Group of Parishes, including
  Kinawley, Templeport and Tomregan *K, E & A*
  P-in-c S J DONOHOE
SWATRAGH *see* Maghera w Killelagh *D & R*
SWORDS (St Columba) w Donabate and Kilsallaghan
  D & G I N D S PHAIR NSM K E LONG
SYDDAN (St David) *see* Kingscourt w Syddan *M & K*
SYDENHAM *see* Belfast St Brendan *D & D*
TAGHMON (St Munn) w Horetown and Bannow *C, F & O*
  I *vacant*
TALLAGHT (St Maelruain) *D & G* I W R H DEVERELL
  NSM A E J BENNETT
TAMLAGHT *see* Derryvullen S w Garvary *Clogh*
TAMLAGHT (St Luke) *see* Ballinderry, Tamlaght and Arboe
  Arm
TAMLAGHTARD (St Gedanus) w Aghanloo *D & R* I R JONES
TAMLAGHTFINLAGAN (St Findlunganus) w Myroe *D & R*
  I H R GIVEN
TANEY (Christ Church) (St Nahi) *D & G* C C N WEST,
  N J PIERPOINT
TARA *see* Navan w Kentstown, Tara, Slane, Painestown etc
  M & K
TARBERT *see* Tralee w Kilmoyley, Ballymacelligott etc *L & K*
TARTARAGHAN (St Paul) w Diamond *Arm* I D HILLIARD
TASHINNY (no dedication) *see* Ardagh w Tashinny, Shrule
  and Kilcommick *K, E & A*
TAUGHBOYNE (St Baithan) w Craigadooish,
  Newtowncunningham and Killea *D & R* I D W T CROOKS
TAUNAGH (no dedication) w Kilmactranny,
  Ballysumaghan and Killery *K, E & A* I *vacant*
TEAMPOL-NA-MBOCHT (Altar) *see* Kilmoe Union
  C, C & R
TEMPLEBREEDY (Holy Trinity) w Tracton and Nohoval
  C, C & R I I M JACKSON
TEMPLECARNE (no dedication) *see* Drumkeeran w
  Templecarne and Muckross *Clogh*
TEMPLECORRAN (St John) *see* Kilroot and Templecorran
  Conn
TEMPLECRONE (St Crone) *see* Gweedore, Carrickfin and
  Templecrone *D & R*
TEMPLEDERRY (no dedication) *see* Nenagh *L & K*
TEMPLEHARRY (no dedication) *see* Cloughjordan w
  Borrisokane etc *L & K*
TEMPLEMARTIN (St Martin) *see* Moviddy Union *C, C & R*
TEMPLEMICHAEL (St John) w Clongish, Clooncumber,
  Killashee and Ballymacormack *K, E & A* I S M SCOTT
TEMPLEMORE (St Mary) w Thurles and Kilfithmone
  C, F & O P-in-c I H Y COULTER
TEMPLEMORE Londonderry (Cathedral of St Columb)
  D & R I R J STEWART
TEMPLEPATRICK (St Patrick) w Donegore *Conn*
  I J J MOULD
TEMPLEPORT (St Peter) *see* Swanlinbar Gp *K, E & A*
TEMPLESCOBIN (St Paul) *see* Enniscorthy w Clone,
  Clonmore, Monart etc *C, F & O*
TEMPLESHANBO (St Colman) *see* Kilanne w Killegney,
  Rossdroit and Templeshanbo *C, F & O*
TEMPLETRINE (no dedication) *see* Kinsale Union *C, C & R*
TEMPO (no dedication) and Clabby *Clogh*
  I M A ARMSTRONG
TERENURE *see* Dublin Rathfarnham *D & G*
TERMONAMONGAN (St Bestius) *see* Derg w
  Termonamongan *D & R*
TERMONEENY (no dedication) *see* Desertmartin w
  Termoneeny *D & R*
TERMONFECKIN (St Feckin) *see* Drogheda w Ardee, Collon
  and Termonfeckin *Arm*
TERMONMAGUIRKE (St Columbkille) *see* Sixmilecross w
  Termonmaguirke *Arm*
THOMASTOWN (no dedication) *see* Clonsast w Rathangan,
  Thomastown etc *M & K*
THURLES (no dedication) *see* Templemore w Thurles and
  Kilfithmone *C, F & O*
TICKMACREVAN (St Patrick) *see* Ardclinis and Tickmacrevan
  w Layde and Cushendun *Conn*

TIMOGUE (St Mogue) *see* Stradbally w Ballintubbert,
  Coraclone etc *C, F & O*
TIMOLEAGUE (Ascension) *see* Kilgariffe Union *C, C & R*
TIMOLIN (St Mullin) *see* Narraghmore and Timolin w
  Castledermot etc *D & G*
TINTERN (St Mary) *see* New w Old Ross, Whitechurch,
  Fethard etc *C, F & O*
TIPPERARY (St Mary) *see* Cashel w Magorban, Tipperary,
  Clonbeg etc *C, F & O*
TOBERMORE *see* Kilcronaghan w Draperstown and Sixtowns
  D & R
TOMREGAN (no dedication) *see* Swanlinbar Gp *K, E & A*
TOOMBE (St Catherine) *see* Ferns w Kilbride, Toombe,
  Kilcormack etc *C, F & O*
TOOMNA (no dedication) *see* Kiltoghart w Drumshambo,
  Annaduff and Kilronan *K, E & A*
TOORMORE *see* Kilmoe Union *C, C & R*
TRACTON *see* Templebreedy w Tracton and Nohoval
  C, C & R
TRALEE (St John the Evangelist) w Kilmoyley,
  Ballymacelligott, Ballyseedy, Listowel and Ballybunnion
  L & K I J C STEPHENS Hon C P G C JONES
TRAMORE *see* Waterford w Killea, Drumcannon and Dunhill
  C, F & O
TRILLICK (Christ Church) *see* Kilskeery w Trillick *Clogh*
TRIM (Cathedral of St Patrick) and Athboy Group, The
  M & K I P D BOGLE
TRORY (St Michael) w Killadeas *Clogh* I M GALLAGHER
TUAM (Cathedral of St Mary) w Cong and Aasleagh
  T, K & A I A J GRIMASON
TUAMGRANEY (St Cronan) *see* Killaloe w Stradbally *L & K*
TUBBERCURRY (St George) w Killoran *T, K & A*
  P-in-c P J NORMAN
TUBRID *see* Drumkeeran w Templecarne and Muckross *Clogh*
TULLAGH (no dedication) *see* Abbeystrewry Union *C, C & R*
TULLAGHBEGLEY (St Ann) *see* Dunfanaghy,
  Raymunterdoney and Tullaghbegley *D & R*
TULLAGHMELAN (no dedication) *see* Clonmel w
  Innislounagh, Tullaghmelan etc *C, F & O*
TULLAMORE (St Catherine) w Durrow,
  Newtownfertullagh, Rahan, Tyrellspass and Killoughy
  M & K I I G DELAMERE OLM Y HUTCHINSON
TULLANISKIN (Holy Trinity) w Clonoe *Arm* I W H BLAIR
TULLOW (no dedication) *D & G* I L J TANNER
TULLOW (St Columba) w Shillelagh, Aghold and
  Mullinacuff *C, F & O* I B J G O'ROURKE
TULLYAUGHNISH (St Paul) w Kilmacrennan and
  Killygarvan *D & R* I H GILMORE
TULLYLISH (All Saints) *D & D* I B J A CRUISE
TULLYNAKILL (no dedication) *see* Killinchy w Kilmood and
  Tullynakill *D & D*
TUNNY (St Andrew) *see* Glenavy w Tunny and Crumlin
  Conn
TURLOUGH (no dedication) *see* Aughaval w Achill,
  Knappagh, Dugort etc *T, K & A*
TYBOHINE (no dedication) *see* Roscommon Gp *K, E & A*
TYDAVNET (St Davnet) *see* Monaghan w Tydavnet and
  Kilmore *Clogh*
TYHOLLAND (St Sillian) *see* Donagh w Tyholland and Errigal
  Truagh *Clogh*
TYNAN (St Vindic) w Middletown and Aghavilly *Arm*
  I M H HAGAN
TYRELLA (St John) *see* Rathmullan w Tyrella *D & D*
TYRELLSPASS (St Sinian) *see* Tullamore w Durrow,
  Newtownfertullagh, Rahan etc *M & K*
UPPER DONAGHMORE (St Patrick) *see* Donaghmore w
  Donaghmore Upper *Arm*
URGLIN (no dedication) *see* Carlow w Urglin and
  Staplestown *C, F & O*
URNEY (Christ Church) w Sion Mills *D & R*
  C J H MCFARLAND
URNEY (no dedication) w Denn and Derryheen *K, E & A*
  I M R LIDWILL
VALENTIA (St John the Baptist) *see* Kenmare w Sneem,
  Waterville etc *L & K*
VIRGINIA *see* Lurgan w Billis, Killinkere and
  Munterconnaught *K, E & A*
WARINGSTOWN (Holy Trinity) *see* Donaghcloney w
  Waringstown *D & D*
WARRENPOINT (no dedication) *see* Clonallon and
  Warrenpoint w Kilbroney *D & D*
WATERFORD (Christ Church Cathedral) w Killea,
  Drumcannon and Dunhill *C, F & O* I M P JANSSON
WATERVILLE *see* Kenmare w Sneem, Waterville etc *L & K*
WESTPORT *see* Aughaval w Achill, Knappagh, Dugort etc
  T, K & A

WEXFORD (St Iberius) and Kilscoran Union *C, F & O*
  I A MINION   **C** M SYKES   **NSM** P A NEILAND
WHITECHURCH   *see* Dublin Whitechurch *D & G*
WHITECHURCH (no dedication)   *see* New w Old Ross,
  Whitechurch, Fethard etc *C, F & O*
WHITEGATE   *see* Cloyne Union *C, C & R*
WHITEHEAD (St Patrick) and Islandmagee *Conn*
  I M F TAYLOR
WHITEHOUSE (St John) *Conn*   **I** E O'BRIEN   **OLM**
  A LOCKE
WHITEROCK   *see* Belfast Whiterock *Conn*

WICKLOW (no dedication) w Killiskey *D & G*
  I J A H KINKEAD   **NSM** K G RUE
WILLOWFIELD (no dedication) *D & D*   **I** C J ATKINSON
  C K E SALMON
WOODBURN (Holy Trinity) *Conn*   **I** T A G MCCANN
WOODLAWN (no dedication)   *see* Aughrim w Ballinasloe etc
  L & K
WOODSCHAPEL (St John) w Gracefield *Arm*   **I** E R MURRAY
**YOUGHAL (St Mary's Collegiate) w Ardmore, Castlemartyr
  and Ballycotton** *C, C & R*   **P-in-c** A D H ORR
ZION   *see* Dublin Zion Ch *D & G*

THE DIOCESE IN EUROPE

Diocesan Office, 14 Tufton Street, London SW1P 3QZ
T: (020) 7898 1155
E: bron.panter@churchofengland.org
W: www.europe.anglican.org

ARCHDEACONS
1. Eastern L S NATHANIEL
2. France P G HOOPER
3. Gibraltar D J WALLER
4. Italy and Malta D J WALLER
5. North West Europe S W VAN LEER
6. Germany and Northern Europe L S NATHANIEL
7. Switzerland A KELHAM

Further information may be obtained from the appropriate archdeacon (the archdeaconry number is given after the name of each country). Mission to Seafarers chaplaincies are listed separately at the end of the section.

Andorra 3
Served from Barcelona

Austria 1
VIENNA (Christ Church) **Chapl** P M S CURRAN, C M WALTNER, **Hon** C R S KINNEY

Azerbaijan 1
BAKU *vacant*

Belgium 5
ANTWERP (St Boniface) **Chapl** A R WAGSTAFF
BRUGES (St Peter) **Chapl** A U NWAEKWE
BRUSSELS (Pro-Cathedral of the Holy Trinity)
  Sen Chapl P D VROLIJK, **Asst Chapl** A E BOLGER, C H LAING, J D MCDONALD, NSM J-B TURAHIRWA, **Assoc Chapl** J A WILKINSON
GHENT (St John) **Chapl** S M MURRAY, **Asst Chapl** O SOPEJU
KNOKKE (St George) **Chapl** A U NWAEKWE
LEUVEN **Chapl** C H LAING, **C** S-J KING
LIÈGE **Chapl** G M DIAKIESE
OSTEND **Chapl** A U NWAEKWE
TERVUREN **Chapl** D G B NEWSTEAD
YPRES (St George) **Chapl** A B MCMULLON

Bosnia and Herzegovina 1
SARAJEVO (St Anthony) *vacant*

Bulgaria 1
Served from Bucharest (Romania)

Croatia 1
Served from Vienna (Austria)

Czech Republic 1
PRAGUE **Chapl** NATHANIAL

Denmark 6
COPENHAGEN (St Alban) w Aarhus **Chapl** M S PRASADAM

Estonia 6
TALLINN (St Timothy and St Titus) **P-in-c** G P PIIR

Finland 6
HELSINKI w Kerava, Kuopio, Mikkeli, Oulu, Pori, Tampere, Turku and White Nile **Chapl** T MÄKIPÄÄ, **Asst Chapl** D L OLIVER

France 2
AIX-EN-PROVENCE *see* Marseille w Aix-en-Provence
AMBERNAC *see* Poitou-Charentes

AQUITAINE (Bertric Burée, Bordeaux, Limeuil, Monteton, Périgueux-Chancelade, Sorges, Ste Nathalène and Doudrac) **Chapl** A D LOMAS, **Asst Chapl** E A MORRIS
ARRAS *see* Lille
BARBEZIEUX ST HILAIRE *see* Poitou-Charentes
BEAULIEU-SUR-MER (St Michael) **P-in-c** A W INGHAM
BORDEAUX *see* Aquitaine
BOULOGNE-SUR-MER *see* Pas de Calais
BRITTANY (Ploërmel, Huelgoat and Rostrene) *vacant*
CAEN *see* Paris St George
CAHORS *see* Midi-Pyrénées and Aude
CALAIS *see* Pas de Calais
CANNES (Holy Trinity) **Chapl** G P WILLIAMS
CAYLUS *see* Midi-Pyrénées and Aude
CHANTILLY (St Peter) **Chapl** S L TILLETT
CHEF BOUTONNE *see* Poitou-Charentes
CIVRAY *see* Poitou-Charentes
DINARD (St Bartholomew) *vacant*
FONTAINEBLEAU *vacant*
GIF SUR YVETTE *see* Versailles
GRATOT HOMÉEL (Christ Church) *see* La Manche
GRENOBLE **Chapl** N FINLAY
HESDIN *see* Pas de Calais
HUELGOAT *see* Brittany
JARNAC *see* Poitou-Charentes
LA MANCHE w Gratot Hommëel and Virey *vacant*
LA ROCHEFOUCAULD *see* Poitou-Charentes
LE GARD *vacant*
LILLE (Christ Church) **P-in-c** D M R FLACH
LIMEUIL *see* Aquitaine
LORGUES w Fayence *vacant*
LYON **Chapl** B L HARDING
MAGNÉ *see* Poitou-Charentes
MAISONS-LAFFITTE (Holy Trinity) **Chapl** C L SULLIVAN
MARSEILLE (All Saints) w Aix-en-Provence **Chapl** C J A JOHNSTON, **C** R I TENEA TELEMAN
MENTON (St John) *vacant*
MIDI-PYRÉNÉES and Aude (Cahors, Caylus, Tarn, Toulouse and Valence d'Agen) *vacant*
MONTETON *see* Aquitaine
NANTES *see* Vendée
NICE (Holy Trinity) w Vence **Chapl** P J E JACKSON
PARIS (St George) **Chapl** M W OSBORNE, **C** J P H JOHN, **C** N RAZAFINDRATSIMA
PARIS (St Michael) **Chapl** J J CLARK
PAS DE CALAIS (Boulogne-sur-Mer, Calais and Hesdin) *vacant*
PARTHENAY *see* Poitou-Charentes
PAU (St Andrew) *vacant*
PÉRIGUEUX-CHANCELADE *see* Aquitaine
PLOËRMEL *see* Brittany
POITOU-CHARENTES (Christ the Good Shepherd) w Ambernac, Barbézieux St Hilaire, Chef Boutonne, Civray, Jarnac, La Rochefoucauld, Magné, Parthenay, St Jean d'Angély, Verteuil and Villejésus *vacant*
PORT GRIMAUD *see* St Raphaël
ROSTRENEN *see* Brittany
ST JEAN D'ANGÉLY *see* Poitou-Charentes
ST PARGOIRE (All Saints) **Chapl** R W SMITH
ST RAPHAËL (St John the Evangelist) w Port Grimaud **Chapl** T D WILSON
STE NATHALÈNE *see* Aquitaine

SORGES   *see* Aquitaine
STRASBOURG   Chapl L M BARWICK
TARN   *see* Midi-Pyrénées and Aude
TOULOUSE   *see* Midi-Pyrénées and Aude
VALENCE D'AGEN   *see* Midi-Pyrénées and Aude
VENCE (St Hugh)   *see* Nice w Vence
**VENDÉE (Puy de Serre, La Chapelle Archard and La
   Chapelle Palluau)   Chapl** H L DOOR
VERNET-LES-BAINS (St George)   P-in-c D T PHILLIPS
VERSAILLES (St Mark)   Chapl D R HANSON
VERTEUIL   *see* Poitou-Charentes
VILLEJÉSUS   *see* Poitou-Charentes
VIREY   *see* La Manche

Georgia 1

TBILISI   *vacant*

Germany 6

BERLIN (St George)   Chapl C W JAGE-BOWLER, **C** J REICH,
   NSM G L M GEORGE
BONN w Cologne   Chapl R A GARDINER
DRESDEN   *see* Berlin
DÜSSELDORF (Christ Church)   Chapl S J WALTON
FREIBURG-IM-BREISGAU   *vacant*
HAMBURG (St Thomas à Becket)   Chapl J A BARNES
HEIDELBERG   Chapl J K NEWSOME
LEIPZIG   Chapl G M REAKES-WILLIAMS
STUTTGART (St Catherine)   Chapl K K WERNER

Gibraltar 3

GIBRALTAR (Cathedral of the Holy Trinity)   (Dean)
   I D TARRANT

Greece 1

ATHENS, GREATER   Chapl L W DOOLAN,
   Asst Chapl C R SACCALI
CORFU (Holy Trinity)   P-in-c J J WILSON
CRETE (St Thomas, the Apostle)   Asst Chapl D B BRYANT-
   SCOTT, **NSM** J D BRADSHAW

Hungary 1

BUDAPEST   P-in-c F M HEGEDUS

Italy 4

AVIANO   *see* Venice
BARI   *see* Naples
BOLOGNA   *see* Florence
BORDIGHERA   *see* Menton
CADENABBIA   *see* Milan
CAPRI   *see* Naples
**FLORENCE (St Mark) w Siena (St Peter) and Bologna
   Asst Chapl** G PANCETTI
GENOVA (The Holy Ghost)   Chapl A W DICKINSON
MACERATA   *see* Rome
MILAN (All Saints)   Chapl V L SIMS, C R R MORLEY
**NAPLES (Christ Church) w Sorrento, Capri and Bari
   Chapl** J A CAVE BERGQUIST
PADOVA   Chapl A OSAROMPKE
PALERMO (Holy Cross)   Chapl J T HADLEY
ROME (All Saints) w Macerata   Chapl R J WARREN
SIENA   *see* Florence
SORRENTO   *see* Naples
TAORMINA (St George)   *vacant*
TRIESTE   *see* Venice
VARESE   Served from Lugano (Switzerland)
VENICE (St George) w Trieste   Chapl M M BRADSHAW
VINCENZA   Served by US Army Base

Latvia 6

RIGA (St Saviour)   Chapl E ZIKMANE, **NSM** V TERAUDKALNS

Luxembourg 5

LUXEMBOURG   Chapl G P READ, **NSM** E H E SWEERTS-
   VERMEULEN

Malta and Gozo 4

**VALLETTA (Pro-Cathedral of St Paul)
   Sen Chapl** S H M GODFREY
SLIEMA (Holy Trinity)   Chapl C M UPTON

Monaco 2

MONTE CARLO (St Paul)   Chapl D J ROPER

Morocco 3

CASABLANCA (St John the Evangelist)   *vacant*
TANGIER (St Andrew)   Chapl D C OBIDIEGWU

The Netherlands 5

AMSTERDAM (Christ Church)   *vacant*
ARNHEM (St Willibrord)   Chapl J M STRENGHOLT,
   NSM D J DE VRIES-SYTSMA
EINDHOVEN   *vacant*
HAARLEM   *vacant*
HEILOO   *vacant*
HAGUE, THE (St John and St Philip)   Chapl M A NIJMEGEN
   see Arnhem
ROTTERDAM (St Mary)   Chapl J L C PRIDMORE, C H SUNIL
TWENTE (St Mary)   Chapl B G RODFORD
UTRECHT (Holy Trinity) w Zwolle   Asst Chapl G N CROWE
VOORSCHOTEN   Chapl R J CREW, C M J THIJS
ZWOLLE   *see* Utrecht

Norway 6

**OSLO (St Edmund) w Bergen, Trondheim , Stavanger,
   Drammen, Moss, Sandefjord, Tromsö and Kristiansand
   Sen Chapl** J E M UDAL, **Asst Chapl** S ROSENTHAL,
   C J K WEISZ

Poland 1

WARSAW w Gdansk   P-in-c D V A BROWN

Portugal 3

ALGARVE (St Vincent)   Chapl R J KEAN, R H HAMILTON
ALMANCIL   *see* Algarve
ESTORIL   *see* Lisbon
GORJÕES   *see* Algarve
LISBON (St George) w Estoril (St Paul)   Chapl E J BENDREY,
   Asst Chapl I R BENDREY
MADEIRA (Holy Trinity)   Chapl M R JARMAN
PORTO (*or* OPORTO) (St James)   *vacant*
PRAIA DA LUZ   *see* Algarve
TAVIRA   *see* Algarve

Romania 1

BUCHAREST (The Resurrection)   *vacant*

Russian Federation 1

**MOSCOW (St Andrew) w Vladivostock
   Chapl** M D ROGERS, **C** G S RUFFLE
ST PETERSBURG   *vacant*

Serbia 1

BELGRADE   Chapl J R FOX

Slovakia

Served from Vienna (Austria)

Slovenia

Served from Vienna (Austria)

Spain 3

ALCOCEBRE   *see* Costa Azahar
ALBOX   *see* Costa Almeria and Costa Calida
ALHAURÍN EL GRANDE   *see* Costa del Sol East
ALMUÑÉCAR   *see* Nerja and Almuñécar
BARCELONA (St George)   Chapl J B CHAPMAN,
   Asst Chapl D H CHAPMAN
BENALMADENA COSTA   *see* Costa del Sol East
CALA D'OR   *see* Palma de Mallorca

CALAHONDA *see* Costa del Sol East
CALPE *see* Costa Blanca
CAMPOVERDE *see* Torrevieja
COIN *see* Costa del Sol East
COSTA ALMERIA Chapl V C ORAM,
    Asst Chapl A W BENNETT
COSTA BLANCA Sen Chapl Q M RONCHETTI,
    Asst Chapl J H BOOKER, R MIDDLETON
COSTA BRAVA Chapl R A SHOCK
COSTA CALIDA *see* Costa Almeria
COSTA DEL SOL EAST Chapl N L STIMPSON
COSTA DEL SOL WEST *vacant*
COSTACABANA *see* Costa Almeria and Costa Calida
DENIA *see* Costa Blanca
EL CAMPELLO *see* Costa Blanca
FORMENTERA *see* Ibiza
FUENGIROLA (St Andrew) *see* Costa del Sol East
FUERTEVENTURA P-in-c R J HORROCKS
GANDIA *see* Costa Blanca
IBIZA Chapl A P GREEN
JÁVEA *see* Costa Blanca
LA MANGA *see* Torrevieja
LA MARINA *see* Torrevieja
LA PALMA *see* Puerto de la Cruz
LA SIESTA *see* Torrevieja
LAGO JARDIN *see* Torrevieja
LANZAROTE Chapl S G EVANS
LAS PALMAS (Holy Trinity) *vacant*
LOS BALCONES *see* Torrevieja
LOS GIGANTES *see* Tenerife Sur
MADRID (St George) Chapl M S EL KISS MIHANNY, C S U IKE
MÁLAGA (St George) Chapl L P DARRANT,
    Asst Chapl D A CAGE
MALLORCA *see* Palma de Mallorca
MENORCA P-in-c P STRUDWICK
MOJÁCAR *see* Costa Almeria
NAZARET *see* Lanzarote
NERJA and Almuñécar Chapl N C THOMAS
PALMA DE MALLORCA (St Philip and St James)
    Chapl I S GUSHA
PLAYA BLANCA *see* Lanzarote
PLAYA DE LAS AMERICAS *see* Tenerife Sur
PLAYA DEL INGLES *see* Las Palmas
PUERTO DE LA CRUZ Tenerife (All Saints)
    Chapl R A CORNE
PUERTO DEL CARMEN *see* Lanzarote
PUERTO POLLENSA *see* Palma de Mallorca
PUERTO SOLLER *see* Palma de Mallorca
ROQUETAS DE MAR *see* Costa Almeria and Costa Calida
SAN PEDRO *see* Costa del Sol West

SAN RAFAEL *see* Ibiza
SANTA EULALIA *see* Ibiza
SOTOGRANDE *see* Costa del Sol West
TENERIFE SUR (St Eugenio) P-in-c E J POOLE
TORREVIEJA Chapl R A SEABROOK
VINAROS *see* Costa Azahar

Sweden 6

GOTHENBURG (St Andrew) w Halmstad, Jönköping and
    Uddevalla Chapl A T M TOLLEFSEN VAN DER LANS
STOCKHOLM (St Peter and St Sigfrid) w Gävle and
    Västerås Chapl N S HOWE

Switzerland 7

ANZERE *see* Montreux
BADEN *see* Zürich
BASLE Asst Chapl R B HILLIARD, A L LOWEN, M D POGSON,
    NSM M KISSELL
BERNE (St Ursula) Chapl H J MARSHALL
CHÂTEAU D'OEX *see* Vevey
GENEVA (Holy Trinity) Chapl D M GREEN
GSTAAD *see* Montreuz
LA CÔTE P-in-c C J COOKE, Asst Chapl J L CHAMBEYRON
LAUSANNE (Christ Church) w Neuchâtel
    Chapl C L BLOOMFIELD
LUGANO (St Edward the Confessor) *vacant*
MONTHEY *see* Montreux
MONTREUX (St John) w Anzere, Gstaad and Monthey
    Chapl P W ORMROD
NEUCHÂTEL *see* Lausanne
ST GALLEN *see* Zürich
VEVEY (All Saints) w Château d'Oex
    Asst Chapl M E BUSSMANN
VILLARS *see* Montreux
ZUG *see* Zürich
ZÜRICH (St Andrew) w Baden, St Gallen and Zug *vacant*

Turkey 1

ANKARA (St Nicholas) *vacant*
ISTANBUL (Christ Church) (Chapel of St Helena) w Moda
    (All Saints) Chapl I W L SHERWOOD
IZMIR (SMYRNA) (St John the Evangelist) w Bornova
    (St Mary Magdalene) Chapl J A D BUXTON

Ukraine 1

KIEV (Christ Church) *vacant*

MISSION TO SEAFARERS CHAPLAINCIES

Belgium 5
ANTWERP *Lay Chapl*
GHENT Chapl S M MURRAY

France 2
DUNKERQUE Chapl P S EDELL

The Netherlands 5
ROTTERDAM and Schiedam Chapl D A WOODWARD
VLISSINGEN *vacant*

CHAPLAINS TO HER MAJESTY'S SERVICES

ROYAL NAVY

Chaplain of the Fleet and Archdeacon for the Royal Navy
Director General Naval Chaplaincy Service
The Ven A HILLIER QHC
Royal Naval Chaplaincy Service Headquarters, Tanner Building, HMS Excellent Whale Island, Portsmouth PO2 8ER
Tel 03001-577544

Chaplains RN

M D ALLSOPP	R H CHURCH	A J F MANSFIELD
P M AMEY	A S CORNESS	J C MONEY
P R ANDREW	R T M J DUCKETT	E A A NORTHEY
O J BALOGUN	M L EVANS	J F PERCIVAL
R W BARBER	J S FRANCIS	S P RASON
N A BEARDSLEY	P F GARVIE	N M J ROBERTSON
J R E BELL	M F GODFREY	W D SWEENEY
J L BELL-WINFROW	M J GOUGH	N THORNHILL
A J P BLAINE	A HILLIER	M WAGSTAFF
P R BRYCE	T M ST J JAMES	E R WILLS
M F CHATFIELD	D J JEAL	

ARMY

Chaplain General HM Land Forces and Archdeacon for the Army
The Ven C M LANGSTON QHC
MOD Chaplains (A), Army Headquarters, 1DL3 Blenheim Building,
Marlborough Lines, Monxton Road, Andover SP11 8HT
Tel (01264) 887064

Chaplains to the Forces

D J ADAMS	A J FELTHAM-WHITE	K PUNSHON
N J D ADLEY	B G FLUX	A C REES
P ALDRED	P T FRANCIS	S A RICHARDS
G D ALLEN	C A GILLHAM	R J RICHARDSON
J M AMEY	S H M GODFREY	J S ROBERTSHAW
P B ARCHIBALD	E G A GORRINGE	P A ROBINSON
K G BARRY	N J GOWER	R J ROBINSON
A R F BATTEY	A J GRANT	I C ROGERS
C D BELL	R A B HALL	C L ROTERS
A S F BENNETT	A B HARDING	M RUTTER
M W BEZERRA SPEEKS	J A HARDING	H D RYDEN
H D BISHOP	D A G HATHAWAY	A T J SALTER
S F BLOXAM-ROSE	L T J HILLARY	G J SCOTT
J R G BRADBURY	T R C HINEY	J P SCOTT
P G BURROWS	P C HULLYER	G C SMITH
J W CALDWELL	P J HUNT	A C STEELE
M W A CHADWICK	J E JEPSON	T M SUMPTER
J S CLARKE	I A KEMP	P H SUMSION
M S R COLES	C D KINCH	J J E SUTTON
G L COLLINGWOOD	P W S KING	A J TEARE
I R COLSON	N P KINSELLA	N S TODD
D P CREES	C M LANGSTON	C A TOME DA SILVA
D D CRITCHLOW	A M LATIFA	A J TOTTEN
A I DALTON	S H LODWICK	S TROTT
D S DEMPSEY	T J MATHEWS	J L VINCENT
R A DESICS	K D MENTZEL	M J WAINWRIGHT
M P R DIETZ	P J MILLS	P C WHITEHEAD
P DIXON	D T MORGAN	A C WHORTON
R J DOWNES	A J NICOLLS	A W WILKINSON
S J H DUNWOODY	A J NORTH	J S WILLIAMS
J DURBIN	T R PLACE	N C WILLIAMS
A J EARL	R PLUCK	S G WILSON
D A EATON	S S PRATT	F J L WINFIELD
H D EVANS	I M R PRICE	W WORLEY
S J FARMER	M O PRITCHARD	

ROYAL AIR FORCE

Chaplain-in-Chief and Archdeacon for the RAF
The Ven J R ELLIS QHC
Chaplaincy Services (RAF), HQ Air Command, RAF High Wycombe HP14 4UE
Tel (01494) 496800   Fax 496343

Chaplains RAF

K S BRUCE	J A HOBSON	M C PERRY
M A J BUCHAN	C J HODDER	P A RENNIE
R L CANNON	J M S HOLLAND	D RICHARDSON
K S CAPELIN-JONES	I A JONES	S J SHAW
A J CHAPMAN	C N LACEY	M D SHELDON
R P CLEMENT	S P LAMOND	P J STEPHENS
A L DYER	C D LAWRENCE	M STEVENS
J R ELLIS	G L LEGOOD	A M TUCKER
G D FIRTH	C A MITCHELL	A W WAKEHAM-DAWSON
R V HAKE	D J NORFIELD	G E WITHERS
C J HARRISON	C J O'DELL	E L WYNN
A D HEWETT	D T OSBORN	

PRISON CHAPLAINS

HM PRISON SERVICE (England and Wales)

Chaplain General to HM Prisons
The Ven J S RIDGE

HMPPS Chaplaincy HQ, Post Point 8.34, Ministry of Justice, 102 Petty France,
London SW1H 9AJ M: 07394-715223

Prisons

Altcourse R E GREENACRE
Ashfield E A PERRY, A THOMSON
Bedford A M BARKER
Belmarsh T G JACQUET
Berwyn A PIERCE-JONES
Birmingham P GILLON
Bristol P F ROBERTS
Brixton A A ADAMOLEKUN, I G THOMPSON
Bronzefield K HARTLEY, M J MCCARRON
Buckley Hall H A EDGERTON, R W A REECE
Bure I COOPER
Cardiff N R SANDFORD
Channings Wood P F HARTOPP
Chelmsford J JONES
Coldingley R D S SANDERS
Dartmoor L H COOPER
Doncaster D C STANDEN
Dorchester R A BETTS
Dovegate A J WALKER
Drake Hall S J MORRIS, E K WYKES
Durham R M L AMOROSO, M D TETLEY
Eastwood Park G A MARTIN, G M TREWEEK, A J WILLIAMS
Elmley N M ASH, J K M NJOROGE
Erlestoke J M CLARK, S A IBBETSON
Exeter V ATKINSON
Frankland R T FARNHAM, A V WEST
Full Sutton G R HOCKEN, A D ROBINSON
Garth R W BUNDAY, D W GOODWIN, G C TURNER
Gartree E V HIGGINS
Grendon and Spring Hill P G HILL, S P Z SMITH,
  M B WHITAKER
Guys Marsh P C BROWNE
Haverigg G JONES, R P SPRATT
Hewell S A WATSON
High Down B FRASER, E J F GBONDA, W M HARVEY
Highpoint M A OSBORNE
Hindley P MAGINN, L J SWEET
Hollesley Bay M R RENNARD
Holme House S BELL, K M BROOKE
Hull N J WHETTON
Humber N P ELY
Huntercombe I D THACKER
Isle of Wight J A SWAINE

Kirklevington Grange K E JAMIE
Leeds J C PARKES
Leyhill B E DAVIS, L G HEWISH
Lincoln A P SMITH
Lindholme C L SMITH
Littlehey A J HUTCHINSON, D J KINDER, M C LAWSON,
  T MCFADDEN, S M ROLFE
Liverpool P N TYERS
Long Lartin S BLAKE, S W NEWNES
Low Newton S K R PARKINSON
Lowdham Grange J M SAVAGE
Maidstone G L BURN
Manchester J E CALLADINE, H R F MARTIN, S PAGE
Moorland M E BALL
New Hall L K GREENWOOD-HAIGH, L E SENIOR
Northumberland T J K CONLIN
Norwich O O SOTONWA
Nottingham M TYACK
Oakwood O T OLUMUYIWA
Onley S K GILLARD-FAULKNER
Parc (Bridgend) D C TILT
Pentonville J W P AITKEN, J DAVIES
Peterborough J A C WIEGMAN
Preston G MILLER
Risley L J SWEET
Send A E DIXON, L J MASON
Stocken R J MACKRILL, T S WRIGHT
Stoke Heath M R KINDER
Styal Y L YATES
Sudbury J C HONOUR
Swinfen Hall S NTOYIMONDO
Thameside G R HARPER
Verne, The G A HEBBERN, E W D TILDESLEY
Wakefield M J BURNS
Wandsworth T CLAPTON
Wayland N P MORROW
Wealstun D T HAYES
Whitemoor P FOSTER
Winchester D J HINKS, C S MCCLELLAND
Wolds, The B WORSDALE
Wormwood Scrubs R W MAYO
Wymott C D F CROMBIE

Young Offender Institutions

Deerbolt K E JAMIE
Feltham M J BOYES
Lancaster Farms D NOBLET
Rochester B N B MUSINDI

Thorn Cross S G VERHEY
Werrington J C CUTTELL, V S PERRETT
Wetherby D E HERTH, A R ROWE

Immigration Centres

Colnbrook J W GEEN

CHANNEL ISLANDS PRISON SERVICE

Guernsey P J GRAYSMITH

NORTHERN IRELAND PRISON SERVICE

Maghaberry J R HOWARD, D JARDINE

HOSPITAL CHAPLAINS

2GETHER NHS FOUNDATION TRUST   H CLARKE
5 BOROUGHS PARTNERSHIP NHS FOUNDATION
TRUST   P LOVATT
ABERDEEN MATERNITY   *see* NHS Grampian
ABERDEEN ROYAL INFIRMARY   *see* NHS Grampian
ABRAHAM COWLEY UNIT Chertsey   *see* Surrey and Borders
Partnership NHS Foundn Trust
ADDENBROOKE'S Cambridge   *see* Cam Univ Hosps NHS
Foundn Trust
AIREDALE GENERAL   *see* Airedale NHS Foundn Trust
AIREDALE NHS FOUNDATION TRUST   D J GRIFFITHS,
J P SMITH, R L MULLIGAN
ALDEBURGH AND DISTRICT COMMUNITY   *see* Suffolk
Coastal Primary Care Trust
ALDER HEY CHILDREN'S NHS FOUNDATION
TRUST   A R BROCKBANK, D J WILLIAMS
ALEXANDRA Redditch   *see* Worcs Acute Hosps NHS Trust
ALNWICK INFIRMARY   *see* Northumbria Healthcare NHS
Foundn Trust
ALTRINCHAM GENERAL   *see* Trafford Healthcare NHS Trust
AMBERSTONE Hailsham   *see* E Sussex Healthcare NHS Trust
AMERSHAM   *see* Bucks Healthcare NHS Trust
ARCHERY HOUSE Dartford   *see* Kent and Medway NHS and
Soc Care Partnership Trust
ASHFIELD COMMUNITY Kirkby-in-Ashfield   *see* Sherwood
Forest Hosps NHS Foundn Trust
ASHFORD   *see* E Kent Hosps Univ NHS Foundn Trust   *and*
Surrey and Borders Partnership NHS Foundn Trust
ASHFORD AND ST PETER'S HOSPITALS NHS FOUNDATION
TRUST   L W GAMLEN
ASHINGTON   *see* Northumbria Healthcare NHS Foundn
Trust
ATKINSON MORLEY   *see* SW Lon and St George's Mental
Health NHS Trust
BARKING, HAVERING AND REDBRIDGE UNIVERSITY
HOSPITALS NHS TRUST   P J WRIGHT, S M HARTLEY
BARNES   *see* SW Lon and St George's Mental Health NHS
Trust
BARNET, ENFIELD AND HARINGEY MENTAL HEALTH NHS
TRUST   T M BARON
BARTLET Felixstowe   *see* Suffolk Coastal Primary Care Trust
BASILDON AND THURROCK UNIVERSITY HOSPITALS NHS
FOUNDATION TRUST   D F BATES
BASSETLAW DISTRICT GENERAL Worksop   *see* Doncaster and
Bassetlaw Teaching Hosps NHS Foundn Trust
BATH AND WEST COMMUNITY NHS TRUST   M JOYCE
BATTLE Reading   *see* R Berks NHS Foundn Trust
BELFAST CITY   *see* Belfast Health and Soc Care Trust
BELFAST HEALTH AND SOCIAL CARE TRUST   D W GAMBLE
BENNION CENTRE Leicester   *see* Leics Partnership NHS Trust
BENSHAM Gateshead   *see* Gateshead Health NHS Foundn
Trust
BERKSHIRE HEALTHCARE NHS FOUNDATION
TRUST   C J STOTT
BERWICK INFIRMARY   *see* Northumbria Healthcare NHS
Foundn Trust
BETHLEM ROYAL Beckenham   *see* S Lon and Maudsley NHS
Foundn Trust
BEXHILL   *see* E Sussex Healthcare NHS Trust
BIDEFORD   *see* N Devon Healthcare NHS Trust
BILLINGE   *see* Wrightington, Wigan and Leigh Teaching
Hosps NHS Foundn Trust
BIRCH HILL   *see* Pennine Acute Hosps NHS Trust
BIRMINGHAM CHILDREN'S HOSPITAL NHS FOUNDATION
TRUST   E BLAIR-CHAPPELL, M A ROBINSON
BIRMINGHAM CITY   *see* Sandwell and W Birm Hosps NHS
Trust
BIRMINGHAM SKIN   *see* Sandwell and W Birm Hosps NHS
Trust
BIRMINGHAM WOMEN'S NHS FOUNDATION
TRUST   P NASH
BISHOP AUCKLAND GENERAL   *see* Co Durham and
Darlington NHS Foundn Trust
BLACK COUNTRY HEALTHCARE NHS FOUNDATION
TRUST   E C LOUIS
BLACKBERRY HILL Bristol   *see* N Bris NHS Trust
BLACKBURN ROYAL INFIRMARY   *see* E Lancs Hosps NHS Trust
BLACKPOOL TEACHING HOSPITALS NHS FOUNDATION
TRUST   H S HOUSTON

BLACKPOOL, FYLDE AND WYRE HOSPITALS NHS
TRUST   C G LORD
BLYTH COMMUNITY   *see* Northumbria Healthcare NHS
Foundn Trust
BODMIN   *see* Cornwall Partnership NHS Foundn Trust
BOLTON GENERAL   *see* Bolton NHS Foundn Trust
BOLTON HOSPITALS NHS TRUST   D SIMPSON
BOLTON NHS FOUNDATION TRUST   B S GASKELL,
C D BINNS, J NICHOLLS
BOOTHAM PARK   *see* York Teaching Hosp NHS Foundn Trust
BOWNESS UNIT Prestwich   *see* Gtr Man W Mental Health
NHS Foundn Trust
BRADFORD TEACHING HOSPITALS NHS FOUNDATION
TRUST   S D LEES
BRADGATE MENTAL HEALTH UNIT Leicester   *see* Leics
Partnership NHS Trust
BRANDON MENTAL HEALTH UNIT Leicester   *see* Leics
Partnership NHS Trust
BRIDLINGTON AND DISTRICT   *see* York Teaching Hosp NHS
Foundn Trust
BRIDPORT COMMUNITY   *see* SW Dorset Primary Care Trust
BRIGHTON AND SUSSEX UNIVERSITY HOSPITALS NHS
TRUST   J M ELLIOTT, J S MCARTHUR-EDWARDS
BRIGHTON GENERAL   *see* Brighton and Sussex Univ Hosps
NHS Trust
BRISTOL GENERAL   *see* Univ Hosps Bris and Weston NHS
Foundn Trust
BRISTOL ROYAL HOSPITAL FOR CHILDREN   *see* Univ Hosps
Bris and Weston NHS Foundn Trust
BRISTOL ROYAL INFIRMARY   *see* Univ Hosps Bris and Weston
NHS Foundn Trust
BROADGREEN Liverpool   *see* R Liverpool and Broadgreen
Univ Hosps NHS Trust
BRONGLAIS GENERAL   *see* Hywel Dda Health Bd
BROOMFIELD Chelmsford   *see* Mid-Essex Hosp Services NHS
Trust
BRYN Y NEUADD Llanfairfechan   *see* NW Wales NHS Trust
BUCKINGHAMSHIRE HEALTHCARE NHS TRUST   C E HOUGH
BUCKLAND Dover   *see* E Kent Hosps Univ NHS Foundn Trust
BURNLEY GENERAL   *see* E Lancs Hosps NHS Trust
BURTON HOSPITALS NHS FOUNDATION TRUST   A C THORP,
H J BAKER
CAERPHILLY DISTRICT MINERS'   *see* Gwent Healthcare NHS
Trust
CALDERDALE AND HUDDERSFIELD NHS FOUNDATION
TRUST   M D ELLERTON
CAMBRIDGE UNIVERSITY HOSPITALS NHS FOUNDATION
TRUST   D P FORD, N CRITCHLOW, P M SHARKEY
CAMBRIDGESHIRE AND PETERBOROUGH NHS FOUNDATION
TRUST   J P NICHOLSON
CANTERBURY St Martin's   *see* Kent and Medway NHS and
Soc Care Partnership Trust
CARDIFF AND VALE NHS TRUST   E J BURKE, R V C LEWIS
CARDIFF ROYAL INFIRMARY   *see* Cardiff and Vale NHS Trust
CASTLE HILL Cottingham   *see* Hull and E Yorks Hosps NHS
Trust
CASTLEFORD NORMANTON AND DISTRICT   *see* Mid Yorks
Hosps NHS Trust
CATERHAM   *see* Surrey and Sussex Healthcare NHS Trust
CAVELL CENTRE Peterborough   *see* Cambs and Pet NHS
Foundn Trust
CEFN COED Swansea   *see* Swansea NHS Trust
CHADWICK LODGE Milton Keynes   P F TURNBULL
CHAPEL ALLERTON Leeds   *see* Leeds Teaching Hosps NHS
Trust
CHARLTON LANE CENTRE Leckhampton   *see* Glos Hosps
NHS Foundn Trust
CHELMSFORD Broomfield   *see* Mid-Essex Hosp Services NHS
Trust
CHELSEA AND WESTMINSTER HOSPITAL NHS FOUNDATION
TRUST   M J LEE
CHELTENHAM GENERAL   *see* Glos Hosps NHS Foundn Trust
CHEPSTOW COMMUNITY   *see* Gwent Healthcare NHS Trust
CHERRY KNOWLE Sunderland   *see* Northumberland, Tyne
and Wear NHS Foundn Trust
CHESTERTON Cambridge   *see* Cam Univ Hosps NHS Foundn
Trust
CHICHESTER St Richard's   *see* W Sussex Hosps NHS Foundn
Trust

CHRISTIE NHS FOUNDATION TRUST
Manchester   A R BRADLEY, F A JENKINSON, K L DUNN
CHURCHILL, THE Oxford   *see* Ox Univ Hosps NHS Foundn Trust
CIRENCESTER   *see* Glos Hosps NHS Foundn Trust
CITY Birmingham   *see* Sandwell and W Birm Hosps NHS Trust
CITY GENERAL Stoke-on-Trent   *see* Univ Hosp of N Staffs NHS Trust
CITY HOSPITALS SUNDERLAND NHS FOUNDATION TRUST   O R OMOLE
CLAYBURY Woodford Bridge   *see* Forest Healthcare NHS Trust Lon
CLAYTON Wakefield   *see* Mid Yorks Hosps NHS Trust
CLEVELAND, SOUTH Middlesbrough   *see* S Tees Hosps NHS Foundn Trust
CLIFTON Lytham St Annes   *see* Blackpool, Fylde and Wyre Hosps NHS Trust
COLINDALE   *see* Enfield Primary Care Trust
COLMAN Norwich   *see* Norfolk Primary Care Trust
CONQUEST Hastings   *see* E Sussex Healthcare NHS Trust
COOKRIDGE Leeds   *see* Leeds Teaching Hosps NHS Trust
CORK UNIVERSITY   D R NUZUM
CORNWALL PARTNERSHIP NHS FOUNDATION TRUST   E C DEELEY, M E PINNOCK
COUNTESS MOUNTBATTEN   I S MCFARLANE
COUNTESS MOUNTBATTEN HOSPICE Southampton   *see* Univ Hosp Southn NHS Foundn Trust
COUNTESS OF CHESTER HOSPITAL NHS FOUNDATION TRUST   E M GARDNER, G M HIBBERT
COUNTY DURHAM AND DARLINGTON NHS FOUNDATION TRUST   K S TROMANS
COVENTRY AND WARWICKSHIRE   *see* Univ Hosps Cov and Warks NHS Trust
COVENTRY AND WARWICKSHIRE PARTNERSHIP NHS TRUST   S P MOULT
CROMER   *see* Norfolk and Nor Univ Hosps NHS Foundn Trust
CROMER AND DISTRICT   *see* Norfolk Primary Care Trust
CROYDON HEALTH SERVICES NHS TRUST   A M S DOVEY
CROYDON MENTAL HEALTH SERVICES Warlingham   *see* S Lon and Maudsley NHS Foundn Trust
CUMBERLAND INFIRMARY   *see* N Cumbria Integrated Care NHS Foundn Trust
DARLINGTON MEMORIAL   *see* Co Durham and Darlington NHS Foundn Trust
DELANCEY Leckhampton   *see* Glos Hosps NHS Foundn Trust
DELLWOOD Reading   *see* R Berks NHS Foundn Trust
DERBYSHIRE CHILDREN'S   *see* Univ Hosps of Derby and Burton NHS Foundn Trust
DERBYSHIRE ROYAL INFIRMARY   *see* Univ Hosps of Derby and Burton NHS Foundn Trust
DEREHAM   *see* Norfolk Primary Care Trust
DERRIFORD   *see* Plymouth Hosps NHS Trust
DEVONSHIRE ROAD Blackpool   *see* Blackpool, Fylde and Wyre Hosps NHS Trust
DEWSBURY AND DISTRICT   *see* Mid Yorks Hosps NHS Trust
DIANA, PRINCESS OF WALES Grimsby   *see* N Lincs and Goole NHS Foundn Trust
DONCASTER AND BASSETLAW TEACHING HOSPITALS NHS FOUNDATION TRUST   A J ARMITT
DONCASTER ROYAL INFIRMARY   *see* Doncaster and Bassetlaw Teaching Hosps NHS Foundn Trust
DORKING   *see* Surrey and Sussex Healthcare NHS Trust
DORSET COUNTY HOSPITAL NHS FOUNDATION TRUST   R A BETTS, R C J R MARTIN
DORSET HEALTHCARE UNIVERSITY NHS FOUNDATION TRUST   M G OATES
DR GRAY'S Elgin   *see* NHS Grampian
DUNSTON HILL Gateshead   *see* Gateshead Health NHS Foundn Trust
DURHAM AND DARLINGTON NHS FOUNDATION TRUST   *see* Co Durham and Darlington NHS Foundn Trust
EAST HAM MEMORIAL   *see* E Lon NHS Foundation Trust
EAST KENT HOSPITALS UNIVERSITY NHS FOUNDATION TRUST   P F HILL
EAST LANCASHIRE HOSPITALS NHS TRUST   A S HORSFALL, D L ANDERSON
EAST LONDON NHS FOUNDATION TRUST   N J COPSEY
EAST SUFFOLK AND NORTH ESSEX NHS FOUNDATION TRUST   C J COOK, L G PEALL, M K LING
EAST SURREY PRIORITY CARE NHS TRUST   N J COPSEY
EAST SUSSEX HEALTHCARE NHS TRUST   G J A COOK, G R ATFIELD, M P TURNBULL
EASTBOURNE GENERAL   *see* E Sussex Healthcare NHS Trust
ENFIELD PRIMARY CARE TRUST   T M BARON

EPSOM St Ebba's   *see* Surrey and Borders Partnership NHS Foundn Trust
ESSEX PARTNERSHIP University NHS Foundation Trust   H A N PLATTS
EVELINA CHILDREN'S London   S M TAYLOR
FAIRFIELD GENERAL   *see* Pennine Acute Hosps NHS Trust
FARNHAM   *see* Surrey and Borders Partnership NHS Foundn Trust
FARNHAM ROAD Guildford   *see* Surrey and Borders Partnership NHS Foundn Trust
FIELDHEAD Wakefield   *see* SW Yorks Partnership NHS Foundn Trust
FINCHLEY MEMORIAL   *see* Enfield Primary Care Trust
FIVE BOROUGHS PARTNERSHIP NHS FOUNDATION TRUST   *see* 5 Boroughs Partnership NHS Foundn Trust
FOREST HEALTHCARE NHS TRUST London   S BEURKLIAN-CARTER
FORSTER GREEN   *see* Belfast Health and Soc Care Trust
FORTH VALLEY NHS TRUST   T NJUGUNA
FREEMAN Newcastle   *see* Newcastle upon Tyne Hosps NHS Foundn Trust
FRENCHAY Bristol   *see* N Bris NHS Trust
FRIARAGE Northallerton   *see* S Tees Hosps NHS Foundn Trust
FRIMLEY HEALTH NHS FOUNDATION TRUST   B D BURBIDGE, C E L SMITH, J J SISTIG
FULBOURN Cambridge   *see* Cam Univ Hosps NHS Foundn Trust
FURNESS GENERAL Barrow-in-Furness   *see* Univ Hosps of Morecambe Bay NHS Foundn Trust
GATESHEAD HEALTH NHS FOUNDATION TRUST   G R ROWLANDS, J ROBINSON
GEORGE ELIOT HOSPITAL NHS TRUST Nuneaton   M J HAMMOND, R J WITCOMBE, S P MOULT
GLANGWILI GENERAL   *see* Hywel Dda Health Bd
GLENFIELD Bennion Centre   *see* Leics Partnership NHS Trust
GLENFIELD Bradgate Mental Health Unit   *see* Leics Partnership NHS Trust
GLENFIELD Leicester   *see* Univ Hosps Leic NHS Trust
GLOUCESTERSHIRE HOSPITALS NHS FOUNDATION TRUST   C A MCCLURE, J R THOMPSON
GLOUCESTERSHIRE ROYAL   *see* Glos Hosps NHS Foundn Trust
GOOLE AND DISTRICT   *see* N Lincs and Goole NHS Foundn Trust
GORSE HILL Leicester   *see* Leics Partnership NHS Trust
GREAT ORMOND STREET HOSPITAL FOR CHILDREN NHS FOUNDATION TRUST   D A MOORE BROOKS, J D LINTHICUM, P J SHERRINGTON
GREAT WESTERN HOSPITALS NHS FOUNDATION TRUST   A GOSDEN, C J OWEN, J A COUTTS
GREATER GLASGOW AND CLYDE NHS   R F JONES
GREATER MANCHESTER WEST MENTAL HEALTH NHS FOUNDATION TRUST   B S GASKELL, G M BERESFORD JONES
GREENACRES Dartford   *see* Kent and Medway NHS and Soc Care Partnership Trust
GRIMSBY   *see* N Lincs and Goole NHS Foundn Trust
GUILDFORD St Luke's   *see* R Surrey NHS Foundn Trust
GUY'S AND ST THOMAS' NHS FOUNDATION TRUST London   G A NEWMAN, J M WATTS, M A K HILBORN, N O TRAYNOR, R A SHAW, S BEURKLIAN-CARTER, S M TAYLOR, W W SHARPE
GWENT COUNTY Griffithstown   *see* Gwent Healthcare NHS Trust
GWENT HEALTHCARE NHS TRUST   A W TYLER, M J MARSDEN
HALTON GENERAL   *see* Warrington and Halton Hosps NHS Foundn Trust
HAM GREEN Bristol   *see* N Bris NHS Trust
HAMPSHIRE HOSPITALS NHS FOUNDATION TRUST   C S WHITEHEAD, J L WILLIAMS, V J PERRICONE
HAROLD WOOD   *see* Barking, Havering and Redbridge Hosps NHS Trust
HARROGATE AND DISTRICT NHS FOUNDATION TRUST   A CLAYTON, D J MCCLINTOCK, D L LOFTHOUSE
HARTSHILL ORTHOPAEDIC   *see* Univ Hosp of N Staffs NHS Trust
HASLAR   *see* Portsm Hosps Univ NHS Trust
HEART OF ENGLAND NHS FOUNDATION TRUST   L M BUSFIELD, M MACLACHLAN
HERGEST UNIT Ysbyty Gwynedd   *see* NW Wales NHS Trust
HERTFORDSHIRE PARTNERSHIP UNIVERSITY NHS FOUNDATION TRUST   R J S ALLEN, V M HARVEY
HEXHAM   *see* Northumbria Healthcare NHS Foundn Trust
HIGHBURY Bulwell   *see* Notts Healthcare NHS Foundn Trust
HILL HOUSE Swansea   *see* Swansea NHS Trust
HINCHINGBROOKE HEALTH CARE NHS TRUST   S GRIFFITH
HOPE Salford   *see* Salford R NHS Foundn Trust

HUDDERSFIELD ROYAL INFIRMARY see Calderdale and Huddersfield NHS Foundn Trust
HULL AND EAST YORKSHIRE HOSPITALS NHS TRUST C R TETLEY
HULL MATERNITY see Hull and E Yorks Hosps NHS Trust
HULL ROYAL INFIRMARY see Hull and E Yorks Hosps NHS Trust
HULTON Bolton see Bolton Hosp NHS Trust
HUMBER NHS FOUNDATION TRUST E ROSE
HURSTWOOD PARK Haywards Heath see Brighton and Sussex Univ Hosps NHS Trust
HYWEL DDA HEALTH BOARD E HOWELLS
IDA DARWIN Cambridge see Cam Univ Hosps NHS Foundn Trust
IMPERIAL COLLEGE HEALTHCARE NHS TRUST M LEGG, M J LEE, R RATCLIFFE
ISLE OF WIGHT NHS TRUST D M NETHERWAY, J K HALLAM, K S BURKE, L J TROMBETTI, S H HOLT
JAMES COOK UNIVERSITY Middlesbrough see S Tees Hosps NHS Foundn Trust
JAMES PAGET UNIVERSITY HOSPITALS NHS FOUNDATION TRUST C E HOWARD, S R ANDREWS
JERSEY GENERAL St Helier see Jersey Gp of Hosps
JERSEY GROUP J A DAVY, T L C BROMLEY
JESSOP WOMEN'S Sheffield see Sheff Teaching Hosps NHS Foundn Trust
JOHN RADCLIFFE Oxford see Ox Univ Hosps NHS Foundn Trust
KELLING Holt see Norfolk Primary Care Trust
KENT AND CANTERBURY see E Kent Hosps Univ NHS Foundn Trust
KENT AND MEDWAY NHS AND SOCIAL CARE PARTNERSHIP TRUST E HURST, K A NELSON, M CLEEVE, P R BECKINSALE, R A BIERBAUM, S A J MITCHELL, T N ALEXANDER-WATTS
KETTERING GENERAL HOSPITAL NHS FOUNDATION TRUST M P CORCORAN, N PURVEY-TYRER
KIDDERMINSTER see Worcs Acute Hosps NHS Trust
KING GEORGE Redbridge see Barking, Havering and Redbridge Hosps NHS Trust
KING'S COLLEGE HOSPITAL NHS FOUNDATION TRUST G O OCHOLA, K A CARPANI, S L SUTHERLAND
KINGS MILL Sutton-in-Ashfield see Sherwood Forest Hosps NHS Foundn Trust
KINGSTON HOSPITAL NHS FOUNDATION TRUST Surrey S M VAN BEVEREN
LANSDOWNE see Cardiff and Vale NHS Trust
LEEDS AND YORK PARTNERSHIP NHS FOUNDATION TRUST B M KIMARU, S J M COWLING-GREEN
LEEDS GENERAL INFIRMARY see Leeds Teaching Hosps NHS Trust
LEEDS TEACHING HOSPITALS NHS TRUST A J HESLOP, B RHODES, D L M YOUNG, I WILLIAMS, S A KASIBANTE
LEICESTER GENERAL see Univ Hosps Leic NHS Trust
LEICESTER GENERAL Brandon Mental Health Unit see Leics Partnership NHS Trust
LEICESTER ROYAL INFIRMARY see Univ Hosps Leic NHS Trust
LEICESTERSHIRE PARTNERSHIP NHS TRUST H A LOMAX, T H GIRLING
LEIGH INFIRMARY see Wrightington, Wigan and Leigh Teaching Hosps NHS Foundn Trust
LEIGHTON Crewe see Mid Cheshire Hosps NHS Foundn Trust
LEWISHAM AND GREENWICH NHS TRUST C F NESTOR, E B KORMI, G C DAVIES, K PARKES, L SEEAR, W J DAVID
LIFECARE Caterham see Surrey and Borders Partnership NHS Foundn Trust
LINCOLN COUNTY see United Lincs Hosps NHS Trust
LITTLE PLUMSTEAD see Norfolk Primary Care Trust
LITTLEMORE Oxford see Ox Health NHS Foundn Trust
LIVERPOOL CARDIOTHORACIC CENTRE see R Liverpool and Broadgreen Univ Hosps NHS Trust
LIVERPOOL WOMEN'S NHS FOUNDATION TRUST L J N PARRY
LLANDOUGH see Cardiff and Vale NHS Trust
LLANDUDNO GENERAL see NW Wales NHS Trust
LLANFRECHFA GRANGE Cwmbran see Gwent Healthcare NHS Trust
LONDON AND SURREY see R Marsden NHS Foundn Trust
LONDON NORTH WEST HEALTHCARE NHS TRUST J M BEVIS-KNOWLES
LOUTH COUNTY see United Lincs Hosps NHS Trust
LUTON AND DUNSTABLE UNIVERSITY HOSPITAL NHS FOUNDATION TRUST E A BRADLEY, P G STANNARD, P H NYATSANZA
MAINDIFF COURT Abergavenny see Gwent Healthcare NHS Trust

MANCHESTER see also Greater Manchester
MANCHESTER AND SALFORD SKIN see Salford R NHS Foundn Trust
MANCHESTER MENTAL HEALTH AND SOCIAL CARE TRUST A G RUSTED
MANCHESTER UNIVERSITY NHS FOUNDATION TRUST A C MCMULLEN, D L MOCK, H W BEARN, R D FIELDING
MANOR Walsall see Walsall Healthcare NHS Trust
MANSFIELD COMMUNITY see Sherwood Forest Hosps NHS Foundn Trust
MATER see Belfast Health and Soc Care Trust
MATTHEW HAY BUILDING Aberdeen see NHS Grampian
MAUDSLEY Denmark Hill see S Lon and Maudsley NHS Foundn Trust
MEADOWBROOK UNIT Salford see Gtr Man W Mental Health NHS Foundn Trust
MEDWAY MARITIME Gillingham see Kent and Medway NHS and Soc Care Partnership Trust
MEDWAY NHS FOUNDATION TRUST D V GOWER, L COOKE, S C SPENCER
MID CHESHIRE HOSPITALS NHS FOUNDATION TRUST C J SANDERSON
MID YORKSHIRE HOSPITALS NHS TRUST S HULME
MIDDLESBROUGH GENERAL see S Tees Hosps NHS Foundn Trust
MID-ESSEX HOSPITAL SERVICES NHS TRUST K M SALA, S M MALAM
MILLBROOK MENTAL HEALTH UNIT Sutton-in-Ashfield see Notts Healthcare NHS Foundn Trust
MILTON KEYNES UNIVERSITY HOSPITAL NHS FOUNDATION TRUST A J FERRIS
MONKWEARMOUTH Sunderland see Northumberland, Tyne and Wear NHS Foundn Trust
MONTAGU Mexborough see Doncaster and Bassetlaw Teaching Hosps NHS Foundn Trust
MORAY Hospitals A L WILLIS
MORPETH COTTAGE see Northumbria Healthcare NHS Foundn Trust
MORRISTON Swansea see Swansea NHS Trust
MOUNT, THE Bishopstoke see Hants Hosps NHS Foundn Trust
MUSGRAVE PARK see Belfast Health and Soc Care Trust
MUSGROVE PARK Taunton see Taunton and Somerset NHS Foundn Trust
NAPSBURY St Albans see Enfield Primary Care Trust
NEVILL HALL Abergavenny see Gwent Healthcare NHS Trust
NEW CROSS Wolverhampton see R Wolv NHS Trust
NEWARK see Sherwood Forest Hosps NHS Foundn Trust
NEWCASTLE Freeman see Newcastle upon Tyne Hosps NHS Foundn Trust
NEWCASTLE GENERAL see Newcastle upon Tyne Hosps NHS Foundn Trust
NEWCASTLE Royal Victoria Infirmary see Newcastle upon Tyne Hosps NHS Foundn Trust
NEWCASTLE St Nicholas see Northumberland, Tyne and Wear NHS Foundn Trust
NEWCASTLE UPON TYNE HOSPITALS NHS FOUNDATION TRUST F M COLLIN, K WATSON
NEWHAM PRIMARY CARE TRUST N J COPSEY
NHS GRAMPIAN I N PALLETT, N C MILNE, S SPENCER
NHS LOTHIAN D A S MACLAREN
NHS TAYSIDE L DAWSON, P T MEAD
NINEWELLS Dundee see NHS Tayside
NORFOLK AND NORWICH UNIVERSITY HOSPITALS NHS FOUNDATION TRUST A V WOODROW, D T THORNTON, J J CHAMBERLIN, J L NURSEY, J M STEWART
NORFOLK COMMUNITY HEALTH AND CARE NHS TRUST E H GARRARD, J M STEWART
NORFOLK PRIMARY CARE TRUST P A ATKINSON
NORTH BRISTOL NHS TRUST A M BUCKNALL, A R GOOD, C L DICKSON, N A HECTOR, R CONWAY, W B M DOWIE
NORTH CUMBRIA INTEGRATED CARE NHS FOUNDATION TRUST I B THOMAS
NORTH DEVON DISTRICT Barnstaple see N Devon Healthcare NHS Trust
NORTH EAST LONDON NHS FOUNDATION TRUST R S ALLEN
NORTH HAMPSHIRE see Hants Hosps NHS Foundn Trust
NORTH MANCHESTER GENERAL see Pennine Acute Hosps NHS Trust
NORTH MIDDLESEX UNIVERSITY HOSPITAL NHS TRUST J G S MORGAN
NORTH STAFFORDSHIRE ROYAL INFIRMARY see Univ Hosp of N Staffs NHS Trust

NORTH SURREY PRIMARY CARE TRUST J C L RUNNACLES
NORTH TYNESIDE GENERAL North Shields *see* Northumbria Healthcare NHS Foundn Trust
NORTH WEST ANGLIA NHS FOUNDATION TRUST E L DAVIS, J M THOMSON, P M DUFFETT-SMITH
NORTH WEST WALES NHS TRUST W ROBERTS
NORTHAMPTON GENERAL HOSPITAL NHS TRUST C L SHAW, G A SARMEZEY
NORTHAMPTONSHIRE HEALTHCARE NHS FOUNDATION TRUST R J T FARMER
NORTHERN DEVON HEALTHCARE NHS TRUST J A CARTWRIGHT
NORTHERN GENERAL Sheffield *see* Sheff Teaching Hosps NHS Foundn Trust
NORTHERN LINCOLNSHIRE AND GOOLE NHS FOUNDATION TRUST E J TOMS, H G SMART
NORTHUMBERLAND, TYNE AND WEAR NHS FOUNDATION TRUST C J WORSFOLD, J GOODE, M C CONNORS, S D MASON
NORTHUMBRIA HEALTHCARE NHS FOUNDATION TRUST C J CLINCH, E A M G BROWN, N WILSON
NORWICH COMMUNITY *see* Norfolk Primary Care Trust
NORWICH, WEST *see* Norfolk and Nor Univ Hosps NHS Foundn Trust
NOTTINGHAM UNIVERSITY HOSPITAL NHS TRUST City Hospital Campus J S PACEY, L M RAYNOR, M S DOERING, P KEY
NOTTINGHAM UNIVERSITY HOSPITAL NHS TRUST Queen's Medical Centre Campus A M BROOKS, G SPENCER, J HEMSTOCK
NOTTINGHAMSHIRE HEALTHCARE NHS FOUNDATION TRUST T W POWNALL-JONES
NUNNERY FIELDS Canterbury *see* E Kent Hosps Univ NHS Foundn Trust
OAKS, THE Moray *see* NHS Grampian
ORSETT *see* Basildon and Thurrock Univ Hosps NHS Foundn Trust
OVERDALE St Helier *see* Jersey Gp of Hosps
OXFORD HEALTH NHS FOUNDATION TRUST G P HARRISON, R H MADZORERA, S J HORNER, S L BUSHELL
OXFORD UNIVERSITY HOSPITALS NHS FOUNDATION TRUST J G S MORGAN, S F SEWELL
OXTED *see* Surrey and Sussex Healthcare NHS Trust
PEACE HOSPICE Watford M J CARTER
PEMBURY Tunbridge Wells *see* Kent and Medway NHS and Soc Care Partnership Trust
PENDERED CENTRE Northampton *see* Northants Healthcare NHS Foundn Trust
PENDLE COMMUNITY Nelson *see* E Lancs Hosps NHS Trust
PENNINE ACUTE HOSPITALS NHS TRUST, THE K R CARMYLLIE, N ALEXANDER
PENNINE CARE NHS FOUNDATION TRUST A G RUSTED
PETERBOROUGH AND STAMFORD HOSPITALS NHS FOUNDATION TRUST J J PRICE
PILGRIM Boston *see* United Lincs Hosps NHS Trust
PINDERFIELDS GENERAL Wakefield *see* Mid Yorks Hosps NHS Trust
PLAISTOW *see* Newham Primary Care Trust
PLYMOUTH HOSPITALS NHS TRUST A P BARTON, J M COLLIS, S J T PEARCE
PONTEFRACT GENERAL INFIRMARY *see* Mid Yorks Hosps NHS Trust
POOLE St Ann's *see* Dorset HealthCare University NHS Foundn Trust
PORTSMOUTH HOSPITALS UNIVERISTY NHS TRUST B R SMITH, D A BANTING, I NEWTON
PRINCE PHILIP Llanelli *see* Hywel Dda Health Bd
PRINCESS ALEXANDRA HOSPITAL NHS TRUST Harlow C C OKEKE, G A NEWMAN, T R WEEKS
PRINCESS ANNE Southampton *see* Univ Hosp Southn NHS Foundn Trust
PRINCESS ELIZABETH Guernsey L S LE VASSEUR
PRINCESS MARINA Northampton *see* Northants Healthcare NHS Foundn Trust
PRINCESS ROYAL Haywards Heath *see* Brighton and Sussex Univ Hosps NHS Trust
PRINCESS ROYAL Hull *see* Hull and E Yorks Hosps NHS Trust
PRIORITY HOUSE Maidstone *see* Kent and Medway NHS and Soc Care Partnership Trust
PRIORY Birmingham J A GRIFFIN
QUEEN ALEXANDRA Portsmouth *see* Portsm Hosps Univ NHS Trust
QUEEN ELIZABETH Birmingham *see* Univ Hosp Birm NHS Foundn Trust
QUEEN ELIZABETH Gateshead *see* Gateshead Health NHS Foundn Trust

QUEEN ELIZABETH HOSPITAL KING'S LYNN NHS FOUNDATION TRUST S L GREEN
QUEEN ELIZABETH THE QUEEN MOTHER Margate *see* E Kent Hosps Univ NHS Foundn Trust
QUEEN VICTORIA Morecambe *see* Univ Hosps of Morecambe Bay NHS Foundn Trust
QUEEN'S Burton-on-Trent *see* Burton Hosps NHS Foundn Trust
QUEEN'S MEDICAL CENTRE Nottingham *see* Qu Medical Cen Nottm Univ Hosp NHS Trust
QUEEN'S MEDICAL CENTRE UNIVERSITY HOSPITAL Nottingham, Department of Psychiatry and Psychiatric Medicine *see* Notts Healthcare NHS Foundn Trust
QUEEN'S PARK Blackburn *see* E Lancs Hosps NHS Trust
QUEEN'S Romford *see* Barking, Havering and Redbridge Hosps NHS Trust
RAIGMORE HOSPITAL NHS TRUST Inverness A A SINCLAIR
RAMPTON Retford *see* Notts Healthcare NHS Foundn Trust
RAMSGATE GENERAL *see* E Kent Hosps Univ NHS Foundn Trust
REDBRIDGE King George *see* Barking, Havering and Redbridge Hosps NHS Trust
RIDGEWOOD CENTRE Frimley *see* Surrey and Borders Partnership NHS Foundn Trust
ROBERT JONES/AGNES HUNT ORTHOPAEDIC AND DISTRICT HOSPITAL NHS TRUST Oswestry S C AIREY
ROCHDALE INFIRMARY *see* Pennine Acute Hosps NHS Trust
ROOKWOOD Llandaff *see* Cardiff and Vale NHS Trust
ROWLEY REGIS Warley *see* Sandwell and W Birm Hosps NHS Trust
ROXBURGHE HOUSE Aberdeen *see* NHS Grampian
ROYAL ABERDEEN CHILDREN'S *see* NHS Grampian
ROYAL ALBERT EDWARD INFIRMARY *see* Wrightington, Wigan and Leigh Teaching Hosps NHS Foundn Trust
ROYAL ALEXANDRA CHILDREN'S Brighton *see* Brighton and Sussex Univ Hosps NHS Trust
ROYAL BELFAST HOSPITAL FOR SICK CHILDREN *see* Belfast Health and Soc Care Trust
ROYAL BERKSHIRE NHS FOUNDATION TRUST R J SIMMONDS
ROYAL BROMPTON AND HAREFIELD NHS FOUNDATION TRUST B MAHILUM, C T BARKER, N K LEE
ROYAL CORNHILL Aberdeen *see* NHS Grampian
ROYAL CORNWALL HOSPITALS TRUST D P WHITTING, J K P S ROBERTSHAW
ROYAL DERBY *see* Univ Hosps of Derby and Burton NHS Foundn Trust
ROYAL DEVON AND EXETER NHS FOUNDATION TRUST J J HORWOOD, S R SWARBRICK, S W COOK
ROYAL FREE LONDON NHS FOUNDATION TRUST C CARSON, P D CONRAD
ROYAL GWENT Newport *see* Gwent Healthcare NHS Trust
ROYAL HALLAMSHIRE Sheffield *see* Sheff Teaching Hosps NHS Foundn Trust
ROYAL HAMPSHIRE COUNTY Winchester *see* Hants Hosps NHS Foundn Trust
ROYAL HOSPITAL HASLAR *see* Portsm Hosps Univ NHS Trust
ROYAL JUBILEE MATERNITY SERVICE *see* Belfast Health and Soc Care Trust
ROYAL LANCASTER INFIRMARY *see* Univ Hosps of Morecambe Bay NHS Foundn Trust
ROYAL LIVERPOOL AND BROADGREEN UNIVERSITY HOSPITALS NHS TRUST C J PETER, G A PERERA
ROYAL MARSDEN NHS FOUNDATION TRUST London and Surrey A E DOERR, L A GREEN
ROYAL NATIONAL ORTHOPAEDIC HOSPITAL NHS TRUST P M REECE
ROYAL OLDHAM *see* Pennine Acute Hosps NHS Trust
ROYAL SHREWSBURY *see* Shrewsbury and Telford Hosp NHS Trust
ROYAL SOUTH HAMPSHIRE *see* Univ Hosp Southn NHS Foundn Trust
ROYAL SURREY NHS FOUNDATION TRUST A J TEARE
ROYAL SUSSEX COUNTY Brighton *see* Brighton and Sussex Univ Hosps NHS Trust
ROYAL UNITED HOSPITALS BATH NHS FOUNDATION TRUST N J K TEGALLY
ROYAL VICTORIA Belfast *see* Belfast Health and Soc Care Trust
ROYAL VICTORIA Folkestone *see* E Kent Hosps Univ NHS Foundn Trust
ROYAL VICTORIA INFIRMARY Newcastle *see* Newcastle upon Tyne Hosps NHS Foundn Trust
ROYAL WOLVERHAMPTON NHS TRUST C W FULLARD, J D DEAKIN, S PETTY
ST ALBANS Napsbury *see* Enfield Primary Care Trust

ST ANDREW'S HEALTHCARE Birmingham, Essex, Northampton, Nottinghamshire M J MARSHALL, P R EVANS
ST ANNE'S CENTRE St Leonards-on-Sea see E Sussex Healthcare NHS Trust
ST ANN'S Poole see Dorset HealthCare University NHS Foundn Trust
ST ANN'S Tottenham see Barnet, Enfield and Haringey Mental Health NHS Trust
ST CADOC'S Caerleon see Gwent Healthcare NHS Trust
ST CLEMENT'S London see E Lon NHS Foundation Trust
ST CROSS Rugby see Univ Hosps Cov and Warks NHS Trust
ST EBBA'S Epsom see Surrey and Borders Partnership NHS Foundn Trust
ST EDMUND'S Northampton see Northn Gen Hosp NHS Trust
ST GEORGE'S HEALTHCARE NHS TRUST London R B REYNOLDS
ST GEORGE'S UNIVERSITY HOSPITALS NHS FOUNDATION TRUST C S W VAN D'ARQUE
ST HELENS AND KNOWSLEY HOSPITALS NHS TRUST P TAYLOR
ST JAMES'S UNIVERSITY Leeds see Leeds Teaching Hosps NHS Trust
ST LUKE'S Bradford see Bradf Teaching Hosps NHS Foundn Trust
ST MARTIN'S Bath see Bath and West Community NHS Trust
ST MARTIN'S Canterbury see Kent and Medway NHS and Soc Care Partnership Trust
ST MARY'S Kettering see Northants Healthcare NHS Foundn Trust
ST MARY'S Portsmouth see Portsm Hosps Univ NHS Trust
ST MICHAEL'S Aylsham see Norfolk Primary Care Trust
ST MICHAEL'S Bristol see Univ Hosps Bris and Weston NHS Foundn Trust
ST NICHOLAS Newcastle see Northumberland, Tyne and Wear NHS Foundn Trust
ST PETER'S Chertsey see Ashford and St Pet Hosps NHS Foundn Trust see N Surrey Primary Care Trust
ST RICHARD'S Chichester see W Sussex Hosps NHS Foundn Trust
ST SAVIOUR see Jersey Gp of Hosps
ST THOMAS' London see Guy's and St Thos' NHS Foundn Trust
ST WOOLOS Newport see Gwent Healthcare NHS Trust
SALFORD ROYAL NHS FOUNDATION TRUST J L JOYCE-HOOD
SALISBURY NHS FOUNDATION TRUST A R SYMES, F E CANHAM
SALKELD DAY Chepstow see Gwent Healthcare NHS Trust
SANDWELL AND WEST BIRMINGHAM HOSPITALS NHS TRUST D H GARNER
SANDWELL GENERAL West Bromwich see Sandwell and W Birm Hosps NHS Trust
SCARBOROUGH GENERAL see York Teaching Hosp NHS Foundn Trust
SCUNTHORPE GENERAL see N Lincs and Goole NHS Foundn Trust
SEACROFT Leeds see Leeds Teaching Hosps NHS Trust
SELBY WAR MEMORIAL see York Teaching Hosp NHS Foundn Trust
SELLY OAK see Univ Hosp Birm NHS Foundn Trust
SHEFFIELD CHILDREN'S NHS FOUNDATION TRUST K A GREEN
SHEFFIELD HEALTH AND SOCIAL CARE NHS FOUNDATION TRUST S H ROSS
SHEFFIELD TEACHING HOSPITALS NHS FOUNDATION TRUST A D WHITEHEAD, J H DALEY, L A YAULL, M J NEWITT, M R COBB
SHERWOOD FOREST HOSPITALS NHS FOUNDATION TRUST E A FRANKLIN
SHOTLEY BRIDGE GENERAL Consett see Co Durham and Darlington NHS Foundn Trust
SHREWSBURY AND TELFORD HOSPITAL NHS TRUST M I FEARNSIDE, P HRYZIUK
SHREWSBURY ROYAL INFIRMARY see Shrewsbury and Telford Hosp NHS Trust
SINGLETON Swansea see Swansea NHS Trust
SOBELL HOUSE Oxford see Ox Univ Hosps NHS Foundn Trust
SOMERSET NHS FOUNDATION TRUST J M FRENCH, K J SCOTT
SOMERSET PARTNERSHIP NHS FOUNDATION TRUST B E PRIORY
SOUTH LONDON AND MAUDSLEY NHS FOUNDATION TRUST I N FISHWICK
SOUTH SHORE Blackpool see Blackpool, Fylde and Wyre Hosps NHS Trust

SOUTH TEES HOSPITALS NHS FOUNDATION TRUST L M OPALA
SOUTH TYNESIDE NHS FOUNDATION TRUST P R BEALING
SOUTH WARWICKSHIRE GENERAL HOSPITALS NHS TRUST H F COCKELL, R C PANTLING, S S MILES
SOUTH WEST DORSET PRIMARY CARE TRUST P J RINGER
SOUTH WEST LONDON AND ST GEORGE'S MENTAL HEALTH NHS TRUST A R BECK, T MATIKAINEN-CASTLEDINE
SOUTH WEST YORKSHIRE PARTNERSHIP NHS FOUNDATION TRUST B M KIMARU, C M GARTLAND
SOUTHAMPTON GENERAL see Univ Hosp Southn NHS Foundn Trust
SOUTHEND UNIVERSITY HOSPITAL NHS FOUNDATION TRUST D R CHILDS
SOUTHERN HEALTH NHS FOUNDATION TRUST E L A D'AETH, J A JONES, V J LAWRENCE
SOUTHLANDS Shoreham-by-Sea see W Sussex Hosps NHS Foundn Trust
SOUTHMEAD Bristol see N Bris NHS Trust
SPRINGFIELD UNIVERSITY see SW Lon and St George's Mental Health NHS Trust
STANDISH Stonehouse see Glos Hosps NHS Foundn Trust
STOKE MANDEVILLE Aylesbury see Bucks Healthcare NHS Trust
STOKE-ON-TRENT CITY GENERAL see Univ Hosp of N Staffs NHS Trust
SUFFOLK COASTAL PRIMARY CARE TRUST N J WINTER
SUNDERLAND ROYAL see City Hosps Sunderland NHS Foundn Trust
SURREY AND BORDERS PARTNERSHIP NHS FOUNDATION TRUST N J COPSEY
SURREY AND SUSSEX HEALTHCARE NHS TRUST S NJOKA
SUSSEX COMMUNITY NHS FOUNDATION TRUST D A KNIGHT
SUSSEX PARTNERSHIP NHS FOUNDATION TRUST G REEVES, S J HOBBS
SWANSEA NHS TRUST D M GRIFFITHS, N R GRIFFIN
TAMESIDE AND GLOSSOP INTEGRATED CARE NHS FOUNDATION TRUST J M HURLSTON
TAMESIDE GENERAL see Pennine Acute Hosps NHS Trust
TAUNTON AND SOMERSET NHS FOUNDATION TRUST G J W EDMUNDS, L A BALE
TEES, ESK AND WEAR VALLEYS NHS FOUNDATION TRUST B O OMOBUDE, C JAY
TELFORD Princess Royal see Shrewsbury and Telford Hosp NHS Trust
TEWKESBURY see Glos Hosps NHS Foundn Trust
THANET MENTAL HEALTH UNIT Margate see Kent and Medway NHS and Soc Care Partnership Trust
TICKHILL ROAD Doncaster see Doncaster and Bassetlaw Teaching Hosps NHS Foundn Trust
TOGETHER NHS FOUNDATION TRUST see 2gether NHS Foundn Trust
TORBAY AND SOUTH DEVON NHS FOUNDATION TRUST A D SUMNER
TRAFFORD HEALTHCARE NHS TRUST C J BROWN
TRANWELL UNIT Gateshead see Northumberland, Tyne and Wear NHS Foundn Trust
TREDEGAR GENERAL see Gwent Healthcare NHS Trust
ULVERSTON see Univ Hosps of Morecambe Bay NHS Foundn Trust
UNITED LINCOLNSHIRE HOSPITALS NHS TRUST A AMELIA, B A HUTCHINSON, B M S CHAMBERS, J FRESHNEY, J M ROWLAND, K M TOMLIN, P BEATTIE
UNIVERSITY Durham see Co Durham and Darlington NHS Foundn Trust
UNIVERSITY HOSPITAL BIRMINGHAM NHS FOUNDATION TRUST R J HILL-BROWN, R M WHARTON
UNIVERSITY HOSPITAL OF NORTH STAFFORDSHIRE NHS TRUST L B VARQUEZ
UNIVERSITY HOSPITAL OF WALES see Cardiff and Vale NHS Trust
UNIVERSITY HOSPITAL SOUTHAMPTON NHS FOUNDATION TRUST K A MACKINNON, P A BOGGUST, S A TAUSON, S M PITKIN
UNIVERSITY HOSPITALS BRISTOL AND WESTON NHS FOUNDATION TRUST J E NORMAN, M A SNOOK, N J ARCHER
UNIVERSITY HOSPITALS COVENTRY AND WARWICKSHIRE NHS TRUST E A JONES, R L HOMER, S F BETTERIDGE, S R TASH
UNIVERSITY HOSPITALS DORSET NHS FOUNDATION TRUST I R PEARCE, J R TAYLOR
UNIVERSITY HOSPITALS OF DERBY AND BURTON NHS FOUNDATION TRUST M HARGREAVES, P A SHORT, S C NEAL, T ROBINSON

UNIVERSITY HOSPITALS OF LEICESTER NHS TRUST   H A LOMAX

UNIVERSITY HOSPITALS OF MORECAMBE BAY NHS FOUNDATION TRUST   I J J DEWAR

UNIVERSITY HOSPITALS OF NORTH MIDLANDS NHS TRUST   C S B ROUTLEDGE, V L FLANAGAN

VICTORIA Blackpool   see Blackpool, Fylde and Wyre Hosps NHS Trust

WALKERGATE Newcastle   see Newcastle upon Tyne Hosps NHS Foundn Trust

WALSALL HEALTHCARE NHS TRUST   J N FIELDER, L A W SWABY

WALSGRAVE GENERAL Coventry   see Univ Hosps Cov and Warks NHS Trust

WALTON COMMUNITY   see N Surrey Primary Care Trust

WANSBECK GENERAL Ashington   see Northumbria Healthcare NHS Foundn Trust

WARNEFORD Leamington Spa   see S Warks Gen Hosps NHS Trust

WARRINGTON AND HALTON HOSPITALS NHS FOUNDATION TRUST   J E DUFFIELD, P J TURNER

WARWICKSHIRE, SOUTH   see S Warks Gen Hosps NHS Trust

WELLS ROAD CENTRE Mapperley   see Notts Healthcare NHS Foundn Trust

WEST CORNWALL   see R Cornwall Hosps Trust

WEST CUMBERLAND   see N Cumbria Integrated Care NHS Foundn Trust

WEST MIDDLESEX UNIVERSITY HOSPITAL NHS TRUST   M W SSERUNKUMA

WEST SUFFOLK NHS FOUNDATION TRUST   D WEBB, R EMMANUEL, S D GRIFFITHS

WESTERN SUSSEX HOSPITALS NHS FOUNDATION TRUST   R E BENNETT

WESTMORLAND GENERAL   see Univ Hosps of Morecambe Bay NHS Foundn Trust

WESTON AREA HEALTH NHS TRUST   L J EVANS

WESTON GENERAL Weston-super-Mare   see Weston Area Health NHS Trust

WESTON PARK Sheffield   see Sheff Teaching Hosps NHS Foundn Trust

WEYMOUTH COMMUNITY   see Dorset Co Hosp NHS Foundn Trust

WHARFEDALE GENERAL Otley   see Leeds Teaching Hosps NHS Trust

WHELLEY   see Wrightington, Wigan and Leigh Teaching Hosps NHS Foundn Trust

WHIPPS CROSS   see Forest Healthcare NHS Trust Lon

WHISTON Prescot   see St Helens and Knowsley Hosps NHS Trust

WHITBY   see York Teaching Hosp NHS Foundn Trust

WHITCHURCH   see Cardiff and Vale NHS Trust

WHITTINGTON HOSPITAL NHS TRUST   A O BADEJO

WILLIAM HARVEY Arundel Unit   see Kent and Medway NHS and Soc Care Partnership Trust

WILLIAM HARVEY Ashford   see E Kent Hosps Univ NHS Foundn Trust

WINWICK Warrington   see 5 Boroughs Partnership NHS Foundn Trust

WIRRAL UNIVERSITY TEACHING HOSPITAL NHS FOUNDATION TRUST   L J N PARRY, M COWAN

WOKING COMMUNITY   see Surrey and Borders Partnership NHS Foundn Trust

WOODEND Aberdeen   see NHS Grampian

WOODLANDS Worsley   see Gtr Man W Mental Health NHS Foundn Trust

WOOLMANHILL Aberdeen   see NHS Grampian

WORCESTER ROYAL   see Worcs Acute Hosps NHS Trust

WORCESTERSHIRE ACUTE HOSPITALS NHS TRUST   D P RYAN

WRIGHTINGTON, WIGAN AND LEIGH TEACHING HOSPITALS NHS FOUNDATION TRUST   A J EDWARDS, C JACKSON, C P TRACEY, J M REYNOLDS, M RYAN

WYCOMBE   see Bucks Healthcare NHS Trust

YEOVIL DISTRICT HOSPITAL NHS FOUNDATION TRUST   J M CUMMINGS, L A SCOTT, R M BURT

YORK Teaching Hospital NHS Foundation Trust   C J HAYES, D M COX, G M WEBB, R J BAILES

YSBYTY GWYNEDD Penrhosgarnedd   see NW Wales NHS Trust

YSBYTY PENRHOS STANLEY Holyhead   see NW Wales NHS Trust

YSTRAD MYNACH Hengoed   see Gwent Healthcare NHS Trust

HOSPICE CHAPLAINS

ACORNS Wolverhampton P H SMITH
ARTHUR RANK Cambridge K C MORRISON
BLUEBELL WOOD CHILDREN'S Sheffield K A GREEN
BLYTHE HOUSE Chapel-en-le-Frith S H COCKSEDGE
BURY H W BEARN
CHESTNUT TREE HOUSE Arundel S J GURR
COMPTON Wolverhampton E I DE JONGE
DOUGLAS MACMILLAN Blurton M L T MCGONIGLE
EARL MOUNTBATTEN Newport J M MYLES
EXETER HOSPISCARE L ASHDOWN
GARDEN HOUSE Letchworth A J FERRIS
GREENWICH AND BEXLEY COTTAGE H O APARANGA
JERSEY G J HOUGHTON
KATHARINE HOUSE Banbury J P JONES
KEMP Kidderminster P J L CODY, S FOSTER
LECKHAMPTON COURT R C PESTELL
LOROS Leicester B DAVIES, C A LACEY, S P J BURNHAM
MARIE CURIE CENTRE Newcastle upon Tyne K J FRANCIS
MARIE CURIE Edinburgh M F CHATTERLEY
MARIE CURIE Liverpool R E PRYCE
MARY ANN EVANS Nuneaton G HANCOCK, P DODDS
NIGHTINGALE HOUSE Wrexham G WINDON
NORTH LONDON J R SHINHMAR, S P YOUNG
OAKHAVEN TRUST J E L ALEXANDER
PHYLLIS TUCKWELL Farnham J L WALKER,
   S M R CUMMING-LATTEY
PILGRIMS Thanet K I R COX
PRIMROSE Bromsgrove D R L WHITE
ROWANS, THE Purbrook C G GULLY

ROWCROFT Torquay G STILL
ST ANDREW'S Airdrie M LITTLE
ST ANN'S Manchester I C ANTHONY
ST BARNABAS HOUSE Worthing S J GURR
ST CLARE Hastingwood A L KOSLA
ST ELIZABETH Ipswich M A H FINCH
ST HELENA Colchester T E WALKER
ST JOSEPH'S Hackney J A ALTY
ST JOSEPH'S Liverpool A R BROCKBANK
ST LEONARD'S York S A WHITTINGTON
ST LUKE'S CHESHIRE Winsford C B MOORE, J T STOPFORD,
   R J GATES
ST LUKE'S Sheffield M W P REEDER
ST MARGARET'S Taunton A E FULTON
ST MICHAEL'S Hereford J GROVES
ST MICHAEL'S St Leonards-on-Sea G L DRIVER
ST NICHOLAS Bury St Edmunds S M CONNELL, S M NUTT
ST PETER AND ST JAMES North Chailey S C M MCLARNON
ST RICHARD'S Worcester C E GRIFFITHS
ST WILFRID'S Chichester J P COOPER
SAM BEARE Weybridge B D PROTHERO
SEVERN Shrewsbury E C PHILLIPS, H J EDWARDS
SOBELL HOUSE Oxford G T G SYKES
STRATHCARRON Denny S M COATES
SUSSEX BEACON Brighton J K T ELDRIDGE
TRINITY IN THE FYLDE Blackpool P E BERRY
TYNEDALE Hexham J L JACKSON
WEALD Tunbridge Wells P C STEPHENS
WHEATFIELDS Leeds D A BUCK

EDUCATIONAL CHAPLAINS

UNIVERSITIES

ABERDEEN D HEDDLE
ABERYSTWYTH S R BELL
ANGLIA RUSKIN N S COOPER, J THORNTON
ASHRIDGE EXECUTIVE EDUCATION L GEOGHEGAN
BATH J N RAWLINSON
BEDFORDSHIRE A F M GOODMAN
BIRMINGHAM S JONES
BISHOP GROSSETESTE
  P G GREEN, J G HESKINS, M J S JACKSON
BOLTON G M SMART
BOURNEMOUTH R M WELLS
BRADFORD A J HOWORTH
BRISTOL E G A DAVIS
BRUNEL P J ASHWIN-SIEJKOWSKI
CAMBRIDGE
  Churchill J RAWLINSON
  Corpus Christi M J BULLIMORE, A P DAVISON
  Downing K J EYEONS
  Emmanuel D C G BAGNALL
  Fitzwilliam G STEVENSON
  Girton T R BONIFACE
  Gonville and Caius C J-B HAMMOND
  King's A R LEPINE
  Magdalene S C ATKINS
  Newnham H D SHILSON-THOMAS
  Queens' M T BAYLISS, T C HARLING
  Selwyn H D SHILSON-THOMAS
  St Catharine's A M BARRETT
  St John's A C R HAMMOND
  Trinity O FABRIKANT-BURKE, J E SUMMERS
  Trinity Hall S J PLANT
  Wolfson R C ROSBOROUGH
CARDIFF D K SHEEN
CARDIFF METROPOLITAN P K FITZPATRICK
CHESTER P J JENNER, G B REEVE, L C RHODES
COVENTRY A M RICHARDS
CUMBRIA C J KENNEDY, A J LOGAN
DE MONTFORT J ARENS
DERBY A P DICKENS
DUNDEE A WALLER
DURHAM G WORT
  Collingwood G WORT
  Grey G WORT
  St Chad's D W RUSHTON
  St Hild and St Bede T M FERGUSON
  St Mary's P Z KASHOURIS
  Trevelyan G WORT
  University S C O BURETTE
  Van Mildert G WORT
EAST ANGLIA A C WOODMAN
EDINBURGH F S BURBERRY, H A HARRIS
ESSEX S L BATTS-NEALE
EXETER H S J ALDERSON
GLOUCESTERSHIRE N D DAVIES, S C WITCOMBE
GREENWICH S COOK
HERIOT-WATT M J H ROUND
HERTFORDSHIRE F C SOUTER
HUDDERSFIELD C A CHESHIRE
HULL J C COWAN
IMPERIAL COLLEGE LONDON A W WILLSON
KEELE S J COUVELA
KENT S C E LAIRD
KINGSTON D BUCKLEY
LANCASTER K J HUGGETT
LEEDS A J COLLEDGE
LEEDS BECKETT R H DOWSON
LEICESTER L S BRIGGS
LONDON
  Central Chaplaincies A W WILLSON

Goldsmiths' College A J CLARKE
King's J O M CRAIG, J L MORGANS
London School of Economics and Political Science J A WALTERS
Queen Mary A SHARPLES
Queen Mary and Westfield N J GOULDING
Royal Holloway and Bedford New O B EDGAR
Royal Veterinary College A S MARSHALL
University C E BRADLEY
LOUGHBOROUGH C D TAYLOR
MANCHESTER H W BEARN, J B EDSON
MANCHESTER METROPOLITAN J B EDSON
NEWCASTLE A GRAY
NORTHAMPTON S N MOUSIR-HARRISON
NORTHUMBRIA AT NEWCASTLE A P BOWSHER
NOTTINGHAM TRENT R H DAVEY
OXFORD
  All Souls J H DRURY
  Balliol B R L KINSEY
  Brasenose J C BALDWIN
  Christ Church C J Y HAYNS
  Exeter A M ALLEN
  Hertford M A SMITH
  Jesus C L DINGWALL-JONES
  Keble N J EVERETT
  Lady Margaret Hall A D FORESHEW-CAIN
  Lincoln A T SHAMEL
  Magdalen S M ALKIRE
  Merton S M JONES, M K MARSHALL, M STAFFORD
  New S BRIDGE, E D LONGFELLOW
  Oriel R J D WAINWRIGHT
  Pembroke A R TEAL
  Queen's K A M PRICE
  St Edmund Hall Z M GUILIANO
  St Hugh's S C HENSON
  St John's E C MACFARLANE
  St Peter's E J PITKETHLY
  Trinity E M PERCY
  University A F GREGORY
  Wadham J R BAUN
  Worcester T KUIN LAWTON, M R C SALISBURY
OXFORD BROOKES S MATHEW
PORTSMOUTH C SHERMAN
READING M D LAYNESMITH
ROBERT GORDON I M POOBALAN
ROEHAMPTON D J ESHUN
ROYAL COLLEGE OF ART A W WILLSON
ROYAL NORTHERN COLLEGE OF MUSIC J B EDSON
ST ANDREWS S J FERGUSON
ST MARK AND ST JOHN C MCILROY, M J PARKMAN
SALFORD H TOMLINSON, K A C WASEY
SHEFFIELD J M S CLINES, S U TENGE-HESLOP
SHEFFIELD HALLAM H R L ROULSTON
STAFFORDSHIRE M WILLIAMS
STIRLING E F J MULLINER
SUNDERLAND C S HOWSON
SURREY D F MYERS
SUSSEX J C GILLESPIE, C F P MCDERMOTT
UNIVERSITY COLLEGE CORK A G MARLEY
UNIVERSITY OF THE ARTS
  Bournemouth R M WELLS
  London M W J DEAN, W A WHITCOMBE
WALES TRINITY ST DAVID E L WHITTICK
WEST LONDON E C FRANCE
WEST OF ENGLAND, BRISTOL J K NICHOLSON
WESTMINSTER J M NOBLE
WINCHESTER C A DAY
WOLVERHAMPTON S SCHOFIELD
YORK C E REID
YORK ST JOHN J E SPECK

COLLEGES OF HIGHER EDUCATION

SOMERSET COLLEGE OF ARTS AND TECHNOLOGY
  P J HUGHES

COLLEGES OF FURTHER EDUCATION

BISHOP BURTON COLLEGE OF AGRICULTURE
  York R F PARKINSON
GOWER COLLEGE SWANSEA A MORGAN

LEICESTER J M SHARP
SWINDON S F FISHER
TRELOAR COLLEGE *Alton* S GOLDING

SCHOOLS

ABINGDON P D B GOODING, S M STEER
ALDENHAM *Hertfordshire* P S GREEN, J C PERRIS
ALL SAINTS' ACADEMY *Cheltenham* K J SAMUEL
ALL SAINTS ACADEMY *Dunstable* T A DAVIS
ALL SAINTS' CHURCH OF ENGLAND PRIMARY
  Peterborough M R MATTHEWS
ALLEYN'S *Dulwich* E A LANDER
ALTON W MATTHEWS
ARCHBISHOP SENTAMU ACADEMY *Hull* A RICHARDS
ARCHBISHOP'S *Canterbury* K MADDY
ARK ALL SAINTS ACADEMY *Camberwell* J G A ROBERTS
ASHFORD R W BELLAMY
BABLAKE *Coventry* J SLAVIC
BACON'S COLLEGE *Rotherhithe* R J HALL, N J TEVERSON
BANCROFT'S *Woodford Green* I MOORE
BAPCHILD AND TONGE CHURCH OF ENGLAND
  PRIMARY S R YOUNG
BAYSGARTH *Barton-upon-Humber* R M JAGGS-FOWLER
BENENDEN *Kent* J W BATESON, T J BATESON
BENNETT MEMORIAL DIOCESAN *Tunbridge Wells* R A KNAPP
BERKHAMSTED *Herts* J E MARKBY
BETHANY *Goudhurst* S L WILLOUGHBY
BIRKENHEAD *Merseyside* M R J TURNER
BISHOP HENDERSON *Taunton* J A JEFFERY
BISHOP LUFFA *Chichester* S P MILLS
BISHOP RAMSEY S E DAND
BISHOP WORDSWORTH'S *Salisbury* S M WOOD
BLOXHAM D C WEAVER
BLUE COAT *Reading* K L WAKEMAN-TOOGOOD
BLUNDELL'S *Tiverton* T C HUNT
BRADFIELD COLLEGE *Berkshire* P M HANSELL
BRAMBLETYE *East Grinstead* K E HIGGS
BRENTWOOD *Essex* A W MCCONNAUGHIE
BRIGHTON COLLEGE R C AMESS
BROMSGROVE P S J HEDWORTH
BRYANSTON *Dorset* J H DAVIS
CANFORD *Wimborne* P A JACK
CANON SLADE *Bolton* T R LILLEY
CANTERBURY CHRIST CHURCH J T LAW, D A STROUD
CATHEDRAL *Llandaff* W A DAVID
CHARTERHOUSE *Godalming* C A CASE
CHELTENHAM COLLEGE A J DUNNING, A F G SAMUEL,
  K J SAMUEL
CHELTENHAM LADIES' COLLEGE J A GOODWIN, H R WOOD
CHICHESTER A I GREEN, K J ROBINSON
CHIGWELL *Essex* G J SCOTT
CHRIST'S HOSPITAL *Horsham* C J HUXLEY-JONES
CITY OF LONDON FREEMEN'S *Ashtead* J R L PRIOR
CLIFTON COLLEGE *Bristol* S J CHAPMAN
COKETHORPE *Witney* I B HOWARD
COLFE'S *London* S P HALL
COTHILL HOUSE *Abingdon* P V PARKER
COVENTRY BLUE COAT CHURCH OF ENGLAND
  C M VICKERS
CRANLEIGH PREPARATORY *Surrey* N H GREEN
CRANLEIGH *Surrey* J A N HARRISON
DAME ALLAN'S *Newcastle* J MCGOWAN
DAUNTSEY'S *Devizes* D R JOHNSON
DEAN CLOSE *Cheltenham* J C G ASH
DENSTONE COLLEGE *Uttoxeter* D EDGE
DOWNE HOUSE *Berkshire* A K H PLATT
DULWICH COLLEGE T BUCKLER
DULWICH PREPARATORY *Cranbrook* D F P RUTHERFORD
DURHAM S A MCMURTARY
DURHAM HIGH B P S VALLIS

EAST GLENDALOUGH S M ZIETSMAN
EASTBOURNE COLLEGE D J MERCERON
ELIZABETH COLLEGE *Guernsey* P A GRAYSMITH
ELLESMERE COLLEGE *Shropshire* P J GRATION
EMANUEL *Wandsworth* S LABRAN
EPSOM COLLEGE A M J HAVILAND
ETON COLLEGE *Berkshire* D M BOND, R E R DEMERY,
  S J N GRAY, P A HESS, C M JONES
FELSTED *Essex* N J LITTLE
FETTES COLLEGE *Edinburgh* A CLARK
FRAMLINGHAM COLLEGE *Woodbridge* B A BAYMAN
GIGGLESWICK A J LADDS
GLENALMOND COLLEGE S A GRAHAM
GODOLPHIN *Salisbury* R T AYERS-HARRIS
GORDON'S *Woking* G J A WRIGHT
GREIG CITY ACADEMY P J HENDERSON
GRESHAM'S *Holt* J O BRANFORD
GREYCOAT HOSPITAL M R OWEN
GUILDFORD M C WOODWARD
HABERDASHERS' ASKE'S *Elstree* M BRANDON
HABERDASHERS' MONMOUTH SCHOOL FOR GIRLS
  C M HAYNES, C R SWARTZ
HAILEYBURY AND IMPERIAL SERVICE COLLEGE
  Hertfordshire C B STOLTZ
HARROW J E POWER, N TIVEY
HARTFORD CHURCH OF ENGLAND HIGH P W HIGHTON
HARTPURY *Gloucester* R M C WHEELER
HEATHFIELD *Ascot* D C CLUES
HIGHGATE *London* R P S EASTON
HURSTPIERPOINT COLLEGE *Hassocks* J H BLOKLAND,
  J M WOMACK
IMMANUEL COLLEGE CHURCH OF ENGLAND
  Bradford S P HACKING
IPSWICH H J CROMPTON-BATTERSBY
JAMES ALLEN'S GIRLS' *Dulwich* C SCHNYDER
JCB ACADEMY E J JONES
KING EDWARD'S *Bath* C L O'NEILL
KING EDWARD'S *Witley* J S RADCLIFFE
KING HENRY VIII *Coventry* A HOGGER-GADSBY
KING WILLIAM'S COLLEGE *Isle of Man* E J SCOTT
KINGHAM HILL *Oxfordshire* T G HUTCHINGS
KING'S *Bruton* G C BEVERLY
KING'S COLLEGE SCHOOL *Wimbledon* J W CROSSLEY
KING'S COLLEGE *Taunton* M A SMITH
KING'S *Dublin* P R CAMPION
KING'S *Ely* R A LANE
KING'S *Rochester* S J PADFIELD
KING'S *Worcester* M R DORSETT
KING'S, THE *Canterbury* L R F COLLINS, M C ROBBINS
KING'S, THE *Peterborough* J S PADDISON
KOINONIA FEDERATION OF ST MARY MAGDALENE CHURCH
  OF ENGLAND SCHOOL AND CHRIST CHURCH CHURCH
  OF ENGLAND PRIMARY SCHOOL D G HUBBUCK
LADY MARGARET *Fulham* H J WHITTAKER
LAMBROOK *School Bracknell* A M SAVAGE
LANCING COLLEGE R K HARRISON
LICENSED VICTUALLERS' *Ascot* N J JARVIS
LIVERPOOL HOPE S SHAKESPEARE
LONDON DESIGN AND ENGINEERING UNIVERSITY
  TECHNICAL COLLEGE V J E MCCARTHY
LOUGHBOROUGH SCHOOLS FOUNDATION E J YORK
MAGDALEN COLLEGE SCHOOL *Oxford* W W BELL
MAIDWELL HALL J V J G WATSON
MALVERN COLLEGE D P IBBOTSON
MALVERN ST JAMES GIRLS' SCHOOL K TAPLIN

MANSHEAD ACADEMY *Luton*   T A DAVIS
MARLBOROUGH COLLEGE   T W G NOVIS
MERCHANT TAYLORS' *Crosby*   D A SMITH
MILL HILL *London*   A C WILSON
MILLFIELD JUNIOR *Somerset*   M C KITTO
MILLFIELD *Somerset*   P C A HARBRIDGE
MONKTON COMBE *Bath*   A G P HUTCHINSON
MONMOUTH   C R SWARTZ
MORETON HALL   A B STRATFORD
NORTHBOURNE PARK *Deal*   D N J HALE
NORWICH   C J CHILD
NORWICH UNIVERSITY OF THE ARTS   M J YOUNG
OAKHAM   T F TREGUNNO
OUNDLE *Peterborough*   M E A COULTER, B J CUNNINGHAM
PANGBOURNE COLLEGE *Berkshire*   N G T JEFFERS
PETERBOROUGH   T B SHERRING
PIPERS CORNER   M J MEARDON
PITSFORD *Northamptonshire*   S TROTT
POCKLINGTON *York*   B MERRINGTON
PORTSMOUTH GRAMMAR   S C HUNT
PREBENDAL *Chichester*   I E SMALE
PRESTFELDE *Shrewsbury*   A C V ALDOUS
QUAINTON HALL *Harrow*   M J STILL
QUEEN ANNE'S *Caversham*   R A ROSS
QUEEN MARGARET'S *York*   R L OWEN
QUEEN MARY'S *Baldersby Park*   P PERCY
RADLEY COLLEGE *Oxfordshire*   P J TAYLOR, D WILSON
REED'S *Cobham*   A C WINTER
REEPHAM HIGH   H C RENGERT, K A F RENGERT
REIGATE GRAMMAR   P M JACKSON
RENDCOMB COLLEGE *Cirencester*   R J EDY
REPTON *Derby*   A J M WATKINSON
RIDDLESWORTH HALL *Norwich*   K A HAWKES
RISHWORTH *Ripponden*   J S BRADBERRY
ROEDEAN *Brighton*   G N RAINEY
ROSSHALL ACADEMY *Glasgow*   J F LYON
ROYAL MASONIC FOR GIRLS *Rickmansworth*   J S QUILL
ROYAL WOLVERHAMPTON   R MAXFIELD
RUGBY   R M HORNER
ST ALBANS   C D PINES
ST ALBAN'S ACADEMY *Birmingham*   G A SYKES
ST ALBANS HIGH SCHOOL FOR GIRLS
   D C FITZGERALD CLARK
ST ANTONY'S LEWESTON *Sherborne*   L A MCCREADIE
ST BEDE'S *Cambridge*   A N M CLARKE
ST BEDE'S *Reigate*   J A PENN
ST CATHERINE'S *Bramley*   B G MCNAIR SCOTT
ST CATHERINE'S *Eastbourne*   D J GARRATT
ST CHAD'S CATHOLIC AND CHURCH OF ENGLAND HIGH
   Runcorn   E L SPEAKE
ST COLUMBA'S *Dublin*   D J OWEN
ST CUTHBERT MAYNE *Torquay*   I N KIYAGA
ST DAVID'S COLLEGE *Llandudno*   T R HALL
ST DUNSTAN'S COLLEGE *Catford*   C J L BOSWELL
ST EDMUND'S *Canterbury*   J K ATKINS
ST EDWARD'S *Oxford*   E A LENNON
ST GABRIEL'S COLLEGE *Camberwell*   S D T HARRIES
ST GEORGE'S *Ascot*   S A L WATTS
ST GEORGE'S *Blackpool*   L H A PEARSON

ST GEORGE'S *Gravesend*   T OLIVER
ST GEORGE'S *Windsor*   J COORE
ST HELEN'S AND ST KATHARINE'S *Abingdon*   E A M BIRCH
ST JOHN'S *Leatherhead*   C M S MOLONEY
ST JOSEPH'S *Wrexham*   L C S STROUD
ST LAWRENCE COLLEGE *Ramsgate*   A J P GOODWIN-HUDSON
ST MARK'S CHURCH OF ENGLAND ACADEMY
   Mitcham   R A BURGE-THOMAS
ST MARY MAGDALENE ACADEMY *London*   A I KEECH,
   S C KORN
ST MARYLEBONE CHURCH OF ENGLAND   J M NOBLE
ST MARY'S *Calne*   J M BEACH
ST MARY'S HALL *Brighton*   A H MANSON-BRAILSFORD
ST MARY'S *Shaftesbury*   L J LANE
ST OLAVE'S GRAMMAR *Orpington*   J E BOWEN
ST PAUL'S *Barnes*   P L F ALLSOP
ST PAUL'S GIRLS' *Hammersmith*   M S KNOX
ST PAUL'S *Hammersmith*   M S KNOX
ST PETER'S *Cambridge*   C N TWEDDELL
ST PETER'S *York*   D A JONES
ST SAVIOUR'S AND ST OLAVE'S *Newington*   I E VIBERT
ST SWITHUN'S *Winchester*   P WALLINGTON
ST TERESA'S *Effingham*   P THOMPSON
SANDWELL *West Bromwich*   J A LEACH
SEAFORD COLLEGE *Petworth*   C N DATCHLER
SEDBERGH   P L SWEETING
SEVENOAKS   N N HENSHAW
SHERBORNE   D CAMPBELL
SHERBORNE GIRLS   C E WINDLE
SHIPLAKE *Henley-on-Thames*   C R BRIGGS
SHREWSBURY   A C V ALDOUS, A F C KEULEMANS
SIR ROBERT WOODARD ACADEMY *Lancing*   H J HUGHES
SOLIHULL   A C HUTCHINSON
STAMFORD   M A S GOODMAN
STOCKPORT GRAMMAR   L E J LEAVER
STOWE *Buckingham*   T D MULLINS
SWINTON PRIMARY *Glasgow*   M J W BENTON-EVANS
TAUNTON   E J GETMAN
TONBRIDGE   D A PETERS
TRINITY *Belvedere*   A S J HEALY
TRINITY *Carlisle*   C J KENNEDY
TUDOR HALL *Banbury*   S M BOURNE, A M RICHARDSON
TWYFORD CHURCH OF ENGLAND HIGH
   Acton   D J BRAMMER
UPPINGHAM *Leicestershire*   J B J SAUNDERS
WELLINGTON COLLEGE *Berkshire*   A J STARK-ORDISH
WELLINGTON *Somerset*   C G GRAHAM
WESTMINSTER   D J WARNKE
WESTMINSTER CITY   S G TAYLOR
WESTONBIRT   H A MONAGHAN
WHITGIFT *School and House Croydon*   F A BAYES
WILLIAM PERKIN CHURCH OF ENGLAND HIGH
   Greenford   D J BRAMMER, A M RICHARDSON
WINCHESTER COLLEGE   R J MAIDMENT, J M WHITE
WORKSOP COLLEGE *Nottinghamshire*   M R ASKEY
WREKIN COLLEGE *Telford*   L R PLUMMER
WYCLIFFE COLLEGE *Gloucestershire*   D A PRESCOTT
WYCOMBE ABBEY *High Wycombe*   P J NASH
WYMONDHAM COLLEGE   I JONES

THEOLOGICAL EDUCATION INSTITUTIONS

Church of Ireland Theological Institute
Braemor Park, Dublin 14, D14 KX24, Republic of Ireland
T: (00353) (1) 492 3506 E: admin@theologicalinstitute.ie
W: www.theologicalinstitute.ie
Dir M J ELLIOTT

College of the Resurrection
Stocks Bank Road, Mirfield WF14 0BW
T: (01924) 490441 E: alewis@mirfield.org.uk
W: www.college.mirfield.org.uk
Prin M C R SOWERBY

Cranmer Hall
St John's College, 3 South Bailey, Durham DH1 3RJ
T: 0191-334 3894 E: enquiries@cranmerhall.com
W: www.cranmerhall.com
Warden P J J PLYMING

Eastern Region Ministry Course
1A The Bounds, Lady Margaret Road, Cambridge CB3 0BJ
T: (01223) 760444 E: admin@ermc.cam.ac.uk
W: www.ermc.cam.ac.uk
Prin A S JENSEN

Emmanuel Theological College
7 Abbey Square, Chester CH1 2HU
T: (01244) 668571
E: info@emmanueltheologicalcollege.org.uk
W: www.emmanueltheologicalcollege.org.uk
Dean M J LEYDEN

Guildford Local Ministry Programme
Church House, 20 Alan Turing Road, Guildford GU2 7YF
T: (01483) 790319 E: admin@cofeguildford.org.uk
W: www.cofeguildford.org.uk/lmp
Prin S B SUMMERS

Lincoln School of Theology
Edward King House, Minster Yard, Lincoln LN2 1PU
T: (01522) 504050 E: clindsay@lincoln.anglican.org
W: www.lincoln.anglican.org/lincoln-school-of-theology

Lindisfarne College of Theology
Church House, St John's Terrace, North Shields NE29 6HS
T: 0191-270 4144 E: enquiries@lindisfarnect.org
W: www.lindisfarnect.org
Prin D J BRYAN

Oak Hill College
Chase Side, London N14 4PS
T: (020) 8449 0467 E: reception@oakhill.ac.uk
W: www.oakhill.ac.uk
Pres J S JUCKES

Oxford Local Ministry Programme
Church House Oxford, Langford Locks, Kidlington
OX5 1GF
T: (01865) 208282 E: phil.cooke@oxford.anglican.org
W: www.oxford.anglican.org
Prin P N TOVEY

**The Queen's Foundation for Ecumenical Theological
Education**
Somerset Road, Edgbaston, Birmingham B15 2QH
T: 0121-454 1527 E: enquire@queens.ac.uk
W: www.queens.ac.uk
Prin C MARSH[1]

Ridley Hall
Ridley Hall Road, Cambridge CB3 9HG
T: (01223) 746580 E: info@ridley.cam.ac.uk
W: www.ridley.cam.ac.uk
Prin M J VOLLAND

Ripon College Cuddesdon (including Portsmouth Pathway
Cuddesdon, and Cuddesdon Gloucester & Hereford)
Cuddesdon, Oxford OX44 9EX
T: (01865) 877404 F: 875431 E: enquiries@rcc.ac.uk
W: www.rcc.ac.uk
Prin THE RT REVD H I J SOUTHERN

St Augustine's College of Theology
52 Swan Street, West Malling ME19 6JX
T: (01732) 252656 E: office@staugustinescollege.ac.uk
W: www.staugustinescollege.ac.uk
Prin A P R GREGORY

St Hild College
Stocks Bank Road, Mirfield WF14 0BW
T: (01924) 481925 E: enquiries@sthild.org
W: www.sthild.org
Prin M T POWLEY

St Mellitus College
24 Collingham Road, London SW5 0LX
T: (020) 7052 0573 E: info@stmellitus.ac.uk
W: www.stmellitus.ac.uk
Dean R J WINFIELD

St Padarn's Institute
54 Cardiff Road, Llandaff, Cardiff CF5 2YJ
T: (029) 2056 3379 E: info@stpadarns.ac.uk
W: www.stpadarns.ac.uk
Prin J DUFF

St Stephen's House
16 Marston Street, Oxford OX4 1JX
T: (01865) 613500 E: enquiries@ssho.ox.ac.uk
W: www.ssho.ox.ac.uk
Prin R WARD

Sarum College
19 The Close, Salisbury SP1 2EE
T: (01722) 424800 E: info@sarum.ac.uk
W: www.sarum.ac.uk
Prin J W WOODWARD

Scottish Episcopal Institute
21 Grosvenor Crescent, Edinburgh EH12 5EE
T: 0131-243 1347 E: institute@scotland.anglican.org
W: www.scotland.anglican.org
Prin A L TOMLINSON

South West Ministry Training Course
13–14 Okehampton Street, Exeter EX4 1DU
T: (01392) 272544 E: admin@swmtc.org.uk
W: www.swmtc.org.uk
Prin M A BUTCHERS

Trinity College
Stoke Hill, Bristol BS9 1JP
T: 0117-968 2803 E: info@trinitycollegebristol.ac.uk
W: www.trinitycollegebristol.ac.uk
Prin S W DOHERTY

Westcott House
Jesus Lane, Cambridge CB5 8BP
T: (01223) 741000 E: info@westcott.cam.ac.uk
W: www.westcott.cam.ac.uk
Prin H E DAWES

Winchester Diocese School of Mission
Old Alresford Place, Old Alresford SO24 9DH
T: (01962) 710981
E: schoolofmission@winchester.anglican.org
W: www.winchester.anglican.org/school-of-mission-team/
Prin M P C COLLINSON

Wycliffe Hall
54 Banbury Road, Oxford OX2 6PW
T: (01865) 274200 F: 274215 E: enquiries@wycliffe.ox.ac.uk
W: www.wycliffe.ox.ac.uk
Prin M F LLOYD

1   Professor Marsh is a lay person.

PROVINCIAL OFFICES

From which further information may be sought.

Anglican Communion Office St Andrew's House, 16 Tavistock Crescent, Westbourne Park, London W11 1AP, UK
T: (020) 7313 3900   E: aco@anglicancommunion.org

Alexandria   E: emadbasilios@gmail.com
See Anglican Communion website for more recent contact details

Australia   Suite 4, Level 5, 189 Kent Street, Sydney NSW 2000, Australia
T: (0061) (2) 8267 2700   F: (0061) (2) 8267 2727   E: gsoffice@anglican.org.au

Bangladesh   Church of Bangladesh, 54/1 Barobag, Mirpur 2, Dhaka 1216, Bangladesh
T: (00880) (2) 902 5876   F: (00880) (2) 805 3729   E: probhudanh@gmail.com

Brazil   Av. Joao Dias 150, Santa Amaro, São Paulo, SP, 04724-000, Brazil
T/F: (0055) (53) 8159 3067   E: mguedes@ieab.org.br

Burundi   BP 2098, Bujumbura, Burundi
T: (00257) (2) 222 4389   E: anglicanburundinews@gmail.com

Canada   80 Hayden Street, Toronto ON M4Y 3G2, Canada
T: (001) (416) 924 9192   E: atperry@national.anglican.ca

Central Africa   Central Africa, PO Box 22317, Kitwe, Zambia
T: (00260) (2) 6735 1081   F: (00260) (2) 6735 1668   E: dioeastzm@zamnet.zm

Central America   Apartado R, Balboa, Republic of Panama
T: (00507) 262 2052   E: invcat@yahoo.com

Ceylon   Bishop's House, 368/3A Bauddhaloka Mawatha, Colombo 7, Sri Lanka
T: (0094) (11) 269 2985   E: ps@churchofceylon.com

Chile   Victoria Subercaseaux 41, RM Casilla 50675, Correo Central, Santiago 8320154, Chile
T: (0056) (2) 638 3009   E: psantibanez@iach.cl

Congo   11 Av Basalakala, Commune de Kalamu, Kinshasa 1, DR Congo
T: (00243) (99) 541 2138   E: hm.kyausa@gmail.com

England   Church House, Great Smith Street, London SW1P 3NZ, UK
T: (020) 7898 1000   E: enquiry@churchofengland.org

Hong Kong   16/F Tung Wai Commercial Building, 109–111 Gloucester Road, Wanchai, Hong Kong
T: (00852) 2526 5355   F: (00852) 2521 2199   E: office1@hkskh.org

Indian Ocean   PO Box 44, Victoria, Mahe, Seychelles
E: stpsecacio@gmail.com

Ireland   Church of Ireland House, Church Avenue, Rathmines, Dublin 6, DO6 CF67, Republic of Ireland
T: (00353) (1) 497 8422   F: (00353) (1) 497 8821   E: chiefofficer@rcbdub.org

Japan   65–3 Yarai-cho, Shinjuku-ku, Tokyo 162–0805, Japan
T: (0081) (3) 5228 3171   F: (0081) (3) 5228 3175   E: general-sec.po@nskk.org

Jerusalem and the Middle East   2 Grigori Afxentiou, Nicosia 1515, PO Box 22075, Cyprus
E: georgia@spidernet.com.cy

Kenya   PO Box 40502, 00100 Nairobi, Kenya
T: (00254) (20) 271 4755   F: (00254) (20) 271 8442   E: ackpsoffice@ackenya.org

Korea   16 Sejong-daero 19-gil, Jung-gu, Seoul 100–120, Korea
T: (0082) (2) 738 8952   E: freevayu@gmail.com

Melanesia   Provincial Headquarters, PO Box 19, Honiara, Solomon Islands
T: (0067) 20470   E: hauriasi_a@comphq.org.sb

Mexico   Acatlán 102 Oriente, Col Mitras Centro, Monterrey, Nuevo Leon, 64460, Mexico
T: (0052) (81) 8333 0992   E: laura.gracia.g@gmail.com

Mozambique and Angola   Caixa Postale 120, Maputo, Mozambique
T: (00258) 860 278 712
See Anglican Communion website for more recent contact details

Myanmar (Burma)   PO Box 11191, 140 Pyidaungsu Yeiktha Road, Dagon, Yangon, Myanmar
T: (0095) (1) 395 279   E: myinthtet@gmail.com

New Zealand (Aotearoa, New Zealand and Polynesia)   PO Box 87188, Meadowbank, Auckland 1742, New Zealand
T: (0064) (9) 521 4439   E: gensecm@anglicanchurch.org.nz

Nigeria   24 Douala Street, Wuse Zone 5, Abuja, Nigeria
T: (00234) (95) 236950   E: generalsecretary@anglican-nig.org

North India   CNI, 16 Pandit Pant Marg, New Delhi 110001, India
T: (0091) (11) 4231 4000   E: rev.dennislall@gmail.com

Pakistan   St John's Cathedral, 1 Sir Syed Road, Peshawar Cantt 25000, Pakistan
T: (0092) (91) 527 6519   E: anthony.lamuel00@gmail.com

Papua New Guinea   Box 673, Lae 411, Morobe Province, Papua New Guinea
T: (00675) 472 4262   E: dpk07jan@gmail.com

Philippines   PO Box 10321, Broadway Centrum, 1112 Quezon City, Philippines
F: (0063) (2) 721 1923   E: flaw997@gmail.com

PROVINCIAL OFFICES

Rwanda BP 2487, Kigali, Rwanda
  F: (00250) 788 590 714   E: frkaremera@ear-acr.org

Scotland 21 Grosvenor Crescent, Edinburgh EH12 5EE, UK
  T: (0131) 255 6357   F: (0131) 346 7247   E: *via website* www.scotland.anglican.org

South America Cro. Gral. Belgrano 946, Hurlingham, Buenos Aires 1686, Argentina
  T: (0053) (114) 452 7555   E: cristindaly@gmail.com

South East Asia PO Box 10811, 88809 Kota Kinablu, Sabah, Malaysia
  E: kenneththien@gmail.com

South India CSI Centre, 5 Whites Road, Royapettah, Chennai 600 041, India
  T: (0091) (44) 2852 1566   E: synodcsi@gmail.com

South Sudan PO Box 110, Juba, South Sudan
  E: provincialsecretary@southsudan.anglican.org

Southern Africa 20 Bishopscourt Drive, Bishopscourt, Claremont, 7708 South Africa
  T: (0027) (21) 763 1300   E: mnzimande@anglicanchurchsa.org.za

Sudan *See Anglican Communion website for latest contact details*

Tanzania PO Box 899, Dodoma, Tanzania
  T: (00255) (26) 232 4574   F: (00255) (26) 232 4565   E: act@anglican.or.tz

Uganda PO Box 14123, Kampala, Uganda
  T: (00256) (414) 272757   F: (00256) (414) 251925   E: pschurchofuganda@gmail.com

USA Episcopal Church Center, 815 Second Avenue, New York NY 10017, USA
  T: (001) (212) 716 6000   F: (001) (212) 490 3298   E: *via website* www.episcopalchurch.org

Wales The Church in Wales, 2 Callaghan Square, Cardiff CF10 5BT, UK
  T: (029) 2034 8200   E: *via website* wwwchurchinwales.org.uk

West Africa PO Box KN 2023, Kaneshie, Accra, Ghana
  T: (00233) (277) 201538   E: morkeiwuley@gmail.com

West Indies Provincial Secretariat, Bamford House, Society Hill, St John, Barbados, West Indies
  T: (001) (246) 423 0842   F: (001) (246) 423 0855   E: cpwi@caribsurf.com

ADDRESSES UNKNOWN

ADAMS, Mark. b 67. d 99. V Norwell w Ossington, Cromwell etc S'well 16–20; AD Newark and S'well 16–20; Hon Can S'well Minster 15–20.

ADAN, Howard Keith. b 62. d 01. PtO Eur from 20.

AFFLECK, Stuart John. b 47. d 70. PtO St E from 20.

ALDER, Mrs Alison Kirstine Ruth. b 62. d 19. NSM Blyth Valley St E from 19.

ALDIS, John Arnold. b 43. d 69. rtd 08.

ALLMAN, Mrs Susan. b 56. d 96. rtd 20.

ANDREW, Donald. b 35. d 66. rtd 00.

ARTISS, Rebecca Jane. b 72. d 18. NSM Four Rivers St E from 18.

ASH, David Nicholas. b 61. d 03. P-in-c Bryn a Mor Miss Area St As from 18.

ASHURST, Mrs Judith Anne. b 57. d 08. rtd 20.

BAILEY, Mark David. b 62. d 90. P-in-c Ardeley, Benington, Cottered w Throcking etc St Alb from 21.

BALL, Stephen Andrew. b 54. d 05. rtd 21.

BARCLAY, Adam John. b 61. d 18. NSM Stanton St E from 18.

BARLING, Michael Keith. b 38. d 66. rtd 03.

BARLOW, Patricia Mary. b 60. d 17. NSM Gt Grimsby St Mary and St Jas Linc from 17.

BARNSLEY, David Edward. b 75. d 03. C Buxton w Burbage and King Sterndale Derby from 20.

BARRON, Kurt Karl. b 60. d 92. PtO S'well from 19.

BARTER, Christopher Stuart. b 49. d 84. rtd 13; PtO Ely from 14.

BAYLEY, Anne Christine. b 34. d 91. PtO Heref 05–19.

BAYLIS (née LOFTS), Mrs Sally Anne. b 55. d 03. rtd 21; PtO S'well from 21.

BAZELY, Stephen William. b 80. d 11. P-in-c Willaston Ches 15–21.

BENNETT, Mark Stephen. b 66. d 10. rtd 21.

BENSON, Richard John. b 55. d 94. rtd 19.

BENTLEY, Lesley. b 55. d 87. rtd 20; PtO Lich from 20.

BINKS, Robert Peter. b 73. d 10. P-in-c Warley Ch Ch and Gt Warley St Mary Chelmsf 14–18.

BLAY, Linda Jean. b 00. rtd 21.

BODDAM-WHETHAM, Paul Nathaniel. b 52. d 12. rtd 21.

BOLAND, Geoffrey. b 56. d 89. rtd 21; PtO Eur from 17.

BONE, Canon Simon Adrian. b 78. d 09. P-in-c Chacewater w St Day and Carharrack etc Truro.

BRADBROOK, Peter David. b 33. d 60. rtd 98; PtO Ches from 00.

BRADLEY, Peter Edward. b 64. d 88. PtO Sheff from 21; Lon from 21.

BRADSHAW, Graham. b 58. d 86. R Aspley Guise w Husborne Crawley and Ridgmont St Alb 00–21.

BRADSHAW, Timothy. b 50. d 76. Tutor Regent's Park Coll Ox from 91; rtd 18.

BRETHERTON, Canon Anthony Atkinson. b 51. d 75. PtO B & W 07–10.

BROSTER, Godfrey David. b 52. d 81. rtd 20.

BROWN, Philip Anthony. b 54. d 91. rtd 20; PtO Cant from 20.

BURROWS, Jean. b 54. d 91. rtd 21.

BURTON, Michael John. b 55. d 88. rtd 20.

BUTLER, Edward Daniel. b 42. d 68. PtO Chich 74–99.

BYSOUTH, Paul Graham. b 55. d 84. rtd 20.

CAMPBELL, Miss Elizabeth Hume. b 53. d 02. rtd 18.

CANNON, Elizabeth Mary. b 50. d 97. rtd 15; PtO Nor from 16; St E from 17.

CAPLE, Stephen Malcolm. b 55. d 88. rtd 19.

CATHIE, Sean Bewley. b 43. d 69. rtd 06; PtO Heref from 09.

CHAPMAN, Mrs Lesley. b 61. d 05. Bp's Adv for Spirituality and Spiritual Direction Newc from 16.

CHIVERS, Canon Christopher Mark. b 67. d 97. PV Westmr Abbey from 12; Hon Can Saldhana Bay S Africa from 14.

CLARK, Michael James. b 71. d 02. Miss Community Development Adv Ex from 19.

CLARKE, Duncan James Edward. b 54. d 78. rtd 20.

CLARKE, Miss Kirsty Ann. b 81. d 15. TV Shaftesbury Sarum 19–20.

CLARKE, The Rt Revd Richard Lionel. b 49. d 75. rtd 20.

CLEMENTS, Mrs Virginia. b 47. d 13. rtd 20.

CLITHEROW, Canon Andrew. b 50. d 79. rtd 20.

CLOCKSIN, Prof William Frederick. b 55. d 94. PtO St Alb 17–21.

COBURN, Dennis Anthony. b 70. d 18. NSM Brandon St E from 18.

COLE, Jennifer Ann. b 52. d 09. PtO B & W 19–20.

COLEMAN, Timothy. b 57. d 89. rtd 21; PtO Chelmsf from 21.

COLES, Preb Alison Elizabeth. b 60. d 97. Bp's Adv on Healthcare Chapl Lich from 19; Preb Lich Cathl from 15.

COLES, Preb Stephen Richard. b 49. d 81. rtd 20; PtO Lon from 20.

COOPER, Gavin Ashley. b 85. d 11. R Stamford St Mary and St Martin Linc 16–20.

COOPER, Sarah Fiona Louise. b 69. d 17. C Perry Barr Birm 17–20.

COTTON-BETTERIDGE, Mrs Fiona Jane Marson. b 56. d 05. NSM Barrow upon Soar w Walton le Wolds Leic from 20; NSM Wymeswold and Prestwold w Hoton from 20.

CRADDOCK, Lesley-Ann. b 58. d 12. P-in-c Dunkeld St And from 20.

CRANKSHAW, Ronald. b 41. d 76. rtd 07; PtO Liv from 16.

CRONIN, Mrs Janie. b 62. d 16. C Rochdale Man 20–21.

CUNLIFFE, The Ven Christopher John. b 55. d 83. rtd 21.

CUNLIFFE, The Ven Helen Margaret. b 54. d 87. rtd 08.

DAVIES, Reginald Charles. b 33. d 64. rtd 20.

DAVIS, Matthew Peter. d 18. Min Area Ldr Tredegar Mon from 21.

DAVIS, Maureen Anne. b 59. d 99. rtd 21.

DAWSON, Peter John. b 44. d 06. rtd 14; PtO Leeds from 14.

DAY, Andrew Christopher. b 62. d 18. NSM Cambridge Gt St Mary w St Mich Ely from 18.

DENERLEY, John Keith Christopher. b 34. d 61. rtd 99; PtO Glouc from 00.

DESBOROUGH, Mrs Margaret Maureen. b 63. d 15. NSM Skirlaugh, Catwick, Long Riston, Rise, Swine w Ellerby etc York 15–20.

DESBOROUGH, Paul. b 63. d 17. P-in-c Sinfin Moor Derby from 21; Bp's Adv for New Housing from 21.

DIXON, Charles William. b 41. d 81. rtd 06.

DODHIA, Hitesh Kishorilal. b 57. d 88. The Mount 98–01.

DONAGHEY, Thomas Alfred. b 67. d 08. V Baxenden Blackb 13–20.

DUGUID, Alison Audrey. b 52. d 02. rtd 20.

DUNN, Derek William Robert. b 48. d 85. Bp's C Acton and Drumbanagher Arm 09; V Choral Arm Cathl from 14.

DUNN, Paul James Hugh. b 55. d 83. V Ham St Rich S'wark 98–17.

ELLIS, John Roland. b 32. d 69. rtd 99; PtO Mon from 12.

ELSTOB, Stephen William. b 57. d 86. rtd 20.

ENWEREM, Christopher Onyemaechi. b 75. d 16. P-in-c Tipton St Matt w St Martin and St Paul Lich 20–21.

EVANS, Canon Colin Rex. b 24. d 57. rtd 90.

EVANS, Daniel Barri. b 70. d 03. TV Hawarden St As from 15; TV Borderlands Miss Area from 17.

EVANS, Michael John. b 53. d 00. rtd 20.

EVANS, Nigel William Reid. b 70. d 01. TR Bucknall Lich 10–18; RD Stoke-on-Trent 17–18.

EZAT, Timothy. b 83. d 12. V Langney Chich 17–20.

FAIRBANK, Brian Douglas Seeley. b 53. d 78. rtd 20.

FERGUSON, Mrs Zoë Marie. b 75. d 12. P-in-c Mundford w Lynford Nor 16–19; P-in-c Hilborough w Bodney 17–19; P-in-c Oxborough w Foulden and Caldecote 17–19.

FERNYHOUGH, Timothy John Edward. b 49. d 83. rtd 20.

FINCH, Mrs Alison. b 59. d 92. rtd 18; NSM Seaton and Beer Ex from 20.

FIRTH, Matthew Paul. b 83. d 09. P-in-c Darlington St Cuth Dur 18–20; P-in-c Darlington H Trin 18–20.

FLOOD, Mrs Jean Anne. b 51. d 08. rtd 19.

FORD, The Rt Revd John Frank. b 52. d 79. Rtd 19; PtO Eur from 20.

FOSTER, Canon David Brereton. b 55. d 81. rtd 21.

FOSTER, Mrs Geraldine. b 55. d 03. rtd 21.

FOSTER, Mrs Jessica Beatrice. b 70. d 15. PtO Birm from 19; Bp's Dom Chapl from 20.

FOSTER, Michael John. b 52. d 79. rtd 20.

FOX (née COULDRIDGE), Mrs Janice Evelyn. b 49. d 92. rtd 05; PtO Worc from 05.

FRENCH, Peter Robert. b 65. d 90. PtO Birm from 18.

FRYDAY, Canon Barbara Yvonne. b 47. d 92. I Clonmel w Innislounagh, Tullaghmelan etc C, F & O from 07; Can Ossory Cathl from 03; Warden of Readers from 08.

FRYMANN, Mrs Janet Elizabeth. b 57. d 12. rtd 20.

GAGE, Aëlla Rupert Fitzhardinge Berkeley. b 66. d 00. PtO Chelmsf from 20.

GHEORGHIU GOULD, Helen Elizabeth-Anne. b 65. d 10. C Valle Crucis Miss Area *St As* from 21.

GIBBS (*née* DE ROBECK), Fiona Caroline. b 74. d 00. V Hedge End St Luke *Win* 19–20; Hon Can Win Cathl 17–20.

GILLIBRAND, Margaret Ann Jane. b 43. d 01. rtd 13.

GILMORE, David Samuel. b 70. d 03. R Soho St Anne w St Thos and St Pet *Lon* 08–10.

GLOVER, Thomas Edward. b 85. d 10. P-in-c Dur St Giles 18–21; P-in-c Shadforth and Sherburn 18–21.

GODFREY, The Rt Revd Harold William. b 48. d 72. V Lastingham w Appleton-le-Moors, Rosedale etc *York* 17–20.

GOLDSMITH, Mrs Ellen Elizabeth. b 48. d 06. rtd 19.

GOODE, John Laurence. b 48. d 83. rtd 20.

GORDON, Martin Lewis. b 73. d 10. V Gen Dio Goma Democratic Republic of Congo from 20.

GORE, Canon John Charles. b 29. d 54. rtd 95.

GOUGH, Andrew Walter. b 55. d 92. rtd 21; PtO *Sarum* from 21.

GRAY, Ms Christine Angela (Kit). b 46. d 87. rtd 10; PtO *Chelmsf* from 12.

GRAY, Canon Philip Charles. b 67. d 93. Hon Can Ho Ghana from 04.

GREENLAND, Paul Howard. b 59. d 00. V Chelmsf St Andr 05–20.

GREENWOOD, Sharon. b 44. d 07. rtd 18; PtO *Cant* from 19.

GRIFFITHS, John. b 57. d 14. C Cockermouth Area *Carl* from 15; rtd 21.

GRUNDY, Judith Michal Towers Mynors. b 54. d 93. rtd 19.

HAMMOND, Kathryn Mary. b 49. d 08. rtd 21; PtO *Cov* from 21.

HANDY, Thomas. b 79. d 09. R S Petherton w The Seavingtons and The Lambrooks *B & W* 14–21.

HARMER, Timothy James. b 47. d 95. rtd 12.

HARMON, Michael Edgar. b 54. d 12. rtd 20.

HARRIS, Joshua Lloyd. b 89. d 19. NSM St Geo-in-the-East w St Paul *Lon* from 19.

HARROP, Stephen Douglas. b 48. d 79. R Harlaxton Gp *Linc* 18–20.

HAY, Nicholas John. b 56. d 88. rtd 21.

HEMPHILL, John James. b 44. d 73. rtd 19.

HENRY, Miss Jacqueline Margaret. b 40. d 87. rtd 02; PtO *Roch* from 09.

HENWOOD (née OAKLEY), Mrs Susan Mary. b 55. d 87. rtd 21.

HERBERT, Canon David Roy. b 51. d 74. rtd 21; Hon Can Ches Cathl from 08.

HETHERINGTON, Mrs Rachel Marie. b 65. d 08. C Abington *Pet* from 21.

HILL, Rosemary. d 17. TV Llantrisant *Llan* from 20.

HISCOX, Jonathan Ronald James. b 64. d 89. C Upper Wylye Valley *Sarum* from 21.

HOLGATE, Audrey Elizabeth. b 60. d 07. rtd 21.

HOLLIS, Mrs Valerie Elizabeth. b 40. d 92. PtO *Ches* from 20.

HOLME, Thomas Edmund. b 49. d 73. rtd 20.

HOLT, Michael. b 38. d 63. rtd 03; PtO *Man* from 03.

HOOPER, The Ven Peter George. b 62. d 06. R Groby and Ratby *Leic* from 15; R Peckleton from 15; Adn France *Eur* from 21.

HUNTLEY, Stuart Michael. b 73. d 08. R Wulfric Benefice *B & W* 15–20.

INCH, Vivian Ann. b 57. d 13. OLM High Wycombe *Ox* 13–16.

IZZARD, David Antony. b 55. d 94. R Radstock w Writhlington *B & W* 16–21; R Kilmersdon w Babington 16–21.

JANSSON, The Very Revd Maria Patricia. b 55. d 01. Dean Waterford *C, F & O* from 11; I Waterford w Killea, Drumcannon and Dunhill from 11; Preb Ossory Cathl from 12.

JENNINGS, Mrs Susan Mary. b 61. d 15. C Girlington, Heaton and Manningham *Leeds* 18–21.

JESSETT, David Charles. b 55. d 79. rtd 19; PtO *Cov* from 19.

JESSIMAN, Timothy Edward. b 58. d 91. rtd 20.

JONAS, Ian Robert. b 54. d 80. rtd 21.

JONES, Alison. b 61. d 10. V Swansea St Nic and St Jude *S & B* 15–20; Can Res Brecon Cathl 18–20; Bp's Officer for Lay Min 18–20; Warden of Readers 18–20.

JONES, Karen Elizabeth. b 64. d 06. C Chacewater w St Day and Carharrack *Truro* 18–19; C Devoran 18–19; C Feock 18–19; C St Stythians w Perranarworthal and Gwennap 18–19.

JUPP, Vincent John. b 64. d 00. rtd 21.

KALENIUK, Nicholas George. b 69. d 09. V Norton and Wollaston *Worc* 17–21.

KEAY, Charles Edward. b 70. d 03. TV Ex St Thos and Em 15–20.

KENNEDY, Gary. b 63. d 03. PtO *Blackb* from 18.

KENNEDY, Brother Philip Bartholomew. b 47. d 98. SSF from 77.

KIRBY, David Graham. b 58. d 86. rtd 20.

KIRBY, Mrs Elizabeth. b 56. d 10. rtd 19.

KITCHEN, Andrew Jonathan. b 79. d 19. C Wrexham *St As* from 20.

KITCHEN, Mrs Rachel Jane. b 75. d 19. C Wrexham *St As* from 20.

KORMOS, Endre. b 86. d 16. C Wallsend St Pet and St Luke *Newc* 16–20.

LAKE, David Michael. b 57. d 01. rtd 20.

LANCHANTIN-PIGGOTT, Mrs Eve Line. b 51. d 07. rtd 21.

LANGSTAFF, The Rt Revd James Henry. b 56. d 81. rtd 21.

LAVARELLO-SMITH, Mrs Lorna Mary. b 64. d 13. S Africa from 16.

LAW, Richard Anthony Kelway. b 57. d 01. rtd 20.

LECKEY, Paul Robert. b 61. d 96. rtd 20.

LEES, Stephen. b 55. d 90. rtd 20.

LEFFLER, Jeremy Paul (Jem). b 62. d 94. rtd 21.

LINDSAY-SMITH, Kevin Roy. b 55. d 05. rtd 15.

LISTER (née AISBITT), Mrs Joanne. b 69. d 93. NSM Mill End and Heronsgate w Hyde *St Alb* 93–96.

LISTER, William Bernard. b 67. d 92. Chapl Florence w Siena *Eur* 12–21.

LLOYD, Derek James. b 78. d 04. Catholic Miss Enabler from 17; CMP from 05.

LOVERN, Mrs Sandra Elaine. b 48. d 07. NSM Chew Magna w Dundry, Norton Malreward etc *B & W* 07–21.

LUDKIN, Miss Linda Elaine. b 50. d 05. rtd 16; PtO *Leeds* from 17.

LUNN, Graham Edward. b 86. d 11. C Beckenham St Jas w St Mich and St Aug *Roch* 16–20.

McCANN, Michael Joseph. b 61. d 91. I Kilroot and Templecorran *Conn* 99–18.

McDONOUGH, Terence. b 57. d 89. rtd 21; PtO *York* from 21.

McKENZIE, Stephen George. b 58. d 05. rtd 19.

MacLEAN, Lawrence Alexander Charles. b 61. d 88. rtd 21.

MARCHANT, John Bennet. b 46. d 06. rtd 21.

MARSDEN, Robert James. b 56. d 94. PtO *Sarum* from 21.

MARSH, John. b 53. d 10. NSM Ewhurst w Okewood and Forest Green *Guildf* from 16.

MARSTON, William Thornton. b 59. d 88. rtd 21.

MASSIAH, Amrela Celeste. b 60. d 07. P-in-c St Phil St Martin Barbados from 16.

MAYLOR, David Charles. b 59. d 91. rtd 20.

MELLOR, Canon Kenneth Paul. b 49. d 73. rtd 14; PtO *Sarum* from 16.

MILTON-THOMPSON, Jonathan Patrick. b 51. d 88. rtd 20.

MOATT, Richard Albert. b 54. d 81. rtd 20.

MOORE, Geoffrey David. b 51. d 07. rtd 20; PtO *Pet* from 21.

MORRIS, John Dudley. b 33. d 60. rtd 98; PtO *Chich* from 98.

MORRIS, William Hazlitt. b 62. d 09. NSM St Martin-in-the-Fields *Lon* 09–19.

MORROW, David. b 63. d 89. rtd 11.

MOUL, Russell Derek. b 56. d 99. rtd 21.

MOULDER, Kenneth. b 53. d 81. rtd 21.

MUSSER, Ms Christine. b 55. d 00. rtd 19.

MWAMBA, The Rt Revd Musonda Trevor Selwyn. b 58. d 84. Hon Asst Bp Chelmsf from 13.

MYERS, Peter Daniel. b 83. d 13. Lect Ethiopian Grad Sch of Th Addis Ababa Ethiopia from 20.

NEAUM, Canon Andrew David Irwin. b 45. d 74. Hon C Boldre w S Baddesley *Win* from 13.

NORMAN, Lynette Dianne. b 52. d 02. I Tanat Valley Miss Area *St As* 17–19.

NORMAN, Michael John. b 61. d 93. rtd 21.

NTAHOTURI, The Most Revd Bernard. b 48. d 73. rtd 18.

O'CONNELL, William Anthony. b 61. d 10. P-in-c Lyddington and Wanborough and Bishopstone etc *Bris* 13–20.

O'MAOIL MHEANA, Patrick John. b 66. d 14. R Airdrie *Glas* 17–20.

ORRIDGE, Harriet Grace. b 72. d 09. P-in-c Saxonwell *Linc* 13–21.

OWEN, Miss Hannah Mair. b 72. d 13. P-in-c Llandybie *St D* 18–19.

OYEBODE, Olukayode Olugboyega. b 57. d 11. rtd 17.

PAIN, The Rt Revd Richard Edward. b 56. d 84. rtd 19.

PALMER, Mrs Kathleen. b 50. d 19. NSM Brandon *St E* from 19.

PALMER, Kay. b 52. d 18. NSM Ipswich St Mary Stoke *St E* from 21.

PARBURY, Mrs Heather Christina Winifred. b 56. d 01. rtd 20; Hon C Brailes *Cov* from 20; Hon C Sutton under Brailes from 20; Hon C Tysoe w Oxhill and Whatcote from 20.

PARKER, Michael. b 54. d 07. rtd 21.

PARKER, Robert Nicolas. b 71. d 98. AD Yardley and Solihull *Birm* from 21; Bp's Ecum Adv from 12.

PARKES, Mrs Celia Anne. b 50. d 09. rtd 20.

PARKIN, Mrs Melanie Joanne. b 75. d 18. C Grantham St Wulfram *Linc* 18–21; C Grantham, Manthorpe 18–21.

PARTRIDGE, Alan Christopher. b 55. d 00. rtd 20; PtO *Ely* from 21.
PATTEN (*née* STARNS), Mrs Helen Edna. b 43. d 87. rtd 03; Hon C Fairlight and Pett *Chich* from 04.
PAYNE, Preb Robert Christian. b 42. d 65. rtd 02.
PENGELLY, Canon Geoffrey. b 50. d 88. rtd 20.
PENNIE, Mrs Fiona Clare. b 64. d 15. C Walton-on-the-Hill *Liv* from 20.
PEREIRA, Melvyn Christopher. b 52. d 04. rtd 20.
PHILBRICK, Craig Edward. b 86. d 19. C Win Ch Ch from 20.
POWELL, Martin. b 71. d 00. P-in-c Moulsecoomb w Bevendean and Coldean *Chich* from 20.
PRIESTNER, Hugh. b 45. d 75. V Offchurch Gp *Cov* from 17.
PURNELL, Marcus John. b 75. d 09. TV March *Ely* 18–20.
RATHBONE, Stephen Derek. b 61. d 00. rtd 20.
RAYMONT, Philip Richard. b 56. d 04. Sen Chapl Guildford Gr Sch Australia 09–21.
READ, James Arthur. b 51. d 87. rtd 20; PtO *Man* from 20.
REEVES, Kenneth William. b 38. d 69. rtd 92; PtO *Nor* from 05.
REID, Donald. b 58. d 85. PtO *Edin* 15–17.
RENDALL, Richard John. b 54. d 92. rtd 21.
REYNOLDS, Marion. b 49. d 06. rtd 21.
RIGBY, Anthony Paul. d 20. NSM Elworth *Ches* from 20.
ROBERTS, Carol Susan Butler. b 63. d 07. PtO *Ban* from 18.
ROBINSON, Mrs Jane Hippisley. b 41. d 91. PtO *Lon* 00–21.
ROBSON, Mrs Julie. b 52. d 12. rtd 17; PtO *Newc* from 18.
ROCKS, James Anthony. b 82. d 11. CMS Brazil from 15.
ROLLINGS, Mrs Tina Petula. b 51. d 13. PtO *Ox* from 18.
ROSS-McNAIRN, Jonathon Edward. b 73. d 11. Lead Chapl Devon and Cornwall Police from 21.
RUSCOE, Canon John Ernest. b 32. d 59. rtd 10.
RUSSELL, Eric Watson. b 39. d 69. rtd 09.
SACRE, Phillip Daniel. b 83. d 14. C Gt Clacton *Chelmsf* 14–19.
SANDAY, Robert Ward. b 55. d 91. rtd 20.
SCOTT-BROMLEY, Ms Deborah Joan. b 58. d 01. V Bordon *Guildf* 05–20.
SEAL (*formerly* MILLER), Mrs Rosamund Joy. b 56. d 94. rtd 21.
SEEAR, Ms Louise. b 57. d 12. Chapl Lewisham and Greenwich NHS Trust from 19; Asst Dir of Ords *Cant* from 16.
SEWELL, John Andrew Clarkson. b 58. d 97. R Redmarley D'Abitot, Bromesberrow, Pauntley etc *Glouc* 17–18.
SHARP, Philip Paul Clayton. b 66. d 06. R Looe and Morval *Truro* 17–21.
SHEDDEN, Canon Valerie. b 56. d 87. rtd 20.
SMALLWOOD, Simon Laurence. b 58. d 92. V Becontree St Geo *Chelmsf* 03–19.
SMITH, Mrs Antoinette. b 47. d 98. rtd 21.
SMITH, Mrs Denise. b 46. d 08. rtd 16; PtO *Man* from 18.
SMITH, The Ven Jonathan Peter. b 55. d 80. rtd 20; PtO *St Alb* from 20.
SMITH, Miss Judith. b 74. d 09. Dir Ch Revitalisation *Leeds* from 21.
SMITH, Paul Allan. b 66. d 00. Can Res Guildf Cathl 17–20.
SOWDEN, Charles William Bartholomew. b 47. d 97. rtd 17.
STANNARD, Brian. b 46. d 88. rtd 04; PtO *Liv* from 16.
STARTIN, Nicola Gail. b 57. d 90. Chapl Haslar Immigration Removal Cen 02–18.
STAZIKER, Catherine. b 61. d 12. PtO *Sheff* from 18; *Roch* from 18; P-in-c Cloughton and Burniston *York* from 21; P-in-c Ravenscar and Staintondale from 21.
STEIN, Ms Ann Elizabeth. b 57. d 07. rtd 21.
STEPHENS, Mrs Joanna Louise. b 69. d 08. V W Hucknall *S'well* 19–20.
STEPHENSON, James Alexander. b 77. d 11. Zambia from 19.
STEPHENSON (*née* BRYAN), Judith Claire. b 57. d 95. Chapl HM Pris Wormwood Scrubs 18–20.

STEVENS, Philip Terence. b 55. d 83. rtd 20.
STEWART, Ms Dorothy Elaine. b 51. d 10. rtd 21.
STONEHOUSE, Ian Michael. b 66. d 16. PtO *Guildf* 20–21.
SWEENEY, Andrew John. b 59. d 11. P-in-c Hythe *Cant* 15–20.
SWIFT, Christopher John. b 54. d 81. rtd 20.
THODY, Charles Michael Jackson. b 62. d 94. Sen Chapl N Lincs and Goole NHS Foundn Trust 12–20.
THOMPSON, Carrie Julia Lucy Jadwiga. b 77. d 04. V Forton *Portsm* 08–20; Chapl St Vincent Sixth Form Coll 08–20.
THORN, Peter. b 50. d 84. rtd 18; PtO *Liv* from 20.
THORNE, Mrs Anne. b 55. d 98. rtd 20; PtO *Ex* from 20.
THORP, Norman Arthur. b 29. d 65. rtd 95.
TINKER, Christopher Graham. b 78. d 04. R Bradwell *Nor* 13–18.
TREMBATH, Martyn Anthony. b 65. d 90. R Ayr *Glas* from 20.
UNDERDOWN, Steven. b 52. d 88. PtO *Roch* from 19.
VAN DER HART, William Richard. b 76. d 04. C Fulham St Dionis *Lon* from 20.
VAUGHAN, Andrew Kenneth. b 64. d 07. C Chatham St Phil and St Jas *Roch* from 21.
WALKER, Canon Lesley Ann. b 53. d 88. Hon Can Truro Cathl from 15; rtd 19.
WARD, Miss Beverley Jayne. b 61. d 02. rtd 20.
WARHURST, Richard. b 76. d 02. R St Bartholomew *Sarum* 15–20.
WARREN, Robert. b 54. d 78. rtd 21.
WATTS, Roger Mansfield. b 41. d 91. rtd 06.
WEBB, Mrs Linda. b 61. d 17. NSM Hulland, Atlow, Kniveton, Bradley and Hognaston *Derby* 17–21.
WEBB, Peter Henry. b 55. d 79. rtd 21.
WEDGE, Christopher Graham. b 67. d 06. PtO *Man* from 19.
WELSBY, George Andrew. b 61. d 98. rtd 21.
WHATELEY, Thomas Roderick (Rod). b 52. d 96. rtd 19; PtO *Eur* from 16.
WHITAKER, Irene Anne. b 57. d 01. rtd 20.
WHITE (*née* DUNCOMBE), Mrs Maureen Barbara. b 42. d 89. rtd 07.
WHITHAM, Ian Scott. b 66. d 01. C Ringwood w Ellingham and Harbridge etc *Win* 17–21.
WHITMARSH, Mrs Pauline. b 45. d 04. rtd 14; PtO *Sarum* from 14.
WIGRAM, Andrew Oswald. b 39. d 64. rtd 05.
WIGRAM, Miss Ruth Margaret. b 41. d 87. rtd 07; PtO *York* from 07.
WILLIAMS, Derek Ivor. b 37. d 05. PtO *Newc* from 07.
WILLIAMS, Stephen James. b 52. d 78. rtd 21.
WILLIAMSON, Robert John. b 55. d 79. rtd 21; PtO *York* from 21.
WILLINGHAM (*formerly* TIMINGS), Mrs Julie Elizabeth. b 54. d 10. PtO *Linc* from 17.
WILTON (*née* ADAMS), Mrs Gillian Linda. b 57. d 87. PtO *Eur* from 19.
WIMSETT, Paul. b 58. d 85. rtd 20; PtO *Ex* from 20.
WINTER, Mrs Mary Elizabeth. b 56. d 11. C Greengates and Thorpe Edge *Leeds* from 20.
WITCOMBE, Michael David. b 53. d 78. rtd 19.
WITHNELL, Roderick David. b 55. d 90. rtd 20.
WOADDEN, Christopher Martyn. b 56. d 87. rtd 20.
WOOD (*née* DROBIG), Mrs Marion. b 76. d 06. R Shaw cum Donnington *Ox* 09–20.
WOOD, Roger Graham. b 49. d 76. rtd 19.
WOODHEAD, Canon Michael. b 51. d 90. rtd 20.
WOODMANSEY, Michael Balfour. b 55. d 83. rtd 20.
WRAY-WEAR, Lucinda Jane. b 61. d 18. NSM Lt Drayton *Lich* from 19; NSM Woore and Norton in Hales from 21.
WRIGHT, Stuart Kendle. b 73. d 08. V Hounslow H Trin *Lon* 19–21.

CLERGY WHO HAVE DIED SINCE THE LAST EDITION

A list of clergy who have died since 14 August 2019, when the compilation of the 2020–2021 edition was completed. The month and year of death (if known) are recorded with each entry.

ABBOTT, Valerie Ann. 03/21
ABRAHAM, David Alexander. 07/21
ADAM, David. 01/20
ADAMS, David John Anthony. 04/20
AINSWORTH-SMITH, Ian Martin. 03/21
AITKEN, William Stuart. 05/20
ALDERSON, Maureen. 02/20
ALEXANDER, James Douglas. 06/21
ALLBUTT, Mavis Miriam. 02/21
ALLCOCK, Peter Michael. 01/21
ALLEN, Peter Henry. 01/21
ALLIN, Philip Ronald. 02/20
ALLISON, Michael John. 03/21
ALLSOP, Anthony James. 10/19
AMOS, Gerald. 09/20
ANDERS, Jonathan Cyril. 07/20
ANDERSON, Brian Glaister. 04/20
ANDERSON, John Robert. 04/21
ANDERSON, Michael John Austen.
  01/21
ANDERTON, Frederic Michael. 04/20
ANDREW, Brian. 09/20
ANDREW, William Hugh. 08/20
ANDREWS, Anthony John. 05/21
ANNIS, Herman North. 07/21
ARCHER, Michael John. 04/21
ARMITAGE, Susan. 02/20
ARMSON, John Moss. 04/20
ARMSTRONG, Christopher John
  Richard. 07/21
ARNOLD, Keith Appleby. 01/21
ASHLEY, Brian. 02/20
ASHTON, Neville Anthony. 02/21
ASHWORTH, Keith Benjamin. 12/19
ASVAT, David Malcolm. 10/20
ATKINSON, Michael Hubert. 12/20
ATWELL, James Edgar. 12/20
AUDEN, Lawson Philip. 01/21
AVENT, Raymond John. 10/19
BACKHOUSE, Colin. 09/19
BAILEY, Richard William. 02/21
BAIRD, William Stanley. 06/21
BAKER, David Jordan. 11/19
BAKER, Kenneth William. 08/20
BAKERE, Ronald Duncan. 04/20
BALE, Edward William Carre. 05/21
BALFOUR, Andrew Crispin Roxburgh.
  07/20
BALL, Christopher Rowland. 07/20
BALL, Peter William. 01/21
BALL, Vernon. 03/20
BANYARD, Douglas Edward. 11/19
BARBER, Paul Everard. 02/21
BARNES, Brian. 03/20
BARRINGTON-WARD, Simon. 04/20
BARTLETT, George Frederick. 01/20
BARTON, John. 01/20
BASKERVILLE, John. 04/21
BASTIDE, Derek. 04/20
BATSON, William Francis Robert. 02/20
BATTY, Mark Alan. 05/20
BATTYE, John Noel. 08/19
BAXENDALE, John Richard. 03/20
BAXTER, David Norman. 08/19
BAXTER, Richard David. 04/20
BAYNES, Timothy Francis de Brissac.
  04/20
BEACOCK, Nicholas Julian. 10/20
BEADLE, David Alexander. 05/20
BEAMER, Neville David. 03/20
BEAN, Douglas Jeyes Lendrum. 04/20
BEAN, John Victor. 10/20
BEAUMONT, Brian Maxwell. 04/20
BEAUMONT, John Philip. 04/20
BEETHAM, Anthony. 06/20
BELITHER, John Roland. 03/21

BELL, Jack Gorman. 12/20
BELL, Paul Joseph. 02/20
BELLAMY, Dorothy Kathleen. 01/21
BENNETT, Roger Sherwood. 06/20
BENSON, John David. 08/20
BENTLEY, David Edward. 03/20
BERRY, Timothy Hugh. 06/21
BESSANT, Brian Keith. 02/20
BETTS, Anthony Clive. 02/20
BILLINGSLEY, Raymond Philip. 10/19
BINGHAM, Norman James Frederick.
  09/19
BINSLEY, Michael. 05/21
BINSLEY, Michael Robert. 05/21
BIRTWISTLE, James. 04/20
BISHOP, Donald. 01/20
BISHOP, Waveney Joyce. 05/20
BLACKALL, Robin Jeremy McRae. 04/21
BLOOMFIELD, John Michael. 06/21
BOAK, Donald Kenneth. 06/21
BOARDMAN, Frederick Henry. 10/20
BOND, Norman. 12/19
BONHAM, Frederick Thomas. 02/21
BONIFACE, Lionel Ernest George. 02/20
BOOKER, Gerald Dennis. 09/19
BOOTS, Claude Donald Roy. 08/21
BOSTON, Jonathan Bertram. 06/21
BOULTER, Robert George. 07/20
BOULTON, Wallace Dawson. 04/20
BOURDEAUX, Michael Alan. 03/21
BOUTFLOWER, David Curtis. 12/20
BOWERS, John Edward. 10/19
BOWLBY, Ronald Oliver. 12/19
BOYES, Michael Charles. 12/20
BOYSE, Felix Vivian Allan. 03/20
BRAIN, Michael Charles. 03/20
BRANDIE, Beaumont Lauder. 05/20
BRATLEY, David Frederick. 04/20
BRAVINGTON, Timothy Frederick
  Desmond. 03/20
BRAY, Kenneth John. 09/19
BRIDGMAN, Gerald Bernard. 05/21
BRIERLEY, John Michael. 10/19
BRIGHTMAN, Peter Arthur. 06/21
BROAD, Hugh Robert. 07/20
BROADBENT, Hugh Patrick Colin.
  11/20
BROADBERRY, Richard St Lawrence.
  09/20
BROTHWELL, Paul David. 08/20
BROUN, Claud Michael. 08/21
BROWN, Arthur William Stawell. 10/20
BROWN, Brian Ernest. 05/20
BROWN, Christopher. 07/20
BROWN, Marcus Clement. 10/20
BRYANT, Donald Thomas. 10/20
BUCKLEY, Michael. 12/19
BUDGETT, Anthony Thomas. 12/19
BUIK, Allan David. 03/20
BULLIVANT, Ronald. 10/19
BUNDAY, Paul. 11/19
BUNYAN, Richard Charles. 04/20
BURDEN, Robert John. 01/21
BURGESS, John Henry William. 06/20
BURGESS, John Mulholland. 10/20
BURGHALL, Kenneth Miles. 05/20
BURLEIGH, David John. 02/21
BURROWS, Clifford Robert. 04/20
BURTON, Christopher Paul. 08/20
BUTLER, Christopher John. 04/21
BUTT, Edward. 09/20
BUTTERWORTH, Roderick. 06/21
BUTTLE, Leslie Albert. 03/20
BYRON-DAVIES, Peter. 01/21
CAMPBELL, Patrick Alistair. 01/20
CAMPLING, Christopher Russell. 12/20

CANSDALE, George Graham. 10/20
CARDEN, Edwin William. 04/20
CAREY, Charles John. 11/19
CARLIN, Philip Charles. 03/20
CARLSSON, Siw Ebba Christina. 03/21
CARNELLEY, Desmond. 12/20
CARNEY, Richard Wayne. 08/20
CARPENTER, William Brodie. 04/20
CARTER, Christopher Franklin. 05/21
CARTER, Ronald George. 11/19
CARTER, Terence John. 04/20
CARTWRIGHT, Samuel. 01/21
CARVER, Elizabeth Ann. 08/20
CATCHPOLE, Roy. 11/20
CATLEY, John Howard. 02/20
CAVAGAN, Raymond. 10/19
CAVEEN, David Francis. 09/20
CAVELL-NORTHAM, Cavell Herbert
  James. 09/19
CHADWICK, Francis Arnold Edwin.
  02/21
CHANTER, Anthony Roy. 02/21
CHAPMAN, Celia. 04/20
CHAPMAN, Patricia Ann. 12/19
CHAPPELL, Frank Arnold. 10/2̄
CHARLES-EDWARDS, David Mervyn.
  03/21
CHARLESWORTH, Ian Peter. 04/20
CHARRETT, Geoffrey Barton. 05/20
CHOWN, William Richard Bartlett.
  04/21
CHUDLEY, Cyril Raymond. 04/21
CLARK, Christopher Austin. 10/19
CLARK, David George Neville. 05/20
CLARK, John Michael. 02/20
CLARKE, Audrey May. 06/21
CLARKE, Christopher George. 08/20
CLARKE, John Philip. 09/20
CLARKE, Robert Sydney. 06/20
CLARKE, Valerie Diane. 12/20
CLAYTON, William Alan. 11/19
CLEMENTS, Anthony John. 07/21
CLEMENTS, Philip Christian. 05/20
CLIFF, Julian Arnold. 06/21
CLOUGH, Anthony McKenzie. 02/20
COGHLAN, Patrick John. 04/20
COLE, David. 11/19
COLEBROOK, Peter Acland. 03/20
COLES (formerly OLDHAM), David
  Christian. 12/19
COLLINGWOOD, John Jeremy
  Raynham. 12/20
COLLINS, Janet May. 04/21
COLLINS, John Gilbert. 01/20
COLLIS, Stephen Thomas. 01/20
COLLYER, David John. 09/20
COMBER, Michael. 09/19
COMER, Michael John. 04/20
CONGDON, John Jameson. 04/21
CONN, Alistair Aberdein. 03/20
CONNELL, Julie. 06/20
CONWAY, Thomas Robertson. 06/21
COOK, Brian Edwin. 08/20
COOK, Christopher. 06/20
COOK, Ian Bell. 01/21
COOK, John Michael. 02/20
COOKE, Kenneth John. 09/20
COOMBS, Peter Bertram. 09/20
COOPER, Malcolm Tydeman. 06/20
COPELAND, Derek Norman. 12/20
COPLAND, Carole Jean. 11/19
COPPING, Raymond. 07/20
CORBETT, Phyllis. 10/19
CORDINGLEY, Brian Lambert. 08/21
CORNWELL, Peter Raphael. 03/21
COTTON, John Horace Brazel. 01/21

COULING, David Charles. 06/20
COUSSENS, Mervyn Haigh Wingfield. 12/19
COWARD, Raymond. 03/20
COZENS, Audrey Lilian. 08/20
CRAIG-WILD, Peter John. 11/19
CRIPPS, Michael Frank Douglas. 10/20
CROCKER, Peter David. 09/20
CROMPTON-THOMAS, Lionel Edrich. 01/21
CROOK, David Creighton. 07/20
CROSS, Alan. 09/20
CROWE, Leonard Charles. 04/20
CROWE, Philip Anthony. 06/21
CROWTHER, Clarence Edward. 06/21
CRUMPTON, Michael Reginald. 03/21
CUMINGS, Llewellyn Frank Beadnell. 12/19
CUNNINGHAM, Philip John. 08/20
CURRAH, Michael Ewart. 02/20
CURTIS, Geoffrey John. 07/21
DAGLISH, John David. 08/19
DALLOW, Gillian Margaret. 06/21
DALTON, Derek. 01/20
DARVILL, George Collins. 10/20
DARWENT, Frederick Charles. 01/20
DAVIDSON, Charles Hilary. 01/21
DAVIES, John Howard. 04/21
DAVIES, Lorys Martin. 02/21
DAVIS, Alan Norman. 03/21
DAVIS, Peter Langdon (Matthias). 05/21
DAWSON, Cyril. 11/20
DAY, Roy Frederick. 06/20
DEAN, Malcolm. 03/20
DEARNLEY, Patrick Walter. 11/20
DEAVE, Gillian Mary. 01/21
DENNIS, John. 04/20
DEWAR, Francis John Lindsay. 04/20
DEWHURST, Gabriel George. 10/20
DILNOT, John William. 10/20
DODD, Jane. 01/20
DOOLAN, Brian James. 12/19
DORRINGTON, Richard Bryan. 05/20
DOWSE, Ivor Roy. 06/21
DOYLE, Eileen Ann. 08/20
DRAYCOTT, Philip John. 07/20
DRUCE, Brian Lemuel. 07/20
DRUMMOND, John Malcolm. 10/19
DRUMMOND, Josceline Maurice Vaughan. 01/20
DRYE, Douglas John. 03/20
DUKE, Alan Arthur. 05/20
DUNN, Christopher George Hunter. 09/19
DUNN, David James. 06/21
DUPUY, Alan Douglas William. 02/20
DUTHIE, John. 10/20
EARDLEY, William Robert. 04/21
EARNSHAW, Alan Mark. 09/20
EAST, William Gordon. 07/20
EASTON, John. 10/20
EASTWOOD, Colin Foster. 03/21
EATON, Barry Anthony Matthew. 02/21
EDE, Dennis. 01/21
EDWARDS, Harry Steadman. 01/21
EDWARDS, Philip John. 06/21
EFIRD, David Hampton. 01/20
ELKINS, Alan Bernard. 04/21
ELLERY, Arthur James Gabriel. 12/19
ELLIOTT, Colin David. 01/20
ELLIOTT, Gordon. 10/20
ELLIOTT, Ian David. 04/21
ELLIOTT, William James. 11/19
ELLIS, Dorothy Pearson. 12/19
ELSDON, Bernard Robert. 06/20
ELVY, Peter David. 08/19
EMMEL, Malcolm David. 02/21
EUSTICE, Peter Lafevre. 09/19
EVANS, Kenneth. 11/19
EVANS, Peter. 12/19
EVANS, Stanley Munro. 12/19
EVANS, Trevor Owen. 06/20
EXLEY, Malcolm. 08/20

FARBRIDGE, Nicholas Brisco. 07/20
FARISH, Alan John. 11/19
FARMER, Lorelie Joy. 03/21
FARMILOE, Trevor James. 12/19
FARTHING, Michael Thomas. 12/19
FARTHING, Ronald Edward. 10/20
FELCE, Brian George. 05/20
FERGUSON, Richard Archie. 07/21
FERMER, Michael Thorpe. 09/20
FIELDGATE, John William Sheridan. 04/21
FILER, Victor John. 03/20
FINDLAY, Brian James. 05/20
FINNEY, David. 01/20
FINNIMORE, Keith Anthony. 02/21
FISHER, Michael John. 04/21
FLETCHER, Keith. 02/20
FLETCHER, Ralph Henry Maurice. 03/20
FLOATE, Herbert Frederick Giraud. 03/21
FOSTER, Thomas Andrew Hayden. 09/19
FOULIS BROWN, Graham Douglas. 06/20
FOWLES, Christopher John. 07/21
FOX, Norman Stanley. 06/20
FRANCIS, Graham John. 01/20
FRANCIS, John. 02/21
FRANCIS, John Sims. 11/19
FRAZER, James Stewart. 10/19
FREEMAN, Pamela Mary. 02/21
FRONDIGOUN, Marjorie Elizabeth. 01/21
FRY, Florence Marion. 05/21
FUDGE, Erik Charles. 11/20
FULLJAMES, Michael William. 05/20
FULLJAMES, Peter Godfrey. 07/20
FYFFE, Timothy Bruce. 01/20
FYLES, Gordon. 04/20
GALE, Christopher. 06/20
GAMMON, William Paul Lachlan. 10/20
GANT, Peter Robert. 11/20
GARNER, Geoffrey Walter. 01/20
GARRATT, Peter James. 07/20
GARTON, Derek John. 02/20
GEAR, John Arthur. 07/21
GEE, Edward. 05/21
GEILINGER, John Edward. 06/20
GELL, Margaret Florence. 08/21
GEORGE, Frederick. 10/20
GIBBONS, William Simpson. 09/19
GILBERT, Frederick Joseph. 12/19
GINN, Richard John. 07/20
GIRLING, David Frederick Charles. 06/21
GITTINGS, Graham. 11/19
GLEESON, Robert Godfrey. 12/20
GODFREY, Simon. 12/20
GOLDSPINK, David. 07/20
GOODCHILD, Penelope Faith. 12/20
GOODERHAM, Daniel Charles. 04/20
GOODING, Ian Eric. 06/20
GOODLAD, Martin Randall. 02/20
GOODWIN, Ronald Victor. 09/20
GORDON, Kenneth Davidson. 06/21
GORE, John Harrington. 11/19
GORICK, David Charles. 02/20
GOWARD, Giles Conrad. 01/21
GRAHAM, Andrew Alexander Kenny (Alec). 05/21
GRAHAM, Gordon Cecil. 01/21
GRAINGER, Bruce. 09/19
GREAVES, John Neville. 06/21
GREEN, Arthur Edward. 12/20
GREEN, Brian Robert. 02/20
GREEN, Christopher Frederick. 10/19
GREEN, Donald Pentney (Brother Donald). 04/21
GREEN, Dorothy Mary. 12/19
GREEN, Gillian. 02/21
GREEN, Janice Anne. 01/21
GREEN, Margaret Elizabeth. 08/20
GREENWOOD, Roy Douglas. 08/20
GREY, Richard Thomas. 08/20

GRICE, Charles. 08/19
GRIEVES, Anthony Michael. 04/21
GRIFFIN, Alan Howard Foster. 11/20
GRIFFITH, Glyn Keble Gethin. 02/21
GRIFFITHS, Alec. 08/20
GRIFFITHS, David. 02/20
GRIFFITHS, Jean Rose. 02/21
GRIGGS, Ian Macdonald. 01/21
GRIGSBY, Peter Edward. 01/20
GROVE, Ronald Edward. 10/20
GURNEY, Ann. 02/21
HACK, Rex Hereward. 10/20
HACKETT, Peter Edward. 05/20
HALL, Denis. 01/21
HALL, Michael Edward. 06/21
HAMMERSLEY, Peter Angus Ragsdale. 06/20
HAMPSON, David. 12/19
HANKINS, Clifford James. 11/19
HANSFORD, Gordon John. 11/20
HANSON, Margaret Patricia. 10/19
HARDINGHAM, Timothy Kenneth. 10/20
HARDY, Brian Albert. 11/19
HARDY, Robert Maynard. 04/21
HARDY, Thomas Woodburn. 12/19
HARLEY, Brian Nigel. 05/21
HARPER, David Laurence. 03/20
HARRIS, John. 09/19
HARRIS, Patrick Burnet. 12/20
HARRISON, John Northcott. 01/20
HARRISON, Robert Peter. 01/20
HARRISON, Ruth Margaret. 04/21
HART, Anthony. 05/20
HART, Dennis William. 05/20
HARVEY, Alan Douglas. 03/20
HASSELL, David Edwin. 07/21
HASTE, James Victor William. 06/21
HATHAWAY, John Albert. 08/19
HAVILAND, Edmund Selwyn. 10/20
HAWKER, Brian Henry. 09/20
HAWKINS, Donald John. 03/20
HAWKINS, Roger David William. 05/21
HAWKINS, Roger Julian. 07/21
HAWNT, John Charles Frederick. 06/21
HAY, John. 11/20
HAYNES, Clifford. 09/20
HAYNES, Michael Thomas Avery. 06/21
HAYWARD, Peter Noel. 02/20
HEAPS, Richard Peter. 08/21
HENEY, William Butler. 12/20
HETLING, William Maurice. 08/21
HEWITT, John Kaffrell. 04/20
HIGGS, Michael John. 04/21
HILL, Martyn William. 06/21
HILLMAN, John Anthony. 03/21
HILLS, Alan Arthur. 02/21
HILLS, Kenneth Hugh. 02/21
HILTON-TURVEY, Geoffrey Michael. 05/20
HINCHEY, Peter John. 09/20
HINDS, Kenneth Arthur Lancelot. 01/21
HIPKINS, Leslie Michael. 12/19
HOBBS, Michael Bedo. 03/20
HODGSON, Thomas Richard Burnham. 09/20
HOEY, Raymond George. 11/19
HOGARTH, Joseph. 02/20
HOLDEN, Geoffrey. 03/21
HOLMES, Jane Margaret. 02/21
HOLMES, Peter Anthony. 04/20
HOOPER, Walter McGehee. 12/20
HOPKINS, Christopher Freeman. 05/20
HOPKINS, Hugh. 11/20
HOPKINS, John Dawson. 10/19
HOPPERTON, Thomas. 11/19
HORSFALL, Keith. 05/20
HOSKIN, Henry Brian. 05/20
HOUGH, Peter George. 01/21
HOWARD, Francis Curzon. 09/20
HOWARD-COWLEY, Joseph Charles. 02/20
HOWARTH, Ronald. 10/19
HUCKLE, Peter. 12/19

HUDSON, John Peter. 10/20
HUGHES, David Anthony. 06/20
HUGHES, Gerald Thomas. 10/19
HUGHES, Martin Conway. 01/20
HUGHES, Robert Elistan-Glodrydd. 12/19
HUGHES, Rodney Thomas. 03/20
HULL, David John. 08/20
HUMPHREYS, Kenneth Glyn. 04/20
HUMPHRIES, Grahame Leslie. 11/20
HUNT, John Stewart. 04/21
HUNTER, John Gaunt. 10/19
HURST, Alaric Desmond St John. 06/20
HUTCHINGS, Colin Michael. 04/20
HUTCHINGS, John Denis Arthur. 05/20
HUTCHINGS, Robert Henry. 04/21
HUTTON-BURY, David. 02/21
HUXTABLE, Christopher Michael Barclay. 10/20
IBALL, Charles Martin John. 06/20
ILLING, Eric James. 02/20
IND, Philip William David. 09/20
INDER, Patrick John. 12/19
INGHAM, John Edmund. 11/19
INGRAM, Brian. 06/20
INNES, Donald Keith. 12/20
IRESON, Gillian Dorothy. 12/19
ISHERWOOD, Samuel Peter. 02/20
JACKSON, Barry. 12/20
JACKSON, David William. 12/19
JACKSON, Frederick George. 07/20
JACKSON, John Edward. 11/19
JACKSON, Michael Richard. 11/19
JACSON, Edward Shallcross Owen. 09/19
JAMES, Henley George. 07/20
JAMESON, Dermot Christopher Ledgard. 04/21
JEFFORD, Peter Ernest. 08/20
JEFFREYS, Timothy John. 08/20
JENNER, Michael Albert. 08/19
JOHN, David Michael. 09/20
JOHNSON, David William. 04/20
JONES, Evan Trefor. 10/19
JONES, Glyndŵr. 04/20
JONES, Jeffrey Lloyd. 12/20
JONES, Kingsley Charles. 07/21
JONES, Leslie Joseph. 09/20
JONES, Neville George. 04/20
JONES, Raymond Alban. 05/20
JONES, Raymond Trevor. 12/19
JONES, William David. 01/21
JORDAN, John Charles. 04/20
JOYCE, Paul David. 12/20
KARRACH, Herbert Adolf. 01/21
KELSEY, Michael Ray. 01/20
KEOGH, Henry James. 02/20
KERSHAW, John Harvey. 11/20
KIDD, Anthony John Eric. 01/20
KIDD, Maurice Edward. 12/19
KINGSTON, Roy William Henry. 05/20
KIRBY, Barbara Anne June (Sister Barbara June). 01/21
KIRBY, Maurice William Herbert. 07/21
KIRK, Geoffrey. 04/20
KIRKHAM, John Dudley Galtrey. 10/19
KLYBERG, Charles John. 01/20
KNIGHT, Terence. 04/20
KNOTT, Christopher Rodney. 02/21
KNOX, Janet. 06/20
LABDON, John. 06/21
LAING, William Sydney. 04/21
LAIRD, Robert George (Robin). 06/20
LAMB, Bryan John Harry. 11/20
LAMBERT, David Nathaniel. 04/20
LAMBERT, Michael Roy. 03/20
LAMBERT, Peter George. 05/20
LANGFORD, Carol Mary. 04/21
LANGFORD, Michael John. 07/20
LANGRELL, Gordon John. 12/19
LAWRENCE, Martin Kenneth. 10/19
LEAKEY, Ian Raymond Arundell. 01/20
LEE, Peter Kenneth. 06/20
LEEMING, Jack. 05/21
LEES, Peter John William. 09/19

LEGGE, Anne Christine. 03/20
LEITCH, Peter William. 06/21
LEWIS, David Tudor. 09/19
LEWIS, Ian. 09/19
LEWIS, John Edward. 07/20
LEWIS, John Hubert Richard. 09/20
LIDDLE, George. 11/20
LIDDLE, Harry. 02/21
LIGHTFOOT, Vernon Keith. 09/20
LIMBERT, Kenneth Edward. 03/20
LINDSAY, Eric Graham. 01/21
LIVERSIDGE, Linda Sheila. 04/20
LLOYD, Barrington. 08/20
LLOYD, Elizabeth Jane. 04/21
LLOYD, Graham. 09/20
LLOYD, Harry James. 04/20
LLOYD, Robert Graham. 08/20
LORAINE, Kenneth. 03/21
LOUIS, Peter Anthony. 07/21
LOWE, David Charles. 12/20
LOWE, Donald. 07/20
LUCAS, John Kenneth. 01/20
LUCAS, Pamela Turnbull. 02/21
LUCAS, Pauline Ada. 04/20
LUCAS, Ronald James. 02/21
LUCAS, William Wallace. 12/19
LUFF, Alan Harold Frank. 04/20
LUNN, David Ramsay. 07/21
McCANN, Hilda. 06/21
MacCARTY, Paul Andrew. 04/21
MACE, Alan Herbert. 02/21
McFARLAND, Alan Malcolm. 06/21
McILROY, Honor Margaret. 09/20
MACKAY, Hedley Neill. 09/19
McMANUS, James Robert. 01/21
MACNEILL, Nicholas Terence. 12/20
MANLEY (née McCARTHY), Sandra Ellen. 12/19
MANN, Nicola Antoinette. 04/21
MANNS, Edwin Ernest. 10/19
MARCHANT, Iain William. 09/19
MARR, Margaret Rose. 11/20
MARSH, Anthony David. 06/20
MARSH, Lawrence Allan. 10/19
MARSH, Robert Christopher. 03/21
MARSHALL, Peter Arthur. 01/21
MARSHALL, Peter Jerome. 06/20
MARTIN, Edward Eldred William. 12/19
MARTIN, Raymond William. 05/21
MASON, John Evans. 07/21
MASON, John Martin. 03/20
MASSEY, William Cyril. 04/21
MATHESON, Ronald Stuart. 11/19
MATTHEWS, Brian. 05/21
MAWER, David Ronald. 11/20
MAYBURY, Doreen Lorna. 11/19
MAYES, John Charles Dougan. 11/20
MAYLAND, Ralph. 04/20
MEADEN, Philip George William. 01/20
MEAKIN, Anthony John. 04/20
MEESE, Dudley Noel. 01/21
✠MEHAFFEY, James. 01/20
MELLOWS, Alan Frank. 04/21
MILES, Patricia Ellen. 07/20
MILLER, Patrick Figgis. 06/20
MILLIGAN, Peter John. 11/19
MILLIGAN, William John (Barney). 01/21
MILLING, David Horace. 04/20
MILLS, Glenys Christine. 04/20
MILLSON, Brian Douglas. 03/21
MINALL, Peter. 05/20
MINNS, John Charles. 12/19
MITCHELL, George Alfred. 03/21
MITCHELL, Patrick Reynolds. 01/20
MITFORD, Bertram William Jeremy (Bill). 06/20
MITSON, John Dane. 09/20
MOLLER, George Brian. 01/21
MOODY, George Henry. 10/19
MOORE, David Roy. 12/19
MOORE, John Michael. 01/21
MORDECAI, Betty. 11/19
MORDECAI, Thomas Huw. 12/20
MORGAN, Ian David John. 10/19
MORPHY, Michael John. 08/19

MORRELL, Nigel Paul. 01/20
MOSELEY, David John Reading. 02/20
MOSELING, Peter. 12/20
MOSLEY, Edward Peter. 10/20
MOUNTFORD, Ian David. 12/19
MUDDIMAN, John Bernard. 12/20
MUMFORD, Hugh Raymond. 09/20
MUNDELL, Christine Elizabeth. 09/19
MUNGAVIN, Gerald Clarence. 12/20
MURPHY, Owen. 04/21
MURPHY, Peter Frederick. 06/21
MURRAY, Gordon Stewart. 01/21
MUST, Albert Henry. 08/19
MYLES, Peter Rodney. 03/20
NADKARNI, Edward Wasant. 01/21
NAISH, Hilary Marilyn. 04/20
NAISMITH, Carol. 10/19
NEALE, John Robert Geoffrey. 07/20
NEVILL, Mavis Hetty. 05/21
NEWALL, Arthur William. 04/21
NEWALL, Richard Lucas. 10/19
NEWELL, Kenneth Ernest. 01/21
NEWSUM, Alfred Turner Paul. 12/19
NICHOLSON, Pamela Elizabeth. 01/20
NICKLIN, John Marcus. 09/19
NICOL, Stephen Trevor. 12/20
NICOLL, Alexander Charles Fiennes Jack. 01/20
NICOLSON, Paul Roderick. 03/20
NIXON, Annette Rose. 02/21
NORTHALL, Malcolm Walter. 12/20
NUNN, Christina Mary. 06/21
NURSER, John Shelley. 11/20
OAKES, Graham. 08/19
OATES, Alexander John. 06/20
ODDIE, William John Muir. 11/19
OGILVIE, Gordon. 09/20
OLIVER, John Michael. 01/21
ORAM, John Ernest Donald. 11/19
ORCHARD, Nigel John. 03/20
ORME, Sydney. 01/21
ORMEROD, Henry Lawrence. 07/21
OSBORNE, Derek James. 08/20
OSMERS, John Robert. 06/21
OSWALD, John Edward Guy. 02/20
OTTEY, Anthony O'Neil. 07/21
PACKER, James Innell. 07/20
PACKER, Roger Ernest John. 01/20
PAGE, Irene May. 02/20
PAGE-CHESTNEY, Michael William. 07/21
PALMER, David Henry. 12/20
PALMER, David Michael. 07/21
PALMER, David Philip. 06/21
PAPWORTH, John. 07/20
PARKER, Margaret. 06/20
PARKER, Robert Lawrence. 04/20
PARKIN, John Anthony. 03/21
PARMENTIER, Martinus Franciscus Georgius. 03/21
PARRY, Derek Nugent Goulding. 07/20
PARRY, Keith Melville. 05/20
PARSONS, George Horace Norman. 06/20
PATON, John David Marshall. 12/19
PAYNE, Rosemary Ann. 02/20
PEARCE, Trevor John. 03/20
PEARSE, Ronald Thomas Hennessy. 08/19
PEEL, Derek. 11/20
PENN, Barry Edwin. 12/19
PEPPER, Leonard Edwin. 01/21
PERKES, Brian Robert Keith. 05/20
PERKINS, Douglas Brian. 05/20
PERRY, Timothy Richard. 03/20
PERRY-GORE, Walter Keith. 10/19
PETERS, David Lewis. 07/20
PETERS, Kenneth. 05/20
PETERS, Michael. 11/20
PHEELY, William Rattray. 04/20
PHILIP, Peter Wells. 01/21
PHILLIPS, Brian Robert. 02/21
PHILLIPS, Elizabeth Beryl. 07/20
PHILPOTT, Ronald. 10/20
PICKERING, Geoffrey Craig. 01/20
PICKERING, Malcolm. 02/20

PIKE, George Richard. 12/19
PILKINGTON, Charles George Willink. 12/19
PINNINGTON, Suzanne Jane. 07/21
PINSENT, Ewen Macpherson. 10/20
PLATT, John Emerson. 12/19
PLATT, Katherine Mary. 04/20
PLATT, William David. 02/21
POCOCK, Gillian Margaret. 09/19
POLKINGHORNE, John Charlton. 03/21
POLLARD, Roger Frederick. 01/21
PONTER, John Arthur. 06/20
POOLEY, Peter Owen. 05/20
POPE, Michael John. 04/20
PORTER, John Dudley Dowell. 06/21
PORTHOUSE, Roger Gordon Hargreaves. 05/21
POTTER, James David. 01/20
POTTS, James. 02/21
POULTON, Arthur Leslie. 09/19
PRAGNELL, Michael John. 07/20
PRESTON, James Martin. 12/19
PRICE, Desmond. 10/20
PRICE, John Richard. 05/20
PRICE, Stanley George. 03/20
PRIOR, David Clement Lyndon. 06/21
PRITCHARD, Brian James Pallister. 03/21
PRITCHARD, Peter Benson. 10/20
PRUDOM, William Haigh. 01/21
PUCKRIN, Christopher. 02/21
PULLAN, Lionel Stephen. 12/19
QUINT, Patricia Mary. 07/21
RABJOHNS, Alan. 10/19
RAVEN, Margaret Hilary. 02/20
RAVENSCROFT, Raymond Lockwood. 05/20
RAWE, Alan Charles George. 12/19
RAY, Joanna Zorina. 03/21
REDDINGTON, Gerald Alfred. 06/20
REED, Richard David. 04/21
REEDER, Angela Lilian. 07/21
REES, Leslie. 06/21
REES, Richard John Edward Williams. 05/21
REEVE, Roger Patrick. 04/21
REEVES, John Graham. 08/20
REID, Herbert Alan. 02/21
RENNARD, Edward Lionel. 12/19
RENNIE, Iain Hugh. 10/19
RICHARDS, Thomas John Wynzie. 03/21
RICHARDS, William Hughes. 04/21
RICHARDSON, John Humphrey. 02/20
RIDLEY, Alfred Forbes. 10/19
RIGBY, Harold. 11/19
RIGBY, Joseph. 02/21
RIMMINGTON, Gerald Thorneycroft. 10/19
RINGROSE, Brian Sefton. 10/20
RINGROSE, Hedley Sidney. 04/21
RITCHIE, Brian Albert. 03/20
RIVETT, Peter John. 03/21
RIX, Patrick George. 11/19
ROAN, William Forster. 04/20
ROBERTS, Andrea Joan. 02/21
ROBERTS, Raymond Harcourt. 09/19
ROBERTSON, Brian Ainsley. 03/20
ROBINSON, Christine. 08/21
ROBINSON, Janet. 11/20
ROBINSON, John Kenneth. 08/20
ROBINSON, Margaret. 07/20
ROBINSON, Raymonde Robin. 08/19
ROBINSON, Roy David. 11/19
ROBSON, Ian Leonard. 07/21
ROBY, Richard James. 05/20
RODGERS, David. 02/21
RODRIGUEZ-VEGLIO, Francis Bonny. 01/21
ROE, Joseph Thorley. 10/20
ROE, Peter Harold. 06/20
ROGAN, John. 04/20
ROGERS, David Arthur. 11/20
ROLFE, Charles Edward. 04/21
ROSE, Paul Rosamond. 04/21

ROSE-CASEMORE, John. 06/20
ROSKILLY, John Noel. 04/21
ROSS, Malcolm Hargrave. 10/20
ROWLANDS, Joseph Haydn. 01/21
ROWLEY-BROOKE, Marie Gordon. 09/20
RUDMAN, Thomas Peter William. 12/19
RUMING, Gordon William. 09/20
RUNDLE, Beryl Rosemary. 02/21
RUSSELL, Harold Ian Lyle. 08/21
RUSSELL, John Arthur. 01/21
RUTT, Celia Mary Avril. 11/19
SALMON, Anthony James Heygate. 08/21
SALWAY, Donald Macleay. 03/21
SANDERS, Nora Irene. 03/20
SATTERLY, Gerald Albert. 12/20
SAUL, Norman Stanley. 02/20
SAUNDERS, Brian Gerald. 02/20
SAUNDERS, Sheila Lilian. 03/21
SAUNT, James Peter Robert. 02/20
SAVAGE, Michael Atkinson. 04/21
SAVILL, David. 12/20
SCHUTTE, Margaret Ann. 12/20
SCOBIE, Geoffrey Edward Winsor. 04/20
SCOTT, Allan George. 01/21
SCOTT, Andrew Charles Graham. 08/21
SCOTT, Beryl May. 08/20
SCOTT, Christopher Michael. 04/21
SCOTT, William Sievwright. 07/20
SEARL, John. 06/21
SEARLE, Charles Peter. 04/20
SEARLE, Hugh Douglas. 10/19
SEARLE-BARNES, Albert Victor. 10/19
SECCOMBE, Marcus John. 04/20
SELF, John Andrew. 05/21
SELLERS, George William. 08/19
SEWELL, John Barratt (Barry). 01/21
SHARP, Alfred James Frederick. 03/20
SHARP, David Malcolm. 01/20
SHARP, Robert. 01/21
SHARPE, Derek Martin Brereton (Pip). 11/20
SHAW, Graham. 04/21
SHEEN, John Harold. 04/20
SHEPHARD, Brian Edward. 05/20
SHEPHERD, Christopher Francis Pleydell. 02/21
SHEPHERD, David. 03/21
SHERWIN, Jane. 03/20
SHILL, Kenneth Leslie. 03/21
SHILLAKER, John. 02/21
SHILVOCK, Geoffrey. 12/19
SHINN, William Raymond. 12/20
SHIPP, Linda Mary. 10/20
SHIRRAS, Edward Scott. 10/20
SHREWSBURY, Michael Buller. 05/20
SHUFFLEBOTHAM, Alastair Vincent. 06/21
SIDDLE, Michael Edward. 04/20
SIDEBOTHAM, Stephen Francis. 07/21
SILK, John Arthur. 02/20
SILKSTONE, Thomas William. 09/20
SILLIS, Eric Keith. 01/20
SILLITOE, William John. 09/20
SIMMONS, Bernard Peter. 01/21
SIMMONS, Eric. 01/21
SIMON, David Sidney. 06/20
SIMPSON, Georgina. 10/20
SIMS, Keith George. 08/20
SINCLAIR, Jane Elizabeth Margaret. 01/21
SISSONS, Gordon. 02/20
SKINNER, John Richard. 12/19
SMART, Haydn Christopher. 11/19
SMITH, Christine. 03/21
SMITH, David Earling. 11/20
SMITH, Eustace. 01/21
SMITH, Grahame Clarence. 10/19
SMITH, John Graham. 05/20
SMITH, John William. 09/19
SMITH, Lawrence Paul. 01/21
SMITH, Peter James. 11/19
SMITH, Philip Lloyd Cyril. 12/19

SMITH, Robert Harold. 02/21
SMITH, Ronald James. 09/20
SMYTH, Robert Andrew Laine (Brother Anselm). 12/19
SNELSON, William Thomas. 12/20
SOPHIANOU, Neofitos Anthony. 04/20
SOUNDY, Philippa Clare. 04/21
SOWDON, Henry Lewis Malcolm. 01/21
SPEAR, Sylvia Grace. 04/20
SPENCER, John Edward. 02/20
SPENCER, Roy Primett. 05/20
STACEY, Victor George. 12/20
STAFFORD, John Ingham Henry. 06/20
STAINSBY, Alan. 11/19
STALLARD, John Charles. 09/20
STAMMERS, Robert Andrew. 03/20
STANDEN McDOUGAL, John Anthony Phelps. 05/20
STARES, Olive Beryl. 05/21
STARK, John Jordan. 01/21
STATHAM, John Francis. 11/20
STELL, Peter Donald. 02/21
STEPHENS, Richard William. 08/21
STEPHENSON, Ian Clarke. 02/21
STERRY, Timothy John. 10/20
STEVENS, Martin Leonard. 01/21
STEVENS, Michael John. 06/20
STEVINSON, Josephine Mary. 05/21
STIDOLPH, Robert Anthony. 05/21
STOKES, Andrew John. 12/20
STOKES, Michael John. 01/20
STONES, John Graham. 12/19
STOWE, Brian. 01/21
STOWE, Nigel James. 01/21
STRACHAN, Donald Philip Michael. 07/21
STRONG, John David. 07/21
STUART, Francis David. 04/20
SULLIVAN, Trevor Arnold. 10/20
SUMMERS, Paul Anthony. 02/20
SURTEES, Timothy John de Leybourne. 07/21
SUTCLIFFE, Peter John. 03/21
SUTHERLAND, Alistair Campbell. 11/20
SWAIN, John Roger. 01/21
SWANBOROUGH, Robert Charles. 09/19
SWANN, Frederick David. 11/19
SWIFT, Richard Barrie. 04/20
SYMONS, Stewart Burlace. 04/21
TALBOTT, Brian Hugh. 06/20
TAVERNOR, William Noel. 09/20
TAYLOR, Averil Mary. 06/20
TAYLOR, Brian. 03/21
TAYLOR, George James Trueman. 02/20
TAYLOR, Humphrey Vincent. 02/21
TAYLOR, John Andrew Wemyss. 06/20
TAYLOR, John Rowland. 04/21
TAYLOR, Roland Haydn. 12/19
TETLEY, Brian. 10/20
THOMAS, Andrew Herbert Redding. 05/20
THOMAS, David Geoffrey. 03/21
THOMAS, John Roger. 12/19
THOMAS, June Marion. 01/21
THOMAS, William Jordison. 01/20
THOMPSON, Edward Ronald Charles. 07/20
THOMPSON, Tom Malcolm. 03/20
THOMPSON-McCAUSLAND, Marcus Perronet. 02/20
THORNEWILL, Mark Lyon. 10/20
THORNTON, David John Dennis. 02/20
TODD, William Moorhouse. 03/20
TOLWORTHY, Colin. 04/20
TOOGOOD, Melanie Lorraine. 05/21
TOWERS, David Francis. 02/21
TOWLSON, George Eric. 07/20
TOWNSHEND, Charles Hume. 07/20
TREBY, David Alan. 02/20
TUCKWELL, Christopher Howard Joseph. 06/20
TURNER, Antony Hubert Michael. 07/20

CLERGY WHO HAVE DIED SINCE THE LAST EDITION

TURNER, Derek John. 10/20
TURNER, Henry John Mansfield. 05/20
TURNER, Leslie. 01/20
TURNER, St John Alwin. 02/21
TWENTYMAN, Trevor Lawrence Holme. 04/20
TYLER, Brian Sidney. 04/20
TYLER (née WAITE), Sheila Margaret. 09/20
TYLER, Thomas May. 12/20
UFFINDELL, David Wilfred George. 05/20
UNDERHILL, Robin. 04/20
UNWIN, Kenneth. 12/20
VALENTINE, Jeremy Wilfred. 08/19
VAN CARRAPIETT, Timothy Michael James. 07/21
van der LINDE, Herbert John. 05/20
VASEY, Arthur Stuart. 10/19
VAUGHAN, Jeffrey Charles. 01/20
VAUGHAN, Peter St George. 04/20
VELLACOTT, Peter Graham. 01/21
VICKERS, Donald. 11/20
VIGEON, Owen George. 05/20
VINCENT, Alfred James. 06/21
VINCENT, David Cyril. 09/20
VIVIAN, Thomas Keith. 07/20
VOLTZENLOGEL, Timothy John. 03/21
WADSWORTH, Michael Philip. 04/21
WAGSTAFF, Robert William. 05/20
WAINE, John. 12/20
WAINWRIGHT, Kevin Frank. 04/20
WAITE, Robin Derek. 04/20
WAIYAKI, Jennie. 09/19
WAKELIN, Alan Frank. 11/20
WALFORD, David John. 05/21
WALFORD, Robin Peter. 01/20
WALKER, Alan Edward. 08/20
WALKER, Harvey William. 12/19
WALTER, Donald Alex. 10/19
WALTERS, Jennifer Betty. 02/20
WALTERS, Peter. 04/20
WALTON, Frank. 04/21
WALTON, Geoffrey Elmer. 07/20
WARD, Lionel Owen. 03/21
WARD, Michael Reginald. 03/21

WAREHAM, Caroline. 06/20
WARING, Graham George Albert. 10/20
WARKE, Robert Alexander. 01/21
WARMAN, Marion Alice. 03/21
WARNER, Robert William. 08/21
WARREN, Alan Christopher. 12/20
WARREN, Cecil Allan. 09/19
WARREN, Gordon Lenham (Bunny). 07/20
WATERS, Gordon Keith. 01/21
WATERSTONE, Albert Thomas. 08/20
WATSON, Gordon Mark Stewart. 03/20
WATSON, Graeme Campbell Hubert. 01/20
WATSON, Henry Stanley. 09/20
WATSON, Jeffrey John Seagrief. 01/21
WATSON, John. 04/20
WATSON WILLIAMS, Richard Hamilton Patrick. 05/20
WATTS, David Henry. 06/20
WEAVER, Brian John. 06/21
WEBB, Rowland James. 01/20
WEBBER, Lionel Frank. 04/21
WEBSTER, Patricia Eileen. 07/20
WELLS, William Alan John. 02/20
WERRELL, Ralph Sidney. 07/20
WHEATLEY, David. 07/21
WHITE, David John. 07/20
WHITE, Richard Alfred. 11/20
WHITEHEAD, Christopher Martin Field. 11/19
WHITEMAN, Cedric Henry. 11/19
WHITTAKER, Derek. 10/19
WHITTAM, Kenneth Michael. 12/19
WHYTE, Duncan Macmillan. 08/20
WIBBERLEY, Anthony Norman. 08/20
WIDDOWS, Edward John. 10/20
WILBY, Jean. 11/19
WILKINSON, Edwin. 08/20
WILKINSON, Stephen Graham. 04/20
WILL, Nicholas James. 12/19
WILLCOX (née THOMPSON), Pauline. 08/19
WILLETTS, Mary Elizabeth Willetts. 01/21

WILLIAMS, John Frederick Arthur. 03/21
WILLIAMS, John Heard. 04/20
WILLIAMS, John Roger. 07/20
WILLIAMS, Stephen Lionel. 04/20
WILLIAMS, Trevor Stanley Morlais. 11/19
WILLIAMS, William Garmon. 04/20
WILLIAMSON, Robert Kerr (Roy). 09/19
WILLOUGHBY, Francis Edward John. 11/20
WILMER, John Watts. 10/19
WILSON, James Andrew Christopher. 10/20
WILSON, James Kenneth. 07/20
WILSON, John Lake. 01/20
WILSON, Peter John. 09/20
WILSON, Thomas Roderick. 10/20
WINFIELD, June Mary. 03/21
WINNARD, Jack. 07/21
WINSTONE, Peter John. 10/19
WINTER, Thomas Andrew. 04/20
WISKEN, Brian Leonard. 10/20
WITHERS, Christine Mary. 05/20
WOLSTENCROFT, Alan. 09/20
WOOD, Brian Frederick. 12/19
WOOD, Geoffrey. 04/20
WOOD, George Albert. 01/20
WOODALL, Reginald Homer. 01/21
WOODGER, John Page. 07/21
WOODHALL, Peter. 12/19
WOODHOUSE, Andrew Henry. 12/19
WOODS, David Arthur. 06/20
WOODSFORD, Andrew Norman. 11/19
WOOLVEN, Ronald. 01/20
WRIGHT, John Gordon. 05/20
WRIGHT, Leslie Vandernoll. 10/19
WRIGHT, Michael. 11/19
WRIGHT, Michael John. 06/21
WRIGHT, Peter Reginald. 06/20
WYATT, Royston Dennis. 01/21
YATES, Keith Leonard. 11/20
YIEND, Paul Martin. 09/19
YOUNG, Iain Clavering. 02/21

MAPS

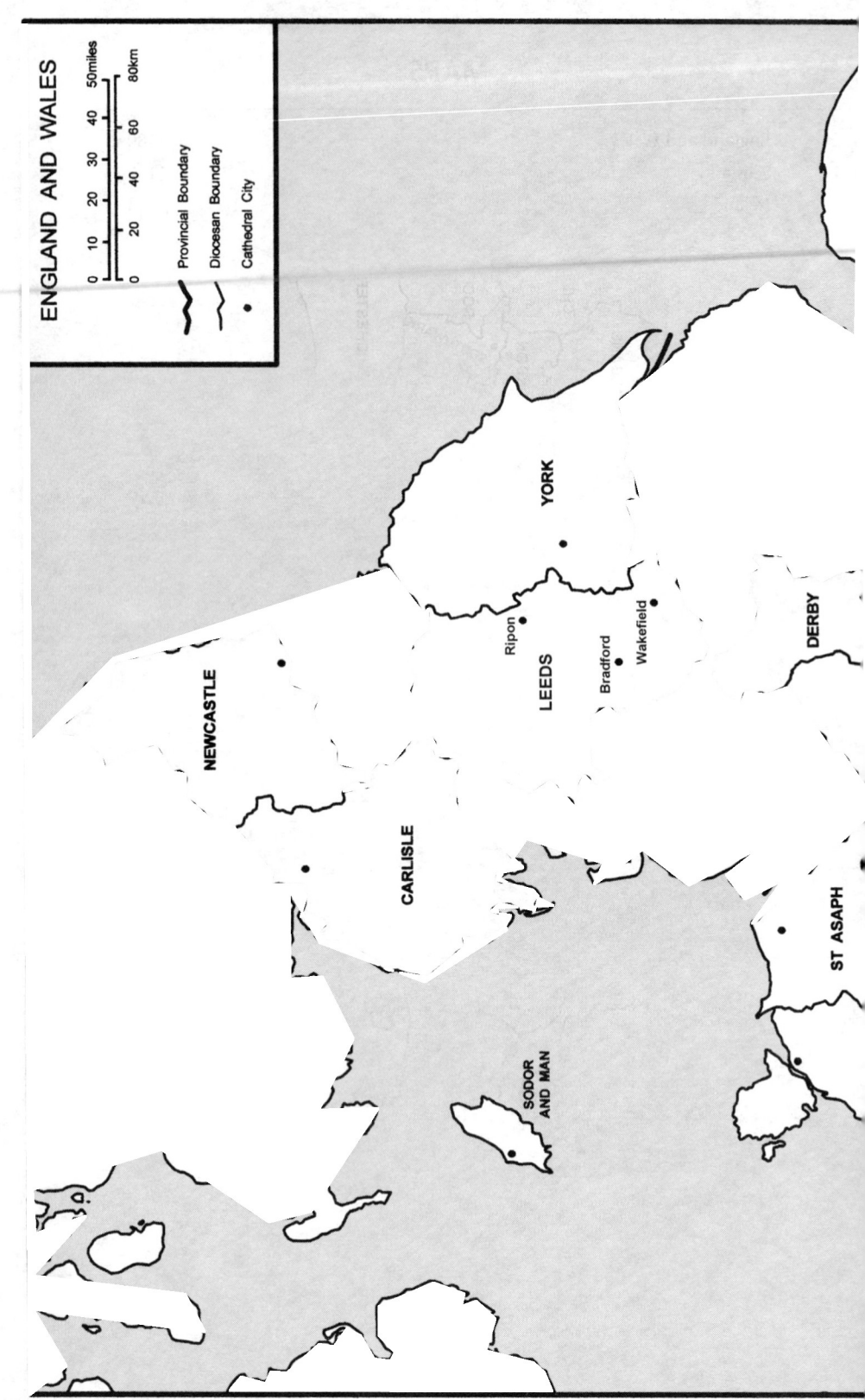

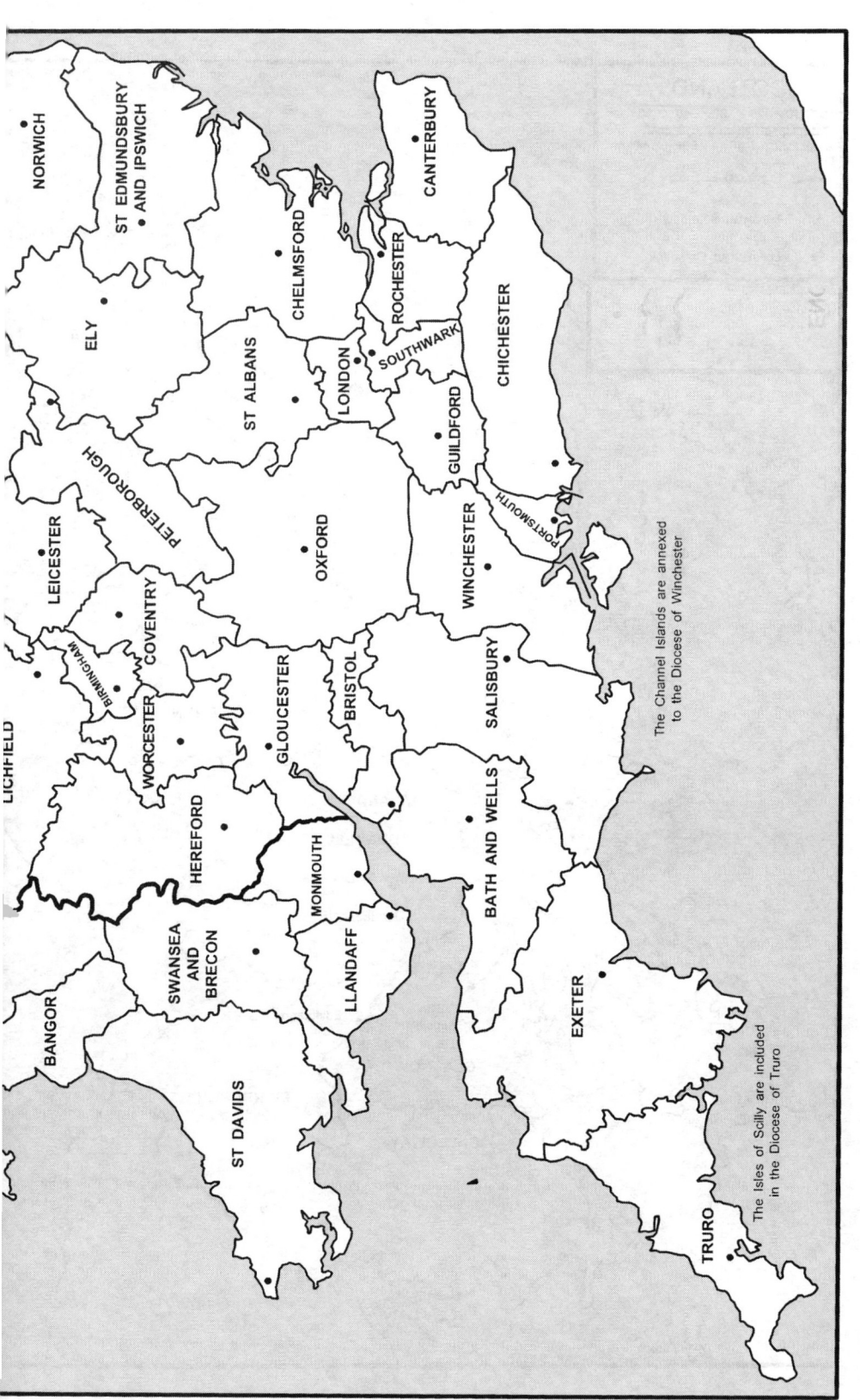

NORWICH

ST EDMUNDSBURY AND IPSWICH

CANTERBURY

CHELMSFORD

ROCHESTER

ELY

ST ALBANS

SOUTHWARK

LONDON

CHICHESTER

GUILDFORD

PETERBOROUGH

LEICESTER

COVENTRY

OXFORD

WINCHESTER

PORTSMOUTH

BIRMINGHAM

LICHFIELD

WORCESTER

GLOUCESTER

BRISTOL

SALISBURY

HEREFORD

BATH AND WELLS

MONMOUTH

SWANSEA AND BRECON

LLANDAFF

BANGOR

ST DAVIDS

EXETER

TRURO

The Channel Islands are annexed to the Diocese of Winchester

The Isles of Scilly are included in the Diocese of Truro

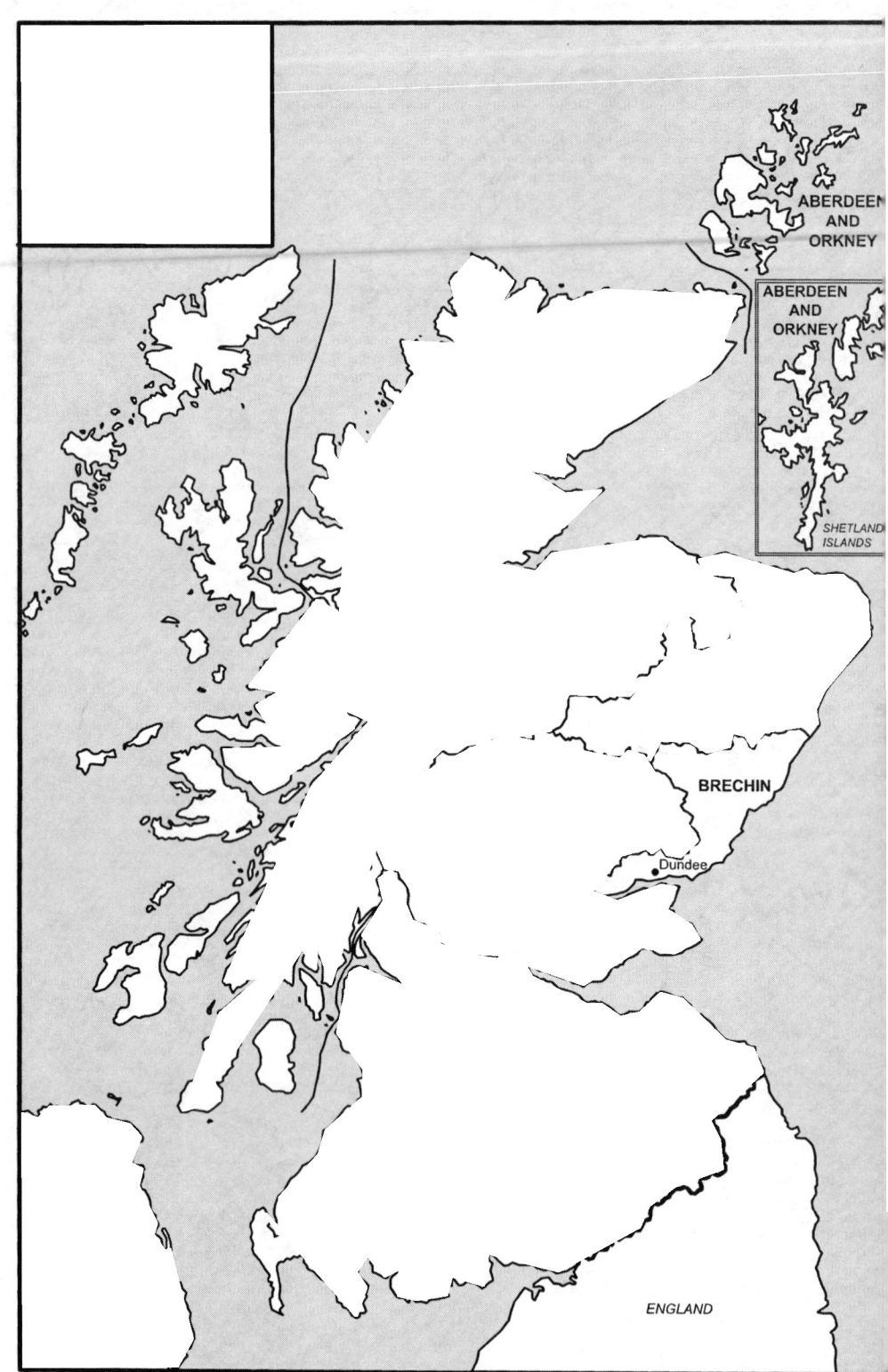

ABERDEEN
AND
ORKNEY

ABERDEEN
AND
ORKNEY

SHETLAND
ISLANDS

BRECHIN

Dundee

ENGLAND

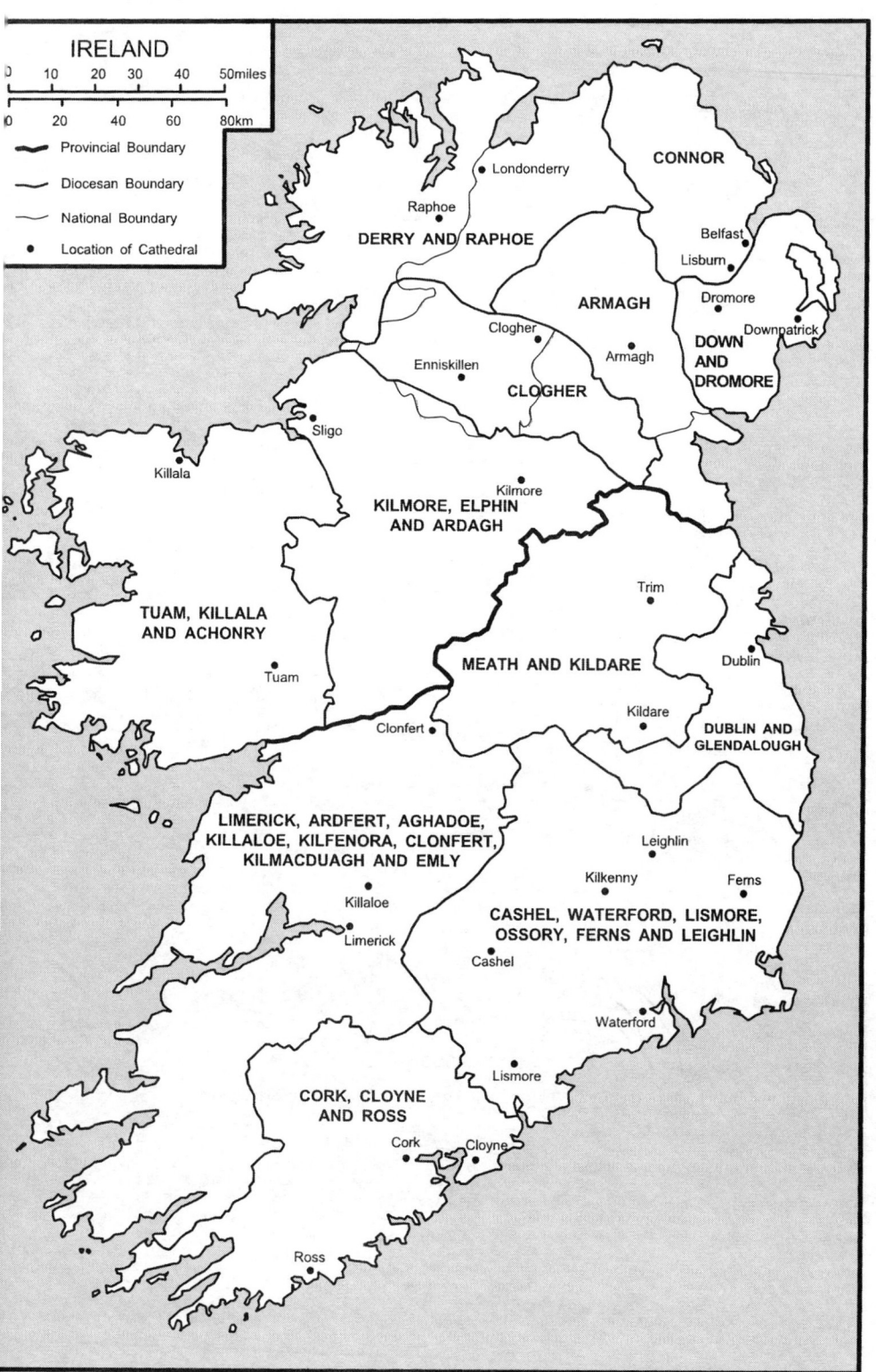

IRELAND

0	10	20 30	40	50miles	
0	20	40	60	80km	

〰 Provincial Boundary

─ Diocesan Boundary

─ National Boundary

● Location of Cathedral

CONNOR

Londonderry

Raphoe

DERRY AND RAPHOE

Belfast

Lisburn

ARMAGH

Dromore

Downpatrick

Clogher

Armagh

DOWN AND DROMORE

Enniskillen

CLOGHER

Sligo

Killala

Kilmore

KILMORE, ELPHIN AND ARDAGH

Trim

TUAM, KILLALA AND ACHONRY

Tuam

MEATH AND KILDARE

Dublin

Clonfert

Kildare

DUBLIN AND GLENDALOUGH

LIMERICK, ARDFERT, AGHADOE, KILLALOE, KILFENORA, CLONFERT, KILMACDUAGH AND EMLY

Leighlin

Kilkenny

Fems

Killaloe

Limerick

CASHEL, WATERFORD, LISMORE, OSSORY, FERNS AND LEIGHLIN

Cashel

Waterford

Lismore

CORK, CLOYNE AND ROSS

Cork

Cloyne

Ross